The Cassell Encyclopaedia Dictionary

The Cassell Encyclopaedia Dictionary

CASSELL

First published 1990 by **Cassell Publishers Limited**
Villiers House, 41/47 Strand
London WC2N 5JE

Cassell's English Dictionary first published 1891
Last complete revision 1962
The Cassell Concise English Dictionary first published 1989

British Library Cataloguing in Publication Data
The Cassell encyclopaedia dictionary.
1. English language – dictionaries
2. Encyclopaedias in English
I. Kerr-Frost, Pandora
423
ISBN 0-304-34027-8

Data processing and typesetting by
Morton Word Processing Ltd, Scarborough
Printed and bound in Great Britain by
The Bath Press, Avon

CONTENTS

ACKNOWLEDGMENTS

Lexicographers	John Bailie Callum Brines Carolyn Donaldson Sarah Harland Pandora Kerr-Frost Kathy Seed
Proof reading	Rod Gray, Bath Proofreading Service
Data Processing	Morton Word Processing Ltd.
Design	Vaughan Allen Richard Earney
Production	Geoffrey Charters
Publisher	Stephen Butcher
Assistant Editor	Steve Cook
Administration	Alison Potter

HOW TO USE THE CASSELL ENCYCLOPAEDIA DICTIONARY

The entry
Each entry in the Encyclopaedia Dictionary begins with an entry-word or head-word in bold type. This is immediately followed by the relevant part of speech and the meaning/meanings, or, in the case of encyclopaedic entries, an account of the person, place etc. to which the head-word refers. The etymology, where relevant, is placed at the very end of the entry in square brackets.

Arrangement of entries
By no means all words defined in the dictionary are headwords. Many words and expressions which are derived from the same root have been grouped or 'nested' together, e.g. **execrable** is under **execrate**. This has the great merit not only of demonstrating at a glance the relationship of the words but of acting as a significant space-saving device. The system allows many more words to be included in the dictionary than would otherwise be the case.

The majority of such words are easy to find since their positions in the dictionary are very close alphabetically to what they would have been if they had been entered as separate headwords. Where this is not the case cross-references have been added for facility of use, e.g. **elision** is cross-referred to **elide**.

Organization of entries
Most headwords have more than one meaning and more than one word derived from them. The words and expressions derived from headwords fall into three categories – idioms/phrases, compounds and direct derivatives.

Idioms consist of phrases including the headword, e.g. **to gain on** or compound words not beginning with the headword, e.g. **old gold**. They are placed immediately after the last meaning of the last part of speech of the headword.

Compounds, which consist of two elements beginning with the headword, are placed immediately after the last meaning of the last idiom. The compound word may be hyphenated, e.g. **cross-bow**, two words, e.g. **emergency landing** or one word, e.g. **eyesight**, according to convention.

Direct derivatives are words formed from the root of the headword or its stem by adding a suffix, e.g. *-ness, -ly*, etc. e.g. **gauntness, ghostly**. These are placed after the last meaning of the last compound.

Derivatives which themselves are derived from derivatives of the headword follow on from the words in the entry from which they are derived. Thus **endless band** follows the direct derivative **endless**.

Labels
Labels in round brackets have been added where necessary. They are divided into two categories – stylistic labels, such as (*offensive*), (*sl.*), (*coll.*) etc. and field labels such as (*Med.*), (*Comput.*) etc. A list of abbreviations of labels appears under *Chief Abbreviations Used* (p.viii).

Cross-references
The word cross-referred to appears in small caps, e.g. **enure** INURE.

Obsolete/archaic words
Obsolete and archaic words or meanings are preceded by a dagger sign : †

CHIEF ABBREVIATIONS USED

All are given here in roman, though most of them may also appear in italics as labels.

a.	adjective
abbr.	abbreviation
abl.	ablative
Abor.	Aboriginal, Aborigines
acc.	accusative; according
adapt.	adaptation
adv.	adverb
A-F	Anglo-French
Afr.	African
aft.	afterwards
Agric.	Agriculture
Alch.	Alchemy
Alg.	Algebra
alln.	allusion
alt.	alternative
Am. Ind.	American Indian
anal.	analogous
Anat.	Anatomy
Ang.-Ind.	Anglo-Indian
Ang.-Ir.	Anglo-Irish
Ang.-Lat.	Anglo-Latin
appar.	apparently
Arab.	Arabic
Aram.	Aramaic
Arch.	Architecture
Archaeol.	Archaeology
Arith.	Arithmetic
Art.	Artistic
Artill.	Artillery
assim.	assimilated, assimilation
Assyr.	Assyrian
Astrol.	Astrology
Astron.	Astronomy
attrib.	attribute, attributive
augm.	augmentative
Austral.	Australian
Austr.-Hung.	Austro-Hungarian
aux.v.	auxiliary verb
Aviat.	Aviation
Bibl.	Bible, biblical
Bibliog.	Bibliography
Biol.	Biology
Boh.	Bohemian
Bot.	Botany
Braz.	Brazilian
Bret.	Breton
Build.	Building
Bulg.	Bulgarian
Byz.	Byzantine
c.	circa, about
Camb.	Cambridge
Campan.	Campanology
Can.	Canada, Canadian
Carib.	Caribbean
Carp.	Carpentry
Cat.	Catalan
Celt.	Celtic
Ceram.	Ceramics
Ch.	Church
Chem.	Chemistry
Chin.	Chinese
Civ. Eng.	Civil Engineering
Class.	Classical
Coal-min.	Coal mining
cogn.	cognate
coll.	colloquial; collateral
collect.	collective
comb.	combination
comb. form	combining form
Comm.	Commerce
comp.	comparative
Comput.	Computing
Conch.	Conchology
cond.	conditional
conf.	confusion
conj.	conjunction
conn.	connected
contr.	contraction
Cook.	Cooking
Copt.	Coptic
Corn.	Cornish
corr.	corruption; corresponding
Cosmog.	Cosmogony
cp.	compare
Cryst.	Crystallography
Dan.	Danish
dat.	dative
def.	definition
deriv.	derivation
derog.	derogatory
dial.	dialect
dim.	diminutive
Diplom.	Diplomatics
dist.	distinct, distinguished
Dut.	Dutch
Dynam.	Dynamics
E	East, Eastern
Eccles.	Ecclesiastical
econ.	Economics
EFris.	East Frisian
e.g.	exempli gratia, for example
Egypt.	Egyptian
Egyptol.	Egyptology
EInd.	East Indian
Elec.	Electricity
ellipt.	elliptical, elliptically
Embryol.	Embryology
emphat.	emphatic
Eng.	English; Engineering
Ent.	Entomology
erron.	erroneously
esp.	especially
Ethn.	Ethnology
euphem.	euphemistic
Eur.	European
Exam.	Examination
exc.	except
F	French
f.	feminine
facet.	facetiously
fem.	feminine
Feud.	Feudal
fig.	figuratively
fl.	floruit, flourished
Flem.	Flemish

foll. the following
For. Foreign
Fort. Fortification
freq. frequentative
Fris. Frisian
fut. future

G German
Gael. Gaelic
gen. genitive
Geneal. Genealogy
Geog. Geography
Geol. Geology
Geom. Geometry
ger. gerund, gerundive
Goth. Gothic
Gr. Greek
grad. gradually
Gram. Grammar

Heb. Hebrew
Her. Heraldry
Hind. Hindi
Hist. History
Hort. Horticulture
Hung. Hungarian
Hydrostat. Hydrostatics
Hyg. Hygiene

Icel. Icelandic
Ichthyol. Ichthyology
ident. identical; identified
i.e. id est, that is
imag. imaginary
imit. imitative
imper. imperative
impers. impersonal
incept. inceptive
incorr. incorrectly
Ind. India, Indian
ind. indicative
indef. art. indefinite article
Indo-Port. Indo-Portuguese
inf. infinitive
influ. influenced
inst. instinctive
instr. instrumental
int. interjection
intens. intensive
Internat. International
interrog. interrogative
intr. intransitive
Ir. Irish
iron. ironical
irreg. irregular
It. Italian

Jap. Japanese
Jav. Javanese
Jewel. Jewellery

L Latin
lat. latitude
LG Low German
Lit. Literature, literary
lit. literal, literally
Lit. crit. Literary criticism
Lith. Lithuanian
loc. locative
Log. Logic

Mach. Machinery
manufact. manufacturing
Math. Mathematics
MDan. Middle Danish
MDut. Middle Dutch
ME Middle English
Mech. Mechanics
Med. Medicine
med. mediaeval
Merc. Mercian
Metal. Metallurgy
Metaph. Metaphysics
Meteor. Meteorology
Mex. Mexican
MF Middle French
MG Middle German
Microsc. Microscopy
Mil. Military
Min. Mineralogy
mistrans. mistranslation
mod. modern
Mus. Music
Myth. Mythology

N North
n. noun
N Am. North American
Nat. Hist. Natural History
Naut. Nautical
Nav. Naval
neg. negative
neol. neologism
neut. neuter
Newsp. Newspaper
nom. nominative
Norm. Norman
North. Northern
Northum. Northumbrian
Norw. Norwegian
NT New Testament
Numis. Numismatics

obj. objective
obs. obsolete
OED the Oxford English Dictionary
OF Old French
OFris. Old Frisian
OHG Old High German
OLG Old Low German
ON Old Norse
ONF Old Norman French
onomat. onomatopoeic
OPers. Old Persian
opp. opposed, opposition
Opt. Optics
orig. origin, originally
Ornith. Ornithology
OS Old Saxon
o.s. old style
OSlav. Old Slavonic
OSp. Old Spanish
OTeut. Old Teutonic

Palaeont. Palaeontology
paral. parallel
Parl. Parliamentary
part. participle, participial
pass. passive
Path. Pathology
perf. perfect

perh.	perhaps	Scand.	Scandinavian
Pers.	Persian	Sci.	Science
pers.	person; personal	Sculp.	Sculpture
Peruv.	Peruvian	Semit.	Semitic
Petrol.	Petrology	Serb.	Serbian
Phil.	Philosophy	Shak.	Shakespeare
Philol.	Philology	Sic.	Sicilian
Phoen.	Phoenician	sing.	singular
phon.	phonetics; phonology	sl.	slang
Phot.	Photography	Slav.	Slavonic
phr.	phrase	Sp.	Spanish
Phys.	Physics	Spens.	Spenser
Phys. Sci.	Physical Science	Stock. Exch.	Stock Exchange
pl.	plural	subj.	subjunctive
poet.	poetry, poetical	suf.	suffix
Pol.	Polish	superl.	superlative
Polit.	Political	Surg.	Surgery
pop.	popular, popularly	Swed.	Swedish
Port.	Portuguese	syl.	syllable
poss.	possessive	Syr.	Syriac
p.p.	past participle		
prec.	the preceding	Teleg.	Telegraphy
pred.	predicatival	Teut.	Teutonic
pref.	prefix	Theat.	Theatre
prep.	preposition	Theol.	Theology
pres.	present	Therap.	Therapeutics
pres.p.	present participle	Therm.	Thermionics
pret.	preterite	tr.	transitive
prev.	previously	trans.	translation
Print.	Printing	Trig.	Trigonometry
priv.	privative	Turk.	Turkish
prob.	probably	TV	Television
pron.	pronoun; pronounced		
prop.	proper, properly	ult.	ultimately
Pros.	Prosody	Univ.	University
Prov.	Provençal	US	United States of America
prov.	provincial		
Psych.	Psychology	usu.	usually
pubd.	published		
		v.	verb
Radiol.	Radiology	var.	variant
redupl.	reduplicate	Venet.	Venetian
ref.	referring, reference	verb.a.	verbal adjective
reflex.	reflexive	Vet.	Veterinary Surgery
rel.	related	v.i.	verb intransitive
Relig.	Religion	viz.	videlicet, namely
rel. pron.	relative pronoun	voc.	vocative
remonstr.	remonstrative	v.t.	verb transitive
Rhet.	Rhetoric		
Rom.	Roman; Romance	W	West; Welsh
Rus.	Russian	WG	West German
		WInd.	West Indian
S	South	wr.	written
Sansk.	Sanskrit		
Sc.	Scottish	Zool.	Zoology

Introduction

THE HISTORY OF THE ENGLISH LANGUAGE

1. **An examination of the European** and some of the Asiatic languages has shown that they can be divided into several groups, the members of which resemble one another because they were derived from the same original tongue. Thus English, with German, Dutch, Norwegian, Danish, etc., belongs to the *Germanic* group of languages. All of these tongues were developed from a primitive language spoken in prehistoric times by the early Germanic tribes. Similarly, French, Italian, Spanish, Portuguese, etc. (called *Romance* languages, because they are derived from the speech of the Romans), are the offspring of Latin, which was one of the Italic family; Irish, Welsh, Scots Gaelic, Manx, and Breton belong to the Celtic group; while Russian, Polish, Serbian, etc., belong to the Slavonic group. Now it is found that not only do the various members of any *one* of these groups of languages exhibit strong resemblances one to another, but that members of *different* groups also show slight marks of kinship: European languages even show likenesses to the languages of India and Persia. These facts have been accounted for by assuming that there existed thousands of years ago a primitive language, called *Indo-European*, which was the common origin of the various groups described above.

2. **The relationship of the various languages** belonging to the Indo-European family is shown by the following (abridged) genealogical tree:

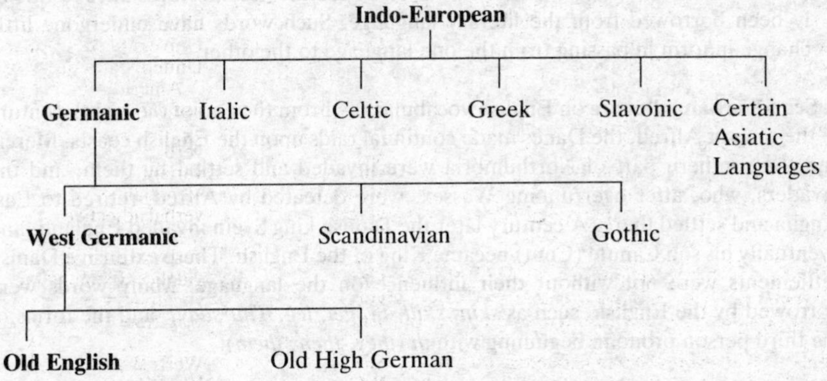

3. **The English language** was brought to this country by the Germanic tribes (Angles, Saxons, and Jutes) who settled here in the fifth and sixth centuries. Old English (i.e., the language spoken in England before the Norman Conquest) differed greatly from our present language in pronunciation, vocabulary, and grammar: in fact, a passage of English written in the time of King Alfred is unintelligible to a modern reader. Old English, like Latin and Greek, had a complicated system of *inflexions*; that is to say, nouns, pronouns, adjectives, verbs, etc., had many different forms according to their grammatical relationship. The vocabulary of the language was almost purely Germanic: very little borrowing from other languages had taken place.

4. **During the last thousand years** English has undergone great changes. Large additions to vocabulary have been made through the influence of invaders who have settled in England (Danes and Normans) and through borrowing from literary sources – especially Latin and Greek. This question of the development of English vocabulary needs detailed treatment.

5. **Latin influence** on English vocabulary. –

(a) Latin began to influence our language while our forefathers were still in their continental homes. The Germanic tribes were in contact with the outposts of Roman civilisation, and borrowed a *few* words, which are still to be found in the different branches of the Germanic group of languages: e.g.–

street (Lat. *strata via*): *cheese* (Lat. *caseum*); *mint* (O.E. *mynet*, Lat. *moneta*).

(b) When the English tribes came to settle in this country, they came in contact with a people (the Britons) that had for long been part of the Roman Empire. It is probable that the educated population of the British towns spoke a form of Latin. Certainly a large number of Latin words were in use among them, and some of these words passed into the language of the new conquerors. Latin borrowings of this period are distinguished by their form, because the Latin spoken in Britain had undergone considerable modification; e.g.–

Chester (Lat. *castra*); *cowl* (O.E. *cugele*, Lat. *cucullus*); *provost* (O.E. *prafost*, Lat. *praepositus*).

(c) In the sixth century, Christianity was reintroduced into this country by Roman missionaries. As the new religion spread, the English language adopted a large number of Latin words to express new ideas connected with the faith; e.g.

Pope (Lat. *papa*), *martyr, mass, monk.*

(d) In later times, especially since the Revival of Learning in the sixteenth century (which led to wide study of Latin and Greek literature), Latin words have frequently been borrowed from the literary language. Such words have undergone little change in form in passing from the one language to the other.

6. **Scandinavian influence** on English vocabulary. – From the end of the eighth century to the time of Alfred, the Danes made continual raids upon the English coasts. Mercia and the southern part of Northumbria were invaded and settled by them, and the invaders, who, after overrunning Wessex, were defeated by Alfred, retired to East Anglia and settled there. A century later the Danish king Svein invaded England, and eventually his son Canute (Cnut) became King of the English. These extensive Danish settlements were not without their influence on the language. Many words were borrowed by the English, such as *skin, skill, ill, get, leg, Thursday,* and the forms of the third person pronoun beginning with *th* (*they, their, them*).

7. **French influence** on English vocabulary. – It is to be noted that French influence is indirectly Latin influence, since the French language is derived from Latin; and also that a very large proportion of English vocabulary is thus, either directly or indirectly, of Latin origin.

(a) After the Norman Conquest the French language, as spoken by the Normans, was the tongue of the ruling classes in this country, and was also used largely by Englishmen. Moreover, from the thirteenth to the fifteenth century much French literature was translated into English. A large number of French words were thus incorporated in our language. Classified examples are –

i. Words for the flesh of animals used for food – *beef, mutton, veal, pork*. (The names of the living animals – *ox, sheep, calf, pig* – are English.)
ii. Words connected with the household – *master, servant, dinner, banquet*.
iii. Words connected with law, government, and property – *court, assize, prison, custom, rent, price*.

iv. Names of titles – *duke, marquis, viscount, baron*.
v. Military terms – *battle, siege, standard, fortress*.
vi. Words for the remoter relationships – *uncle, aunt, nephew, niece, cousin*.

(b) The Norman conquerors of England spoke the French dialect of Normandy and Picardy. When the Angevin dynasty came to the throne of England in the twelfth century, the dialect of central France became the language of the Court, and the incorporation of French words in English continued. Some words were borrowed twice, first from one dialect and then from the other –

catch – chase; warden – guardian; wage – gage.

(c) In the reign of Charles II there was close intimacy between the English and the French courts, and a knowledge of French language and literature was fashionable in England. Many French words thus passed into English, and the process has continued ever since that time –

campaign, memoir, prestige.

8. **Greek influence** on English vocabulary. – The Greek element in the English language is chiefly of modern origin, and is used mainly to express scientific ideas. New words from this source are constantly being introduced because it is very easy to coin words from Greek roots –

telegraph, philology, geology, gramophone, cybernetics.

9. **The effect of the mixed nature of the English vocabulary.** As an instrument of expression, the English language has been enormously improved by its borrowings from other tongues. It surpasses most other languages in its wealth of synonymous words and hence in its power of drawing precise and subtle distinctions. Very often we have a choice between a native English word and a synonym of Latin or French origin –

almighty – omnipotent; blessing – benediction; bloom – flower; calling – vocation; manly – virile; womanly – feminine.

In the course of centuries, many of these originally equivalent terms have acquired slightly divergent meanings, and our means of expression have consequently been increased.

10. **A Glossary of foreign loan-words and phrases.** Terms borrowed from foreign tongues which have gradually become naturalised, losing their identity (and often their original spelling and pronunciation) are now recorded in most English dictionaries as fully-fledged words. There exists however, a wealth of expressions which inhabit a lexical no-man's-land, having a place in current English usage, but without the full status of naturalised words. A glossary of such words appears at the end of this *Introduction*.

11. **The alphabet**. The sounds of spoken language are represented in writing by means of symbols known as the letters of the alphabet. In a perfect alphabet, every letter would be a phonetic symbol representing one sound and one only, and each sound would have its appropriate symbol. Judged by this standard, the English alphabet is obviously defective. We have not enough symbols to represent all the sounds, and hence –

(a) The same symbol may represent many different sounds; e.g. –

"a" in *rat, tall, many, mane, want, bare*.
"o" in *hot, woman, whose, hero, son*.

(b) The same sound may be represented by various symbols; e.g. –

hit, nymph, busy, women, sieve. (All these words contain the vowel sound of *hit*.)
fate, champagne, pail, vein, they, reign, gauge, dahlia, steak. (All these words contain the diphthongal sound of *fate*.)

On the other hand, some letters are superfluous; e.g. –

"q" (*qu* might equally well be written *kw*), "x" (=*ks* or *gs*), "c" (=*k* or *s*).

In pointing out the deficiencies of the English alphabet, we are really calling attention to the fact that modern English spelling is not phonetic; that is, it does not accurately and consistently represent the sounds of speech. The spelling of Old English was very nearly phonetic. How is it, then, that the spelling of to-day is so defective as a symbolic representation of the spoken language?

12. **The history of English spelling.** The answer is, briefly, that modern spelling was fixed in the fifteenth century, and, so far as it represents any pronunciation at all, it represents the pronunciation of that century. Before that time the scribes had observed no uniformity in the matter of spelling, but when printing was invented and books began to multiply, it was found necessary to adhere to some definite system. Thus the early printers produced a system of spelling which has persisted, with few changes, ever since. When it is added that English pronunciation has undergone many and far-reaching changes since Caxton's time, one reason for the lack of correspondence between the written word and the spoken sound will become clear. The symbol *gh* for instance, which is now silent in *sought, bought,* etc., and which, in *laugh, enough,* etc., has the sound of "f", originally represented one and the same sound in all these words. Again, the symbols *ee* in *seed* or *ei* in *receive* in the fifteenth century represented a different sound from that of *ea* in *bead*, though these three symbols now all represent the same sound.

A further reason for the chaotic state of modern English spelling is to be found in the fact that even as early as the fifteenth century there were many anomalies, due largely to French scribes who had introduced symbols from their own language to represent English sounds. This explains the use of *c* for *s* in *city, mice,* etc., *gu* for *g* in *guest, guess,* etc., *qu* for O.E. *cw* in *quick, queen,* etc., and *ou* or *ow* for the diphthongal sound in *house, cow,* etc.

Further confusion resulted from attempts to make the spelling of certain words indicate their etymology. The Norman-French words *dette* and *doute*, for example, retained this spelling when they were first introduced. They were later written *debt* and *doubt* in order to show their connection with the Latin *debitum* and *dubitum*. The *b* has never been pronounced.

A SUMMARY OF SPELLING RULES

I. Plurals of nouns:

(a) In most words add -s: cat, cats.
(b) In words ending in s, x, z, ch, sh (i.e. the sibilants) add -es: bosses, taxes, topazes, churches, bushes, brushes.
(c) After f preceded by a long vowel change f to v: e.g. thief, thieves; wolf, wolves. But *not* after oo: e.g. roofs, hoofs, proofs.
(d) y becomes ies when preceded by a consonant: e.g. lady, ladies; penny, pennies. But y becomes ys when preceded by a vowel: e.g. boy, boys; donkey, donkeys; holiday, holidays.
(e) Words ending in o take -es:
e.g. potatoes, tomatoes, heroes, echoes.
But a few take just -s:
e.g. pianos, dynamos, cantos, sopranos.
(f) Some words have the same form in the singular and plural:
sheep, deer, grouse, swine, salmon, trout, etc.
(g) Some words have a plural form but take a singular verb: news, mathematics, statistics, means, politics, innings
e.g. The news is bad; he played a good innings; politics is in his blood.

2. The doubling of the final consonant of some words can be decided by the position of the stress:

(a) Words ending in VOWEL plus CONSONANT double the final consonant when the stress falls on the end of the word.
e.g. transfér transférred or transférring;
begín, begínning, begínner;
occúr, occúrring, occúrred.
(b) All words of one syllable ending in VOWEL plus CONSONANT observe this rule, since the stress is bound to fall on them:
e.g. rot, rotten, rotter, rotting;
stop, stopper, stopping, stopped;
sob, sobbing, sobbed.
(c) In words where the stress does not fall on the final VOWEL PLUS CONSONANT, do not double the final consonant:
e.g. rívet, ríveted, ríveting;
díffer, díffered, díffering.
Note however the exception: worship, worshipped, worshipping.

3. When the last syllable ends in a VOWEL PLUS L the final 'l' is doubled, wherever the stress:

travel, traveller, travelling, travelled;
level, levelling, levelled;
control, controlling, controlled, controller.
Note the exception in: paralleled.

4. Words ending in mute (silent) e:

(a) In words ending in e, drop the e coming before a vowel:
e.g. give, giving; love, lovable.
But retain the e before a consonant:

e.g. care, careful; love, lovely.

Note exceptions: true, truly; whole, wholly; nine, ninth; argue, argument.

(b) Retain the e in words ending in -ce or -ge before a, o, u:

e.g. change, changeable; courage, courageous;
peace, peaceable; notice, noticeable.

5. Words beginning or ending in -all, -ful, -fil, or beginning in well, in such words drop one -l when combined with another word:

e.g. almost, already, faithful, doubtful, skilful, fulfil, welcome.

6. Words spelt with -ie with the sound *ee* (*see*). In words spelt with *ie* sounded as *ee* in 'see', put i before e except after c:

e.g. belief, chief, *but* receive, ceiling.

Note however: seize, weird, weir, counterfeit. In words like *ancient, either, their, foreign,* the sound is not like *ee*.

WORDS COMMONLY MIS-SPELT

absence
accident
accommodation
achieve
acknowledgement (*or* -gment)
acquiesce
address
adviser
advisory
aggravate
agreeable
all right
already
altogether (*totally*)
ancillary
anxiety
apologise (*or* -ize)
argument
ascend
ascension
ascendancy (*or* -ency)
atrophy
auxiliary
awful

bachelor
beginning
beige
believe
benefit, benefited
bureau
bureaucracy
business

calendar
cancel, cancelled
cannon (*gun*)
canon (*law, church*)
category
ceiling
chaos
college
commitment
committee
comparison
competence (*competency*)
complement (*completion*)
compliment (*flattery*)
conscientious
consciousness
correspondence
courteous
courtesy
credible
currant (*fruit*)
current (*electric*)

deceit
defer, deferred
difficult
definite
despatch (dispatch)
desperate
differ, differed
disastrous
discipline
disseminate
doubt
draft (*rough note*)
draught (*drink*)

eighth
embarrass
equip, equipped
especially
essential
exhaustion
extrovert (extravert)
existence

familiar
favour
favourable
February
fictitious
financial
financier
forty
fulfil, fulfilled

gauge
grammar
gramophone
guardian
guerrilla
guild

harass
height
honorary
humour
humorous
hungrily
hurriedly
hygiene
hypothesis

immediately
immigrant
independent
influential
install
instil, instilled
intelligible
interfere
introvert

jeopardy
jewel, jewelled
jewellery (*or* jewelry)
judgement (*or* judgment)

kaleidoscope
knack
knobbly
knowledgeable

labour
laborious
laundry
legible
leisurely
level, levelled
livelihood
luscious

manoeuvre
marriage
medicine
Mediterranean
meridional
miniature
minutia (*pl.* -iae)
moustache
movable
movement
myxomatosis

necessary
niece
nought
nutritious

occasionally
occur, occurred
offer, offerred
omit, omitted
omission

parallel
paralleled
parliament
planning
pleasant
practice (*noun*)
(to) practise (*verb*)
preceding
privilege
proceeding
professor
proficient
pronunciation
proprietor
proprietary
psychiatrist

pusillanimous

queue
quiet
quotient

recommend
refer, referred
repetition
replaceable
replacement
resuscitation
rheumatism
rhinoceros
rhododendron

sanctuary
scarcely
scholastic
seize
separate
sincerely
skilful
successful
summary
supersede
synonym

tendentious
tenterhooks
thoroughfare
transfer, transferred
truly
twelfth

unconscionable
unctious
unmistakable
unparalleled
until
unwieldy

vaccination
valuable
vigour
vigorous

Wednesday
wholly
woollen
worship, worshipped
wreathe (*verb*)
wring

yeoman

zoology
zoological

COMMON PREFIXES AND SUFFIXES

PREFIXES

a-, an- not, without *asexual*.
aero- aircraft *aerodrome*; air *aerobic*.
agro- agriculture *agrobiology*.
ambi- two, both *ambidextrous*.
Anglo- English, British *Anglo-Catholic*.
ante- before *antenatal*.
anthropo- human being *anthropology*.
anti- against, opposite, opposing *anti-establishment*.
arch- chief, highest *archbishop*.
astro- star *astrophysics*.
audio- sound, hearing *audiovisual*.
auto- self, oneself *autobiography*; automatic *autopilot*; automotive, automobile *autocross*.
bi- two, twice *bicycle*.
biblio- book *bibliophile*.
bio- life, living material *biology*.
by(e)- secondary *by-product*.
cardi(o)- heart *cardiovascular*.
centi- hundred *centipede*; hundredth part *centimetre*.
chron(o)- time *chronology*.
circum- round *circumnavigate*.
co- together *cooperate*.
con-, col-, com-, cor- with, together *conjoin*.
contra- against *contraception*.
counter- against, opposite *counter-clockwise*; matching *counterpart*.
crypto- secret, hidden *cryptofascist*.
cyclo- circle *cyclorama*.
de- to do the opposite *decentralize*; to remove *deseed*; to make less *devalue*.
deca- ten *decathlon*.
deci- tenth part *decilitre*.
demi- half, part *demigod*.
derm- skin *dermatitis*.
di- two, double *dioxide*.
dis- opposite, not *dishonest*; to remove *dismember*.
electro- electricity, electrical *electromagnetic*.
en-, em- to cause to be *enlarge*; to put in or on *endanger*.
equi- equal *equidistant*.
Eur(o)- European *Eurasian*; European Economic Community *Eurocurrency*.
ex- former *ex-president*.
extra- beyond, outside *extraterrestrial*.
fore- before *foretell*; front, front part *foreleg*.
geo- earth *geography*.
gyn(o)-, gynaec(o)- female, woman *gynaecology*.
haem(o)- blood *haemorrhage*.
hemi- half hemisphere.
hetero- different, other *heterosexual*.
hex(a)- six *hexagram*.
hol(o)- complete, whole *holistic*.
homo- same, alike *homogeneous*.
hydro- water *hydroelectric*; hydrogen *hydrochloric*.
hyper- more than normal, excessive *hyperactive*.
hypo- less than normal, low, too low *hypothermia*.
in-, il-, im-, ir- not *insensitive*.
infra- below, beneath *infrared*.
inter- between *intercity*.
intra- in, within *intravenous*.
iso- equal, uniform, the same *isobar*.
kilo- thousand *kilogram*.
macro- large, large-scale *macroclimate*.
mal- bad, badly *malnutrition*.
matri- mother *matriarch*.
mega- million *megaton*; large, extremely large *megalith*.
micro- small, small-scale *microcomputer*.
milli- thousandth part *millilitre*.
mini- small *mini-skirt*.
mis- bad, badly *misbehave*; not *mistrust*.
mono- single, one *monoplane*.
multi- many, several *multiracial*.
neo- new, recent *neo-Georgian*.
neuro- nerve, nervous system *neuroscience*.
non- not *nonsmoker*.
oct-, octa-, octo- eight *octopus*.
omni- all *omnivore*.
osteo- bone *osteoarthritis*.
out- beyond, exceeding, surpassing *outlive*; forth *outpouring*; outside, external *outlying*.
over- above *overlord*; outer *overcoat*; too much *overeat*.
paed(o)- child, *paediatrician*.
palaeo- old, archaic, early *Palaeolithic*.
pan- all *pan-American*.
para- beside *parallel*; beyond *paranormal*; abnormal *paranoia*; resembling *paratyphoid*; associated, supplementary *paramedical*.
patri- father *patriarch*.
pent(a)- five *pentagon*.
photo- light *photosensitive*; photography *photocopy*.
physi(o)- nature, living things *physiology*; physical *physiotherapy*.
poly- many *polyglot*.
post- after *postdate*.
pre- before *prehistoric*.
pro- favouring *pro-American*; substitute for *pro-consul*.
prot(o)- first, original *prototype*.
pseud(o)- false *pseudonym*.
psych(o)- mind *psychoanalysis*.
quadr(i)- four *quadruped*.
quasi- partly, seemingly *quasi-judicial*.
radio- radiation *radiology*; radioactive, radioactivity *radioisotope*.
re- again *rewrite*.
retro- back, backwards *retrogress*.
self- oneself, itself *self-discipline*.
semi- half *semicircle*; partly *semi-conscious*.
socio- social, society *sociology*.
step- related by remarriage *stepsister*.
sub- below, under *subsoil*; less than, incompletely *subhuman*; subordinate, subdivision *subcontinent*.
super- above, greater, exceeding, more, superior *superpower*.
syn-, sym- together, with *synthesis*.
techno- technology, technical *technocracy*.
tele- over a distance *telecommunications*.

tetra- four *tetrahedron*.
theo- gods, God *theology*.
thermo- heat *thermometer*.
trans- across *transatlantic*.
tri- three *triangle*.
ultra- above, beyond *ultraviolet*.
un- not *unhappy*; to do the opposite *unknot*.
under- below, underneath *underpass*; insufficient *underfunding*; less important *undersecretary*.
uni- one *unicycle*.
vice- one next below *vice-president*.

SUFFIXES

-able,- ible that can be *washable*; having the quality of *comfortable*. **-ability, -ibility.**
-ade fruit drink *lemonade*.
-aholic, -oholic (one) addicted to *workaholic*.
-ana, -iana objects etc. belonging to *Victoriana*.
-arch ruler, leader, governor *monarch*. **-archy.**
-arian believer in, supporter of *vegetarian*; one connected with *librarian*.
-athon, -thon large-scale contest or event *swimathon*.
-cide killing, killer *fungicide*. **-cidal.**
-cracy government, rule *democracy*; dominant or ruling class *aristocracy*.
-crat supporter of (the type of government) *democrat*; member of (a dominant class) *aristocrat*. **-cratic.**
-dom state or condition of being *boredom*; realm, domain *kingdom*.
-ectomy surgical removal *mastectomy*.
-ee one to whom something is done *payee*; one who is *absentee*; small version of *bootee*.
-eer one engaged in *profiteer*.
-er one who or that which does or is *employer*; one engaged in *lawyer*; one coming from *Londoner*.
-ese (people or language) of or from *Chinese*; language associated with *journalese*.
-esque in the style of *statuesque*.
-ess female *lioness*.
-ette small version of *kitchenette*; female *majorette*; imitation *satinette*.
-fold times *two-fold*.
-form having the form of *cruciform*.
-free without *lead-free*.
-friendly helpful to, supporting *user-friendly*.
-ful amount that fills something *bucketful*; full of *colourful*; having or causing *peaceful*.
-fy -IFY.
-gram drawn or written record *cardiogram*; message, greeting *kissogram*.
-graph instrument that records *seismograph*; something recorded or represented *autograph*. **-graphic. -graphy.**
-hood time or condition of being *childhood*.
-iana -ANA.
-ible, -ibility -ABLE.
-ics science, study *electronics*.
-ify to make or become *purity*; to fill with *terrify*.
-ise -IZE.
-ish like, similar to *childish*; somewhat *baldish*.
-ism state, condition *heroism*; doctrine, movement, system, theory *Buddhism*; discrimination on ground of *racism*.
-ist follower or practitioner of a doctrine, science etc. *botanist*.
-ite (person) of or from, or that adheres to or supports *Israelite*; mineral *calcite*.
-itis disease *bronchitis*.
-ize, -ise to make or become *neutralize*.
-kin small version of *lambkin*.
-latry worship *idolatry*.
-less without *harmless*.
-let small version of *piglet*.
-like resembling *ladylike*.
-ling small, young, or lesser version of *duckling*.
-logy science, theory *biology*; writing, treatise *trilogy*. **-logist.**
-meter instrument for measuring *barometer*.
-monger dealer in *fishmonger*.
-nik one connected with *beatnik*.
-oholic -AHOLIC.
-oid like, resembling *planetoid*.
-ology, -ologist -LOGY.
-or -ER.
-osis action, process *metamorphosis*; diseased condition *thrombosis*.
-ped foot *quadruped*. **-pedal.**
-phile, -phil lover of *Anglophile*. **-philia** love of, attraction or tendency towards *necrophilia*. **-philiac.**
-phobe one who hates or fears *xenophobe*. **-phobia** hatred or fear of *claustrophobia*. **-phobic.**
-phone speaker of (a language) *Francophone*; sound *xylophone*.
-proof resisting, protecting against *heatproof*.
-scape view, scene *landscape*.
-scope instrument for viewing *microscope*. **-scopy.**
-ship condition, state, position *membership*; skill *craftsmanship*.
-some characterized by, full of *troublesome*; group of so many *foursome*.
-speak language, jargon *computerspeak*.
-thon -ATHON.
-tomy surgical incision *lobotomy*.
-ward, -wards towards *upward*.
-ware articles *silverware*.
-ways in the direction, manner, or position of *sideways*.
-wise in the direction, manner, or position of *clockwise*; concerning *money-wise*.
-y having, full of, covered with *dirty*; inclined to *sleepy*; like *wintry*; affectionate term used esp. with children *doggy*.

ENGLISH IRREGULAR VERBS

* = *obsolete*. *A = *obsolete, but still used adjectivally*. † = *becoming obsolete*. R = *rare*. S = *slang*.

Infinitive	Past Tense	Past Participle
abide	abode	abode
arise	arose	arisen
awake	awoke *awaked	awoke *or* awaked
be *Pres. Indic.* am art is are	was were	been
bear	bore *bare	borne *or* born
beat	beat	beaten
become	became	become
befall	befell	befallen
beget	begot *begat	begotten
begin	began	begun
behold	beheld	beheld
bend	bent *bended	bent *A bended
bereave	bereaved *or* bereft	bereaved *or* bereft
beseech	besought R beseeched	besought R beseeched
bestride	bestrode *bestrid	bestridden *bestrid
bid	bade †bid	bidden *bid
bide	bode *or* bided	bided
bind	bound	bound *A bounden
bite	bit	bitten
bleed	bled	bled
blow	blew	blown S blowed
break	broke *brake	broken
breed	bred	bred
bring	brought	brought
build	built *builded	built *builded
burn	burnt *or* burned	burnt *or* burned
burst	burst	burst
buy	bought	bought
Pres. Indic. can	could	—
cast	cast	cast
catch	caught	caught
chide	chid	chidden *chid
choose	chose	chosen
cleave (*v.t.* to split)	cleft *clove	cleft *A cloven
cleave (*v.i.* to cling)	cleaved *clave	cleaved
cling	clung	clung
clothe	clothed †clad	clothed †clad
come	came	come
cost	cost	cost
creep	crept	crept
crow	crowed *or* †crew	crowed
cut	cut	cut
dare	dared *durst	dared
deal	dealt *dealed	dealt *dealed
dig	dug **digged*	dug **digged*
do	did	done
draw	drew	drawn
dream	dreamt *or* dreamed	dreamt *or* dreamed
drink	drank *drunk	drunk *A drunken
drive	drove	driven
dwell	dwelt	dwelt *dwelled
eat	ate	eaten
fall	fell	fallen
feed	fed	fed
feel	felt	felt
fight	fought	fought
find	found	found
flee	fled	fled
fling	flung	flung

Infinitive	Past Tense	Past Participle
fly	flew	flown
forbear	forbore	forborne
forbid	forbade *or* forbad	forbidden *forbid
foresee	foresaw	foreseen
forget	forgot	forgotten *forgot
forgive	forgave	forgiven
forsake	forsook	forsaken
freeze	froze	frozen
geld	gelded *or* gelt	gelded *or* gelt
get	got *gat	got *or* gotten
gild	gilt	gilt
gird	girded *or* girt	girded *or* girt
give	gave	given
go	went	gone
grind	ground	ground
grow	grew	grown
hang	hung	hung
have hast has	had	had
hear	heard	heard
heave	heaved *or* *hove	heaved *hove
hew	hewed	hewn *or* hewed
hide	hid	hidden *hid
hit	hit	hit
hold	held	held
hurt	hurt	hurt
keep	kept	kept
kneel	knelt *kneeled	knelt *kneeled
knit	knitted *or* knit	knitted *or* knit
know	knew	known
lade	laded	laded *or* †laden
lay	laid	laid
lead	led	led
lean	leant *or* leaned	leant *or* leaned
leap	leapt *or* leaped	leapt *or* leaped
learn	learnt *or* †learned	learnt *or* †learned
leave	left	left
lend	lent	lent
let	let	let
lie	lay	lain
light	lit *or* lighted	lit *or* lighted
lose	lost	lost
make	made	made
Pres. Indic. may	might	—
mean	meant	meant
meet	met	met
melt	melted	melted *A molten
mistake	mistook	mistaken
mow	mowed	mowed *or* mown
Pres. Indic. must	—	—
pay	paid	paid
pen	penned *or* pent	penned *or* pent
put	put	put
quit	quitted *or* quit	quitted *or* quit
—	*quoth	—
read	read	read
rend	rent	rent
rid	rid	rid
ride	rode	ridden *rode
ring	rang	rung
rise	rose	risen
rive	rived	riven *or* rived
run	ran	run

Infinitive	Past Tense	Past Participle
saw	sawed	sawn R sawed
say	said	said
see	saw	seen
seek	sought	sought
sell	sold	sold
send	sent	sent
set	set	set
shake	shook	shaken *shook
Pres. Indic. shall	should	—
shape	shaped	shaped *shapen
shave	shaved	shaved *A shaven
shear	sheared *shore	sheared *A shorn
shed	shed	shed
shew	shewed	shewn *or* shewed
shine	shone	shone
shoe	shod	shod
shoot	shot	shot
show	showed	shown *or* showed
shrink	shrank *or* shrunk	shrunk *A shrunken
shrive	shrove	shriven
shut	shut	shut
sing	sang †sung	sung
sink	sank †sunk	sunk *A sunken
sit	sat *sate	sat *sate
slay	slew	slain
sleep	slept	slept
slide	slid	slid
sling	slung	slung
slink	slunk *slank	slunk
slit	slit	slit
smell	smelt *or* smelled	smelt *or* smelled
smite	smote	smitten
sow	sowed	sown *or* sowed
speak	spoke *spake	spoken
speed	sped *or* speeded	sped *or* speeded
spell	spelt *or* spelled	spelt *or* spelled
spend	spent	spent
spill	spilt *or* spilled	spilt *or* spilled
spin	spun	spun
spit	spat †spit	spat †spit
split	split	split
spoil	spoilt *or* spoiled	spoilt *or* spoiled
spread	spread	spread
spring	sprang R sprung	sprung
stand	stood	stood
stave	staved *or* stove	staved *or* stove
steal	stole	stolen
stick	stuck	stuck
sting	stung	stung
stink	stank	stunk
strew	strewed	strewed *A strewn
stride	strode	stridden
strike	struck	struck *A stricken
string	strung	strung
strive	strove	striven *strove
*strow	*strowed	*strown *or* *strowed
swear	swore	sworn
sweep	swept	swept
swell	swelled	swollen *or* swelled
swim	swam	swum
swing	swung	swung
take	took	taken
teach	taught	taught
tear	tore	torn
tell	told	told
think	thought	thought
thrive	thrive *or* throve	thrived *or* thriven
throw	threw	thrown
thrust	thrust	thrust

Infinitive	Past Tense	Past Participle
tread	trod	trodden
understand	understood	understood
undo	undid	undone
upset	upset	upset
wake	woke *or* waked	waked *or* woken
wax	waxed	waxed *waxen
wear	wore	worn
weave	wove R weaved	woven *A wove
weep	wept	wept
wet	wetted *or* wet	wetted *or* wet
will	would	—
win	won	won
wind	wound	wound
withdraw	withdrew	withdrawn
withstand	withstood	withstood
work	worked *or* wrought	worked *or* wrought
wring	wrung	wrung
write	wrote	written

A GLOSSARY OF FOREIGN LOAN-WORDS AND PHRASES

à bas [F.]. Down! down with!
ab initio [L.]. From the beginning.
ab ovo [L.]. From the egg, from beginning.
ad astra [L.]. To the stars.
à demi [F.]. By halves.
ad hoc [L.]. For this particular purpose, specially.
ad infinitum [L.]. To infinity.
ad nauseam [L.] So as to disgust or nauseate.
ad rem [L.]. To the point.
advocatus diaboli [L.]. The devil's advocate.
affaire d'honneur [F.]. An affair of honour, a duel.
à fond [F.]. To the bottom, thoroughly.
à jamais [F.]. For ever.
à la [F.]. According to; in the style of.
à la carte [F.]. By the bill of fare.
à la mode [F.]. In fashion.
al fresco [It.]. In the open air.
allons! [F.]. Come, let us be off!
Alma Mater [L., fostering mother]. One's school, college, or university.
alter ego [L.]. One's second self.
alter idem [L.]. Another exactly similar.
amende honorable [F.]. Public apology, public amends.
à merveille [F.]. Admirably, perfectly.
amicus curiæ [L.]. A friend of the court, an adviser with no personal interest.
amour-propre [F.]. Self-esteem, vanity.
anno Domini [L.]. In the year of our Lord.
anno mundi [L.]. In the year of the world.
annus mirabilis [L.]. A year of wonders.
ante bellum [L.]. Before the war.
ante meridiem [L.]. Before noon.
à outrance [F.]. To the end, to extremities.
à pied [F.]. On foot.
à plaisir [F.]. At pleasure, at will.
a posteriori [L.]. From effect to cause; inductive.
a priori [L.]. From cause to effect; deductive.
Arcades ambo [L.]. Two of similar tastes, etc.
argumentum ad hominem [L.]. An appeal to personal interests, etc.
ars est celare artem [L.]. The art is to conceal art.
ars longa, vita brevis [L.]. Art is long, life short.
artium magister [L.]. Master of Arts.
assez bien [F.]. Moderately well.
à tout prix [F.]. At any price.
à travers [F.]. Across, through.
au contraire [F.]. On the contrary.
au courant de [F.]. Fully informed about.
au fait [F.]. Familiar, well-acquainted with.
au fond [F.]. At bottom.
au gratin [F.]. (Cooked) with bread-crumbs or grated cheese.
au naturel [F.]. In its natural state.
au pied de la lettre [F.]. Literally, precisely.
au revoir [F.]. Till we meet again.
au sérieux [F.]. Seriously.
aux armes! [F.]. To arms!
avant-propos [F.]. Preface, preliminary remarks.
à votre santé! [F.]. To your health!

Bachelier ès lettres, sciences [F.]. Bachelor of Letters, of Science.
ballon d'essai [F.]. A feeler.
beaux esprits [F.]. Men of wit.
beaux yeux [F.]. Fine eyes, good looks.
bel esprit [F.]. A brilliant mind, man of parts.
ben trovato [It.]. Well invented.
ben venuto [It.]. Welcome.
bête noire [F.]. A bugbear, one's aversion.
bien aimé [F.]. (*fem.* aimée) Well-beloved.
bien entendu [F.]. To be sure, of course.
blague [F.]. Humbug.
bona fide [L.]. In good faith.
bonjour [F.]. Good day.
bon marché [F.]. A cheap shop; a bargain.
bon mot [F.]. A witty saying.
bonne-bouche [F.]. A dainty morsel.
bon soir [F.]. Good evening.
bon ton [F.]. Fashion, good style.
bon vivant [F.]. One fond of good living.
bon voyage [F.]. A pleasant journey, farewell.

çà ira [F.]. That will go, that's the thing.
canaille [F.]. The rabble.
carpe diem [L.]. Enjoy the day, seize the present opportunity, improve the time.
casus belli [L.]. A ground of war.
cause célèbre [F.]. A notable case or trial.
cela va sans dire [F.]. That goes without saying.
ce n'est que le premier pas qui coûte [F.]. It is only the first step that is troublesome.
c'est-à-dire [F.]. That is to say.
ceteris paribus [L.]. Other things being equal.
chacun à son goût [F.]. Every one to his taste.
chef-d'œuvre [F.]. A masterpiece.
chemin de fer [F.]. A railway.
cherchez la femme [F.]. Look for the woman, there's a woman at the bottom of it.
che sarà, sarà [It.]. What will be, will be.
ci-devant [F.]. Formerly, of a past time.
circa [L.]. About.
cogito, ergo sum [L.]. I think, therefore I exist.
comme il faut [F.]. As it should be, correct.
communiqué [F.]. An official report.
compos mentis [L.]. Sound of mind.
compte rendue [F.]. An official report.
con amore [It.]. With affection, with zeal.
con spirito [It.]. With animation.
consummatum est [L.]. It is finished.
corpus delicti [L.]. The substance of the offence.
coup de grâce [F.]. A finishing stroke.
coup de main [F.]. A sudden attack, enterprise, or undertaking.
coup d'état [F.]. A stroke of policy; a sudden, esp. unconstitutional, change of government.
coup d'œil [F.]. A rapid glance.
coûte que coûte [F.]. Cost what it may.
crème de la crème [F.]. The very best.
cui bonop [L.]. For whose advantage?
cum privilegio [L.]. With privilege.

d'accord [F.]. Agreed; in time.
dame d'honneur [F.]. A maid of honour.

de bonne grâce [F.]. With good will, willingly.
de die in diem [L.]. From day to day.
de facto [L.]. In reality, actually.
défense de fumer [F.]. Smoking not allowed.
de gustibus non est disputandum [L.]. There is no disputing about tastes.
Dei gratia [L.]. By the grace of God.
déjeuner à la fourchette [F.]. Luncheon.
de jure [L.]. By right.
de luxa [F.]. Luxurious.
Deo gratias [L.]. Thanks be to God.
Deo volente [L.]. God willing.
de profundis [L.]. Out of the depths.
de rigueur [F.]. According to strict etiquette.
dernier ressort [F.]. A last resource.
de trop [F.]. Superfluous, not wanted.
deus ex machina [L.]. A god from the machine (in the Gr. theatre) a romantic *dénouement*.
dies iræ [L.]. The Day of Judgment.
Dieu et mon droit [F.]. God and my right.
Dieu vous garde! [F.]. God protect you!
divide et impera [L.]. Divide and govern.
dolce far niente [It.]. Sweet idleness.
Domine, dirige nos [L.]. O Lord direct us (the motto of the City of London).
Dominus illuminatio mea [L.]. The Lord is my light (the motto of Oxford Univ.).
Dominus vobiscum [L.]. The Lord be with you.
dulce et decorum est pro patria mori [L.]. It is sweet and glorious to die for one's country.
dum spiro, spero [L.]. While I breathe, I hope.

ecce homo [L.]. Behold the man!
ecce signum [L.]. Behold the proof.
édition de luxe [F.]. A sumptuous edition.
embarras de richesse [F.]. A superfluity of anything wanted or desirable.
en arrière [F.]. In the rear, behind.
en avant [F.]. Forward.
en bloc [F.]. In the mass.
en déshabillé [F.]. In undress; in one's true colours.
en effet [F.]. Substantially, in effect.
en famille [F.]. With one's family, at home.
enfant terrible [F.]. A precocious youngster.
en fête [F.]. In festivity.
en garçon [F.]. As a bachelor.
en grand tenue [F.]. In full dress.
en masse [F.]. In a body.
en passant [F.]. By the way.
en rapport [F.]. In sympathy with.
en règle [F.]. In order, as it should be.
en revanche [F.]. In return, as compensation.
en route [F.]. On the way.
en suite [F.]. In a set, in succession.
entente cordiale [F.]. A good understanding.
entre nous [F.]. Between ourselves, in confidence.
e pluribus unum [L.]. One out of or composed of many. (Motto of the U.S.A.).
esprit de corps [F.]. Animating spirit of a collective body; pride in one's school, regiment, etc.
et tu Brute! [L.]. And thou too Brutus (the last words of Caesar).
ex cathedra [L.]. From the chair, with authority.
ex gratia [L.]. As an act of favour.
ex nihilo nihil fit [L.]. Out of nothing, nothing comes.
ex òfficio [L.]. By virtue of one's office.
ex post facto [L.]. After the deed is done.

façon de parler [F.]. Manner of speaking.
factum est [L.]. It is done.
fait accompli [F.]. An accomplished fact.
far niente [It.]. Doing nothing.
faute de mieux [F.]. In default of something better.
faux pas [F.]. A blunder, a slip.
fecit [L.]. He (or she) made or drew it.
flat lux [L.]. Let there be light.
fidei defensor [L.]. Defender of the faith.
fille de chambre [F.]. A chamber-maid.
floreat [L.]. May (it) flourish.
force majeure [F.]. Superior power, circumstances not under one's control.

garde du corps [F.]. A body-guard.
gardez bien [F.]. Take good care, be careful.
gens d'affaires [F.]. Business people.
gens de lettres [F.]. Literary men.
gloria in excelsis Deo [L.]. Glory to God in the highest.
gloria Patri [L.]. Glory be to the Father.
grâce à Dieu [F.]. Thanks be to God.
grande passion [F.]. A serious love-affair.

Heimweh [G.]. Home-sickness.
homme de bien [F.]. A man of worth.
homme d'esprit [F.]. A wit, a genius.
homo sum; humani nihil a me alienum puto [L.]. I am a man, and I consider nothing that concerns mankind a matter of indifference.
honi soit qui mal y pense [F.]. Shame be to him who thinks evil of it (motto of the Order of the Garter).
honoris causa or **gratia** [L.]. For the sake of honour, honorary.
hors concours [F.]. Not for competition.
hors de combat [F.]. Disabled.
humanum est errare [L.]. To err is human.

ich dien [G.]. I serve (Prince of Wales's motto).
idée fixe [F.]. A fixed idea, monomania.
il n'y a pas de quoi [F.]. There is no need, don't mention it.
il va sans dire [F.]. It goes without saying.
in æternum [L.]. For ever.
in articulo mortis [L.]. At the moment of death.
in camera [L.]. In the judge's chamber, not in open court.
inconnu [F.]. (*fem.* -nue) Unknown.
in curia [L.]. In open court.
in Deo speravi [L.]. In God have I trusted.
in esse [L.]. In actual being.
in excelsis [L.]. In the highest.
in extremis [L.]. At the point of death.
in flagrante delicto [L.]. In the very act.
infra dignitatem (infra dig.) [L.]. Beneath one's dignity.
in hoc signo vinces [L.]. By this sign thou shalt conquer (motto of Constantine the Great).
in infinitum [L.]. For ever.
in initio [L.]. In the beginning.
in loco parentis [L.]. In the place of a parent.
in medias res [L.]. Into the very midst of the business.

in memoriam [L.]. To the memory of.
in nomine [L.]. In the name (of).
in pace [L.]. In peace.
in propria persona [L.]. In one's own person.
in puris naturalibus [L.]. In a state of nature; naked.
in re [L.]. In the matter of.
in sæcula sæculorum [L.]. For ever and ever.
in situ [L.]. In (its original or proper) position.
in tenebris [L.]. In the dark, in doubt.
inter alia [L.]. Among other things.
in toto [L.]. Entirely.
in vacuo [L.]. In a vacuum, in empty space.
in vino veritas [L.]. Drunkenness makes a man let out the truth.
ipso facto [L.]. By the fact itself.

jacta alea est [L.]. The die is cast.
je ne sais quoi [F.]. I know not what, something indefinable.
je suis prêt [F.]. I am ready.
jeune premier [F.]. A stage lover.
jeunesse dorée [F.]. The gilded youth.
jubilate Deo [L.]. Oh be joyful in the Lord.

labor omnia vincit [L.]. Labour overcomes all difficulties.
lasciate ogni speranza, voi ch' entrate [It.]. All hope abandon ye who enter here.
le beau monde [F.]. The world of fashion, society.
les convenances [F.]. The proprieties.
l'État, c'est moi [F.]. The State! I am the State.
le tout ensemble [F.]. The general effect.
l'homme propose et Dieu dispose [F.]. Man proposes and God disposes.
l'inconnu [F.]. The unknown.
lux mundi [L.]. The light of the world.

magnum bonum [L.]. A great good.
magnum opus [L.]. A great undertaking, the great work of a man's life.
maître d'hôtel [F.]. A house steward; head waiter.
mal à propos [F.]. Unseasonably.
mala fide [L.]. In bad faith, treacherously.
mal de mer [F.]. Sea-sickness.
mal entendu [F.]. Misunderstood.
manu forti [L.]. With the strong hand.
manu propria [L.]. With one's own hand.
mardi gras [F.]. Shrove Tuesday.
marque de fabrique [F.]. A trade-mark.
mauvaise honte [F.]. False shame.
mauvais sujet [F.]. A worthless fellow.
mauvais ton [F.]. Bad style.
mea culpa [L.]. By my fault.
mens sana in corpore sano [L.]. A sound mind in a sound body.
mon Dieu! [F.]. Good heavens! gracious!
moyen age [F.]. The Middle Ages.
multum in parvo [L.]. Much in little.
mutatis mutandis [L.]. The necessary changes being made.

ne plus ultra [L.]. Nothing further; perfection.
nil desperandum [L.]. Never despair.
n'importe [F.]. It is of no consequence.
noblesse oblige [F.]. Rank imposes obligations.
non compos mentis [L.]. Not of sound mind, mentally deranged, lunatic.
non mi ricordo [It.]. I do not remember.
non sequitur [L., it does not follow]. An illogical inference; an irrelevant conclusion.
nota bene [L.]. Note well.
nous avons changé tout cela [F.]. We have changed all that.
nous verrons [F.]. We shall see.
nouveau riche [F.]. (*pl.* nouveaux riches) A newly-rich man, a parvenu.
nulli secundus [L.]. Second to none.

œuvres [F.]. Works.
omnia mutantur, nos et mutamur in illis [L.]. All things are subject to change, and we change with them.
omnia vincit amor [L.]. Love conquers all things.
onus probandi [L.]. The burden of proving.
ora e sempre [It.]. Now and always.
ora et labora [L.]. Pray and work.
ora pro nobis [L.]. Pray for us.
orate pro anima [L.]. Pray for the soul (of).
O tempora! O mores! [L.]. Alas for the times and the manners!

parbleu! [F.]. An exclamation of surprise, etc.
par excellence [F.]. Pre-eminently.
par exemple [F.]. For instance.
pari passu [L.]. At the same rate or pace.
parole d'honneur [F.]. Word of honour.
pas de deux [F.]. A dance for two.
pas possible! [F.]. Impossible!
pas seul [F.]. A dance for one person.
pax Romana [L.]. The peace of the Roman Empire.
pax vobiscum [L.]. Peace be with you.
per aspera ad astra [L.]. Through rough ways to the stars; through suffering to renown.
per contra [L.]. On the contrary.
per mensem [L.]. Monthly.
per saltum [L.]. At a leap.
per se [L.]. By itself.
persona grata [L.]. An acceptable person.
pièce de résistance [F.]. The most substantial dish at a meal.
pied-à-terre [F.]. A footing, a temporary lodging.
pis aller [F.]. A makeshift.
plein air [F.]. The open air.
post obitum [L.]. After death.
pour ainsi dire [F.]. So to speak.
pour encourager les autres [F.]. To encourage the others.
pour faire rire [F.]. To raise a laugh.
preux chevalier [F.]. A brave knight.
prima facie [L.]. At first sight.
primus inter pares [L.]. First among equals.
pro bono publico [L.]. For the public good.
pro forma [L.]. As a matter of form.
pro patria et rege [L.]. For country and king.
pro rata [L.]. In proportion.
pro tanto [L.]. For so much, to that extent.
pro tempore [L.]. For the time being.

quelque chose [F.]. Something; a trifle.
que voulez-vous? [F.]. What would you have?
quid pro quo [L.]. Something in return.
qu'importe? [F.]. What does it matter?
qui s'excuse, s'accuse [F.]. He who excuses himself accuses himself.

qui va là? [F.]. Who goes there?
quod dixi, dixi [L.]. What I have said, I have said.
quod erat demonstrandum (Q.E.D.) [L.]. Which was to be proved.
quod vide (q.v.) [L.]. Which (thing) see.
quo jure? [L.]. By what right?
quo modo? [L.]. By what means?
quot homines, tot sententiæ [L.]. As many minds as men, so many men, so many minds (sometimes incorr. quoted TOT HOMINES, etc.).
quo vadis? [L.]. Whither goest thou?

raison d'être [F.]. The reason for a thing's existence.
reculer pour mieux sauter [F.]. To retire in order to advance better.
reductio ad absurdum [L.]. Proof by demonstrating the absurdity of the contrary.
répondez s'il vous plaît (R.S.V.P.) [F.]. Please reply.
requiescat in pace (R.I.P.) [L.]. May he rest in peace.
res angusta domi [L.]. Matters straitened at home, poverty.
res judicata [L.]. An issue that has been settled in a court.
revenons à nos moutons [F.]. Let us return to our sheep, let us come back to our subject.

sans doute [F.]. Doubtless.
sans pareil [F.]. Unequalled.
sans peur et sans reproche [F.]. Without fear and without blame.
sans souci [F.]. Free from care.
sauve qui peut [F.]. Save himself who can.
savoir faire [F.]. Tact, skill.
savoir vivre [F.]. Good breeding.
semper eadem [L. pl.]. (*sing.* idem) Always the same.
semper fidelis [L.]. Always faithful.
Senatus Populusque Romanus (S.P.Q.R.) [L.]. The Roman Senate and People.
se non è vero, è ben trovato [It.]. If it is not true, it is cleverly invented.
sic transit gloria mundi [L.]. So earthly glory passes away.
s'il vous plaît [F.]. If you please.
sine cura [L.]. Without charge or office.
sine die [L.]. Without any day (being fixed).
sine qua non [L.]. An indispensable condition.
si vis pacem, para bellum [L.]. If you want peace be ready for war.
statim [L.]. At once.
Sturm und Drang [G.]. Storm and stress.
sub judice [L.]. Under consideration.
sub pœna [L.]. Under penalty (of).
sub silentio [L.]. Without notice being taken.
succès d'estime [F.]. A success with more credit than profit.
sui generis [L.]. Of its (his, or her) own kind.
sui juris [L.]. Of his (or her) own right.

tabula rasa [L.]. A smooth tablet ("a clean slate").
tædium vitæ [L.]. Weariness of life.
tant mieux [F.]. So much the better.
tant pis [F.]. So much the worse.
tantum quantum [L.]. Just as much as (is required).
tempus fugit [L.]. Time flies.
terra incognita [L.]. An unknown land.
tour de force [F.]. A feat of strength or skill.
tout à coup [F.]. Suddenly.
tout à fait [F.]. Wholly, entirely.
tout à l'heure [F.]. Instantly.
tout de suite [F.]. Immediately.
tout ensemble [F.]. The general effect.

ultra vires [L.]. Beyond one's (legal) powers.
urbi et orbi [L.]. To the city and the world.

vade in pace [L.]. Go in peace.
vanitas vanitatum, et omnia vanitas [L.]. Vanity of vanities, all is vanity.
veni, vidi, vici [L.]. I came, I saw, I conquered.
verbatim et literatim [L.]. Word for word and letter for letter.
verbum satis sapienti (verb. sap.) [L.]. A word is enough to the wise.
via media [L.]. A middle course.
vigilate et orate [L.]. Watch and pray.
vivat rex (regina)! [L.]. Long live the king (queen)!
vive la République! [F.]. Long live the Republic!
vive l'Empereur! [F.]. Long live the Emperor.
voilà [F.]. See there, there it is.
voilà tout [F.]. That's all.
vox (*pl.* **voces**) **populi** [L.]. The voice of the people, popular feeling.
vox populi vox Dei [L.]. The voice of the people is the voice of God.

Weltgeist [G.]. The world-spirit.
Weltschmerz [G.]. World-sorrow, pessimism.

Zeitgeist [G.]. The spirit of the age.

A[1], **a**, the first letter in the English alphabet, and in most others derived from the Phoenician. In English it has five sounds: (1) open as in *far, father, mikado,* marked in this dictionary ah; (2) short as in *fat, man, ample,* marked a; (3) long, as in *fate, fame,* marked ā; (4) broad as in *fall, appal,* spelt aw; (5) the long sound modified by the letter *r*, as in *fair, bear,* marked eə. In unaccented syllables **a** is often slurred and obscured, as in *separate* (adj.), *amidst,* marked ə. **A** is used as a symbol to denote the first of a series; the first known quantity in an algebraic expression; the sixth note of the diatonic scale of C major, corresponding to *la* in tonic sol-fa notation; the scale of a composition in which the keynote is **A**; the reference pitch to which instruments of an orchestra are tuned; in Britain formerly, a film certified as suitable for all but requiring parental consent for children under 14. **from A to B,** from one point or position to another. **from A to Z,** from beginning to end. **Al,** *a.* first class in Lloyd's Register of ships; first class. **A-bomb,** *n.* an atomic bomb, as distinct from a hydrogen bomb. **A-level**, *n.* (a pass in) an examination in a subject at the Advanced level of the General Certificate of Education. **A-road,** *n.* a trunk road or a main road. **A-team,** *n.* the first or best team in a sport; a team of skilled capable people brought together for a specific task.

A[2], (*abbr.*) academy, academician; ampere; angstrom; Associate.

a[1], **an**, *a.* a weakened form of one, sometimes called the indefinite article, used before singular substantives to denote an individual of a class. *A* is used before words beginning with a consonant, *h* aspirate, or *eu* or *u,* with the sound of *yu,* also before *one. An* is used before vowels and sometimes before *h* in an unaccented syllable, e.g. *an historian*. In such phrases as *50 pence a pound, twice a week,* it has a distributive force. Also used before collective phrases like *a hundred men a dozen eggs, a few, a good many,* i.e. a hundred of men etc. [OE *an,* one]

a[2], (*abbr.*) acre; alto; anno (in the year); ante (before); are (metric unit of area).

a-, *pref.* (1) (*prep.*), as in *aboard, adying, afoot*. [OE *on, an*]; (2) (*intens.*) away, out, as in *arise, awake*. [OE *ar-* or *a-*; cp. G *er-*]; (3) (*intens.*) of, from, as in *akin, athirst*. [OE *of, af*]; (4) (*prep.*) from, as in *avert*. [L *a, ab*]; (5) (*prep.*) directly, as in *aspect, ascent,* or indirectly through F *à*, as in *achieve,* from *à chef,* L *ad caput*. [L *ad-*, to]; (6) (*prep.*) out of, utterly, as in *amend* (F *amender,* L *ēmendāre* (or *exmendāre*). [L *ex-, e-*]; (7) not, without, as in *achromatic, amoral*. [Gr. *a-, an-*]

AA, (*abbr.*) Alcoholics Anonymous; anti-aircraft; Automobile Association.

AAA, (*abbr.*) Amateur Athletic Association; American Automobile Association.

Aalborg, *n.* (Danish **Ålborg**) port in Denmark 32 km/20 mi inland from the Kattegat, on the south shore of the Limfjord; population (1988) 155,000. One of Denmark's oldest towns, it has a castle and the fine Budolfi church. It is the capital of Nordjylland county in Jylland (Jutland); the port is linked to Nørresundby on the north side of the fjord by a tunnel built 1969.

Aalto, *n.* **Alvar** (1898–1976), Finnish architect and designer. One of Finland's first modernists, his architectural style was unique, characterized by asymmetry, curved walls, and contrast of natural materials. Buildings include the Hall of Residence, Massachusetts Institute of Technology, Cambridge, Massachusetts 1947–49; Technical High School, Otaniemi (1962–65); Finlandia Hall, Helsinki (1972). He also invented a new form of laminated bent plywood furniture in 1932.

AAM, (*abbr.*) air-to-air missile.

A and M, (*abbr.*) Ancient and Modern (hymns).

aardvark, *n.* the African ant-eater, *Orycteropus capensis*. **aardwolf**, *n.* a hyena-like carnivorous mammal, *Proteles lalandi,* of southern Africa. [Dut. *aarde,* earth, *varken,* pig]

Aarhus, *n.* (Danish **Århus**) second city of Denmark, on the east coast overlooking the Kattegat; population (1988) 258,000. It is the capital of Aarhus county in Jylland (Jutland), and a shipping and commercial centre.

Aaron[1], *n.* in the Bible, the elder brother of Moses and co-leader of the Israelites in their march from Egypt to the Promised Land of Canaan. He made the Golden Calf for the Israelites to worship when they despaired of Moses' return from Mount Sinai.

Aaron[2], *n.* **Hank** (1934–), US baseball player. He played for 23 years with the Milwaukee (later Atlanta) Braves (1954–74) and the Milwaukee Brewers (1975–76), hitting a major-league record 755 home runs and 2297 runs batted in. He was elected to the Baseball Hall of Fame (1982).

Aaronic, -ical, *a.* of or pertaining to Aaron[1], his descendants, or the Jewish priesthood. **Aaron's beard,** *n.* pop. name for *Hypericum calycinum,* or large-flowered St-John's wort, and for *Saxifraga sarmentosa,* a Chinese herb with hanging stems bearing clusters of hairy leaves. **Aaron's rod,** *n.* pop. name for certain plants that flower on long stems, e.g. great mullein and golden rod.

Ab, *n.* the fifth ecclesiastical month, or 11th civil month, of the Jewish year (corresponding roughly with August). [Heb.]

AB, (*abbr.*) able-bodied seaman; (US) Bachelor of Arts.

ab-[1], *pref.* off, from, away, apart, as in *abrogate, abuse* (cp. Gr. *apo,* Eng. *of, off,* G *ab*); in L and F derivatives often assimilated to subsequent consonant or reduced to *a,* as in *assoil, avert, avocation, abstract*. [L *ab*]

ab-[2], *pref.* to, as in *abbreviate*. [L *ad-*, to, assim. to consonant *b*]

aback, *adv.* backwards; behind; by surprise; with the sails pressed against the mast. [ME *abak,* OE *onbæc* (*on-*, on, *bæc,* back)]

abactinal, *a.* pertaining to that part of a radiate animal that is opposite the mouth. [L *ab-*, from, away, Gr. *aktis aktinos,* a ray]

abacus, *n.* (*pl.* **-ci, -cuses**) a counting-frame; an apparatus made of beads sliding on wires for facilitating arithmetical calculations; a flat stone crowning the capital of a column and supporting the architrave. **abacist,** *n.* an arithmetician. [L *abacus,* Gr. *abax -akos,* atablet]

Abadan, *n.* Iranian oil port on the east side of the Shatt-al-Arab; population (1986) 294,000. Abadan is the chief refinery and shipping centre for Iran's oil industry, nationalized 1951. This measure was the beginning of the worldwide movement by oil-producing countries to assume control of profits from their own resources.

abaddon, *n.* a destroyer, the angel of the Bottomless Pit, Apollyon (Rev. ix.11); Hell, the Bottomless Pit. [Heb. *ābad,* he perished]

abaft, *adv.*, *prep.* in, on or towards the hinder part of a ship; behind. [*a-*, on; OE *beæftan*]

†**abalienate,** *v.t.* to transfer to the ownership of

another, to alienate. **abalienation,** *n.*

abalone, *n.* an edible gasteropod mollusc of the genus *Haliotis*. [Am. Sp. *abulōn*]

abandon, *v.t.* to give up, yield; to desert or forsake; to surrender oneself unreservedly, e.g. to indolence or vice. *n.* freedom from conventional restraint, careless freedom of manner. **abandoned,** *a.* deserted; wholly given up to wickedness, profligate. **abandonee,** *n.* (*Law*) one to whom anything is abandoned, e.g. an underwriter to whom salvage is formally surrendered. **abandonment,** *n.* the act of abandoning; self-surrender to a cause, passion or vice; relinquishment of property, desertion (of a relation, friend, servant). [OF *abandoner,* to leave at liberty, from *à bandon,* at liberty; low L *ad-,* to, *bandum,* jurisdiction, proclamation, OHG BAN]

à bas, *int.* (F) down with.

abase, *v.t.* to lower, to humble, degrade. **abasement,** *n.* the act of abasing, a state of humiliation, degradation. [OF *abaissier* (F *abaisser*), to lower, from late L *abassāre* (AD-, *bassāre*), late L *bassus,* low]

abash, *v.t.* to embarrass or put to shame by exciting a sense of guilt, mistake or inferiority. **abashment,** *n.* confusion produced by shame, consternation. [OF *esbaïr* (F *ébahir*), pres.p. *esbaïssant;* OF *es-* (L *ex-*) *baïr,* to express amazement, BAH]

abasia, *n.* lack of power to coordinate the movements of the muscles in walking. [Gr. *a-,* not; *basis,* movement]

abask, *adv.* in the sunshine, basking.

abate, *v.t.* to diminish, reduce, lessen, deduct; †to beat down, destroy. *v.i.* to become less, diminish, fail. **abatable,** *a.* **abatement,** *n.* **abater,** *n.* [OF *abatre,* to beat down; *à* (L *ad*) *batre;* late L *batere,* L *batuere,* beat]

abatis, abattis, *n.* a defence made of felled trees with their boughs directed outwards. **abattised,** *a.* furnished with an abattis. [F *abatis,* from OF *abatre,* to beat down]

abatjour, *n.* (F) a skylight.

abattoir, *n.* a public slaughter-house. [F]

abaxial, *a.* facing away from the stem. [AB-[1], AXIS]

abb, *n.* yarn for a weaver's woof or weft, sometimes warp-yarn. **abb-wool,** *n.* wool suitable for a weaver's warp. [OE *ab, aweb, awefan* (*a-* intens., *wefan,* to weave)]

abba, *n.* father (in the invocation *Abba, father*); an episcopal title in the Syriac and Gothic churches. [Aram. *abba,* O Father]

abbacy, *n.* the office and jurisdiction of an abbot. **abbat,** *n.* ABBOT. **abbatial**, *a.* pertaining to an abbey or an abbot. [late L *abbatia,* from *abbas,* ABBOT]

Abbado, *n.* **Claudio** (1933–), Italian conductor, long associated with La Scala, Milan. Principal conductor of London Symphony Orchestra from 1979, he also worked with the European Community Youth Orchestra from 1977.

Abbas I, *n.* **the Great** (*c.* 1557–1629), shah of Persia from 1588. He expanded Persian territory by conquest, defeating the Uzbeks near Herat in 1597 and also the Turks. The port of Bandar-Abbas is named after him. At his death his empire reached from the river Tigris to the Indus. He was a patron of the arts.

Abbas II, *n.* **Hilmi** (1874–1944), last khedive (viceroy) of Egypt, 1892–1914. On the outbreak of war between Britain and Turkey in 1914, he sided with Turkey and was deposed following the establishment of a British protectorate over Egypt.

Abbasid dynasty, *n.* dynasty of the Islamic empire who reigned as caliphs in Baghdad 750–1258. They were descended from Abbas, the prophet Muhammad's uncle, and some of them, such as Harun al-Rashid and Mamun (reigned 813–33), were outstanding patrons of cultural development. Later their power dwindled, and in 1258 Baghdad was burned by the Tatars.

abbé, *n.* an ecclesiastic without a cure; a cleric in minor orders; generally a mere title without any definite office or responsibility. [F *abbé,* an abbot, L *abbas -atem*]

abbess, *n.* the lady superior of an abbey. [OF *abaesse,* L *abatissa* fem. of *abbas,* ABBOT]

abbey, *n.* a monastic community governed by an abbot or abbess; a building either now or formerly inhabited by a body of monks or nuns; a church attached to an abbey. **abbey land,** *n.* land now, or formerly, attached to an abbey. [OF *abeie, abaie,* as prec.]

Abbey Theatre, *n.* playhouse in Dublin associated with the Irish literary revival of the early 1900s. The theatre, opened in 1904, staged the works of a number of Irish dramatists, including Lady Gregory, Yeats, J M Synge, and Sean O'Casey. Burned down in 1951, the Abbey Theatre was rebuilt 1966.

abbot, *n.* a monk; the superior of a monastery; the superior of an abbey. **abbot of misrule,** (*Sc.*) **abbot of unreason,** *n.* a leader in mediaeval burlesque. **abbotship,** *n.* the state or office of an abbot. [L *abbas,* Gr. *abbas abbatos,* Syriac *abba,* father]

Abbott and Costello, *n.* Stage names of William Abbot (1895–1974) and Louis Cristillo (1906–1959). US comedy duo. They moved to the cinema from vaudeville, and their films, including *Buck Privates* (1941) and *Lost in a Harem* (1944), were showcases for their routines.

abbreviate, *v.t.* to shorten, abridge, reduce to a smaller compass. **abbreviate**, *a.* shortened, cut short. **abbreviation,** *n.* the act of abridging or contracting; the abridged or shortened form, e.g. of a word; an abridgment. **abbreviator,** *n.* one who abridges or curtails; an officer in the Roman Chancery who abridges the petitions granted by the Pope. **abbreviatory,** *a.* abbreviating or tending to abbreviate, shortening. **abbreviature,** *n.* an abbreviation, an abridgment. [L *abbreviātus,* p.p. of *abbreviāre,* to shorten (*ab-, ad-, brevis,* short)]

A B C[1], *n.* the alphabet; rudiments, first principles. [the first letters of the alphabet]

ABC[2], (*abbr.*) American Broadcasting Company; Associated British Cinemas; Australian Broadcasting Commission.

Abd el-Krim, *n.* **el-Khettabi** (1881–1963), Moroccan chief known as the 'Wolf of the Riff'. With his brother Muhammad, he led the Riff revolt against the French and Spanish invaders, inflicting disastrous defeat on the Spanish at Anual in 1921, but surrendered to a large French army under Pétain in 1926. Banished to the island of Réunion, he was released in 1947 and died in voluntary exile in Cairo.

Abderian, *a.* pertaining to Abdera; given to laughter. **Abderite**, *n.* an inhabitant of Abdera; a stupid person. **the Abderite,** Democritus, the laughing philosopher. [*Abdera,* a town of Thrace, the inhabitants of which were regarded as very stupid]

abdicate, *v.t.* to resign, to formally renounce, to give up. *v.i.* to abandon or relinquish a throne, or other dignity or privilege. **abdicable,** *a.* **abdicant,** *a.* abdicating, renouncing. *n.* one who abdicates, an abdicator. **abdication,** *n.* the act of abdicating. **abdicator,** *n.* [L *abdicātus,* p.p. of *abdicāre* (*ab-,* from, and *dicāre,* to declare)]

Abdication crisis, *n.* the constitutional upheaval of the period 16 Nov. 1936 to 10 Dec. 1936 was brought about by the English king, Edward VIII's decision to marry Mrs Wallis Simpson, an American divorcee. The marriage of the 'Supreme Governer' of the Church of England to a divorced person was considered unsuitable and the king was finally forced to abdicate on 10 Dec. and left for voluntary exile in France. He married Wallis Simpson on 3 June 1937.

abdomen, *n.* that portion of the trunk which lies between the thorax and the pelvis; the belly; the posterior division of the body in the higher Arthropoda. **abdominal**, *a.* belonging to the abdomen; of fish, having the ventral fins under the abdomen. **abdominal regions,** *n.pl.* certain portions of the body near to or including the belly, arbitrarily marked off for convenience in anatomical study. **abdominally,** *adv.* **abdominous**, *a.* having a large abdomen, corpulent, potbellied. [L]

abduce, *v.t.* to draw from one part to another by an abductor; to lead away. **abducent,** *a.* having the property of drawing back or away (applied to muscles, the function of which is to draw away or pull back the parts to which they belong. The abducent muscles are opposed in their action to the adductor or adducent muscles). [L *abdūcere, ab-*, from, *dūcere,* to lead, draw]

abduct, *v.t.* to take away (esp. a woman or child) by guile or force; to kidnap. **abduction,** *n.* a leading or drawing away; separation of parts or a bone after a fracture, or of sides of a wound; the illegal taking away of a person, esp. a child or a woman by fraud or force. **abductor,** *n.* one who, or that which, abducts; a muscle which draws or pulls back any part of the body. [L *abducere,* p.p. *abductus*]

Abdul-Hamid II *n.* (1842–1918), last sultan of Turkey (1876–1909). In 1908 the Young Turks under Enver Pasha forced Abdul-Hamid to restore the constitution of 1876, and in 1909 insisted on his deposition. He died in confinement. For his part in the Armenian massacres suppressing the revolt of 1894–96 he was known as the Great Assassin and still motivates Armenian violence against the Turks.

Abdullah[1] *n.* **ibn Hussein,** (1882–1951), king of Jordan from 1946. He worked with the British guerrilla leader T. E. Lawrence in the Arab revolt of World War I. Abdullah became king of Transjordan (1946); on the incorporation of Arab Palestine (after the 1948–49 Arab-Israeli War) he renamed the country the Hashemite Kingdom of Jordan. He was assassinated.

Abdullah[2], *n.* **Sheikh Muhammad** (1905–82), Indian politician, known as the 'Lion of Kashmir'. He headed the struggle for constitutional government against the Maharajah of Kashmir, and in 1948 became prime minister of Kashmir. He agreed to the accession of the state to India to halt ethnic infiltration, but was dismissed and imprisoned from 1953 (with brief intervals) until 1966, when he reaffirmed the right of the people 'to decide the future of the state'. He became chief minister of Jammu and Kashmir 1975, accepting the sovereignty of India.

abeam, *adv.* on a line at right angles to the keel of a ship. [BEAM]

abear, *v.t.* to endure, put up with; to behave (oneself). [OE *aberan*]

abecedarian, *n.* one who teaches or is learning the alphabet. *a.* alphabetical; having verses distinguished by letters alphabetically arranged like the 119th Psalm; a member of an 18th-cent. Anabaptist sect that rejected all worldly knowledge, even of the alphabet. **abecedary,** *n.* or *a.* [late L *abecedarium,* alphabet, from A B C D]

abed, *adv.* in bed, gone to bed.

Abel[1], *n.* in the Old Testament, second son of Adam and Eve; as a shepherd, he made burnt offerings of meat to God which were more acceptable than the fruits offered by his brother Cain; he was killed by the jealous Cain.

Abel[2], *n.* **Frederick Augustus** (1827–1902), British scientist and inventor, who developed explosives. As a chemist to the War Department, he introduced a method of making gun-cotton and was joint inventor with Dewar of cordite. He also invented the Abel close-test instrument for determining the flash point of petroleum.

Abel[3], *n.* **John Jacob** (1857–1938), US biochemist, discoverer of adrenaline. He studied the chemical composition of body tissues, and this led, in 1898, to the discovery of adrenaline, the first hormone to be identified, which Abel called epinephrine. He later became the first to isolate amino acids from blood.

Abel[4], *n.* **Niels Henrik** (1802–29), Norwegian mathematician who demonstrated that the general quintic equation could not be solved algebraically. Despite a life of poverty and ill-health he also looked at elliptic functions, integral equations, infinite series and binomial theorem. He died of tuberculosis shortly before the arrival of an offer of a position at the University of Berlin.

Abelard, *n.* **Peter** (1079–1142), French scholastic philosopher noted for his work on logic and theology and for his love affair with Heloise. Details of his controversial life are contained in the autobiographical *Historia Calamitatum Mearum/The History of My Misfortunes*.

abele, *n.* the white poplar. [Dut. *abeel,* OF *abel, aubel,* late L *albellum,* L *albus,* white]

aber, *n.* a celtic term for the mouth of ariver, found as a prefix in place names, e.g. *Aberdeen.*

Abercrombie, *n.* **Leslie Patrick** (1879–1957), pioneer of British town planning. He is known for his work of replanning British cities after damage in World War II (such as the Greater London Plan, 1944) and for the new town policy.

Aberdeen[1], *n.* city and seaport on the E coast of Scotland, administrative headquarters of Grampian region; population (1986) 214,082. Shore-based maintenance and service depots for the North Sea oil rigs; a rough-haired Scotch terrier. **Aberdonian,** *n.* a native or inhabitant of Aberdeen, supposedly noted for thrift. *a.* belonging to Aberdeen.

Aberdeen[2], *n.* **George Hamilton Gordon, 4th Earl of Aberdeen** (1784–1860), British Tory politician, prime minister (1852–55), resigned because of the Crimean War losses. Although a Tory, he supported Catholic emancipation and followed Robert Peel in his conversion to free trade.

Aberdeenshire, *n.* former county in E Scotland, merged in 1975 in Grampian region.

aberdevine, *n.* the siskin. [etym. doubtful]

Aberdonian ABERDEEN[1].

Aberfan, *n.* mining village in Mid Glamorgan, Wales. Coal waste overwhelmed a school and houses in 1966; of 144 dead, 116 were children.

†**aberr,** †**aberre,** *v.i.* to wander; to err. [L *aberrāre, ab-*, from, *errāre,* to wander]

aberrance, -cy, *n.* a wandering from the right way. **aberrant,** *a.* wandering from the right way; deviating from the normal type. **aberration,** *n.* deviation from the normal course or standard; departure from rule; deviation from type; the difference between the true and observed position of a heavenly body; deviation of focused rays preventing them from uniting in a point. [ABERR]

abet, *v.t.* (*past, p.p.* **abetted**) to encourage or aid (a person or cause) by word or deed; to countenance, stimulate or instigate (chiefly in a bad sense). **abetment,** *n.* the act of abetting, countenancing or encouraging. **abetter,** (*Law*) **abettor,** *n.* one who encourages or instigates another; an accessory. [OF *abeter,* to instigate, deceive; AD-, *beter,* see BAIT]

abeyance, *n.* the state of being held back, suspended; dormancy, quiescence. **in abeyance,** (*Law*) waiting for an occupant or owner. [OF *abeance* (*à,* to, *béer,* late L *baddāre,* to gape)]

abhor, *v.t.* (*past, p.p.* **abhorred**) to hate extremely, loathe, detest; to shrink from with horror. **abhorrence, -ency,** *n.* extreme hatred, aversion, repugnance, loathing. **abhorrent,** *a.* exciting repugnance, loathing, hatred; opposed to, inconsistent with; †drawing back with loathing or fear. **abhorrently,** *adv.* **abhorrer,** *n.* one who abhors or detests – nickname of the court party in the reign of Charles II who signed the address of abhorrence against the Whigs (1679). [L *abhorrēre,* to shrink from (AB-, *horrēre,* to bristle, shudder)]

Abib, *n.* the first month of the ancient Hebrew calendar, corresponding to Nisan. [Heb. *ābīb,* a full green ear of corn]

abide[1], *v.i.* to dwell or live in a place; to stay, wait; to continue, remain firm. *v.t.* to await, encounter, withstand; to submit to; to endure, bear, tolerate. **to abide by,** to remain beside, adhere to, act upon (terms). **abidance,** *n.* continuance. **abider,** *n.* one who abides or continues. **abiding,** *a.* continuing, permanent, durable. *n.* continuance, residence. **abiding-place,** *n.*

place of abode. **abidingly,** *adv.* [OE *abīdan* (A-, *bīdan,* to bide)]

abide², ABY.

Abidjan, *n.* port and capital of the Republic of Ivory Coast, W Africa; population (1982) 1,850,000. Products include coffee, palm oil, cocoa, and timber (mahogany). To be replaced as capital by Yamoussoukro.

Abies, *n.* a genus of conifers, containing the silver firs, spruces, larches and cedars. **abietic,** *a.* pertaining to or derived from trees of this genus. **abiet-,** *comb. form.* stem of various chemical terms relating to substances so derived, e.g. **abietin,** *n.*, **abietite,** *n.* [L]

abigail, *n.* a waiting-maid (I Sam. xxv); a lady's maid; †a waiting gentlewoman. [Heb.]

ability, *n.* physical, mental or moral power; capacity, competence; wealth, means; (*pl.*) intellectual gifts. [OF *ableté,* see ABLE]

ab initio, *adv.* from the beginning. [L]

abiogenesis, *n.* the theory that living matter can be produced from that which has no life; spontaneous generation. **abiogenetic,** *a.* **abiogenetically,** *adv.* **abiogenist,** *n.* one who holds the hypothesis of abiogenesis. **abiogenous,** *a.* produced by abiogenesis. [Gr. *a-,* priv., *bios,* life, GENESIS]

abiotic, *a.* not living, not produced by living organisms. [Gr. *a-,* priv., *biotikos,* from *bios,* life]

abject, *a.* cast away; sunk to a low condition; servile, degraded, morally debased; mean, low. †*n.* a person of the lowest condition, and morally despicable. **abjectedness, abjection,** *n.* the act of casting away; the state of being cast away; abasement. **abjectly,** *adv.* **abjectness,** *n.* [L *abjectus,* cast away, p.p. of *abjicere* (*jacere,* to cast)]

abjure, *v.t.* to renounce, recant, retract or abrogate anything upon oath. *v.i.* to take an oath of abjuration. †**to abjure the realm** or **commonwealth,** to take an oath to quit the country within a given time. **abjuration,** *n.* the act of forswearing, abjuring or renouncing on oath; a denial or renunciation on oath. **abjuratory,** *a.* **abjurement,** *n.* **abjurer,** *n.* [L *ab-,* from, *jurāre,* to swear]

Abkhazia, *n.* autonomous republic in the NW corner of the republic of Georgia in SW USSR. Inhabited traditionally by Abkhazis, an ethnic group converted from Christianity to Islam in the 17th century, today two thirds of the population of 526,000 are of Georgian origin. In Mar.–Apr. and July 1989, Abkhazis demanded succession from Georgia and reinstatement as a full Union republic; violent inter-ethnic clashes erupted in which at least 20 people died.

ablactate, *v.t.* to wean from the breast. **ablactation,** *n.* the weaning of a child from the breast; grafting by inarching. [L *ab-,* from, away, *lactāre,* suckle (*lac, lactis,* milk)]

ablation, *n.* removal, carrying away; wearing away. **ablate,** *v.t.* **ablative,** *a.* taking away, separating, subtractive. *n.* the case in Latin and other languages expressing separation, instrumentality, and other relations expressed in English by the prepositions from, by, with etc. **ablative absolute,** *n.* in Latin grammar, a construction with noun and participle, noun and adjective, in the ablative case, expressing time or circumstances: corresponds to the English nominative absolute. **ablatival,** *a.* [L *ab-,* from, *lātus,* p.p. of *fero,* I bear]

ablator, *n.* an instrument for excising diseased parts; an instrument for removing the tails of sheep.

ablaut, *n.* a vowel change in the middle of a word to indicate modification in meaning, as *sit, set; rise, raise; ring, rang, rung.* [G *ab-,* off, *Laut,* sound]

ablaze, *adv., a.* on fire, in a blaze; brilliant; excited.

able, *a.* having sufficient physical, mental, moral or spiritual power, or acquired skill, or sufficient pecuniary and other resources to do something indicated; gifted, vigorous, active. †*v.t.* to make able, enable; to vouch for, warrant. **able-bodied,** *a.* having a sound, strong body; experienced, skilled (applied to a sailor who is classed as AB, and called an **able-seaman**). **ableism,** *n.* discrimination in favour of able-bodied people. **ableist,** *a.* **ably,** *adv.* in an able manner; with ability. [OF *hable, able* (F *habile*), L *habilis,* handy (*habēre,* to have, hold)]

-able, *suf.* able, or likely, to; fit, suitable for, that may be, full of, as in *movable, comfortable, eatable, saleable, reasonable.* **-ably,** *suf.* **-ability,** *suf.* [F *-able,* L *-abilis*]

ablegate, *n.* a papal envoy sent with insignia to new cardinals etc. [L *ablegatus,* one sent away]

ablet, ablen, *n.* the bleak, a small freshwater fish. [F *ablette,* from late L *abula* (*albula,* dim. of L *alba*), white]

ablings, ablins, aiblins, *adv.* (*Sc., North.*) possibly, perhaps. [ABLE, with suf. -LING(S)]

abloom, *a., adv.* blooming, in a state of bloom.

abluent, *a.* cleansing, washing away. *n.* that which washes off or carries off impurities. [L *ab-,* away, *luere,* to wash, pres.p. *abluens -tis*)]

ablush, *adv., pred.a.* blushing, ruddy.

ablution, *n.* (*often pl.*) the act of washing, cleansing or purifying by means of water or other liquids; a ceremonial or symbolical washing or cleansing; the state of being washed; the water used for washing; a building containing washing facilities as in a military camp. **ablutionary,** *a.* [ABLUENT]

ABM, (*abbr.*) antiballistic missile.

abnegate, *v.t.* to deny, to refuse, to renounce, to abjure. **abnegation,** *n.* denial, renunciation; self-sacrifice. **abnegative,** *a.* implying denial, negative. **abnegator,** *n.* [L *ab-,* from, away, *negāre,* to deny (p.p. *abnegātus*)]

abnormal, *a.* not according to rule, anomalous, departing from the ordinary type. **abnormality,** *n.* irregularity, deformity. **abnormally,** *adv.* **abnormity,** *n.* departure from the ordinary type, rule or standard. [F *anormal,* assim. to L *abnormis* (*ab-,* from, *norma,* rule); see NORMAL]

Abo, *n.* (*offensive*) an aboriginal native of Australia. [ABORIGINE]

Åbo, *n.* Swedish name for the Finnish town of Turku.

aboard, *adv.* on board, on a ship or boat. *prep.* into a ship. **to fall aboard,** to strike the side of. **to get aboard,** to get foul of. **to lay a ship aboard,** to place a ship alongside an enemy in order to board.

abode¹, past of ABIDE, dwelt, stayed. *n.* stay; continuance for a longer or shorter period in any place; residence; a habitation. **to make abode,** to dwell, reside.

†**abode²,** *v.t.* to bode, presage. *n.* prediction, boding. **abodement,** *n.* a foreboding; an omen. [OE *ābēodan,* to announce, to bode]

aboil, *adv.* a-boiling, boiling, on the boil.

abolish, *v.t.* to do away with, put an end to, destroy; to annul, cancel or revoke (used of laws, customs, institutions or offices). **abolishable,** *a.* **abolisher,** *n.* **abolishment,** *n.* **abolition,** *n.* the act of abolishing or doing away with; the state of being abolished. **abolitionism,** *n.* **abolitionist,** *n.* one who entertains views in favour of abolition, esp. one who favoured the abolition of slavery during the movement against it in the 18th and 19th cents. [F *abolir* (*aboliss-*), L *abolescere, abolēre* (*ab-,* from, *olēre,* to grow)]

abomasum, -masus, *n.* (*pl.* **-sa, -si**) the fourth stomach in a ruminating animal. [L *ab-,* from, *omāsum,* paunch]

abominate, *v.t.* to loathe, to detest, to hate exceedingly. **abominable,** *a.* very loathsome, hateful or odious, physically or morally. **abominable snowman,** *n.* the yeti. **abominableness,** *n.* **abominably,** *adv.* **abomination,** *n.* the act of doing something hateful; the state of being greatly hated or loathed; an object of extreme hatred, loathing or aversion. [L *abōminātus,* p.p. of *abōminārī* (*ab-,* from, OMEN), to dislike]

aboon, *adv.* (*Sc.*) above.

†**abord,** *v.t.* to approach; to accost. *n.*approach; accosting. [F *aborder* (*à bord;* see ABOARD)]

aborigine, *n.* an indigenous or original inhabitant of a continent, country or district, esp. Australia; (*pl.*) the earliest fauna and flora of an area. **aboriginal,** *a.* original, indigenous, inhabiting a place from the earliest times. *n.* an original inhabitant (esp. of Australia); a member of the original fauna or flora. **aboriginally,** *adv.* from the beginning, from the first; originally. [L *aborigines* (*ab-*, from, *origine,* the beginning)]

abort, *v.i.* to miscarry, bring forth prematurely; to undergo partial or entire arrest of development. *v.t.* to give birth to before the proper time; to induce the abortion of; to terminate prematurely or in the early stages. **abortient**, *a.* (*Bot.*) barren, sterile. [L *abort-*, p.p. stem of *aborīri* (*ab-*, off, away, *orīri,* to arise, grow)]

abortifacient, *n.* a device or drug to induce abortion. **abortion,** *n.* the act of miscarrying; the production of a foetus before the proper time; a procedure to induce the premature production of a foetus; the product of a miscarriage; anything which fails instead of coming to maturity; a monster, a misshapen creature. **contagious abortion,** a contagious or infectious disease, esp. brucellosis, which causes abortion in some farm animals. **abortionist,** *n.* one who performs abortions. **abortive**, *a.* brought forth in an immature state; imperfectly formed; procuring or intended to procure abortion; fruitless, ineffectual, failing in its effect. *n.* an immature birth; a drug causing or intended to cause abortion. **abortively,** *adv.* **abortiveness,** *n.* †**abortment,** *n.* an untimely birth; abortion.

ABO system, *n.* a system for typing human blood according to the presence or absence of certain antigens.

Aboukir Bay, Battle of, also known as the **Battle of the Nile,** naval battle between the UK and France, in which Admiral Nelson defeated Napoleon's fleet at the Egyptian seaport of Aboukir on 1 Aug. 1798.

aboulia, abulia, *n.* abnormal loss of will-power. [Gr. *a-*, priv., *boulē,* will]

abound, *v.i.* to overflow; to be rich (in), to be copiously supplied (with); to be in great plenty. **abounding,** *a.* plentiful, copious. *n.* abundance. [OF *abunder, abonder,* L *abundāre,* to overflow (*ab-*, away, *unda,* a wave)]

about, *prep.* around, surrounding, on the outside or surface of; near in time, space, number, quantity or quality; on the point of; concerning, in connection with. *adv.* around, circuitously, nearly; here and there; in different directions. **about face, (right-)about turn,** turn right round, face the opposite way. **to bring about,** to cause to happen; to effect. **to come about,** to come to pass, to happen. **to go about,** to prepare to do; to change the course of a ship or boat, to tack. **about-sledge,** *n.* the largest hammer used by smiths. [OE *ābūtan, onbūtan* (*on-*, on, *be,* by, *ūtan,* outside)]

above, *prep.* over, at or to a higher point than; in excess of, superior to, more important than, beyond; previous, preceding. *adv.* overhead; in a higher place or position; previously; in heaven. *n.* the upper part; the aforesaid; heaven. **above all,** principally; before everything else. **above-board,** *adv., pred.a.* openly, without trickery. **above-ground,** *a.* alive, unburied. **above par,** *a.* at a premium; of superior quality. [OE *ābūfan* (*an,* on, *be,* by, *ūfan,* over)]

Abp., (*abbr.*) archbishop.

abracadabra, *n.* a cabbalistic word used as a charm: when written in triangular form – the first line containing the whole word, the others successively omitting first and last letters, till the last consists only of the final A – it was worn as an amulet, and was considered to ward off or cure certain diseases; hence a word-charm, a jingle or nonsensical phrase. [etym. doubtful]

abrade, *v.t.* to rub or wear away by friction. **abradant,** *a.* abrasive. [L *abrādere* (*ab-*, off, *rādere,* to scrape)]

Abraham, *n.* (*c.* 2300 BC) according to the Old Testament, founder of the Jewish nation. Jehovah promised him heirs and land for his people in Canaan, renamed him Abraham ('father of many nations') and once tested him by a command (later retracted) to sacrifice his son Isaac or, in the Koran, Ishmael.

Abraham, Plains of, plateau near Québec, Canada, where the British commander Wolfe defeated the French under Montcalm, 13 Sept. 1759, during the French and Indian War (1754–63).

Abrahamic, -mitic, -mitical, *a.* pertaining to the patriarch Abraham or the dispensation under which he lived. **to sham Abraham,** to feign sickness, in allusion to the Abraham men. **Abraham man, Abramman,** *n.* originally, a lunatic beggar from Bethlehem Hospital, London; an impostor who wandered about the country and feigned lunacy to excite compassion.

abranchial, abranchiate, *a.* without gills. *n.* an animal that at no period possesses gills. [Gr. *a-*, priv., *branchia,* gills]

abrasion, *n.* the act of rubbing away or wearing down; the state of being rubbed away or worn down; a superficial lesion of the skin; the substance worn or rubbed off. **abrasive**, *a.* tending to rub or wear away; of a person's manner, causing friction or irritation. *n.* a substance, as emery, used for grinding or rubbing down. [L *abrādere, abrāsio*]

abraum, *n.* a red clay used to deepen the colour of mahogany. [G]

abraxas, *n.* a word denoting a power which presides over 365 others, and used by the Basilidians (a Gnostic sect, 2nd cent.) to denote their supreme god; a gem with this word, or the mystical image corresponding thereto, engraved on it. [late Gr.]

abreaction, *n.* the ridding oneself of a complex by reliving in feeling or action repressed fantasies or experiences. **abreact,** *v.t.*

abreast, *adv.* side by side with the fronts in line; up to the standard (of); up-to-date, aware (of). [OE *a-*, on, BREAST]

abrégé, *n.* (*F.*) an abridgment. [F, p.p. of *abréger,* L *abbreviāre,* to ABBREVIATE]

abreption, *n.* complete severance. [L *abreptus,* torn away]

abridge, *v.t.* to shorten, curtail, epitomize; to deprive (a person of). **abridger,** *n.* **abridgment,** *n.* the act of abridging; the state or process of being abridged; a condensed form, an epitome, a compend, an abstract, a summary. [OF*abregier, abrigier,* L *abbreviāre,* to shorten]

abroach, *adv.* broached, pierced; in aposition to allow the enclosed liquor to run out freely. *a.* tapped or opened.

abroad, *adv.* widely, at large, far and wide; beyond the bounds of a house or country; in or to a foreign country; before the public generally. **all abroad,** at a loss, astray.

abrogate, *v.t.* to annul by an authoritative act; to repeal, make void. **abrogation,** *n.* the act of abrogating; repeal. **abrogative,** *a.* tending to abrogate. **abrogator,** *n.* [L *abrogātus,* p.p. of *abrogāre* (*ab-*, away, *rogāre,* to ask, propose a law)]

abrupt, *a.* broken, very steep, precipitous; sudden, disconnected; brusque, curt; (*Bot.*) truncated; as if cut off below or above. **abruption,** *n.* a sudden or violent breaking off; the state of being broken off. **abruptly,** *adv.* **abruptness,** *n.* [L *abruptus,* p.p. of *abrumpere* (*ab-*, off, *rumpere,* to break)]

Abruzzi, *n.* mountainous region of S central Italy, comprising the provinces of L'Aquila, Chieti, Pescara and Teramo; area 10,800 sq km/4169 sq miles; population (1988) 1,258,000; capital L'Aquila. Gran Sasso d'Italia, 2914 m/9564 ft, is the highest point of the Apennines.

ABS, (*abbr.*) anti-lock braking system.

abs-, *pref.* away, off, from, as in *abstain, absterge, abstruse.* [L AB-, away, from]

Absalom, *n.* in the Old Testament, favourite son of King David; when defeated in a revolt against his father he fled on a mule, but was caught up by his hair in a tree branch and killed by Joab, one of David's officers.

abscess, *n.* a gathering of pus in any tissue or organ, accompanied by pain and heat. **abscessed,** *a.* [L *abscessus,* p.p. of *abscēdere* (*abs-*, away, *cēdere,* to go)]

abscind, *v.t.* to cut off. **abscission,** *n.* the act of cutting off; the state or condition of being cut off. [L *abscindere* (*ab-*, from, *scindere,* to cut)]

abscissa, *n.* (*pl.* **-ssae**, **-ssas**) one of the two coordinates by which a point is referred to a system of fixed rectilinear axes. [L *abscissa linea,* from p.p. of *abscindere,* to cut]

abscond, *v.t.* to go away secretly; to go out of the jurisdiction of a court, or hide oneself to avoid legal proceedings. †*v.t.* to hide, conceal. **abscondence,** *n.* act of absconding, concealment. **absconder,** *n.* one who absconds, a fugitive from justice. [L *abscondere* (*abs-*, away, *condere,* to hide, from *con-*, *cum-*, with, and *-dere,* to put)]

abseil, *v.i.* to descend a vertical or steeply sloping surface, as a rock face, using a rope attached at the top and wound round the body. [G *abseilen (ab-,* down, *Seil,* rope)]

absent[1]**,** *a.* away from or not present in a place; wanting, not existing; inattentive to what is passing around one. **absent-minded,** *a.* inattentive, abstracted in mind. **absent-mindedly,** *adv.* inattentively, abstractedly. **absent-mindedness,** *n.* inattentiveness, abstraction of mind from immediate objects or business. **absence,** *n.* the state of being absent. **absence of mind,** inattention to what is passing. **absentee,** *n.* one who is habitually absent from duty, work or home; a landlord who lives away from his/her estate. *a.* habitually absent from duty or from one's estate. **absenteeism,** *n.* usu. applied to unjustified failure of workers to report for work. **absently,** *adv.* [L *absentem,* acc. of *absens,* pres.p. of *abesse,* to be away]

absent[2]**,** *v.refl.* to keep oneself away. [L *absentāre* (*absens*)]

absidal, *a.* apsidal.

absinthe, *n.* wormwood; a liqueur flavoured with wormwood. **absinthian,** *a.* absinthic. **absinthinate,** *v.t.* to impregnate with wormwood. **absinthic,** *a.* pertaining to or derived from wormwood; hence, bitter. **absinthin,** *n.* the bitter principle in *Artemisia absinthium* (wormwood). [F, from L *absinthium,* Gr. *apsinthion*]

absolute, *a.* independent, unlimited, under no restraint; self-existent; arbitrary, despotic; highly accomplished, perfect; unconditioned; applied to a grammatical case not determined by any other word in a sentence; (*Phil.*) existing independently of any other cause; (*Chem.*) free from mixture; measured from vacuum, as 'the absolute pressure of steam'. **Absolute,** the Self-existent, the First Cause or God of theism. **absolute magnitude,** *n.* the magnitude of a star at a distance of 32·6 light years (10 parsecs) from the Earth. **absolute majority,** *n.* a number of votes polled which exceeds the combined total for all other candidates. **absolute music,** *n.* music which does not endeavour to illustrate or depict, as contrasted with programme music. **absolute temperature,** *n.* temperature measured from the absolute zero. **absolute zero,** *n.* the zero of the absolute scale of temperature, equal to −273·1° C. **absolutely,** *adv.* totally, unconditionally; used to express agreement or assent. **absoluteness,** *n.* **absolutism,** *n.* despotic government; the theological doctrine of absolute predestination; the doctrine of the Absolute. **absolutist,** *n.* one who is in favour of arbitrary government; a metaphysician who holds the theory of the Absolute. *a.* pertaining to absolutism or despotism. **absolutistic,** *a.* absolutist. [OF *absolut,* L *absolūtus,* p.p. of *absolvere,* to ABSOLVE]

absolution, *n.* acquittal, remission, forgiveness; the declaration of pardon of sins by a priest to a penitent or a congregation after private or general public confession. [see foll.]

absolve, *v.t.* to set free, release, pardon, acquit; to pronounce forgiveness of sins to a penitent. **absolver,** *n.* one who absolves or pardons. **absolvitor,** *n.* (*Sc. Law*) a favourable verdict; an acquittal. [L *absolvere* (*ab-*, from, *solvere,* to loosen)]

absonant, *a.* discordant, inharmonious, unreasonable. [L *ab-*, from, *sonantem,* acc. of *sonans,* pres.p. of *sonāre,* to sound]

absorb, *v.t.* to suck up, drink in; to imbibe by capillarity; to incorporate; to fully occupy the attention, to engross; to take in and transform (radiant energy) without transmission or reflection. **absorbable,** *a.* **absorbability,** *n.* **absorbed,** *a.* fully engrossed. **absorbent,** *a.* absorbing, capable of or tending to absorb, absorptive. *n.* a vessel in an organism which takes nutritive matter into the system; a substance which has the power of absorbing gases or liquids. **absorbent cotton,** *n.* (*N Am.*) cotton-wool. **absorber,** *n.* that which absorbs; the part of a caloric-engine that absorbs heat. **absorbing,** *a.* occupying one's complete attention. **absorption,** *n.* the act of absorbing; the process of being absorbed. **absorption spectrum,** *n.* the spectrum produced when electromagnetic radiation passes through a selectively absorbing medium. **absorptive,** *a.* having power to absorb, tending to absorb, absorbent. [F *asorber,* from L *absorbēre* (*ab-*, off, away, *sorbēre,* to suck up]

absquatulate, *v.i.* (*N Am., sl.*) to run away, make off quickly, scram.

abstain, *v.i.* to keep oneself away, refrain (from); to refrain from intoxicating liquorsvoluntarily; to refrain from voting. **abstainer,** *n.* [F *abstenir,* from L *abstinēre* (*abs-*, away, *tenēre,* to hold)]

abstemious, *a.* sparing, not self-indulgent, esp. in the use of food and strong liquors; moderate, temperate, inclined to abstinence. **abstemiously,** *adv.* **abstemiousness,** *n.* [L *abstemius* (*abs-*, from, *tēmum,* strong drink, a word extant only in derivatives, *tēmētum, tēmulentus*)]

abstention, *n.* the act of abstaining or refraining, esp. from exercising one's right to vote.

absterge, *v.t.* to wipe clean, to cleanse; to purge by medicine. **abstergent,** *a.* wiping clean, making clean by wiping; having cleansing qualities. *n.* (something) that cleanses, esp. a medicine which cleanses or purges. **abstersion,** *n.* the act of cleansing or purgation. **abstersive,** *a.* having cleansing, purifying qualities; abstergent. *n.* that which wipes, cleanses or purges away. **abstersiveness,** *n.* [L *abstergēre* (*abs-*, away, *tergēre,* to wipe)]

abstinence, *n.* the act or practice of refraining from some indulgence; continence, fasting. **abstinency,** *n.* the habit of abstaining. **abstinent,** *a.* practising abstinence. *n.* an abstainer. **abstinently,** *adv.* [L *abstinens,* pres.p. of *abstinēre;* see ABSTAIN]

abstract[1]**,** *v.t.* to draw or take away, remove; (*euphem.*) to steal; to separate mentally, to consider apart from other things; to epitomize, summarize; to separate by chemical distillation; to extract. [L *abstractus,* p.p. of *abstrahere* (*abs-*, from, *trahere,* to draw)]

abstract[2]**,** *a.* abstracted; separated from particular things, ideal; existing in the mind only; abstruse; theoretical; geometrical or non-representational in design. *n.* an abstract term; a summary, an epitome; an abstract work of art. **abstract of quantities,** apportionment of quantity and cost of materials in a building. **abstract of title,** an epitome of the evidences of ownership; an extract. **in the abstract,** without reference to individual cases, abstractly, ideally, theoretically. **abstract nouns** or **terms,** *n.pl.* names of qualities, in contradistinction to concrete terms which are names of things. **abstract numbers,** *n.pl.* numbers used without reference to particular objects. **abstracted,** *a.* absent-minded, inattentive, withdrawn in thought. **abstractedly,** *adv.* absent-mindedly; in the abstract, separately. **abstractedness,** *n.*

abstract expressionism, *n.* US movement in abstract art that emphasized the act of painting, the expression inherent in paint itself, and the interaction of artist, paint, and canvas. Abstract expressionism first emerged in New York in the early 1940s. Gorky, Kline, Pollock and Rothko are associated with the movement.

abstraction, *n.* the act of abstracting or separating; taking away; (*euphem.*) stealing; the state of being engrossed in thought; the process of considering separately the quality of an object; a mental conception so formed; an abstract idea; the faculty by which people form abstract ideas; an abstract work of art. **abstr-**

active, *a.* possessing the power or quality of abstracting; tending to abstraction. **abstractively,** *adv.* **abstractly,** *adv.* **abstractness,** *n.* [as prec.]

abstruse, *a.* hidden from observation or knowledge; off the beaten track of human thought; recondite, profound. **abstrusely,** *adv.* **abstruseness, †abstrusity,** *n.* [L *abstrūsus,* p.p. of *abstrūdere* (*abs-,* away, *trūdere,* to push)]

absurd, *a.* incongruous; contrary to or inconsistent with reason; nonsensical, logically contradictory; ridiculous. **absurdity,** *n.* the quality or state of being absurd; folly; an absurd notion, statement or action. **absurdly,** *adv.* **absurdness,** *n.* [F *absurde,* from L *absurdus* (*ab-,* away, *surdus,* deaf)]

absurd, theatre of the, THEATRE.

ABTA, (*abbr.*) Association of British Travel Agents.

Abu Bakr or **Abu-Bekr,** *n.* (573–634), 'Father of the virgin', name used by Abd-el-Ka'aba from about 618 when the prophet Mohammed married his daughter Aisha. He was a close adviser to Mohammed in the period 622-32. On the prophet's death, he became the first caliph, adding Mesopotamia to the Muslim world and instigating expansion into Iraq and Syria.

Abu Dhabi, *n.* sheikdom in SW Asia, on the Arabian Gulf, capital of the United Arab Emirates. Formerly under British protection, it has been ruled since 1971 by Sheik Zayed Bin al-Nahayan, who is also president of the Supreme Council of Rulers of the United Arab Emirates.

Abuja, *n.* newly built city in Nigeria which is planned to replace Lagos as capital. Shaped like a crescent, it was designed by the Japanese architect Kenzo Tange.

abulia ABOULIA.

Abu Musa, *n.* a small island in the Persian Gulf. Formerly owned by the ruler of Sharjah, it was forcibly occupied by Iran in 1971.

abundance, *n.* fullness; plenteousness to overflowing; a more than sufficient quantity or number (of); copiousness, affluence. **abundant,** *a.* overflowing; in great supply; plentiful, fully sufficient, more than sufficient, ample. **abundant number,** *n.* a number, the sum of whose aliquot parts exceeds the number itself. **abundantly,** *adv.* [OF *abondance,* from L *abundantia* (*abundant-,* stem of pres.p. of *abundāre,* to ABOUND)]

Abú Nuwás, *n.*, **Hasan ibn Háni** (762–*c.* 815), Arab poet. His work was based on old forms, but the new freedom with which he used them, his eroticism, and his ironic humour, have contributed to his reputation as perhaps the greatest of Arab poets.

abuse[1], *v.t.* to put to an improper use, misuse; to reproach coarsely; to use in an illegitimate sense, to pervert the meaning of; to maltreat, act cruelly to; to violate; to deceive. **abusable,** *a.* capable of being abused. **abuser,** *n.* [OF *abuser,* L *abūsus,* p.p. of *abūtī* (*ab-,* from, amiss, *utī,* to use)]

abuse[2], *n.* improper treatment or employment, misuse; a corrupt practice or custom; insulting or scurrilous language; perversion from the proper meaning; physical maltreatment; violation. **abusive,** *a.* practising abuse; given to the use of harsh language or ill-treatment; opprobrious; misapplied. **abusively,** *adv.* **abusiveness, †abusion,** *n.*

Abu Simbel, *n.* former site of two ancient temples in S Egypt, built during the reign of Ramses II and commemorating him and his wife Nefertari; before the site was flooded by the Aswan High Dam, the temples were moved, in sections, 1966–67.

abut, *v.i.* (*past, p.p.* **abutted**) to be contiguous; to border (on or upon); to form a point or line of contact; of a building, to lean (on or upon). *v.t.* to border. **abutment,** *n.* the state of abutting; that which abuts or borders; a pier or wall, or the part of a pier or wall, against which an arch rests. **abuttal,** *n.* abutment, esp. the abutting part of a piece of land. **abutter,** *n.* one who or that which abuts; the owner of property that abuts. [OF *abouter, abuter,* (*à* to, *but,* end), cp. F *abouter,* to join end to end]

†aby, abye, *v.t.* to redeem, to pay the penalty for; to endure; to atone. *v.i.* to make restitution; to expiate; to endure, to abide. [OE *a-,* intens., away, BUY]

abysm, *n.* an older form of ABYSS, still used poetically. **abysmal,** *a.* pertaining to an abyss; profound, immeasurable; extremely bad. **abysmally,** *adv.* [OF *abisme* (F *abîme*), late L *abyssimus,* superl. of *abyssus*]

abyss, *n.* a vast physical depth, chasm or cavity, as the depth of the sea, or the bowels of the earth; primeval chaos; anything profound and unfathomable, as ignorance or degradation; the middle of an escutcheon. **abyssal,** *a.* pertaining to an abyss; pertaining to the lowest depths of the sea beyond 300 fathoms (about 550 m). [L *abyssus,* Gr. *abussos* (*a-,* without, *bussos,* depth), bottomless]

Abyssinia, *n.* former name of Ethiopia. **Abyssinian,** *a.* belonging to Abyssinia or its inhabitants. *n.* an inhabitant of Abyssinia or Ethiopia; a member of its Church. **Abyssinian gold,** *n.* an alloy of copper and zinc, plated thinly with gold. **Abyssinian pump,** *n.* a pump with well-tube attached to the suction-tube, for use in an Abyssinian well. **Abyssinian well,** *n.* a tube driven into strata of moderate hardness for obtaining water.

ac-, *pref.* AD-, assim. to *c, k, qu,* e.g. *accommodate, accord acquire.*

-ac, *suf.* pertaining to, e.g. *cardiac, demoniac.* (Adjectives so formed are often used as nouns.) [Gr. *-akos*]

AC, (*abbr.*) alternating current; ante Christum (before Christ); appellation contrôlée.

Ac, (*chem. symbol*) actinium.

a/c, (*abbr.*) account.

ACA, (*abbr.*) Associate of the Institute of Chartered Accountants.

Acacia, *n.* an extensive genus of trees with pinnated leaves or else phyllodia, and small flowers in balls or spikes: some species yield catechu and others gum-arabic; (**acacia**) any plant of this genus. **acacia-tree,** *n.* the N American locust-tree or false acacia, *Robinia pseudacacia.*

academic, *a.* pertaining to an academy, college or university; scholarly, theoretic, professorial, unpractical; pertaining to the Platonic school. *n.* a member of an academy, college or university; a person belonging to the academy of Plato, or adhering to the Academic philosophy. **academical,** *a.* academic; unpractical. *n.pl.* academical dress, cap and gown. **academically,** *adv.*

academy, *n.* the members of the philosophical school founded by Plato; a place of study, a high school; a seminary for higher education; a society or association for promoting literature, science or art, established by Government or by private individuals, the members of which are entitled Academicians; the Royal Academy. **academe,** *n.* (*poet.*) an academy [incorrect philologically; probably derived from a misunderstanding of Milton's 'Grove of Academe' (Academos)]. **academician,** *n.* a person belonging to an academy or association for the promotion of science, literature or art; a Royal Academician. **academicism,** *n.* the system of teaching in an academy or high school; academical mannerism; the professorial method. **academism,** *n.* the tenets of the Academic philosophy; Platonism. **academist,** *n.* an Academic philosopher, a member of an academy. [F *académie,* L *acadēmia,* Gr. *akadēmeia* (the gymnasium in the suburbs of Athens where Plato taught, named after the hero *Akadēmos*)]

Academy, French, *n.* (French **Académie Française**), literary society founded by Richelieu in 1635; it is especially concerned with maintaining the purity of the French language; membership is limited to 40 'immortals' at a time.

Academy Award, *n.* annual cinema award given from 1927 onwards by the American Academy of Motion Pictures, nicknamed 'Oscar' (1931).

Academy of Sciences, Soviet, society founded 1725 by Catherine the Great in what is now called Leningrad; it has been responsible for such achievements as Sputnik, and has branches in Ukraine (welding, cybernetics), Armenia (astrophysics), and Georgia (mechanical engineering).

Acadian, *a., n.*, belonging to Nova Scotia. [F *Acadie*, Nova Scotia]

acajou, *n.* the cashew-nut tree, *Anacardium occidentale;* a gummy substance derived from this tree; a wood resembling mahogany; mahogany. [F *acajou*, Brazil. Sp. *acaju*]

-acal, *suf.* adjectives ending in *-ac* being often used as nouns, *-al* was added to distinguish the adjective, e.g. *demoniacal, maniacal; -al* is also added to adjectives to show a less intimate connection with the original noun, e.g. *cardiacal*. [Gr. *akos*, -AK, -AL]

Acalephae, *n.pl.* a class of marine animals containing the sea-nettles, jelly-fish etc. **acaleph**, *n.* any individual of the Acalephae. **acalephan,** *a.* belonging to the Acalephae. *n.* an acaleph. **acalephoid**, *a.* resembling the Acalephae. [Gr. *akalēphē,* a nettle]

acalycine, *a.* without calyx or flower-cup. **acalycinous**, *a.* [mod. L *acalycinus,* from Gr. *a-*, priv., *kalux,* cup]

Acanthopterygii, *n.pl.* a large order of fishes, having the dorsal fin or fins entirely, and the other fins partially, supported by spinous rays: the common perch is a good example. **acanthopterygian,** *a.* belonging to the Acanthopterygii. *n.* any individual of the Acanthopterygii. **acanthopterygious,** *a.* [Gr. *akantha* (see foll.), *pterux,* a wing, *pterugion,* a little wing]

Acanthus, *n.* a genus of prickly-leaved plants; the plant bear's-breech; a conventional ornament resembling the foliage of the acanthus, used to decorate the capitals of the Corinthian and Composite orders. **acanthaceous**, *a.* armed with spines or prickles. **acanthine**, *a.* pertaining to or resembling the acanthus; prickly; ornamented with the acanthus leaf. **acanthoid**, **acanthous,** *a.* prickly, spinous. **acantho-,** *comb.form* (*Bot.*) spiny, having thorns or thorn-like processes. [L *acanthus,* Gr. *akanthos* (*akantha,* a thorn, *akē,* a point)]

a cappella, *a., adv.* (It.) withoutinstrumental accompaniment. [It. *a cappella,* in chapel style]

acapsular, *a.* having no capsule. [CAPSULE]

Acapulco, *n.* (or **Acapulco de Juarez**) port and holiday resort in Mexico; population (1985) 638,000.

acardiac, *a.* without a heart. *n.* a foetus destitute of a heart. [Gr. *akardios* (*a-*, priv., *kardia,* heart)]

acarodomatium, *n.* an abode for mites found in certain plants which benefit by their presence. [Gr. *akari,* a mite; *domation,* a little house]

acarpous, *a.* producing no fruit; sterile, barren. [Gr. *akarpos* (*a-*, priv., *karpos,* fruit)]

Acarus, *n.* a genus of Arachnida, comprising the mites and ticks. **acaricide**, *n.* a substance that kills mites, a remedy for the itch. **Acarida**, **Acarina**, *n.pl.* the order including the mites and ticks. **acarid, acaridan**, **acaridean**, *n., a.* (one) of the Acarida. **acaroid**, *a.* [Gr. *akari,* a mite (*a-*, priv., *keirein,* to cut)]

ACAS, (*abbr.*) Advisory, Conciliation and Arbitration Service, an independent organization set up by the UK government 1975 to advise and arbitrate in industrial disputes between staff and employers.

acatalectic, *a.* not breaking off short; complete; having the full number of metrical feet. *n.* a verse having the complete number of feet. [late L *acatalēcticus,* Gr. *akatalēktos* (*a-*, priv., CATALECTIC)]

acatalepsy, *n.* incomprehensibleness; the sceptical doctrine that things are unknowable; mental confusion. **acataleptic**, *a.* incomprehensible; not to be known with certainty. [Gr. *akatalēpsia* (*a-*, priv., *kata,* down, *lēpsis,* a taking hold)]

acauline, -lose, -lous, *a.* without apparent stem, stemless. **acaulescence**, *n.* the occasional apparent suppression of the stem. **acaulescent,** *a.* acauline. [Gr. *a-*, priv., *kaulos,* stalk, stem]

acc., (*abbr.*) according; account; accusative.

accablé, *a.* crushed, overwhelmed. [F, p.p. of *accabler,* to overwhelm (fem. *accablée*)]

Accadian, AKKADIAN under AKKAD.

accede, *v.i.* to come to (a certain view), to agree to, assent; to join, give one's adhesion to; to come to (an office or dignity). **accedance,** *n.* [L *accēdere* (*ac-*, *ad-*, to, *cēdere,* to come)]

accelerando, *a., adv.* with increasing speed. [It.]

accelerate, *v.t.* to hasten; to increase the rate of progress or velocity of; to bring nearer in point of time. *v.i.* to increase in velocity or rate of progress, to move faster. **acceleratedly,** *adv.* **acceleration,** *n.* the act of accelerating, or the state of being accelerated; progressive increase of velocity or rate of progress; rate of increase ofvelocity, measured by time-units. **accelerative,** *a.* **accelerator,** *n.* that which accelerates; a device for increasing the supply of petrol into the carburettor, thus causing the engine to run at an accelerated speed; any chemical or apparatus for speeding up the appearance or development of a picture or an exposed sensitized plate or print; an electrical appliance for accelerating charged particles such as electrons or protons to high velocities or energies. **accelerator nerve,** *n.* a nerve that accelerates the frequency of the heart-beat. **acceleratory,** *a.* **accelerometer**, *n.* an instrument for measuring acceleration. [L *accelerāre,* to hasten (*ac-*, *ad-*, to, *celer,* swift); -ATE]

†**accend,** *v.t.* to light, to set on fire. †**accendibility**, *n.* †**accendible,** *a.* capable of being set on fire or burnt; inflammable.†**accension**, *n.* the act of setting on fire; the state of being set on fire; inflammation, heat. **accensor,** *n.* one who lights and trims the tapers in the Roman Catholic Church. [L *accendere* (*ac-*, *ad-*, to, *-cendere,* to kindle, cp. *candēre,* to glow with heat)]

accent[1]**,** *n.* a particular prominence given to a syllable by means of stress or higher musical pitch; manner of speaking or pronunciation expressive of feeling, or peculiar to an individual, a locality or a nation; a mark used in writing or printing to direct the stress of the voice; musical stress, metrical or rhythmical stress; distinctive emphasis or intensity; (*pl.*) words, language. [F *accent,* L *accentum,* acc. of *accentus* (*ad-*, to, *cantus,* singing)]

accent[2]**,** *v.t.* to lay stress upon a syllable or word, or a note or passage of music; to mark with emphasis, make conspicuous; to mark with an accent; †to utter, to pronounce. **accentual,** *a.* pertaining to accent; rhythmical; accented verse as distinguished from that governed by quantity. **accentuate,** *v.t.* to pronounce or mark with an accent; to lay stress on, to emphasize. **accentuation,** *n.* the application of accent; stress, emphasis; mode of pronunciation.

accentor, *n.* the hedge-warbler or hedge-sparrow.

accept, *v.t.* to consent to take (something offered); to view with favour; to admit the truth of, acknowledge; to agree to, to admit, to take responsibility for; to promise to pay (a bill of exchange) when due. **accepted mason,** *n.* an approved and admitted Freemason. **acceptable,** *a.* **acceptability**, **acceptableness,** *n.* **acceptably,** *adv.* **acceptance,** *n.* the act of receiving; favourable reception; agreement to terms or proposals; admission to favour; generally received meaning of an expression; an accepted bill of exchange; the act of subscribing, or the subscription to, a bill of exchange. **acceptancy,** *n.* acceptance; willingness to accept. **acceptant,** *a.* willingly receiving. *n.* one who accepts. **acceptation,** *n.* the act of accepting; favourable reception; the recognized sense or meaning of an expression. **accepter,** *n.* one who accepts; †one who shows partiality (e.g. a judge who is influenced by personal considerations), a respecter of persons. **acceptor,** *n.* one who accepts a bill of exchange; an impurity added to a semiconductor to increase the number of positively charged current carriers and hence the conductivity. [F *accepter,* L *acceptāre,* freq. of *accipere* (*ac-*, *ad-*, to, *capere,* to take)]

access, *n.* admission to a place or person; freedom to obtain or use something; approach; the means of approach, passage, channel; increase, addition; attack by disease or emotion. *v.t.* to gain access to, esp. to retrieve (data) from (computer storage); to place (data) in (computer storage). *a.* designating or pertaining to radio and television programmes made by the general public. **access road,** *n.* a road that gives access to a particular place. **access time,** *n.* the time interval between requesting data and its delivery from computer storage. **accessary**, *n.*, *a.* (an) accessory. **accessible**, *a.* capable of being approached or reached; easy of access; approachable, attainable. **accessibility**, *n.* **accessibly,** *adv.* **accession**, *n.* the act of going or coming to; agreeing or consenting to; coming to the throne, an office or a dignity; an increase, addition; an improvement or addition to property by growth or labour expended. **accession-book,** *n.* a register of additions to the stock of books in a library. **accession-number,** *n.* the serial number given to a volume in the accession-book on its arrival in the library. **accessory**, *a.* contributive, helpful to some effect, aiding, or acting in subordination to a principal; accompanying, additional; guilty, not as the chief actor, but *before the fact,* by counselling or commanding the act, or *after the fact,* by assisting or concealing the offender. *n.* one who abets or countenances anything that is wrong; an accomplice; something added merely for ornament; any secondary accompaniment. [L *accessus,* p.p. of *accēdere;* see ACCEDE]

acciaccatura, *n.* (*pl.* **-ras, -re**) a short grace note played rapidly. [It. *acciaccare,* to crush together]

accidence, *n.* that part of grammar which deals with the inflection (i.e. the accidents) of words; an elementary grammar; the rudiments of a subject. [L *accidentia,* pl. neuter n. or the same word taken as fem. sing.; see foll.]

accident, *n.* an event proceeding from an unknown cause; the unforeseen effect of a known cause; something unexpected; a casualty, a mishap; a property or quality of a thing not essential to our conception of it; a mere accessory, an attribute. **accidental**, *a.* occurring by chance, unexpectedly; not according to the usual order of things; adventitious, non-essential. *n.* a non-essential property; an accident; a sharp, flat or natural sign occurring in music before a particular note, not in the key-signature. **accidental colours,** *n.pl.* the complementary colours seen after looking fixedly on a bright-coloured object, and then on a white or light-coloured surface. **accidental lights, accidentals,** *n.pl.* effects of light and shade in a painting, caused, not by daylight, but by the artificial introduction of light. **accidental point,** *n.* the point in which a straight line drawn from the eye parallel to another given straight line intersects the plane of a picture. **accidentalism,** *n.* accidental character; accidental effect. **accidentality**, *n.* **accidentally,** *adv.* **accidentalness,** *n.* [F *accident,* L *accidens -entis,* pres.p. of *accidere* (*ac-, ad-,* to, *cadere,* to fall)]

accidie ACEDIA.

Accipiter, *n.* a genus of raptorial birds, containing the hawks. **accipitral,** *a.* **accipitrine**, *a.* belonging to or resembling hawks; rapacious, predatory; keen-sighted. [L *accipiter* (*accipere,* to take, accept)]

accite, *v.t.* to summon, to cite. [late L *accītāre* (*ad-, cītāre,* to CITE)]

acclaim, *v.t.* to applaud loudly, welcome with enthusiasm, announce with enthusiasm. *v.i.* to shout applause. *n.* a shout of joy; acclamation. **acclamation**, *n.* a demonstration of joy or applause made by a multitude. **acclamatory**, *a.* [L *acclāmāre* (*ac-, ad-,* to, *clāmāre,* to shout)]

acclimatize, -ise, (*N Am.*) **acclimate**, *v.t.* to habituate to a new climate or environment; to adapt for existence and propagation in a new climate. **acclimatization, -isation,** *n.* the act or process of acclimatizing; the state of being acclimatized; the modification of the constitution of an organic being which enables it to exist in aclimate other than its own. **acclimatation, acclimation,** *n.* acclimatization by nature, spontaneous accommodation to new conditions as distinguished from acclimatization by humans. [F *acclimater*]

acclivity, *n.* an upward slope; the talus of a rampart. **acclivitous,** *a.* characterized by an acclivity or acclivities. †**acclivous**, *a.* rising with a slope, ascending. [L *acclīvitātem,* acc. of *acclīvitas* (*ac-, ad-, clīvus,* a slope)]

accolade, *n.* the ceremony of conferring knighthood by an embrace, putting hand on neck, or a gentle stroke with the flat of a sword; a brace uniting several staves; an award or honour, (an expression of) praise and approval. [F *accolade,*It. *accolata,* fem. p.p. of *accolare* (L *ac-, ad-, collum,* neck), to embrace about the neck]

accommodate, *v.t.* to make suitable, correspondent or consistent; to fit, adapt to, settle or adjust; to bring into harmony or concord, reconcile; to supply or furnish; to provide lodging for. **accommodating,** *a.* obliging, complying, yielding to others' desires. **accommodatingly,** *adv.* **accommodation,** *n.* the act of accommodating; adjustment, adaptation, reconciliation, compromise; the act of supplying a want; the state of being accommodated; fitness, state of adaptation; anything that supplies a want in respect of ease, convenience, food, lodging etc.; a loan; changing the focus of the eye. **accommodation address,** *n.* an address to which mail may be sent, used by a person or business unable or unwilling to give a permanent address. **accommodation bill** or **note,** *n.* a bill or note drawn for the purpose of raising money, and not for value received. **accommodation ladder,** *n.* a light ladder fixed outside a vessel at the gangway. **accommodation land,** *n.* land bought by a speculator to be leased out for building purposes. **accommodation unit,** *n.* a dwelling. **accommodative,** *a.* **accommodativeness,** *n.* [L *accommodāre* (*ac-, ad-, commodus,* fitting; COM-, with, *modus,* measure)]

accompany, *v.t.* to go with, escort, attend as a companion; to live with; to exist along with, to characterize; to play the instrumental accompaniment for; †to cohabit. *v.i.* to play the accompaniment. **accompanier,** *n.* **accompaniment,** *n.* something super-added to or attendant upon another thing; something which gives greater completeness to; the part or parts performed by instruments accompanying the soloist. **accompanist,** *n.* the performer who plays the instrumental accompaniment. [F *accompagner*]

accomplice, *n.* a partner, esp. in crime; a partaker in guilt. **accompliceship,** *n.* **accomplicity**, *n.* complicity, assistance in crime. [F *complice,* L *complicem,* nom. *complex (com-,* together, *plicāre,* to fold); *ac* is either indef. art. *a* or due to erroneous assimilation to *accomplish*]

accomplish, *v.t.* to fill up, to complete, to finish; to carry out, fulfil, achieve. **accomplishable,** *a.* **accomplished,** *a.* complete, finished; highly skilled, consummate; having the graces and social skills perfecting one for society. **accomplisher,** *n.* **accomplishment,** *n.* the act of accomplishing or fulfilling; the state of being accomplished; something achieved; an acquirement, attainment, esp. a social skill. [OF *acomplir* (mod. F *accomplir,* pres.p. *accomplissant*) from late L *accomplēre* (*ac-, ad-, complēre,* to fill up)]

accompt, *v.*, *n.* ACCOUNT. **accomptant** ACCOUNTANT.

accord, *v.t.* to cause to agree; to adapt, to make consistent, to adjust, to grant. *v.i.* to agree, to be in correspondence or harmony. *n.* agreement, harmony, assent, adjustment of a difference; harmonious correspondence; a treaty. **of one's own accord,** voluntarily. **with one accord,** with the assent of all. **accordance, -ancy,** *n.* **accordant,** *a.* agreeing, consonant, harmonious, in tune. **accordantly,** *adv.* **accorder,** *n.* **according,** *part.a.*, *adv.* agreeing, corresponding (to), consentient, harmonious; agreeably with, precisely, just. **according as,** agreeably, in proportion to. **according to,** agreeably to, in relation to; as stated by; depending on. **accordingly,** *adv.* suitably, in accordance; therefore, consequently. [OF *acorder,* late L *accordāre* L (*cor, cordis,* heart)]

accordion, *n.* a small portable keyed instrument in which the notes are produced by bellows action on metallic reeds. **accordion-pleating,** *n.* pleats with very narrow folds resembling the bellows of an accordion. **accordionist,** *n.* a player on the accordion. [It. *accordare,* to tune; -ION]

accost, *v.t.* †to come side by side with, to border, to adjoin; to approach and speak to, to address; of a prostitute, to solicit. †*v.i.* to be contiguous; to sail along the coast. *n.* address, salutation, greeting. †**accostable,** *a.* [F *accoster,* late L *accostāre* (*ac-, ad-,* to, *costa,* a rib, side)]

accouchement, *n.* confinement, lying-in, delivery. **accoucheur,** *n.* a person who assists women at childbirth. **accoucheuse,** *n.fem.* [F *accoucher* and -MENT]

account, *v.t.* to reckon, compute, count; to regard as, to deem, consider. *v.i.* to give a reckoning, reason, explanation or answer. *n.* reckoning, counting, computation; a recital, description, narrative, explanation; a statement of receipts and expenditure showing the balance; a register of debit and credit; a statement of goods or services supplied with calculation of money due, a bill; on the Stock Exchange, the fortnightly period from one settlement to another; credit relations, business relations; a business arrangement involving the establishing of a record of debit and credit; an amount of money deposited at a bank; profit, advantage; behalf, sake. **for account of,** to be sold on behalf of, to be accounted for to. **in account with,** having business relations with. **of no account,** valueless, negligible. **on account,** as an interim payment. **on account of,** for the sake of, because of. **on no account,** by no means. **to account for,** to render an account of; to afford an explanation of; to tell the cause of. **to bring** or **call to account,** to require an explanation from; to reprimand. **to find one's account in,** to find advantage, profit in. **to give a good account of,** to be successful, do (oneself) credit. **to hold to account,** to hold responsible. **to take account of, to take into account** TAKE. **account-book,** *n.* a register of business transactions. **account day,** *n.* a day of reckoning. **accountable,** *a.* liable to be called on to render an account of; responsible. **accountability,** *n.* liability to be called on to give an account of; responsibility. **accountableness,** *n.* [OF *aconter,* late L *acomptāre* (*ac-, ad-,* to, *com-,* together, *putāre,* to reckon)]

accountant, *n.* one whose occupation is the keeping of accounts; a public officer charged with the duty of keeping and inspecting accounts; one liable to render account; †the defendant in an action of account. **accountant-general,** *n.* the principal accountant in large mercantile houses, companies or public offices. **accountancy,** *n.* **accountantship,** *n.*

accouplement, *n.* the act of coupling together; the state of being coupled together; that which serves to connect; a tie or brace. [F]

accoutre, *v.t.* to dress, to equip; to array in military dress; to equip for military service. **accoutrement,** *n.* a soldier's equipment, excepting arms and dress; (*usu. pl.*) dress, outfit, equipment. [med. F *accoustrer* (F *accoutrer*), prob. from *à* prep. and *coustre, coutre,* a sacristan]

Accra, *n.* capital and port of Ghana; population of Greater Accra region (1984) 1,420,000. The port trades in cacao, gold, and timber. Industries include engineering, brewing, and food processing. Osu (Christiansborg) Castle is the presidential residence.

accredit, *v.t.* to confer credit on, vouch for, sanction; to send with credentials (as an ambassador). **accreditation,** *n.* **accredited,** *a.* recognized officially, generally accepted; conforming to an official standard of quality. **accredited milk,** *n.* milk that has passed bacterial-content tests and has been produced by a periodically examined herd. [F *accréditer* (*à crédit;* see CREDIT)]

accrescence, *n.* continued growth, increase; something which grows on a thing, anaccretion. **accrescent,** *a.* [L *accrescere,* to grow]

accrete, *v.i.* to grow together; to combine round a nucleus. *a.* (*Bot.*) grown together by adhesion (of parts normally separate). **accretion,** *n.* increase by organic growth; increase in growth by external additions; the growing together of parts naturally separate, as the fingers; the result of such growth; the part added; (*Law*) the accession or adhesion of foreign matter to something (chiefly used of land deposited from a river or the sea). [L *accrētus,* p.p. of *accrēscere,* to grow (*ac-, ad-,* to, *crēscere*)]

accrue, *v.i.* to grow, to increase; to arise, to fall, come to (as a natural growth). **accrual,** *n.* [OF *acreue,* growth, orig. p.p. of *acroître* (L *accrēscere*), to grow]

acct., (*abbr.*) account; accountant.

acculturate, *v.t., v.i.* to adopt the values and traits of another culture. **acculturation,** *n.* [L *ac-, ad-,* to, CULTURE, -ATE]

accumulate, *v.t.* to heap up, pile one thing above another; to bring together by degrees, to amass; to take several university degrees at a time. *v.i.* to grow in size, number or quantity, by repeated additions. **accumulation,** *n.* the act of accumulating or amassing; the process of taking a number of university degrees; the state of being accumulated; that which is accumulated; a mass. **accumulative,** *a.* accumulating, amassing. **accumulatively,** *adv.* **accumulator,** *n.* one who or that which accumulates; one who takes university degrees by accumulation; an apparatus for storing hydraulic or electric energy, esp. a rechargeable electric cell or battery; a bet, usu. on four or more races, in which the winnings from one race are staked on the next; a location in a computer where numbers are stored or arithmetic operations are performed. [L *accumulātus,* p.p. of *accumulāre,* to heap up (*ac-, ad-,* to, *cumulāre*)]

accurate, *a.* careful, exact, in precise accordance with rule or standard of truth; without error or defect. **accuracy,** *n.* exactness; correctness resulting from care; precision; conformity to a standard; precision of fit. **accurately,** *adv.* **accurateness,** *n.* [L *accūrātus,* p.p. of *accūrāre* (*ac-, ad-, cūrāre,* from *cūra,* care)]

accurse, *v.t.* to call down curses on. **accursed, accurst,** *a.* lying under a curse; execrable, detestable; excommunicated; fated. [OE *a-,* intens., *cursian,* to curse]

accusative, *a.* of or belonging to the objective case of declinable words in inflected languages; also applied to the word that represents the object in uninflected languages. (It in many respects agrees with the objective case in English, which is often called the accusative.) *n.* the grammatical case defined above. **accusatival,** *a.* pertaining to the accusative. **accusatively,** *adv.* [F *accusatif,* L *accūsātīvus* (ACCUSE), lit. trans. of Gr. *aitiatikē,* the case of accusing or of effect]

accuse, *v.t.* to charge with a crime, offence or fault, to indict; to lay the blame formally (on a person or thing). **accusable,** *a.* liable to be charged with a crime or fault, blameworthy, censurable. **accusal,** *n.* **accusation,** *n.* the act of accusing; the state of being accused; a charge brought against one. **accusatory,** *a.* containing or involving an accusation. **accusatorial,** *a.* involving accusation or indictment in a case in which judge and prosecutor are distinct (contrasted with inquisitorial). **accusatorially,** *adv.* **accused,** *a.* **the accused,** the defendant or defendants in a criminal case. **accuser,** *n.* **accusingly,** *adv.* [OF *acuser,* L *accūsāre* (*ac-, ad-,* to, *cause,* reason, cause, lawsuit)]

accustom, *v.t.* to habituate (usually in *pass.* or *reflex.,* oneself to, or to do), to make familiar by use. †*v.i.* to be used or wont. †**accustomary,** *a.* **accustomed,** *a.* often practised, usual, familiar, ordinary, habitual. **accustomedness,** *n.* [CUSTOM]

AC/DC, *a.* (*sl.*) bisexual. [*a*lternating *c*urrent, *d*irect *c*urrent]

ace, *n.* the single point on cards or dice; a card or domino with but one mark upon it; a trifle, a very small amount; a hair's-breadth; a fighter-pilot who has brought down ten or more hostile aircraft; a person of first rank in sport etc. [OF *as,* L *as,* a unit]

-acea, *suf.* used analogously to form names of classes or orders of animals, e.g. *Cetacea, Crustacea* etc. [L *suf.,* pl. neut. of *-āceus* (-āc and *-cus*)]

-aceae, *suf.* used to form names of orders or families of plants, e.g. *Rosaceae.* [L *suf.,* fem. pl. qualifying *plantae;* see -ACEA]

-acean, *suf.* forms singular nouns or adjectives corresponding to collective nouns in -acea, e.g. (a) crustacean, cetacean. [L -ACEA, *-āceus*]

acedia, *n.* an abnormal mental condition characterized by listlessness, fatigue and lack of interest in things. [Gr., heedlessness]

aceldama, *n.* a field near Jerusalem purchased by the chief priests with the 30 pieces of silver returned by Judas, and used as a burial-place (Acts i.19); hence any place stained by slaughter. [Gr. *akeldama,* cp. Syr. *ōkēl damō,* the field of blood]

acentric, *a.* without centre; not about a centre. [Gr. *a-,* priv., *kentron,* centre]

-aceous, *suf.* of the nature of, belonging to, like; forming adjectives from nouns in natural science, e.g. *crustaceous, cretaceous, farinaceous, filaceous.* [L *suf.* -ACEA and -OUS]

acephal-, *pref.* headless: combining form to various scientific terms, chiefly botanical and zoological. **acephalous,** *a.* without a head; having no superior or head; short of the beginning (as in a verse or manuscript); (*Zool.*) with no distinct head, as in one division of the Mollusca; (*Bot.*) with lateral instead of terminal style. **acephalan,** *a., n.* [Gr. *akephalos* (*a-,* priv., *kephalē,* head)]

Acer, *n.* a genus of trees and shrubs of N temperate regions with over 115 species, including the sycamores and maples.

acerb, *a.* sour, with a rough and astringent taste, as of unripe fruit. **acerbic,** *a.* sour, astringent; bitter or harsh in speech or manner. **acerbically,** *adv.* [L *acerbus,* bitter]

acerbity, *n.* sourness, with roughness or astringency, as of unripe fruit; bitterness of suffering; harshness of speech, action or temper. [F *acerbité,* L *acerbitātem,* acc. of *acerbitas* (*acerbus,* bitter)]

acerose, *a.* (*Bot.*) needle-sharp. [L *acer,* sharp]

acervate, *a.* heaped up; growing into heaps or clusters. **acervation,** *n.* the act of heaping up, accumulation. [L *acervātus,* p.p. of *acervāre* (*acervus,* a heap), to heap up]

acescent, *a.* turning sour, rather sour, subacid. **acescence,** *n.* [L *acescere,* inceptive of *acēre,* to be sour]

acet-, *comb. form* of the nature of vinegar; acetic; acetic acid. [L *acētum,* vinegar (*acēre,* to be sour)]

acetabulum, *n.* (*pl.* **-la, -lums**) an ancient Roman vessel for holding vinegar; a cavity in any bone designed to receive the protuberant head of another bone, e.g. the socket of the hip-joint in man; the socket in which the leg of an insect is inserted; one of the suckers on the arms of a cuttlefish; the cup-shaped fructification of many lichens; the receptacle of certain fungi. [L *acētābulum,* from *acētum,* vinegar, *-abulum,* dim. of *-abrum,* a vessel or holder]

acetaldehyde, *n.* a volatile liquid aldehyde used in the manufacture of organic compounds. [ACET-, ALDEHYDE]

acetarious, *a.* used in salads. [L *acētāria,* salad plants, neut. pl. of *acētāris,* a., pertaining to vinegar]

acetic, *n.* pertaining to vinegar, akin to vinegar; sour. **acetic acid,** *n.* the acid which imparts sourness to vinegar. **acetate,** *n.* a salt of acetic acid; cellulose acetate; a photographic film or a textile made from cellulose acetate. **acetated,** *a.* treated with acetic acid. **acetify,** *v.t.* to convert into vinegar; to render sour. *v.i.* to become sour. **acetification,** *n.* the process of making into vinegar, or of rendering sour. **acetous, -ose,** *a.* having the character of vinegar, sour; causing acetification. [ACET-]

acetone, *n.* an inflammable liquid obtained by distilling acetated or organic substances and used in the manufacture of chloroform and as a solvent; a ketone. [from prec.]

acetyl, *n.* the radical of acetic acid. **acetylcholine,** *n.* a chemical released at nerve endings that transmits nerve impulses. **acetylsalicylic acid,** *n.* aspirin. [ACET-, -YL]

acetylene, *n.* a gas composed of carbon and hydrogen, which burns with an intensely brilliant flame; ethyne. [ACET-, -YL, -ENE]

Achaea, *n.* in ancient Greece, and also today, an area of the N Peloponnese; the **Achaeans** were the predominant society during the Mycenaean period and are said by Homer to have taken part in the siege of Troy.

Achaean League, *n.* union in 275 BC of most of the cities of the N Peloponnese, which managed to defeat Sparta, but was itself defeated by the Romans, 146 BC.

Achaemenid dynasty, *n.* dynasty ruling the Persian Empire (550–330 BC), and named after Achaemenes, ancestor of Cyrus the Great, founder of the empire. His successors included Cambyses, Darius I, Xerxes and Darius III, who, as the last Achaemenid ruler, was killed after defeat in battle against Alexander the Great in 330 BC.

acharnement, *n.* (F) bloodthirsty fury, ferocity; gusto.

Achates, *n.* character in the *Aeneid,* an epic poem by the Roman poet Virgil from the 1st century BC. Achates was the friend of the hero Aeneas, hence a *fidus Achates* (Latin 'faithful'). The name is proverbial for a faithful companion.

ache, *v.i.* to suffer pain or distress. *n.* continuous pain (in contradistinction to a twinge); distress. [OE *acan*]

Achebe, *n.* **Chinua** (1930–), Nigerian novelist, whose themes include the social and political impact of European colonialism on African people, and the problems of newly independent African nations. His first novel, *Things Fall Apart* (1958), was widely acclaimed; *Anthills of the Savannah* (1987) is also set in a fictional African country.

achene, achaene, *n.* a small dry carpel, with a single seed, which does not open when ripe. **achenial,** *a.* [Gr. *a-,* priv., *chainein,* to gape]

Acheron, *n.* a fabled stream in the infernal regions; the infernal regions, the underworld. **Acherontic,** *a.* of or pertaining to Acheron, infernal; gloomy; about to die, moribund. [L from Gr. *Acheron* (*achos,* grief, *rhoos,* stream), river of sorrow]

Acheson, *n.* **Dean (Gooderham)** (1893–1971), US politician; as undersecretary of state (1945–47) in Truman's Democratic administration, he was associated with George C. Marshall in preparing the Marshall Plan, and succeeded him as secretary of state (1949–53).

Acheulian, *a.* of or pertaining to the period of Lower Palaeolithic culture, typified by remains discovered in St Acheul, and placed by archaeologists between the Chellean and the Mousterian epochs. [St *Acheul,* France]

achieve, *v.t.* to perform, accomplish, finish; to attain, acquire, or bring about by an effort. **achievable,** *a.* **achievement,** *n.* the act of accomplishing; the thing achieved; a heroic deed, an exploit; a complete heraldic composition; a funeral escutcheon. **achiever,** *n.* [OF *achever,* from phrase *venir à chef,* late L *ad caput venīre,* to come to a head]

Achilles, *n.* Greek hero of Homer's *Iliad.* He was the son of Peleus, king of the Myrmidons in Thessaly, and the sea nymph Thetis, who rendered him invulnerable, except for the heel by which she held him, by dipping him in the river Styx. Achilles killed Hector in the Trojan War and was himself killed by Paris who shot a poisoned arrow into Achilles' heel. **Achillean,** *a.* like Achilles; heroic, invulnerable; invincible. **Achilles heel,** *n.* a person's vulnerable point, the heel being the part where Achilles was said to be vulnerable, his mother Thetis holding him by the heel when she dipped him in the river Styx to make himinvulnerable. **Achilles' tendon,** *n.* the tendon or ligature connecting the muscles of the calf to the heel-bone.

achilous, *a.* (*Bot.*) without lips. [Gr. *a-,* *cheilos,* lip]

achlamydeous, *a.* having neither calyx nor corolla, as the willows. [Gr. *a-,* priv., *chlamus -udos,* a cloak]

achromatic, *a.* colourless; transmitting light without decomposing it into its primary colours. **achromatically,** *adv.* **achromatism, achromaticity,** *n.* the quality or state of being achromatic. **achromatize, -ise,** *v.t.* to deprive of colour. **achromatopsy,** *n.* colour blindness. [Gr. *achrōmatos* (*a-,* priv., *chrōma -atos,* colour)]

acicular, *a.* resembling a needle in shape or sharpness. **acicularly,** *adv.* **aciculate, -ated,** *a.* having needle-like bristles; marked with fine, irregular streaks. [L *acicula,* a small needle, -AR[1]]

acid, *a.* sour, tart, sharp to the taste; sharp or sour in manner or speech; having the properties of an acid, reacting as an acid; of rocks which have a large proportion of silica. *n.* a sour substance; a compound of hydrogen in which the hydrogen can be replaced by a metal, or with a basic metallic oxide, to form a salt of that metal and water; (*sl.*) LSD. **to put on the acid,** (*Austral.*) to scrounge, to cadge. **acid cloud,** *n.* an area of mist or low cloud containing high concentrations of pollutant acids harmful to crops etc. **acid house, Acid House,** *n.* a youth cult concerned with highly electronically synthesized disco or pop music (and the taking of psychedelic drugs); such disco or pop music. **acid rain,** *n.* precipitation made acidic and thus harmful to crops etc. by the release of (industrial) pollutants, esp. sulphur and nitrogen compounds, into the atmosphere. **acid rock,** *n.* rock music featuring bizarre amplified instrumental effects. **acid test,** *n.* (*coll.*) an absolute and definite test; a critical ordeal. **acidic,** *a.* acid. **acidify,** *v.t.* to render acid or sour; to convert into an acid. *v.i.* to become acid. **acidifiable,** *a.* capable of being rendered acid. **acidification,** *n.* the act or process of acidifying; the state of being acidified. **acidimeter,** *n.* instrument for measuring the strength of acids. **acidimetry,** *n.* **acidity, acidness,** *n.* the quality of being acid; sourness, tartness, sharpness. [L *acidus,* sour (*acēre,* to be sour)]

acidosis, *n.* condition characterized by the appearance of acetone bodies in the urine and bloodstream. **acidotic,** *a.*

acidulous, *a.* a little sour or acid, moderately sharp to the taste, subacid. **acidulate,** *v.t.* to render slightly acid; to flavour with an acid. **acidulated,** *a.* rendered slightly acid; flavoured with acid; soured, embittered in temper. [L *acidulus,* dim. of *acidus*]

acierate, *v.t.* to turn into steel. **acierage,** *n.* the process of electroplating a metal with iron or steel. [F *acier,* late L *aciārium,* L *acies,* edge]

acinus, *n.* (*pl.* **-ni**) a bunch of fleshy fruit, especially a bunch of grapes; a fruit consisting of several drupels, as the raspberry; small stones as in grapes, strawberries etc.; a racemose gland. **aciniform,** *a.* clustered like grapes. [L *acinus,* a berry growing in a cluster]

-acious, *suf.* abounding in, characterized by, inclined to; added to verbal stems to form adjectives, e.g. *loquacious, tenacious.* [L *-ax -ācis* and -OUS]

-acity, *suf.* the quality of: forms nouns of quality from adjectives in -ACIOUS. [F *-acité,* L *ācitas -tātem*]

ack-ack, *n.* anti-aircraft. [morse names of letters formerly used by signallers]

ack dum, *adv.* at once, quickly. [Hind.]

ack-emma, *n.* morning, a.m. [see ACK-ACK]

acknowledge, *v.t.* to own the truth of, to own, to confess, to admit; to recognize the authority of; to give a receipt for; to express appreciation or gratitude for. **acknowledgeable,** *a.* **acknowledgment,** *n.* the act of acknowledging; recognition, confession, admission; receipt for money or goods; an expression of gratitude; something given or done in return for a service or message. [OE *on,* KNOWLEDGE, or from obs. n. *acknowledge* (*acknowe,* OE *on, cnāwan,* to know)]

-acle, *suf.* diminutive of nouns, e.g. *tabernacle, miracle.* [L *-āculum*]

aclinic, *a.* not dipping, situated where the magnetic needle does not dip. **aclinic line,** *n.* the magnetic equator. [Gr. *a-,* priv., *klinein,* to bend, see -IC]

acme, *n.* the top or highest point, the culmination; the maturity of life; the crisis or turning-point of a disease. [Gr. *akmē,* an edge]

acne, *n.* a pimple or tubercle; a skin disease characterized by pimples or tubercles. [prob. Gr. *aknesis,* without itch]

acock, *adv.* in a cocked fashion; defiantly.

†**acold,** *a.* cold, chilly. [OE prob. *ācōlod,* pp. of *ācōlian,* to cool]

acolyte, *n.* an assisting officer in the Roman Catholic Church; an attendant, ministrant; a faithful follower. [late L *acolythus, acolitus,* from Gr. *akolouthos,* a follower]

Aconcagua, *n.* an extinct volcano in the Argentine Andes, the highest peak in the Americas. Height 6960 m/22,834 ft. It was first climbed by Vines and Zeebruggen in 1897.

aconite, *n.* a plant of the genus *Aconitum,* esp. *A. napellus,* the common monk's-hood or wolf's-bane; a poison drug used medicinally, obtained from the root of this plant. **aconitic,** *a.* **aconitine,** *n.* an alkaloid substance derived from the genus *Aconitum.* [F *aconit,* L *aconītum,* Gr. *akonīton*]

acorn, *n.* the fruit of the oak. **acorn-barnacle, acorn-shell,** *n. Balanus crenatus;* a multi-valve cirriped allied to the barnacles. **acorned,** *a.* (*Her.*) bearing acorns as a charge. [OE *æcern* (*æcer,* a field), fruit of the field, i.e. of the open country]

Acorus, *n.* an aromatic herb of the order Orontiaceae, once used for strewing on floors, now for flavouring beer and in the manufacture of perfumes.

acosmism, *n.* denial of the existence of the universe as apart from the Creator. [Gr. *a-,*priv., *kosmos,* the world]

acotyledon, *n.* any plant of the class Acotyledones; a plant without distinct seed-lobes. **acotyledonous,** *a.* having no cotyledons; pertaining to a plant without visible seed-lobes. [mod. L *acotylēdones,* from Gr. *a-,* priv., COTYLEDON]

acoustic, -ical, *a.* pertaining to the ear, constituting part of the physical apparatus for hearing; pertaining to hearing, sound or acoustics; pertaining to musical instruments whose sound is not electronically amplified. *n.* a remedy for deafness. **acoustically,** *adv.* **acoustician,** *n.* one who investigates the phenomena of sound; one skilled in acoustics. **acousticon,** *n.* an appliance to aid hearing. **acoustics,** *n.* the science of sound and its phenomena, and of the phenomena of hearing; (*pl.*) the properties of a room or building that determine sound quality. [F *acoustique,* from Gr. *akoustikos* (*akouein,* to hear)]

acquaint, *v.t.* to make aware of, inform, to communicate intelligence of. *v.reflex.* to give(oneself) knowledge of or acquaintance with. **acquaintance,** *n.* knowledge of any person or thing; the state of knowing, or becoming known to, a person; a person, or the persons collectively, whom one knows, but with whom one is not intimate. **acquaintanceship,** *n.* the state of being acquainted; the relation of mutual acquaintance. **acquainted,** *a.* known to another or each other; familiar (with). [OF *acointer,* late L *adcognitāre* (*ad-,* to, *cognitum,* p.p. of *cognoscere,* to know; *co-, cum-,* with, *gnoscere, noscere,* to know)]

acquest, *n.* a thing acquired, an acquisition; (*Law*) †the action of acquiring; property gained otherwise than by inheritance. [OF *acquest,* from late L *acquīsītum*); see ACQUIRE]

acquiesce, *v.i.* to submit or remain passive; to assent, to accept tacitly, to concur (in). **acquiescence,** *n.* **acquiescent,** *a.* submissive; accepting, assenting. **acquiescently,** *adv.* **acquiescingly,** *adv.* [Fr. *acquiescer,* L *acquiēscere* (*ac-, ad-,* to, *quiēscere,* to rest, from *quies,* rest)]

acquire, *v.t.* to gain, or obtain possession of, by one's own exertions or abilities; to come into possession of. **acquired characteristic,** *n.* a characteristic of an organism that is attained through environmental influences rather than genetically. **acquired immune deficiency syndrome** AIDS. **acquired taste,** *n.* something which one learns to like. **acquirable,** *a.* capable of being acquired. **acquirability,** *n.* **acquirement,** *n.* the act of acquiring; the object gained; a personal attainment of body or mind. [OF *aquerre, acquerre,* from L *acquīrere* (*ac-, ad-,* to, *quaerere* to seek)]

acquisition, *n.* the act of acquiring; the object acquired; a gain, an acquirement. **acquisitive,** *a.* capable of making, or disposed to make acquisitions. **acquisitively,** *adv.* **acquisitiveness,** *n.* the quality of being acquisitive; desire of possession; a phrenological organ supposed to denote such desire.

acquist, *n.* ACQUEST.

acquit, *v.t.* (*past, p.p.* **acquitted**) to release from an obligation, suspicion or charge; †to pay (a debt); to declare not guilty. *v.reflex.* to discharge (oneself) of (the duties of one's position); to conduct (oneself) in a particular way. **acquittal,** *n.* discharge or release from a promise, debt or other obligation; discharge of duty; performance; a deliverance from a charge by legal process. **acquittance,** *n.* the act of releasing from a charge or debt; a receipt in full; discharge of duty. **acquitter,** *n.* [OF *acquiter,* late L *aquitāre* (AC-, *quiētāre,* to settle)]

Acre, *n.* (or **'Akko**) seaport in Israel; population (1983) 37,000. Taken by the Crusaders (1104), it was captured by Saladin (1187) and retaken by Richard I (the Lionheart, 1191). Napoleon failed in a siege (1799); Gen. Allenby captured it 1918; and it became part of Israel in 1948.

acre, *n.* a measure of land containing 4840 sq. yd. (0·4 ha); a piece of tilled or enclosed land; a field (still surviving in place names). **acreage,** *n.* the area of any piece of land in acres; acres taken collectively or in the abstract. [OE *æcer,* a field (cp. OSax. *accar,* OHG *achar,* L *ager,* Gr. *agros,* Sansk. *ajras*)]

acrid, *a.* sharp, pungent, biting to the taste; irritating, corrosive; bitterly irritating to the feelings; of irritating temper and manners. **acridness, acridity**, *n.* sharpness, pungency, bitterness of manner or speech. **acritude,** *n.* [L *ācer ācris,* sharp, pungent, probably assim. to ACID]

acriflavine, *n.* an aniline dye, solutions of which form a strong antiseptic. [L *ācer,* sharp; *flavus,* yellow]

Acrilan®, *n.* a type of acrylic fibre or fabric used for clothing, carpets etc.

acrimony, *n.* sharpness, bitterness of temper, manner or speech. **acrimonious**, *a.* bitter and irritating in temper or manner. **acrimoniously,** *adv.* **acrimoniousness,** *n.* [L *ācrimōnia* (*ācer ācris,* -MONY), sharpness]

acro-, *comb. form* situated on the outside, beginning, termination, extremity, point or top, e.g. *acrobat, acrogenous*. [Gr. *akros,* outermost, at the top]

acrobat, *n.* a performer of daring gymnastic feats, as a tumbler or a tight-rope walker; a person who rapidly changes his or her opinions or loyalties. **acrobatic**, *a.* pertaining to an acrobat or the performances of an acrobat. **acrobatically,** *adv.* after the manner of an acrobat. **acrobatics,** *n.pl.* the feats performed by an acrobat; any agile performance. **acrobatism,** *n.* the feats or occupation of an acrobat. [F *acrobate,* Gr. *akrobatos* (ACRO-, *batos,* verb.a. of *bainein,* to go)]

acrogen, *n.* a cryptogam, a plant distinguished by growth from growing points at the extremity of the stem; one of the higher cryptogams (mosses, club-mosses and ferns). **acrogenous**, *a.* of the nature of an acrogen; increasing at the summit. [Gr. ACRO-, *genēs,* born]

acrolith, *n.* a statue having only the head and extremities of stone. [Gr. ACRO-, *lithos,* stone]

acromegaly, *n.* a disease the chief feature of which is the enlargement of the face and extremities of the limbs. **acromegalic**, *a.* [Gr. *akron,* a point; *megas megalou,* great]

acronychal, acronycal, *a.* vespertine; taking place in the evening or at nightfall. **acronychally,** *adv.* at the acronychal time; in an acronychal manner; at sunset or nightfall. [Gr. ACRO-, *nux nuktos,* night]

acronym, *n.* a word formed from initials, e.g. *NATO, laser*. **acronymic**, *a.* [ACRO-, Gr. *onoma,* name]

acropetal, *a.* in the direction of the apex. **acropetally,** *adv.* [Gr. *akron,* a point; L*petere,* to seek]

acrophobia, *n.* a morbid dread of high places.

acropolis, *n.* the citadel or elevated part of a Greek town, esp. that of Athens. [Gr. ACRO-, *polis,* city]

across, *adv., prep.* transversely, from side to side, crosswise, forming a cross with, opposed to, athwart; upon (e.g. *come across,* to come upon accidentally); over (e.g. *across the Channel*). **across-the-board,** *a.* affecting or applying in all cases. [OE *a-,* on, CROSS]

acrostic, *n.* a composition in which the lines are so disposed that their initial letters taken in order constitute a word or short sentence; an abecedarian poem. *a.* relating to or containing an acrostic. **acrostical,** *a.* **acrostically,** *adv.* in the manner of an acrostic composition. [Gr. *akrostichis* (ACRO-, *stichos,* a row)]

acroterium, acroterion, **acroter,** *n.* (*pl.* **-teria, -ters**) a pedestal on a pediment, for the reception of a figure; (*usu. pl.*) a pinnacle. **acroterial,** *a.* pertaining to or having the character of acroteria. [Gr. *akrotērion*]

acrylic, *n.* a synthetic textile fibre; paint containing an acrylic resin; a painting executed in acrylic paint. **acrylic acid,** *n.* an acid used in the manufacture of acrylic resins. **acrylic resin,** *n.* a resin consisting of a polymer of acrylic acid or one of its derivatives, used in making paints, adhesives, and for cast and moulded goods.

act, *n.* that which is done or being done, a deed, process of doing, operation; the exertion of physical, mental or moral power; a thesis publicly maintained by a candidate for a degree; one of the principal divisions of a play, usually subdivided into smaller portions called scenes; a statute, law or edict of a legislative or judicial body; an instrument in writing proving the truth of some transaction; †real, as distinguished from possible existence, actuality, reality. *v.t.* to perform; to play the part of; to impersonate. *v.i.* to exert power, to produce an effect; to be in action or motion; to carry out a purpose or determination; to behave, to demean oneself; to perform as (if) an actor. **in the (very) act,** in the actual commission of some deed. **to act up,** (*coll.*) to behave badly; to function badly, to give trouble. **to get in on the act,** (*coll.*) to become involved in an undertaking, esp. so as to benefit. **act of Congress,** in the US, a bill or resolution passed by both houses of Congress, the Senate and the House of Representatives, which then becomes law unless it is vetoed by the president. If vetoed, it may still become a law if it is returned to Congress again and passed by a majority of two-thirds in each house. **act of God,** the operation of uncontrollable natural forces in causing an event. **act of Parliament,** in Britain, a change in the law originating in Parliament and called a statute. Such acts may be either public (of general effect), local, or private. Before an act receives the royal assent and becomes law it is a 'bill'. The body of English statute law comprises all the acts passed by Parliament: the existing list opens with the Statute of Merton, passed in 1235. An act (unless it is stated to be for a definite period and then to come to an end) remains on the statute book until it is repealed. **actable,** *a.* capable of being performed on the stage; practically possible. **acting,** *a.* performing dramatically; operating; doing temporary duty. *n.* performance, execution, action; dramatic performance. **actor,** *n.* a performer; one who represents a character on the stage; a doer. **actress**, *n. fem.* a female actor. [F *acte,* or directly from L *actus,* a doing, and *actum* (pl. *acta*), a thing done, from *agere,* to do, to drive]

ACTH ADRENOCORTICOTROPHIC HORMONE.

actinia, *n.* (*pl.* **-niae, -nias**), a sea-anemone of the genus *Actinia*.

actinic, *a.* pertaining to rays; pertaining to the chemical rays of the sun. **actinic rays,** *n.pl.* electromagnetic rays capable of affecting photographic emulsions, including X-rays, ultraviolet, infrared rays etc. **actinism**, *n.* the property in rays of light by which chemical changes are produced; the radiation of light or heat; **actinograph**, *n.* an instrument which registers thevariations of chemical influence in solar rays. **actinometer**, *n.* an instrument for measuring the heating power of the sun's rays. **actinometric**, *a.* **actinometry**, *n.* **actinotherapy**, *n.* the treatment of disease by exposure to actinic radiation.

actinium, *n.* a radioactive metallic element, at. no 89; chem. symbol Ac, found in pitchblende. **actinide**, **actinoid**, *n.* any of a series of radioactive elements beginning with actinium and ending with lawrencium.

actin(o)-, *comb. form* radiate; stellate; pertaining to the rays of the sun; stem of many terms in physics and natural history, e.g. *actinal, actino-chemistry, actinograph*. [Gr. *aktis aktinos,* a ray]

Actinozoa, *n.pl.* a class of radiated animals, containing the sea-anemones and coral polyps. **actinozoon, -zoan**, *n.* an animal of this class.

action, *n.* the state or condition of acting or doing; activity; anything done or performed; a deed, an exploit; a battle, an engagement; combat, fighting; the mechanism or movement of a compound instrument; gesture, gesticulation; the trained motion of a horse; agency, operation, impulse; the working of an organ; the representation of passion in painting and sculpture; the things done, events or series of events constituting the main subjects of a play, poem or other work of fiction; a legal process or suit; (*coll.*) the principal or most lively activity. **action committee,** *n.* a committee formed to take positive action to achieve an end. **action painting,** *n.* abstract expression using spontaneous actions of smearing, throwing etc. to apply paint. **action radius,** *n.* the distance an aircraft can cover without running short of fuel before returning to its base or starting-point. **action replay,** *n.* the repetition, often in slow motion, of a small piece of film showing an important or decisive (sporting) incident. **action-taking,** *a.* litigious. **actionable,** *a.* furnishing ground for an action at law. **actionably,** *adv.* so as to be actionable. [F *action,* L *actiōnem,* acc. of *actio,* a doing, performance; see ACT]

Action Française, *n.* French extreme nationalist political movement founded 1899, first led by Charles Maurras (1868–1952); stressed the essential unity of all French people in contrast to the socialist doctrines of class warfare. Its influence peaked in the 1920s.

Actium, Battle of, *n.* naval battle in which Augustus defeated the combined fleets of Mark Antony and Cleopatra in 31 BC. The site is at Akri, a promontory in W Greece.

active, *a.* possessed of the power of acting, exerting the power of acting; communicating action or motion; exerting influence; quick in movement, nimble, agile; continually employed, busy, assiduous (opposed to idle or indolent); characterized by action, work or the performance of business; in actual operation; of a volcano, still liable to erupt; applied to intransitive verbs, or transitive verbs that attribute the action expressed to the subject whence it proceeds (the *active voice* is opposed to the *passive voice,* in which the action is viewed in relation to the thing affected). **activate,** *v.t.* to make active; to make radioactive; to make (more) reactive. **activated carbon,** *n.* carbon in the form of an absorbent powder used for purifying liquids and gases. **activation,** *n.* **activator,** *n.* **actively,** *adv.* in an active manner. **activism,** *n.* the policy of decisive action. **activist,** *n.* one who takes decisive, sometimes militant, action in support of a (political or social) cause. **activity**, *n.* the quality or state of being active; exertion of energy; energy, liveliness; a pursuit, occupation, recreation. [F *actif -ve,* L *activus*]

Acton, *n.* **Eliza** (1799–1859), English cookery writer and poet, whose *Modern Cookery for Private Families* (1845) influenced Mrs Beeton.

acton, *n.* a vest or jacket of quilted cotton, worn under mail; later, a jacket of leather or other material protected with plates or mail. [OF *auqueton* (F *hoqueton*), Sp. *alcoton* (*algodon*), Arab. *al-qūtun,* the cotton]

actor, actress ACT.

Actors' Studio, *n.* theatre workshop in New York City, established 1947 by Cheryl Crawford and Elia Kazan. Under Lee Strasberg, who became artistic director (1948), it became known for the study of Stanislavsky's method acting.

actual, *a.* existing in act or reality; real, existing, present, current. **actuality**, *n.* the state of being actual; reality; realism. **actualize, -ise,** *v.t.* to make actual; to describe realistically. **actualization, -isation,** *n.* a making real or actual; realization. **actually,** *adv.* [F *actuel,* L *actuālis* (*actus,* verb.n. of *agere,* to act); see ACT, -AL]

actuary, *n.* an officer of a mercantile or insurance company, skilled in statistics, especially on the expectancy of life and the average proportion of losses by fire and other accidents. **actuarial**, *a.* of or belonging to actuaries or their profession. [L *actuārius,* amanuensis, account-keeper]

actuate, *v.t.* to excite to action, to put in action, to furnish the motive of. **actuation,** *n.* a putting in action, communication of motion; effectual operation. **actuator,** *n.* [med. L *actuātus,* p.p. of *actuāre* (*actus*)]

acuity, *n.* sharpness, acuteness (of a point, an acid, disease or wit). [F *acuité,* med. L *acuitātem* (*acus,* needle, *acuere,* to sharpen)]

aculeus, *n.* (*Zool.*) a sting; (*Bot.*) a prickle. **aculeate, -ated,** *a.* furnished with a sting; prickly; set with prickles; pointed, incisive, pungent. [L *acūleus,* a sting (dim. of *acus,* a needle)]

acumen, *n.* acuteness of mind, shrewdness, keen penetration. [L *acūmen* (*acuere,* to sharpen)]

acuminate, *a.* tapering to a point. *v.t.*, to sharpen, to point, to give keenness or poignancy to. **acuminated,** *part.a.* brought to a point; sharp, stinging. **acumination,** *n.* the act of making sharp; termination in a sharp point. **acuminose,** *a.* (*Bot.*) terminating gradually in a flat, narrow end, inclined to be acuminate. [L *acuminatus,* pointed]

acupressure, *n.* massage using the fingertips applied to the points of the body used in acupuncture.

acupuncture, *n.* a system of medical treatment in which the body surface is punctured by needles at specific points to relieve pain, cure disease or produce anaesthesia. **acupuncturist** , *n.* a practitioner in acupuncture. [L *acus,* needle, PUNCTURE]

acute, *a.* terminating in a sharp point; sharp, keen, penetrating; quick to perceive minute distinctions; of pain, sharp, piercing; shrill, high in pitch; applied also to the accent (′) marking such sounds; of an illness, attended with violent symptoms, and coming speedily to a crisis; less than a right angle. *n.* an acute accent. **acutely,** *adv.* **acuteness,** *n.* [L *acūtus* (*acuere,* to sharpen)]

acut(i)-, *comb. form* sharp, acute, as in *acutangular, acutifoliate, acutiform.* [L *acūtus,* sharp]

-acy, *suf.* forming nouns of quality, state,condition etc.; e.g. *fallacy, infancy, magistracy, piracy*. [L *-ācia, ātia,* Gr. *-ateia*]

ad, *n.* (*coll.*) short for ADVERTISEMENT.

AD, (*abbr.*) in the year of our Lord. [L *anno Domini*]

ad-, *pref.* to, at, into; signifying motion towards, direction to, adherence etc. e.g. *adduce, adhere, adjacent, admire.* (This prefix undergoes many alterations to assimilate it with the initial consonant of the root, examples of which will be found in their respective places.) [L *ad,* to, at]

-ad, *suf.* pertaining to (in collective numerals, feminine patronymics, titles of poems, names of botanical families); e.g. *monad, myriad, Iliad, naiad, liliad.* [Gr. *-ad,* nom. *-as,* gen. *-ados*]

ADA, *n.* computer programming language, developed and owned by the US Department of Defence, designed for use in situations where the computer directly controls a process or machine, such as a military aircraft. The language took over five years to specify, and only became commercially available in the late 1980s. It is named after Ada Lovelace, regarded as the world's first computer programmer.

adage, *n.* a proverb; a pithy maxim handed down from old time. [F *adage,* L *adagium* (*ad-,* to, *agium,* a saying, from *aīo,* I say)]

adagio, *adv.* (*Mus.*) slowly, gracefully. *a.* slow, graceful. *n.* a slow movement of a soft, tender, elegiac character. **adagietto**, *n.* a slow, graceful movement but somewhat quicker than adagio. **adagissimo**, *adv.* very slowly. [It. *ad agio,* at leisure]

Adam[1], *n.* in the Old Testament, founder of the human race. Formed by God from the dust and given the breath of life, Adam was placed in the Garden of Eden, where Eve was given to him as a companion. With her, he tasted the forbidden fruit of the Tree of Knowledge of Good and Evil, and they were expelled from the Garden; the unregenerate state of man. **Adam's ale,** *n.* water. **Adam's apple,** *n.* the lime, the orange or the shaddock, from the idea that it was the forbidden fruit; a protuberance on the forepart of the throat formed by the thyroid cartilage. **adamic, -ical,** *a.* pertaining to Adam, resembling Adam; naked. **adamically,** *adv.* [Heb. *ā-dām,* man]

Adam², *n.* family of Scottish architects and designers. **William Adam** (1689–1748) was the leading Scottish architect of his day, and his son **Robert Adam** (1728–92) is considered one of the greatest British architects of the late 18th century. He transformed the prevailing Palladian fashion in architecture to a neo-classic style. He designed interiors for many great country houses (Harewood House, Yorkshire; Luton Hoo, Luton;). With his brother **James Adam** (1732–94), also an architect, he speculatively developed the the Adelphi near Charing Cross, London, largely rebuilt (1936). *a.* pertaining to a decorative style of architecture and furniture designed by Robert and James Adam.

adamant, *n.* a stone of impenetrable hardness; the lodestone, the diamond. *a.* made of adamant, pertaining to adamant; hard, destitute or incapable of feeling. **adamancy,** *n.* **adamantine,** †**adamantean,** *a.* made of adamant; incapable of being broken. **adamantly,** *adv.* [OF *adamaunt,* L *adamas -antem,* Gr. *adamas* (*a-*, priv., *damaō,* I tame)]

Adam de la Halle, *n.* (*c.* 1240–*c.* 90), French poet and composer. His *Jeu de Robin et Marion*, written in Italy about 1282, is a theatrical work with dialogue and songs set to what were apparently popular tunes of the day. It is sometimes called the forerunner of comic opera.

Adamite, *n.* a descendant of Adam; one of a sect who professed to reestablish a state of innocence, and went naked. **adamitic, -ical,** *a.* pertaining to the Adamites. **adamitism,** *n.*

Adams¹, *n.* **Ansel** (1902–84), US photographer, known for his printed images of dramatic landscapes and organic forms of the American West. He was associated with the Zone System of exposure estimation.

Adams², *n.* **Gerry (Gerard)** (1948–), Northern Ireland politician, president of Provisional Sinn Féin (the political wing of the IRA). He was elected a member of Parliament (1983) but declined to take up his Westminster seat. He has been criticised for failing to denounce IRA violence. In the 1970s, because of his connections with the IRA, he was interned and later released.

Adams³, *n.* **John** (1735–1826), 2nd president of the US (1797–1801), and vice president (1789–97). Born at Quincy, Massachusetts. He was a member of the Continental Congress, 1774–78, and signed the Declaration of Independence. In 1779 he went to France and negotiated the treaties that ended the War of American Independence. In 1785 he became the first US ambassador in London.

Adams⁴, *n.* **John Coolidge** (1947–), US composer and conductor, director of the New Music Ensemble (1972–81), and artistic adviser to the San Francisco Symphony Orchestra from 1978. His works include *Electric Wake* (1968), *Heavy Metal* (1971), *Bridge of Dreams* (1982), and the opera *Nixon in China* (1988).

Adams⁵, *n.* **John Couch** (1819–92), English astronomer, who deduced the existence of the planet Neptune in 1845.

Adams⁶, *n.* **John Quincy** (1767–48), 6th president of the US (1825–29). Eldest son of President John Adams, he was born at Quincy, Massachusetts, and became US minister in The Hague, Berlin, St Petersburg and London. In 1817 he became Monroe's secretary of state, formulated the Monroe doctrine (1823), and succeeded him in the presidency, despite receiving fewer votes than his main rival, Andrew Jackson. As president, Adams was an advocate of strong federal government.

Adams⁷, *n.* **Neil** (1958-), English judo champion. He won two junior and five senior European titles (1974–85), eight senior national titles, and two Olympic silver medals (1980, 1984). In 1981 he was world champion in the 78 kg class.

Adams⁸, *n.* **Richard** (1920–), British novelist. A civil servant (1948–72), he wrote *Watership Down* (1972), a tale of a rabbit community, which is read by adults and children. Later novels include *The Plague Dogs* (1977) and *Girl on a Swing* (1980).

Adams⁹, *n.* **Roger** (1889–1971), US organic chemist, known for his painstaking analytical work to determine the composition of naturally-occurring substances such as complex vegetable oils and plant alkaloids.

Adams¹⁰, *n.* **Samuel** (1722–1803), US politician, second cousin of President John Adams; he was the chief prompter of the Boston Tea Party. He was also a signatory of the Declaration of Independence, and anticipated the French emperor Napoleon in calling the British a 'nation of shopkeepers'.

Adamson, *n.* **Robert R.** (1821–1848), Scottish photographer who, with David Octavius Hill, produced 2500 calotypes (mostly portraits) in five years from 1843.

Adana, *n.* capital of Adana (Seyhan) province, S Turkey; population (1985) 776,000. It is a major cotton-growing centre and Turkey's fourth largest city.

adapt, *v.t.* to fit, to adjust, to make suitable, to remodel. *v.i.* to become fit or suitable. **adaptability,** *n.* **adaptable,** *a.* capable of being adapted. **adaptation,** *n.* the act of adapting; the state of being adapted; that which is adapted. **adaptedness,** *n.* **adapter, -or,** *a.* one who adapts; an accessory for connecting a plug etc., fitted with terminals of one type to a supply point fitted with terminals of another type, or for connecting several appliances to a single supply point. **adaptogen,** *n.* a biological substance which helps regulate the nervous system and endocrine glands and controls the effects of stress. **adaptive,** *a.* tending to adapt; suitable. **adaptively,** *adv.* [F *adapter,* L *adaptāre* (*ad-*, to, *aptare,* from *aptus,* fit)]

Adar, *n.* the sixth civil month, or ecclesiastical 12th month of the Jewish year (corresponding to part of February and March). [Heb. *ādār*]

adaxial, *a.* (*Bot.*) facing the stem. [AD-, AXIS¹]

ADB, (*abbr.*) Asian Development Bank.

ADC, (*abbr.*) aide-de-camp.

add, *v.t.* to set or put together; to join, to unite; to put into one total; to annex, to subjoin. *v.i.* to serve as an increment (to); to perform the operation of addition. **to add up,** to produce a correct total when added; to amount to; to make sense, show a consistent pattern. **add-on,** *n.* something supplementary; a computer peripheral. **adder¹,** an adding machine; a circuit in a calculator or computer that adds binary numbers. **addibility,** *n.* **addible,** *a.* capable of being added. **addition,** *n.* the act of adding; the state of being added to; the thing added; the process of collecting two or more numbers or quantities into one sum; the title or designation given to a person beyond his name and surname; anything added to a coat of arms as a mark of honour; a dot placed at the right side of a musical note to indicate that it is to be lengthened one half. **in addition,** as well as, also. **additional,** *a.* added; supplementary. *n.* that which is added. **additionally,** *adv.* **additive,** *a.* that may be or is to be added. **additively,** *adv.* [L *addere* (*ad-*, to, *dare,* to put)]

Addams¹, *n.* **Charles** (1912–88), US cartoonist, creator of the Gothically ghoulish Addams family in the *New Yorker* magazine. There was a successful television series based on the cartoon in the 1960s.

Addams², *n.* **Jane** (1860–1935), US sociologist and feminist, who in 1889 founded and led the social settlement of Hull House, Chicago, one of the earliest community centres. She was Vice-President of the National American Woman Suffrage Association (1911–14), and in 1915 led the Woman's Peace Party and the first Women's Peace Congress. She shared a Nobel prize in 1931.

addax, *n.* a species of antelope, *Oryx nasomaculata.* [African]

addendum, *n.* (*pl.* **-da**) a thing to be added, an addition; an appendix. [L *addendum,* ger. of *addere* (ADD)]

adder¹ ADD.

adder², *n.* the common viper, *Pelias berus;* applied, with epithet, to some of the foreign Viperidae, as puff-adder, death-adder; †a serpent; †a dragon. **adder-bolt,** *n.* the dragon-fly. **adder's tongue,** *n.* the fern-genus *Ophioglossum*. **adderwort,** *n.* bistort or snake-weed, *Polygonum bistorta*. [OE *nædre* (*n* has disappeared through mistaken division of *a naddre* as *an addre*)]

addict¹, *v.t.* to apply habitually, to habituate. *v.reflex.* to devote (oneself) to, make (oneself) a slave to (a vice). **addicted,** *part.a.* wholly devoted; given over (to), prone. **addictedness,** *n.* **addiction,** *n.* the act of addicting or devoting; the state of being addicted or devoted; propensity, proclivity. [L *addictus,* p.p. of *addicere* (*ad-,* to, *dicere,* to say)]

addict², *n.* one who is addicted to some habit, esp. the taking of drugs; a slave to a vice.

Addis Ababa, *n.* (or **Adis Abeba**) capital of Ethiopia; population (1984) 1,413,000. It was founded 1887 by Menelik, chief of Shoa, who ascended the throne of Ethiopia in 1889. His former residence, Menelik Palace, is now occupied by the government; the city is the headquarters of the Organization of African Unity.

Addison, *n.* **Joseph** (1672–1719), British writer. In 1704 he celebrated Marlborough's victory at Blenheim in a poem, 'The Campaign', and subsequently held political appointments, including under-secretary of state and secretary to the Lord-Lieutenant of Ireland in 1708. In 1709 he contributed to the *Tatler*, begun by Richard Steele, with whom he was co-founder in 1711 of the *Spectator*.

Addison's disease, *n.* a disease characterized by undersecretion of steroid hormones from the adrenal cortex, causing weakness, weight loss and browning of the skin. [the physician Thomas *Addison,* 1793–1860]

additament, *n.* something added. [L *additāmentum* (*additus,* p.p. of *addere;* see ADD]

addition ADD.

addle, *a.* putrid, bad, as an egg; empty, idle, vain, muddled, confused. *n.* foul and putrid water; the dry lees of wine. *v.t.* to make addle or addled; to confuse (mentally); to spoil. *v.i.* to grow putrid (as an egg). **addle-headed, addle-brained, addle-pated,** *a.* terms applied to one whose brain seems muddled. **addleplot,** *n.* a marplot. **addled,** *part.a.* rendered or become putrid, as an egg; confused in one's wits etc. **addlement,** *n.* [OE *adela,* mire, filth]

address, *v.t.* to direct an oral or written communication to; to accost or speak to; to write the address or direction on; to court or make suit to. *v.reflex.* to prepare (oneself) to, apply (oneself) to. *v.i.* to present a formal address. *n.* the act of addressing oneself to a person or persons; a discourse; any speech or writing in which one person or body makes a communication to another person or body; tact, skill, adroitness; bearing in conversation; (*pl.*) courtship; the direction of a letter; the name of the place where one lives; a number that identifies a location in a computer memory where a particular piece of data is stored. **to address oneself to,** to speak to. **to pay one's addresses to,** to court. **addressable,** *a.* (*Comput.*) able to be accessed by means of an address. **addressee,** *n.* one to whom a parcel or communication is addressed. **addresser, -or,** *n.* one who addresses; one who directs a communication. **Addressograph®,** *n.* a machine for addressing envelopes, wrappers etc. [F *adresser,* late L *addrictiare* (*ad-,* to, *drictum, directum,* DIRECT)]

adduce, *v.t.* to bring forward as a proof or illustration, to cite, to quote. **adducent,** *a.* bringing or drawing to a given point (used of the adductor muscles). **adducer,** *n.* **adducible,** *a.* capable of being adduced. **adduct,** *v.t.* to draw (a body part) inwards or towards another part. **adduction,** *n.* the act of leading or drawing to or together, bringing forward or citing. **adductive,** *a.* tending to lead or draw to or together. **adductor,** *n.* a muscle which brings one part of the body towards or in contact with another part. [L *addūcere* (*ad,* to, *dūcere,* to lead)]

-ade, *suf.* forms nouns denoting action, e.g. *cannonade, ambuscade;* person or body involved in action, e.g. *brigade, cavalcade;* product of action, e.g. *masquerade;* sweet drink, e.g. *lemonade*. [F *-ade* (cp. *-ada* in Sp. and Prov.), L *-āta,* f. sing. p.p. of verbs in *-āre*]

adeem, *v.t.* (*Law*) to cancel a bequest. [L *adimere,* to take away]

Adelaide¹, *n.* capital and industrial city of South Australia; population (1986) 993,100. Industries include oil refining, shipbuilding, and the manufacture of electrical goods and cars. Grain, wool, fruit, and wine are exported. Founded in 1836, Adelaide was named after William IV's queen.

Adelaide², *n.* (1792–1849), queen consort of William IV of England. Daughter of the Duke of Saxe-Meiningen, she married William, then Duke of Clarence, in 1818. No children of the marriage survived infancy.

adelphous, *a.* having the stamens in groups or bundles. [Gr. *adelphos,* a brother]

ademption, *n.* a taking away; (*Law*) the revocation of a grant. [L *ademptiōnem,* n. of action, from *adimere* (*ad-,* to, *emere,* to take)]

aden-, adeni-, adeno- *comb. form* connected with a gland or glands; glandular; in medical terms, e.g. *adenitis, adenotomy*. [Gr. *adēn,* an acorn, a gland]

Aden, *n.* (Arabic **'Adan**) capital of South Yemen, on a rocky peninsula at the SW corner of Arabia, commanding the entrance to the Red Sea; population (1984) 318,000. It comprises the new administrative centre Madinet al-Sha'ab; the commercial and business quarters of Crater and Tawahi, and the harbour area of Ma'alla. The city's economy is based on oil refining, fishing, and shipping. A British territory from 1839, Aden became part of independent South Yemen in 1967.

Adenauer, *n.* **Konrad** (1876–1967), German Christian Democrat politician, chancellor of West Germany (1949–63). With the French president de Gaulle he achieved the postwar reconciliation of France and Germany and strongly supported all measures designed to strengthen the Western bloc in Europe.

adenine, *n.* one of the four purine bases in DNA and RNA.

adenitis, *n.* inflammation of the lymphatic glands.

adenoid, *a.* having the form of a gland, glandular. *n.pl.* adenoid tissue; a spongy growth at the back of the nose and throat, impeding respiration and speech. **adenoidal,** *a.*

adenoma, *n.* (*pl* **-mas, -mata**) a benign tumour formed of glandular tissue.

adenopathy, *n.* disease of a gland or glands; a general affection attacking mainly the lymphatic glands.

adenosine, *n.* a compound of adenine and the sugar ribose that forms part of RNA and various compounds that provide energy in cells. **adenosine triphosphate** ATP. [*adenine* and *ribose*]

adept, *n.* one who was supposed to have obtained the elixir of life and the philosopher's stone; an occultist; one completely versed in any science or art. *a.,* thoroughly versed, well skilled. **adeption,** *a., n.* **adeptly,** *adv.* [L *adeptus,* p.p. of *adipisci* (*ad-,* to, *apisci,* to attain)]

adequate, *a.* equal to a requirement, sufficient, proportionate, commensurate. **adequately,** *adv.* **adequateness, adequacy,** *n.* [L *adaequātus,* p.p. of *adaequāre* (*ad-,* to, *aequāre,* to make equal, from *aequus,* equal)]

Ader, *n.* **Clement** (1841–1925), French aviation pioneer whose steam-driven aeroplane, the *Éole*, made the first powered take-off in history (1890), but it could not fly. In 1897, with his *Avion III*, he failed completely, despite false claims made later.

à deux, *a., adv.* (F) of or between two (people).

adhere, *v.i.* to stick (to); to remain firmly attached (to); to continue to support or to follow; †to be coherent, consistent; to agree. [L *adhaerēre* (*ad-,* to, *haerēre,* to stick)]

adherence, *n.* the state or quality of adhering; firm attachment. **adherent,** *a.* sticking; tenaciously attached. *n.* one who adheres; a partisan, a follower. [F *adhérence,* L *adhaerentia,* verbal n., from *adhaerens -ntem,* pres.p. of *adhaerēre*]

adhesion, *n.* the act or state of sticking, attaching oneself to, or joining; the union of structures or tissues that are normally separate; the fusion of two surfaces, as the two opposing surfaces of a wound in healing. **adhesive**, *a.* having the power of adhering; sticky, clinging. *n.* a substance used for sticking things together. **adhesively,** *adv.* **adhesiveness,** *n.* the power of sticking; (*Phrenol.*) stickiness; the propensity to form attachments with people. [ADHERE]

adhibit, *v.t.* to apply, to add, to append, to use, employ. **adhibition**, *n.* application, employment, use. [L *adhibit-,* stem in *adhibit -us,* p.p. of *adhibēre* (*ad-,* to, *habēre,* to hold)]

ad hoc, *a.*, *adv.* for a particular purpose, specially. [L]

ad hominem, *a.*, *adv.* (*L*) directed to or against the person, not disinterested. [L, to the man]

adiabatic, *a.* impervious, esp. to heat, without loss or gain of heat. **adiabatically,** *adv.* in an adiabatic manner. [Gr. *adiabatos* (*a-,* not, *dia,* through, *batos,* passable, from *baino,* I go); -IC]

Adiantum, *n.* a genus of ferns, containing the maidenhair. [Gr. *adianton*]

adiaphorism, *n.* indifference in religion or ethics, latitudinarianism. **Adiaphorist,** *n.* one who holds that dogmas or rites are matters of indifference; a moderate Lutheran; a latitudinarian. *a.* pertaining to the Adiaphorists; theologically indifferent. [Gr. *adiaphoros,* not different (*a-,* not, *dia,* apart, *pherein,* to bear); -ISM]

adieu, *int.*, *n.* (*pl.* **adieux**, **adieus**) God be with you, good-bye, farewell. [F *à,* to, *Dieu,* God]

Adi Granth, *n.* (or **Guru Granth Sahib**) the holy book of Sikhism.

ad infinitum, *adv.* to infinity, without end. [L]

adipocere, *n.* a greyish-white fatty or soapy substance, into which the flesh of dead bodies buried in moist places is converted. **adipocerous**, *a.* of the nature of adipocere. [F *adipocire* (L *adeps -ipem,* fat, F *cire,* L *cera,* wax)]

adipose, *a.* pertaining to animal fat, fatty. *n.* animal fat, esp. the fat on the kidneys. **adipose fin,** *n.* the fatty dorsal fin of some fishes,as of the Salmo family. **adipose tissue,** *n.* the vesicular structure in which fat is deposited. **adipescent**, *a.* growing fat. **adipic**, *a.* derived from fat. **adiposity**, *n.* [L *adeps -ipem,* fat]

adit, *n.* an approach, entrance, passage; a more or less horizontal entrance to a mine. [L *aditus,* approach (*ad-,* to, *īre,* to go)]

Adj., Adjt., (*abbr.*) adjutant.

adj., (*abbr.*) adjective; adjustment.

adjacent, *a.* lying near (to); contiguous; neighbouring, bordering. **adjacency,** *n.* the state of lying adjacent or near to, that which lies near to; †(*pl.*) environs, precincts. **adjacently,** *adv.* [L *adjacentem,* pres.p. of *adjacēre* (*ad-,* to, at, *jacēre,* to lie)]

Adjani, *n.* **Isabelle** (1955–), French film actress of Algerian-German descent. She played the title role in Truffaut's *L'Histoire d'Adele H/The Story of Adele H* (1975) and has since appeared in international productions including *La Locataire/The Tenant*; *Nosferatu Phantom der Nacht* (1979); *Ishtar* (1987).

adjective, *a.* added to; dependent; forming an adjunct to a noun substantive. *n.* a part of speech joined to a substantive to define and limit its signification. **adjectival**, *a.* **adjectivally, adjectively,** *adv.* [F *adjectif -ve,* L *adjectīvus, adjectus,* p.p. of *adjicere* (*ad-,* to, *jacere,* to throw); -IVE]

adjoin, *v.t.* to join or add, to unite; to be contiguous to. *v.i.* to be contiguous. **adjoining,** *a.* adjacent, contiguous; neighbouring. [OF *ajoindre,* L *adjungere* (*ad-,* to, *jungere,* to join)]

adjourn, *v.t.* to put off or defer till a later period; to suspend (a meeting) in order to meet at a later period or elsewhere; to postpone till a future meeting. *v.i.* to cease proceedings till a later period; to move elsewhere. **adjournment,** *n.* the act of adjourning; the time during which or to which business or a meeting (esp. of a public body) is postponed. [OF *ajorner,* late L *adjornāre,* appoint a day (*jurnus,* day, L *diurnus*)]

adjudge, *v.t.* to award by a judicial decision, to decide, pronounce, condemn. **adjudgment,** *n.* the act of judging; adjudging; the judgment or verdict given. [OF *ajüger,* L *adjūdicāre;* see ADJUDICATE]

adjudicate, *v.t.* to judge, to determine, decide, pronounce on. *v.i.* to sit as a judge; to act as a judge in a competition. **adjudication,** *n.* the act of adjudicating; the decision or judgment of a judge or court. **adjudicator,** *n.* [L *adjūdicāre* (*ad-,* to, *jūdicāre,* to judge)]

adjunct, *n.* any thing joined to another without being an essential part of it; an attribute, qualifying addition; (*Gram.*) an extension of the subject or predicate; (*Logic*) a non-essential attribute; an associate. *a.* added to, or conjoined with any person or thing. **adjunction,** *n.* a joining to; the act of joining; a thing joined. **adjunctive**, *a.* joining, having the quality of joining. *n.* anything joined to another. **adjunctively, adjunctly,** *adv.* by way of adjunct, in connection with. [L *adjunctus,* p.p. of *adjungere* (*ad-,* to, *jungere,* to join)]

adjure, *v.t.* to charge upon oath, or upon pain of the divine displeasure; to entreat with great earnestness. **adjuration,** *n.* the act of adjuring; an appeal under penalty of a curse; a solemn entreaty. **adjuratory,** *a.* containing or characterized by an adjuration. [L *adjūrāre,* to swear to (*ad-,* to, *jūrāre,* to swear); late L, to put to an oath]

adjust, *v.t.* to put together, to order, arrange; to fit, adapt to, to make correspondent, to accommodate, to settle, to assess (an insurance claim). *v.i.* to adopt or conform to a new situation, environment etc. **adjustable,** *a.* **adjuster,** *n.* one who or that which adjusts; a person who assesses settlements in respect of insurance claims. **adjustment,** *n.* the act of adjusting; the state of being adjusted; settlement, arrangement; a settlement of claims, liabilities etc. [OF *ajuster,* late L *adjuxtāre,* bring together (*ad-,* to, *juxta,* near)]

adjutage, ajutage, *n.* a tube fitted as mouthpiece to a fountain or the pipe from a vessel. [F *ajutage* (*ajouter,* to join on; see ADJUST)]

adjutant, *n.* an assistant; an officer in each regiment who assists the commanding officer in matters of business, duty and discipline. **adjutant bird,** *n.* a large wading bird of the stork family, native of India, where it is protected as a scavenger. **adjutancy,** *n.* the office of adjutant. [L *adjutans,* pres.p. of *adjūtāre,* freq. of *adjūvāre,* see below]

adjuvant, *a.* helping. *n.* an assistant, helper, auxiliary; an auxiliary ingredient in a prescription. [L *adjūvāre* (*ad-,* to, *jūvāre,* to help); -ANT]

Adler[1], *n.* **Alfred** (1870–1937), Austrian psychologist. Adler saw the 'will to power' as more influential in accounting for human behaviour than the sexual drive theory. Over this theory he parted company with Freud after a ten-year collaboration.

Adler[2], *n.* **Larry** (1914–), US musician, a virtuoso performer on the harmonica.

ad libitum, ad lib., *adv.* at pleasure, to any extent; (*Mus.*) at will to change time or omit passages. **ad-lib,** *v.t.* (*past, p.p.* **ad-libbed**) to deliver (as a speech) without notes or preparation. *v.i.* to extemporize. *a.* improvised, extempore. *n.* an improvised speech, line etc. [L]

Adm., (*abbr.*) admiral.

admass, *n.* the mass viewers and listeners to whom television and radio advertising is directed. [ADVERTISEMENT, MASS[2]]

admeasure, *v.t.* to measure out, to apportion. **admeasurement,** *n.* the act of measuring; the dimensions ascertained; apportionment of shares. [OF *amesurer,* late L *admensūrāre*]

admin, *n.* (*coll.*) administration, administrative work.

adminicle, *n.* an aid, support, auxiliary evidence. **adminicular**, *a.* auxiliary, corroborative. [L *adminiculum,* a prop, (*manus,* hand)]

administer, *v.t.* to manage or conduct as chief agent; to superintend the execution of (as laws); to tender (as an oath); to dispense, supply; to manage and dispose of (the estate of a deceased person); to give as medicine. *v.i.* to minister to; to act as administrator. **administrable,** *a.* **administrant,** *a., n.* **administration,** *n.* the act of administering; the executive functions of government; the executive; the management and distribution of the estate of a deceased person, esp. an intestate; (*N Am.*) government. **administrative,** *a.* pertaining to administration; executive. **administratively,** *adv.* in an administrative manner; with regard to administration. **administrator,** *n.* one who administers, manages, dispenses or furnishes; (*Law*) one who administers the estate of an intestate. **administratorship,** *n.* **administratrix,** *n. fem.* (*pl.* **-trices**) a female administrator. [OF *aministrer,* L *administrāre*]

admirable, *a.* worthy of admiration; excellent, highly satisfactory. **Admirable Crichton,** *n.* one who distinguishes himself in many spheres. Taken from James Crichton (1560–93), a Scottish adventurer famous for his accomplishments and attainments. **admirability, admirableness,** *n.* **admirably,** *adv.* [ADMIRE]

admiral, *n.* the commander of a fleet or a division of a fleet. This rank in England has four grades: Admiral of the Fleet, Admiral, Vice-Admiral and Rear-Admiral; †the ship of an admiral; a flag-ship; the commander of a fishing-fleet; *Vanessa atalanta,* the red, and *Limenitis sibylla,* the white admiral butterfly. †**admiral-ship,** *n.* a flag-ship, the largest and most important ship of a fleet. **admiralship,** *n.* the office or position of an admiral. [OF *amiral,* Arab. *amir,* a prince (Latinized as *amīrālis,* and through confusion with *admirāri,* converted into *admirālis*)]

Admiral's Cup, *n.* sailing series first held in 1957 and held biennially. National teams consisting of four boats compete over three inshore courses (in the Solent) and two offshore courses (378 km/235 miles across the Channel from Cherbourg to the Isle of Wight and 1045 km/650 miles from Plymouth to Fastnet lighthouse off Ireland, and back). The highlight is the Fastnet race.

admiralty, *n.* the office of admiral. **Board of the Admiralty,** *n.* in Britain, the controlling department of state for the Royal Navy from the reign of Henry VIII until 1964, when most of its functions – apart from that of management – passed to the Ministry of Defence. **The Admiralty,** *n.* the Government department that deals with the British navy; the Lords Commissioners who administer naval affairs in Great Britain; the building where they transact business. **Admiralty Court,** *n.* the chief court for the trial of maritime causes.

admire, *v.t.* †to wonder at; to regard with wonder, mingled with pleasing emotions; to look with pleasure on; to have a high opinion of. *v.i.* to feel admiration, to wonder, to be astonished. **admiration,** *n.* †wonder; wonder excited by anything pleasing or excellent; pleased contemplation. **admirer,** *n.* one who feels admiration; one who has a high opinion of; a suitor, lover **admiringly,** *adv.* [F *admirer,* L *admīrāri* (*ad-,* at, *mīrāri,* to wonder)]

admissible, *a.* fit to be considered as an opinion or as evidence; (*Law*) allowable as evidence; qualified for entrance to an office. **admissibility,** *n.* the quality of being admissible. **admissibly,** *adv.* **admission,** *n.* the act of admitting; the state of being admitted; permission to enter; concession in argument; acknowledgment. **admissive,** *a.* tending to admit, implying admission. [late L *admissibilis,* from *admissus,* p.p. of *admittere,* to ADMIT]

admit, *v.t.* (*past, p.p.* **admitted**) to let in; to permit to enter, as a place, an office, or the mind; to accept as valid; to concede, to acknowledge. **admittable,** *a.* admissible. **admittance,** *n.* the act of admitting; entrance given or permitted; the ease of flow of an alternating current, the reciprocal of impedance. **admittedly,** *adv.* [OF *amettre,* L *admittere* (*ad-,* to, *mittere,* to send)]

admix, *v.t.* to mix, to mingle. **admixture,** *n.* the act of mixing; something added to something else; an alloy; a foreign element. [L *ad-,* to, MIX (formed like L *admiscere,* p.p. *admixtus*)]

admonish, *v.t.* †to put in mind, exhort; to reprove gently; to warn, caution; to apprise, instruct. **admonisher,** *n.* **admonishment,** *n.* the act of admonishing; an admonition. **admonition,** *n.* (a) gentle reproof; friendly caution; counsel. **admonitive,** *a.* implying admonition. **admonitively,** *adv.* **admonitor,** *n.* **admonitory,** *a.* [OF *amonester,* late L *admonestāre,* L *admonēre,* (*ad-,* to, *monēre,* to advise)]

adnate, *a.* (*Biol.*) growing or grown to another part along its whole surface; attached to the stem. **adnascence,** *n.* **adnascent,** *a.* **adnation,** *n.* adhesion of different parts, esp. different whorls of the inflorescence. [L *adnātus* (*agnātus*) (*ad-,* to, *nātus, gnātus,* born)]

ad nauseam, *adv.* to the point of producing disgust or nausea. [L]

adnominal, *a.* pertaining to an adnoun; adjectival; attached to a noun. [L *adnōmen* (var. of *agnōmen*); -AL]

adnoun, *n.* an adjective; an adjective used substantively. [L *ad-,* to, NOUN (formed like *adverb*)]

ado, *n.* doing, business, activity; trouble, difficulty, fuss, bustle. [Scand. *at,* to, DO]

-ado, *suf.* forms nouns, e.g. *desperado, renegado, tornado* (*bravado, gambado, strappado,* and some other terms, are malformations of words in -ade). [Sp. and Port. *-ado,* L *-ātus,* in p.p. of verbs in *āre*]

adobe, *n.* a sun-dried brick; a clay used in making such bricks; a building made of adobe bricks. [Sp. *adobe,* from *adobar,* to daub, plaster, late L *adobāre*]

adolescent, *a.* growing up; advancing to maturity. *n.* a person in the age of adolescence. **adolescence,** *n.* the growing youth; the period between childhood and adulthood. [F *adolescent,* L *adolēscens -ntem,* pres.p. of *adolēscere,* to grow up]

Adonai, *n.* the Lord. [Heb. *ădōnāi,* my lords; see ADONIS]

Adonis, *n.* in Greek mythology, a beautiful youth beloved by the goddess Aphrodite. He was killed while boar-hunting but was allowed to return from the lower world for six months every year to rejoin her. The anemone sprang from his blood; a beau, a dandy; a handsome young man; a genus of Ranunculaceae, popularly called pheasant's eye; a butterfly. *Polyommatus adonis,* called also mazarine, or Clifton blue. **adonic,** *a.* pertaining to Adonis; of a metre composed of a dactyl and spondee (¯ ˘ ˘/¯ ¯). **adonize, -ise,** *v.t.* to adorn, to dandify. *v.i.* to adorn oneself.

adopt, *v.t.* to take into any relationship, as child, heir, citizen, candidate etc.; to take (a child) as one's own; to embrace, to espouse (as a principle, cause etc.); to choose for or take as one's own. **adopted,** *part.a.* taken as one's own, accepted into some intimate relation such as that of one's child. †**adoptedly,** *adv.* (*Shak.*) by adoption. **adopter,** *n.* one who or that which adopts. **adoption,** *n.* the act of adopting. **adoptional,** *a.* pertaining to adoption. **Adoptionism,** *n.* the tenets of the Adoptionists. **Adoptionist,** *n.* a member of a Christian sect (of the 8th cent.) which held that Christ was the Son of God by adoption only. †**adoptious,** *a.* **adoptive,** *a.* due to or by reason of adoption; fitted to adopt. **adoptively,** *adv.* [F *adopter,* L *adoptāre* (*ad-,* to, *optāre,* to choose)]

adore, *v.t.* to pay divine honours to; to regard with the utmost respect and affection. *v.i.* to offer worship. **adorable,** *a.* worthy of divine honours; worthy of the utmost love and respect; charming, delightful, fascinating. **adorableness,** *n.* **adorably,** *adv.* in a manner worthy of adoration; delightfully. **adoration,** *n.* divine worship; homage to one high in station or esteem. **adorer,** *n.* one who adores, a worshipper, a votary, an admirer, lover. **adoringly,** *adv.* [OF *aörer, aourer* (F *adorer*), L *adōrāre* (*ad-,* to, *ōrāre,* to pray, from *os oris,* the mouth)]

adorn, *v.t.* to decorate, ornament, embellish; to add attractiveness to. †*n.* adornment. **adorner,** *n.* **adorning,** *n.* adornment. **adorningly,** *adv.* **adornment,** *n.* an adorning, decoration, ornament, embellishment.

[OF *aörner* (F *adorner*), L *adornāre* (*ad-*, to, *ornāre*, to deck)]

adown, *adv.* down from a higher to a lower place. *prep.* upon or along in a descending direction. [OE *of-dune,* off the down or hill]

adrenal, *a.* near the kidneys. **adrenal gland,** *n.* a small gland adjacent to each kidney that secretes adrenalin and steroid hormones. **adren(o)-,** *comb. form* adrenal; adrenalin. [L *ad-,* to; *renes,* kidneys]

adrenalin, adrenaline, *n.* a hormone secreted by the adrenal glands; a crystalline substance derived from the adrenal glands of cattle and sheep, used for checking bleeding. **adrenocorticotrophic hormone**, *n.* a hormone produced by the pituitary gland that stimulates the activity of the adrenal cortex.

Adrian IV, *n.* (Nicholas Breakspear, *c.* 1100–59), Pope (1154–59), the only British pope. He secured the execution of Arnold of Brescia; crowned Frederick I Barbarossa as German emperor; refused Henry II's request that Ireland should be granted to the English crown in absolute ownership; and was at the height of a quarrel with the emperor when he died.

Adrianople, *n.* older name of the Turkish town Edirne, after the Emperor Hadrian, who rebuilt it about AD 125.

Adriatic Sea, *n.* large arm of the Mediterranean Sea, lying NW to SE between the Italian and the Balkan peninsulas. The western shore is Italian; the eastern Yugoslav and Albanian. The sea is about 805 km/500 miles long, and its area is 135,250 sq km/52,220 sq miles.

adrift, *adv.* in a drifting condition; at the mercy of the wind and waves; wandering, at a loss.

adroit, *a.* dexterous, active, clever, ready in mental or bodily resource. **adroitly,** *adv.* **adroitness,** *n.* [F *à,* to, *droit,* right, late L *drictum* (L *directum*); see DIRECT]

adry, *adv.*, *pred.a.* dry, athirst.

adscititious, *a.* assumed, adopted, derived from without, suplemental. **adscititiously,** *adv.* [L *adscitus* (*ascītus*) p.p. of *adscīscere,* adopted, received from others (*ad-* to, *scīt-,* part. stem of *scīscere,* to acknowledge, freq. of *scīre,* to know)]

adscript, *a.* written after (opposed to subscript); attached to the soil (said of feudal serfs). *n.* one held to service, a serf. **adscription,** *n.* ascription; attachment, as a feudal inferior. [L *adscriptus,* p.p. of *adscrībere* (*ad-,* to, *scrībere,* to write]

adsorb, *v.t.* to take up and cause to adhere in a thin film on the surface. *v.i.* to concentrate and adhere to the surface of a solid. **adsorbent,** *n.* a solid substance that adsorbs gases, vapours or liquids that contact it. **adsorption,** *n.* concentration of a substance on a surface. [AD-, SORB]

aduki bean, adsuki, adzuki, *n.* a bean, *Phaseolus angularis,* with small reddish-brown edible seeds, grown esp. in China and Japan. [Jap. *azuki*]

adulate, *v.t.* to fawn upon, to flatter servilely. **adulation,** *n.* the act of fawning or flattering servilely; servile flattery. **adulator,** *n.* **adulatory,** *a.* [L *adūlātus,* p.p. of *adūlārī,* to flatter]

Adullam, *n.* a biblical city with nearby caves in which David and those who had some grievance took refuge (1 Samuel 22). **Adullamite,** *n.* a person who is disaffected or who secedes from a political party; the term was used to describe about 40 British Liberal MPs who voted against their leaders to defeat the 1866 Reform Bill. **adullamy**, *n.* defection, ratting.

adult, *a.* grown to maturity; grown up, full-grown; of or for adults; (*euphem.*) containing sexually explicit material, pornographic. *n.* one grown to maturity. **adult education,** *n.* part-time, usu. non-vocational courses for people over school-leaving age. **adulthood, adultness,** *n.* [L *adultus,* p.p. of*adolescere,* to grow up (*ad-,* to, *olescere,* freq. of *olēre,* to grow)]

adulterate¹, *v.t.* to corrupt or debase anything by mixing with it a baser substance. *a.* adulterated; spurious, debased by admixture. **adulterant,** *n.*, *a.* that which adulterates or is used to adulterate; adulterating. **adulterately,** *adv.* **adulterateness,** *n.* **adulteration,** *n.* the act or result of adulterating; the state of being adulterated; an adulterated substance. **adulterator,** *n.* one who adulterates. **adulterine¹,** *a.* spurious, counterfeit, illegal, unlicensed. [L *adulterātus,* p.p. of *adulterāre,* commit adultery, corrupt (*ad-* to, *alterāre,* to change, from *alter,* other), cp. *adulter,* an adulterer, a debaser of the coinage]

adultery, *n.* marital infidelity; illicit sexual intercourse on the part of a married person. **adulterate²,** *a.* adulterous; born of an adulterous union. **adulterer,** *n.* a man guilty of adultery. **adulteress,** *n.* a woman guilty of adultery. **adulterine²,** *a.* born of adultery; relating to adultery. *n.* a child born of adultery. †**adulterize, -ise,** *v.i.* **adulterous,** *a.* pertaining to or guilty of adultery. **adulterously,** *adv.* [L *adultērium* (superseding older *avoutrie,* from OF *avouterie,* L *adulter*); see ADULTERATE]

adumbrate, *v.t.* to shadow, forth, toindicate faintly as if by a shadow; to typify, foreshadow; to overshadow. **adumbrant,** *a.* **adumbration,** *n.* the act of shadowing forth; a faint, imperfect representation. **adumbrative,** *a.* faintly representing. [L *adumbrāre,* to cast a shadow(*ad-,* to, *umbrāre,* to shadow, from *umbra,*shadow)]

adust, *a.* burnt, scorched, parched, sunburnt; gloomy in features or temperament. [L *adūstus,* p.p. of *adūrere,* to burn (*ad-,* to, *ūrere,* burn)]

Aduwa, Battle of, defeat of the Italians by the Ethiopians at Aduwa in 1896 under Emperor Menelik II. It marked the end of Italian ambitions in this part of Africa until Mussolini's reconquest in 1935.

adv., (*abbr.*) adverb; adverbial; adversus (against); advocate.

ad valorem, *a.*, *adv.* of a tax, in proportion to the value of the goods. [L, according to value]

advance, *v.t.* to bring or move forward or upwards; †to extol; †to influence; †to impel; to promote; to supply before or on credit; to put forward for attention; to raise. *v.i.* to move forward, to progress, to rise. *n.* the act or process of moving forward; promotion, improvement; a rise (in price); the first step, movement towards; (*pl.*) amorous overtures; payment beforehand, a loan. *a.* being before in time or place; beforehand. **in advance,** beforehand; in front. **advance(d) guard,** *n.* a detachment which precedes the advance of the main body of an army. **advance note,** *n.* a draft for payment of one month's wages given to a member of a ship's crew when signing on. **advanced,** *a.* in the front rank; far on; before one's age; extreme (opinions). **advanced gas-cooled reactor** AGR. **Advanced level** A-LEVEL. **advancer,** *n.* one who advances; a promoter; a moneylender. [OF *avancer,* pop. L *abanteāre,* from *abante* (*ab-,* away, *ante,* before)]

advancement, *n.* the act of advancing; the state of being advanced; preferment; furtherance, improvement; the application beforehand of property to which children are prospectively entitled; the property so applied.

advantage, *n.* favourable condition or circumstance; gain, profit, superiority of any kind; a consideration super-added to one going before, and giving it increased force; the victory resulting from such aids; in tennis, the next point or game won after deuce points or games. *v.t.* to benefit, to further, to promote the interests of. **to advantage,** so as to display the best points. †**advantaged,** *a.* (*Shak.*) placed at advantage. **advantageous**, *a.* conferring advantage; profitable, beneficial. **advantageously,** *adv.* **advantageousness,** *n.* [F *avantage*]

advection, *n.* the transfer of heat by the horizontal movement of air. [L *advectus,* p.p. of *advehere* (*ad-,* towards, *vehere,* to carry)]

advent, *n.* the Incarnation of Christ; the Second Coming; the season including the four Sundays before Christmas; any important arrival; a coming. **Adventist**, *n.* one who believes that the Second Coming of Christ is imminent. Expectation of the Second Coming of Christ is found in New Testament writings generally. Adventist views are held by the Seventh-Day Adventists, Christadelphians, Jehovah's Witnesses, and the Four Square Gospel Alliance. [OF *advent, auvent,* L *adventus,* arrival (*ad-*, to, *venire,* to come)]

adventitious, *a.* extraneous; foreign; accidental, casual; (*Law*) coming otherwise than by direct succession; (*Biol.*) occurring in an unusual location. **adventitiously,** *adv.* **adventitiousness,** *n.* [L *adventicius,* coming from abroad]

adventure, *n.* hazard, risk; an enterprise in which hazard or risk is incurred; any novel or unexpected event; a speculation. *v.t.* to risk, to hazard, to put in danger. *v.i.* to venture; to dare. **adventure holiday,** *n.* a holiday centred round outdoor activities having an element of danger, as rock-climbing and canoeing. **adventure playground,** *n.* a children's playground containing old or waste objects that can be used in creative play. **adventurer,** *n.* one who seeks adventures; one who seeks to gain social position by false pretences. **adventuresome**, *a.* adventurous. **adventuresomeness,** *n.* **adventuress,** *n.* a female adventurer, a woman who seeks to gain socialposition by false pretences. **adventurism,** *n.* hasty, ill-considered, opportunistic action, esp. in politics. **adventurous,** *a.* fond of adventure; venturesome, daring, rash; involving risk; perilous, hazardous. **adventurously,** *adv.* **adventurousness,** *n.* [OF *aventure,* L *adventūra,* fut.p. of *advenīre;* see ADVENT]

adverb, *n.* a word or phrase qualifying a verb, an adjective or another adverb. **adverbial**, *a.* **adverbially,** *adv.* [F *adverbe,* L *adverbium* (*ad-*, to, *verbum,* word)]

adversary, *n.* an opponent, an enemy, a foe. *a.* (*Law*) opposed, hostile. **adversarious**, *a.* **adversative**, *a.* denoting opposition or antithesis. *n.* a word or proposition expressing opposition. [OF *aversier,* L*adversarius;* see ADVERSE]

adverse, *a.* acting in a contrary direction; hostile, inimical, unpropitious; opposite in position. **adversely,** *adv.* **adverseness,** *n.* **adversifoliate,** *a.* having opposite leaves. **adversity**, *n.* adverse circumstances, misfortune, calamity, trouble. [OF *avers, advers,* L *adversus,* p.p. of *advertĕre* (*ad-*, towards, *vertere,* to turn)]

advert[1], *v.t.* to attend to, to turn attention to, refer to. *v.i.* to take heed, pay heed; to refer (to). **advertence, -ency,** *n.* attention, notice, regard. **advertent,** *a.* attentive, heedful. **advertently,** *adv.* [F *avertir,* late L *advertĕre,* L *advertĕre* (*ad-*, to, *vertĕre,* to turn)]

advert[2], *n.* (*coll.*) short for ADVERTISEMENT.

advertise, *v.t.* to inform; to give public notice of; to make publicly known; to publicly describe (a product or service) in order to promote awareness or increase sales. *v.i.* to give public notice to issue advertisements. **advertisement**, *n.* the act of advertising; a public notice; a paid announcement by journal, radio, television etc. **advertiser,** *n.* one who or a journal which advertises. **advertising,** *n.* publicity; advertisements; the business of securing publicity. [F *avertiss-*, stem of *avertir, avertissement,* L *advertere;* see ADVERT[1]]

Advertising Standards Authority, organization founded by the UK advertising industry (1962) to promote higher standards of advertising in the media (excluding television and radio, which have their own authority). It is financed by the advertisers, who pay 0.1% supplement on the cost of advertisements. It recommends to the media that advertisements which might breach the British Code of Advertising Practice are not published, but has no statutory power.

advertorial, *n.* a newspaper feature which is commissioned and often supplied by an advertiser, though appearing in the form of an editorial or impartial report. [ADVERTISEMENT, EDITORIAL]

advice, *n.* counsel, opinion as to a course of action; a formal or official notice; (*usu. pl.*)information or notice; news. [OF *avis,* L *ad-*, to, *vīsum,* seen (*vidēre,* to see)]

advise, *v.t.* to counsel; to communicate intelligence to; to inform, to notify. *v.i.* to give advice; (*chiefly N Am.*) to consult; †to deliberate, to reflect. **advised,** *a.* acting with deliberation; well considered, deliberate. **advisable,** *a.* capable of being advised; right, proper, befitting, expedient. **advisability**, *n.* **advisableness, advisably,** *adv.* **advisedly**, *adv.* with mature deliberation. †**advisedness**, *n.* †**advisement,** *n.* consideration, deliberation. **adviser, -or,** *n.* one who advises, esp. in a professional capacity; (*N Am.*) a supervisor of studies. **advisership,** *n.* **advising,** *n.* advice, counsel. **advisory,** *a.* having power to advise; containing advice. [OF *aviser,* late L *advisāre;* see ADVICE]

advocaat, *n.* a sweet thick liqueur containing raw egg and brandy. [Dut.]

advocate, *n.* one who defends or promotes a cause; one who pleads a cause in a civil or criminal court; an intercessor. *v.t.* to plead in favour of, recommend. **faculty of advocates,** the professional organization for Scottish advocates, the equivalent of English barristers, incorporated in 1532 under James V. **advocacy,** *n.* a pleading for; judicial pleading; the office of advocate; support. **advocateship,** *n.* the office of an advocate or intercessor; advocacy. **advocatory,** *a.* pertaining to advocacy. [L *advocātus* p.p. (used as n.) of *advocāre* (*ad-*, to, *vocāre,* to call)]

advouter, *n.* an adulterer.

advowee, *n.* a person possessed of an advowson; the patron of an ecclesiastical benefice. [OF *avoué,* L *advocātus*]

advowson, *n.* the right of presentation to a vacant benefice in the Church of England. [OF *avoson,* L *advocatiōnem* (ADVOCATE, -ION)]

advt., (*abbr.*) advertisement.

adynamia, *n.* lack of power, nervous debility, physical prostration. **adynamic,** *a.* pertaining to adynamia; weak, asthenic; without force. [Gr. *adunamia* (*a-*, not, *dunamis,* power)]

adytum, *n.* (*pl.* **-ta**) a shrine; theinnermost and most sacred part of a temple; an inner chamber. [L *adytum,* Gr. *aduton* (*a-*, not, *dutos,* verb.a. from *duein,* to enter)]

adze, *n.* a cutting tool with an arched blade at right angles to the handle. *v.t.* to shape by means of an adze. [OE *adesa*]

adzuki bean ADUKI BEAN.

ae, *adj.* (*Sc.*) one, a.

-ae, *suf.* forming plural of unnaturalized Latin words, e.g. *laminae, Rosaceae, Homeridae.* [L]

AEA, (*abbr.*) Atomic Energy Authority.

AEC, (*abbr.*) Atomic Energy Commission (US).

aedile, *n.* a magistrate in ancient Rome who had charge of public and private buildings; hence, a municipal officer. **aedileship,** *n.* [L *aedīlis* (*aedes,* a building), -ILE]

Aegean civilization, *n.* the cultures of Bronze Age Greece, including the Minoan civilization of Crete and the Mycenaean civilization of the E Peloponnese.

Aegean Islands, *n. pl.* the islands of the Aegean Sea, but more specifically a region of Greece comprising the Dodecanese islands, the Cyclades islands, Lesvos, Samos and Chios; population (1981) 428,500; area 9122 sq km/3523 sq miles.

Aegean Sea, *n.* branch of the Mediterranean between Greece and Turkey; the Dardanelles connect it with the Sea of Marmara. The numerous islands in the Aegean Sea include Crete, the Cyclades, the Sporades and the Dodecanese. There is political tension between Greece and Turkey over sea limits claimed by Greece around such islands as Lesvos, Chios, Samos and Kos.

aegis, *n.* a shield (esp. that of Minerva); protection, a protective influence. [L *aegis,* Gr. *aigis*]

aegrotat, *n.* a note certifying that a student is sick; a degree awarded to a student unable to sit the relevant examinations because of illness. [L *aegrotat,* he is sick (*aeger,* sick)]

Aelfric, *n.* (*c.* 955–1020), English writer, author of two collections of homilies and the *Lives of the Saints*, written in vernacular Old English prose.

-aemia, (*esp. N Am.*) **-emia**, *comb. form* pertaining to or denoting blood, esp. a specified condition of the blood. [Gr. *haima,* blood]

Aeneas, *n.* in classical legend, a Trojan prince who became the ancestral hero of the Romans. According to Homer, he was the son of Anchises and the goddess Aphrodite. During the Trojan War he owed his life several times to the intervention of the gods. Virgil's epic poem the *Aeneid* is based on this legend.

Aeneid, *n.* epic poem by Virgil, written in 12 books of hexameters and composed during the last 11 years of his life (30–19 BC). It celebrates the development of the Roman Empire through the legend of Aeneas. After the fall of Troy, Aeneas wanders for seven years and becomes shipwrecked off Africa. He is received by Dido, queen of Carthage, and they fall in love. Aeneas, however, renounces their love and sails on to Italy where he settles as founder of Latium and the Roman state. [L *Aenēida,* acc. of *Aenēis,* Gr. a., pertaining to *Aenēas*]

Aeolian, *a.* of or belonging to Aeolia; pertaining to Aeolus (god of the winds); aerial; formed by the action of the wind. **Aeolian harp,** *n.* a wind-blown instrument, consisting of a shallow soundbox supporting gut strings at low tension and tuned to the same pitch. It produces an eerie harmony that rises and falls with the changing pressure of the wind. It was common in parts of central Europe during the 19th century. **Aeolian mode,** *n.* (*Mus.*) the ninth of the church modes. [L *Aeolius,* a. from *Aeolis* (Gr. *Aiolis*), or *Aeolus* (Gr. *Aiolos*), -AN]

Aeolic, *a.* of or belonging to Aeolia. **Aeolic dialect,** *n.* one of the three great dialects of the Greek language. [Gr. *aiolikos* (a. from Aeolis)]

aeolipyle, -pile, *n.* an apparatus for demonstrating the force of steam generated in a closed chamber and escaping through a small aperture. [F *aeolipyle,* L *Aeoli pylae,* Gr. *Aiolou pulai,* gates of Aeolus]

aeolotropy, *n.* change of physical qualities consequent on change of position, as of the refracting properties of Iceland spar. **aeolotropic,** *a.* [Gr. *aiolos,* changeful, *tropia,* turning]

aeon, *n.* an age of the universe; a cosmic cycle; a period of immense duration; an age personified; an emanation from or phase of the Deity. **aeonian,** *a.* eternal, everlasting. [L *aeon,* Gr. *aiōn*]

Aepyornis, *n.* a genus of gigantic fossil birds much larger than the ostrich, found in Madagascar. [Gr. *aipus,* tall, *ornis,* bird]

Aequi, *n. pl.* an Italian people, originating around the river Velino, who were turned back from their advance on Rome in 431 BC and were conquered in 304 BC, during the Samnite Wars. They subsequently adopted Roman customs and culture.

aerate, *v.t.* to subject to the action of atmospheric air; to charge with carbon dioxide; to oxygenate (the blood) by respiration. **aerated,** *part.a.* exposed to the action of the air, charged with air; charged with carbon dioxide gas; effervescent. **aeration,** *n.* the act of aerating. **aerator,** *n.*

AERE, (*abbr.*) Atomic Energy Research Establishment.

aerial, *a.* belonging to the air; resembling, produced by, operating in or inhabiting the air; growing in the air; airy, thin, gaseous; atmospheric; high, elevated; imaginary, immaterial, refined; of, for or using aircraft, effected by or operating from or against aircraft. *n.* a collector or radiator of electromagnetic waves for radio, television etc. **aerial-perspective,** *n.* the representation of distance and space on a plane surface. **aerial photograph,** *n.* a photograph made from an aeroplane for military or surveying purposes. **aerial railway,** *n.* a wire or cable stretched from point to point across rivers, valleys etc. for transporting loads. **aerial surveying,** *n.* a method of surveying by the use of aerial photographs. **aerial torpedo,** *n.* a large, winged bomb for aircraft use. **aerially,** *adv.* **aerialist,** *n.* a trapeze artist or tight-rope walker. **aeriality,** *n.* airiness, unsubstantiality. [L *aērus,* Gr. *aerios* (*āer,* air), -AL]

aerie, aery, eyrie, eyry, *n.* the nest of any bird of prey, esp. of an eagle; the young of a bird of prey; a human dwelling or retreat perched on a rock; (*Shak.*) a family of children of high birth. [med. L *aeria,* F *aire* (from L *ārea,* a spot of level ground, or *ātrium,* an open hall)]

aeriferous, *a.* bearing air, carrying air.

aeriform, *a.* of the form or nature of air; gaseous.

aer(o)- *comb. form* pertaining to the air oratmosphere; aerial, atmospheric; e.g. *aeroplane, aerodynamics, aeronaut.* [Gr. *aēr aeros,* the air]

aerobatics, *n.pl.* aerial acrobatics; stunting in an aeroplane.

aerobe, *n.* an organism that requires oxygen for life. **aerobic,** *a.* using or requiring oxygen, occurring in the presence of oxygen; of or involving aerobes; pertaining to aerobics. **aerobically,** *adv.* **aerobics,** *n.pl.* physical exercises designed to improve heart and lung function, esp. (*often sing. in constr.*) a system of exercises consisting of routines of rhythmic dance-like movements and stretches, usu. performed to music.

aerobiology, *n.* the study of air-borne microorganisms.

aerobioscope, *n.* a mechanism for determining the number of forms of microorganisms in a given volume of air.

aerocamera, *n.* a special form ofcamera used vertically for photographing the ground from an aeroplane.

aerodensimeter, *n.* a pressure gauge for gases.

aerodrome, *n.* an area, with any buildings attached, for the operation of aircraft; an air-station. [Gr. *dromos,* race, racecourse]

aerodynamics, *n.* the science which deals with the forces exerted by gases in motion. **aerodynamic,** *a.* of or involving aerodynamics;designed so as to minimize wind resistance. **aerodynamically,** *adv.*

aerodyne, *n.* a generic term for heavier-than-air aircraft.

aeroembolism, *n.* the formation of nitrogen bubbles in the blood and tissues, caused by too rapid a reduction in atmospheric pressure (see CAISSON DISEASE).

aerofoil, *n.* a wing-like structure constructed to obtain reaction on its surfaces from the air; a plane or flying surface of an aeroplane.

aerogram, *n.* a radiogram, a wireless message; (*or* **aerogramme**) an air letter.

Aerograph®**,** *n.* an instrument for spraying paint.

aerography, *n.* the description of the properties etc. of the air.

aerolite, -lith, *n.* a stone which falls through the air to the earth; a meteoric stone. **aerolitic,** *a.* [Gr. *lithos,* a stone]

aerology, *n.* the department of science that deals with the atmosphere. **aerological,** *a.* **aerologist,** *n.*

†**aeromancy,** *n.* divination by means of aerial phenomena; forecasting the weather.

aerometer, *n.* an instrument for measuring the weight and density of air and gases.

aeronaut, *n.* one concerned with thenavigation of balloons or airships. **aeronautic, -ical,** *a.* pertaining to aerial navigation. **aeronautics,** *n.* the science or art which deals with aerial navigation. [Gr. *nautēs,* a sailor]

aeronomy, *n.* the science of the upper atmosphere of the earth and other planets.**aeronomist,** *n.*

aerophyte, *n.* a plant which grows entirely in the air, as distinguished from one growing on the ground.

aeroplane, (*N Am.*) **airplane,** *n.* a mechanically-driven heavier-than-air flying-machine with fixed wings as lifting surfaces.

aerosol, *n.* a suspension of fine particles in air or gas, as in smoke or mist; a substance dispersed as an aerosol from a pressurized metalcontainer; such a container.

aerospace, *n.* the earth's atmosphere and the space beyond; the science or industry concerned with aerospace. *a.* pertaining to aerospace, to travel or operation in aerospace, or to vehicles used in aerospace. **aerospaceplane,** *n.* an aerospace vehicle. **aerospace vehicle,** *n.* a vehicle that can operate in both the earth's atmosphere and outer space.

aerostat, *n.* an aircraft supported in the air statically. i.e. lighter-than-air. **aerostatic,** *a.* of or pertaining to aerostatics; pneumatic; aeronautic. **aerostatics,** *n.* the science which deals with the equilibrium and pressure of air and gases; aeronautics. [F *aérostat* (Gr. *statos,* verb. a., standing)]

aerostation, *n.* aerial navigation; aeronautics.
aerotherapy, *n.* the treatment of disease by fresh or suitably medicated air.
aeruginous, *a.* of the nature of or resembling verdigris, copper rust. [L *aerūginōsus,* rusty (*aerūgo -inis,* verdigris, from *aes aeris,* copper)]
aery, *a.* (*Milton*) aerial, ethereal, unsubstantial, visionary. [L *āerius* (*āer,* the air)]
Aeschines, *n.* (lived 4th century BC) orator of ancient Athens, a rival of Demosthenes.
Aeschylus, *n.* (*c.* 525–*c.* 456 BC), Greek dramatist, widely regarded as the founder of Greek tragedy. By the introduction of a second actor he made true dialogue and dramatic action possible. Aeschylus wrote some 90 plays between 499 and 458 BC of which seven survive. These are: *The Suppliant Women* peformed about 490, *The Persians* (472), *Seven against Thebes* (467), *Prometheus Bound* (about 460) and the *Oresteia* trilogy (458).
Aesculapius, *n.* the Greek god of medicine; a physician. **Aesculapian,** *a.* of or belonging to Aesculapius; medicinal. [L]
aesculin, *n.* a kind of glucoside found in the bark of the horse chestnut (*Aesculus hippocastanum*). [L *æsculus,* the Italian oak]
Aesir, *n. pl.* principal gods of Norse mythology - Odin, Thor, Balder, Loki, Freya and Tyr, whose dwelling place was Asgard.
Aesop, *n.* traditional writer of Greek fables. According to Herodotus he lived in the reign of Amasis of Egypt (mid-6th century BC) and was a slave of Iadmon, a Thracian. The fables, for which no evidence of his authorship exists, are anecdotal stories using animal characters to illustrate moral or satirical points.
aesthesia, -thesis, (*esp. N Am.*) **esthesia, -thesis,** *n.* capacity to feel or sense, sensibility. **aesthesiometer,** *n.* an instrument for testing the sensibility of the skin. [see ANAESTHESIA]
aesthete , (*esp. N Am.*) **esthete,** *n.* one who professes a special appreciation of the beautiful, and endeavours to carry his or her ideas into practice. **aesthetic, -ical,** *a.* pertaining to aesthetics; appreciating the beautiful in nature and art; in accord with the laws of the beautiful, or with principles of taste. **Aesthetic movement,** *n.* English artistic movement of the late 19th century, dedicated to the doctrine 'art for art's sake' – that is, art as self-sufficient, not needing to justify its existence by serving any particular use. **aesthetically,** *adv.* **aestheticism,** *n.* the quality of being aesthetic; devotion to the study of the beautiful. **aestheticize, -ise,** *v.t.* **aesthetics,** *n.* the theory or philosophy of the perception of the beautiful. [Gr. *aisthētēs,* one who perceives]
aestho-physiology, (*esp. N Am.*) **estho-physiology,** *n.* the science dealing with the physical organs of sensation. [Gr. *aisth-* (stem of *aisthanomai,* I perceive), PHYSIOLOGY]
aestival, (*esp. N Am.*) **estival,** *a.* of or belonging to the summer; produced in the summer. **aestivate,** *v.i.* to remain in a place during the summer; of an animal, to fall into a summer sleep or torpor. **aestivation,** *n.* the internal arrangement of a flower-bed, prefloration; the act of remaining torpid in the summer. [L *aestīvālis,* from *aestīvus* (*aestus,* heat)]
aether etc. ETHER etc.
aethrioscope, *n.* an instrument for measuring radiation towards a clear sky, andfor indicating the presence of invisible aqueousvapour in the atmosphere. [Gr. *aithrios,*clear, -SCOPE]
aetiology, (*esp. N Am.*) **etiology,** *n.* an account of the cause of anything, assignment of a cause; the philosophy of causation; the science of the causes of disease. **aetiological,** *a.* pertaining to aetiology. **aetiologically,** *adv.* [L *aetiologia,* Gr. *aitiologia* (*aitia,* a cause, -LOGY)]
Aetolia, *n.* district of ancient Greece on the NW of the gulf of Corinth. The **Aetolian League** was a confederation of the cities of Aetolia which, following the death of Alexander the Great, became the chief rival of Macedonian power and the Achaean League.

AF, (*abbr.*) audio frequency.
af-, *pref.* AD-, assim. to *f,* e.g. *afford.*
afar, *adv.* from, at or to a (great) distance.
AFC, (*abbr.*) Air Force Cross; Association Football Club.
AFD, (*abbr.*) accelerated freeze drying, a common method of food preservation.
†**afeard,** *part.a.* afraid, frightened. [OE p.p. of *afǣran* (*a-,* intens., *fǣran,* to frighten)]
affable, *a.* easily approached; courteous, complaisant, benign. **affability,** *n.* the quality of being affable; courtesy of manners. **affableness,** *n.* **affably,** *adv.* [L *affābilis* (*af-, ad-,* to, *fāri,* to speak), -ABLE]
affair, *n.* any kind of business; that which is to be done; a thing, concern, matter or object of slight importance; a love intrigue; (*pl.*) public or private business; (*pl.*) finances; (*pl.*) circumstances. [OF *afaire* (*à,* to, *faire,* to do, L *facere*)]
affect[1]**,** *v.t.* to tend towards, aim at, to be drawn towards; to be fond of, fancy, love, like; to practise, use, assume; to frequent, haunt; to feign, to pretend, to make a pretence of. **affectation,** *n.* an aiming at, a striving after; artificial appearance, assumption, pretence. **affected,** *a.* given to false show; pretending to what is not natural or real. **affectedly,** *adv.* **affectedness,** *n.* **affectible,** *a.* that may be affected or influenced. **affectibility,** *n.* **affecting,** *a.* touching, moving; fitted to excite emotion. **affectingly,** *adv.* [F *affecter,* L *affectāre,* freq. of *afficere* (*ad-,* to, *facere,* to do, act)]
affect[2]**,** *v.t.* to act upon, exert an influence upon; to attack, impress, touch, move, have effect upon; †to appoint, assign specially. [L *afficere*]
affection, *n.* the state of being affected, esp. in the emotions; feeling, disposition, attachment, fondness, love; a state of the body due to any cause, malady, disease; a relation, mode of being, attributes. †*v.t.* to have regard for, like, love. **affectional,** *a.* pertaining to the affections; having affections. **affectionate,** *a.* of a loving disposition; tenderly disposed; indicating or expressing love. **affectionately,** *adv.* **affectionateness,** *n.* †**affectioned,** *a.* disposed, inclined, partial; emotional, passionate; affectionate. **affective,** *a.* †influencing the affections; pertaining to the affections, emotional. [F *affection,* L *affectiōnem*]
†**affeer,** *v.t.* to fix or settle a fine; (*Shak.*) to confirm. [OF *afeurer,* late L *afforāre,* to fix the price (*ad-,* to, *forum,* market)]
afferent, *a.* bringing or conducting inwards or towards, esp. conducting nerve impulses towards the brain or spinal cord. [L *afferre* (*ad-,* to, *ferre,* to bring), -ENT]
affettuoso, *adv.* (*Mus.*) with feeling. [It.]
affiance, *v.t.* to promise solemnly in marriage. *n.* faith, trust, confidence; plighting of faith, contract of marriage, betrothal; †affinity; †implicit trust. **affianced,** *a.* promised in marriage, betrothed. [OF *afiancer;* late L *affidare,* to trust]
affiche, *n.* a poster, placard. [F *afficher,* to fasten (L *af-, ad-,* to, *ficher,* L *fīgicāre,* from *figere*)]
affidavit, *n.* a voluntary affirmation sworn before a person qualified to administer an oath. [late L, he made oath, from *affidāre;* see AFFIANCE]
affiliate, *v.t.* to adopt; to receive as a member or branch; to attribute to; to assign (an illegitimate child) to the father. *v.i.* to become connected or associated, combine. *n., a.* (of) a person etc. who is affiliated. **affiliable,** *a.* capable of being affiliated or assigned. **affiliation,** *n.* the act of affiliating; adoption; the assignment of an illegitimate child to the father. **affiliation order,** *n.* a legal order requiring the father of an illegitimate child to make maintenance payments. [L *affiliāre,* to adopt (*ad-,* to, *filius,* a son)]
affined, *a.* joined in affinity; bound, obliged. [F *affiné* (L *affinis,* related to)]
affinity, *n.* relationship, relationship by marriage as opposed to consanguinity or relationship by blood; connection; resemblance due to common origin; physical attraction; the object of this attraction; chemical attraction, the property by which elements unite to

form new compounds. [F *affinité,* L *affīnitātem* (*af-, ad-,* to, *finis,* end, border)]

affirm, *v.t.* to assert positively or solemnly; to allege confidently; to aver; (*Log.*) to state affirmatively. *v.i.* to make a solemn affirmation in lieu of oath. **affirmable,** *a.* **affirmance,** *n.* confirmation, ratification, assertion. **affirmation**, *n.* the act of affirming anything; that which is affirmed; a solemn declaration made under penalties, in lieu of oath. **affirmative,** *a.* relating to or containing an affirmation; confirmatory, positive. *n.* that which affirms. **in the affirmative,** yes. **affirmatively,** *adv.* [OF *afermer,* L *affirmāre* (*af-, ad-,* to, *firmāre,* from *firmus,* strong)]

affix, *v.t.* to fix, fasten, attach; to annex, to subjoin. **affix**, *n.* an addition; a word or syllable added to the beginning or the end of, or inserted in a word or root to produce a derived word or inflection, a prefix, suffix or infix. **affixture**, *n.* the act of affixing; attachment. [med. L *affixāre,* freq. of L *affīgere* (*af-, ad-,* to, FIX)]

afflation, *n.* the act of blowing or breathing upon; inspiration. **afflatus**, *n.* inspiration; poetic impulse. [L *afflatiōnem,* from *afflāre* (*af-, ad-,* to, *flāre,* to blow)]

afflict, *v.t.* to inflict bodily or mental pain on; to cast down; to trouble. **afflicted,** *a.* **afflictingly,** *adv.* **affliction,** *n.* the state of being afflicted; calamity, trouble, misery, distress; mental orbodily ailment. **afflictive,** *a.* causing affliction; distressing. **afflictively,** *adv.* [OF *aflit,* L *afflictus,* p.p. of *afflīgere* (*af-, ad-,* to, *flīgere,* dash, strike)]

affluent, *a.* flowing; abundant, copious; wealthy. *n.* a tributary. **affluently,** *adv.* **affluence,** *n.* the state of flowing in, influx; abounding flow; abundance, wealth. [F *affluent,* L *affluentem,* pres.p. of *affluere* (*af-, ad-,* to, *fluere,* flow)]

afflux, *n.* a flowing to or in; that which flows; a concourse of people, an accession. [med. L *affluxus* (*fluere*)]

afford, *v.t.* to yield the means; to be able to bear the expense of; to share, furnish, supply. **affordable,** *a.* [OE *ge-forthian* (*ge-,* intens., *forthian,* to further)]

afforest, *v.t.* to convert into forest. **afforestation,** *n.* the act of converting waste or other land into forest. [med L *afforestāre* (*af-, ad-,* to, *foresta*]

affranchise, *v.t.* to make free; to set at liberty physically or morally. **affranchisement**, *n.* the act of making free; emancipation. [F *affranchir* (*af- franchiss-*) (*à,* to, *franchir,* to free)]

affray, *v.t.* to frighten, to scare; †to rouse out of sleep. *n.* commotion, tumult; a fight between two or more persons in a public place. [OF *effreër, esfreër,* late L *exfridāre* (*ex-,* intens., OHG *fridu,* cp. OE *frith,* peace)]

affreightment, *n.* (a contract for) the hiring of a ship for conveyance of goods by sea. [F *affrètement,* from *affréter,* to freight a ship]

affrettando, affrettate, **affrettore**, *adv.* (*Mus.*) hastening the time. [It. *affrettare,* to hasten]

affright, *v.t.* to frighten, to terrify. †*part.a.* frightened. *n.* fright, terror; a cause of fright or terror. **affrightedly,** *adv.* [ME *afright,* p.p., OE*āfyrhted,* p.p. (*ā-,* intens., *fyrhtan,* to frighten)]

affrite AFREET.

affront, *v.t.* to insult openly; to confront, esp. in a hostile way, †to accost; to makeashamed; to offend. *n.* a hostile encounter; an insult; contemptuous, rude treatment. **affrontingly,** *adv.* [OF *afronter,* late L *affrontāre, af-, ad-,* to, against, *frontem,* acc. of *frons,* forehead)]

affusion, *n.* a pouring on of liquid; baptism; a remedy in fever. [L *affundere* (*af-, ad-,* to, *fundere, fus-,* to pour)]

Afghan, *a.* belonging to Afghanistan. *n.* an inhabitant of Afghanistan. The dominant group, particularly in Kabul, are the Pathans. The Tadzhiks, a smaller ethnic group, are predominantly traders and farmers in the province of Herat and around Kabul; the Hazaras, another farming group, are found in the southern mountain ranges of the Hindu Kush. **Afghan hound,** *n.* dog resembling the saluki, though less thickly coated, first introduced to Britain by army officers serving on the North-West Frontier in the late 19th century. **Afghan Wars,** *n. pl.* three wars waged between Britain and Afghanistan to counter the threat to British India from expanding Russian influence in Afghanistan. [Pushtoo *afghāni*]

Afghanistan, *n.* Republic of (*Jamhuria Afghanistan*), mountainous, landlocked country in S central Asia, bounded by the USSR to the north, Iran to the West and Pakistan to the south and east. **area** 652,090 sq km/251,707 sq miles. **capital** Kábul. **towns** Kandahár, Herát. **physical** mountainous, with rivers and desert areas. **exports** dried fruit, rare minerals, natural gas (piped to USSR), karakul lamb skins, Afghan coats. **population** (1988) 10,000,000–12,000,000 (more than 5 million have become refugees since 1979); annual growth rate 0.6%. **language** Pushtoo. **religion** Muslim: 80% Sunni, 20% Shi'ite.

aficionado, *n.* (*pl.* **-dos**) a keen follower or fan. **aficionada**, *n.fem.* (*pl.* **-das**). [Sp. *aficionar,* from *aficiōn,* affection]

afield, *adv.* to or in the field; away, at a distance, abroad.

afire, *adv., pred.a.* on fire.

aflame, *adv., pred.a.* flaming; in or into flame.

aflatoxin, *n.* a carcinogenic toxin produced in badly stored peanuts, maize etc. by the mould *Aspergillus flavus*. [*A*spergillus *fla*vus, TOXIN]

AFL-CIO, (*abbr.*) American Federation of Labor and Congress of Industrial Organizations.

afloat, *a., adv.* floating; in a floating condition; at sea, aboard ship; out of debt, solvent, unembarrassed; in full swing; in circulation, current; moving about, adrift.

AFM, (*abbr.*) Air Force Medal.

afoot, *adv.* on foot; in motion, in action.

afore, *adv., prep.* before, in front of; †in or towards the front part of a ship. **afore-cited,** *a.* already cited. **afore-going,** *n., a.* the preceding; preceding. †**aforehand,** *adv.* beforehand; previously. *a.* provided, prepared, previously fitted, ready. **aforementioned,** *a.* before-mentioned. **aforenamed,** *a.* before-named. **aforesaid,** *a.* said or mentioned before. **aforethought,** *a.* premeditated, prepense. †**aforetime,** *adv.* at a former time; previously. *n.* time past. [OE *onforan* (ON prep., *foran,* in front)]

a fortiori, *adv.* (*L*) with still more reason; much more; still more conclusively.

afoul, *a., adv.* fouled, entangled, in collision.

afraid, *a.* filled with fear, terrified; apprehensive; regretfully admitting or of the opinion. [p.p. of AFFRAY]

afreet, afrit, affrite, *n.* a demon or monster of Muslim mythology. [Arab. *ifrīt*]

afresh, *adv.* again, anew, freshly.

Africa, *n.* second largest of the continents, three times the area of Europe. **area** 30,097,000 sq km/11,620,451 sq miles. **largest cities** Cairo, Algiers, Lagos, Kinshasa, Abidjan, Tunis, Cape Town, Nairobi. **physical** dominated by a central plateau, which includes the world's largest desert (Sahara); Nile and Zaïre rivers, but generally there is a lack of rivers, and also of other inlets, so that Africa has proportionately the shortest coastline of all the continents; comparatively few offshore islands; 75% is within the tropics; Great Rift Valley; immensely rich fauna and flora. **exports** has 30% of the world's minerals; crops include coffee (Kenya), cocoa (Ghana, Nigeria), cotton (Egypt, Uganda). **population** (1984) 537,000,000; annual growth rate 3%. **language** Hamito-Semitic in the north; Bantu below the Sahara; Khosan languages with 'click' consonants in the far south. **religion** Islam in the north; animism below the Sahara, which survives alongside Christianity (both Catholic and Protestant) in many central and southern areas.

African, *a.* pertaining to Africa. *n.* a native of Africa, a person, wherever born, who belongs ethnologically to one of the African races. **Afric,** *a.* (*poet.*) African. **African art,** *n.* the art of sub-Saharan Africa, from prehistory onwards, ranging from the art of ancient civilizations to the new styles of post- imperialist African nations. Among the best-known examples of historic African art are bronze figures from Benin and Ife (in modern Nigeria) dating from about 1500 and, also on the W coast, in the same period, bronze or brass figures for weighing gold, made by the Ashanti. **African green,** *n.* a pigment obtained from copper. **African oak,** *n.* a wood from Sierra Leone resembling oak or mahogany, sometimes called African teak or African mahogany. **African violet,** *n.* a tropical African plant, *Saintpaulia ionantha,* with velvety leaves and pink, white or violet flowers. **Africanism,** *n.* a characteristic of Africa or of the African culture or language. **Africanize, -ise,** *v.t.* to make African; to bring under Black African influence or control. **Africanization, -isation,** *n.* [L *Africa*]

African National Congress, multiracial nationalist organization formed in South Africa (1912) to extend the franchise to the whole population and end all racial discrimination there. Although nonviolent, it was banned by the government 1960, and in exile in Mozambique developed a military wing, Umkhonto we Sizwe, which has engaged in sabotage and guerrilla training. The ANC is now based in Lusaka, Zambia, and its leader in exile is Oliver Tambo; former ANC leaders include Albert Luthuli, Nelson Mandela, and Solomon Plaatje. State president F. W. de Klerk announced the lifting of the ban in Jan. 1990 and the intention to release from prison its leaders including Nelson Mandela.

Afridi, *a.* of a race of Afghans living in the mountain region north of Peshawar. *n.* a member of this race. [native name]

Afrikaans, *n.* along with English, an official language of the Republic of South Africa. Spoken mainly by the Afrikaners, descendants of Dutch and other 17th century colonists, it is a variety of the Dutch language, modified by circumstance and the influence of German, French and other immigrant and local languages. It became a standardized written language about 1875.

Afrika Korps, *n.* the German army in the western desert of N Africa (1941–43) in World War II, commanded by Field Marshal Rommel. They were driven out of N Africa by May 1943.

Afrikander, *n., a.* a South African breed of sheep and of cattle. **Afrikander Bond,** *n.* a political association (founded 1879–80) for promotion of South African interests and eventual independence of South Africa as United States of South Africa. [Dut. *Afrikaender, Afrikaner*]

Afrikaner, *n.* (formerly known as **Boer**) inhabitant of South Africa descended from the original Dutch and Huguenot settlers of the 17th century. Comprising approximately 60% of the white population in the Republic, they were originally farmers but have now become mainly urbanized. Their language is Afrikaans. [Dutch]

afrit AFREET.

Afro-, *comb. form* pertaining to Africa or Africans.

Afr(o)-, *n., a.* (of) a hairstyle characterized by thick, bushy, curly hair.

Afro-American, *n., a.* (of) an American of African descent.

Afro-Caribbean, *n.* a person of African descent from the West Indies. Afro-Caribbeans are the descendants of W Africans kidnapped by European slave traders, and shipped to the West Indies. Since World War II many Afro-Caribbeans have migrated to Europe, especially Britain and the Netherlands, and also to North America.

afrormosia, *n.* any tree of the African genus *Afrormosia,* with dark hard wood used for furniture; this wood. [L *Afr-, Afer,* African, *Ormosia,* genus name]

aft, *a., adv.* towards or at the stern of a vessel; abaft. [OE *æftan*]

after, *adv., prep., conj.* in the rear; behind; in pursuit of, according to; following (in time), next to; subsequently to, at the time subsequent. *a.* later, subsequent; located (further) towards the rear or stern, posterior. **a long way after,** in feeble imitation (of a painter, musician, writer etc.). **after-birth,** *n.* the placenta, the secundine; †a later birth; late-born offspring; posthumous birth. **after-care,** *n.* care or supervision following a person's discharge from hospital, prison etc. **after-clap,** *n.* an unexpected subsequent event. **after-crop,** *n.* a second crop in the same year. **after-damp,** *n.* choke damp; carbon dioxide gas resulting from the combustion of fire-damp in coal-mines. **after-effect,** *n.* an effect that follows some time after the cause. **after-game,** *n.* a game played to reverse the issue of the first. **after-glow,** *n.* glow in the western sky after sunset; (*coll.*) a feeling of pleasure after an enjoyable experience. **after-grass,** *n.* the grass which springs up after a first crop has been mown. **after-guard,** *n.* the seamen stationed on the poop of a ship to attend to the after sails. **after-image,** *n.* the image that remains for a moment after looking away from an object at which one has been gazing steadily. **afterlife,** *n.* life after death. **after-light,** *n.* later knowledge. **after-mast,** *n.* mast fitted aft. **afternoon,** *n.* the time between midday and evening. **afternoon-buyer,** *n.* a purchaser who waits till after the market dinner, in the hope of cheaper prices. **after-pains,** *n.pl.* the pains which follow childbirth, and by which the after-birth is expelled. **after-piece,** *n.* a short piece acted after a more important play. **afters,** *n.pl.* (*coll.*) what follows the main course at a meal. **after-shave,** *n.* a cosmetic lotion applied to the face after shaving. **after-taste,** *n.* a taste that persists after eating or drinking; an impression or feeling that remains. **afterthought,** *n.* reflection after the act; a belated explanation. **afterward, afterwards,** *adv.* subsequently; at a later period. [OE *æfter* (*af,* off, *ter,* comp. suf.; cp. Gr. *apo-ter-o*)]

aftermath, after-grass; consequences. [OE *mæth,* a mowing]

aftermost, *a.* nearest the stern. [OE *æftemæst,* superlative]

AG, (*abbr.*) adjutant-general; attorney general; joint-stock company (G *Aktiengesellschaft*).

Ag, (*chem. symbol*) silver. [L *argentum*]

ag-, *pref.* AD-, assim. to *g,* e.g. *aggravate, aggrieve*.

aga, agha, *n.* a Turkish civil or military officer of high rank. [Turk. *agha,* a master]

agacerie, *n.* (F) blandishment, charm, allurement.

Agadir, *n.* resort and seaport in S Morocco, near the mouth of the river Sus. Population (1984) 110,500. It was rebuilt after being destroyed by an earthquake in 1960.

Agadir Incident, *n.* international crisis provoked by Kaiser Wilhelm II of Germany. By sending the gunboat *Panther* to demand territorial concessions from the French, he hoped to drive a wedge into the Anglo-French entente. In fact, German aggression during the second Moroccan crisis merely served to reinforce Anglo-French fears of Germany's intentions. The crisis gave rise to the term 'gunboat diplomacy'.

again, *adv.* a second time, once more, moreover, in addition; on the other hand, in return, in answer. **again and again,** *adv.* with frequent repetition, repeatedly. [OE *ongean* (*on,* prep., on or in, *gagn, gegn,* in a direct line with, opposite)]

against, *prep.* in opposition to, opposite to, in contrast to; in contact with, in preparation or provision for. **against the grain,** contrary to inclination, reluctantly, with aversion. [AGAIN]

Aga Khan IV, *n.* (1936–), spiritual head (*imam*) of the **Ismaili** Muslim sect. He succeeded his grandfather in 1957.

agalite, *n.* a fine kind of talc used in the manufacture of paper. [Gr. *agē,* wonder, -LITE]

agalmatolite, *n.* a soft stone of greyish, greenish or yellowish tint. [Gr. *agalma,* image, *lithos,* a stone]

Agamemnon, *n.* in Greek mythology, a Greek hero, son of Atreus, king of Mycenae. He married Clytemnestra, and their children included Electra, Iphigenia and Orestes. He led the capture of Troy, received Priam's daughter Cassandra as a prize, and was murdered by Clytemnestra and her lover, Aegisthus, on his return home. His children Orestes and Electra later killed the guilty couple.

agami, *n.* the trumpeter, *Psophia crepitans,* a South American bird, allied to the crane. [native name in Guiana]

agamic, agamous, *a.* characterized by absence of sexual action, asexual, parthenogenetic. **agamically,** *adv.* [Gr. *agamos* (*a-*, not, *gamos,* marriage)]

agamogenesis, *n.* asexual reproduction. **agamogenetic**, *a.* pertaining to agamogenesis, generated or reproduced asexually. **agamogenetically,** *adv.* agamically. [Gr. *agamos,* GENESIS]

Agapanthus, *n.* a genus of ornamental plants with bright blue flowers, of the order Liliaceae. [Gr. *agapē,* love, *anthos,* a flower]

agape[1], *adv., pred.a.* on the gape, in an attitude or condition of wondering expectation.

agape[2], *n.* (*pl.* **-pae**) a 'love-feast', a kind of feast held by the primitive Christians in connection with the Lord's Supper. [Gr. *agapē,* brotherly love]

agapemone, *n.* abode of love; a religious community of men and women established 1846. [Gr. *agapē,* AGAPE[2], *monē* a dwelling]

agar-agar, agar, *n.* a gelatinous substance obtained from seaweeds and used for the artificial cultivation of bacteria. [Malay]

agaric, *n.* a mushroom; the name of several species of fungus. *a.* fungoid. [L *agaricum,* Gr. *agarikon*]

Agassiz, *n.* **Jean Louis** (1807–73), Swiss naturalist who emigrated to the US and became one of the foremost scientists of the 19th century. He established his name through work on the classification of the fossil fishes. Although he is credited with the discovery of the ice ages he did not believe that species themselves changed, and thus opposed Darwin.

†**agast,** *v.t.* (*Spens.*) to terrify, to frighten. *v.i.* to take fright. [OE *gǣstan*]

agastric, *a.* without a distinct alimentary canal. [Gr. *a-*, priv., *gastēr,* the belly]

agate[1], *n.* any semi-pellucid variety of chalcedony, marked with bands or clouds, or infiltrated by other minerals, and used for seals, brooches etc.; a dwarf, in allusion to the small figures cut in agates for seals; (*N Am.*) ruby or $5\frac{1}{2}$ point type; drawplate used for drawing gold wire, so called because there is an agate in the middle of it. [F *agathe,* It. *àgata,* L *achātes,* Gr. *achatēs*]

agate[2], *adv.* (*North.*) on the way; a-going.

Agave, *n.* a genus of spiny-leaved plants, including the century plant. [L *agave,* Gr. *agauē*]

agaze, *adv.* at gaze; in a gazing attitude.

†**agazed,** *part.a.* affrighted, dumbfounded. [prob. var. of *agast,* AGHAST]

age, *n.* a period of existence; duration of existence; a period or stage of life; the latter portion of life; senility; (*legal*) maturity, majority; an epoch, a generation; an aeon. (*usu. pl.*) (*coll.*) a long time. *v.i.* to grow old. *v.t.* to cause to grow old or to show signs of age. **age of consent,** the age at which a person's consent is legally valid, esp. a female's consent to sexual intercourse; beneath that age (16 in English and Scottish law) to have carnal knowledge of her is a criminal offence. **age of discretion,** the age when one is judged able to using one's discretion, in English law, 14. **of age,** having reached the age of 18. **aged**, *a.* of a certain age, old. **the aged**, old people. **agedness,** *n.* the state of being old, the state of having attained a certain age. **ageism,** *n.* discrimination on grounds of age. **ageist,** *a.* supporting ageism. **ageless**, *a.* never growing aged, never coming to an end. [OF *aage, edage,* late L *aetāticum* (L *aetas -atis,* from *aevitas aevum,* an age)]

-age, *suf.* appertaining to, aggregate of: forms abstract or collective nouns, e.g. *baronage, courage, foliage;* notes act of doing or thing done, e.g. *passage, voyage.* [OF *-age,* late L *-āticum,* neut. of adj. in *-āticus*]

agee, *adv.* (*Sc.*) to one side; awry. [*a-*, on, GEE, to move aside]

agency AGENT.

agenda, *n.* a memorandum-book; a list of the business to be transacted; (*pl.*) things to be done, engagements to be kept. [L, pl. of *agendum,* neut. ger. of *agere,* to do]

agent, *n.* one who or that which exerts power; something that produces an effect, thematerial cause or instrument; a deputy, one acting in place of another; one who transacts business on behalf of another; a spy. †*a.* acting, in contradistinction to *patient*. **agent orange,** *n.* a herbicide containing dioxin as an impurity, used as a defoliant in the Vietnam war (from the orange marking on the container). **agency,** *n.* the office or business of an agent; causative action, instrumentality, active working, operation; place ofbusiness, office, commercial organization. **agential**, *a.* of or pertaining to an agent or agency. [L *agentem,* acc. of *agens,* pres.p. of *agere,* to do]

agent provocateur, *n.* (*pl.* **agents provocateurs**) a person employed to detect suspected political offenders by leading them on to some overt action. [F]

Ageratum, *n.* a genus of low plants of the aster family. [Gr. *ageraton,* an aromatic herb]

agger, *n.* a mound; the rampart of a Roman camp. [L, from *aggere* (AD-, *gerere,* to carry)]

agglomerate, *v.t.* to heap up or collect into a ball or mass. *v.i.* to gather in a mass. **agglomerate**, *a.* heaped up. *n.* a mass; a mass of volcanic fragments united by heat. **agglomeration,** *n.* the act of agglomerating; a mass, a heap. **agglomerative,** *a.* [L *agglomerāre* (*ag-, ad-,* to, *glomus -meris,* a ball)]

agglutinate, *v.t.* to glue together; to turn into glue; to cause to adhere; to compound, e.g. simple words into compounds; to cause (bacteria, blood cells etc.) to collect into clumps. *v.i.* to unite, cohere; to form compound words. **agglutinate**, *a.* glued together; (*Philol.*) consisting of simple words, or roots, combined into compounds. **agglutination,** *n.* the act of gluing or cementing; the formation of simple words or roots into compound terms; the clumping together of red blood cells, bacteria etc. **agglutinative,** *a.* [L *agglutināre* (*ag-, ad-,* to, *gluten -inis,* glue)]

aggrandize, -ise, *v.t.* to enlarge; to make great in power, wealth, rank or reputation; to exalt. **aggrandization, -isation,** *n.* aggrandizement. **aggrandizement, -isement,** *n.* the act of aggrandizing; the state of being aggrandized. [F *agrandir* (lengthened stem *-iss-*), to greaten (L *ad-,* to, *grandis*)]

†**aggrate,** *v.t.* to gratify. [It. *aggratare,* late L *aggrātāre,* see AGREE]

aggravate, *v.t.* to add weight to; to render less tolerable; to make worse or more severe; (*coll.*) to exasperate, to provoke, to irritate. **aggravating,** *a.* provoking; rendering less excusable. **aggravatingly,** *adv.* in an aggravating manner; in an exasperating manner. **aggravation,** *n.* the act of aggravating; the state of being aggravated; that which aggravates; an addition to a burden, wrong, crime, abuse or charge. [L *aggravātus,* p.p. of *aggravāre* (*ad-,* to, *gravāre,* to make heavy, *gravis,* heavy)]

aggregate[1], *v.t.* to collect together; to bring together into a mass or whole. *v.i.* to form an aggregate; to unite. [L *aggregātus,* p.p. of *aggregāre* (*ag-, ad-,* to, *grex gregis,* a flock)]

aggregate[2], *a.* collected together; formed of separate parts combined into a mass or whole; consisting of florets united together; collected into a mass; consisting of individuals united in a compound organism; composed of distinct minerals. *n.* a mass formed by the union of individual particles; the total, the whole; particles to be bonded together to form concrete. **in the aggregate,** collectively. **aggregation,** *n.* the act of collecting together; the state of being aggregated; an aggregate. **aggregative,** *a.*

aggress, *v.i.* to begin an attack or quarrel. *v.t.* to attack, to assault. **aggression,** *n.* (an) unprovoked attack or injury; violation of a country's territorial integrity or sovereignty by another country; hostile attitude or outlook. **aggressive,** *a.* involving an act of aggression; making the first attack; offensive, pugnacious. **aggressively,** *adv.* **aggressiveness,** *n.* **ag-**

gressor, *n.* one who begins a quarrel. [F *aggresser,* late L *aggressāre,* freq. of *aggredior* (*ad-, gradior,* I walk)]

aggrieve, *v.t.* to cause grief, annoyanceor pain to; to perpetrate injustice against. [OF *agrever,* L *ad-, gravāre,* to weigh down (*gravis,* heavy)]

aggro, *n.* (*coll.*) aggressive, annoying behaviour; trouble-making. [short for AGGRAVATION]

agha AGA.

aghast, *a.* terrified, frightened, appalled; struck with terror. [p.p. of obsolete *v.* AGAST, to frighten; OE *gǣstan*]

agile, *a.* having the faculty of moving quickly and gracefully; mentally quick, nimble, active. **agilely,** *adv.* **agility,** *n.* [L *agilis,* nimble (*agere,* to do)]

Agincourt, Battle of, battle in which Henry V of England defeated the French on 24 Oct. 1415, St Crispin's Day. The village of Agincourt (modern **Azincourt**) is south of Calais, in N France.

agio, *n.* the difference in value between one kind of currency and another; money-changing; the charge for changing notes for cash, or one kind of money for another. **agiotage,** *n.* money-changing; speculation in stocks; stock-jobbing. [It. *agio,* ease]

agist, *v.t.* to afford pasture to the cattle of others at a certain rate; to lay a public rate on land or landowners. **agistment,** *n.* the action or practice of agisting; the pasture, or right to the pasture, of a forest; rate levied on, or profit made from, the agistment of cattle. [OF *agister* (*à,* to, *gister, géter,* to lodge)]

agitate, *v.t.* to shake or move briskly; to excite, to disturb, to perturb; to consider, discuss, debate; to bring forward for public discussion. *v.i.* to arouse public feeling or opinion for or against something. **agitation,** *n.* the act of agitating; the state of being agitated; commotion, perturbation; excited discussion, public excitement. **agitator,** *n.* one who or that which agitates; one who excites or keeps up political agitation; a mechanical contrivance for shaking and mixing. [L *agitātus,* p.p. of *agitāre,* freq. of *agere,* to drive]

agitato, *adv.* (*Mus.*) in an agitated manner; (*coll., facet.*) anxious, upset. [It.]

agitprop, *n.* political propaganda, esp. pro-Communist. [Rus. *agitatsiya,* agitation, and *propaganda*]

aglet, aiglet, aiguillette, *n.* the metal tag of a lace; a spangle; a tag-like ornament on a uniform. [F *aiguillette,* dim. of *aiguille,* needle (late L *acūcula,* L *acicula,* dim. of *acus,* needle)]

agley, *adv.* (*Sc.*) astray, awry.

aglow, *adv.* in a glow.

AGM, (*abbr.*) annual general meeting.

agmatology, *n.* the department of surgery dealing with fractures. [Gr. *agma,* a fragment, *logos,* a discourse]

agnail, *n.* a sore at the root of toe- or fingernail, a whitlow; **hang-nail** and (*Sc.*) **anger-nail** are terms invented by false etymology,mistaking *nægl* (a nail of iron or other hard substance, or a hard excrescence) for fingernail. [OE *angnægl* (*ang,* tight, painful, *nægl,* nail)]

agnate, *n.* a descendant from the same male ancestor; a relative on the father's side. *a.* related on the father's side; hence, allied, akin. **agnatic,** *a.* pertaining to descent on the father's side. **agnation,** *n.* relationship on the father's side; descent from a common male ancestor, in contradistinction to cognation or descent from the same female ancestor. [F *agnat,* L *agnātus* (*ad-, gnātus,* born, p.p. of (*g*)*nascī* to be born)]

Agnew, *n.* **Spiro** (1918–), US vice-president (1969–73). A Republican, he was governor of Maryland (1966–69), and vice-president under Nixon. He resigned in 1973, shortly before pleading 'no contest' to a charge of income-tax evasion.

agnomen, *n.* surname appended to the cognomen among the Romans; an additional name or epithet; a nickname. †**agnomination,** *n.* the bestowal of an agnomen; paronomasia; alliteration. [L *ad-,* to, (*g*)*nōmen,* name]

agnostic, *n.* one who is uncertain about the existence of a God; one who denies that humans have any knowledge except of material phenomena. *a.* pertaining to agnostics or their teachings. **agnostically,** *adv.* **agnosticism,** *n.* the teachings of the agnostics; the state of being agnostic. [Gr. *agnōstos,* ignorant of, unknown, unknowable (*a-,* not, *gno-,* know)]

agnus castus, *n.* an aromatic shrub, *Vitex agnus castus,* formerly supposed to be a preservative of chastity. [L *agnus,* Gr. *agnos,* name of tree (mistaken for adj. chaste), L *castus,* chaste]

Agnus Dei, *n.* a figure of a lamb bearing a flag or cross; a cake of wax stamped with such a figure of a lamb and blessed by the Pope; a part of the Mass beginning with the words *Agnus Dei;* a musical setting of this part of the Mass. [L, The Lamb of God]

ago, *a., adv.* gone by, bygone, passed, passed away; since. [ME *agone,* p.p. of v. *ago-* (*a-,* forth, GO)]

agog, *adv.* in a state of eager expectation; astir. [perhaps from OF *en gogues* (*gogue,* mirth, fun)]

agogic, *a.* of or characterized by variations of stress in speech or musical rhythm, by the lengthening of a syllable or note. **agogics,** *n. sing.* variation of stress by lengthening of duration. [Gr. *agogē,* tendency]

-agogue *comb. form* a leader, a leading, as in*demagogue, pedagogue, synagogue.* [Gr. *agōgos,* leading]

agoing, *adv.* in a state of motion.

†**agone** AGO.

agonic, *a.* having no dip, applied to an imaginary line on the earth's surface, drawn through the two magnetic poles. [Gr. *agōnios,* without an angle (*a-,* not, *gōnia,* angle)]

agonistic, -ical, *a.* pertaining to contests in public games or athletic exercises; combative, argumentative. **agonistically,** *adv.* [Gr. *agōnistikos,* of or pertaining to an *agōnistēs,* competitor in the athletic games (*agōn,* a gathering or assembly, from *agein,* to lead)]

agonize, -ise, *v.t.* to subject to extreme pain; to torture. *v.i.* to suffer agony; to make desperate or convulsive efforts. **agonizing, -ising,** *a.* causing or suffering agony. **agonizingly, -isingly,** *adv.* [L *agonizare*]

agony, *n.* anguish of mind; extreme physical pain; a paroxysm of pain or pleasure; the death struggle; a painful struggle or contest; the mental anguish of Christ in Gethsemane. **to pile on the agony,** (*coll.*) to exaggerate, describe in the most sensational terms. **agony aunt,** *n.* the person in charge of an agony column; a woman who gives sympathetic advice. **agony column,** *n.* the column in a newspaper devoted to advertisements for missing friends and other matters of a personal kind; the part of a newspaper or magazine dealing with readers' problems. [L *agōnia,* from Gr. *agōnia,* contest (from *agōn,* see AGONISTIC)]

agora[1], *n.* the public square, forum or market-place of an ancient Greek town. **agoraphobia,** *n.* abnormal dread of open spaces. **agoraphobic,** *a., n.* [Gr. *agora*]

agora[2], *n.* (*pl.* **agorot**) a monetary unit of Israel equal to one-hundredth of a shekel. [Heb. *ăgōrāh*]

Agostini, *n.* **Giacomo** (1943–), Italian motorcyclist. He won a record 122 grands prix and 15 world titles. His world titles were at 350 cc and 500 cc and he was five times a dual champion.

agouti, agouty, *n.* (*pl.* **-tis, -ties**) a small W Indian and S American rodent, *Dasyprocta agouti.* [Native Indian, *aguti*]

AGR, (*abbr.*) advanced gas-cooled reactor, a type of nuclear reactor widely used in Britain. The AGR uses a fuel of enriched uranium dioxide in stainless steel cladding and a moderator of graphite. Carbon dioxide gas is pumped through the reactor core to extract the heat produced by the fission of the uranium. The heat is transferred to water in a steam generator, and the steam drives a turbogenerator to produce electricity.

agr., agric., (*abbr.*) agriculture, agricultural.

Agra, *n.* city of Uttar Pradesh, republic of India, on the river Jumna, 160 km/100 miles SE of Delhi; population (1981) 747,318. A commercial and university centre, it was the capital of the Mogul empire (1527–1628), from which period dates the Taj Mahal.

agraffe, *n.* a sort of hook, used as a clasp or fastening; a cramp used by builders to fix objects to walls. [F *agrafe* (*à, grappe,* late L *grappa,* OHG *chrapfo,* hook)]

agraphia, *n.* loss of the cerebral power of expressing one's ideas in writing. **agraphic,** *a.* [Gr. *a-*, not, *graphein,* to write)]

agrarian, *a.* the epithet of an ancient Roman law pertaining to the division of conquered territory; hence, pertaining to landed property or cultivated land; growing wild in the fields. *n.* a person in favour of the redistribution of landed property. **agrarian crime, agrarian outrage,** *n.* crime or outrage arising out of disputes about land. **agrarianism,** *n.* a redistribution of land; political agitation concerning land or land-tenure. **agrarianize, -ise,** *v.t.* to apportion (land) by an agrarian law; to imbue with agrarianism. **agrarianization, -isation,** *n.* [L *agrārius,* pertaining to land (*ager,* land)]

agree, *v.i.* to be of one mind; to live in concord; to consent, to accede; to settle by stipulation; to harmonize with, to coincide; to do well (with); to suit; to be in grammatical concord. *v.t.* to make agreeable or harmonious; to concert, to settle, to reconcile, arrange, render consistent. [OF *agréer,* late L *aggrātāre* (*ad-*, to, *grātāre,* to make agreeable, from *grātus,* pleasing)]

agreeable, *a.* affording pleasure, pleasing, pleasant; favourable, disposed to; corresponding, comfortable, suitable to. **agreeability**, **agreeableness,** *n.* **agreeably,** *adv.* [as prec.]

agreement, *n.* a coming into accord; mutual conformity, understanding, accordance; grammatical concord; a contract duly executed and legally binding.

agrestic, *a.* rural, rustic; clownish, uncouth. [L *agrestis* (*ager,* a field)]

agreutic, *a.* skilful in hunting; subsisting by the chase. [Gr. *agreuein* to hunt]

agribusiness, *n.* the businesses involved in farming and marketing farm produce taken as a whole. [AGRICULTURE, BUSINESS]

Agricola, *n.* **Gnaeus Julius** (AD 37–93), Roman general and politician. Born in Provence, he became Consul of the Roman Republic AD 77, and then governor of Britain AD 78–85. He extended Roman rule to the Firth of Forth in Scotland and won the battle of Mons Graupius. His fleet sailed round the N of Scotland and proved Britain an island.

agriculture, *n.* the science and practice of cultivating the soil, growing crops and rearing livestock. **agricultural**, *a.* pertaining tothe culture of the soil. **agriculturalist, agriculturist**, *n.* one engaged in agriculture. [L *agricultūra* (*ager agri,* field, *cultūra,* CULTURE)]

agrimony, *n.* any plant of the genus *Agrimonia,* one species of which (*Agrimonia eupatoria*) was formerly valued as a tonic; also applied to other plants, e.g. hemp agrimony and wild agrimony. [late L *agrimōnia,* L *argemōnia,* Gr. *argemōnē*]

agrimotor, *n.* a motor tractor used in agriculture. [L *ager agri,* field; MOTOR]

Agrippa, *n.* **Marcus Vipsanius** (63–12 BC), Roman general. He commanded the victorious fleet at Actium and married Julia, daughter of Augustus.

†**agrise,** *v.i.* to shudder, to fear, loathe. *v.t.* to terrify. [*a-*, intens., GRISE]

agro-, *comb. form* pertaining to fields, soil or agriculture. [Gr. *agros,* land]

agrobiology, *n.* the study of plantnutrition etc., in relation to soil management. **agrobiological**, *a.* **agrobiologist,** *n.* [AGRO-, BIOLOGY]

agrochemical, *n.* a chemical for use on the land or in farming. *a.* of or producing agrochemicals.

agronomy, *n.* the management of land. **agronomic, -ical,** *a.* of or pertaining to agronomy. **agronomics,** *n.* science of land management as a branch of economics. **agronomist,** *n.* a rural economist; one skilled in agronomy. [Gr. *agronomos,* an overseer (*agros,* land, *nomos,* dispensing, from *nemein,* to dispense)]

aground, *adv.*, *pred.a.* on the ground; on the shallow bottom of any water. [*a-*, on, GROUND]

agt., (*abbr.*) agent.

agterskot, *n.* (*S Afr.*) a percentage paid to (fruit) farmers after the first payment has been made.

ague, *n.* a malarial fever, marked by successive hot and cold paroxysms, the latter attended with shivering; any fit of shivering or shaking. **ague-cake,** *n.* a tumour of the spleen which sometimes accompanies ague. **agued,** *part.a.* (*Shak.*) affected with ague; shaking with fear. **aguish,** *a.* of the nature of or subject to ague; quaking; shivering; intermittent. †**aguishly,** *adv.* [OF *ague,* fem.a., L *acūta,* sharp]

AH, (*abbr.*) in the year of the Hegira (AD 622), from which is dated the Muslim era. [L *anno Hegirae*]

ah, *int.* an exclamation expressive of various emotions, according to the manner in which it is uttered, e.g. sorrow, regret, fatigue, relief, surprise, admiration, appeal, remonstrance, aversion, contempt, mockery. [OF *a,* L *ah*]

aha, *int.* an exclamation of surprise, triumph or mockery. [*a* combined with HA]

Ahab, *n.* (*c.* 875–854 BC), king of Israel. His empire included the suzerainty of Moab, and Judah was his subordinate ally, but his kingdom was weakened by constant wars with Syria. By his marriage with Jezebel, princess of Sidon, Ahab introduced into Israel the worship of the Phoenician god Baal, thus provoking the hostility of Elijah and the prophets. Ahab died in battle against the Syrians at Ramoth Gilead.

Ahasuerus, *n.* (latinized Hebrew form of the Persian Khshayarsha, Greek **Xerxes**), name of several Persian kings in the Bible, notably the husband of Esther. Traditionally it was also the name of the Wandering Jew.

ahead, *adv.*, *pred.a.* in advance; forward, onward; at the head, in front. **to go ahead,** to make rapid progress; to start.

aheap, *adv.* in a heap, all of a heap.

ahem, *int.* an exclamation used to attract attention or merely to gain time. [HEM[2]]

ahimsa, *n.* the Hindu and Buddhist doctrine of nonviolence towards all living things. [Sansk. *ahiṁsā,* without injury]

Ahmadiyya, *n.* Islamic religious movement founded by Mirza Ghulam Ahmad (1839–1908). His followers reject the doctrine that Mohammed was the last of the prophets and accept Ahmad's claim to be the Mahdi and Promised Messiah. In 1974 the Ahmadis were denounced by their coreligionists as non-Muslims.

Ahmad Shah, *n.* (1724–1773), first ruler of Afghanistan. Elected king in 1747, he had made himself master of the Punjab by 1751. He defeated the Mahrattas at Panipat in 1761, and then the Sikhs.

Ahmedabad, Ahmadabad, *n.* capital of Gujarat, India; population (1981) 2,515,195. It is a cotton-manufacturing centre, and has many edifices of the Hindu, Muslim and Jain faiths.

ahoy, *int.* (*Naut.*) a word used in hailing. [HOY[2]]

Ahriman, *n.* in Zoroastrianism, the supreme evil spirit, lord of the darkness and death, waging war with his counterpart Ahura Mazda (Ormuzd) until a time when human beings choose to lead good lives and Ahriman is finally destroyed.

ahull, *adv.* with the sails furled and the helm lashed on the leeside. [*a-*, prep., HULL]

Ahura Mazda, *n.* (or **Ormuzd**) in Zoroastrianism, the spirit of supreme good. As god of life and light, he will finally prevail over his enemy, Ahriman.

Ahvaz, *n.* industrial capital of the province of Khuzestan, W Iran; population (1986) 590,000.

AI, (*abbr.*) artificial insemination; (*Comput.*) artificial intelligence.

ai, *n.* a three-toed sloth, *Bradypus tridactylus,* from S America. [Braz. Sp. *aï,* sound of its cry]

aiblins ABLINGS.

Aich's Metal, *n.* an alloy of zinc, iron and copper, resistant to water and used for sheathing ships' bottoms. [J. *Aich,* inventor]

AID, (*abbr.*) Agency for International Development (US); artificial insemination by donor.

aid, *v.t.* to assist, to help. *n.* help, assistance, succour, relief; an aide-de-camp; a contribution by a vassal for the ransom of his lord, on the occasion when the lord's eldest son was made a knight, or to furnish a dowry for his eldest daughter; a subsidy granted by Parliament to the sovereign; an exchequer loan; anything, as an apparatus, by which assistance is rendered. **in aid of,** in support of, so as to help; (*coll.*) intended for. †**aidance,** *n.* aid, assistance, help. †**aidant,** *a.* helping, assisting, helpful. †**aider,** *n.* one who or that which aids; an assistant, helper; a help, assistance. †**aidless,** *a.* helpless. [OF *aider,* L *adjutāre,* freq. of *adjuvāre* (*ad-,* to, *juvāre,* to help]

Aidan, St, *n.* (*c.* 600–651), Irish monk from Iona who converted Northumbria to Christianity and founded Lindisfarne monastery on Holy Island. His feast day is 31 Aug.

aide, *n.* an assistant, a help. **aide-de-camp,** *n.* (*pl.* **aides-de-camp**) an officer who receives and transmits the orders of a general. **aide-memoire,** *n.* an aid to memory, a memorandum, a memorandum-book. [F]

Aidoo, *n.* **Ama Ata** (1940–), Ghanaian writer of plays, *Dilemma of a Ghost* (1965), novels, *Our Sister Killjoy* (1977), and short stories.

AIDS, *n.* a condition in which the body's immune system is attacked by a virus, leaving the body defenceless against disease. [*a*cquired *i*mmune *d*eficiency *s*yndrome]

aiglet AGLET.

aigrette, *n.* the egret or lesser white heron; a tuft of feathers like that of the egret; a spray of gems worn on the head; any light feathery tuft or spray. [F *aigrette*]

aiguille, *n.* a slender, needle-shaped peak of rock; an instrument used in boring holes for blasting. **aiguillesque,** *a.* shaped like an aiguille. [F, see AGLET]

aiguillette AGLET.

Aigun, Treaty of, treaty between Russia and China signed in 1858 at the port of Aigun in China on the Amur River. It ceded the left bank to Russia, but has since been repudiated by China.

AIH, (*abbr.*) artificial insemination by husband.

Aiken¹, *n.* **Conrad (Potter)** (1899–1973), US poet and novelist, whose *Collected Poems* appeared in 1953.

Aiken², *n.* **Howard** (1900–), US mathematician. In 1939, in conjunction with engineers from IBM, he started work on the design of an automatic calculator using standard business machine components. In 1944 they completed one of the first computers, the Automatic Sequence Controlled Calculator (known as the Mark 1), a programmable computer controlled by punched paper tape and using punched cards.

aikido, *n.* a Japanese martial art using throws, locks and twisting techniques to turn an opponent's momentum against him- or herself. [Jap.]

ail, *v.t.* †to trouble; to cause pain or uneasiness of body or mind to. *v.i.* to be in pain, trouble or ill-health. **ailing,** *part.a.* affected with illness, sick, suffering. **ailment,** *n.* a (slight) disorder or illness, sickness, indisposition. [OE *eglan* (Goth. *agljan*), from *egle,* troublesome (Goth. *aglus,* difficult, hard)]

aileron, *n.* the hinged portion on the rear edge of the wing-tip of an aeroplane for purposes of control. [F, tip of a wing)]

aim, *v.t.* to direct as one's course, effect or intention; to endeavour; to point at a target with a (missile or weapon); to level (a gun) at a target; to direct (a blow). *v.i.* to take aim; to form plans, intend; to direct a course. *n.* the act of aiming; the point or object aimed at; direction of a missile; purpose, intention, design. **aimer,** *n.* one who aims, directs or purposes. **aimful,** *a.* full of aim or purpose. **aimfully,** *adv.* **aimless,** *a.* purposeless, objectless. **aimlessly,** *adv.* **aimlessness,** *n.* [OF *aësmer,* late L *adaestimāre* (perh. confused with OF *esmer,* L *aestimāre,* to reckon)]

Aino AINU.

ain't, (*coll.*) are not; is not, am not; have not, has not. [contr. of *aren't, are not*]

Ainu, *n.* aboriginal people of Japan, whose language is unrelated to any other. In the 4th century AD, they were driven N by ancestors of the modern Japanese; some 16,000 still inhabit the island of Hokkaido in N Japan. Others settled in Sakhalin on the Kuril islands, which were divided between Russia and Japan in the 18th century. Sakhalin was occupied by Soviet troops in 1945, and became part of the USSR two years later. The Ainu population in Sakhalin at that time numbered 1500. [native name]

air, *n.* the mixture of oxygen and nitrogen enveloping the earth, the atmosphere; open space; a light wind, a breeze; manner, appearance, mien, gesture; (*usu. pl.*) affectation, haughtiness; (the operation of, or transportation by) aircraft; the medium of broadcasting, airwaves; a tune, melody, either solo or in harmony. *v.t.* to expose to open or fresh air; to ventilate, to dry or warm (as clothes) by exposing to heat; to show off, to parade. *v.i.* to become aired; to take the air; to show oneself off. **castles in the air,** somethingvisionary, chimerical, impossible. **in the air,** projected, dreamed-of, anticipated; chimerical. **to go on the air,** to broadcast. **to take air,** to become public. **to take the air,** to go for an airing. **air bag,** *n.* a safety device in a car consisting of a bag that inflates automatically in a collision, cushioning the passengers against the impact. **air-ball,** *n.* an inflated ball, a toy. **air base,** *n.* a place used as a base for operations or the housing of aircraft. **air-bed,** *n.* a bed or mattress inflated with air. **air-bladder,** *n.* a vesicle containing air, esp. the swimming-bladder of fishes. **airborne,** *a.* of troops etc., carried by air. **air-brake,** *n.* a brake worked by atmospheric pressure. **air-brick,** *n.* a perforated brick or iron grating for admitting air through a wall. **air-bridge,** *n.* a service by air transport between two places. **air-brush,** *n.* a device for spraying paint by compressed air. *v.t.* to paint with an air-brush. **airbus,** *n.* a large passenger jet aeroplane used for short intercity flights. **air-chamber,** *n.* a chamber filled with air, in an animal or plant; AIR VESSEL. **Air Chief Marshal,** *n.* an officer in the RAF corresponding in rank to general in the Army. **Air Commodore,** *n.* an officerin RAF corresponding in rank to brigadier in the army. **air-condition,** *v.t.* to equip (as a building) with an air-conditioning system. **air-conditioned,** *a.* **air-conditioner,** *n.* **air-conditioning,** *n.* an apparatus for, or the process of, purifying the air circulating in a room or building and controlling its temperature and humidity. **air-cool,** *v.t.* to cool (an engine) by circulating air. **air-corridor,** *n.* a path for air traffic in an area where flying is restricted. **aircraft,** *n.* collective term for all types of flying-machines, both heavier and lighter than air. **aircraft carrier,** *n.* a ship designed for the housing and servicing of aircraft, with a deck where they can take off and alight. **aircraftman,** *n.*, **aircraftwoman,** *n.fem.* a person of lowest rank in the RAF. **aircrew,** *n.* the crew of a aircraft. **air cushion,** *n.* a cushion or pillow inflated to make it resilient; the body of air supporting a hovercraft. **air-drain,** *n.* a dry area round a wall for preventing damp. **air drop,** *n.* a delivery of supplies or troops by parachute from an aircraft. **air-drop,** *v.t.* **air eddy,** *n.* an eddy in the air-currents of the atmosphere. **air-engine,** *n.* any engine driven by the compression and expansion of heated air. **airfield,** *n.* a field specially prepared for the landing and taking-off of aircraft. **air-force,** *n.* the branch of a country's armed forces organized for warfare in the air. **air fountain,** *n.* a mechanism for producing a jet of water by the elastic force of compressed air. **airframe,** *n.* the structure and external surfaces of an aircraft or rocket, excluding the engines. **airgun,** *n.* a gun from which missiles are projected by compressed air. **air-head,** *n.* (*sl.*) a stupid or empty-headed person, a fool. **air-hole,** *n.* an opening to admit air; a flaw in a casting; an air pocket. **air hostess,** *n.* a woman employed to attend to the comfort of passengers on aeroplanes. **air-jacket,** *n.* an inflated jacket for supporting the wearer in water. **air-lane,** *n.* a path regularly used by aircraft. **air letter,** *n.* (a letter on) a single sheet of lightweight paper to be folded and sent by airmail, aerogram. **air-lift,** *n.* the transport of supplies, goods etc. by air. **air-line,** *n.* a commercial organization operating regular transport by air, straight line through the air; a bee-line. **airliner,** *n.* a passenger-carrying aeroplane flying along a regular air route. **air-lock,** *n.* a pneumatic chamber allowing entrance to or exit from a caisson without loss of air-pressure; an obstruction in a pipe caused by a bubble of air. **airmail,** *n.* mail conveyed by aircraft; the postal system of conveying mail by air. **airman,** *n.* **airwoman,** *n.fem.* aviator, pilot of an aeroplane or airship. **Air Marshal,** *n.* an officer in the RAF corresponding in rank to lieutenant-general in the army. **air mechanic,** *n.* a mechanic employed in the repair of aircraft. **air-miss,** *n.* a near-collision of aircraft. **air-pilot,** *n.* a pilot who steers and controls the machinery of an aircraft. **airplane** AEROPLANE. **air-plant,** *n.* an epiphyte. **air pocket,** *n.* an area of rarefied atmosphere where an aircraft is apt to drop unexpectedly. **air-poise,** *n.* an instrument for weighing air. **airport,** *n.* a circular aperture in the side of a ship to admit light and air; a station for passenger aeroplanes, furnished with Customs etc. **air-post** AIR MAIL. **air power,** *n.* the strength of a country in military aircraft. **air-pump,** *n.* an instrument for exhausting the air from a receiver. **air raid,** *n.* an attack on a town, camp etc. by hostile aircraft. **Air Raid Precautions,** official regulations for the prevention of air raids, or for minimizing the damage caused by them. **air rifle,** *n.* a rifle from which missiles are projected by compressed air. **air sac,** *n.* a tiny air cell in the lungs, an alveolus; an air-filled space connecting with the lungs in birds. **air screw,** *n.* the propeller of an aircraft. **air-shaft,** *n.* a vertical passage into a mine for the purpose of ventilation. **airship,** *n.* a lighter-than-air flying-machine driven by an engine. **air-sickness,** *n.* nausea caused by the motion of aircraft. **air-sick,** *a.* **air side,** *n.* the part of an airport complex beyond the passport control. **air-space,** *n.* the atmosphere above (a certain part of) the earth, esp. above a particular country. **air speed,** *n.* the speed of an aeroplane or airship relative to the air, as distinct from its speed relative to the ground. **air-strip,** *n.* a strip of even ground for taking-off and landing of aircraft. **air terminal,** *n.* a building where passengers assemble to be taken to an airport. **air-thermometer,** *n.* a thermometer in which a column of air replaces a column of mercury. **air-threads,** *n.pl.* the floating threads of the gossamer spider. **airtight,** *a.* so tight as to prevent the passage of the air. **airtime,** *n.* broadcasting time, esp. on radio, allotted to a particular topic, record etc. **air-to-air,** *a.* between aircraft in flight; launched from one aircraft at another. **air-to-surface,** *a.* launched from an aircraft at a target on the earth's surface. **air-traffic control,** *n.* the ground-based organization which determines the altitudes, routes etc. to be used by aircraft in a particular area. **air-trap,** *n.* a trap to prevent the escape of foul air from a sewer. **air-vessel,** *n.* a vessel in which air is compressed, in order that its elasticity may be employed as a moving or regulating power, used in a forcing pump to render the discharge of water continuous; any vessel containing air, esp. one of the respiratory tubes or tracheae of insects or the spiral vessels of plants; an air-chamber. **Air Vice-Marshal,** *n.* an officer in the RAF corresponding in rank to major-general in the army. **airwaves,** *n.pl.* (radio) broadcasting channels. **air-way,** *n.* a tunnel in a mine, fitted with valve-like doors, for the passage of air in one direction; a fully organized air route. **airer,** *n.* a clothes-horse. **airing,** *n.* exposure to the free action of the air, or to a fire or heat; a walk or ride in the open air. **airing cupboard,** *n.* a heated cupboard fitted with racks for airing, esp. sheets and other household linen. **airless,** *a.* not open to the air; close, musty; calm, still. **airworthy,** *a.* of an aeroplane, examined and passed as fit for flying. **airworthiness,** *n.* **airy,** *a.* of or belonging to the air; consisting of or open to the air; aerial, lofty, light, unsubstantial as air; sprightly, visionary, unreal. **airy-fairy,** *a.* (*coll.*) fanciful, unrealistic. **airily,** *adv.* **airiness,** *n.* [OF *air,* L *āer-em,* Gr. *aēr* (*aēmi,* I blow)]

Airedale (terrier), *n.* large terrier dog with a rough red-brown coat. It originated about 1850 in the Aire and Wharfedale districts of Yorkshire, England, as a cross of the otter hound and Irish and Welsh terriers.

airt, *n.* (*Sc.*) a point of the compass; a direction. [Gael. *aird*]

Airy, *n.* **George Biddell** (1801–1892), English astronomer. At Greenwich he installed a transit telescope for accurately measuring time by the stars. The position of this instrument defines the Greenwich meridian, internationally accepted as the line of zero longitude in 1884.

Aisha, *n.*, favourite wife of Mohammed.

aisle, *n.* a wing or lateral division of a church; hence, a passage between the seats in a place of worship; an avenue; (*chiefly N. Am.*) a corridor, gangway. **aisled,** *a.* furnished with aisles. [OF *ele,* L *āla* (*axilla*) wing]

ait, *n.* a small island, esp. one in a river or lake. [OE *īggath, īgeoth* (*īg*), island]

aitch, *n.* the letter *h.* [phonetic spelling]

aitchbone, *n.* the rump bone; the cut of beef over this bone (also *erroneously* edge-bone). [OF *nache,* sing. of *naches,* the buttocks, L *naticas -icae,* dim. of *nates* (for loss of *n,* cp. ADDER)]

Ajaccio, *n.* capital and second largest port of Corsica; population (1982) 55,279. Founded by the Genoese in 1492, it was the birthplace of Napoleon; it has been French since 1768.

ajar¹, *a., adv.* partly open, as a door or (less usually) a window. [*a-,* prep., *char* (OE *on cerre, on cyrre,* on cyrre, on the turn)]

ajar², *adv.* in a jarring state, at discord. [AGEE]

Ajax, *n.* Greek hero in Homer's Iliad. Son of Telamon, king of Salamis, he was second only to Achilles among the Greek heroes in the Trojan War. When Agamemnon awarded the armour of the dead Achilles to Odysseus, Ajax is said to have gone mad with jealousy, and then committed suicide in shame.

ajee, *adv.* (*Sc.*) to one side, awry; ajar. [AGEE]

Ajman, *n.* smallest of the seven states that make up the United Arab Emirates; area 250 sq km/96 sq miles; population (1980) 36,000.

ajoupa, *n.* a W Indian hut constructed on piles and roofed with leaves.

ajutage ADJUTAGE.

Akbar, *n.* **Jellaladin Muhammad** (1542–1605), Mughal emperor of N India from 1556, when he succeeded his father. He gradually established his rule throughout the whole of India N of the Deccan. He is considered the greatest of the Mughal emperors, and the firmness and wisdom of his rule won him the title 'Guardian of Mankind'; he was a patron of the arts.

A Kempis, Thomas THOMAS À KEMPIS.

Akhenaton, *n.* another name for Ikhnaton, pharaoh of Egypt.

Akhetaton, *n.* capital of ancient Egypt established by the monotheistic pharaoh Ikhnaton as the centre for his cult of the Aten, the sun's disk; it is the modern Tell el Amarna 300 km/190 miles S of Cairo. His palace had formal enclosed gardens. After his death it was abandoned, and the Amarna tablets (q.v.), found in the ruins, were probably discarded by his officials.

Akhmatova, *n.* **Anna,** Pen name of Anna Andreevna Gorenko (1889–1966), Russian poet. Among her works are the cycle *Requiem* (1963) (written in the 1930s), which deals with the Stalinist terror, and *Poem without a hero* (1962) (begun 1940).

Akihito, *n.* (1933–), emperor of Japan from 1989, succeeding his father Hirohito (Showa). His reign is called the Heisei ('achievement of universal peace') era.

akimbo, *adv.* with the hands resting on the hips and the elbows turned outwards. [ME *in kenebowe,* in a keen (sharp) bow]

akin, *a.* allied by blood relationship; allied in properties or character. [*a-,* prep., KIN]

Akkad, *n.* northern Semitic people who conquered the Sumerians in 2350 BC and ruled Mesopotamia. The ancient city of Akkad in central Mesopotamia, founded by Sargon I, was an imperial centre in the 3rd millennium BC; the site is unidentified, but it was on the Euphrates. **Akkadian,** *n.* a member of this people;

the language of this people.

Akkaia, *n.* alternative form of ACHAEA.

Aksai Chin, *n.* part of Himalayan Kashmir lying to the east of the Karakoram range. Occupied by China but claimed by India.

Aksum, *n.* ancient Greek-influenced Semitic kingdom which flourished 1st–6th centuries AD and covered a large part of modern Ethiopia as well as the Sudan. The ruins of its capital, also called Aksum, lie NW of Aduwa, but the site has been developed as a modern city.

Al, (*chem. symbol*) aluminium.

al-, *pref.* AD-, assim. to *l*, e.g. *alliteration*.

-al, *suf.* belonging to, capable of, like, e.g. *annual, equal, mortal;* forming substantives, e.g. *animal, canal, hospital.* [L *-ālis,* suf., or noun ending *-ālis, -al, -āles, -ālia*]

Ala., (*abbr.*) Alabama.

ala, *n.* (*pl.* **alae**) a wing or wing-like anatomical or plant part. **alar, alary,** *a.* pertaining to a wing; wing-like; wing-shaped. **alate, -ated,** *a.* having wings or wing-like processes. [L *āla,* wing]

à la, *prep.* in the fashion of, after the manner of, after; of food, prepared with or in the style of. **à la française, grècque, l'anglaise** etc., in the French, Greek, English etc. style. [F]

Alabama, *n.* state of southern US; nickname Heart of Dixie/Camellia State. **area** 134,700 sq km/51,994 sq miles **capital** Montgomery. **towns** Birmingham, Mobile, Huntsville, Tuscaloosa. **physical** the state comprises the Cumberland Plateau in the north; the Black Belt, or Canebrake, which is excellent cotton-growing country, in the centre; and south of this, the coastal plain of Piny Woods. The main river is the river Alabama. **products** cotton no longer prime crop, though still important; soybeans, peanuts, wood products, coal, iron, chemicals, textiles, paper. **population** (1987) 4,149,000.

alabaster, *n.* massive gypsum, and other kinds of sulphate or carbonate of lime, either white or delicately shaded. *a.* made of alabaster; white and translucent like alabaster. **alabastrine,** *a.* made of or resembling alabaster. [OF *alabastre,* L *alabaster -astrum,* Gr. *alabastros -on, alabastos,* said to be from the name of a town in Egypt]

à la carte, *a., adv.* (according to a menu) having each dish priced separately. [F, by the bill of fare]

alack, *int.* an exclamation of sorrow. **alackaday,** *int.* shame on the day! alas, the day!. [*a,* ah, LACK, ah! lack, or ah! loss]

alacrity, *n.* briskness, eagerness; vivacity, sprightliness, cheerful ardour. [L *alacritās* (*alacer,* brisk)]

Aladdin, *n.* in the *Arabian Nights*, a poor boy who obtains a magic lamp: when the lamp is rubbed, a jinn (genie, or spirit) appears and fulfils its owner's wishes.

Alain-Fournier, *n.* pen name of Henri-Alban Fournier (1886–1914), french novelist. His haunting semi-autobiographical fantasy *Le Grand Meaulnes/The Lost Domain* (1913) was a cult novel of the 1920s and 1930s. His life is intimately recorded in his correspondence with his brother-in-law Jacques Rivière.

Alamein, El, Battles of, in World War II, two decisive battles in the western desert, N Egypt. In the **First Battle of El Alamein** 1–27 Jul. 1942 the British 8th Army under Auchinleck held the German and Italian forces under Rommel. In the **Second Battle of El Alamein** 23 Oct.–4 Nov. 1942 Montgomery defeated Rommel.

Alamo, the, mission fortress in San Antonio, Texas, US; besieged 23 Feb.–6 Mar. 1836 by Santa Anna and 4000 Mexicans; they killed the garrison of about 180, including Davy Crockett and Jim Bowie.

alamode, à la mode, *adv., a.* fashionable. *n.* a thin kind of black silk. **alamode beef,** *n.* beef braised and served with a thick gravy. **alamodality,** *n.* the quality of being according to the prevailing mode or fashion. [F *à la mode,* in the fashion]

Alamogordo, *n.* town in New Mexico, US. The first atom bomb was exploded nearby at Trinity Site 16 July 1945. It is now a test site for guided missiles.

alamort, all amort, *adv.* to the death. *a.* sick to the point of death; dejected. [F *à la mort,* to the death]

Alanbrooke, *n.* **Alan Francis Brooke, 1st Viscount Alanbrooke** (1883–1963), British army officer, chief of staff in World War II and largely responsible for the strategy that led to the German defeat.

alar, alary ALA.

Alarcón, *n.* **Pedro Antonio de** (1833–1891), Spanish journalist and writer. The acclaimed *Diario/Diary* was based upon his experiences as a soldier in Morocco. His *El Sombrero de tres picos/The Three-Cornered Hat* (1874) was the basis of Manuel de Falla's ballet.

Alaric, *n.* (*c.* 370–410), king of the Visigoths. In 396 he invaded Greece and retired with much booty to Illyria. In 400 and 408 he invaded Italy, and in 410 captured and sacked Rome, but he died the same year on his way to invade Sicily.

alarm, *n.* a summons to arms; warning of approaching danger; terror mingled with surprise; a device for waking persons from sleep or arousing attention; (*Fencing*) a challenge. *v.t.* to rouse to a sense of danger; to inspire with apprehension of coming evil. **alarm-bell,** *n.* a bell rung to sound an alarm. **alarm-clock,** *n.* a clock that can be set to sound a loud peal at a particular hour. **alarm-cord,** *n.* a cord pulled by passengers to stop a train. **alarm-gun,** *n.* a gun fired to give notice of danger. **alarm-post,** *n.* a rendezvous in case of alarm. **alarm-watch,** *n.* a watch fitted with an alarm; ALARM-CLOCK. **alarming,** *part.a.* exciting apprehension; terrifying. **alarmingly,** *adv.* **alarmist,** *n.* one who needlessly raises alarm; a panic-monger. **alarum,** *n.* (*poet.*) an alarm; an alarm-clock or alarm-watch. [OF *alarme,* It. *all'arme,* to arms!]

alas, *int.* an exclamation of sorrow, grief, pity or concern. [OF *a,* ah! *las!* wretched (L *lassus,* wearied, wretched)]

Alaska, *n.* largest state of the US, on the NW extremity of North America, separated from the lower 48 states by British Columbia. **area** 1,531,100 sq km/591,005 sq miles. **capital** Juneau. **towns** Anchorage, Fairbanks, Fort Yukon, Holy Cross, Nome. **physical** much of Alaska is mountainous and includes Mount McKinley, 6,194 m/20,329 ft, the highest peak in North America, surrounded by a national park. Reindeer thrive in the Arctic tundra and elsewhere there are extensive forests. **products** oil, natural gas, coal, copper, iron, gold, tin, fur, salmon fisheries and canneries, lumber. **population** (1987) 538,000, including about 50,000 American Indians, Aleuts, and Inuits.

Alastor, *n.* an avenging spirit, nemesis. [Gr. *a,* not, *last-* (*lathein,* to forget)]

alate, alated ALA.

alb, *n.* a kind of surplice with close sleeves worn by priests when celebrating Mass, and by certain consecrated kings. [OF *albe,* late L *alba* (fem. a., *albus,* white)]

Alba, *n.* Celtic name for Scotland; also an alternate spelling for Alva, Ferdinand Alvarez de Toledo, duke of Alva, Spanish politician and general.

albacore, *n.* a large species of tunny; loosely applied to allied species. [Port. *albacor* (Arab. *al,* the, *bukr,* a young camel, a heifer)]

Alba Iulia, *n.* (German **Karlsburg**) a city on the River Mures, W central Romania, founded by the Romans in the 2nd century AD. The Romanian kings were crowned here. Population (1985) 64,300.

Alban, St, *n.* (d. 303 AD), first Christian martyr in England. In 793 King Offa founded a monastery on the site of Alban's martyrdom, and round this the city of St Albans grew up.

Albania, *n.* Socialist People's Republic of (*Republika Popullore Socialiste e Shqipërisë*), a country in SE Europe, bounded to the W and SW by the Mediterranean sea, to the N and E by Yugoslavia, and to the SE by Greece. **area** 28,748 sq km/11,097 sq miles. **capital** Tiranë. **towns** Shkodër, Vlorë, chief port Durrës. **physical** mainly mountainous, with rivers flowing E–W, and a small coastal plain. **exports** crude oil, bitumen, chrome, iron ore, nickel, coal, copper wire, tobacco, fruit. **population** (1987) 3,080,000; annual growth rate 2.1%. **language** Albanian. **religion** Muslim 70%, although since 1967 Albania is officially a secular state, **Albanian,** *a.* pertaining to Albania or its inhabitants. *n.* a native of Albania; the language of Albania.

Albany, *n.* a city of the State of New York, named in honour of James, Duke of York and Albany, afterwards James II. **Albany-beef,** *n.* (*N Am.*) the flesh of the sturgeon, caught in the Hudson River as far up as Albany. **Albany doctor,** *n.* (*W Austral.*) a sea breeze.

albata, *n.* an alloy like silver; German silver. [L *albāta,* fem. of *albātus,* whitened, from *albus*]

albatross, *n.* †the frigate-bird; the English name of a genus of Tubinares or petrels; *Diomedea exulans,* the largest known sea-bird, the great albatross. [Port. *alcatraz, alcatruz,* Arab. *al,* the, *quadras,* bucket, the pelican (corrupted through assimilation to L *albus,* white)]

albedo, *n.* (*pl.* **-dos**) the fraction of incident light reflected by a planet or other body or surface. [late L, whiteness (L *albus,* white)]

Albee, *n.* **Edward** (1928–), US playwright. His internationally performed plays are associated with the theatre of the absurd and include *The Zoo Story* (1960), *The American Dream* (1961), *Who's Afraid of Virginia Woolf?* (1962) (filmed with Elizabeth Taylor and Richard Burton as the quarrelling, alcoholic, academic couple, 1966), *Tiny Alice* (1965), and *A Delicate Balance* (1966).

albeit, †**albe,** *conj.* although, even though, notwithstanding. [ME *al be it*]

Albéniz, *n.* **Isaac** (1860–1909), Spanish composer and pianist, born in Catalonia. He composed the suite *Iberia* and other piano pieces, making use of traditional Spanish tunes.

Alberoni, *n.* **Giulio** (1664–1752), Spanish-Italian priest and politician. Born in Parma, Italy. Philip V made him prime minister of Spain in 1715. In 1717 he became a cardinal. He introduced many reforms, but was forced to flee to Italy in 1719, when his foreign policies failed.

albert, *n.* a short kind of watch-chain, fastened to a waistcoat buttonhole. [from foll.]

Albert, *n.* Prince Consort (1819–1861), husband of British Queen Victoria from 1840; a patron of arts and science. Albert was the second son of the Duke of Saxe-Coburg-Gotha and first cousin to Queen Victoria. He planned the Great Exhibition of 1851, which made a handsome profit (£186,000); Albert popularized the Christmas tree in England. He was regarded by the British people with groundless suspicion because of his German connections. He died of typhoid.

Albert I, *n.* (1875–1934), king of the Belgians from 1909, the younger son of Philip, Count of Flanders, and the nephew of Leopold II. In 1900 he married Duchess Elisabeth of Bavaria. In World War I he commanded the Allied army that conquered the Belgian coast in 1918, re-entering Brussels in triumph on 22 Nov. He was killed while mountaineering.

Alberta, *n.* province of W Canada. **area** 661,200 sq km/ 255,223 sq miles. **capital** Edmonton. **towns** Calgary, Lethbridge, Medicine Hat, Red Deer. **physical** the Rocky Mountains; dry, treeless prairie in the centre and south; towards the north this merges into a zone of poplar, then mixed forest. The valley of the Peace River is the most northerly farming land in Canada (except for Inuit pastures), and there are good grazing lands in the foothills of the Rockies. **products** coal; wheat, barley, oats, sugar beet in the south; more than a million head of cattle; oil and natural gas. **population** (1986) 2,375,000.

Alberti, *n.* **Leon Battista** (1404–1472), Italian Renaissance architect and theorist, noted for his recognition of the principles of classical architecture and their modification for Renaissance practice in *On Architecture* (1452).

albescent, *a.* becoming or passing into white; whitish. **albescence,** *n.* [L *albēscere* to grow white (*albus*), -ENT]

Albigenses, *n. pl.* heretical sect of Christians (associated with the Cathars) who flourished in S France near Albi and Toulouse during the 11th–13th centuries. They adopted the Manichean belief in the duality of good and evil and pictured Jesus as being a rebel against the cruelty of an omnipotent God. **albigensian,** *a.* [L from *Albigeoi,* inhabitants of the town of Albi (L *Albiga*)]

albino, *n.* a human being, or animal, having the colour pigment absent from the skin, the hair and the eyes, so as to be abnormally light in colour; a plant in which little or no chlorophyll isdeveloped. **albiness,** *n. fem.* **albinism,** *n.* [Port. a white negro (L *albus,* white)]

Albinoni, *n.* **Tomaso** (1671–1751), Italian baroque composer and violinist, whose work was studied and adapted by Bach. He composed over 40 operas.

Albion, *n.* ancient name for Britain used by the Greeks and Romans. It was mentioned by Pytheas of Massilia (4th century BC), and is probably of Celtic origin, but the Romans, having in mind the white cliffs of Dover, assumed it to be derived from *albus* (white).

albite, *n.* white feldspar, soda feldspar. **albitic,** *a.* pertaining to or of the nature of albite. [L *albus,* white, -ITE]

Alboin, *n.* (6th cent.), king of the Lombards about 561–573. At that time the Lombards were settled north of the Alps. Early in his reign he attacked the Gepidae, a Germanic tribe occupying Romania, killing their king and taking his daughter Rosamund to be his wife. About 568 he invaded Italy, conquering the country as far as Rome. He was murdered at the instigation of his wife, whom he had forced to drink from a wine-cup made from her father's skull.

Ålborg, *n.* alternative form of AALBORG, Denmark.

Albufeira, *n.* fishing village and resort on the Algarve coast of S Portugal, 43 km/27 miles W of Faro.

album, *n.* a blank book for the insertion of autographs, poetry, drawings or the like; (*N Am.*) a visitors' book; a collection of pieces of recorded music issued on one or more long-playing records, cassettes etc. [L *album,* neut. of *albus,* white]

albumen, *n.* the white of an egg; albumin; the substance interposed between the skin and embryo of many seeds; the endosperm or perisperm. **albumenize, -ise,** *v.t.* to coat (a photographic paper or plate) with an albuminous solution. [L *albumen -inis,* white of egg (*albus,* white)]

albumin, *n.* any of several water-soluble proteins existing in animals, in the white of egg, in blood serum and in plants. **albuminize, -ise,** *v.t.* to convert into albumen. **albuminoid, -oidal,** *a.* resembling or of the nature of albumen. *n.* a protein; a fibrous protein, as collagen or keratin. **albuminous, -ose,** *a.* consisting of, resembling or containing albumen. **albuminuria,** *n.* the presence of albumen in the urine; the morbid condition causing this. [as prec.]

Albuquerque, *n.* **Alfonso de** (1453–1515), viceroy and founder of the Portuguese East Indies (1508–15), when the king of Portugal replaced him by his worst enemy and he died at sea on the way home; his ship *Flor del Mar* was lost between Malaysia and India with all his treasure.

alburnum, alburn, *n.* the sapwood in exogenous stems, between the inner bark and heart-wood. **alburnous,** *a.* of or pertaining to alburnum. [L *alburnum* (*albus,* white)]

alcade ALCAYDE.

Alcaeus, *n.* (*c.* 611–*c.* 580 BC), Greek lyric poet. Born at Mytilene in Lesvos, he was a member of the aristocratic party and went into exile when the popular party triumphed. He wrote odes, and the Alcaic stanza is named after him.

alcahest ALKAHEST.

alcaic, *a.* of or pertaining to Alcaeus, a lyric poet born in Mitylene, *c.*600 BC, or to a kind of verse he invented. *n.* (*usu. in pl.*) Alcaic strophes. [L *alcaicus,* Gr. *alkaikos* (*Alkaios,* prop. name)]

alcalde, *n.* the judge or major of a Spanish town. [Sp., from Arab. *al,* the, *qādī,* judge]

alcayde, alcade, alcaide, *n.* the governor of a fortress in Spain, Portugal etc.; the warden of a prison, a gaoler. [Sp. *alcaide, alcayde,* Arab. *al,* the, *qāīd,* leader, commander (*qāda,* lead)]

Alcazarquivir, Battle of, battle on 4 Aug. 1578 between the forces of Sebastian, king of Portugal (1554-1578), and those of the Berber kingdom of Fez. Sebastian's death on the field of battle paved the way for the incorporation of Portugal into the Spanish kingdom of Philip II.

alchemy, *n.* the chemistry of the Middle Ages, the search for an alkahest, the philosophers' stone, and the panacea; a metallic compound imitating gold; magic power of transmutation. **alchemic, -ical**, *a.* of or pertaining to alchemy. **alchemically,** *adv.* **alchemist,** *n.* one who studies or practises alchemy. **alchemistic,** *a.* **alchemize, -ise,** *v.t.* to transmute. [OF *alchemie, alquimie,* med. L *alchimia,* Arab. *al,* the, *kimia* (late Gr. *chemeia,* prob. Egyptian art, confused with *chumeia,* a mingling, from *cheein,* to pour)]

alchymy etc. ALCHEMY.

Alcibiades, *n.* (450–404 BC), Athenian general. Handsome and dissolute, he became the archetype of capricious treachery for his military intrigues against his native state with Sparta and Persia; the Persians eventually had him assassinated. He was brought up by Pericles and was a friend of Socrates, whose reputation as a teacher suffered from the association.

Alcock, *n.* **John William** (1892–1919), British aviator. On 14 June 1919 in a Vickers-Vimy biplane, he and Lt Whitten-Brown made the first nonstop transatlantic flight. Alcock died after an aeroplane accident in the same year.

alcohol, *n.* pure spirit, rectified spirit, spirits of wine; a colourless liquid produced by fermenting sugars and constituting the intoxicating agent in various drinks; any of a class of compounds analogous to common alcohol that contain one or more hydroxyl groups; any intoxicating drink containing alcohol. **alcohol abuse,** *n.* excessive use of alcohol. **alcohol lamp,** *n.* (*N Am.*) a spirit-lamp. **alcoholate,** *n.* a crystalline compound in which alcohol acts as water of crystallization. **alcoholic,** *n.* an addict to alcohol. *a.* of or pertaining to alcohol. **alcoholism,** *n.* the action of (excessive) alcohol on thehuman system; the state of being affected by alcohol; addiction to or excessive use of alcohol. **alcoholize, -ise,** *v.t.* to rectify; to mix, saturate with alcohol. **alcoholization, -isation,** *n.* the act or process of rectifying any spirit; mixing or saturation with alcohol; alcoholism. **alcoholometer, alcoometer,** *n.* an instrument for measuring the proportion of pure alcohol in a liquor. **alcoholometrical, alcoometrical,** *a.* pertaining to the process of alcoholometry. **alcoholometry, alcoometry,** *n.* the act, art or process of ascertaining the quantity of pure alcohol in a liquor. [med. L *alcohol,* Arab. *al-koh'l* (*al,* the, *koh'l,* powder to stain the eyelids)]

Alcoholics Anonymous, *n.* voluntary self-help organization established in 1934 in the US to combat alcoholism; organizations now exist in many other countries.

alcoran, *n.* the Koran. **alcoranist,** *n.* one who adheres to the letter of the Koran. [KORAN]

Alcott, *n.* **Louisa M(ay)** (1832–1888), US author of the children's classic *Little Women* (1869), which drew on her own home circumstances, the heroine Jo being a partial self-portrait. *Good Wives* (1869) was among its sequels.

alcove, *n.* a vaulted recess; a recess in a wall; a bower, a summer-house. [F *alcôve,* Sp. *alcoba,* Arab. *alqobbah,* the vault]

Alcuin, *n.* (735–804), English scholar. Born in York, he went to Rome in 780, and in 782 took up residence at Charlemagne's court in Aachen. From 796 he was abbot of Tours. He disseminated Anglo-Saxon scholarship, organized education and learning in the Frankish empire, gave a strong impulse to the Carolingian Renaissance, and was a prominent member of Charlemagne's academy.

alcyon HALCYON.

alcyonarian, *a.* belonging to the Alcyonaria, a group of marine invertebrates including the sea-pens and various coral polyps. *n.* any individual of that group. [Gr. *alkuonion,* a marine organism which resembles the nest of *alcuōn,* the alcyon, or HALCYON)]

Ald., (*abbr.*) alderman.

Aldebaran, *n.* brightest star in the constellation Taurus, and marking the eye of the 'bull'. It is a red giant 68 light years away, shining with a true luminosity of about 100 times that of the Sun. It is the 13th-brightest star in the sky.

aldehyde, *n.* a volatile liquid that can be obtained from alcohol by oxidation, acetaldehyde, ethanal; any of an extensive class of organic compounds of the same type. **aldehydic**, *a.* [abbr. of L *alcohol dehydrogenatum,* alcohol deprived of hydrogen]

al dente, *a.* esp. of cooked pasta, firm when bitten. [It., to the teeth]

alder, *n.* a well-known English tree (*Alnus glutinosa*) growing in moist places; applied also, with distinguishing epithet, to many plants whose leaves more or less resemble those of the alder. [OE *alr, aler, alor* (cp. Icel. *ôlr,* OHG *elira,* L *alnus*)]

alderman, *n.* a civic dignitary next in rank below the mayor; (*coll.*) a long clay, i.e. a long clay pipe, a 'churchwarden'. **aldermanic,** *a.* pertaining or relating to an alderman. **aldermanlike, aldermanly,** *a.* like or befitting an alderman. **aldermanry,** *n.* a district having its own alderman, a ward; the dignity or office of alderman. **aldermanship,** *n.* the office or dignity of alderman. [OE *ealdor, alder,* a chief (cp. OLD) MAN]

aldermanate, *n.* aldermanry; aldermen collectively. [med. L *aldermannātus,* from *aldermannus*]

Aldermaston, *n.* site of the Atomic Weapons Establishment (AWE) in Berkshire, England. During 1958–63 the Campaign for Nuclear Disarmament (CND) made it the focus of an annual Easter protest march.

Alderney, *n.* an animal of that breed of cattle originating on Alderney Island. [name of island]

aldine, *a.* of, belonging to or printed by Aldus Manutius (a celebrated Venetian printer of the 16th cent.) or his family; type modelled on that used by him. [*Aldus,* -INE]

Aldington, *n.* **Richard** (1892–1962), British imagist poet, novelist and critic, who was married to Hilda Doolittle from 1913 to 1937. He wrote biographies of D. H. Lawrence and T. E. Lawrence. His novels include *Death of a Hero* (1929) and *All Men are Enemies* (1933).

Aldiss, *n.* **Brian** (1925–), English science-fiction writer, anthologist and critic. His novels include *Non-Stop* (1958), *The Malacia Tapestry* (1976), and the 'Helliconia' trilogy. *Trillion Year Spree* (1986) is a history of science fiction.

aldosterone, *n.* a steroid hormone produced by the adrenal glands that regulates saltlevels. [*ald*ehyde, *ste*rol (as *cholesterol*) -ONE]

aldrin, *n.* an extremely poisonous chlorine-containing insecticide. [the G chemist Kurt *Alder,* 1902–58]

ale, *n.* an intoxicating drink made from malt by fermentation; †a rural festival or merry-making, at which ale was drunk. **ale-bench,** *n.* a bench inor before a public-house. **ale-house,** *n.* a tavern licensed to sell ale. **ale-taster,** *n.* an ale-conner. **ale-wife**[1], *n.* a woman who keeps an ale-house (see also ALEWIFE[2]). [OE *ealu*]

aleatory, *a.* depending upon an uncertain event. **aleatoric**, *a.* [L *āleātōrius,* from *āleātor,* a dice-player (*ālea,* dice)]

ale-conner, *n.* an examiner or inspector of ale. [OE *cunnere; cunnian,* to know; see CAN]

alecost, *n.* the plant costmary formerly used to flavour ale.

alee, *adv.*, *pred.a.* on the lee side; to leeward. [ON *á hlé,* a sea-phrase (*á,* on, *hlé,* shelter)]

alegar, *n.* vinegar made from ale; malt vinegar. [ALE, F *aigre,* sharp, sour]

alembic, *n.* a vessel made of glass or copper formerly used for distilling. [F *alambique,* Arab. *al-anbīq,* the still, Gr. *ambix -ikos,* a cup]

Alemmanic, *n.* the group of High German dialects of Alsace, Switzerland, and SW Germany. [late L *Alemanni,* Germanic people]

Alentejo, *n.* a region of E central Portugal divided into the districts of Alto Alentejo and Baixo Alentejo. The chief towns are Evora, Neja and Portalegre.

aleph, *n.* the first letter of the Hebrew alphabet. **aleph-null,** *n.* the cardinal number indicating the number of elements in the set of all positive integers; the smallest infinite cardinal number.

Aleppo, *n.* (Syrian **Halab**) ancient city in NW Syria; population (1981) 977,000. There has been a settlement on the site for at least 4000 years.

alert, *a.* watchful, vigilant; brisk, sprightly. *n.* an alarm; a surprise; warning by siren or otherwise of a threatened air-raid. *v.t.* to warn; to put on guard; to arouse. **on the alert,** on the watch; on one's guard; ready, prepared. **alertly,** *adv.* **alertness,** *n.* [F *alerte, allerte, à l'erte,* It. *all'erta,* on one's guard (*à la,* to the, *erta,* fem. p.p. of *ergere,* L *ērigere,* to erect)]

Aletsch, *n.* most extensive glacier in Europe, 23.6 km/14.7 miles long, beginning on the southern slopes of the Jungfrau in the Bernese Alps, Switzerland.

aleuron, aleurone, *n.* a protein found in the form of grains in ripening seeds. [Gr. *aleuron,* flour (*aleō,* I grind)]

Aleutian Islands, *n. pl.* volcanic island chain in the N Pacific, stretching 1900 km/1200 miles SW of Alaska, of which it forms part. Population 6000 Inuit (Eskimo), most of whom belong to the Greek Orthodox Church, plus a large US military establishment. There are 14 large and over 100 small islands, running along the Aleutian Trench. The islands are mountainous, barren and treeless; they are ice-free all the year round, but are often foggy.

A-level A.

alevin, *n.* a young fish, esp. a young salmon. [F, from OF *aleuer,* to rear, from L *allevare* (*ad-,* to, *levāre,* to raise)]

alewife[2], *n.* a N American fish, *Clupea serrata,* resembling the shad but smaller (see also ALE). [perhaps N Am. Indian]

Alexander, *n.*, three kings of Scotland:

Alexander I, *n.* (*c.* 1078–1124), king of Scotland from 1107, known as 'the Fierce'.

Alexander II, *n.* (1198–1249), king of Scotland from 1214, when he succeeded his father William the Lion. Alexander supported the English barons in their struggle with King John after Magna Carta. By the treaty of Newcastle (1244) he acknowledged Henry III of England as his liege lord.

Alexander III, *n.* (1241–1285), king of Scotland from 1249, son of Alexander II. In 1263 he extended his authority over the Western Isles, which had been dependent on Norway, and strengthened the power of the central Scottish government. He died as the result of a fall from his horse, leaving his granddaughter Margaret, the Maid of Norway, to become queen of Scotland.

Alexander, *n.* three tsars of Russia:

Alexander I, *n.* (1777–1825), tsar from 1801. Defeated by Napoleon at Austerlitz (1805), he made peace at Tilsit (1807), but economic crisis led to a break with Napoleon's continental system, and the opening of Russian ports to British trade; this led to Napoleon's ill-fated invasion of Russia. After the Congress of Vienna in 1815, Alexander hoped through the Holy Alliance with Austria and Prussia to establish a new Christian order in Europe. He gave a constitution to Poland.

Alexander II, *n.* (1818–1881), tsar from 1855. He embarked on reforms of the army, the government, and education, and is remembered as 'the Liberator' for his emancipation of the serfs (1861). However, the revolutionary element remained unsatisfied, and Alexander became increasingly autocratic and reactionary. He was assassinated by nihilists.

Alexander III, *n.* (1845–1894), tsar from 1881, when he succeeded his father, Alexander II. He pursued a reactionary policy, persecuting the Jews and promoting Russification. He married Dagmar (1847–1928), daughter of Christian IX of Denmark and sister of Queen Alexandra of the UK, in 1866.

Alexander, *n.* eight popes, including:

Alexander III, *n.* **(Orlando Barninelli)** (d. 1181), Pope 1159–81. His authority was opposed by Frederick I Barbarossa, but Alexander eventually compelled him to render homage (1178). He supported Henry II of England in his invasion of Ireland, but imposed penance on him after the murder of Thomas Becket.

Alexander VI, *n.* **(Rodrigo Borgia)** (1431–1503), Pope 1492–1503. He was of Spanish origin, and bribed his way to the papacy, where he furthered the advancement of his illegitimate children, who included Cesare and Lucrezia Borgia. When Savonarola preached against his corrupt practices Alexander had him executed, and he is said to have died of poison he had prepared for his cardinals. He was a great patron of the arts.

Alexander I, Karageorgevich, *n.* (1888–1934), regent of Serbia (1912–21) and king of Yugoslavia (1921–34), as dictator from 1929; assassinated, possibly by Italian Fascists.

Alexander Nevski, St, *n.* (1220–1263), Russian military leader, son of the grand duke of Novgorod; in 1240 he defeated the Swedes on the banks of the Neva (hence Nevski), and in 1242 defeated the Teutonic Knights on frozen Lake Peipus.

Alexander Obrenovich, *n.* (1876–1903), king of Serbia from 1889 while still a minor, on the abdication of his father, King Milan. He took power into his own hands in 1893, and in 1900 married a widow, Draga Mashin. In 1903 Alexander and his queen were murdered, and Peter I Karageorgevich was placed on the throne.

Alexander Severus, *n.* (AD 208–235), Roman emperor from 222, when he succeeded his cousin Heliogabalus. He was born in Palestine. His campaign against the Persians in 232 achieved some success, but in 235, while proceeding to defend Gaul against German invaders, he was killed in a mutiny.

Alexander the Great, *n.* (356–323 BC), king of Macedonia and conqueror of the large Persian empire. As commander of the vast Macedonian army he conquered Greece (336). He defeated the Persian king Darius in Asia Minor (333), then moved on to Egypt, where he founded Alexandria. He defeated the Persians again in Assyria (331), then advanced further east to reach the Indus. He conquered the Punjab before diminished troops forced his retreat.

Alexander, *n.* **Samuel** (1859–1938), Australian philosopher, who originated the theory of emergent evolution: that the space-time matrix evolved matter; matter evolved life; life evolved mind; and finally God emerged from mind.

alexanders, *n.* (*pl.* **alexanders**) a European plant, *Smyorium olusatrum,* formerly used as a vegetable. [OE *alexandre,* med. L *alexandrum,* prob. from L *holus atrum* black vegetable]

Alexandra[1], *n.* (1872–1918), last tsarina of Russia (1894–1917). She was the former Princess Alix of Hessen, and granddaughter of Queen Victoria. She married Nicholas II and, from 1907, fell under the spell of Rasputin, brought to the palace to try to cure her son of haemophilia. She was shot with the rest of her family by the Bolsheviks in the Russian Revolution.

Alexandra[2], *n.* (1936–), princess of the UK. Daughter of the Duke of Kent and Princess Marina, she married Angus Ogilvy (1928–), younger son of the earl of Airlie. They have two children, James (1964–) and Marina (1966–).

Alexandria, *n.* (or **El Iskandariya**) city, chief port, and second largest city of Egypt, situated between the

Mediterranean and Lake Maryut; population (1986) 5,000,000. It is linked by canal with the Nile and is an industrial city (oil refining, gas processing, and cotton and grain trading). Founded in 331 BC by Alexander the Great, Alexandria was for over 1000 years the capital of Egypt.

Alexandria, Library of, library in Alexandria, Egypt, founded in 330 BC by Ptolemy I Soter. It was the world's first state-funded scientific institution, and comprised a museum, teaching facilities and a library that contained 700,000 scrolls, including much ancient Greek literature. It was destroyed (641) following the Arab conquest.

Alexandria, School of, the writers and scholars of Alexandria, who made the city the chief centre of culture in the Western world from about 331 BC–AD 642. They include the poets Callimachus, Apollonius Rhodius and Theocritus; Euclid, pioneer of geometry; Eratosthenes, the geographer; Hipparchus, who developed a system of trigonometry; the astronomer Ptolemy, who gave his name to the Ptolemaic system of astronomy that endured for over 1000 years; and the Jewish philosopher Philo. The Gnostics and Neoplatonists also flourished in Alexandria.

alexandrine, *n.* iambic verse with six feet. [F *alexandrin,* etym. doubtful]

alexandrite, *n.* a dark green chrysoberyl. [the Rus. czar *Alexander I,* 1777–1825]

Alexeev, *n.* **Vasiliy** (1942–), Soviet weightlifter who broke 80 world records (1970–77), a record for any sport. He was Olympic super-heavyweight champion twice, world champion seven times, and European champion on eight occasions.

alexia, *n.* the loss of power to understand written or printed words; word-blindness. [Gr. *a-,* not; *lexis,* speech, but confused with L *legere,* to read]

alexin, *n.* a substance present in blood serum, which, combining with an antibody or antiserum, gives protection against disease. [Gr. *alexein,* to ward off]

alexipharmic, *a.* preserving against poison. *n.* an antidote. [F *alexipharmaque,* Gr. *alexipharmakon* (*alexō, I* ward off, *pharmakon,* poison)]

Alexius, *n.*, five emperors of Byzantium, including:

Alexius I, *n.* **(Comnenus)** (1048–1118), Byzantine emperor (1081–1118). The Latin (W European) Crusaders helped him repel Norman and Turkish invasions, and he devoted great skill to buttressing the threatened empire. His daughter Anna Comnena chronicled his reign.

Alexius III, *n.* **(Angelos)** (d. *c.* 1210), Byzantine emperor (1195–1203). He gained power by deposing and blinding his brother Isaac II, but Isaac's Venetian allies enabled him and his son Alexius IV to regain power as co-emperors.

Alexius IV, *n.* **(Angelos)** (1182–1204), Byzantine emperor from 1203, when, with the aid of the army of the Fourth Crusade, he deposed his uncle Alexius III. He soon lost the support of the Crusaders (by that time occupying Constantinople), and he was overthrown and murdered by another Alexius, Alexius Mourtzouphlus (son-in-law of Alexius III) in 1204, an act which the Crusaders used as a pretext to sack the city the same year.

alfalfa, *n.* general term for lucerne. [Sp.]

Alfa Romeo, *n.* Italian car-manufacturing company, known for its racing cars. In 1985 the company was bought by Fiat.

Alfieri, *n.* **Vittorio, Count Alfieri** (1749–1803), Italian dramatist. The best of his 28 plays, most of them tragedies, are *Saul* (1782) and *Mirra* (1786).

Alfonsín Foulkes, *n.* **Raúl Ricardo** (1927–), Argentinian politician, president (1983–89), leader of the Radical Union Party (UCR). As president from the country's return to civilian government, he set up an investigation of the army's human-rights violations. Economic problems forced him to seek help from the International Monetary Fund and introduce austerity measures.

Alfonso, *n.* 13 kings of León, Castile, and Spain, including:

Alfonso VII, *n.* (*c.* 1107–1157), king of León and Castile from 1126, who attempted to unite Spain. Although he protected the Moors, he was killed trying to check a Moorish rising.

Alfonso X, *n.* called **el Sabio** 'the Wise' (1221–1284), king of Castile from 1252. His reign was politically unsuccessful but he contributed to learning: he made Castilian the official language of the country, and commissioned a history of Spain and an encyclopaedia, as well as several translations from Arabic, concerning, among other subjects, astronomy and games.

Alfonso XI, *n.* **'the Avenger'** (1311–1350), king of Castile from 1312 who ruled cruelly, repressed a rebellion by his nobles, and defeated the last Moorish invasion in 1340.

Alfonso XII, *n.* (1857–1885), king of Spain from 1875, son of Isabella II. He assumed the throne after a period of republican government following his mother's flight and effective abdication in 1868.

Alfonso XIII, *n.* (1886–1941), king of Spain (1886–1931). He assumed power in 1906 and married Princess Ena, granddaughter of Queen Victoria of the UK, in the same year. He abdicated soon after the fall of the Primo de Rivera dictatorship (which he supported), and Spain became a republic. His assassination was attempted several times.

Alfonso, *n.* six kings of Portugal, including:

Alfonso I, *n.* (1094–1185), king of Portugal from 1112, who made Portugal independent from León.

Alfred the Great, *n.* (*c.* 848–*c.* 900), king of Wessex from 871. He defended England against Danish invasion, founded the first English navy, and put into operation a legal code. He encouraged the translation of works from Latin (some of which he translated himself), and promoted the development of the Anglo-Saxon Chronicle.

alfresco, *adv., a.* in the open air, open-air. [It. *al fresco,* in the fresh]

alg., (*abbr.*) algebra.

alga, *n.* (*pl.* **algae**) a seaweed or other plant belonging to the Algae.

Algae, *n.pl.* a major group of simple aquatic or subaquatic plants, including the seaweeds, that lack differentiation into stems, roots and leaves. **algal,** *a.* pertaining to seaweeds or other Algae. **algin,** *n.* a jelly-like substance obtained from seaweed. **alginate,** *n.* a salt of alginic acid used as a stabilizing and thickening agent in pharmaceuticals, food and plastics. **alginic,** *a.* pertaining to or obtained from seaweed. **alginic acid,** *n.* an insoluble acid found in some Algae, as kelp. **algist,** *n.* a botanist who specializes in Algae. **algoid,** *a.* of the nature of or like Algae. **algological,** *a.* **algology,** *n.* the branch of botany dealing with Algae. **algologist,** *n.* an algist. **algous,** *a.* pertaining to, resembling or full of seaweed. [L]

Algarve, *n.* ancient kingdom in S Portugal, the modern district of Faro, a popular holiday resort; population (1981) 323,500.

†algate, †algates, *adv.* every way; any way; by all means, at any rate. [ON *alla gôtu,* every way (GATE)]

algebra, *n.* universal arithmetic in which letters are used as symbols for quantities, and signs represent arithmetical processes. **algebraic, -ical,** *a.* of or relating to algebra; involving or employing algebra. **algebraically,** *adv.* **algebraist, algebrist,** *n.* one who is versed in algebra. **algebraize, -ise,** *v.t.* to reduce to an algebraic form; to solve by means of algebra. [Arab. *al-jebr,* the reunion of parts]

Algeciras Conference, *n.* a conference held Jan. 1906 when the European powers of France, Germany, Britain, Russia and Austria-Hungary, together with the US, Spain, the Low Countries, Portugal, and Sweden, met to settle the question of Morocco. The conference was prompted by increased German demands in what had traditionally been seen as a French area of influence, but resulted in a reassertion of Anglo-French friendship, and the increased isolation of Germany.

Algeria, *n.* Democratic and Popular Republic of (*al-Jumhuriya al-Jazairiya ad-Dimuqratiya ash-Shabiya*), country in N Africa, bounded to the E by Tunisia and Libya, to the SE by Niger, to the SW by Mali, to the NW by Morocco, and to the N by the Mediterranean sea. **area** 2,381,741 sq km/919,352 sq miles. **capital** al-Jazair (Algiers). **towns** Qacentina/Constantine; ports are Ouahran/Oran, Annaba. **physical** coastal plains, mountain plateau, desert. **exports** oil, natural gas, iron, wine, olive oil. **population** (1988 est.) 23,850,000 (83% Arab, 17% Berber); annual growth rate 3.0%. **language** Arabic (official); Berber, French. **religion** Sunni Muslim.

-algia, *comb. form* denoting pain (in a particular place), e.g. *neuralgia*. [Gr. *algos,* pain]

algid, *a.* cold, esp. in ague. **algidity**, *n.* a state of coldness. [F *algide,* L *algidus* (*algēre,* to be cold)]

Algiers, *n.* (Arabic **al-Jazair**, French **Alger**) capital of Algeria, situated on the narrow coastal plain between the Atlas mountains and the Mediterranean; population (1984) 2,442,300.

Algiers, Battle of, the bitter conflict in Algiers (1954–62) between the Algerian nationalist population and the French army and French settlers. The conflict ended with Algerian independence 1962.

algin, algist, algoid, algology, algous etc. ALGA.

Algol[1], *n.* in computing, an early high-level programming language, developed in the 1950s and 1960s for scientific applications. A general-purpose language, Algol is best suited for mathematical work and has an algebraic style. Although no longer in common use, it has greatly influenced more recent languages such as ADA and Pascal. [*algo*rithmic language]

Algol[2], *n.* an eclipsing binary, a pair of rotating stars in the constellation Perseus, one of which eclipses the other every 69 hours, causing its brightness to drop by two thirds. It is also known as Beta Persei.

algolagnia, *n.* sexual gratification derived from inflicting or suffering pain. **algolagnic,** *n., a.* [Gr. *algos,* pain, *lagneia,* lust]

algometer, *n.* an instrument for estimating degrees of sensitiveness to pain. [Gr. *algos,* pain, *metron,* measure]

Algonquian, Algonquin, Algonkian, *n.* a family of New American Indian languages; a member of a tribe speaking an Algonquian language. [Can. F *Algonquin*]

algorithm, *n.* a rule or set procedure for solving a mathematical problem. [med. L *algorismus,* Arab. *al-Khwārizmi,* the native of Khwarism, a 9th-cent. Arab mathematician]

alguazil, *n.* in Spain, an inferior officer of justice; a constable. [Sp. *alguazil* (*-cil*), Arab. *alwazir,* the vizier]

algum, *n.* a tree mentioned in the Bible, prob. sandalwood. [Heb. *algūm* (wrongly *almug,* I Kings x.11)]

Alhambra, *n.* fortified palace in Granada, Spain, built by Moorish kings mainly between 1248 and 1354. The finest example of Moorish architecture, it stands on a rocky hill. **alhambraesque**, *a.* resembling the Alhambra or its style of architecture. [Arab. *al-hamra',* the red house]

Alhazen, *n.* **Ibn al Haytham** (*c.* 965–1038), Arabian scientist, author of the *Kitab al Manazir/Book of Optics*, translated into Latin as *Perspectiva*. For centuries it remained the most comprehensive and authoritative treatment of optics in both East and West.

ali-, *comb. form* pertaining to a wing. [L *ala,* wing]

Ali[1], *n.* **(Ali Pasha)** (1741–1822), Turkish politician, known as *Arslan* ('the Lion'). An Albanian, he was appointed pasha (governor) of the Janina region (now Ioánnina, Greece) in 1788. His court was visited by the British poet Byron. He was murdered by the sultan's order.

Ali[2], *n.* **Muhammad** (born Cassius Marcellus Clay) (1942–), US boxer. Olympic light-heavyweight champion 1960, he went on to become world professional heavyweight champion (1964), and was the only man to regain the title twice. He was known for his quickness and extroversion.

Ali[3], *n.* (*c.* 600–661), 4th caliph of Islam. He was born in Mecca, the son of Abu Talib, uncle to the prophet Mohammed, who gave him his daughter Fatima in marriage. On Mohammed's death (632), Ali had a claim to succeed him, but this was not conceded until 656. After a stormy reign, he was assassinated. Around Ali's name has raged the controversy of the Sunnites and the Shi'ites, the former denying his right to the caliphate and the latter supporting it.

alia, *n.pl.* other things. [L neut. pl. of a. *alius,* other]

Alia, *n.* **Ramiz** (1925–), Albanian communist politician, head of state from 1982 and party leader from 1985. He has slightly modified the isolationist policies of his predecessor Hoxha.

alias, *adv.* otherwise (named or called). *n.* a second name, an assumed name. [L]

alibi, *n.* the plea (of a person accused) of having been 'elsewhere' when the offence was committed, the evidence to support such a plea; (*coll.*) an excuse (for failing to do something). [L, elsewhere, loc. of *alius* (cp. *ibi, ubi*)]

Alicante, *n.* seaport and tourist resort in Valencia, SE Spain; population (1986) 266,000. The wine and fruit trade passes through the port; a red, sweet wine from this town.

alicyclic, *a.* of an organic compound, having aliphatic properties but containing a ring of carbon atoms. [*ali*phatic, *cyclic*]

alidad, alidade, *n.* an arm or index showing degrees on a circle in an astrolabe, quadrant, theodolite etc. [F *alidade,* med. L *alhidada,* Arab. *al- 'idādah* (*al,* the, *'adad,* upper arm)]

alien, *a.* belonging to another or others; of foreign extraction; estranged; averse, repugnant (to); incongruous. *n.* a foreigner; a foreign-born non-naturalized resident. †*v.t.* to alienate. **alienability,** *n.* capable of being alienated. **alienable,** *a.* that may be alienated. **alienee,** *n.* (*Law*) one to whom the ownership of property is transferred. [OF *alien,* L *aliēnus,* a stranger, or of a stranger (*alius,* another)]

Alien and Sedition Acts, laws passed by the US Congress in 1798, when war with France seemed likely. The acts lengthened the period of residency required for US citizenship, gave the president the power to expel 'dangerous' aliens, and severely restricted criticism of the government. They were controversial because of the degree of power exercised by central government; they are now also seen as an early manifestation of US xenophobia.

alienate, *v.t.* to estrange; to transfer to the ownership of another. *a.* estranged. **alienation,** *n.* of alienating; state of being alienated; mental disorder; feeling estranged from one's social environment. **alienator,** *n.* [OF *aliéner*]

alienism, *n.* the state of being an alien; the treatment and study of mental illness. **alienist,** *n.* one skilled in the treatment or engaged in the study of mental illness.

aliform, *a.* shaped like a wing. [ALI-]

alight[1], *v.i.* to get down, descend, dismount; to reach the ground, to settle; to light on, happen on, meet with; †to stop, arrive. [OE *ālīhtan* (*a-,* intens., *līhtan,* to jump down from a horse)]

alight[2], *pred.a.* on fire; illuminated. [p.p. of *alīhtan, onlīhtan,* to shine upon, light up (confused with forms like ABLAZE, AFIRE)]

align, aline, *v.t.* to range or place in a line; to place in a position of agreement with others. *v.i.* to fall into line. **alignment,** *n.* the act of ranging in line or being ranged; objects arranged in a line or lines; the ground-plan of a road or earthwork; agreement or alliance with others; the act of taking a side or associating with a party, cause, etc. [F *aligner* (*à,* to, *ligner,* from L *līneāre,* to line, from *līnea,* a line)]

alike, *a.* similar. *adv.* equally, in the same manner, similarly. [OE *onlīc* (*on-,* on, *līc,* like); also OE *gelīc* (*ge-,* together, *līc,* like); cp. OHG *gelīh* (G *gleich*) and Icel. *ālīkr*]

aliment, *n.* nutriment, food; support, sustenance; (*Sc.*) alimony; mental nutriment. *v.t.* †to nourish; to make provision for the maintenance of. **alimental,** *a.* pertaining to aliment; nutritive. **alimentally,** *adv.* **alimentary,** *a.* pertaining to aliment or nutrition; nutritious, nourishing; sustaining, supporting. **alimentary-canal,** *n.* the great tube or duct from mouth to anus conveying food to the stomach and carrying off solid excreta from the system. **alimentation,** *n.* the act or quality of affording nourishment; the state of being nourished. **alimentative,** *a.* connected with the function of nutrition. [L *alimentum* (*alere,* to nourish]

alimony, *n.* maintenance; payment of means of support, esp. the proportional part of a person's income allowed for the support of a spouse on legal separation, or for other causes. [L *alimōnia* (*alere,* to nourish)]

aline etc. ALIGN.

Ali Pasha, *n.* **Mehmed Emin** (1815–1871), grand vizier (chief minister) of the Ottoman empire (1855–56, 1858–59, 1861, and 1867–71), noted for his attempts to westernize the Ottoman Empire.

aliped, *n.* a wing-footed creature, e.g. a bat. [L *ala,* wing; *pes pedis,* foot]

aliphatic, *a.* fatty; belonging or pertaining to a class of organic compounds containing open chains of carbon atoms in the molecular structure, not aromatic. [Gr. *aleiphar,* an unguent]

aliquot, *a.* pertaining to a number that is contained an integral number of times by a given number. *n.* an integral factor, an aliquot part. **aliquot part,** *n.* a part that is a division of the whole without remainder, as 50p of £1, 10 g of 1 kg. [F *aliquote,* late L *aliquota,* (fem. a. from *aliquot,* several, so many)]

alive, *pred.a., adv.* living, existent; in force or operation; astir, lively; sensible of (an idea). **alive and kicking,** in a very lively state, all alive. **all alive,** alive, lively, frisky. **look alive!** look sharp, make haste. [ME *on live,* OE *on life* (*on,* prep., *līfe,* dat. of *lif,* LIFE)]

alizarin, *n.* the red colouring matter of madder. [F *alizari* (prob. Arab.)]

alkahest, alcahest, *n.* a word invented, probably by Paracelsus (early 16th cent.), to signify the universal solvent of the alchemists. [Imitation Arab.]

alkali, *n.* (*pl.* **-lis, -lies**) a compound of hydrogen and oxygen with sodium, potassium or other substances, which is soluble in water, and produces caustic and corrosive solutions capable of neutralizing acids and changing the colour of vegetable substances; any water-soluble chemical base; alkaline products, such as caustic potash and caustic soda. **alkali-cellulose** VISCOSE. **alkali-flat, alkali-land,** *n.* any one of several wide waste districts in Colorado and Nevada, covered with an alkaline efflorescence. **alkali-metals,** *n.pl.* metals, the hydroxides of which are alkalis: these arepotassium, sodium, caesium, lithium, rubidium, francium. **alkalescence, -cy,** *n.* the state or condition of becoming alkaline, tendency to become alkaline. **alkalescent,** *a.* becoming or tending to become alkaline; slightly alkaline. *n.* an alkalescent substance. **alkalifiable,** *a.* capable of being converted into an alkali. **alkalify,** *v.t.* to convert into an alkali. *v.i.* to be converted into an alkali. **alkalimetry,** *n.* the measurement of the strength of alkalis. **alkalimetrical,** *a.* **alkaline,** *a.* having the properties of an alkali. **alkaline-earth,** *n.* (an oxide of) any of the alkaline-earth metals. **alkaline-earth metals,** *n.pl.* the metals calcium, strontium, magnesium, radium and beryllium. **alkaline-metals,** *n.pl.* ALKALI-METALS. **alkalize, -ise,** *v.t.* to render alkaline. **alkalization, -isation,** *n.* the act of rendering alkaline. **alkaloid,** *a.* resembling an alkali in properties. *n.* any of a large group of natural organic nitrogenous bases derived from plants, some of which are used as medicinal drugs. [F *alcali,* Arab. *al-qalī,* calcined ashes of saltwort]

alkane, *n.* any of a series of aliphatic hydrocarbons including methane, ethane, butane and octane. [ALKYL]

alkanet, *n.* a dye material obtained from *Anchusa tinctoria;* the plant itself. [Sp. *alcana,* Arab. *al henna,* HENNA]

al-Khalil, *n.* Arabic name for Hebron in the Israeli-occupied West Bank.

alkoran ALCORAN, KORAN.

al Kūt, *n.* alternative term for Kūlt al Imāra.

alkyl, *n.* general name for a monovalent hydrocarbon radical of the alkane series, e.g. methyl, ethyl, butyl. **alkylation,** *a.* the introduction of an alkyl into a compound. [ALC(OHOL), -YL]

all, *a.* the whole (quantity, duration, extent, amount, quality or degree) of; the greatest possible; any whatever; every one of. *n.* the whole, everything, every one. *adv.* wholly, entirely, completely; each, apiece. **after all,** after everything has been taken into account. **all aboard,** take your seats. **all about it,** the whole of the matter. **all ages,** of a race in which horses of all ages are entered. **all along,** throughout. **all and some, all and sundry,** all (taken distributively). **all but,** almost. **all in all,** all things in all respects. **all of,** as much, far etc. as, no less than. **all one,** the same in all respects. **all over,** (*coll.*) completely, everywhere; finished (in the phrases *all over with, is all over*). **all right** RIGHT. **all the better,** so much the better. **all the same,** nevertheless; in spite of what has been said. **all there,** sharp in intellect, alert, quick. †**all-to,** wholly, completely, (the *to* is the OE intens. pref. *to-* corresponding to the G. *zer-;* and, in course of time, the fact that *to-* belonged to the verb was lost sight of, and it was incorporated with *all*). **all told** TELL. **all up with,** no more hope for. **and all,** (*coll.*) too, withal. **and all that,** with all the rest of it. **at all,** in any respect; to the extent; in any degree; of any kind; whatever. (The compounds of *all* are exceedingly numerous, and only the more important are inserted here.) **all-American,** *a.* typifying US ideals, as *all-American boy.* **All Blacks,** *n.pl.* the New Zealand international Rugby Union team. **all clear,** *n.* a signal indicating that danger has passed or that one can proceed safely. **All-father,** *n.* the Father of all; applied to Odin, Jupiter and the Deity. **all-fired,** *a.* (*N Am.*) a euphemism for 'hell-fired'; infernal. **All Fools' Day,** *n.* the 1st of April, from the custom of practising then on the credulity of one's neighbours. **all-fours,** *n.* a game of cards named from the four cards by which points are counted; a game of dominoes in which points are scored only when the pips at both ends make up some multiple of four; the four legs of a quadruped, the arms and legs of a human being. **to run on all fours,** to go evenly; to be analogous to. **all-hail,** *int.* a phrase expressive of respect or welcome. *n.* a salutation of respect and welcome. **All-Hallows,** *n.* All Saints' Day. **All-Hallows' Eve,** *n.* Hallowe'en. **all-important,** *a.* of utmost importance. **all in,** *a.* including everything; (*coll.*) exhausted. **all-in wrestling,** *n.* a form of wrestling with almost no restrictions. **all out,** *a., adv.* with maximum effort. **all-overish,** *a.* (*coll.*) feeling generally unwell. **all-purpose,** *a.* suitable for all purposes. **all-round,** *a.* good in all respects. **all-rounder,** *n., adv.* one whose merits, acquirements or skill are not limited to one or two pursuits; one generally competent or versatile. **all-round traverse,** a machine gun fired so that it can be fired in any direction. **All Saints,** *n.pl.* the saints collectively. **All Saints' Day,** *n.* a church festival (1 Nov.) in honour of the saints collectively. **All Souls,** *n.pl.* the souls of the pious dead. **All Souls' Day,** *n.* the day (2 Nov.) on which the Roman Catholic Church commemorates all the faithful departed. **all speed,** *n.* the greatest possible speed, **all-standing,** (*coll.*) unexpectedly, taken by surprise; in one's clothes, as in *to turn in all-standing.* **all-star,** *a.* composed of star performers. **all-time,** *a.* exceeding all others, as yet unsurpassed. **all-time high,** or **low,** *n.* a record high or low level. **all together,** *adv.* in a body, altogether. **all-up,** *a.* expressing the total weight of an aircraft with its burden when in the air. [OE *eal* (sing.), *ealle* (pl.), old Mercian form *alle;* (OHG *al*)]

alla, *n.* (*New Zealand*) the sea-mullet. [Maori]

Allah, *n.* the name of God among the Muslims. [Arab. *allah,* contr. of *al-ilāh,* the god (cp. Heb. *ĕlōah*)]

Allahabad, *n.* sacred city in Uttar Pradesh, India, 580 km/360 miles SE of Delhi, at the junction of the Ganges and Jumna and a 'mystic' third river, the Saraswati; population (1981) 642,000. Every 12 years a major pilgrimage and fair takes place, the participants washing away sin and sickness by bathing in the rivers. 15 million people attended the festival of the jar of nectar of immortality, Khumbha-mela Jan.-Mar. 1989.

allantois, *n.* (*pl.* **-toides**) a foetal membrane acting as an organ of respiration and excretion in reptiles, birds and mammals. **allantoic,** *a.* [Gr. *allantoeidēs,* sausage-shaped]

allay, *v.t.* to quiet, to still; to put down, to repress; to temper, to abate, to alleviate; †to dilute, to weaken. †*v.i.* to sink, to subside, to grow calm. **allaying,** *n.* dilution, mitigation. †*a.* diluting, tempering. **allayment,** *n.* mitigation, alleviation. [*a-,* intens. pref., LAY (ME form *alleyen;* confused with *aleggen,* to alleviate, and also with *aleye,* allege, and *allay,* alloy)]

Allbutt, *n.* **Sir Thomas Clifford** (1836–1925), British physician. He invented a compact medical thermometer, proved that angina is caused by narrowing of the coronary artery, and studied hydrophobia and tetanus.

allegation, *n.* the act of alleging; an assertion without proof; a specific charge; a statement of what one undertakes to prove. [as foll.]

allege, *v.t.* to adduce as an authority, to plead as an excuse; to affirm positively but without or before proof. **allegedly,** *adv.* [*adlēgiāre,* Latinization of OF *esligier,* late L *exlītigāre* (L *lītigāre,* to contend at law); treated as if from *allēgāre,* to send, bring forward]

allegiance, *n.* the obligation of a subject to his sovereign or government; respect, devotion, fealty. [ME *legeance,* OF *ligeance* (LIEGE); *a-* (L *ad-*) prefixed through confusion with obs. *allegance* (L *allegātio*)]

allegory, *n.* a description of one thing under the image of another; an instance of such description, an extended metaphor, an emblem, an allegorical representation. **allegoric, -ical,** *a.* pertaining to an allegory; resembling an allegory. **allegorically,** *adv.* **allegorist,** *n.* a writer of allegories. **allegorize, -ise,** *v.t.* to convert into an allegory, to interpret allegorically. *v.i.* to use allegory, to speak or write in a figurative manner. [L *allegōria,* Gr. *allegoria;* speaking otherwise than one seems to speak]

allegro, *a.* (*Mus.*) brisk, lively, merry. *adv.* briskly, quickly. *n.* a movement in allegro time or manner. **allegramente,** *adv.* joyfully. **allegretto,** *adv.* somewhat briskly. [It.]

allele, *n.* an allelomorph. **allelic,** *a.* [G *Allel,* short for ALLELOMORPH]

allelomorph, *n.* any of two or more contrasted characteristics, inherited as alternatives, and assumed to depend on genes in homologous chromosomes; any of two or more genes determining such alternative characteristics. **allelomorphic,** *a.* [Gr. *allelon,* of one another; *morphē,* form]

alleluia HALLELUJAH.

allemande, *n.* any of various German dances of the 17th and 18th cents.; the music for or suitable for this (occurring as a movement in a suite). [F, fem. of *allemand,* German]

Allen, *n.* **Woody** (adopted name of Allen Stewart Konigsberg) (1935–), US film director and actor, known for his cynical, witty, often self-deprecating parody and off-beat humour. His films include *Sleeper* (1973), *Annie Hall* (1977) (for which he won three Academy Awards), and *Hannah and her Sisters* (1986), all of which he directed, wrote, and appeared in. From the late 1970s, Allen has mixed his output of comedies with straight dramas in which he does not appear, such as *Interiors* (1978) and *Another Woman* (1988).

Allende (Gossens), *n.* **Salvador** (1908–1973), Chilean left-wing politician. Elected president 1970 as the candidate of the Popular Front alliance, Allende never succeeded in keeping the electoral alliance together in government. His failure to solve the country's economic problems or to deal with political subversion allowed the army, backed by the CIA, to stage the 1973 coup which brought about the death of Allende and many of his supporters.

allergy, *n.* an abnormal response or reaction to some food or substance innocuous to most people; hypersensitiveness to certain substances inhaled or touched; (*coll.*) an aversion, antipathy. **allergen,** *n.* a substance that induces allergy. **allergenic,** *a.* **allergic,** *a.* caused by allergy; having an allergic response (to); (*coll.*) averse (to). **allergist,** *n.* a specialist in the treatment of allergy. [Gr. *allos,* other; ENERGY]

alleviate, *v.t.* to lighten, lessen, mitigate, extenuate. **alleviation,** *n.* the act of alleviating; relief, mitigation. **alleviative,** *n.* that which alleviates. **alleviator,** *n.* **alleviatory,** *a.* [late L *alleviātus,* p.p. of *alleviāre* (*al-, ad-,* to, *levāre* to lift)]

alley¹, *n.* a passage, a walk; a bordered walk; a narrow street or lane; a narrow enclosure for playing at skittles etc. **alleyed,** *a.* formed into alleys, laid out as an alley. [OF *alee* (*aller,* to go)]

alley² ALLY².

All-Hallows ALL.

alliaceous, *a.* pertaining to the plant-genus *Allium,* which contains the onion and garlic; having the taste or smell of garlic. [L *allium,* garlic, -ACEOUS]

alliance, *n.* the state of being allied; union by marriage, affinity; union by treaty or league; a treaty or league; union or connection of interests; the parties allied; (*Bot.*) Lindley's name for a group of a natural order. [OF *aliance*]

Alliance, the, loose union (1981–87) formed by the British Liberal Party and Social Democratic Party (SDP) for electoral purposes.

allied, Allies etc. ALLY.

Allied Mobile Force, (AMF) permanent multinational military force established 1960 to move immediately to any NATO country under threat of attack. Its headquarters are in Heidelberg, West Germany.

Allies, the, in World War I, the 23 countries allied against the Central Powers (Germany, Austria-Hungary, Turkey and Bulgaria), including France, Italy, Russia, the UK and Commonwealth, and, in the later part of the war, the US; and in World War II, the 49 countries allied against the Axis (Germany, Italy and Japan), including France, the UK and Commonwealth, the US, and the USSR.

alligation, *n.* the act of binding together; an arithmetical rule or process for finding the value of a mixture of various ingredients of different qualities and prices. [L *alligāre* (*ad-,* to, *ligāre,* to bind)]

alligator, *n.* an animal of the genus *Alligator,* that differs from the crocodiles esp. in having a broader snout; a genus of saurians from America and China. **alligator-apple,** *n.* the fruit of *Anona palustris,* a W Indian tree. **alligator-gar,** *n.* the garpike of the southern states of the US. **alligator-pear,** *n.* an avocado. **alligator-tortoise,** *n.* the snapping-turtle. **alligator-wood,** *n.* the timber of *Guarea swartzii,* a W Indian tree. [Sp. *ellagarto,* the lizard (L *lacerta*)]

allign etc. ALIGN.

allineation, *n.* alignment; (*Astron.*) the alignment of two or more objects with a certain point. [L *ad-,* to, *lineat-,* part. stem of *lineāre,* to draw a line]

alliterate, *v.i.* to commence with the same letter or sound; to practise alliteration. **alliteration,** *n.* commencement of two or more words or accented syllables, in close connection, with the same letter or sound. **alliterative,** *a.* pertaining to alliteration. **alliteratively,** *adv.* [L *ad-,* to, *litera,* a letter]

Allium, *n.* a genus of plants containing garlic, leeks, onions etc. [L]

allo-, *comb. form* different, other, as in *allomorph, allopathy.* [Gr. *allos,* other]

allocate, *v.t.* to assign, allot, apportion; to localize. **alloca'tion,** *n.* the act of allocating; the admission of an item in an account; the item so admitted. [late L *allocātus,* p.p. of *allocāre* (*ad-,* to, *locāre,* to place, *locus,* a place)]

allocution, *n.* a formal address, esp. one delivered by the Pope to the bishops and clergy, or to the Church generally. [L *allocūtiōnem* (*ad-,* to, *loqui,* to speak)]

allodium, *n.* landed property held in absolute ownership. **allodial,** *a.* pertaining to allodium; held independently, in contradistinction to feudal. **allodialism,** *n.* the system of absolute proprietorship of land. **allodialist,** *n.* one who holds allodial land. **allodially,** *adv.* [med. L *allodium,* OFrankish *alod* (*al,* all or whole, *ōd,* estate, cp. OHG *ōt*)]

allogamy, *n.* (*Bot.*) cross-fertilization. **allogamous,** *a.* reproducing by cross-fertilization. [Gr. ALLO-, -GAMY]

allograph, *n.* a signature written by one person on behalf of another.

allomorph, *n.* any of the two or more forms of a morpheme; any of two or more crystalline forms of a substance. **allomorphic,** *a.* [Gr. ALLO- *morphē,* form]

allonge, *n.* a slip of paper attached to a bill of exchange to hold further signatures; a fly-leaf. [F *allonge,* a lengthening]

allopathy, *n.* the treatment of disease by including effects of a different kind from those produced by the disease; ordinary medical practice, as opposed to homoeopathy. **allopathic,** *a.* pertaining to or practising allopathy. **allopathically,** *adv.* **allopathist,** *n.* one who practises allopathy. [Gr. ALLO-, -PATHY]

allophone, *n.* any of the two or more forms of a phoneme. **allophonic,** *a.* [Gr. ALLO-, -PHONE]

allophylian, *a.* of another race than Aryan or Semitic; (sometimes) Turanian. *n.* one of non-Aryan and non-Semitic race. [Gr. *allophulos,* alien (*allos,* other, *phulē,* tribe)]

allot, *v.t.* (*past, p.p.* **allotted**) to distribute, to grant, to bestow, to assign as one's share. **allotment,** *n.* the act of allotting; the share assigned; a small plot of land let for cultivation. **allottee,** *n.* the person to whom allotment is made. [AF *aloter* (*a-,* L *ad-,* to, LOT)]

allotropy, *n.* variation of physicalproperties without change of substance; thus, diamond, graphite and charcoal are allotropic forms of carbon. **allotrope,** *n.* one of the forms in which a substance exhibiting allotropy exists. **allotropic,** *a.* pertaining to allotropy; existing in diverse states. **allotropically,** *adv.* in an allotropic manner. **allotropism,** *n.* allotropy. [Gr. *allotropia,* from *allotropos* (ALLO-, *tropos,* turn, manner, from *trepein,* to turn)]

allow, *v.t.* †to praise, sanction, approve; to admit, permit; to assign, set aside for a purpose; †to bestow, concede; to take into account, give credit for. **to allow for,** to make allowance or deduction for. **to allow of,** to accept, to admit. **allowable,** *a.* **allowableness,** *n.* **allowably,** *adv.* **allowance,** *n.* the act of allowing; †praise, approbation; permission; a deduction; a fixed quantity or sum allowed. *v.t.* to put upon allowance. **to make allowance** or **allowances for,** to take (mitigating circumstances) into account. [OF *alouer,* from two verbs whose meanings were oftenconfused, (1) L *allaudāre,* to praise, (2) low L *allocāre,* to place, to admit as proved]

alloy, *n.* an inferior metal mixed with one of greater value; a mixture of metals; an amalgam; any base admixture; the standard of purity, the quality of gold and silver. *v.t.* to mix with a baser metal; to mix metals; to mix with anything base or inferior. [formerly *alay* or *allay,* OF *alai,* from *aleier,* to combine, L *alligāre* (*ad-,* to, *ligāre,* to bind)]

allseed, *n.* name of various many-seeded plants.

allspice, *n.* (a spice prepared from) the berry of the pimento, said to combine the flavour of cinnamon, cloves and nutmeg; other aromatic shrubs.

Allston, *n.* **Washington** (1779–1843), US painter, a pioneer of the Romantic movement in the US with his sea- and landscapes. His handling of light and colour earned him the title 'the American Titian'. He also painted classical, religious, and historical subjects.

allude, *v.i.* to make indirect reference (to), to hint at; (*loosely*) to mention, to refer to. **allusion,** *n.* a reference to anything not directly mentioned; a hint. **allusive,** *a.* containing an allusion; hinting at an implied meaning, characterized by allusion. **allusively,** *adv.* **allusiveness,** *n.* [L *allūdere* (*ad-,* to, *lūdere,* to play)]

allure, *v.t.* to attract or tempt by the offer of some real or apparent good; to entice; to fascinate, to charm. *n.* charm, sex appeal. **allurement,** *n.* the act of alluring or enticing; that which allures; a bait, an enticement. **alluring,** *a.* luring, enticing, attractive. **alluringly,** *adv.* [OF *alurer, aleurrer* (*à,* to, *leurrer,* to lure)]

allusion, etc. ALLUDE.

alluvia, alluvial ALLUVIUM.

alluvion, *n.* the wash of the sea against the land; (*Law*) the formation of new land by the action of flowing water. [F *alluvion,* L *alluviōnem,* acc. of *alluvio,* a washing against; see ALLUVIUM]

alluvium, *n.* (*pl.* **alluvia**) earth, sand, gravel, stones or other transported matter which has been washed away and thrown down by rivers, floods or similar causes. **alluvial,** *a.* pertaining to alluvium; deposited from flowing water. [L, neut. of a. *alluvius* (*ad-,* to, *luere,* to wash)]

ally[1], *v.t.* to unite by treaty, confederation, marriage or friendship. **allied,** *a.* united, associated; of the same type, related. **Allied,** *a.* of the Allies. [OF *alier,* L *alligāre* (*ad-,* to, *ligāre,* to bind)]

ally[2], *n.* one united by treaty, confederation, marriage or friendship; something akin to another in structure or properties; an auxiliary. **the Allies,** in World War I, the nations united against the central European powers; in World War II, the nations united against the Axis powers.

ally[3], alley, *n.* a superior kind of marble or taw. [said to be dim. from ALABASTER]

Allyson, *n.* **June** (stage name of Ella Geisman) (1917–), US film actress, popular in musicals and straight drama in the 1940s and 1950s. Her work includes *Music for Millions* (1945), *The Three Musketeers* (1948), and *The Glenn Miller Story* (1954).

alma, almah, *n.* an Egyptian dancing-girl. [Arab. *'almah,* learned, knowing]

Alma-Ata, *n.* formerly (to (1921)) **Vernyi,** capital of the Republic of Kazakh, USSR; population (1987) 1,108,000. Industries include engineering, printing, tobacco processing, textile manufacturing, and leather products.

almacantar, almucantar, *n.* an instrument for determining time and latitude; a smaller circle of the celestial sphere parallel to the horizon, a parallel of altitude. [F *almicantarat* or *almucantarat,* med. L *almi-* or *almucontarath,* Arab. *al-muquantarāt,* pl. of *muquantarah,* sun-dial, from *quantarah,* a bridge]

Almadan, *n.* mining town in Ciudad Real province, Castilla-La Mancha, central Spain. It has the world's largest supply of mercury, worked since the 4th century BC. Population (1981) 9700.

almagest, *n.* the great astronomical treatise of Ptolemy; hence, any work on astrologyor alchemy. [OF *almageste,* Arab. *almajistī,* Gr. *megistē,* the greatest]

alma mater, *n.* name used by an ex-student for his college or school. [L, fostering mother]

almanac, †**almanack,** *n.* a register of the days of the year, with astronomical data and calculations, civil and ecclesiastical festivals etc. [F *almanach,* med. L *almanac* (etym. doubtful)]

almandine, *n.* a precious deep red garnet. [formerly *alabandine,* L *alabandina,* from *Alabanda,* a city of Caria]

Almansa, Battle of, in the War of the Spanish Succession, battle 25 Apr. 1707 in which British, Portuguese and Spanish forces were defeated by the French under the Duke of Berwick at a Spanish town in Albacete, about 80 km/50 miles NW of Alicante.

Alma-Tadema, *n.* **Laurence** (1836–1912), Dutch painter who settled in the UK in 1870. He painted romantic, idealized scenes from Greek, Roman and Egyptian life in a distinctive, detailed style.

Almeida, *n.* **Francisco de** (*c.* 1450–1510), first viceroy of Portuguese India (1505–08). He was killed in a skirmish with the Hottentots at Table Bay, S Africa.

almighty, *a.* omnipotent; possessed of unlimited ability, strength or power. *a., adv.* (*sl.*) mighty, great, exceedingly. **the Almighty,** God. **almighty dollar,** *n.* (*coll.*) money; feverish love of money. **almightiness,** *n.* [OE *ealmihtig* (ALL, MIGHTY)]

Almohad, *n.* a Berber dynasty (1130–1269) founded by the Berber prophet Mohammed ibn Tumart (*c.* 1080–1130). They ruled much of Morocco and Spain, which they took by defeating the Almoravids; they later took the area which today forms Algeria and Tunis. Their policy of religious 'purity' involved the forced conversion and massacre of the Jewish population of Spain. They were themselves defeated by the Christian kings of Spain in 1212, and in Morocco in 1269.

almond, *n.* a small widely cultivated tree of the rose family, *Prunus amygdalus;* the edible kernel of the fruit of the almond-tree; anything shaped like an almond, hence a tonsil. **almond-tumbler,** *n.* a kind of tumbler pigeon. **almond-willow,** *n.* a British willow with almond-shaped leaves, *Salix amygdalina.* [OF *almande,* L *amygdala,* Gr. *amygdalē*]

almond-furnace, *n.* a furnace used to separate metals from cinders and other dross. [corruption of *Allemand,* German]

almoner, *n.* an official distributor of alms or bounty; a hospital official who assesses the amount of payments to be made by patients for their treatment; a former name for a medico-social worker attached to a hospital. **Hereditary Grand Almoner, Lord High Almoner,** officials who superintended the distribution of the royal alms in England. **almonry,** *n.* a place where alms are distributed; the residence of an almoner. [OF *aumoner,* late L *almosinarius* (see ALMS)]

Almoravid, *n.* a Berber dynasty (1056–1147) founded by the prophet Abdullah ibn Tashfin, ruling much of Morocco and Spain in the 11th–12th centuries. They came from the Sahara and in the 11th century began laying the foundations of an empire covering the whole of Morocco and parts of Algeria; their capital was the newly founded Marrakesh. In 1086 they defeated Alfonso VI of Castile to gain much of Spain. They were later overthrown by the Almohads.

almost, *adv.* nearly, very nearly, well-nigh; (*used elliptically or colloquially as a.*) closely approaching; e.g. *almost night, his almost impudence.*

alms, *n.pl.* anything given out of charity to the poor; charity. †**alms-basket,** *n.* a basket containing alms to be distributed. †**to live on the alms-basket,** to live on charity. **alms-deed,** *n.* an act of charity. **alms-giving,** *n.* the giving of alms. **almshouse,** *n.* a house where poor persons are lodged and provided for by charitable endowment; (*N Am.*) a workhouse. **almsman,** *n.* a man supported by alms. **almswoman,** *n. fem.* [OE *ælmesse,* L *eleēmosyna,* Gr. *eleēmosunē* (*eleēmōn,* a from *eleos,* pity)]

almucantar ALMACANTAR.

almug ALGUM.

Aloe, *n.* a genus of succulent plants, with bitter juice; any of various other plants, e.g. the American aloe (see CENTURY plant); the inspissated juice of plants of the genus *Aloe,* a purgative drug. **Aloe vera,** *n.* a Mediterranean aloe whose juice is used in various medical and cosmetic preparations. **aloetic,** *a.* pertaining to the aloe or aloes; consisting entirely or chiefly of aloes. *n.* an aloetic medicine. [L *aloë,* Gr. *aloē*]

aloft, *adv.* on high; above the ground; in the rigging, at the mast-head. **to go aloft,** (*coll.*) to go to heaven, to die. [Icel. *a lopt,* in the air (cp. LIFT)]

alogical, *a.* not logical, not rational.

alone, *pred.a.* single, solitary, by oneself or itself; without equal, unique. *adv.* only, merely, simply; solely. [ME *al one* (ALL, ONE)]

along¹, *adv.* lengthwise, in a line with the length, in progressive motion; onward. *prep.* by the side of, from end to end, over or through lengthwise. **all along,** *adv.* throughout, all the time. **along with,** in company or together with. **along-ships,** *adv.* lengthwise, fore and aft. **alongshore,** *adv.* in a line with, and nearly parallel to, the shore; along and on the shore. **alongshoreman,** *n.* a fisherman engaged in coastal fishing. **alongside,** *prep., adv.* beside, by the side (of); side by side. **alongside of,** side by side with. [OE *andlang* (*and,* against, *lang,* long; cp. OHG *ant-,* Gr. *anti*]

along², *adv.* (*dial.*) pertaining, belonging, chargeable. **along of, all along of,** (*dial.*) because of, owing to, attributable to. [OE *gelang* (*ge-,* intens., *lang,* long)]

aloof, *adv.* away at a distance from, apart; †(*Naut.*) to windward. *a.* distant or unsympathetic in manner. **to stand, keep aloof,** to take no part in, keep away; to remain by oneself, remain unsympathetic. **aloofness,** *n.* the state of keeping aloof. [*a-,* on, ME *loof* (cp. Dut. *to loef,* to windward) see LUFF]

alopecia, *n.* baldness. [Gr. *alopekia,* fox-mange]

aloud, *adv.* loudly; with a loud voice; audibly.

alow, *adv.* †low down, downwards; †in a low voice; in or into the lower part of a ship, opposed to aloft.

alp, *n.* a high mountain; pasture ground on the side of mountain; a formidable obstacle. **Alps,** *n.pl.* see separate article. **alphorn, alpenhorn,** *n.* a very long wooden horn used by herdsmen in the Swiss Alps. **Alpine,** *a.* pertaining to the Alps or to any high mountains; growing on the Alps or on any high mountain; growing above the tree line; pertaining to ski events such as slalom and downhill racing. **alpinism,** *n.* mountain-climbing. **alpinist,** *n.* one devoted to Alpine climbing. [L *Alpes,* pl., etym. doubtful]

alpaca, *n.* the domesticated llama of Peru; the wool of the domesticated llama; cloth made from this wool. [Sp. *alpaca* (Arab. *al-,* the, Peruv. Sp. *paco*]

alpenhorn ALP.

alpenstock, *n.* a long stick shod with iron, used in mountaineering. [G *alpen,* of the Alps, *Stock,* stick]

alpha, *n.* the first letter of the Greek alphabet, used to designate numerical sequence; the chief or brightest star in a constellation. **alpha and omega,** the beginning and the end. **alpha particle,** *n.* a positively-charged particle emitted by certain radioactive substances, e.g. radium. It has been identified as a doubly-ionized helium atom. **alpha plus,** *a.* superlatively good. **alpha-rays,** *n.pl.* rays consisting of streams of alpha particles. **alpha rhythm, alpha wave,** *n.* the pattern of electrical activity of the brain associated with a person awake but at rest. [Gr. *alpha,* Heb. *āleph,* an ox, a leader]

alphabet, *n.* the letters or characters used to represent a language, arranged in order; rudiments, a long and complete series. *v.t.* to arrange in the order of the alphabet; to designate by letters of the alphabet. **alphabetic, -ical,** *a.* pertaining to the alphabet, arranged alphabetically. **alphabetically,** *adv.* **alphabetize, -ise,** *v.t.* [L *alphabētum,* Gr. *alpha, bēta,* (Heb. *bēth,* a house), the first two letters]

Alpha Centauri, *n.* the brightest star in the constellation of Centaurus. It is actually a triple star (see binary star); the two brighter stars orbit each other every 80 years, and the third, Proxima Centauri, 4.3 light years away, is the closest star to the Sun. Alpha Centauri is the third brightest star in the sky.

alphanumeric, -ical, alphameric, -ical, *a.* consisting of or using both letters and numbers. [ALPHA(BET), NUMERIC]

Alpine ALP.

Alps, *n. pl.* mountain chain, the barrier between N Italy and France, Germany and Austria. **famous peaks** include *Mont Blanc* the highest at 4807 m/15,777 ft, first climbed by Jacques Balmat and Michel Paccard 1786; *Matterhorn* in the Pennine Alps 4477 m/14,694 ft, first climbed by Edward Whymper 1865 (four of the party of seven were killed when the rope broke during their descent); *Eiger* in the Bernese Alps/Oberland, 3970 m/13,030 ft, with a near-vertical rock wall on the north face, first climbed 1858; *Jungfrau* 4166 m/13,673 ft, and *Finsteraarhorn* 4274 m/14,027 ft. **famous passes** include *Brenner* the lowest, Austria/Italy; *Great St Bernard* the highest, 2472 m/8113 ft, Italy/Switzerland (by which Napoleon marched into Italy 1800); *Little St Bernard* Italy/France (which Hannibal is thought to have used), and *St Gotthard* S Switzerland, which Suvorov used when ordered by the tsar to withdraw his troops from Italy. All have been superseded by all-weather road/rail tunnels. The Alps extend into Yugoslavia with the Julian and Dinaric Alps.

already, *adv.* beforehand, before some specified time,

in anticipation. [ALL, *adv.* READY]

alright, a nonstandard spelling of all right (see RIGHT).

Alsace, *n.* region of France; area 8300 sq km/3204 sq miles; population (1986) 1,600,000. It consists of the *départements* of Bas-Rhin and Haut-Rhin, and its capital is Strasbourg.

Alsace-Lorraine, *n.* area of NE France, lying west of the river Rhine. It forms the modern French regions of Alsace and Lorraine. The former iron and steel industries are being replaced by electronics, chemicals, and precision engineering. The German dialect spoken does not have equal rights with French, and there is autonomist sentiment. Alsace-Lorraine formed part of Celtic Gaul in Caesar's time, was invaded by the Alemanni and other Germanic tribes in the 4th century, and remained part of the German Empire until the 17th century. In 1648 part of the territory was ceded to France; in 1681 Louis XIV seized Strasbourg. The few remaining districts were seized by France after the Revolution. Conquered by Germany in 1870–71 (chiefly for its iron ores), it was regained by France (1919), then again annexed by Germany (1940–44), when it was liberated by the Allies.

Alsatia, *n.* province west of the Rhine; cant name for the precinct of White Friars, London, formerly a sanctuary for debtors andcriminals; an asylum for lawbreakers. **Alsatian,** *a.* belonging to Alsace, or to old White Friars. *n.* a native of Alsatia; a large, intelligent, German wolf-like dog; an adventurer; a bohemian. [L form of *Elsass*, F *Alsace*]

alsike, *n.* a species of clover, *Trifolium hybridum.* [*Alsike,* place in Sweden]

alsirat, *n.* the bridge over the abyss, finer than a hair or a razor's edge, which all must pass to reach the Muslim paradise. [Arab. *al-sirat,* the road, way; prob. from L *strāta*]

also, *adv., conj.* likewise, in like manner, even as, besides; in addition, as well. **also-ran,** *n.* an unplaced horse in a race; (*coll.*) an unimportant person, a failure. [ALL, *adv.*, so]

alt, *n.* (*Mus.*) high tone; the higher register of sounds; exaltation of mind. [Prov.; L *altum,* high]

alt., (*abbr.*) alternate; altitude; alto.

Alta, (*abbr.*) Alberta (Canada).

Altai, *n.* territory of the Russian Soviet Federal Socialist Republic in SW Siberia; area 261,700 sq km/101,043 sq miles; population (1985) 2,744,000. The capital is Barnaul. **Altaian,** *a.* a term applied to the peoples, and to the languages of the peoples (Turanian or Ural-Altaic), lying near the Altai mountains and the Arctic ocean. *n.* a member of this group. **Altaic,** *a.* Altaian. [F *altaïen,* from the *Altai* (mountains in Asia)]

Altair, *n.* brightest star in the constellation of Aquila. It is a white star 16 light years away and forms the so-called Summer Triangle with the stars Deneb (in Cygnus) and Vega (in Lyra). It is the 12th brightest star in the sky.

Altamira¹, *n.* cave near the Spanish village of Santillana del Mar in Santander province where in 1879 palaeolithic wall paintings were discovered.

Altamira², *n.* an Amazonian town in the state of Pará, NE Brazil, situated at the junction of the Trans-Amazonian Highway with the Xingu river, 700 km SW of Belam. In Feb. 1989 world attention focused on the devastation of the Amazon rainforest following a protest against the building of six dams by what amounted to the largest gathering of Brazilian Indians and environmentalists in modern times.

altar, *n.* a sacrificial block; a place ofsacrifice, commemoration or devotion; the communion-table; a southern constellation, also called Ara. **to lead to the altar,** to marry. **altar-bread,** *n.* wafer bread used in the celebration of the Eucharist. **altar-cloth,** *n.* the linen cloth which covers an altar; an altar-frontal. **altar-frontal** ANTEPENDIUM. **altar-piece,** *n.* a picture or ornamental sculpture over the altar (or communion-table) in a church. **altar-plate,** *n.* the plate used in the celebration of the Eucharist. **altar-rails,** *n.pl.* the low railings separating the altar from the main body of the church. **altar-screen,** *n.* the reredos wall or screen at the back of an altar. **altar-slab,** *n.* the slab forming the top of an altar. **altar-stone,** *n.* an altar-slab; a portable altar on which Mass is said. **altar-table** ALTAR-SLAB. **altar-tomb,** *n.* a raised funeral monument resembling an altar. **altar-wise,** *adv.* after the manner, or in the position of an altar. [L *altāre* (*altus,* high)]

altazimuth, *n.* an instrument for measuring altitude and azimuth. [*alt-* (for ALTITUDE), AZIMUTH]

Altdorfer, *n.* **Albrecht** (*c.* 1480–1538), German painter and printmaker, active in Regensburg, Bavaria. Altdorfer's work, influenced by the linear, classical style of the Italian Renaissance, often depicts dramatic landscapes that are out of scale with the figures in the paintings. His use of light creates tension and effects of movement. Many of his works are of religious subjects.

alter, *v.t.* to cause to vary or change in some degree; to modify. *v.i.* to undergo some change. **alterable,** *a.* capable of being altered. **alterability,** *n.* **alteration,** *n.* the act of altering; the change made. **alterative,** *a.* tending to produce alteration. *n.* a medicine which alters the processes of nutrition and reduces them to a healthy state. [F *altérer,* late L *alterāre* (*alter,* other, same root as *al-ius*)]

altercate, *v.i.* to dispute hotly; to wrangle. **altercation,** *n.* wrangling; a vehement dispute. [L *altercāt-,* part. stem of *altercāri*]

alter ego, *n.* a second self; a trusted friend; a plenipotentiary. [L, another I]

alternate¹, *v.t.* to arrange or perform by turns; to cause to succeed by turns or reciprocally; to interchange. *v.i.* to happen by turns; to change repeatedly from one condition or state to another; (*Elec.*) to change from positive to negative and back again in turns. **alternant,** *a.* alternating; (*Min.*) consisting of alternatinglayers. **alternating,** *a.* (*Elec.*) changing from positive to negative and back. **alternating current,** *n.* an electric current that changes from positive to negative regularly and frequently. **alternation,** *n.* the act of alternating; the state of being alternate; antiphonal reading or singing. [L *alternatus,* p.p. of *alternāre,* to do by turns (*alternus,* every other, from *alter,* other)]

alternate², *a.* done or happening by turns, first one and then the other; reciprocal; every other, every second; of plant parts, placed on opposite sides of an axis at successive levels; of angles, succeeding regularly on opposite sides of a straight line. **alternately,** *adv.*

alternative, *a.* offering a choice of two things; being the other of two things open to choice; denoting or pertaining to a life-style, practice, art form etc. which functions outside and constitutes an alternative to conventional or institutionalized methods or systems. *n.* the permission or opportunity to choose between two things; either of two courses which may be chosen. **alternative medicine,** *n.* any system of medicine or medical treatment, as homoeopathy or osteopathy, that does not use orthodox practices or substances. **alternatively,** *adv.* [as prec.]

alternator, *n.* a dynamo for generating an alternating electric current.

Althing, *n.* the parliament of Iceland, established about 930 and the oldest in the world.

although, *conj.* though, notwithstanding, however. [ALL, *adv.*, THOUGH]

Althusser, *n.* **Louis** (1918–). French philosopher and Marxist, born in Algeria, who from 1968 argued that the idea that economic systems determine family and political systems is too simple. He attempted to show how the ruling class ideology of a particular era is a crucial form of class control.

alti- *comb. form* high, highly, height. [L *alto-* etc., from *altus,* high]

altimeter, *n.* an instrument that indicates height above a given datum, usu. sea-level.

Altiplano, *n.* the densely populated upland plateau of the Andes of South America, stretching from Ecuador to NW Argentina. Height 3000-4000 m/10,000-13,000 ft.

altiscope, *n.* an apparatus for enabling one to see over intervening objects by means of lenses and mirrors arranged in a telescopic tube.

altisonant, *a.* loud, noisy, high-sounding.

altissimo, *adv.* (*Mus.*) in the second octave above the treble stave. [It. superl. of ALTO]

altitude, *n.* vertical height; elevation of an object above its base; height above sea; the elevation of a heavenly body above the horizon. [L *altitūdo* (*altus,* high)]

Altman, *n.* **Robert** (1922–), US film director. His an,iwar comedy *M.A.S.H.* (1970) was a critical and commercial success; subsequent films include *McCabe and Mrs Miller* (1971), *Nashville* (1975), and *Popeye* (1980). He has a distinctive style as a director.

alto, *n.* the highest adult male voice, countertenor; the lowest female voice, contralto;a singer possessing such a voice; the part of the music sung by persons possessing the alto voice. **alto-clarinet, alto-viola,** *n.* musical instruments of alto pitch. **alto-clef,** *n.* the C clef when on the third line of the stave. [It., high (viz. *canto* singing)]

altogether, *adv.* wholly, completely, entirely; inclusive of everything; on the whole, in view of all things. **the altogether,** (*coll.*) the nude. [ALL, *adv.*, TOGETHER]

alto-relievo, *n.* high relief, standing out from the background by more than half thetrue proportions of the figures carved. [It. *alto-rilievo*]

altruism, *n.* devotion to the good of others (opposed to egoism). **altruist,** *n.* one who practises altruism. **altruistic,** *a.* **altruistically,** *adv.* [F *altruisme,* It. *altrui* (F *autrui*), L *alteri huic* (to this other)]

ALU, (*abbr.*) (*Comput.*) arithmetic and logic unit, in a computer, the part of the CPU (central processing unit) that performs the basic arithmetic and logical operations on data.

alula, *n.* the bastard-wing. [L, dim. of *ală,* wing]

alum, *n.* a double sulphate salt of aluminium and potassium; any of a series of double salts including this; a family of analogous compounds; (*Min.*) name of various minerals, alums or pseudo-alums. [OF *alum* (F *alun*), L *alumen*]

alumina, *n.* the oxide of aluminium occurring as corundum and a constituent of all clays. [L *alumen*]

aluminium, *n.* a white, ductile metallic element with good resistance to corrosion, used as a basis for many light alloys. **aluminium-bronze,** *n.* a compound of aluminium and copper. **aluminize, -ise,** *v.t.* to coat with aluminium. [see prec.]

aluminous, *a.* composed of or pertaining to alum or alumina.

aluminum, *n.* (*N Am.*) aluminium.

alumnus, *n.* (*pl.* **-ni**) a pupil or student in relation to his place of education; (*N Am.*) a graduate, old scholar. **alumna,** *n. fem.* (*pl.* **-nae**). [L, foster-child]

Alva, or **Alba,** *n.* **Ferdinand Alvarez de Toledo, Duke of Alva** (1508–1582), Spanish politician and general. He commanded the Spanish armies of the Holy Roman emperor Charles V and his son Philip II of Spain, and in 1567 was appointed governor of the Netherlands, where he set up a reign of terror to suppress the revolt against increased taxation, reductions in local autonomy, and the Inquisition. In 1573 he retired, and returned to Spain.

Alvarado, *n.* **Pedro de** (*c.* 1485–1541), Spanish conquistador. In 1519 he accompanied Hernándo Cortés in the conquest of Mexico. In 1523–24 he conquered Guatemala.

Alvarez, *n.* **Luis Walter** (1911–1988), US physicist who led the research team that discovered the Xi-zero atomic particle (1959). He worked on the US atomic bomb project for two years, at Chicago and Los Alamos, during World War II. Nobel prize 1968.

Alvárez Quintero, *n.* **Serafin** (1871–1938) and **Joaquin** (1873–1945), Spanish dramatists. The brothers, born near Seville, always worked together and from 1897 produced some 200 plays, principally dealing with Andalusia. Among them are *Papá Juan: Centenario* (1909) and *Los Mosquitos* (1928).

alveolus, *n.* (*pl.* **-li**) a little cavity; the cell of a honeycomb; the conical chamber of a belemnite; the conical body found therein; a tooth socket; an air sac in the lungs. **alveolar,** *a.* pertaining to or having alveoli or an alveolus; pertaining to the sockets of the teeth; socket-shaped; produced with the tip of the tongue touching the roof of the mouth behind the front teeth. **alveolate,** *a.* honey-combed; deeply pitted. [L *alveolus,* dim. of *alveus,* a cavity]

alvine, *a.* pertaining to the belly or to the intestines. [L *alvīnus* (*alvus,* the belly)]

always, alway, *adv.* all the while; without intermission; uninterruptedly, regularly; on all occasions; while one lives; in all cases; in any event. [OE *ealne weg,* acc. (ALL, WAY)]

Alyssum, *n.* a genus of cruciferous plants, including *Alyssum saxatile,* (*pop.*) gold dust; a related plant, *Lobularia maritima,* sweet alyssum. [Gr. *alusson*]

Alzheimer's disease, *n.* a degenerative disease of the central nervous system characterized by a deterioration of mental faculties resembling premature mental senility or dementia. [the G physician Alois *Alzheimer,* 1864–1915]

AM, (*abbr.*) amplitude modulation; anno mundi (in the year of the world); associate member; (*chiefly N Am.*) Master of Arts. [L *Artium Magister*]

Am., (*abbr.*) America, American.

Am, (*chem. symbol*) americium.

am, *1st pers. sing. pres. ind. of the v.* to BE. [OE *am, eom,* from *es-m* (cp. Sansk. *asmi,* Gr. *eimi,* L *sum*); from the root *es,* to be, also come *art* and *are,* OE *eart, earth* (cp. Icel. *est, ert,* Sansk. *asī,* Gr. *essi,* L *es*), and Merc. *earun* (cp. Northumb. *aron,* OE *sindon,* Icel. *erum,* Gr.*eisin,* L *sunt*); (see also BE, WAS)]

a.m., (*abbr.*) ante meridiem (before noon).

amabile, *adv.* (*Mus.*) amiably, tenderly, sweetly. [It., amiable]

amadou, *n.* a German tinder, prepared from a dried fungus steeped in saltpetre, used as a match and a styptic. [F *amadou,* OProv. *amador,* L *amātōrem,* a lover (*amāre,* to love)]

amah, *n.* in the East, a wet-nurse, nanny. [Port.]

amain, *adv.* energetically, violently, in full force, at full speed, at once. [OE *a-,* on, *mægen,* might]

Amal, *n.* a radical Lebanese Shi'ite military force, established by Musa Sadr in the 1970s; their headquarters are at Borj al-Barajneh. The movement split into extremist and moderate groups 1982, but both sides agreed on the aim of increasing Shi'ite political representation in Lebanon. Amal guerrillas were responsible for many of the attacks and kidnappings in Lebanon during the 1980s.

Amalekite, *n.* in the Old Testament, member of an ancient Semitic people of SW Palestine and the Sinai peninsula. According to Exodus 17 they harried the rear of the Israelites after their crossing of the Red Sea, were defeated by Saul and David, and finally crushed in the reign of Hezekiah.

amalgam, *n.* a mixture of any other metal with mercury; a compound of different things. **amalgamate,** *v.t.* to mix, unite, combine, to compound into one mixture; to combine another metal with mercury. *v.i.* to combine, to blend, to merge into one. **amalgamation,** *n.* the act of amalgamating; the blending of different things; a homogeneous union. **amalgamative,** *a.* tending to combine. [F *amalgame,* med. L *amalgama,* prob. from Gr. *malagma,* an emollient, a plaster (*malassein,* to soften)]

Amanita, *n.* a genus of fungi, distinguished by a ring, or *volva,* round the stem, warty patches on the cap, and by the clear white colour of the gills. Many of the species are brightly coloured and highly poisonous.

amanuensis, *n.* (*pl.* **-ses**) a person employed to write what another dictates or to copy manuscripts. [L *amanuensis,* a. (viz. *servus*), a scribe (*ā mānu,* by hand, *-ensis,* suf. pertaining to)]

Amanullah Khan, *n.* (1892–1960), emir (ruler) of Afghanistan (1919–29). Third son of Habibullah Khan, he seized the throne on his father's assassination and concluded a treaty with the British, but his policy of westernization led to rebellion in 1928. Amanullah had to flee, abdicated in 1929, and settled in Rome, Italy.

amaracus, *n.* an aromatic plant, marjoram or dittany. [L *amāracus,* Gr. *amarakos*]

amaranth, †**amarant**, *n.* an imaginary flower supposed never to fade; a purple colour; any of a genus of plants, *Amaranthus,* that includes love-lies-bleeding and prince's feather. **amaranthine**, **amarantine**, *a.* pertaining to amaranth; unfading. [L *amarantus,* Gr. *amarantos* (*a-,* not, *marainein,* to wither)]

Amarna tablets, *n. pl.* a collection of Egyptian clay tablets with cuneiform inscriptions, found in the ruins of the ancient Akhetaton on the east bank of the Nile. The majority of the tablets, which comprise royal archives and letters of 1411–1375 BC, are in the British Museum.

Amaryllis, *n.* a genus of autumn-flowering bulbous plants. [Gr. *Amarullis,* name of a country-girl]

amass, *v.t.* to make or gather into a heap; to collect together, to accumulate. [F *amasser* (*à,* to, *masse,* mass, L *ad, massam*)]

Amaterasu, *n.* in Japanese mythology, the sun-goddess, grandmother of Jimmu Tenno, first ruler of Japan, from whom the emperors claimed to be descended.

amateur, *n.* one who cultivates anything as a pastime, as distinguished from one who does so professionally; one who competes in a sport for enjoyment rather than payment; one who is fond of an art, pastime etc., a devotee; one who dabbles or is unskilled in a subject. *a.* pertaining to an amateur as *amateur gardener;* not professional; not receiving payment as *amateur boxer.* **amateurish,** *a.* not up to the professional standard. **amateurishness,** *n.* the quality of being amateurish; inferior standard of execution. **amateurism,** *n.* state, condition or practice of an amateur; dilettantism. [F *amateur,* L *amātōrem* (*amāre,* to love)]

Amati, *n.* Italian family of violin-makers, who worked in Cremona, about 1550–1700. Niccolo Amati (1596–1684) taught Andrea Guarneri and Antonio Stradivari.

amative, *a.* disposed to loving. **amativeness,** *n.* disposition to loving; erotic propensity. [L *amāre,* to love]

amatol, *n.* an explosive consisting of a mixture of ammonium nitrate and trinitrotoluene. [AM(MONIUM), TOL(UENE)]

amatory, *a.* pertaining to love; causing or designed to cause love. **amatorial**, *a.* pertaining to love or courtship. **amatorially,** *adv.* [L *amātorius* (*amātor,* a lover)]

amaurosis, *n.* partial or total blindness from disease of the optic nerve, usu. without visible defect. **amaurotic**, *a.* affected with amaurosis. [Gr. *amaurōsis* (*amauroein,* to darken, from *amauros,* dark)]

amaze, *v.t.* to astound, to overwhelm with wonder, to bewilder. †*n.* extreme astonishment, wonder, bewilderment, amazement. **amazedly**, *adv.* **amazedness**, *n.* **amazement,** *n.* overwhelming surprise; the state of being amazed. **amazing,** *a.* **amazingly,** *adv.* [OE *āmasian* (*a-,* intens. pref.), to confound (*Skeat*); see also MAZE]

amazon, *n.* in Greek mythology, a member of a group of legendary female warriors living near the Black Sea, who cut off their right breasts to use the bow more easily (the Amazons attacked Theseus and besieged him at Athens, but were defeated, and Theseus took the Amazon Hippolyta captive; she later gave birth to Hippolytus); a female warrior; a tall, strong woman, virago. **amazon-ant,** *n. Formica rufescens,* the neuters of which enslave the young of other species. **amazonian, Amazonian**, *a.* of or pertaining to the fabled Amazons, hence, war-like, strong; pertaining to the river Amazon, named from the female warriors recorded there by the early Spaniards. [Gr. *amazōn* (foreign word explained by Greeks as *a-* not, *mazos,* breast, from legend that they cut away the right breast to use the bow more freely)]

Amazon, *n.* South American river, the world's second longest, 6570 km/4080 mi, and the largest in volume of water. Its main headstreams, the Marañón and the Ucayali, rise in central Peru and unite to flow eastwards across Brazil for about 4000 km/2500 mi. It has 48,280 km/30,000 mi of navigable waterways, draining 7,000,000 sq km/2,750,000 sq mi, nearly half the South American land mass. It reaches the Atlantic on the Equator, its estuary 80 km/50 mi wide, discharging a volume of water so immense that 64 km/40 mi out to sea fresh water remains at the surface.

ambage, ambages, *n.* circumlocution; roundabout expression; equivocation; the use of ambiguous language intended to mystify or deceive. **ambagious**, *a.* [F *ambage, ambages,* L *ambāges* (*amb-,* about, *agere,* to drive)]

ambassador, *n.* a minister of high rank, representing his or her country at a foreign court or government, being styled **ordinary** when resident, and **extraordinary** when sent on a special mission; a representative, messenger. **ambassador-at-large,** *n.* a US ambassador not accredited to a particular foreign government. **ambassador plenipotentiary,** *n.* an ambassador armed with full powers to sign treaties etc. **ambassadorial**, *a.* **ambassadress**, *n. fem.* a female ambassador; the wife of an ambassador. †**ambassage**, *n.* EMBASSY. [F *ambassadeur,* OSp. *ambaxador,* late L *ambaxiāre, ambactiāre* (*ambactia,* a mission, office, from Celt. **ambactus**, a servant, from *amb-,* about, and Celt. root *ag-,* to drive, cognate with L *agere*)]

amber, *n.* a yellowish translucent fossil resin, found chiefly on the southern shores of the Baltic, used for ornaments, mouthpieces of pipes, and in the manufacture of some varnishes; †ambergris; †a love-charm made of amber. *a.* made of or coloured like amber. **amber fauna,** *n.* animals whose remains are found preserved in amber. **amber flora,** *n.* plants found preserved in amber. **amber-seed,** *n.* the seed of the plant *Abelmoschus moschatus,* used to perfume pomatum etc. **amber-tree,** *n.* a plant of the genus *Anthospermum,* containing evergreen shrubsfragrant when bruised. [F *ambre,* Arab. *'anbar,* ambergris]

ambergris, *n.* a light, fatty, inflammable substance, ashy in colour, found floating in tropical seas, a secretion from the intestines of the cachalot or spermaceti whale; used in perfumery, formerly in cookery and medicine. [F *ambre gris,* grey amber]

ambidextrous, -terous, *a.* using both hands with equal facility; double-dealing. **ambidexter,** *a.* ambidextrous. *n.* †one who can use both hands with equal facility; a double-dealer; one who accepts bribes from both sides. **ambidexterity**, *n.* **ambidextrously,** *adv.* **ambidextrousness,** *n.* [med. L *ambidexter* (*ambi-,* both, on both sides, *dexter,* right-handed)]

ambient, *a.* surrounding, encompassing on all sides, circumfused, investing. **ambience, ambiance,** *n.* the surrounding atmosphere or influence, environment. [L *ambiens -entis* pres.p. of *ambīre* (*amb-,* on both sides, about, *īre,* to go)]

ambiguous, *a.* susceptible of two or more meanings; of doubtful meaning, equivocal, obscure; of uncertain position or classification. **ambiguously,** *adv.* **ambiguousness,** *n.* **ambiguity,** *n.* the state or an instance of being ambiguous; uncertainty of meaning. [L *ambiguus,* doubtful, from *ambigere* (*amb-,* both ways, *agere,* to drive)]

ambit, *n.* bounds, precincts, scope. [L *ambitus,* a going about (see AMBIENT)]

ambition, *n.* a desire for power, success, superiority or excellence; strong desire to achieve anything (advantageous or creditable); the object of such desire. **ambitious,** *a.* actuated by or indicating ambition; full of or displaying ambition. **ambitiously,** *adv.* **ambitiousness,** *n.* [F *ambition,* L *ambitiōnem,* soliciting for votes, *ambīre* (*amb-,* about, *īre,* to go)]

ambivalence, -cy, *n.* the simultaneous existence in the mind of two incompatible feelings or wishes. **ambivalent,** *a.* [L *ambo,* both, *valens,* being worth]

amble, *v.i.* to move (as a horse or mule) by lifting the two feet on one side alternately with the two feet on the other; to ride an ambling horse; to move easily, or like an ambling horse. *n.* the pace described above; an easy pace; a pace like that of an ambling horse; a leisurely-walk, a stroll. **ambler,** *n.* an ambling horse; a person whose gait resembles that of an ambling horse. **ambling,** *a.* [OF *ambler,* L *ambulāre,* to walk]

amblyopia, *n.* dimness of vision. **amblyopic,** *a.* affected with or pertaining to amblyopia. [Gr. *ambluōpos,* a. (*amblus,* dull, *ōps ōpos,* eye)]

ambo, ambon, *n.* (*pl.* **ambos, ambones**) a pulpit or reading-desk in early mediaeval churches. [late L *ambo -ōnem,* Gr. *ambōn*]

amboyna-wood, *n.* the wood of *Pterospermum indicum,* which is finely variegated. [from name of island]

Ambrose, St, *n.* (*c.* 340–397), one of the early Christian leaders and writers known as the Fathers of the Church. He was bishop of Milan, Italy, and wrote on theological subjects. Feast day 7 Dec.

ambrosia, *n.* the fabled food of the gods; anything very pleasant to the taste or the smell; bee-bread; (**Ambrosia**) a genus of composite plants, allied to wormwood. **ambrosial,** *a.* containing the qualities of ambrosia; delicious,fragrant; ethereal, divine. **ambrosially,** *adv.* [Gr. *ambrosia,* fem. of a. *ambrosios,* from *ambrotos* (*a-,* not, *brotos,* mortal)]

Ambrosian, *a.* pertaining to St Ambrose or his teaching. **Ambrosian chant,** *n.* the plainsong of the Milanese liturgy.

ambry, aumbry, *n.*† a cupboard, a locker, a chest; a niche or cupboard in a church for books and sacred vessels; †a meat-safe, a store-closet. Also confused with *almonry,* e.g. *Almry* or *Ambry* Close, Westminster. [OF *armarie,* late L *armāria,* chest or cupboard, L *armārium* (*arma,* arms, tools, gear)]

ambs-ace, ames-ace, *n.* both aces, the lowest possible throw at dice; bad luck, misfortune, worthlessness. [OF *ambes as,* L *ambas as*]

ambulance, *n.* a moving hospital which follows an army in the field; a vehicle for the transport of wounded, injured or sick people. **ambulance-chaser,** *n.* (*coll.*) one who seeks to make profit from another's tragedy, grief etc., esp. a lawyer who offers to pursue a claim for damages on behalf of accident victims. [F *ambulance,* L *ambulans -ntem,* pres.p. of *ambulāre,* to walk]

ambulate, *v.i.* to walk about. **ambulation,** *n.* the act of walking. **ambulant,** *a.* walking or moving about; able to walk. [L *ambulat-,* part. stem of *ambulāre,* see prec.]

ambulatory, *a.* pertaining to walking; fitted for walking; not confined or confining to bed; movable, temporary. *n.* a place to walk in, such as a corridor or a cloister. [as prec.]

ambuscade, *n.* an ambush. a lying in wait to attack an enemy; the force placed in ambush. *v.i.* to lie in ambush; *v.t.* to place in ambush. [F *embuscade,* Sp. *emboscada* or It. *imboscata,* from late L *imboscāre* (see AMBUSH)]

ambush, *n.* the concealment of forces to entrap an enemy; the locality chosen; the force employed; any lying in wait. *v.t.* to place in ambush; to lie in wait for, to attack from ambush. *v.i.* to lie in wait. [OF *embusche,* from v. *embuscher,* late L *imboscāre,* to set in ambush (*in,* in, *boscus,* a bush, thicket)]

AMDG, (*abbr.*) to the greater glory of God. [L *ad majorem Dei gloriam*]

ameba AMOEBA.

ameer, amir, *n.* the title of several Muslim rulers in India and Afghanistan. [Arab. *amīr,* nobleman, prince (*amara,* he commanded)]

ameliorate, *v.t.* to make better; to improve. *v.i.* to grow better. **amelioration,** *n.* the act of making better; the state of being made better; improvement. **ameliorative,** *a.* **ameliorator,** *n.* [F *améliorer,* OF *ameillorer* (*à,* to, *meillorer,* from late L *meliōrāre,* from *melior,* better)]

amen, *int.* truly, verily; so be it; may it be as has been asked, said or promised. *n.* the word 'Amen', an expression of assent; a concluding word; a title applied to Christ. [L *āmēn,* Gr. *amēn,* Heb. *ā-mēn,* certainty, truth, certainly, verily (*āman,* to strengthen, confirm)]

amenable, *a.* liable to be called to account; answerable, liable; easy to lead, readily persuaded, tractable, responsive. **amenability,** *n.* the quality or state of being amenable; tractableness. **amenableness,** *n.* **amenably,** *adv.* [F *amener* (*à,* to, *mener,* to lead, bring, from late L *mināre,* from L *minārī,* to threaten)]

†**amenage,** *v.t.* to domesticate,tame. [OF *amenager* (*à,* to, *ménage,* see MANAGE)]

amend, *v.t.* to alter (a person or thing) for the better, to improve; to reform, to correct; to formally alter (a bill or resolution). *v.i.* to abandon evil courses, grow better. **amendable,** *a.* **amendment,** *n.* a change for the better; improvement in health; reformation; something added to a bill or motion; a correction of error in a writ or process. **amends,** *n.* reparation, satisfaction, compensation; †improvement in health. [OF *amender,* L *ēmendāre* (*e-, ex-,* out of, *menda,* fault)]

Amenhotep, *n.* four Egyptian pharaohs, including:

Amenhotep III, *n.* (*c.* 1400 BC–), king of Egypt who built great monuments at Thebes, including the temples at Luxor. Two portrait statues at his tomb were known to the Greeks as the colossi of Memnon; one was cracked, and when the temperature changed at dawn it gave out an eerie sound, then thought supernatural. His son **Amenhotep IV** changed his name to Ikhnaton.

amenity, *n.* the quality of being pleasant or agreeable; a feature or facility conducive to the attractiveness of something; (*pl.*) pleasing manners, civilities; attractions, charms. [L *amoenitātem* (*amoenus,* pleasant, allied to *amāre,* to love)]

amenorrhoea, *n.* the abnormal cessation of menstruation. [Gr. *a-,* not, *men,* a month, *rhoia,* flow]

ament[1]**, amentum,** *n.* (*pl.* **-ta**) a catkin. **amentaceous,** *a.* [L *amentum,* a thong or strap]

amentia, *n.* severe (congenital) mental deficiency. **ament**[2], *n.* a person with amentia. [L *a-, ab-,* from, *mens -tis,* mind]

Amer., (*abbr.*) America, American.

amerce, *v.t.* to punish by fine; to exact something from; to punish. **amercement,** †**amerciament,** *n.* the infliction of an arbitrary fine; the fine inflicted. **amerciable,** *a.* liable to amercement. [AF *amercier, à merci,* at the mercy of the court (*à,* at, *merci,* MERCY)]

America, *n.* the western hemisphere of the earth, containing the continents of North America and South America, with Central America in between. This great land mass extends from the Arctic to the Antarctic, from beyond 75° N to past 55° S. The area is about 42,000,000 sq km/16,000,000 sq miles, and the estimated population is over 500,000,000.

American, *a.* pertaining to the continent of America, esp. to the US. *n.* †an American Indian; a native or inhabitant of N, S or Central America; a citizen of the US; the English language as spoken in the United States. **American aloe,** *n.* the century plant. **American blight,** *n.* woolly aphis. **American football,** *n.* a football game somewhat resembling rugby, played with an oval ball and teams of 11 players. **American Indian,** *n.* see separate article, below. **American plan,** *n.* inclusive terms at a hotel etc. **Americanism,** *n.* attachment to or political sympathy with the US; anything characteristic of the US, esp. a word or phrase peculiar to or borrowed from the US. **Americanize, -ise,** *v.t.* to naturalize as an American; to assimilate political customs or institutions to those of the US. *v.i.* to become American in character, manners or speech.

American Ballet Theater, founded 1939 as 'Ballet Theater' with co-directors Lucia Chase and Richard Pleasant, then from 1945 Oliver Smith. Aiming to present the best of traditional along with the best of ballets with numerous guest celebrities, they established one of the best repertoires in the world.

American Civil War CIVIL WAR, AMERICAN.

American Independence, War of, the revolt (1775–83) of the British North American colonies that resulted in the establishment of the US. It was caused by colonial resentment at the contemporary attitude that commercial or industrial interests of any colony should be subordinate to those of the mother country, and the unwillingness of the colonists to pay for a permanent army.

American Indian, *n.*, an aboriginal of the Americas. They were called Indians by Columbus because he believed he had found, not the New World, but a new route to India. They are thought to have entered North America from Asia via the former landbridge, Beringia (from Siberia to Alaska), 60,000–35,000 BC.

American Samoa SAMOA, AMERICAN.

American System, the, in US history, a federal legislative programme following the War of 1812 that was designed to promote an integrated national economy. It introduced tariffs to protect US industry from foreign competition, internal improvements to the transport network, and a national bank to facilitate economic growth.

America's Cup, *n.* international yacht-racing trophy named after the US schooner *America*, owned by J. L. Stevens, who won a race around the Isle of Wight in 1851.

americium, *n.* an artificially-created, metallic radioactive element at. no. 95; chem. symbol Am.

Amerind, *n.* an American Indian. **Amerindian**, *a.* [contr. American Indian]

Ames, *n.* **Adelbert** (1880–1955), US scientist, who studied optics and the psychology of visual perception.

ames-ace AMBS-ACE.

amethyst, *n.* a violet-blue variety of crystalline quartz, supposed by the ancients to prevent intoxication. **amethystine**, *a.* composed of, containing or resembling amethyst. [L *amethystus,* Gr. *amethustos,* a remedy against drunkenness (*a-*, not *methuein,* to be drunken, from *methu,* strong drink)]

Amethyst Incident, *n.* UK–China episode arising when on 20 Apr. 1949 a British frigate, HMS *Amethyst*, sailing on the Chang Jiang River was fired on by communist Chinese forces. The ship was trapped for 14 weeks before breaking free and completing the journey to the sea. The temporary detention of this British vessel has been interpreted as an attempt by the Chinese to assert their sovereignty over what had been considered an international waterway.

Amhara, *n.* a person of Amhara culture from the central Ethiopian plateau. They comprise approximately 25% of Ethiopia's population. **Amharic,** *n.* the official language of Ethiopia. [*Amhara,* a province of Ethiopia]

amiable, *a.* friendly, kindly-disposed, lovable; possessed of qualities fitted to evoke friendly feeling. **amiably,** *adv.* **amiability,** *n.* [OF *amiable,* L *amicābilis* (AMICABLE), (confused with OF *amable,* L *amābilis,* lovable (*amāre,* to love)]

amiantus, amianthus, †**amiant,** *n.* a variety of asbestos, a fibrous kind of chrysotile of a greenish colour. **amianthoid**, *a.* resembling amianthus. *n.* a kind of asbestos. [L *amiantus,* Gr. *amiantos,* undefiled (*a-*, not, *miainein,* to stain)]

amic, *a.* of, pertaining to or derived from ammonia. [AM(MONIA)]

amicable, *a.* friendly; designed to be friendly; resulting from friendliness. **amicable suit,** *n.* (*Law*) a suit promoted by arrangement in order to obtain an authoritative decision on some point of law. **amicability**, *n.* **amicableness,** *n.* **amicably,** *adv.* [L *amicābilis* (*amicāre,* to make friendly, *amīcus,* friend)]

amice[1], *n.* a loose wrap; a vest or flowing garment; a square piece of white linen worn on the neck and shoulders at Mass by Roman Catholic priests. [early form, *amyte,* OF *amit,* L *amictus,* p.p. of *amicīre* (*amb-*, around, *jacere,* to cast)]

amice[2], *n.* a pilgrim's hood or cap, an ecclesiastical cape or other garment; a college badge or hood worn on the left arm by canons in France. [OF *aumuce,* Sp. *almucio* (perh. from Arab. *al-*, the, and G *Mütze,* cap)]

amicus curiae, *n.* (*pl.* **-ci curiae**) a disinterested counsellor. [L, friend of the court]

amid, amidst, *prep.* in the midst or middle; among. **amidships,** *adv.* in the middle part of a ship. [ME *amiddes,* OE *on middan,* in the middle (adverbial *s* is properly a sign of gen. case)]

Amida Buddha, *n.* the 'Buddha of immeasurable light'. Japanese name for **Amitābha**, the transhistorical Buddha venerated in Pure Land Buddhism, who presides over the Western Paradise where, through his infinite compassion, believers hope to be reborn.

amide, *n.* any of various organic compounds constituted as if obtained from ammonia by the substitution of one or more univalent organic acid radicals for one or more atoms of hydrogen; any of various compounds formed by substitution of another element or radical for an atom of hydrogen in ammonia. **amidic**, *a.* **amido-,** *comb. form.* containing the characteristic amide group of ammonia with one hydrogen atom replaced by an acid radical. [AM(MONIA), -IDE]

amidin, *n.* the soluble matter of starch; starch in solution. [F *amid-* (as in *amidon*), from L *amylum,* starch]

amidol, *n.* a compound of phenol used as a soluble crystalline powder in the development of bromide plates in photography. [AMIDON]

amidst AMID.

Amies, *n.* **Hardy** (1909–), British couturier, one of Queen Elizabeth II's dressmakers. Noted from 1934 for his tailored clothes for women, he also designed for men from 1959.

Amin Dada, *n.* **Idi** (1925–), Ugandan politician, president (1971–79). He led the coup that deposed Milton Obote in 1971, expelled the Asian community (1972), and exercised a reign of terror over his people. He fled when insurgent Ugandan and Tanzanian troops invaded the country 1979.

amine, *n.* any of various organic compounds derived from ammonia by the substitution of one or more univalent hydrocarbon radicals for one or more atoms of hydrogen. **aminic**, *a.* **amino**, *a.* containing the characteristic amine group of ammonia with one hydrogen atom replaced by a hydrocarbon radical. **amino acid,** *n.* an organic acid containing one or more amino groups, esp. any of those that occur as the constituents of proteins. [AM(MONIA), -INE]

amir AMEER.

Amis[1], *n.* **Kingsley** (1922–), English novelist and poet. His works include *Lucky Jim* (1954), a comic portrayal of life in a provincial university, and *Take a Girl Like You* (1960). He won the Booker Prize in 1986 for *The Old Devils*. He is the father of Martin Amis.

Amis[2], *n.* **Martin** (1949–), English novelist. His works include *The Rachel Papers* (1974) and *Money* (1984).

amiss, *a.* faulty, beside the mark, unsatisfactory, wrong. *adv.* wrongly, astray, in a faulty manner, unsatisfactorily. [MISS[2]]

amissibility, *n.* liability to be lost. **amission**, *n.* loss. [Fr. *amissibilité*]

amity, *n.* friendship, concord, mutual good feeling, friendly relations. [F *amitié,* late L *amīcitātem* (*amīcus,* friendly, from *amāre,* to love)]

Amman, *n.* capital and chief industrial centre of Jordan; population (1980) 1,232,600. It is an important communications centre, linking historic trade routes across the Middle East.

ammeter, *n.* an instrument for measuring the strength of the electric current in a circuit. [AM(PERE), -METER]

ammo, *n.* (*coll.*) short for AMMUNITION.

Ammon, *n.* in Egyptian mythology, the king of the gods, the equivalent of Zeus or Jupiter. The name is also spelt Amen/Amun, as in the name of the pharaoh Tutank*hamen*.

ammonal, *n.* an explosive composition containing aluminium mixed with charcoal and an oxidizing agent. [AMMONIA]

ammonia, *n.* a pungent volatile gas, powerfully alkaline, a compound of nitrogen and hydrogen first obtained from sal ammoniac; ammonium hydroxide. **ammonia water, aqueous ammonia, liquid ammonia,** *n.* ammonium hydroxide. **ammoniac, -acal,** *a.* pertaining to or possessing the properties of ammonia. **ammoniated,** *a.* combined with ammonia. **ammonify,** *v.t.* to treat or combine with (a compound of) ammonia. **ammonification**, *n.* **ammonium**, *n.* the ion or radical derived from ammonia by addition of a hydrogen ion or atom. **ammonium hydroxide,** *n.* a solution of ammonia in water. [adopted from L SAL AMMŌNIACUS, salt of Ammon, Gr. *ammōniakos,* of (Jupiter) Ammon; see sal ammoniac under SAL]

ammonite, *n.* the shell of a genus of fossil cephalopods, curved like the ram's horn on the statue of Jupiter Ammon. [med. L *cornu Ammonis,* horn of Ammon]

ammonium AMMONIA.

ammunition, *n.* military stores or supplies; (now only) powder, shot, shell etc.; offensive missiles generally. *v.t.* to supply with ammunition. *a.* for ammunition. **ammunitioned,** *a.* provided with ammunition. [F *amunition* (MUNITION), formed by vulgar confusion of *la munition* with *l'amunition*]

amnesia, *n.* loss of memory. **amnesiac**, **amnesic**, *n.* a person suffering from amnesia. *a.* pertaining to amnesia. **amnestic**, *a.* [Gr. *amnēsia*]

amnesty, *n.* an act of oblivion, passed after an exciting political period; a general overlooking or pardon. *v.t.* to grant amnesty to. [L from Gr. *amnēstia,* from *amnēstos,* forgotten (*a-*, not, *mna-omai,* I remember)]

Amnesty International, *n.* human-rights organization established in the UK in 1961 to campaign for the release of political prisoners worldwide. It is politically unaligned. Nobel prize 1977.

amniocentesis, *n.* the removal ofa sample of amniotic fluid from the womb, by insertion of a hollow needle, in order to test for chromosomal abnormalities in the foetus. [Gr. AMNION, *kentesis,* pricking, puncture]

amnion, *n.* (*pl.* **-ions, -nia**) the innermost membrane with which the foetus in the womb is surrounded. **amnios**, *n.* the fluid of the rudimentary embryo-sac. **Amniota**, *n.pl.* the group of vertebrates (reptiles, birds and mammals), which possess an amnion in the foetal state. **amniotic**, *a.* pertaining to, characterized by, contained in or of the nature of an amnion. **amniotic fluid,** *n.* the fluid contained by the amnion in which the foetus is suspended. [Gr., caul, dim. of *amnos,* a lamb]

amoeba, (*N Am.*) **ameba,** *n.* (*pl.* **-bas, -bae**) a microscopic organism of the simplest structure, consisting of a single protoplasmic cell, which is extensile and contractile, so that the shape is continually changing. **amoeban,** *a.* amoebic; answering alternately; antiphonal. **amoebic,** *a.* amoeba-like, caused by an amoeba. **amoebiform**, *a.* amoeba-like; varying in shape, protean. **amoeboid**, *a.* amoeba-like. [Gr. *amoibē,* change]

amok AMUCK.

among, amongst, *prep.* mingled with, in the number of; in the midst of; surrounded by. [ME *amonges,* OE *onmang, on gemange* (*on,* prep., *gemang,* crowd) in a crowd, allied to *mengan,* to mingle]

amontillado, *n.* a kind of medium dry sherry. [Sp.]

amoral, *a.* not concerned with morals, non-moral. **amoralism,** *n.* **amoralist,** *n.* a non-moral person. [Gr. *a-*, not, MORAL]

amoret, *n.* a sweetheart; a paramour; a love-knot; a love-poem; (*pl.*) dalliance. [OF *amorete,* dim. of *amour,* love (L *amōr-*, *amāre,* to love)]

amorist, *n.* a lover, a gallant, a philanderer; one who makes a study of love.

Amorites, *n. pl.* ancient people of Semitic or Indo-European origin, who were among the inhabitants of Canaan at the time of the Israelite invasion. They provided a number of Babylonian kings.

amorous, *a.* naturally inclined to love; in love; lecherous; relating to, or belonging to, love. **amorously,** *adv.* **amorousness,** *n.* [OF *amoros,* L *amōrōsus* (cp. AMORET)]

amorphous, *a.* shapeless; irregularly shaped; (*Biol.*) not conforming to a normal standard; not crystalline, uncrystallized; ill-arranged, unsystematic, unorganized. **amorphism,** *n.* lack of regular form; absence of crystallization. **amorphousness,** *n.* the quality of being amorphous. [Gr. *amorphos,* shapeless (*a-*, not, *morphē,* form)]

†**amort,** *a.* lifeless, inanimate. *adv.* in a state of death or depression. [F *à la mort,* to the death, corrupted to *all amort* (ALAMORT)]

amortize, -ise, *v.t.* to deaden, to destroy; †to kill; to alienate in mortmain; to extinguish by a sinking fund. **amortization, -isation,** *n.* the act or the right of alienating lands in mortmain. [F *amortir,* to bring to death, possibly from a late L *admortīre* (*ad-*, to, *mortem,* death)]

Amos, *n.* book of the Old Testament or Jewish Bible written *c.* 750 BC. One of the prophets, Amos was a shepherd who foretold the destruction of Israel because of the people's abandonment of their faith.

amount, *v.i.* to run into an aggregate by the accumulation of particulars; to mount up (to), to add up (to); to be equivalent (to); †to ascend, as a hill. *n.* the sum total, effect, substance, result, significance; a (numerical) quantity. [OF *amonter* (*a mont,* to a mountain, L *ad montem*)]

amour, *n.* a love affair; an affair of gallantry; an amorous intrigue. **amourette,** *n.* (F, dim. of *amour*) a petty love affair. [OF *amur, amour,* L *amōr -em,* love]

amour propre, *n.* (*F*) self-esteem. [F dim. of *amour*]

amp, *n.* short for AMPERE, AMPLIFIER.

Ampelopsis, *n.* a genus of vine-creeper, including the Virginia creeper. [Gr. *ampelos,* vine; *opsis,* appearance]

ampere, *n.* a unit by which an electric current is measured; the current sent by 1 volt through a resistance of 1 ohm. **ampere-hour,** *n.* the quantity of electricity delivered in 1 hour by a 1-ampere strength current. **amperemeter** AMMETER. **ampere turn,** *n.* the product of the number of turns in the coil of wire of an electromagnet and the number of amperes flowing through. **amperage,** *n.* the strength of an electric current measured in amperes. [the F physicist André M. *Ampère,* 1775–1836]

Ampère's rule, *n.* rule developed by André Ampère connecting the direction of an electric current and its associated magnetic currents. Travelling along a current-carrying wire in the direction of the current (from the positive to the negative terminal of a battery), and facing a magnetic needle, the north pole of the needle is deflected to the left-hand side.

ampersand, *n.* the sign '&'. [a corruption of *and per se,* 'and' by itself makes 'and']

amphetamine, *n.* (a derivative of) a synthetic drug which has a stimulant action on the brain. [*a*lpha, *m*ethyl, *ph*enyl, *e*thyl, *amine*]

amphi- *comb. form* both, of both kinds, on both sides, around, e.g. *Amphibia, amphibrach, amphitheatre.* [Gr. *amphi,* prep., on both sides]

Amphibia, *n.pl.* a class of vertebrate animals, between reptiles and fishes, which in their early stage breathe by gills; (**amphibia**) animals which can live either on land or water. **amphibian,** *n.* any amphibious animal, an animal of the Amphibia; an aircraft, tank or other vehicle adapted for both land and water. *a.* pertaining to the Amphibia; amphibious. **amphibious,** *a.* capable of living both on land and in water; designed for operation on land and in water; pertaining to or trained for the invasion of foreign shores via the sea; of mixed nature. **amphibiousness,** *n.* [Gr. *amphibia,* sing. *amphibios,* living in both elements (AMPHI-, *bios,* life)]

amphibiology, *n.* the department of science which treats of the Amphibia. **amphibiological**, *a.*

amphibole, *n.* any of a group of minerals including hornblende and tremolite. **amphibolite**, *n.* a rock consisting essentially of amphibole. **amphibolitic**, *a.*

amphibology, *n.* ambiguous expression, a sentence susceptible of two interpretations; ambiguity; equivocation. **amphibological**, *a.* **amphibologically,** *adv.* [F *amphibologie,* late L *amphibologia* (L *amphibolia*), Gr. *amphibolia* (AMPHI-, *ballein,* to throw), -LOGY]

amphiboly, *n.* a fallacy occurring when a sentence, composed of unambiguous words, is itself susceptible of a double meaning. **amphibolous,** *a.* doubtful, ambiguous. [AMPHIBOLOGY]

amphibrach, *n.* a metrical foot of three syllables, the middle one long and the first and third short, as *in-hū-*

man. [Gr. *amphibrachus,* (*brachus,* short)]

Amphictyons, *n.pl.* delegates from 12 of the states of ancient Greece, forming an assembly or council. **Amphictyonic,** *a.* of or pertaining to the Amphictyons. **Amphictyony,** *n.* the council of amphictyons; a confederation of states for common benefit. [Gr. *amphiktuones* (AMPHI-, *ktuones*), dwellers about, neighbours]

amphigam, *n.* one of the lower cryptogams, having no distinct sexual organs. [F *amphigame,* Gr. *gamos,* marriage]

amphigory, amphigouri, *n.* a meaningless rigmarole, a verse-composition containing no sense. [F *amphigouri*]

amphimacer, *n.* a metrical foot consisting of three syllables, one short between two long. [G. *amphimakros* (*makros,* long)]

amphimixis, *n.* sexual reproduction; the fusion of gametes. [Gr. *mixis,* a mingling]

Amphioxus, *n.* a genus of lancelets with one species, a lancelet. [Gr. *oxus,* sharp]

Amphipoda, *n.pl.* an order of sessile-eyed Crustacea, having two kinds of feet, one for walking and one for swimming. **amphipod,** *a.* amphipodous. *n.* any animal of the Amphipoda. **amphipodous,** *a.* [Gr. *pous podos,* foot]

amphiprostyle, *n.* a temple having a portico at each end. [F from L *amphiprostylus,* Gr. *amphiprostulos* (*prostulos,* PROSTYLE)]

amphisbaena, *n.* a fabled snake said by the ancients to have two heads, and to be able to move in either direction; a serpentiform genus of lizards, having the tail short and blunt. [Gr. *amphisbaina* (*amphis,* both ways, *bainein,* to go)]

amphitheatre, *n.* an oval or circular building with rows of seats rising one above another round an open space; a place of public contest; a semicircular gallery in a theatre; a valley surrounded by hills. **amphitheatrical,** *a.* [Gr. *amphitheatron* (see AMPHI-, THEATRE)]

amphitryon, *n.* a host; the giver of a banquet. [from the foster-father of Heracles in classical legend]

amphora, *n.* an ancient two-handled vessel for holding wine, oil etc.; an ancient liquid measure containing about 6 gallons. (27·3 l) among the Romans, and about 9 gallons (41 litres) among the Greeks. **amphotic,** *a.* (*Med.*) resembling the sound made by blowing into an amphora. [L *amphora,* Gr. *amphoreus* (*phoreus,* a bearer, from *pherein,* to bear)]

amphoteric, *a.* of two (opposite) kinds; able to react as both an acid and a base. [Gr. *amphoteros,* each of two]

ample, *a.* of large dimensions; wide, great, fully sufficient, liberal. **ampleness,** *n.* **amply,** *adv.* [F *ample,* L *amplus*]

amplexicaul, *a.* (*Bot.*) embracing or clasping the stem. [L *amplexus,* p.p. of *amplector,* I embrace, *caulis,* a stem]

amplexifoliate, *a.* having leaves which embrace the stem. [as prec.]

ampliate, *v.t.* to enlarge, extend, amplify. **ampliative,** *a.* enlarging a simple conception. [L *ampliāre* (see AMPLE)]

amplify, *v.t.* to enlarge or dilate upon; to increase, make greater; to increase the strength of (a signal), esp. the loudness of (sound). *v.i.* to speak or write diffusely; to expatiate. **amplification,** *n.* enlargement or extension; diffuseness; increase in strength of a signal or sound; an enlarged representation. **amplifier,** *n.* a complete unit which performs amplification of signals; an electrical or electronic circuit or system to amplify signals. [L *amplificare* (see AMPLE)]

amplitude, *n.* extent, size, bulk; greatness, abundance; dignity; the angular distance ofa heavenly body, at its rising or setting, from the east or the west point of the horizon; the magnitude of the variation from a main position or value of a vibration or oscillation, or of an alternating current or wave. **amplitude modulation,** *n.* (transmission of a signal by) modulation of the amplitude of a radio carrier wave in accordance with the characteristics of the signal carried; broadcasting using this system of transmission. [L *amplitudo* (see AMPLE)]

ampoule, *n.* a sealed phial containing one dose of a drug. [F]

ampulla, *n.* (*pl.* **-llae**) a nearly globular flask with two handles, used by the ancient Romans; a vessel for holding consecrated oil, wine etc.; (*Biol.*) the dilated end of any vessel; a spongiole of a root. **ampullaceous,** *a.* resembling a globular flask; bottle-shaped; swelling. [L]

amputate, *v.t.* to cut off from an animal body. **amputation,** *n.* the act of amputating. **amputator,** *n.* [L *amputātus,* p.p. of *amputāre* (*amb-,* about, *putāre,* to prune, lop)]

amrita, *n.* the ambrosia of the gods in Hindu mythology. [Sansk.]

Amritsar, *n.* industrial city in the Punjab, India; population (1981) 595,000. It is the holy city of Sikhism, with the Guru Nanak University (named after the first Sikh guru) and the Golden Temple from which armed demonstrators were evicted by the Indian army under Gen. Dayal in 1984, 325 being killed. Subsequently, Indian prime minister Indira Gandhi was assassinated in reprisal. In 1919 it was the scene of the Amritsar Massacre. **Amritsar Massacre,** *n.* (also called **Jallianwallah Bagh massacre**) the killing of 379 Indians (and wounding of 1200) in Amritsar in the Punjab 1919, when British troops under Gen. Edward Dyer (1864–1927) opened fire without warning on an angry crowd of some 10,000, assembled to protest against the arrest of two Indian National Congress (see CONGRESS PARTY) leaders.

Amsterdam, *n.* capital of the Netherlands; population (1988) 1,031,000. Canals cut through the city link it with the North Sea and the Rhine, and as a port it is second only to Rotterdam. There is shipbuilding, printing, food processing, banking and insurance.

amt, (*abbr.*) amount.

AMU, (*abbr.*) atomic mass unit.

amuck, amok, *adv.* in **to run amuck,** to attack indiscriminately, actuated by a frenzied desire for blood; hence to run wild or headlong. [Malay *amoq,* engaging furiously in battle]

amulet, *n.* anything worn about the person as an imagined preservative against sickness, witchcraft etc. [F *amulette,* L *amulētum,* a talisman]

Amundsen, *n.* **Roald** (1872–1928), Norwegian explorer who in 1903–06 was the first person to navigate the Northwest Passage. Beaten to the North Pole by Peary in 1910, he reached the South Pole ahead of Scott in 1911.

Amur, *n.* river in E Asia. Formed by the Argun and the Shilka, the Amur enters the Sea of Okhotsk. At its mouth at Nikolaevsk it is 16 km/10 miles wide. For much of its course of over 4400 km/2730 miles it forms, together with its tributary, the Ussuri, the boundary between the USSR and China.

amuse, *v.t.* †to divert with false promises, beguile; to divert attention from serious business by anything entertaining; to please with anything light and cheerful; to entertain. **amusement,** *n.* that which amuses; play, diversion; excitement of laughter; the state of being amused. **amusement arcade,** *n.* a covered space containing coin-operated game and gambling machines. **amusing,** *a.* entertaining, diverting, laughable. **amusingly,** *adv.* **amusive,** *a.* affording entertainment; tending to excite laughter; tending to amusement. [OF *amuser,* to cause to muse (*à,* to, *muser,* to stare), see MUSE]

amygdalic, *a.* pertaining to plants of the genus *Amygdalus;* obtained from almonds. **amygdalin,** *n.* a crystalline substance extracted from bitter almonds, and found amorphous in the leaves of the cherry laurel. **amygdaloid,** *a.* almond-shaped. *n.* an igneous rock containing almond-shaped nodules of some mineral. [L *amygdala,* Gr. *amugdalē,* an almond, -IC]

amyl, *n.* a monovalent alcohol radical. **amylaceous,** *a.* pertaining to or of the nature of starch. **amylase,** *n.* any of various enzymes that break down starch and glycogen. **amylene,** *n.* a hydrocarbon, with anaesthetic properties. **amyloid,** *a.* resembling or containing

starch; starchy. *n.* a non-nitrogenous starchy substance. [L *amylum,* starch]
an[1],, *a.* [A, AN]
†**an**[2], *conj.* if. [AND]
an., (*abbr.*) in the year. [L ANNO]
an-, *pref.* (1) on, as in *anent, anon;* (2) AD- before *in,* as in *annex, announce;* (3) see ANA-; (4) A-, not, as in *anaesthetic, anarchy.*
-an, *suf.* of, belonging to, pertaining to, e.g. *human, pagan, publican, Christian, Unitarian, European* etc. [L *-ānus* (sometimes through F *-ain,* retained in *captain, chaplain* or F *-en,* or through It., Sp. or Port. *-ano*)]
ana, *n.* literary gossip, usu. of a personal or local kind. [-ANA]
ana-, an-, *pref.* up, back, backwards; as in *anachronism, anagram, analogy, aneurism* again, as in *anabaptism.* [Gr. *ana,* upon, up, backwards]
-ana, -iana, *suf.* things about, sayings of, anecdotes concerning, objects relating to, as in *Boxiana, Tunbrigiana, Johnsoniana, Shakespeareana, Virgiliana.* [L *-āna,* neut. pl. of -ANUS]
anabaptism, *n.* a second baptism; the doctrine of the Anabaptists. **anabaptist,** *n.* one who rebaptizes; a member of a German sect which arose in the 16th cent. and advocated baptism only of adults and sought to establish utopian communities; applied (as a term of reproach) to the modern Baptists who adhere to this doctrine. *a.* of or pertaining to anabaptism. **anabaptistical,** *a.* [L *anabaptismus,* Gr. *anabaptismos* (see ANA-, BAPTISM)]
Anabas, *n.* a genus of fishes including the climbing perch that can leave the water. [Gr. *anabas,* part. of *anabainein* (ANA- *bainein,* to walk)]
anabasis, *n.* a military advance; the expedition of Cyrus the Younger into Asia, narrated by Xenophon. [Gr. *anabasis,* going up (*anabainein,* see prec.)]
anabatic, *a.* of wind or air currents, moving upwards. [Gr. *anabatikos,* ascending (*anabainein,* see ANABAS)]
anabolism, *n.* building up of complex substances by assimilation of nutriment, using energy. **anabolic,** *a.* **anabolic steroids,** *n.pl.* synthetic steroid hormones that cause rapid growth in body tissues, esp. skeletal muscle, and are sometimes (illegally) taken by athletes. [Gr. *anabolē,* rising up]
anabranch, *n.* (*Austral.*) a tributary rejoining the main stream of a river and thus forming an island.
anacharis, *n.* a N American waterweed which suddenly appeared in Britain in 1842, and spread with great rapidity. [Gr. *charis,* grace]
anachronism, *n.* the reference of an event, custom or circumstance to a wrong period or date; anything out of date or incongruous with the present. **anachronic,** *a.* wrong in date, characterized by anachronism. **anachronically,** *adv.* **anachronistic,** *a.* pertaining to or involving an anachronism. **anachronistically,** *adv.* [F *anachronisme,* L *anachronismus,* Gr. *anachronismos* (*anachronizein,* to refer to a wrong time)]
anaclastic, *a.* pertaining to refraction; produced by refraction. **anaclastic glasses,** *n.pl.* vessels with thin bottoms that spring in or out with a crackling sound as one sucks out the air or blows into them. **anaclastics,** *n.* the science which treats of refraction; dioptrics. [Gr. *anaklastos* (*klaein,* to bend)]
anacoluthon, *n.* (*pl.* **-tha**) want of sequence in a sentence; such a change of structure in a sentence as renders it ungrammatical. [Gr. *anakolouthon* (*an-,* not, *akolouthos,* following, from *keleuthos,* road)]
anaconda, *n.* a python from Sri Lanka; *Eunectes murinus,* a large S American boa; any large snake which kills its prey by constriction. [Sinhalese, *henakandāya*]
anacreontic, *a.* pertaining to the Greek poet Anacreon, or the metre used by him; erotic, convivial. *n.* an erotic or convivial poem. [L *Anacreonticus,* from Gr. *Anakreōn*]
anacrusis, *n.* (*pl.* **-ses**) an upward beat at the beginning of a verse, consisting of an unstressed syllable or syllables. [Gr. *anakrousis* (*krouein,* to strike)]
anadem, *n.* a garland or fillet; a chaplet or crown of flowers. [L *anadēma,* Gr. *anadēma* (*ana-, deein,* to bind)]
anadromous, *a.* of fish, ascending rivers to deposit spawn. [Gr. (*dromos,* running)]
anaemia, (*esp. N Am.*) **anemia,** *n.* want of blood, deficiency of blood; lack of haemoglobin or of red corpuscles. **anaemic,** *a.* of, relating to or suffering from anaemia; lacking vitality; pale. [Gr. *anaimia* (*an-* not, *haima,* blood)]
anaerobe, *n.* an organism that thrives best, or only, in the absence of oxygen. **anaerobic,** *a.* [Gr. *a-,* not, *aer,* air, *bios,* life]
anaesthesia, (*esp. N Am.*) **anesthesia,** *n.* loss of feeling; insensibility. **anaesthesis,** *n.* anaesthesia. **anaesthetic,** *a.* producing anaesthesia. *n.* a substance which produces anaesthesia (during surgical operations). **anaesthetically,** *adv.* by way of an anaesthetic, so as to cause anaesthesia. **anaesthetist,** *n.* one who administers an anaesthetic. **anaesthetize, -ise,** *v.t.* to administer an anaesthetic to. **anaesthetization, -isa'tion,** *n.* the process of effecting anaesthesia. [Gr. *anaisthēsia* (AN-, not, *aisthe-,* stem of *aisthanomai,* I feel)]
anaglyph, *n.* a figure cut or embossed in low relief. **anaglyphic, anaglyptic,** *a.* of or pertaining to an anaglyph; wrought in low relief. **anaglypta,** *n.* a type of thick white wallpaper with a heavily embossed pattern. **anaglyptics,** *n.pl.* the art of working in low relief. [Gr. *anagluphē* (*gluphein,* to carve)]
anagnorisis, *n.* recognition; the denouement in a drama. [L, from Gr. *anagnōrisis* (*gnōrizein,* to recognize)]
anagoge, -gogy, *n.* mystical, allegorical or spiritual interpretation; †spiritual enlightenment. **anagogic, -ical,** *a.* pertaining to anagoge; mysterious, elevated, spiritual. **anagogically,** *adv.* [L; Gr. *anagōgē* (*agein,* to lead)]
anagram, *n.* a word or sentence formed by transposing the letters of another word or sentence; †change, transposition. **anagrammatical,** *a.* of, pertaining to or containing an anagram. **anagrammatically,** *adv.* **anagrammatism,** *n.* the art or practice of making anagrams. **anagrammatist,** *n.* one who makes anagrams. **anagrammatize, -ise,** *v.t.* to transpose so as to form into an anagram. [F *anagramme,* Gr. *anagramma* (*graphein,* to write)]
anal, *a.* pertaining to or situated near the anus.
anal., (*abbr.*) analogous, analogy; analyse, analysis.
analects, analecta, *n.pl.* †crumbs which fall from the table; literary gleanings; **(Analects)** the most important of the four books that contain the teachings and ideas of Confucianism. **analectic,** *a.* [L, from Gr. *analekta* (*legein,* to gather)]
analeptic, *a.* restorative, increasing the strength. *n.* a restorative medicine. [Gr. *analēptikos* (*lambanein,* to take)]
analgesia, *n.* loss of sensibility to pain. **analgesic,** *n.* a drug that relieves pain. *a.* insensible to pain. [Gr., painlessness]
analogous, *a.* presenting some analogy or resemblance. **analogously,** *adv.* [L *analogus* Gr. *analogos* according to proportion]
analogue, (*esp. N Am.*) **analog,** *n.* an analogous word or thing; a parallel; an anatomical part which agrees with another in function, but not in origin. *a.* pertaining to information having a continuous range of values; measuring or displaying information on a continuous scale. **analogue computer,** *n.* a computer in which directly measurable, varying physical quantities, as current or voltage, represent the numbers on which arithmetical operations are to be performed. [F *analogue,* Gr. *analogon* (see ANALOGOUS)]
analogy, *n.* similitude of relations, conformity, similarity; reasoning from a parallel case; the relation between anatomical parts agreeing in function but not in origin; (*Math.*) proportion, or the similitude of ratios; imitation of existing words or linguistic patterns in forming new words, inflectional forms etc. **analogic, -ical,** *a.* of, pertaining to, or involving analogy. **analogically,** *adv.* **analogist,** *n.* one who is occupied with analogy. **analogize, -ise,** *v.t.* to represent or explain by analogy. *v.i.* to reason from analogy. [L *analogia,*

Gr. *analogia* (*logos,* word, relation, proportion, whence *logia*)]

analyse, (*esp. N Am.*) **analyze,** *v.t.* to take to pieces, resolve into the constituent elements; to examine minutely; to determine the elements of a chemical compound; (*Lit.*) to examine critically; to resolve a sentence into its grammatical elements; to psychoanalyse. **analysable,** *a.* **analysand,** *n.* one undergoing psychoanalysis. **analyser,** *n.* one who or that which analyses; (*Optics*) an apparatus in the polariscope exhibiting the fact that the light has been polarized. [F *analyser,* v. from n. *analyse,* analysis (L, from Gr. *analusis* (*luein,* to loosen); or direct from n. *analyse*)]

analysis, *n.* (*pl.* **-ses**) the process of analysing; separation into constituent elements; resolution of a chemical compound into its elements to ascertain composition, purity etc.; resolution of mathematical problems by reducing them to equations. [Gr. *analusis*]

analyst, *n.* one who analyses; a psychoanalyst.

analytic, -ical, *a.* pertaining to analysis; resolving anything into its constituent parts; using separate words instead of inflections. **analytical geometry,** *n.* geometry that uses coordinates to determine the position of a point. **analytically,** *adv.* **analytics,** *n.* the science of analysis.

anamnesis, *n.* (*pl.* **-ses**) recollection; the doctrine of recollection of a previous existence; a patient's medical history. **anamnestic,** *a.* [Gr. *anamnēsis,* remembrance (*anamimnēskein,* to remember)]

anamorphosis, *n.* a distorted projection of any object so contrived that if looked at from one point of view, or reflected from a suitable mirror, it will appear properly proportioned; (*Bot.*) degeneration causing change of appearance; abnormal alteration of form. [Gr. *anamorphōsis,* n. of *anamorphoein,* to transform (*morphē,* form)]

ananas, anana, *n.* the pineapple plant or its fruit. [Port. *ananás,* Guaraní *anānā* (*s* mistaken for pl.)]

Ananda, *n.* (5th cent. BC), favourite disciple of the Buddha. At his plea, a separate order was established for women. He played a major part in collecting the teachings of the Buddha after his death.

anandrous, *a.* lacking stamens. [Gr. *anandros,* without a husband (*an-,* priv., *anēr andros,* male)]

anapaest, (*esp. N Am.*) **anapest,** *n.* a metrical foot consisting of three syllables, the first two short and the third long, a reversed dactyl. **anapaestic,** *a.* composed of anapaests. *n.* an anapaestic line or verse. [L *anapaestus,* Gr. *anapaistos,* reversed (*paiein,* to strike)]

anaphora, *n.* the commencement of successive sentences or clauses with the same word or words; use of a word, such as a pronoun, to refer to a preceding word or phrase without repetition; the rising of the constellations of the Zodiac by the daily course of the heavens. **anaphoric,** *a.* pertaining to anaphora; referring to a preceding word or phrase. **anaphorically,** *adv.* [L, from Gr. *anaphorē,* a carrying back (*pherein,* to bear)]

anaphrodisiac, *n.* an agent abolishing or decreasing sexual desire. [AN-[4]; Gr. *aphrodisiakos,* venereal]

anaphylaxis, *n.* a condition of increased or extreme sensitivity to a foreign substance introduced into the body following previous contact. **anaphylactic,** *a.* [ANA-; Gr. *phulassein,* to guard]

anaplasty, *n.* plastic surgery. **anaplastic,** *a.* [Gr. *anaplastos,* that can be moulded]

anaptotic, *a.* becoming uninflected again (a term applied to languages, English for example, in which the inflections have been replaced by particles). [Gr. *ana-,* again, *aptōtos,* indeclinable; or *ana,* back, *ptotikos* (see APTOTE)]

anarch, *n.* (*poet.*) a promoter of anarchy or leader of revolt. [Gr. *anarchos,* without a ruler (*an-,* without, *archos,* ruler)]

anarchy, *n.* absence of government; want of settled government; disorder, lawlessness; political anarchism or the utopian society resulting from this. **anarchic, -ical,** *a.* **anarchically,** *adv.* **anarchism,** *n.* the principles of anarchy; a theory of government based on the free agreement of individuals rather than on submission to law and authority. **anarchist,** *n.* one who aims at producing anarchy; one opposed to all forms of government, a supporter of anarchism. [Gr. *anarchia,* as prec.]

anarthrous, *a.* without the (Greek) article; (*Physiol.*) without joints. [Gr. *an-,* without, *arthron,* joint]

anasarca, *n.* dropsy in the cellular tissue. **anasarcous,** *a.* puffy, affected with anasarca. [Gr. *ana,* up, *sarx sarca,* flesh]

Anastasia, *n.* (1901–1918), Russian Grand Duchess, youngest daughter of Nicholas II. She was murdered with her parents but it has been alleged that Anastasia escaped. Those who claimed her identity included Anna Anderson (1902–1984). Alleged by some to be a Pole, Franziska Schanzkowski, she was rescued from a Berlin canal 1920. The German Federal Supreme Court found no proof of her claim in 1970.

anastatic, *a.* raised, in relief; with the characters or illustrations in relief. **anastatic-printing,** *n.* a process in which copies of engravings etc. are printed from facsimiles produced in relief on zinc plates. [Gr. *anastatos,* caused to stand up (*ana,* up, *sta-,* stand)]

anastigmat, anastigmat lens, *n.* a lens free from astigmatism, which refers every point on the scene accurately to a corresponding point image. **anastigmatic,** *a.* free from astigmatism. [Gr. *stigmē,* a dot]

anastomose, *v.i.* to communicate by anastomosis; to interosculate, to intercommunicate. *v.t.* to join by anastomosis. **anastomosed,** *a.* joined by anastomosis. **anastomosis,** *n.* (*pl.* **-ses**) the uniting of vessels, such as veins, arteries, sap-vessels etc., by connecting branches; the surgical joining of two hollow parts. **anastomotic,** *a.* of or pertaining to anastomosis; (*Med.*) tending to remove obstructions from vessels. *n.* a medicine which removes obstructions from vessels. [F *anastomoser,* v. from mod. L *anastomōsis,* from Gr. *anastomoein,* to provide with a mouth (*stoma*)]

anastrophe, *n.* inversion of the natural order of the words in a sentence or clause. [Gr. (*ana,* back, *strephein,* to turn)]

anat., (*abbr.*) anatomical, anatomy.

anathema, *n.* (*pl.* **-mas, -mata**) the formal act by which a person or thing is cursed, excommunication; the person or thing cursed; a curse, denunciation; an object of loathing; a thing consecrated to sacred use. **anathematize, -ise,** *v.t.* to excommunicate, to curse, to put under a ban. *v.i.* to curse. [L, an excommunicated person, from Gr. *anathema* (*ana,* up, *tithēmi,* I put)]

anathema maranatha, *n.* an intensified imprecation. [Syriac *māran ethā,* the Lord has come, I Cor. XVI. 22 (connected by early criticism with the preceding *anathema*)]

anatomy, *n.* the art of dissecting an organized body so as to discover its structure, and the make-up, arrangement and inter-relation of its parts; the science of the structure of organized bodies; treatise on the science or art of anatomy; the act of dissecting; †a subject, or any part of a subject, for dissection; †a model of a dissected body; the physical structure of an animal or plant or of one of its parts; a skeleton; a withered, emaciated person; a minute examination, reduction to parts or elements, analysis. **anatomic, -ical,** *a.* pertaining to or connected with anatomy. **anatomically,** *adv.* **anatomize, -ise,** *v.t.* to dissect; to make a dissection of; to examine minutely, analyse. **anatomist,** *n.* one who practises or is skilled in anatomy. [F *anatomie,* L *anatomia,* Gr. *anatomia,* abstract n. (*anatomē,* cutting up, from *temnein,* to cut)]

anatta, anatto, annatto, *n.* an orange-red dye from Central America, used to colour cheese. [? native Am.]

Anaximander, *n.* (610–*c.* 547 BC), Greek astronomer and philosopher. He is thought to have been the first to determine solstices and equinoxes, to have invented the sundial, and to have produced the first geographical map. He believed that the universe originated as a formless mass (*apeiron,* 'indefinite') containing within itself the contraries of hot and cold, and wet and dry, from which land, sea and air were formed out of the union and separation of these opposites.

anbury, ambury, *n.* a soft wart on a horse's neck; the disease called 'fingers and toes' in turnips. [? OE *ang-*, pain (cp. AGNAIL), BERRY]

anc., (*abbr.*) ancient.

ANC, (*abbr.*) African National Congress.

-ance, *suf.* noting state or action, as *distance, fragrance, parlance, riddance*. [F *-ance,* L *-antia* and *-entia*]

ancestor, *n.* one from whom a person is descended; a progenitor; an organism of low type from which others of higher type have been developed. **ancestral**, *a.* pertaining to ancestors; derived from or possessed by ancestors. **ancestress**, *n. fem.* a female ancestor. **ancestry**, *n.* a line of ancestors; high birth, honourable lineage; ancient descent. [OF *ancestre,* L *antecessor,* one who goes before (*ante,* before, *cēdere,* go)]

anchithere, *n.* an extinct animal, between the palaeothere and the horse. [Gr. *anki,* near, *thērion,* a wild beast]

anchor, *n.* a heavy hooked iron instrument dropped from a ship to grapple the bottom and prevent drifting; anything shaped like an anchor; something that holds an object in place; a source of security or confidence. *v.t.* to secure by means of an anchor; to fix firmly. *v.i.* to come to anchor; to take up a position; to settle, rest, to sit down. **at anchor,** held by an anchor; at rest. **to cast anchor,** to drop the anchor into the sea; to fix one's self. **to weigh anchor,** to raise the anchor preparatory to sailing. **anchor-ground,** *n.* ground for anchoring. **anchor-hold,** *n.* the hold which an anchor takes. **anchor-ice,** *n.* ground ice, formed at the bottom of lakes, rivers or the sea. **anchorman, woman,** *n.* in sport, the last team member to compete, esp. in a relay race; a television or radio broadcaster who introduces and links the various reports etc. making up a (news) programme. **anchor-watch,** *n.* a watch set on board ship whilst at anchor; the people composing such a watch. **anchored,** *a.* held by an anchor; firmly fixed; applied to a heraldic cross, the extremities of which are bent back like the flukes of an anchor. **anchorless**, *a.* without an anchor or firm hold; drifting. [OE *ancor,* L *ancora,* Gr. *agkūra,* an anchor]

anchorage, *n.* a place suitable for anchoring in; the hold on the sea-bottom by an anchor; duty paid for permission to anchor; a source of security.

Anchorage, *n.* port and largest town of Alaska, US, at the head of Cook Inlet; population (1984) 244,030. Established in 1918, Anchorage is an important centre of administration, communication and commerce. Industries include salmon canning, and coal and gold are mined.

anchorite, anchoret, *n.* a religious recluse, a hermit; one of the early Christianrecluses; a person of solitary habits. **anchoress, ancress**, *n.* a female anchorite. **anchoritic, -ical**, **anchoretic, -ical**, *a.* pertaining to an anchorite, or a reclusive life. [F *anachorète,* L *anachōrēta,* Gr. *anachōrētēs (ana-, chōreein,* to withdraw, retire)]

anchovy, *n.* a small fish, *Engraulis encrasicholus* of the herring family, caught in the Mediterranean, pickled for exportation, and used in sauces etc. **anchovy pear,** *n. Grias cauliflora,* a W Indian fruit, which is eaten as a pickle. **anchovy-toast,** *n.* toast spread with anchovies. [Sp. *anchova,* perhaps Basque *anchua,* a dried fish]

anchylose, ankylose, *v.t.* to stiffen (a joint) by anchylosis; to consolidate (two separate bones). *v.i.* to become stiff; to grow together. **anchylosis, ankylosis**, *n.* the formation of a stiff joint by the union of bones or fibrous tissue; the coalescence of two bones. [Gr. *ankulōsis,* stiffening of joints, from *ankuloein,* to crook (*ankulos,* crooked)]

ancient[1], *a.* of or belonging to long past time; past, former, esp. of the times before the Middle Ages, that is before the end of the Western Empire, (AD 476); very old; antiquated. *n.pl.* those who lived in former (esp. Classical) times. **the Ancient of Days,** the Deity. **ancient history,** *n.* history of ancient times, esp. to the end of the Western Empire, AD 476; (*coll.*) information, gossip etc. that is widely known. **ancient lights,** *n.pl.* windows that have acquired by long usage (not less than 20 years) the right to light from adjoining property. **anciently,** *adv.* in ancient times; of old; in a very old-fashioned manner. **ancientness,** *n.* the quality or state of being ancient. †**ancientry,** *n.* ancientness; ancestry. [OF *ancien,* late L *antiānus,* old (*ante,* before), -AN, assim. to -ENT]

ancient[2], *n.* (*Hist.*) a flag, a standard; a standard-bearer, an ensign. [corr. of ENSIGN]

ancillary, *a.* subservient, subordinate; auxiliary, supplementary; pertaining to female servants. *n.* one who assists or supplements [L *ancillāris* (*ancilla,* a maid)]

ancipital, *a.* (*Biol.*) having two sharp edges. **ancipitous,** *a.* †doubtful; (*Bot.*) ancipital. [L *anceps -ipitis,* two-headed (*an-*, AMBI-, *caput -itis,* head)]

†**ancle** ANKLE.

ancon, *n.* (*pl.* **-nes**) the elbow; the corner or quoin of a wall, cross-beam or rafter; a bracket, a console; a support to a cornice; a breed of sheep with short legs. [L, from Gr. *akōn,* a bend]

Ancona, *n.* a strain of laying poultry. [town in Italy]

ancress ANCHORITE.

-ancy, *suf.* expressing quality or state, e.g. *constancy, elegancy, infancy, vacancy*. [-ANCE]

and, *conj.* the copulative which joins words and sentences; plus; †if, whether, as if, though. [OE *and, ond, end,* cp. OHG *anti* (cognate with L *ante,* before, Gr. *anti,* against); OE *and-*, over against as in *andswarian,* answer; *and,* and if, was often shortened to *an*]

Andalusia, *n.* (Spanish **Andalucía**) fertile autonomous region of S Spain, including the provinces of Almería, Cádiz, Córdoba, Granada, Huelva, Jaén, Málaga, and Seville; area 87,300 sq km/33,698 sq miles; population (1986) 6,876,000. Málaga, Cádiz and Algeciras are the chief ports and industrial centres. The Costa del Sol on the south coast is famous for its tourist resorts, including Marbella and Torremolinos.

Andaman and Nicobar Islands, two groups of islands in the Bay of Bengal, between India and Burma, forming a Union Territory of the Republic of India; area 8300 sq km/3204 sq miles; population (1981) 188,000. The economy is based on fishing, timber, rubber, fruit and rice. The Andamans consist of five principal islands (forming the Great Andaman), the Little Andaman, and about 204 islets; area 6340 sq km/2447 sq miles; population (1981) 158,000. They were used as a penal settlement 1857–1942. The Nicobars, consisting of 19 islands (7 of which are uninhabited), are 120 km/75 miles south of Little Andaman; area 1953 sq km/754 sq miles; population (1981) 30,500. The main items of trade are coconut and areca nut. They were British, 1869–1947.

andante, *adv., a.* (*Mus.*) moderately slow. *n.* a moderately slow movement or piece. **andante affettuoso,** *adv.* (*Mus.*) slowly and tenderly. **andante con moto**, *adv.* slowly but with movement. **andante grazioso,** *adv.* slowly and gracefully. **andante maestoso,** *adv.* slowly and majestically. **andante sostenuto,** *adv.* slow, but sustained. **andantino**, *adv., a.* rather quicker than andante. *n.* a movement or piece of this character. [It.]

Andean Group, *n.* (Spanish **Grupo Andino**) S American organization aimed at economic and social cooperation between member states. It was established under the Treaty of Cartagena (1969), by Bolivia, Chile, Colombia, Ecuador and Peru; Venezuela joined in 1973, but Chile withdrew in 1976. The organization is based in Lima, Peru.

Andean Indian, *n.* indigenous inhabitant of the Andes Mountains in S America. The Incas extended their control over much of the Andean region, 1200–1525. Pachacuti (1438–1463), the ninth Inca and first emperor, imposed the Quechua language in order to unify the different conquered groups. It is now spoken by over 10,000,000 people, and is a member of the Andean-Equatorial family.

Andersen, *n.* **Hans Christian** (1805–1875), Danish writer. His fairy tales such as 'The Ugly Duckling', 'The Emperor's New Clothes', and 'The Snow Queen', gained him international fame and have been translated into many languages.

Anderson[1], *n.* **Carl David** (1905–), US physicist, who discovered the positive electron (positron) in 1932; he shared a Nobel prize in 1936.

Anderson[2], *n.* **Elizabeth Garrett** (1836–1917), the first English woman to qualify in medicine. Refused entry into medical school, Anderson studied privately and was licensed by the Society of Apothecaries in London in 1865. She was physician to the Marylebone Dispensary for Women and Children (later renamed the Elizabeth Garrett Anderson Hospital), now staffed by women and serving women patients.

Anderson[3], *n.* **Marian** (1902–), US contralto, whose voice is remarkable for its range and richness. She toured Europe (1930), but in 1939 she was barred from singing at Constitution Hall, Washington, DC, because she was black. In 1955 she sang at the Metropolitan Opera, the first black singer to appear there. In 1958 she was appointed an alternate delegate to the United Nations.

Anderson[4], *n.* **Sherwood** (1876–1941), US writer of sensitive, experimental and poetic stories of small-town Midwestern life, *Winesburg, Ohio* (1919).

Anderson shelter, *n.* an air-raid shelter formed of arched corrugated steel. [Sir J. *Anderson,* 1882–1958, Home Secretary, 1939–40]

Andes, *n. pl.* the great mountain system or *cordillera* that forms the western fringe of S America, extending through some 67° of latitude and the republics of Colombia, Venezuela, Ecuador, Peru, Bolivia, Chile and Argentina. The mountains exceed 3600 m/12,000 ft for half their length of 6500 km/4000 miles. Most of the individual mountains are volcanic, with some still active.

Andhra Pradesh, *n.* state in E central India. **area** 276,800 sq km/106,845 sq miles. **capital** Hyderabad. **towns** Secunderabad. **products** rice, sugar cane, tobacco, groundnuts and cotton. **population** (1981) 53,404,000. **languages** Telugu, Urdu, Tamil.

andiron, *n.* a horizontal bar raised on short legs, with an ornamental upright in front, placed on each side of the hearth to support logs in a wood fire; a fire-dog. [OF *andier*]

Andorra, *n.* Principality of (*Principat d'Andorra*), landlocked country in the E Pyrenees, bounded to the north by France and to the south by Spain. **area** 470 sq km/181 sq miles **capital** Andorra-la-Vella. **physical** mountainous, with narrow valleys. **exports** main industries tourism and smuggling. **population** (1988) 51,400 (25% Andorrans, 75% immigrant Spanish workers). **language** Catalan (official) 30%; Spanish 59%, French 6%. **religion** Roman Catholic.

André, *n.* **Carl** (1935–), US sculptor, a minimalist, who often uses industrial materials and basic geometrical forms. An example is the notorious *Equivalent VIII* (1976), a simple rectangle of bricks (Tate Gallery, London).

Andrea del Sarto, *n.* (Andrea d'Agnola) (1486–1531), Italian Renaissance painter active in Florence, one of the finest portraitists and religious painters of his time. His style is serene and noble, characteristic of High Renaissance art.

André le Chapelain, *n.* (Latin **Andreas** *Capellanus*), 12th cent. French priest and author. He wrote *De Arte Honest Amandi/The Art of Honest Love*, a seminal work in courtly love literature, at the request of Marie de France, while he was chaplain at her court in Troyes, E France.

Andress, *n.* **Ursula** (1936–), Swiss actress specializing in glamour leads. Her international career started with *Dr No* (1962). Other films include *She* (1965), *Casino Royale* (1967), *Red Sun* (1971), and *Clash of the Titans* (1981).

Andrew[1], *n.* a body-servant, a valet. [personal name]

Andrew[2], St, *n.* New Testament apostle, martyred on an X-shaped cross (**St Andrew's cross**). He is the patron saint of Scotland. Feast day 30 Nov.

Andrew[3], *n.* (full name **Andrew Albert Christian Edward**) (1960–), prince of the United Kingdom, duke of York, second son of Queen Elizabeth II. He married Sarah Ferguson in 1986. They have two daughters, Princess Beatrice (b. 1988) and Princess Eugenie (b. 1990). He is a naval helicopter pilot.

Andrews, *n.* **John** (1813–1885), Irish chemist, who conducted a series of experiments on the behaviour of carbon dioxide under varying temperature and pressure. In 1869 he introduced the idea of a critical temperature: 30.9° C in the case of carbon dioxide, beyond which no amount of pressure would liquefy the gas.

Andrić, *n.* **Ivo** (1892–1974), Yugoslavian novelist and nationalist. He became a diplomat, and was ambassador to Berlin (1940). *Na Drini ćuprija/The Bridge on the Drina* (1945) is an epic history of a small Bosnian town. Nobel prize 1961.

andr(o)-, *comb. form.* pertaining to the male sex, or to male flowers. [Gr. *anēr andros,* a man, a male]

Androcles, *n.* traditionally, a Roman slave who fled from a cruel master into the African desert, where he withdrew a thorn from the paw of a crippled lion. Recaptured and sentenced to combat a lion in the arena, he found his adversary was his old friend. The emperor Tiberius was said to have freed them both.

androecium, *n.* (*pl.* **-cia**) the stamens of a flower collectively. [Gr. *aner,* a man, *oikion,* a house]

androgen, *n.* a male sex hormone; any substance with male sex hormone activity. **androgenic,** *a.*

androgyne, *n.* a hermaphrodite; an effeminate man; an androgynous plant. **androgynous,** *a.* presenting the characteristics of both sexes in the same individual; bearing both stamens and pistils in the same flower or on the same plant. **androgyny,** *n.* hermaphroditism, the presence of male and female organs in one individual. [F *androgyne,* L *androgynus,* Gr. *androgunos,* male and female in one (*gunē,* woman)]

android, *n.* a robot having human form. [Gr. ANDR(O)-, -OID]

Andromache[1], *n.* in Greek mythology, the faithful wife of Hector and mother of Astyanax. After the fall of Troy she was awarded to Neoptolemus, Achilles' son; she later married a Trojan seer called Helenus. Andromache is the heroine of Homer's *Iliad* and the subject of a play by Euripides.

Andromache[2], *n.* tragedy by Euripides, first produced about 426 BC. Hermione, wife of Neoptolemus, seeks revenge on Andromache, her husband's lover, whom she blames for her own childlessness, but fails in her attempt to kill Andromache and her son. Neoptolemus is murdered by Orestes, a former suitor of Hermione.

Andromeda, *n.* a major constellation of the northern hemisphere, visible in autumn with as its main feature the Andromeda galaxy; a genus of heaths. **Andromeda Galaxy,** *n.* a galaxy 2.2 million light years away in the constellation of Andromeda, and the most distant object visible to the naked eye. It is the largest member of the Local Group of galaxies. Like the Milky Way, it is a spiral orbited by several companion galaxies but contains about twice as many stars. It is about 200,000 light years across. **andromed, andromede,** *n.* one of a system of meteors radiating from a point in the constellation Andromeda. [Gr. name of the daughter of Cepheus and Cassiopeia rescued by Perseus]

andropetalous, *a.* a term applied to flowers made double by the conversion of stamens into petals.

androphagous, *a.* man-eating, cannibal. [Gr. *androphagos* (*phagos,* eating, from *phagein,* to eat)]

Andropov, *n.* **Yuri** (1914–1984), Soviet communist politician, president (1983–84). As chief of the KGB (1967–82), he established a reputation for efficiently suppressing dissent.

androsterone, *n.* a male sex hormone occurring in the testes and in urine. [Gr. ANDR(O)-, *sterol* (as *cholesterol*)]

-androus, *suf.* having male organs or stamens, e.g. *diandrous, monandrous.* [L *-andrus,* Gr. *-andros,* male (*anēr andros,* man)]

ane, *n., a., pron.* (*Sc.*) one, a, an.

-ane, *suf.* forming adjectives, e.g. *humane, mundane, urbane;* names of hydrocarbons, *methane, pentane, hexane.* [L *-ānus,* cp. -AN; also formed to range with -ENE, -INE and -ONE in chemical terminology for hydrocarbons]

anecdote, *n.* the relation of an isolated fact or incident; a short, pithy narrative; a passage of private life. **anecdotage**, *n.* anecdotes collectively; garrulous old age (as if from DOTAGE). **anecdotal**, *a.* pertaining to or consisting of anecdotes. **anecdotic**, **-ical,** *a.* pertaining to anecdotes; in the habit of relating anecdotes. **anecdotist,** *n.* one given to relating anecdotes. [med. L *anecdota,* Gr. *anekdota,* things unpublished (*an-* not, *ekdotos,* published, from *ek-,* out, *didōmi,* I give)]

anechoic, *a.* free from echoes. [Gr. *an-,* not, *echoic* (ECHO)]

anele, *v.t.* to anoint with oil; to give the sacrament of extreme unction to. [ME *anelien,* OE *o-,* on, ME *elien,* to oil (*ele,* L *oleum,* oil)]

anelectric, *a.* †non-electric; parting readily with electricity. *n.* †a non-electric substance or body; a body which does not become electrified by friction.

anemia ANAEMIA.

anem(o)-, *comb. form.* wind. [Gr. *anemos,* wind]

anemograph, *n.* an instrument which automatically records the velocity and direction of the wind. **anemographic**, *a.* of or pertaining to an anemograph. [Gr.]

anemometer, *n.* an instrument for measuring the velocity of wind, a wind gauge. **anemometric**, *a.* **anemometry**, *n.* [Gr.]

Anemone, *n.* a genus of plants with brilliantly-coloured flowers; esp. *Anemone nemorosa,* sometimes called the wind-flower, common in Britain; (**anemone**) a plant or flower of this genus. See also SEA-ANEMONE under SEA. [Gr. *anemōnē,* wind-flower (*anemos,* wind)]

anemophilous, *a.* wind-fertilized; having the pollen carried away by the wind. [Gr. *philos,* loving]

anencephaly, *n.* a congenital defect in which part or all of the brain is missing. **anencephalic**, *a.* [Gr. *an-,* not, ENCEPHALON]

anent, *prep.* concerning, touching, in respect of. [OE *on-efen* (*on,* in, *efen,* even, equal), even with, on a level with]

-aneous, *suf.* belonging to, e.g. *extraneous, instantaneous.* [L *-āneus*]

aneroid, *a.* operating without liquid. *n.* an aneroid barometer. **aneroid barometer,** *n.* a barometer which measures the pressure of air by its action on a springy metallic box from which the air has been partially exhausted. [F *anëroide* (Gr. *a-,* priv., *nēros,* wet, -OID)]

anesthesia, anesthetic etc. ANAESTHESIA.

Aneto, Pico, *n.* highest peak of the Pyrenees mountains, rising to 3,400 m/11,052 ft in the Spanish province of Huesca.

aneurysm, aneurism, *n.* an abnormal dilatation in an artery, particularly of the aorta. **aneurysmal, -ismal**, *a.* [Gr. *aneurusma,* a widening (*an, ana,* up, *eurunein,* to widen, from *eurus,* wide)]

anew, *adv.* again; once again; afresh.

anfractuose, -tuous, *a.* winding, sinuous, tortuous. **anfractuosity**, *n.* circuitousness, tortuousness; a winding depression separating convolutions of the brain; intricacy. [L *anfractuōsus,* winding, L *anfractus* (*an-, ambi-,* around, *frangere,* to break)]

Angad, *n.* (1504–1552), Indian religious leader, second guru (teacher) of Sikhism (1539–52), succeeding Nanak. He popularized the alphabet known as *Gurmukhi,* in which the Sikh scriptures are written.

angary, angaria, *n.* (*Law*) the confiscation or destruction by a belligerent of neutral property, esp. shipping, subject to claim for compensation. [Gr. *angareia,* duty of a mounted courier]

angel, *n.* a messenger from God; a ministering spirit; a guardian or attendant spirit; a benign, innocent or adorable creature; a title applied to some ministers; an old English gold coin, orig. the *angel-noble,* varying in value from 33p upwards, and bearing the figure of the archangel Michael; a conventional representation of the heavenly messenger; (*coll.*) a financial backer, esp. of a theatrical production. **angels on horseback,** oysters rolled in bacon. **angel dust,** *n.* the hallucinogenic drug phencyclidine. **angel-fish,** *n.* a fish allied to the rays and sharks, named from the wing-like expansion of the pectoral fins; any of several brightly-coloured tropical fishes with laterally compressed bodies; a small tropical American fish with black and silver stripes, often kept in aquariums. **angel (food) cake,** *n.* a light sponge cake made with egg whites. †**angel-gold**, *n.* standard gold. **angel-noble** ANGEL. **angel-shot,** *n.* a kind of chain shot. **angel-water,** *n.* angelica-water, a perfume or cosmetic in which angelica was a chief ingredient. **angelhood,** *n.* **angelic**; **-ical,** *a.* resembling or of the nature of an angel. **angelic doctor,** *n.* title or epithet applied to St Thomas Aquinas. **angelically,** *adv.* **angelolatry,** *n.* angel-worship. **angelology**, *n.* the doctrine of angelic beings. [OE *ængel, engel,* L *angelus,* Gr. *angelos,* a messenger; soft *g* due to OF *angele*]

Angel Falls, *n.* highest waterfalls in the New World, on the river Caroní in the tropical rainforest of Bolivar Region, Venezuela; total height 978 m/3210 ft. Named after the aviator and prospector James Angel who flew over the falls and crash-landed nearby 1935.

Angelica, *n.* a genus of umbelliferous plants, including *arch-angelica,* used in medicine, and as a preserve or sweetmeat; (**angelica**) candied angelica root; (**angelica**) angelica-water. [med. L *herba angelica*]

Angelico, *n.* **Fra** (Guido di Pietro) (*c.* 1400–1455), Italian painter of religious scenes, active in Florence. He was a monk and painted a series of frescoes at the monastery of San Marco, Florence, begun after 1436. He also produced several altarpieces in a simple style.

Angelou, *n.* **Maya** (born Marguerite Johnson) (1928–), US novelist, poet, playwright and short-story writer. Her powerful autobiographical work, *I Know Why the Caged Bird Sings* (1970) and its sequels, tell of the struggles towards physical and spiritual liberation of a black woman growing up in the US South.

angelus, *n.* a short devotional exercise in the Roman Catholic Church in honour of the Incarnation; the angelus-bell. **angelus-bell,** *n.* a bell rung early in the morning, at noon, and in the evening, as a signal to say the angelus. [first word of opening, *Angelus domini*]

anger, *n.* rage, fierce displeasure, passion, excited by a sense of wrong; †physical pain, inflammation. *v.t.*to make angry, to excite to wrath; to enrage. *v.i.* to become angry. **angerly,** *adv.* angrily; like an angry person. **angry**, *a.* wrathful, expressing anger; hot-tempered, choleric; inflamed, painful; suggesting anger, threatening. **angrily,** *adv.* [Icel. *angr,* grief, sorrow]

Anger, *n.* **Kenneth** (1932–), US avant-garde film-maker, brought up in Hollywood. His films, which dispense with conventional narrative, often portray homosexual iconography and a personal form of mysticism. They include *Fireworks* (1947), *Scorpio Rising* (1964), and *Lucifer Rising* (1973).

anger-nail AGNAIL.

Angevin, *a.* relating to the reigns of the English kings Henry II, and Richard I (also known, with the later English kings up to Richard III, as the PLANTAGENETS); derived from Anjou, the region in France controlled by English kings at this time. The **Angevin Empire** comprised the territories (including England) that belonged to the Anjou dynasty.

angina, *n.* quinsy; angina pectoris. **anginal,** *a.* [L *angīna* (*angere,* to strangle)]

angina pectoris, *n.* a heart condition marked by paroxysms of intense pain due to over-exertion when the heart is weak or diseased. [L *pectoris,* of or in the chest]

angi(o)-, *comb. form.* vascular; pertaining to the vessels of organisms. [Gr. *angeion,* a vessel (dim. of *angos,* a chest)]

angiocarpous, *a.* having the fruit in an envelope not

constituting part of the calyx. [Gr. ANGI(o)-, *karpos,* fruit]

angiography, *n.* X-ray photography of the blood vessels. **angiograph**, **angiogram,** *n.* a photograph made by angiography.

angioma, *n.* (*pl.* **-mas, -mata**) a tumour composed of blood or lymph vessels. **angiomatous,** *a.*

angiosperm, *n.* a plant of the class Angiospermae, that has its seed enclosed in a vessel or ovary. **angiospermous**, *a.* having the seeds enclosed in an ovary. [Gr. L ANGI(O)-, *sperma,* seed]

Angle, *n.* member of a Germanic tribe that invaded Britain in the 5th century and settled in Northumbria, Mercia and East Anglia (see ANGLO-SAXON). **Anglian,** *a.* of or pertaining to the Angles. *n.* an Angle. [L *anglus,* OE *engle,* the people of *Angul,* district of Holstein, so-called from its shape (see ANGLE[2])]

angle[1], *n.* a fish-hook; a rod and line for fishing. *v.i.* to fish with rod and line; (*fig.*) to fish (for), to try to elicit, as a compliment; to get something by craft. *v.t.* to fish (a stream) with rod and line. †**angle-rod,** *n.* a fishing rod. **angler,** *n.* one who fishes with a rod. **angler-fish,** *n. Lophius piscatorius,* a small British fish which attracts its prey by filaments attached to its head. **angling,** *n.* the art or practice of fishing with a rod and line; trying to find out by craft. [OE *angel, ongul,* fish-hook (cp. L *oncus,* hook, Gr. *ankōn,* a bend)]

angle[2], *n.* a corner; the inclination of two lines towards each other; the space between the lines or planes inclined to each other; an angular projection; a point of view from which something is considered, an approach. *v.t.* to move, place, turn, direct at an angle; to present (a report, news story etc.) in a particular way or from a particular point of view. *v.i.* to proceed or turn at an angle. **angle of application,** the angle between the line along which a force is directed and the lever on which it acts. **angle of incidence,** the angle made by a ray of light meeting a surface and a line perpendicular to the surface. **angle of inclination,** the angle made by an inclined plane and the horizon. **angle of refraction,** the angle at which a ray of light is turned from its direct course in passing through a given medium. **angle of repose,** the slope at which a mass of loose material comes to rest if left to itself. **angle of vision,** the angle at which objects are seen and which determines their apparent magnitudes. **angle-bead,** *n.* a vertical bead, usually of wood, fixed to an exterior angle, flush with the plaster. **angle-iron,** *n.* an angular piece of iron used to strengthen framework of any kind. **anglemeter,** *n.* an instrument for measuring angles; a clinometer. **angle-staff**, ANGLE-BEAD. **angle-tie,** *n.* a piece of timber placed across an angle in roofing. **angle-wise,** *adv.* in the manner of an angle, angularly. **angled,** *a.* having an angle or angles; biased. [OF *angle,* L *angulum,* from same root as prec.]

angler ANGLE[1].

Anglican, *a.* English (as opposed to Roman); of or belonging to the Church of England or any church in communion with it. *n.* a member of the Anglican church. **Anglican Communion,** *n.* family of Christian churches including the Church of England, the US Episcopal Church, and those holding the same essential doctrines, that is the Lambeth Quadrilateral 1888 Holy Scripture as the basis of all doctrine, the Nicene and Apostles' Creeds, Holy Baptism and Holy Communion, and the historic episcopate. **Anglicanism,** *n.* the teachings and practices of the Anglican church. [med. L *Anglicānus,* from *Anglicus* (*Anglus,* ANGLE)]

anglice, *adv.* in English. [L]

Anglicism, *n.* an English idiom; an English custom or characteristic; English political principles; attachment to what is English. **Anglicist, Anglist,** *n.* a student or specialist in English language, literature or culture. **Anglicize, -ise,** *v.t.* to make English; to give an English form to; to turn into English. [L *Anglicus,* English]

Anglo-, *comb. form.* English; of or belonging to England or the English; partially English (the meaning completed by another word). [L *Anglus*]

Anglo-American, *n.* an American of English parentage or descent. *a.* of or belonging to such Americans, or to England and the US.

Anglo-Catholic, *a.* Catholic of the English communion; Anglican but of Catholic not Protestant tendencies. *n.* an English Catholic opposed to Romanizing principles; a High Church member. **Anglo-Catholicism,** *n.* Anglican Catholicism; the doctrine that the English church is a branch of the Catholic church but not of the Roman church.

Anglo-French, *a.* pertaining to England and France. *n.* the French language of mediaeval England.

Anglo-Indian, *n.* an English person born, or long resident, in India; a person of mixed British and Indian blood. *a.* of or belonging to such people, or to England and India.

Anglo-Irish, *a.* of or between Britain and N or S Ireland; of the Anglo-Irish people. *n.* Irish people of English Protestant descent.

Anglo-Irish Agreement, *n.* (also called *Hillsborough Agreement*) a concord reached in 1985 between the UK and Irish premiers, Margaret Thatcher and Garret FitzGerald. One sign of the improved relations between the two countries was increased cross-border cooperation between police and security forces across the border with Northern Ireland. However, the agreement was rejected by Northern Ireland Unionists as a step towards a renunciation of British sovereignty. In Mar. 1988 talks led to further strengthening of the agreement.

Anglo-Israelites, *n.pl.* a sect claiming that the English are the lost Ten Tribes.

Anglo-mania, *n.* excessive fondness for English manners and customs. **Anglo-maniac,** *n.*

Anglophile, -phil, *n.* an admirer of England or of the English. **Anglophilia,** *n.* **Anglophilic,** *a.*

Anglophobe, *n.* a hater of England or of the English. **Anglophobia,** *n.* fear or distrust of England.

Anglophone, *n.* a person who speaks English. *a.* of or belonging to an English-speaking nation.

Anglo-Saxon, *a.* of or belonging to the English race or language as distinct from Continental Saxons; of the whole English people before the Norman Conquest; of English people of Teutonic descent; of English-speaking people generally. *n.* one of several Germanic invaders (Angles, Saxons, and Jutes) who conquered much of Britain between the 5th and 7th cents. (see ANGLE, SAXON, JUTE, HEPTARCHY); Old English. **Anglo-Saxondom**, *n.* Anglo-Saxons collectively. **Anglo-Saxonism,** *n.* anything peculiar to the Anglo-Saxon race; belief in the superiority of the Anglo-Saxon race.

Anglo-Saxon art, *n.* the painting and sculpture of England from the 7th cent. to 1066. Sculpted crosses and ivories, manuscript painting, and gold and enamel jewellery survive. The relics of the Sutton Hoo ship burial (7th century) and the *Lindisfarne Gospels* (about 690) (both British Museum, London) have typical Celtic ornamental patterns, but in manuscripts of S England a different style emerged in the 9th century, with delicate, lively pen-and-ink figures and heavily decorative foliage borders.

Anglo-Saxon Chronicle, *n.*, a history of England from the Roman invasion to the 11th century, in the form of a series of chronicles written in Old English by monks, begun in the 9th century (during the reign of King Alfred), and continuing to the 12th century.

Angola[1], *n.* People's Republic of (*República Popular de Angola*) a country in SW Africa, bounded to the W by the Atlantic Ocean, to the N and NE by Zaïre, to the E by Zambia, and to the S by Namibia. **area** 1,246,700 sq km/481,226 sq miles. **capital** and chief port Luanda. **towns** Lobito and Benguela, also ports. **physical** elevated plateau, desert in the south. **exports** oil, coffee, diamonds, palm oil, sisal, iron ore, fish. **population** (1988 est) 9,387,000 (largest ethnic group Ovimbundu); annual growth rate 2.5%. **language** Portuguese (official); Umbundu,

Kimbundu. **religion** Roman Catholic 46%, Protestant 12%, animist 42%.

Angora, Angola[2], *n.* a goat with long silky hair; the hair itself, or a fabric made therefrom; a long-haired variety of the domestic cat; a breed of rabbit with long, fine fur; a yarn or fabric made from Angora rabbit hair. [*Angora* (a town in Asia Minor), L *Ancyra,* Gr. *Ankura*]

angostura, angustura, *n., a.* a febrifugal bark, used also in the preparation of bitters. [*Angustura,* a town on the Orinoco (now called Ciudad Bolivar)]

angry, angrily ANGER.

Angry Young Men, a group of British writers who emerged about 1950 after the creative hiatus which followed World War II. They included Kingsley Amis, John Wain, John Osborne and Colin Wilson. Also linked to the group were Iris Murdoch and Kenneth Tynan.

angst, *n.* a nonspecific feeling of anxiety and guilt produced esp. by considering the imperfect human condition. [G *Angst,* Dan. *anqst*]

Ångström, *n.* **Anders Jonas** (1814–1874), Swedish physicist, who worked in spectroscopy and solar physics. **Ångström unit,** *n.* a unit of length used to express the wavelengths of different kinds of radiations, equivalent to 1/254,000,000 in. (10^{-10}m).

Anguilla, *n.* island in the E Caribbean. **area** 160 sq km/ 62 sq miles. **capital** The Valley. **exports** lobster, salt. **population** (1988) 7000. **language** English and Creole.

anguine, *a.* pertaining to or resembling a snake; snaky. [L *anguīnus* (*anguis*)]

anguish, *n.* excessive pain or distress of body or mind. *v.t.* to afflict with extreme pain or grief. [OF *anguisse, angoisse,* the sense of choking, L *angustia,* tightness, narrowness (*angustus,* narrow; *angere,* to stifle, choke)]

angular, *a.* having angles or sharp corners; forming an angle; in an angle; measured by an angle; bony, lacking in plumpness or smoothness; stiff, formal, unaccommodating, crotchety. **angular party,** *n.* (*coll.*) one composed of an odd number of people. **angular velocity,** *n.* rate of rotation about an axis, measured by the angle turned through per unit time, usu. radians per second. **angularity**, *n.* **angularly,** *adv.* **angulate,** *a.* angular, formed with angles or corners. *v.t.* to make angular. **angulation,** *n.* the making of angles; angular form or structure. **angulose, -lous,** *a.* angular, having angles or corners. [L *angulāris* (*angulus,* ANGLE)]

Angus, *n.* former county and modern district on the E coast of Scotland, merged in 1975 in Tayside region.

angustifoliate, *a.* having the leaves narrow. [L *angustus,* narrow, *folium,* a leaf]

anharmonic, *a.* (*Math.*) not harmonic. [F *anharmonique* (Gr. *an-,* not, *harmonikos,* HARMONIC)]

anhelation, *n.* the act of panting; difficult respiration; (*fig.*) aspiration. [F *anhélation,* L *anhelatiōnem* (L *anhēlāre,* to pant)]

Anhui, *n.* (formerly **Anhwei**) province of E China, watered by the Chang Jiang (Yangtze river). **area** 139,900 sq km/54,000 sq miles. **capital** Hefei. **products** cereals in the north, and cotton, rice and tea in the south. **population** (1986) 52,170,000.

anhydride, *n.* a chemical substance formed from another, esp. an acid, by removing the elements of water. [ANHYDROUS]

anhydrite, *n.* a colourless, or thorhombic mineral, calcium sulphate, anhydrous gypsum.

anhydrosis, *n.* deficiency of perspiration.

anhydrous, *a.* having no water in the composition; esp. destitute of water of crystallization. [Gr. *anudros* (*an-,* not, *hudōr,* water)]

anigh, *adv., prep.* near; near to. [NIGH; formed in imitation of *adown, afar* etc.]

†anight, †anights, *adv.* at night, by night, of a night. [OE *on niht; on niht* and *nihtes* (adv. gen. sing.) have coalesced in *a-nights*]

anil, *n.* the indigo-plant; indigo. [F, from Sp. *añil,* Arab. *an-nīl* (*al-,* the *nīl,* from Sansk. *nīlī,* indigo, from *nīlas,* blue)]

anile, *a.* of or resembling an old woman; old-womanish; feeble-minded. **anility**, *n.* the state of being old-womanish, dotage. [L *anīlis* (*anus,* an old woman)]

aniline, *n.* a chemical base used in the production of many beautiful dyes, and originally obtained from indigo, now chiefly from nitrobenzene. [ANIL]

anima, *n.* (*Psych.*) a person's true inner self; the feminine aspect of the male personality. [L, mind, soul]

animadvert, *v.i.* to direct the attention to; to criticize or censure (with *on* or *upon*). **animadversion**, *n.* criticism, comment, censure, reproof. [L *animadvertere* (*animus,* the mind; *ad-,* to, *vertere,* to turn)]

animal, *n.* an organized being possessing life, sensation and the power of voluntary motion; one of the lower animals as distinct from humans, esp. a mammal or quadruped; a human being whose animal nature is abnormally strong, a brute; (*coll.*) a person, thing or organization. *a.* of, belonging to or derived from animals, their nature or functions; carnal; pertaining to animals as distinguished from vegetables or minerals. **animal charcoal,** *n.* charcoal made from animal substances. **animal flower,** *n.* an actinozoon, e.g. a sea-anemone. **animal food,** *n.* animal substances used as food. **animal-free,** *a.* not containing or using animal products. **animal heat, animal warmth,** *n.* the warm temperature characterizing the bodies of living animals. **animal husbandry,** *n.* the breeding and care of domestic animals. **animal kingdom,** *n.* animals generally, viewed as one of the three great divisions of natural objects. **animal liberation,** *n.* a movement aimed at securing animal rights. **animal magnetism,** *n.* the quality of being attractive esp. to members of the opposite sex; MESMERISM; power to sexually attract. **animal rights,** *n.* the bestowing on animals of various rights usu. attributed only to humans. **animal spirits,** *n.pl.* †nerve-force, the principle of sensation and volitional movement; animal courage; liveliness of disposition. **animalism,** *n.* the exercise of the animal faculties; the theory which views mankind as merely animal; sensuality. **animalist,** *n.* a believer in animalism; a supporter of animal rights. **animality**, *n.* animal nature; the phenomena of animal life, animal life as distinct from vegetable life. **animalize, -ise,** *v.t.* to make into an animal; to make into animal substance; to brutalize. **animalization, -isation,** *n.* the act or process of animalizing. **animally,** *adv.* physically, as opposed to intellectually; †with respect to the *anima,* psychically. [L, n. from neut. a. *animāle,* having breath (*anima,* breath)]

animalcule, animalculum, *n.* (*pl.* **-cules, -cula**) an animal so small as to be invisible to the naked eye. **animalcular,** *a.* pertaining or relating to animalcules. **animalculism,** *n.* the theory that animalcules are the germs of life and the cause of disease. **animalculist,** *n.* one who makes animalcules a special study; an adherent of animalculism. [L *animalculum,* dim. of *animal*]

animalism, animality ANIMAL.

animate, *v.t.* to give life or spirit to; to vivify, to inspire; to stir up; to give the appearance of movement to; to produce as an animated cartoon. *a.*, living, endowed with life; lively. **animated,** *part.a.* possessing life; full of life or spirits; vivacious, lively; moving as if alive. **animated cartoon,** *n.* a film produced by photographing a series of drawings or objects, each varying slightly in position from the preceding one, to give the illusion of movement. **animated graphics,** *n.pl.* computer graphics featuring moving pictures or shapes. **animated nature,** *n.* the animal kingdom. **animatedly,** *adv.* in a lively manner, vivaciously. **animating,** *a.* life-giving, quickening,inspiring. **animatingly,** *adv.* **animation,** *n.* the act of animating; state of being animated, vitality; life, vivacity; (the techniques used in the production of) an animated cartoon. **animative,** *a.* having the power to impart life or spirit. **animator,** *n.* an artist who prepares material for animated cartoons. [L *animātus,* p.p. of *animāre,* to give life to, -ATE]

animé, *n.* a West Indian resin, used for varnish; other resins. [F, animated, i.e. alive with insects]

animism, *n.* the doctrine that vital phenomena are produced by an immaterial soul distinct from matter; the attribution of a living soul to inanimate objects and to natural phenomena; a spiritual (not a materialist) theory of the universe. **animist,** *n.* a believer in animism. **animistic,** *a.* [L *anima*]

animosity, *n.* enmity tending to show itself in action. [F *animosité,* L *animōsitātem* (*animōsus,* spirited)]

animoso, *adv.* (*Mus.*) with spirit. [It.]

animus, *n.* spirit actuating feeling, usu. of a hostile character; animosity; the masculine part of the female personality. [L, mind, spirit, passion]

anion, *n.* (*Elec.*) an ion that moves towards the anode; a negatively charged ion. [Gr. *ana,* up, *iōn,* going]

anise, *n.* an umbelliferous plant, *Pimpinella anisum,* cultivated for its aromatic seeds, which are carminative, anciently confused with the dill. **aniseed,** *n.* the seed of the anise, used as a flavouring. **anisette,** *n.* a liqueur made from aniseed. [F, from L *anīsum,* Gr. *anison, anēthon,* anise, or dill]

aniso-, *comb. form.* odd, unequal, unsymmetrical. [Gr. *anisos,* unequal, uneven (*an-,* not, *isos,* equal)]

anisomeric, *a.* not isomeric; not having the same proportions. [Gr. *meros,* a part]

anisometric, *a.* of unequal measurement.

anisotropy, *n.* aeolotropy. **anisotropic,** *a.*

Ankara, *n.* (formerly **Angora**) capital of Turkey; population (1985) 2,252,000. Industries include cement, textiles and leather products. It replaced Istanbul (then in Allied occupation) as capital in 1923.

anker, *n.* a measure for wine and spirits of nearly 9 imperial gall. (41 l); a keg containing that quantity. [Dut.]

ankh, *n.* a keylike cross being the emblem of life, or male symbol of generation. [Egypt., life or soul]

ankle, *n.* the joint by which the foot is united to the leg; the part of the leg between foot and calf. **ankle-deep,** *a., adv.* so deep as to cover the ankles. **ankle-high,** *a., adv.* so high as to cover the ankles. **ankle-jacks,** *n.pl.* boots reaching above the ankles. **anklet,** *n.* a fetter, strap or band for the ankle; an ornamental chain or band worn round the ankle. [OE *anclēow,* perh. cogn. with Dut. *anklaauw* (cp. *klaaw,* claw); mod. *ankle* may be from OFris. *ankel,* Dut. *enkel* (cp. L *ang-,* bend, crook, root of *angulus*)]

ankus, *n.* an elephant goad. [Hind.]

ankylose, ankylosis ANCHYLOSE.

ann., (*abbr.*) annals; annual.

anna, *n.* a former monetary unit and coin of India, Burma and Pakistan, equal to one-sixteenth of a rupee. [Hind. *ana*]

Anna Comnena, *n.* (1083–after 1148), Byzantine historian, daughter of the emperor Alexius I, who was the historian of her father's reign. After a number of abortive attempts to alter the imperial succession in favour of her husband, Nicephorus Bryennius (*c.* 1062–1137), she retired to a convent to write her major work, the *Alexiad.* It describes the Byzantine view of public office, as well as the religious and intellectual life of the period.

Anna Karenina, *n.* a novel by Leo Tolstoy, published 1873–77. It describes a married woman's love affair with Vronski, a young officer, which ends with her suicide.

annals, *n.pl.* a narrative of events arranged in years; historical records; in the Roman Catholic Church, Masses said for the space of a year. **annalist,** *n.* one who writes annals. **annalistic,** *a.* [L *annāles* annual (*annus,* year)]

Annapurna, *n.* mountain 8075 m/26,502 ft in the Himalayas, Nepal. The north face was climbed by a French expedition (Maurice Herzog) in 1950 and the south by a British one in 1970.

annates, *n.pl.* the first year's revenue ofRoman Catholic ecclesiastics on their appointment to a benefice, paid to the Pope; (*Sc. Law*) the half-year's revenue of a deceased minister's incumbency due to the executors. [F *annate,* med. L *annāta,* fruits of a year (*annus* year)]

annatto ANATTA.

Anne[1], *n.* (full name **Anne Elizabeth Alice Louise**) (1950–), princess of the UK, second child of Queen Elizabeth II, declared Princess Royal 1987. She is an excellent horsewoman, winning a gold medal at the 1976 Olympics, and is actively involved in global charity work, especially for children. In 1973 she married Captain Mark Phillips (1949–), of the Queen's Dragoon Guards; they separated in 1989. Their son Peter (1977–) was the first direct descendant of the Queen not to bear a title. They also have a daughter Zara.

Anne[2], *n.* (1665–1714), queen of Great Britain and Ireland (1702–14). Second daughter of James, Duke of York, who became James II, and Anne Hyde. She succeeded William III on the throne in 1702. Events of her reign include the War of the Spanish Succession, Marlborough's victories at Blenheim, Ramillies, Oudenarde and Malplaquet, and the union of the English and Scottish parliaments in 1707. She was succeeded by George I.

Anne[3] **of Austria,** *n.* (1601–1666), queen of France from 1615 and regent (1643–61). Daughter of Philip III of Spain, she married Louis XIII of France and on his death became regent for their son, Louis XIV, until his majority.

Anne[4] **of Cleves,** *n.* (1515–1557), fourth wife of Henry VIII of England. She was the daughter of the Duke of Cleves, and was recommended to Henry as a wife by Thomas Cromwell, who wanted an alliance with German Protestantism against the Holy Roman Emperor. Henry did not like her looks, had the marriage declared void after six months, and pensioned her.

Anne[5] **of Denmark,** *n.* (1574–1619), queen consort of James VI of Scotland (later James I of Great Britain, 1603). She was the daughter of Frederick II of Denmark and Norway, and married James in 1589. Anne was suspected of Catholic leanings, and was notably extravagant.

anneal, *v.t.* †to bake, as tiles; †to enamel by encaustic process; to temper, as glass or metals, by subjecting them to intense heat, and then allowing them to cool slowly; (*fig.*) to temper; to render tough. **annealing,** *n.* the burning of metallic colours into glass etc.; the tempering of glass or metals etc. [OE *onælan* (*ælan,* to burn), whence ME *anelen,* later confused with OF *neeler,* to enamel, late L *nigellāre,* to blacken (*nigellus,* dim. of *niger,* black)]

annectent, *a.* connecting, linking. [L *annectere,* to knit or bind to]

Annelida, *n.pl.* a class of invertebrate animals, including the earthworm, with elongated bodies composed of annular segments. **annelid,** *n.* one of the Annelida. **annelidan,** *a.* of or pertaining to the Annelida. *n.* an annelid. [mod. L, F *annelés,* ringed, OF *annel,* ring, L *annelus,* dim. of *anulus,* ring]

annex, *v.t.* to unite to, add on to; to take possession of (as territory); to append as a condition, qualification or consequence; (*coll.*) to steal. **annexable,** *a.* able to be annexed. **annexation,** *n.* the act of annexing; something annexed (often with the idea of unlawful acquisition). **annexe, annex,** *n.* an appendix; a supplementary or subsidiary; building; (*Sc. Law*) an appurtenance. [F *annexer,* L *annexum,* p.p. of *annectere* (*ad-,* to, *nectere,* to bind)]

annihilate, *v.t.* to reduce to nothing; to blot out of existence; to destroy the organized existence of; to reduce to constituent elements or parts. *v.i.* (*Phys.*) to undergo annihilation. **annihilation,** *n.* the act of annihilating; the state of being annihilated; complete destruction of soul and body; the combining of an elementary particle and its antiparticle with the spontaneous transformation into energy. **annihilationism,** *n.* the doctrine that the wicked are annihilated after death. **annihilationist,** *n.* one who holds this doctrine. **annihilator,** *n.* FIRE-ANNIHILATOR. [L *annihilātus,* p.p. of *annihilāre* (*ad-,* to, *nihil,* nothing)]

anniversary, *a.* recurring at the same date in succeeding years. *n.* the annual return of any remarkable date;

the celebration of such annually recurring date. [L *anniversārius* (*annus,* year, *versus,* p.p. of *vertere,* to turn)]

Anno Domini, *phr.* in the year of our Lord (abbr. AD); reckoned from the Christian era. *n.* (*coll.*) old age. [L]

annotate, *v.t.* to make notes or comments upon. *v.i.* to write notes or comments. **annotation,** *n.* the act of annotating; an explanatory note. **annotator,** *n.* [L *annotātus,* p.p. of *annotāre,* (*ad-,* to, *notāre,* to mark)]

announce, *v.t.* to make known, to proclaim; to declare officially, or with authority; to make known the approach or arrival of. **announcement,** *n.* **announcer,** *n.* the person who announces the items of a broadcasting programme, reads news summaries etc. [OF *anoncer,* L *annuntiāre* (*ad-,* to, *nuntiāre,* to report, bear a message, *nuntius,* messenger)]

annoy, *v.t.* to tease, to molest, to trouble, to put to inconvenience by repeated or continued acts. *v.i.* to cause annoyance. †*n.* discomfort, vexation, annoyance. **annoyance,** *n.* the act of annoying; the state of being annoyed; that which annoys. **annoying,** *a.* **annoyingly,** *adv.* [OF *anoier, anuier,* to molest, annoy, from *anoi, anui,* annoyance, vexation, L *in odio,* in hatred]

annual, *a.* returning or happening every year; reckoned by, or done or performed in a year; (*Bot.*) lasting but a single year or season. *n.* a book published every year, a year-book; a plant which lives for a year only; in the Roman Catholic Church, an anniversary Mass for the dead. **annual ring,** *n.* a ring of wood seen in the cross-section of a plant stem or root, indicating one year's growth. †**annualist,** *n.* one who edits or writes for an annual. **annualize, -ise,** *v.t.* to adjust or calculate according to a yearly rate. **annually,** *adv.* year by year, yearly. [F *annuel,* late L *annuālis* (L *annālis,* years, from *annus,* year)]

annuity, *n.* a sum of money payable annually; an investment insuring fixed annual payments. **annuitant,** *n.* one who receives an annuity. [F *annuité,* med. L *annuitātem* (*annuus,* yearly)]

annul, *v.t.* (*past, p.p.* **annulled**) to render void, cancel, abolish; to destroy the validity of. **annulment,** *n.* the act of annulling; revocation; abolition. [OF *anuller,* late L *annullāre* (*ad-,* to, *nullus,* none)]

annular, *a.* ring-shaped, ringed. **annular eclipse,** *n.* an eclipse of the sun in which the silhouette of the moon obscures only the central portion of the sun's surface and leaves a ring of light showing round the moon. **annular space,** *n.* the ring-like space between an inner and an outer cylinder. **annularly,** *adv.* **annulate, -lated** *a.* wearing, marked, distinguished by or furnished with, rings; composed of rings or ring-like segments. **annulation,** *n.* the state of being annulate; ring-like structure or markings. **annulet,** *n.* a little ring; (*Arch.*) a small fillet encircling a column. **annulus,** *n.* (*pl.* **-li**) a ring-shaped structure or part. [L *annulāris* (*annulus,* ring, dim. of *ānus,* a round shape]

Annuloida, *n.pl.* one of Huxley's primary groups of animals, containing flukes, tape-worms and rotifers. **annuloid** *a.* ring-shaped; of or pertaining to the Annuloida *n.* any individual of the Annuloida. [as prec.]

Annulosa, *n.pl.* one of Huxley's primary groups of animals, containing those whose body is enclosed in a kind of external ringed skeleton. **annulose,** *a.* ringed; of or belonging to the Annulosa. [ANNULAR]

annunciate, *v.t.* to announce, proclaim approach or arrival; to bring tidings of. **annunciation,** *n.* the act of announcing; the announcement of the Incarnation made by the angel Gabriel to the Virgin Mary; the church festival (Lady Day, 25 March) in honour of that event. **annunciator,** *n.* one who or that which announces; an indicator for electric bells or telephones to show who has rung or spoken; an officer in the Greek church who gives notice of holy days. [ANNOUNCE]

annus mirabilis, *n.* (*pl.* **anni, mirabiles**) a remarkable year (usu.applied in English history to 1666, year of the Great Fire of London etc.). [L, year of wonders]

anode, *n.* the positive electrode or pole in an electrolytic cell; the negative electrode of a primary cell delivering current; the positive electrode which collects electrons in an electronic valve. **anode circuit,** *n.* the circuit that includes the anode and cathode in an electronic valve, as distinct from grid or filament heating circuits. **anode converter,** *n.* a rotary machine for supplying anode voltage. **anode current,** *n.* the current circulating in the anode circuit of an electronic valve. **anode rays,** *n.pl.* (*Radio*) rays of positively charged particles issuing from the anode of a thermionic valve. **anodal, anodic,** *a.* **anodize, -ise,** *v.t.* to give a protective surface coating of an oxide to (a metal) by making it the anode of an electrolytic cell. [Gr. *anodos,* a way up]

anodyne, *a.* assuaging pain; alleviating distress of mind, soothing to the feelings. *n.* a medicine which assuages pain; anything which alleviates distress of mind or soothes the feelings. [late L *anōdynus* Gr. *anōdunos* (*an-,* not, *odunē,* pain)]

anoint, *v.t.* to smear with oil or an unguent; esp. to pour oil on as a religious ceremony; to consecrate with oil; (*coll.*) to belabour, thrash soundly. **anointed,** *a.* smeared with oil or unguent; consecrated. *n.* a consecrated person. [OF *enoint,* anointed, p.p. of *enoindre* (L *in-, ungere,* to smear, p.p. *unctus*)]

anomaly, *n.* (an) irregularity; (a) deviation from the common or established order, abnormality; the angular distance of a planet or satellite from its last perihelion or perigee. **anomalistic,** *a.* irregular, abnormal. **anomalistic month,** *n.* the time in which the moon passes from perigee to perigee. **anomalistic year,** *n.* the time occupied by the earth (or other planet) in passing from perihelion to perihelion: it is slightly longer than a tropical or sidereal year. **anomalous,** *a.* deviating from rule; irregular, abnormal. **anomalously,** *adv.* **anomalousness,** *n.* [L *anōmalia,* Gr. *anōmalia,* unevenness, *anōmalos* (*an-,* not, *ōmalos* even)]

anomie, anomy, *n.* the breakdown or absence of moral and social standards in an individual or society. [F *anomie,* Gr. *anomia,* lawlessness (*a-,* priv., *nomos,* law)]

anomo-, *comb. form.* irregular, as in *anomocarpous, anomorhomboid.* [Gr. *a,* not, *nomos,* rule]

anon, *adv.* immediately, thereupon; soon after; in a little while. [OE *on ān,* in one moment]

anon., (*abbr.*) anonymous.

anonaceous, *a.* pertaining to the pineapple. [mod. L *anōna,* ANANAS]

anonymous, *a.* nameless; having no name attached; of unknown or unavowed authorship or origin; lacking distinctive characteristics, nondescript. **anonym,** *n.* a person whose name is not made known; a pseudonym. **anonymity,** *n.* **anonymized, -ised,** *a.* made anonymous. **anonymized screening,** *n.* the testing of unidentified (blood) samples, as for the presence of the HIV virus, without the patient's knowledge. **anonymously,** *adv.* **anonymousness,** *n.* [Gr. *anōnumos* (*an-,* not, *onoma,* name)]

Anopheles, *n.* a genus of mosquitoes including the malarial mosquito *Anopheles maculipennis.* [Gr.]

Anoplura, *n.* an order of parasitic insects including the human louse. [Gr.]

anorak, *n.* a warm waterproof jacket, usu. with a hood. [Greenland Eskimo *ánorâq*]

anorexia, *n.* loss of appetite; anorexia nervosa. **anorexia nervosa,** *n.* a psychological disorder characterized by an aversion to eating and fear of gaining weight. **anorectic,** *a.* suffering from anorexia (nervosa); causing loss of appetite. *n.* a substance that causes loss of appetite. **anorexic,** *a.* anorectic. *n.* a person suffering from anorexia (nervosa). [Gr. *orexis,* longing]

anosmia, *n.* absence of the sense of smell. **anosmatic,** *a.* lacking the sense of smell. [mod. L, from Gr. *an-,* priv., and *osmē,* smell]

another, *pron., a.* an other one, one more; one of the same kind; a different one; any other. **you're another,** (*sl., dated*) you are a liar, fool or rascal. **another place,** *n.* the other House (of Parliament).

†**another-guess,** *a.* of another sort or fashion. [corr. of *another-gates* or *another-gets,* of another gate or way]

anotta ANATTA.

Anouilh, *n.* **Jean** (1910–1987), French playwright. His plays, influenced by the neo-classical tradition, include *Antigone* (1942), *L'Invitation au château/Ring Round the Moon* (1947), *Colombe* (1950), and *Becket* (1959), about Thomas à Becket and Henry II.

anourous, *a.* destitute of a tail. [Gr. *an-*, not, *oura,* tail]

anoxia, *n.* deficiency of oxygen to the tissues. **anoxic,** *a.* [AN-, OXYGEN]

ansa, *n.* (*pl.* **ansae**) a handle on a vase; the parts of Saturn's rings which appear to extend like handles beyond the sphere. **ansate,** *a.* having a handle. [L, handle]

Anschluss, *n.* the union of Austria with Germany, accomplished by the German chancellor Hitler on 12 Mar. 1938. [G, annexation]

anserine, *a.* of or belonging to the goose; goose-like, stupid, silly. [L *anserīnus,* pertaining to a goose (*anser*)]

Ansermet, *n.* **Ernest** (1883–1969), Swiss conductor with Diaghilev's Russian Ballet (1915-23). In 1918 he founded the Swiss Romande Orchestra, conducting many first performances of Stravinsky.

ANSI, (*abbr.*) American National Standards Institution, the US national standards body. It sets official procedures in (amongst other areas) computing and electronics.

Anson, *n.* **George, 1st Baron Anson** (1697–1762), English admiral who sailed around the world (1740–44). In 1740 he commanded the squadron attacking the Spanish colonies and shipping in South America; he returned home by circumnavigating the world, with £500,000 of Spanish treasure; his chaplain's *Voyage Round the World* (1748) is a classic. He carried out reforms at the Admiralty.

answer, *n.* a reply to a charge, objection, appeal or question; a solution of a problem; something done in return; a practical reply; (*Law*) a counter-statement to a bill of charges. *v.t.* to reply or respond to; to be sufficient for or suitable to; to be opposite to; to solve. *v.i.* to reply, to respond; to suit, to correspond. **to answer back,** to reply rudely or cheekily. **to answer for,** to be responsible or answerable for. **to answer to,** to correspond, to suit; to accord, to own. **answerable,** *a.* liable to be called to account; capable of being answered; †correspondent. †**answerably,** *adv.* proportionally, correspondingly, conformably. **answerer,** *n.* one who answers (to a question etc.). [OE *andswaru,* a reply (*and-*, against, *swar-*, stem of *swerian,* to swear)]

ant., (*abbr.*) antonym.

ant, *n.* a small, social, hymenopterous insect of the family Formicidae. **ant-bear,** *n.* the giant ant-eater of S America; an aardvark. **ant-catcher** ANT-THRUSH. **ant-cow** APHIS. **ant-eater,** *n.* a genus of edentate mammals, with long extensile tongues, which they thrust into ant-hills and withdraw covered with ants; the porcupine ant-eater, an echidna; an aardvark; an ant-thrush. **ant-eggs,** *n.pl.* the popular name for the pupae of ants. **ant-fly,** *n.* a winged ant; a perfect male or female. **ant-hill,** *n.* the mound or hillock raised by a community of ants. **ant-lion,** *n.* a genus of neuropterous insects, the larvae of which construct a kind of pitfall for ants and other insects. **ant-thrush,** *n.* a tropical bird, allied to the thrush, which feeds chiefly on ants. **anting,** *n.* the placing by birds of ants in their plumage. [OE *æmette,* grad. contracted to *amte, ante, ant*]

an't AIN'T.

-ant, *suf.* forming adjectives, as *distant, elegant, trenchant;* denoting an agent, one who or thing which produces effect, as in *accountant, merchant.* [Lat. *-antem,* acc. sing. of pres.p. in *-ans*]

ant-, *pref.* against, as in *antagonist, Antarctic.* [ANTI-]

Antabuse®, *n.* brand name of disulfiram, a drug used in the treatment of alcoholism.

antacid, *a.* counteracting acidity. *n.* a medicine that counteracts acidity of the stomach.

antae, *n.pl.* square pilasters on each side of a door, or at the angles of a building. [L]

antagonist, *n.* an opponent; one who contends or strives with another; a muscle which counteracts another, and is in turn counteracted by it; a drug that counteracts the action of another or of a substance occurring naturally in the body. **antagonism,** *n.* opposition; conflict, active disagreement; (an) opposing force, action or principle. **antagonistic,** *a.* **antagonistically,** *adv.* **antagonize, -ise,** *v.t.* †to compete with, to contend against; to counteract, to make antagonistic, put in active opposition; to arouse hostility or opposition in. *v.i.* to act in opposition. [late L *antagōnista,* Gr. *antagōnistēs,* an adversary, from *antagōnizesthai, (ant-, anti-,* against, *agōnizesthai,* to struggle)]

Antakya, *n.* (or **Hatay**) city in SE Turkey, site of the ancient Antioch; population (1985) 109,200.

antalkali, *n.* something that neutralizes an alkali. **antalkaline,** *a.* counteracting the effect of an alkali. *n.* a medicine that counteracts the effect of an alkali.

Antalya, *n.* Mediterranean port on the W coast of Turkey and capital of a province of the same name; population(1985) 258,000. The port trades in agriculture and forest produce.

Antananarivo, *n.* (formerly **Tananarive**) capital of Madagascar, on the interior plateau, with a rail link to Tamatave; population (1986) 703,000.

antaphrodisiac, *a.* counteracting or preventing sexual desire. *n.* a medicine or agent that allays sexual desire.

Antarctic, *a.* opposite to the Arctic; southern; of or belonging to the S Pole or the region within the Antarctic Circle. *n.* Antarctica. **Antarctic Circle,** *n.* a parallel of the globe, 23° 28′ distant from the S Pole, which is its centre. **Antarctic Peninsula,** *n.* mountainous peninsula of W Antarctica extending *c.* 1930 km/1200 miles N toward South America. Originally named Palmer Land after a US navigator, Captain Nathaniel Palmer, who was the first to explore the region in 1820. Claimed by Britain (1832), Chile (1942) and Argentina (1940), its name was changed to the Antarctic Peninsula in 1964. [ME *antartik,* OF *antartique,* L *antarcticus* (ANT-, ARCTIC)]

Antarctica, *n.* the Antarctic continent. **area** 13,727,000 sq km/5,300,000 sq miles. **physical** the continent, once part of Gondwanaland, is a vast plateau, of which the highest point is the Vinson Massif in the Ellsworth mountains, 5139 m/16,866 ft high. The Ross Ice Shelf is formed by several glaciers coalescing in the Ross Sea, and Mount Erebus on Ross Island is the world's southernmost active volcano. There is less than 50 mm/2 in. of rainfall a year (less than the Sahara). Little more than 1% is ice-free, the temperature falling to –70°C/–100°F and below, and in places the ice is 5000 m/16,000 ft deep, comprising over two-thirds of the world's fresh water. Each annual layer of snow preserves a record of global conditions, and where no melting at the surface of the bedrock has occurred the ice can be a million years old. It covers extensive mineral resources, including iron, coal, and with indications of uranium and other strategic metals, as well as oil. There are only two species of flowering plants, plus a number of mosses, algae and fungi. Animal life is restricted to visiting whales, seals, penguins and other seabirds. Fossils of apes resembling humans have been found. **population** settlement is limited to scientific research stations with changing personnel.

Antarctic Treaty, *n.* agreement signed in 1959 between 12 nations with an interest in Antarctica (including Britain), and today with 35 countries party to it. It came into force in 1961 for a 30 year period. Its provisions (covering the area S of latitude 60°S) neither accepted nor rejected any nation's territorial claims, but barred any new ones; imposed a ban on military operations and large-scale mineral extraction, and allowed for free exchange of scientific data from bases. Since 1980 the Treaty has been extended to conserve marine resources within the larger area bordered by the Antarctic Convergence.

Antares, *n.* brightest star in the constellation of Scorpius. It is a red supergiant several hundred times larger than the Sun, lies about 400 light years away, and fluctuates slightly in brightness. It is the 15th brightest star in the sky.

antarthritic, *a.* tending to prevent or relieve gout. *n.* a medicine which prevents or relieves gout.

antasthmatic, *a.* tending to prevent or relieve asthma. *n.* a medicine which prevents or relieves asthma.

ante, *n.* the stake which a poker-player puts down after looking at his cards, but before drawing; (*coll.*) amount paid, price. *v.t.* to stake; to pay. **to up the ante,** to increase the (asking) price or cost. [L, before]

ante-, *pref.* before. [L prep. and adv.]

antebellum, *a.* existing before the war, esp. the American Civil War. [L *ante,* before, *bellum,* war]

antecede, *v.t.* to precede; to go before or in front of. **antecedence,** *n.* a going before in point of time; precedence, anteriority; (*Astron.*) an apparent motion contrary to the true motion. **antecedent,** *a.* going before in time, prior, anterior, presumptive, a priori. *n.* that which goes before; the word to which a relative pronoun refers; the conditional clause of a hypothetical proposition; the first term of a mathematical ratio; (*pl.*) past circumstances. **antecedently,** *adv.* **antecessor,** *n.* one who goes before; (*Law*) a previous possessor. [L *antecēdere* (*ante-,* before, *cēdere,* to go)]

antechamber, *n.* an anteroom. [F *antichambre*]

antechapel, *n.* the part of a chapel between the western wall and the choir screen.

antedate, *n.* a date preceding the actual date. *v.t.* to date before the true date; to cause to happen prematurely; to happen earlier, precede; to anticipate.

antediluvian, *a.* of or pertaining to the period before the biblical Flood; old-fashioned, antiquated. *n.* one who lived before the Flood; a very old or old-fashioned person. [L*dilūvium,* flood]

antelope, *n.* an animal of the genus *Antilope,* containing ruminants akin to the deer and the goat. [OF *antelop* late L *antalopus,* late Gr. *antholops*]

antelucan, *a.* of or pertaining to the time just before daybreak. [L *antelucānus* (*ante-,* before, *lux,* light)]

ante meridiem, *phr.* before noon (abbr. a.m.). [L]

antemundane, *a.* existing or occurring before the creation of the world.

antenatal, *a.* happening or existing before birth; dealing with pregnancy or pregnantwomen.

antenna, *n.* (*pl.* **-nnae, -nnas**) a sensory organ occurring in pairs on the heads of insects and crustaceans; a palp, a feeler; a filament in the male flowers of orchids that ejects the pollen when touched; an aerial. **antennal, antennary,** *a.* pertaining to the antennae. **antenniferous,** *a.* bearing antennae. **antenniform,** *a.* shaped like an antenna. [L, sail-yard]

antenuptial, *a.* happening before marriage.

antependium, *n.* a covering for the front of an altar; a frontal. [late L (*ante-, pendēre,* to hang)]

antepenult, antepenultimate, *a.* pertaining to the last syllable but two; last but two. *n.* the last (syllable) but two. [L *antepaenultimus* (L *paene,* almost, *ultimus,* latest, last)]

anteprandial, *a.* happening, done or taken before dinner. [L *prandium,* dinner]

anterior, *a.* going before, more to the front, preceding, prior. **anteriority,** *n.* **anteriorly,** *adv.* [L, comp. of *ante,* before]

antero-, *comb. form.* front, in front; used in the formation of technical adjectives and adverbs, as **anterolateral,** *a.* situated on the front side; **antero-posterior,** *a.* running or continued from the front to the back; **antero-posteriorly,** *adv.* from front to back. [ANTERIOR]

anteroom, *n.* a room leading into orforming an entrance to another.

anth-, *pref.* against, opposite to; used before aspirates, e.g. *anthelion, anthelmintic.* [ANTI-]

anthelion, *n.* (*pl.* **-lia**) a mock sun, a luminous ring projected on a cloud or fog-bank opposite the sun. [late Gr. neut. of *anthēlios,* opposite to sun (*hēlios,* sun)]

anthelmintic, *a.* destroying or remedial against parasitic, esp. intestinal, worms. *n.* a remedy for intestinal worms. [Gr. ANTH-, *helmins -minthos,* a worm]

anthem, *n.* a hymn in alternate parts; a portion of Scripture or of the Liturgy set to music; a song of gladness or triumph. **anthem-wise,** *adv.* in the manner of an anthem; antiphonally. [OE *antefn,* late L *antiphōna, see* ANTIPHON]

Anthemis, *n.* a genus of composite plants including the camomile, *Anthemis nobilis.* **anthemium,** *n.* (*pl.* **-mia**) a palmette, honeysuckle or conventional leaf or floral design. [Gr. *anthos,* a flower]

anther, *n.* the pollen-bearing organ of flowering plants. **anther-dust,** *n.* pollen. **anther-valve,** *n.* the opening through which the pollen is discharged. **antheral,** *a.* pertaining to an anther or anthers. **antheriferous,** *a.* bearing anthers. **antheroid,** *a.* having the nature or appearance of an anther. [MF *anthere,* L *anthēra,* medicine made of flowers, Gr. *anthēra,* fem. a., flowery (*anthos,* a bud)]

antheridium, *n.* (*pl.* **-dia**) the male spore-bearing organ, analogous to an anther, of cryptogams. [mod. L *anthēra,* see prec.; Gr. *-idion,* dim. ending]

antherozoid, *n.* a motile male gamete produced in an antheridium. [ANTHER, Gr. *zōon,* -(O)ID]

anthocyanin, *n.* any of a class of scarlet to blue plant pigments. [Gr. *anthos,* a flower, *kuanos,* blue]

anthology, *n.* a collection of flowers or beauties; a collection of small choice poems from classic authors, esp. a famous Greek collection; any collection of selected poems or other literary pieces; a collection of songs, paintings etc. **anthological,** *a.* **anthologist,** *n.* the compiler of an anthology. **anthologize, -ise,** *v.t.* to compile or put into an anthology. [Gr. *anthologia,* a gathering of flowers (*anthos,* flower, *legein,* to collect)]

Anthony[1], *n.* the smallest in a litter of pigs. **St Anthony's fire,** popular name for erysipelas, from the tradition that those stricken by the pestilence of erysipelas, or sacred fire, in 1089, were cured through the intercession of St Anthony. [St *Anthony,* the patron saint of swineherds]

Anthony[2], **St,** *n.* (*c.* 251–356), also known as Anthony of Thebes. Founder of Christian monasticism. Born in Egypt, at the age of 20 he renounced all his possessions and lived in a tomb, and at 35 sought further solitude on a mountain in the desert.

Anthony[3], *n.* **Susan B(rownell)** (1820–1906), US pioneering feminist, who also worked for the anti-slavery and temperance movements. Her campaigns included demands for equality of pay for female teachers, the married women's property act, and women's suffrage. In 1869, with Elizabeth Cady Stanton, she founded the National Woman Suffrage Association.

Anthozoa, *n.pl.* the Actinozoa. **anthozoan,** *n.* [Gr. *anthos,* a flower, *zōon,* animal]

anthracene, *n.* a crystalline substance with blue fluorescence obtained from tar, used in the manufacture of dyes. [Gr. *anthrax,* coal]

anthracite, *n.* a non-bituminous coal, burning with intense heat, without smoke, and with little flame. **anthracite stove,** *n.* a stove for domestic heating specially constructed to burn anthracite coal. **anthracitic,** *a.* **-tous,** *a.* bearing anthracite; composed of anthracite; characterized by the presence of anthracite. [L *anthracītes,* Gr. *anthrakitēs,* resembling coals (*anthrax,* coal, carbon)]

anthrax, *n.* †a carbuncle; an infectious, often fatal bacterial disease of sheep and cattle transmissible to humans; a malignant pustule in humans derived from animals suffering from this. [L from Gr., a carbuncle, also coal]

anthrop(o)-, *comb. form.* human; pertaining to mankind. [Gr. *anthrōpos,* a man]

anthropocentric, *a.* centring in human beings; regarding mankind as the measure and aim of the universe.

anthropogeny, anthropogenesis, *n.* the science or study of the origin of human beings. **anthropogenic,**

-genetic, *a.*
anthropogeography, *n.* the geography of the distribution of the races of mankind.
anthropography, *n.* the science which investigates the geographical distribution of human beings; ethnography.
anthropoid, *a.* resembling human beings, of human form; of a person, apelike. *n.* a creature, esp. one of the higher apes, resembling a human being in form.
anthropolite, -lith, *n.* a human fossil.
anthropology, *n.* the science ofhuman beings in the widest sense; the study of human beings, or mankind, as to body, mind, evolution, race and environment. **anthropological**, *a.* of or pertaining to anthropology; dealing with the natural history of mankind. **anthropologically,** *adv.* in an anthropological way. **anthropologist,** *n.* one versed in anthropology.
anthropometry, *n.* the scientific measurement of the human body. **anthropometric, -ical**, *a.*
anthropomorphous, -morphic, *a.* possessed of a form resembling that of a human being; pertaining to anthropomorphism. **anthropomorphism,** *n.* the attribution of a human form or character to the Deity, or of human characteristics to the lower animals. **anthropomorphist,** *n.* one who attributes the human form or human characteristics to the Deity, or other things. **anthropomorphize, -ise,** *v.t.* to give a human shape or attribute human characteristics to. [Gr. *anthrōpomorphos (anthrōpos,* man, *morphē,* form)]
anthropophagous, *a.* feeding on human flesh, cannibal. **anthropophagy,** *n.* the practice of eating human flesh; cannibalism.
Anthropopithecus, *n.* the genus of apes, including the chimpanzee and the gorilla, which most resembles man.
anthroposophy, *n.* a system of esoteric philosophy enunciated by Rudolf Steiner (1861–1925), who defined it as 'the knowledge of the spiritual human being ... and of everything which the spirit man can perceive in the spiritual world.' [Gr. *anthrōpos,* a man, and *sophia,* knowledge]
anti, *prep.* opposed to. *n.* an opponent of a policy, political party etc.
anti-, *pref.* opposite, opposed to, against, instead of, in exchange, acting against, counteracting, as in *antibilious, anti-phlogistic, antiseptic, anti-social;* the opposite of, an opponent of, one of a contrary kind, the reverse of. [Gr.]
anti-abolitionist, *n.* one opposed to the abolition of slavery.
anti-aircraft, *a.* employed against hostile aircraft.
antiar, *n.* the upas-tree; the poison obtained from it. **antiar resin,** *n.* a resin obtained from the upas-tree. [Javanese, *antjar*]
antiballistic missile, *n.* a missile designed to intercept and destroy a ballistic missile in flight.
antibiosis, *n.* antagonistic association between two organisms or between one organism and a substance produced by the other. **antibiotic**, *a.* inimical to life, esp. bacteria. *n.* a substance produced by a micro-organism which inhibits the growth of or kills another microorganism. [ANTI-, BIO-]
antibody, *n.* a substance produced in the blood in response to the presence of an antigen and capable of counteracting toxins.
antic, *a.* †grotesque, odd, ludicrous, whimsical. *n.* †a merry-andrew, a buffoon; (*usu. pl.*) anything antic or grotesque; (*usu. pl.*) an odd trick, a ludicrous gesture; †a grotesque figure placed as an ornament on a building. *v.t.* †to make antic or grotesque. *v.i.* †to perform antics. [It, *antico,* L *antīquus,* ancient]
anticancer, *a.* used in the treatment of cancer.
Antichrist, *n.* in Christian theology, the opponent of Christ, by whom he is finally to be conquered (the idea of conflict between Light and Darkness is present in Persian, Babylonian, and Jewish literature, and influenced early Christian thought); an opponent of Christ. **antichristian**, *a.* opposed to Christ or to Christianity; pertaining to Antichrist. *n.* one opposed to Christ or to Christianity; an adherent of Antichrist. **antichristianism,** *n.* [OF *antecrist,* L *antechristus,* Gr. *antichristos*]
anticipate, *v.t.* to use in advance; to deal with or be before (another); to forestall; to cause to happen earlier; to hasten; to look forward to, consider or deal with anything before the proper time. *v.i.* †to occur in advance; to speak, write or do something in expectation of something occurring later. **anicipant,** *a.* anticipating, expecting. *n.* one who anticipates. **anticipation,** *n.* the act of anticipating; preconception, expectation, presentiment; the occurrence of symptoms before the normal period; the introduction of a note before the chord about to be played. **anticipative,** *a.* anticipating; containing an anticipation. **anticipatively,** *adv.* **anticipator,** *n.* **anticipatory,** *a.* [L *anticipātus,* p.p. of *anticipāre* (*ante-*, before, *capere,* to take)]
anticlerical, *a.* opposed to (the political influence of) the clergy. **anticlericalism,** *n.*
anticlimax, *n.* the opposite of climax; a descent or decrease in impressiveness; bathos. **anticlimactic**, *a.*
anticlinal, *a.* (*Geol.*) forming a ridge so that the strata lean against each other and in opposite directions; (*Anat.*) having an upright spine towards which the spines on both sides slope. *n.* an anticlinal axis, fold or line from which the strata dip in opposite directions. **anticline**, *n.* (*Geol.*) an anticlinal fold; a saddleback. [Gr. *klinein,* to lean]
anticlockwise, *a., adv.* in the reverse direction from that taken by the hands of a clock.
anticoagulant, *n., a.* (a drug) that hinders blood clotting.
Anti-Comintern Pact, *n.* (also called Anti-Communist Pact) agreement signed between Germany and Japan 25 Nov. 1936, opposing communism as a menace to peace and order. The pact was signed by Italy (1937) and by Hungary, Spain and the Japanese puppet state of Manchukuo in 1939. While directed against the USSR, the agreement also had the effect of giving international recognition to Japanese rule in Manchuria.
anti-constitutional, *a.* opposed to the constitution of the country, or to sound constitutional principles.
anticonvulsant, *n., a.* (a drug) used in treating or controlling (epileptic) convulsions.
Anti-Corn Law League, in UK history, an extra-parliamentary pressure group formed in 1838, led by the Liberals Cobden and Bright, which argued for free trade and campaigned successfully against duties on the import of foreign corn to Britain imposed by the Corn Laws, which were repealed in 1846.
anticyclone, *n.* the rotary outward flow of air from an atmospheric region of high pressure. **anticyclonic**, *a.*
antidepressant, *n., a.* (a drug) used in treating or preventing mental depression.
antidote, *n.* a medicine designed to counteract poison or disease; anything intended to counteract something harmful or unpleasant. **antidotal**, *a.* [L *antidotum,* Gr. *antidoton,* aremedy, neut. of *antidotos,* given against (ANTI, *didōmi,* I give)]
antifreeze, *n.* a substance added to the water in car radiators to lower the freezing point.
anti-friction, *n., a.* (a substance) that reduces friction. **anti-friction metal,** *n.* any of various alloys used for high-speed bearings.
antigen, *n.* a substance introduced into the body which stimulates the production of antibodies. [Gr. *gennaein,* to engender]
Antigone, *n.* in Greek legend, a daughter of Jocasta, by her son Oedipus; tragedy by Sophocles written about 411 BC, in which Antigone buries her brother Polyneices in defiance of the Theban king Creon, but in accordance with the wishes of the gods. Creon imprisons Antigone in a cave, but after a warning that he has defied the gods, he goes to the cave and finds that Antigone has hanged herself.
Antigonus, *n.* (382–301 BC), a general of Alexander the Great, after whose death (323) he made himself master of Asia Minor. He was defeated and slain by Seleucus I

at the battle of Ipsus.

†**antigropelos,** *n.pl.* waterproof leggings. [coined from Gr. *anti,* against, *hugros,* wet, *pēlos* mud]

Antigua and Barbuda, State of, three islands (Antigua, Barbuda and uninhabited Redonda) in the E Caribbean. **area** Antigua 280 sq km/108 sq miles, Barbuda 161 sq km/62 sq miles, plus Redonda 1 sq km/0.4 sq miles. **capital** and chief port St John's. **physical** tropical island country. **exports** sea-island cotton, rum. **population** (1986) 81,500; annual growth rate 1.3%. **language** English. **religion** Christian.

antihelix, anthelix, *n.* (*pl.* **-helices**, **-helixes**) the curved elevationwithin the helix of the ear. [Gr. *anthelix* (*helix,* a spiral, the outer ear)]

anti-hero, *n.* (*pl.* **-roes**) a principal character in a play, novel etc. who lacks noble or traditional heroic qualities. **anti-heroic**, *a.*

antihistamine, *n.* a drug that counteracts the effects of histamine in allergic reactions.

antiknock, *n.* a compound which is added to petrol to prevent knocking.

antilibration, *n.* the weighing of one thing against another. [L *librātiōnem,* balancing, weighing (*librāre,* to balance)]

Antilles, *n. pl.* the whole group of West Indian islands, divided north-south into the **Greater Antilles** (Cuba, Jamaica, Haiti-Dominican Republic, Puerto Rico) and **Lesser Antilles**, sub-divided into the Leeward Islands (Virgin Islands, St Kitts-Nevis, Antigua and Barbuda, Anguilla, Montserrat and Guadeloupe) and the Windward Islands (Dominica, Martinique, St Lucia, St Vincent and the Grenadines, Barbados and Grenada).

antilogarithm, antilog, *n.* the number represented by a logarithm. **antilogarithmic**, *a.*

antilogy, *n.* contradiction in terms or in ideas. [Gr. *antilogia* (*logia,* speaking)]

antimacassar, *n.* a covering for chairs, sofas etc. to prevent their being soiled by (macassar) oil on the hair, or as an ornament.

anti-marketeer, *n.* an opponent of Britain's membership of the European Economic Community.

antimasque, antimask, *n.* a grotesque interlude between the acts of a masque.

antimatter, *n.* hypothetical matter composed of antiparticles.

antimony, *n.* a bright bluish-white brittle metallic element, at. no. 51; chem. symbol Sb, occurring native, and of great use in the arts and medicine. **antimonial**, *a.* pertaining to or containing antimony. *n.* a medicine containing antimony. **antimonial wine,** *n.* sherry in which tartar emetic has been dissolved, used medicinally. **antimoniate**, *n.* a salt of antimonic acid. **antimonic**, *a.* of or pertaining to antimony; applied to compounds in which antimony combines as a pentavalent element. **antimonic acid,** *n.* containing two equivalents of antimony and five of oxygen. **antimonious**, *a.* containing or composed of antimony; applied to compounds in which antimony combines as a trivalent element. [med. L *antimōnium,* prob. from Arab.]

anti-national, *a.* opposed to the interest of one's country, or the national party.

anting ANT.

antinode, *n.* (*Phys.*) a region of maximum vibration between two nodes.

Antinomian, *a.* opposed to the moral law; of or pertaining to the Antinomians. *n.* one who holds that the moral law is not binding on Christians; one of a German sect of the 16th cent. said to hold this opinion. **antinomianism,** *n.* rejection of the moral law. [med. L *Antinomi,* name of sect (Gr. *anti,* against, *nomos,* law)]

antinomy, *n.* a contradiction between two laws; a conflict of authority; intellectual contradiction, opposition between laws or principles that appear to be equally founded in reason; paradox. [L from Gr. *antinomia*]

Antioch, *n.* ancient capital of the Greek kingdom of Syria, founded in 300 BC by Seleucus Nicator in memory of his father Antiochus, and famed for its splendour and luxury. Under the Romans it was an early centre of Christianity. The site is now occupied by the Turkish town of Antakya.

Antiochus, *n.* 13 kings of Syria of the Seleucid dynasty, including:

Antiochus I, *n.* (*c.* 324–*c.* 261 BC), king of Syria from 281 BC, son of Seleucus I, one of the generals of Alexander the Great. He earned the title of Antiochus Soter or Saviour by his defeat of the Gauls in Galatia (278 BC).

Antiochus II, *n.* (*c.* 286–*c.* 246 BC), king of Syria (261–246 BC), son of Antiochus I. He was known as Antiochus Theos, the Divine. During his reign the eastern provinces broke away from the Graeco-Macedonian rule and set up native princes. He made peace with Egypt by marrying the daughter of Ptolemy Philadelphus, but was a tyrant among his own people.

Antiochus III, *n.* **the Great** (*c.*241–187 BC), king of Syria from 223 BC, nephew of Antiochus II. He secured a loose suzerainty over Armenia and Parthia (209), overcame Bactria, received the homage of the Indian king of the Kabul valley, and returned by way of the Persian Gulf (204). He took possession of Palestine, entering Jerusalem (198). He crossed into NW Greece, but was decisively defeated by the Romans at Thermopylae (191) and at Magnesia (190). He had to abandon his domains in Anatolia, and perished at the hands of the people of Elymais.

Antiochus IV, *n.* (*c.* 215–164 BC), king of Syria from 175 BC, known as Antiochus Epiphanes, the Illustrious; second son of Antiochus III. He occupied Jerusalem about 170 BC, seizing much of the Temple treasure, and instituted worship of the Greek type in the Temple in an attempt to eradicate Judaism. This produced the revolt of the Jewish people under the Maccabees, and Antiochus died before he could suppress it.

Antiochus VII, *n.* **Sidetes,** king of Syria from 138 BC. The last strong ruler of the Seleucid dynasty, he took Jerusalem in 134 BC, reducing the Maccabees to subjection, and fought successfully against the Parthians.

Antiochus XIII, *n.* **Asiaticus** (1st cent. BC), king of Syria (69–65 BC), the last of the Seleucid dynasty. During his reign Syria was made a Roman province by Pompey the Great.

Antiochus, *n.* four kings of Commagene (69 BC–AD 72), affiliated to the Seleucid dynasty, including:

Antiochus IV, *n.* **Epiphanes** (1st cent. AD), king of Commagene, son of Antiochus III. He was made king in 38 by Caligula, who deposed him immediately. He was restored in 41 by Claudius, and reigned as an ally of Rome against Parthia. He was deposed on suspicion of treason in 72.

antipapal, *a.* opposed to the pope or to papal doctrine.

antiparticle, *n.* an elementary particle with the same mass as but opposite charge to another particle. Collision of a particle with its antiparticle produces mutual annihilation.

antipasto, *n.* (*pl.* **-tos**) hors d'oeuvre. [It. *anti-,* before, *pasto,* food]

antipathic, *a.* of contrary character or disposition; (*Med.*) exhibiting or exciting contrary symptoms, allopathic. [F *antipathique* (*antipathie,* ANTIPATHY)]

antipathy, *n.* contrariety of nature or disposition; hostile feeling towards; aversion, dislike. **antipathetic**, **-ical**, *a.* having an antipathy or contrariety to. **antipathetically,** *adv.* [L, from Gr. *antipatheia* (*pathein,* to suffer)]

antipersonnel, *a.* of a weapon etc., designed to kill or injure people.

antiperspirant, *n.*, *a.* (a substance) used to reduce perspiration.

antiphlogistic, *a.* opposed to the doctrine of phlogiston; (*Med.*) allaying inflammation, cooling. *n.* a remedy which allays inflammation.

antiphon, *n.* a sentence sung by one choir in response to another; a series of such responsive sentences or versicles; a short sentence said or sung before the psalms, canticles etc., in the Roman Catholic Church, an anthem; an answer. **antiphonal**, *a.* consisting of antiphons; sung alternately. *n.* an antiphonary. **anti-**

phonally, *adv.* **antiphonary**, *n.* a book containing a collection of antiphons. **antiphony**, *n.* opposition of sound; alternate chanting or singing by a choir divided into two parts; an antiphon. [late L *antiphōna,* Gr. *antiphōna,* pl. of *antiphōnon,* an anthem (*anti-*, in return, *phōnē,* voice)]

antiphrasis, *n.* the use of words in a sense contrary to their ordinary meaning. **antiphrastic**, *a.* [late L, from Gr. *antiphrasis* (*anti-*, contrary, *phrazein,* to speak)]

antipodes, *n.pl.* those who dwell directly opposite to each other on the globe, so that the soles of their feet occupy diametrically opposite positions; a place on the surface of the globe diametrically opposite to another, esp. Australasia; a pair of places diametrically opposite; the direct opposite of some other person or thing. **antipodal**, *a.* pertaining to the antipodes; situated on the opposite side of the globe. **antipode**, *n.* one who lives on the opposite side of the globe. **antipodean**, *a.* pertaining to the antipodes. [L, from Gr. *antipodes,* sing. *antipous (anti-*, against, *pous,* foot)]

antipole, *n.* the opposite pole; the direct opposite.

antipope, *n.* a pope elected in opposition to the one canonically chosen.

antipyretic, *a.* preventing or allaying fever. *n.* a medicine to prevent or allay fever. [Gr. *puretos,* fever]

antiquary, *n.* a student, investigator, collector or seller of antiquities or antiques; a student of ancient times. **antiquarian**, *a.* pertaining to the study of antiquities; of paper, of the size 52½ ins (133·35 cm) by 30½ ins (77·47 cm). *n.* an antiquary. **antiquarianism,** *n.* **antiquarianize, -ise,** *v.i.* [L *antiquarius*]

antiquated, *a.* old-fashioned, out of date, obsolete. [as prec.]

antique, *a.* ancient, old, that has long existed; old-fashioned, antiquated. *n.* a relic of antiquity; a piece of furniture, ornament etc., made in an earlier period and valued by collectors. **the antique,** *n.* the ancient style in art. [F *antique,* L *antīquus, anticus* (*ante-*, before)]

antiquity, *n.* the state of having existed long ago; the state of being ancient; great age; ancient times; the ancients; manners, customs, events etc. of ancient times; (*usu. pl.*) a relic of ancient times. [as prec.]

Antirrhinum, *n.* a genus of plants that includes the snapdragon. [L, from Gr. *antirrhinon* (*anti-*, instead of, *rhis, rhinos,* nose)]

anti-sabbatarian, *n., a.* (one) opposed to sabbatarian views.

antiscorbutic, *n., a.* (a medicine or remedy) used in treating or preventing scurvy.

anti-scriptural, *a.* opposed to Scripture.

anti-Semitism, *n.* literally, prejudice against Semitic people (see SEMITE), but in practice it has meant prejudice or discrimination against, and persecution of, the Jews as an ethnic group. Anti-Semitism was a tenet of Hitler's Germany, and in the Holocaust of 1933–45 about 6 million Jews died in concentration camps. It is a form of racism. **anti-Semite**, *n.* **anti-Semitic**, *a.*

antiseptic, *a.* counteracting sepsis, or putrefaction; free from contamination; lacking interest, warmth or excitement, sterile. *n.* a substance which counteracts putrefaction, which inhibits the growth of microorganisms. **antisepsis,** *n.* the principle of antiseptic treatment.

antiserum, *n.* (*pl.* **-rums, -ra**) serum containing antibodies.

anti-social, *a.* opposed to the interest of society, or to the principles on which society is constituted; unsociable.

antistatic, *n., a.* (an agent) that counteracts the effects of static electricity.

antistrophe, *n.* the returning of the Greek chorus, exactly answering to a previous strophe, except that the movement was from left to right, instead of from right to left; the poem or choral song recited during this movement; any choral response; the rhetorical figure of retort; an inverted grammatical construction. **antistrophic**, *a.* [L, from Gr. *antistrophē* (*strophē,* a turning, a verse)]

antitetanus, *a.* preventing tetanus. **antitetanic**, *a.* **antitetanin**, *n.* an antitoxin used for curing or preventing tetanus.

antitheism, *n.* opposition to belief in a god. **antitheist,** *n.* **antitheistic**, *a.*

antithesis, *n.* (*pl.* **-ses**) sharp opposition or contrast between words, clauses, sentences or ideas; a counter proposition; opposition, contrast; the direct opposite. **antithetic**, **-ical**, *a.* pertaining to or marked by antithesis; contrasted; sharply opposed. **antithetically,** *adv.* [Gr. (*thesis,* a setting, from *tithēmi,* I place)]

antitoxin, *n.* an antibody or antiserum formed in the body which neutralizes the action of toxins.

antitrade, *n., a.* (a wind) blowing in an opposite direction to that of the trade-winds.

anti-trinitarian, *n., a.* (one) opposed to the doctrine of the Trinity. **anti-trinitarianism,** *n.*

anti-trust, *a.* (*N Am.*) opposing trusts or monopolies which adversely affect trust.

antitype, *n.* that which is represented by a type or symbol; an opposite type. **antitypal**, *a.* of the nature of an antitype. **antitypical**, *a.* [Gr. *antitupos,* answering to, as an impression to a die (*tupos,* a blow, a stamp, cognate with *tuptein,* to strike)]

antivenin, *n.* serum obtained from animals immunized against snake venom, used as an antidote against snake-bite. [L *venenum,* poison]

anti-vivisection, *n.* (active) opposition to vivisection. **anti-vivisectionist,** *n., a.*

antler, *n.* a branch of the horns of a stag or other deer; either of the branched horns of a deer. **antlered,** *part.a.* furnished with antlers; branched like stags' horns. [OF *antoillier,* late L *antoculārem* (*ramum*), the branch (orig., the lowest or brow antler) which is in front of the eye (*ante-*, before, *oculus,* eye)]

Antofagasta, *n.* port of N Chile, capital of a region of the same name. The area of the region is 125,300 sq km/48,366 sq miles, its population (1982) 341,000. The population of the town of Antofagasta is 175,000. Nitrates from the Atacama desert are exported.

Antonello da Messina, *n.* (*c.* 1430–1479), Italian painter, born in Messina, Sicily, a pioneer of the technique of oil painting, which he is said to have introduced to Italy from N Europe. Flemish influence is reflected in his technique, his use of light, and sometimes in his imagery. Surviving works include bust-length portraits and sombre religious paintings.

Antonine Wall, *n.* Roman line of fortification built 142–200 AD. The Roman Empire's NW frontier, between the Clyde and Forth rivers, Scotland.

Antoninus Pius, *n.* (86–161 AD), Roman emperor who had been adopted 138 as Hadrian's heir, and succeeded him later that year. He enjoyed a prosperous reign, during which he built the Antonine Wall. His daughter married Marcus Aurelius Antoninus.

Antonioni, *n.* **Michelangelo** (1912–), Italian film director, famous for his subtle analysis of neuroses and personal relationships of the leisured classes. His work includes *L'Avventura* (1960), *Blow Up* (1966), and *The Passenger* (1975).

antonomasia, *n.* the substitution of an epithet for a proper name, as *the Corsican* for Napoleon; the use of a proper name to describe one of a class, as a *Cicero* for an orator. **antonomastic**, *a.* characterized by antonomasia. **antonomastically,** *adv.* [L, from Gr. *antonomasia, antonomazein,* to name instead (*anti-*, instead, *onomazein,* to name)]

antonym, *n.* a term expressing the reverse of some other term, as 'good' to 'bad'. [Gr. *antōnumia* (*anti-*, instead of, *onuma,* a name)]

Antrim, *n.* county of Northern Ireland. **area** 2830 sq km/1092 sq miles. **towns** Belfast (county town), port of Larne. **products** potatoes, oats, linen, synthetic textiles. **population** (1981) 642,000.

antrum, *n.* a natural anatomical cavity, particularly one in bone. [Gr. *antron,* a cave]

Antwerp, *n.* (Flemish **Antwerpen**, French **Anvers**) port in Belgium on the river Scheldt, capital of the province of Antwerp; population (1988) 476,000. One of the world's busiest ports, it has shipbuilding, oil-refining, petrochemical, textile, and diamond-cutting industries. The home of Rubens is preserved, and many of his works are in the Gothic cathedral. The province of Antwerp has an area of 2900 sq km/1119 sq miles, and a population (1987) 1,588,000.

Anubis, *n.* in Egyptian mythology, the jackal-headed god of the dead.

anus, *n.* the lower, excretory opening of the intestinal tube; the inferior aperture of a monopetalous flower. **anal,** *a.* [L, a rounding, ring]

anvil, *n.* the iron block on which smiths hammer and shape their work; anything resembling a smith's anvil in shape or use; esp. a bone in the ear, the incus. †*v.t.* (*past, p.p.* **anvilled**) to fashion on an anvil. *v.i.* to work at an anvil. **on the anvil,** in preparation. [OE *onfilti* (etym. doubtful)]

anxious, *a.* troubled or solicitous about some uncertain or future event; †inspiring anxiety; distressing, worrying; eagerly desirous (to do something). **anxiety,** *n.* the state of being anxious; trouble, solicitude or mental distress. **anxiously,** *adv.* [L *anxius* (*angere,* to choke)]

any, *a., pron.* one indefinitely; some or any number indefinitely; whichever, whatever; †either; (*coll.*) anything, in *I'm not taking any*. **anybody,** *n., pron.* any person, any one; a person of little importance; (*pl.*) persons of no importance. **anyhow,** *adv., conj.* at any rate; in any way; in any case; imperfectly, haphazardly. **anyone,** *n., pron.* any person, anybody. **anyplace,** *adv.* (*N Am.*) anywhere. **anything,** *n., pron.* any thing (in its widest sense) as distinguished from any person. **anyway,** *adv., conj.* anyhow. †**anywhen,** *adv.* at any time. **anywhere,** *adv.* in any place. **anywhither,** *adv.* to or towards any place. **anywise,** *adv.* in any manner, case, or degree; anyhow. [OE *ænig* (*ān,* one, *-ig,* adj. ending)]

Anzac, *n.* a soldier in the Australian or New Zealand forces, in the war of 1914–18. **Anzac button,** *n.* (*Austral.*) a nail used to hold up the trousers. [from initials of Australian (and) New Zealand Army Corps]

Anzio, Battle of, *n.* in World War II, the beachhead invasion of Italy 22 Jan.–23 May 1944 by Allied troops; failure to use information gained by deciphering German signals (see ULTRA) led to Allied troops being stranded for a period after German attacks. Anzio is a seaport and resort on the W coast of Italy, 53 km/33 miles SE of Rome; population (1984) 25,000. It is the site of the Roman town of Antium, and the birthplace of Emperor Nero.

Anzus, *n.* a pact for the security of the Pacific, formed in 1952 by Australia, New Zealand and the US. [acronym]

a/o, (*abbr.*) account of.

AOB, (*abbr.*) any other business.

AOC, (*abbr.*) Air Officer Commanding.

aorist, *n.* a Greek tense expressing indefinite past time. *a.* aoristic. **aoristic,** *a.* indefinite in point of time; pertaining to an aorist tense. [Gr. *aoristos,* unlimited (*a-,* not, *horizein,* to limit)]

aorta, *n.* the largest artery in the body; the main trunk of the arterial system proceeding from the left ventricle of the heart. **aortic,** *a.* of or pertaining to the aorta. [late L, from Gr. *aortē* (*aerein,* to lift)]

Aouita, *n.* **Said** (1960–), Moroccan runner. Outstanding at middle and long distances, he won the 1984 Olympic and 1987 World Championship 5000 metres title, and has set many world records.

Aoun, *n.* **Michel** (1935–), Lebanese soldier and Maronite Christian politician. As commander of the Lebanese army, in 1988 he was made president without Muslim support, his appointment precipitating a civil war between Christians and Muslims. His unwillingness to accept a 1989 Arab League sponsored peace agreement increased his isolation.

à outrance, *adv.* to the end; to the death. [F]

Aouzu Strip, *n.* disputed teritory 100 km wide on the Chad–Libya frontier, occupied by Libya in 1973. Lying to the N of the Tibesti massif, the area is rich in uranium and other minerals.

AP, (*abbr.*) Associated Press.

ap-, *pref.* AD-, assim. to *p* e.g. *appear, approve.*

apace, *adv.* at a quick pace; speedily, fast.

Apache, *n.* a member of a N American Indian people related to the Navajo of the SW US and N Mexico, who now number about 10,000; a (Parisian) ruffian who robs and maltreats people, a hooligan. [Mex. Sp.]

apanage, appanage, *n.* lands or office assigned for the maintenance of a royal house; a dependency; a perquisite; a necessary adjunct or attribute. [OF *apaner,* to nourish, med. L *apānāre* (*ap-, ad-,* to, *pānis,* bread)]

apart, *adv.* to one side; separately with regard to place, purpose or things; independently; parted, at a distance; separate; into two or more pieces or parts. [F *à part,* to one side, singly, L *ad partem*]

apartheid, *n.* (a policy of) racial segregation. [Afrikaans, APART, -HOOD]

apartment, *n.* a portion of a house; a single room in a house; (*pl.*) a suite of rooms, lodgings; (*chiefly N Am.*) a flat. [F *appartement,* med. L *appartīmentum,* from *appartīre,* to apportion (*ad-,* to, *partīre,* to divide)]

apathy, *n.* absence of feeling or passion; insensibility; indifference; mental indolence. **apathetic,** *a.* characterized by apathy; insensible, unemotional, indifferent. **apathetically,** *adv.* [F *apathie,* L *apathia,* Gr. *apatheia* (*a-,* not, *pathein,* to suffer)]

apatite, *n.* a common mineral, calcium phosphate. [G *Apatit,* Gr. *apatē,* deceit, from its resemblance to other minerals]

Apatosaurus, *n.* the large plant-eating dinosaur, formerly called *Brontosaurus,* which flourished about 145 million years ago. Up to 21 m/69 ft long and 30 tonnes in weight, it stood on four elephant-like legs and had a long tail, long neck, and small head. It probably snipped off low-growing vegetation with peg-like front teeth, and swallowed it whole to be ground by pebbles in the stomach.

APB, (*abbr.*) all-points bulletin.

ape, *n.* a tailless monkey; one of the Simiidae (a gorilla, chimpanzee, orang-outan or gibbon); a mimic, a servile imitator. *v.t.* to imitate or mimic. **apery,** *n.* mimicry; apish behaviour. **apish,** *a.* of the nature of or befitting an ape. **apishly,** *adv.* **apishness,** *n.* [OE *apa* (cp. Dut. *aap,* Icel. *api,* OHG *affo*)]

apeak, *adv., pred.a.* (*Naut.*) in a vertical or nearly vertical position; pointed upwards. [F *à pic,* vertically, vertical (*à,* at, *pic,* summit)]

Apeldoorn, *n.* commercial city in Gelderland province, E central Netherlands. Population (1982) 142,400. Het Loo, which is situated nearby, has been the summer residence of the Dutch royal family since the time of William of Orange.

Apennines, *n.* a chain of mountains stretching the length of the Italian peninsula. A continuation of the Maritime Alps, from Genoa it swings across the peninsula to Ancona on the E coast, and then back to the W coast and into the 'toe' of Italy. The system is continued over the Strait of Messina along the N Sicilian coast, then across the Mediterranean sea in a series of islands to the Atlas mountains of North Africa. The highest peak is Gran Sasso d'Italia at 2914 m/9560 ft.

apepsy, apepsia, *n.* indigestion, dyspepsia. [Gr. *apepsia* (*a-,* not, *peptein,* to digest)]

aperçu, *n.* a concise exposition, an outline, a brief summary; an insight. [F, p.p. of *apercevoir,* to perceive]

aperient, aperitive, *a.* laxative, purgative, deobstruent. *n.* a laxative medicine. [L *aperīre,* to open]

aperiodic, *a.* not occurring regularly; (*Phys.*) not having a periodic motion, not oscillatory. *n.* (*Radio.*) an untuned circuit. **aperiodic aerial,** *n.* an aerial which has no natural or inherent tuning to any particular wavelength.

aperitif, *n.* a short drink, usu. alcoholic, taken as an appetizer. [F]

aperitive APERIENT.

†**apert,** *a., adv.* open, manifest; openly, in public. [OF *apert,* L *aperīre,* to open]

aperture, *n.* an opening, a hole, a gap, a passage; (the diameter of) the space through which light passes in an optical instrument; the diameter of a lens. [L *apertura*]

apery APE.
apetalous, *a.* without petals. [Gr. *apetalous,* leafless (*a-*, not, *petalon,* leaf)]
APEX, *n.* a discounted fare on some air or sea journeys paid for at least 28 days before departure. [acronym for *A*dvance *P*urchase *Ex*cursion]
apex, *n.* (*pl.* **apices**, **apexes**) the tip, top, vertex or summit of anything; the culmination, climax. **apical**, *a.* pertaining to an apex; placed at the summit. **apically,** *adv.* at the apex; towards the apex. [L]
aphaeresis, apheresis, *n.* the taking away of a letter or syllable at the commencement of a word; (*Med.*) the removal of something that is noxious. [L, from Gr. *aphairēsis* (*aph, apo,* away, *airein,* to take)]
aphasia, *n.* (partial) loss of the power of articulate speech. **aphasic,** *a.* [Gr., speechlessness]
aphelion, *n.* (*pl.* **-lia**) the point most distant from the sun in the orbit of a planet or a comet. [L *aphēlium,* Gr. *aph' hēlion,* away from the sun]
apheliotropic, *a.* bending or turning away from the sun. **apheliotropically,** *adv.* **apheliotropism**, *n.* [Gr. *tropikos,* turning]
aphesis, *n.* a form of aphaeresis, in which an unaccented vowel at the beginning of a word is gradually lost. **aphetic**, *a.* pertaining to aphesis. **aphetize, -ise,** *v.t.* to shorten by aphesis. [Gr., from *aphienai* (*aph-, apo-,* away, *ienai,* to let go)]
aphid, *n.* plant-louse; any of a group of minute insects very destructive to vegetation, comprising among others the green-fly, black fly, American blight etc. **aphidian**, *a.* of or pertaining to aphids or aphides. *n.* an aphid or plant-louse. [back formation from *aphides* (see APHIS)]
aphis, *n.* (*pl.* **aphides**) an aphid, esp. of the genus *Aphis.* [genus name coined by Linnaeus]
aphonia, aphony, *n.* inability to speak; loss of voice. **aphonic**, *a.* [Gr., from *aphōnos,* voiceless (*a-*, not, *phōnē,* voice)]
aphorism, *n.* a detached, pithy sentence, containing a maxim or wise precept. **aphorismic**, *a.* **aphorist,** *n.* one who writes or utters aphorisms. **aphoristic**, *a.* **aphoristically,** *adv.* **aphorize, -ise,** *v.i.* to utter or write aphorisms. [Gr. *aphorismos,* a definition, from *aphorixein (aph-, apo-,* off, *horizein,* to mark)]
aphrodisiac, *a.* exciting sexual desire. *n.* a drug provocative of sexual desire. **aphrodisian,** *a.* [Gr. *aphrodisiakos,* from *aphroditios,* from *Aphroditē,* see foll.
Aphrodite, *n.* in Greek mythology, the goddess of love (Roman Venus, Phoenician Astarte, Babylonian Ishtar); said to be either a daughter of Zeus (in Homer) or sprung from the foam of the sea (in Hesiod). She was the unfaithful wife of Hephaestus, the god of fire, and the mother of Eros.
aphthae, *n.pl.* the minute specks seen in the mouth and tongue in thrush. [L, from Gr. *aphthai* (prob. cogn. with *haptein,* to set on fire, inflame)]
aphyllous, *a.* without leaves. [Gr. *aphullos* (*a-*, not, *phullon,* leaf)]
Apia, *n.* capital and port of Western Samoa, on the north coast of Upolu island, in the W Pacific; population (1981) 33,000. It was the home of the writer Robert Louis Stevenson.
apian, *a.* pertaining to bees. [L *apianus,* from *apis,* a bee]
apiarian, *a.* relating to bees or bee-keeping. *n.* an apiarist. **apiarist**, *n.* one who rears bees; a bee-keeper. **apiary**, *n.* a place where bees are kept. [L *apiārium,* neut. of *apiārius,* pertaining to bees (*apis,* bee)]
apical etc. APEX[2].
apicular, *a.* of or belonging to a little apex; situated at the tip. **apiculate**, **-ated,** *a.* (*Bot.*) terminating abruptly in a little point. [mod. L *apiculus,* dim. of APEX]
apiculture, *n.* bee-keeping; bee-rearing. [L *apis,* a bee]
apiece, *adv.* for or to each, severally. [*a piece,* for one piece]
Apis, *n.* ancient Egyptian god with a bull's head, linked with Osiris (and later merged with him into the Ptolemaic god Serapis); his cult centres were Memphis and Heliopolis, where sacred bulls were mummified.
apish etc. APE.
APL, *n.* a computer programming language designed for mathematical applications. [*a p*rogramming *l*anguage]
aplanatic, *a.* of a lens etc., free from spherical aberration. [Gr. *aplanētos* (*a-*, priv., *planaein,* to wander)]
aplasia, *n.* defective or arrested development in a body tissue or organ. **aplastic**, *a.* [A-(7); Gr. *plasis,* formation]
aplenty, *adv.* in plenty, in abundance.
aplomb, *n.* the state of being perpendicular; self-possession, coolness. [F *aplomb,* perpendicular (*à plomb,* by the plummet)]
aplustre, *n.* the ornament above the stern of an ancient ship. [Gr. *aphlaston*]
apnoea, (*N Am.*) **apnea,** *n.* a cessation of respiration. [mod. L, from Gr. *apnoia,* from *apnoos,* breathless (*a-*, not, *pnoē,* breath)]
apo-, *pref.* away, detached, separate; as in *apology, apostrophe.* [Gr. *apo,* away, from]
Apo, Mount, *n.* active volcano and highest peak in the Philippines, rising to 2954 m/9692 ft on the island of Mindanao.
Apoc., (*abbr.*) Apocalypse; Apocrypha, apocryphal.
apocalypse, *n.* the revelation granted to St John the Divine; the book of the New Testament in which this is recorded; any revelation or prophetic disclosure; a vast decisive event or confrontation; **(Apocalypse)** in literature, a movement (favouring Biblical symbolism) which developed from Surrealism 1938, and included G. S. Fraser, Henry Treece, J. F. Hendry, Nicholas Moore and Tom Scott. **apocalyptic, -ical**, *a.* pertaining to the revelation of St John; of the nature of a revelation or apocalypse; prophesying disaster or doom. **apocalyptically,** *adv.* [L *apocalypsis,* Gr. *apokalupsis,* from *apokaluptein,* to uncover (*apo-*, off, *kaluptein,* to cover)]
apocarpous, *a.* having the carpels wholly or partly distinct. [APO-, Gr. *karpos,* fruit]
apocope, *n.* a cutting off or dropping of the last letter or syllable of a word. [L, from Gr. *apokopē* (*apo-*, away, *koptein,* to cut)]
apocrypha, *n.* writings or statements of doubtful authority; **(Apocrypha)** a collection of 14 books in the Old Testament, included in the Septuagint and the Vulgate, but not written in Hebrew originally, nor reckoned genuine by the Jews, nor inserted in the Authorized Version of the Bible. **apocryphal,** *a.* pertaining to the apocrypha; spurious, fabulous. **apocryphally,** *adv.* [Gr. *apokrupha,* neut. pl., things hidden, from *apokruptein* (*apo,* away, *kruptein,* to hide)]
apod, *n.* a footless creature, a bird, fish or reptile in which the feet or corresponding members are absent or undeveloped. **apodal,** *a.* footless; having no ventral fin. [Gr. *apous* (*a-*, not, without, *pous podos,* foot)]
apodictic, apodeictic, *a.* clearly demonstrative; established on uncontrovertible evidence. **apodictically, apodeictically,** *adv.* [L *apodīcticus,* Gr. *apodeiktikos* (*apodeiknunai,* to show)]
apodosis, *n.* the consequent clause in a conditional sentence, answering to the protasis. [L, from Gr. *apodosis,* a giving (*apodidonai,* to give back)]
apodyterium, *n.* the apartment in ancient baths or palaestras where the clothes were taken off. [L, from Gr. *apodutērion* (*apo-*, off, *-duein,* put, dress)]
apogamy, *n.* (*Bot.*) the absence of sexual reproductive power, the plant perpetuating itself from an unfertilized female cell. **apogamous,** *a.* **apogamously,** *adv.* [Gr. *apo-*, away from, *gamos,* marriage]
apogee, *n.* the point in the orbit of the moon or any planet or satellite which is at the greatest distance from the earth; the most distant point in the orbit of a satellite from the planet round which it revolves; the furthest point, the highest point, the culmination. **apogean,** *a.* [F *apogée,* late L *apogæum,* Gr. *apogaion,* neut. a., away from the earth (APO-, *gaia,* earth)]
apolar, *a.* (*Biol.*) without poles or fibrous processes. [*a-*, not, without, POLAR]

apolaustic, *a.* devoted to pleasure; self-indulgent. [Gr. *apolaustikos* (*apolauein,* to enjoy)]

apolitical, *a.* uninterested in political affairs, politically neutral; without political significance.

Apollinaire, *n.* **Guillaume** (pen name of Guillaume Apollinaire de Kostrowitsky) (1880–1918), French poet of aristocratic Polish descent. He was a leader of the *avant garde* in Parisian literary and artistic circles. His novel *Le Poète assassiné/The Poet Assassinated* (1916), followed by the experimental poems *Alcools/Alcohols* (1913) and *Calligrammes/Word Pictures* (1918), show him as a representative of the cubist and futurist movements.

Apollo, *n.* in Greek and Roman mythology, the god of sun, music, poetry, prophecy, agriculture and pastoral life, and leader of the Muses. He was the twin child (with Artemis) of Zeus and Leto. Ancient statues show Apollo as the embodiment of the Greek ideal of male beauty.

Apollo asteroid, *n.* a member of a group of asteroids whose orbits cross that of the Earth. They are named after the first of their kind, Apollo, discovered 1932, and then lost until 1973. Apollo asteroids are so small and faint that they are difficult to see except when close to Earth (Apollo is about 2 km across).

Apollonius, *n.* (*c.* 261–*c.* 190 BC), Greek mathematician and astronomer, who studied in Alexandria. His eight-book treatise *Conic Sections* earned him the title 'the Great Geometer'; also known as Apollonius of Perga.

Apollonius of Rhodes, *n.* (*c.* 220–180 BC), Greek poet, author of the epic *Argonautica*, which tells the story of Jason and the Argonauts.

Apollo of Rhodes, the Greek statue of Apollo generally known as the Colossus of Rhodes.

Apollo project, *n.* US space project to land a person on the Moon, achieved in July 1969, when Neil Armstrong was the first to set foot there. The programme was announced in 1961 by President Kennedy. The world's most powerful rocket, Saturn V, was built to launch the Apollo spacecraft, which carried three astronauts. When the spacecraft was in orbit around the Moon, two astronauts descended to the lunar surface in a lunar module. The first Apollo mission carrying a crew, Apollo 7 (Oct. 1968), was a test flight in orbit around the Earth. After three other preparatory flights, Apollo 11 made the first lunar landing. Five more manned landings followed, the last in 1972. The total cost of the programme was over $24 billion.

Apollo-Soyuz test project, a joint US-Soviet mission begun 1972 to link a Soviet and a US spacecraft in space. The project culminated in the docking of an Apollo 18 and Soyuz 15 craft, both of which were launched 15 July 1975.

Apollyon, *n.* the destroyer; the Devil. [L, from Gr. *apolluōn,* pres.p. of *apolluein,* to destroy]

apologetic, -ical, *a.* excusing, explanatory, vindicatory. **apologetically,** *adv.* **apologetics,** *n.sing.* defensive argument; especially the argumentative defence of Christianity. [F *apologétique,* L *apologēticus,* Gr. *apologētikos* (*apologeesthai,* to speak in defence)]

apologia *n.* a vindication, formal defence, excuse. [L, from Gr.]

apologist, apologize APOLOGY.

apologue, *n.* a fable designed to impress some moral truth upon the mind; esp. a beast-fable or a fable of inanimate things. [F, from L *apologus,* from Gr. (*apo-*, off, *logos,* speech)]

apology, *n.* a defence, vindication; an explanation, excuse; a regretful acknowledgment of offence; a wretched substitute for the real thing. **apologist,** *n.* one who defends or apologizes by speech or writing; a professed defender of Christianity. **apologize, -ise,** *v.i.* to make an apology or excuse for. [L *apologia,* from Gr. (*apo-*, off, *legein,* to speak)]

apomecometer, *n.* an instrument for measuring the height of buildings etc. [Gr. *apo,* from, *mekos,* length]

apomixis, *n.* reproduction without fertilization. **apomictic,** *a.* **apomictically,** *adv.* [Gr. APO-, *mixis,* mixing]

apoop, *adv.* on or against or towards the poop of a ship.

apophthegm, apothegm, *n.* a terse pointed saying, a maxim expressed in few but weighty words. **apophthegmatic,** *a.* pertaining to, or using apophthegms; sententious, pithy. **apophthegmatically,** *adv.* [Gr. *apophthegma* (*apo-*, off, out, *phthengesthai,* to speak)]

apoplexy, *n.* a sudden loss of sensation and of power of motion, generally caused by rupture or obstruction of a blood vessel in the brain. **apoplectic,** *a.* pertaining to or tending to cause apoplexy; predisposed to apoplexy; violently angry. *n.* a person liable to or afflicted with apoplexy. [F *apoplexie,* late L, from Gr. *apoplēxia* (*apoplēssein,* to cripple with a blow)]

aport, *adv.* on or towards the port side of a ship.

aposiopesis, *n.* a stopping short for rhetorical effect. [L, from Gr., from *aposiōpaein* (*apo-*, off, away, *siōpein,* to be silent)]

apositic, *a.* causing *apositia* or aversion to food; tending to weaken appetite. [Gr. *apositikos,* exciting distaste for food]

apostasy, *n.* renunciation of religious faith, moral allegiance or political principles; in the Roman Catholic Church, renunciation of religious vows. [L, from Gr. *apostasia,* previously *apostasis* (*apo-*, away, *stasis,* a standing, from *sta-*, stem of *histēmi,* I stand)]

apostate, *n.* one who apostatizes. *a.* unfaithful to creed or principles; rebel, rebellious. **apostatic, -ical,** *a.* **apostatize, -ise,** *v.i.* to abandon one's creed, principles or party; to commit apostasy. [OF *apostate,* late L *apostata,* Gr. *apostatēs*]

a posteriori, *a., adv.* reasoning from consequences, effects, things observed to causes; inductive, as opposed to a priori or deductive. [L]

apostil, *n.* a marginal note, gloss, annotation. [F *apostille* (etym. doubtful)]

apostle, *n.* one of the 12 men appointed by Christ to preach the gospel; a first Christian missionary to any region, or one who has pre-eminent success; the leader of a reform; a supporter. **apostle bird,** *n.* the grey-crowned babbler. **Apostles' Creed,** *n.* a Christian creed, each clause of which is said to have been contributed by one of the Apostles. **apostle-spoons,** *n.pl.* (tea)spoons, the handles ending in figures of the Apostles – formerly a frequent present of sponsors in baptism. **apostleship,** *n.* **apostolate,** *n.* the office of apostle; leadership; propagation of a doctrine. **apostolic, -ical,** *a.* pertaining to the Apostles; derived directly from or agreeable to the doctrine or practice of the Apostles; of the character or nature of an apostle; pertaining to the Pope as St Peter's successor, papal. *n.* †the Pope; a bishop; †a member of a sect who claimed to follow the doctrines of the Apostles. **Apostolic Fathers,** *n.pl.* those Christian Fathers or writers contemporaneous with the Apostles or their immediate disciples. **Apostolic See,** *n.* the Papacy. **apostolic succession,** *n.* uninterrupted transmission of spiritual authority through bishops, from the Apostles. **apostolically,** *adv.* [OF *apostle, apostre,* L *apostolus,* Gr. *apostolos,* a messenger (*apo-*, away, and *stellein,* to send)]

Apostles, *n.pl.* discussion group founded in 1820 at Cambridge University, England; members have included the poet Tennyson, the philosophers G. E. Moore and Bertrand Russell, the writers Lytton Strachey and Leonard Woolf, the economist Keynes, and the spies Guy Burgess and Anthony Blunt.

apostrophe[1]**,** *n.* a rhetorical figure in which the speaker addresses one person in particular, or turns away from those present to address the absent or dead. **apostrophic,** *a.* **apostrophize, -ise,** *v.t.* to address in or with apostrophe. [L, from Gr. *apostrophē,* a turning away (*apostrephein,* to turn away)]

apostrophe[2]**,** *n.* the sign (') used to denote the omission of a letter or letters, and as the sign of the English possessive case. **apostrophize, -ise,** *v.t.* to mark an omission of a letter or letters from a word by inserting an apostrophe. [F *apostrophe,* from L *apostrophus,* from Gr. *apostrophos,* turned away]

apothecary, *n.* one who prepares and sells medicines; a druggist or pharmaceutical chemist; a licentiate of the Apothecaries' Society. **apothecaries' measure,** *n.* a system of liquid capacity measure formerly used in pharmacy, based on the minim, fluid drachm and fluid ounce. **apothecaries' weight,** *n.* a system of weights formerly used in pharmacy, based on the grain, scruple, drachm, and troy ounce. [OF *apotecaire,* late L *apothēcārius,* from *apothēca,* a storehouse, Gr. *apothēkē* (*apo-,* away, *tithēmi,* I put)]

apothecium, *n.* the spore-case in lichens. [mod. L, from Gr. *apothēkē,* see prec.]

apothegm APOPHTHEGM.

apotheosis, *n.* (*pl.* **-ses**) deification; transformation into a god; canonization; enrolment among the saints; a deified ideal. **apotheosize, -ise,** *v.t.* to deify, to exalt, to glorify. [L, from Gr. *apotheōsis* (*apo-, theoō,* I deify, from *theos,* a god)]

apozem, *n.* a decoction or infusion. [F *apozème,* late L *apozema,* Gr. *apozema* (from *apo-,* off or away, *zeein,* to boil)]

app., (*abbr.*) apparent, apparently; appendix; appointed; apprentice.

appal, (*esp. N Am.*) **appall,** *v.i.* (*past, p.p.* **appalled**) †to grow pale, to grow faint or feeble. *v.t.* †to make pale; †to enfeeble, impair; to inspire with terror; to terrify; to dismay. **appalling,** *a.* **appallingly,** *adv.* [OF *apalir, apallir,* to grow pale, to make pale]

Appalachians, *n.pl.* mountain system of E North America, stretching about 2400 km/1500 miles from Alabama to Québec, composed of very ancient eroded rocks. The chain includes the Allegheny, Catskill and Blue Ridge mountains, the latter having the highest peak, Mount Mitchell, 2045 m/6712 ft. The eastern edge has a fall line to the coastal plain where Philadelphia, Baltimore and Washington stand.

Appaloosa, *n.* a N American breed of horse with a spotted coat. [prob. from the *Palouse* Indians]

appanage APANAGE.

apparat, *n.* the apparatus of the Soviet Communist party. **apparatchik,** *n.* a member of the Soviet apparat. [Rus.]

apparatus, *n.* (*pl.* **apparatuses, apparatus**) equipment or arrangements generally; the instruments employed in scientific or other research; materials for critical study; the organs by which any natural process is carried on; the administrative workings of a (political) system or organization. **apparatus criticus,** *n.* critical equipment, the materials employed, as variant readings etc., in literary criticism and investigation. [L *ad-,* to, *parare,* to prepare]

apparel, *n.* dress, attire, clothes; ornamental embroidery on ecclesiastical vestments; †the outfit of a ship. *v.t.* (*past, p.p.* **apparelled**) to dress, to clothe; to equip, to fit out; to adorn, to embellish, to ornament. †**apparelment,** *n.* outfit; equipment. [OF *aparail,* n., and *apareiller,* v., to dress (*à,* L *ad-,* to, *pareiller,* to assort, make fit, from *pareil,* like, late L *pariculum,* dim. of *par,* equal)]

apparent, *a.* to be seen, visible, in sight; plain, obvious, indubitable; appearing (in a certain way), seeming. **apparent horizon** HORIZON. **apparently,** *adv.* †manifestly, evidently; to external appearances; seemingly, as distinguished from actually. [OF *aparant, aparent,* L *appārentem,* p.p. of *appārēre,* to come into sight]

apparition, *n.* the state of becoming visible; a strange appearance; a spectre, phantom, ghost; the visibility of a star, planet or comet. **apparitional,** *a.* [F, from L *appāritiōnem,* from *appārēre,* see APPEAR]

apparitor, *n.* one of the public servants of the ancient Roman magistrates; a petty officer in a civil or ecclesiastical court; a beadle, usher orsimilar functionary. [L, see APPEAR]

appeal, *v.t.* †to accuse; to impeach; to challenge; to invoke as a judge; to refer (a case) to a higher court. *v.i.* to refer to a superior judge, court or authority; to refer to some person or thing as corroboration; to invoke aid, pity, mercy etc.; to have recourse (to); to apply (to); to attract or interest. *n.* †a calling to account; the act of appealing; the right of appeal; reference or recourse to another; entreaty; a request for aid, esp. for money for charitable purposes; power of attracting or interesting. **to appeal to the country** COUNTRY. **appealable,** *a.* that may be appealed against; that can be appealed to. **appealing,** *a.* of the nature of an appeal, suppliant; having appeal, arousing interest. **appealingly,** *adv.* **appealingness,** *n.* [OF *apeler,* to invoke, L *appellāre* (*ad-,* to, *pellere,* to drive)]

appear, *v.i.* to become or be visible; to present oneself; to come before the public; to be manifest; to seem. **appearance,** *n.* the act of appearing; the thing seen; the act of appearing formally or publicly; a phenomenon; a phantom; mien, aspect; external show, pretence; (*pl.*) the aspect of circumstances. **to keep up appearances,** to keep up an outward show; to conceal the absence of something desirable. [OF *aper-,* stem of *aparoir,* to appear (pres. subj. *apere*), L *appārēre* (*ad-,* to, *pārēre,* to come into sight)]

appease, *v.t.* to quiet, to pacify, to calm, to assuage, to allay; to conciliate by acceding to demands. **appeasable,** *a.* **appeasement,** *n.* the act of appeasing; the state of being appeased; the thing that appeases, satisfies or makes peace; the endeavour to preserve peace by giving way to the demands of an aggressor power. [OF *apeser, apaisier* (*à,* to, *pais,* peace, L *ad pacem, pax*)]

Appel, *n.* **Karel,** Dutch painter and sculptor, founder of Cobra (1948), a group of European artists that developed an expressive and dynamic form of abstract painting, with thick paintwork and lurid colours.

appellant, *a.* appealing, challenging; relating to appeals. *n.* one who appeals to a higher tribunal or authority; one who makes an appeal. **appellate,** *a.* pertaining to or dealing with appeals. **appellation,** *n.* a name, designation; naming, nomenclature. **appellative,** *a.* common as opposed to proper; designating a class. *n.* an appellation, a name; a common as opposed to a proper noun. **appellatively,** *adv.* [F *appellant,* see APPEAL]

append, *v.t.* to hang to or upon; to add or subjoin. **appendage,** *n.* something added or appended; a subordinate or subsidiary organ or process, as a limb or branch. **appendant,** *a.* attached, annexed, joined on. *n.* that which is attached or annexed; an appendix, a corollary. [L *appendere* (*ad-,* to, *pendere,* to hang)]

appendicectomy, appendectomy, *n.* the excision of the vermiform appendix.

appendicitis, *n.* inflammation of the vermiform appendix.

appendicle, *n.* a small appendage. **appendicular,** *a.* of or of the nature of an appendicle. **appendiculate,** *a.* furnished with small appendages. [L *appendicula,* dim. of *appendix*]

appendix, *n.* (*pl.* **-dixes, -dices**) something appended; an adjunct or concomitant; a supplement to a book or document containing useful material; a small process arising from, or the prolongation of, any organ, esp. the vermiform appendix of the intestine. [L, see APPEND]

apperception, *n.* perception of one's own mental processes; consciousness of one's self; understanding and assimilation of a new perception in terms of previous experiences. [F *apperception,* mod. L *appercipere* (*ad-,* to, *percipere,* see PERCEIVE)]

appertain, *v.i.* to belong (as a part to a whole, as a possession, or as a right or privilege); to relate (to); to be suitable or appropriate. [OF *apartenir,* late L *appertinēre* (*ad-,* to, *pertinēre,* to pertain)]

appetence, -ency, *n.* instinctive desire, craving, appetite; natural propensity; affinity. **appetent,** *a.* longing, eagerly desirous; pertaining to desire and volition. [F *appétence,* L *appetentia,* from *appetent-, appetens,* pres.p. of *appetere* (*ad-,* to, *petere,* to seek)]

appetite, *n.* inclination, disposition; the desire to satisfy a natural function; desire, relish for food. **appetitive,** *a.* possessed of or characterized by appetite. **appetize, -ise,** *v.t.* to give an appetite to; to make (one) feel hungry or relish one's food. **appetizer, -iser,** *n.* a whet; stimulant to appetite, esp. food or drink served before or at the beginning of a meal. **appetizing, -ising,** *a.* stimulating appetite or hunger. [OF *apetit,* L *appetitus*]

applaud, *v.i.* to express approbation, esp. by clapping the hands. *v.t.* to approve, commend praise in an audible and significant manner. **applause** *n.* the act of applauding; praise loudly expressed. **applausive,** *a.* praising by acclamation, approbative. **applausively,** *adv.* in an applausive manner. [L *applaudere* (*ad-,* together, *plaudere,* to clap)]

apple, *n.* the round, firm, fleshy fruit of the apple-tree; any similar fruit; the fruit of the forbidden tree in the Garden of Eden; a tree, genus *Malus,* that bears apples; anything resembling an apple in shape or colour. **apple of discord,** the golden apple contended for as prize of beauty by Juno, Minerva and Venus; a cause of contention. **apple of one's eye,** the pupil, formerly supposed to be a solid body; anything very dear or precious. **apple of Sodom,** a mythical fruit, said to resemble an apple, but turning to ashes, also called *Dead Sea apple* or *Dead Sea fruit;* anything disappointing. **to upset the apple-cart,** to disrupt plans or arrangements. **apple-brandy,** *n.* spirit made from apples. **apple-butter,** *n.* a preserve (or sauce) made of apples stewed in cider. **apple-cheese,** *n.* apple-pomace compressed. **apple-dumpling,** *n.* an apple covered with pastry and baked or boiled. **apple-faced, apple-cheeked,** *a.* having a chubby face or cheeks. **Apple Island,** *n.* (*Austral.*) Tasmania. **apple-jack,** *n.* (*N Am.*) apple-brandy. **apple-john,** *n.* a variety of late apple, good for keeping, but shrivelling up outside. **apple-pie,** *n.* a pie consisting of apples enclosed in a crust. **apple-pie bed,** a bed whose sheets are so doubled as to prevent one stretching one's full length. **apple-pie order,** perfect order. **apple-pomace,** *n.* pulp left after apples have been pressed in cider-making. **apple-pudding,** *n.* a pudding consisting of apples enclosed in a pastry. **apple-sauce,** *n.* sauce made from apples; (*N Am., coll.*) insincere praise, nonsense. **apple-toddy,** *n.* toddy in which roasted apples are used instead of lemon-peel. **apple-wife, apple-woman,** *n.* a woman who sells apples in the street. †**apple-yard,** *n.* an orchard. [OE *æpl, æppel* (OHG *aphul,* G *Apfel*)]

Appleseed, *n.* **Johnny,** character in US folk legend who wandered through the country for 40 years sowing apple seeds from which apple trees grew. The legend seems to be based on a historical figure, the US pioneer John Chapman (1774–1845).

Appleton layer, *n.* a band containing ionized gases in the Earth's upper atmosphere, above the Kennelly–Heaviside layer. It can act as a reflector of radio signals, although its ionic composition varies with the sunspot cycle. [the British physicist, Sir E. *Appleton,* 1892–1965]

appliance, applicant etc. APPLY.

appliqué, *n.* ornamental work laid on some other material. **appliquéd,** *part.a.* treated with work of this kind. [F, p.p. of *appliquer,* to apply]

apply, *v.t.* to put or lay on; to put close to; to administer (as an external remedy); to employ, to devote; to make suitable, adapt, conform to. *v.i.* to agree, to harmonize, to be relevant; to have recourse (to); to study; to offer oneself (for a job, position etc.). **appliance,** *n.* the act of applying; anything applied as a means to an end; an apparatus, device or contrivance. **applicable,** *a.* capable of being applied; fit, suitable, appropriate. **applicability,** *n.* **applicant,** *n.* one who applies; a petitioner; (*N Am.*) a person remarkable for application to study. **applicate,** *a.* applied to practical use. *n.* a straight line drawn across a curve so as to bisect its diameter. **application,** *n.* the act of applying; the thing applied; the use to which something is put; (a) petition, request; close attention; study. **applications program,** *n.* a computer program that performs a specific task for a user. **applicative,** *a.* characterized by application; practical. **applied,** *a.* practical; put to practical use. **applied science,** *n.* science of which the abstract principles are put to practical use in solving problems. [OF *aplier,* L *applicāre* (*ad-,* to, *plicāre,* to fold together, fasten)]

appoggiatura, *n.* a grace-note before a significant note. [It.]

appoint, *v.t.* to decree, ordain, fix, prescribe; to nominate, designate; to make an appointment or assignation with (a person) or at (a time); to assign, to grant (a thing to a person). *v.i.* to decree, ordain. **appointed,** *a.* furnished, equipped. **appointee,** *n.* one who receives an appointment; (*Law*) one in whose favour an appointment is executed. **appointment,** *n.* the act of appointing; the office or situation assigned; that which is appointed or fixed; an engagement or assignation; allowance, decree, ordinance; (*pl.*) equipment, accoutrements, apparel (of a ship); (*Law*) the official declaration of the destination of any specific property. [OF *apointer* (*à,* to, *point,* the point)]

Appomattox, *n.* a village in Virginia, US, scene of the surrender on 9 Apr. 1865 of the Confederate army under Robert E. Lee to the Union army under Ulysses S. Grant, which ended the American Civil War.

apport, *n.* in spiritualistic terminology, a material object brought without material agency. [L *apportāre* to bring]

apportion, *v.t.* to mete out in just proportions; to divide in suitable proportion. **apportionment,** *n.* the act of apportioning; the state of being apportioned. [OF *apportionner*]

apposite, *a.* fit, apt, appropriate. **appositely,** *adv.* **appositeness,** *n.* **apposition,** *n.* the act of putting together or side by side; juxtaposition, addition; (*Gram.*) the placing together of two words, esp. of two substantives, one being a complement to the other. **appositional,** *a.* relating to apposition. [L *appositus,* p.p. of *appōnere* (*ad-,* to, *pōnere,* to place, put)]

appraise, *v.t.* to set a price on; to value; to estimate the worth of. **appraisable,** *a.* **appraisal,** *n.* an authoritative valuation; an estimate of worth. **appraisement,** *n.* the act of appraising; estimated value or worth. **appraiser,** *n.* one who appraises; a person authorized to fix the value of property. [PRAISE]

appreciate, *v.t.* to form an estimate of the value, merit, quality or quantity of; to estimate aright; to be sensible of (delicate impressions); to esteem highly; to raise in value. *v.i.* to rise in value. **appreciable,** *a.* capable of being appreciated. **appreciably,** *adv.* in a way that can be estimated, to an appreciable extent. **appreciation,** *n.* the act of appreciating; an estimate;a critical study; adequate recognition; a rise in value. **appreciative,** *a.* capable of, expressing appreciation; esteeming favourably. **appreciatively,** *adv.* **appreciator,** *n.* **appreciatory,** *a.* [L *appretiātus,* p.p. of *appretiāre,* to fix a price on (*ad,* to, *pretium,* a price)]

apprehend, *v.t.* to take hold of; to grasp, to seize, to arrest; to seize, grasp or lay hold of mentally; to fear, to dread; to anticipate. *v.i.* to understand. **apprehensible,** *a.* **apprehension,** *n.* the act of laying hold of, seizing or arresting; the mental faculty which apprehends; conception, idea; fear, dread of what may happen. **apprehensive,** *a.* characterized by or fitted for (mental) apprehension; perceptive, sensitive, discerning; anticipative of something unpleasant or harmful, fearful, anxious. **apprehensively,** *adv.* **apprehensiveness,** *n.* [F *appréhender,* L *apprehendere* (*ad-,* to, *prehendere,* to seize)]

apprentice, *n.* one bound by indentures to serve an employer for a term of years in order to learn some trade or craft which the employer agrees to teach; a learner, a tyro, a novice. *v.t.* to bind as an apprentice. **apprenticeship,** *n.* the state or position of an apprentice; service or training of an apprentice; the term for which an apprentice is bound to serve. [OF *aprentis,* from *apprendre,* to learn (L *apprehendere,* see prec.)]

apprise, *v.t.* to inform, to make aware, to bring to the knowledge or notice of. [F *appris,* p.p. of *apprendre,* see APPREHEND]

apprize, *v.t.* to put a price on; to estimate the worth of.

[OF *aprisier,* to appraise (*à,* to, *prisier,* to prize or praise, perhaps from *à prix,* cp. *mettre à prix*)]

appro, *n.* short for APPROVAL.

approach, *v.i.* to come, go or draw near or nearer; to approximate. *v.t.* to come near to; to resemble; (*Mil.*) to make approaches or entrenchments; (*coll.*) to come near or address with a view to securing something, as a favour or intimate relations. *n.* the act of drawing near; approximation, resemblance; avenue, entrance, access; (*usu. pl.*) works thrown up by a besieging force to protect it in its advance; (*Golf*) a stroke that should take the ball on to the green. **to graft by approach,** to bring together branches which are to be grafted, to inarch. **approachable,** *a.* capable of being approached; easy to deal with; friendly. **approachability,** *n.* [OF *aprochier,* late L *appropiāre* (*ad-,* to, *propius,* compar. of *prope,* near)]

approbate, *v.t.* (*chiefly N Am.*) to express approval of; (*Sc. Law*) to approve formally as valid.

approbation, *n.* the act of approving; approval, commendation, praise; probation, trial. **approbatory,** *a.* containing, expressing or implying approval.

approof, *n.* proof, trial, experience; approval. [OF *aprove,* proof, trial, L *approbāre* (cp. APPROVE)]

appropinquate, *v.i.* to draw near to, to approach. **appropinquation,** *n.* the act of coming or bringing near. **appropinquity,** *n.* nearness, contiguity, propinquity. [L *appropinquātus,* p.p. of *appropinquāre,* to draw near (*ad-,* towards, *propinquus, prope,* near)]

appropriate[1], *v.t.* to take as one's own; to take possession of; to devote to or set apart for a special purpose or use; to annex the fruits of a benefice to a spiritual corporation. **appropriable,** *a.* **appropriation,** *n.* the act of appropriating; the state of being appropriated; that which is appropriated; a sum of money or a portion of revenue appropriated to a specific object. **appropriative,** *a.* appropriating; involving appropriation; tending to appropriate. **appropriator,** *n.* one who appropriates; a religious corporation owning a benefice. [L *appropriātus,* p.p. of *appropriāre* (*ad-,* to, *proprius,* one's own)]

appropriate[2], *a.* annexed or attached to; set apart for a particular person or use; suitable, fit, becoming. **appropriately,** *adv.* **appropriateness,** *n.* fitness, suitability.

approve, *v.t.* to esteem, accept or pronounce as good; to commend, sanction, confirm; to demonstrate practically. *v.i.* to express or to feel approbation. **approvable,** *a.* **approval,** *n.* approbation, sanction. **on approval, on appro,** on trial to ascertain if suitable; of goods, to be returned if not suitable. **approved,** *a.* tried, proved, tested; regarded with approval; officially sanctioned. **approved school,** *n.* formerly, a state boarding school for juvenile offenders (boys under 15, girls under 17). **approvement,** *n.* (*Law*) the improvement of commons by enclosure for purposes of husbandry. **approver,** *n.* one who approves, sanctions or commends; one who confesses a crime and gives evidence against his/her associates. **approving,** *a.* **approvingly,** *adv.* [OF *aprover,* L *approbāre* (*ad-,* to, *probāre,* to test, try)]

approx., (*abbr.*) approximate, approximately.

approximate[1], *v.t.* to draw or bring near; to cause to approach. *v.i.* to draw near, to approach. **approximation,** *n.* the act of approximating or approaching; approach, proximity; (*Math.*) a coming or getting nearer to a quantity sought, when no process exists for ascertaining it exactly; something approximate; a mathematical value that is sufficiently accurate for a purpose though not exact; communication of a disease by contact. **approximative,** *a.* of an approximate character; drawing or coming nearer; approaching. **approximatively,** *adv.* [L *approximātus,* p.p. of *approximāre* (*ad-,* to, *proximus,* very near, superl. of *prope,* near)]

approximate[2], *a.* very close to; closely resembling; nearly approaching accuracy; (*Biol.*) set very close together. *n.* an approximate result, an approximate number or quantity. **approximately,** *adv.* [from prec.]

appui, *n.* the stay (of a horse) upon the bridle-hand of its rider; (*Mil.*) defensive support. **point of appui, point d'appui,** *n.* (*Mil.*) any particular point or body upon which troops are formed. [F, from *appuyer,* late L *appodiāre,* to lean upon (*ad-,* upon, *podium,* a support, from Gr. *podion,* base, *pous podos,* foot)]

appulse, *n.* a striking against; the approach of a planet or a fixed star to the meridian, or to conjunction with the sun or the moon. **appulsion,** *n.* a driving against. [L *appulsus,* approach, *appellere* (*ad-,* to, *pellere,* to drive)]

appurtenance, *n.* that which belongs to something else; an adjunct, an accessory, an appendage. **appurtenant,** *a.* pertaining to, belonging to, pertinent. *n.* an appurtenance. [OF *apurtenaunce,* late L *appertinēntia,* from *appertinēre* (APPERTAIN)]

APR, (*abbr.*) annual percentage rate (of credit etc.).

Apr., (*abbr.*) April.

apraxia, *n.* (partial) loss of the ability to execute voluntary movements. [Gr., inaction (*a-,* priv., *praxis,* action)]

après-ski, *n., a.* (of or intended for) the social time following a day's skiing. [F]

apricot, *n.* a stone-fruit allied to the plum; the tree, *Prunus armeniaca,* on which it grows. [formerly *apricock,* Port. *albricoque,* Sp. *albaricoque,* Arab. *alburqūq* (*al,* the, corr. of Gr. *praikokion,* from L *praecoqua,* apricots, neut. pl. of *praecoquum,* from *praecox,* early ripe), assim. to F *abricot*]

April, *n.* the fourth month of the year. **April-fool,** *n.* a victim of a practical joke on 1 April. **April-fool day, April-Fools' day,** *n.* the first day of April, when it is customary in W Europe and the US to expose people to ridicule by causing them to believe some falsehood or to go on a fruitless errand. **April shower,** *n.* a sudden, brief shower of rain (common in the month of April). [OF *avrill,* L *Aprīlis* (prob. from *aperīre,* to open)]

a priori, *adv.* from the cause to the effect; from abstract ideas to consequences; deductively. *a.* deductive; derived by reasoning from cause to effect; prior to experience; abstract and unsupported by actual evidence. **apriority,** *n.* [L, from what is before]

apron, *n.* a garment worn in front of the body to protect the clothes, or as part of a distinctive dress, e.g. of bishops, Freemasons; anything resembling an apron in shape or function, as a leather covering for the legs in an open carriage; the fat skin covering the belly of a roast goose or duck; a covering for the vent of a cannon; a strip of lead carrying drip into a gutter; the extension of the stage in some theatres beyond the proscenium; a platform of planks at the entrance to a dock; the surfaced area on an airfield; an extensive deposit of sand, gravel etc. **apron-string,** *n.* the string of an apron. **tied to the apron-strings,** unduly controlled (by a wife, mother etc.). **aproned,** *a.* wearing an apron. **apronful,** *n.* as much as can be held in an apron. [OF *naperon,* a large cloth, dim. of *nape,* a tablecloth, L *nappa,* a cloth (cp. formation of ADDER[2])]

apropos, *adv.* opportunely, seasonably; by the way. *a.* opportune, seasonable; appropriate; bearing on the matter in hand; to the point. **apropos of,** *prep.* as bearing upon the subject; as suggested by. [F *àpropos,* L *ad prōpositum,* to the thing proposed (*prōpōnere,* to propose)]

apse, apsis, *n.* (*pl.* **apses apsides** (*usu.* **apse**) a semicircular, or polygonal, and generally dome-roofed, recess in a building, esp. in a church; a tribune, a bishop's throne; a reliquary (from this being situated in the apse in ancient churches); (*usu.* **apsis**) one of two points at which a planet or satellite is at its greatest or least distance from the body round which it revolves; the imaginary line joining these points is called the **line of the apsides**. **apsidal**, *a.* pertaining to or of the shape of an apse or apsis. [L *apsis, absis,* Gr. *apsis, apsis -idos,* fastening, felloe of a wheel, curve (*aptein,* to fasten, join)]

apt, *a.* fit, suitable, proper, relevant; having a tendency (to), likely; quick, ready; qualified. **aptly,** *adv.* **apt-**

ness, *n.* [L *aptus,* p.p. of obs. v. *apere,* to fasten (used as p.p. of *apiscī,* to reach)]
apteral, *a.* wingless; (*Arch.*) without columns at the sides. [Gr. *apteros* (*a-,* not, without, *pteron,* a wing)]
apterous, *a.* wingless; having only rudimentary wings; (*Bot.*) without membranous wing-like expansions. [Gr. *apteros* (*a,* not, *pteron,* a wing)]
apteryx, *n.* the kiwi, a bird from New Zealand, about the size of a goose, with rudimentary wings. [Gr. *a-,* not, *pteron,* a wing]
aptitude, *n.* fitness, suitability, adaptation; a tendency towards, or proneness to something. [F, from med L *aptitūdo,* n. of quality from *aptus,* APT]
aptote, *n.* an indeclinable noun. **aptotic,** *a.* without grammatical inflexion. [L *aptōtum,* Gr. *aptōtos -on* (*a-,* not, *ptōtos,* falling, cp. *ptōsis,* case, from *piptein,* to fall)]
Apuleius, *n.* **Lucius** (*c.* AD 160), Roman lawyer, philosopher and author of *Metamorphoses*, or *The Golden Ass*.
Apulia, *n.* English form of Puglia, region of Italy.
apyretic, *a.* without fever. [Gr. *apuretos* (a-, not, *puretos,* fever)]
apyrexy, *n.* the intermission or abatement of a fever. [L, from Gr. *apurexia* (*a-,* not, *puressein,* to be feverish)]
aq., (*abbr.*) water. [L *aqua*]
Aqaba, Gulf of, a gulf extending for 160 km/100 miles between the Negev and the Red Sea; its coastline is uninhabited except at its head, where the frontiers of Israel, Egypt, Jordan and Saudi Arabia converge. Here are the two ports Eilat (Israeli Elath) and Aqaba, Jordan's only port.
aqua, *n.* water, liquid, solution. [L]
aqu(a)-, aqu(i)-, *comb. form.* pertaining to water. [L *aqua*]
aquaculture, aquiculture, *n.* hydroponics, the cultivation of aquatic organisms for human use.
Aquae Sulis, *n.* Roman name of the city of Bath in W England.
aqua fortis, aquafortis, *n.* nitric acid. **aquafortist,** *n.* (*Art*) one who etches or engraves with aqua-fortis. [L *fortis,* strong]
aqualung, *n.* a portable diving apparatus, strapped on the back and feeding air to the diver as required.
aquamarine, *n.* a bluish-green variety of beryl, named from its colour. *a.* bluish-green. [L *aquamarina,* sea-water]
aquaplane, *n.* a board on which one is towed, standing, behind a motor-boat. *v.i.* to ride on an aquaplane; of a car etc., to slide on a film of water on a road surface.
aqua regia, *n.* a mixture of nitric and hydrochloric acids, capable of dissolving gold and platinum. [royal water, from its use in dissolving gold, the royal (L *regius*) metal]
aquarelle, *n.* a kind of painting in Chinese ink and very thin transparent water-colours; the design so produced. **aquarellist,** *n.* one who paints in aquarelle. [F, from It. *acquerella,* dim. of *acqua* (L *aqua*), water]
aquarist, *n.* the keeper of an aquarium.
aquarium, *n.* (*pl.* **-riums, -ria**) an artificial tank, pond or vessel in which aquatic animals and plants are kept alive; a place in which such tanks are exhibited.
Aquarius, *n.* a zodiacal constellation in the southern hemisphere near Pegasus. It is represented as a man pouring water from a jar. The Sun passes through Aquarius from late Feb to early Mar. In astrology, the dates for Aquarius are between about 20 Jan. and 18 Feb.
aquatic, *a.* of or pertaining to water; living or growing in or near water. *n.* an aquatic animal or plant. **aquatics,** *n.pl.* sports or athletic exercises on or in the water. [L *aquaticus*]
aquatint, *n.* a method of etching on copper; a design so produced. [F *aqua-tinte,* It. *acqua tinta* (L *aqua,* water, *tincta,* dyed, from *tingere,* to dye)]
aquavit, *n.* an alcoholic spirit flavoured with caraway seeds. [Scand. *akvavit,* from med. L *aqua vitae*]
aqua vitae, *n.* unrectified alcohol; strong spirits, brandy etc. [L, water of life]
aqueduct, *n.* an artificial channel, esp. an artificial channel raised on pillars or arches for the conveyance of (drinking) water from place to place; a small canal, chiefly in the heads of mammals. [L *aquaeductus* (*aquae,* of water, *ductus,* conveyance, from *ducere,* to lead)]
aqueous, *a.* consisting of, containing, formed in or deposited from water; watery. **aqueous humour,** *n.* the watery fluid in the eye between the cornea and the lens. **aqueous rocks,** *n.pl.* rocks deposited in water; sedimentary rocks. [L *aqueus*]
aquiculture AQUACULTURE.
aquifer, *n.* a water-bearing layer of rock, gravel etc. **aquiferous,** *a.* conveying, bearing or yielding water.
aquiform, *a.* in the form or state of water; liquid.
Aquila, *n.*, a constellation of the equatorial region of the sky. Its brightest star is the first-magnitude Altair, flanked by the stars Beta and Gamma Aquilae. It is represented by an eagle.
Aquilegia, *n.* a genus of acrid plants, order Ranunculaceae, commonly known as columbine. [L *aquila,* an eagle]
aquiline, *a.* of or pertaining to an eagle; eagle-like; esp. of noses, hooked, curved, like an eagle's bill. [L *aquilinus,* eagle-like (*aquila,* an eagle)]
†**aquilon,** *n.* the north-east wind. [OF, from L *aquilo -ōnem*]
Aquinas, *n.* **St Thomas** (*c.* 1226–1274), Neapolitan philosopher and theologian. His *Summa Contra Gentiles/Against the Errors of the Infidels* (1259–64) argues that reason and faith are compatible. His most significant contribution to philosophy was to synthesize the philosophy of Aristotle and Christian doctrine.
Aquino, *n.* **(Maria) Corazón** (born Cojuangco) (1933–), president of the Philippines from 1986, when she was instrumental in the nonviolent overthrow of President Marcos. She has sought to rule in a conciliatory manner, but has encountered opposition from left (communist guerrillas) and right (army coup attempts), and her land reforms have been seen as inadequate.
Aquitaine, *n.* region of SW France; capital Bordeaux; area 41,300 sq km/15,942 sq miles; population (1986) 2,718,000. It comprises the *départements* of Dordogne, Gironde, Landes, Lot-et-Garonne, and Pyrénées-Atlantiques. Red wines (Margaux, St Julien) are produced in the Médoc district, bordering the Gironde. Aquitaine was an English possession (1152–1452).
aquosity, *n.* wateriness. [med. L *aquōsitas,* from *aquōsus,* watery]
Ar, (*chem. symbol*) argon.
ar, (*abbr.*) in the year of the reign. [L *anno regni*]
ar., (*abbr.*) arrival, arrive(s).
ar-, *pref.* AD-, assim, to *r,* e.g. *arrest, arrogate.*
-ar¹, *suf.* belonging to, of the nature of, e.g. *angular, linear, lunar, regular* [L *-ārem, -āris*]; thing pertaining to, e.g. *altar, exemplar, pillar.* [L *-āre, -ār*]
-ar², *suf.* -er, -ary, the agent, e.g. *bursar, mortar, vicar.* [OF *-ier* (F *-aire*), L *-ārius, -ārium*]
-ar³, *suf.* -er, the agent, doer, e.g. *beggar, liar.* [-ER¹]
ARA, (*abbr.*) Associate of the Royal Academy.
Arab, *n.* a member of a Semitic people orig. inhabiting Arabia and now much of the Middle East; an Arabian horse; (**arab, street arab**) an outcast or vagrant child. *a.* Arabian. **Arabian,** *a.* of or pertaining to Arabia or to Arabs. *n.* a native of Arabia. **Arabian-bird,** *n.* the phoenix; something unique. **Arabian Nights,** *n.* a famous collection of stories; a collection of fantastic stories. **Arabic,** *a.* pertaining to Arabia, the Arabs, or to Arabic. *n.* see ARABIC LANGUAGE below. **Arabic numerals,** *n.pl.* the figures, 1,2,3 etc. **arabist,** *n.* a student of the Arabic language or culture. [F *Arabe,* L *Arab -em* (nom. *Arabs*), Gr. *Araps -abos*]
Arab., (*abbr.*) Arabia, Arabian, Arabic.
araba, *n.* an oriental wheeled carriage. [Arab. and Pers. *arābah*]
Arab Emirates, UNITED ARAB EMIRATES.
arabesque, *a.* Arabian in design; in the style of ara-

besque. *n.* surface decoration composed of flowing line fancifully intermingled, usu. representing foliage in a conventional manner, without animal forms; a posture in ballet-dancing with one leg raised behind and the arms extended. [F]

Arabian Nights, *n.pl.* tales in oral circulation among Arab storytellers from the 10th cent., and probably having roots in India. They are also known as *The Thousand and One Nights* and include 'Ali Baba', 'Aladdin', 'Sinbad the Sailor', and 'The Old Man of the Sea'.

Arabian sea, *n.* the NW branch of the Indian Ocean.

Arabic language, *n.* a Hamito-Semitic language of W Asia and North Africa, originating among the Arabs of the Arabian peninsula. Arabic script is written from right to left.

Arabis, *n.* a genus of cruciferous plants largely grown on rockwork, also called rock-cress. [med. L *Arabs -bis,* Arab; prob. from its liking for stony places]

Arab-Israeli Wars, *n.pl.* a series of wars between Israel and various Arab states in the Middle East since the founding of the state of Israel in 1948.

Arabistan, *n.* former name of the Iranian province of Khuzestan, revived in the 1980s by the 2 million Sunni Arab inhabitants who demand autonomy. Unrest and sabotage (1979–80) led to a pledge of a degree of autonomy by Ayatollah Khomeini.

arable, *a.* capable of being ploughed; fit for tillage. [L *arābilis* (*arāre,* to plough)]

Arab League, *n.* an organization of Arab states established in Cairo (1945) to promote Arab unity, especially in opposition to Israel. The original members were Egypt, Syria, Iraq, Lebanon, Transjordan (Jordan 1949), Saudi Arabia and Yemen. In 1979 Egypt was suspended and the league's headquarters transferred to Tunis in protest against the Egypt–Israeli peace, but Egypt was readmitted as a full member in May 1989.

†**Araby,** *a.* Arabic. *n.* an Arab; an Arab horse; Arabia. [OF *arabi*]

araceous, *a.* belonging to the *Arum* genus of plants. [ARUM]

Arachis, *n.* a small genus of low Brazilian leguminous herbs including the peanut, *Arachis hypogeae*. **arachis oil,** *n.* peanut oil. [Gr. *arachos,* a leguminous plant]

Arachne, *n.* (Greek 'spider') in Greek mythology, a Lydian woman who was so skilful a weaver that she challenged the goddess Athena to a contest. Athena tore Arachne's beautiful tapestries to pieces and Arachne hanged herself. She was transformed into a spider, and her weaving became a cobweb.

arachnid, *n.* any individual of the class Arachnida, which contains the spiders, scorpions and mites. **arachnidan, -dean,** *a.* of or belonging to the arachnids. *n.* an arachnid. **arachnoid,** *a.* resembling the Arachnida; (*Bot.*) cobweb-like, covered with long, filamentous hairs; of or belonging to the Arachnida. *n.* the transparent membrane lying between the pia mater and the dura mater, that is the middle of the three membranes enveloping the brain and spinal cord. **arachnology,** *n.* the scientific study of spiders or of the Arachnida generally. **arachnologist,** *n.* one versed in arachnology. [Gr. *arachnē,* a spider]

araeometer, areometer, *n.* an instrument for determining the specific gravity or relative density of liquids, a hydrometer. **araeometry,** *n.* the measurement of the specific gravity ofliquids, hydrometry. [Gr. *araios,* thin, -METER]

Arafat, *n.* **Yasser** (1929–), Palestinian nationalist politician, cofounder of al-Fatah (1956) and president of the Palestine Liberation Organization (PLO) from 1969. In the 1970s his activities in pursuit of an independent homeland for Palestinians made him a prominent figure in world politics, but in the 1980s the growth of factions within the PLO effectively reduced his power. He was forced to evacuate Lebanon in 1983, but remained leader of most of the PLO.

Arago, *n.* **Dominique** (1786–1853), French physicist and astronomer who made major contributions to the early study of electromagnetism. In 1820 he found out that iron enclosed in a wire coil could be magnetized by the passage of an electric current. Later in 1824 he was the first to observe the ability of a floating copper disk to deflect a magnetic needle, the phenomenon of magnetic rotation.

Aragón, *n.* autonomous region of NE Spain including the provinces of Huesca, Teruel and Zaragoza; area 47,700 sq km/18,412 sq miles; population (1986) 1,215,000. Its capital is Zaragoza, and products include almonds, figs, grapes and olives. Aragón was an independent kingdom (1035–1479).

Aragon, *n.* **Louis** (1897–1982), French poet and novelist. Beginning as a Dadaist, he became one of the leaders of surrealism, published volumes of verse and in 1930 joined the Communist Party. Taken prisoner in World War II he escaped to join the Resistance, experiences reflected in the poetry of *Le Crève-coeur* (1942) and *Les Yeux d'Elsa* (1944).

aragonite, *n.* a carbonate of lime, dimorphous with calcite, first found in Aragon, Spain.

Arago's disk, *n.* an apparatus illustrating the action of induced currents by means of a magnet pivoted over a revolving copper disc. [the physicist and inventor Dominique François Jean *Arago,* 1786–1853]

arak ARRACK.

Aral Sea, *n.* inland sea in the USSR; the world's fourth largest lake; divided between Kazakhstan and Uzbekistan; former area 62,000 sq km/24,000 sq miles, but decreasing. Water from its tributaries, the Amu Darya and Syr Darya, has been diverted for irrigation and city use, and the sea is disappearing, with long-term consequences for the climate.

ARAM, (*abbr.*) Associate of the Royal Academy of Music.

Aramaean, *a.* pertaining to ancient Aram, or Syria, or its language. *n.* a Syrian; the Syrian language. **Aramaic,** *a.* of or belonging to Aram; applied to the ancient northern branch of the Semitic family of languages, including Syriac and Chaldean. *n.* Syriac. [L *aramaeus,* Gr. *Aramaios*]

Aran, *a.* knitted in a style that originated in the Aran Islands off the W coast of Ireland, typically with a thick cream-coloured wool.

Araneida, *n.pl.* the typical order of the class Arachnida. **araneidan,** *a.* of or belonging to the Araneida, or spiders. *n.* a spider. **araneiform,** *a.* shaped like a spider. [L *arānea,* a spider]

araphorostic, *a.* not sewed, seamless. [Gr. *arrhaphos* (*a-,* not, *rhaptein,* to sew)]

Ararat, *n.* a double-peaked mountain on the Turkish-Iranian border; the higher, Great Ararat, 5156 m/17,000 ft, was the reputed resting place of Noah's Ark after the Flood.

Araucaria, *n.* a genus of coniferous plants, one species of which (*A. imbricata*), the monkey-puzzle, is common in England as an ornamental tree. **araucarian,** *a.* [*Arauco,* in Chile]

Arawak, *n.* an indigenous American people of the Caribbean and Amazon basin. They lived mainly by shifting cultivation in tropical forests. They were driven out of the Lesser Antilles by another American Indian people, the Caribs, shortly before the arrival of the Spanish in the 16th century.

arbalest, arbalist, †**arblast** (ah'blahst), *n.* a steel crossbow for throwing arrows and other missiles. **arbalester, arbalister,** †**arblaster** *n.* a man armed with an arbalest. [OF *arbaleste,* L *arcuballista* (*arcus,* a bow, *ballista,* a military engine for hurling missiles)]

Arbenz Guzmán, *n.* **Jácobo** (1913–1971), Guatemalan social democratic politician and president from 1951 until his overthrow in 1954 by rebels operating with the help of the US Central Intelligence Agency.

Arbil, *n.* Kurdish town in a province of the same name in N Iraq. Occupied since Assyrian times, it was the site of a battle in 331 BC at which Alexander the Great defeated the Persians under Darius III. In 1974 Arbil became the capital of a Kurdish autonomous region set up by the Iraqi government. Population (1985) 334,000.

arbiter, *n.* a judge; a person appointed to decide between contending parties; an umpire; one who has power to decide according to his or her absolute pleasure [L *arbiter* (*ar-, ad-,* to, *biter,* a comer, from *bītere,* to go, go to see)]

arbitrage, *n.* traffic in bills of exchange or stocks so as to take advantage of rates of exchange in different markets. **arbitrageur**, *n.*

arbitrament, *n.* power or liberty of deciding; decision by authority; the award given by arbitrators.

arbitrary, *a.* determined by one's own will or caprice, capricious; (apparently) random, irrational; subject to the will or control of no other. **arbitrarily**, *adv.* **arbitrariness,** *n.*

arbitrate, *v.t.* to hear and judge as an arbitrator; to decide, to settle. *v.i.* to act as arbitrator or umpire. **arbitral,** *a.* of or pertaining to arbitration. **arbitration,** *n.* the hearing or determining of a dispute by means of an arbitrator. **arbitrator,** *n.* an umpire, an arbiter; a person chosen or appointed to arbitrate. **arbitratorship,** *n.* [L *arbitrari,* to give judgment]

arbitress, *n.* a female arbiter; a woman who has absolute power. [OF *arbitresse,* fem. of *arbitre,* L *arbiter*]

arbor[1]**,** *n.* a tree, as distinguished from a plant or shrub; the main support or chief axis of a piece of mechanism; a spindle; (*Biol.*) name of many things of a tree-like appearance; (*N Am.*) an arbour. **Arbor Day,** *n.* a spring holiday in the US. **arbor-Dianae**, *n.* Diana's tree; an arborescent precipitate made by introducing mercury into a solution of nitrate of silver. **arbor-Saturni**, *n.* Saturn's tree; the arborescent appearance presented when zinc is suspended in a solution of acetate of lead. **arbor-vitae**, *n.* the tree of life; the popular name of several evergreens of the genus *Thuja;* a dendriform appearance in a vertical section of the cerebellum. **arboraceous**, *a.* resembling a tree; woody, wooded. **arboreal**, *a.* pertaining to trees; connected with or living in trees. **arboreous**, *a.* wooded, arboreal, arborescent. **arboretum**, *n.* a botanical garden for the rearing and exhibition of rare trees. **arborization, -isation,** *n.* tree-like appearance; tree-like formation or markings in crystalline substances; a tree-like appearance in distended veins caused by inflammation. **arborous,** *a.* of or belonging to trees; formed by trees. [F *arbre,* L *arbor,* tree]

arbor[2] ARBOUR.

arborescent, *a.* having tree-like characteristics; branching like a tree; dendritic. **arborescence,** *n.* **arborescently,** *adv.* [L *arborēscens -tem,* pres.p. of *arborēscere,* to grow into a tree]

arboriculture, *n.* the systematic culture of trees and shrubs. **arboricultural**, *a.* **arboriculturist**, *n.*

arbour, (*esp. N Am.*) **arbor,** *n.* a bower formed by trees or shrubs closely planted or trained on lattice-work; a shady retreat. [formerly *herber* or *erber,* OF *herbier,* L *herbārium* (*herba,* a herb, grass), assim. to ARBOR]

Arbuckle, *n.* **(Roscoe Conkling) 'Fatty'** (1887–1933), big-framed US silent-film comedian, also a writer and director. His successful career in such films as *The Butcher Boy* (1917) and *The Hayseed* (1919) ended in 1921 after a sex-murder scandal. Although acquitted, he was spurned by the public and his films banned.

Arbuthnot, *n.* **John** (1667–1735), Scottish physician, attendant on Queen Anne (1705–14). He was a friend of Pope, Gray and Swift, and was the chief author of the satiric *Memoirs of Martinus Scriblerus*. He created the national character of John Bull, a prosperous farmer, in his *The History of John Bull* (1712), pamphlets advocating peace with France.

Arbutus, *n.* a genus of evergreen shrubs and trees, of which *A. unedo,* the strawberry-tree, is cultivated as an ornamental tree in Britain. [L]

ARC, (*abbr.*) Agricultural Research Council.

arc, *n.* a portion of the circumference of a circle or other curve; something curved in shape; that part of a circle which a heavenly body appears to pass through above or below the horizon, and called respectively the **diurnal** and **nocturnal arcs,** the luminous arc or bridge across a gap between two electrodes when an electric current is sent through them. *v.i.* (*past, p.p.* **arced, arcked**) to form an (electric) arc. **arc-lamp,** *n.* an electric lamp in which such an arc or bridge is the source of illumination. **arc-weld,** *v.t.* to weld (metal) by means of an electric arc. **arc welding,** *n.* [OF *arc,* L *arcum arcus,* a bow]

ARCA, (*abbr.*) Associate of the Royal College of Art.

arcade, *n.* a series of arches sustained by columns or piers; a walk arched over; a covered passage with shops on each side. **arcaded,** *a.* furnished with or formed like an arcade. [F, from It. *arcata,* arched, fem. p.p. of *arcare,* to bend, arch (*arco,* a bow, L *arcum arcus,* a bow)]

Arcadian, *a.* of or pertaining to Arcadia, a district of the Peloponnesus, the ideal region of rural happiness; hence, ideally rustic or pastoral. *n.* an inhabitant of Arcadia; an ideal rustic. **arcadianism,** *n.* ideal rustic condition; pastoral simplicity. [L *Arcādius*]

arcane, *a.* secret, esoteric. [see foll.]

arcanum, *n.* (*pl.* **-na**) anything hidden; a mystery, a secret; esp. one of the supposed secrets of the alchemists; an elixir, a miraculous remedy. [L, neut. of a. *arcānus,* from *arcēre,* to shut up (*arca,* a chest)]

Arc de Triomphe, arch in the Place de l'Etoile, Paris, France, begun by Napoleon (1806) and completed in 1836. It was intended to commemorate the French victories of 1805–06. Beneath it rests France's 'Unknown Soldier'.

Arch, *n.* **Joseph** (1826–1919), English Radical Member of Parliament and trade unionist, founder of the National Agricultural Union (the first of its kind) in 1872. He was born in Warwickshire, the son of an agricultural labourer. Entirely self-taught, he became a Methodist preacher, and was Liberal-Labour MP for NW Norfolk.

arch[1]**,** *n.* a curved structure so arranged that the parts support each other by mutual pressure; anything resembling this, a vault, a curve; a curved anatomical structure, as of the bony part of the foot; an archway; the vault of heaven, the sky. *v.t.* to cover with or form into an arch or arches; to overarch, to span. *v.i.* to assume an arched form. **arch-board,** *n.* the part of a ship's stern over the counter. **arch-brick,** *n.* a wedge-shaped brick employed in building arches. †**arch-buttress,** *n.* a flying buttress. **Arches-Court, Court of Arches,** *n.* the ecclesiastical court of appeal for the province of Canterbury, formerly held in the church of St Mary-le-Bow, or of the Arches. **arch-stone,** *n.* a wedge-shaped stone used in building arches; a keystone. **archway,** *n.* an arched entrance or vaulted passage. **arch-wise,** *adv.* in the shape of an arch or vault. **arching,** *a.* forming an arch, curved. *n.* arched structure. [OF *arche,* L *arca,* chest (confs. with *arc,* L *arcus,* a bow)]

arch[2]**,** *a.* chief, pre-eminent, principal (in this sense generally in composition with a hyphen). **arch-enemy,** *n.* a principal enemy; esp. Satan, the devil. **arch-fiend,** *n.* the chief fiend; Satan, the devil. **arch-flamen,** *n.* a chief flamen or priest; an archbishop. **arch-foe,** *n.* principal foe. **arch-heresy,** *n.* extreme heresy. **arch-heretic,** *n.* a chief heretic; the founder of a heresy. **arch-hypocrite,** *n.* one notorious for hypocrisy. **arch-pastor,** *n.* a chief pastor. **arch-prelate,** *n.* a chief prelate, archbishop. **arch-priest,** *n.* a chief priest; a kind of dean or vicar to a bishop; a rural dean. [ARCH-, used as a separate word]

arch[3]**,** *a.* clever, cunning, mischievous, mirthful, roguish, sly. **archly,** *adv.* **archness,** *n.* [ARCH[2]]

arch., (*abbr.*) archaic; architect, architecture.

arch-, archi-, *pref.* chief, principal; leading, pre-eminent; first; e.g. *archangel, archbishop, archchamberlain, archdeacon, archidiaconal, architect, arch-knave, arch-founder*. [OE *erce-, aerce-, arce-,* L *archi-,* Gr. *archi-* (*archos,* chief, *archein,* to be first, *archē,* beginning)]

Archaean or **Archaeozoic,** *n.* earliest period of geological time; the first part of the Precambrian era, from the formation of Earth up to 2.5 billion years ago. Traces of life have recently been found in Archaean rocks. [Gr. *archaios*, ancient]

archaeo-, *pref.* pertaining to past time (*archē*, beginning); primitive. [Gr. *archaios*, ancient, primitive]

archaeol., (*abbr.*) archaeology.

archaeology, *n.* the science or special study of antiquities, esp. of prehistoric remains. **archaeologic, -ical**, *a.* of or pertaining to archaeology. **archaeolog'ically**, *adv.* **archaeologist**, *n.*

Archaeopteryx, *n.* a fossil genus containing the oldest known bird; the bird itself. [Gr. *pteron*, a wing, a bird]

Archaeozoic, *a.* pertaining to the earliest geological era, the dawn of life on the earth.

archaic, *a.* pertaining to antiquity; belonging to an earlier period, no longer in general use; old-fashioned, antiquated. **archaism**, *n.* an old-fashioned habit or custom; an archaic word or expression; affectation or imitation of ancient style or idioms. **archaist**, *n.* one who affects the archaic, an imitator of ancient style; an antiquary. **archaistic**, *a.* imitating or affecting the archaic; tending to archaism. [Gr. *archaikos*, primitive, ancient (*archaios*, old, *archē*, beginning)]

archaize, -ise, *v.i.* to imitate or affect ancient manners, language or style. *v.t.* to make archaic. [Gr. *archaizein*, to be old-fashioned, copy the ancients]

archangel, *n.* a chief angel; an angel of the highest rank; a kind of dead-nettle; a kind of fancy pigeon. **archangelic**, *a.* [OF *archangel*, L *archangelus*, Gr. *archangelos*]

archbishop, *n.* a chief bishop; a metropolitan; the spiritual head of an archiepiscopal province. **archbishopric**, *n.* the office of archbishop; the district under the jurisdiction of an archbishop. [L *archiepiscopus*]

archdeacon, *n.* a chief deacon; a church dignitary next below a bishop in the care of the diocese. **archdeaconry**, *n.* the portion of a diocese over which an archdeacon exercises jurisdiction; the rank or office of an archdeacon; an archdeacon's residence. **archdeaconship**, *n.* [L *archidiāconus*, Gr. *archidiakonos*]

archdiocese, *n.* the see of an archbishop.

archduke, *n.* a chief duke, esp. a son of an Emperor of Austria. **archducal**, *a.* of or pertaining to an archduke. **archduchess**, *n.* the wife of an archduke; a daughter of an Emperor of Austria. **archduchy**, *n.* the territory ruled over by an archduke. [OF *archeduc*]

archegonium, *n.* (*pl.* **-nia**) the female sex organ in mosses, ferns and some conifers. [Gr. *archegonos*, originator of a race]

archer, *n.* one who uses the bow and arrow; a bowman; the constellation of Sagittarius; archer-fish. **archer-fish**, *n.* a fish, *Toxotes jaculator*, from the E Indies, that has the power of projecting water from its mouth to a considerable distance. **archer-god**, *n.* Cupid, conventionally represented with a bow and arrows. **archeress**, *n.* a female archer. **archery**, *n.* the act or art of shooting with bow and arrow. [A-F *archer*, OF *archier*, late L *arcārius*, archer (*arcus*, a bow)]

Archer, *n.* **Jeffrey** (1940–), English writer and politician. A Conservative Member of Parliament (1969–74), he lost a fortune in a disastrous investment, but recouped it as a best-selling novelist. Works include *Not a Penny More, Not a Penny Less* (1975) and *First Among Equals* (1984). In 1985 he became deputy chair of the Conservative Party but resigned Nov. 1986 after a scandal involving an alleged payment to a prostitute.

archetype, *n.* the primitive or original type, model or pattern on which anything is formed, or assumed to be formed. **archetypal, -typical**, *a.* pertaining to an archetype; primitive, original. **archetypally, -typically**, *adv.*

archidiaconal, *a.* of, or pertaining to, or holding the office of an archdeacon. **archidiaconate**, *n.* the office or territory of an archdeacon. [L *archidiāconus*, an archdeacon]

archiepiscopal, *a.* of or pertaining to an archbishop or an archbishopric. **archiepiscopate**, *n.* the office, dignity, or jurisdiction of an archbishop, an archbishopric; an archbishop's tenure of office. [L *archiepiscopus*, Gr. *archiepiskopos*, an archbishop]

archil, *n.* a popular name for some lichens of the genus *Roccella;* a purple or violet dye prepared from these lichens. [ORCHIL]

Archilochian, *a.* pertaining to the Greek satiric poet Archilochus (*c.* 714–676 BC), or to the metre he introduced; severe, bitter. *n.* a verse supposed to have been invented by Archilochus.

archimage, *n.* a chief magician; a wizard, an enchanter.

archimandrite, *n.* the superior of a monastery or convent in the Greek Church, corresponding to an abbot in the Roman Catholic Church. [late L *archimandrīta*, late Gr. *archimandritēs* (*archi-*, chief, *mandra*, an enclosure, a monastery)]

Archimedean, *a.* of, pertaining to, or invented by Archimedes, a Greek mathematician (*c.* 287–212 BC). **Archimedean screw, Archimedes' screw**, *n.* an instrument for raising water, formed by winding a tube into the form of a screw round a long cylinder; a type of ship's propeller.

Archimedes, *n.* (*c.* 287–212 BC), Greek mathematician, who made important discoveries in geometry, hydrostatics and mechanics. He formulated a law of fluid displacement (Archimedes' principle), and is credited with the invention of the Archimedes screw, a cylindrical device for raising water.

Archimedes' principle, *n.* in physics, law stating that an object totally or partly submerged in a fluid displaces a volume of fluid that weighs the same as the apparent loss in weight of the object (which equals the upthrust on it).

archipelago, *n.* (*pl.* **-goes, -gos**) the Aegean Sea; any sea or water studded with islands; these islands collectively. **archipelagic, -gian**, *a.* of or pertaining to an archipelago. [It. *arcipelago* (*arci-*, Gr. *archi-*, chief, *pelago*, gulf, pool, L *pelagus*, Gr. *pelagos*, sea)]

Archipenko, *n.* **Alexander** (1887–1964), Russian-born abstract sculptor, who lived in France from 1908 and in the US from 1923. He pioneered cubist works composed of angular forms and spaces, and later experimented with clear plastic and sculptures incorporating lights.

architect, *n.* one who plans and draws the designs of buildings, and superintends their erection; a contriver, a designer of some complex work; the Creator. **architective**, *a.* of or pertaining to architecture. **architecture**, *n.* the art of building edifices or constructions of any kind; the art or profession of designing buildings; architectural work; building; style of building; construction; the design and structural arrangement of the hardware components of a computer. **architectural**, *a.* **architecturally**, *adv.* in an architectural style; with regard to architecture. [L *architectus*, Gr. *architektōn* (ARCHI-, *tektōn*, a builder, allied to *technē*, art)]

architectonic, -ical, *a.* of or pertaining to architecture; constructive; of or pertaining to an architect; directive, controlling; pertaining to the organization of knowledge. **architectonics**, *n.* the science of architecture; the systematization of knowledge; construction or systematic design in a literary or other artistic work. [L *architectonicus*, Gr. *architektonikos;* see prec.]

architrave, *n.* the lowest portion of the entablature of a column, immediately resting on the column itself; the ornamental moulding round a door or window. **architrave cornice**, *n.* an entablature comprising architrave and cornice only, without a frieze. [L *trabem*, nom. *trabs*, a beam]

archive, *n.* (*usu. pl.*) a place in which (historical) records are kept; (historical) records officially preserved. **archival**, *a.* **archivist**, *n.* one who has charge of archives; a keeper of records. [F *archive*, *archif*, late L *archīvum*, *archīum*, Gr. *archeion*, public office (*archē*, government)]

archivolt, *n.* the inner contour of an arch; the mouldings and ornaments on this inner contour. [It. *archivolto*, *arcovolta* (*arco*, L *arcus*, arch, *volta*, vault, *volto*, arched)]

archly etc. ARCH3.

archology, *n.* the philosophy of the origin of things; the science of government. [Gr. *archē*, a beginning, rule]

archon, *n.* the chief magistrate of Athens; after the time of Solon one of the nine chief magistrates of Athens; a ruler, a chief; in Gnostic theology, a creator or demiurge. **archonship,** *n.* the office of an archon; the time during which he held office. [Gr. *archōn*, ruler, pres.p. of *archein*, to rule]

archway ARCH[1].

ARCM, (*abbr.*) Associate of the Royal College of Music.

ARCS, (*abbr.*) Associate of the Royal College of Science.

Arctic, the, *n.* region north of the Arctic Circle. There is no Arctic continent, merely pack ice (which breaks into ice floes in summer) surrounding the Pole and floating on the Arctic Ocean. Pack ice is carried by the south-flowing current into the Atlantic Ocean as icebergs. In winter the Sun disappears below the horizon for a time (and in summer, which only lasts up to two months, remains above it), but the cold is less severe than in parts of E Siberia or Antarctica. Land areas in the Arctic have mainly stunted tundra vegetation, with an outburst of summer flowers. Animals include reindeer, caribou, musk ox, fox, hare, lemming, wolf, polar bear, seal and walrus. There are few birds, except in summer, when insects, especially mosquitoes, are plentiful. The aboriginal people are the Inuit of the Alaskan/Canadian Arctic and Greenland. The most valuable resource is oil. The International Arctic Sciences Committee was established in 1987 by the countries with Arctic coastlines to study ozone depletion and climatic change. **Arctic Circle,** *n.* a parallel of the globe, 23° 28′ distant from the North Pole, which is its centre. **Arctic fox,** *n.* a small species of fox, with beautiful fur, found in N America within the Arctic Circle. **Arctic Ocean**, *n.* ocean surrounding the North Pole; area 14,000,000 sq km/5,400,000 sq miles. Because of the Siberian and North American rivers flowing into it, it has comparatively low salinity and freezes readily. [OF *artique*, L *articus* from Gr. *arktikos*, belonging to the Great Bear (*arktos*, bear)]

Arcturus, *n.* the bright star in the constellation Boötes, the fourth-brightest star in the sky; †the constellation Boötes; †the Great Bear. [L, from Gr. *arktouros* (*arktos*, bear, *ouros*, guardian)]

arcuate, -ated, *a.* curved like a bow; arched. **arcuately,** *adv.* **arcuation,** *n.* the act of bending; the state of being bent; arched work in building; the method of propagating trees by bending down twigs and pegging them into the ground. [L *arcuātus*, p.p. of *arcuāre*, to curve like a bow (*arcus*, bow)]

-ard, *suf.* noting disposition or character, with augmentative force; e.g. *drunkard, sluggard*. [OF *-ard, -art*, G *-hart, -hard*]

Ardea, *n.* a genus of birds including herons, bitterns and egrets. [L, a heron]

Arden, *n.* **John** (1930–), English playwright. His early plays *Serjeant Musgrave's Dance* (1959) and *The Workhouse Donkey* (1963) show the influence of Brecht. Subsequent works, often written in collaboration with his wife, Margaretta D'Arcy, show increasing concern with the political situation in Northern Ireland and a dissatisfaction with the professional and subsidized theatre world.

Ardennes, *n.* a wooded plateau in NE France, SE Belgium and N Luxembourg, cut through by the river Meuse; also a *département* of Champagne-Ardenne. There was heavy fighting here in World War I and World War II.

ardent, *a.* burning; on fire; glowing, fierce, intense, eager, zealous, fervid. **ardent-spirits,** *n.pl.* alcoholic spirits (orig. meaning inflammable, combustible spirits). **ardency,** *n.* **ardently,** *adv.* [OF *ardant*, pres.p. of *ardoir*, to burn, L *ardēre*, to burn]

ardente, *a.* (*Mus.*) ardent, fiery. [It.]

ardour, *n.* fierce heat; flame; heat of passion; warmth of emotion. [OF *ardor*, L *ardorem*]

arduous, *a.* steep and lofty, hard to climb; involving much labour, strenuous, energetic; laborious, difficult. **arduously,** *adv.* **arduousness,** *n.* [L *arduus*, steep, difficult]

are[1], *n.* a metric unit of area equal to 100 square metres (1076·44 sq. ft.). [F, from L *area*]

are[2], *pl. pres. ind. of the verb* to be. [see AM, BE]

area, *n.* any clear or open space; the sunken court, partly enclosed by railings, giving access to the basement of some dwelling-houses; space left open round a basement to obviate damp; the extent of a surface; a particular extent of surface, a region, a tract of country; a section of a larger space or surface or of a building etc.; a limited extent of the surface of any organism, distinguished from that which surrounds it; a sphere of interest or study. **area-bell,** *n.* a bell rung from the handle at an area-gate. **area-gate,** *n.* a gate at the entrance into an area giving access to the basement of a house. **area-sneak,** *n.* a thief who sneaks in at area-gates. **area-steps,** *n.pl.* steps leading from the street down to the basement. [L]

Areca, *n.* a genus of palms, esp. *A catechu*, which yields the betel-nut. [Port., from Tamil *adaikāy* (*adai*, clustering, *kāy*, nut)]

Arecibo, *n.* the site in Puerto Rico of the world's largest single-dish radio telescope, 305 m/1000 ft in diameter. It is built in a natural hollow, and uses the rotation of the Earth to scan the sky. It has been used both for radar work on the planets and for conventional radio-astronomy, and is operated by Cornell University, US.

arefy, *v.t.* to make dry, to dry up, to parch. **arefaction**, *n.* the act or process of drying; the state or condition of being dried. [L *ārefacere*, to make dry (*ārēre*, to be dry, *facere*, to make)]

arena, *n.* the floor of an amphitheatre where combats took place, originally strewn with sand to absorb the blood; an amphitheatre; a field of conflict; a sphere of action. **arenaceous**, *a.* sandy; in the form of sand; composed partly or entirely of sand. **arenose**, *a.* full of grit or sand. [L *arēna, harēna*, sand]

Arenaria, *n.* the genus typified by the sandworts, tiny herbaceous plants allied to chickweed. [L fem. of a. *arēnārius*, belonging to the sand]

aren't, *contr. form.* short for are not; am not (in questions).

areo- *comb. form.* pertaining to the planet Mars; e.g. **areocentric**, *a.* centring in Mars. **areography**, *n.* the description of the physical features of Mars. **areology**, *n.* the scientific study of Mars. [Gr. *areos*, pertaining to *Arēs*, Mars]

areola, *n.* (*pl.* **-lae**) a very small defined area; one of the interstices in organized tissue; any minute space enclosed by lines or markings; a slightly depressed spot; a dark circle round the human nipple; a similar circle round a pustule; (*Bot.*) a cell-nucleus. **areolar,** *a.* of, pertaining to, or consisting of areolae. **areolar tissue,** *n.* loose fibrous connective tissue, the cellular tissue underlying the skin. **areolate**, *a.* marked or marked off by intersecting lines. **areola'tion**, *n.* the state of being areolate. **areole**, *n.* an areola. [L dim. of *area*]

areometer etc. ARAEOMETER.

Areopagus, *n.* the highest court at Athens (which sat on Mars' Hill); any important tribunal. **areopagite**, *n.* a member of the Areopagus. [L *arēopagus*, Gr. *Areios pagos* (*Areios*, belonging to *Arēs* or Mars, *pagos*, a hill)]

Arequipa, *n.* city in Peru at the base of the volcano El Misti; population (1988) 592,000. Founded by Pizarro 1540, it is the cultural focus of S Peru, and a busy commercial (soap, textiles) centre.

Ares, *n.* in Greek mythology, the god of war (Roman Mars). The son of Zeus and Hera, he was worshipped chiefly in Thrace.

†aret, arette, *v.t.* to reckon, to count, to impute; to deliver, entrust. [OF *areter, aretter* (*à*, to, *reter*, L *reputāre*, to count, reckon)]

arête, *n.* a sharp ascending ridge of a mountain. [F *arête* (OF *areste*), L *arista*, an ear of corn, a spine]

Aretino, *n.* **Pietro** (1492–1556), Italian writer, born in Arezzo. He earned his living, both in Rome and Venice, by publishing satirical pamphlets while under the protection of a highly placed family. His *Letters* (1537–57) are a unique record of the cultural and political events of his time, and illustrate his vivacious, exuberant character. He also wrote poems and comedies. Aretino began as a protégé of Pope Leo X, but left Rome after the publication of his lewd verses. He settled in Venice, and quickly became known as the 'Scourge of Princes' with his vicious satires on powerful contemporaries; he was also well paid for not taking up his pen.

†**argal,** *adv.* therefore. *n.* a clumsy piece of reasoning. [corr. of L *ergo*]

argala, *n.* the adjutant-bird, a gigantic stork from India. [Hind. *hargālā*]

argali, *n.* (*pl.* **-lis, -li**) the wild rock-sheep of Asia. [Mongol.]

argand, argand lamp, *n.* a lamp having a circular hollow wick or gas-burner, which admits air so as to secure more complete combustion and brighter light. [Aimé *Argand,* 1755–1803, Swiss inventor]

Argand diagram, *n.* a method for representing complex numbers by cartesian coordinates (x, y). The x axis represents the real numbers, and the y axis the non-real, or 'imaginary', numbers. [J.-R. *Argand,* 1768–1822, F mathematician]

argent, *n.* †silver; (*Her.*) the white colour representing silver. *a.* of or resembling silver; silvery-white. **argentiferous,** *a.* producing silver. **argentometer,** *n.* (*Phot.*) an instrument for gauging the amount of silver put into a sensitizing bath. [F, from L *argentum*]

Argentina, *n.* Republic of (*República Argentina*), a country in S America, bounded by Chile to the S and W, Bolivia to the NW, and Paraguay, Brazil, Uruguay and the Atlantic Ocean to the E. **area** 2,780,092 sq km/1,073,116 sq miles. **capital** Buenos Aires. **towns** Rosario, Córdoba, Tucumán, Mendoza, Santa Fé; ports are La Plata and Bahía Blanca. **physical** mountains in the W, forest in the N and E, pampas (treeless plains) in the central area; rivers Colorado, Paraná, Uruguay, Rio de la Plata estuary. **territories** Tierra del Fuego; disputed claims to S Atlantic islands; part of Antarctica. **exports** beef, livestock, cereals, wool, tannin, groundnuts, linseed oil, minerals (coal, copper, molybdenum, gold, silver, lead, zinc, barium, uranium), and the country has huge resources of oil, natural gas, hydroelectric power. **population** (1986) 31,060,000 (mainly of Spanish or Italian origin, only about 30,000 American Indians surviving); annual growth rate 1.6%. **language** Spanish. **religion** Roman Catholic (state-supported).

Argentina, La, *n.* (Antonia Merce) (1890–1936), Spanish dancer, choreographer and director. She took her artistic name from the land of her birth. She toured the world as a concert artist with Vicente Escudero and her techniques of castanet playing were revolutionary.

Argentine, Argentinian, *a.* of or pertaining to Argentina. *n.* a native of Argentina.

argentine, *a.* of or containing silver; silvery. *n.* silver, electro-plate, imitation silver; a small fish with silvery scales; a pearly lamellar variety of calcite. [F *argentin,* L *argentinus*]

argie-bargie ARGY-BARGY.

argil, *n.* white clay, potter's earth. **argillaceous,** *a.* of the nature of clay; containing a large amount of clay. **argilliferous,** *a.* producing or yielding clay. [F *argille,* L *argilla,* Gr. *argillos,* white clay (*argēs,* white)]

Argive, *a.* of or pertaining to Argos; hence, Greek. *n.* a native of Argos; a Greek. [L *Argīvus,* Gr. *Argeios* (*Argos,* city of Argolis, in the Peloponnesus)]

argol, *n.* an impure acid potassium tartrate deposited from wines; crude cream of tartar. [ME *argoile*]

argon, *n.* an inert gas, at. no. 18; chem. symbol Ar, one of the gaseous constituents of the atmosphere, discovered in 1894. [Gr. *argos,* neut. *argon,* not working (*a-,* not, *ergon,* work)]

Argonaut, *n.* one of the legendary heroes who accompanied Jason in the ship *Argo* to seek the Golden Fleece; (**argonaut**) (the popular name of a genus of cephalopod molluscs containing) the paper-nautilus. **argonautic,** *a.* of or pertaining to the Argonauts or their expedition. *n.* one of Jason's companions; an Argonaut; (*pl.*) a poem on the quest of the Golden Fleece. [L *argonauta,* Gr. *argonautēs*]

Argos, *n.* city in ancient Greece, at the head of the Gulf of Nauplia, which was once a cult centre of the goddess Hera.

argosy, *n.* a large vessel for carrying merchandise; a carrack; (*fig.*) a richly-laden ship; anything of great value. [prob. It. *una Ragusea* (*nave*), a Ragusan (ship)]

argot, *n.* thieves' slang; the phraseology of a class; slang generally. **argotic,** *a.* slangy. [F]

argue, *v.t.* to prove, to show, to evince; to (try to) exhibit or prove by reasoning; to convince by logical methods; to discuss, debate. *v.i.* to bring forward reasons, to discuss; to reason in opposition, to dispute. **arguable,** *a.* capable of being argued. **argufy,** *v.i.* (*coll.*) to argue. **argufier,** *n.* (*coll.*) one who argues; a contentious person. [OF *arguer,* late L *argūtāre* (freq. of *arguere,* to prove, make clear)]

argument, *n.* proof; (a) reason, series of reasons or demonstration put forward; process of reasoning; (a) debate, discussion; an abstract or summary of a book; the subject of a discourse; a mathematical variable whose value determines that of a dependent function. **argumentation,** *n.* the act or process of reasoning; methodical reasoning; a systematic argument. **argumentative,** *a.* consisting of or pertaining to argument; controversial; having a natural tendency to argue, disputatious. **argumentatively,** *adv.* **argumentativeness,** *n.*

argute, *a.* shrill, sharp; quick, keen, shrewd. **arguteness,** *n.* [L *argūtus,* shrill, p.p. of *arguere,* ARGUE]

argy-bargy, argie-bargie, *n.* (*coll.*) (a) dispute, argument. [Sc., Eng. dial. *argy,* to argue]

argyle, *n.* a dinner-table receptacle for keeping gravy hot. [etym. doubtful]

Argyll[1], *n.* earls and dukes of Argyll, line of Scottish peers who trace their descent from the Campbells of Lochow. The earldom dates from 1457. They include:

Argyll[2], *n.* **Archibald Campbell, 5th Earl of** (1530–1573), adherent of the Scottish presbyterian, John Knox. A supporter of Mary Queen of Scots from 1561 on her return from France, he commanded her forces during the days following her escape from Lochleven Castle in 1568. He revised his position and became Lord High Chancellor of Scotland in 1572.

Århus, *n.* alternative form of Aarhus, Denmark.

aria, *n.* an air; a song for one voice supported by instruments. [It.]

Ariadne, *n.* in Greek mythology, the daughter of Minos, king of Crete. When Theseus came from Athens as one of the sacrificial victims offered to the Minotaur, she fell in love with him and gave him a ball of thread which enabled him to find his way out of the labyrinth.

Arian[1], *a.* pertaining to Arius or his doctrine. *n.* a follower of Arius of Alexandria (see ARIUS below). **Arianism,** *n.* the system of doctrine held by Arius and his followers. **Arianize, -ise,** *v.t.* to convert to Arianism. *v.i.* to become an Arian; to propagate Arianism. [L *Ariānus* (*Arīus, Arius,* Gr. *areios, Arios,* prop. name)]

Arian[2] ARYAN.

-arian, *suf.* belonging to, believing in; one who belongs to, believes in, or is associated with; e.g. *humanitarian, sabbatarian, sexagenarian, trinitarian.* [L *-ārius*]

Ariane, *n.* a series of launch vehicles built by the European Space Agency to place satellites into Earth orbit (first flight 1979). The launch site is at Kouru in French Guiana.

Arias Sanchez, *n.* **Oscar** (1940–), Costa Rican politician, president from 1860. Secretary-general of the left-wing National Liberation Party (PLN). He advocated a neutralist policy and in 1987 was the leading promoter of the Central American Peace Plan.

arid, *a.* dry, parched, wanting in moisture; barren, bare; dry, uninteresting. **aridity, aridness,** *n.* the quality or state of being dry or parched; dryness, drought; absence of moisture. **aridly,** *adv.* [L *āridus* (*ārēre,* to dry)]

ariel, *n.* a W Asiatic and African gazelle. [Arab. *aryil, ayyil,* stag]

Aries, †Ariete, *n.* a zodiac constellation, in the northern hemisphere near Auriga, seen as representing the legendary ram whose golden fleece was sought by Jason and the Argonauts. Its most distinctive feature is a curve of three stars of decreasing brightness. The Sun passes through Aries from late Apr. to mid-May. In astrology, the dates for Aries are between about 21 Mar. and 19 Apr.

arietta, *n.* a short lively air, tune or song. [It., dim. of ARIA]

ariette, *n.* an arietta. [F, from It. *arietta*]

aright, †arights, *adv.* right, rightly, properly, becomingly; without failure or mistake. [*a-,* on, RIGHT (*rights,* from *rihtes,* gen.)]

aril, *n.* an accessory seed-covering, more or less incomplete, formed by a growth near the hilum. **arillate, arilled,** *a.* furnished with an aril. **arillode,** *n.* a false aril, proceeding from the placenta. [mod. L *arillus,* med. L *arilli,* Sp. *arillos,* raisins]

Ariosto, *n.* **Ludovico** (1474–1533), Italian poet, born in Reggio. He wrote Latin poems and comedies on Classical lines, including, the epic poem *Orlando Furioso* (1516, 1532).

ariot, *adv.* riotously.

-arious, *suf.* connected with, belonging to; forming adjectives, e.g. *gregarious, vicarious.* [L *-ārius*]

aripple, *a.* rippling.

arise, *v.i.* (*past,* **arose**, *p.p.* **arisen**) to assume an upright position from an attitude of repose, to get up; to rise from the dead; to appear, to come into being, notoriety etc.; to originate, to take rise; to take place, occur (as a result). [OE *ārīsan* (*a-,* intens., *rīsan*)]

arista, *n.* (*pl.* **-tae, -tas**) an awn; a bristle or bristle-like process; a bristle on the antennae of various flies. **aristate,** *a.* awned; furnished with an arista. [L]

Aristarch, *n.* a severe critic. **aristarchian,** *a.* pertaining to Aristarchus; severely critical. [L *Aristarchus,* Gr. *Aristarchos,* a Greek grammarian, *c.* 217–145 BC]

Aristarchus of Samos, *n.* (*c.* 310–264 BC), Greek astronomer. The first to argue that the Earth moves round the Sun, he was ridiculed for his beliefs.

Aristides, *n.* (*c.* 530–468 BC), Athenian politician. He was one of the ten Athenian generals at the battle of Marathon (490 BC) and was elected chief Archon, or magistrate. Later he came into conflict with the democratic leader Themistocles, and was exiled about 483 BC. He returned to fight against the Persians at Salamis in 480 BC and in the following year, commanded the Athenians at Plataea.

aristo, *n.* (*pl.* **-tos**) short for ARISTOCRAT.

aristocracy, *n.* government by the best citizens or by the nobles; a state so governed; a ruling body of nobles; the nobility; the best of any class or group. **aristocrat,** *n.* a noble; a member of an aristocracy; (*rare*) one who favours aristocratic government. **aristocratic, -ical,** *a.* pertaining or relating to an aristocracy; grand, stylish. **aristocratically,** *adv.* [L *aristocratia,* Gr. *aristokratia* (*aristos,* the best, *kratein,* to rule, hence *kratia,* rule)]

Aristophanes, *n.* (*c.* 448–380 BC), Greek dramatist. Of his 11 extant plays (of a total of over 40), the early comedies are remarkable for the violent satire with which he ridiculed the democratic war leaders. He also satirized contemporary issues such as the new learning of Socrates in *The Clouds* (423), and the power of women in *Lysistrata* (411). The chorus plays a prominent role, frequently giving the play its title, as in *The Wasps* (422), *The Birds* (414), and *The Frogs* (405). **Aristophanic,** *a.*

Aristotle, *n.* (384–322 BC), Greek philosopher, who advocated reason and moderation. Aristotle maintained that sense experience is our only source of knowledge, and that by reasoning we can discover the essences of things, that is, their distinguishing qualities. In his works on ethics and politics, Aristotle suggested that human happiness consists in living in conformity with nature. He derived his political theory from the recognition that mutual aid is natural to humankind, and refused to set up any one constitution as universally ideal. Of Aristotle's works some 22 treatises survive, dealing with logic, metaphysics, physics, astronomy, meteorology, biology, psychology, ethics, politics and literary criticism. **Aristotelian, -ean,** *n., a.* **Aristotelianism,** *n.*

arith., (*abbr.*) arithmetic, arithmetical.

arithmancy, *n.* divination by means of numbers. [more correctly **arithmomancy**, (Gr. *arithmos,* number, -MANCY)]

arithmetic, *n.* the science of numbers; computation by figures; arithmetical knowledge; a treatise on computation by figures. *a.* of or pertaining to arithmetic. **arithmetic and logic unit,** *n.* (*Comput.*) the section of a central processing unit where arithmetic operations are carried out. **arithmetic of series,** *n.* trigonometry. **arithmetic mean,** *n.* the average value of a set of numbers or terms, found by dividing the sum of the terms by the number. **arithmetic progression,** *n.* a series of numbers that increase or decrease consecutively by a constant quantity. **arithmetical,** *a.* arithmetic. **arithmetically,** *adv.* in an arithmetical manner; according to the principles of arithmetic. **arithmetician,** *n.* one skilled in arithmetic; a professor of arithmetic. [OF *arismetique,* late L *arismetica,* L *arithmētica,* Gr. *arithmētikē techne,* art of counting (*arithmeein,* to count, *arithmos,* number)]

arithmocracy, *n.* government by a mere numerical majority. **arithmocratic,** *a.* having the nature of an arithmocracy. [Gr. *arithmos,* number, -CRACY]

arithmometer, *n.* a calculating machine.

-arium, *suf.* thing connected with or used for; place for; as in *aquarium, herbarium, sacrarium.* [L, neut. of a. in *-ārius* (-ARY)]

Arius, *n.* (*c.* 256–336), Egyptian priest whose ideas gave rise to Arianism, a Christian belief which denied the complete divinity of Jesus. He was condemned at the Council of Nicaea (325).

a rivederci, arrivederci, *int.* (*It.*) goodbye, to our next meeting.

Ariz., (*abbr.*) Arizona.

Arizona, *n.* state in SW USA; nickname Grand Canyon State. **area** 294,100 sq km/113,523 sq miles. **capital** Phoenix. **towns** Tucson, Scottsdale, Tempe, Mesa, Glendale, Flagstaff. **physical** Colorado Plateau in the north and east, desert basins and mountains in the south and west; Colorado River; Grand Canyon. **products** cotton under irrigation, livestock, copper, molybdenum, silver, electronics, aircraft. **population** (1987) 3,469,000 including over 150,000 American Indians (Navajo, Hopi, Apache), who still own a quarter of the state.

Arjan, *n.* Indian religious leader, fifth guru (teacher) of Sikhism from 1581. He built the Golden Temple in Amritsar and compiled the *Adi Granth,* the first volume of Sikh scriptures. He died in Muslim custody.

Arjuna, *n.* Indian prince, one of the two main characters in the Hindu epic *Mahābhārata.*

ark, *n.* a chest, a box; a sacred repository; esp. one for the scrolls of the Torah; a refuge; a ship, a boat, esp. a large flat-bottomed vessel used in the US for transporting produce. **Ark, Ark of the Covenant,** the wooden coffer containing the tables of the Law etc. in the Jewish tabernacle. **(Noah's) ark,** *n.* the vessel in which Noah and his family were saved from the Deluge; a toy model of this with toy animals. **arkite,** *a.* pertaining to Noah's ark. *n.* an inmate of the ark. [OE *arc* (cp. Goth. *arka,* Icel. *örka,* L *arca*)]

Ark., (*abbr.*) Arkansas.

Arkansas, *n.* state in S central USA; nickname Wonder State/Land of Opportunity. **area** 137,800 sq km/53,191 sq miles. **capital** Little Rock. **towns** Fort Smith, Pine Bluff, Fayetteville. **physical** Ozark mountains in the west; lowlands in the east; Arkansas River; many lakes. **products** cotton, soya beans, rice, oil, natural gas, bauxite, timber, processed foods. **population** (1986) 2,372,000.

Arkwright, *n.* **Richard** (1732–1792), English inventor and manufacturing pioneer. He developed a machine for spinning cotton, the 'spinning frame' in Preston, Lancashire (1768). He installed steam power in his Nottingham works (1790).

Arlen, *n.* **Michael** (adopted name of Dikran Kuyumjian) (1895–1956), Bulgarian novelist of Armenian descent, who became a naturalized British subject in 1922. His greatest success was the cynical *The Green Hat* (1924), the story of a *femme fatale*. He died in New York.

arles, *n.pl.* (*sometimes used as sing.*) (*Sc., North.*) earnest-money; money paid at the hiring of a servant to clinch the engagement. **arles-penny,** *n.* earnest-money. [L *arrha* (perh. through an OF *erle* or *arle* from a dim. *arrhula*)]

arm[1], *n.* the upper limb of the human body on either side, from the shoulder to the hand; anything resembling the human arm; a sleeve; a projecting branch, as of the sea, mountain, river, nerve, machine, instrument or the like; the fore-limb of any of the lower mammals; a flexible limb or appendage, with arm-like functions, in invertebrates; the parts of an anchor which bear the flukes; the parts of a yard on each side of the mast; the part of a chair etc. on which the arm rests; a division of a service or organization; power, authority. *v.t.* to offer the arm to; to take by the arm; to put one's arms round; †to take in the arms. **an arm and a leg,** (*coll.*) a great amount of money. **arm in arm, arm-in-arm,** with the arms interlinked. **with open arms,** enthusiastically. **arm-band,** *n.* a band of material encircling the coat-sleeve, usu. black to indicate mourning. **armchair,** *n.* a chair with arms to support the elbows. †**arm-gaunt,** *a.* a Shakespearian adjective of uncertain meaning, *perhaps* with gaunt limbs. **armhole,** *n.* the armpit; the hole in a garment to admit the arm. **armpit,** *n.* the hollow under the arm at the shoulder. **arm's length,** *n.* the length of one's arm. **at arm's length,** at a distance. **armful,** *n.* as much as the arm or arms can hold. **armless,** *a.* without arms or branches. [OE *earm* (cp. Dut. *arm,* L *armus,* shoulder, Gr. *harmos,* joint, shoulder)]

arm[2], *n.* a weapon; any branch of the military service; (*pl.*) war; (*pl.*) the military profession; (*pl.*) armour; (*pl.*) †heraldic bearings. *v.t.* to furnish or equip with offensive or defensive arms or weapons; to furnish with a protective covering; to prepare for war; to equip with tools or other appliances; to furnish (a magnet) with an armature; to make ready (a bomb etc.) for explosion. *v.i.* to take arms; to prepare for war. **to arms!** take your weapons; prepare for battle. **under arms,** bearing arms; ready for service; in battle array. **up in arms,** in revolt; on the aggressive defensive. **arms race,** *n.* rivalry between nations, esp. US and USSR, in building up stocks of (nuclear) weapons. **armed,** *a.* equipped with weapons or armour; prepared for war; furnished with claws, teeth, horns etc., or with natural armour; furnished with thorns, prickles etc.; equipped with anything required for action or defence; provided with an armature; furnished with heraldic devices, represented with claws, teeth etc. **arming,** *n.* the act of equipping with weapons or means of defence; equipment for any purpose; furnishing with heraldic devices. **arming-press,** *n.* a press used in stamping and lettering the covers of books. **armless,** *a.* destitute of weapons of offence or defence. [F *armes,* L *arma,* weapons]

armada, *n.* an armed fleet, esp. the fleet sent by Philip II of Spain against England in 1588; any large (armed) force. [Sp., fem. of *armado,* armed, p.p. of *armar* (L *armāre*)]

Armadillo, *n.* (*pl.* **-llos**) the name of several small burrowing edentate animals, native to S America, encased in bony armour, and capable of rolling themselves into a ball; a genus of isopod crustaceans, allied to the wood-louse. [Sp., dim. of *armado* (see ARMADA)]

Armageddon, *n.* in the New Testament (Revelation 16), the site of the final battle between the nations which will end the world; it has been identified with Megiddo in Israel.

Armagh, *n.* county of Northern Ireland. **area** 1250 sq km/483 sq miles. **towns** county town Armagh; Lurgan, Portadown, Keady. **physical** flat in the north, with many bogs; low hills in the south; Lough Neagh. **products** chiefly agricultural: apples, potatoes, flax. **population** (1981) 119,000.

Armagnac, *n.* a dry brandy from S W France. [region of France]

armament, *n.* the act of arming a fleet or army for war; the munitions of war, esp. the guns of a warship; an armed force. [L *armamentum*]

armature, *n.* weapons, armour; means of defence in general; the supportive framework for a model in clay etc.; a piece of soft iron placed in contact with the poles of a magnet to preserve and increase its power; the revolving part of an electric motor or dynamo; the moving part of an electromagnetic device. [L *armatura*]

Armenia, *n.* constituent republic of the Soviet Union from 1936. **area** 29,800 sq km/11,506 sq miles. **capital** Yerevan. **towns** Leninakan. **physical** mainly mountainous (including Mt Ararat), wooded. **products** copper, molybdenum, cereals, cotton, silk. **population** (1987) 3,412,000; 90% Armenian, 5% Azerbaijani, Russian 2%, Kurd 2%. **language** Armenian. **religion** traditionally Armenian Christian.

Armenian, *a.* of or pertaining to Armenia. *n.* a native of Armenia; the Armenian language (see below); a member of the Armenian Church. **Armenian bole,** *n.* a pale red medicinal earth from Armenia. **Armenian stone,** *n.* a blue carbonate of copper, formerly given in epilepsy. [L, from Gr. *Armenia*]

Armenian church, *n.* the form of Christianity adopted in Armenia in the 3rd cent. The Catholicos, or exarch, is the supreme head, and Echmiadzin, near Yerevan, is his traditional seat.

Armenian language, *n.* one of the main divisions of the Indo-European language family. Old Armenian, the classic literary language, is still used in the liturgy of the Armenian church. Contemporary Armenian, with modified grammar and enriched with words from other languages, is used by a group of 20th-cent. writers.

Armenian massacres, *n.pl.* a series of massacres of Armenians by Turkish soldiers between 1895 and 1915. Reforms promised to Armenian Christians by Turkish rulers never materialized; unrest broke out and there were massacres by Turkish troops in 1895. Again in 1909 and 1915, the Turks massacred altogether more than a million Armenians, and deported others into the N Syrian desert, where they died of starvation; those who could fled to Russia or Persia, and only some 100,000 were left.

armet, *n.* a kind of helmet consisting of a rounded iron cap, a spreading protection for the back of the neck, and visor, beaver and gorget in front, which superseded the basinet in the 15th cent. [F *armet,* OF *armette,* dim. of *arme*]

armiger, *n.* an esquire; one entitled to heraldic bearings. **armigerous,** *a.* entitled to heraldic bearings. [L (*arma,* arms, *gerere,* to bear)]

armilla, *n.* a bracelet, an armlet; an old astronomical instrument for ascertaining the recurrence of the solstices and the equinoxes; the round ligament of the wrist. **armillary,** *a.* pertaining to bracelets; consisting of parts resembling bracelets. **armillary sphere,** *n.* a skeleton celestial globe or sphere consisting of metallic circles mechanically fixed to represent the celestial equator, the ecliptic, the colures etc. [L *armilla,* bracelet (*armus,* the shoulder)]

Arminius[1], *n.* **Jacobus** (Latinized name of Jakob Harmensen) (1560–1609), Dutch Protestant priest who founded Arminianism, a school of Christian theology opposed to Calvin's doctrine of predestination. His views were developed by Simon Episcopius (1583–1643). Arminianism is the basis of Wesleyan Methodism in the UK. **Arminian,** *a.* of or pertaining to Arminius. *n.* a follower of Arminius.

Arminianism, *n.*

Arminius [2], *n.* (17 BC–21 AD), German chieftain. An ex-soldier of the Roman army, he annihilated a Roman force led by Varus in the Teutoburger Forest area in 9 AD, and saved Germany from becoming a Roman province. He thus ensured that the empire's frontier did not extend beyond the Rhine.

armipotent, *a.* powerful or mighty in arms (an epithet of Mars). [L *armipotens* (*arma,* arms, *potens,* powerful)]

armistice, *n.* a cessation of arms for a stipulated time during war; a truce. **Armistice Day,** *n.* 11 Nov., the day on which an armistice was signed in 1918. Since the 1939–45 war, Remembrance Day (in Britain, the Sunday nearest to 11 Nov.) is solemnly observed to commemorate the fallen in both wars. [F *armistice* (L *arma,* arms, *-stitium,* from *sistere,* to stop)]

armlet, *n.* a small ornamental band worn on the arm; a badge on a band around the arm; armour for the arm; a small arm of the sea.

armoire, *n.* a chest, a cupboard. [F, from L *armārium* (see AMBRY)]

Armoric, *a.* of or pertaining to Brittany, the ancient Armorica. *n.* the language of Armorica. **Armorican,** *a.* Armoric. *n.* a Breton.

armory [1], *n.* the science of heraldry. **armorial,** *a.* pertaining or relating to heraldic arms. *n.* a book containing coats of arms. **armorist,** *n.* one learned in heraldry; one skilled inblazoning arms. [OF *armoierie,* from *armoier,* a blazoner, *armoier,* to blazon]

armory [2] ARMOURY.

armour, (*esp. N Am.*) **armor,** *n.* a defensive covering worn by a person in combat, esp. a mediaeval warrior; a protective covering of animals or plants; the iron or steel plating of a warship; the watertight dress of a diver; heraldic bearings; steel plates to protect a motor-car, tank, aircraft or other vehicle from projectiles; collectively tanks and other armoured vehicles. *v.t.* to furnish with armour; to furnish with protective covering, esp. armour-plating. **armour-bearer,** *n.* one who carried the weapons of a warrior; an esquire. **armour-clad,** *a.* ironclad. **armour-plate,** *n.* a plate of iron or steel for covering the sides of ships of war, tanks etc.; armour-plating. **armour-plated,** *a.* covered with plates of iron or steel; iron-clad. **armour-plating,** *n.* (a defensive covering of) iron or steel plates. **armoured,** *a.* clad in armour; protected; of a ship, ironclad. **armoured car, train,** *n.* a motor-car or train protected by steel plates. **armoured column,** *n.* a military force equipped with armoured vehicles, tanks etc. **armoured concrete,** *n.* FERRO-CONCRETE. **armourer,** *n.* one who made armour; a manufacturer of arms; a non-commissioned officer in charge of the arms of a regiment, ship etc. **armoury,** *n.* armour or arms; a place for keeping arms, an arsenal; the craft or skill of an armourer; (*N Am.*) an armourer's workshop; (*N Am.*) a drill-hall. [OF *armure, armeüre,* L *armātūra* (see ARMATURE)]

armozeen, *n.* a thick plain silk, generally black, used for clerical robes. [F *armoisin,* OF *armesin,* taffeta]

armpit ARM [1].

Armstrong [1], *n.* **Edwin Howard** (1890–1954), US radio engineer, who developed superheterodyne tuning for reception over a very wide spectrum of radio frequencies and frequency modulation for static-free reception.

Armstrong [2], *n.* **Louis ('Satchmo')** (1901–1971), US jazz trumpet player and singer, born in New Orleans. His Chicago recordings in the 1920s with the Hot Five and Hot Seven made him known for his warm and pure trumpet tone, his improvisation and gravelly voice. From the 1930s he became equally widely known as a singer and entertainer.

Armstrong [3], *n.* **Neil Alden** (1930–), US astronaut. In 1969, he was the first person to set foot on the Moon, and said, 'That's one small step for a man, one giant leap for mankind'. The Moon landing was part of the Apollo project.

Armstrong [4], *n.* **Robert, Baron Armstrong of Ilminster** (1927–), British civil servant, cabinet secretary in Margaret Thatcher's government. He achieved notoriety as a key witness in the 'Spycatcher' trial in Australia 1987. After Oxford University he joined the civil service and rose rapidly to deputy-secretary rank. In 1970 he became Prime Minister Heath's principal private secretary; Thatcher later made him cabinet secretary and head of the home civil service. He achieved considerable attention as a witness in the 'Spycatcher' trial in Australia when he admitted to having been sometimes 'economical with the truth'. He retired in 1988 and was made a life peer.

Armstrong [5], *n.* **William George** (1810–1900), English engineer, who developed a revolutionary method of making gun barrels in 1855, by building a breech-loading artillery piece with a steel and wrought-iron barrel (previous guns were muzzle loaded and had cast bronze barrels). By 1880 the 150 mm/16 in. **Armstrong gun** was the standard for all British ordnance.

army, *n.* a body of people organized for land warfare; a multitude, a host; an organized body (e.g. the *Salvation Army*). **army ant,** *n.* any of various ants which travel in vast numbers destroying animals and plants. **army-broker,** *n.* a broker whose business is closely connected with the army. **army-corps,** *n.* a main division of an army. **Army Council,** *n.* a committee composed of military and civil officials of the War Office. **army list,** *n.* an official list of the officers of an army. [F *armée,* fem. p.p. of *armer,* to arm (L *armāre*)]

Arnauld, *n.* a French family closely associated with Jansenism, a Christian church movement in the 17th cent. **Antoine Arnauld** (1560–1619) was a Paris advocate and pamphleteer, strongly critical of the Jesuits. Many of his 20 children were associated with the abbey of Port Royal, which became the centre of Jansenism. His youngest child, **Antoine** (1612–94), the 'great Arnauld', was religious director of the nuns there.

Arne, *n.* **Thomas Augustus** (1710–1778), English composer, whose musical drama *Alfred* (1740) includes the song 'Rule Britannia!'.

Arnhem, Battle of, in World War II, airborne operation by the Allies, 17–26 Sept. 1944, to secure a bridgehead over the Rhine, thereby opening the way for a thrust towards the Ruhr and a possible early end to the war. It was only partly successful, with 7600 casualties. Arnhem is a city in the Netherlands, on the Rhine SE of Utrecht; population (1988) 297,000. It produces salt, chemicals, and pharmaceuticals. The English poet Sir Philip Sidney died here in 1586.

arnica, *n.* a tincture prepared from *Arnica montana,* mountain tobacco, and used as an application for bruises, sprains etc.; (**Arnica**) a genus of compositous plants including this; a plant of that genus. [etym. unknown]

†**aroint, aroynt,** *int., v.* avaunt! begone! [etym. doubtful]

Arnim, *n.* **Ludwig Achim von** (1781–1831), German Romantic poet and novelist. Born in Berlin, he wrote short stories, a romance, *Gräfin Dolores/Countess Dolores* (1810), and plays, but left the historical novel *Die Kronenwächter* (1817) unfinished. With Clemens Brentano he collected the German folk-songs in *Des Knaben Wunderhorn/The Boy's Magic Horn* (1805–8).

Arnold [1], *n.* **Benedict** (1741–1801), US soldier and traitor to the American side in the War of American Independence. A merchant in New Haven, Connecticut, he joined the colonial forces but in 1780 plotted to betray the strategic post at West Point to the British. Maj. André was sent by the British to discuss terms with him, but was caught and hanged as a spy. Arnold escaped to the British, who gave him an army command.

Arnold [2], *n.* **Matthew** (1822–1888), English poet and critic. His poems, characterized by their elegiac mood and pastoral themes, include *The Forsaken Merman* (1849), *Thyrsis* (1867) (commemorating his friend Arthur Hugh Clough), *Dover Beach* (1867) and *The Scholar Gypsy* (1853). Arnold's critical works include *Essays in Criticism* (1865 and 1888), and *Culture and*

Anarchy (1869), which attacks 19th-century philistinism.

aroma, *n.* the fragrance in a plant, spice, fruit, wine etc.; an agreeable odour or smell; a subtle pervasive quality. **aromatherapy,** *n.* the use of (massage with) essential plant oils to promote physical and mental well-being and in healing. **aromatherapist,** *n.* [late L, from Gr. *arōma,* a spice]

aromatic, *a.* of or pertaining to an aroma; fragrant, spicy; belonging or pertaining to a class of organic compounds containing a benzene ring in the molecular structure. *n.* a fragrant drug, a spice; (*pl.*) a benzene-type additive to motor fuel. **aromatically,** *adv.* **aromaticity,** *n.* **aromatize, -ise,** *v.t.* to render aromatic or fragrant; to perfume, to scent. **aromatization, -isation,** *n.* the act of rendering aromatic; the state of being so scented. [F *aromatique,* L *arōmaticus,* Gr. *arōmatikos*]

aroo, *int.* goodbye, au revoir. [Austral.]

arose, *pret.* ARISE.

around, *prep.* surrounding; round about; on all sides of; along the circuit of. *adv.* all round; in a circle; about, here and there, in all directions.

arouse, *v.t.* to raise, stir up, awaken; to excite, stimulate.

arow, *adv.* in a row; one after the other; in succession.

ARP, (*abbr.*) air raid precautions.

Arp, *n.* **Hans/Jean** (1887–1966), French abstract painter and sculptor. He was one of the founders of Dada about 1917, and later associated with the surrealists. His innovative wood sculptures use organic shapes in bright colours.

arpeggio, *n.* (*pl.* **-ggios**) a method of playing a chord on a keyed instrument by striking the notes in rapid succession instead of simultaneously; a chord so played. [It. *arpeggiare,* to play the harp (*arpa,* a harp)]

arquebus HARQUEBUS.

arrack, arak, *n.* a distilled spirit from the East; esp. one distilled from coconut or rice. [Arab. *'araq,* juice, essence, sweat (*'arqua,* he sweated)]

arrah, *int.* (*Ir.*) an expletive expressing mild excitement.

arraign, *v.t.* to cite before a tribunal to answer a criminal charge; to accuse; to charge with fault; to find fault with. **arraigner,** *n.* **arraignment,** *n.* the act of arraigning; accusation, charge; the state of being so arraigned. [OF *araisnier,* late L *arratiōnāre* (*ad-,* to, *ratio -ōnem,* reason)]

arrange, *v.t.* to draw up in rank or ranks; to adjust, to settle, to put in proper order; to adapt (a musical composition) for other instruments or voices; to plan or settle circumstances in readiness for. *v.i.* to come to arrangement; to make a settlement. **arrangement,** *n.* the act of arranging, the state of being arranged; the manner in which things are arranged; settlement, disposition, preparation; a grouping or combination of things in a particular way; (*pl.*) dispositions in advance, preparations; the adaptation of a musical composition for instruments or voices for which it was not written. [OF *arangier* (*à,* to, *rangier,* to range, from *rang,* rank or file; cp. OHG *hring*)]

arrant, *a.* notorious, downright, unmitigated; complete, thorough. **arrantly,** *adv.* shamelessly, infamously. [var. of ERRANT (as in 'an outlawe or a theef erraunt', i.e. wandering or roving thief)]

arras, *n.* a kind of tapestry made at Arras in Artois; a rich fabric of coloured tapestry; wall hangings. **arrased,** *a.* furnished or hung with arras. **arrasene,** *n.* a mixed thread of wool and silk used in embroidery.

Arras, Battle of, battle of World War I, April–May 1917. It was an effective but costly British attack on German forces in support of a French offensive, which was only partially successful, on the Siegfried Line. British casualties totalled 84,000 as compared to 75,000 German casualties. In World War II the town of Arras was captured in 1940 by the Germans in their advance on Dunkirk.

Arras, Congress and Treaty of, a meeting in N France (1435) between representatives of Henry VI of England, Charles VII of France, and Philip the Good of Burgundy, to settle the Hundred Years' War.

array, *v.t.* to put in readiness (as troops), to marshal; to arrange, order; to dress up, to deck, to equip; (*Law*) to set (a jury) in order for a trial. *n.* order, esp. of battle; the summoning and arming of a military force, esp. of the militia; a military force; an imposing or orderly arrangement or disposition; state of preparation; (*poet.*) dress, attire; (*Law*) the order of empanelling a jury; the panel of jurors; an arrangement of numbers or mathematical symbols in rows and columns; a collection of elements that form a unit. [A-F*arayer,* OF *araier* (Prov. *aredar,* early Rom. and It. *arredare*), from *a-, ad-,* to, LG *rēde,* ready (cp.OE *rǣde*)]

arrear, *adv.* †to or in the rear, backward. *n.* the state of being behindhand; (*usu. pl.*) that which is behindhand, unpaid, or unsatisfied. **in arrears,** unpaid, unsatisfied. **arrearage,** *n.* arrear, backwardness; that which is in arrears, outstanding or kept back; arrears, items overdue. [OF *arere* (cp. F *arrière*), backward (L *ad-,* towards, *retro,* behind)]

arrect, *a.* of the ears of an animal, pricked up, pointed up; alert, attentive. [L *arrectus,* p.p. of *arrigere,* to erect (*ad-,* to, *regere,* direct)]

arrest, *v.t.* to stop, check; to seize and fix (the sight, mind etc.); to stay (legal proceedings etc.); to apprehend, esp. to apprehend and take into legal custody; to seize by legal authority. *n.* a stoppage, stay, check; seizure, detention, esp. by legal authority. **arrest of judgment,** staying of a judgment after a verdict. **under arrest,** in legal custody. **arrested development,** *n.* development arrested at some stage of its progress. †**arrestation,** *n.* the act of arresting; arrest; stopping. **arrester,** *n.* one who or that which arrests; a contrivance for cutting off a force (e.g. lightning); (*usu.* **arrestor**) (*Sc. Law*) the person who arrests a debt or property in another's hands. **arresting,** *a.* striking, catching the attention. **arrestive,** *a.* tending to arrest (e.g. the conj. *but*). **arrestment,** *n.* the act of arresting; stop, stay, check; (*Law*) seizure of property by legal authority, esp. (*Sc. Law*) the process by which a creditor detains the effects of a debtor, which are in the hands of third parties, till the money owing is paid. **arrestor** ARRESTER. **arrestor-hook,** *n.* a device that enables an aircraft landing on a carrier-ship to check speed by catching on a cable. [OF *arester,* late L *adrestāre* (*ad-,* to, at, *restāre,* to stay, stop, from *re-,* back, *stāre,* stand)]

arret, *n.* formerly, an authoritative sentence or decision of the King or Parliament of France; an authoritative pronouncement, a decree. [OF*arest,* from *arester* (see ARREST)]

arrhythmia, *n.* an irregularity or alteration in the rhythm of the heartbeat. **arrhythmic,** *a.* [Gr. *a-,* priv., *rhuthmos,* RHYTHM]

arrière, *n.* (*F*) the rear; the rear of an army. **arrière-fief,** *n.* a fief held by a feudatory; a sub-fief. **arrière-pensée,** *n.* (*F*) a mental reservation; an unrevealed intention. **arrière-tenant,** *n.* the tenant of a mesne-lord or feudatory; a sub-tenant. **arrière-vassal,** *n.* the holder of an arrière-fief. [F (see ARREAR)]

arris, *n.* (*pl.* **arris, arrises**) the line in which two straight or curved surfaces forming an exterior angle meet each other. **arris-gutter,** *n.* a wooden gutter shaped like the letter **V**. **arris-wise,** *adv.* diagonally, ridge-wise; so as to present a sharp edge. [OF *areste,* ARÊTE]

arrive, *v.i.* to come to, reach a place, position, state of mind etc.; to gain, compass, reach to or attain an object; to come about, to occur; (*coll.*) to attain notoriety, become eminent, make one's fortune. †*v.t.* to reach, attain. **arrival,** *n.* the act of coming to a journey's end or destination; the coming to a position, state of mind etc.; a person who or thing which has arrived; (*coll.*) a new-born child; a cargo to be delivered when a ship comes into port. [OF *ariver,* late L *arrībāre, arrīpāre* (*ad rīpam,* to shore)]

arrivederci A RIVEDERCI.

arriviste, *n.* a social climber, a parvenu; a self-seeker, esp. in politics. [F]

arrogance, -ancy, *n.* the act or quality of being arrogant; undue assumption. [F *arrogance,* L *arrogantia* (see foll.)]

arrogant, *a.* claiming or assuming too much; insolent, assuming, overbearing, haughty. **arrogantly,** *adv.* [F *arrogant,* L *arrogantem,* pres.p. of *arrogāre* (see ARROGATE)]

arrogate, *v.t.* to make unduly exalted claims or baseless pretensions to a thing for oneself or for someone else. **arrogation,** *n.* the act of claiming or assuming unwarrantably; undue pretension. [L *arrogātus,* p.p. of *arrogāre* (*ad-,* to, *rogāre,* to ask)]

arrondissement, *n.* a territorial division of a French department; a ward in Paris. [F]

arrow, *n.* a slender, straight missile shot from a bow; anything resembling an arrow in shape or function. **arrow-grass,** *n.* (*Bot.*) the popular name of the genus *Triglochin;* a kind of pampas grass. **arrowhead,** *n.* the pointed head of an arrow; a mark shaped like an arrowhead, indicating direction; a plant of the genus *Sagittaria,* the leaves of which resemble arrowheads. **arrow-headed,** *a.* shaped like the head of an arrow; sagittate, cuneiform. **arrowroot,** *n.* a nutritious starch extracted from the tubers of several species of *Maranta;* the food prepared from this substance; a plant of the genus *Maranta,* which includes *M. arundinacea,* the tubers of which were used to absorb poison from wounds, esp. those made by poisoned arrows. **arrow-stitch,** *n.* a triangular series of stitches for securing the ends of whalebone in stays. **arrowlet,** *n.* a little arrow; the feathery seeds of dandelion, thistle etc. **arrowy,** *a.* consisting of arrows; resembling an arrow or arrows in form or motion; darting, swift; sharp, piercing. [OE *arewe, earh* (Goth. *arhwazna;* allied to L *arcus,* a bow)]

arroyo, *n.* (*pl.* **-yos**) (*N Am.*) a dried-up watercourse, a rocky ravine. [Sp.]

arse, (*esp. N Am.*) **ass**, *n.* (*taboo*) the buttocks, the rump, the hind parts; (*sl.*) the fag-end; (*taboo*) the anus. **to arse about** or **around,** (*taboo sl.*) to mess around, act in a stupid or irritating manner. **arsehole,** (*esp. N Am.*) **asshole,** *n.* (*taboo*) the anus; (*sl.*) a stupid or worthless person. **arselicker,** *n.* (*sl.*) a sycophant, toady. **arselicking,** *n., a.* [OE *ærs, ears* (Icel. and MHG *ars;* cp. Gr. *orrhos*)]

arsenal, *n.* a place for the storage, or manufacture and storage, of naval and military weapons and ammunition - also *fig.* [It. *arsenale, arzenà, darsena,* Arab. *dār aççinā'ah* (*dār,* house, *al,* the, *çinā'ah,* art, trade)]

arsenic[1], *n.* a brittle, semi-metallic steel-grey element, at.no. 33; chem. symbol As; the trioxide of this element, a virulent poison. [OF *arsenic,* L *arsenicum,* Gr. *arsenikon (a. arrenikos -on,* male, masculine, used as masculine metal), Arab. *az-zernikh* (*al,* the, *zernikh,* orpiment, Pers. *zerni,* orpiment, *zar,* gold)]

arsenic[2], *a.* of or containing arsenic; esp. applied to compounds in which arsenic combines as a pentavalent element. **arsenical,** *a.* pertaining to arsenic; having arsenic in the composition. **arsenious**, *a.* of or containing arsenic; esp. applied to compounds in which arsenic combines as a trivalent element. **arsine**, *n.* hydrogen arsenide, a very poisonous gas.

arsis, *n.* (*pl.* **-ses**) the stressed syllable in metre; the stressed note in barred music. [L from Gr. *arsis,* a raising, (*airein,* to lift)]

arson, *n.* the wilful setting on fire of another's house or other property, or to one's own with intent to defraud the insurers. [OF *arson,* late L *arsio -ōnem* (*ardēre,* to burn, p.p. *arsus*)]

†**art**[1], *v.* the second pers. sing. pres. ind. of the verb TO BE.

art[2], *n.* skill, human skill or workmanship, as opposed to nature; skill applied to the creation of (visual) beauty and aesthetic objects; (any of) the fine arts, esp. the arts of representation and design; (visual) works of art; perfection of workmanship for its own sake; the practical application of science; a body of rules for putting principles into practice; an industrial pursuit; a craft, a profession; acquired skill; a knack; craft, cunning, artifice; (*pl.*) the humanities or liberal arts, the learning of the schools; (*pl.*) the subjects studied in a nonscientific or nontechnical university course; (*pl.*) the faculty concerned with such subjects. **be** (or **have**) **art and part,** (*Sc. Law*) accessory by contrivance or participation; participating, sharing in any way. **Bachelor of Arts, Master of Arts,** titles conferred on those who have attained certain degrees of proficiency in the humanities. **Art Deco**, *n.* a style of decorative art of the 1920s and 1930s characterized by bold geometrical forms. **art form,** *n.* an established form in music or literature; a medium of artistic expression. **art-house,** *a.* pertaining to films produced for aesthetic or artistic purposes rather than commercial success. **Art Nouveau**, *n.* see separate article below. **art paper,** *n.* paper coated with a composition of china clay, making it suitable for fine printing. **art union,** *n.* an association for the promotion and the encouragement of artists; (*Austral.*) a lottery. **artwork,** *n.* the illustrative material in a magazine, book etc. **artful,** *a.* crafty, cunning; characterized by art or skill; artificial, unreal. **artfully,** *adv.* **artfulness,** *n.* **artless**, *a.* guileless, simple, unaffected; without art; unskilful, clumsy; uncultured, natural. **artlessly,** *adv.* **artlessness,** *n.* **artsman,** *n.* †one instructed in the liberal or the fine arts; †an artist; (*dated*) one who has graduated in Arts. **arty** *a.* (*coll.*) self-consciously or pretentiously aping the artistic. **arty crafty,** *a.* more showily artistic than functional. **arty party,** *n.* (*dated*) a poseur, one who pretends to artistic taste. [OF *art,* L *ars artem* (stem *ar-,* to fit)]

art., (*abbr.*) article; artificial; artillery.

Artaud, *n.* **Antonin** (1896–1948), French theatre director. Although his play, *Les Cenci/The Cenci* (1935), was a failure, his concept of the Theatre of Cruelty (q.v.), intended to release feelings usually repressed in the unconscious, has been an important influence on modern dramatists such as Camus and Genet and on directors and producers. Declared insane in 1936, Artaud was confined in an asylum.

artefact, artifact, *n.* a product of human skill or workmanship; esp. a simple object of archaeological importance or interest. [L *ars artis,* art, *factus,* made]

Artemis, *n.* in Greek mythology, the goddess (Roman Diana) of chastity, the Moon, and the hunt. She is the sister of Apollo. Her cult centre was at Ephesus.

Artemisia, *n.* a genus of composite plants, containing wormwood, southern-wood etc. [L, from Gr. *artemisia* (*Artemis,* Diana)]

artery, *n.* any of the membranous pulsating vessels, conveying blood from the heart to all parts of the body; a main channel of communication or transport. **arterial**, *a.* pertaining to or contained in an artery or arteries; pertaining to the oxygenated blood that circulates in the arteries; resembling an artery; ramifying. **arterial road,** *n.* a main road for swift, long-distance traffic between the chief industrial centres. **arterialize, -ise,** *v.t.* to convert venous into arterial blood by exposing to the action of oxygen in the lungs; to endow with arteries. **arterialization, -isation,** *n.* the process of converting venous into arterial blood. **arteriole**, *n.* a small branch of an artery. **arteriosclerosis**, *n.* thickening and loss of elasticity in the walls of the arteries. **arteriosclerotic**, *a.* **arteriotomy**, *n.* the opening of an artery for the purpose of bleeding; the dissection of arteries. **arteritis**, *n.* inflammation occurring in the arteries. [L *artēria,* Gr. *artēria* (prob. from *aeirein,* to raise)]

Artesian, *a.* of or pertaining to Artois; resembling the wells said to have been first dug there. **artesian well,** *n.* a well in which water is obtained by boring through an upper retentive stratum to a subjacent water-bearing stratum, the water being forced to the surface by natural pressure. [F *Artésien,* from *Artois,* an old province of France]

Artex®, *n.* a textured paint covering for ceilings and walls. *v.t.* to give a textured surface to.

artful etc. ART[2].

arthralgia, *n.* pain in a joint. **arthralgic,** *a.*

arthritic, *a.* pertaining to or affecting the joints; of or suffering from arthritis. *n.* a person with arthritis. **ar-**

thritis, *n.* (painful) inflammation of one or more joints causing stiffness. [L *arthrīticus,* Gr. *arthrītikos,* from *arthron,* a joint (orig. through OF *artetique,* afterwards corrected)]

arthr(o)-, *comb. form.* pertaining to joints; characterized by joints. [Gr. *arthron,* a joint]

arthrology, *n.* a treatise on the joints.

arthropathy, *n.* (a) disease of the joints.

Arthropoda, *n.pl.* a phylum of invertebrate animals with segmented bodies and jointed limbs, including the insects, arachnids and crustaceans. **arthropodal, arthropodous,** *a.* of or belonging to the Arthropoda. **arthropod**, *n.* a member of the Arthropoda. [Gr. *pous podos,* a foot]

arthrosis, *n.* (*pl.* **-ses**) a joint uniting two bones, an articulation.

Arthur[1], *n.* (6th cent. AD), legendary English 'king' and hero in stories of Camelot and the quest for the Holy Grail. Arthur is said to have been born at Tintagel and be buried at Glastonbury. He may have been a Romano-British leader against pagan Saxon invaders.

Arthur[2], *n.* **Chester Alan** (1830–1886), 21st president of the US. He was born in Vermont, son of a Baptist minister, and became a lawyer and Republican political appointee in New York. In 1880, Arthur was chosen as Garfield's vice president, and was his successor when Garfield was assassinated the following year. Arthur held office until 1885.

Arthur[3], *n.* **Duke of Brittany** (1187–1203), grandson of Henry II of England and nephew of King John, who is supposed to have had him murdered, 13 Apr. 1203, as a rival for the crown.

Arthur[4], *n.* **Prince of Wales** (1486–1502), eldest son of Henry VII of England. He married Catherine of Aragon in 1501, when he was 16 and she was 15, but died the next year.

artic, *n.* short for ARTICULATED LORRY under ARTICULATE[1].

artichoke, *n.* a composite plant, *Cynara scolymus,* somewhat like a large thistle: the receptacle and fleshy bases of the scales are eaten as a vegetable; JERUSALEM ARTICHOKE. [It. *articiocco, articioffo* (OSp. *alcarchofa*); Arab. *al-kharshūf*]

article, *n.* a distinct member or portion; a point of faith or duty; a prose composition, complete in itself, in a newspaper, magazine, encyclopaedia etc.; an item, a piece, a distinct detail; a distinct statement, clause or provision in an agreement, statute, indictment, code or other document; an item of trade, use or property; a commodity, a thing, an object; a name for the adjectives, *a, an, the,* when these are considered to form a separate part of speech; (*pl.*) a formal agreement; (*pl.*) terms, conditions. *v.t.* to draw up in the form of articles; to bind (an apprentice), indenture; to indict. **articles of association,** *n.pl.* the statutes of a limited liability company. **Articles of War,** *n.pl.* a code of discipline for the British Army. **Thirty-nine Articles,** *n.pl.* the thirty-nine statements subscribed to by the clergy of the Church of England. **articled,** *a.* bound under article of apprenticeship, esp. of a lawyer's clerk. [F *article,* L *articulus,* dim. of *artus,* joint]

articular, *a.* pertaining or relating to the joints. **Articulata**, *n.pl.* Cuvier's name for the third subkingdom of animals, comprising insects, crustaceans, centipedes and worms. [L *articulāris* (see ARTICLE)]

articulate[1], *v.t.* to connect by means of a joint; to join together in proper order; to joint; to divide into distinct words and syllables; to utter distinctly; to express clearly and coherently; to article. *v.i.* to form a joint (with); to utter intelligible sounds; to speak distinctly. **articulated,** *a.* **articulated lorry,** *n.* a long lorry with separate tractor and trailer sections connected so as to allow the tractor to turn at an angle to the remainder. **articulation,** *n.* the process or method of jointing; the act or process of speaking; articulate sound, utterance, speech; a consonant; a joint; a jointed structure; the space between two natural joints; a segment of a jointed body; (*Bot.*) the point at which a deciduous member separates from the plant. **articulator,** *n.* one who pronounces words; one who articulates skeletons. **articulatory,** *a.* pertaining to articulation. [as prec.]

articulate[2], *a.* jointed; formed by the distinct and intelligent movements of the organs of speech; able to express oneself clearly and coherently; expressed in this manner; (*Biol.*) composed of segments; of or belonging to the Articulata. **articulately,** *adv.* **articulateness,** *n.*

artifact ARTEFACT.

artifice, *n.* anything contrived by art; human skill; cunning, trickery; a contrivance; a trick. **artificer**, *n.* one who practises an art; a craftsman; a maker, a contriver; a mechanic employed to make and repair military stores. [F *artifice,* L *artificium* (*ars artis,* art, *-ficium,* suf. from *facere,* to make)]

artificial, *a.* made or produced by art; not natural, not real; affected in manner; factitious, feigned, fictitious. **artificial aerial,** *n.* a structure used in place of an aerial to test wireless apparatus. **artificial day,** *n.* (*Astron.*) that part of the day between sunrise and sunset. **artificial horion,** *n.* a small trough containing mercury, the surface of which affords a reflected image of a heavenly body, used in taking altitudes etc. in places where there is no visible horizon; an instrument that indicates an aircraft's position with respect to the horizontal. **artificial insemination,** *n.* artificial injection of semen into a female. In human beings from the husband (AIH), or from an anonymous donor (AID). **artificial intelligence,** *n.* the ability of a computer, robot etc. to perform as an intelligent being; the area of study dealing with the development of machines capable of imitating intelligent human-like mental processes. **artificial lines,** *n.pl.* lines so drawn as to represent logarithmic lines and tangents. **artificial manure,** *n.* chemical manure, manure composed of other than animal dung. **artificial respiration,** *n.* a method of reviving a person who has lost consciousness through drowning etc. **artificial silk,** *n.* synthetically produced filaments that resemble natural silk in appearance. **artificial sunlight,** *n.* a medium for producing sunlight effects by artificial sources of radiation. **artificial system,** *n.* (*Nat. Hist.*) a system of classification not based on natural affinity. **artificially,** *adv.* **artificiality**, *n.* **artificialize, -ise,** *v.t.* to render artificial. **artificialness,** *n.* [as prec.]

artillery, *n.* implements of war; engines or devices for casting missiles; guns, cannons, ordnance, with their equipment; the science and practice of gunnery; the branch of the military service in charge of the ordnance; any immaterial weapon; thunder and lightning. **artillery train,** *n.* cannon mounted and fitted with all equipment, ready for going into action. **artilleryman, artillerist,** *n.* an artillery soldier; one practically acquainted with the principles of gunnery. **artilleryship,** *n.* the management of ordnance; artillery practice. [OF *artillerie, artiller,* to fortify, equip, late L *artillātor,* a maker of machines (*articula, ars,* art)]

artiodactyl, -yle, *a.* having an even number of toes. *n.* an ungulate with an even number of toes. **Artiodactyla**, *n.pl.* a division of the Ungulata, containing those with an even number of toes. [Gr. *artios,* of even number, *daktulos,* finger, toe]

artisan, *n.* one trained to practise a manual art; a handicraftsman, a mechanic. [F, prob. from It. *artigiano* (L *artītus,* p.p. of *artīre,* to instruct in arts)]

artist, *n.* †one skilled in the learned arts; †one proficient in any art requiring skill; a mechanic, artisan, craftsman; one who practises any of the fine arts, esp. that of painting; a craftsman who applies the principles of taste; any artistic performer, an artiste; (*sl.*) one who frequently practises, or is proficient in, a particular, esp.dubious, activity. **artistic, ical**, *a.* of or pertaining to art or artists. **artistically,** *adv.* [F *artiste,* It. *artista,* late L *artista* (*ars artis* art)]

artiste, *n.* a public performer, an actor, dancer, musician, acrobat etc.; a highly proficient cook, hairdresser etc. [F]

artless, arty etc. ART.

Art Nouveau, *n.* an art style of about 1890–1910 in Europe, marked by sinuous lines and stylized flowers and foliage. Also called *Jugendstil* (Germany), *Stile Liberty* (Italy). Exponents included the illustrator Beardsley, the architect and furniture designer C. R. Mackintosh, and the glass and jewellery designer René Lalique.

Arts and Crafts movement, an English social movement, largely anti-machine in spirit, based in design and architecture and founded by William Morris in the latter half of the 19th cent. It was supported by the architect A. W. Pugin and by John Ruskin and stressed the importance of manual processes.

Arts Council of Great Britain, a British arts organization, incorporated 1945, which aids music, drama, and visual arts with government funds.

arty., (*abbr.*) artillery.

Aruba, *n.* island in the Caribbean, the westernmost of the Lesser Antilles; an overseas part of the Netherlands. **area** 193 sq km/75 sq miles. **population** (1985) 61,000.

Arum, *n.* a genus of plants, containing the wake-robin or cuckoo-pint. **arum lily,** *n.* an ornamental plant of the same genus. [L, from Gr. *aron*]

Arunachal Pradesh, *n.* state of India, in the Himalayas on the borders of Tibet and Burma. **area** 83,600 sq km/32,270 sq miles. **capital** Itanagar. **products** rubber, coffee, spices, fruit, timber. **population** (1981) 628,000. **language** 50 different dialects.

arundinaceous, *a.* resembling a reed; reedy. **arundineous,** *a.* abounding in reeds; reedy. [L *arundo -inis,* a reed, -ACEOUS]

Arunta, *n.* a member of an aboriginal tribe of central Australia. [native name]

aruspex HARUSPEX.

Arvand River, *n.* Iranian name for the Shatt al-Arab waterway.

arvo, *n.* (*Austral. coll.*) afternoon.

-ary¹, *suf.* pertaining to, connected with; belonging to, engaged in; thing connected with, used in; a place for, as in *elementary, necessary, voluntary; antiquary, statuary; aviary, granary*. [L *-ārius -ārium*]

-ary², *suf.* equivalent to -AR and sometimes to -ARY¹; e.g. *exemplary, military, contrary*. [L *-āris*]

Aryan, Arian, *a.* of or belonging to an ancient race of Europe or Central Asia, from whom many of the Indian and most of the European races are descended; of the Indo-European or Indo-Germanic race; of or speaking the Indo-European or Indo-Iranian languages; in Nazi terminology, non-Semitic. *n.* the old Aryan language; a member of the Aryan race; a non-semitic Caucasian, esp. a Nordic. **Aryanize, -ise,** *v.t.* to imbue with Aryan characteristics. [Sansk. *ārya,* noble, a worshipper of the gods of the Brahmins; the earlier *Arian* (from L *ariānus*) of Aria, eastern Persia (Gr. *Areia, Aria,* prob. from OPers. *Ariya,* a national name)]

Arya Samaj, *n.* a Hindu religious sect founded by Dayanand Saraswati (1825–88) about 1875. He renounced idol-worship and urged a return to the purer principles of the Rig Veda (Hindu scriptures). The movement believes that caste should be determined by merit rather than birth.

aryl, *n.* a general name for a monovalent aromatic hydrocarbon radical, e.g. phenyl. **arylation,** *n.* the introduction of an aryl radical into a compound. [AR(OMATIC), -YL]

AS, (*abbr.*) Anglo-Saxon; antisubmarine.

As, (*chem. symbol*) arsenic.

as¹, *adv., conj.* in the same manner; in or to the same degree; equally with; thus; for instance; while, whilst; since, because, that. *rel. pron.* that, who, which; in the role, position, or state of. **as for, as regards, as to,** regarding, concerning. **as from, as of,** from (the specified time or date).**as if, as though,** as it would be if. **as it is,** in the present state, actually. **as it were,** in a certain way, to some extent, so to speak. **as was,** (*coll.*) in a previous state. [OE *eal swā,* all so, quite so (ME *alswa, also, als, as*)]

as², *n.* a Roman copper coin, originally of 12 oz (340 g) but frequently reduced. [L]

as- *pref.* AD-, assim. to *s,* as *assimilate, assume*. [AD-]

ASA, (*abbr.*) Advertising Standards Authority; Amateur Swimming Association; American Standards Association; Association of Southeast Asia.

asafoetida, asafetida, *n.* a gum, with a strong smell of garlic, obtained from *Narthex asafetida* and allied plants, used in medicine and cookery. [med. L *asa* (Pers. *aza,* mastic), *foetida,* stinking]

Asante, Ashanti, *n.* a person of Asante culture from central Ghana, west of Lake Volta. The Asante language belongs to the Kwa branch of the Niger–Congo family.

a.s.a.p., (*abbr.*) as soon as possible.

ASAT, (*abbr.*) antisatellite weapon.

asbestos, *n.* a mineral, esp. a variety of hornblende, of flax-like fibrous structure, practically incombustible, and resistant to chemicals; †a fabulous stone, the heat of which, once kindled, was supposed to be unquenchable. *a.* made of asbestos, or like asbestos in nature. **asbestic,** *a.* pertaining to or of the nature of asbestos. **asbestine,** *a.* made of or like asbestos; incombustible. **asbestoid,** *a.* of the form of asbestos; fibrous. *n.* a fibrous mineral, also called byssolite. **asbestosis,** *n.* a lung disease caused by breathing in asbestos particles. [Gr. inextinguishable (*a-,* not, *sbestos,* from*sbenunai,* to quench)]

Ascaris, *n.* a genus of intestinal nematode worms, parasitic in man and the lower animals. **ascarid,** *n.* a worm of the genus *Ascaris*. [Gr. *askaris*]

ascend, *v.i.* to go or come from a lower to a higher place, position or degree; to rise, to be raised; to slope upwards; to proceed from a lower to a higher plane of thought, quality, degree, rank; to go back in order of time; (*Astron.*) to move towards the zenith; to come above the horizon; (*Mus.*) to rise in pitch. *v.t.* to climb or go up, to go to a higher position upon; to go to the top, summit or source of; to mount. **ascendable,** *a.* capable of being ascended; accessible. **ascendancy, -ency, -ance, -ence,** *n.* controlling influence; governing power. **ascendant, -ent,** *a.* moving upwards, rising; predominating, ruling; (*Astrol.*) just above the eastern horizon; (*Astron.*) moving towards the zenith. *n.* ascent, slope, acclivity; one who precedes genealogically, an ancestor; superiority, supremacy; (*Astrol.*) the point of the ecliptic which is rising in the eastern point of the horizon at the moment of a person's birth; the horoscope. **house of the ascendant,** the space from 5° of the zodiac above to 25° below the ascendant. **in the ascendant,** dominant, predominant, supreme; (*coll.*) ascending, rising. **lord of the ascendant,** *n.* the heavenly body rules in the ascendant or when the latter is just rising above the horizon. [L *ascendere* (*ad-,* to, *scandere,* to climb)]

ascension, *n.* the act of ascending; the ascent of Christ to Heaven; Ascension Day; the rising of a celestial body. **Ascension Day,** *n.* the day on which the Ascension of Jesus Christ is commemorated – the Thursday but one before Whitsuntide, Holy Thursday. **ascensional,** *a.* pertaining or relating to ascension. **ascensive,** *a.* ascending; on an ascending scale; (*Gram.*) intensive. [as prec.]

Ascension, *n.* a British island of volcanic origin in the S Atlantic, a dependency of St Helena since 1922; population (1982) 1625. The chief settlement is Georgetown.

ascent, *n.* the act or process of ascending, upward motion; an eminence; a slope; a way by which one may ascend; a movement back in time or ancestry; advancement, rise.

ascertain, *v.t.* to find out or learn by investigation, examination or experiment; to make sure of; to find out. **ascertainable,** *a.* **ascertainment,** *n.* [OF *acertainer, acertener* (*à,* to, CERTAIN)]

ascetic, *a.* of or pertaining to the ascetics or their mode of life; severely abstinent, austere; practising rigorous self-discipline. *n.* one of the early hermits who practised rigorous self-denial and mortification; hence, any person given to rigorous self-denial and mortification; (*pl.*) asceticism; an ascetical treatise. **ascetical,** *a.* concerned with the attainment of spiritual perfection by means of self-discipline. **ascetically,** *adv.* **asceticism,** *n.* the mode of life of an ascetic. [Gr. *askētikos,* given to exercises, *askētēs,* an athlete, a monk (*askeein,* to work, exercise)]

Ascham, *n.* **Roger** (*c.*1515–1568), English scholar and royal tutor, author of *The Scholemaster* (1570) on the art of education.

asci, pl. of ASCUS.

ascidian, *n.* a tunicate of the order Ascidiacea. [as foll.]

ascidium, *n.* (*pl.* **-dia**) a pitcher- or flask-shaped plant part, as the leaf of the pitcher plant. [L, from Gr. *askidion,* a small leather bottle (*askos,* a wine-skin)]

ASCII, *n.* in computing, a coding system in which numbers (between 0 and 127) are assigned to letters, digits, and punctuation symbols. For example, 45 represents a hyphen and 65 a capital A. The first 32 codes are used for control functions, such as carriage return and backspace. Strictly speaking, ASCII is a seven-bit code, although an eighth bit is often used to provide parity or to allow for extra characters. The system is widely used for the storage of text and for the transmission of data between computers. [acronym for *A*merican *S*tandard *C*ode for *I*nformation *I*nterchange]

ascites, *n.* dropsy of the belly or abdomen. **ascitic, -ical,** *a.* suffering from abdominal dropsy. [Gr. *askites*]

ascititious ADSCITITIOUS.

Asclepiad, *n.* a kind of verse invented by Asclepiades, a Greek poet of the 3rd cent. BC, consisting of a spondee, two (or three) choriambs and an iambus. **Asclepiadean,** †**Asclepiadic,** *a.* of or pertaining to the metre called Asclepiad.

asclepiad, *n.* a plant of the genus *Asclepias,* or order Asclepiadaceae, containing the milkweeds, swallow worts etc., principally from N America. [Gr. *asklēpias -ados, Asklēpios,* Aesculapius]

Ascomycetes ASCUS.

ascorbic acid, *n.* vitamin C, occurring in vegetables, fruits etc.

Ascot, *n.* English racecourse where the main meeting is the Royal meeting every June and the leading race is the Ascot Gold Cup. It does not stage any of the classic races. It is situated near Windsor and was founded by Queen Anne in 1711.

ascribe, *v.t.* to attribute, to impute, to assign, to claim (something) for (someone). **ascribable,** *a.* [L *ascrībere (ad-,* to, *scrībere,* to write)]

ascription, *n.* the act of attributing; that which is ascribed. **ascriptitious,** *a.* additional; ascribed to (usu. on insufficient evidence). [L *ascrīptio (ascrīptus,* p.p. of *ascrībere*)]

ascus, *n.* (*pl.* **asci**) a cell in which spores are formed in an ascomycete. **ascomycete,** *n.* a fungus of the Ascomycetes. **Ascomycetes,** *n.pl.* a large class of fungi, including *Penicillium* and yeasts, having spores formed in asci. [Gr. *askos,* wine-skin, bladder, bag]

asdic, *n.* instruments and apparatus for detecting the presence and position of submarines. [acronym for *A*llied *S*ubmarine *D*etection *I*nvestigation *C*ommittee]

-ase, *suf.* denoting an enzyme, e.g. *zymase.* [F, from DIASTASE]

ASEAN, (*abbr.*) Association of South-East Asian Nations.

aseismatic, *a.* proof against earthquake shocks, protect from such shocks. [SEISMIC]

asepsis, *n.* freedom from blood-poisoning; the condition of being aseptic; the process of making aseptic. **aseptic,** *a.* not liable to or free from putrefaction; preventing putrefaction or infection; free from a tendency to blood-poisoning. *n.* an aseptic substance. **asepticism,** *n.* treatment by aseptic or antiseptic principles. **asepticize, -ise,** *v.t.* to treat by these methods, to render aseptic. [Gr. *a-,* not; SEPSIS]

asexual, *a.* without sex, sexual organs or sexual functions; of reproduction, without union of gametes; without sexual content or interest. **asexuality,** *n.* **asexually,** *adv.* [Gr. *a-,* not, SEXUAL]

Asgard, *n.* in Scandinavian mythology, the place where the gods lived. It was reached by a bridge called Bifrost, the rainbow.

ASH, (*abbr.*) Action on Smoking and Health.

ash[1], *n.* the residuum left after the burning of anything combustible; powdery mineral matter ejected from volcanoes; (*pl.*) the remains of anything burnt; (*pl.*) the remains of a cremated dead body preserved in an urn or coffin; (*pl.*) a buried corpse, a dead body; (*pl.*) a symbol of grief or repentance. **The Ashes,** *n.pl.* a term used by the *Sporting Times* in 1882 in a mock In Memoriam to the demise of English cricket after the successful visit of the Australians. Since then English and Australian teams visiting one another have endeavoured to 'bring back the ashes'. **to lay in ashes,** to destroy utterly. **ash-bin,** *n.* a receptacle for household refuse. **ash-blond,** *n.* a very pale blond colour; a person with hair of this colour. *a.* of or having hair of this colour. **ash-blonde,** *n.fem.* **ash-cake,** *n.* a corn-cake baked in hot ashes. **ash-can,** *n.* (*N Am.*) a dustbin. **ash-coloured,** *a.* of a colour between brown and grey. **ash-fire,** *n.* a slow fire used in chemical operations. **ash-furnace,** *n.* a furnace used in glass-making. **ash-heap,** *n.* a collection of ashes and other refuse. **ash-hole,** *n.* a receptacle for ashes beneath a furnace. **ash-pan,** *n.* a pan beneath a furnace or grate for the reception of ashes. **ash-pit,** *n.* an ash-hole. **ashtray,** *n.* a small container for tobacco ash, cigarette butts etc. **Ash Wednesday,** *n.* the first day of Lent, so called from the Roman Catholic practice of sprinkling the foreheads of the people with ashes on that day. **ashery,** *n.* a place where pearl-ash is manufactured; a receptacle for ashes. **ashy,** *a.* of or composed of ashes; covered with ashes; whitish-grey; pale. **ashy-pale,** *a.* very pale, ashen. [OE *æsce, asce, axe* (cp. Icel. *aska,* Goth. *azgō*)]

ash[2], *n.* a forest tree, *Fraxinus excelsior,* with grey bark, pinnate leaves and tough, close-grained wood; the wood of the ash-tree. *a.* made from ash. **ash-key,** *n.* the winged seed-vessel of the ash. **ash-leaf kidney,** *n.* an early potato with leaves like those of the ash. [OE *æsc* (cp. Icel. *askr,* OHG *asc,* cp. G *Esche*)]

ashake, *adv.* on the shake.

ashamed, *a.* affected with shame; abashed by consciousness of error or guilt. **ashamedly,** *adv.* [p.p. of *ashame,* obs. v. (*a-,* intens., SHAME), OE *asceamod*]

Ashanti ASANTE.

Ashbee, *n.* **C(harles) R(obert)** (1863–1942), British designer, architect, and writer, one of the major figures of the Arts and Crafts movement. He founded a 'Guild and School of Handicraft' in the East End of London in 1888, but later modified his views, accepting the importance of machinery and design for industry.

Ashcan school, *n.* a group of US painters active about 1908–14, whose members included Robert Henri (1865–1929), George Luks (1867–1933), William Glackens (1870–1938), Everett Shinn (1876–1953) and John Sloan (1871–1951). Their style is realist; their subjects centred on modern city life, the poor and the outcast.

Ashcroft, *n.* **Peggy** (1907–), English actress. Her many leading roles include Desdemona in *Othello* (with Paul Robeson), Juliet in *Romeo and Juliet* (1935) (with Laurence Olivier and John Gielgud), and appearances in the British TV play *Caught on a Train* (1980) (BAFTA award), the series *The Jewel in the Crown* (1984) and the film *A Passage to India* (1985).

Ashdown, *n.* **(Jeremy John Durham) 'Paddy'** (1941–), British politician. Originally a Liberal MP, he became leader of the Social and Liberal Democrats in 1988. He served in the Royal Marines as a commando, leading a Special Boat Section in Borneo, and was a member of the Diplomatic Service (1971–76).

ashen[1], *a.* ash-coloured; pale; between brown and grey.

ashen[2], *a.* of or pertaining to the ash-tree; made of ash.

Ashes, the, ASH[1].

ashet, *n.* (*Sc., North.*) a large flat plate or dish for meat. [F *assiette*]

Ashford, *n.* **Daisy** (1881–1972), English author of *The Young Visiters* (1919), a classic of unconscious humour written when she was nine.

ashine, *adv.* shining.

ashiver, *adv.* in a shiver.

Ashkenazi, *n.* (*pl.* **-zim**) a Jew of German or E European descent, as opposed to Sephardi, of Spanish, Portuguese, or N African descent. [Heb. *Ashkenaz*]

Ashkenazy, *n.* **Vladimir** (1937–), Soviet-born pianist and conductor. His keyboard technique differs slightly from standard Western technique. In 1962 he was joint winner of the Tchaikovsky Competition with John Ogdon. He excels in Rachmaninov, Prokofiev and Liszt.

Ashkhabad, *n.* capital of Republic of Turkmenistan, USSR; population (1987) 382,000. 'Bukhara' carpets are made here.

ashlar, ashler, *n.* square-hewn stone used in a building; masonry built of this; thin masonry built as a facing to rubble or brick work; rough-hewn stone as it leaves the quarry. **ashlar-work,** *n.* masonry of hewn as opposed to unhewn stones. **ashlared,** *a.* covered with ashlar. **ashlaring,** *n.* the quartering to which laths are nailed in garrets, in order to cut off the angle between roof and floor; ashlar masonry. [OF *aiseler,* L. *axilla,* dim. of *axis,* axis, board, plank]

Ashley, *n.* **Laura** (born Mountney) (1925–1985), Welsh designer, who established and gave her name to a neo-Victorian country style in clothes and furnishings beginning in 1953. She started an international chain of shops.

Ashmole, *n.* **Elias** (1617–1692), English antiquary, whose collection forms the basis of the Ashmolean Museum, Oxford.

ashore, *adv.* to the shore; on the shore; on land.

Ashton, *n.* **Frederick** (1904–1988), British dancer and choreographer. He studied with Massine and Rambert before joining the Vic-Wells Ballet in 1935 as chief choreographer, creating several roles for Margot Fonteyn. He was director of the Royal Ballet, London, 1963–70.

Asia, *n.* largest of the continents, forming the eastern part of Eurasia to the east of the Ural mountains, one third of the total land surface of the world. **area** 44,000,000 sq km/17,000,000 sq miles. **largest cities** (over 5 million) Tokyo, Shanghai, Osaka, Beijing, Seoul, Calcutta, Bombay, Jakarta, Bangkok, Tehran, Hong Kong. **physical** five main divisions: (1) Central triangular mountain mass, including the Himalayas; to the N the great Tibetan plateau, bounded by the Kunlun mountains, to the N of which lie further ranges, as well as the Gobi Desert. (2) The SW plateaux and ranges, forming Afghanistan, Baluchistan, Iran. (3) The northern lowlands, from the central mountains to the Arctic Ocean, much of which is frozen for several months each year. (4) The eastern margin and islands, where much of the population is concentrated. (5) The southern plateau and river plains, including Arabia, the Deccan, and the alluvial plains of the Euphrates, Tigris, Indus, Ganges, and Irrawaddy. The climate shows great extremes and contrasts, the heart of the continent becoming bitterly cold in winter and very hot in summer. This, with the resulting pressure and wind systems, accounts for the Asiatic monsoons, bringing heavy rain to all SE Asia, China, and Japan, between May and October. **population** (1984) 2,778,000,000, the most densely populated of the continents; annual growth rate 1.7%. **language** predominantly tonal languages (Chinese, Japanese) in the east, Indo-Iranian languages in central India and Pakistan (Hindi/Urdu), and Semitic (Arabic) in the SW. **religion** Hinduism, Islam, Buddhism, Christianity, Confucianism, Shintoism.

Asia Minor, *n.* historical name for Anatolia, the Asian part of Turkey.

Asian, *a.* of, pertaining to or belonging to Asia or its people. *n.* (a descendant of) a native or inhabitant of Asia, esp. (in Britain) of the Indian sub-continent. **Asian flu,** *n.* a severe type of influenza caused by a virus isolated during an epidemic in Asia in 1957. [L *Asiānus,* Gr. *Asiānos,* from *Asia*]

Asian Development Bank, (ADB) a bank founded in 1966 to stimulate growth in Asia and the Far East by administering direct loans and technical assistance. Members include 30 countries within the region and 14 countries of W Europe and North America. The headquarters are in Manila, Philippines.

Asia-Pacific Economic Cooperation Conference, (APEC) trade group comprising 12 Pacific Asian countries, formed Nov. 1898 to promote multilateral trade and economic cooperation between member states. Its members are the US, Canada, Japan, Australia, New Zealand, South Korea, Brunei, Indonesia, Malaysia, the Philippines, Singapore and Thailand.

Asiatic, *a.* Asian. [L *Aiāticus,* Gr. *Asiātikos*]

aside, *adv.* at, to or towards one side; away. *n.* something spoken aside so as to be audible only to the person addressed, esp. by an actor, which the others on the stage are not supposed to hear; an indirect effort, a digression. [formerly *on side*]

Asiento, Treaty of, an agreement between the UK and Spain (1713), whereby British traders were permitted to introduce 144,000 black slaves into the Spanish-American colonies in the course of the following 30 years. In 1750 the right was bought out by the Spanish government for $100,000.

Asimov, *n.* **Isaac** (1920–), US science-fiction writer and writer on science, born in the USSR. He has published about 200 books, and is possibly best known for his *I, Robot* (1950) and the 'Foundation' trilogy (1951–53), continued in *Foundation's Edge* (1983).

asinego, *n.* a little ass; a fool, a duffer. [Sp. *asnico,* dim. of *asno,* ass]

asinine, *a.* of, pertaining to or resembling asses; stupid, obstinate. **asininity,** *n.* asinine behaviour, obstinate stupidity. [L *asinīnus* (*asinus,* an ass)]

-asis, *suf.* forming names of diseases; e.g. *elephantiasis.* [L *-ăsis,* Gr. *-āsis*]

asitia, *n.* pathological distaste for food, want of appetite. [Gr., want of food]

ask, *v.t.* to request; to seek to obtain by words; to solicit, to demand, to state (a price required); to question, to inquire of; to inquire concerning; to request to be informed about; to invite; (*dated*) to publish (the banns of marriage). *v.i.* to make a request, petition or demand; to inquire. **to ask for,** to behave in such a way as toinvite (trouble etc.). **asker,** *n.* one who asks or inquires; a petitioner, a suppliant, a beggar. **asking,** *n.* petitioning; expressed wish; solicitation; (*dated*) the publication of the banns of marriage. **asking price,** *n.* the price set by a seller. [OE *ascian*]

askance, askant, *adv.* obliquely, sideways, askew, squintingly; with mistrust, suspicion or disapproval. †*v.t.* to turn away. [etym. doubtful]

askari, *n.* an E African native soldier. [Ar. *askar,* an army]

askew, *adv.* askance, asquint; in an oblique direction. *a.* oblique, awry, skew. [SKEW]

†**aslake,** *v.t.* to cause to become slack; to assuage, to appease. *v.i.* to become slack; to be slaked, become cool. [OE *aslacian*]

aslant, *adv., a.* in a slanting or oblique direction. *prep.* across in a slanting direction; oblique.

asleep, *adv., pred.a.* in or into a state of sleep; (*euphem.*) dead.

ASLEF, (*abbr.*) Associated Society of Locomotive Engineers and Firemen.

AS Level, *n.* examinations introduced in the UK in 1988 as the equivalent to 'half an A Level' as a means of broadening the sixth form (age 16–18) curriculum, and including more students in the examination system. [*A*dvanced *S*upplementary]

aslope, *a.* sloping, oblique. *adv.* with a slope; aslant, obliquely, crosswise. [OE *aslopen,* p.p. of *aslūpan,* to slip away; or *a-,* on, SLOPE]

ASM, (*abbr.*) air-to-surface missile.

Asmara, Asmera, *n.* capital of Eritrea, Ethiopia; 64

km/40 miles SW of Massawa on the Red Sea; population (1984) 275,385. Products include beer, clothes and textiles.

asmoulder, *adv.* smouldering.

asocial, *a.* not social; antisocial. [Gr. *a-*, priv., SOCIAL]

Asoka, *n.* (reigned 264–228 BC), Indian emperor, who was a Buddhist convert. He had edicts enjoining the adoption of his new faith carved on pillars and rock faces throughout his dominions, and many survive. In Patna there are the remains of a hall built by him.

asp[1]**, aspic,** *n.* a small venomous hooded serpent, *Naja haje,* the Egyptian cobra; a European viper, *Vipera aspis;* any venomous serpent. [L *aspis,* Gr. *aspis*]

asp[2] ASPEN.

asparagus, *n.* a culinary plant, the tender shoots of which are eaten. [L, from Gr. *asparagos* (etym. doubtful)]

Aspasia, *n.* (*c.* 440 BC), Greek courtesan, the mistress of the Athenian politician Pericles. As a 'foreigner' from Miletus, she could not be recognized as his wife, but their son was later legitimized. The philosopher Socrates visited her salon, a meeting place for the celebrities of Athens. Her free thinking led to a charge of impiety, from which Pericles had to defend her.

aspect, *n.* look, view; looking, way of looking; (*Astrol.*) the situation of one planet with respect to another; the direction in which something is turned, phase; appearance, expression. **aspectable,** *a.* visible; worthy to be looked upon. [L *aspectus,* p.p. of *aspicere,* to behold (*ad-*, to, at, *spicere,* to look)]

aspen, asp,[2] *n. Populus tremula,* the trembling poplar, remarkable for its quivering leaves. *a.* belonging to the aspen; made of the wood of the aspen; like an aspen, trembling, quaking; (of a tongue) always wagging. [OE *æspe* (cp. OHG *aspâ,* G. *Espe*)]

asper, *n.* a small Turkish silver coin, now only money of account. [F *aspre* or It. *aspero,* late Gr. *aspron,* white money (*aspros -on,* white, perh. from L *asper,* rough)]

asperate, *v.t.* to roughen; to make rough. **asperation,** *n.* a making rough; roughness. [L *asperātus,* p.p. of *asperāre,* to roughen (*asper,* rough)]

asperge, *v.t.* to besprinkle, esp. with holy water. *n.* an aspergillum. **asperges,** *n.* the sprinkling of the congregation with holy water by the celebrant of High Mass. **aspergillum,** *n.* (*pl.* **-lla, -llums**) the brush used to sprinkle holy water; a genus of lamellibranchs. **Aspergillus,** *n.* a genus of fungi including many moulds that grow on decaying organic matter, named from their resemblance to the aspergillum. [F *asperger,* L *aspergere* (*ad-*, to, *spargere,* to sprinkle)]

asperity, *n.* roughness of surface; a rugged excrescence; harshness of sound; severity, bleakness; harshness of manner, acrimony. [OF *asprete,* L *asperitātem,* nom. *asperitas* (*asper,* rough)]

aspermia, *n.* total absence of semen. [as foll.]

aspermous, *a.* (*Bot.*) without seed; destitute of seed. [Gr. *a-*, not, *sperma,* seed]

asperse, *v.t.* to scatter or strew upon, to besprinkle; to spread disparaging reports about, to defame. **aspersion,** *n.* calumny, slander, a false report or insinuation; the act of sprinkling; that which is sprinkled. **aspersive, aspersory,** *a.* **aspersively,** *adv.* **aspersorium,** *n.* the vessel from which holy water is sprinkled. [L *aspersus,* p.p. of *aspergere* (see ASPERGE)]

asphalt, asphalte, *n.* mineral pitch, a dark brown or black form of bitumen; bituminous limestone, or an artificial substitute (often made with tar), used for roofing, road surfacing etc. *v.t.* to cover, surface or line with asphalt. **asphaltic,** *a.* pertaining to asphalt; consisting of or containing asphalt. [late L *asphaltum,* Gr. *asphalton* (foreign in origin)]

aspheterism, *n.* communism; the negation of private property. **aspheterize, -ise,** *v.i.* to practise this doctrine. [Gr. *a-*, not, *spheteros,* one's own, -ISM]

asphodel, *n.* a mythical undying flower, said to bloom in the Elysian fields; a plant of the liliaceous genus *Asphodelus,* comprising the king's spear. [Gr. *asphodelos* (etym. doubtful), see also DAFFODIL]

asphyxia, asphyxy, *n.* stoppage of the pulse; suspended animation, produced by a lack of oxygen in the blood; suffocation. **asphyxial, asphyxiant,** *a.* of or pertaining to asphyxia. **asphyxiate,** *v.t.* to affect with asphyxia; to suffocate. **asphyxiation,** *n.* the act of asphyxiating or the process of being asphyxiated; suffocation. **asphyxiator,** *n.* one who or that which asphyxiates; a kind of fire extinguisher employing carbon dioxide; an apparatus for testing drains by means of smoke. [Gr. *asphuxia* (*a-*, not, *sphuzein,* to throb, pulsate)]

aspic[1] ASP[1].

aspic[2]**,** *n.* a savoury jelly used as a garnish or in which game, hard-boiled eggs, fish etc., may be embedded; a dish of meat etc. moulded in aspic. [F, etym. doubtful]

Aspidistra, *n.* a liliaceous genus of plants including the parlour palm. [Gr. *aspis,* a shield; *astron,* star]

aspirant ASPIRE.

aspirate, *v.t.* to pronounce with a full breath; to prefix the letter *h* or its equivalent; to draw out (gas) from a vessel; to remove (blood etc.) by suction. *a.* aspirated; pronounced with a breathing. *n.* a letter pronounced with the sound of *h.* **aspiration,** *n.* the act of breathing; the act of aspirating; an aspirated sound. **aspirator,** *n.* one or that which aspirates; an instrument for drawing air or gas through a tube; an appliance enabling one to breathe in poison gas; (*Med.*) an instrument for evacuating a cavity by means of an exhausted receiver; a winnowing- or fanning-machine. [L *aspīrātus,* p.p. of *aspīrāre* (see ASPIRE)]

aspire, *v.i.* to long, desire eagerly; to seek to attain; (*fig.*) to rise, to mount up. †*v.t.* to long for ardently; to mount up, to reach. **aspirant,** *a.* aspiring, aiming at a higher position. *n.* one who aspires; a candidate. **aspiration,** *n.* the act of aspiring; steadfast desire; a seeking for better things. **aspiring,** *a.* eagerly desirous of some high object, ambitious tapering upwards, soaring. **aspiringly,** *adv.* **aspiringness,** *n.* [L *aspīrāre* (*ad-*, to, *spīrāre,* to breathe, blow)]

aspirin, *n.* (*Med.*) (a tablet containing) acetylsalicylic acid, used as a pain-killer.

asplenium SPLEENWORT under SPLEEN.

Asplund, *n.* **(Erik) Gunnar** (1885–1940), Swedish architect. His early work, for example at the Stockholm South Cemetery (1914), was in the neo-classical tradition. Later buildings, such as the Stockholm City Library (1924–27) and Gothenburg City Hall (1934–37), developed a refined modern-classical style, culminating in the Stockholm South Cemetery Crematorium (1935–40).

asprawl, *adv.* in a sprawling attitude.

aspread, *adv.* spread out.

asquat, *adv.* in a squatting attitude.

asquint, *adv.* with a squint; obliquely; with distrust, suspicion; with crafty designs, furtively. [*a-*, on, and a word corresponding to Dut. *schuinte,* slope, slant]

Asquith, *n.* **Herbert Henry, 1st Earl of Oxford and Asquith** (1852–1928), British Liberal politician, prime minister (1908–16). As chancellor of the exchequer he introduced old-age pensions in 1908. He limited the powers of the House of Lords and attempted to give Ireland Home Rule.

ass[1]**,** *n.* (*pl.* **asses**) a quadruped, *Equus asinus,* allied to the horse, but of smaller size, with long ears and a tufted tail; (also *pron.* ahs) a stupid, obstinate person. **to make an ass of,** to treat as an ass, to render ridiculous. **to make an ass of oneself,** to stultify oneself, play the fool. **asses' bridge,** *n.* the fifth proposition of Euclid, Bk.I.; the *pons asinorum.* †**ass head,** *n.* a person of dull intellect, a block-head. [OE *assa, esol* (cp. Dut. *ezel,* G. *Esel,* Goth. *asilus,* L *asinus*)]

ass[2] ARSE.

Assad, *n.* **Hafez al** (1930–), Syrian Ba'athist politician. He became prime minister after the bloodless military coup 1970, and in 1971 was the first president to be elected by popular vote. He was re-elected in 1978. He is a Shia (Alawite) Muslim.

assafetida, ASAFOETIDA.

assagai, assegai, *n.* a slender lance of hard wood, chiefly applied to the missile lances of the southern

African tribes. *v.t.* to wound or kill with an assagai. [Arab. *azzaghayah* (*al*, the, Berber *zaghayah*); either through F *azagaye* or Port. *azagaia*]

assai, *adv.* (*Mus.*) very; as *largo assai,* very slow. [It., enough]

assail, *v.t.* to attack violently by physical means or with argument, abuse, censure, entreaty or hostile influence, temptation, snares and the like; to dash against; to approach with intent to overcome; †to tempt; †to woo. **assailable,** *a.* **assailant,** *a.* assailing, attacking. *n.* one who assails. [OF *asailer, assailler,* late L *adsalīre* (*ad,* to, at, *salīre,* to leap)]

Assam, *n.*, state of NE India. **area** 78,400 sq km/30,262 sq miles. **capital** Dispur. **towns** Shilling. **products** half India's tea is grown here, and half its oil produced; rice, jute, sugar, cotton, coal. **population** (1981) 19,903,000, including 12,000,000 Assamese (Hindus), 5,000,000 Bengalis (chiefly Muslim immigrants from Bangladesh), and Nepalis; and 2,000,000 native people (Christian and traditional religions). **language** Assamese.

assassin, *n.* one of a body of Muslim fanatics, in the time of the Crusades, who were sent forth to murder secretly the Christian leaders; one who kills by surprise or secret assault (generally for money or for fanatical, political etc. motives). **assassinate,** *v.t.* to kill by surprise or secret assault; to murder (as a political or religious leader) by sudden violence; to injure or destroy (a person's character or reputation). **assassination,** *n.* **assassinator,** *n.* [F *assassin* or It. *assassino,* med. L *assassīnus,* Arab. *hashshāshin,* hashish-eaters]

assault, *n.* the act of assailing; a violent attack with material or immaterial weapons; the charge of an attacking body on a fortified post; (*Law*) a threatening word or act; an attempt at rape. *v.t.* to make a violent onset or attack on, with material or immaterial weapons; to attack (a fortified post) by sudden rush; to storm; (*Law*) to attack with threatening words or with blows; to attempt to rape. **assault and battery,** *n.* (*Law*) an assault with action as well as words. **assault-at-arms,** *n.* an attack in fencing; a display of military exercises. **assault course,** *n.* an obstacle course used for training soldiers. **assaultable,** *a.* [OF *asaut, assaut,* L *ad-,* to, at, *saltus,* a leap (ASSAIL)]

assay, *n.* a trial, examination; the scientific determination of the quantity of metal in an ore, alloy, bullion or coin; the chemical analysis of a substance to determine its content; a metal or other substance analysed; a trying, attempt, endeavour. *v.t.*, to try, to test; to determine the amount of metal in (an ore, alloy, bullion or coin); to subject to chemical analysis; to try to do, attempt; †to taste food or drink before it is offered to a sovereign or noble. *v.i.* to attempt, to endeavour. **assay-balance,** *n.* a very delicate balance, used in assaying. **assay-master,** *n.* an officer of the Mint, appointed to assay bullion and coin. **assay ton,** *n.* a weight of 29,166·66 grams. **assayer,** *n.* one who assays bullion; †an officer whose duty it was to taste food and drink before his lord. **assaying,** *n.* the act or process of determining the amount of a particular substance in a compound. [OF *assai,* L *exagium,* from *exagere, exigere,* to weigh, try (*ex-*, out, *agere,* to drive, deal)]

assegai ASSAGAI.

assemblance[1]**,** *n.* appearance, show. [SEMBLANCE]

assemble, *v.t.* to call together; to bring together into one mass or heap; to fit together the component parts. *v.i.* to meet or come together; to gather, to congregate. *n.* (*Mil.*) an assembly. **assemblage,** *n.* a gathering, assembling; a concourse; a collection; (*Carp.*) a putting together. †**assemblance**[2]**,** *n.* assemblage, assembly. **assembler,** *n.* a person who, or thing that, assembles; a computer program that automatically translates assembly language into machine code; assembly language. **assembly,** *n.* the act of assembling; the state of being assembled; a body of people met together for some common purpose; a deliberative, legislative or religious body; a lower house in some legislatures; (*Mil.*) the second beat of the drum summoning soldiers to prepare to march; the conversion of assembly language into machine code. **assembly language,** *n.* a low-level computer language in which instructions written in mnemonics correspond directly to instructions in machine code. **assembly line,** *n.* a serial collection of workers and machines operating from stage to stage in assembling some product. **assemblyman,** *n.* a member of a legislative assembly. **assembly-room,** *n.* a room in which public assemblies, balls, concerts etc. are held. **Westminster Assembly,** *n.* the body of divines appointed in 1643 by the Long Parliament to assist in revising the government and liturgy of the Church of England. [OF *assembler,* late L *assimulāre ad-,* to, *simul,* together)]

assent, *v.i.* to agree to or sanction something proposed; to admit a statement as true. *n.* the act of admitting, agreeing to or concurring in; sanction; agreement, acquiescence. **assentation,** *n.* the action of assenting, esp. with obsequiousness or servility. **assentient,** *a.* assenting to. *n.* one who assents or agrees. **assentingly,** *adv.* **assentor,** *n.* one who gives assent, esp. one who signs the nomination of a Parliamentary candidate after the proposer and seconder. [OF *asenter,* L *assentīre* (*ad-*, to, *sentīre,* to feel)]

assert, *v.t.* to affirm, to declare positively; to maintain; to insist on (a claim, right etc.); to put (oneself) forward, insist on one's rights etc. **assertable,** *a.* **assertion,** *n.* the act of asserting; a positive statement, an affirmation. **assertive,** *a.* characterized by assertion, dogmatic. **assertively,** *adv.* **assertiveness,** *n.* **assertor,** *n.* one who maintains or defends; an advocate; one who makes an assertion. [L *assertus,* p.p. of *asserere,* to add to, take to oneself (*ad-,* to *serere,* to join, bind)]

assess, *v.t.* to fix by authority the amount of (a tax fine etc. for a person or community); to value (property, income etc.) for the purpose of taxation; to value; to estimate, to judge. **assessable,** *a.* capable of being assessed; liable to be assessed. **assessably,** *adv.* **assessment,** *n.* the act of assessing; the amount assessed; a scheme of rating or taxation; an official valuation for those purposes; (an) estimation, appraisal. **assessment centre,** *n.* a centre where juvenile offenders are sent whilst their situation is assessed. **assessment-work,** *n.* (*Mining*) work done each year on a claim, to maintain title. **assessor,** *n.* one who shares another's rank and sits beside him; one who makes an assessment; one who sits near and advises a judge or magistrate on technical points, commercial usage, navigation etc.; one who evaluates insurance claims. **assessorship,** *n.* [OF *assesser,* late L *assessāre,* freq. of *assidēre* (*ad-*, to, *sedēre,* to sit)]

assets, *n.pl.* goods sufficient to satisfy a testator's debts and legacies; property or effects that may be applied for this purpose; the effects of an insolvent debtor; all the property of a person or company which may be liable for outstanding debts; property in general. **asset,** *n.* a useful or valuable resource. **asset-stripping,** *n.* the practice of buying a company and selling off its assets to make a profit. [A-F *asetz,* OF *asez,* enough, late L *ad satis,* sufficiency (*satis,* enough)]

asseverate, *v.t.* to affirm with solemnity; to assert positively. **asseveration,** *n.* the act of asseverating; a solemn affirmation; an emphatic declaration or confirmation, an oath. [L *assevērātus,* p.p. of *assevērāre* (*ad-*, to, *sevērus,* earnest, serious)]

assiduous, *a.* constant in application; diligent. **assiduously,** *adv.* **assiduousness,** *n.* **assiduity,** *n.* constant or close application to the matter in hand, perseverance, diligence; (*pl.*) persistent endeavours to please, constant attentions. [L *assiduus,* from *assidēre* (see ASSESS)]

assiege, *v.t.* to besiege. *n.* a siege. [OF *asegier,* late L *assediāre* (*ad-*, to, *sedium,* siege)]

assiento, *n.* a contract or convention between the King of Spain and other powers for furnishing slaves for the Spanish dominions in America, esp. that between Great Britain and Spain at the peace of Utrecht

(1713). [Sp., a contract]

assign, *v.t.* to allot, to apportion; to designate for a specific purpose; to name, to fix; to point out, to ascribe, to attribute; (*Law*) to transfer, to surrender. *n.* one to whom a property or right is transferred; †an appurtenance, an appendage. **assignable,** *a.* capable of being transferred, designated or pointed out as source or reason. **assignation,** *n.* (appointment of a particular time or place for) meeting, esp. an illicit one between lovers; the act of assigning; attribution of origin; an appointment; a transference of property or right. **assignee,** *n.* an agent, a representative; (*Law*) one to whom a right or property is transferred; (*Austral. Hist.*) a convict assigned as a servant. **assignees in bankruptcy,** *n.pl.* people to whom a bankrupt's estate is assigned and who manage it for the benefit of the creditors. **assignment,** *n.* the act of assigning; allotment, allocation; a specific task or mission; a position or job to which one is assigned; a specification of reasons; attribution; a legal transference of right or property; the instrument by which such transference is effected; the right or property transferred; (*Austral. Hist.*) the formal assignment of a convict to private service. **assignment in bankruptcy,** the transference of a bankrupt's estate to assignees for the benefit of his creditors. **assignor,** *n.* one who transfers a right or property. [OF *assigner,* L *assignāre* (*ad-,* to, *signāre,* to mark)]

assignat, *n.* paper money issued by the Revolutionary Government of France (1790–96) on the security of State lands. [F]

assimilate, *v.t.* to make similar or alike; to liken, to compare; to take as nutriment and convert into living tissue, to incorporate in the substance of an organism; to take in (information) and comprehend; to absorb into a population or group; to incorporate; to adapt (a speech sound) so as to resemble an adjacent sound. *v.i.* to become similar; to be incorporated in the substance of a living organism; to become absorbed or incorporated. **assimilable,** *a.* capable of being assimilated. **assimilability,** *n.* the capability of being assimilated. **assimilation,** *n.* the act or process of assimilating; the state of being assimilated; comparison; the process by which an organism converts nourishment into its own substance. **assimilative,** *a.* having the power of assimilating; (*rare*) capable of being assimilated. **assimilator,** *n.* one who or that which assimilates. **assimilatory,** *a.* tending to assimilate. [L *assimilāre* (*ad-, similis,* like), -ATE]

assise, *n.* a geological formation consisting of parallel beds with the same organic remains throughout. [F (ASSIZE)]

assist, *v.t.* to help, to aid, to give support or succour to; to act as a subordinate to. *v.i.* to give help or aid; to be present (at). **assistance,** *n.* help, aid, support, succour, furtherance. **assistant,** *a.* aiding, helping, auxiliary. *n.* one who assists another; an auxiliary. **assisted,** *a.* helped, aided. **assisted reproduction,** *n.* a collective term for all methods of human fertilization and reproduction involving medical intervention e.g. artificial insemination, gameto intra-fallopian transfer. **assistor,** *n.* (*Law*) an assistant, one who aids or is accessory. [F *assister,* L *assistere* (*ad-,* to, *sistere,* to place, from *stāre,* to stand)]

Assisted Places Scheme, in UK education, a scheme established in 1980 by which the government assists parents with the cost of fees at independent schools on a means-tested basis.

assize, *n.* †a formal session or sitting; †a decree or edict made at such sitting; †ordinance, regulation, esp. respecting weight and price, hence standard of quantity, price or quality, esp. of bread and ale; a trial in which sworn assessors decide questions of fact; an action so tried or decided; (*pl.*) from 1815 to 1971, the sessions held periodically by the judges of the Supreme Court in each county in England for the administration of civil and criminal justice. †*v.t.* to fix by a legal ordinance the weight, measure or price of; to assess, to rate. **assizer,** *n.* †one who had charge of an assizes of weights, measures or prices; (*Sc. Law*) a jury member. [OF *asise,* orig. fem. p.p. of *asseoir,* sit at (L *assidēre,* see ASSESS)]

assoc., (*abbr.*) associate, associated, association.

associate, *v.t.* to join, to unite, to combine, to connect; to bring together in the mind; to connect (oneself) as a partner, supporter, friend, companion etc. *v.i.* to unite or combine for a common purpose; to keep company or mix (with). *a.*, connected, joined; confederate, allied; in the same group or category; having subordinate status. *n.*, a confederate, an ally; a partner, colleague, coadjutor; a person having partial membership or a subordinate status in an association or institution; something generally found with another. **associateship,** *n.* **associability,** *n.* **associable,** *a.* †companionable; capable of being (mentally) associated; (*Physiol.*) liable to be affected by sympathy with other parts. **association,** *n.* the act of combining for a common purpose; a society formed for the promotion of some common object; fellowship, intimacy, connection; mental connection of ideas, memories, sensations etc.; memory, thought or feeling connected with some object, place etc. and recalled to the mind in connection therewith; a plant community growing in a uniform habitat and forming part of a larger ecological unit; the formation of loosely held aggregates of molecules, ions etc. **Association Football,** *n.* football played between two teams of eleven players, with a round ball which may not be touched with the hands except by the goalkeepers. **deed of association,** *n.* a legal instrument in which the particulars of a limited liability company must be recorded on its formation. **associational,** *a.* **associationism,** *n.* (*Psych.*) the theory which accounts for mental and moral phenomena by association of ideas. **associationist,** *n.* **associative,** *a.* tending to associate. [L *associāre* (*ad-,* to, *sociāre,* to join, from *socius,* an ally), -ATE]

Association of Southeast Asian Nations, (ASEAN) a regional alliance formed in Bangkok 1967; it took over the nonmilitary role of the Southeast Asia Treaty Organization in 1975. Its members are Indonesia, Malaysia, the Philippines, Singapore, Thailand, and (from 1984) Brunei; its headquarters are in Jakarta, Indonesia.

assoil, *v.t.* to pardon, to absolve from sin; to atone for, expiate; to discharge, acquit; to get rid of, to dispel; to discharge (a duty). **assoilzie,** *v.t.* (*Sc. Law*) to acquit. [OF *assoile,* pres. sing. of *assoldre,* L *absolvere* (*ab-,* away, *solvere,* to loosen)]

assonant, *a.* corresponding in sound; rhyming in the accented vowels, but not in the consonants; also, correspondence of consonant sounds with different vowels. *n.* an assonant word. **assonance,** *n.* the quality of being assonant; a word or syllable answering to another in sound; correspondence or resemblance in other respects. [F, from L *assonāre -ātum* (*ad-,* to, *sonāre,* to sound; *sonus,* sound)]

assort, *v.t.* to arrange or dispose in sorts or lots; to arrange into different classes; to furnish with articles so arranged. *v.i.* to suit, to agree, to match; to be in congruity or harmony. **assorted,** *a.* arranged in sorts; of various sorts. **assortment,** *n.* a collection of things assorted; a collection of things of various kinds; the act of assorting; the state of being assorted. [OF *assorter* (*F assortir*) (*à,* to, *sorte,* sort, manner, kind, L *sors, sortis*)]

asst., (*abbr.*) assistant.

assuage, *v.t.* to sweeten, allay, mitigate; tosoothe, to lessen the violence of; to appease, satisfy. †*v.i.* to abate, subside. **assuagement,** *n.* the act of assuaging; mitigation, abatement; something that assuages; a pain-relieving medicine or application. **assuasive,** *a.* assuaging, mitigating, soothing. *n.* a soothing medicine or application. [OF *assouagier,* L *assuāviāre* (*suāvis,* sweet)]

†assuefaction, *n.* the act of accustoming; the state of being accustomed. **†assuetude,** *n.* the state of being accustomed. [L *assuēfacere,* to make accustomed (*assuētus,* p.p. of *assuēscere,* to accustom]

assume, *v.t.* to take to oneself; to receive, adopt; to take upon oneself, to put on, to undertake; to arrogate, appropriate, pretend to, to claim; to take for granted; to pretend, feign. *v.i.* to be arrogant or pretentious; to claim more than is one's due. **assumed,** *a.* usurped, pretended; feigned, false; taken for granted. **assumedly**, *adv.* **assuming,** *a.* arrogant, haughty. *n.* assumption, presumption. [L *assūmere,* to take to oneself (*ad-,* to, *sūmere* to take)]

assumpsit, *n.* (*Law*) an oral or unsealed contract, founded on a consideration; an action to enforce this. [L, he has taken upon him]

assumption, *n.* the act of assuming; the thing assumed; a supposition, a postulate; arrogance; ascent to heaven, esp. the reception of the Virgin Mary into heaven; the feast (15 Aug.) in honour of this event; (*Law*) an oral or unsealed contract. **assumptive,** *a.* assumed; taken to oneself; taken for granted; arrogant. [L *assūmptus,* p.p. of *assūmere,* ASSUME]

assure, *v.t.* to make safe, secure or certain; to give confidence to, to encourage; to tell positively; to ensure, guarantee; to insure the payment of compensation in case of loss of (esp. life), to insure. **assurance,** *n.* the act of assuring; positive declaration; certainty, security; self-reliance, intrepidity; audacity, impudence; insurance, esp. a contract to pay a given sum on a person's death in return for an annual premium; (*Law*) evidence of the conveyance of property. **assured,** *a.* safe; made certain, confident, convinced; self-confident, full of assurance; insured. *n.* one whose life is insured; the beneficiary of an assurance policy. **assuredly**, *adv.* **assuredness**, *n.* **assurer,** *n.* one who or that which gives assurance; an insurer, an underwriter; one who takes out a policy of assurance. **assuror,** *n.* (*Law*) an assurer, an underwriter. **assuring,** *a.* creating assurance, inspiring confidence. **assuringly,** *adv.* [OF *aseürer,* late L *adsēcūrāre* (*ad-,* to, *sēcūrus,* safe)]

assurgent, *a.* rising, rising aggressively; (*Bot.*) pointing upwards; rising in a curve. [L *assurgere* (*ad-,* to, against, *surgere,* to rise)]

Assyria, *n.* empire in the Middle East *c.* 2500–612 BC, in N Mesopotamia (now Iraq); capital Nineveh. It was initially subject to Sumeria and intermittently to Babylon. The Assyrians adopted in the main the Sumerian religion and structure of society. At its greatest extent the empire included Egypt and stretched from the E Mediterranean coast to the Persian Gulf. **Assyrian**, *a.* of or pertaining to the ancient empire of Assyria. *n.* a native of Assyria; the language of Assyria. **Assyriology**, *n.* the study of the history, language and antiquities of Assyria. **Assyriological**, *a.* **Assyriologist,** *n.*

assythment, *n.* (*Sc.*) satisfaction for an injury; compensation. [Sc. *assyth, assythe,* ME *aseth,* OF *aset* (F *assez*) enough, from late L *ad satis* (cp. ASSETS, -MENT)]

AST, (*abbr.*) Atlantic Standard Time.

astable, *a.* not stable; of an electrical circuit, switching between two states. [Gr. *a-,* not, STABLE¹]

Astaire, *n.* **Fred** (stage name of Frederick Austerlitz) (1899–1987), US dancer, actor, singer and choreographer, who starred in numerous films, including *Top Hat* (1935), *Easter Parade* (1948), and *Funny Face* (1957), many of which contained inventive sequences he designed himself. He made ten classic films with the most popular of his dancing partners, Ginger Rogers. He later played straight dramatic roles, in films such as *On the Beach* (1959).

astarboard, *adv.* towards the right side of the ship (looking forward).

astare, *adv.* staring, prominent, glaring.

Astarte, *n.* alternative name for the Babylonian and Assyrian goddess Ishtar.

astatic, *a.* not remaining fixed; not influenced by the earth's magnetism. [Gr. *astatos* (*a-,* not, *sta-,* stem of verb, stand)]

astatine, *n.* a radioactive element, at.no. 85; chem. symbol At, formed in minute amounts by radioactive decay or made artificially. [Gr. *astatos,* unstable (see ASTATIC)]

Aster, *n.* a genus of compositous plants with showy, daisy-like heads; a star-shaped figure seen in a cell during mitosis. **China aster** CHINA. [L, from Gr. *astēr,* a star]

-aster, *suf.* after the manner of, somewhat after the manner of; as in *criticaster, poetaster.* [L, diminutive and contemptuous termination]

asteria, *n.* a precious stone mentioned by Pliny; perhaps the asteriated sapphire. **asteriated,** *a.* exhibiting asterism. [L]

Asterias, *n.* a genus of Echinoderms, containing the common starfish. **asterid,** *n.* any individual of the Asteridae or starfishfamily. [Mod. L, from Gr. *asterias,* starry]

asterisk, *n.* a mark (*) used in printing to call attention to a note, to mark omission etc.; a star-shaped device placed over the paten in the Greek Church to prevent anything touching the Elements. *v.t.* to mark with an asterisk. [L *asteriscus,* Gr. *asteriskos*]

asterism, *n.* a constellation; a small cluster of stars; †an asterisk; three asterisks placed thus () to draw attention to something important; the star-like figure visible in some mineral crystals, as in the asteriated sapphire. [Gr. *asterismos*]

astern, *adv., a.* in, at or towards the stern of a ship, behind a ship; in the rear, behind.

asteroid, *a.* having the figure or appearance of a star; resembling a starfish. *n.* any of the small celestial bodies that orbit the sun, esp. between the orbits of Mars and Jupiter, a planetoid, a minor planet. **asteroidal**, *a.*

Asterolepis, *n.* a genus of giganticganoid fishes from the Old Red Sandstone of the Devonian period. [Gr. *astēr,* star, *lepis,* scale]

asthenia, *n.* absence of strength; debility, diminution or loss of vital power. **asthenic,** *a.* [mod. L, Gr. *astheneia,* from *asthenes,* weak (*a-,* without, *sthenos,* strength)]

asthma, *n.* chronic shortness of breath; a disorder of respiration characterized by wheezing, constriction of the chest, and usu. coughing. **asthmatic,** *a.* of or pertaining to, affected with or good for asthma; wheezy, puffing. *n.* a person affected with asthma. **asthmatical,** *a.* **asthmatically,** *adv.* [Gr. *asthma -matos,* from *azein,* to breathe hard (*aein,* to blow)]

astigmatism, *n.* a defect of the eye or of a lens as a result of which a point source of light tends to be focused as a line. **astigmatic,** *a.* of or pertaining to, or characterized by, astigmatism. [Gr. *a-,* not, *stigma,* point]

astir, *a.* in motion; in commotion, in excitement; out of bed. [*a,* on, STIR]

astomatous, *a.* mouthless; of or pertaining to the Astomata, a group of ciliate Protozoa without a determinate mouth. **astomous,** *a.* astomatous; (*Bot.*) without a deciduous operculum. [Gr. *a-,* without, *stoma stomatos,* a mouth]

Aston, *n.* **Francis William** (1877–1945), English physicist, who developed the mass spectrometer, which separates isotopes by projecting their ions (charged atoms) through a magnetic field.

astonish, *v.t.* to strike with sudden surprise or wonder; to amaze, to surprise. **astonishing,** *a.* **astonishingly,** *adv.* **astonishment,** *n.* the act of astonishing; the state of being astonished; amazement; †stupefaction, stupor; an object causing amazement. **†astony,** *v.t.* to stun, to paralyse, to astound. **†astonied,** *a.* stunned, dazed, bewildered, astonished. [earlier *astony,* ME *astone,* OF *estoner* (F *étonner*), to amaze (L *ex-,* out, *tonāre,* to thunder)]

Astor, *n.* prominent US and British family. **John Jacob Astor** (1763–1848) was a US millionaire. **Waldorf Astor**, 2nd Viscount Astor (1879–1952), was Conservative member of parliament for Plymouth (1910–19), when he succeeded to the peerage. He was chief proprietor of the British *Observer* newspaper. His wife was Nancy Witcher Langhorne (1879–1964) **Lady Astor**, the first woman member of parliament to take a seat in the House of Commons (1919), when she succeeded her husband for the constituency of Plymouth. She was also a temperance fanatic and political hostess. Government policy was said to be decided at Cliveden, their country home.

astound, *v.t.* †to stun, to stupefy; to strike with amazement; to shock with alarm, wonder, or surprise. **astounding,** *a.* **astoundingly,** *adv.* **astoundment,** *n.* [ME *astoned,* p.p. of *astone*]

astraddle, *adv.* in a straddling position; astride.

astragal, *n.* the astragalus; (*Arch.*) a small semicircular moulding or bead, round the top or the bottom of a column; a moulding round a cannon or round a large pipe. **astragalus,** *n.* the ball of the ankle-joint; the bone which the tibia articulates below; (**Astragalus**) a large genus of leguminous plants, containing the milk-vetch. [L *astragalus,* Gr. *astragalos*]

astrakhan, *n.* the tightly curled, usu. black or grey fleece obtained from lambs orig. from Astrakhan; a fabric with a pile in imitation of this.

astral, *a.* of or pertaining to the stars; starry; star-shaped; pertaining to one's astral body or to the material of which the astral body is composed. *n.* an astral-lamp. **astral-body,** *n.* a kind of spiritual body which occultists claim to be able to project to a distance, and so to exercise the power of bilocation; the ethereal or spiritual body round which the physical body is built up, the spirit. **astral-lamp,** *n.* a lamp similar in character to an argand lamp, and throwing a shadowless light on the table. **astral-spirits,** *n.pl.* spirits formerly believed to inhabit the heavenly bodies. [L *astrālis* (*astrum,* Gr. *astron,* a star)]

astray, *adv., pred. a.* out of or away from the right way. [prob. OF *estraié,* p.p. of *estraier,* to stray (L *extra-,* out of bounds, *vagāre,* to wander)]

astrict, *v.t.* to bind up, to compress, to render costive; to bind by legal or moral obligation; to restrict, limit; (*Sc. Law*) to restrict in tenure. **astriction,** *n.* an act of binding or drawing closely; constriction, constipation, restriction; the use of or result of using devices to stop haemorrhage, as styptics or ligatures; (*Sc. Law*) obligation to have corn ground at a particular mill. **astrictive,** *a.* possessing the quality of astricting; binding; astringent. *n.* an astringent. [L *astrictus,* p.p. of *astringere* (*ad-,* to, *stringere,* to bind)]

astride, *adv., pred. a.* in a striding position; with legs on either side. *prep.* astride of.

astringe, *v.t.* to bind together, to compress, to constrict, to render costive. **astringent,** *a.* causing contraction of body tissues; styptic; binding, astrictive; stern, severe, harsh. *n.* an astringent substance. **astringently,** *adv.* **astringency,** *n.* the quality of being astringent; sternness, severity, harshness. [L *astringere,* see ASTRICT]

astro-, *comb. form.* pertaining to the heavenly bodies, planets or stars; e.g. *astrology, astronomy.* [Gr. *astron,* a star]

astrobiology, *n.* a branch of biology concerned with the search for life beyond the earth.

astrodome, *n.* a dome window in an aircraft to enable astronomical observations to be made; a large sports stadium covered by a translucent domed roof.

astrography, *n.* the mapping of the heavens.

astrol., (*abbr.*) astrologer, astrology.

astrolabe, *n.* an instrument formerly used in astrology and in astronomical observations for taking altitudes. [OF *astrelabe,* med. L *astrolabium* (L *lab-,* stem of v. to take)]

astrolatry, *n.* worship of the stars. [Gr. *latreia,* worship]

astrology, *n.* †practical astronomy (the derivatives were also formerly used in corresponding senses); a spurious science that professes to establish a connection between the changing aspects of the heavenly bodies and the changing course of human life, thence claiming to predict events and to be competent to advise on life's conduct. **astrologer,** *n.* one versed in astrology. **astrological, astrologic,** *a.* **astrologically,** *adv.* [F *astrologie,* L *astrologia* (Gr. *logos,* discourse)]

astron., (*abbr.*) astronomer, astronomy.

astronautics, *n.* the science of aerial navigation. **astronaut,** *n.* one who travels into space beyond the earth's atmosphere in a suitable projectile. [Gr. *nautēs,* a sailor]

astronomy, *n.* the science which studies all the phenomena of the heavenly bodies. **astronomer,** *n.* one who studies or is versed in astronomy. **astronomer-royal,** *n.* the officer in charge of a royal or national observatory in Great Britain. **astronomic, -ical,** *a.* of or pertaining to astronomy; enormously large or great. **astronomical clock,** *n.* a pendulum clock which gives sidereal time. **astronomical unit,** *n.* a unit of length equal to the mean distance of the earth from the sun, about 93 million miles (150 million km), used for measuring distances in the solar system. **astronomical-year,** *n.* a year determined by astronomical observations, as opposed to a civil year. **astronomically,** *adv.* [OF *astronomie,* L *astronomia,* Gr. from *astronomos,* star-arranging, a. (*nemein,* to distribute, arrange)]

†astrophel, *n.* an unidentified herb mentioned by Spenser. [perhaps corrupted from Gr. *astrophyllon,* star-leaf]

astrophotometer, *n.* an instrument for measuring the intensity of sidereal light.

astrophysics, *n. sing.* the study of stellar physics. **astrophysical,** *a.* relating to stellar physics. **astrophysicist,** *n.*

Astroturf®, *n.* an artificial grass surface, esp. for sports fields.

astrut, *adv.* in a strutting manner.

Asturias¹, *n.* **Miguel Ángel** (1899–1974), Guatemalan author and diplomat. He published poetry, Guatemalan legends, and novels, such as *El Señor Presidente/The President* (1946), *Men of Corn* (1949), and *Strong Wind* (1950), attacking Latin-American dictatorships and 'Yankee imperialism'. Nobel prize 1967.

Asturias², *n.* autonomous region of N Spain; area 10,600 sq km/4092 sq miles; population (1986) 1,114,000. Half of Spain's coal is produced from the mines of Asturias. Agricultural produce includes maize, fruit and livestock. Oviedo and Gijon are the main industrial towns.

astute, *a.* acute, discerning, shrewd; clever, wily, cunning. **astutely,** *adv.* **astuteness,** *n.* [L *astūtus,* crafty, cunning (*astus,* craft, cunning)]

astylar, *a.* (*Arch.*) without columns or pilasters. [*a,* not, Gr. *stulos,* a pillar]

Asunción, *n.* capital and port of Paraguay, on the Paraguay river; population (1984) 729,000. It produces textiles, footwear and food products.

asunder, *adv.* apart, separately, in different pieces or places. [OE *onsundran*]

Aswan, *n.* winter resort town in Upper Egypt; population (1985) 183,000. It is near the High Dam (1960–70), which keeps the level of the Nile constant throughout the year without flooding. It produces steel and textiles.

asylum, *n.* a place of refuge for criminals and debtors, a sanctuary; an institution affording relief and shelter to the afflicted, unfortunate or destitute, esp. (formerly) an institution for the treatment of the mentally ill; protection from extradition given by one country to a person, esp. a political refugee, from another; (a) shelter, (a) refuge. [L, from Gr. *asūlon,* neut. of *asūlos,* inviolable (*a-,* not, *sulē,* a right of seizure)]

asymmetry, *n.* want of symmetry, or of proportion; (*Math.*) incommensurability. **asymmetric, -ical,** *a.* out of proportion. **asymmetrically,** *adv.* [Gr. *asummetria* (*a-,* not, *summetria,* SYMMETRY)]

asymptomatic, *a.* not exhibiting symptoms of disease. [Gr. *a-,* not, **symptomatic** (see SYMPTOM]

asymptote, *n.* a straight mathematical line continually approaching some curve but never meeting it within a finite distance. **asymptotic, -ical,** *a.* [Gr. *asumptōtos,* not coinciding (*a-,* not, *sum-, sun-,* together, *ptōtos,* falling, from *piptein,* to fall)]

asynartete, *a.* disconnected; consisting of two members differing in rhythm. *n.* such a verse as described above. [Gr. *asunartētos* (*a-,* not, *sun-,* with, *artaein,* to knit together)]

asynchronous, *a.* not coincident in point of time. **asynchronism, asynchrony,** *n.* want of coincidence in time. [*a-*, not, SYNCHRONOUS]

asyndeton, *n.* a rhetorical figure by which the conjunction is omitted, as 'I came, I saw, I conquered'. [Gr. *asundeton* (*a-*, not, *sun-*, with, *deein,* to bind)]

asyntactic, *a.* ill-arranged, irregular, ungrammatical. [Gr. *asuntaktos* (*a-*, not, *sun-*,together, *tassein,* to range)]

At, (*chem. symbol*) astatine.

at, *prep.* denoting nearness or precise position in time or space; denoting position or situation as regards occupation, condition, quality or degree, effect, relation, value; denoting direction to or towards. **at it,** at work, engaged, busy. **at that,** moreover. [OE *æt* (cp. Icel. *at,* OHG *az,* L *ad*)]

at., (*abbr.*) atomic.

at-, *pref.* AD-, assim. to *t,* e.g. *attain, attend.*

atabal, *n.* a Moorish kettle-drum. [Sp., from Arab. *at tabl,* the drum]

Atacama, *n.* desert in N Chile; area about 80,000 sq km/31,000 sq miles. Inland are mountains, and the coastal area is rainless and barren. There are silver and copper mines, and extensive nitrate deposits.

Atahualpa *n.* (*c.* 1502–1533), last emperor of the Incas of Peru. He was taken prisoner (1532) when the Spaniards arrived, and agreed to pay a huge ransom, but was accused of plotting against the conquistador Pizarro and sentenced to be burned. On his consenting to Christian baptism, the sentence was commuted to strangulation.

ataraxia, ataraxy, *n.* impassiveness, calmness, indifference, stoicism. **ataractic,** *a.* calming, tranquillizing. *n.* a tranquillizing drug. [Gr. *ataraxia* (*a-*, not, *tarassein,* to disturb)]

Atatürk, *n.* **Kemal** (name assumed 1934) by Mustafa Kemal Pasha (1881–1938), Turkish politician and general, first president of Turkey from 1923. After World War I he established a provisional rebel government and in 1921–22 the Turkish armies under his leadership expelled the Greeks who were occupying Turkey. He is the founder of the modern republic, which he ruled as virtual dictator, with a policy of consistent and radical westernization.

ataunto, *adv.* with all sails set. **all ataunto,** *adv.* all in good shape and condition. [OF *autant,* so much]

atavism, *n.* recurrence of some characteristic of a more or less remote ancestor; recurrence of a disease after the lapse of some generations; reversion to a primitive or ancestral form. **atavistic,** *a.* [F *atavisme,* L *atavus,* an ancestor]

ataxia, ataxy, *n.* loss of the power of co-ordination of the muscles, resulting in irregular, jerky movements; disorder, confusion. **locomotor ataxia** LOCOMOTION. **ataxic,** *a.* of or pertaining to ataxy; irregular. [Gr. *ataxia* (*a-*, not, *taxis,* order, from *tassein,* to arrange)]

ATB, *n.* a bicycle with wide tyres and a large range of gears, designed for riding off the road. [*a*ll-*t*errain *b*icycle]

ATC, (*abbr.*) air-traffic control; Air Training Corps.

ate, *pret.* EAT.

-ate, *suf.* (1) forming nouns of office or function, e.g. *curate, episcopate, aldermanate;* participial nouns, e.g. *delegate, mandate;* chemical names for salts of acids, e.g. *acetate, carbonate;* (2) forming participial adjectives, e.g. *desolate, situate* (cp. *desolated, situated,* in which the p.p. gives rise to a causative verb); and other adjectives formed by analogy, e.g. roseate, ovate; (3) forming verbs, e.g. *desolate, separate,* corresponding to adjectives in same form, or others produced on the same model, e.g. *fascinate, isolate, felicitate.* [L *-ātus* in nouns of state, or *-ātus, -āta, -ātum,* p.p. of 1st conj., through F *-at,* as in *prélat, sénat*]

ateleo-, atelo-, *comb. form* indicating incomplete development or imperfection of structure. [Gr. *atelēs,* imperfect (*a-*, not, *telos,* end, completion)]

ateleocephalous, *a.* with an imperfect skull.

atelier, *n.* a workshop, an artist's studio. [F, OF *astelier,* from *astelle,* small plank or splint]

atelocardia, *n.* imperfect development of the heart.

a tempo, *adv., a.* (*Mus.*) in the original tempo or time.

athalamous, *a.* of or pertaining to lichens, the thallus of which have no conceptacles or spore-shields. [Gr. *a-*, not, *thalamos,* a bed]

Athanasian, *a.* of or pertaining to Athanasius (see below). *n.* a follower of Athanasius; one holding his views with respect to the Trinity. **Athanasian creed,** *n.* a creed stating the doctrine of the Trinity and the Incarnation, with damnatory clauses, formerly attributed to Athanasius.

Athanasius, St, *n.* (298–373), Christian bishop of Alexandria, supporter of the doctrines of the Trinity and incarnation. He was a disciple of St Anthony the hermit, and an opponent of Arianism in the great Arian controversy. Arianism was officially condemned at the Council of Nicaea (325), and Athanasius was appointed bishop of Alexandria (328). The Athanasian creed was not actually written by him, although it reflects his views.

athanasy, *n.* deathlessness, immortality. [L *athanasia,* from Gr. (*a-*, not, without, *thanatos,* death)]

atheism, *n.* disbelief in the existence of a God or gods; godlessness, wickedness; disregard of God and God's laws. **atheist,** *n.* one who disbelieves, or denies the existence of a God. *a.* atheistic, godless, impious. **atheistic, -ical,** *a.* **atheistically,** *adv.* [F *athéisme,* from Gr. *atheos* (*a-*, not, *theos,* God)]

†**atheling,** *n.* a member of a noble family, often restricted to a prince of the royal blood or to the heir-apparent. [OE *ætheling (æthel,* noble family, *-ing,* one belonging to)]

Athelney, Isle of, an area of firm ground in marshland near Taunton in Somerset, England, in 878 the headquarters of King Alfred when he was in hiding from the Danes. The legend of his burning the cakes is set here.

Athelstan, *n.* (*c.* 895–939), king of the Mercians and West Saxons. Son of Edward the Elder and grandson of Alfred the Great, he was crowned king (925) at Kingston-upon-Thames. He subdued parts of Cornwall and Wales, and in 937 defeated the Welsh, Scots and Danes at Brunanburh.

Athena, *n.* in Greek mythology, the goddess (Roman Minerva) of war, wisdom and the arts and crafts, who was supposed to have sprung fully grown from the head of Zeus. Her chief cult centre was Athens, where the Parthenon was dedicated to her.

Athenaeum, *n.* the temple of Athene in ancient Athens, where professors taught and orators and poets declaimed; hence, a literary or scientific club or institution; a literary club-room, a public reading-room or library. [L, from Gr. *Athēnaion*]

Athenian, *n., a.* (a native or inhabitant) of Athens.

Athens, *n.* (Greek **Athinai**) capital city of modern Greece and of ancient Attica; population (1981) 885,000, metropolitan area 3,027,000. Situated 8 km/5 miles NE of its port of Piraeus on the Gulf of Aegina, it is built around the rocky hills of the Acropolis 169 m/555 ft and the Areopagus 112 m/368 ft, and is overlooked from the NE by the hill of Lycabettus 277 m/909 ft. It lies in the south of the central plain of Attica, watered by the mountain streams of Cephissus and Ilissus.

ather, *n.* the beard of barley. [Gr.]

atherine, *n.* a small fish of the family Atherinidae. [mod. L *atherīna,* Gr. *atherinē,* some kind of smelt]

athermancy, *n.* the power of stopping radiant heat. **athermanous,** *a.* impermeable by radiant heat. [Gr. *athermantos* (*a-*, not, *thermainein,* to heat, from *thermē,* heat)]

atheroma, *n.* the deposition of fatty material on the inner coat of the arteries. **atheromatosis,** *n.* **atheromatous,** *a.* [L, a tumour containing gruel-like matter, from Gr. *athērōma,* from *athērā,* gruel]

atherosclerosis, *n.* arteriosclerosis characterized by deposits of fatty material in the arteries. **atherosclerotic,** *a.* [ATHEROMA, SCLEROSIS]

athirst, *a.* thirsty, oppressed with thirst; eager, eagerly desirous. [OE *ofthyrst, ofthyrsted,* p.p. of *ofthyrstan,* to be thirsty]

athlete, *n.* a competitor in the public games of ancient Greece and Rome; one trained to perform feats of strength and activity; esp. one trained to compete in events, as running, weight-throwing and jumping, requiring strength, agility, speed or stamina; a powerful, vigorous person. **athlete's foot,** *n.* a fungal infection of the foot. **athletic,** *a.* of or for athletes or athletics; physically strong and active; muscular, robust. **athletic support,** *n.* a jockstrap. **athletically,** *adv.* **athleticism,** *n.* the practice of athletics; devotion (esp. excessive) to athletics; the state of being athletic. **athletics,** *n. sing.* the practice of physical exercises by which muscular strength is developed; the type of competitive sporting events engaged in by athletes. [L *athlēta,* Gr. *athlētēs,* from *athlein,* to contend (*athlon, aethlion,* a prize)]

-athon, *suf.* denoting an event or contest that continues for a long time, e.g. *talkathon, danceathon.* [from *marathon*]

athwart, *prep.* from side to side of, across; against, opposing. *adv.* transversely, from side to side, crosswise; so as to thwart. **athwart-hawse,** *adv., a.* of a ship, (lying) across the stem of another ship at anchor. **athwart-ships,** *adv.* from side to side of the ship. [*a-*, on, THWART]

atibar, *n.* gold dust found on the coast of southern Africa. [etym. doubtful]

-atic, *suf.* forming adjectives, e.g. *aquatic, fanatic, lunatic.* [F *-atique,* L *-āticus*]

-atile, *suf.* forming adjectives chiefly denoting possibility or quality, e.g. *fluviatile, volatile.* [F *-atile,* L *-ātilis*]

atilt, *adv., pred. a.* tilted up; as if thrusting at an antagonist. **to run atilt,** to attack.

atimy, *n.* loss of honour; loss of civil right. [Gr. *atimia* (*a-*, not, *timē,* honour)]

-ation, *suf.* forming abstract nouns from verbs, e.g. *agitation, appreciation, ovation.* [L *-ātio -ōnis*]

-ative, *suf.* forming adjectives, e.g. *demonstrative, representative, talkative.* [L *-atīvus, -a, -um*]

Atlanta, *n.* capital and largest city of Georgia, USA; population (1980) 422,000, metropolitan area 2,010,000. There are Ford and Lockheed assembly plants, and it is the headquarters of Coca-Cola.

Atlantean[1], *a.* of or like the Titan Atlas, very strong.

Atlantean[2], *a.* of Atlantis.

atlantes ATLAS.

Atlantic, *n.* the Atlantic Ocean (see below). *a.* of or pertaining to the Atlas mountains in N Africa; of or occurring in or near the Atlantic Ocean.

Atlantic, Battle of the[1], a continuous battle fought in the Atlantic Ocean throughout World War II (1939–45) by the sea and air forces of the Allies and Germany. The number of U-boats destroyed by the Allies during the war was nearly 800. At least 2200 convoys of 75,000 merchant ships crossed the Atlantic, protected by US naval forces. Before the US entry into the war in 1941, destroyers were supplied to the British under the Lend-Lease Act of 1941.

Atlantic, Battle of the[2], the German campaign during World War I to prevent merchant shipping from delivering food supplies from the US to the Allies, especially the UK. By 1917, some 875,000 tons of shipping had been lost. The odds were only turned by the belated use of naval convoys and depth charges to deter submarine attack.

Atlantic Charter, *n.* a joint declaration by Great Britain and the US laying down 'certain principles as a basis for a better future for the world'. The eight points of the Charter cover freedom from fear, want and aggression and ensure political and commercial liberty. The Charter was signed in 1941, and was accepted by nine other European countries. [ATLANTIS]

Atlantic Ocean, *n.* ocean lying between Europe and Africa to the east and the Americas to the west, probably named after Atlantis; area of basin 81,500,000 sq km/31,500,000 sq miles; including the Arctic Ocean, and Antarctic seas, 106,200,000 sq km/41,000,000 sq miles. The average depth is 3 km/2 miles; greatest depth the Milwaukee Depth in the Puerto Rico Trench 8650 m/28,389 ft. The Mid-Atlantic Ridge, of which the Azores, Ascension, St Helena, and Tristan da Cunha form part, divides it from north to south. Lava welling up from this central area annually increases the distance between South America and Africa. The North Atlantic is the saltiest of the main oceans, and it has the largest tidal range. In the 1960s–1980s average wave heights have increased by 25%, the largest from 12 m/40 ft to 18 m/60 ft.

Atlantis, *n.* the legendary island in the West whose site is occupied by the Atlantic Ocean. [Gr.]

atlas, *n.* a collection of maps in a volume; a collection of charts or plates in a volume; a large size of drawing paper; (*pl.* **atlantes**) a colossal statue of a man used to support an entablature; the first cervical vertebra, on which the skull is supported. **atlas-beetle,** *n.* a large lamellicorn beetle (*Chalcosoma atlas*) from the East. **atlas-moth,** *n. Attacus atlas,* a large moth from China. [Gr. *Atlas -antos,* a Titan, see foll.]

Atlas, *n.* in Greek mythology, one of the Titans who revolted against the gods; as a punishment, Atlas was compelled to support the heavens on his head and shoulders. Growing weary, he asked Perseus to turn him into stone, and he was transformed into Mount Atlas.

Atlas Mountains, *n.pl.* mountain system of NW Africa, stretching 2400 km/1500 miles from the Atlantic coast of Morocco to the Gulf of Gabes, Tunisia, and lying between the Mediterranean on the north and the Sahara on the south. The highest peak is Mount Toubkal 4165 m/13,670 ft.

ATM, (*abbr.*) automated teller machine.

atm., (*abbr.*) atmosphere; atmospheric.

atman, *n.* in Hinduism, the innermost self, the soul. [Sansk. *ātman,* breath, soul]

atm(o)-, *comb. form.* pertaining to vapour or to the atmosphere. [Gr. *atmos,* vapour]

atmology, *n.* the branch of physics which treats of the laws and phenomena of aqueous vapour.

atmolysis, *n.* the separation of gases in combination.

atmometer, *n.* an instrument for measuring the moisture exhaled in a given time from any humid surface.

atmosphere, *n.* the gaseous envelope of any of the celestial bodies; that surrounding the earth; a gaseous envelope surrounding any substance; the air in any given place; a unit of pressure corresponding to the average pressure of the earth's atmosphere at sea level and equal to a pressure of about 15 lb/sq. in. (101,325 N/m^2); mental or moral environment; a prevailing emotional etc. mood. **atmospheric, -ical,** *a.* of or pertaining to the atmosphere; of the nature of air; existing in the atmosphere, or produced by the atmosphere. **atmospheric engine,** *n.* an engine the piston of which is driven down by the pressure of the atmosphere and forced up by steam. **atmospheric railway,** *n.* a pneumatic railway. **atmospherically,** *adv.* **atmospherics,** *n.pl.* (audible radio interference produced by) electromagnetic waves generated by an electric discharge between two clouds or from a cloud to earth. [ATM(O)-, Gr. *sphaira,* a ball]

at. no., (*abbr.*) atomic number.

atoll, *n.* a coral island, consisting of an annular reef surrounding a lagoon. [Maldive *atollon, atoll*]

atom, *n.* the smallest conceivable portion of anything; a body or particle of matter originally thought to be incapable of further divison; the smallest particle taking part in chemical action, the smallest particle of matter possessing the properties of an element. **atom bomb,** *n.* a bomb in which the explosion is due to atomic energy released when atoms of uranium, plutonium etc. undergo nuclear fission. **atom smasher,** *n.* (*coll.*) an accelerator for increasing the energy of charged particles. **atomic,** *a.* consisting of separate atoms; pertaining or relating to an atom or atoms; pertaining to or using atomic energy or atom bombs; extremely small. **atomic bomb** ATOM BOMB. **atomic clock,** *n.* an electronic apparatus which makes use of molecular or atomic resonances to generate precise intervals of time. **atomic energy,** *n.* the energy liberated when the nucleus of an atom undergoes change, e.g. by fission of uranium or by fusion of hydrogen, nuclear energy. **atomic number,** *n.* the number of protons in the nucleus of an atom. The atomic number determines the chemical properties of an atom. **atomic philosophy,** *n.* the doctrine of the formation of all things from atoms possessing gravity and motion. **atomic pile,** *n.* a nuclear reactor. **atomic theory,** *n.* the theory that all combinations take place between the ultimate particles of matter, either atom for atom, or in a definite proportion. **atomic volume,** *n.* the volume occupied by the mass of an element equal to its atomic weight. **atomic warfare,** *n.* warfare with nuclear weapons. **atomic weight,** *n.* the weight of an atom of an element expressed on a scale in which the weight of an atom of carbon-12 is 12. **atomically,** *adv.* **atomicity,** *n.* the number of atoms in a molecule of an element or of a compound; the combining capacity of an element or radical; valency. **atomism,** *n.* the atomic philosophy; the atomic theory. **atomist,** *n.* **atomize, -ise,** *v.t.* to reduce to atoms; to reduce to fine particles or to a spray. **atomization,-isation,** *n.* **atomizer, iser,** *n.* an instrument for reducing a liquid, as a disinfectant or perfume, into spray. [Gr. *atomos,* indivisible]

atomy¹, *n.* a minute particle, an atom; a diminutive being.

atomy², *n.* a skeleton, an anatomical preparation; an emaciated person, a living skeleton. [*anatomy,* first syl. mistaken for article *an*]

Aton, *n.* in ancient Egypt, the sun's disk as an emblem of the single deity whose worship was enforced by Ikhnaton.

atonal, *a.* (*Mus.*) without a fixed key.**atonality,** *n.* [ATONIC]

at one, †at-on, aton, *adv.* in harmony, at one, in a state of reconciliation; of the same opinion; †with the same result; †together. **at-oneness,** *n.* the condition of being at one, reconcilement, harmony. [AT, ONE]

atone, *v.i.* to make expiation or satisfaction for some crime, sin or fault. †*v.t.* to make at one; to bring into concord; to conciliate, to appease; to expiate. **atonable,** *a.* able to be expiated. **atonement,** *n.* the act of atoning; reparation, expiation, amends, reconciliation; the propitiation of God by the expiation of sin; the Redemption. **atoningly,** *adv.* [AT ONE]

Atonement, Day of, a Jewish holy day (**Yom Kippur**) held on the tenth day of Tishri (Sept.–Oct.), the first month of the Jewish year. It is a day of fasting, penitence and cleansing from sin, ending the Ten Days of Penitence that follow *Rosh Hashanah*, the Jewish New Year.

atonic, *a.* without an accent, unaccented; lacking physiological or muscular tone. *n.* an unaccented word in Greek; a medicine to allay excitement. **atony,** *n.* lack of physiological, esp. muscular, tone; enervation; lack of intellectual energy. [med. L *atonicus,* Gr. *atonos,* without tone (*a-*, not, *tenein,* to stretch)]

atop, *adv.* on or at the top. **atop of,** *prep.* on or at the top of.

-ator, *suf.* -OR, e.g. *commentator.*

-atory, *suf.* -ORY, forming adjectives, e.g. *commendatory*.

ATP, (*abbr.*) adenosine triphosphate, nucleotide molecule found in all cells. It can yield large amounts of energy, used to drive many biological processes, including muscle contraction and the synthesis of complex molecules needed by the cell. ATP is formed during photosynthesis in plants, or by the breakdown of food molecules during metabolism in animals.

atrabiliar, -ary, *a.* atrabilious. **atrabiliary-capsules,** *n.pl.* a name formerly given to the renal glands or capsules, from the blackish fluid they contain. [F *atrabiliaire,* mod. L *ātrabīliārius*]

atrabilious, *a.* †of or affected by black bile; melancholic, hypochondriacal; splenetic, bitter-tempered. **atrabiliousness,** *n.* [L *ātra bīlis,* black bile]

†atramental, *a.* of or pertaining to ink; inky, black. [L *ātrāmentum,* blacking, ink (*āter,* black)]

atremble, *pred. a.* in a trembling condition.

atrip, *pred. a.* of an anchor, just drawn out of the ground at right angles to it; of the top sails, hoisted as high as possible on the masts. [*a-*, on, TRIP]

atrium, *n.* (*pl.* **atria, atriums**) the court or portico in an ancient Roman house; a covered court or portico; a body cavity; esp. either of the two upper chambers of the heart into which the veins pour the blood. **atrial,** *a.* [L]

atrocious, *a.* savagely and wantonly cruel, characterized by heinous wickedness; stern, fierce, violent; very bad, execrable. **atrociously,** *adv.* **atrocity,** *n.* excessive cruelty or other flagrant wickedness; an atrocious act; a bad blunder; a barbarism. [L *atrox -ōcis* (*āter,* black)]

atrophy, *n.* a wasting of the body, or (one of) its organs, through want of nourishment or disease; mental or spiritual starvation. *v.t.* to affect with atrophy, to cause to waste away. *v.i.* to waste away. **atrophied,** *a.* [F *atrophie,* L *atrophia,* from Gr., from *atrophos,* ill-fed (*a-*, not, *trephein,* to nourish)]

atropine, *n.* an organic base obtained from deadly nightshade, *Atropa belladonna*. **atropism,** *n.* atropine poisoning. [Gr. *atropos,* inflexible, name of one of the Fates]

att., (*abbr.*) attorney.

attaboy, *int.* (*chiefly N Am., coll.*) an exclamation of encouragement.

attach, *v.t.* to fasten on, connect; to affix; to lay hold on, arrest, indict, esp. to seize (a person or goods) by a writ of attachment; to appoint to an organization, military, police etc. unit, temporarily; to join to in sympathy or feelings; to attract and cause to adhere to oneself; to attribute. *v.i.* to adhere; (*Law*) to apply. **attachable,** *a.* capable of being attached; liable to attachment. **attached,** *a.* arrested; joined, fastened; joined in function, taste, feeling or affection; incident, connected; (*Zool.*) stationary, as opposed to free; (*Arch.*) joined to a wall; not standing clear. **attachment,** *n.* the act of attaching; the means by which anything is attached; connection; fidelity, affection, devotion; the thing attached; (*Law*) apprehension, esp. for contempt of court; theseizure of goods or estate to secure a debt or demand; the writ or precept by which such apprehension or seizure is effected. [OF *atachier* (F *attacher*), from *a,* to, Genevese *tache* (cp. Port. *tacha,* nail, Eng. *tack,* LG *takk*)]

attaché, *n.* one attached to the suite of an ambassador. **attaché case,** *n.* a leather case for carrying papers etc. [F]

attack, *v.t.* to fall upon with force; to assault; to assail by hostile words, writings etc.; to begin (a work) with determination; of a physical agent, disease etc., to exert a destructive influence on; to take offensive action against. *v.i.* to make an attack; to take offensive action in a game or sport. *n.* the act of attacking; an onset, an assault; violent abuse or injury; the beginning of active work on something; a fit of illness; the commencement of destructive action; a (crisp and decisive) manner of beginning a musical piece or passage; an offensive or scoring move in a game or sport; the players in a team who attack. **attackable,** *a.* [F *attaquer,* It. *attaccare,* to join (battle) (see ATTACH)]

attain, *v.i.* to arrive at some object. *v.t.* to reach, gain; to arrive at; to accomplish. **attainable,** *a.* **attainability,** *n.* **attainableness,** *n.* **attainment,** *n.* the act of attaining; that which is attained; a personal acquirement. [OF *ateign-*, pres. stem of *ataindre,* to reach, attain (L *ad-*, to, *tangere,* to touch)]

attainder, *n.* the act or process of attainting a criminal; the forfeiture of civil rights as the legal consequence of a sentence of death or outlawry for treason or felony; an act or bill of attainder; condemnation; †dishonouring accusation; †taint of dishonour. **Act** or **Bill of attainder,** one introduced into the British Parliament for attainting a person without judicial process. [OF *ataindre,* to ATTAIN (meaning modified by confusion with *taindre,* to dye, stain)]

attaint, *v.t.* to condemn or subject to attainder; †to accuse; to infect; to taint, stain; †to dim, sully. †*part.a.* under an attainder, attainted; corrupted, infected; exhausted, overcome. *n.* †a hit; †a stain, blot; conviction of or process against a jury for returning a false verdict; attainder. †**attainture,** *n.* attainder; dishonour, stain.

attar, *n.* a fragrant essence, or essential oil, esp. of roses. †**attargul,** *n.* the essential oil obtained from roses by distillation. [Pers. *'atar,* essence, Arab. *'utūr,* aroma]

attemper, *v.t.* †to qualify or modify by admixture; to moderate the temperature of; †to soften, mollify; to mix in just proportions; †to fit or make suitable; †to attune; †to temper. †**attemperance,** *n.* temperance, moderation; natural temperament. †**attemperate,** *v.t.* to attemper. *a.* temperate; regulated, proportioned. †**attemperment,** *n.* the act of tempering; the state of being tempered. [OF *atemprer,* L *attemperāre* (*ad-,* to, *temperāre,* to temper, moderate)]

attempt, *v.t.* to try, endeavour to do, achieve, effect etc.; †to try to influence; †to attack; to make trial of; †to try to seduce. *n.* an endeavour, effort, undertaking; an effort as contrasted with attainment; an assault (on life, honour etc.). **to attempt the life of,** to try to kill. **attemptable,** *a.* **attemptability,** *n.* [OF *atempter,* undertake, L *attemptāre, attentāre* (*ad-,* to, *tentāre,* strive after)]

Attenborough, *n.* **Richard** (1923–), English film actor and director. His films include *Brighton Rock* (1947) and *10 Rillington Place* (1970) (as actor), and *Oh! What a Lovely War* (1968), *Gandhi* (1982) and *Cry Freedom* (1987) (as director).

attend, *v.t.* †to turn the thoughts towards; to apply the mind to; to accompany, escort; to look after, wait upon; to be present at; to go regularly to (church, a school etc.); †to wait for, to expect. *v.i.* to pay attention, apply the mind; to apply one's efforts; to be present; to be in attendance; to wait upon or for a person. **attendance,** *n.* the act of attending; service, presence; (the number of) persons attending; †a train of servants. **to dance attendance on,** to wait upon obsequiously. **in attendance,** waiting, attendant on. **attendance-officer,** *n.* an official whose duty it is to see that children attend school. **attendance register,** *n.* the list of pupils at a school read out at roll call. **attendant,** *a.* accompanying, waiting on, ministering to; following as a consequence; present. *n.* one who, that which attends or accompanies; a servant. †**attendment,** *n.* meaning; intent; (*pl.*) environment, surroundings. [OF *atendre,* to wait, L *attendere* (*ad-,* to, *tendere,* to stretch)]

attent, *a.* intent, attentive. *n.* attention. [as prec.]

attention, *n.* the act or state of attending; the mental faculty of attending; (*usu. pl.*) an act of courtesy, kindness or love, watchful care, close observation, notice; a military attitude of readiness. [as prec.]

attentive, *a.* heedful, intent, regardful; polite, courteous. **attentively,** *adv.* **attentiveness,** *n.*

attenuate, *v.t.* to make thin or slender; to dilute, diminish the density of; to reduce the strength, intensity or force of, to weaken; to extenuate. *v.i.* to become thin or weak. **attenuate,** *a.* slender; tapering; thin in consistency. **attenuated,** *a.* **attenuation,** *n.* the act of attenuating; diminution of thickness, density, strength or force; emaciation; reduction in strength of radiation as it passes through the medium between the source and destination. **attenuation constant,** *n.* a constant determining the connection between the current sent out and received. **attenuator,** *n.* a circuit to provide attenuation of the current, voltage or power of a signal. [L *attenuātus,* p.p. of *attenuāre* (*ad-,* to, *tenuis,* thin)]

Atterbury, *n.* **Francis** (1662–1732), English bishop and Jacobite politician. In 1687 he was appointed a royal chaplain by William III. Under Queen Anne he received rapid promotion, becoming bishop of Rochester (1713). His Jacobite sympathies prevented his further rise, and in 1722 he was sent to the Tower of London and subsequently banished. He was a friend of the writers Pope and Swift.

attest, *v.t.* to testify, esp. in a formal manner; to vouch for; to affirm to be true or valid; to put (a person) on oath or solemn declaration. *v.i.* to bear witness. *n.* evidence, attestation. **attestation,** *n.* the act of attesting; evidence, proof; formal confirmation; formal verification; the administration of an oath, esp. of the oath of allegiance. **attested,** *a.* certified as being free from the tuberculosis bacillus. **attestor,** *n.* one who attests or vouches for. [F *attester,* L *attestārī* (*ad-,* to, *testis,* a witness)]

Attic, *a.* of or belonging to Attica or its capital, Athens; classical, refined; witty. *n.* a native of Attica; an Athenian; the Attic dialect. **Attic base,** *n.* a base consisting of an upper torus, a scotia and lower torus, with fillets between them. **Attic bird,** *n.* the nightingale. **Attic dialect,** *n.* the dialect of ancient Athens; the chief literary dialect. **Attic faith,** *n.* inviolable faith. **Attic order,** *n.* an architectural order of small square pillars at the uppermost part of a building. **Attic salt,** or **wit,** *n.* refined, delicate wit, for which the Athenians were famous. **Atticism,** *n.* attachment to Athens; idiom and style characteristic of Attic Greek; concise and elegant expression. **Atticize, -ise,** *v.i.* to conform to the idiom of Attica or Athens, or to Greek habits or modes of thought; to side with the Athenians. [L *Atticus,* Gr. *Attikos*]

attic, *n.* a low storey placed above an entablature or cornice; the top storey of a house; a room in this storey; (*sl.*) the head, the brain, the 'upper storey'. **attic storey,** *n.* an upper storey of a house, usu. the highest storey below the garret. [F *attique,* as prec.]

Attica, *n.* (Greek **Attiki**) a region of Greece comprising Athens and the district around it; area 3381 sq km/1305 sq miles; population (1981) 342,000. It is noted for its language, art and philosophical thought in Classical times. It is a prefecture of modern Greece with Athens as its capital.

Attila, *n.* (*c.* 406–453), king of the Huns from 434, called the 'Scourge of God'. He embarked on a career of vast conquests ranging from the Rhine to Persia. In 451 he invaded Gaul, but was defeated on the Catalaunian Fields by the Roman and Visigothic armies under Aëtius (died 454) and Theodoric I. In 452 he led his Huns into Italy and only the personal intervention of Pope Leo I prevented the sacking of Rome.

Attila Line, *n.* a line dividing Greek and Turkish Cyprus, so called because of a fanciful identification of the Turks with the Huns.

attire, *v.t.* to dress; to array in apparel. *n.* dress, clothes; †a woman's head-dress; (*Her.*) the horns of a stag or buck. **attired,** *a.* dressed, decked, arrayed; (*Her.*) furnished with horns. **attiring,** *n.* dress, apparel, trappings. [OF *atirer* (*à,* to, *tire,* a row) (see TIER²)]

Attis, *n.* in classical mythology, a Phrygian god whose death and resurrection symbolized the end of winter and the arrival of spring. Beloved by the goddess Cybele, who drove him mad as a punishment for his infidelity, he castrated himself and bled to death.

attitude, *n.* the posture in which a figure is represented in painting or sculpture; bearing or gesture, expressing action or emotion; a mental position or mood as regards someone or something; posture or disposition of a person, animal or object; behaviour indicating opinion and sentiment; the position of an aircraft or spacecraft in relation to a plane of reference. **to strike an attitude,** to assume an exaggerated or theatrical attitude. **attitude of mind,** habitual mode of thinking and feeling. **attitudinize, -ise,** *v.i.* to practise or assume attitudes; to pose; to behave or act affectedly. [F, from It. *attitudine,* L *aptitūdinem* (*aptus,* fitted)]

Attlee, *n.* **Clement (Richard), 1st Earl** (1883–1967), British Labour politician. In the coalition government during World War II he was Lord Privy Seal (1940–42), dominions secretary (1942–43), and Lord President of the Council (1943–45), as well as deputy prime minister from 1942. As prime minister (1945–51) he introduced a sweeping programme of nationalization and a whole new system of social services.

attn., (*abbr.*) attention, for the attention of.

atto-, *pref.* a million million millionth part of, 10^{-18}. [Dan. or Norw. *atten,* eighteen]

attorn, *v.t.* to assign, transfer. *v.i.* to transfer service or fealty to a new lord. [OF *atorner* (*à,* to, *tourner,* L *tornāre,* to turn)]

attorney[1], *n.* a legally authorized agent or deputy; formerly, a qualified practitioner in the Common Law courts, who prepared the case for the barristers or counsel, as distinguished from a solicitor who practised in a court of equity, the title is now Solicitor of the Supreme Court; (*N Am.*) a lawyer, a barrister, a solicitor, esp. one qualified to act for another in legal proceedings. **District Attorney** DISTRICT. **Attorney-General,** *n.* (*pl.* **Attorneys-General, Attorney-Generals**) principal law officer of the Crown and head of the English Bar; (*US*) the chief law officer of the government and head of the Department of Justice. **Attorney-Generalship,** *n.* the office or dignity of the Attorney-General. **attorneyship,** *n.* the office of an attorney; agency, proxy. [OF *atorné,* p.p. *atorner*]

attorney[2], *n.* †appointment of a legal representative; the authority or function soconceded. **power, letter, warrant of attorney,** a written authority by which one person authorizes another to act in his or her stead. [OF *atornée,* fem. n. from p.p.]

attract, *v.t.* to draw to or cause to approach (in a material or immaterial sense); to cause to approach by some influence; to entice, to allure; to draw the notice of. *v.i.* to exert the power of attraction, to be attractive. **attractable,** *a.* that may be attracted. **attractability**, *n.* capability of being attracted. **attracting,** *a.* **attractingly,** *adv.* **attractor,** *n.* **attraction,** *n.* the action or power of attracting; an attracting quality or characteristic; a force causing two objects, molecules etc. to be drawn together or to resist separation; that which attracts. **attraction of gravity,** the mutual action between two bodies by which they tend to approach each other; the force by which this action is exerted. **attraction of cohesion,** the attraction by which the atoms of a body are kept together. **attractive,** *a.* having the power of attracting; alluring. **attractively,** *adv.* **attractiveness,** *n.* [L *attractus,* p.p. of *attrahere* (*ad-,* to, *trahere,* to draw)]

attrib., (*abbr.*) attribute, attributed (to); attributive, attributively.

attribute, *n.* a quality ascribed or imputed to any person or thing, as an essential characteristic; a characteristic; a symbol or other object recognized as peculiar or characteristic; an attributive word; (*Log.*) that which may be predicated of any subject. **attribute**, *v.t.* to ascribe; to impute as belonging or due to; to ascribe as consequence. **attributable**, *a.* **attribution**, *n.* the act of attributing; that which is ascribed; function, authority etc. formally assigned; (*Log.*) predication. **attributive**, *a.* characterized by attributing; (*Log.*) assigning an attribute to a subject; (*Gram.*) expressing an attribute without actual predication. *n.* a word denoting an attribute, now generally restricted to adjectives. **attributively,** *adv.* [L *attribūtus -um,* p.p. of *attribuere,* to assign (*ad-,* to, *tribuere,* to give)]

attrist, *v.t.* to cause to be sad. [F *attrister,* to sadden (*à,* to, *triste,* L *tristis,* sad)]

attrite, *a.* rubbed down; subjected to the action of friction; penitent through fear of consequences. **attrited,** *a.* worn down by friction. **attriteness,** *n.* **attrition**, *n.* the act or process of rubbing down or away; abrasion; wearing away by friction; (*Theol.*) sorrow for sin on account of the punishment due to it; a constant wearing down or weakening, as of an adversary. [L *attrītus,* p.p. of *atterere* (*ad-,* to, *terere,* to rub)]

attune, *v.t.* to bring to the right pitch; to make tuneful; to bring into accord; to accustom, acclimatize. *n.* (*rare*) tuneful accord; harmony. [*at-,* AD-, TUNE]

atty, (*abbr.*) attorney.

ATV, (*abbr.*) all-terrain vehicle; Associated Television.

Atwood, *n.* **Margaret (Eleanor)** (1939–), Canadian novelist, short-story writer, and poet. Her novels, which often treat feminist themes with wit and irony, include *The Edible Woman* (1969), *Life Before Man* (1979), *Bodily Harm* (1981), *The Handmaid's Tale* (1986), and *Cat's Eye* (1989).

at. wt., (*abbr.*) atomic weight.

atypical, *a.* not typical, not conforming to type. **atypically,** *adv.* [Gr. *a-,* not, TYPIC]

AU, (*abbr.*) Ångström unit; astronomical unit.

Au, (*chem. symbol*) gold. [L *aurum*]

aubade, *n.* music performed at daybreak; a poem or musical piece announcing or greeting dawn. [F, from Sp. *albada* (*alba,* dawn)]

Auber, *n.* **Daniel François Esprit** (1782–1871), French operatic composer who studied under the Italian composer and teacher Cherubini. He wrote about 50 operas, including *La Muette de Portici/The Mute Girl of Portici* (1828) and the comic opera *Fra Diavolo* (1830).

auberge, *n.* (F) an inn; a place of entertainment for travellers. **aubergiste,** *n.* a keeper of an auberge, an inn-keeper. [F *auberge,* OF *alberge, helberge,* OHG *heri-berga,* army shelter (cp. G *Herberg,* inn, and Eng. HARBOUR)]

aubergine, *n.* the egg-plant, *Solanum esculentum;* its ovoid, characteristically dark purple fruit used as a vegetable and in stews; a dark purple colour. [F, dim. of *auberge, alberge,* Sp. *alberchigo,* apricot]

Aubrey, *n.* **John** (1626–1697), English antiquary. His *Brief Lives* (1898) (edited by A. Clark) contains gossip and anecdotes on celebrities of his time. Aubrey was the first to claim Stonehenge as a Druid temple.

Aubrietia, *n.* a genus of rock plants of the family Cruciferae.

auburn, *a.* †yellowish; reddish-brown; golden-brown. [OF *auborne,* L *alburnus,* whitish (*albus,* white)]

Auckland, *n.* the largest city in New Zealand, situated in N North Island; population (1987) 889,000. It fills the isthmus that separates its two harbours (Waitemata and Manukau), and its suburbs spread north across the Harbour Bridge. It is the country's chief port and leading industrial centre, having iron and steel plants, engineering, car assembly, textiles, food-processing, sugar-refining and brewing.

au courant, *a.* fully informed, up-to-date with the situation. [F]

auction, *n.* a public sale by a person licensed for the purpose, in which each bidder offers a higher price than the preceding; †property put up to auction. *v.t.* to sell by auction. **auction bridge,** *n.* a development of bridge in which the players bid for the advantage of choosing trump suit. **auction-mart,** *n.* a place where goods are sold by public auction. †**auctionary,** *a.* pertaining to an auction. **auctioneer,** *n.* a person who sells goods by auction, one licensed to conduct auctions. *v.t., v.i.* to sell by auction. [L *auctio -ōnem,* an increase, auction (*auctus,* p.p. of *augēre,* to increase)]

auctorial, *a.* pertaining to an author or his occupation. [L *auctor,* -IAL]

aucupation, *n.* the art of bird-catching. [L *auceps,* bird-catcher]

audacious, *a.* bold, daring, spirited; impudent, shameless. **audaciously,** *adv.* boldly, impudently. **audaciousness,** *n.* **audacity**, *n.* courage, daring, gallantry; effrontery. [L *audax -acis* (*audēre,* to dare)]

Auden, *n.* **W(ystan) H(ugh)** (1907–1973), English poet. He wrote some of his most original poetry, such as *Look, Stranger!* (1936), in the 1930s when he led the influential left-wing literary group that included MacNeice, Spender and Day Lewis. He moved to the US in 1939, became a citizen (1946), and adopted a more conservative and Christian viewpoint, such as in *The Age of Anxiety* (1947).

audible, *a.* capable of being heard; clear or loud enough to be heard. **audibility**, *n.* **audibleness,** *n.* **audibly,** *adv.* [med. L *audibilis* (*audīre,* to hear)]

audience, *n.* the act of hearing, attention; reception at a formal interview granted by a superior to an inferior; an assemblage of hearers or spectators; the readers of a book; the people who regularly watch or listen to a particular television or radio programme, performer etc. **audience-chamber,** *n.* a chamber in which formal audiences are granted. **audience-court,** *n.* an ecclesiastical court (now abolished), at first presided over by the archbishop, afterwards by auditors on his behalf. **audient,** *a.* hearing, listening. *n.* a hearer, esp. one not yet admitted to the Church, a catechumen. [F *audience,* L *audientia (audiens -ntem,* pres.p. of *audīre*)]

audile, *a.* pertaining to sound or hearing; characterized by mental pictures of sounds. *n.* a person whose recollection is based mainly on terms of sounds. [L *audīre,* to hear]

audio, *a.* of or pertaining to sound or its reproduction, transmission or broadcasting; pertaining to or using audio-frequencies. *n.* the (electronic) reproduction and transmission of sound. [L *audīre,* to hear]

audio-, *comb. form.* pertaining to hearing; pertaining to sound or sound reproduction.

audio-frequency, *n.* a frequency in the range corresponding to that of audible sound waves.

audiology, *n.* the science of hearing. **audiological**, *a.* **audiologist,** *n.*

audiometer, *n.* an application of the telephone for testing the sense of hearing. **audiometric,** *a.* **audiometry**, *n.*

audiotypist, *n.* a typist trained to type directly from material on a dictating machine. **audiotyping,** *n.*

audiovisual, *a.* directed at or involving hearing and sight as in *audiovisual aids*.

audiphone, *n.* an instrument which, when pressed against the teeth, enables people with some types of deafness to hear by conveying sound-waves to the auditory nerves. [L *audīre,* to hear, Gr. *phōnē,* sound]

audit, *n.* †a hearing, an audience; an official examination of accounts; a formal receipt of rents at stated periods; any formal review orsolemn rendering of accounts; the Day of Judgment. *v.t.* to examine officially and pronounce as to the accuracy of (accounts). **audit ale,** *n.* ale of special quality formerly brewed for the day of audit at English universities. **audit-house, audit-room,** *n.* a house or room appendant to cathedrals for the transaction of business. **audit-office,** *n.* the office in which public accounts are audited. [L *audītus,* hearing (*audīre,* to hear)]

Audit Commission, an independent body in the UK established by the Local Government Finance Act 1982. It administers the District Audit Service (established 1844) and appoints auditors for the accounts of all UK local authorities. The Audit Commission consists of 15 members: its aims include finding ways of saving costs, and controlling illegal local-authority spending.

audition, *n.* the act or faculty of hearing; something heard, a sound; a trial performance by a singer, musician, actor etc. applying for a position or role. *v.t.* to test by an audition. *v.i.* to give a trial performance. **auditive**, *a.* pertaining to hearing.

auditor, *n.* a hearer, one of an audience; an audient, a catechumen; one appointed to audit accounts; the president of an audience court. **auditorship,** *n.* **auditorial**, *a.* auditory; of or pertaining to an audit of accounts. **auditorially,** *adv.*

auditorium, *n.* (*pl.* **-riums, -ria**) the part of a building occupied by the audience; the nave of a church; the reception-room in a monastic building.

auditory, *a.* of or pertaining to the organs or sense of hearing, perceived by the ear. *n.* †an audience, people assembled to hear; †a place for hearing, an auditorium.

Audubon, *n.* **John James** (1785–1851), US naturalist. In 1827, he published the first part of his *Birds of North America*, with a remarkable series of colour plates. Later, he produced a similar work on North American quadrupeds.

au fait, *a.* familiar, well-acquainted with; up to the mark. [F, to the point]

auf Wiedersehen, *int.* (*G*) farewell, goodbye.

Aug., (*abbr.*) August.

Augean, *a.* pertaining to Augeas (mythical king of Elis, whose stable, containing 3000 oxen, had not been cleaned for 30 years, till Hercules, by turning the river Alpheus through it, did so in a day); filthy. [L *Augeas,* Gr. *Augeias*]

auger, *n.* a carpenter's tool, somewhat resembling a very large gimlet, worked with both hands, for boring holes in wood; a similar instrument of larger size, for boring into soil or rock. **auger-hole,** *n.* a hole drilled with an auger. **auger-shell,** *n.* the long pointed shell of the mollusc genus *Teredra*. **auger worm,** *n.* the teredo, or boring-worm. [OE *nafugār* (*nafu,* the nave of a wheel, *gār,* a borer)]

auges, *n.* (*Astron.*) two points in a planet's orbit, the apogee and the perigee. [L summit]

aught, *n.* anything whatever; a whit, a jot or tittle; (*erroneously*) the figure 0, a naught. *adv.* in any respect. [OE *āwiht* (*ā,* one, *wiht,* a creature)]

augite, *n.* a greenish, brownish-black or black variety of aluminous pyroxene. **augitic**, *a.* [L, from Gr. *augitēs,* prob. a turquoise (*augē,* lustre)]

augment, *v.t.* to increase, to make larger or greater in number, degree, intensity etc.; to extend, to enlarge; to prefix a grammatical augment to; to make an honourable addition to (a coat of arms). *v.i.* to increase, to become greater in size, number, degree etc. **augment**, *n.* a grammatical prefix (*a*) used in the older Aryan languages to denote past time. In Greek, when the prefix (*ĕ*) remains distinct, the augment is called *syllabic;* when it forms, with a following vowel, a long vowel or diphthong, it is called *temporal*. **augmentation,** *n.* the act of augmenting; the state of being augmented; the thing added; increase, addition; an honourable addition to a coat of arms; the reproduction of a melody or passage in notes of greater length than those in which it was first treated. **process of augmentation,** (*Sc. Law*) action in the Court of Teinds by a parish clergyman for increase of stipend. **Augmentation court,** *n.* a court created by Henry VIII to deal with suits arising from his suppression of monasteries. **augmentative**, *a.* having the power or quality of augmenting; of an affix, increasing the force of a word; of a word, extending the force of an idea. *n.* an augmentative element or word. [F *augmenter,* L *augmentum,* an increase (*augēre,* to increase)]

Augrabies Falls, *n.* falls in the Orange River, NW Cape Province, South Africa. Height 148 m/480 ft.

Augsburg, Confession of, a statement of the Protestant faith as held by the German Reformers composed by Philip Melanchthon. Presented to Charles V, Holy Roman Emperor, at the conference known as the Diet of Augsburg (1530), it is the creed of the modern Lutheran church.

augur, *n.* a religious official among the Romans who professed to foretell future events from omens derived chiefly from the actions of birds, inspection of the entrails of slaughtered victims etc.; a soothsayer, a diviner. *v.t.* to foretell from signs or omens; to betoken, portend. *v.i.* to make predictions of future events from signs or omens; to be a sign or foreboding. **augural**, *a.* pertaining to an augur or to augury. **augurship,** *n.* **augury**, *n.* the art or practice of the augur; divination from the actions of birds; an augural ceremony; an omen, prognostication, foreboding. [L (prob. *avis, aui,* a bird, *-gur,* telling, connected with *garrīre,* to talk, *garrulus,* talkative; Sansk. *gar,* to shout)]

August, *n.* the eighth month of the year, named in honour of Augustus Caesar.

august[1], *a.* majestic, stately, inspiring reverence and admiration; dignified, worshipful. **augustly,** *adv.* **augustness,** *n.* [L *augustus,* honoured, venerable]

august[2] AUGUSTE.

Augustan, *a.* of or belonging to Augustus Caesar (63 BC–AD 14), or his age in which Latin literature reached its highest development; hence, classical, refined, distinguished by correct literary taste; of or belonging to Augusta Vindelicorum (Augsburg, Bavaria), where Luther and Melanchthon, in 1530, drew up their confession of the Protestant faith. *n.* a writer of the Augustan period of any literature.

auguste, august, *n.* a clown with maladroit antics. [G]

†**Augustin,** †**Augustine**, *n.* an Augustinian friar. **Augustinian**, *a.* of or pertaining to St Augustine (354–430), Bishop of Hippo (396–430), or to his doctrine of grace and predestination. *n.* an adherent of these doctrines; one of an order of friars named after him. [F *Augustin,* L *Augustīnus* (see also AUSTIN)]

Augustine, St, *n.* first archbishop of Canterbury, England. He was sent from Rome to convert England to Christianity by Pope Gregory I. He landed at Ebbsfleet, Thanet, and baptized Ethelbert, King of Kent in 597. He was consecrated bishop of the English at Arles in the same year, and appointed archbishop in 601. Feast day 26 May.

Augustine of Hippo, St, *n.* (354–430), one of the early Christian leaders and writers known as the Fathers of the Church. He was converted to Christianity by Ambrose in Milan and became bishop of Hippo (modern Annaba, Algeria) in 396. Among Augustine's many writings are his *Confessions*, a spiritual autobiography, and the influential *De Civitate Dei/The City of God* vindicating the Christian church and divine providence in 22 books.

Augustinian AUGUSTIN.

Augustus, *n.* (63 BC–AD 14), title of Octavian (Gaius Julius Caesar Octavianus), first of the Roman emperors. He joined forces with Mark Antony and Lepidus in the Second Triumvirate. Following Mark Antony's liaison with the Egyptian Queen Cleopatra, Augustus defeated her troops at Actium in 31 BC. As emperor (from 27 BC) he reformed the government of the empire, the army, and Rome's public services, and was a patron of the arts. The period of his rule is known as the Augustan Age.

auk, *n.* a northern sea-bird with rudimentary wings, esp. the great auk (now extinct), the little auk and the razor-bill. [Swed. *alka,* a puffin]

aularian, *a.* of or pertaining to a hall. *n.* the member of an English university hall as distinguished from the member of a college. [late L *aulārius,* from *aula,* hall (Gr. *aulē*)]

auld, *a.* (*Sc., North.*) old. **auld lang syne,** old long since, long ago. **Auld Reekie,** old smoky, Edinburgh. **auldfarrant,** *a.* old-favouring; old-fashioned; favouring the ways of grown-up people, precocious. **auldwarld**, *a.* old-world, ancient.

aulic, *a.* pertaining to a royal court; courtly. *n.* the ceremony observed in the Sorbonne in granting the degree of Doctor of Divinity. **aulic council,** *n.* the personal council of the sovereign in the old German empire; formerly also a council at Vienna in charge of the Austrian War Department. [F *aulique,* L *aulicus,* Gr. *aulikos* (*aulē,* a court)]

†**aumail,** *v.t.* to enamel. *n.* enamel. [OF *esmal, esmail* (perhaps from OHG *smelzan,* to smelt)]

†**aumbry** AMBRY.

au naturel, *a., adv.* in the natural state; uncooked or plainly cooked; (*coll. euphem.*) naked.

Aung San, *n.* (1914–1974), Burmese politician. As leader of the Anti-Fascist People's Freedom League he became vice-president of the executive council Sept. 1946. During World War II he had collaborated first with Japan and then with the UK.

aunt, *n.* the sister of one's father or mother; one's uncle's wife; (*coll.*) a woman friend of a child, esp. a benevolent, practical woman; †a prostitute, a procuress. **Aunt Sally,** *n.* a game at fairs, in which a figure with a pipe in its mouth is set up, and the players endeavour to break the pipe by throwing sticks at it; an object of ridicule. **aunthood**, *n.* **auntie, aunty,** *n.* a familiar form of AUNT; a familiar term for an elderly woman. **auntship,** *n.* [OF *aunte,* L *amita;* till 17th cent. *naunt* is common (*my naunt for mine aunt;* cp. F *tante,* prob. *ta ante*)]

au pair, *n.* a person, esp. a girl, from a foreign country who performs domestic tasks in exchange for board and lodging. *v.i.* to work as an au pair. [F, on equal terms]

aura, *n.* a subtle emanation from any body; a distinctive atmosphere or quality; a sensation (as of a current of cold air rising to the head) that precedes an attack in epilepsy, hysteria etc.; the air-current caused by a discharge of electricity from a sharp point. **aural**[1], *a.* of or pertaining to an aura. [L, from Gr. *aura,* breath, breeze]

aural[2], *a.* of or pertaining to the ear; received by the ear. **aurally,** *adv.* **auriform**, *a.* having the form of an ear. **auriscope,** *n.* an instrument for examining the internal ear. **aurist,** *n.* a specialist in ear diseases. [L *auris,* the ear]

Aurangzeb, Aurungzebe (1618–1707), Mughal emperor of N India from 1658. Third son of Shah Jehan, he made himself master of the court by a palace revolution. His reign was the most brilliant period of the Mughal dynasty, but by despotic tendencies and Muslim fanaticism he aroused much opposition. His latter years were spent in war with the princes of Rajputana and Mahrattas.

aurated, *a.* containing gold; gilded or resembling gold in colour. [L *aurātus,* p.p. of *aurāre,* to gild (*aurum,* gold)]

aureate, *a.* golden, gold-coloured; brilliant, splendid; of language or literary style, over-elaborate and embellished. [late L *aureātus, aureus,* golden]

Aurelia, *n.* †a chrysalis, a pupa; a genus of phosphorescent marine jellyfish. **aurelian,** *a.* of or pertaining to *Aurelia* or an aurelia; golden. *n.* one who studies entomology, esp. a lepidopterist, one who studies butterflies and moths. [It., silkworm, fem. of *aurelio,* shining, golden (L *aurum,* gold)]

Aurelian (Lucius Domitius Aurelianus), *n.* (*c.* 214–275 AD), Roman emperor from 270. A successful soldier, he was chosen emperor by his troops on the death of Claudius II. He defeated the Goths and Vandals, defeated and captured Zenobia of Palmyra, and was planning a campaign against Parthia when he was murdered. The **Aurelian Wall**, a fortification surrounding Rome, was built by him in 271. It was made of concrete, and substantial ruins exist. The **Aurelian Way** ran from Rome through Pisa and Genoa to Antipolis (Antibes) in Gaul.

Aurelius Antoninus, Marcus MARCUS AURELIUS ANTONINUS.

aureole, aureola, *n.* the crown which is the special reward of virgins, martyrs and doctors; the glory attaching to such a crown; the gold disc surrounding the head in early pictures, and denoting glory, a nimbus; a luminous envelope surrounding the body, a vesica piscis; a glorifying halo, glory; the halo round the moon in total eclipses of the sun, a corona; a halo of radiating light round the sun or moon. [L *aureola,* golden, fem. of *aureolus,* from *aurum,* gold (*aureola corona,* golden crown)]

au revoir, *int.* (*F*) farewell, goodbye.

auric AURUM.

Auric, *n.* **Georges** (1899–1983), French composer. He was one of the musical group called *Les Six*. Auric composed a comic opera, several ballets and incidental music to films of Jacques Cocteau.

auricle, *n.* the external ear, that part which projects from the head; any process shaped like the lobe of the ear; an atrium of the heart. **auricled,** *a.* having an auricle or auricles. [L, external ear, dim. of *auris,* ear]

auricula, *n.* a garden flower, *Primula auricula,* sometimes called bear's ear, from the shape of its leaves. [AURICLE]

auricular, *a.* of, pertaining to, using or known by the sense of hearing; whispered in the ear, hence secret; shaped like an auricle; of or pertaining to an atrium of the heart. *n.* an auricular organ; a tuft of feathers covering the auditory orifice in birds. **auricularly,** *adv.* by whispering in the ear; secretly; by means of the ear; by means of auricles. **auriculate,** *a.* having ears, or appendages resembling ears.

auriferous, *a.* yielding or producing gold. [L *aurifer* (*aurum,* gold, *-fer,* producing)]

aurific, *a.* having the power of changing other substances into gold; producing gold. [L *aurum,* gold, *-ficus,* making (*facere,* to make)]

Auriga, *n.* constellation of the northern hemisphere, represented as a man driving a chariot. Its brightest star is first-magnitude Capella; Epsilon Aurigae is an eclipsing binary star, with a period of 27 years, the longest of its kind (last eclipse 1983).

Aurignacian, *a.* pertaining to the period of Upper Palaeolithic culture typified by human remains and implements etc. of stone, horn and bone found in the cave of Aurignac, Haute-Garonne. [grotto of *Aurignac,* France]

Auriol, *n.* **Vincent** (1884–1966), French socialist politician. He was president of the two Constituent Assemblies of 1946 and first president of the Fourth Republic in 1947–54.

auriscope, aurist AURAL.

aurochs, *n.* (*pl.* **aurochs**) the extinct wild ox, *Bos urus* or *primigenius,* of Central Europe; erroneously applied to the European bison, *Bos bonasus,* strictly preserved in Lithuania. [G *Aurochs* (*Auerochs*), OHG *ur-ohso* (cp. OE *ūr*), whence L *ūrus*]

aurora, *n.* (*pl.* **-ras, -rae**) morning twilight, dawn; the colour of the sky at sunrise; (**Aurora**) the Roman goddess of the dawn; a beginning or early period; a peculiar illumination of the night sky common within the polar circles, consisting of streams of light ascending towards the zenith, called **aurora borealis**, or **aurora australis** according to whether it is seen in the northern or southern hemisphere. **auroral,** *a.* of or pertaining to the dawn or to the rise or beginning of anything; rosy, roseate; eastern; of or pertaining to an aurora. [L, the goddess of the dawn]

aurum, *n.* (*poet.*) gold. **aurum fulminans**, *n.* fulminate of gold. **aurum mosaicum**, *n.* bisulphide of tin, a bronze powder. **aurum potabile**, *n.* a cordial consisting of volatile oil containing minute particles of gold. **auric,** *a.* of or pertaining to gold; applied to compounds in which gold is trivalent. **aurous,** *a.* of or pertaining to gold; applied to compounds in which gold is univalent. [L]

Auschwitz, *n.* (Polish **Oswiecim**) town near Krakow in Poland, the site of a camp used by the Nazis in World War II to exterminate Jews as part of the 'final solution'. Each of the four gas chambers could hold 6000 people.

auscultation, *n.* the act of listening; listening with the ear or stethoscope to the sounds made by the internal organs, to judge their condition. **auscultator**, *n.* **auscultatory**, *a.* **auscultate**, *v.t.* to examine by auscultation; to detect by means of an instrument where land mines have been laid. [L *auscultātiō -nem,* from *auscultāre,* to listen (*aus auris,* the ear)]

Ausgleich, *n.* the compromise between Austria and Hungary, 8 Feb. 1867, that established the Austro-Hungarian Dual Monarchy under Habsburg rule. It endured until the collapse of Austria-Hungary in 1918.

Auslese, *n.* a usu. sweetish white wine from Germany or Austria made from selected ripe grapes. [G, choice, selection]

Ausonian, *a.* (*poet.*) of or pertaining to ancient Italy, Italian. [L *Ausonia*]

†**auspex,** *n.* in ancient Rome, one who took the auspices; a protector, a favourer; one who saw that marriage ceremonies were rightly performed. [L (*avis,* bird, *spex,* an observer, from *specere,* to observe)]

†**auspicate,** *v.t.* to betoken, to prognosticate; to inaugurate, initiate. *v.i.* to augur. [L *auspicātus,* p.p. of *auspicāre,* to take omens]

auspice, *n.* an omen drawn from the actions of birds; (*often pl.*) a (favourable) portent, sign or omen; (*usu. pl.*) patronage, protection. **under the auspices of,** under the leadership,encouragement or patronage of. **auspicious**, *a.* having favourable omens; auguring good fortune; conducive to prosperity or success; †kind, benignant. **auspiciously,** *adv.* **auspiciousness,** *n.* [F *auspice,* L *auspicium*]

Aussie, *n.*, *a.* (*coll.*) (an) Australian.

Austen, *n.* **Jane** (1775–1817), English novelist, noted for her domestic novels of manners. All her novels are set within the confines of middle-class provincial society, and show her skill at drawing characters and situations with delicate irony. These include *Sense and Sensibility* (1811), *Pride and Prejudice* (1813), *Mansfield Park* (1814), *Emma* (1816), and published posthumously, *Persuasion* (1817) and *Northanger Abbey* (1818).

Auster, *n.* (*poet.*) the south wind. [L]

austere, *a.* harsh, tart or rough to the taste; severe, stern, rigorous; ascetic, abstemious; sober, simple, unadorned. **austerely,** *adv.* **austereness,** *n.* **austerity**, *n.* harshness to the taste or feelings; sternness, severity; self-denial, asceticism; lack of adornment; (*pl.*) ascetic or penitential practices. [OF, from L *austērus,* from Gr. *austēros,* dry, harsh (*auein,* to dry, parch)]

Austerlitz, Battle of, battle on 2 Dec. 1805 in which the French forces of Emperor Napoleon defeated those of Alexander I of Russia and Francis II of Austria at a small town in Czechoslovakia, formerly in Austria, 19 km/12 miles E of Brno. Its Czech name is *Slavkov*.

Austin[1], *n., a.* Augustin, Augustinian. [syncopated form of AUGUSTIN]

Austin[2], *n.* **Herbert, 1st Baron Austin** (1866–1941), English industrialist, who began manufacturing cars in 1905 at Northfield, Birmingham, notably the 'Austin Seven' of 1921.

Austin[3], *n.* **Alfred** (1835–1913), British poet. He made his name with the satirical poem *The Season* (1861), which was followed by plays and volumes of poetry little read today; from 1896 he was Poet Laureate.

austral, *a.* of or pertaining to, or situated in or towards the south; southern. **austral signs,** *n.pl.* the last six signs of the zodiac. [L *australis* (AUSTER, south wind)]

Australasian, *a.* of or pertaining to Australasia, a general name for Australia, New Zealand, Tasmania and the surrounding islands. *n.* a native or inhabitant of Australasia. [F *Australasie,* L *australis, Asia*]

Australia, *n.* Commonwealth of, the smallest continent and largest island in the world, situated S of Indonesia, between the Pacific and Indian oceans. **area** 7,682,300 sq km/2,966,136 sq miles. **capital** Canberra. **towns** Adelaide, Alice Springs, Brisbane, Darwin, Melbourne, Perth, Sydney. **physical** the world's driest continent, arid in north and west, Great Dividing Range in the east; NE peninsula has rainforest; rivers N–S and Darling River and Murray system E–S; Lake Eyre basin and fertile Nullarbor Plain in south. **territories** Norfolk Island, Christmas Island, Cocos Islands, Ashmore and Cartier Islands, Coral Sea Islands, Heard Island and McDonald Islands, Australian Antarctic Territory. **exports** cereals, meat and dairy products, wool (30% of world production), fruit, wine, nuts, sugar, honey, bauxite (world's largest producer), coal, iron, copper, lead, tin, zinc, opal, mineral sands, uranium, machinery, transport equipment. **population** (1988) 16,250,000; annual growth rate 1.6%. **language** English. **religion** Anglican 36%, other Protestant 25%, Roman Catholic 33%.

Australia Day, *n.* public holiday in Australia, the anniversary of Captain Phillip's arrival on 26 Jan. 1788 to found Port Jackson (now Sydney), the first colony.

Australian, *a.* of or belonging to Australia. *n.* a native or inhabitant of Australia. **Australian crawl,** *n.* a style of swimming popular in Australia. **Australian kelpie,** *n.* a smooth-haired breed of sheep-dog. **Australian rules,** *n.* a variety of rugby football played in Australia. **Australian terrier,** *n.* a short-legged breed of terrier, small and wire-haired. **Australianism,** *n.* an Australian idiom or characteristic. **australioid, australoid**, *a.* terms used by Huxley and Lubbock (Lord Avebury) respectively to denote resemblance to the type of the Aborigines of Australia. **australite**, *n.* a lump of smooth black glass, meteoric in origin, found in parts of Australia. [AUSTRAL]

Australian Aborigine, *n.* indigenous inhabitant of the continent of Australia. The Aborigines speak several hundred different languages, the most important being

Aranda (Arunta), spoken in central Australia, and Murngin, spoken in Arnhem Land. In recent years there has been a movement for the recognition of Aborigine rights, campaigning against racial discrimination in housing, education, wages and inadequate medical facilities.

Australian Antarctic Territory, the islands and territories south of 60° S, between 160° E and 45° E longitude, excluding Adélie Land; area 6,044,000 sq km/ 2,332,984 sq miles of land, and 75,800 sq km/29,259 sq miles of ice shelf. The population on the Antarctic continent is limited to research personnel.

Australian art, *n.* art in Australia dates back to early Aboriginal works some 15,000 years ago. These are closely linked with religion and mythology, and include rock and bark paintings. True Aboriginal art is now rare. European-style art developed in the 17th century, with landscape painting predominating.

Australian Capital Territory, territory ceded to Australia by New South Wales in 1911 to provide the site of Canberra, with its port at Jervis Bay, ceded 1915; area 2400 sq km/926 sq miles; population (1987) 261,000.

Austral Islands, *n.* alternative name for Tubuai Islands, part of French Polynesia.

Australopithecus, *n.* a genus of fossil primates whose remains have been found in Southern Africa. **australopithecine,** *n., a.* (an individual) of the genus *Australopithecus* or a related genus. [L *australis,* southern, Gr. *pithēkos,* ape]

Australorp, *n.* an Australian utility type of Black Orpington fowl.

Austria, *n.* Republic of (*Republik Österreich*), a landlocked country in central Europe, bounded by Hungary to the E, Yugoslavia to the SE, Italy to the SW, Switzerland to the W, Germany to the NW and Czechoslovakia to the NE. **area** 83,920 sq km/32,393 sq miles. **capital** Vienna. **towns** Graz, Linz, Salzburg, Innsbruck. **physical** mountainous, with the Danube river basin in the east. **exports** minerals, manufactured goods. **population** (1987) 7,576,000; annual growth rate 0%. **language** German. **religion** Roman Catholic 90%.

Austrian, *n., a.* (a native or inhabitant) of Austria.

Austrian Succession, War of the, war fought (1740–48) between Austria, supported by England and Holland, on the one side, and Prussia, France and Spain on the other.

†**austringer,** *n.* a keeper of goshawks. [OF *ostruchier, austruchier* (*ostour,* mod. F *autour,* the goshawk)]

Austro-1, *comb. form.* southern. [AUSTER]

Austro-2, *comb. form.* Austrian.

Austro-Hungarian empire, *n.* the Dual Monarchy established by the Habsburg Franz Joseph in 1867 between his empire of Austria and his kingdom of Hungary. In 1910 it had an area of 261,239 sq km/ 100,838 sq miles with a population of 51 million. It collapsed autumn 1918. There were only two king-emperors: Franz Joseph (1867–1916) and Charles (1916–18).

autacoid, *n.* (*Physiol.*) an internal secretion, a hormone or chalone. [Gr. *autos,* self; *akos,* a drug; *eidos,* form]

autarch, *n.* an absolute sovereign, an autocrat. **autarchy,** *n.* absolute sovereignty, autocracy. **autarchic, -ical,** *a.* [Gr. *archein,* to rule]

autarky, *n.* self-sufficiency, esp. national economic self-sufficiency. [Gr. *autarkeia*]

authentic, *a.* entitled to acceptance or belief; trustworthy, credible; of undisputed origin, genuine; really proceeding from the professed source; †vested with all legal formalities and legally attested; (*Mus.*) having the notes between the keynote or tonic and the octave above. **authentical,** *a.* **authentically,** *adv.* **authenticalness,** *n.* **authenticate,** *v.t.* to render authentic or valid; to establish the truth or credibility of; to verify the authorship of. **authentication,** *n.* **authenticator,** *n.* **authenticity,** *n.* [OF *autentique,* L *authenticus,* Gr. *authentikos* vouched for, *authentēs,* one who does things himself (AUTO-)]

author, *n.* the originator, producer or efficient cause of anything; the composer of a literary work; one whose profession is writing, esp. books; the works of an author; an authority, an informant. **author-craft,** *n.* skill in literary composition; literary work. **authoress,** *n. fem.* a female author. **authorial,** *a.* authorism. *n.* **authorless,** *a.* without an acknowledged author; anonymous. **authorship,** *n.* the profession of a writer of books; the personality of an author; origin of a literary work. [OF *autour,* L *auctor -em* (*auctus.* p.p. of *augere,* to make to grow)]

authority, *n.* legitimate power to command or act; (*often pl.*) a person or body exercising this power; power, weight or influence, derived from character, station, mental superiority and the like; weight of testimony, credibility; delegated power or right to act; the author or the source of a statement; the standard book or work of reference on any subject; an expert, one entitled to speak with authority on any subject. **authoritarian,** *n.* one who places obedience to authority above personal liberty. **authoritative,** *a.* imperative, commanding; possessed of authority, founded on sufficient authority. **authoritatively,** *adv.* **authoritativeness,** *n.* [F *autorité,* L *auctoritātem* (*auctor*)]

authorize, -ise, *v.t.* to give authority to, to empower; to establish by authority; to sanction; to warrant legally; to justify, afford just ground for; to make or prove legitimate; to vouch for, to confirm. **authorized, -ised,** *a.* **Authorized Version,** *n.* the English translation of the Bible published in 1611. **authorizable, -isable,** *a.* **authorization,** *n.* the act of authorizing; establishment by authority; a document etc. that authorizes something.

autism, *n.* abnormal absorption in fantasy, delusions etc., accompanied by withdrawal from reality; a disorder of mental development marked by lack of social communication and inability to form relationships. **autistic,** *a.* [Gr. *autos,* self, -ISM]

auto, *n.* (*chiefly N Am.*) short for AUTOMOBILE.

auto., (*abbr.*) automatic.

auto-, *comb. form.* self, from within or by oneself; one's own, independently, e.g. *automatic,* self-regulating; *automotive,* self-propelling. [Gr. *autos,* self]

Autobahn, *n.* a road designed and reserved for motor traffic, a motorway in Germany. [G]

autobiography, *n.* a memoir of one's life, written by oneself; the writing of one's own memoirs. **autobiographer,** *n.* one who writes an account of his or her own life. **autobiographic, -ical,** *a.* **autobiographically,** *adv.* [AUTO-, BIOGRAPHY]

autocar, *n.* a vehicle driven by its own mechanical power, a motor-car.

autocarpous, *a.* consisting of pericarp only.

autocephalous, *a.* having an independent head or chief; esp., of a church, having its own bishop. **autocephaly,** *n.* [Gr., having an independent head]

autochrome, *a.* of a photographic colour process in which the screen plate is coated with an emulsion sensitive to all colours in an almost equal degree.

autochthon, *n.* (*pl.* **-thons, -thones** a person supposedly sprung from the soil; one of the original or earliest known inhabitants; an aboriginal animal or plant. **autochthonal, -nic,** *a.* **autochthonous,** *a.* native, indigenous; occurring, formed or originating in the place where found. **autochthonism,** *n.* birth from the soil or original occupation of a region. **autochthony,** *n.* the condition of being autochthonous. [Gr., sprung from the land itself]

autoclave, *n.* a sealed vessel used for chemical reactions at high temperature and pressure; an apparatus using super-heated steam for sterilizing, cooking etc. *v.t.* to put in an autoclave; to sterilize etc. in an autoclave.

autocracy, *n.* absolute government; controlling power. [Gr. *autokrateia* (AUTO-, *krateein,* to rule)]

autocrat, *n.* a sovereign of uncontrolled authority; a dictatorial person. **autocratic, -ical,** *a.* pertaining to autocracy; absolute, despotic. **autocratically,** *adv.*

autocratrix, †**-atrice**, *n.* a female autocrat; an Empress of Russia in her own right. [F *autocrate,* Gr. *autokratēs*]
autocross, *n.* the sport of motor racing on grass.
Autocue®, *n.* a device that displays the text to be spoken by a person on television.
autocycle, *n.* a push-bicycle with motor attachment.
auto-da-fé, *n.* (*pl.* **autos-da-fé**) a sentence pronounced by the Inquisition; the execution of this judgment; the burning of a heretic. [Port., action for the faith]
autodidact, *n.* a self-taught person. **autodidactic**, *a.* [Gr. *autodidaktos* (AUTO-, *didaskein,* to teach)]
autoerotism, -ticism, *n.* self-produced sexual pleasure or emotion, e.g. masturbation. **autoerotic**, *a.*
autofocus, *n.* a facility in some cameras for automatically focusing the lens.
autogamy, *n.* self-fertilization. **autogamous,** *a.*
autogenous, -genic, *a.* self-engendered, self-produced, independent; (*Physiol.*) developed from distinct and independent centres; originating from sources within the same body. **autogeny**, *n.* (*Biol.*) a kind of spontaneous generation. [Gr. *autogenēs* (AUTO-*genēs,* produced, *gen-,* stem of *gignesthai,* to be begotten)]
autogiro, -gyro, *n.* an aircraft in which the lifting surfaces are the freely-rotating blades of a large horizontal air-screw.
autograph, *n.* a person's own handwriting, esp. his or her signature; a manuscript in an author's own handwriting; a copy produced by autography. *a.* written by the author. *v.t.* to write with one's own hand; to reproduce by autography; to sign. **autographic, -ical**, *a.* written by one's own hand; of or pertaining to autographs or autography. **autographically,** *adv.* **autography**, *n.* writing with one's own hand; one's own handwriting; a process of reproducing handwriting or drawing in facsimile. [L *autographus,* Gr. *autographos* (AUTO-, *graphein,* to write)]
autogravure, *n.* a process of photo-engraving similar to autotype. [AUTO-, F *gravure,* engraving]
Autoharp®, *n.* a zither-like instrument having dampers which stop selected strings from sounding and allow chords to be played.
auto-immune, *a.* of or caused by antibodies that attack the normally present molecules, cells etc. of the organism producing them. **auto-immunity,** *n.* **auto-immunization, -isation,** *n.*
auto-intoxication, *n.* reabsorption of toxic matter produced by the body.
autolatry, *n.* worship of self.
autolysis, *n.* the breakdown of cells by the action of enzymes produced in the cells themselves. **autolyse**, (*chiefly N Am.*) **-lyze,** *v.t.* to cause autolysis in. *v.i.* to undergo autolysis. **autolytic,** *a.* [Gr. *lysis,* loosening]
automat, *n.* (*N Am.*) a restaurant equipped with automatic machines for supplying food etc.; a vending machine. [AUTOMATIC]
automate AUTOMATION.
automatic, *a.* self-acting, self-regulating; acting as an automaton, having the power of movement within itself; of a firearm, repeatedly ejecting the empty shell, introducing a new one and firing, until the trigger is released; carried on unconsciously; involuntary, reflex; merely mechanical. *n.* an automatic firearm; a motor vehicle with automatic transmission. **automatic pilot,** *n.* a device which automatically maintains an aircraft or spacecraft on a predetermined course. **automatic signalling,** *n.* a signalling system whereby the passing of a train automatically puts the signals behind it at danger. **automatic telephone,** *n.* a telephone system in which connection between two subscribers is obtained by electrical means without the interposition of an operator. **automatic transmission,** *n.* power transmission in a motor vehicle in which the gears change automatically. **automatic writing,** *n.* writing performed without the consciousness of the writer. **automatically,** *adv.* **automaticity,** *n.* [Gr. *automatos,* acting of itself (AUTO-, *-matos,* allied to Sansk. *matas,* thought, known)]
automation, *n.* the use of self-regulating or automatically programmed machines in the manufacture of goods. **automate,** *v.t.* to make automatic. *v.i.* to apply automation. **automated teller machine,** an electronic machine operated by a bank or building society from which a customer can obtain money or account details on the insertion of a special card. [AUTOMATIC]
automatism, *n.* the quality of being automatic; involuntary action; the theory that animals are automatons performing their functions as mere machines without conscious control, as the result of natural laws; unconscious action, automatic routine; the faculty of initiating movement. **automatist,** *n.* **automatize, -ise,** *v.t.* to reduce to the condition of an automaton; to make automatic. [AUTOMATIC]
automaton, *n.* (*pl.* **-tons, -ta**) that which has the power of spontaneous motion; a piece of machinery simulating human or animal action; a man or lower animal whose actions are merely mechanical. **automatous,** *a.* acting spontaneously; of the nature of an automaton.
automobile[1], *a.* self-moving. **automobilism,** *n.* [F (AUTO-, L *mōbilis*)]
automobile[2], *n.* (*chiefly N Am.*) a motor-car. **automobilist,** *n.*
automorphic, *a.* characterized by automorphism. **automorphically,** *adv.* **automorphism,** *n.* the attribution of one's own characteristics to another. [Gr. *automorphos,* self-formed]
automotive, *a.* self-propelling; pertaining to motor vehicles.
Autonomisti, *n.* semi-clandestine amalgam of Marxist student organizations, linked with guerrilla groups and such acts as the kidnapping and murder of Italian premier Aldo Moro by the Red Brigades (1978).
autonomy, *n.* the right of self-government; an independent state or community; freedom to act as one pleases; in Kantian philosophy, freedom of the will; organic independence. **autonomous,** *a.* of or possessing autonomy; self-governing; independent; having organic independence. **autonomously,** *adv.* **autonomic,** *a.* autonomous; independent; (*Biol.*) occurring involuntarily, spontaneous; pertaining to or mediated by the autonomic nervous system. **autonomic nervous system,** *n.* the part of the vertebrate nervous system that regulates the involuntary actions of the heart, glands and some muscles. **autonomist,** *n.* an advocate of autonomy. **autonomize, -ise,** *v.t.* to render independent; to make self-governing. [Gr. *autonomia,* independence]
autonym, *n.* a real name, as opp. to a pseudonym. [Gr. *autos,* self, *onoma,* name]
autophagy, *n.* sustenance of life by the absorption of the tissues.
autopilot AUTOMATIC PILOT under AUTOMATIC.
autoplasty, *n.* reparation of a lesion by healthy tissue from the same body. **autoplastic,** *a.*
autopsy, *n.* personal observation; dissection; a post-mortem examination; a critical examination. *v.t.* to perform a post-mortem examination on. **autoptic, -ical,** *a.* seen by one's own eyes; based on personal examination. **autoptically,** *adv.* [Gr. *autopsia* (AUTO-, *opsis,* sight)]
autoroute, *n.* a motorway in France. [F]
autoschediasm, *n.* something hastily improvised. **autoschediastic, -ical,** *a.* hastily improvised. **autoschediaze,** *v.t.* to improvise. [AUTO-, Gr. *schediasma,* from *autoschediazein,* to act or speak offhand (*autoschedios,* off-hand, on the spur of the moment)]
autosome, *n.* a chromosome other than a sex chromosome. **autosomal,** *a.* [Gr. *autos,* self, *soma,* body]
autostrada, *n.* a motorway in Italy. [It.]
autosuggestion, *n.* suggestion arising from oneself, esp. the unconscious influencing of one's own beliefs, physical condition etc. **autosuggestive,** *a.*
autotheism, *n.* †the self-subsistence of God; deification of self. **autotheist,** *n.* one who deifies him- or herself. [Gr. *autotheos,* very God (Gr. *theos,* God)]

autotomy, *n.* voluntary separation of a part of the body, e.g. the tail, as in certain lizards; self-amputation. [Gr. *autos,* self, *tomos,* cutting]

autotoxic, *a.* self-poisoning. **autotoxication,** *n.*

autotrophic, *a.* self-nourishing; of or pertaining to organisms capable of manufacturing organic foods from inorganic sources, as by photosynthesis.

autotype, *n.* a true impress; a facsimile; a photographic printing process for reproducing photographs in monochrome pictures. *v.t.* to reproduce by the autotype process. **autotypography,** *n.* a process by which drawings on gelatine can be transferred to soft metallic plates, which are later printed from. **autotypy,** *n.* the process of reproducing in autotype.

autovac, *n.* a vacuum device for raising petrol from a low tank to a level from which it will flow into the carburettor.

autumn, *n.* the season of the year between summer and winter (astronomically, it extends from the autumnal equinox, 21 Sept., to the winter solstice, 21 Dec.; popularly, it comprises September, October and often November); the early stages of decline of human life; the fruits of harvest. **autumn-bells,** *n.* the Calathian violet, *Gentiana pneumonanthe.* **autumn crocus,** *n.* meadow-saffron. **autumnal,** *a.* of or pertaining to, characteristic of or produced in autumn; pertaining to the declining period of life. *n.* a plant which flowers in autumn. **autumnal equinox,** *n.* the time when the sun crosses the equator southwards (this happens about 21 Sept.). [OF *autompne,* L *autumnus*]

autunite, *n.* a mineral consisting of a hydrous phosphate of uranium and calcium. [town of *Autun,* France]

Auvergne, *n.* ancient province of central France and a modern region (*départements* Allier, Cantal, Haute-Loire, and Puy-de-Dôme); area 26,000 sq km/10,036 sq miles; population (1986) 1,334,000. Its capital is Clermont-Ferrand. It lies in the heart of the Central Plateau and is mountainous, composed chiefly of volcanic rocks in several masses.

aux., (*abbr.*) auxiliary.

auxiliary, *a.* helping, aiding; subsidiary to; applied to verbs used in the conjugation of other verbs. *n.* one who or that which helps or assists; a verb used in the conjugation of other verbs; (*Math.*) a quantity introduced with the view of simplifying some complex operation; (*pl.*) foreign or allied troops in the service of a nation at war. †**auxiliar,** *a., n.* auxiliary. [L *auxiliārius,* from *auxilium,* help (*augēre,* to increase)]

auxin, *n.* a growth-promoting plant hormone. [Gr. *auxein,* to grow]

auxometer, *n.* an optical instrument for measuring magnifying power. [Gr. *auxein,* to grow, METER]

AV, (*abbr.*) audio-visual; Authorized Version.

av., (*abbr.*) average; avoirdupois; (**av., Av.**) avenue.

ava, *n.* KAVA. [native name]

avail, *v.i.* to be of value, use, profit or advantage; to be helpful; to be effectual, sufficient. *v.t.* to be of use or advantage to; (*N Am.*) to inform, to assure of. *n.* worth, value, profit, advantage, use; (*pl.*) profits, proceeds.**of no avail, without avail,** ineffectual. **to avail oneself of,** (*N Am.*) **to avail of,** to take advantage of, make use of. **to little avail,** ineffectually. **available,** *a.* capable of being employed; at one's disposal; at hand, valid. **availability,** *n.* the quality of being available; (*N Am.*) a qualification in a candidate which implies strong probability of his success. **availableness,** *n.* **availably,** *adv.* [OF *vail,* 1st pers. pres. sing of *valoir,* L *valēre* to be worth]

avalanche, *n.* a mass of snow, ice and debris falling or sliding from the upper parts of a mountain; a sudden inundation; the cumulative production of charged particles resulting from the collisions of a single charged particle with matter to produce further particles which in turn collide etc. [Swiss-F (F *avalance,* descent), from *avaler,* to descend to the valley (*à val* L *ad vallem,* to the valley)]

†**avale,** *v.t.* to cause to descend, come down or fall; to let down, to lower; to doff; to humble, to depress. *v.i.* to dismount; to come down; to sink. [F *avaler,* see prec.]

Avalokiteśvara, *n.* in Mahāyāna Buddhism, one of the most important bodhisattvas, seen as embodying compassion. Known as *Guanyin* in China, *Kwannon* in Japan, he is one of the attendants of Amida Buddha.

Avalon, *n.* in Celtic legend, the island of the blessed or paradise; and in the Arthurian legend the land of heroes, to which the dead king was conveyed. It has been associated with Glastonbury in SW England.

avant, *adv., a.* (*F*) before, in front. **avant-brace** VAMBRACE. **avant-courier,** *n.* a forerunner, a precursor; (*pl.*) scouts, skirmishers. [F, before, now principally found in the form *van-* or *vant-*]

avant-garde, *a.* as a forerunner in music, art etc.; in advance of contemporary artistic taste or trend. *n.* the people who create or take up avant-garde or experimental ideas, esp. in the arts. **avant-gardism,** *n.* **avant-gardist,** *n.*

avarice, *n.* an excessive craving after wealth; greediness of gain; eager desire to get and keep. **avaricious,** *a.* **avariciously,** *adv.* [OF, from L *avāritia,* from *avārus,* greedy (*avēre,* to wish, desire)]

avast, *int.* (*Naut.*) stay! stop! desist! [prob. from Dut. *hou' vast,* or *houd vast.* hold fast]

avatar, *n.* the descent of a deity to the earth; in Hindu mythology, the incarnation of a deity; a manifestation, phase. [Sansk. *avatara,* descent]

†**avaunt,** *v.t.* to raise, to advance. *v.i.* to come forward, to depart. *adv.* to the front, forward. *int.* be off! away with you! begone! *n.* a dismissal; a defiance. [AVANT]

ave, *int.* hail! welcome! farewell! (in allusion to the classical custom of greeting the dead). *n.* an Ave Maria; one of the small beads on a rosary on which prayers are counted; a shout of welcome or adieu. **ave-bell,** *n.* the bell rung when the Ave Maria should be repeated. **Ave Maria, Ave Mary,** *n.* the Hail Mary; the angelical salutation (Luke i.28) with that of St Elisabeth (i.42), to which a prayer is added, the whole being used as a form of devotion; the ave-bell. [L, hail (*avēre,* to fare well)]

ave., Ave., (*abbr.*) avenue.

Avebury1**,** *n.* **John Lubbock, 1st Baron Avebury** (1834–1913), British banker. A Liberal (from 1886 Liberal Unionist) member of Parliament (1870–1900), he was largely responsible for the Bank Holidays Act 1871 introducing statutory public holidays.

Avebury2**,** *n.* Europe's largest stone circle (diameter 412 m/1352 ft), Wiltshire, England. It was probably constructed in the Neolithic period 3500 years ago, and is linked with nearby Silbury Hill. The village of Avebury was built within the circle, and many of the stones were used for building material.

Avedon, *n.* **Richard** (1923–), US photographer. A fashion photographer with *Harper's Bazaar* magazine in New York in the mid-1940s, he later became one of the highest-paid commercial photographers.

avenaceous, *a.* of, pertaining to or resembling oats. [L *avēnāceus,* from *avēna,* oats]

avenge, *v.t.* to vindicate by punishing a wrong-doer; to exact satisfaction for (an injury etc.); to inflict punishment on account of. *v.i.* to execute vengeance. **avengeful,** *a.* **avengement,** *n.* **avenger,** *n.* one who avenges or vindicates; a vindicator, a revenger. **avenger of blood,** *n.* the name given in the Mosaic law to the person on whom it devolved to punish murder by death. [OF *avengier* (*à,* to, *vengier,* L *vindicāre,* to claim, to revenge)]

avens, *n.* a plant of the genus *Geum,* as the wood avens or herb bennet. *G. urbanum,* and the water avens, *G. rivale;* the mountain avens, *Dryas octopetala.* [OF *avence* (etym. doubtful)]

aventail, aventayle, *n.* the movable part of a helmet in front, which may be lifted to admit fresh air. [OF *esventail* (L *ex-,* out, *ventus,* wind)]

aventre, *v.t.* to throw forward or thrust (a spear). [perh. F *à,* to, *ventre,* belly]

aventurine, aventurin, *n.* a gold-spangled glass made first at Murano (the process was accidentally discovered, whence the name); a quartz of similar appearance spangled with scales of mica or some other mineral. [F, from It. *avventurino* (*avventura,* chance)]

avenue, *n.* a way or means of access or approach; an approach to a country house or similar building; a broad alley bordered with trees; the rows of trees bordering such an alley; a fine wide thoroughfare. [F, fem. p.p. of *avenir,* to come to, L *advenīre* (*ad-,* to, *venīre,* to come)]

aver, *v.t.* (*past, p.p.* **averred**) to assert or declare positively; (*Law*) to prove; to allege, declare. **averrable,** *a.* capable of being affirmed with certainty. **averment,** *n.* the act of averring; affirmation, positive assertion; (*Law*) an affirmation alleged to be true, and followed by an offer to verify. [F *avérer,* late L *āverāre* (*ad,* to *verum,* truth)]

average, *n.* any charge payable by the owner of goods over and above the freight, often called **petty** (formerly **accustomed**) **average**; loss arising from damage to ship or cargo at sea; apportionment of such loss among the parties interested (if the damage was unavoidable, such apportionment is called a **particular average,** and falls upon the respective owners or insurers in proportion to their shares of the particular interests affected; if intentional (as by cutting away masts etc.), it is called a **general average**); a number or quantity intermediate to several different numbers or quantities; a mean; the rate, proportion, degree, quantity, level or number generally prevailing. *v.t.* to calculate the average of; to take the ordinary standard of; to divide proportionately to the number involved; to be or consist of on an average; to do, have or take as a mean rate or value. *v.i.* to be or amount to as an average. *a.* ascertained by taking a mean proportion between given quantities; medium, ordinary. **on an average,** taking the mean deduced from a number of examples. **average adjuster,** *n.* an assessor who deals with claims for losses at sea. **averagely,** *adv.* [F *avarie* (etym. doubtful; cp. Sp. *averia,* It. *avaria,* Dut. *avarij, haverij,* G *Haferei*)]

avernian, *a.* of or pertaining to Lake Avernus in Campania, near which was the fabled entrance to the lower world; infernal. [L *Avernus,* -IAN]

averrable AVER.

Averroes, *n.* (Arabic **Ibn Rushd**) (1126–1198), Arabian philosopher, who argued for the eternity of matter, and denied the immortality of the individual soul. His philosophical writings, including commentaries on Aristotle and Plato's *Republic*, became known to the West through Latin translations. He influenced Christian and Jewish writers, and reconciled Islamic and Greek thought. **Averroist,** *n.* one of a sect named after Averroes. **Averroism,** *n.*

†**averruncate,** *v.t.* to turn away, to avert; (*erroneously*) to weed, to root up. †**averruncation,** *n.* the act of turning away or averting; (*erroneously*) the act of rooting up. **averruncator,** *n.* an instrument for pruning trees, consisting of two blades, working like shears, at the end of a rod. [L *āverruncātus,* p.p. of *āverruncāre,* to ward off, remove; wrongly taken as meaning to weed out, as if from *eruncāre*]

averse, *a.* turned away mentally; feeling repugnance or dislike; unwilling, disinclined, reluctant (to). **aversely,** *adv.* **averseness,** *n.* **aversion,** *n.* an averted state of feeling or mind; disinclination, dislike, repugnance; an object of dislike. **aversion therapy,** *n.* therapy designed to stop undesirable behaviour by associating it with an unpleasant sensation (as an electric shock). [L *aversus,* p.p. of *āvertere* (*a-, ab-,* away, *vertere,* to turn)]

avert, *v.t.* to turn away; to ward off. **avertible,** *a.* [F *avertir,* late L *avertēre,* L *āvertere,* to turn away (*avertir* seems to have represented both *advertere* and *āvertere,* the meaning being differentiated later)]

Avery, *n.* **'Tex'** (Frederick Bean) (1907–1980), US cartoon-film director who used violent, sometimes surreal humour. At Warner Brothers he helped develop the characters Bugs Bunny and Daffy Duck before moving to MGM in 1942 where he created, among others, Droopy and Screwball Squirrel.

Avesta, *n.* the sacred scriptures of Zoroastrianism. **Avestan,** *a.* of the Avesta. *n.* the Iranian language of the Avesta, ZEND. [Pers.]

avian, *a.* of or pertaining to birds. **aviary,** *n.* a large cage or building in which birds are kept. **aviarist,** *n.* [L *avis,* a bird, -AN]

aviation, *n.* the art of flying or travelling in the air; all matters to do with aircraft or flying in an aircraft; the design and manufacture of aircraft. **aviate,** *v.i.* to fly, to travel in an aircraft. **aviator,** *n.* a person who flies an aircraft; †a flying-machine. **aviatrix,** *n. fem.* [L *avis,* a bird]

aviculture, *n.* the breeding and rearing of birds.

avid, *a.* greedy, covetous; ardently desirous; extremely eager, hungry. **avidly,** *adv.* **avidity,** *n.* [L *avidus,* greedy (*avēre,* to crave)]

avifauna, *n.* the birds in any district taken collectively. **avifaunal,** *a.*

Avignon, *n.* city in Provence, France, capital of Vaucluse *département,* on the river Rhône NW of Marseille; population (1982) 174,000. It was an important Gallic and Roman city, and has 14th-cent. walls, a 12th-cent. bridge (only half still standing), a 13th-cent. cathedral, and the palace built (1334–42) during the residence here of the popes. Avignon was papal property 1348–1791.

avionics, *n. sing.* (the science concerned with) the development and use of electronic and electric equipment in aircraft and spacecraft. [*avi*ation electr*onics*]

†**aviso,** *n.* advice, intelligence. [Sp., advice, L *advīsum* (see ADVICE)]

avitaminosis, *n.* (*pl.* **-ses**) disease resulting from vitamin deficiency.

avizandum, *n.* (*Sc. Law*) private consideration. **to take** (a case) **to avizandum,** to consider privately with a view to judgment. [med. L, gerund of *avizāre,* to consider]

AVM, (*abbr.*) Air Vice-Marshal.

avocado, *n.* (*pl.* **-dos**) (also **avocado pear**) the pear-shaped fruit of a West Indian tree, *Persea gratissima;* this tree; a dull green colour. [Sp., 'advocate', a popular substitute for Aztec *ahuacatl*]

avocation, *n.* †the condition of being called away, diversion, distraction; a minor employment or occupation; ordinary employment, calling, vocation, business. [L *āvocātiōnem,* from *āvocāre* (*ā-, ab-,* away, *vocāre,* to call)]

avocet, avoset, *n.* a wading bird allied to the snipes and stilts, having a long slender bill curved upwards. [F *avocette,* It. *avosetta*]

Avogadro's hypothesis, in chemistry, the law stating that equal volumes of all gases, when at the same temperature and pressure, have the same numbers of molecules. This law was first propounded by Count Amadeo Avogadro.

Avogadro's number, constant, the number of carbon atoms in 12 g of the carbon-12 isotope (6.022045×10^{23}). The relative atomic mass of any element, expressed in grams, contains this number of atoms. It is named after Amadeo Avogadro.

avoid, *v.t.* to keep at a distance from, to shun; to keep away from; to escape, evade; (*Law*) to defeat, to invalidate, to quash; †to empty by excretion. †*v.i.* to become void or vacant; to depart, retreat, escape. **avoidable,** *a.* capable of being avoided. **avoidably,** *adv.* **avoidability,** *n.* **avoidance,** *n.* the act of making void or annulling; the act of shunning or avoiding; †the act or process of becoming void or vacant. **avoidless,** *a.* (*poet.*) incapable of being avoided; inevitable. [A-F *avoider,* OF *esvuidier* (*es-,* out, *vuidier,* to void, from *vuit, vuide,* empty)]

avoirdupois, *n.* a system of weights based on the unit of a pound of 16 ounces, equal to 7000 grains (0·4536 kg); (*chiefly N Am.*) weight, heaviness. [OF *avoir* (*aveir*) *de pois,* things of weight (*avoir, aveir,* goods, property, L *habēre,* to have, *de,* of, *pois, peis,* L *pensum,* weight)]

Avon[1], *n.* county in SW England. **area** 1340 sq km/517 sq miles. **towns** administrative headquarters: Bristol, Bath, Weston-super-Mare. **products** aircraft and other engineering, tobacco, chemicals, printing, dairy products. **population** (1987) 951,000.

Avon[2], *n.* any of several rivers in England and Scotland. The Avon in Warwickshire is associated with Shakespeare.

avoset AVOCET.

avouch, *v.t.* to affirm, vouch for, guarantee as certain; to own, acknowledge, avow; to maintain, to justify. *v.i.* to vouch, give assurance or guarantee. †*n.* evidence, testimony, guarantee. **avouchable,** *a.* [OF *avochier,* L *advocāre* (*ad,* to, *vocāre,* to call)]

†**avoure,** *n.* avowal, answer. [see foll.]

avow, *v.t.* to own, to acknowledge, to admit (of one's free will); to state, allege, declare; †to vow, promise with a vow. †*n.* a vow, solemn promise; avowal, sanction. **avowable,** *a.* **avowal,** *n.* an open declaration, a free admission. **avowed,** *a.* acknowledged; self-acknowledged. **avowedly,** *adv.* [OF *avouer,* L *advocāre,* to call upon, to call in as patron (*ad-,* to, *vocāre,* to call), more or less identified with sense of *a,* to, and *vouer,* L *votāre,* to vow (*vōtum,* a vow)]

avowry, *n.* †patronage, advocacy; a patron, a protector; (*Law*) the plea whereby a person who distrains for rent avows and justifies the act. [OF *avoerie, avouerie,* office of the *avoueur* or patron]

avulsion, *n.* the act of tearing away or violently separating; a fragment torn off; (*Law*) sudden removal of land (without change of ownership) by flood, alteration in the course of a river or the like. **avulsive,** *a.* [L *āvulsiōnem,* from *āvellere* (*a-, ab-,* from, *vellere,* to pluck)]

avuncular, *a.* of, pertaining to or resembling an uncle. [L *avunculus,* a maternaluncle]

AWACS, (*abbr.*) Airborne Warning and Control System.

await, *v.* to watch for, lie in wait for; to wait for, look out for, expect; to be in store for. *v.i.* to lie in wait; to wait; to be in store. †*n.* a lying in wait; ambush. [ONF *awaitier* (OF *agaitier*), to lie in wait for (*à,* to, *waitier, gaitier,* see WAIT)]

awake, *v.i.* to wake from sleep, cease sleeping; to become conscious of or alive to something; to become active or alert. *v.t.* to arouse from sleep, or from lethargy or inaction; to excite to action or new life. *a.* not asleep; roused from sleep; active, vigilant, aware, alive (to). **awakable,** *a.* **awaken,** *v.t.* to arouse, awake; to arouse to a sense of sin. *v.i.* to awake. **awakenable,** *a.* **awakening,** *a.* rising as if from sleep; fitted to inspire activity, rousing. *n.* a rising from sleep, lethargy or moral indifference. **awakenment,** *n.* an awakening. [two OE verbs were early confused, *awæcnan* (*a-,* on, WAKE[1]), *awōc, awacen;* and *awacian, awacode* (*awæcnan* gave us *awaken* and*awakened, awacian* gave *awake, awaked*). Both verbs were intr., meaning, to arise from sleep, cease sleeping; the tr. senses were supplied by *āweccan,* to rouse, which was gradually superseded by *awake*]

awanting, *a.* wanting, missing, absent. [*ā-,* on, wanting, taken as a single word, as if from adv. *awant*]

award, *v.t.* to adjudge, to assign by judicial sentence; †to decide authoritatively, after due deliberation and examination; to grant or confer, esp. as a prize for merit or as something needed. *n.* the decision of judge, arbitrator or umpire; the document embodying the terms of such decision; that which is awarded. [A-F *awarder,* OF *esguarder,* from *es-,* L *ex-,* out of, OLG *wardēn* (OHG *wartēn*), watch, guard (cp. WARD)]

aware, *a.* apprised, cognizant, conscious; †excited to caution; watchful, vigilant. **awareness,** *n.* [OE *gewær* (*ge-,* intens., *wær,* aware, wary) (cp. OHG *gawar,* G *gewahr*)]

awash, *adv.* on a level with the water; at the mercy of the waves. *a.* covered with water. **awash with,** full of, having an abundance of.

Awash, *n.* a river which rises to the S of Addis Ababa in Ethiopia and flows NE to Lake Abba on the frontier with Djibouti. Although deep inside present day Ethiopia, the Awash River is considered by Somalis to mark the eastern limit of Ethiopian sovereignty prior to the colonial division of Somaliland in the 19th cent.

awaste, *adv.* on the waste.

awave, *a.* on the wave, waving.

away, *adv.* implying motion from a place, person, cause or condition; absent, in the other direction, at another place; continuously, constantly; straightaway, directly. Used elliptically as a verb, be off! begone! (to) go away. *a.* absent; distant; played on an opponent's ground. *n.* a (football) match played or won at an opponent's ground. **away back,** long ago. **away with,** take away; (with negative phrase) bear, endure, tolerate. **cannot away with,** cannot endure. **to do away with** DO. **to make away with** MAKE. **far and away, out and away,** beyond comparison. [OE *onweg,* on the way]

awe[1], *n.* dread mingled with veneration; solemn, reverential wonder. *v.t.* to inspire with solemn fear or reverence; to restrain by profound respect or reverential fear. **to keep in awe,** to restrain by fear. **aweless,** *a.* not feeling awe or dread; †not inspiring awe. **awelessness,** *n.* **awesome,** *a.* full of or displaying awe; inspiring awe. **awesomely,** *adv.* **awesomeness,** *n.* **awe-stricken, awe-struck,** *a.* overwhelmed with awe. [Icel. *agi* (cp. OE *ege,* fear, also *ōga,* terror)]

awe[2], *n.* a float-board of a water-wheel. [etym. unknown]

Awe, *n.* longest (37 km/23 miles) of the Scottish freshwater lochs, in Strathclyde, SE of Oban. It is drained by the river Awe into Loch Etive.

aweary, *a.* tired, weary.

a-weather, *adv.* to the weather side, as opposed to the lee side; towards the wind. **aweather of,** *prep.* on the weather side of.

aweel, *adv.* (*Sc.*) well; well then. [*ah well* (cp. F *eh bien*)]

aweigh, *adv.* (*Naut.*) raised vertically just off the bottom; atrip.

awful, *a.* inspiring awe; worthy of profound reverence; dreadful, fearful, appalling; filled with awe; extremely disagreeable, frightful, terrible, monstrous; (*coll.*) often used as an intensive. **awfully,** *adv.* in an awful manner; (*coll.*) exceedingly, very. **awfulness,** *n.* [AWE[1]]

awheto, aweto, *n.* (*New Zealand*) a vegetable-eating caterpillar that, when dried, yields a tattoo dye. [Maori]

awhile, *adv.* for some time; for a little; (*loosely*) a while. [OE *àne while*]

awing, *adv.* on the wing, flying.

awkward, *a.* unhandy, ill-adapted for use; †froward, perverse, cross-grained; lacking dexterity, bungling, clumsy; ungraceful, ungainly; embarrassed, ill at ease; embarrassing; not easy to manage or deal with. **awkwardly,** *adv.* **awkwardness,** *n.* [ME *awk,* contrary, untoward (Icel. *afug, ofug,* turned the wrong way), -WARD(s)]

awl, *n.* a tool with a cylindrical tapering blade, sharpened at the end, for making holes for stitches in leather. **awl-bird,** *n.* (*dial.*) *Picus viridis,* the green woodpecker. **awl-shaped,** *a.* (*Bot.*) subulate. **awlwort,** *n.* a plant of the genus *Subularia,* esp. *S. aquatica,* a British species, named from the shape of the leaves. [OE *ǣl* (cp. OHG *ala,* G *Ahle*)]

awn, *n.* the beard of corn and grasses, one of the bristles springing from a bract in the inflorescence of grasses. **awned,** *a.* **awnless,** *a.* [Icel. *ögn,* chaff, a husk (cp. OHG *agana,* G *Ahne*)]

awning, *n.* a covering of tarpaulin, canvas or other material used as a protection from sun or rain, as above the deck of a ship; the part of the poop-deck which is continued forward beyond the bulk-head of the cabin; a shelter. **awned,** *part.a.* fitted with an awning. [etym. doubtful, perhaps from F *auvent,* penthouse]

awoke, *past* AWAKE.

AWOL, *a., adv.* absent without authorization from one's post or position of duty. *n.* a member of the armed forces who is absent without authorization. [*a*bsent without leave]

a-work, *adv.* at work.

awrong, *adv.* wrongly.

awry, *adv.* wrily, obliquely, crookedly; erroneously, amiss. *a.* crooked, distorted, oblique; wrong.

axe, (*esp. N Am.*) **ax,** *n.* (*pl.* **axes**) an instrument for cutting or chopping consisting of an iron head with a sharp edge, fitted to a wooden handle or helve; the headsman's axe; execution; a celt probably used as an axe. *v.t.* to chop or cut with an axe; to dismiss (staff) for reasons of economy; to make drastic reductions in (expenditure, services etc.). **the axe,** *n.* dismissal from employment; drastic reduction in expenditure. **to have an axe to grind,** to have an ulterior motive; to have a grievance to air. **to put the axe on the helve,** to solve a doubt or a puzzle. **axe-head,** *n.* the cutting portion of the axe. **axe-man,** *n.* a woodman; a warrior armed with a battle-axe; a psychopath who kills with an axe. †**axe-stone,** *n.* jade, nephrite, from which prehistoric man used to make many stone implements. [OE *æx* (cp. Icel *öx,* OHG *acchus,* G *Axt,* L *ascia,* Gr. *axinē*)]

axel, *n.* a jump in ice-skating incorporating one and a half turns. [*Axel* Paulsen, 1855–1938, Norw. skater]

Axelrod, *n.* **Julius** (1912–), US neuropharmacologist, who shared the 1970 Nobel prize for medicine with the biophysicists Bernard Katz and Ulf von Euler for his work on neurotransmitters (the chemical messengers of the brain).

axial, axile, etc. AXIS.

axil, *n.* the hollow where the base of a leaf joins the stem or where a branch leaves the trunk. **axilla,** *n.* (*pl.* **-llas, -llae**) the armpit. **axillar, axillary,** *a.* pertaining to the armpit; pertaining to or arising from the axil. [L *axilla,* an armpit]

axiom, *n.* a self-evident or generally accepted truth; (*Math.*) a self-evident proposition, assented to as soon as enunciated. **axiomatic, -ical,** *a.* self-evident, containing an axiom or axioms; full of maxims. **axiomatically,** *adv.* [F *axiome,* L *axiōma,* from Gr. (*axioō,* I esteem, from *axios,* worthy)]

axis[1], *n.* (*pl.* **axes**) a real or imaginary straight line round which a body revolves, or round which its parts are arranged, or to which they have a symmetrical relation; a fixed reference line used, as on a graph, in locating a point; the second cervical vertebra; the central stem, core or main skeletal support of (a part of) an organism; the central shaft of growth of a plant, the stem is the **ascending** and the root the **descending axis;** an imaginary line round which a crystal can be symmetrically built up; (*Geol.*) a central ridge; (*Math.*) a straight line in a plane figure about which it is conceived to revolve to generate a solid; a line dividing a regular figure into two symmetrical parts; a ray of light passing through the centre of or falling perpendicularly on a lens; the straight line from the lens of the eye to the object seen; (*pl.*) the sloping timbers of a roof, the principals; (**Axis**) see separate article below. **axis of a balance,** the line on which a balance turns. **axis of oscillation,** a straight line passing through the point about which a pendulum oscillates, at right angles to the plane of motion. **axis of the equator,** the polar diameter of the earth, the axis of revolution. **axial,** *a.* pertaining to an axis; forming an axis. **axial pitch,** *n.* (*Mech.*) the pitch of a screw measured in a direction parallel with the axis. **axiality,** *n.* the quality of being axial. **axially,** *adv.* in the direction of the axis. **axile,** *a.* situated in the axis of anything. [L, the axle (cp. Gr. *axōn,* Sansk. *aksha,* OE *eax*)]

axis[2], **axis deer,** *n.* a S Asian deer with a white-spotted coat. [L, an Indian wild animal]

Axis, *n.* the alliance of Nazi Germany and Fascist Italy before and during World War II. The **Rome–Berlin Axis** was formed in 1936, when Italy was being threatened with sanctions because of its invasion of Abyssinia. It became a full military and political alliance May 1939. A 10-year alliance between Germany, Italy and Japan (**Rome–Berlin–Tokyo Axis**) was signed Sept. 1940, and was subsequently joined by Hungary, Bulgaria, Romania and the puppet states of Slovakia and Croatia. The Axis collapsed with the fall of Mussolini and the surrender of Italy in 1943.

axle, *n.* the pin or bar on which a wheel revolves or which revolves with the wheel; the thin ends of the axle-tree; the axle-tree; †the pole of the earth or heavens. **axle-box,** *n.* a case in which the ends of axles revolve; a metal cover for the hub. **axle-pin,** *n.* a linchpin. **axle-tree,** *n.* the beam or bar connecting wheels, on the ends of which the wheels revolve; †a spindle, axis. **axled,** *a.* furnished with an axle. [Icel. *öxull* (cp. Goth. *ahsuls,* OTeut. *ahsā,* Sansk. *aksha,* L *axis,* Gr. *axōn*)]

Axminster, *n.* a variously coloured and patterned woven carpet with a tufted pile. [*Axminster,* town in Devon where a type of patterned carpet was originally woven]

axolotl, *n.* a salamander of the genus *Ambystoma* that retains the larval form when fully grown; esp. a small Mexican salamander, *Ambystoma mexicanum.* [Aztec *a-, atl,* water, *xolotl,* servant]

axon, *n.* the projection from a nerve cell that typically conducts impulses away from the cell. [Gr. *axon,* axis]

Axum, *n.* alternative transliteration of Aksum, an ancient kingdom in Ethiopia.

ay, aye[1], *adv., int.* yes. *n.* an affirmative vote in the House of Commons; (*pl.*) those who vote in the affirmative. **aye, aye, sir,** (*Naut.* or *facet.*) yes, sir; very well, sir. [perh. an alt. form of YEA; or from I, expressing assent]

Ayacucho, *n.* the capital of a province of the same name in the Andean mountains of central Peru; population (1988) 94,200. The last great battle in the war of independence against Spain was fought near here in Dec. 1824.

ayah, *n.* a Hindu nurse for children; a lady's maid. [Hind.]

ayatollah, *n.* a leader of the Shiite Muslims in Iran. [Pers. *āyatollāh,* sign of God, from Arab. (*aya,* sign, *allah,* God)]

Ayckbourn, *n.* **Alan** (1939–), English playwright. His prolific output, characterized by his acute ear for comic dialogue, includes *Absurd Person Singular* (1973), the trilogy *The Norman Conquests* (1974), *A Woman in Mind* (1986), *A Small Family Business* (1987), *Man of the Moment* (1988), and scripts for television.

aye[1], AY.

aye[2], *adv.* always, ever; in all cases, on all occasions. **for aye, for ever and aye,** for ever, to all eternity. [ME *a33, ai, ei,* Icel. *ei, ey* (cogn. with OE *ā,* Goth. *aiw,* L *ævum,* Gr. *aei*)]

aye-aye, *n.* a small lemur found in Madagascar, *Daubentonia madagascariensis.* [F, from Malagasy *aiay,* from its cry]

Ayer, *n.* **A(lfred) J(ules)** (1910–1989), English philosopher. He wrote *Language, Truth and Logic* (1936), an exposition of the theory of 'logical positivism', presenting a criterion by which meaningful statements (essentially truths of logic, as well as statements derived from experience) could be distinguished from meaningless metaphysical utterances (for example, claims that there is a God, or that the world external to our own minds is illusory).

Ayers Rock, *n.* a vast ovate mass of pinkish rock in Northern Territory, Australia; 335 m/1100 ft high and 9 km/6 miles round.

Ayesha, *n.* (611–678), third and favourite wife of the prophet Mohammed, who married her when she was nine. Her father, Abu Bakr, became caliph on Mohammed's death in 632, and she bitterly opposed the later succession to the caliphate of Ali, who had once accused her of infidelity.

Aylesbury, *n.* a breed of table ducks. [town in Bucks]

ayond, ayont, *prep.* (*Sc., North.*) beyond.

Ayrshire, *n.* former county of SW Scotland, with a 113 km/70 miles coastline on the Firth of Clyde. In 1975 the major part was merged in the region of Strathclyde, the remaining sector, approximately south of the Water of Girvan and including Girvan itself, became part of Dumfries and Galloway. It is the name of a breed of cattle highly prized for dairy purposes.

Ayurveda, *n.* ancient Hindu system of medicine, the main principles of which are derived from the Vedas, that is still practised in India in Ayurvedic hospitals and dispensaries. **Ayurvedic,** *a.* of or pertaining to the Hindu philosophy of medicine and healing as set down in the Ayurveda. [Sansk. *āyur,* life, *veda,* knowledge]

az., (*abbr.*) azimuth.

azalea, *n.* a genus of shrubby plants with showy and occasionally fragrant flowers. [Gr., fem. of *azaleos,* dry (either from dry wood or its liking for dry soil)]

Azaña, *n.* **Manuel** (1880–1940), Spanish politician and first prime minister (1931–33) of the second Spanish republic. He was last president of the republic during the Civil War (1936–39), before the establishment of a dictatorship under Francisco Franco.

azarole, *n.* the Neapolitan medlar, *Crataegus azarolus,* or its fruit. [F *azerole,* Arab. *az-zu'rūr*]

Azerbaijan, *n.* constituent republic (Azerbaydzhan Soviet Socialist Republic) of the USSR from 1936. **area** 86,600 sq km/33,436 sq miles. **capital** Baku. **towns** Kirovabad. **physical** Caspian Sea; the country ranges from semi-desert to the Caucasus mountains. **products** oil, iron, copper, fruit, vines, cotton, silk, carpets. **population** (1987) 6,811,000; 78% Azerbaijani, 8% Russian, 8% Armenian. **language** Turkic. **religion** traditionally Shi'ite Muslim.

Azerbaijan, Iranian, *n.* two provinces of NW Iran, Eastern Azerbaijan (capital Tabriz), population (1986) 4,114,000, and Western Azerbaijan (capital Orúmiyeh), population 1,972,000. Like the people of Soviet Azerbaijan, the people are Muslim (Shiah) ethnic Turks, descendants of followers of the Khans from the Mongol Empire.

Azhar, El, *n.* Muslim university and mosque in Cairo, Egypt. Founded in 970 by Jawhar, commander in chief of the army of the Fatimid caliph, it is claimed to be the oldest university in the world. It became the centre of Islamic learning, with several subsidiary foundations, and is now primarily a school of Koranic teaching.

azidothymidine AZT.

Azilian, *n.* an archaeological period following the close of the Old Stone (Palaeolithic) Age, and regarded as one of the cultures of the Mesolithic Age. It was first recognized by Piette at Mas d'Azil, a village in Ariège, France. *a.* pertaining to this period.

azimuth, *n.* an arc of the heavens extending from the zenith to the horizon, which it cuts at right angles; horizontal angle or direction, point of the compass, bearing; (**azimuth, true azimuth**) the arc of the horizon intercepted between the north (or, in the southern hemisphere, the south) point of the horizon and the point where the vertical circle passing through a heavenly body cuts the horizon; (**azimuth, magnetic azimuth**) the arc intercepted between the true azimuth and the magnetic meridian. **azimuth circle,** *n.* a circle passing through the zenith and cutting the horizon perpendicularly. **azimuth compass,** *n.* an instrument for finding the magnetic azimuth. **azimuth dial,** *n.* a dial having the gnomon at right angles to the plane of the horizon, the shadow indicating the sun's azimuth. **azimuthal,** *a.* of or pertaining to the azimuth; in azimuth. **azimuthally,** *adv.* in azimuth; in a circle parallel to the horizon. [F *azimut,* Arab. *assamūt* (*al,* the, *sumut,* ways or points, sing. *samt*)]

azo-, *comb. form.* nitrogen. [see AZOTE]

azoic, *a.* having no trace of life; (*Geol.*) destitute of organic remains, in the time that antedates life. [Gr. *azōos,* lifeless (*a-,* not, *zoē,* life)]

azonic, *a.* not pertaining to a definite region, not local. [Gr. *azōnikos* (*a-,* not, without, *zōnē,* region)]

Azores, *n.pl.* a group of nine islands in the N Atlantic, an autonomous region of Portugal; area 2247 sq km/867 sq miles; population (1987) 254,000. They are outlying peaks of the Mid-Atlantic Ridge, and are volcanic in origin. The capital is Ponta Delgada on the main island, San Miguel.

azorite, *n.* a variety of zirconium found in the Azores. [from the place]

azote, *n.* an old name for nitrogen, from its fatal effects upon animal life. **azotic,** *a.* **azotize, -ise,** *v.t.* to render nitrogenous, to deoxygenize. [F *azote* (Gr. *a-,* not, *zōt-,* as in *zōtikos,* fit for maintaining life)]

Azov, *n.* (Russian **Azovskoye More**) inland sea of the USSR forming a gulf in the NE of the Black Sea; area 37,555 sq km/14,500 sq miles. Principal ports include Rostov-on-Don, Kerch and Taganrog. Azov is an important source of freshwater fish.

AZT, *n.* an antiviral drug that suppresses the activity of the virus that causes AIDS and is used to alleviate some of the AIDS symptoms. [*azidothymidine*]

Aztec, *n.* a member of a Mexican American Indian people who migrated from further north in the 12th century, and in 1325 began reclaiming lake marshland to build their capital, Tenochtitlán, on the site of modern Mexico City. Under Montezuma I (reigned from 1440), they created an empire in central and southern Mexico. *a.* of, or pertaining to, this people; loosely applied to Mexican antiquities generally. [*Azteca,* native name]

azure, *n.* lapis-lazuli; the deep blue of the sky; the vault of heaven; a bright blue pigment or dye; (*Her.*) the blue of coats of arms, represented in engraving by horizontal lines. *a.* resembling the clear bright blue of the sky; clear, unclouded; (*Her.*) blue. *v.t.* to colour azure or bright clear blue. **azure-spar, -stone,** *n.* lazulite. **azurine,** *n.* the blue roach *Leuciscus caeruleus.* **azurite,** *n.* blue carbonate of copper; †lazulite. **azurn,** *a.* (*poet.*) azure. [OF *azur,* med. L *azura,* Arab. *lazward,* Pers. *lājward, lāzhward,* lapis lazuli]

azygous, *a.* (*Biol.*) unpaired, occurring singly, not as one of a pair. **azygously,** *adv.* [Gr. *azugos,* unyoked (*a-,* not, *zugon,* a yoke)]

azyme, *n.* the Passover cake of unleavened bread. **Azymite,** *n.* one who uses unleavened bread in the Eucharist; a name given by the Greek Church to members of the Western Church and to Armenians and Maronites. **azymous,** *a.* unleavened. [L *azȳmus,* Gr. *azumos* (*a-,* not, without, *zumē,* leaven)]

B

B[1], **b**[1], the second letter in the English, Aryan and other alphabets, corresponding in power to the Greek Beta (ß) and the Phoenician and Hebrew Beth, representing a flat labial mute; (*pl.* **Bs, B's, Bees**) used as a symbol to denote the second of a series; the second known quantity in an algebraic expression; (*Mus.*) the seventh note of the diatonic scale of C major; one of a second class or order; one of the human blood groups. **not to know B from a bull's foot,** to be grossly ignorant or illiterate. **B road,** *n.* a road of secondary importance.

B[2], (*abbr.*) Bachelor; Baron; bel; Belgium; of pencil lead, black; British.

B[3], (*chem. symbol*) boron.

b[4], (*abbr.*) barrel; billion; book; born; bottle; bowled.

BA, (*abbr.*) Bachelor of Arts; British Academy; British Airways; British America; British Association (for the Advancement of Science); Buenos Aires.

Ba, (*chem. symbol*) barium.

B.A.A., (*abbr.*) British Airports Authority.

baa, *n.* the cry or bleat of a sheep. *v.t.* to cry or bleat as a sheep. [from the sound]

Baabda, *n.* capital of the province of Jebel Lubnan in central Lebanon and site of the country's presidential palace. Situated to the SE of Beirut, it is the headquarters of the Christian military leader, Michel Aoun.

Baader, *n.* **Andreas** (1943–77), West German extreme left-wing guerrilla. A former left-wing student activist, he formed, with Ulrike Meinhof, the Red Army Faction, an underground urban guerrilla organization that carried out a succession of terrorist acts in West Germany during the 1970s. Sentenced to life imprisonment in April 1977, he apparently took his own life in Oct 1977, following the failure of the Faction's hostage-swap attempt at Mogadishu airport.

Baader-Meinhof gang, *n.* popular name for the West German guerrilla group the *Rote Armee Fraktion* ('Red Army Faction'), active from 1968 against what it perceived as US imperialism. Its two leaders were Andreas Baader and Ulrike Meinhof, who died in prison under mysterious circumstances.

Baal, *n.* a divine title given to their chief male gods by the Phoenicians, or Canaanites. Their worship as deities of fertility, often orgiastic and of a phallic character, was strongly denounced by the Hebrew prophets; a false god. **Baalism**, *n.* worship of Baal; idolatry. **Baalist, Baalite,** *n.* a worshipper of Baal; an idolater. [Heb. *ba'al,* lord]

Baalbek, *n.* city of ancient Syria, in modern Lebanon, 60 km/36 miles NE of Beirut, 1150 m/3000 ft above sea level. Originally a centre of Baal worship. The Greeks identified Baal with Helios, the sun, and renamed Baalbek **Heliopolis**. Its ruins, including Roman temples, survive; the Temple of Bacchus, built in the 2nd century AD, is still almost intact.

baas, *n.* boss, overseer. [Dut. S Afr.]

Ba'ath Party, *n.* socialist party aiming at the extended union of all Arab countries, active in Iraq and Syria.

Bab, *n.* **Mirza Ali Mohammad** (1819–1850), Persian religious leader, born in Shiraz, founder of Babism. In 1844 he proclaimed that he was a gateway to the Hidden Imam, a new messenger of Allah who was to come. He gained a large following whose activities caused the Persian authorities to fear a rebellion, and who were therefore persecuted. The Bab was executed for heresy.

baba, *n.* a small cake soaked in rum (**rum baba**). [F from Pol. *baba,* old woman]

babacoote, *n.* the indri, a short-tailed woolly lemur, *Lichanotus brevicaudatus,* from Madagascar. [Malagasy *ba-bako-to*]

Babangida, *n.* **Ibrahim** (1941–), Nigerian politician and soldier. After training in the UK and the US, he became head of the Nigerian army in 1983 and in 1985 led a coup against President Buhari, assuming the presidency himself.

Babbage, *n.* **Charles** (1792–1871), English mathematician credited with being the inventor of the computer. He designed an analytical engine, a general-purpose computing device for performing different calculations according to a program input on punched cards (an idea borrowed from the Jacquard loom). This device was never built, but it embodied many of the principles on which modern digital computers are based.

Babbit, *n.* a dull, complacent business man (or other person) with orthodox views and little interest in cultural values. [after the leading character in the novel (1922) by Sinclair Lewis]

babbit metal, babbit's metal, *n.* an alloy of tin, antimony and copper, used in bearings to diminish friction. [Isaac *Babbit,* 1799–1862, American inventor]

Babbitt, *n.* **Milton** (1916–), US composer. After studying with Sessions he developed a personal style of serialism influenced by jazz. He is a leading composer of electronic music using the 1960 RCA Mark II synthesizer, which he helped to design.

babble, *v.i.* to talk childishly or inopportunely; to prattle; of streams, birds etc.; to make inarticulate sounds; of hounds, to give tongue without reason. *v.t.* to prate; to utter; to blab. *n.* prattle; shallow, foolish talk; confused murmur, as of a running brook. **babblement,** *n.* idle, foolish talk; senseless, indiscreet talk; babble, as of streams. **babbler,** *n.* an unintermitting and shallow talker; a gossip; one who tells secrets; a name for the long-legged thrushes. [from *ba ba,* the earliest attempts of a child to speak, -LE (cp. Dut. *babbelen,* F *babiller,* G *pappelen* etc.)]

babe, *n.* a young child, a baby; a foolish or childish person; (*sl., sometimes derog.*) a girl, woman. [prob. from obs. *baban,* imit. from childish speech (cp. BABBLE)]

Babel[1], *n.* the city and tower described in Gen. xi, the place where the confusion of tongues is said to have occurred; a lofty structure; a visionary project; noisy confusion, tumult, disorder. [Heb., confusion, Babylon (perh. from Assyr. *bab-ilu,* the Gate of God)]

Babel[2], *n.* **Isaak Emmanuilovich** (1894–1939/40), Russian writer. Born in Odessa, he was an ardent supporter of the Revolution and fought with Budyenny's cavalry in the Polish campaign of 1921–22, an experience which inspired *Konarmiya/Red Cavalry* (1926). His other works include *Odesskie rasskazy/Stories from Odessa* (1924), which portrays the life of the Odessa Jews.

Baber, *n.* title given to Zahir ud-din Muhammad, founder of the Mughal Empire in N India.

Babeuf, *n.* **François Noël** (1760–97), French revolutionary journalist, a pioneer of practical socialism. In 1794 he founded a newspaper in Paris, later known as the *Tribune of the People*, in which he demanded the equality of all people. He was guillotined for conspiring against the Directory (see FRENCH REVOLUTION).

Babington, *n.* **Anthony** (1561–86), English traitor who hatched a plot to assassinate Elizabeth I and replace her by Mary, Queen of Scots; its discovery led to Mary's execution and his own.

babiroussa, babirussa, *n.* the wild hog of eastern

Asia, in the male of which the upper canines grow through the lip and turn backwards like horns. [Malay *babī rūsa,* hog like a deer (*babi,* hog, *rusa,* deer)]

Babism, *n.* religious movement founded by Mirza Ali Mohammad ('the Bab'). An offshoot of Islam, its main difference is the belief that Mohammed was not the last of the prophets. The movement split into two groups after the death of the Bab: Baha'ullah, the leader of one of these groups, founded the Baha'i faith.

Babi Yar, *n.* site of a massacre of Jews by the Germans in 1941, near Kiev, USSR.

baboo, babu, *n.* a term used in Lower Bengal for a Hindu gentleman, corresponding to English Mr; an Indian clerk who writes English; a Bengali with a superficial English education. [Hind. *babu*]

baboon, *n.* †a grotesque decorative figure; the popular name of a large division of monkeys, with long dog-like snout, great canine teeth, callosities on the buttocks, and capacious cheek-pouches; an epithet of abuse. **baboonery,** *n.* an assemblage of baboons; behaviour like that of a baboon. [F *babuin,* mod. *babouin* (etym. unknown)]

babouche, babuche, *n.* a Turkish heelless slipper. [Arab.]

babuina, *n.* a female baboon. [fem. of mod. L *babuinus,* F *babouine*]

baby, *n.* an infant; a child in arms; †a grotesque decorative figure; a foolish, childish person; (*coll.*) a girl; a pet project. *v.t.* to make a baby of, to treat like a baby. **to hold the baby,** (*coll.*) to be left to bear the brunt of something; to be landed with something. **baby boomer,** *n.* (*coll.*) one born during an upswing in the birth-rate, esp. in the years following World War II. **baby-carriage,** *n.* (*N Am.*) a perambulator, pram. **baby-farmer,** *n.* one who takes in infants to nurse for payment. **baby grand,** *n.* a small grand piano. **Babygro®**, *n.* an all-in-one baby garment made of a stretch fabric. **baby-minder,** *n.* one who looks after infants when their parents are at work etc. **baby ribbon,** *n.* narrow ribbon. **baby-sitter,** *n.* a person who looks after a child while the parents are out. **baby-sit,** *v.i.* **baby-snatcher,** *n.* one who abducts an infant; a person who marries or goes out with someone much younger. **baby- walker,** *n.* a frame on wheels for supporting a baby learning to walk. **babyhood,** *n.* infancy. **babyish,** *a.* **babyishness,** *n.* **babyism,** *n.* [dim. of BABE]

Babylon, *n.* the ancient capital of the Chaldaean empire on the left bank of the Euphrates, whose hanging gardens were one of the seven wonders of the world; the mystical city mentioned in the Apocalypse; Rome; the papacy; a great and dissolute city. **Babylonian**, *a.* of or pertaining to Babylon; gigantic, magnificent, luxurious; popish, scarlet (from the fancied identification of the Scarlet Woman (Rev. xvii. 4) with Rome). **Babylonic**, **Babylonish,** *a.*[L *Babylōn,* Gr. *Babulōn,* Heb. *Bābel*]

Bacall, *n.* **Lauren**, stage name of Betty Joan Perske (1924–), striking US actress who became an overnight star when cast by Howard Hawks opposite Humphrey Bogart in *To Have and Have Not* (1944). She and Bogart married in 1945, and starred together in *The Big Sleep* (1946). Her other films include *The Cobweb* (1955) and *Harper* (1966).

bacca, baccy, *n.* short for TOBACCO.

baccalaureate, *n.* the French examination providing the school-leaving certificate and qualification for university entrance, also available on an international basis as an alternative to English A Levels; the university degree of bachelor. [med. L *baccalaureus,* as if from *bacca lauri,* laurel berry, late L *baccalāris,* BACHELOR]

baccara, baccarat, *n.* a gambling card game between banker and punters. [F *baccara*]

baccate, *a.* berried, bearing berries; berry-like. [L *baccātus* (*bacca,* berry)]

bacchanal, *a.* of or pertaining to Bacchus, the god of wine, or his festivities; hence characterized by drunken revelry. *n.* a votary of Bacchus; hence, a drunken reveller; a song or dance, or (*pl.*) a festival, in honour of Bacchus; an orgy. **bacchanalia,** *n.pl.* the festival of Bacchus; bacchanals; drunken revelry. **bacchanalian,** *a.* of or pertaining to bacchanals; bacchanal. *n.* a bacchanal; a drunken reveller. **bacchanalianism,** *n.* **bacchant,** *n.* a votary of Bacchus; hence, a drunken reveller. *a.* worshipping Bacchus; fond of drinking. **bacchante,** *n.* a priestess of Bacchus. **bacchantic,** *a.* **bacchic,** *a.* pertaining or relating to Bacchus or his worship; hence, frenzied; riotously festive. [L *bacchānālis* (*Bacchus,* Gr. *Bakchos,* the god of wine)]

bacchius, *n.* a metrical foot of three syllables, two long and one short. [L, from Gr. *bakcheios*]

Bacchus, *n.* in Greek and Roman mythology, the god of fertility and of wine.

bacci-, *comb. form* pertaining to a berry or berries. [L *bacca,* a berry]

bacciferous, *a.* bearing berries.

bacciform, *a.* berry-shaped.

baccivorous, *a.* berry-eating.

bach[1] BACHELOR.

bach[2], *n.* (*N. Zealand*) a small cottage or habitable hut.

Bach[1], *n.* **Carl Philip Emmanuel** (1714–88), German composer, son of J.S. Bach. He introduced a new 'homophonic' style, lighter and easier to follow, which influenced Mozart, Haydn, and Beethoven.

Bach[2], *n.* **Johann Christian** (1735–82), German composer, the 11th son of J.S. Bach, who became well known in Italy as a composer of operas. In 1762 he was invited to London, where he became music master to the royal family. He remained in England until his death, enjoying great popularity both as a composer and performer.

Bach[3], *n.* **Johann Sebastian** (1685–1750), German composer. His appointments included positions at the courts of Weimar and Anhalt-Köther, and from 1723 until his death, he was musical director at St Thomas's choir school in Leipzig. Bach was a master of counterpoint, and his music epitomizes the Baroque polyphonic style. His orchestral music includes the six *Brandenburg Concertos*, other concertos for clavier and for violin, and four orchestral suites. Bach's keyboard music, for clavier and for organ, his fugues and his choral music are of equal importance. He also wrote chamber music and songs.

Bach[4], *n.* **Wilhelm Friedemann** (1710–84), German composer, who was also an organist, improviser, and master of counterpoint. He was the eldest son of J.S. Bach.

Bacharach, *n.* a wine from the Rhine. [from *Bacharach,* a town on the Rhine]

Bachelard, *n.* **Gaston** (1884–1962), French philosopher and scientist who argued for a creative interplay between reason and experience. He attacked both Cartesian and positivist positions, insisting that science was derived neither from first principles nor directly from experience.

bachelor, *n.* an unmarried man; (also **bachelor girl**) an unmarried woman; a man or woman who has taken the first degree of a university below master or doctor; †a young knight who followed the banner of another. **knight bachelor,** a knight of the oldest order of knighthood; one knighted but not belonging to any of the special orders. **bachelor's buttons,** *n.pl.* the double variety of *Ranunculus acris;* applied also to several other plants with button-like flowers. **bachelorhood, bachelorship,** *n.* the state or condition of a bachelor; the position of bachelor of arts. **bachelorism,** *n.* a peculiarity of a bachelor. **bach**[1], *n.* (*coll.*) a bachelor. *v.i.* to live as a bachelor. [OF *bacheler,* late L *baccalāris* (cp. *baccalārius,* a farm labourer, perh. from late L *bacca,* L *vacca,* a cow)]

bachle, bauchle, *n.* (*Sc.*) an old worn-out shoe. [etym. doubtful]

bacillus, *n.* (*pl.* **-lli**) a microscopic, rod-like (disease-causing) bacterium. **bacillar,** *a.* shaped like a rod. **bacillary,** *a.* of, pertaining to or consisting of little rods; of, pertaining to or caused by bacilli. **bacilliform**, *a.* rod-shaped. [late L, a little rod, dim. of *bacu-*

lus, a stick]

back[1], *n.* the hinder part of the human body, from the neck to the lower extremity of the spine; the corresponding portion in the lower vertebrates, and the analogous part in the invertebrates; the surface of any object opposite to the face or front; the outer surface of the hand, the convex part of a book, the thick edge of a knife etc.; the hinder part, the rear, the part away from the actor or speaker; the ridge or upper surface of a hill; the keel of a ship; (*Mining*) a diagonal parting in coal; that side of an inclined mineral ore nearest the surface; one of the players whose duty it is to defend the goal in football (**half** and **three-quarter backs** are stationed nearer the front). *a.* situated behind or in the rear; coming back, turned back, reversed; behind in time; remote, distant, inferior. *adv.* in a direction to the rear; to the place from which one came; to a former state, position or condition; behind, not advancing, behindhand; in return, in retaliation; in a position behind, away from the front; in a state of check; in time past; again; in returning. *v.t.* to furnish with a back or backing; to be at the back of; to support materially or morally, to second, to uphold; to bet in favour of; to mount or get on the back of; to write on the back of, to countersign, to endorse; to cause to move back; to push back; to reverse the action of. *v.i.* to retreat, to recede; to move in a reversed direction. **at the back of one's mind,** not consciously thought of. **back and belly,** all over, completely. **back and forth,** backwards and forwards, up and down. **back of,** (*N Am.*) behind. **back to front,** in reverse; the wrong way round. **behind one's back,** secretly, surreptitiously. **on one's back,** floored; at the end of one's tether; laid up. **on the back burner,** put aside for the moment; not of immediate importance. **on the back of,** weighing as a heavy burden on; in addition to. **the back of beyond,** an extremely remote place. **to back down, out,** to move backwards; to retreat from a difficult situation. **to back into,** to knock into someone or something with a backward motion; (*Rail.*) to run backwards into a station or siding. **to back the field,** to bet against all the horses except one. **to back the wrong horse,** to make a bad choice. **to back up,** to support; in cricket and other games, to render support to a team-mate; to duplicate a computer data file as security against damage to the original. **to back water,** to reverse the motion of the oars when rowing. **to bend, lean, fall over backwards,** to go to extreme lengths to please or accommodate someone. **to break the back of,** to overburden; to perform the greater part of (a piece of work). **to put one's back into,** to make a strenuous effort to perform (a task). **to put, get the back up,** to offer resistance; to cause resentment; to feel resentment and show it. **to see the back of,** to get rid of. **to turn the back,** to turn away, to flee. **to turn the back (up)on,** to abandon, to forsake. **with one's back to the wall,** to be in a critical position. **back-band,** *n.* a strap or chain put across the cart saddle of a horse to support the shafts. **back-bencher,** *n.* (*Pol.*) a member of Parliament without portfolio. **backbite,** *v.t., v.i.* to slander, censure or speak ill of. **back-biter,** *n.* **back-blocks,** *n.pl.* (*Austral.*) the interior parts of the continent or a station, esp. those far from a river. **back-blocker,** *n.* one who lives there. **back-board,** *n.* a board forming the back of anything; a board attached to the rim of a water-wheel to prevent the water running off the floats; a board strapped across the back to prevent stooping. **back-bond,** *n.* (*Sc. Law*) a deed by which a party holding a title acknowledges that it is held in trust for a certain purpose. **backbone,** *n.* the bony framework of the back, the spine; the spinal column; a main support or axis; strength of character, firmness, decision. **to the backbone,** thoroughly. **backboned,** *a.* **back-boxes,** *n.pl.* (*Print.*) the boxes on the top of the upper case, usu. appropriated to small capitals. **back-breaking,** *a.* physically exhausting. **back-cast,** *n.* a reverse; a relapse. *a.* thrown backwards. **back-chat,** *n.* (*coll.*) flippant retort, answering back. **back-cloth,** *n.* the curtain at the back of a stage; background. **back-comb,** *v.t.* to comb backwards with short, sharp strokes, making (the hair) fuzzy. **back-country,** *n.* thinly populated districts. **backdate,** *v.t.* to apply retrospectively from a particular date (e.g. a pay rise). **back-door,** *n.* a back or private entrance; an indirect or circuitous way. *a.* clandestine. **back-draught,** *n.* a backward draught of air; a hood for producing back-draught in a fire. **back-end,** *n.* (*coll.*, dial.) late autumn. **backfall,** *n.* a throw or fall on the back in wrestling. **back-fire,** *n.* (*Motor*) premature combustion in the cylinder; a controlled fire set to make a barrier of scorched earth against the advance of a forest fire. *v.i.* to emit a loud noise as a result of premature combustion in the cylinder; (*coll.*) to fail and have the opposite effect. **back-formation,** *n.* the formation of a new word as if it were formed, e.g. by contraction, from an existing one (as *burgle* from *burglar*). **back-friend,** *n.* †a false or pretended friend; a reliable friend; a backer. **background,** *n.* the ground or surface behind the chief objects of contemplation; that part of a picture, stage-scene or description which represents this; the setting; (*fig.*) inferior position; obscurity; a person's upbringing, education and history. **background radiation,** *n.* low-level radiation present in the soil and atmosphere. **back hair,** *n.* the long hair at the back of a woman's head. **back-hand,** *n.* handwriting sloped backwards; the hand turned backwards (as at tennis) to take a ball at the left. **back-handed,** *a.* with the back of the hand; directed backwards; indirect. **back-hander,** *n.* a blow with the back of the hand; a drink out of one's proper turn; a bribe. **back-lash,** *n.* jarring reaction in a piece of mechanism. **back-light,** *n.* (*Cinema*) a light projected on a subject from a source behind the camera. **back-lock,** *n.* a trick in wrestling. **backlog,** *n.* (*N Am.*) a large log placed at the back of the fire; reserves or arrears of unfulfilled orders; an accumulation of business. **back marker,** *n.* the competitor at the back in a race. **back-number,** *n.* a past issue of a newspaper or magazine; an out-of-date person or thing. **back pack,** *n.* a rucksack; the oxygen supply etc. carried by an astronaut. *v.i.* to hike with a rucksack. **back-pages,** *n.pl.* pages on the left-hand side of an open book. **back passage,** *n.* (*coll.*) the rectum. **back-pay,** *n.* arrears of pay. **back-pedal,** *v.i.* to press back the pedals of a cycle; to reverse a course of action; to restrain one's enthusiasm. **back-piece,** *n.* a piece of armour for the back; a piece forming the back of anything. **back-plate,** *n.* armour for the back, corresponding to the breastplate in front; the piece forming the back of anything. **back-pressure,** *n.* resistance to the working of the piston, caused by waste steam or atmospheric pressure. **backroom boys,** *n.pl.* (*coll.*) scientists and others who work in the background unrecognized. **back-scratcher,** *n.* a hand-shaped appliance with out-stretched fingers for scratching the back; a flatterer. **back-scratching,** *n.* flattery; toadyism. **back seat,** *n.* the seat at the back of anything, such as a car or theatre; a position of less importance. **to take a back seat,** *n.* to accept an inferior role; to withdraw from the forefront. **back-seat driver,** *n.* a passenger in a car who offers unwanted advice; one who offers advice on matters which do not concern him or her. **backset,** *n.* a setback, a reverse; a counter current. **back settlement,** *n.* an outlying settlement; (*pl.*) the backwoods. **back-settler,** *n.* a backwoodsman. **backside,** *n.* the back or hinder portion of anything; (*coll.*) the buttocks. **back-sight,** *n.* a sight taken backwards in land surveying; the sight of a rifle near the stock. **back-slang,** *n.* a peculiar kind of slang in which ordinary words are pronounced backwards (as, *Cool the eslop* (or *slop*), Look, the police). **backslide,** *v.i.* to fall into wrongdoing or false opinions; to relapse. **backslider,** *n.* **back-spacer,** *n.* a typewriter key for moving the carriage backwards. **back-speed,** *n.* the second-speed gear of a lathe. **back spin,** *n.* in tennis, golf etc., the spin of a ball against the direction it is moving, imparted to dull the bounce. **backstage,** *a.* behind the scenes; out of public view. **backstairs,** *n.pl.* stairs at the back of a house; the private stairs in a house or palace for the use of servants etc. *a.* clandestine, underhand, scandalous. **back-stays,** *n.pl.* rope or stays extending with a slant aft from the mast-heads to the sides of a ship, and serving, with the shrouds, to support the mast under press of sail. **back-stitch,** *n.* a method of sewing with stitches that are made to overlap. *v.t., v.i.* to sew in this manner. **back street,** *n.* a street away from the centre of the town; *pl.* the poorer streets of a town. **back-street abortion,** *n.* an abortion performed by an unqualified person. **back-string,** *n.* a string at the back; the fastener of a pinafore. **back-stroke,** *n.* a return stroke; a swimming stroke. †**backsword,** *n.* a sword with only one sharp edge; a single-stick; hence, a backswordman. †**backsword-man,** *n.* one skilled in the use of the backsword. **backtrack,** *v.i.* to retrace one's steps; to reverse an opinion, attitude etc. **backup,** *n.* support; reinforcement, reserve. **backveld,** *n.* (*S Afr.*) country far removed from towns. *a.* remote, rural, primitive. **backwash,** *n.* the wash from the oars of a boat in front; the dragging motion of a receding wave; a backward current; eddy or swirl caused by a ship's propeller; reaction; aftermath; the rush of air from an aircraft engine. **backwater,** *n.* water dammed back or that has overflowed; a piece of water without current fed by the back flow of a river; a backward current of water; a creek or lagoon separated from the sea by a narrow strip of land and communicating therewith by barred outlets; the wash thrown back by a water-wheel or the paddles or screws of steamboats. **back-way,** *n.* a way leading to the back; a roundabout way; a bypath. **backwoods,** *n.pl.* remote, uncleared forest land; (*derog.*) a remote, uncultured area. **backwoodsman,** *n.* a settler in the backwoods; a back-settler; (*coll.*) a peer who rarely attends the House of Lords. **backed,** *a.* (chiefly in comb.) provided with a back; supported, seconded, betted on; endorsed, accepted. **backer,** *n.* one who backs or supports, by money or credit; one who bets on a horse or an event; a book-maker, a bookie; (*Build.*) a small slate laid on the back of a large one at certain points. **backing,** *n.* supporting, seconding; the thing or the body of persons which forms a back or support; money supplied for a project by an investor; musical accompaniment, esp. for a popular song; a piece forming the back or lining the back; putting back; backward motion, esp. of the wind in an opposite direction to that of the sun; opaque varnish put on back of a negative to obviate halation; perfecting a sheet printed on one side by printing on the other; putting the shoulder on a book before putting the cover on; (*pl.*) refuse from wool or flax after dressing it. **backing group,** *n.* one that provides a musical backing. [OE *bæc*]

back[2], *n.* a large tub used in brewing, distilling, dyeing etc. [Dut. *bak,* trough, tub, F *bac,* ferry-boat, punt, late L *baccus,* ferry-boat]

backet, *n.* (*Sc.*) a shallow wooden trough or hod for carrying coals, mortar and the like. [F *baquet,* dim. of *bac,* BACK[2]]

backgammon, *n.* a game played by two persons on a table with draughtsmen, the moves being determined by throwing dice; the highest win in backgammon. *v.t.* to defeat at backgammon. [BACK, GAME]

backing BACK[1].

backsheesh BAKSHEESH.

backwards, backward, *adv.* with the back foremost; towards the back or rear; behind, towards the starting-point; towards past time; towards a worse state or condition, in reverse order; †the wrong way, perversely, contrariwise. **backward,** *a.* directed to the back or rear; directed the way from which one has come; reversed, reluctant, unwilling; esp. of the season, crops etc., behind in time, late; behind in progress; towards or into past time. †*n.* time past. **backward(s) and forward(s),** to and fro; uncertain, vacillating. **backwardation,** *n.* (*Stock Exchange*) a consideration paid by a seller of stock for the privilege of delaying its delivery. **backwardly,** *adv.* in a backward direction; in a reluctant or negligent manner. **backwardness,** *n.* [orig. *abackward*]

baclava, BAKLAVA.

bacon, *n.* the back and sides of a pig, cured by salting and drying with or without wood-smoke; †a rustic, a chawbacon. **to bring home the bacon,** (*coll.*) to succeed; to provide a living. **to save one's bacon,** to escape from injury or loss. **bacon-chops, bacon-slicer, chawbacon,** *n.* (*sl.*) a rustic, a clod-hopper; a clownish fellow. **bacon-like,** *a.* in a state of fatty degeneration. **bacony,** *a.* [OF, from OHG *bacho* (MHG *backe*), buttock, ham]

Bacon[1], *n.* **Francis** (1561–1626), English politician, philosopher, and essayist. He became Lord Chancellor in 1618, and the same year confessed to bribe-taking, was fined £40,000 (which was paid by the king), and spent four days in the Tower of London. Although he admitted taking the money, he claimed that he had not always given the verdict to his paymasters. His works include *Essays* (1597), notable for pith and brevity; *The Advancement of Learning* (1605), a seminal work discussing scientific method; the *Novum Organum* (1620), in which he redefined the task of natural science, seeing it as a means of empirical discovery and a method of increasing human power over nature; and *The New Atlantis* (1626), describing a Utopian state in which scientific knowledge is systematically sought and exploited.

Bacon[2], *n.* **Francis** (1909–), British painter, born in Dublin. He came to London in 1925 and taught himself to paint. He practised abstract art, then developed a distorted expressionist style, with tortured figures presented in loosely defined space. Since 1945 he has focused on studies of figures, as in his series of screaming popes based on the portrait of Innocent X by Velázquez.

Baconian, *a.* of or pertaining to Francis Bacon or his inductive philosophy; experimental, inductive. *n.* a follower of the inductive system of natural philosophy; (*pop.*) a believer in the conceit that Bacon was really the author of Shakespeare's works.

bactericide, *n.* an agent that destroys bacteria.

bacteri(o)-, *comb. form* pertaining to bacteria.

bacteriology, *n.* the scientific study of bacteria. **bacteriological,** *a.* **bacteriologist,** *n.*

bacteriolysis, *n.* the destruction of bacteria. **bacteriolytic,** *a.* [Gr. *lusis,* dissolution]

bacteriophage, *n.* a virus which destroys bacteria. **bacteriophagic,** *a.* [Gr. *phagein,* to eat]

bacteriostasis, *n.* inhibition of the growth of bacterial cells. **bacteriostatic,** *a.* [Gr. *stasis,* standing]

bacterium, *n.* (*pl.* **-ria**) a member of a class (Schizomycetes) of microscopic unicellular organisms found in soil, water and as saprophytes or parasites in organic bodies. **bacterial,** *a.* [Gr. *baktērion,* dim. of *baktron,* a stick]

bacteroid, *a.* of the nature of or resembling a bacterium.

Bactria, *n.* former region of central Asia (now Afghanistan, Pakistan and Soviet Central Asia) which was partly conquered by Alexander the Great. During the 6rd–3th centuries BC it was a centre of E–W trade and cultural exchange. **Bactrian,** *n., a.* (one) of the two species of camel with two humps, found in Asia.

baculine, *n.* characterized by the stick, cane or flogging. [L *baculum,* a stick]

bad, *a.* (*comp.* **worse,** *superl.* **worst**) not good, worthless; defective, faulty, incorrect; ill, evil, hurtful, wicked, morally depraved; noxious, painful, dangerous, pernicious; in ill-health, sick; injured, diseased; (*Law*) invalid; (*N Am. sl.*) very good. *n.* that which is bad; a bad state or condition. **to go bad,** to decay. **to go to the bad,** to go to ruin, to go to the dogs. **to the bad,** to ruin; to the wrong side of an account. **bad blood,** *n.* angry feeling, enmity. **bad debt,** *n.* a debt that cannot be recovered. **bad egg, lot, penny,** *n.* a bad speculation; a ne'er-do-well. **bad form,** *n.* bad manners; lack of breeding. **bad grace,** *n.* unwillingness, reluctance. **bad hat,** *n.* a rogue, ne'er-do-well. **bad lands,** *n.pl.* tracts of arid country in the western States of America; unsafe parts of a country. **bad mouth,** *v.t.* (*coll.*) to abuse, to criticize. **bad shot,** *n.* a wrong guess. **bad word,** *n.* criticism of someone; (*coll.*) a swear-word. **baddie, baddy,** *n.* (*coll.*) a criminal or wrong-doer, esp. an evil character in fiction, cinema, television or radio. **baddish,** *a.* rather bad. **badly,** *adv.* (comp. **worse,** superl. **worst**) in a bad manner; improperly, wickedly, evilly; unskilfully, imperfectly; defectively; faultily; dangerously, disastrously; (*coll.*) very much, by much. **to want something badly,** to want something very much. **badness,** *n.* the quality of being bad; inferiority; incorrectness, faultiness; wickedness; worthlessness. [etym. doubtful]

bade, *past* BID.

Baden, *n.* former state of SW Germany, which had Karlsruhe as its capital. Baden was captured from the Romans in 282 by the Alemanni; later it became a margravate, and in 1806 a grand duchy. A state of the German empire (1871–1918), then a republic, and under Hitler a *Gau* (province), it was divided between the *Länder* of Württemberg-Baden and Baden in 1945, and in 1952 made part of Baden-Württemberg.

Baden-Powell, *n.* **Robert Stephenson Smyth, 1st Baron Baden-Powell** (1857–1941), British general, founder of the Scout Association. He fought in defence of Mafeking (now Mafikeng) during the Second South African War. After 1907 he devoted his time to developing the Scout movement, which rapidly spread throughout the world. He was created a peer in 1929.

Baden-Württemberg, *n.* administrative region (German *Land*) of West Germany. **area** 35,800 sq km/ 13,819 sq miles. **capital** Stuttgart. **towns** Mannheim, Karlsruhe, Freiburg, Heidelberg, Heilbronn, Pforzheim, Ulm. **physical** Black Forest; Rhine boundary south and west; source of the Danube; see also Swabia. **population** (1988) 9,390,000. **products** wine, jewellery, watches, clocks, musical instruments, textiles, chemicals, iron, steel, electrical equipment, surgical instruments.

Bader, *n.* **Douglas** (1910–82), British fighter pilot. He lost both legs in a flying accident in 1931, but had a distinguished flying career in World War II. He was knighted (1976) for his work with disabled people.

badge¹, *n.* a distinctive mark, sign or token; an emblem sewn on clothing; (*Her.*) a cognizance; (*Naut.*) an ornament on the quarters of small vessels, near the stern; a feature or quality that characterizes. *v.t.* to mark with or as with a badge. [etym. unknown]

badge² BAG².

badger¹, *n.* a plantigrade animal about the size of a fox, with thick body and short legs, *Meles vulgaris,* found in Britain, Europe and Asia; hence, a painter's brush, or angler's fly, made of badgers' hair. *v.t.* to worry, to tease, to annoy like dogs baiting a badger. **badger-baiting, badger-drawing,** *n.* the setting of dogs to draw a badger from its earth or from a barrel. **badger-dog,** *n.* the German dachshund, with long body and short legs, used to draw badgers. †**badger-legged,** *a.* having legs of unequal length, as those of the badger were popularly supposed to be. [etym. doubtful (prob. in allusion to white mark on face)]

badger², *n.* (*dial.*) a huckster; a corn-dealer; a travelling provision-dealer. [etym. doubtful]

badigeon, *n.* a mixture of plaster and freestone used by sculptors to repair defects in stone, and by builders to present the appearance of stone; a mixture of sawdust and glue, used to conceal defects in woodwork. [F, etym. unknown]

badinage, *n.* light good-humoured, playful talk; banter. [F, from *badiner,* to jest (*badin,* silly, late L *badāre,* to gape)]

badminton, *n.* a game resembling lawn-tennis, but played, usu. indoors, with shuttlecocks instead of balls; a kind of claret-cup. [name of country seat of Duke of Beaufort]

Badoglio, *n.* **Pietro** (1871–1956), Italian soldier and Fascist politician. A veteran of campaigns against the peoples of Tripoli and Cyrenaica, in 1935 he became commander in chief in Ethiopia, adopting ruthless measures to break patriot resistance, and being created viceroy of Ethiopia and duke of Addis Ababa in 1936. He succeeded Mussolini as prime minister of Italy from July 1943 to June 1944.

Baedeker, *n.* **Karl** (1801–59), German publisher of foreign-travel guides; these are now based in Hamburg (before World War II in Leipzig).

Baekeland, *n.* **Leo Hendrik** (1863–1944), US chemist, the inventor of Bakelite, the first commercial plastic. He later made a photographic paper, Velox, which could be developed in artificial light.

baff, *v.t.* (*Sc.*) a blow with something soft; (*Golf*) to strike the ground with a club and send the ball up in the air. **baffing-spoon,** *n.* (*Golf*) a baffy. **baffy,** *n.* a club for lofting. [perh. from OF *baffe,* a blow; or merely imitative]

Baffin, *n.* **William** (1584–1622), English explorer and navigator. In 1616, he and Robert Bylot explored Baffin Bay, NE Canada, and reached latitude 77° 45′6 N, which for 236 years remained the 'furthest north'.

baffle, *v.t.* †to disgrace; to scoff at; to frustrate, elude, escape, circumvent; to thwart, defeat; to confound. *v.i.* to struggle ineffectually. *n.* a defeat; (*Acous.*) a rigid appliance that regulates the distribution of sound-waves from a producer. **baffle-board,** *n.* a device to prevent the carrying of noise. **baffle-plate,** *n.* (*Eng.*) a plate used to direct the flow of fluid. **baffler,** *n.* **baffling,** *a.* bewildering; thwarting; of winds, variable, shifting. **bafflingly,** *adv.* [perh. F *beffler,* to deceive, mock, or *bafoüer,* to hoodwink; (OF *befel,* mockery, It. *beffa,* Prov. *bafa,* a scoff, perh. from *baf!* an imitative int.)]

baft¹, *n.* a cheap coarse fabric. [prob. Pers., wrought, woven]

baft², *adv.* †behind; abaft, astern. [OE *beæftan* (*be,* by, *æftan,* behind)]

BAFTA, (*abbr.*) British Academy of Film and Television Arts.

bag¹, *n.* a pouch, small sack or other flexible receptacle; a measure of quantity, varying with different commodities; the contents of such a measure; a game-bag, the result of a day's sport or of a hunting expedition; a purse, a money-bag; an udder; a sac or bag-like receptacle in animal bodies containing some secretion; (*pl.*) loose clothes, esp. trousers; (*pl.*) (*coll.*) quantities; (*sl.*) a slovenly, bad tempered or ugly woman, often in *old bag. v.t.* to put into a bag; to put into a game-bag; hence, to shoot, to catch; (*coll.*) to take, seize, appropriate. *v.i.* to swell as a bag; to hang loosely; (*Naut.*) to drop away from the direct course. **bag and baggage,** with all belongings; entirely, completely. **bag of bones,** a living skeleton, someone very thin. **bag o' moonshine,** (*coll.*) nonsense. **the whole bag of tricks,** everything; all means or expedients. **to give one the bag to hold,** to slip off, leave in the lurch. **to let the cat out of the bag,** to reveal the secret. **bag-fox,** *n.* a fox brought alive to the meet and turned out of a bag. **bag lady,** *n.* (*coll.*) a female vagrant. **bagman,** *n.* (*coll.*) a travelling salesman; a vagrant; (*N Am. sl.*), one who collects and transports money for gangsters. **bag-swinger,** *n.* (*Austral.*) a book-maker. **bag-wash,** *n.* a system of laundry-work by which a comprehensive charge is made for a bagful of garments. **bag-wig,** *n.* a wig fashionable in the 18th cent. in which the back hair was enclosed in a bag. **bagful,** *n.* as much as a bag will hold. **bagging,** *n.* cloth, canvas or other material for bags. **baggy,** *a.* loose; bulging out like a bag; of trousers etc., stretched by wear. **bagginess,** *n.* looseness. [etym. doubtful; perh. Icel. *baggi*]

bag², (*dial.*) **badge²,** *v.t.* to cut (wheat, grass etc.) with a hook. **bagging-hook,** *n.* a kind of sickle or hook used in bagging. [etym. unknown]

bagasse, *n.* the refuse products in sugar-making; cane-trash. [Sp. *bagazo,* residue]

bagatelle, *n.* a trifle, a trumpery amount; a game played on a nine-holed board, with nine balls and a cue; a light piece of music. [F, from It. *bagatelle,* a trifle (perh. dim. of *baga,* baggage)]

Bagehot, *n.* **Walter** (1826–77), British writer and economist, author of *The English Constitution* (1867), a classic analysis of the British political system. He was editor of *The Economist* magazine (1860–1877).

bagel, *n.* a doughnut-shaped bread roll. [Yiddish, *beygel*]

baggage, *n.* portable belongings, esp. the tents, furniture, utensils and other necessaries of an army; luggage; a woman of loose character; a playful arch young woman. *a.* used for carrying or looking after or conveying baggage. **baggage-car,** *n.* (*N Am.*) a railway luggage-van. **baggage-man, -master,** *n.* (*N Am.*) a guard in charge of passengers' luggage. **baggage-train,** *n.* the part of an army that convoys the baggage. [OF *bagage* (*baguer,* to tie up, or *bagues,* bundles; It. *baga,* a wine-skin; see also BAG[1])]

Baggara, *n.* a Bedouin people of the Nile Basin, principally in Kordofan, Sudan, W of the White Nile. They are Muslims, traditionally occupied in cattle-breeding and big-game hunting.

baggit, *n.* (*Sc.*) a salmon that has just spawned. [prob. Sc. form of BAGGED, see BAG[1]]

Baghdad, *n.* historic city and capital of Iraq, on the Tigris; population (1985) 4,649,000. Industries include oil refining, distilling, tanning, tobacco processing, and the manufacture of textiles and cement. Founded 762, it became Iraq's capital in 1921.

bagman BAG[1].

bagnio, *n.* (*pl.* **-nios**) a bathing-house, a bath; an Oriental prison for slaves; a brothel. [It. *bagno,* L *balneum,* a bath]

bagpipe, *n.* a musical instrument of great antiquity, now chiefly used in the Scottish Highlands, consisting of a wind-bag and several reed-pipes into which the air is pressed by the player.

baguette, -guet, *n.* a precious stone cut into a rectangular shape; a narrow stick of French bread. [F rod, from L *baculum*]

bah, *int.* an expression of contempt. [perh. from F *bah!*]

bahadur, *n.* a ceremonious title formerly given in India to European officers. [Hind., brave]

Bahadur Shah II, *n.* (1775–1862) last of the Mughal emperors of India. He reigned, though in name only (including under the British), as king of Delhi (1837–57), when he was hailed by the mutineers (see INDIAN MUTINY) as an independent emperor at Delhi. After the mutiny he was deported to Rangoon, Burma, with his family.

Baha'i, *n.* religion founded in the 19th century from a Muslim splinter group, Babism, by the Persian Baha'ullah. The most important principle of his message was that all great religious leaders are manifestations of the unknowable God and all scriptures are sacred. There is no priesthood: all Baha'is are expected to teach, and to work towards world unification. There are about 4.5 million Baha'is worldwide. **Bahaism,** *n.* **Bahaist,** *n.* [Pers. *baha'i,* lit. of glory]

Bahamas, *n.* Commonwealth of the. **area** 13,864 sq km/5352 sq miles. **capital** Nassau on New Providence. **physical** comprises 700 tropical coral islands and about 1000 cays. **population** (1986) 236,171; annual growth rate 1.8%. **exports** cement, pharmaceuticals, petroleum products, crawfish, rum, pulpwood; over half the islands' employment comes from tourism. **language** English. **religion** 26% Roman Catholic, 21% Anglican, 48% other Protestants.

Baha'ullah, *n.* title of Mirza Hosein Ali (1817–92), Persian founder of the Baha'i religion. Baha'ullah, 'God's Glory', proclaimed himself as the prophet the Bab had foretold.

Bahrain, *n.* State of (*Dawlat al Bahrayn*). **area** 688 sq km/266 sq miles. **capital** Manama on the largest island (also called Bahrain). **towns** oil port Mina Sulman. **physical** 33 islands, flat and hot. **population** (1988 est.) 421,000 (two thirds are nationals); annual growth rate 4.4%. **exports** oil and natural gas. **language** Arabic, Farsi, English. **religion** Muslim (Shi'ite 60%, Sunni 40%).

baignoire, *n.* a box at the theatre on the lowest tier at the level of the stalls. [F, orig. a vessel for bathing in, from *baigner,* to bathe]

Baikal, *n.* (Russian **Baykal Ozero**) largest freshwater lake in Asia 31,500 sq km/12,150 sq miles and deepest in the world (up to 1740 m/5710 ft), in S Siberia, USSR. Fed by more than 300 rivers, it is drained only by the Lower Angara. Baikal has sturgeon fisheries and rich fauna.

Baikonur, *n.* the main Soviet launch site for spacecraft, at Tyuratam, near the Aral Sea.

bail[1], *n.* the temporary release of a prisoner from custody on security given for his or her due surrender when required; the money security, or the person or persons giving security, for the due surrender of a prisoner temporarily released; security, guarantee. *v.t.* to procure the liberation of by giving sureties; to admit to or release on bail; to deliver (goods) in trust on an expressed or implied contract. **to bail out,** to procure release on bail from prison. **to give leg-bail,** to run away. **to stand bail,** to secure freedom until trial for an accused on payment of surety. **bail-bond,** *n.* a bond entered into by a prisoner upon release on bail, and his sureties. **bailsman,** *n.* one who gives bail. **bailable,** *a.* entitled to be admitted to bail; admitting of bail. **bailment,** *n.* delivery of goods; delivery in trust; the bailing of a prisoner. [OF *bail,* safe keeping, from *bailler,* L *bāiulāre,* to carry, to guard (*bāiulus,* a porter)]

bail[2], *n.* a hoop or ring; the arched support for an awning or hood; the handle of a kettle. [ME *beyl,* Icel. *beygla,* hoop, guard of a sword-hilt]

bail[3], *n.* a division between the stalls of a stable; (*Austral.*) a framework for securing the head of a cow while she is being milked; (*pl.*) (*Cricket*) the crosspieces laid on the top of the wicket; †the outer line of fortifications, a palisade; †the wall of the outer courtyard in a feudal castle, a bailey. *v.i.* to surrender by throwing up the arms. **bailer,** *n.* (*Cricket*) a ball that hits off the bails. †*v.t.* to confine. [OF *bail* (etym. doubtful, perh. from *baillier,* to enclose)]

bail[4], bale[3], *v.t.* to throw (water) out of a boat with a shallow vessel; to empty a boat of water. **to bail out** BALE[3]. **bailer,** *n.* one who or that which bails water out of a boat etc. [obs. n. *bail,* a bucket, bailer, F *baile,* a bucket (prob. from late L *bacula,* dim. of *baca, bacca,* a shallow vessel)]

bailee, *n.* one to whom goods are entrusted for a specific purpose. [BAIL[1]]

bailey , *n.* the wall enclosing the outer court of a feudal castle; the outer court itself; any other courts or enclosures of courts, the *outer bailey* or the *inner bailey.* **Old Bailey,** the Central Criminal Court standing at the outer boundary of the old wall of London. [BAIL[3] (perh. from med. L *balium*)]

Bailey, *n.* **Donald Coleman** (1901–85), English engineer, inventor in World War II of the portable **Bailey bridge**, made of interlocking, interchangeable, adjustable and easily transportable units.

bailie, *n.* †a Scottish magistrate with duties corresponding to those of an English sheriff; now a Scottish municipal magistrate corresponding to an English alderman. **water-bailies,** *n.pl.* (*Sc.*) constables specially employed in carrying out the Tweed Fisheries Acts. [ME *bailli,* OF *bailli* (prev. *baillis, baillif*), BAILIFF]

bailiff, *n.* an officer appointed for the administration of justice in a certain bailiwick or district; †a king's administrative officer (still used in *High Bailiff of Westminster, Bailiff of Dover Castle*); a foreign magistrate of similar standing (e.g. *Bailly* or first civil officer of the Channel Isles); a sheriff's officer who executes writs and distrains; an agent or steward to a landowner. [OF *baillif* (nom. *baillis*), late L *bāiukīvus* (see BAIL[1])]

bailiwick, *n.* the district within which a bailie or bailiff possesses jurisdiction. [BAILIE, -WICK]

bailment BAIL[1].

bailor, *n.* (*Law*) one who entrusts another person, called the bailee, with goods for a specific purpose.[BAIL[1]]

Bainbridge, *n.* **Beryl** (1933–), English novelist, originally an actress, whose works have the drama and economy of a stage-play. They include *The Dressmaker* (1973), *The Bottle Factory Outing* (1974), and the collected short stories in *Mum and Mr Armitage* (1985).

bain-marie, *n.* a vessel of boiling water into which saucepans are put to warm; a double saucepan. [F (L *balneum Mariae,* the bath of Mary, i.e. the Virgin)]

Bairam, *n.* the name of two Muslim festivals following the Ramadan, the *Lesser* lasting three days, the *Greater,* which falls seventy days later, lasting four days. [Turk., from Pers. *bairām*]

Baird, *n.* **John Logie** (1888–1946), Scottish electrical engineer, who pioneered television. In 1925 he gave the first public demonstration of television, and in 1926 pioneered fibre optics, radar (in advance of Robert Watson-Watt), and 'noctovision', a system for seeing at night by using infrared rays.

bairn, *n.* (*Sc.*) a child of either sex. [OE *bearn* (cp. Icel. *barn,* Goth. *barn,* OTeut. *beran,* to bear)]

†**baisemain,** *n.* (*usu. pl.*) kissing hands; compliments, respects. [F *baiser,* to kiss, *main,* hand]

bait, *v.t.* to furnish (a hook, gin, snare etc.) with real or sham food; to tempt, entice, allure; to give food to (a horse) on a journey, to feed; to set dogs to worry (an animal); to worry, harass, torment. *v.i.* to stop on a journey for rest or refreshment. *n.* an attractive morsel put on a hook, gin, snare etc., to attract fish or animals; worms, insects, grubs, small fish etc., so used; food, refreshment on a journey; a halt for refreshment; a temptation, allurement. **live bait,** small fish used alive for bait. **baiting,** *n.* (*usu. in comb.*) worrying with dogs, as *badger-baiting, bear-baiting, bull-baiting.* [Icel. *beita,* to cause to bite (*bita,* to bite)]

baize, *n.* a coarse woollen stuff something like flannel. [F *baies,* pl. fem of a. *bai* (L *badius*), chestnut-coloured]

bake, *v.t.* to cook by dry conducted (as opposed to radiated) heat, to cook in an oven or on a heated surface; to dry and harden by means of fire or by the sun's rays; †to harden by means of extreme cold. *v.i.* to cook food by baking; to undergo the process of baking; to become dry and hard by heat. **to bake blind** BLIND. **bakehouse,** *n.* a house or building in which baking is carried on. **bake-meat, baked-meat,** *n.* pastry, a pie. **bakestone,** *n.* a stone or metal plate on which muffins and cakes are baked. **baked,** *a.* **half-baked,** *a.* (*coll.*) raw, uncouth, half-witted, soft. **baked Alaska,** *n.* a dessert of ice-cream covered with meringue baked in an oven. **baked beans,** *n.pl.* haricot beans baked and usu. tinned in tomato sauce. **baker,** *n.* one whose occupation is to bake bread, biscuits etc. †**baker-foot,** *n.* a distorted foot. †**baker-kneed, baker-legged,** *a.* having the right knee-joint inclined inwards. **baker's dozen,** *n.* thirteen. **baker's itch,** *n.* a kind of psoriasis affecting the hands of bakers. **bakery,** *n.* the trade or calling of a baker; a bakehouse; a baker's establishment. **baking,** *n.* the action of the verb **to bake,** the quantity baked at one operation. **baking-powder,** *n.* a powder of bicarbonate of soda and tartaric acid used as a raising agent. [OE *bacan*]

Bakelite®, *n.* a synthetic resin much used for insulating purposes and in the manufacture of plastics, paints and varnishes. [L.H. BAEKELAND]

Baker[1], *n.* **Benjamin** (1840–1907), English engineer, who designed (with English engineer John Fowler 1817–1898) London's first underground railway (the Metropolitan and District) in 1869, the Forth Bridge, Scotland, 1890, and the original Aswan Dam on the River Nile, Egypt.

Baker[2], *n.* **Kenneth (Wilfrid)** (1934–), British Conservative politician, education secretary (1986–89), and chair of the Conservative Party from 1989.

Baker III, *n.* **James (Addison)** (1930–), US Republican politician. Under President Reagan, he was White House Chief of Staff (1981–85) and Treasury secretary (1985–88). After managing Bush's successful presidential campaign in 1988, Baker was appointed secretary of state in 1989.

Bakke, *n.* **Allan** (1940–), US student who, in 1978, gave his name to a test case claiming 'reverse discrimination' when appealing against his exclusion from medical school, since less well-qualified blacks were to be admitted as part of a special programme for ethnic minorities. He won his case against quotas before the Supreme Court, although other affirmative action for minority groups was still endorsed.

baklava, *n.* a cake made from layered pastry strips with nuts and honey. [Turkish]

baksheesh, bakhshish, *n.* a gratuity, a tip (used without the article). [Pers., a present]

Bakst, *n.* **Leon** (assumed name of Leon Rosenberg) (1886–1924), Russian painter and theatrical designer. He used intense colours and fantastic images from Oriental and folk art, with an Art Nouveau tendency to graceful surface pattern. His designs for Diaghilev's touring *Ballets Russes* made a deep impression in Paris (1909–14).

Baku, *n.* capital city of the Azerbaijan Republic, USSR, and industrial port (oil refining) on the Caspian Sea; population (1987) 1,741,000. Baku is a centre of the Soviet oil industry, and is linked by pipelines with Batumi on the Black Sea.

Bakunin, *n.* **Mikhail** (1814–76), Russian anarchist, active in Europe. In 1848 he was expelled from France as a revolutionary agitator. In Switzerland in the 1860s he became recognized as the leader of the anarchist movement. In 1869 he joined the First International (a coordinating socialist body) but, after stormy conflicts with Karl Marx, was expelled in 1872.

Balaclava, Battle of, in the Crimean War, an engagement on 25 Oct. 1854 near a town in Ukraine, 10 km/6 miles SE of Sevastopol. It was the scene of the ill-timed **Charge of the Light Brigade** of British cavalry against the Russian entrenched artillery. Of the 673 soldiers who took part, there were 272 casualties. **Balaclava helmets** were knitted hoods worn here by soldiers in the bitter weather.

Balakirev, *n.* **Mily Alexeyevich** (1837–1910), Russian composer. He wrote orchestral and piano music, songs, and a symphonic poem *Tamara,* all imbued with the Russian national character and spirit. He was leader of the group known as The Five and taught its members, Mussorgsky, Cui, Rimsky-Korsakov, and Borodin.

balalaika, *n.* a three-stringed triangular-shaped musical instrument resembling a guitar. [Rus.]

balance, *n.* (*often pl.*) a pair of scales; other instrument used for weighing; a zodiacal constellation, Libra; the seventh sign of the zodiac, which the sun enters at the autumnal equinox; a contrivance for regulating the speed of a clock or watch; equipoise, equality of weight or power; the amount necessary to make two unequal amounts equal; an impartial state of mind; that which renders weight or authority equal; the difference between the debtor and creditor side of the account; harmony of design, perfect proportion; (*coll.*) the remainder, the residue. *v.t.* to weigh; to compare by weighing; to compare; to bring to an equipoise, equalize, to steady; to adjust an account, to make two amounts equal; to sway backwards and forwards. *v.i.* to be in equipoise, to have equal weight or force; to oscillate; in dancing, to move to and fro in an opposite direction to that of one's partner. **balance of mind,** sanity. **balance of payments,** the difference over a period of time between the total payments (for goods and services) to, and total receipts from, abroad. **balance of power,** a condition of equilibrium among sovereign states, supposed to be a guarantee of peace. **balance of trade,** the difference between the imports and exports of a country. **in the balance,** in an uncertain or undecided state. **on balance,** taking all factors into consideration. **to hold the balance,** to have the power of deciding. **to lose one's balance,** to tumble; to be upset mentally. **to strike a balance,** to reckon up the balance on a statement of credit and indebtedness. **balance-fish,** *n.* the hammer-headed shark. **balance-knife,** *n.* a table-knife with a handle weighted so as to keep the blade from touching the cloth. **balance-reef,** *n.* the closest reef, a lower fore-and-aft sail. **balance-sheet,** *n.* a tabular statement of accounts, showing receipts and expenditure. **balance-step,** *n.* the goose-step. **balance-wheel,** *n.* the wheel regulating the beat in watches. **balanceable,** *a.* capable of being balanced. **balanced,** *a.* having good balance; sane, sensible (*often in comb.*, as *well-balanced*). **balanced motor,** *n.* a single-cylinder motor fitted with two fly-wheels rotating in opposite directions so as to reduce vibration; a motor in which the explosion takes place between two pistons in one cylinder. **balancer,** *n.* one who or that which balances; an acrobat; an organ in lieu of the posterior wing on each side of the Diptera. **balancer meal,** *n.* poultry meal mixed with various nutritive ingredients. [F, from L *bilancem* (nom. *bilanx*), two-scaled, in *libra bilanx* (*bi-*, two, *lanx*, a flat plate)]

Balanchine, *n.* **George** (1904–83), Russian-born choreographer. After leaving the USSR in 1924, he worked with Diaghilev in France. Moving to the US in 1933, he became a major influence on modern dance, starting the New York City Ballet in 1948. His many works include *Apollon Musagète* (1928) and *The Prodigal Son* (1929) for Diaghilev, several works for music by Stravinsky such as *Agon* (1957) and *Duo Concertante* (1972), and musicals such as *On Your Toes* (1936) and *The Boys from Syracuse* (1938).

balanid, *n.* (*Zool.*) a member of the Balanidae, or acorn shells. **balaniferous,** *a.* acorn-bearing. **balanite,** *n.* a precious stone. **Balanoglossus**, *n.* a genus of worm-like animals. **balanoid**, *a.* acorn-shaped. [Gr. *balanos,* an acorn]

balas, *n.* a rose-red variety of the spinel ruby. [OF *balais,* low L *balascius,* Arab. *balakhsh,* Pers. *Badakhshān* (L *Balaxia*), name of district near Samarkand where found]

balata, *n.* the dried gum of the bully-tree, used for insulating telegraph wires. [Am. Sp., of Carib. origin]

balboa, *n.* the unit of currency in Panama. [Vasco Nuñez de BALBOA]

Balboa, *n.* **Vasco Núñez de** (1475–1517), Spanish conquistador, the first European to see the Pacific Ocean, on 29 Sept. 1513, from the isthmus of Darien (now Panama). He was made admiral of the Pacific and governor of Panama, but was removed by Spanish court intrigue, imprisoned and executed.

Balbriggan, *n.* knitted cotton hose and other goods. [*Balbriggan,* in Co. Dublin, where it is made]

Balcon, *n.* **Michael** (1896–1977), British film producer, responsible for the 'Ealing Comedies' of the 1940s and early 1950s, such as *Kind Hearts and Coronets* (1949), and *The Lavender Hill Mob* (1951).

balcony, *n.* a gallery or platform projecting from a house or other building; in theatres, a tier of seats between the dress-circle and the gallery; (*N Am.*) dress-circle. **balconied**, *a.* [It. *balcone, balco,* OHG *balcho,* a scaffold (cogn. with BALK)]

bald, *a.* without hair upon the crown of the head; applied to some rapacious birds which have no feathers on the head; bare, treeless, leafless; of horses, streaked or marked with white; trivial, meagre; destitute of ornament or grace; undisguised, shameless. **bald-coot, baldicoot,** *n.* the coot, *Fulica atra,* from its broad white frontal plate; bald-head. **bald-faced,** *a.* having the face marked with white. **bald-head,** *n.* one who is bald; a variety of pigeon. **bald-headed,** *a.* with a bald head. **go at it bald-headed,** attack or undertake something boldly, regardless of consequences. **bald-pate,** *n.* one who is bald; a variety of duck and pigeon. *a.* bald. **bald-pated,** *a.* having no hair on the head. **bald-rib,** *n.* a joint of pork cut from nearer the rump than the spare-rib; a lean person. **baldly,** *adv.* in a bald manner; nakedly, shamelessly, inelegantly; plainly. **baldness,** *n.* [ME *balled,* etym. doubtful (perh. from Celt. *bal,* white mark on animal's face; cp. W *ceffyl bàl,* a horse with white forehead, W and Gael. *bal,* spot mark)]

baldachin, -quin, **baldachino**, *n.* †a kind of rich brocade of silk and gold; a canopy over an altar, throne or doorway, generally supported by pillars, but sometimes suspended from above, formerly of the material described above. [F and Sp. *baldaquin,* It. *baldacchino* (*Baldaco, Bagdad,* whence it originated)]

Balder, *n.* in Norse mythology, the son of Odin and Freya and husband of Nanna, and the best, wisest, and most loved of all the gods. He was killed, at Loki's instigation, by a twig of mistletoe shot by the blind god Hodur.

balderdash, *n.* confused speech or writing; a jumble of words; rubbish, nonsense. [etym. doubtful]

baldric, *n.* a richly ornamented girdle or belt, passing over one shoulder and under the opposite, to support dagger, sword, bugle etc. **baldric-wise,** *adv.* worn like a baldric. [ME *baudrik, baudry,* OF *baudrei* (cp. MHG *balderich* and low L *baldringus,* perh. from L *balteus,* a belt)]

Baldwin[1], *n.* **James** (1924–87), US writer, born in Harlem, New York, who portrayed the condition of black Americans in contemporary society. His works include the novels *Go Tell It on the Mountain* (1953), *Another Country* (1962), and *Just Above My Head* (1979); the play *The Amen Corner* (1955); and the autobiographical essays *Notes of a Native Son* (1955) and *The Fire Next Time* (1963).

Baldwin[2], *n.* **Stanley, 1st Earl Baldwin of Bewdley** (1867–1947), British Conservative politician, prime minister 1923–24, 1924–29, and 1935–37; he weathered the general strike (1926), secured complete adult suffrage (1928), and handled the abdication crisis of Edward VIII (1936).

Baldwin I, *n.* (1058–1118), king of Jerusalem. A French nobleman, who joined his brother Godfrey de Bouillon on the First Crusade in 1096, he established the kingdom in 1100. It was destroyed by Islamic conquest in 1187.

bale[1], *n.* evil, mischief, calamity; pain, sorrow, misery. **baleful,** *a.* full of evil; pernicious, harmful, deadly; †full of pain, misery, sorrow. **balefully,** *adv.* **balefulness,** *n.* [OE *bealo* (cp. OS and OFris. *balu,* OHG *balo*), evil]

bale[2], *n.* a package, a certain quantity of goods or merchandise, wrapped in cloth or baling-paper and corded for transportation. *v.t.* to pack in a bale or bales. **bale-goods,** *n.pl.* goods done up in bales, as distinguished from those packed in barrels, boxes etc. **baling,** *n.* the process of putting goods into bales. **baling-paper,** *n.* (*N Am.*) stout paper for packing. **baling-press,** *n.* a press used to compress goods before putting them into bales. [OF *bale* (prob. from MHG *balla, palla*)]

bale[3], **bail**[4], **to bale out,** to abandon an aeroplane in the air and descend by parachute; to help out of a difficulty. [BAIL[4]]

Balearic Islands, *n.pl.* (Spanish **Baleares**) Mediterranean group of islands forming an autonomous region of Spain; including Majorca, Minorca, Ibiza, Cabrera, and Formentera. **area** 5000 sq km/1930 sq miles. **capital** Palma de Mallorca. **population** (1986) 755,000. **products** figs, olives, oranges, wine, brandy, coal, iron, slate; tourism is important.

baleen, *n.* whalebone. *a.* of whalebone. [OF *baleine,* L *balaena,* a whale]

balefire, *n.* †a great fire in the open; †a funeral pyre; a beacon-fire; a bonfire. [OE *bǣl* (cp. Icel. *bāl,* a great fire, OTeut. *balom*)]

Balewa TAFAWA BALEWA.

Balfour, *n.* **Arthur James, 1st Earl of Balfour** (1848–1930), British Conservative politician, prime minister (1902–05) and foreign secretary (1916–19), when he issued the Balfour Declaration and was involved in peace negotiations after World War I.

Balfour Declaration, *n.* a letter, dated 2 Nov. 1917, from the British foreign secretary, A.J. Balfour, to Lord Rothschild (chair, British Zionist Federation) stating: 'HM government view with favour the establishment in Palestine of a national home for the Jewish people' but without prejudicing non-Jewish peoples; it led to the foundation of Israel in 1948.

Bali, *n.* island of Indonesia, E of Java, one of the Sunda Islands. **area** 5800 sq km/2240 sq miles. **capital** Denpasar. **physical** volcanic mountains. **population** (1980) 2,470,000. **products** gold and silver work, woodcarving, weaving, copra, salt, coffee.

Baliol *n.* **John de** (*c.* 1250–1314), king of Scotland 1292–96. As an heir to the Scottish throne on the death of Margaret, the Maid of Norway, his cause was supported by the English king, Edward I, against 12 other claimants. Having paid homage to Edward, he was proclaimed king but soon rebelled and gave up the kingdom when English forces attacked Scotland.

balistite, *n.* a powerful explosive containing nitroglycerine. [BALLISTA]

balistraria, *n.* a cruciform aperture or loophole in the wall of a fortress, through which arbalesters shot. [med. L, fem. of *ballistrārius,* as prec.]

balk, baulk, *n.* a ridge of land left unploughed; †a dividing ridge; a ridge left unploughed inadvertently; a beam of timber; †a tie-beam of a house; the head-line of a fishing-net; the part of a billiard table behind a transverse line; an obstacle, a hindrance, a check; a disappointment. *v.t.* to pass over intentionally; to refuse; to avoid, let slip; to check, hinder; to disappoint; to evade, frustrate; to dispute, argue contentiously. *v.i.* to turn aside, to swerve, to refuse a leap. **to make a balk,** (*Billiards*) to leave one's own ball and the red inside the balk when the opponent's is in hand. **balked,** *a.* foiled, disappointed. **balker,** *n.* **balking,** *n., a.* **balky,** *a.* of a horse, prone to balk or swerve. **balkiness,** *n.* [OE *balca,* a ridge (prob. cogn. with Icel. *bālkr*, a beam, partition)]

Balkanize, -ise, *v.t.* to split (a region) into a number of smaller and often mutually hostile states, as occurred in the *Balkan* peninsula, SE Europe, during the 19th and early 20th cents. **Balkanization, -isation,** *n.*

Balkans, *n.pl.* peninsula of SE Europe, stretching into the Mediterranean between the Adriatic and Aegean Seas, comprising Albania, Bulgaria, Greece, Romania, Turkey-in-Europe, and Yugoslavia. It is joined to the rest of Europe by an isthmus 1200 km/750 miles wide between Rijeka on the W and the mouth of the Danube on the Black Sea to the E.

Balkan Wars, *n.pl.* two wars (1912–13 and 1913) which resulted in the expulsion by the Balkan states of Ottoman Turkey from Europe except for a small area around Istanbul.

ball¹, *n.* a spherical body of any dimensions, a globe; such a body, differing in size, make and hardness, used in games; a game with a ball; a throw or cast of the ball in games; a globular body of wood, ivory or other substance used for voting by ballot; a bullet (not now usually spherical) or larger globular projectile for ordnance, esp. a solid projectile; †a symbol of authority, an orb; a planetary or celestial body (usu. with qualifying adjective); anything made, rolled or packed into a spherical shape; things or parts of things with spherical or rounded outlines. (*pl.*) (*sl.*) testicles. *v.t.* to clog (as a horse's foot with a collection of snow). *v.i.* to gather into a ball; to become clogged; of bees, to cluster round the queen when they swarm. **ball and socket,** an instrument made of brass with a universal screw, capable of being turned in any direction. **ball and socket joint,** a joint formed by a ball playing in a socket, and admitting of motion in any direction; applied to joints like those of the human hip and shoulder. **ball of fire,** (*coll.*) a dynamic or lively individual. **ball of the eye,** the pupil, the apple of the eye; the eye itself. **ball of the foot,** the rounded part of the base of the great toe. **ball of the thumb,** the corresponding part of the hand. **on the ball,** alert; in control. **the ball's in your court,** it's your move, it's your turn to act. **three balls,** a pawnbroker's sign. **to balls up, to make a balls of,** (*sl.*) to make a mess of; to botch, do badly. **to keep the ball rolling,** to keep the conversation, debate, work or game from flagging. **ball-bearing,** *n.* (*usu. pl.*) a bearing containing loose metallic balls for lessening friction; axle-bearing of this kind; one of the metal balls used in such a bearing. **ball-cartridge,** *n.* a cartridge containing a bullet. **ball-cock, -tap,** *n.* a self-acting tap which is turned off or on by the rising or falling of a hollow ball on the surface of the water in a cistern, boiler etc. **ball-flower,** *n.* (*Arch.*) an ornament like a ball enclosed within three or four petals of a flower. **ballgame,** *n.* a game played with a ball; (*N Am.*) baseball. **a different ballgame,** (*coll.*) something quite different. **ball lightning,** *n.* floating luminous balls sometimes seen during thunderstorms. **ballpark,** *n.* a park or field where ballgames are played; (*N Am.*) a baseball field. **ball-point pen,** *n.* a fountain pen with a tiny ball in place of a nib. **ball-proof,** *a.* impenetrable by bullets. **ball-valve,** *n.* a valve opened or closed by the rising of a ball. **balled,** *a.* formed into a ball. **balls!** *int.* (*sl.*) nonsense. [ME *balle,* Icel. *böllr,* OTeut. *balluz*]

ball², *n.* a social assembly for dancing. **to have a ball,** (*coll.*) to have a good time. **to open the ball,** to lead off in the first dance; to commence operations. **ballroom,** *n.* a room used for balls. [F *bal,* OF *baler,* to dance, late L *ballāre* (prob. from Gr. *ballizein,* to dance)]

Ball¹, *n.* **John,** English priest, one of the leaders of the Peasants' Revolt in 1381, was known as 'the mad priest of Kent'. A follower of John Wycliffe and a believer in social equality, he was imprisoned for disagreeing with the archbishop of Canterbury, and was probably excommunicated. During the revolt, he was released from prison, and when in Blackheath, London, preached from the text 'When Adam delved and Eve span, who was then the gentleman?' When the revolt collapsed he escaped but was captured near Coventry and executed.

Ball², *n.* **Lucille 'Lucy'** (1911–89), US comedy actress. From 1951–57 she starred with her husband, Cuban bandleader Desi Arnaz, in *I Love Lucy*, the first US television show filmed before an audience. It was followed by *The Lucy Show* (1962–68) and *Here's Lucy* (1968–74).

ballad, *n.* light simple song; a popular song, generally of a personal or political character, and printed as a broadside; a simple spirited poem usu. narrating some popular or patriotic story; a proverb in the form of a rhymed couplet. †*v.i.* to compose ballads. *v.t.* to make (someone) the subject of a ballad or ballads; to satirize ballad-wise. **ballad-farce, ballad-opera,** *n.* a play in which ballads are introduced into the spoken dialogue. **ballad-maker,** *n.* a writer of ballads. **ballad-monger,** *n.* one who sells ballads; a contemptuous epithet for a composer of ballads. **ballad-opera** BALLAD-FARCE. **ballad-singer,** *n.* one who sings ballads, esp. in the streets. †**ballader, balladeer, balladist,** *n.* one who composes or sings ballads. **balladry,** *n.* the ballad style of composition; ballads collectively. **ballad-wise,** *adv.* in the form of a ballad. [OF *balade,* Prov. *balada,* a dancing song (late L *ballāre,* see prec.)]

ballade, *n.* a poem consisting of three eight-lined stanzas rhyming *a b a b b c b c,* each having the same line as a refrain, and with an envoy of four lines; an old form revived in the 19th cent. **ballade royal,** *n.* stanzas of seven or eight decasyllabic lines, rhyme royal. [F, see prec.]

Ballance, *n.* **John** (1839–93), New Zealand politician, born in N Ireland; prime minister (1891–93).

Ballard, *n.* **J(ames) G(raham)** (1930–), British novelist, whose works include science fiction on the theme of disaster, such as *The Drowned World* (1962), and *High-Rise* (1975), and the partly autobiographical *Empire of the Sun* (1984), dealing with his internment in China during World War II.

ballast, *n.* stones, iron or other heavy substances placed in the bottom of a ship or boat to lower the centre of gravity and make her steady; gravel or other material laid as foundation for a railway, or for making roads; that which tends to give intellectual or moral stability; (*coll.*) solid foods, food containing carbohydrate. *v.t.*

to furnish with ballast; to lay or pack with ballast; †to load; to steady. **in ballast,** without a cargo, having only ballast in the hold; used for ballasting. **ballastage**, *n.* a toll paid for the privilege of taking ballast. **ballasting,** *n.* the act of ballasting; material for ballast; ballast. [*ballast* in most Eur. languages; oldest form prob. OSwed. and ODan. *barlast,* mere load (*bar,* bare, *last,* load)]

ballerina, *n.* (*pl.* **-rine, -rinas**) a female ballet dancer; a female dancer taking a leading part in a ballet.

Ballesteros, *n.* **Severiano 'Seve'** (1957–), Spanish golfer who came to prominence in 1976 and has been dominant in Europe, as well as winning leading tournaments in the US. He has won the British Open three times: 1979, 1984, 1988.

ballet, *n.* a dramatic representation, consisting of dancing and pantomime; an artistic exhibition of dancing. **ballet-girl,** *n.* a girl who takes a subordinate part in a ballet. **ballet-master, -mistress,** *n.* the director of a ballet. **balletomane**, *n.* an enthusiast for the ballet. [F, dim. of *bal,* BALL²]

ballista, *n.* (*pl.* **-ae, -as**) a military engine used in ancient times for hurling stones, darts and other missiles. [L, from Gr. *ballein,* to throw]

ballistic, *a.* of or pertaining to the hurling and flight of projectiles. **ballistic missile,** *n.* (*Mil.*) a missile guided over the first part of its course but then descending according to the laws of ballistics. **ballistic pendulum,** *n.* an instrument for measuring the velocity of projectiles. **ballistics,** *n.sing.* the science of the flight of projectiles. **ballistite,** *n.* a propellant explosive based on nitroglycerine and nitrocellulose. [as prec.]

ballocks, BOLLOCKS.

balloon, *n.* a spherical or pear-shaped bag of paper, silk or other light material, which when filled with heated air or hydrogen gas rises and floats in the air (to the larger kinds a car is attached, capable of containing several persons, and these balloons are used for scientific observations, reconnoitring etc.); †an inflated ball driven to and fro by blows with the arm; †an old game played with such a ball; an inflatable rubber bag used as a child's toy; a ball or globe surmounting a pillar, cupola etc.; (*Chem.*) a spherical glass receiver, used in distilling; a frame or trellis on which trees or plants are trained; the shape into which fruit trees are trained; a line enclosing the words or thoughts of a cartoon character; anything inflated or hollow. *v.i.* to go up in a balloon; to swell out. **captive balloon,** a balloon held by a rope. **like a lead balloon,** utterly useless, a complete failure. **pilot balloon,** a small balloon sent up in advance to show the direction and strength of the wind. **when the balloon goes up,** when the action begins, when the troubles start. **balloon angioplasty,** *n.* a technique for treating blocked arteries, in which a tiny balloon is inserted into the blockage and inflated. **balloon barrage,** *n.* a line or series of captive balloons employed as a defence against enemy aircraft. **balloon-fish,** *n.* popular name for fishes belonging to the genus *Diodon,* which are able to distend their bodies with air. **balloon tyre,** *n.* a low-pressure tyre, large in section. **ballooner,** *n.* a balloonist; a balloon-like sail; a dress or other object that swells out like a balloon. **ballooning,** *n.* the practice of making balloon ascents; aeronautics; (*N Am.*) the practice of running up stock above its value. **balloonist,** *n.* one who makes balloon ascents; an aeronaut. [It. *ballone,* a large ball, from *balla* (see BALE²)]

ballot, *n.* a ball used for secret voting; hence, a ticket, paper or other instrument used to give a secret vote; the method or system of secret voting; the total votes recorded; drawing of lots by means of balls or otherwise. *v.t.* †to vote upon by ballot; to select by drawing lots; to ask to vote secretly. *v.i.* to vote secretly. **to ballot for,** to choose by secret voting. **ballot-box,** *n.* a box into which ballots are put in voting, or from which balls are taken in drawing lots. **ballot-paper,** *n.* the voting-paper used in voting by ballot. [It. *ballotta,* dim. of *balla* (see BALE²)]

bally, *a.* (*sl., euphem.*) bloody. [perh. from *Ballyhooly*]

ballyhoo, *n.* noisy and unprincipled propaganda; a great fuss about nothing. [etym. doubtful]

ballyrag, *v.t.* to revile, abuse, assail with violent language; to victimize with practical jokes. *v.i.* to use violent or abusive language; to engage in horseplay. [also *bullyrag* (etym. unknown)]

balm, *n.* the fragrant juice, sap or gum of certain trees or plants; fragrant ointment or oil; anything which soothes pain, irritation or distress; perfume, fragrance; a plant of the genus *Balsamodendron,* which yields balm; the popular name of several fragrant garden herbs. *v.t.* to anoint or impregnate with balm; †to embalm; to soothe, to assuage. **Balm of Gilead**, the gum of *Balsamodendron gileadense,* used as antiseptic and vulnerary; a quack imitation of this. **balm-cricket,** *n.* the cicada. **balmy,** *a.* producing balm; impregnated with or having the qualities of balm; soft, soothing, healing; fragrant, mild; (*sl.*) rather idiotic, daft, silly. **balmily,** *adv.* **balminess,** *n.* [OF *basme,* L *balsamum,* BALSAM (spelling gradually reassimilated to L *bal-*)]

Balmer *n.* **Johann** (1825–98), Swiss physicist and mathematician who developed formulae capable of deriving the wavelengths of the hydrogen atom spectrum. The simplicity of his formula, which involves only the manipulation of integers, had a central role in the development of spectral theory.

Balmoral, *n.* a castle in Scotland, in Grampian region, a residence of the British royal family; a kind of Scottish cap; a kind of petticoat; (*pl.*) ankle boots for men and women, laced in front.

balneology, *n.* the science of treating diseases by bathing and medicinal springs. [L *balneum,* a bath]

baloney, boloney, *n.* (*sl.*) idiotic talk, nonsense. [thought to be from Bologna sausage]

balsa, *n.* an American tropical tree, *Ochroma lagopus,* with light, strong wood used for rafts, model aircraft etc. [Sp.]

balsam, *n.* a vegetable resin with a strong fragrant odour, balm; a tree yielding a resin of this kind; popular name of the genus *Impatiens;* a medicinal preparation made with oil or resin for anointing wounds or soothing pain; a preservative essence supposed by alchemists to pervade all organic bodies; resins mixed with volatile oils, CANADA BALSAM; anything that possesses healing or soothing qualities. *v.t.* to impregnate or perfume with balsam; to heal, soothe; to embalm. **balsam-apple,** *n.* a tropical plant of the gourd family bearing a highly coloured fruit; (*erroneously*) the common garden balsam. **balsam-fir,** *n.* a N American fir, *Abies balsamea,* which yields Canada Balsam. **balsamic**, **balsamous,** *a.* having the qualities of balsam; mitigating, assuaging pain, soothing; like a warm, soothing oily medicine. **balsamically,** *adv.* **balsamiferous**, *a.* **Balsamodendron,** *n.* a genus of trees which exude balm. **balsamy,** *a.* balsam-like; balmy. [L *balsamum*]

balsamine, *n.* the English name of *Impatiens balsamina;* (*erroneously*) the balsam-apple. [F, from Gr. *balsaminē*]

Baltic, *a.* pertaining to the Baltic Sea in N Europe or its bordering provinces; of, or denoting Baltic as a group of languages. *n.* BALTIC SEA; a branch of the Indo-European languages comprising Latvian, Lithuanian and Old Prussian. **Baltoslav,** *n.* **Baltoslavic, -slavonic,** *n.* a subfamily of Indo-European languages containing Baltic and Slavonic. [L *Baltia,* Scandinavia]

Baltic, Battle of the, naval battle fought off Copenhagen on 2 Apr. 1801, in which a British fleet under Sir Hyde Parker, with Nelson as second-in-command, annihilated the Danish navy.

Baltic Sea, *n.* large shallow arm of the North Sea, extending NE from the narrow Skagerrak and Kattegat, between Sweden and Denmark, to the Gulf of Bothnia between Sweden and Finland. Its coastline is 8000 km/5000 miles long, and its area, including the gulfs of Riga, Finland and Bothnia, is 422,300 sq km/163,000 sq miles. Its shoreline is shared by Denmark, Germany, Poland, USSR, Finland, and Sweden.

Baltimore, *n.* industrial port and largest city in Maryland, US, on the W shore of Chesapeake Bay, NE of Washington DC; population (1980) 2,300,000. Industries include shipbuilding, oil refining, food processing, and the manufacture of steel, chemicals, and aerospace equipment.

Baltimore, Baltimore bird, *n.* a N American bird of the starling family, *Cterus baltimorii,* with black head and orange plumage (called also Baltimore oriole, Baltimore hang-nest etc.). [named after colours of Lord *Baltimore,* proprietary of Maryland]

Baltistan, *n.* a region in the Karakoram range of NE Kashmir held by Pakistan since 1949. The home of Balti Muslims of Tibetan origin. The chief town is Skardu, but Ghyari is of greater significance to Muslims as the site of a mosque built by Sayyid Ali Hamadani, a Persian who brought the Shia Muslim religion to Baltistan in the 14th century.

Baluch, Baluchi, *n.* inhabitant of Baluchistan, SW Asia. The common religion is Islam, and they speak Baluchi (a member of the Iranian branch of the Indo-European language family).

Baluchistan, *n.* mountainous desert area, comprising a province of Pakistan, part of the Iranian province of Sistán and Balúchestan, and a small area of Afghanistan. The Pakistani province has an area of 347,200 sq km/134,019 sq miles, and a population (1985) 4,908,000; its capital is Quetta. Sistán and Balúchestan has an area of 181,600 sq km/70,098 sq miles, and a population (1986) 1,197,000; its capital is Zahedan. The port of Gwadar in Pakistan is strategically important, on the Indian Ocean and the Strait of Hormuz.

baluster, *n.* a small column, usu. circular, swelling towards the bottom, and forming part of a series called a balustrade; a post supporting a hand-rail, a banister; a small pillar, swelling in the middle, in a two-light window. **balustered,** *a.* **balustrade**, *n.* a range of balusters, resting on a plinth, supporting a coping or rail, and serving as a protection, barrier, ornament etc. [F *balustre,* It. *balausta, balaustra,* L *balaustium,* Gr. *balaustion,* flower of the wild pomegranate (from supposed resemblance to its calyx-tube)]

Balzac, *n.* **Honoré de** (1799–1850), French novelist. His first success was *Les Chouans/The Chouans* and *La Physiologie du mariage/The Physiology of Marriage* (1829), inspired by Scott. This was the beginning of the long series of novels *La Comédie humaine/The Human Comedy*. He also wrote Rabelaisian *Contes drôlatiques/Ribald Tales* (1833).

bam, (*sl.*) *v.t.* to cheat, hoax, bamboozle. *v.i.* to hoax. *n.* a hoax, a mystification; a cock-and-bull story. [perh. abbr. from BAMBOOZLE]

Bamako, *n.* capital and port of Mali on the River Niger; population (1976) 404,022. It produces pharmaceuticals, chemicals, textiles, tobacco and metal products.

bambino, *n.* (*pl.* **-nos, -ni**) a child, a baby; esp. an image of the infant Jesus in the crib, exhibited at Christmas in Roman Catholic churches. [It., a baby]

bamboo, *n.* (*pl.* **-boos**) any of a genus, *Bambusa*, of giant tropical grasses; the stem of such grass used as a stick, thatch, building material etc. *v.t.* to beat with a bamboo. **bamboo curtain,** *n.* the barrier set up between Communist China and the rest of the world. [etym. doubtful; perh. from Canarese *bănbŭ, banivu*]

bamboozle, *v.t.* to mystify for purposes of fraud; to cheat, to swindle; to bewilder, confuse, *v.i.* to practise trickery. *n.* bamboozlement. **bamboozlement,** *n.* the act or process of bamboozling; a tricky deception, a hoax. [etym. doubtful; cp. BAM]

Ban¹, *n.* (*Hist.*) a title given to the governor of certain districts in Hungary and Croatia, who takes command in time of war. [Pers., lord]

ban², *v.t.* (*past, p.p.* **banned**) to curse, anathematize; to scold, to chide; to interdict, to proscribe. *v.i.* to utter curses. *n.* a public proclamation; an edict of excommunication, an interdict; a curse, a formal anathematization; an imprecation, execration, a formal prohibition; a proclamation of outlawry; denunciation, proscription, outlawry; (*pl., now spelt* BANNS) proclamation of intended marriage. [OE *bannan,* to summon, OTeut. *bannan,* to proclaim, root *ba-* (cp. L *fārī,* to speak, Gr. *phēmi,* I speak)]

banal, *a.* †of or belonging to compulsory feudal service; commonplace, trite, petty. **banality**, *n.* a commonplace, trite remark; commonplaceness, triviality. [F *banal,* from *ban* (late L *bannum*), BAN²]

banana, *n.* a tropical and subtropical tree, *Musa sapientum,* closely allied to the plantain; the fruit of this, a large, elongated berry, growing in clusters, very nutritious. **to be, go bananas,** (*sl.*) to be or go insane. **Bananaland,** *n.* (*coll.*) Queensland. **banana republic,** *n.* (*offensive*) a small tropical country, politically unstable, economically dependent on the export of fruit, and dominated by foreign capital. **banana skin,** *n.* any episode or occurrence which leads to humiliation or embarrassment, esp. in a political context. **banana split,** *n.* a dessert consisting of a banana sliced length-wise and filled with ice-cream, cream etc. [through Sp. or Port. from native name in Guinea]

banausic, *a.* mechanical, merely fit for a mechanic. **banausocracy**, *n.* government by the uncultured, vulgar elements of society. [Gr. *banausikos,* from *banausos,* working by fire, mechanical (*baunos,* a furnace)]

Banbury-cake, *n.* a kind of cake filled with mincemeat, supposed to be made at Banbury in Oxfordshire. **Banbury-man,** *n.* an overzealous Puritan; a puritanical rogue; a hypocrite.

banc, banco¹, *n.* the Bench. **in banc, in banco,** a term applied to sittings of a Superior Court of Common Law as a full court, as distinguished from the sittings of the judges at Nisi Prius or on circuit. [L (*in*) *banco* (*bancus,* a bench)]

banco², *a.* a term applied to bank money of account, as distinguished from ordinary currency. [It., bank, as prec.]

Bancroft, *n.* **George** (1800–91), US diplomat and historian. A Democrat, he was secretary of the navy in 1845, when he established the US Naval Academy at Annapolis, Maryland, and as acting secretary of war (May 1846) was instrumental in bringing about the occupation of California and war with Mexico. He wrote a *History of the United States* (1834–76).

band¹, *n.* that which binds, confines or restrains; a fillet, a tie, a chain; one of the cords on which a book is sewn; a bond, a tie, a uniting influence; †a pledge; †a league; (*pl.*) fetters, manacles. †**in bands,** in prison. [ME *band,* Icel. *band* (OTeut. *bindan,* to bind)]

band², *n.* a flat slip or band (BAND¹), used to bind together, encircle or confine, or as part of an article of apparel; the collar of a shirt, a collar or ruff; (*pl.*) a pair of linen strips hanging down in front from the collar and forming part of clerical, legal or academical dress; a bandage; (*Ent.*) a transverse stripe; (*Geol.*) a band-like stratum; a space between any two ribs on the fruit of umbellifers; a broad, endless strap for communicating motion; a slip of canvas used to strengthen the parts of a sail most liable to pressure; a specific range of frequencies or wavelengths; a track of a record or magnetic tape; a division of pupils according to ability. **Band-Aid®**, *n.* a small adhesive plaster with a medicated gauze pad. **band-aid,** *a.* of measures etc., temporary. **bandbox,** *n.* a box of cardboard or other thin material for holding collars, hats, millinery etc., originally used for bands or ruffs; a flimsy affair. **like something out of a bandbox,** immaculately smart. **band brake,** *n.* (*Mech.*) a flexible band that grips the periphery of a drum or wheel. **band-fish,** *n.* a Mediterranean fish of the genus *Cepola,* from their ribbon-like shape. **band-saw,** *n.* an endless steel saw, running rapidly over wheels. **band-wheel,** *n.* a wheel worked by means of an endless strap. **bandwidth,** *n.* the range of frequencies used for a particular radio transmission; the range of frequencies within which an amplifier (or other electronic device) operates most efficiently. [late ME *bande,* F *bande,* a strip, Prov. and It. *benda,* OHG *binda* (OTeut. *bindan,* as prec.)]

band[3], *n.* an organized company; a confederation; an assemblage of people or of the lower animals; a company of musicians trained to play together; the musicians attached to a regiment or ship. **Band of Hope,** a name given about 1850 to any association of children pledged to total abstinence. **when the band begins to play,** when things get lively; when trouble begins. **band-master,** *n.* the leader of a band of musicians. **bandsman,** *n.* a member of a band of musicians. **band-stand,** *n.* an elevated platform for the use of a band of musicians. **band-wagon,** *n.* the musicians' wagon in a circus parade. **to climb on the band-wagon,** to try to be on the winning side. [F *bande* (Prov., Sp. and It. *banda,* a sash, ribbon), prob. from OHG *Bant*]

band[4], *v.t.* to bind or fasten with a band; to mark with a band; to form into a band, troop or society. *v.i.* to unite, to assemble. [F *bander,* from *bande;* or from the nouns BAND[1] and [2]]

band[5] BANDY[1].

Band, the, a North American rock group (1961–76). They acquired their name when working as Bob Dylan's backing band, and made their solo debut 1968 with *Music from Big Pink*. Their unostentatious ensemble playing and strong original material set a new trend.

Banda, *n.* **Hastings Kamuzu** (*c.* 1902–), Malawi politican, president from 1966. He led his country's independence movement, was prime minister of Nyasaland from 1963, and became the first president of the one-party republic.

bandage, *n.* a strip of flexible material used to bind up wounds, fractures etc.; the operation of bandaging; a strip of flexible material used to cover up something; (*Arch.*) a tie or bond. *v.t.* to bind up with a bandage. [BAND[2]]

bandanna, bandana, *n.* a silk handkerchief of Indian manufacture, having white or yellow spots on a coloured ground; a cotton handkerchief thus printed. [Hind. *bāndhnū,* a mode of spot-dyeing]

Bandaranaike[1], *n.* **Sirimavo** (born **Ratwatte**) (1916–), Sri Lankan politician, who succeeded her husband Solomon Bandaranaike to become the world's first woman prime minister (1960–65 and 1970–77), but was expelled from parliament in 1980 for abuse of her powers while in office. She was largely responsible for the new constitution (1972).

Bandaranaike[2], *n.* **Solomon West Ridgeway Dias** (1899–1959), Sri Lankan nationalist politician. In 1951 he founded the Sri Lanka Freedom Party and in 1956 became prime minister, pledged to a socialist programme and a neutral foreign policy. He failed to satisfy extremists and was assassinated by a Buddhist monk.

Bandar Seri Begawan, (formerly **Brunei Town**) capital of Brunei; population (1983) 57,558.

b. and b., (*abbr.*) bed and breakfast.

bandeau, *n.* (*pl.* **-deaux**) a narrow band or fillet for the head; a bandage. [F, from OF *bandel,* dim. of *bande,* BAND[2]]

bandelet, *n.* a small stripe or band; a small flat moulding round a column. [F *bandelette,* dim. of OF *bandel,* dim of *bande,* BAND[2]]

banderilla, *n.* a little dart ornamented with ribbons, which bull-fighters stick in the neck of the bull. [Sp., dim. of BANNER]

banderol, banderole, *n.* a long narrow flag with a cleft end flying at a mast-head; any small ornamental streamer; the small square of silk hanging from a trumpet; a flat band with an inscription, used in the decoration of buildings of the Renaissance period. [F *banderole,* dim. of *bandière, bannière,* BANNER]

bandicoot, *n.* a large Indian rat (*Mus giganteus*); the marsupial genus *Perameles,* which has some resemblance to this. [Telugu *pandi-kokku,* pig-rat]

bandit, *n.* (*pl.* **-itti, dits**) one who is proscribed, an outlaw; a brigand; a member of an organized band of marauders infesting the mountainous districts of the south and south-east of Europe. **banditti,** *n.sing.* a company of bandits. [It. *bandito,* p.p. of *bandire,* to proscribe, low L *bandīre, bannīre* (see BAN[2])]

bandog, *n.* a large fierce dog, kept chained, a mastiff, a bloodhound. [orig. *band-dog,* from BAND[1]]

bandoleer, bandolier, *n.* †a leather belt worn over the right shoulder and across the breast; such a belt used to support the musket and 12 charges of powder and shot in small wooden boxes; a similar belt with little leather loops to receive cartridges; (*usu. pl.*) the cases or boxes containing charges. [F *bandouillere,* It. *bandoliera,* or Sp. *bandolera* (*bandola,* dim. of *banda,* BAND[2])]

bandoline, *n.* a gummy substance applied to the hair to keep it smooth and flat. [F]

bandore, *n.* an old musical instrument somewhat resembling a lute. [Sp. *bandurria, bandola,* or Port. *bandurra, mandore,* L *pandūra,* Gr. *pandoura*]

Bandung, *n.* commercial city and capital of Jawa Barat province on the island of Java, Indonesia; population (1980) 1,463,000. Bandung is the third largest city in Indonesia and was the administrative centre when the country was the Netherlands East Indies.

Bandung Conference, *n.* the first conference (1955) of the Afro-Asian nations, proclaiming anti-colonialism and neutrality between East and West.

bandy[1], *v.t.* to beat or throw to and fro as at the game of tennis or bandy; to toss to and fro or toss about like a ball; to give and take, to exchange (esp. blows, arguments etc.); to band together, make into a faction. *v.i.* to throw a ball about; to contend, to wrangle; to be factious, to strive, fight. *n.* †a game like tennis; a return stroke at tennis; the game of hockey; a club, bent and rounded at the lower end, used in this game for striking the ball. **to bandy words,** to wrangle. **bandy ball,** *n.* bandy or hockey. [etym. doubtful; cp. F *bander,* to bandy at tennis, perh. from *bande, side*]

bandy[2], *a.* crooked, bent. **bandy-legged,** *a.* having crooked legs. [etym. doubtful]

bane, *n.* poison (chiefly in comb., as *henbane, rat's bane* etc.); that which causes ruin; ruin, destruction, mischief, woe. †*v.t.* to kill, esp. by poison; to harm, to injure. **baneberry,** *n.* a popular name for *Actaea spicata* or herb Christopher; the black berries of this, which are very poisonous. **banewort,** *n.* a poisonous plant; the lesser spearwort; the deadly nightshade. **baneful,** *a.* poisonous, harmful, destructive. **banefully,** *adv.* **banefulness,** *n.* [OE *bana,* a murderer (cp. Icel. *bani,* death, slayer, OHG *bano,* Gr. *phonos,* murder, carnage)]

Banffshire, *n.* former county of NE Scotland, now in Grampian region.

bang[1], *v.t.* to beat with loud blows; to thrash, to thump; to handle roughly, to drub; to slam (a door), fire (a gun), beat (a musical instrument) with a loud noise; to cut (the front hair) square across; to beat, to surpass; (*sl.*) to have sexual intercourse with. *v.i.* to resound with a loud noise; to jump or bounce up noisily. *n.* a resounding blow, a thump; a sudden explosive noise; impulsive motion, a dash; (*sl.*) an act of sexual intercourse; the front hair cut straight across. *adv.* with a violent blow or noise; suddenly, abruptly, all at once. **to bang away at,** to do something violently or noisily. **to go (off) with a bang,** to go very well, to succeed. **bang-tail,** *n.* a horse with tail cut off square. **bang-up,** *a.* (*sl.*) fine, first-rate. **banger,** *n.* (*sl.*) a very fine and exceptional specimen; a sausage; a cudgel; (*coll.*) a decrepit old car; a small explosive firework. †**bangster**, *n.* a bully; a victor. [Icel. *banga,* to beat (cp. LG *bangen,* to beat, G *bengel,* to cudgel)]

bang[2] BHANG.

bangalay, *n.* a variety of eucalyptus tree. [Austral. Abor.]

Bangalore, *n.* capital of Karnataka state, S India; population (1981) 2,914,000. Industries include electronics, aircraft and machine tools construction, and coffee.

Bangkok, *n.* capital and port of Thailand, on the river Chao Phraya; population (1987) 5,609,000. Products include paper, ceramics, cement, textiles, and aircraft. It is the headquarters of the South-East Asia Treaty Organization.

Bangladesh, *n.* country in S Asia. **area** 144,000 sq km/55,585 sq miles. **capital** Dhaka (formerly Dacca). **towns** ports Chittagong, Khulna. **physical** flat delta of rivers Ganges and Brahmaputra; annual rainfall of 2540 mm/100 in; some 75% of the land is less than 3 m/10 ft above sea level and vulnerable to flooding and cyclones. **population** (1987) 104,100,000; annual growth rate 2.7%. **exports** jute (50% of world production), tea. **language** Bangla (Bengali). **religion** Sunni Muslim 85%, Hindu 14%.

bangle, *n.* a ring-bracelet or anklet. **bangled,** *a.* adorned with bangles. [Hind. *bangrī,* a wrist-ring of glass]

Bangui, *n.* capital and port of the Central African Republic on the River Ubangi; population (1988) 597,000. Industries include beer, cigarettes, office machinery, and timber and metal products.

banian BANYAN.

banish, *v.t.* to condemn to exile; to drive out or away, to expel. **banishment,** *n.* the act of banishing; the state of being banished; exile, expatriation, expulsion. [OF *banir* (lengthened stem *baniss-*), late L *bannīre* (see BAN[2])]

banister, *n.* a shaft or upright supporting a hand-rail at the side of a staircase; (*pl.*) the whole railing protecting the outer side of a staircase. [corr. of BALUSTER]

banjo, *n.* (*pl.* **-jos, -joes**) a stringed musical instrument, having a head and neck like a guitar and a body like a tambourine, and played with the fingers; (*Austral. sl.*) a shoulder of mutton. **banjoist,** *n.* [Negro pronun. of BANDORE]

Banjul, *n.* capital and chief port of Gambia, on an island at the mouth of the river Gambia; population (1983) 44,536. Known as Bathurst until 1973. It was established as a settlement for freed slaves in 1816.

bank[1], *n.* a raised shelf or ridge of ground; a mound with steeply sloping sides; a shelving elevation of sand, gravel etc., in the sea or in a river; the margin or shore of a river; the ground near a river; †the seashore; an embankment; the sides of a road, cutting or any hollow; an incline on a railway; a bed of shell-fish; a long flat-topped mass, as of ice, snow, cloud or the like; the face of the coal in a mine; the surface of the ground at the top of a mine-shaft. *v.t.* to form a bank to; to confine within a bank or banks; to embank; to bring to land; to fortify with earth-works; (*Aviat.*) to incline inwards at a high angle in turning; to confine (the escapement of a watch); †to coast, to skirt. *v.i.* to rise into banks; (*Watchmaking*) to rest against the banking-pins. **to bank up,** to make up (a fire) by putting on and pressing down fuel. **bank engine,** *n.* a locomotive employed to assist trains up inclines. **bank fish,** *n.* fish from the Newfoundland bank. **bank-martin, -swallow,** *n.* the sand-martin. **bankside,** *n.* the sloping side of a bank; †the shore of a river, lake or sea; (**Bankside**) the district bordering the Thames at Southwark. **bank-smack,** *n.* a Newfoundland fishing smack. **banksman,** *n.* a workman who superintends unloading at a pit-mouth. **banker[1],** *n.* a bank-smack; a horse good at jumping on and off high banks; (*Austral.*) a swollen river. **bankless,** *a.* not defined or limited by a bank. [ME *banke* (Icel. *bakki,* OTeut. *bankon;* cp. *bankiz,* a bench)]

bank[2], *n.* an establishment which deals in money, receiving it on deposit from customers and investing it; (*Gaming*) the money which the proprietor of the table, or player who plays against the rest, has before him or her; any store or reserve of material or information, as in *blood bank. v.i.* to keep a bank; to act as a banker; to be a depositor in a bank; (*Gaming*) to form a bank, to challenge all comers; (*coll.*) to count or depend (on). *v.t.* to deposit in a bank; to realize, convert into money. **to break the bank,** to win the limit set by the management of a gambling house for a particular period. **bank-bill,** *n.* (*formerly*) a bill drawn by one bank on another, payable on demand or at some specified time; (*N Am.*) a bank note. **bankbook,** *n.* a passbook in which the cashier enters the debits and credits of a customer. **bank credit,** *n.* permission to draw on a bank to a certain amount. **bank holiday,** *n.* a day on which all banks are legally closed, observed as a national holiday. **bank note,** *n.* a note issued by a bank and payable on demand. **bank rate,** *n.* the rate at which the Bank of England is prepared to discount bills of exchange (see MINIMUM LENDING RATE). **bank-stock,** *n.* the capital stock of a bank. **bankable,** *a.* capable of being banked; guaranteed to produce a profit. **banker[2],** *n.* a proprietor of a bank; one involved in banking; one who keeps the bank at a gaming-table; the dealer in certain card games. **banker's card,** *n.* a card issued by a bank guaranteeing payment of cheques up to a certain limit. [F *banque,* It. *banca,* a bench, Teut. *bank,* BANK[1]]

bank[3], *n.* †a long seat; a platform or stage; a seat of justice; the bench for rowers, or a tier of oars, in a galley; a bench or table used in various trades; (*Print.*) the table on which sheets are laid; the raised floor of a glass-furnace; (*Organ*) a row of keys. [OF *banc,* Teut. *bank,* BANK[1] (cp. BENCH)]

banker[1] BANK[1].

banker[2] BANK[2].

banker[3], *n.* a sculptor's revolving table; a bench used by bricklayers or stonemasons. [prob. corr. of It. *banco,* a statuary's table]

banket, *n.* a gold-bearing conglomerate. [S Afr. Dut., hardbake]

Bank for International Settlements (BIS), a bank established in 1930 to handle German reparations settlements from World War I. The BIS (based in Basel, Switzerland) is today an important centre for economic and monetary research and assists cooperation of central banks. Its financial activities are essentially short term.

Bankhead, *n.* **Tallulah** (1903–68), US actress, noted for her wit and flamboyant lifestyle. Her stage appearances include *Dark Victory* (1934), *The Little Foxes* (1939), and *The Skin of Our Teeth* (1942).

Bank of England, UK central bank founded by Act of Parliament in 1694. It was entrusted with note-issue in 1844, and nationalized in 1946. It is banker to the UK government and assists in implementing financial and monetary policies through intervention in financial and foreign exchange markets.

bankrupt, *n.* a person who, becoming insolvent, is judicially required to surrender his or her estates to be administered for the benefit of his or her creditors; an insolvent debtor. *a.* judicially declared bankrupt; insolvent; (*fig.*) without credit; at the end of one's resources. *v.t.* to render (a person) bankrupt; to render insolvent; to reduce to beggary, or to discredit. **bankruptcy,** *n.* the state of being bankrupt; the act of declaring oneself bankrupt; (*fig.*) utter ruin; loss of reputation. **bankruptcy laws,** *n.pl.* laws requiring a bankrupt to surrender his or her property for the benefit of his or her creditors to ensure his or her discharge. [earlier *banqueroute,* It. *banca rotta,* bank broken (BANK[2], L *rupta,* p.p. of *rumpere,* to break), assimilated to L *rupt-*]

banksia, *n.* an Australian flowering shrub or tree (genus *Banksia*) of the family Proteaceae. [Sir Joseph *Banks,* 1744–1820]

banlieue, *n.* the territory outside the walls but within the jurisdiction of a town or city; suburbs, precincts. [F, from L *banleuca* (BAN[1], *leuca,* a league)]

banner, *n.* the standard of a feudal lord, used as a rallying-point in battle; hence (*fig.*) **to join, follow, fight under the banner of;** an ensign or flag painted with some device or emblem; a flag, generally square, painted or embroidered with the arms of the person in whose honour it is borne; an ensign or symbol of principles or fellowship; the vexillum of a papilionaceous flower; †a banderole. **banner headline,** *n.* a headline in heavy type running across the entire page of a newspaper. **banner-screen,** *n.* a fire-screen suspended from a pole or mantelpiece by its upper edge. **bannered,** *a.* furnished with banners; borne on a banner. [OF *baniere* (late L *bannum, bandum,* standard, Goth. *bandwa,* sign, token, perh. from same root as BAND, BIND)]

banneret, *n.* †a knight entitled to lead a company of vassals under his banner, ranking above other knights and next below a baron; a title conferred for deeds done in the king's presence on a field of battle; a title borne by certain officers in Switzerland and in some of the old Italian republics. [OF *baneret* (*baniere,* see prec., *-et, -ate,* L *-ātus*)]

bannerette, *n.* a small banner. [OF *banerete*]

bannerol, *n.* a banner about a yard square, borne at the funeral of eminent personages and placed over the tomb. [BANDEROLE]

Bannister, *n.* **Roger Gilbert** (1929–), English athlete, the first person to run the mile in under four minutes. He achieved this feat at Oxford, England, on 6 May 1954 in a time of 3 min. 59.4 sec.

bannock, *n.* a flat round cake made of pease- or barley-meal or flour, usu. unleavened, and baked on an iron plate over the fire. [Gael. *bannach* (perh. from L *pānicium,* from *pānis,* bread)]

Bannockburn, Battle of, battle in central Scotland, near Stirling, on 24 June 1314, when Robert I (also known as Robert the Bruce) defeated the English under Edward II.

banns, *n.pl.* proclamation in church of an intended marriage, so that any impediment thereto may be made known and inquired into. **to forbid the banns,** to allege an impediment to an intended marriage. [BAN[2]]

banquet, *n.* a sumptuous feast, usu. of a ceremonial character, followed by speeches. *v.t.* to entertain at a sumptuous feast. *v.i.* to take part in a banquet, to feast luxuriously. **†running banquet,** a repast taken between meals; a snack. **banqueter,** *n.* the giver of a banquet; one entertained at a banquet; a feaster, a carouser. [F dim. of *banc,* bench (cp. It. *banchetto,* dim. of *banco,* table)]

banquette, *n.* a bank behind a parapet on which soldiers mount to fire; the long seat behind the driver in a French diligence; built-in cushioned seating along a wall. [F, from It. *banchetta,* dim. of *banca,* a bench, BANK[1]]

banshee, *n.* a supernatural being, supposed by the peasantry in Ireland and the Scottish Highlands to wail round a house when one of the inmates is about to die. [Ir. *bean sidhe,* OIr. *ben sīde,* woman of the fairies]

bant BANTING.

bantam, *n.* a small domestic fowl, of which the cocks are very pugnacious; a small and conceited or very pugnacious person. **bantam-weight,** *n.* a boxer not exceeding 8 st. 6 lb. (53·5 kg) in weight if professional, or between 8 st. and 8 st. 7 lb. (51–54 kg) if amateur. [name from *Bantam* in Java, whence they were said (prob. wrongly) to have been first brought]

banter, *v.t.* to ridicule good-humouredly; to rally, to chaff. *v.i.* to indulge in good-natured raillery. *n.* good-natured raillery, chaff. [etym. unknown]

banting, *n.* the reduction of obesity by abstinence from fat, starch and sugar. **bant,** *v.i.* (*coll.*) to practise this method. [W. Banting, 1797–1878, inventor]

Banting, *n.* **Frederick Grant** (1891–1941), Canadian physician who discovered the hormone insulin in 1921 when, experimentally, he tied off the ducts of the pancreas in order to determine the function of the islets of Langerhans. He was helped by Charles Best and John J.R. Macleod, with whom he shared the 1923 Nobel Prize for Medicine.

bantling, *n.* a little child, a brat; †bastard. [prob. from G *Bänkling,* a bastard (*Bank,* a bench, whence bench-begotten)]

Bantu, *n.* a group of languages of S and Central Africa including Swahili, Xhosa, and Zulu; a member of the peoples inhabiting these areas; an official name for Black S Africans; (*pl.* **-tu, -tus**) (*offensive*) a Bantu speaker. *a.* relating to these languages or peoples. **Bantustan,** *n.* (*coll.*) a name formerly applied to semi-autonomous regions of the Republic of S Africa reserved for Black people. [Bantu, *Ba-ntu,* people]

banxring, *n.* a Javanese squirrel-like tree-shrew, *Tupaia javanica*. [Javanese, *bangsring*]

banyan, banian, *n.* a Hindu merchant or shop-keeper, esp. in Bengal, a native broker or hawker; a loose morning-gown or jacket; the banian-tree. **banian-day,** *n.* a day when sailors have no meat (in allusion to the vegetarian diet of Hindus). **banian-hospital,** *n.* a hospital for animals, named in reference to caste reverence for animal life. **bānian-, banyan-tree,** *n.* the Indian fig-tree, *Ficus indica,* the branches of which drop shoots to the ground, which taking root support the parent branches and in turn become trunks, so that one tree covers a very large extent of ground. The name was originally given to a tree near Gombroon, on the Persian Gulf, under which banians or traders had built a pagoda. [Port. *banian,* a trader, Arab. *banyan,* Gujarati *vaniyo,* one of the trading caste, Sansk. *vanij,* a merchant]

banzai, *int.* Japanese battle-cry, patriotic salute or cheer. [Jap. *banzai,* 10,000 years, forever]

baobab, *n.* an African tree, *Adansonia digitata,* called also monkey-bread. [prob. native]

BAOR, (*abbr.*) British Army of the Rhine.

bap, *n.* a large soft roll. [etym. unknown]

Baphomet, *n.* an idol or symbol which the Knights Templars were accused of worshipping. **baphometic,** *a.* [F, corrupted from *Mahomet*]

Baptist, *n.* member of any of several Protestant and evangelical Christian sects practising baptism by immersion of believers only on profession of faith. Baptists seek their authority in the Bible. Baptism originated among English Dissenters who took refuge in the Netherlands in the early 17th cent., and spread by emigration and, later, missionary activity. Of the world total of approximately 31 million, some 26.5 million are in the US and 265,000 in the UK.

baptize, -ise, *v.t.* to sprinkle with or immerse in water as a sign of purification and consecration, esp. into the Christian Church; to consecrate, purify, initiate; to christen, to give a name or nickname to; to name (a ship) at launching; to initiate into or to introduce to for the first time. *v.i.* to administer baptism. **baptism,** *n.* the act of baptizing; the ceremony of sprinkling with or immersion in water, by which a person is admitted into the Christian Church; a ceremonial naming of ships, church bells etc.; an initiation (ceremony). **baptism of blood,** martyrdom before baptism. **baptism of fire,** the baptism of the Holy Ghost, martyrdom; a soldier's first experience of actual war. **baptismal,** *a.* conferred at baptism. **baptismally,** *adv.* **baptist,** *n.* one who baptizes; (**Baptist**) a special title of St John, the forerunner of Christ (see also above); **baptistery, baptistry,** *n.* the place where baptism is administered, originally a building adjoining the church; the tank used for baptism in Baptist churches; (*poet.*) baptism. [OF *baptiser,* L *baptizāre,* Gr. *baptizein,* (*baptein,* to dip)]

bar[1], *n.* a piece of wood, iron or other solid material, long in proportion to breadth; a pole; a transverse piece in a gate, window, door, fire-grate etc.; a connecting piece in various structures; a straight stripe, a broad band; an ingot of gold or silver cast in a mould; (*pl.*) the ridged divisions in a horse's palate; the part of the wall of a horse's hoof that bends inwards; any thing that constitutes a hindrance or obstruction; a bank of silt, sand or gravel deposited at the mouth of a river or harbour; a rail or barrier, a space marked off by a rail or barrier; (*Law Courts*) the barrier at which prisoners stand during trial; the railing separating ordinary barristers from Queen's Counsel, hence the profession of a barrister; barristers collectively; any tribunal; the barrier cutting off a space near the door in both Houses of Parliament, to which non-members are admitted; the counter in a public house, hotel or other house or place of refreshment, across which liquors etc. are sold; the room containing this; (*Mus.*) a vertical line drawn across the stave to divide a composition into parts of equal duration, and to indicate periodical recurrence; the portion contained between two such lines; a strip of metal mounted parallel to a rail, which holds points or makes a signal when depressed by the wheels of a train; two horizontal lines across a shield; a metal strip attached to a medal, indicative of an additional award; (*Law*) a plea or objection of sufficient force to stop an action; any physical or moral barrier or obstacle; a counter or place where foods, goods or services are sold or provided. *v.t.* (*past, p.p.* **barred**) to fasten with a bar or bars; to obstruct, to exclude; to take exception to; to hinder, to prevent; to mark with or form into bars; (*Law*) to stay by objection; to cancel a claim or right; (*Betting*) to exclude; (*sl.*) to object to, dislike. **to be called within the bar,** to be made a Queen's Counsel. **to call to the bar,** to admit as a barrister. **trial at bar,** a trial before all the judges of a court, a trial in the Queen's Bench division. **bar-bell,** *n.* a metal bar with heavy disks at each end used for weightlifting and exercising. **bar chart, -graph,** *n.* a graph containing vertical or horizontal bars representing comparative quantities. **bar code,** *n.* a compact arrangement of lines of varied lengths and thicknesses which is machine-readable, printed on supermarket goods, books etc., giving coded details of price, quantity etc. **bar-iron,** *n.* iron wrought into malleable bars. **bar-keeper,** *n.* a bartender; a toll-bar keeper. **barmaid,** *n.* a female bartender. **barman,** *n.* a male bartender. **bar-parlour,** *n.* a small room adjoining or containing a bar in a public house. **bar-posts,** *n.pl.* posts sunk in the ground to admit movable bars serving the purpose of a gate. **bar-room,** *n.* the room in a public house in which the bar is situated. **bar-shoe,** *n.* a horse-shoe with a bar across the hinder part, to protect the frog. **bar-shot,** *n.* a bar with half a cannon-shot at each end, formerly used to injure masts and rigging. **bar-sinister** BEND SINISTER. **bartender,** *n.* one who serves at the bar of a public house, hotel etc. **bar-tracery,** *n.* window tracery characteristic of later Gothic in which the stonework resembles a twisted bar, as distinguished from *plate tracery,* in which the apertures were cut in solid slabs of stone. **barred,** *a.* furnished or secured with a bar or bars; obstructed by a bar; striped, streaked. **barring,** *n., a.* **barring-out,** *n.* a rebellion by schoolboys who shut the master out of the school, and keep him out till certain demands are conceded. [OF *barre,* late L *barra* (etym. unknown)]

bar[2], *n.* the maigre, a large European fish. [F]

bar[3], *n.* a unit of atmospheric pressure which is equivalent to 10^6 dynes per square centimetre (10^5 newtons per square metre). [Gr. *baros,* weight]

bar[4], *prep.* except, apart from. **bar none,** without exception. **bar one,** except one. **barring accidents,** apart from accidents.

bar., (*abbr.*) baritone; barometric; barrel; barrister.

bar- BAR(O)-.

Barabbas, *n.* in the New Testament, a condemned robber released by Pilate at Passover instead of Jesus to appease a mob.

baralipton, *n.* second word in the mnemonic lines representing the first figure of a syllogism (cp. BARBARA). [formed on L]

barathrum, *n.* a pit or chasm outside Athens into which condemned criminals were thrown; the abyss (of hell); anything insatiable. [L, from Gr. *barathron*]

barb[1], *n.* †the beard of man, or the analogous growth in the lower animals; the appendages on the mouth of the barbel and other fishes; part of a woman's head-dress, still worn by some nuns; a recurved point, as in a fish-hook or arrow; a point, a sting; a biting or pointed remark or comment; one of the lateral filaments from the shaft of a feather; (*Bot.*) a hooked hair. *v.t.* †to shave, to trim; to furnish (fish-hooks, arrows etc.) with barbs. **barbed wire,** *n.* a wire armed with sharp points, used for fences, to protect front-line trenches, to enclose prison camps. [F *barbe,* L *barba,* beard]

barb[2], *n.* a fine breed of horse; a fancy breed of pigeons (both orig. from Barbary). [F *barbe* (from the country, *Barbarie*)]

†**barb**[3], *n.* armour for the breast and flanks of a horse. **barbed,** *a.* covered with armour. [corr. of BARD[2]]

Barbados, *n.* island in the Caribbean, one of the Lesser Antilles. **area** 430 sq km/166 sq miles. **capital** Bridgetown. **physical** most easterly island of the West Indies; surrounded by coral reefs. **population** (1985) 253,000; annual growth rate 0.3%. **exports** sugar, rum, oil. **language** English. **religion** Christian.

barbara, *n.* a mnemonic word used to designate the first mood of the first figure of syllogisms, containing three universal affirmatives, e.g. all A is B; all C is A; ∴ all C is B. [L, barbarous things]

barbarian, *n.* a savage, a person belonging to some uncivilized race; one destitute of pity or humanity; (*formerly*) one not Greek, one not Greek or Roman, one outside the Roman Empire; one outside the pale of Christian civilization; a foreigner having outlandish manners and language. *a.* rude, uncivilized, savage; cruel, inhuman. **barbaric,** *a.* of or pertaining to barbarians; rude, uncouth, uncivilized. **barbarism,** *n.* an impropriety of speech, a foreign idiom; absence of civilization, brutality, cruelty; lack of culture or refinement; a concrete instance of this defect. **barbarity,** *n.* brutality, inhumanity, cruelty; an act of brutality or cruelty; the state or quality of being barbaric; a barbarism. **barbarize, -ise,** *v.t.* to render barbarous; to corrupt (a language). *v.i.* to utter a barbarism in speech; to grow barbarous. **barbarization, -isation,** *n.* the act of barbarizing; the state of being barbarized. **barbarous,** *a.* foreign in speech, barbarian; hence, harsh-sounding; rude, uncivilized; uncultured, unpolished; cruel; uncouth. **barbarously,** *adv.* **barbarousness,** *n.* [L *barbarus,* Gr. *barbaros* (prob. a word imitative of unintelligible speech)]

Barbarossa, *n.* nickname 'red beard' given to the Holy Roman emperor Frederick I, and also to two brothers who were Barbary pirates. **Horuk** was killed by the Spaniards in 1518; **Khair-ed-Din** took Tunis in 1534 and died in Constantinople 1546.

Barbarossa, operation, *n.* German code name for the plans to invade the USSR during World War II in 1941.

Barbary, *n.* an extensive region in the north of Africa; †a Barbary horse or pigeon, a barb. **Barbary ape,** *n.* a tailless ape, *Macaca sylvana* found in the north of Africa, with a colony on the rock of Gibraltar. **Barbary gum,** *n.* a gum obtained from *Acacia gummifera.* **Barbary hen** GUINEA-HEN. **Barbary-horse** BARB[2]. [Arab. *Berber,* a native of Barbary (perh. from Gr. *barbaria,* country of the barbarians)]

barbate, *n.* (*Bot., Zool.*) bearded; having small tufts of hair. [L *barbātus*]

barbecue, *n.* a framework on which meat is smoked; a very large grill or gridiron; an animal broiled or roasted whole; a social picnic at which food is prepared outdoors over a charcoal fire; food so cooked; an open floor for drying coffee-beans. *v.t.* to smoke or dry (meat etc.) on a framework over a fire; to broil or roast whole. [Sp. *barbacoa,* Haitian *barbàcoa*]

barbel, *n.* a European freshwater fish, *Barbus vulgaris,* allied to the carp, named from the fleshy filaments which hang below the mouth; the small fleshy filament hanging from the mouth of some fishes, probably organs of touch. **barbelled, barbeled,** *a.* furnished with barbels. [OF *barbel,* late L *barbellum* (nom. *-us*), dim. of *barbus,* barbel (*barba,* beard)]

barber, *n.* one who shaves and cuts beards and hair. *v.t.* to shave or dress the hair of. †**barber-monger,** *n.* one who constantly frequented the barber's shop; a fop. **barber's block,** *n.* a round block on which wigs were made up and displayed; a fop. **barbershop,** *n., a.* a type of close harmony singing for male voices, usu. quartets. **barber's itch, rash,** *n.* sycosis, an inflammation of the roots of the hair. **barber's pole,** *n.* a pole usu. striped spirally, exhibited as a sign in front of a barber's shop. †**barber-surgeon,** *n.* a barber who practised surgery, as was the custom till the reign of Henry VIII. [A-F *barbour,* OF *barbeor* (L *barbātōr -em,* from *barba,* beard)]

Barber, *n.* **Samuel** (1910–81), US composer of works in a restrained neo-classical style, including *Adagio for Strings* (1936) and the opera *Vanessa* (1958).

barberry, berberry, *n.* a shrub of the genus *Berberis,* esp. *B. vulgaris;* the red acid berry of this tree. [late L *barbaris* or *berberis* (etym. doubtful)]

barbet, *n.* a tropical bird allied to the toucans, having tufts of hair at base of its bill. [prob. OF *barbet,* L *barbātus,* bearded (*barba,* beard)]

barbette, *n.* a mound of earth in a fortification on which guns are mounted to be fired over the parapet; a platform for a similar purpose on a warship. **guns en barbette,** guns so mounted as to allow of their being fired over a parapet without embrasures or port-holes. **barbette-cruiser,** *n.* a cruiser equipped with barbettes. [F, dim. of *barbe,* beard]

barbican, *n.* an outer fortification to a city or castle, designed as a cover to the inner works; esp. over a gate or bridge and serving as a watch-tower. [OF *barbacan* (etym. doubtful)]

Barbican, the, an arts and residential complex in the City of London. The Barbican Arts Centre (1982) contains theatres, cinemas, exhibitions and concert halls.

Barbie, *n.* **Klaus** (1913–), German Nazi, a member of the SS from 1936. During World War II he was involved in the deportation of Jews from the occupied Netherlands (1940–42) and in tracking down Jews and Resistance workers in France (1942–45). He was arrested 1983 and convicted of crimes against humanity in France in 1987.

Barbirolli, *n.* **John** (1899–1970), English conductor. He made a name as a cellist, and in 1937 succeeded Toscanini as conductor of the New York Philharmonic Orchestra. He returned to England in 1943, where he remained conductor of the Hallé Orchestra, Manchester until his death.

barbituric, *a.* term applied to an acid obtained from malonic and uric acids. **barbitone,** (*N Am.*) **barbital,** *n.* a derivative of barbituric acid used as a sedative, veronal. **barbiturates,** *n.pl.* (*Med.*) compounds with hypnotic and sedative properties derived from barbituric acid. [G *Barbitursäure*]

Barbizon school, *n.* French school of landscape painters of the mid-19th century, based at Barbizon in the forest of Fontainebleau. Members included J.F. Millet, Diaz de la Peña (1807–76), and Théodore Rousseau (1812–67). They aimed to paint fresh, realistic scenes, sketching and painting their subjects in the open air.

barbola, *n.* the attachment of small flowers etc. in paste to embellish vases etc. [etym. unknown]

Barbour, *n.* **John** (*c.* 1316–95), Scottish poet whose chronicle-poem *The Brus* is among the earliest Scottish poetry.

Barbuda, *n.* one of the islands which form the state of Antigua and Barbuda.

barbule, *n.* a hooked or serrated filament given off from the barb of a feather. [L *barbula,* dim. of *barba,* beard]

barcarole, -rolle, *n.* a song sung by Venetian gondoliers; a composition of a similar kind. [F *barcarolle,* It. *barcarola,* from *barcaruola,* a boat song (*barca,* a boat)]

Barcelona, *n.* capital, industrial city (textiles, engineering, chemicals), and port of Catalonia, NE Spain; population (1986) 1,694,000. As the chief centre of anarchism and Catalonian nationalism it was prominent in the overthrow of the monarchy (1931), and was the last city of the republic to surrender to Franco in 1939.

bard[1], *n.* a Celtic minstrel; one of an order whose function it was to celebrate heroic achievements, and to perpetuate historical facts and traditions in verse; hence, a poet generally; (*Welsh*) a poet honoured at the Eisteddfod. **Bard of Avon,** Shakespeare. **bardic,** *a.* **bardish,** *a.* **bardism,** *n.* the sentiments, maxims or system of the bards. **bardling,** *n.* a young bard, a tyro; a poetaster. **bardolatry,** *n.* the worship of Shakespeare. [Gael. and Ir. *bàrd*]

†**bard[2],** *n.* (*usu. pl.*) protective armour for a war-horse; armour for men-at-arms. *v.t.* to caparison; to adorn with trappings; to cover with slices of bacon before roasting (from an old sense of the noun). [F *barde,* armour for a horse (perhaps from Sp. and Port. *albarda,* a pack-saddle, Arab. *al-barda'ah*)]

Bardeen, *n.* **John** (1908–), US physicist, who won a Nobel prize in 1956, with Walter Brattain and William Shockley, for the development of the transistor in 1948. In 1972, he was the first double winner of a Nobel prize in the same subject (with Leon Cooper and John Schrieffer) for his work on superconductivity.

Bardot, *n.* **Brigitte** (1934–), French film actress, whose sensual appeal did much to popularize French cinema internationally. Her films include *Et Dieu créa la Femme/And God Created Woman* (1950) and *Shalako* (1968).

Bardo Thodol, *n.* also known as the *Book of the Dead*, a Tibetan Buddhist text giving instructions to the newly dead about the Bardo, or state between death and rebirth.

bare, *a.* unclothed, naked, nude; with the head uncovered as a mark of respect; destitute of natural covering, as hair, fur, flesh, leaves, soil etc.; napless; unarmoured, unarmed, defenceless; unsheathed; poor, indigent, ill-furnished, empty; simple, mere, unsupported, undisguised, open; bald, meagre; unadorned. *v.t.* to strip, to make bare; to uncover, unsheathe; to make manifest. **bareback,** *a., adv.* without a saddle. **bare-backed,** *a.* with the back unclothed; without a saddle. **barefaced,** *a.* having the face bare or uncovered; unconcealed, impudent, shameless; beardless, whiskerless. **barefacedly,** *adv.* **barefacedness,** *n.* **barefoot,** *a., adv.* with the feet naked. **barefoot doctor,** *n.* a villager, esp. in Asia, who has been trained in basic health care to meet the simple medical needs of the community. **bare-footed,** *a.* **bare-headed,** *a.* **bare poles,** *n.pl.* masts with no sails set. **barely,** *adv.* nakedly, poorly; hardly, scarcely; baldly, openly, plainly, explicitly. **bareness,** *n.* the quality of being bare; poverty, meanness; †leanness. **barish,** *a.* rather bare; poorly covered. [OE *bær* (cp. OHG *par,* G *bar,* Dut. *baar*)]

Barebones Parliament, *n.* the English assembly called by Oliver Cromwell to replace the 'Rump Parliament' in July 1653. It consisted of 140 members nominated by the army and derived its name from one of its members, Praise-God Barbon. Although they attempted to pass sensible legislation (civil marriage; registration of births, deaths, and marriages; custody of lunatics), their attempts to abolish tithes, patronage, and the court of chancery, and to codify the law led to the resignation of the moderates and its dissolution in Dec. 1653.

barège, *n.* a light gauzy dress fabric originally made at Barèges, Hautes-Pyrénées, France.

Barenboim, *n.* **Daniel** (1942–), Israeli pianist and conductor, born in Argentina. Pianist/conductor with the English Chamber Orchestra from 1964, he became conductor of the New York Philharmonic Orchestra in 1970 and musical director of the Orchestre de Paris in 1975. Appointed artistic director of the Opéra Bastille, Paris, July 1987, he was dismissed from his post a few months before its opening in July 1989. He is a celebrated interpreter of Mozart and Beethoven.

Barents, *n.* **Willem** (*c.* 1550–97), Dutch explorer and navigator. He made three expeditions to seek the Northeast Passage; he died on the last voyage. The Barents Sea, part of the Arctic Ocean N of Norway, is named after him.

baresark, BERSERK.

barette, *n.* (*N Am.*) a hair-clasp.

bargain, *n.* haggling, discussions as to terms; an agreement between two parties, generally concerning a sale; the thing bought or sold; an advantageous purchase. †*v.i.* to agree to buy or sell, to transfer for a consideration. *v.i.* to haggle over terms; to make a contract or agreement for purchase or sale. **a bad bargain,** a purchase or sale adverse to the party under consideration. **bargain and sale,** a method of conveyance. **Dutch bargain, wet bargain,** a bargain concluded over a glass of liquor. **into the bargain,** over and above what is stipulated. **to bargain for,** to count on, to expect. **to be off one's bargain,** to be released from a purchase or engagement. **to make the best of**

a bad bargain, to do the best one can in adverse circumstances. **to strike a bargain,** to come to terms. **bargain-basement, -counter,** *n.* basement or counter in a store where goods are sold which have been marked down in price. **bargainee,**, *n.* the person who accepts a conveyance of bargain and sale; the purchaser. **bargainer,** *n.* a trafficker, a haggler; †a bargainor. **bargainor,** *n.* one who transfers real property by bargain and sale; the seller. [OF *bargaigner,* to trade, to haggle]

bargan, barragan, *n.* a boomerang. [Austral. Abor.]

barge, *n.* a flat-bottomed freight-boat, with or without sails, used principally on canals or rivers; the second boat of a man-of-war; a large ornamental state or pleasure boat, an ornamental houseboat. *v.i.* to lurch (into), rush (against). **bargeman,** *n.* **barge-master,** *n.* **barge-pole,** *n.* the pole with which a barge is propelled or kept clear of banks etc. **not fit to be touched with a barge-pole,** not fit to come near on account of dirt, disease or ill temper. **bargee,** *n.* a bargeman. [OF *barge,* late L *barga,* var. for *barca,* BARK3]

barge-, *comb. form.* **barge-board,** *n.* a projecting horizontal board at the gable-end of a building, concealing the barge-couples and warding off the rain. **barge-couples,** *n.pl.* two beams mortised and tenoned together to increase the strength of a building. **barge-course,** *n.* the tiling projecting beyond the principal rafters in a building; a wall-coping formed of bricks set on edge. **barge-stones,** *n.pl.* stones set on the sloping or stepped edge of a gable-end. [med. L *bargus,* a kind of gallows]

barghest, -gest, -gaist, *n.* a dog-like goblin whose apparition portends calamity or death. [G *Berggeist,* mountain demon]

Bari, *n.* capital of Puglia region, S Italy, and industrial port on the Adriatic; population (1988) 359,000. It is the site of Italy's first nuclear power station; the part of the town known as Tecnopolis is the Italian equivalent of Silicon Valley.

baric, BARIUM.

Barikot, *n.* a garrison town in Konar province, E Afghanistan, near the Pakistan frontier. Besieged by mujaheddin rebels in 1985, the relief of Barikot by Soviet and Afghan troops was one of the largest military engagements of the Afghan war during Soviet occupation.

barilla, *n.* an impure alkali obtained from the ash of *Salsola soda* and allied species; an impure alkali obtained from kelp; a plant, *Salsola soda,* common on the seashore in Spain, Sicily and the Canaries. [Sp.]

Barisal, *n.* river port and capital city of Barisal region, S Bangladesh; population (1981) 142,000. It trades in jute, rice, fish, and oilseed.

baritone, *n.* a male voice intermediate between a bass and a tenor; a singer having such a voice; the smaller bass sax-horn in B flat or C; (*Gr. gram.*) a word unaccented on the last syllable. *a.* having a compass between tenor and bass; of or pertaining to such a compass; (*Gr. gram.*) unaccented on the last syllable. **baritone-clef,** *n.* the F clef on the middle line of the bass stave. [F *baryton,* It. *baritono,* Gr. *barutonos* (*barus,* heavy, *tonos,* tone)]

barium, *n.* a metallic divalent element, at. no. 56; chem. symbol Ba, the metallic base of baryta. **barium meal,** *n.* a mixture of barium-sulphate, administered to allow X-ray examination of a patient's stomach or intestines. **baric,** *a.* containing barium. [BARYTA, -IUM]

bark1, *v.i.* to utter a sharp, explosive cry, like that of a dog; to speak in a peevish, explosive manner; to cough. †*v.t.* to burst forth with. *n.* a sharp, explosive cry, orig. of dogs, hence of other animals; the report of a firearm; a cough. **to bark up the wrong tree,** to be on a false scent; to accuse the wrong person. **barker,** *n.* one who or that which barks; a dog; a clamorous assailant; an auction tout; a vocal advertiser for a circus, fun-fair etc.; (*sl.*) a pistol, a cannon. **barking,** *n., a.* **barking-bird,** *n.* the *Pteroptochus tarnu,* from S America, named from its cry. **barking-iron,** *n.* (*sl.*) a pistol. [OE *beorcan* (cp. Icel. *berkja*)]

bark2, *n.* the rind or exterior covering of a tree, formed of tissues parallel to the wood; spent bark, tan; an outer covering. *v.t.* to strip the bark from (a tree); to cut a ring in the bark so as to kill (the tree); to steep in a solution of bark, to tan; to graze, to abrade (the shins, elbows etc.); to cover with or as with bark, to encrust; to strip or scrape off. **bark-bed,** *n.* a hot-bed formed of spent bark. **bark-bound,** *a.* having the bark so close as to hinder the growth. **bark-mill,** *n.* a mill for crushing bark. **bark-pit,** *n.* a pit in which hides are tanned. **bark-tree,** *n.* the popular name of the genus *Cinchona.* **barker,** *n.* one who strips the bark from a tree. **barky,** *a.* covered with bark; of the nature of or resembling bark. [Scand. (Swed. *bark,* Icel. *bōrkr* etc.)]

bark3, barque, *n.* (*Poet.*) a ship or boat, esp. a small sailing vessel; (*usu.* **barque**) a sailing-vessel with three or more masts, square-rigged on the fore and main masts, schooner rigged on the mizzen or other masts. **barkentine** BARQUENTINE. **barque-rigged,** *a.* rigged like a barque. [F *barque,* Prov., Sp. or It. *barca,* a small ship or boat]

Barker1, *n.* **Clive** (1952–), British horror writer, whose *Books of Blood* (1984–85) are in the sensationalist tradition of horror fiction.

Barker2, *n.* **George** (1913–), British poet noted for his vivid imagery, as in *Calamiterror* (1937), *The True Confessions of George Barker* (1950), and *Collected Poems* (1930–50).

Barlach, *n.* **Ernst** (1870–1938), German expressionist sculptor, painter, and poet. His simple, evocative figures carved in wood (for example in St Catherine's, Lübeck, 1930–32) often express melancholy.

barley1, *n.* the grain or the plant of the genus *Hordeum,* a hardy, awned cereal, used for soups, malt liquors and spirits, animal feeds etc. **pearl-barley,** barley stripped of the husk and ground to a small white lump. †**barley-break,** *n.* an old rustic game, played round stacks of grain (see also BARLEY2). **barley-broth,** *n.* broth made with barley; strong beer. **barley-corn,** *n.* a grain of barley; a measure, the third part of an inch (about 0·8 cm) **John Barleycorn,** *n.* barley personified as the grain from which malt liquor is made; malt liquor. **barley-mow,** *n.* stack of barley. **barley-sugar,** *n.* a hard confection, prepared by boiling down sugar, formerly with a decoction of barley. **barley-water,** *n.* a soothing drink made from pearl-barley. **barley-wine,** *n.* a kind of wine prepared by the ancient Greeks from barley; a strong kind of ale. [OE *bærlic; bær-* (cp. Icel. *barr,* OTeut. *bariz*) *-lic,* -LY]

barley2, *int.* (*Sc., North.*) parley, truce (a word called out in various games, signifying 'quarter'). **barley-break** (see prec.) may be derived from this. [perh. corr. of F *parlez,* speak]

barm1, *n.* the frothy scum which rises to the surface of malt liquor in fermentation, used as a leaven; yeast. **barmy,** *a.* of or full of barm or yeast; frothing, fermenting; crazy, cracked, silly (cp. BALMY: (*sl.*)). [OE *beorma* (cp. Dan. *bārme,* Fris. *berme,* G *Bärme*)]

†**barm2,** *n.* a bosom, lap. **barm-cloth,** *n.* an apron. [OE *barm* (*beran,* to wear)]

Barmecide, *n.* one who gives illusory benefits. *a.* barmecidal. **Barmecide feast,** *n.* short commons. **barmecidal,** *a.* unreal, unsatisfying, illusory. [name of a family who ruled at Baghdad, one of whom is said in the *Arabian Nights* to have invited a beggar to an imaginary feast]

bar mitzvah, *n.* a Jewish boy who has reached the age of religious responsibility, usu. on his 13th birthday; the ceremony and celebration marking this event. [Heb., son of the law]

barn, *n.* a covered building for the storage of grain and other agricultural produce; a barn-like building; (*N Am.*) a stable, a cowshed. **barn dance,** *n.* a dance, originally US, somewhat like a schottische. **barn door,** *n.* the large door of a barn; a target too big to be easily missed. *a.* of fowls, reared at the barndoor. **barn-owl,** *n.* the white, church and screech owl, *Strix flammea.* **barnstorm,** *v.i.* to tour the country giving theatrical performances; (*N Am.*) to tour rural areas giving political speeches at election time. **barnstormer,** *n.* a strolling-player. **barnyard,** *n.* the yard adjoining a barn; a farmyard, a barton. †*v.t.* to put into a barn, to garner. [OE *bern: berern* (*bere,* barley, *aern,* house)]

Barnabas, St, *n.* in the New Testament, a 'fellow labourer' with St Paul; he went with St Mark on a missionary journey to Cyprus, his birthplace. Feast day 11 June.

Barnaby, *n.* Barnabas. **Barnaby-Bright,** *n.* St Barnabas's Day, 11 June; according to the Old Style, the longest day. [F *Barnabé,* L *Barnabas*]

barnacle, *n.* (also **bernacle**) the barnacle-goose; the popular name of the cirripede crustacean that lives attached to rocks, ship bottoms etc.; a constant attendant. **barnacle-goose,** *n.* a species of wild goose, *Anas leucopsis,* formerly supposed to be developed from the common barnacle, *Lepas anatifera.* [OF *bernaque* (etym. doubtful, perhaps from L *Hibernicae, Hiberniculae,* Irish goose)]

barnacles, *n.pl.* a kind of twitch put on the nostrils of a restive horse while being shod; an instrument of torture used in a similar manner; (*coll.*) a pair of spectacles, goggles. [OF *bernac,* flat-nosed (etym. unknown)]

Barnard, *n.* **Christiaan Neethling** (1922–), South African surgeon who performed the first human heart transplant in 1967 in Cape Town. The patient, 54-year-old Louis Washkansky, lived for 18 days.

Barnardo, *n.* **Thomas John** (1845–1905), British philanthropist, who was known as Dr Barnardo, although not medically qualified. He opened the first of a series of homes for destitute children in 1867 in Stepney, E London.

Barnard's star, *n.* second-closest star to the Sun, 6 light years away in the constellation Ophiuchus. It is a faint red dwarf of 9th magnitude, visible only through a telescope.

Barnet, Battle of, in the English Wars of the Roses, the defeat of Lancaster by York on 14 Apr. 1471 in Barnet, Hertfordshire (now NW London).

barney, *n.* (*coll.*) a humbug, a cheating; an unfair contest, esp. a prize-fight of a disreputable kind; a lark, a spree. [etym. unknown]

Barnum, *n.* **Phineas T(aylor)** (1810–91), US showman. In 1871, after an adventurous career, he established the 'Greatest Show on Earth' (which included the midget 'Tom Thumb') comprising circus, menagerie, and an exhibition of 'freaks', conveyed in 100 rail cars. He coined the phrase 'there's a sucker born every minute'.

bar(o)-, *comb. form* weight, pressure. [Gr. *baros,* weight]

barograph, *n.* an aneroid barometer recording the variations of atmospheric pressure. **barogram,** *n.* the record produced by a barograph.

barogyroscope, *n.* a gyrostat used for demonstrating the rotation of the earth.

barology, *n.* the science of weight.

barometer, *n.* an instrument used for measuring the atmospheric pressure, thus indicating probable weather change, and also for measuring altitudes reached; any indicator of change (e.g. in public opinion). **barometric, -ical,** *a.* of or pertaining to the barometer; measured or indicated by a barometer. **barometrically,** *adv.* **barometry,** *n.* the art or practice of taking barometrical observations. [Gr. *baros,* weight]

barometrography, *n.* the branch of meteorology which deals with the measurement of atmospheric pressure.

baron, *n.* one who held land by military service from the king; a Great Baron, attending the Great Council or summoned to Parliament; a noble, a peer; a member of the lowest rank of nobility; a title of the judges of the Court of Exchequer; †a freeman of the Cinque Ports; †a member of Parliament for any of these Ports; (*Law, Her.*) a husband; a powerful head of a business or financial organization. **baron of beef,** a joint consisting of the two sirloins. **baronage,** *n.* the whole body of barons, the peerage; the dignity of a baron; the land from which a baron derives his title, a barony; a published list of barons. **baroness,** *n.* the wife or widow of a baron; a lady who holds the baronial dignity in her own right. **baronial,** *a.* **barony,** *n.* the lordship, or fee, of a baron; the rank or dignity of a baron; a subdivision of a county of Ireland; a large manor in Scotland. [OF *barun, baron,* acc. of *ber,* man, husband; late L *baro,* a man (L *bāro,* a simpleton)]

baronet, *n.* a hereditary titled order of commoners ranking next below barons, instituted by James I in 1611. *v.t.* to confer a baronetcy on. **baronetage,** *n.* baronets collectively; the dignity of a baronet; a list of the baronets. **baronetcy** (-si), *n.* the title or rank of a baronet. [dim. of BARON (BARON, -ET)]

Barons' Wars, *n.pl.* civil wars in England: **1215–17** between King John and his barons, over his failure to honour Magna Carta; **1264–67** between Henry III (and the future Edward 1) and his barons (led by Simon de Montfort); **1264** 14 May **Battle of Lewes** at which Henry III was defeated and captured; **1265** 4 Aug. Simon de Montfort was defeated by Edward I at Evesham and killed.

baroque, *n.* orig., an irregularly shaped pearl; a style of artistic or architectural expression prevalent esp. in 17th-cent. Europe, characterized by extravagant ornamentation; a similar style in music or literature. *a.* baroque in style; grotesque; gaudy; flamboyant. [F, Port. *barroco,* Sp. *barrueco,* a rough or imperfect pearl (etym. doubtful)]

baroscope, *n.* a weather glass.

barothermograph, *n.* an instrument combining a barometer and a thermometer.

Barotseland, *n.* former kingdom in Western Province of Zambia.

barouche, *n.* a double-seated four-wheeled horse-drawn carriage, with a movable top, and a seat outside for the driver. [G *Barutsche,* It. *baroccio,* L *birotus,* two-wheeled]

barque BARK3.

barquentine, barkentine, *n.* a three-masted vessel, with the foremast square-rigged, and the main and mizen fore-and-aft rigged. [BARK3, either after BRIGANTINE or from Sp. *bergantine,* a small ship]

†**barracan, baracan,** *n.* a coarse cloth resembling camlet; a thin silky material. [F, from Arab. *barrakān,* a camlet cloak (Pers. *barak,* a garment made of camel's hair)]

barrack1, *n.* a temporary hut; (*pl.*) buildings used to house troops; any large building resembling barracks. *v.t.* to provide with barracks; to put in barracks. *v.i.* to lodge in barracks. **barrack-master,** *n.* an officer in charge of barracks. [F *baroque,* It. *baracca* or Sp. *barraca* (etym. doubtful)]

barrack2, *v.i.* to jeer; (*Austral.*) to cheer (for). *v.t.* to shout or cheer derisively at (e.g. a sports side); (*Austral.*) to shout support or encouragement for (a team). [Austral. Abor. *borak,* nonsense, or perh. Ir., to boast]

barracoon, *n.* a fortified African slave-house. [Sp. *barracon, barraca* (see BARRACK1)]

barracouta, *n.* a large edible fish of the Pacific. [var. of BARRACUDA.]

barracuda, *n.* (*pl.* **-da, -das**) a predatory tropical fish, dangerous to man. [Sp. *baracuta,* etym. unknown]

barrad, *n.* an Irish conical cap. [Ir. *baireud, bairread,* F *barrette,* BARRET]

barragan, barragon, *n.* a modern stuff supposed to be like barracan. [Sp. *barragan,* BARRACAN]

Barragán, *n.* **Luis** (1902–88), Mexican architect, known for his use of rough wooden beams, cobbles, lava, and adobe, his simple houses with walled gardens, and his fountains.

barrage1, *n.* the formation of an artificial bar or dam to raise the water in a river; the bar or dam so formed. [F, from *barre,* BAR, -AGE]

barrage2, *n.* (*Mil.*) a screen of artillery fire behind which troops can advance, or which can be laid down to hinder an enemy advance; heavy or continuous questioning or criticism. **box barrage,** a barrage surrounding a particular area. **creeping barrage,** a barrage that moves forward or backward at prearranged intervals. **balloon barrage,** disposition of anchored balloons to prevent hostile aircraft making machine-gun attacks.

barramundi, burramundi, *n.* a variety of perch found in Queensland rivers. [Austral. Abor.]

barranca, *n.* (*N Am.*) a deep gorge, with steep sides. [Sp.]

Barrancabermeja, *n.* a port and oil refining centre on the Magdalena River in the department of Santander, NE Colombia. A major outlet for oil from the De Mares fields which are linked by pipeline to Cartagena on the Caribbean coast.

Barranquilla, *n.* seaport in N Colombia, on the river Magdalena; population (1985) 1,120,900. Products include chemicals, tobacco, textiles, furniture and footwear.

Barras, *n.* **Paul François Jean Nicolas, Count Barras** (1755–1829), French revolutionary. He was elected to the National Convention in 1792, and helped to overthrow Robespierre (1794). In 1795 he became a member of the Directory (see FRENCH REVOLUTION). In 1796 he brought about the marriage of his former mistress, Joséphine de Beauharnais, with Napoleon, and assumed dictatorial powers. After Napoleon's coup d'état (19 Nov. 1799), Barras fell into disgrace.

barrator, -er, *n.* one who out of malice or for his own purposes stirs up litigation or discord; †a quarrelsome person, a bully; †a buyer or seller of church benefices. **barratry,** *n.* (*Law*) fraud or criminal negligence on the part of a master of a ship to the owners' detriment; the offence of vexatiously exciting or maintaining lawsuits; traffic in church or public offices. **barratrous,** *a.* [OF *barateor,* a fraudulent dealer, trickster (*barat,* fraud, perh. of Celtic origin; cp. OIr. *mrath, brath,* O Bret. *brat,* W *brad,* betrayal, treachery; sense influenced by Icel. *barātta,* strife)]

Barrault, *n.* **Jean Louis** (1910–), French actor and director. His films include *La Symphonie fantastique* (1942), *Les Enfants du Paradis* (1944), and *La Ronde* (1950).

barre, *n.* a wall-mounted horizontal rail used for ballet exercises. [F, bar]

Barre, *n.* **Raymond** (1924–), French politician, member of the centre-right Union pour la Démocratie Française; prime minister (1976–81), when he also held the Finance Ministry portfolio and gained a reputation as a tough and determined budget-cutter (nicknamed Monsieur Economy).

barrel, *n.* a cask; a cylindrical wooden vessel bulging in the middle, formed of staves held together by hoops, and with flat ends; the capacity or contents of such a vessel; anything resembling such a vessel, as the tube of a firearm, through which the bullet or shot is discharged; the belly and loins of a horse, ox etc.; a measure of capacity for liquid and dry goods, varying with the commodity; a revolving cylinder or drum round which a chain or rope is wound; the revolving cylinder studded with pins in a musical box or barrel-organ; (*Physiol.*) the cavity behind the drum of the ear; (*N Am. sl.*) money to be used for political campaigning. *v.t.* to draw off into, or put or stow in barrels. *v.i.* (*N Am.*) to drive fast. **to have someone over a barrel,** to have power over someone; to have someone at a disadvantage. **to scrape the barrel,** to get the last remaining bit; to obtain the last scrap. **barrel-bellied,** *a.* having a protuberant belly. **barrel-bulk,** *n.* (*Naut.*) a measure of 5 cu. ft. used in estimating the capacity of a vessel for freight. **barrel campaign,** *n.* (*N Am.*) an election fought by means of bribery. **barrel-drain,** *n.* a cylindrical drain. **barrel-organ,** *n.* a musical instrument in which the keys are mechanically acted on by a revolving cylinder (barrel) studded with pins. **barrel roll,** *n.* a manoeuvre in aerobatics in which an aircraft rolls about its longitudinal axis. **barrel-vault,** *n.* (*Arch.*) a semi-cylindrical vault. **barrelled,** *a.* packed in barrels; barrel-shaped; having a barrel or barrels. [F *baril* (etym. doubtful)]

barren, *a.* incapable of producing offspring; not producing; bearing no fruit; unfertile, producing no vegetation; fruitless, unprofitable; not productive intellectually, uninventive, dull. *n.* a tract of barren land, esp. in the US, elevated land on which small trees grow but not timber. **barrenly,** *adv.* **barrenness,** *n.* **barrenwort,** *n.* the English name of the genus *Epimedium,* esp. *E. alpinum,* with purple and yellow flowers. [MG *barain, baraine,* OF *baraine* (masc.), *brahain* (etym. unknown)]

barret, *n.* a little flat cap; a biretta. [F *barrette, biretta*]

barretter, *n.* (*Elec.*) an appliance for keeping current in a circuit at constant strength. [etym. unknown]

barricade, barricado, *n.* a hastily-formed rampart erected across a street or passage to obstruct an enemy or an attacking party; (*Naut.*) a wooden rail across the fore-part of the quarter-deck in ships of war; any bar or obstruction. *v.t.* to block or fortify with a barricade; to obstruct in any way by physical obstacles. [F *barricade,* Sp. *barricada,* p.p. of *barricare* (*barrica,* a barrel)]

barrico, *n.* (*pl.* **-coes**) a small cask, a keg. [Sp. *barrica*]

Barrie, *n.* **J(ames) M(atthew)** (1860–1937), Scottish playwright and novelist, author of *The Admirable Crichton* (1902) and the children's fantasy *Peter Pan* (1904).

barrier, *n.* that which hinders approach or attack; an enclosing fence; a limit, a boundary; the gate where customs are collected, in foreign towns; the starting-point (barred cells) in ancient races; the palisade enclosing a tournament ground, the lists; the railing across which tilters thrust with their spears; (*fig.*) any material or immaterial obstruction. *v.t.* to close (in) or shut (off) with a barrier. *a.* pertaining to an obstruction or separating agent, often protective, as in *barrier contraceptive.* **barrier cream,** *n.* a cream used to protect the hands from dirt, oils and solvents. **barrier-gate,** *n.* a gate in a barrier. **barrier ice,** *n.* ice-floe, ice-pack. **barrier-pillar,** *n.* a large pillar of coal supporting the roof of a mine. **barrier-reef,** *n.* a coral reef running nearly parallel to the land, with a lagoon between. [A-F *barrere,* OF, *barriere,* late L *barrāria* (*barra,* bar)]

barring, *prep.* (*coll.*) except, omitting. [BAR[1]]

barrio, *n.* (*pl.* **-rios**) a Spanish-speaking community or district, usu. sited in the poorer areas of cities in the Southwestern US. [Sp., district]

barrister, *n.* a member of the legal profession who has been admitted to practise as an advocate at the bar; a counsellor-at-law. **revising barrister,** a barrister formerly appointed to hold an annual court for the revision of the register of Parliamentary voters. **barristership,** *n.* [orig. *barrester,* prob. from BAR or F *barre* (the bar was orig. a division among the Benchers in the Inns of Court)]

barrow[1], *n.* a hill; a prehistoric grave-mound, a tumulus. [OE *beorg* (cp. G *Berg,* OTeut. *bergoz*)]

barrow[2], *n.* a shallow cart with two wheels pushed by hand; †a bier. **barrow-boy,** *n.* a street trader in fruit, vegetables or other goods with a barrow. **barrowful,** *n.* as much as a barrow will hold. [OE *bearwe,* from *beran,* to carry (see BEAR)]

†**barrow[3],** *n.* a castrated boar (later called **barrow-hog** or **barrow-pig**. [OE *bearg* (cp. Dut. *barg,* G *Barch,* OTeut. *barguz*)]

barrow[4], *n.* a long flannel garment without sleeves, for infants. **barrow-coat,** *n.* a child's coat. [perh. from OE *beorgan,* to protect]

Barrow[5], Clyde BONNIE AND CLYDE.

Barrow[6], *n.* **Isaac** (1630–77), British mathematician, theologian, and classicist. His *Lectiones geometricae* (1670) contains the essence of the theory of calculus, which was later expanded by Newton and Leibniz.

Barry, *n.* **Charles** (1795–1860), English architect of the neo-Gothic Houses of Parliament at Westminster, London, 1840–60, in collaboration with Pugin.

Barrymore, *n.* US family of actors, the children of British-born Maurice Barrymore and Georgie Drew, both stage personalities. **Lionel Barrymore**

(1878–1954) first appeared on the stage with his grandmother, Mrs John Drew, in 1893. He played numerous film roles from 1909, including *A Free Soul* (1931), Academy Award, and *Grand Hotel* (1932), but was perhaps best known for his annual radio portrayal of Scrooge in Dickens's *A Christmas Carol*. **Ethel Barrymore** (1879–1959) played with the British actor Henry Irving in London in 1898 and in 1928 opened the Ethel Barrymore Theatre in New York; she also appeared in many films from 1914, including *None but the Lonely Heart* (1944), Academy Award. **John Barrymore** (1882–1942) was a flamboyant personality who often appeared on stage and screen with his brother and sister. In his early years he was a Shakespearean actor. From 1923 he acted almost entirely in films, including *Dinner at Eight* (1933), and became a screen idol, nicknamed 'the Profile'.

Barstow, *n.* **Stan** (1928–), English novelist. Born in W Yorkshire, his novels describe northern working-class life including *A Kind of Loving* (1960).

Bart, *n.* **Jean** (1651–1702), French naval hero. The son of a fisherman, he served in the French navy, and harassed the British fleet in many daring exploits.

barter, *v.t.* to give (anything except money) in exchange for some other commodity; to exchange. *v.i.* to traffic by exchanging one thing for another. *n.* traffic by exchanging one commodity for another; a trade, a truck; (*Arith.*) the rule for reckoning quantities of a commodity in terms of another on the principle of exchange. **to barter away,** to dispose of by barter; to part with for a consideration (usually an inadequate one). **barterer,** *n.* [OF *bareter,* from *baret,* cheat (see BARRATOR)]

Barth[1], *n.* **Heinrich** (1821–65), German geographer and explorer who in explorations of North Africa between 1844 and 1855 established the exact course of the river Niger.

Barth[2], *n.* **John** (1930–), US novelist, born in Baltimore, influential in experimental writing in the 1960s. Chief works include *The Sot-Weed Factor* (1960), *Giles Goat-Boy* (1966), and *Lost in the Funhouse* (1968), interwoven fictions based on language games.

Barth[3], *n.* **Karl** (1886–1968), Swiss Protestant theologian. Socialist in his political views, he attacked the Nazis. His *Church Dogmatics* (1932–62) makes the resurrection of Jesus the focal point of Christianity.

Barthes, *n.* **Roland** (1915–80), French critic. He was an influential theorist of semiology, the science of signs and symbols. One of the French 'new critics', he attacked traditional literary criticism in his early works, including *Sur Racine/On Racine* (1963), and set out his own theories in *Eléments de sémiologie* (1964). He also wrote an autobiographical novel, *Roland Barthes sur Roland Barthes* (1975).

Bartholomew, *n.* one of the twelve Apostles. **Black Bartholomew,** Bartholomew-day in 1662 when the penal clauses of the English Act of Uniformity came into force. **Bartholomew-day, -tide,** *n.* the festival held in his honour on 24 August (also known as †**Bartlemy**). **Bartholomew Fair,** *n.* a fair formerly held annually about this date at Smithfield, notorious for its roughness and licence. **Bartholomew pig,** *n.* roast pig sold piping-hot at this fair. [L *Bartholomaeus,* Gr. *Bartholomaios*]

Bartholomew, Massacre of St, see ST BARTHOLOMEW, MASSACRE OF.

Bartholomew, St, *n.* in the New Testament, one of the apostles. Legends relate that after the Crucifixion he took Christianity to India, or that he was a missionary in Anatolia and Armenia, where he suffered martyrdom by being flayed alive. Feast day 24 Aug.

bartizan, *n.* a battlement on top of a house or castle; a small overhanging turret projecting from the angle on the top of a tower. **bartizaned,** *a.* [a modern formation from the spelling *bertisene* (or *bretising*) (see BRATTICE)]

Bartók, *n.* **Béla** (1881–1945), Hungarian composer. Regarded as a child prodigy, he studied music at the Budapest Conservatory, later working with Kodály in recording and transcribing local folk music for a government project. This led him to develop a personal musical language combining folk elements with mathematical concepts of tone and rhythmic proportion. His large output includes six string quartets, a ballet *The Miraculous Mandarin* (1919), which was banned because of its subject matter, concertos, an opera, and graded teaching pieces for piano. He died in the US, having fled from Hungary in 1940.

Bartolommeo, *n.* **Fra,** also called Baccio della Porta (*c.* 1472–*c.* 1517), Italian religious painter of the High Renaissance, active in Florence. His painting of the *Last Judgment* (1499, Museo di S Marco, Florence) influenced Raphael.

barton[1], *n.* the part of an estate which the lord of the manor kept in his own hand; a farm-yard. [OE *beretūn* (*bere,* barley, *tūn,* enclosure)]

barton[2], BURTON.

Barton[3], *n.* **Edmund** (1849–1920), Australian politician. He was leader of the federation movement from 1896 and first prime minister of Australia (1901–03).

Baruch, *n.* **Bernard (Mannes)** (1870–1965), US financier. He was a friend of British prime minister Churchill and a self-appointed, unpaid adviser to US presidents Wilson, F.D. Roosevelt, and Truman. He strongly advocated international control of nuclear energy.

barwood, *n.* a red wood from W Africa used for dyeing.

baryon, *n.* any member of the heavier class of subatomic particles that have a mass equal to or greater than that of the proton. [Gr. *barus,* heavy]

Baryshnikov, *n.* **Mikhail** (1948–), Soviet dancer, now in the US. He joined the Kirov Ballet in 1967 and soon gained fame worldwide as a soloist. After defecting 'on artistic, not political grounds' while in Canada in 1974, he danced with various companies, becoming director of the American Ballet Theatre in 1980.

barysphere, *n.* the solid, heavy core of the earth, probably consisting of iron and other metals. [Gr. *barus,* heavy]

baryta, *n.* the monoxide of barium. **barytes,** *n.* native sulphate of barium, heavy spar (used as white paint). **barytic,** *a.* [Gr. *barutēs,* weight (*barus,* heavy)]

barytone, BARITONE.

basal BASE[2].

basal metabolic rate, the amount of energy needed by an animal just to stay alive. It is measured when the animal is awake but resting, and includes the energy required to keep the heart beating, sustain breathing, repair tissues, and keep the brain and nerves functioning. Measuring the animal's consumption of oxygen gives an accurate value for BMR, because oxygen is needed to release energy from food.

basalt, *n.* a dark igneous rock of a black, bluish or leaden grey colour, of a uniform, compact texture, consisting of augite, felspar and iron intimately blended, olivine also being often present; a black stone-ware first used by Wedgwood. **basaltic,** *a.* of or of the nature of basalt; columnar, like basalt; resembling basalt. **basaltiform,** *a.* [L *basaltēs,* from Gr. *basanītēs (lithos)* touchstone]

basan, bazan, *n.* a sheepskin for bookbinding, tanned in oak or larch bark, as distinguished from roan which is tanned in sumach. [F *basane,* prob. from Prov. *bazana,* Sp. *badana,* Arab. *bitānah,* lining; see also BASIL[2]]

basanite, *n.* a velvet-black variety of quartz; Lydian-stone, touchstone. [L *basanītes,* (*lapis*), Gr. *basanos* touchstone]

bas-bleu, *n.* BLUESTOCKING. [F]

bascinet, BASINET.

bascule, *n.* an apparatus on the principle of the lever, in which the depression of one end raises the other; a bascule-bridge. **bascule-bridge,** *n.* a kind of drawbridge balanced by a counterpoise which falls or rises as the bridge is raised or lowered. [F, a see-saw (*battre,* to bump, or *bas,* down, *cul,* the rump]

base[1], *a.* low, of little height; occupying a low position; †low in the social scale; †illegitimate, bastard; low in the moral scale; unworthy, despicable; menial, inferior in quality; alloyed, debased, counterfeit; (*Law*) †by servile tenure; †by tenure at the will of a lord; †bass[3]. **base-born,** *a.* born out of wedlock; of humble birth; of base origin or nature. **base-court,** *n.* the outer court of a mansion, the servants' court, the back-yard, the farm-yard. **base-hearted,** *a.* having a base, treacherous heart. **base-heartedness,** *n.* the quality of being base-hearted. **base metals,** *n.pl.* those which are not precious metals. **base-tenant,** *n.* a tenant holding land as a villein; a tenant holding at the will of his lord; †**bass**[3]. **basely,** *adv.* in a low, selfish, unworthy or despicable manner. **baseness,** *n.* [F *bas,* late L *bassus,* short, stout (a cognomen)]

base[2], *n.* the lowest part on which anything rests; fundamental principle, ground-work; the part of a column between the bottom of a shaft and the top of the pedestal; a plinth with its mouldings constituting the lower part of the wall of a room; a pedestal; the bottom of anything; the extremity of a part by which it is attached to the trunk; the side on which a plane figure stands or is supposed to stand; (*Mil.*) the imaginary line connecting the salient angles of two adjacent bastions; the protuberant rear portion of a gun, between the knot of the cascabel and the base-ring; that line or place from which a combatant draws reinforcements of men, ammunition etc.; (*Her.*) the width of a bar parted off from the lower part of a shield by a horizontal line; that with which an acid combines to form a salt; the place from which a commencement is made in some ball-games; the starting-post; any substance used in dyeing as a mordant; the original stem of a word; the line from which trigonometrical measurements are calculated; the number on which a system of calculations depends; the datum or basis for any process of reckoning measurement or argument; an old popular game, still played by boys, and often called 'prisoner's base'; (†*pl.*) a skirt attached to a man's doublet and reaching to the knee; armour occupying this position. *v.t.* to make a foundation for; to lay on a foundation; to found, to secure. †**to bid base,** to challenge in the game of prisoner's base; to challenge. **to make first base,** (*N Am. coll.*) to complete the initial stage in a process; to seduce. **baseball,** *n.* the national ballgame of America, akin to English rounders, also called 'ball-game'; the ball used in this. **base-burner,** *n.* an iron stove fed at the top, the fire being confined to the base or lower part. **base-line,** *n.* the base; the common section of a picture and the geometrical plane; the back line at each end of a tennis court. **base-plate,** *n.* a foundation-plate. **base rate,** *n.* the rate of interest on which a bank bases its lending rates. **basal,** *a.* pertaining to, situated at or constituting the base of anything; fundamental *n.* a basal part. **basal metabolism,** *n.* the amount of energy consumed by an individual in a resting state for functions such as respiration and blood circulation. **baseless,** *a.* without a base or foundation; groundless. **baselessness,** *n.* **basement,** *n.* the lowest or fundamental portion of a structure; the lowest inhabited storey of a building, esp. when below the ground level. **basic,** *a.* of, pertaining to or constituting a base, fundamental; without luxury, extras etc. (*Chem.*) having the base in excess; (of igneous rock) with little silica present in its composition; (*Metal.*) prepared by the basic process. **basic process,** *n.* a method of making steel or homogeneous iron by means of a Bessemer converter lined with non-siliceous materials. **basic slag,** *n.* a by-product of the manufacture of steel, used as manure. **basicity,** *n.* the combining power of an acid. **basilar,** *a.* (*Bot., Zool.*) growing from, or situated near, the base. [F *base,* L and Gr. *basis* (*bainein,* to go, step, stand)]

Basel, Basle, *n.* (French **Bâle**) financial, commercial, and industrial city in Switzerland; population (1987) 363,000. Basel was a strong military station under the Romans. In 1501 it joined the Swiss confederation, and later developed as a centre for the Reformation.

bash[1], *v.t.* to strike, so as to smash. *v.i.* to strike violently. *adv.* with force; with a smash or bang. *n.* a heavy blow, a bang; a social entertainment. **to have a bash at,** to attempt. **basher,** *n.* a rough, a hooligan. [imit. like *bang,* or Scand. (cp. Swed. *basa,* Dan. *baske,* to beat)]

bash[2], *v.t.* to dismay, abash. *v.i.* †to be dismayed; to be abashed. **bashful,** *a.* †without self-possession, daunted; shamefaced, shy; characterized by excessive modesty. **bashfully,** *adv.* **bashfulness,** *n.* [ABASH]

bashaw, PASHA.

bashi-bazouk, *n.* (*Hist.*) a Turkish irregular soldier, once noted for lawlessness and atrocious brutality. [Turk., one whose head is turned]

Bashkir, *n.* autonomous republic of the USSR, with the Ural Mountains on the E. **area** 143,600 sq km/55,430 sq miles. **capital** Ufa. **population** (1982) 3,876,000. **products** minerals, oil.

Bashō, *n.* pen name of Matsuo Munefusa (1644–94), Japanese poet. He was master of the *haiku,* a 17-syllable poetic form with lines of 5, 7, and 5 syllables, which he infused with subtle allusiveness and made the accepted form of poetic expression in Japan. His most famous work is *Oku-no-hosomichi/The Narrow Road to the Deep North* (1694), an account of a visit to northern Japan, which consists of haikus interspersed with prose passages.

basi-, *comb. form.* pertaining to or forming the base, or at the base of. [L *basis,* BASE[2]]

basic BASE[2].

BASIC, *n.* Beginner's All-purpose Symbolic Instruction Code, a computer-programming language, developed in 1964, originally designed to take advantage of time-sharing computers (where many people can use the computer at the same time). Most versions use an interpreter program, which allows programs to be entered and run with no intermediate translation, although recent versions have been implemented as a compiler. The language is relatively easy to learn, and is popular among users of microcomputers.

Basic English, *n.* a simplified form of English devised and promoted by C.K. Ogden in the 1920s and 1930s as an international auxiliary language; as a route into Standard English for foreign learners; and as a reminder to the English-speaking world of the virtues of plain language. Its name derives from the letters of *B*ritish, *A*merican, *S*cientific, *I*nternational, *C*ommercial.

basicranial, *a.* of or at the base of the cranium.

basidium, *n.* (*pl.* **-a**) (*Bot.*) a mother-cell carried on a stalk and bearing spores characteristic of various fungi. **Basidiomycetes,** *n.* a group of fungi (including many toadstools and mushrooms) in which the spores are borne on basidia. [BASE[2]]

Basie, *n.* **'Count' (William)** (1904–84) US band leader, pianist, and organist who developed the big-band sound and a simplified, swinging style of music. He led impressive groups of musicians in a career spanning more than 50 years.

basifugal, *a.* growing away from the base.

basil[1], *n.* the popular name of the genus *Ocymum,* species of which are used as culinary herbs, e.g. the sweet basil, *O. basilicum.* [OF *basile,* L *basilisca* (*basiliscus* BASILISK); the botanical name *basilicum* is from Gr. *basilikon,* royal]

basil[2], *n.* the skin of a sheep tanned in bark, used for bookbinding. [prob. a corr. of F *basane,* see BASAN]

Basil, St, *n.* (*c.*330–379), Cappadocian monk, known as 'the Great', founder of the Basilian monks. Elected bishop of Caesarea in 370, Basil opposed the heresy of Arianism. He wrote many theological works and composed the 'Liturgy of St Basil', in use in the Eastern Orthodox Church. Feast day 2 Jan.

Basil II, *n.* (*c.*958–1025) Byzantine emperor from 976. His achievement as emperor was to contain, and later decisively defeat, the Bulgarians, earning for himself the title 'Bulgar-Slayer' after a victory (1014). After the battle he blinded almost all 15,000 of the defeated, leaving only a few men with one eye to lead their fellows home. The Byzantine empire reached its greatest extent at the time of his death.

basilar BASE[2].
basilateral, *a.* at the side of a base.
Basilian, *a.* pertaining to the monastic order instituted by St Basil in the Greek Church. *n.* a member of the order.
basilica, *n.* (*pl.* **-cas**) †a royal residence; a large oblong building with double colonnades and an apse, used as a court of justice and an exchange; such a building used as a Christian church; a church built on the same plan; one of the seven principal churches of Rome founded by Constantine the Great (4th cent.). **basilical,** *a.* †royal, kingly. **basilican,** *a.* **basilicum,** *n.* a name given to several ointments from their reputed sovereign virtues. [F *basilique,* L *basilicus,* Gr. *basilikos,* royal (*basileus,* king]
Basilicata, *n.* mountainous region of S Italy, comprising the provinces of Potenza and Matera; area 10,000 sq km/3860 sq miles; population (1988) 622,000. Its capital is Potenza. It was the Roman province of Lucania.
basilisk, *n.* a fabulous reptile, said to be hatched by a serpent from a cock's egg – its look and breath were reputed fatal. COCKATRICE; †a large cannon, generally of brass; a tropical American lizard named from its inflatable crest. [L *basiliscus,* Gr. *basiliskos,* kingly]
basin, *n.* a hollow (usu. circular) vessel for holding water, esp. for washing; a bowl; the quantity contained by such a vessel, a basinful; a pond, a dock, a reservoir; a land-locked harbour; the scale-dish of a balance; a tool used in grinding convex lenses; the tract of country drained by a river and its tributaries; a hollow; a depression in strata in which beds of later age have been deposited; a circumscribed formation in which the strata dip on all sides inward. †**basin-wide,** *a.* as wide or large as a basin (of eyes). **basinful,** *n.* as much as a basin will hold; (*coll.*) as much work or trouble as one can cope with. [OF *bacin* (F *bassin*), late L *bacchīnus* (*bacca,* a water-vessel)]
basinet, basnet, *n.* a light helmet, almost round, and generally without a visor. [OF *basinet,* dim. of *bacin,* basin]
basiophil, *a.* having an affinity for basic stains.
basiophthalmite, *n.* the lowest joint in the eye-stalk in Crustaceans.
basipetal, *a.* proceeding in the direction of the base.
basipodite, *n.* the second segment of the leg of an arthropod.
basis, *n.* (*pl.* **-ses**) the base or foundation; the fundamental principle, ground-work, ingredient or support. [L, BASE[2]]
basitemporal, *a.* of or pertaining to the base of the temples.
bask, *v.t.* to expose to natural or artificial warmth (*chiefly refl.*). *v.i.* to expose oneself to the influence of genial warmth; to sun; (*fig.*) to luxuriate in love, good fortune etc. **basking-shark,** *n.* the sun-fish or sail-fish, the largest species of shark. [prob. from OScand. *bathask* (*batha sik,* bathe oneself; cp. Icel. *bathast*)]
Baskerville, *n.* **John** (1706–75), English printer and typographer, who experimented in casting types from 1750 onwards. The Baskerville typeface is named after him.
basket, *n.* a wickerwork vessel of plaited osiers, twigs or similar flexible material; as much as will fill a basket; a basketful; a basket-hilt; (*Arch.*) the vase of a Corinthian column with its carved foliage; the net or hoop used as a goal in basketball. *v.t.* to put in a basket. **the pick of the basket,** the best of the lot. **basketball,** *n.* (*Sport*) a game consisting in dropping a large ball into suspended nets or hoops; the ball used in the game. **basket-chair,** *n.* a wickerwork chair. **basket-fish,** *n.* a starfish of the genus *Astrophyton*. **basket-hilt,** *n.* the hilt of a sword, so called because it is made something like a basket to defend the swordsman's hand. **basket-hilted,** *a.* having a basket-hilt. †**basket-justice,** *n.* a justice who bought his position and took bribes to recoup himself. **basket-stitch,** *n.* in knitting, alternate purl and plain stitches which create a basketwork pattern. **basket-stones,** *n.pl.* fragments of the stems of the fossil Crinoidea. **basket weave,** *n.* a form of textile weave resembling chequered basketwork. **basket-woman,** *n.* a woman who carries about goods for sale in a basket. **basketwork,** *n.* wickerwork. **basketful,** *n.* as much as would fill a basket. **basketry,** *n.* BASKETWORK. [etym. doubtful]
Basle, BASEL.
basmati rice, *n.* a type of rice with a slender grain, delicate fragrance and nutty flavour.
bason[1], BASIN.
bason[2], *n.* a bench with a slab or iron plate and a fire underneath for felting hats. *v.t.* to harden the felt in hat-making. [etym. doubtful]
basophil, -phile, *n.* a white blood cell with basophilic contents. **basophilic**, *a.* (of cells) readily stained with basic dyes.
Basov, *n.* **Nikolai Gennadievich** (1912–), Soviet physicist who in 1953, with his compatriot Alexander Prokhorov, developed the microwave amplifier called a maser. They were awarded the Nobel Prize in Physics (1964), which they shared with Charles Townes of the US.
Basque, *n.* a member of a people occupying both slopes of the western Pyrenees; the language spoken by this people. *a.* of or pertaining to this. **basque,** *n.* a woman's jacket, extended below the waist, forming a kind of skirt. **basqued,** *a.* furnished with a basque or short skirt. [F, from late L *Vasco,* dweller in Vasconia, a region of W Pyrenees]
Basque Country, *n.* homeland of the Basque people in the W Pyrenees. The Basque Country includes the Basque Provinces of N Spain and the French arrondissements of Bayonne and Maulaon. The Basques are a pre-Indo-European people who largely maintained their independence until the 19th century and speak their own Euskara tongue.
Basque Provinces, *n.pl.* (Spanish **Vascongadas**, Basque **Euskadi**) autonomous region of NW Spain, comprising the provinces of Vizcaya, Alava, and Guipuzcoa; area 7300 sq km/2818 sq miles; population (1986) 2,133,000.
Basra, *n.* (Arabic **al-Basrah**) principal port in Iraq, in the Shatt-al-Arab delta, 97 km/60 miles from the Persian Gulf; population (1985) 617,000. Exports include wool, oil, cereal, and dates.
bas-relief, *n.* low relief; a kind of sculpture in which the figures project less than one-half of their true proportions above the plane forming the background; a carving in low relief. [F, from It. *basso-rilievo*]
bass[1], *n.* the inner fibre of the lime-tree or any similar vegetable fibre; an article made from this fibre. **bass broom,** *n.* a coarse-fibred broom made from bass. **bass-wood,** *n.* the American lime-tree, *Tilia americana;* its wood. [BAST]
bass[2], basse, *n.* †the common perch, *Perca fluviatilis;* a sea-fish, *Labrax lupus,* called also sea-wolf and sea-dace, common in European waters. **black bass,** *Perca huro,* from Lake Huron. **sea bass,** (*N Am.*) a serranoid food-fish, *Centropristis striatus,* common on the Atlantic shores of the US; also called blackfish, bluefish, rock-bass etc. **striped bass,** (*N Am.*) the rockfish, *Roccus lineatus* and *R. sexatilis*. [OE *bars* (cp. Dut. *baars,* G *Bars, Barsch;* see BRISTLE)]
bass[3], *n.* the lowest part in harmonized musical compositions; the deepest male voice; the lowest tones of an instrument; one who sings the bass part; a bass string; a bass instrument esp. bass guitar or double-bass. *a.* of or pertaining to the lowest part in harmonized musical composition. *v.t.* to utter in a bass voice. **bass-bar,** *n.* a bar of wood fixed lengthwise in the belly of stringed instruments to enable them to resist pressure. **bass clef,** *n.* (*Mus.*) the F clef on the fourth line. **bass drum,** *n.* a large drum with a low pitch played in an orchestra or band. **bass-viol,** *n.* a stringed instrument for playing bass; a violon-cello. DOUBLE-BASS, THOROUGH-BASS. [earlier *base,* (see BASE[1])]
Bassein, *n.* port in Burma, in the Irrawaddy delta, 125 km/78 miles from the sea; population (1983) 355,588. Bassein was founded in the 13th century.

Basse-Normandie, *n.* or **Lower Normandy**, coastal region of NW France lying between Haute-Normandie and Brittany (Bretagne). It includes the *départements* of Calvados, Manche, and Orne; area 17,600 sq km/ 6794 sq miles; population (1986) 1,373,000. Its capital is Caen. Apart from stock farming, dairy farming and the production of textiles, the area is noted for its Calvados (apple brandy).

basset[1], *n.* an obsolete game of cards, said to have been first played at Venice. [F *basette,* It. *bassetta, bassetto,* rather low (dim. of *basso,* low)]

basset[2], *n.* a short-legged dog used to drive foxes and badgers from their earths. also **basset hound**. [F, dim. of *bas, basse,* low]

basset[3], *n.* the outcrop of strata at the surface of the ground. *a.* tending to crop out. *v.i.* to crop out at the surface. [etym. doubtful]

Basseterre, *n.* capital and port of St Kitts-Nevis, in the Leeward Islands; population (1980) 14,000. Industries include data processing, rum, clothes and electrical components.

basset-horn, *n.* a tenor clarinet with a recurved mouth. [F *cor de bassette,* It. *corno di bassetto*]

bassinet, *n.* an oblong wicker basket with a hood at the end used as a cradle; a pram of similar shape. [F, dim. of *bassin,* BASIN]

basso, *n.* bass. **basso-continuo**, *n.* **basso-profundo**, *n.* the lowest male voice. **basso-ripieno**, *n.* the bass of the grand chorus, which comes in only occasionally. [It.]

bassoon, *n.* a wooden double-reed instrument, the bass to the clarinet and oboe; an organ-stop of similar tone, a similar series of reeds on a harmonium etc. **bassoonist,** *n.* [F *basson* (*bas, basse,* -ON, or perhaps *bas son,* low sound)]

basso-rilievo, *n.* (*pl.* **-vos**) bas-relief. [It., low relief]

bassorin, *n.* an insoluble mucus found in Bassora gum and the gums of cherry, plum etc. [*Bassora,* in Asia Minor]

bast, *n.* the inner bark of the lime or linden-tree; any similar fibrous bark; a rope, mat etc., made from this fibre (see also BASS[1]). [OE *bæst*]

bastard, *n.* an illegitimate child or person; anything spurious, counterfeit or false; †a kind of Spanish wine; an impure coarse brown sugar; (*sl., often considered taboo*) an obnoxious or disagreeable person; (*sl., often considered taboo*) any person in general; (*sl., often considered taboo*) something annoying or unpleasant. *a.* born out of wedlock, illegitimate; spurious, not genuine; having the resemblance of something of a higher quality or kind, inferior; of abnormal shape or size. **bastard title,** *n.* a short title preceding the title-page of a book. **bastard type,** *n.* (*Print.*) a fount of type with a face too large or too small in proportion to its body. **bastard-wing,** *n.* three or four quill-like feathers placed at a small joint in the middle of a bird's wing. **bastardize, -ise,** *v.t.* to declare one a bastard; to debase. †*v.i.* to beget bastards. **bastardization, -isation,** *n.* the action of declaring or of making illegitimate. †**bastardly,** *a.* spurious, counterfeit, debased. **bastardy,** *n.* illegitimacy; fornication. [OF *bast* (F *bât*), pack-saddle, late L *bastum* (cp. BANTLING)]

baste[1], *v.t.* to moisten (a roasting joint etc.) with liquid fat, gravy etc. [etym. unknown]

baste[2], *v.t.* to beat with a stick, to thrash, cudgel. [perh. from the prec., or from Scand. (Swed. *basa,* to flog, cp. Icel. *beysta,* and see BASH)]

baste[3], *v.t.* to sew slightly, to tack, to fasten together with long stitches. [OF *bastir* (F *bâtir*), to baste (perh. from OHG *bestan,* to patch, *bast,* BAST, or from late L *bastīre,* to build, construct]

Bastille, *n.* the State prison in Paris, destroyed in 1789 in an initial attack by a mob that set the French Revolution in motion; (**bastille**) a fortified tower; (*Mil.*) a small wooden fort; one of a series of huts defended by entrenchments; a prison, a workhouse. [F, from late L *bastīlia,* pl. of *bastīle* (*bastīre,* to build)]

bastinado, *n.* (*pl.* **-dos, does**) a method of corporal punishment or torture inflicted with a stick on the soles of the feet; a rod, a stick, a cudgel. *v.t.* to beat with a stick, esp. on the soles of the feet. [Sp. *bastonada* (*baston,* a stick)]

bastion, *n.* a projecting work at the angle or in the line of a fortification, having two faces and two flanks; (*fig.*) a rampart, a defence. **bastioned,** *a.* **last bastion,** one of a small set of people or things left defending a principle, way of life etc. [F, from It. *bastione* (*bastia,* a building), from late L *bastire,* to build]

Basutoland, *n.* former name for Lesotho.

bat[1], *n.* †a club, a stout piece of wood; a wooden instrument with a cylindrical handle and broad blade used to strike the ball at cricket or similar games; a blow with a bat or club; a batsman; a sheet of wadding used for filling quilts; (*Coal-mining*) interstratified shale; (*dial. and sl.*) beat, rate of speed; condition. *v.t.* (*past, p.p.* **batted**) to strike with a bat. *v.i.* to take an innings as batsman. **off his/her own bat,** by his/her own exertions. **bat-fowling,** *n.* a method of taking birds by holding a light before a net, and beating their roosting-places with bats or clubs. **batsman,** *n.* one who uses the bat at cricket and other ball games; (*Aviat.*) the person on an airfield or aircraft carrier who guides landing aircraft by waving a round, plainly visible bat in each hand. **batlet,** *n.* a small bat, a flat wooden mallet used for beating linen. [etym. doubtful; perh. from OF *batte,* a club (*battre,* to beat)]

bat[2], *n.* a small nocturnal mouse-like mammal, having the digits extended to support a wing-membrane stretching from the neck to the tail, by means of which it flies. **blind as a bat,** having very poor eyesight. **like a bat out of hell,** (*coll.*) extremely quickly. **to have bats in the belfry,** (*coll.*) to be crazy; to suffer from delusions. **bats,** *a.* (*coll.*) batty. **batty,** *a.* batlike; (*coll.*) mentally unstable; crazy. [ME *bakke,* from Scand. (Dan. *aften-bakke,* evening-bat, Icel. *blaka,* to flutter, flap)]

bat[3], *n.* (*only in comb.*) a pack-saddle, **bat-horse,** *n.* a sumpter-horse carrying officers' baggage during a campaign. **batman,** *n.* a man in charge of a bat-horse and its load; the military servant of an officer; †a man in charge of the cookery utensils of a company of soldiers in the field. **bat-money, bat-pay,** *n.* an allowance for carrying baggage in the field. **bat-needle,** *n.* a packing-needle. [F *bât,* a pack-saddle, OF *bast,* late L *bastum,* perh. from Gr. *bastazein,* to carry]

bat[4], *v.t.* to blink. **not bat an eyelid, eyelash,** not to blink; to show no surprise or emotion.

†**batable,** *a.* debatable, subject to contention. **Batable Ground,** *n.* the Debatable Land on the Scottish Border. [DEBATABLE]

Bataan, *n.* peninsula in Luzon, the Philippines, which was defended against the Japanese in World War II by US and Filipino troops under Gen MacArthur 1 Jan.–9 Apr. 1942. MacArthur was evacuated, but some 67,000 Allied prisoners died on the Bataan Death March to camps in the interior.

Batak, *n. pl.* several distinct but related peoples of N Sumatra in Indonesia. Numbering approximately 2.5 million the Batak speak languages belonging to the Austronesian family.

batata, *n.* a plant with a tuberous root, from the West Indies, the sweet potato. [Sp. and Port., from native American]

Batavian, *a.* of or pertaining to the ancient Batavians or the modern Dutch. *n.* one of the ancient Batavi; a Dutchman. [L *Batavia,* from *Batavi*]

batch[1], *n.* as much bread as is produced at one baking; hence, any quantity produced at one operation; sort, lot, set, crew. *v.t.* to collect into batches; to group (items) for computer processing. **batch processing,** *n.* a system by which a number of jobs submitted by users are run through a computer as a single batch. [ME *bacche* (OE *bacan,* to bake)]

batch[2], *n.* (*Austral.*) a holiday cottage.

bate[1], *v.t.* to abate, diminish; let down, humble; to blunt, satiate; to reduce, moderate, restrain; to deduct; to take away, deprive, remove. *v.i.* to fall away, diminish; to decrease, dwindle, fall off in strength or intensity. **with bated breath,** with breath held in check; in suspense, anxiously. [aphetic form of **abate**]

bate[2], *n.* alkaline lye used in tanning; the vat containing this; the process of steeping. *v.t.* to steep in bate. [from Swed. *beta,* maceration, tanning (cp. G *beizen,* to steep, tan)]

†**bate**[3], *v.i.* †to contend, strive; to beat the wings, flutter impatiently; to be restless or impatient. *n.* strife, contention. [OF *batre,* late L *batere,* L *battuere;* or abbr. of DEBATE]

bateau, *n.* (*pl.* **bateaux**) a long, light, flat-bottomed river-boat, tapering at both ends, used by French-Canadians. **bateau-bridge,** *n.* a floating bridge supported by *bateaux.* [F (cogn. with BOAT]

Bateman, *n.* **H(enry) M(ayo)** (1887–1970) Australian cartoonist, lived in England. His cartoons were based on themes of social embarrassment and confusion, in such series as *The Man who. ...* (as in *The Guardsman who dropped his rifle*).

Bates[1], *n.* **Alan** (1934–), English actor. A versatile male lead in over 60 plays and films, his roles include *Zorba the Greek* (1965); *Far from the Madding Crowd* (1967); *Women in Love* (1970); *The Go-Between* (1971); *The Shout* (1978) and *Duet for One* (1986).

Bates[2], *n.* **H(enry) W(alter)** (1825–92), English naturalist and explorer, who identified 8000 new species of insects. He made a special study of camouflage in animals, and his observation of insect imitation of species unpleasant to predators is known as 'Batesian mimicry'.

bath[1], *n.* the act of washing or immersing the body in water or other fluid; the water or other fluid used for bathing; a wash, a lotion; the vessel for containing water for bathing; a room or building for bathing in; a hydropathic establishment; a town having medicinal springs used for bathing; the action of immersing any substance in a solution for scientific, art or trade purposes; the vessel containing such solution; the solution itself. *v.t.* to wash or put (usu. a child) in a bath. **bath-oil,** *n.* (perfumed) oil for use in bath-water. **bath robe,** *n.* (*esp. N Am.*) a dressing-gown. **bathroom,** *n.* an apartment containing a bath or shower; (*esp. N Am.*) a lavatory. **bath salts,** *n.pl.* perfumed crystals used for softening bath water. **bath-tub,** (*esp. N Am.*) tub, a vessel for containing water for bathing. [OE *bœth (cp. Icel. bath,* G *Bad,* OTeut. *bathom;* cogn. with L *fovere*)]

Bath[2], *n.* a city in Somerset, famous for its hot springs. **to go to Bath,** (*sl.*) to go begging; to go to Jericho, to blazes etc. **bath brick,** *n.* a preparation of calcareous earth in the form of a brick, used for cleaning knives and metal work. **bath bun,** *n.* a rich bun, generally without currants. **bath chair,** *n.* a wheeled chair for invalids. **bath chap,** *n.* a small pig's cheek cured for the table. **Bath Oliver,** *n.* a special kind of biscuit invented by Dr W. Oliver, 1695–1764, of Bath. **bath stone,** *n.* a white building-stone quarried from the oolite near Bath. [as prec.]

bath[3], *n.* a liquid measure among the ancient Hebrews, containing about 6½ gallons. [Heb.]

Bath, Order of the, British order of knighthood, believed to have been founded in the reign of Henry IV (1399–1413). Formally instituted in 1815, it included civilians from 1847 and women from 1970. There are three grades: Knights of the Grand Cross (GCB), Knights Commanders (KCB), and Knights Companions (CB).

bathe, *v.t.* to immerse in or as in a bath; to plunge or dip; to suffuse, to moisten, to wet copiously; to cleanse (a wound) by applying water. *v.i.* to swim in a body of water for pleasure; (*esp. N Am.*) to take a bath. *n.* the act of taking a bath (esp. in the sea, a river etc.). **bathing-costume, -dress, -suit,** *n.* a garment for swimming or sunbathing in. **bathing hut,** *n.* a hut for bathers to undress and dress in. **bathing-machine,** *n.* (*formerly*) a kind of covered carriage to bathe from. **bather,** *n.* one who bathes, esp. one who bathes in the sea, a river or a swimming-bath. **bathers,** *n.* (*Austral.*) a swimming costume or swimming trunks. [OE *bathian* (from *bœth,* a bath; cp. Icel. *batha.* G *baden*)]

bath mitzvah, (also **bas, bat**), *n.* a Jewish girl who has reached the age (usu. 13 years) of religious responsibility; the celebrations marking this event. [Heb., daughter of the law]

batho-, bathy-, prefixes used in compound words employed in oceanography etc. [Gr. *bathus,* deep]

batholite, -lith, *n.* a great mass of intrusive igneous rock, esp. granite. **batholitic, -lithic,** *a.* [Gr. *bathos,* depth, *lithos,* a stone]

bathometer, *n.* an instrument used to ascertain the depths reached in soundings. [Gr. *bathos,* depth]

Báthory, *n.* **Stephen** (1533–86), king of Poland, elected by a diet convened in 1575 and crowned in 1576. Báthory proved extremely sucessful in driving the Russian troops of Ivan the Terrible out of his country. His military successes brought potential conflicts with Sweden, but he died before these could develop.

bathos, *n.* ridiculous descent from the sublime to the commonplace in writing or speech; anticlimax. **bathetic,** *a.* characterized by bathos.

Bathurst, *n.*, former name (until 1973) of Banjul, capital of the Gambia.

bathybius, *n.* a slimy matter dredged up from the bottom of the Atlantic, formerly supposed to be a primitive form of life. [mod. L, from Gr. *bathus,* deep, *bios,* life]

bathymetry, *n.* the art or method of taking deep soundings. **bathymetric, bathymetrical,** *a.* of or pertaining to sounding, or to the depth at which life is found in the sea. **bathymetrically,** *adv.* [Gr. *bathus,* deep]

bathyscaph, -scaphe, -scape, *n.* a submersible vessel for deep-sea observation and exploration. [Gr. *skaphē,* light boat]

bathysphere, *n.* a strong steel deep-sea observation chamber. [as prec.]

batik, *n.* a method of printing designs on fabric by masking areas to be left undyed with wax; fabric produced by this method. [Malay, from Jav., painted]

bating, *prep.* leaving out of the question; excepting.

Batista, *n.* **Fulgencio** (1901–73), Cuban dictator during 1933–44 and 1952–59, whose authoritarian methods enabled him to jail his opponents and amass a large personal fortune. He was overthrown by rebel forces led by Fidel Castro in 1959.

batiste, *n.* a fine cotton or linen fabric. *a.* made of batiste. [F perh. after *Baptiste* of Cambray, the original maker]

batlet BAT.

batman BAT[3].

baton, †**batoon,** *n.* a staff or club; a truncheon used as a badge or symbol of authority or as an offensive weapon; a short stick transferred between successive team-mates in a relay-race; a knobbed staff carried and swung into the air at the head of a parade or twirled by majorettes etc. a diminutive of the bend sinister, used in English coats of arms as a badge of bastardy; the wand used by a conductor in beating time. *v.t.* †to cudgel; to strike with a policeman's baton or truncheon. **baton charge,** *n.* a charge by police or troops with batons. **baton gun,** *n.* a gun which fires rubber or plastic bullets to control rioters. **baton sinister,** *n.* the baton signifying illegitimacy (pop. called the *bar sinister;* cp. BEND SINISTER). [F *bâton,* OF *baston*]

Batrachia, *n.pl.* an order of reptiles including those breathing by gills; an order of Amphibia containing those animals which have gills and a tail only in the larval stage; according to Brongniart, the last of the four orders of reptiles. **batrachian,** *a.* of or pertaining to the Batrachia. *n.* any individual of the Batrachia. **batrachoid,** *a.* [mod. L, from neut. pl. of a. *batrachīos,* Gr. *batracheia,* frog-like (*batrachos,* frog)]

†**battalia,** *n.* order of battle, battle array; an army, or portions of it, which is arranged in order of battle. **in battalia,** in order of battle. [It. *battaglia*]

battalion, *n.* a main division of an army; an assemblage of companies of infantry; the tactical and administrative unit of infantry, consisting of from four to eight companies, and generally about 1000 strong on a war footing. *v.t.* to form into battalions. [F *bataillon,* It. *battaglione* (*battaglia,* see prec.)]

battels, *n.pl.* (*Univ. of Oxford*) provisions from the college buttery; the account for these; college accounts generally. **battel,** *v.i.* to have an account for battels; to get one's provisions at the college buttery. †**batteler,** *n.* one who receives his provisions from the college buttery; a name formerly applied to a class of students at Oxford below commoners. [etym. doubtful]

batten[1], *n.* a strip of sawn wood used for flooring; a piece of wood for clamping together the boards of a door; a scantling, ledge, clamp; a thin piece of wood nailed on masts etc. to prevent chafing, or to fasten down the edges of tarpaulins over the hatches. *v.t.* to fasten or strengthen with battens. **to batten down the hatches,** to secure the hatches of a ship; to prepare for action, trouble, danger etc. **battening,** *n.* the act of attaching battens to a wall for nailing up laths; the battens so affixed. [BATON]

batten[2], †*v.t.* to fatten up; to make fertile. *v.i.* to grow fat; to thrive, to prosper; to feed on gluttonously; to revel in. [prob. from Icel. *batna,* to get better, recover (*bati,* advantage, improvement; cp. Dut. *baten,* to avail, to profit; cp. BOOT[2])]

batten[3], *n.* the movable bar of a loom which strikes the weft in. [F *battant,* pres.p of *battre,* to strike]

Batten[4], *n.* **Jean** (1909–82), New Zealand aviator, who made the first return solo flight by a woman (Australia–Britain 1935), and established speed records.

batter[1], *v.t.* to strike with successive blows so as to bruise, shake, demolish; to wear or impair by beating or rough usage; to subject to hard, crushing attack; to attack with engines of war, formerly with a battering-ram, now with artillery; to bombard. *v.i.* to hammer (at) a door. *n.* in cooking, a mixture of several ingredients, esp. eggs, flour and milk, well beaten together, adhesive paste; liquid mud; a blow. **battered baby,** *n.* an infant or young child who has suffered violent injury at the hands of an adult or parent. **battering-charge,** *n.* the heaviest charge for a siege-gun. **battering-engine, -machine,** *n.* an engine used for battering down walls or ramparts. **battering-gun, -piece,** *n.* a siege-gun. **battering-ram,** *n.* an ancient military engine used for battering down walls, and consisting of a heavy beam shod with iron, which was originally in the form of a ram's head. **battering-train,** *n.* a train of artillery for siege purposes. [OF *battre,* to beat, late L *battere,* L *battuere*]

batter[2], *v.i.* to incline (as walls, parapets, embankments etc.) from the perpendicular with a receding slope. *n.* a receding slope (of a wall etc.); a talus. **battering,** *a.* sloping inwards. [etym. doubtful; perh. from F *abattre,* to beat down, depress]

battery, *n.* an assailing by blows; (*Law*) an unlawful attack by beating, or even touching in a hostile manner; (*Mil.*) a number of pieces of artillery for combined action, with men, transport and equipment; the tactical unit of artillery; a ship's armament; the fortified work, or the part of a ship, in which artillery is mounted; a connected series of electric cells, dynamos or Leyden jars, forming a source of electric energy; any apparatus for providing voltaic electricity; a combined series of lenses or prisms; a combination of instruments and general apparatus for use in various arts or sciences; articles of metal, esp. beaten copper and brass; an embankment; a series of nesting-boxes in which hens are confined to increase laying. **cross batteries,** two batteries commanding the same point from different directions. **enfilading battery,** a battery that rakes a whole line with its fire. **floating battery,** an armoured vessel, heavily armed, for bombarding fortresses. **masked battery,** a battery concealed from the enemy's observation. **to turn one's battery against oneself,** to use a man's own arguments to confute him. **battery-piece,** *n.* a siege-gun. **battery-wagon,** *n.* a vehicle used for transporting tools and material for a battery. [F *batterie* (battre, see BATTER[1])]

batting, *n.* cotton fibre prepared for quilting. [etym. doubtful, see BAT[1]]

battle, *n.* a fight or hostile engagement between opposing armies etc.; fighting, hostilities, war. *v.i.* to fight, to contend (with or against); (*esp. Austral.*) to struggle for a living. †*v.t.* to assail in battle, to fight against. **line of battle,** the arrangement of troops in readiness for a general engagement; the line formed by warships in preparation for battle. **pitched battle,** a general engagement the time and place of which have been settled beforehand. **half the battle,** an immense advantage. **to have the battle,** to be victorious. **to join battle,** to commence a general combat. **wager of battle, trial by battle,** legal decision of a case by single combat. **battle-array,** *n.* the order of troops prepared for engagement. **battle-axe, -ax,** *n.* a weapon like an axe, formerly used in battle; a halberd; (*coll.*) a formidable woman. **battle-cry,** *n.* a war-cry, a slogan. **battle-cruiser,** *n.* a large, heavily-armed cruiser. **battle-dress,** *n.* comfortable, loose-fitting uniform worn by soldiers in battle. **battle fatigue** SHELL SHOCK. **battle-field,** *n.* the scene of a battle. **battle-piece,** *n.* a pictorial, rhetorical or poetical description of a battle. **battle-plane,** *n.* a large, fighting aircraft. **battle-royal,** *n.* a cock-fight in which more than two game cocks are engaged; a general engagement; a free fight, a general row. **battle-ship,** *n.* a warship; a ship adapted by armament for line of battle as opposed to a cruiser. **battled[1],** *a.* drawn up in line of battle; fought, contested. **battled[2],** *a.* embattled, protected with battlements. [OF *batayle,* late L *battuālia,* neut. pl. of a. *battuālis,* fighting (*battuere,* to beat)]

battledore, *n.* a wooden bat used for washing; the light racket used to strike a shuttlecock; the game in which this is used; †a card or hornbook containing the alphabet etc. **battledore and shuttlecock,** *n.* the game of battledore. [etym. doubtful; prob. from Prov. *batedor,* a washing-beetle (*batre,* to beat, *-dor,* -TOR)]

battlement, *n.* a parapet with openings or embrasures, on the top of a building, originally for defensive purposes, afterwards used as an ornament; a roof having a battlement; (*fig.*) the indented crest of mountains; the heights of the heavens. **battlemented,** *a.* [OF *batailles,* battlements, or temporary turrets of timber; prob. confused with OF *batillement,* a redoubt (*bastiller,* to fortify)]

battue, *n.* driving game from cover by beating the bushes; a shoot on this plan; a beat up, wholesale slaughter. [F (fem. p.p. of *battre,* to beat)]

battuta, *n.* a bar; the beating of time. [It., a beat]

baubee, BAWBEE.

bauble, *n.* a short stick or wand having a head with asses' ears carved at the end of it, carried by the fools or jesters of former times; a gew-gaw, a showy trinket; a piece of childish folly; a mere toy; a thing of no value; a foolish, childish person. [OF *babel, baubel,* a child's plaything; perh. confused with ME *babyll, babulle,* a stick with a thong (*bablyn,* to waver, oscillate, from *bab* or *bob*)]

baud, *n.* (*pl.* **baud, -s**) a unit which measures the rate of telegraphic transmission: one equals one bit of data per second. [from J.M.E. *Baudot,* d. 1903, F inventor]

baudekin, baudkin, BALDACHIN.

Baudelaire, *n.* **Charles Pierre** (1821–67), French poet, whose work combined rhythmical and musical perfection with a morbid romanticism and eroticism, finding beauty in decadence and evil. His first book of verse was *Les Fleurs du mal/Flowers of Evil* (1857).

Baudouin, *n.* (1930–), king of the Belgians from 1951. In 1950 his father, Leopold III, abdicated and Baudouin was known until his succession in July 1951 as *Le Prince Royal.* In 1960 he married Fabiola de Mora y Aragó (1928–), member of a Spanish noble family.

baudric, BALDRIC.

Bauhaus, *n.* a radical German school of architecture and the arts founded in 1919 and dedicated to achieving a functional synthesis of art, design and technology. [G, lit. building house]

Bāul, *n.* member of Bengali mystical sect that emphasizes freedom from compulsion, from doctrine, and from social caste; they avoid all outward forms of religious worship. Not ascetic, they aim for harmony between physical and spiritual needs.

baulk BALK.

Baum, *n.* **L(yman) Frank** (1856–1919), US writer, best known for the children's fantasy *The Wonderful Wizard of Oz* (1900).

Bausch, *n.* **Pina** (1940–), German dance choreographer and director of the unique Wuppertal Tanztheater. Her works incorporate dialogue, elements of psychoanalysis, comedy and drama. She never accepts requests to restage her creations.

bauxite, *n.* a clay which is the principal source of aluminium. [*Les Baux,* near Arles]

Bavaria, *n.* (German **Bayern**) administrative region (German *Land*) of West Germany. **area** 70,600 sq km/27,252 sq miles. **capital** Munich. **towns** Nuremberg, Augsburg, Würzburg, Regensburg. **population** (1988) 11,083,000. **products** beer, electronics, electrical engineering, optics, cars, aerospace, chemicals, plastics, oil-refining, textiles, glass, toys. **religion** 70% Roman Catholic, 26% Protestant.

bavin, *n.* a bundle of brushwood; brushwood, firewood for baking bread. [etym. unknown]

Bawa, *n.* **Geoffrey** (1919–), Sri Lankan architect, formerly a barrister. His buildings are a contemporary interpretation of vernacular traditions, and include houses, hotels, and gardens. More recently he has designed public buildings such as the New Parliamentary Complex, Kotte, Colombo, Sri Lanka (1982), and Ruhuru University, Matara, Sri Lanka (1984).

bawbee, *n.* an old Scots copper coin equivalent to about a halfpenny; a halfpenny. [prob. from Alexander Orrock of Sille*bawbe,* fl.1514, Sc. mint-master]

†**bawcock,** *n.* a fine fellow. [F *beau coq*]

bawd[1], *n.* †a procurer; a go-between, a pander; a procuress, a brothel-keeper; a prostitute. †*v.i.* to pander. **bawdy,** *a.* dirty; of or befitting a bawd; obscene, lewd. *n.* bawdiness. **bawdy-house,** *n.* a brothel. **bawdily,** *adv.* lasciviously; obscenely. **bawdiness,** *n.* obscenity, lewdness. **bawdry,** *n.* the practice of a bawd; fornication; obscene talk. [etym. doubtful]

bawd[2], *n.* a hare. [etym. doubtful]

bawl, *v.i.* to cry loudly, howl, bellow; to shout at the top of one's voice. *v.t.* to shout aloud; to utter with bawling; to cry for sale. *n.* a loud, prolonged shout or cry. **to bawl out,** (*coll.*) to reprove fiercely. [med. L *baulāre,* to bark; or Icel. *baula,* to low, ON *baula,* a cow]

bawley, *n.* a small fishing-smack. [etym. unknown]

bawn, *n.* the courtyard of a castle; an enclosure for cattle. [etym. unknown]

Bax, *n.* **Arnold Edward Trevor** (1883–1953), English composer. His works were often based on Celtic legends and include seven symphonies, *The Garden of Fand* (a symphonic poem), and *Tintagel* (an orchestral tone poem). He was Master of the King's Musick (1942–53).

Baxter, *n.* **George** (1804–67); English engraver and printmaker; inventor in 1834 of a special process for printing in oil colours, which he applied successfully in book illustrations.

bay[1], *n.* an arm or inlet of the sea extending into the land with a wide mouth; a recess or cirque in a range of hills; (*N Am.*) an arm of a prairie extending into woods. **bay-floe, bay-ice,** *n.* new ice formed in bays or sheltered waters. **bay-salt,** *n.* coarse-grained crystals of salt obtained by slow evaporation, originally of seawater, now of a saturated solution of chloride of sodium. **Bay State,** *n.* (*N Am.*) Massachusetts (formerly the colony of Massachusetts Bay). **bay-wood,** *n.* a coarse mahogany from Honduras or Campeachy Bay. [F *baie,* low L *baia*]

bay[2], *n.* an opening or recess in a wall; a main compartment or division, like the interval between two pillars; a division of a barn or other building; an internal recess in a room formed by the outward projection of the walls; (*Rail.*) a platform with a cul-de-sac, forming the terminus of a side-line; a compartment or division in a ship or in the fuselage of an aircraft. **bay-window,** *n.* an angular window structure forming a recess in a room, distinguished from an *oriel* by havings its walls carried down to the ground, and from a bow-window, which is curved, not angular, in ground-plan. **sick bay,** *n.* a ship's hospital. [F *baie,* OF *baée,* fem. p.p. of *baer,* to gape, late L *baddāre* (fem. p.p. *badāta*)]

bay[3], *n.* a dam or embankment retaining water. *v.t.* to dam, hold (back) water. [etym. doubtful]

bay[4], *n.* barking; the prolonged hoarse bark of a dog; the barking of a pack that has tracked down its prey; hence, the final encounter between hounds and their prey; the position of a hunted animal defending itself at close quarters. *v.i.* to bark hoarsely, as a hound at its prey. *v.t.* to bark at; to bring to bay; to express by barking. **at bay,** in a position of defence, in great straits, in the last extremity. **to stand at bay, hold (hounds) at bay,** to keep back the assailing dogs or other form of attack. **to bring** or **drive to bay,** to come to close quarters with the animal hunted; to reduce to extremities. [OF *abai,* barking, from *abaier* (F *aboi, aboyer*)]

bay[5], *n.* the bay-tree or bay-laurel; (*N Am.*) a place covered with bay trees; (*pl.*) *Laurus nobilis,* leaves or twigs of this tree, woven into a garland as a reward for a conqueror or poet; fame, renown. **bayberry,** *n.* the berry of the bay; (*N Am.*) the fruit of *Myrica cerifera* or wax myrtle of North America; the plant itself. **bayberry tallow,** *n.* a kind of tallow obtained from the berries of the wax myrtle. **bay-cherry,** *n.* the cherry laurel, *Cerasus laurocerasus*. **bay-leaf,** *n.* a leaf from the bay-tree, dried and used in cooking to flavour sauces, stews etc. **bay-rum,** *n.* an aromatic, spirituous liquid, used in medicines and cosmetics, and prepared by distilling rum in which bay leaves have been steeped. **bay-tree,** *n.* the bay, *Laurus nobilis*. **baywood,** *n.* wood of the mahogany tree, *Swietenia mahogani*. [OF *baie,* L *baca,* berry]

bay[6], *a.* reddish-brown in colour, approaching chestnut. *n.* a horse of that colour. [F *bai,* L *badius* (cp. Gael. and Ir. *buidhe,* yellow)]

bay[7], *n.* the second branch of a stag's horn, the next to the brow antler. [abbr. of *bay-antler,* OF *besantlier* (*bes,* second, ANTLER)]

bayadère, *n.* a Hindu dancing-girl. [F, from Port. *bailadeira,* a dancing girl (*bailar,* to dance)]

†**bayard,** *a.* bay-coloured. *n.* a bay horse; name of the wondrous horse of Renaud de Montauban in the *chanson de geste* (*fig.* in allusion to proverbial sayings in which Bayard figures as a type of chivalry); one blinded with self-conceit. **bayardly,** *a.* done in a blind or stupid manner. *adv.* blindly, self-confidently. [OF *baiard,* from *bai,* BAY[6]]

Bayard, *n.* **Pierre du Terrail (Chevalier)** (1473–1524), French soldier. He served under Charles VIII, Louis XII, and Francis I, and was killed in action at the crossing of the Sesia in Italy. His heroic exploits in battle and in tournaments, his chivalry and magnanimity won him the name of 'knight without fear and without reproach'.

Bayern, BAVARIA.

Bayesian statistics, *n.* a form of statistics that uses the knowledge of prior probability together with the probability of actual data to determine posterior probabilities, using Bayes' theorem.

Bayes' theorem, *n.* in statistics, a theorem relating the probability of particular events taking place to the probability that events conditional upon them have occurred.

Bayeux Tapestry, *n.* a linen hanging 70 m/231 ft long and 50 cm/20 in wide, made about 1067–70, which gives a vivid pictorial record of the invasion of England by William I (the Conqueror) in 1066. It is an embroidery rather than a true tapestry, sewn with woollen threads in blue, green, red, and yellow, containing 72 separate scenes with descriptive wording in Latin. It is exhibited at the museum of Bayeux in Normandy, France.

Bayliss, *n.* **William Maddock** (1860–1924), English physiologist, who discovered the hormone secretin with E.H. Starling in 1902. Secretin plays an important part in digestion. During World War I, he introduced the use of saline (salt water) injections to help the injured recover from shock.

Bay of Pigs, inlet on the S coast of Cuba about 145 km/90 miles SW of Havana, the site of an unsuccessful invasion attempt by 1500 US-sponsored Cuban exiles during 17–20 Apr 1961; 1173 were taken prisoner.

bayonet, *n.* a weapon for stabbing or thrusting, attached by a band to the muzzle of a rifle, so as to convert that into a kind of pike; (*pl.*) infantry; military force; a kind of clutch; a type of connection used to secure light-bulbs, camera lenses etc. in which pins are engaged in slots in a cylindrical fitting. *v.t.* to stab with a bayonet; to compel by military force. **Spanish bayonet,** a species of yucca with lanceolate leaves. **bayonet catch, joint,** *n.* device for securing in place two cylindrical parts by means of a turn. [etym. doubtful, said to be from *Bayonne,* France]

bayou, *n.* (*N Am.*) the outlet of a lake or river; a sluggish watercourse. [Fr. *boyau,* a gut]

bazaar, *n.* an Eastern market-place, where goods of all descriptions are offered for sale; a sale of useful or ornamental articles often handmade or second-hand in aid of charity; a shop where a variety of (ornamental) goods are sold. [Pers. *bāzār*]

Bazaine, *n.* **Achille François** (1811–88), marshal of France. From being a private soldier in 1831 he rose to command the French troops in Mexico (1862–67), and was made a marshal in 1864. In the Franco-Prussian War Bazaine commanded the Third Corps of the Army of the Rhine, allowed himself to be taken in the fortress of Metz, and surrendered on 27 Oct 1870 with nearly 180,000 men. For this he was court-martialled in 1873 and imprisoned, but in 1874 escaped to Spain.

Bazalgette, *n.* **Joseph** (1819–90), British civil engineer who, as Chief Engineer to the London Board of Works, designed London's sewer system, a total of 155 km/83 miles of sewers, covering an area of 256 sq km/ 100 sq miles. It was completed in 1865. He also designed the Victoria Embankment (1864–70), which was built over the river Thames and combined a main sewer, a water frontage, an underground railway, and a road.

bazooka, *n.* an anti-tank or rocket-firing gun. [after a crude pipe instrument]

BB, (*abbr.*) Boys' Brigade; (on lead pencils) double black.

BBC, (*abbr.*) British Broadcasting Corporation.

BC, (*abbr.*) before Christ; British Columbia; British Council.

BCE, (*abbr.*) before the Common Era.

B cell, B lymphocyte, *n.* a type of immune cell that is responsible for producing antibodies. Each B cell produces just one type of antibody, specific for a single antigen.

BCG, (*abbr.*) Bacillus Calmette-Guérin, used in anti-tuberculosis vaccine.

BD, (*abbr.*) Bachelor of Divinity.

bdellium, *n.* a popular name of several species of *Balsamodendron,* which produces gum-resin; the gum-resin of these trees. [L, from Gr. *bdellion, bdella, bdolchon,* Heb. *bedōlakh,* perh. a pear]

BDS, (*abbr.*) Bachelor of Dental Surgery.

be, *inf., pres. subj.* and *imper. v.* to exist, to live, to have a real state or existence, physical or mental; to become, to remain, continue; to happen, occur, come to pass; to have come or gone to or to occupy a certain place; to have a certain state or quality; (most commonly used as a copula, asserting connection between the subject and the predicate). **the be-all and end-all,** the sole object or idea in view. **be-all,** *n.* all that is to be; the consummation, the finality. [OE *bēon* (cp. Sansk. *bhū-*, Gr. *phuein,* L *fui,* OTeut. *beo-*; see also AM, WAS)]

Be, (*chem. symb.*) beryllium.

be- *pref.* about, by; e.g. (1) *besmear,* to smear all over, *bedaub,* to daub about, *before,* about the front of, *below,* on the low side of, *besiege,* to sit around; (2) making intransitive verbs transitive or reflective; e.g. *bemoan, bespeak, bethink;* (3) forming verbs from nouns or adjectives, as *befool, befriend, benumb;* (4) having a privative force, as in *behead, bereave;* (5) compounded with nouns, signifying to call this or that, as *bedevil, belady, bemadam;* (6) intensive, e.g. *becrowd, bedrug, bescorch;* (7) making adjectives, e.g. *bejewelled, bewigged.* [OE *be-*, *bī, by*]

BE, (*abbr.*) bill of exchange; Bachelor of Engineering; Board of Education.

beach, *n.* shingle; a sandy or pebbly seashore; the strand on which the waves break. *v.t.* to haul or run (a ship or boat) on a beach. **raised beach,** an ancient beach or shore, of lake or sea, left high and dry by elevation of the land or recession of the water. **beachcomber,** *n.* a long wave rolling in from the ocean; a settler in the Pacific Islands, living by pearl-fishing and other means; a loafer in these conditions; a wrecker, a water-rat. **beach-grass,** *n.* a coarse grass, *Arundo arenaria,* growing on the sea-shore. **beachhead,** *n.* a position held on the beach of a hostile coast. **beachmaster,** *n.* an officer who directs the process of disembarking troops. **beached,** *a.* having a beach; †covered with beach or shingle; run aground on a beach. **beachy,** *a.* like a beach; pebbly, shingly. [etym. unknown]

Beach Boys, the, US pop group formed 1961. They began as exponents of vocal-harmony surf music with Chuck Berry guitar riffs (hits include 'Surfin' USA', in 1963, 'Help Me, Rhonda', 1965) but the compositions, arrangements, and production by Brian Wilson (1942–) became highly complex under the influence of psychedelic rock, peaking with 'Good Vibrations' (1966).

beacon, *n.* a burning cresset fixed on a pole or on a building; a signal-fire on an eminence; a conspicuous hill; a watch-tower; a lighthouse; a fixed signal to give warning of a shoal or rock, or to indicate the fairway; a transmitter concentrating its radiation in a narrow beam, to act as a guide to aircraft; anything which gives notice of danger. *v.t.* to light up with beacon-fires; to mark with beacons; to lead, to guide. *v.i.* to shine like a beacon. **beaconage,** *n.* money paid for the maintenance of beacons, buoys etc.; a system of lighting shoals etc. [OE *bēacen* (cp. OS *bōkan.* OHG *Bouhhan*]

bead, *n.* †a prayer; †(*pl.*) prayers, formerly counted on the rosary or paternoster; a small globular perforated body of glass, coral, metal or other material; a bead-like drop threaded on a string to form a rosary; the same used as an ornament; a bead-like drop of a liquid, a bubble; the front sight of a gun; a narrow semi-circular moulding; an ornament resembling a string of beads; (*pl.*) a necklace; a rosary. *v.t.* to ornament with beads or beading; to thread beads. *v.i.* to form beads. **Baily's beads,** a phenomenon resembling a string of beads observed on the sun in total eclipses, first described by the astronomer Francis *Baily* in 1836. **to draw a bead upon,** to aim at. **to tell** or **say one's beads,** to count the rosary, to say one's prayers. **bead-frame,** *n.* an abacus. **bead-house,** *n.* a house of prayer; an almshouse. **bead-roll,** *n.* a list of names (originally of benefactors) to be prayed for. **beadsman, bedesman, beadswoman, bedeswoman,** *n.* one appointed to pray for another; an almsman or almswoman. **bead-tree,** *n.* the pride of India, *Melia azedirach,* and other trees, the seeds of which are used as rosary beads. **bead-work,** *n.* ornamental work in beads. **beading,** *n.* the formation of beads; bead-work; a bead-moulding. **beady,** *a.* of eyes, small and bright like beads; covered with beads or bubbles, foaming. [OE *bed-* (only in comb.), *gebed,* prayer (*biddan,* to pray)]

beadle, *n.* a messenger, crier or usher of a court; a petty officer of a church, parish, college, city company etc. **beadledom,** *n.* beadles collectively; the characteristics of beadles; stupid officiousness. **beadleship,** *n.* [OE *bydel,* a herald, or OF *bedel* (F *beadeau*); OTeut. *budiloz,* from *buidan,* to announce]

beadsman, beadswoman BEAD.

beagle, *n.* a small dog originally bred for hunting hares by members of the hunt on foot; one who scents out or hunts down; an officer of the law. [etym. unknown]

beak, *n.* the pointed bill of a bird; anything pointed like the bill of a bird, as the mandibles of a turtle or an octopus; the prow of an ancient war-galley, often sheathed with brass, and used as the modern ram; a promontory of land etc.; a spout; any beak-like process; (*sl.*) a magistrate, a headmaster or headmistress. *v.t.* to seize or strike with the beak (esp. in cock-fighting). **beaked,** *a.* having a beak or beak-like process; (*Bot.*) rostrate; (*Zool.*) having a beak-like process; (*Her.*) having the beak and legs of a different tincture from the body. **beak-head,** *n.* the prow of an ancient war-galley; (*Naut.*) a small platform at the fore part of the upper deck; the part of a ship in front of the fo'c'sle, fastened to the stem; (*Arch.*) a Norman moulding shaped like a bird's beak. [F *bec,* low L *beccus,* prob. of Celtic origin]

beaker, *n.* a large wide-mouthed drinking-vessel; the contents of a beaker; an open-mouthed glass vessel with a lip, used in scientific experiments. **Beaker Folk,** *n.pl.* a prehistoric people inhabiting Britain and Europe during the Bronze Age, named from the beakers found in their burial sites. [Icel. *bikarr* (cp. G *Becher,* late L *bīcārium,* from Gr. *bīkos*)]

beal, bull, *n.* a sweet honey drink. [Austral. Abor.]

beam, *n.* a large, long piece of timber squared on its sides, esp. one supporting rafters in a building; the part of a balance from which the scales are suspended; the pole of a carriage; the part of a loom on which the warp is wound; a cylinder on which cloth is wound as it is woven; the main piece of a plough to which the handles are fixed; the main trunk of a stag's horn; a ray or collection of rays of light or radiation; the heavy iron lever which transmits motion in a beam-engine; a transverse piece of timber, supporting the deck and staying the sides of a ship; the width of a ship or boat; the shank of an anchor. *v.t.* to send forth, to radiate, to emit in rays; to send forth by beam-transmission. *v.i.* to send forth rays of light; to shine radiantly; to smile brightly. **off** or **on the beam,** off or on the course indicated by a radio beam; off or on the mark. **on the beam,** (*Naut.*) at right-angles to the keel. **on the port** or **starboard beam,** away upon the left or right of the ship. **to be on one's beam-ends,** to be thrown so much to one side that the beams are in the water; to be penniless, quite destitute. **beam-compass,** *n.* an instrument for describing large circles, consisting of a beam of wood or brass, with sliding sockets bearing steel or pencil points. **beam-ends,** *n.pl.* the ends of the beams of a ship. **beam-engine,** *n.* an engine with a beam connecting piston-rod and crank, in contradistinction to one in which the piston-rod is applied directly to the crank. **beam-filling,** *n.* masonry brought up from the level of the under to the upper sides of the beams; cargo between the beams. **beam transmission,** *n.* a method of short-wave radio transmission in which the energy radiated is concentrated by a reflector system of wires within a limited angle for reception in a particular zone. **beam-tree,** *n.* the white-beam, *Pyrus aria,* the timber of which is used for axle-trees. **beamy,** *a.* massive, shining, radiant, brilliant; antlered; broad in the beam (of ships). **beaming,** *a.* bright, shining. [OE *bēam* (cp. OHG *boum,* G *Baum,* Dut. *boom*]

bean, *n.* the kidney-shaped seed in long pods of *Faba vulgaris* and allied plants; the seeds of other plants in some way resembling those of the common bean. **full of beans,** energetic and vigorous. **old bean,** (*dated sl.*) old fellow, old chap. **beanbag,** *n.* a small cloth bag filled with dried beans used in games; a large cushion filled with foam or polystyrene beads. **bean-counter,** *n.* (*sl.*) a financial expert or adviser; an accountant. **bean-feast,** *n.* an annual dinner given by an employer to his workmen; a celebration. **bean-fed,** *a.* fed on beans; in good condition. **bean-fly,** *n.* an insect of purple colour found on beans. **bean-goose,** *n.* a migratory goose, *Anser segetum.* **beanpole,** *n.* a tall, thin pole used to support bean plants; (*coll.*) a tall thin person. **bean sprouts,** *n.pl.* the young shoots of mung beans used as a vegetable in Chinese cooking, and in salads. **bean-stalk,** *n.* stem of the bean. **bean-straw,** *n.* the haulm of bean plants. **bean-tree,** *n.* a popular name for several trees bearing seeds in pod, esp. the carob-tree, *Ceratonia siliqua.* **bean-trefoil,** *n.* a popular name for the leguminous genus *Anagyris,* the laburnum, *Cytisus laburnum,* and the buck-bean or bog-bean, *Menyanthes trifoliata.* **beano,** *n.* (*coll.*) a treat, a spree, a bean-feast. [OE *bēan* (cp. Dut. *boon,* Icel. *baun,* OHG *pona,* G *Bohne*)]

bear[1], *n.* a plantigrade mammal with a large head, long shaggy hair, hooked claws and a stumpy tail; a rough unmannerly man; either of the northern constellations, the Great or the Little Bear; one who sells stock for future delivery in the expectation that prices will fall, a speculator for the fall. *v.i.* to speculate for a fall in stocks. *v.t.* to produce a fall in the price of (stock etc.). **bear-baiting,** *n.* the sport of baiting a chained bear with dogs. **bear-berry,** *n.* the genus *Arctostaphylos,* a procumbent heath; (*erroneously*) the barberry. **bear-garden,** *n.* a place in which bears were kept and baited; hence, a rude, turbulent assembly. **bear-leader,** *n.* (*coll.*) a travelling tutor. **bear's-breech,** *n.* the genus *Acanthus.* **bear's ear,** *n.* the common auricula, *Primula auricula.* **bear's foot,** *n.* stinking hellebore, *Helleborus foetidus.* **bear's-grease,** *n.* the fat of bears, formerly much used as a pomade. **bearskin,** *n.* the skin of a bear; a shaggy woollen cloth, used for overcoats; the tall fur cap worn by the Foot Guards and some other regiments in the British Army. **bear-ward,** *n.* a bear-herd; (*coll.*) a tutor, a bear-leader. **bearish,** *a.* bear-like; rough, rude, uncouth; in the stock market characterized by a fall in prices. [OE *bera* (cp. Dut. *beer;* Icel. *bera, björn,* G *Bär*)]

bear[2], *v.t.* (*past* **bore**, *p.p.* **borne**) to carry, to wear, to show or display (as armorial bearings); to bring; to sustain, to support the weight of (material or immaterial things); to be responsible for, to wield, to suffer, to endure; to thrust, to press; to bring forth, to give birth to; to produce, to yield. *v.i.* to behave; to suffer, to be patient; to imply, to take effect, to have relation to; to incline, take a certain direction (as to the point of the compass) with respect to something else. **to bear against,** to rest upon; to be in contact with. **to bear arms,** to be a soldier; (*Her.*) to be entitled to a coat of arms. **to bear a hand,** to lend assistance. **to bear away,** to carry off; to win; to change the course of a ship when close-hauled, and put her before the wind. **to bear down,** to overwhelm, to crush, to subdue; to use the abdominal muscles to assist in giving birth. **to bear down on,** to sail in the direction of; to approach purposefully. **to bear hard,** to press, to urge; †to resent; to have a grudge against. †**to bear in hand,** to flatter with pretences; to deceive. **to bear in mind,** to remember; **to bear on,** to press against. **to bear out,** to confirm, to justify. **to bear up,** to endure cheerfully; to put the helm up so as to bring the vessel before the wind. **to bear up for,** to sail before the wind towards. **to bear upon,** to be relevant to. **to bring to bear,** to apply, bring into operation. **to bear with,** to put up with, to endure. **borne in upon one,** become one's firm conviction, realized by one. **bearable,** *a.* **bearably,** *adv.* **bearer,** *n.* one who or that which bears, carries or supports; one who assists to carry a corpse to the grave or to hold the pall; a porter; one who holds or presents a cheque; a bringer of anything; the holder of any rank or office; a support; the pieces supporting the winders of a stair; an animal or plant producing its kind; in India, Africa etc. a personal or domestic servant. **bearing,** *n.* endurance, toleration; mien, deportment, carriage, manner, behaviour, relation, connection; the space between the two fixed extremities of a piece of timber, or between one of the extremities and a post or wall; a carrier or support for moving parts of any machine; any part of a machine that bears the friction; (*Her.*) a charge, a device; relation, relevance, aspect; the direction in which an object lies from a ship; (*pl.*) relative position. **to lose one's bearings,** to be uncertain of one's position. **bearing-cloth,** *n.* the robe in which an infant is carried to the font. **bearing-rein,** *n.* a fixed rein for holding a horse's head up. [OE *beran* (cp. Goth *bairan*, OHG *beran*, L *ferre*, Gr. *pherein*)]

†**bear**[3] BIER.

bear[4], *n.* (*Sc.*) barley. **bear-bind, bear-bine,** *n.* bindweed, the field convolvulus; the large *Polygonum convolvulus*. [OE *bere*, barley]

beard, *n.* the hair on the lower part of a man's face, esp. on the chin; analogous hairy appendage in animals; (*Print.*) the part of a type above and below the face to allow for ascending and descending letters; the barb of an arrow; †the tail of a comet when it is in front of the nucleus; the hairy appendages in the mouth of some fishes, gills of some bivalves etc.; a byssus; the bristles of a feather; the awn of grasses; hairs occurring in tufts. *v.t.* to furnish with or as with a beard; to chip or plane away; to oppose with resolute effrontery; to defy. **old man's beard,** the wild clematis or traveller's joy. **bearded,** *a.* furnished with a beard or similar appendage; barbed, hooked, jagged. **beardie,** *n.* (*Austral.*) a variety of cod-fish. **beardless,** *a.* without a beard; hence, youthful, immature. **beardlessness,** *n.* [OE]

Beardsley, *n.* **Aubrey (Vincent)** (1872–98), British illustrator, whose meticulously executed black-and-white work displays the sinuous line and decorative mannerisms of Art Nouveau and was often charged with being grotesque and decadent. He became known through the *Yellow Book* magazine and his drawings for Oscar Wilde's *Salome* (1893).

bearskin BEAR[1].

beast, *n.* any of the animals other than man; a quadruped, esp. a large wild one; an animal to ride or drive; a domestic animal, esp. ox or cattle; a brutal person; an objectionable person; an objectionable thing. **the beast,** Antichrist (Rev. xiii.I); (*fig.*) man's carnal instincts. **beast-fable,** *n.* a story in which animals are the dramatis personae, much prevalent in the earlier forms of literature. **beast-like,** *a.* **beastly,** *a.* like a beast in form or nature; brutal, filthy, coarse; disgusting, offensive; disagreeable. †*adv.* in a beastly manner; (*coll.*) exceedingly, very. **beastliness,** *n.* †**beastlihead,** *n.* the nature or condition of a beast. [OF *beste*, L *bestia*]

beastings, BEEST.

beat, *v.t.* (*past* **beat,** *p.p.* **beaten**) to strike with repeated blows, to thrash; to bruise or break by striking or pounding; to work (metal etc.) by striking; to strike, as bushes, in order to rouse game; to mix or agitate by beating; to strike or impinge on, to dash against (of water, wind etc.); to conquer, overcome, master; to tread, as a path; to play (an instrument or tune) by striking; to indicate time with a baton. *v.i.* to strike against some obstacle; to pulsate, throb; to knock; to move rhythmically; to mark time in music; (*Naut.*) to make way against the wind. *n.* a stroke or blow; a stroke upon the drum, the signal given by such a blow; a pulsation, a throb; a certain assigned space regularly traversed at intervals by patrols, police etc.; hence, sphere, department, range; the rise or fall of the hand or foot in regulating time; variously applied by different writers to melodic graces or ornament; a periodic variation in amplitude caused by the combination of oscillations of different frequencies. *a.* a shortened form of **beaten**. **dead-beat,** overcome, worn out. **to beat about,** to tack. **to beat about the bush,** to approach a matter in a roundabout way; to shilly-shally. **to beat a retreat,** to retire. **to beat back,** to compel to retire. **to beat down,** to throw or cast down; to force down (price) by haggling. **to beat hollow,** to excel or surpass in a great degree. **to beat in,** to crush. **to beat into,** to knock into by dint of blows: to instil. **to beat it,** (*sl.*) to go away. **to beat off,** to drive away by blows. **to beat one's brains,** to puzzle, to ponder laboriously. **to beat out,** to extend by beating, to hammer out; to extinguish by beating. **to beat the bounds,** to mark the boundary of a parish by striking it with light rods. **to beat the clock,** to complete a task within the allotted time. **to beat the tattoo,** (*Mil.*) to beat to quarters. **to beat time,** (*Mus.*) to regulate or measure the time by a motion of the hand or foot. **to beat up,** to bring to a fluid or semi-fluid mass by beating; to make way against wind or tide; to injure seriously by beating. **to beat up for,** to make great endeavours to procure. **to beat up for recruits,** to collect recruits. **to beat up and down,** to run first one way, then another, as a hunted animal. **beat generation,** (*orig. N Am.*) a bohemian movement of poets, writers etc. of the 1950s who rejected prevailing social and cultural values; young people of the 1950s and early 1960s characterized by unconventional attitudes and self-conscious bohemianism in behaviour and dress. **beatnik,** *n.* (often *derog.*) a member of this movement. **beat music,** *n.* popular music characterized by a pulsating rhythm. **beaten,** *a.* subjected to repeated blows; defeated, vanquished, weary, exhausted; trodden smooth, plain or bare; prostrated by the wind. **beater,** *n.* one who beats; a man employed to rouse game, esp. grouse or pheasant; an instrument for beating, pounding or mixing. **beating,** *n.* the action of striking repeated blows; punishment or chastisement by blows; pulsation, throbbing; overthrow, defeat; sailing against the wind. **to take a beating,** to suffer verbal or physical punishment. **to take some, a lot of beating,** to be difficult to improve upon. [OE *bēatan* (cp. OHG *pōzan*)]

†**beath,** *v.t.* to foment to heal; (Spens.) to bathe. [OE *bethian*, to foment]

beatify, *v.t.* to render supremely blessed or happy; in the Roman Catholic Church, to declare (deceased person) blessed. **beatific,** *a.* making one blessed; expressing happiness. **beatific vision,** *n.* vision of the glories of heaven. **beatifically,** *adv.* **beatification,** *n.* the act of rendering blessed; the Pope's declaration that a deceased person is blessed in heaven and that definite forms of public reverence should be paid to him/her – the first step towards canonization. **beatitude,** *n.* supreme felicity; heavenly bliss; esp. the special blessedness announced in the Sermon on the Mount. [L *beātificāre*, (*beātus*, happy, *facere*, to make)]

Beatitudes, *n.* in the New Testament, the sayings of Jesus reported in Matthew vi. 1–12; Luke vi. 20–38, depicting the spiritual qualities which characterize members of the Kingdom of God.

Beatles, the, an English pop group (1960–70). The members, all born in Liverpool, were John Lennon (1940–80, rhythm guitar, vocals), Paul McCartney (1942– , bass, vocals), George Harrison (1943– , lead guitar, vocals), and Ringo Starr (formerly Richard Starkey, 1940– , drums). Using songs written by Lennon and McCartney, they brought the Mersey beat to prominence with worldwide hits including 'She Loves You' (1963), 'I Want To Hold Your Hand' (1963), and 'Can't Buy Me Love' (1964).

beatnik BEAT.

Beaton[1], *n.* **Cecil** (1904–80), English portrait and fashion photographer, designer, illustrator, diarist, and conversationalist. He produced portrait studies and also designed scenery and costumes for ballets, and sets for plays and films.

Beaton[2], *n.* **David** (1494–1546), Scottish nationalist cardinal and politician, adviser to James V. Under Mary, Queen of Scots, he was opposed to the alliance with England and persecuted reformers such as George Wishart, who was condemned to the stake; he was killed by Wishart's friends.

Beatrix, *n.* (1936–), queen of the Netherlands. The eldest daughter of Queen Juliana, she succeeded to the throne on her mother's abdication 1980. In 1966, she married the West German diplomat, Claus von Amsberg (1926–), who was created Prince of the Netherlands. Her heir is Prince Willem Alexander (1967–).

Beatty, *n.* **Warren** (stage name of Warren Beaty) (1937–), US film actor and director, popular for such films as *Bonnie and Clyde* (1967) and *Heaven Can Wait* (1978). His more recent productions include *Reds* (1981) and *Ishtar* (1987).

beau, *n.* (*pl.* **beaus, beaux**) a man unduly attentive to dress and social fashions and etiquette; a fop, a dandy; a suitor, lover, sweetheart. *v.t.* to act as beau to; to escort. **beau geste**, *n.* (F) gracious gesture. **beau-ideal,** *n.* †ideal beauty; the highest conceivable type of excellence. **beau-monde**, *n.* the fashionable world. †**beau-pere**, *n.* a respectful term of address for a father, clergyman or elderly man; a companion. **beauish,** *a.* after the manner of a beau; like a beau; foppish. [OF *beau, bel,* L *bellus,* fine, pretty (perh. *benlus,* dim. of *benus,* related to *bene,* well, *bonus,* good)]

Beauclerk, *n.* family name of the Dukes of St Albans; descended from King Charles II by his mistress Eleanor Gwyn.

Beaufort, *n.* **Henry** (1375–1447), English priest, bishop of Lincoln from 1398, Winchester from 1405. As chancellor of England, he supported his half-brother Henry IV, and made enormous personal loans to Henry V to finance war against France. As a guardian of Henry VI from 1421, he was in effective control of the country until 1426. In the same year he was created a cardinal. In 1431 he crowned Henry VI as king of France in Paris.

Beaufort scale, *n.* system of recording wind velocity, devised in 1806 by Sir Francis *Beaufort*, 1774–1857. It is a numerical scale ranging from 0 to 17, calm being indicated by 0 and a hurricane by 12; 13–17 indicate degrees of hurricane force.

Beaujolais, *n.* a usu. red, light Burgundy wine. [F, district in the Lyonnais, SE France]

Beaumarchais, *n.* **Pierre Augustin Caron de** (1732–99), French dramatist. His great comedies *Le Barbier de Seville/The Barber of Seville* (1775) and *Le Mariage de Figaro/The Marriage of Figaro* (1778, but prohibited until 1784) form the basis of operas by Rossini and Mozart.

Beaumont, *n.* **Francis** (1584–1616), English dramatist and poet. From about 1608 he collaborated with John Fletcher. Their joint plays include *Philaster* (1610), *The Maid's Tragedy* (*c.* 1611), and *A King and No King* (*c.* 1611). *The Woman Hater* (*c.* 1606) and *The Knight of the Burning Pestle* (*c.* 1607) are ascribed to Beaumont alone.

Beaune, *n.* a usu. red Burgundy wine. [name of place in Côte-d'Or, France]

Beauregard, *n.* **Pierre** (1818–93), US Confederate general whose opening fire on Fort Sumter, South Carolina, started the American Civil War in 1861.

beauty, *n.* that quality or assemblage of qualities which gives the eye or the other senses intense pleasure; or that characteristic in a material object or an abstraction which gratifies the intellect or the moral feeling; a beautiful person, esp. a woman; beautiful women generally; a beautiful feature or characteristic; embellishment, grace, charm; a particular aspect that gives satisfaction or (*ironically*) the reverse; a very fine example of its kind; (*coll.*) an egregious person; a scamp. *v.t.* to adorn; to beautify. **beauty parlour,** *n.* a shop specializing in beauty treatments. **beauty queen,** *n.* a woman picked as the most attractive in a beauty contest. **beauty-sleep,** *n.* sleep before midnight. **beauty specialist,** *n.* one who makes a speciality of beauty treatment. **beauty-spot,** *n.* a patch or spot placed upon the face to heighten some beauty; a foil; (*coll.*) a beautiful place or landscape. **beauty treatment,** *n.* improvement of women's appearance by artificial means. **beaut,** *n.* (*sl., esp. Austral.*) something or someone outstanding. *int.* great, excellent. **beauteous,** *a.* (*poet.*) endowed with beauty; beautiful. **beauteously,** *adv.* **beauteousness,** *n.* **beautician,** *n.* one who administers beauty treatment. **beautiful,** *a.* full of beauty; possessing the attributes that constitute beauty; satisfactory, palatable, delicious; (*ironically*) egregious. *n.* (*poet.*) one who or that which is beautiful. **the beautiful,** the abstract notion of the qualities constituting beauty. **beautifully,** *adv.* **beautifulness,** *n.* **beautify,** *v.t.* to make beautiful. *v.i.* to grow beautiful. **beautifier,** *n.* one who or that which beautifies. †**beautiless,** *a.* [OF *biaute, beïtet* (late L *bellus,* see BEAU)]

Beauvoir, *n.* **Simone de** (1908–86), French socialist, feminist, and writer, who taught philosophy at the Sorbonne university in Paris during 1931–43. Her book *Le Deuxième sexe/The Second Sex* (1949) is a classic text that became a seminal work for many feminists.

beaux arts, *n.pl.* (F) fine arts.

beaux esprits BEL ESPRIT.

beauxite, BAUXITE.

beaver¹, *n.* an amphibious rodent mammal, *Castor fiber,* with broad tail, soft fur and habits of building huts and dams; the fur of this animal; a hat made of such fur; †a felted cloth for overcoats; (*sl.*) a man with a beard. **to beaver away at,** to work hard at. **beaver board,** *n.* a building board of wood-fibre material. **beaver-dam,** *n.* an obstruction placed across a stream by beavers. **beaver-rat,** *n.* the musquash or musk-rat. **beaver-tree, beaver-wood,** *n.* (*N Am.*) the sweet-bay or laurel-magnolia, *Magnolia glauca.* **beaverteen** (after VELVETEEN), *n.* a twilled cotton fabric with looped filling or pile. [OE *beafer* (cp. Dut. *bever,* G *Biber,* L *fiber*)]

beaver², *n.* the lower part of a visor; the visor of a helmet. **beavered,** *a.* provided with a beaver; wearing a beaver hat. [OF *bavière,* bib, from *baver,* to foam, slaver (*bave,* froth, slaver)]

Beaverbrook, *n.* **William Maxwell Aitken, 1st Baron Beaverbrook** (1879–1964), British newspaper proprietor and politician, born in Canada. Between World War I and II he used his newspapers, especially the *Daily Express*, to campaign for Empire free trade and against Prime Minister Baldwin.

bebop, *n.* a variety of jazz music which developed in the 1940s, distinguished from the earlier jazz tradition by its harsher melodies, dissonant harmonies and faster tempos. (see BOP). [imit. of the rhythm]

becall, *v.t.* to miscall, abuse, call names.

becalm, *v.t.* to render calm or still; to quiet, to tranquillize, to soothe; to deprive (a ship) of wind.

became, *past* BECOME.

because, *conj.* by cause of, by reason of, on account of, for; for this reason, inasmuch as. [*be-*, by, CAUSE]

beccafico, *n.* a small migratory songbird of the genus *Sylvia* and eaten as a delicacy on the continent. [It., fig-pecker (*beccare,* to peck, *fico,* fig)]

béchamel, *n.* a white sauce made with cream or milk and flavoured with onions and herbs. [after Louis de *Béchamel,* d. 1704, its F inventor]

bechance, *v.i.* to chance, to happen. *v.t.* to befall. †*adv.* by chance.

becharm, *v.t.* to charm, to fascinate.

bêche-de-mer, *n.* the sea-slug or trepang, *Holothuria edulis,* an echinoderm eaten by the Chinese. **beching boat,** *n.* (*Austral.*) a boat engaged in this trade. [Fr, sea-spade]

Bechuanaland, *n.* former name until 1966 of Botswana.

beck¹, *n.* a bow or curtsy; a mute signal of assent or command; a nod, a gesture of the finger or hand; the slightest indication of will. *v.i.* to make a mute signal; to make obeisance, to curtsy. *v.t.* to call by a beck. **beck and call,** absolute control. [BECKON]

beck², *n.* a brook, a rivulet; esp. a mountain or moorland stream. [Icel. *bekkr* (Swed. *bäck,* G *Bach*)]

Becker, *n.* **Boris** (1967–), West German lawn-tennis player. In 1985 he became the youngest winner of a singles title at Wimbledon at the age of 17 years. He has won the title three times and helped West Germany to win the Davis Cup in 1988.

becket¹, *n.* (*Naut.*) anything used to confine loose ropes, tackle or spars, as a large hook, a rope with an eye at one end; a bracket, pocket, loop etc. [etym.

doubtful]

Becket[2], *n.* **St Thomas** (1118–70), English priest and politician. He was chancellor to Henry II (1155–62), when he was appointed archbishop of Canterbury. The interests of the church soon conflicted with those of the crown, and Becket was assassinated; he was canonized in 1172.

Beckett, *n.* **Samuel** (1906–89), Irish novelist and dramatist, who wrote in French and English. *En attendant Godot/Waiting for Godot* (1952) is possibly the best-known example of Theatre of the Absurd. This genre is taken to further extremes in *Fin de Partie/Endgame* (1957) and *Happy Days* (1961). Nobel Prize for Literature (1969).

Beckmann, *n.* **Max** (1884–1950), German expressionist painter, who fled the Nazi regime in 1933 for the US. After World War I his art was devoted to themes of cruelty in human society, portraying sadists and their victims with a harsh style of realism.

beckon, *v.i.* to make a signal by a gesture of the hand or a finger or by a nod. *v.t.* to summon or signal to by a motion of the hand, a nod etc. [OE *bēacnian, bīecnian* (*beacen*, a sign, BEACON)]

becloud, *v.t.* to cover with or as with a cloud; to obscure.

become, *v.i.* (*past* **became**, *p.p.* **become**) to pass from one state or condition into another; to come into existence; to come to be. *v.t.* to be suitable to, to befit, to be proper to or for; to be in harmony with; to look well upon. **becoming,** *a.* befitting, suitable, proper; in harmony or keeping with; graceful in conduct, attire etc. **becomingly,** *adv.* **becomingness,** *n.* [OE *becuman* (BE-, *cuman,* to come; cp. Goth. *bikwiman,* G *bekommen*)]

becquerel, *n.* (*symb.* Bq) a unit which measures the activity of a radioactive source. [A.H. BECQUEREL]

Becquerel, *n.* **Antoine Henri** (1852–1908), French physicist, who discovered penetrating, invisible radiation coming from uranium salts, the first indication of radioactivity, and shared a Nobel prize with the Curies in 1903.

becurl, *v.t.* to curl; to deck with curls.

bed, *n.* an article of domestic furniture to sleep upon; hence, marriage, conjugal rights, childbirth and, with qualifying adjective, the grave; the resting-place of an animal; the flat surface on which anything rests; a plot of ground in a garden; the channel of a river; the bottom of the sea; a horizontal course in a wall; a stratum, a layer of rock; hence, an aggregation of small animals disposed in a bed-like mass; a layer of oysters; the central portion of a gun-carriage; the foundation of a road, street or railway; the bottom layer or support on which a mechanical structure or machine is laid. *v.t.* (*past, p.p.* **bedded**) to put in bed; to plant in a bed or beds; to have sexual intercourse with; to fix in a stratum or course; to place in a matrix of any kind, to embed. *v.i.* to go to bed. **bed and board,** lodgings and food; connubial relations. **bed and breakfast,** in a hotel etc., overnight accommodation with breakfast. **bed of justice,** orig. a state-bed round which the French king held receptions; a formal session of Parlement under the French kings, for the compulsory registration of royal edicts. **bed of roses,** a comfortable place. **to be brought to bed,** to be delivered of a child. **to bed out,** to plant out in beds. **to get out of bed on the wrong side,** to begin the day in a foul mood. **to keep one's bed,** to remain in bed (from sickness etc.). **to lie in the bed one has made,** to suffer for one's own misdeeds or mistakes. **to make a bed,** to put a bed in order after it has been used. **to make up a bed,** to prepare sleeping accommodation at short notice. **to take to one's bed,** to be confined to bed (from sickness etc.). **bedbug,** *n.* a bloodsucking insect which infests filthy bedding. **bed-chair,** *n.* a chair with a movable back, to support an invalid in bed. **bed-chamber,** *n.* a sleeping apartment; a bedroom. **lord, groom, gentleman of the bed-chamber,** officers of the Royal Household who wait upon a male sovereign. **ladies, women of the bedchamber,** ladies who wait on a female sovereign. **bed-clothes,** *n.pl.* sheets, blankets and coverlets for a bed. **bed-fast,** *a.* confined to bed. **bed-fellow,** *n.* one who sleeps in the same bed with another. **bed-hangings,** *n.pl.* hangings or curtains for a bed. **bed-linen,** *n.* sheets and pillow cases for a bed. **bed-maker,** *n.* one who makes beds; a person at English universities who makes the beds and sweeps the rooms. **bed-mate,** *n.* a bed-fellow. **bed-moulding,** *n.* the moulding under a projection, as the corona of a cornice. **bed-pan,** *n.* a warming-pan; a chamber-utensil for use in bed. **bed-plate,** *n.* (*Eng.*) the cast-iron or steel plate used as the base plate of an engine or machine. **bedpost,** *n.* one of the upright supports of a bedstead. †**bed-presser,** *n.* a great lazy person. **bed-quilt,** *n.* a counterpane, a coverlet. **bed-rid, bed-ridden,** *a.* confined to bed through age or sickness. **bedrock,** *n.* the rock underlying superficial formations; hence, bottom, foundation, fundamental principles; the lowest possible state. **bed-roll,** *n.* bedding rolled up so as to be carried by a camper etc. **bed-room,** *n.* †room in a bed; a sleeping apartment. **bed-side,** *n.* place by, or companionship by a bed. *a.* pertaining to the sick-chamber. **bedside manner,** *n.* suave manner in attending a patient. **bed-sitting-room, bed-sitter, -sit,** *n.* bedroom and sitting-room combined. **bedsore,** *n.* a sore produced by long confinement to bed. **bedspread,** *n.* a counterpane, coverlet. †**bed-staff,** *n.* (*pl.* **-staffs, -staves**) a stick used in some way about a bed; often mentioned as a ready weapon. **bedstead,** *n.* the wooden or metal framework on which a mattress is placed. **bedstraw,** *n.* straw covered with a sheet and used as a bed or palliasse; English name of the genus *Galium*. **bed-swerver,** *n.* one unfaithful to marriage vows. **bed-tick,** *n.* a bag or oblong case into which the feathers, hair, straw, chaff etc., of a bed are put. **bedtime,** *n.* the usual hour for going to bed. **bedward,** *adv.* in the direction of bed; towards bedtime. **bedder,** *n.* a plant for bedding-out; (*Camb. Univ.*) a charwoman, a bed-maker. **bedding,** *n.* a bed with the clothes upon it; bed-clothes; litter for domestic animals; a bottom layer or foundation; stratification; the line or plane of stratification. **bedding-plane,** *n.* plane of stratification; top or bottom surface of a stratum. **bedding-plants, bedding-out plants,** *n.pl.* plants intended to be set in beds. [OE *bed, bedd* (cp. Goth. *badi, G Bett;* perh. from Indo-Eur. *bhodh-,* whence L *fodere,* to dig, from idea of dug-out, lair)]

BEd., (*abbr.*) Bachelor of Education.

bedabble, *v.t.* to sprinkle, to wet; to splash, stain.

bedad, *int.* (*Ir.*) begad (an attenuated *by God*). [BY, DAD]

bedaub, *v.t.* to daub over, to besmear, to bedizen.

bedazzle, *v.t.* to confuse by dazzling. **bedazzlingly,** *adv.*

†**bede, bedesman,** etc. BEAD.

Bede, *n.* (*c.* 673–735), English theologian and historian, known as the Venerable Bede, active in Durham and Northumbria. He wrote many scientific, theological, and historical works. His *Historia Ecclesiastica Gentis Anglorum/Ecclesiastical History of the English People* (731) is an important source for early English history.

bedeck, *v.t.* to deck out, to adorn.

bedeguar, *n.* a mossy growth on rose-briers. [F *bédéguar,* Pers. and Arab. *bādāwar,* wind-brought, some thorny plant]

bedel, *n.* an officer at the Universities of Oxford and Cambridge who performs ceremonial functions (Cambridge spelling, **bedell**). [BEADLE]

bederel BEDRAL.

bedevil, *v.t.* to treat with diabolical violence or ribaldry; to bewitch; to torment; to confound, confuse; to obstruct. **bedevilment,** *n.* demoniacal possession; a state of utter confusion or disorder; bewildering trouble.

bedew, *v.t.* to moisten or sprinkle with dew-like drops.

Bedfordshire, *n.* county in central S England. **area** 1,240 sq km/479 sq miles. **towns** administrative headquarters Bedford; Luton, Dunstable. **population** (1987) 526,000. **products** cereals, vegetables, agricultural machinery, electrical goods.

bedim, *v.t.* to render dim; to obscure.

bedizen, *v.t.* to deck out in gaudy vestments or with tinsel finery. **bedizenment,** *n.* bedizening; gaudy attire, finery.

bedlam, *n.* a lunatic asylum; a scene of wild uproar; madness, lunacy; †a madman, a lunatic. *a.* of or belonging to a madhouse; mad, foolish, lunatic. †**bedlam-beggar,** *n.* an inmate of old Bedlam, discharged cured or relieved, furnished with a badge and allowed to beg. **bedlamite,** *n.* a bedlam-beggar; a madman, a lunatic. *a.* mad, lunatic. [from the priory of St Mary of *Bethlehem,* incorporated as a royal foundation for lunatics, 1547]

Bedlington, *n.* a grey, crisp-haired terrier. [town in Northumberland]

Bedouin, -duin, *n.* a nomadic Arab, as distinguished from one living in a town; a gipsy, a wanderer. *a.* pertaining to the wandering Arabs; nomad. [F *bédouin,* Arab. *badawīn,* (*pl.*) *badawīy,* wild, wandering (*badw,* a desert)]

bedowrie shower, *n.* (*Austral.*) a red dust-storm.

bedraggle, *v.t.* to soil by trailing in the wet or mire.

bedral, bederel, betherel, corr. of BEADLE, *n.* (*Sc.*) a kind of beadle in Scottish churches.

Beds., (*abbr.*) Bedfordshire.

bee, *n.* a four-winged insect which collects nectar and pollen and is often kept in hives for the honey and wax it produces; any closely allied insect, e.g. *carpenter-bee, bumble-bee, mason-bee;* a busy worker; (*N Am.*) a social meeting for work usually on behalf of a neighbour. **spelling-bee,** a social contest in spelling. **the bee's knees,** (*coll.*) someone or something wonderful, admirable. **to have a bee in one's bonnet,** to have a crazy fancy or be cranky on some point. **bee-bird,** *n.* the spotted fly-catcher, *Muscicapa grisola;* (*N Am.*) the king-bird, *Tyrannus tyrannus.* **bee-bread,** *n.* a mixture of honey and pollen, on which bees feed their larvae; local name of several plants yielding nectar. **bee-cuckoo,** *n.* an African bird, *Cuculus indicator,* called also the honey-guide. **bee-eater,** *n.* a tropical Old World bird of the genus *Merops,* esp. *M. apiaster.* **bee-fold,** *n.* an enclosure for beehives. **bee-glue,** *n.* the substance with which bees fill up crevices in their hives. **beehive,** *n.* a receptacle (usually of wood or straw and dome-shaped) for bees. *a.* shaped like a beehive. **beehive-houses, beehive-huts,** *n.pl.* dwellings in which a roof of dry-stone masonry covers a single chamber formed by stone walls, each course being set successively inward (common in Lewis). **bee-line,** *n.* the shortest route between two places, that which a bee is assumed to take. **to make a bee-line for,** to make straight for. **bee-master, bee-mistress,** *n.* one who keeps bees. **bee-moth,** *n.* the wax-moth, *Galleria cereana,* which lays its eggs in hives, the larvae feeding on the wax. **bee-orchis,** *n.* a British orchid, *Ophrys apifera,* the flower of which resembles a bee. **bee-skep,** *n.* a straw beehive. **beeswax,** *n.* the wax secreted by bees for their cells, used to make polishes. *v.t.* to rub or polish with beeswax. **beeswing,** *n.* the second crust, a fine filmy deposit in an old port wine; old port. [OE *bēo, bī* (cp. Dut. *bij,* G *Biene*)]

Beeb, *n.* (*coll.*) an informal, humorous name for the BBC.

beech, *n.* a forest tree of the genus *Fagus;* esp. *F. sylvatica,* the common beech, a well-known forest tree with smooth bark and yielding nuts or mast; the wood of this tree. **beech-drops,** *n.pl.* (*N Am.*) the popular name of several plants parasitic on the roots of the beech. **beech-fern,** *n.* popular name of *Polypodium phegopteris,* **beech-mast,** *n.* the fruit of the beech-tree. **beech-nut,** *n.* the nut of the beech, two of which lie in the prickly capsule. **beech-oil,** *n.* oil expressed from beech-mast. **beech-wheat** BUCK WHEAT. **beechen,** *a.* of or pertaining to the beech; made of beech-wood. **beechy,** *a.* abounding in beech-trees. [OE *bēce, bōece (cp. Dut. beuk,* G *buche,* Gr. *phēgos,* L *fāgus*)]

Beecher, Harriet, unmarried name of Harriet Beecher STOWE, author of *Uncle Tom's Cabin.*

Beecher, *n.* **Lyman** (1775–1863), US Presbyterian minister, one of the most influential pulpit orators of his time. He was the father of Harriet Beecher Stowe and Henry Ward Beecher. As pastor from 1847 of Plymouth church, Brooklyn, New York, he was a leader in the movement for the abolition of slavery.

Beeching, *n.* **Richard, Baron Beeching** (1913–85), British scientist and administrator. He was chair of British Railways Board (1963–65), producing the controversial *Beeching Report* of 1963 planning concentration on inter-city passenger traffic and a freight system.

beef, *n.* the flesh of the ox, cow or bull, used as food; an ox (*usu. in pl.,* **beeves**), esp. one fatted for the market; flesh, muscle; (*sl. pl.* **beefs**) a complaint. *v.i.* to grumble, to grouse. **to beef up,** (*coll.*) to strengthen, reinforce. **beefcake,** *n.* (*sl.*) men with muscular physiques, esp. as displayed in photographs. **beef-eater,** *n.* one who eats beef; a well-fed servant; an African bird of the genus *Buphaga,* allied to the starling; (**Beefeater**) a Yeoman of the Guard, instituted in 1485; a warder of the Tower of London. **beefburger,** a kind of hamburger. **beefsteak,** *n.* a thick slice of meat from the hindquarters of an ox. **beef-tea,** *n.* the nutritive juice extracted from beef by simmering. **beef-wood,** *n.* the popular name of the timber of the *Casuarina,* the *Stenocarpus salignus,* and *Banksia compar,* three Australian trees, and of that of a Jamaican shrub. **beefy,** *a.* like beef; fleshy; stolid; muscular. **beefiness,** *n.* fleshiness; weight, stolidity. [OF *boef,* L *bovem* (nom. *bos,* cp. Gr. *bous,* Gael. *bō,* Sansk. *go,* cp. cow)]

beehive BEE.

Beelzebub, *n.* a god worshipped (as *Baal-zebub*) in Ekron (II Kings i.2); the prince of evil spirits, Satan; an evil spirit. [L *Beelzebūb,* Gr. *beelzeboub,* Heb. *ba' al-z'būb,* lord of flies]

been, *p.p.* BE.

beep, *n.* a short sound as made by a car horn or an electronic device, usu. as a warning. *v.i.* to make such a sound. *v.t.* to cause (e.g. a car horn) to sound.

beer[1], *n.* an alcoholic drink brewed from fermented malt, hops, water and sugar; any malt liquor prepared by brewing, including ale and porter; other fermented liquors, as *ginger-beer, spruce-beer* etc. **small beer,** weak beer; poor stuff: things of no account. **beer and skittles,** enjoyment or pleasure; all one could wish. **beer-barrel,** *n.* a barrel used to contain beer. **beer-engine, -pump,** *n.* a machine for pumping up beer from the cellar to the bar. **beer-garden,** *n.* a garden or outdoor area with tables where beer and other refreshments may be consumed. **beer-money,** *n.* a money allowance in lieu of beer; a tip. **beery,** *a.* abounding in beer; like beer; under the influence of beer; fuddled. **beeriness,** *n.* a condition approaching intoxication. [OE *bēor* (cp. Dut. and G *Bier*)]

beer[2], *n.* (*Weaving*) about forty threads gathered together from the ends of a warp, to help in opening or dividing the warp; in Scotland called the porter. [BIER]

beest, *n.* the first milk drawn from a cow after calving. **beestings** *n.pl.* beest. [OE *bēost* (OHG *Biost,* Dut. *biest*)]

beeswax, beeswing BEE.

beet, *n.* a plant or genus of plants, comprising red beet, used as a salad, and white beet, used in sugar-making, cultivated for its esculent root; (*N Am.*) beetroot. **beet-radish, beet-rave,** *n.* the common beet, *Beta vulgaris,* when raised for salad. **beetroot,** *n.* the root of this used as a salad; the red colour of beetroot. *a.* [OE *bēte,* L *beta*]

Beethoven, *n.* **Ludwig van** (1770–1827), German composer. In a career which spanned the transition from classicism to romanticism, his mastery of musical expression in every genre made him the dominant influence in 19th-cent. music, especially the symphony. His works include piano and violin concertos, piano sonatas, string quartets, sacred music and nine symphonies. From 1801 he was hampered by deafness but continued his composition.

beetle[1], *n.* a maul; a heavy wooden mallet for driving stones, stakes or tent-pegs into the ground, hammering down paving-stones and other ramming and crushing operations. *v.t.* to beat with a beetle. **as deaf as a beetle,** very deaf; stupidly deaf. **beetlebrain,** *n.* (*coll.*) an idiot. **beetlebrained,** *a.* [OE *bȳtel, bȳtl,* OTeut. *bautilos,* from *bautan,* to beat (cp. OE *beatan,* to beat)]

beetle[2], *n.* an insect of the order Coleoptera, the upper wings of which have been converted into hard wing-cases, the under ones being used for flight, if it is able to fly; the name is popularly confined to those of black colour and large size, and applied to other insects resembling these, such as the cockroach; a game in which the players attempt to complete a beetle-shaped drawing according to the throw of a dice; *v.i.* (prob. coined by Shakespeare) to jut out, to hang over. *a.* projecting, overhanging, scowling. **to beetle along, off** etc., to hurry, scuttle along. **beetle-browed,** *a.* having projecting or overhanging brows. **beetle-crusher,** *n.* (*sl.*) a large foot; a heavy boot; a policeman; a soldier. **beetling,** *a.* jutting, overhanging, prominent. [OE *bitela, bitula,* from *bitan,* to bite]

Beeton, *n.* **Mrs** (Isabella Mary Mayson) (1836–65), British writer on cookery and domestic management. Wife of a publisher, she produced *Beeton's Household Management* (1859), the first comprehensive work on domestic science.

beetroot BEET.

beeves BEEF.

BEF, (*abbr.*) British Expeditionary Force.

befall, *v.t.* (*past* **befell**, *p.p.* **befallen**) to happen to. *v.i.* to happen. [OE *befealtan* (BE-, *fallan,* FALL)]

befit, *v.t.* to be suitable to or for; to become; to be incumbent upon; †to fit. **befitting,** *a.* **befittingly,** *adv.*

befog, *v.t.* to involve in a fog; to obscure, to confuse.

befool, *v.t.* to make a fool of; to dupe, delude.

before, *prep.* in front of, in time, space, rank or degree; in presence or sight of; under the cognizance of; under the influence or impulsion of; in preference to. *adv.* ahead, in front; beforehand, already, in the past. *conj.* earlier than; sooner than, rather than. †*a.* anterior, prior. **before the mast,** in the fo'c'sle; applied to common sailors who live in the fo'c'sle in front of the foremast. **before the wind,** with the wind right aft. **before Christ,** before the birth of Christ (e.g. '1000 BC'). **before-cited,** *a.* cited in a preceding part. **before God,** *a.* with the knowledge or in the sight of God. **beforegoing,** *a.* preceding. **before-mentioned,** *a.* mentioned before. **beforehand,** *adv.* in anticipation, in advance, before the time. **to be beforehand,** to forestall; to be earlier than expected. **before-time,** *adv.* formerly; in the olden time. [OE *beforan* (*be-, bi-,* by, *foran,* adv., before, *fore,* prep. before, above, OTeut. *fora,* for)]

befortune, *v.i.* to befall, bechance.

befoul, *v.t.* to render dirty, to soil.

befriend, *v.t.* to favour, help; to countenance.

befringe, *v.t.* to furnish or decorate with or as with a fringe.

befuddle, *v.t.* to confuse, baffle; to stupefy with drink.

beg[1], *v.i.* (*past, p.p.* **begged**). to ask for alms, to live by asking alms; (of a dog) to sit up on the hind quarters expectantly. *v.t.* to ask or supplicate in charity; to ask earnestly, to crave, entreat. **to beg off,** to seek to be released from some obligation. **to beg the question,** to assume the thing to be proved. **to go a-begging,** to be acceptable to nobody; to be left after everyone has eaten etc. **beggar,** *n.* one who begs; one who lives by asking alms; one in indigent circumstances; †a suppliant, a petitioner; (*coll.*) a fellow; youngster. *v.t.* to reduce to want; to impoverish; to exhaust, to outdo. **a good beggar,** a successful pleader or collector for charitable objects. **to beggar description,** to go beyond one's power of expression. **beggar-my-neighbour,** *n.* a game of cards; the making of profits at the expense of others. **beggarly,** *a.* like a beggar; mean, poverty-stricken; poor, contemptible. *adv.* in the manner of a beggar. **beggarliness,** *n.* the quality of being beggarly. **beggary,** *n.* the state or condition of a habitual beggar; extreme indigence. [etym. doubtful; perh. from OF *begard,* a lay brother, corr. to the BEGUINES]

beg[2] BEY.

begad, *int.* by God.

began, *past* BEGIN.

begem, *v.t.* to cover or set as with gems.

beget, *v.t.* (*past,* **begot,** *p.p.* **begotten**) to engender, to generate, to procreate; to cause to come into existence. †*v.i.* to acquire. **begetter,** *n.* one who begets, a father; an originator.

beggar, etc. BEG[1].

Beghard, *n.* a lay brother, belonging to a 13th-cent. Flemish religious order like the Beguines, in France called *Beguins*. [med. L *Beghardus,* from F *Beguine,* or directly from *Bègue,* see BEGUINE[1]]

Begin, *n.* **Menachem** (1913–), Israeli politician, born in Poland. He was a leader of the extremist Irgun Zvai Leumi organization in Palestine from 1942; prime minister of Israel (1977–83), as head of the right-wing Likud party; and in 1978 shared a Nobel Peace Prize with President Sadat of Egypt for work on the Camp David Agreements for a Middle East peace settlement.

begin, *v.i.* (*past* **began**, *p.p.* **begun**) to come into existence, to arise, to start; to commence. *v.t.* to be the first to do, to do the first act of, to enter on, to commence. †*n.* a beginning. **to begin with,** to take first; firstly. **beginner,** *n.* one who originates anything; one who is the first to do anything; a young learner or practitioner; the actor or actors who appear first on the stage at the start of a play. **beginning,** *n.* the first cause, the origin; the first state or commencement; first principles, rudiments. [OE *beginnan* (cp. Dut. and G *beginnen,* begin, OE *ginan,* to yawn, Aryan *ghī,* L *hiāre,* to gape)]

begird, *v.t.* to encircle with or as with a girdle. [OE *begierdan,* BE-, GIRD[1]]

begirdle, *v.t.* to encompass like a girdle or belt.

begone, *imper. v.* get you gone, go away, depart.

begonia, *n.* a genus of tropical plants cultivated chiefly for their ornamental foliage. [Michael *Begon,* 1638–1710]

begot, *past,* **begotten,** *p.p.* BEGET.

begrime, *v.t.* to blacken or soil with grime.

begrudge, *v.t.* to grudge; to envy (a person) the possession of.

beguile, *v.t.* to deceive, cheat; to deprive of or lead into by fraud; to charm away tedium or weariness, to amuse; to bewitch. **beguilement,** *n.* the act of beguiling; a wile, temptation, deceit. **beguiler,** *n.* one who beguiles, a deceiver, a cheat. **beguiling,** *a.* deceiving, charming, wiling away. **beguilingly,** *adv.* so as to beguile. [BE-, *guile,* obs. v., deceive (see GUILE)]

Beguine[1], *n.* a member of certain sisterhoods which arose in the Netherlands in the 12th cent. (some of which still exist); the members are not bound by perpetual vows, and may leave the community when they please. **beguinage**, *n.* a house or establishment for Beguines. [the founder Lamberthe Bègue, late 12th cent.]

beguine[2], *n.* music or dance in bolero rhythm, of S American or W Indian origin. [F]

begum, *n.* a queen, princess or lady of high rank in some Muslim countries. [Hind. *bigam,* Turk. *bigīm,* princess, fem. of *beg,* BEY]

begun, *p.p.* BEGIN.

behalf, *n.* interest, lieu, stead. **on his behalf, on behalf of,** on account of, for the sake of; representing. [OE *be healfe,* by the side, blended with *on healfe,* on the side of]

Behan, *n.* **Brendan** (1923–64), Irish dramatist. His early experience of prison and knowledge of the workings of the IRA (recounted in his autobiography *Borstal Boy*, 1958), provided him with two recurrent themes in his plays. *The Quare Fellow* (1954) was followed by the tragicomedy *The Hostage* (1958), first written in Gaelic.

behave, †*v.t.* to handle, to exercise, to employ. *v.r.* to conduct, to demean. *v.i.* to conduct oneself or itself; to conduct oneself well, to display good manners; to act as regards, to conduct oneself towards. **well-behaved,** having good manners. **behaviour,** (*esp. N Am.*) **behavior,** *n.* outward deportment, carriage; manners, conduct, demeanour; the manner in which a thing acts; †good manners; †personality. **behaviour therapy,** *n.* a method of treating neurotic disorders (e.g. a phobia) by gradually conditioning the patient to react normally. **behavioural,** *a.* of or relating to behaviour. **behavioural science,** *n.* the scientific study of human beings and other organisms. **behaviourism,** *n.* the guiding principle of certain psychologists who hold that the proper basis of psychological science is the objective study of behaviour under stimuli. **behaviourist,** *n.* a proponent of behaviourism. [BE- HAVE]

behead, *v.t.* to cut the head off, to kill by decapitation; (*Geol.*) to cut off and capture the upper portion of (another stream) by gradual erosion in a backward direction. [OE *behēadian* (*be-*, by, *hēafod,* head)]

beheld, *pret., p.p.* BEHOLD.

behemoth, *n.* the animal described in Job xl.15-24, probably the hippopotamus; a huge person or thing. [Heb., from Egyp. *p-ehe-mau,* water-ox]

behest, *n.* a command; an injunction. [OE *behœs (behatan,* to promise)]

behind, *prep.* at the back of; inferior to; after, later than; in the rear of. *adv.* at the back, in the rear; towards the rear; in the past; back-wards, out of sight, on the further side of; in reserve; in arrears. *n.* the back part of a person or garment; the posteriors. **behind one's back,** without one's knowledge. **behind the scenes,** out of sight, without being obvious, private, secret. **behindhand,** *a.* dilatory, tardy; backward, unfinished; in arrear. [OE *behindan* (BE-, *hindan,* adv., at the back)]

Behn, *n.* **Aphra** (1640–89), English novelist and playwright, the first professional English writer. She was often criticized for her sexual explicitness, and tended to present her novels and plays from a woman's point of view. In 1688 her novel *Oronooko*, an attack on slavery, was published.

behold, *v.t.* (*past, p.p.* **beheld**) †to fix the eyes upon; look attentively at, observe with care; to see; view; to consider. *v.i.* to look. *int.* lo!, see. **beholder,** *n.* one who beholds; a spectator. **beholden**, (orig. p.p. of BEHOLD) *a.* obliged, indebted, under obligation of gratitude (with *to*). †**beholding** BEHOLDEN. [OE *bihaldan* (BE-, *healdan,* hold, keep)]

behoof, †**behove**, *n.* advantage, use, profit, benefit. [OE *behōf* (*behōflīc,* useful) (cp. Dut. *behoef,* G *Behuf; be-*, Goth. *hafjan,* OE *hebban,* to heave, cp. L *capere,* to take)]

behove, †**behoove**, *v.t.* to befit, to be due to, to suit. *v.i.* to be needful to; due to; to be incumbent. †**behoveful,** *a.* needful, necessary. [OE *bihōvian, behōfian* (see BEHOOF)]

Behrens, *n.* **Peter** (1868–1940), German architect. He pioneered the adaptation of architecture to modern industry, and designed the AEG turbine factory in Berlin (1909), a landmark in industrial design. He influenced Le Corbusier and Gropius.

Behring, *n.* **Emil von** (1854–1917), German physician who discovered that the body produces antitoxins, substances able to counteract poisons released by bacteria. Using this knowledge, he was able to develop new treatments for diseases such as diphtheria.

Beiderbecke, *n.* **Bix (Leon Bismarck)** (1903–31), US jazz cornetist, composer, and pianist. He was greatly inspired by the classical composers Debussy, Ravel and Stravinsky. A romantic soloist with Paul Whiteman's orchestra, his reputation grew after his early death.

beige, *n.* a fabric made of undyed and unbleached wool. *a.* grey; more recently, a brownish yellow. [F]

Beijing, *n.* (formerly **Peking**) capital of China; part of its NE border is formed by the Great Wall of China; population (1982) 9,230,500. Industries include textiles, petrochemicals, steel and engineering. The Forbidden City, built 1406–20 as Gu Gong (Imperial Palace) of the Ming emperors, and the Summer Palace are here. Founded 3000 years ago, Beijing was the 13th-cent. capital of Kublai Khan. Later replaced by Nanking, it was again capital from 1421, except 1928–49, when it was renamed Peiping.

bein, *a.* (*Sc.*) comfortable; well-off; well-fed, lazy. **beinness,** *n.* comfort; comfortable circumstances. [etym. doubtful]

being, *n.* the state of existing; lifetime; existence; nature, essence; a thing or person existing. *conj.* seeing that, since. *a.* existing, present. **Supreme Being,** God. **the time being,** the present. [BE-]

Beirut, *n.* (or **Beyrouth**) capital and port of Lebanon, devastated by civil war in the 1970s and 1980s and occupied by armies of neighbouring countries; population 702,000 (1980).

bejabers, *int.* an exclamation of surprise, regarded as exclusive to the Irish. [a modification of *by Jesus!*]

bejade, *v.t.* to tire out.

bejan, *n.* (*Sc.*) a freshman at Aberdeen and St Andrews Universities (borrowed from Paris University). [F *béjaune* (*bec jaune,* yellow beak, nestling)]

bekah, *n.* a Hebrew weight of $\frac{1}{4}$ ounce (Exodus xxxviii.26). [Heb.]

bekko-ware, *n.* Chinese pottery veined with colour like tortoise-shell. [Jap. *bekko,* tortoise-shell]

bel, *n.* a measure for comparing the intensity of noises, currents etc. the logarithm to the base 10 of the ratio of one to the other is the number of bels. [A.G. *Bell,* 1847–1922, inventor of the telephone]

belabour, *v.t.* to cultivate with labour, to labour at; to beat, to thrash; to dwell unduly on; to assault verbally.

belar, belah, *n.* a variety of casuarina tree. [Austral. Abor.]

belated, *a.* very late; behind time; too late; benighted. **belatedness,** *n.*

belaud, *v.t.* to praise excessively.

Belaunde Terry, *n.* **Fernando** (1912–), president of Peru (1963–68 and 1980–85). He championed land reform and the construction of roads to open up the Amazon valley. He maintained good relations with the US, and was forced to flee there in 1968 after being deposed by a military junta. His second term in office was marked by rampant inflation, huge foreign debts, military intervention, and terrorism.

belay, *v.t.* to fasten a running rope by winding it round a cleat or belaying-pin; to turn a rope round an object; to secure a climber to a rope. *n.* a turn of a rope round an object; that around which a climber's rope is belayed. *int.* Stop enough. **belaying-pin,** *n.* a stout pin to which running ropes may be belayed; a projection round which a rope can be tied or hitched. [OE *belecgan,* (to lay round, envelop; (nautical use perh. from Dut. *beleggan,* to cover, belay)]

bel Canto, (It.) *n.* a style of operatic singing characterized by purity of tone and exact phrasing. [lit., beautiful singing]

belch, *v.t.* to expel from the mouth with violence; to eject, to throw out; to utter in a noisy or drunken manner. *v.i.* to eject wind by the mouth from the stomach; to eructate; †to issue out, as by eructation. *n.* an eructation; an eruption, a burst (of smoke or fire). [OE *bealcan*]

belcher, *n.* a blue and white spotted neckerchief. [Jim *Belcher,* the boxer, 1781–1811]

beldam, †**beldame**, *n.* a grandmother, a remote ancestress; an old woman; a hag, a witch. [F *belle, bel,* expressing relationship, DAM[1], mother]

beleaguer, *v.t.* to besiege; to harass. **beleaguerment,** *n.* siege, blockade, harassment. [Dut. *belegeren,* besiege (*be-*, around, *leger,* a bed, a camp)]

belemnite, *n.* a conical, sharply pointed fossil shell of a genus of cephalopods, allied to the cuttle-fish; any individual of this genus. **belemnitic,** *a.* of, pertaining to or characterized by belemnites. [Gr. *belemnon,* a dart (*ballein,* to throw)]

bel esprit, *n.* (*pl.* **beaux esprits**) a person of genius; a wit. [F, fine mind]

Belfast, *n.* industrial port (shipbuilding, engineering, electronics, textiles, tobacco) and capital of Northern Ireland since 1920; population (1985) 300,000. From 1968 it has been heavily damaged by guerrilla activities.

belfry, *n.* †a movable wooden tower formerly used in besieging a place; †a shed for cattle; a bell-tower attached to or separate from a church or other building; the chamber for the bells in a church-tower; the frame on which a ship's bell is hung. [OF *berfrei, berfroi,* MHG *bercfrit* (*berc.* protection, shelter, *fride,* OHG *Fridis,* peace), a protection tower, a siege tower]

Belg., (*abbr.*) Belgian; Belgium.

belga, *n.* a former Belgian unit of exchange, equivalent to 5 francs. [L, *Belgicus,* Belgian]

Belgian, *a.* of or pertaining to Belgium or to the Belgians. *n.* a native of Belgium; a kind of canary. **Belgian hare,** *n.* a large breed of domestic rabbit, dark-red in colouring. **Belgic** *a.* or *n.* of the ancient Belgae or of Belgium. [L *Belga, Belgicus*]

Belgian Congo, *n.* former name (1908–60) of ZAIRE.

Belgium, *n.* Kingdom of (French *Royaume de Belgique,* Flemish *Koninkrijk België*), a country in northern Europe, bounded to the NW by the North Sea, to the SW by France, to the E by Luxembourg and West Germany, and to the NE by the Netherlands. **area** 30,600 sq km/11,815 sq miles. **capital** Brussels. **towns** Ghent, Liège, Charleroi, Bruges, Mons, Namur, Leuven; ports are Antwerp, Ostend, Zeebrugge. **physical** mostly flat, with hills and forest in SE. **population** (1987) 9,880,000 (comprising Flemings and Walloons); annual growth rate 0.1%. **exports** iron, steel, textiles, manufactured goods, petrochemicals. **language** in the north (Flanders) Flemish (a Dutch dialect, known as *Vlaams*) 55%; in the south (Wallonia) Walloon (a French dialect which is almost a separate language) 44%; 11% bilingual; German (E border) 0.6%; all are official. **religion** Roman Catholic.

Belgrade, *n.* (Serbo-Croat **Beograd**), capital of Yugoslavia and Serbia, and Danube river port linked with the port of Bar on the Adriatic; population (1981) 1,470,000. Industries include light engineering, food processing, textiles, pharmaceuticals and electrical goods.

Belgravian, *a.* of or belonging to Belgravia, a fashionable district in the West End of London; fashionable. *n.* one of the aristocracy. [*Belgrave* Square]

Belial, *n.* the Devil, Satan; one of the fallen angels. **son of Belial, man of Belial,** *n.* a worthless, wicked man. [Heb. *b'li-yaal,* worthlessness]

belie, (*pres.p.* **belying,** *past, p.p.* **belied**) *v.t.* to tell lies about, to slander; to misrepresent; to be faithless to; to fail to perform or justify; †to counterfeit, to imitate; †to fill with lies. [OE *belēogan* (BE-, *lēogan,* to lie)]

belief, *n.* reliance, confidence; the mental act or operation of accepting a fact or proposition as true; the thing so believed; opinion, persuasion; religion, faith. **the Belief,** the Apostles' Creed. [BE-, OE *lēafa, gelēafa* (cp. G *Glaube*)]

believe, *v.t.* to have confidence in or reliance on; to give credence to; to accept as true; be of opinion that. *v.i.* to think; to have faith; to exercise the virtue of faith. **believe it or not,** although it may seem incredible, the statement is true. **to believe in,** to trust in, to rely on. **to make believe,** to pretend. **believable,** *a.* capable of being believed; credible. **believableness,** *n.* the quality of being believable. **believer,** *n.* one who believes; a convert to Christianity or any other religion. **believing,** *a.* exercising belief or the virtue of faith. **believingly,** *adv.* in a believing manner; with faith. [as prec.]

belike, *adv.* likely, possibly, perhaps.

Belisarius, *n.* (*c.* 505–565), Roman general under Emperor Justinian I.

Belisha beacon, *n.* a flashing orange globe on a post to indicate a street-crossing for pedestrians. [L *Hore-Belisha,* 1893–1957, British politician]

belittle, *v.t.* to make little; to dwarf; to depreciate or undermine verbally.

Belize, *n.* a country in Central America. **area** 22,963 sq km/8,864 sq miles. **capital** Belmopan. **towns** port Belize City. **physical** half the country is forested. **population** (1987) 176,000 (including Maya minority in the interior); annual growth rate 2.5%. **exports** sugar, citrus, rice, lobster. **language** English (official), but Spanish is widely spoken. **religion** Roman Catholic 60%, Protestant 35%, Hindu and Muslim minorities.

Belize City, *n.* chief port of Belize, and capital until 1970; population (1980) 40,000. It was destroyed by a hurricane (1961) and it was decided to move the capital inland, to Belmopan.

Bell, *n.* **Alexander Graham** (1847–1922), British scientist, and inventor of the telephone. He patented his invention in 1876, and later experimented with a type of phonograph and in aeronautics invented the tricycle undercarriage.

bell, *n.* a hollow body of cast metal, usually in the shape of an inverted cup with recurved edge, so formed as to emit a clear musical sound when struck by a hammer; hence, used for many objects in nature and art of a similar form; the vase, basket or cushion of a Corinthian capital; the cry of a stag at rutting time; a bell-shaped corolla; the catkin containing the female flowers of the hop; the bell struck on board ship every half-hour to indicate the time; a space of half an hour. *v.i.* of stags at rutting time, to bellow; to be in flower (of hops). *v.t.* to furnish with a bell; to utter loudly. **one to eight bells,** a watch of four hours. **sound, clear as a bell,** sound or clear, free from any flaw. **to bear away the bell,** to carry off the prize. **to bear the bell,** to be first. **to bell the cat,** to be a ringleader in a hazardous movement; to grapple with a dangerous opponent (in allusion to the fable of the mice wishing to put a bell on the cat). **to curse by bell, book and candle,** to excommunicate solemnly by a ceremony in which these objects were used symbolically. **bell-animalcules,** *n.pl.* the infusorial family Vorticellidae, which have a bell-shaped body on a flexible stalk. **bell-bird,** *n.* a S American bird, *Procnias carunculata,* with a note like the toll of a bell; an Australian bird, *Myzantha melanophrys,* with a tinkling note. **bell-bottomed,** *a.* (of trousers) with wide, bell-shaped bottoms. **bell-boy, bell-hop,** *n.* (*N Am.*) an hotel page-boy. **bell-buoy,** *n.* a buoy to which a bell is attached, rung by the motion of the waves. **bell-cot, bell-cote,** *n.* a small turret for a bell or bells. **bell-crank,** *n.* a crank adapted to communicate motion from one bell-wire to another at right angles to it. **bell-faced,** *a.* having a convex face (as a hammer). **bell-flower,** *n.* a bell-shaped flower or plant with such flowers, belonging to the genus *Campanula.* **bell-founder, -founding, -foundry,** *n.* the caster, the casting and the manufactory of bells. **bell-gable, -turret,** *n.* a gable or turret in which bells are hung. **bell-glass,** *n.* a bell-shaped glass for protecting plants. **bell-hanger,** *n.* one who hangs or fixes bells. **bell-hanging,** *n.* the act or process of fixing bells. **belljar,** *n.* a bell-shaped glass cover used in laboratories to protect apparatus or contain gases in experiments etc. **bellman,** *n.* a public crier who attracts attention by ringing a bell. **bell-metal,** *n.* an alloy of copper and tin, usually with a little zinc, used for bells. **bell-pull,** *n.* a cord or handle by which a bell is rung. **bell-punch,** *n.* a ticket punch in which a bell is rung each time it is used. **bell push,** *n.* a button which operates an electric bell. **bell-ringer,** *n.* one whose business it is to ring a church or public bell at stated times. **bell-rope,** *n.* the rope by which a bell is rung. **bell-shaped,** *a.* shaped like a bell; campanulate. **bell-telegraph,** *n.* a telegraph instrument in which needles are replaced by two bells, signals on one of which represent dots and on the other dashes, of the Morse system. **bell-tent,** *n.* a conical tent. **bell-turret,** *n.* BELL-GABLE. **bell-wether,** *n.* the sheep that wears a bell and leads a flock; (*fig.*) a leader. **bell-wort,** *n.* any plant of the family Campanulaceae. [OE *belle* (*bellan,* to bellow)]

belladonna, *n.* deadly nightshade or dwale, *Atropa belladonna;* a drug prepared from the leaves and root of this plant. [It., a fine lady]

Bellay, *n.* **Joaquim du** (*c.* 1522–60), French poet and prose-writer, who published the great manifesto of the new school of French poetry, the Pléiade: *Défense et illustration de la langue française* (1549).

belle[1], *n.* a beautiful woman; reigning beauty. [F, from L. *bella,* fem. of *bellus,* fine, pretty]

belle[2], (F) fem. of BEAU. **belle amie**, *n.* a female friend; mistress. **belle vue**, *n.* a fine sight. **belle époque**, *n.* the period of security and comfort enjoyed by the wealthy before the outbreak of World War I. [lit., fine period]

belles-lettres, (F) *n.pl.* polite literature, the humanities, pure literature. **belletrist,** *n.* a person devoted to belles-lettres. **belletristic,** *a.* pertaining to belles-lettres.

bellicose, *a.* warlike; inclined to war or fighting. **bellicosity**, *n.* inclination to war. [L *bellicosus* (*bellum,* war)]

bellied BELLY.

belligerent, *a.* carrying on war; of or pertaining to persons or nations carrying on war; aggressive. *n.* a nation, party or individual engaged in war. **belligerence,** *n.* the state of being at war. **belligerency,** *n.* belligerence; the status of a belligerent. [F *belligérant,* L *belligerans -ntem,* pres.p. of *belligerāre* (*bellum,* war, *gerere,* to wage)]

Bellini, *n.* family of Italian painters, founders of the Venetian school. The greatest is **Giovanni Bellini** (*c.* 1430–1516), who produced varied devotional pictures of the Madonna. He introduced softness in tone, harmony in composition, and a use of luminous colour that greatly influenced the next generation of painters (especially Giorgione and Titian). He worked in oil rather than tempera.

Bellini, *n.* **Vincenzo** (1801–35), Italian composer, born in Catania, Sicily. His best-known operas include *La sonnambula* (1831), *Norma* (1831), and *I puritani* (1835).

Bellona, *n.* the goddess of war; (*fig.*) a tall, high-spirited woman. [L, the Roman goddess of war (*bellum,* war)]

Bellow, *n.* **Saul** (1915–), US novelist. Canadian-born of Russian descent, he settled in Chicago with his family at the age of nine. His works include the picaresque *The Adventures of Augie March* (1953), the philosophically speculative *Herzog* (1964), *Humboldt's Gift* (1975), *The Dean's December* (1982) and *More Die of Heartbreak* (1987). Nobel Prize 1976.

bellow, *v.i.* to emit a loud hollow sound (as a bull); to raise an outcry or clamour, to bawl, to vociferate; to emit a loud hollow sound (as the sea, the wind, artillery etc.). *v.t.* to utter with a loud hollow voice. *n.* the roar of a bull, or any similar sound. [OE *bellan*]

bellows, *n.pl.* or *n.sing.* an instrument or machine for supplying a strong blast of air to a fire or a wind instrument; the expansible portion of a photographic camera; (*fig.*) the lungs. **pair of bellows,** a two-handled bellows for fanning fire. **bellows-fish,** *n.* the Cornish name of the trumpet-fish or sea-snipe, *Macrorhamphosus scolopax;* (*N Am.*) the fishing-frog, *Lophius piscatorius*. [ME *belu, belw* (pl. *belwes, belowes*), Icel. *belgr* (cp. OE *bœlig*), a bag (see BELLY)]

belly, *n.* that part of the human body in front which extends from the breast to the insertion of the lower limbs; the corresponding part in the inferior vertebrates; the part containing the stomach and bowels; the stomach, the womb; that part of the body which demands food; hence, appetite, gluttony; the front or lower surface of an object; anything swelling out or protuberant; a cavity, a hollow surface; the interior; the bulging part of a violin or a similar instrument. *v.t.* to cause to swell out, to render protuberant. *v.i.* to swell or bulge out, to become protuberant. **belly-ache,** *n.* a pain in the stomach; *v.i.* (*coll.*) to express discontent, to whine. **belly-band,** *n.* a band passing under the belly of a horse, ass or other beast of burden to keep the saddle in place. **belly-bound,** *a.* (*sl.*) constipated, costive. **bellybutton,** *n.* (*coll.*) the navel. **belly dance,** *n.* an erotic solo dance involving undulating movements of the abdomen. **belly flop,** *n.* an awkward dive into the water on to the front of the body and flat against the surface. *v.i.* to perform a belly flop. **belly-furniture, -timber,** *n.* (*sl.*) food, provisions. †**belly-god,** *n.* a glutton. **belly landing,** *n.* landing without using the landing-wheels. **belly-laugh,** *n.* a deep, hearty laugh. **bellied,** *a.* having a belly (*in comb.*); corpulent; (*Bot.*) ventricose. **bellyful,** *n.* as much as fills the belly, as much food as satisfies the appetite; (*coll.*) sufficiency, more than enough. **bellying,** *a.* swelling, protuberant, bulging out of sails with wind. [OE *bœlig, bylig,* a leather bag (OTeut. *balgiz*), *balgan,* to swell out]

Belo Horizonte, *n.* industrial city (steel, engineering, textiles) in SE Brazil, capital of the fast-developing state of Minas Gerais; population (1980) 1,442,500. Built in the 1890s, it was Brazil's first planned modern city.

belomancy, *n.* divination by means of arrows. [Gr. *belos,* an arrow, -MANCY]

belong, *v.i.* to be appropriate, to pertain; to be the property, attribute, appendage, member, right, duty, concern or business of; to be connected with; to be a native or resident of. **belonging,** *n.* anything belonging to one (*usu. in pl.*); a quality or endowment; (*coll., pl.*) one's possessions. [ME *bilongen, belongen* (BE-, LONG[3])]

Belorussia, BYELORUSSIA.

beloved, *a.* loved greatly. *n.* one greatly loved.

below, *prep.* beneath; under in place; down stream from; on the inferior side of; inferior in rank, degree or excellence; unworthy of, unsuitable to. *adv.* in or to a lower place, rank or station, below; on earth (as opp. to heaven); in hell (as opp. to earth); downstairs; down stream; lower on the same page, or on a following page. **below one's breath,** in a whisper.

bel paese, *n.* a mild Italian cream cheese. [It. lit., beautiful country]

Belsen, *n.* site of a Nazi concentration camp in Lower Saxony, West Germany.

Belshazzar, *n.* in the Old Testament, the last king of Babylon, son of Nebuchadnezzar. During a feast (known as Belshazzar's Feast) the king saw a message, interpreted by Daniel as prophesying the fall of Babylon and death of Belshazzar, all of which is said to have happened that same night when the city was invaded by the Medes and Persians (539 BC).

belt, *n.* a broad, flat strip of leather or other material worn around the waist or over the shoulder, esp. one worn as a badge of rank or distinction; anything resembling such a belt in shape; a broad strip or stripe; a strait; a zone or region; a flat endless strap passing round two wheels and communicating motion from one to the other; (*coll.*) a blow. *v.t.* to encircle with or as with a belt; to fasten on with a belt; to invest with a belt; to deck with a zone of colour; to thrash with a belt. **to hit below the belt,** to act unfairly in contest (from boxing). **to tighten one's belt,** to make economies, to reduce expenditure. **under one's belt,** secured in one's possession. **belt out,** *v.i.* to sing or emit a sound vigorously or with enthusiasm. **belt up,** *v.i.* (*sl.*) to stop talking (often *imp.*), to fasten with a belt. **belted,** *a.* wearing a belt, esp. as a mark of rank or distinction; furnished with a belt of any kind; affixed by a belt; surrounded as with a belt. **belted earl,** *n.* an earl wearing (or entitled to wear) his distinctive cincture. **belting,** *n.* belts collectively; material for belts; a series of belts fixed round chimney-stacks to strengthen them; (*sl.*) a beating. [OE (cp. *Balz,* L *balteus*)]

Beltane, *n.* May-day (o.s.), one of the old Scottish quarter-days; a Celtic festival celebrated by bonfires on May-day. [Gael. *beailtainn* (prob. conn. with OE *bœl,* a blaze, Gr. *phalios,* bright)]

beluga, *n.* the great white or hausen sturgeon, *Acipenser huso,* from the Black and Caspian Seas; the white whale, *Delphinapterus leucas*. [Rus., white]

belvedere, *n.* a turret, lantern or cupola, raised above the roof of a building to command a view; a summer-house built on an eminence for the same purpose. [It. (*bel*, fine, *vedere*, to see)]

belying BELIE.

bema, *n.* the sanctuary, presbytery or chancel of a church; the platform from which Athenian orators spoke. [Gr.]

Bemba, *n.* people of Bemba origin. Their homeland is the northern province of Zambia, though many reside in urban areas such as Lusaka and Copperbelt. The Bemba language belongs to the Bantu branch of the Niger-Congo family.

bemean, *v.t.* to render mean, to lower or debase.

bemire, *v.t.* to cover or soil with mire. **bemired,** *p.p.* stuck or sunk in mire.

bemoan, *v.t.* to moan over, to deplore. *v.i.* to moan, to lament. [OE *bimœnan* (*mœnan,* MOAN)]

bemuddle, *v.t.* to muddle completely.

bemuse, *v.t.* to make utterly confused or dazed, as by drinking alcohol.

ben[1]**,** *n.* a mountain-peak. [Gael. *beinn*]

ben[2]**,** *prep.* (*Sc.*) in or into the inner apartment of. *adv.* within, into or towards the inner part of a house. *n.* the inner room. see BUT[2]. [Sc., from ME *binne,* OE *binnan* (cp. Dut. and G *binnen*)]

Benares, *n.* a transliteration of Varanasi, holy city in India.

Ben Bella, *n.* **Ahmed** (1916–), Algerian leader of the National Liberation Front (FLN) from 1952; he was prime minister of independent Algeria (1962–65), when he was overthrown by Boumédienne and detained till 1980. He founded a new party, Mouvement pour la Démocratie en Algérie (1985).

bench, *n.* a long seat or form; a seat where judges and magistrates sit in court; hence judges or magistrates collectively, or sitting as a court; a tribunal; the office of judge; (*pl.*) groups of seats in the Houses of Parliament; other official seats and those who have a right to occupy them; (*N Am.*) a level tract between a river and neighbouring hills; a terrace or ledge in masonry, quarrying, mining, earthwork etc.; a carpenter's or other mechanic's work-table; a platform for exhibiting dogs. *v.t.* to furnish with benches; †to seat upon a bench; to exhibit (dogs) at a show; (*N Am.*) to remove a player from a game. †*v.i.* to sit on a bench (as in a court of justice). **Queen's** (or **King's**) **Bench,** the court formerly presided over by the Sovereign; now one of the divisions of the Supreme Court. **the Bench of Bishops,** the Episcopate collectively, esp. those who rank as peers. **to be raised to the bench,** to be made a judge. **treasury bench, front bench, Conservative benches** etc., seats appropriated to certain officers, parties or groups in Parliament. †**bench-hole,** *n.* a privy. **bench-mark,** *n.* a mark cut in some durable material in a line of survey for reference at a future time; anything that serves as a standard of comparison or point of reference. **bench-plane,** *n.* the jack-plane, the trying-plane or the smoothing plane. **bench-show,** *n.* a dog-show, in which the dogs are exhibited on benches or platforms. **bench-table,** *n.* a low seat of stone in churches and cloisters. **bench-warrant,** *n.* a warrant issued by a judge, as distinct from a magistrate's warrant. **bencher,** *n.* one who sits upon a bench, †esp. in a tavern, a tavern-haunter; †one who sits officially on a bench; one of the senior members of an Inn of Court who collectively govern the Inn, and have power of 'calling to the bar'. [OE *benc* (cp. Swed. *bänk,* G *Bank,* It. *banca,* OTeut. *bankiz,* see BANK[3])]

bend, (*past, p.p.* **bent**, *exc.* in **bended knees**), *v.t.* to bring into a curved shape (as a bow) by pulling the string; to render curved or angular; to deflect; to direct to a certain point; to apply closely; bring into operation; to incline from the vertical; to subdue; to fasten, to make fast; to tie into a knot; †to direct, aim (a weapon). *v.i.* to assume the form of a curve or angle; to incline from an erect position, to bow, stoop; to surrender, submit; to turn in a new direction; †to drink hard. *n.* a bending curve or flexure; incurvation; a sudden turn in a road or river; an inclination; †a glance; (*Her.*) an ordinary formed by two parallel lines drawn across from the dexter chief to the sinister base point of an escutcheon; a similar ordinary from the sinister chief to the dexter base point is a mark of bastardy, and is called **bend sinister** (cp. BAR[1], BATON); a knot; (*pl.*) the crooked timbers which make the ribs or sides of a ship; (*pl.*) caisson disease; a shape or size in tanned leather, half a butt. **bend-leather,** *n.* the stoutest kind of leather. **on bended knees,** *adv.* with the knees bent; as a suppliant. **to be round the bend,** (*coll.*) to be crazy, insane. **to bend a sail,** to extend or make it fast to its proper yard or stay. **to bend the brows,** to frown. **to bend the elbow,** (*coll.*) to be fond of drinking alcohol. **bender,** *n.* (*sl.*) an old sixpence; (*sl.*) a bout of heavy drinking. **bendy,** *a.* [OE *bendan* (Icel. *benda,* to join, strain, OTeut. *bandjan*)]

beneath, *prep.* below, under, in point of place or position; unworthy of. *adv.* in a lower place, below. [OE *beneothan* (*be-,* by, *neo than,* adv. below, cp. *nither,* below, OTeut. *nithar,* G *nieden*)]

benedicite, *int.* bless you, good gracious. *n.* the invocation of a blessing; grace before meat; the Song of the Three Holy Children, one of the canticles in the Prayer Book; (*Mus.*) a setting of this. [L, bless ye! imper. of *benedīcere* (*bene,* well, *dīcere,* to speak)]

benedick, benedict, *n.* a newly married man (from *Benedick,* a character in *Much Ado About Nothing*). [L *benedictus,* blessed (see prec.)]

Benedictine, *a.* of or pertaining to St Benedict, or to the Benedictine order. *n.* a monk or nun of this order; a liqueur first made by Benedictine monks. [F *bénédictin,* L *benedictus*]

Benedictine order, *n.* religious order of monks and nuns in the Roman Catholic Church, founded by St Benedict at Subiaco, Italy, in the 6th cent. St Augustine brought the order to England. At the beginning of the 14th cent. it was at the height of its prosperity, and had a strong influence on mediaeval learning.

Benedict, St, *n.* (*c.* 480–*c.* 547), founder of Christian monasticism in the West, and of the Benedictine order. He founded the monastery of Monte Cassino, Italy. Here he wrote out his rule for monastic life, and was visited shortly before his death by the Ostrogothic king Totila, whom he converted to the Christian faith. Feast day 11 July.

benediction, *n.* the act of blessing or invoking a blessing; grace before or after meals; blessedness, grace, blessing; a blessing pronounced officially; a Roman Catholic devotion including a blessing with the Host. **benedictional,** *n.* a book containing the episcopal benedictions formerly in use. **benedictory,** *a.* of or relating to or expressing benediction. **benedictus**, *n.* the hymn of Zacharias (Luke i.68), used as a canticle in the Church of England; in the Roman Catholic Church, a portion of the Mass following the Sanctus; (*Mus.*) a setting of either of these. [L *benedictio -ōnem* (see BENEDICITE)]

benefaction, *n.* the conferring of a benefit; a benefit conferred; a gift or endowment for charitable purposes. **benefactor**, *n.* one who gives another help or friendly service; one who gives to a religious or charitable institution; †a well-doer. **benefactress**, *n.* a female benefactor. [L *benefactio -ōnem,* from *benefacere* (see BENEFICE)]

benefice, *n.* †an estate held by feudal tenure; an ecclesiastical living. **beneficed,** *a.* possessed of a benefice. [L *beneficium* (*bene,* well, *-ficium,* a doing, from *facere*)]

beneficent, *a.* kind, generous, doing good; characterized by benevolence. **beneficently,** *adv.* **beneficence,** *n.* the habitual practice of doing good; active kindness; charity. **beneficial**, *a.* advantageous, helpful; remedial; (*Law*) of or belonging to usufruct; enjoying the usufruct of. **beneficially,** *adv.* **beneficiary**, *a.* holding or held by feudal tenure. *n.* one who receives a favour; a feudatory; the holder of a benefice; one who benefits under a trust.

benefit, *n.* †a kindness, a favour, a benefaction; †a natural gift; profit, advantage, gain; a theatrical, music-hall or other performance, the receipts from which, with certain deductions, are given to some person or charity; (*Law*) the advantage of belonging to some privileged order; exemption from the jurisdiction of the ordinary courts; money or services provided under government social security or private pension schemes etc. *v.t.* to do good to; to be of advantage or profit to. *v.i.* to derive advantage. **benefit of clergy,** CLERGY. **benefit of the doubt,** the assumption of innocence in the absence of clear evidence of guilt. **benefit club** or **society**, *n.* a society whose members, in return for a certain periodical payment, receive certain benefits in sickness or old age. [OF *bienfait,* L *benefactum,* neut. p.p. of *benefacere* (see BENEFICE)]

Benelux, *n.* name given to Belgium, the Netherlands and Luxembourg, and to the Customs union formed between these three countries in 1947. [first letters of *Be*lgium, *Ne*therlands, *Lux*embourg]

Beneš, *n.* **Eduard** (1884–1948), Czech politician. President of the republic from 1935 until forced to resign by the Germans, he headed a government in exile in London during World War II. Returning home as president in 1945, he resigned again in 1948.

benevolent, *a.* disposed to do good; kind, charitable, generous. **benevolently,** *adv.* **benevolence,** *n.* disposition to do good; charitable feeling, goodwill; a forced loan formerly levied by English kings, but abolished by the Bill of Rights (1689). [OF *benevolent,* L *bene volens -tem,* well wishing (*velle,* to wish)]

BEng., (*abbr.*) Bachelor of Engineering.

Bengal, *n.* former province of British India, divided (1947) into West Bengal, a state of India, and East Bengal, from 1972 Bangladesh. The famine in 1943, caused by a slump in demand for jute and a bad harvest, resulted in over 3 million deaths.

Bengali, *a.* of or pertaining to Bengal, its people or language. *n.* a native of Bengal; the Indo-European language of Bengal. **Bengal light,** *n.* a firework giving a vivid and sustained light. [native name Bangālī]

Benghazi, *n.* (or **Banghazi**) historic city and industrial port in N Libya on the Gulf of Sirte; population (1982) 650,000. It was controlled by Turkey between the 16th century and 1911, and by Italy (1911–42).

Ben-Gurion, *n.* **David** (adopted name of David Gruen) (1886–1973), Israeli socialist politician, the country's first prime minister (1948–53, and again in 1955–63). He was born in Poland.

benighted, *p.p.* overtaken by night. *a.* involved in moral or intellectual darkness; ignorant; uncivilized.

benign, *a.* kind-hearted, gracious, mild; favourable, propitious; genial, agreeable, salubrious; not malignant; mild. **benignly,** *adv.* **benignant**, *a.* gracious, kind, benevolent; favourable, propitious. **benignantly,** *adv.* **benignity**, *n.* kindly feeling; kindness, a favour bestowed. [OF *benigne,* L *benignus,* prob. orig. *benigenus* (*bene,* well, *-genus,* born, cp. *indigenus*)]

Benin¹, *n.* People's Republic of (*République Populaire du Bénin*) a country in W Africa. **area** 112,622 sq km/ 43,472 sq miles. **capital** Porto Novo. **towns** Abomey, Natitingou; chief port Cotonou. **physical** flat, humid, with dense vegetation. **population** (1988 est.) 4,444,000; annual growth rate 3%. **exports** cocoa, groundnuts, cotton, palm oil. **language** French (official); Fan 47%. **religion** animist 65%, Christian 17%, Muslim 13%.

Benin², *n.* former African kingdom (1200–1897), now part of Nigeria.

benison, *n.* a blessing. [OF *beneison,* L *benedictio -ōnem,* BENEDICTION]

benjamin¹, *n.* benzoin. **benjamin-tree,** *n.* name of three trees, *Styrax benzoin,* which yields the resin called benzoin, *Benzoin odoriferum,* a N American shrub, also *Ficus benjamina*. [corr. of BENZOIN]

Benjamin², *n.* the youngest son; the darling of a family. [alluding to Gen. xlii. 4]

Benjamin³, *n.* a kind of overcoat once in fashion. [tailor's name; or perh. from Romany *bengari,* waistcoat]

Benn, *n.* **Tony** (Anthony Wedgwood) (1925–), English Labour politician, the most influential figure on the party's left wing. He was minister of technology (1966–70) and of industry (1974–75), but his campaign against entry to the European Community led to his transfer to the Department of Energy (1975–79).

bennet¹, *n.* herb bennet, *Geum urbanum;* some other plants. [ME *herbe beneit,* prob. from OF *herbe beneite,* L *herba benedicta,* blessed herb *benedictus,* p.p. of *benedīcere,* see BENEDICITE)]

bennet², BENT².

Bennett¹, *n.* **(Enoch) Arnold** (1867–1931), English novelist. Coming from one of the 'five towns' of the Potteries which formed the setting of his major books, he became a London journalist in 1893, and editor of *Woman* in 1896. His books include *Anna of the Five Towns* (1904), *Sacred and Profane Love* (1905), *The Old Wives' Tale* (1908), and the trilogy *Clayhanger, Hilda Lessways*, and *These Twain* (1910–15).

Bennett², *n.* **Alan** (1934–), English playwright. His works (set in his native north of England), treat subjects such as senility, illness and death, with macabre comedy. His work includes TV films, for example, *An Englishman Abroad* (1982), the cinema film, *A Private Function* (1984) and plays *Forty Years On* (1968) and *Getting On* (1971).

Bennett³, Richard Rodney (1936–), British composer of jazz, film music including *Far from the Madding Crowd* (1967), *Nicholas and Alexandra* (1971), *Murder on the Orient Express* (1974) (all three scores receiving Oscar nominations), symphonies and operas, including *The Mines of Sulphur* (1963), and *Victory* (1970).

Ben Nevis, *n.* highest mountain in the British Isles (1342 m/4406 ft), in the Grampians, Scotland.

bent¹, *n.* inclination, bias; disposition, propensity; tension, extent, capacity. *a.* curved; intent (on), resolved (to); (*sl.*) dishonest; crooked; (*sl.*) stolen; (*sl.*) homosexual. **to the top of one's bent,** to one's utmost capacity, to one's full tension. **bentwood,** *n.* wood steamed and curved in moulds for making furniture. *a.* made using bentwood. *p.p.* see BEND. [BEND]

bent², *n.* stiff, rush-like grass; old grass-stalks; grassy ground, unenclosed pasture; a heath; a slope, a rising ground. **take to the bent,** flee to the open country. **bent-grass,** *n.* the genus *Agrostis*. [OE *beonet* (cp. OHG *binuz,* G *Binse*)]

benthal, *a.* of or pertaining to the depths of the ocean beyond 1000 fathoms. [Gr. *benthos,* sea-depths]

Bentham, *n.* **Jeremy** (1748–1832), English philosopher, legal and social reformer, founder of utilitarianism. The essence of his moral philosophy is found in the pronouncement of his *Principles of Morals and Legislation* (written 1780, published 1789), that the object of all legislation should be 'the greatest happiness for the greatest number'.

Benthamism, *n.* the Utilitarian philosophy based on the principle of the greatest happiness of the greatest number. **Benthamite**, *n.* a follower of Jeremy Bentham; a Utilitarian.

benthon, benthos, *n.* the sedentary animal and plant life on the ocean bed. **benthoscope**, *n.* a submersible sphere for studying deep-sea life, a bathysphere. [Gr. *benthos,* the depths of the sea]

bentonite, *n.* an absorbent clay used in various industries as a filler, bonding agent etc.

benumb, *v.t.* to render torpid or numb; to deaden, to paralyse. **benumbment,** *n.* the act of benumbing; the state of being benumbed; torpor. [formerly *benum* OE *benumen,* p.p. of *beniman* (*niman,* see NUMB)]

Benz, *n.* **Karl** (1844–1929), German automobile engineer, who produced the world's first petrol-driven motor-car. He built his first model engine in 1878 and the petrol driven car in 1885.

Benzedrine®, *n.* amphetamine.

benzene, *n.* an aromatic hydrocarbon obtained from coal tar and some petroleum fractions, used in industry in the synthesis of organic chemical compounds, as a solvent and insecticide. **benzene ring,** *n.* a closed chain of six carbon atoms each bound to a hydrogen atom in the benzene molecule. **benzine**, *n.* a mixture of liquid hydrocarbons, distilled from petroleum, used esp. as a solvent and motor fuel. **benzocaine**, *n.* a drug used as a local anaesthetic. **benzodiazepine**, *n.* any of a group of synthetic drugs used as sedatives and tranquillizers. **benzol**, **-zole**, *n.* unrefined benzene used as a fuel; an obsolete name for benzene. **benzoline**, *n.* impure benzene; benzine. **benzyl**, *n.* an organic radical derived from benzene.

benzoin, *n.* a resin obtained from *Styrax benzoin,* used in medicine and in perfumery, called also gum benzoin, popularly corrupted to benjamin and gum benjamin; a N American genus of Lauraceae; a camphor obtained from bitter-almond oil. **benzoic**, *a.* pertaining to or derived from benzoin. **benzoic acid,** *n.* an acid present in benzoin and other natural resins, used in medicines, dyes, as a food preservative and in organic synthesis. [F *benjoin,* Sp. *benjui* (It. *bengivi*), Arab. *lubān jāwi,* Javanese frankincense (*lu-* mistaken for It. article *lo* and dropped)]

Ben Zvi, *n.* **Izhak** (1884–1963), Israeli politician, president (1952–63). He was born in Atpoltava, Russia, and became active in the Zionist movement in the Ukraine. In 1907 he went to Palestine but was deported together with Ben Gurion in 1915 and, with him, served in the Jewish Legion under Gen. Allenby, who commanded the British forces in the Middle East.

Beograd, *n.* the Serbo-Croatian form of BELGRADE, capital of Yugoslavia.

Beowulf, *n.* an Anglo-Saxon poem (composed *c.* 700), the only complete surviving example of Germanic folk-epic. It is extant in a single manuscript copied *c.* 1000 in the Cottonian collection of the British Museum.

bequeath, *v.t.* †to transfer, hand over; to leave by will or testament; to transmit to future generations. **bequeathable,** *a.* †**bequeathal, bequeathment,** *n.* the act of bequeathing; a legacy. **bequest**, *n.* the act of bequeathing; that which is bequeathed; a legacy. [OE *becwethan* (BE-, *cwethan,* to say, cp. QUOTH)]

berate, *v.t.* to rebuke or scold vehemently.

Berber, *n.* a member of the Hamitic peoples of N Africa; their language. *a.* of or belonging to this people or their language. [BARBARY]

berberis, *n,* any of the barberry genus of shrubs. **berberine**, *n.* an alkaloid obtained from barberry roots. [see BARBERRY]

berberry BARBERRY.

berceuse, *n.* a lullaby, cradle-song; lulling music. [Fr., a cradle-rocker]

bereave, *v.t.* (*past, p.p.* **bereaved, bereft**,) to deprive, rob or spoil of anything; to render desolate (*usu. in p.p.* **bereaved,** of the loss of near relatives by death). **bereavement,** *n.* the state of being bereaved; the loss of a near relative or friend by death. [OE *berēafian* (BE-, *rēafian,* to rob; cp. G *berauben*)]

Berenice's hair, *n.* †the star Canopus; a small northern constellation, near the tail of Leo. [from the myth that the hair of *Berenice,* wife of Ptolemy Euergetes, king of Egypt (3rd cent. BC), was placed in a constellation]

beret, berret, *n.* a round, brimless flat cap fitting the head fairly closely. [F *béret,* Bearnais *berreto,* late L *birretum,* BIRETTA]

Berg, *n.* **Alban** (1885–1935), Austrian composer who studied under Schoenberg, and was associated with him as one of the leaders of the serial, or 12-tone, school of composition. His output includes orchestral, chamber, vocal music, and two operas, *Wozzeck* (1925), a grim story of working-class life, and an unfinished opera, *Lulu.*

berg¹**,** ICEBERG.

berg²**,** *n.* a South African word for mountain, often used in place names. **berg wind,** *n.* a hot dry wind in South Africa blowing from the north to the coast. [G *Berg* Dut. S Afr. *berg,* hill]

bergamask, *n.* a rustic dance associated with the people of Bergamo in Italy.

bergamot¹**,** *n.* the bergamot orange, *Citrus bergamia,* which yields a fragrant essential oil used in perfumery; the oil itself; †a snuff scented with the oil; a kind of mint, *Mentha citrata,* which yields an oil somewhat similar. [prob. from *bergamo,* in Italy]

bergamot²**,** *n.* a juicy kind of pear. [F *bergamotte,* It. *bergamotta,* Turk. *beg-armūdi,* prince's pear]

Bergen, *n.* industrial port (shipbuilding, engineering, fishing) in SW Norway; population (1980) 207,500. Founded in 1070, Bergen was a member of the Hanseatic League.

Bergius, *n.* **Friedrich Karl Rudolph** (1884–1949), German research chemist who invented processes for converting coal into oil, and wood into sugar.

Bergman¹**,** *n.* **Ingmar** (1918–), Swedish film producer and director. His work deals with complex moral, psychological, and metaphysical problems and is often heavily tinged with pessimism. His films include *Wild Strawberries* (1957), *Persona* (1966) and *Fanny and Alexander* (1982).

Bergman²**,** *n.* **Ingrid** (1917–82), Swedish actress, whose early films include *Casablanca* and *For Whom the Bell Tolls* (both 1943). By leaving her husband for film producer Roberto Rossellini, she broke an unofficial code of Hollywood 'star' behaviour and was ostracized for many years. She was re-admitted to make the award-winning *Anastasia* (1956).

bergmehl, *n.* a diatomaceous earth that is used, in Norway, to be mixed with flour and eaten. [G, mountain flour]

bergschrund, *n.* a crevasse or fissure between the base of a steep slope and a glacier or *nevé.* [G *Berg,* mountain, *schrund,* crack, gap]

Bergson, *n.* **Henri** (1859–1941), French philosopher, who believed that time, change, and development were the essence of reality. He thought that time was not a succession of distinct and separate instants, but a continuous process in which one period merged imperceptibly into the next.

Bergsonian, *a.* pertaining to the French philosopher Henry Bergson's theory of creative evolution and the life force. *n.* a follower of Bergson.

Beria, *n.* **Lavrenti** (1899–1953), Soviet politician, who became head of the Soviet police force and minister of the interior in 1938. On Stalin's death in 1953, he was shot after a secret trial.

beriberi, *n.* a degenerative disease prevalent in S and E Asia due to a deficiency of vitamin B_1. [Sinhalese *beri,* weakness]

Bering, *n.* **Vitus** (1681–1741), Danish explorer, the first European to sight Alaska. He died on Bering Island in the Bering Sea, both named after him, as are Bering Strait and Beringia.

Bering Sea, *n.* section of the N Pacific between Alaska and Siberia, from the Aleutian Islands N to Bering Strait.

Bering Strait, *n.* strait between Alaska and Siberia, linking the N Pacific and Arctic oceans.

Berio, *n.* **Luciano** (1925–), Italian composer. His style has been described as graceful serialism, and he has frequently experimented with electronic music and taped sound. His works include nine *Sequenzas/ Sequences* for various solo instruments or voice, *Sinfonia* for voices and orchestra (1969), *Points on the curve to find ...* (1974), and a number of dramatic works.

berk, burk, *n.* (*sl.*) an idiot.

Berkeleian, *a.* of or pertaining to Berkeley or his philosophy, which denied that the mind, being entirely subjective, could know the external world objectively. *n.* an adherent of the Berkeleian philosophy. [Bishop *Berkeley,* 1685–1753]

Berkeley, *n.* **Busby** (1895–1976), US film director, famous for his ingeniously extravagant sets and his use of female dancers to create large-scale pattern effects through movement and costume, as in *Gold Diggers of 1933.*

berkelium, *n.* an artificially produced radioactive element, at. no. 97; chem. symbol Bk.

Berks., (*abbr.*) Berkshire.

Berkshire or **Royal Berkshire,** *n.* county in S central England. **area** 1259 sq km/486 sq miles. **towns** administrative headquarters Reading; Eton, Slough, Maidenhead, Ascot, Bracknell, Newbury, Windsor. **population** (1987) 741,000. **products** general agricultural and horticultural, electronics, plastics, pharmaceuticals.

Berlin[1], *n.* industrial city (machine tools, electrical goods, paper and printing) within East Germany, with a Western sector; population (1984) East Berlin 1,197,000; West Berlin 1,848,500. East Berlin is the capital of East Germany; the Berlin Wall dividing the city was built in 1961.

Berlin[2], *n.* **Irving** (Adopted name of Israel Baline) (1888–1989), Russian-born American composer, whose hits include 'Alexander's Ragtime Band', 'Always', 'God Bless America', and 'White Christmas', and the musicals *Top Hat* (1935), *Annie Get Your Gun* (1950), and *Call Me Madam* (1953). He also wrote the scores of films such as *Blue Skies* and *Easter Parade*.

berlin, *n.* †a four-wheeled carriage having a hooded seat behind. **Berlin wool,** *n.* a fine kind of wool used for knitting, embroidery etc. [from the city of *Berlin*]

Berlin blockade, *n.* in June 1948, the closing of entry to Berlin from the west by Soviet forces. It was an attempt to prevent the other Allies (US, France, and Britain) unifying the western part of Germany. The British and US forces responded by sending supplies to the city by air for over a year (the **Berlin airlift**). In May 1949 the blockade was lifted; the airlift continued until Sept. The blockade marked the formal division of the city into Eastern and Western sectors.

Berlin, Congress of, congress of the European powers (Russia, Turkey, Austria-Hungary, Britain, France, Italy, and Germany) held at Berlin in 1878 to determine the boundaries of the Balkan states after the Russo-Turkish war. Prime Minister Disraeli attended as Britain's chief envoy, and declared on his return to England that he had brought back 'peace with honour'.

Berlinguer, *n.* **Enrico** (1922–84), Italian Communist who freed the party from Soviet influence. By 1976 he was near to the premiership, but the Red Brigade murder of Aldo Moro, the prime minister, revived the socialist vote.

Berlin Wall, *n.* the dividing line between East and West Berlin (1961–89). Beginning 13 Aug. 1961, it was reinforced by the Russians with armed guards and barbed wire to prevent the escape of unwilling inhabitants of E Berlin to the rival economic and political system of W Berlin. The interconnecting link between E and W Berlin was CHECKPOINT CHARLIE, where both sides exchanged captured spies. Escapers were shot on sight. On 9 Nov. 1989 the East German government opened its borders to try to halt the mass exodus of its citizens to the west via other east bloc countries, thus making the wall obsolete.

Berlioz, *n.* **(Louis) Hector** (1803–69), French Romantic composer and the founder of modern orchestration. Much of his work was inspired by drama and literature and has a theatrical quality. He wrote symphonic works such as *Symphonie fantastique* and *Roméo et Juliette*, dramatic cantatas including *La Damnation de Faust* and *L'Enfance du Christ*, sacred music and three operas, *Béatrice et Bénédict*, *Benvenuto Cellini*, and *Les Troyens*.

berm, *n.* a narrow ledge at the foot of the exterior slope of a parapet; the bank of a canal opposite the towing-path. [F *berme*, G *Berme* (Dut. *berm*)]

Bermuda, *n.* British colony in the NW Atlantic. **area** 54 sq km/21 sq miles. **capital** and chief port Hamilton. **population** (1988) 58,100. **products** Easter lilies, pharmaceutical; tourism and banking are important. **language** English. **religion** Christian.

Bermuda shorts, *n.* tight-fitting knee-length shorts. [after the BERMUDA Islands]

Bern, *n.* (French **Berne**) capital of Switzerland and of Bern canton, in W Switzerland on the Aar; population (1987) 300,000. It joined the Swiss confederation (1353) and became the capital in 1848. Industries include textiles, chocolate, pharmaceuticals, light metal, and electrical goods.

bernacle, BARNACLE.

Bernadette, *n.* **St** (1844–79), French saint, born in Lourdes in the French Pyrenees. In Feb. 1858 she had a vision of the Virgin Mary in a grotto, and it became a centre of pilgrimage. Many sick people who were dipped in the water of a spring there were said to have been cured. Feast day 16 Apr.

Bernadotte[1], *n.* **Count Folke** (1895–1948), Swedish diplomat and president of the Swedish Red Cross. In 1945 he conveyed the Nazi commander Himmler's offer of capitulation to the British and US governments, and in 1948 was United Nations mediator in Palestine, where he was assassinated by Stern Gang guerrillas. He was a nephew of Gustaf VI of Sweden.

Bernadotte[2], *n.* **Jean-Baptiste Jules** (1764–1844), marshal in Napoleon's army, who in 1818 became Charles XIV of Sweden. Hence, Bernadotte is the family name of the present royal house of Sweden.

Bernard, *n.* **Claude** (1813–78), French physiologist and founder of experimental medicine. Bernard first demonstrated that digestion is not restricted to the stomach, but takes place throughout the small intestine. He discovered the digestive input of the pancreas, several functions of the liver, and the vasomotor nerves which dilate and contract the blood vessels and thus regulate body temperature.

Bernardine, *a.* of or pertaining to St Bernard of Clairvaux or the Cistercian order. *n.* a Cistercian monk.

Bernard of Clairvaux, St (1090-1153), Christian founder in 1115 of Clairvaux monastery in Champagne, France. He reinvigorated the Cistercian order, preached the Second Crusade in 1146, and had the scholastic philosopher Abelard condemned for heresy. He is often depicted with a beehive. Feast day 20 Aug.

Bernard of Menthon St (or **Bernard of Montjoux**), (923–1008), Christian priest, founder of the hospices for travellers on the Alpine passes that bear his name. The large, heavily built St Bernard dogs formerly used to find travellers lost in the snow were also called after him. He is the patron saint of mountaineers. Feast day 28 May.

Bernese Oberland, *n.* or **Bernese Alps**, the mountainous area in the S of Berne canton which includes some of the most famous peaks, such as the Jungfrau, Eiger, and Finsteraarhorn. Interlaken is the chief town.

Bernhard, *n.* **Prince of the Netherlands** (1911–), formerly Prince Bernhard of Lippe-Biesterfeld, he married Princess Juliana in 1937. When Germany invaded the Netherlands in 1940, he escaped to England and became liaison officer for the Dutch and British forces, playing a part in the organization of the Dutch Resistance. In 1976 he was widely censured for his involvement in the purchase of Lockheed aircraft by the Netherlands.

Bernhardt, *n.* **Sarah** (stage name of Rosine Bernard) (1845–1923), French actress who dominated the stage of her day, frequently performing at the Comédie-Française in Paris. She excelled in tragic roles, including Cordelia in Shakespeare's *King Lear*, the title role in Racine's *Phèdre*, and the male roles of Hamlet and of Napoleon's son in Rostand's *L'Aiglon*.

Bernini, *n.* **Giovanni Lorenzo** (1598–1680), Italian sculptor, architect, and painter, a leading figure in the development of the Baroque style. His work in Rome includes the colonnaded piazza in front of St Peter's Basilica (1656), fountains (as in the Piazza Navona), and papal monuments. His sculpture includes *The Ecstasy of St Theresa*, 1645–52 (Sta Maria della Vittoria, Rome), and numerous portrait busts.

Bernoulli, *n.* Swiss family of mathematicians. **Jakob** (1654–1705) discovered Bernoullian numbers, a series of complex fractions used in higher mathematics. **Johann** (1667–1748), brother of Jakob, found the equation to the catenary (1690) and developed exponential calculus (1691). Johann's son **Daniel** (1700–82) made important contributions in hydrodynamics (the study of fluids).

Bernoulli effect, *n.* a drop in hydraulic pressure, such as that in a fluid flowing through a constriction in a pipe. It is also responsible for the pressure differences on each surface of an aerofoil, which gives lift to the wing of an aircraft. The effect was named after DANIEL BERNOUILLI.

Bernstein, *n.* **Edouard** (1850–1932), German socialist thinker, proponent of reformist rather than revolutionary socialism, whereby a socialist society could be achieved within an existing parliamentary structure, merely by workers' parties obtaining a majority.

Bernstein, *n.* **Leonard** (1918–), US composer, conductor, and pianist. He has conducted major orchestras throughout the world. His works, which established a vogue for realistic, contemporary themes, include symphonies such as *The Age of Anxiety* (1949); ballets such as *Fancy Free* (1944); scores for musicals including *Wonderful Town* (1953) and *West Side Story* (1957); and *Mass* (1971) in memory of President J. F. Kennedy.

berretta, BIRETTA.

Berri, *n.* **Nabih** (1939–), Lebanese politician and soldier, leader of Amal ('Hope'), the Syrian-backed Shi'ite nationalist movement. He was minister of justice in government of President Gemayel from 1984. In 1988 Amal was disbanded after defeat by the Iranian-backed Hezbollah ('Children of God') during the Lebanese civil wars.

Berrigan, *n.* **Daniel** (1921–) and **Philip** (1924–), US Roman Catholic priests. The brothers, opponents of the Vietnam War, broke into the draft-records offices at Catonsville, Maryland, to burn the files with napalm, and were sentenced in 1968 to three and six years' imprisonment, but went underground. Subsequently Philip Berrigan was tried with others in 1972 for allegedly conspiring to kidnap President Nixon's adviser Henry Kissinger and blow up government offices in Washington, DC, and sentenced to two years' imprisonment.

berry, *n.* any smallish, round, fleshy fruit; one of the eggs of a fish or lobster; (*Bot.*) a many-seeded, inferior, indehiscent, pulpy fruit, the seeds of which are loosely scattered through the pulp (a def. excluding the strawberry); a coffee bean; cereal grain. *v.i.* to bear or produce berries; to swell, to fill; to go berry-gathering. **in berry,** bearing her eggs (of a hen lobster). **berried,** *a.* having or bearing berries; (of a hen lobster) bearing eggs. [OE *berige* (cp. Icel. *ber,* Goth. *basi,* G *Beere*]

Berry, *n.* **Chuck (Charles Edward)** (1926–), US rock-and-roll singer, prolific songwriter, and guitarist. His characteristic guitar riffs became staples of rock music, and his humorous storytelling lyrics were also influential. He had a string of hits in the 1950s beginning with 'Maybellene' (1955).

Berryman, *n.* **John** (1914–72), US poet, whose complex and personal works include *Homage to Mistress Bradstreet* (1956), *77 Dream Songs* (1964, Pulitzer Prize), and *His Toy, His Dream, His Rest* (1968).

bersagliere, *n.* (*pl.* **-ri**) a sharpshooter; one of a crack corps in the Italian army. [It., from *bersaglio,* a mark]

berserk, berserker, baresark, *n.* a Norse warrior possessed of preternatural strength and fighting with desperate fury and courage; a bravo. *a., adv.* frenzied; filled with furious rage. **to go berserk,** to lose control of one's actions in violent rage. [Icel. *berserkr* (etym. doubtful, prob. bearsark, bear-coat)]

berth, *n.* sea-room; a convenient place for mooring; a place for a ship at a wharf; a room in a ship where any number of officers mess and reside; a situation on board ship; a permanent job or situation of any kind; a sleeping-place on board ship; a sleeping-place in a railway carriage. *v.t.* to moor; to furnish with a berth. **to give a wide berth to,** to keep away from; to steer clear of. **berthage,** *n.* room or accommodation for mooring ships; dock dues. [etym. doubtful; perh. from OE *gebyrian,* to suit (cp. G *gebühren*), or from BEAR[2]]

Berthelot, *n.* **Pierre Eugène Marcellin** (1827–1907), French chemist and politician, who carried out research into dyes and explosives, and proved that hydrocarbons and other organic compounds can be synthesized from inorganic materials.

Bertholet, *n.* **Claude Louis** (1748–1822), French chemist, who carried out research on dyes and bleaches (introducing the use of chlorine as a bleach) and determined the composition of ammonia.

Berthon boat, *n.* a collapsible, canvas lifeboat. [after E. L. *Berthon,* 1813–99, its inventor]

Bertillon, *a.* of or pertaining to Bertillon or his system. **Bertillon system,** a method of recording personal measurements and other characteristics, esp. for the purpose of identifying criminals. [Alphonse *Bertillon,* 1853–1914, F anthropologist]

Bertolucci, *n.* **Bernardo** (1940–), Italian director, whose work combines political and historical satire with an elegant visual appeal. His films include *The Spider's Stratagem* (1970), *Last Tango in Paris* (1972), and *The Last Emperor* (1987), for which he received an Academy Award.

Bertrand de Born (*c.* 1140–*c.* 1215), Provençal troubadour. He was viscount of Hautefort in Périgord, accompanied Richard Lionheart to Palestine, and died a monk.

Berufsverbot, (G) *n.* in West Germany, the policy of preventing political extremists from becoming government employees.

Berwickshire, *n.* former county of SE Scotland, a district of Borders region from 1975.

beryl, *n.* a gem nearly identical with the emerald, but varying in colour from pale green to yellow or white; a silicate of aluminium and beryllium, occurring usually in hexagonal prisms. **berylline,** *a.* resembling a beryl. [OF, from L *bēryllus,* Gr. *bērullos* (Sansk. *vaidūrya*)]

beryllium, *n.* a light metallic element, at. no. 4; chem. symbol Be, used as a component in nuclear reactors and to harden alloys etc.

Berzelius, *n.* **Jöns Jakob** (1779–1848), Swedish chemist, whose accurate determination of atomic and molecular weights helped to establish the laws of combination and the atomic theory. He invented (1813–14) the system of chemical symbols now in use and did valuable work on catalysts.

bescreen, *v.t.* to screen, to conceal, to hide from view; to envelop in shadow.

bescribble, *v.t.* to scribble about or over; to write in a scribbling style.

beseech, *v.t.* (*past, p.p.* **besought**), to ask earnestly, implore, entreat, supplicate. **beseeching,** *a.* **beseechingly,** *adv.* [BE-, ME *sechen, seken* (cp. Dut. *bezoeken, G besuchen*)]

beseem, *v.t.* to be fit, suitable, proper for or becoming to. *v.i.* to be seemly or proper. (*usu. impersonal in either voice*). **beseeming,** *a.* becoming, fitting. †*n.* appearance, look, becomingness, fitness. **beseemingly,** *adv.* **beseemingness,** *n.* **beseemly,** *a.* seemly, suitable, becoming, proper.

beseen, *p.p.* seen, looking, appearing; dressed, furnished, accomplished. **well-beseen,** †good-looking, of fair appearance; accomplished, well versed. [p.p. of obs. v. *besee,* from OE *biseon, beseōn,* to look about, to pay regard to]

beset, *v.t.* (*past, p.p.* **beset**) to set or surround (with); to surround, to invest, to occupy; to set upon, to fall upon; to encompass, to assail. **beset,** *p.p.* set or encumbered (with difficulties, snares etc.). **besetment,** *n.* the state of being beset; a besetting sin or weakness. [OE *bisettan,* to surround (BE-, *settan,* to SET)]

beshrew, *v.t.* to deprave, to make evil; †(*playfully*) to curse. [ME *bischrewen* (BE-, *schrewen,* to curse; see SHREW]

beside, *prep.* by the side of, side by side with; in comparison with; near, hard by, close to; away from, wide of. *adv.* besides. **beside oneself,** out of one's wits. **beside the point, question,** irrelevant. **besides,** *prep.* in addition to, over and above; other than, except. *adv.* moreover, further, over and above, in addition; otherwise. [OE *be sīdan,* by side]

besiege, *v.t.* to surround a place with intent to capture it by military force; to invest; to crowd round; to assail importunately. **besieger,** *n.* one who besieges a place. **besiegingly,** *adv.* [ME *bisegen, besegen* (BE-, *segen,* OF *asegier,* late L *assediāre,* from *ad-,* to, *sedium,* sitting, from *sedēre,* to sit)]

besmear, *v.t.* to cover or daub with something unctuous or viscous; to soil, to defile.

besmirch, *v.t.* to soil, discolour; to sully, bedim.

besom, *n.* a broom made of twigs or heath bound round a handle; (*fig.*) anything that sweeps away impurity; (*Sc.*) a term of reproach for a woman. †*v.i.* to sweep. †*v.t.* to sweep; to sweep away. [OE *besma* (cp. Dut. *bezem,* G *Besen*)]

besot, *v.t.* to make sottish; to stupefy, to muddle; to cause to dote upon. **besotted,** *a.* intoxicated, muddled, infatuated. **besottedly,** *adv.* blindly, infatuatedly.

besought, *p.p.* BESEECH.

bespangle, *v.t.* to cover over with or as with spangles.

bespatter, *v.t.* to spatter over or about; (*fig.*) to load with abuse.

bespeak, †*v.i.* (*past,* **-spoke**, *p.p.* **-spoken**) to speak; to speak out. *v.t.* to speak for, to arrange for, to order beforehand; to ask; to request; to give evidence of; to betoken, to foreshow; †to speak to. *n.* the bespeaking of a particular play; an actor's benefit. **bespoke** for BESPOKEN, *p.p.* ordered beforehand. *a.* made-to-measure; of a suit etc., made to a customer's specific requirements; making or selling such articles. [OE *besprecan* (BE-, *sprecan,* SPEAK), cp. OHG *bisprācha,* detraction, G *besprechen,* to talk over]

bespeckle, *v.t.* to speckle over, to variegate.

bespectacled, *a.* wearing spectacles.

bespoke, bespoken BESPEAK.

bespread, *v.t.* to spread over; to spread with; to adorn. [ME *bispreden, bespreden* (BE-, *spreden,* to spread)]

besprinkle, *v.t.* to sprinkle or scatter over; to bedew. [ME *besprengil* (BE-, *sprenkel,* freq. of *sprengan*)]

Bessarabia, *n.* territory in SE Europe, annexed by Russia in 1812, which broke away at the Russian Revolution to join Romania. The cession was confirmed by the Allies, but not by Russia, in a Paris treaty of 1920; Russia reoccupied it in 1940 and divided it between the Moldavian and Ukrainian republics. Romania recognized the position in the 1947 peace treaty.

Bessel, *n.* **Friedrich Wilhelm** (1784–1846), German astronomer and mathematician, the first person to find the approximate distance to a star by direct methods when he measured the parallax of 61 Cygni in 1838. In mathematics, he introduced the series of functions now known as Bessel functions.

Bessemer, *n.* **Henry** (1813–98), British civil engineer, who invented a method of converting molten pig-iron into steel (the Bessemer process).

Bessemer process, *n.* a process invented in 1856 for the elimination of carbon and silicon by forcing air into melted cast iron. **Bessemer iron** or **steel**, *n.* iron or steel manufactured by this process. **Bessemerize, -ise,** *v.t.*

best[1], *a.* of the highest excellence; surpassing all others; most desirable. *v.t.* to get the better of; to cheat, outwit. *adv.* superlative of WELL; in the highest degree; to the most advantage; with most ease; most intimately. *n.* the best thing; the utmost; (*collect.*) the best people. **at best,** as far as can be expected. **to get** or **have the best of,** to get or have the advantage. **to make the best of,** to make the most of; to be content with. **to the best of,** to the utmost extent of. **best man,** *n.* a groomsman. **the best part,** the largest part, the most. **best people,** *n.pl.* those considered the most select socially. **bestseller,** *n.* a popular book which has sold in large numbers; a writer of such a book. **bestsell,** *v.i.* to be or become a bestseller. **Sunday-best,** *n.* best clothes. [OE *betst* (cp. BETTER), superlative of GOOD]

Best[2], *n.* **Charles Herbert** (1899–1978), Canadian physiologist, one of the team of Canadian scientists including Frederick Banting, whose researches resulted in 1922 in the discovery of insulin as a treatment for diabetes.

bestead[1], *v.t.* to help; to profit; to be of service to. *v.i.* to avail.

bested, bestead[2], *p.p.* situated, circumstanced (usu. with adv. *ill, hard, hardly, sore* etc.). [ME *bistad,* p.p. of *bisteden* (BE-, *stad,* from Icel. *staadr,* p.p. of *stethja,* to stop, fix, appoint)]

bestial, *a.* of or pertaining to the inferior animals, esp. the quadrupeds; resembling a beast; brutish, sensual, obscene, sexually depraved. *n.* (*Sc.*) cattle. **bestiality,** *n.* bestial behaviour; sexual relations between a person and an animal. **bestialize, -ise,** *v.t.* to make bestial; to reduce to the level of a beast. **bestially,** *adv.* **bestiary,** *n.* one who fought with beasts in the Roman amphitheatre; †a moralized natural history of animals. [OF *bestial,* L *bestiālis* (*bestia,* a beast)]

bestick, *v.t.* to stick about, to bedeck; to transfix. **bestuck,** *p.p.* adorned; pierced.

bestir, *v.t.* to rouse into activity. [OE *bestyrian* (BE-, *styrian,* STIR)]

bestow, *v.t.* to stow, to lay up; to stow away, to lodge, provide with quarters; to expend, to lay out; to give as a present. **bestowal,** *n.* disposal, location; gift. **bestowment,** *n.* bestowal.

bestrew, *v.t.* to strew over; to bescatter; to lie scattered over. [OE *bestrēowian* (BE-, *strēowian,* STREW)]

bestride, *v.t.* to sit upon with the legs astride; to bestraddle; to span, overarch. [OE *bestridan* (BE-, STRIDE)]

bet, *n.* a wager; a sum staked upon a contingent event. *v.t.* (*past, p.p.* **bet, betted**) to wager; to stake upon a contingency. *v.i.* to lay a wager. **you bet,** (*sl.*) certainly, of course, depend upon it. **better**[2], *n.* one who makes bets. [perh. from ABET]

beta, *n.* the second letter of the Greek alphabet; the second star in a constellation; the second of a series of numerous compounds and other enumerations. **beta-blocker,** *n.* a drug that reduces the heart-rate, esp. used to treat high blood-pressure, but also used illegally by some sports competitors to improve their concentration and performance. **beta particle,** *n.* a negatively-charged particle emitted by certain radioactive substances. Identified as an electron. **beta rays,** *n.pl.* rays consisting of a stream of beta particles or electrons. **beta rhythm, wave,** *n.* the normal electrical activity of the brain. **betratron**, BETA, ELECTRON, *n.* (*Phys.*) an electrical apparatus for accelerating electrons to high energies. [Gr.]

betake, *v.r.* (*past* **betook**, *p.p.* **betaken**) to take oneself to; to have recourse to.

betel, *n.* *Piper betle,* a shrubby plant with evergreen leaves, called also **betel-pepper** and **betel-vine**; its leaf, used as a wrapper to enclose a few slices of the areca nut with a little shell lime, which are chewed by the peoples of SE Asia. **betel-nut,** *n.* the nut of the areca palm. **betel-tree,** *n.* *Areca catechu,* so called because its nut is chewed with betel-leaves. [Port., from Malayālam, *vettila*]

Betelgeuse, *n.* a red supergiant star in the constellation of Orion, over 300 times the diameter of the Sun, about the same size as the orbit of Mars. It lies 650 light years away and is the tenth-brightest star in the sky, although its brightness varies.

betê noire, *n.* a bugbear, pet aversion. [F, black beast]

beth, *n.* the second letter of the Hebrew alphabet. [Heb. *bēth,* house]

bethankit, *n.* (*Sc.*) grace after meat. [BE-, THANK].

bethel, *n.* a Nonconformist chapel; a mission-room; a seamen's church, esp. afloat. [Heb. *bēthēl,* house of God]

betherel BEDRAL.

bethesda, *n.* a Nonconformist chapel. [Heb. *bethesda,* house of mercy or place of the flowing of water]

bethink, †*v.t.* to think, to recollect; to contrive, to plan. *v.r.* to consider, think; to collect one's thoughts; to meditate. [OE *bithencan* (cp. Dut. and G *bedenken*)]

Bethlehem, *n.* (Hebrew **Beit-Lahm**) town on the W bank of the river Jordan, S of Jerusalem. Occupied by Israel in 1967; population (1980) 14,000. In the New Testament it was the birthplace of Jesus and associated with King David.

Bethmann Hollweg, *n.* **Theobald von** (1856–1921), German politician, imperial chancellor (1909–17), largely responsible for engineering popular support for World War I in Germany, but his power was gradually superseded by a military dictatorship under Ludendorff.

bethrall, *v.t.* to enslave, to bring into subjection.

betide, *v.t.* to happen to; (*erron.*) to betoken. *v.i.* to happen, to come to pass. [ME *betiden* (BE-, OE *tīdan,* TIDE)]

betimes, †betime, *adv.* at an early hour or period; in good time, in time; in a short time, soon.

betitle, *v.t.* to entitle; to adorn with a title or titles.

Betjeman, *n.* **John** (1906–84), English poet and essayist, originator of a peculiarly English light verse, nostalgic and delighting in Victorian and Edwardian architecture. His *Collected Poems* appeared in 1968 and a verse autobiography *Summoned by Bells* in 1960. He was knighted in 1969 and became Poet Laureate in 1972.

betoken, *v.t.* to be a type of; to foreshow, to be an omen of, to indicate. [ME *bitacnen* (see BE-, TOKEN, OE *getacnian*)]

beton, *n.* concrete made with sand or stone and hydraulic lime or cement. [F *béton,* Port. *betun,* cement, L *bitūmen,* mineral pitch]

betony, *n.* a labiate plant, *Stachys betonica,* with purple flowers. [OF *betonie,* late *betonia,* L *vettonica* (*Vettones,* a Sp. tribe)]

betook, *past.* BETAKE.

betray, *v.t.* to give up; to deliver up a person or thing treacherously; to be false to; to lead astray; to disclose treacherously; to disclose against one's will or intention; to reveal incidentally. **betrayal,** *n.* a treacherous giving up or violation of a trust; a revelation or divulging. **betrayer,** *n.* one who betrays; a traitor. [ME *betraien* (BE-, *traien,* to betray), OF *traïr,* late L *trādere* (*trans-,* over, *dāre,* to give)]

betroth, *v.t.* to contract two persons in an engagement to marry; to engage, affiance; †to engage oneself to. **betrothal, betrothment,** *n.* the act of betrothing; the state of being betrothed; affiance. **betrothed,** *a.* engaged to be married; affianced. *n.* a person engaged to be married. [ME *bitreuthien* (BE-, *treuthe,* OE *trēowth,* TRUTH]

better[1], *a.* superior, more excellent; more desirable; greater in degree; improved in health. *v.t.* to make better; to excel, to surpass, to improve on. *v.i.* to become better, to improve. *adv.* comp. of WELL. In a superior, more excellent or more desirable manner; more correctly or fully; with greater profit; in a greater or higher degree; more. *n.pl.* social superiors. **better off,** in better circumstances. **for better (or) for worse,** whatever the circumstances. **for the better,** in the way of improvement. **the better part of,** the most. **to better oneself,** to get on, to get a better job. **to get the better of,** to defeat, to outwit. **to think better of,** to reconsider. **better half,** *n.* (*facet.*) a spouse, esp. a wife. **betterment,** *n.* amelioration; an improvement of property; improvements made on new lands. **bettermost,** *a.* best; of the highest quality. [OE *bet, bett,* adv., *betera,* a., comparative of GOOD (Goth. *batiza,* Icel. *betri,* Dut. *beter,* G *besser*)]

better[2] BET.

Betterton, *n.* **Thomas** (*c.* 1635–1710), British actor. A member of the Duke of York's company after the Restoration, he attracted the attention of Charles II. He was greatly admired in many Shakespeare parts, including Hamlet and Othello.

bettong, *n.* a small prehensile-tailed kangaroo. [Austral. Abor.]

betty, *n.* †a burglar's jemmy; a man who busies himself with household duties. [dim. of *Elizabeth*]

between, *prep.* in, on, into, along or across the place, space or interval of any kind separating two points, lines, places or objects; intermediate in relation to; related to both of; related so as to separate; related so as to connect, from one to another; among; in shares among, so as to affect all. *n.* an interval of time; (*pl.*) an intermediate size and quality of sewing-needles. *adv.* intermediately; in an intervening space or time; in relation to both of; to and fro; during or in an interval. **go-between,** an intermediary. **between-decks,** *n.* the space between two decks. **between-maid** TWEENY under TWEEN. **betweenwhiles, betweentimes,** *adv.* now and then; at intervals. **between ourselves,** in confidence. **betwixt and between,** neither one thing nor the other; half and half; middling. [OE *betwēonum* (*be,* by, *twēonum,* dat. of *twēon,* twain, adj. corr. to distributive numeral *twā,* two)]

betwixt, *prep., adv.* (*archaic*) between. [OE *betweox* (*be,* by, with either a dat. *tweoxum, tweohsum,* or an acc. pl. neut. *twiscu,* from OTeut. *twiskjo,* twofold)]

Beuys, *n.* **Joseph** (1921–86), German sculptor and performance artist. By the 1970s he had gained an international reputation. His sculpture makes use of unusual materials such as felt and fat. He was strongly influenced by his wartime experiences.

BeV, (*abbr.*) Billion Electron-Volt(s) in the US: equivalent to gigaelectronvolt(s), GeV.

Bevan, *n.* **Aneurin** (1897–1960), British Labour politician. Son of a Welsh miner, and himself a miner at 13, he became member of Parliament for Ebbw Vale (1929–60). As minister of health (1945–51), he inaugurated the National Health Service (NHS); he was minister of labour during Jan.–Apr. 1951, when he resigned (with Harold Wilson) on the introduction of NHS charges and led a Bevanite faction against the government. He was noted as an orator.

bevatron, *n.* an electrical apparatus for accelerating protons to high energies.

bevel, *a.* oblique, sloping, slanting; at more than a right angle. *n.* a tool consisting of a flat rule with a movable tongue or arm for setting off angles; a slope from the right angle, an inclination of two planes, except one of 90°. *v.t.* to cut away to a slope, to give a bevel angle to. *v.i.* to recede from the perpendicular, to slant. **bevel-edge,** *n.* the oblique edge of a chisel or similar cutting tool. **bevel-gear, -gearing,** *n.* gear for transmitting motion from one shaft to another by means of bevel-wheels. **bevel-wheels,** *n.pl.* cogged wheels whose axes form an angle (usually 90°) with each other. **bevelling,** *n.* reducing to an oblique angle; the angle so given; (*Naut.*) a bevelled surface or part. *a.* slanting, having an obtuse angle. **bevelment,** *n.* the process of bevelling; the replacement of the edge of a crystal by two similar planes equally inclined to the adjacent faces. [prob. from an OF *bevel* or *buvel* (F *beveau*)]

beverage, *n.* any drink other than water. **bevvied,** *a.* (*sl.*) drunk. **bevvy,** *n.* (*sl.*) alcoholic drink. [OF *beverage,* from *bevre, beivre* (cp. F *boire*), to drink, from L *bibere,* to drink, -AGE]

Beveridge, *n.* **William Henry, 1st Baron Beveridge** (1879–1963), British economist. A civil servant, he acted as Lloyd George's lieutenant in the social legislation of the Liberal government before World War I. The *Beveridge Report* (1942) formed the basis of the welfare state in Britain.

Bevin, *n.* **Ernest** (1881–1951). British Labour politician. Chief creator of the Transport and General Workers' Union, he was its general secretary (1921–40), when he entered the war cabinet as minister of labour and National Service. He organized the 'Bevin boys', chosen by ballot to work in the coal mines as war service, and was foreign secretary in the Labour government (1945–51).

bevy, *n.* a flock of larks or quails; a herd of roes; a company of women. [etym. unknown]

bewail, *v.t.* to wail over, to lament for. *v.i.* to express grief. **bewailing,** *n.* loud lamentation. *a.* that bewails or laments. **bewailingly,** *adv.* mournfully, with lamentation. **bewailment,** *n.* the act of bewailing.

beware, *v.i.* to be wary, to be on one's guard; to take care. *v.t.* to be wary of, on guard against; to look out for. [ME *be war,* be cautious, OE *wær* wary (cp. WARE[2], v. from OE *warian,* to guard)]

beweep , *v.t.* to weep over or for; to moisten with or as with tears. *v.i.* to weep.

bewet, *v.t.* to wet profusely; to bedew.

Bewick, *n.* **Thomas** (1753–1828), British wood engraver, excelling in animal subjects. His illustrated *General History of Quadrupeds* (1790) and *History of British Birds* (1797, 1804) display his skill.

bewig, *v.t.* to adorn with a wig. **bewigged,** *a.* (*fig.*) perked up, bureaucratic, bound with convention or red tape.

bewilder, *v.t.* to perplex, confuse, lead astray. **bewildering,** *a.* causing one to lose his way, physically or mentally. **bewilderingly,** *adv.* **bewilderment,** *n.* the state of being bewildered. [BE-, *wilder, wildern,* a wilderness]

bewitch, *v.t.* to practise witchcraft against a person or thing; to charm, to fascinate, to allure. **bewitching,** *a.* alluring, charming. **bewitchingly,** *adv.* **bewitchment,** *n.* fascination, charm. [ME *bewicchen* (BE-, OE *wiccian,* to practise witchcraft, from *wicca,* a wizard)]

bewray, *v.t.* to reveal, to disclose. **bewrayingly,** *adv.* [BE-, OE *wrēgan,* to accuse]

bey, †**beg,** *n.* a governor of a Turkish town, province or district. **beylic,** *n.* the district governed by a bey. [Turk. *bēg*]

beyond, *prep.* on, to or towards the farther side of; past, later than; exceeding in quantity or amount, more than; surpassing in quality or degree, outside the limit of; in addition to, over and above. *adv.* at a greater distance than; farther away. *n.* that which lies beyond human experience or after death. **the back of beyond,** an out-of-the-way place. [OE *begeondan* (BE-, *geond,* across, *-an,* from)]

Beza, *n.* **Théodore** (properly **De Bèsze**) (1519–1605), French church reformer. He settled in Geneva, Switzerland, where he worked with the Protestant leader Calvin and succeeded him in 1564–1600 as head of the reformed church there. He wrote in defence of the burning of Servetus (1554) and translated the New Testament into Latin.

bezant, *n.* a gold coin struck at Constantinople by the Byzantine emperors, varying greatly in value; (*Her.*) a gold roundel borne as a charge. [OF *besant,* L *Byzantius nummus,* coin of Byzantium]

bezel, *n.* a sloping edge like that of a cutting tool; one of the oblique sides of a cut gem; the groove by which a watch-glass or a jewel is held. [OF *bisel* (F *bizeau*)]

Bezier curve, *n.* a curved line that connects a series of points (or 'nodes') in the smoothest possible way. The shape of the curve is governed by a series of complex mathematical formulae. They are used in computer graphics and CAD.

bezique, *n.* a game of cards of French origin. [F *besigue* (etym. doubtful)]

bezoar, *n.* †an antidote; a calculous concretion found in the stomach of certain animals and supposed to be an antidote to poisons. **bezoar-goat,** *n.* the Persian wild goat, the best-known example of an animal producing the bezoar. **bezoar-stone,** *n.* [F, through Port. or Sp. from Arab. *bāzahr, bādizahr,* Pers. *pādzahr,* counter-poison]

†**bezonian,** *n.* a beggar, a low fellow. [It. *bisogno,* want, poverty (etym. unknown)]

†**bezzle,** *v.t.* to plunder, rob, make away with; to squander. *v.i.* to drink, to tipple; to revel. †**bezzled,** *part. a.* drunk, tipsy. [ME *besil,* OF *besiler* (abbr. from *embesillier,* EMBEZZLE)]

bf, (*abbr.*) bloody fool; bold face (print); brought forward.

Bhagavad-Gītā, *n.* (Hindu 'the Song of the Blessed') religious and philosophical Sanskrit poem, dating from around 300 BC, forming an episode in the sixth book of the *Mahābhārata,* one of the two great Hindu epics. It is the supreme religious work of Hinduism.

bhang, bang, *n.* an intoxicating or stupefying liquor or drug made from the dried leaves of hemp, *Cannabis indica.* [Hind.]

bhangra, *n., a.* (of) a type of popular music combining Western and Asian, esp Punjabi, forms. [Hindi]

bharal, burhel, *n.* a wild blue-coated sheep of the Himalayas. [Hind.]

bheesti, *n.* a servant who supplies water to an Indian house. [Hind.]

Bhindranwale, *n.* **Sant Jarnail Singh** (1947–84), Indian Sikh fundamentalist leader, who campaigned for the creation of a separate state of Khalistan during the early 1980s, precipitating a bloody Hindu-Sikh conflict in the Punjab. He was killed in the siege of the Golden Temple in Amritsar.

Bhopal, *n.* industrial city (textiles, chemicals, electrical goods, jewellery); capital of Madhya Pradesh, central India; population (1981) 672,000. Nearby Bhimbetka Caves, discovered 1973, have the world's largest collection of prehistoric paintings which are about 10,000 years old. In 1984 some 2000 people died after an escape of poisonous gas from a factory owned by the US company Union Carbide; the long-term effects are yet to be discovered.

bhp, (*abbr.*) brake horsepower.

Bhumibol Adulyadej, *n.* (1927–), king of Thailand from 1946. Educated in Bangkok and Switzerland, he succeeded on the assassination of his brother, formally taking the throne 1950. In 1973 he was active, with popular support, in overthrowing the military government of Field Marshal Kittikachorn and ending a sequence of army-dominated regimes in power from 1932.

Bhutan, *n.* Kingdom of (*Druk-yul*). **area** 46,500 sq km/ 17,954 sq miles. **capital** Thimbu. **physical** occupies S slopes of the Himalayas, and is cut by valleys of tributaries of the Brahmaputra. **population** (1988) 1,400,000; annual growth rate 2%. **exports** timber, minerals. **language** Dzongkha (a Tibetan dialect), Nepali, and English (all official). **religion** Mahayana Buddhist, 35% Hindu.

Bhutto¹, *n.* **Benazir** (1953–), Pakistani politician, leader of the Pakistan People's Party (PPP) from 1984 (in exile until 1986), and prime minister of Pakistan from 1988. She is the first female leader of a Muslim state.

Bhutto², *n.* **Zulfiqar Ali** (1928–79), Pakistani politician, president 1971–73 and then prime minister until the 1977 military coup led by Gen. Zia ul Haq. In 1978 he was sentenced to death for conspiracy to murder a political opponent, and was hanged.

Bi (*chem. symb.*) bismuth.

bi- *pref.* double twice; doubly; with two; in two; every two, once in every two, lasting for two (used even with Eng. words, e.g. *bi-weekly, bi-monthly,* but chiefly with words from L, esp. scientific terms). [L *bi-, dui-,* double (cp. *duo,* two, Gr. *di-, duō,* Sansk. *doi*]

biacuminate, *a.* having two tapering points.

Biafra, Republic of, an African state proclaimed in 1967 when fears that Nigerian central government was increasingly in the hands of the rival Hausa tribe led the predominantly Ibo Eastern Region of Nigeria to secede under Lt-Col Odumegwu Ojukwu, an Oxford-educated Ibo. On the proclamation of Biafra, civil war ensued with the rest of the federation. In a bitterly fought campaign federal forces had confined the Biafrans to a shrinking area of the interior by 1968, and by 1970 Biafra ceased to exist.

biangular, *a.* having two angles.

biannual, *a.* half-yearly, twice a year.

biarticulate, *a.* (*Zool.*) two-jointed.

bias, *n.* a weight formerly placed on the side of a bowl to impart oblique motion; the motion so imparted; hence, a leaning of the mind, inclination, prejudice, prepossession. *a.* slanting, oblique. *adv.* obliquely, athwart, awry; on slant. *v.t.* to cause to incline to one side; to prejudice, to prepossess. **bias binding,** *n.* a strip of material cut slantwise used for binding hems in sewing. **bias(s)ing,** *pres.p.* **bias(s)ed,** *past, p.p.* [F *biais,* oblique or obliquity]

biathlon, *n.* an athletic event combining cross-country skiing and rifle shooting. [BI-, Gr. *athlon,* a contest]

biaxial, biaxal, *a.* having two (optical) axes.

bib, *v.t., i.* to drink; to drink frequently; to tipple. *n.* a cloth or piece of shaped plastic put under a child's chin to keep the front of the clothes clean; the front section of a garment (e.g. an apron, dungarees) above the waist; the whiting-pout, *Gadus luscus*, a food fish with a chin barbel. **best bib and tucker,** (*coll.*) best clothing, outfit. **bibcock,** *n.* a tap with the nozzle bent downwards. **bibber,** *n.* a tippler. **bibbing,** *n.* tippling. [prob. from L *bibere,* to drink]

Bib., (*abbr.*) Bible; Biblical.

bibacious, *a.* addicted to drinking.

bibelot, *n.* a knick-knack. [F]

Biber, *n.* **Heinrich von** (1644–1704), Bohemian composer, Kapellmeister at the Archbishop of Salzburg's court. A virtuoso violinist, he composed a wide variety of musical pieces including the *Nightwatchman Serenade.*

†**bibl**[1], (*abbr.*) bibliographical; bibliography.

Bibl., bibl[2], (*abbr.*) Biblical.

Bible, *n.* the sacred writings of the Christian religion comprising the Old and New Testament; a copy of the Scriptures, a particular edition; a text-book, an authority. **Breeches Bible,** the Geneva Bible of 1560 in which the word *breeches* was used for *aprons* in Gen. iii.7. **Douay Bible,** an English version of the Vulgate made at the Roman Catholic college of Douai (1582–1609). **Geneva Bible,** an English translation, without the Apocrypha, and with the chapters divided into verses, published at Geneva (1560). **Mazarine Bible,** a Bible printed by Gutenberg (1450), the first book printed from movable types. **Bible-basher, -thumper,** *n.* an aggressive preacher; an ardent exponent of the Bible. **Bible belt,** *n.* those regions of the southern US characterized by fervent religious fundamentalism. **Bible-Christian,** *n.* a member of a sect founded (1815) by W. O. Bryan, a Cornish Wesleyan. **Bible-class,** *n.* a class for studying the Bible. **Bible-clerk,** *n.* (*Univ.*) a student who reads the Lessons in chapel. **Bible-reader, Bible-woman,** *n.* one employed as a lay missioner. **Bible Society,** *n.* a society for the distribution of the Bible. **biblical,** *a.* of or pertaining to the Bible. **biblically,** *adv.* **biblicism,** *n.* strict adherence to the letter of the Bible. **biblism,** *n.* adherence to the Bible as the only rule of faith. **biblicist,** *n.* **biblist,** *n.* one who takes the Bible as the only rule of faith; a biblical scholar or student. [F, from late L *biblia* (used as fem. sing.), Gr. *biblia,* neut. pl. writings, *biblion,* dim. of *biblos,* a book (*bublos,* papyrus)]

Biblical criticism, *n.* study of the content and origin of the Bible. **Lower** or **textual criticism** is directed to the recovery of the original text; **higher** or **documentary criticism** is concerned with questions of authorship, date, and literary sources; **historical criticism** seeks to ascertain the actual historic content of the Bible, aided by archaeological discoveries and the ancient history of neighbouring peoples.

biblio- *comb. form.* pertaining to books. [Gr. *biblion,* a book]

bibliography, *n.* the methodical study of books, authorship, printing, editions, forms etc.; a book dealing with this; a systematic list of books of any author, printer or country, or on any subject. **bibliographer,** *n.* one skilled in bibliography; one who writes about books. **bibliographical,** *a.* of or pertaining to bibliography. [Gr. *bibliographia* (BIBLIO, -GRAPHY)]

bibliolatry, *n.* excessive admiration of a book or books; excessive reverence for the letter of the Bible. **bibliolater,** *n.* a person addicted to bibliolatry. **bibliolatrous,** *a.* addicted to bibliolatry. [BIBLIO-, -LATRY]

bibliology, *n.* scientific study of books; bibliography; biblical study. **bibliological,** *a.* pertaining to bibliology.

bibliomancy, *n.* divination by books or verses of the Bible.

bibliomania, *n.* a mania for collecting and possessing books. **bibliomaniac,** *n.* one who has such a mania.

bibliopegy, *n.* the art of binding books. **bibliopegic,** *a.* relating to the art of bookbinding. **bibliopegist,** *n.* one who collects bindings; a bookbinder. [Gr. *-pēgia,* from *pēgnunai,* to fix]

bibliophile, *n.* a lover of books. **bibliophilism,** *n.* love of books; book-fancying. **bibliophilist,** *n.* [BIBLIO-, -PHILE]

bibliophobia, *n.* a dread or hatred of books.

bibliopole, *n.* a bookseller. **bibliopolic, bibliopolical,** *a.* of or pertaining to booksellers or to bookselling. **bibliopolist,** *n.* a bookseller. **bibliopoly,** *n.* bookselling. [L *bibliopōla,* Gr. *bibliopōlēs* (*pōlēs,* seller)]

bibliotheca, *n.* †the Bible; a library; a bibliography. **bibliothecal,** *a.* of or pertaining to a library. [L, from Gr. *bibliothēkē (thēkē* a repository)]

bibulous, *a.* readily absorbing moisture; addicted to alcohol. **bibulously,** *adv.* [L *bibulus* (*bibere*)]

bicameral, *a.* having two legislative chambers or assemblies. [BI-, L *camera,* CHAMBER]

bicarbonate, *a.* a salt of carbonic acid. **bicarbonate of soda,** *n.* (*coll. contr.* **bicarb**,) sodium bicarbonate used in baking as a raising agent or as an antacid.

bice, *n.* a pale blue or green pigment made from smalt. [F *bis* (fem. *bise*), It. *bigio,* greyish]

bicentenary, *a.* consisting of or pertaining to 200 years. *n.* the 200th anniversary. **bicentennial,** *a.* occurring every 200 years; lasting 200 years. *n.* a bicentenary.

bicephalous, *a.* having two heads; two-headed. [Gr. *kephalē,* the head]

biceps, *a.* having two heads, points or summits, esp. of muscles having two attachments. *n.* the large muscle in front of the upper arm; the corresponding muscle of the thigh. **bicipital,** *a.* two-headed; of or pertaining to the biceps muscle. [L *caput,* head)]

Bichat, *n.* **Marie François Xavier** (1771–1802), French physician and founder of histology. He studied the organs of the body, their structure, and the ways in which they are affected by disease. This led to his discovery and naming of 'tissues', a basic medical concept. He argued that disease does not affect the whole organ but only certain of its constituent tissues.

bichromate, *n.* a salt containing dichromic acid.

bicker, *v.i.* †to skirmish, fight; to dispute, quarrel, wrangle, squabble over petty issues; to quiver, glisten, flicker. *n.* †a quarrel, contention; strife, fighting; rattling, pattering, noise as of bickering, a skirmish; altercation, disagreement, wrangling. [ME *bickere,* prob. freq. of *biken,* to thrust]

biconcave, *a.* concave on both sides.

biconvex, *a.* convex on both sides.

bicorporal, *a.* having two bodies, bicorporate, bicorporated.

bicorporate, *a.* double-headed; (*Her.*) having two bodies with a single head.

bicuspid, *a.* having two points or cusps. *n.* a bicuspid tooth, one of the premolars in man. **bicuspidate,** *a.* two-pointed.

bicycle, *n.* a two-wheeled pedal-driven vehicle, with the wheels one behind the other and usually with a saddle for the rider mounted on a metal frame. *v.i.* to ride on a bicycle. **tandem bicycle,** a bicycle for two persons. **bicycle clip,** *n.* a thin metal clip worn around the ankles by cyclists to prevent their trousers from catching on the chain. **bicycle pump,** *n.* a hand pump for filling bicycle tyres with air. **bicyclist,** *n.* one who rides a bicycle.

bid, *v.t.* (*past* **bid,** *p.p.* **bid, bidden**) to command; to invite, to ask; to announce, to declare; to offer, to make a tender of (a price, esp. at an auction). *v.i.* to make an offer at an auction; to tender. *n.* an offer of a price, esp. at an auction; the call at bridge whereby a player contracts to make as many tricks as he names. **to bid defiance,** to defy, proclaim a challenge. **to bid farewell, welcome,** to salute at parting or arrival. **to bid fair,** to seem likely, to promise well. **to bid up,** to raise the price of a commodity at auction by a succession of overbids. **biddable,** *a.* obedient, willing. **bidder,** *n.* one who makes an offer at an auction. **bidding,** *n.* †prayer, the act of praying, esp. with a rosary; invitation, command; a bid at an auction. **bidding-prayer,** *n.* †praying of prayers; prayer in which the congregation is exhorted to pray for certain objects. [two verbs blended (1) OE *beodan,* to offer, inform, command (cp. Dut. *bieden,* G *bieten,* Goth. *biudan*), (2) *biddan* to press, beg, pray (cp. Dut. *bidden,* G *bitten,* Goth. *bidjan*)]

biddy, *n.* (*dial.*) a fowl; (*derog.*) an old woman. [corr. of *Bridget*]

biddy-biddy, *n.* a New Zealand grassland plant related to the rose; the burrs of this plant. [Maori *piripiri*]

bide, *v.t.* (*past* **bided, bode**, *p.p.* **bided**) to abide, await; to endure, suffer; (*arch. exc. in* **bide one's time,** await an opportunity). *v.i.* to abide, stay; to continue, to remain. **biding,** *n.* awaiting, abiding; stay, residence; abode, abiding-place. [OE *bīdan* (cp. Dut. *beiden,* OHG *bītan*)]

bident, *n.* a two-pronged fork. **bidentate, bidentated,** *a.* having two teeth or toothlike processes.

bidet, *n.* a small horse; a low basin for bathing the genital and anal area. [F]

Biedermeier, *n.* early-19th-century Germanic style of art and furniture, derogatorily named after Gottlieb Biedermeier, a fictional character embodying bourgeois taste.

bield, *n.* (*Sc.*) protection, shelter, *a.* (*Sc.*) comfortable, cosy. **bielding,** *n.* (*Sc.*) protection, shelter. **bieldy,** *a.* (*Sc.*) protective, sheltering. [ME *belde,* OE *bieldo,* boldness (Goth. *balthei,* OHG *Bald*)]

biennial, *a.* happening every two years; lasting two years; taking two years to reach maturity, ripen its seeds and die. *n.* a biennial plant. **biennially,** *adv.* **biennium,** *n.* a period of two years.

bier, *n.* †a handbarrow; a stand or litter on which a corpse is placed, or on which the coffin is borne to the grave; †the corpse on a bier; a tomb. †**bier-balk,** *n.* a path along which there is a right of way for funerals only. [OE *bǣr* (*beran,* to bear; cp. BARROW¹)]

Bierstadt, *n.* **Albert** (1830–1902), US landscape painter. His spectacular panoramas fell out of favour after the American Civil War. A classic work is *Thunderstorm in the Rocky Mountains* (1859, Museum of Fine Arts, Boston).

bifacial, *a.* having two faces.

bifarious, *a.* double; ranged in two rows.

biff, *v.t.* (*coll.*) to strike, to cuff. *n.* a blow. [onomat.]

Biffen, *n.* **(William) John** (1930–), British Conservative politician. In 1971 Biffen was elected to Parliament for a Shropshire seat. Despite being to the left of Margaret Thatcher, he held key positions in government from 1979, including leadership of the House of Commons from 1982, but was dropped after the general election of 1987.

biffin, *n.* a deep-red cooking-apple much cultivated in Norfolk; a baked apple of this kind, flattened into a cake. [*beefing,* from BEEF, from the colour]

bifid, *a.* split into two lobes by a central cleft; two-cleft. **bifidity, bifidly,** *adv.* [L *bifidus,* from BI-, *findere,* to split]

bifocal, *a.* with two foci. **bifocal lenses,** *n.pl.* spectacle lenses divided for near and distant vision.

bifold, *a.* twofold, double.

bifoliate, *a.* having two leaves.

biform, biformed, *a.* having or partaking of two forms.

bifurcate, *v.i.* to divide into two branches, forks or peaks. **bifurcate,** *a.* divided into two forks or branches. **bifurcation,** *n.* division into two parts or branches; the point of such division; either of the forks or branches. [med. L *bifurcātus,* p.p. of *bifurcārī,* from L *bifurcus,* two-pronged (BI-, *furca,* a fork, prong)]

big¹, *a.* large or great in bulk; grown up; pregnant, advanced in pregnancy; important; magnanimous, boastful, pompous, pretentious. *adv.* (*coll.*) boastfully; pretentiously. **too big for one's boots, britches,** unduly self-important. **to talk big,** to boast. **Big Bang,** *n.* the deregulation of the London Stock Exchange in 1986 which allowed foreign institutions access to the London money markets, and ended various restrictive practices in the provision of financial services; (*fig.*) any fundamental change in organization. **big bang theory,** in cosmology, the theory that the universe evolved from a cataclysmic explosion of superdense matter and is still expanding. (cp. STEADY STATE THEORY). **big-bellied,** *a.* corpulent; heavily pregnant. **Big Ben,** *n.* the great bell and clock in the Houses of Parliament in Westminster. **big-boned,** *a.* of large frame. **Big Brother,** *n.* a sinister and ruthless person or organization that exercises totalitarian control [from George Orwell's novel *1984* (1949)]. **big business,** *n.* large corporations and enterprises, used collectively esp. when regarded as exploitative. **big deal,** *int.* (*sl.*) a derisory exclamation or response. **big dipper,** *n.* (orig. *N Am.*) ROLLER COASTER. **big end,** *n.* the crankpin end of the connecting-rod in an internal-combustion engine. **big game,** *n.* large animals hunted or fished for sport. **big gun,** *n.* (*sl.*) an important person. **big-head,** *n.* (*coll.*) a conceited individual. **big-horn,** *n.* the Rocky Mountain sheep, *Ovis montana.* **big-mouth,** *n.* (*sl.*) a loud, indiscreet, boastful person. **big noise, shot,** *n.* (*coll.*) a person of importance. **big stick,** *n.* (*coll.*) brutal force. **big talk,** *n.* boasting, bragging. **big time,** *n.* (*coll.*) the highest rank in a profession, esp. in entertainment. **big top,** *n.* a large circus tent. **big-wig,** *n.* (*coll.*) a man of importance (from the large wigs formerly worn). **bigness,** *n.* the quality of being big. [etym. doubtful]

big², *v.t.* (*Sc.*) to build. **bigging,** *n.* the action of building; a building. [Icel. *byggja,* to dwell in, to build (cp. OE *būian, būan,* to dwell, cultivate)]

biga, *n.* a two-horse chariot. [L]

bigamy, *n.* marriage with a second person while a legal spouse is living; (*Eccles. Law*) a second marriage; marriage of or with a widow or widower. **bigamist,** *n.* one who commits bigamy. **bigamous,** *a.* pertaining to or involving bigamy. **bigamously,** *adv.* [F *bigamie,* from OF *bigame,* bigamist, med. L *bigamus* (*bi-,* two, Gr. *gamos,* marriage)]

Big Bertha, *n.* any of three large German howitzer guns that were mounted on railway wagons during World War I.

Big Dipper, *n.* North American nickname for the Plough, the seven brightest and most prominent stars in the constellation Ursa Major.

bigg, big³, *n.* (*Sc.*) four-rowed barley, a variety of *Hordeum hexastichon.* [Icel. *bygg* (OE *bēow,* grain, barley, cp. Gr. *phuein,* Sansk. *bhū,* to grow)]

†**biggin¹,** *n.* a child's cap, a night-cap; the coif of a serjeant-at-law. [F *béguin*]

bigging, biggin'² BIG².

Biggin Hill, *n.* airport in the SE London borough of Bromley. It was the most famous of the Royal Air Force stations in the Battle of Britain in World War II.

bight, *n.* a bending, a bend; a small bay, the space between two headlands; the loop of a rope. [OE *byht* (*būgan,* to bend)]

Bignonia, *n.* a genus of plants, containing the trumpet flower. [after Abbé *Bignon,* 1662–1743, librarian to Louis XIV]

bigot, *n.* a person unreasonably and intolerantly devoted to a particular creed, system or party. **bigoted,** *a.* affected with bigotry. **bigotedly,** *adv.* **bigotry,** *n.* the character, conduct or mental condition of a bigot. [etym. unknown]

Bihar, *n.* (or **Behar**) state of NE India. **area** 173,900 sq km/67,125 sq miles. **capital** Patna. **population** (1981) 69,823,000. **products** copper, iron, coal, rice, jute, sugarcane, grain, oilseed. **language** Hindi, Bihari.

Bijapur, *n.* ancient city in Karnataka, India. It was founded around AD 1489 by Yusuf Adil Shah (died 1511), the son of Murad II, as the capital of the Muslim kingdom of Biafra. The city and kingdom was annexed by the Mughal emperor Aurangzeb in 1686.

bijou, *n.* (*pl.* **bijoux**) a jewel, a trinket; anything that is small, pretty or valuable. **bijouterie,** *n.* jewellery, trinkets. [F, prob. Celtic (Bret. *bizou,* from *biz,* Corn. *bis,* W *bys,* finger)]

bike¹, *n.* a wasps', bees' or hornets' nest; a swarm, a crowd, a rabble. [Sc. and North.; etym. unknown]

bike², *n.* (*coll.*) a bicycle; a motorcycle. *v.i.* to ride a bicycle. **biker,** *n.* (*coll.*) a motorbike enthusiast.

bike³, *n.* (*Austral. sl.*) a prostitute.

bikini¹, *n.* a brief, two-piece swimming costume. [BIKINI atoll]

Bikini[2], *n.* atoll in the Marshall Islands, W Pacific, where the US carried out atom-bomb tests 1946–63. Radioactivity will last there for 100 years.

Biko, *n.* **Steve (Stephen)** (1946–77), South African civil rights leader. An active opponent of apartheid, he was arrested in Sept. 1977 and died in detention six days later.

bilabial, *a.* two-lipped; of or denoting a consonant produced with two lips, e.g. b, p, w. *n.* a bilabial consonant. **bilabiate,** *a.* (*Bot.*) having two lips.

bilateral, *a.* having, arranged on, or pertaining to two sides; affecting two parties. **bilaterally,** *adv.* with or on two sides. [BI-, L *laterālis* (*latus -eris,* side)]

Bilbao, *n.* industrial port (iron and steel, chemicals, cement, food) in N Spain, capital of Biscay province; population (1986) 378,000.

bilberry, *n.* the fruit of a dwarf moorland shrub, *Vaccinium myrtillus,* called also whortleberry and blaeberry; the plant; other species of *Vaccinium.* [prob. from Scand. (cp. Dan. *böllebaer*)]

†**bilbo,** *n.* a rapier, a sword; (*fig.*) a bully, a swashbuckler. [from *Bilbao,* in Spain, where the best weapons were made]

†**bilboes,** *n.pl.* a long iron bar, with sliding shackles for the feet, used to fetter prisoners. [etym. doubtful]

Bildungsroman, *n.* (G.) a novel dealing with the emotional and spiritual education of its central figure.

bile, *n.* a bitter yellowish fluid secreted by the liver to aid digestion; a medical disorder caused by faulty secretion of bile; (*fig.*) anger, choler. **bile-pigment,** *n.* colouring matter existing in bile. **biliary,** *a.* of or pertaining to the bile, to the ducts which convey the bile, to the small intestine, or to the gall-bladder. **bilious,** *a.* biliary; produced or affected by bile; (*fig.*) peevish, ill-tempered. **biliously,** *adv.* **biliousness,** *n.* [F, from L *bīlis,* bile, anger]

bilge, *n.* the bulging part of a cask; the bottom of a ship's floor; that part on which a ship rests when aground; the dirt which collects in the bottom of the hold; bilge-water; (*sl.*) worthless nonsense. *v.i.* to spring a leak; to bulge or swell. *v.t.* to stave in, to cause to spring a leak. **bilge-keel,** *n.* a timber fixed under the bilge to hold a vessel up when ashore and to prevent rolling. **bilge-pump,** *n.* a pump to carry off bilge-water. **bilge-water,** *n.* the foul water that collects in the bilge of a ship. [corr. of BULGE]

Bilharzia, *n.* a genus of trematode worms that are parasitic in the blood of birds, humans and other mammals. **bilharzia, -iasis, -iosis,** *n.* a disease caused by the worm, characterized by blood loss and tissue damage, which is endemic to Asia, Africa and S America. (Also known as SCHISTOSOMIASIS.) [after Theodor *Bilharz,* 1825–62, the parasitologist]

bilingual, *a.* knowing, speaking or composed of two languages; written in two languages. **bilingually,** *adv.* in two languages. **bilinguist,** *n.* one who knows or speaks two languages. [L *bilinguis* (BI-, *lingua,* tongue)]

bilious, biliary, etc. BILE.

bilirubin, *n.* the chief pigment of the bile, a derivative of haemoglobin. [L *bilis,* bile, *ruber,* red]

biliteral, *a.* a philological term applied to roots consisting of two letters.

bilk, *v.t.* to spoil an opponent's score at cribbage; to cheat, to defraud; to evade payment of; to escape from, to elude. *n.* spoiling an opponent's score in cribbage; (*sl.*) a swindler. [etym. doubtful]

bill[1], *n.* the horny beak of birds or of the platypus; a beak-like projection or promontory; the point of the fluke of an anchor. *v.i.* to lay the bills together (as doves); to exhibit affection. **to bill and coo,** to kiss and fondle; to make love. **billed,** *a.* furnished with a beak or bill (usually in comb., as *hard-billed, tooth-billed,* etc.). [OE *bile*]

bill[2], *n.* an obsolete weapon resembling a halberd; a bill-hook. **bill-hook,** *n.* a thick, heavy knife with a hooked end, used for chopping brushwood etc. **billman,** *n.* a soldier armed with a bill. [OE *bil, bill* (cp. G *Bille*)]

bill[3], *n.* a statement of particulars of goods delivered or services rendered; an obsolete name for a PROMISSORY NOTE; a draft of a proposed law; an advertisement or public announcement printed and distributed or posted up; (*Law*) a written statement of a case; a petition to the Scottish Court of Session; (*N Am.*) a bank-note; †a list, an inventory; †a document of any kind. *v.t.* to announce by bills or placards, to cover with bills or placards; to put into a programme; to present an account for payment (to). **bill of exchange,** a written order from one person to another to pay a sum on a given date to a designated person. **bill of fare,** a list of dishes, a menu; (*fig.*) a programme. **bill of health,** a document certifying the health of a ship's company (hence (*fig.*) a **clean bill of health**). **bill of lading,** a master of a ship's acknowledgment of goods received; a list of goods to be shipped. **bill of mortality,** the official return of the deaths (and births) of a district, first published for about 100 parishes in London in 1592 (hence **within the bills of mortality,** within this area). **bill of rights,** a summary of rights and liberties claimed by a people and guaranteed by the state, esp. the English statute of 1689 and the first ten amendments to the US Constitution protecting the freedom of the individual. **bill of sale,** a legal document for the transfer of personal property. **bill of sight,** permission for a merchant to land goods for inspection of which the quantity or quality are unknown to him. **bill of store,** a licence from the customs authorities to ship dutiable goods for consumption on the voyage without payment of duties; a licence to reimport goods formerly exported. **to fill the bill,** to prove satisfactory, to be what is required. **to find a true bill, to ignore a bill,** (*Law*) said of a grand jury when they decide that there is (or is not) sufficient evidence against a prisoner to warrant his/her trial. **to head, top the bill,** to have one's name at the top of a playbill; to be the star attraction. **billboard,** *n.* (*N Am.*) a street hoarding. **bill-broker, -discounter,** *n.* one who deals in bills of exchange and promissory notes. **bill-chamber,** *n.* a department of the Scottish Court of Session for summary proceedings on petition. **bill-fold,** *n.* (*N Am.*) a wallet for notes. **billhead,** *n.* a business form with the name and address of the firm etc. at the top. **billposter, -sticker,** *n.* a person who sticks bills on walls, etc. **billed,** *a.* named in a programme or advertisement. **billing,** *n.* sending out invoices; the relative position of a performer or act in a programme or advertisement. [A-F and ME *bille,* late L *billa,* corr. of *bulla,* a writing, a sealed writing; formerly, a stud or seal)]

billabong, *n.* an effluent from a river; a creek that fills seasonally. [Austral. Abor. *billa,* river, *bong,* dead]

billet[1], *n.* a small paper, a note; a ticket requiring a householder to furnish food and lodgings for a soldier or others; the quarters so assigned; (*coll.*) a situation, an appointment. *v.t.* to quarter soldiers or others. [A-F *billette,* dim. of *bille,* BILL.]

billet[2], *n.* a small log or faggot for firing; a bar, wedge or ingot of gold or silver; (*Arch.*) a short cylindrical piece placed lengthwise at regular intervals in a hollow moulding in Norman work; (*Her.*) a rectangle set on end. [F *billete* (*billot*), dim. of *bille,* a log of wood (etym. unknown)]

billet-doux, *n.* (*pl.* **billets-doux**) a love-letter. [F, a sweet letter]

billiards, *n.pl.* a game with balls, which are driven about on a cloth-lined table with a cue. **billiard-cue,** *n.* a tapering stick used to drive the balls. **billiard-marker,** *n.* one who marks the points made by players; an apparatus for registering these. [F *billard,* a stick, a cue, dim. of *bille,* BILLET[2]]

billingsgate, *n.* scurrilous abuse, foul language. [after *Billingsgate,* the former London fish market]

billion, *n.* formerly in Britain, one million million, i.e. 1,000,000,000,000 or 10^{12}; in the US (and now in Britain and elsewhere this usage is the more common) one thousand million, i.e. 1,000,000,000 or 10^9; (*pl.*) any very large number. **billionaire,** *n.* [F, coined from *million,* with pref. BI-]

billon, *n.* base metal, esp. silver alloyed with copper. [F, base metal, orig. mass, from *bille,* see BILLET[2]]

billow, *n.* a great swelling wave of the sea; (*fig.*) the sea; anything sweeping onward like a mighty wave. *v.i.* to surge; to rise in billows. **billowy,** *a.* characterized by, of the nature of, or like billows. [Icel. *bylgja,* a billow (cp. OE *ballgan,* to swell)]

billy, billie, *n.* (*Sc., N*) fellow, comrade, mate; brother; (*esp. Austral.*) a metal can or pot for boiling water etc. over a campfire. (*N Am.*) a policeman's club. **billy-can,** *n.* (*esp. Austral.*) a billy. **billy goat,** *n.* a male goat. [prob. from the personal name]

billyboy, *n.* a Humber or east-coast boat of river-barge build; a bluff-bowed north-country trader. [etym. unknown]

Billy Bunter, *n.* a fat, bespectacled schoolboy who featured in stories by Frank Richards, set at Greyfriars School. His adventures, in which he attempts to raise enough money to fund his passion for eating, appeared in the children's paper *Magnet* between 1908 and 1940, and subsequently in books in the 1940s and on television during 1952–62.

billycock, *n.* a round, low-crowned felt hat; a wide-awake. [etym. doubtful]

Billy the Kid, nickname of William H. Bonney (1859–81), US outlaw, a leader in the Lincoln County cattle war in New Mexico, who allegedly killed his first man at 12 and 22 people in total. He was sentenced to death for murdering a sheriff, but escaped (killing two guards), and was finally shot by Sheriff Pat Garrett while trying to avoid recapture.

bilobed, bilobate, *a.* having or divided into two lobes.

bilocation, *n.* the state or faculty of being in two places at once.

bilocular, *a.* having two cells or compartments.

biltong, *n.* strips of lean meat dried in the sun. [S Afric. Dut. *bil,* bullock, *tong* tongue]

Bimana, *n.pl.* animals with two hands, as in the higher primates and man. **bimanal, bimanous,** *a.* two-handed; of or belonging to the Bimana. [BI-, L *manus,* a hand]

bimbashi, *n.* a Turkish or Egyptian army officer. [Turk.]

bimbo, *n.* (*sl.*) an attractive person, esp. a woman, who is naive or of limited intelligence; a foolish or stupid person; a whore. [It., a child]

bimensal, bimestrial, *a.* continuing for two months; occurring every two months.

bimeridian, *a.* pertaining to or recurring at midday and midnight.

bimetallism, *n.* the employment of two metals (gold and silver) in the currency of a country, at a fixed ratio to each other, as standard coin and legal tender. **bimetallist,** *n.* a supporter or advocate of bimetallism. **bimetallic,** *a.* composed of two metals; of or pertaining to bimetallism. **bimetallic strip,** *n.* a strip of two metals bonded together which expand by different amounts when heated. [F *bimétallique*]

bimillenary, *n.* a period of two thousand years.

bimonthly, *a.* occurring once in two months; lasting two months.

bin, *n.* (*pres.p.* **binning,** *past, p.p.* **binned**) a box or other receptacle for corn, bread, wine etc.; wine from a particular bin; a large canvas receptacle into which hops are picked; a container for rubbish; (*sl., derog.*) a lunatic asylum. *v.t.* to stow in a bin. **bin-end,** *n.* a bottle of wine sold off cheaply because there are so few left of the bin. **bin-liner,** *n.* a plastic bag used to line a rubbish bin. [OE *binn* (perh. from L *benna,* of Celtic origin)]

binary, *a.* consisting of a pair or pairs; double, dual. **binary compound,** *n.* a chemical compound of two elements. **binary fission,** *n.* the division of a cell into two parts. **binary form,** *n.* a musical composition having two themes or sections. **binary notation,** *n.* a number system using the base two (instead of base ten), numbers being represented as combinations of one and zero: because the two digits can be represented electronically as on and off, the system is used in computers. **binary star, system,** *n.* a system of two stars revolving around a common centre of gravity. [L *bīnārius,* from *bīnī,* two each]

binaural, *a.* relating to, having or using two ears; employing two channels in recording or transmitting sound.

bind, *v.t.* (*past, p.p.* **bound**) to tie, or fasten together, to or on something; to put in bonds, confine; to wrap or confine with a cover or bandage; to form a border to; to cover, secure or strengthen, by means of a band; to sew (a book) and put into a cover; to tie up; to cause to cohere; to make constipated; to oblige to do something by contract; to oblige, to engage, to compel; to confirm or ratify. *v.i.* to cohere; to grow stiff and hard; to tie up; to be obligatory; (*sl.*) to complain. *n.* a band or tie; a bine; a sign which groups notes together; a tie or brace; indurated clay mixed with oxide of iron; (*coll.*) an annoying or frustrating predicament, a bore. **to bind down,** to restrain by formal stipulations. **to bind over,** to place under legal obligation. **bind-weed,** *n.* a plant of the genus *Convolvulus;* several other climbing plants. **binder,** *n.* one who binds; a book-binder; one who binds sheaves; that which binds or fastens; a straw band for binding sheaves of corn; a cover or folder for loose papers, correspondence etc.; a clip; a tie-beam; a bandage; a cementing agent; a principal part of a ship's frame, as the keel, transom, beam, knee etc. **bindery,** *n.* a book-binder's workshop. **binding,** *a.* obligatory. *n.* the act of binding; that which binds; the state of being bound; the act, art or particular style of bookbinding; a book-cover, braid or other edging. **bindingly,** *adv.* **bindingness,** *n.* [OE *bindan* (cp. Goth. *bindan,* G *binden,* Aryan *bhendh*)]

bine, *n.* a flexible shoot or stem, esp. of the hop (cp. WOODBINE). [BIND]

binervate, *a.* having two nerves or leaf-ribs.

Binet-Simon scale, *n.* an intelligence test employing graded tasks for subjects (usually children) according to age. [after Alfred *Binet,* 1857–1911, and Theodore *Simon,* 1873–1961, F psychologists]

bing, *n.* a heap, a pile; (*Mining*) a heap of alum or of metallic ore; a measure (8 cwt.) of lead ore. [Icel. *bingr* (cp. Swed. *binge*)]

binge, *n.* (*coll.*) a drinking spree; overindulgence in anything. [etym. doubtful; perh. dial. *binge,* to soak]

bingo[1], *n.* (*sl.*) brandy. [coined from B (brandy) and STINGO]

bingo[2], *n.* a game in which random numbers are called out and then marked off by players on a card with numbered squares, the winner being the first to mark off all or a predetermined sequence of numbers; an exclamation made by the winner of a bingo game; an exclamation expressing the suddenness of an event. [etym. doubtful]

bink, *n.* (*Sc.*) a bench; a shelf, a dresser; a bank. [ME *benk,* BENCH]

binnacle, *n.* the case in which the ship's compass is kept. [formerly *bittacle,* Sp. *bitacula,* L *habitāculum,* a dwelling-place (*habitāre,* to dwell, freq. of *habēre,* to have, hold)]

binocular, *a.* having two eyes; suited for use by both eyes. *n.* a binocular microscope. **binoculars,** *n.pl.* a field or opera glass with tubes for both eyes.

binomial, *a.* binominal; of or pertaining to binomials; *n.* a mathematical expression consisting of two terms united by the signs + or −. **binomial theorem,** *n.* a formula discovered by Newton by which a binomial quantity can be raised to any power without actual multiplication. **binominal,** *a.* having two names, the first denoting the genus, the second the species. [L *nomen,* a name]

bint, *n.* (*sl. derog.*) a girl or woman. [Arab., lit. daughter]

binturong, *n.* a SE Asian arboreal mammal with a prehensile tail.

bio-, *comb. form.* pertaining to life or living things. [Gr. *bios,* life]

bioastronautics, *n.sing.* the study of the effects of

space travel on living organisms.

biochemistry, *n.* the chemistry of physiological processes occurring in living organisms. **biochemical,** *a.* **biochemist,** *n.*

biocide, *a.* chemical which kills living organisms. **biocidal,** *a.*

biocoenosis, *n.* the relationship between plants and animals that are ecologically interdependent.

biodegradable, *a.* capable of being broken down by bacteria.

bioengineering, *n.* the provision of aids such as artificial limbs, hearts etc. to restore body functions; the design, construction and maintenance of equipment used in biosynthesis.

bioethics, *n.sing.* the study of ethical issues arising from advances in medicine and science.

biofeedback, *n.* a method of regulating involuntary body functions, e.g. heartbeat, by conscious mental control.

biogenesis, biogeny, *n.* the doctrine that living matter originates only from living matter. **biogenetic,** *a.*

biogeography, *n.* the study of the distribution of plant and animal life over the globe.

biograph, *n.* an early name for the cinematograph.

biography, *n.* the history of the life of a person; literature dealing with personal history. **biographer,** *n.* a writer of biography. **biographic, biographical,** *a.* of, pertaining to or containing biography. **biographically,** *adv.* [late Gr. *biographia*]

Bioko, *n.* island in the Bight of Bonny, West Africa, part of Equatorial Guinea; area 2,017 sq km/786 sq miles; produces coffee, cacao and copra; population (1983) 57,190. Formerly a Spanish possession, as Fernando Po, it was known (1973–79) as Macías Nguema Bijogo.

biology, *n.* the science of physical life or living matter in all its phases. **biologic, biological,** *a.* pertaining to biology. **biological clock,** *n.* the inherent mechanism that regulates cyclic physiological processes in living organisms. **biological control,** *n.* the control of pests etc. by using other organisms that destroy them. **biological warfare,** *n.* warfare involving the use of disease germs. **biologist,** *n.*

bioluminescence, *n.* the production of light by living organisms such as insects, marine animals and fungi.

biomass, *n.* the total weight of living organisms in a unit of area.

biomedicine, *n.* the study of the medical and biological effects of stressful environments, esp. space travel.

biometry, *n.* the statistical measurement of biological data. **biometrics,** *n.sing.* **biometric,** *a.* **biometrical,** *a.*

bionics, *n.sing.* the science of applying knowledge of biological systems to the development of electronic equipment; the replacement of parts of the body or enhancement of physiological functions by electrical or mechanical equipment. **bionic,** *a.* of or pertaining to bionics; (science fiction) having exceptional powers through the electronic augmentation of physical processes.

bionomics, *n.sing.* ecology. **bionomic,** *a.*

biont, *n.* a living organism. **biontic,** *a.* **-biont,** *n. comb. form* belonging to a specific environment. **-biontic,** *a. comb. form.* [prob. from Gr. *biount-, biōn, pres.p.* of *bioun,* to live from *bios,* life]

biophysics, *n.sing.* the application of physics to living things.

biopic, *n.* a film, usu. giving a glamorized and uncritical account of the life of a celebrity. [*Bio*graphical *Pic*ture]

bioplasm, *n.* protoplasm; the germinal matter whence all organic matter is developed. **bioplast,** *n.* a nucleus of germinal matter.

biopsy, *n.* (*pl.* **-sies**) the removal and diagnostic examination of tissue or fluids from a living body.

biorhythms, *n.pl.* supposed biological cycles governing physical, emotional and intellectual moods and performance.

bioscope, *n.* a cinematograph; a S African word for CINEMA.

-biosis, *comb. form* a specific mode of life. **-biotic,** *a. comb. form.* [Gr. *biōsis,* way of life]

biosphere, *n.* the portion of the earth's surface and atmosphere which is inhabited by living things.

biosynthesis, *n.* the production of chemical compounds by living organisms. **biosynthetic,** *a.*

biota, *n.* the flora and fauna of a region.

biotechnology, *n.* the use of microorganisms and biological processes in industry.

biotin, *n.* a vitamin of the B complex (also known as vitamin H) found esp. in liver and egg yolk. [G. *biotos,* sustenance]

biparous, *a.* bringing forth two at a birth; producing two at once. [L *parere,* to produce]

bipartite, *a.* comprising or having two parts; affecting or corresponding to two parties (e.g. as an agreement); divided into two corresponding parts from the apex almost to the base (of leaves). **bipartisan,** *a.* involving or supported by two or more (political) parties. **bipartisanship, bipartition,** *n.* division into two.

biped, *a.* having two feet. *n.* an animal having only two feet, as man and birds. **bipedal,** *a.* [L *pes, pedis,* a foot]

bipetalous, *a.* having two petals in a flower.

bipinnaria, *n.* a starfish larva with two bands of cilia.

bipinnate, bipinnated *a.* the term applied to pinnated leaflets of a pinnate leaf.

biplane, *n.* an aircraft with two wings one above the other.

bipolar, *a.* having two poles or opposite extremities.

biquadratic, *a.* raised to the fourth power; of or pertaining to the fourth power. *n.* the fourth power, the square of a square. **biquadratic equation,** *n.* an equation containing the fourth power of the unknown quantity.

birch, *n.* a genus of northern forest trees, *Betula,* with slender limbs and thin, tough bark; the wood of any of these trees; a birch-rod; (*Austral.*) a variety of beech tree; (*N Am.*) a canoe made from the bark of *Betula papyracea;* a rod made from birch twigs for flogging. *a.* birchen. *v.t.* to chastise with a birch-rod; to flog. **birchen,** *a.* composed of birch. **birching,** *n.* a flogging. [OE *birce, beorc* (cp. OHG *biricha,* Sansk. *bhurja,* Icel. *björk,* Sc. *birk*)]

bird[1], *n.* any feathered vertebrate animal; (*sl.*) a girl, young woman; (*sl.*) a prison term; (*coll.*) a person. **a bird in the hand is worth two in the bush,** possession is better than expectation. **birds of a feather,** persons of similar tastes or proclivities. **strictly for the birds,** worthless, not serious. **to get the bird,** to be hissed, hence fired or dismissed. **to kill two birds with one stone,** to achieve two aims with a single effort. **bird of paradise,** *n.* any of the New Guinea Paradisidea which have brilliantly coloured plumage. **bird of passage,** *n.* a migratory bird: a person who travels frequently and rarely stays long in one place. **bird of peace,** *n.* (*fig.*) the dove. **bird of prey,** *n.*, a bird such as the hawk or vulture which feeds on carrion or hunts other animals for food. **birdbath,** *n.* a small usu. ornamental basin for birds to bathe in. **bird-brained,** *a.* (*coll.*) stupid, silly. **birdcage,** *n.* a wire or wicker cage for holding birds. **birdcall,** *n.* the cry of a bird; an instrument for imitating the cry of birds. **bird-catcher,** *n.* a professional trapper of birds. **bird-catching,** *n.*, *a.* (applied to some plants (of) the trapping of birds and insects). **bird-fancier,** *n.* one who collects, breeds or rears birds. **bird-lime,** *n.* a sticky substance used to snare birds. **bird-seed,** *n.* special seed (hemp, canary, millet etc.) given to cagebirds. **bird's-eye,** *a.* of, belonging to or resembling a bird's eye; having eye-like marking; seen from above, as by the eye of a bird esp. in **bird's-eye view,** *n.* a kind of tobacco in which the ribs of the leaves are cut with the fibre; a popular name for several plants with small, round, bright flowers; the germander speed-well. **bird's-eye primrose,** *n.* an English wild plant, the mealy primrose, *Primula farinosa.* **bird's-foot, bird-foot,** *n.* a popular name for certain plants etc., e.g. *Cheilanthes radiata,* a small fern widely distributed. **bird's-foot sea-star,** *n.* a British echinoderm, *Palmipes membranaceus.* **bird's-foot**

trefoil, *n.* a British wild flower, *Lotus corniculatus.* **bird's-nest,** *n.* the nest of a bird; an edible bird's-nest; a cask or other shelter for the lookout man at the masthead. *v.i.* to search for birds'-nests. **bird's-nest fern,** *n.* name of several exotic ferns. **bird's-nest orchid,** *n. Neottia nidus-avis,* a British orchid. **bird's-tongue,** *n.* a popular name for several plants, probably from the shape of their leaves. **bird-nesting,** *n.* seeking birds' nests to steal the eggs. **bird strike,** *n.* a collision of a bird with an aircraft. **bird table,** *n.* a small elevated platform for wild birds to feed from. **bird-watcher,** *n.* one who observes wild birds in their natural habitat. **bird-watching,** *n.* **birdie**, *n.* a little bird (used as a term of endearment); a hole in golf made in one under par. **birding,** *n.* bird-catching; fowling, bird-watching. *a.* pertaining to or used in fowling, bird-catching or bird-watching. **birding-piece,** *n.* a fowling-piece. [OE *brid,* a bird, the young of any bird (etym. doubtful)]

Bird[2], *n.* **Isabella** (1832–1904), British traveller and writer who wrote extensively of her journeys in the US, Persia, Tibet, Kurdistan, China, Japan, and Korea.

Birdseye, *n.* **Clarence** (1886–1956), US inventor who pioneered food refrigeration processes. While working as a fur trader in Labrador in 1912–16 he was struck by the ease with which food could be preserved in an Arctic climate. Back in the US he found that the same effect could be obtained by rapidly freezing prepared food between two refrigerated metal plates.

birefringence, *n.* the formation of two unequally refracted rays of light from a single unpolarized ray. **birefringent,** *a.*

bireme, *n.* a Roman galley with two banks of oars. *a.* having two banks of oars. [L *birēmis* (BI-, *rēmus,* oar)]

biretta, *n.* a square cap worn by clerics of the Roman Catholic and Anglican Churches. [It. *berretta,* late L *birretum* (*birrus, byrrhus,* a mantle with a hood, prob. from Gr. *purrhos,* flame-coloured)]

biriani, biryani, *n.* an Indian dish of spiced rice mixed with meat or fish. [Urdu]

birk, BIRCH.

Birkenhead, *n.* **Frederick Edwin Smith, 1st Earl of Birkenhead** (1872–1930), British Conservative politician. A flamboyant character, known as 'FE', he joined with Baron Carson in organizing armed resistance in Ulster to Irish Home Rule; he was Lord Chancellor (1919–22), and a much criticized secretary for India during 1924–28.

birkie, *n.* (*Sc., sometimes derog.*) a man, a fellow; a card game. *a.* (*Sc.*) gay, spirited; active. [etym. doubtful]

birl, *v.i.* to spin round, to rotate noisily. *v.t.* to spin; to throw, toss. [probably onomat.]

birle, *v.t.* (*Sc.*) to ply with drink. *v.i.* to carouse. †**birler,** *n.* (*Sc.*) one who carries round drink. **birling,** *n.* the pouring out of drink; carousing. [OE *byrelian,* to give drink (*byrele, byrle,* cup-bearer)]

Birmingham[1], *n.* industrial city in the West Midlands, second largest city of the UK; population (1986) 1,006,527, metropolitan area 2,632,000. Industries include motor vehicles, machine tools, aerospace control systems, plastics, chemicals, food.

Birmingham[2], *n.* industrial city (iron, steel, chemicals, building materials, computers, cotton textiles) and commercial centre in Alabama, US; population (1980) 847,500.

Biro®, *n.* (*pl.* **-ros**) a type of ballpoint pen.

Biro, *n.* **Lazlo** (1900–85), Hungarian-born Argentinian who invented a ballpoint pen in 1944. His name became generic for ballpoint pens in the UK.

birostrate, birostrated, *a.* having two beaks or beak-like processes.

birr, *n.* momentum, rush; strength, exertion; emphasis in pronunciation, energetic stress; a whirring sound. [Icel. *byrr,* a favourable wind]

birse, *n.* (*Sc.*) bristle. **to lick the birse,** to pass a bunch of hog's bristle through the mouth, as in the ceremony of being made a soutar or citizen of Selkirk. **to set up the birse,** to raise someone's anger; to put someone's back up. [OE *byrst* (see BRISTLE)]

birsle, *v.t.* (*Sc.*) to scorch, to toast. [etym. doubtful]

birth, *n.* the act of bringing forth; the bearing of offspring; the act of coming into life or being born; that which is brought forth; parentage, extraction, lineage, esp. high extraction, high lineage; condition resulting from birth; origin, beginning, product, creation. **birth certificate,** *n.* an official document giving particulars of one's birth. **birth control,** *n.* the artificial control of reproduction, esp. by means of contraceptives. **birthday,** *n.* the day on which one was born, or its anniversary. *a.* pertaining to the day of one's birth, or to its anniversary. **birthday-book,** *n.* a kind of diary with spaces for noting the birthdays of relatives and friends. **birthday honours,** *n.pl.* knighthoods, peerages and other honours conferred on the sovereign's birthday. **birthday present,** *n.* a present given on one's birthday. **birthday-suit,** (*coll.*) *n.* bare skin; nudity. **birthmark,** *n.* a mark or blemish formed on the body of a child at or before birth. **birthplace,** *n.* the place at which someone or something was born. **birthrate,** *n.* the percentage of births to the population. **birthright,** *n.* rights belonging to an eldest son, to a member of a family, order or people, or to a person as a human being. [ME *byrthe,* Icel. *byrthr, burthr* (OTeut. *beran,* to bear]

Birtwistle, *n.* **Harrison** (1934–), English avant-garde composer. He has specialized in chamber music: for example, his chamber opera *Punch and Judy* (1967) and *Down by the Greenwood Side* (1969).

bis, *adv.* encore, again; twice (indicating that something occurs twice). [F, It., L *bis,* twice]

Biscay, Bay of, bay of the Atlantic Ocean between N Spain and W France, known for rough seas and exceptionally high tides.

Biscayan, *a.* pertaining to Biscay. *n.* a native of Biscay; †a heavy musket mounted on a pivot; †a ball from this. [*Biscay,* province of Spain]

biscuit, *n.* thin flour-cake baked until it is highly dried; pottery moulded and baked in an oven, but not glazed. *a.* light brown in colour. **to take the biscuit,** (*coll.*) to be the best of the lot; to be incredible. [OF *bescoit* (F **biscuit**), L *bis coctus;* twice cooked (*coctus* p.p. of *coquere*)]

bise, *n.* a keen, dry, northerly wind prevalent in Switzerland and adjacent countries. [F (med. L and Prov. *bisa,* OHG *bīsa*)]

bisect, *v.t.* to divide into two (equal) parts. *v.i.* to fork. **bisection,** *n.* division into two (generally equal) parts; division into two branches. **bisector,** *n.* one who bisects; a bisecting line. [BI-, L *sectum,* p.p. of *secāre* to cut]

biserial, biseriate, *a.* arranged in two rows.

bisexual, *a.* having both sexes combined in one individual; attracted sexually to both sexes; of or relating to both sexes. **bisexual,** *n.* **bisexuality**, *n.*

bishop[1], *n.* a spiritual superintendent in the early Christian Church; a dignitary presiding over a diocese, ranking beneath an archbishop, and above the priests and deacons; a beverage composed of wine, oranges and sugar; a piece in chess, having the upper part shaped like a mitre. [OE *biscop,* L *episcopus,* Gr. *episkopos,* an overlooker, an inspector] **bishop's-cap,** *n.* the genus *Mitella,* or mitre-wort. **bishop's court,** *n.* an ecclesiastical court held in the cathedral of each diocese. **bishop's weed,** *n. Aegopodium podagraria;* the umbelliferous genus *Ammi.* **bishopric,** *n.* the diocese, jurisdiction or office of a bishop. [OE *bisceoprīce* (*rice,* dominion, cp. G *Reich*]

bishop[2], *v.t.* to tamper with the teeth (of a horse) so as to conceal its age. [from proper name]

Bishop[3], *n.* **Ronald Eric** (1903–89), British aircraft designer. He joined the de Havilland Aircraft Company (1931) as an apprentice, and designed the Mosquito bomber, the Vampire fighter, and the Comet jet airliner.

bisk BISQUE[1].

bismar, *n.* (*Sc.*) a steelyard in Orkney and Shetland and NE Scotland. [*Sc.* from Dan. *bismer*]

Bismarck, *n.* **Otto Eduard Leopold, Prince von Bismarck** (1815–98), German politician, prime minister of Prussia (1862–90) and chancellor of the German Empire (1871–90). He pursued an aggressively expansionist policy, with wars against Denmark (1863–64), Austria (1866), and France (1870–71), which brought about the unification of Germany.

Bismarck Archipelago, *n.* group of over 200 islands in SW Pacific Ocean, part of Papua New Guinea; area 49,660 sq km/19,200 sq miles. Largest island New Britain.

bismillah, *int.* in the name of Allah. [Arab.]

bismuth, *n.* a reddish white crystalline metallic element (at. no. 83; chem. symb. Bi), used in alloys and in medicine. [G, more commonly *Wismut*]

bison, *n.* a large bovine mammal with a shaggy coat and a large hump; the European bison, now very rare; the American bison, commonly called buffalo, once found in great numbers in the mid-Western prairies. [L, from OTeut. *wisand* (cp. OE *wesend,* OHG *wismit,* G *Wisent*)]

bisque¹, *n.* a rich soup made by boiling down fish, birds or the like.

bisque², *n.* in tennis, golf etc. a stroke allowed at any time to the weaker party to equalize the players. [F, etym. doubtful]

bisque³, *n.* a kind of unglazed white porcelain used for statuettes. [BISCUIT].

Bissau, *n.* capital and chief port of Guinea-Bissau, on an island at the mouth of the Geba river; population (1988) 125,000. Originally a fortified slave-trading centre, Bissau became a free port 1869.

bissextile, *a.* of or pertaining to leap-year. *n.* leap-year. [L *bissextīlis annus,* the bissextile year (a term applied to every fourth year, because then the sixth day before the calends of March was reckoned twice)]

bistort, *n.* a plant with a twisted root, and spike of flesh-coloured flowers, *Polygonum bistorta,* called also *snakeweed*. [L *bistorta* (*bis,* twice, *torta tortus,* p.p. of *torquere,* to twist)]

bistoury, *n.* a small instrument used for making incisions; a scalpel. [F *bistouri,* etym. doubtful]

bistre, *n.* a transparent brownish yellow pigment prepared from soot. *a.* coloured like this pigment. **bistred,** *a.* coloured with or as with bistre. [F, etym. doubtful]

bistro, *n.* (*pl.* **-tros**) a small bar or restaurant. [F]

bisulcate, *a.* (*Zool.*) having cloven hoof.

bit¹, *n.* †a bite, a piece bitten off; †as much as can be bitten off at once; hence, a small portion; a morsel, a fragment; the smallest quantity, a whit, a jot; a brief period of time; a small coin (usually with the value expressed, as a **threepenny-bit**); (*N Am.*) an eighth of a dollar. (*coll.*) a poor little thing; somewhat or something of. **a bit,** a little; rather, somewhat. **a bit of muslin, bit of stuff,** (*sl.*) a young woman. **bit by bit,** gradually, piece-meal. **every bit,** quite, entirely. **to do one's bit,** to do one's share. **bit (-part),** *n.* a small role in a play. **bit-player,** *n.* an actor who plays small parts. **bittock** , *n.* (*Sc.*) a little bit; a small portion; a short distance. **bitty,** *a.* scrappy, disjointed, piecemeal; lacking unity. [OE *bita,* a bit, a morsel (cp. OFris. *bita,* Dut. *beet,* bit, OHG *bizzo,* biting, G *Bisse*), from *bitan,* to bite]

bit², *n.* a bite, the act of biting; the iron part of the bridle inserted in the mouth of a horse; the cutting part of a tool; the movable boring-piece in a drill; the part of the key at right angles to the shank; short sliding piece of tube in a cornet for modifying the tone etc. *v.t.* to furnish with, or accustom (a horse) to, a bit; to restrain. **a bit and a sup,** something to bite and drink. **to draw bit,** to stop a horse by pulling the reins; (*fig.*) to stop to slacken speed. **to take the bit in one's teeth,** to hold the bit between the teeth; to become unmanageable. [OE *bite,* bite, biting (cp. OFris. *bit, biti,* Dut. *beet,* OHG *biz,* a piece bitten off, G *Bisz,* biting)]

bit³, *n.* in binary notation, either of two digits, one or zero, a unit of information in computers and information theory representing either of two states, such as *on* and *off*. [*B*inary Dig*it*]

bitch, *n.* the female of the dog; a female of allied species; (*sl., derog.*) an offensive, malicious or spiteful woman; (*sl.*) a complaint; (*sl.*) an awkward problem. *v.i.* (*sl.*) to moan, complain. *v.t.* (*sl.*) to mess up, botch. **bitchy,** *a.* of or like a bitch, spiteful; ill-tempered. **bitchily,** *adv.* **bitchiness,** *n.* [OE *bicce* (etym. doubtful)]

bite, *v.t.* (*past* **bit**, *p.p.* **bitten**) to seize, nip, rend, cut, pierce or crush anything with the teeth; to cut, to wound; to affect with severe cold; to cause to smart; to inflict sharp physical or mental pain on; to wound with reproach or sarcasm; to hold fast, as an anchor or screw; to corrode; to cheat, to trick. *v.i.* to have a habit, or exercise the power, of biting; to sting, to be pungent; to take a bait; to act upon something (of weapons, tools etc.). *n.* the act of biting; a wound made by the teeth; a mouthful, a small quantity; a piece seized or detached by biting; a hold, a grip; †a cheat, a trick, a fraud; a trickster; one who cheats. **to bite in,** to corrode or eat into by means of a chemical agent, esp. to eat out the lines of an engraving with acid. **to bite off,** to seize with the teeth and detach. **to bite off more than one can chew,** to undertake more than one can manage. **to bite someone's head off,** (*coll.*) to snap at someone; to be irritable. **to bite the bullet,** to submit to an unpleasant situation; to face up to something. **to bite the dust,** to be slain in battle, to die. **to bite the lip,** to press the lip between the teeth so as to prevent the expression of one's feelings. **to bite the hand that feeds one,** to be ungrateful. **biter,** *n.* one who or that which bites; (*fig.*) a trickster, a cheat. **the biter bit,** the cheater cheated. **biting,** *a.* sharp, keen; acrid, pungent; stinging, caustic, sarcastic. **bitingly,** *adv.* **bitten with,** infected by (a passion, mania etc.). **bitten,** *a.* [OE *bītan* (cp. Icel. *bīta,* OTeut. *bītan,* G *beissen,* L *fid- findere,* to cut)]

Bithynia, *n.* district of NW Asia which became a Roman province in 74 BC.

bitt, *n.* a strong post fixed in pairs on the deck of a ship for fastening cables, belaying ropes etc. *v.t.* to put around a bitt. hence prob. **bitter end,** *n.* the loose end of a belayed rope; the last extremity. [etym. doubtful]

bitten, *p.p.* BITE.

bitter, *a.* sharp or biting to the taste; acrid, harsh, virulent, piercingly cold; painful, distressing, mournful. *n.* anything bitter; bitterness; (*coll.*) bitter beer; *pl.* liquors flavoured with bitter herbs etc., used as appetizers or stomachics. *v.t.* to make bitter. **to the bitter end** BITT. **bitter-almond,** *n.* a bitter variety of the common almond, *Amygdalus communis*. **bitter-cup,** *n.* a cup made of quassia wood which imparts a bitter taste to water poured into it. **bitter-sweet,** *a.* sweet with a bitter after-taste; pleasant with admixture of unpleasantness or sadness. *n.* a kind of apple; woody nightshade, *Solanum dulcamara*. **bitter-sweeting,** *n.* the bitter-sweet apple. **bitter-vetch,** *n.* a popular name for some species of the genus *Vicia*. **bitterwort,** *n.* the yellow gentian, *G lutea;* other species of *Gentiana*. **bitterish,** *a.* **bitterly,** *adv.* **bitterness,** *n.* [OE *biter* (prob. from *bitan,* to bite)]

bittern¹, *n.* the liquid obtained when sea-water is evaporated to extract the salt. [BITTER].

bittern², *n.* a wading bird smaller than a heron; the genus *Botaurus,* esp. *B stellaris,* the common bittern. [ME *bitore,* OF *butor* (etym. doubtful; prob. from the bird's cry)]

bittock BIT¹.

bitumen, *n.* any of various solid or sticky mixtures of hydrocarbons that occur naturally or as a residue from petroleum distillation, e.g. tar, asphalt. **bitume**, *v.t.* to smear with bitumen. **bituminiferous**, *a.* yielding bitumen. **bituminize, -ise**, *v.t.* to impregnate with or convert into, bitumen. **bituminization, -isation,** *n.* the art, process, or state of conversion into bitumen. **bituminous**, *a.* of the nature of, resembling, or impregnated with bitumen. [L]

bivalent, *a.* having a valency of two; (of homologous chromosomes) associated in pairs.

bivalve, *a.* having two shells or valves which open and shut. *n.* a mollusc which has its shell in two opposite directions connected by a ligament and hinge, as the oyster; a bivalve seed-capsule. **bivalved, bivalvular,** *a.* bivalve.

bivious, *a.* leading two different ways. [L *via,* a way]

bivouac, *n.* †a night watch by an army against sudden attack; a temporary encampment in the field without tents etc.; the scene of such an encampment. *v.i.* (*past, p.p.* **bivouacked**) to remain in the open air without tents or other covering. [F, from G *Beiwache,* a watch, keeping guard]

biweekly, *a., adv.* occurring once a fortnight; occurring twice a week. *n.* a periodical appearing every two weeks.

biz, *n.* (*coll.*) business, work, employment. [short for BUSINESS]

bizarre, *a.* odd, whimsical, fantastic, eccentric; of mixed or discordant style; irregular, in bad taste. **bizarrely,** *adv.* **bizarreness,** *n.* [F (cp. Sp. *bizarro,* handsome, gallant; It. *bizzarro*]

Bizet, *n.* **Georges (Alexandre César Léopold)** (1838–75), French composer of operas, among them *Les Pêcheurs de perles/The Pearl Fishers* (1863), and *La jolie Fille de Perth/The Fair Maid of Perth* (1866). He also wrote the concert overture *Patrie* and incidental music to Daudet's *L'Arlésienne*. His operatic masterpiece *Carmen* was produced a few months before his death in 1875.

Bjelke-Patterson, *n.* **Joh(annes)** (1911–), Australian right-wing politician, leader of the Queensland National Party (QNP) and premier of Queensland 1968–87.

Bk, (*chem. symb.*) berkelium.

bk, (*abbr.*) bank; book.

BL, (*abbr.*) Bachelor of Law; Bachelor of Letters; Barrister-at-Law; British Legion; British Library.

blab, *v.t.* to tell or reveal indiscreetly; to betray. *v.i.* to talk indiscreetly, to tell tales or secrets; to tattle. *n.* a chatterer, babbler; a tell- tale; babbling, tale-telling. **blabber,** *n.* one who blabs; a tell-tale, a tattler. [ME *blobbe*]

black[1]**,** *a.* intensely dark in colour (the opposite of white); destitute of light; obscure; dirty; angry; dark-skinned, of or pertaining to the Negro race (often offensive but accepted in many countries); wearing black clothes, uniform or armour; sombre, gloomy, dirty; denoting total absence of colour due to absence or entire absorption of light; atrociously wicked; disastrous, dismal, mournful; subject to a trade-union ban. *n.* the darkest of all colours (the opposite of white); a black pigment or dye; a member of a dark-skinned race, a Negro, W Indian, Austral. Aborigine etc (often offensive but accepted in many countries esp. **Black**); mourning garments; a minute particle of soot or dirt; *v.t.* to blacken; to soil; to place under a trade-union ban. **black-and-blue,** *a.* discoloured by beating; livid. **black-and-white,** *n.* printed or written matter; a photograph, drawing etc., in black and white or shades of grey; visual images reproduced in black and white, esp. by photography or television. *a.* monochrome as opposed to colour (television); divided into two extremes, not admitting of compromise. **black art,** *n.* magic, necromancy [from idea that NECROMANCY was connected with L *niger,* black]. **blackball,** *n.* vote of rejection in a ballot. *v.t.* to vote against; to exclude; to dislike, bar. [from the black ball sometimes used to indicate a vote against in a ballot]. **black-beetle,** *n.* a cockroach, *Blatta orientalis*. **black belt,** *n.* a belt awarded for highest proficiency in judo, karate etc.; one entitled to wear this. **blackberry,** *n.* the common bramble, *Rubus fruticosus* or *discolor;* its fruit. **blackberrying,** *n.* gathering blackberries. **blackbird,** *n.* a species of European thrush, the male of which has black plumage and an orange beak; any of several dark plumaged American birds; a captive African or Polynesian. **black-birding,** *n.* the kidnapping of Africans or Polynesian natives for slavery. **blackboard,** *n.* a board painted black used by teachers and lecturers to write and draw on. **black body,** *n.* a hypothetical body which absorbs all radiation falling upon it, and reflects none. **black book,** *n.* a book on the black art; a book recording the names of persons liable to censure or punishment. **to be in someone's black books,** to be in disgrace. **black box,** *n.* a closed unit in an electronic system whose circuitry remains hidden from the user and is irrelevant to understanding its function; (*coll.*) FLIGHT RECORDER. **black bread,** *n.* rye bread. **black-browed,** *a.* dark, gloomy; threatening, forbidding. **black buck,** *n.* a common Indian antelope. **black butt,** *n.* any of several Australian Eucalyptus trees used as timber. **black cap,** *n.* formerly a cap worn by judges in full dress, and put on when pronouncing sentence of death; the popular name of many English birds having the top of the head black, esp. the **black-cap warbler,** *Curruca atricapilla*. **black coat,** *n.* a familiar name for a clergyman. **black-cock,** *n.* the male of the black grouse or black game; the heathcock, *Tetrao tetrix*. **black cod,** (*New Zealand*) a local variety of cod-fish. **black coffee,** *n.* coffee without milk or cream. **black comedy,** *n.* a play or film in which grotesque humour or farce serves to underline and expose true reality. **black-currant,** *n.* a well-known garden bush, *Ribes nigrum,* and its fruit. **black earth,** *n.* a fertile soil covering regions in southern USSR north of the Black Sea. **black economy,** *n.* illegal and undeclared economic activity. **black eye,** *n.* an eye of which the iris is very dark; discoloration produced by a blow upon the parts round the eye. **black-face,** *n.* a black-faced sheep or other animal. **black-fellow,** *n.* (*derog., offensive*) an Aboriginal of Australia. **black-fish,** *n.* a salmon just after spawning; a popular name for several species of fish; in Australia, a small species of whale. **black flag,** *n.* a flag of black cloth used as a sign that no quarter will be given or taken, as an ensign by pirates, and as the signal for an execution. **blackfly,** *n.* a black aphid that infests beans and other plants. **Blackfoot,** *n.* one of a tribe of North American Indians, called Blackfeet from their dark moccasins. **black friar,** *n.* a Dominican friar; (*pl.*) the quarter of a town where the Dominicans had their convent (the name still survives in London and some other places). **black game,** *n.* BLACK-COCK. **blackguard,** *n.* †a body of menials in charge of the kitchen utensils in a royal household; *pl.* †a low, worthless rabble; a low, worthless fellow; a scoundrel. *a.* of or pertaining to the lowest class; scurrilous, abusive. *v.t.* to revile in scurrilous language. *v.i.* to act the part of a blackguard; to behave in a riotous or indecent manner. **blackguardism,** *n.* the language or actions of a blackguard. **blackguardly,** *a., adv.* **black-head,** *n.* various birds with dark plumage on the head; a pimple with a black head. **black-hearted,** *a.* wicked; having a wicked heart. **black-hole,** *n.* a punishment cell; the guardroom; a hypothetical celestial region formed from a collapsed star, surrounded by a strong gravitational field from which no matter or energy can escape. **black ice,** *n.* a thin layer of transparent ice on roads. **black-jack,** *n.* a large leather jug for beer; (*N Am.*) a loaded stick, a bludgeon; pontoon or a similar card game. **blacklead,** *n.* plumbago or graphite, made into pencils, also used to polish ironwork. *v.t.* to colour or rub with blacklead. **blackleg,** *n.* a gambler and cheat, a swindler, esp. on the turf; a workman who works for an employer when his comrades are on strike, a scab. **black-letter,** *n.* the Old English or Gothic as distinguished from the Roman character; *a.* written or printed in this character. **black light,** *n.* invisible infrared or ultraviolet light. **blacklist,** *n.* a list of persons in disgrace, or who have incurred censure or punishment. *v.t.* to ban or prohibit books etc. **black magic** BLACK ART. **blackmail,** *n.* a tribute formerly exacted by free-booting chiefs in return for protection or immunity from plunder; (*fig.*) any payment extorted by intimidation or pressure. *v.t.* to levy blackmail on. **blackmailer,** *n.* one who levies blackmail. **Black Maria,** *n.* a prison van. **black mark,** *n.* a note of disgrace put against one's name. **black market,** *n.* illegal buying and selling of rationed goods. **black-martin,** *n.* the swift, *Cypselus* *apus*. **black mass,** *n.* a travesty of the Mass performed by diabolists. **black monks,** *n.pl.* the Benedictines, from the colour of their habit. **blackout,** *n.* the extinguishing or concealment of lights against air attack; a temporary loss of consciousness, sight or memory; an electrical power failure or cut; an interruption or suppression of broadcasting, communications etc. *v.t.* to cause a blackout; to censor or suppress (a broadcast etc.). *v.i.* to suffer a temporary loss of consciousness, sight or memory. **black-pudding,** *n.* a kind of sausage made with blood, rice and chopped fat. **Black Rod,** *n.* the chief usher of the Lord Chamberlain's department, of the House of Lords and of the Garter. **black sheep,** *n.* a bad member of a group or family. **blacksmith,** *n.* a smith who works in iron. **black-snake,** *n.* (*N Am.*) a large non-poisonous snake; any of several Old World venomous snakes. **black spot,** *n.* an area of a road where accidents are common; any dangerous area. **blackstrap,** *n.* an inferior kind of port wine; a mixture of rum and treacle. **blackthorn,** *n.* the sloe, *Prunus spinosa,* so called from the dark colour of the bark; a walking-stick or cudgel of its wood. **black tie,** *a.* denoting an occasion when a dinner jacket and black bow tie should be worn. **black tracker,** (*Austral.*) an Aboriginal used in tracking escaped criminals or lost travellers. **black velvet,** *n.* a mixture of stout and champagne or cider. **blackwash,** *n.* (*Med.*) a lotion made from lime-water and mercury. **Black Watch,** *n.* the 42nd Highland Regiment, from the colour of their tartan. **blackwater fever,** *n.* a form of malaria disease in which the urine is very dark in colour. **black widow,** *n.* a venomous American and Far Eastern spider, of which the female has a black body. **blackish,** *a.* **blacken,** *v.t.* to make black, to darken; to sully, to defame. *v.i.* to become black. **blacking,** *n.* the action of making black; a composition for giving a shining black polish to boots and shoes, harness etc. **blackness,** *n.* [OE *blæc* (OHG *blah, blach;* perh. cognate with Gr. *phlegein,* L *flagrāre* to burn)]

Black[2], *n.* **Joseph** (1728–99), Scottish physicist and chemist, who in 1754 discovered carbon dioxide (which he called 'fixed air'). By his investigations in 1761 of latent heat and specific heat, he laid the foundation for the work of his pupil James Watt.

Black and Tans, *n.pl.*, nickname of a specially raised force of military police employed by the British in 1920–21 to combat the Sinn Feiners (Irish nationalists) in Ireland; the name was derived from the colours of the uniforms.

Blackburn, *n.* industrial town (engineering) in Lancashire, England, 32 km/20 miles NW of Manchester; population (1981) 88,000.

Black Country, *n.* central area of England, around and to the north of Birmingham. Heavily industrialized, it gained its name in the 19th century from its belching chimneys, but pollution laws have given it a changed aspect.

Black Death, *n.* modern name (first used in England in the early 19th century) for the great epidemic of bubonic plague that ravaged Europe in the 14th century, killing between one third and one half of the population. The cause of the Black Death was the bacterium *Pasteurella pestis*, transmitted by rat fleas.

Blackfoot, *n.* member of a Plains Indian people who now live predominantly in Saskatchewan, Canada. Their name is derived from their black moccasins, and their language belongs to the Algonquian family.

Black Forest, *n.* (German **Schwarzwald**) mountainous region of coniferous forest in Baden-Württemberg, West Germany. Bounded west and south by the Rhine, which separates it from the Vosges, it has an area of 4,660 sq km/1,800 sq miles and rises to 1,493 m/4,905 ft in the Feldberg. Parts of the forest have recently been affected by acid rain.

Black Hole of Calcutta, incident in Anglo-Indian history: according to tradition Suraj-ud-Dowlah, the nawab of Bengal, confined 146 British prisoners on the night of 20 June 1756 in one small room, of whom only 23 allegedly survived. Later research reduced the deaths to 43, a result of negligence rather than intention.

Black Monday, *n.* a worldwide stockmarket crash that began 19 Oct. 1987, prompted by the announcement of worse-than-expected US trade figures and the response by US Secretary of the Treasury Baker who indicated that the sliding dollar needed to decline further. This caused a world panic as fears of the likely impact of a US recession were voiced by the major industrialized countries. The total paper loss on the London Stock Exchange and other City of London institutions was £94 billion. The expected world recession did not, however, occur.

Blackmore, *n.* **R(ichard) D(oddridge)** (1825–1900), English novelist, author of *Lorna Doone* (1869), a romance set on Exmoor, SW England, in the late 17th century.

Black Muslim, *n.* member of a religious group founded (1929) in the US and led from 1934 by Elijah Muhammad (1897–1975) (then Elijah Poole) after a vision of Allah. Its growth from 1946 as a black separatist organization was due to Malcolm X (1926–65), son of a Baptist minister, who in 1964 broke away and founded his own Organization for Afro-American Unity, preaching 'active self-defence'.

Black National State, *n.* an area in the Republic of South Africa set aside for development to self-government by black Africans in accordance with apartheid. Before 1980 these areas were known as black homelands or **bantustans**. They make up less than 14% of the country; tend to be in arid areas, though some have mineral wealth; and may be in scattered blocks. Those that have so far reached nominal independence are Transkei (1976), Bophuthatswana (1977), Venda (1979), and Ciskei (1981). They are not recognized outside South Africa because of their racial basis, and 11 million blacks live permanently in the country's white-designated areas.

Blackpool, *n.* seaside resort in Lancashire, England, 45 km/28 miles north of Liverpool; population (1981) 148,000. Amusement facilities include 11 km/7 miles of promenades, known for their 'illuminations' of coloured lights, fun fairs, and a tower 152 m/500 ft high.

Black Power, *n.* a movement towards black separatism in the US during the 1960s, embodied in the **Black Panther Party** founded 1966 by Huey Newton and Bobby Seale. Its ultimate aim was the establishment of a separate black state in the US established by a black plebiscite under the aegis of the UN. Following a National Black Political Convention in 1972, a National Black Assembly was established to exercise pressure on the Democratic and Republican parties.

Black Prince, *n.* name given to Edward, Prince of Wales, eldest son of Edward III of England.

Black Sea, *n.* (Russian **Chernoye More**) inland sea in SE Europe, linked with the seas of Azov and Marmara, and via the Dardanelles with the Mediterranean. Uranium deposits beneath it are among the world's largest.

Black September, *n.* a guerrilla splinter group of the Palestine Liberation Organization formed in 1970. Operating from bases in Syria and the Lebanon, it was responsible for the kidnap attempts at the Munich Olympics in 1972 which led to the deaths of 11 Israelis, and more recent hijack and bomb attempts carried out by individuals such as Leila Khaled.

Blackshirts, *n.pl.* term widely used to describe fascist paramilitary organizations. Originating with Mussolini's fascist Squadristi in the 1920s, it was also applied to the Nazi SS (Schutzstaffel) and to the members of Oswald Mosley's British Union of Fascists.

Black Stone, *n.* in Islam, sacred stone built into the east corner of the Kaaba which is a focal point of the *hajj*, or pilgrimage, to Mecca. There are a number of stories concerning its origin, one of which states that it was sent to Earth at the time of the first man, Adam; Mohammed declared that it was given to Abraham by Gabriel. It has been suggested that it is of meteoric origin.

Blackstone, *n.* **William** (1723–80), English jurist, who published his *Commentaries on the Laws of England* 1765–70. Called to the Bar in 1746, he became professor of law at Oxford in 1758, and a Justice of the Court of Common Pleas in 1770.

Black Stump, the, in Australia, an imaginary boundary between civilization and the outback, as in the phrase *this side of the black stump*.

Black Thursday, *n.* name given to the day of the Wall Street stock market crash 29 Oct. 1929, which was followed by the worst economic depression in US history.

Blackwell, *n.* **Elizabeth** (1821–1910), First British woman to qualify in medicine, in 1849.

blad, blaud, *v.t.* (*Sc.*) to hit a thumping blow. *v.i.* to strike smartly. *n.* a thumping blow; a thumping piece. [prob. onomat.]

bladder, *n.* a membranous bag in the animal body which receives the urine; any similar membranous bag (usually with distinctive epithet, as *gall-*, *swim-bladder* etc.); †a morbid vesicle, a pustule; an inflated pericarp; a vesicle; the prepared (urinary) bladder of an animal; the membrane of this bladder used for airtight coverings; a wind-bag; anything inflated and hollow. **bladder-fern,** *n.* the genus *Cystopteris*. **bladder-kelp,** *n.* BLADDER-WRACK. **bladder-nut,** *n.* the fruit of the bladder-tree, *Staphylea trifoliata*. **bladder-tree,** *n.* [BLADDER-NUT]. **bladder-wort,** *n.* the genus *Utricularia*. **bladder-wrack,** *n.* the sea-weed, *Fucus vesiculosus*, which has air-bladders in its fronds. **bladdered,** *a.* put or packed in a bladder; (*fig.*) inflated, puffed up; (*sl.*) very drunk. **bladdery,** *a.* of the nature of a bladder; containing bladders. [OE *blœdre* (cp. OHG *blātara*, G *Blatter*, a bladder, OE *blāwan*, L *flāre*, to blow)]

blade, *n.* a leaf of a plant; the culm and leaves of a grass or cereal; the expanded part of the leaf as distinguished from the petiole; the corresponding part of a petal; any broad, flattened part, as of a paddle, bat, oar etc.; the thin cutting part of a knife, sword etc.; the front part of the tongue; a sword; a dashing, reckless fellow. *v.i.* to put forth blades. **blade-bone,** *n.* the shoulder-blade in man and the lower mammals. **bladed,** *a.* [OE *blœd* (OHG *plat*, G *Blatt*, OTeut. stem *blo-*, to blow, cp. L *flos*, a flower)]

blaeberry, bleaberry, *n.* (*Sc. and North.*) the bilberry or whortleberry; similar fruits or plants. [Icel. *blā*, *blār*, livid, dark blue (OHG *blāo*, G *blau*), whence *blāber*, bilberry]

blaes, *n.* a hardened shale found in coal measures, which is burned and powdered to make surface for tennis courts. [Sc. *blae*, blue]

blague, *n.* pretentiousness, humbug. [F]

blah, blah blah, *n.* foolish talk, chatter, exaggeration. [onomat.]

blain, *n.* a pustule, a blister or sore [CHILBLAIN]. *v.t.* to affect with blains. [OE *blegen* (cp. Dut. *blein*, Dan. *blegn*)]

Blake, *n.* **William** (1757–1827), English painter, engraver, poet, and mystic, a leading figure in the Romantic period. His visionary, symbolic poems include *Songs of Innocence* (1789) and *Songs of Experience* (1794). He engraved the text and illustrations for his works and hand-coloured them, mostly in watercolour. He also illustrated works by others, including the poet Milton, and created a highly personal style.

blame, *v.t.* to censure, to find fault with, to reproach; to hold responsible; †to reprove, to bring into discredit. *n.* the act of censuring; the expression of censure; responsibility, accountability, †culpability, demerit; a fault; †injury. **to be to blame,** to be culpable. **blame it,** a mild oath. **blamable,** *a.* deserving blame; culpable. **blamableness,** *n.* **blamably,,** *a.* **blamelessly,** *adv.* **blamelessness,** *n.* **blameworthy,** *a.* deserving blame. **blameworthiness,** *n.* [OF *blasmer*, L *blasphemāre*, BLASPHEME]

Blamey, *n.* **Thomas Albert** (1884–1951), the first Australian field marshal. Born in New South Wales, he served at Gallipoli, Turkey, and on the Western Front in World War I. In World War II he was commander in chief of the Allied Land Forces in the SW Pacific during 1942–45.

Blanc, *n.* **Louis** (1811–82), French socialist and journalist. In 1839 he founded the *Revue du progrès*, in which he published his *Organisation du travail*, advocating the establishment of cooperative workshops and other socialist schemes. He was a member of the provisional government of 1848 (see REVOLUTIONS OF 1848) and from its fall lived in Britain until 1871.

blanch, *a.* white; (*Her.*) argent. *v.t.* to whiten by taking out the colour; to bleach, to make pale; to take off the outward covering of (as of almonds, walnuts etc.); to whiten (as plants) by the deprivation of light; to plunge (vegetables, fruit, meat etc.) briefly into boiling water; to palliate, whitewash. *v.i.* to lose colour; to become white. [OF fem. of *blanc*, white]

blancmange, *n.* milk (usu. sweetened) thickened with cornflour or gelatine to form a jelly-like dessert. [OF *blanc-manger, -mangier* (*blanc*, see prec., L *manducāre* to chew, to eat)]

blanco, *n.* a substance used by the armed forces to whiten or colour uniform belts, webbing etc. [*Blanco*, a trademark, F *blanc*, white]

bland, *a.* mild, soft, gentle; genial, balmy; dull, insipid. **blandly,** *adv.* **blandness,** *n.* [L *blandus*, agreeable]

blandish, *v.t.* to flatter gently; to coax, to cajole. **blandishment,** *n.* flattering speech or action; cajolery, charm, allurement. **blandiloquence,** ELOQUENCE, *n.* (*coll.*) smooth, ingratiating talk; a flattering speech. [OF *blandiss-*, stem of *blandir*, L *blandīrī*, to flatter (*blandus*, see prec.)]

blank, *a.* empty, void, vacant; not written or printed on; not filled up; confused, dispirited, nonplussed; pure, unmixed, downright, sheer. *n.* the white point in the centre of a target; †the range of one's aim; a blank space in a written or printed document; a blank form; a lottery ticket that draws no prize; a piece of metal before stamping; a level range for a firearm [POINT-BLANK]; (*fig.*) aim, range; a vacant space, a void; an uneventful space of time; a meaningless thing. *v.t.* to render blank; to nonplus, confuse, dumbfounder; to block out; (*int.*) a mild execration. **blank-cartridge,** *n.* cartridge containing no bullet. †blank charter, *n.* a blank paper given to the agents of the Crown in the reign of Richard II, with liberty to fill it up as they pleased. **blank cheque,** *n.* a cheque with the amount left for the payee to insert; complete freedom of action. **blank credit,** *n.* permission to draw on a person or firm to a certain amount. **blank verse,** *n.* unrhymed verse, esp. the iambic pentameter or unrhymed heroic. **blankly,** *adv.* **blankness,** *n.* [F *blanc*, white (It. *blanco*, L *blancus*, OHG *blanch*, OTeut. *blankoz*, shining)]

blanket, *n.* a coarse, loosely-woven woollen material, used for bed-coverings or for covering animals; *a.* covering all conditions or cases, as in *blanket medical screening*. *v.t.* to cover with or as with a blanket; to toss in a blanket; to bring under one coverage; to apply over a wide area. **born on the wrong side of the blanket,** illegitimate. **blanket bath,** *n.* a wash given to a bedridden person. **blanket stitch,** *n.* a reinforcing stitch for the edge of blankets and other thick material. **wet blanket,** *n.* a person who is a damper to conversation or enjoyment. **blanketing,** *n.* material for blankets; tossing in a blanket. [OF *blankete, blanquette*, dim. of *blanc*, see BLANK]

Blanqui, *n.* **Louis Auguste** (1805–81), French revolutionary politician. He formulated the theory of the 'dictatorship of the proletariat', used by Karl Marx, and spent a total of 33 years in prison for insurrection. He became a martyr figure for the French workers' movement.

Blantyre-Limbe, *n.* the chief industrial and commercial centre of Malawi, in the Shire highlands; population (1985) 355,000. It produces tea, coffee, rubber, tobacco, and textiles.

blare, *v.i.* to roar, bellow; to sound as a trumpet. *v.t.* to utter with trumpet-like sound. *n.* sound as of a trumpet; roar, noise, bellowing. [prob. imitated from the sound (cp. Dut. *blaren,* MHG *blēren,* G *plarren*)]

blarney, *n.* smooth, flattering speech; cajolery. *v.t.* to wheedle, to cajole. *v.i.* to talk in a wheedling way. **blarney-stone,** *n.* an inscribed stone in the wall of an old castle at Blarney, near Cork, Ireland, whoever kisses which will have a cajoling tongue.

blasé, *a.* dulled in sense or emotion; worn out through over-indulgence, used-up. [F *p.p.* of *blaser,* to cloy]

blash, *n.* (*Sc. and North.*) a splash or watery burst, watery stuff; (*fig.*) wishy-washy talk. *v.t.* and *i.* to splash or dash. **blashy,** *a.* splashing, showery; watery, thin. [prob. onomat.]

Blashford-Snell, *n.* **John** (1936–), British explorer and soldier. His expeditions have included the first descent and exploration of the Blue Nile (1968); the journey N to S from Alaska to Cape Horn, crossing the Darien Gap between Panama and Colombia for the first time (1971–72); and the first complete navigation of the Zaïre river, Africa (1974–75).

Blasis, *n.* **Carlo** (1797–1878), Italian ballet teacher of French extraction. He was successful as a dancer in Paris and in Milan, where he established a dancing school in 1837. His celebrated treatise on the art of dancing, *Traité élémentaire, théoretique et pratique de l'art de la danse* (1820), forms the basis of classical dance training.

blaspheme, *v.t.* to utter profane language against (God or anything sacred); to abuse. *v.i.* to utter blasphemy, to rail. **blasphemous**, *a.* uttering or containing blasphemy; grossly irreverent or impious. **blasphemously,** *adv.* **blasphemy**, *n.* profane language towards God or about sacred things; impious irreverence; irreverent or abusive speaking about any person or thing held in high esteem. [OF *blasfemer,* L *blasphēmāre,* Gr. *blasphēmein,* from *-phemos,* evil-speaking]

blast, *n.* a violent gust of wind; the sound of a trumpet or the like; any pernicious or destructive influence on animals or plants; a flatulent disease in sheep; the strong current of air used in iron-smelting; a blowing by gunpowder or other explosive; the charge of explosive used; a violent gust of air caused by the explosion of a bomb. *v.t.* to blow or breathe on so as to wither; to injure by some pernicious influence; to blight, to ruin; to blow up with gunpowder or other explosive; to curse (often used as an imprecation). **in, at full blast,** hard at work. **blast-furnace,** *n.* a furnace into which a current of air is introduced to assist combustion. **blast-off,** *n.* the launch of a rocket-propelled missile or space vehicle; (*coll.*) the start of something. **blast off,** *v.i.* **blast-pipe,** *n.* a pipe conveying steam from the cylinders to the funnel of a locomotive to aid the draught. **blasted,** *a.* blighted, confounded, cursed. **blaster,** *n.* **blasting,** *n., a.* [OE *blǣst* (cp. OHG *blāst,* Goth. *-blesan,* to blow)]

-blast, *comb. form.* used in biological terms indicating an embryonic cell or cell layer; e.g. *mesoblast, statoblast.* [Gr. *blastos,* a bud, a germ]

blastema, *n.* protoplasm; the initial matter from which any part is developed; the thallus or frond of lichens; the budding or sprouting part of a plant. [Gr., a sprout]

blasto- [see -BLAST] *comb. form.* pertaining to germs or buds; germinal.

blastocyst, *n.* the modified blastula in mammals.

blastoderm, *n.* the germinal membrane enclosing the yolk of an impregnated ovum which divides into layers that develop into embryonic organs. [Gr. *derma,* skin]

Blastoidea, *n.* an order of bud-like calcareous fossil Echinoderms. **blastoid,** *a.*

blastomere, *n.* one of the cells formed during the primary divisions of an egg.

blastula, *n.* (*pl.* **-las, -lae**) a hollow sphere composed of a single layer of cells, produced by the cleavage of an ovum. **blastular,** *a.* **blastulation,** *n.*

blatant, *a.* loud, clamorous; very obvious, palpable. **blatancy,** *n.* quality of being blatant. **blatantly,** *adv.* [etym. doubtful; prob. coined by Spenser (perh. from Sc. *blaitand,* bleating)]

blate, *a.* (*Sc., North.*) †livid, pale; bashful, sheepish. [*Sc.* and *North.*, from OE *blāt*]

blather, blatherskite BLETHER.

Blatta, *n.* (*Zool.*) a genus of Orthoptera comprising the cockroach. [L cockroach]

blatter, *v.i.* to talk volubly and senselessly; to patter (as rain or hail); to rush in a clattering way. *n.* a clatter; a rushing noise. †**blatterer,** *n.* a babbler; a blusterer. [L *blaterāre,* to babble]

blaud BLAD.

Blaue Reiter, der, ('the Blue Rider') a group of German expressionist painters based in Munich, some of whom had left die Brücke. They were interested in the value of colours, in folk art, and in the necessity of painting 'the inner, spiritual side of nature', but styles were highly varied. Wassily Kandinsky and Franz Marc published a book of their views in 1912 and there were two exhibitions (1911, 1912).

blawort, *n.* the harebell, *Campanula rotundifolia;* the corn bluebottle, *Centaurea cyanus.* [*blae* (see BLAEBERRY), WORT]

blaze[1]**,** *n.* a bright glowing flame; a glow of bright light or colour; an outburst of display, glory, splendour; an outburst of passion; (*pl.*) the flames of hell. *v.i.* to burn with a bright flame; to shine, to glitter; to be bright with colour; to be eminent or conspicuous from character, talents etc. *v.t.* to make resplendent; †to pour forth (as flame). **like blazes,** furiously. **Old Blazes,** (*sl.*) the devil. **to blazes,** to perdition, to the devil. **to blaze away,** of a fire, to burn brightly and strongly; to fire continuously (with guns); to work continuously and enthusiastically. **to blaze out,** to cause to flare away; to subside with a flare. **to blaze up,** of a fire, suddenly to burst into flames; to burst into anger. **blazer,** *n.* a flannel jacket of bright colour worn at cricket, lawn-tennis etc; a jacket used in school uniform. **blazing,** *a.* emitting flame or light; radiant, lustrous; very angry. **blazing scent,** *n.* a hot scent. [OE *blœse, blase,* a blaze, a torch (cp. MHG *Blas,* a torch, G *blass,* pale)]

blaze[2]**,** *n.* a white mark on the face of a horse or other animal; a white mark made on a tree by chipping off bark; (*N Am.*) the path or boundary indicated by a line of such marks. *v.t.* to mark (a tree); to indicate a path or boundary by such marks. [Icel. *blesi* (cp. G *Blässe*)]

blaze[3]**,** *v.t.* to proclaim; to blazon; to depict, emblazon. [Icel. *blāsa,* to blow (cp. Dut. *blazen,* G *blasen*), from OTeut, *bloesan,* to blow (cp. L *flāre*)]

blazer BLAZE[1].

blazon, *n.* †a shield; armorial bearings; a coat of arms; a banner bearing a coat of arms; the art of describing and explaining coats of arms; renown, reputation (of virtues or good qualities), proclamation, revelation. *v.t.* to describe or depict according to the rules of heraldry; to depict in brilliant hues; to decorate with heraldic devices; to describe in fit terms; to publish vauntingly; to proclaim, to trumpet. **blazonment,** *n.* the act of blazoning; the act of diffusing abroad. **blazonry,** *n.* a heraldic device; the art of depicting or describing a coat of arms; armorial bearings; brilliant display. [F *blason,* a coat of arms (some of the later senses prob. influenced by BLAZE[3])]

bldg., (*abbr.*) building.

-ble, *suf.* tending to, able to, fit to (forming verbal adjectives); e.g. *conformable, durable, flexible, suitable, visible.* [-ABLE; -IBLE]

bleaberry BLAEBERRY.

bleach, *v.t.* to make white by exposure to the sun or by chemical agents. *v.i.* to grow white; to become pale or colourless. **bleach-field,** *n.* a field in which bleaching is carried on. **bleaching-clay,** *n.* kaolin, used for sizing cotton goods. **bleaching-powder,** *n.* chloride of lime, a whitish powder consisting of chlorinated calcium hydroxide. **bleacher,** *n.* one who or that which bleaches, a vessel used in bleaching. **bleachery,** *n.* [OE *blǣcan* (OTeut. *blaikjan,* cp. G *bleichen,* and OE *blāc,* pale)]

bleak[1]**,** *a.* †pale, pallid, wan; bare of vegetation; cold, chilly, desolate, cheerless. **bleakish,** *a.* **bleakly,** *adv.*

bleakness, *n.* [OE *blāc* (see prec.)]

bleak², *n.* a small European river fish, *Leuciscus alburnus,* with silvery scales. [Icel. *bleikr* (OTeut. *blaikjōn,* white, cp. BLEACH), or OE *blāc,* as prec.]

blear, *a.* dim, indistinct, misty. *v.t.* to make (the eyes) dim; to blur with or as with tears. **blearedness,** *n.* dimness, dullness; haziness; indistinctness. **bleary,** *a.* **bleary-eyed,** *a.* [etym. doubtful]

bleat, *v.i.* to cry like a sheep, goat or calf. *v.t.* to utter in a bleating tone; to say feebly and foolishly. *n.* the cry of a sheep, goat or calf; a complaint, whine. [OE *blœtan* (cp. Dut. *blaten,* OHG *plāzan,* G *blöken*)]

bleb, *n.* a small blister or bladder; a bubble in glass or anything similar. [cp. BLOB, BLUBBER; imit. of action of making a bubble with the lips]

bleed, *v.i.* (*past, p.p.* **bled**) to emit, discharge or run with blood; to emit sap, resin or juice from a cut or wound; to be wounded; to die from a wound; to lose money; to have money extorted; (*coll.*) to feel acute mental pain. *v.t.* to draw blood from; (*coll.*) to extort money from; (*Bookbinding*) to cut margins too much and trench on the print. **bled,** *a.* **bled-off,** (*Print*) illustration pages so arranged that the outside edges of the illustration are cut off in trimming when binding. to extract liquid, air or gas from a container or closed system (such as hydraulic brakes). **bleeding heart,** *n.* any of various plants belonging to the genus Dicentra, characterized by heart shaped flowers. **bleeder,** *n.* one who bleeds; one who exhibits the blood condition known as haemophilia; (*sl.*) a contemptible person. **bleeding,** *n.* haemorrhage; the operation of letting blood, or of drawing sap from a tree. *a.* running with blood; (*sl.*) bloody; accursed. [OE *blēdan* (cp. BLOOD)]

bleep, *n.* an intermittent, high-pitched sound from an electronic device. *v.i.* to emit this sound. **to bleep out,** (*coll.*) to substitute offensive words in recorded speech with bleeps. **bleeper,** *n.* a small radio receiver emitting a bleeping sound, often carried by doctors, policemen, business men allowing them to be contacted. a bleeper. [onomat.]

blemish, *v.t.* †to mar, to spoil; to impair, tarnish, sully. *n.* a physical or moral defect or stain; an imperfection, a flaw, a fault. †**blemishment,** *n.* [OF (blemir, blesmir, from *blaisme, blesme, blême,* pale (etym. doubtful)]

blench¹, *v.t.* †to elude, to shirk; to flinch from. *v.i.* to shrink back, to draw back; to turn aside, to flinch. †*n.* a side-glance. [OE *blencan,* to deceive (perh. causal to a v. *blinkan,* to BLINK)]

blench², *v.i.* to become pale. *v.t.* to make pale. [var. of BLANCH]

blench³, blench farm [BLANCH]

blend¹, *v.t.* to blind, to make blind. [OE *blendan*]

blend², *v.t.* to mix, to mingle (esp. teas, wines, spirits, tobacco etc. so as to produce a certain quality). *v.i.* to become mingled or indistinguishably mixed; to form an harmonious union or compound; to pass imperceptibly into each other. *n.* a mixture of various qualities (of teas, wines, spirits, tobacco etc.). **blender,** *n.* a type of electric liquidizer used in the preparation of food esp. for mixing and pureéing. [OE *blendan*]

blende, *n.* a native sulphide of zinc. [G, from *blenden,* to deceive, because it yielded no lead]

Blenheim, *n.* a breed of spaniels; a variety of apple (*also* **Blenheim orange**). [Duke of Marlborough's seat near Woodstock, Oxfordshire]

Blenheim, Battle of, battle on 13 Aug. 1704 in which English troops under Marlborough defeated the French and Bavarian armies near the Bavarian village of Blenheim (now in West Germany) on the left bank of the Danube.

blennorrhoea, *n.* (*Path.*) excessive discharge of mucus, esp. from the genital and urinary organs. [Gr. *blennos,* mucus, *rheein,* to flow]

blenny, *n.* a genus of small, spiny-finned sea-fishes; a member of this genus. [L *blennius,* Gr. *blennos,* from the mucous coating of the scales]

blent, *a.* mingled. [Gr. *blepharon,* eyelid]

blepharitis, *n.* inflammation of the eye-lids.

blepharo- *comb. form* pertaining to the eyelids. [Gr. *blepharon,* eyelid]

Blériot, *n.* **Louis** (1872–1936), French aviator who, in a 24-horsepower monoplane of his own construction, made the first flight across the English Channel on 25 July 1909.

blesbok, *n.* the S African white-faced antelope, *Alcelaphus albifrons*. [S Afr. Dut. *bles,* blaze, *bok,* buck]

bless¹, *v.t.* to consecrate, to hallow; to invoke God's favour on, to render happy or prosperous, as by supernatural means; to wish happiness to; to extol, magnify, worship. **God bless me** or **bless me!** an ejaculation of surprise etc. **to bless oneself,** to make the sign of the cross (as a defence against evil spirits). **to bless one's stars,** to be very thankful. **without a penny to bless oneself with,** penniless (with allusion to the cross on a silver penny). **blessed, blest,** *a.* consecrated by religious rites; worthy of veneration; happy; fortunate, beatified, enjoying the bliss of heaven; joyful, blissful; (*euphem.*) cursed. *n.* (*collect.*) the saints in heaven. **blessedly,** *adv.* fortunately, happily. **blessedness,** *n.* the state of being blessed, esp. by Heaven; happiness, bliss. **single blessedness,** the state of being unmarried. **blessing,** *n.* consecration; divine favour; an invocation of divine favour or happiness; a cause of happiness; a gift; grace before or after meat. **to ask a blessing,** to say grace before meat. [OE *blētsian, bledsian, blœdsian;* orig. to redden with blood, to bless (*blōd,* BLOOD)]

bless², *v.t.* to wave about, brandish; to brandish round. [a Spenserian adaptation]

blet, blett, *v.i.* (of fruit) to become internally rotten as a pear which ripens after being picked. [OF *blette,* soft, mellow]

blether, blather, *v.i.* to talk nonsense volubly. *n.* voluble nonsense; one who blathers, a prattler. **bletherskate, blatherskite,** *n.* one who talks blatant nonsense. [Icel. *blathra,* to talk nonsense (*blathr,* nonsense)]

blew, *past* BLOW¹.

blewits, *n.* an edible mushroom with a purplish top. [prob. from BLUE]

Bligh, *n.* **William** (1754–1817), British admiral. Bligh accompanied Captain Cook on his second voyage (1772–74), and in 1787 commanded HMS *Bounty* on an expedition to the Pacific. On the return voyage the crew mutinied (1789), and Bligh was cast adrift in a boat with 18 men. He was appointed governor of New South Wales in 1805, where his discipline again provoked a mutiny (1808). He returned to Britain, and was made an admiral in 1811.

blight, *n.* any baleful atmospheric influence affecting the growth of plants; diseases caused in plants by fungoid parasites and various insects, mildew, smut, rust, aphides etc.; a close and overcast state of the weather; any obscure malignant influence; an area of urban decay. *v.t.* to affect with blight; to exert a baleful influence; to mar, frustrate. **blight bird,** *n.* the white-eye or silver-eye. **blighter,** *n.* (*sl.*) a nasty fellow, a blackguard. **blightingly,** *adv.* [etym. doubtful]

Blighty, *n.* (*sl.*) soldier's name for Britain, home; (*Mil.*) a wound that invalids one home. [Urdu *Bilati,* provincial removed at some distance]

blimey, *int.* exclamation of astonishment. [abbrev. God *blind me*]

blimp, *n.* a small airship used for observation; (*Cinema*) a sound-proof covering to drown the sound of the camera mechanism; (*coll.*) someone who is narrow-minded and conservative; a die-hard army officer. **blimpish,** *a.* [from Colonel *Blimp,* the cartoon character created by David Low, 1891–1963]

blind, *a.* unseeing; destitute of sight either naturally or by deprivation; unseen, dark, admitting no light, having no outlet; of, pertaining to or for the use or benefit of, the sightless; destitute of understanding, judgment or foresight; undiscerning, obtuse; reckless, heedless; drunk; purposeless, random; imperfectly addressed [of letters, applied also to the Post officials (called **blind-officers, blind-readers**) who deal with such letters];

(*Bot.*) having no buds, eyes or terminal flower; abortive (of a bud). *n.* a blind person; *pl.* blind persons collectively; anything which obstructs the light or sight; a blinker for a horse; (*coll.*) a pretence, a pretext; a window-screen or shade, esp. one on rollers for coiling up, or of slats on strips of webbing; (*sl.*) a drunken fit. *v.t.* to make blind, to deprive of slight (permanently or temporarily); to darken, make dim; (*coll.*) to deceive; to darken the understanding. *v.i.* (*Motor.*) to drive blindly and recklessly; (*sl.*) to swear. **to bake blind,** to bake pastry intended for a pie or flan before adding the filling. **to fly blind,** (*Aviat.*) to fly by the use of instruments only. **blind alley,** *n.* a street, road or alley walled-up at the end. **blind-blocking, -tooling,** *n.* (*Bookbinding*) ornamentation done by impressing hot tools without gold-leaf. **blind-coal,** *n.* a flameless anthracite. **blind date,** *n.* a social engagement arranged between two people previously unknown to one another. **blind-ditch,** *n.* a concealed ditch. **blind-door, -window,** *n.* door or window that is walled-up. **blind drunk,** *adv.* too drunk to be able to see straight. **blind-fish,** *n.* a fish without functional eyes found in underground streams, e.g. the *Amblyopsis speloeus* of Mammoth Cave, Kentucky. **blindfold,** *v.t.* to cover the eyes, esp. with a bandage; to dull or obstruct the understanding; *a.* having the eyes bandaged; devoid of foresight. **blind-lantern,** *n.* a dark lantern. **blind-man's-buff,** *n.* a game in which a player has his eyes bandaged, and has to catch and identify one of the others. **blind screening** (also **anonymized screening**), *n.* the testing of unidentified samples (of blood) without the patient's knowledge. **blind side,** *n.* the direction in which one is most easily assailed; a weakness, a foible. **blind spot,** *n.* a part of the retina insensitive to light, owing to the passage through it of the optic nerve; (*Radio.*) a point within the service area of a station where signals are received very faintly; a tendency to overlook faults etc.; a failure of understanding or judgment; a weakness. **blind-stitch,** *n.* sewing that does not show, or that shows at the back only. *v.t.*, *v.i.* to sew in this manner. **blind-story,** *n.* a series of arches below the clerestory, admitting no light; a triforium. **blind-wall,** *n.* a wall with no opening in it. **blind-worm,** *n.* an aberrant British lizard, *Anguis fragilis,* called also the slow-worm, erroneously supposed to be blind, from the small size of its eyes. **blindage,** *n.* a screen for troops, a mantelet. **blinder,** *n.* one who or that which blinds; (*N Am.*) a horse's blinker. **blindly,** *adv.* **blindness,** *n.* sightlessness; lack of intellectual or moral perception; ignorance, folly, recklessness. [OE (also Dut. Swed., G, etc.)]

blink, *v.i.* to move the eyelids; to open and shut the eyes; to look with winking eyelids, to look unsteadily; to shine fitfully; to peep, to wink, to twinkle. *v.t.* to shut the eyes to; evade, to shirk. *a,* blinking, twinkling. *n.* a gleam, a glimmer, a twinkle; a glance, a twinkling (cp. ICE-BLINK). **on the blink,** (*coll.*) not functioning properly (of a machine). †**blinkard,** *n.* one who blinks; a person with imperfect sight; an obtuse or foolish person. **blinked,** *a.* affected with blinking. **blinker,** *n.* one who blinks; (*pl.*) spectacles to cure squinting, or to protect the eyes from cold, dust etc.; leather screens to prevent a horse from seeing sideways. **blinkered,** *a.* wearing blinkers; not understanding what is going on around one; having a distorted or biased view or opinion. **to wear blinkers,** (*fig.*) not to see or understand what is going on around one. **blinking,** *a.* (*coll.*) a euphemism for BLOODY used for emphasis. [ME *blenken* (cp. Dut. and G *blinken;* OE *blencan,* see BLENCH[1])]

blintz(e), *n.* a thin, stuffed pancake. [Yiddish *blintse,* from Rus. *blin*]

blip, *n.* (*coll.*) an irregularity in the linear trace on a radar screen indicating the presence of an aircraft, vessel etc.; an intermittent, high-pitched sound from an electronic device, a bleep.

blirt, *v.i.* (*Sc.*) to weep violently. *v.t.* to disfigure with weeping. *n.* a violent burst of tears; a gust of wind and rain. [prob. onomat.]

bliss, *n.* happiness of the highest kind; the perfect joy of heaven; heaven. **blissful,** *a.* full of bliss; causing bliss. **blissfully,** *adv.* in a blissful manner. **blissfully ignorant of,** quite unaware of. **blissfulness,** *n.* the state of being blissful. [OE *blis, bliss, blīths* (*blīthe,* happy); sense influenced by BLESS[1]]

Bliss, *n.* **Arthur (Drummond)** (1891–1975), English composer, who became Master of the Queen's Musick in 1953. Works include *A Colour Symphony* (1922), music for ballets *Checkmate* (1937), *Miracle in the Gorbals* (1944), and *Adam Zero* (1946); an opera *The Olympians* (1949); and dramatic film music, including *Things to Come* (1935).

blister, *n.* a pustule or thin vesicle raised on the skin by some injury or vesicatory, and containing a watery fluid or serum; any similar swelling on a plant, metal, a painted surface etc.; a vesicatory; anything applied to raise a blister. *v.i.* to rise in blisters; to be covered with blisters; (*Austral. coll.*) to overcharge, to demand an exorbitant sum. *v.t.* to raise blisters on, esp. by a vesicatory; to criticize spitefully; (*sl.*) to bore; to damn. **blister-fly,** *n.* the Spanish fly, *Cantharis vesicatoria,* used to raise blisters. **blister pack,** *n.* a type of clear plastic and cardboard packaging for small products. **blister-plaster,** *n.* a plaster for raising a blister. **blister-steel,** *n.* steel having a blistered surface, the result of absorption of carbon in its conversion from iron. **blistered,** *a.* affected with blisters; †ornamented with puffs. **blistery,** *a.* full of blisters. [ME *blister, blester,* perh. from OF *blestre,* Icel. *blāstr,* a blowing, a swelling (*blāsa,* to blow)]

blithe, *a.* gay, cheerful, joyous; merry, sprightly. **blithely,** *adv.* **blitheness,** *n.* **blithesome,** *a.* blithe; cheery. **blithesomeness,** *n.* [OE *blīthe* (cp. OHG *blīdi,* Icel. *blīthr,* Dut. *blijde*)]

blithering, *a.* (*sl.*) nonsensical, contemptible. [BLETHER]

blitz[1], *n.* (*coll.*) intense enemy onslaught, esp. an air raid; an intensive campaign; intensive activity or action. *v.t.* to make an enemy onslaught on; to mount an intensive campaign; to subject to intensive activity. [G *Blitz* lightning]

Blitz[2], *n.* name given in Britain to the attempted saturation bombing of London by the Germans between Sep. 1940 and May 1941 during World War II.

Blitzkrieg, *n.* (German **'lightning war')** a swift military campaign, as used by Germany at the beginning of World War II (1939–41).

Blixen, *n.* **Karen,** born Karen Dinesen (1885–1962), Danish writer. Her autobiography *Out of Africa* (1937) is based on her experience of running a coffee plantation in Kenya. She wrote fiction, mainly in English, under the pen name Isak Dinesen.

blizzard, *n.* a snow-squall; a furious storm of snow and wind. [etym. doubtful; perhaps fashioned on BLOW, BLAST etc.]

bloat, *v.t.* to cause to swell; to puff up; to make vain or conceited. *v.i.* to swell; to grow turgid. †*a.* soft, flabby; swollen, esp. with self-indulgence. *n.* a cattle disease, hoove. **bloated,** *a.* swollen, inflated, pampered, puffed up with pride. **bloatedness,** *n.* the quality of being bloated. [ME *bloat, blowt,* soft (prob. var. of *blote,* see BLOATER)]

bloater, *n.* a herring partially cured by steeping in dry salt and smoking. [ME *blote,* soft, soaked (Icel. *blautr*), whence *bloat,* to cure, *bloat,* or *bloated,* herring, bloater]

blob, *n.* a globular drop of liquid; a spot of colour; †a pustule; (*Naut.*) the round mass forming the base of an iron post; any vague, soft form. **blobber-lipped,** *a.* having swollen, pouting lips. [BLEB]

bloc, *n.* a combination of parties, or of nations. [F]

Bloch[1], *n.* **Ernest** (1880–1959), US composer, born in Geneva, Switzerland. He went to the US in 1916 and became founder-director of the Cleveland Institute of Music (1920–25). Among his works are the lyrical drama *Macbeth* (1910), *Schelomo* for cello and orchestra (1916), five string quartets, and *Suite Hébraique*, for viola and orchestra (1953). He often used themes based on Jewish liturgical music and folk song.

Bloch[2], *n.* **Konrad** (1912–), US chemist whose research, lasting more than a decade, concerned cholesterol. Making use of the radioisotope carbon-14, Bloch was able to follow the complex steps by which the body chemically transforms acetic acid into cholesterol. For his ability in this field Bloch shared the 1964 Nobel Prize in Physiology or Medicine with Feodor Lynen (1911–).

block, *n.* a solid mass of wood or stone; a log, a tree-stump; the piece of wood on which criminals were beheaded; death by beheading; a compact or connected group of buildings, esp. when bounded by intersecting streets, regarded in the US as a method of measuring distances; a mould on which a thing is shaped; a piece of wood or metal on which figures are engraved for printing from; a cliché taken from such a block; a solid unshaped mass of any material; (*Cricket*) the position in which a batsman blocks balls; a block-hole; a pulley, or system of pulleys, mounted in a frame or shell; (*Parl.*) a notice of opposition to a Bill (*see below*); an obstruction, a hindrance, an impediment or its effects; a blockhead; (*sl.*) the head. *v.t.* to enclose, to shut up; to stop up, to obstruct; to impede progress or advance; to stop a train by a block-signal; to shape a hat on the block; to subject to a blockade; (*Bookbinding*) to emboss a cover by impressing a device; (*Cricket*) to stop a ball dead without attempting to hit it; (*Parl.*) to give notice of opposition to a Bill, thus preventing its being proceeded with at certain times; (*fig.*) to block up, to obstruct. **to block in,** to sketch roughly the broad masses of a picture or drawing. **to block out,** to mark out work roughly. **to block up,** to confine. **barber's block,** a head-shaped piece of wood for mounting wigs upon. **block-book,** *n.* a book printed from wooden blocks on which the letters or pictures have been cut in relief. **block-booking,** *n.* the reserving of a number of seats or places at a single booking. **block-buster,** *n.* (*coll.*) a very heavy and effective aerial bomb; a very successful and profitable film or book; a particularly effective or successful thing or person. **block-busting,** *a.* **block-chain,** *n.* an endless chain on bicycles and other vehicles. **blockhead,** *n.* a stupid, dull person. **block-hole,** *n.* (*Cricket*) a mark made a yard in front of the wicket. **blockhouse,** *n.* a detached fort covering some strategical point; a one-storeyed timber building, with loop-holes for musketry; a house of squared timber. **block-letters,** *n.pl.* wood type of large size used in printing; imitation in handwriting of printed capital letters. **block-machine,** *n.* a machine for making tackle-blocks. **block-plan,** *n.* a sketch-plan showing the outline and relative situation of buildings without detail. **block-printing,** *n.* printing from engraved wooden blocks. **block release,** *n.* the short-term release of employees for formal study or training. **block-signal,** *n.* a signal to stop a train when the next section of the line is not clear. **block-system,** *n.* a system by which a railway line is divided into sections, and no train is allowed to pass into any section till it is signalled clear. **block-tin,** *n.* tin cast into ingots. **blockish,** *a.* stupid; dull; rough, clumsy. **blockishly,** *adv.* blockishness, *n.* [prob. from F *bloc* (OHG *bloh,* or MHG *bloch,* G *Block*)]

blockade, *n.* the investment of a place by sea or land, so as to compel surrender by starvation or prevent communication with the outside; imprisonment by weather or other causes. *v.t.* to block up, esp. by troops or ships. **paper blockade,** a blockade that has been proclaimed but not rendered effective. **blockade-runner,** *n.* a vessel that runs or attempts to run into a blockaded port; the owner, captain or any of the sailors of such a vessel. [as prec.]

Bloemfontein, *n.* capital of the Orange Free State and judicial capital of the Republic of South Africa; population (1985) 204,000. Founded in 1846, the city produces canned fruit, glassware, furniture, and plastics.

Blok, *n.* **Alexander Alexandrovich** (1880–1921), Russian poet who, as a follower of the French Symbolist movement, used words for their symbolic rather than actual meaning. He backed the 1917 Revolution, as in his most famous poems *The Twelve* (1918), and *The Scythians* (1918), the latter appealing to the West to join in the revolution.

bloke, *n.* (*coll.*) a man, a fellow. [etym. unknown]

Blomberg, *n.* **Werner von** (1878–1946), German soldier and Nazi politician, minister of defence (1933–35) and minister of war and head of the Wehrmacht (army) 1935–38 under Hitler's chancellorship. He was discredited by his marriage to a prostitute and dismissed in Jan. 1938, enabling Hitler to exercise more direct control over the armed forces. In spite of his removal from office, Blomberg was put on trial for war crimes in 1946 at Nuremberg.

Blomdahl, *n.* **Karl-Birger** (1916–68), Swedish composer of ballets and symphonies in expressionist style. His opera *Aniara* (1959) incorporates electronic music and is set in a spaceship.

blond, blonde (used with fem. substantives), *a.* fair or light in colour; having light hair and a fair complexion. *n.* one who has light hair and a fair complexion (the form **blonde** is used of women). **blonde lace,** *n.* a kind of lace, orig. made of raw silk. [F (Sp. *blondo,* It. *biondo,* late L *bludus*), prob. of Teut. origin]

blood[1]**,** *n.* the red fluid circulating by means of veins and arteries, through the bodies of man and other vertebrates; any analogous fluid in the invertebrates; lineage, descent; honourable or high birth, family relationship, kinship; slaughter, muder, bloodshed; the guilt of murder; temperament, passion; vitality, mettle; a man of a fiery spirit, a rake, a dandy, a dissipated character; the juice of anything, esp. if red; sap; the supposed seat of the emotions; the sensual nature of man; blood shed in sacrifice. *v.i.* to cause blood to flow from, to bleed; to inure to blood (as a hound); (*fig.*) to exasperate; to stain with blood; to render bloody. **bad blood,** resentment, ill-feeling. **blood and thunder,** sensational literature; (*sl.*) a mixture of port wine and brandy. **flesh and blood,** the carnal nature of man; human nature. **half-blood,** connection through one parent only; a half-breed. **in cold blood,** not in anger; deliberately. **new blood,** new entrants to a community or group who add freshness or vigour. **the blood,** Royal blood; the royal family. **whole blood,** connection by both parents. **blood bank,** *n.* the place where blood for transfusion is stored. **blood-bought,** *a.* bought or redeemed by blood, or at the expense of life. **blood-brother,** *n.* a brother by both parents. **blood count,** *n.* a calculation of the number of red and white corpuscles in a sample of blood. **blood curdling,** *a.* harrowing exciting. **blood donor,** *n.* one from whom blood is taken for transfusion. **blood-feud,** *n.* a feud arising out of murder or homicide; a vendetta. **blood-frozen,** *a.* having the blood chilled. **blood groups,** *n.pl.* the four groups into which human beings have been classified for purposes of blood-transfusion. **blood-guilt, blood-guiltiness,** *n.* murder or homicide. **blood-guilty,** *a.* guilty of murder or homicide. **blood-heat,** *n.* the ordinary heat of blood in a healthy human body (about 98° F or 37°C). **blood-horse,** *n.* a horse of good breed or pedigree. **bloodhound,** *n.* a variety of hound remarkable for keenness of scent, used for tracking fugitives; (*fig.*) one who relentlessly pursues an opponent; a detective, a spy. **blood-letting,** *n.* the act, process or art of taking blood from the body; phlebotomy; bloodshed, (*coll.*) excessive financial demands. **blood-money,** *n.* money paid for evidence of information leading to a conviction on a capital charge; money paid to the next of kin as compensation for the murder of a relative. **blood-orange,** *n.* an orange having pulp and juice of a reddish hue. **blood plasma,** *n.* blood from which all red corpuscles have been removed. **blood poisoning,** *n.* a diseased condition set up by the entrance of septic matter into the blood. **blood pressure,** *n.* pressure of the blood on the walls of the containing arteries. **blood rain,** *n.* rain tinted reddish from contact with dust particles in the air. **blood-red,** *a.* red as blood. **blood-relation,** *n.* a relation by descent, not merely by marriage. **blood-shed,** *n.* the act of shedding blood; murder; slaughter in war. **bloodshot,** *a.* red and inflamed; (of the eye) suffused with blood. **blood-spavin,** *n.* a dilatation of the vein inside the hock of a horse. **blood sports,** *n.pl.* sports entailing the killing of animals, such as fox-hunting. **blood-stain,** *n.* a stain produced by blood. **blood-stained,** *a.* stained by blood; guilty of bloodshed. **blood stock,** *n.* collective term for thoroughbred horses. **blood-stone,** *n.* heliotrope, a variety of quartz with blood-like spots of jasper; other stones similarly spotted, which, like heliotrope, were supposed to staunch bleeding when worn as amulets; red iron-ore. **blood stream,** *n.* the circulatory movement of the blood in the body. **blood-sucker,** *n.* any animal which sucks blood, esp. the leech; an extortioner. **blood-tax,** *n.* conscription; compulsory military service. **blood test,** *n.* the examination of a sample of blood for medical disorders. **bloodthirsty,** *a.* eager to shed blood; delighting in sanguinary deeds. **bloodthirstiness,** *n.* blood-transfusion, *n.* transference of blood from the vein of a healthy person to the vein of one whose blood is deficient in quantity or quality. **blood-vessel,** *n.* a vessel in which blood circulates in the animal body; an artery or a vein. †**blood-wite,** *n.* a fine for shedding blood paid to the king, in addition to the wergild paid to the family. **bloodwood, blood-tree,** *n.* a term applied to several varieties of trees that exude a bright red gum. **blood-worm,** *n.* a small red earth-worm used by anglers. **blood-wort,** *n.* a popular name for various plants, either from their red leaves or roots, or from the notion that they were efficacious in staunching blood. **bloodied,** *a.* stained with blood. †**bloodily,** *adv.* **bloodiness,** *n.* the state or condition of being bloody; abounding with blood, as a battle-field. **bloodless,** *a.* without blood; without effusion of blood; spiritless; unfeeling. **bloodlessly,** *adv.* **bloody,** *a.* of or pertaining to blood; stained or running with blood; attended with bloodshed; cruel, murderous; (*sl.*) damned, devilish; very, exceedingly (prob. from the bloods or hooligans of rank in the seventeenth or eighteenth century); (*sl.*) annoying, wretched etc. **bloody-bones,** *n.* a bugbear, a fright [RAWHEAD AND BLOODY BONES]. **bloody-faced,** *a.* having the face stained with blood; sanguinary. **bloody flux,** *n.* an old popular name for dysentery. **bloody-hand,** *n.* (*Her.*) the Ulster badge borne by baronets. **bloody-minded,** *a.* of a cruel disposition; of an obstinate or unhelpful disposition. **bloody nose,** *n.* a bleeding nose. **bloody sweat,** *n.* the sweating sickness; transudation of blood through the pores, esp. used of the agony of Christ in Gethsemane. [OE *blōd* (cp. Goth. *blōth,* G *Blut,* Icel. *blōth,* Dut. *bloed*)]

Blood[2], *n.* **Thomas** (1618–80), Irish adventurer, known as Colonel Blood, who attempted to steal the crown jewels from the Tower of London, England, 1671.

bloom[1], *n.* a blossom, a flower; the delicate dust on newly gathered plums, grapes etc.; the yellow sheen on well-tanned leather; lustre, efflorescence; a lens-coating that increases its transparency; a kind of currant; flush, glow, prime, perfection. *v.i.* to blossom, to come into flower; to be at the highest point of perfection or beauty. **bloomer**[1], *n.* a plant that blooms (esp. in *comb.,* as an *early-bloomer*); (*sl.*) a mistake, a foolish blunder. **in bloom,** flowering, blossoming. **blooming,** *a.* in a state of bloom, flourishing; bright, lustrous; (*sl.*) euphemistically for bloody. **bloomingly,** *adv.* **bloomless,** *a.* **bloomy,** *a.* full of blooms, flowery. [Icel. *blōm,* a blossom (cp. OHG *bluomo,* G *Blume*), from the root *blō-,* to blow, to flourish (cp. L *flos, florēre)*]

bloom[2], *n.* a mass of iron that has undergone the first hammering. *v.t.* to hammer or squeeze the ball, or lump of iron, from the puddling furnace into a bloom. **bloomery,** *n.* the apparatus for making blooms out of puddled iron; a furnace for making malleable iron by a direct process. [OE *blōma*]

Bloom[3], *n.* **Claire** (1931–), British actress. Born in London, she first made her reputation on the stage in Shakespearean roles. Her films include *Richard III* (1956) and *The Brothers Karamazov* (1958), and television appearances include *Brideshead Revisited* (1980).

bloomer, *n.* a style of dress for ladies, consisting of a shorter skirt, and loose trousers gathered round the ankles; a woman wearing such a dress; a broad-brimmed straw hat for women. [the American Mrs *Bloomer,* who introduced it *c.* 1850]

Bloomsbury Group, *n.* a group of writers and artists based in Bloomsbury, London, between the world wars. The group included the artists Duncan Grant and Vanessa Bell, and the writers Lytton Strachey and Leonard and Virginia Woolf.

blore, *n.* a violent gust or blast. [prob. onomat.]

blossom, *n.* the flower of a plant, esp. considered as giving promise of fruit; a flower; the mass of flowers on a fruit-tree; promise of future excellence or development; a promising person. *v.i.* to put forth flowers; to bloom; to flourish. **blossomless,** *a.* **blossomy,** *a.* full of blossoms. [OE *blōstma, blōstm* (prob. cognate with BLOOM[1])]

blot[1], *n.* a spot or stain of ink or other discolouring matter; a blotting out by way of correction; a dark patch; blemish, disgrace, disfigurement, defect; a fault; a disgraceful action. *v.t.* (*past, p.p.* **blotted**) to spot or stain with ink or other discolouring matter; to obliterate; to dry with blotting-paper; to apply blotting-paper to; to darken, to disfigure, to sully. *v.i.* to make blots, to become blotted. **to blot one's copybook,** (*coll.*) to commit an indiscretion; to spoil one's good record. **to blot out,** to obliterate, to efface. **blotter,** *n.* one who or that which blots; a scribbler; a paper pad or book for absorbing superfluous ink from paper after writing; a blotting-pad. **blottesque,** *a.* characterized (as a painting) by masses of colour heavily laid on. **blotting,** *n., a.* **blotting-paper,** *n.* absorbent paper for drying up ink. **blotting-book, -pad,** *n.* a book or pad made up of this. [etym. doubtful]

blot[2], *n.* an exposed piece at backgammon; a weak point, a failing; a mark, a butt. **to hit a blot,** to take an exposed piece at backgammon; to detect a fault. [etym. doubtful (prob. conn. with Dan. *blot,* bare, naked)]

blotch, *n.* a pustule, boil, botch; a blot; a patch; a clumsy daub. *v.t.* to blot. **blotched,** *a.* marked with blotches. **blotchy,** *a.* full of blotches. [prob. from BLOT[2]]

blotto, *a.* (*sl.*) unconscious with drink.

blouse, *n.* a light, loose, upper garment. [F (etym. unknown)]

blouson, *n.* a short, loose jacket fitted or belted in at the waist. [F]

blow[1], *v.i.* (*past* **blew,** *p.p.* **blown**) to move as a current of air; to send a current of air from the mouth; to pant, to puff; to sound, to give forth musical notes (as a horn); to eject water and air from the spiracles (as cetaceans); to boast, talk big; (*sl.*) to squander money, to spend. *v.t.* to drive a current of air upon; to inflate with air; to drive by a current of air; to put out of breath; to sound a wind instrument or a note on it; to taint by depositing eggs upon (as flies); to shatter by explosives; to spread, as a report; to inflate, to puff up, to enlarge; (*sl.*) curse, confound. *n.* a blowing, a blast of air; a breath of fresh air; an egg (of a flesh-fly); oviposition (of flesh-flies); a single operation of the Bessemer converter; a boast; boastfulness. **blow it!** confound it. **I'll be blowed!** *int.* (*sl.*) I'll be confounded etc. **to blow hot and cold,** to vacillate; to do one thing at one time, and its opposite at another. **to blow in,** to make an unexpected visit. **to blow it, something,** (*coll.*) to lose a chance or advantage by committing a blunder. **to blow off,** to escape with a blowing noise, as steam; to discharge (steam, energy, anger etc.). **to blow one's own trumpet,** to boast, to sing one's own praises. **to blow out,** to extinguish by blowing; to clear by means of blowing. **to blow over,** to pass away, to subside. **to blow the gaff,** (*sl.*) to let out a secret. **to blow up,** to inflate, to scold, to censure severely; to ruin; to explode, to fly in fragments. †**to blow upon,** to make stale or common; to bring into discredit; to expose. **blow-ball,** *n.* the downy head of the dandelion and allied plants. **blowdry,** *n.* a method of styling hair while drying it with a small hairdryer. **blow-fly,** *n.* the meat-fly. **blow-hole,** *n.* an air-hole; a hole in the ice to which seals and whales come to breathe; (*pl.*) the spiracles of a cetacean. **blow-job,** *n.* (*sl.*) fellatio. **blow-lamp, -torch,** *n.* lamp used in soldering, brazing etc.; burner used to remove paint. **blow-line,** *n.* (*Angling*) a light line with real or artificial bait at the end, allowed to float over the surface of water with the wind. **blow moulding,** *v.i.* a method of manufacturing plastic goods. **blow-out,** *n.* (*sl.*) a hearty meal; a celebration; an explosion of oil and gas from an oil well; the puncturing of a tyre; the burning out of an electrical fuse or a valve. **blow-pipe,** *n.* a tube used for increasing combustion by directing a current of air into a flame; a pipe used in glass-blowing; a tube used by American Indians for shooting darts by means of the breath. **blow-torch,** BLOW-LAMP. **blow up,** *n.* the enlargement of part or whole of a photograph; (*coll.*) a burst of danger, a heated argument. **blower,** *n.* one who or that which blows; a cetacean, a whale; a contrivance for creating an artificial current of air; an escape of gas in a mine; the fissure through which this escapes; (*coll.*) a telephone, speaking-tube etc. **blowing,** *n, a.* **blowing-machine,** *n.* a machine for creating a current of air. **blowy,** *a.* windy; exposed to the wind. [OE *blāwan* (cp. OHG *bllāhan,* G *blāhen,* L *flāre*)]

blow², *v.i.* to blossom; to bloom, to flourish. *n.* the state of blossoming; bloom; a display of blossoms. [OE *blōwan* (OHG *bluojan,* G *blūhen,* cp. L *florēre,* see also BLOOM¹)]

blow³, *n.* a stroke with the fist or any weapon or instrument; an act of hostility; a severe shock; a sudden and painful calamity. **to come to blows,** to fight. [etym. doubtful]

Blow⁴, *n.* **John** (1648–1708), British composer. He taught Purcell, and wrote church music, for example the anthem 'I Was Glad when They Said unto Me' (1697). His masque *Venus and Adonis* (1685) is sometimes called the first English opera.

blowze, blowse, *n.* †a wench, a beggar's wench; a red-faced, bloated woman; a woman with disordered hair. **blowzed, blowsed,** *a.* red-faced, bloated, dishevelled, slatternly. **blowzy, blowsy,** *a.* having a bloated face, untidy, sluttish. [conn. with BLUSH]

blub, *v.i.* (*sl.*) to weep, shed tears. [short for BLUBBER]

blubber, *n.* the fat underlying the skin in whales and other cetaceans, from which train-oil is prepared; weeping; (*Naut.*) a sea-nettle or jelly-fish. *a.* having swollen, pouting lips; blobber-lipped. *v.i.* to weep in a noisy manner. *v.t.* to wet and disfigure with weeping; to utter with sobs and tears. [prob. imit. in origin (cp. BABBLE, BLEB, BUBBLE)]

Blucher, *n.* (*usu. in pl.*) a strong leather half-boot. [from Field-Marshal von BLÜCHER]

Blücher, *n.* **Gebhard Leberecht von** (1742–1819), Prussian field marshal, popular as 'Marshal Forward'. He took an active part in the patriotic movement, and in the War of German Liberation defeated the French as commander in chief at Leipzig (1813), crossed the Rhine to Paris (1814), and was made prince of Wahlstadt (Silesia). In 1815 he was defeated by Napoleon at Ligny, but played a crucial role in the British commander Wellington's triumph at Waterloo, near Brussels.

bludgeon, *n.* a short, thick stick, sometimes loaded; a black-jack. *v.t.* to strike with this; to coerce verbally, or by physical force. [etym. doubtful]

blue, *a.* of the colour of the cloudless sky or deep sea; applied also to smoke, vapour, distant landscape, steel, skim-milk etc.; †livid; dressed in blue; belonging to the political party which adopts blue for its colour (in Britain, usually the Conservative); (*coll.*) miserable, low-spirited; learned, pedantic (of women); (*sl.*) obscene, smutty. *n.* a blue colour; a blue pigment; a blue powder used by laundresses; a blue jacket or cap worn as colours; a blue substance, object or animal (as explained by context); a blue-coat boy; the sky; the sea; a man who plays for his university in sport or athletics; (*Austral.*) a summons. *v.t.* to make blue; to treat with laundress's blue; *v.t.* (*sl.*) to squander money. **light-blue, dark-blue,** the respective colours of Eton and Harrow schools, and of Cambridge and Oxford Universities in their athletic contests. **old blue,** a former University athlete. **out of the blue,** unexpected, unpredicted. **the Blue,** one of the three former divisions of the British Navy. **the Blues,** the Royal Horse Guards; the Conservatives; a form of melancholy, Black American folk-song originating in the deep south, usu. consisting of 3, 4-bar phrases in 4/4 time. **the blues,** low spirits, depression [contr. of BLUE DEVILS]. **to burn blue,** to burn (as candles) with a blue flame, as an omen of death, or indicating the presence of ghosts or evil spirits. **to look blue,** to look frightened or depressed. **true blue,** staunch, faithful, genuine. **blue baby,** *n.* a baby with a bluish discolouration of the skin due to a shortage of oxygen in the blood. **bluebell,** *n.* the blue bell of Scotland, *Campanula rotundifolia;* the wild hyacinth of England, *Scilla nutans.* **blueberry,** *n.* (*N Am.*) the genus *Vaccinium;* (*Austral.*) the native currant. **blue-black,** *a.* of a blue colour that is almost black; black with a tinge of blue. **blue-bird,** *n.* a small American bird, *Sylvia sialis;* (*fig.*) a symbol of happiness. **blue blood,** *n.* aristocratic descent. **blue blooded,** *a.* **blue bonnet,** *n.* a flat Scottish cap, or bonnet, of blue wool; hence a peasant or soldier wearing such a bonnet; (*Sc.*) a popular name for species of *Centaurea* and scabious. **Blue book,** *n.* an official report of Parliament (bound in volumes which have blue covers); (*N Am.*) a list of Government officials with their salaries etc. **blue-bottle,** *n.* the blue cornflower, *Centaurea cyanus;* applied also loosely to other blue flowers; the meat-fly or blow fly, *Musca vomitoria;* †a beadle, a policeman. **blue-cap,** *n.* a blue-bonnet; a salmon in its first year; the blue titmouse, *Parus coeruleus.* **blue cat,** *n.* a Siberian cat, valued for its slaty-blue fur. **blue cheese,** *n.* a cheese threaded by blue veins of mould induced by the insertion of copper wires during its making. **blue chip,** *n.* an issue of stocks or shares believed to be dependable in maintaining or increasing its value; hence, anything of worth and stability. **blue chip,** *a.* **blue-coat,** *n.* a coat of blue, formerly the dress of the poor classes; hence (often) of almoners and children in charity schools; hence, any individual of these classes. **blue-coat boy,** *n.* a boy wearing the blue coat of a charity school, esp. a scholar of Christ's Hospital. **blue-cod,** *n.* (*N Zealand*) an edible salt-water fish. **blue-collar,** *a.* pertaining to manual work and manual workers in contrast to desk work and office employees (see WHITE-COLLAR). **blue-devils,** *n.pl.* low spirits, depression (the blues); the illusions of delirium tremens. **blue eye,** †a livid contusion round the eye from a blow, an old-fashioned name for a black eye; †a dark circle round the eye from weeping; an eye with a blue iris; (*Austral.*) the blue-faced honey-eater. **blue-eyed,** *a.* having an eye with a blue iris. **blue-eyed boy, girl,** someone especially favoured by a person or group. **blue film, movie,** *n.* a sexually explicit or pornographic film. **blue funk,** *n.* (*sl.*) abject terror. **blue-gown,** *n.* the dress of an almoner or licensed beggar in Scotland; an almoner, a licensed beggar. **blue-grass,** *n.* (*N Am.*) the rich grass of the limestone lands of Kentucky and Tennessee (blue-grass country); a kind of folk music originating from these regions. **Blue-grass State,** *n.* Kentucky. **blue-gum tree,** *n.* an Australian tree, *Eucalyptus globulus.* **bluejacket,** *n.* a sailor in the British Navy. **blue-john,** [prob. from F *bleujaune,* blue-yellow], *n.* blue fluorspar. **blue-light,** *n.* a composition burning with a blue flame used at sea as a night-signal. **Blue Mantle,** *n.* one of the four pursuivants in the College of Arms. **blue moon,** *n.* a very rare or unknown occurrence, never. **blue mould,** *n.* a blue coloured fungus which grows on rotting food and other vegetable matter, and is induced in blue cheese. **blue movie,** BLUE FILM. **blue-nose,** *n.* (*N Am.*) a native of Nova Scotia. **blue pencil,** *v.t.* (*coll.*) to censor, edit or mark with corrections (trad. using a blue pencil). **Blue**

Peter, *n.* a small blue flag, with a white square in the centre used as a signal for sailing. **blue pill,** *n.* an antibilious pill made from mercury. **blue pointer,** *n.* (*Austral.*) a voracious shark with a blue back. **blueprint,** *n.* a plan or drawing printed on specially sensitized paper: the print is composed of white lines on a blue background, and is much used for scale and working drawings of engineering designs, electrical circuits etc.; any original plan or guideline for future work; a prototype. **blue ribbon,** *n.* the ribbon of the Garter; hence, the greatest distinction, the first prize; a total abstainer's badge. **blue-ribbonism,** *n.* the tenets or practice of total abstinence. **blue-ribbonite,** *n.* one who wears a blue ribbon as a badge of total abstinence, a member of the Blue Ribbon Army. **blue rock,** *n.* a kind of domestic pigeon. **blue ruin,** *n.* bad gin. **blue-sky,** *a.* (*coll.*) purely theoretical, speculative or experimental; lacking specific goals (as of a research project). **blue-sky laws,** *n.pl.* American legislation against a form of fraud involving stocks and shares. **bluestocking,** *a.* wearing blue worsted stockings, applied (contemptuously) to a literary society that met at Montagu House, London, the latter part of the 18th cent.; hence (of women) affecting learning or literary tastes. *n.* a woman affecting learning or literary tastes. **bluestone,** *n.* a dark building-stone found in Australia and New Zealand; sulphate of copper. **blue vitriol,** *n.* hydrous sulphate of copper. **blue water,** *n.* the open sea. **blueing,** *n.* (*N Am.*) laundress's blue. **bluely,** *adv.* **blueness,** *n.* **bluey, bluish,** *a.* **bluishly,** *adv.* **bluishness,** *n.* [prob. from F *bleujaune,* blue-yellow]

Blue Arrow, *n.* UK company whose attempted purchase of the US company Manpower Inc in 1987 prompted an investigation by the Serious Fraud Squad.

Bluebeard, *n.* folktale character, popularized by the writer Charles Perrault in France about 1697, and historically identified with Gilles de Rais. He murdered six wives for disobeying his command not to enter a locked room, but was himself killed before he could murder the seventh.

Bluefields, *n.* one of three major port facilities on the E coast of Nicaragua, situated on an inlet of the Caribbean Sea.

Blue Mountains, *n.pl.* part of the Great Divide, New South Wales, Australia, ranging 600–1,100 m/ 2,000–3,600 ft and blocking Sydney from the interior until the crossing (1813) by surveyor William Lawson, Gregory Blaxland and William Wentworth.

Blue Nile, *n.* (Arabic **Bahr el Azraq**) river rising in the mountains of Ethiopia. Flowing W then N for 2000 km/1250 miles it eventually meets the White Nile at Khartoum. The river is dammed at Roseires where a hydro-electric scheme produces 70% of Sudan's electricity.

Blue Ridge Mountains, a range extending from West Virginia to Georgia, US, and including Mount Mitchell 2,045 m/6,712 ft; part of the Appalachians.

bluff[1], *a.* having a broad, flattened face or front; abrupt, blunt, frank, outspoken. **bluff-bowed, bluff-headed,** *a.* (*Naut.*) having vertical or nearly vertical bows. *n.* a cliff or headland with a broad, precipitous front. **bluffly,** *adv.* **bluffness,** *n.* **bluffy,** *a.* having bold headlands; blunt, off-handed. [naut., etym. doubtful (cp. MDut. *blaf,* flat, broad)]

bluff[2], *n.* a blinker for a horse; a game of cards, called also poker; (*sl.*) an excuse, a blind; the action of bluffing at cards; boastful language; empty threats or promises. *v.t.* to hoodwink; to impose upon one's adversary (at cards) by making him believe one's hand is stronger than it is, and inducing him to throw up the game; (*fig.*) to treat rivals, political opponents, or foreign powers in this way. [etym. doubtful (cp. Dut. *bluffen,* to brag, boast)]

Blum, *n.* **Léon** (1872–1950), French politician. He was converted to socialism by the Dreyfus affair (1899), and in 1936 became the first socialist prime minister of France. He was again premier for a few weeks in 1938. Imprisoned under the Vichy government in 1942 as a danger to French security, he was released by the Allies in 1945. He again became premier for a few weeks in 1946.

blunder, *v.i.* to err grossly; to act blindly or stupidly; to flounder, to stumble. *v.t.* to utter thoughtlessly, to mismanage. *n.* a gross mistake, a stupid error. **to blunder upon,** to find or succeed by luck. **blunderhead,** *n.* a dunderhead; a muddleheaded fellow. **blunderer,** *n.* one who habitually blunders. **blundering,** *a.* **blunderingly,** *adv.* [etym. doubtful]

blunderbuss, *n.* a short gun, of large bore, widening at the muzzle. [Dut. *donderbus,* thunder-gun]

blunge, *v.t.* to mix (clay, powdered flint etc. with water) in a pug-mill. **blunger,** *n.* [prob. onomat.]

†**blunket,** *a.* grey; sky-coloured. [prob. cognate with BLANKET]

blunt, *a.* dull, stupid, obtuse; without edge or point; abrupt, unceremonious; rough, unpolished; †bare, naked. *n.* a short, thick make of sewing-needle; *v.t.* to make less sharp, keen, or acute; to deaden, to dull. *v.i.* to become blunt. **blunt-witted,** *a.* dull of understanding. **bluntish,** *a.* **bluntly,** *adv.* **bluntness,** *n.* [etym. doubtful]

Blunt, *n.* **Anthony** (1907–83), British art historian and double agent. As a Cambridge lecturer, he recruited for the Soviet secret service, and, as a member of the British Secret Service (1940–45), passed information to the Russians. In 1951 he assisted the defection to the USSR of the British agents Guy Burgess and Donald Maclean (1913–83). He was author of many respected works on French and Italian art.

blur, *n.* a smear, a blot, a stain; a dim, misty effect. *v.t.* to smear, to blot; to stain, to sully; to render misty and indistinct; to dim. **blurriness,** *n.* **blurry,** *a.* [etym. doubtful]

blurb, *n.* a description of a book, usually printed on the dust-jacket intended to advertise and promote it. [etym. unknown]

blurt, *v.i.* †to puff out the lips contemptuously; to burst into tears. *v.t.* to utter abruptly (*usu.* with *out*). *n.* an impetuous outburst. [prob. an imitative word]

blush, *v.i.* to become red in the face from shame or other emotion, to assume a bright-red colour; to be ashamed; to bloom. *v.t.* †to make red; to express by blushing. *n.* the reddening of the face produced by shame, modesty or any similar cause; a crimson or roseate hue; a flush of light. **at the first blush, at first blush,** at the first glance; at first sight. **to put to the blush,** to cause to blush; to make ashamed. **blush-rose,** *n.* a white rose with pink tinge. **blusher,** *n.* one who blushes; a cosmetic for reddening the cheeks. **blushful,** *a.* full of or suffused with blushes; modest, self-conscious. **blushfully,** *adv.* **blushing,** *a.* that blushes; modest; ruddy, roseate; blooming. **blushingly,** *adv.* **blushless,** *a.* [OE *āblisian* (cp. Dut. *blozen* to blush, Dan. *blus,* a blaze, a torch, OE *bœlblys,* a fire-blaze)]

bluster, *v.i.* to blow boisterously; to be agitated (as water by wind); to make a loud boisterous noise; to play the bully, to swagger, to boast. *v.t.* to disarray, to dishevel. *n.* boisterous, blowing, inflated talk, swaggering; empty vaunts and threats. **blusterer,** *n.* one who or that which blusters. **blustering,** †**blusterous, blustery,** *a.* blowing boisterously; tempestuous; hectoring, boastful. **blusteringly,** *adv.* [onomat.; cp. BLAST]

Blyth, *n.* **Charles 'Chay'** (1940–), British sailing adventurer who rowed across the Atlantic with Captain John Ridgeway in 1966 and sailed solo around the world in a westerly direction during 1970–71. In 1973–74 he sailed around the world with a crew in the opposite direction, and in 1977 he made a record-breaking transatlantic crossing from Cape Verde to Antigua.

Blyton, *n.* **Enid** (1897–1968), British writer of children's books. She created the character Noddy and the adventures of the 'Famous Five' and 'Secret Seven', but has been criticized by educationalists for social, racial, and sexual stereotyping.

BM, (*abbr.*) British Museum; Bachelor of Music;

(surveying) bench mark.
BMA, (*abbr.*) British Medical Association.
BMC, (*abbr.*) British Medical Council.
BMR, (*abbr.*) basal metabolic rate.
B Mus, (*abbr.*) Bachelor of Music.
BMW, (*abbr.*) Bayerische Motoren Werke, a kind of car. [G, Bavarian motor works]
BMX, (*abbr.*) bicycle motocross, bicycle stunt riding over an obstacle course, (**BMX**®) a bicycle designed for this.
Bn., (*abbr.*) Baron, battalion; billion.
bo, boh, *int.* an exclamation intended to surprise or frighten; **to say bo to a goose,** to open one's mouth, to speak. **bo-beep,** *n.* a childish game in which a player suddenly looks out from a hiding-place and cries 'bo!' to startle his or her playmates. [imit.]
BO, (*abbr.*) body odour; box office.
Boa, *n.* a genus of large S American serpents which kill their prey by crushing (popularly applied also to the pythons, which are from the Old World); a long fur or feather tippet worn round the neck. **boa-constrictor,** *n.* a Brazilian serpent, the best-known species of the genus Boa; any very large snake which kills its prey by constriction. [L (etym. unknown)]
Boadicea BOUDICCA.
boanerges, *n.* a loud, vociferous preacher or orator. [Gr., from Heb. *b'ney regesh,* sons of thunder (Mark iii.17)]
boar, *n.* the uncastrated male of the domesticated or the wild swine. **boar's foot,** *n.* the green hellebore, *Helleborus viridis*. **boar-spear,** *n.* a spear used in boar-hunting. **wild boar,** *n.* the male of *Sus scrofa,* wild in Europe, Asia and Africa. **boarish,** *a.* swinish, brutal; sensual, cruel. [OE *bār* (cp. Dut. *beer,* Gr. *bār*]
board, *n.* a piece of timber of considerable length, and of moderate breadth and thickness; a flat slab of wood, used as a table, for exhibiting notices, and other purposes; a table or frame on which games (as chess, draughts etc.) are played; a thick substance formed of layers of paper etc., pasted or squeezed together; a piece of stout pasteboard or millboard used as one of the sides of a bound book; a table, esp. for meals; a table spread for a meal; food served at table; daily provisions; one's keep, or money in lieu of keep; a council table; the members of a council; the persons who have the management of some public trust or business concern; the side of a ship; a passage driven across the grain of the coal; (*pl.*) the stage; (*Austral.*) the floor of a shearing-shed, the shearers there employed. *v.t.* to furnish or cover with boards; to provide with daily meals (and now *usu.* with lodging); to board out; to attack and enter (a ship) by force; to go on a ship, to embark; †to border upon; (*fig.*) to accost, to make up to. *v.i.* to have one's meals (and *usu.* lodging) at another person's house. **above board,** open, unconcealed, openly. **across the board,** inclusive of all categories or types. **bed and board,** conjugal relations. **board and lodging,** meals and sleeping-quarters. **by the board,** overboard, by the ship's side; ignored, rejected or disused. **on board,** in or into a ship, train, bus or aeroplane. **to sweep the board,** to win a total victory, as in a game. **board-room,** *n.* the meeting place of a company's board of directors. **board sailing,** *n.* sailing on a surf board propelled by a sail mounted with a steering bar; windsurfing. **board-sailing,** *v.i.* **to board out,** to place at board; to take one's meals out. **board game,** *n.* a game, such as chess, which is played with pieces or counters on a special board. **board-school,** *n.* a school managed by a Board, as established by the Elementary Education Act, 1870. **board-wages,** *n.pl.* wages given to servants in lieu of food. **board-walk,** *n.* a seaside promenade made of planks. **boarder,** *n.* one who has his food at the house of another; a scholar who is boarded and lodged at a school; (*Naut.*) one who boards an enemy's ship. **boarding,** *n.* the action of the verb TO BOARD; a structure of boards. **boarding-clerk,** *n.* a clerk in the Customs or in a mercantile firm, who communicates with the masters of ships on their arrival in port. **boarding-house,** *n.* a house in which board may be had. **boarding officer,** *n.* officer who boards a ship to examine bill of health etc. **boarding-out,** *n.* the obtaining of state meals at another person's house; the placing of pauper children in the houses of poor people, by whom they are treated as their own. **boarding pass,** *n.* a ticket authorising one to board an aeroplane, ship etc. **boarding-school,** *n.* a school in which pupils are boarded as well as taught. [OE *bord,* board, plank, table (cp. Dut. *boord,* MHG and G *Bort,* Icel. *borth*); *bord,* in the sense of border, rim, ship's side, appears to be a distinct word which was early associated; and at later periods the F *bord* (from Teut.) influenced the development of meaning]
boast, *n.* proud, vain glorious assertion, a vaunt, a brag; an occasion of pride; laudable exultation. *v.i.* to brag, to praise oneself, to speak ostentatiously or vaingloriously. *v.t.* to extol, to speak of with pride; to have as worthy of pride. **boaster,** *n.* one who boasts, a bragger, a braggadocio. **boastful,** *a.* full of boasting; vainglorious. **boastfully,** *adv.* **boastfulness,** *n.* **boastingly,** *adv.* [etym. doubtful]
boat, *n.* a small vessel, generally undecked and propelled by oars or sails; applied also to fishing vessels, packets, and passenger steamers; a vessel or utensil resembling a boat, a sauce-boat. *v.t.* to transport in a boat. *v.i.* to take boat, to row in a boat. **in the same boat,** in the same circumstances or position. **ship's boat,** a boat carried on board ship. **to rock the boat,** to disrupt existing conditions, to cause trouble. **boat-bill,** *n.* the S American genus *Cancroma,* allied to the herons, esp. *C. cochlearia,* from the shape of the bill. **boat-fly,** *n.* a boat-shaped water-bug, *Notonecta glauca*. **boat-hook,** *n.* a pole with an iron point and hook, used to push or pull a boat. **boat-house,** *n.* a house by the water in which boats are kept. **boatman,** *n.* a man who lets out boats on hire; a man who rows or sails a boat for hire. **boat people,** *n.pl.* refugees (usu. Vietnamese) who flee from their countries in small boats. **boat-race,** *n.* a race between rowing-boats. **boat-train,** *n.* a train conveying passengers to or from a ship. **boatable,** *a.* (*N Am.*) that may be traversed by boat; navigable. **boatage,** *n.* charges for carriage by boat. **boater,** *n.* one who boats; a man's stiff straw hat. **boatful, boat-load,** *n.* as much or as many as a boat will hold. [OE *bāt;* etym. obscure, prob. from Teut. (whence Icel. *bātr*, Dut. *boot,* and perh. F *bateau* etc.)]
boatel, botel, *n.* a floating hotel, a moored ship functioning as a hotel; a water-front hotel accommodating boaters. [BOAT, HOTEL]
Boat Race, *n.* annual British rowing race between the crews of Oxford and Cambridge universities. It is held during the Easter vacation over a 6.8 km/4.25 mile course on the river Thames between Putney and Mortlake, SW London.
boatswain, bos'n, *n.* the foreman of the crew (in the RN a warrant officer) who looks after the ship's boats, rigging, flags, cables etc. **boatswain's mate,** *n.* his chief assistant.
bob¹, *n.* a weight or pendant at the end of a cord, chain, plumb-line, pendulum etc.; a knot of worms used in fishing for eels; a knot or bunch of hair, a short curl, a bob-wig; the docked tail of a horse; †a chorus or refrain; a short line at the end of a stanza; a shake, a jog; a short jerking action, a curtsy; (*sl.*) a shilling or 5 pence; a peal of courses or set of changes in bell-ringing. *v.t.* to move with a short jerking motion; to cut short (as a horse's tail); to rap, to strike lightly; †to cheat, swindle. *v.i.* to have a short jerking motion; to move to and fro or up and down; to dance, to curtsy; to catch at cherries; to fish for eels with a bob. **rag-tag and bob-tail,** the rabble. **to bob up,** to emerge suddenly. **treble bob, bob major, bob minor,** peals in which the bells have a jerking or dodging action; in the first the treble bell is dominant; the others are rung on eight and six bells respectively. **bob-cherry,** *n.* a child's game with cherries suspended on a string. **bob-sled,** *n.* a conveyance formed of two sleds or sleighs coupled together, used to transport large timber. **bob-**

sleigh, *n.* a sleigh with two pairs of runners, one behind the other often used for racing. **bob-tail,** *n.* a tail (of a horse) cut short; a horse or dog with its tail cut short; a lewd woman; a worthless fellow. **bob-tail wig,** *n.* a short wig. **bob-tail, bob-tailed,** *a.* having the tail cut short. **bob-wig,** *n.* a wig having the bottom turned up in bobs or curls, in contradistinction to a full-bottomed wig. **bobbish,** *a.* (*coll.*) well, in good health; brisk. **bobble,** *n.* a fabric or wool ball used as decorative trimming, a pom-pom. [etym. doubtful; prob. onomat.]

bob[2], *n.* a person, a fellow. **dry-bob,** (*Eton*) a boy who devotes himself to cricket, tennis etc., as opposed to a **wet-bob,** who devotes himself to boating. **light-bob,** a light infantry man. [prob. from *Robert*]

Bobadil, *n.* a braggart. [character in Jonson's *Every Man in His Humour*]

bobbers, *n.pl.* a name given to the men who unload trawlers.

bobbery, *n.* a row; a fuss. [Hind. *bāp re!* O father!]

bobbie (-by) pin, *n.* (*esp. N Am.*) a hair-grip.

bobbin, *n.* a wooden pin with a head on which thread for making lace, cotton, yarn, wire etc., is wound and drawn off as required; a piece of wood with a string for actuating a door-latch; a reel, spool. **bobbin-lace, -work,** *n.* work woven with bobbins. **bobbinet,** *n.* machine-made cotton net, orig. imitated from bobbin-lace. [F *bobine* (etym. unknown)]

bobby, *n.* (*coll.*) a policeman. [from Sir *Robert* Peel, who introduced the new police, 1828]

bobby sox, socks, *n.* (*N Am.*) ankle socks usu. worn by young girls. **bobby soxer,** *n.* an adolescent girl.

bobolink, *n.* an American song-bird, *Dolichonyx oryzivorus,* called also reed-bird and rice-bird. [earlier *Bob Lincoln* or *Bob o' Lincoln,* from the cry]

bobstay, *n.* a chain or rope for drawing the bowsprit downward and keeping it steady. [etym. unknown]

bob-tail etc. BOB[1].

Boccaccio, *n.* **Giovanni** (1313–75), Italian poet, author of a collection of tales called the *Decameron* (1348–53).

Boccherini, *n.* **(Ridolfo) Luigi** (1743–1805), Italian composer and cellist. He studied in Rome, made his mark in Paris in 1768, and was court composer in Prussia and Spain. Boccherini composed some 350 instrumental works, an opera, and oratorios.

Boccioni, *n.* **Umberto** (1882–1916), Italian painter and sculptor. One of the founders of the Futurist movement, he was a pioneer of abstract art.

Boche, *n.* (*offensive*) a German; (*sl.*) nonsense, rubbish. *a.* German. [F sl.]

bock, *n.* a large beer-glass; a large glass of beer. [a mistaken sense, from F, the G *Bock,* goat, used to describe a strong kind of beer, being taken for a measure]

bod, *n.* (*coll.*) a person. [contr. BODY]

bode[1], *v.t.* to foretell, to presage, to give promise of, to forebode. *v.i.* to portend (well or ill). †**bodeful,** *a.* ominous, portentous. **bodement,** *n.* an omen, a presage; prognostication. **boding,** *a.* presaging, ominous. *n.* an omen, presentiment, prediction. **bodingly,** *adv.* ominously, forebodingly. [OE *bodian* (*bod,* a message, *boda,* a messenger), cp. Icel. *botha,* to announce]

†**bode[2],** ABODE, ABIDE[1].

Bode, *n.* **Johann Elert** (1747–1826), German astronomer, director of the Berlin observatory. He published the first atlas of all stars visible to the naked eye, *Uranographia* (1801).

bodega, *n.* a wine-shop. [Sp., from L *apotheca,* Gr. *apothēkē;* seeAPOTHECARY]

Bodhidharma *n.* (6th century AD) Indian Buddhist. He entered China from S India *c.* 520, and was the founder of Zen, the school of Mahāyāna Buddhism in which intuitive meditation, prompted by contemplation, leads to enlightenment.

bodice, *n.* †a quilted inner garment for the upper part of the body (worn by both sexes); †a corset; †a pair of stays; formerly an inner vest worn by women over the corset; a tight-fitting outer vest for women; the upper part of a woman's dress. [orig. *pair of bodies*]

†**bodikin,** *n.* a little body. **od's bodikins,** by God's dear body. [BODY, KIN]

†**bodkin,** *n.* †a small dagger; an instrument for piercing holes; a large-eyed and blunt-pointed needle for leading a tape or cord through a hem, loop etc.; a pin for fastening up women's hair; an awl-like tool for picking out letters in correcting set-up type; (*coll.*) a third person wedged in between two others. **to ride or sit bodkin,** to ride or sit thus. [etym. unknown]

Bodichon, *n.* **Barbara** (born Leigh-Smith) (1827–91), English feminist and campaigner for women's education and suffrage. She wrote *Women and Work* (1857), and was a founder of the magazine *The Englishwoman's Journal* in 1858.

Bodin, *n.* **Jean** (1530–96), French political philosopher, whose six-volume *De la République* (1576) is considered the first work on political economy.

bodle, *a.* an old Scots copper coin; anything of little value. [perh. from *Bothwell,* an old mint-master]

Bodleian, *a.* of or pertaining to Thomas Bodley. *n.* the Bodleian Library.

Bodley, *n.* **Thomas** (1545–1613), English scholar and diplomat after whom the Bodleian Library in Oxford is named. After retiring from Queen Elizabeth I's service in 1597, he restored the library, which was opened in 1602. He was knighted in 1604.

Bodoni, *n.* **Giambattista** (1740–1813), Italian printer who managed the printing-press of the Duke of Parma and produced high-quality editions of the classics. He designed several typefaces, including one bearing his name, which is in use today.

body, *n.* the material frame of man or the lower animals; the trunk; the upper part of a dress BODICE; a corpse, a dead body; the main or central part of a building, ship, document, book etc.; the part of a motor-car in which the driver and passengers sit; a collective mass of persons, things or doctrine, precepts etc.; matter, substance, as opposed to spirit; a human being, a person, an individual; a society, a corporate body, a corporation; a military force; (*Phil.*) matter, substance, that which has sensible properties; (*Geom.*) any substance, simple or compound; a figure of three dimensions; strength, substantial quality. a figure-hugging woman's top resembling a swimsuit or leotard fastened beneath the crotch (and worn under a skirt or trousers). *v.t.* to clothe with a body; to embody. **heavenly body,** a sun, star, planet or other mass of matter, distinct from the earth. **of good body,** having substantial quality (as of wine), as opposed to thinness, flimsiness, transparency and the like. **to body forth,** to give mental shape to; to exhibit, to typify. **body blow,** *n.* in boxing, a punch landing between the breast bone and navel; a harsh disappointment or set-back, a severe shock. **body builder,** *n.* one who develops his/her muscles through exercise; an exercising machine and/or eating high-protein food. **body building,** *n., a.* **body-colour,** *n.* a pigment having a certain degree of consistence and tingeing power as distinct from a wash; a colour rendered opaque by the addition of white. **bodyguard,** *n.* a guard for the person of a sovereign or dignitary; retinue, following. **body language,** *n.* a form of non-verbal communication by means of conscious or unconscious gestures, postures and facial expressions. **body politic,** *n.* organized society; the State. **body-servant,** *n.* a valet. **body-snatcher,** *n.* one who steals a body from a grave for the purpose of dissection; a resurrection-man; (*sl.*) a bailiff; a police officer. **body stocking,** *n.* a clinging all-in-one undergarment often of a sheer material. **bodywork,** *n.* the metal shell of a motor vehicle. **bodied,** *a.* having a body; embodied. **bodiless,** *a.* **bodily,** *a.* of, pertaining to or affecting the body or the physical nature; corporeal. *adv.* corporeally, united with matter; wholly, completely, entirely. [OE *bodig*]

Boeing, *n.* **William Edward** (1881–1956), US industrialist, and founder of the Boeing Airplane Company 1917. Its military aircraft include the flying fortress bombers used in World War II, and the Chinook helicopter; its commercial craft include the jetfoil, and the

Boeing 747 and 707 jets.

Boeotia, *n.* ancient district of central Greece, of which Thebes was the chief city; the **Boeotian League** (formed by 10 city states in the 6th century BC) superseded Sparta in the leadership of Greece in the 4th century. **Boeotian,** *a.* stupid, dull.

Boer, *n.* a S African of Dutch birth or extraction. [Dut. *boer,* countryman, farmer (see BOOR)]

Boer War, *n.* war between the Dutch settlers in South Africa and the British (see SOUTH AFRICAN WARS).

boffin, *n.* a scientist, esp. one employed by the Services or the government. [uncert.]

Bofors gun, *n.* an automatic anti-aircraft gun [from *Bofors* the Swedish munition works]

bog, *n.* a marsh, a morass; wet, spongy soil, a quagmire; (*sl.*) a bog-house. *v.t.* to sink or submerge in a bog. **to bog down,** to overwhelm, as with work; to hinder. **bog-asphodel,** *n.* the genus *Narthecium,* esp. Lancashire bog-asphodel, *N. ossifragum.* **bog-bean** BUCK-BEAN. **bog-berry,** *n.* the cranberry. **bog-butter,** *n.* a fatty hydrocarbon found in peat-bogs. **bog-house,** *n.* (*sl.*) a privy, lavatory. **bog-land,** *n.* boggy soil, derogatorily applied to Ireland, hence **bog-lander,** *n.* (*offensive*) an Irishman. **bog-moss,** *n.* the genus *Sphagnum.* **bog-oak,** *n.* oak found preserved in bogs, black from impregnation with iron. **bog-timber, bog-wood,** *n.* timber found preserved in bogs. **bog-trotter,** *n.* a person used to traversing boggy country; (*offensive*) an Irishman. **bog-violet,** *n.* the butter-wort the genus *Pinguicula.* **boggy,** *a.* of or characterized by bogs; swampy. **bogginess,** *n.* **boglet,** *n.* a little bog. [Ir. *bogach*]

Bogarde, *n.* **Dirk** (stage-name of Derek van den Bogaerde) (1921–), British film actor, who appeared in comedies and adventure films such as *Doctor in the House* (1954) and *Campbell's Kingdom* (1957), before acquiring international recognition for complex roles in films such as *The Servant* (1963). He distinguished himself in films made with director Joseph Losey, such as *Accident* (1967), and with Luchino Visconti in *Death in Venice* (1971).

Bogart, *n.* **Humphrey** (1899–1957), US film actor, who achieved fame with his portrayal of a gangster in *The Petrified Forest* (1936). He became a cult figure as the romantic, tough 'loner' in such films as *The Maltese Falcon* (1941) and *Casablanca* (1943). He won an Academy Award for his role in *The African Queen* (1952).

Bogdanovich, *n.* **Peter** (1939–), US film director, screenwriter, and producer, formerly a critic. *The Last Picture Show* (1971) was followed by two films that attempted to capture the style of old Hollywood, *What's Up Doc?* (1972) and *Paper Moon* (1973). Both made money but neither was a critical success.

bogey1, **Colonel Bogey**, *n.* a fair score or allowance for a good player, orig. an ideal opponent against whom a solitary player could pit himself; one stroke over par on a hole. [imag. person]

bogey2, BOGIE1.

boggard, boggart, *n.* a hobgoblin; a ghost. [North. dial., conn. with BOGLE, BOGY etc.]

boggle, BOGLE *v.i.* to shrink back, start with fright; to hesitate, make difficulties; equivocate; to bungle. (*coll.*) to be astounded; (*coll.*) to be unable to imagine or understand.

bogie1, **bogy**1, *n.* †a long, low truck on four small wheels; a plate-layer's truck or trolley; a revolving under-carriage. **bogie-car, -engine,** *n.* a railway-carriage or locomotive-engine mounted on these. [etym. doubtful]

bogie2, **bogy**2, *v.i.* to bathe, to swim. *n.* a bathe. **bogie-hole,** *n.* a swimming-hole. [Austral. Abor.]

bogle, *n.* a hobgoblin, a spectre; a scarecrow, a bugbear. [Sc., perh. from W *bwg,* a goblin]

Bogomils, *n.pl.* heretics who originated in 10th-cent. Bulgaria and spread throughout the Byzantine empire. They take their name from Bogomilus, or Theophilus, who taught in Bulgaria 927–950. Despite persecution, they were only expunged by the Ottomans after the fall of Constantinople in 1453.

Bogotá, *n.* capital of Colombia, South America; 2,640 m/8,660 ft above sea level on the edge of the plateau of the E Cordillera; population (1985) 4,185,000. It was founded in 1538.

bogus, *a.* sham, counterfeit, spurious, fictitious. [etym. doubtful]

bogy1, **bogy**2, BOGIE1, BOGIE2.

bogy3, **bogey**3, *n.* a spectre, a bugbear. **old Bogy,** Nick, the Devil. **bogy (-gey) man,** *n.* an evil person or spirit, used to menace children. [BOGLE]

bohea, *n.* a name given in the 18th cent. to the finest kind of black tea; now applied to inferior qualities. [Chin. *Wu-i* or *Bu-i* hills, in China]

Bohemia, *n.* kingdom of central Europe from the 9th cent., under Habsburg rule (1526–1918), when it was included in Czechoslovakia. The name Bohemia derives from the Celtic Boii, its earliest known inhabitants.

Bohemian1, *a.* of or pertaining to Bohemia or its people or their language. *n.* a native or inhabitant of Bohemia; a Czech; the Czech language.

bohemian2, *n.* a gipsy; one who leads a free, irregular life, despising social conventionalities. *a.* of or characteristic of the gipsies or of social bohemians. **bohemianism,** *n.* the habits or conduct of a social bohemian. **bohemianize, -ise,** *v.i.* to live in an unconventional way. [F *bohémien,* gipsy (because the gipsies were supposed to come from Bohemia)]

Bohlen, *n.* **Charles 'Chip'** (1904–74), US diplomat. Educated at Harvard, he entered the foreign service in 1929. Interpreter and adviser to presidents Roosevelt at Tehran and Yalta, and Truman at Potsdam, he served as ambassador to the USSR during 1953–57.

Bohr1, *n.* **Aage** (1922–), Danish physicist who produced a new model of the nucleus in 1952, known as the collective model. For this work, he shared the 1975 Nobel Physics prize.

Bohr2, *n.* **Niels Henrik David** (1885–1962), Danish physicist. He founded the Institute of Theoretical Physics in Copenhagen, of which he became director in 1920. Nobel prize (1922). In 1952, he helped to set up CERN in Geneva.

boiar, BOYAR.

boil1, *v.i.* to be agitated by the action of heat, as water or other fluids; to reach the temperature at which these are converted into gas; to be subjected to the action of boiling, as meat etc., in cooking; to bubble or seethe like boiling water (also of the containing vessel); to be agitated with passion. *v.t.* to cause a liquid to bubble with heat; to bring to the boiling point; to cook by heat in boiling water; to prepare in a boiling liquid; *n.* an act of boiling; the state of boiling; boiling-point. **to boil away,** to evaporate in boiling. **to boil down,** to lessen the bulk of by boiling; to condense. **to boil over,** to bubble up, so as to run over the sides of the vessel; to be effusive. **boiled,** *a.* **boiled shirt,** *n.* (*coll.*) a dress shirt. **boiler,** *n.* one who boils; a vessel in which anything is boiled; the large vessel in a steam-engine in which water is converted into steam; a tank in which water is heated for domestic use; formerly a vessel for boiling clothes in a laundry, a copper. **boiler-iron, -plate,** *n.* rolled iron $\frac{1}{4}$ to $\frac{1}{2}$ in. (about 0·5 to 1·0 cm) thick for making boilers. **boiler-suit,** *n.* a combined overall garment, esp. for dirty work. **boiler-tube,** *n.* one of a system of tubes by which heat is transmitted to the water in a boiler. **boiling,** *a.* in a state of ebullition by heat; inflamed, greatly agitated. *n.* the action of boiling. **the whole boiling (lot),** *n.* (*sl.*) the whole lot. **boiling-point,** *n.* the temperature at which a fluid is converted into the gaseous state; esp. the boiling-point of water at sea-level (212°F, 100°C). [OF *boillir* (F *bouillir*), L *bullīre*), to bubble (*bulla,* a bubble)]

boil2, *n.* a hard, inflamed, suppurating tumour. [OE *bȳl* (cp. Dut. *buil,* G *Beule*)

Boileau, *n.* **Nicolas** (1636–1711), French poet and critic. After a series of contemporary satires, his *Epîtres/Epistles* (1669–77) led to his joint appointment with Racine as royal historiographer in 1677. Later works include *L'Art poétique/The Art of Poetry* (1674) and the mock-heroic *Le Lutrin/The Lectern* (1674–83).

boisterous, †boistous, *a.* †rough, coarse, cumbrous; wild, unruly, intractable; stormy, roaring, noisy; tumultuous, rudely violent. **boisterously,** *adv.* **boisterousness,** *n.* [ME *boistous,* rough]

Bokassa, *n.* **Jean-Bédel** (1921–), president and later self-proclaimed emperor of the Central African Republic (1966–79). Commander in chief from 1963, in Dec. 1965 he led a military coup which gave him the presidency, and on 4 Dec. 1977 he proclaimed the Central African Empire with himself as emperor for life. His regime was characterized by arbitrary state violence and cruelty. In exile during 1979–86, he was tried and imprisoned.

Bol, *n.* **Ferdinand** (1610–80), Dutch painter, a pupil and for many years an imitator of Rembrandt. There is uncertainty in attributing some works between them. After the 1660s he developed a more independent style and prospered as a portraitist.

bolas, *n.* a missile, used by the S American Indians, formed of balls or stones strung together and flung round the legs of the animal aimed at. [Sp. and Port., pl. of *bola,* ball]

bold, *a.* courageous, daring, confident, fearless; planned or executed with courage; vigorous, striking; audacious, forward, presumptuous; steep, prominent, projecting (of a cliff or headland). **bold as brass,** wholly impudent or audacious. **to make** or **be so bold,** to venture, to presume. **bold-face,** *a.* of type, heavy, conspicuous. **bold-faced,** *a.* impudent, shameless. **bold-spirited,** *a.* courageous, daring. **boldly,** *adv.* impudently with effrontery. **boldness,** *n.* courage, enterprise, audacity; effrontery, shamelessness. [OE *beald, bald* (cp. OHG *pald,* G *bald,* quickly),]

Boldrewood, *n.* **Rolf**, pen name of Thomas Alexander Browne (1826–1915), Australian writer, born in London, he was taken to Australia as a child in 1830. He became a pioneer squatter, and a police magistrate in the goldfields. His books include *Robbery Under Arms* (1888).

bole[1], *n.* the stem or trunk of a tree. [Icel. *bolr* (Dan. *bul,* log, G *Bohle,* plank, board)]

bole[2], *n.* a brownish, yellowish or reddish, soft unctuous clay, containing more or less iron oxide. **bole armeniac**, **†armoniac**, *n.* an astringent earth brought from Armenia, formerly used as an antidote and a styptic etc.; †a bolus. [late L *bōlus,* Gr. *bōlos,* a clod of earth]

bole[3], *n.* (*Sc.*) a small recess in a wall; a small unglazed window. [etym. unknown]

bolection, *n.* a projecting moulding. [etym. unknown]

bolero, *n.* a lively Spanish dance; (*Mus.*) the air to which it is danced;, a short jacket worn over a bodice. [Sp.]

Boletus, *n.* a genus of fungi having the under surface of the pileus full of pores instead of gills. **boletic**, *a.* of or pertaining to the boletus. [L and Gr. *bōlites* (perh. from *bōlos,* a lump)]

Boleyn, *n.* **Anne** (1507–36), queen of England. Second wife of King Henry VIII, she was married to him in 1533 and gave birth to the future Queen Elizabeth I in the same year. Accused of adultery and incest with her half-brother (a charge invented by Thomas Cromwell), she was beheaded.

bolide, *n.* a large meteor; usually one that explodes and falls in the form of aerolites. [F, from L *bolidem -lis,* Gr. *bolis,* missile (*ballein,* to throw)]

bolin, bowline see BOW[3].

Bolingbroke[1], *n.* **Henry of Bolingbroke** title of Henry IV of England.

Bolingbroke[2], *n.* **Henry John, Viscount Bolingbroke** (1678–1751), British Tory politician and philosopher. He was foreign secretary 1710–14 and a Jacobite conspirator.

bolivar[1], *n.* (*pl.* **-vars, -vares**) the standard unit of currency in Venezuela [from Simon *Bolivar,* 1783–1830]

Bolívar[2], *n.* **Simón** (1783–1830), South American nationalist, leader of revolutionary armies, known as **the Liberator**. He fought the Spanish colonial forces in several uprisings and eventually liberated his native Venezuela (1821), Colombia and Ecuador (1822), Peru (1824), and Bolivia (a new state named after him, formerly Upper Peru) in 1825.

Bolivia, *n.* Republic of (*República de Bolivia*). **area** 1,098,581 sq km/424,052 sq miles. **capital** La Paz (seat of government), Sucre (legal capital and seat of judiciary). **towns** Santa Cruz, Cochabamba. **physical** high plateau between mountain ridges; forest and lowlands in the E. **population** (1988 est.) 7,000,000; (Quechua 25%, Aymara 17%, Mestizo 30%, European 14%); annual growth rate 2.7%. **exports** tin (second largest world producer), other non-ferrous metals, oil, gas (piped to Argentina), agricultural products. **language** Spanish (official); Aymara, Quechua. **religion** Roman Catholic (state-recognized).

Bolkiah, *n.* **Hassanal** (1946–), sultan of Brunei from 1967, following the abdication of his father, Omar Ali Saifuddin (1916–86). On independence, in 1984, Bolkiah also assumed the posts of prime minister and defence minister.

boll[1], *n.* †a bowl; a rounded seed-vessel or pod. **boll-weevil,** *n.* a weevil (*Anthonomus grandis*) that infests the flowers and bolls of the cotton plant. [BOW[1]]

boll[2], **bow,** (*Sc.*) *n.* a measure of capacity varying from two to six bushels (about 0.07 to 0.2 cm.) for grain. [perh. from Icel. *bolli* (cp.Dan. *bolle,* OE *bolla*)]

Böll, *n.* **Heinrich** (1917–85), West German novelist. A radical Catholic and anti-Nazi, he attacked Germany's political past and the materialism of its contemporary society. His many publications include poems, short stories, and novels which satirize German society, for example *Billard um Halbzehn/Billiards at Half-Past Nine* (1959) and *Gruppenbild mit Dame/Group Portrait with Lady* (1971). Nobel Prize for Literature (1972).

Bollandist, *n.* one of the Jesuit continuators of the *Acta Sanctorum,* commenced by Bolland. [John *Bolland,* Flemish Jesuit, 1596–1665]

bollard, *n.* (*Naut.*) a large post or bitt on a wharf, dock or on ship-board for securing ropes or cables; a short post preventing motor-vehicle access. [perh. from BOLE[1]]

bollocks, *n.pl.* (*sl.*) testicles; (often *int.*) rubbish, nonsense, a mess. *v.i.* to make a mess of. **bollocking,** *n.* (*sl.*) a strong rebuke. [OE *beallucas,* testicles]

Bologna, *n.* industrial city and capital of Emilia-Romagna, Italy, 80 km/50 miles north of Florence; population (1988) 427,000. It was the site of an Etruscan town, later of a Roman colony, and became a republic in the 12th century. It came under papal rule 1506, and was united with Italy 1860. **Bologna-bottle, -flask,** *n.* an unannealed bottle which flies in pieces when scratched. **Bologna-phosphorus,** *n.* a phosphorescent preparation of Bologna-spar. **Bologna-sausage,** *n.* a large kind of sausage, first made at Bologna, POLONY. **Bologna-spar, -stone,** *n.* native sulphate of baryta, with phosphorescent properties, found near Bologna. **Bolognese**, *a.* belonging or native to Bologna. *n.* a native or resident of Bologna.

bolometer, *n.* an extremely sensitive instrument for measuring radiant heat. **bolometric**, *a.* [Gr. *bole,* a ray of light; -GRAF]

boloney, BALONEY.

Bolshevik, -vist, *n.* a member of the Russian majority Social Democratic party which came to power under Lenin in 1917 and which advocated the destruction of capitalist political and economic institutions, and the setting up of a socialist state with power in the hands of the workers; a revolutionary; (*often offensive*) a political troublemaker. **Bolshevism,** *n.* **bolshie, -shy**, *n.* (*coll.*) a Bolshevik; (*often offensive*) a political agitator. *a.* (*sl.*) stubborn and argumentative. [Rus. *bolsheviki,* majority party]

bolster, *n.* a long under-pillow, used to support the pillows in a bed; a pad, cushion or anything resembling a pad or cushion, in an instrument, machine, ship, architecture or engineering; a punching-tool. *v.t.* to support with or as with a bolster; to belabour with bolsters; to pad, stuff. *v.i.* to fight with bolsters. **to bolster up,** to support, to prevent from falling; to save from deserved chastisement, criticism or disgrace; to aid, abet, countenance. **bolstering,** *n.* prop, support; padding, stuffing; a fight with bolsters. [OE (OHG *polstar,* G *Polster,* Icel. *bolstr*)]

bolt[1], *n.* a short thick arrow with a blunt or thick head; a discharge of lightning; †a kind of fetter for the leg; the act of gulping food without chewing; a measured roll of woven fabric, esp. canvas; a bundle of osiers or reeds, measuring about 3 ft. (0.9 m) in circumference; a sliding piece of iron for fastening a door, window etc.; a metal pin for holding objects together, frequently screw-headed at one end to receive a nut; that portion of a lock which engages with the keeper to form a fastening; a sudden start, a sudden flight; the act of suddenly breaking away; (*N Am.*) sudden desertion from a political party. *v.t.* to shut or fasten by means of a bolt or iron; to fasten together with a bolt or bolts; to gulp, to swallow hastily and without chewing; (*N Am.*) to desert (a political party). *v.i.* to start suddenly forward or aside; to run away (as a horse); (*N Am.*) to break away from a political party. **a bolt from the blue,** lightning from a cloudless sky, an unexpected sudden event. **to bolt in, bolt out,** to shut in; to exclude. **bolt-head,** *n.* the head of a bolt; a globular flask with a long, cylindrical neck, used in distilling. **bolt-hole,** *n.* a hole by which or into which one escapes; an escape; a means of escape. **bolt-rope,** *n.* a rope sewed round the margin of a sail to prevent its being torn. **boltsprit,** *n.* bowsprit. **bolt upright,** *a.* straight upright. **bolter,**[1] *n.* (*N Am.*) one that bolts or runs; a horse given to bolting; one who suddenly breaks away from his party; (*Austral. Hist.*) a runaway convict. **bolting,** *n.* sudden flight; (*N Am.*) political desertion; fastening with bolts; a bundle of straw; swallowing without chewing. [OE (cp. Dut. *bout,* G *Bolz*)]

bolt[2], **boult**, *n.* a sieve for separating bran from flour. *v.t.* to pass through a bolt or bolting cloth; to examine, to try. **to bolt out,** to separate by sifting. **bolter,** *n.* a sieve; a bolting-cloth; a sifting-machine. **bolting,** *n.* the act or process of sifting; †private arguing of cases for practice. **bolting-cloth,** *n.* a fine cloth used in sifting meal. **bolting-hutch,** *n.* a tub or box into which flour or meal is bolted; a receptacle for refuse. **bolting-machine, -mill,** *n.* a machine or mill for sifting flour or meal. [OF *bulter, buleter* (*buletel,* a sieve), It. *burattare* (*buratto,* a sieve, late L *burra,* a coarse cloth)]

Bolt[3], *n.* **Robert (Oxton)** (1924–), British dramatist, noted for his historical plays, especially *A Man for All Seasons* (1960), about Thomas More (filmed 1967), and for his screenplays, including *Lawrence of Arabia* (1962) and *Dr Zhivago* (1965).

Boltzmann's constant, *n.* in physics, the constant that relates the kinetic energy (energy of motion) of a gas atom or molecule to temperature. Its symbol is k and its value is 1.380662×10^{-23} joules per Kelvin. It is equal to the gas constant, R, divided by Avogadro's number.

bolus, *n.* medicine in a round mass larger than a pill; a round lump of anything; anything mentally unpalatable. [late L (*bōlus,* Gr. *bōlos,* a clod, lump]

bomb, *n.* an explosive device triggered by impact or a timer usu. dropped from the air, thrown or placed by hand; (*coll.*) a great success; (*coll.*) a large amount of money; (*coll.*) of a play etc., utter failure, a flop. *v.t.* to attack, destroy or harm with bombs. *v.i.* to throw, drop or detonate bombs; (*coll.*) to fail utterly, to flop. **the bomb,** the atom or hydrogen bomb; nuclear arms. **volcanic bomb,** a roundish solid mass of lava ejected from a volcano. **bomb crater,** *n.* crater caused by the explosion of a bomb. **bomb disposal,** *n.* the detonation or diffusing of an unexploded bomb rendering it harmless. **bomb-ketch, bomb-vessel,** *n.* a small strongly-built vessel formerly used to carry mortars for naval bombardments. **bomb-proof,** *a.* applied to a shelter etc., affording safety from the explosion of a bomb. *n.* a bomb-proof structure. **bomb-shell,** *n.* a bomb thrown by artillery; a total (often unpleasant) surprise. **bomb-sight,** *n.* device for aiming a bomb from an aircraft. [F *bombe,* Sp. *bomba,* L *bombus,* Gr. *bombos* a humming noise]

bombard, *v.t.* to attack with shot and shell; to assail with arguments or invective; to subject atoms to a stream of high-speed particles. *n.*, the earliest form of cannon; a bombardment; a bomb-ketch; a leather jug for liquor; a toper; a deep-toned wooden instrument of the bassoon family. †**bombardman,** *n.* a pot-boy. **bombardier**, *n.* †an artilleryman employed in serving mortars and howitzers; a noncommissioned artillery officer ranking as corporal. **bombardier-beetle,** *n.* the genus *Brachinus,* which, when disturbed, emits fluid from the abdomen, with blue vapour and a perceptible report. **bombardment,** *n.* the act of bombarding; an attack upon a place with shot and shell. **bombardon, bombardone**, *n.* a brass instrument related to the tuba; a bass-reed stop on the organ. **bomber,** *n.* one who throws, drops, places or triggers bombs; an aircraft used for bombing. **bomber jacket,** *n.* a waist-length jacket elasticated at the wrists and waist. [see prec.]

bombasine, bombazine, *n.* a twilled dress fabric of silk and worsted cotton and worsted or of worsted alone. [F *bombasin* late L *bombācinus* (*bombax,* L *bombyx,* Gr. *bombux,* silk, cotton, orig. silk-worm)]

bombast, *n.* †cotton-wool, esp. used as padding; padding, stuffing; inflated speech, fustian; high-sounding words. †*a.* turgid, bombastic. *v.t.* (*usu.* , †to stuff out, to inflate; to fill out with imposing language. **bombastic**, *a.* of the nature of bombast; inflated, turgid; given to inflated language. **bombastically,** *a.* in an inflated, grandiloquent style. [OF *bumbace,* cotton, late L *bombax -ācem* (L *bombyx,* see prec.)]

Bombax, *n.* a genus of W Indian silk-cotton trees. [L *bombyx*]

Bombay[1], *n.* former province of British India. Together with a number of interspersed princely states, it was included in the domain of India in 1947, and the major part became in 1960 the two new states of Gujarat and Maharashtra. The capital was the city of Bombay.

Bombay[2], *n.* industrial port (textiles, engineering, pharmaceuticals, diamonds), commercial centre, and capital of Maharashtra, W India; population (1981) 8,227,000. It is the centre of the Hindi film industry.

Bombay bowler, *n.* a small, light pith helmet.

Bombay duck, *n.* a small E Indian fish, *Harpodon nehereus,* when salted and dried eaten as a relish; called also bummalo. [Mahratti *bombil,* name of the fish]

bombe, *n.* an ice-cream dessert moulded into a rounded, bomb shape. [F]

bombé, *a.* protruding or round-fronted, as of furniture. [F]

bomber BOMB.

bombora, *n.* (*Austral.*) dangerous broken water, usu. at the base of a cliff.

Bombyx, *n.* a genus of moths, containing the silkworm, *Bombyx mori.* **bombycid**, *a.* [Gr., see BOMBASINE]

bona fide, *adv.* in good faith. *a.* genuine. **bona fides**, *n.* good faith, sincerity. [L]

bonanza, *n.* a rich mine; a successful enterprise; a run of luck. *a.* very successful; highly profitable. **bonanza farm,** *n.* a big farm in the West worked by the best modern appliances and securing large profits. [N Am., from Sp., fair weather, prosperity]

Bonaparte, *n.* Corsican family of Italian origin, which gave rise to the Napoleonic dynasty (see NAPOLEON I, NAPOLEON II, and NAPOLEON III). Other well-known members were the brothers and sister of Napoleon I:

Bonapartism, *n.* attachment to the dynasty founded in France by Napoleon Bonaparte. **Bonapartist,** *n.* an adherent of the Bonaparte dynasty. *a.* of, pertaining to or supporting the Bonaparte dynasty.

†**bona-roba,** *n.* a showy wanton; a harlot. [It. *buona-*

roba (*buona,* good, *roba,* dress)]

Bonar Law, LAW, ANDREW BONAR.

Bonaventura, St, *n.* (John of Fidanza) (1221–74), Italian Roman Catholic theologian. He entered the Franciscan order in 1243, became professor of theology at Paris, France, and in 1256 general of his order. In 1273 he was created cardinal and bishop of Albano. His eloquent writings earned him the title of the 'Seraphic Doctor'. Feast day 15 July.

bonbon, *n.* a sweet esp. of fondant; a Christmas cracker. [F (*bon,* good, L *bonus*)]

bonce, *n.* a large playing-marble; the game played with these; (*sl.*) the head. [etym. unknown]

bond[1], *n.* that which binds or confines, as a cord or band; (*pl.*) chains, imprisonment, captivity; a withe for tying a faggot; that which restrains or cements; a binding agreement or engagement; that which impedes or enslaves; (*pl.*) trammels; a mode of overlapping bricks in a wall so as to tie the courses together (as with English bond and Flemish bond); (*Law*) a deed by which one person (the obligor) binds himself, his or her heirs, executors and assigns, to pay a certain sum to another person (the obligee), his/or her heirs etc.; a document by which a government or a public company undertakes to repay borrowed money, a debenture. *v.t.* to put into a bonded warehouse; to mortgage; to bind or connect (as bricks or stones) by overlapping or by clamps. **in bond,** in a bonded warehouse and liable to customs duty. **bond-creditor,** *n.* a creditor secured by bond. **bond-holder,** *n.* a person holding a bond or bonds granted by a private person or by a government. **bond paper,** *n.* a good quality paper. **bond-stone,** *n.* a stone going through a wall, a bonder. **bond-timber,** *n.* pieces of timber built into a stone or brick wall to strengthen it. **bonded,** *a.* bound by a bond; put in bond. **bonded debt,** *n.* a debt secured by bonds issued by a corporation as distinguished from floating debts. **bonded goods,** *n.pl.* goods stored, under the care of customs officers, in warehouses until the duties are paid. **bonded warehouse,** *n.* see BONDED GOODS. **bonder,** *n.* one who puts or holds goods in bond; a stone or brick reaching a considerable distance through a wall so as to bind it together. **bonding,** *n.* the storing of goods in bond; the act of strengthening by bonders; the adherence of two surfaces glued together; any union or attachment, esp. the emotional one formed between a parent and his/her newborn child. [var. of BAND[1]]

bond[2], *a.* in serfdom or slavery. **bond-maid,** *n.* a slave-girl. **bond-servant,** *n.* a slave. **bond-service,** *n.* villainage. **bond-slave,** *n.* an emphatic term for a slave. **bondsman, bondman,** *n.* a slave; a surety. **bondswoman, bondwoman,** *n. fem.* a female slave. **bondage,** *n.* slavery, captivity, imprisonment; subjection, restraint, obligation. **bondager,** *n.* (*Sc.*) a cotter bound to render certain services to a farmer; a female worker paid by a cotter to render certain services on his behalf to a farmer. [OE *bōnda, bunda,* a husbandman, Icel. *bōndi* (*būa,* to till); influenced in meaning by prec.]

bond[3], *n.* a league of confederation, see AFRIKANDER. [Dut., from *binden,* to bind (cp. G *Bund*)]

Bond, *n.* **Edward** (1935–), British dramatist, whose work has aroused controversy because of the savagery of some of his themes, for example the brutal killing of a baby, symbol of a society producing unwanted children, in *Saved* (1965). His later works include *Black Mass* (1970) about apartheid, *Bingo* (1973), and *The Sea* (1973).

Bondfield, *n.* **Margaret Grace** (1873–1953), British socialist who became a trade-union organizer to improve working conditions for women. She was a Labour Member of Parliament in 1923–24 and during 1926–31, and was the first woman to enter the cabinet – as minister of labour, 1929–31.

bone, *n.* the hard material of the skeleton of mammals, birds, reptiles and some fishes; any separate and distinct part of such a skeleton; the substance of which the skeleton consists; applied to many articles made (or formerly made) of bone or ivory, whalebone etc.; a stiffening material for garments; a small joint of meat; (*pl.*) dice; a domino; castanets, two pieces of bone held between the fingers of each hand, and used as a musical accompaniment; the performer on these; the body; mortal remains. *a.* of or pertaining to bone; made of bone. *v.t.* to take out the bones of (for cooking); (*sl.*) to steal; to stiffen a garment. **a bone of contention,** a subject of dispute. **body and bones,** altogether. **to bone up,** (*sl.*) to study hard, to swot. **to have a bone to pick with someone,** to have a cause of quarrel with or complaint against someone. **to make no bones,** to act or speak without hesitation or scruple; to present no difficulty or opposition. **to point a bone,** (*Austral.*) in aboriginal magic, to will the death of an enemy; to put a jinx on someone. **to the bone,** to the inmost part. **bone-breaker,** *n.* one who or that which breaks bones; the osprey. †**bone-ache,** *n.* pain in the bones. **bone-ash,** *n.* the mineral residue of bones burnt in the air. **bone-bed,** *n.* (*Geol.*) a bed largely made up of bones of animals. **bone-black,** *n.* animal charcoal used as a deodorizer and as a pigment. **bone-cave,** *n.* a cave, containing remains of prehistoric or recent animals. **bone china,** *a.* porcelain made with china clay (kaolin) and bone-ash (calcium phosphate). **bone-dry,** *a.* quite dry. **bone-dust,** *n.* bones ground for manure. **bone-earth,** *n.* BONE-ASH. **bone-grafting,** *n.* introduction of a piece of bone obtained elsewhere to replace bone lost by injury or disease. **bonehead,** *n.* (*sl.*) a dolt. **bone-lace,** *n.* a kind of thread-lace originally made with bone bobbins. **bone meal,** *n.* bone-dust used as animal feed or fertilizer. **bone-oil,** *n.* a fetid oil obtained in the dry distillation of bones. **bone-setter,** *n.* †a surgeon; a non-qualified practitioner who sets fractured and dislocated bones. **bone-shaker,** *n.* an old-fashioned bicycle without india-rubber tyres; any delapidated or old-fashioned vehicle. **bone-spavin,** *n.* a bony excrescence on the inside of a horse's hock. **boned,** *a.* possessed of bones (*in comb.*); deprived of bones (for cooking). **big-boned,** *a.* of large and massive build. **boneless,** *a.* without bones; without backbone, having no stamina. **bonelessness,** *n.* **boner,** *n.* (*N Am.*) gross mistake, a howler. **boning,** *n.* the removing of bones from poultry, fish etc.; the operation of levelling or judging of the straightness of a surface by the eye. **boning-rod,** *n.* one of a line of poles set up some distance apart, and used in judging the level of a surface by the eye. **bony,** *a.* of, pertaining to or of the nature of bone or bones; big-boned. **bony pike,** *n.* the American genus *Lepidosteus.* **boniness,** *n.* [OE *bān* (cp. Dut. *been,* OHG *pein, bein,* G *bein*)]

bonfire, *n.* a large fire lit in the open air on occasion of some public rejoicing; a fire for burning up garden rubbish. [BONE, FIRE]

bong, *a.* dead. [Austral. Abor.]

bongo, *n.* (*pl.* **-gos, -goes**), **bongo drum,** (*pl.* **drums**) a small Cuban hand drum often played in pairs [S Am. Sp. *bongó*]

†**bongrace,** *n.* a kind of sunshade worn on the front of the bonnet; a broad-brimmed hat for women; (*Naut.*) a bow-grace or junk-fender. [F *bonne-grace* (*bonne,* good, *grace,* GRACE)]

Bonhoeffer, *n.* **Dietrich** (1906–45), German Lutheran theologian and opponent of Nazism. Involved in an anti-Hitler plot, he was executed by the Nazis in Flossenburg concentration camp. His *Letters and Papers from Prison* (1953) advocate the idea of 'religionless' Christianity.

bonhom(m)ie, *n.* good-nature, geniality. [F *bon,* good, *homme,* man]

boniface, *n.* a generic name for an innkeeper; mine host. [name of the innkeeper in Farquhar's *The Beaux' Stratagem*]

Boniface, *n.* name of nine popes, including:

Boniface VIII, *n.* Benedict Caetani (*c.* 1228–1303). Pope from 1294. He clashed unsuccessfully with Philip IV of France over his taxation of the clergy, and also with Henry III of England.

Boniface, St, *n.* (680–754) English Benedictine monk, known as the 'Apostle of Germany'; originally named Wynfrith. After a missionary journey to Frisia in 716, he was given the task of bringing Christianity to Germany by Pope Gregory II in 718, and was appointed archbishop of Mainz in 746. He returned to Frisia in 754 and was martyred near Dockum. Feast day 5 June.

boning, etc. BONE.

bonito, *n.* the striped tunny, *Thynnus pelamys;* some other species of the mackerel family. [Sp., etym. doubtful]

bonjour, good day. [F]

bonk, *v.t.* (*coll.*) to hit; (*sl.*) to have sexual intercourse with. *v.i.* to have sexual intercourse. [imit.]

bonkers, *a.* crazy; tipsy with alcohol.

†**bon mot,** *n.* (*pl.* **bon mots**) a witticism. [F, lit. good word]

Bonn, *n.* industrial city (chemicals, textiles, plastics, aluminium), capital of West Germany, 18 km/11 miles SSE of Cologne, on the left bank of the Rhine; population (1988) 292,000.

Bonnard, *n.* **Pierre** (1867–1947), French post-impressionist painter. With other members of les Nabis, he explored the decorative arts (posters, stained glass, furniture). He painted domestic interiors and nudes.

bonne, *n.* a nursemaid; a maid (of French nationality). [F]

Bonner, *n.* **Yelena** (1923–), Soviet human-rights campaigner. Disillusioned by the Soviet invasion of Czechoslovakia in 1968, she resigned from the Communist Party (CPSU) after marrying her second husband Dr Andrei Sakharov in 1971, and became active in the dissident movement. She was banished to internal exile in Gorky in 1984–86.

bonnet, *n.* a head-covering without a brim for men and boys; (*esp. Sc.*) a flat cap; a head-covering tied beneath the chin, of various shapes and materials, formerly worn by women out of doors and now usu. by babies; a confederate, a decoy; a protective covering to a machine etc.; a chimney-cowl; the front part of a motor-car covering the engine; an additional piece of canvas laced to the bottom of a sail to enlarge it. *v.t.* to put a bonnet on a person; to knock a man's hat over his eyes. *v.i.* †to take off the bonnet or cap as a salute. **Balmoral bonnet,** a flat cap like a Scottish bonnet. **Glengarry bonnet, glengarry,** a pointed cap with flowing ribbons behind. **poke bonnet,** an old-fashioned bonnet that covered the sides of the face. **Scotch** or **Lowland bonnet,** a round, flat, woollen cap, like a beret, with a tassel in the middle. **bonnet-piece,** *n.* a gold coin of James V of Scotland, on which the king is represented as wearing a bonnet instead of a crown. **bonnet rouge,** *n.* the red cap of liberty worn by revolutionaries. **bonneted,** *a.* wearing a bonnet or cap. [OF *bonet,* stuff of which caps were made (whence *chapel de bonet,* abbr. into *bonet*), low L *bonnētus*]

Bonneville Salt Flats, bed of a prehistoric lake in Utah, US, of which the Great Salt Lake is the surviving remnant. It has been used for motor speed records.

Bonnie and Clyde, Bonnie Parker (1911–34) and Clyde Barrow (1900–34), infamous US criminals who carried out a series of small-scale robberies in Texas, Oklahoma, New Mexico, and Missouri between Aug. 1932 and May 1934. They were eventually betrayed and then killed in a police ambush.

bonny, *a.* beautiful, handsome, pretty; healthy-looking. **bonnily,** *adv.* bonniness, *n.* [F *bonne,* good]

bonsai, *n.* (*pl.* **-sai**) a potted tree or shrub cultivated into a dwarf variety by skilful pruning of its roots; the art or practice of cultivating trees and shrubs in this manner. [Jap. *bon,* bowl, *sai,* to grow]

bonsella, *n.* (*S Afr.*) a tip, a present.

bonspiel, *n.* (*Sc.*) a curling-match. [etym. unknown]

bon ton, *n.* fashion, good style. [F]

bonus, *n.* something over and above what is due; a premium given for a privilege or in addition to interest for a loan; an extra dividend; a distribution of profits to policy-holders in an insurance company; a gratuity over and above a fixed salary or wages. **bonus share, bonus issue,** *n.* a share or number of shares issued free to the holder of a paid-up share in a joint-stock company. *v.t.* to give a bonus to; to promote by bonuses. [L *bonus,* a good (man)]

Bonus Expeditionary Force, in US history, a march on Washington DC by unemployed ex-servicemen during the great Depression to lobby Congress for immediate cash payment of a promised war veterans' bonus.

bon vivant, *n.* (*fem.* **bonne vivante**) one fond of good living. [F]

bon voyage, a pleasant journey, farewell. [F]

bony, etc. BONE.

bonza, bonzer, *a.* (*Austral. sl.*) excellent. [Austral. Abor.]

bonze, *n.* a Buddhist priest in Japan, China and adjacent regions. [Jap. *bonzō,* Chin. *fan seng,* religious person (through F *bonze,* Port. *bonzo,* or directly)]

boo, booh, *int.* and *n.* a sound imitating the lowing of oxen, used as an expression of contempt, aversion and the like. *v.i.* to low as an ox, to groan. *v.t.* to groan at, to hoot. **boo-hoo,** *n.* an ejaculation of contempt; the sound of noisy weeping. *v.i.* to weep noisily; to bellow, to roar, to hoot. [onomat.].

boob[1]**, boo boo,** *n.* (*coll.*) an error, a blunder. *v.t.* to err, commit a blunder. [BOOBY]

boob[2]**,** *n.* (*pl.* **-bs**) (*usu. in pl., sl.*) a woman's breast. **boob tube,** *n.* (*sl.*) a woman's elasticated, strapless top.

booby, *n.* a dull, stupid fellow; a dunce; a gannet, esp. *Sula fusca.* **booby hatch,** *n.* a small kind of companion for the half-decks of merchant ships. **booby-prize,** *n.* the prize, usu. a worthless one, given in ridicule to the player who makes the lowest score, esp. in whist-drives. **booby-trap,** *n.* a practical joke consisting of e.g. placing books or the like on the top of a door left ajar, so that the whole tumbles on the head of the first person entering; a bomb so disposed that it will explode when some object is touched. **boobyish,** *a.* stupid, foolish, awkward. [Sp. *bobo,* a blockhead; also, a kind of bird (prob. from L *balbus,* stammering)]

boodle, *n.* (*sl.*) money, capital, stock in trade; a fund for bribery; bribery, plunder, graft; a pack, crew, lot. [etym. doubtful; perh. from Dut. *boedel,* estate, possession]

boogie-woogie, (*contr.***) boogie,** *n.* (*Mus., Dancing*) a jazz piano style of a rhythmic and percussive nature based on 12-bar blues.

book, *n.* †a writing, a document, a charter; a collection of sheets printed, written on or blank, bound in a volume; a literary composition of considerable extent; one of its principal divisions; a libretto; a set of tickets, cheques, forms of receipt, stamps or the like, fastened together; (*Turf*) bets on a race or at a meeting taken collectively; (*fig.*) anything that can be read or that conveys instruction; (*Cards*) the first six tricks gained by a side at whist etc. *n.pl.* a set of accounts. *v.t.* to enter or register in a book; to reserve by payment in advance (as a seat in a conveyance, theatre or the like); to hand in or to receive for transmission (as a parcel, goods etc.); (of police) to take name etc. prior to making a charge. **Book of Hours,** *n.* in medieval Europe, a collection of liturgical prayers for the use of the faithful, especially at home. Books of Hours appeared in England in the 13th cent., and contained short prayers and illustrations, with each prayer suitable for a different hour of the day, in honour of the Virgin Mary. The enormous demand for Books of Hours was a stimulus for the development of Gothic illumination. A notable example is the *Très Riches Heures du Duc de Berry,* illustrated in the early 15th cent. by the Limbourg brothers. **by the book,** with exact information. **like a book,** formally, pedantically, as if one were reciting from a book. **reference book,** *n.* a book for occasional consultation, not for continuous reading, as an encyclopaedia, gazetteer, or the like. **The Book, The Book of God,** the Bible. **book of fate, book of life,** the record of souls to be saved. **to be on the books,** to have one's name on the official list. **in one's black books,** in bad favour with anyone. **to bring to book,** to convict, call to account. **without book,** from memory; without authority. **book-account,** *n.* an account or register of debit or credit in a book. **bookbinder,** *n.* one who binds books. **bookbindery,** *n.* a place for binding books. **bookbinding,** *n.* **book-case,** *n.* a case with shelves for books; a book-cover. **book-club,** *n.* an association of persons who buy and lend each other books; a business which sells to its members a choice of books at below publishers' prices. **book-cover,** *n.* a pair of boards (usu. cloth- or leather-covered) for binding a book; case for periodicals, music etc. **book-debt,** *n.* a debt for articles supplied, entered in an account-book. **book-ends,** *n.pl.* props placed at the ends of a row of books to keep them upright. **book-holder,** *n.* (*Theat.*) a prompter. **book-hunter,** *n.* a collector of rare books. **book-keeper,** *n.* one who keeps the accounts in a merchant's office etc. **book-keeping,** *n.* the art or practice of keeping accounts. †**bookland,** *n.* land taken from the folcland or common land and granted by *bōc* (see BOOK) or charter to a private person. **book-learned,** *a.* **book-learning,** *n.* learning derived from books; theory, not practical knowledge or experience. **book louse,** *n.* (*pl.* **book lice**) an insect, belonging to the Corrodentia, found amongst books, papers etc. **book-maker,** *n.* one who makes or compiles books; one who takes bets, principally in relation to horse races, and pays out to winners as a profession. **book-making,** *n.* the compilation of books; the making of a betting-book. **bookman,** *n.* a literary man; a bookseller. **book-mark(er),** *n.* a piece of ribbon, paper, leather etc. put in a book to mark a place. †**book-mate,** *n.* a school-fellow. †**book-oath,** *n.* an oath taken on the Bible. **book-plate,** *n.* a label with a name or device, pasted in a book to show the ownership. **book-post,** *n.* the postal system for conveying books. **book-rest, -stand,** *n.* a support for a book. **bookseller,** *n.* one whose trade it is to sell books. **bookshop,** *n.* a shop where books are sold. **bookstall, -stand,** *n.* a stall or stand at which books and periodicals are sold. **book-store,** *n.* a bookshop. **book token,** *n.* a gift token exchangeable for books. **book value,** *n.* the value of an asset, commodity or enterprise as it is recorded on paper (not always the same as its market value). **bookwork,** *n.* study of textbooks, as opposed to practice and experiment. **bookworm,** *n.* any worm or insect which eats holes in books; an avid reader. **bookable,** *a.* **booked,** *a.* registered; entered in a book; (*coll.*) caught, arrested. **booker,** *n.* one who books, makes a booking. **bookful,** †*a.* full of knowledge derived from books. *n.* all that a book contains. **bookie,** *n.* (*coll.*) short for bookmaker. **booking,** *n.* a reservation. **booking-clerk,** *n.* one who issues tickets or takes bookings. **booking-office,** *n.* an office where tickets are issued or bookings are made. **bookish,** *a.* learned, studious; acquainted with books only. **bookishly,** *adv.* **bookishness,** *n.* **booklet,** *n.* a little book, a pamphlet. **booksie,** *a.*, *adv.* (*coll.*) would-be literary. **booky,** *a.* (*coll.*) bookish. [OE *bōc,* a book, document, charter (cp. OHG *buoh,* G *Buch*) (possibly conn. with OE *bōece,* G *Buche,* Gr. *phages,* L *fāgus,* a beech)]

Booker Prize, *n.* British literary prize of £20,000 awarded annually (from 1969) by the Booker company (formerly Booker McConnell) to a novel published in the UK during the previous year.

Book of the Dead, an ancient Egyptian book, known as the *Book of Coming Forth by Day*, and buried with the dead as a guide to reaching the kingdom of Osiris, the god of the underworld.

Books of Hours, HOURS, BOOKS OF.

Book Trust, *n.* British association of authors, publishers, booksellers, librarians, and readers, to encourage the reading and production of better books. Founded as the National Book Council in 1925, it was renamed the National Book League in 1944 and renamed Book Trust in 1986.

Boole, *n.* **George** (1814–64), English mathematician, whose work *The Mathematical Analysis of Logic* (1847) established the basis of modern mathematical logic, and whose **Boolean algebra** can be used in designing computers.

boom¹, *n.* a loud, deep, resonant sound; a sudden demand for a thing; a rapid advance in prices; a burst of commercial activity and prosperity; *v.i.* to make a loud, deep, resonant sound; to rush with violence; to go off with a boom; to become very important, prosperous or active. *v.t.* to utter with a booming sound. **boom town,** *n.* a town undergoing rapid expansion or enjoying sudden commercial prosperity. **booming,** *n.*, *a.* [imit. (cp. BOMB)]

boom², *n.* a long spar to extend the foot of a particular sail; a bar, chain or line of connected spars forming an obstruction to the mouth of a harbour; a line of floating timber enclosing an area of water for lumber; the logs so enclosed; a movable overhead pole carrying a microphone used in television, film, video tape recordings. **boomslang,** *n.* a poisonous S African tree-snake. [Dut. *boom,* a tree (cp. BEAM)]

boomer, *n.* (*Austral.*) a large kangaroo; (*coll.*) anything of a large size.

boomerang, *n.* an Aboriginal Australian missile weapon, consisting of a curved flat stick so constructed that it returns to the thrower; an action, speech or argument that recoils on the person who makes it. *v.i.* [Australian Abor.]

boon¹, *n.* a prayer, a petition, an entreaty; a favour, a gift; a benefit, a blessing. [Icel. *bōn* (cp. OE *bēn*)]

†**boon²,** *a.* †good; †advantageous, fortunate; jolly, convivial; close, intimate. **boon companion,** *n.* one who is convivial or congenial; a close or special friend. [F *bon,* good]

boondocks, *n.pl.* (*N Am.*) remote or uncultivated country; (*sl.*) a provincial area [Tagalog *bundok,* mountain]

Boone, *n.* **Daniel** (1734–1820), US pioneer, who explored the Wilderness Road (East Virginia/ Kentucky) in 1775 and paved the way for the first westward migration of settlers.

boong, *n.* (*Austral. offensive*) an Aborigine.

boongarry, *n.* the N Queensland tree-kangaroo. [Austral. Abor.]

boor, *n.* a peasant, a rustic; a rude, awkward or insensitive person. **boorish,** *a.* clumsy, insensitive, unmannerly. **boorishly,** *adv.* **boorishness,** *n.* [Dut. *boer* (G *bauer,* from Goth. *baüan,* to till); the OE *gebūr* (*būan,* to dwell, to till) gave the rare ME *boueer*]

Boorman, *n.* **John** (1933–), British film director who, after working in television, subsequently directed successful films both in Hollywood (*Deliverance* 1972, *Point Blank* 1967) and in Britain (*Excalibur* 1981, *Hope and Glory* 1987).

boost, *v.t.*, *v.i.* to push or shove upwards; to advertise widely; to promote or encourage; to enlarge or increase, e.g. the voltage in an electric circuit; to elevate or raise, e.g. the pressure of an internal combustion engine. **booster,** *n.* a contrivance for intensifying the strength of an alternating-current; an auxiliary motor in a rocket that usu. breaks away when exhausted; any thing or person which boosts; a supplementary vaccination. [etym. doubtful]

boot¹, *n.* a covering (usually of leather) for the foot and part of the leg; an instrument of torture applied to the leg and foot, formerly used in Scotland to extort confessions; †an outside space or compartment on a coach; (*pl.*) a hotel servant who cleans boots, runs errands etc.; a luggage compartment in a motor car; (*sl.*) summary dismissal, e.g. from employment; a heavy sports shoe, e.g. football boot; (*sl.*) a kick; *v.t.* to equip with boots; to kick; to start a computer program running. **boot and saddle** (F *boute-selle,* put the saddle on), (*Mil. command*) Mount. **the boot is on the other foot, leg,** the situation is reversed. **to bet one's boots,** to be absolutely certain. **to boot out,**

(*sl.*) to eject, dismiss, sack. **to get the boot,** to be dismissed; to get the sack. **to put, stick the boot in,** (*sl.*) to cause further upset or harm to one already in distress. **boot-black,** *n.* a person who cleans and polishes shoes. **boot boy,** *n.* a hooligan, a bovver boy. **boot-jack,** *n.* a device for removing boots. **bootlace,** *n.* a string for fastening boots. **bootleg,** *a.* illicit, smuggled, e.g. of alcohol. *n.* an illicit or smuggled commodity. *v.i.* **bootlegger,** *n.* one who makes, deals in or transports an illicit commodity esp. liquor. **bootlegging,** *n.* **bootlicker,** *n.* a sycophant. **boot-maker,** *n.* one who makes boots. **boot strap,** *n.* a looped strap on a boot-top enabling it to be pulled up. **to pull oneself up by the bootstraps,** to achieve or improve one's situation by one's own efforts. **boot-top,** *n.* the upper part of a boot, esp. of top-boots. **boot-tree,** *n.* a block inserted into a boot to stretch it or keep it in shape. **booted,** *a.* having boots on. **booted and spurred,** equipped for riding. **bootee,** *n.* a short boot; a knitted boot for infants. **bootless**[1], *a.* [OF *bote* (F *botte*), etym. doubtful]

†**boot**[2], *n.* profit, gain, advantage; anything given in addition to what is stipulated. *v.t.* to benefit, to profit. **to boot,** into the bargain, besides, in addition. **bootless**[2], *a.* profitless, unavailing. **bootlessly,** *adv.* **bootlessness,** *n.* [OE *bōt* (bētan, to amend, help, cp. Goth. *bōtjan,* to profit, G *Busse,* making good, atonement)]

Boötes, *n.* constellation of the northern hemisphere representing a herdsman driving a bear (Ursa Major) around the pole. Its brightest star is Arcturus.

booth[1], *n.* †a temporary dwelling covered with boughs or other light material; a tent; a stall, tent or other temporary erection at a fair, in a market, polling station etc., a compartment or structure containing a telephone, a table in a restaurant etc. **polling-booth,** *n.* a temporary structure for voting in at elections. [MDan. *bōth,* Dan. *bod* (Icel. *buth,* from *būa,* to dwell), related to Ir. and Gael. *both, bothan,* a hut, a bothy]

Booth[2], *n.* **John Wilkes** (1839–65), US actor and fanatical Confederate who assassinated President Lincoln on 14 Apr. 1865; he escaped with a broken leg and was later shot in a barn in Virginia when he refused to surrender.

Booth[3], *n.* **William** (1829–1912), British founder of the Salvation Army in 1878, and its first 'general'.

Boothby, *n.* **Robert John Graham, Baron Boothby** (1900–86), Scottish politician. He became a Unionist Member of Parliament in 1924 and was parliamentary private secretary to Churchill (1926–29). He advocated Britain's entry into the European Community, and was a noted speaker.

Boothe Luce, *n.* **Clare** (1903–87), US journalist, playwright, and politician. She was managing editor of the magazine *Vanity Fair* (1933–34), and wrote several successful plays, including *The Women* (1936) and *Margin for Error* (1939).

booty, *n.* spoil taken in war; property carried off by thieves; gain, a prize. **to play booty,** to join with confederates so as to victimize another player; to play to lose. [prob. from Icel. *bȳti,* barter, through F *butin* or MDut. *būte* (Dut. *buit,* booty, spoil), with influence from *bot,* BOOT[2]]

booze, boose, *n.* (*coll.*) drink; a drinking bout. *v.i.* to drink to excess, to tipple. **booze-up,** *n.* a drinking session. **boozer,** *n.* a heavy drinker; (*sl.*) a public house. **boozy, boosy,** *a.* drunk, tipsy; addicted to boozing. [ME *bousen,* to drink deeply; perh. from MDut. *būsen* (*buize,* a drinking-cup, cp. Dut. *buis,* OF *buse, buise,* a conduit)]

bop, *n.* an innovative style of jazz music dating from the 1940s, *v.i.* **bopper,** *n.* a fan of bop; any follower of popular music, one who dances to it. [contr. BEEBOP]

bo-peep BO.

Bophuthatswana, *n.* Republic of southern Africa. **area** 40,330 sq km/15,571 sq miles. **capital** Mmbatho or Sun City, a casino resort frequented by many white South Africans. **population** (1985) 1,622,000. **exports** platinum, chrome, vanadium, asbestos, manganese. **language** Setswana, English. **religion** Christian.

bora[1], *n.* a keen dry, north-east wind in the Upper Adriatic. [It. *borea,* L *boreas,* the north wind]

bora[2], *n.* ritual initiation rites and ground where they are performed. [Austral. Abor.]

†**borachio,** *n.* a leather wine-bag; a drunkard. [Sp. *borracha,* wine-bag, *borracho,* drunkard, or It. *boraccia,* a goat-skin for wine]

Bora-Bora, *n.* one of the 14 Society Islands of French Polynesia. Situated 225 km/140 miles NW of Tahiti. Area 39 sq km/15 sq miles. Exports include mother-of-pearl, fruit and tobacco.

boracic BORAX.

boracite, *n.* native borate of magnesia.

borage, *n.* a hairy, blue-flowered plant of the genus *Borago,* formerly esteemed as a cordial, and now much used to flavour claret-cup etc. [F *bourrache* (OF *borrace*), or late L *borrāgo*]

Borah, *n.* **William Edgar** (1865–1940), US Republican politician. Born in Illinois, he was a senator for Idaho from 1906. An arch-isolationist, he was one of those chiefly responsible for the US repudiation of the League of Nations.

borak, *n.* chaff, banter. **to poke borak at,** to ridicule, to pull someone's leg. [Austral. Abor.]

borax, *n.* a native salt used as a flux and a solder, and as a detergent. **boracic, boric,** *a.* of, pertaining to or derived from borax or boron. **boracic, boric acid,** *n.* an acid obtained from borax. **borate,** *n.* a salt of boric acid. [low L (OF *boras*), from Arab. *būrāq*]

borazon BORON.

bordar, *n.* a villein of the lowest rank, doing manual service for a cottage which he held at his lord's will. [med. L *bordārius,* cottager, from *borda,* a hut (prob. from Teut. *bord*)]

†**bordel, bordello,** *n.* a brothel. [OF, hut, brothel]

Bordeaux[1], *n.* port on the Garonne, capital of Aquitaine, SW France, a centre for the wine trade, oil refining, aeronautics and space industries; population (1982) 640,000. Bordeaux was under the English crown for three centuries until 1453. In 1870, 1914, and 1940 the French government was moved here because of German invasion.

Bordeaux[2], *n.* a red French wine; claret. **Bordeaux mixture,** *n.* a preparation of sulphate of copper and lime for destroying fungi and other garden pests.

border[1], *n.* brim, edge, margin; boundary line or region; frontier, frontier region, esp. the boundary between England and Scotland with the contiguous regions; (*N Am.*) the frontier of civilization; an edging designed as an ornament; an edging to a plot or flower-bed. *v.t.* to put a border or edging to; to form a boundary to. *v.i.* to lie on the border; to be contiguous. **borderland,** *n.* land near the border between two countries or districts. **border-line,** *n.* a line of demarcation. **border-line case,** *n.* a case of mental disturbance bordering on insanity. **border-plant,** *n.* a decorative plant for flower borders. **Border terrier,** *n.* a type of small rough-haired terrier. **bordered,** *a.* **borderer,** *n.* one who dwells on a border or frontier, esp. on that between England and Scotland. **bordering,** *n.* an ornamental border. **bordering upon,** adjoining; resembling. **borderless,** *a.* without a border, limitless. [OF *bordure,* low L *bordātūra* from *bordāre,* to edge, from *bordus* (Teut. *bord*)]

Border[2], *n.* **Allan** (1955–), Australian cricketer, captain of the Australian team from 1985. He has played for New South Wales and Queensland, and in England for Gloucestershire and Essex. He made his test debut for Australia 1978–79.

bordereau, *n.* (*pl.* **-eaux**) a letter, memorandum, invoice or other document. [F, dim. of *bord,* as prec.]

Borders, *n.* region of Scotland. **area** 4700 sq km/1815 sq miles. **towns** administrative headquarters Newtown St Boswells; Hawick, Jedburgh. **population** (1987) 102,000. **products** knitted goods, tweed, electronics, timber.

bordure, *n.* †a border; (*Her.*) the border of an

escutcheon, occupying one-fifth of the shield. [F (see BORDER)]

bore[1], *v.t.* to perforate or make a hole through; to hollow out. *v.i.* to make a hole; to push forward persistently; to thrust the head straight forward (of a horse); to push a horse, boat or other competitor out of the course; to drive a boxing adversary on to the ropes by sheer weight. *n.* a hole made by boring; the diameter of a tube; the cavity of a gun-barrel. **bore-hole,** *n.* a shaft or pit cut by means of a special tool. **borer,** *n.* a person, tool or machine that bores or pierces; a horse that bores; popular name for *Myxine glutinosa,* the glutinous hag or blind fish, the genus *Teredo* or shipworm, the annelid genus *Terebella,* and some insects that bore holes in wood. **boring,** *n.* the action of the verb TO BORE; a hole made by boring; (*pl.*) chips or fragments made by boring. [OE *borian* (*bor,* Icel, *borr,* gimlet, *bora,* Dut. *boren,* to bore, cp. L *forāre,* to bore, Gr. *pharanx,* a chasm)]

bore[2], *n.* a tidal wave of great height and velocity, caused by the meeting of two tides or the rush of the tide up a narrowing estuary. [prob. from Icel. *bāra,* a billow]

bore[3], *n.* a tiresome person, a wearisome twaddler. *v.t.* to weary with twaddle or dullness. **boredom,** *n.* the characteristic behaviour of bores; the condition of being bored; bores collectively. **boring,** *a.* **boringly,** *adv.* [etym. doubtful]

bore[4] BEAR[2].

boreas, *n.* the god of the north wind; (*Poet.*) the north wind. **boreal,** *a.* pertaining to the north or the north wind; northern; living near the north; sub-arctic. [L, from Gr. *Boreas, Borras*]

borecole, *n.* a curled variety of winter cabbage; kail. [Dut. *boerenkool,* peasant's cabbage (BOER)]

boree, *n.* a kind of wattle-tree affording firewood. [Austral. Abor.]

boreen, *n.* (*Ir.*) a lane, a bridle-path; an opening in a crowd. [Ir. *bothar,* pron. bō'ér, *-een,* dim. suf.]

borer BORE[1].

Borg, *n.* **Bjorn** (1956–), Swedish lawn tennis player who won the men's singles title at Wimbledon five times (1976–80), a record since the abolition of the challenge system in 1922.

Borges, *n.* **Jorge Luis** (1899–1986), Argentinian poet and short-story writer. In 1961 he became director of the National Library in Buenos Aires, and was professor of English at the university there. He is known for his fantastic and paradoxical work *Ficciones/Fictions* (1944).

Borgia[1], **Cesare** (1476–1507), Italian general, illegitimate son of Pope Alexander VI. Made a cardinal at 17 by his father, he resigned to become captain-general of the papacy. Ruthless and treacherous in war, he was an able ruler of conquered territory (the model of Machiavelli's *The Prince*), but his power crumbled on the death of his father. He was a patron of artists, incl. Leonardo da Vinci.

Borgia[2], *n.* **Lucrezia** (1480–1519), Duchess of Ferrara from 1519. She was the illegitimate daughter of Pope Alexander VI and sister of Cesare Borgia. She was married at 12 and again at 13 to further her father's ambitions, both marriages being annulled by him. Her final marriage was to the son and heir of the Duke of Ferrara. She made the court a centre of culture.

boring BORE[1].

Boris Godunov GODUNOV.

Bormann, *n.* **Martin** (1900–45), German Nazi leader. He rose to high positions in the Nazi Party, becoming party chancellor in May 1941. He was believed to have escaped the fall of Berlin in May 1945, and was tried in his absence and sentenced to death at Nuremberg (1945–46), but a skeleton uncovered in Berlin in 1972 was officially recognized as his by forensic experts in 1973.

born, *p.p., a.* brought into the world; brought forth, produced; having certain characteristics from birth. **born again,** regenerate. **born to,** destined to. **born with a silver spoon in one's mouth,** born in luxury. [orig. p.p. of BEAR[2]]

Born, *n.* **Max** (1882–1970), German physicist, who received a Nobel Prize in 1954 for fundamental work on the quantum theory.

borne, *p.p.* BEAR[2].

Borneo, *n.* third largest island in the world, one of the Sunda Islands in the W Pacific; area 754,000 sq km/290,000 sq miles. It comprises the Malaysian territories of Sabah and Sarawak; Brunei; and, by far the largest, the Indonesian territory of Kalimantan. It is mountainous and densely forested. In coastal areas the people are mainly of Malaysian origin, with a few Chinese, and the interior is inhabited by the indigenous Dayaks.

bornite, *n.* a valuable copper ore found in Cornwall and elsewhere. [I. von *Born* 1742–91, Austrian mineralogist]

Borodin, *n.* **Alexander Profir'yevich** (1833–87), Russian composer. Born in St Petersburg, the illegitimate son of a Russian prince, he became by profession an expert in medical chemistry, but in his spare time devoted himself to music. His principal work is the opera *Prince Igor*; left unfinished, it was completed by Rimsky-Korsakov and Glazunov, and includes the Polovtsian Dances.

Borodino, Battle of, a battle NW of Moscow in which French troops under Napoleon defeated the Russians under Kutusov on 7 Sept. 1812.

boron, *n.* the element, at. no. 5; chem. symbol B, present in borax and boracic acid. **borazon,** *n.* a substance compounded of boron and nitrogen that for industrial use is harder than a diamond. **boride,** *n.* a compound containing boron. [BORAX]

borough, *n.* a town possessing a municipal corporation; a town which sends a representative to Parliament. **to own or purchase a borough,** to control or purchase the control of a Parliamentary borough (before the Reform Act of 1832). **close** or **pocket borough,** a borough owned by a person or persons. **county borough,** a borough of more than 50,000 inhabitants ranking under the Local Government Act of 1888 as an administrative county. **rotten borough,** a borough (before 1832) having only a nominal constituency. **borough-English,** *n.* a custom existent in some parts of England by which the youngest son inherits all lands and tenements. **borough-monger,** *n.* one who buys or sells the representation of a borough. **borough-reeve,** *n.* the chief municipal officer in certain unincorporated boroughs before the Municipal Corporations Act of 1835. [OE *burgh, burg.* OTeut. *bergan,* to shelter (OE *beorgan*); cp. G *Burg,* castle, Sc. *burgh*]

borrow, *v.t.* to obtain and make temporary use of; to obtain under a promise or understanding to return; to adopt, to assume, to derive from other people; to copy, imitate, feign; (*Golf*) to play a ball uphill in order that it may roll back. **borrowed,** *a.* obtained on loan; not genuine; hypocritical. **borrowing days,** *n.pl.* the last three days of March (o.s.) supposed in Scottish folk-lore to have been borrowed from April and to be particularly stormy. [OE *borgian,* from *borg, borh,* a pledge. OTeut. *bergan,* to protect (cp. G *borgen,* to borrow, also BOROUGH)]

borsch, -t, bortsch, -t, *n.* Russian beetroot soup. [Rus. *borshch*]

borstal, *n.* a place of detention and corrective training for juvenile offenders, now called **youth custody centre. Borstal system,** *n.* a system of treating juvenile offenders by education and technical instruction. [named from the first system of its kind at the institute in *Borstal,* near Rochester in Kent]

borstall, *n.* a steep track on a hillside. [OE *beorh,* a hill, *steall,* place, stead, or *stigol,* stile]

bort, boart, *n.* small fragments split from diamonds in roughly reducing them to shape, used to make diamond powder. [etym. doubtful (perh. OF *bort,* bastard)]

borzoi, *n.* (*pl.* **-zois**) a Russian wolfhound. [Rus.]

boscage, boskage, *n.* wood, woodland; underwood or ground covered with it; thick foliage; wooded landscape. [OF *boscage,* late L *boscum,* a bush]

Bosch[1], *n.* **Hieronymus** (Jerome) (1460–1516), Netherlandish painter. His fantastic visions of weird and hellish creatures, as shown in *The Garden of Earthly Delights* (*c.* 1505–10, Prado, Madrid) show astonishing imagination and complex imagery. His religious subjects focused not on the holy figures but on the mass of ordinary witnesses, placing the religious event in a contemporary Netherlandish context and creating cruel caricatures of human sinfulness.

Bosch[2], *n.* **Juan** (1909–), president of the Dominican Republic (1962–63). His left-wing *Partido Revolucionario Dominicano* won a landslide victory in the 1962 elections. In office, he attempted agrarian reform and labour legislation. Opposed in the US, he was overthrown by the army. His achievement was to establish a democratic political party after three decades of dictatorship.

bosey, *n.* (*Cricket*) a googly. [Eng. cricketer *Bosanquet*]

bosh, *n.* empty talk, nonsense, folly *int.* stuff! rubbish! humbug! *v.t.* (*sl.*) to spoil, to humbug, make a fool of. [Turk.]

bosjes-man BUSHMAN.

bosk, *n.* a bush, a thicket, a small forest. **bosky,** *a.* bushy, woody; covered with boscage; **boskiness,** *n.* the quality of being bosky. [ME *boske,* var. of *busk,* BUSH (mod. lit. *bosk,* prob. from BOSKY)]

bosket, bosquet, *n.* a grove; a plantation of small trees and underwood in a garden or park. [F *bosquet,* It. *boschetto,* dim. of *bosco,* a wood]

Bosnia and Herzegovina (Serbo-Croat **Bosna-Hercegovina**), constituent republic of Yugoslavia. **area** 51,000 sq km/19,725 sq miles. **capital** Sarajevo. **population** (1986) 4,360,000, including 1,630,000 Muslims, 1,320,000 Serbs, and 760,000 Croats. **language** Serbian variant of Serbo-Croat. **religion** Sunni Muslim, Serbian Orthodox, and Roman Catholic.

Bosnian Crisis, *n.* period of international tension in 1908 when Austria attempted to capitalize on Turkish weakness after the Young Turk revolt by annexing provinces of Bosnia and Herzegovina. Austria obtained Russian approval in exchange for conceding Russian access to the Bosporus straits.

bosom, *n.* the breast of a human being esp. of a woman; that part of the dress which covers this; the breast as the seat of emotions or the repository of secrets; secret counsel or intention; embrace; intimate relations; affection; the surface of water or of ground; a hollow, a cavity, the interior of anything. *v.t.* to put into or hide in the bosom; to embosom; to receive into intimate companionship. **bosom of one's family,** midst of one's family. **in one's bosom,** clasped in one's embrace; in one's inmost feelings. **bosom friend,** dearest and most intimate friend. [OE *bōsm* (cp. OHG *puosam,* G *Busen,* etym. unknown)]

boson, *n.* a particle, or member of a class of particles, with an integral or zero spin, which behaves in accordance with the statistical relations laid down by Bose and Einstein. [after S. N. *Bose,* 1894–1974, Indian physicist]

Bosporus, *n.* (Turkish **Karadeniz Boğazi**) strait 27 km/17 miles long joining the Black Sea with the Sea of Marmara and forming part of the water division between Europe and Asia. Istanbul stands on its W side. The **Bosporus Bridge** (1973) links Istanbul and Turkey-in-Asia (1621 m/5320 ft). In 1988 a second bridge across the straits was opened, linking Asia and Europe.

boss[1], *n.* a protuberant part; an ornamental stud; the knob in the centre of a shield; (*Arch.*) an ornamental projection at the intersection of the ribs in vaulting. *v.t.* to press out, emboss; to furnish with bosses. **bossed,** *a.* embossed, ornamented with bosses. **bossy,** *a.* having a boss or bosses, studded with bosses. [OF *boce* (F *bosse*), It. *bozza,* a swelling; perh. from OHG *bōzan,* to strike]

boss[2], *n.* a foreman, manager; a chief leader or master; the manager or dictator of a party machine. *a.* chief, best, most highly esteemed; first-rate, excellent. *v.t.* to manage, to direct, to control. **bossy,** *a.* managing; domineering. [Dut. *baas,* master, orig. uncle]

boss[3], *n.* a miss, a bad shot, a bungle; a short-sighted person; one who squints. *v.t.* to miss, to bungle. *v.i.* to make a miss. **boss-eyed,** *a.* (*coll.*) having but one eye; having one eye injured; squinting. **bosser,** *n.*

boss[4], *a.* (*Sc.*) hollow, empty. [etym. doubtful]

bossa nova, *n.* a Brazilian dance resembling the samba; the music for such a dance. [Port. *bossa,* trend, *nova,* new]

boston[1], *n.* a game of cards somewhat resembling whist; a slow waltz. [after *Boston,* Mass., US]

Boston[2], *n.* industrial and commercial centre, capital of Massachusetts, US; population (1980) 563,000; metropolitan area 2,800,000. It is a publishing centre, and Harvard University and Massachusetts Institute of Technology are nearby. A centre of opposition to British trade restrictions, it was the scene of the Boston Tea Party.

Boston Tea Party, US colonists' protest (1773) against the British tea tax before the War of American Independence.

Boswell[1], *n.* a biographer; a minute and rather slavish biographer. **Boswellian,** *a.* resembling James Boswell in style. **Boswellism,** *n.* Boswell's style of biography. **Boswellize, -ise,** *v.i.* to write biography in Boswell's style.

Boswell[2], *n.* **James** (1740–95), Scottish biographer and diarist. He was a member of Samuel Johnson's London Literary Club, and in 1773 the two men travelled to Scotland together, as recorded in Boswell's *Journal of the Tour to the Hebrides* (1785). His *Life of Samuel Johnson* was published in 1791.

Bosworth, Battle of, last battle of the Wars of the Roses, fought on 22 Aug. 1485 near the village of Market Bosworth, 19 km /12 miles W of Leicester, England. Richard III, the Yorkist king, was defeated and slain by Henry of Richmond, who became Henry VII.

bot, bott, *n.* a parasitic worm, the larva of the genus *Oestrus.* **the bots, botts,** a disease caused by these in horses; an analogous disease in cattle and in sheep. **bot-fly,** *n.* a fly of the genus *Oestrus;* a gadfly. [etym. unknown]

bot., (*abbr.*) botany, botanical, botanist; bought; bottle.

botany, *n.* the science which treats of plants and plant-life. **Botany Bay** (in New South Wales, named by Capt. Cook after the abundance of botanical specimens found there), *n.* a convict settlement established there in 1787, on whose site Sydney now stands; (*fig.*) transportation. **Botany Bay dozen,** (*Austral. Hist.*) 25 lashes with the cat-o'-nine-tails. **Botany-wool, -yarn,** *n.* wool from Botany Bay, and yarn made from it. **botanic, botanical,** *a.* of or pertaining to botany. **botanic garden,** *n.* (*often in pl.*) a garden laid out for the scientific culture and study of plants. **botanically,** *adv.* **botanist,** *n.* **botanize, -ise,** *v.i.* to collect plants for scientific study; to study plants. *v.t.* to explore botanically. [F *botanique,* late L *botanicus,* Gr. *botanikos,* pertaining to plants, from *botanē,* a plant, *boskein,* to feed]

botargo, *n.* (*pl.* **-gos, -goes**) a relish made of the roes of the mullet and tunny. [It., from Arab. *butarkhah,* Copt. *outarakhon* (*ou-,* a, Gr. *tarichion,* dim. of *tarichos,* dried fish)]

botch[1], *n.* a clumsy patch; a bungled piece of work. *v.t.* to mend or patch clumsily; to put together in an unsuitable or unskilful manner; to ruin. **botcher**[1], *n.* a mender, a patcher, a bungler. **botchery,** *n.* the results of botching; clumsy workmanship. **botchy,** *a.* characterized by botching or bungling. [etym. doubtful (cp. PATCH)]

botch[2], *n.* an ulcerous swelling. **botchy,** *a.* marked with botches or excrescences. [OF *boce* (see BOSS[1])]

botcher[2], *n.* a young salmon, a grilse. [local; etym. doubtful]

botel, BOATEL.

Botero, *n.* **Fernando** (1932–), Colombian painter.

He studied in Spain and gained an international reputation for his paintings of fat, vulgar figures, often of women, parodies of conventional sensuality.

both, *a., pron.* the one and also the other, the two. *adv.* as well the one thing as the other; equally in the two cases. [Icel. *bāthir, bāthi* (*bā-thir,* both they or the); OE *ba* gave the earlier *bo*]

Botha[1], *n.* **Louis** (1862–1919), South African soldier and politician, a commander in the Second South African War. In 1907 Botha became premier of the Transvaal and in 1910 of the first Union government. On the outbreak of World War I in 1914 he rallied South Africa to the Commonwealth, suppressed a Boer revolt under Gen. de Wet, and conquered German South West Africa.

Botha[2], *n.* **P(ieter) W(illem)** (1916–), South African politician. Prime minister from 1978, he initiated a modification of apartheid, which later slowed in the face of Afrikaner (Boer) opposition. In 1984 he became the first executive state president. In 1989 he unwillingly resigned both party leadership and presidency after suffering a stroke, and was succeeded by F.W. de Klerk.

Botham, *n.* **Ian (Terrence)** (1955–), English cricketer, a prolific all-rounder. His 373 test wickets, 109 catches, and 5,057 runs in 94 appearances by the end of the 1988 English season were a record until surpassed by Richard Hadlee (New Zealand) in 1989. He has played county cricket for Somerset and Worcestershire as well as playing in Australia.

Bothe, *n.* **Walther** (1891–1957), German physicist, who showed in 1929 that the cosmic rays bombarding the Earth are composed not of photons but of more massive particles. Nobel prize for physics 1954.

bother, *v.t.* to tease, to vex; to annoy, to pester. *v.i.* to make a fuss, to be troublesome; to worry oneself; to take trouble. *int.* an exclamation of annoyance. *n.* worry, disturbance, fuss. **botheration,** *n.* the act of bothering; bother. **bothersome,** *a.* troublesome, annoying. [etym. doubtful]

Bothwell, *n.* **James Hepburn, 4th Earl of Bothwell** (*c.* 1536–78), Scottish nobleman, husband of Mary, Queen of Scots, 1567–70, alleged to have arranged the explosion that killed Darnley, her previous husband, in 1567.

bothy, bothie, *n.* (*esp. Sc.*) a rough kind of cottage; a hut, a hovel; esp. a lodging place for unmarried labourers on a Scottish farm. [etym. doubtful; cp. BOOTH]

bo-tree, bodhi tree, *n.* the peepul or peepla tree; the tree, *Ficus religiosa,* under which Gautama is said to have received the enlightenment which constituted him the Buddha. It is held sacred by the Buddhists and planted beside their temples. [Sinhalese *bo,* Pāli, *bodhi,* perfect knowledge]

botryoid, botryoidal, *a.* in form resembling a bunch of grapes. [Gr. *botruoeides* (*botrus,* a bunch of grapes, -OID)]

bots, bott BOT.

Botswana, *n.* landlocked country in central S Africa. **area** 582,000 sq km/225,000 sq miles. **capital** Gaborone. **physical** desert in SW, plains in E, fertile lands and swamp in N. **population** (1988) 1,210,000 (80% Bamangwato, 20% Bangwaketse); annual growth rate 3.8%. **exports** diamonds, copper, nickel, meat. **language** English (official); Setswana (national). **religion** Christian (majority).

Botticelli, *n.* **Sandro** (1445–1510), Florentine painter of religious and mythological subjects. He was patronized by the ruling Medici family, for whom he painted *Primavera* (1478) and *The Birth of Venus* (about 1482–84) (both in the Uffizi, Florence). From the 1490s he was influenced by the religious fanatic Savonarola and developed a harshly expressive and emotional style.

bottine, *n.* a buskin; a light kind of boot for women and children. [F, dim. of *botte,* boot]

bottle[1], *n.* a vessel with a narrow neck for holding liquids (usu. of glass); the quantity in a bottle; (*sl.*) temerity, courage, strength of will. *v.t.* to put into bottles. **the bottle,** drinking. **to hit the bottle,** (*sl.*) to drink a great deal of alcoholic drinks. **to bottle-feed,** to feed a baby from a bottle instead of the breast. **to bottle up,** to conceal; to restrain, repress (one's emotions). **bottle bank,** *n.* a public repository for empty glass jars and bottles which are to be recycled. **bottle-brush,** *n.* a brush for cleaning bottles; the genus *Equisetum; Hipparis vulgaris;* (*Austral.*) a genus of trees bearing brush-like flowers. **bottle gas,** *n.* butane gas in liquid form supplied in containers for use in eating, cooking etc. **bottle-glass,** *n.* coarse green glass for making bottles. **bottle-green,** *n.* dark green, like bottle-glass. **bottle-head,** *n.* a species of whale (see BOTTLE-NOSE). **bottle-holder,** *n.* one who attends a boxer in a boxing match, a supporter, a second, a backer. **bottle-imp,** *n.* an imp supposed to be sealed up in a bottle. **bottle-neck,** *n.* a constricted outlet. **bottle-nose,** *n.* the bottle-nosed whale, *Hyperoödon bidens. a.* bottle-nosed. **bottle-nosed,** *a.* having a large thick nose. **bottle-party,** *n.* a drinking party to which each person brings his/her own alcoholic drink. **bottle-tree,** *n.* (*Austral.*) an Australian tree with a bulbous trunk resembling the shape of a bottle. **bottle-washer,** *n.* a person or machine that washes bottles; a general factotum, an understrapper. **bottled,** *a.* stored in jars or bottles; bottle-shaped; (*sl.*) drunk. **bottler,** *n.* [OF *boteile, botele,* late L *buticula,* dim. of *butis, buttis,* a cask, a BUTT[2]]

bottle[2], *n.* a bundle of hay or straw. [OF *botel,* dim. of *botte*]

bottom, *n.* the lowest part of anything, the part on which anything rests; the posteriors; the buttocks; the seat of a chair; the bed or channel of any body of water; an alluvial hollow; low-lying land; the lowest point; a deep cavity, an abyss; the inmost part, the furthest point of a recess, gulf or inland sea; the end of a table remote from a host, chairman etc.; the lowest rank; the keel of a ship, the part near and including the keel, the hull; a ship as receptacle for cargo; †a skein or ball of thread; (*pl.*) dregs of liquor, sediment; foundation, base; source, basis; stamina, power of endurance. *v.t.* to put a bottom to; †to wind, as a skein; to examine exhaustively, to sound, to fathom. *v.i.* to be based or founded (on). *a.* of or pertaining to the bottom; lowest; fundamental. **at bottom,** in reality; at heart. **on one's own bottom,** independently. **to bottom out,** to drop to, and level out at, the lowest point, as of prices. **bottom dollar,** *n.* one's last coin. **bottom drawer,** *n.* a drawer in which a woman keeps her new clothes etc. before marriage. **bottom-heat,** *n.* heat supplied beneath the surface by decomposing manure or by means of a greenhouse furnace. **bottom-lands,** *n.pl.* (*N Am.*) rich flat lands on the banks of rivers in the western states. **bottom line,** *n.* the concluding line in a statement of accounts, giving net profit or loss figures; the final word on; the crux of a matter. **bottom-up,** *a., adv.* upside-down. **bottomed,** *a.* (*usu. in comb.*) having a bottom, as *flat-bottomed;* based; well-grounded. **bottomless,** *a.* without a bottom; having no seat; fathomless, unfathomable. **bottomless pit,** *n.* hell; (*coll.*) a very hungry or greedy person. **bottom-most,** *a.* lowest of all. **bottomry,** *n.* borrowing money on the security of a ship. *v.t.* to pledge a ship in this manner. [OE *botm* (cp. Icel. *botn,* OHG *podam,* G *Boden,* L *fundus,* Gr. *puthmēn,* Sansk. *budhnā*)]

botulism, *n.* a form of food-poisoning caused by eating preserved food infected by *Bacillus botulinus.* [L *botulus,* a sausage]

Boucher, *n.* **François** (1703–70), French Rococo painter, court painter from 1765. He was much patronized for his light-hearted, decorative scenes, for example *Diana Bathing,* 1742 (Louvre, Paris).

bouclé, *n.* a looped yarn; the thick, curly material woven from such yarn. *a.* [F curly]

Boudicca, *n.* (died AD 60) queen of the Iceni (native Britons), often referred to by the Latin form *Boadicea.* Her husband, King Prasutagus, had been a tributary of the Romans, but on his death AD 60 the territory of the

Iceni was violently annexed, Boudicca was scourged and her daughters raped. Boudicca raised the whole of SE England in revolt, and before the main Roman armies could return from campaigning in Wales she burned London and Colchester. Later the British were virtually annihilated somewhere between London and Chester, and Boudicca poisoned herself.

Boudin, *n.* **Eugène** (1824–98), French painter, a forerunner of impressionism, noted for his fresh seaside scenes painted in the open air.

boudoir, *n.* a small, elegantly furnished room, used as a lady's private apartment. [F, from *bouder,* to sulk]

bouffant, *a.* full, puffed out, as a hairstyle. [Fr.]

bouffe OPERA BOUFFE.

bougainvillaea, -vilia, *n.* a genus of tropical plants belonging to the Nyctaginaceae, the red or purple bracts of which almost conceal the flowers. [Louis Antoine de BOUGAINVILLE]

Bougainville, *n.* **Louis Antoine de** (1729–1811), French navigator who made the first French circumnavigation of the world in 1766–69 and the first systematic observations of longitude.

bough, *n.* a large arm or branch of a tree. [OE *bōg, bōh* (cp. Icel. *bōgr,* Dan. *boug,* OHG *buog,* G *Bog,* Dut. *boeg,* all meaning shoulder of man or quadruped; Gr. *pēchos,* forearm)]

bought, *p.p.* BUY.

boughten, (irreg. part. from BOUGHT), *a.* (*poet.*) bought.

bougie, *n.* a wax candle; a smooth, flexible, slender cylinder used for exploring or dilating passages in the human body. [F, from *Bougie,* Arab. *Bijiyah,* town in Algeria with trade in wax candles]

Bouguereau, *n.* **Adolphe William** (1825–1905), French academic painter of historical and mythological subjects. He was respected in his day but his style is now thought to be insipid.

bouillabaisse, *n.* a rich fish stew or chowder, popular in the south of France. [F]

bouilli, *n.* meat gently simmered. [F, p.p. of *bouillir,* to boil]

bouillon, *n.* broth, soup; a fleshy excrescence on a horse's foot; a puffed flounce. [see prec.]

Bou Kraa, *n.* the principal phosphate mining centre of Western Sahara, linked by conveyor belt to the Atlantic coast near La'youn.

Boulanger1, *n.* **Lili (Juliette Marie Olga)** (1893–1918), French composer, the younger sister of Nadia Boulanger. At the age of 19, she won the *Prix de Rome* with the cantata *Faust et Halkne* for voices and orchestra.

Boulanger2, *n.* **Nadia (Juliette)** (1887–1979), French music teacher and conductor. A pupil of Fauré, and admirer of Stravinsky, she included among her composition pupils at the American Conservatory in Fontainebleau (from 1921) Aaron Copland, Roy Harris, Walter Piston, and Philip Glass.

boulder, *n.* a water-worn, rounded stone, a cobble; a large rounded block of stone transported to a lesser or greater distance from its parent rock; an erratic block; a large detached piece of ore. **boulder-clay, -drift,** *n.* a clayey deposit of the glacial period. **boulder-formation,** *n.* a formation of mud, sand and clay containing boulders. **boulder period,** *n.* the Ice Age, the glacial period. [ME (*bulderston,* Swed. dial. *bullersten,* from *bullra,* to make a noise (cp. Dan. *buldre,* to roar, rattle)]

boule, -lle, BUHL.

boules, *n.pl.* a French game resembling bowls, played with metal balls. [F balls]

boulevard, *n.* a public walk on the rampart of a demolished fortification; a broad street planted with trees; (*esp. N Am.*) an arterial road, trunk road. **boulevardier, -dist,** *n.* one who haunts the boulevards (of Paris); a man-about-town. [F, perh. from G *Bollwerk,* BULWARK]

Boulez, *n.* **Pierre** (1925–), French composer and conductor. He studied with Messiaen and has promoted contemporary music with a series of innovative *Domaine Musical* concerts and recordings in the 1950s, as conductor of the BBC Symphony and New York Philharmonic orchestras during the 1970s, and as founder-director of IRCAM, a music research studio in Paris opened in 1976. His music, strictly serial and expressionistic in style, includes the cantatas *Le Visage nuptial* (1946–52) and *Le Marteau sans maître* (1955), both to texts by René Char; *Pli selon pli* (1962) for soprano and orchestra; and *Répons* (1981) for soloists, orchestra, tapes and computer-generated sounds.

boulter, *n.* a fishing-line with a number of hooks attached. [etym. unknown]

Boulting, *n.* **John** (1913–85) and **Roy** (1913–), British director-producer team that was particularly influential in the years following World War II. Their films include *Brighton Rock* (1947), *Lucky Jim* (1957), and *I'm All Right Jack* (1959). They were twins.

Boulton, *n.* **Matthew** (1728–1809), British factory-owner, who helped to finance James Watt's development of the steam engine.

Boumédienne, *n.* **Houari**, adopted name of Mohammed Boukharouba (1925–78), Algerian politician who brought the nationalist leader Ben Bella to power by a revolt (1962), and superseded him as president (1965–78) by a further coup.

bounce, *v.i.* to rebound; to bound like a ball; to come or go unceremoniously; to exaggerate, to brag; (of a cheque) to be returned to drawer. *v.t.* †to drive or hit against; to slam, to bang; (*fig.*) to bully; (*N Am.*) to discharge suddenly from employment; (*N Am.*) to throw or turn out. *n.* a heavy, noisy blow; rebound; a leap, a spring; swagger, self-assertion; impudence; a boastful lie; (*N Am.*) dismissal from employment. **bouncer,** *n.* anything large and bouncing; a boaster, a swaggerer; a bouncing lie; a fine specimen of anything; someone employed to eject (undesirable) people from a public place. **bouncing,** *a.* big, heavy; stout, strong; bustling, noisy. **bouncingly,** *adv.* with a bounce. **bouncy,** *a.* vivacious, bouncing. [prob. imit.]

bound1, *n.* a leap, a spring, a rebound. *v.i.* to leap, to spring; to rebound, to bounce. †*v.t.* to cause (a horse) to leap. **by leaps and bounds,** with astonishing speed. **bounder,** *n.* one who or that which leaps; (*sl.*) an ill-bred person; (*dated*) a scoundrel. [F *bondir,* to bound, orig. to resound, L *bombitāre,* to hum, buzz (*bombus,* see BOMB)]

bound2, *n.* a limit, a boundary; limitation, restriction; territory. *v.t.* to set bounds to; to confine; to form the boundary of. **boundary,** *n.* a mark indicating limit; the limit thus marked. **boundary-rider,** *n.* (*Austral.*) a man who keeps the boundary fences of a station in repair. **out of bounds,** of an area, topic or person, forbidden, prohibited. **bounded,** *a.* having bounds. **boundless,** *a.* without bounds; limitless. **boundlessly,** *adv.* **boundlessness,** *n.* [OF *bonde, bodne,* late L *bodena* (etym. doubtful)]

bound3, *a.* under obligation; compelled, obliged, certain (*with inf.*); in a cover, esp. in a cover of leather or other permanent material as distinguished from paper covers. **bound up with,** intimately associated with; having identical aims or interests with. **bounden,** *a.* bound; enslaved; obliged; under obligation. **bounden duty,** *n.* obligatory duty. [past, p.p. of BIND]

bound4, *a.* prepared, ready; starting, destined; directing one's course. **homeward bound,** on the way home. [ME *boun,* Icel. *būinn,* p.p. of *būa,* to till, to get ready; *-d* added in assim. to other participles]

Boundary Peak, *n.* highest mountain in Nevada state, US, rising to 4006 m/13,143 ft on the Nevada-California frontier.

bounty, *n.* †goodness, gracious liberality; an act of generosity, a gift; a premium for joining the army or navy, or to encourage commerce or industry. **Queen's (King's) Bounty,** a grant made to the mother of three or more children at a birth. **Queen Anne's Bounty,** a provision made in the reign of Queen Anne for augmenting poor church livings. **bounteous,** *a.* full of bounty; liberal, beneficent; generously given. **bounteously,** *adv.* **bounteousness,** *n.* **bountiful,** *a.* full of bounty; liberal, munificent; plenteous, abundant. **Lady Bountiful,** a wealthy woman charitable in her neighbourhood. **bountifully,** *adv.* †**bountihead,** *n.* bounteousness, goodness; virtue, generosity. [OF *bonté, bontet,* L *bonitātem -as,* goodness, from *bonus,* good]

Bounty, Mutiny on the, naval mutiny in the Pacific in 1789 against British captain William Bligh.

bouquet, *n.* a nosegay, a bunch of flowers; the perfume exhaled by wine. **bouquet garni,** *n.* a bunch (trad. five sprigs) of herbs for flavouring meat dishes and soups. [F, OF *bosquet,* It. *boschetto,* BOSKET]

bouquetin, *n.* the ibex; an Alpine animal of the goat family. [F *bouquetin,* prob. for *bouc-estain* (G *Steinbock*)]

Bourbon[1], *n.* a member of the royal family that formerly ruled France; (*N Am.*) an obsolete and unteachable Democrat, a reactionary; (*N Am.*), a kind of whisky made of wheat or Indian corn. **Bourbon biscuit,** *n.* one consisting of two chocolate-flavoured pieces with chocolate cream between. **Bourbonism,** *n.* adherence to the Bourbon dynasty. **Bourbonist,** *n.* [French town]

Bourbon[2], *n.* **Charles, Duke of Bourbon** (1490–1527), constable of France, honoured for his courage at the Battle of Marignano (1515). Later he served the Holy Roman emperor Charles V, and helped to drive the French from Italy. In 1526 he was made duke of Milan, and in 1527 allowed his troops to sack Rome. He was killed by a shot the artist Cellini claimed to have fired.

Bourbon, duchy of, originally a seigneury (feudal domain) created in the 10th century in the county of Bourges, central France, held by the Bourbon family. It became a duchy 1327.

bourdon, *n.* †a low undersong or accompaniment; a bass stop on an organ; a bass reed in a harmonium; the drone of a bagpipe. [F, prob. imit.]

bourg, *n.* a town built under the shadow of a castle; a market town. [F, from late L *burgus,* WG *burg* (cp. OE *burh,* Eng. BOROUGH)]

bourgeois[1], *n.* a French citizen; (*sometimes derog.*) one of the mercantile, shop-keeping or middle class. *a.* of or pertaining to the bourgeoisie; middle-class or industrial as distinguished from the working-class; commonplace, humdrum, unintellectual; materialistic, middle-class in outlook. **bourgeoisie,** *n.* (*sometimes derog.*) mercantile or shop-keeping class; middle class as opposed to the proletariat. [as prec.]

bourgeois[2], *n.* a kind of type between brevier and long-primer. [prob. from a French printer]

Bourgeois, *n.* **Léon Victor Auguste** (1851–1925), French politician. Entering politics as a Radical, he was prime minister in 1895, and later served in many cabinets. He was one of the pioneer advocates of the League of Nations. Nobel peace prize (1920).

bourgeon BURGEON.

Bourgogne, *n.* region of France, which includes the *départements* of Côte-d'Or, Nièvre, Sâone-et-Loire, and Yonne; area 31,600 sq km/12,198 sq miles; population (1986) 1,607,000. Its capital is Dijon. It is famous for its wines, such as Chablis and Nuits-Saint-Georges, and for its cattle (the Charolais herdbook is maintained at Nevers). A former independent kingdom and duchy (see BURGUNDY), it was incorporated into France in 1477.

Bourguiba, *n.* **Habib ben Ali** (1903–), Tunisian politician, first president of Tunisia (1957–87). Educated at the University of Paris, he became a journalist and was frequently imprisoned by the French for his nationalist aims as leader of the Néo-Destour party. He became prime minister (1956), president (for life from 1974) and prime minister of the Tunisian republic (1957), and was overthrown in a coup in 1987.

bourguignon, *a.* of meat dishes, stewed with (Burgundy) wine. [F Burgundian]

bourn[1], *n.* a small stream.

bourn[2], **bourne,** *n.* a bound, a limit, a goal. [F *borne,* OF *bodne,* BOUND[2]]

Bournonville, *n.* **August** (1805–79), Danish dancer and choreographer. He worked with the Royal Danish Ballet for most of his life, giving Danish ballet a worldwide importance. His ballets, many of which have been revived in the last 50 years, include *La Sylphide* (1836) (music by Lövenskjöld) and *Napoli* (1842).

bourree, *n.* a folk-dance from the Auvergne and Basque provinces; a musical composition in this rhythm. [F]

bourse, *n.* a foreign exchange for the transaction of commercial business; a stock exchange, esp. that of Paris. [F, lit. purse]

bourtree, *n.* (*Sc., North.*) the elder-tree, *Sambucus nigra.* [etym. unknown]

bouse, BOOZE.

boustrophedon, *a.* written alternately from left to right and from right to left. [Gr., as an ox turns in ploughing (*bous,* ox, *strophē,* a turning, *-don,* adv. suf.)]

bout, *n.* a turn, a round, a set-to; trial, essay, attempt; a spell of work; a fit of drunkenness or of illness. [earlier *bought*]

†**boutade,** *n.* an outburst, a sudden fit of violence. [F, from *bouter,* to thrust]

boutique, *n.* a fashionable clothes shop; any small specialist shop; a shop within a department store, hotel, airport lounge etc. [F, shop]

bouton, *n.* a pimple, pustule, boil; the hollow at the end of the tongue of the honey-bee. [F, button]

Bouts, *n.* **Dierick** (*c.* 1420–75), early Netherlandish painter. Born in Haarlem, he settled in Louvain, painting portraits and religious scenes influenced by Rogier van der Weyden. *The Last Supper*, 1464–68 (St Pierre, Louvain) is considered one of his finest works.

bouts-rimés, *n.pl.* a game in which a list of rhymed endings is handed to each player to fill in and complete the verse. [F, rhymed endings]

Bouvines, Battle of, a victory for Philip II (Philip Augustus) of France in 1214, near the village of Bouvines in Flanders, over the Holy Roman emperor Otto IV and his allies. The battle, one of the most decisive in mediaeval Europe, ensured the succession of Frederick II as emperor, and confirmed Philip as ruler of the whole of N France and Flanders; it led to the renunciation of all English claims to the region.

bouzouki, *n.* a Greek stringed instrument similar to the mandolin [mod. Gr. *mpouzouki*]

bovine, *a.* of or resembling oxen; sluggish; dull, stupid. **bovine spongiform encephalopathy,** a fatal degenerative disease of the brain in cattle, similar to scrapie in sheep. [L *bovīnus* (*bos bovis,* ox)]

Bovril®, *n.* a concentrated beef extract used for flavouring stews etc.

bovver, *n.* (*sl.*) a boisterous or violent commotion, a street fight. **bovver boots,** *n.pl.* (*sl.*) heavy workboots worn as weapons by teenage thugs. **bovver boy,** *n.* (*sl.*) a member of a violent teenage gang; a hooligan. [from BOTHER]

bow[1], *n.* a curve, a rainbow; a stringed weapon for discharging arrows; the doubling of a string in a slip-knot; a single-looped knot; an ornamental knot in which neckties, ribbons etc. are tied; a necktie, ribbon or the like, tied in such a knot; a name for various simple contrivances in shape like a bow; a saddle-bow, an oxbow; the appliance with which instruments of the violin family are played; a single stroke of such an appliance. *v.t.* to play with or use the bow on (a violin etc.). **to draw the long bow,** to exaggerate; to tell lies. **to have two strings to one's bow,** to have more resources, plans or opportunities than one. **bow and string beam, bridge** or **girder,** a structure in the form of a bent bow, with a horizontal beam or girder in the position of the string. **bow-bent,** *a.* bent like a bow. †**bow-boy,** *n.* the Archer, Cupid. **bow-compasses,** *n.pl.* compasses with the legs jointed, so that the points can be turned inwards. **bow-hand,** *n.* the hand that holds the bow in archery or in playing a stringed instrument. **bow-head,** *n.* the Greenland right whale. **bow-legged,** *a.* having the legs bowed or bent. **bowman**[1], *n.* one who shoots with the bow, an archer. **bow-net,**

n. a cylinder of wickerwork with one narrow entrance, for catching lobsters; a net attached to a bow or arch of metal. **bow-pen, bow-pencil,** *n.* bow-compassess fitted with a pen or pencil. **bow-saw,** *n.* a saw fitted in a frame like a bowstring in a bow. **bowshot,** *n.* the distance to which an arrow can be shot. **bowstring,** *n.* the string by which a bow is stretched; the string with which persons were executed in Turkey. *v.t.* to strangle with a bowstring. **bow-window,** *n.* a bay-window segmentally curved. **bowyer,** *n.* a bow-maker; a setter of bows. [OE *boga* (cp. OHG *bogo,* G *Bogen,* OTeut. *beugan,* to bend (see BOW[2])]

bow[2], *v.i.* to bend forward as a sign of assent, submission or salutation; to incline the head; to kneel; to bend under a yoke; hence, to submit, to yield. *v.t.* to cause to bend; to incline, to influence; to crush; to express by bowing; to usher (in or out). *n.* an inclination of the body or head, as a salute or token of respect. **bowed,** *a.* bent, crooked; bent down. [OE *būgan,* OTeut. *beugan,* to bend, stem *bug-* (cp. L *fugere,* Gr. *pheugein,* Sansk. *bhuj*)]

bow[3], *n.* (*often in pl.*) the rounded fore-end of a ship or boat; the rower nearest this. **on the bow,** (*Naut.*) within 45° of the point right ahead. **bow-cap,** *n.* a metal plate fitted on the nose of a submarine or an aeroplane. **bow-chaser,** *n.* a gun in the bow of a vessel pointing forward. **bow-grace,** *n.* a kind of junk fender round the bows and sides of a ship to prevent injury from floating ice or timber. **bowline,** *n.* a rope fastened to the middle part of the weather side of a sail to make it stand close to the wind. **bowline knot,** *n.* a safe kind of knot. **on a bowline,** close-hauled; sailing close to the wind. **bowman,**[2] *n.* the rower nearest the bow. **bow-oar,** *n.* the rower nearest the bow; his oar. **bowsprit,** †**boltsprit,** *n.* (*Naut.*) a spar running out from the bows of a vessel to support sails and stays. **bower,** *n.* the name given to two anchors (**best bower** and **small bower**) carried in the bows; the cable attached to either. [cogn. with BOUGH]

Bow[4], *n.* **Clara** (1905–65), US silent-film actress, known as the 'It' girl after her vivacious performance in *It* (1927). Her other films included *Wings* (1927) and *The Wild Party* (1929). Scandals about her romances and her mental and physical fragility led to the end of her career, and she spent many of her post-career years in sanatoriums.

Bow bells, *n.pl.* the bells of St. Mary le Bow, Cheapside. **to be born within the sound of Bow bells,** to be born in the City of London; to be a true Cockney.

bowdlerize, -ise, *v.t.* to expurgate (a book). **bowdlerism, bowdlerization, -isation,** *n.* the act or practice of expurgating. [Thomas *Bowdler* who in 1818 published an expurgated Shakespeare]

bowel, *n.* one of the intestines, a gut; (*pl.*) the entrails, the intestines; (*fig.*) the seat of tender emotions; pity, compassion; the interior, the centre. *v.t.* to disembowel. [OF *boel* (It. *budello*), late L *botellus,* dim. of *botulus,* a sausage]

bower[1], *n.* (*poet.*) a dwelling; an inner room, a boudoir; an arbour, a shady retreat, a summer-house; the run of a bower-bird. **bower-bird,** *n.* the name given to several Australian birds of the starling family, which build bowers or runs, adorning them with feathers, shells etc. **bowery,** *a.* of the nature of a bower; leafy. **The Bowery,** *n.* a district in New York formerly notorious for political graft, now for its numerous bars, shops and cheap hotels. [OE *būr,* a chamber, a college (*būan,* to dwell); cp. Dan. *buur,* and G *bauer,* a cage]

bower[2], *n.* one of the two knaves in euchre. The knave of trumps is the **right,** and the other of the same colour the **left bower**. [G *Bauer,* a peasant, the knave (cp. BOER)]

bower[3] BOW[3].

Bowie[1], *n.* **David,** stage name of David Jones (1947–), British pop singer and songwriter, born in Brixton, London. He became a glitter-rock star with the album *The Rise and Fall of Ziggy Stardust and the Spiders from Mars* (1972), and collaborated in the mid-1970s with the electronic virtuoso Brian Eno (1948–) and Iggy Pop. He has also acted in plays and films, including Nicolas Roeg's *The Man Who Fell to Earth* (1976).

Bowie[2], *n.* **James 'Jim'** (1796–1836), US frontiersman and folk hero. A colonel in the Texan forces during the Mexican War, he is said to have invented the single-edge, guarded hunting and throwing knife known as a **Bowie knife**. He was killed in the battle of the Alamo.

bowl[1], *n.* a hollow (usually hemispherical) vessel for holding liquids; a basin; the contents of such a vessel; a drinking-vessel; a basin-shaped part or concavity. [OE *bolla,* Teut. stem *bul-,* to swell]

bowl[2], *n.* a solid ball, generally made of wood, used to play with, either spherical or slightly biased or one sided; (*pl.*) a game with bowls; (*dial.*) skittles. (*N. Am.*) ten-pin bowls. *v.i.* to play at bowls; to roll a bowl along the ground; to deliver the ball at cricket; to move rapidly and smoothly (usu. with *along*). *v.t.* to cause to roll or run along the ground; to deliver (as a ball at cricket); to strike the wicket and put a man out; †to pelt. **to bowl out,** to get a player out at cricket by bowling the bails off; (*sl.*) to find out; to convict. **to bowl over,** to knock over; to throw into a helpless condition. **bowler[1],** *n.* one who plays at bowls; the player who delivers the ball at cricket. **bowling,** *n.* playing at bowls; the act of delivering a ball at cricket. **bowling-alley,** *n.* a covered space for playing skittles or ten-pin bowls. **bowling-crease,** *n.* the line from behind which the bowler delivers the ball at cricket. **bowling-green,** *n.* a level green on which bowls are played. [F *boule,* L *bulla,* a bubble]

bowler[2], bowler hat, *n.* an almost-hemispherical stiff felt hat. [BOWL[1]]

bowline BOW[3].

bowman[1] BOW[1]; **bowman[2]** BOW[3].

bowsprit BOW[3].

Bow-street, *n.* a street in London where the principal police-court is situated. **Bow-street officer, runner,** *n.* old name for a detective police officer.

bow-window BOW[1].

bow-wow, *int., n.* an exclamation imitating the bark of a dog. *n.* the bark of a dog; (*childish*), a dog. [imit.]

bowyang, *n.* (*Austral.*) a strap or string below the knee to prevent trousers from dragging.

bowyer BOW[1].

box[1], *n.* a genus of small evergreen shrubs, *Buxus,* esp. the common box-tree; box-wood. **box-tree,** *n.* the common box, *Buxus sempervirens*. **box-wood,** *n.* the wood of the box-tree. **boxen,** *a.* of, made of or resembling box. [OE *box,* L *buxus,* Gr. *puxos*]

box[2], *n.* a case or receptacle usually with a lid and rectangular or cylindrical, adapted for holding solids, not liquids; the contents of such a case; a compartment partitioned off in a theatre, tavern, coffee-house, or for animals in a stable, railway-truck etc.; the driver's seat on a coach; a hut, a small house; one of the compartments into which a type-case is divided; a case for the protection of some piece of mechanism from injury; a protective pad for the genitals worn by cricketers. *v.t.* to enclose in or furnish with a box; to deposit a document in court; (*Austral.*) to allow sheep that should be kept separate to run together. **in the box seat,** in the most advantageous position, best placed. **in the wrong box,** mistaken, out of place. **the box,** television; a television set. **to box-haul,** *v.t.* (*Naut.*) to veer (a ship) in a particular manner when near the shore. **to box off,** to box-haul; to partition off. **to box the compass,** to name the points of the compass in proper order; to go right round (in direction, political views etc.) and end at the starting point. **to box up,** to shut in; to squeeze together. **box-bed,** *n.* a bedstead with sides, roof and sliding panels of wood; a bedstead that folds up like a box. **box-car,** *n.* (*N Am.*) a goods van. **box-cloth,** *n.* a tough, closely woven cloth. **box-coat,** *n.* a heavy overcoat worn by coachmen. **box-day,** *n.* (*Sc. Law*) a day in vacation appointed for the lodgment of papers. **box-drain,** *n.* a square drain. **box girder,** *n.* a rectangular or square hollow girder. **box-hat,** *n.* a silk hat. **box-iron,** *n.* a smoothing-iron with a cavity for a heater. **box junction,** *n.* a road junction with a box-shaped area painted with criss-crossed yellow lines into which traffic is prohibited from entering until there is a clear exit. **box-key,** *n.* a T-shaped implement for turning a water cock. **box kite,** *n.* a box-shaped kite composed of open-ended connected cubes. **box mattress, box spring mattress,** *n.* a mattress consisting of spiral springs contained in a wooden frame and covered with ticking. **box number,** *n.* a number in a newspaper office to which replies to advertisements may be sent. **box-office,** *n.* an office in a theatre or concert-hall for booking seats. **box-pleat,** *n.* a double fold or pleat. **box-room,** *n.* a room for storing. **box-spanner,** *n.* a tubular spanner with the ends shaped to fit the nuts and turned by a tommy-bar inserted into a transverse hole. **box-tree, box-gum,** *n.* (*Austral.*) a variety of Eucalyptus tree. **boxer¹,** *n.* one who puts or packs things up in boxes. **Boxing Day,** *n.* the first week-day after Christmas, when Christmas-boxes, i.e. presents in acknowledgement of services rendered throughout the year, are given. **boxful,** *n.* the quantity of things that a box will hold. [from prec.]

box³, *n.* †a blow; a blow with the open hand on the ear or side of the head. *v.t.* to strike (on the ear etc.) with the open hand. *v.i.* to fight or spar with fists or with gloves. **boxer²,** *n.* one who boxes; a pugilist; a member of a secret society in China, ostensibly devoted to athletics, which took the leading part in the movement for the expulsion of foreigners, which came to a head in the rising of 1900; a large, smooth-haired mastiff derived from the German bulldog; (*Austral.*) one who organizes a game of two-up. **boxer shorts,** *n.pl.* men's baggy underpants resembling the shorts worn by boxers. **boxing,** *n.* the sport of fist fighting with gloves. **boxing gloves,** *n.pl.* a pair of protective leather mittens worn by boxers. [etym. doubtful (perh. imit.)]

Boxer, *n.* member of the *I Ho Ch'üan* ('Society of Harmonious Fists'), Chinese nationalists who in 1900 at the instigation of the empress dowager besieged the foreign legations in Beijing and murdered European missionaries and thousands of Chinese Christian converts (the **Boxer Rebellion**). An international punitive force was dispatched, Beijing was captured 14 Aug. 1900, and China agreed to pay a large indemnity.

boy, *n.* a male child; a lad, a son; a slave; (*offensive*) a native, a native servant or labourer; (*offensive*) any male servant; (*pl.*) grown up sons; (*pl. coll.*) a group of male friends. **oh boy,** (*int.*) an exclamation of surprise, appreciation, delight or derision. **old boy,** a familiar kind of address. **boy friend,** *n.* (*coll.*) a man or boy in whom a girl is especially interested. **Boys' Brigade,** *n.* an organization founded in Britain in 1883 for the training and welfare of boys. **boy's love,** *n.* southernwood. **boy's play,** *n.* play such as boys engage in; trifling. **boyhood,** *n.* the state of being a boy; the time of life at which one is a boy. **Scout,** *orig.* **Boy Scout,** *n.* a member of an organization founded in 1908 for the development of good citizenship, character and resourcefulness among boys. **boyish,** *a.* characteristic of or suitable to a boy; puerile. **boyishly,** *adv.* **boyishness,** *n.* [etym. doubtful; perh. from EFris. *boi,* young gentleman (cp. Dut. *boef,* knave, MHG *buobe,* G *Bube*)]

boyar, boyard, *n.* a member of the old Russian nobility; a landed proprietor. [Rus. *boyāre,* pl. of *boyārin* (from OSlav. *bol* great, or Rus. *boi,* war)]

boycott, *v.t.* to combine to ostracize (a person) on account of his political opinions; to refuse to have dealings with. *n.* the action of boycotting. **boycottee,** *n.* **boycotter,** *n.* **boycottism,** *n.* [first used in 1880 to describe the action of the Land League towards Capt. *Boycott,* an Irish landlord]

Boycott¹, *n.* **Charles Cunningham** (1832–97), English land agent in County Mayo, Ireland, who strongly opposed the demands for agrarian reform by the Irish Land League (1879–81), with the result that the peasants refused to work for him; hence the word 'boycott'.

Boycott², *n.* **Geoffrey** (1940–), England cricketer born in Yorkshire, England's most prolific run-maker with 8114 runs in test cricket. He was banned as a test player in 1982 for taking part in matches against South Africa.

Boyd-Orr, *n.* **John** (1880–1971), British nutritionist and health campaigner. He was awarded the Nobel peace prize in 1949 in recognition of his work towards alleviating world hunger.

Boyer, *n.* **Charles** (1899–1978), French film actor, who made his name in Hollywood in the 1930s as a screen 'lover' in films such as *Mayerling* (1937) and *The Garden of Allah* (1936).

boyla, *n.* a sorcerer. [Austral. Abor.]

Boyle's law, *n.* in physics, law stating that the volume of a given mass of gas at a constant temperature is inversely proportional to its pressure. It was discovered in 1662 by Robert Boyle.

Boyne, *n.* a river in the Irish Republic. Rising in the Bog of Allen in County Kildare, it flows 110 km/69 miles NE to the Irish Sea near Drogheda.

Boyne, Battle of the, battle fought 1 Jul. 1690 in E Ireland, in which James II was defeated by William III and fled to France. It was the decisive battle of the War of English Succession, confirming a Protestant monarch. It took its name from the river Boyne.

boysenberry, *n.* an edible hybrid fruit related to the loganberry and the raspberry. [after Rudolph *Boysen*]

BP, (*abbr.*) British Petroleum; British Pharmacopeia.

bp, (*abbr.*) boiling point; of alcoholic density, below proof; bishop; bills payable; baptized; birthplace.

bpi, (*abbr.*) of computer tape, bits per inch.

Bq (*chem.* symbol) becquerel.

BR (*abbr.*) British Rail.

Br (*chem. symbol*) bromine.

Br. (*abbr.*) British; Brother.

bra, short for BRASSIÈRE. **bra-burning,** *a.* exceptionally feministic, from the practice of burning brassieres as a token of women's independence. **braless,** *a.* not wearing a bra.

Brabançonne, La, *n.* national anthem of Belgium, written and composed during the revolution of 1830.

Brabant, *n.* (Flemish **Braband**) former duchy of W Europe, comprising the Dutch province of North Brabant, and the Belgian provinces of Brabant and Antwerp. They were divided when Belgium became independent in 1830. The present-day Belgian province of Brabant has an area of 3400 sq km/1312 sq miles, and a population (1987) of 2,222,000.

Brabham, *n.* Grand Prix racing team started 1962 by the top Australian driver, Jack Brabham. Their first car, designed by Ron Tauranac, gained its first win 1964, and in 1966 Brabham won the world title in his own Repco-powered car. It was the first time anyone had won the world title in a car bearing their own name.

brace, *n.* †armour for the arms; †a coat of armour; †warlike preparation; that which clasps, tightens, connects or supports; (*pl.*) straps to support the trousers; a strap connecting the body of a coach to the springs; a sign in writing, printing or music uniting two or more words, lines, staves etc.; two taken together, a couple, a pair; a timber or scantling to strengthen the framework of a building; a rope attached to a yard for trimming the sail; a leather thong on the cord of a drum regulating the tension of the skin; a cord of a drum; a wire dental appliance for straightening crooked teeth. *v.t.* to encompass; to gird; to bind or tie close; to tighten or make tense; to strengthen, to fill with energy or firmness; to trim sails by means of braces. **brace and bit,** a tool used by carpenters for boring, consisting of a kind of crank in which a bit or drill is fixed. **to splice the main brace,** (*Naut. sl.*) to serve an extra rum ration. **bracer,** *n.* that which braces; (*coll.*) a stiff drink; a defence for the arm, used in archery, fencing etc. [OF *brasseure,* L *brachium,* arm]

bracing, *a.* imparting tone or strength. [OF *brace, brasse,* L *brāchia,* the arms, Gr. *brachiōn,* the arm]

bracelet, *n.* an ornamental ring or band for the wrist or arm; (*pl.*) (*sl.*) handcuffs. [OF *bracel*]

†**brach,** *n.* a bitch hound. [OF *brachet, braquet,* dim. of *brac,* OHG *bracco* (G *Bracke*), a dog that hunts by scent]

brachial, *a.* of or belonging to the arm; resembling an arm. **brachiate**, *a.* having branches in pairs, nearly at right angles to a stem and crossing each other alternately. *v.i.* of various arboreal mammals, to move along by swinging from each arm alternately. **brachiation,** *n.* [L *brāchiālis (brāchium,* arm)]

brachio-, *comb. form.* having arms or arm-like processes. [Gr. *brachiōn,* an arm]

brachiopod, *n.* (*pl.* **-pods, -poda**,) a bivalve mollusc with tentacles on each side of the mouth. **brachiopodous**, *a.* of or resembling the brachiopoda. [Gr. *pous podos,* foot]

Brachiopoda, *n.* phylum of marine clamlike creatures with about 300 species. They are suspension feeders, ingesting minute food particles from water. A single internal organ, the iophophore, handles feeding, aspiration, and excretion.

brachiosaurus, *n.* an herbivorous dinosaur characterized by the length of its front legs and its huge size.

brachy-, *comb. form.* short. [Gr. *brachus,* short]

brachycephalic, *a.* short-headed; having a skull in which the breadth is at least four-fifths of the length; belonging to a race distinguished by skulls of that proportion. **brachycephaly, brachycephalism**, *n.* the state of being brachycephalic. [Gr. *kephalē,* head]

brachylogy, *n.* concision of speech; abridged or condensed expression; inaccuracy caused by excess of brevity.

†**brack,** *n.* a flaw or tear in a cloth or dress [BREAK]

bracken, *n.* a fern, esp. the brake-fern, *Pteris aquilina*. [Swed. *bräken* fern]

bracket, *n.* a projection with horizontal top fixed to a wall, a shelf with a stay underneath for hanging against a wall; an angular support; the cheek of a gun-carriage, holding the trunnion; a gas pipe projecting from a wall; a mark used in printing to enclose words or mathematical symbols. *v.t.* to furnish with a bracket or brackets; to place within brackets; to connect (names of equal merit) in honour list; to associate, categorize or group like things together. (*Artill.*) to find the range of a target by dropping shots alternately short of and over it. **bracketing,** *n.* a skeleton support for mouldings. [formerly *bragget,* Sp. *bragueta,* dim. of *braga,* L *brāca,* sing. of *bracae, braccae,* breeches (the sense affected by confusion with L *brāchium,* arm)]

brackish, *a.* partly fresh, partly salt; of a saline taste. **brackishness,** *n.* [formerly *brack,* Dut. *brak*]

bract, *n.* a small modified leaf or scale on the flower-stalk. **bracteal**, *a.* of the nature of a bract. **bracteate**, *a.* formed of metal beaten thin; furnished with bracts. **bracteole**, *n.* a small bract. **bracteolate**, *a.* furnished with bracteoles. **bractless,** *a.* [L *bractea,* a thin plate]

Bracton, *n.* **Henry de** (d. 1268), English judge, writer on English law, and chancellor of Exeter cathedral from 1264. He compiled an account of the laws and customs of the English, *De Legibus et Consuetudinibus Angliae*, the first of its kind.

brad, *n.* a thin, flattish nail, with a small lip or projection on one side instead of a head. [ME *brad,* Icel. *broddr;* a spike (cp. OE *brord*)]

bradawl, *n.* a small boring-tool. [AWL]

Bradbury[1], *n.* **Malcolm** (1932–), British novelist and critic, noted for his comic and satiric portrayals of academic life. His best-known work is *The History Man* (1975), set in a provincial English university. Other works include *Rates of Exchange* (1983).

Bradbury[2], *n.* **Ray** (1920–), US writer, born in Illinois. He was one of the first science-fiction writers to make the genre 'respectable' to a wider readership. His work shows nostalgia for small-town Midwestern life, and includes *The Martian Chronicles* (1950), *Something Wicked This Way Comes* (1962), and *Fahrenheit 451* (1953).

Bradford, *n.* industrial city (engineering, machine tools, electronics, printing) in West Yorkshire, England, 14 km/9 miles W of Leeds; population (1981) 281,000. From the 13th century, Bradford developed as a great wool- and, later, cloth-manufacturing centre, but the industry declined from the 1970s with Third World and Common Market competition. The city has received a succession of immigrants, Irish in the 1840s, German merchants in the mid-19th century, then Poles and Ukrainians, and more recently West Indians and Asians.

brady-, *comb. form.* slow. [Gr. *bradus,* slow]

bradycardia, *n.* a slow heartbeat.

bradypeptic, *a.* of slow digestion.

bradypod, *n.* one of the sloth tribe. [Gr. *pous podos,* foot]

brae, *n.* a slope bounding a river valley; a hill. [Icel. *brā,* eyelid, brow (cp. OE *brœw*)]

brag, *v.i.* to boast. *v.t.* to boast; to challenge; to bully. *n.* a boast; boasting; a game of cards. *adv.* proudly, conceitedly. †**bragly,** *adv.* finely, briskly, nimbly. [etym. doubtful] **braggadocio,** *n.* the name given by Spenser to Vainglory personified; an empty boaster; empty boasting. **braggart**, *n.* a boastful fellow. *a.* given to bragging; boastful. †**braggartism,** *n.* boastfulness, bragging. **bragging,** *n., a.* †**braggingly,** *adv.* [F *bragard,* from *braguer,* to brag]

Brahma[1], Brahmaputra, *n.* a variety of domestic fowl. [*Brahmaputra,* name of river]

Brahma[2], *n.* the chief Hindu divinity, the Creator God. **Brahman**, *n.* Brahmin.

Brahmin, *n.* a member of the highest Hindu caste, the priestly order; (*N Am.*) a person of superior intellectual or social status, a highbrow; a breed of Indian cattle. **Brahminic, Brahminical**, *a.* of or pertaining to Brahmins or to Brahminism. **Brahminee** (1), *n.* a female Brahmin. **Brahminee** (2), *a.* pertaining to the Brahmin caste. **Brahminism** *n.* [Sansk. *brāhmana,* from *brahman,* worship]

braid[1], *n.* anything plaited or interwoven; a narrow band; a woven fabric for trimming or binding. †*a.* deceitful. *v.t.* to intertwine, to plait; to dress the hair in plaits or bands; to tie the hair with ribbon or bands; to trim or bind with braid. **braided,** *a.* †**braiding,** *n.* the action of plaiting or interweaving; embroidery. [OE *brœgd, brœd,* trick, deceit, from *bregdan, bredan,* to move to and fro, weave (cp. Icel. *bregtha,* OHG *brettan*)]

†**braid[2],** *v.t.* to upbraid, to reproach. [BRAID[1], or from obs. v. *abraid,* upbraid]

braid[3], (*Sc.*) BROAD.

braidism, *n.* hypnotism, mesmerism. [Dr James *Braid* 1795–1860, who applied and explained the system in 1842]

brail, *n.* a piece of leather with which to bind up a hawk's wing; (*pl.*) ropes used to gather up the foot and leeches of a sail before furling. *v.t.* to fasten up (the wing of a hawk) with a brail; to haul up by means of the brails. [OF *brail, braiel,* L *brācāle,* breech-girdle (*bracoe,* breeches)]

Braille, *n.* a system of writing or printing for the blind, by means of combinations of points stamped in relief. **Braille music, type,** *n.* music or symbols designed on this system. **Braille writer,** *n.* an instrument for stamping paper with these. [Louis *Braille* (1809–52), inventor]

brain, *n.* the soft, whitish, convoluted mass of nervous substance contained in the skull of vertebrates; any analogous organ in the invertebrates (*sing.* the organ, *pl.* the substance); the seat of intellect, thought etc.; the centre of sensation; intellectual power; (*coll.*) an intelligent person. *v.t.* to dash out the brains of; to kill in this way; †to conceive in the brain. **to have something on the brain,** to be obsessed with it. **brain child,** *n.* a plan or project which is the product of creative thought. **brain-coral,** *n.* coral resembling the convolutions of the brain. **brain death,** *n.* the cessation of brain function, taken as an indication of death. **brain-fag,** *n.* nervous exhaustion. **brain-fever,** *n.* inflammation of the brain; fever with brain complications. **brain-pan,** *n.* the skull. **brain-sick,** *a.* of diseased brain or mind; flighty, one-sided, injudicious; produced by a diseased brain. **brain stem,** *n.* the stalk-shaped part of the brain which connects it to the spinal cord. **brain storm,** *n.* a sudden, violent mental disturbance. **brainstorming,** *n.* (*esp. N Am.*) intensive discussion, e.g. to generate ideas. **brains trust,** *n.* a bench of persons before the microphone answering impromptu selected questions from an audience. **brain teaser,** *n.* a perplexing problem or puzzle. **brain-washing,** *n.* the subjection of a victim to sustained mental pressure, or to indoctrination, in order to extort a confession or to induce him to change his views. **brain-wash,** *v.t.* **brain-wave,** *n.* (*coll.*) a (sudden) brilliant idea. **braininess,** *n.* cleverness, intelligence. †**brainish,** *a.* headstrong, ambitious. **brainless,** *a.* destitute of brain; silly, witless. **brainy,** *a.* having brains; acute, clever. [OE *brægen* (Dut. *brein,* perh. conn. with Gr. *brechmos,* forehead)]

braird, *n.* the first shoots of corn or grain. *v.i.* to sprout. [OE *brerd,* brim, border, edge, point]

braise, *v.t.* to cook slowly in little liquid in a tightly closed pan. [F *braiser,* from *braise,* hot charcoal]

brake[1], *n.* bracken. [BRACKEN]

brake[2], *n.* an instrument for breaking flax or hemp; an implement like scissors for peeling the bark of withes for baskets; a heavy harrow for breaking up clods; †an instrument of torture; a framework in which restive horses are confined during shoeing; a light carriage in which horses are broken to harness; a large wagonette (in this sense also spelt BREAK). *v.t.* to crush flax or hemp. [MLG *brake* or ODut. *bracke* (Dut. *braak*), a flax-brake, Dut. *breken,* to break]

brake[3], *n.* an appliance to a wheel to check or stop motion; a brake-van; the handle of a pump. *v.t.* to retard by means of a brake. **brake-block,** *n.* a block applied to a wheel as a brake. **brakeman,** (*N Am.*) **brakesman,** *n.* a man in charge of a brake, a railway guard. **brake horsepower,** *n.* the measurement of an engine's power calculated from its resistance to a brake. **brake light,** *n.* the red light on the rear of a vehicle which indicates braking. **brake-van,** *n.* a railway carriage containing a brake; a guard's van. **brakeless,** *a.* without a brake. [etym. doubtful; perh. from prec. or from OF *brac,* an arm, lever]

brake[4], *n.* a mass of brushwood, a thicket. **braky,** *a.* full of bracken or brake; rough, thorny. [etym. doubtful; perh. from MLG *brake,* tree-stumps, or conn. with BREAK]

Bramah, *n.* **Joseph** (1748–1814), British inventor of a flushing water-closet (1778), an 'unpickable' lock (1784) and the hydraulic press (1795). The press made use of Pascal's principle and employed water as the hydraulic fluid; it enabled the 19th-cent. bridge-builders to lift massive girders.

Bramante, *n.* **Donato** (*c.* 1444–1514), Italian Renaissance architect and artist. Inspired by classical designs, he was employed by Pope Julius II in rebuilding part of the Vatican and St Peter's in Rome.

bramble, *n.* the blackberry, or any allied thorny shrub. **bramble finch, brambling,** *n.* the mountain finch, *Fringilla montifringilla.* **bramble-net,** *n.* a net to catch birds. **brambled,** *a.* overgrown with brambles. **brambly,** *a.* full of brambles. [OE *brembel, brēmel,* dim. of OTeut. word corr. to OE *brom,* broom (cp. Dut. *braam,* blackberry, OHG *Brāma,* bramble, G *Brombeere,* blackberry)]

bran, *n.* the husks of ground corn separated from the flour by bolting. **bran-mash,** *n.* bran soaked in water. [OF, etym. doubtful]

brancard, *n.* a horse-litter. [F, a litter, from *branche,* BRANCH]

branch, *n.* a shoot or limb of a tree or shrub, esp. one from a bough; any offshoot, member, part or subdivision of an analogous kind; a child, a scion; anything considered as a subdivision or extension of a main trunk, as of mountain-range, river, road, railway, family, genus, system of knowledge, legislature, commercial organization etc.; a rib in a Gothic vault. *v.i.* to shoot out into branches or subdivisions; to diverge from a main direction; to divide, to ramify. *v.t.* †to embroider with flowers or foliage; to divide into branches; to subdivide. **to branch out,** to broaden one's interests or activities. **branch-work,** *n.* sculptured foliage. **branched,** *a.* having branches. **brancher,** *n.* that which shoots out into branches; a young hawk or other bird when it leaves the nest and takes to the branches. **branchless,** *a.* **branchlet,** *n.* a small branch, a twig. **branchy,** *a.* full of branches, ramifying. [F *branche,* late L *branca,* a paw]

branchia, branchiae, *n.pl.* the gills of fishes and some amphibia. **branchial,** *a.* pertaining to or of the nature of gills. **branchiate,** *a.* characterized by gills. **branchiform,** *a.* shaped like gills. [L *branchia, -iae,* Gr. *branchia,* pl. of *branchion*]

branchio-, *comb. form.* pertaining to gills.

branchiopod, *n.* (*pl.* **branchiopoda**) an individual of a group of molluscoid animals with gills on the feet. **branchiopodous,** *a.* [Gr. *pous podos,* foot]

Brancusi, *n.* **Constantin** (1876–1957), Romanian sculptor; active in Paris from 1904, a pioneer of abstract forms and conceptual art. He was one of the first sculptors of the 20th cent. to carve directly from his material, and he developed increasingly simplified natural or organic forms.

brand, *n.* a piece of burning wood; a piece of wood partially burnt; a torch; a mark made by or with a hot iron, an instrument for stamping a mark; a trade-mark, hence a particular kind of manufactured article; a kind of blight; a sword; a stigma; class, quality. *v.t.* to mark with a brand; to imprint on the memory; to stigmatize. **a brand from the burning,** a person rescued or converted from sin or irreligion. **brand-iron,** *n.* a gridiron, an andiron, †a trivet; (*fig.*) †a sword. **brand name,** *n.* a trade name for the commodities of a particular manufacturer. **brand-new,** *a.* as if just from the furnace, quite new. **branding-iron,** *n.* an iron to brand with. **branded,** *a.* **brander,** *n.* a branding-iron, a gridiron. *v.t.* to cook on a gridiron; to broil or grill. †**brandise,** *n.* a trivet. [OE (cp. OTeut. *brandoz,* from *bran-,* pret. stem of *brinnan,* to burn, OHG *Brant,* brand, sword)]

brand-, bran-new BRAND.

Brandenburg, *n.* a former Prussian and German province, capital Potsdam. It was divided in 1945 between Poland and East Germany.

brandish, *v.t.* to wave or flourish about (as a weapon etc.). *n.* a flourish; waving. [F *brandir* (pres.p. *brandissant*), from OTeut. *brandoz,* see prec.]

brandling, *n.* a small red worm with vivid rings, used as bait in angling; a salmon parr. [BRAND, -LING]

Brando, *n.* **Marlon** (1924–), US actor whose casual mumbling speech and use of method acting earned him a place as one of the most distinctive screen actors. His films include *A Streetcar Named Desire* (1951), *Julius Caesar* (1953), *The Godfather* and *Last Tango in Paris* (both 1972).

brandreth, *n.* a wooden stand for a barrel, a rick etc.; a fence round a well. [Icel. *brand-reith,* a grate (*brandr,* BRAND, *reith,* a vehicle)]

Brandt[1], *n.* **Bill** (1905–83), British photographer, who produced a large body of richly-printed and romantic black-and-white studies of people, London life and social behaviour.

Brandt[2], *n.* **Willy** (adopted name of Karl Herbert Frahm) (1913–), West German socialist politician, federal chancellor (1969–74). He played a key role in the remoulding of the Social Democratic Party (SDP) as a moderate social force (chair 1964–87). As mayor of West Berlin (1957–66) he became internationally known during the Berlin Wall crisis of 1961. Nobel Peace prize (1971).

brandy, *n.* a spirit distilled from wine. *v.t.* to mix with brandy; to furnish or refresh with brandy. [formerly *brandwine,* Dut. *bran-dewijn,* burnt or distilled wine (*brandt,* p.p. of *branden,* to burn)] **brandy-ball,** *n.* a kind of sweet. **brandy glass,** *n.* a balloon-shaped glass with a short stem. **brandy-pawnee,** *n.* brandy and water. [Hind. *pāni,* water] **brandy-snap,** *n.* thin, crisp, wafer-like gingerbread, usually scroll-shaped. †**brandy-wine,** *n.* [BRANDY]

brangle, *n.* a wrangle, a quarrel. *v.i.* to wrangle, to quarrel, to dispute. †**branglement,** *n.* a brangle, a squabble. [F *branler,* to shake (etym. doubtful)]

brank, *n.* buckwheat, *Fagopyrum esculentum.* [etym. unknown]

branks, *n.* (*Sc.*) a kind of gag or bridle for punishing scolds; a bridle; a muzzle. [etym. doubtful]

brank-ursine, *n.* the acanthus or bear's-breech. [med. L *branca ursīna,* bear's paw]

†**bransle,** *n.* a kind of dance. [F, var. of *branle,* see BRAWL[2]]

Branson, *n.* **Richard** (1950–), British businessman and entrepreneur, whose Virgin company developed quickly, diversifying from retailing records to the airline business.

brant BRENT[2].

Braque, *n.* **Georges** (1882–1963), French painter who, with Picasso, founded the Cubist movement around 1908–10. Braque soon began to work with collages and invented a technique of gluing paper, wood and other materials to canvas. His later work became more decorative.

brash[1], *n.* loose, disintegrated rock or rubble. *a.* (*N Am.*) tender, brittle. **brash-ice,** *n.* broken ice. **brashy,** *a.* crumbly, rubbly. [etym. doubtful]

brash[2], *n.* a slight indisposition arising from disorder of the alimentary canal. **water-brash,** a belching of water from the stomach; heartburn; a dash of rain. [onomat.]

brash[3], *a.* impertinent, cheeky; vulgarly assertive or pushy; impudent. [etym. unknown]

brasier, BRAZIER[2].

Brasília, *n.* capital of Brazil from 1960, some 1000 m/3000 ft above sea level; population (1980) 411,500. It was designed by Lucio Costa (1902–63), with Oscar Niemeyer as chief architect, as a completely new city to bring life to the interior.

Braşov, *n.* (Hungarian **Brassó,** German **Krondstadt**) industrial city (machine tools, industrial equipment, chemicals, cement, woollens) in central Romania at the foot of the Transylvanian Alps; population (1983) 331,240. It belonged to Hungary until 1920.

brass, *n.* a yellow alloy of copper and zinc; anything made of this alloy; a brazen vessel; an engraved sepulchral tablet of this metal; musical wind-instruments of brass; (*also pl.*) the section in an orchestra composed of brass instruments; (*sl.*) money; effrontery, impudence. *a.* made of brass. **the brass,** those in authority; officers, brass hats. **top brass,** those in highest authority; the highest-ranking officers. **brass band,** *n.* a band performing chiefly on brass instruments. **brass-bounder,** *n.* (*sl.*) a midshipman; a ship's officer in the mercantile marine. **brass farthing,** *n.* (*coll.*) the lowest measure of value. **brass hat,** *n.* (*coll.*) a staff officer. **brass neck,** *n.* (*coll.*) impudence, audacity. **brass plate,** *n.* a plate of brass engraved with name, trade or profession etc. fixed at doors etc. **brass rubbing,** *n.* the transfer of an image from a brass tablet to paper by placing the paper over the original and rubbing it with crayon or chalk; the image copied by this method. **brass tacks,** (*coll.*) details; the essential facts of a matter. **brassily,** *adv.* **brassiness,** *n.* **brassy,** *a.* resembling brass; unfeeling, impudent, shameless; debased, cheap, pretentious. *n.* a wooden golf club faced with brass. [OE *brœs*]

brassard, *n.* a badge worn on the arm, an armband, armlet. [F *bras,* arm]

brasserie, *n.* a (usu. small) restaurant which serves beer as well as wine etc. [F, from *brasser,* OF *bracer* to brew, from *brace,* malt]

brassica, *n.* any plant belonging to the genus *Brassica* of the cruciferae family (turnip, cabbage etc.). [L, cabbage]

brassière, *n.* an undergarment for supporting the breasts. [F]

brassy BRASS.

brat, *n.* a child, usu. one who is badly behaved or ragged and dirty. **Brat pack, brat pack,** *n.* a group of precociously successful young performers or practitioners in any field, esp. a group of young American film actors and directors in the 1980's. [etym. doubtful]

Bratislava, *n.* (German **Pressburg**) an industrial port (engineering, chemicals, oil-refining) in Czechoslovakia, on the Danube; population (1981) 381,000. It was the capital of Hungary (1526–1784). Now capital of the Slovak Socialist Republic and 2nd largest city in Czechoslovakia.

brattice, *n.* †a temporary breastwork; a partition for ventilation in a mine; a partition; a lining of timber. **brattice-cloth,** *n.* a stout tarred cloth used instead of boards for bratticing. **brattice-work,** *n.* **bratticing,** *n.* brattice-work; (*Arch.*) open carved work. [ME *bretasce, brutaske,* OF *bretesce, breteske,* prob. from G *Brett,* board]

bratwurst, *n.* a kind of German sausage. [G *brat-,* roasted, fried, *Wurst,* sausage]

Braun, *n.* **Eva** (1910–45), German Nazi, born in Munich. Secretary to Hitler's photographer and personal friend, Heinrich Hoffmann, she was Hitler's mistress for years, and married him in the air-raid shelter of the Chancellery in Berlin on 29 Apr. 1945. They then committed suicide together.

bravado, *n.* (*pl.* **-oes**) an insolent menace; ostentatious defiance; swaggering behaviour. [Sp. *bravada*]

brave, *a.* daring, courageous; gallant, noble; showy, merry; excellent, fine. *n.* †a bully, a bravo; †a toast, a brag; a N Am. Indian warrior. *v.t.* to defy, to challenge; to meet with courage. *v.i.* to swagger, to show off. **to brave it out,** to bear oneself defiantly in the face of blame or suspicion. **bravely,** *adv.* **bravery,** *n.* courage; †bravado; display, splendour; finery. [F *bravo,* It. *bravo,* gallant, fine (etym. unknown)]

bravo[1], *n.* (*pl.* **-oes**), a hired assassin; a bandit, a desperado. [It.]

bravo[2], *int.* (*pl.* **-voes, vos**; *fem.* **-va**; *superl.* **-vissimo, -ma**) capital! well done! *n.* a cry of approval; a cheer. [It.]

bravura, *n.* (*Mus.*) brilliance of execution; a display of daring and skill in artistic execution; a piece of music that calls out all the powers of an executant. *a.* [It., bravery]

braw, (*Sc.*) BRAVE.

brawl[1], *v.i.* to quarrel noisily; to babble (as running water); (*Law*) to create a disturbance in a consecrated place or building. *v.t.* to utter loudly; †to overpower with noise. *n.* a noisy quarrel, disturbance, a tumult. **brawler,** *n.* **brawling,** *a.* **brawlingly,** *adv.* [etym. doubtful; prob. imit.]

brawl[2], *n.* a French dance like a cotillion. [F *branle* (*branler,* BRANGLE]

brawn, *n.* muscle, flesh; the flesh of a boar; a potted meat dish usu. made from pig's head; strength, muscularity. †**brawned,** *a.* brawny, muscular. †**brawner,** *n.* a boar fattened for the table. **brawny,** *a.* muscular, strong, hardy. **brawniness,** *n.* [OF *braon,* flesh for roasting, WG *Brâdo,* from *brâdan,* to roast]

braxy, *n.* splenic apoplexy in sheep; the flesh of a sheep which has died of this disorder. *a.* affected by this disease, or belonging to a sheep that has died through disease or accident. **braxied,** *a.* [etym. doubtful]

bray[1], *v.t.* to pound or grind small, esp. with pestle and mortar; to beat fine. **brayer,** *n.* a wooden muller used to temper printing-ink. [OF *breier* (F *broyer*), perh. conn. with BREAK]

bray[2], *v.i.* to make a harsh, discordant noise, like an ass. *v.t.* to utter harshly or loudly (often with *out*). *n.* a loud cry; the cry of the ass; a harsh, grating sound. [OF *braire,* low L *bragīre* (cogn. with L *fragor,* a crashing noise)]

braze[1], *v.t.* to solder with an alloy of brass and zinc. [OF *braser,* to harden by fire]

braze[2], *v.t.* to cover or ornament with brass; to colour like brass. [BRASS] **brazen** *a.* made of brass; resembling brass; shameless, impudent. *v.t.* to face impudently (often with *out*); to harden, make shameless. **brazen**

age, *n.* the third of the mythological ages, the age of violence. **brazen-face,** *n.* an impudent person. **brazen-faced,** *a.* impudent, shameless. **brazenly,** *adv.* **brazenness, brazenry,** *n.* **brazier**[1], *n.* a worker in brass. **braziery,** *n.* brasswork. [OE *bræsen,* from *bræs,* brass]

brazier[2], *n.* a large pan to hold lighted charcoal. [F *brasier,* from *braise,* live coals]

brazil[1], **brazil wood,** *n.* a red dyewood produced by the genus *Caesalpinia,* which gave its name to the country in S America. **brazil-nut,** *n.* the triangular, edible seed of *Bertholletia excelsa*. [etym. unknown]

Brazil[2], *n.* Federative Republic of (*República Federativa do Brasil*), country in S America. **area** 8,511,965 sq km/3,285,618 sq miles. **capital** Brasília. **towns** São Paulo, Belo Horizonte, Curitiba, Fortaleza; ports are Rio de Janeiro, Recife, Pôrto Alegre, Salvador. **physical** the densely forested Amazon basin covers the N half of the country with a network of rivers; the S is fertile; enormous energy resources, both hydroelectric (Itaipú dam on the Paraná, and Tucurui on the Tocantins) and nuclear (uranium ores). **population** (1988) 144,262,000 (including 200,000 Indians, survivors of 5 million, especially in Rondonia and Mato Grosso, mostly living on reserves); annual growth rate 2.2%. **exports** coffee, sugar, cotton, textiles, motor vehicles, iron, chrome, manganese, tungsten and other ores, as well as quartz crystals, industrial diamonds. **language** Portuguese; 120 Indian languages. **religion** Roman Catholic 89%, Indian faiths.

Brazzaville, *n.* capital of the Congo, industrial port (foundries, railway repairs, shipbuilding, shoes, soap, furniture, bricks) on the river Zaïre, opposite Kinshasa; population (1980) 422,500. It was the African headquarters of the Free (later Fighting) French during World War II.

BRCS, (*abbr.*) British Red Cross Society.

breach, *n.* the act of breaking; a break, a gap; †an inlet of the sea; violation, whether by a definite act or by omission, of a law, duty, right, contract or engagement; a rupture of friendship or alliance; alienation, quarrel; a gap, esp. one made by guns in a fortification; the breaking of waves; a whale's leap from the water. *v.t.* to make a breach or gap in. *v.i.* to leap from the water (as a whale). **breach of faith,** violation of trust. **breach of promise,** failure to keep a promise to marry. **breach of the peace,** violation of the public peace; a riot, an affray. [OE *brice, bryce* (*brecan,* to BREAK]

bread, *n.* a food, made of flour or other meal kneaded into dough, generally with yeast, made into loaves and baked; (*sl.*) money; livelihood. *v.t.* to dress with bread-crumbs before cooking. **bread and circuses,** free food and entertainment, esp. to placate the population. **bread and wine,** the Lord's Supper, Holy Communion; the eucharistic elements. **bread buttered on both sides,** fortunate circumstances; ease and prosperity. **on the bread line,** in extreme poverty. **to break bread,** to take food; to dispense or partake of Holy Communion. **bread-and-butter,** *n.* a slice of buttered bread; livelihood. *a.* plain, practical; routine, basic; giving thanks for hospitality (of a letter). **bread-basket,** *n.* a basket for holding bread; (*sl.*) the stomach; rich grain lands. **bread-board,** *n.* a board on which bread is sliced. **bread-corn,** *n.* corn for making bread. **bread-crumb,** *n.* a fragment of the soft part of bread; (*pl.*) bread crumbled for culinary purposes. **bread-fruit,** *n.* the farinaceous fruit of a S Sea tree, *Artocarpus incisa*. **bread-poultice,** *n.* a poultice made of hot soaked bread. **bread-room,** *n.* a place for keeping bread, esp. on board ship. **bread-root,** *n.* a N Am. plant with an edible carrot-like root, *Psoralea esculenta*. **bread-sauce,** *n.* a sauce made with bread-crumbs, milk and onions. **bread-stuff,** *n.* material for bread. **bread-winner,** *n.* the member of a family who supports it with his or her earnings; a trade, art, tool or machine that supports a family. **breaded,** *a.* dressed with bread-crumbs. **breadless,** *a.* without bread, without food. [OE *brēad,* piece of a loaf (cp. OHG *prōt,* G *Brot*)]

breadth, *n.* measure from side to side; a piece of material of full breadth; width, extent, largeness; broad effect; liberality, catholicity, tolerance. **breadthways, -wise,** *adv.* by way of the breadth, across. [OE *brædu,* later *brede*]

break, *v.t.* (*past* **broke**, *earlier* **brake**, *p.p.* **broken**, **broke**) to part by violence; to rend apart, to shatter, to rupture, to disperse to, to impair; to destroy the completeness or continuity of; to subdue, to tame, to train; to ruin financially; to cashier, to reduce to the ranks; to disable, to wear out, to exhaust the strength or resources of; to disconnect, to interrupt; to intercept, to lessen the force of; to infringe, to transgress, to violate; †to carve (a deer). *v.i.* to separate into two or more portions; to burst, to burst forth; to appear with suddenness; to become bankrupt; to decline in health; to change direction; to twist, as a ball at cricket; to make the first stroke at billiards; to alter the pace (as a horse); to alter (as a boy's voice at the age of puberty). *n.* the act of breaking; an opening, gap, breach; interruption of continuity in time or space; a line in writing or printing noting suspension of the sense; irregularity; the twist of a ball at cricket; the vertical face of forecastle head or poop of a ship; a number of points scored continuously in billiards; the point where one voice register changes to another, as bass to tenor; the corresponding point in musical instruments; (*coll.*) a lucky opportunity. **break of day,** dawn. **to break a head,** to injure someone. **to break a way,** to make a way by forcing obstacles apart. **to break away,** to remove by breaking; to start away; to revolt. **to break bread with,** to be entertained at table by; to take Communion with. **to break camp,** to take down one's tent in preparation for leaving. **to break cover,** to dart out from a hiding-place. **to break down,** to destroy, to overcome; to collapse, to fail; to analyse costs etc. into component parts. **to break even,** to emerge without gaining or losing. **to break free** or **loose,** to escape from captivity; to shake off restraint. **to break ground,** to plough, to dig (esp. uncultivated or fallow ground); to open trenches; to commence operations; (*Naut.*) to begin to weigh anchor. **to break in,** to tame, to train to something; to wear in (e.g. shoes). **to break into,** to enter by force; to interrupt. **to break news,** to reveal gently. **to break off,** to detach from; to cease, to desist. **to break open,** to force a door or cover; to penetrate by violence. **to break out,** to burst loose, to escape; to burst forth (as a war); to appear (as an eruption on the skin; said also of the individual and of feelings, passions etc.). **to break service, to break someone's serve,** to win a game of tennis in which the opposing player served. **to break the back,** to break the keel of a ship; (*fig.*) to get through the greater part of. **to break the heart,** to overwhelm with grief. **to break the ice,** to prepare the way; to take the first steps. **to break the mould,** to make unique; to effect a fundamental change. **to break up,** to disintegrate; to lay open (as ground); to dissolve into laughter; to disband, to separate; to start school holidays. **to break upon the wheel,** to torture or execute by stretching upon a wheel, and breaking the limbs with an iron bar. **to break wind,** to emit wind from the bowels. **to break with,** to cease to be friends with; to quarrel with. **break-away,** *n.* (*Austral.*) a stampede of cattle or sheep; an animal that breaks away from the herd; any person, thing or group which breaks away from a main body. *a.* **break-club,** *n.* an obstacle that might break a golf club accidentally hitting it. **break dancing,** *n.* an energetic type of modern dancing characterized by spinning on various parts of the body (the hands, back etc.); *v.i.* to dance in this manner. **break-down,** *n.* down-fall, collapse; total failure resulting in stoppage; an analysis. **break-head,** *n.* the reinforced head of a ship fitted for breaking its way through ice. **break-joint,** *n.* a disposition of stones or bricks so that the joints do not fall immediately over each other. **break-neck,** *a.* endangering the neck, hazardous of speed, very fast. **break-through,** *n.* an outcrop; penetration of enemy lines; an advance, a discovery. **break-up,** *n.* disruption, dispersal into parts or elements; disintegration, decay, dissolution; dispersal. **breakwater** *n.* a pier, mole or anything similar, to break the force of the waves and protect shipping. **breakable,** *a.* capable of being broken. **breakage,** *n.* the act of breaking; the state of being broken; loss or damage from breaking; an interruption; change in quality of voice from one register to another. **breaker**[1], *n.* one or that which breaks; a heavy wave breaking against the rocks or shore. **breaking,** *n., a.* **breaking and entering,** illegal forced entry into premises for criminal purposes. **breaking point,** *n.* the limit of endurance. [OE *brecan* (cp. Goth. *brican,* OHG *prechan,* G *brechen,* from OTeut, stem *brek-,* cp. L *frangere*)]

breaker[2], *n.* a keg, a water-cask. [Sp. *barrica*]

breakfast, *n.* the first meal of the day. *v.i.* to take breakfast. *v.t.* to provide with or entertain at breakfast. [BREAK, FAST]

Breakspear, *n.* **Nicholas,** original name of Adrian IV, the only English pope.

bream[1], *n.* a freshwater fish of the genus *Abramis,* esp. *A. brama,* the carp-bream. [OF *bresme* (F *brême*), (cp. MHG *brahsem,* G *Brassen;* perh. from stem *breh-,* to glitter),

bream[2], *v.t.* to clear (a ship's bottom) of ooze, seaweed, shell-fish etc. by burning. [etym. doubtful]

breast, *n.* one of the organs for the secretion of milk in women; the rudimentary part corresponding to this in men; the fore-part of the human body between the neck and the abdomen; the analogous part in the lower animals; the upper fore-part of a coat or other article of dress; the working coal-face; (*fig.*) source of nourishment; the seat of the affections; the affections; the front, the fore-part. *v.t.* to apply or oppose the breast to; to stem, to oppose, to face. **to breast-feed,** to feed a baby from the breast instead of the bottle. **to breast up a hedge,** to cut the face of it so as to lay bare the stems. **to make a clean breast,** to confess all that one knows. **breast-bone,** *n.* the flat bone in front of the chest to which certain ribs are attached, the sternum. **breast-deep,** *a., adv.* as deep as the breast is high. **breast-drill,** *n.* a drill worked against the breast. **breast-harness,** *n.* harness attached to a breast-band instead of a collar. **breast-high,** *a., adv.* as high as the breast; (*Hunting*) of scent, so high that the hounds race with heads erect. **breast-knot,** *n.* a knot of ribbons worn on the breast. **breast-pin,** *n.* a pin worn on the breast or in a scarf; a brooch. **breast-plate,** *n.* armour worn upon the breast; a piece of embroidered linen, adorned with precious stones, worn on the breast of the Jewish high priest; the upper part of the shell of a turtle or tortoise; an inscribed plate on a coffin. **breast-plough,** *n.* a kind of small hand-plough used in paring turf. **breast-pocket,** *n.* inside pocket of a man's jacket. **breast-rail,** *n.* the upper rail on a balcony. **breast stroke,** *n.* a swimming stroke involving wide circling motions of the arms and legs while facing forward on one's breast. **breast-summer, bressummer,** *n.* a beam supporting the front of a building after the manner of a lintel. SUMMER[2]. **breast-wall,** *n.* a retaining wall. **breast-wheel,** *n.* a water-wheel which receives the water at the level of its axis. **breast-work,** *n.* a hastily constructed parapet thrown up breast-high for defence; the parapet of a building; a railing or balustrade across a ship. **breasted,** *a.* having a breast; decorated on the breast. [OE *brēost,* OTeut. *breustom* (G *Brust,* Dut. *borst*)]

breath, *n.* the air drawn in and expelled by the lungs in respiration; the act or power of breathing; a single respiration; phonetically, the expulsion of air without vibrat- ing the vocal cords; a very slight breeze; (*fig.*) the time of a single respiration; respite; an instant; a whiff, an exhalation; a rumour, a whisper, a murmur. **below, under one's breath,** in a whisper. **to catch one's breath,** to cease breathing momentarily; to regain even breathing after exertion or a shock. **to save one's breath,** (*coll.*) to avoid talking to on purpose. **to take breath,** to pause. **to take one's breath away,** to astonish. **breathtaking,** *a.* astonishing, marvellous. **breath test,** *n.* a test to determine the amount of alcohol in the breath. **breathalyse, -yze,** *v.i.* to test for the level of alcohol in a driver's breath with a breathalyser. **breathalyser, -yzer,** *n.* an instrument containing crystals for measuring the level of alcohol in the breath. **breathful,** *a.* full of breath or wind; alive; odorous. **breathless,** *a.* out of breath; dead, lifeless; panting; without a movement of the air; excited, eager. **breathlessly,** *adv.* **breathlessness,** *n.* **breathy,** *a.* aspirated; giving the sound of breathing. **breathiness,** *n.* [OE *braeth,* OTeut. *braethoz,* steam, or from stem *brae-* (Indo-Eur. *bhrē-*), to heat, burn]

breathe, *v.i.* to inhale or exhale air, to respire; to live; to take breath; to move or sound like breath. *v.t.* to inhale or exhale (as air); to emit, to send out, by means of the lungs; to utter; to utter softly; to express, to manifest; to allow breathing space to; to make breathe by means of exercise; to blow into (as a wind instrument). **to breathe again, breathe freely, easily,** to be relieved from fear or anxiety. **to breathe down someone's neck,** to cause someone discomfort with one's close supervision or constant attention. **to breathe one's last,** to die. **breathable,** *a.* that may be breathed. **breathableness,** *n.* **breather,** *n.* one who or that which breathes; an exercise to try the lungs; a rest in order to gain breath; a vent in an airtight container. **breathing,** *a.* living; lifelike. *n.* the action of breathing; a respite; an aspirate; (*Gr. Gram.*) either of the two signs ['] or ['] placed over the first vowel of a word to mark the presence or absence of the aspirate. **breathing-place, -space,** *n.* a pause, place or opening for breathing. **breathing-time,** *n.* time for recovering one's breath; a pause. **breathing-while,** *n.* a moment, an instant. [from prec.]

breccia, *n.* a rock composed of angular, as distinguished from rounded, fragments cemented together in a matrix. **brecciated,** *a.* formed into breccia. [It., gravel, rubble (cp. F *brèche,* OHG *Brecha,* breaking, *brechan,* to BREAK]

Brecht, *n.* **Bertolt** (1898–1955), German dramatist and poet, who aimed to destroy the 'suspension of disbelief' usual in the theatre and to express Marxist ideas. He adapted John Gay's *Beggar's Opera* as *Die Dreigroschenoper/The Threepenny Opera* (1928), set to music by Kurt Weill. Later plays include *Mutter Courage/Mother Courage* (1941), set in the Thirty Years' War, and *Der kaukasische Kreidekreis/The Caucasian Chalk Circle* (1949).

Brecknockshire, *n.* former county of Wales, merged in Powys in 1974.

bred, *p.p.* BREED.

†**brede,** BRAID[1].

Breda, Treaty of, 1667 treaty that ended the Second Anglo-Dutch War (1664–67). By the terms of the treaty, England gained New Amsterdam, which was renamed New York.

breech, *n.* (*pl.* **breeches**) the buttocks, the posteriors; the hinder part of anything; the portion of a gun behind the bore; (*pl.*) a garment worn by men, covering the loins and thighs, and reaching just below the knees. *v.t.* to clothe or cover with or as with breeches; to whip upon the buttocks. **to wear the breeches,** to rule, to head the household. **breech birth, delivery,** *n.* a birth in which the baby's buttocks or feet emerge first. **breech-block,** *n.* a movable piece to close the breech of a gun. **breeches-buoy,** *n.* a life-saving device run on a rope stretched from a wrecked vessel to a place of safety. **breech-loader,** *n.* a fire-arm loaded at the breech. **breech-loading,** *a.* loaded at the breech. **breeching,** *n.* a strong leather strap passing round the haunches of a shaft-horse; a stout rope securing a gun to a ship's side. **breechless,** *a.* without breeches. [OE *brēc,* pl. of *brōc* (MHG *Bruoch,* breeches)]

breed, *v.t.* (*past, p.p.* **bred**) to bring forth; to give birth to; to raise (cattle etc.), to rear; to give rise to, to yield, to produce; to engender, to cause to develop; to train up, to educate, to bring up. *v.i.* to be pregnant; to produce offspring; to come into being, to arise, to spread; to be produced or engendered. *n.* a line of descendants from the same parents or stock; family, race, offspring. **to breed in and in,** to breed always with or from near relatives. **to breed true,** always to produce young in harmony with the parental type. †**breed-bate,** *n.* a quarrelsome person [*bate,* contention, DEBATE]. **breeder,** *n.* one who breeds, esp. one who breeds cattle and other animals. **breeder reactor,** *n.* a nuclear reactor which produces more plutonium than it consumes. **breeding,** *n.* the act of giving birth to; the raising of a breed; bringing-up, nurture, rearing; education, deportment, good manners. **breeding ground,** *n.* a favourable environment or atmosphere for generating or nurturing ideas, bacteria etc. [OE *brēdan* (cp. G *Bruten,* OE *brōd,* BROOD)]

breeks, (*Sc.*) BREECHES, see BREECH.

breeze¹, *n.* a gentle gale, a light wind; a disturbance, a row; a whisper, rumour. (*coll.*) something which can be done or got with ease. *v.i.* to blow gently or moderately; to move in a lively way; (*coll.*) to do or achieve something easily. **to breeze up,** to begin to blow freshly; to sound louder on the breeze; to approach in a carefree or lively manner. **breezeless,** *a.* undisturbed by any breeze; still, calm. **breezy,** *a.* open, exposed to breezes, windy; lively, brisk, jovial. **breeziness,** *n.* [Sp. *brisa* the NE wind, prob. from F BISE]

breeze², **brize,** *n.* a gad-fly. [OE *briosa* (etym. doubtful)]

breeze³, *n.* small cinders and cinder-dust; small coke, siftings of coke. **breeze block, brick,** *n.* a brick or block made of breeze and cement. [F *braise,* live coals (see BRAZIER)]

bregma, *n.* (*pl.* **-mata**), the point on the skull where the coronal and sagittal sutures meet. [Gr. *brechein,* to moisten]

Brehon, *n.* an ancient hereditary Irish judge. **Brehon law,** *n.* the native Irish code of laws, abolished in the reign of James I. [OIr. *breitheamh,* a judge (*brieth,* judgment)]

breloque, *n.* an ornament attached to a watch-chain. [F (etym. unknown)]

Bremen¹, *n.* industrial port (iron, steel, oil refining, chemicals, aircraft, shipbuilding, cars) in West Germany, on the Weser 69 km/43 miles from the open sea; population (1988) 522,000.

Bremen², *n.* administrative region (German *Land*) of West Germany, consisting of the cities of Bremen and Bremerhaven; area 400 sq km/154 sq miles; population (1988) 652,000.

bremsstrahlung, *n.* the electromagnetic radiation caused by an electron colliding with or slowed down by the electric field of a positively charged nucleus. [G *bremsen,* to brake, *Strahlung,* radiation]

bren, brent¹, [obs. forms of BURN¹, BURNT]

Bren gun, *n.* a type of light machine-gun. [first letters of *Br*no (Czechoslovakia) and *En*field]

Brennan¹, *n.* **Christopher (John)** (1870–1932), Australian symbolist poet, influenced by Baudelaire and Mallarmé. Although one of Australia's greatest poets, he is virtually unknown outside his native country. His complex, idiosyncratic verse includes *Poems* (1914) and *A Chant of Doom and Other Verses* (1918).

Brennan², *n.* **Walter** (1894–1974), US actor, often seen in Westerns as the hero's sidekick. His work includes *The Westerner* (1940), *Bad Day at Black Rock* (1955), and *Rio Bravo* (1959).

Brenner, *n.* **Sidney** (1927–), South African scientist, one of the pioneers of genetic engineering. Brenner discovered messenger RNA (a link between DNA and ribosomes, where proteins are synthesized) in 1960.

Brenner Pass, *n.* lowest of the Alpine passes, 1370 m/ 4495 ft; it leads from Trentino–Alto Adige, Italy, to the Austrian Tirol, and is 19 km/12 miles long.

brent¹ BREN.

brent², †**brant,** *a.* steep, precipitous, lofty; smooth, without wrinkles. [OE *brant*]

brent-goose, *n.* the smallest of the wild geese, *Bernicla brenta,* which visits Britain in the winter. [etym. doubtful; cp. Swed. *brandgås,* G *Brandgans*]

Brenton, *n.* **Howard** (1942–), British dramatist, noted for *The Romans in Britain* (1980), and a translation of Brecht's *The Life of Galileo.*

brer, *n.* brother. [Black Am. contr. of BROTHER]

Brescia, *n.* (ancient **Brixia**) historic and industrial city (textiles, engineering, firearms, metal products) in N Italy, 84 km/52 miles E of Milan; population (1988) 199,000. It has mediaeval walls and two cathedrals (12th and 17th century).

Breslau, *n.* German name of Wroclaw.

bressummer BREAST-SUMMER under BREAST.

Brest, *n.* naval base and industrial port (electronics, engineering, chemicals) on **Rade de Brest** (Brest Roads), a great bay at the western extremity of Bretagne, France; population (1983) 201,000. Occupied as a U-boat base by the Germans (1940–44), the town was destroyed by Allied bombing and rebuilt.

Brest-Litovsk, Treaty of, treaty signed 3 Mar. 1918 between Russia and Germany, Austria-Hungary, and their allies. Under it, Russia agreed to recognize the independence of the Baltic states, Georgia, Ukraine, and Poland, and pay heavy compensation. Under the Nov. 1918 Armistice that ended World War I, it was annulled.

Bretagne, *n.* (English **Brittany**) region of NW France in the Breton peninsula between the Bay of Biscay and the English Channel; area 27,200 sq km/10,499 sq miles; population (1986) 2,764,000. Its capital is Rennes, and includes the *départements* of Côte-du-Nord, Finistère, Ille-et-Vilaine, and Morbihan. It is a farming region.

brethren, *n.pl.* [BROTHER]

Brétigny, Treaty of, treaty made between Edward III of England and John II of France in 1360 at the end of the first phase of the Hundred Years' War, under which Edward received Aquitaine and its dependencies in exchange for renunciation of his claim to the French throne.

Breton¹, *n.* a native of, or the language of, Brittany. *a.* belonging to Brittany.

Breton², *n.* **André** (1896–1966), French author, among the leaders of Dada. *Les Champs magnétiques/ Magnetic Fields* (1921), an experiment in automatic writing, was one of the most notable products of the movement He was also a founder of surrealism, publishing *Le Manifeste de surréalisme/Surrealist Manifesto* (1924). Other works include *Najda* (1928), the story of his love affair with a medium.

Breton language, *n.* a member of the Celtic branch of the Indo-European language family; the language of Brittany in France, related to Welsh and Cornish, and descended from the speech of Celts who left Britain as a consequence of the Anglo-Saxon invasions of the 5th and 6th centuries. Officially neglected for centuries, Breton is now a recognized language of France.

Bretton Woods, *n.* township in New Hampshire, US, where the United Nations Monetary and Financial Conference was held in 1944 to discuss post-war international payments problems. The agreements reached on financial assistance and measures to stabilize exchange rates led to the creation of the International Bank for Reconstruction and Development in 1945 and the International Monetary Fund.

bretwalda, *n.* ruler of the Britons or of Britain; a title given to some of the Anglo-Saxon kings who held supremacy or precedence over the rest. [OE *walda,* ruler]

Breuer¹, *n.* **Marcel** (1902–), Hungarian-born architect and designer, who studied and taught at the Bauhaus. His tubular steel chair (1925) was the first of its kind. He moved to England, then to the US, where he was in partnership with Gropius (1937–40). His buildings show an affinity with natural materials; the best known is the Bijenkorf, Rotterdam (with Elzas) (1953).

Breuer², *n.* **Josef** (1842–1925), Viennese physician, one of the pioneers of psychoanalysis. He applied it successfully to cases of hysteria, and collaborated with

Freud in *Studien über Hysterie/Studies in Hysteria* (1895).

Breuil, *n.* **Henri** (1877–1961), French prehistorian, professor of historic ethnography and director of research at the Institute of Human Palaeontology, Paris, from 1910. He established the genuine antiquity of Palaeolithic cave art and stressed the anthropological approach to the early human history.

breve, *n.* †a brief; a sign (˘) used in printing to mark a short vowel; a note of time equal to two semibreves. [BRIEF]

brevet, *n.* an official document conferring certain privileges; a warrant conferring nominal rank of an officer without the pay; the wing-badge a flying member of the RAF may put on his uniform. *a.* conferred by brevet; honorary, nominal. *v.t.* to confer (a certain rank) by brevet. [F, dim. of *bref,* a letter (cp. BRIEF]

breveté, *a.* patented. [F]

brevi-, *comb. form.* short. [L *brevis*]

breviary, *n.* †a brief statement; in the Roman Catholic Church, a book containing the divine office. [L *breviārium* (*brevis,* short)]

breviate, *a.* abbreviated, short. *n.* a short summary, an abridgement; a note; a lawyer's brief. *v.t.* to abridge; to curtail. [L *breviātus,* p.p. of *breviāre,* to shorten, from *brevis,* short]

brevier, *n.* a size of type between bourgeois and minion, in which breviaries were thought to be formerly printed. [BREVIARY]

breviped, *a.* short-footed, short-legged. [L *pes, pedis,* foot]

brevipennate, *a.* having short wings. [L *penna,* wing]

brevirostrate, *a.* having a short bill or beak. [L *rōstrum,* a beak]

brevity, *n.* briefness, shortness; conciseness. [L *brevitas -tātem*]

brew, *v.t.* to make (beer, ale etc.) by boiling, steeping and fermenting; to convert into (beer, ale etc.) by such processes; to prepare other beverages by mixing or infusion; to prepare; to concoct; to contrive, to plot; to bring about. *v.i.* to make beer etc. by boiling, fermenting etc.; to undergo these or similar processes; to be in preparation. *n.* the action, process or product of brewing; the quantity brewed at one process; the quality of the thing brewed. **to brew up,** (*coll.*) to make tea. **brewage,** *n.* a mixture; a concocted beverage; the process of brewing. **brewer,** *n.* one whose trade is to brew malt liquors. **brewer's droop,** *n.* (*sl.*) temporary sexual impotence in men due to overindulgence in alcohol. **brewer's yeast,** *n.* a yeast used in brewing and as a source of vitamin B. **brewery, brewhouse,** *n.* a place where beer is brewed. **brewster,** *n.* †a female brewer; †a brewer. **Brewster Sessions,** *n.pl.* sessions for granting licences to sell alcoholic liquors. [OE (brēowan (cp. OHG *briuwan,* G *brauen;* cp. L *dēfrutum,* new wine boiled down)]

brewis, *n.* broth; liquor in which meat and vegetables have been boiled. [OF *brouetz,* dim. of *bro,* OHG *brod*]

Brezhnev, *n.* **Leonid Ilyich** (1906–82), Soviet leader. A protégé of Stalin and Khrushchev, he came into power as general secretary of the Soviet Communist Party (CPSU) during 1964–82 and was president during 1977–82. Domestically he was conservative, abroad the USSR as a military and political superpower was established during the Brezhnev era, extending its influence in Africa and Asia.

Brian[1], *n.* known as **Brian Boru** ('Brian of the Tribute') (926–1014), king of Ireland from 976, who took Munster, Leinster, and Connacht, to become ruler of all Ireland. He defeated the Norse at Clontarf, thus ending Norse control of Dublin, although he was himself killed. His exploits were celebrated in several chronicles.

Brian[2], *n.* **Havergal** (1876–1972), English composer of 32 symphonies in visionary romantic style, including the *Gothic* (1919-27) for large choral and orchestral forces.

Briand, *n.* **Aristide** (1862–1932), French radical socialist politician. He was prime minister in 1909–11, 1913, 1915–17, 1921–22, 1925–26, and 1929, and foreign minister during 1925–32. In 1925 he concluded the Locarno Pact and in 1928 the Kellogg Pact; in 1930 he outlined a scheme for a United States of Europe.

briar BRIER.

Briareus, *n.* a giant of Greek mythology, said to have had a hundred hands; a many-handed person. **Briarean,** *a.* of or pertaining to Briareus; many-handed. [Gr. mythol.]

bribe, *n.* a gift or consideration of any kind offered to any one to influence his judgment or conduct; an inducement; a seduction. *v.t.* to influence action or opinion by means of a gift or other inducement. *v.i.* to practise bribery. **bribable,** *a.* **bribability,** *n.* **bribee,** *n.* one who receives a bribe. **bribeless,** *a.* incapable of being bribed. **briber,** *n.* one who offers or gives bribes. **bribery,** *n.* the act of giving or receiving bribes. [OF *bribe,* a piece of bread given to a beggar]

bric-a-brac, *n.* fancy ware, curiosities, knick-knacks. [F phrase *de bric et de broc,* by hook or by crook]

brick, *n.* a block of clay and sand, usually oblong, moulded and baked, used in building; a brick-shaped block of any material; a child's block for toy building; a brick-shaped loaf; (*sl.*) a good person. *a.* made of brick. *v.t.* to lay or construct with bricks; to imitate brickwork in plaster. **like a ton of bricks,** with great force. **to brick up,** to block up with brickwork. **to drop a brick,** to say the wrong thing, to commit a blunder. **to make bricks without straw,** to perform the impossible. **brickbat,** *n.* a broken piece of brick, esp. for use as a missile; (*coll.*) a critical remark. **brick-clay, brick-earth,** *n.* clay used for making brick; a clayey earth in the London basin. **brick-dust,** *n.* powdered brick, *n.* tinged with this; coloured like this. **brick-field,** *n.* a field in which brick-making is carried on. **brickfielder,** (*Austral.*) *n.* a hot wind from the interior laden with dust. **brick-kiln,** *n.* a kiln for baking bricks. **bricklayer,** *n.* one who lays or sets bricks. **brick-nogging,** *n.* brickwork built into a timber framework. **brick-red,** *a.* the colour of a red brick. **brick-tea,** *n.* tea compressed into bricks. **brickwork,** *n.* builder's work in brick; bricklaying; a brickyard. **bricken,** *a.* (*formerly*) made of brick. **brickie,** *n.* (*coll.*) a bricklayer. **bricking,** *n.* brickwork. **bricky,** *a.* full of or composed of bricks; resembling bricks. [F *brique,* a fragment (cp. MDut. *brick, bricke*), from the Teut. root *brek-,* BREAK]

brickle, *a.* fragile, frail; ticklish, troublesome. [parallel form to BRITTLE]

bricole, *n.* †a kind of military catapult; the rebound of a ball from a wall or cushion; in tennis or billiards; an indirect stroke. [F *bricole,* late L *briccola* (etym. doubtful)]

bride[1], *n.* a woman newly married or on the point of being married. †*v.i.* to play the bride. †*v.t.* to marry. **bride-ale** (see BRIDAL), *n.* an old English marriage feast; a bride-cup. **bride-cake,** *n.* the cake distributed to the guests at a wedding, wedding cake. **bride-cup, -bowl,** *n.* a cup or bowl handed round at a wedding; a cup of spiced wine or ale prepared for a newly married couple. **bridegroom** *n.* a man about to be married or recently married. **bride(s)maid, bride(s)man,** *n.* the unmarried friends of the bride and groom who attend them at their wedding. **bridewort,** *n.* meadowsweet. **bridal** *n.* the nuptial ceremony or festival; a wedding; marriage. *a.* of or pertaining to a bride or a wedding. [OE *brȳd* (cp. OHG *Prut,* G *Braut,* from OTeut. *brūdiz*]

bride[2], *n.* the foundation net-work of lace; a bonnet-string. [F *bride,* BRIDLE]

bridewell, *n.* a house of correction, a prison. [from a prison near St Bride's (Bridget's) Well, near Fleet Street, London]

bridge[1], *n.* a structure thrown over a body of water, a ravine, another road etc. to carry a road or path across; anything more or less resembling a bridge in form or function; the upper bony part of the nose; the thin wooden bar over which the strings are stretched in a violin or similar instrument; a support for a billiard cue in an awkward stroke; a partial deck extending from side to side of a steam-vessel amidships; an electrical circuit used for the accurate measurement of electrical quantities, e.g. resistance; a partial denture. *v.t.* to span or cross with or as with a bridge. **to cross a bridge when one comes to it,** to cope with a difficulty only when it occurs. **bridgehead,** *n.* a fortification protecting the end of a bridge nearest the enemy. **bridge-of-boats,** *n.* a bridge supported on a number of boats moored abreast. **bridgeable,** *a.* **bridgeless,** *a.* without a bridge. **bridging,** *n.* the structure of a bridge; the act of making or forming a bridge. **bridging loan,** *n.* a short-term loan with a high interest rate which covers a financial transaction until a long-term loan is arranged. [OE *brycg* (cp. OHG *Brucca,* G *brücke,* from Teut. *brugj-*)]

bridge[2], *n.* a card game resembling whist. **auction, contract, bridge** AUCTION, CONTRACT. **bridge-marker,** *n.* a device for registering the points made at bridge. **bridge-scorer,** *n.* one who keeps the score at bridge. [etym. doubtful]

Bridge[3], *n.* **Frank** (1879–1941), English composer, the teacher of Benjamin Britten. His works include the orchestral *The Sea* (1912), and *Oration* (1930) for cello and orchestra.

Bridget, St, *n.* (453–523), a patron saint of Ireland, also known as St Brigit or St Bride. She founded a church and monastery at Kildare, and is said to have been the daughter of a prince of Ulster. Feast day 1 Feb.

Bridgetown, *n.* port and capital of Barbados, founded 1628; population (1987) 8000. Sugar is exported through the nearby deep-water port.

Bridgewater, *n.* **Francis Egerton, 3rd Duke of Bridgewater** (1736–1803), pioneer of British inland navigation. With James Brindley as his engineer, he constructed (1762–72) the Bridgewater canal from Worsley to Manchester, and thence to the Mersey, a distance of 67.5 km/42 miles.

bridle, *n.* a head-stall, bit and bearing or riding rein, forming the head-gear of a horse or other beast of burden; a curb, a check, a restraint; a rope by which the bowline of a ship is fastened to the leech of a sail; a mooring cable; *v.t.* to put a bridle on; to control with a bridle; to hold in, to check, to control. *v.i.* to hold up the head and draw in the chest in pride, scorn or resentment (with *up*). **bridle-hand,** *n.* the hand that holds the bridle; the left hand. **bridle-path, -road, -way,** *n.* a horse-track, a path for horsemen. **bridled,** *a.* wearing a bridle. [OE *brīdel,* cogn. with *bregdan* (see BRAID[1])]

bridoon, *n.* the snaffle and rein of a military bridle. [F *bridon* (see BRIDE[2])]

Brie, *n.* a soft white cheese orig. produced in France. [F *Brie,* a region in NE France]

brief, *n.* short in duration; expeditious; short, concise; curt. *n.* a papal letter of a less solemn character than a bull; instructions; a short statement; †a writ, a summons; a summary of facts and points of law given to counsel in charge of a case; (*N Am.*) pleadings. (*pl.*) close fitting pants, underpants or knickers without legs. *v.t.* to reduce to the form of a counsel's brief; to instruct or retain a barrister by brief; to give detailed instructions. **in brief,** briefly. **brief-case,** *n.* a small leather handbag for carrying papers. **briefing,** *n.* the imparting of instructions or information. **briefless,** *a.* having no briefs; without clients. **briefly,** *adv.* **briefness,** *n.* [OF *bref,* L *breve, brevis* (cp. Gr. *brachus*)]

brier, briar[1], *n.* a thorny or prickly shrub, esp. of a wild rose; the stem of a wild rose on which a garden rose is grafted. **sweet brier,** *n.* a wild rose with fragrant leaves. **brier-rose,** *n.* the dog-rose or the field-rose. **briery, briary,** *a.* full of briers; thorny. [OE *brēr, brœr* (etym. doubtful)]

brier, briar[2], *n.* the white or tree heath, *Erica arborea;* a tobacco-pipe made from the root of this. **brier-root,** *n.* the root of the white heath. [F *bruyère,* heath]

brig[1], Sc., North. form of BRIDGE[1].

brig[2], *n.* a square-rigged vessel with two masts; a US Navy prison; (*sl.*) any prison. [short for BRIGANTINE]

Brig., (*abbr.*) Brigade; Brigadier.

brigade, *n.* a subdivision of an army, varying in composition in different countries and at different dates; a division of the Horse or Field Artillery; an organized body of workers, often wearing a uniform. *v.t.* to form into one or more brigades; to combine into a brigade; to associate as into a brigade. **Boys' Brigade** BOY. **Fire Brigade** FIRE. **Household Brigade** HOUSEHOLD. **brigade-major,** *n.* a staff officer who assists a brigadier in his command. **brigadier,** *n.* the officer in command of a brigade; the rank below that of major-general. [F, from It. *brigata,* a troop, *brigare,* to quarrel, late L *briga,* strife]

brigalow, *n.* a variety of acacia tree. [Austral. Abor.]

brigand, *n.* a robber, a bandit, an outlaw. **brigandage, brigandry,** *n.* the practices of brigands; highway robbery. **brigandine,** *n.* a brigand's armour. **brigandish,** *a.* **brigandism,** *n.* [F, prob. from It. *brigante,* pres.p. of *brigare,* see prec.]

brigantine, *n.* a two-masted vessel square-rigged on both masts but with a fore-and-aft mainsail, and mainmast much longer than the foremast. [F *brigantin, brigandin,* It. *brigantino,* a pirate-ship, *brigante,* BRIGAND]

bright, *a.* lighted up, full of light; emitting or reflecting abundance of light; shining; unclouded; cheerful, happy, sanguine; witty, clever; †clear, evident; †illustrious, noble. *adv.* brightly. **bright and early,** very early in the morning. **bright-eyed and bushy-tailed,** radiant with health and vigour. **the bright lights,** the area of a city where places of entertainment are concentrated; the city. **brighten,** *v.t.* to make bright; to make happy, hopeful etc. *v.i.* to become bright; of the weather, to clear up. **brightly,** *adv.* **brightness,** *n.* [OE *beorht,* OTeut, *berhtoz,* shining]

Bright, *n.* **John** (1811–89), British Liberal politician, a campaigner for free trade, peace, and social reform. A Quaker mill-owner, he was among the founders of the Anti-Corn Law League in 1839, and was largely instrumental in securing the passage of the Reform Bill of 1867.

Bright's disease, *n.* a term including several forms of kidney disease, associated with albuminuria. [Dr R. *Bright* (1789–1858)]

†**brigue,** *n.* strife, intrigue. †*v.t.* to ensnare; to obtain by intrigue. †*v.i.* to intrigue. [F, from med. L *briga*]

brill[1], *n.* a flat seafish, *Rhombus vulgaris,* allied to and like the turbot. [etym. unknown]

brill[2], *a.* (*coll.*) short for BRILLIANT, used as a general term of approbation.

Brillat-Savarin, *n.* **Jean Anthelme** (1755–1826), French gastronome, author of *La Physiologie du Goût* (1825), a compilation of observations on food and drink regarded as the first great classic of gastronomic literature. Most of his professional life was spent as a politician.

brilliant, *a.* shining, sparkling; lustrous; illustrious, distinguished; extremely clever and successful. *n.* a diamond or other gem of the finest cut, consisting of lozenge-shaped facets alternating with triangles; the smallest type used in English printing. **brilliance, brilliancy,** *n.* **brilliantine** (-tēn), *n.* a cosmetic for rendering the hair glossy. **brilliantly,** *adv.* [F *brillant,* pres.p. of *briller,* to shine; perh. from late L *beryllāre,* to sparkle (*beryillus,* a gem)]

brim, *n.* the upper edge, margin or brink of a vessel, hollow or body of water; the rim of a hat. *v.t.* to fill to the brim. *v.i.* to be full to the brim. **to brim over,** to overflow. **brimful,** *a.* **brimless,** *a.* without a brim. **brimmed,** *a.* housing a brim; brimful. **brimmer,** *n.* †a vessel filled to the brim; a bumper. **brimming,** *a.* [etym. doubtful (cp. G *Gebräme,* border, *Bräme,* brim, edge) (OE *brim,* the sea, water, is prob. not the same word)]

brimstone, *n.* sulphur, esp. in the Biblical sense of the lake of brimstone; the sulphur butterfly; (*fig.*) a spitfire, a termagant. **brimstone butterfly,** *n.* an early sulphur, *Gonepteryx rhamni.* **brimstone moth,** *n.* a sulphur-coloured moth, *Rumia crataegata.* [ME *bren,* *brennen,* to burn, STONE]

brindle, brindled *a.* tawny, with bars of darker hue; streaked, spotted. [Shak. *brinded,* prob. variant of BRANDED]

Brindley, *n.* **James** (1716–72), British canal builder, the first to employ tunnels and aqueducts extensively, in order to reduce the number of locks on a direct-route canal. His 580 km/360 miles of canals included the Bridgewater (Manchester-Liverpool) and Grand Union (Manchester-Potteries) canals.

brine, *n.* water strongly impregnated with salt; the sea; tears. *v.t.* to treat with brine, to pickle. **brine-pan,** *n.* a shallow vessel or pit in which brine is evaporated in the manufacture of salt. **brine-pit,** *n.* a pit or well of salt water. †**brinish,** *a.* **briny,** *a.* full of brine; very salt. **the briny,** (*coll.*) the sea. [OE *brȳne* (cp. Dut. *brijn,* brine, pickle)]

Brinell, *n.* **Johann Auguste** (1849–1925), Swedish engineer, who devised the Brinell hardness test in 1900.

Brinell hardness test, a test for the hardness of a substance according to the area of indentation made by a 10-mm/0.4-in hardened steel or sintered tungsten carbide ball under standard loading conditions in a test machine. It is equal to the load (kg) divided by the surface area (mm^2), and is named after its inventor Johann Brinell.

bring, *v.t.* (*pres., p.p.* **brought**) to cause to come along with oneself; to bear, to carry, to conduct, to lead; to induce, to prevail upon, to influence, to persuade; to produce, to yield result in. **to bring about,** to cause, to bring to pass; to reverse the ship. **to bring back,** to recall to memory. **to bring down,** to humble, to abase; to shoot, to kill; to lower (a price); to carry on (a history) to a certain date; to depose, to overthrow. **to bring down the house,** to create tumultuous applause. **to bring forth,** to bear, to produce, to give birth to; to cause. **to bring forward,** to produce, to adduce; to carry on a sum from the bottom of one folio to the top of the next (in book-keeping). **to bring home to,** to prove conclusively; to convince. **to bring in,** to produce, to yield; to introduce (as an action or Bill); to return (as a verdict). **to bring off,** to bring away (from a ship, the shore etc.); to procure the acquittal of; to accomplish. **to bring on,** to cause to begin; to introduce for discussion; to cause to develop (more quickly). **to bring out,** to express, to exhibit, to illustrate; to introduce to society; to launch (as a company); to produce upon the stage; to publish; to expose. **to bring over,** to convert; to cause to change sides. **to bring round,** to revive; to convert. **to bring to,** to restore to health or consciousness; to check the course of (a ship). **to bring to pass,** to cause to happen. **to bring under,** to subdue. **to bring up,** to educate, to rear; to lay before a meeting; to vomit; to come to a stop; to continue a further stage; to cast anchor. **to bring up the rear,** to come last. [OE *bringan* (cp. Goth. *briggan,* OHG *pringan,* G *bringen*)]

brinjall, *n.* (*esp. in India and Africa*) an aubergine. [Sansk. *vātingan,* Port. *bringella, beringela,* from Arab. *bādhinjān,* from Pers. *bādingān*]

brink, *n.* the edge or border of a precipice, pit, chasm or the like; the margin of water; the verge. **brinkmanship** *n.* the art of maintaining one's position on the brink of a decision or crisis. [Scand. (Icel. *brekka,* ON *brenka*)]

brio, *n.* spirit, liveliness. **brioso,** *adv.* with a spirit, vigorously. [It., vivacity]

brioche, *n.* a kind of bread; a sponge-cake. [F]

briolet, *n.* a pear- or drop-shaped diamond cut with long triangular facets. [F *briller,* to sparkle]

briony, BRYONY.

briquette, briquet, *n.* a block of compressed coal-dust; a slab of artificial stone. *v.t.* to compress (mineral matter etc.) into bricks by heat. [F]

Brisbane, *n.* industrial port (brewing, engineering, tanning, tobacco, shoes; oil pipeline from Moonie), capital of Queensland, E Australia, near the mouth of Brisbane river, dredged to carry ocean-going ships; population (1986) 1,171,300

Brisbane, *n.* **Thomas Makdougall** (1773–1860), Scottish soldier, colonial administrator, and astronomer. After serving in the Napoleonic Wars under Wellington, he was governor of New South Wales 1821–25, and Brisbane in Queensland is named after him. He catalogued over 7000 stars.

brisk, *a.* lively, animated, active; keen, stimulating, bracing; sharp-witted, fast, brief, *v.t.* to make brisk. *v.i.* to move briskly. **briskly,** *adv.* **briskness,** *n.* †**brisky,** *a.* [etym. doubtful (W *brisg,* quick-footed, and F *brusque* have been suggested)]

brisket, *n.* that part of the breast of an animal which lies next to the ribs; this joint of meat. **brisket-bone,** *n.* the breast-bone. [etym. doubtful]

brisling, bristling,, *n.* a small herring, a sprat. [Norw. *brisling,* from LG *Bretling,* from *bret,* broad, like OE *brād,* broad]

Brissot, *n.* **Jacques Pierre** (1754–93), French revolutionary leader, born in Chartres. He became a member of the legislative assembly and the National Convention, but his party of moderate republicans, the Girondins, or Brissotins, fell foul of Robespierre and Brissot was guillotined.

bristle, *n.* a short, stiff, coarse hair, particularly on the back and sides of swine; (*pl.*) a beard cropped short; stiff hairs on plants. *v.t.* †to cause to stand up (as hair); to cover with bristles. *v.i.* to stand erect (as hair); to show indignation or defiance (with *up*); to be thickly beset (with difficulties, dangers etc.). **bristling,** *a.* **bristling with,** full of, with many of. **bristled,** *a.* having bristles. **bristly,** *a.* thickly covered with or as with bristles, (*coll.*) quick to anger, touchy. **bristliness,** *n.* [ME *bristle, brustel, brustle,* OE *byrst,* OTeut. root *bors-*]

Bristol, *n.* industrial port (aircraft engines, engineering, microelectronics, tobacco, chemicals, paper, printing), administrative headquarters of Avon, SW England; population (1986) 391,000; (*pl., sl.*) breasts. [rhyming slang, *Bristol City,* titty, breast] **Bristol-board,** *n.* a thick smooth white cardboard. **Bristol diamond, Bristol stone,** *n.* transparent rock-crystal, found in the Clifton limestone. **Bristol fashion,** in good order. **Bristol milk,** *n.* cream sherry.

Brit[1], *n.* (*coll. abbr., some. derog.*) a Briton.

Brit[2], (*abbr.,*) Britain; British.

brit[3], *n.* the spawn and young of the herring and the sprat. [local dial; etym. unknown]

Britain, Great Britain *n.* England, Wales and Scotland. **Britannia,** *n.* Britain; Britain personified; a female figure emblematic of Britain. **Britannia metal,** *n.* a white alloy of tin, copper and antimony. **Britannic,** *a.* British. **British,** *a.* of or pertaining to ancient Britain, to Great Britain or its inhabitants or to the British Commonwealth. **the British,** British people or soldiers. **British warm,** *n.* a short military overcoat. **Britisher,** *n.* a Briton, a British subject or a native of Britain. **Britishism, Briticism,** *n.* an idiom employed in Britain and not in the US or elsewhere. **Briton,** *n.* a member of the people inhabiting S Britain at the Roman invasion; a native of Britain or of the British Commonwealth. [ME *Bretayne,* OF *Bretaigne,* L *Britannia,* OE *Breten, Breoten, Brytten, Breoton-lond* (Celtic *Britto, Brython,* name of the people)]

British Columbia, *n.* province of W Canada on the Pacific. **area** 947,800 sq km/365,851 sq miles. **capital** Victoria. **towns** Vancouver, Prince George, Kamloops, Kelowna. **physical** Rocky Mountains and Coast Range; the coast is deeply indented; rivers include the Fraser and Columbia; there are more than 80 lakes; more than half the land is forested. **population** (1986) 2,889,000. **products** fruit and vegetables; timber and wood products; fish; coal, copper, iron, lead; oil and natural gas, and hydroelectricity.

British Commonwealth of Nations, former official name of the Commonwealth.

British Council, *n.* semi-official organization set up 1935 (royal charter 1940) to promote a wider knowledge of the UK, excluding politics and commerce, and to develop cultural relations with other countries.

British Empire, *n.* the various territories all over the world conquered or colonized by Britain from about 1600, most now independent or lost to other powers; the British Empire was at its largest at the end of World War I, with over 25% of the world's population and area. The Commonwealth is composed of former and remaining territories of the British Empire.

British Empire, Order of the, a British order of chivalry, instituted by George V in 1917. There are military and civil divisions, and the ranks are GBE, Knight Grand Cross or Dame Grand Cross; KBE, Knight Commander; DBE, Dame Commander; CBE, Commander; OBE, Officer; MBE, Member. In 1974 awards for civilian gallantry previously made within the order were replaced by the Queen's Gallantry Medal (QGM), which ranks after the George Cross and George Medal.

British Expeditionary Force, a British army serving in France in World War I (1914–18). Also the 1939–40 army in Europe in World War II, which was evacuated from Dunkirk, France.

British Honduras, *n.* former name of Belize, a country in Central America.

British Indian Ocean Territory, British colony in the Indian Ocean directly administered by the Foreign and Commonwealth Office. It consists of the Chagos Archipelago some 1900 km/1200 miles NE of Mauritius. **area** 60 sq km/23 sq miles. **population** (1982) 3,000. **products** copra, salt fish, tortoiseshell.

British Isles, *n. pl.* group of islands off the NW coast of Europe, consisting of Great Britain (England, Wales and Scotland), Ireland, the Channel Islands, Orkney and Shetland, the Isle of Man, and many others which are included in various counties, such as the Isle of Wight, Scilly Isles, Lundy Island, and the Inner and Outer Hebrides. The islands are divided from Europe by the North Sea, Strait of Dover, and the English Channel, and face the Atlantic to the west.

British Legion, *n.* organization to promote the welfare of British veterans of war service and their dependants. Established under the leadership of D. Haig in 1921 (royal charter 1925) it became the **Royal British Legion** in 1971; it is nonpolitical. The sale on Remembrance Sunday of Flanders poppies made by disabled members raises much of its funds.

British Library, *n.* the national library of the UK. Created in 1973, it comprises the reference division (the former library departments of the British Museum, being rehoused at the Euston Road, London, site); lending division at Boston Spa, Yorkshire, from which full text documents and graphics can be sent, using a satellite link, to other countries; and bibliographic services division (incorporating the British National Bibliography).

British Museum, *n.* largest museum of the UK. Founded in 1753 with the purchase of Hans Sloane's library and art collection, and the subsequent acquisition of the Cottonian, Harleian, and other libraries, the British Museum was opened at Montagu House, Bloomsbury, London, in 1759.

British Somaliland, *n.* a British protectorate over 176,000 sq km/67,980 sq miles of territory on the Somali coast of Africa from 1884 until the independence of Somalia in 1960. British authorities were harassed by a self-proclaimed messiah known as the 'Mad Mullah' from 1901 until 1910.

British Standards Institute, the UK national standards body. Although government funded, the institute is independent. The BSI interprets international technical standards for the UK, and also sets its own. For consumer goods, it sets standards which products should reach (the BS standard), as well as testing products to see that they conform to that standard (as a result of which the product may be given the BSI 'kite' mark).

British Telecom, *n.* a British company that formed part of the Post Office until 1980, and was privatized in 1984. It is responsible for telecommunications, including the telephone network, and radio and television broadcasting. Previously a monopoly, it now faces commercial competition for some of its services. It operates Britain's viewdata network called Prestel.

British Thermal Unit, imperial unit (symbol Btu) of heat, now replaced in the SI system by the joule (1 Btu is approximately 1,055 joules). Burning 1 cubic foot of natural gas releases about 1,000 Btus of heat.

British Virgin Islands, part of the Virgin Islands group in the West Indies.

Brittain, *n.* **Vera** (1894–1970), English socialist writer, a nurse to the troops overseas 1915–19, as told in her *Testament of Youth* (1933); *Testament of Friendship* (1950) commemorated Winifred Holtby. She married political scientist Sir George Catlin (1896–1979); their daughter is Shirley Williams.

Brittan, *n.* **Leon** (1939–), British Conservative politician and lawyer. Chief secretary to the Treasury (1981–83), home secretary (1983–85), secretary for trade and industry (1985–86, resigned over his part in the Westland affair) and senior European Commissioner from 1988.

Brittany, *n.* English name for Bretagne.

Britten, *n.* **(Edward) Benjamin** (1913–76), English composer. He often wrote for the individual voice, for example the role of Peter Pears in the opera *Peter Grimes* (1945), based on verses by Crabbe. Among his many works are the *Young Person's Guide to the Orchestra* (1946); the chamber opera *The Rape of Lucretia* (1946); *Billy Budd* (1951); *A Midsummer Night's Dream* (1960); and *Death in Venice* (1973).

brittle, *a.* liable to break or be broken, fragile; not malleable; *n.* a brittle sweet (e.g. peanut brittle). **brittle-bone disease,** *n.* a disease which causes the bones to break easily. **brittle star,** *n.* a type of starfish with long flexible arms. **brittleness,** *n.* [OE *brēotan,* to break]

britzka, *n.* an open carriage with a calash top. [Pol. *bryczka,* dim. of *bryka,* a wagon]

Briza, *n.* a genus of grasses comprising quaking-grass, maidenhair grass etc. [Gr. *brizein,* to nod]

BRM, *n.* (British Racing Motors) racing-car manufacturer founded 1949 by Raymond Mays (1899–). Their early days in Grand Prix racing were a disaster and it was not until 1956 that they started having moderate success. Their first Grand Prix win was 1959, and in the next thirty years they won 17 Grands Prix. Their world champions include Graham Hill.

Brno, *n.* industrial city in central Czechoslovakia (chemicals, arms, textiles, machinery), population (1984) 380,800. Now third largest city in Czechoslovakia, Brno was formerly capital of the Austrian crownland of Moravia.

bro., Bro., (*abbr.*) brother; Brother.

broach, *n.* a tapering iron instrument; a roasting-spit; an awl; a mason's chisel, a boring-bit; a first horn on the head of a young stag; a spire rising from a tower without a parapet. *v.t.* to pierce (as a cask), so as to allow liquor to flow; to tap; to open, to moot, to make public; †to transfix, to spit; of a ship, to turn suddenly to windward. **to broach to,** to veer to windward so as to present a ship's broadside to the sea. [F *broche,* a spit, late L *brocca,* a sharp stick (L *broccus,* projecting like teeth)]

broad, *a.* wide, large, extended across; extensive, expansive; of wide range, general; expanded, open, clear; tolerant, liberal; rough, strong, rustic; coarse, obscene; bold, vigorous, free in style or effect. *n.* a large, fresh-water lake formed by the broadening of a river; the broad portion of a thing; (*N Am. sl.*) a woman; a prostitute; *adv.* in breadth; broadly, widely. **broad as long,** equal upon the whole; the same either way. **broad arrow,** *n.* a mark resembling an arrowhead cut or stamped on British Government property. **broadaxe,** *n.* a battle-axe; an axe for hewing timber. **broad band,** *a.* receiving, transmitting or involving a wide range of frequencies. **†broad-blown,** *a.* full-blown, in full bloom. **broad bean,** *n.* a leguminous plant with edible seeds in a pod, *Faba vulgaris.* **broadcast,** *a.* scattered by the hand (as seed); widely disseminated; transmitted by radio or television. *n.* broadcast sowing; anything transmitted to the public by radio or television. *adv.* by scattering widely *v.t.* to sow by scattering with the hand; to transmit by radio or television; to disseminate widely. **broadcaster,** *n.* **Broad Church,** *n.* a party in the Church of England interpreting formularies and dogmas in a liberal sense. *a.* of or pertaining to the Broad Church. **broadcloth,** *n.* a fine, wide, dressed black cloth, used for men's coats etc.; poplin. **broadleaf,** *n.* (*New Zealand*) the Maori *paukatea* tree; *a.* having a broad leaf. **broadleafed,** *a.* **broadloom,** *n.* carpet woven on a wide loom. *a.* **broad-minded,** *a.* tolerant, having an open mind. **broadsheet,** *n.* a large sheet printed on one side only; a large format newspaper. **broadside,** *n.* the side of a ship above the water; a volley from all the guns on one side of a ship of war; a broadsheet; a political attack on a person or policy. **broadsilk,** *n.* silk in the piece as distinguished from ribbons. **broad-spectrum,** *a.* of antibiotics etc., wide-ranging. **broadsword,** *n.* a sword with a broad blade; a soldier armed with this. **broad-spoken,** *a.* plain spoken; using a dialect or coarse language. **broadway,** *n.* a wide road, a main thoroughfare; (**Broadway**) New York's theatre and restaurant district. **broadways, -wise,** *adv.* in the direction of the breadth. **broaden,** *v.t.* to become broader, to spread. *v.t.* to make broader. **broadly,** *adv.* **broadness,** *n.* coarseness, indelicacy. [OE *brād,* Teut. *braid-* (cp. G *breit*)]

Broadmoor, *n.* special hospital (established 1863) in Crowthorne, Berkshire, England, for those formerly described as 'criminally insane'.

Broads, Norfolk, *n. pl.* area of some twelve interlinked freshwater lakes in E England, created about 600 years ago by the digging out of peat deposits; they are noted for wildlife and boating facilities.

broadside, broadsword BROAD.

Broadway, *n.* major avenue in New York running from the tip of Manhattan NW and crossing Times Square at 42nd Street, at the heart of the theatre district, where Broadway is known as 'the Great White Way'.

Brobdingnagian, *a.* gigantic, huge. *n.* a giant. [*Brobdingnag,* a country of giants in Swift's *Gulliver's Travels*]

brocade, *n.* silken stuff with raised figures. *v.t.* to weave or work with raised patterns; to decorate with brocade. **brocaded,** *a.* [Sp. *brocadoi,* It. *broccato,* p.p. of *broccare* (*brocca;* see BROACH)]

brocard, *n.* an elementary principle of law; (F) a sarcastic jest. [F, low L *brocarda, Brocard* or *Burchard,* Bishop of Worms, compiler of *Regulae ecclesiasticae*]

broccoli, brocoli, *n.* a variety of cauliflower. [It. pl. of *broccolo,* a sprout, dim. of *brocco,* a skewer, BROACH]

broché, *a.* brocaded, woven with a raised design. [F, stitched]

brochette, *n.* a skewer; small pieces of food grilled together on a skewer (like a kebab).

brochure, *n.* a small pamphlet. [F, from *brocher,* to stitch]

brock, *n.* a badger; a dirty fellow, a stinker. **brocked,** *a.* (*Sc.*) speckled, black and white. [OE *broc.* (W, Corn. and Bret. *broch,* Ir. *broc;* prob. from *breac,* spotted, cp. Gr. *phorkos,* grey)]

brocket, *n.* a stag in its second year with its first horns, which are straight and unbranched. [F *brocard,* from *broche* BROACH]

brodekin, brodkin, *n.* a high boot: a buskin. [F *brodequin*]

broderie anglaise, *n.* open embroidery on cambric or linen. [F]

Brodsky, *n.* **Joseph** (1940–), Russian poet, who emigrated to the US in 1972. His work, often dealing with themes of exile, is admired for its wit and economy of language, particularly in its use of understatement. Many of his poems, written in Russian, have been translated into English (*A Part of Speech,* 1980). More recently he has also written in English. Nobel prize (1987).

brogue, *n.* (*formerly*) a coarse, rough shoe, usually of untanned leather; a sturdy shoe; dialectal pronunciation, esp. Irish; †(*pl.*) trousers, breeches. *v.t.* to utter in a brogue. [Gael. and Ir. *brōg,* shoe, sandal, OIr. *broce* (prob. from OCelt. *brācca,* whence L *braccae,* BREECH]

†broider, etc. EMBROIDER.

broil[1], *n.* a tumult, disturbance, contention. [F *brouiller,* to tumble, trouble, confound (It. *brogliare,* to disturb, *broglio,* confusion)]

broil[2], *v.t.* to cook on a gridiron; to scorch; to grill. *v.i.* to be very hot; to grow hot; to be in the heat; to be subjected to heat; to burn, to be inflamed. *n.* broiled meat. **broiler,** *n.* one who or that which broils; a gridiron: a chicken 8–10 weeks old for broiling or roasting. [etym. doubtful]

broke[1], *part.a.* BROKEN.

broke[2], *n.* †a piece; †broken meat; (*pl.*) short wool sorted, or broken, from the fleece. *adv.* (*sl.*) ruined, penniless. [OE *broc,* affliction, *gebroc,* a fragment, affliction, from *brecan,* to break]

broken *a.* in pieces; not whole or continuous; weakened, infirm; crushed, humbled; transgressed, violated; interrupted, incoherent, ejaculatory; shattered, bankrupt, ruined; (*Painting*) reduced by the addition of some other colour. **broken-backed,** *a.* having the back broken; drooping at stem and stern from injury to the keel. **broken-down,** *a.* decayed; worn-out; ruined in health, in character or financially. **broken English,** *n.* halting or defective English as spoken by a foreigner. **broken-hearted,** *a.* crushed in spirit by grief or anxiety. **broken home,** *n.* the home of children with separated or divorced parents. **broken meat(s),** *n.* remains of food. **broken water,** *n.* choppy water. **broken-winded,** *a.* having defective respiratory organs; habitually short of breath. **brokenly,** *adv.* with breaks, jerkily, spasmodically. [p.p. of BREAK]

broker, *n.* †a petty dealer, a pawnbroker; an agent, a factor, a middleman, †a pimp, a pander; one who buys and sells for others; a dealer in second-hand furniture. **brokerage,** *n.* the business or commission of a broker; a broker's commission on sales etc. **broking,** *n.* the trade of broker. [ME and A-F *brocour,* late L *broccātor,* from *broccāre,* to BROACH]

brolly, *n.* (*coll.*) an umbrella, a gamp. [corr. of UMBRELLA]

brome grass, *n.* a grass of the genus *Bromus,* esp. *B. inermis,* a cultivated fodder-grass. [Gr. *bromos,* a kind of oats]

bromine, *n.* a non-metallic, dark red, liquid element; at. no. 35; chem. symbol Br. with a strong, irritating odour. **bromal,** *n.* a liquid like chloral produced by the action of bromine upon alcohol. **bromate,** *n.* a salt of bromic acid. **bromic** *a.* of or pertaining to bromine; having bromine in its composition. **bromide,** *n.* a combination of bromine with a metal or a radical, esp. bromide of potassium, which is used as a sedative; (*coll.*) a commonplace remark, a platitude. **bromide paper,** *n.* a sensitized paper used in printing a photograph from a negative. **bromide process,** *n.* in photography, printing from negatives or enlarging on paper coated with silver bromide emulsion. **bromidic,** *a.* (*coll.*) dull, commonplace. **bromism** *n.* the condition produced by long treatment with bromide of potassium. **bromize, -mise,** *v.t.* to treat with bromine; to prepare a photographic plate with a bromide. [Gr. *brōmos,* a stench]

brom(o)-, *comb. form.* pertaining to bromine.

bronchi , bronchia, *n.pl.* the main divisions of the windpipe; the ramifications into which these divide within the lungs. **bronchial,** *a.* **bronchial tubes,** *n.pl.* the bronchia. [L, from Gr. *bronchos, bronchia*]

bronchiectasis, *n.* abnormal dilation of the bronchial tubes.

bronchio-, broncho-, *comb. forms.* pertaining to the windpipe or the tubes into which it divides beneath.

bronchiole, *n.* any of the tiny branches of the bronchi.

bronchitis, *n.* inflammation of the bronchia. **bronchitic,** *a.*

bronchocele, *n.* abnormal swelling of the thyroid

gland, goitre.

bronchopneumonia, *n.* pneumonia originating in the bronchial tubes.

bronchoscope, *n.* an instrument which is inserted in the bronchial tubes for the purpose of examination or extraction. **bronchoscopic,** *a.* **bronchoscopically,** *adv.* **bronchoscopy,** *n.*

bronchotomy, *n.* the operation of opening the windpipe, tracheotomy.

bronco, *n.* (*pl.* **-cos**) a native half-tamed horse of California or New Mexico. **bronco-buster,** BURSTER, *n.* a breaker-in of broncos. [Sp., rough, rude]

Bronson, *n.* **Charles** (stage name of Charles Bunchinsky) (1922–), US film actor. His films are mainly violent thrillers such as *Death Wish* (1974). He was one of *The Magnificent Seven* (1960).

Brontë, *n.* family of English writers, including the three sisters **Charlotte** (1816–55), **Emily Jane** (1818–48) and **Anne** (1820–49), and their brother **Patrick Branwell** (1817–48). Their best-known works are Charlotte Brontë's *Jane Eyre* (1847) and Emily Brontë's *Wuthering Heights* (1847). Later works include Anne's *The Tenant of Wildfell Hall* (1848) and Charlotte's *Shirley* (1849) and *Villette* (1853).

Brontosaurus, *n.* a genus of huge fossil dinosaurian reptiles, notable for their small head and diminutive brain-cavity. [Gr. *brontē,* thunder; *sauros,* a lizard]

bronze, *n.* a brown alloy of copper and tin, sometimes with a little zinc or lead; a brown colour, like that of bronze; a work of art in bronze; a bronze medal. *a.* made of or the colour of bronze. *v.t.* to give a bronze-like appearance to (wood, metal, plaster etc.); to brown, to tan. *v.i.* to become brown or tanned. **bronze medal,** *n.* a medal made of bronze awarded for third place in a contest. **bronze-powder,** *n.* a metallic powder used in printing, painting etc. for imparting a metallic colour and lustre. **bronze-wing,** *n.* an Australian pigeon, *Phaps chalcoptera.* **bronzed,** *a.* overlaid with bronze; coloured like bronze, sun to brown, to tan. *v.i.* to become brown or tanned. **bronzed,** *a.* overlaid with bronze; coloured like bronze, sun tanned. **bronzing,** *n.* the process of imparting a bronze-like appearance or of becoming bronzed. **bronzite,** *n.* a bronze-like variety of diallage. **bronzy,** *a.* like bronze; tinged with bronze. [F, from It. *bronzo,* bronze, *bronzino,* made of bronze, L *Brundusīnium,* made at *Brundusium,* Brindisi]

Bronze Age, *n.* period of early history and prehistory when bronze was the chief material used for tools and weapons. It lies between the Stone Age and the Iron Age and may be dated 5000–1200 BC in the Middle East and about 2000–500 BC in Europe. Recent discoveries in Thailand suggest that the Far East, rather than the Middle East, was the cradle of the Bronze Age.

Bronzino, *n.* **Agnolo** (1503–72), Italian painter active in Florence, court painter to Cosimo I, Duke of Tuscany. He painted in an elegant, Mannerist style, and is best known for portraits and the allegory *Venus, Cupid, Folly and Time* (about 1545, National Gallery, London).

brooch, *n.* an ornamental clasp with a pin, for fastening some part of a woman's dress. †*v.t.* to adorn as with a brooch. [BROACH]

brood, *n.* a family of birds hatched at once; offspring, progeny; †the act of breeding or hatching; parentage, lineage; a race, a species; a swarm, a crowd. *v.i.* to sit on eggs; to hover with outspread wings; to hang close over (as clouds); to meditate moodily. *v.t.* to sit upon eggs to hatch them; to cherish under the wings; to prepare by long meditation, to hatch; to cherish moodily. **brood-hen, -mare,** *n.* a hen or a mare kept for breeding. **brooder,** *n.* a cover for sheltering young chickens. **broodiness,** *n.* **broody,** *a.* inclined to sit on eggs; sullen, morose; inclined to brood over matters. [OE *brōd,* from Teut. root *bro-,* to warm]

brook¹, *n.* a small stream, a rivulet. **brooklime,** *n.* a kind of speedwell, *Veronica becca-bunga,* growing in watery places. **brooklet,** *n.* a little brook, a streamlet. **brooky,** *a.* abounding in brooks. [OE *brōc* (etym. doubtful cp. Dut. *broek,* a marsh, a pool, G *Bruch,* a bog)]

brook², *v.t.* to endure, to support, to put up with. [OE *brūcan,* from OTeut. root *bruk-,* to use, to enjoy (cp. L *fruī,* to enjoy)]

Brook, *n.* **Peter** (1925–), British theatrical producer and director. Known for his experimental productions with the Royal Shakespeare Company in England, he began working with the Paris-based Le Centre International de Créations Théâtrales in 1970. Films he has directed include *Lord of the Flies* (1962) and *Meetings with Remarkable Men* (1979).

Brooke¹, *n.* **James** (1803–68), British administrator who became rajah of Sarawak, on Borneo, 1841.

Brooke², *n.* **Peter Leonard** (1934–), British Conservative politician. The son of a former home secretary, Lord Brooke of Cumnor, he entered the House of Commons in 1977. He was appointed chairman of the Conservative Party by Margaret Thatcher in 1987. He was made Northern Ireland secretary in 1989.

Brooke³, *n.* **Rupert Chawner** (1887–1915), English poet, symbol of the World War I 'lost generation'. His poems, the best-known being the five war sonnets (including 'Grantchester' and 'The Great Lover'), were published posthumously.

Brookeborough, *n.* **Basil Brooke, Viscount Brookeborough** (1888–1973), Unionist politician of Northern Ireland. He entered Parliament in 1929, held ministerial posts (1933–45), and was prime minister of Northern Ireland (1943–63). He was a staunch advocate of strong links with Britain.

Brooklands, *n.* former UK motor racing track near Weybridge, Surrey. One of the world's first purpose-built circuits, it was opened in 1907 as a testing ground for early motor-cars. It was the venue for the first British Grand Prix (then known as the RAC Grand Prix) 1926. It was sold to aircraft builders Vickers in 1946.

Brookner, *n.* **Anita** (1928–), British novelist and art historian, whose novels include *Hotel du Lac* (1984), winner of the Booker prize, *A Misalliance* (1986), and *Latecomers* (1988).

Brooks¹, *n.* **Louise** (1906–85), US actress, known for her roles in silent films such as *Die Büchse der Pandora/Pandora's Box* and *Das Tagebuch einer Verlorenen/Diary of a Lost Girl* (both 1929), and directed by G. W. Pabst. She retired from the screen in 1938.

Brooks², *n.* **Mel** (assumed name of Melvin Kaminsky) (1926–), US film director, whose comic films include *Blazing Saddles* (1974) and *History of the World Part I* (1981).

broom, *n.* a shrub with yellow flowers belonging to the genus *Sarothamnus* or *Cytisus,* esp. *C. scoparius;* the allied genus *Genista;* a besom for sweeping, orig. made of broom; a long-handled brush. *v.t.* to sweep with a broom. **new broom,** a newly appointed person who sweeps away old practices or attitudes. **broom-corn,** *n.* the common millet, *Sorghum vulgare,* and sugar millet, *S saccharatum,* from the tufts of which brooms are made. **broom-rape,** *n.* the parasitic genus *Orobanche.* **broom-stick, -staff,** *n.* the handle of a broom. **broomy,** *a.* broom-like; abounding in broom. [OE *brōm, broom,* OTeut, *braemoz* (cp. BRAMBLE)]

bros., Bros., (*abbr.*) brothers, Brothers.

brose, *n.* a kind of porridge made by pouring water on oatmeal or oatcake, with seasoning. **Athol brose,** *n.* a mixture of whisky and honey. [BREWIS]

broth, *n.* the liquor in which anything, esp. meat, has been boiled; thin soup; a medium for growing cultures (e.g. of bacteria). **a broth of a boy,** a high-spirited fellow. [OE from Teut. root *bru-,* to boil (cp. OE *brēowan,* to brew)]

brothel, *n.* premises where prostitutes sell their services. [OE *brothen,* p.p. of *brēothan,* to go to ruin (confused with BORDEL)]

brother, *n., pl.* **brothers,** and in more solemn senses **brethren,** a son of the same parents or parent; one closely connected with another; an associate; one of the same community, country, city, church, order, profession or society; a fellow-countryman, fellow citizen etc.; a fellow-man, a fellow-creature; (*Bibl.*) kinsman, cousin. **half-brother,** brother on one side only; having the same father or the same mother only. **brother-german,** *n.* brother on both sides. **brother-in-arms,** *n.* fellow-soldier. **brother-in-law,** *n.* (*pl.* **brothers-in-law**) the brother of one's husband or wife, one's sister's husband. †**brother-love,** *n.* brotherly love. **brotherhood**, *n.* the relationship of a brother; a fraternity, an association for mutual service; brotherly affection or feeling. **brotherless,** *a.* **brotherlike,** *a.* **brotherly,** *a.* becoming to a brother; fraternal. *adv.* fraternally. **brotherliness,** *n.* [OE *brōthor* (cp. G *bruder,* L *frāter,* Gr. *phratēr,* Sansk. *bhrātr,* W *brawd*)]

brougham, *n.* a close, four-wheeled carriage drawn by one horse; an early motor vehicle with an open driver's seat. [Lord *Brougham,* 1778–1868]

Brougham, *n.* **Henry Peter, 1st Baron Brougham and Vaux** (1778–1868), British Whig politician and lawyer. From 1811 he was chief adviser to the Princess of Wales (afterwards Queen Caroline), and in 1820 he defeated the attempt of George IV to divorce her. He was lord chancellor (1830–34), supporting the Reform Bill.

brought, *past, p.p.* BRING.

brouhaha, *n.* a tumult, a row. [F]

Brouwer, *n.* **Adriaen** (1605–38), Flemish painter who studied with Frans Hals. He excelled in scenes of peasant revelry.

brow, *n.* the ridge over the eye; the forehead; the countenance generally; (*fig.*) aspect, appearance; the projecting edge of a cliff or hill; the top of a hill; a ship's gangway; (*N Am.*) an inclined roadway for drawing up logs to a lumber-mill. *v.t.* to be at the edge of; to form a brow to. **to knit the brows,** to frown. **brow-antler,** *n.* the lowest tine of a deer's horn. **brow-beat,** *v.t.* to bear down arrogantly; to bully. **brow-beaten,** *a.* intimidated. [OE *brū* (cp. Icel. *brūn,* Lith. *bruwis,* Rus. *brove,* Gr. *ophrus,* Sansk. *bhrū*)]

brown¹, *a.* of the colour produced when wood or paper is scorched; dusky, dark, suntanned. *v.t.* to make brown; to give a brown lustre to (gun-barrels etc.). *v.i.* to become brown; to get sunburnt. *n.* a brown colour; a compound colour produced by a mixture of red, black and yellow; pigment of this colour; a brown butterfly; brown clothes. **to do brown,** (*sl.*) to take in, to deceive. **brown bear,** *n.* a brown coloured bear common to Europe, Asia and N America. **brown Bess,** *n.* the old flint-lock musket of the British Army. **brown-bill,** *n.* a kind of halberd formerly used by English foot-soldiers. **brown bomber,** *n.* (*coll.*) a member of the New South Wales parking police. **brown bread,** *n.* bread made from whole-meal; bread in which bran is mixed with the flour. **brown coal,** *n.* lignite. **brown fat,** *n.* a dark fatty tissue which generates body heat. **brown goods,** *n.pl.* household appliances, usu. brownish in colour, such as TV sets, record players etc. as opposed to *white goods*. **brown paper,** *n.* coarse, unbleached paper for packing parcels etc. **brown rice,** *n.* husked rice left unpolished. **brownstone,** *n.* (*N Am.*) a dark-brown sandstone; a building of this material. **brown study,** *n.* reverie, day-dream. **brown sugar,** *n.* coarse, half-refined sugar. **brown trout,** *n.* a common European trout with a dark spotted back. **brown ware,** *n.* a coarse, cheap kind of pottery. **browned,** *a.* **browned off,** *adv.* disappointed; bored, fed up. **Brownie, Brownie Guide,** *n.* a junior Girl Guide from 8 to 11 years of age. **Brownie point,** *n.* (sometimes *derog.*) a supposed mark to one's credit for some achievement. **brownie,** *n.* (*Austral.*) a kind of currant loaf; (*orig. N Am.*) a kind of nutty, dark chocolate cake cut into flat squares; a kindly domestic elf. **browning,** *n.* colouring material for gravy. **brownish,** *a.* **brownness,** *n.* [OE *brūn* (cp. Icel. *brunn,* G *braun,* Gr. *phrūnos,* a toad; F *brun* and It. *bruno* are from Teut.)]

Brown², *n.* **'Capability' (Lancelot)** (1715–83), English landscape gardener. He acquired his nickname because of his continual enthusiam for the 'capabilities' of natural landscapes.

Brown³, *n.* **Charles Brockden** (1771–1810), US novelist and magazine editor. He is called the 'father of the American novel' for his *Wieland* (1798), *Ormond* (1799), *Edgar Huntly* (1799), and *Arthur Mervyn* (1800). His works also pioneered the Gothic and fantastic tradition of US fiction.

Brown⁴, *n.* **Earle** (1926–), US composer who pioneered graphic notation and mobile form during the 1950s. He was an associate of Cage.

Brown⁵, *n.* **Ford Madox** (1821–93), British painter, associated with the Pre-Raphaelite Brotherhood. His pictures include *The Last of England* (1855, Birmingham Art Gallery) and *Work* (1852–65, City Art Gallery, Manchester), packed with realistic detail and symbolic incident.

Brown⁶, *n.* **George, Baron George-Brown** (1914–85), British Labour politician. He entered Parliament in 1945, was briefly minister of works (1951), and contested the leadership of the party on the death of Gaitskell, but was defeated by Harold Wilson. He was secretary for economic affairs (1964–66) and foreign secretary (1966–68). He was created a life peer in 1970.

Brown⁷, *n.* **(James) Gordon** (1951–), British Labour politician. He entered Parliament in 1983, rising quickly to the opposition front bench, with a reputation as an outstanding debater.

Brown⁸, *n.* **John** (1800–59), US slavery abolitionist. With 18 men, he seized, on the night of 16 Oct. 1859, the government arsenal at Harper's Ferry in W Virginia, apparently intending to distribute weapons to runaway slaves who would then defend the mountain stronghold, which Brown hoped would become a republic of former slaves. On 18 Oct. the arsenal was stormed by US Marines under Col. Robert E. Lee. Brown was tried and hanged on 2 Dec., becoming a martyr and the hero of the popular song 'John Brown's Body' (*c.* 1860).

Brown⁹, *n.* **John** (1825–83), Scottish servant and confidant of Queen Victoria from 1858.

Brown¹⁰, *n.* **Robert** (1773–1858), Scottish botanist, a pioneer of plant classification and the first to describe and name the cell nucleus.

Browne¹, *n.* **Robert** (1550–1633), English Puritan religious leader, founder of the Brownists. He was imprisoned several times in 1581–82 for attacking Episcopalianism. He founded a community in Norwich, East Anglia and in the Netherlands which continued on Nonconformist lines, developing into modern Congregationalism.

Browne², *n.* **Thomas** (1605–82), English author and physician. Born in London, he travelled widely in Europe before settling in Norwich in 1637. He is noted for his personal richness of style in *Religio Medici/The Religion of a Doctor* (1643), a justification of his profession; *Vulgar Errors* (1646), an examination of popular legend and superstition; *Urn Burial* and *The Garden of Cyrus* (1658); and *Christian Morals* (1717). He was knighted in 1671.

Brownian movement, *n.* continuous random motion of particles in a fluid medium (gas or liquid) as they are subject to impact from the molecules of the medium. This was observed in 1827 by the Scottish botanist Robert Brown but not convincingly explained until Einstein in 1905.

Browning¹, *n.* **Elizabeth Barrett** (1806–61), English poet. In 1844 she published *Poems* (including 'The Cry of the Children'), which led to her friendship and secret marriage with Robert Browning in 1846. The *Sonnets from the Portuguese* (1847) were written during their courtship. Later works include *Casa Guidi Windows* (1851) and the poetic novel *Aurora Leigh* (1857).

Browning², *n.* **Robert** (1812–89), English poet, married to Elizabeth Barrett Browning. His work is characterized by the use of dramatic monologue and an interest in obscure literary and historical figures. It includes the play *Pippa Passes* (1841), and the poems

'The Pied Piper of Hamelin' (1842), 'My Last Duchess' (1842), 'Home Thoughts from Abroad' (1845), and 'Rabbi Ben Ezra' (1864).

Brownism, *n.* the Congregationalist scheme of Church government formed by Robert Browne and adopted in a modified form by the Independents. **Brownist,** *n.* [Robert BROWNE[1]]

Browns Ferry, *n.* site of a nuclear power station on the Alabama River, central Alabama. A nuclear accident in 1975 resulted in the closure of the plant for 18 months. This incident marked the beginning of widespread disenchantment with nuclear power in the US.

Brownshirts, *n.* the SA (*Sturm-Abteilung*), or Storm Troops, the private army of the German Nazi party; so called from the colour of their uniform.

browse, *v.t.* to nibble and eat off (twigs, young shoots etc.). *v.i.* to feed on twigs, young shoots etc.; to graze; to read in a desultory way, to leaf through; to look through, among articles in an idle manner. *n.* the tender shoots of trees and shrubs fit for cattle to feed on; the act of browsing. **browser,** *n.* [F *brouster, brouter* (MHG *Broz,* a bud, OS *brustian,* to bud, cp. OE *brēotan,* to break)]

browst, *n.* a brewing. [prob. from *brow-*, p.p. stem of BREW]

BRS, (*abbr.*) British Road Services.

Bruce[1], *n.* **Robert de, 5th Lord of Annandale** (1210–95), Scottish noble, one of the unsuccessful claimants to the throne at the death of Alexander II (1290). His grandson was Robert I (the Bruce).

Bruce[2], *n.* **Stanley Melbourne, 1st Viscount Bruce of Melbourne** (1883–1967), Australian National Party politician, prime minister (1923–29). He was elected to parliament in 1918. As prime minister he introduced a number of social welfare measures.

Bruce[3], *n.* **Robert the,** title of Robert I of Scotland.

Bruce[4], *n.* one of the most important Scottish noble houses. Robert I and his son, David II were both kings of Scotland descended from Robert de Bruis (died 1094), a Norman knight who came to England with William the Conqueror in 1066.

Bruce[5], *n.* **James** (1730–94), Scottish explorer, the first European to reach the source of the Blue Nile (1770), and to follow the river downstream to Cairo (1773).

brucellosis, *n.* an infectious bacterial disease in animals which is also contagious to man (also called *contagious abortion, Malta* or *undulant fever*). [after bacteriologist Sir David *Bruce* 1855–1931]

brucine, *n.* a poisonous alkaloid found in the seed and bark of *nux vomica* and other species of *Strychnos*. [James *Bruce* 1730–94]

Brücke, die, *n.* (**'the Bridge'**), German Expressionist art movement (1905–13), formed in Dresden. Ernst Ludwig Kirchner was one of its founders and Emil Nolde a member 1906–07. Influenced by African art, they strove for spiritual significance, using raw colours to express different emotions. In 1911 the Blaue Reiter took over as the leading group in German art.

bruckle, *a.* fragile, brittle, precarious, ticklish. [OE *brucol* (in *scipbrucol,* shipwreck), from *bruc-,* stem of *brekan,* to break]

Bruckner, *n.* **(Joseph) Anton** (1824–96), Austrian Romantic composer. He was cathedral organist at Linz (1856–68), and from 1868 he was professor at the Vienna Conservatoire. His works include many choral pieces, and ten symphonies, the last unfinished. His compositions were influenced by Wagner and Beethoven.

Bruderhof, *n.* Christian Protestant sect with beliefs similar to the Mennonites. They live in groups of families (single persons are assigned to a family), marry only within the sect (divorce is not allowed), and retain a 'modest' dress for women (cap or headscarf, and long skirts).

Brueghel, *n.* family of Flemish painters, the eldest of whom, **Pieter Brueghel** (*c.* 1525–69), was one of the greatest artists of his time. He painted satirical and humorous pictures of peasant life, many of which include symbolic details illustrating folly and inhumanity, and a series of Months (five survive), including *Hunters in the Snow* (Kunsthistorisches Museum, Vienna).

Bruges, *n.* (Flemish **Brugge**) historic city in NW Belgium; capital of W Flanders province, 16 km/10 miles from the North Sea, with which it is connected by canal; population (1985) 117,700.

Bruin, *n.* familiar name for the brown bear. [Dut., lit. brown]

bruise, *v.t.* to crush, indent or discolour, by a blow from something blunt and heavy; to injure without breaking skin or bone; to batter, pound, grind up; to hurt, disable. *v.i.* to box; to display the effects of a blow. *n.* an injury caused by something blunt and heavy; a contusion. **bruiser,** *n.* one who or that which bruises; (*coll.*) a large strong man, a prize-fighter. [OE *brȳsan,* to bruise (combined later with OF *bruiser, brisier* (etym. doubtful), to break)]

bruit, *n.* noise, tumult, rumour, report; an abnormal sound heard in auscultation. *v.t.* to rumour, to noise abroad. [F, noise, from *bruire,* to roar]

brûlé, *a.* cooked with brown sugar. [F]

brulye, brulzie, bruilzie, *n.* (*Sc.*) an affray, a disturbance. [BROIL[1]]

Brum, (*abbr.*) BRUMMAGEM, Birmingham. **Brummy, -mmie,,** *n.* (*coll.*) a person from Birmingham.

brumby, *n.* (*Austral.*) a wild horse.

brume, *n.* mist, fog, vapour. **brumal,** *a.* pertaining to winter; winterly. **brumous,** *a.* wintry, foggy. [F *brume,* fog, L *brūma,* winter (contr. of *brevima, brevissima,* shortest)]

brummagem, the local vulgar form of the name of the city of *Birmingham*. *n.* an article manufactured there; a counterfeit coin etc. *a.* sham, spurious.

Brummell, *n.* **George Bryan** (1778–1840), British dandy and leader of fashion, known as Beau Brummell. A friend of the Prince of Wales, the future George IV, he later quarrelled with him and was driven by gambling losses to exile in France in 1816.

brunch, *n.* (*coll.*) a meal which combines a late breakfast with an early lunch. [BREAKFAST, LUNCH]

Brundtland, *n.* **Gro Harlem** (1939–), Norwegian Labour politician, prime minister in 1981 and from 1986. Educated at Oslo and Harvard universities, she entered politics with the Norwegian Labour Party and became its leader in 1981. The *Brundtland Report* (1987) was produced by the World Commision on Environment and development, chaired by her.

Brunei, *n.* (Negara Brunei Darussalam) a country on the N coast of Borneo. **area** 5,765 sq km/2,225 sq miles. **capital** and chief port Bandar Seri Begawan. **physical** 75% of the area is forested; the Limbang valley splits Brunei in two, and its cession to Sarawak 1890 is disputed by Brunei. **population** (1986) 226,300 (65% Malay, 25% Chinese; few Chinese granted citizenship); annual growth rate 12%. **exports** liquefied natural gas (world's largest producer) and oil, both expected to be exhausted by 2000. **language** 50% Malay (official), 26% Chinese (Hokkien), English. **religion** Muslim.

Brunel[1], *n.* **Isambard Kingdom** (1806–59), British engineer and inventor. In 1833 he became engineer to the Great Western Railway. He built the Clifton Suspension Bridge over the Avon and the Saltash Bridge over the Tamar. His ship-building designs include the *Great Western* (1838), the *Great Britain* (1845) and the *Great Eastern* (1858) which laid the first transatlantic telegraph cable.

Brunel[2], *n.* **Marc Isambard** (1769–1849), British engineer and inventor, who constructed the Rotherhithe tunnel under the Thames from Wapping to Rotherhithe (1825–43).

Brunelleschi, *n.* **Filippo** (1377–1446), Italian Renaissance architect who pioneered the scientific use of perspective. He was responsible for the construction of the dome of Florence cathedral (completed in 1438), a feat thought to be impossible by many of his contemporaries.

brunette, *n.* a girl or woman of dark hair and complexion. *a.* brown-haired; of dark complexion. [F, fem. dim of *brun,* brown]

Bruno[1], *n.* **Giordano** (1548–1600), Italian philosopher. His sceptical attitude to Catholic doctrines caused him to flee Italy in 1577. After visiting Geneva and Paris, he lived in England (1583–85), where he wrote some of his finest work. After returning to Europe, he was arrested by the Inquisition in Venice in 1593, and burned at the stake for his adoption of Copernican astronomy and his heretical religious views.

Bruno[2], **St,** *n.* (1030–1101), German founder of the monastic Catholic Carthusian order. He was born in Cologne, became a priest and controlled the cathedral school at Rheims (1057–76). Withdrawing to the mountains near Grenoble after an ecclesiastical controversy, he founded the monastery of Chartreuse in 1084. Feast day 6 Oct.

Brunswick, *n.* (German **Braunshweig**) industrial city in Lower Saxony, West Germany (chemical engineering, precision engineering, food processing); population (1985) 253,478. It was one of the chief cities of N Germany in The Middle Ages, and a member of the Hanseatic League. It was capital of the duchy of Brunswick from 1671.

brunt, *n.* the shock, impetus or stress of an attack, danger or crisis. **to bear the brunt,** to take the main force (e.g. of an attack). [etym. doubtful; perh. conn. with Icel. *bruna,* to advance like fire]

bruscamente, *adv.* (*Mus.*) strongly accented; roughly. [It.]

brush[1], *n.* an instrument for sweeping or scrubbing, generally made of bristles, twigs or feathers; an instrument consisting of hair or bristle attached to a handle, for colouring, white-washing, painting etc.; a hair-pencil; a brushing; an attack, a skirmish; a bushy tail, as of a fox; a piece of metal or carbon or bundle of wires or plates, forming a good electrical conductor; a brush-like discharge of electric sparks; a painter, a style in painting; a brush-like appearance produced by polarized light; brushwood, underwood, a thicket of small trees; loppings, faggots of brushwood. *v.t.* to sweep or scrub with a brush; to remove by brushing; to touch lightly, as in passing. *v.i.* to move with a sweeping motion; to pass lightly over. **the brush,** (*fig.*) the art of painting. **to brush aside, off,** to dismiss curtly. **to brush up,** to clean by brushing; to revive, to tidy one's appearance; to refresh one's memory. **brush fire,** *n.* a fast spreading fire which consumes dry brush and scrub. **brush kangaroo,** *n.* the wallaby. **brush-off,** *n.* (*coll.*) a brusque rebuff. **brush-pencil,** *n.* an artist's brush. **brush-up,** *n.* a brushing. **brush-wheel,** *n.* a circular revolving brush. **brushwood,** *n.* a thicket, underwood; low scrubby thicket; loppings. **brush-work,** *n.* a painter's manipulation of the brush; style of manipulation of the brush. **brushed,** *a.* cleaned or smoothed with a brush; having a raised nap (of a fabric). **brusher,** *n.* **brushy,** *a.* resembling a brush; rough, shaggy; covered with brushwood. [OF *broce, brosse,* brushwood, late L *bruscia,* a thicket (prob. from OHG *Bursta,* bristle); and OF *brosse, broisse,* a brush, broom (perh. of similar origin)]

brush[2], *n.* (*Austral.*) a young woman, a girl.

brusque, *a.* rough, blunt, unceremonious. **brusquely,** *adv.* **brusqueness,** *n.* **brusquerie,** *n.* [F, from It. *brusco,* sharp, sour; etym. doubtful]

Brussels, *n.* (Flemish **Brussel**, French **Bruxelles**) capital of Belgium, industrial city (lace, textiles, machinery, chemicals); population (1985) 980,200 (80% French-speaking, the suburbs Flemish-speaking. *a.* made at or derived from Brussels. *n.* a Brussels carpet. **Brussels carpet,** *n.* a kind of carpet with a backing of linen and wool face. **Brussels lace,** *n.* a kind of pillow-lace. **brussels sprouts,** *n.pl.* the small sprouts springing from the stalks of a variety of cabbage, and used as a vegetable. [the capital of Belgium]

brut, *a.* of wine, dry, unsweetened. [F]

brute, *a.* stupid, irrational; beastlike, sensual; unconscious, material. *n.* an irrational animal; a beast; the animal nature in man; one resembling a brute in cruelty, want of intelligence etc. **brutehood,** *n.* the condition of brutes. **brutal,** *a.* resembling a brute; savage, cruel; coarse, unrefined, sensual. **brutally,** *adv.* **brutality, brutalism,** *n.* the quality of being brutal; a brutal action. **brutalize, -ise,** *v.t.* to render brutal; *v.i.* to become brutal. **brutalization, -isation,** *n.* **brutify,** *v.t.* to brutalize; to render brutal. **brutification,** *n.* **brutish,** *a.* like a brute; animal, bestial. **brutishly,** *adv.* **brutishness,** *n.* [F *brut, brute,* L *brūtus,* stupid]

Brutus[1], *n.* **Marcus Junius** (*c.* 78–42 BC), Roman soldier, a supporter of Pompey (against Caesar) in the Civil War. Pardoned by Caesar and raised to high office by him, he nevertheless plotted Casear's assassination to restore the purity of the republic. When he was defeated (with Cassius) by Mark Antony, Caesar's lieutenant, at Philippi in 42 BC, he committed suicide.

Brutus[2], *n.* a method of dressing the hair in which it is brushed back from the forehead and the head covered with curls; a kind of wig. [after BRUTUS[1]]

bruxism, *n.* the unconscious habit of grinding the teeth. [Gr. *brychein,* to gnash]

bryology, *n.* the science of mosses; mosses collectively. **bryologist,** *n.* a student of mosses. [Gr. *bruun,* a mossy seaweed]

bryony, *n.* a genus of climbing plants, esp. *Bryonia dioica,* white or common bryony; a similar plant, black bryony, *Tamus communis.* [L *bryōnia,* Gr. *bruōnia* (*bruein,* to teem, swell)]

Bryophyta, *n.* a division of the higher cryptogams consisting of the liverworts and mosses. **bryophyte,** *n.* a member of this group. [Gr. *bruon,* moss, *phuton,* a plant]

bryozoon, *n.* (*pl.* **-zoa, -zōa**) one of the lowest class of the mollusca, called also polyzoa. [Gr. *bruon,* moss, *zōon, zōa,* animal, -als]

Brython, *n.* a member of the Celtic people occupying S Britain at the time of the Roman invasion, as distinguished from the Goidels, the Scoto-Irish or Gaelic race. **Brythonic,** *a.* [W *Brython,* BRITON]

BS, (*abbr.*) British Standard(s).

b.s., (*abbr.*) balance sheet; bill of sale.

B.Sc., (*abbr.*) Bachelor of Science.

BSE (*abbr.*) bovine spongiform encephalopathy.

BSI, (*abbr.*) British Standards Institution.

BST (*abbr.*) British Standard Time; British Summer Time.

Bt., (*abbr.*) Baronet; bought.

btu, BTU, B.Th.U., (*abbr.*) British Thermal Unit.

bu., (*abbr.*) bushel.

bub[1] , *n.* (*N Am. sl.*) a boy.

bub[2], *n.* (*sl.*) drink; beer. [prob. imit.]

bubble, *n.* a vesicle of water or other liquid filled with air or other gas; a cavity in a solidified material, such as ice, amber, glass etc.; (*fig.*) anything unsubstantial or unreal; a chest, a fraud; a swindling project. *a.* visionary, unreal; fraudulent, fictitious. *v.i.* to rise up in or as in bubbles; to make a noise like bubbling water. *v.t.* to cheat, to delude. **to bubble over,** to boil over with laughter, anger, etc. **bubble and squeak,** meat and vegetables fried together. **bubble bath,** *n.* a foaming bath preparation. **bubble-car,** *n.* a midget motor-car with rounded line and transparent top. **bubble chamber,** *n.* an apparatus for tracking the path of a charged particle by the stream of bubbles left in its wake. **bubble-gum,** *n.* a kind of chewing-gum that can be blown up into a bubble. **bubble memory,** *n.* a data-storage system in computers composed of tiny areas of bubbles of magnetism. **bubble pack** BLISTER PACK. **bubbler,** *n.* a cheat; a fish found in the Ohio, named from the peculiar noise it makes. **bubbly,** *a.* full of bubbles; excited, vivacious. *n.* (*coll.*) champagne. **bubbly-jock,** *n.* (*coll., esp. Sc.*) a turkey-cock. [imit. cp. BLEB, BLUBBER]

bubo, *n.* (*pl.* **-boes**) an inflamed swelling of the lymphatic glands, esp. in the groin or armpit. **bubonic,** *a.* **bubonic plague,** *n.* a type of plague characterized by buboes. **bubonocele,** *n.* hernia of the groin. [-CELE] †**bubukle,** *n.* (*Shak.*) a red pimple. [late L, from Gr. *boubōn,* the groin, a swelling in the groin]

buccal, *a.* pertaining to the cheek or the mouth. [L

bucca, cheek]

buccaneer, *n.* one of the piratical rovers who formerly infested the Spanish Main; a filibuster. *v.i.* to act the part of a buccaneer. **buccaneering,** *a.* [F *boucanier,* orig. a hunter of wild oxen, from *boucan* (from a Brazilian word), a gridiron or frame on which flesh was barbecued]

buccinator, *n.* the flat, thin muscle forming the wall of the cheek, used in blowing. [L *buccināre,* to blow the trumpet (*buccina,* trumpet)]

Bucentaur, *n.* the state barge of the Venetian Republic; †a large decorated barge. [It. *bucentoro,* etym. unknown]

Bucephalus, *n.* a riding-horse, a hack. [name of the charger of Alexander the Great]

Bucer, *n.* **Martin** (1491–1551), German protestant reformer, regius professor of divinity at Cambridge Univ. from 1549, who tried to reconcile the views of his fellow protestants Luther and Zwingli and the significance of the eucharist.

Buchan, *n.* **John, Baron Tweedsmuir** (1875–1940), Scottish politician and author. Called to the bar in 1901, he was Conservative MP for the Scottish universities (1927–35) and governor-general of Canada (1934–40). He published adventure stories which won wide popularity, incl. *Prester John* (1910), *The Thirty-Nine Steps* (1915), *Greenmantle* (1916), *Huntingtower* (1922), *The Three Hostages* (1924) and *The House of the Four Winds* (1935).

Bucharest *n.* (Romanian **Bucuresti**) capital and largest city of Romania, population (1983) 1,995,000. It became the capital in 1861.

Buchenwald, *n.* site of a Nazi concentration camp (1937–45) at a village NE of Weimar, East Germany.

Buchmanism, *n.* the name applied to an undenominational evangelical religious movement of American origin, brought by F. Buchman to Britain where it became known as the Oxford Group, now more usually Moral Rearmament. **Buchmanite,** *n.* a member of this group.

buck¹, *n.* the male of the fallow-deer, reindeer, goat, hare and rabbit; a dashing young fellow; (*offensive*) a male Indian or Negro; (*N Am. sl.*) a dollar; (*sl.*) cheek; a marker in poker which indicates the next dealer; an object used as a reminder. *v.i.* to buck-jump. **to buck up,** to hurry; to improve; to beecome cheerful or lively. **to make a fast buck,** to make money quickly and easily, but not always strictly legally. **to pass the buck,** (*sl.*) to shift responsibility to someone else. **buck-eye,** *n.* the horse-chestnut of the US; (*offensive*) a native of Ohio. **buck-handled,** *a.* with a buckthorn handle. **buckhorn,** *n.* the horn of a buck; the material of a buck's horn used for knife-handles etc. **buck-hound,** *n.* a small variety of the stag-hound. **buck-jump,** *n.* a jump by a vicious or unbroken horse, with the feet drawn together and the back arched to unseat the rider. *v.i.* to jump as described above. **buck-jumper,** *n.* a horse given to buck-jumping. **buck-shot,** *n.* a kind of shot larger than swan-shot. **buck-skin,** *n.* the skin of a buck; a soft yellowish leather made from deer and sheepskins; (*pl.*) buckskin breeches; *a.* made of buckskin. **buckthorn,** *n.* the genus *Rhamnus,* esp. *R. catharticus,* berries of which yield sap-green. **bucktooth,** *n.* a large, protruding tooth. **bucked,** *a.* invigorated; pleased. **bucker,** *n.* a buck-jumper. **buckish,** *a.* †lascivious; foppish. **buckishly,** *adv.* [OE *bucc,* a buck, *bucca,* a he-goat (distinction between the two words doubtful) (cp. Dut. *bok,* G *Bock,* F *bouc,* a he-goat, W *bwch,* a buck, all from Teut.)]

buck², *n.* a lye in which linen etc. is soaked before washing; clothes washed at one operation. *v.t.* to soak or wash in lye; to drench, to soak. †**buck-basket,** *n.* a basket to hold dirty linen. [etym. doubtful (cp. G *Beuche,* Swed. *byk,* lye, F *buer,* to steep in lye, and perh. OE *būc,* a pitcher)]

buck³, *n.* a large basket for trapping eels. [etym. doubtful]

buck⁴, *n.* (*dial., N Am.*) the body of a wagon or cart. **buck-board,** *n.* a projecting board or ledge over the wheels of a cart; (*N Am.*) a light four-wheeled vehicle. **buck-cart, -wagon,** *n.* vehicles fitted with buckboards. [perh. OE *būc,* belly, body, trunk]

buck⁵, *n.* (*coll.*) talk, chatter; swagger. **not so much of your buck,** don't swagger. [Hind.]

Buck⁶, *n.* **Pearl S.** (1892–1973), US novelist. Daughter of missionaries to China, she wrote novels about Chinese life, such as *East Wind – West Wind* (1930) and *The Good Earth* (1931). Nobel prize for Literature (1938).

buckbean, *n.* a water-plant having pinkish-white flowers, of the genus *Menyanthes,* esp. *M. trifoliata* (also called the bog bean). [etym. doubtful]

bucket, *n.* a vessel with a handle, for drawing or carrying water; a scoop or receptacle for lifting mud, gravel, coal, grain etc. in a dredger or elevator; as much as a bucket will hold; the piston of a pump; a whip socket; a holder attached to a saddle for a carbine, rifle etc. *v.t.* to lift or draw in buckets; (*sl.*) to cheat; to ride (a horse) hard; to hurry or jerk while rowing. *v.i.* to hurry the forward swing of an oar; (*coll.*) to rain heavily. **to kick the bucket,** (perh. from OF *buquet,* a beam) (*sl.*) to die. **bucket-seat,** *n.* a round-backed seat for one person in a motor or aeroplane. **bucket-shop,** *n.* the office of unofficial brokers who deal in trashy stock; a place where cheap airline tickets are sold. [conn. accidentally with *bucket,* from expression *bucketful* of people] **bucketful,** *n.* as much as will fill a bucket. [etym. doubtful (perh. OE *būc,* pitcher, or OF *buket, buquet,* tub, pail)]

buckie, *n.* a spiral shell, e.g. the whelk; an obstinate, perverse person. [etym. doubtful]

Buckingham¹, *n.* **George Villiers, 1st Duke of Buckingham** (1592–1628), English courtier, adviser to James I and later Charles I. After Charles's accession, Buckingham attempted to form a Protestant coalition in Europe which led to war with France, but he failed to relieve the Protestants besieged in La Rochelle in 1627. This added to his unpopularity with Parliament, and he was assassinated.

Buckingham², *n.* **George Villiers, 2nd Duke of Buckingham** (1628–87), English politician, a member of the Cabal under Charles II. A dissolute son of the 1st Duke, he was brought up with the royal children. His play *The Rehearsal* satirized the style of the poet Dryden, who portrayed him as Zimri in *Absalom and Achitophel.*

Buckingham Palace, *n.* the London home of the British sovereign, built in 1703 for the duke of Buckingham, but bought by George III in 1762 and reconstructed by Nash (1821–36). A new front was added in 1913.

Buckinghamshire *n.* country in SE central England. **area** 1880 sq km/726 sq miles. **towns** administrative headquarters Aylesbury; Buckingham, High Wycombe, Beaconsfield, Olney. **population** (1987) 621,000. **products** furniture, especially beech; agricultural.

buckle, *n.* a link of metal, with a tongue or catch, for fastening straps etc.; a bow, a curl, a twist; the state of being crisped, curled or twisted. *v.t.* to fasten with or as with a buckle; to bend, to twist; to equip, to confine; to join in matrimony; to prepare (oneself) resolutely. *v.i.* to bend, to be put out of shape; to be married. **to buckle to, down,** to set to work, to set about energetically. **to buckle under,** to give way under stress. **buckler,** *n.* a small round shield; a protection, a protector; (*Biol.*) a hard protective covering; a carapace; the interior segment of a trilobite. *v.t.* to defend with or as with a buckler. **buckler-fern,** *n.* one of the shield ferns. [OF *bocle* (F *boucle,* L *buccula,* cheek-strap of helmet, buckle (*bucca,* cheek)]

Buckley, *n.* **William** (1780–1856), Australian convict, who escaped from Port Phillip and lived (1803–35) among the Aborigines before giving himself up; hence 'Buckley's chance' meaning an 'outside chance'.

buckram, *n.* a strong coarse kind of linen cloth, stiffened with gum; a stiff, precise manner; appearance of strength. *a.* made of buckram; starched, stiff, precise. *v.i.* to stiffen with or as with buckram. [OF *boucaran, boquerant* (It. *bucherane, buchirano*); etym. unknown]

Bucks., (*abbr.*) Buckinghamshire.

buckshee, *n.* (*sl.*) something for nothing, a windfall; something in addition to the agreed allowance. *a.* free, gratuitous. [BAKSHEESH]

buckthorn BUCK[1].

buckwheat, *n.* a cereal plant, *Polygonum fagopyrum,* the three-cornered seeds of which are given to horses and poultry, and in the US are used for cakes. [*beechwheat,* from the shape of its seeds (OE *boc,* beech)]

bucolic, *a.* (often *derog.*) pastoral, rustic. *n.* a pastoral poem, a pastoral poet. **bucolically,** *adv.* [L *būcolicus,* Gr. *boukolikos,* from *boukolos,* a herdsman (*bous,* ox, *kol-,* stem of v. to drive)]

bud, *n.* the germ of a branch, cluster of leaves or flower, usu. arising from the axil of a leaf; an unexpanded leaf or flower; a gemmule which develops into a complete animal; something undeveloped. *v.i.* to put forth buds; to begin to grow; to develop. *v.t.* to graft (on) by inserting a bud under the bark; to produce by germination. **in bud,** about to flower or put forth leaves. **to nip in the bud,** to put a stop to at the outset. **budded,** *a.* in bud. **budding,** *n.* grafting with a bud; asexual reproduction from a parent cell, as in yeast; (*Zool.*) gemmation. *a.* having buds; beginning to develop; promising; aspiring. **budless,** *a.* **budlet**, *n.* a little bud. [etym. doubtful]

Budapest, *n.* capital of Hungary, industrial city (chemicals, textiles) on the Danube; population (1985) 2,089,000. Buda, on the right bank of the Danube, became the Hungarian capital in 1867 and was joined with Pest, on the left bank, in 1872.

Buddha, *n.* the title given to Gautama, the founder of Buddhism, by his disciples. **Buddhism,** *n.* the religious system founded in India in the 5th cent. BC by Sakyamuni, Gautama or Siddartha, with currently about 250 million followers worldwide: its chief doctrine teaches that good or evil deeds meet an appropriate reward or punishment either in this life or (through reincarnation) in a long succession of lives. **esoteric Buddhism** THEOSOPHY. **Buddhist,** *n.* a follower of Buddha. *a.* of or connected with Buddhism. **Buddhistic, -ical**, *a.* [Sansk. *buddha,* enlightened (p.p. of *budh,* to awake, to know)]

buddle, *n.* an oblong inclined vat in which ore is washed. *v.t.* to wash (ore) by means of a buddle. [etym. unknown]

Buddleia, *n.* a genus of shrubs of the family Loganiaceae. [Adam *Buddle,* d. 1715]

buddy, *n.* (*pl.* **-ddies**) (*coll.*) close friend, pal; one who visits and counsels (in a voluntary capacity) someone suffering from AIDS.

budge[1], *v.i.* to stir; to move from one's place. *v.t.* to cause (something heavy) to move. [F *bouger,* to stir (cp. Prov. *bolegar,* to disturb oneself, It. *bulicare,* to bubble up, L *bullīre,* to boil)]

budge[2], *n.* a kind of fur made of lambskin with the wool outwards. †*a.* wearing budge; pedantic, stiff, formal. [etym. doubtful]

Budge, *n.* **Donald** (1915–), US tennis player, the first person to perform the Grand Slam when he won Wimbledon, French, US, and Australian championships in 1938.

budgeree, budgery, *a.* good, excellent. [Austral. Abor.]

budgerigar, *n.* the Australian green parrakeet, *Melopsittacus undulatus.* [Austral. Abor.]

budget, *n.* a small leather bag, the contents of such a bag; a bundle, a collection of news; an estimate of receipts and expenditure, esp. the annual financial statement of the Chancellor of the Exchequer in the House of Commons. *v.i.* to prepare a budget or estimate (for). *v.t.* to make provision for in a budget. **budget account,** *n.* an account which allows one to regularize payments as prescribed in a budget. **budgetary,** *a.* [F *bougette,* dim. of *bouge,* a wallet, L *bulga,* of Gaulish origin (cp. OIr. *bolg, bolc,* a bag)]

budgie, short for BUDGERIGAR.

Buenos Aires, *n.* capital and industrial city of Argentina, on the south bank of the River Plate; population (1980) 9,927,000.

buff[1], *n.* a blow, a buffet. **buffer,** *n.* a mechanical apparatus for deadening or sustaining the force of a concussion; an apparatus fixed to railway carriages for this purpose; the fender of a ship; a fellow; a chemical compound which maintains the balance of acidity/alkalinity in a solution; a short-term storage unit in a computer. *v.t.* to add or treat with a buffer; to protect with a buffer. **old buffer,** a doddering old man. **buffer state,** *n.* a small neutral state separating two larger rival states and tending to prevent hostilities. **buffered,** *a.* [OF *bufe, buffe,* a blow]

buff[2], *n.* soft, stout leather prepared from the skin of the buffalo; the skins of other animals similarly prepared; †a soldier's coat of buff; the colour of buff leather, light yellow; (*coll.*) the bare skin; an instrument for polishing with; an expert on or devotee of a subject. *v.t.* to polish with a buff; to give a velvety surface to leather. **in the buff,** (*coll.*) naked. **the Buffs,** the third regiment of the line (later the East Kent) from the colour of their facings. **buff-coat, -jerkin,** *n.* stout garment of buff leather orig. worn as a defence against sword-cuts. **buff-stick, buff-wheel,** *n.* a stick or wheel covered with buff leather or a similar material, used for polishing metals. **buffy,** *a.* coloured like buff. [contr. of *buffe* or *buffle,* F *buffle,* buffalo]

buffalo, *n.* (*pl.* **-loes**) the name of various kinds of ox, *Bos bubalus, B caffer,* and the American bison. **buffalo-grass,** *n.* prairie grass of various kinds. **buffalo-robe,** *n.* the skin of the American bison dressed with the hair on. [Port. *bufalo* or It. *buffalo,* L *būfalus, būbalus,* Gr. *boubalos*]

buffer BUFF[1].

buffet[1], *n.* a blow with the hand or fist, a cuff; a blow of fate, a disaster, a misfortune. *v.t.* to strike with the hand; to thump, to cuff; to beat back, to contend with. *v.i.* to struggle, to contend. **buffeting,** *n.* repeated blows; (air) turbulence, strife. [OF *bufet,* dim. of *bufe,* BUFF[1]]

buffet[2], *n.* a cupboard or sideboard for the display of plate, china etc.; a refreshment bar;, dishes of food set out on a table from which diners help themselves. [F, etym. unknown]

buffo, *n.* a singer in a comic opera. *a.* burlesque, comic. [It., comic, burlesque]

Buffon, *n.* **Comte de** (1707–78), French naturalist and author of the 18th century's most significant work of natural history, the 44 volume *Histoire naturelle* (1749–1804), 36 of which he completed before his death. In *The Epochs of Nature*, one of the volumes, he questioned for the first time the received biblical chronology and raised the Earth's age from the traditional figure of 6000 years to the seemingly colossal estimate of 75,000 years.

buffoon, *n.* one who indulges in low jests and antics; a vulgar, clowning fool. **buffoonery,** *n.* [F *bouffon,* It. *buffone,* from *buffa,* a jest (*buffare,* orig. to puff out the cheeks)]

bug[1], *n.* a hobgoblin, a bugbear. **bugaboo**, *n.* a bogy; a source of worry. **bug-bear,** *n.* a hobgoblin invoked to frighten naughty children; an imaginary object of terror; a nuisance. [perh. from W *bwg,* ghost]

bug[2], *n.* †a loose name for various insects; any coleopterous insect; a blood-sucking, evil-smelling insect, *Cimex lectularius,* found in bedsteads etc.; any individual of the order Hemiptera, to which this belongs; a virus; a viral infection; a secreted radio receiver; a technical hitch, a flaw; an obsession, a temporary craze or fashion; a self-important person, a swell. *v.t.* to plant a hidden microphone; to pester or irritate. **big bug,** an important, aristocratic or wealthy person. **bug-bane,** *n.* a herb of the ranunculaceous genus *Cimifuga,* formerly used as a specific against insect pests. **bughouse,** *n.* (*sl.*) an asylum. *a.* mad, crazy. **bugged,** *a.* **buggy,**[1] *a.* infested with bugs. [etym. doubtful (perh. OE *budda,* beetle, influenced by BUG[1])]

Bugatti, *n.* racing and sports-car company, founded by the Italian Ettore Bugatti (1881–1947). The first car was produced 1908, and one of the great Bugattis was the Type 35, produced 1924. Bugatti cars are credited with more race wins than any other.

bugger, *n.* a sodomite; a beast; something difficult, disliked, unwanted etc., a nuisance; (*esp. N Am.*) term of affection used to a child etc. *int.* (*often considered taboo*) used to indicate annoyance, frustration etc. *v.t.* to commit a sodomous act; to have anal intercourse with; (*sl.*) to exhaust; (*sl.*) to destroy or spoil. **bugger all,** (*sl.*) nothing. **to bugger about,** (*sl.*) to muddle about, to interfere with a thing. **to bugger off,** (*sl.*) to leave. **buggery,** *n.* sodomy, anal intercourse. [F *bougre,* L *Bulgarus,* one of a sect of Bulgarian heretics, 11th cent. to whom homosexual practices were attributed]

buggy[1] BUG[2].

buggy[2], *n.* a light, four-wheeled or two-wheeled vehicle, having a single seat; a pushchair, a baby buggy; any such light vehicle or carriage (e.g. beach buggy). [etym. doubtful]

bugle[1], *n.* a hunting-horn, orig. made from the horn of a wild ox; a small military trumpet used to sound signals for the infantry. *v.t.* to sound by bugle; to call by bugle. *v.i.* to sound a bugle. **bugle-horn,** *n.* a bugle. **bugler,** *n.* one who plays a bugle; a soldier who transmits signals on a bugle. **buglet,** *n.* a small bugle. [short for BUGLE-HORN, OF *bugle,* a wild ox. L *būculus,* dim. of *bos bovis,* ox]

bugle[2], *n.* a long, slender glass bead, usu. black, for trimming dresses. [etym. unknown]

bugle[3], *n.* name of plants of the genus *Ajuga,* esp. *A. reptans.* **bugle-weed,** *n.* an American plant, *Lycopus virginicus,* used as a remedy for blood-spitting. [F, from late L *būgula*]

bugloss, *n.* name of plants of the borage family with rough, hairy leaves; *Echium vulgare,* viper's bugloss; *Lycopsis arvensis,* small or wild bugloss. [F *buglosse,* L *būglōssa,* Gr. *buglōssos* (*bous,* ox, *glōssa,* tongue)]

buhl, boulle, boule, *n.* brass, tortoise-shell etc. cut into ornamental patterns for inlaying; work so inlaid. [from André *Buhl,* or *Boule,* 1642–1732]

build, *v.t.* (*past, p.p.* **built**) to construct, to erect, to make by putting together parts and materials; to put (into a structure); to establish. *v.i.* to erect a building or buildings; to make a nest. *n.* form, style or mode of construction; shape, proportions, figure. **to build on, upon,** to found or rely on (as a basis). **to build up,** to establish or strengthen by degrees; to block up; to erect many buildings in an area. **build-up,** *n.* a creation of favourable publicity; the leading to the climax in a speech etc. **builder,** *n.* one who builds; a master-builder or contractor who erects buildings under the direction of the architect. **builder's merchant,** *n.* a trades person who supplies building materials to builders. **building,** *n.* the act of constructing or erecting; an erection, an edifice. **building society,** *n.* an organization lending money to contributors enabling them to purchase dwelling-houses. **built,** *a.* constructed, erected, fashioned, formed (in *comb.* as *well-built*). **built-in,** *a.* part of the main structure, e.g. cupboards, wardrobe; fixed, included. **built-up,** *a.* having many buildings (of an urban area). [OE *bold,* a house (whence ME *bulden, bilden,* to build), from Teut. *bu-,* to dwell]

buirdly, *a.* (*Sc.*) stalwart, stout, burly. [S, earlier *buirly,* BURLY]

Bukharin, *n.* **Nikolai Ivanovich** (1888–1938), Russian politician and theorist. A moderate, he was the most influential Bolshevik thinker after Lenin. Executed on Stalin's orders for treason in 1938, he was posthumously rehabilitated in 1988.

Bulawayo, *n.* industrial city and railway junction in Zimbabwe; population (1982) 415,000. It lies at an altitude of 1,355 m/4,450 ft on the river Matsheumlope, a tributary of the Zambezi, and was founded on the site of the kraal (enclosed village), burned down in 1893, of the Matabele chief Lobenguela. It produces agricultural and electrical equipment.

bulb, *n.* a subterranean stem or bud sending off roots below and leaves above, as in the onion or lily; a bulbil; a spherical dilatation of a glass tube, as in the thermometer; an electric-light globe; a spherical swelling of any cylindrical organ or structure. *v.i.* to take or grow into the form of a bulb. **bulbar, bulbed,** *a.* having the form of a bulb. **bulbiferous,** *a.* producing bulbs. **bulbiform,** *a.* **bulbil,** *a.* a small bulb developed at the side of a larger one, or in an axil. **bulbo-,** *comb. form.* bulb-like; pertaining to the bulb; as in **bulbo-tuber,** *n.* a corm. TUBER **bulbo-medullary,** *a.* pertaining to the bulb of the spinal marrow. MEDULLARY **bulbous, bulbose,** *a.* of or pertaining to a bulb; bulb-shaped. [F *bulbe,* L *bulbus,* Gr. *bolbos,* onion]

bulbul, *n.* an Eastern bird of the genus *Pycnonotus* belonging to the thrush family; a singer, a poet. [Pers.]

Bulgakov, *n.* **Mikhail Afanasyevich** (1891–1940), Russian novelist and playwright. His novel *The White Guard* (1924), dramatized as *The Days of the Turbins* (1926), deals with the Revolution and the civil war.

Bulganin, *n.* **Nikolai** (1895–1975), Russian military leader and politician. He helped to organize Moscow's defence in World War II, became a marshal of the USSR in 1947, and was minister of defence (1947–49) and (1953–55). On the fall of Malenkov he became prime minister (chair of Council of Ministers) in 1955 until ousted by Khrushchev in 1958.

Bulgaria, *n.* People's Republic of (*Narodna Republika Bulgaria*), a country in SE Europe. **area** 110,912 sq km/42,812 sq miles. **capital** Sofia. **towns** Plovdiv, Rusé; Burgas and Varna are Black Sea ports. **physical** Balkan and Rhodope mountains; river Danube in the north. **population** (1988) 8,970,000 (including 900,000–1,500,000 ethnic Turks, concentrated in the S and NE); annual growth rate 0.5%. **exports** textiles, chemicals, non-ferrous metals, timber, minerals, machinery. **language** Bulgarian, Turkish. **religion** Eastern Orthodox Christian 90%, Sunni Muslim 10%. **Bulgarian,** *n.* the language or people of Bulgaria. *a.* belonging to Bulgaria.

bulge, *n.* the protuberant part of a cask; a swelling on a flat or flattish surface; a temporary increase in volume or numbers; bilge. *v.i.* to swell irregularly; to be protuberant. *v.t.* to swell out (a bag); to push out of shape. **bulger,** *n.* (*Golf*) a brassy or driver with a convex face. **bulginess,** *n.* **bulging,** *a.* protuberant. **bulgy,** *a.* swollen so as to be clumsy. [OF *boulge, bouge,* L *bulga;* see BUDGET]

Bulge, Battle of the, or **Ardennes offensive,** in World War II, Hitler's plan, codenamed 'Watch on the Rhine', for a breakthrough by his field marshal Rundstedt aimed at the US line in Ardennes 16 Dec. 1944–28 Jan. 1945. There were 77,000 Allied casualties and 130,000 German, including Hitler's last powerful reserve, his Panzer elite.

bulimia (nervosa), bulimy, *n.* a medical condition characterized by abnormal hunger, the sufferer alternately overeating and then inducing vomiting. [Gr. *boulimia* (*bous,* ox, *limos,* hunger)]

bulk[1], *n.* cargo; magnitude of three dimensions; size, great size, mass; the greater portion, the main mass; a ship's hold or hull; anything of great size; the trunk of the body, esp. if large. *v.i.* to appear relatively big or important; to amount. *v.t.* to pile in heaps; to pack in bulk; to measure the bulk of. **in bulk,** cargo loose in the hold; in large quantities. **to break bulk,** to begin to unload or unpack. **bulk buying,** *n.* the purchase of goods in large quantities in order to obtain cheaper prices; the purchase by one customer of the whole of a producer's output. **bulk carrier,** *n.* a vessel or vehicle which carries a large, undivided cargo. **bulkily,** *adv.* **bulkiness,** *n.* **bulky,** *a.* of great bulk or dimensions; large. [prob. from Icel. *būlki,* a heap, a cargo, confused with *bouk,* OE *būc,* belly]

bulk[2], *n.* a framework projecting in front of a shop for displaying goods. [etym. doubtful; Skeat proposed MDan. *bulk,* a balk]

bulkhead, *n.* an upright partition dividing a ship into compartments.

bull[1], *n.* the uncastrated male of any bovine mammal, esp. of the domestic species, *Bos taurus;* the male of some other large animals, as the elk, the elephant, the whale; one who speculates for a rise in stocks (see also BEAR); the constellation and sign Taurus; a bull's-eye, a hit in the bull's eye; (*sl.*) rubbish, nonsense. *a.* of large size; thickset; coarse; male. *v.i.* to speculate for a rise (in stocks); of a cow, to low when in season. *v.t.* to produce a rise in (stocks etc.). **a bull in a china shop,** an indelicate or tactless person, a blunderer. **to take the bull by the horns,** to grapple with a difficulty boldly. **bull artist,** *n.* (*Austral.*) a swanker, a blowhard. **bull-baiting,** *n.* the baiting of a bull with dogs. **bull-beef,** *n.* the flesh of a bull; coarse, stringy beef. **bull-board,** *n.* a game like quoits played on board ship with a disk thrown on to numbered squares. **bull-calf,** *n.* a male calf; a stupid fellow. **bulldog** *n.* a powerful breed of dogs formerly used to bait bulls; one who possesses obstinate courage; one of the proctor's attendants at Oxford and Cambridge; a gun or pistol of a certain pattern. **bull-dog ant,** *n.* a large red or black Australian ant with poisonous bite. **Bulldog clip,**® *n.* a metal spring clip for fastening papers together or onto a board. **bullfight,** *n.* a Spanish sport in which a bull is baited and then killed. **bull-fighter,** *n.* **bullfinch,** *n.* an English song-bird with handsome plumage, belonging to the genus *Pyrrhula;* a high, quick-set hedge with a ditch on one side. **bull-frog,** *n.* a large American frog with a deep voice, *Ranma pipiens*. **bullhead,** *n.* the miller's thumb, a small river-fish *Cottus gobio,* with a big head; a small shark; an edible freshwater fish. **bull-headed,** *a.* with a massive head; stupid; obstinate, impetuous. **bull horn,** *n.* a loudspeaker. **bull-puncher,** *n.* (*Austral.*) a cattle-driver. **bull-pup,** *n.* a young bulldog. **bull-ring,** *n.* an arena for a bullfight; a place where bulls used to be baited. **bull-roarer,** *n.* a thin slat of wood that produces a formidable noise when swung rapidly with a string, now a plaything orig. used in religious rites of e.g. Australian aborigines, N Am. Indians. **bull's-eye,** *n.* a boss of glass in the middle of a blown sheet; a sweetmeat; a hemispherical disk of glass in the side or deck of a ship to give light below; a hemispherical lens in a lantern; a lantern with such a lens; a small round window; the centre of a target; something that achieves its aim. **bullshit,** *n.* (*sl.*) rubbish, deceptive nonsense. *v.i.* to talk rubbish, to attempt to deceive with nonsense. **bull-terrier,** *n.* a cross between a bulldog and a terrier, but now an acknowledged breed. **bull-trout,** *n.* a variety of sea-trout, *Salmo eriox*. **bullish,** *a.* resembling a bull; obstinate; on the stock-market, a tendency towards rising share prices. **bullishly,** *adv.* **bullishness,** *n.* **bullock,** *n.* †a castrated bull; an ox; a bovine animal. [OE *bule* in *bule-hide* (see also BULLOCK, from *bulluc*) from *bellan,* to bellow]

bull[2], *n.* a leaden seal appended to a Papal edict; a Papal edict. [L *bulla,* a knob, a seal]

bull[3], *n.* †a jest; a ludicrous contradiction in terms, supposed to be characteristic of the Irish. [etym. unknown (cp. OF *boul,* fraud, trickery)]

bull[4], *n.* drink made by putting water into an empty spirit cask to acquire the flavour of the liquor. [etym. unknown]

bull[5], BEAL.

Bull[6], *n.* **John,** typical Englishman, especially as represented in cartoons. The name came into use after the publication of Dr John Arbuthnot's *History of John Bull* (1712) advocating the Tory policy of peace with France.

Bull[7], *n.* **John** (*c.* 1562–1628), British composer, organist, and virginalist. Most of his output is for keyboard, and includes 'God Save the King'. He also wrote sacred vocal music.

bulla, *n.* a round pendant worn by Roman children; a watery vesicle; a genus of freshwater mollusca. **bullate,** *a.* blistered, puckered; having bleb-like excrescences. [L]

bullace, *n.* a wild plum, *Prunus insititia,* having two varieties, one with white, the other with dark fruit. [OF *beloce,* late L *pilota,* L *pila,* a ball]

bulldoze, *v.i.* to level ground using a bulldozer; to force or bully. **bulldozer,** *n.* a power-operated machine with a large blade, employed for removing obstacles, levelling ground and spreading material; a person who bulldozes, a bully.

Buller, *n.* **Redvers Henry** (1839–1908), British commander against the Boers in the South African War (1899–1902). He was defeated at Colenso and Spion Kop, but relieved Ladysmith; he was superseded by Lord Roberts.

bullet, *n.* a metal ball or cone used in fire-arms of small calibre; †a cannon-ball; a small round ball; a round missile; a fisherman's sinker. **to get the bullet,** (*sl.*) to be dismissed, get the sack. **bullet-head,** *n.* a round-shaped head; (*esp. N Am.*) an obstinate fellow. **bullet-headed,** *a.* **bullet-proof,** *a.* impenetrable to bullets. [F *boulette,* dim. of *boule,* ball, L *bulla,* a round object]

bulletin, *n.* an official report of some matter of public interest, e.g. of the condition of an invalid; a brief news item on radio or television, a news bulletin. *v.t.* to announce by bulletin. **bulletin board,** *n.* a notice-board. **bulletinist,** *n.* [F, from It. *bulletino,* dim. of *bulletta,* a passport, a lottery-ticket, dim. of *bulla;* see BULL[2]]

bullion, *n.* uncoined gold and silver in the mass; solid gold or silver; fringe made of gold or silver wire. *a.* made of solid gold or silver. **bullionist,** *n.* an advocate for a metallic currency. [perh. from F *bouillon,* boiling, soup, med. L *bulliōnem,* acc. of *bullio* (*bullīre,* to boil); or from F *billon,* an ingot, influenced by this]

Bull Run, Battles of, in the American Civil War, two victories for the Confederate army under Gen. Robert E. Lee at Manassas Junction, NE Virginia: **1st Battle of Bull Run** 21 July 1861; **2nd Battle of Bull Run** 29–30 Aug. 1862.

bully[1], *n.* a blustering, overbearing fellow; a cowardly tyrant; a bravo, a swashbuckler, a hired ruffian; †a dashing fellow. *a.* jolly, first-rate, capital. *v.t.* to treat in a tyrannical manner; to tease, oppress, terrorize. *v.i.* to act as a bully. **bully for you,** (*sometimes iron.*) well done! bravo! **bully boy,** *n.* a thug; a hired ruffian. [etym. doubtful; perh. from Dut. *boel,* a lover (cp. MHG *Buole,* G *Buhle*)]

bully[2], **bully-off,** *n.* in football, a scrimmage; in hockey, the starting of a game. *v.t.* to start a game of hockey.

bully[3], *n.* tinned beef, also called **bully beef,** [BULL[1] or BOUILLI]

bullyrag, BALLYRAG.

bulrush, *n.* a tall rush growing in water, *Scirpus lacustris,* or *Typha latifolia,* the reed-mace or cat's-tail; (*Bibl.*) the papyrus. **bulrushy,** *a.* [etym. doubtful; perh. BOLE[1], whence 'strong-stemmed,' or BULL[1], big (cp. BULL-FROG etc.)]

bulwark, *n.* a rampart or fortification; a mole, a breakwater; any shelter, protection, screen; that part of the sides of a ship which rises above the upper deck. *v.t.* to furnish with or protect as with bulwarks. [formed like Dut. *bolwerk* and G *Bollwerk,* from words represented by BOLE[1], or the MHG v. *boln,* to throw, and WORK]

bum[1], *v.i.* to make a humming noise; to boom. [onomat.; cp. BOOM[1]]

bum[2], *n.* the buttocks; a bumbailiff. [etym. doubtful; cp. BUMP] **bumbailiff** *n.* an under bailiff. [cp. F *pousse-cul*]

bum[3], **bummer** *n.* (*N Am.*) an irregular forager in the American Civil War; an idler, a loafer; a rascal, a blackleg; (*coll.*) a tramp; (*coll.*) a scrounger; (*coll.*) a devotee of a particular form of recreation *a.* (*coll.*) useless, broken; worthless. *v.i.* (*coll.*) to live like a tramp; to idle; to scrounge *v.t.* (*coll.*) to acquire by scrounging. [G *Bummler,* a loafer]

bumbaze, *v.t.* to confound, to bamboozle. [perh. from Dut. *bazen,* to astonish; see also BAMBOOZLE]

bumble[1], *n.* a beadle; a jack-in-office. **bumbledom,** *n.* fussy officialism, esp. of parochial officers; parish officers collectively. [from *Bumble,* the beadle in Dickens' *Oliver Twist*]

†**bumble**[2], *v.i.* to buzz, to boom. *v.t.* to grumble at; to bustle and blunder. *n.* a jumble, a confused heap; a blunderer, an idler. **bumble-bee,** *n.* a large bee belonging to the genus *Bombus;* a humble-bee. **bumble-foot,** *n.* a club-foot. **bumble-puppy,** *n.* †a childish game with marbles; whist played unscientifically. [imit.; cp. BOOM[1]]

bumbo, *n.* punch made with rum or gin. [cp. It. *bombo,* childish word for drink]

bumboat, *n.* a boat used to carry provisions to vessels.

bumf, bumph, *n.* (*sl.*) toilet paper; (*derog.*) official documents; any unwanted paperwork. [BUM[2], FODDER]

bumkin, *n.* a small boom projecting from each bow to extend the foresail; a similar boom for the mainsail or the mizzen.

bum(m)alo, *n.* Bombay duck; a small Asiatic fish, dried and used as a relish. [Mahratti *bombīl, bombīla*]

bummaree, *n.* a middleman in the Billingsgate and Smithfield markets; a porter at Smithfield. [etym. unknown]

bummer BUM[3].

bummock, *n.* (*Sc.*) a large brewing of ale. [etym. unknown]

bump[1], *n.* a thump, a dull, heavy blow, an impact or collision; a swelling; a protuberance on the skull, said by phrenologists to indicate distinct faculties or affections; a touch in a bumping-race; a sudden movement of an aircraft caused by currents. *v.t.* to cause to strike forcibly against anything hard or solid; to hurt by striking against something; to hit (against); in boat racing, to strike the boat in front with the prow of one's own boat. *v.i.* to strike heavily; to collide; to move along with a bump or succession of bumps. *adv.* with a bump; with a sudden shock. **to bump into,** to meet unexpectedly; to encounter accidentally. **to bump off,** (*coll.*) *v.t.* to murder. **to bump start,** to start a motor vehicle by pushing it while engaging the gears; to jump start. **to bump up,** to increase (prices); to raise. **bumper,** *n.* one or that which bumps; a glass filled to the brim, esp. for drinking a toast; the fender of a motor-car; a buffer; (*coll.*) anything very large or wonderful or full; a crowded house at the theatre; in whist, a score of two games to nothing; (*Austral.*) a cigarette-butt. *a.* (*coll.*) extraordinary, startling, fine; full to the brim. **bumpiness,** *n.* **bumpy,** *a.* full of bumps, uneven, jolty. [onomat.]

bump[2], *n.* the cry of the bittern. *v.i.* to cry like a bittern. [onomat.]

bumph BUMF.

bumpkin, *n.* a country lout; a clumsy, thickheaded fellow; a bashful person. [prob. BUMKIN]

bumptious, *a.* disagreeably self-assertive. **bumptiously,** *adv.* **bumptiousness,** *n.* [facetious, from BUMP[1]]

bun[1], *n.* a small sweet cake; a compact ball of hair worn at the back of the head. **hot cross bun,** *n.* a bun marked with a cross and trad. sold on Good Friday. **bun-fight,** *n.* a crowded tea-party; a disturbance at an assembly. [perh. OF (prov.) *bugne,* fritters]

bun[2], *n.* (*Sc.*) a hare's tail. [etym. unknown; perh. from Gael. *bun,* a root]

bun[3], *n.* playful name for the squirrel; also for the rabbit. [etym. unknown]

Buna®, *n.* (*sl.*) a type of artificial rubber.

bunce, *n.* (*sl.*) extra profit. [etym. unknown]

bunch, *n.* a cluster of several things of the same kind growing or tied together; a tuft, a knot, a bow; a lot, a collection, a pack, a herd. *v.t.* to tie up or form into a bunch; to gather into folds. *v.i.* to come or grow into a cluster or bunch. **bunchy,** *a.* forming a bunch; growing in bunches. [prob. onomat.]

Bunche, *n.* **Ralph** (1904–71), US diplomat. Grandson of a slave, he was principal director of the UN Department of Trusteeship (1947–54), and UN undersecretary acting as mediator in Palestine (1948–49) and as special representative in the Congo (1960). He was awarded the Nobel Peace Prize (1950).

bunco BUNKO.

buncombe BUNKUM.

bund, *n.* an embankment, a dam or causeway. [Hind.]

Bundelas, *n.* Rajput clan prominent in the 14th cent., which gave its name to the Bundelkhand in N central India. The clan had replaced the Chandelā in the 11th cent. and continued to resist the attacks of other Indian rulers until coming under British control after 1812.

Bundesrat, *n.* the federal council of the former German Empire, now of the Federal Republic of Germany; federal council of Switzerland. [G *Bund,* confederation, *Rat,* council]

bundle, *n.* a number of things or a quantity of anything bound together loosely; a package, a parcel; a set of rods, wires, fibres, nerves etc., bound together; 20 hanks of linen thread; a group of characteristics; (*sl.*) a large amount of money, a bundle of bank notes. *v.t.* to tie up in a bundle; to throw hurriedly together. *v.i.* to prepare for departure, to pack up, to start hurriedly (in, off, away or out); to sleep (with a person of the opposite sex) without undressing, an old custom in parts of Britain and N America. **to bundle off,** to send away hurriedly or unceremoniously; to dismiss. **to bundle up,** to gather into a bundle; to clothe warmly. **to go a bundle on,** to like enormously, to be enthusiastic for. [*bund-,* p.p. stem of OTeut. *bindan,* to BIND (cp. MDut. *bondel,* G *Bündel*)]

bundook, *n.* a musket or rifle, a gun. [Hind.]

bundu, *n.* (*S Afr.*) the back of beyond, the far interior.

bung, *n.* a large cork stopper for a bung-hole; †a purse; a cut-purse, a pickpocket. *v.t.* to stop with a bung; (*fig.*) to close, to shut up; to throw, to sling. **to go bung,** (*Austral. coll.*) to go bankrupt. **bung-hole,** *n.* the hole in the bulge of a cask through which it is filled. [cp. MDut. *bonghe, bonde, bonne* (Dut. *bon*), L *puncta,* an orifice (fem. p.p. of *pungere,* to prick)]

bungalow, *n.* a one-storied house. [Hind. *bānglā,* of Bengal]

bungle, *v.t.* to botch; to manage clumsily or awkwardly. *v.i.* to act clumsily or awkwardly; to fail in a task. *n.* botching; mismanagement. **bungler,** *n.* **bungling,** *a.* clumsy, awkward, unskilful. **bunglingly,** *adv.* [prob. imit., cp. BOGGLE, BUMBLE[2]]

bunion, *n.* a swelling on the foot, esp. of the joint of the great toe. [perh. from It. *bugnone, bugno,* a boil or blain (cp. OF *bugne,* see BUN[1]]

bunk[1], *n.* a box or recess serving for a bed; a sleeping-berth; (*N Am.*) a piece of timber on a sled to support heavy timber. *v.i.* to sleep in a bunk. **bunk bed,** *n.* one of a pair of narrow beds built one above the other. **bunker** *n.* (*Sc.*) a bench, a bank; a sandy hollow or other obstruction on a golf course; a container or bin usu. for coal or fuel, e.g. on a ship; an underground shelter with gun emplacements. **bunkered,** *a.* in golf, having hit one's ball into a bunker. [etym. doubtful]

bunk[2], *v.i.* (*sl.*) to make off, to bolt. *n.* a bolt; a making off, an escape. **to bunk off,** (*sl.*) to play truant. **to do a bunk,** (*sl.*) to run away. [etym. unknown]

bunk[3] BUNKUM.

Bunker Hill, Battle of, the first considerable engagement in the War of American Independence, 17 June 1775, near a small hill in Charlestown (now part of Boston), Massachusetts, US; although the colonists were defeated they were able to retreat to Boston and suffered fewer casualties than the British.

bunko, bunco, *n.* (*N Am. sl.*) a swindling game or confidence trick. *v.t.* to swindle in this or a similar manner. **bunko-steerer,** *n.* a decoy in bunko.

bunkum, buncombe, **bunk,** *n.* political clap-trap; tall talk, humbug. [from *Buncombe* County, N Carolina, the representative of which made a speech in Congress, 1820, merely to please his constituents]

bunny, *n.* a childish name for a rabbit. **bunny girl,** *n.* a waitress in a night-club who wears a sexually provocative costume including rabbit ears and tail. **bunny-hug, bunny-hugging,** *n.* a romping kind of dance in which the partners closely embrace each other. [BUN[3], -Y]

Bunsen, *n.* **Robert Wilhelm von** (1811–99), German chemist, credited with the invention of the Bunsen burner. His name is also given to the carbon–zinc electric cell, which he invented in 1841 for use in arc-lamps. In 1859 he discovered two new elements, caesium and rubidium.

Bunsen burner, lamp, *n.* a burner or lamp in which air is mingled with gas to produce an intense flame.

bunt¹, *n.* the middle part of a sail, formed into a cavity to hold the wind; the baggy part of a fishing-net. **bunt-line,** *n.* a rope passing from the foot-rope of a square sail and in front of the canvas to prevent bellying. [etym. doubtful]

bunt², *n.* a fungus, *Tilletia caries,* which attacks wheat. **bunted, bunty,** *a.* [etym. doubtful]

bunt³, *v.t., v.i.* to hit, push, butt. [cp. BUTT⁴, BOUNCE]

bunter, *n.* (*Geol.*) new Red Sandstone. [G *bunter Sandstein*]

bunting¹, *n.* a group of birds, the Emberizinae, allied to the larks; the grey shrimp, *Crangon vulgaris.* [etym. doubtful]

bunting², *n.* a thin woollen stuff of which flags are made; a flag; flags collectively (e.g. strung up as decoration). [etym. doubtful]

Buñuel, *n.* **Luis** (1900–83), Spanish surrealist film director. He collaborated with Salvador Dali in *Un Chien Andalou* (1928), and established his solo career with *Los Olvidados/The Young and the Damned* (1950). His works are often controversial and anticlerical, with black humour and erotic imagery.

bunya-bunya, bunya, *n.* a large conifer with edible seeds. [Austral. Abor.]

Bunyan, *n.* **John** (1628–88). English author. A Baptist, he was imprisoned in Bedford (1660-72) for preaching. During a second jail sentence in 1675 he started to write *Pilgrim's Progress*, the first part of which was published in 1678. Other works include *Grace Abounding* (1666), *The Life and Death of Mr Badman* (1680), and *The Holy War* (1682).

bunyip, *n.* the fabulous rainbow-serpent that lives in pools; an impostor. **bunyip peerage,** a nickname for the attempt to introduce an aristocracy in Australia in 1853. [Austral. Abor.]

buoy, *n.* an anchored float indicating a fairway, reef, shoal etc. *v.t.* to place a buoy upon, to mark with a buoy. **life-buoy,** *n.* a float to sustain a person in the water. **to buoy up,** to keep afloat, to bear up, bring to the surface. **buoyage,** *n.* the act of providing with buoys. **buoyancy,** *n.* ability to float; loss of weight due to immersion in a liquid; (*fig.*) power of resisting or recovering from depression, elasticity; lightheartedness; tendency to rise (of stocks, prices etc.). **buoyant,** *a.* tending to float; tending to keep up; elastic, light; easily recovering from depression. **buoyantly,** *adv.* [OF *boie* or Dut. *boei,* L *boia,* a fetter]

bur¹, burr², *n.* any prickly or spinous fruit, calyx or involucre; the involucre of the burdock; the catkin or cone of the hop; a knot of excrescence on a tree; hence the series of markings left in the timber, which are valuable for the effect in polished veneer etc.; the husk of the chestnut; someone or thing hard to get rid of; a lump in the throat; a small drill used by dentists and surgeons. **burdock,** *n.* a coarse plant with prickly flower-heads, of the genus *Arctium,* esp. *A. lappa.* **bur-thistle,** *n.* the spear-thistle, *Carduus lanceolatus.* [cp. Dan. *borre,* burdock]

bur², BURR¹.

Burbage, *n.* **Richard** (*c.* 1567–1619), English actor, thought to have been Shakespeare's original Hamlet, Othello, and Lear. He also appeared in first productions of works by Ben Jonson, Thomas Kyd, and John Webster. His father **James Burbage** (*c.* 1530–97) built the first English playhouse, known as 'the Theatre'; his brother **Cuthbert Burbage** (*c.* 1566–1636) built the original Globe Theatre in London in 1599.

Burberry®, *n.* a type of weatherproof cloth or clothing; a raincoat.

burble¹, *v.i.* to bubble, gurgle, †to flow with a gurgling noise. *v.i.* to simmer, to bubble with mirth or other emotion; to talk inconsequently or excitedly. [imit., cp. BUBBLE]

burble², *v.t.* (*Sc.*) to muddle, confuse. *n.* disorder, confusion. [perh. from F *barbouiller*]

burbot, *n.* the eel-pout, *Lota vulgaris,* a flat-headed freshwater fish. [F *bourbotte* (*bourbe,* late L *borba,* Gr. *borboros,* mud)]

†burd, *n.* (*poet.*) lady, maiden. **burd-alone, burd-alane,** *n.* the last surviving child of a family. [etym. doubtful; cp. perh. BRIDE]

burden, burthen, *n.* something borne or carried; a load; a load of labour, sin, sorrow, care, obligation, duty, taxation, expense, fate etc.; the principal theme, the gist of a composition of any kind; the carrying capacity of a vessel; tonnage; †an accompaniment; a refrain, a chorus. *v.t.* to load; to lay a burden on; to oppress, to encumber. **the burden of proof,** the obligation of proving a contention or assertion. **†burdenous,** *a.* heavy; onerous, oppressive. **burdensome,** *a.* hard to bear; grievous, oppressive. **burdensomely,** *adv.* **burdensomeness,** *n.* [OE *byrthen,* OS *burthinnia,* from Teut. stem *bur-,* of *beran,* to BEAR]

burdock BUR¹.

bureau, *n.* (*pl.* **bureaux**) a writing table with drawers for papers; a chest of drawers; an office; a public office; a Government department. **bureau de change,** *n.* an office or kiosk (e.g. in an airport, railway station) for exchanging currencies. [F, an office, a desk, orig. baize, OF *burel,* dim. of *bure,* drugget, L *burra,* a coarse red cloth, fem. of *burrus* (perh. from Gr. *purrhos,* red)]

bureaucracy, *n.* government by departments of state; centralization of government; officials as a body; officialism. **bureaucrat,** *n.* a government official; a bureaucratist. **bureaucratic,** *a.* pertaining to or constituting a bureaucracy; tending towards bureaucracy. **bureaucratically,** *adv.* **bureaucratism,** *n.* **bureaucratist,** *n.* one who advocates or supports bureaucracy. **bureaucratization, -isation,** *n.* the process of bureaucratizing. **bureaucratize, -ise,** *v.t.* to make into a bureaucracy. [as prec.]

burette, buret, *n.* a graduated glass tube for measuring small quantities of liquid. [F, dim. of *buire,* a vase (cp. *boire,* to drink)]

burg, *n.* a fortress; a walled town. [G (cp. BOROUGH)]

burgage, *n.* a tenure by which lands or tenements in towns or cities were held for a small yearly rent; property so held. [med. L *burgāgium,* from *burgus,* G *Burg*]

burganet, burgonet, *n.* a light helmet for foot-soldiers; a helmet with a visor. [OF (bourguignotte, from *Bourgogne,* Burgundy]

burgee, *n.* a kind of small coal suitable for furnaces; a triangular or swallow-tailed flag. [etym. and connection of the two senses doubtful]

Burgenland, *n.* federal state of SE Austria, extending from the Danube south along the west border of the Hungarian plain; area 4000 sq km/1544 sq miles; population (1987) 267,000. It is a largely agricultural region adjoining the Neusiedler See, and produces timber, fruit, sugar, wine, lignite, antimony, and limestone. Its capital is Eisenstadt.

burgeois, BOURGEOIS².

burgeon, bourgeon, *v.t.* to sprout, to bud; to begin to grow. *n.* (*poet.*) a bud, a shoot. [OF *borjon,* prob. from OTeut. stem *bur-* (*beran,* to BEAR)]

burger, *n.* a flat round cake of minced meat or vegetables, e.g. *hamburger, beefburger,* which is grilled or fried; a burger served in a bread roll or bun often with a topping, e.g. *cheese burger, chilli burger.* [ham*burger*]

Burges, *n.* **William** (1827–81). British Gothic revivalist architect. His chief works are Cork Cathedral (1862–76), additions to and remodelling of Cardiff Castle (1865), and Castle Coch near Cardiff (1875). His style is characterized by sumptuous interiors with carving, painting, and gilding.

burgess¹, *n.* an inhabitant of a borough possessing full municipal rights, a citizen; a freeman of a borough; †a member of Parliament for a borough or a University. **burgess-ship,** *n.* the status of a burgess. [OF *burgeis,* see BOURGEOIS[1]]

Burgess[2], *n.* **Anthony** (pen name of Anthony John Burgess Wilson) (1917–), British novelist, critic, and composer. His prolific work includes *A Clockwork Orange* (1962), set in a future London terrorized by teenage gangs, and the panoramic *Earthly Powers* (1980). His vision has been described as bleak and pessimistic, but his work is also comic and satiric, as in his novels featuring the poet Enderby.

Burgess[3], *n.* **Guy (Francis de Moncy)** (1910–63), British spy, a diplomat recruited by the USSR as agent; linked with Kim Philby, Donald Maclean (1913–83), and Anthony Blunt.

Burgess Shale Site, the site of unique fossil-bearing rock formations in Yoho National Park, British Columbia, Canada. The shales in this corner of the Rocky Mountains contain more than 120 species of marine invertebrate fossils. Although discovered in 1909 by Charles Walcott, the Burgess Shales have only recently been used as evidence in the debate concerning the evolution of life.

burgh[1], *n.* a Scottish town holding a charter; a borough. **burgh of barony,** a borough having a charter from the sovereign, but holding its land from a feudal lord. **burgh of regality,** a borough holding its charter of incorporation from the sovereign, with regal or exclusive criminal jurisdiction within its boundaries. **Parliamentary burgh,** a place delimited in 1832 which is entitled to send a representative to Parliament, and is municipally on the same footing as a Burgh Royal. **police burgh,** a burgh constituted by a sheriff and having the police commissioners for local authority. **Burgh Royal,** a burgh holding its municipal authority by royal charter. **burghal**, *a.* pertaining to a burgh. **burgher**, *n.* a citizen or inhabitant of a burgh, borough or corporate town, esp. of a Continental town. **burghership,** *n.* the position and privileges of a burgher. [Sc. (see BOROUGH)]

Burgh[2], *n.* **Hubert de** (died 1243), English justiciar and regent of England. He began his career in the administration of Richard I, and was promoted to the justiciarship by King John and remained in that position under Henry III from 1216 until his dismissal. He was a supporter of King John against the barons, and ended French intervention in England by his defeat of the French fleet in the Strait of Dover in 1217. He reorganized royal administration and the Common Law.

Burghley, *n.* **William Cecil, Baron Burghley** (1520–98), English politician, chief adviser to Elizabeth I as secretary of state from 1558 and Lord High Treasurer from 1572. He was largely responsible for the religious settlement of 1559, and took a leading role in the events preceding the execution of Mary, Queen of Scots, in 1587.

burglar, *n.* one who breaks into premises with intent to commit a felony, esp. theft. **burglarious**, *a.* **burglariously,** *adv.* **burglarize, -ise,** *v.t.* (*N Am.*) to enter or rob burglariously. **burglary,** *n.* **burgle,**, *v.i.* to commit burglary. [Ang.-Lat. *burglātor, burgātor,* perh. from ME *burgh-breche,* breach of a borough]

burgomaster, *n.* the chief magistrate of a municipal town in Austria, Germany, Holland or Flanders. [Dut. *burgemeester,* see BURG]

burgonet BURGANET.

burgoo, *n.* a kind of oatmeal porridge or thick gruel used by sailors; (*N Am.*) a thick soup or stew. [etym. doubtful]

Burgoyne, *n.* **John** (1722–92), British general and dramatist. He served in the American War of Independence and surrendered (1777) to the colonists at Saratoga, New York State, in one of the pivotal battles of the war. He wrote comedies, among them *The Maid of the Oaks* (1775) and *The Heiress* (1786). He figures in George Bernard Shaw's play *The Devil's Disciple*.

burgrave, *n.* the commandant of a castle or fortified town; a hereditary noble ruling such a town and the adjacent domain. [G (BURG, *Graf,* count)]

Burgundy, *n.* ancient kingdom and duchy in the valleys of the rivers Saône and Rhône, France; red or white wine made in Burgundy. **Burgundy mixture,** *n.* a preparation of soda and copper sulphate used for spraying potatoes in order to destroy disease germs.

burial, *n.* the act of burying, esp. of a dead body in the earth; interment; a funeral. **burial-ground, -place** *n.* a place for burying the dead. **burial-mound,** *n.* a tumulus. **burial-service,** *n.* a religious service (esp. of the Church of England) for the burial of the dead. [OE *byrgels,* a tomb, a burying-place (*byrgan,* to bury)]

burin, *n.* the cutting-tool of an engraver on copper; a triangular steel tool used by marble-workers; an early Stone Age flint tool. [F, prob. from OHG *Bora,* a borer, through It. *borino*]

burk, BERK.

burke[1], *v.t.* †to kill secretly by suffocation; to smother, to hush up; to shirk publicity by supressing. [from *Burke,* an Irishman who (1828) killed many persons by smothering, to sell their bodies for dissection]

Burke[2], *n.* **Edmund** (1729–97), British Whig politician and political theorist, born in Dublin, Ireland. In Parliament from 1765, he opposed the government's attempts to coerce the American colonists, for example in *Thoughts on the Present Discontents* (1770), and supported the emancipation of Ireland, but denounced the French Revolution, for example in *Reflections on the Revolution in France* (1790).

Burke[3], *n.* **John** (1787–1848), first publisher, in 1826, of *Burke's Peerage*.

Burke[4], *n.* **Martha Jane** (*c.* 1852–1903), real name of US heroine Calamity Jane.

Burke[5], *n.* **Robert O'Hara** (1820–61), Australian explorer who made the first south-north crossing of Australia (from Victoria to the Gulf of Carpentaria), with William Wills (1834–61). Both died on the return journey, and only one of their party survived.

Burke[6], *n.* **William** (1792–1829), Irish murderer. He and his partner **William Hare**, living in Edinburgh, dug up the dead to sell for dissection. They increased their supplies by murdering at least 15 people. Burke was hanged on the evidence of Hare. Hare is said to have died a beggar in London in the 1860s.

Burke's Peerage, *n.* popular name of the *Genealogical and Heraldic History of the Peerage, Baronetage, and Knightage of the United Kingdom*, first issued by John Burke in 1826. The most recent edition was in 1970.

burk(h)ah, *n.* the long veil or veiled, loose overgarment worn by Muslim women. [Hind.]

Burkina Faso, *n.* ('Land of Upright Men'), country in W Africa. **area** 274,122 sq km/105,811 sq miles. **capital** Ouagadougou. **towns** Bobo-Doiulasso. **physical** landlocked plateau, savannah country; headwaters of the river Volta. **population** (1988) 8,530,000; annual growth rate 2.4%. **exports** cotton, groundnuts, livestock, hides, skins. **language** French (official); about 50 native languages. **religion** animist 53%, Sunni Muslim 36%, Roman Catholic 11%.

burl[1], *n.* a knot or lump in wool or cloth; a knot in wood. *v.t.* to dress (cloth) by removing knots or lumps. **burling-comb, -iron, -machine,** *n.* contrivances for clearing wool of burls. [OF *bourle* (prob. dim. of *bourre,* from late L *burra,* a woollen pad)]

burl[2], **birl**[2], *n.* (*Sc., New Zealand, Austral., coll.*) a spin (in a motor vehicle); an attempt, a try. [prob. from BIRL[1]]

burlap, *n.* a coarse kind of canvas used for sacking, upholstering etc. [etym. doubtful (cp. Dut. *boenlap,* rubbing-clout)]

burlesque, *a.* †jocular, ludicrous; drolly or absurdly imitative; mock-serious or mock-heroic. *n.* mockery, grotesque imitation; literary or dramatic representation caricaturing other work; (*N Am.*) a form of theatrical variety show characterized by lewd humour, singing and dancing and strip-tease. *v.t.* to produce a grotesque imitation of; to travesty. **burlesquely,** *adv.* [F, from It. *burlesco* (*burla,* a trick, banter)]

burletta, *n.* a comic opera; a musical farce. [It., dim. of *burla,* see prec.]

Burlington, *n.* **Richard Boyle, 3rd Earl of** (1694–1753), British architectural patron and architect;

one of the premier exponents of Palladianism in Britain. His buildings, such as Chiswick House in London (1725–29), are characterized by absolute adherence to the Classical rules. His major protégé was William Kent.

burly, *a.* †stately, dignified, imposing; †goodly, excellent; bluff, domineering; stout, lusty, corpulent. **burliness,** *n.* [ME *burliche,* prob. from an OE *būrlīc,* suitable for a lady's BOWER]

Burma *n.* country in SE Asia (since 1989 officially called Myanma). **area** 678,000 sq km/261,789 sq miles. **capital** and chief port Rangoon. **towns** Mandalay, Karbe. **physical** over half is forested; rivers Irrawaddy and Chindwin; mountains in N, W and E. **population** 37,150,000 (1985); annual growth rate 1.9%. **exports** rice, rubber, jute, teak, jade, rubies, sapphires. **language** Burmese. **religion** Hinayan Buddhist; pagan.

Burmese, Burman, *n.* the language, people of Burma. *a.* belonging to Burma.

burn[1], *v.t.* (*past, p.p.* **burnt**, sometimes **burned**) to consume, destroy, scorch or injure by fire; to subject to the action of fire; to produce an effect (on anything) similar to the action of fire; to treat with heat for some purpose of manufacture etc.; to corrode, eat into; to combine with oxygen; to make use of the nuclear energy of uranium etc.; to cauterize. *v.i.* to be on fire; to be or become intensely hot; to emit light, to shine; to act with destructive effect; to be bright, to glow with light or colour; to glow, to rage, to be inflamed. *n.* the effect of burning; a burnt place; a firing of a space-rocket engine to obtain thrust. **to burn a hole in one's pocket,** describing money one is keen to spend immediately. **to burn away,** to consume entirely by fire. **to burn down,** to reduce to ashes. **to burn in,** to render indelible by or as by burning. **to burn off,** to remove paint by means of softening with a lamp-flame or hot iron. **to burn one's boats, bridges,** to commit oneself to something without possibility of retreat. **to burn one's fingers,** to hurt oneself by meddling. **to burn out,** to consume the inside or contents of; (*coll.*) to exhaust or render inoperative through overwork or overheating; to eradicate or expel by burning. **to burn up,** to destroy, to get rid of, by fire; to blaze, to flash into a blaze; to drive fast; **to go for the burn,** (*coll.*) to try to achieve the burning sensation in the muscles produced by strenuous exercise, to exercise hard. **burn up,** *n.* (*coll.*) a fast drive in a motor vehicle; the consumption of nuclear fuel in a reactor. **burned up,** *a.* (*N Am. sl.*) angry. **burnable,** *a.* **burner,** *n.* that part of a lamp or gas-jet from which the flame issues. **burning,** *a.* in a state of heat; ardent, glowing; vehement, exciting; flagrant. **burning bush,** *n.* the bush that burned and was not consumed (Exod. iii.2), adopted as an emblem by the Scottish Presbyterian churches in memory of the persecutions; *Dictamnus fraxinella,* various species of *Euonymus,* and other shrubs with vivid foliage, fruit etc. **burning-glass,** *n.* a convex lens used for causing intense heat by concentrating the sun's rays. **burning-mirror, -reflector,** *n.* a concave mirror, or a combination of plane-mirrors arranged to act as a burning-glass. **burning-point,** *n.* the temperature at which volatile oils ignite, FLASHPOINT. **burning question, issue** *n.* one that excites heated discussion or that demands immediate solution. **burning shame,** *n.* a flagrant shame; †a shame that causes one to blush. **burnt-ear,** *n.* a disease in grain caused by a smut or fungus, *Uredo segetum.* **burnt offering, burnt sacrifice,** *n.* an offering or sacrifice to a deity by fire, esp. one offered to God by the Jews. **burnt-sienna** SIENNA. **burnt umber** UMBER. [OE *bœrnan,* tr., and *biernan,* intr., from Teut. *brennan* (cp. G *brennan*)]

burn[2], *n.* (*chiefly Sc.*) a small stream, a brook. [OE *burna* (cp. Dut. *born,* Goth. *brunna,* G *Brunnen,* Eng. BOURN[1])]

Burne-Jones, *n.* **Edward Coley** (1833–98), British painter. Influenced by William Morris and the Pre-Raphaelite Rossetti, he was inspired by legend and myth, as in *King Cophetua and the Beggar Maid* (1880–84, Tate Gallery, London), but moved towards Symbolism. He also designed tapestries and stained glass.

burnet[1], *n.* brown-flowered plants of the genera *Poterium* and *Sanguisorba,* **burnet-fly, -moth,** *n.* a crimson-spotted, greenish-black moth, *Zygaena filipendulae.* **burnet-rose,** *n.* the Scottish wild rose. **burnet saxifrage,** *n.* a plant, *Pimpinella saxifraga,* with leaves like burnet. [OF *burnete,* BRUNETTE]

Burnet[2], *n.* **Gilbert** (1643–1715), British historian and bishop, author of *History of His Own Time* (1723–24). His Whig views having brought him into disfavour, he retired to The Hague on the accession of James II, and became the confidential adviser of William of Orange, with whom he sailed to England in 1688. He was appointed bishop of Salisbury in 1689.

Burnett, *n.* **Frances Eliza Hodgson** (1849–1924), English writer, living in the US from 1865, whose novels for children include the rags-to-riches tale *Little Lord Fauntleroy* (1886) and the sentimental *The Secret Garden* (1909).

Burney, *n.* **Frances (Fanny)** (1752–1840), English novelist and diarist, daughter of the musician Dr Charles Burney (1726–1814). She achieved success with *Evelina*, published anonymously in 1778, became a member of Dr Johnson's circle, received a post at court from Queen Charlotte, and in 1793 married the émigré General D'Arblay. She published two further novels, *Cecilia* (1782), and *Camilla* (1796), and her diaries and letters appeared in 1842.

Burnham, *n.* **Forbes** (1923–85), Guyanese Marxist-Leninist politician. He was prime minister during 1964–80, leading the country to independence in 1966 and declaring it the world's first cooperative republic 1970. He was executive president (1980–85). Resistance to the US landing in Grenada 1983 was said to be due to his forewarning the Grenadans of the attack.

burnish, *v.t.* to polish, esp. by rubbing. *v.i.* to become bright or glossy. *n.* polish, gloss, lacquer. **burnisher,** *n.* one who burnishes; tool for burnishing. [OF *burnir, brunir,* to brown, to polish]

burnous, -nouse, *n. sing.* a mantle or cloak with a hood, worn by Arabs. [F, from Arab. *burnus*]

Burns[1], *n.* **John** (1858–1943), British labour leader, sentenced to six weeks' imprisonment for his part in the Trafalgar Square demonstration on 'Bloody Sunday' 13 Nov. 1887, and leader of the strike in 1889 securing the dockers' tanner (wage of 6d per hour). An Independent Labour member of parliament 1892–1918, he was the first person from the labouring classes to be a member of the Cabinet, as president of the Local Government Board (1906–14).

Burns[2], *n.* **Robert** (1759–96), Scottish poet, notable for his use of the Scots dialect at a time when it was not considered suitably 'elevated' for literature. Burns's first volume, *Poems, Chiefly in the Scottish Dialect*, appeared in 1786. In addition to his poetry Burns wrote or adapted many songs, including 'Auld Lang Syne'.

burnt, *past, p.p.* BURN[1].

burp, *n.* a belch. *v.i.* to belch. *v.t.* to make a baby burp by massaging or patting on the back. [onomat.]

burr[1], *n.* †circle; a washer on a rivet; a nebulous disk or halo surrounding the moon; the round, knobby base of a deer's horn; a rough ridge or edge left on metal or other substance after cutting, punching etc.; the roughness made by the graver on a copper plate; a triangular hollow chisel; a clinker, a mass of semi-vitrified brick; a rough sounding of the letter *r;* a whirring noise; a burr-stone, hence a whetstone; siliceous rock occurring in bands or masses among softer formations; an electric rotary filing tool. *v.t.* to pronounce with a rough sounding of the *r. v.i.* to speak with a burr; to speak indistinctly. **burr-stone,** *n.* a coarse siliceous rock used for millstones. **burry**, *a.* characterized by burrs; rough, prickly. [etym. doubtful]

burr[2] BUR[1].

Burr[3], *n.* **Aaron** (1756–1836), US politician. He was on George Washington's staff during the War of Independence. He tied with Thomas Jefferson in the presidential election of 1800, but Alexander Hamilton influenced the House of Representatives to vote Jefferson in, Burr becoming vice-president. He killed Hamilton in a duel in 1804, became a social outcast, and had to leave the US for some years following the 'Burr conspiracy', which implicated him variously in a scheme to conquer Mexico, or part of Florida, or to rule over a seceded Louisiana.

Burr[4], *n.* **Raymond** (1917–), Canadian character actor who played Perry Mason in the television series of the same name and in several films. He played the murderer in Alfred Hitchcock's *Rear Window* (1954), and his other films include *The Adventures of Don Juan* (1948) and *Godzilla* (English-language version 1956).

burro, *n.* (*pl.* **-rros**) (*mainly N Am.*) a donkey. [Sp.]

Burroughs[1], *n.* **Edgar Rice** (1875–1950), US novelist, born in Chicago. He wrote *Tarzan of the Apes* (1914), the story of an aristocratic child lost in the jungle and reared by apes, and many other thrillers.

Burroughs[2], *n.* **William S.** (1914–), US novelist, born in St Louis, Missouri. He dropped out and, as part of the beat generation, wrote *Junkie* (1953), *The Naked Lunch* (1959), *The Soft Machine* (1961), and *Dead Fingers Talk* (1963). Later novels include *Queer* (1986).

Burroughs[3], *n.* **William Steward** (1857–98), US industrialist, who invented the first hand-operated adding machine to give printed results.

burrow, *n.* a hole in the ground made by rabbits, foxes etc., for a dwelling-place. *v.i.* to excavate a burrow for shelter or concealment; to live in a burrow; to hide oneself; to bore or excavate. *v.t.* to make by means of excavating; to nestle into; to dig deep while searching (e.g. in a pocket). **burrow-duck,** *n.* the sheldrake, *Anas tadorna*. **burrower,** *n.* **burrowing-owl,** *n.* an American owl, *Noctua cunicularia*. **burrows-town,** *n.* borough town, a town which is a borough. *a.* townish. [prob. var. of BOROUGH]

bursa[1], *n.* (*pl.* **-sas, -sae**) a synovial sac found among tendons in the body and serving to reduce friction. **bursal,** *a.* **bursar** *n.* a treasurer, esp. of a college; one who holds a bursary. **bursarial,** *a.* **bursarship,** *n.* **bursary,** *n.* the treasury of a college or a monastery; an exhibition in a Scottish university; a scholarship. **burse,** *n.* †a purse; †an exchange or bourse; an exhibition, a bursary or the fund for maintaining such; a receptacle for the cloth used to cover the sacred Elements. **bursiculate,** *a.* **bursiform,** *a.* **bursitis,** *n.* inflammation of a bursa. [med. L, bag, purse, from Gr. *bursa,* wine-skin]

Bursa[2], *n.* city in NW Turkey, with a port at Mudania; population (1985) 614,000. It was the capital of the Ottoman Empire (1326–1423).

burst, *v.t.* (*past, p.p.* **burst**) to break, split or rend asunder with suddenness and violence. *v.i.* to be broken suddenly from within; to fly open; to issue or rush forth with suddenness and energy or force. *n.* a sudden and violent breaking forth; a sudden explosion; an outbreak; a spurt, a vigorous fit of activity; a drinking-bout, a spree; a volley of bullets. **to burst in,** to enter suddenly; to interrupt. **to burst out,** to break out; to exclaim. **burst up, bust up,** *v.i.* (*coll.*) to go bankrupt; to collapse; *n.* a collapse; a quarrel. **burster,** *n.* one who goes bankrupt or collapses. **bursting at the seams,** being too full for comfort. [OE *berstan,* OTeut. *brestan* (cp. Dut. *bersten*. MHG *bresten,* G *bersten*)]

Burt, *n.* **Cyril Lodowic** (1883–1971), British psychologist. A specialist in child and mental development, he argued in *The Young Delinquent* (1925) the importance of social and environmental factors in delinquency. After his death it was discovered that he falsified some of his experimental results in an attempt to prove his theory that intelligence is largely inherited.

burthen BURDEN.

Burton[1], *n.* a kind of beer. **gone for a burton,** (*orig. Aviat. sl.*) dead; absent, missing. [Burton-on-Trent]

burton[2], **barton,** *n.* a small tackle consisting of two or three pulleys. [etym. doubtful]

Burton[3], *n.* **Richard Francis** (1821–90), British traveller, master of 35 oriental languages, and translator of the *Arabian Nights* (1885–88). In 1853 he made the pilgrimage to Mecca in disguise; in 1856 he was commissioned by the Foreign Office to explore the sources of the Nile, and (with Speke) reached Lake Tanganyika in 1858.

Burton[4], *n.* **Richard** (stage name of Richard Jenkins) (1925–84), Welsh actor. He was remarkable for his voice, as in the radio adaptation of Dylan Thomas's *Under Milk Wood*, and for his marital and acting partnership with Elizabeth Taylor, with whom he appeared in the films *Cleopatra* (1962) and *Who's Afraid of Virginia Woolf?* (1966). His later works include *Equus* (1977) and *1984* (1984).

Burton[5], *n.* **Robert** (1577–1640), English philosopher, who wrote an analysis of depression, *Anatomy of Melancholy* (1621), a compendium of information on the medical and religious opinions of the time, much used by later authors. Born in Leicester, he was educated at Oxford, and remained there for the rest of his life as a fellow of Christ Church.

Burundi, *n.* Republic of (*Republika y'Uburundi*), a country in E central Africa. **area** 27,834 sq km/10,744 sq miles. **capital** Bujumbura. **towns** Kitega. **physical** grassy highland. **population** (1988) 5,130,000 (of whom 15% are the Nilotic Tutsi, still holding most of the land and political power, and the remainder the Bantu Hutu); annual growth rate 2.8%. **exports** coffee, cotton, tea, nickel, hides, livestock; there are also 500 million tonnes of peat reserves in the basin of the Akanyaru river. **language** Kirundi (a Bantu language) and French (official); Kiswahili. **religion** Roman Catholic over 50%, with a Sunni Muslim minority.

bury, *v.t.* to place (a corpse) under ground, to inter, to consign to the grave (whether earth or sea); to perform funeral rites for; to put under ground; to consign to obscurity, oblivion etc.; to hide, to cover up, to embed; (*used only in p.p.*) to occupy deeply, engross, absorb. **to bury the hatchet,** to forget and forgive, to effect a reconciliation (in allusion to an American Indian custom of burying a tomahawk when peace was concluded). **burying,** *n.* burial. **burying-ground, -place,** *n.* BURIAL-GROUND under BURIAL. [OE *byrgan* (cp. BURIAL)]

bus., (*abbr.*) business.

bus, 'bus, *n.* (*pl.* **buses**) an omnibus; (*sl.*) an aeroplane, car etc; a series of conductors in a computer which carry information or power. *v.i.* to go by omnibus. *v.t.* to transport by bus. **to miss the bus,** (*coll.*) to miss an opportunity, to be too late. **busbar,** *n.* in an electric system, a conductor or series of conductors connecting several circuits; in computers, a bus. **busboy, girl,** *n.* (*N Am.*) a restaurant employee who assists the waiters or waitresses. **bus fare,** *n.* the payment for a bus journey made by a passenger. **bus lane,** *n.* a traffic lane restricted to the use of buses (i.e. the lane closest to the verge or pavement). **busman,** *n.* the conductor or driver of an omnibus. **busman's holiday,** *n.* (*coll.*) holiday spent doing one's everyday work. **bus shelter,** *n.* a shelter erected at a bus stop to protect waiting passengers against the weather. **bus stop,** *n.* a place marked by a sign at which buses stop to pick up or let off passengers. **busing, bussing,** *n. sing.* (*N Am.*) the practice of transporting children by bus to schools outside their areas to achieve evenly balanced racial numbers in classrooms.

busby, *n.* †a kind of large bushy wig; the tall fur cap worn by hussars; a bearskin hat worn by the Guards. [etym. doubtful]

bush[1], *n.* a thick shrub; a clump of shrubs; a thicket; a bunch of ivy used as a tavern-sign; uncleared land, more or less covered with wood, esp. in Australasia; anything resembling a bush; the hinterland, the interior, the wild; a thick growth of hair; †a fox's tail. †the sign of a tavern. *v.t.* to set with bushes in order to prevent poaching; to cover in (seed) with a bush-harrow. *v.i.* to grow bushy. **to beat about the bush,** to take circuitous methods. **to take to the bush,** to take refuge in the back-woods; to become a bushranger. **bush-baby,** *n.* a small nocturnal African primate, *Galago maholi;* a lemur, a galago. **bushbuck,** *n.* a small bush-dwelling African antelope. **bush-cat,** *n.* the servil. **bush craft,** *n.* a working knowledge of the ways of the bush. **bush fire,** *n.* a usu. fast spreading fire in the bush. **bush-harrow,** *n.* a harrow with bushes interwoven in the bars. **bush hawk,** *n.* a predatory bird of New Zealand belonging to the hawk family. **bush jacket, shirt,** *n.* a belted upper garment of a lightweight material equipped with large pockets. **bush-lawyer,** *n.* (*Austral.*) an irregular legal practitioner. **bushman** *n.* one who lives in the Australian bush; (**Bushman**) *n.* a member of a disappearing nomadic tribe in S Africa. **bushmanship,** *n.* **bushmaster** *n.* a large and poisonous rattlesnake in S America. **bushranger,** *n.* one who has taken to the Australian bush and lives by robbing travellers etc. **bush-rope,** a wild, vine-like plant in tropical forests. **bush-telegraph,** *n.* the rapid dissemination of rumours, information etc. **bushveld, bos(ch)veld,** *n.* wooded S African grasslands. **bushwhacker,** *n.* (*N Am.*) a backwoodsman; a bush-fighter; an implement for cutting brushwood; an (*Austral.*) inhabitant of the outback, a country bumpkin. **bushwhacking,** *n.* clearing a way in the bush; ambushing; living in the manner of a bushwhacker. **bushed,** *a.* (*Austral.*) lost in the bush; (*sl.*) confused; (*sl.*) exhausted. **bushiness,** *n.* **bushy,** *a.* abounding with bushes; shrubby, thick; growing like a bush. [ME *bush, busk,* Icel. *buskr* (cp. Dan. *busk,* OHG *Busc,* G *Busch*) late L *boscus*]

bush², **bushing** *n.* the metal lining of an axle-hole or similar orifice. *v.t.* to furnish with a bush; to line with metal. **bush-metal,** *n.* an alloy of copper and tin used for bearings etc; gunmetal. [prob. from MDut. *busse* (Dut. *bus*), late L *buxis,* a box (cp. BOX²)]

Bush, *n.* **George** (1924–), US Republican president from 1989. He was director of the Central Intelligence Agency (CIA) during 1976–81 and US vice president (1981–89). Evidence came to light in 1987 linking him with the Irangate scandal. His responses as president to the Soviet leader Gorbachev's diplomatic initiatives were criticized as inadequate but sending US troops to depose his former ally, General Noriega of Panama, proved a popular move at home.

bushel¹, *n.* a dry measure of 8 gal. (36·37 litres). **to hide one's light under a bushel,** to conceal one's skills or talents. **bushelful,** *n.* [OF *boissel* (F *boisseau*), late L *boisselus, buscellus,* dim. of *busta* (*buxida, buxis,* BOX)]

bushel², *v.t.* to mend or alter. *v.i.* to mend or alter clothes. **busheller, bushelman, bushelwoman,** *n.* [N Am. (cp. G *bosseln*)]

bushido, *n.* the code of honour of the Japanese Samurai. [Jap.]

busily, *adv.* BUSY.

business, *n.* †the state of being busy; employment, occupation, trade, profession; serious occupation, work; duty, concern, province; commercial, industrial or professional affairs; commercial activity; buying and selling, bargaining; a particular matter demanding attention; a commercial establishment; a shop, with stock, fixtures etc.; (*Theat.*) action, as distinct from speech; (*coll.*) an affair, a matter, a concern, a contrivance. **like nobody's business,** vigorously; zealously. **man of business,** a business man, an agent, an attorney. **to mean business,** to be in earnest. **to mind one's own business,** to attend to one's own affairs; to refrain from meddling. **to send someone about his/her business,** to send someone off brusquely or summarily. **business card,** *n.* a card printed with a company's name, address and phone number, and the identity of the employee or executive who carries it. **business end,** *n.* the point (of a tool or weapon). **business hours,** *n.* fixed hours of work or for transaction of business in a shop, office etc. (esp. 9 am to 5 pm). **businessman, -woman,** *n.* one who deals with matters of commerce etc. **business studies,** *n. pl.* a college or university course comprising courses relating to business. **business suit,** *n.* a lounge suit. **businesslike,** *a.* suitable for or befitting business; methodical, practical; prompt, punctual; energetic. [OE *bisigness* (BUSY, -NESS)]

busk¹, *n.* a stiffening bone or plate in a corset; a corset. **busked,** *a.* [MF *busque* (F *busc*), etym. doubtful]

busk², *v.i.* to perform in the street or in a public place, esp. beside a queue in order to collect money. **busker,** *n.* an itinerant singer or actor, a street performer. [prob. Sp. *buscar,* to seek]

buskin, *n.* a kind of high-boot reaching to the calf or knee; the thick-soled boot worn by actors in Athenian tragedy; the tragic vein; tragedy. **buskined,** *a.* wearing buskins; tragic, lofty, sublime. [cp. Sp. *borcegui,* It. *borzacchino,* F *brodequin,* OF *bousequin* (etym. doubtful)]

Busoni, *n.* **Ferruccio (Dante Benvenuto)** (1866–1924), Italian pianist, composer, and music critic. Much of his music was for the piano, but he also composed several operas including *Doktor Faust*, completed by a pupil after his death.

†**buss¹**, *n.* a loud kiss. *v.t.* to kiss. [onomat. (ME *bass,* cp. F *baiser,* L *bāsiāre,* to kiss, from *bāsium,* a kiss)]

buss², *n.* a herring-boat with two or three masts. [OF *busse* (cp. Dut. *buis,* med. L *bussa,* MHG *Buze,* G *Büse*)]

bust¹, *n.* a sculptured representation of the head, shoulders and breast of a person; the upper front part of the body, the breast, the bosom, esp. of a woman. **busted,** *a.* having breasts. **busty,** *a.* (*coll.*) having ample breasts. [F *buste,* It. *busto,* late L *bustum,* etym. unknown]

bust², *v.i.* (*coll.*) to break or burst. *v.t.* (*sl.*) to raid or arrest, esp for a drug offence. *n.* (*sl.*) a drinking spree. **a bust up,** a quarrel. **to go bust,** to go bankrupt. **buster,** *n.* something big, something astonishing; a spree; a dashing fellow; (*Austral.*) a gale; (*coll., sometimes derog.*) a form of address to a boy or man; (*sl.*) something or person that breaks or destroys. [dial., var. of BURST]

Bustamante, *n.* **(William) Alexander** (born Clarke) (1884–1977), Jamaican socialist politician. As leader of the Labour Party, he was the first prime minister of independent Jamaica (1962–67).

bustard, *n.* a large bird allied to the plovers and the cranes, belonging to the genus *Otis;* the great bustard, *O. tarda,* was formerly indigenous to Britain. [prob. from OF *bistarde,* confused with *oustarde,* both derivations from L *avis tarda,* slow bird (*a. slow,* perh. due to perversion of Gr. *ōtis*)]

bustle¹, *n.* activity with noise and excitement; stir, agitation, fuss. *v.i.* to be active, esp. with excessive fuss and noise; to make a show of activity. *v.t.* to hurry; to hustle, to cause to move quickly or work hard. **bustler,** *n.* [prob. onomat., or var. of *buskle,* from BUSK¹]

bustle², *n.* a pad, cushion or framework, worn under a woman's dress to expand the skirts behind. [etym. doubtful; perh. from prec.]

busy, *a.* fully occupied; actively employed; closely engaged, diligent; characterized by activity, unresting, always at work; fussy, officious, meddlesome. *v.i.* to occupy oneself (about, in etc.). *v.t.* †to make or keep busy. *n.* (*sl.*) a detective. **busy Lizzie,** *n.* a popular flowering house plant belonging to the genus *Impatiens.* **busybody,** *n.* an officious person; a meddler; a mischief-maker. **busily,** *adv.* **busyness,** *n.* the state of being busy. [OE *bysig* (*bisgian,* to occupy, to worry)]

but, *prep.* except, barring; (*Sc.*) apart from, outside of; *conj.* yet still; notwithstanding which; except that; otherwise than, not that; on the contrary, nevertheless, however. *n.* a verbal objection; (*Sc.*) an outer room. *adv.* only; (*Sc.*) outwards. *v.t.* to make a verbal objection. **a but and ben,** (*Sc.*) a two-roomed cottage BEN. **all but,** almost, very nearly. **but and ben,** (*Sc.*) out and in. **but for, that,** were it not for, not that. **but me**

no buts, bring forward no objections. [OE *būtan, būte* (BE-, *utan,* OUT), outside, beyond, except]

butadiene, *n.* the gas used in making synthetic rubber. [L *butyrum,* butter]

butane, *n.* an inflammable gaseous compound; a hydrocarbon of the paraffin series found in petroleum.

butch, *a.* (*sl.*) masculine in manner or appearance; *n.* (*derog. sl.*) a lesbian with masculine manners or appearance; the more dominant or masculine partner in a lesbian relationship; a tough, aggressive man. [prob. a contr. of BUTCHER]

butcher, *n.* one whose trade it is to slaughter domestic animals for food; one who sells the flesh of such animals; one who delights in killing; a salmon-fly. (*pl., rhyming sl.*) a look (from butcher's hook). *v.t.* to slaughter animals for food; to put to death in a wanton or sanguinary fashion; to spoil by bad playing, acting, reading, editing etc.; to criticize savagely. **butcher-bird,** *n.* a shrike. **butcher's knife,** *n.* a carving-knife. **butcher's-broom,** *n.* a prickly, evergreen British shrub, the knee-holly. **butcher('s) meat,** *n.* the flesh of animals killed for food, sold fresh by butchers. **butcherly,** *adv.* **butchery,** *n.* the business of a butcher; a slaugher-house; cruel and remorseless slaughter, carnage. [OF *bochier,* orig. a purveyor of goat's flesh (F *bouchier*), *boc,* a he-goat]

Bute, *n.* **John Stuart, 3rd Earl of Bute** (1713–92), British Tory politician, prime minister (1762–63). On the accession of George III in 1760, he became the chief instrument in the king's policy for breaking the power of the Whigs and establishing the personal rule of the monarch through Parliament.

butene, BUTYLENE under BUTYL.

Buthelezi, *n.* **Chief Gatsha** (1928–), Zulu leader and politician, chief minister of KwaZulu, a black 'homeland' in the Republic of South Africa from 1970. He is founder and president of **Inkatha** (1975), a paramilitary organization for attaining a nonracial democratic political system.

butler¹, *n.* a servant in charge of the wine, plate etc.; a head servant. **butlership,** *n.* **butlery,** *n.* a butler's pantry; a buttery. [OE *butuiller,* (OF *bouteillier*), med. L *buticulārius,* from *buticula,* BOTTLE¹]

Butler², *n.* **Joseph** (1692–1752), British priest, who became dean of St Paul's in 1740 and bishop of Durham in 1750; his *Analogy of Religion* (1736) argued that it is no more rational to accept deism, arguing for God as the first cause, than revealed religion (not arrived at by reasoning).

Butler³, *n.* **Josephine** (born Gray) (1828–1906), British social reformer. She promoted women's education and the Married Women's Property Act, and campaigned against the Contagious Diseases Acts of 1862–70, which made women in garrison towns liable to compulsory examination for venereal disease. As a result of her campaigns the acts were repealed in 1883.

Butler⁴, *n.* **Richard Austen, Baron Butler** (1902–82), British Conservative politician, known from his initials as Rab. As minister of education (1941–45), he was responsible for the Education Act 1944; he was chancellor of the Exchequer (1951–55), Lord Privy Seal (1955–59), and foreign minister (1963–64). As a candidate for the premiership, he was defeated by Harold Macmillan in 1957 (under whom he was home secretary, 1957–62), and by Douglas-Home in 1963. He was master of Trinity College, Cambridge, during 1965–78.

Butler⁵, *n.* **Samuel** (1612–80), English satirist. His poem *Hudibras*, published in three parts in 1663, 1664 and 1678, became immediately popular for its biting satire against the Puritans.

Butler⁶, *n.* **Samuel** (1835–1902), English author, who made his name in 1872 with his satiric attack on contemporary utopianism, *Erewhon* ('nowhere' reversed), but is now remembered for his autobiographical *The Way of All Flesh,* written 1872–85 but not published until 1903.

Butlin, *n.* **William 'Billy'** (1899–1980), British holiday-camp entrepreneur. Born in South Africa, he went in early life to Canada, but later entered the fair business in the UK. He originated a chain of camps that provide accommodation, meals, and amusements at an inclusive price.

butment, ABUTMENT.

butt¹, *n.* the hinder, larger or blunter end of anything, esp. of a tool, weapon and the like; the stout part of tanned ox-hides; the square end of a piece of timber coming against another piece; the joint so formed; the bole of a tree; the base of a leaf-stalk. *v.i.* to abut, to meet with the end against (of timber, planks etc.); to meet end to end. **butt-end,** *n.* the thick and heavy end; the remnant. **butt-hinge,** *n.* a kind of hinge screwed to the edge of the door and the abutting edge of the casing. **butt-joint,** *n.* a joint in which the pieces come square against each other. **butt-weld,** *n.* a weld formed by forcing together flat iron or steel bars. [prob. Eng. (cp. Icel. *buttr,* short, *būtr,* a log, Dan. *but,* Swed. *butt,* Dut. *bot,* stumpy)]

butt², *n.* a large cask; a measure of 126 gall. (572·8 litres) of wine, or 108 gall. (490·98 litres) of beer. [OF *boute* (F *botte*), late L *butis, buttis,* a cask]

butt³, *n.* a goal; a target, a mark for shooting; hence the mound behind targets, the shelter for the marker, and (*pl.*) the distance between the targets, the shooting-range; aim, object; a target for ridicule, criticism or abuse. [F *but,* a goal]

butt⁴, *v.i.* to strike, thrust or push with the head or as with the head; *v.t.* to strike or drive away with or as with the head or horns. **to butt in,** to interfere, interrupt. **butter¹,** *n.* an animal which butts. [OF *boter* (F *bouter*), to push, thrust; senses modified by BUTT¹ in verbal sense and by ABUT]

butte, *n.* (*N Am.*) an abrupt, isolated hill or peak. [prob. from F *butte,* OF *bute,* fem. form of *but,* see BUTT³]

butter¹ BUTT⁴.

butter², *n.* the fatty portion of milk or cream solidified by churning; applied also to various substances of the consistency or appearance of butter; gross flattery. *v.t.* to spread or cook with butter; to flatter grossly. **to butter up,** (*coll.*) to flatter. **butter bean,** *n.* a variety of lima bean. **butter-bird,** *n.* a Jamaican name for the bobolink. **butter-boat,** *n.* a vessel for sauce. **butter-bur, -dock,** *n.* the sweet coltsfoot. **buttercup,** *n.* popular name for the genus *Ranunculus,* esp. those species with yellow cup-shaped flowers. **butterfat,** *n.* the fat in milk from which butter is made. **butter-fingered,** *a.* apt to let things fall, as if the hands were greasy. **butter-fingers,** *n.sing.* one who is butter-fingered. **butterfly,** *n.* (*pl.* **-flies**) an insect with erect wings and knobbed antennae belonging to the diurnal Lepidoptera; a showily dressed, vain, giddy or fickle person; a swimming stroke performed on the front and characterized by simultaneous wide, upward strokes of the arms. (*pl., coll.*) nervous tremors. [OE *buttorfleoge*] **butterflies in the stomach,** (*coll.*) nervous tremors in the stomach. **butterfly-nut, -screw,** *n.* a screw with a thumb-piece, a wing nut. **buttermilk,** *n.* that part of the milk which remains when the butter is extracted. **butter-muslin,** *n.* a fine loosely woven, cotton material used for protecting food from insects. **butter-nut,** *n.* the N American white walnut-tree, *Juglans cinerea,* and its fruit; the S American genus *Caryocar.* **butter-print, butter-stamp,** *n.* a piece of carved wood to mark butter. **butter-scotch,** *n.* a kind of toffee. **butter-tree,** *n.* E Indian and African trees, *Bassia butyracea,* and *B. parkii,* which yield a sweet buttery substance. **butter-wife, butter-woman,** *n.* a woman who sells butter. **butterwort,** *n.* a British bog-plant belonging to the genus *Pinguicula.* **buttered,** *a.* **butteriness, buttery¹,** *a.* having the qualities or appearance of butter. [OE *butere,* L *būtyrum,* Gr. *bouturon* (*bous,* an ox, *turos,* cheese)]

butterbump, *n.* another name for the bittern. [earlier *bitterbump,* from *bittern*]

buttercup BUTTER.

Butterfield, *n.* **William** (1814–1900), English architect. His work is Gothic Revival characterized by vigorous, aggressive forms and multicoloured striped and patterned brickwork, as in the church of All Saints, Margaret Street, London, and Keble College, Oxford.

buttery[1] BUTTER[2].

buttery[2], *n.* a room in which liquor and provisions are kept; the room in which ale, bread, butter etc. are kept; esp. in a university. **buttery-hatch,** *n.* the half-door over which provisions are served out from the buttery. [OF *boterie, bouterillerie;* see BOTTLE]

buttock, *n., usu. in pl.,* one of the protuberant parts of the rump, the posteriors; a manoeuvre in wrestling. *v.t.* in wrestling, to throw by means of the buttock or hip. **buttock-mail,** *n.* a fine imposed in the Church for the sin of fornication. [BUTT[1], -OCK]

button, *n.* a knob or disk used for fastening or ornamenting garments; a small bud; a small handle, knob, fastener, catch etc. for securing doors, actuating electrical apparatus etc.; the knob on a foil. *a.* of mushrooms, blooms etc., having a small round shape. *v.t.* to fasten or furnish with buttons; to secure by means of buttons or a buttoned garment. *v.i.* to fasten up the clothes with buttons. **not to care a button,** to be quite indifferent about something. **not worth a button,** of no value. **the button,** a button which, when pushed, puts the apparatus for nuclear war into operation. **to button up,** to arrange, to settle satisfactorily; to keep silent; to silence. **buttonhole,** *n.* a hole, slit or loop to admit a button; a small bouquet for the buttonhole of a coat. *v.t.* to hold by the buttonhole; to detain in conversation; to make buttonholes. **buttonholer,** *n.* (*coll.*) one who detains in conversation. **buttonhook,** *n.* a hook for drawing buttons through buttonholes. **button-mould,** *n.* a disk of metal or other substance to be covered with cloth, so as to form a button. **button-through,** *a.* of a garment, having button fastenings from top to bottom. **buttoned,** *a.* **buttonless,** *a.* **buttonlessness,** *n.* **buttons,** *n.sing.* (*coll.*) a page in buttoned livery. **buttony,** *a.* like a button; having many buttons. [OF *boton* (F *bouton*), perh. from late L *botto -ōnem,* from *bottare* or *buttare,* to thrust, sprout]

buttress, *n.* a structure built against a wall to strengthen it; a prop, support; a spur or supporting ridge of a hill. *v.t.* to support by or as by a buttress. [prob. from OF *bouterez,* pl. of *bouteret,* a prop (*bouter,* to push against)]

butty[1], *n.* (*dial.*) a partner, companion, a mate; a middleman in the mining districts. **butty-gang,** *n.* a body of workmen who undertake a job and are paid in a lump sum. **butty-system,** *n.* the letting of work to a body of men who divide the proceeds. [etym. doubtful; perh. a corr. of BOOTY]

butty[2], *n.* (*dial.*) a sandwich, a snack. [from BUTTERY[1] or BUTTERED under BUTTER]

butyl, *n.* any of four isomeric forms of the chemical group C_4H_9. **butylene,** *n.* a colourless gas, formula C_4H_8.

butyraceous, *a.* of the nature or consistency of butter. **butyrate**, *n.* a salt of butyric acid. **butyric**, *a.* of or pertaining to butter. **butyric acid,** *n.* a colourless acid occurring in butter and other fats. **butyrine**, *n.* an oily liquid, obtained by the action of butyric acid on glycerine. **butyro-**, *comb. form.* **butyro-acetic**, *a.* applied to a combination of butyric and acetic acid. [L *būtyrum*]

buxom, *a.* †obedient, submissive; †pliant, flexible; blithe, jolly, full of health and spirits; plump and comely (of women). **buxomly,** *adv.* **buxomness,** *n.* [ME *buhsum,* from OE *būgan,* to bow, to bend]

Buxtehude, *n.* **Diderik** (1637–1707), Danish composer and organist at Lübeck, Germany, who influenced Bach and Handel. He is remembered for his organ works and cantatas, written for his evening concerts or *Abendmusiken*.

buy, *v.t.* (*past, p.p.* **bought**,) to purchase; to procure by means of money or something paid as a price; to gain by bribery; to redeem; (*sl.*) to believe. **a good buy,** (*coll.*) a bargain, a good thing to have bought. **to buy in,** to buy back for the owner (at an auction); to obtain a stock of anything by purchase; (*Stock Exch.*) to purchase stock and charge the extra cost to the person who had undertaken to deliver it. **to buy into,** to purchase a share of or interest in (e.g. a company). **to buy off,** to pay a price for release or non-opposition; to get rid of by a payment. **to buy out,** to purchase the release of a member of the forces from service; to buy a majority share in or complete control over (e.g. a property, a company), thereby dispossessing the original owner(s); to buy off; †to redeem. *n.* **buy-out**. **to buy over,** to gain over by a bribe. **to buy up,** to purchase all the available stock of. **buyable,** *a.* **buyer,** *n.* one who buys; esp. one who buys stock for a mercantile house. **buyer's market,** *n.* one favourable to buyers, i.e. when supply exceeds demand. [OE *bycgan* (cp. Goth. *bugjan,* OS *buggean*)]

buzz[1], *n.* a sibilant hum, like that of a bee; a confused, mingled noise; stir, bustle, movement; report, rumour; a telephone call; a euphoric feeling, a boost. *v.i.* to make a noise like humming or whirring; to whisper, to circulate a rumour; to signal by electric buzzer. *v.t.* to tell in a low whisper; to spread abroad secretly; (*Aviat.*) to interfere with by flying very near to. to make a telphone call to; to telegraph morse code; (*sl.*) to throw with some violence. **to buzz about,** to hover or bustle about in an annoying manner. **buzz-bomb,** *n.* a flying bomb. **buzz off,** *int.* go away! **buzz-saw,** *n.* a circular saw. **buzzword,** *n.* a vogue word adopted from the jargon of a particular subject or discipline. **buzzer,** *n.* a buzzing insect; a whisper; a steam or electric apparatus for making a loud humming noise; an electric warning apparatus that makes a buzzing sound; a morse transmitter. **buzzing,** *a.* **buzzingly,** *adv.* [onomat.]

buzz[2], *n.* a bur; a fuzzy seed-vessel; a fuzzy beetle, *Rhizotrogus solstitialis;* an angler's fly made in imitation of this. [prob. onomat.]

buzzard[1], *n.* any large nocturnal insect; a stupid blunderer. [BUZZ[1], -ARD]

buzzard[2], *n.* a kind of falcon, esp. *Buteo vulgaris;* a block-head, a dunce. †*a.* stupid, ignorant. [OF *busard,* L *buteo*]

BVM., (*abbr.*) *Beata Virgo Maria,* Blessed Virgin Mary. [L]

bwana, *n.* sir, master. [Swahili, from Arab. *abūna,* our father]

BWR, (*abbr.*) Boiling Water Reactor.

by, *prep.* near, at, in the neighbourhood of, beside, along, through, via; with, through (as author, maker, means, cause); according to, by direction, authority or example of; in the ratio of; to the amount of; during, not later than, as soon as; concerning, with regard to; sired by. *adv.* near at hand; in the same place; aside, in reserve; past. *a.* side, subordinate, secondary, of minor importance; private, secret, clandestine, sly. *n.* BYE. **by and by,** soon, presently; later on; the future; time to come. **by and large,** on the whole. **by oneself,** alone, without help; of one's own initiative. **by the by(e), by the way,** casually, apart from the main subject. **to abide by,** be faithful to; to observe. **to come by,** to obtain. **to do by,** to behave towards. **to set store by,** to value. **to stand by,** to aid, to support; to do nothing; to be ready to act. **by-bidder,** *n.* one who bids at an auction with the view of running up the price. **by-blow,** *n.* a side-blow; a bastard. **by-business,** *n.* a secondary business. **by-election,** *n.* an election caused by the death or resignation of a member. **by-end,** *n.* private interest. **bygone,** *a.* past. *n.* a past event; (*pl.*) the past; past injuries. **let bygones be bygones,** let us think no more of past injuries. **by-lane,** *n.* a lane leading off the main road. **bylaw** BYLAW. **byline,** *n.* a sideline; the name of the author of a newspaper or magazine article printed beside it. **bypass,** *n.* a pipe passing round a tap or valve, so as to leave a gas-burner etc. alight; a road for the purpose of diverting traffic from crowded areas; a cutting-out of undesirable radio frequencies. *v.t.* to avoid, evade; to go around; to cause to use a bypass; to supply a bypass. **by-pass surgery,** *n.* an operation performed to by-pass blocked or damaged arteries as a cure for certain heart conditions. **by-path,** *n.* a private or unfrequented path. **by-play,** *n.*

action carried on aside while the main action is proceeding. **by-product,** *n.* a secondary product. **by-purpose,** *n.* an incidental purpose, esp. in manufacture. **byroad,** *n.* a road little frequented. **bystander,** *n.* one standing near; an onlooker, an eyewitness. **bystreet,** *n.* an out-of-the-way or little frequented street. **byway,** *n.* a bypath; a secret or obscure way; a short cut; an out-of-the-way side of a subject. **byword,** *n.* a common saying; a proverb; an object of general contempt; a nickname. **bywork,** *n.* work done apart from one's regular occupation. [OE *be, bi* (cp. OHG Bī, *pī,* G *bei,* Goth. *bi,* L *ambi,* Gr. *amphi*)]

Byblos, *n.* ancient Phoenician city (modern Jebeil), 32 km/20 miles N of Beirut, Lebanon. Known to the Assyrians and Babylonians as Gubla. It had a thriving export of cedar and pinewood to Egypt as early as 1500 BC. In Roman times called Byblos, it boasted an amphitheatre, baths, and a temple dedicated to an unknown male god, and was noted for its celebration of the resurrection of Adonis, worshipped as a god of vegetation.

bye¹, *n.* a subsidiary object; something of an incidental or secondary kind; in cricket, a run scored when the ball passes the batsman and wicket-keeper; in golf, holes left over after end of contest and played as a new game; a goal at lacrosse; an individual left without a competitor when the rest have been drawn in pairs; an odd man, the case of being odd man; an event not in the list of sports. [BY]

bye², bye-bye, *int.* (*coll.*) good-bye.

bye-byes, *n.* a childish word for sleep, bedtime, bed.

Byelorussia, *n.* (Russian **Belaruskaya** or 'White Russia') constituent republic of western USSR since 1919. **area** 207,600 sq km/80,154 sq miles. **capital** Minsk. **population** (1987) 10,078,000; 79% Byelorussian, 12% Russian, 4% Polish, 2% Ukrainian, 1% Jewish. **products** peat, agricultural machinery, fertilizers, glass, textiles, leather, salt, electrical goods, meat, dairy produce.

bylaw, byelaw *n.* a private statute made by the members of a corporation or local authority; rules adopted by an incorporated or other society. [formerly *birlaw, burlaw,* from Icel. *baer, byr,* village (cp. *baejar-lög,* a town-law, Dan. *bylov,* municipal law)]

Byng, *n.* **John** (1704–1757), British admiral. Byng failed in the attempt to relieve Fort St Philip when in 1756 the island of Minorca was invaded by France. He was court-martialled and shot. As the French writer Voltaire commented, it was done 'to encourage the others'.

Byrd¹, *n.* **Richard Evelyn** (1888–1957), US aviator and explorer. The first to fly over the North Pole (1926), he also flew over the South Pole (1929), and led five overland expeditions in Antarctica.

Byrd², *n.* **William** (1543–1623), British composer. His church choral music (set to Latin words, as he was a firm Catholic) represents his most important work. He also composed secular vocal and instrumental music.

Byrds, the, a US pioneering folk-rock group (1964–73). Remembered for their 12-string guitar sound and the hits 'Mr Tambourine Man', 1965 (a version of Bob Dylan's song) and 'Eight Miles High' (1966), they moved towards country rock in the late 1960s.

byre, *n.* a cow-house. [OE *byre,* a hut; prob. var. of *būr,* BOWER]

†**byrlaw,** *n.* (*Sc.*) the local custom or popular jurisprudence of a village, township or district, dealing with minor matters of dispute without reference to the law courts. **byrlaw-court, -man,** *n.* [BYLAW]

Byron, *n.* **George Gordon, 6th Baron Byron** (1788–1824), English poet, who became the symbol of Romanticism and political liberalism throughout Europe in the 19th century. His reputation was established with the first two cantos of *Childe Harold* (1812). Later works include *The Prisoner of Chillon* (1816), *Beppo* (1818), *Mazeppa* (1819), and, most notably, *Don Juan* (1819–24). He left England in 1816, spending most of his later life in Italy. **Byronic,** *a.* like Lord Byron or his poetry; theatrical, moody; affecting volcanic passion, gloom or remorse. **Byronically,** *adv.* **Byronism,** *n.*

byssus, *n.* a textile fabric of various substances; the fine linen of the Scriptures; the tuft of fibres by which molluscs of the genus *Pinna* attach themselves to other bodies; the thread-like stipe of some fungi. **byssaceous, bussoid,** *a.* consisting of fine threads. **byssal,** *a.* referring to a mollosc's byssus. **byssiferous,** *a.* producing a byssus. **byssine,** *a.* made of fine flax; like byssus. **byssinosis,** *n.* a lung disease contracted by cotton workers. [L, from Gr. *bussos,* a fine flax]

byte, *n.* in a computer, a series of usu. eight binary digits treated as a unit.

byzant, BEZANT.

Byzantine , *a.* of or pertaining to Byzantium or Istanbul (formerly Constantinople); hierarchical, inflexible; convoluted, complex; belonging to the style of architecture developed in the Eastern Empire, characterized by the round arch, the circle, the dome and ornamentation in mosaic. *n.* an inhabitant of Byzantium; a bezant. **Byzantine Church,** *n.* the Greek or E Church. **Byzantine Empire,** *n.* the E or Greek Empire (AD 395–1453). **Byzantinesque,** *a.* **Byzantinism,** *n.* **Byzantinist,** *n.* a specialist in Byzantine history, arts etc. [L *Byzantīnus*]

Byzantine style, *n.* a style in the visual arts and architecture, which originated in Byzantium (4th–5th centuries) and spread to Italy, throughout the Balkans, and to Russia, where it survived for many centuries. It is characterized by heavy stylization, strong linear emphasis, the use of rigid artistic stereotypes, and rich colours, particularly gold. Byzantine artists excelled in mosaic work and manuscript painting. In architecture the dome supported on pendentives was widely used.

Byzantium, *n.* ancient Greek city on the Bosporus (modern Istanbul), founded as a colony of the Greek city of Megara, near Corinth about 660 BC. In AD 330 the capital of the Roman Empire was transferred there by Constantine the Great, who renamed it Constantinople.

bz., bz, (*abbr.*) benzene.

C

C[1], **c**[1], the third letter and the second consonant of the English alphabet, is borrowed in shape from the Latin. Before *a, o, u, l* and *r* it is sounded like guttural mute *k*, and before *e, i* and *y* like the soft sibilant *s* (when it has this sound before other letters it is marked ç). C is used as a symbol to denote the third serial order; (*Alg.*) the third quantity known; (*Mus.*) the first note of the diatonic scale, corresponding to the Italian *do;* the natural major mode; common time; (*Roman numeral*) 100. **C$_3$**, *n.* (*Mil.*) lowest category of a medical board. *a.* of a person, of low physique.

C[2], (*abbr.*) capacitance; catholic; Celsius; century; Conservative; coulomb.

C[3], (*chem. symbol*) carbon.

C[4], *n.* a general-purpose computer-programming language popular on minicomputers and microcomputers. Developed in the early 1970s from an earlier language called BCPL, C is closely associated with the operating system Unix. It is good for writing fast and efficient systems programs, such as operating systems (which control the operations of the computer).

c[2], (*abbr.*) caught; cent; centi-; chapter; cubic.

c., (*abbr.*) about. [L *circa*]

CA, (*abbr.*) chartered accountant; Consumers' Association.

Ca, (*chem. symbol*) calcium.

CAA, (*abbr.*) Civil Aviation Authority.

Caaba, KAABA.

CAB, (*abbr.*) Citizens' Advice Bureau.

cab[1], *n.* a public covered carriage with two or four wheels; a taxi; the guard, or covered part, of a locomotive which protects the driver and fireman from the weather; the driver's compartment in a lorry, crane etc. **to call a cab**, to hail a taxi. **cabman**, *n.* a cab-driver. **cab-rank**, *n.* a row of cabs on a stand. **cab-runner, -tout**, *n.* a person employed to fetch cabs or unload luggage. **cab-stand**, *n.* a place where cabs are authorized to stand for hire. **cabbie, cabby**, *n.* (*coll.*) a cab-driver. **cabless**, *a.* [short for CABRIOLET]

cab[2], *n.* a Jewish measure of capacity containing nearly 3 pt. (1.7 l). [Heb. *qab*, a hollow vessel]

cabal, *n.* a small body of persons closely united for some secret purpose; a junto, a clique; a plot, conspiracy; the five ministers of Charles II who signed the Treaty of Alliance in 1672, the initials of whose names (Clifford, Ashley, Buckingham, Arlington and Lauderdale) happened to form the word *cabal. v.i.* (*past, p.p.* **caballed**) to intrigue secretly with others for some private end. **caballer**, *n.* [CABBALA]

cabala, CABBALA.

caballero, *n.* a Spanish gentleman; a stately kind of Spanish dance. [Sp. from L *caballārius* (*caballus*, horse)]

caballine, *a.* pertaining to horses; equine. [L *caballīnus*, horse]

cabaret, *n.* a public-house, a tavern; an entertainment or floor show consisting of singing, dancing etc.; (*N Am.*) a restaurant or nightclub where such entertainment is provided. [F (etym. unknown)]

cabbage[1], *n.* the plain-leaved, hearted varieties of *Brassica oleracea;* the terminal bud of palm-trees; (*coll.*) an inert or apathetic person. **cabbage-butterfly**, *n.* two kinds of butterfly the larvae of which cause injury to cabbages, *Pieris brassicae, P. rapae.* **cabbage-leaf**, *n.* (*sl.*) a bad cigar. **cabbage lettuce**, *n.* a kind of lettuce with a firm heart as a cabbage. **cabbage-moth**, *n.* a nocturnal moth, *Mammestra brassicae,* whose larvae feed on the cabbage. **cabbage-palm** CABBAGE-TREE. **cabbage-rose**, *n.* a double red rose *Rosa centifolia,* with large, compact flowers. **cabbage-stump**, *n.* the stem of a cabbage. **cabbage-tree**, *n.* a palm with an edible terminal bud. **cabbage white** CABBAGE BUTTERFLY. **cabbage-worm**, *n.* the larva of the cabbage-moth and other insects. **cabbagy**, *a.* [F *caboche,* great head, L *caput,* head (F *choux cabus,* cabbage cole)]

cabbage[2], *n.* (*formerly*) the shreds and clippings made by tailors, and taken by them as perquisites. *v.t.* to purloin (esp. cloth left after cutting out a garment); (*dated, sl.*) to pilfer; to crib. [perh. from F *cabas,* a basket (cp. Norman *cabasser,* to steal), late L *cabātium* (L *capax -ācem,* holding)]

cabbala, *n.* a traditional exposition of the Pentateuch attributed to Moses; mystic or esoteric doctrine. **cabbalism**, *n.* the system of the cabbala; occult doctrine. **cabbalist**, *n.* one skilled in the Jewish cabbala, or in mystic learning. **cabbalistic, -ical**, *a.* pertaining to the Jewish cabbala; mysterious, occult. **cabbalistically**, *adv.* [med. L, from Heb. *qabbālāh,* tradition, received doctrine (*qābal,* to receive)]

caber, *n.* a pole, the roughly-trimmed stem of a young tree, used in the Highland sport of tossing the caber. [Gael. *cabar*]

cabin, *n.* a small hut or house; a temporary shelter; a little room; a room or compartment in a ship or aircraft for officers or passengers; a driver's cab. *v.i.* to live in a cabin. *v.t.* to shelter or confine in or as in a cabin; to coop in. **cabin-boy**, *n.* a boy who waits on the officers of a ship or passengers in the cabin. **cabin class**, *n.* in a passenger ship, a class between tourist and first. **cabin crew**, *n.* the crew in an aircraft responsible for looking after passengers. **cabin cruiser**, *n.* a motor-boat with living accommodation. **cabin-passenger**, *n.* one who pays for accommodation in the superior part of a ship. [F *cabane,* late L *capanna,* a hut]

cabinet, *n.* a closet, a small room; a private room; a piece of furniture with drawers, shelves etc., in which to keep curiosities or articles of value; an outer case for a television set etc.; a cabinet photograph; a council room; the secret council of a sovereign; a kind of deliberative committee of the principal members of the British Government; a meeting of such a committee. **Cabinet council**, *n.* a meeting of the Cabinet for consultation. **cabinet edition**, *n.* an edition of a book at a moderate price, inferior to a library edition and superior to a popular edition. **cabinet lock**, *n.* a lock suitable for a desk, drawer, box and the like. **cabinet-maker**, *n.* one who makes the finer kinds of household furniture. **cabinet-making**, *n.* **Cabinet Minister**, *n.* a member of the Cabinet. **cabinet photograph**, *n.* a photographic print measuring about 6 × 4 in. (about 10 × 15 cm). **cabinet pudding**, *n.* a sort of bread-and-butter pudding, with dried fruit. **cabinet-work**, *n.* cabinet-making; a piece of such furniture. [dim. of CABIN, or from F *cabinet*]

cable, *n.* a strong rope, more than 10 in. (25.4 cm) round; one-tenth of a nautical mile; the rope or chain to which an anchor is fastened; a nautical unit of length, about 202 yds. (185 m); a wire rope; an electrical circuit of one or more conductors insulated and in a sheath; (*Arch.*) a cable-like moulding; a cablegram; cable television. *v.t.* to fasten with a cable; to send (a message) by cable; to inform by cablegram; to fill the lower part of the flutings in a column with convex mouldings. **cable car**, *n.* a passenger cabin suspended from an overhead cable and moved by it; a carriage on a cable railway. **cablegram,** *n.* a telegraphic message by submarine cable, communications satellite etc. **cablegrammic**, **cablegraphic**, *a.* **cable-laid,** *a.* twisted like a cable. **cable-moulding,** *n.* (*Arch.*) a cable-like bead or moulding; (*Goldsmithing*) a cable-like ornament. **cable railway,** *n.* a funicular railway. **cable stitch,** *n.* a plaited stitch in knitting. **cable television,** *n.* a television service transmitted by an underground cable connected to subscribers' television sets. **cableway,** *n.* a transport system for freight or passengers using containers or cable cars suspended from overhead cables. **cablet**, *n.* a small cable, less than 10 in. (25.4 cm) round. **cabling,** *n.* decoration of columns by means of convex mouldings in the fluting. [ult. from L *caplum, capulum,* from *capere,* to take hold of (cp. OF *cable,* It. *cappio,* Dut. *Kabel*)]

†**cabob,** KEBAB.

caboched, caboshed, **cabossed**, *a.* (*Her.*) borne full-faced and showing no other feature, as the heads of some animals. [from obs. v. *caboche,* F *cabocher* (L *caput,* head; cp. CABBAGE[1])]

cabochon, *n.* a precious stone polished, and having the rough parts removed, but without facets. **en cabochon,** polished, but without facets. **cabochon-shaped,** *a.* [F *caboche* (see prec.)]

caboodle, *n.* (*coll.*) crowd, lot. **the whole caboodle,** all the lot. [BOODLE]

caboose, *n.* the cook's house or galley; (*N Am.*) the guard's van in a goods train; (*N Am.*) a car for the use of workmen or train crew. [prob. from MDut. *kabuys* (etym. unknown; perh. from a form *kabanhuys,* cabin-house)]

Cabot, *n.* **Sebastian** (1474–1557), Italian navigator and cartographer, the second son of Giovanni Caboto. He explored the Brazilian coast and the River Plate for Charles V (1526–30).

cabotage, *n.* coasting; coasting-trade; the restriction of a country's internal air traffic to carriers belonging to that country. [F, from *caboter,* to coast (etym. doubtful)]

Caboto, *n.* **Giovanni** (or John Cabot) (1450–98), Italian navigator. Commissioned with his three sons by Henry VII of England to discover unknown lands, he arrived at Cape Breton Island on 24 June 1497, thus becoming the first European to reach the North American mainland (he thought he was in NE Asia). In 1498 he sailed again, touching Greenland, and probably died on the voyage.

Cabral, *n.* **Pedro Alvarez** (1460–1526), Portuguese explorer. He set sail from Lisbon for the East Indies in Mar. 1500, and accidentally reached Brazil by taking a course too far W. He claimed the country for Portugal 25 Apr., as Spain had not followed up Vicente Pinzón's landing there earlier in the year. Continuing around Africa, he lost seven of his fleet of 13 ships (Diaz being one of those drowned), and landed in Mozambique. Proceeding to India, he negotiated the first Indo-Portuguese treaties for trade, and returned to Lisbon in July 1501.

cabriole, *a.* of table and chair legs, shaped in a reflex curve. [F, a caper]

cabriolet, *n.* (also erron. **cabriole**) a covered carriage drawn by two horses; a type of motor-car with a folding top. [F, dim. of *cabriole,* a caper (see CAPRIOLE)]

ca' canny, *int.* (*Sc.*) go warily! *n.* a worker's policy of going slowly. [CALL, CANNY]

cacao, *n.* a tropical American tree, *Theobroma cacao,* from the seeds of which chocolate and cocoa are prepared. **cacao-butter** COCOA BUTTER. [Sp., from Mex. *cacauatl*]

cachaemia, cachemia, *n.* a bad state of the blood. [Gr. *kakos,* bad, *haima,* blood]

cachalot, *n.* a member of a genus of whales having teeth in the lower jaw, esp. the sperm whale. [F, from Gascon *cachaon,* a big tooth]

cache, *n.* a hole in the ground or other place in which provisions, goods or ammunition are hidden; the hiding of stores; the stores hidden. *v.t.* to hide or conceal in a cache. **cachepot,** *n.* an ornamental holder for a plant-pot. [F, from *cacher,* to hide]

cachectic CACHEXIA.

cachet, *n.* a paper capsule in which nauseous or other drugs can be administered; a seal; a stamp, a characteristic mark; a sign of authenticity; a mark of excellence; prestige. **lettre de cachet,** a royal warrant for the imprisonment or exile of a person without trial, in France before the Revolution. [F from *cacher,* to conceal]

cachexia, cachexy, *n.* loss of weight, weakness etc., of body resulting from chronic disease. **cachectic**, *a.* [L, from Gr. *kachexia* (*kakos,* bad, *hexis,* habit)]

cachinnate, *v.i.* to laugh immoderately. **cachinnation,** *n.* loud or immoderate laughter. **cachinnatory,** *a.* [L *cachinnāre* (onomat.)]

cacholong, *n.* a white or opaque variety of opal or quartz. [Kalmuck *kaschtschilon,* beautiful stone]

cachou, *n.* a small pill-like sweetmeat for perfuming the breath. [F, from Malay *cachu* (see CATECHU)]

cachucha, *n.* a lively kind of Spanish dance in triple time. [Sp.]

cacique, cazique, *n.* a chief of the aborigines of the W Indies or the neighbouring parts of America; a local political leader in this area. **caciquism,** *n.* [Sp., from Haitian]

cack, *n.* (*dial.*) excrement. **cack-handed,** *a.* (*sl.*) left-handed; inept. [L *cacāre,* to defecate]

cackle, *n.* the cackling of a hen; silly chatter. *v.i.* to make a noise like a hen after laying an egg; to chatter in a silly manner; to giggle. **to cut the cackle,** to get down to business. **cackler**, *n.* **cackling**, *n.* [ME *kakelen;* onomat. (cp. Dut. *kakelen,* G *gackeln*)]

caco-, *comb. form.* bad, malformed, evil to the senses. [Gr. *kako-, kakos,* evil, bad]

cacodemon, *n.* an evil spirit; a nightmare; an evil person.

cacodyl, *n.* a stinking organic compound of arsenic and methyl. **cacodylic**, *a.* [Gr. *kakōdēs,* stinking (CACO-, *od-*, root of *ozein,* to smell), -YL]

cacoepy, *n.* false pronunciation of words. [Gr. *epos,* a word]

cacoethes, *n.* a bad habit; an irresistible propensity. **cacoethes scribendi**, *n.* an itch for writing [L from Gr. *kakoēthes* evil habit, neut. of a. *kakoēthēs,* ill-disposed (CACO- *ēthos,* disposition, character)]

cacogastric , *a.* dyspeptic; characterized by a disordered stomach.

cacography, *n.* bad spelling; bad writing.

cacolet, *n.* a mule-chair used for the transport of the sick or wounded. [F dial., prob. Basque]

cacology, *n.* bad choice of words; incorrect pronunciation. [Gr. *kakologia,* from *kakologos,* speaking evil (CACO-, *logos,* from *legein,* to speak)]

cacomorphia, *n.* malformation, deformity.

cacoon, *n.* the large, flat, polished seed of a tropical climbing plant of the bean family, having pods as much as 8 ft. (2.4 m) long, used for making snuff-boxes and other small articles; a purgative seed of a climbing plant of the gourd family, also used as an antidote for poisons. [prob. African]

cacophony, *n.* a rough, discordant style; (*Mus.*) a discord. **cacophonous,** *a.* harsh-sounding, discordant. [F *cacophonie,* Gr. *kakophōnia,* from *kakophōnos,* harsh-sounding]

cacophthalmia, *n.* malignant inflammation of the eyes.

cactus, *n.* (*pl.* **-ti**, **-tuses**) a genus of succulent spiny plants. **cactaceous,** *a.* **cactal,** *a.* allied to the cactuses. **cactoid,** *a.* [L, from Gr. *kaktos,* a prickly Sicilian plant]

CAD[1], (*abbr.*) compact audio disk.

CAD[2], *n.* (*abbr.*) computer-aided design, the use of computers for creating and editing design drawings. CAD also allows such things as automatic testing of designs and multiple or animated three-dimensional views of designs. CAD systems are widely used in architecture, electronics and engineering, for example in the motor vehicle industry where cars designed with the assistance of computers are now commonplace. A related development is CAM (computer-assisted manufacture).

cad, *n.* a low, vulgar fellow; a bounder; an ill-mannered person, a person guilty of ungentlemanly conduct; one employed on odd jobs at school or university sports; †a bus conductor. **caddish,** *a.* [prob. short for Sc. *cadie, caddie,* Engl. CADET]

cadastre, *n.* a register of property as a basis of taxation; an official register of the ownership of land. **cadastral,** *a.* [F, from late L *capistratum,* register of *capita,* heads, for the land tax in Roman provinces]

cadaver, *n.* a corpse, dead body. **cadaveric,** *a.* (*Med.*) cadaverous. **cadaverous,** *a.* corpse-like; deathly pale. **cadaverously,** *adv.* **cadaverousness,** *n.* [L]

caddice, CADDIS[1].

caddie, caddy, cadie, *n.* one who attends on a golfer; †a messenger or errand-boy; (*N. Zealand*) a straw-hat; (*Austral.*) a slouch hat, a trilby. *v.i.* to act as a caddie. **caddie car, cart,** *n.* a two-wheeled cart for carrying golf clubs.

caddis[1], *n.* the larva of any species of *Phryganea,* esp. of the may-fly. **caddis-fly,** *n.* **caddis-worm,** *n.* [etym. doubtful]

†**caddis[2],** *n.* a kind of worsted yarn; caddis ribbon. **caddis ribbon,** *n.* a tape of this stuff used for garters etc. [A-F *cadace,* OF *cadaz,* the coarsest part of silk, and OF *cadis,* a kind of woollen serge]

caddy[1], *n.* a small box in which tea is kept. [Malay *kātī,* a weight of $1\frac{1}{2}$ lb (0.68 kg)]

caddy[2] CADDIE.

cade[1], *n.* a barrel of 500 herrings or of 1000 sprats. [F, from L *cadus,* Gr. *kados,* a pail, jar, cask]

†**cade[2],** *a.* domesticated; brought up by hand. *n.* a pet lamb. *v.t.* to bring up tenderly, to coddle. [etym. doubtful]

Cade, *n.* **Jack** (*d.* 1450), English rebel. He was a prosperous landowner, but led a revolt in Kent against the misgovernment of Henry VI (1450), defeated the royal forces at Sevenoaks, and occupied London. After being promised reforms and pardon, the rebels dispersed, but Cade was hunted down and killed.

cadence, *n.* the sinking of the voice, esp. at the end of a sentence; modulation of the voice, intonation; local modulation or accent; rhythm, poetical rhythm or measure; rhythmical beat or movement; (*Mus.*) close of a movement or phrase; a cadenza. *v.t.* to put into rhythmical measure. **cadenced,** *a.* **cadency,** *n.* †cadence; (*Her.*, *Geneal.*) the state of a cadet; descent from a younger branch. **cadent,** *a.* †falling; (*Astron.*) going down; having rhythmical cadence. **cadenza,** *n.* a vocal or instrumental flourish of indefinite form at the close of a movement. [F, from It. *cadenza,* late L *cadentia* (*cadere,* to fall)]

cadet, *n.* a younger son; the younger branch of a family; †a volunteer who served in hope to gain a commission; a pupil in a military or naval academy; a member of a reactionary party in the Russian revolution. **cadetship,** *n.* [F, from Prov. *capdet,* late L *capitellum,* dim. of L *caput,* head]

cadge, *v.t.* to get by begging. *v.i.* to peddle; to beg. **cadger,** *n.* one who cadges; a carrier, a man who collects farm produce for sale in town; a huckster, a street hawker; a beggar; a tramp. [etym. doubtful; perh. a var. of CATCH]

cadi, *n.* the judge of a Persian, Arab or Turkish town or village. [Arab *qādī* (cp. ALCAYDE)]

cadie CADDIE.

Cádiz, *n.* Spanish city and naval base, capital and seaport of the province of Cádiz, standing on Cádiz Bay, an inlet of the Atlantic, 103 km/64 miles south of Seville; population (1986) 154,000. After the discovery of the Americas (1492), Cádiz became one of the most important ports in Europe. Francis Drake burned a Spanish fleet here (1587) to prevent the sailing of the Armada.

Cadmean, Cadmian, *a.* of or belonging to Cadmus, the mythical founder of Thebes, and inventor of letters; Theban. **Cadmean victory,** *n.* a victory that ruins the victor; a moral victory.

cadmium, *n.* a bluish-white metallic element, at. no. 51; chem. symbol Cd. **cadmium-yellow,** *n.* a pigment prepared from cadmium sulphide. **cadmic,** *a.* **cadmiferous,** *a.* [obs. *cadmia,* CALAMINE, L, from Gr. *kadmia, -meia,* Cadmean (earth)]

cadre, *n.* a framework, a scheme; the skeleton of a regiment; the permanent establishment or nucleus of a regiment; a group of usu. Communist activists; a member of such a group. [F, from It. *quadro,* L *quadrum,* square]

caduceus, *n.* (*pl.* **-cei**) the winged staff of Mercury, borne by him as messenger of the gods. **caducean,** *a.* [L *cādūceus,* Doric Gr. *karukion* (*kērux,* a herald)]

caduciary, *a.* (*Law*) heritable; subject to forfeiture. [as foll.]

caducous, *a.* (*Bot.*) falling off quickly or prematurely. **caducity,** *n.* [L *cadūcus,* easily falling (*cadere,* to fall)]

Cadwalader, *n.* (7th cent.), Welsh hero. The son of Cadwallon, king of Gwynedd, N Wales, he defeated and killed Eadwine of Northumbria in 633. About a year later he was killed in battle.

caecum, (*esp. N Am.*) **cecum,** *n.* (*pl.* **-ca**) the blind gut, the first part of the large intestine which is prolonged into a blind pouch; any blind tube. **caecal,** *a.* pertaining to the caecum; having a blind end. **caecally,** *adv.* **caeciform,** *a.* **caecitis,** *n.* inflammation of the caecum. [L *caecus,* blind]

Caedmon, *n.* (7th cent.), earliest-known English poet. According to the Northumbrian historian Bede, when Caedmon was a cowherd at the Christian monastery of Whitby, he was commanded to sing by a stranger in a dream, and on waking produced a hymn on the Creation. The original poem is preserved in some manuscripts. Caedmon became a monk and may have composed other religious poems.

Caenozoic CENOZOIC.

Caen stone, *n.* a soft, yellowish, oolitic building-stone from Caen. [*Caen,* Normandy]

Caernarvonshire, *n.* former county of N Wales, merged in Gwynedd (1974).

†**caerule,** CERULEAN.

Caesar[1], *n.* powerful family of ancient Rome, which included Gaius Julius Caesar, whose grand-nephew and adopted son Augustus assumed the name of Caesar and passed it on to his adopted son Tiberius; the title of the Roman emperors down to Hadrian, and of the heirs presumptive of later emperors; the Emperor (i.e. of the Holy Roman Empire), the German Kaiser; an autocrat; the temporal (as distinguished from the spiritual) power; (*coll.*) a Caesarean section. **Caesar's wife,** *n.* a woman of spotless reputation. **Caesarian, -rean,** *a.* of or belonging to Caesar; imperial. *n.* a follower of Caesar; a supporter of autocratic government; (*esp. N Am.* **Cesarian, -rean**) a Caesarean section. **Caesarian** (esp. N. Am. **Cesarian**) **section, birth,** *n.* the delivery of a child through the walls of the abdomen (as Julius Caesar is said to have been brought into the world). **Caesarism,** *n.* absolute government; imperialism. **Caesarist,** *n.* [L, cognomen of Caius Julius *Caesar*]

Caesar[2], *n.* **Gaius Julius** (*c.* 102–44 BC), Roman statesman and general. He formed with Pompey and Crassus the First Triumvirate in 60 BC. He conquered Gaul (58–50) and invaded Britain in 55 and 54. He fought against Pompey (49–48) defeating him at Pharsalus. After a period in Egypt Caesar returned to Rome as dictator from 46. He was assassinated by conspirators on the Ides of March 44.

Caesarea, *n.* ancient city in Palestine (now Qisarya). It was built by Herod the Great (22–12 BC), who also constructed a port (*portus Augusti*). It was the administrative capital of the province of Judaea.

Caesarea Mazaca, *n.* ancient name for the Turkish city of Kayseri.

caesious, *a.* bluish or greenish grey. [L *caesius*]

caesium, (*esp. N Am.*) **cesium,** *n.* a highly-reactive, silvery-white metallic element, at. no. 55; chem. symbol Cs, similar to sodium in many properties. Named after the bluish-green lines of its spectrum. [as prec.]

caespitose, cespitose, *a.* growing in tufts; matted; turfy. [mod. L *caespitōsus,* from L *caespes -item,* turf]

caesura, cesura, *n.* (*Classic pros.*) the division of a metrical foot between two words, esp. in the middle of a line; (*Eng. pros.*) a pause about the middle of a line. **caesural,** *a.* [L, from *caesus,* p.p. of *caesere,* to cut]

Caetano, *n.* **Marcello** (1906–80), Portuguese right-wing politician. Professor of administrative law at Lisbon from 1940, he succeeded the dictator Salazar as prime minister from 1968 until his exile after the revolution of 1974. He was granted political asylum in Brazil.

cafard, *n.* depression, low spirits. [F]

café, cafe, *n.* a coffee-house; a coffee-bar; a restaurant; coffee. **café au lait**, *n.* coffee with milk. **café chantant**, *n.* a place of musical and other entertainment, indoors or in the open air, where refreshments are served. **café noir**, *n.* coffee without milk. **cafeteria**, *n.* a restaurant in which customers fetch their own food from the counter. [F]

caffeic, *a.* derived from coffee.

caffeine, *n.* a vegetable alkaloid derived from the coffee and tea plants.

Caffre, KAFIR.

caftan, *n.* a kind of long belted tunic worn in the East; a woman's long loose dress. [Turk. *qaftān*]

cage, *n.* a box or enclosure wholly or partly of wire, wicker-work or iron bars, in which birds or other animals are kept; an open framework resembling this; a prison, a lock-up; the cabin of a lift; (*Mining*) an iron structure used as a lift in a shaft; an outer work of timber enclosing another. *v.t.* to shut up in a cage; to confine. **cage aerial,** *n.* an aerial constructed like a cage by fixing a number of conductors parallel-wise to circular spreaders. **cagebird,** *n.* a cageling; a type of bird normally kept in a cage. **cageling,** *n.* a bird kept in a cage. [OF, from L *cavea* (*cavus,* hollow)]

Cage, *n.* **John** (1912–), US composer. A pupil of Schoenberg and Cowell, he joined others in reacting against the European art music tradition in favour of a more realistic idiom open to non-Western attitudes. Working in films during the 1930s he assembled and toured a percussion orchestra incorporating ethnic instruments and noise-makers, for which the *First Construction in Metal* (1930) was composed. He also invented the prepared piano to tour as accompanist with the dancer Merce Cunningham, a lifelong collaborator. His effect on contemporary musical thinking is summed up by the piano piece *4 minutes 33 seconds* (1952), in which a performer holds an audience in expectation without playing a note.

cagey, cagy, *a.* (*sl.*) wary, shrewdly knowing; sly. **cagily,** *adv.* **caginess, cageyness,** *n.*

Cagliari, *n.* capital and port of Sardinia, Italy, on the Gulf of Cagliari; population (1988) 222,000.

Cagney, *n.* **James** (1899–1986), US actor who moved to films from Broadway. Usually associated with gangster roles in films such as *The Public Enemy* (1931), he was an actor of great versatility, playing Bottom in *A Midsummer Night's Dream* (1935) and singing and dancing in *Yankee Doodle Dandy* (1942).

cagoule, *n.* a lightweight long anorak, usu. hooded. [F, a monk's hood]

cahier, *n.* a number of sheets of paper loosely put together; the report of a committee.[F (OF *quayer,* see QUIRE[1])]

cahoots, *n.pl.* (*sl.*) partnership, collusion.

Cahora Bassa, *n.* the largest hydro-electric scheme in Africa, created as a result of the damming of the Zambezi river to form a 230 km/144 mile-long reservoir in W Mozambique.

cailleach, cailliach, *n.* (*Highland*) an old woman, a crone. [Gael., from *caille,* a veil]

caiman CAYMAN.

Cain[1], *n.* a murderer, a fratricide. **to raise Cain,** (*sl.*) to make a disturbance, to make trouble. **Cainite,** *n.* a son of Cain; one of a heretical sect (2nd cent.) who reverenced Cain and other bad Scriptural characters. [*Cain,* brother of Abel, Gen. iv., who murdered Abel from motives of jealousy, as Abel's sacrifice was more acceptable to God than his own.]

Cain[2], *n.* **James M(allahan)** (1892–1977), US novelist. He was the author of thrillers, including *The Postman Always Rings Twice* (1934), *Mildred Pierce* (1941), and *Double Indemnity* (1943).

†**cain, kain**, *n.* (*Sc.*) rent paid in kind, esp. poultry. [Celt. *cáin,* law, tribute]

Caine, *n.* **Michael,** stage-name of Maurice Micklewhite (1933–), British actor, noted for his dry, laconic Cockney style. His long cinematic career includes the films *Alfie* (1966), *California Suite* (1978), *Educating Rita* (1983), and *Hannah and her Sisters* (1986).

Cainozoic, *n., a.* the tertiary period, belonging to the third geological period. [Gr. *kainos,* recent, -ZOIC]

caïque, *n.* a light boat used on the Bosporus; a small Levantine sailing vessel. [Turk. *qāiq*]

ça ira, that will go, that's the thing. [F]

caird, *n.* (*Sc.*) a travelling tinker; a vagrant. [Gael. *ceard,* an artificer]

cairn, *n.* a pyramidal heap of stones, esp. one raised over a grave or to mark a summit, track or boundary; a cairn terrier. **cairn terrier,** *n.* a small rough-haired terrier orig. from Scotland. [Gael., Ir., W *carn*]

cairngorm, *n.* a yellow or brown variety of rock crystal, from the Cairngorm mountains on the borders of Banff, Aberdeen and Inverness shires. [Gael., lit. blue stone, name of a mountain]

Cairo, *n.* (Arabic **El Qahira**), capital of Egypt, on the east bank of the Nile 13 km/8 miles above the apex of the Delta and 160 km/100 miles from the Mediterranean; the largest city in Africa and in the Middle East; population (1985) 6,205,000, Greater Cairo (1987) 13,300,000. El Fustat (Old Cairo) was founded by Arabs about AD 64, Cairo itself about 1000 by the Fatimid ruler Gowhar. The Great Pyramids and Sphinx are at nearby Giza.

caisson, *n.* an ammunition-chest or wagon; a large, watertight case or chamber used in laying foundations under water; a similar apparatus used for raising sunken vessels; a floating vessel used as a dock-gate; a sunken panel in ceilings etc. **caisson disease,** *n.* symptoms resulting from a sudden return from high air pressure to normal pressure conditions; the bends. [F (*caisse,* L *capsa,* see CASE)]

caitiff, *n.* †a poor wretch; a despicable wretch; a cowardly fellow. *a.* cowardly, base, despicable. [ONorth. F *caitif,* L *captīvus,* CAPTIVE]

cajole, *v.t.* to persuade, beguile, or deceive by flattery or fair speech; to wheedle, to coax; to beguile (into or out of something). *v.i.* to use artful flattery. **cajoler,** *n.* **cajolement, cajolery**, *n.* **cajolingly,** *adv.* [F *cajoler;* etym. doubtful]

Cajun, *n.* member of a French-speaking community of Louisiana, US, descended from French-Canadians who in the 18th century were driven there from Nova Scotia (then known as Acadia, from which the name Cajun comes). **Cajun music** has a lively beat and features steel guitar, fiddle, and accordion. **Cajun cooking** is characterized by hot spicy sauces. [var. of ACADIAN]

cajuput, *n.* a tree of the genus *Melaleuca,* the species of which yield a volatile oil. [Malay *kāyu, pūtih,* white wood]

cake, *n.* a small mass of dough baked; a composition of flour, butter, sugar and other ingredients, baked usu. in a tin; (*Sc.*) oatcake; a flat mass of food or any solidified or compressed substance. *v.t.* (*usu. pass.*) to make into a cake. *v.i.* to assume a cake-like form. **cakes and ale,** a good time. **like hot cakes,** with great speed; with energy. **piece of cake,** (*coll.*) something achieved without effort. **slice of the cake,** a share in the benefits. **to take the cake,** (*iron., sl.*) to come out first; to take first prize. **cake-walk,** *n.* (*N Am.*) a Negro dance; a form of dance using high marching steps; (*sl.*) something easily accomplished. [Icel. *kaka* (cp. Dan. *kåge,* Dut. *koek,* G *Kuchen*)]

Cal., (*abbr.*) California; Calorie (kilocalorie).

cal., (*abbr.*) calendar; calibre; (small) calorie.

CAL, (*abbr.*) computer-assisted learning, the use of

computers in education and training, where the computer displays instructional material to a student and asks questions about the information given. The student's answers determine the sequence of the lessons.

calabar CALABER.

Calabar bean PHYSOSTIGMA. [name of a port in Nigeria]

calabash, *n.* a kind of gourd or pumpkin; the calabash-tree, *Crescentia cujete;* the shell enclosing the fruit of this, used for drinking-vessels and other domestic utensils, and tobacco-pipes. **calabash-pipe**, *n.* [F *calebasse,* Sp. *calabaza* (Cat. Sp. *carabassa,* Sic. It. *caravazza*); perh. from Pers. *kharbuz,* a melon]

calaber, calabar, *n.* the fur of a grey squirrel, esp. the Siberian squirrel. [prob. from F *Calabre, Calabria*]

calaboose, *n.* (*N Am. coll.*) a prison. [Negro-French *calabouse,* Sp. *calabozo*]

calabrese, *n.* a form of green broccoli. [It., of Calabria, see foll.]

Calabria, *n.* mountainous earthquake region occupying the 'toe' of Italy, comprising the provinces of Catanzaro, Cosenza and Reggio; capital Catanzaro; area 15,100 sq km/5,829 sq miles; population (1988) 2,146,000. Reggio is the industrial centre.

caladium, *n.* a genus of plants belonging to the arum family, with starchy tuberous roots used in the tropics for food. [Malay *kélādy*]

calamanco, *n.* (*pl.* **-coes**) a Flemish woollen stuff with a fine gloss, and checkered in the warp, much in use in the 18th cent.; (*usu. pl.*) a garment of this stuff. [etym. doubtful; cp. Dut. *kalamink,* F *calmande,* Sp. *calamaco*]

calamander, *n.* a hard wood, from India and Sri Lanka. [etym. doubtful]

calamary, *n.* a cuttle-fish of the genus *Loligo* or the family *Teuthidae;* a squid, a pen-fish (named either from its pen-shaped skull or its inky fluid) [L *calamārius* (*calamus,* a pen)]

calamine, *n.* (*formerly*) native zinc carbonate; a pinkish powder of this or zinc oxide used in a lotion to soothe the skin. [F, from med. L *calamīna* (prob. corr. of L *cadmīa,* see CADMIUM)]

calamint, *n.* an aromatic herb. *Calamintha officinalis,* and the genus it belongs to. [MF *calament,* late L. *calamentum*]

calamite, *n.* a fossil coal-plant, allied to the mare's tails or equisetums; a variety of tremolite. [mod. L *calamītes,* from L *calamus,* a reed]

calamity, *n.* extreme misfortune, adversity, disaster, misery; distress. **calamity Jane,** *n.* (*coll.*) a person who heralds or brings disaster. **calamitous,** *a.* causing or characterized by great or widespread distress or unhappiness. **calamitously,** *adv.* **calamitousness,** *n.* [F *calamité,* L *calamitas -atem* (cp. *in-columis,* safe)]

Calamity Jane, *n.* (nickname of Martha Jane Burke) (*c.* 1852–1903), US heroine of Deadwood, South Dakota, mining camps. She worked as a teamster, transporting supplies to the camps, adopted male dress and, as an excellent shot, promised 'calamity' to any aggressor. Her renown was spread by many fictional accounts of the 'wild west' that featured her exploits.

calamus, *n.* (*pl.* **-mi**) the sweet flag, *Acorus calamus;* a fragrant Eastern plant; a genus of palm trees producing enormously long canes; a genus of fishes comprising the porgies; the quill of a feather. [L, from Gr. *kalamos,* a reed]

calando, *a., adv.* (*Mus.*) gradually becoming softer and slower. [It.]

calandria, *n.* a sealed cylindrical vessel with tubes passing through it, used as a heat-exchanger, e.g. in nuclear reactors. [Sp., lark]

calash, *n.* a light pleasure-carriage, with low wheels and removable top; (*Canada*) a two-wheeled vehicle for two, with seat for the driver on the splash-board; a woman's silk hood supported by a framework of whalebone. [F *calèche,* G *Kalesche,* from Slav. (Boh. *kolésa,* Rus. *kolaska*)]

calc-, *comb. form.* lime. **calc-sinter,** *n.* travertine. **calc-spar**, *n.* calcite. **calc-tuff,** *n.* a porous deposit of carbonate of lime. [G *Kalk,* L *calx -cis*]

calcaneum, *n.* (*pl.* **-nea**) the bone of the heel. **calcaneal**, *a.*

calcar[1], *n.* the reverberatory furnace in which the first calcination is made in glass-making. [L *calcāria,* lime-kiln]

calcar[2], *n.* (*Bot.*) a spur-like process. **calcarate,** *a.* [L, from *calx -cem,* heel]

calcareo-, *comb. form.* (*Geol.*) calcareous. **calcareo-argillaceous,** *a.* composed of clay with a mixture of lime. **calcareo-bituminous,** *a.* **calcareo-siliceous,** *a.* **calcareo-sulphurous,** *a.* [as foll.]

calcareous, -ious, *a.* of the nature of lime or limestone. **calcareous-spar,** *n.* calcite. **calcareous-tufa,** *n.* CALC-TUFF under CALC-. **calcareously,** *adv.* **calcareousness,** *n.* [L *calcārius,* see CALC-].

calceolaria, *n.* slipperwort; a genus of plants with slipper-like flowers. **calceolate**, *a.* (*Bot.*) shaped like a slipper. [L *calceolus,* dim. of *calceus,* a shoe (*calx -cem,* the heel)]

calcic, *a.* pertaining to or composed in whole or in part of lime. **calciferous**, *a.* (*Chem.*) yielding or containing calcium salts. **calcific**, *a.* **calciform,** *a.* *v.i.* to become calcified. **calcify**, *v.t.* to convert into lime. **calcification,** *n.*

calciferol, *n.* vitamin D_2. [*calci*ferous, *ergo*sterol]

calcine, *v.t.* to reduce to quick-lime or powder by heat; to expel water and other volatile matter, to desiccate by heat; to purify or refine; to burn to ashes. *v.i.* to undergo calcination. **calcination**, *n.* **calciner,** *n.*

calcio-, *comb. form.* **calcio-ferrite**, *n.* a phosphate of calcium and iron. **calcio-thorite,** *n.* a variety of thorite containing calcium.

calcite, *n.* native crystallized carbonate of lime. **calcitic**, *a.*

calcium, *n.* a silver-white metallic element, at. no. 20; chem. symbol Ca; usually met with in the form of its oxide, lime. **calcium carbonate,** *n.* a white crystalline compound occurring in limestone, chalk, marble etc. **calcium chloride,** *n.* chloride of lime, bleaching-powder. **calcium-light**, *n.* lime-light.

calcography, etc. CHALCOGRAPHY.

calc-sinter, -spar, -tuff CALC-.

calculate, *v.t.* to compute, to reckon up, to estimate; to ascertain beforehand by mathematical process; to plan beforehand; to adjust, to arrange. *v.i.* to reckon, to form an estimate; to rely (upon); (*N Am.*) to think, to suppose. **calculable,** *a.* that may be calculated. **calculated,** *a.* pre-arranged, intended; cold-blooded; suitable, well-adapted (to). **calculating,** *a.* that calculates; shrewd, acting with forethought. **calculating machine,** *n.* a mechanical device which performs one or more of the fundamental arithmetical operations. **calculation,** *n.* the act of reckoning or computing in numbers; the result of such process; computation, reckoning; estimate, opinion, inference; careful planning, esp. selfish. **calculative,** *a.* pertaining to calculation; disposed to calculate. **calculator,** *n.* one who calculates; a series of tables for use in calculating; an electronic device, usu. small and portable, which can carry out mathematical calculations [L *calculāre* (CALCULUS)]

calculus, *n.* (*pl.* **-li**) a stony, morbid concretion formed in various organs of the body; (*Math.*) a method of calculation cp. DIFFERENTIAL CALCULUS, INTEGRAL CALCULUS. **calculous,** *a.* affected with or of the nature of a calculus. [L, a pebble, dim. of CALX]

Calcutta, *n.* the largest city of India, on the Hooghly, the most westerly mouth of the Ganges, some 130 km/80 miles N of the Bay of Bengal. It is the capital of West Bengal; population (1981) 9,166,000. Chiefly a commercial and industrial centre (engineering, shipbuilding, jute, and other textiles). Calcutta was the seat of government of British India (1773–1912).

caldarium, *n.* a Roman hot bath or hot bath-room. [L, from *calidus,* hot]

Calder, *n.* **Alexander** (1898–1976), US abstract sculptor, the inventor of mobiles, suspended shapes that move in the lightest current of air. In the 1920s he began making wire sculptures with movable parts; in the 1960s he created stabiles, large coloured sculptures of sheet metal.

caldera, *n.* a large, deep volcanic crater. [Sp., cauldron]

Calderón de la Barca, *n.* **Pedro** (1600–81), Spanish dramatist and poet. After the death of Lope de Vega, he was considered to be the leading Spanish dramatist. Most famous of some 118 plays is the philosophical *La Vida es sueño/Life is a Dream* (1635).

caldron CAULDRON.

Caldwell, *n.* **Erskine (Preston)** (1903–87), US novelist, whose *Tobacco Road* (1932) and *God's Little Acre* (1933) are earthy and vivid presentations of poverty-stricken Southern sharecroppers.

Caledonian, *a.* (*poet.*) of or pertaining to Scotland; Scottish; denoting a mountain-building movement in the Palaeozoic era. *n.* a Scotsman. [L *Calēdonia,* N Britain]

calefacient, *a.* (*Med.*) causing or exciting heat or warmth. *n.* a medicine for increasing the heat of the body. **calefaction,** *n.* **calefactive,** *a.* **calefactor,** *n.* a small cooking-stove. **calefactory,** *a.* producing or communicating heat. *n.* a room in which monks used to warm themselves. †**calefy**, *v.t.* to make warm; *v.i.* to grow warm. [*calefaciens -ntem,* pres.p. of *calefacere,* to warm (*calēre,* to be warm, *facere,* to make)]

calembour, *n.* a pun. [F]

calendar, *n.* a register or list of the months, weeks, and days of the year, with the civil and ecclesiastical holidays, festivals and other dates; a table giving the times of sunrise and sunset, with other astronomical phenomena, an almanac; the system by which the beginning, length and subdivisions of the civil year are defined, esp. the Gregorian calendar adopted in England in 1752; a list or register, a roll, esp. a catalogue of documents in chronological order with digests of the contents; a list of courses etc. offered by a university. *v.t.* to register; to insert in a list; to arrange, digest and catalogue documents. **calendar line** DATE LINE. **calendar month, year,** *n.* a month, or year, according to the calendar, as distinct from *lunar month* etc. **calendric, -ical,** *a.* [OF *calendier,* L *calendārium,* an account-book]

calender[1], *n.* a press or machine in which cloth or paper is passed between rollers to make it glossy. *v.t.* to glaze by passing between rollers. **calenderer, calendrer,** *n.* **calendry**, *n.* [F *calandre,* med. L *celendra,* L *cylindrus,* Gr. *kulindros,* a roller]

calender[2], *n.* one of an order of mendicant dervishes. [Pers. *galandar*]

calends, kalends, *n.pl.* the first day of any month in the old Roman calendar; † the beginning. **at the Greek calends,** never (the Greeks had no calends). [L *calendae,* name of first day of month (old v. *calāre,* to proclaim, cp. Gr. *kalein*)]

calendula, *n.* a marigold, or the genus of plants to which it belongs. [L, dim. of *calendae,* CALENDS]

calenture, *n.* a fever or delirium incident to sailors within the tropics; fever, ardour, fury. [F, from Sp. *calentura* (L *calens -ntis,* pres.p. of *calēre* to be hot)]

calescence, *n.* increasing warmth or heat. [L *calescere,* to grow hot]

calf[1], *n.* (*pl.* **calves**) the young of any bovine animal, esp. of the domestic cow; leather made from calfskin; the young of some large animals, as of the elephant, rhinoceros, whale etc; a stupid, childish fellow; a small island (or iceberg) near a larger one. *v.i.* (*past, p.p.* **calved**) to give birth to a calf. **Golden Calf**, the idol set up by the Israelites (Ex. xxxii); Mammon-worship, the pursuit of riches. **in calf, with calf,** of the above animals, pregnant. **calf-bound,** *a.* bound in calfskin. **calf-love,** *n.* attachment between a boy and a girl. **calfskin,** *n.* calf-leather used in bookbinding and for boots and shoes. **calf's teeth**, *n.pl.* milk teeth. **calfhood,** *n.* **calfish**, *a.* like a calf; raw, inexperienced. [OE *cealf* (cp. Icel. *kālfr,* Goth *kalbō,* G *Kalb*)]

calf[2], *n.* (*pl.* **calves,**) the thick fleshy part of the leg below the knee. **calfless,** *a.* **-calved,** *a.* (*in comb.*, as *thick-calved*). [Icel. *kālfl,* prob. conn. with prec.]

Calgary, *n.* city in Alberta, Canada, on the Bow river, in the foothills of the Rockies; at 1048 m/3440 ft it is one of the highest Canadian towns; population (1986) 671,000. It is the centre of a large agricultural region, and the oil and financial centre of Alberta and W Canada. Founded as Fort Calgary by the North West Mounted Police (1875), it was reached by the Canadian Pacific Railway (1885), and developed rapidly after the discovery of oil in 1914.

Calhoun, *n.* **John Caldwell** (1782–1850), US politician, born in South Carolina. He was vice-president (1825–29) under John Quincy Adams and (1829–33) under Andrew Jackson. Throughout he was a defender of the states' rights against the federal government, and of the institution of black slavery.

Cali, *n.* city in SW Colombia, in the Cauca Valley 975 m/3200 ft above sea level, founded in 1536. Cali has textile, sugar and engineering industries. Population (1985) 1,398,276.

Caliban, *n.* a man having bestial propensities; a savage, a boor. [character in Shakespeare's *Tempest*]

calibre, (*esp. N Am.*) **caliber**, *n.* the internal diameter of the bore of a gun or any tube; quality, capacity, compass; ability, character, standing. **calibrate,** *v.t.* to ascertain the calibre of; to test the accuracy of an instrument against a standard; to graduate (as a gauge). **calibration,** *n.* the act of calibrating; the testing by experiment of the accuracy of a graduated scale. **calibrator,** *n.* **-calibred,** *a.* (*in comb.*). [F *calibre,* It. *calibro* (etym. doubtful; perh. from *qālib,* a mould)]

caliciform, CALYCIFORM under CALYX.

calicle, *n.* (*Biol.*) a small cup-shaped body or organ. **calicular,** *a.* [L *caliculus* dim. of CALIX]

calico, *n.* (*pl.* **-coes, -cos**) cotton cloth formerly imported from the East; white or unbleached cotton cloth; printed cotton cloth. **calico-ball,** *n.* a ball at which ladies wear cotton dresses. **calico-printing**, *n.* the business or art of printing patterns on calico. [*Calicut* on the Malabar coast]

calid, *a.* warm, tepid, hot. **calidity**, †**caliduct,** *n.* a pipe for the conveyance of heat by means of steam, hot air etc. [L *calidus,* warm]

calif, califate CALIPH.

California, *n.* Pacific state of the US; nickname the Golden State, originally because of its gold mines, but more recently because of its sunshine. **area** 411,100 sq km/158,685 sq miles. **capital** Sacramento. **towns** Los Angeles, San Diego, San Francisco, San José, Fresno. **physical** Sierra Nevada (including Yosemite and Sequoia National Parks, Lake Tahoe and Mount Whitney, 4418 m/14,500 ft, the highest mountain in the lower 48 states); and the Coast Range; Death Valley 86 m/282 ft below sea level; Colorado and Mojave deserts (Edwards Air Force base is in the latter); Monterey Peninsula; Salton Sea; offshore in the Pacific there are huge underwater volcanoes with tops 8 km/5 miles across. **products** leading agricultural state with fruit (peaches, citrus, grapes in the valley of the San Joaquin and Sacramento rivers), nuts, wheat, vegetables, cotton, rice, all mostly grown by irrigation, the water being carried by immense concrete-lined canals to the Central Valley and Imperial Valley; beef cattle, timber, fish, oil, natural gas, aerospace, electronics (Silicon Valley), food-processing, films and television programmes. There are also great reserves of energy (geothermal) in the hot water which lies beneath much of the state. **population** (1987) 27,663,000, most populous state of the US, 66% non-Hispanic white; 20% Hispanic; 7.5% Black; 7% Asian (including many Vietnamese).

California current, *n.* the cold ocean current in the East Pacific Ocean flowing southwards down the west coast of North America. It is part of the North Pacific gyre (a vast, circular movement of ocean water).

California jack, *n.* a card game resembling all-fours. [CALIFORNIA, see above, JACK, the knave].

California poppy ESCHSCHOLTZIA.

californium, *n.* an artificially-produced radioactive element, at. no. 98; chem. symbol Cf.

†**caliginous,** *a.* misty, murky; obscure, gloomy. [L *cālīginōsus,* misty (*cāligo -inem,* mist, obscurity)]

Caligula, *n.* **Gaius Caesar** (AD 12–41), Roman emperor, son of Germanicus and successor to Tiberius in AD 37. Caligula was a cruel tyrant and was assassinated by an officer of his guard. Believed to have been mentally unstable, he is remembered for giving a consulship to his horse Incitatus.

calipash, *n.* that part of a turtle next to the upper shell, containing a dull green gelatinous substance. [perh. var. of CARAPACE]

calipee, *n.* that part of a turtle next to the lower shell, containing a light yellow substance. [coined to jingle with prec.]

calipers CALLIPERS.

caliph, calif, *n.* the chief ruler in certain Muslim countries, who is regarded as the successor of Mohammed. **caliphate, califate,** *n.* the office or dignity of a caliph; his term of office; the dominion of a caliph. [F *calife,* med. L *calīpha,* Arab. *khalīfah,* successor]

†**caliver,** *n.* a light kind of musket fired without a rest; a soldier armed with a caliver. [CALIBRE]

calix, *n.* (*pl.* **-lices**) a cup-like body cavity or organ. [L, cp. CALYX]

Calixtin, -tine, *n.* one of a Hussite sect who contended that the cup as well as the bread should be administered to the laity at the Sacrament, a Utraquist; one of the followers of the Lutheran George Calixtus (1586–1656), also called Syncretists. [F *Calixtin,* med. L *Calixtini,* pl. (*calix,* cup)]

calk¹ CAULK.

calk², *v.t.* to copy (a drawing etc.) by rubbing the back with colouring matter, and tracing the lines with a style on to paper beneath. [F *calquer,* It. *calcare,* L *calcāre,* to tread (*calx -cis,* heel)]

calk³, *n.* a calkin. *v.t.* to furnish with a calkin; to rough-shoe; to knock down the edges of (an iron plate or the head or point of a rivet) so as to make them fit closely. **calking-iron,** *n.* an instrument used for this purpose.

calkin, *n.* a sharp projection on a horseshoe to prevent slipping; irons nailed on shoes or clogs. [OF *calcain,* L *calcāneum,* the heel (*calx*)]

call¹, *v.t.* to name, to designate; to describe as; to regard or consider as; to summon; to cite; to invite; to command; to invoke; to appeal to; to rouse from sleep; to nominate; to lure (as birds), to attract by imitating their cry; (*Comput.*) to transfer control to (a subroutine) by means of a code (**calling sequence**). *v.i.* to speak in a loud voice; to cry aloud, to shout; to pay a short visit; in bridge, to make a bid; in poker, to ask an opponent to show his or her cards; in whist, to show by special play that trumps are wanted; to ring up on the telephone. *n.* a loud cry; a vocal address or supplication; the cry of an animal, esp. of a bird; a whistle to imitate the cry of an animal; the act of calling at a house or office on one's way; a short, formal visit; a summons, an invitation; an invitation to become minister to a congregation; a summons or signal on a bugle, whistle or telephone; a requirement of duty; duty, necessity, justification, occasion; a demand for payment of instalments due (of shares etc.); the option of claiming stock at a certain time at a price agreed on. **at call, on call,** at command; available at once. **call of nature,** a need to urinate or defecate. **to call back,** to revoke, to withdraw; to visit again; to call later by telephone. **to call down,** to invoke. **to call for,** to desire the attendance of; to appeal, demand; to signal for (trumps); to visit any place to bring (some person or thing) away; to require, necessitate. **to call forth,** to elicit; to summon to action. **to call in,** to summon to one's aid; to withdraw (money) from circulation; to order the return of; to pay a short visit (on, upon, at etc.). **to call in question,** to dispute. **to call into being,** to give existence to, create. **to call into play,** to put in operation. **to call names,** to abuse. **to call off,** to summon away, to divert; to cancel. **to call on,** to invoke, to appeal to; to pay a short visit to; to demand explanation, payment etc. **to call one's own,** to regard as one's possession, to own. **to call out,** to bawl; to challenge to a duel; to summon (as troops etc.) to service; to elicit; to order (workers) to strike. **to call over,** to read aloud. **to call the roll,** to call over a list of names to ascertain that all are present. **to call the tune** TUNE. **to call to mind,** to recall. **to call to the Bar,** to admit as a barrister. **to call up,** to bring into view or remembrance; to rouse from sleep; to require payment of; to summon by telephone; (*Mil., Nav.*) to mobilize; to summon to appear (before). **to call upon,** to invoke, to appeal to; to pay a short visit to. **within call,** within hearing. **call-bird,** *n.* a bird that decoys others by its note. **call-box,** *n.* a public telephone booth. **call-boy,** *n.* a boy who calls actors when they are wanted on the stage; one who transmits the orders of the captain of a (river) steamer to the engineer. **call-day, -night,** *n.* in the Inns of Court, dates on which benchers are called to the Bar. **call-girl,** *n.* a prostitute who makes appointments by telephone. **calling card,** *n.* (*N Am.*) a visiting card. **call-loan, -money,** *n.* money lent on condition that repayment may be demanded without notice. **call-note,** *n.* the call of an animal, esp. a bird, to its mate or young. **call number,** *n.* a set of numbers and/or letters identifying the position of a book in a library. **call sign,** *n.* a set of numbers and/or letters identifying a radio transmitter or station. **callable,** *a.* **caller,** *n.* one who calls, esp. one who pays a call or visit. **calling,** *n.* the action of the verb TO CALL; habitual occupation, trade, profession; a vocation; a solemn summons to duty, renunciation, faith etc.; duty; the body of persons employed in a particular occupation, business or vocation. [Icel. *kalla*]

†**call²,** CAUL.

Callaghan¹, *n.* **(Leonard) James** (1912–), British Labour politician. As chancellor of the exchequer (1964–67), he introduced corporation and capital-gains tax, and resigned following devaluation. He was home secretary (1967–70) and prime minister (1976–79) in a period of increasing economic stress.

Callaghan², *n.* **Morley** (1903–), Canadian novelist and short story writer, whose realistic novels include *Such Is My Beloved* (1934), *More Joy In Heaven* (1937), and *Close To The Sun Again* (1977).

calla lily, *n.* the arum lily, *Richardia* (or *Calla*) *aethiopica.*

Callanetics, *n.sing.* a system of exercises using small precise movements to increase muscle tone. [*Callan* Pinckney, its inventor]

callant, *n.* (*Sc.*) a youth, a lad. [Dut. *kalant,* a customer, a blade]

Callao, *n.* chief commercial and fishing port of Peru, 12 km/7 miles SW of Lima; population (1988) 318,000. Founded in 1537, it was destroyed by an earthquake in 1746. It is Peru's main naval base, and produces fertilizers.

Callas, *n.* **Maria** (adopted name of Maria Kalogeropoulos) (1923–77), US lyric soprano, born in New York of Greek parents. With a voice of fine range and a gift for dramatic expression, she excelled in operas including *Norma, Madame Butterfly, Aïda, Lucia di Lammermoor* and *Medea.*

caller¹ CALL¹.

caller², *a.* cool, refreshing; of fish, freshly caught.

Callicrates, *n.* (5th cent. BC), Athenian architect (with Ictinus) of the Parthenon.

callid, *a.* cunning, crafty. **callidity,** *n.* [L *callidus*]

calligraphy, *n.* the art of beautiful handwriting; (*coll.*) handwriting. **calligraph,** *n., v.t.* **calligrapher, calligraphist,** *n.* **calligraphic,** *a.* [Gr. *kalligraphia*]

Callimachus, *n.* (310–240 BC), Greek poet and critic known for his epigrams. Born in Cyrene, he taught in Alexandria where he is reputed to have been head of the great library.

calling CALL¹.

Calliope, *n.* the ninth Muse, of eloquence and heroic poetry; (*Astron.*) one of the asteroids; (**calliope**) a series of steam-whistles toned to produce musical notes, and played by a key-board. [Gr.]

callipers, calipers, *n.pl.* compasses with bow legs for measuring convex bodies, or with points turned out for measuring calibres. *v.t.* to measure by means of callipers. **calliper (splint),** *n.* a form of splint for the leg which takes pressure off the foot when walking. **calliper-square,** *n.* a rule for measuring diameters, internal or external. [short for *calibre-compasses*]

callisthenic, *a.* promoting strength and beauty. **callisthenics,** *n.pl.* gymnastics (esp. for girls) productive of strength and beauty. [Gr. *kallos,* beauty, *sthenos,* strength (anal. with *kallisthenes,* adorned with strength)]

Callisto, *n.* second-largest moon of Jupiter, 4800 km/3000 miles in diameter, orbiting every 16.7 days at a distance of 1.9 million km/1.2 million miles from the planet. Its surface is covered with large craters.

callous, *a.* hardened, indurated; unfeeling, unsympathetic. **callously,** *adv.* **callousness,** *n.* **callosity**, *n.* hardened or thick skin, caused by friction, pressure, disease or other injury; a callus; insensibility, want of feeling. [L *callōsus,* hard or thick-skinned]

callow, *a.* unfledged, downy; immature, like the down of a fledgeling; youthful, inexperienced; of land, bare; low-lying and liable to floods. *n.* a meadow liable to floods. **callowness,** *n.* [OE *calu,* Teut. *kalwoz,* L *calvus* bald]

calluna, *n.* the ling, *Calluna vulgaris*. [Gr. *kallunein,* to beautify, to sweep (*kalos,* beautiful)]

callus, *n.* a hardening of the skin from pressure or friction; (*Med.*) a bony formation serving to unite a fracture; (*Bot.*) a hard formation. *v.t.*, *v.i.* to make or form a callus. [L]

calm, *a.* still, quiet, serene; tranquil, undisturbed. *n.* the state of being calm; (*Naut.*) entire absence of wind. *v.t.* to still, to quiet, to soothe. *v.i.* to become calm (with *down*). **calmative,** *a.* tending to calm. *n.* (*Med.*) a sedative medicine. **calmed,** *a.* rendered calm; becalmed. **calmly,** *adv.* **calmness,** *n.* †**calmy,** *a.* [F *calme,* Sp. and It. *calma,* prob. from late L *cauma,* Gr. *kauma,* heat (*kaiein,* to burn)]

calmato, *a.*, *adv.* (*Mus.*) quiet, quietly. [It.]

Calmette, *n.* **Albert** (1863–1933), French bacteriologist. A student of Pasteur, he developed (with Camille Guérin, 1872–1961) the BCG vaccine against tuberculosis in 1921.

calomel, *n.* mercurous chloride, an active purgative. [F]

calore, *n.* (*Mus.*) passion, warmth. **caloroso**, *a.*, *adv.* passionately. [It.]

Calor gas®, *n.* a type of bottled gas for cooking etc. [L *calor,* heat]

caloric, *a.* pertaining to heat or calories. *n.* †the supposed fluid cause of heat; heat. **caloric-engine,** *n.* Ericsson's hot-air engine. **calorescence**, (on analogy of CALESCENCE), *n.* the change of non-luminous into luminous heat-rays. **caloricity**, *n.* the faculty in living beings of developing heat. **calorifacient**, *a.* esp. of foods, heat-producing. **calorify,** *v.t.* to make hot. [F *calorique,* L *calor,* heat]

calorie, calory, *n.* unit of heat. **(small) calorie** is the quantity of heat required to raise the temperature of 1 gram of water by 1° C; the **kilocalorie** or **Calorie,** equalling 1000 calories, is used in measuring the energy content of food. Now officially superseded by the *joule* (1 joule = 4.1868 calories). **calorific,** *a.* producing heat, thermal. **calorific value,** *n.* the amount of heat produced by the complete combustion of a given amount (usu. 1 kg) of fuel. **calorifically,** *adv.* **calorimeter**, *n.* an instrument for measuring actual quantities of heat, or the specific heat of a body. **calorimetric**, *a.* **calorimetry**, *n.* [as. prec.]

calotte, *n.* a small skull-cap worn by Roman ecclesiastics; a cap-like crest on a bird's head; anything cap-shaped; a recess hollowed out in the upper part of a room, chapel etc. to diminish the apparent height. [F, perh. dim. of *cale,* CAUL]

calotype, *n.* a photographic process invented by Fox Talbot and now disused; a Talbotype. [Gr. *kalos,* beautiful, TYPE]

caloyer, *n.* a Greek monk, esp. of the order of St Basil. [F, from It. *caloiero,* mod. Gr *kalogēros* (*kalos,* beautiful, *-gēros,* aged)]

calp, *n.* the local name of a dark limestone common in Ireland. [etym. unknown]

calpac, calpack, *n.* a high, triangular felt cap worn in the East. [Turk. *qalpaq*]

calque, *n.* a loan translation, a literal translation into English of a foreign idiom. [F, tracing, from L *calcāre,* to tread]

caltha, *n.* a genus of ranunculaceous marsh plants containing the marsh marigold, *Caltha palustris*. [L]

caltrop, *n.* an instrument formed of four iron spikes joined at the bases, thrown on the ground to impede the advance of cavalry; a name for several trailing plants, with spiny fruit, that entangle the feet; the star-thistle, the genus *Tribulus* etc. **water-caltrops,** water weeds – *Potamogeton densus, P. crispus, Trapa natans*. [OE *calcatrippe, calcetreppe,* a thistle (cp. OF *kauketrape, cauchetrepe*), prob. from late L (L *calx -cem,* heel, late L *trappa,* OHG *trapo,* TRAP)]

calumba, *n.* the root of *Cocculus palmatus,* of Mozambique, used as a tonic and antiseptic. [*Colombo,* Sri Lanka, whence it was wrongly supposed to come]

calumet, *n.* the tobacco-pipe of the N American Indians, used as a symbol of peace and friendship. [Norm. F (preserved in French-Canadian); parallel to OF *chalemel* (F *chalumeau*), from L *calamellus,* dim. of CALAMUS]

calumniate, *v.t.* to slander; to charge falsely with something criminal or disreputable. *v.i.* to utter calumnies. **calumniation,** *n.* the act of calumniating. **calumniator,** *n.* **calumniatory,** *a.* **calumnious,** *a.* **calumniously,** *adv.* **calumniousness,** *n.* **calumny**, *n.* a malicious misrepresentation of the words or actions of another; slander; a false charge. [L *calumniātus,* p.p. of *calumniāri* (*calvī,* to deceive]

calvados, *n.* apple brandy made in Normandy. [*Calvados* department]

Calvary, *n.* the place where Christ was crucified (two chief sites are suggested: one is where the Church of the Sepulchre now stands, the other is the hill beyond the Damascus gate); a life-size representation of the Crucifixion, usu. in the open air; a representation of the successive scenes of the passion. **Calvary-cross,** *n.* a cross mounted on three steps. [L *Calvāria,* a skull (*calvus,* bald); trans. of Gr. *Golgotha,* Heb. *gogolthā,* the skull]

calve, *v.i.* to bring forth a calf; to bring forth young; of icebergs, to detach and cast off a mass of ice. *v.t.* to bear, bring forth. [OE *cealfian* (*cealf,* CALF[1])]

†**calvered,** *a.* of salmon etc., prepared in a particular way when fresh. [from obs. v. *calver,* etym. unknown]

Calvin[1], *n.* **John** (1509–64), French-born Swiss Protestant church reformer and theologian. He was a leader of the Reformation in Geneva and set up a strict religious community there. His theological system is known as Calvinism, and his church government as Presbyterianism. Calvin wrote (in Latin) *Institutes of the Christian Religion* (1536) and commentaries on the New Testament and much of the Old Testament.

Calvin[2], *n.* **Melvin** (1911–), US chemist who, using radioactive carbon-14 as a tracer, determined the biochemical processes of photosynthesis, in which green plants use chlorophyll to convert carbon dioxide and water into sugar and oxygen. Nobel Prize 1961.

Calvinism, *n.* Christian doctrine as interpreted by John Calvin and adopted in Scotland, parts of Switzerland, and the Netherlands. Its central doctrine is predestination, under which certain souls (the elect) are predestined by God through the sacrifice of Jesus to salvation, and the rest to damnation. Although Calvinism is rarely accepted today in its strictest interpretation, the 20th century has seen a neo-Calvinist revival through the work of Karl Barth. **Calvinist,** *n.* **Calvinistic, -ical,** *a.*

calvity, calvities, *n.* baldness. [L *calvities,* baldness (*calvus,* bald)]

calx, *n.* (*pl.* **calces**) ashes or fine powder remaining from metals, minerals etc. after they have undergone calcination; (*Eton.*) a goal (from the goal marked with lime or chalk). [L *calx -cis,* lime]

calycanthus, *n.* a genus of N American shrubs.

calyc(i)-, *comb. form* calyx.

calyciferous, *a.* bearing a calyx.

calycifloral, -florate, -florous, *a.* having the petals and stamens growing upon the calyx.

calyciform, *a.* having the form of a calyx.

calycine, calycinal, *a.* of, belonging to, or in the form of a calyx.

calycle, calyculus, *n.* a little calyx; a row of small leaflets at the base of the calyx on the outside; the outer covering of a seed. **calycular, calyculate,** *a.* [L *calyculus,* dim. of CALYX]

calypso, *n.* a W Indian narrative song made up as the singer goes on.

Calypso, *n.* in Greek mythology, a sea nymph who waylaid the homeward-bound Odysseus for seven years.

calyptr-, *comb. form.* furnished with a hood; resembling a hood.

calyptra, *n.* (*Bot.*) a hood or cover. **calyptrate,** *a.* **calyptriform,** *a.* [Gr. *kaluptra,* a veil (*kaluptein,* to cover, conceal)]

calyx, *n.* (*pl.* **calyces**), the whorl of leaves or sepals (usu. green) forming the outer integument of a flower; a calix. **calycled,** *a.* having a calyx. [L, from Gr. *kalux* (cp. *kaluptein,* L *cēlāre,* to cover, conceal)]

CAM[1], (*abbr.*) content-addressable memory.

CAM[2], *n.* computer-aided manufacture, the use of computers to control production processes; in particular, the control of machine tools and robots in factories. In some factories, the whole design and production system has been automated by linking CAD (computer-aided design) to CAM.

cam, *n.* an eccentric projection attached to a revolving shaft for the purpose of giving linear motion to another part or follower. **camshaft,** *n.* a shaft bearing cams which operate the valves of internal-combustion engines. [var. of COMB[1]]

camaraderie, *n.* comradeship; good fellowship and loyalty among intimate friends. [F, from *camarade,* COMRADE]

Camargo, *n.* **Marie-Anne de Cupis** (1710–70), French ballerina of Spanish descent. The first ballerina to attain the 'batterie' (movements involving beating the legs together) previously danced only by men. She caused a scandal by shortening her skirt to expose her ankles, showing her brilliant footwork and giving more liberty of movement.

Camargue, *n.* the marshy area of the Rhône delta, S of Arles, France: area about 780 sq km/300 sq miles. Bulls and horses are bred there, and the nature reserve, which is known for its bird life, forms the southern part.

camarilla, *n.* †an audience chamber; a band or company of intriguers; a private cabinet; a cabal. [Sp. dim. of *camara,* CHAMBER]

camber, *n.* the condition of being slightly convex above; the curvature given to a road surface to make water run off it; a piece of timber bent with a camber; a small dock for discharging timber; the part of a dockyard where timber is cambered. *v.t., v.i.* to bend, to arch. **camber-beam,** *n.* **camber-keeled,** *a.* **camber-slip,** *n.* a slightly curved strip of wood used in making flat arches. **camber-windowed,** *a.* **cambered, cambering,** *a.* [F *cambre,* from *cambrer,* L *camerāre,* to vault (*camera,* chamber)]

Camberwell beauty, *n.* a butterfly, *Vanessa antiopa.* [*Camberwell,* in SE London]

cambist, *n.* one skilled in the science of exchange; a bill-broker; a money-changer. **cambism, †cambistry,** *n.* [F *cambiste,* late L *cambium,* exchange]

cambium, *n.* the viscid substance consisting of cellular tissue which appears, in the spring, between the wood and bark of exogenous trees. [late L, exchange]

Cambodia, *n.* State of, country in SE Asia, bordered to the N and NW by Thailand, N by Laos, E and SE by Vietnam, and SW by the South China Sea. **area** 181,035 sq km/69,880 sq miles. **capital** Phnom Penh. **towns** Battambang, and the seaport Kompong Som. **physical** mostly forested; flat, with mountains in S; Mekong River runs N–S. **exports** rubber, rice. **population** (1985 est.) 7,280,000; annual growth rate 2.6%. **language** Khmer (official), French. **religion** Theravada Buddhist.

Cambrai, Battles of, two battles in World War I at Cambrai in NE France; in the **First Battle**, Nov.–Dec. 1917, the town was almost captured by the British when large numbers of tanks were used for the first time; in the **Second Battle**, 26 Aug.–5 Oct. 1918, the town was taken during the final British offensive.

cambrel, *n.* a bent piece of wood used by butchers for hanging up carcases. [etym. doubtful]

Cambrian[1], *a.* of or belonging to Wales. *n.* a Welshman. [L *Cambria, Cumbria,* Celt. *Cymry,* Welsh, *Cymru,* Wales]

Cambrian[2], *n.* period of geological time 590–505 million years ago; the first period of the Palaeozoic era. All invertebrate animal life appeared, and marine algae was widespread. The earliest fossils with hard shells, such as trilobites, date from this period. [as prec.]

cambric, *n.* a kind of very fine white linen; handkerchiefs. [orig. made at *Cambray*]

Cambridge, *n.* city in England, on the river Cam (a river sometimes called by its earlier name, Granta), 80 km/50 miles north of London; population (1989) 101,000. It is the administrative headquarters of Cambridgeshire. The city is centred on Cambridge University (founded 12th cent.). **Cambridge blue,** *n., a.* pale blue.

Cambridgeshire, *n.* county in E England. **area** 3410 sq km/1316 sq miles. **towns** administrative headquarters Cambridge; Ely, Huntingdon, Peterborough. **products** mainly agricultural. **population** (1987) 642,000.

Cambs., (*abbr.*) Cambridgeshire.

Cambyses, *n.* (6th cent. BC), emperor of Persia (529–522 BC). Succeeding his father Cyrus, he assassinated his brother Smerdis and conquered Egypt in 525. Here he outraged many of the local religious customs, and was said to have become mad. He died in Syria on his journey home, probably by suicide.

camcorder, *n.* a video camera and recorder combined in one unit.

Camden, *n.* **William** (1551–1623), English antiquary. He published his topographical survey *Britannia* in 1586, and was headmaster of Westminster School from 1593. The **Camden Society** (1838) commemorates his work.

Camden Town Group, school of British painters (1911–13), based in Camden Town, London, in part inspired by W.R. Sickert. The work of Spencer Gore (1878–1914) and Harold Gilman (1876–1919) is typical of the group, rendering everyday town scenes in post-impressionist style.

came[1], *n.* a strip of lead used in framing glass in lattice windows. [Sc., earlier *calm*]

came[2], *past* COME.

camel, *n.* a large, hornless, humpbacked ruminant with long neck and padded feet, used in Africa and the East as a beast of burden; two species, the Arabian camel, *Camelus dromedarius,* with one hump, and the Bactrian, *C. bactrianus,* with two; a great hulking fellow; a watertight float attached to a boat to raise it in the water; a pale brownish-yellow colour. *a.* of this colour; made of camel-hair fabric. **to swallow a camel,** (alln. to Matt. xxiii.24) to believe an incredibility; to accept something intolerable. **camel-backed,** *a.* humpbacked. **camel-brown,** *n.* an angler's fly. **camel corps,** *n.* troops mounted on camels. **camel-hair,** *n.* camel's hair used as a material for various fabrics; a painter's brush made of hairs from squirrels' tails. **cameleer,** *n.* a camel-driver. **camelish,** *a.* obstinate. **camelry,** *n.* troops mounted on camels. [OE, from L *camēlus,* Gr. *kamēlos,* from Semitic (Heb. *gāmāl,* Arab. *jāmāl*)]

cameleon CHAMELEON.

cameline, *n.* camlet.

camellia, *n.* a genus of evergreen shrubs with beautiful flowers. [G.J. *Kamel,* a Moravian Jesuit, and Eastern traveller]

†**camelopard,** *n.* the giraffe. [L *camēlopardus -pardălis,* Gr. *kamēlopardis* (CAMEL, PARD[1])]

Camelot, *n.* legendary capital of King Arthur.

camembert, *n.* a soft rich cheese from Normandy. [F, name of village]

cameo, *n.* a precious stone with two layers of colours, the upper being carved in relief, the lower serving as background; used also of similar carvings on shells; a piece of jewellery using such carving; a short literary piece; a small part in a play or film which allows an actor to display his or her skill. *a.* of a cameo or cameos; small and perfect. [It. *cammé,* late L *cammaeus;* etym. unknown]

camera, *n.* the private chamber of a judge; an apparatus for taking photographs which records an image (or a series of images in a movie camera) on a light-sensitive surface; an apparatus which records (moving) images and converts them to electrical signals for TV transmission. **in camera** in private, the public being excluded from the court. **off camera,** not being filmed. **on camera,** being recorded on film. **camera crew,** *n.* a group of people, including cameraman, sound recordist etc., needed to make a television film (usu. on location). **camera lucida,** *n.* an instrument (used for copying drawings etc.) by which the rays of light from an object are reflected by a prism, to produce an image of the object on paper placed below. **cameraman,** *n.* a person who operates a movie or television camera. **camera obscura,** *n.* a dark box, or chamber, admitting light through a pinhole or a double-convex lens, at the focus of which an image is formed of external objects on paper, glass etc. **camera-shy,** *a.* unwilling to be photographed or filmed. **camerated,** *a.* arched; (*Zool.*) divided into chambers. [L vault, from Aryan *kam-,* to cover over (cp. Gr. *kamara,* anything with a vaulted roof)]

camerlengo, -lingo, *n.* a papal treasurer. [It., chamberlain].

Cameron[1], *n.* **Charles** (1746–1812), British architect. He trained under Isaac Ware in the Palladian tradition before being summoned to Russia in 1779. He created the palace complex at Tsarskoe Selo (Pushkin), planned the town of Sofia, and from 1803 as Chief Architect of the Admiralty executed many buildings, including the Naval Hospital and barracks at Kronstadt.

Cameron[2], *n.* **Julia Margaret** (1815–79), British photographer. She made lively, revealing portraits of the Victorian intelligentsia using a large camera, five-minute exposures, and wet plates. Her subjects included Darwin and Tennyson.

Cameronian, *n.* a follower of Richard Cameron (d. 1680), a noted Scottish Presbyterian Covenanter, or of his doctrines; a member of the Reformed Presbyterian Church; (*pl.*) the Cameronian Regiment, the 26th Regiment, later the 1st Batt. Scottish Rifles. [*Cameron,* -IAN]

Cameroon, *n.* United Republic of (*République du Cameroun*), country in W Africa, bounded NW by Nigeria, NE by Chad, E by the Central African Republic, S by Congo, Gabon and Equatorial Guinea, and W by the Atlantic Ocean. **area** 465,054 sq km/179,511 sq miles. **capital** Yaoundé. **towns** chief port Douala. **physical** desert in the far N in the Lake Chad basin, dry savanna plateau in the intermediate area, and in the S dense tropical rainforest. **exports** cocoa, coffee, bananas, cotton, timber, rubber, groundnuts, gold, aluminium. **population** (1988 est.) 11,082,000; annual growth rate 2.7%. **language** French and English in pidgin variations (official), but there has been some discontent with the emphasis on French; there are 163 indigenous peoples with many African languages. **religion** Roman Catholic 35%, animist 25%, Muslim 22%, Protestant 18%.

camion, *n.* a heavy lorry; a dray. [F, a lorry]

†**camis, camus,** *n.* a thin, loose linen dress; a shirt, a chemise. [Sp. and Port. *camisa,* late L *camisia,* CHEMISE]

camisade, †**camisado,** *n.* a night assault or surprise, in which the soldiers wore their shirts over their armour as a means of recognition. [F *camisade,* Sp. *camisada, camiçada,* from prec.]

Camisard, *n.* one of the French Calvinist insurgents in the Cevennes after the revocation of the Edict of Nantes. [F, from prec.]

camisole, *n.* an under-bodice. **cami-knickers,** *n.pl.* camisole and knickers in one piece. [F, from Sp. *camisola,* dim. of *camisa,* see CAMIS]

camlet, *n.* a fabric orig. of camel's hair, now a mixture of silk, wool and hair (applied at different times to various substances); a garment of camlet. [F *camelot,* Arab. *khamlat, khaml,* an Eastern fabric]

cammock, *n.* the rest-harrow, *Ononis arvensis;* applied locally to other yellow-flowered plants. [OE *cammoc;* etym. doubtful]

Camoens, Camões, *n.* **Luís Vaz de** (1524–80), Portuguese poet and soldier. He went on various military expeditions, and was shipwrecked in 1558. His poem, *Os Lusiades/The Lusiads*, published 1572, tells the story of the explorer Vasco da Gama and incorporates much Portuguese history; it has become the country's national epic. His posthumously published lyric poetry is also now valued.

camomile, chamomile, *n.* an aromatic creeping plant belonging to the genera *Anthemis* or *Matricaria,* esp. *A. nobilis;* applied also to some other plants. **camomile tea,** *n.* [F *camomille,* late L *camomilla,* Gr. *chamaimēlon,* lit. earth-apple]

Camorra, *n.* Italian secret society formed about 1820 by criminals in the dungeons of Naples, and continued once they were outside. It dominated politics from 1848, was suppressed in 1911, but many members eventually surfaced in the US Mafia. The Camorra still operates in the Naples area. **Camorrist,** *n.* [It., a blouse]

camouflage, *n.* disguise, esp. the concealment of guns, camps, buildings, vehicles etc., from the enemy by means of deceptive painting, a covering of boughs and the like; concealment of one's actions. *v.t.* to disguise. [F *camouflet,* a smokepuff]

camouflet, *n.* a cavity formed underground by the exploding of a bomb. [as prec.]

camp[1], *n.* the place where an army is lodged in tents or other temporary structures; a station for training troops; a body of troops in tents; an army on campaign; military life; temporary quarters of gipsies, holidaymakers, refugees etc.; the occupants of such quarters; (*Austral.*) a halting-place for cattle; a body of adherents; a side; a ruined prehistoric fort. *v.t.* to encamp troops. *v.i.* to encamp. **to camp out,** *v.i.* to lodge in a camp in the open; to sleep outdoors. *v.t.* to place troops in camp. **camp-bed,** *n.* a light folding bedstead. **camp-ceiling,** *n.* a concave ceiling or one with sloping sides (as in a garret). **camp-chair,** *n.* a folding chair. **camp-colour,** *n.* a flag for marking out a camping ground. †**camp-fever,** *n.* an epidemic to which troops in camp are liable, esp. typhus. **camp-fire,** *n.* an open fire at the centre of a camp. **camp-follower,** *n.* a civilian who follows an army in the field; a hanger-on. **camp-meeting,** *n.* a religious meeting in the open air or in a tent, often prolonged for days. **camp-site,** *n.* a place set aside, or suitable, for camping. **camp-stool,** *n.* a folding stool. **camper,** *n.* one who camps; a vehicle having living accommodation in the back. [F *camp* (cp. *champ*), It. or Sp. *campo,* L *campus,* a field]

camp[2], *a.* affectedly homosexual; effeminate; bizarre. *v.i.* to behave in a camp manner. *n.* camp behaviour. **high camp,** deliberately exaggerated camp. **to camp it up,** to act in an exaggeratedly camp manner. **campy,** *a.* [etym. unknown]

Campagna, *n.* the flat country around Rome. [L *Campania*]

campaign, *n.* †an open tract of country; the operations and continuance of an army in the field; any analogous operations or course of action, esp. a course of political propaganda. *v.i.* to serve on a campaign. **campaigner,** *n.* [F *campagne,* the open country, a campaign. It. *campagna,* L *campania,* a plain, *campus,* a field (cp. CHAMPAGNE, CHAMPAIGN)]

Campaign for Nuclear Disarmament, a non-political British organization advocating worldwide abolition of nuclear weapons. It was founded in 1958.

campanero, *n.* the Brazilian bell-bird. [Sp., bell-man (*campana,* bell)]

Campania, *n.* agricultural region (wheat, citrus, wine, vegetables, tobacco) of S Italy, including the volcano Vesuvius; capital Naples; industrial centres Benevento, Caserta and Salerno; area 13,600 sq km/5250 sq miles; population (1988) 5,732,000. There are ancient sites at Pompeii, Herculaneum and Paestum.

campanile, *n.* (*pl.* **-niles, -nili**) a bell-tower, esp. a detached one; a steeple. [It., from *campana,* bell]

campanology, *n.* the principles of bell-ringing, founding etc. **campanologer, -gist,** *n.* **campanological,** *a.*

campanula, *n.* a genus of plants with bell-shaped flowers, containing the bluebell of Scotland, the Canterbury bell etc. **campanulaceous,** *a.* **campanular, -ulate,** *a.* (*Bot., Zool.*) bell-shaped.

Campbell[1], *n.* family name of Dukes of Argyll; seated at Inveraray Castle, Argyll.

Campbell[2], *n.* **Colin, 1st Baron Clyde** (1792–1863), British field marshal. He commanded the Highland Brigade at Balaclava in the Crimean War, and as commander in chief during the Indian Mutiny raised the siege of Lucknow and captured Cawnpore.

Campbell[3], *n.* **Donald Malcolm** (1921–67), British car and speedboat enthusiast, son of Malcolm Campbell, who simultaneously held the land-speed and water-speed records. In 1964 he set the world water-speed record of 444.57 kph/276.3 mph on Lake Dumbleyung, Australia, with the turbo-jet hydroplane *Bluebird,* and achieved the land-speed record of 648.7 kph/403.1 mph at Lake Eyre salt flats, Australia. He was killed in an attempt to raise his water-speed record on Coniston Water, England.

Campbell[4], *n.* **Malcolm** (1885–1948), British racing driver who at one time held both land- and water-speed records. His car and boat were both called *Bluebird.*

Campbell[5], *n.* **Mrs Patrick** (born Beatrice Stella Tanner) (1865–1940), British actress, whose roles included Paula in Pinero's *The Second Mrs Tanqueray* (1893) and Eliza in *Pygmalion,* written for her by G.B. Shaw, with whom she had an amusing correspondence.

Campbell[6], *n.* **Roy** (1901–57), South African poet, who established his reputation with *The Flaming Terrapin* (1924). Born in Durban, he became a professional jouster and bull-fighter in Spain and Provence, France. He fought for Franco in the Spanish Civil War, and was with the Commonwealth forces in World War II.

Campbell-Bannerman, *n.* **Henry** (1836–1908), British Liberal politician, prime minister (1905–08). He granted self-government to the South African colonies, and passed the Trades Disputes Act of 1906.

Campbellite, *n.* a member of a sect founded by Campbell, called the Disciples of Christ. [Alexander *Campbell,* 1788–1866, of Virginia, a religious teacher]

Camp David, *n.* official country home of US presidents in the Appalachian mountains, Maryland; it was originally named Shangri-la by F.D. Roosevelt, but was renamed Camp David by Eisenhower (after his grandson).

Camp David Agreements, two framework agreements signed at Camp David, US, in 1978 by the Israeli prime minister Begin and president Sadat of Eygpt, at the instance of US president Carter, covering an Egypt–Israel peace treaty and phased withdrawal of Egypt from Sinai, which was completed in 1982, and an overall Middle East settlement including the election by the Palestinians of the West Bank and Gaza Strip of a 'self-governing authority'.

Campeachy wood, *n.* logwood. [*Campeche,* on W coast of Mexico]

Camperdown, *n.* (Dutch **Kamperduin**), village on the NW Netherlands coast, off which a British fleet defeated the Dutch on 11 Oct. 1797 in the Revolutionary Wars.

campestral, *a.* pertaining to or growing in the fields or open country. [L *campester -tris,* pertaining to a field (*campus,* a field)]

camphene, camphine, *n.* an illuminating oil distilled from turpentine. [see foll.]

camphor, *n.* a whitish, translucent, volatile, crystalline substance with a pungent odour, obtained from *Camphora officinarum, Dryobalanops aromatica* and other trees, used as an insect repellent, in liniment (**camphorated oil**), and in the manufacture of celluloid. †*v.t.* to camphorate. **camphor-laurel, -tree,** *n. Cinnamomum camphora.* **camphor-wood,** *n.* the wood of this or of an Australian timber-tree, *Callitris robusta.* **camphoraceous,** *a.* **camphorate,** *n.* **camphorate,** *v.t.* to wash or impregnate with camphor. **camphoric,** *a.*

Campin, *n.* **Robert** (active 1406–44), Netherlandish painter of the early Renaissance, active in Tournai, one of the first northern masters to use oil. He has been identified as the *Master of Flémalle,* and several altarpieces are attributed to him. Rogier van der Weyden was his pupil.

campion, *n.* British flowering plants of the genus *Lychnis.* [etym. doubtful; perh. from F *campagne* or L *campus,* a field]

Campion[1], *n.* **Edmund** (1540–81), English Jesuit and Roman Catholic martyr. He took deacon's orders in the English church, but fled to Douai, France, where in 1571 he recanted Protestantism. In 1573 he became a Jesuit in Rome, and in 1580 was sent to England as a missionary. He was betrayed as a spy in 1581, imprisoned in the Tower of London, and hanged, drawn, and quartered as a traitor.

Campion[2], *n.* **Thomas** (1567–1620), English poet and musician. He was the author of the critical *Art of English Poesie* (1602), and four *Bookes of Ayres,* for which he composed both words and music.

Campo-Formio, Treaty of, peace settlement during the Revolutionary Wars in 1797 between Napoleon and Austria, by which France gained the region of modern Belgium and Austria was compensated with Venice and part of modern Yugoslavia.

campshed, *v.t.* to line (a river bank) with piles and planks to prevent it from being worn away. **campshedding, -sheeting, -shot,** *n.* [etym. unknown]

campus, *n.* the buildings and grounds of a university or college, or (*N Am.*) a school; a geographically separate part of a university; the academic world in general. [L, a field]

CAMRA, (*abbr.*) Campaign for Real Ale.

Camu-Camu, camu-camu, *n.* a S American shrub with a fruit rich in vitamin C.

camus CAMIS.

Camus, *n.* **Albert** (1913–60), Algerian-born French writer. A journalist in France, he was active in the Resistance during World War II. His novels, which owe much to existentialism, include *L'Etranger/The Outsider* (1942), *La Peste/The Plague* (1948), and *L'Homme Révolté/The Rebel* (1952). Nobel Prize 1957.

camwood, *n.* barwood, a hard red wood from W Africa. [perh. from African name *kambi*]

Can., (*abbr.*) Canada; Canadian.

can[1], *n.* a metal vessel for holding liquid; a vessel of tinned iron in which meat, fruit, fish etc. are hermetically sealed up for preservation; a canful; (*coll.*) a shallow metal container for film; (*sl.*) prison; (*sl.*) a lavatory; (*pl., sl.*) headphones. *v.t.* (*past, p.p.* **canned**) to put up in cans for preservation. **can it!,** (*sl.*) stop doing that! **in the can,** of film, processed and ready for showing; (*fig.*) arranged; tidied up. **to carry the can,** to take responsibility, accept blame. **can-buoy,** *n.* a conical buoy to mark out shoals and rocks. **can-opener,** *n.* a tin-opener. **canful,** *n.* **canned,** *a.* preserved in a can; (*sl.*) drunk; of music, recorded in advance; of laughter, not spontaneous. **canner,** *n.* **cannery,** *n.* [OE *canne* (cp. Dut. *kan,* OHG *chann,* G *Kanne*)]

can[2], *aux. v.* (*pres* **can, canst,** *neg.* **cannot**, *past* **could, couldst**, OE *cūthe,* ME *coude*) to be able to; to be allowed to; to be possible to. [OE *cunnan,* to know, pl. *cunnon* (cp. Dut. *kunnen,* OHG *chunnan,* G *können,* KEN, KNOW, L *gnoscere,* Gr. *gignōskein*)]

Canaan, *n.* an ancient region between the Mediterranean and the Dead Sea, in the Bible the 'Promised Land' of the Israelites. Occupied as early as the 3rd millennium BC by the Canaanites, a Semitic-speaking people who were known to the Greeks of the 1st millennium BC as Phoenicians. The capital was Ebla (the modern Tell Mardikh, Syria). **Canaanitic**, **Canaanitish**, *a.* [Heb. *k'naan,* western Palestine]

Canada, *n.* Dominion of, a country occupying the northern part of the North American continent, bounded to the south by the US, to the north by the Arctic, to the east by the Atlantic Ocean, to the northwest by Alaska and to the west by the Pacific Ocean. **area** 9,971,000 sq km/3,849,803 sq miles. **capital** Ottawa. **towns** Toronto, Montréal, Vancouver, Edmonton, Calgary, Winnipeg, Québec, Hamilton. **physical** St Lawrence Seaway, Mackenzie river; Great Lakes; Arctic Archipelago; Rocky Mountains; Great Plains or Prairies; Canadian Shield. **exports** wheat, timber, pulp, newsprint, fish (especially salmon), furs (ranched fox and mink exceed the value of wild furs), oil, natural gas, aluminium, asbestos, coal, copper, iron, nickel, motor vehicles and parts, industrial and agricultural machinery, fertilizers. **population** (1987) 25,600,000 (including 300,000 North American Indians, of whom 75% live on over 2000 reserves in Ontario and the four western provinces; some 300,000 Métis (people of mixed race) and 19,000 Inuit (or Eskimo), of whom 75% live in the Northwest Territories). Over half Canada's population lives in Ontario and Québec. Annual growth rate 1.1%. **language** English, French (both official) (about 70% speak English, 20% French, and the rest are bilingual); there are also North American Indian languages and the Inuit Inuktitut. **religion** Roman Catholic 40%, Protestant 35%.

Canada balsam, *n.* a pale resin obtained from *Abies balsamea* and *A. canadensis,* used in medicine and to mount microscopic objects.

Canada goose *n.* a large N American wild goose, *Branta canadensis,* grey and brown in colour.

Canadian, *n.* a native or citizen of Canada. *a.* belonging to or pertaining to Canada.

canaille, *n.* the rabble, the mob. [F, from It. *canaglia, cane,* L *canis,* a dog]

canakin, CANNIKIN.

canal, *n.* an artificial watercourse, esp. one used for navigation; (*Physiol., Bot.*) a duct; (*Zool.*) a siphonal groove; (*Arch.*) a fluting, a groove. *v.t.* to make a canal across; to canalize. **canals of Mars,** linear markings on the surface of the planet Mars, supposed by some astronomers to be waterways, or zones of vegetation produced by periodical diffusion of moisture. **canal boat,** *n.* a long narrow boat used on canals. **canal rays,** *n.* positive rays; a steady flow of positively electrified particles which take part in the electrical discharge in a rarefied gas. **canalize, -ise,** *v.t.* to make a canal across or through; to convert a river into a navigable waterway; to give a desired direction to; to channel. **canalization, -isation,** *n.* the construction of canals. [F, from L *canālis*]

Canaletto, *n.* **Antonio** (Giovanni Antoni Canal) (1697–1768), Italian painter celebrated for his paintings of views (*vedute*) of Venice (where he lived for some years) and of the Thames and London 1746–56.

canaliculate, -ated, *a.* (*Physiol.*) minutely grooved; striated. [mod. L *canāliculātus* (*canāliculus,* dim. of *canālis,* see prec.)]

canape, canapé, *n.* a thin piece of bread or toast spread with cheese, fish etc. [F]

canard, *n.* an absurd story, a hoax, a false report; an aircraft having a tailplane mounted in front of the wings. [F, lit. a duck]

Canaries current, *n.* the cold ocean current in the North Atlantic Ocean flowing SW from Spain along the NW coast of Africa. It meets the northern equatorial current at a latitude of 20° N.

Canary, *n.* †a lively dance, orig. from the Canary Islands; a light sweet wine made there; a well-known cage-bird *Fringilla canaria*. *a.* bright yellow. **canary-coloured,** *a.* **canary-creeper, canariensis**, *n.* a climbing-plant with yellow flowers. **canary-seed**, *n.* the seed of *Phalaris canariensis,* the **canary-grass,** used as food for canaries. [F *Canarie,* Sp. *Canāria,* L *Canāria Insula,* Isle of Dogs (*canis,* a dog)]

Canary Islands, *n.pl.* (Spanish **Canarias**) a group of volcanic islands 100 km/60 miles off the NW coast of Africa, forming the Spanish provinces of Las Palmas and Santa Cruz de Tenerife; area 7300 sq km/2818 sq miles; population (1986) 1,615,000.

canasta, *n.* a card game similar to rummy, played by two to six players.

canaster, *n.* a coarse kind of tobacco, so called from the rush baskets in which it was orig. brought from America; such a rush-basket. [Sp. *canastra,* through L, from Gr. *kanastron,* basket (cp. CANISTER)]

Canberra, *n.* the capital of Australia (since 1908), situated in the Australian Capital Territory enclosed within New South Wales, on a tributary of the Murrumbidgee; area (Australian Capital Territory incl. the port at Jervis Bay 2432 sq km/939 sq miles; population (1986) 285,800.

cancan, *n.* a French stage dance performed by female dancers, involving high kicking of the legs. [F, etym. doubtful]

cancel, *v.t.* (*past, p.p.* **cancelled**) to obliterate by drawing lines across; to annul, countermand, revoke, neutralize; to suppress; (*Math.*) to strike out common factors; to mark (a stamp, ticket) to prevent reuse. *n.* a cancelling, countermanding; the deletion and reprinting of a part of a book; a page or sheet substituted for a cancelled one. **pair of cancels,** a stamp for defacing tickets. **to cancel out,** to cancel one another; to make up for. **cancellate, -lated, -lous,** *a.* (*Bot., Zool.*) cross-barred; reticulated; of bones, formed of cancelli. **cancellation,** *n.* **canceller,** *n.* **cancelli,** *n.pl.* a rail of lattice-work between the choir and the body of a church; the reticulation in the spongy part of bones. [F *canceller,* L *cancellāre* (*cancellus,* a grating, *cancelli,* crossbars, lattice)]

Cancer[1], *n.* the fourth of the 12 signs of the zodiac, the Crab; one born under this sign; (**cancer**) a malignant spreading growth affecting different parts of the human body; (**cancer**) a vice or other evil of an inveterate spreading kind. **Tropic of Cancer** TROPIC[1]. **cancer stick,** *n.* (*sl.*) a cigarette. **canceration,** *n.* **cancered, cancerous,** *a.* **cancriform**, *a.* crab-like; of the form of a cancer. **cancroid,** *a.* crab-like; having some of the qualities of cancer. *n.* a crustacean belonging to the crab family; a disease resembling cancer. [L *cancer a crab*]

Cancer[2], *n.* the faintest zodiac constellation (its brightest stars are fourth magnitude), through which the sun passes during late July and early Aug. It is represented as a crab, and its main feature is the star cluster Praesepe, pop. known as the Beehive. It is in the northern hemisphere near Ursa Major.

candela, *n.* a unit of luminous intensity. [L *candēla,* candle]

candelabrum, -bra, *n.* (*pl.* **-bra, -bras**) a tall lampstand; a high, ornamental candlestick, usually branched. [L (*candēla,* CANDLE)]

candescent, *a.* glowing with or as with white heat. **candescence,** *n.* [L *candescens -entem,* pres.p. of *candescere,* to glow, to become white (*candēre,* to glow)]

C and G, (*abbr.*) City and Guilds.

candid, *a.* †white; †pure, innocent; frank, sincere, open, ingenuous; unbiased; outspoken, freely critical. **candid camera**, *n.* a small camera for taking photographs of people without their knowledge. **candidly,** *adv.* **candidness,** *n.* [L *candidus,* white (see prec.)]

candida, *n.* a genus of yeastlike fungi, esp. *Candida albicans,* which causes thrush. [L, fem. of *candidus,* white]

candidate, *n.* one who seeks or is proposed for some office or appointment (so named because such persons in ancient Rome wore white togas); a person considered suitable or worthy for an office or dignity; a person taking an examination. *v.i.* (*N Am.*) to be a candidate. **candidacy,** *n.* **candidature, candidateship,** *n.* [L *candidātus,* white-robed (see prec.)]

candied CANDY.

candle, *n.* a cylindrical body of tallow, wax etc. with a wick in the middle, used as an illuminant; candlepower. *v.t.* to test eggs by holding before a candle. **not fit to hold a candle to,** not to be named in comparison with. **not worth the candle,** not worth the trouble. **Roman candle,** a firework consisting of a tube from which coloured fireballs are discharged. **standard candle** CANDELA. **to burn the candle at both ends,** to expend one's energies or waste resources in two ways at once. **candleberry(-myrtle),** *n.* a N American shrub, *Myrica cerifera,* yielding wax used for candlemaking. **candle-bomb,** *n.* a small bubble filled with water, which, when placed in the flame of a candle, bursts by the expansion of the steam. **candle-coal,** *n.* CANNEL-COAL. **candle-ends,** *n.pl.* fragments. **candleholder,** *n.* CANDLESTICK. **candlelight,** *n.* the light of a candle; evening. **Candlemas,** *n.* the feast of the Purification of the Virgin (2 Feb.), when candles are blessed and carried in procession. **candle-nut,** *n.* the fruit of *Aleurites triloba,* which furnishes a kind of wax. **candle-power,** *n.* intensity of light emitted, expressed in candelas. **candlestick,** *n.* a utensil for holding a candle. **candle-tree,** *n.* a tree growing in the Moluccas, *Aleurites tribola,* and other trees, the nuts or fruit of which yield illuminants. **candlewick,** *n.* a cotton fabric with a pattern of raised tufts. [OE *candel,* L *candēla* (*candēre,* to glow, shine)]

candock, *n.* the water-lily, esp. the yellow water-lily. [CAN[1], DOCK[1]]

candour, *n.* †whiteness; †integrity, innocence; candidness, sincerity, openness; freedom from malice or bias. [L *candor*]

C and W, (*abbr.*) Country and Western.

candy, *n.* sugar crystallized by boiling and evaporation; (*N Am.*) sweetmeats. *v.t.* to preserve with sugar, to coat with crystallized sugar; to crystallize. *v.i.* to become candied. **candy-floss,** *n.* coloured spun sugar on a stick. **candy-store,** *n.* (*N Am.*) a sweet-shop. **candy-stripe,** *n.* a pattern of alternate stripes of white and a colour. **candied,** *a.* preserved in or coated with sugar; crystalline, glistening; flattering, honeyed. [orig. *sugar-candy,* F *sucre candi,* Arab. and Pers. *qand,* sugar *qandi,* candied]

candytuft, *n.* a herbaceous plant, *Iberis umbellata;* any plant of the genus *Iberis,* esp. *I. sempervivum,* the perennial candytuft. [from the island *Candia*]

cane, *n.* a slender, hollow, jointed stem of the bamboo, sugar-cane or other reeds or grasses; the thin stem of the rattan or other palms; such a stem or a bamboo used as a walking-stick or an instrument of punishment; a (slender) walking-stick; the stem of a raspberry and other plants. *v.t.* to beat with a cane; to thrash (a lesson, with *into*); to put a cane bottom to (as a chair). **cane-brake,** *n.* (*N Am.*) a thicket of canes; a genus of grasses. **cane-chair,** *n.* a chair with a seat of cane splints. **cane-mill,** *n.* a mill for grinding sugarcanes. **cane-sugar,** *n.* sugar made from canes as distinguished from beet-sugar; sucrose. **cane-trash,** *n.* the refuse of sugar-cane. **cany,** *a.* **caning,** *n.* a beating with a cane; a thorough defeat. [OF *cane* (F *canne*), L *canna,* Gr. *kanna,* prob. Semit. (cp. Arab. *qanāh,* Heb. *qāneh*)]

canella, *n.* a genus of W Indian plants, with aromatic bark, comprising *Canella alba,* the wild cinnamon. [med. L, dim. of *canna,* cane]

canephorus, *n.* (*pl.* **-ri**) a sculptured figure of a maiden or youth carrying a basket on head. [Gr. *kanēphoros* (*kaneon,* basket, *-phoros,* bearing, *pherein,* to carry)]

canescent, *a.* hoary, approaching to white. **canescence,** *n.* [L *cānēscere,* to grow grey (*cānus,* white)]

Canetti, *n.* **Elias** (1905–), Bulgarian-born writer. He was exiled from Austria as a Jew in 1938, and settled in England in 1939. His books, written in German, include the novel *Die Blendung/Auto da Fé* and an autobiography. He is concerned with crowd behaviour and the psychology of power. Nobel prize 1981.

cangue, cang, *n.* a heavy wooden collar or yoke, formerly fixed round the neck of criminals in China. [F *cangue,* Port. *cango* (conn. with *canga,* yoke)]

canicular, *a.* of or pertaining to the dog-star; excessively hot; (*coll.*) pertaining to a dog. [L *canīculāris* (*canīcula,* a little dog, the dog-star, dim. of *canis*)]

canine, *a.* of or pertaining to dogs; dog-like. *n.* a canine tooth. **canine teeth,** *n.pl.* two pointed teeth in each jaw, one on each side, between the incisors and the molars. [L *canīnus* (*canis,* dog)]

Canis Major, *n.* a brilliant constellation of the southern hemisphere, representing one of the two dogs following at the heel of Orion. Its main star is Sirius, the 'dog star', and the brightest star in the sky.

Canis Minor, *n.* a small constellation of the equatorial region, representing the second of the two dogs of Orion (see CANIS MAJOR). Its brightest star is Procyon.

canister, *n.* a metal case or box for holding tea, coffee etc.; canister-shot; in the Roman Catholic Church, the box in which the eucharistic wafers are kept before consecration; †a reed basket. **canister-shot,** *n.* bullets packed in metal cases which burst when fired, called also case-shot. [L *canistrum,* Gr. *kanastron,* a basket (*canna,* a reed)]

canker, *n.* a corroding ulceration in the human mouth; a fungous excrescence in a horse's foot; a fungus growing on and injuring fruit trees; †the dog-rose; †a cancer; anything which corrupts or consumes. *v.t.* to infect or rot with canker, to eat into like a canker; to infect, corrode. *v.i.* to become cankered, infected or corrupt. **†canker-fly,** *n.* an insect preying on fruit. **canker-rash,** *n.* a form of scarlet fever in which the throat is ulcerated. **canker-weed,** *n.* ragwort, esp. the common species, *Senecio jacobaea.* **canker-worm,** *n.* a caterpillar that feeds on buds and leaves; (*chiefly N Am.*) the larva of the geometer moths. **cankered,** *a.* corroded by canker; cross, peevish. **cankerous,** *a.* corroding, destroying. [OE *cancer,* North.F *cancre* (F *chancre*), L *cancrum,* acc. of CANCER]

canna[1], *n.* a genus of ornamental plants with bright coloured flowers. [L *canna,* CANE]

canna[2] (*Sc.*) CANNOT under CAN[2].

cannabis, *n.* any of a genus, *Cannabis,* of plants containing the Indian hemp; a narcotic drug obtained from the leaves and flowers of plants of the genus, esp. *C. sativa* and *C. indica.* **cannabis resin,** *n.* cannabin. **cannabic,** *a.* **cannabin,** *n.* a sticky resin, the active principle of the drug cannabis. **cannabine,** *a.* of or pertaining to hemp. [Gr. *kannabis*]

cannach, *n.* (*Sc.*) the cotton-grass. [Gael. *cánach*]

canned, cannery, *a.* CAN[1].

cannel, cannel-coal, *n.* a hard, bituminous coal, burning with a bright flame. [var. of CANDLE]

cannelloni, *n.* an Italian dish, rolls of sheet pasta filled with meat etc. and baked. [It., augm. pl. of *cannello.,* stalk from *canna,* cane]

cannelure, *n.* (*Arch.*) a flute, a channel; a groove round a projectile. [F, a groove]

cannibal, *n.* a human being that feeds on human flesh; an animal that feeds on its own kind. *a.* pertaining to cannibalism; like a cannibal; ravenous, bloodthirsty. **cannibalism,** *n.* the act or practice of feeding on one's own kind; barbarity, atrocity. **cannibalistic,** *a.* **†cannibally,** *adv.* **cannibalize, -ise,** *v.t.* to dismantle a machine for its spare parts to be built into a similar machine. [Sp. *Canibales,* var. of *Caribes,* Caribbeans]

cannikin, canikin, canakin, *n.* a little can or cup.

cannily, canniness CANNY.

Canning, *n.* **George** (1770–1827), British Tory politician, foreign secretary (1807–10) and prime minister (1827) in coalition with the Whigs. He was largely responsible during the Napoleonic Wars for the seizure of the Danish fleet and British intervention in the Spanish peninsula.

cannon[1], *n.* a piece of ordnance; a heavy mounted gun; artillery, ordnance; a hollow sleeve or cylinder revolving independently on a shaft. **cannon-ball,** *n.* a solid shot fired from a cannon. **cannon-bit,** *n.* a smooth round bit for a horse. **cannon-bone,** *n.* the metacarpal or metatarsal bone of a horse, ox etc. **cannon-fodder,** *n.* (*iron.*) soldiers, esp. infantrymen. **cannon-proof,** *a.* proof against artillery. **cannon-shot,** *n.* †a cannon-ball; the range of a cannon. **cannonade,** *n.* a continued attack with artillery against a town, fortress etc. *v.t.* to attack or batter with cannon. *v.i.* to discharge heavy artillery. **cannoneer, †cannonier,** *n.* a gunner, an artilleryman. **cannonry,** *n.* cannon collectively; cannonading. [F *canon,* a law, decree, a great gun, It. *cannone,* a great tube (*canna,* a pipe, a cane, L *canna,* CANE)]

cannon[2], *n.* (*Billiards*) a stroke by which two balls are hit successively. *v.i.* to make a cannon; to come into violent contact (*against* or *with*). [corr. of obs. *carom,* short for *carambole,* F, from Sp. *carambola* (etym. doubtful)]

cannot CAN[2].

cannula, *n.* a small tube introduced into a body cavity to withdraw a fluid. **cannular,** *a.* **cannulate,** *v.t.* to insert a cannula into. [L, dim. of *canna,* CANE]

canny, *a.* knowing, shrewd, wise; quiet, gentle; comely, good; artful, crafty; prudent, cautious; frugal, thrifty; safe to have dealings with (cp. UNCANNY); †lucky, prosperous; †gifted with occult power. **to ca' canny,** to go gently; not to work too well. **cannily,** *adv.* **canniness,** *n.* [CAN[2]]

canoe, *n.* a kind of light boat formed of the trunk of a tree hollowed out, or of bark or hide, and propelled by paddles; a light narrow boat propelled by paddles. *v.i.* to go in a canoe. **to paddle one's own canoe,** to be independent. **canoeist,** *n.* [Sp. *canoa,* from Haitian]

canon, *n.* a rule, a regulation, a general law or principle; a standard, test or criterion; a decree of the Church; the largest size of type, equivalent to 48 pt.; the ring or loop by which a bell is suspended; the catalogue of canonized saints; the portion of the Mass in which the words of consecration are spoken; a list of the books of Scriptures received as inspired; the books themselves; the list of an author's recognized works; a rule of discipline or doctrine; a resident member of a cathedral chapter; a member of a religious body, from the fact that some cathedral canons lived in community; a musical composition in which the several parts take up the same subject in succession; the strictest species of imitation. **canon law,** *n.* ecclesiastical law as laid down by popes and councils. **canoness,** *n.* a member of a female community living by rule but not bound by vows. **canonic, -ical,** *a.* pertaining to or according to canon law; included in the canon of Scripture; authoritative, accepted, approved; belonging or pertaining to a cathedral chapter; (*Mus.*) in canon form. **Canonical Epistles,** *n.pl.* the Epistles of Peter, James, John and Jude. **canonical hours,** *n.* 8 am to 6 pm during which marriages may legally be celebrated. **canonically,** *adv.* **canonicals,** *n.pl.* the full robes of an officiating clergyman as appointed by the canons. **canonicate,** *n.* the dignity or office of a canon. **canonicity,** *n.* the quality of being canonical, esp. the authority of a canonical book. **canonist,** *n.* one versed in canon law. **canonistic, -ical,** *a.* **canonize, -ise,** *v.t.* to enrol in the canon or list of saints; to recognize officially as a saint; to recognize as canonical; to sanction as conforming to the canons of the Church. **canonization, -isation,** *n.* **canonry,** *n.* the dignity, position or benefice of a canon. [OE, from L, from Gr. *kanōn,* a rule (*kanē, kanna,* CANE)]

cañon CANYON.

canoodle, *v.t.* (*coll.*) to fondle, to cuddle. *v.i.* to fondle and cuddle amorously. [etym. unknown]

Canopus, *n.* the bright star in the constellation Carina, the 2nd-brightest star in the sky; name of an ancient Egyptian city; a Canopic vase. **Canopic,** *a.* **Canopic vase, jar,** *n.* an Egyptian vase with a lid shaped like a god's head, for holding the viscera of embalmed bodies. [L, from Gr. *Kanōpos*]

canopy, *n.* a rich covering of state suspended over an altar, throne, bed etc.; or borne over some person, relics, or the Host, in procession; a shelter, a covering, the sky; an ornamental projection over a niche or doorway; (*Aviat.*) the transparent roof of the cockpit; the fabric portion of a parachute; in a forest, the topmost layer of branches and leaves. *v.t.* to cover with or as with a canopy. **canopied,** *a.* [F, *canapé,* a tent or pavilion (now, a sofa), med. L *canōpeum,* L *cōnōpēum,* Gr. *kōnōpeion,* a bed with mosquito-curtains (*kōnōps,* a gnat)]

canorous, *a.* tuneful, melodious, resonant. [L *canōrus* (*canere,* to sing)]

Canossa, *n.* a ruined castle 19 km/12 miles SW of Reggio, Italy. The Holy Roman Emperor Henry IV did penance here before pope Gregory VII in 1077 for having opposed him in the question of investitures.

Canova, *n.* **Antonio** (1757–1822), Italian neo-classical sculptor, based in Rome from 1781. His highly-finished marble portrait busts and groups soon proved popular, and he received commissions from popes, kings and emperors. He made several portraits of Napoleon.

Cánovas del Castillo, *n.* **Antonio** (1828–97), Spanish politician and chief architect of the political system known as the *turno politico* through which his own conservative party, and that of the liberals under Práxedes Sagasta, alternated in power. Elections were rigged to ensure the appropriate majorities. Cánovas was assassinated in 1897 in an attack carried out by anarchists.

canst, *2nd pers. sing.,* CAN[2].

†canstick, *contr. form of* CANDLESTICK.

cant[1], *n.* †a monotonous whining; the peculiar dialect or jargon of beggars, thieves etc.; slang; (*often derog.*) a method of speech or phraseology peculiar to any sect or party; hypocritical sanctimoniousness; hypocritical talk. *a.* pertaining to or of the nature of cant. *v.i.* to speak whiningly or insincerely; to talk cant. **canter**[1], *n.* **canting,** *n.* cant. *a.* whining, hypocritical. **canting arms, heraldry,** *n.* armorial bearings containing a punning device or other allusion to the name of the family. **canting crew,** *n.* the brotherhood or fraternity of vagabonds, thieves, sharpers etc. **cantingly,** *adv.* **cantish,** *a.* [L *cantāre,* to sing, freq. of *canere*]

cant[2], *n.* a slope, a slant; an inclination; a jerk producing a slant or upset; an external angle; a bevel; a slanting position. *v.t.* to tip, to tilt; to throw with a jerk; to bevel, give a bevel to. *v.i.* to tilt or slant over; (*Naut.*) to swing round. **cant-board,** *n.* a sloping board. **cant dog, hook,** *n.* a metal hook on a pole, used esp. for handling logs. **cant-rail,** *n.* a bevelled plank placed along the top of the uprights in a railway carriage to support the roof. **canted,** *a.* [Dut. *kant* (cp. OF *cant,* It. *canto,* med. L *cantus,* corner, and perh. L *canthus,* Gr. *kanthos,* corner of the eye, felloe of a wheel; course of derivation uncertain)]

cant[3], *a.* (*Sc., North.*) strong, lusty; keen, lively, brisk. **canty,** *a.* lively, cheerful. **cantiness,** *n.* [etym. doubtful; perh. from CANT[2], edge, angle, corner (cp. Dut. *kant,* great, clever)]

can't, *contr. form of* CANNOT.

Cantab., (*abbr.*) of Cambridge. [L *Cantabrigiensis*)]

cantabile, *a.* (*Mus.*) in an easy, flowing style. *n.* a piece in the cantabile style. [It., able to be sung (L *cantare,* to sing, freq. of *canere*)]

Cantabria, *n.* autonomous region of N Spain (coextensive with the province of Santander); area 5289 sq km/2043 sq miles; population (1981) 511,000; capital Santander.

Cantabrigian, *a.* of or relating to the town or Univ. of Cambridge, England or Massachusetts. *n.* a member of Cambridge or Harvard Univ. [L *Cantabrigia,* Cambridge]

cantal, *n.* a hard strong-flavoured French cheese. [name of a department in the Auvergne]

cantaloup, *n.* a small, round, ribbed musk-melon, first raised at Cantalupo near Rome.

cantankerous, *a.* disagreeable, cross-grained; quarrelsome, crotchety. **cantankerously,** *adv.* **cantankerousness,** *n.* [etym. doubtful; perh. from ME *contak,* contention]

cantar, *n.* an Oriental measure of weight, varying from 100 to 130 lb. (45.4—59.0 kg); a Spanish liquid measure, varying from 2½ to 4 galls. (13.6—18.2 l). [It. *cantaro* (Turk. *qantār*), L *cantharus,* Gr. *kantharos,* a tankard]

cantata, *n.* a poem, short lyrical drama or (usu.) a biblical text, set to music, with solos and choruses. [It.]

cantatore, *n.* (*Mus.*) a male professional singer. **cantatrice,** *n.* a female professional singer. [It.]

canteen, *n.* a place in a barracks, factory or office where refreshments are sold at low prices to the soldiers or employees; a soldier's mess tin; a chest or box in which the mess utensils, cutlery etc., are carried; a chest for cutlery; a water-bottle. **dry, wet canteen,** *n.* canteen where alcoholic liquors are not, or are, sold. [F *cantine,* It. *cantina,* cellar (perh. from CANTO, a side, a corner)]

canter[1] CANT[1].

canter[2], *n.* an easy gallop; a Canterbury gallop. *v.t.* to cause (a horse) to go at this pace. *v.i.* to ride at a canter; to move at this pace. **in, at a canter,** easily. [short for CANTERBURY]

Canterbury, *n.* a city in Kent, seat of the metropolitan see of all England; a light stand with divisions for music portfolios etc. **Canterbury bell,** *n.* name of plants belonging to the genus *Campanula,* esp. the exotic *C. medium.* **Canterbury gallop, pace,** *n.* phrases applied to the easy, ambling pace at which pilgrims went to the shrine of St Thomas à Becket at Canterbury. [OE *Cantwaraburh* (*Cantware,* people of Kent)]

Canterbury, Archbishop of, primate of all England, archobishop of the Church of England, and first peer of the realm, ranking next to royalty. He crowns the sovereign, has a seat in the House of Lords, and is a member of the Privy Council. He is appointed by the prime minister. His seat is Lambeth Palace, London, with a second residence at the Old Palace, Canterbury.

Canterbury Tales, *n.pl.* an unfinished collection of stories in prose and verse (*c.* 1387) by Geoffrey Chaucer, told by a group of pilgrims on their way to Thomas Becket's tomb at Canterbury. The tales and preludes are notable for their vivid character portrayal and colloquial language.

cantharides, *n.pl.* Spanish flies dried and used as a blister or internally, also used as an aphrodisiac. **cantharidin, -dine,** *n.* the active principle of cantharides. [L, pl. of CANTHARIS]

cantharis, *n.* Spanish fly, a coleopterous insect having vesicatory properties; applied to similar beetles. [L, from Gr. *kantharis,* blistering-fly]

canthus, *n.* the angle made by the meeting of the eyelids. [L, from Gr. *kanthos*]

canticle, *n.* a brief song, a chant; applied to certain portions of Scripture appointed in the Prayer Book to be said or sung in churches. **The Canticles,** the Song of Solomon. [L *canticulum,* dim. of *canticum,* song (*cantus,* song, *canere,* to sing)]

cantilena, *n.* a ballad; plain-song. [F *cantilène,* L *cantilēna,* a song (*cantillāre,* CANTILLATE)]

cantilever, *n.* a projecting beam, girder or bracket for supporting a balcony or other structure. **cantilever bridge,** *n.* a bridge formed with cantilevers, resting in pairs on piers of masonry or ironwork, the ends meeting or connected by girders. **cantilever spring,** *n.* a laminated spring supported at the middle and bearing the weight on shackles at either end. [perh. CANT[2] (or from CANTLE), LEVER]

cantillate, *v.t.* to chant; to intone, as in Jewish synagogues. **cantillation,** *n.* [L *cantillāre,* to sing low (*cantare,* freq. of *canere,* to sing)]

cantina, *n.* a bar, wine shop, esp. in Spanish-speaking countries. [Sp.]

cantle, *n.* a fragment, a piece; the projection at the rear of a saddle. *v.t.* to cut into pieces, divide. †**cantlet,** *n.* a morsel, fragment. [O North.F *cantel* (med. L *cantellus,* dim. of *cantus* CANT[2])]

canto, *n.* (*pl.* **-tos**) one of the principal divisions of a poem; †a song; the upper voice part in concerted music. **canto fermo,** *n.* plainsong; the main theme, which is treated contrapuntally. [It., from L *cantus,* CANT[1]]

canton[1], *n.* †a corner; a division of a country, a small district; a political division of Switzerland; (*Her.*) a small division in the corner of a shield. **canton,** *v.t.* to divide into parts. **cantoned,** *a.* having projecting corners. **cantonal,** *a.* [OF, a corner, a district, It. *cantone,* from *canto,* CANT[2]]

canton[2], *v.t.* to billet troops, to provide with quarters. **cantonment,** *n.* temporary or winter quarters for troops; a permanent military station in British India.

†**canton**[3], var. of CANTO.

Canton, *n.* former name of Guangzhou in China.

Cantonese, *a.* of the city of Canton, or its inhabitants, or the dialect of Chinese spoken there; of a highly-spiced style of cookery originating there. *n.* a native or inhabitant of Canton; the Cantonese dialect.

cantor, *n.* †a singer; a precentor; the Jewish religious official who sings the liturgy. **cantorial,** *a.* pertaining to the precentor or to the north side of the choir. **cantoris,** *a.* (sung) by the cantorial side of the choir. [L, precentor (*cant-,* freq. stem of *canere,* to sing)]

†**cantrip,** *n.* (*Sc.*) a spell, an incantation, a charm; a trick, a piece of mischief. [etym. doubtful]

Cantuarian, *a.* of or pertaining to Canterbury or its archiepiscopal see. **Cantuar,** (*abbr.*) Cantuarensis the official signature of the Archbishop of Canterbury. [late L *Cantuarius* (OE *Cantware,* see CANTERBURY)]

cantus firmus CANTO FERMO under CANTO.

canty CANT[3].

Canuck, *n.* (*chiefly N Am., coll.*) a Canadian; (*Canada*) a French Canadian; a small rough Canadian horse. [N Am. Ind.]

Canute, *n.* (*c.* 995–1035), king of England from 1016, Denmark from 1018 and Norway from 1028. Having invaded England with his father Sweyn, king of Denmark, in 1013, Canute defeated Edmund Ironside in 1016, invaded Scotland, and conquered Norway. According to legend, deflated his flattering courtiers by showing that the sea would not retreat at his command.

canvas, *n.* a coarse unbleached cloth, made of hemp or flax, formerly used for sifting, now for sails, tents, paintings, embroidery etc.; sails; the sails of a ship; a sheet of canvas for oil-painting; a picture; a covering for the ends of a racing-boat. *a.* made of canvas. **under canvas,** in a tent or tents; with sails set. **canvas-back,** *n.* a N American sea-duck. **canvas town,** *n.* a large encampment. [ONorth.F *canevas,* late L *canabācius* (L *cannabis,* Gr. *kannabis,* hemp)]

canvass, *n.* close examination, discussion; the act of soliciting votes. *v.t.* to examine thoroughly, to discuss; to solicit votes, interest, orders etc. from *v.i.* to solicit votes etc. **canvasser,** *n.* [from prec., orig. to sift through canvas]

cany CANE.

canyon, cañon, *n.* a deep gorge or ravine with precipitous sides, esp. of the type of those formed by erosion in the western plateaux of the US. [Sp. *cañon,* a tube, a conduit, a cannon, from *caña,* L *canna,* CANE]

canzone, *n.* a Provençal or Italian song. **canzonet, -netta,** *n.* a short air of song; a light air in an opera. [It., from L *cantio -ōnem,* singing (*cant-,* freq. stem of *canere,* to sing)]

caoutchouc, *n.* India-rubber, the coagulated juice of certain tropical trees, which is elastic and waterproof. [Carib. *cahuchu*]

CAP, (*abbr.*) Common Agricultural Policy.

cap[1], *n.* a covering for the head, a brimless head-covering for a man or a boy; a woman's head-dress, usu. for indoor wear; a natural or artificial covering resembling this in form or function; a special form of head-dress distinguishing the holder of an office, membership of a sports team etc.; a percussion cap; a particular size of paper; cap-paper; the top part of anything; a coping; a block pierced to hold a mast or spar above another; (*Arch.*) a capital; (also **Dutch cap**) a form of contraceptive device; a porcelain crown set on the stump of a tooth. *v.t.* (*past, p.p.* **capped**) to cover the top with a cap; to put a cap on; (*Sc. Univ.*) to confer a degree upon; to put a percussion cap on (a gun); to protect or cover with or as with a cap; to be on the top of; to complete, to surpass. *v.i.* to take one's cap off (to). **cap and bells,** the insignia of a jester. **cap and gown,** full academic dress. **cap in hand,** in a humble or servile manner. **cap of liberty,** a conical or Phrygian cap given to a manumitted slave; the symbol of republicanism. **cap of maintenance,** a cap of state carried before the sovereign at the coronation, and before some mayors. **if the cap fits,** if the general remark applies to you, take it to yourself. **percussion cap,** a small cylinder containing detonating powder for igniting the explosive in a gun, cartridge, shell, torpedo etc. **to cap a story,** to tell another story that is still more to the point. **to cap it all,** (*coll.*) as a finishing touch. **to cap verses,** to reply to a verse quoted by quoting another that rhymes or is otherwise appropriate. **to send the cap round,** to make a collection. **to set one's cap at,** of a woman, to endeavour to captivate. **cap-paper**. *n.* coarse paper used by grocers for wrapping up sugar etc. **cap-sheaf,** *n.* (*N Am.*) the top sheaf of a stack of corn. **cap sleeve,** *n.* a short sleeve just covering the shoulder. **capstone,** *n.* the top stone; a coping; the horizontal stone of a cromlech or dolmen; the uppermost bed in a quarry; a kind of fossil echinite. **capful,** *n.* as much as a cap will hold. **capful of wind,** a light gust. **capper,** *n.* **capping,** *a.* that caps or forms the cap (of). *n.* that which covers or protects anything. [OE *cæppe,* late L *cappa,* later *cāpa* (cp. OF *capel, chapel,* F *chapeau,* and CAPE[1], COPE[1])]

cap[2], *n.* (*Sc.*) a wooden drinking-bowl; a measure, the fourth part of a peck, about 140 cu.in. (2.25 l). [OE *copp,* cup, or Icel. *koppr,* cup]

cap[3], (*abbr.*) capital (letter); chapter. [L *caput,* head]

capable, *a.* susceptible (of); competent, able, skilful, qualified, fitted. **capably,** *adv.* **capability,** *n.* the quality of being capable; capacity; (*pl.*) resources, abilities, intellectual attainments. [F, from late L *capābilis* (formed from *capere,* to hold, on anal. of *capax -ācis,* see foll.)]

capacious, *a.* able to contain much; wide, large, extensive; comprehensive, liberal. **capaciously,** *adv.* **capaciousness,** *n.* **capacitate,** *v.t.* to make capable of; to qualify; to render competent. [L *capax -ācis* (*capere,* to hold, contain), -ACIOUS]

capacity, *n.* power of containing or receiving; room, cubic extent; power to absorb; capability, ability; opportunity, scope; relative position, character or office; legal qualification; a term used to denote the output of a piece of electrical apparatus. **to capacity,** (full) to the limit. **capacity coupling,** *n.* the coupling of two circuits by a condenser to transfer energy from one to the other. **capacity reaction,** *n.* reaction from the output to the input circuit of an amplifier through a path with a condenser. **capacitance,** *n.* the ability of a conductor, system etc. to store electric charge; the amount stored, measured in farads. **capacitor,** *n.* a device for storing electric charge in a circuit. [as prec.]

cap-à-pie, *adv.* from head to foot (armed or accoutred). [OF *cap a pie,* head to foot (L *caput,* head, *pes pedis,* foot)]

caparison, *n.* (*often pl.*) housings, often ornamental, for a horse or other beast of burden; outfit, equipment. *v.t.* to furnish with trappings; to deck out. [MF *caparasson,* Sp. *caparazon,* med. L *caparo,* a cowl (late L *cāpa,* CAPE)]

cape[1], *n.* a covering for the shoulders, attached to another garment or separate. **caped,** *a.* [F (through Sp. *capa* or It. *cappa*), from late L *cappa,* CAP[1]]

cape[2], *n.* a headland projecting into the sea. **the Cape,** the Cape of Good Hope; the province of South Africa containing it. **Cape ant-eater** AARDVARK. **Cape cart,** *n.* a hooded, two-wheeled vehicle. **Cape doctor,** *n.* a south easterly wind in the Cape. **Cape Dutch,** *n.* an architectural style characterized by high ornamental front gables, typical of early buildings at the Cape; †Afrikaans. **Cape gooseberry,** *n.* a tropical plant with a small yellow edible fruit; this fruit. [F *cap,* It. *capo,* L *caput,* head]

Cape Canaveral, *n.* a promontory on the Atlantic coast of Florida, US, 367 km/228 miles N of Miami, used as a rocket launch site by NASA.

Cape Cod, *n.* a peninsula in SE Massachusetts, US, where in 1620 the English Pilgrims landed at Provincetown.

Cape Horn, *n.* the most southerly point of S America, in the Chilean part of the archipelago of Tierra del Fuego; notorious for gales and heavy seas.

Čapek, *n.* **Karel (Matelj)** (1890–1938), Czech writer whose works often deal with social injustice in an imaginative, satirical way. *R.U.R.* (1921) is a play in which robots (a term he coined) rebel against their controllers; the novel *Valka s Mloky/War With the Newts* (1936) is a science-fiction classic.

capelin, caplin, *n.* a small Newfoundland fish like a smelt, used as bait for cod. [F and Sp. *capelan*]

Capella, *n.* brightest star in the constellation Auriga, and the sixth brightest star in the sky. It consists of a pair of yellow giant stars 45 light years away orbiting each other every 104 days.

capellmeister, KAPELLMEISTER.

Cape of Good Hope South African headland forming a peninsula between Table Bay and False Bay, Cape Town. The first European to sail round it was Bartholomew Diaz in 1488.

Cape Province, *n.* (Afrikaans **Kaapprovinsie**) largest province of the Republic of South Africa, named after the Cape of Good Hope. **area** 641,379 sq km/247,638 sq miles, excluding Walvis Bay **capital** Cape Town. **towns** Port Elizabeth, East London, Kimberley, Grahamstown, Stellenbosch. **physical** Orange river, Drakensberg, Table Mountain (highest point Maclear's Beacon 1087 m/3567 ft); Great Karoo Plateau, Walvis Bay. **products** fruit, vegetables, wine; meat, ostrich feathers; diamonds, copper, asbestos, manganese. **population** (1985) 5,041,000, officially including 2,226,200 Coloured; 1,569,000 Black; 1,264,000 White; 32,120 Asian.

caper[1], *n.* a frolicsome leap, a frisky movement; eccentric behaviour. *v.i.* to leap; to skip about. **to cut capers,** to caper; to act in a ridiculous manner. **caperer,** *n.* a person that capers; a caddis-fly. [short for CAPRIOLE]

caper[2], *n.* a prickly shrub, *Capparis spinosa; (pl.)* the flower-buds of this, used for pickling. **English capers,** *n.pl.* the fruit of the nasturtium, used for pickling. **caper sauce,** *n.* a white sauce flavoured with capers, eaten with boiled mutton etc. [L *capparis,* Gr. *kapparis* (cp. PEA, L *pisum,* for loss of the *s*)]

capercailzie, -caillie, *n.* the wood-grouse, *Tetrao urogallus,* called also the mountain cock or cock of the wood. [Gael. *capull coille,* the cock of the wood (*capull,* L *caballus,* horse, Gael. *coille,* wood)]

Capernaite, *n.* (*Theol. polemics*) a believer in transubstantiation. **Capernaitic,** *a.* [*Capernaum,* in Galilee]

capernoitie, *n.* (*Sc.*) the head, the noddle. **capernoited, capernoity,** *a.* wrong-headed, cracked. **capernoitedness,** *n.* [etym. unknown]

Capet, *n.* **Hugh** (938–996), king of France from 987, when he claimed the throne on the death of Louis V. He founded the **Capetian dynasty**, of which various branches continued to reign until the French Revolution, for example, Valois and Bourbon.

Cape Town, *n.* (Afrikaans **Kaapstad**) port and oldest town in South Africa, situated in the SW on Table Bay; population (1985) 776,617. Industries include horticulture and trade in wool, wine, fruit, grain and oil. It is the legislative capital of the Republic of South Africa, and capital of Cape Province, and was founded in 1652.

Cape Verde, *n.* Republic of (*República de Cabo Verde*), group of islands in the Atlantic, off the coast of Senegal. **area** 4033 sq km/1557 sq miles. **capital** Praia. **physical** archipelago of ten islands 565 km/350 miles W of Senegal. **exports** bananas, coffee. **population** (1988) 359,000 (including 100,000 Angolan refugees); annual growth rate 1.9%. **language** Creole dialect of Portuguese. **religion** Roman Catholic 80%.

capias, *n.* a judicial writ ordering an officer to arrest. [L, take thou, or thou mayst take]

capibara CAPYBARA.

capillary, *a.* resembling a hair in tenuity; having a minute bore; pertaining to the hair, pertaining to the capillary vessels or capillary attraction etc. *n.* one of the minute blood-vessels in which the arterial circulation ends and the venous begins. **capillary attraction, repulsion,** *n.* the cause which determines the ascent or descent of a fluid in a hair-like tube. **capillarity,** *n.* **capillose,** *a.* hairy. *n.* (*Min.*) sulphide of nickel, capillary pyrites. [L *capillāris,* relating to hair (*capillus,* hair)]

capital[1], *n.* the head of a pillar. [prob. from ONorth.F *capitel* (F *chapiteau*), late L *capitellum,* dim. of L *caput -itis,* head]

capital[2], *a.* principal, chief, most important; excellent, first-rate; involving or affecting the head or the life; punishable by death; fatal, injurious to life; of letters, initial; hence, of a larger size and a shape distinguishing chief letters; relating to the main fund or stock of a corporation or business firm; a capital letter; a head city or town; a metropolis; wealth appropriated to reproductive employment; a principal or fund employed in earning interest or profits. **capital transfer tax,** a tax levied on the transfer of capital, either by gift or inheritance. **circulating capital** FLOATING CAPITAL. **fixed capital,** buildings, machinery, tools etc. used in industry. **floating capital,** raw material, money, goods etc. **to make capital out of,** to make profit from, turn to one's advantage. **capital assets** FIXED CAPITAL. **capital expenditure,** *n.* expenditure on buildings, equipment etc. **capital gain,** *n.* profit made from the sale of shares or other property. **capital goods,** *n.pl.* raw materials and tools used in the production of consumers' goods. **capital levy,** *n.* (*Fin.*) a levy on capital. **capital murder,** *n.* a murder involving the death penalty. **capital punishment,** *n.* the death penalty. **capital sentence,** *n.* a sentence of death. **capital ship,** *n.* a warship of the most powerful kind. **capitalism,** *n.* the economic system under which individuals employ capital and employees to produce wealth. **capitalist,** *n.* one who possesses capital. **capitalistic,** *a.* **capitalize, -ise,** *v.t.* to convert into capital; to use as capital; to calculate or realize the present value of periodical payments; to write or print with a capital letter; to use to one's advantage. **capitalization, -isation,** *n.* **capitally,** *adv.* excellently. [F, from L *capitālis, capitāle,* relating to the head, chief (*caput -itis,* head)]

capitan, *n.* (*Hist.*) the chief admiral of a Turkish fleet. **capitan galley,** *n.* **capitan pacha,** *n.* **capitano,** *n.* [Sp. *capitán,* It. *capitano,* captain]

capitate, -ated, *a.* having a head; having the inflorescence in a head-like cluster. [L *capitātus,* headed (*caput,* head)]

capitation, *n.* †enumeration by the head; a tax, fee or grant per head. **capitation grant, allowance,** *n.* a subsidy or allowance calculated on the number of persons passing an examination or fulfilling specified conditions. [F, from late L *capitātio -ōnem* (*caput -itis,* head)]

Capitol, *n.* the great national temple of ancient Rome, situated on the *Capitoline* Hill, dedicated to Jupiter; the building in which the US Congress meets; (*N Am.*) the senate-house of a state. **Capitolian, Capitoline,** *a.* of or pertaining to the Roman Capitol. **Capitoline games,** *n.pl.* games in honour of Capitoline Jove. [L *Capitōlium*]

capitular, *a.* of or pertaining to an ecclesiastical chapter; (*Bot.*) growing in small heads. *n.* a member of a chapter; a statute passed by a chapter. **capitularly,** *adv.* in the form of an ecclesiastical chapter. [med. L *capitulāris,* relating to a *capitulum,* or chapter]

capitulary, *n.* a collection of ordinances, esp. those of the Frankish kings. [med. L *capitulārium,* a book of decrees, from *capitulāre,* a writing divided into chapters, *capitulāris*]

capitulate, *v.i.* †to treat, to bargain; to stipulate; to make terms of surrender, to surrender on stipulated terms. *v.t.* to surrender on stipulated terms. **capitulation,** *n.* the act of capitulating; the document containing the terms of surrender; (*pl.*) the articles under which foreigners in dependencies of Turkey and other states were formerly granted extraterritorial rights. **capitulator,** *n.* [med. L *capitulāre,* to divide into chapters, to propose terms]

capitulum, *n.* (*pl.* **-la**) a small head; a close cluster or head of sessile flowers; a head-shaped anatomical part; the body of a barnacle or cirriped which is carried on a peduncle. [L, dim. of *caput,* head]

capiz, *n.* a bivalve mollusc, *Placuna placenta,* found in the Philippines, having a translucent lining to the shell which is used in lampshades etc. [native name]

†**caple, capul,** *n.* (*poet.*) a horse. [ult. from L *caballus,* horse (cp. Icel. *kapall,* Ir. and Gael. *capall*)]

caplin CAPELIN.

capnomancy, *n.* divination by smoke. [Gr. *kapnos,* smoke, -MANCY]

capo, *n.* the head of a branch of the Mafia; a capotasto. [It., head]

Capodimonte, *n.* village, N of Naples, Italy, where porcelain known by the same name was first produced under King Charles III of Naples about 1740. The porcelain is usually white, painted with colourful folk figures, landscapes or flowers.

capon, *n.* a castrated cock, esp. fattened for cooking; (*sl.*) a eunuch. *v.t.* to caponize. **caponize, -ise,** *v.t.* to castrate. [OE *capun,* L *capo -ōnem*]

Capone, *n.* **Al(phonse)** (1898–1947), US gangster, born in Brooklyn, New York, the son of an Italian barber. During the Prohibition period Capone built up a criminal organization in the city of Chicago. He was imprisoned (1931–39) for income-tax evasion, the only charge that could be sustained against him. His nickname was 'Scarface'.

caponiere, -ier, *n.* a covered passage across the ditch of a fortified place. [F *caponnière,* Sp. *caponera-* orig. a capon-coop. see prec.]

caporal, *n.* a coarse kind of French tobacco. [F, a corporal]

Caporetto, *n.* former name of Kobarid, Yugoslavia.

capot, *n.* the winning of all the tricks at piquet by one player. *v.t.* to win all the tricks from. [F]

capotasto, *n.* a bar fitted across the fingerboard of a guitar, to alter the pitch of all the strings simultaneously. [It. *capo tasto,* head stop]

capote, *n.* a long cloak or overcoat, usu. with a hood. [F, dim. of CAPE[1]]

Capote, *n.* **Truman** (pen name of Truman Streckfuss Persons) (1924–84), US novelist. He wrote *Breakfast at Tiffany's* (1958); set a trend with *In Cold Blood* (1966), reconstructing a Kansas killing; and mingled recollection and fiction in *Music for Chameleons* (1980).

Cappadocia, *n.* an ancient region of Asia Minor, in E central Turkey. It was conquered by the Persians in 584 BC but in the 3rd century BC became an independent kingdom. The region was annexed as a province of the Roman Empire in AD 17.

cappuccino, *n.* white coffee, esp. from an espresso machine, often with whipped cream or powdered chocolate. [It., see CAPUCHIN]

capric, *a.* pertaining to a goat. **capric acid,** *n.* an acid, having a slight goat-like smell, contained in butter, coconut oil, and other compounds. [L *caper -pri,* a goat]

capriccio, *n.* †a frisky movement, a prank, a caper; †a caprice; (*Mus.*) a lively composition more or less free in form. **capriccioso,** *adv.* (*Mus.*) in a free, fantastic style. [It., from *capro,* a goat]

caprice, *n.* a sudden impulsive change of opinion or humour; a whim, a freak; disposition to this kind of behaviour; a freakish or playful work of art. **capricious,** *a.* influenced by caprice; whimsical, uncertain, fickle, given to unexpected and incalculable changes. **capriciously,** *adv.* **capriciousness,** *n.* [F, from prec.]

Capricorn, Capricornus, *n.* zodiac constellation in the southern hemisphere near Sagittarius. It is represented as a fish-tailed goat, and its brightest stars are third magnitude. The Sun passes through it late Jan to mid-Feb. In astrology, the dates for Capricornus are between about 22 Dec. and 19 Jan. **Tropic of Capricorn** TROPIC¹. [L *capricornus,* goat-horned (*caper,* goat, *cornu,* a horn)]

caprification, *n.* the practice of suspending branches of the wild fig on the cultivated fig, that the (female) flowers of the latter may be pollinated by wasps parasitic on the flowers of the former. **capriform,** *a.* having the form of a goat. **caprine,** *a.* like a goat. [L *caprificātio -nem,* from *caprificāre,* to ripen figs, *caprificus,* the wild fig (*caper,* goat, *ficus,* fig)]

caprifig, *n.* the wild fig of S Europe and Asia Minor, used in caprification. [L *caprificus;* see prec.]

capriole, *n.* a leap made by a horse without advancing. *v.i.* to leap or caper without advancing. [F *capriole* (now *cabriole*), a caper, It. *capriola,* (dim. of *capra,* she-goat)]

Capri pants, Capris, *n.pl.* women's tight-fitting trousers, reaching to above the ankle. [*Capri,* island off SW Italy]

Caprivi, *n.* **Georg Leo, Count von Caprivi** (1831–99), German imperial chancellor (1890–94).

Caprivi Strip, *n.* NE access strip for Namibia to the Zambezi river.

caproic, *a.* pertaining to a goat. **caproic acid,** *n.* an acid contained, like capric and butyric acids, in butter etc. [L *caper,* a goat, -IC (specially differentiated from CAPRIC)]

capsicum, *n.* a genus of the potato family, with mild or pungent fruit and seeds; the fruit of a capsicum used as a vegetable or ground as the condiments chilli, cayenne etc. **capsicine,** *n.* the active principle in capsicum pods. [prob. formed irregularly from L *capsa,* a case]

capsid¹, *n.* any bug of the family Miridae, feeding on plants. [Gr. *kapsis,* gulp, from *kaptein,* to gulp down]

capsid², *n.* the outer casing of some viruses, made of protein. [L *capsa,* case]

capsize, *v.t.* to upset, to overturn. *v.i.* to be upset. *n.* an overturn. **capsizal,** *n.* [etym. unknown; perh. from Sp. *capuzar,* to sink by the head]

capstan, *n.* a revolving pulley or drum, either power- or lever-driven, with a belt or cable running over it. Used to increase the force exerted by the cable or belt. **capstan lathe,** *n.* one with a revolving turret, so that several different tools can be used in rotation. [Prov. and F *cabestan,* L *capistrāre,* to fasten (*capistrum,* a halter, from *capere,* to hold)]

capsule, *n.* a metallic cover for a bottle; (*Physiol.*) an envelope or sac; (*Bot.*) a dry dehiscent seed-vessel; (*Chem.*) a shallow saucer; a small envelope of gelatine containing medicine. **capsular,** *a.* †**capsulate, -ated,** *a.* **capsuliform,** *a.* **capsulize, -ise,** *v.t.* to enclose in a capsule; to put (information) into a very condensed form. [F, from L *capsula,* dim. of *capsa,* a case]

capt., (*abbr.*) captain.

captain, *n.* a leader, a commander; in the army, a rank between major and lieutenant; in the navy, a rank between commodore and commander; (*N Am.*) a headwaiter or the supervisor of bell boys in a hotel; (*N Am.*) a police officer in charge of a precinct; the master of a merchant ship; the head of a gang, side or team; a foreman; the chief boy or girl in a school; the manager of a Cornish mine; a general, a strategist, a great soldier; a veteran commander. *v.t.* to act as captain to; to lead, to head. **Captain of the Fleet,** the adjutant-general of a naval force. **Captain Cookers,** *n.pl.* (*New Zealand, coll.*) wild boars (descended from swine landed there by Capt. Cook). †**captain-general,** *n.* a commander-in-chief. **captain's chair,** *n.* a wooden chair with back and arms in one semicircular piece, supported on wooden shafts. **captaincy,** *n.* **captainship,** *n.* **captainless,** *a.* [OF *capitain,* late L *capitaneus,* chief, *capitānus,* a chief (L *caput -itis,* head)]

Captain Marvel, *n.* US comic-book character created 1940 by C(larence) C(harles) Beale (1910–89). Captain Marvel is a 15-year-old schoolboy, Billy Batson, who transforms himself into a superhuman hero.

captation, *n.* an endeavour to obtain by means of artful appeals to feeling or prejudice. [L *captātio -ōnem* (*captāre,* freq. of *capere,* to take, seize)]

caption, *n.* †seizure, capture; †a quibble, a fallacious argument; (*Law, esp. Sc.*) apprehension by judicial process; the heading or descriptive preamble of a legal document; the wording under an illustration, the legend; the heading of a chapter, section or newspaper article; a subtitle or other printed or graphic material in a television or cinematograph film. [L *captio -oñem* (*capere,* to take)]

captious, *a.* sophistical, quibbling; fault-finding, carping, cavilling; †capacious. **captiously,** *adv.* **captiousness,** *n.* [L *captiōsus,* from prec.]

captivate, *v.t.* †to take captive; to fascinate, to charm. **captivating,** *a.* **captivation,** *n.* the act of fascinating; a fascination, a charm. [L *captīvātus,* p.p. of *captīvāre* (*captīvus,* CAPTIVE)]

captive, *n.* one taken prisoner, held in confinement or bondage, or fascinated; *a.* taken prisoner; held in bondage; held in control; pertaining to captivity; captivated, fascinated; unable to move away or otherwise exercise choice, as in a *captive audience, market* etc. *v.t.* †to take prisoner, to enslave; to captivate. **captive balloon,** *n.* a balloon held by a rope from the ground. **captive time,** *n.* time during which a person is not working but must be available if needed. †**captivated,** *a.* **captivity,** *n.* **captor,** *n.* **captress,** *n.* (*fem.*) **capture,** *n.* the act of seizing as a prisoner or a prize; the person or thing so taken. *v.t.* to make a capture of; to seize as a prize; to succeed in describing in words or by drawing (a likeness etc.). **capturer,** *n.* [F *captif,* fem. *captive,* L *captīvus* (*captus,* p.p. of *capere,* to take)]

capuche, *n.* a hood, esp. the long pointed hood of the Capuchins. [F, from It. *capuccio,* a cowl (*cappa,* CAP¹)]

Capuchin, *n.* a member of the Franciscan order of monks in the Roman Catholic church, instituted by Matteo di Bassi (d. 1552), an Italian monk who wished to return to the literal observance of the rule of St Francis; their rule was drawn up in 1529. The brown habit with the pointed hood (French *capuche*) that he adopted gave his followers the name. The order was recognized by the pope in 1619, and has been involved in missionary activity. **capuchin monkey,** *n.* an American monkey, *Cebus capucinus.* **capuchin pigeon,** *n.* a sub-variety of the Jacobin pigeon. [It. *cappuccino,* dim. of *capuccio,* from prec.]

capul CAPLE.

caput, *n.* (*pl.* **capita**) the head, the top part; the peridium of some fungi. [L]

caput mortuum, *n.* (*Alch.*) the residuum after distillation or sublimation; worthless residuum. [L, lit. dead head]

capybara, capibara, *n.* a S American mammal, *Hydrochaerus capybara,* the largest living rodent, allied to the guinea-pig. [Tupi]

CAR, (*abbr.*) Central African Republic.

Car., (*abbr.*) Carolina; Charles. [L *Carolus*]

car, *n.* a motor-car; (*poet.*) a wheeled vehicle, a chariot; (*Ir.*) a jaunting-car; (*N Am.*) any railway coach or wagon; (*N Am.*) a lift cage; the pendent carriage of an airship; in Britain, used of certain types of passenger railway carriages, as in *dining-car, Pullman-car.* **car-bomb,** *n.* an explosive device hidden in a parked car, which destroys the car and anything nearby. **car-boot sale,** *n.* a sale of second-hand goods, from the boot of a car. **car-coat,** *n.* a short coat which can be worn comfortably in a car. **car-fare,** *n.* (*N Am.*) a bus etc. fare. **car ferry,** *n.* a ferry-boat built so that motor vehicles can be driven on and off it. **car hop,** *n.* (*N Am.*) a waiter or waitress at a drive-in restaurant. **carman,**

n. one who drives a van or (*Ir.*) a jaunting-car; a carter, a carrier. **car-park,** *n.* a place where cars may be left for a limited period. **car port,** *n.* an open-sided shelter for a car beside a house. **car-wash,** *n.* an establishment with equipment for the automatic washing of cars. **carful,** *n.* as many people as a car will hold. [ONorthF *carre,* late L *carra* (L *carrus,* a four-wheeled vehicle mentioned by Caesar, Bret. *carr,* cp. W *car,* Ir. *carr*)]

carabine, carabineer etc. CARBINE.

caracal, *n.* the Persian lynx, *Felis caracal.* [Turk. *qarah qalaq,* lit. black ear]

Caracalla, *n.* **Marcus Aurelius Antoninus** (AD 186–217), Roman emperor. So-called from the celtic cloak (*caracalla*) that he wore. He succeeded his father Septimius Severus in 211, ruled with cruelty and extravagance, and was assassinated.

Caracas, *n.* chief city and capital of Venezuela; situated on the Andean slopes, 13 km/8 miles south of its port La Guaira on the Caribbean coast; population of metropolitan area (1981) 1,817,000. Founded 1567, it is now a major industrial and commercial centre, notably for oil companies.

carack CARRACK.

caracol, -cole, *n.* a half turn or wheel made by a horse or horseman; a winding staircase. *v.i.* to perform a caracol or half turn; to caper. *v.t.* to make (a horse) caracol. [F *caracole,* It. *caracollo,* wheeling of a horse, Sp. *caracol,* a spiral shell, a snail (etym. doubtful; cp. Gael. *carach,* circling, winding)]

†**caract,** *n.* a mark; character. [OF *caracte,* through L, from Gr. *charaktos,* graven, stamped]

Caractacus, *n.* (d. *c.* AD 54), British chieftain, who headed resistance to the Romans in SE England AD 43–51, but was defeated on the Welsh border. Shown in Claudius's triumphal procession, he was released in tribute to his courage and died in Rome.

carafe, *n.* a wide-mouthed glass jar for holding wine or water at table; as much wine or water as a carafe will hold. [F, It., *caraffa* (cp. Sp. and Port. *garrafa*), Arab. *gharafa,* to draw water]

carambola STAR-FRUIT.

carambole, *n.* (*Billiards*) a cannon. *v.i.* to make a cannon. [F, from Sp. *carambola,* the red ball and a certain stroke at billiards]

caramel, *n.* burnt sugar for colouring spirits; a kind of sweetmeat; the colour of caramel, a pale brown. *v.t., v.i.* **caramelize, -ise,** to turn into caramel. [F, from Sp. *caramello*]

carapace, *n.* the upper body-shell of the tortoise family; any analogous covering in the lower animals. [F, from Sp. *carapacho;* etym. doubtful]

carat, *n.* a weight (standardized as the International Carat of 0.200 g) used for precious stones, esp. diamonds; a proportional measure of one 24th part, used to describe the fineness of gold. [F, from It. *carato,* Arab. *qīrāt,* prob. from Gr. *keration,* fruit of the locust-tree (dim. of *keras -atos,* a horn)]

Caravaggio, *n.* **Michelangelo Merisi da** (1573–1610), Italian early Baroque painter, active in Rome (1592–1606), then in Naples and finally Malta. His life was as dramatic as his art (he had to leave Rome after killing a man). He created a forceful style, using contrasts of light and shade and focusing closely on the subject figures, sometimes using dramatic foreshortening.

caravan, *n.* a company of merchants or pilgrims, travelling together (esp. in desert regions) for mutual security; a travelling house, a carriage for living in drawn by horse or motor-car; a showman's covered wagon; (*N Am.*) a trailer. *v.i.* to live, esp. temporarily in a caravan. **caravaneer,** *n.* the leader of an Eastern caravan. **caravanner,** *n.* **caravanning,** *n.* [F *caravane,* or directly from Pers. *karwān*]

caravanserai, -sera, -sary, *n.* an Oriental inn with a large courtyard for the accommodation of caravans; a large hotel. [Pers. *karwān, -sarāy*]

caravel, carvel, *n.* a name applied at different times to various kinds of ships; e.g. a swift Spanish or Portuguese merchant vessel; a Turkish frigate. [F *caravelle,* It. *caravella,* late L *carabus,* Gr. *karabos*]

caraway, *n.* a European umbelliferous plant, *Carum carvi.* **caraway-seeds,** *n.pl.* the small dried fruit of this, used as a flavouring. [Arab. *karawiyā* (perh. through med. L *carvi*)]

carbamate, *n.* a salt or ester of carbamic acid, esp. carbaryl, an insecticide.

carbamide UREA.

carbide, *n.* a compound of carbon with a metal, esp. **calcium carbide,** used for generating acetylene.

carbine, carabine, *n.* a short rifle used by cavalry. **carbineer, carabinier,** *n.* a soldier armed with a carbine. [F *carabin* (now *carabine*); perh. from OF *calabrin,* late L. *Calabrīnus,* a Calabrian; or from late L *chadabula,* a kind of ballista, Gr. *katabolē* (*kataballein,* to throw down with missiles)]

carb(o)-, *comb. form.* of, with, containing, or pertaining to carbon. [CARBON]

carbo-cyclic, *a.* denoting a compound which includes a closed ring of carbon atoms.

carbohydrate, *n.* an organic compound of carbon, hydrogen and oxygen. Usually there are two atoms of hydrogen to every one of oxygen as in starch, glucose etc.

carbolic, *a.* derived from coal or coal-tar. **carbolic acid,** *n.* an antiseptic and disinfectant acid. **carbolize, -ise,** *v.t.* to impregnate with carbolic acid.

carbon, *n.* a non-metallic element found in nearly all organic substances, in carbon dioxide, and the carbonates, and uncombined in diamond, graphite and charcoal; a pencil of fine charcoal used in arc-lamps; carbon-paper; a carbon-copy. **carbon-copy,** *n.* a typewritten duplicate. **carbon dating,** *n.* a method of calculating the age of organic material (wood, bones etc.) by measuring the decay of the isotope carbon-14. **carbon dioxide,** *n.* a gaseous combination of one atom of carbon with two of oxygen, a normal constituent of the atmosphere and of expired breath. **carbon fibre,** *n.* a very strong thread of pure carbon, used for reinforcing plastics, metals etc. **carbon monoxide,** *n.* a gas containing one atom of oxygen for each atom of carbon; it is poisonous and a constituent of motor-car exhaust gases. **carbon-paper,** *n.* a dark-coated paper for taking impressions of writing, drawing etc. **carbon printing, process,** *n.* a permanent black and white photographic process, the shades of which are produced by lamp-black. **carbon steel,** *n.* any of several steels containing carbon in varying amounts. **carbon tetrachloride,** *n.* a colourless toxic liquid, used as a dry-cleaning solvent. **carbonaceous,** *a.* like coal or charcoal; containing carbon; abounding in or of the nature of coal. **carbonate,** *n.* a salt of carbonic acid. *v.t.* to impregnate with carbonic acid; to aerate (water etc.); to form into a carbonate. **carbonic,** *a.* pertaining to carbon, containing carbon. **carbonic acid,** *n.* a weak acid; the compound formed by carbon dioxide and water. **carbonic-acid gas,** *n.* carbon dioxide. **carboniferous,** *a.* producing coal or carbon; (*Geol.*) see separate article below. **Carboniferous age, period,** *n.* the geological epoch during which these strata were deposited. **Carboniferous formation, system,** *n.* **Carboniferous strata,** *n.pl.* **carbonize, -ise,** *v.t.* to convert into carbon by the action of fire or acids; to cover with carbon-paper, charcoal, lamp-black, or the like. **carbonization, -isation,** *n.* [F *carbone,* L *carbo -ōnem,* a coal]

carbonade, -nnade, *n.* a beef stew made with beer.

carbonado[1], *n.* a carbonade; †flesh, fish or fowl scored across, and grilled on coals. [F *carbonade,* Sp. *carbonada,* from Sp. *carbon,* coal]

carbonado[2], *n.* a black, opaque diamond of poor quality, used industrially in drills etc. [Port., carbonated]

Carbonari, *n.pl.* members of a secret republican society in Italy and France in the early part of the 19th cent.; hence, republican revolutionists. **carbonarism,** *n.* [It., charcoal burners]

carbonate, carbonic CARBON.

Carboniferous, *n.* a period of geological time 360–286

million years ago, the fifth period of the Palaeozoic era. In the US it is regarded as two periods: the Mississippian (lower) and the Pennsylvanian (upper). Typical of the lower-Carboniferous rocks are shallow-water limestones, while upper-Carboniferous rocks have delta deposits with coal (hence the name). Amphibians were abundant, and reptiles evolved.

carbora, *n.* the koala. [Austral. Abor.]

Carborundum®, *n.* a silicon carbide used for grinding-wheels etc.

carboy, *n.* a large globular bottle of green or blue glass, protected with wickerwork, used for holding corrosive liquids. [Pers. *qarābah*]

carbuncle, *n.* a precious stone of a red or fiery colour; a garnet cut in a concave cabochon; (*Her.*) a carbuncle borne as a charge; a hard, painful boil without a core, caused by bacterial infection; (*coll.*) an ugly building etc. which defaces the appearance of the landscape. **carbuncled,** *a.* **carbuncular,** *a.* [ME *charbucle, carbuncle,* OF *charboucle* (ONorth.F *carbuncle*), L *carbunculus,* a small coal, a gem]

carburet, *n.* the compound formed by the combination of carbon with another element. *v.t.* (*past, p.p.* **carburetted**) to combine (another element) with carbon. **carburation, -retion**, *n.* **carburettor,** *n.* an apparatus designed to vaporize a liquid and to mix it intimately with air in proportions to ensure ready ignition and complete combustion. **carburize, -ise,** *v.t.* to carburet; to impart carbon to (wrought iron). **carburization, -isation,** *n.*

carcajou, *n.* the glutton or wolverine. [N Am.F (prob. Indian)]

carcake, *n.* a cake eaten on Shrove Tuesday in parts of Scotland. [Sc., CARE, OE *caru,* grief]

†**carcanet,** *n.* a jewelled necklet or collar. [*carcan,* an iron collar used for punishment, F *carcan,* late L *carcannum,* from Teut. (cp. OHG *querca,* the throat)]

carcass, -case, *n.* the trunk of a slaughtered beast without the head and offal; the dead body of a beast; (*derog.* or *facet.*) the human body dead or alive; the framework of a building, ship etc.; a mere body, mere shell, or husk; †a perforated shell filled with combustibles. **carcass meat,** *n.* raw meat as sold in a butcher's shop. [A-F *carcois,* med. L *carcosium,* afterwards modified by MF *carquasse* (F *carcasse*), It. *carcassa,* a shell or bomb (etym. doubtful)]

Carchemish, *n.* (now Karkamis, Turkey) centre of the Hittite New Empire (*c.* 1400–1200 BC) on the Euphrates, 80 km/50 miles NE of Aleppo, and taken by Sargon II of Assyria in 717 BC. Nebuchadnezzar II of Babylon defeated the Egyptians here in 605 BC.

carcinogen, *n.* a substance that can give rise to cancer. **carcinogenic,** *a.* [CARCINOMA, -GEN]

carcinology, *n.* that part of zoology which deals with the crustacea. **carcinological**, *a.* **carcinologist,** *n.* [Gr. *karkinos,* a crab]

carcinoma, *n.* (*pl.* **-mata, -mas**) the disease cancer; a malignant tumour. **carcinomatous,** *a.* **carcinosis**, **carcinomatosis**, *n.* the spread of cancer through the body. [L, from Gr. *karkinōma,* cancer (*karkinos,* a crab)]

card¹, *n.* one of a pack of oblong pieces of pasteboard, marked with pips and pictures, used in playing games of chance or skill; a flat, rectangular piece of stiff pasteboard for writing or drawing on or the like; a visiting-card, a ticket of admission, an invitation; a programme, a menu, a list of events at races, regattas etc., and various other senses denoted by a prefixed substantive; †a chart, †the piece of card on which the points are marked in the mariner's compass; (*pl.*) a game or games with cards; card-playing; (*sl.*) a character, an eccentric; (*pl., coll.*) a worker's employment documents; (*Comput.*) a punched card. **house of cards** HOUSE. **on the cards,** possible; not improbable. **to get one's cards,** to be dismissed or made redundant. **to lay, put, one's cards on the table,** to disclose one's situation, plans etc. **to play one's cards well,** to be a good strategist. **to play with one's cards close to one's chest** PLAY. **to show one's cards,** to reveal one's plan. **to speak by the card,** to speak with exactness. **to throw up the cards,** to give up the game. **cardboard,** *n.* fine pasteboard for making light boxes and other articles, pasteboard. *a.* without substance or reality. **card-carrying,** *a.* being a full member of (a political party etc.). **card-case,** *n.* a case to hold visiting-cards. **card catalogue, index,** *n.* a catalogue or index in which each item is entered on a separate card. **cardphone,** *n.* a public telephone where a special card (*phonecard*) is inserted rather than coins. **card punch,** (*Comput.*) a device which can take data from a store or processor and transfer it to punched cards. **card-rack,** *n.* a rack for visitors' cards. **card reader,** (*Comput.*) a device which can read the data on punched cards and convert it to a form in which it can be stored or processed. **card-sharp, -sharper,** *n.* one who swindles by means of card games or tricks with cards. **card-table,** *n.* a table to play cards on. **card vote,** *n.* a ballot where the vote of each delegate counts for the number of his constituents. **visiting card** VISIT. [F *carte,* It. *carta,* late L *carta,* L. *charta,* Gr. *chartē, chartēs,* a leaf of papyrus]

card², *n.* an iron toothed instrument for combing wool or flax. *v.t.* to comb (wool, flax or hemp) with a card; to raise a nap; to tear the flesh with a card by way of punishment or torture. **card-thistle,** *n.* the teazel. **carder,** *n.* one who cards wool; a species of wild bee, *Bombus muscorum.* **carding,** *a.* **carding-engine, -machine,** *n.* a machine for combing out and cleaning wool, cotton, etc. **carding-wool,** *n.* short-stapled wool. [F *carde,* a teazel, a wool-card, It. *card,* late L *cardus,* L *carduus,* a thistle]

cardamine , *n.* a genus of cruciferous plants comprising the cuckoo-flower or lady-smock. [Gr. *kardaminē*]

cardamom, *n.* a spice obtained from the seed capsules of various species of *Amomum* and other genera. [L *cardamōmum,* Gr. *kardamōmon* (*kardamon,* cress, *amōmon,* an Indian spice-plant)]

Cárdenas, *n.* **Lázaro** (1895–1970), Mexican centre-left politician and general, president (1934–40). In early life a civil servant, Cárdenas took part in the revolutionary campaigns (1915–29) that followed the fall of President Díaz (1830–1915). As president of the republic, he attempted to achieve the goals of the revolution by building schools, distributing land to the peasants, and developing transport and industry. He was minister of defence (1943–45).

cardiac, *a.* of or pertaining to the heart; heart-shaped; of or pertaining to the upper orifice of the stomach; cordial, strengthening. *n.* a cordial or stimulant for the heart; a person suffering from heart disease. **cardiac arrest,** *n.* cessation of the heartbeat. †**cardiacal**, *a.* **cardial,** *a.* **cardialgy**, **-algia**, *n.* an affection of the heart; heartburn. **cardialgic**, *a.* [F *cardiaque,* L *cardiacus,* Gr. *kardiakos* (*kardia,* the heart)]

cardi(e), *n.* short for CARDIGAN.

Cardiff, *n.* capital of Wales (from 1955), and administrative headquarters of South and Mid Glamorgan, at the mouth of the Taff, Rhymney and Ely rivers; population (1983) 279,800. Besides steelworks, there are automotive component, flour milling, paper, cigar and other industries.

Cardiff Arms Park, Welsh rugby union ground officially known as the National Stadium, situated in Cardiff. The stadium became the permanent home of the Welsh national team in 1964 and has a capacity of 64,000.

cardigan, *n.* a knitted jacket buttoned up the front. [7th Earl of *Cardigan*, 1797–1868]

Cardiganshire, *n.* former county of Wales, which was in 1974 merged, together with Pembroke and Carmarthen, into Dyfed.

Cardin, *n.* **Pierre** (1922–), French fashion designer; the first women's designer to show a collection for men, in 1960.

cardinal, *a.* fundamental, chief, principal; of the colour of a cardinal's cassock, deep scarlet; (*Zool.*) pertaining to the hinge of a bivalve. *n.* one of the ecclesiastical princes of the Roman Church who elect a new pope, usu. from among their own number; orig. one in charge of a cardinal church at Rome; a short cloak (orig. of scarlet) for women; a cardinal-bird; (*coll.*) mulled red wine. **cardinal-bird,** *n.* a N American red-plumaged song-bird, *Cardinalis virginianus*. **cardinal bishop,** *n.* the highest rank of cardinal. **cardinal church,** *n.* (*Hist.*) the name given in early ages to the principal or parish churches of Rome. **cardinal deacon,** *n.* the third rank of cardinal. **cardinal-flower,** *n.* the scarlet lobelia, *Lobelia cardinalis*. **cardinal numbers,** *n.pl.* the simple numbers 1, 2, 3 etc., as distinguished from 1st, 2nd, 3rd etc. **cardinal points,** *n.pl.* the four points of the compass: north, south, east and west. **cardinal priest,** *n.* the second rank of cardinal. **cardinal signs,** *n.pl.* Aries, Libra, Cancer, Capricorn; the two solstitial and the two equinoctial points of the ecliptic. **cardinal's hat,** *n.* the official emblem of the cardinalate, a flat red hat with fifteen tassels on each side. **cardinal virtues,** *n.pl.* (*Phil.*) Prudence, Temperance, Justice and Fortitude; (*Theol.*) Faith, Hope and Charity. **cardinalate**, **cardinalship,** *n.* the office or dignity of a cardinal. **cardinally,** *adv.* fundamentally; †(*punningly*) carnally. [F, from L *cardinālis* (*cardo -inis,* a hinge)]

cardio-, *comb. form.* pertaining to the heart.

cardiograph, *n.* an instrument for registering the movement of the heart. **cardiogram**, *n.* a reading from a cardiograph. **cardiography**, *n.* the use of this; a description of the heart.

cardioid, *n.* (*Math.*) a heart-shaped curve. [Gr. *kardioeides* (*kardia,* heart, -OID)]

cardiology, *n.* knowledge of the heart; a treatise on the heart.

cardiovascular, *a.* relating to the heart and blood-vessels.

carditis, *n.* inflammation of the heart.

cardoon, *n.* a kitchen-garden plant, *Cynara cardunculus,* allied to the artichoke. [F *cardon* (It. *cardone,* or Sp. *cardon*), late L *cardus,* L *carduus,* thistle]

Cardwell, *n.* **Edward, Viscount Cardwell** (1813–86), British Liberal politician. He entered Parliament as a supporter of the Conservative prime minister Peel in 1842, and was secretary for war under Gladstone (1868–74), when he carried out many reforms, including the abolition of the purchase of military commissions and promotions.

care, *n.* †sorrow, grief, trouble; solicitude, anxiety, concern; a cause of these; caution, serious attention, heed; oversight, protection; object of regard or solicitude. *v.i.* to be anxious or solicitous; to be concerned about; to provide (for), attend (upon); to have affection, respect or liking (for); to be desirous, willing or inclined (to). **in care,** in the guardianship of the local authority. **who cares?** (*coll.*) I don't care. **carefree,** *a.* free from responsibility, light-hearted. **care-laden,** *a.* **care-worn,** *a.* **caretaker,** *n.* a person in charge of an unlet house or chambers, or other building, *a.* interim. **carer,** *n.* one who cares; one who looks after someone, e.g. an invalid, dependent relative etc. **caring,** *a.* showing care or concern; providing medical care or social services, as in *caring professions*. **careful,** *a.* †full of care, sorrowful; solicitous; watchful, cautious, circumspect; provident, painstaking, attentive, exact; done with care. **carefully,** *adv.* **carefulness,** *n.* **careless,** *a.* free from care, without anxiety, unconcerned; heedless, thoughtless, inaccurate; inattentive, negligent (of); negligently done; †neglected. **carelessly,** *adv.* **carelessness,** *n.* [OE *caru* (cp. OS and Goth. *kara,* sorrow, OHG *charōn,* to lament), from Teut. *karā-*]

CARE, (*abbr.*) Cooperative for American Relief Everywhere.

careen, *v.t.* to turn (a ship) on one side in order to clean or caulk her. *v.i.* to heel over under press of sail. **careenage,** *n.* the act of, a place for, or the expense of careening. [F *cariner* (now *caréner*), ult. from L *carīna,* a keel]

career, *n.* †a race-course; †the lists at a tournament; †a charge, an encounter; a running, a swift course; course or progress through life; the progress and development of a nation, party etc; a way of making a living in business, professional or artistic fields etc. *a.* having a specified career, professional as *career diplomat*. *v.i.* to move in a swift, head-long course; to gallop at full speed. **careers master, mistress or teacher,** *n.* a teacher who gives advice on careers. **career girl, woman,** *n.* one who pursues a full-time career. **careerism,** *n.* **careerist,** *n.* one who makes personal advancement his or her main objective. [F *carière,* late L *carrāria via,* a road for cars (L *carrus,* CAR)]

carême, *n.* Lent. [F]

caress, *n.* an embrace, a kiss; an act of endearment. *v.t.* to fondle, to stroke affectionately; to pet, to court, to flatter. **caressing,** *a.* **caressingly,** *adv.* [F *caresse,* It. *carezza,* late L *cāritia* (L *carus,* dear)]

caret, *n.* a mark (‸) used to show that something, which may be read above or in the margin, has been left out. [L, is wanting (*carēre,* to need)]

Carew, *n.* **Thomas** (*c.* 1595– *c.* 1640), English poet. He was a gentleman of the privy chamber to Charles I in 1628, and a lyricist as well as craftsman of the school of Cavalier Poets.

carex, *n.* (*pl.* **carices**) a genus of grass-like plants of the sedge family. [L]

Carey, *n.* **Peter** (1943–), Australian novelist. He has combined work in advertising with a writing career since 1962, and his novels include *Bliss* (1981), *Illywhacker* (Australian slang for 'con man') (1985), and *Oscar and Lucinda* (1988), which won the Booker prize.

carfuffle, *n.* commotion, disorder. [etym. unknown]

cargo, *n.* the freight of a ship or aircraft; such a load. **cargo boat,** *n.* one designed to carry freight. **cargo cult,** *n.* a religion popular in some Polynesian islands, according to which the ancestors will come back in cargo boats or aeroplanes, bringing wealth for the islanders. [Sp., a load, a loading, med. L *carricum,* late L *carricāre,* to load (*carrus,* CAR)]

Carib, *n.* a member of a group of American Indian aboriginal people of South America and the islands of the West Indies in the Caribbean Sea. In 1796 the English in the West Indies deported most of them to Roatan Island off Honduras. They have since spread extensively in Honduras and Nicaragua. **Caribbean**, *a.* of or pertaining to the W Indies or their inhabitants. [Sp. *caribe* (see CANNIBAL)]

Caribbean Community, *n.* (CARICOM) organization for economic and foreign policy coordination in the Caribbean region, established by the Treaty of Chaguaramas (1973). The leading member is Trinidad and Tobago; headquarters Georgetown, Guyana; others are Antigua, Barbados, Belize, Dominica, Grenada, Guyana, Jamaica, Montserrat, St Christopher Nevis, Anguilla, St Lucia and St Vincent. From 1979 a left-wing Grenadan coup led to a progressive regional subgroup including St Lucia and Dominica.

Caribbean Sea, *n.* part of the Atlantic Ocean between the N coasts of South and Central America and the West Indies, about 2740 km/1700 miles long and between 650 km/400 miles–1500 km/900 miles wide. It is here that the Gulf Stream turns towards Europe.

caribou, *n.* the N American reindeer. [French-Canadian, prob. from native Ind.]

caricature, *n.* a representation of a person or thing exaggerating characteristic traits in a ludicrous way; a burlesque, a parody; a laughably inadequate person or thing. *v.t.* to represent in this way; to burlesque. **caricaturable**, *a.* **caricatural,** *a.* **caricaturist**, *n.* [It. *caricatura* (assim. to F *caricature*), from *caricare,* late L *carricāre* (see CARGO)]

CARICOM, (*abbr.*) see CARIBBEAN COMMUNITY.

caries, *n.* decay of the bones or teeth; decay of vegetable tissue. **cariogenic**, *a.* producing caries. **carious,** *a.* [L]

carillon, *n.* a set of bells so arranged as to be played by the hand or by machinery; an air played on such bells; a musical instrument (or part of one) to imitate such bells. [F, from med. L *quadrilo -ōnem,* a quaternion (of four bells)]

carina, *n.* (*Zool., Bot.*) a ridge-like structure. **carinal,** *a.* **carinate, -ated,** *a.* [L, a keel]

Carina, *n.* constellation of the southern hemisphere, representing a ship's keel. Its brightest star is Canopus; it also contains Eta Carinae, a massive and highly luminous star embedded in a gas cloud. It has varied unpredictably in the past; some astronomers think it is likely to explode as a supernova within 10,000 years.

caring CARE.

Carinthia, *n.* (German **Kärnten**) alpine federal province of SE Austria, bordering Italy and Yugoslavia in the south; capital Klagenfurt; area 9500 sq km/3667 sq miles; population (1987) 542,000. It was an independent duchy from 976, and a possession of the Habsburg dynasty (1276–1918).

carioca, *n.* a S American dance like the samba; music for this dance; (*coll.*) a native or inhabitant of Rio de Janeiro. [Port.]

cariogenic CARIES.

cariole CARRIOLE.

Carissimi, *n.* **Giacomo** (1605–74), Italian composer, a pioneer of the oratorio.

†**cark,** *v.t.* to burden, to harass, to worry. *v.i.* to be anxious, to fret, to worry. *n.* care, distress, anxiety. **carking,** *a.* burdening, distressing, wearisome. [ONorth.F *carkier* (cp. OF *chargier*), late L *carcāre, carricāre* (see CARGO)]

carl, carle, *n.* (*Sc.*) a countryman; a man of low birth; a strong, sturdy fellow. [Icel. *karl* (cp. OE *hūscarl* and CHURL)]

Carl Gustaf XVI, *n.* (1946–), king of Sweden from 1973. He succeeded his grandfather Gustaf VI, his father having been killed in an air crash in 1947. Under the new Swedish constitution which became effective on his grandfather's death, the monarchy was effectively stripped of all power at his accession.

carline¹, *n.* (*Sc.*) an old woman, a witch. [Icel. *kerling,* fem. of prec.]

carline², *n.* any of a genus of plants allied to the thistle, commonest species *Carlina vulgaris*. [F, from late L *Carlīna, Carolīna,* fem. of *Carolīnus,* Charlemagne]

Carlist, *n.* a supporter of the claims of the Spanish pretender Don Carlos de Bourbon (1788–1855), and his descendants, to the Spanish crown. The Carlist revolt continued, especially in the Basque provinces, until 1839. In 1977 the Carlist political party was legalized and Carlos Hugo de Bourbon Parma (1930–) renounced his claim as pretender and became reconciled with King Juan Carlos. **Carlism,** *n.*.

carlock, *n.* isinglass from the bladder of the sturgeon. [Rus. *karluku*]

Carlos, *n.* four kings of Spain. See CHARLES.

Carlos, *n.* **Don** (1545–68), Spanish prince. Son of Philip II, he was recognized as heir to the thrones of Castile and Aragon, but became mentally unstable and had to be placed under restraint following a plot to assassinate his father. His story was the subject of plays by Schiller, Alfieri, Otway, and others.

Carlos I, *n.* (1863–1908), king of Portugal, of the Braganza-Coburg line, from 1889 until he was assassinated in Lisbon with his elder son Luis. He was succeeded by his younger son Manoel.

Carlovingian CAROLINGIAN under CAROLINE.

Carlow, *n.* a county in the Republic of Ireland, in the province of Leinster; county town Carlow; area 900 sq km/347 sq miles; population (1986) 41,000. Mostly flat except for mountains in the south, the land is fertile, and dairy farming is important.

Carlson, *n.* **Chester** (1906–68), US scientist, who invented xerography. A research worker with Bell Telephone, he was sacked from his post in 1930 during the Depression, and set to work on his own to develop an efficient copying machine. By 1938 he had invented the Xerox photocopier.

Carlsson, *n.* **Ingvar (Gösta)** (1934–), Swedish socialist politician, leader of the Social Democratic Party, deputy prime minister (1982–86) and prime minister from 1986.

Carlucci, *n.* **Frank (Charles)** (1930–), US politician, a pragmatic moderate. A former diplomat and deputy director of the CIA, he was national security adviser (1986–87) and defence secretary from Nov. 1987 under Reagan, supporting Soviet-US arms reduction.

Carlyle, *n.* **Thomas** (1795–1881), Scottish essayist and social historian. His work included *Sartor Resartus* (1836), describing his loss of Christian belief, *French Revolution* (1837), *Chartism* (1839), and *Past and Present* (1843). He was a friend of J.S. Mill and Ralph Waldo Emerson. **Carlylese,** *n.* the irregular, vehement, vividly metaphorical style and phraseology of Thomas Carlyle.

carmagnole, *n.* a lively song and dance popular among the French revolutionists of 1793; a French revolutionist; the bombastic style of the writings of the first French Revolution. [F, an upper garment worn during the Revolution, said to be named from *Carmagnole* in Piedmont]

Carmarthenshire, *n.* a former county of S Wales, and formerly also the largest Welsh county. It bordered on the Bristol Channel, and was merged in 1974, together with Cardigan and Pembroke, into Dyfed. The county town was Carmarthen, population (1981) 12,302.

Carmelite, *n.* one of an order of mendicant friars, founded in the 12th cent. on Mount Carmel (also *White Friars*); a nun of this order; a fine woollen stuff, usu. grey. *a.* belonging or pertaining to this order.

Carmichael, *n.* **'Hoagy'** (Hoagland Howard) (1899–1981), US jazz composer, pianist, singer and actor. His songs include 'Stardust' (1927), 'Rockin' Chair' (1930), 'Lazy River' (1931), and 'In the Cool, Cool, Cool of the Evening' (1951) (Academy Award).

Carmina Burana, *n.* a medieval lyric miscellany compiled from the work of wandering 13th-cent. scholars and including secular (love songs and drinking songs) as well as religious verse. A cantata (1937) by Carl Orff is based on the material.

carminative, *a.* expelling flatulence *n.* a medicine that expels flatulence. [L *carminātus,* p.p. of *carmināre,* to card wool]

carmine, *n.* a beautiful red or crimson pigment obtained from cochineal. *a.* coloured like this. [F or Sp. *carmin* (med. L *carmīnus, carmesīnus*), Sp. *carmesi,* Arab. *quirmazī,* CRIMSON]

carnage, *n.* †dead bodies slain in battle; butchery, slaughter, esp. of men. [F, from It. *carnaggio,* late L *carnāticum* (L *caro carnis,* flesh)]

carnal, *a.* †bodily; fleshly, sensual; sexual, unregenerate, as opp. to *spiritual;* temporal, secular; †murderous. **carnal knowledge,** *n.* sexual intercourse. **carnal-minded,** *a.* worldly-minded. **carnal-mindedness,** *n.* **carnalism,** *n.* sensualism. **carnalist,** *n.* **carnality,** *n.* the state of being carnal. **carnalize, -ise,** *v.t.* to sensualize; to materialize. **carneous, -nose, †-nous,** *a.* resembling flesh; fleshy. [L *carnālis* (*caro carnis,* flesh)]

carnallite, *n.* a white or reddish hydrous chloride of magnesium and potassium found in German and Iranian salt-mines. [from the mineralogist Von *Carnall*]

Carnarvon, *n.* alternate spelling of CAERNARVON.

carnassial, *n.* in the Carnivora, a large tooth adapted for tearing flesh. *a.* relating to such a tooth.

carnation¹, *n.* a light rose-pink; a flesh tint; a part of a painting representing human flesh. *a.* of this colour. **carnationed,** *a.* [F, from L *carnātio -ōnem* (*caro,* see CARNAL)]

carnation², *n.* the cultivated clove-pink, *Dianthus caryophyllus*. [perh. a corr. of INCARNATION or CORONATION]

carnauba, *n.* a Brazilian palm, *Copernicia;* its yellow wax, used in polishes. [Port.]

Carnegie¹, *n.* family name of the earls of Northesk and Southesk and of the Duke of Fife, who is descended from Queen Victoria.

Carnegie², *n.* **Andrew** (1835–1919), US industrialist and philanthropist, born in Scotland, who developed the Pittsburgh iron and steel industries. He endowed public libraries, education and various research trusts.

Carnegie[3], *n.* **Dale** (1888–1955), US author and teacher, a former YMCA public-speaking instructor, who wrote *How to Win Friends and Influence People* (1938).

carnelian, CORNELIAN.

carnet, *n.* a document allowing the transport of vehicles or goods across a frontier; a book of vouchers, tickets etc. [F, notebook]

carnify, *v.t.* to convert to flesh; to convert (bone or tissue) into fleshy substance. *v.i.* to alter in this way. **carnification,** *n.*

carnival, *n.* Shrovetide; the season immediately before Lent, in many Roman Catholic countries devoted to pageantry and riotous amusement; riotous amusement, revelry; a fun-fair. [It. *carnevale,* the eve of Ash Wednesday, late L *carnelevāmen* (*caro carnem,* flesh, *levāre,* to remove), altered into It, carne vale (flesh, farewell)]

Carnivora, *n.pl.* a large order of mammals subsisting on flesh. **carnivore,** *n.* a carnivorous animal or plant. **carnivorous,** *a.* feeding on flesh; also applied to insectivorous plants. [L *carnivorus,* neut. *-um,* neut. pl. *-a* (*caro carnis,* flesh, -VOROUS)]

carnoso-, *comb. form* pertaining to flesh, fleshy.

Carnot[1], *n.* **Marie François Sadi** (1837–94), French president from 1887, grandson of Lazare Carnot. He successfully countered the Boulangist anti-German movement and in 1892 the scandals arising out of French financial activities in Panama. He was assassinated by an Italian anarchist at Lyons.

Carnot[2], *n.* **Lazare** (1753–1823), French general and politician. A member of the National Convention in the French Revolution, he organized the armies of the republic. He was war minister (1800–01) and minister of the interior in 1815 under Napoleon. His work on fortification, *De la défense de places fortes* (1810), became a military textbook.

Carnot[3], *n.* **Nicolas Leonard Sadi** (1796–1832), French scientist and military engineer, son of Lazare Carnot, who founded thermodynamics; his pioneering work was *Réflexions sur la puissance motrice du feu/On the Motive Power of Fire.*

Carnot cycle, *n.* changes in the physical condition of a gas in a reversible heat engine, necessarily in the following order: (1) isothermal expansion (without change of temperature), (2) adiabatic expansion (without change of heat content), (3) isothermal compression, and (4) adiabatic compression.

carnotite, *n.* a vanadate of uranium and potassium, noted as an important source of radium. [A. *Carnot,* d.1920, F mine inspector]

carny, -ney, *v.i.* (*dial., coll.*) to act in a wheedling manner. *v.t.* to wheedle, coax. [etym. unknown]

Caro, *n.* **Anthony** (1924–), British sculptor, noted for bold, large abstracts, using ready-made angular metal shapes, often without bases. Works include *Fathom* (outside the Economist Building, London).

carob, *n.* the Mediterranean locust-tree, *Ceratonia siliqua,* or its fruit, with an edible pulp, used as a substitute for chocolate. [F *carobe,* Arab. *kharrūb,* bean-pods]

carol, *n.* †a ring-dance; †a song, usu. with dancing; a joyous hymn, esp. in honour of the Nativity; joyous warbling of birds. *v.i.* (*past, p.p.* **carolled**) to sing carols; to warble. *v.t.* to celebrate in songs. **caroller,** *n.* [OF *carole,* prob. from L *choraula,* a dance, L and Gr. *choraulēs,* a flute-player (Gr. *choros,* dance, *aulos,* a flute)]

Carol, *n.* two kings of Romania:

Carol I, *n.* (1839–1914), first king of Romania, (1881–1914). A prince of the house of Hohenzollern-Sigmaringen, he was invited to become prince of Romania, then under Turkish suzerainty in 1866. In 1877, in alliance with Russia, he declared war on Turkey, and the Congress of Berlin (1878) recognized Romanian independence.

Carol II, *n.* (1893–1953), king of Romania (1930–40). Son of King Ferdinand, he married Princess Helen of Greece and they had a son, Michael. In 1925 he renounced the succession and settled in Paris with his mistress, Mme Lupescu. Michael succeeded to the throne in 1927, but in 1930 Carol returned to Romania and was proclaimed king. In 1938 he introduced a new constitution under which he became practically absolute. He was forced to abdicate by the pro-Nazi Iron Guard in Sept. 1940, and went to Mexico and married his mistress in 1947.

Carolina, *n.* two separate states of the US; see NORTH CAROLINA and SOUTH CAROLINA.

Caroline, *a.* (also **Carolean**, **Carolinian**) pertaining to the reigns of Charles I and II of Britain; pertaining to Charlemagne; of a script (**Caroline minuscule**) developed during the reign of Charlemagne. **Carolingian**, **Carlovingian**, *a.* of or belonging to the dynasty of French kings founded by Charlemagne. *n.* a member of this dynasty. [L *Carolus,* Charles]

Caroline of Anspach, (1683–1737), queen of George II of Great Britain. The daughter of the Margrave of Brandenburg-Anspach, she married George, Electoral Prince of Hanover, in 1705, and followed him to England in 1714 when his father became King George I. She was the patron of many leading writers and politicians.

Caroline of Brunswick, (1768–1821), queen of George IV of Great Britain, who unsuccessfully attempted to divorce her on his accession to the throne in 1820.

Carolines, *n.pl.* a scattered archipelago in Micronesia, Pacific Ocean, consisting of over 500 coral islets; area 1200 sq km/463 sq miles. The chief islands are Ponape, Kusai and Truk in the eastern group, and Yap and Belau in the western.

Carolingian dynasty, *n.* a Frankish dynasty descending from Pepin the Short (d. 768) and named after his son Charlemagne; its last ruler was Louis V of France (reigned 966–87), who was followed by Hugh Capet.

carom, CANNON[2].

caromel, CARAMEL.

Carothers, *n.* **Wallace** (1896–1937), US chemist, who carried out research into polymerization. By 1930 he had discovered that some polymers were fibre-forming, and in 1937 produced nylon.

carotid, *a.* of or related to either of the arteries (one on each side of the neck) supplying blood to the head. *n.* a carotid artery. [Gr. *karōtides,* the two neck arteries (*karoein,* to stupefy, from *karos,* sleep, torpor)]

carouse, *n.* †a bumper; a toast; a carousal. *v.i.* to drink a bumper or toast; to drink freely. †*v.t.* to drink, to quaff. **carousal,** *n.* a drinking bout. **carouser,** *n.* **carousingly,** *adv.* in a carousing manner. [G *gar aus,* completely (referring to emptying a bumper)]

carousel, (*esp. N Am.*) **carrousel**, *n.* (*N Am.*) a merry-go-round; a rotating conveyor belt for luggage at an airport; a rotating container which delivers slides to a projector. [F *carrousel,* tournament, merry-go-round]

carp[1], *v.i.* to talk querulously; to find fault, to cavil. **carping,** *a.* **carpingly,** *adv.* [Icel. *karpa,* to boast (confused with L *carpere,* to pluck at, to slander)]

carp[2], *n.* a freshwater fish of the genus *Cyprinus,* esp. *C. cyprio,* the common carp, a pond-fish. [OF *carpe,* late L *carpa,* from Teut. (cp. Dut. *karper,* OHG *charpo,* G *Karpfen*)]

Carpaccio, *n.* **Vittorio** (1450/60–1525/26), Italian painter, known for scenes of his native Venice. His series *The Legend of St Ursula* (1490–98) (Accademia, Venice) is full of detail of contemporary Venetian life. His other great series is the lives of saints George and Jerome (1502–07) (S Giorgio degli Schiavone, Venice).

carpal CARPUS.

Carpathian Mountains, *n.pl.* Central European mountain system, forming a semi-circle through Czechoslovakia-Poland-USSR-Romania, 1450 km/900 miles long. The central **Tatra mountains** on the Czech-Polish frontier include the highest peak, Gerlachovka, 2663 m/8737 ft.

Carpeaux, *n.* **Jean-Baptiste** (1827–75), French sculptor, whose lively naturalistic subjects include *La*

Danse (1865–69) for the Opéra, Paris.

carpel, *n.* the female reproductive organ of a flower, comprising ovary, style and stigma. **carpellary,** *a.* [cp. F *carpelle,* mod. dim. of Gr. *karpos,* fruit]

carpenter, *n.* an artificer who prepares and fixes the wood-work of houses, ships etc; a wood-worker; (*chiefly N Am.*) a joiner. *v.i.* to do carpenter's work. *v.t.* to make by carpentry. **carpenter-ant, -bee, -bird, -moth,** *n.* insects and birds that bore into wood. **carpenter('s) scene,** *n.* a front scene played whilst more elaborate scenery is being arranged at the back of the stage; a painted background behind this screening the stage-carpenters. **carpentry,** *n.* the trade of a carpenter; carpenter's work, esp. the kind of wood-work prepared at the carpenter's bench. [ONorth.F *carpentier* (F. *charpentier*), late L *carpentārius,* from *carpentāre,* to work in timber (*carpentum,* a wagon, from Celt., cp. OIr. *carpat,* OBret. *cerpit*)]

Carpenter, *n.* **John** (1948–), US director of horror and science fiction films. His career began with *Dark Star* (1974) and *Halloween* (1978), and continued with such films as *The Thing* (1981) and *They Live* (1988).

carpet, *n.* a woollen or other thick fabric, usu. with a pattern, for covering floors and stairs. *v.t.* to cover with or as with a carpet; (*coll.*) to reprimand. **on the carpet,** under consideration; (*coll.*) being reprimanded. **to sweep under the carpet,** to conceal or ignore deliberately (an object, happening etc.). **carpet-bag,** *n.* a travelling-bag orig. made with sides of carpet. **carpet-bagger,** *n.* (*chiefly N Am.*) an adventurer, esp. political. **carpet-baggery,** *n.* **carpet-beater,** *n.* a racket-shaped cane utensil for beating carpets. **carpet-bedding,** *n.* the formal arrangement of dwarf foliage plants. **carpet-bombing,** *n.* bombing of a whole area, rather than of selected targets. **carpet-dance,** *n.* an informal dancing-party. **carpet-knight,** *n.* one who has seen no service; a stay-at-home soldier. †**carpet-monger,** *n.* a carpet-knight. **carpet-rod,** *n.* a rod for holding down stair-carpet. **carpet-shark,** *n.* a shark of the genus *Orectolobus,* with two dorsal fins and the back patterned like a carpet. **carpet-slippers,** *n.pl.* comfortable slippers made of tapestry. **carpet-snake,** *n.* an Australian snake, *Morelia variegata.* **carpet-sweeper,** *n.* an apparatus equipped with revolving brushes and dustpans, used for sweeping carpets. **carpet-tack,** *n.* a nail for fastening down a carpet. **carpet tiles,** *n.pl.* small squares of carpeting which can be laid like tiles to cover a floor. **carpeting,** *n.* the action of covering as with carpet; the stuff of which carpets are made; (*coll.*) a dressing-down. **carpetless,** *a.* [OF *carpite,* late L *carpita, carpeta,* a thick cloth, from L *carpere,* to pluck (cp F *charpie,* late L *carpia,* lint, made by plucking rags)]

carphology, *n.* delirious plucking of the bedclothes in fever. [Gr. *karphologia* (*karphos,* twig, *legein,* to pluck)]

Carpini, *n.* **Johannes de Plano** (1182–1252), Franciscan friar and traveller. Sent by Pope Innocent IV on a mission to the Great Khan, he visited Mongolia (1245–47) and wrote a history of the Mongols.

carpo-¹, *comb. form.* pertaining to the wrist. **carpometacarpal**, *a.* of or pertaining to the carpus and the metacarpus. [Gr. *karpos,* the wrist]

carpo-², *comb. form.* pertaining to fruit. [Gr. *karpos,* fruit]

carpolite, *n.* (*Geol.*) a fossil fruit.

carpology, *n.* that part of botany which treats of fruits.

carpophagous, *a.* fruit-eating.

carpus, *n.* (*pl.* **-pi**) the wrist, the part of the human skeleton joining the hand to the forearm; the corresponding part in animals, in horses the knee. **carpal,** *a.* of the wrist. *n.* a wrist bone. [L, from Gr. *karpos,* the wrist]

Carracci, *n.* Italian family of painters in Bologna, noted for murals and ceilings. The foremost of them, **Annibale Carracci** (1560–1609), decorated the Farnese Palace, Rome, with a series of mythological paintings united by simulated architectural ornamental surrounds (completed 1604).

carrack, *n.* a large merchant ship; a galleon. [OF *carraque,* late L *carraca, carrica* (prob. conn. with *carricāre,* see CARGO)]

Carradine, *n.* **Richmond Reed ('John')** (1906–88), US film actor who often played sinister roles. He appeared in many major Hollywood films, such as *Stagecoach* (1939) and *The Grapes of Wrath* (1940), but was later seen mostly in 'B' horror films, including *House of Frankenstein* (1944).

carrageen, -gheen, *n.* Irish moss, a nutritious seaweed, *Chondrus crispus,* found on N Atlantic shores; carrageenan. **carrageenan, -g(h)eenin,** *n.* an extract of carrageen used in food-processing. [*Carragheen,* Co. Waterford, Ireland, where it is particularly plentiful]

carraway, CARAWAY.

carrel, -ell, *n.* a cubicle for private study in a library. [var. of CAROL]

Carrel, *n.* **Alexis** (1873–1944), US surgeon born in France, whose experiments paved the way for organ transplantation. Working at the Rockefeller Institute, Carrel devised a way of joining blood vessels end to end (anastomosing). This was important in the development of transplant surgery, as was his work on keeping organs viable outside the body. He was awarded the Nobel Prize for Medicine in 1912.

Carrhae, Battle of, battle in which the invading Roman general Crassus was defeated and killed by the Parthians in 53 BC. The ancient town of Carrhae is near Haran, Turkey.

carriage, *n.* carrying, transporting, conveyance, esp. of merchandise; the cost of conveying; manner of carrying; mien, bearing, behaviour; conducting, management; carrying (of a motion, Bill etc.); †things carried, burden, baggage, luggage, impedimenta; means of carrying; a conveyance, a wheeled vehicle, esp. a horse-drawn vehicle kept for pleasure; the sliding or wheeled portion of machinery carrying another part; the bed of a printing press on which a form is laid; the wheeled framework of a vehicle as distinguished from the body; the wheeled support of a cannon; a passenger vehicle in a train. **carriage and pair,** *n.* a four-wheeled private vehicle drawn by two horses. **carriage clock,** *n.* a portable clock in an oblong metal case with a handle on top. **carriage dog,** *n.* (*dated*) a Dalmatian. **carriage-drive,** *n.* a road through a park or pleasure grounds. **carriage-folk,** *n.* the kind of people who own a carriage. **carriage forward,** *adv.* the cost of carriage to be paid by the receiver. **carriage free,** *a.* carried without charge to the purchaser. **carriage rug,** *n.* a rug to cover the knees. **carriage trade,** *n.* trade from well-off customers. **carriageway,** *n.* that part of a road used for vehicular traffic. **carriageable,** *a.* practicable for wheeled carriages. **carriageful,** *n.* as many as a carriage will hold. **carriageless,** *a.* [ONorth.F *cariage* (F *charriage*), from *carier,* to CARRY]

†**carrick,** *a.* **carrick bend,** *n.* a particular knot for splicing two ropes together. [CARRACK]

carrier, *n.* one who carries, esp. one who conveys goods and merchandise for hire; a frame for holding photographic plates or magic-lantern slides; a framework on a bicycle for holding luggage; applied also to various parts of machines or instruments which act as transmitters or bearers; a person who transmits an infectious disease without personally suffering from the disease; a carrier bag; an electron or hole that carries charge in a semiconductor; an aircraft carrier. **common carrier,** (*Law*) a person or company transporting goods or merchandise for hire. **carrier bag,** *n.* a strong paper or plastic bag with handles. **carrier pigeon,** *n.* a breed of pigeons trained to carry communications. **carrier rocket,** *n.* one which carries, e.g. a satellite into orbit. **carrier wave,** *n.* an electromagnetic wave which is modulated for the radio etc. transmission of a signal.

Carrington, *n.* **Peter Alexander Rupert, 6th Baron Carrington** (1919–), British Conservative politician. He was defence secretary (1970–74), and led the opposition in the House of Lords (1964–70) and (1974–79).

While foreign secretary (1979–82), he negotiated independence for Zimbabwe, but resigned after failing to anticipate the Falklands crisis. He was secretary-general of NATO (1984–88).

carriole, *n.* a small open carriage; a light, covered cart; in Canada, an ornamental sledge. [F, from It. *carriola* (*carro,* a car, L *carrus,* CAR)]

carrion, *n.* dead, putrefying flesh; garbage, filth. *a.* feeding on carrion; putrid; loathsome. **carrion-crow,** *n.* a species of crow, *Corvus corone,* that feeds on small animals and carrion; †the vulture. [ME and OF *caroigne,* late L *carōnia,* a carcass (*caro carnis,* flesh)]

Carroll, *n.* **Lewis** (pen name of Charles Lutwidge Dodgson) (1832–98), English mathematician and writer of children's books. He wrote the children's classics *Alice's Adventures in Wonderland* (1865), and its sequel *Through the Looking Glass* (1872), published under the pen name Lewis Carroll. He also published mathematics books under his own name.

carrom CARAMBOLE.

carronade, *n.* a short naval cannon of large bore, orig. made at Carron, near Falkirk, Scotland.

carron oil, *n.* a mixture of linseed oil and lime-water, formerly used at the Carron ironworks in Scotland for scalds and burns.

carrot, *n.* a plant with an orange-coloured tapering root, *Daucus carota,* used as a vegetable; (*pl., coll.*) (a person with) red hair; an incentive. **carroty,** *a.* of the colour of a carrot; red, red-haired. [F *carrotte,* L *carōta,* Gr. *karōton* (prob. from *kara,* head]

carrousel CAROUSEL.

carry, *v.t.* to convey, to bear, to transport from one place to another by lifting and moving with the thing carried; to transfer, as from one book, page or column to another; to convey or take with one; to conduct; to bring, to enable to go or come; to support; to effect, to accomplish; to bear, to stand (as sail); to wear (as clothes); to bear or hold in a distinctive way; to extend in any direction in time or space (back, up etc.); to imply, to import, to contain; to have in or on (esp. as armament); to take by assault; to be pregnant with. *v.i.* to act as bearer; of a firearm etc., to propel a projectile to a distance; to be propelled, as a missile; to bear the head in a particular manner, as a horse; (*Hunting*) of a hare etc., to run on ground that sticks to the feet. *n.* the act of carrying; (*dial.*) the drift or motion of the clouds; the range of a firearm; (*N Am.*) a portage. **to carry all before one,** to bear off all the honours; to succeed. **to carry away,** to excite, to deprive of self-control; (*Naut.*) to break or lose (as a rope or spar). **to carry coals to Newcastle,** to bring things to a place where they abound; to lose one's labour. **to carry it off,** to brave it out. **to carry off,** to remove; to win; to do successfully; to deprive of life. **to carry on,** to manage; to continue; to behave in a particular way, esp. to flirt outrageously; to make a fuss. **to carry oneself,** to behave (in a particular way). **to carry out,** to perform; to accomplish. **to carry over, forward,** to transfer to another page or column, or to a future occasion. **to carry through,** to accomplish; to bring to a conclusion in spite of obstacles. **to carry weight,** to be handicapped; of an argument etc., to be cogent. **to carry with one,** to bear in mind, to convince. **carry-all,** *n.* a bag; (*N Am.*) a four-wheeled pleasure-carriage for several persons; (*N Am.*) a hold-all. **carry-cot,** *n.* a light portable cot for a baby. **carrying,** *a.* **carryings-on,** *n.pl.* course of behaviour (usu. of a questionable kind). **carrying trade,** *n.* the transport of goods, esp. by water. [ONorth.F *carier,* late L *carricāre carrus,* CAR]

Carry on films, a series of low-budget British comedies with an emphasis on unsubtle double entendre. Probably the most successful film run in post-war Britain. The first was *Carry on Sergeant* (1958) and the series continued for 20 years with titles like *Carry on Nurse, Carry on Spying, Carry on Screaming* and *Carry on Doctor*.

carse, *n.* (*Sc.*) low fertile land, usu. near a river. **carse-land,** *n.* [prob. pl. of obs. *carr,* fen or boggy ground, from Icel. (cp. Dan. *kær,* Swed. *kærr,* Norw. *kjær,* pool, marsh, fen)]

Carson[1], *n.* **Christopher 'Kit'** (1809–68), US frontiersman, guide and Indian agent, who later fought for the Federal side in the Civil War. Carson City was named after him.

Carson[2], *n.* **Edward Henry, Baron Carson** (1854–1935), Irish politician and lawyer, who played a decisive part in the trial of the writer Oscar Wilde. In the years before World War I he led the movement in Ulster to resist Irish Home Rule by force of arms if need be.

Carson[3], *n.* **William (Willie)** (1942–), British jockey, born in Scotland, who has ridden three Epsom Derby winners as well as the winners of most major races in England and abroad.

cart, *n.* †a carriage, a chariot; a strong two-wheeled vehicle for heavy goods etc.; a light two-wheeled vehicle (usu. with attrib., as **dog-cart, spring-cart** etc.). *v.t.* to carry or convey in a cart; †to expose in a cart as a punishment; (*sl.*) to defeat badly; (*coll.*) to carry or pull with difficulty. *v.i.* to use carts for cartage. **in the cart,** (*sl.*) in a fix, a predicament. **to cart off,** (*coll.*) to remove by force. **cart-horse,** *n.* one of a breed of horses for drawing heavy carts. **cart-load,** *n.* as much as will fill a cart; a load of hay etc. **cart-road, -way,** *n.* a rough road on a farm etc. **cartwheel,** *n.* the wheel of a cart; a large coin; a somersault taken sideways. **cart-whip,** *n.* a long whip suitable for driving a team of horses. **cartwright,** *n.* one whose trade is to make carts. **cartage,** *n.* the act of carting; the price paid for carting. **carter,** *n.* [Icel. *kartr* (OE *craet* may be cogn.)]

Cartagena, *n.* (or **Cartagena de los Indes**) port, industrial centre and capital of the department of Bolívar, NW Colombia; population (1985) 531,000. Plastics and chemicals are produced here.

carte[1], †a card; a bill of fare; a carte-de-visite. carte du jour, the menu of the day. **carte-blanche**, *n.* a signed sheet of paper given to a person to fill up as he or she pleases; unlimited power to act. **carte-de-visite**, *n.* a visiting card; a photographic likeness on a small card. [F *carte*, see CARD[1]]

carte[2], quarte, *n.* the fourth regular movement in fencing. [F *quarte,* It. *quarta,* fourth]

cartel, *n.* a challenge in writing; an agreement between hostile states concerning the exchange of prisoners; an agreement (often international) among manufacturers to keep prices up; in politics, an alliance between two parties to further common policies. **cartelize, -ise,** *v.t., v.i.* to form a cartel. [F, from It. *cartella,* dim. of *carta,* CARD[1]]

Carter[1], *n.* **Angela** (1940–), English writer of the magic realist school. Her novels include *The Magic Toyshop* (filmed by David Wheatley, 1987) and *Nights at the Circus* (1984). She co-wrote the script for the film *The Company of Wolves* (1984), based on one of her stories.

Carter[2], *n.* **Elliott (Cook)** (1908–), US composer. His early music shows the influence of Stravinsky, but after 1950 it became increasingly intricate and densely written in a manner resembling Ives. He invented 'metrical modulation' which allows different instruments or groups to stay in touch while playing at different speeds. He has written four string quartets, the *Symphony for Three Orchestras* (1967), and the song cycle *A Mirror on Which to Dwell* (1975).

Carter[3], *n.* **Jimmy (James Earl)** (1924–), 39th president of the US (1977–81), a Democrat. In 1976 he narrowly wrested the presidency from Ford. Features of his presidency were the return of the Panama Canal Zone to Panama, the Camp David Agreements for peace in the Middle East, and the Iranian seizure of US embassy hostages. He was defeated by Reagan in 1980.

Carter Doctrine, *n.* the assertion in 1980 by President Carter of a vital US interest in the Persian Gulf region (prompted by the Soviet invasion of Afghanistan): any outside attempt at control would be met by force if necessary.

Cartesian, *a.* of or pertaining to the French philosopher Descartes (1596–1650), or his philosophy or mathematical methods. *n.* an adherent of his philosophy. **Cartesian coordinates,** *n.pl.* in coordinate geometry, a system used to represent vectors or to denote the position of a point on a plane (two dimensions) or in space (three dimensions) with reference to a set of two or more axes. The Cartesian coordinate system can be extended to any finite number of dimensions (axes), and is used thus in theoretical mathematics. It is named after Descartes. **Cartesianism,** *n.* [mod. L *Cartesius*]

Carthage, *n.* an ancient Phoenician port in N Africa, 16 km/10 miles N of modern Tunis, Tunisia. An important trading centre, from the 6th cent. BC it was in conflict with Greece, and then with Rome, and was destroyed in 146 BC at the end of the Punic Wars. About 45 BC Roman colonists settled in Carthage, and it rose to be the wealthy and important capital of the province of Africa. After its capture by the Vandals in AD 439 it was little more than a pirate stronghold. From 533 it formed part of the Byzantine Empire until its final destruction by the Arabs in 698.

Carthusian[1], *a.* of or belonging to Charterhouse School, founded on the site of a Carthusian monastery. *n.* a scholar or pensioner of the London Charterhouse. [med. L *Cartusiānūs, Chartreuse,* in Dauphiné]

Carthusian[2], *n.* a member of a Roman Catholic order of monks and, later, nuns, founded by St Bruno in 1084 at Chartreuse, near Grenoble, France. Living chiefly in unbroken silence, they ate one vegetarian meal a day and supported themselves by their own labours; the rule is still one of severe austerity.

Cartier[1], *n.* **Georges Étienne** (1814–73), French-Canadian politician. He fought against the British in the rebellion of 1837, was elected to the Canadian parliament in 1848, and was joint prime minister with John A. Macdonald (1858–62). He brought Québec into the Canadian federation in 1867.

Cartier[2], *n.* **Jacques** (1491–1557), French navigator who was the first European to sail up the St Lawrence river in 1534. He named the site of Montréal.

Cartier-Bresson, *n.* **Henri** (1908–), French photographer, considered the greatest of photographic artists. His documentary work was achieved in black and white, using a small format camera. He was noted for his ability to structure the image and to capture the decisive moment.

cartilage, *n.* an elastic, pearly-white animal tissue, gristle; a cartilaginous structure. **cartilaginoid,** *a.* **cartilaginous,** *a.* of, like or pertaining to cartilage. **cartilaginous fishes,** *n.pl.* fishes with a cartilaginous skeleton, as sharks and rays. [F, from L *cartilāgo -āginem;* etym. unknown]

Cartland, *n.* **Barbara** (1904–), English romantic novelist. She published her first book *Jigsaw* in 1921, and since then has produced a prolific stream of stories of chastely romantic love, usually in idealized or exotic settings, for a mainly female audience (such as *Love Climbs In* (1978) and *Moments of Love* (1981).

cartogram, *n.* a map showing statistical information in diagrammatic form. [see foll.]

cartography, *n.* the art or business of making maps and charts. **cartographer,** *n.* **cartographic,** *a.* **cartology,** *n.* the science of maps and charts. [F *carte,* CARD[1]]

cartomancy, *n.* divination or fortune-telling by cards. [It. *carta,* playing-card, -MANCY]

carton, *n.* a cardboard box; a white disc within the bull's eye of a target; a shot which hits this; a box made of waxed paper for holding liquids. *v.t.* to put into a carton. **cartonnage,** *n.* layers of linen hardened with glue, used for the casing of mummies. [F, pasteboard, cardboard; It. *cartone* (*carta,* CARD[1])]

cartoon, *n.* a design on strong paper for painting tapestry, mosaic, stained-glass etc.; a full-page illustration, esp. comic, dealing with a social or political subject; a comic strip; an animated film. **cartoonist,** *n.* [F]

cartouche, *n.* †a cartridge; a scroll on the cornice of a column; an ornamental tablet in the form of a scroll, for inscriptions etc.; an elliptical figure containing the hieroglyphics of Egyptian royal or divine names or titles. [F, from It. *cartocchio* (*carta,* CARD[1])]

cartridge, *n.* a case of paper, pasteboard, metal etc., holding the exact charge of a gun; a removable, sealed container holding film for a camera or magnetic tape for a tape recorder; a removable part of the pick-up arm of a record player, containing the stylus etc.; a replaceable container holding ink for a pen. **blank-cartridge,** *n.* one containing only the explosive. **ball-cartridge,** *n.* one containing the bullet as well. **cartridge-belt,** *n.* a belt with pockets for cartridges. **cartridge-box,** *n.* a box for storing or carrying cartridges. **cartridge-clip,** *n.* a removable container for cartridges in an automatic firearm. **cartridge-paper,** *n.* a stout, rough-surfaced paper, orig. used for cartridge-making, now for drawing, strong envelopes etc. [corr. of *cartouche*]

cartulary, *n.* the register, or collection of documents, relating to a monastery or church; the place where this is kept. [late L *ch-, cartulārium* (L *cartula,* dim. of *carta,* CARD[1]))]

Cartwright, *n.* **Edmund** (1743–1823), British inventor. He patented the power loom in 1785, built a weaving mill (1787), and patented a wool-combing machine in 1789.

carucate, *n.* a measure of land, as much as could be tilled with one plough in a year. [late L *carrūcāta,* fem. p.p. of *carrūcāre,* to plough (L *carrūca,* a plough, from *carrus,* CAR)]

caruncle, *n.* a small, morbid, fleshy excrescence; a wattle or the like; (*Bot.*) a protuberance round or near the hilum. **caruncular,** *a.* **carunculate, -ated,** *a.* [F *caruncule,* L *caruncula,* dim. of *caro carnem,* flesh]

Caruso, *n.* **Enrico** (1873–1921), Italian operatic tenor. In 1902 he starred in Monte Carlo, in Puccini's *La Bohème*. He is chiefly remembered for performances as Canio in Leoncavallo's *Pagliacci*, and the Duke in Verdi's *Rigoletto*.

carve, *v.t.* (*p.p.* **carved** or **carven**) to cut; to cut into slices, as meat at table; to apportion; to make or shape by cutting; to cut or hew (some solid material) into the resemblance of some object; to cut (a design, inscription, representation etc.); to adorn by cutting. *v.i.* to exercise the profession of a sculptor or carver; to carve meat; †(*Shak.*) to show great courtesy and affability. **to carve out,** (*Law*) to create a small estate out of a larger one; to take (a piece) from something larger; to create by one's own effort. **to carve up,** to divide by, or as if by, carving. **carver,** *n.* one who carves; a large table-knife for carving; (*pl.*) a carving-knife and fork; a dining-chair with arms. **carving,** *n.* the action of the verb TO CARVE; carved work. **carving-knife,** *n.* a knife to carve meat at table; (*N Am.*) a butcher-knife. [OE *ceorfan,* from Teut. *kerf-* (cp. Dut. *kerven,* G *kerben*), cogn. with Gr. *graphein,* to write]

carvel, *n.* a caravel. **carvel-built,** *a.* (*Naut.*) having the planks flush at the edges, as distinct from *clinker-built*.

Carver[1], *n.* **George Washington** (1864–1943), US agricultural chemist. Born a slave in Missouri, he devoted his life to improving the economy of the US South and the condition of blacks. He advocated the diversification of crops, promoted peanut production, and was a pioneer in the field of plastics.

Carver[2], *n.* **Raymond** (1939–88), US story writer and poet, author of vivid stories of contemporary US life. *Cathedral* (1983) collects many of his stories; *Fires* (1985) also has essays and poems.

Cary, *n.* **(Arthur) Joyce (Lunel)** (1888–1957), British novelist. In 1918 he entered the Colonial Service, and Nigeria, where he had served, gave a background to such novels as *Mister Johnson* (1939). Other books include *The Horse's Mouth* (1944).

caryatid, *n.* (*pl.* **-tids, -tides**) a figure of a woman in long robes, serving to support an entablature. **caryatic,** *a.* **caryatic-order,** *n.* an order in which the entablature is supported by caryatids. [L *Caryātis,* Gr. *Karuatis -idos,* a priestess of Artemis at Caryae, in Laconia]

caryo-, *comb. form.* nut, kernel. [Gr. *karuon,* a nut]

caryophyllaceous, *a.* belonging to the order Caryophyllaceae, typified by the clove-pink; having a corolla with five petals with long claws, as the clove-pink. [Gr. *karuophullon* (*phullon,* a leaf)]

caryopsis, *n.* (*pl.* **-ses**, **-sides**) a fruit with a single seed, to which the pericarp adheres throughout, as in grasses. [Gr. *opsis,* appearance]

carz(e)y, kars(e)y, kazi, *n.* (*sl.*) a lavatory. [It. *casa,* house]

Casablanca, *n.* (Arabic **Dar el-Beida**) port, commercial and industrial centre on the Atlantic coast of Morocco; population (1981) 2,409,000. It trades in fish, phosphates and manganese. The Great Hassan II Mosque, completed 1989, is the world's largest; it is built on a platform (40,000 sq m/430,000 sq ft) jutting out over the Atlantic, with walls 60 m/200 ft high, topped by a hydraulic sliding roof, and a minaret 175 m/574 ft high.

Casablanca Conference, *n.* a World War II meeting of the US and UK leaders Roosevelt and Churchill, 14–24 Jan. 1943, at which the Allied demand for the unconditional surrender of Germany, Italy and Japan was issued.

Casals, *n.* **Pablo** (1876–1973), Catalan cellist, composer, and conductor. As a cellist, he is renowned for his interpretations of J.S. Bach's unaccompanied suites. He left Spain in 1939 to live in Prades, in the French Pyrenees, where he founded an annual music festival. He wrote instrumental and choral works, including the Christmas oratorio *The Manger*.

Casanova (de Seingalt), *n.* **Giovanni Jacopo** (1725–98), Italian adventurer, spy, violinist, librarian and, according to his *Memoirs*, one of the world's great lovers. From 1774 he was a spy in the Venetian police service. In 1782 a libel got him into trouble, and after more wanderings he was in 1785 appointed Count Waldstein's librarian at his castle of Dûx in Bohemia, where he wrote his *Memoirs* (published 1826–38, although the complete text did not appear until 1960–61).

casbah, kasbah, *n.* in a N African city, the citadel or the (older) area round it. [Arab. *qasba,* citadel]

cascade, *n.* a small waterfall; anything resembling a cascade, as a loose, wavy fall of lace, a firework imitating a waterfall; a sequence of actions or processes, each triggered or fuelled by the previous one. *v.i.* to fall in or like a cascade. **cascade amplifier,** *n.* a series of electrical amplifiers so connected that the output of each stage is amplified by the succeeding stage. [F, from It. *cascata,* p.p. of *cascare,* to fall]

Cascais, *n.* fishing port and resort town on the Costa do Sol, 25 km/16 miles W of Lisbon, Portugal.

cascara, *n.* a birch-bark canoe; the bark of the Californian *Cascara sagrada,* used as an aperient. [Sp.]

cascarilla, *n.* the aromatic bark of *Croton eleutheria*. [Sp., dim. of prec.]

case[1], *n.* that which contains or encloses something else; a box, covering or sheath; an oblong frame, with divisions, for type (see also LOWER CASE under LOW[1], UPPER-CASE under UPPER); a cloth cover for a book; a glass box for exhibits; the outer cover of an instrument, seed-vessel, pupa, projectile etc. *v.t.* to cover with or put into a case; †to skin. **case-bottle,** *n.* a bottle shaped to fit into a case. **case-bound,** *a.* of a book, hardback. **case-harden,** *v.t.* to harden the outside surface, esp. of iron, by converting into steel; to make callous. **case-knife,** *n.* a knife carried in a sheath. **case-shot,** *n.* small projectiles put in cases to be discharged from cannon shrapnel. **case-worm,** *n.* the caddis-worm. **casing,** *n.* the action of the verb TO CASE; something that encases; an outside covering. [ONorth.F *casse* (F *châsse*), L *capsa* (*capere,* to receive, to hold)]

case[2], *n.* that which happens or befalls; an event, a condition of things, position, state, circumstances; an instance; a question at issue; change in the termination of a declinable word to express relation to some other word in the sentence; used also of such relation in uninflected languages; (*sl.*) an eccentric or difficult character; a cause or suit in court; a statement of facts or evidence for submission to a court; the evidence and arguments considered collectively; a cause that has been decided and may be quoted as a precedent; the condition of a sick person; the patient; a particular instance of any disease; a solicitor's or social worker's client. *v.t.* (*sl.*) to reconnoitre with a view to burglary. **in any case,** in any event, whatever may happen. **in case,** if, supposing that, lest. **in case of,** in the event of. **in good case,** in good condition. **in that case,** if that should happen. **it's a case with,** (*sl.*) it's all up with. **case-book,** *n.* a book describing (medical or legal) cases for record or for instruction. **case-history,** *n.* a record of a patient's ancestry and personal history made for clinical purposes. **case law,** *n.* (*Law*) law as settled by precedent. **case-load,** *n.* the number of cases assigned to a medical or social worker. **case of conscience,** *n.* a matter in which conscience must make the decision between two principles. **case study,** *n.* a case-history; study or analysis of a case-history. **case-work,** *n.* medical or social work concentrating on individual cases. **case-worker,** *n.* [OF *cas,* L *cāsus,* p.p. of *cadere,* to fall]

casein, *n.* the albuminoid or protein in milk, forming the basis of cheese. **vegetable casein,** *n.* a similar albuminoid found in leguminous plants. **caseic,** *a.* obtained from cheese. **caseic acid,** *n.* lactic acid. **caseous,** *a.* of or like cheese; resembling cheese; cheesy. [L *caseus,* cheese, -IN[1]]

casemate, *n.* a bomb-proof vault or chamber in a fortress or ship, containing an embrasure. **casemated,** *a.* [F, from It. *casamatta* (etym. doubtful)]

casement, *n.* a window or part of a window opening on hinges; (*poet.*) a window; a hollow moulding. **casemented,** *a.* having casements [from CASE[1] or from It. *casamento,* a building or frame of a building, med. L *casamentum*]

Casement, *n.* **Roger David** (1864–1916), Irish nationalist. While in the British consular service he exposed the ruthless exploitation of the people of the Belgian Congo and in Peru, for which he was knighted in 1911 (degraded 1916). He was hanged for treason by the British for his part in the Irish republican Easter Rising.

casern, -erne, *n.* one of a series of temporary buildings for soldiers between the ramparts and the houses of a fortified town; a barrack. [F *caserne,* Sp. *caserna* (*casa,* a house, L *casa,* cottage)]

cash[1], *n.* ready money; coin, specie, bank-notes. *a.* involving cash, paid for, or paying in cash. *v.t.* to turn into or exchange for cash. **cash down,** money paid on the spot. **cash on delivery,** a system by which goods are paid for on delivery. **hard cash,** actual coin; ready money. **in cash,** having money. **out of cash,** having no money. **to cash in, to cash in one's checks,** to hand over in exchange for money; (*sl.*) to die. **to cash in on,** (*coll.*) to seize a chance to profit from. **to cash up,** to add up the money taken (in a shop etc.) at the end of the day. **cash-account,** *n.* an account of cash paid, received, or in hand. **cash-and-carry,** *a.*, *adv.* sold for cash, without a delivery service. *n.* a shop which trades in this way. **cash-balance,** *n.* the balance on the debtor side of a cash-account. **cash-book,** *n.* a book in which money transactions are entered. **cash crop,** *n.* one grown for sale, not for consumption. **cash desk,** *n.* the desk in a shop where payments are made by customers. **cash dispenser,** *n.* an electronic machine operated by a bank, which dispenses cash on insertion of a special card. **cash flow,** *n.* (the balance of) the flow of money into and out from a business in the course of trading. **cash payment,** *n.* payment by ready money. **cash price,** *n.* the price for ready money. **cash register,** *n.* a calculating till used in a retail shop. **cashless,** *a.* moneyless; without ready money; of financial transactions, made without using cash, e.g. by computer transfer etc. [F *casse,* box (see CASE[1])]

cash[2], *n.* a name applied by Europeans to various Eastern (esp. Chinese) coins of low value. [Tamil *kasu,* a small coin (confused with CASH[1])]

Cash, *n.* **Johnny** (1932–), US country singer, songwriter, and guitarist. His early hits, recorded for Sun Records in Memphis, Tennessee, include the million-selling 'I Walk the Line' (1956). Many of his songs have become classics.

cashew, *n.* the kidney-shaped fruit of a tropical tree, *Anacardium occidentale.* **cashew-nut,** *n.* **cashew-tree,** *n.* [F *acajou,* Braz. *acaju* (see also ACAJOU)]

cashier[1], *n.* one who has charge of the cash or of money transactions. [F *caissier*]

cashier[2], *v.t.* to dismiss from the service, to discharge; to get rid of; (*rare*) to deprive (a person) of his cash. [Dut. *casseren* (cp. F *casser,* L *quassāre,* to shatter, later blended with senses of *cassāre,* to annul)]

cashmere, *n.* a material for shawls, made from the hair of the Cashmere goat; a shawl of this material; a fine woollen dress fabric. [*Kashmīr,* state to the north of the Indian subcontinent]

casing CASE[1].

casino[1], *n.* a public dancing-room; an establishment, or part of one, used esp. for gambling. [It., dim. of *casa,* house, L *casa,* cottage]

casino[2] CASSINO.

cask, *n.* a barrel; the quantity contained in a cask; †a casket; †a casque. [perh. from Sp. *casco,* a cask, a skull, a potsherd]

casket, *n.* a small case for jewels etc.; (*chiefly N Am.*) a coffin. *v.t.* to enclose in a casket. [etym. doubtful; perh. dim. of prec.]

Caslavska, *n.* **Vera** (1943–), Czechoslovak gymnast, the first of the great modern-day stylists. She won a record 21 world, Olympic and European gold medals (1959-68); she also won eight silver and three bronze medals.

Caspian Sea, *n.* the world's largest inland sea, divided between Iran and the USSR. Area about 400,000 sq km/155,000 sq miles, with a maximum depth of 1000 m/3250 ft. The chief ports are Astrakhan and Baku. It is now approximately 28 m/90 ft below sea level due to drainage in the north, and the damming of the Volga and Ural rivers for hydroelectric power.

casque, *n.* a helmet; a horny cap or protuberance on the head of some birds. [F, from Sp. *casco,* CASK]

Cassandra, *n.* one who prophesies evil; one who takes gloomy views of the future; a prophet who is not listened to. [daughter of Priam, king of Troy, who had the gift of prophecy but was not believed]

cassareep, *n.* the boiled down juice of the cassava, used as a condiment. [Carib.]

cassata, *n.* a type of ice-cream containing nuts and candied fruit. [It.]

cassation, *n.* abrogation; reversal of a judicial sentence. **court of cassation,** *n.* the highest court of appeal in France and Belgium. [late L *cassatiō -ōnem* (*cassāre,* to make void)]

Cassatt, *n.* **Mary** (1845–1926), US Impressionist painter and printmaker. In 1868 she settled in Paris. Her popular, colourful pictures of mothers and children show the influence of Japanese prints, for example *The Bath* (1892) (Art Institute, Chicago).

cassava, *n.* a W Indian plant, the manioc, of the genus *Manihot;* a nutritious floor obtained from its roots; bread made from this flour. [Haitian *caçábi*]

casserole, *n.* a stew-pan; an earthenware etc. cooking-pot with a lid; the food cooked in such a pot. *v.t.* to cook in such a pot. [F (*casse,* etym. obscure)]

cassette, *n.* a small plastic container with magnetic tape or film, to be inserted into a tape deck or camera. [F, casket]

cassia, *n.* a coarse kind of cinnamon, esp. the bark of *Cinnamomum cassia;* a genus of leguminous plants, including the senna. **cassia-bark,** *n.* [L, from Gr. *kasia,* Heb. *qetsī'āh,* cassia-bark (*qātsa',* to bark or peel)]

cassimere, *n.* a thin, fine-twilled cloth for men's clothes. [CASHMERE]

Cassini, *n.* **Giovanni Domenico** (1625–1712), Italian-French astronomer, who discovered four moons of Saturn and the gap in the rings of Saturn now called the **Cassini division.**

cassino, casino[2], *n.* a game at cards for two or four players. [CASINO[1]]

Cassiopeia, *n.* a prominent constellation of the northern hemisphere, representing the mother of Andromeda. It has a distinctive W-shape, and contains one of the most powerful radio sources in the sky, Cassiopeia A, the remains of a supernova (star explosion), as well as open and globular clusters.

cassis, *n.* a cordial made from blackcurrants. [F, blackcurrant]

cassiterite, *n.* native stannic dioxide, common tin-ore. [Gr. *kassiteros,* tin, -ITE]

Cassius, *n.* **Gaius** (d. 42 BC), Roman soldier, one of the conspirators who killed Julius Caesar in 44. He fought at Carrhae 53, and with the republicans against Caesar at Pharsalus 48, was pardoned and appointed praetor, but became a leader in the conspiracy of 44, and after Caesar's death joined Brutus. He committed suicide after his defeat at Philippi 42 BC.

Cassivelaunus, *n.* chieftain of the British tribe, the Catuvellauni, who led the British resistance to Caesar in 54 BC.

cassock, *n.* †a long loose coat or gown (for either sex); a long, close-fitting garment worn by clerics, choristers, vergers etc.; a soutane. **cassocked,** *a.* wearing a cassock. [F *casaque,* It. *casacca* (etym. doubtful; perh. from *casa,* house, L *casa,* cottage)]

cassolette, *n.* a vessel in which perfumes are burned; a perfume-box with perforated lid. [F, dim. of *cassole* (*casse,* see CASSEROLE)]

Casson, *n.* **Hugh** (1910–), British architect, professor at the Royal College of Art (1953–75), and president of the Royal Academy (1976–84). His books include *Victorian Architecture* (1948).

cassoulet, *n.* a dish consisting of haricot beans stewed with bacon, pork etc. [F]

cassowary, *n.* an E Indian genus (*Casuarius*) of large cursorial birds. [Malay *kasuwārī*]

cast[1], *v.t.* (*past, p.p.* **cast**) to throw, fling, hurl (now chiefly poet. or archaic except in certain uses); to drive, to toss; to cause to fall, to emit; to throw off, to shed, to throw by reflection; to allot, to assign (as the parts in a play); to condemn, to reject; to drop (as young) prematurely; to add up, compute, calculate; (*Law*) to defeat; to found, to mould. *v.i.* to throw a fishing-line; to reckon accounts; to consider, to scheme, to contrive; to take form or shape (in a mould); to warp. **to cast about,** to look hither and thither for something; to consider; to devise a means. **to cast aside,** to reject; to give up. **to cast away,** to reject; to lavish. **to cast back,** to turn (one's mind) back to the past. **to cast down,** to throw down; to deject, to depress, to destroy. **to cast forth,** to throw away; to emit. **to cast in one's lot with,** to share the fate or fortunes of. **to cast in one's teeth,** to upbraid one with. **to cast off,** to discard; to estimate the number of words in a manuscript; to untie, to unmoor (a boat); to let loose (as dogs); in knitting, to finish by closing loops and making a selvedge. **to cast on,** in knitting, to form new stitches. **to cast oneself on,** to take refuge with. **to cast out,** to expel. **to cast up,** to reckon, to add; to vomit; to throw in one's teeth. **casting,** *n.* the action of the verb TO CAST; anything formed by casting or founding; esp. a metal object as distinguished from a plaster cast. **casting-net,** *n.* a net thrown into the water and drawn in again. **casting voice, vote,** *n.* the deciding vote of a president when the votes are equal. [Icel. *kasta,* to throw]

cast[2], *n.* the act of casting or throwing; a throw; the thing thrown; the distance thrown; the allotment of parts in a play, the set of actors allotted; a throw of dice; the number thrown; chance; feathers, fur etc. ejected from the stomach by a bird of prey; the end portion of a fishing line, usu. of gut or gimp, carrying hooks etc.; an adding up, a computation; a motion or turn of the eye; direction of glance; a twist, a squint; †plan, design; tinge, characteristic quality or form; †a pair (of hawks); a mould; the thing moulded, the shape. *a.* thrown; (*Law*) condemned; made by founding or casting. **cast-iron,** *n.* iron melted and run in moulds; *a.* made of cast-iron; rigid, unyielding, unadaptable; hard, indefatigable. **cast-off,** *a.* laid aside, rejected. **cast-steel,** *n.* steel melted and run into moulds. **caster,** *n.* one who or that which casts. **castor**[2], **-ter,** *n.* a small vessel for holding condiments at table; a cruet-stand; a small swivelled wheel attached to the leg of a table, sofa, chair etc. **caster-, castor-sugar,** *n.* white powdered sugar for table use. [from prec.]

Castagno, *n.* **Andrea del** (*c.* 1421–57), Italian Renaissance painter, active in Florence. In his frescoes in Sta Apollonia, Florence, he adapted the pictorial space to the architectural framework and followed Masaccio's lead in perspective.

Castalian, *a.* of or pertaining to Castalia, a spring on Mount Parnassus sacred to the Muses; poetical. [L, from Gr. *Kastalia*]

castanet, *n.* (*usu. pl.*) a small spoon-shaped concave instrument of ivory or hard wood, a pair of which is fastened to each thumb and rattled as an accompaniment to music. [Sp. *castaneta,* dim. of *castaña,* L *castanea,* chestnut]

castaway, *a.* rejected, useless; shipwrecked. *n.* an outcast; a reprobate; a shipwrecked person.

caste, *n.* one of the hereditary classes of society in India; any hereditary, exclusive class; the class system; the dignity or social influence due to position; a term used to describe specialized individuals among insects, e.g. queen bee, worker bee etc. **to lose caste,** to descend in the social scale; to lose favour or consideration. **caste mark,** *n.* a red mark on the forehead showing one's caste. **casteless,** *a.* [Port. *casta,* fem. of *casto,* lineage, L *castus,* pure, unmixed (cp. CHASTE)]

castellan, *n.* the governor of a castle. **castellany,** the lordship or jurisdiction of a castellan. [ONorth.F *castellain* (F *châtelain*), late L *castellānus* (see CASTLE)]

castellated, *a.* having turrets and battlements; having castles; resembling a castle. **castellation,** *n.* [med. L *castellātus,* p.p. *castellāre,* to build a castle (see CASTLE)]

Castelo Branco, *n.* **Camilo** (1825–90), Portuguese novelist. His work fluctuates between mysticism and Bohemianism, and includes *Amor de perdição/Love of Perdition* (1862), written during his imprisonment for adultery, and *Novelas do Minho* (1875), stories of the rural north.

caster CAST[2].

castigate, *v.t.* to chastise, to punish; to correct. **castigation,** *n.* **castigator,** *n.* one who castigates; a corrector. **castigatory,** *a.* [L *castigātus,* p.p. of *castigāre,* to chasten (*castus,* CHASTE)]

Castiglione, *n.* **Baldassare, Count Castiglione** (1478–1529), Italian author and diplomat, who described the perfect Renaissance gentleman in *Il Cortegiano/The Courtier* (1528).

Castile, *n.* a kingdom founded in the 10th cent., occupying the central plateau of Spain. Its union with Aragon in 1479 was the foundation of the Spanish state. It comprised the two great basins separated by the Sierra de Gredos and the Sierra de Guadarrama, known traditionally as Old and New Castile. The area now forms the modern regions of Castilla-León and Castilla-La Mancha.

Castile soap, *n.* a fine, hard soap, whose main constituents are olive oil and soda. [Castile, in Spain]

Castilian, *a.* of or pertaining to Castile. **Castilian language**, *n.* a member of the Romance branch of the Indo-European language family originating in NW Spain, in the provinces of Old and New Castile. It is the basis of present-day standard Spanish and is often seen as the same language, the terms *castellano* and *español* being used interchangeably in both Spain and the Spanish-speaking countries of the Americas.

Castilla, *n.* **Ramón** (1797–1867), president of Peru (1841–51) and (1855-62). He dominated Peruvian politics for over two decades, bringing political stability. Income from guano exports was used to reduce the national debt and improve transport and educational facilities. He abolished black slavery and the head tax on Indians.

Castilla-La Mancha, *n.* an autonomous region of central Spain; area 79,200 sq km/30,571 sq miles; population (1986) 1,665,000. It includes the provinces of Albacete, Ciudad Real, Cuenca, Guadalajara and Toledo. Irrigated land produces grain and chickpeas, and merino sheep graze here.

Castilla-León, *n.* an autonomous region of central Spain; area 94,100 sq km/36,323 sq miles; population (1986) 2,600,000. It includes the provinces of Ávila, Burgos, León, Palencia, Salamanca, Segovia, Soria, Valladolid, and Zamora. Irrigated land produces wheat and rye. Cattle, sheep and fighting bulls are bred in the uplands.

casting CAST[1].

castle, *n.* a fortified building, a fortress; a mansion that was formerly a fortress; the mansion of a noble or prince; a piece at chess in the shape of a tower, a rook. *v.i.* in chess, to move the king two squares to the right or left and bring up the castle to the square the king has passed over. *v.t.* to treat (the king) thus. **castles in the air** or **in Spain,** visionary projects. **The Castle,** Dublin Castle; the former centre of the governmental system. **castle-builder,** *n.* a dreamer, a visionary. †**castleguard,** *n.* a tenure by which a tenant was bound to defend his lord's castle. **castle-nut,** *n.* a nut with notched extension for a locking-pin. **castled,** *a.* having a castle. **castlery,** *n.* the tenure or government of a castle; the territory attached to it. [ONorth.F *castel* (OF *chastel, château*), L *castellum,* dim. of *castrum,* a fort]

Castle, *n.* **Barbara, Baroness Castle** (born Betts) (1911–), British Labour politician, a cabinet minister in the Labour governments of the 1960s and 1970s. She led the Labour group in the European Parliament (1979–89).

Castle Hill rising, Irish convict revolt in New South Wales, Australia, 4 Mar. 1804; a number were killed while parleying with the military under a flag of truce.

Castlemaine[1], *n.* a town in Victoria, Australia, about 105 km/65 miles NW of Melbourne, on the Loddon. Site of the earliest gold strikes in 1851, its population rose to 30,000 at that period. It survives as an agricultural marketing centre.

Castlemaine[2], *n.* **Lady** (born Barbara Villiers) (1641–1709), mistress of Charles II of England (1660–70) and mother of his son the Duke of Grafton (1663–90).

Castlereagh, *n.* **Robert Stewart, Viscount Castlereagh** (1769–1822), British Tory politician. As chief secretary for Ireland (1797–1801), he suppressed the rebellion of 1798, and helped the younger Pitt secure the union of England, Scotland and Ireland in 1801. As foreign secretary (1812–22) he coordinated European opposition to Napoleon and represented Britain at the Congress of Vienna (1814–15).

castor[1], *n.* a beaver hat; a mammalian genus, containing the beaver; (also **castoreum**) an oily compound secreted by the beaver, used in medicine and perfumery. [F, from L, from Gr. *kastōr,* prob. Eastern in origin (cp. Sansk. *kastūrī,* musk)]

castor[2] CAST[2].

Castor, *n.* second-brightest star in the constellation Gemini, and the 23rd-brightest star in the sky. Along with Pollux, it forms a prominent pair at the eastern end of Gemini.

Castor and Pollux, the twins; stars in the constellation Gemini; St Elmo's Fire, seen on ships during a storm (when two lights appear). [Gr., twin sons of Tyndarus and Leda]

castoreum CASTOR[1].

castor-oil, *n.* an oil, used as a cathartic and lubricant, obtained from the seeds of Palma Christi or **castor-oil plant** (*Ricinus communis,* also grown as a house plant).

castrametation, *n.* the act or art of arranging a camp.

[F *castrametation* (L *castra,* a camp, *mētāri,* to measure or lay out)]

castrate, *v.t.* to cut away the testicles, to geld; to deprive of generative power; to emasculate, to deprive of force or vigour; to expurgate unduly. **castration,** *n.* [L *castrātus,* p.p. of *castrāre*]

castrato, *n.* (*pl.* **-ti**), a male soprano; a male emasculated for the purpose of retaining the pitch of his voice. [It., p.p. of *castrare* (L *castrāre*)]

Castries, *n.* port and capital of St Lucia, on the NW coast of the island; population (1988) 53,000. It produces textiles, chemicals, wood products, tobacco and rubber products.

Castro, *n.* **Cipriano** (1858–1924), Venezuelan dictator (1899–1908), known as 'the Lion of the Andes'. When he refused to pay off foreign debts in 1902, British, German, and Italian ships blockaded the country. He presided over a corrupt government. There were frequent rebellions during his rule, and opponents of his regime were exiled or murdered.

Castro (Ruz), *n.* **Fidel** (1927–), Cuban Communist politician, prime minister (1959–76) and president from 1976. He led two unsuccessful coups against the right-wing Batista regime and led the revolution that overthrew the dictator in 1959. From 1979 he was also president of the non-aligned movement, although promoting the line of the USSR, which subsidized his regime. The Castro regime introduced a centrally planned economy based on the production for export of sugar, tobacco and nickel. Aid for developmemt has been provided by the USSR while Cuba joined COMECON in 1972. By nationalizing US-owned businesses in 1960 Castro gained the enmity of the US, which came to a head in the Cuban missile crisis of 1962. His regime became socialist and he espoused Marxism-Leninism until in 1974 he rejected Marx's formula 'from each according to his ability and to each according to his need' and decreed that each Cuban should 'receive according to his work'.

casual, *a.* happening by chance; accidental, trivial; occasional, unmethodical; careless; unconcerned, apathetic; informal. *n.* a tramp; a frequenter of casual wards; (*pl.*) flat-heeled shoes that slip on without lacing; (*pl.*) informal clothes; an occasional worker; (*coll.*) a (football) hooligan. **casual labour,** *n.* workers employed irregularly. **casual ward,** *n.* (*Hist.*) a ward in a workhouse for tramps or occasional paupers. **casualism,** *n.* the doctrine that all things exist or happen by chance. **casualist,** *n.* **casually,** *adv.* **casualness,** *n.* [F *casuel,* L *cāsuālis* (*cāsus,* CASE[2])]

casualty, *n.* an accident, esp. one attended with personal injury or loss of life; one who is killed or injured in war or an accident. **casualty ward, department,** *n.* the ward in a hospital for receiving the victims of accidents. [see prec.]

casuarina, *n.* a genus of trees of the E Indies with jointed leafless branches. [mod. L, from Malay *kasuwāri,* cassowary, from a supposed resemblance of the branches to cassowary plumage]

casuist, *n.* one who studies doubtful questions of conduct, esp. one who discovers exceptions; a sophist, a hair-splitter. **casuistic, -ical**, *a.* **casuistically,** *adv.* **casuistry,** *n.* that part of ethics or theology which deals with cases of conscience. [F *casuiste* (L *cāsus,* CASE[2])]

casus belli, a ground of war. **casus foederis**, a case provided for by treaty. [L]

CAT, (*abbr.*) college of advanced technology.

cat[1], *n.* any species of the genus *Felis,* comprising the lion, tiger, leopard etc., esp. *F. domestica,* the domestic cat; any cat-like animal; a strong tackle used to hoist the anchor to the cat-heads; various parts of this tackle; the game of tip-cat, the doubly-tapered stick used in this game; a cat-o'-nine-tails; a double tripod which always falls on its feet, as a cat is said to do; (*coll.*) a spiteful woman; (*sl.*) a man, esp. fashionable. *v.t.* (*past, p.p.* **catted**) to draw to the cat-head; (*coll.*) to vomit. *v.i.* (*coll.*) to be sick. **care killed the cat,** cheer up; don't worry (referring to the cat's proverbial nine lives). **cat-and-dog,** quarrelsome. **Cat-and-Mouse Act,** popular name of an Act passed in 1913, permitting of the release and rearrest of hunger-strikers. **to let the cat out of the bag,** to give away a secret, to be indiscreet. **to rain cats and dogs,** to pour. **to see which way the cat jumps,** to wait until the public has made up its mind; to sit on the fence. **to whip the cat,** (*Austral. coll.*) to cry over spilt milk. **cat-beam,** *n.* the broadest beam in a ship. **cat-bird,** *n.* an American thrush, *Mimus carolinesis*. **cat-block,** *n.* a block used to cat the anchor. **cat burglar,** *n.* a thief who enters a house by climbing up the outside. **catcall,** *n.* a squeaking instrument, used in theatres to condemn plays; any similar sound; one using a catcall; *v.i.* to make a noise like a catcall; *v.t.* to deride with a catcall. **cat-door, -flap,** *n.* a small flap set into a door to allow a cat to pass through. **cat-eyed,** *a.* able to see in the dark. **cat-fish,** *n.* a N American river-fish belonging to the genus *Pimelodus;* applied to various other fishes. **cat-head,** *n.* a beam projecting from a ship's bows to which the anchor is secured; (*Geol.*) a kind of nodule containing a fossil. *v.t.* to cat (the anchor). **cat-holes,** *n.pl.* two holes at the stern of a ship for a cable or hawser. **cat-house,** *n.* (*sl.*) a brothel. **cat-ice,** *n.* thin white ice over shallow places where the water has receded. **cat-lap,** *n.* (*coll.*) weak drink, slops. **cat-lick,** *n.* (*coll.*) a perfunctory wash. **cat litter,** *n.* an absorbent material spread on a tray for a cat to urinate or defecate on. **cat-mint,** *n.* a European labiate plant, *Nepeta cataria*. **cat-nap,** *n.* a short sleep. **cat-nip,** *n.* cat-mint. **cat-o'-nine-tails,** *n.* a whip or scourge with nine lashes, formerly used as an instrument of punishment in the Army and Navy. **cat's brains,** *n.* sandstone veined with chalk. **cat's cradle,** *n.* a childish game with string. **cat's-eye,** *n.* a precious stone, from Sri Lanka, Malabar etc., a vitreous variety of quartz; (**Cat's eye**®) a reflector stud on a road. **cat's-foot,** *n.* the ground-ivy, *Nepeta glechoma;* the mountain cudweed, *Antennaria dioica*. **cat's meat,** *n.* horse-flesh, used as food for cats. **cat's paw,** *n.* a dupe used as a tool (in allusion to the fable of the monkey who used the cat's paw to pick chestnuts out of the fire); a light wind which just ripples the surface of the water; a turn in the bight of a rope to hook a tackle on. **cat's-tail,** *n.* the horse-tail, *Equisetum;* several species of *Typha;* a catkin. **cat-suit,** *n.* a one-piece trouser-suit. **cat's whisker,** *n.* (*Radio.*) a very fine wire in contact with a crystal receiver to rectify current and cause audibility. **cat-walk,** *n.* a narrow walkway high above the ground, as above the stage in a theatre. **cathood,** *n.* **catlike,** *a.* **cattery,** *n.* a place where cats are bred or boarded. **cattish,** *a.* **catty,** *a.* spiteful, malicious. [OE (cp. Dut. *kat,* Icel, *köttr,* G *Kater, Katze,* Ir. and Gael. *cat,* late L *cattus*)]

cat., (*abbr.*) catalogue; catamaran; catechism.

cat(a)-, cath-, *pref.* down; against; away; wrongly; entirely; thoroughly; according to. [Gr. *kata,* down, downwards]

catabolism KATABOLISM.

catacaustic, *a.* formed by reflected rays. *n.* a caustic curve formed by reflection.

catachresis, *n.* the abuse of a trope or metaphor; the wrong use of one word for another. **catachrestic**, *a.* **catachrestically,** *adv.* [L, from Gr. *katachrēsis* (*chrēsthai,* to be used)]

cataclasis, *n.* (*Geol.*) the crushing of rocks by pressure. **cataclastic**, *a.* [Gr, *klais,* a breaking]

cataclasm, *n.* a violent disruption; a rending asunder. [Gr. *kataklasma,* from *kataklân* (*klân,* to break)]

cataclysm, *n.* a deluge, esp. the Noachian Flood; a terrestrial catastrophe; a vast and sudden social or political change. **cataclysmal, -mic,** *a.* **cataclysmist**, *n.* one who ascribes changes in the earth's surface to cataclysms. [F *cataclysme,* Gr. *kataklasmos,* from *katakluzein* (*kluzein,* to wash)]

catacomb, *n.* a subterranean burying-place, with niches for the dead; (*pl.*) the subterranean galleries at Rome; similar excavations at Syracuse, Paris etc.; a cellar, esp. a wine-cellar. [F *catacombe,* It. *catacomba,* late L

Catacumbas (etym. doubtful; prob. a place name, but not applied to the Roman catacombs when in use)]

catacoustics, *n.sing.* the science of echoes or reflected sounds.

catadioptric, *a.* reflecting and refracting light.

catadromous, *n.* of fish, descending periodically to spawn (in the sea or the lower waters of a river). [Gr. *katadromos* (*-dromos,* running, from *dramein,* to run)]

catafalque, *n.* a temporary stage or tomb-like structure for the coffin during a state funeral service; a kind of hearse. [F *catafalque,* It. *catafalco* (etym. unknown)]

Catalan, *a.* of or pertaining to Catalonia. *n.* a native, or the language, of Catalonia. **Catalan forge,** *n.* a kind of blast furnace used in Catalonia. **Catalan language**, *n.* a member of the Romance branch of the Indo-European language family, an Iberian language closely related to Provençal in France. It is spoken in Catalonia in NE Spain, the Balearic Isles, Andorra and a corner of SW France.

Catalaunian Fields, *n.pl.* a plain near Troyes, France, scene of the defeat of Attila the Hun by the Romans and Goths under the Roman general Aëtius (d. 454) in 451.

catalectic, *a.* having the metrical foot at the end of a line incomplete. [late L *catalēcticus,* Gr. *katalēktikos,* from *katalēgein* (*lēgein,* to leave, cease)]

catalepsy, *n.* a sudden trance or suspension of voluntary sensation; (*Phil.*) apprehension; mental comprehension. **cataleptic**, *a.* affected by or subject to catalepsy; relating to mental apprehension. *n.* a person subject to attacks of catalepsy. [med. L *catalēpsia,* Gr. *katalēpsis* (*lambanein,* to seize)]

Catal Hüyük, *n.* a Neolithic site (6000 BC) discovered by James Mellaart in 1961 in Anatolia, SE of Konya. It was a fortified city, and had temples with wall paintings, and there were rich finds including jewellery, obsidian and mirrors. Together with finds at Jericho, it demonstrated much earlier development of urban life in the ancient world than previously imagined.

catallactic, *a.* pertaining to exchange. **catallactics,** *n. sing.* political economy. [Gr. *katallatikos* (*katalassein,* to exchange)]

catalogue, *n.* a methodical list, arranged alphabetically or under class-headings; (*N Am.*) a university calendar. *v.t.* to enter in a list; to make a complete list of. **catalogue raisonné,** *n.* a catalogue in which a description of the items is given. **cataloguer,** *n.* [F, from late L *catalogus,* Gr. *katalogos,* from *katalegein* (*legein,* to choose, state)]

Catalonia, *n.* (Spanish **Cataluña**) an autonomous region of NE Spain; area 31,900 sq km/12,313 sq miles; population (1986) 5,977,000. It includes Barcelona (the capital), Gerona, Lérida and Tarragona. Industries include wool and cotton textiles, and hydroelectric power is produced.

catalpa, *n.* a genus of trees, chiefly N American, with long, thin seed-pods. [Carolina Ind.]

catalysis, *n.* the force supposed to be exerted by one substance upon a second, whereby the latter is decomposed, while the former remains unchanged; the effect so produced. **catalyse**, (*esp. N Am.*) **-yze,** *v.t.* to subject to catalysis. **catalyst**, *n.* any substance that changes the speed of a chemical reaction without itself being changed. **catalytic**, *a.* relating to or effected by catalysis. *n.* a medicine supposed to act by the destruction of morbid agencies in the blood. **catalytic converter,** *n.* a device fitted to the exhaust pipe of a motor vehicle to remove toxic impurities from the exhaust gases. **catalytic cracker,** *n.* an industrial apparatus used to break down the heavy hydrocarbons of crude oil and yield petrol, paraffins etc. [Gr. *katalusis,* from *kataluein* (*luein,* to loosen)]

catamaran, *n.* a raft or float used as a surf-boat in the E and W Indies; a raft made by lashing two boats together; a double-hulled boat; an obsolete kind of fire-ship; (*coll.*) a vixenish woman. [Tamil *katta-maram* (*katta,* tie, *maram,* wood)]

catamenia, *n.pl.* the menses. **catamenial,** *a.*

catamite, *n.* a boy kept for homosexual purposes. [L *Catamītus,* corr. from Gr. *Ganymēdes,* Jove's cupbearer]

catamount, catamountain, cat-o'-mountain, *n.* (*N Am.*) the puma; †the leopard, panther etc.; †a fierce, outlandish person. [prob Eng. in orig.]

Cat and Mouse Act, popular name for the Prisoners, Temporary Discharge for Health, Act (1913); an attempt by the UK Liberal government under Asquith to reduce embarrassment caused by the incarceration of suffragettes accused of violent offences against property.

Catania, *n.* industrial port in Sicily; population (1988) 372,000. It exports local sulphur.

cataphonics, *n.sing.* catacoustics. **cataphonic,** *a.*

cataphract, *n.* a scaly plate. **cataphracted,** *a.* covered with scaly plates, as some fishes.

cataphyll, *n.* a simplified or rudimentary leaf. **cataphyllary**, *a.* [Gr. *phullon,* leaf]

cataphysical, *a.* against the laws of nature.

cataplasm, *n.* a poultice, a plaster.

cataplexy, *n.* temporary paralysis or a hypnotic condition affecting animals supposedly shamming dead. **cataplectic**, *a.*

catapult, *n.* an ancient military engine for hurling darts or stones; hence, a toy for propelling small stones. *v.t.* to throw or shoot with or as with a catapult; to assist the take-off of an aircraft by giving an initial acceleration with a spring or other device. *v.i.* to shoot with a catapult. [L *catapulta,* Gr. *katapeltēs* (*pallein,* to hurl)]

cataract, *n.* a large, rushing waterfall; a deluge of rain; a violent rush of water; a kind of governor worked by a flow of water; a disease of the eye in which the crystalline lens or its envelope becomes opaque and vision is impaired or destroyed. **cataractous**, *a.* (*Med.*) affected with cataract. [F *cataracte,* L *cataracta,* Gr. *katarrhaktēs* (from *katarassein,* to dash down, or *katarrhēgnunai,* to break or rush down)]

catarrh, *n.* a running or discharge of the mucous membrane, esp. from the nose; a cold in the head or chest. **catarrhal, -rhous,** *a.* [F *catarrhe,* late L *catarrhus,* Gr. *katarrhoos,* from *katarrheein* (CATA-, *rheein,* to flow)]

catarrhine, *a.* a term applied to the Old World monkeys, from the close, oblique position of their nostrils. *n.* a monkey of the Old World. [Gr. *rhin rhinos,* the nostril]

†**catasta,** *n.* a block on which slaves were exposed for sale; a stage or rack for torture. [L, from Gr. *katastasis* (*sta-,* stem of *histanai,* to stand)]

catastasis, *n.* the part in the ancient drama leading up to the catastrophe; (*Rhet.*) the exordium. [see prec.]

catastrophe, *n.* the change which brings about the conclusion of a dramatic piece; a final event; a great misfortune; a violent convulsion of the globe, producing changes in the relative extent of land or water. **catastrophic**, *a.* **catastrophism,** *a.* the view that geological changes have been produced by the action of catastrophes. **catastrophist,** *n.* [Gr. *katastrophē* (*strephein,* to turn)]

catatonia, *n.* a syndrome often associated with schizophrenia, marked by periods of catalepsy; (*loosely*) catalepsy, or a state of apathy or stupor. **catatonic**, *a.* [Gr. *tonos,* a stretching, tension]

catawampus, *n.* something very fierce; vermin. **catawampous,** *a.* **catawamptiously,** *adv.* [N Am. sl.]

catawba, *n.* a grape-vine, *Vitis abrusca;* wine made therefrom. [a S Carolina river named after *Katahba* Indians]

catch, *v.t.* (*past, p.p.* **caught**) to grasp, to seize, esp. in pursuit; to take in a snare, to entrap; to take by angling or in a net; to intercept (as a ball) when falling; to dismiss (a batsman) by this; to check, to interrupt, to come upon suddenly; to surprise; to detect: to take hold of (as fire); to receive by infection or contagion; to be in time for; to grasp, perceive, comprehend; to attract, gain over, fascinate. *v.i.* to become fastened or attached suddenly; to communicate; to ignite; to spread epidemically; to take hold; to become entangled. *n.* the act of seizing or grasping; anything that seizes, takes hold, or checks; the basket, the amount of fish caught; seizing and holding the ball at cricket; a contrivance for checking motion; an acquisition; an opportunity; an advantage seized; (*coll.*) a person worth capturing matrimonially; profit; trap; a surprise; a snare; a play upon words; a part-song in which each singer in turn catches up, as it were, the words of his predecessor. **to catch at,** to attempt to seize. **to catch a tartar,** to meet with a formidable opponent unexpectedly; to get into difficulties of one's own making. **to catch it,** to get a scolding. **to catch napping** NAP. **to catch on,** to hit the public taste; to grasp, to understand. **to catch one's eye,** to attract attention. **to catch out,** to discover (someone) in error or wrong-doing; in cricket, to dismiss (a batsman); by catching a ball. **to catch up,** to overtake; to make up arrears. **catch-all,** *a.* of a rule etc., which covers all situations, or any not previously covered. **catch-crop,** *n.* a quick-growing green crop sown between main crops; a crop which springs up on fallow land from seed dropped from the previous year's crop. **catch-drain,** *n.* an open drain along the side of a hill or canal to catch the surplus water. **catch-fly,** a book name for species of lychnis and silene, from their glutinous stems which often retain small insects. **catch-penny,** *a.* worthless, made only to sell. **catch-phrase,** *n.* a phrase which comes into fashion for a time and is much (or over-) used. **catch-pit,** *n.* a pit in a drain, to catch sediment and prevent clogging. **catch-points,** *n.pl.* railway points placed on an up-gradient and so set as to derail any vehicle accidentally descending the gradient. **catch-22,** *n.* a situation from which escape is impossible because rules or circumstances frustrate effort in any direction. **catchweed,** *n.* goose-grass or cleavers. **catchword,** *n.* a popular cry; an actor's cue; a word printed under the last line of a page, being the first word of the next; the first word in a dictionary entry. **catchable,** *a.* catcher, *n.* **catching,** *a.* that catches; infectious; taking, attractive. **catchment,** *n.* a surface on which water may be caught and collected. **catchment-area,** *n.* (also **-basin**) an area the rainfall in which feeds a river-system; the area from which a particular school, hospital etc. officially takes its pupils, patients etc. **catchy,** *a.* catching; easy to catch (as a tune); tricky, deceptive; irregular, fitful. [O North. F *cachier* (cp. OF *chacier,* TO CHASE[1]), prob. from a late L *captiāre* (L *captāre,* to chase, freq. of *capere,* to take)]

Catcher in the Rye, The, a 1951 novel of a young man's growing up and his fight to maintain his integrity in a 'phoney' adult world; written by J.D. Salinger, it became an international student classic.

catchpole, *n.* a constable; a bum-bailiff. [med. L *chassipullus,* chase-fowl (CHASE[1], *pullus,* fowl)]

catchup, catsup, KETCHUP.

†**cate,** CATES.

Cateau-Cambresis, Treaty of, treaty that ended the dynastic wars between the Valois of France and the Habsburg Empire, 2–3 Apr. 1559.

catechize, -ise, *v.t.* to instruct by means of questions and answers; to instruct in the Church Catechism; to question closely. **catechizer, -iser,** *n.* **catechetic, -ical,** *a.* consisting of questions and answers, pertaining to catechism. **catechetically,** *adv.* **catechetics,** *n.pl.* that part of Christian theology which deals with oral instruction. **catechism,** *n.* a form of instruction by means of question and answer; esp. the authorized manuals of doctrine, the Church Catechism published by the Church of England, and the Longer and Shorter Catechisms by the Presbyterians; a series of interrogations. **catechismal**, *a.* **catechist,** *n.* one who teaches by catechizing; one who imparts elementary instruction, esp. in the principles of religion. **catechistic, -ical**, *a.* **catechistically,** *adv.* [L *catēchizāre,* Gr. *katēchizein, katēcheein,* to din into the ears (*ēchein,* to sound, *ēcho,* ECHO)]

catechu, *n.* a brown astringent gum, furnished chiefly by *Acacia catechu*. **catechuic**, *a.* [Malay *kāchu*]

catechumen, *n.* one who is under Christian instruction preparatory to receiving baptism; a beginner in any art or science. [F *catéchumène,* L *catēchūmenus,* Gr. *katēchoumenos* (*katēcheein,* see CATECHIZE)]

categorem, *n.* a categorematic word. **categorematic**, *a.* applied to a word capable of being employed by itself as a logical term.

category, *n.* an order, a class, a division; one of the ten predicaments or classes of Aristotle, to which all objects of thought or knowledge can be reduced; one of Kant's twelve primitive forms of thought, contributed by the understanding, apart from experience. **categorial**, *a.* **categorical**, *a.* pertaining to a category or the categories; absolute, unconditional; explicit, direct. **categorical imperative,** *n.* (*Kantian ethics*) the absolute command of the reason as interpreter of the moral law. **categorically,** *adv.* **categorize, -ise,** *v.t.* to place in a category. [L *catēgoria,* Gr. *katēgoria,* a statement, from *katēgoros,* an accuser (CATA-, AGORA, the assembly)]

catelectrode, *n.* the negative pole of an electric battery; a cathode.

catena, *n.* (*pl.* **-nae**) a chain; a connected series. **Catena Patrum**, *n.* a series of extracts from the writings of the Fathers. **catenate**, *v.t.* to chain, to link together. **catenation,** *n.* [L, see foll.]

catenary, *n.* a curve formed by a chain or rope of uniform density hanging from two points of suspension not in one vertical line. *a.* relating to a chain, or to a catena. **catenarian**, *a.* of the nature of or resembling a chain. [L *catēnārius* (*catēna,* a chain)]

cater[1], *v.i.* to supply food, amusement etc. (for). *v.t.* to provide food etc. for (a party etc.). **caterer,** *n.* **cateress,** *n. fem.* **catering,** *n.* the trade of a caterer; the provisions etc. for a social function. [ME *catour,* a caterer, earlier *acatour,* OF *acateor* (*acat, achat,* a purchasing, late L *accaptāre,* to purchase, freq. of *accipere,* to receive)]

†**cater[2],** *n.* the number four on cards or dice; change-ringing on nine bells (four couples of bells changing places in the order of ringing). **cater-cornered,** *a.* not square (applied to a house built at a corner, and therefore more or less oblique in plan; and to a sheet of paper not cut square). [F *quatre,* L *quatuor,* four]

cateran, *n.* a Highland freebooter; †a Highland irregular soldier. [Gael. *ceathairne,* peasantry]

cater-cousin, *n.* someone on very intimate terms with one. [prob. from CATER[1] (not from CATER[2])]

caterpillar, *n.* the larva of a lepidopterous insect; (**Caterpillar®**) a device whereby motor vehicles are fitted with articulated belts in lieu of wheels for operation on difficult ground. **Caterpillar track®**, *n.* an articulated belt revolving round two or more wheels, to propel a vehicle over soft or rough ground. **Caterpillar tractor®**, *n.* a tractor fitted with an articulated belt. [etym. doubtful; perh. a corr. of ONorth.F *catepelose* (OF *chatepelose*). hairy-cat (*chate,* fem. of *chat,* cat, *pelose,* L *pilōsus,* hairy, assim. to PILL[2]]

caterwaul, *v.i.* to make a noise as cats in the rutting season. *n.* such a noise. [CAT[1], WAUL]

†**cates** , *n.pl.* provisions; dainties, delicacies. [earlier *acates,* OF *acat,* a purchase (see CATER[1])]

catgut, *n.* cord made from the intestines of animals and used for strings of musical instruments, and for surgical sutures; a kind of coarse cloth.

cath- CAT(A)-.

Cathar, *n.* member of a sect in medieval Europe usually numbered among the Christian heretics. They started about the 10th century in the Balkans where they were called Bogomils, spread to SW Europe where they were often identified with the Albigenses, and by the middle of the 14th century had been destroyed or driven underground by the Inquisition. They believed in reincarnation for everyone except their members. **catharism,** *n.* **catharist,** *n.* [med. L *catharistae,* Gr. *katharistai,* from *katharizein* (*katharos,* clean)]

Catharine CATHERINE.

catharsis, *n.* purgation of the body; the purging of the emotions by tragedy (according to Aristotle's *Poetics*); (*Psych.*) the bringing out and expression of repressed ideas and emotions. **cathartic,** *a.* cleansing the bowels; purgative; causing or resulting in catharsis. *n.* a purgative medicine. **cathartical,** *a.* **cathartically,** *adv.* **carthartin**, *n.* the active principle of senna. [Gr. *katharsis* from *kathairein* (*katharos,* clean)]

cathedra, *n.* the bishop's throne in a cathedral; hence, a professorial chair. **ex cathedra**, with authority. [L, from Gr. (CATH-, *hedra,* a seat)]

cathedral, *n.* the principal church in a diocese, containing the bishop's throne. **cathedral church,** *n.* a cathedral. [as prec.]

Cather, *n.* **Willa (Sibert)** (1876–1947), US novelist. Born in Virginia, she moved as a child to Nebraska. Her novels and short stories frequently explore life in the pioneer West, for example in *Death Comes for the Archbishop* (1927), set in New Mexico. Other chief works are *My Antonia* (1918) and *A Lost Lady* (1923).

Catherine, *n.* **Catherine pear,** *n.* a small variety of pear. [F *Catherine,* mod. L *Catharīna,* earlier *Katerina,* Gr. *Aikaterina* (assim. to *katharos,* pure)]

Catherine I, *n.* (1683–1727), empress of Russia from 1724. A Lithuanian peasant girl, born Martha Skavronsky, she married a Swedish dragoon and eventually became the mistress of Peter the Great. In 1703 she was rechristened as Katarina Alexeievna, and in 1711 the tsar divorced his wife and married Catherine. She accompanied him in his campaigns, and showed tact and shrewdness. In 1724 she was proclaimed empress, and after Peter's death in 1725 she ruled capably with the help of her ministers. She allied Russia with Austria and Spain in an anti-English bloc.

Catherine II, *n.* (**the Great**) (1729–96), empress of Russia from 1762, and daughter of the German prince of Anhalt-Zerbst. In 1745, she married the Russian grand duke Peter. Catherine was able to dominate him, and six months after he became tsar in 1762 she ruled alone. During her reign Russia extended its boundaries to include territory from Turkey in 1774, and profited also by the partitions of Poland.

Catherine de' Medici, (1519–89), French queen consort of Henry II, whom she married in 1533, and mother of Francis II, Charles IX and Henry III. At first outshone by Henry's mistress Diane de Poitiers (1490–1566), she became regent 1560–63 for Charles IX, and was politically powerful until his death in 1574.

Catherine of Alexandria, St, Christian martyr. According to legend she disputed with 50 scholars, refusing to give up her faith and marry Emperor Maxentius. Her emblem is a wheel, on which her persecutors tried to kill her (the wheel broke and she was beheaded). Feast day 25 Nov.

Catherine of Aragon, (1485–1536), first queen of Henry VIII of England, 1509–33, and mother of Mary I; Henry divorced her without papal approval.

Catherine of Braganza, (1638–1705), queen of Charles II of England, 1662–85. The daughter of John IV of Portugal (1604–56), she brought the Portuguese possessions of Bombay and Tangier as her dowry. Her childlessness and practice of her Catholic faith were unpopular, but Charles resisted pressure for divorce. She returned to Lisbon 1692.

Catherine of Siena, (1347–80), catholic mystic, born in Siena, Italy. She attempted to reconcile the Florentines with the Pope, and persuaded Gregory XI to return to Rome from Avignon in 1376. In 1375 she is said to have received on her body the stigmata, the impression of Jesus' wounds. Her *Dialogue* is a classic mystical work. Feast day 29 Apr.

Catherine of Valois, (1401–37), queen of Henry V of England, whom she married in 1420, and the mother of Henry VI. After the death of Henry V, she secretly married Owen Tudor (*c.* 1400–61) about 1425, and their son became the father of Henry VII.

catherine wheel, *n.* a firework that rotates like a wheel; an ornamental circular window with spoke-like mullions or shafts; a cartwheel somersault. [referring to the martyrdom of St Catherine, see above]

catheter, *n.* a tube used to introduce fluids to, or withdraw them from, the body, esp. to withdraw urine from the bladder. **catheterize, -ise,** to introduce a catheter into. [L, from Gr. *kathetēr,* from *cathienai,* to let down (*ienai* to send)]

cathetometer, *n.* an instrument consisting of a telescope mounted on a vertical graduated support, used for measuring small vertical distances. [L *cathetus,* a straight line perpendicular to another]

cathexis, *n.* concentration of mental or emotional energy on a single object. **cathectic,** *a.* [Gr. *kathexis,* retention]

cathode, *n.* the negative electrode, the source of electrons in an electronic valve. **cathode ray,** *n.* a stream of electrons emitted from the surface of a cathode during an electrical discharge. **cathode ray tube,** a vacuum tube in which a beam of electrons, which can be controlled in direction and intensity, is projected on to a fluorescent screen thus producing a point of light. **cathodic, -dal,** *a.* [Gr. *kathodos,* descent]

catholic, *a.* universal, general, comprehensive; liberal, large-hearted, tolerant; of or pertaining to the whole Christian church; not heretical; in the Middle Ages, of the Western or Latin Church; since the Reformation, of the Roman Church, as opposed to the Protestant churches; occasionally used of the Anglican Church, as claiming continuity from the old, undivided Christian church. *n.* a Roman Catholic; an Anglo-Catholic. **Catholic and Apostolic Church,** the Irvingite Church. **Old Catholics,** the German Catholics who separated from the Roman Communion in 1870. **Roman Catholic,** a member of the Roman Church. **Catholic Emancipation,** *n.* the removal (1780–1829) of restrictions and penal laws from Roman Catholics in the United Kingdom. **Catholic Epistles,** *n.pl.* certain epistles addressed to the Church at large, including those of Peter, James, Jude and the 1st of John (sometimes also the 2nd and 3rd). **Catholic King,** *n.* the King of Spain. **catholicly, -cally**, *adv.* **catholicism,** *n.* (Roman) Catholic christianity. **catholicity**, *n.* the quality of being catholic (in all senses). **catholicize, -ise**, *v.t.* to make Catholic. *v.i.* to become Catholic. **catholico-**, *comb. form.* [F *catholique,* L *catholicus,* Gr. *katholikos,* from *kath'holou,* on the whole, universally (CATH-, *holou,* gen. of *holos,* the whole)]

catholicon, *n.* a universal medicine; a panacea; †a treatise of a general kind. [F, from Gr. *katholikon,* neut. of *katholikos,* see prec.]

Catiline, *n.* **(Lucius Sergius Catilina)** (*c.* 108–62 BC), Roman politician. Twice failing to be elected to the consulship in 64/63 BC, he planned a military coup, but Cicero exposed his conspiracy. He died at the head of the insurgents. His name is applied to any conspirator, esp. against the state. **catilinarian,** *a.* **catilinism,** *n.*

cation, *n.* the positive ion which in electrolysis is attracted towards the cathode. **cationic**, *a.* [Gr. *katienai,* to go down]

catkin, *n.* the pendulous unisexual inflorescence of the willow, birch, poplar etc. [prob. from Dut. *katteken,* kitten, dim. of *katte* (CAT[1], -KIN)]

Catlin, *n.* **George** (1796–1872), US painter and explorer. From the 1830s he made a series of visits to the Great Plains, painting landscapes and scenes of American Indian life.

catling, *n.* a little cat; the smaller kind of catgut; hence, †a lute-string. [CAT[1], -LING[1]]

Cato, *n.* **Marcus Porcius** (234–149 BC), Roman politician. Appointed censor (senior magistrate) in 184, he excluded from the Senate those who did not meet his high standards. He was so impressed by the power of Carthage, on a visit in 157, that he ended every speech by saying 'Carthage must be destroyed.' His farming manual is the earliest surviving work in Latin prose.

Catonian, *a.* resembling either of the Catos; grave, severe. [L *Catōniānus,* from *Cato* (the Censor, and Uticensis)]

catoptric, *a.* pertaining to a mirror or reflector, or to reflection. **catoptrics,** *n.sing.* the science of reflected light. **catoptromancy**, *n.* divination by looking into a mirror placed in a vessel of water. [Gr. *katoptrikos,* from *katoptron,* a mirror (CAT(A)-, *optesthai,* to see)]

Cato Street Conspiracy, an unsuccessful plot hatched in Cato Street, Edgware Road, London, to murder the Tory foreign secretary Castlereagh and his ministers on 20 Feb. 1820. The leader, the Radical Arthur Thistlewood (1770–1820), who intended to set up a provisional government, was hanged with four others.

Cat scanner, *n.* a machine which produces diagnostic X-ray photographs of sections of the body with the assistance of a computer. **Cat scan,** *n.* [Computed *a*xial *t*omography]

catsup, KETCHUP.

cattalo, *n.* (*pl.* **-loes, -los**) a cross between domestic cattle and American bison, very hardy. [from *catt*le + buff*alo*]

cattle, *n.* domesticated animals, esp. oxen and cows; often extended to sheep and pigs; (*sl.*) horses; objectionable people. **cattle-cake,** *n.* a concentrated processed food for cattle. **cattle-feeder,** *n.* a mechanical device for regulating the supply of food to cattle. **cattle grid,** *n.* a trench in a road, covered by a grid which hinders cattle from passing over it but leaves the road free for traffic. **cattle-guard,** *n.* (*N Am.*) a cattle grid. **cattle-leader,** *n.* a nose-grip used for leading dangerous beasts. **cattle-lifter, -reiver,** a cattle-stealer. **cattle-man,** *n.* one who looks after cattle; (*N Am.*) one who breeds and rears cattle, a ranch-owner. **cattle-plague,** *n.* the name given to several diseases to which cattle are subject, such as foot-and-mouth disease, rinderpest etc. **cattle-run,** *n.* (*N Am.*) grazing ground. **cattle rustler,** *n.* (*N Am.*) a cattle-thief **cattle-show,** *n.* an exhibition of cattle at which prizes are given. **cattle truck,** *n.* a railway van for conveying cattle; very crowded, uncomfortable living or travelling conditions. [ONorth.F *catel* (OF *chatel*), late L *captāle,* L *capitāle,* neut. of *capitālis,* CAPITAL[2] (cp. CHATTEL)]

cattleya, *n.* a genus of beautifully-coloured epiphytic orchids. [Wm. *Cattley,* English horticulturist]

catty[1], *n.* an E Indian weight of 1½ lb. (0.68 kg). [Malay (cp. CADDY[1])]

catty[2] CAT[1].

Catullus, *n.* **Gaius Valerius** (*c.* 84–54 BC), Roman lyric poet, born in Verona of a well-to-do family. He moved in the literary and political society of Rome and wrote lyrics describing his unhappy love affair with Clodia, probably the wife of the consul Metellus, calling her Lesbia. His longer poems include two wedding-songs. Many of his poems are short verses to his friends.

Caucasian, *a.* of or pertaining to Mount Caucasus or the district adjoining; belonging to one of the main ethnological divisions of mankind, native to Europe, W Asia, and N Africa, with pale skin. *n.* a member of this race.

Caucasus, *n.* a series of mountain ranges between the Caspian and Black Seas, USSR; 1200 km/750 miles long. The highest is Elbruz, 5633 m/18,480 ft.

Cauchy, *n.* **Augustin Louis** (1789–1857), French mathematician, noted for his rigorous methods of analysis. His prolific output included work on complex functions, determinants and probability, and on the convergence of infinite series. In calculus, he refined the concepts of the limit and the definite integral. Although bigoted in his religion and conceited in his work, he published in 1843 a defence of academic freedom of thought which was instrumental in the abolition of the oath of allegiance soon after the fall of Louis Phillipe in 1848.

caucus, *n.* (*N Am.*) a preparatory meeting of representatives of a political party to decide upon a course of action; a party committee controlling electoral organization; party policy; the system of organizing a political party as a machine. *v.i.* to hold a caucus. *v.t.* to control by means of a caucus. **caucusdom,** *n.* **caucuser,** *n.* [etym. doubtful; perh. Algonkin *kaw-kaw-asu,* a counsellor]

caudal, *a.* pertaining to the tail or the posterior part of the body. **caudally,** *adv.* **caudate,** *a.* having a tail or tail-like process. **caudiform,** *a.* tail-shaped. [L *caudālis* (*cauda,* tail)]

caudex, *n.* (*pl.* **-dices**) the stem and root of a plant, esp. of a palm or tree-fern. **caudicle,** *n.* the strap which connects pollen masses to the stigma in orchids. [L, trunk or stem]

caudillo, *n.* in Spanish-speaking countries, a military leader or head of state. [Sp., from late L *capitellum,* little head, from L *caput,* head]

caudle, *n.* a warm drink of wine and eggs formerly given to invalids. *v.t.* to give as a caudle to; to comfort, refresh. [ONorth.F *caudel,* med. L *caldellium,* dim. of *caldum* (L *calidum,* neut. of *calidus,* warm)]

caught CATCH.

caul, *n.* the rear part of a woman's cap; †a net for the hair; a membrane enveloping the intestines, the omentum; a part of the amnion, sometimes enclosing the head of a child when born. [OF *cale,* a little cap; etym. doubtful]

cauldrife , *a.* (*Sc.*) cold, chilly; chilling, lifeless. [*cauld,* COLD, RIFE]

cauldron, caldron, *n.* a large kettle or deep, bowl-shaped vessel with handles, for boiling. [ONorth.F *caudron* (F *chaudron*), L *caldārium*]

caulescent, *a.* having a stem or stalk visible above the ground. [L *caulis,* stalk, -ESCENT]

cauliflower, *n.* a variety of cabbage with an edible white flowering head. **cauliflower ear,** *n.* a permanently swollen or misshapen ear, usu. caused by boxing injuries. [earlier *cole-, colie-florie,* from ONorth.F. *col* (cp. OF *chol,* F *chou, chou-fleur*), from L *caulis,* stem]

caulis, *n.* (*pl.* **caules**) the stem or stalk; any of the four principal stalks from which spring the volutes in a Corinthian capital. **caulide,** *n.* a small, or rudimentary, stem or stalk. **cauliferous,** *a.* having a stalk. **cauline,** *a.* pertaining to the stem. [L, a stalk]

caulk, calk, *v.t.* to stuff the seams (of a ship) with oakum. **caulking-iron,** *n.* a blunt chisel used by caulkers. **caulker,** *n.* [OF *cauquer* (L *calcāre,* to tread, from *calx,* the heel)]

causa vera, a true cause. [L]

cause, *n.* that which produces or contributes to an effect; (*Phil.*) the condition or aggregate of circumstances and conditions that is invariably accompanied or immediately followed by a certain effect; the person or other agent bringing about something; the reason or motive that justifies some act or mental state; a ground of action; a side or party; a movement, agitation, principle or propaganda; a matter in dispute; (*Law*) the grounds for an action; a suit, an action. *v.t.* to act as an agent in producing; to effect; to produce; to make or induce (to do). **efficient cause,** the power immediately producing an effect. **final cause,** the end or aim, esp. the ultimate object of the universe. **first cause,** the Creator. **to make common cause,** to unite for a definite purpose. **cause célèbre,** *n.* a famous or notorious law-suit. **cause list,** *n.* a list of cases due to come up for trial. †**causable,** *a.* **causal,** *a.* relating to or expressing cause; due to a cause or causes. **causally,** *adv.* **causality,** *n.* the operation of a cause; relation of cause and effect; the theory of causation. **causation,** *n.* the act of causing; connection between cause and effect; (*Phil.*) the theory that there is a cause for everything. **causationism,** *n.* the doctrine that all things are due to the agency of a causal force. **causationist,** *n.* **causative,** *a.* that causes; effective as a cause; (*Gram.*) expressing cause. **causatively,** *adv.* **causeless,** *a.* having no cause or creative agent; without just reason. **causelessly,** *adv.* †**causer,** *n.* [F, from L *causa*]

'cause, (*coll.*) BECAUSE.

causerie, *n.* a chatty kind of essay or article. **causeur,** *n.* a talker, a tattler. [F *causer,* to chat]

causeway, causey, *n.* a raised road across marshy ground or shallow water; a raised footway beside a road; †a paved roadway; a path or road of any kind. *v.t.* to make a causeway for or across. [ONorth.F *caucié* (OF *chaucié,* F *chaussée*), late L *calciāta via* (L *calcāre,* to tread, from *calx -cis,* heel) WAY]

causidical, *a.* pertaining to a legal advocate or advocacy. [L *causidicus,* a pleader]

caustic, *a.* burning, hot, corrosive; bitter, sarcastic. *n.* a substance that burns or corrodes organic matter. **caustic curve,** *n.* (*Math.*) a curve to which the rays of light reflected or refracted by another curve are tangents. **caustic potash,** *n.* potassium hydroxide, an alkaline solid used in the manufacture of soap, detergents etc. **caustic soda,** *n.* sodium hydroxide, an alkaline solid used in the manufacture of rayon, paper, soap etc. **caustically,** *adv.* **causticity**, *n.* [L *causticus,* Gr. *kaustikos* (*kaien,* to burn, fut. *kaus-*)]

†**cautel,** *n.* a trick, a stratagem. †**cautelous,** *a.* treacherous, tricky. [F *cautèle,* L *cautēla* (*caut-,* stem of *cavēre,* to beware)]

cauterize, -ise, *v.t.* to burn or sear (a wound etc.) with a hot iron or caustic; (*fig.*) to sear. **cauterization, -isation,** *n.* **cautery, cauter,** *n.* burning with a hot iron, electricity or a caustic; an instrument for effecting such burning; a caustic. [F *cautériser* late L *cautērizāre,* from prec.]

Cauthen, *n.* **Steve** (1960–), US jockey. He has ridden in England since 1979 and has twice won the Derby, on Slip Anchor in 1985 and on Reference Point in 1987. He rode Affirmed to the US Triple Crown in 1978 at the age of 18 and won 487 races in 1977. He was UK champion jockey in 1984, 1985 and 1987.

caution, *n.* wariness, prudence; care to avoid injury or misfortune, providence; advice to be prudent, a warning; a reprimand and injunction; (*Sc. Law*) bail, security, pledge; (*sl.*) something extraordinary, a strange person; a formal warning to a person under arrest that what is said may be taken down and used in evidence. *v.t.* to warn; to administer a caution to. **caution-money,** *n.* money lodged by way of security or guarantee. **cautionary,** *a.* given as security; containing, or serving as, a caution; cautious. **cautioner,** *n.* (*Sc. Law*) one who is bound as security for another. **cautious,** *a.* heedful, careful, wary. **cautiously,** *adv.* **cautiousness,** *n.* [F, from L *cautio -ōnem* (*cautus,* p.p. of *cavēre,* to take heed)]

Cauvery, or **Kaveri,** *n.* river of S India, rising in the W Ghats and flowing 765 km/475 miles SE to meet the Bay of Bengal in a wide delta. A major source of hydroelectric power since 1902 when India's first hydropower plant was built on the river.

Cavaco Silva, *n.* **Anibal** (1939–), Portuguese politician, finance minister (1980–81), and prime minister and Social Democratic Party (PSD) leader from 1985. Under his leadership Portugal joined the European Community (EC) in 1985 and the Western European Union (WEU) in 1988.

Cavafy, *n.* **Constantinos** (pen name of Konstantínos Pétrou) (1863–1933), Greek poet. An Alexandrian, he threw light on the Greek past, recreating the classical period with zest. He published only one book of poetry, and remained almost unknown until translations appeared in 1952.

cavalcade, *n.* a company or train of riders on horseback; or (loosely) motor-cars; a procession. [F, from It. *cavalcata,* fem. of *cavalcato,* p.p. of *cavalcar* (late L *caballicāre,* from L *caballus,* a horse)]

cavalier, *n.* a horseman, a knight; a gallant; a lady's man; a lover; a partisan of Charles I; a Royalist. *a.* knightly, warlike, gallant; off-hand, haughty, supercilious. *v.i.* to play the cavalier to a lady. **cavalierish,** *a.* **cavalierly,** *adv.* in a haughty or off-hand manner. [F, from It. *cavaliere* (L *caballārius,* from *caballus* horse)]

Cavalier poets, *n.pl.* poets of Charles II's court, including Thomas Carew, Robert Herrick, Richard Lovelace and Sir John Suckling. They wrote witty, light-hearted love lyrics.

Cavalli, *n.* **(Pietro) Francesco** (1602–76), Italian composer, organist at St Mark's, Venice, and the first to make opera a popular entertainment with such works as *Xerxes* (1654), later performed in honour of Louis XIV's wedding in Paris. Twenty-seven of his operas survive.

cavally, cavalla, *n.* a species of tropical fish, known also as horse-mackerel. [Sp. and Port. *cavalla,* mackerel (It. *caballo,* L *caballus,* horse)]

cavalry, *n.* horse soldiers trained to act as a body; one of the arms of the service. **cavalry twill,** *n.* a strong woollen twill fabric, used esp. for trousers. [F *cavallerie,* It. *cavalleria* (*cavaliere,* CAVALIER)]

Cavan, *n.* agricultural inland county of the Republic of Ireland, in the province of Ulster; area 1890 sq km/730 sq miles; population (1986) 54,000.

cavass KAVASS.

cavatina, *n.* a short, simple and smooth song; a similar instrumental composition. [It.]

cave[1], *n.* a hollow place in the earth; a den; (*Hist.*) the secession of a discontented faction from their party; the body of seceders (see ADULLAMITE); (*sl.*) a caving-in. *v.t.* to hollow out; to cause to cave in. *v.i.* to give way, to cave in; to secede from a political party; to dwell in a cave; to explore caves as a sport. **to cave in,** *v.i.* to fall in; to give in, to yield. [perh. *calve in* (cp. Flem. *inkalven,* Dut. *afkalven*)] **cave-bear,** *n.* an extinct species of bear, *Ursus spelaeus*. **cave-earth,** *n.* the earth forming the floor of a cave. **cave-hyaena,** *n.* an extinct species of hyaena, *H. spelaea*. **cave-lion,** *n.* a lion that used to inhabit caves, *Felis spelaea*. **caveman,** *n.* (also **-dweller**) a prehistoric man who dwelt in caves; (*facet.*) a man of primitive instincts. **caver,** *n.* **caving,** *n.* the sport of exploring caves. [F from L *cava,* neut. pl. of *cavus,* hollow (cp. Gr. *kuar,* a cavity)]

cave[2], *int.* Look out! **cave canem**, beware of the dog. [L, beware]

Cave, *n.* **Edward** (1691–1754), British printer, founder under the pseudonym Sylvanus Urban of *The Gentleman's Magazine* (1731–1914), the first periodical to be called a magazine. Dr Samuel Johnson was an influential contributor (1738–44).

caveat, *n.* (*Law*) a process to stop procedure; (*N Am.*) a notice of intention to apply for a patent; a warning, a caution. **caveat actor**, let the doer beware. **caveat emptor**, let the purchaser beware. **caveator**, *n.* one who enters a caveat. [L, let him beware]

Cavell, *n.* **Edith Louisa** (1865–1915), British matron of a Red Cross hospital in Brussels, Belgium, in World War I, who helped Allied soldiers escape to the Dutch frontier. She was court-martialled by the Germans and condemned to death. Her last words were: 'Patriotism is not enough. I must have no hatred or bitterness towards anyone.'

cavendish, *n.* a kind of tobacco softened and pressed into cakes. [perh. from the maker's name]

Cavendish[1], *n.* family name of dukes of Devonshire; the family seat is at Chatsworth, Derbyshire.

Cavendish[2], **Spencer,** HARTINGTON, SPENCER COMPTON CAVENDISH.

Cavendish[3], *n.* **Frederick Charles, Lord Cavendish** (1836–82), British administrator, second son of the 7th duke of Devonshire. He was appointed chief secretary to the lord-lieutenant of Ireland in 1882. On the evening of his arrival in Dublin he was murdered in Phoenix Park with Burke, the permanent Irish undersecretary, by members of the Irish Invincibles, a group of Irish Fenian extremists founded in 1881.

Cavendish[4], *n.* **Henry** (1731–1810), British physicist. He discovered hydrogen, which he called 'inflammable air' 1766, and determined the compositions of water and of nitric acid.

Cavendish-Bentinck, *n.* family name of Dukes of Portland.

Cavendish experiment, *n.* measurement of the gravitational attraction between lead and gold spheres, which enabled Henry Cavendish to calculate a mean value for the mass and density of Earth, using Newton's Law of Universal Gravitation.

cavern, *n.* a cave; a deep hollow place in the earth. *v.t.* to shut or enclose in a cavern; to hollow out. **caverned,** *a.* **cavernous,** *a.* hollow or huge, like a cavern; full of caverns. [F *caverne,* L *caverna* (*cavus,* see CAVE[1])]

cavey CAVY.

caviar, -are, *n.* the salted roes of various fish, esp. the sturgeon. **caviare to the general,** something too refined to be generally appreciated. [cp. It. *caviale*, Turk *havyār*]

cavicorn, *a.* having hollow horns. *n.* a hollow-horned ruminant, one of the Cavicornia. [L *cavus*, hollow, *cornu*, horn]

cavie, *n.* (*Sc.*) a hen-coop; a fowl-house. [prob. from MDut. *kēvie*, ult. from late L *cavea* (L *cavus*, hollow)]

cavil, *n.* a frivolous objection. *v.i.* (*past, p.p.* **cavilled**) to argue captiously. *v.t.* to object to frivolously. †**cavillation,** *n.* **caviller,** *n.* **cavilling,** *a.* **cavillingly,** *adv.* [OF *caviller*, L *cavillāri* (*cavilla*, jeer, mockery)]

cavitation, *n.* the formation of a cavity or partial vacuum between a solid and a liquid in rapid relative motion, e.g. on a propeller. [as foll.]

cavity, *n.* a hollow place or part; a decayed hole in a tooth. **cavity wall,** *n.* one consisting of two rows of bricks with a space between. [F *cavité* (L *cavus*, CAVE[1])]

cavo-rilievo, *n.* (*pl.* **-vi**) sculpture made by hollowing out a flat surface and leaving the figures standing out to the original level. [It., hollow relief]

cavort, *v.i.* to prance about; to bustle about in an important manner. [perh. corr. of CURVET]

Cavour, *n.* **Camillo Benso, Count** (1810–61), Italian nationalist politician. Editor of *Il Risorgimento* from 1847. Prime minister of Piedmont (1852–59) and (1860–61), he enlisted the support of Britain and France for the concept of a united Italy achieved in 1861, having expelled the Austrians in 1859 and assisted Garibaldi in liberating S Italy in 1860.

cavy, cavey, *n.* a S American rodent; any of the genus *Cavia*, esp. *C. cobaya*, the guinea-pig. [French Guiana native *cabiai*]

caw, *v.i.* to cry like a rook. *n.* the cry of a rook. **to caw out,** to utter in a cawing tone. [imit.]

cawk, *n.* an opaque, compact variety of baryta. [North. var. of CHALK, or perh. from Dut. *kalk*]

cawker CAULKER.

Cawnpore, *n.* former spelling of Kanpur, Indian city.

†**caxon,** *n.* an obsolete style of wig. [prob. from a pers. name]

Caxton[1], *n.* a black-letter book printed by William Caxton; type of the same pattern as Caxton's. [see foll.]

Caxton[2], *n.* **William** (*c.* 1422–91), first English printer. He learned the art of printing in Cologne, Germany (1471) and set up a press in Belgium, where he produced the first book printed in English, his own version of a French romance, *Recuyell of the Historyes of Troye* (1474). Returning to England in 1476 he established himself in London, where he produced the first book printed in England, *Dictes or Sayengis of the Philosophres* (1477).

cay, key, *n.* a reef, a shoal. [Sp. *cayo*, med. L *caium*, prob. from Celt (cp. W *cae*, a hedge, a field, Bret. *kaé*, an enclosure, an embankment)]

cayenne, Cayenne pepper, *n.* the powdered fruit of various species of capsicum, a very hot, red condiment. [Tupi, *kýonha*, assim. to *Cayenne*, in French Guiana]

Cayenne, *n.* capital and chief port of French Guiana, on Cayenne island at the mouth of the river Cayenne; population (1982) 38,135.

Cayley[1], *n.* **Arthur** (1821–95), British mathematician, who developed matrix algebra, used by Heisenberg in his elucidation of quantum mechanics.

Cayley[2], *n.* **George** (1773–1857), British aviation pioneer, inventor of the first piloted glider in 1853, and the caterpillar tractor.

cayman, caiman, *n.* a tropical American alligator. [Carib *acáyouman*]

Cayman Islands, *n.pl.* British island group in the West Indies. **area** 260 sq km/100 sq miles. **exports** seawhip coral, a source of prostaglandins; shrimps; honey; jewellery. **population** (1988) 22,000. **language** English. **GNP** $10,900 per head of population.

cayuse, *n.* a small Indian horse. [N Am. Ind.]

cazique CACIQUE.

CB, (*abbr.*) cavalry brigade; Chief Baron; citizen's band; Common Bench Reports and Scott's Reports; Companion of the Order of the Bath; confined to barracks; county borough.

Cb, (*chem. symbol*) columbium.

CBC, (*abbr.*) Canadian Broadcasting Corporation.

CBE, (*abbr.*) Commander of the Order of the British Empire.

CBI, (*abbr.*) Confederation of British Industry.

CBS, (*abbr.*) Columbia Broadcasting System.

CC, (*abbr.*) chamber of commerce; closed-circuit; county council(lor); cricket club.

c.c., (*abbr.*) carbon copy; cubic centimetre.

CCD, (*abbr.*) charge coupled device.

CCTV, (*abbr.*) closed-circuit television.

CD, (*abbr.*) civil defence; compact disk; corps diplomatique. [F., diplomatic corps]

Cd, (*chem. symbol*) cadmium.

cd, (*abbr.*) candela.

Cdr, (*abbr.*) commander.

CD-ROM, *n.* (*Comput.*) a storage device, consisting of a metal disk with a plastic coating, on which information is etched in the form of microscopic pits. A CD-ROM typically holds about 550 megabytes of data. CD-ROMs cannot have information written on to them by the computer, but must be manufactured from a master.

CDU, *n.* abbreviation for the centre-right Christian Democratic Union in the Federal Republic of Germany.

CE, (*abbr.*) chief engineer; Church of England; civil engineer; Common (or Christian) Era; Council of Europe.

Ce, (*chem. symbol*) cerium.

Ceanothus, *n.* a genus of ornamental flowering N American shrubs of the buckthorn family. [Gr. *keanothos*, a kind of thistle]

cease, *v.i.* to come to an end, to leave off; to desist (from). *v.t.* to put a stop to; to discontinue. *n.* the end; extinction; a stopping. **without cease,** without intermission. **cease fire,** *n., int.* a command to stop firing; an agreement to stop fighting. **ceaseless,** *a.* incessant, unceasing. **ceaselessly,** *adv.* **ceaselessness,** *n.* [F *cesser*, L *cessāre*, freq. of *cēdere* (p.p. *cessus*), to go, to yield]

Ceauşescu, *n.* **Nicolae** (1918–89), Romanian politician, leader of Romanian Communist Party (RCP), in power (1965–89). He pursued a policy line independent of and critical of the USSR. He appointed family members, including his wife, to senior state and party posts, and governed in a personalized and increasingly repressive manner, zealously implementing schemes that impoverished the nation. He was overthrown in a bloody revolutionary coup in Dec. 1989 and executed, along with his wife Elena, on Christmas Day 1989.

Cebu, *n.* chief city and port of the island of Cebu in the Philippines; population (1980) 490,000; area 5086 sq km/1964 sq miles.

Cecil[1], *n.* **Robert, 1st Earl of Salisbury** (1563–1612), secretary of state to Elizabeth I of England, succeeding his father, Lord Burghley; he was afterwards chief minister to James I, who created him earl of Salisbury (1605).

Cecil[2], *n.* **Henry Richard Amherst** (1943–), Scottish-born racehorse trainer with stables at Warren Place, Newmarket. The most successful English trainer of all time in terms of prize money, he has been the top trainer eight times.

Cecilia, *n.* Christian patron saint of music, martyred in Rome in the 2nd or 3rd cent., who is said to have sung hymns while undergoing torture. Feast day 22 Nov.

cecity, *n.* blindness (physical or mental). [L *caecitas*, from *caecus*, blind]

CEDA, *n.* (*Confederación Española de Derechas Autonomas*) a federation of right-wing parties under the leadership of José Maria Gil Robles founded during the Second Spanish Republic 1933 to provide a right-wing coalition in the Spanish Cortes. Supporting the Catholic and Monarchist causes, the federation was uncommitted as to the form of government.

cedar, *n.* any of a genus, *Cedrus,* of evergreen coniferous trees with durable and fragrant wood, including the **cedar of Lebanon,** *Cedrus libani,* and many others; the wood of any of these trees. **cedared,** *a.* covered with cedars. **cedarn**, *a.* (*poet.*) made of cedar-wood; consisting of cedars. [OF *cedre,* L *cedrus,* Gr. *kedros*]

cede, *v.t.* to give up, to surrender; to yield, grant. [L *cēdere,* to yield]

cedilla, *n.* a mark (¸) placed under a c in French, Spanish etc., to show that it has the sound of *s*. [Sp. *çedilla,* It. *zediglia,* dim. of Gr. *zēta,* Z]

cedrela, *n.* a genus of E and W Indian and Australian trees. **cedrelaceous**, *a.* [Latinized from Sp. *cedrela,* dim. of *cedro,* CEDAR]

cee, *n.* the third letter of the alphabet, C, c; anything shaped like this letter. **cee-spring, C-spring,** *n.* a C-shaped carriage-spring.

Ceefax®, *n.* one of Britain's two teletext systems (the other is Oracle), or 'magazines of the air', developed by the BBC and first broadcast in 1973. [*see, facts*]

CEGB, (*abbr.*) Central Electricity Generating Board.

ceil, *v.t.* to line the roof of (a room), esp. with plaster. **ceiling,** *n.* the inner, upper surface of an apartment; the plaster or other lining of this; the maximum height to which an aircraft can climb; the upper limit of prices, wages etc. **ceiling price,** *n.* the maximum price for commodities etc. fixed by law. **ceilinged,** *a.* having a ceiling. [prob. from F *ciel,* heaven, L *caelum* (influenced by L *caelāre,* to emboss; cp. late L *caelātūra,* a vaulted roof)]

ceilidh, *n.* an informal gathering, esp. in Scotland or Ireland, for music, dancing etc. [Gael.]

ceinture, *n.* the belt of leather, stuff or rope worn round the waist outside the cassock. [F, girdle]

celadon, *n., a.* a soft, pale green colour; a glaze of this colour on pottery. [F perh. after the character of that name in D'Urfé's *Astrée*]

celandine, *n.* the name of two plants with yellow flowers, the **greater celandine,** *Chelidonium majus,* related to the poppy, and the **lesser celandine,** *Ranunculus ficaria,* also called the pile-wort or figwort. [OF *celindoine,* L *chelidonia,* Gr. *chelidonion,* swallow-wort, neut. of *chelidonios* (*chelidōn,* swallow)]

celarent, *n.* (*Log.*) a mnemonic word applied to the mood of the first figure in which the major premise and the conclusion are universal negatives, and the minor premise a universal affirmative. [L, they might hide]

celation, *n.* (*Law*) concealment (of birth etc.). [L *celare,* to conceal]

-cele, *comb. form.* a tumour or hernia. [Gr. *kēlē,* a tumour]

Celebes, *n.* English name for Sulawesi, an island of Indonesia.

celebrate, *v.t.* to praise, extol; to make famous; to commemorate; to observe; to perform, to say or sing (as Mass), to administer (as Communion). *v.i.* to officiate at the Eucharist; to mark an occasion with festivities. **celebrated,** *a.* famous, renowned. **celebration,** *n.* **celebrator,** *n.* **celebratory,** *a.* **celebrant,** *n.* the priest who officiates, esp. at the Eucharist. **celebrity,** *n.* fame, renown; a celebrated personage. [L *celebrātus,* p.p. of *celebrāre* (*celeber -bris,* frequented, populous)]

celeriac, *n.* a turnip-rooted variety of celery.

celerity, *n.* speed, swiftness, promptness. [F *célérité,* L *celeritas -tātem* (*celer,* swift, cp. Gr. *kelēs,* a runner)]

celery, *n.* a plant, *Apium graveolens,* the blanched stems of which are eaten cooked or as a salad vegetable. **celery fly,** *n.* a small, two-winged fly, *Acadia heraclei,* the larvae of which destroy the leaves of celery and parsnips. [F *céleri,* prov. It. *seleri, seleni,* from L, from Gr. *selinon,* parsley]

celesta, *n.* a keyboard instrument in which steel plates are struck by hammers. [F *céleste,* CELESTIAL]

celestial, *a.* pertaining to heaven or the heavens; spiritual, angelic, divine. *n.* an inhabitant of heaven; a native of China. **Celestial Empire,** *n.* the old Chinese empire (from the trans. of a native name meaning that the empire is divinely established). **celestial sphere,** *n.* an imaginary sphere with the observer at its centre and all heavenly objects on its surface. **celestially,** *adv.* [OF, from L *caelestis;* -AL]

Celestial Police, *n.* a group of astronomers in Germany (1800–15), who set out to discover a supposed missing planet thought to be orbiting the Sun between Mars and Jupiter, a region now known to be occupied by types of asteroid. Although they did not discover the first asteroid (found 1801), they discovered the second (1802), third (1804) and fourth (1807).

Celestine, Celestinian, *n.* one of a monastic order founded about 1254 by Pietro di Morone, afterwards Pope Celestine V. [L *Celestīnus*]

celestine, -tite, *n.* a native sulphate of strontium. [perh. from It. *celestino,* sky-blue]

celiac COELIAC.

celibate, *n.* an unmarried or sexually inactive person. *a.* unmarried; devoted or vowed to a single life; fitted for a single life; abstaining from sexual activity. **celibatarian**, *a.* **celibacy,** *n.* single life; the unmarried state; abstention from sexual activity. [orig. the unmarried state, from F *célibat,* L *caelibātus* celibacy (*caelebs -libem,* unmarried)]

Céline, *n.* **Louis Ferdinand** (pen name of Louis Destouches) (1884–1961), French novelist, whose writings (the first of which was *Voyage au bout de la nuit/Journey to the End of the Night*, 1932) were controversial for their cynicism and misanthropy.

cell, *n.* a small room, esp. one in a monastery or prison; a small religious house dependent on a larger one; the retreat of a hermit; (*poet.*) a humble dwelling; the grave; a small cavity; a cavity in the brain, formerly supposed to be the seat of a particular faculty; a compartment in a comb made by bees; the unit-mass of living matter in animals or plants; the cup-like cavity containing an individual zoophyte in a compound organism; a subsidiary unit of a political organization, esp. a proscribed or revolutionary one; a division of a galvanic battery, or a battery having only one pair of metallic plates; see CELLULAR RADIO under CELLULE. **cellphone,** *n.* a telephone apparatus suitable for use with the cellular radio system. **celled,** *a.* **celliferous**, *a.* **celliform,** *a.* [OF *celle,* L *cella* (cp. *cēlāre,* to hide)]

cella, *n.* the central chamber in a temple. [L, CELL]

cellar[1], *n.* a vault for stores under ground; a place for storing wine; a stock of wine; an underground chamber beneath a house used for storing coal etc. *v.t.* to put in a cellar; to store in a cellar. **cellarage,** *n.* cellars collectively; space for, or charge for storage in, cellars. **cellarer,** *n.* a monk in charge of the stores; an officer of a chapter in charge of the provisions. **cellaret**, *n.* a small case with compartments for holding bottles; a sideboard for storing wine. **cellaring,** *n.* cellars or cellar space. **cellarman,** *n.* one employed in a wine or beer cellar. [OF *celier* (F *cellier*), L *cellārium*]

cellar[2], SALT-CELLAR.

Cellini, *n.* **Benvenuto** (1500–71), Italian sculptor and goldsmith working in the Mannerist style; author of an arrogant autobiography (begun 1558). Among his works are a graceful bronze *Perseus* (1545–54) (Loggia dei Lanzi, Florence) and a magnificent gold salt cellar made for Francis I of France (1540–43) (Kunsthistorisches Museum, Vienna), topped by nude reclining figures.

'cello, VIOLONCELLO.

Cellophane®, *n.* a transparent material made of viscose, chiefly used for wrapping.

cellule, *n.* a little cell or cavity. **cellular,** *a.* of, pertaining to, or resembling a cell or cells; pertaining to a monastic cell; (*Physiol.*) composed of cells; of textiles, woven with a very open texture. *n.* a cellular plant having no distinct stem or leaves; a cryptogamic plant having spiral vessels. **cellular radio,** *n.* a type of radio communication, used esp. for car telephones, which connects directly to the public telephone network and uses a series of transmitting stations, each covering a small area or cell. **cellular telephone,** *n.* **cellulate**, **-lated**, *a.* formed of cells. **cellulation,** *n.* **cellulifer-**

ous, *a*. **cellulite**, *n*. subcutaneous fat which gives the skin a dimpled appearance. **cellulitis**, *n*. inflammation of subcutaneous tissue, caused by bacterial infection. [L *cellular,* dim. of *cella,* CELL]

cellulo-, *comb. form*. composed of cells.

Celluloid®, *n*. a flammable thermoplastic made from cellulose nitrate, camphor and alcohol, used e.g. in cinema film; cinema film.

cellulose, *n*. a carbohydrate of a starchy nature that forms the cell walls of all plants. *a*. containing or consisting of cells. **cellulose acetate,** *n*. any of several chemical compounds formed e.g. by the action of acetic acid on cellulose, used in the manufacture of photographic film, varnish, some textile fibres etc. **cellulose nitrate,** *n*. cellulose treated with nitric acid, used in making plastics, explosives etc. **cellulosity**, *n*.

Celosia, *n*. a genus of plants of the armaranth family, containing *Celosia cristata,* the cockscomb. [Gr. *kelos,* burnt]

Celsius, *a*. denoting a temperature scale in which the freezing point of water is designated 0° and the boiling point 100°. [Anders *Celsius*, 1701–44, Swed. astronomer, who invented it]

celt, *n*. a prehistoric cutting or cleaving implement of stone or bronze. [late L *celtis,* a chisel, a hypothetical word from a reading *celte* (perh. *certe*) in the Vulgate book of Job]

Celt, Kelt, *n*. a people whose first known territory was in central Europe about 1200 BC, in the basin of the upper Danube, the Alps and parts of France and S Germany. In the 6th cent. they spread into Spain and Portugal where they intermarried with Iberians and were known as Celtiberi. Over the next 300 years, they also spread into the British Isles, N Italy (sacking Rome 390 BC), Greece and the Balkans, though they never established a united empire, probably because they were divided into numerous tribes. Their conquests were made by emigrant bands which made permanent settlements in these areas, as well as in the part of Asia Minor later known as Galatia. In the 1st cent. BC they were defeated by the Roman empire and by Germanic tribes, and confined to W Europe, especially Britain and Ireland. They developed a transitional culture between the Bronze and Iron Ages, 9th–5th cents. BC (the Hallstatt culture, from its site SW of Salzburg). They farmed and raised cattle, and were pioneers of iron working, reaching their peak in the period from the 5th cent. to the Roman conquest (the La Tène culture). They were known for their warring, feasting, and gold, bead and enamel ornaments. Classical authors named the fair, tall people of N Europe Celts and only gradually distinguished them from Germanic peoples. **Celtic,** *a*. pertaining to the Celts. *n*. the Celtic languages. **Celtic cross,** *n*. a Latin cross with a circle round the intersection of the arms. **Celtically,** *adv*. **Celticism,** *n*. a custom peculiar to the Celts. **Celticize, -ise,** *v.i.* to become Celtic. *v.t.* to make Celtic. **Celtologist**, *n*. a student of Celtic antiquities, philology etc. **Celtomaniac,** *n*. **Celtophil**, **-phile,** *n*. [F *Celte,* L *Celtae,* pl., Gr. *Keltoi, Keltai*]

Celtic art, *n*. a style of art that originated in about 500 BC, probably on the Rhine, and spread westwards to Gaul and the British Isles, and southwards to Italy and Turkey. Metalwork using curving incised lines and inlays of coloured enamel and coral survived at La Tène, a site at Lake Neuchâtel, Switzerland. Celtic manuscript illumination and sculpture from Ireland and Anglo-Saxon Britain of the 6th–8th cents. has intricate spiral and geometric ornament, as in *The Book of Kells* (Trinity College, Dublin) and the *Lindisfarne Gospels* (British Museum, London).

Celtic languages, *n.pl.* a branch of the Indo-European family, divided into two groups: the **Brythonic** or P-Celtic (Welsh, Cornish, Breton and Gaulish) and the **Goidelic** or Q-Celtic (Irish, Scottish and Manx Gaelic). Celtic languages once stretched from the Black Sea to Britain, but have been in decline for centuries, limited to the so-called 'Celtic Fringe' of W Europe.

Celtic League, *n*. nationalist organization based in Ireland, aiming at an independent Celtic federation. It was founded in 1975 with representatives from Alba (Scotland), Breizh (Brittany), Eire, Kernow (Cornwall), Cymru (Wales) and Ellan Vannin (Isle of Man).

cembalo, *n*. (*pl*. **-li, -los**) a harpsichord. [It.]

cement, *n*. an adhesive substance, esp. one used in building for binding masonry and brickwork and hardening like stone; any analogous material, paste, gum or mucilage for sticking things together; a substance for stopping teeth; (also **cementum**) the bony substance forming the outer layer of the root of a tooth; (*fig.*) a bond of union. *v.t.* to unite with or as with cement; to line or coat with cement; to unite firmly and closely. *v.i.* to cohere. **cementation**, *n*. the act of cementing; the conversion of iron into steel by heating the former in a mass of charcoal. [OF *ciment,* L *caementum* (prob. short for *caedimentum,* from *caedere,* to cut)]

cemetery, *n*. a public burial-ground that is not a churchyard. [L *caemētērium,* Gr. *koimētērion,* orig. dormitory (*koīmaein,* to put to sleep)]

cenacle, *n*. the room, or a representation of it, in which the Last Supper took place; a former French literary coterie. [L *cenaculum,* a dining-room]

cenobite, COENOBITE.

cenotaph, *n*. a sepulchral monument raised to a person buried elsewhere; an empty tomb. **The Cenotaph,** the monument in Whitehall, London, commemorating those in the British armed forces who died in the wars of 1914–18 and 1939–45. [F *cénotaphe,* L *cenotaphium,* Gr. *kenotaphion* (*kenos,* empty, *taphos,* tomb)]

Cenozoic, Caenozoic, *n*. era of geological time that began 65 million years ago and is still in process. It is divided into the Tertiary and Quaternary periods. The Cenozoic marks the emergence of mammals as a dominant group, including humans, and the formation of the mountain chains of the Himalayas and the Alps.

cense, *v.t.* to perfume with incense; to worship with incense. **censer**, *n*. a vessel for burning incense; a thurible; a vessel for burning perfumes. [from obs. n. *cense,* incense, or short for V. INCENSE [1]]

censor, *n*. a Roman officer who registered the property of the citizens, imposed the taxes, and watched over manners and morals; a public officer appointed to examine books, plays etc., before they are published, to see that they contain nothing immoral, seditious or offensive; a public servant whose duty it is in war-time to see that nothing is published, or passes through the post, that might give information to the enemy; the superego, an unconscious mechanism in the mind that excludes disturbing factors from the conscious; one given to reproof or censure of other people. *v.t.* to control any sort of publication in this way; to expurgate or delete objectionable matter from. **censor morum**, *n*. a censor of morals. **censorial**, **†-rian**, *a*. **censorious,** *a*. expressing or addicted to criticism or censure. **censoriously,** *adv*. **censoriousness,** *n*. **censorship,** *n*. [L, from *censēre,* to tax, to appraise]

censure, *n*. †opinion; disapproval, condemnation; an expression of this; blame, reproach. *v.t.* †to form or give a judgment or opinion on; to blame; to find fault with. †*v.i.* to form an opinion (of). **censurable,** *a*. **censurableness,** *n*. **censurably,** *adv*. [F, from L *censūra* (*censēre,* see prec.)]

census, *n*. an official enumeration of the inhabitants of a country; the statistical result of such enumeration; any similar official enumeration, as a *traffic census*. [L, from *censēre* (see CENSOR)]

cent, *n*. a hundred; (a coin of the value of) a hundredth part of the basic unit of many currencies (e.g. of the American dollar); an insignificant coin. **per cent,** by the hundred. **centage,** *n*. rate per hundred; percentage. **cental,** *n*. a weight of 100 lb (45·4 kg) used for grain. [L *centum*]

centaur, *n*. a Greek mythological figure, half man, half horse; any incongruous union of diverse natures; a fine horseman; a constellation in the southern hemisphere (Centaurus). **centauress,** *n. fem*. **centauromachy**, *n*. a battle of centaurs. [L *centauros,* Gr. *kentauros;* etym.

doubtful]

Centaurus, *n.* a large bright constellation of the southern hemisphere, represented as a centaur. It contains the closest star to the Sun, Proxima Centauri. Omega Centauri, the largest and brightest globular cluster of stars in the sky, is 16,000 light years away. Centaurus A, a peculiar galaxy 15 million light years away, is a strong source of radio waves and X-rays.

centaury, *n.* the name of various plants once used medically; the lesser centaury, *Erythraeum centaurium;* (*N Am.*) the genus *Sabbatia.* **yellow centaury,** *Chlora perfoliata.* [L *centaurēa, centaurēum,* Gr. *kentaureion* (nom. *kentaureios* after the Centaur Cheiron)]

CentCom, (*abbr.*) Central Command, a US military strike force.

centenarian, *n.* a person who has reached the age of 100 years. **centenary**, *a.* relating to a hundred; recurring once in a hundred years. *n.* a hundred years; the hundredth anniversary of any event, or the celebration of this. **centennial**, *a.* pertaining to a hundredth anniversary; a hundred or more years old; completing a hundred years. *n.* a centenary. [L *centēnārius,* from *centēni,* a hundred each (*centum,* CENT)]

center CENTRE.

centering, *n.* the woodwork or framing on which an arch or vault is constructed. [CENTRE]

centesimal, *a.* hundredth; by fractions of a hundred. *n.* a hundredth part; (*coll.*) a tiny part. **centesimally,** *adv.* [L *centēsimus,* -AL]

centi-, *comb. form.* a hundred; a hundredth part; esp. denoting a hundredth part of a metric unit, as in *centigram, centilitre, centimetre.* [L *centum,* a hundred]

centifolious, *a.* hundred-leaved. [L *foliōsus, folium,* leaf]

centigrade, *a.* divided into 100 degrees; applied esp. to the Celsius scale of temperature.

centime, *n.* a French, Belgian etc. coin worth a hundredth part of a franc.

centipede, *n.* an animal of the Arthropoda with many segments, each with a pair of legs. [L *centipeda* (*pes pedis,* foot)]

centner, *n.* a German weight equal to 110¼ lb (50 kg); (*N Am.*) 100 lb (45·4 kg). [G, from L *centēnārius,* CENTENARY]

CENTO, (*abbr.*) Central Treaty Organization.

cento, *n.* a composition of verses from different authors, arranged in a new order; a string of quotations, scraps and tags. [L, a patchwork]

centr- CENTRO-.

central, *a.* relating to, containing, proceeding from, or situated in the centre; principal, of chief importance. **central nervous system,** that part of the nervous system of vertebrates consisting of the brain and spinal cord. **central processing unit,** central processor. **central fire,** *a.* of a cartridge, having the fulminate placed at a central point instead of being distributed near the rim. **central forces,** *n.pl.* the centrifugal and centripetal forces. **central heating,** *n.* a system of warming buildings from one furnace by steam or hot-water pipes or other devices. **central processor,** *n.* the part of a computer which performs arithmetical and logical operations on data. **central reservation,** *n.* the strip of ground that separates the carriageways of a motorway. **centralism,** *n.* a system or policy of centralization. **centralist,** *n.* **centrality**, *n.* the quality of being central. **centralize, -ise,** *v.t.* to bring to a centre; to concentrate; to bring under central control. *v.i.* to come to a centre. **centralization, -isation,** *n.* the act of centralizing; the system or policy of carrying on the government or any administrative organization at one central spot. **centrally,** *adv.* **centralness,** *n.* [L *centrālis* (*centrum,* CENTRE)]

Central African Republic, (*République centrafricaine*), a landlocked country in Central Africa, bordered NE and E by the Sudan, S by Zaïre and the Congo, W by Cameroon, and NW by Chad. **area** 622,436 sq km/240,260 sq miles. **capital** Bangui. **physical** most of the country is on a plateau, with rivers flowing N and S. The N is dry and there is rainforest in the SW. **exports** diamonds, uranium, coffee, cotton, timber. **population** (1988) 2,860,000; annual growth rate 2.3%. **language** Sangho, French (both official). **religion** animist over 50%; Christian 35%, both Catholic and Protestant; Muslim 10%.

Central America, *n.* the part of the Americas that links Mexico with the isthmus of Panama, comprising Belize, Costa Rica, El Salvador, Guatemala, Honduras, Nicaragua, and Panama.

Central American Common Market, ODECA (*Organización de Estados Centro-americanos*), established in 1960 by El Salvador, Guatemala, Honduras (seceded 1970) and Nicaragua; Costa Rica joined in 1962.

Central Command, *n.* (*US*) a military strike force consisting of units from the US army, navy and air force, which operates in the Middle East and North Africa. Headquarters in Fort McDill, Florida. It was established in 1979, following the Iranian hostage crisis and the Soviet invasion of Afghanistan, and was known as the Rapid Deployment Force until 1983.

Central Criminal Court, in the UK, Crown Court in the City of London, able to try all treasons and serious offences committed in the City or Greater London. First established in 1834, it is popularly known as the Old Bailey after part of the medieval defences of London; the present building is on the site of Newgate Prison.

Central Intelligence Agency, (CIA) US intelligence organization established in 1947 by President Truman. It has actively intervened overseas, generally to undermine left-wing regimes or to protect US financial interests, for example in Zaïre (when it was still the Congo) and Nicaragua. William Webster became director in 1987. From 1980 all covert activity by the CIA has by law to be reported to Congress, preferably beforehand, and must be authorized by the president.

Central Powers, *n. pl.* originally the signatories of the Triple Alliance in 1882; Germany, Austria and Hungary. During World War I, Italy remained neutral before joining the Allies.

Central Region, *n.* region of Scotland, formed 1975 from the counties of Stirling, S Perth and W Lothian. **area** 2600 sq km/1004 sq miles. **towns** administrative headquarters Stirling; Falkirk, Alloa, Grangemouth. **products** agriculture; industries including brewing and distilling, engineering, electronics. **population** (1987) 272,000.

Central Treaty Organization, military alliance which replaced the Baghdad Pact in 1959. It collapsed when the withdrawal of Iran, Pakistan and Turkey in 1979 left the UK as the only member.

Centre, *n.* a region of N central France; area 39,151 sq km/15,112 sq miles; population (1986) 2,324,000. It includes the *départements* of Cher, Eure-et-Loire, Indre, Indre-et-Loire, Loire-et-Cher and Loiret. Its capital is Orléans.

centre, (*esp. N Am.*) **center**, *n.* the middle of anything; the middle or central object; the point round which anything revolves, the pivot or axis; the principal point; the nucleus, the source from which anything radiates or emanates; the head or leader of an organization; a political party or group occupying a place between two extremes (**left centre,** the more radical portion, and **right centre,** the more conservative of this); (*Austral.*) Central Australia; the main mass of troops between the wings; the framing on which an arch or vault is constructed, the centering. *v.t.* to place on a centre; to collect to a point; to find the centre of. *v.i.* to be fixed on a centre; to be collected at one point. *a.* at or of the centre. **centre of attraction,** one who draws general attention; (*Phys.*) the point towards which bodies gravitate. **centre of buoyancy,** the centre of gravity of the liquid displaced by a floating body. **centre of gravity,** the point about which all the parts of a body exactly balance each other. **centre of inertia, mass,** a point through which a body's inertial force acts (coincident with the centre of gravity).

centre-bit, *n.* a carpenter's tool consisting of a bit fixed in a brace, for boring large round holes. **centre-board,** *n.* a sliding keel which can be raised or lowered; a boat fitted with this. **centrefold,** *n.* (an illustration or article occupying) the two facing pages at the centre of a newspaper or magazine. **centre-forward,** *n.* (*Football*) a player occupying the middle of the front line. **centre-piece,** *n.* an ornament for the middle of a table, ceiling etc. **centre-second(s),** *a.* of a seconds hand, fitted on its own arbor with those of the hour and minute hands. **centre spread** CENTREFOLD. **centric, -ical,** *a.* central. **centrically,** *adv.* **centricity**, *n.* **centrism,** *n.* **centrist,** *n.* one holding moderate political opinions. [F *centre,* L *centrum,* Gr. *kentron,* a spike (*kentein,* to prick)]

centrepede, *n.* a ladder made of a single upright with crosspieces nailed on at intervals.

centri- CENTRO-.

-centric, *comb. form* having a specified centre, as *heliocentric*.

centrifugal, *a.* tending to fly or recede from the centre; of an inflorescence, expanding first at the summit, and last at the base. **centrifugal force,** *n.* the tendency of a revolving body to fly off from the centre. **centrifugal machine,** *n.* a machine utilizing this force for drying or separating purposes. **centrifuge**, *n.* a centrifugal machine for separating liquids of different density, such as cream and milk. **centrifugally,** *adv.* [L *fugere,* to fly from]

centripetal, *a.* tending to approach the centre; of an inflorescence, expanding first at the base, and then at the end or centre. **centripetal force,** *n.* the force which draws a revolving body towards the centre. **centripetally,** *adv.* [L *petere,* to seek]

centro-, centr(i)-, *comb. form.* central, centrally. [L *centrum,* centre]

centrobaric, *a.* pertaining to the centre of gravity.

centrode, *n.* a locus traced out by the successive positions of an instantaneous centre of pure rotation. [Gr. *hodos,* a path]

centrolineal, *a.* converging to a centre.

centrosome, *n.* a small body of protoplasm near a cell nucleus. [Gr. *sōma,* body]

centumvir, *n.* (*pl.* **-viri**) one of the judges appointed by the praetor to decide common causes among the Romans. **centumviral,** *a.* **centumvirate**, *n.* the office or position of a centumvir; the rule of the centumviri. [L (*centum,* hundred, *vir,* man)]

centuple, *n.* a hundredfold. *a.* hundredfold. *v.t.* to multiply a hundredfold. **centuplicate**, *v.t.* to multiply a hundredfold. **centuplicate**, *n.* a centuple. *a.* centuple. **in centuplicate,** *adv.* a hundredfold. **centuplication,** *n.* [F, from late L *centuplum,* nom. *-us,* L *centuplex* (*centum,* a hundred)]

centurion, *n.* a Roman military officer commanding a company of a hundred men. [L *centurio*]

century, *n.* an aggregate of a hundred things; a hundred; a period of a hundred years; a division of the Roman people for the election of magistrates etc.; a division of a legion, consisting originally of a hundred men; a hundred runs in cricket. **century plant,** *n.* the American aloe, *Agave americanus,* erroneously supposed to flower only once in 100 years. **centurial,** *a.* [F *centurie,* L *centuria* (*centum,* a hundred)]

ceorl, *n.* in feudal times, an English freeman, below the thane and above the serf. [CHURL]

cep, *n.* a type of edible mushroom with a brown shiny cap. [F *cèpe,* from L *cippus,* a stake, post]

cephal- CEPHAL(O).

cephalalgia, -algy, *n.* headache. **cephalalgic,** *a.* pertaining to headache. *n.* a medicine for headache. [Gr. *algia,* pain]

cephalaspis, *n.* a genus of fossil ganoids. [Gr. *aspis,* a shield]

cephalic, *a.* pertaining to the head. *n.* a remedy for pains in the head. **cephalic index,** *n.* the ratio of a transverse to the longitudinal diameter of the skull.

-cephalic, -cephalous, *comb. forms.* headed, see HYDROCEPHALOUS, MICROCEPHALOUS, BRACHYCEPHALIC, ORTHOCEPHALIC. [Gr. *kephalē,* the head]

cephalitis, *n.* inflammation of the brain.

cephal(o)-, *comb. form.* pertaining to the head. [Gr. *kephalē,* the head]

cephaloid, *a.* shaped like a head.

cephalopod, *n.* a mollusc having a distinct head with prehensile and locomotive organs attached.

cephalothorax, *n.* the anterior division of the body, consisting of the coalescence of head and thorax in spiders, crabs and other arthropods.

cephalotomy, *n.* the dissection of the head.

cephalous, *a.* having a head.

Cepheus, *n.* a constellation of the N polar region, representing King Cepheus of Gr. mythology, husband of Cassiopeia and father of Andromeda. It contains the Garnet Star, Mu Cepher, a red supergiant of variable brightness that is one of the reddest-coloured stars known, and Delta Cephei, prototype of the Cepheid variables.

ceramic, keramic, *a.* of or pertaining to pottery; applied to any material made by applying great heat to clay or another non-metallic mineral. *n.* such a substance. **ceramics,** *n.pl.* the art of pottery. **ceramist,** *n.* [Gr. *keramikos* (*keramos,* potter's earth, pottery)]

cerasin, *n.* the insoluble part of the gum of the cherry and plum trees. [L *cerasus,* cherry]

cerastes, *n.* a horned viper. [L, from Gr. *kerastēs* (*keras,* horn)]

cerated, *a.* waxed; covered with wax. [L *cērātus,* p.p. of *cērāre,* to cover with wax (*cēra,* wax)]

cerato-, *comb. form.* horned; horny; having processes like horns. [Gr. *keras keratos,* a horn]

ceratoid, *a.* horny; horn-like.

ceratophyte, *n.* a coral polyp with a horny axis.

ceratotome, *n.* an instrument for cutting the cornea. [Gr. *-tomos,* cutting (*temnein,* to cut)]

ceraunoscope, *n.* an apparatus for imitating thunder and lightning, used by the ancients in their mysteries. [Gr. *keraunoskopeion* (*keraunos,* thunderbolt, *skopeein,* to look at)]

Cerberus, *n.* a three-headed dog, fabled to guard the entrance of Hades. **sop to Cerberus,** a propitiatory bribe. [L, from Gr. *Kerberos*]

cercaria, *n.* a trematode worm or fluke in its second larval stage. [mod. L, from Gr. *kerkos,* tail]

cere, *n.* the naked, wax-like skin at the base of the bill in many birds. *v.t.* to cover with wax. **cerecloth,** *n.* a cloth dipped in melted wax, used to wrap embalmed bodies in. **cerement,** *n.* a cerecloth; (*pl.*) graveclothes. **cereous,** *a.* waxen, waxy; like wax. **cerin,** *n.* a crystalline substance obtained from cork, from which it is extracted by means of ether or soluble alcohol. [F *cire,* L *cēra* (cp. *cērāre,* to wax)]

cereal, *a.* pertaining to wheat or other grain. *n.* any edible grain; a breakfast food made from a cereal. **cerealian,** *a.* **cerealin**, *n.* a nitrogenous substance found in bran. [L *cereālis* (*Ceres,* the goddess of corn)]

cerebellum, *n.* (*pl.* **-lla**) a portion of the brain situated beneath the posterior lobes of the cerebrum; responsible for balance and muscular coordination. **cerebellar, cerebellous,** *a.* [L, dim. of *cerebrum,* brain)]

cerebro-, *comb. form.* relating to the brain.

cerebrospinal, *a.* pertaining to the brain and to the spinal cord. **cerebrospinal meningitis,** *n.* inflammation of the brain and spinal cord, spotted fever.

cerebrovascular, *a.* pertaining to the brain and its blood-vessels. **cerebrovascular accident,** *n.* a paralytic stroke.

cerebrum, *n.* (*pl.* **-bra**) the chief portion of the brain, filling the upper cavity of the skull. **cerebral,** *a.* of or pertaining to the brain or the intellect; intellectual rather than emotional; of sounds, made by touching the roof of the mouth with the tip of the tongue. **cerebral cortex,** *n.* the much-folded mass of grey matter forming the outer layer of the cerebrum and responsible for intelligent behaviour. **cerebral haemorrhage,** *n.* bleeding into brain tissue from a cerebral artery. **cerebral hemisphere,** *n.* one of the two great divisions of the cerebrum. **cerebral palsy,** *n.* a disability caused by brain damage before or during birth, characterized by lack of balance and muscular coordination, often with speech impairment. **cerebralism,** *n.* the theory that mental operations arise from activity of the brain. **cerebrate,** *v.i.* to think. **cerebration,** *n.* the action of the brain, whether conscious or unconscious. **cerebric,** *a.* cerebral. **cerebric acid,** *n.* a fatty compound obtained from nerve tissue. **cerebrin,** *n.* a name given to several substances obtained from brain matter. **cerebritis,** *n.* inflammation of the cerebrum. [L, brain]

cerement CERE.

ceremonial, *a.* relating to or performed with ceremonies or rites. *n.* the prescribed order for a ceremony or function; a polite usage or formality; observance of etiquette; in the Roman Catholic Church, the rules for rites and ceremonies; the book containing these. **ceremonialism,** *n.* fondness for or adherence to ceremony. **ceremonialist,** *n.* **ceremonially,** *adv.* [as foll.]

ceremony, *n.* a prescribed rite or formality; a usage of politeness; formality, punctilio. **master of ceremonies,** one whose duty it is to see that due formalities are observed on public or state occasions; person responsible for the running of a dance etc. **to stand on ceremony,** to be rigidly conventional. **ceremonious,** *a.* punctiliously observant of ceremony according to prescribed form. **ceremoniously,** *adv.* **ceremoniousness,** *n.* [OF *ceremonie,* L *caerimōnia* (cp. Sansk. *karman,* an action, a rite)]

cereous, cerin CERE.

Ceres[1], *n.* the largest asteroid, 1020 km/634 miles in diameter. It is a rock that orbits the Sun every 4.6 years at an average distance of 420,000,000 km/ 260,000,000 miles. Its mass is about 1/60th that of the Moon.

Ceres[2], *n.* in Roman mythology, the goddess of agriculture (Greek Demeter).

cerinthian, *a.* pertaining to Cerinthus, an early heretic, who taught a mixture of Gnosticism, Christianity and Judaism. [*Cerinthus,* -IAN]

ceriph, SERIF.

cerise, *n.* cherry colour. *a.* cherry-coloured. [F, cherry, L *cerasus,* Gr. *kerasos*]

cerium, *n.* a malleable grey metallic element of the rare earth group, at.no. 58; chem. symbol Ce, found in cerite. **cerite,** *n.* a siliceous oxide of cerium. [after the planet *Ceres*]

cermet, *n.* an alloy of a heat-resistant ceramic and a metal. [*ceramic, metal*]

CERN, (*abbr.*) European organization for nuclear research, founded 1954, with laboratories at Meyrin, near Geneva in Switzerland. [F, *Conseil européen pour la recherche nucléaire*]

cero-, *comb. form.* pertaining to or composed of wax. [L *cēra* or Gr. *kēros,* wax]

cerography, *n.* the art of writing or engraving on wax; painting in wax-colours; encaustic painting. **cerographic, -ical,** *a.* **cerographist,** *n.*

ceromancy, *n.* divination from the forms assumed by melting wax dropped into water.

ceroplastic, *a.* modelled in wax; modelling in wax. **ceroplastics,** *n.pl.* the art of modelling in wax.

cert CERTAIN.

certain, *a.* sure, convinced, assured, absolutely confident; established beyond a doubt, undoubtedly existing; absolutely determined, regular, fixed; sure to happen, inevitable; sure to do, reliable, unerring; not particularized, indefinite. *n.* an indefinite number or quantity. **for certain,** assuredly. **cert,** *n.* (*sl.*) a certainty. **certainly,** *adv.* assuredly; beyond doubt; without fail; admittedly, yes. **certainty,** *n.* that which is certain; absolute assurance. †**certes,** *adv.* certainly or bound to happen, assuredly. [OF *certein,* L *certus,* -AN]

certificate[1], *n.* a written testimony or voucher, esp. of character or ability. [CERTIFY]

certificate[2], *v.t.* to give a certificate to; to license by certificate. **certificated,** *a.* possessing a certificate from some examining body. **certification,** *n.*

certify, *v.t.* to assure, to testify to in writing; to give certain information of or to; to certify as insane. **certified milk,** *n.* milk guaranteed free from tubercle bacillus. **certifiable,** *a.* **certifier,** *n.* [F *certifier,* L *certificāre* (*certus,* certain, facere, to make)]

certiorari, *n.* a writ issuing from a superior court calling for the records of or removing a case from a court below. [L to be certified]

certitude, *n.* the quality of being certain; certainty, conviction.

cerulean, *a.* of a sky-blue colour; sky-coloured. **cerulein, -lin,** *n.* the colouring matter of indigo dissolved in sulphuric acid with potash added to the solution; a colouring matter obtained from coal-tar and other substances. [L *caeruleus* (prob. for *caelulus,* from *caelum,* the sky), -AN]

cerumen, *n.* the wax-like secretion of the ear. **ceruminous,** *a.* [L *cēra,* wax]

ceruse, *n.* white lead; a cosmetic made from this. †*v.t.* to apply ceruse to as a cosmetic. **cerusite, cerussite,** *n.* a native carbonate of lead. [F *céruse,* or directly from L *cērussa* (cp. *cēra,* wax), prob. from Gr. *kēroussa* (cp. *kērous,* waxy, from *kēros,* wax)]

Cervantes (Saavedra), *n.* **Miguel de** (1547–1616), Spanish novelist, playwright and poet, whose masterpiece *Don Quijote* (in full *El ingenioso hidalgo Don Quijote de la Mancha*) was published in 1605. A spurious second part of *Don Quijote* prompted Cervantes to bring out his own authentic second part in 1615.

cervelat, *n.* a kind of smoked sausage made from pork or beef. [F, from It. *cervellata*]

cervical, *a.* of or pertaining to the neck or cervix. **cervical smear,** *n.* a specimen of cells taken from the cervix of the uterus to test for the presence of cancer. **cervico-,** *comb. form.* pertaining to or connected with the neck or cervix. [CERVIX]

cervine, *a.* pertaining to the deer family; of or like deer. [L *cervīnus* (*cervus,* a hart)]

cervix, *n.* a necklike part of the body, esp. the passage between the uterus and the vagina. [L *cervix -icis,* a neck]

César, *n.* adopted name of César Baldaccini (1921–), French sculptor who uses iron and scrap metal and, in the 1960s, crushed car bodies. His subjects are imaginary insects and animals.

Cesarian, -rean CAESARIAN under CAESAR.

cesium CAESIUM.

cespitose CAESPITOSE.

cess[1], *v.t.* to tax, to assess. *n.* (*obs. exc. in Ireland*) a local rate. [prob. short for ASSESS]

cess[2], *n.* (*Ir., sl.*) luck. **bad cess to you,** ill luck befall you. [Irish slang; perh. short for SUCCESS]

cessation, *n.* the act of ceasing; pause, rest. **cessavit,** *n.* a process for the recovery of possession of lands from a tenant who has failed to pay rent for two years. [L *cessātio* (*cessāre,* CEASE)]

cesser, *n.* cessation. [F, from L *cessāre,* CEASE]

cessio bonorum, *n.* a surrender by a debtor of property to creditors. [L, surrender of goods]

cession, *n.* a yielding, a surrender, a ceding of territory, or of rights or property; the surrender of a benefice by its holder before accepting another; a cessio bonorum. **cessionary,** *n.* one who is the recipient of an assignment, an assign or assignee. [F, from L *cessio -ōnem* (cess-, part. stem of *cēdere,* CERE)]

cesspit, *n.* a pit for night-soil; a midden. [formed on anal. of foll.]

cesspool, *n.* a deep hole in the ground for sewage to drain into; any receptacle for filth. [etym. doubtful (perh. It. *cesso,* a privy, from L *sēcessus,* from *sēcēdere,* to retire)]

cestoid, *a.* ribbon-like. **cestode, -toid,** *n.* an intestinal worm of the group Cestoidea, a tape-worm. [L *cestus,* Gr. *kestos,* a girdle, -OID]

Cestr., (*abbr.*) of Chester (bishop of Chester's signature). [L *cestrensis*]

cestus[1], *n.* the girdle of Venus; the classic marriage girdle. [L, from Gr. *kestos* a girdle]

cestus[2], *n.* a heavy boxing-glove, made with thongs

and armed with lead or iron, used by the Romans. [L *caestus,* from *caesus,* p.p. of *caedere,* to strike, or prec.]

cesura, CAESURA.

CET, (*abbr.*) Central European Time.

cet-, *comb. form.* of or relating to spermaceti. [L *cētus,* a whale, Gr. *kētos,* a sea-monster]

Cetacea, *n.pl.* a group of marine mammalia, containing the whales, manatees etc. **cetacean,** *a.* of or pertaining to the Cetacea. *n.* any individual of the Cetacea. **cetaceous,** *a.*

cetane, *n.* an oily, colourless hydrocarbon found in petroleum. **cetane number,** *n.* a measure of the ignition quality of diesel fuel. [CET-, -ANE]

ceteosaur, -saurus , *n.* a large fossil saurian. [Gr. *kētos kēteos,* a whale, *sauros,* a lizard]

ceterach, *n.* a genus of polypodiaceous ferns, the fronds of which are covered with scales on the back. [med. L, from Pers *saytarak*]

Cetewayo or **Cetshwayo,** *n.* (*c.* 1829–84), king of Zululand, South Africa (1873–83), whose rule was threatened by British annexation of the Transvaal in 1877. Although he defeated the British at Isandhlwana in 1879, he was later that year defeated by them at Ulundi. Restored to his throne in 1883, he was then expelled by his subjects.

cet. par., (*abbr.*) other things being equal. [L *ceteris paribus*]

Ceylon, former name of SRI LANKA.

Cézanne, *n.* **Paul** (1839–1906), French post-impressionist painter, a leading figure in the development of modern art. He broke away from the impressionists' spontaneous vision to develop a style that captured not only light and life, but the structure of natural forms, in landscapes, still lifes, portraits and his series of bathers.

Cf, (*chem. symbol*) californium.

cf., (*abbr.*) compare. [L *confer*]

cfc, (*abbr.*) chlorofluorocarbon.

c.f.i., (*abbr.*) cost, freight and insurance.

C.G., (*abbr.*) captain-general; captain of the guard; coast-guard; Coldstream Guards; commissary-general; consul-general.

cg, (*abbr.*) centigram.

CGM, (*abbr.*) conspicuous gallantry medal.

CGS, (*abbr.*) centimetre-gram-second; chief of general staff.

CGT, (*abbr.*) capital gains tax; *Confédération générale du travail* (the French TUC).

CH, (*abbr.*) Companion of Honour; Confederatio Helvetica (L, Switzerland); court-house; custom-house.

ch, (*abbr.*) chain (in knitting); chairman; champion (of dogs); chapter; chestnut (of horses); chief; child; choir organ; church.

cha, *n.* (*Anglo-Indian, sl.*) tea. [Hind.]

chablis, *n.* a white wine made at Chablis, in central France. [place-name]

cha-cha, cha-cha-cha, *n.* a ballroom dance of W Indian origin. [Am. Sp.]

chacma, *n.* a S African baboon. [Hottentot]

chaco, SHAKO.

chaconne, *n.* a Spanish dance in triple time; the music for this. [F, from Sp. *chacona,* prob. from Basque *chucun,* pretty]

chad, *n.* (*pl.* **chad**) the small piece of paper removed when a hole is punched in a punched card, paper tape etc.

Chad, *n.* Republic of (*République du Tchad*), a landlocked country in central N Africa, bounded to the north by Libya, to the east by the Sudan, to the south by the Central African Republic, and to the west by Cameroon, Nigeria and Niger. **area** 1,284,000 sq km/ 495,624 sq miles. **capital** N'djamena. **physical** savanna and part of Sahara Desert in the N; rivers in the S flow N to Lake Chad in the marshy E. **exports** cotton, meat, livestock, hides, skins, bauxite, uranium, gold, oil. **population** (1987) 5,241,000; annual growth rate 2.3%. **language** French (official), Arabic. **religion** Muslim (north); Christian, animist (south).

Chad, Lake, *n.* a lake on the NE boundary of Nigeria. It varies in extent between rainy and dry seasons from 50,000 sq km/20,000 sq miles to 20,000 sq km/7000 sq miles. The Lake Chad basin is being jointly developed by Cameroon, Chad, Niger and Nigeria.

chador, *n.* a large veil, worn over the head and body by Muslim women. [Pers. *chaddar*]

Chadwick, *n.* **James** (1891–1974), British physicist. In 1932 he discovered the particle in an atomic nucleus which became known as the neutron because it has no electric charge.

chaet(o)-, *comb. form.* characterized by bristles or a mane. [Gr. *chaite,* hair, mane]

chaetodon, *n.* a genus of fishes with bristly teeth and brilliant colouring. [Gr. *odous odontos, tooth*]

chaetopod, *n.* a group of marine worms with bristles in foot-like appendages. [Gr. *pous podos,* foot]

chafe, *v.t.* †to make warm; †to inflame; to make warm by rubbing; to rub so as to make sore, to fret; to gall, to irritate. *v.i.* to be worn by rubbing; to fret. *n.* a sore caused by rubbing; irritation, a fit of rage, passion. †**chafer**[1], *n.* one who chafes; a chafing-dish. **chafery**, *n.* a forge in which iron is heated and welded into bars. **chafing,** *a.* that chafes. **chafing-dish,** *n.* a vessel for making anything hot; a small portable grate for coals. **chafing-gear,** *n.* battens, mats, yarn etc. put upon rigging to prevent its being chafed. [OF *chaufer* (F *chauffer*), L *calefacere* (*calēre,* to glow, *facere,* to make)]

chafer[2], *n.* a beetle, a cockchafer. [OE *ceafor,* prob. from Teut. *kaf-,* to gnaw (cp. Dut. *kever,* G *Käfer*)]

chaff[1], *n.* the husks of grain; hay or straw cut fine for fodder; the scales and bracts of grass and other flowers; winnowings; anything worthless; thin strips of metal foil thrown from an aeroplane to confuse enemy radar. **chaff-cutter,** *n.* a machine for cutting straw and hay for fodder. **chaffy,** *a.* like or full of chaff; light, worthless. [OE *ceaf* (cp. Dut. *kaf,* OHG *cheva*)]

chaff[2], *n.* banter; teasing. *v.t.* to banter; to tease. *v.i.* to indulge in banter or teasing. [CHAFF[1], or from CHAFE]

chaffer, *v.i.* to dispute about price; to haggle; to bargain; to chatter. *v.t.* to buy or sell. *n.* the act of bargaining; chaffering, haggling. **chafferer,** *n.* [ME *chaffare, chapfare* (OE *cēap,* bargain, *far,* a journey)]

chaffinch, *n.* a common British small bird, *Fringilla coelebs*. [CHAFF[1] (from its frequenting barn-doors), FINCH]

Chagall, *n.* **Marc** (1887–1985), French painter and designer, born in Russia. Much of his highly-coloured, fantastic imagery was inspired by the village life of his boyhood. He designed stained glass, tapestries and stage sets.

chagrin, *n.* vexation, disappointment, mortification; ill-humour. *v.t.* to vex, to disappoint; to put out of humour. [F, from Turk. *saghrī,* SHAGREEN (from the sense of rubbing or chafing)]

chai CHAL.

Chain, *n.* **Ernst Boris** (1906–79), German biochemist who worked on the development of penicillin. After the discovery of penicillin by Alexander Fleming, Chain worked to isolate and purify it. He also discovered penicillinase, an enzyme which destroys penicillin. He shared the 1945 Nobel Prize for Medicine.

chain, *n.* a series of links or rings fitted into or connected with each other, for binding, connecting, holding, hauling or ornamenting; a measure of 100 links, or 66 ft. (20·12 m), used in land surveying; (*pl.*) bonds, fetters, bondage, restraint; a connected series, a sequence, a range; a series of atoms linked together in a molecule; (*pl.*) strong plates of iron bolted to a ship's sides and used to secure the shrouds; a group of shops, hotels etc. under the same ownership and run in a similar style. *v.t.* to fasten or bind with or as with a chain or chains. **chain armour,** *n.* chain mail. **chain-belt,** *n.* a chain used as a belt to transmit power. **chain-bridge,** *n.* a suspension bridge. **chain-coupling,** *n.* a coupling for railway luggage vans as a safeguard in case of breakage of the ordinary coupling. **chain-gang,** *n.* a gang of convicts working in chains. **chain letter,** *n.* a circular letter each recipient of which forwards a copy to friends and others. **chain-mail,** *n.* armour of interwoven links. **chain-moulding,** *n.* an ornamental band carved with link-work. **chain-pier,** *n.* a pier on the principle of the suspension bridge. **chain-plate,** *n.* one of the flat iron bars bolted to a ship's side to secure the shrouds, also called channel plates. **chain-pump,** *n.* a machine for raising water, consisting of an endless chain fitted with buckets or discs which return upwards through a tube. **chain reaction,** *n.* a self-perpetuating chemical or nuclear reaction, producing energy etc., which initiates another, identical reaction. **chainsaw,** *n.* a power saw whose teeth are in a continuous revolving chain. **chain-shot,** *n.* two cannon-balls connected by a chain to destroy spars and rigging. **chain-smoke,** *v.i.* (*coll.*) to smoke continuously, lighting one cigarette from another. **chain-smoker,** *n.* **chain-stitch,** *n.* an ornamental stitch resembling a chain; a loop-stitch (made by a sewing-machine). **chain-store,** *n.* one of a series of retail stores under the same ownership and selling the same kind of wares. **chain-wales,** *n.pl.* CHANNEL². **chain-wheel,** *n.* a toothed wheel which receives or transmits power by means of an endless chain. **chain-work,** *n.* needlework with open spaces like the links of a chain; sewing with chain-stitches. **chainless,** *a.* **chainlet,** *n.* [OF *chaëne,* L *catēna*]

chair, *n.* a movable seat with a back for one person; a seat of authority or office; a professorship; a chairmanship or mayoralty; (the seat of) the person presiding at a meeting; a Bath chair; a sedan; an iron socket to support and secure the rails in a railway. *v.t.* to carry publicly in a chair in triumph; to install as president of a meeting or society; to act as chairman. **to take the chair,** to preside at a meeting. **chair-bed,** *n.* a bed that folds up and becomes a chair. **chairman,** *n.* a chairperson; a man who draws a Bath chair; (*Hist.*) one of a pair of men who carried a sedan. **Chairman of Committees,** a member of either House who is appointed to preside over the House when it is in committee. **chairmanship,** *n.* **chairperson,** *n.* the president of a meeting or the permanent president of a society, committee etc. **chairwoman,** *n. fem.* [OF *chaëre,* L *cathedra,* Gr. *kathedra* (see CATHEDRA)]

chaise, *n.* a light travelling or pleasure carriage of various patterns. **chaise longue,** *n.* a chair with support for the legs. [F, corr. of *chaire,* CHAIR]

chal, (fem.) chai, *n.* a person, a fellow. [Romany]

chalaza, *n.* one of the two twisted albuminous threads holding the yolk in position in an egg; an analogous part of a plant ovule. [Gr., hailstone]

chalcedony, calcedony, *n.* a cryptocrystalline variety of quartz. **chalcedonic,** *a.* **chalcedonyx,** *n.* a variety of agate. [L *chalcēdonius,* Gr. *chalkēdōn,* etym. doubtful]

chalco-, *comb. form.* of or pertaining to copper or brass. [Gr. *chalkos*]

chalcography, the art or process of engraving on brass or copper. chalcographer, -ist, *n.* **chalcographic,** *a.*

chalcopyrite, *n.* a copper sulphoferrite, yellow or copper pyrites, a copper ore.

Chaldean, -dee, *a.* of or belonging to ancient Chaldea or its language. *n.* the language of Chaldea; a native of Chaldea. **chaldaic,** *n., a.* [L *Chaldeus* Gr. *Chaldaios,* -AN]

chaldron, *n.* a measure (36 bushels; about 1·3 cu. m) for coals. [OF *chauderon* (F *chaudron*), see CAULDRON]

chalet, *n.* a small house or villa on a mountain-side; a Swiss cottage; a small flimsy dwelling used esp. for holiday accommodation. [Swiss F, prob. dim. of *casella,* dim. of It. or L *casa,* cottage]

chalice, *n.* a cup or drinking vessel; the cup used in the Eucharist; (*poet.*) a flower-cup. †**chaliced,** *a.* having a cell or cup; cup-shaped. [OF, from L CALIX]

chalk, *n.* soft white limestone or massive carbonate of lime, chiefly composed of marine shells; a piece of this or of a coloured composition prepared from it, used for writing and drawing; a public-house score. *v.t.* to rub, mark or write with chalk; to manure with chalk. **a long chalk,** a great deal; a score or point in a game. **French chalk,** a kind of steatite or soap-stone. **red chalk,** a clay coloured with peroxide of iron; ruddle. **to chalk it up,** to give or take credit for something. **to chalk out,** to sketch out, to plan. **to walk one's chalks,** to be off, to depart without ceremony. **to walk the chalk,** to follow a straight course as by walking along a chalk-line, orig. a test of sobriety. **chalk-bed,** *n.* a stratum of chalk. **chalk-pit,** *n.* a chalk quarry. **chalk-stone,** *n.* a chalky concretion in the joints; occurring in chronic gout. **chalk-stripe,** *n.* a pattern of narrow white stripes on a dark-coloured background. **chalky,** *a.* containing or resembling chalk; containing or resembling chalk-stones. **chalkiness,** *n.* [OE *cealc* (cp. Dut., Dan., Swed., and G *kalk*), from L *calx -cis,* lime]

challenge, *n.* a summons or defiance to fight a duel; an invitation to a contest of any kind; the cry of hounds on finding scent; a calling in question; exception taken to a juror or voter; the call of a sentry in demanding the counter-sign; a difficult task which stretches one's abilities. *v.t.* to invite or defy to a duel; to invite to a contest of any kind; to call on to answer; to demand, to invite, to claim; to object to, to dispute, contest; to stimulate, stretch. **challenge cup,** *n.* a cup competed for annually by football teams, yacht clubs etc. **challengeable,** *a.* **challenged,** *a.* handicapped as in *visually challenged.* **challenger,** *n.* [OF *chalenge,* L *calumnia,* CALUMNY]

challis, *n.* a light woollen fabric; formerly a fabric of silk and wool, for ladies' dresses. [perh. a pers. name]

chalumeau, *n.* a reed, a shepherd's pipe. [F, from OF *chalemel,* L *calamellus,* see CALUMET]

chalybeate, *a.* impregnated with iron. *n.* a mineral water or spring so impregnated. **Chalybean,** *a.* pertaining to the Chalybes, an ancient people of Asia Minor, famous as makers of steel. [L *chalbys,* Gr. *chalups -ubos,* steel, -ATE]

†**cham,** *n.* the ruler of Tartary; an autocrat. [KHAN]

chamade, *n.* the beat of a drum or sound of a trumpet demanding or announcing a surrender or parley. [F, from Port. *chamada* (*chamar,* to summon, L *clāmāre,* to call)]

chamber, *n.* a room, esp. a sleeping room; the place where a legislative assembly meets; the assembly itself; a hall of justice; an association of persons for the promotion of some common object; a hollow cavity or enclosed space; the space between the gates of a canal lock; that part of the bore of a gun or other firearm where the charge lies; a judge's private room in a court; (*pl.*) the office or apartments of a barrister in an Inn of Court; a suite of apartments; a chamber-pot. **Chamber of Agriculture, of Commerce,** boards or committees appointed to promote the interests of agriculture or business in a district. **Chamber of Horrors,** *n.* a room at Madame Tussaud's waxwork exhibition devoted to famous criminals; (*fig.*) a place full of horrifying objects. **chamber concert,** *n.* one where chamber music is given. **chamber council,** *n.* a secret council. **chamber-counsel,** *n.* a secret thought; a lawyer who gives opinions etc. but does not plead. †**chamber-fellow,** *n.* one who sleeps in the same room. **chambermaid,** *n.* a woman who cleans the bedrooms at a hotel. **chamber-master,** *n.* one who makes up materials at home and sells the goods to shops. **chamber music,** *n.* music adapted for performance in a room, as distinguished from that intended for theatres, churches etc. **chamber orchestra,** *n.* a small orchestra suitable for playing chamber music. **chamber-pot, -utensil,** *n.* a bedroom receptacle for slops and urine. **chamber-practice,** *n.* the practice of a chamber-counsel. **chambered,** *a.* enclosed; divided into compartments or sections. †**chamberer,** *n.* a valet; a lady's maid; a dissipated person; an intriguer. †**chambering,** *n.* licentious behaviour; intrigue. [OF, from L *camera,* from Aryan *kam-,* to cover (cp. Gr. *kamara,* a vault, Icel. *hamr,* a covering)]

Chamberlain¹, *n.* **(Arthur) Neville** (1869–1940), British Conservative politician, son of Joseph Chamberlain. He was prime minister (1937–40); his policy of appeasement towards the fascist dictators Mussolini and Hitler (Munich Agreement, 1938) failed to prevent the outbreak of World War II.

Chamberlain[2], *n.* **(Joseph) Austen** (1863–1937), British Conservative politician, elder son of Joseph Chamberlain. As foreign secretary (1924–29) he negotiated the Pact of Locarno (Nobel Peace Prize 1925) and signed the Kellogg-Briand pact in 1928.

Chamberlain[3], *n.* **Joseph** (1836–1914), British politician, reformist mayor of and MP for Birmingham. In 1886 he disagreed with Gladstone's policy of Home Rule for Ireland, resigned from the Cabinet and led the revolt of the Liberal-Unionists.

chamberlain, *n.* an officer in charge of the household of a sovereign or nobleman; a male servant in charge of suites of chambers; the treasurer of a city or corporation; †a servant at an inn with duties like those of a head waiter and a chambermaid. **Lord Chamberlain (of the Household),** one of the principal British officers of State, controlling the servants of the royal household above stairs, and the licensing of theatres and plays. **Lord Great Chamberlain of England,** a British hereditary officer of State in charge of the Palace of Westminster and performing ceremonial functions. **chamberlainship,** *n.* [OF, from OHG *chamberling* (L *camera,* CHAMBER, -LING)]

Chambers, *n.* **William** (1726–96), British architect, popularizer of Chinese influence (as in the Pagoda, Kew Gardens, London) and designer of Somerset House, London.

Chambertin, *n.* a dry red Burgundy wine. [a vineyard near Dijon]

chambré, *a.* of wine, warmed to room temperature. [F p.p. of *chambrer,* to keep in a room]

chameleon, *n.* a lizard having the power of changing colour and formerly fabled to live on air; a changeable person. **chameleonic,** *a.* **chameleon-like,** *a., adv.* [L *chamaeleon,* Gr. *chamaileōn* (*chamai,* on the ground, dwarf, *leōn,* a lion)]

chamfer, *n.* in carpentry, an angle slightly pared off; a bevel, a groove, a fluting. *v.t.* to groove; to bevel off. [OF *chanfrein* (*chant,* CANT[2], L *frangere,* to break)]

chamfron, *n.* armour for a horse's head. [OF *chanfrain* (F *chanfrein*), etym. unknown]

chamlet, CAMLET.

chamois, *n.* (*pl.* **chamois**) a goat-like European antelope, *Antilope rupicapra.* **chamois-leather, chamois,** *n.* a soft, pliable leather, orig. prepared from the skin of the chamois. [F, prob. from Swiss Romanic (cp. It. *camozza,* G *Gemse*); prob. Teut. but etym. doubtful]

chamomile CAMOMILE.

champ[1], *vt., vi.* to bite with a grinding action or noise; to chew, to crunch. *n.* champing; the noise of champing. **to champ at the bit,** to be impatient. [earlier *cham;* prob. imit.]

champ[2], *n.* (*coll.*) short for CHAMPION.

champac, *n.* a kind of magnolia, much venerated in India. [Hind. *champak*]

champagne, *n.* a light sparkling wine made in the province of Champagne, France; a pale yellow colour. **fine champagne**, liqueur brandy. [place-name]

champaign, *n.* flat, open country; level country; †a field of battle. *a.* flat; open, unenclosed. [OF *champaigne* (see CAMPAIGN)]

champers, (*coll.*) CHAMPAGNE.

champerty, *n.* †apportionment of land; †a partnership in power; maintenance of a party in a suit on condition of sharing the property at issue if recovered. [earlier *champarty,* ONorth.F *campart,* L *campi pars,* part of the field (assim. to PARTY[1])]

champignon, *n.* †a mushroom; the fairy-ring agaric, *Agaricus oreades.* [F, prob. from late L *campinio -ōnem* (*campus,* field)]

champion, *n.* †a warrior; one who engages in single combat on behalf of another; one who argues on behalf of or defends a person or a cause; the acknowledged superior in any athletic exercise or trial of skill; the person, animal or exhibit that defeats all competitors; †one who maintained a cause by wager of battle. *v.t.* to challenge to combat; to defend as a champion; to support a cause. *a.* superior to all competitors; (*dial.*) first-class, supremely excellent. **championless,** *a.* **championship,** *n.* the fact of being a champion; the act of championing or defending; a contest to find a champion. [OF, from late L *campio -ōnem,* a fighter in a duel (L *campus,* field)]

Champlain, *n.* **Samuel de** (1567–1635), French pioneer, soldier and explorer in Canada. Having served in the army of Henry IV and on an expedition to the W Indies, he began his exploration of Canada in 1603. He founded and named Québec (1608) and was appointed lieutenant governor of French Canada in 1612.

champlevé, *n.* enamelling by the process of inlaying vitreous powders into channels cut in the metal base; a plate so treated. [F *champ,* a field, *levé,* raised]

Champollion, *n.* **Jean François, le Jeune** (1790–1832), French egyptologist who in 1822 deciphered Egyptian hieroglyphics with the aid of the Rosetta Stone.

Chanc., (*abbr.*) chancellor; chancery. **Chanc. Ex.,** (*abbr.*) Chancellor of the Exchequer.

chance, *n.* fortune, luck, the course of events; event, issue, result; undesigned result or occurrence; accident, risk, possibility, opportunity; (*usu. pl.*) likelihood, probability; fate, the indeterminable course of events, fortuity. *v.t.* (*coll.*) to risk. *v.i.* to happen, to come to pass. *a.* fortuitous, unforeseen. **by chance,** as things fall out; accidentally; undesignedly. **†how chance?** how was it that? **on the (off-) chance,** on the possibility; in case. **the main chance,** the most important issue; gain; self-interest. **to chance it,** to take the risk. **to chance upon,** to come upon accidentally. **to stand** (or **have**) **a good chance,** to have a reasonable prospect of success. **chance-comer,** *n.* one who comes by chance. **chanceful,** *a.* fortuitous, accidental; (*poet.*) eventful; †hazardous, risky. **chancer,** *n.* (*sl.*) a person who takes risks in order to make a profit. **chancy,** *a.* risky, doubtful. [OF *cheance,* late L *cadentia* (*cadens -tis,* pres.p. of *cadere,* to fall)]

chancel, *n.* the eastern part of a church, formerly cut off from the nave by a screen. [OF (see CANCEL)]

chancellery, -ory, *n.* a chancellor's court or council and official establishment; the building or room in which a chancellor has his office; the office or department attached to an embassy or consulate. [OF *chancelerie,* late L *cancellāria* (see CHANCELLOR)]

chancellor, *n.* the president of a court, public department, or university; an officer who seals the commissions etc. of an order of knighthood; a bishop's law-officer or a vicar-general. **Chancellor of the Duchy of Lancaster,** the representative of the Crown as holder of the Duchy of Lancaster. **Chancellor of the Exchequer,** the principal finance minister of the British Government. **Lord (High) Chancellor,** the highest officer of the British Crown, the keeper of the Great Seal, president of the Chancery division of the Supreme Court (formerly the High Court of Chancery), and Speaker of the House of Lords **chancellorship,** *n.* **chancellory** CHANCELLERY. [OF *chancelier, cancelier,* late L *cancellārius* (L *cancellus,* a grating, see CANCEL)]

chance-medley, *n.* (*Law*) homicide by misadventure, as accidental homicide in repelling an unprovoked attack; inadvertency; pure chance or luck. [A-F *chance medlée* (CHANCE, *medler,* var. of *mesler,* to mix; cp. MEDDLE)]

chancery, *n.* the court of the Lord Chancellor, before 1873; the highest English court of justice next to the House of Lords, comprising a court of common law and a court of equity, now a division of the High Court of Justice; (*N Am.*) a court of equity; a court or office for the deposit of records. **to get into chancery,** to get into a hopeless predicament; in boxing, to get one's head under an opponent's arm. [OF *cancellerie,* CHANCELLERY]

chancre, *n.* a hard syphilitic lesion. **chancrous,** *a.* **chancroid,** *n.* a soft ulcer caused by venereal infection. [F, cp. CANCER, CANKER]

chancy CHANCE.

chandelier, *n.* a hanging branched frame for a number of lights. [OF *chandelier,* candlemaker, candlestick (see foll.)]

chandler, *n.* one who makes or sells candles; a retail dealer in oil, groceries and other commodities. **chandlery,** *n.* the establishment or the stock in trade of a chandler. [OF *chandelier,* L *candēlārius* (*candēla,* CANDLE)]

Chandler, *n.* **Raymond** (1888–1959), US crime writer, who created the 'private eye' hero Philip Marlowe, in such novels as *The Big Sleep* (1939), *Farewell, My Lovely* (1940) and *The Long Goodbye* (1954).

Chandragupta Maurya, *n.* ruler of N India (*c.* 321–*c.* 297 BC), founder of the Maurya dynasty. He overthrew the Nanda dynasty (325) and then conquered the Punjab in 322 after the death of Alexander the Great, expanding his empire to the borders of Persia. He is credited with having united most of India under one administration.

Chanel, *n.* **Coco (Gabrielle)** (1883–1971), French fashion designer, creator of the 'little black dress', informal cardigan suit and perfumes.

change, *v.t.* to make different, to alter; to give up or to substitute for something else; to give or take an equivalent for in other coin; to exchange. *v.i.* to become different; to be altered in appearance; to pass from one state or phase to another; to become tainted; to deteriorate. *n.* alteration, variation; shifting, transition the passing of the moon from one phase to another; alteration in order, esp. of ringing a peal of bells; substitution of one thing for another; small coin or foreign money given in return for other coins; balance of money paid beyond the value of goods purchased; exchange; an exchange; novelty, variety. **change of front,** (*Mil.*) a wheeling movement; a change of attitude, a reversal of policy. **change of life,** the menopause. **on change** (not **'change**) where merchants meet or transact business. **to change colour,** to turn pale; to blush. **to change down,** in driving etc. to change to a lower gear. **to change hands,** to pass from one person's ownership to another's. **to change one's clothes,** to put on different clothes. **to change one's mind,** to form a new plan or opinion. **to change one's tune,** to adopt a humble attitude; to become sad or vexed. **to change sides,** to desert one's party. **to change up,** in driving etc., to change to a higher gear. **to get no change out of,** not to be able to take any advantage of. **to ring the changes,** to try all ways of doing something; to swindle by counterfeit money, or in changing a coin. **to take one's change,** to exact revenge; to get even with someone. **changeover,** *n.* an alteration or reversal from one state to another; in a relay race, the passing of the baton from one runner to the next. **change-ringing,** *n.* a form of bell-ringing in which a set of bells is rung repeatedly but in slightly varying order. **changeable,** *a.* liable to change; inconstant, fickle, variable; †shot with different colours. **changeability,** *n.* **changeableness,** *n.* **changeably,** *adv.* **changeful,** *a.* full of change; changeable. **changefully,** *adv.* **changefulness,** *n.* **changeless,** *a.* free from change; unchanging. **changeling,** *n.* anything substituted for another; a child substituted for another, esp. an elf-child; a waverer, a fickle person. **changer,** *n.* one who changes anything; a money-changer. **changing,** *a.* [OF *changer,* late L *cambiāre* (*cambium,* exchange, L *cambire;* etym. doubtful)]

Chang Tiang, *n.* the longest river (formerly Yangtze Kiang) of China, flowing about 6300 km/3900 miles from Tibet to the Yellow Sea.

channel[1], *n.* the bed of a stream or an artificial watercourse; the deep part of an estuary; a fairway; a narrow piece of water joining two seas; a tube or duct, natural or artificial, for the passage of liquids or gases; means of passing, conveying or transmitting; a furrow, a groove, a fluting; a gutter; a course, line, or direction; a band of frequencies on which radio and television signals can be transmitted without interference from other channels; a path for an electrical signal; in a computer, a route along which data can be transmitted. *v.t.* to cut a channel or channels in; to cut (a way) out; to groove. **The Channel,** the English Channel. **channelize, -ise,** *v.t.* to channel. **channelization, -isation,** *n.* [OF *chanel,* var. of CANAL]

channel[2], *n.* a plank fastened horizontally to the side of a ship to spread the lower rigging. **channel plate,** *n.* CHAIN PLATE under CHAIN. [CHAIN, WALE[2]]

Channel, English, *n.* a stretch of water between England and France, leading in the west to the Atlantic Ocean, and in the east via the Strait of Dover to the North Sea; also known as La Manche (French 'the sleeve') from its shape.

Channel Islands, *n.pl.* a group of islands in the English Channel, off the coast of Normandy. **islands** Jersey, Guernsey, Alderney, Great and Little Sark, with the lesser Herm, Brechou, Jethou, and Lihou. **exports** flowers, early potatoes, tomatoes, butterflies. **population** (1981) 128,878. **language** official language French (Norman French) but English more widely used. **religion** chiefly Anglican.

Channel swimming, *n.* a popular test of endurance since Capt. Matthew Webb (1848–83) first swam from Dover to Calais in 1875. His time was 21 hr. 45 min. for the 34 km/21 mile journey.

Channel tunnel, *n.* a tunnel being built beneath the English Channel, linking Britain with mainland Europe. It will comprise twin rail tunnels 50 km/31 miles long and 7.3 m/24 ft in diameter located 40 m/130 ft beneath the seabed. Specially designed shuttle trains carrying cars and lorries will run every few minutes between terminals at Folkestone, Kent, and Sangatte W of Calais, France. The latest estimated cost is £6 billion. It is scheduled to be operational in 1993.

chanson, *n.* a song. **chansonette,** *n.* a little song. [F, from L *cantio -ōnis* (*cant-,* part. stem of *canere,* to sing)]

Chanson de Roland, an early 12th-cent. epic poem which describes the Romantic legend based on the life of Roland, one of the 12 Paladins or peers of Charlemagne, killed by the Basques at Roncesvalles.

chant, *v.t.* †to sing; to celebrate in song; to recite to music or musically, to intone. *v.i.* to sing in an intoning fashion. *n.* song, melody; a composition consisting of a long reciting note and a melodic phrase; a psalm, canticle or other piece sung in this manner; a musical recitation or monotonous song. **to chant a horse,** to sell it fraudulently by concealing its defects or overpraising it. **to chant the praises of,** to praise monotonously. **chanter,** *n.* †a singer; a chantry priest, a chorister; one who chants; a precentor; the pipe on a bagpipe that plays the tune; (*sl.*) a horse-coper. [F *chanter,* L *cantāre,* freq. of *canerer,* to sing]

chantage, *n.* black mailing. [F, as prec.]

chanterelle[1], *n.* an edible fungus, *Cantharellus cibarius.* [F, from mod. L *cantharellus,* dim. of *cantharus,* cup]

chanterelle[2], *n.* the highest string upon stringed instruments. [F, from It. *cantarella* (L *cantāre,* CHANT)]

chanteuse, *n.* a female nightclub singer. [F (fem.), singer]

chantey, SHANTY[2].

chanticleer, *n.* a name for a cock, esp. as the herald of day. [OF *chantecler* (F *chanteclair*), *chanter,* CHANT, *cler,* CLEAR]

chantry, *n.* an endowment for a priest or priests to say mass daily for some person or persons deceased; the chapel or the part of a church used for this purpose; the body of priests who perform this duty. **chantry-priest,** *n.* [OF *chanterie* (*chanter,* CHANT, -ERY)]

chanty, SHANTY[2].

chaos, *n.* the void, the confusion of matter said to have existed at the Creation; confusion, disorder. **chaotic,** *a.* **chaotically,** *adv.* [L, from Gr. *chaos* (*chaskein,* to gape)]

chap[1], *v.t.* to cause to crack or open in long slits; (*Sc.*) to strike, to beat. *v.i.* to crack or open in long slits. *n.* (*usu. pl.*) a longitudinal crack, cleft or seam on the surface of the skin, the earth etc. **chapped,** *a.* **chappy,** *a.* [ME *chappen* (MDut. *cappen,* Dut. *kappen,* Dan. *kappe*), relations of these obscure]

chap[2], **chop**, *n.* (*pl.*) the jaws (usu. of animals), the mouth and cheeks; the lower part of the cheek. **to lick one's chops,** to relish in anticipation. **chap-fallen,** *a.* having the lower jaw depressed; downcast, dejected, dispirited. [from prec.]

chap[3], *n.* †a buyer, a customer; (*coll.*) a man, a fellow. [CHAPMAN]

chaparejos, CHAPS.

chaparral, *n.* a thicket of low evergreen oaks, or of thick bramble-bushes and thorny shrubs. [Sp., from *chaparra,* evergreen oak]

chapati, -tti, *n.* in Indian cookery, a round, thin loaf of unleavened bread. [Hind. *capati*]

chap-book, *n.* a small book, usually of wonderful tales, ballads or the like, formerly hawked by chapmen. [formed on analogy of CHAPMAN]

chape, *n.* the catch or piece by which an object is attached, as the frog of a sword-belt, the back-piece of a buckle etc.; the transverse guard of a sword; the hook or tip of a scabbard. *v.t.* †to furnish with a chape. [F, from late L *cāpa,* CAP[1]]

chapeau, *n.* (*pl.* **chapeaux**) in heraldry, a hat. **chapeau bras,** *n.* a small, three-cornered, flat silk hat carried under the arm by men in full dress in the latter part of the 18th cent (F *bras,* arm). [F, from OF *chapel,* L *cappellum,* dim. of *cappa,* CAP[1]]

chapel, *n.* a place of worship connected with and subsidiary to a church; a part containing an altar in a church; a place of worship other than a church or cathedral, esp. one in a palace, mansion or public institution; a Nonconformist place of worship; a service, or the sort of service, at a chapel; a printing-office (from the legend that Caxton set up his printing press in Westminster Abbey); a printers' or journalists' trade union, or a branch of it. *a.* belonging to a Nonconformist church. **chapel of ease,** a subordinate church in a parish. **father, mother of chapel,** the president of a branch of a printers' or journalists' trade union. **chapelry,** *n.* the district or jurisdiction of a chapel. [OF *chapele* (F *chapelle*), from late L *cappella,* dim. of *cappa, cāpa,* CAP[1] (after the *cāpa* or cloak of St Martin, which was preserved in the first chapel)]

Chapel Royal, *n.* in the UK, the royal retinue of priests, singers and musicians (including Tallis, Byrd, and Purcell) of the English court from 1135.

chaperon(e), *n.* †a kind of hood or cap; a married or elderly woman who attends a young unmarried lady in public places. *v.t.* to act as chaperon to. **chaperonage,** *n.* the duties or position of a chaperon. [F, a hood, dim. of *chape,* a cope (see CAP[1])]

chapiter, *n.* the upper part of the capital of a column; †a chapter or article. [OF *chapitre,* L *capitulum,* dim. of *caput -itis,* head]

chaplain, *n.* a clergyman who officiates at court, in the house of a person of rank, or in a regiment, ship or public institution. **chaplaincy,** *n.* **chaplainship,** *n.* [OF *chapelain,* late L *cappellānus*]

chaplet, *n.* a wreath or garland for the head; a string of beads one-third the number of a rosary; a necklace; a bird's crest; a toad's string of eggs; a round moulding carved into beads, olives or the like. [OF *chapelet,* dim. of CHAPE]

†**chapman,** *n.* one who buys and sells; an itinerant merchant, a pedlar, a hawker. [OE *cēapmann* (*cēap,* CHEAP, *mann,* MAN), cp. Dut. *koopman,* G *Kaufmann*]

Chaplin, *n.* **Charles Spencer ('Charlie')** (1889–1977), English actor-director. He made his reputation as a tramp with smudge moustache, bowler hat, and cane in silent films from the mid-1910s, including *The Rink* (1916), *The Kid* (1921), and *The Gold Rush* (1925). His works often contrast buffoonery with pathos, and later films combine dialogue with mime and music, such as *The Great Dictator* (1940), and *Limelight* (1952).

Chapman[1], *n.* **Frederick Spencer** (1907–71), British explorer, mountaineer and writer, who explored Greenland, the Himalayas and Malaya. He accompanied Gino Watkins on the British Arctic Air Routes Expedition (1930–31), recalled in *Northern Lights* (1932), and in 1935 he joined a climbing expedition to the Himalayas. For two years he participated in a government mission to Tibet described in *Lhasa, the Holy City* (1938), before setting out to climb the 7315 m/24,000 ft peak, Chomollari.

Chapman[2], *n.* **George** (1559–1634), English poet and dramatist. His translations of Homer (completed 1616) were celebrated; his plays include the comedy *Eastward Ho!* (with Jonson and Marston) (1605), and the tragedy *Bussy d'Amboise* (1607).

chappie, (*coll.*) CHAP[3].

chaps, *n.pl.* leather leggings worn by cowboys. [Sp. *chaparajos*]

chapter, *n.* a division of a book; a part of a subject; a piece of narrative, an episode; a division of Acts of Parliament arranged in chronological order for reference; the general meeting of certain orders and societies; the council of a bishop, consisting of the clergy attached to a cathedral or collegiate church; a meeting of the members of a religious order; a chapter-house. *v.t.* to divided into chapters. **chapter and verse,** full and precise reference in order to verify a fact or quotation. **chapter of accidents,** a series of accidents; an unfortunate coincidence. **to the end of the chapter,** throughout, to the end. **chapterhouse,** *n.* the place in which a chapter is held. [CHAPITER]

char[1], *n.* a small fish (genus *Salvelinus*) of the salmon family, found in the Lake District and N Wales; the American brook-trout, *S. fontinalis*. [perh. Celtic; cp. Ir. *cear,* red]

char[2], **chare**, *n.* a turn of work, an odd job; a charwoman. *v.i.* (*past, p.p.* **charred**) to work by the day; to do small jobs. **charwoman, -lady,** *n.* a woman employed to do cleaning. [OE *cierr, cyrr,* a turn, from *cierran,* to turn (cp. Am. CHORE)]

char[3], *v.t.* (*past, p.p.* **charred**) to reduce to charcoal; to burn slightly, to blacken with fire. *v.i.* to become blackened with fire. [back-formation from CHARCOAL]

char[4], CHA.

charabanc, *n.* (*dated*) a coach for day-trippers. [F, carriage with benches]

character, *n.* a mark made by cutting, engraving or writing; a letter, a sign; (*pl.*) letters distinctive of a particular language; style of handwriting; peculiar distinctive qualities or traits; the sum of a person's mental and moral qualities; moral excellence, moral strength; reputation, standing; good reputation; a certificate of capacity, moral qualities and conduct (esp. of a servant); position, rank, capacity; a person, a personage; a personality created by a novelist, poet or dramatist; a part in a play; an actor's part; (*coll.*) an eccentric person; a characteristic (of a species etc.); an inherited characteristic; (*Comput.*) a symbol, e.g. a letter, punctuation mark etc., that can be used in representing data. †*v.t.* to inscribe; to engrave; to characterize. **generic characters,** those which constitute a genus. **specific characters,** those which constitute a species. **character actor,** *n.* one who specializes in portraying eccentric or complicated characters. **character assassination,** *n.* the destruction of a person's good reputation by, e.g. the spreading of malicious rumour. **charactered,** *a.* invested with definite character. **characteristic,** *n.* that which marks or constitutes the character; the whole-number or integral part of a logarithm. **characteristic, -ical,** *a.* constituting or exhibiting typical qualities. **characteristically,** *adv.* **characterize, -ise,** *v.t.* to give character to, to stamp, to distinguish; to describe; to be characteristic of. **characterization, -isation,** *n.* **characterless,** *a.* without definite character; ordinary, commonplace; without a written character. †**charactery,** *n.* characterization; a mark, an impression. [F *caractère* (or OF *characte,* see CARACT), L *charactēr,* Gr. *charactēr* (*charassein,* to furrow, engrave)]

charade, *n.* a kind of riddle based upon a word the key to which is given by description or action representing each syllable and the whole word; (*pl.*) a game based on such riddles; a ridiculous pretence, a travesty. [F, from Sp. and Port. *charrada* (*charro,* a peasant), or Prov. *charrada* (*charra,* to chatter)]

charcoal, *n.* wood partially burnt under turf; an impure form of carbon prepared from vegetable or animal substances; a stick of charcoal used for drawing; a drawing made with such a stick; a dark grey colour. [etym. doubtful]

Charcot, *n.* **Jean-Martin** (1825–93), French neurologist who studied diseases of the nervous system. He became known for his work on hysteria, sclerosis, locomotor ataxia, and senile diseases.

chard, *n.* a variety of beet, *Beta vulgaris sicla,* with stalks and leaves eaten as a vegetable. [F *carde;* L *carduus,* a thistle]

Chardin, *n.* **Jean-Baptiste-Siméon** (1699–1779), French painter of naturalistic still lifes and quiet domestic scenes that recall the Dutch tradition. His work is a complete contrast to that of contemporary Rococo painters. He developed his own technique using successive layers of paint to achieve depth of tone and is generally considered one of the finest exponents of the genre.

Chardonnet, *n.* **Hilaire Bernigaud** (1839–1924), French chemist who developed artificial silk in 1883, the first artificial fibre.

chare CHAR[2].

charge, *v.t.* †to lay a load or burden on; to fill; to put the proper load or quantity of material into (any apparatus), as to load (a gun), to accumulate electricity in (a battery) etc.; to saturate (water) with gas; to rush on and attack; to put (weapons) in an attacking position; to lay on or impose; to enjoin, to command, to exhort; to entrust, to accuse; to debit to; to ask a price for; to give directions to, as a judge to a jury etc., or a bishop to his clergy. *v.i.* to make an attack or onset; (*coll.*) to demand high prices or payments. *n.* a load, a burden; an office, duty or obligation; care, custody; the thing or person under one's care, a minister's flock; command, commission; an entry on the debit side of an account; price demanded, cost; accusation; attack, onset; the quantity with which any apparatus, esp. a firearm, is loaded; instructions, directions, esp. those of a judge to a jury, or of a bishop to his clergy; anything borne on an escutcheon; the electrical property of matter, negative or positive; the amount or accumulation of electricity, e.g. in a battery. **charge coupled device,** (CCD) (*Comput.*) a data storage device built into a chip which usually consists of alternate layers of metal, silicon dioxide, and silicon. CCDs are used by astronomers and in television cameras to detect solid photons of light and to record visual images. Each CCD contains large numbers of light-sensitive electric circuits known as picture elements (or pixels). Each pixel stores an electronic charge proportional to the amount of light reaching it from the image focused on to the CCD. Following each exposure, additional circuits are used to control the transfer of the acquired data to computers for analysis. An image can then be built up on photographic film. **in charge,** on duty; responsible (for). **to give in charge,** to commit to the care of another; to hand over to the custody of a policeman. **to return to the charge,** to begin again. **to take in charge,** to arrest, to take into custody. **charge account,** *n.* a credit account at a shop. **charge hand,** *n.* a workman in charge of several other men. **charge nurse,** *n.* a nurse in charge of a ward. **charge-sheet,** *n.* a list of offenders taken into custody, with their offences, for the use of a police-magistrate. **chargeable,** *a.* liable to be charged or accused; liable to a monetary demand; liable to be an expense (to); imputable; capable of being properly charged (to); burdensome, costly; rateable. **chargeability,** *n.* chargeable expense. †**chargeful,** *a.* involving expense; costly. **chargeless,** *a.* free from charge. **charger,** *n.* one who charges; a war-horse; a cavalry horse; †a large dish. [F *charger,* L *carricāre,* (*carrus,* CAR)]

chargé d'affaires, chargé, *n.* (*pl.* **chargés d'affaires**) a diplomatic agent acting as deputy to an ambassador; an ambassador to a court of minor importance. [F, charged with affairs]

Charge of the Light Brigade, a disastrous charge of British Light Brigade of cavalry against the Russian entrenched artillery on 25 Oct. 1854 during the Crimean War at Balaclava.

charily, etc. CHARY.

chariot, *n.* (*chiefly poet.*) a car, a vehicle, a stately kind of vehicle; (*Hist.*) a light, four-wheeled pleasure carriage used in the 18th cent.; (*Hist.*) a carriage used in war, public triumphs and racing. *v.t.* (*poet.*) to convey in a chariot. *v.i.* (*poet*) to ride in a chariot. **chariot-race,** *n.* a race in chariots. **charioteer,** *n.* a chariot-driver. **charioteering,** *n.* the act, art or practice of driving a chariot. [OF *chariot,* augm. of *char,* CAR]

charisma, *n.* a divinely given power or talent; personal magnetism or charm enabling one to inspire or influence other people; a quality which inspires admiration or devotion. **charismatic,** *a.* [Gr *charis,* grace]

charity, *n.* love of one's fellow, one of the theological virtues; liberality to the poor; alms-giving; alms; an act of kindness; kindness, goodwill; liberality of judgment; leniency, tolerance of faults and offences; a foundation or institution for assisting the poor, the sick, or the helpless. **cold as charity,** cold-hearted, unsympathetic. †**charity-boy, -girl,** *n.* one brought up in a charity school or similar institution. **Charity Commissioners,** *n.pl.* members of a board instituted in 1853 for the control of charitable foundations. †**charity school,** *n.* an endowed school for the education of poor children, who usu. wore a distinctive dress. **charitable,** *a.* full of, pertaining to, or supported by charity; kind; liberal to the poor; benevolent, kindly, lenient, large-hearted; dictated by kindness. **charitableness,** *n.* **charitably,** *adv.* [OF *charité, charitet,* L *caritas -tātis* (*carus,* dear)]

charivari, *n.* a mock serenade of discordant music, intended to insult and annoy; a confusion of sounds, a hubbub; a satirical journal. [F, from late L *caribaria,* headache]

charlady CHAR[2].

charlatan, *n.* an empty pretender to skill or knowledge; a quack; an impostor. **charlatanic, -ical,** *a.* **charlatanically,** *adv.* **charlatanish,** *a.* **charlatanism, -tanry,** *n.* [F, from It. *ciarlatano* (*ciarlare,* to prattle)]

Charlemagne, *n.* **Charles I, the Great** (742–814), king of the Franks from 768 and Holy Roman Emperor from 800. By inheritance (his father was Pepin the Short) and extensive campaigns of conquest, he united most of W Europe by 804, when after 30 years of war the Saxons came under his control. He reformed the legal, judicial and military systems, established schools, promoted Christianity, commerce, agriculture, arts and literature. In his capital Aachen, scholars gathered from all over Europe.

Charles, *n.* seven rulers of the Holy Roman Empire:

Charles I, *n.* better known as the emperor Charlemagne.

Charles II, *n.* **the Bald** (823–877), Holy Roman Emperor from 875 and (as Charles II) king of France from 843. Younger son of Louis I (the Pious), he warred against his eldest brother, Emperor Lothair I. The Treaty of Verdun (843) made him king of the West Frankish Kingdom (modern France and the Spanish Marches).

Charles III, *n.* **the Fat** (839–888), Holy Roman Emperor 881–87; he became king of the West Franks in 885, thus uniting for the last time the whole of Charlemagne's dominions, but was deposed.

Charles IV *n.* (1316–78), Holy Roman Emperor from 1355 and king of Bohemia from 1346. Son of John of Luxembourg, king of Bohemia, he was elected king of Germany in 1346 and ruled all Germany from 1347. He was the founder of the first German university in Prague (1348).

Charles V, *n.* (1500–58), Holy Roman Emperor 1519–56. Son of Philip of Burgundy and Joanna of

Castile, he inherited vast possessions which led to rivalry from Francis I of France, whose alliance with the Ottoman Empire brought Vienna under siege in 1529 and 1532. Charles was also in conflict with the Protestants in Germany until the Treaty of Passau (1552), which allowed the Lutherans religious liberty.

Charles VI, *n.* (1685–1740), Holy Roman Emperor from 1711, father of Maria Theresa, whose succession to his Austrian dominions he tried to ensure, and himself claimant to the Spanish throne, 1700, thus causing the War of the Spanish Succession.

Charles VII, *n.* (1697–1745), Holy Roman Emperor from 1742, opponent of Maria Theresa's claim to the Austrian dominions of Charles VI.

Charles, *n.* ten kings of France, including:

Charles I, *n.* better known as Charlemagne.

Charles II, *n.* **the Bald**; see CHARLES II, Holy Roman Emperor.

Charles III, *n.* **the Simple** (879–929), king of France 893–922, son of Louis the Stammerer. He was crowned at Reims. In 911 he ceded what later became the duchy of Normandy to the Norman chief Rollo.

Charles IV, *n.* **the Fair** (1294–1328), king of France from 1322, when he succeeded Philip V as the last of the direct Capetian line.

Charles V, *n.* **the Wise** (1337–80), king of France from 1364. He was regent during the captivity of his father, John II, in England (1356–60), and became king on John's death. He reconquered nearly all France from England (1369–80).

Charles VI, *n.* **the Mad** or **the Well-Beloved** (1368–1422), king of France from 1380, succeeding his father Charles V, he was under the regency of his uncles until 1388. He became mentally unstable in 1392, and civil war broke out between the dukes of Orleans and Burgundy. Henry V of England invaded France in 1415, conquering Normandy, and in 1420 forcing Charles to sign the Treaty of Troyes, recognizing Henry as his successor.

Charles VII, *n.* (1403–61), king of France from 1429. Son of Charles VI, he was excluded from the succession by the Treaty of Troyes, but recognized by the South of France. In 1429 Joan of Arc raised the siege of Orléans and had him crowned at Reims. He organized France's first standing army and by 1453 he had expelled the English from all of France except Calais.

Charles VIII, *n.* (1470–98), king of France from 1483, when he succeeded his father, Louis XI. In 1494 he unsuccessfully tried to claim the Neapolitan crown, and when he entered Naples in 1495 was forced to withdraw by a coalition of Milan, Venice, Spain and the Holy Roman Empire. He defeated them at Fornovo, but lost Naples. He died while preparing a second expedition.

Charles IX, *n.* (1550–74), king of France from 1560. Second son of Henry II and Catherine de' Medici, he succeeded his brother Francis II at the age of ten, but remained under the domination of his mother for ten years while France was torn by religious wars. In 1570 he fell under the influence of the Huguenot leader Admiral Coligny (1517–72); alarmed by this, Catherine instigated his order for the Massacre of St Bartholomew, which led to a new religious war.

Charles X, *n.* (1757–1836), king of France from 1824. Grandson of Louis XV and brother of Louis XVI and Louis XVIII, he was known as the Count of Artois before his accession. He fled to England at the beginning of the French Revolution, and when he came to the throne on the death of Louis XVIII, he attempted to reverse the achievements of the Revolution. A revolt ensued in 1830, and he again fled to England.

Charles, *n.* (Spanish **Carlos**) four kings of Spain:

Charles I, *n.* (1500–58), see CHARLES V, Holy Roman Emperor.

Charles II, *n.* (1661–1700), king of Spain from 1665; second son of Philip IV, he was the last of the Spanish Habsburg kings. Mentally handicapped from birth, he bequeathed his dominions to Philip of Anjou, grandson of Louis XIV, which led to the War of the Spanish Succession.

Charles III, *n.* (1716–88), king of Spain from 1759. Son of Philip V, he became duke of Parma in 1732, and in 1734 conquered Naples and Sicily. On the death of his half-brother Ferdinand VI (1713–59), he became king of Spain, handing over Naples and Sicily to his son Ferdinand (1751–1825). During his reign Spain was twice at war with Britain: during the Seven Years' War, when he sided with France and lost Florida; and when he backed the Americans in the War of Independence and regained it. At home he carried out a programme of reforms and expelled the Jesuits.

Charles IV, *n.* (1748–1819), king of Spain from 1788, when he succeeded his father, Charles III, but left the government in the hands of his wife and her lover, the minister Manuel de Godoy (1767–1851). In 1808 Charles was induced to abdicate by Napoleon's machinations in favour of his son Ferdinand VII (1784–1833), who was subsequently deposed by Napoleon's brother Joseph. Charles was awarded a pension by Napoleon, and died in Rome.

Charles, *n.* two kings of Britain:

Charles I, *n.* (1600–1649), king of Great Britain and Ireland from 1625, son of James I of England (James VI of Scotland). He accepted the Petition of Right in 1628, but then dissolved Parliament and ruled without one, 1629–40. His advisers were Strafford and Laud, who persecuted the Puritans and provoked the Scots to revolt. The Short Parliament, summoned 1640, refused funds, and the Long Parliament later that year rebelled. Charles declared war on Parliament in 1642 but surrendered in 1646 and was beheaded 1649. He was the father of Charles II.

Charles II, *n.* (1630–85), king of Great Britain and Ireland from 1660, when Parliament accepted the restoration of the monarchy; son of Charles I. His chief minister Clarendon arranged his marriage in 1662 with Catherine of Braganza, but was replaced 1667 with the Cabal of advisers. His plans to restore Catholicism in Britain led to war with the Netherlands (1672–74) and a break with Parliament, which he dissolved in 1681. He was succeeded by James II.

Charles, *n.* (Swedish **Carl**) 15 kings of Sweden. The first six were local chieftains.

Charles VIII, *n.* king of Sweden from 1448. He was elected regent of Sweden in 1438, when Sweden broke away from Denmark and Norway. He stepped down in 1441 when Christopher III of Bavaria (1418–48) was elected king, but after his death became king. He was twice expelled by the Danes and twice restored.

Charles IX, *n.* (1550–1611), king of Sweden from 1604, the youngest son of Gustavus Vasa. In 1568 he and his brother John led the rebellion against Eric XIV (1533–77); John became king as John III, and attempted to Catholicize Sweden, and Charles led the opposition. John's son Sigismund, king of Poland and a Catholic, succeeded to the Swedish throne in 1592, and Charles led the Protestants. He was made regent in 1595, and deposed Sigismund in 1599. Charles was elected king of Sweden 1604. He was involved in unsuccessful wars with Russia, Poland and Denmark. He was the father of Gustavus Adolphus.

Charles X, *n.* (1622–60), king of Sweden from 1654, when he succeeded his cousin Christina. He waged war with Poland and Denmark, and in 1657 invaded Denmark by leading his army over the frozen sea.

Charles XI, *n.* (1655–97), king of Sweden from 1660, when he succeeded his father Charles X. His mother acted as regent until 1672 when Charles took over the government. He was a remarkable general, and reformed the administration.

Charles XII, *n.* (1682–1718), king of Sweden from 1697, when he succeeded his father, Charles XI. From 1700 he was involved in wars with Denmark, Poland and Russia. He won a succession of victories, until in 1709 while invading Russia, he was defeated at Poltava in the Ukraine, and forced to take refuge in Turkey until 1714. He was killed while besieging Fredrikshall.

Charles XIII, *n.* (1748–1818), king of Sweden from

1809, when he was elected; he became the first king of Sweden and Norway in 1814.

Charles XIV, *n.* **(Jean Baptiste Jules Bernadotte)** (1763–1844), king of Sweden and Norway from 1818. A former marshal in the French army, in 1810 he was elected crown prince of Sweden, under the name of Charles John (*Carl Johan*). Loyal to his adopted country, he brought Sweden into the alliance against Napoleon in 1813, as a reward for which Sweden received Norway. He was the founder of the present dynasty.

Charles XV, *n.* (1826–72), king of Sweden and Norway from 1859, when he succeeded his father Oscar I. A popular and liberal monarch, his main achievement was the reform of the constitution.

Charles, *n.* (full name **Charles Philip Arthur George)** (1948–), prince of the United Kingdom, heir to the British throne, and Prince of Wales since 1958 (invested 1969). He is the first-born child of Queen Elizabeth II and the Duke of Edinburgh. He studied at Trinity College, Cambridge, 1967–70, before serving in the RAF and Royal Navy. He is the first royal heir since 1659 to have an English wife, Lady Diana Spencer, daughter of the 8th Earl Spencer. They have two sons: Prince William, born 1982, and Prince Henry, born 1984.

Charles, *n.* **(Karl Franz Josef)** (1887–1922), emperor of Austria and king of Hungary from 1916, the last of the Habsburg emperors. He succeeded his great-uncle, Franz Josef, in 1916, but was forced to withdraw to Switzerland in 1918, although he refused to abdicate. In 1921 he attempted unsuccessfully to regain the crown of Hungary and was deported to Madeira, where he died.

Charles Albert, *n.* (1798–1849), king of Sardinia from 1831. He showed liberal sympathies in early life, and after his accession introduced some reforms. On the outbreak of the 1848 revolution he granted a constitution and declared war on Austria. His troops were defeated at Custozza and Novara. In 1849 he abdicated in favour of his son Victor Emmanuel and retired to a monastery, where he died.

Charles Augustus, *n.* (1757–1828), grand duke of Saxe-Weimar in Germany. He succeeded his father in infancy, fought against the French in 1792–94 and 1806, and was the patron and friend of the writer Goethe.

Charles Edward Stuart, *n.* (1720–88), British prince, known as the Young Pretender or Bonnie Prince Charlie, grandson of James II. In the Jacobite rebellion of 1745 Charles won the support of the Scottish Highlanders and his army invaded England, but was beaten back by the Duke of Cumberland and routed at Culloden in 1746.

Charles Martel, *n.* (*c.* 688–741), Frankish ruler (Mayor of the Palace) of the east of the Frankish kingdom from 717 and the whole kingdom from 731. His victory against the Moors (732) between Poitiers and Tours earned him his nickname of Martel, 'the Hammer', and halted the Islamic advance into Europe. An illegitimate son of Pepin of Heristal (Pepin II, Mayor of the Palace (*c.* 640–714), he was grandfather of Charlemagne.

Charles the Bold, Duke of Burgundy (1433–77), son of Philip the Good, he inherited Burgundy and the Low Countries from him in 1465. He waged wars attempting to free the duchy from dependence on France and restore it as a kingdom. He was killed in battle.

Charles, *n.* **Jacques Alexandre César** (1746–1823), French physicist, who studied gases and made the first ascent in a hydrogen-filled balloon in 1783. His work on the expansion of gases led to the formulation of Charles' law.

Charles, *n.* **(Mary) Eugenia** (1919–), Dominican politician, prime minister from 1980.

Charles, *n.* **Ray** (1930–), US singer, songwriter and pianist, whose first hits were 'I've Got A Woman' (1955), 'What'd I Say' (1959), and 'Georgia on My Mind' (1960). He has recorded gospel, blues, rock, soul, country, and rhythm and blues.

Charles's law, *n.* a law stated by Jacques Charles in 1787, and independently by Joseph Gay-Lussac (1778–1850) in 1802, which states that the volume of a given mass of gas at constant pressure increases by 1/273 of its volume at 0°C for each °C rise of temperature, that is, the coefficient of expansion of all gases is the same. The law is only approximately true and the coefficient of expansion is generally taken as 0.003663 per °C.

Charles's wain, *n.* seven stars in the constellation the Great Bear, also called the Plough. [OE *Carles wægn,* the wain of *Carl* (Charlemagne); perh. from confusion of *Arcturus* (the neighbouring constellation) with *Arturus* and association of King Arthur and Charlemagne]

Charleston, *n.* a strenuous dance in 4/4 time with characteristic kicking outwards of the lower part of the legs. [Charleston, S Carolina]

Charlie, *n.* (*sl.*) an utterly foolish person, often in *a proper Charlie*. [var. of *Charles*]

charlock, *n.* the wild mustard, *Sinapis arvensis*. [OE *cerlic*]

charlotte, *n.* a kind of pudding made of fruit and thin slices of the crumb of bread. **charlotte russe,** *n.* custard or whipped cream enclosed in sponge cake. [F perh. from the fem. name; *russe,* Russian]

Charlotte Amalie, *n.* capital and tourist resort of the US Virgin Islands; population (1980) 11,756.

Charlotte Augusta, *n.* **Princess** (1796–1817), only child of George IV and Caroline of Brunswick, and heir to the British throne. In 1816 she married Prince Leopold of Saxe-Coburg (later Leopold I of the Belgians), but died in childbirth 18 months later.

Charlotte Sophia, *n.* (1744–1818), British queen consort. The daughter of the German duke of Mecklenburg-Strelitz, she married George III of Great Britain and Ireland in 1761, and bore him nine sons and six daughters.

Charlottetown, *n.* capital of Prince Edward Island, Canada; population (1986) 16,000. The city trades in textiles, fish, timber, vegetables and dairy produce. It was founded by the French in the 1720s.

Charlton[1], *n.* **Jack** (1935–), English footballer, older brother of Robert (Bobby) and nephew of Jackie Milburn. He spent all his playing career with Leeds United and played more than 750 games for them.

Charlton[2], *n.* **Robert 'Bobby'** (1937–), English footballer, younger brother of Jack Charlton, who scored a record 49 goals in 106 appearances. He spent most of his playing career with Manchester United.

charm[1], *n.* a spell, an enchantment; a thing, act or formula having magical power; an article worn to avert evil or ensure good luck, an amulet; a power or gift of alluring, pleasing or exciting love or desire; a pleasing or attractive feature; a trinket worn on a bracelet. *v.t.* to enchant, to fascinate, to bewitch; to attract, to delight; (*coll.*) to please; (*usu. pass.*) to protect with occult power; to remove by charms (with *away*). *v.i.* to use charms. **like a charm,** perfectly. **charmer,** *n.* one who uses charms; one who fascinates. **charmful,** *a.* full of charms; charming. **charming,** *a.* highly pleasing; delightful. **charmingly,** *adv.* **charmingness,** *n.* **charmless,** *a.* [OF *charme,* L *carmen,* a song]

charm[2], *n.* a blended noise or confusion of voices, as of birds or children. [from obs. v. *chirm,* OE *cirman,* to shout]

charnel-house, *n.* a place where dead bodies or the bones of the dead are deposited. [OF *charnel,* carnal, a cemetery, late L *carnāle,* a graveyard, neut. of *carnālis,* CARNAL]

Charon, *n.* the son of Erebus and Nox, who ferried departed spirits across the Styx into Hades; a ferryman. [Gr. *Charōn*]

Charpentier[1], *n.* **Gustave** (1860–1956), French composer who wrote an opera about Paris working-class life, *Louise* (1900).

Charpentier[2], *n.* **Marc-Antoine** (1645–1704), French composer. He wrote sacred music including a number of masses; other works include instrumental theatre music and the opera *Médée* (1693).

charpoy, *n.* a light Indian bedstead. [Urdu *chārpāi,* Pers. *chahārpāi,* four-footed]

charqui, *n.* beef cut into strips and dried in the sun, jerked beef. **charqued,** *a.* [Quechua *charqui*]

charr, CHAR[1].

chart, *n.* a map of some part of the sea, with coasts, islands, rocks, shoals etc., for the use of sailors; a statement of facts in tabular form; a projection of relative facts, statistics or observations in the form of a graphic curve; a skeleton map for special purposes, e.g. *heliographic chart;* (*often pl.*) a weekly list of best-selling records. *v.t.* to make a chart; to map. **chartaceous,** *a.* resembling paper. **chartless,** *a.* without a chart. [F *charte,* L *charta, carta,* Gr. *chartē,* a sheet of papyrus (cp. CARD[1])]

charter, *n.* a deed, an instrument; an instrument in writing granted by the sovereign or Parliament, incorporating a borough, company or institution, or conferring certain rights and privileges; privilege, exemption; a charter-party; the People's Charter, embodying the demands of the Chartists. *a.* of an aircraft, hired; of a flight, made in a hired aircraft. *v.t.* to establish by charter; to license by charter; to hire or let by charter-party; (*coll.*) to hire. **charter-land,** *n.* land held by charter; professionally qualified to the standards set by a chartered professional body, as in *chartered accountant.* [OF *chartre,* late L *chartula,* dim. of prec.]

Charter 88, *n.* British political campaign begun in 1988, calling for a written constitution to prevent what it termed the development of 'an elective dictatorship'. Those who signed the Charter, including many figures from the arts, objected to what they saw as the autocratic premiership of Prime Minister Margaret Thatcher.

Charterhouse, *n.* †a Carthusian monastery; a hospital and school founded in London on the site of a Carthusian monastery, now removed. [A-F *chart rouse* (see CHARTREUSE)]

charter-party, *n.* an agreement in writing concerning the hire and freight of a vessel. [F *charte partie,* divided document]

Chartism, *n.* a radical British democratic movement, mainly of the working classes, which flourished around 1838–50. It derived its name from the People's Charter, a programme comprising six points: universal male suffrage, equal electoral districts, vote by ballot, annual parliaments, abolition of the property qualification for, and payment of, Members of Parliament. **Chartist,** *n.* [L *charta,* -ISM]

chartography, etc. CARTOGRAPHY.

chartreuse, *n.* a pale green or yellow liqueur made by the monks at la Grande Chartreuse.

Chartreuse, La Grande, the original home of the Carthusian order of Roman Catholic monks, established by St Bruno around 1084, in a remote valley 23 km/14 miles NNE of Grenoble (in the modern *département* of Isère), France. The present buildings date from the 17th cent.

chartulary CARTULARY.

charwoman CHAR[2].

chary, *a.* wary, prudent, cautious, frugal, sparing. **charily,** *adv.* **chariness,** *n.* [OE *cearig* (*cearu, caru,* care, sorrow, OTeut. *Karā*) cp. OHG *charag,* G. *karg,* sparing]

Charybdis, *n.* a dangerous whirlpool off the coast of Sicily, opposite Scylla, a rock on the Italian shore; one of a pair of alternative risks. [L, from Gr. *Charubdis*]

Chas., (*abbr.*) Charles.

chase[1], *v.t.* to pursue; to hunt; to drive away; to put to flight. *v.i.* to ride or run rapidly. *n.* earnest pursuit; the hunting of wild animals; that which is chased; an open hunting-ground or preserve for game; in real tennis where the ball completes its first bound. **to chase up,** (*coll.*) to pursue or investigate in order to obtain information etc. **chase-gun, bow-chaser, stern-chaser,** *n.* a gun mounted at the bow or stern, used for attack or defence. **chaser,** *n.* a chase-gun; a horse used for steeplechasing; a drink of one kind taken after one of another kind. [OF *chacier,* late L *captiāre* (see CATCH)]

chase[2], *v.t.* to engrave, to emboss; to cut the worm of (a screw). **chaser,** *n.* an enchaser; a tool used in screw cutting. **chasing,** *n.* the art of embossing metals; the pattern embossed. [earlier *enchase,* F *enchâsser* (*en,* L *in, châsse,* L *capsa,* CASE[1])]

chase[3], *n.* a rectangular iron frame in which type is locked for printing. [F *châsse,* L *capsa,* CASE[1]]

chase[4], *n.* a wide groove; the part of a gun in front of the trunnions. [F *chas,* late L *capsum,* an enclosure (cp. *capsa,* CASE[1]), from *capere,* to hold]

chasm, *n.* a cleft, a fissure, a rent, a yawning gulf; a break of continuity; a breach or division between persons or parties; a gap or void. **chasmed,** *a.* having chasms. **chasmy,** *a.* abounding with chasms. [L and Gr. *chasma,* from *chaskein,* to gape]

chasse, *n.* a liqueur after coffee. [F *chasse-café,* chase-coffee (*chasser,* to chase)]

chassé, *n.* a gliding step in dancing. *v.i.* to perform this step. *v.t.* (*sl.*) to dismiss. [F, chasing, gliding (*chasser,* see prec.)]

chassepot, *n.* a breech-loading needle-gun in use in France, 1866–74. [name of its F inventor Antoine *Chassepot,* 1833–1905]

chasseur, *n.* a huntsman; a light-armed French soldier; an attendant on persons of rank, wearing a military uniform. *a.* cooked in a sauce of white wine and mushrooms. [F, from *chasser,* to chase, hunt]

chassis, *n.* (*pl.* **chassis**) the base-frame of a gun in a barbette or battery; the framework of a motor-car, aeroplane etc.; a framework supporting a piece of electronic equipment. [F, *châssis* late L *capsum* (cp. CHASE[4])]

chaste, *a.* abstaining from all sexual intercourse, or from sex outside marriage; modest, innocent, virginal; free from obscenity; pure in style; simple, unadorned, unaffected. **chastely,** *adv.* **chastity,** *n.* the state of being chaste; virginity; purity of taste and style; celibacy. [OF, from L *castus,* pure]

chasten, *v.t.* to punish with a view to reformation; to correct; to discipline; to purify, to refine, to subdue. **chastener,** *n.* [from obs. v. *chasty,* OF *chastier,* L *castīgāre* (*castus,* chaste), or from prec., -EN]

chastise, *v.t.* to punish, esp. physically; to correct an offence or wrong; to chasten; to refine; to revise and correct. **chastisement,** *n.* **chastiser,** *n.* [ME *chastien,* chasten, later *chasty* (see prec.), -IZE (formation obscure)]

chastity CHASTE.

chasuble, *n.* a sleeveless vestment worn by a priest over the alb while celebrating Mass. [F, from med. L *casubla, casubula,* dim. of *casa,* a little house]

chat[1], *v.i.* (*past, p.p.* **chatted**) to talk easily and familiarly; to gossip. **to chat up,** (*sl.*) to chat to in order to establish a (sexual) relationship. **chatline,** *n.* a telephone service where callers unknown to each other are connected for informal conversation. **chat show,** *n.* a television show in which a host(ess) interviews celebrities informally. **chatty[1],** *a.* **chattiness,** *n.* [short for CHATTER]

chat[2], *n.* the name of various birds, mostly Sylviadae or warblers, e.g. *whinchat.* [from prec.]

chateau, *n.* (*pl.* **-teaux**) a castle; a country house in French-speaking countries. [F, from OF *castel,* CASTLE]

Chateaubriand, *n.* **François René, vicomte de** (1768–1848), French author. In exile from the French Revolution (1794–99), he wrote *Atala* (1801) (written after his encounters with North American Indians); and the autobiographical *René,* which formed part of *Le Génie du Christianisme/The Genius of Christianity* (1802).

chatelaine, *n.* a chain worn on a woman's belt, to which may be attached a watch, keys, trinkets, etc. [F, mistress of chateau]

chatoyant, *a.* having a changeable lustre or colour, like that of a cat's eye in the dark. *n.* a stone with changing lustre like the cat's eye. [F, pres. p. of *chatoyer* (*chat,* cat)]

chattel, *n.* (*usu. pl.*) moveable property; any article of property except such as is freehold. [OF *chatel,* CATTLE]

chatter, *v.i.* to utter rapid, inharmonious sounds like a magpie, jay etc.; to make a noise by or like the rattling together of the teeth; to talk idly and thoughtlessly; to jabber, to prattle. *n.* sounds like those of a magpie, jay etc.; idle talk. **chatterbox,** *n.* an incessant talker. **chatterer,** *n.* one who chatters; name given to birds belonging to the family Ampelidae. **the chattering classes,** (*derog.*) a set of people who spend much time in discussion rather than in action; people who regard themselves as having informed opinions and ideas, e.g. about the arts or politics. [onomat.]

Chatterton, *n.* **Thomas** (1752–70), English poet, whose mediaeval-style poems and brief life were to inspire English Romanticism. Born in Bristol, he studied ancient documents he found in the Church of St Mary Redcliffe, and composed poems he ascribed to a 15th-century monk, 'Thomas Rowley', which were accepted as genuine. He committed suicide in London, after becoming destitute.

chatty[1] CHAT[1].

chatty[2], *n.* an Indian earthen pitcher or water-pot. [Hind. *chātī*]

Chatwin, *n.* **Bruce** (1940–89), English writer. His works include *The Songlines* (1987), written after living with nomadic Aborigines, and *Utz* (1988), a novel about a manic porcelain collector in Prague.

Chaucer, *n.* **Geoffrey** (*c.* 1340–1400), English poet. Author of *The Canterbury Tales*, (about 1387), a collection of tales told by pilgrims on their way to the Thomas Becket shrine, he was the most influential English poet of the Middle Ages. The popularity of his work assured the dominance of southern English in literature. Chaucer's other work includes the French-influenced *Romance of the Rose* and an adaptation of Boccaccio's *Troilus and Criseyde*.

Chaucerian, *a.* pertaining or relating to the poet Chaucer; resembling his style. *n.* a student of Chaucer. **Chaucerism**, *n.* a characteristic or mannerism of Chaucer or imitated from Chaucer. [Geoffrey *Chaucer* see prec.]

chaudfroid, *n.* a dish of cold meat in an aspic sauce. [F, lit. hot-cold]

chaudron, CHALDRON.

chauffeur, *n.* a person employed to drive a motor-car. *v.t., v.i.* to act as driver (for). **chauffeuse**, *n. fem.* [F *chauffer,* to heat]

chausses, *n.pl.* a kind of trunk-hose; armour for the leg. [F, from med. L *calcias,* pl. of *calcia,* leggings, breeches (L *calceus,* shoe)]

chauvinism, *n.* exaggerated patriotism of an aggressive kind; jingoism, an exaggerated and excessive attachment to any cause, such as sexism. **chauvinist,** *n.* one who believes his own race, sex etc. to be superior and despises all others, as in *male chauvinist*. **chauvinistic**, *a.* [F *chauvinisme,* from Nicolas *Chauvin,* an old soldier devotedly attached to Napoleon]

chaw, *v.t.* to chew. *n.* a quid of tobacco. **to chaw up,** (*N Am., sl.*) to defeat completely, to smash up. **chaw-bacon,** *n.* (*coll.*) a yokel. [CHEW]

†**chawdron,** *n.* intestines; entrails of an animal used as food. [ME *chaudoun,* OF *chaudun,* prob. from a late L *caldūnum* (cp. *caldūna,* perh. from L *caldus, calidus,* warm)]

chay, *n.* (*coll.*) a chaise, see also SHAY. [corr. of CHAISE (taken as a pl.)]

Chayefsky, *n.* **(Sidney) 'Paddy'** (1923–81), US writer. He established his reputation with the television plays *Marty* (1955) (for which he won an Oscar when he turned it into a film), and *Bachelor Party* (1957). He also won Oscars for *The Hospital* (1971) and *Network* (1976).

chay root, chaya root, *n.* the root of an Indian plant, *Oldenlandia umbellata,* which furnishes a red dye. [Tamil *saya*]

ChB, (*abbr.*) Bachelor of Surgery. [L *Chirurgiae Baccalaureus*]

cheap, *a.* low in price; worth more than its price or cost; easy to get; easily got; of small value or esteem. **on the cheap,** cheaply; in a miserly way. **cheap and nasty,** low in price and quality. **to get cheap,** to purchase at a low price; to obtain easily. **to hold cheap,** to despise. **to make oneself cheap,** to behave with undignified familiarity. **cheap-jack,** *n.* a travelling hawker, esp. one who sells by Dutch auction. *a.* cheap; inferior. **cheap-skate,** *n.* (*coll.*) a miserly person. **cheapen,** *v.t.* to beat down the price or value of; to depreciate. *v.i.* to become cheap; to depreciate. **cheapener,** *n.* one who bargains or haggles. **cheapish,** *a.* **cheaply,** *adv.* **cheapness,** *n.* [ME phrase *good cheap* (cp. F *bon marché*), OE *ceap,* price, barter]

cheat, *n.* a fraud, an imposition; a swindle, a fraudulent card-game; a trickster, a swindler. *v.t.* to defraud, to deprive of; to deceive; to impose upon. *v.i.* to act as a cheat. **cheater,** *n.* one who cheats or defrauds. [short for ESCHEAT]

check[1], *n.* a sudden stoppage, arrest or restraint of motion; the person, thing or means of arrest; a reverse, a repulse; a pause, a halt; restraint, repression; a mark put against names or items in going over a list; a token by which the correctness or authenticity of a document etc. may be ascertained; a test for accuracy etc.; a token serving for identification; a pass entitling to readmission to a theatre; a term in chess when one player obliges the other to move or guard his king; the situation of such a king; (*N Am.*) a bill at a restaurant etc.; (*N Am.*) a token at cards; (*N Am.*) a left-luggage ticket. *v.t.* to arrest; to cause to stop; to repress, to curb; to rebuke; to test the accuracy of, esp. by comparison with a list; in chess, to put an opponent's king in check; to ease off (as a rope). *v.i.* to pause, to halt; to agree, correspond (with). *int.* a call when an opponent's king is exposed (see CHECKMATE); a term expressing agreement or identicalness. **to check in,** to register on arrival at a hotel, at work etc. **to check out,** to leave a hotel,, place of work etc.; to test for accuracy, to investigate. **to check up,** to investigate, to test (often with *on*). **to hand, pass in one's checks,** to die. **check-action,** *n.* a device for preventing the hammer in a piano from striking twice. **check bit, digit,** *n.* in computing, a bit or digit used to detect error. **check-in,** *n.* a place where one's arrival is registered. **check-list,** *n.* one used in checking for accuracy, completeness etc.; an inventory. **check-nut,** *n.* a cap screwed over a nut to keep it from working loose. **check-out,** *n.* a cash desk at a supermarket. **checkpoint,** *n.* a place (as at a frontier) where documents etc. are checked. **check-receiver,** *n.* a device for checking the quality of radio transmission. **check-rein,** *n.* a bearing-rein; a branch rein coupling horses in a team. **check-string,** *n.* a cord by which the occupant of a closed carriage signals to the driver. **check-taker,** *n.* a collector of tickets etc. **check-up,** *n.* a general examination (esp. medical). **check-valve,** *n.* a valve that allows a flow in only one direction. **checker**[1], *n.* [OF *eschec,* Arab. *shāg,* Pers. *shāh,* a king]

check[2], *n.* a chequered pattern; a cross-lined pattern; a chequered fabric. **checked,** *a.* [short for *checker*[2], CHEQUER]

check[3], (*N Am.*) CHEQUE. **checking account,** *n.* (*N Am.*) a current account.

checker[1] CHECK[1].

checker[2] CHEQUER.

checkmate, *n.* in chess, the winning movement when one king is in check and cannot escape from that position; a complete defeat; a position from which there is no escape. *int.* the call when an opponent's king is put into this position. *v.t.* to give checkmate to; to defeat utterly, to frustrate. [OF *eschec mat,* Pers. *shāh māt,* the king is dead; see CHECK[1]]

Cheddar, *n.* a hard, strong-flavoured yellow cheese. **Cheddar-pink,** *n.* a pink, *Dianthus caesius,* found on the limestone rocks at Cheddar. [village in Somerset, near the Mendip Hills]

cheek, *n.* the side of the face below the eye; (*coll.*) impudence, sauciness; effrontery, assurance; impudent speech; one of two corresponding sides of a frame, machine, or implement; a side-post of a door, the side of a pulley; (*sl.*) a buttock. *v.t.* to be impudent to. *v.i.* to be saucy. **cheek by jowl,** side by side; in the closest proximity. **cheek-bone,** *n.* the prominence of the malar bone. **cheek-tooth,** *n.* a molar tooth. **cheeker,** *n.* **cheeky,** *a.* impudent, saucy. **cheekily,** *adv.* **cheekiness,** *n.* [OE *cēace,* from Teut. (cp. Dut. *kaak,* Swed. *kāk*)]

cheep, *v.i.* to chirp feebly (as a young bird). *n.* the feeble cry of a young bird. **cheeper,** *n.* a young game bird. [onomat.]

cheer, *n.* disposition, the frame of mind, esp. as shown by the face; entertainment, good fare, a state of gladness or joy; a shout of joy or applause; †the face, the countenance; the expression of the face. *v.t.* to make glad or cheerful (often with *up*); to applaud, to encourage, to incite (as dogs). *v.i.* to grow cheerful (with *up*); to utter cheers. **cheer-leader,** *n.* (*N Am.*) a girl who leads organized cheering at a rally, football game etc. **cheerful,** *a.* contented, hopeful; full of good spirits; lively, animated; willing. **cheerfully,** *adv.* **cheerfulness,** *n.* **cheering,** *a.* **cheeringly,** *adv.* **cheerio, cheer-ho,** *int.* good-bye, au revoir; a drinking toast. **cheerless,** *a.* dull, gloomy, dispiriting. **cheerlessness,** *n.* **cheerly,** *adv.* (*Naut.*) cheerfully, heartily. **cheers,** *int.* a drinking toast; thank-you; good-bye. **cheery,** *a.* lively, sprightly, full of good spirits, genial. **cheerily,** *adv.* (*Naut.*) **cheeriness,** *n.* [ME and OF *chere,* the face, look, late L *cara,* face, perh. from Gr. *kara,* head]

cheese[1], *n.* the curd of milk pressed into a solid mass and ripened by keeping; a cylindrical or spherical block of this; the unripe fruit of the mallow; anything of cheese-like form. **hard cheese,** (*coll.*) hard luck. **say cheese,** used by photographers to encourage people to smile. **to make cheeses,** to whirl round and sink suddenly so as to make the petticoats stand out. **cheese-board,** *n.* a board on which cheese is served at table; the variety of cheeses on such a board. **cheeseburger,** *n.* a hamburger with a slice of cheese on top. **cheesecake,** *n.* a kind of tart made of pastry or crumbs with a filling of cream cheese, sugar etc.; (pictures of) young and shapely women, esp. scantily clad or nude. **cheesecloth,** *n.* thin cotton cloth loosely woven; butter muslin. **cheese-cutter,** *n.* a knife with broad curved blade. **cheese-fly,** *n.* a fly, *Piophila casei,* bred in cheese. **cheese-hopper,** *n.* the larva of the cheese-fly. **cheese-mite,** *n.* a minute acarid, *Acarus domesticus,* infesting old cheese and other food-stuffs. **cheese-monger,** *n.* one who deals in cheese. **cheese-paring,** *a.* niggardly, mean, miserly. *n.* (*pl.*) scraps of cheese; (*pl.*) odds and ends; meanness, stinginess. **cheese-plate,** *n.* a small plate used for cheese at the end of a meal; (*facet.*) a large button. **cheese-press, -wring,** *n.* the press in which the curds are pressed in making cheese. **cheese-rennet,** *n.* the lady's bedstraw, *Galium verum,* used to coagulate milk. **cheese straw,** *n.* a long, thin, cheese-flavoured biscuit. **cheese-taster,** *n.* a gouge-like knife for scooping pieces of cheese as samples. **cheese-vat,** *n.* the vat in which curds are pressed. **cheese-wood,** *n.* an Australian tree with a hard wood of a cheese colour. **cheesy,** *a.* resembling or tasting like cheese. **cheesiness,** *n.* [OE *cēse* (cp. Dut *kaas,* G *Käse,* L *cāseus*)]

cheese[2], *n.* (*sl.*) the real thing, the correct thing. **big cheese,** (*sl.*) an important person. [etym. doubtful]

cheese[3], *v.t.* (*sl.*) stop. **cheesed off,** (*coll.*) bored, annoyed. [etym. unknown]

cheetah, *n.* the hunting leopard, *Cynaelurus jubatus.* [Hind. *chītā* (Sansk. *chitraka,* spotted)]

Cheever, *n.* **John** (1912–82), US writer. His short stories and novels include *The Wapshot Chronicle* (1937), *Bullet Park* (1969), *World of Apples* (1973), and *Falconer* (1977).

chef, *n.* a head or professional cook. **chef de cuisine,** a head cook. [F, CHIEF]

chef-d'oeuvre, *n.* (*pl.* **chefs-**) a masterpiece. [as prec., F *oeuvre,* work]

cheil(o)- CHIL(O)-.

cheir(o)- CHIR(O)-.

cheiroptera, *n.pl.* a group of mammals with membranes connecting their fingers and used as wings, consisting of the bats. **cheiropteran,** *n.* **cheiropterous,** *a.* [CHIR(O)-, Gr. *pteron,* wing, *ptera,* wings]

Cheka, *n.* secret police operating in the USSR 1918–23. It originated from the tsarist Okhrana and became successively the OGPU (GPU) 1923–34, NKVD 1934–46, and MVD 1946–53, before its present form, the KGB. [names of initial letters of Rus. *Chrezvichainaya Kommissiya,* extraordinary commission]

Chekhov, *n.* **Anton (Pavlovich)** (1860–1904), Russian dramatist and writer. He began to write short stories and comic sketches as a medical student. His plays concentrate on the creation of atmosphere and delineation of internal development, rather than external action. His first play *Ivanov* (1887) was a failure, as was *The Seagull* (1896) until revived by Stanislavsky in 1898 at the Moscow Arts Theatre, for which Chekhov went on to write his major plays *Uncle Vanya* (1899), *The Three Sisters* (1901) and *The Cherry Orchard* (1904).

chela[1], *n.* (*pl.* **-lae**) a claw (as of a lobster or crab), a modified thoracic limb. **chelate,** *a.* [Gr. *chēlē*]

chela[2], *n.* a student or novice in esoteric Buddhism. [Hind. *chēlā,* servant, pupil]

cheli-, *comb. form.* pertaining to a claw or claws.

chelicer, *n.* (*pl.* **-rae**) one of the claw-like antennae of scorpions and spiders. **cheliceral,** *a.* [F *chélicère,* mod. L *chelicera* (Gr. *chēlē,* claw, *keras,* horn)]

chelidonic, *a.* pertaining to the celandine or swallowwort. **chelidonine,** *n.* [L *chelīdonium,* Gr. *chelidonion,* from *chelidōn,* swallow]

chelifer, *n.* a genus of arachnids or spiders, resembling small tailless scorpions. **cheliferous,** *a.* [L *-fer,* bearing]

cheliform, *a.* like a claw in form or shape.

cheliped, *n.* one of the pair of legs carrying chelae.

Chellean, *a.* of or pertaining to the period of Lower Palaeolithic culture typified by the remains found at Chelles in the valley of the Marne. [*Chelles,* 13 km E of Paris, -AN]

Chelonia, *n.pl.* an order of reptiles containing the turtles and tortoises. **chelonian,** *n., a.* [L, from Gr. *chelōnē,* tortoise]

Chelsea bun, *n.* a bun made of a roll of sweet dough with raisins. **Chelsea ware,** *n.* a type of 18th-cent. china. [name of a district in London]

Chelsea porcelain factory, thought to be the first porcelain factory in England. Based in SW London, it dates from the 1740s and produced softpaste porcelain in imitation of Chinese high-fired porcelain. Later items are distinguishable by the anchor mark on the base.

Chelyabinsk, *n.* industrial town and capital of Chelyabinsk region, W Siberia, USSR; population (1987) 1,119,000. It has iron and engineering works, and makes chemicals, motor vehicles and aircraft.

chem(i)-, chemic(o)-, chem(o)- *comb. forms.* chemical.

chemical, *a.* pertaining to chemistry, its laws, or phenomena; of or produced by chemical process. *n.* a substance or agent produced by or used in chemical processes. **chemical change,** *n.* a change involving the formation of a new substance. **chemical engineering,** *n.* the branch of engineering concerned with the design and building of industrial chemical plants. **chemical reaction,** *n.* the process of changing one substance into another. **chemical symbol,** *n.* a letter or letters used to represent an atom of a chemical element. **chemical warfare,** *n.* war waged using poisonous chemicals (gases, sprays etc.). **chemically,** *adv.* [F *chimique,* or mod. L *chymicus* (see ALCHEMY)]

chemico-electric, *a.* pertaining to or produced by chemistry in conjunction with electricity.

chemiluminescence, *n.* luminescence occurring as a result of a chemical reaction, without production of heat.

chemin de fer, a variety of baccarat. [F, railway]

chemise, *n.* a body garment of linen or cotton worn next to the skin by women. **chemisette,** *n.* a woman's light bodice; lace-work worn in the opening of a dress below the throat. [F, from late L *camisia* (cp. OE *ham,* Goth. *af-hamōn,* to unclothe)]

chemism, *n.* chemical attraction or affinity considered as a form of energy.

chemist, *n.* one versed in chemistry; one qualified to dispense drugs, a pharmacist. **analytical chemist,** a chemist who carries out the process of analysis by chemical means. [F *chimiste,* mod. L *chimista, chymista, alchimista,* ALCHEMIST]

chemistry, *n.* the science which investigates the elements of which bodies are composed, the combination of these elements, and the reaction of these chemical compounds on each other (**inorganic chemistry** deals with mineral substances, **organic chemistry** with animal and vegetable substances); the practical application of this science; any process or change conceived as analogous to chemical action, esp. emotional attraction. [as prec.]

chemitype, *n.* a process by which a drawing or impression from an engraved plate is obtained in relief, to be employed in printing.

chemmy, *n.* CHEMIN DE FER.

chemo-, *comb. form.* CHEM(I).

chemolysis, *n.* chemical decomposition or analysis. **chemolytic,** *a.* [Gr. *lusis,* loosening, from *luein,* to loosen]

chemoreceptor, *n.* a sensory nerve-ending which responds to a chemical stimulus.

chemosynthesis, *n.* the production of organic material by some bacteria, using chemical reactions.

chemotaxis, *n.* the property possessed by some mobile cells of being drawn towards or repelled by certain chemical substances.

chemotherapy, *n.* treatment of disease, esp. cancer, by drugs.

chemurgy, *n.* that branch of chemistry which is devoted to the industrial utilization of organic raw material, esp. farm products. [Gr. *ergos,* working]

Chengdu, *n.* (formerly **Chengtu**) ancient city, capital of Sichuan province, China; population (1986) 2,580,000. It is an important rail junction and has railway workshops, textile, electronics and engineering industries.

chenille, *n.* round tufted or fluffy cord of silk or worsted; a pile fabric made with similar yarn. [F, hairy caterpillar, L *canicula,* little dog, dim. of *canis,* dog]

cheongsam, *n.* a Chinese woman's long, tight-fitting dress with slit sides. [Chin.]

cheque, *n.* a draft on a banker for money payable to bearer or order. **crossed cheque,** a cheque marked as negotiable only through a banker. **cheque-book,** *n.* a book containing forms for drawing cheques. **cheque-book, journalism,** *n.* sensational journalism, using stories bought at high prices. **cheque card,** *n.* a card issued by a bank, guaranteeing payment of cheques up to a specified limit. [CHECK]

chequer, (*N Am.*) **checker,** *n.* †a chess-board; (*pl.*) a chess-board used as the sign of an inn; (*usu. pl.*) a pattern made of squares in alternating colours, like a chess-board; (*pl., N Am.*) the game of draughts. *v.t.* to form into a pattern of little squares; to variegate; to diversify, to fill with vicissitudes. **checker-board,** *n.* (*N Am.*) a draught-board; a chess-board. **chequered flag,** *n.* one with black and white squares used to signal the winner in a motor race. **chequer-work,** *n.* work executed in diaper pattern or checkers. [OF *eschekier,* chessboard, late L *scaccarium,* EXCHEQUER]

Chequers, *n.* country home of the prime minister of the UK. It is an Elizabethan mansion in the Chiltern hills near Princes Risborough, Buckinghamshire, and was given to the nation by Lord Lee of Fareham under the Chequers Estate Act 1917, which came into effect Jan. 1921.

Cherenkov, *n.* **Pavel** (1904–), Soviet physicist. In 1934, he discovered **Cherenkov radiation**; this occurs as a bluish light when charged atomic particles pass through water or other media at a speed in excess of that of light. He shared a Nobel prize in 1958 with his colleagues Ilya Frank and Igor Tamm.

cherimoya, *n.* a Peruvian tree, *Anona cherimolia,* with pulpy fruit. [Quechua]

cherish, *v.t.* to hold dear, to treat with affection, to caress; to foster, to promote; to hold closely to, cling to. **cherishable,** *a.* **cherishingly,** *adv.* [OF *cherir* (pres.p. *cherissant*), from *cher,* L *cārus,* dear]

Chernenko, *n.* **Konstantin** (1911–85), Soviet politician, leader of the Soviet Communist Party (CPSU) and president (1984–85). He was a protégé of Brezhnev and from 1978 a member of the Politburo.

Chernobyl, *n.* a town in the Ukraine, USSR. In Apr. 1986, a leak, caused by overheating, occurred in a non-pressurized boiling-water nuclear reactor. The resulting clouds of radioactive isotopes were traced as far away as Sweden; over 250 people were killed, and thousands of square kilometres contaminated.

chernozem, *n.* a dark-coloured, very fertile soil found in temperate climates. [Rus., black earth]

Cherokee, *n.* a North American Indian people, formerly living in the mountain country of Alabama, the Carolinas, Georgia and Tennessee. Sequoyah (*c.* 1770–1843), devised the syllabary used for writing down the Indian languages. They now live mainly in North Carolina and Oklahoma, where they established their capital at Tahlequah. Their language belongs to the Iroquoian family.

cheroot, *n.* a cigar with both ends cut square off. [Tamil *shuruttu,* a roll of tobacco]

cherry, *n.* a small stone-fruit of the plum family; the tree, *Prunus cerasus,* on which it grows; the wood of this. *a.* of the colour of a red cherry; ruddy. **two bites at a cherry,** a bungling attempt; a second chance. **cherry-bag,** *n.* the common cherry-laurel. **cherry-bob,** *n.* a pair of cherries joined by their stems. **cherry-bounce,** *n.* cherry brandy mixed with sugar. **cherry brandy,** *n.* brandy in which cherries have been steeped. **cherry-cheeked,** *a.* ruddy-cheeked. **cherry-pie,** *n.* a pie made with cherries; the hairy willow-herb; the garden heliotrope. †**cherry-pit,** *n.* a childish game in which cherry-stones are pitched into a small hole. **cherry-ripe,** *n.* the cry of persons hawking cherries. **cherry-stone,** *n.* the endocarp of the cherry. **cherry-tree,** *n.* the tree, *Prunus cerasus,* on which the cherry grows. **cherry-wood,** *n.* the wood of the cherry-tree; the wood of the wild guelder-rose, *Viburnum opulus.* [ME *chery,* ONorth.F. *cherise* (OF *cerise*), L *cerasus,* Gr. *kerasos;* (for loss of *s,* cp. PEA)]

Cherry Orchard, The, a play by Anton Chekhov, first produced 1904. Its theme, the demise of the way of life of a landowning family, is symbolized by the felling of a cherry orchard after it has been sold to an entrepreneur.

chert, *n.* hornstone; impure flinty rock. **cherty,** *a.* resembling or containing chert. [orig. unknown]

cherub, *n.* (*pl.* **-s, -bim, -bims**) a celestial spirit next in order to the seraphim; a beautiful child; in art, the winged head of a child. **cherubic,** *a.* of or pertaining to cherubs; angelic; full-cheeked and ruddy. **cherubically,** *adv.* **cherubin,** *n.* a cherub. [Heb. *k'rūb, k'rūv,* pl. *k'rūvīm*]

chervil, *n.* a garden pot-herb and salad-herb, *Chaerophyllum sativum.* [OE *caerfille,* L *chaerephylla,* pl., Gr. *chairephullon* (*chairein,* to rejoice, *phullon,* leaf)]

Chesapeake Bay, *n.* the largest of the inlets on the Atlantic coast of the US, bordered by Maryland and Virginia. Its wildlife is threatened by urban and industrial development.

Cheshire, *n.* county in NW England. **area** 2320 sq km/ 896 sq miles. **towns** administrative headquarters Chester; Warrington, Crewe, Widnes, Macclesfield, Congleton. **physical** chiefly a fertile plain; Mersey, Dee, and Weaver rivers. **products** textiles, chemicals, dairy products. **population** (1987) 952,000. **to grin like a cheshire cat,** to laugh all over one's face. **Cheshire cheese,** *n.* a red cheese made in Cheshire.

chesnut, CHESTNUT.

chess[1], *n.* a game played by two persons with 16 pieces each on a board divided into 64 squares. **chess-board,** *n.* the board on which chess is played. **chess-man,** *n.* one of the pieces used in chess. **chess-player,** *n.* one who plays or is well-skilled in chess. [OF *esches,* pl. of *eschec,* CHECK[1]]

†**chess**[2], *n.* (*usu. pl.*) one of the parallel baulks of timber used in laying a pontoon-bridge. [etym. doubtful; perh. from prec.]

chessel, *n.* a cheese-mould.

chest, *n.* a large box; a case for holding particular commodities; the quantity such a case holds; the coffer, treasury or funds of an institution; the fore part of the human body from the neck to the belly. *v.t.* †to deposit in a chest; to put into a coffin. **chest of drawers,** a movable wooden frame containing drawers. **to get off one's chest,** to unburden oneself (of a secret etc.); to admit, declare. **chest-note,** *n.* a deep note sounded from the chest, the lowest singing register. **chest-protector,** *n.* a thick scarf or wrap of flannel worn over the chest to prevent colds. **-chested,** *comb. form.* having a chest of a specified kind. **chesty,** *a.* (*coll.*) suffering from, or subject to, bronchitis etc. [OE *cest,* L *cista,* Gr. *kistē*]

Chesterfield[1], *n.* a loose kind of overcoat; a deeply upholstered sofa. [6th Earl of *Chesterfield*]

Chesterfield[2], *n.* **Philip Dormer Stanhope, 4th Earl of Chesterfield** (1694–1773), English politician and writer, author of *Letters to his Son* (1774) – his illegitimate son, Philip Stanhope (1732–68).

Chesterton, *n.* **G(ilbert) K(eith)** (1874–1936), English novelist, essayist, and satirical poet, author of a series of novels featuring the naive priest-detective 'Father Brown'. Other novels include *The Napoleon of Notting Hill* (1904) and *The Man Who Knew Too Much* (1922).

chestnut, *n.* a tree of the genus *Castanea,* esp. the Spanish or sweet chestnut, *C. vesca,* or its edible fruit; hence, a reddish-brown colour; a horse of this colour; (*coll.*) a stale joke or anecdote; in horses, a knob on the inside of the forelegs, a castor. *a.* reddish-brown. [formerly *chesten, chesteine,* OF *chastaigne* (F *châtaigne*), L *castanea,* Gr. *kastanea* (prob. a place-name), NUT]

chetah, CHEETAH.

Chetnik, *n.* member of a Serbian nationalist group that operated underground during the German occupation of Yugoslavia during World War II. Led by Col. Draza Mihailovič, the Chetniks initially received aid from the Allies, but this was later transferred to the communist partisans led by Tito.

cheval de frise, *n.* (*pl.* **chevaux**) a kind of fence, consisting of a bar armed with two rows of long spikes, for checking attacks by cavalry etc. [F, a Friesland horse]

cheval-glass, *n.* a large swing glass mounted on a frame. [F *cheval,* a horse, a support, GLASS]

chevalier, *n.* †a cavalier, a knight; a member of some foreign orders of knighthood or of the French Legion of Honour. **chevalier d'industrie,** *n.* an adventurer, a swindler. [F, (*cheval,* L *caballus,* horse)]

Chevalier, *n.* **Maurice** (1888–1972), French singer and actor. He began as dancing partner to the revue artiste Mistinguett at the Folies-Bergère, and made numerous films including *Innocents of Paris* (1929), which revived his song 'Louise', *The Merry Widow* (1934), and *Gigi* (1958).

chevelure, *n.* a head of hair; a luminous nebulosity round the nucleus of a comet. [F, from OF *cheveleūre,* L *capillātūra* (*capillātus,* haired, from *capillus,* a hair)]

Chevening, *n.* residence near Sevenoaks, Kent, bequeathed to the nation by the 7th Earl of Stanhope for royal or ministerial use.

cheverel, *n.* leather made from kidskin; a soft, yielding nature. *a.* made of kidskin; yielding, pliant. [OF *chevrele,* dim. of *chèvre,* L *capra,* a goat]

chevet, *n.* an apse. [F, pillow]

cheville, *n.* a peg for a violin, guitar, lute etc.; a meaningless word put into a sentence. [F, a peg]

chevin, *n.* the chub. [F *chevin, chevanne* (cp. *chef,* head)]

cheviot, *n.* a sheep bred on the *Cheviot* Hills; rough cloth made from the wool of such sheep.

†**chevisance,** *n.* a resource, a shift; provisions, booty, profit, gain; a borrowing of money. [OF, from *chevissant,* pres.p of *chevir,* to bring to a head, finish (*chef,* head)]

chevrette, *n.* a thin goatskin leather used for gloves. [F, dim. of *chèvre,* L *capra,* the goat]

Chevreul, *n.* **Michel-Eugene** (1786–1889), French chemist who studied the composition of fats and identified a number of fatty acids, including 'margaric acid', which became the basis of margarine.

chevron, *n.* (*Her.*) an honourable ordinary representing two rafters meeting at the top; inverted, the distinguishing mark on the coat-sleeves of non-commissioned officers; (*Arch.*) zig-zag moulding. **chevronel,** *n.* (*Her.*) a bar like a chevron but only half the width. **chevrony,** *a.* [F, rafter, from L *capreoli,* used of a pair of rafters]

chevrotain, -tin, *n.* a small animal allied to the musk-deer. [F, dim. of OF *chevrot,* dim. of *chèvre,* she-goat, L *capra*]

chevy, chivy , *v.t.* to chase about; to hunt. *v.i.* to scamper about. *n.* a hunt, a chase; the game of prisoners' base. [prob. from the ballad of *Chevy Chase*]

chew, *v.t.* to masticate, to grind with the teeth; to ruminate on, to digest mentally. *v.i.* to masticate food; to chew tobacco or gum; to meditate. *n.* that which is chewed in the mouth; a mouthful; a quid of tobacco. **to chew over,** to discuss. **to chew the cud,** CUD. **to chew the rag, fat,** (*sl.*) to grumble, to complain. **chewing-gum,** *n.* a preparation of flavoured insoluble gum for chewing. **chewy,** *a.* (*coll.*) firm-textured, suitable for chewing. [OE *cēowan,* from Teut. (cp. Dut. *kaauwen,* OHG *kiuwan,* G *kauen*)]

†**chewet,** *n.* a chough; a chatterer. [F *chouette,* a chough, a daw]

Chewings fescue, *n.* (*New Zealand*) a notable fodder-grass. [agriculturist's name]

chez, *prep.* at the house of. [F]

chiack, *v.t.* (*Austral., coll.*) to cheek, to poke fun at. *n.* teasing.

Chian, *a.* of or pertaining to Chios. *n.* an inhabitant of Chios.

Chiang Ching, *n.* former name of the Chinese actress Jiang Qing, third wife of Mao.

Chiang Ching-kuo, *n.* (1910–88), Taiwanese politician, son of Chiang Kai-shek. Prime minister from 1971, he became president in 1978.

Chiang Kai-shek, *n.* (Pinyin **Jiang Jie Shi**) (1887–1975), Chinese Guomindang (Kuomintang) general and politician, president of China (1928–31) and (1943–49), and of Taiwan from 1949, where he set up a breakaway right-wing government on his expulsion from the mainland by the communist forces. He was a commander in the civil war that lasted from the end of imperial rule (1911) to the Second Sino-Japanese War and beyond, having split with the communist leader Mao Zedong in 1927.

Chianti, *n.* a dry white or red wine from Tuscany. [It.]

chiaroscuro, *n.* the treatment of light and shade; effects of light and shade; a drawing in black and white; relief, contrast (in a literary work etc.). *a.* obscure; half-revealed. [It. (*chiaro,* L *clārus,* clear, bright, *oscuro,* L *obscūrus,* dark)]

chiasm, *n.* the crossing or decussation of the optic nerves. [Gr. *chiasma* (*chiazein,* to mark with a χ)]

chiasmus, *n.* inversion of order in parallel phrases, as *you came late, to go early would be unreasonable.* [Gr. *chiasmos,* crossing (as prec.)]

chiaster, *n.* a species of sponge found in the W Indies; a star-like spicule in some sponges. [Gr. *chi,* χ, *astēr,* star]

Chiba, *n.* industrial city (paper, steel, textiles) in Kanton region, E Honshu island, Japan, 40 km/25 miles west of Tokyo; population (1987) 793,000.

chibouk, chibouque, *n.* a long Turkish pipe for smoking. [Turk. *chibūq*]

chic, *n.* smartness, style; the best fashion or taste. *a.* stylish; fashionable. [F, etym. unknown]

chica¹, *n.* a red colouring-matter used by S American Indians to stain the skin. [native name from the Orinoco]

chica², *n.* an old Spanish dance of an erotic character, forerunner of the fandango, bolero and cachucha. [Sp.]

Chicago, *n.* financial and industrial (iron, steel, chemicals, textiles) city in Illinois, US, on Lake Michigan; population (1980) 3,005,000, metropolitan area 7,581,000. The famous stockyards are now closed.

chicane, *n.* the use of mean petty subterfuge; artifice, stratagem; a hand of cards containing no trumps; an artificial obstacle on a motor-racing track. *v.i.* to use chicane; to cheat. **chicanery,** *n.* the employment of chicane, esp. legal trickery; pettifogging. [F, etym. doubtful (perh. from med. Gr. *tzukanion,* Pers. *chaugān,* a polo club)]

chicano, *n.* a Spanish-speaking American of Mexican descent in the SW US. The term was originally used for those who became US citizens because of the Mexican War. [from Sp. *mejicano,* Mexican]

chicha, *n.* a fermented drink made from maize. [Haitian]

Chichen Itzá, *n.* Mayan city in Yucatán, Mexico, which flourished 11th–13th cent. Excavated (1924–40) by Sylvanus Griswold Morley, the remains include temples with sculptures and colour reliefs, an observatory, and a sacred well into which sacrifices, including human beings, were cast.

Chichester, *n.* **Francis** (1901–72), English sailor and navigator. In 1931, he made the first E-W crossing of the Tasman Sea in *Gipsy Moth,* and in 1966–67 circumnavigated the world in his yacht *Gipsy Moth IV*.

chick, *n.* a young bird about to be hatched or newly hatched; (*coll.*) a little child; (*coll., sometimes derog.*) a young woman. **chickabiddy,** *n.* a term of endearment for a child. **chickweed,** *n.* a small weed, *Stellaria media*. [see foll.]

chicken, *n.* the young of the domestic fowl; a fowl for the table; a person of tender years; (*coll.*) a coward. *a.* (*coll.*) cowardly. **Mother Cary's chicken,** the stormy petrel. **no chicken,** older than he or she appears. **to chicken out,** (*coll.*) to lose one's nerve. **to count one's chickens before they are hatched,** to make plans which depend on something uncertain. **chicken-breasted,** *a.* pigeon-breasted, having a contracted chest through malformation of the breast-bone. **chicken-feed,** *n.* (*coll.*) trifling matter; an insignificant sum of money. **chicken-hazard,** *n.* a game at dice for trumpery stakes. **chicken-hearted,** *a.* timid, cowardly. **chicken-pox,** *n.* a pustulous, contagious disease, usually occurring in childhood. **chicken-snake,** *n.* (*N Am.*) any snake that preys on chickens and hen's eggs. **chicken-wire,** *n.* wire netting with a small hexagonal mesh. **chicken yard,** *n.* (*N Am.*) a fowl-run. [OE *cīcen,* pl. *cīcenu* (cp. Dut. *kieken,* G *Küchlein,* Eng. COCK¹)]

chickling, *n.* the cultivated vetch; also commonly called the **chickling vetch**. [formerly *chicheling,* dim. of *chiche,* OF *chiche,* L *cicer*]

chick-pea, *n.* a dwarf species of pea, *Cicer arietinum*. [earlier *chich,* later *chich-pease,* see prec. and PEA]

chickweed CHICK.

Chiclayo, *n.* capital of Lambayeque department, NW Peru; population (1988) 395,000.

chicle, *n.* the juice of the sapodilla, used in the making of chewing-gum. [Nahuatl *tzictli*]

chicory, *n.* the succory, a blue-flowered plant, *Cichorium intybus,* or its root, which, when roasted and ground, is used as a coffee additive; endive. [F *chichorée, cichorée,* L *cichorium,* Gr. *kichōrion, kichōrē,* succory]

chide, *v.t.* (*past* **chided, chid**, *p.p.* **chided, chid, chidden**) to find fault with, to reprove, to blame; †to drive by chiding; †to fret against; †to dispute with. *v.i.* to scold, to fret, to make complaints; to make a complaining or brawling sound. *n.* chiding, bickering, a reproof; murmur, gentle noise. **chider,** *n.* **chidingly,** *adv.* [OE *cīdan*]

chief, *a.* principal, first; highest in authority; most important, leading, main. *n.* a leader or commander, esp. the leader of a tribe or clan; the prime mover; the principal agent; the head of a department; the principal thing; the largest part; (*Her.*) the upper third of a shield. **chief of staff,** *n.* the senior officer of a division of the armed forces. **to hold land in chief,** to hold it directly from the sovereign by honourable personal service. **chief justice,** *n.* in several countries, the judge presiding over the highest court. **chiefdom,** *n.* **chiefery, chiefry,** *n.* the institution of chiefs of clans. †a small rent paid to the lord in chief. **chiefess,** *n. fem.* †**chiefest,** *a.* first, most important. *adv.* firstly, chiefly. **chiefless,** *a.* without a chief or leader. **chiefly,** *adv.* principally, especially; for the most part. **chiefship,** *n.* **-in-chief,** *comb. form.* leading, most important, as **commander-in-chief**. [OF *chef,* L *caput,* head]

chieftain, *n.* a general, a leader; the head of a tribe or a Highland clan. **chieftainess,** *n. fem.* **chieftaincy, -ry, -ship,** *n.* [OF *chevetain,* late L *capitānus,* CAPTAIN]

chield, *n.* (*Sc.*) a man; a lad; a fellow. [var. of CHILD]

chiff-chaff, *n.* a European warbler, *Phylloscopus rufa*. [onomat.]

chiffon, *n.* a gauzy semitransparent fabric; (*pl.*) trimmings, esp. of dresses. *a.* made of chiffon; of puddings, having a fine, light consistency. **chiffonier,** *n.* a movable piece of furniture serving as a cupboard and sideboard. [F (*chiffe,* a rag)]

Chifley, *n.* **Joseph Benedict 'Ben'** (1885–1951), Australian Labour prime minister (1945–49). He united the party in fulfilling a welfare and nationalization programme (1945–49) (although he failed in an attempt to nationalize the banks, 1947) and initiated an immigration programme and the Snowy Mountains hydroelectric project.

chigger, CHIGOE.

chignon, *n.* a coil or knot of long hair at the back of the head. [F, earlier *chaignon* (*chaignon du col,* nape of the neck), var. of *chaînon,* ring or link (*chaîne,* CHAIN)]

chigoe, *n.* a small W Indian and S American flea, *Pulex penetrans*. [W Indian form of Sp. *chico,* small]

chihuahua, *n.* a very small dog with big eyes and pointed ears. [town in Mexico]

chilblain, *n.* a blain, or inflamed state of the hands or feet caused by bad circulation and cold. **chilblained,** *a.* **chilblainy,** *a.*

child, *n.* (*pl.* **children**) a descendant in the first degree; a boy; a girl; an infant; a young person; a son or daughter; one young in experience, judgment or attainments; (*pl.*) descendants; the inhabitants of a country; disciples; a person whose character is the result (of a specified environment etc.). †*v.t.* to give birth to. †*v.i.* to bring forth a child or children. **second childhood,** dotage. **with child,** pregnant. **childbearing,** *a.* bringing forth children. *n.* the act of bearing children. **childbed,** *n.* the state of a woman in labour, or bringing forth a child. **child benefit,** *n.* a sum of money paid regularly by government to the parent of a child. **childbirth,** *n.* the time or act of bringing forth a child. **child-minder,** *n.* a person who looks after another (working) person's children. **child-proof,** *a.* of bottle tops, locks etc., designed to be impossible for a child to operate or damage. **child's-play,** *n.* easy work. **childe,** *n.* a scion of a noble family, esp. one not yet admitted to knighthood. †**childed,** *a.* provided with a child. **childhood,** *n.* the state of being a child; the period from birth till puberty. †**childing,** *a.* childbearing, fruitful; in childbirth. **childish,** *a.* of or befitting a child; silly, puerile. **childish-minded,** *a.* **childishly,** *adv.* **childishness,** *n.* **childless,** *a.* without child or offspring. **childlessness,** *n.* **childlike,** *a.* resembling or befitting a child; docile, simple, innocent. †**childly,** *a., adv.* †**childness,** *n.* childishness. [OE *cild,* from Teut. (cp. Goth. *kilthei,* the womb, Dan. *kuld,* Swed. *kull,* a litter)]

Childe, *n.* **Gordon** (1892–1957), Australian archaeologist, director of the London Institute of Archaeology (1946–57). He discovered the prehistoric village of

Skara Brae in the Orkneys, and published *The Dawn of European Civilization* (1939).

Childermas day, *n.* the festival of Holy Innocents (28 Dec.). [OE *cildru, mæsse,* MASS[1]]

Childers, *n.* **(Robert) Erskine** (1870–1922), Irish Sinn Féin politician, author of the spy novel *The Riddle of the Sands* (1903). He was executed as a Republican guerrilla.

Children's Crusade, *n.* a Crusade by some 10,000 children from France, the Low Countries and Germany, in 1212, to recapture Jerusalem. Motivated by religious piety, many of them were sold into slavery or died of disease.

Chile, *n.* Republic of (*República de Chile*), a S American country, bounded to the north by Peru and Bolivia, to the east by Argentina, and to the south and west by the Pacific Ocean. **area** 736,905 sq km/284,445 sq miles. **capital** Santiago. **towns** Concepción, Viña del Mar, Temuco; ports are Valparaiso, Antofagasta, Arica, Iquique. **physical** Andes mountains along E border, Atacama Desert in N, arable land and forest in the S. **territories** Easter Island, Juan Fernandez Island, half of Tierra del Fuego, and part of Antarctica. **exports** copper, iron, nitrate (Chile is the chief mining country of South America), pulp and paper. **population** (1988) 12,680,000 (the majority mestizo, of mixed American Indian and Spanish descent); annual growth rate 1.6%. **language** Spanish. **religion** Roman Catholic.

Chilean Revolution, *n.* in Chile, the presidency of Salvador Allende (1970–73), the Western hemisphere's first democratically elected Marxist-oriented president of an independent state.

chiliad, *n.* a thousand; a thousand years. [Gr. *chilias -ados* (*chilioi,* a thousand)]

chiliagon, *n.* (*Geom.*) a figure having a thousand angles. [-GON]

chiliahedron, *n.* (*Geom.*) a figure having a thousand angles and sides. [Gr. *hedra,* a seat, a base]

†**chiliarch,** *n.* the commander of a thousand men. †**chiliarchy,** *n.* a body of a thousand men. [Gr. *chiliarchēs* (*chilioi,* thousand, *archos,* from *archein,* to rule)]

chiliasm, *n.* the doctrine of the millennium. **chiliast,** *n.* **chiliastic,** *a.* [Gr. *chiliasmos,* from *chilias*]

chill , *n.* coldness, a fall in bodily temperature; a cold; a cold, shivering sensation preceding fever or ague; a check, a discouragement; discouragement, depression. *v.t.* to make cold; to preserve meat etc. by cold; to cool (metal) suddenly so as to harden; to depress, to dispirit, to discourage; to take the chill off wine etc. *v.i.* to become cold. *a.* cold; causing a sensation of coolness; unfeeling; unemotional; coldly formal; depressing. **to chill out,** (*sl.*) to relax to a marked extent, sometimes under the influence of drugs; to hang around aimlessly as on street corners. **to take the chill off,** to warm slightly. **chiller,** *n.* a chilled container for food or drink; (*coll.*) a frightening novel, film etc. **chilling,** *a.* making cold; depressing, distant in manner. **chillingly,** *adv.* **chillness,** *n.* **chilly,** *a.* rather cold; susceptible of cold; cold or distant in manner. **chilliness,** *n.* [OE *ciele, cele,* from Teut. (cp. Icel. *kala,* to freeze, Dut. *kil,* chilly, L *gelu,* frost)]

chilli, *n.* (*pl.* **-(l)lies**) the dried ripe pod of red pepper, *Capsicum fastigiatum,* and other species. **chilli con carne,** *n.* a Mexican dish of minced meat with beans in a chilli sauce. [Nahuatl]

chil(o)-, *comb. form.* lip-shaped, labiate. [Gr. *cheilos,* a lip]

chilopod, *n.* a member of an order Chilopoda comprising the centipedes. [Gr. *pous, podos,* foot]

chilostomatous, *a.* having a movable lip-like operculum. [Gr. *stoma -atos,* mouth]

Chiltern Hundreds, *n.pl.* certain Crown lands in Buckinghamshire and Oxfordshire, the nominal stewardship of which is granted to a Member of Parliament who wishes to vacate his or her seat. **to apply for the Chiltern Hundreds,** to resign membership of the House of Commons.

chimaera, CHIMERA.

Chimbote, *n.* largest fishing port in Peru; population (1981) 216,000.

chime[1], *n.* the harmonic or consonant sounds of musical instruments or bells; a number of bells tuned in diatonic succession; the sounds so produced; harmony, accord; tune, rhythm; correspondence of relation. *v.i.* to sound in harmony or accord; of bells, to ring; to strike the hour etc.; to accord, to agree; to be in rhyme. *v.t.* to ring a series of bells; to ring a chime on bells; to cause to sound in harmony; to recite musically or rhythmically. **to chime in,** to join in; to express agreement. [ME *chimbe,* OF *chimble,* L *cymbalum,* Gr. *kumbalon,* CYMBAL]

chime[2], chimb, *n.* the edge of a cask or tub formed by the ends of the staves. [ME *chimb* (cp. Dut. *kim,* G *Kimme,* OE *cimb-īren*)]

chimer, chimere, *n.* a bishop's outer robe. [OF *chamarre* (etym. unknown)]

chimera, chimaera, *n.* a fabulous fire-eating monster, with a lion's head, a serpent's tail, and the body of a goat; any incongruous conception of the fancy; an imaginary terror; a genus of cartilaginous fishes; a hybrid of genetically quite dissimilar tissues. **chimerical**, *a.* purely imaginary. **chimerically,** *adv.* [L *chimaera,* Gr. *chimaira,* she-goat, a monster, fem. of *chimaros,* goat]

chimney, *n.* †a fireplace, a hearth; the flue, vent or passage through which smoke escapes from a fire into the open air; a glass tube placed over the flame of a lamp to intensify combustion; a vent from a volcano; a vertical or nearly vertical fissure in rock. **chimney-breast,** *n.* the projecting part of the wall of a room containing the fireplace. **chimney-cap,** *n.* a cowl. **chimney-corner,** *n.* a nook or seat beside the fire, esp. inside a wide, old-fashioned fireplace. **chimney-jack,** *n.* a rotating cap or cowl. **chimney-piece,** *n.* a mantelpiece. **chimney-pot,** *n.* a tube of pottery or sheet-metal carried up above the chimney-shaft to prevent smoking; (*coll.*) a tall silk hat. **chimney-stack,** *n.* a series of chimney-stalks united in a block of masonry or brickwork; a tall factory chimney. **chimney-stalk, -top,** *n.* the part of the chimney-stack carried up above the roof. **chimney-swallow,** *n.* the common swallow. **chimney-sweep,** *n.* a brush with long, jointed handle for sweeping chimneys; one whose business is to sweep chimneys. [OF *chiminée,* late L *camīnāta* (L *camīnus,* hearth, stove, flue)]

chimpanzee, *n.* a large intelligent African anthropoid ape, *Pan troglodytes.* [native name from Angola]

Chimu, *n.* South American civilization that flourished in Peru about 1250–1470, when it was conquered by the Incas. It produced fine work in gold, realistic portrait pottery, savage fanged images in clay, and possibly a system of writing or recording by painting beans in particular patterns. Aqueducts were built carrying water many miles, and the maze-like city of Chan Chan, 36 sq km/14 sq miles, on the coast near Trujillo.

chin, *n.* the front part of the lower jaw. **to keep one's chin up,** (*coll.*) to remain cheerful in adversity. **chinwag,** *n.* (*coll.*) chat, talk. **chinless,** *a.* (*coll.*) having a receding chin; weak-spirited, ineffectual. [OE *cin*]

china, *n.* porcelain, first brought from China; porcelain ware. *a.* made of porcelain. **china-clay,** *n.* kaolin. **china-closet,** *n.* a cupboard for storing china-ware. **china-ware,** *n.* articles made of china. [as prec.]

China[1], *a.* of or belonging to China. **China aster,** a garden flower, *Callistephus chinensis.* **china-grass,** *n.* the fibre of *Bohmeria nivea,* used for making ropes and cordage. **China ink,** *n.* a black, solid which, when mixed with water, yields a black indelible ink. **Chinaman,** (*n. derog.*) a native of China, or one of Chinese blood. **China pink,** *n.* a variety of garden flower, *Dianthus chinensis.* **china-root,** *n.* the root of a Chinese plant, *Smilax china,* used medicinally. **China rose,** *n.* a garden name for several varieties of the rose. **China tea,** *n.* a smoky-flavoured tea from China. **Chinatown,** *n.* the Chinese quarter of a town. **Chinese**, *n.* a native of China, or one of Chinese blood; the language of the

Chinese. *a.* of or belonging to China. **Chinese cabbage, leaves,** *n.* a vegetable with crisp leaves, like a cabbage. **Chinese chequers,** *n.* a board game like draughts. **Chinese gooseberry** KIWI FRUIT. **Chinese lantern,** *n.* a collapsible lantern made of thin paper. **Chinese wall,** *n.* an agreement among different departments of a large (financial) institution not to exchange sensitive information in order to avoid conflicts of interest or malpractice by members of staff. **Chinese white,** *n.* an opaque white paint. [English name for the Far-Eastern country]

China², *n.* People's Republic of (*Zhonghua Renmin Gonghe Guo*), a country in SE Asia, bounded N by Mongolia, NW and NE by the USSR, SW by India and Nepal, S by Bhutan, Burma, Laos and Vietnam, SE by the South China Sea, and E by the East China Sea, North Korea and the USSR. **area** 9,139,300 sq km/ 3,528,684 sq miles. **capital** Beijing (Peking). **towns** Chongqing (Chungking), Shenyang (Mukden), Wuhan, Nanjing (Nanking), Harbin; ports Tianjin (Tientsin), Shanghai, Qingdao (Tsingtao), Lüda (Lüta), Guangzhou (Canton). **physical** two-thirds of China is mountains (in the N and SW) or desert; the east is irrigated by rivers Huang He (Yellow River), Chang Jiang (Yangtze-Kiang), Xi Jiang (Si Kiang). **exports** tea, livestock and animal products, silk, cotton, oil, minerals (China is the world's largest producer of tungsten), chemicals, light industrial goods. **population** (1989) 1,112,000,000 (of whom the majority are Han or ethnic Chinese; the 67 million of other ethnic groups, including Tibetan, Uigur, and Zhuang, live in border areas). The number of people of Chinese origin outside China, Taiwan, and Hong Kong is estimated at 15–24 million. Annual growth rate 1.2%. **language** Chinese. **religion** officially atheist, but traditionally Taoist, Confucianist, and Buddhist; Muslim 13 million; Catholic 3–6 million (divided between the 'patriotic' church established 1958 and the 'loyal' church subject to Rome); Protestant 3 million.

China Sea, *n.* an area of the Pacific Ocean bordered by China, Vietnam, Borneo, the Philippines and Japan. Various groups of small islands and shoals, including the Paracels, 500 km/300 miles east of Vietnam, have been disputed by China and other powers because they lie in oil-rich areas.

chinch, *n.* (*N Am.*) the bed-bug; a fetid insect, destructive to corn. [Sp. *chinche*]

chinchilla, *n.* (the fur of) a genus (*Chinchilla*) of S American rodents. [Sp., dim. of *chinche,* see prec.]

chin-chin, *n.* (*coll.*) a familiar form of salutation or health-drinking. [Chin. *ts'ing ts'ing*]

chinchona, CINCHONA.

chin-cough, *n.* whooping-cough. [earlier and still dial. *chink-, kink-cough* (CHINK⁴, COUGH)]

chindit, *n.* a commando in Burma during World War II. [Burmese *chinthey,* a griffin]

chine¹, *n.* the backbone or spine of any animal; part of the back (of a pig) cut for cooking; a ridge. *v.t.* to cut or break the backbone of. **chined,** *a.* (*usu. in comb.*) having a backbone; backboned. [OF *eschine* (F *échine*), perh. from OHG *skina,* a needle]

chine², *n.* (*S Eng. dial.*) a deep and narrow ravine. [OE *cinu,* a chink, cleft (cp. Dut. *keen*)]

Chinese, *n.* an inhabitant of China or a person of Chinese descent. The Chinese comprise approximately 25% of the world's population, and the Chinese language is the largest member of the Sino-Tibetan family.

Chinese art, *n.* the painting and sculpture of China. From the Bronze Age to the Cultural Revolution, Chinese art shows a stylistic unity unparalleled in any other culture. From about the 1st cent. AD Buddhism inspired much sculpture and painting. The **Han dynasty** (206 BC–AD 220) produced outstanding metalwork, ceramics, and sculpture. The **Song dynasty** (960–1278) established standards of idyllic landscape and nature painting in a delicate calligraphic style.

Chinese language, *n.* a language or group of languages of the Sino-Tibetan family, spoken in China, Taiwan, Hongkong, Singapore and Chinese communities throughout the world. Varieties of spoken Chinese differ greatly, but share a written form using thousands of ideographic symbols which have changed little in 2000 years. Nowadays, *putonghua* ('common speech'), based on the educated Beijing dialect known as 'Mandarin' Chinese, is promoted throughout China as the national spoken and written language.

Chinese Revolution, *n.* a series of major political upheavals in China (1911–49). A nationalist revolt overthrew the imperial dynasty in 1912. Led by Sun Yat-sen (1923–25), and by Chiang Kai-shek (1925–49), the nationalists, or Guomindang, came under increasing pressure from the growing communist movement. The 10,000 km/6000 miles **Long March** of the communists (1934–35) to escape from the nationalist forces saw Mao Zedong emerge as leader. After World War II, the conflict expanded into open civil war (1946–49), until the Guomindang were defeated at Nanking. This effectively established communist rule in China under the leadership of Mao.

Chink¹, Chinkie, *n., a.* (*offensive*) Chinese.

chink², *n.* a narrow cleft or crevice; a small longitudinal opening; a slit. *v.t.* to stuff up chinks. *v.i.* to split, to crack. [etym. doubtful]

chink³, *n.* a jingling sound as of coin. *v.t.* to cause to jingle. *v.i.* to emit a jingling sound. [onomat.]

chink⁴, kink, *v.i.* to gasp or lose one's breath in coughing or laughing. *n.* a gasp of this kind. [prob. from an OE *cincian* (11th cent. *cincung,* noun of action); cp. Dut. *kinken,* to cough]

chino, *n.* (*pl.* **-nos**) a tough, twilled cotton fabric, (*pl.*) trousers, often off-white, made of this fabric. [Am. Sp.]

Chino-, *comb. form.* Chinese, or relating to China.

Chinook, *n.* a jargon of Indian and European words used in intercourse between traders and Indians in the region of the Columbia River; a warm west wind from the Pacific Ocean occurring in the Rocky Mountains. [native name of Indian tribe]

chintz, *n.* printed cotton cloth with floral devices etc., usu. glazed. **chintzy,** *a.* [formerly *chints,* pl., Hind. *chīnt* (Sansk. *chitra,* variegated)]

chip, *n.* a small piece of wood, stone etc. detached or chopped off; a thin strip of wood; a thin fragment; (*pl.*) thin slices of fried potato; wood or wood-fibre cut into thin strips for making hats or baskets; a playing-counter used in card games; a very small piece of semiconducting material, esp. silicon, with an integrated circuit printed on it. *v.t.* (*past, p.p.* **chipped**) to cut into chips; to cut or break chips off; to crack. *v.i.* to break or fly off in chips; to play a chip-shot. **chip off the old block,** a son resembling his father. **to chip at,** (*Austral.*) to jeer at, to nag. **to chip in,** (*sl.*) to cut into a conversation; to contribute (money). **to have a chip on one's shoulder,** to nourish a grievance. **chip-bonnet, -hat,** *n.* a bonnet or hat made of chip. **chip-shot,** *n.* in football or golf, a short high shot. **chip-board,** *n.* a thin board made of compressed wood fragments. **chippy,** *a.* (*sl.*) seedy; (*sl.*) unwell after a bout of drinking; (*sl.*) irritable. *n.* (*coll.*) a fish-and-chip shop; (*coll.*) a carpenter. **chippiness,** *n.* [dim. of CHOP (cp. *click, clack; clink, clank; drip, drop*)]

chip², *v.t.* (*Wrestling*) to trip up. *n.* (*Wrestling*) a trip; a particular kind of throw. [cp. Icel. *kippa,* to scratch, to pull, Dut. *kippen,* to catch]

chipmunk, *n.* a N American rodent, *Tamias lysteri,* like the squirrel. [N Am. Ind.]

chipolata, *n.* a small sausage. [F, from It. *cipolla,* onion]

Chippendale¹, *a.* applied to furniture of the style introduced by Chippendale about the middle of the 18th cent.; also to a contemporaneous style of book-plates.

Chippendale², *n.* **Thomas** (*c.* 1718–79), English furniture designer. He set up his workshop in St Martin's Lane, London in 1753. His book *The Gentleman and Cabinet Maker's Director* (1754), was a significant contribution to furniture design. He favoured Louis XVI, Chinese, Gothic and Neo-Classical styles, and worked mainly in mahogany.

chipper, *a.* (*coll.*) energetic and cheerful; smart. [etym. doubtful]

Chirac, *n.* **Jacques** (1932–), French conservative politician, prime minister (1974–76) and (1986–88). He established the neo-Gaullist Rassemblement pour la République (RPR) 1976, and became mayor of Paris in 1977.

chiragra, *n.* gout in the finger-joints. **chiragrical,** *a.* [L, from Gr. *cheiragra* (*agra,* a hunt, a catch)]

Chirico, *n.* **Giorgio de** (1888–1978), Italian painter born in Greece, the founder of Metaphysical painting, a style that presaged surrealism in its use of enigmatic imagery and dreamlike settings. Early examples date from 1910.

chir(o)-, *comb. form.* manual; having hands or hand-like organs. [Gr. *cheir,* hand]

chirognomy, *n.* judgment of character from the lines in the hand.

chirograph, *n.* a written or signed document. **chirographer**, *n.* an officer in the Court of Common Pleas who engrossed fines. **chirographic, -ical**, *a.* pertaining to or in handwriting. **chirography**, *n.* the art of writing or engrossing; character and style in handwriting. [F *chirographe,* L *chirographum,* Gr. *cheirographon*]

chirology, *n.* the art or practice of conversing by signs made with the hands or fingers; finger-speech. **chirologist,** *n.*

chiromancy, *n.* divination by means of the hand; palmistry. **chiromancer,** *n.* **chiromantic**, *a.*

Chiron, *n.* an outer asteroid discovered by Charles Kowal in 1977, orbiting between Saturn and Uranus. It appears to have a dark surface resembling that of asteroids in the inner solar system, probably consists of a mixture of ice and dark stony material, and may have a diameter of about 200 km/120 miles.

chiropodist, *n.* one skilled in the care of the hands and feet, esp. in the removal of corns etc. **chiropody,** *n.* [Gr. *pous podos,* foot]

chiropractic, *n.* spinal manipulation as a method of curing disease. **chiropractor**, *n.* [Gr. *praktikos,* practical, effective]

chiroptera, CHEIROPTERA.

chirp, *v.i.* to make a quick, sharp sound (as birds and their young, insects etc.); to talk cheerfully; to speak faintly. *v.t.* to utter or sing with a sharp, quick sound. *n.* a sharp, quick sound of a bird; a sound resembling this. **chirpingly,** *adv.* in a chirping manner. **chirpy,** *a.* cheerful; vivacious. **chirpiness,** *n.* [imit.]

chirr, *v.i.* to make a trilling monotonous sound like that of the grasshopper. [imit.]

chirrup, *v.i.* to chirp, to make a twittering sound. **chirruper,** *n.* **chirrupy,** *a.* cheerful, chatty. [CHIRP]

†**chirurgeon,** *n.* a surgeon. †**chirurgeonly,** *adv.* †**chirurgery,** *n.* [OF *cirurgien,* from *cirurgie,* L *chīrurgia,* Gr. *cheirourgia* (CHEIR-, *ergein,* to work)]

chisel, *n.* an edged tool for cutting wood, iron or stone, operated by pressure or striking. *v.t.* to cut, pare or grave with a chisel; (*sl.*) to take advantage of, to cheat. **chiselled,** *a.* cut with or as with a chisel; clear-cut. **chiseller,** *n.* [ONorth.F (OF *cisel,* F *ciseau*), late L *cīsellus,* forceps (L *-cisum,* from *caedere,* to cut)]

chisleu, *n.* the third month of the civil, and the ninth of the ecclesiastical Jewish year, corresponding roughly to December. [Heb.]

Chissano, *n.* **Joaquim** (1939–), Mozambique politician, president from 1986.

chit[1], *n.* a child; a young thing; (*derog.*) a young girl. [cp. KIT]

chit[2], **chitty**, *n.* a voucher; a receipt; a memorandum. [Hind. *chitthī* (Sansk. *chitra,* mark)]

chit-chat, *n.* trifling talk; chat, gossip. *v.i.* to chat, gossip. [CHAT[1]]

chitin, *n.* the horny substance that gives firmness to the integuments of crustaceans, arachnidans, and insects. **chitinous,** *a.* [F *chitine,* Gr. *chitōn,* a tunic]

chiton, *n.* a robe; a lady's dress made in Greek fashion; a mollusc of the genus *Chiton,* having an imbricated shell. [Gr. *chitōn,* tunic]

Chittagong, *n.* a city and port in Bangladesh, 16 km/10 miles from the mouth of the Karnaphuli river, on the Bay of Bengal; population (1981) 1,388,476. Industries include steel, engineering, chemicals and textiles.

chitter, *v.i.* to shiver, to tremble, to chatter, as the teeth; to twitter, as birds. [CHATTER (cp. CHIP[1], CHOP[1] etc.)]

chitterlings, *n.pl.* the smaller intestines of animals, esp. as prepared for food. [etym. doubtful, cp. G *Kutteln,* entrails]

chivalry, *n.* the knightly system of the Middle Ages; the ideal qualities which inspired it, nobleness and gallantry of spirit, courtesy, respect for and defence of the weak; gallantry, devotion to the service of women; †knights collectively; †horsemen, cavalry; †a knightly exploit. **flower of cavalry,** a pattern knight; the finest type of knighthood; the choicest in a body of armed knights. **chivalric**, *a.* pertaining to chivalry; gallant. **chivalrous,** *a.* gallant, noble; courteous. **chivalrously,** *adv.* [OF *chevalerie,* from L *caballārius,* CHEVALIER]

chive, cive, *n.* a small onion-like herb, *Allium schoenoprasum.* [F *cive* or North.F *chive,* L *cepa,* onion]

chivy CHEVY.

chlamyd-, *comb. form.* (*Bot., Zool.*) having a mantle or envelope.

Chlamydia, *n.* a genus of disease-causing microorganisms resembling both bacteria and viruses; a sexually-transmitted disease caused by one of the Chlamydia.

chlamys, *n.* (*pl.* **-ydes**) a Greek cloak or mantle; the floral envelope of a plant. [Gr. *chlamus -udos,* a cloak]

chlor- CHLOR(O)-.

chloral, *n.* a narcotic liquid made from chlorine and alcohol; chloral hydrate. **chloral-hydrate,** *n.* a white crystalline substance obtained from chloral, used as a hypnotic and anaesthetic. **chloralism,** *n.* the morbid effects on the system of taking chloral freely. **chloralize,** *v.t.* to treat with chloral. [CHLOR-, AL(COHOL)]

chloramphenicol, *n.* an antibiotic used to treat typhoid etc.

chlorate, *n.* a salt of chloric acid.

Chlorella, *n.* a genus of green freshwater algae.

chloric, *a.* pertaining to pentavalent chlorine. **chloric acid,** *n.* an acid containing hydrogen, chlorine and oxygen.

chloride, *n.* a compound of chlorine with another element. **chloride of lime,** a compound of chlorine with lime, used as a disinfectant and for bleaching. **chloridate, -dize, -dise,** *v.t.* to treat or prepare (as a photographic plate) with a chloride.

chlorine, *n.* a yellow-green, poisonous, gaseous element, at.no. 17; chem. symbol Cl, obtained from common salt, used as a disinfectant and for bleaching. **chlorinate**, *v.t.* **chlorination**, *n.* the extraction of gold by exposure of ore to chlorine gas; the sterilization of water with chlorine.

chlorite, *n.* a green silicate mineral. **chloritic**, *a.*

chlor(o)-, *comb. form.* of a green colour; (denoting a chemical compound in which chlorine has replaced some other element. [Gr. *chlōros,* green]

chlorodyne, *n.* a formerly popular anodyne composed of chloroform, prussic acid and Indian hemp. [Gr. *odunē,* pain]

chloroform, *n.* a volatile fluid formerly used as an anaesthetic. *v.t.* to administer chloroform to; to render insensible with chloroform. [F *chloroforme* (CHLOR(O)-, *form*(yl), see FORMIC)]

chlorometer, *n.* an instrument for testing the bleaching power of chloride of lime. **chlorometric**, *a.* **chlorometry,** *n.*

chlorophyll, *n.* the green colouring-matter of plants which absorbs the energy from sunlight, used in producing carbohydrates from water and carbon dioxide. [Gr. *phullon,* a leaf]

chloroplast, *n.* a plastid containing chlorophyll.

chlorosis, *n.* etiolation, a blanching of plants through the non-development of chlorophyll; a disease affecting young persons due to deficiency of iron in the blood. **chlorotic,** *a.*

chlorpromazine, *n.* a tranquillizing drug.

ChM, (*abbr.*) Master of Surgery. [L *Chirurgiae Magister*]

choc, *n.* (*coll.*) short for CHOCOLATE. **choc-ice,** *n.* a bar of (vanilla) ice-cream coated with chocolate.

chock, *n.* a wood block, esp. a wedge-shaped block used to prevent a cask or other body from shifting. *v.t.* to wedge, support, make fast, with a chock or chocks; to place a boat on the chocks. *adv.* as close as possible; tightly, fully. **boat chocks,** blocks for wedging up a boat on a ship's deck. **chock-a-block,** chock-full. **chock-full,** *adv.* quite full; full to overflowing. **chock-stone,** *n.* (*Mountaineering*) a stone wedged in a chimney or crack. **chocker,** *a.* (*coll.*) full up; crammed; (*sl.*) annoyed. [prob. from O.North.F *choque,* a log (prob. influenced by CHOKE)]

chocolate, *n.* an edible paste made from the roasted, ground seeds of the cacao tree; a sweetmeat made of or coated with this paste; a drink made of this paste dissolved in hot water or milk; a dark brown colour. *a.* made of or flavoured with chocolate. **milk chocolate,** chocolate prepared with milk. **plain chocolate,** chocolate that is less creamy and sweet than milk chocolate. **chocolate-box,** *a.* sentimentally pretty. **chocolate-cream,** *n.* a sweet confection enclosed in chocolate. [F *chocolat,* Sp. *chocolate,* Nahuatl *chocolatl* (*choco,* cacao, *latl,* water)]

choctaw, *n.* (*Skating*) a change of foot and from one edge to the other. [name of N Am. Ind. tribe fancifully applied]

choice, *n.* the power or act of choosing; the person or thing chosen; the things to be selected from; selection, preference; care in selecting; the best and preferable part. *a.* selected, picked, chosen with care; of great value; careful, fastidious. **for choice,** for preference. **Hobson's choice**, no alternative. [*Hobson,* a Cambridge livery-stable keeper who insisted on every customer's taking the first horse inside the stable door or none at all] **to have no choice,** to have no option; to have no preference. †**choice-drawn,** *a.* selected with special care. †**choiceful,** *a.* fickle, changeable, varied. **choicely,** *adv.* **choiceness,** *n.* [OF *chois,* from *choisir,* to choose]

choir, *n.* a band of singers, esp. in a church or chapel; the part of the church or chapel allotted to the singers; the part of a cathedral or large church where service is performed, the chancel; an organized body of singers; a body of dancers or of singers and dancers. *v.i.* to sing together. *v.t.* to sing (a hymn, anthem etc.) as in a choir. **choirboy,** *n.* a boy singer in a church choir. **choir organ,** properly **chair organ**, *n.* the least powerful section of a compound organ, used chiefly for accompaniments. **choir-screen,** *n.* a screen of latticework, wood or other open work separating the choir from the nave. [ME *queir, quere,* OF *cuer,* L *chorum -us,* Gr. *choros,* a band of dancers and singers]

Choiseul, *n.* **Étienne François, duc de Choiseul** (1719–85), French politician. Originally a protégé of Mme de Pompadour, the mistress of Louis XV, he became minister for foreign affairs in 1758, and held this and other offices until 1770. He banished the Jesuits, and was a supporter of the Enlightenment philosophers Diderot and Voltaire.

choke, *v.t.* to block or compress the windpipe (of), so as to prevent breathing; to suffocate (as by gas, water etc.); to smother, to stifle; to repress, to silence (often with *back, down*); to stop up, to block; to obstruct, to clog. *v.i.* to have the windpipe stopped; to be wholly or partially suffocated; to be blocked up. *n.* the action of choking; a noise of suffocation in the throat; an inductance coil constructed to prevent high-frequency currents from passing; the constriction of a choke-bore; a device to prevent the passage of too much air to a carburettor. **to choke off,** to discourage, to suppress. **to choke up,** to fill up until blocked. **choke-bore,** *n.* a gun-barrel the bore of which narrows towards the muzzle. **choke-damp,** *n.* carbon dioxide generated in mines, wells etc.; suffocating vapour. **choke-full** CHOCK-FULL. **choke-pear,** *n.* a kind of pear with a rough, astringent taste; a sarcasm which puts one to silence. †**choke-weed,** *n.* a species of broomrape, *Orobanche rapum,* a parasite on roots. **choked,** *a.* (*coll.*) disappointed; angry. **choker,** *n.* one who or that which chokes; (*sl.*) a tie; a cravat; a clerical collar; a necklace that fits closely round the neck. **choky[1],** *a.* that chokes; having a sensation of choking. [OE *ā-cēocian* (etym. doubtful)]

choko, *n.* (*Austral.*) a succulent vegetable like a cucumber. [Am. Sp. *chocho*]

choky[1] CHOKE.

choky[2], chokey, *n.* (*coll.*) a lock-up, police-station; a prison. [Hind. *chaukī*]

chol- CHOL(E)-.

cholaemia, *n.* a morbid accumulation of bile in the blood.

cholagogue, *n.* a medicine which promotes the flow of bile. [F, from mod. L *cholagōgum,* Gr. *cholagōgon* (*agōgos,* leading, from *agein,* to lead)]

chol(e)-, *comb. form.* of or pertaining to bile. [Gr. *cholē,* gall bile]

choler, *n.* bile, the humour supposed to cause irascibility of temper; anger; tendency to anger. **choleric,** *a.* full of choler; irascible, passionate. [ME and OF *colere,* L *cholera,* Gr. *cholera* (*cholē,* bile)]

cholera, Asiatic cholera, *n.* an acute, often fatal, bacterial infection, spread by contaminated water supplies in which severe vomiting and diarrhoea cause dehydration. **choleraic**, *a.* **choleroid,** *a.* **cholerine**, *n.* summer cholera, a mild form of cholera; the first stage of cholera; the supposed cause of epidemic cholera. [L, see prec.]

choleric CHOLER.

cholesterol, (*formerly***) cholesterin,** *n.* a white solid alcohol occurring in gall-stones, nerves, blood etc., thought to be a cause of arteriosclerosis. **cholesteric,** *a.* [Gr. *stereos,* stiff, solid]

choli, *n.* an Indian woman's garment, a short tight-fitting bodice worn under a sari. [Hind. *colī*]

choliamb, *n.* a scazon. **choliambic,** *a.* [L *chōliambus,* Gr. *chōliambos* (*cholos,* lame, IAMBUS)]

cholic, *a.* pertaining to or obtained from bile.

choline, *n.* a substance occurring naturally in the body, important for the synthesis of lecithin etc.

chomp, CHAMP[1].

Chomsky, *n.* **Noam** (1928–), US professor of linguistics. He proposed a theory of transformational generative grammar, which attracted widespread interest because of the claims it made about the relationship between language and the mind, and the universality of an underlying language structure. He is also a leading spokesman against imperialist tendencies of the US government.

chondr(i)-, chondro- *comb. form* composed of or pertaining to cartilage. [Gr. *chondros,* cartilage]

chondrify, *v.t.* to be converted into cartilage. **chondrification,** *n.*

chondrine, *n.* gelatine from the cartilage of the ribs, joints etc.

chondrite, *n.* a meteorite containing stony granules.

chondritis, *n.* inflammation of cartilage.

chondro- CHONDRI-.

chondrography, -ology, *n.* a treatise on cartilages.

chondroid, *a.* like cartilage.

chondrometer, *n.* a steelyard or balance for weighing grain.

chondropterygian, *n.* a cartilaginous fish, one of a section of fishes (as the sharks, lampreys and sturgeons) in which the skeleton and fin spines are cartilaginous. *a.* pertaining to this section. [Gr. *pterux,* a fin]

Chongjin, *n.* capital of North Hamgyong province on the NE coast of North Korea; population (1984) 754,000.

Chongqing, *n.* (or **Chungking**, also known as **Pahsien**) city in Sichuan province, China, which stands at the confluence of the Chang Jiang and the Jialing Jiang; population (1984) 2,733,700. Industries include iron, steel, chemicals, synthetic rubber and textiles.

Choonhavan, *n.* **Major-General Chatichai** (1922–), Thai politician, prime minister of Thailand from 1988. He has promoted a peace settlement in neighbouring Cambodia as part of a broader vision of transforming Indochina into a thriving, open-trading zone. A field marshal's son, he fought in World War II and the Korean War. After a successful career as a diplomat and businessman, he moved into politics and became leader of the conservative Chat Thai party and, in 1988, prime minister.

choose, *v.t.* (*past* **chose**, *p.p.* **chosen**) to take by preference, to select from a number; to feel inclined, to prefer (to do something rather than something else); to decide willingly (to do). *v.i.* to make one's choice; to have the power of choice. **cannot choose but,** have no alternative but. **to pick and choose,** to make a careful choice, to be over-particular. **chooser,** *n.* **choosy, -sey,** *adv.* (*coll.*) hard to please, particular. **choosingly,** *adv.* [OE *cēosan,* from Teut. (cp. Dut. *kiezen,* G *kiesen,* Icel. *kjōsa*)]

chop¹, *v.t.* (*past, p.p.* **chopped**) to cut off suddenly; to strike off; to cut short or into parts; to strike (a ball) with backspin; (*coll.*) to reduce or abolish. *v.i.* to do anything with a quick motion like that of a blow. *n.* the act of chopping; a cutting stroke; a piece chopped off; a rib (of a sheep or pig) chopped off and cooked separately; (*pl.*) broken waves of the sea. **the chop,** (*sl.*) dismissal (from a job etc.). **to chop in,** to intervene suddenly in a conversation. **to chop up,** to cut into small pieces, to mince. **chop-house,** *n.* a restaurant specializing in chops and steaks. **chopper,** *n.* one who or that which chops; a butcher's cleaver; an axe; (*Radio*) an interrupter, usually a rotating commutator; (*sl.*) a helicopter; (*coll.*) a motorcycle or bicycle with very high handlebars. **chopping,** *n.* the action of the verb TO CHOP. *a.* that chops; choppy. **chopping-block,** *n.* a wooden block on which anything is chopped. **chopping-knife,** *n.* a large knife for chopping or mincing. **choppy,** *a.* full of cracks or clefts; of the sea, rough, with short quick waves. [var. of CHAP¹]

chop², *v.t.* to exchange, to barter. *v.i.* to shift suddenly, as the wind. *n.* change. **to chop and change,** to vary continuously; to fluctuate. **to chop logic,** to wrangle pedantically. **choppy,** *a.* variable, continually changing. [etym. doubtful (perh. from prec. or from CHAPMAN)]

chop³ CHAP².

chop⁴, *n.* in India and China, a seal or official stamp; a passport, a permit; (*coll.*) brand, quality. **first chop,** (*sl.*) first-rate. [Hind. *chhap,* print, stamp]

chop-chop, (*coll.*) at once, quickly. [Pidgin Eng. *chop,* fast]

chopin, *n.* a Scottish wine-quart. [prob. from F *chopine,* from *chope* (cp. G *Schoppen,* a half-litre)]

†**chopine,** *n.* a high shoe or patten formerly worn by women. [OF and Sp. *chapin* (Sp. *chapa,* a metal plate)]

†**chopping,** *a.* fine, strapping. [CHOP¹]

Chopin¹, *n.* **Frédéric (François)** (1810–49), Polish composer and pianist. He made his debut as a pianist at the age of eight. As a performer, Chopin revolutionized the technique of pianoforte-playing, and concentrated on solo piano pieces. His compositions for piano are characterized by their lyrical and poetic quality.

Chopin², *n.* **Kate** (1851–1904), US novelist and story writer. Her novel *The Awakening* (1899) is now regarded as a classic of feminist sensibility.

chopsticks, *n.pl.* two small sticks of wood or ivory used by the Chinese to eat with. [rendering of Chinese *k'wâi-tsze,* quick ones; see CHOP-CHOP]

chop suey, *n.* a Chinese dish of shredded meat and vegetables served with rice. [Chin. *chap sui,* odds and ends]

choragus, *n.* the leader or director of the chorus in the ancient Greek theatrical performances; the deputy of the professor of music at Oxford; the leader of a band or chorus; a leader. **choragic,** *a.* **choragic monument,** *n.* a monument in honour of the choragus who produced the best musical or theatrical entertainment at the festival of Bacchus. [L *chorāgus,* Gr. *chorēgos* (*choros,* chorus, *agein,* to lead)]

choral¹, *a.* belonging to or sung by a choir or chorus; chanted or sung. **chorally,** *adv.* **choralist,** *n.* a singer in a chorus. [med. L *chorālis* (L *chorus,* Gr. *choros*)]

choral², chorale, *n.* a simple choral hymn or song, usually of slow rhythm and sung in unison. [G *Choral* (in *choralgesang,* choral song)]

chord¹, *n.* the string of a musical instrument; a straight line joining the extremities of an arc or two points in a curve; (*Anat.*) CORD. **chordal,** *a.* **Chordata,** *n.* a phylum of the animal kingdom, animals with a backbone or notochord. **chordate,** *n., a.* (a member) of the Chordata. [L *chorda,* Gr. *chordē* (CORD, before 16th cent.)]

chord², *n.* the simultaneous and harmonious sounding of notes of different pitch; any harmonious combination, as of colours. **chordal,** *a.* [ACCORD]

chore, *n.* a small regular task; a daily or other household job; a boring task. [CHAR²]

chorea, *n.* a nervous disorder characterized by irregular convulsive movements of an involuntary kind, St Vitus's dance. [L, from Gr. *choreia* (*choros,* dance)]

choree, *n.* a trochee; a metrical foot consisting of a long syllable followed by a short one. **choreic,** *a.* [L *chorēus,* Gr. *choreios,* pertaining to a *choros*]

choreograph, *v.t.* to compose or arrange the steps of (a stage dance or ballet). *n.* the composer or designer of a ballet. **choreographer,** *n.* **choreographic,** *a.* **choreography,** *n.* [Gr. *choreia* (*choros,* dance)]

chorepiscopal, *a.* (*Eccles. Hist.*) pertaining to a country bishop. [L *chōrepiscopus,* Gr. *chōrepiskopos* (*chōra, chōras,* country, *episkopos,* BISHOP¹]

choriamb, -ambus, *n.* (*pl.* **-ambs, -ambi**) a metrical foot of four syllables, of which the first and fourth are long, and the second and third short. **choriambic,** *a.* pertaining to or of the nature of a choriamb. *n.* a choriamb. [L, from Gr. *choriambos* (CHOREE, IAMB, IAMBUS)]

choric CHORUS.

chorion, *n.* the outer membrane which envelops the foetus in the womb; the external membrane of a seed. **chorionic,** *a.* **chorionic villus sampling,** a diagnostic test for detecting abnormalities in a foetus, whereby small pieces of the chorion are removed and examined. **choroid,** *a.* resembling the chorion. *n.* the vascular portion of the retina. [Gr.]

choripetalous, chorisepalous CHORI(S)-.

chori(s)-, *comb. form* (*Bot.*) separate. **choripetalous,** *a.* having free petals; polypetalous. **chorisepalous,** *a.* [Gr. *chōri* (*chōris,* before a vowel), apart]

chorister, †**chorist,** *n.* a singer; one who sings in a choir, a choirboy; one of a band or flock of singers; (*N Am.*) the leader of a choir or congregation, a precentor. [med. L *chorista,* from *chorus,* CHOIR]

chorography, *n.* the art or practice of describing and making maps of particular regions or districts. **chorographer,** *n.* **chorographic, -ical,** *a.* **chorographically,** *adv.* [F *chorographie,* Gr. *chōrographia, chōra,* a land, a region]

choroid CHORION.

chorology, *n.* the science of the geographical distribution of plants and animals. **chorological,** *a.* [Gr. *chōra,* a district]

chortle, *v.i.* to make a loud chuckle. *v.t.* to utter with a loud chuckle. [coined by 'Lewis Carroll' (cp. CHUCKLE and SNORT)]

chorus, *n.* a band of dancers and singers in the ancient Greek drama; the song or recitative between the acts of a Greek tragedy; (the speaker of) the prologue and epilogue in an Elizabethan play; a band of persons singing or dancing in concert; a concerted piece of vocal music; the refrain of a song in which the company joins the singer. **chorus girl,** *n.* a young woman who sings or dances in the chorus in a musical comedy etc. **choric,** *a.* pertaining to a chorus; like the chorus in a Greek play. [L, from Gr. *choros*]

chose, *past,* **chosen,** *p.p.* CHOOSE.

chota hazri, *n.* a light, early breakfast. **chota peg,** *n.*

whisky and soda. [Hind.]

Chou En-lai, *n.* former name for Chinese politician Zhou Enlai.

chough, *n.* a large black bird of the crow family with a red bill. [imit. (cp. Dut. *kaauw,* Dan. *kaa,* OF *choue*)]

chouse, *v.t.* to trick, to swindle, to cheat. *n.* a swindle. [Turk. *chiaus,* an interpreter, from an interpreter attached to the Turkish embassy in London who in 1609 perpetrated great frauds]

choux pastry, *n.* a rich light pastry made with eggs. [F, *pl.* of *chou,* cabbage]

chow, *n.* (*coll.*) food; a chow-chow (dog); (*Austral., dated, derog.*) a Chinese. [Chin.]

chow-chow, *n.* an orig. Chinese breed of dog with thick coat and curled tail; a kind of mixed vegetable pickle; preserved fruit and ginger in syrup. [Chin.]

chowder, *n.* a thick soup or stew made of fish, bacon etc.; a picnic where chowder is eaten. *v.t.* to make a chowder of. [F *chaudière,* pot, L *caldāria* (see CALDARIUM)]

chow mein, *n.* a Chinese dish of meat and vegetables served with fried noodles. [Chin., fried noodles]

chowry, *n.* a flapper for driving away flies. [Hind. *chaunri*]

Chr., (*abbr.*) Christ(ian).

chrematistic, *a.* concerning money-making. **chrematistics,** *n. sing.* political economy so far as it relates to the production of wealth. [Gr. *chrēmatistikos,* from *chrēmatizein,* to traffic, make money (*chrēmatos,* money)]

chrestomathy, *n.* a selection of passages with notes etc., to be used in learning a language. **chrestomathic,** *a.* learning or teaching good and useful things. [Gr. *chrēstomatheia* (*chrēstos,* good *matheia,* learning, from *manthanein,* to learn)]

Chrétien de Troyes, *n.* medieval French poet, born in Champagne about the middle of the 12th cent. His epics, which include *Le Chevalier de la Charrette*; *Perceval*, written for Philip, Count of Flanders; *Erec*; *Yvain*; and other Arthurian romances, introduced the concept of the Holy Grail.

chrism, *n.* consecrated oil, used in the Roman and Greek Churches in administering baptism, confirmation, ordination and extreme unction. **chrismal,** *a.* **chrismatory,** *n.* a vessel for holding chrism. †**chrisom,** *n.* a white cloth, anointed with chrism, formerly placed over the face of a child after baptism; hence, a child just baptized, or one that died within a month of its baptism. **chrisom-child,** *n.* one who died before a month old. [OE *crisma,* L and Gr. *chrisma* (Gr. *chriein,* to anoint)]

†**chrison** CHRISM.

Christ, *n.* the Anointed One, a title given to Jesus the Saviour, and synonymous with the Hebrew Messiah. *int.* (*taboo*) expressing anger, annoyance etc. †**Christ-cross-row,** *n.* the alphabet, prob. from the cross being placed at the beginning in the horn-books. **Christ's-thorn,** *n.* name of several shrubs identified with that from which the crown of thorns was made. **Christhood,** *n.* **Christless,** *a.* without faith in or without the spirit of Christ. **Christlessness,** *n.* **Christlike,** *a.* **Christlikeness,** *n.* **Christly,** *a.* **Christward, -wards,** *adv.* [OE *Crist,* L *Christus,* Gr. *Christos* (*chriein,* to anoint)]

Christadelphian, *n., a.* (a member) of a millenarian Christian sect, calling themselves the brethren of Christ, and claiming apostolic origin. [Gr. *Christos, adelphoi,* brethren]

christen, *v.t.* to receive into the Christian Church by baptism; to baptize; to name; to nickname. *v.i.* to administer baptism. **christening,** *n.* [OE *cristnian,* from *cristen*]

Christendom, *n.* †baptism; †Christianity; that portion of the world in which Christianity is the prevailing religion; Christians collectively. [OE *cristen* (see prec.)]

Christian, *n.* one who believes in or professes the religion of Christ; one belonging to a nation or country of which Christianity is the prevailing religion; one whose character is consistent with the teaching of Christ; (*dated, coll.*) a civilized person as distinguished from a savage; a human being as distinguished from a brute. *a.* pertaining to Christ or Christianity; professing the religion of Christ; Christlike; civilized. **Christian Democrat,** *n.* a member of a moderate Roman Catholic Church party in Belgium, France, Italy, Germany etc. **Christian era,** *n.* the chronological period since the birth of Christ. **Christian name,** *n.* a name given in baptism. **Christian Science,** *n.* a system based on the belief that diseases are the result of wrong thinking and can be healed without medical treatment. **Christian Scientist,** *n.* **Christianity**, *n.* see separate article below. **christianize, -ise,** *v.t.* to convert to Christianity. *v.i.* to be converted to Christianity. **christianization, -isation,** *n.* **christianlike,** *a.* **christianly,** *a., adv.* **Christiano-,** *comb. form.* [L *Christiānus*]

Christian, *n.* ten kings of Denmark and Norway, including:

Christian I, *n.* (1426–81), king of Denmark from 1448, and founder of the Oldenburg dynasty. In 1450 he established the union of Denmark and Norway that lasted until 1814.

Christian IV, *n.* (1577–1648), king of Denmark and Norway from 1588. He sided with the Protestants in the Thirty Years' War (1618–48), and founded Christiania (now Oslo, capital of Norway). He was succeeded by Frederick II in 1648.

Christian VIII, *n.* (1786–1848), king of Denmark 1839–48. He was unpopular because of his opposition to reform. His attempt to encourage the Danish language and culture in Schleswig and Holstein led to an insurrection there shortly after his death. He was succeeded by Frederick VII.

Christian IX, *n.* (1818–1906), king of Denmark from 1863. His daughter Alexandra married Edward VII of the UK and another, Dagmar, married Tsar Alexander III of Russia; his second son, George, became king of Greece. In 1864 he lost the duchies of Schleswig and Holstein after a war with Austria and Prussia.

Christian X, *n.* (1870–1947), king of Denmark and Iceland from 1912, when he succeeded his father Frederick VIII. He married Alexandrine, Duchess of Mecklenburg-Schwerin, and was popular for his democratic attitude. During World War II he was held prisoner by the Germans in Copenhagen. He was succeeded by Frederick IX.

Christiania, Christie, *n.* a turn in skiing in which the skis are kept parallel, used esp. for stopping or turning sharply. [former name of Oslo, Norway]

Christianity, *n.* a world religion derived from the teaching of Jesus Christ in the first third of the 1st cent., with a present-day membership of about 1 billion. Its main divisions are the Roman Catholic, Orthodox and Protestant churches. **beliefs** An omnipotent God the Father is the fundamental concept, together with the doctrine of the Trinity, that is, the union of the three persons of the Father, Son and Holy Spirit in one Godhead. Christians believe that Jesus died for the sins of the people, and his divinity is based on the belief of his resurrection after death, and his ascension into Heaven. The main commandments are to love God and to love one's neighbour as oneself.

Christian Science, *n.* a sect, the Church of Christ, Scientist, established in the US by Mary Baker Eddy in 1879. Christian Scientists believe that since God is good and is spirit, matter and evil are not truly real. Consequently they refuse all medical treatment. The sect has its own daily newspaper, the *Christian Science Monitor*.

Christie[1], *n.* **Agatha** (1890–1976), English detective novelist who created the characters Hercule Poirot and Miss Jane Marple. Her prolific output included the novels *The Murder of Roger Ackroyd* (1926) and *Ten Little Indians* (1939), and the play *The Mousetrap* (1952).

Christie[2], *n.* **Julie** (1940–), British film actress, who became a star in the 1960s following her award-winning performance in *Darling* (1965). She also appeared in *Doctor Zhivago* (1965); *The Go-Between* (1971);

Don't Look Now (1973); *Memoirs of a Survivor* (1982); and *Power* (1986).

Christie[3] CHRISTIANIA.

Christina, *n.* (1626–89), queen of Sweden (1632–54). Succeeding her father Gustavus Adolphus at the age of six, she assumed power in 1644, but disagreed with the former regent Oxenstjerna. Refusing to marry, she eventually nominated her cousin Charles Gustavus (Charles X) as her successor. As a secret convert to Roman Catholicism, which was then illegal in Sweden, she had to abdicate in 1654, and went to live in Rome, twice returning to Sweden unsuccessfully to claim the throne.

Christine de Pisan, *n.* (1364–1430), French poet and historian. Her works include love lyrics, philosophical poems, a poem in praise of Joan of Arc, a history of Charles V, and various defences of women, including *La cité des dames/The City of Ladies*.

Christmas, *n.* the festival of the nativity of Jesus Christ celebrated on 25 Dec.; Christmastide. *a.* pertaining or appropriate to Christmas or its festivities. *v.i.* (*coll.*) to celebrate Christmas. *v.t.* to decorate with Christmas tokens. **Christmas-box,** *n.* †a box in which presents were collected at Christmas; a present or tip given at Christmas, esp. to tradesmen. **Christmas bush,** *n.* (*Austral.*) a tree that comes into flower about Christmastime, with bright red blooms. **Christmas cactus,** *n.* a S American branching cactus which produces red flowers in winter. **Christmas card,** *n.* an ornamental card sent as a Christmas greeting. **Christmas carol,** *n.* a song of praise sung at Christmas. **Christmas day,** *n.* the festival of Christmas. **Christmas eve,** *n.* the day before Christmas day. **Christmas number,** *n.* a special number of a magazine or other periodical issued at Christmastime. **Christmas pudding,** *n.* a rich pudding made at Christmastime. **Christmas rose,** *n.* a white-flowered hellebore, *Helleborus niger,* flowering in winter. **Christmastide, -time,** *n.* the season of Christmas. **Christmas tree,** *n.* an evergreen or artificial tree kept indoors and decorated at Christmastide. **Christmasy, -massy,** *a.* [OE *cristes mæsse*]

Christo, *n.* (adopted name of **Christo Javacheff**) (1935–), US sculptor, born in Bulgaria, active in Paris in the 1950s and in New York from 1964. He is known for his wrapped works: structures such as bridges and buildings, and even areas of coastline, are temporarily wrapped in synthetic fabric tied down with rope. The *Running Fence* (1976) across California was another temporary work.

Christo-, *comb. form.* pertaining to Christ. [L *Christus,* Gr. *Christos*]

Christolatry, *n.* the worship of Christ regarded as a form of idolatry.

Christology, *n.* the doctrine of the person of Christ. **Christological**, *a.* **Christologist,** *n.*

Christophany, *n.* an appearance of Christ to mankind.

Christophe, *n.* **Henri** (1767–1820), West Indian slave, one of the leaders of the revolt against the French 1791, who was proclaimed king of Haiti in 1811. His government distributed plantations to military leaders. He shot himself when his troops deserted him because of his alleged cruelty.

Christopher, St, *n.* the patron saint of travellers. His feast day on 25 July was dropped from the Roman Catholic liturgical calendar in 1969.

chrom- CHROM(O)-.

chromat- CHROMAT(O)-.

chromate, *n.* a salt of chromic acid.

chromatic, *a.* relating to colour; coloured; including notes not belonging to the diatonic scale. **chromatic printing,** *n.* colour printing. **chromatic scale,** *n.* a succession of notes a semitone apart. **chromatic semitone,** *n.* the interval between a note and its flat or sharp. **chromatically,** *adv.* **chromaticity,** *n.* **chromatics,** *n.sing.* the science of colour. [Gr. *chrōmatikos*]

chromatin, *n.* the portion of the nucleus of a cell, consisting of nucleic acids and protein, which readily takes up a basic stain.

chromat(o)-, *comb. form.* pertaining to colour. [Gr. *chrōma chrōmatos,* colour]

chromatography, *n.* a technique for separating or analysing the components of a mixture which relies on the differing capacity for adsorption of the components (in a column of powder, strip of paper etc.). **chromatogram,** *n.* the visual record produced by separating the components of a mixture by chromatography.

chromatophore, *n.* a movable pigment cell in some animals.

chromatoscope, *n.* an instrument for combining rays of different colours into one compound colour; a light-reflecting telescope for studying the scintillations of stars.

chromatrope, *n.* a rotating magic-lantern slide for producing a kaleidoscopic effect.

chrome, *n.* chromium; a pigment containing chromium. *v.t.* to plate with chromium; to treat with a chromium compound. **chrome-colour,** *n.* a colour prepared from a chromium salt. **chrome-green,** *n.* a dark green pigment obtained from oxide of chromium. **chrome steel,** *n.* a kind of steel containing chromium. **chrome-yellow,** *n.* chromate of lead; a brilliant yellow pigment. [F, from Gr. *chrōma,* colour]

chromite, *n.* a mineral consisting of chromium and iron oxide.

chromium, *n.* a bright steel-grey metallic element, at. no. 24; chem. symbol Cr, remarkable for the brilliance of colour of its compounds, used as a protective plating. **chromium-plated,** *a.* electroplated with chromium to give a shiny appearance; showy. **chromic,** *a.* pertaining to or containing chromium.

chromo, CHROMOLITHOGRAPH.

chrom(o)-, *comb. form* pertaining to colour. [Gr. *chrōma,* colour]

chromogen, *n.* an organic colouring matter; a dye obtained from naphthalene; an animal or vegetable matter which alters in colour under certain conditions.

chromograph, *n.* an apparatus for reproducing writing or drawing in colours by lithography from an impression on gelatine; a hectograph. *v.t.* to make copies in this way.

chromolithograph, *n.* a picture printed in colours by lithography. **chromolithographic**, *a.* **chromolithographer**, *n.* **chromolithography,** *n.*

chromophotography, *n.* colour photography.

chromosome, *n.* any of the rod-shaped structures in a cell nucleus that carry the genes which transmit hereditary characteristics. **chromosomal**, *a.* [Gr. *sōma,* body]

chromosphere, *n.* the gaseous envelope of the sun through which light passes from the photosphere.

chromotypography, *n.* colour printing at an ordinary press.

chronic, *a.* relating to time; applied to diseases of long duration, or apt to recur; (*coll.*) very bad, severe. *n.* a chronic invalid. **chronically,** *adv.* **chronicity**, *n.* [F *chronique,* L, late L *chronicus,* Gr. *chronikos* (*chronos,* time)]

chronicle, *n.* a register or history of events in order of time; a history, a record. *v.t.* to record in a chronicle; to register. **Chronicles,** *n.pl.* the two books of the Old Testament immediately following I and II Kings. **chronicler,** *n.* [ME and OF *cronique,* late L *chronica,* sing., from Gr. *kronika,* neut. p. (see prec.)]

chrono-, *comb. form* pertaining to time or dates. [Gr. *chronos,* time]

chronogram, *n.* a device by which a date is given by taking the letters of an inscription which coincide with Roman numerals and printing them larger than the rest: thus, GEORGIVS DVX BVCKINGAMIAE (1 + 5 + 500 + 5 + 10 + 5 + 100 + 1 + 1000 + 1) = 1628 when the Duke was murdered by Felton. **chronogrammatic**, *a.*

chronograph, *n.* an instrument for measuring and registering minute portions of time with great precision; a stop-watch. **chronographer**, *n.* a chronicler; a chronologist. **chronography,** *n.* a description of past events. **chronographic**, *a.* pertaining to a chronograph.

chronology, *n.* the science of computing time; an arrangement of dates of historical events; a tabular list of dates. **chronologer, -gist,** *n.* **chronological**, *a.* **chronological age,** *n.* age in years, as opposed to mental etc. age. **chronologically,** *adv.*

chronometer, *n.* an instrument such as a sundial, clock or watch that measures time, esp. one that measures time with great exactness, such as is used to determine the longitude at sea by the difference between its time and solar time. **chronometric, -ical**, *a.* **chronometrically,** *adv.* **chronometry,** *n.*

chronopher, *n.* an instrument for sending time-signals to a distance by electricity. [Gr. *phoros,* carrying (*pherein,* to carry)]

chronoscope, *n.* an instrument for measuring the velocity of projectiles.

chrys- CHRYSO-.

chrysalis, -alid, *n.* (*pl.* **-lises, -lides**, **-lids**) the last stage through which a lepidopterous insect passes before becoming a perfect insect; the pupa, the shell or case containing the imago; an undeveloped or transitional state. [L *chrysalis, chrysallis,* Gr. *chrusallis* (*chrusos,* gold)]

chrysanth, *n.* short for CHRYSANTHEMUM.

Chrysanthemum, *n.* a genus of composite plants containing the ox-eye daisy, the corn-marigold and the garden chrysanthemum, *Chrysanthemum sinense;* (**chrysanthemum;** often shortened to **chrysanth**) any of the cultivated varieties of the last-named. [L *chrȳsanthemum,* Gr. *chrusanthemon,* marigold (CHRYS-, *anthemon,* flower)]

chryselephantine, *a.* made partly of gold and partly of ivory; overlaid with gold and ivory. [Gr. *chryselephantinos*]

chrys(o)-, *comb. form* golden; of a bright yellow colour. [Gr. *chrusos,* gold]

chrysoberyl, *n.* a gem of a yellowish-green colour, composed of beryllium aluminate. [L *chrȳsobēryllus,* Gr. *chrusobērullos*]

chrysocolla, *n.* a green, lustrous, opaline silicate of copper; (*Anc. Hist.*) gold-solder (composition doubtful). [L, from Gr. *chrusokolla* (*kolla,* glue)]

chrysolite, *n.* a green-coloured translucent orthorhombic mineral; olivine. [OF *crisolit,* L *chrȳsolithus,* Gr. *chrusolithos* (*-lithos,* stone)]

chrysoprase, *n.* an apple-green variety of chalcedony; in the New Testament, a variety of beryl. [ME and OF *crisopace,* L *chrȳsoprasus,* Gr. *chrusoprasos* (*prason,* a leek)]

chthonian, chthonic, *a.* of or pertaining to the underworld; Tartarean. [Gr. *chthŏnios* (*chthōn chthonos,* earth)]

chub, *n.* (*pl.* in general **chub;** in particular **chubs**) a coarse river-fish, *Leuciscus cephalus,* also called the chevin; applied to various American fishes. **chub-faced,** *a.* having a plump face, chubby. **chubby,** *a.* fat, plump (esp. in the face). **chubbiness,** *n.* [etym. unknown]

Chubb®, *n.* name of a tumbler-lock. [from the inventor, Charles *Chubb,* 1772–1846]

Chubu, *n.* mountainous coastal region of central Honshu island, Japan; population(1986) 20,694,000; area 66,774 sq km/25,791 sq miles. Chief city is Nagoya.

chuck¹, *n.* the call of a hen to her chickens. *v.i.* to make such a noise. *v.t.* to call, as a hen does her chickens. [onomat.]

chuck², *n.* a slight tap or blow under the chin; a toss or throw. *v.t.* to strike gently under the chin; to fling, to throw. **the chuck,** (*sl.*) dismissal (from a job etc.). **to chuck away,** (*coll.*) to discard; to waste. **to chuck out,** (*sl.*) to eject forcibly from a public meeting, licensed premises etc. **to chuck up,** (*sl.*) to abandon. **chuck-farthing,** *n.* a game in which a farthing or other piece of money is pitched into a hole. **chucker-out,** *n.* a bouncer. [earlier *chock;* prob. imit. (cp. F *choquer,* Dut. *schokken*)]

chuck³, *n.* an appendage to a lathe for holding the work to be turned, or to a drill for holding the bit; a cut of beef from the neck and shoulder; (*coll.*) food. *v.t.* to fix on a lathe by means of a chuck. **chuck key,** *n.* an instrument for tightening or loosening a chuck. **chuck steak,** *n.* **chuck wagon,** *n.* (*N Am.*) a wagon carrying food, cooking utensils etc. [CHOCK]

chuck⁴, *n.* †darling, dear; (*Sc., North.*) a chick, a fowl. [var. of CHICK]

chuckle, *v.i.* to laugh to oneself; to make a half-suppressed sound of laughter; to exult to oneself; to call (as a hen). *n.* such a laugh or call. [CHUCK¹]

chuckle-head, *n.* a stupid person. **chuckle-headed,** *a.* [prob. var. of CHUCK³]

†**chuff¹**, *n.* a dull, stupid thick-headed fellow; a churlish fellow. *a.* chuffy. †**chuffy,** *a.* rough, rude, clownish. †**chuffily,** *adv.* [etym. unknown]

chuff², *v.i.* to make a short puffing sound, as of a steam locomotive; to move while making such sounds. *n.* such a sound; (also **chuff-chuff**) a child's word for a steam locomotive. [onomat.]

chuffed, *a.* (*coll.*) pleased, happy. [E dial. *chuff*]

chug, *n.* a short dull explosive sound, as of an internal-combustion engine. *v.i.* (*past, p.p.* **chugged**) to make such a noise; to move while making such a noise. [onomat.]

Chugoku, *n.* southwestern region of Honshu island, Japan; population(1986) 7,764,000; area 31,881 sq km/12,314 sq miles. Chief city is Hiroshima.

chukka, chukker, *n.* name of each of the periods into which a polo game is divided. [Hind.]

chum, *n.* one who lives in the same room with another; a comrade and close companion. *v.i.* (*past, p.p.* **chummed,** *dated*) to occupy the same rooms with another. **new chum,** (*Austral.*) a newcomer to Australia, a new immigrant. **chummery,** *n.* **chummy,** *a.* [etym. doubtful]

chump, *n.* a short, thick piece of wood, a thick end-piece; (*sl.*) a head; (*sl.*) a silly fellow; a cut of meat from the loin and hindleg. **off one's chump,** crazy. **chump chop,** *n.* a thick chop from the chump. [recent; parallel to CHUNK (perh. influenced by CHOP¹ and LUMP)]

chunder, *v.i.* (*Austral., sl.*) to vomit. [etym. unknown]

Chun Doo-hwan, *n.* (1931–), South Korean military ruler who seized power 1979; president (1981–88) as head of the newly formed Democratic Justice Party.

chunk, *n.* a short, thick lump of anything; a large portion. **chunky,** *a.* containing or consisting of chunks; (*coll.*) small and sturdy. [prob. var. of CHUCK³]

Chunnel, *n.* short for CHANNEL TUNNEL.

chunter, *v.i.* (*coll.*) to talk at length and irrelevantly. [onomat.]

chupatty, CHAPATI.

church, *n.* a building set apart and consecrated for Christian worship; a body of Christian believers worshipping in one place, with the same ritual and doctrines; Christians collectively; a section of Christians organized for worship under a certain form; the whole organization of a religious body or association; the clergy as distinct from the laity; divine service; ecclesiastical authority or influence; (*N Am.*) the communicants of a congregation. *v.t.* †to say the thanksgiving service for a woman after childbirth; (*Sc.*) to take or escort to church (esp. a bride on her first attendance after marriage). *a.* of or pertaining to church; ecclesiastical. **Church of England,** see separate entry. **Church of Scotland,** see separate entry. **Free Church of Scotland,** see separate entry. **to go into the church,** to take Holy Orders. **church-ale,** *n.* a periodical merry-making in connection with a church. **Church Army,** *n.* an organization in the Church of England based on the Salvation Army. **church-burial,** *n.* burial according to the rites of the church. **Church Commissioners,** *n.pl.* a body of administrators who manage the finances and property of the Church of England. **church-goer,** *n.* a regular attendant at church. **church-going,** *n.* the practice of regularly attending divine service. *a.* calling to divine service; habitually attending divine service. **church-land,** *n.* land belonging to the church. **church-living,** *n.* a benefice. **churchman,** *n.* a cleric, an ecclesiastic; a member of the Church of England; an episcopalian. **churchmanly,** *a.* **churchmanship,** *n.* **churchwoman,** *n. fem.* **church member,** *n.* one in communion with a church. **church membership,** *n.* **Church militant,** *n.* Christians on earth, regarded as warring against evil. **church mouse,** *n.* a type of extreme poverty. **church music,** *n.* sacred music, such as is used in church services. †**church-outed,** *a.* excommunicated. **church-owl,** *n.* the barn-owl. **church-rate,** *n.* a rate (now voluntary) for the support of a parish church. **church service,** *n.* service in a church; the Book of Common Prayer with the daily lessons added. **church-text,** *n.* Gothic or black-letter used in monumental inscriptions. **Church triumphant,** *n.* Christians in heaven. **churchwarden,** *n.* one of two officers, chosen annually at the Easter vestry, to protect church property, to superintend the performance of divine worship etc. and to act as the legal representatives of the parish generally; (*coll.*) a long clay pipe with a large bowl. **churchward, -wards,** *adv.* towards the church. **churchway,** *n.* a pathway leading to or round a church. **churchwork,** *n.* work on or for a church; work in connection with the church; religious efforts. **churchyard,** *n.* the ground adjoining the church consecrated for the burial of the dead. **churchyard cough,** *n.* one that is premonitory of death. †**churching,** *n.* the act of returning public thanks in church after childbirth. **churchism,** *n.* preference for and adherence to the principles of a church, esp. of the establishment. **churchless,** *a.* without a church. **churchlike,** *a.* befitting the church or clerics. **churchly,** *a.* **churchy,** *a.* making a hobby of church-work and church matters; aggressively devoted to the church and intolerant of dissenters. **churchify,** *v.t.* **churchiness,** *n.* [OE *circe, cirice,* WG *kîrika,* Gr. *kuriakon,* neut. of a. *kuriakos* (*kurios,* lord)]

Churchill[1], *n.* **Caryl** (1938–), British playwright, whose predominantly radical and feminist works include *Cloud Nine* (1979), *Top Girls* (1982), and *Serious Money* (1987).

Churchill[2], *n.* **Randolph (Henry Spencer)** (1849–1895), British Conservative politician, chancellor of the Exchequer and leader of the House of Commons 1886, father of Winston Churchill.

Churchill[3], *n.* **Winston (Leonard Spencer)** (1874–1965), British Conservative politician. In Parliament from 1900, as a Liberal until 1923, he held a number of ministerial offices, including 1st Lord of the Admiralty (1911–15) and chancellor of the Exchequer (1924–29). Absent from the cabinet in the 1930s, he returned in Sept. 1939 to lead a coalition government (1940–45), negotiating with Allied leaders in World War II; he was again prime minister (1951–55). Nobel Prize for Literature 1953.

Church in Wales, the Welsh Anglican church; see WALES, CHURCH IN.

Church of England, the established form of Christianity in England, a member of the Anglican Communion. It was dissociated from the Roman Catholic Church in 1534. There were approximately 1,100,000 regular worshippers in 1988.

Church of Scotland, the established form of Christianity in Scotland, first recognized by the state in 1560. It is based on the Protestant doctrines of the reformer Calvin and governed on Presbyterian lines. The Church went through several periods of episcopacy in the 17th cent., and those who adhered to episcopacy after 1690 formed the Episcopal Church of Scotland, an autonomous church in communion with the Church of England. In 1843, there was a split in the Church of Scotland (the Disruption), in which almost a third of its ministers and members left and formed the Free Church of Scotland. Its membership in 1988 was about 850,000.

churinga, *n.* (*Austral.*) a sacred amulet. [Abor.]

churl, *n.* †a serf or villein; a man of low birth; a peasant; a surly person; a niggard. **churlish,** *a.* **churlishly,** *adv.* **churlishness,** *n.* **churly,** *a.* churlish. [OE *ceorl,* from Teut. (cp. Icel. *karl,* OHG *charal,* G *Kerl*)]

churn, *n.* a vessel in which milk or cream is agitated or beaten in order to produce butter; the block or chuck on a porcelain-turner's lathe, on which the articles are turned by thin iron tools; a large can for carrying milk long distances. *v.t.* to agitate in a churn for the purpose of making butter; to agitate with violence or continued motion (often with *up*). *v.i.* to perform the operation of churning; of waves, to foam, to swirl about. **to churn out,** to produce rapidly and prolifically, usu. without concern for excellence. **churn-dash, -dasher,** *n.* the contrivance for agitating the milk in a churn. **churn-staff,** *n.* the staff used with the old plunge churn. **churning,** *n.* the action of the verb TO CHURN; the butter made at one operation. [OE *cyrin,* from Teut. (cp. Icel. *kirna,* Dut. *karn*)]

churr, *n.* the deep, trilling cry of the night-jar. *v.i.* to make this cry. [imit.]

chut, *int.* expressing impatience. [F]

chute, *n.* an inclined trough for conveying water, timber, grain etc. to a lower level; an inclined watercourse; a toboggan-slide; short for PARACHUTE. [F *chute* (late L *caduta,* fem. of *cadūtus,* p.p., from L *cadere,* to fall), influenced by SHOOT]

chutney, *n.* a hot seasoned condiment or pickle. [Hind. *chatnī*]

chutzpah, *n.* barefaced audacity. [Yiddish]

chyle, *n.* the milky fluid separated from the chyme by the action of the pancreatic juice and the bile, absorbed by the lacteal vessels, and assimilated with the blood. **chylaceous,** *a.* **chylify,** *v.t.* to convert into chyle. *v.i.* to be turned into chyle. **chylification,** *n.* **chyliferous,** *a.* **chylific,** *a.* **chylous,** *a.* **chylo-,** *comb. form.* [F, from L *chȳlus,* Gr. *chulos* (stem *chu-, cheu-, cheein,* to pour)]

chyme, *n.* the pulpy mass of digested food before the chyle is separated from it. **chymify,** *v.t.* to form into chyme. *v.i.* to become chyme. **chymification,** *n.* **chymous,** *a.* **chymo-,** *comb. form.* [L *chȳmus,* Gr. *chumos* (as prec.)]

chypre, *n.* a strong sandalwood perfume. [F, Cyprus]

CI, (*abbr.*) Channel Islands.

Ci, (*abbr.*) curie.

CIA, (*abbr.*) Central Intelligence Agency (US).

Ciano, *n.* **Galeazzo** (1903–44), Italian Fascist politician. Son-in-law of Mussolini, he was foreign minister (1936–43), when his loyalty became suspect. He voted against Mussolini at the meeting of the Grand Council 25 July 1943 that overthrew the dictator, but was later tried for treason and shot by the Fascists.

ciao, *int.* expressing greeting or leave-taking. [It.]

Cibachrome, *n.* in photography, a process of printing directly from transparencies. Distinguished by rich, saturated colours, it can be home-processed and the colours are highly resistant to fading. It was introduced in 1963.

ciborium, *n.* (*pl.* **-ria**) a baldachin canopy or shrine; a pyx or cup with arched cover for the reservation of the Eucharist; a shrine or tabernacle to receive this. [med. L, from Gr. *kibōrion,* cup-shaped seed-vessel of the Egyptian water-lily]

cicada, *n.* (*pl.* **dae**) a genus of homopterous insects with stridulating organs; any individual of the genus. [L]

cicala, cigala, *n.* (*pl.* **-le**) a cicada. [It. and Prov. (cp. F *cigale*)]

cicatrice CICATRIX.

cicatricle, -cule, *n.* the germinating point in the yolk of an egg, or the vesicle of a seed. [L *cicātrīcula,* dim. of CICATRIX]

cicatrix, *n.* (*pl.* **-trices**) the mark or scar left after a wound or ulcer has healed; a mark on a stem or branch of a plant where a leaf was attached. **cicatrice,** *n.* **cicatricial,** *a.* **cicatricose,** *a.* **cicatrize, -ise,** *v.t.* to heal a wound or ulcer by inducing the formation of a cicatrix. *v.i.* to skin over. **cicatrization, -isation,** *n.* **cicatrose,** *a.* full of scars; scarry. [L]

cicely, *n.* the name of several plants of the parsley family. [L *seselis,* Gr. *seseli, seselis* (perh. confused with *Cicely, Cecilia*)]

Cicero, *n.* (106–43 BC), Roman orator, writer and statesman. His speeches, and philosophical and rhetorical works are models of Latin prose, and his letters provide a picture of contemporary Roman life. As consul in 63 BC he exposed Catiline's conspiracy in four major orations.

cicerone, *n.* (*pl.* **-roni**) a guide; one who explains the curiosities and interesting features of a place to strangers. *v.t.* to conduct in this manner. [It., from *Cicero -ōnem,* the Roman orator, 106–43 BC]

Ciceronian, *a.* resembling the style of Cicero; easy, flowing. *n.* an admirer or imitator of the style of Cicero. **Ciceronianism,** *n.* [L, *Ciceroniānus* (see prec.)]

Cicestr., (*abbr.*) of Chichester, used as the Bishop of Chichester's signature. [L *Cicestriensis*]

cicisbeo, *n.* (*pl.* **-bei**) the recognized gallant of a married woman. **cicisbeism,** *n.* the system (18th cent.) that recognized this. [It. (etym. doubtful)]

cicuta, *n.* a genus of umbelliferous plants comprising the British water-hemlock. [L]

CID, (*abbr.*) Criminal Investigation Department.

Cid, *n.* **Rodrigo Diaz de Bivar** (1040–99), Spanish soldier, nicknamed *El Cid* ('the lord') by the Moors. Born in Castile of a noble family, he fought against the king of Navarre, and won his nickname *el Campeadar* (the Champion) by killing the Navarrese champion in single combat. Essentially a mercenary, fighting both with and against the Moors, he died while defending Valencia against them, and in subsequent romances became Spain's national hero. [Sp., from Arab, *sayyid*]

-cide, *comb. form* a person or substance that kills, as *fratricide, insecticide;* a killing, as *homicide*. [F, from L *-cidium* (*caedere,* to kill)]

cider, *n.* the juice of apples expressed and fermented; (*N Am.*) an unfermented apple-juice drink. **cider-brandy,** *n.* apple-brandy. **cider-mill,** *n.* a mill in which cider is made; a machine for grinding or crushing apples. **cider-press,** *n.* a press for squeezing the juice from crushed apples. †**ciderkin**, *n.* a liquor made from the crushed mass of apples, after the juice has been expressed for cider. [OF *sidre* (F *cidre*), late L *sicera,* Gr. *sikera,* Heb. *shēkār,* strong drink (*shākar,* to drink to intoxication)]

ci-devant, *a.* former, of a past time. *n.* a French aristocrat during the Revolution. **ci-gît**, here lies (inscribed on gravestones). [F, formerly]

Cie., (*abbr.*) Company, Co. (F *Compagnie*).

cierge, *n.* a wax candle used in religious processions in the Roman Catholic Church. [earlier *cerge, serge,* OF *cerge* (F *cierge*), L *cēreus* (*cēra,* wax)]

Cierva, *n.* **Juan de la** (1895–1936), Spanish engineer. In trying to produce an aircraft that would not stall and could fly slowly, he invented the autogiro, the forerunner of the helicopter, but differing from it in having unpowered rotors that revolve freely.

c.i.f., (*abbr.*) cost, insurance, freight.

cig, *n.* (*coll.*) short for CIGARETTE.

cigala CICADA.

cigar, (*formerly*) **segar**, *n.* a roll of tobacco leaf for smoking. **cigar-holder,** *n.* a mouthpiece for a cigar. **cigar-shaped,** *a.* cylindrical, with tapering ends. **cigar-store,** *n.* (*N Am.*) a tobacconist's shop. **cigarette**, *n.* cut tobacco or aromatic herbs rolled in paper for smoking. **cigarette-card,** *n.* a picture card enclosed in cigarette packets. **cigarette-holder,** *n.* a mouthpiece for holding a cigarette. **cigarette machine,** *n.* a machine for making cigarettes; a vending machine for cigarettes. **cigarette-paper,***n.* thin paper, usu. rice-paper, for wrapping the tobacco in cigarettes. **cigarillo**, *n.* a very small cigar. [Sp. *cigarro* (perh. from *cigarra,* cicada)]

cilice, *n.* hair-cloth; a hair shirt. **cilicious**, *a.* [OE *cilic,* Gr. *kilikion,* of Cilician goat's hair]

cilium, *n.* (*pl.* **-lia**) an eyelash; a flagellum in a unicellular organism. **ciliary,** *a.* **ciliate, -ated,** *a.* **ciliation,** *n.* **ciliato-, ciliati-, cilio-,** *comb. forms* pertaining to the eyelids; furnished with microscopic hairlike processes. **ciliform**, *a.* [L, eyelash]

Cimabue, *n.* **Giovanni (Cenni de Peppi)** (*c.* 1240–1302), Italian painter, active in Florence, traditionally styled the 'father of Italian painting'. Among the works attributed to him are *Madonna and Child* (Uffizi, Florence), a huge Gothic image of the Virgin which nevertheless has a new softness and solidity that leads forwards to Giotto.

Cimbric, *a.* pertaining to the Cimbri, a tribe formerly inhabiting Jutland. *n.* the language of the Cimbri. **Cimbrian,** *n., a.*

†**cimeter,** SCIMITAR.

cimex, *n.* (*pl.* **cimices**) any of a genus (*Cimex*) of insects, containing the bed-bug.

cimices CIMEX.

Cimino, *n.* **Michael** (1943–), US film director, who established his reputation with *The Deer Hunter* (1978) (which won five Academy Awards). His other films include *Heaven's Gate* (1981), and *The Year of the Dragon* (1986).

Cimmerian, *a.* of or pertaining to the Cimmerii or their country, which was variously localized and fabled to be in a state of perpetual darkness; profoundly dark. [L *Cimmerius,* Gr. *Kimmerios*]

cimolite, *n.* a friable white clay resembling fuller's earth, first found at Cimolus in the Cyclades. [L *Cimōlia,* Gr. *Kimōlia,* pertaining to *Kimōlos*]

C.-in-C., (*abbr.*) Commander-in-Chief.

cinch, *n.* (*N Am.*) a broad kind of saddle-girth; a firm grip or hold; (*sl.*) a certainty; (*sl.*) an easy task. *v.t.* to furnish or fasten with a cinch; to hold firmly; (*sl.*) to make certain of. **to cinch up,** to tighten a cinch. [Sp. *cincha,* L *cingula,* from *cingere,* to gird]

cinchona, *n.* a genus of S American trees whose bark (Peruvian bark) yields quinine. **cinchonaceous**, *a.* **cinchenic**, *a.* **cinchonine**, *n.* an organic alkaloid contained in Peruvian bark. **cinchonism**, *n.* the disturbed condition of the body caused by overdoses of quinine. **cinchonize, -ise**, *v.t.* to treat with quinine. [from the Countess of Chinchon, wife of a Viceroy of Peru in the 17th cent.]

Cincinnatus, *n.* **Lucius Quintus** (lived 5th century BC), early Roman general. Appointed dictator in 458 BC he defeated the Aequi (an Italian people) in a brief campaign, then resumed life as a yeoman farmer. The name is applied to any great man summoned from retirement to save the state in a crisis.

cincture, *n.* a belt, a girdle, a band; an enclosure; the fillet at the top and bottom of a column. *v.t.* to gird, to encircle. [L *cinctūra* (*cinctus,* p.p. of *cingere,* to gird)]

cinder, *n.* a coal that has ceased to burn but retains heat; a partly-burnt coal or other combustible; light slag; (*pl.*) the refuse of burnt coal or wood; the remains of anything that has been subject to combustion; scoriae ejected from a volcano. **cinder-bed,** *n.* a loose bed of oyster-shells in the Middle Purbeck series. **cinder-path, -track,** *n.* a racecourse or footpath made up with cinders. **cinder-sifter,** *n.* **cindery,** *a.* [OE *sinder* (cp. Icel. *sindr,* G *Sinter,* slag or dross)]

Cinderella, *n.* a traditional European fairy tale, of which about 700 versions exist, including one by Charles Perrault. Cinderella is an ill-treated youngest daughter who is enabled by a fairy godmother to attend the royal ball. She captivates Prince Charming but must flee at midnight, losing a tiny glass slipper by which the prince later identifies her. **Cinderella dance,** *n.* a dance ending at midnight.

cine-, ciné-, *comb. forms* cinema; cinematographic, as *cine-projector*.

cineaste, *n.* a cinema enthusiast; a person who makes films. [F]

cine-camera, ciné-, *n.* a camera for taking motion pictures.

cine-film, *n.* film suitable for use in a cine-camera.

cinema, *n.* a theatre where cinematographic films are shown; films collectively; the making of films as art-form or industry. **cinema-goer,** *n.* one who goes regularly to the cinema. **Cinemascope**®, *n.* a method of film-projection on a wide screen to give a three-dimensional effect. **cinematic**, *a.* [see foll.]

cinematograph, *n.* an apparatus for projecting very rapidly on to a screen a series of photographs, so as to create the illusion of continuous motion. **cinematographer**, *n.* **cinematographic**, *a.* **cinematography,** *n.* [F *cinématographe,* from Gr. *kinēma -atos,* movement, -GRAPH]

cinéma vérité, *n.* cinema which approaches a documentary style by using realistic settings, characters etc. [F, lit. cinema truth]

cinenchyma, *n.* (*Bot.*) lactiferous tissue. [Gr. *kinein,* to move, *enchuma,* infusion (*en,* in, *chu-, cheu-, cheein,* to pour)]

Cinerama®, *n.* a wide-screen process devised in 1937. Originally three 35-mm cameras and three projectors were used to record and project a single image. Three aspects of the image were recorded and then projected on a large curved screen with the result that the images blended together to produce an illusion of vastness.

cineraria, *n.* a variety of garden or hot-house plants, of the genus *Senecio.* [L *cinerārius,* ash-coloured (*cinis -eris,* ashes)]

cinerary, *a.* pertaining to ashes. **cinerary-urn,** *n.* an urn used to contain the ashes of the dead. **cinerarium,** *n.* a place for the deposit of human ashes after cremation. **cineration,** *n.* reduction to ashes. **cinerator,** *n.* a furnace for cremating corpses. **cinerious**, *a.* ash-coloured, ash-grey. [see prec.]

Cingalese, *n.* SINHALESE.

cingulum, *n.* (*pl.* **-la**) (*Anat., Zool.*) a band of various kinds; the girdle of a priest's alb. [L, from *cingere,* to gird]

cinnabar, *n.* a native mercuric sulphide; vermilion; a large moth with red and black markings. *a.* vermilion in colour. **cinnabaric**, *a.* [late L *cinnabaris,* Gr. *kinnabari* (Oriental in orig.)]

cinnamon, *n.* the aromatic inner bark of an E Indian tree, *Cinnamomum zeylanicum,* used as a spice; applied also to other trees and their bark; a light brownish-yellow colour. **cinnamon-stone,** *n.* a cinnamon-coloured variety of garnet. **cinnamon toast,** *n.* toast spread with cinnamon and sugar. **cinnamate**, *n.* **cinnamic**, *a.* **cinnamomic**, **-monic**, *a.* [F *cinnamome,* L *cinnamōmum,* Gr. *kinamōmon,* Heb. *qinnāmōn*]

cinque, cinq, *n.* five; the five at cards or dice. **Cinque Ports,** see separate entry below. †**cinque-spotted,** *a.* having five spots. [OF *cink* (F *cinq*), L *quinque*]

cinquecento, *n.* the revived classical style of art and literature that characterized the 16th cent., esp. in Italy. **cinquecentist,** *n.* [It. (short for *mil cinque cento,* 1500)]

cinquefoil, *n.* a plant belonging to the genus *Potentilla;* (*Arch.*) an ornamental foliation in five compartments, used in tracery etc. **cinque-foiled,** *a.* [OF (cp. F *quintefeuille*), L *quinquefolium* (*quinque,* five, *folium,* leaf)]

Cinque Ports, *n.pl.* group of ports in S England, originally five, Sandwich, Dover, Hythe, Romney and Hastings, later including Rye, Winchelsea and others. Probably founded in Roman times, they rose to importance after the Norman conquest, and until the end of the 15th cent. were bound to supply the ships and men necessary against invasion.

CIO, (*abbr.*) Congress of Industrial Organizations (US).

cipher, cypher, *n.* the arithmetical symbol 0; a character of any kind used in writing or printing; a monogram, a device; a code or alphabet used to carry on secret correspondence, designed to be intelligible only to the persons concerned; anything written in this; a key to it; a person or thing of no importance; the continued sounding of an organ-pipe through a defective valve. *v.i.* to do arithmetic. *v.t.* to express in cipher; to work by means of arithmetic; of an organ, to continue sounding when the key is not pressed. **cipher-key,** *n.* a key for reading writing in cipher. [OF *cifre* (F *chiffre*), Arab. *çifr,* empty]

cipolin, cipollino, *n.* a green Italian marble with white zones like the section of an onion. [F *cipolin,* It. *cipollino* (*cipolla,* onion)]

cippus, *n.* a small, low, inscribed, monumental column. [L, a post, the stocks]

circ, *n.* (*Archaeol.*) a stone circle. [var. of CIRQUE]

circa, *prep.* about, around. *adv.* about, nearly, often used instead of *circiter* with dates. [L]

circadian, *a.* recurring or repeated (approximately) every 24 hours, as some biological cycles. [CIRCA, and L *diēs,* day]

Circassian, *a.* pertaining to the inhabitants, or country, of Circassia. *n.* a type of light cashmere of silk and mohair. [name of a region in the Caucasus]

Circe, *n.* an enchantress; a woman who seduces. **Circean**, *a.* [L, from Gr. *Kirkē,* mythic enchantress, fabled to have turned the companions of Ulysses into swine]

circensian, *a.* pertaining to the Roman circus. [L *circensis*]

circinate, *a.* (*Bot.*) rolled up (like the leaves of ferns). [L *circinātūs,* p.p. of *circināre* (*circinus,* pair of compasses)]

circle, *n.* a ring, a round figure; (*loosely*) a round body, a sphere; a round enclosure; a number of persons gathered in a ring; any series ending as it begins, and perpetually repeated; a period, a cycle; a complete series; a number of persons or things considered as bound together by some bond; a class, a set, a coterie, an association of persons having common interests; a sphere of action or influence; a territorial division (esp. in Germany); the arena of a circus; a tier of seats at a theatre; a plane figure bounded by a curved line, called the cirumference, every point in which is equidistant from a point within the figure called the centre; an inconclusive argument in which two or more statements are brought forward to prove each other. *v.t.* to move round; to surround. *v.i.* to form a circle; to revolve; to be passed round. **dress circle,** the principal tier of seats in a theatre, in which evening dress is optional. **great circle,** a circle dividing a sphere into two equal parts. **lesser, small circle,** a circle dividing a sphere into two unequal parts. **Polar circles,** the Arctic and Antarctic parallels of latitude. **stone circle,** a ring of prehistoric monoliths. **to circle in,** to confine. **to come full circle,** to come round to where one started. **to go, run, round in circles,** to be very active without achieving much. **to square the circle,** to undertake an impossible task; to construct geometrically a square of an area equal to that of a given circle. **circled,** *a.* having the form of a circle; encircled; marked with a circle or circles. **circler,** *n.* **circlet**, *n.* a little circle; a ring or circular band worn on the finger, head etc. *v.i.* to move in small circles. **circlewise,** *adv.* [OE *circul* (ME and OF *cercle*), L *circulus,* dim. of *circus,* ring]

circs, *n.* (*coll.*) short for CIRCUMSTANCES.

circuit, *n.* the act of revolving or moving round, a revolution; the line enclosing a space, the distance round about; the space enclosed in a circle or within certain limits; formerly the periodical visitation of judges for holding assizes; the district thus visited; the barristers making the circuit; among Methodists, a group of churches associated together for purposes of government and organization of the ministry; a continuous electrical communication between the poles of a battery; a series of conductors, including the lamps, motors etc., through which a current passes; a motor-racing track; a series of sporting tournaments visited regularly by competitors; a group of theatres or cinemas under the same ownership, putting on the same entertainment in turn. **short circuit** SHORT. **circuit board,** *n.* (*Comput.*) a board on which an electronic circuit is built, with a connector to plug into a piece of equipment. **circuit-breaker,** *n.* a device which stops the electric current in the event of e.g. a short circuit. **circuit training,** *n.* a form of athletic training consisting of repeated cycles of exercises. **circuitous**, *a.* indirect, roundabout. **circuitously,** *adv.* **circuitousness,** *n.* **circuitry,** *n.* electric or electronic circuits collectively; the design of such a circuit. **circuity**, *n.* indirect procedure. [F, from L *circuitus,* a going round, from *circumīre* (*circum,* round, *īre,* to go)]

circulable CIRCULATE.

circular, *a.* in the shape of a circle; round; pertaining to a circle; forming part of a circle; moving in a circle; cyclic; of a letter, addressed in identical terms to a number of persons; consisting of an argument in a circle. *n.* a letter or printed notice of which a copy is sent to many persons. **circular instruments,** *n.pl.* (*Geom.*) instruments graduated for the whole circle. **circular letter,** *n.* a notice, advertisement or appeal printed or duplicated for sending to a number of persons. **circular lines,** *n.pl.* lines of sines, tangents, secants etc. on the plane scale and sector. **circular note,** *n.* a letter of credit addressed to several bankers. **circular numbers,** *n.pl.* those whose powers terminate in the same digits as the roots. **circular saw,** *n.* a rotating disk notched with teeth for cutting timber etc. **circular scanning,** *n.* (*TV*) a method of scanning in which the spot follows a spiral path. **circular ticket,** *n.* a ticket for a circular tour. **circular tour,** *n.* a journey to a number of places ending at the starting-point. **circularity,** *n.* the state of being circular. **circularize, -ise,** *v.t.* to send circulars to. **circularly,** *adv.* [ME and A-F *circuler,* OF *circulier,* L *circulāris* (*circulus,* CIRCLE)]

circulate, *v.i.* to move round; to pass through certain channels, as blood in the body, the sap of plants etc.; to pass from point to point or hand to hand as money; to be diffused, to travel. *v.t.* to cause to pass from point to point or hand to hand; to spread, to diffuse. **circulating,** *a.* that circulates; current; (*Math.*) recurring. **circulating decimal,** *n.* a decimal which cannot be expressed with perfect exactness in figures, and in which one or more figures recur continually in the same order. **circulating library,** *n.* a lending library. **circulating medium,** *n.* the currency of a country. **circulable,** *a.* **circulation,** *n.* the act of circulating; the state of being circulated; the motion of the blood in a living animal, by which it is propelled by the heart through the arteries to all parts of the body, and returned to the heart through the veins; the analogous motion of sap in plants; the free movement of water, air etc.; distribution of books, newspapers, news etc.; the amount of distribution, the number of copies sold; a medium of exchange, currency. **circulative,** *a.* tending to circulate; promoting circulation. **circulator,** *n.* one who or that which circulates; a circulating decimal. **circulatory,** *a.* circular, circulating. [L *circulāre*]

circum-, *pref.* round, round about; surrounding; indirectly; pertaining to the circumference. [L, round, round about, surrounding]

circumambient, *a.* going round about; surrounding. **circumambiency,** *n.* [L *ambiēns -entem,* pres.p. of *ambīre,* to go round (*ambi-,* about, *īre,* to go)]

circumambulate, *v.t.* to walk or go round about. *v.i.* to walk about, to beat about the bush. **circumambulation,** *n.* **circumambulatory,** *a.* [L *ambulāre,* to walk]

circumbendibus, *n.* (*facet.*) a roundabout or indirect way; a circumlocution.

circumcise, *v.t.* to remove surgically or by ritual the prepuce or foreskin in the male, or the clitoris in the female; to render spiritual and holy; to purify. **circumcision,** *n.* the operation of circumcising, a Jewish and Muslim rite in males; spiritual purification; the festival of the Circumcision of Christ, on 1 Jan. [OF *circonciser,* L *circumcīdere* (*cædere,* to cut)]

circumdenudation, *n.* (*Geol.*) denudation round a spot which remains as an elevated tract.

circumduct, *v.t.* to lead about or round; (*Law*) to nullify; (*Sc., Law*) to declare elapsed. **circumduction,** *n.* the act of circumducting; a leading about; nullifying or cancelling. [L *circumductus,* p.p. of *circumdūcere* (*dūcere,* to lead)]

circumference, *n.* the line that bounds a circle; a periphery; the distance round a space or a body; circuit. **circumferential,** *a.* [L *circumferentia* (*ferre,* to bear)]

circumflex, *n.* a mark (ˆ or in Gr. ͂) placed above a vowel to indicate accent, quality, or contraction. *a.* marked with such accent; (*Anat.*) bent, turning, or curving round something. *v.t.* to mark or pronounce with a circumflex. **circumflexion, -flection,** *n.* [L *circumflexus* (*flexus,* p.p. of *flectere,* to bend)]

circumfluent, *a.* flowing round on all sides. **circumfluence,** *n.* **circumfluous,** *a.* flowing around; flowed round. [L *circumfluens -entem,* pres.p. of *circumfluere* (*fluere,* to flow)]

circumfuse, *v.t.* to pour round, as a fluid; to surround, to bathe in or with. **circumfusion,** *n.* [L *circumfūsus,* p.p. of *circumfundere* (*fundere,* to pour)]

circumgyrate, *v.i.* to turn, roll or spin round. **circumgyration,** *n.* **circumgyratory,** *a.*

circumjacent, *a.* lying round; bordering. [L *circumjacēns -entem,* pres.p. of *circumjacēre* (*jacēre,* to lie)]

circumlittoral, *a.* adjacent to the shore; pertaining to the zone immediately outside of the littoral. [L *lītus -oris,* the shore]

circumlocution, *n.* periphrasis; the use of roundabout, indirect or evasive language; the use of many words where few would suffice. **Circumlocution Office,** *n.* a type of bureaucratic red-tape and roundabout procedure (from Dickens's *Little Dorrit*). **circumlocutional,** *a.* **circumlocutionary,** *a.* **circumlocutionist,** *n.* **circumlocutory,** *a.* [L *circumlocūtio -ōnem*]

circumlunar, *a.* situated, or moving, around the moon.

circummeridian, *a.* (*Astron.*) occurring near or pertaining to what is near the meridian.

circumnavigate, *v.t.* to sail completely round. **circumnavigation,** *n.* **circumnavigator,** *n.* [L *circumnāvigāre*]

circumnutate, *v.i.* to nod or turn successively to all points of the compass, as the tips of growing plants. **circumnutation,** *n.*

circumoral, *a.* surrounding the mouth. [L *ōs ōris,* mouth]

circumpolar, *a.* (*Geog.*) situated round or near the pole; (*Astron.*) revolving about the pole (not setting).

circumscribe, *v.t.* to write or draw around; to limit, to define by bounds, to restrict; (*Log.*) to define; (*Geom.*) to surround with a figure that touches at every possible point. **circumscriber,** *n.* **circumscription,** *n.* the act of circumscribing; the imposing of limitations; a boundary line; a circular inscription; a definition; a geometrical figure that encloses and touches at every possible point. **circumscriptive,** *a.* **circumscriptively,** *adv.* [L *circumscrībere* (*scrībere,* to write)]

circumsolar, *a.* revolving round or situated near the sun.

circumspect, *a.* looking on all sides; cautious, wary. **circumspection, circumspectness,** *n.* **circumspective,** *a.* **circumspectly,** *adv.* [L *circumspectus,* prudent, p.p. of *circumspicere* (*specere,* to look)]

circumstance, *n.* something attending or relative to a fact or case; an incident, an event; a concomitant; abundance of detail (in a narrative), circumstantiality; ceremony, pomp, fuss; (*pl.*) the facts, relations, influences and other conditions that affect an act or an event; the facts, conditions etc. that affect one's living. *v.t.* to place in a particular situation. **easy circumstances,** prosperity. **in, under, the circumstances,** in the particular situation for which allowance should be made. **straitened circumstances,** indigence. **circumstanced,** *a.* situated; †conditioned by circumstances. [OF, from L *circumstantia,* from *-stāns -ntem,* pres.p. of *circumstāre* (*stāre,* to stand)]

circumstantial, *a.* depending on circumstances; incidental, not essential; detailed, minute. †*n.* something incidental; a non-essential. **circumstantial evidence,** *n.* evidence inferred from circumstances which usually attend facts of a particular nature. **circumstantiality,** *n.* **circumstantially,** *adv.* **circumstantiate,** *v.t.* to provide evidence for; to describe in detail.

circumterrestrial, *a.* situated, or moving, around the earth.

circumvallate, *v.t.* to surround or enclose with a rampart. **circumvallation,** *n.* [L *circumvallāre* (*vallāre,* from *vallum,* a rampart)]

circumvent, *v.t.* to go round, avoid; to deceive, to outwit, to cheat, to get the best of. **circumvention,** *n.* [L *circumventus,* p.p. of *circumvenīre* (*venīre,* to come)]

†**circumvolve,** *v.t.* to roll round or about; to en-

compass. *v.i.* to revolve. **circumvolution**, *n.* the act of rolling round; a winding about, a coil, a convolution; a revolution; a winding or tortuous movement; (*Arch.*) the spiral in a volute. [L *circumvolvere* (*volvere*, to roll)]

circus, *n.* the Circus Maximus in ancient Rome; any similar building; a circle of buildings at the intersection of streets; a travelling company of clowns, acrobats, trained animals etc.; the place, usu. a circular tent, where they perform; such a performance; a set of people who travel together and put on performances, as a *flying circus;* (*coll.*) a scene of noisy, disorganized activity. [L, a ring]

ciré, *n.* satin with a waxed surface. [F, waxed]

cirque, *n.* a circular space; (*poet.*) a circus or arena; a circular recess among hills. [F]

cirrate CIRRUS.

cirrhosis, *n.* a disease of the liver in which it becomes yellowish and nodular because of the death of liver cells and the growth of fibrous tissue. **cirrhotic**, *a.* [Gr. *kirrhos*, yellow]

cirri-, cirro-, *comb. form* having fringe-like appendages.

cirriferous, *a.* (*Bot.*) producing tendrils.

cirriped, -pede, *n.* any individual of the Cirripedia, a class of marine animals related to the Crustacea, having cirriform feet and comprising the barnacles and acorn-shells.

cirrocumulus, *n.* a cloud broken up into small fleecy masses.

cirrostratus, *n.* a horizontal or slightly inclined sheet of cloud more or less broken into fleecy masses.

cirrus, *n.* (*Bot.*) a tendril; (*Zool.*) a slender locomotive filament; a barbule; (*Meteor.*) a lofty feathery cloud. **cirrate**, **cirrose**, **cirrous,** *a.* **cirriform**, *a.* [L, a curl]

cis-, *pref.* on this side of. [L, on this side of]

cisalpine, *a.* on the Roman side of the Alps; south of the Alps.

Cisalpine Gaul, *n.* region of the Roman province of Gallia (N Italy) S of the Alps. **Transalpine Gaul**, the region N of the Alps, comprised Belgium, France, the Netherlands and Switzerland.

cisatlantic, *a.* on the speaker's side of the Atlantic, as distinct from *transatlantic*.

ciselure, *n.* graving; chased work. [F, from *ciseler*, to carve (*ciseau*, CHISEL)]

Ciskei, Republic of, a Bantu homeland in South Africa, which became independent 1981, although this is not recognized by any other country. **area** 7700 sq km/ 2974 sq miles. **capital** Bisho. **products** pineapples, timber, metal products, leather, textiles. **population** (1984) 903,681. **language** Xhosa.

cis-Leithan, *a.* Austrian, non-Hungarian. [river *Leitha*]

cislunar, *a.* between the moon and the earth.

cismontane, *a.* on the north side of the mountains (this as regards France and Germany).

cispadane, *a.* on this side of the Po (L *Podus*), as regards Rome, south of the Po.

cispontine, *a.* on the north side of the Thames, in London. [L *pons -tem*, bridge]

cissoid, *a.* (*Geom.*) contained within two intersecting curves. [Gr. *kissoeides*, like ivy]

cissy, sissy, *a.* (*derog.*) effeminate. *n.* an effeminate person. [*sis*, short for SISTER; perh. also *Cecily*, girl's name]

cist, *n.* a tomb consisting of a kind of stone chest formed of rows of stones, with a flat stone for cover; a casket or chest, esp. one used for carrying the sacred utensils in the Greek mysteries. [L *cista*, Gr. *kistē*, chest]

Cistercian, *n.* a member of a monastic order founded in 1098, and named from the first convent, Cîteaux, in France. *a.* pertaining to the Cistercians. [med. L *Cistercium*, Cîteaux]

cistern, *n.* a tank for storing water; a reservoir; a water-tank for a water-closet. [OF *cisterne*, L *cisterna* (*cista*, a chest)]

cistus, *n.* (*pl.* **-tuses, -ti**) the rock-rose, a plant of a genus (*Cistus*) with ephemeral flowers somewhat like a wild rose. [L, from Gr. *kistos*]

cistvaen, KISTVAEN.

†**cit,** *n.* (*derog.*) a townsman. [short for CITIZEN]

citable CITE.

citadel, *n.* a castle or fortified place in a city; a stronghold; a final retreat; a Salvation Army hall. [F *citadelle*, It. *cittadella*, dim. of *cittade*, L *cīvitās -tātem*, CITY]

cite, *v.t.* to quote, to allege as an authority; to quote as an instance; to refer to; to summon to appear in court. **citable,** *a.* †**cital,** *n.* a summons, a citation; a reproof, a recital. **citation,** *n.* a summons; mention in dispatches etc.; a quotation; an official commendation, for bravery etc. [F *citer*, L *citāre*, freq. of *ciēre*, to rouse]

cithara, *n.* an instrument somewhat resembling a harp. **citharist,** *n.* **citharistic,** *a.* [L, from Gr. *kithara*]

cither, cithern, **cittern**, *n.* a mediaeval kind of guitar with wire strings. [from prec.]

citified CITY.

citizen, *n.* a member of a state in the enjoyment of political rights; a burgess or freeman of a city or town; a dweller in a town; a civilian. *a.* having the character of a citizen; town-bred. **citizen's arrest,** *n.* one made by a member of the public. **citizens' band,** *n.* a band of radio frequencies designated for use by private citizens for communication between individuals. **citizenhood,** *n.* **citizenry,** *n.* citizens collectively. **citizenship,** *n.* the state of being a citizen. [ME *citesein*, A-F *citeseyn*, OF *citeain* (*cité*, CITY, -AN)]

citole, *n.* a stringed musical instrument. [OF, prob. from L CITHARA]

citr- CITR(O)-.

citrate, *n.* a salt of citric acid. **citric**, *a.* derived from the citron. **citric acid,** *n.* the acid found in lemons, citrons, limes, oranges etc. [CITRON]

citrine, *a.* like a citron; greenish-yellow. *n.* (*Min.*) a yellow, pellucid variety of quartz. **citrinous,** *a.* lemon-coloured.

citr(o)-, *comb. form.* citric. [L *citrus*, CITRON]

citron, *n.* a tree, *Citrus medica,* bearing large lemon-like fruit. [F, from late L *citro -ōnem*, L *citrus*]

citronella, *n.* a fragrant oil used to drive away insects.

citrus, *n.* any of a genus (*Citrus*) of trees and shrubs containing the orange, lemon, citron etc. **citrous,** *a.*

cittern CITHER.

city, *n.* a town incorporated by a charter; the inhabitants of a city; (*pop.*) a large and important town; a cathedral town. *a.* pertaining to a city; characteristic of a city. **City technology college,** in Britain, a planned network of some 20 schools, financed jointly by government and industry, designed to teach technological subjects in inner-city areas to students aged 11–18. **Eternal City,** Rome. **the Celestial City,** Heaven. **the City,** the part of London governed by the Lord Mayor and Corporation; the banks and financial institutions located there. **city article,** *n.* an article in a newspaper dealing with commerce or finance. **City company,** *n.* a London livery company representing one of the mediaeval guilds. **city desk,** *n.* the editorial department of a newspaper dealing with financial news; (*N Am.*) the department of a newspaper dealing with local news. **city editor,** *n.* one in charge of a city desk. **city fathers,** *n.pl.* men in charge of the administration of a city. **City man,** *n.* one engaged in commerce or finance. **citied,** *a.* containing cities (*usu. in comb.*, as *many-citied*). **citified,** *a.* townish; having the peculiarities of dwellers in cities. **cityless,** *a.* **cityward, -wards,** *adv.* [OF *cité*, L *cīvitātem*, acc. of *cīvitās* (*cīvis*, a citizen)]

civet, *n.* a resinous musky substance obtained from the anal pouch of the genus *Viverra,* and used as a perfume. *v.t.* to perfume with civet. **civet-cat,** *n.* a carnivorous quadruped from Asia and Africa, belonging to the genus *Viverra*. [F *civette*, Arab. *zabād*]

civic, *a.* pertaining to a city or citizens; urban; municipal; civil. **civic centre,** *n.* a group of buildings including the town hall and local administrative offices. **civic crown,** *n.* a garland of oak-leaves awarded to a Roman soldier who saved the life of a comrade in battle, often used in architecture. **civically,** *adv.* **civicism,** †**civism,** *n.* citizenship; patriotism; (*Hist.*) allegiance to the doctrines of the French Revolution. **civics,** *n. sing.* the study of citizenship and municipal government. [L *cīvicus* (*cīvis,* a citizen)]

civil, *a.* pertaining to citizens; domestic, not foreign; municipal, commercial, legislative; well-regulated; civilized, polite, courteous; †grave, sober; pertaining to social, commercial and administrative affairs, not warlike, not military or naval; (*Law*) pertaining to private matters, not criminal. **civil action, process,** *n.* an action or process in civil law. **civil architecture,** *n.* the construction of buildings for the purposes of civil life. **civil aviation,** *n.* civilian, non-military airlines and their operations. **civil day,** *n.* a day in the civil year, 24 hours. **civil defence,** *n.* a civilian service for the protection of lives and property in the event of enemy attack. **civil disobedience,** *n.* a concerted plan in a political campaign taking the form of refusal to pay taxes or perform civil duties. **civil engineer,** *n.* **civil engineering,** *n.* the science of constructing docks, railways, roads etc. **civil law,** *n.* the law dealing with private rights, not criminal matters; Roman law. **civil liberties,** *n.pl.* personal freedoms, e.g. freedom of speech, within the framework of the state. **civil list,** *n.* the yearly sum granted for the support of a sovereign or ruler; the officers of a government who are paid from the public treasury. **civil list pension,** a small pension granted by the state to selected artists, writers, musicians etc. **civil magistrate,** *n.* a magistrate not dealing with ecclesiastical matters. **civil marriage,** *n.* one performed by a civil official, not by a clergyman. **civil rights,** *n.pl.* the rights of an individual or group within a state to certain freedoms, e.g. from discrimination. **civil servant,** *n.* a member of the civil service. **civil service,** *n.* the non-military branch of the public service, dealing with public administration. **civil state,** *n.* the entire body of the citizens, as distinct from the military, ecclesiastical and naval establishments. **civil suit,** *n.* (*Law*) a suit for a private claim or injury. **civil war,** *n.* a war between citizens of the same country. **civil year,** *n.* the legal year (in any given state), as distinct from an *astronomical year*. **civilian,** *n.* a person engaged in civil life, not belonging to the army or navy; †(*Law*) a student or professor of civil law. *a.* engaged in civil pursuits. **civilianize, -ise,** *v.t.* **civility,** *n.* the quality of being civil; politeness, courtesy. **civilly,** *adv.* [F, from L *cīvīlis* (*cīvis,* citizen)]

civilize, -ise, *v.t.* to reclaim from barbarism; to instruct in the arts and refinements of civilized society. **civilizable, -isable,** *a.* **civilization, -isation,** *n.* the act or process of civilizing; the state of being civilized; refinement, social development; civilized society. **civilizer, -iser,** *n.* [F *civiliser* (CIVIL, -IZE)]

Civil War, American, a war (1861–65) between the Southern or Confederate States of America and the Northern or Union States. The former wished to maintain their 'states' rights', in particular the institution of slavery, and claimed the right to secede from the Union; the latter fought initially to maintain the Union, and later (1863) to emancipate the slaves.

Civil War, English, in British history, the struggle in the middle years of the 17th cent. between the king and the royalists (Cavaliers) on the one side and the Parliamentarians (Roundheads) on the other.

Civil War, Spanish, a war (1936–39) precipitated by a military revolt led by Gen. Franco against the Republican govt. Inferior military capability led to the gradual defeat of the Republicans by 1939.

†**civism** CIVIC.

civvies, *n.pl.* (*Army coll.*) civilian clothes. **Civvy Street,** *n.* civilian life.

Cl, (*chem. symbol*) chlorine.

cl., (*abbr.*) centilitre; class.

clachan, *n.* a small village or hamlet in the Highlands. [Gael., orig. a circle of stones (*clach,* a stone)]

clack, *v.i.* to make a sharp, sudden noise like a clap or crack; to chatter rapidly and noisily. *v.t.* to cause to emit a sudden, sharp noise; to knock together. *n.* a sudden, sharp sound frequently repeated; rapid and noisy chattering; a contrivance in a corn-mill that strikes the hopper and facilitates the descent of the corn; a bell that gives notice when more grain is needed to feed the hopper; a kind of ball-valve; a noisy tongue; a chatterbox. †**clack-dish,** *n.* a dish with a movable lid, formerly used by beggars to attract attention. **clack-valve,** *n.* a valve hinged by one edge. **clacker,** *n.* one who or that which clacks; a clack-valve. **clackety,** *a.* [prob. imit. (cp. Icel. *klaka,* to twitter, F *claquer*)]

clad, *p.p.* CLOTHE.

cladding, *n.* a protective coating, e.g. of stone on a building or insulating material on a hot-water pipe. [*clad,* past of CLOTHE]

clad(o)-, *comb. form.* (*Bot., Zool.*) branching; pertaining to branches or branchlets. **clade,** *n.* a group of organisms sharing a unique characteristic because of evolution from a common ancestor. **cladistics,** *n. sing.* a method of classifying organisms based on clades. [Gr. *klados,* a twig, a shoot]

claes, (*Sc.*) CLOTHES.

claim, *v.t.* to demand, or challenge, as a right; to assert that one has or is (something) or has done (something); to affirm, to maintain; to be deserving of; †to proclaim, to call. *v.i.* †to cry out, to call; †to assert claims. *n.* a real or supposed right; a title; a piece of land allotted to one; a piece of land marked out by a settler or miner with the intention of buying it when it is offered for sale; †a loud call. **claim-jumper,** *n.* one who seizes on land claimed by another. **claim-jumping,** *n.* **claimable,** *a.* **claimant,** *n.* one who makes a claim. [OF *claim-,* stem of *clamer,* L *clāmāre,* to call out]

Clair, *n.* **René**, (pseudonym of René-Lucien Chomette) (1898–1981), French film-maker, originally a poet, novelist, and journalist. His *Sous les Toits de Paris/Under the Roofs of Paris* (1930) was one of the first sound films.

clairaudience, *n.* the faculty of hearing voices and other sounds not perceptible to the senses. **clairaudient,** *n., a.* [F *clair,* clear, L *clārus;* AUDIENCE]

clair-obscure, CHIAROSCURO. [F *clair-obscur*]

clairvoyance, *n.* the power of perceiving objects not present to the senses; unusual sensitivity or insight. **clairvoyant,** *n.* one having the power of clairvoyance. *a.* pertaining to or having the power of clairvoyance. **clairvoyante,** *n. fem.* [F *clair,* L *clārus,* clear, *voir,* L *vidēre,* to see]

clam¹, *v.t.* (*dial.*) to smear with anything viscous. *v.i.* to be sticky or clammy. [OE *clǣman* (confused with ME *clam,* sticky, see CLAMMY)]

clam², *n.* a clamp or vice; a clutch; the lining of a vice. [OE *clamm,* bond, fetter (allied to CLAMP¹)]

clam³, *n.* a name for several edible bivalves; esp. (*N Am.*) *Venus mercenaria,* the hard, and *Mya arenaria,* the soft clam; (*coll.*) a taciturn person. **to clam up,** to become silent. **clambake,** *n.* (*N Am.*) a beach party at which clams are cooked and eaten; any noisy gathering. **clam-shell,** *n.* the shell of a clam. [prob. from prec.]

clamant, *a.* crying or begging earnestly; clamorous. **clamantly,** *adv.* [L *clāmans -ntem,* pres.p. of *clāmāre,* to cry out]

clamber, *v.i.* to climb any steep place with hands and feet, to climb with difficulty; to tower, ascend. *v.t.* to climb up with difficulty. *n.* a climb. [prob. formed from OE *climban,* to climb (cp., however, Icel. *clambra,* to pinch together, clamp, and G *klammern,* to clamp)]

clamjamphrie, *n.* (*Sc.*) rubbish; an affair of no value; nonsense; a rabble, a contemptible lot. [etym. doubtful]

clammy, *a.* moist, damp; sticky; of weather, humid. **clammily,** *adv.* **clamminess,** *n.* [perh. from OE *clām,* clay, confused with CLAM¹]

clamour, *n.* a loud and continuous shouting or calling out; a continued and loud expression of complaint, demand or appeal; popular outcry. *v.t.* to shout (down); to utter or express with loud noise. *v.i.* to cry out loudly and earnestly; to demand or complain importunately; to make a loud noise. **clamorous,** *a.* **clamorously,** *adv.* **clamorousness,** *n.* [OF, from L *clāmor* (*clāmāre,* to cry out)]

clamp[1], *n.* anything rigid which strengthens, fastens or binds; a piece of timber or iron used to fasten work together; a frame with two tightening screws to hold pieces of wood together; a back batten fastened crosswise to several boards to prevent them from warping; (*Naut.*) the internal planking under the shelf on which the deck beams rest; a wheel-clamp. *v.t.* to unite, fasten or strengthen with a clamp or clamps; to immobilize with a wheel-clamp. **to clamp down (on),** to impose (heavier) restrictions (on). **clamp-down,** *n.* **clamper,** *n.* [not in early use; etym. doubtful (cp. Dut. *klampe* (now *klamp*), G *Klampe,* OE *clam*)]

clamp[2], *n.* a pile of bricks for burning; a heap, mound or stack of turf, rubbish, potatoes etc. *v.t.* to pile into a heap; to store in a clamp. [perh. from prec. (cp. Dut. *klamp*)]

clamp[3], *n.* a heavy footstep or tread. *v.i.* to tread heavily and noisily. **clamper[1],** *n.* [imit., cp. CLUMP]

clamper[2], *v.t.* (*Sc.*) to botch up. [prob. from CLAMP[1]]

clan, *n.* a tribe or number of families bearing the same name, descended from a common ancestor, and united under a chieftain representing that ancestor; a large extended family; a clique, a set. **clannish,** *a.* united closely together, as the members of a clan; of or pertaining to a clan; cliquish. **clannishly,** *adv.* **clannishness,** *n.* **clanship,** *n.* the system or state of clans. **clansman,** *n.* a member of a clan. [Gael. *clann* (perh. from L *planta*)]

clandestine, *a.* secret, surreptitious, underhand. **clandestinely,** *adv.* **clandestineness,** *n.* [F *clandestin,* L *clandestīnus* (*clam,* in secret)]

clang, *v.t.* to strike together, so as to cause a sharp, ringing sound. *v.i.* to emit a sharp, ringing sound; to resound. *n.* a sharp, ringing noise, as of two pieces of metal struck together. **clanger,** *n.* (*coll.*) a foolish mistake; a social blunder. **clangour,** *n.* a sharp, ringing sound or series of sounds. **clangorous,** *a.* **clangorously,** *adv.* [L *clangere* (cp. Gr. *klangē,* a clang)]

clank, *v.t.* to strike together so as to make a heavy rattling sound. *v.i.* to make such a sound. *n.* a sound as of solid metallic bodies struck together (usu. denotes a deeper sound than *clink,* and a less resounding one than *clang*). [onomat., or perh. from Dut. *klank*]

clannish, etc. CLAN.

clap[1], *v.t.* (*past, p.p.* **clapped**) to strike together noisily; to strike quickly or slap with something flat; to shut hastily; to put or place suddenly or hastily; to applaud, by striking the hands together. *v.i.* †to knock loudly; to move quickly; to shut (as a door) with a bang; to strike the hands together in applause. *n.* the noise made by the collision of flat surfaces; a sudden loud noise; a peal of thunder; applause shown by clapping; a heavy slap. **to clap eyes on,** to catch sight of. **to clap on,** to add hastily. †**to clap up,** to make hastily; to conclude (as a bargain) hastily; to imprison hastily. †**clap-dish,** *n.* a clack-dish. **clap-net,** *n.* a folding net for snaring birds or catching insects. **clapped-out,** *a.* (*sl.*) finished, exhausted; (*sl.*) of no more use. **claptrap,** *n.* showy words or deeds designed to win applause or public favour; pretentious or insincere nonsense. *a.* deceptive, unreal. **clapper,** *n.* one who or that which claps; the tongue of a bell; the clack of a mill-hopper; a noisy rattle for scaring birds. **like the clappers,** (*sl.*) extremely fast. **clapper-board,** *n.* a pair of hinged boards clapped together at the start of a take during film shooting to help in synchronizing sound and vision. [ME *clappen* (perh. from OE), cp. Dut. and G *klappen,* Icel. *klappa*]

clap[2], *n.* (*sl.*) gonorrhoea. [F *clapoir,* a venereal sore]

clap-board, *n.* a cask stave; (*N Am.*) a feather-edged board used to cover the roofs and sides of houses. *v.t.* (*N Am.*) to cover with clap-boards. **clap-boarding,** *n.* [formed from obs. *clapholt,* LG *klappholt*]

clapperclaw, *v.t.* to beat, to scratch, to drub, to revile. [CLAPPER (CLAP[1]), CLAW]

Clapton *n.* **Eric** (1945–), English blues and rock guitarist, singer and composer, member of the groups Yardbirds and Cream in the 1960s. One of the pioneers of heavy rock and an influence on younger musicians, he later adopted a more subdued style.

claptrap CLAP[1].

claque, *n.* a body of hired applauders; the system of engaging applauders. **claquer, claqueur,** *n.* [F, from *claquer,* to clap]

clarabella, *n.* an organ stop with open wooden pipes giving a powerful fluty tone. [L *clārus,* clear, *bellus,* pretty]

Clare, *n.* county on the west coast of the Republic of Ireland, in the province of Munster; area 3188 sq km/ 1231 sq miles; population (1981) 87,500. Shannon airport is here.

Clare, *n.* **John** (1793–1864), English poet. His work includes *Poems Descriptive of Rural Life* (1820), *The Village Minstrel* (1821) and *Shepherd's Calendar* (1827). Clare's work was largely rediscovered in the 20th century.

Clare, St *n.* (*c.* 1194–1253), Christian saint. Born in Assisi, Italy, she became at 18 a follower of St Francis, who founded for her the convent of San Damiano. Here she gathered the first members of the **Order of Poor Clares**. In 1958 she was proclaimed by Pius XII the patron saint of television, since in 1252 she saw from her convent sickbed the services celebrating Christmas in the basilica of St Francis in Assisi. Feast day 12 Aug.

clarence, *n.* a closed four-wheeled carriage for four passengers, and a seat for the driver. [Duke of *Clarence,* later William IV]

Clarenceux, *n.* (*Her.*) the second King-of-Arms. [Duke of *Clarence,* son of Edward III, who first held this office]

clarendon, *n., a.* (*Print.*) a condensed type with heavy face. [*Clarendon* Press, Oxford]

Clarendon, Constitutions of, in English history, a series of resolutions agreed by a council summoned by Henry II at Clarendon in Wiltshire (1164). The Constitutions aimed at limiting the secular power of the clergy, and were abandoned after the murder of Thomas Becket. They form an important early English legal document.

clare-obscure, CHIAROSCURO.

claret, *n.* a light red Bordeaux wine; any light red wine resembling Bordeaux; an artificial claret-coloured fancy-fly; (*sl.*) blood. **to tap the claret,** to strike the nose and make it bleed. **claret-coloured,** *a.* reddish-violet. **claret-cup,** *n.* a beverage composed of iced claret, brandy, lemon, borage etc. [OF *clairet,* dim. of *clair,* L *clārus,* CLEAR]

clarify, *v.t.* to clear from visible impurities; to make transparent; to make lucid or perspicuous. *v.i.* to become transparent. **clarification,** *n.* **clarifier,** *n.* one who or that which clarifies; a vessel in which sugar is clarified. [OF *clarifier,* L *clārificāre* (*clārus,* clear, *facere,* to make)]

clarinet, *n.* a keyed single-reed instrument. **clarinettist,** *n.* [F *clarinette,* dim. of *clarine* (L *clārus,* clear)]

clarion, *n.* a kind of trumpet, with a narrow tube, and loud and clear note; sound of or as of a clarion; an organ stop giving a similar tone. *a.* loud and clear. *v.t.* to announce as with a clarion; to trumpet. **clarionet,** *n.* a clarinet. [OF *claron,* med. L *clārio -ōnem* (L *clārus,* clear)]

clarity, *n.* clearness; †glory, splendour. [ME and OF *clarté,* L *clāritas -tātem* (L *clārus*)]

Clarke[1], *n.* **Arthur C(harles)** (1917–), English science fiction and non-fiction writer, who originated the plan for the modern system of communications satellites (1945). His works include *Childhood's End* (1953) and the screen play of *2001: A Space Odyssey* (1968).

Clark[2], *n.* **Joe (Joseph) Charles** (1939–), Canadian Progressive Conservative politician, born in Alberta. He became party leader in 1976, and in May 1979 defeated Trudeau at the polls to become the youngest prime minister in Canada's history. Following the rejection of his government's budget, he was defeated in a second election in Feb. 1980. He became Secretary of State for External Affairs (foreign minister) in the Mulroney government (1984–).

Clark[3], *n.* **Mark (Wayne)** (1896–1984), US general in World War II. In 1942 he became chief of staff for ground forces, led a successful secret mission by submarine to get information in N Africa preparatory to the Allied invasion, and commanded the 5th Army in the invasion of Italy.

Clarke orbit, *n.* an alternative name for geostationary orbit, an orbit 35,900 km/22,300 miles high, in which satellites circle at the same speed as the Earth turns. This orbit was first suggsted by space writer Arthur C. Clarke in 1945.

clarkia, *n.* a plant of a genus (*Clarkia*) of herbaceous annuals of the order *Onagraceae* having a showy purple flower. [William *Clark,* 1770–1838]

Clarkson, *n.* **Thomas** (1760–1846), British philanthropist. From 1785 he devoted himself to a campaign against slavery. He was one of the founders of the Anti-Slavery Society (1823) and was largely responsible for the abolition of slavery in British colonies (1833).

clarty, *a.* (*Sc., North.*) muddy, dirty, miry. [*clart,* sticky mud (etym. unknown)]

clary, *n.* name of several labiate plants of the genus *Salvia,* esp. *S. sclarea,* a garden pot-herb. **clary-water, -wine,** *n.* a cordial compounded of brandy, sugar, clary-flowers, cinnamon and ambergris. [OE *slaridge,* med. L *sclarea*]

clash, *v.i.* to make a loud noise by striking against something; to come into collision; to disagree; to conflict; to interfere. *v.t.* to cause one thing to strike against another so as to produce a noise. *n.* the noise produced by the violent collision of two bodies; opposition, contradiction; conflict; disharmony of colours. [imit., cp. CLACK, CRASH and CRACK[1]]

clasp, *n.* a catch, hook or interlocking device for fastening; a fastening; a buckle or brooch; a close embrace; a grasp; a metal bar attached to a ribbon carrying a medal commemorating a battle or other exploit. *v.t.* to fasten or shut with or as with a clasp or buckle; to fasten (a clasp); to cling to by twining; to embrace; to grasp. *v.i.* to cling (to). **clasp-knife,** *n.* a pocket-knife in which the blade shuts into the hollow part of the handle. **clasper,** *n.* one who or that which clasps; one of a pair of organs in some insects and fishes by which the male holds the female. [ME *claspen, clapsen* (cp. OE *clyppan,* to grasp, embrace)]

class, *n.* a number of persons or things ranked together; social rank; the system of social caste; a number of scholars or students taught together; (*N Am.*) the students taken collectively who expect to graduate at the same time; a division according to quality; (*sl.*) high quality; a number of individuals having the same essential or accidental qualities; a division of animals or plants next above an order. *v.t.* to arrange in a class or classes. *a.* (*sl.*) of good quality. **-class,** *a.* (*in comb.*) e.g. *first-class, second-class* etc. **in a class of one's, its, own,** of matchless excellence. **no class,** (*sl.*) altogether inferior. †**the classes,** the wealthy as opposed to the masses. **class-book,** *n.* a text-book used in a class. **class conscious,** *a.* oversensitive to social differences. **class-consciousness,** *n.* **class-list,** *n.* a classified list of candidates issued by examiners; a select list of books etc. **class-man,** *n.* one who takes honours at an examination, as opposed to a *passman.* **class-mate, -fellow,** *n.* one who is or has been in the same class. **class war, warfare,** *n.* overt antagonism between the social classes in a community. **classable,** *a.* capable of being classed. **classism,** *n.* discrimination on the ground of social class. **classist,** *n., a.* **classless,** *a.* not divided into classes; not belonging to any class. **classy,** *a.* (*sl.*) genteel; of superior quality. [F *classe,* L *classis* (*calāre,* to call, summon)]

classic, *n.* a Greek or Latin author of the first rank; an author of the first rank; a literary work by any of these; a recognized masterpiece; †one versed in Greek and Latin literature; a follower of classic models as opposed to romantic; (*pl.*) ancient Greek and Latin literature; the study of these. *a.* pertaining to the literature of the ancient Greeks and Romans; in the style of these; of the first rank in literature or art; harmonious, well-proportioned; pure, refined, restrained; of standard authority; of the features, clear-cut, regular; of clothes, simple and well cut, that will not become dated. **classic ground,** *n.* a spot having illustrious associations. **classic orders,** *n.pl.* (*Arch.*) Doric, Ionic, Corinthian, Tuscan and Composite. **classic races,** *n.pl.* the five principal horse-races in England, being the 2000 Guineas, 1000 Guineas, Derby, Oaks and St Leger. [L *classicus* (*classis,* see prec.)]

classical, *a.* belonging to or characteristic of the ancient Greeks and Romans or their civilization or literature; of education, based on a study of Latin and Greek; of any of the arts, influenced by Roman or Greek models, restrained, simple and pure in form; of music, composed esp. in the 18th and 19th cents., simple and restrained in style; (*loosely*) of orchestral music, opera etc. rather than pop, jazz etc.; of physics, not involving relativity or quantum mechanics. **classicalism,** *n.* **classicality,** *n.* **classically,** *adv.* **classicism,** *n.* a classic style or idiom; devotion to or imitation of the classics; classical scholarship; advocacy of classical education. **classicist,** *n.* **classicize, -ise,** *v.t.* to make classic. *v.i.* to affect or imitate the classic style. **classico-,** *comb. form.*

classify, *v.t.* to distribute into classes or divisions; to assign to a class. **classifiable,** *a.* **classification,** *n.* **classificatory,** *a.* **classified,** *a.* arranged in classes; of information, of restricted availability, esp. for security reasons; of printed advertisements, arranged according to the type of goods or services offered or required. **classifier,** *n.*

clastic, *a.* (*Geol.*) fragmentary; composed of materials derived from the waste of various rocks. [Gr. *klastos,* broken (*klaein,* to break)]

clat, *v.i.* to chatter. *n.* a chatterbox. [CLATTER]

clatter, *v.i.* to emit or make a sharp rattling noise; to fall or move with such a noise; to talk idly and noisily. *v.t.* to cause to emit a rattling sound. *n.* a continuous rattling noise; loud, tumultuous noise; noisy, empty talk. [OE *clatrian* (cp. Dut. *klateren,* LG *klätern*)]

Claude Lorrain, *n.* **(Claude Gellée)** (1600–82), French landscape painter, active in Rome from 1627. His subjects are mostly mythological and historical, with insignificant figures lost in great expanses of poetic scenery, as in *The Enchanted Castle* (1664) (National Gallery, London).

Claude Lorraine glass, *n.* a convex mirror, usually of dark or tinted glass, for giving a concentrated view of a landscape in low tones. [after *Claude Lorrain (Lorraine)*]

Claudian[1], *a.* pertaining to or of the period of the Roman emperors of the Claudian gens (Tiberius, Caligula, Claudius and Nero; AD 14–68).

Claudian[2], *n.* or **Claudius Claudianus** (*c.* 370–404), last of the great Latin poets of the Roman empire. He was probably born at Alexandria, and wrote official panegyrics, epigrams, and the epic *The Rape of Proserpine.*

Claudius (10 BC–54 AD), nephew of Tiberius, made Roman emperor by his troops in 41, after the murder of Caligula, though more inclined to scholarly pursuits. During his reign the Roman Empire was considerably extended, and in 43 he took part in the invasion of Britain. He was long dominated by his third wife, Messalina, whom ultimately he had executed, and is thought to have been poisoned by his fourth wife, Agrippina the Younger.

clause, *n.* a complete grammatical sentence; a subdivision of a compound or complex sentence; a separate and distinct portion of a document; a particular stipulation. **clausal,** *a.* [OF, from L *clausa,* fem. p.p. of *clau-*

dere, to close, to enclose]

Clause 28, *n.* in British law, a controversial clause in the Local Government Bill 1988 (now section 28 of the Local Government Act 1988) which prohibits local authorities promoting homosexuality by publishing material, or by promoting the teaching in state schools of the acceptability of homosexuality as a 'pretended family relationship'. It became law despite widespread opposition.

Clausewitz, *n.* **Karl von** (1780–1831), Prussian officer and writer on war, born near Magdeburg. He is known mainly for his book *Vom Kriege/On War* (1833).

Clausius, *n.* **Rudolf Julius Emanuel** (1822–88), German physicist, one of the founders of the science of thermodynamics. In 1850, he enunciated its second law: heat cannot of itself pass from a colder to a hotter body.

claustral, *a.* pertaining to a cloister or monastic foundation; cloister-like; retired. **claustration**, *n.* the act of shutting up in a cloister. [late L *claustrālis* (*claustrum*)]

claustrophobia, *n.* a morbid dread of being in a confined space. **claustrophobic,** *n., a.* [L *claustra,* a bolt, Gr. *phobos,* fear]

claut, *n.* (*Sc.*) a kind of hoe, scraper or rake; (*Sc.*) a rakeful. *v.t.* (*Sc.*) to rake or scrape. [etym. doubtful (perh. related to CLAW)]

clavate, *a.* (*Biol.*) club-shaped; (*Anat.*) applied to a kind of articulation. **claviform**, *a.* **clavigerous**, *a.* club-bearing. [L *clāvātus,* p.p. of *clāvāre;* or formed from *clāva,* a club]

clave, *past* CLEAVE[1].

clavecin, *n.* †a harpsichord; a set of keys for playing carillons. [F, from It. *clavicembalo* or med. L *clavicymbalum* (L *clāvis,* key, *cymbalum,* CYMBAL)]

Claverhouse, *n.* **John Graham, Viscount Dundee** (1649–89), Scottish soldier. Appointed by Charles II to suppress the Covenanters from 1677, he was routed at Drumclog (1679), but three weeks later won the battle of Bothwell Bridge by which the rebellion was crushed. Until 1688 he was engaged in continued persecution and became known as 'Bloody Clavers', regarded by the Scottish people as a figure of evil. Then his army joined the first Jacobite rebellion and defeated the loyalist forces in the pass of Killiecrankie, where he was mortally wounded.

clavichord, *n.* one of the first stringed instruments with a keyboard, a predecessor of the pianoforte. [L *clāvis,* key, *chorda,* string]

clavicle, *n.* the collar-bone. **clavicular**, *a.* [L *clāvicula,* dim. of *clāvis,* key (med. L, collar-bone)]

clavicorn, *n.* one of a group of pentamerous beetles with club-shaped antennae. [L *clāva,* club; *cornu,* horn]

clavier, *n.* the keyboard of an organ, pianoforte etc.; a keyboard instrument. [F (L *clāvis,* a key)]

claviform, clavigerous CLAVATE.

claw, *n.* the sharp hooked nail of a bird or beast; the foot of any animal armed with such nails; the pincer of a crab, lobster or crayfish; anything resembling the claw of one of the lower animals; an implement for grappling or holding; the hand; a grasp, a clutch. *v.t.* to tear or scratch with the claws; to clutch or drag with or as with claws; †to tickle, to stroke; to flatter. **to claw away, off,** to beat to windward off a lee shore. **to claw back,** to get back by clawing or with difficulty; to take back part (as of a benefit or allowance) by extra taxation etc. **to claw up,** (*dial., sl.*) to beat soundly. **claw hammer,** *n.* a hammer furnished at the back with claws to extract nails; (*sl.*) a dress coat (from its shape). **clawed,** *a.* furnished with claws; damaged by clawing. **clawless,** *a.* [OE *clawu* (cp. Dut. *klaauw,* G *Klaue*)]

Clay, *n.* **Cassius Marcellus,** original name of boxer MUHAMMAD ALI.

clay, *n.* heavy, sticky earth; †the human body; a corpse; the grosser part of human nature; a hydrous silicate of aluminium, with a mixture of other substances; (*coll.*) a clay pipe. *v.t.* to cover, manure, or purify and whiten (as sugar), with clay; to puddle with clay. **clay-cold,** *a.* cold and lifeless as clay. **clay-pan,** *n.* (*Austral.*) a hollow (often dry in summer) where water collects. **clay-pigeon,** *n.* (*Sport*) a clay disk thrown into the air as a target. **clay pipe,** *n.* a pipe made of baked clay, usu. long; a churchwarden. **clay-pit,** *n.* a pit from which clay is dug. **clay-slate,** *n.* an argillaceous, easily-cloven sedimentary rock; roofing-slate. **claystone,** *n.* a felstone of granular texture. **clayey,** *a.* **clayish,** *a.* [OE *clǣg,* Teut. (cp. Dut. and G *klei,* OE *clam,* Gr. *gloios,* L *gluten*)]

claymore, *n.* a two-edged sword used by the Scottish Highlanders; (*incorrectly*) a basket-hilted broadsword. [Gael. *claidheamh mor,* great sword (cp. W *cleddyf,* OIr. *claideb,* sword, L *clādes,* slaughter, W *mawr,* Ir. *mor,* Corn. *maur,* great)]

clean, *a.* free from dirt, stain, alloy, blemish, imperfection, disease, ceremonial defilement, awkwardness or defect; pure, holy, guiltless; free from evidence of criminal activity; of a driving licence, free from endorsements or penalty points; free from sexual references, smut, innuendo etc.; producing relatively little radioactive fallout; (*sl.*) not carrying or containing a gun, drugs, illegal or incriminating articles etc.; (*Print.*) needing no correction, as a proof; empty, having no fish, as a whaler; smart, dexterous, unerring; clear, unobstructed; complete. *v.t.* to make clean; to cleanse, to purify. *adv.* quite, completely; without qualification, absolutely; dexterously, cleverly. **to clean down,** to brush or wipe down. **to clean out,** to strip; (*sl.*) to deprive of all money. **to clean up,** to put tidy; to collect all the money, profits etc. **to come clean,** to confess. **clean bill** BILL OF HEALTH, under BILL[2]. **clean-bred,** thoroughbred. **clean-cut,** *a.* sharply defined; clear-cut. **clean fish,** *n.* not unfit for food as at or about spawning time. **clean-handed,** *a.* free from blame in any matter. **clean-limbed,** *a.* having well-proportioned limbs. **clean-shaped, †-timbered,** *a.* well-proportioned. **clean-shaven,** *a.* without beard or moustache. **clean sheet, slate,** *n.* a new start, all debts etc. written off. **clean skin,** *n.* (*Austral.*) unbranded horses or cattle; (*Austral., sl.*) a person without a criminal record. **cleanable,** *a.* **cleaner,** *n.* one who or that which cleans; (*pl.*) a dry-cleaners' shop. **to take to the cleaners,** (*sl.*) to deprive of all one's money, goods etc. **cleanly[1],** *adv.* in a clean manner. **cleanness,** *n.* [OE *clǣne,* Teut. (cp. Dut. and G *klein,* small)]

cleanly[2], *a.* clean in person and habits. **cleanlily,** *adv.* **cleanliness,** *n.* [OE *clǣnlic, a.*]

cleanse, *v.t.* to make clean, to purge, to purify; (*Bibl.*) to cure. **cleanser,** *n.* [OE *clǣnsian*]

clear, *a.* free from darkness, dullness or opacity; luminous, bright; transparent, translucent; serene, unclouded; brightly intelligent; lucid, evident; indisputable, perspicuous, easily apprehended; irreproachable; unembarrassed, unentangled; free, unshackled; unobstructed; distinctly audible; certain, unmistaken; free from deduction, net, not curtailed. *adv.* clearly, completely; quite entirely; apart, free from risk of contact. *v.t.* to make clear; to free from darkness, dimness, opacity, ambiguity, obstruction, imputation or encumbrance; to empty; to remove, to liberate, to disengage; to acquit, to exonerate; to pay off all charges; to gain, to realize as profit; to pass or leap over without touching; to obtain authorization for; to pass (a cheque or bill) through a clearing house. *v.i.* to become clear, bright or serene; †to become free from embarrassment or entanglements; (*Naut.*) to sail. **a clear day,** a complete day. **in the clear,** freed from suspicion. **to clear a ship,** to pay the charges at the custom-house and receive permission to sail. **to clear a ship for action,** to remove all encumbrances from the deck ready for an engagement. **to clear away,** to remove; to remove plates etc., after a meal; to disappear; to melt away. **to clear land,** to remove trees and brushwood in order to cultivate. **to clear off,** to remove; (*coll.*) to depart. **to clear out,** (*coll.*) to eject; (*coll.*) to depart; to melt away. **to clear the air,** to remove misunderstandings or suspicion. **to clear the land,** to have good sea-room. **to clear up,** to become bright and clear; to elucidate; to tidy up. **to get clear** GET. **clear-cut,** *a.* regular, finely outlined, as if chiselled. **clear days,** *n.pl.* time reckoned apart from the first day and the last. **clear-headed,** *a.* acute, sharp, intelligent. **clear-seeing,** *a.* clear-sighted. †**clear-shining,** *a.* shining brightly. **clear-sighted,** *a.* acute, discerning, far-seeing. **clear-sightedness,** *n.* **clear-starch,** *v.t.* to stiffen and dress with colourless starch. **clear-starcher,** *n.* **clear-story** CLERESTORY. **clear-stuff,** *n.* boards free from knots or shakes. **clearway,** *n.* a road on which parking is forbidden. **clearwing,** *n.* one of the *Sesiadae,* a genus of moths with translucent wings. **clearage,** *n.* **clearer,** *n.* **clearly,** *adv.* in a clear manner; distinctly, audibly, plainly, evidently, certainly, undoubtedly. **clearness,** *n.* the state of being clear; perspicuity, distinctness to or of apprehension. [OF *cler* (F *clair*), L *clārus*]

clearance, *n.* the act of clearing; the state of being cleared; clear profit; authorization; the removal of people, buildings etc. from an area; (*Banking*) the clearing of cheques or bills; a certificate that a ship has been cleared at the custom-house; the distance between the moving and the stationary part of a machine. **clearance sale,** *n.* a sale of stock at reduced prices to make room for new stock.

clear-cole, *v.t.* to treat with a preparation of size and whiting. [F, *claire colle,* clear glue or size]

clearing, *n.* the act of making clear, freeing or justifying; a tract of land cleared for cultivation; (*Banking*) the passing of cheques etc. through a clearing house. **clearing bank,** *n.* one which is a member of a clearing house. **clearing house,** *n.* a financial establishment where cheques, transfers, bills etc. are exchanged between member banks, so that only outstanding balances have to be paid; a person or agency acting as a centre for the exchange of information etc.

cleat, *n.* a strip of wood secured to another one to strengthen it; a strip fastened on steps to obviate slipping; (*Naut.*) a piece of wood or iron for fastening ropes upon; †a wedge. *v.t.* to fasten or strengthen with a cleat. [ME *clete,* a wedge (cp. Dut. *kloot,* G *Klosz,* a ball or clod)]

cleave[1], *v.i.* (*past* **cleaved,** †**clave**) to stick, to adhere; to be attached closely; to be faithful (to). [OE *clifian,* from Teut. *kli-* (cp. G *kleben,* Dut. *kleven,* Swed. *klibba*)]

cleave[2], *v.t.* (*past,* **clove**, **cleft**, *p.p.* **cloven**, **cleft**) to split asunder with violence, to cut through, to divide forcibly; to make one's way through. *v.i.* to part asunder; to split, to crack. **cleavable,** *a.* **cleavage,** *n.* the act of cleaving; the particular manner in which a mineral with a regular structure may be cleft or split; the way in which a party etc. splits up; the hollow between a woman's breasts, esp. as revealed by a low-cut dress or top. **line, plane of cleavage,** the line or plane of weakness along which a mineral or a rock tends to split. **cleaver,** *n.* one who or that which cleaves; a butcher's instrument for cutting meat into joints. [OE *clēofan,* Teut. *kleuth-* (cp. Dut. *klieven,* G *klieben,* Gr. *gluphein,* to hollow out, carve)]

cleavers, clivers, *n.* a loose-growing plant with hooked prickles that catch in clothes. [prob. from CLEAVE[1]]

cleek, *v.t.* (*past* **claucht**, **claught**, **cleekit**) (*Sc., North.*) to catch hold of suddenly, to seize. *n.* (*Sc., North.*) a large hook for hanging things up or for fishing; (*Golf*) an iron-headed club. [ME *cleche,* later *cleach*]

Cleese, *n.* **John** (1939–), English actor and comedian. For television he has written for the satirical *That Was the Week That Was* and *The Frost Report*, and the comic *Monty Python's Flying Circus* and *Fawlty Towers*. His films include *A Fish Called Wanda* (1988).

clef, *n.* a character at the beginning of a stave denoting the pitch and determining the names of the notes according to their position on the stave. [F, from L *clāvis,* key]

cleft[1], *past., p.p.* of **cleave**[2]. **cleft-footed,** *a.* having the hoof divided. **cleft palate,** *n.* congenital fissure of the hard palate. **cleft stick,** *n.* a stick split at the end. **in a cleft stick,** in a situation where going forward or back is impossible; in a tight place, a fix.

cleft[2], *n.* a split, a crack, a fissure; a morbid crack in the pastern of a horse; †the fork of the human body. [earlier *clift,* cogn. with CLEAVE[2] (cp. Icel., Dut. and G *kluft*)]

cleg, *n.* a gadfly, a horsefly. [Icel. *kleggi*]

Cleisthenes, *n.* ruler of Athens. Inspired by Solon, he is credited with the establishment of democracy in Athens in 507 BC.

cleisto-, *comb. form* (*Bot.*) closed. [Gr. *kleistos* (*kleiein,* to close)]

cleistogamic, *a.* having flowers that never open and are self-fertilized. [*Gr. gamos,* marriage]

clem, *v.t.* (*past, p.p.* **clemmed**) (*dial.*) to pinch, as hunger. *v.i.* (*dial.*) to starve, to famish. [cp. CLAM[2] and Dut. and G *klemmen,* to pinch]

clematis, *n.* a plant of a genus (*Clematis*) of ranunculaceous plants, comprising the common traveller's joy, old man's beard or virgin's bower, *C. vitalba.* [late L, from Gr. *klēmatis*]

Clemenceau, *n.* **Georges** (1841–1929), French politician and journalist (prominent in defence of Dreyfus). After World War I he presided over the Peace Conference in Paris that drew up the Treaty of Versailles, but failed to secure for France the Rhine as a frontier.

Clemens, *n.* **Samuel Langhorne,** real name of the US writer Mark Twain.

clement, *a.* gentle; merciful; of weather, mild. **clemency,** *n.* [L *clēmēns -entis*]

Clement VII, *n.* (1478–1534), Pope (1523–34). He refused to allow the divorce of Henry VIII of England and Catherine of Aragon. Illegitimate son of a brother of Lorenzo di Medici, the ruler of Florence, he commissioned monuments for the Medici chapel in Florence from the Renaissance artist Michelangelo.

Clement of Rome, St (late 1st century AD), one of the early Christian leaders and writers known as the Fathers of the Church. According to tradition he was the third or fourth bishop of Rome, and a disciple of St Peter.

Clementine, *a.* pertaining to St Clement or to Pope Clement V (1305–14). *n.pl.* the decretals and constitutions of Clement V.

clementine, *n.* a small, bright orange citrus fruit with a sweet flavour. [F]

clench, *v.t.* to rivet; to fasten firmly by bending the point of (with a hammer); to grasp firmly; to close or fix firmly (as the hands or teeth). **clencher** CLINCHER. [ME *clenchen,* from OE *clencan,* extant only in *beclencan* (cp. OHG *klenkan,* also CLING, CLINCH)]

Cleon, *n.* Athenian demagogue and military leader in the Peloponnesian War. After the death of Pericles, to whom he was opposed, he won power as representative of the commercial classes and leader of the party advocating a vigorous war policy. He was killed fighting the Spartans at Amphipolis.

Cleopatra, *n.* (*c.* 68–30 BC), queen of Egypt from 51 BC. In 49 BC the Roman general Julius Caesar arrived in Egypt and she became his mistress, bore him a son, Caesarion, and accompanied him to Rome. After Caesar's murder 44 BC she returned to Alexandria and resumed her position as queen of Egypt. From 40 BC one of Caesar's successors, Mark Antony, lived with her. Rome declared war on Egypt 32 BC and scored a decisive victory in the naval Battle of Actium the following year; Mark Antony and Cleopatra killed themselves.

Cleopatra's Needle, *n.* either of two ancient Egyptian granite obelisks erected at Heliopolis in the 15th cent. BC by Thothmes III, and removed to Alexandria by the Roman emperor Augustus about 14 BC. They have no connection with Cleopatra's reign. One of the pair was taken to London (1878) and erected on the Victoria Embankment; it is 21 m/68.5 ft high. The other was given by the khedive of Egypt to the US, and erected in Central Park, New York, 1881.

†**clepe,** *v.t.* to call, to name. *v.i.* to call, to cry. [OE *clipian*]

clepsydra, *n.* an instrument used by the ancients to

measure time by the dropping of water from a graduated vessel through a small opening. [L, from Gr. *klepsudra* (*kleptein*, to steal, *hudōr*, water)]

clerestory, *n.* the upper part of the nave, choir or transept of a large church containing windows above the roofs of the aisles. [CLEAR, STORY²]

clergy, *n.* the body of men set apart by ordination for the service of the Christian Church; ecclesiastics collectively; the clergy of a church, district or country. **clergiable,** *a.* for which benefit of clergy might be pleaded. **clergyman,** *n.* a member of the clergy; an ordained Christian minister, esp. of the Established Church. **clergywoman,** *n.* (*coll., dated*) the wife or other female relative of a clergyman, esp. one who tries to manage the affairs of the parish. [OF *clergie* (*clerc*, late L *clēricus*, Gr. *klērikos*, pertaining to the clergy), from *klērikos*, a lot or inheritance, with reference to Deut. xviii.2 and Acts i.17]

cleric, *a.* clerical. *n.* a member of the clergy; one subject to canon law. **clerico-,** *comb. form.* [late L *clēricus*, see prec.]

clerical, *a.* relating to the clergy, or to a clerk, copyist or writer; *n. pl.* clerical dress. **clerical collar** DOG-COLLAR. **clerical error,** *n.* an error in copying. **clericalism,** *n.* undue influence of the clergy. **clericalist,** *n.* **clericalize, -ise,** *v.t.* **clericality**, *n.* **clerically,** *adv.* [late L *clēricālis*, from prec.]

clerihew, *n.* a satirical or humorous poem, usu. biographical, consisting of four rhymed lines of uneven length. [E. *Clerihew* Bentley, 1875–1956]

clerisy, *n.* learned or professional people considered as a class. [G *Klerisei*, ult. from L *clēricus* (see CLERGY)]

clerk, *n.* a cleric, a clergyman; the lay officer of a parish church; one employed in an office, bank, shop etc. to assist in correspondence, book-keeping etc.; one who has charge of an office or department, subject to a higher authority, as a board etc.; (*N Am.*) a shop assistant; (*N Am.*) a hotel receptionist; †a scholar, one able to read and write. *v.i.* to be a clerk. **clerk in holy orders,** an ordained clergyman. **clerk of the course,** an official in charge of administration of a motor- or horse-racing course. **Clerk of the Peace,** an officer who prepares indictments and keeps records of the proceedings at sessions of the peace. **Clerk of the Weather,** (*coll.*) the imaginary controller of the weather; the meteorological office. **clerk of (the) works,** *n.* a surveyor appointed to watch over the performance of a contract and test the quality of materials etc. **Town clerk,** the chief officer of a corporation, usu. a solicitor. **clerkdom**, *n.* **clerkish,** *a.* **clerkly,** *a.* **clerkship,** *n.* scholarship; the office or position of a clerk. [OE *clerc*, from OF *clerc* or late L *clēricus* (see CLERGY)]

Clermont-Ferrand, *n.* city, capital of Puy-de-Dôme *département*, in the Auvergne region of France; population (1983) 155,000. It is a centre for agriculture, and its rubber industry is the largest in France.

cleromancy, *n.* divination by casting lots with dice. [Gr. *klēros*, a lot]

cleuch, cleugh, *n.* (*Sc.*) a rocky gorge or ravine with steep sides. [CLOUGH]

cleve, *n.* (*Devon*) the steep side of a hill. [var. of CLIFF]

Cleveland¹, a county in NE England. **area** 580 sq km/ 224 sq miles. **towns** administrative headquarters Middlesbrough; Stockton on Tees, Billingham, Hartlepool. **products** steel, chemicals. **population** (1987) 555,000.

Cleveland², *n.* largest city of Ohio, US, on Lake Erie at the mouth of the river Cuyahoga; population (1981) 574,000, metropolitan area 1,899,000. Its chief industries are iron and steel and petroleum refining.

Cleveland³, *n.* **(Stephen) Grover** (1837–1908), 22nd and 24th president of the US, 1885–89 and 1893–97; the first Democratic president elected after the Civil War, and the only president to hold office for two non-consecutive terms. He attempted to check corruption in public life, and in 1895 initiated arbitration proceedings that eventually settled a territorial dispute with Britain concerning the Venezuelan boundary.

clever, *a.* dexterous, skilful; talented; very intelligent; expert, ingenious; †agreeable. **cleverdick,** *n.* (*coll.*) one who shows off his or her own cleverness. **cleverish,** *a.* **cleverly,** *adv.* **cleverness,** *n.* [etym. doubtful; conn. with OE *clifer*, a claw, *clifian*, to seize (cp. EFris. *klüfer*)]

clevis, *n.* a forked iron at the end of a shaft or beam, or an iron loop, for fastening tackle to. [etym. doubtful; prob. conn. with CLEAVE²]

clew, *n.* the lower corner of a square sail; the aftermost corner of a staysail; the cords by which a hammock is suspended. *v.t.* to truss up to the yard. **clew-garnets,** *n.pl.* tackles attached to the clews of the main and fore sails, by which they are trussed up to the yards. **clew-lines,** *n.pl.* similar tackles for the smaller square sails. [OE *clīwen* (cp. Dut. *kluwen*, G *Knäuel*); see also CLUE]

clianthus, *n.* a plant of an Australian genus (*Clianthus*), with clusters of red flowers. [Gr. *kleos*, glory, *anthos*, flower]

cliché, *n.* (*Print.*) a stereotype, esp. a stereotype or electrotype from a block; (*Phot.*) a negative; a hackneyed phrase, a tag; anything hackneyed or overused. **clichéd, cliché'd,** *a.* [F, p.p. of *clicher*, to stereotype (var. of *cliquer*)]

click, *v.i.* to make a slight, sharp noise, as small hard bodies knocking together; of horses, to strike shoes together. *v.t.* to cause to click. *v.i.* (*coll.*) to fall into place, to make sense; to be successful; to become friendly with someone, esp. of the opposite sex. *n.* a slight sharp sound; a sharp clicking sound used in some languages of southern Africa; the detent of a ratchet-wheel; a catch for a lock or bolt; a latch. **clicker¹,** *n.* a horse that clicks. [imit., cp. CLACK, Dut. *klikken*, F *cliquer*]

clicker², *n.* †a tout; one who stood at the door to invite passers-by to enter a shop; one who cuts out the leather for shoe-makers; (*Print.*) a foreman in charge of a companionship of compositors. [from prec. or from obs. v. *click*, var. of CLEEK, to clutch, seize]

†clicket, *n.* a latch; a latch-key; a valve, a catch etc., shutting with a click. [OF *cliquet* (*cliquer*, to click)]

client, *n.* (*Rom. Ant.*) a plebeian who placed himself under the protection of a noble (called his patron); one who employs a lawyer as his agent or to conduct a case; one who entrusts any business to a professional man; a dependant; a customer; a person who is receiving help from a social work or charitable agency. **clientage, clientelage**, *n.* one's clients collectively; the system of patron and client; the condition of a client. **cliental,** *a.* **clientless,** *a.* **clientship,** *n.* [L *cliēns -ntis* (*cluere*, to hear, to obey)]

clientele, *n.* clients or dependants collectively; followers or adherents; customers, patients, frequenters etc.; clientship. [L *clientēla* (more recently readopted from F *clientèle*, pron. klēātel)]

cliff, *n.* a steep, precipitous rock; a precipice. **cliff-hanger,** *n.* a story, film etc. that has one in suspense till the end; a highly dramatic, unresolved ending to an instalment of a serial. **cliff-hanging,** *a.* **cliffy,** *a.* having cliffs; craggy. [OE *clif* (cp. Dut. and Icel. *klif*, G *Klippe*)]

Cliff, *n.* **Clarice** (1899–1972), English pottery designer. Her Bizarre ware, characterized by brightly coloured floral and geometric decoration on often geometrically shaped china, became increasingly popular in the 1930s.

Clift, *n.* **(Edward) Montgomery** (1920–66), US film and theatre actor. A star of the late 1940s and 1950s in films such as *Red River* (1948) and *A Place in the Sun* (1951), he was disfigured in a car accident in 1957 but continued to make films. He played the title role in *Freud* (1962).

climacteric, *n.* a critical period in human life; a period in which some great change is supposed to take place in the human constitution, or in the fortune of an individual (the periods are said to be found by multiplying 7 by 3, 5, 7 and 9, the 63rd year being called the **grand climacteric;** to these the 81st year is sometimes added). *a.* of or pertaining to a climacteric; critical;

(*Med.*) occurring late in life. **climacterical**, *a.* climacteric. [L *clīmactēricus,* Gr. *klimaktērikos* (*klimaktēr,* the step of a ladder, a critical period in life; cp. *klimax,* CLIMAX)]

climactic CLIMAX.

climate, *n.* a region considered with reference to its weather; the temperature of a place, and its meteorological conditions generally, with regard to their influence on animal and vegetable life; a prevailing character. †*v.i.* to inhabit, to dwell. **climatic**, *a.* **climatically,** *adv.* **climatology**, *n.* the science of climate; an investigation of climatic phenomena and their causes. **climatological**, *a.* **climature**, *n.* climate. [F *climat,* late L *clima -atos,* Gr. *klima- atos,* a slope, a region (*klinein,* to slope)]

climax, *n.* a rhetorical figure in which the sense rises gradually in a series of images, each exceeding its predecessor in force or dignity; the highest point, culmination; a stable final stage in the development of a plant or animal community; an orgasm. *v.i.* to reach a climax. *v.t.* to bring to a culminating point. **climactic**, *a.* [L, from Gr. *klimax,* a ladder (*klinein,* to slope)]

climb, *v.t.* (*past, p.p.* **climbed, †clomb**) to ascend, esp. by means of the hands and feet; to ascend by means of tendrils. *v.i.* to ascend; to slope upwards; to rise in rank or prosperity. *n.* an ascent; the act of climbing or ascending. **to climb down,** to descend (using hands and feet); to abandon one's claims, withdraw from a position, opinion etc. **climbable,** *a.* **climber,** *n.* one who or that which climbs; a creeper or climbing plant; one of the Scansores or climbing birds. **climbing,** *n.* mountaineering. *a.* that climbs. **climbing-boy,** *n.* a boy formerly sent up a chimney as a chimney-sweep. **climbing-frame,** *n.* a framework of bars for children to climb on. **climbing-irons,** *n.pl.* a set of spikes fastened to the legs to assist in climbing. **climbing-perch,** *n.* the anabas, a fish that climbs river-banks and trees. [OE *climban* (cp. *clifian,* CLEAVE[1], Dut. and G *klimmen*)]

clime, *n.* (*poet.*) a region, a country; a climate. [late L *clima,* CLIMATE]

clinanthium, *n.* the receptacle of a composite flower. [Gr. *klinē,* a couch, *anthos,* a flower]

clinch, *v.t.* to secure a nail by hammering down the point; to drive home or establish (an argument etc.); to make a rope-end fast in a particular way. *v.i.* to hold an opponent by the arms in boxing etc.; (*coll.*) to embrace. *n.* the act of clinching; a mode of fastening large ropes by a half-hitch; a grip, a hold-fast; a pun. **clinch-nail,** *n.* a nail with a malleable end adapted for clinching. **clincher,** *n.* one who or that which clinches; a conclusive argument or statement. **clincher-built** CLINKER-BUILT. [var. of CLENCH]

cline, *n.* a gradation of forms seen in a single species over a given area. [Gr. *klinein,* to bend, slope]

cling, *v.i.* (*past, p.p.* **clung**) to adhere closely and tenaciously, esp. by twining, grasping or embracing; to be faithful (to). †*v.t.* to shrivel, wither; to clasp. *n.* (*N Am.*) a clingstone. **to cling together,** to form one mass; to resist separation. **Clingfilm®,** *n.* a kind of thin polythene film which clings to itself or anything else, used for airtight wrapping. **clingstone,** *n.* a kind of peach in which the pulp adheres closely to the stone. **clingy,** *a.* clinging; showing great emotional dependence. **clinginess,** *n.* [OE *clingan* (cp. Dan. *klynge,* to cluster, Swed. *klänge,* to climb)]

clinic, *n.* medical and surgical instruction, esp. in hospitals; a private hospital, or one specializing in one type of ailment or treatment; a specialist department in a general hospital, esp. for out-patients; a session in which advice and instruction are given on any topic. **clinical,** *a.* pertaining to a patient in bed, or to instruction given to students in a hospital ward; detached, unemotional. **clinical baptism,** *n.* baptism administered to a sick or dying person. **clinical thermometer,** *n.* one for observing the temperature of a patient. **clinically,** *adv.* **clinician**, *n.* a doctor who works with patients, as opposed to a teacher or researcher. **clinique**, CLINIC. [F *clinique,* L *clinicus,* Gr. *klinikos* (*klinē,* a bed, *klinein,* to slope, recline)]

clink[1], *n.* a sharp, tinkling sound, as when two metallic bodies are struck lightly together. *v.i.* to make this sound. *v.t.* to cause to clink. **clinkstone,** *n.* phonolite; a feldspathic rock that clinks when struck. [imit.; cp. CLANK, Dut. *klinken*]

clink[2], *n.* (*sl.*) a gaol, a lock-up; †a particularly dismal sort of cell. [prob. from the name of a Southwark gaol (perh. from CLINCH)]

clinker[1], *n.* †a Dutch sun-baked brick; vitrified slag; fused cinders; bricks run together in a mass by heat; (*sl.*) a sounding blow, a thumping lie etc. [MDut. *klinckaert* (*klinken,* to CLINK)]

clinker[2], *n.* (*North.*) a clinch-nail. **clinker-built,** *a.* (*Naut.*) built with overlapping planks fastened with clinched nails (cp. CARVEL-BUILT). [from obs. v. *clink,* CLINCH]

clinometer, *n.* an instrument for measuring angles of inclination. **clinometric, -ical**, *a.* [Gr. *klinein,* to slope, -METER]

†clinquant, *a.* shining, resplendent; dressed in tinsel. *n.* tinsel, gaudy finery. [F, pres.p. of *clinquer,* to CLINK]

Clio, *n.* the muse of epic poetry and history; a genus of minute molluscs found in the polar seas. [Gr. *Kleiō* (*kleiein,* to celebrate)]

clip[1], *v.t.* (*past, p.p.* **clipped**) to cut with shears or scissors; to trim; to cut away; to pare the edges of (as coin); to cut short by omitting (letters, syllables etc.); to cancel (a ticket) by snipping a piece out; to hit sharply. *v.i.* to run or go swiftly. *n.* a shearing or trimming; the whole wool of a season; a blow; an extract from a film; (*sl.*) a (fast) rate. **to clip the wings of,** to put a check on the ambitions of. **clip joint,** *n.* (*sl.*) a night-club etc. which overcharges. **clipper,** *n.* one who or that which clips; a fast-sailing vessel with a long sharp bow and raking masts; a fast-goer; (*pl.*) a tool for clipping hair, nails etc. **clipper-built,** *a.* (*Naut.*) built like a clipper. **clippie,** *n.* (*coll.*) a bus conductress. **clipping,** *n.* a piece clipped off; (*esp. N Am.*) a press-cutting; the action of the verb. **clipping-bureau,** *n.* (*N Am.*) a press-cutting agency. [Icel. *klippa*]

clip[2], *v.t.* to clasp, to embrace; to encircle, to surround closely. *n.* an appliance for gripping, holding or attaching; a cartridge clip. **clipboard,** *n.* a flat board with a spring clip at one end, to hold paper for writing. [OE *clyppan*]

clip-clop CLOP.

clique, *n.* an exclusive set; a coterie of snobs. **cliquish,** *a.* **cliquishness,** *n.* **cliquism,** *n.* **cliquy,** *a.* [F, from *cliquer,* to CLICK]

clish-clash, *n.* (*Sc.*) gossip. *v.i.* (*Sc.*) to gossip. **clishmaclaver,** *n.* (*Sc.*) gossip. [redupl. of CLASH]

clitellum, *n.* (*pl.* **-lla**) the thick central part of the body of an earthworm. **clitellar,** *a.* [mod. L, from L *clitellae,* a pack-saddle]

clitoris, *n.* (*pl.* **-ides**) a small erectile body situated at the apex of the vulva and corresponding to the penis in the male. **clitoral,** *a.* [Gr. *kleitoris* (*kleiein,* to shut)]

clitter-clatter, *n.* idle talk; noisy chatter. [redupl. of CLATTER]

Clive, *n.* **Robert, Baron Clive of Plassey** (1725–74), British general and administrator, who established British rule in India by victories over the French at Arcot in the Carnatic (a region in SE India) 1751 and over the nawab of Bengal, Suraj-ud-Dowlah, at Calcutta and Plassey (1757). On his return to Britain his wealth led to allegations that he had abused his power.

Cllr, (*abbr.*) councillor.

cloaca, *n.* a sewer; the excretory cavity in certain animals, birds, insects etc.; a receptacle for filth; a sink of iniquity. **cloacal,** *a.* [L]

cloak, †cloke, *n.* a loose, wide, outer garment; a covering; a disguise, a blind, a pretext. *v.t.* to cover with or as with a cloak; to disguise; to hide. *v.i.* to put on one's cloak. **cloak-and-dagger,** *a.* of a story, involving mystery and intrigue. **†cloak-bag,** *n.* a portmanteau, a travelling-bag. **cloak-room,** *n.* a room where cloaks, small parcels etc. can be deposited; a lavatory. **cloak-**

ing, *n.* disguise, concealment; a rough, woollen material for cloaks. [ME and OF *cloke*, med. L *cloca*, a bell, a horseman's cape (cp. CLOCK[1])]

cloam, *n.* (*dial.*) earthenware, clay pottery. [OE *clām*, mud, clay]

clobber, *n.* a kind of coarse paste used by cobblers to conceal cracks in leather; (*sl.*) clothes; (*sl.*) belongings, equipment. *v.t.* (*sl.*) to beat; to criticize harshly. **clobberer,** *n.* [etym. doubtful; perh. from Gael. *clabar*]

cloche, *n.* an orig. bell-shaped glass cover put over young or tender plants to preserve them from frost; a close-fitting hat shaped like a cloche. [F, a bell]

clocher, *n.* a bell-tower, a belfry. [F *clocher*, ONorth.F *clockier, cloquier* (see foll.)]

clock[1], *n.* an instrument for measuring time, consisting of wheels actuated by a spring, weight or electricity; (*coll.*) a taximeter or speedometer. *v.t.* to time using a clock; (*sl.*) to hit; (*sl.*) to see, notice. **against the clock,** of a task etc., requiring to be finished by a certain time. **round the clock,** continuously through the day and night. **to clock in, on, out, off,** to register on a specially constructed clock the times of arrival at, and departure from, work. **to clock up,** to register (a specified time, speed etc.). **what's o'clock? what o'clock is it?** (contr. of What hour of the clock is it?), what is the time? **clock-bird,** *n.* (*Austral.*) the kookaburra. **clock golf,** *n.* a putting game played on lawns. **clock-maker,** *n.* one who makes clocks. **clock radio,** *n.* an alarm clock combined with a radio, which uses the radio instead of a bell. †**clock-setter,** *n.* one who regulates clocks. **clock-watcher,** *n.* one who is careful not to work any longer than necessary. **clock-watching,** *n.* **clockwise,** *adv.* as the hands of a clock, from left to right; **clockwork,** *n.* the movements of a clock; a train of wheels producing motion in a similar fashion. **like clockwork,** with unfailing regularity: mechanically, automatically. [ONorth.F *cloque*, med. L *clocca, cloca*, a bell; or MDut. *clocke* (Dut. *klok*, cp. G *glocke*, a bell, a clock); prob. orig. from Celt. (cp. OIr. *cloc*, W and Corn. *cloch*, Gael. *clag*)]

†**clock[2],** *n.* (*dial., chiefly North.*) a beetle; the dung-beetle. [etym. unknown]

clock[3], *n.* an ornamental pattern on the side of the leg of a stocking. **clocked,** *a.* [etym. doubtful]

clocking, *n.* (*Sc.*) brooding, hatching. *a.* (*Sc.*) brooding, sitting. **clocking-time,** *n.* hatching-time. **clocking-hen,** *n.* [*dial. v. clock*, var. of CLUCK]

clod, *n.* a lump of earth or clay; a mass of earth and turf; any concreted mass; the shoulder part of the neck-piece of beef; a piece of earth, mere lifeless matter; a clod-hopper. †*v.t.* to pelt with clods. *v.i.* to clot. †**clod-breaker,** *n.* a rustic. **clod-crusher,** *n.* an instrument for pulverizing clods. **clod-hopper,** *n.* an awkward rustic; a bumpkin; a clumsy person. **clod-pate, -poll,** *n.* a stupid, thick-headed fellow; a dolt, a boor. **clod-pated,** *a.* **cloddish,** *a.* loutish, coarse, clumsy. **cloddishness,** *n.* **cloddy,** *a.* abounding in clods; (*fig.*) earthy, base, worthless. [var. of CLOT]

clog, *n.* a block of wood attached to a person or animal to hinder free movement; anything that impedes motion or freedom; a kind of shoe with a wooden sole; a boot with a metal rim, a kind of sabot. *v.t.* (*past, p.p.* **clogged**) to encumber or hamper with a weight; to hinder; to obstruct; to choke up; †to form clots on. *v.i.* to be obstructed or encumbered with anything heavy or adhesive. **clog-dance,** *n.* a dance in which the performer wears clogs in order to produce a loud accompaniment to the music. **cloggy,** *a.* clogging; adhesive, sticky. **clogginess,** *n.* [etym. unknown (perh. Scand., cp. Norw. *klugu*, a knotty log)]

cloisonné, *a.* partitioned, divided into compartments. *n.* cloisonné enamel. **cloisonné enamel,** *n.* enamel-work in which the coloured parts are separated by metallic partitions. [F, partitioned, from *cloison*, a partition (ult. from L *clausus*, p.p. of *claudere*, to close)]

cloister, *n.* a place of religious seclusion; a religious house or convent; a series of covered passages usu. arranged along the sides of a quadrangle in monastic, cathedral or collegiate buildings; hence, a piazza. *v.t.* to shut up in or as in a cloister or convent. †**cloister-garth,** *n.* a yard or grass-plot surrounded with cloisters, often used as a burial-ground. **cloistered,** *a.* (*fig.*) out of things; sheltered from the world, reality etc. †**cloisterer,** *n.* one who lives in a cloister. †**cloistress,** *n. fem.* a nun. **cloistral,** *a.* [OF *cloistre* (F *cloître*), L *claustrum* (*claudere*, to shut, p.p. *clausus*)]

cloke CLOAK.

clone, *n.* a number of organisms produced asexually from a single progenitor; any such organism; (*coll.*) an exact copy. *v.t.* to produce a clone of. **clonal,** *a.* [Gr. *klōn*, a shoot]

clonk, *v.i.* to make a short dull sound, as of two solid objects striking each other. *v.t.* (*coll.*) to hit. *n.* such a dull sound. [onomat.]

clonus, *n.* a spasm with alternate contraction and relaxation. **clonic,** *a.* [Gr. *klonos*, violent commotion]

cloot, *n.* (*Sc., North.*) a cloven hoof or one part of it. **Cloots, Clootie,** *n.* (*Sc., North.*) the Devil. [perh. from Icel. *klo*, claw]

clop, clip-clop, *n.* the sound of a horse's hoof striking the ground. *v.i.* (*past, p.p.* **clopped**) to make such a sound. [onomat.]

close[1], *v.t.* to shut to; to fill (up) an opening; to enclose, to shut in; to bring or unite together; †to include; to be the end of, conclude; to complete, to settle. *v.i.* to shut; to coalesce; to come to an end, to cease; to agree, to come to terms; to grapple, to come to hand-to-hand fighting. *n.* the act of closing; an end, a conclusion; a grapple, a hand-to-hand struggle. **to close down,** of factories, works etc., to shut, to cease work; (*Radio*) to go off the air. **to close in,** to shut in, to enclose; to come nearer; to get shorter. **to close on, upon,** to shut over; to grasp; to shut (one's eyes) to; to agree, to come to terms. **to close up,** to block up, fill in; to come together. **to close with,** to accede to, to agree or consent to; to unite with; to grapple with. **closed circuit,** *n.* a circuit with a complete, unbroken path for the current to flow through. **closed-circuit television,** a television system for a restricted number of viewers in which the signal is transmitted to the receiver by cable. **closed shop,** *n.* a workplace where an employer may hire only union members and retain only union members in good standing. **closing time,** *n.* the hour at which a shop, office or other establishment is declared closed for work or business. **closer,** *n.* one who or that which closes or concludes; a worker who sews the seams in the sides of boots; the last stone or brick in the horizontal course of a wall. [ME *closen*, OF *clos*, p.p. of *clore*, L *claudere*, to shut (p.p. *clausus*)]

close[2], *a.* closed, shut fast; confined, shut in; pronounced with the lips or mouth partly shut; solid, dense, compact; near together in time or space; intimate, familiar; concise, compressed, coherent; nearly alike; attentive; following the original closely; to the point, apt, accurate, precise, minute; without ventilation, oppressive, stifling; of the weather, warm and damp; restricted, limited, reserved; difficult to obtain, scarce, as money; retired, secret, reticent; parsimonious, penurious. *adv.* near, close to; closely, tightly, thickly or compactly. *n.* an enclosure; a place fenced in; the precincts of a cathedral or abbey; a small enclosed field; a narrow passage or street; a blind alley. **close by, to, upon,** within a short distance; very near; hard by. **close-banded,** *a.* in close order or array; thickly ranged. **close borough,** *n.* a borough for which the right of returning a member to Parliament was practically in the hands of one person. **close breeding,** *n.* breeding between animals closely akin. **close corporation,** *n.* one which fills up its own vacancies. **close-curtained,** *a.* with curtains drawn close round. **close file,** *n.* a row of people standing or moving one immediately behind the other. **close-fisted,** †**-handed,** *a.* niggardly, miserly, penurious. **close-fistedness,** *n.* **close-fitting,** *a.* of clothes, fitting tightly to the outline of the body. **close harmony,** *n.* a kind of singing in which all the parts lie close together.

close-hauled, *a.* (*Naut.*) kept as near as possible to the point from which the wind blows. **close-pent,** *a.* shut close. **close quarters,** *n.pl.* strong bulkheads formerly erected across a ship for defence against boarders; direct contact. **to come to close quarters,** to come into direct contact, esp. with an enemy. **close season,** *n.* the breeding season, during which it is illegal to kill certain fish or game. **close shave,** *n.* a narrow escape. **close-stool,** *n.* a night-stool. **close-tongued,** *a.* reticent, silent. **close-up,** *n.* a view taken with the camera at very close range. **close vowel,** *n.* one pronounced with a small opening of the lips, or with the mouth-cavity contracted. **closely,** *adv.* **closeness,** *n.* [as prec.]

closet, *n.* a small room for privacy and retirement; a water-closet; (*chiefly N Am.*) a cupboard. *a.* secret; private. *v.t.* †to shut up; to admit into or receive in a private apartment for consultation etc. **to be closeted with,** to hold a confidential conversation with. **to come out of the closet,** to declare or make public one's inclinations, intentions etc., esp. to declare one's homosexuality. **closet play,** *n.* a play suitable for reading, not acting. [dim. of OF *clos,* as prec.]

closure, *n.* the act of shutting; the state of being closed; the power of terminating debate in a legislative or deliberative assembly. *v.t.* to apply this power to a debate, speaker or motion. [OF, from L *clausūra* (*clausus,* p.p. of *claudere,* to close)]

clot, *n.* a clod, a lump, a ball; a small coagulated mass of soft or fluid matter, esp. of blood; (*sl.*) a silly fellow. *v.t.* (*past, p.p.* **clotted**) to make into clots. *v.i.* to become clotted. **clotted cream,** *n.* cream produced in clots on new milk when it is simmered, orig. made in Devonshire. **clotty,** *a.* [OE *clott, clot* (cp. G *Klotz,* CLEAT, CLOD)]

cloth, *n.* a woven fabric of wool, hemp, flax, silk or cotton, used for garments or other coverings (the name of the material is expressed except in the case of wool); any textile fabric, material; a piece of this; a tablecloth; the dress of a profession, esp. the clerical, from their usu. wearing black cloth; (*Theat.*) a curtain, esp. a painted curtain, let up and down between stage and auditorium. **American cloth,** an enamelled fabric with a surface resembling that of polished leather. **cloth of gold, silver,** *n.* a fabric of gold or silver threads interwoven with silk or wool. **cloth binding,** *n.* book covers in linen or cotton cloth. **cloth-cap,** *a.* (*sometimes derog.*) belonging to or characteristic of the working class. **cloth-eared,** *a.* (*coll.*) deaf; inattentive. **cloth hall,** *n.* a cloth exchange. **cloth-measure,** *n.* the measure by which cloth was sold, in which the cloth-yard is divided into quarters and nails. **cloth-shearer,** *n.* one who shears cloth and frees it from superfluous nap. **cloth-worker,** *n.* a maker of cloth. **cloth-yard,** *n.* a former measure for cloth, 37 in. (0·94 m). **cloth-yard shaft,** *n.* an arrow a cloth-yard long. [OE *clāth* (cp. G *Kleid*)]

clothe, , *v.t.* (*past, p.p.* **clothed, clad** *v.t.* (*past, p.p.* **clothed, clad**) to furnish, invest or cover with or as with clothes. †*v.i.* to wear clothes. **clothes,** *n.pl.* garments, dress; bed-clothes. **clothes-basket,** *n.* a basket for clothes to be washed. **clothes-brush,** *n.* a brush for removing dust from clothes. **clothes-horse,** *n.* a frame for drying clothes on; (*coll.*) a fashionably-dressed person. **clothes-line,** *n.* a line for drying clothes on. †**clothes-man,** *n.* a man who deals in clothes, esp. **old-clothes-man,** in old clothes. **clothes-moth,** *n.* the genus *Tinea,* the larvae of which are destructive to cloth. **clothes-peg, -pin,** *n.* a cleft peg used to fasten clothes on a line. **clothes-press,** *n.* a cupboard for storing clothes. **clothes-prop,** *n.* a pole for supporting a clothes-line. **clothes-wringer,** *n.* a machine for wringing clothes after washing. **clothing,** *n.* clothes, dress, apparel. [OE *clāthian* (CLAD is from ONorthum. *clǣthan*)]

clothier, *n.* a manufacturer of cloth; one who deals in cloth or clothing. [orig. *clother*]

cloture, *n.* (*N Am.*) closure of debate in a legislative body. [F]

cloud, *n.* a mass of visible vapour condensed into minute drops or vesicles, and floating in the upper regions of the atmosphere; a volume of smoke or dust resembling a cloud; the dusky veins or markings in marble, precious stones etc.; a dimness or patchiness in liquid; a kind of light woollen scarf; a veil which obscures or darkens; obscurity, bewilderment, confusion of ideas; suspicion, trouble; any temporary depression; a great number, a multitude of living creatures, or snow, arrows etc., moving in a body. *v.t.* to overspread with clouds, to darken; to mark with cloud-like spots; to make gloomy or sullen; to sully, to stain. *v.i.* to grow cloudy. **in the clouds,** mystical, unreal; absent-minded. **on cloud nine,** very happy, elated. **under a cloud,** in temporary disgrace or misfortune. **cloudberry,** *n.* a low mountain and moorland shrub, *Rubus chamaemorus,* with strawberry-like fruit. †**cloud-born,** *a.* born of a cloud. †**cloud-built,** *a.* visionary, imaginary. **cloud-burst,** *n.* a sudden and heavy fall of rain. **cloud-capped,** *a.* with summit or summits veiled with clouds; very lofty. **cloud-castle,** *n.* a daydream, a visionary scheme. **cloud chamber,** *n.* an apparatus in which high-energy particles are tracked as they pass through a vapour. **cloud-compelling,** *a.* having power to gather or disperse clouds. **cloud-cuckoo-land,** *n.* a utopia, a fantastic scheme for social, political or economic reform. **cloud-drift,** *n.* floating, cloudy vapour. **cloud-eclipsed,** *a.* hidden by clouds. **cloud-rack,** *n.* shattered cloud. **cloudscape,** *n.* a view or picture of clouds; picturesque cloud effects. **cloud-wrapt,** *a.* enveloped in clouds; abstracted, absent-minded. †**cloudage,** *n.* cloudiness; a mass of clouds. **cloudless,** *a.* unclouded; clear, bright. **cloudlessly,** *adv.* **cloudlessness,** *n.* **cloudlet,** *n.* a little cloud. **cloudwards,** *adv.* **cloudy,** *a.* consisting of or overspread with clouds; marked with veins or spots; obscure, confused; dull, gloomy, sullen; wanting in clearness. **cloudily,** *adv.* **cloudiness,** *n.* [prob. from OE *clūd,* a rounded mass, conn. with CLOD]

Clouet[1], *n.* **Jean** (known as **Janet**) (1486–1541), French artist, court painter to Francis I. His portraits, often compared to Holbein's, show an outstanding naturalism, particularly his drawings.

Clouet[2], *n.* **François** (*c.* 1515–72), French portrait painter, who succeeded his father Jean Clouet as court painter. He worked in the Italian style of Mannerism. His half-nude portrait of Diane de Poitiers, *The Lady in her Bath* (National Gallery, Washington), is also thought to be a likeness of Marie Touchet, mistress of Charles IX (1550–74).

clough, *n.* a ravine; a narrow valley. [OE *clōh*]

Clough, *n.* **Arthur Hugh** (1819–61), British poet. Many of his lyrics are marked by a melancholy scepticism that reflects his struggle with his religious doubt.

clour, *n.* (*Sc.*) a heavy bump on the head; (*Sc.*) a blow on the head. *v.t.* (*Sc.*) to hit with such a blow. [conn. with Icel. *klōr*]

clout, *n.* a piece of cloth, rag etc., used to patch or mend; a rag; a mark for archers; an iron plate on an axle-tree to keep it from being rubbed; (*coll.*) a blow with the open hand, esp. on the head; (*coll.*) power, influence. *v.t.* to patch, to mend roughly; to cover with a piece of cloth etc.; to tip or plate with iron; to join clumsily; to stud or fasten with clout-nails; (*coll.*) to strike with the open hand. **clout-nail,** *n.* a short nail with a large head for fastening wagon-clouts on, or to stud the soles of heavy boots and shoes. **clouted**[1], *a.* patched; mended clumsily; studded with clout-nails. [OE *clūt* (cogn. with CLOT)]

clouted[2], *a.* CLOTTED under CLOT.

clove[1], *n.* one of the dried, unexpanded flower-buds of the clove-tree, used as a spice; (*pl.*) a spirituous cordial flavoured with this. **clove-gillyflower** (F *clou de girofle,* see below), **-pink,** *n.* any sweet-scented double variety of *Dianthus caryophyllus*. **clove-tree,** *n.* the tree, *Caryophyllus aromaticus*. [F *clou,* L *clavus,* a nail (*clou de girofle,* a clove), prob. assim. in sound to CLOVE[2]]

clove[2], *n.* a small bulb forming one part of a compound bulb, as in garlic, the shallot etc. [OE *clufu* (from *cluf-*, cogn. with *clēofan*, to CLEAVE[2])]

clove[3], *past*, CLEAVE. **clove-hitch**, *n.* a safe kind of rope-fastening round a spar or another rope. **cloven**, *a.* divided into two parts; cleft. **cloven-footed, -hoofed**, *a.* having the hoof divided in the centre, as have the ruminants. **cloven hoof**, *n.* an emblem of Pan or the Devil; an indication of guile or devilish design.

clover, *n.* a trefoil used for fodder. **to be, live in clover**, to be in enjoyable circumstances; to live luxuriously. **cloverleaf**, *n.* a traffic device in which one crossing road passes over the other, and the connecting carriageways, having no abrupt turns, make the shape of a four-leaved clover. [OE *clāfre* (cp. Dut. *klaver*, Dan. *klōver*, G *Klee*)]

Clovis, *n.* (465–511), Merovingian king of the Franks from 481. He succeeded his father Childeric as king of the Salian (northern) Franks, defeated the Gallo-Romans (Romanized Gauls) near Soissons (486), ending their rule in France, and defeated the Alemanni, a confederation of Germanic tribes, near Cologne (496). He embraced Christianity and subsequently proved a powerful defender of orthodoxy against the Arian Visigoths, whom he defeated at Poitiers (507). He made Paris his capital.

clown, *n.* a rustic, a countryman; a clumsy, awkward lout; a rough, ill-bred person; a buffoon in a circus or pantomime. *v.i.* to play silly jokes, to act the buffoon. **clownery**, *n.* **clownish**, *a.* **clownishly**, *adv.* **clownishness**, *n.* **clownswort**, *n.* the hedge stachys, *Stachys sylvatica*, used in herbalism. [cp. Icel. *klunni*, CLUMP or CLOT]

cloy, *v.t.* †to spike a gun; †to prick a horse in shoeing; †to wound with a sharp weapon; †to fill up; to satiate, to glut; to tire with sweetness, richness or excess. **cloyless**, *a.* that does not or cannot cloy. **cloyment**, *n.* surfeit, satiety. [etym. doubtful; perh. from OF *cloyer* (F *clouer*), to nail]

club[1], *n.* a piece of wood with one end thicker and heavier than the other, used as a weapon; a stick bent and (usually) weighted at the end for driving a ball; (*pl.*) one of the four suits at cards (in England denoted by a trefoil); a round, solid mass. *v.t.* (*past, p.p.* **clubbed**) to beat with a club; to gather into a clump. **to club the musket**, to seize by the barrel and use it as a club. **club-foot**, *n.* a short deformed foot. **club-footed**, *a.* **club-grass**, *n.* club-jointed grass of the genus *Corynephorus*. **club-haul**, *v.t.* to tack (a ship) by letting go the lee anchor as soon as the wind is out of the sails in order to escape from a lee-shore. **club-headed**, *a.* having a club-shaped head or top. **club-law**, *n.* government by force. **club-moss**, *n.* species of moss belonging to the genus *Lycopodium*, with seed-vessels pointing straight upwards. **club root**, *n.* a disease of plants of the *Brassica* (cabbage) genus in which the lower part of the stem becomes swollen and misshapen owing to the attacks of larvae. **club-rush**, *n.* name of various species of the genus *Scirpus*. **club sandwich**, *n.* one made with three slices of bread and two different fillings. **club-shaped**, *a.* clavate, claviform. **clubbed**, *a.* club-shaped. [ME *clubbe, clobbe*, prob. from Icel. *klubba, klumba*, aclub, a cudgel]

club[2], *n.* an association of persons combined for some common object, as of temporary residence, social intercourse, literature, politics, sport etc., governed by self-imposed regulations; the house or building in which such an association meets; the body of members collectively; share or proportion contributed to a common stock; joint charge or effort. *v.t.* (*past, p.p.* **clubbed**) to gather into a clump; to contribute for a common object; (*Mil.*) to work (troops) into an inextricable mass. *v.i.* to join (together) for a common object. **in the club**, (*sl.*) pregnant. **club car**, *n.* (*N Am.*) a railway-coach designed like a lounge, usu. with a bar. **clubhouse**, *n.* the house occupied by a club, or in which it holds its meetings; the establishment maintained by the members of a social or sports club, at which they meet, drink, dine or lodge temporarily. **clubland**, *n.* the district round St James's and Pall Mall where the principal London clubs are situated. **club-man, -woman**, *n.* a member of a club. **club-room**, *n.* a room in which a club or society meets. **clubbable**, *a.* having the qualities necessary for club life; sociable. **clubber**, *n.* a member of a club; one who uses a club. **clubdom**, *n.* [as prec.]

Club of Rome, informal international organization, set up after a meeting at the Accademia dei Lincei, Rome, in 1968, which aims to promote greater understanding of the interdependence of global economic, political, natural and social systems.

cluck, *n.* the guttural call of a hen; any similar sound. *v.i.* to utter the cry of a hen to her chickens. *v.t.* to call, as a hen does her chickens. [OE *cloccian*, imit.]

clue, *n.* a ball of thread; a thread to guide a person in a labyrinth, like that given by Ariadne to Theseus to guide him back through the labyrinth at Crete; anything of a material or mental nature that serves as guide, direction or hint for the solution of a problem or mystery. **I haven't a clue**, I have no idea whatever; I am quite in the dark. **to clue in, up**, (*sl.*) to inform. **clueless**, *a.* ignorant; stupid. [CLEW]

Cluj, *n.* (German **Klausenberg**) city in Transylvania, Romania, located on the river Somes; population (1985) 310,000. It is a communications centre for Romania and the Hungarian plain. Industries include machine tools, furniture and knitwear.

clumber, *n.* a variety of spaniel. [*Clumber*, Duke of Newcastle's seat, Notts.]

clump, *n.* a thick cluster of trees, shrubs or flowers; a thick mass of small objects or organisms; a thick piece of leather fastened on to a boot-sole; a heavy blow. *v.i.* to tread in a heavy and clumsy fashion; to form or gather into a clump or clumps. *v.t.* to make a clump of; (*sl.*) to beat. **clump-boot**, *n.* a heavy boot for rough wear. **clumpy**, *a.* [cp. CLUB (Icel. *klubba, klumba*), also G *Klumpen*, Dut. *klomp*]

clumsy, *a.* awkward, ungainly, ill-constructed; rough, rude, tactless. **clumsily**, *adv.* **clumsiness**, *n.* [ME *clumsed*, p.p. of *clumsen*, to benumb (cp. CLAM, CLAMMY)]

clunch, *n.* a lump; the lower and harder beds of the Upper Chalk formation, occasionally used for building purposes; a local name for fire-clay occurring under a coal seam. [prob. var. of CLUMP (cp. BUMP[1], BUNCH; HUMP, HUNCH)]

clung, *past, p.p.* CLING.

Cluniac, *n.* one of a reformed branch of Benedictines founded at Cluny, Saône-et-Loire, France, in the 10th cent. *a.* pertaining to this order. [med. L *Cluniacus*, from *Cluny*]

clunk, *v.i.* to make a short, dull sound, as of metal striking a hard surface. *n.* such a sound. **clunky**, *a.* (*coll.*) heavy unwieldy. [onomat.]

clupeoid, *n.* a fish belonging to the Clupeoidea, a division of fishes, including the Clupeidae, or herring family, and related families. *a.* herring-like. **clupeiform**, *a.* **clupeoidean**, *n., a.* [L *clupea*, a small river-fish, -OID]

cluster, *n.* a number of things of the same kind growing or joined together; a bunch; a number of persons or things gathered into or situated in a close body; a group, a crowd. *v.i.* to come or to grow into clusters. *v.t.* to bring or cause to come into a cluster or clusters. **cluster bomb**, *n.* a bomb which explodes to scatter a number of smaller bombs. **clustered column, pillar**, *n.* a pier consisting of several columns or shafts clustered together. [OE *clyster* (prob. from the same root as CLOT)]

clutch[1], *n.* a snatch, a grip, a grasp; the paw or talon of a rapacious animal; the hands; a device for connecting and disconnecting two revolving shafts in an engine; a gripping device; the throat of an anchor; (*pl.*) claws, tyrannical power. *v.t.* to seize, clasp or grip with the hand; to snatch. **cone clutch**, a friction clutch consisting of a cone sliding into a conical cavity in the engine flywheel. **disc, plate clutch**, a clutch which operates as a result of friction between the surfaces of discs.

clutch bag, *n.* a woman's handbag, without a handle, carried in the hand. **clutch shaft,** *n.* (*Motor.*) a shaft which engages or disengages a clutch. [ME *cloche, cloke,* a claw (OE *clyccan,* to bring together, clench)]

clutch[2], *n.* a sitting (of eggs); a brood (of chickens); a group, set (of people or things). [var. of obs. *clekch,* from *cleck,* to hatch]

clutter, *v.i.* to make a confused noise; to bustle. *n.* a confused noise; bustle, confusion; a mess, confusion; irrelevant echoes on a radar screen from sources other than the target. **to clutter up,** to fill untidily. [var. of *clotter,* freq. of CLOT]

Clwyd, *n.* county in N Wales. **area** 2420 sq km/934 sq miles. **towns** administrative headquarters Mold; Flint, Denbigh, Wrexham; seaside resorts Colwyn Bay, Rhyl, Prestatyn. **physical** rivers Dee and Clwyd; Clwydian Range with Offa's Dyke along the main ridge. **products** dairy and meat products, optical glass, chemicals, limestone, microprocessors, plastics. **population** (1987) 403,000. **language** 19% Welsh, English.

cly, *v.t.* to seize; to get hold of; to steal. *n.* something stolen. **cly-faker,** *n.* a pickpocket. [cogn. with CLAW]

Clyde, *n.* a river in Strathclyde, Scotland; 170 km/103 miles long. The Firth of Clyde and Firth of Forth are linked by the Forth and Clyde canal, 56 km/35 miles long. The shipbuilding yards have declined in recent years.

clypeus, *n.* the shield-like part of an insect's head, which joins the labrum. **clypeal, -eate, -eiform,** *a.* **clypeo-,** *comb. form.* [L, a shield]

†**clyster,** *n.* an enema. **clyster-pipe,** *n.* a pipe used for injections; the nozzle of an enema syringe; an apothecary. [L, from Gr. *klustēr* (*kluzein,* to wash out)]

Clytemnestra, *n.* in Greek mythology, the wife of Agamemnon.

Cm, (*chem. symbol*) curium.

cm, (*abbr.*) centimetre(s).

Cmd., (*abbr.*) Command paper (before 1956).

CMG, (*abbr.*) Companion of (the Order of) St Michael and St George.

Cmnd., (*abbr.*) Command paper (since 1956).

CND, (*abbr.*) Campaign for Nuclear Disarmament.

cnida, *n.* (*pl.* **-dae**) the stinging-cell of the Coelenterata (jellyfish etc.). **cnido-,** *comb. form.* [Gr. *knidē,* a nettle]

Cnossus, *n.* alternative form of KNOSSOS.

CNS, (*abbr.*) central nervous system.

Cnut, *n.* alternative spelling of CANUTE.

c/o, (*abbr.*) care of.

co-, *pref.* with, together, jointly, mutually; joint, mutual; as in *coacervate, coalesce, cooperate; coeternal, coefficient, coequal; coheir, co-mate, copartner.* [L, the form of *cum,* together used before vowels etc.]

CO, (*abbr.*) Colonial Office (before 1966); commanding officer; Commonwealth Office (since 1966); conscientious objector.

Co[1], (*chem. symbol*) cobalt.

Co.[2], (*abbr.*) company; county.

coacervate, *a.* heaped up; accumulated; (*Bot.*) clustered. **coacervation,** *n.* [L *coacervāre* (*acervus,* heap)]

coach, *n.* a large, closed four-wheeled, horse-drawn vehicle, used for purposes of state, for pleasure, or (with regular fares) for travelling; a railway carriage; a long-distance bus; a tutor who prepares for examinations; one who trains sports players; a room near the stern in a large ship of war; (*Austral.*) a decoy. *v.t.* to prepare for an examination; to train; to instruct or advise in preparation for any event. *v.i.* to travel in a coach; to read with a tutor. **coach-box,** *n.* the seat on which the driver of a horse-drawn coach sits. **coach-builder,** *n.* one who builds or repairs the bodywork of road or rail vehicles. **coach-built,** *a.* of vehicles, built individually by craftsmen. **coach-driver,** *n.* the driver of a long-distance bus. †**coach-fellow,** *n.* a horse yoked in the same carriage with another; a comrade, a mate. **coach-house,** *n.* an outhouse to keep a coach or carriage in. **coachman,** *n.* the driver of a horse-drawn coach; a livery servant who drives a carriage; (*Angling*) a kind of artificial fly. **coachmanship,** *n.* **coach-office,** *n.* the booking-office of a stage coach. **coach-whip,** *n.* a whip used by a driver of a coach; a harmless N American tree-snake, *Herpetodryas flagelliformis.* **coachwork,** *n.* the bodywork of a road or rail vehicle. **coachee,** *n.* a coachman, a driver. **coachful,** *n.* as many as will fill a coach. [F *coche,* Magyar *kocsi,* belonging to *Kocz,* village in Hungary]

coact, *v.t.* to compel, to control. *v.i.* to act in concert. **coaction,** *n.* **coactive,** *a.* having a restraining or impelling power; acting together or in concert. **coactively,** *adv.* [L *coactus,* p.p. of *coagere, cōgere,* to compel (co-, *agere,* to drive)]

coadapted, *a.* adapted to one another; mutually adapted or suited. **coadaptation,** *n.*

coadjacent, *a.* mutually near, contiguous. **coadjacence, -ency,** *n.*

coadjutor, *n.* an assistant, a helper, esp. to a bishop; a colleague. **coadjutorship,** *n.* **coadjutrix,** *n. fem.* [L *coadjūtor* (*juvāre,* to help)]

coadunate, *a.* (*Physiol.*) joined together, connate; (*Bot.*) adnate. **coadunation,** *n.* [L *coadūnāre* (co-, AD-, *unus,* one)]

coagent, *n.* one who or that which acts with another. *a.* acting with. **coagency,** *n.*

coagulate, *v.t.* to cause to curdle; to convert from a fluid into a curd-like mass. *v.i.* to become curdled. **coagulable,** *a.* **coagulant,** *n.* a substance which causes coagulation. **coagulation,** *n.* **coagulative,** *a.* **coagulator,** *n.* **coagulometer,** *n.* **coagulum,** *n.* (*pl.* **-la**) a coagulated mass; a coagulant; a blood-clot. [from obs. a. *coagulate,* coagulated, or directly from L *coāgulātus,* p.p. of *coāgulāre,* from *coāgulum,* dim. n. of *coagere* (co-, *agere,* to drive, impel)]

coaita, *n.* the red-faced spider-monkey. [Tupí *coatá*]

coak, *n.* a dowel let into the end of a piece of wood to be joined to another; (*Naut.*) the metal pin-hole in a sheave. [It. *cocca,* a notch]

coal, *n.* a black solid opaque carbonaceous substance of vegetable origin, obtained from the strata usu. below the surface, and used for fuel; a piece of wood or other combustible substance, ignited, burning or charred; a cinder. *v.t.* to supply with coals. *v.i.* to take in a supply of coals. **to blow a coal,** to fan a quarrel; to stir up strife. **to carry coals,** to put up with insults. **to carry coals to Newcastle,** to do anything superfluous or unnecessary. **to haul over the coals,** to call to account; to reprimand. **to heap coals of fire,** to return good for evil. **coal-backer,** *n.* a coal-porter. **coal-bed, -seam,** *n.* a stratum of or containing coal. **coal-black,** *a.* as black as coal; jet-black. **coal-box,** *n.* a coal-scuttle. **coal-brand,** *n.* smut in wheat. **coal-brass,** *n.* the iron pyrites of the coal-measures. **coal-bunker,** *n.* a receptacle for coals, usu. in a steamship. **coal-cellar,** *n.* a basement for storing coal. **coal-dust,** *n.* powdered coal. **coal-face,** *n.* the exposed surface of a coal-seam. **coal-factor,** *n.* a middle-man between colliery-owners and customers, formerly between colliery-owners or shippers and coal-sellers. **coal-field,** *n.* a district where coal abounds. **coal-fired,** *a.* of a furnace, heating system etc., fuelled by coal. **coal-fish,** *n.* the black cod, *Gadus carbonarius.* **coal-flap, -plate,** *n.* an iron cover for the opening in a pavement etc. for putting coal into a cellar. **coal-gas,** *n.* impure carburetted hydrogen obtained from coal and used for lighting and heating. **coal-heaver,** *n.* one employed in carrying, loading or discharging coals. **coal-hole,** *n.* a small cellar for keeping coals. **coal-master,** *n.* (*formerly*) one who works a coal-mine. **coal-measures,** *n.pl.* the upper division of the carboniferous system. **coal-merchant,** *n.* a retail seller of coal. **coal-mine,** *n.* a mine from which coal is obtained. **coal-miner,** *n.* **coal-naphtha,** *n.* naphtha produced as a by-product in the distillation of coal-gas from coal. **coal-oil,** *n.* (*N Am.*) petroleum. **coal-owner,** *n.* (*formerly*) the owner of a colliery. **coal-pit,** *n.* a coal-mine; (*N Am.*) a place where charcoal is burnt. **coal-plant,** *n.* a plant whose remains form coal; a plant of the carboniferous age.

coal-screen, *n.* a large screen or sifting-frame for separating large and small coals. **coal-scuttle,** *n.* a utensil for holding coals for present use. **coal-scuttle bonnet,** a poke-bonnet with a projecting front, like an inverted coal-scuttle. **coal-seam** COAL-BED. **coal-ship,** *n.* a ship employed in carrying coals. **coal-tar,** *n.* tar produced in the destructive distillation of bituminous coal. **coal-tit** COALMOUSE. **coal-vase,** *n.* a coal-scuttle. **coal-whipper,** *n.* a person or machine for raising coal out of the hold of a ship. **coaling station,** *n.* a port where steamships may obtain coal, esp. one established by a government for the supply of coal to warships. **coaler,** *n.* a ship that transports coal. **coalless,** *a.* **coaly,** *a.* [OE *col* (cp. Dut. *kool,* Icel. and Swed. *kol,* G *Kohle*)]

coalesce, *v.i.* to grow together; to unite into masses or groups spontaneously; to combine; to fuse into one; to form a coalition. **coalescence,** *n.* concretion. **coalescent,** *a.* [L *coalescere* (co-, *alescere,* incept. of *alere,* to nourish)]

coalition, *n.* a union of separate bodies into one body or mass; a combination of persons, parties or states, having different interests. **coalition government,** *n.* a government in which two or more parties of varying politics unite for a common policy. **coalitionist,** *n.* [see prec.]

coalmouse, colemouse, *n.* (*pl.* **-mice**) a small dark bird, *Parus ater,* called also the coal-tit or coal-titmouse. [OE *colmāse* (*col,* coal, *māse;* cp. OHG *meisa,* WG *maisa, ua* bird)]

coamings, *n.pl.* (*Naut.*) the raised borders round hatches etc. for keeping water from pouring into the hold. [etym. doubtful]

coaptation, *n.* the adaptation of parts to each other. [L *coaptātio -ōnem,* from *coaptāre*]

coarctate, *a.* (*Bot., Ent.*) pressed together. **coarctation,** *n.* [L *coarctātus,* p.p. of *coarctāre* (*artāre,* from *artus,* confined)]

coarse, *a.* common; of average quality; of inferior quality; large in size or rough in texture; rude, rough, vulgar; unpolished, unrefined, indelicate; indecent. **coarse-fibred, -grained,** *a.* having a coarse grain; unrefined, vulgar. **coarse fish,** *n.* any freshwater fish not of the salmon family. **coarse fishing,** *n.* **coarsely,** *adv.* **coarsen,** *v.t.* to make coarse. *v.i.* to grow or become coarse. **coarseness,** *n.* **coarsish,** *a.* [prob. from *in course,* ordinary (cp. MEAN[3], PLAIN[1])]

coast, *n.* that part of the border of a country which is washed by the sea; the seashore; a toboggan-slide; a swift rush downhill on cycle or motor-car, without using motive power or applying brakes; †a side; †a side of meat; †border, limit; tract, region. *v.t.* to sail by or near to; to keep close to; †to accost. *v.i.* to sail near or in sight of the shore; to sail from port to port in the same country; to slide down snow or ice on a toboggan or sleigh; to descend an incline on a cycle or a mechanically propelled vehicle without applying motive power or brakes; to proceed without any positive effort. **the Coast,** (*N Am.*) the Pacific coast of the US. **the coast is clear,** the road is free; the danger is over. **coast-to-coast,** *a.* from coast to coast, across a whole continent. **coastguard,** *n.* one of a body of people who watch the coast to save those in danger, give warning of wrecks, and prevent the illegal landing of persons and goods. **coastlander,** *n.* a dweller on the coast. **coast-line,** *n.* **coastal,** *a.* of, pertaining to or bordering on a coast-line. **coaster,** *n.* a coasting-vessel; a small tray for a bottle or decanter on a table; a small mat under a glass. **coasting,** *a.* pertaining to the coast; that coasts. **coasting-trade,** *n.* trade between the ports of the same country. **coasting-vessel,** *n.* **coastward, -wards,** *adv.* **coastwise,** *adv.* [OF *coste* (F *côte*), L *costa,* a rib, a side]

coat, *n.* an upper outer garment with sleeves; †a petticoat; the hair or fur of any beast; the natural external covering of an animal; any integument, tunic or covering; a layer of any substance covering and protecting another. *v.t.* to cover; to overspread with a layer of anything. **coat of arms,** (*Her.*) a herald's tabard; an escutcheon or shield of arms; armorial bearings. **coat of mail,** armour worn on the upper part of the body, consisting of iron rings or scales fastened on a stout linen or leather jacket. **great-coat** GREAT. **red-coat** RED. **to trail one's coat, coat-tails,** to invite attack. **to turn one's coat,** to change sides, hence **turn-coat** (see TURN). **coat-armour,** *n.* (*Her.*) a loose vestment embroidered with armorial bearings, worn by knights over their armour; heraldic bearings. †**coat-card,** (*now*) **court-card,** *n.* one of the figured cards in the pack, so called from the coats or dresses in which they are represented. **coat-hanger,** *n.* a utensil for hanging up coats, dresses etc. **coated,** *a.* **coatee,** *n.* a short coat for a woman or esp. a baby. **coating,** *n.* a covering, layer or integument; the act of covering; a substance spread over as a cover or defence; cloth for coats. **coatless,** *a.* [OF *cote* (F *cotte*), med. L *cota, cotta,* OHG *chozza,* fem. *choz, chozzo,* a coarse, shaggy stuff or a garment of this]

coati, coatimundi, *n.* a racoon-like carnivorous animal with a long, flexible snout, from S America; also a Central American and Mexican species. [Tupí (*coa,* a cincture, *tim,* a nose)]

co-author, *n.* one who writes a book together with someone else.

coax, *v.t.* to persuade by fondling or flattery; to wheedle, to cajole. *v.i.* to practise cajolery in order to persuade. **coaxer,** *n.* **coaxingly,** *adv.* [formerly *cokes,* from *cokes,* a fool, a gull]

coaxal, -ial, *a.* having a common axis. **coaxial cable, coax**, *n.* a cable with a central conductor within an outer tubular conductor.

cob, *n.* a lump or ball of anything; a spider, from its round body (cp. COBWEB); a short stout horse for riding; a kind of wicker basket; a cobnut; a sea-gull; a cob-swan; †a Spanish dollar; a kind of breakwater; the top or head of anything; the spike of Indian corn; a mixture of clay and straw used for building walls in the west of England. *v.t.* (*past, p.p.* **cobbed**) to punish by flogging on the breech with a belt or flat piece of wood. †**cob-loaf,** *n.* a small round loaf; a coarse, rough, loutish fellow. **cobnut,** *n.* a variety of the cultivated hazel. **cobstone** COBBLE[2]. **cob-swan,** *n.* a male swan. **cob-wall,** *n.* a wall built of mud or clay, mixed with straw. **cobby,** *a.* [etym. doubtful]

cobalt, *n.* a reddish-grey, or greyish-white, brittle, hard metallic element, at. no. 27; chem. symbol Co. **cobalt-bloom,** *n.* acicular arsenate of cobalt; erythrite. **cobalt-blue,** *n.* a deep blue pigment of alumina and cobalt. **cobaltic**, *a.* **cobaltiferous**, *a.* **cobaltous,** *a.* **cobalto-,** *comb. form.* [G *Kobold,* a mine-demon, because the mineral was at first troublesome to the miners]

Cobb, *n.* **Ty(rus Raymond),** nicknamed 'the Georgia Peach' (1886–1961), US baseball player, one of the greatest batters and base runners of all time. He played for Detroit and Philadelphia (1905–28), and won the American League batting average championship 12 times. He holds the all-time record for runs scored, 2254, and batting average, .367. He had 4191 hits in his career, a record that stood for almost 60 years.

cobber, *n.* (*Austral., sl.*) a pal, a chum. [E dial. *cob,* to take a liking to]

Cobbett, *n.* **William** (1763–1835), British Radical politician and journalist, who published the weekly *Political Register* (1802–35). He spent much time in North America. His crusading essays on farmers' conditions were collected as *Rural Rides* (1830).

cobble[1], *v.t.* to mend or patch (as shoes); to make or do clumsily. **cobbler,** *n.* one who mends shoes; a mender or patcher; a clumsy workman; (*N Am.*) a cooling drink of wine, sugar, lemon and ice; (*Austral.*) a dirty sheep at shearing-time; (*pl.*) (*sl.*) nonsense. **cobbler's wax,** *n.* a resinous substance used for waxing thread. [etym. unknown]

cobble[2], *n.* a rounded stone or pebble used for paving; a roundish lump of coal. *v.t.* to pave with cobbles. [COB]

cobbra, *n.* (*Austral.*) the skull, the head. [Abor.]

Cobden, *n.* **Richard** (1804–65), British Liberal politician and economist, co-founder with John Bright of the Anti-Corn Law League (1839). A member of Parliament from 1841, he opposed class and religious privileges and believed in disarmament and free trade. **Cobdenism**, *n.* the doctrines of Richard Cobden, esp. Free Trade, pacifism and non-intervention. **Cobdenite,** *n.* an adherent of Cobdenism.

cobelligerent, *a.* waging war jointly with another. *n.* one who joins another in waging war.

coble, *n.* a flat, square-sterned fishing-boat with a lugsail and six oars. [W *ceubal* (*ceuo,* to hollow or excavate)]

Cobol, *n.* a high-level computer language for commercial use. [acronym for *co*mmon *b*usiness *o*rientated *l*anguage]

cobra, cobra de capello, *n.* any viperine snake of the genus *Naja,* from Africa and tropical Asia, which distends the skin of the neck into a kind of hood when excited. [Port., snake of (with) a hood]

cobstone COBBLE[2].

coburg, *n.* a loaf of bread with one or more cuts on top that spread out when baking; a type of sponge cake; a thin worsted fabric. [town in Germany]

Coburn, *n.* **James** (1928–), US film actor, popular in the 1960s and 1970s. His films include *The Magnificent Seven* (1960), *Our Man Flint* (1966), and *Cross of Iron* (1977).

cobweb, *n.* the web or net spun by a spider for its prey; the material or a thread of this; anything flimsy and worthless; a fine-spun argument; old musty rubbish. *a.* light, thin, flimsy, worthless. **to blow away the cobwebs,** to refresh oneself in the open air. **cobwebbed,** *a.* covered with or full of cobwebs; (*Bot.*) covered with thick, matted pubescence. **cobwebby,** *a.* [COB (OE *-coppe,* found in *attorcoppe,* poison-spider), WEB (COB, a spider, may, however, be from COBWEB)]

coca, *n.* the dried leaf of *Erythroxylon coca,* a Peruvian plant chewed as a narcotic stimulant; the plant itself. **cocaine**, *n.* an alkaloid contained in coca leaves, used as a stimulant and medicinally as a local anaesthetic. *n.* **cocainism,** *n.* (physical and mental symptoms resulting from) addiction to cocaine. **cocainize, -ise,** *v.t.* **cocainization, -isation,** *n.* **cocainomania**, *n.* a morbid craving for cocaine; a form of insanity resulting from cocainism. [Sp., from Quechua *cuca*]

Coca-Cola®, *n.* a sweetened, fizzy drink, originally flavoured by coca and cola nuts, containing caramel and caffeine. Invented in 1886, Coca-Cola was sold in every state of the US by 1895 and in 155 countries by 1987.

coccagee, *n.* a kind of cider apple. [Ir. *cac a'ghéidh,* goose-dung]

coccidiosis, *n.* a parasitic disease of the intestines, liver etc., found in rabbits, fowls etc.

cocciferous, *a.* bearing berries. [L *coccum,* berry]

coccolite, *n.* a white or green variety of pyroxene. [Gr. *kokkos,* grain]

coccolith, *n.* a small round body found in Atlantic ooze, and prob. extinct plankton. [Gr. *kokkos,* grain, berry]

cocculus, *n.* a genus of menispermaceous climbing plants. **cocculus indicus**, *n.* the fruit of *Anamirta cocculus,* an Asian climber, an acrid narcotic. [mod. L, dim. of foll.]

coccus, *n.* (*pl.* **-cci**) one of the dry one-seeded carpels into which a fruit breaks up; a spore mother-cell in cryptogams; a spherical bacterium; a genus of hemipterous insects, including many forms hurtful to plants. **coccal,** *a.* **coccoid,** *a.* [mod. L, from Gr. *kokkos,* grain]

coccyx, *n.* (*pl.* **-xes, -ges**) the lower solid portion of the vertebral column, the homologue in man of the tail of the lower vertebrates. **coccygeal**, *a.* **coccyg(eo)-,** *comb. form.* [L, from Gr. *kokkux -ugos,* the cuckoo (from the resemblance to a cuckoo's bill)]

Cochabamba, *n.* a city in central Bolivia, SE of La Paz; population (1985) 317,000. Its altitude is 2550 m/ 8370 ft; it is important for agricultural trading and oil refining.

cochin-china, *n.* a breed of domestic fowls from Cochin-China in Vietnam.

cochineal, *n.* a dye-stuff made from the dried bodies of the female cochineal insect, used in dyeing, as a food colouring and in the manufacture of scarlet and carmine pigments. **cochineal-fig,** *n.* the cactus, *Opuntia cochinellifera,* on which the cochineal insect is principally found. **cochineal insect,** *n.* the insect, *Coccus cacti,* from which this dye is obtained. [F *cochenille,* Sp. *cochinilla,* L *coccineus, coccinus* (*coccum,* a berry, scarlet)]

cochlea, *n.* (*pl.* **-leae**) the anterior spiral division of the internal ear. **cochlean,** *a.* **cochlear,** *a.* (*Bot.*) used of a form of aestivation, in which one large part covers all the others. **Cochlearia**, *n.* a genus of plants including the horseradish and common scurvy-grass. **cochleariform**, *a.* **cochleate**, **-ated**, *a.* circular, spiral; (*Bot.*) twisted like a snail-shell. [L, from Gr. *kochlias,* a snail, a screw, *kochlon,* a shellfish]

Cochran, *n.* **C(harles) B(lake)** (1872–1951), British impresario who promoted entertainment ranging from wrestling and roller-skating to Diaghilev's *Ballets Russes.*

cock[1], *n.* the male of birds, particularly of domestic fowls; a male salmon; a vane in the form of a cock; a weathercock; †cock-crowing; †a leader, a chief; a good fellow; a short spout a tap, a valve for regulating the flow through a spout or pipe; (*sl.*) the penis; the hammer of a gun or pistol, which, striking against a piece of flint or a percussion-cap, produces a spark and explodes the charge; the gnomon of a dial; the needle of a balance; the piece which covers the balance in a clock or watch; (*sl.*) nonsense. **cock-a-doodle-doo**, the crow of the domestic cock; a nursery name for the bird. **cock-a-hoop,** strutting like a cock; triumphant, exultant. *adv.* exultantly, with crowing and boastfulness, uppishly. **cock-and-bull,** applied to silly, exaggerated stories or canards. **cock of the north,** the brambling. **cock of the walk,** a masterful person; a leader, a chief. **cock of the wood,** the capercailzie. **old cock,** (*coll.*) a familiar form of address. **to live like fighting cocks,** to have the best food and plenty of it. **cock-bill,** *v.t.* (*Naut.*) to hang (the anchor) from the cathead before letting go. **a-cock-bill,** *adv.* with the anchor in this position. **cock-brained,** *a.* rash, giddy, flighty. **cock-crow, -crowing,** *n.* the crow of a cock; early dawn. **cock-eye,** *n.* (*sl.*) an eye that squints. **cock-eyed,** *a.* (*sl.*) having squinting eyes; irregular, ill-arranged; askew; eccentric. **cock-fight, -fighting,** *n.* a battle or match of game-cocks. **cock-horse,** *n.* a stick with a horse's head at the end, on which children ride. **a-cock-horse,** *adv.* on horseback; in an elevated position; proudly, exultingly. *a.* mounted, as on horseback; proud, exultant, upstart. **cock-laird,** *n.* a landed proprietor who cultivates his own estate. **cock-lobster,** *n.* a male lobster. **cockloft,** *n.* an upper loft, a garret. †**cock-master,** *n.* an owner or breeder of game-cocks. **cock-match,** *n.* a cock-fight. **cock-nest,** *n.* one built by a male bird, as the wren, for roosting. **cockpit,** *n.* a pit or area where game-cocks fight; a part of the lower deck of a man-of-war, used as a hospital in action; that portion of the fuselage of an aircraft where the pilot and crew (if any) are accommodated; the driver's compartment of a racing car. **cockpit of Europe,** Belgium. **cock-robin,** *n.* a male robin; †(*sl.*) an easy-going fellow. **cockscomb,** *n.* the comb of a cock; a fool's cap; the yellow-rattle, *Rhinanthus cristagalli;* a garden plant, *Celosia cristata* (also applied to other plants and shrubs) (see also COXCOMB). **cock's-foot,** *n.* a pasture-grass, *Dactylis glomerata.* **cock's-head,** *n.* sainfoin, from the shape of the pod. **cock-shot, -shy,** *n.* a rough-and-ready target for sticks or stones; a throw at a mark; a butt. **cock-sparrow,** *n.* a male sparrow; a pert presuming fellow. **cock-spur,** *n.* the spur of a cock; (*Angling*) a kind of caddis; various plants. **cockspur-burner,** *n.* a gas-burner pierced with three holes. **cockspur-hawthorn, -thorn,** *n.* a shrub, *Crataegus crusgalli,* from N America. **cock-sure,** *a.*

perfectly sure; absolutely certain; self-confident, arrogantly certain. **cocksurely,** *adv.* **cocksureness,** *n.* **cockish,** *a.* COCKY. [OE *cocc* (cp. F *coq*), low L *coccum,* acc. of *coccus,* onomat. (cp. Gr. *kokku,* cuckoo)]

cock[2], *n.* the act of turning or sticking anything upward; the turn so given, as of a hat, a nose, a knowing turn of the eye etc. *v.t.* to set erect; to cause to stick up; to set (the hat) jauntily on one side; to turn up (the nose), to turn (the eye) in an impudent or knowing fashion; to raise the trigger of. *v.i.* to stick or stand up, to project; to hold up the head; to strut, to swagger, to bluster. **at half cock,** unprepared. **to cock a snook,** to put the thumb to the nose with the fingers spread out. **to cock up,** (*sl.*) to ruin, spoil, by incompetence. **cocked hat,** *n.* a pointed triangular hat; †a hat with the brim turned up. **knocked into a cocked hat,** doubled up in a fight; thunder-struck, amazed; utterly discomfited. **cock-up,** *n.* a turn up of the tip of the nose; (*sl.*) a bungled failure. [from prec.]

cock[3], *n.* a small conical pile of hay. *v.t.* to put into cocks. [cp. Dan. *kok,* a heap, Icel. *kokkr,* a lump, a ball]

cock[4], *n.* a small boat. **cock-boat,** *n.* a small ship's boat. [ME *cog, cogge,* OF *coque, cogue*]

cockabondy, *n.* (*Angling*) an artificial fly of a fancy kind. [W *coch a bon ddu,* 'red with black trunk']

cock-a-bully, *n.* a variety of New Zealand fish. [Maori *kopapu*]

cockade, *n.* a knot of ribbons worn in the hat as a badge; a rosette worn in the hat by the male servants of naval and military officers etc. **cockaded,** *a.* [F *coquarde,* saucy, from *coq* (cp. COCK[1])]

cockaigne, *n.* a fabled country of luxury and idleness; (*punningly*) cockneydom; London. [OF *coquaigne* (F *cocagne*), perh. from *coquer,* to cook, or conn. with G *Kuchen,* cake]

cock-a-leekie, cockie-leckie, cocky-leeky, *n.* soup made from a fowl boiled with leeks. [Sc. COCK[1], LEEK]

cockalorum, *n.* a self-important little man; a game of leap-frog in which one side presents a chain of backs for the others to jump upon. [COCK[1]]

cockatoo, *n.* a large crested parrot, usu. white, from the Indian Archipelago and Australia; (*Austral.*) a small farmer. **cockatoo fence,** *n.* (*Austral.*) a fence made of logs. **cockatoo grass,** *n.* pasture grass frequented by cockatoos. **cockatiel,** *n.* a small cockatoo or parrot. [Malay *kakatūa*]

cockatrice, *n.* the basilisk; †anything deadly; (*Her.*) a cock with a serpent's tail. [OF *cocatrice,* late L *caucātrix,* the treader (trans. of Gr. *ichneumōn,* from *ichneuein,* to trace)]

cockchafer, *n.* a large brown beetle, *Melolontha vulgaris,* that makes a whirring noise in flying.

Cockcroft, *n.* **John Douglas** (1897–1967), British physicist. In 1932, he and E. T. S. Walton succeeded in splitting the nucleus of the atom for the first time. In 1951 they were jointly awarded a Nobel prize.

Cocker, *n.* **according to Cocker,** properly, correctly. [Edward *Cocker,* 1631–75, a teacher and arithmetician]

cocker, *v.t.* to pamper, to fondle, to indulge. [etym. doubtful; perh. from COCK[1] (in allusion to the call of a hen to her chicken); cp. MDan. *kokre,* to keep on calling]

cockerel, *n.* a young cock; (*sl.*) a spirited youth. [ME *cokerelle*]

Cockerell[1], *n.* **Charles** (1788–1863), English architect who built mainly in a neo-classical style derived from antiquity and from the work of Christopher Wren. His buildings include the Ashmolean Museum and Taylorian Institute in Oxford (1841–45).

Cockerell[2], *n.* **Christopher** (1910–), British engineer, who invented the hovercraft (1959).

cocker spaniel, *n.* a small spaniel used in shooting snipe etc. [COCK[1], SPANIEL]

†**cocket,** *n.* a custom-house seal; a customs' receipt for duty on exported goods; the entry-office in the custom-house. [perh. corr. of L *quo quietus est,* 'by which he is quit,' at the end of the document]

cockie-leckie, COCK-A-LEEKIE.

cockle[1], *n.* the corn-cockle or darnel; an unidentified weed, the lolium or tares of the Bible; (*Geol.*) schorl (considered useless). **cockle-burr,** *n.* [OE *coccel*]

cockle[2], *n.* a bivalve belonging to the mollusc genus *Cardium,* esp. *C. edule;* its ribbed shell; a shallow skiff. **cockles of the heart,** the feelings. **cockle-boat,** *n.* a small and shallow skiff. **cockle-hat,** *n.* a pilgrim's hat bearing a shell. **cockle-shell,** *n.* the shell of any species of *Cardium,* worn as the badge of a pilgrim; a small boat. [F *coquille,* a shell, L *conchylia,* Gr. *konchulion,* dim. of *konchē,* a mussel]

cockle[3], *v.i.* to pucker up. *v.t.* to curl, pucker up, crease or make to bulge. *n.* a pucker, crease or wrinkle (on paper). **cockly,** *a.* (*dial.*) [F *coquiller,* to blister, to pucker]

cockle[4], *n.* (also **cockle stove**) a heating-stove with a kind of radiator; (also **cockle-oast**) the furnace of an oast-house. [etym. doubtful; perh. from Dut. *kākel,* G *Kachel,* a stove-tile]

cockney, *n.* a native of London (traditionally, a person born within sound of the bells of St-Mary-le-Bow, Cheapside); the London accent; one who speaks with it; a city resident. *a.* pertaining to a cockney. **cockneydom,** *n.* **cockneyese,** *n.* **cockneyfy,** *v.t.* **cockneyish,** *a.* **cockneyism,** *n.* **cockneyize, -ise,** *v.t., v.i.* [ME *cokeney* (*coken,* gen. pl., *ey,* OE *aeg*), a cock's egg, a term applied to small yolkless eggs, occasionally laid by fowls; hence applied to a foolish or effeminate person, a townsman]

cockroach, *n.* an orthopterous insect (familiarly known as the black beetle), *Blatta orientalis,* resembling a beetle, and a pest in kitchens. [Sp. *cucaracha* (assim. to COCK[1], ROACH[3])]

cock-shut, *n.* nightfall. [prob. COCK[1], SHOOT, a glade suitable for catching woodcocks in nets]

cockswain, COXSWAIN.

cocktail, *n.* a horse with tail docked very short, usu. a half-bred horse; hence, a half-bred fellow; a beetle, *Ocypus olens;* a drink taken before a meal, usu. gin or other spirit with bitters and flavourings; an appetizer consisting of a mixture of cold foods; any mixture of assorted ingredients, e.g. drinks, drugs. *a.* underbred; pertaining to cocktails. **cocktail stick,** *n.* a thin pointed stick for lifting snack foods. **cock-tailed,** *a.* with docked tail or tail cocked up. [COCK[2], TAIL[1] (a tail that cocks up, or like a cock's)]

cock-up COCK[2].

cocky[1], *a.* impudent, uppish, pert, saucy. **cockily,** *adv.* **cockiness,** *n.* [COCK[1]]

cocky[2], *n.* (*Austral., sl.*) a small farmer. [COCKATOO]

cocky-leeky, COCK-A-LEEKIE.

Cockyolly bird, *n.* (*coll.*) a nursery name for a small bird, a dicky-bird.

coco, cocoa[1], **coker,** *n.* a tropical palm tree, *Cocos nucifera.* **coco-, cocoanut,** *n.* the fruit of this, a large, rough, hard-shelled nut with a white edible lining and a sweet liquid known as **coconut milk. coconut butter,** *n.* the solid oil obtained from the lining of the coconut. **coconut matting,** *n.* coarse matting made from the fibrous husk of the nut. **coconut shy,** *n.* a kind of skittles in which the aim is to knock coconuts off sticks. [Port. and Sp. *coco,* a bugbear, a grimace (COKER is a commercial term to distinguish it from the foll.)]

cocoa[2], *n.* a preparation from the seeds of *Theobroma cacao;* a drink made from this. **cocoa-bean,** *n.* the cacao seed. **cocoa butter,** *n.* a buttery substance extracted from the cacao nut in the manufacture of cocoa. **cocoa-nibs,** *n.pl.* the crushed cotyledons of *T. cacao.* **cocoa-powder,** *n.* a brown powder formerly used in large guns. [corr. of CACAO]

cocoon, *n.* a silky covering spun by the larvae of certain insects in the chrysalis state; any analogous case made by other animals; any protective covering; a preservative coating sprayed onto machinery etc. *v.t.* to wrap in, or as if in, a cocoon. *v.i.* to make a cocoon. **cocoonery,** *n.* a place for silkworms when feeding and forming cocoons. [F *cocon,* dim. of *coque,* a shell, L *concha,* Gr. *konchē*]

Cocos Islands, *n. pl.* (or Keeling Islands) group of 27 small coral islands in the Indian Ocean, about 2770 km/1720 miles NW of Perth, Australia; area 14 sq km/ 5.5 sq miles; population (1986) 616. They are owned by Australia.

cocotte, *n.* a prostitute; a woman from the demi-monde; a small dish in which food is cooked and served. [F]

Cocteau, *n.* **Jean** (1889–1963), French poet, dramatist, and film director. A leading figure in European modernism, he worked with Picasso, Diaghilev and Stravinsky. He produced many volumes of poetry, ballets such as *Le Boeuf sur le toit/The Nothing Doing Bar* (1920), plays, for example, *Orphée/Orpheus* (1926), and a mature novel of bourgeois French life, *Les Enfants terribles/Children of the Game* (1929), which he made into a film in 1950.

†**coction,** *n.* the act of boiling; digestion; (*Med.*) the alteration in morbid matter that fits it for elimination. **coctile**, *a.* baked, as a brick. [L *coctio* (*coquere,* to cook)]

COD, (*abbr.*) cash on delivery.

cod[1], *n.* a large deep-sea food-fish, *Gadus morrhua*. **codling**, *n.* a young cod. **codfish,** *n.* **cod-liver oil,** *n.* oil from the liver of the cod, rich in vitamins A and D. [etym. doubtful]

cod[2], *n.* a husk or pod; †the scrotum; †a testicle; a small bag; a pillow. **cod-piece,** *n.* a baggy appendage in the front of breeches or of the tight hose worn in the 15th and 16th cents to cover male genitals. †**codding,** *a.* lecherous. [OE *cod, codd,* a bag]

cod[3], *n.* (*sl.*) a man, a fellow; (*sl.*) a hoax. *a.* (*sl.*) intended to deceive or burlesque. *v.t.* (*past, p.p.* **codded**) (*sl.*) to hoax, to impose upon. [etym. unknown]

coda, *n.* (*Mus.*) an adjunct to the close of a composition to enforce the final character of the movement. **codetta,** *n.* a short coda. [It., from L *cauda,* tail]

†**codding** COD[2].

coddle, *v.t.* to treat as an invalid or baby, to pamper; to cook (esp. eggs) gently in water. *n.* one that coddles him- or herself or other people. [prob. short for CAUDLE]

code, *n.* a collection of statutes; a digest of law; a body of laws or regulations systematically arranged; (*Mil., Nav.*) a system of signals; a series of characters, letters or words used for the sake of brevity or secrecy; a collection of rules or canons; the principles accepted in any sphere of art, taste, conduct etc. *v.t.* to put into a code. **code name, number,** *n.* a short name or number used for convenience or secrecy. **codify,** *v.t.* to reduce to a systematic body; to put into a code. **codification,** *n.* **codifier,** *n.* [F, from L *cōdex -icem,* see CODEX]

codeclination, *n.* (*Astron.*) the North-polar distance of anything, the complement of its declination.

codeine, *n.* an alkaloid obtained from opium and used as a narcotic and analgesic. [Gr. *kōdeia,* head, poppy-head]

codex, *n.* (*pl.* **codices**) a manuscript volume, esp. of the Bible or of texts of classics; (*Med.*) a list of prescriptions. [L *cōdex, caudex,* a tree-trunk, a wooden tablet, a book]

codger, *n.* (*coll.*) a miser; an odd old person. [prob. var. of CADGER]

codicil, *n.* an appendix to a will, treaty etc. **codicillary,** *a.* [MF *codicile* (now *codicille*), L *cōdicillus,* dim. of CODEX]

codify etc. CODE.

codilla, *n.* the coarsest parts of hemp or flax. [prob. dim. of It. *coda,* L *cauda,* tail]

codling[1] COD[1].

codling[2], **-lin,** *n.* a long, tapering kind of apple; an apple for baking; a baked apple. **codlings and cream,** the hairy willow-herb, *Epilobium hirsutum*. **codling-moth,** *n.* the moth *Carpocapsa pomonella,* whose larvae feed on apples and cause them to fall prematurely. [ME *querdling* (perh. Ir. *queirt,* apple-tree, -LING)]

codon, *n.* a small bell; the bell-shaped orifice of a trumpet; a set of three nucleotides in DNA or RNA that specifies a particular amino acid. [Gr. *kōdōn,* bell]

codonostome, *n.* (*Zool.*) the bell-shaped aperture of a medusa. [Gr. *stoma,* mouth]

codswallop, *n.* (*sl.*) nonsense. [etym. doubtful]

Cody[1], *n.* **Samuel Franklin** (1862–1913), US aviation pioneer. He made his first powered flight on 16 Oct. 1908 at Farnborough, England, in a machine of his own design. He was killed in a flying accident.

Cody[2], *n.* **William Frederick** (1846–1917), US scout and performer, known as **Buffalo Bill** from his contract to supply buffalo carcases to railway labourers (over 4000 in 18 months). From 1883 he toured the US and Europe with a Wild West show.

Coe, *n.* **Sebastian** (1956–), English middle-distance runner. He was Olympic 1500 metre champion 1980 and 1984. Between 1979 and 1981 he broke eight individual world records at 800 m, 1000 m, 1500 m, and one mile.

coed, co-ed, *n.* (*chiefly N Am.*) a girl being educated in a coeducational establishment; a coeducational school. *a.* coeducational.

coeducation, *n.* education of the two sexes together. **coeducational,** *a.*

coefficient, *n.* anything cooperating; the cofactor of an algebraical number; in 4*ab*, 4 is the **numerical** and *ab* the **literal coefficient**; (*Phys.*) a number denoting the degree of a quality. **differential coefficient,** the ratio of the change of a function of a variable to the change in that variable.

coehorn, *n.* a small mortar for throwing grenades. [from the inventor Baron *Coehoorn,* 1632–1704]

coel- COEL(O)-.

coelacanth, *n.* the only known living representative of the fossil group of fish Crossopterygii, first captured off S Africa in 1953. [Gr. *koilos,* hollow, *akantha,* spine]

coelenterate, *a.* of or belonging to the Coelenterata, *n.* any individual of the Coelenterata, a subdivision of the Metazoa, containing the sponges, jellyfish, etc. [Gr. *koilos,* hollow, *enteron,* an intestine]

coeliac, (*esp. N Am.*) **celiac**, *a.* pertaining to the abdomen. **coeliac disease,** *n.* a condition involving defective digestion of fats. [L *coeliacus,* Gr. *koiliakos* (*koilia,* bowels, *koilos,* hollow)]

coel(o)-, (*esp. N Am.*) **cel(o)-,** *comb. form* (*Biol.*) hollow. [Gr. *koilos,* hollow]

coelom, (*esp. N Am.*) **celom**, *n.* (*pl.* **-ms, -mata**) a body cavity; in animals above the Coelenterata, the space between the body wall and the intestines. [Gr. *koilōma,* cavity]

coemption, *n.* concerted action among buyers for forestalling the market by purchasing the whole quantity of any commodity.

coenaesthesis, (*esp. N Am.*) **cenesthesis**), *n.* (*Psych.*) the collective consciousness of the body, as distinguished from the impressions of the separate senses. [COEN-, Gr. *aisthesis,* sensation, from *aisthanomai,* I perceive]

coen(o)-, cen(o)-, *comb. form* common. [Gr. *koinos,* common]

coenobite, cenobite, *n.* a monk living in community. **coenobitic, -ical,** *a.* **coenobitism,** *n.* [late L *coenobīta,* from Gr. *koinobion,* a convent (COENO-, *bios,* life)]

coenogamy, *n.* sexual promiscuity.

coequal, *a.* equal with another; of the same rank, dignity etc. *n.* one of the same rank. **coequality**, *n.* **coequally,** *adv.*

coerce, *v.t.* to restrain by force; to compel to obey; to enforce by compulsion. *v.i.* to employ coercion (in government). **coercible,** *a.* **coercibleness,** *n.* **coercion**, *n.* compulsion of a free agent; government by force. **Coercion Act,** *n.* an Act that conferred special power on the executive in Ireland in time of disturbance. **coercionary,** *a.* **coercionist,** *n.* **coercive,** *a.* having power or authority to coerce; compulsory. *n.* a means of coercion. **coercively,** *adv.* [L *coercēre* (co-, *arcēre,* to enclose, cp. *arca,* a chest)]

coessential, *a.* of the same essence. **coessentiality,** *n.* **coessentially,** *adv.*

coetaneous, *a.* of the same age with another; beginning to exist at the same time; coeval. [L *coaetāneus* (co-, *aetās -ātis,* age)]

coeternal, *a.* equally eternal with another. **coeternally,** *adv.* **coeternity,** *n.*

Coetzee, *n.* **J(ohn) M.** (1940–), South African author whose novel *In the Heart of the Country* (1975) dealt with the rape of a white woman by a black man. In 1983 he won the Booker Prize for *Life and Times of Michael K.*

coeval, *a.* of the same age; of the same date of birth or origin; existing at or for the same period. *n.* a contemporary. **coevality,** *n.* **coevally,** *adv.* [L *coaevus* (co-, *aevum,* an age)]

coexecutor, *n.* a joint executor. **coexecutrix,** *n. fem.* (*pl.* **-trices**).

coexist, *v.i.* to exist together with. **coexistence,** *n.* mutual toleration by regimes with differing ideologies or systems of government. **coexistent,** *a.*

coextension, *n.* equal extension. **coextensive,** *a.* **coextensively,** *adv.*

C of E, (*abbr.*) Church of England.

coffee, *n.* a beverage made from the ground roasted seeds of a tropical Asiatic and African shrub, *Coffea arabica;* a cup of coffee; the last course at dinner consisting of coffee; the seeds of the tree; the tree itself; a pale brown colour, like milky coffee. **coffee bar,** *n.* a cafe where coffee, snacks etc. are served. **coffee-bean, -berry,** *n.* a coffee seed. **coffee bush,** *n.* (*N. Zealand*) the karamu. **coffee-cup,** *n.* a small cup from which coffee is drunk. **coffee-grounds,** *n.pl.* the sediment or lees of coffee-berries after infusion. **coffee-house,** *n.* a house where coffee and other refreshments are sold, esp. in 18th cent. London. **coffee-mill,** *n.* a machine for grinding coffee-beans. **coffee morning,** *n.* a party, held at mid-morning, where coffee is served. **coffee-pot,** *n.* a vessel in which coffee is made. **coffee-room,** *n.* a refreshment room in a hotel. **coffee shop** COFFEE BAR. **coffee-stall,** *n.* a street stall where non-alcoholic beverages and snacks are sold throughout the night. **coffee table,** *n.* a low table in a sitting room. *a.* suitable for display on a coffee table, esp. of or being large and expensively produced illustrated books. **coffee-tavern,** *n.* a temperance refreshment house. [Turk. *qahveh,* Arab. *qahweh*]

coffer, *n.* a chest or box for holding valuables; (*pl.*) a treasury, funds, financial resources; a sunk panel in a ceiling etc. †*v.t.* to enclose in a coffer. **coffer-dam,** *n.* a water-tight enclosure which exposes a river bed etc., used in laying foundations of piers, bridges etc. **coffered,** *a.* enclosed in a coffer; ornamented with coffers. †**cofferer,** *n.* a treasurer; an officer of the royal household next below the controller. [OF *cofre,* L *cophinus,* Gr. *kophinos* (doublet of COFFIN)]

coffin, *n.* the box in which a corpse is enclosed for burial or cremation; a coffin-ship; the hoof of a horse below the coronet; (*Print.*) a frame for the imposing stone of a hand-press or the carriage of a machine. *v.t.* to put into a coffin; to put out of sight. **coffin-bone,** *n.* the spongy bone in a horse's hoof around which the horn grows. **coffin-joint,** *n.* the joint above the coffin-bone. **coffin-nail,** *n.* (*sl.*) a cigarette. **coffin-plate,** *n.* a metal plate recording name etc., fastened on the lid of a coffin. **coffin-ship,** *n.* an unseaworthy vessel. [OF *cofin,* L *cophinus,* as prec.]

coffle, *n.* a travelling gang, esp. of slaves. [Arab. *qāfilah,* caravan]

C of I, (*abbr.*) Church of Ireland.

C of S, (*abbr.*) Church of Scotland.

cog¹, *n.* a tooth or projection in the rim of a wheel or other gear for transmitting motion to another part; a person playing a small and unimportant part in any enterprise. *v.t.* to furnish with cogs; (*North. dial.*) to stop the revolutions of a wheel by means of a block or wedge. **hunting cog,** an extra cog in the larger member of cogged gear, securing a constant change of cogs engaging with each other. **cog-wheel,** *n.* a wheel furnished with cogs. **cogged,** *a.* [from Scand. (cp. Swed. *kugge,* Norw. *kug*)]

cog², *v.t.* to handle (dice) in a fraudulent way; to wheedle; to seduce by flattery. *v.i.* to cheat at dicing; to cheat, deceive; to cajole, to wheedle. [perh. conn. with prec. (cp. Norw. *kogga,* Swed. *kugga,* to dupe, cheat)]

cog³, cogge, *n.* a broad round-shaped vessel used in the Middle Ages both for burden and war; a small boat. [OF *cogue* (cp. COCK⁴, Dut. *cogge,* G *Kock*)]

cog⁴ COGUE.

cog., (*abbr.*) cognate.

cogent, *a.* powerful, constraining, convincing. **cogently,** *adv.* **cogency,** *n.* [L *cōgentum,* acc. pres.p. of *cōgere,* to compel (co-, *agere,* to drive)]

coggie, *n.* (*Sc.*) a small wooden bowl. [dim. of COGUE]

coggle¹, *n.* a pebble or cobble; a small boat. [etym. doubtful; perh. onomat. (but cp. G *Kugel,* Dut. *kōgel*)]

coggle², *v.i.* (*Sc.*) to be unsteady or unstable. **coggly,** *a.* [etym. doubtful]

cogitate, *v.i.* to think, to reflect, to meditate. *v.t.* to meditate, devise; (*Phil.*) to form an idea or conception of. **cogitable,** *a.* capable of being thought; conceivable by the reason. **cogitation,** *n.* **cogitative,** *a.* meditative. **cogitatively,** *adv.* **cogitativeness,** *n.* [L *cōgitātus,* p.p. of *cōgitāre,* to think (co-, *agitāre,* freq. of *agere,* to drive)]

cognac, *n.* French brandy of fine quality, esp. that distilled in the neighbourhood of *Cognac,* in SW France.

cognate, *a.* akin, related; of common origin; of the same kind or nature; derived from the same linguistic family or from the same word or root. *n.* (*Law*) a blood relation, as distinct from *agnate,* which is through the father only; (*Sc. Law*) a relative on the mother's side; a cognate word. **cognately,** *adv.* **cognateness,** *n.* **cognation,** *n.* [L *cognātus* (co-, *gnātus, nātus,* p.p. of *gnasci, nasci,* to be born)]

cognition, *n.* the act of apprehending; the faculty of perceiving, conceiving, and knowing, as distinguished from the feelings and the will; a sensation, perception, intuition, or conception; (*Law*) cognizance. **cognitional,** *a.* **cognitive,** *a.* [L *cognitio -ōnem,* from *cognoscere,* to learn (co-, *gnoscere,* cognate with KNOW)]

cognizance, -isance, *n.* knowledge, notice, recognition; (*Law*) judicial notice; knowledge not requiring proof; acknowledgment; jurisdiction; (*Her.*) a badge, a coat, a crest. **cognizant, -isant,** *a.* having cognizance or knowledge (of); (*Law*) competent to take judicial notice of. [OF *conoissance* (L *cognoscere,* see COGNITION), assim. to L *cog-*]

cognize, -ise, *v.t.* (*Phil.*) to have knowledge or perception of. **cognizer, -iser,** *n.* **cognizable, -isable,** *a.* knowable; (*Law*) liable to be tried and determined. **cognizably, -isably,** *adv.* [formed from COGNIZANCE]

cognomen, *n.* a surname; the last of the three names of an ancient Roman citizen; a title, a name; a nickname. †**cognominal,** *a.* **cognominally,** *adv.* †**cognominate,** *v.t.* †**cognomination,** *n.* a cognomen. [L (co-, *gnōmen, nōmen,* name, from *gno-,* stem of *gnoscere*)]

cognosce, *v.t.* (*Sc. Law*) to examine; to decide judicially; to pronounce insane. **cognoscible,** *a.* that may be known; (*Sc. Law*) cognizable. **cognoscibility,** *n.* the quality of being cogniscible. [L *cognoscere,* to know (see COGNITION)]

cognoscente, *n.* (*pl.* **-ti**) a connoisseur. [It., from L *cognoscens -tem,* pres.p. of *cognoscere,* see prec.)]

cognovit, *n.* (*Law*) an acknowledgment by a defendant of the justice of the plaintiff's claim, thus allowing judgment to go by default. [L, he has acknowledged, perf. tense of *cognoscere,* COGNOSCE]

cogue, cog⁴, *n.* (*Sc.*) a small wooden vessel for milking; a wooden cup. [etym. unknown]

cohabit, *v.i.* to live together, esp. as husband and wife (without being legally married). **cohabitant, cohabiter,** *n.* **cohabitation,** *n.* [F *cohabiter,* L *cohabitāre* (co-, *habitāre,* to dwell, freq. of *habēre,* to hold)]

coheir, *n.* a joint heir. **coheiress,** *n. fem.*

cohere, *v.i.* to stick together; to hold together, remain united; to be logically consistent. **coherence, -ency,** *n.* **coherent,** *a.* that coheres; remaining united; logically connected, consistent; of electromagnetic waves, having the same frequency or phase. **coherently,** *adv.* **coherer,** *n.* an early device for detecting electromagnetic waves. [L *cohaerēre* (co-, *haerēre,* to stick)]

coheritor, *n.* a coheir.

cohesion, *n.* coherence; the state of cohering; consistency; the force uniting molecules of the same nature; (*Bot.*) union of organs usu. separated. **cohesive,** *a.* **cohesively,** *adv.* **cohesiveness,** *n.* [F *cohésion* (L *cohaes,* port. stem. of *cohaerare,* COHERE)]

coho, *n.* a Pacific salmon. [etym. unknown]

cohort, *n.* the tenth port of a Roman legion, containing three maniples or six centuries; a body of soldiers; (*coll.*) a colleague or accomplice; a set of people in a population sharing a common attribute, e.g. age or class. [F *cohorte,* L *cohors -tem,* orig. an enclosure (co-, *hort-,* cp. *hortus,* garden, Gr. *chortos,* GARTH, GARDEN)]

cohortative, *a.* in Hebrew grammar, a lengthened form of the imperfect tense, signifying *let me, let us,* etc.

COHSE, (*abbr.*) Confederation of Health Service Employees.

COI, *n.* (*abbr.*) Central Office of Information.

coif, *n.* a close-fitting cap; the cap worn by sergeants-at-law. *v.t.* to cover with a coif. **coifed,** *a.* [OF *coife,* low L *cofia,* a cap, prob. from MHG *kupfe* (*kopf,* the head)]

coiffeur, *n.* a hairdresser. **coiffeuse,** *n.fem.* **coiffure,** *n.* a head-dress; method of dressing the hair. [F, from *coiffer,* to dress the hair (*coiffe,* OF *coife,* COIF)]

coign, *n.* †a corner; a quoin. **coign of vantage,** a projecting corner affording a good view. [COIN]

coil[1], *v.t.* to wind (as a rope) into rings; to twist. *v.i.* to wind itself, as a snake or creeping plant. *n.* a series of concentric rings into which anything is coiled up, a length of anything coiled up; a single turn of anything coiled up; a coiled lock of hair; a wire wound round a bobbin to form a resistance or an inductance; a metal or plastic coil inserted in the uterus as a contraceptive device. **to coil up,** to twist into rings or a spiral shape; to be twisted into such a shape. [OF *coillir* (F *cueillir*), L *colligere* (COL-[1], *legere* to gather)]

coil[2], *n.* noise, turmoil, confusion, bustle; a fuss. [prob. from prec.]

coin, *n.* a piece of metal stamped and current as money; money, esp. coined money; †a corner, a coign; †a wedge, a quoin. *v.t.* to mint or stamp (as money); to invent, to fabricate. *v.i.* to make counterfeit money. **false coin,** an imitation of coined money in base metal; a spurious fabrication. **to coin a phrase,** to use a supposed new expression, (usu. a cliché). **to coin money, to coin it in,** (*sl.*) to make money rapidly. **coin-box,** *n.* a coin-operated telephone. **coin-op, -operated,** *a.* of a machine, operated by inserting a coin. **coiner,** *n.* one who coins money, esp. one who makes counterfeit coin. [OF, a wedge, hence a stamp on a coin, from L *cuneus,* a wedge]

coinage, *n.* the act of coining; the pieces coined; the monetary system in use; invention, fabrication; something invented. [OF *coignaige* (COIN-, -AGE)]

coincide, *v.i.* to correspond in time, place, relations etc.; to happen at the same time; (*Geom.*) to occupy the same position in space; to agree, to concur. **coincidence,** *n.* the act, fact, or condition of coinciding; a remarkable instance of apparently fortuitous concurrence. **coincident,** *a.* that coincides. **coincidently,** *adv.* **coincidental,** *a.* coincident; characterized by or of the nature of coincidence. [F *coincider,* med. L *coincidere* (co-, IN-[1], *cadere,* to fall)]

coinhere, *v.i.* to inhere together. **coinherence,** *n.* **coinherent,** *a.*

coinheritance, *n.* a joint inheritance. **coinheritor,** *n.* a coheir.

coinstantaneous, *a.* occurring at precisely the same instant.

Cointreau®, *n.* a colourless orange-flavoured liqueur. [F]

coir, *n.* coconut fibre; ropes or matting manufactured therefrom. [Malay *kāyar,* cord]

coition, *n.* conjunction; copulation; †said of the moon when in the same sign and degree of the zodiac as the sun. **coitus,** *n.* the act of copulation. **coitus interruptus,** *n.* coitus deliberately interrupted before ejaculation into the vagina. [L *coitio -ōnem,* from *coīre* (co-, *īre,* to come)]

Coke®, *n.* short for COCA-COLA.

coke[1], *n.* (*sl.*) short for COCAINE.

coke[2], *n.* coal from which gas has been extracted. *v.t.* to convert into coke. [prob. the same as ME *colke,* the core of an apple; etym. doubtful]

Coke[1], *n.* **Edward** (1552–1634), Lord Chief Justice of England (1613–17). Against Charles I he drew up the Petition of Right (1628). His *Institutes* are a legal classic, and he ranks as the supreme common lawyer.

Coke[2], *n.* **Thomas William** (1754–1842), English pioneer and promoter of the improvements associated with the Agricultural Revolution. His innovations included regular manuring of the soil, the cultivation of fodder crops in association with corn, and the drilling of wheat and turnips.

coker coco.

Col.[1], (*abbr.*) colonel; Colorado; Colossians.

col.[2], (*abbr.*) column.

col[3], *n.* a depression in a mountain ridge; a saddle or elevated pass; an area of low pressure between two anticyclones. [F, from L *collum,* neck]

col-[1] *pref.* form of COM- before *l.*

col-[2] COL(I)-.

cola, kola, *n.* a tropical African tree bearing a nut which is used as a condiment and digestive and tonic; a soft drink flavoured with cola-nuts. **cola-nut, -seed,** *n.* the fruit of this. [W African native]

colander, cullender, *n.* a culinary strainer having the bottom perforated with small holes; a similar contrivance used in casting small shot. [ult. from med. L *cōlātōrium* (*cōlāre,* to strain)]

colatitude, *n.* the complement of the latitude; the difference between the latitude and 90°.

Colbert[1], *n.* **Claudette** (Stage name of Claudette Lily Cauchoin) (1905–), French-born film actress, who lived in Hollywood from childhood. She was ideally cast in sophisticated, romantic roles, but had a natural instinct for comedy and appeared in several of Hollywood's finest, including *It Happened One Night* (1934) and *The Palm Beach Story* (1942).

Colbert[2], *n.* **Jean-Baptiste** (1619–83), French politician, chief minister to Louis XIV, and controller-general (finance minister) from 1665. He reformed the Treasury, promoted French industry and commerce by protectionist measures, and tried to make France a naval power equal to England or the Netherlands, while favouring a peaceful foreign policy.

colcannon, *n.* an Irish dish consisting of potatoes and greens stewed together and mashed. [etym. doubtful]

Colchicum, *n.* a genus of bulbous plants, containing the meadow saffron, the corm and seeds of which are used in medicine. **colchicīne,** *n.* an alkaloid got from meadow saffron, used to treat gout. [L, from Gr. *Kolchikon* (*Kolchis,* on the Black Sea)]

colcothar, *n.* red peroxide of iron used as a polishing powder. [Arab. *qolqotār,* perh. corr. of Gr. *chalchanthos* (*chalkos,* copper, *anthos,* a flower)]

cold, *a.* low in temperature, esp. in relation to normal or bodily temperature; lacking heat or warmth; causing a sensation of loss of heat; suffering from a sensation of lack of heat; without ardour or intensity, indifferent; unconcerned, received with indifference, unwelcomed; sad, dispiriting, dispirited; not hasty or violent, spiritless; (*Hunting*) not affecting the scent strongly; unaffected by the scent; bluish in tone, as opposed to warm tones such as red, yellow etc.; frigid; dead; (*sl.*) unconscious. *adv.* finally, absolutely; without rehearsal. *n.* absence of warmth; the sensation produced by absence of warmth; COMMON COLD. **in cold blood,** without passion or excitement. **to catch (a) cold,** to contract a cold; (*coll.*) to run into difficulties. **to have cold feet,** (*sl.*) to be afraid. **to leave cold,** (*coll.*) to fail to excite or interest. **to throw cold water on,** to discourage. **cold-blooded,** *a.* having a body temperature which varies with that of the environment; unfeeling, unimpassioned. **cold-bloodedly,** *adv.* **cold-bloodedness,** *n.* **cold-calling,** *n.* the practice of sales representatives etc. of making unsolicited and unexpected calls in order to sell products or services. **cold cathode,** *n.* one which emits electrons at normal temperatures. **cold chisel,** *n.* a chisel for cutting cold metals. **cold coil,** *n.* a tube carrying a stream of cold water round in inflamed part. **cold comfort,** *n.* poor consolation, depressing resassurance. **cold cream,** *n.* a cooling ointment of oil and wax for chaps, used also as a cosmetic. **cold cuts,** *n.pl.* cold sliced meat. **cold-drawn,** *a.* of wire etc., drawn in a cold state. **cold fish,** *n.* (*coll.*) an unemotional person. **cold frame,** *n.* a glass frame to protect seedlings etc., without actual heat. **cold front,** *n.* (*Meteor.*) the front edge of an advancing mass of cold air. **cold hammer,** *v.t.* to hammer (metals) in a cold state. **cold-hearted,** *a.* unfeeling, indifferent. **cold-heartedly,** *adv.* **cold-heartedness,** *n* **cold-livered,** *a.* unemotional. **cold pig,** *n.* wakening a person for a joke by drenching him or her with cold water. **cold-served,** *a.* served up cold. **cold shoulder,** *n.* a rebuff; studied indifference; lit., cold shoulder of mutton. *v.t.* to treat with studied coolness or neglect. **cold sore,** HERPES SIMPLEX. **cold steel,** *n.* cutting weapons, such as sword and bayonet, as opposed to fire-arms. **cold-storage,** *n.* preservation of perishable foodstuffs by refrigeration; abeyance. **cold sweat,** *n.* sweating accompanied by chill, caused esp. by fear. **cold turkey,** *n.* (*coll.*) the physical and psychological symptoms caused by sudden and complete withdrawal of drugs from an addict. **cold war,** *n.* a state of psychological tension between two countries without actual hostilities. **cold without,** *n.* (*sl.*) spirits and cold water, without sugar. **coldish,** *a.* **coldly,** *adv.* **coldness,** *n.* [OE *ceald,* from Teut. *kal-* (cp. Icel. *kaldr,* Dut. *koud,* G *kalt*)]

Cold Harbor, Battle of, in the American Civil War, an engagement near Richmond, Virginia, 1–12 June 1864, in which the Confederate Army under Lee repulsed Union attacks under Grant.

Colditz, *n.* a town in East Germany, near Leipzig, site of a castle used as a high-security prisoner-of-war camp (Oflag IVC) in World War II. Among daring escapes was that of British Capt. Patrick Reid and others Oct. 1942. It became a museum in 1989.

cold-short, *a.* of metals, brittle when cold. [prob. from Swed. *kallskör* (Norw. and Dan. *koldskjör*), from *kall* or *kold.* COLD, and *skor,* brittle]

Cold War, *n.* the tensions from about 1945 between the USSR and Eastern Europe on the one hand, and the US and Western Europe on the other. The Cold War was been exacerbated by propaganda, covert activity by intelligence agencies, and economic sanctions, and intensified at times of conflict. Arms reduction agreements between the US and USSR in the late 1980s, and a diminution of Soviet influence in Eastern Europe, symbolized by the opening of the Berlin Wall 1989, led to a reassessment of positions.

cole, *n.* †the cabbage, and other edible plants of the genus *Brassica;* the rape. **cole-rape,** *n.* a turnip. **cole-seed,** *n.* rape-seed. **coleslaw,** *n.* a salad made of shredded raw cabbage. **colewort,** *n.* the common cabbage. [L *caulis,* a stalk, a cabbage]

Cole[1], *n.* **Old King,** legendary British king, supposed to be the father of St Helena, who married the Roman emperor Constantius, father of Constantine; he is also supposed to have founded Colchester. The historical Cole was possibly a North British chieftain named Coel, of the 5th cent., who successfully defended his land against the Picts and Scots. The nursery rhyme is only recorded from 1709.

Cole[2], *n.* **Thomas** (1801–48), US painter, founder of the Hudson River school of landscape artists.

Coleman, *n.* **Ornette** (1930–), US alto saxophonist and jazz composer. In the late 1950s he rejected the established structural principles of jazz for free avant-garde improvisation.

colemouse COALMOUSE.

coleopter, -teran, *n.* any individual of the Coleoptera or beetles, an order of insects having the fore wings converted into sheaths for the hinder wings. **coleopterist,** *n.* **coleopterous,** *a.* [Gr. *koleos,* a sheath, *pteron,* a wing]

coleorhiza, *n.* (*pl.* **-zae**) the root-sheath in the embryo of grasses and other endogens. [Gr. *koleos,* sheath, *rhiza,* root]

Coleridge, *n.* **Samuel Taylor** (1772–1834), English poet, one of the founders of the Romantic movement. A friend of Southey and Wordsworth, he collaborated with the latter on *Lyrical Ballads* (1798). His poems include 'The Ancient Mariner', 'Christabel', and 'Kubla Khan'; critical works include *Biographia Literaria* (1817).

Coleridge-Taylor, *n.* **Samuel** (1875–1912), English composer, the son of a West African doctor and an English mother. He wrote the cantata *Hiawatha's Wedding Feast* (1898), a setting in three parts of Longfellow's poem. He was a student and champion of traditional black music.

cole-tit COALMOUSE.

Colette, *n.* **Sidonie-Gabrielle** (1873–1954), French writer. At 20 she married Henri Gauthier-Villars, a journalist known as 'Willy'. Her four 'Claudine' novels, based on her own early life, were written under her husband's direction and signed by him. Divorced in 1906, she was a striptease and mime artist for a while, but continued to write, for example, *Chéri* (1920), *La Fin de Chéri/The End of Chéri* (1926), and *Gigi* (1944).

coley COAL-FISH.

col(i)-, colo-, *comb. form.* colon.

colibri, *n.* a kind of humming-bird. [F, from Carib]

colic, *n.* acute pains in the bowels, gripes, stomach-ache. **colicky,** *a.* [F *colique,* L *colicus,* Gr. *kolikos* (see COLON[2])]

coliseum, COLOSSEUM.

colitis, *n.* inflammation of the colon.

coll, *v.t.* to embrace by taking round the neck. *n.* an embrace. [from F *col,* L *collum,* the neck, or from *acole,* see ACCOLADE]

collaborate, *v.t.* to work jointly with another, esp. in literary and scientific pursuit; to cooperate with an enemy in occupation of one's own country. **collaboration,** *n.* **collaborator,** *n.* one who collaborates. [COL-[1], L *labōrāre,* to LABOUR (modelled on L *collabōrātor*)]

collage, *n.* a picture made of pieces of paper, fabric etc., glued on to a surface; any collection of diverse things or ideas. **collagist,** *n.* [F, from Gr. *kolla,* glue]

collagen, *n.* a fibrous protein that yields gelatin when boiled. [Gr. *kolla,* glue, -GEN]

collapse, *v.i.* to fall in, as the sides of a hollow vessel; to shrink together; to break down, to suffer from physical or nervous prostration; to come to nothing. *n.* a falling in, as the sides of a hollow vessel; complete failure; general prostration. **collapsed,** *a.* **collapsible,** *a.* liable to collapse; made so as to fall together easily (for ease in packing). [L *collapsus,* p.p. of *collābī* (COL-[1], *lābī,* to glide down, to lapse)]

collar, *n.* something worn round the neck, either as a separate article of dress, or as forming part of some garment; a leather loop round a horse's neck to which the traces are attached; a broad metal or leather ring for a dog's neck; meat pickled and rolled; anything shaped like a collar or ring; the chain or other ornament for the neck worn by the knights of an order; a ring or round flange; an astragal, a cincture; (*Naut.*) an eye in the end of a shroud or stay; a rope in the form of a wreath to which a stay is confined; (*Angling*) a cast with flies attached. *v.t.* to seize by the collar; to put a collar on; (*Football*) to grasp and hold; to capture; to pickle and roll (as meat); (*coll.*) to seize; (*sl.*) to steal. **collar of SS, esses,** a chain worn as badge by adherents of the House of Lancaster, and still a part of certain official costumes. **to slip the collar,** to free oneself. **collar-beam,** *n.* a tie-beam. **collar-bone,** *n.* the clavicle. **collar-harness,** *n.* harness attached to the collar, as opposed to *breast-harness* in which the weight is borne by a breast-band. **collar-stud,** *n.* a metal or bone stud to hold a collar to a shirt etc. **collar-work,** *n.* uphill work for a horse or (*fig.*) for a person; drudgery. **collared,** *a.* wearing a collar; of meat, pickled and rolled; (*coll.*) seized, arrested. **collarless,** *a.* [OF *colier,* L *collāre,* a band for the neck (*collum,* neck)]

collard, *n.* a kind of cabbage that does not grow into a head. [COLEWORT under COLE]

collarette, *n.* a small collar worn by women. [F *collerette,* dim. of *collier,* see COLLAR]

collate, *v.t.* to bring together in order to compare; to examine critically (esp. old books and manuscripts in order to ascertain by comparison points of agreement and difference); to place in order (as printed sheets for binding); to present to a benefice (used when a bishop presents to a living in his own diocese). **collation,** *n.* the act of collating; a light meal (from treatises being read in monasteries at meal-times). **collator,** *n.* one who collates manuscripts, books or sheets for binding; one who confers; a bishop who collates to a benefice. [L *collātus,* p.p. of *conferre,* to bring together (COL-, *latus,* orig. *tlatus,* conn. with *tollere,* to bear, Gr. *tlētos,* borne)]

collateral, *a.* being by the side; side by side; parallel; subsidiary, concurrent, subordinate; having the same common ancestor but not lineally related (as the children of brothers). *n.* a collateral relation; collateral security. **collateral security,** *n.* security for the performance of any contract over and above the main security. **collaterally,** *adv.* [late L *collaterālis* (COL-[1], *laterālis,* from *latus -eris,* side)]

collation COLLATE.

colleague[1], *n.* one associated with another in any office or employment. **colleagueship,** *n.* [F *collègue,* L *collēga* (COL-, *legere,* to choose)]

colleague[2], *v.t.* to join as ally. [OF *colleguer,* L *colligāre* (COL-[1], *ligāre,* to bind)]

collect[1], *n.* a brief comprehensive form of prayer, adapted for a particular day or occasion. [F *collecte,* *u*late L *collecta,* a summing-up]

collect[2], *v.t.* to gather together into one body, mass or place; to gather (money, taxes, subscriptions, books, curiosities etc.) from a number of sources; to concentrate, to bring under control; to bring a horse under control; to gather from observation, to infer; to call for, to fetch. *v.i.* to come together; to meet together. *a., adv.* (*N Am.*) of a telephone call, paid for by the recipient. **to collect on,** (*sl.*) to make money out of. **to collect oneself,** to recover one's self-possession. **collectable, -ible,** *a.* **collected,** *a.* gathered, brought together; cool, self-possessed, composed. **collectedly,** *adv.* **collectedness,** *n.* **collectible,** *n.* something that is considered worth collecting, esp. because of its likely increase in value. **collector,** *n.* one who collects; a gatherer of rarities of art etc.; one who collects rents etc.; the terminal of a transistor. **collectorate, -ship,** *n.* [as prec.]

collectanea, *n.pl.* a number of passages from various authors; a miscellany, a note or commonplace book. **collectaneous,** *a.* [L, neut. pl. of *collectāneus,* gathered together (see prec.)]

collection, *n.* the act of collecting; that which is collected; an assemblage of natural objects, works of art etc.; money contributed for religious, charitable or other purposes; an accumulation; †deduction, inference; (*pl.*) an examination at the end of term at Oxford, Durham etc. [OF, from L *collectio -ōnem* (see COLLECT[2])]

collective, *a.* tending to collect; collected, aggregated, formed by gathering a number of things or persons together; formed by the aggregation of numerous flowers (as the fruit of the mulberry, pineapple etc.); collectivized. *n.* a cooperative or collectivized organization or enterprise. **collective bargaining,** *n.* the method whereby employer and employees determine the conditions of employment. **collective note,** *n.* a diplomatic note signed by all the powers concerned. **collective noun,** *n.* a noun in the singular number expressing an aggregate of individuals. **collective ownership,** *n.* ownership of land, capital, and other means of production by those engaged in the production. **collective security,** *n.* a policy of mutual aid against aggression. **collective unconscious,** *n.* in Jungian theory, the part of the unconscious mind which is inherited and contains universal thought patterns and memories. **collectively,** *adv.* **collectivism,** *n.* the economic theory that industry should be carried on with a collective capital, as opposed to *individualism.* **collectivist,** *n., a.* **collectivity,** *n.* **collectivize, -ise,** *v.t.* to organize on collectivist lines. **collectivization, -isation,** *n.* [COLLECT[2], IVE]

colleen, *n.* (*Ir.*) a girl, a lass. [Ir. *cailīn,* dim. of *caile,* a country-woman]

college, *n.* a body or community of persons, having certain rights and privileges, and devoted to common pursuits; an independent corporation of scholars, teachers, and fellows forming one of the constituent bodies of a university; a similar foundation independent of a university; an institution for higher education, esp. in affiliation with a university; a large and important secondary school, often applied pretentiously to a private school; †a charitable foundation, such as a hospital, a large almshouse etc.; †(*sl.*) a debtors' prison. **College of Arms, Herald's College,** see separate entry. **College of Cardinals, Sacred College,** in the Roman Catholic Church, the papal council of cardinals. **college of education,** a training college for teachers. **College of Justice,** (*Sc.*) the supreme civil courts. **college pudding,** *n.* a small baked pudding for one person. **colleger,** *n.* a pupil on the foundation of a school, esp. at Eton. **collegial,** *a.* constituted as a college. **collegian,** *n.* a member of a college; a student at a university; †(*sl.*) a prisoner for debt. [MF *college,* L *collēgium* (*collēga,* COLLEAGUE[1])]

College of Arms, Heralds' College, *n.* an English heraldic body formed in 1484 by Richard III incorporating the heralds attached to the Royal Household; reincorporated by Royal Charter of Philip and Mary in 1555. There are three Kings of Arms, six Heralds, and four Pursuivants, who specialize in genealogical and heraldic work. The College establishes the right to bear Arms, and the Kings of Arms grant Arms by letters patent. In Ireland the office of Ulster King of Arms was transferred in 1943 to the College of Arms in London and placed with that of Norroy King of Arms, who now has jurisdiction in Northern Ireland as well as in the north of England.

collegiate, *a.* pertaining to a college; containing a college; instituted or regulated as a college. *v.t.,* to constitute as a college or collegiate foundation. **collegiate church,** *n.* a church which, though not a cathedral, has an endowed chapter of canons; (*Sc., N Am.*) a Presbyterian church under a joint pastorate. **collegiate school,** *n.* a school organized to resemble a college. [L (collēgiātus, member of a college) (*collēgium,* COLLEGE)]

collegium, *n.* (*pl.* **-gia**) an ecclesiastical body not under state control. [L, see prec.]

collenchyma, *n.* plant tissue composed of elongated cells thickened at the angles, occurring immediately under the epidermis in leaf-stalks, stems etc. **collenchymatous,** *a.* [Gr. *kolla,* glue, *enchuma,* infusion (EN-, *cheein,* to pour)]

collet, *n.* a band or ring; a flange or socket; the part of a ring in which a stone is set. [F, dim. of *col,* L *collum,* the neck]

collide, *v.i.* to come into collision or conflict. †*v.t.* to bring into collision. [L *collīdere* (COL-, *lædere,* to strike, hurt)]

collie, *n.* a Scottish sheep-dog; a breed of show-dogs. [perh. COALY, black]

collier, *n.* one who works in a coal-mine; a ship employed in the coal trade; one of her crew; †a charcoal-burner. **colliery,** *n.* a coal-mine. [ME *col,* COAL, -IER]

Collier, *n.* **Lesley** (1947–), British ballerina, a principal dancer of the Royal Ballet from 1972.

colligate, *v.t.* to bind together; to bring into connection. **colligation,** *n.* alliance, union; (*Log.*) the mental process by which isolated facts are brought together into one concept. **colligative,** *a.* (*Chem.*) of a physical property, dependent on the concentration of particles present rather than their nature. [L *colligātus,* p.p. of *colligāre* (COL-, *ligāre,* to bind)]

collimate, *v.t.* to adjust the line of sight in a telescope; to make the axes of lenses or telescopes collinear. **collimation,** *n.* adjustment to the line of sight. **line of collimation,** the correct line of sight, the optical axis (the amount of deviation from this line is called the **error of collimation**). **collimator,** *n.* an instrument for determining the error of collimation; a tube attached to a spectroscope for making parallel the rays falling on the prism. [L *collīmāre,* a misreading for *collīneāre,* to aim (COL-, *līneāre,* from *līnea,* a line)]

collinear, *a.* (*Geom.*) in the same straight line.

collingual, *a.* having the same language.

Collingwood[1], *n.* **Cuthbert, Baron Collingwood** (1748–1810), British admiral, who served with Horatio Nelson in the West Indies against France and blockaded French ports (1803–05); after Nelson's death he took command at the Battle of Trafalgar.

Collingwood[2], *n.* **Robin George** (1889–1943), English philosopher, who believed that any philosophical theory or position could only be properly understood within its own historical context and not from the point of view of the present. His aesthetic theory is outlined in *Principles of Art* (1938).

Collins[1], *n.* a letter of thanks after a visit. [Mr *Collins* in Jane Austen's *Pride and Prejudice*]

Collins[2], *n.* **Michael** (1890–1922), Irish Sinn Féin leader, a founder and director of intelligence of the Irish Republican Army in 1919, minister for finance in the Provisional government of the Irish Free State in 1922, commander of the Free State forces and for ten days head of state; killed in the civil war.

Collins[3], *n.* **Phil** (1951–), English pop singer, drummer and actor. A member of the group Genesis from 1970, he has also pursued a successful solo career from 1981, with hits (often new versions of old songs) including 'In the Air Tonight' (1981) and 'Groovy Kind of Love' (1988).

Collins[4], *n.* **(William) Wilkie** (1824–89), English novelist, author of mystery and suspense novels, including *The Woman in White* (1860) (with its fat villain Count Fosco), often called the first English detective novel, and *The Moonstone* (1868) (with Sergeant Cuff, one of the first detectives in English literature).

collins, *n.* a drink made of spirits mixed with soda water, fruit juice, ice etc.

collision, *n.* the act of striking violently together; the state of being dashed or struck violently together; opposition, antagonism, conflict; clashing of interests; harsh combination of sounds, consonants etc. **collision course,** *n.* a course which will result inevitably in a collision. **collision mat,** *n.* a mat put over the side of a boat to cover a hole made by collision. [L *collisio -ōnem;* see COLLIDE]

collocate, *v.t.* to place together; to arrange; to station in a particular place. **collocation,** *n.* [L *collocātus,* p.p. of *collocāre*]

collocutor, *n.* one who takes part in a conversation or conference. [late L, from *colloquī,* to confer (*loquī,* to talk)]

Collodi, *n.* **Carlo** (pen name of Carlo Lorenzini) (1826–90), Italian journalist and writer, who in 1881–83 wrote *The Adventure of Pinocchio*, the children's story of a wooden puppet who became a human boy.

collodion, *n.* a gummy solution of pyroxylin in ether and spirit, formerly used in photography and medicine. **collodioned,** *a.* **collodionize, -ise,** *v.t.* **collodio-,** *comb. form.* [Gr. *kollōdēs* (*kolla,* glue)]

collograph, *n.* a duplicator or copying machine in which the medium is a film of gelatine; a collotype. [Gr. *kolla,* glue]

collogue, *v.i.* to talk confidentially or plot together. †*v.t.* to wheedle, to flatter. [perh. from F *colloque,* a conference, or from L *colloquī* (see COLLOQUY), influenced by COLLEAGUE[2]]

colloid, *a.* like glue; applied (1) to uncrystallizable liquids or semisolids; (2) to amorphous minerals; (3) to degeneration of the albuminous substance of cells into jelly-like matter. *n.* an uncrystallizable, semisolid substance, capable of only very slow diffusion or penetration. **colloidal,** *a.* **colloidize, -ise,** *v.t.* [Gr. *kolla,* glue, -OID]

collop, *n.* a slice of meat; a thick fold of flesh; a small piece or slice of anything. **Scotch collops,** *n.pl.* meat chopped up and cooked with savoury ingredients. [etym. doubtful]

colloquium, *n.* (*pl.* **-quia**) an academic conference; a seminar. [L, from *colloquī* (COL-, *loquī,* to talk)]

colloquy, *n.* a conference, conversation or dialogue between two or more persons; a court or presbytery in the Presbyterian Churches. **colloquial,** *a.* pertaining to or used in common or familiar conversation; not used in correct writing or in literature. **colloquialism,** *n.* **colloquially,** *adv.* **colloquist,** *n.* a collocutor. [COLLOQUIUM]

collotype, *n.* a method of lithographic printing in which the film of gelatine constituting the negative is used to print from; a print obtained in this way. [Gr. *kolla,* glue]

collude, *v.i.* to play into each other's hands; to act in concert, to conspire. **colluder,** *n.* [L *collūdere* (COL-, *lūdere,* to play)]

collusion, *n.* secret agreement for a fraudulent or deceitful purpose, esp. to defeat the course of law. **collusive,** *a.* **collusively,** *adv.* [F, from L *collūsio -ōnem* (*collūdere,* see prec.)]

colluvies, *n.* filth; a mixed mass of refuse. [L, from *colluere* (COL-, *luere,* to wash)]

†**colly,** *v.t.* to besmear with smut or soot; to blacken. *n.* the smut, grime, or soot of coal or burnt wood; the blackbird. [prob. from OE *colgian,* from *col,* COAL]

collyrium, *n.* (*pl.* **-ria**) an eye-salve, an eye-wash. [L, from Gr. *kollurion,* a poultice (*kollura,* a roll of coarse bread)]

collywobbles, *n.* (*coll.*) a stomach-ache; extreme nervousness. [poss. COLIC, WOBBLE]

Colo., (*abbr.*) Colorado.

colo-, COL(I)-.

Colocasia, *n.* a genus of plants of the arum family. [L, from Gr. *kolokasia*]

colocynth, *n.* the bitter cucumber or bitter apple, *Citrullus colocynthis,* or its fruit; an extract obtained from the pulp of this plant and used as a purgative. **colocynthin,** *n.* the bitter principle contained in colocynth. [L *colocynthis,* Gr *kolokunthis*]

Cologne[1], *n.* a city of Germany (see below); eau-de-Cologne. **Cologne earth,** *n.* a native pigment similar to Vandyke brown. **Cologne water** EAU-DE-COLOGNE. [F, from L *Colōnia* (Roman name *Colōnia Agrippīna*)]

Cologne[2], *n.* (German **Köln**) industrial and commercial port in North Rhine-Westphalia, West Germany, on the left bank of the Rhine, 35 km/22 miles from Düsseldorf; population (1988) 914,000. To the north is the Ruhr coalfield, on which many of Cologne's industries are based. They include motor vehicles, railway wagons, chemicals and machine tools.

Colombia, *n.* Republic of (*República de Colombia*), a country in S America, bounded N and W by the Caribbean and the Pacific, and having borders with Panama to the NW, Venezuela to the E and NE, Brazil to the SE and Peru and Ecuador to the SW. **area** 1,141,748 sq km/440,715 sq miles. **capital** Bogotá. **towns** Medellin, Cali, Bucaramanga; ports Barranquilla, Cartagena. **physical** the Andes mountains run N–S; plains in the E; Magdalena River runs N to the Caribbean. **exports** emeralds (world's largest producer), coffee (second largest world producer), bananas, cotton, meat, sugar, oil, skins, hides. **population** (1985) 29,482,000 (68% mestizo, 20%

white); annual growth rate 2.2%. **language** Spanish. **religion** Roman Catholic.

Colombo[1], *n.* the capital and principal seaport of Sri Lanka, on the west coast near the mouth of the Kelani; population (1981) 588,000, Greater Colombo about 1,000,000. It trades in tea, rubber and cacao. It has iron and steel works, and an oil refinery.

Colombo[2], *n.* **Matteo Realdo** (*c.* 1516–59), Italian anatomist who discovered pulmonary circulation, the process of blood circulating from the heart to the lungs and back.

Colombo Plan, *n.* plan for cooperative economic development in S and SE Asia, established 1951. The member countries meet annually to discuss economic and development plans such as irrigation, hydro-electric schemes and technical training.

colon[1], *n.* a grammatical point (:) used to mark the start of a list or long quotation etc,; also used in expressing an arithmetical ratio. [Gr. *kōlon,* a member, limb, clause]

colon[2], *n.* the largest division of the intestinal canal, extending from the caecum to the rectum. **colonic,** *a.* **colonitis,** *n.* colitis, inflammation of the colon. [L, from Gr. *kolon*]

Colón, *n.* second largest city in Panama, at the Caribbean end of the Panama Canal; population (1980) 60,000.

colonel, *n.* the commander of a regiment or of a battalion. **colonelcy, -ship,** *n.* [F, from It. *colonello,* dim. of *colonna,* column (formerly *coronel,* also from F, due to confusion with *corona,* crown)]

colonial, *a.* of or pertaining to a colony, esp. to those of the British Empire or to those in America that became the US in 1776. *n.* an inhabitant of a colony. **colonial goose,** *n.* (*Austral., coll.*) baked leg of mutton boned and stuffed. **Colonial Office,** *n.* (*Hist.*) the government department dealing with colonies. **colonialism,** *n.* an idiom or habit peculiar to colonials; a policy of tight control over, or exploitation of, colonies. **colonialist,** *n.* **colonially,** *adv.*

colonize, -ise, *v.t.* to found a colony in; to settle in; to people with colonists; of animals and plants, to establish a population in (a new environment). *v.i.* to found a colony or colonies. **colonist,** *n.* a colonizer; a settler in or inhabitant of a colony. **colonization, -isation,** *n.* **colonizationist, -isationist,** *n.* a supporter of colonization; (*N Am.*) one who favours the state-assisted settlement in Liberia of black emigrants from the US. **colonizer, -iser,** *n.* [L *colōnus,* orig. a farmer]

colonnade, *n.* a series or range of columns at certain intervals. [F, from It. *colonnata* (*colonna,* L *columna,* a COLUMN)]

colony, *n.* a settlement founded by emigrants in a foreign country, and remaining subject to the jurisdiction of the parent state; a group of people of the same nationality in a foreign town; a group of people following the same occupation in a town, esp. when they live in the same quarter; a body of organisms living or growing together. **crown colony** CROWN. **the Colonies,** (*Hist.*) those constituting the British Empire; those in America which became the United States. [F, *colonie,* L *colōnia* (*colōnus,* a farmer, from *colere,* to till)]

colophon, *n.* a device or inscription at the end of a book, giving the printer's name, place, date of publication etc.; a publisher's identifying symbol. [late L, from Gr. *kolophōn,* a summit]

colophony, *n.* a dark-coloured resin obtained from turpentine. **colophonate,** *n.* **colophonic,** *a.* [L *colophōnia* (*rēsīna*), from *Colophōn* in Asia Minor, where first obtained]

†**coloquintida,** COLOCYNTH. [med. L]

Colorado, *n.* state of the central W US; nickname Centennial State. **area** 269,700 sq km/104,104 sq miles. **capital** Denver. **towns** Colorado Springs, Aurora, Lakewood, Fort Collins, Greeley, Pueblo. **physical** Great Plains in the east; the main ranges of the Rocky Mountains; high plateaux of the Colorado Basin in the west. **products** cereals, meat and dairy products, oil, coal, molybdenum, uranium, iron, steel, machinery. **population** (1986) 3,267,000.

Colorado beetle, *n.* a small yellow black-striped beetle, *Doryphora decemlineata,* very destructive to the potato. [Sp.]

coloration, *n.* the act of colouring; method of putting on or arranging colours; (*Biol.*) particular marking, arrangement of colours. **colorant,** *n.* a substance used to impart colour, a pigment etc. [F, from L *colōrāre,* to colour]

coloratura, *n.* (*Mus.*) the ornamental use of variation, trills etc.; a singer, esp. a soprano, capable of singing such ornamented music. [It. *coloratura,* L *colōrātura,* from *colōrāre,* see prec.]

colorific, *a.* having the power of imparting colour to other bodies; highly-coloured. [F *colorifique* (L *color -ōrem,* -FIC)]

colorimeter, *n.* an instrument for measuring the hue, brightness, and purity of colours. **colorimetry,** *n.* [L *color,* colour]

Colosseum, *n.* amphitheatre in ancient Rome, begun by the emperor Vespasian to replace the one destroyed by fire during the reign of Nero, and completed by his son Titus in AD 80. It was 187 m/615 ft long and 49 m/160 ft high, and seated 50,000 people. Early Christians were martyred there by lions and gladiators. It could be flooded for mock sea battles. The name is applied to other amphitheatres and places of entertainment. [L, neut. a. from COLOSSUS]

colossus, *n.* (*pl.* **-ssi, -ssuses**) a statue of gigantic size; a gigantic statue of Apollo at Rhodes, which stood astride the harbour and was counted as one of The Seven Wonders of the World (it fell in 224 BC as the result of an earthquake); a man of great power or genius. **colossal,** *a.* pertaining to or resembling a colossus; huge; of sculpture, twice life-size. **colossally,** *adv.* **colossus-wise,** *adv.* in the manner of a colossus; astride. [L, from Gr. *kolossos*]

colostomy, *n.* the surgical formation of an artificial anus by an incision made into the colon. [Gr. *stoma,* mouth]

colostrum, *n.* the first milk secreted after parturition; beestings. [L]

colotomy, *n.* surgical incision into the colon.

colour[1], (*esp. N Am.*) **color,** *n.* the sensation produced by waves of resolved light upon the optic nerve; that property of bodies by which rays of light are resolved so as to produce certain effects upon the eye; any one of the hues into which light can be resolved, or a tint (a hue mixed with white), or a shade (mixed with black); that which is used for colouring, a pigment, a paint; colouring, effect of colour, and of light and shade in drawings and engravings; the complexion or hue of the face, esp. a healthy hue, ruddiness; any tint or hue, as distinguished from black or white; (*Law*) appearance, or *prima facie* right; (*pl.*) a flag, standard, or ensign borne in an army or fleet; (*pl.*) coloured ribbons etc. worn as a badge of party, membership of a league, society, club etc.; (*pl.*) coloured dresses; (*fig.*) semblance, appearance, esp. false appearance; pretence, excuse, pretext; timbre, quality of tone; general character tone, quality; mood, temper, emotional quality; vividness, animation. **complementary colours,** colours which together make up white; thus any of the primary colours is complementary to the other two. **false colours,** pretence. **fast colours,** colours that do not wash out. **off-colour,** *a.* faulty in colour, as a gem; faulty; out of sorts; slightly obscene. **primary colours,** the fundamental colours from which others can be obtained by mixing (for paints red, blue and yellow; for transmitted light red, blue, green). **prismatic colours,** those into which pure white light is resolved when dispersed, for example, in a prism or raindrop. **secondary colours,** colours produced by combinations of two primary colours. **to change colour,** to turn pale; to blush. **to join the colours,** to enlist. **to show one's colours,** to throw off disguise; to reveal one's opinions, feelings or designs. **water-colour** WATER. **with flying colours,** brilliantly, successfully; with signal credit. **colour bar,** *n.* a social, political, or other discrimination against non-Caucasian people. **colour-blind,** *a.* **colour-blindness,** *n.* total or partial inability to distinguish different colours, esp. the primary colours; DALTONISM. **colour-box,** *n.* a box for holding artists' colours, brushes etc. **colour-code,** *n.* a system of marking different things, e.g. electric wires, in different colours for ease of identification. **colour-fast,** *a.* dyed with fast colours. **colour-line,** *n.* a social distinction between white and non-white people in a community. **colourman,** *n.* one who deals in colours, brushes etc. **colour printing,** *n.* reproduction in two or more colours. **colour-scheme,** *n.* a set of colours used together in decorating. **colour-sergeant,** *n.* a non-commissioned officer in the infantry ranking above an ordinary sergeant. **colour supplement,** *n.* a (usu. weekly) supplement to a newspaper printed in colour and containing articles on lifestyle, entertainment etc. **colour-variation,** *n.* the range of variability of colour among animals of one species. **colourway,** *n.* a particular colour scheme, e.g. in a fabric. **colourable,** *a.* specious, plausible; apparent, not real. **colourableness,** *n.* **colourably,** *adv.* **colouration** COLORATION. **Coloured,** *a.* (sometimes *derog.* or *offensive*) of other than Caucasian race; in S Africa, of mixed race. *n.* a person of non-Caucasian or (in S Africa) of mixed race. **coloured,** *a.* having a colour; esp. marked by any colour except black or white; having a specious appearance; (*Bot.*) of any colour except green. **colourful,** *a.* having bright colour(s); interesting; exotic. **colouring,** *n.* the act of giving a colour to; the colour applied; the art or style of using colour; a false appearance; the colour of a person's skin, hair etc. **colourist,** *n.* one who colours; a painter distinguished for management of colour. **colouristic,** *a.* **colourize, -ise,** *v.t.* to put (e.g. a black-and-white film) into colour, esp. using computers. **colourization, -isation,** *n.* **colourless,** *a.* without colour; pale; neutral-tinted, subdued in tone, dull; lacking in life and vigour; bald, tame. **colourlessly,** *adv.* **colourlessness,** *n.* **coloury,** *a.* of hops, certain coffees etc., having a good colour. [OF *color,* L *colōrem,* acc. of *color*]

colour², *v.t.* to give colour to; to tinge, to paint, to dye; to paint with distemper; to give a new colour to; hence, to put in a false light, to misrepresent or disguise. *v.i.* to become coloured; to turn red, to blush.

-colous, *comb. form.* (*Biol.*) inhabiting (a certain environment). [L *colere,* to inhabit]

colporteur, *n.* one who travels about selling religious books, tracts etc. for some society. **colportage,** *n.* [F, from *colporter* (*col,* neck, *porter,* to carry)]

colposcope, *n.* an instrument for examining the cervix and upper vagina. **colposcopy,** *n.* [Gr. *kolpos,* womb]

Colt®, *n.* an early type of American revolver. [inventor, S. *Colt,* 1814–62]

colt, *n.* a young horse, esp. a young male from its weaning till about the age of four; a young, inexperienced fellow; (*Naut.*) a rope's end knotted and used for punishment; in sport, a member of a junior team; (*Cricket*) one who plays for the first time for his country. †*v.i.* to frisk like a colt. †*v.t.* to make pregnant; †to cheat; to beat with a rope's end. **colt's-foot,** *n.* a coarse-leaved, yellow-flowered weed, *Tussilago farfara,* formerly much used in medicine. **colthood,** *n.* **coltish,** *a.* [OE; etym. unknown]

colter, COULTER.

Coltrane, *n.* **John (William)** (1926–67), US jazz saxophonist, a member of the Miles Davis quintet. His performances were noted for experimentation, and his quartet was highly regarded for its innovations in melody and harmony.

coluber, *n.* a genus of innocuous snakes. **colubriform,** *a.* shaped like the genus *Coluber;* belonging to the group Colubriformes, which contains the innocuous snakes. **colubrine,** *a.* relating to serpents; resembling snakes, esp. the genus *Coluber;* †cunning. [L]

Colum, *n.* **Padraic** (1881–1972), Irish poet and playwright. He was associated with the foundation of the Abbey Theatre, Dublin, where his plays *Land* (1905), and *Thomas Muskerry* (1910), were performed. His *Collected Poems* (1932) show his gift for lyrical expression.

Columba, St, *n.* (521–597), Irish Christian abbot, missionary to Scotland. He was born in County Donegal of royal descent, and founded monasteries and churches in Ireland. In 563 he sailed with 12 companions to Iona, and built a monastery there that was to play an important part in the conversion of Britain. Feast day 9 June.

Columban, St, *n.* (543–615), Irish Christian abbot. He was born in Leinster, studied at Bangor, and about 585 went to the Vosges, France, with 12 other monks and founded the monastery of Luxeuil. He preached in Switzerland, then went to Italy, where he built the abbey of Bobbio in the Apennines. Feast day 23 Nov.

columbarium, *n.* (*pl.* **-ria**) a pigeon house; a place of interment among the ancient Romans, fitted with niches like pigeon-holes to receive the cinerary urns; a hole left in a wall to receive the end of a timber. †**columbary,** *n.* a pigeon-house, a dove-cote. [L, neut. of *columbārius* (*columba,* dove)]

Columbia, District of, seat of the federal government of the US, bordering the capital, Washington; area 178 sq km/69 sq miles. Situated on the Potomac River, it was ceded by Maryland as the national capital site 1790.

Columbian, *a.* pertaining to the United States of America. **Columbian press,** *n.* a kind of printing-press first made in America. [Christopher *Columbus,* 1451–1506, discoverer of America]

Columbia Pictures, *n.* a US film production and distribution company founded in 1924. It grew out of a smaller company founded in 1920 by Harry and Jack Cohn and Joe Brandt. Under Harry Cohn's guidance, Columbia became a major studio by the 1940s, producing such commercial hits as *Gilda* (1946). After Cohn's death in 1958 the studio remained successful, producing international films such as *Lawrence of Arabia* (1962).

Columbine, *n.* the female dancer in a pantomime, the sweetheart of Harlequin. [It. *Colombina,* a comedy character]

columbine, *a.* pertaining to or resembling a dove or pigeon. *n.* a plant with five-spurred flowers, supposed to resemble five doves clustered together, constituting the genus *Aquilegia.* [OF *columbin,* late L *columbīna* (*columba,* a dove)]

columbium, NIOBIUM.

Columbus, *n.* **Christopher** (Spanish **Cristobal Colon**) (1451–1506), Italian navigator and explorer who made four voyages to the New World: 1492 to San Salvador Island, Cuba and Haiti; 1493–96 to Guadaloupe, Montserrat, Antigua, Puerto Rico and Jamaica; 1498 to Trinidad and the mainland of South America; 1502–04 to Honduras and Nicaragua.

columella, †**columel,** *n.* the central pillar of a univalve shell, or of corals; the axis of fruit; the central column in the capsule of mosses. [L, dim. of *columna,* see foll.]

column, *n.* a pillar or solid body of wood or stone, of considerably greater length than thickness, usu. consisting of a base, a shaft and a capital, used to support or adorn a building, or as a solitary monument; anything resembling such a column, as the mercury in a thermometer, a cylindrical mass of water, or other liquid, a vertical mass of smoke etc.; a perpendicular line of figures; a perpendicular section of a page; hence (*pl.*) the contents of a newspaper; a regular article in a newspaper or magazine; a support; a solid body into which the filaments in some plants are combined; a body of troops in deep files; a line of ships behind each other. **column-inch,** *n.* a print measure, 1 in. (2.54 cm) deep and one column wide. **column-rule,** *n.* a rule used in printing to divide columns of type. **columnar,** *a.* **columned,** *a.* **columniation,** *n.* the employment or the grouping of columns in a building; arrangement in columns. **columniform,** *a.* **columnist,** *n.* a regular writer on general subjects in a newspaper. [earlier *co-*

lompne, OF *colompne, F colombe,* L *columna* (cogn. with *collis,* hill, *celsus,* high)]

colure, *n.* (*Astron.*) one of two great circles passing through the equinoctial points, and cutting each other at right angles at the poles. [L *colūrus,* Gr. *kolouros* (*kol-os,* docked, *ouros,* tail)]

colza, *n.* rape; rape-seed. **colza-oil,** *n.* oil expressed from this, and used as an illuminant. [F *colza, colzat,* LG *Kôlsôt* (Dut. *koolsaad*)]

Com., (*abbr.*) commander; commission(er); committee; Commonwealth.

com., (*abbr.*) commerce; committee; common; commune.

com-, *pref.* with; together; in combination; completely. [L, the combining form *cum-* (chiefly before *b, f, m, p*)]

coma[1], *n.* a state of absolute unconsciousness, characterized by the absence of any response to external stimuli or inner need. **comatose,** *a.* in a coma; (*coll.*) sleepy, sluggish. [late L, from Gr. *kōma -atos* (cp. *koimaein,* to put to sleep)]

coma[2], *n.* (*pl.* **-mae**), *n.* the nebulous covering of the nucleus of a comet; the assemblage of branches constituting the head of a forest tree; the tuft of hairs terminating certain seeds. [L, from Gr. *komē,* the hair]

Comaneci, *n.* **Nadia** (1961–), Romanian gymnast. She won three gold medals at the 1976 Olympics at the age of 14, and was the first gymnast to record a perfect score of 10 in international competition.

comate, comose, *a.* (*Bot.*) bearing a tuft of hair at the end. [COMA[2]]

comb[1], *n.* a toothed instrument for separating and dressing the hair; an ornamental toothed contrivance for fastening ladies' hair when dressed; a rake-shaped instrument with a short handle for cleaning wool or flax; a row of points for collecting electricity; the red, fleshy tuft on the head of a fowl, esp. the cock; the crest of a bird; the cellular substance in which bees deposit their honey; the crest of a wave; a ridge. *v.t.* to separate, dress, or arrange with a comb; to curry a horse; to dress (flax, hemp, wool etc.); to make a thorough search of; †to beat. *v.i.* to form a crest and roll over as waves. **to comb out,** to remove with a comb; to find and remove; to search thoroughly. **comb-out,** *n.* a thorough search. **-combed,** *comb. form.* **comber[1],** *n.* one who or that which combs; a combing-machine for dressing cotton or wool; a wave that forms a long crest and rolls over. **combing,** *n.* a cleaning or dressing with a comb; (*pl.*) hair removed by a comb. [OE *camb,* from Teut. *kambo-* (cp. Dut. *kam,* Icel. *kambr,* G *Kamm;* Gr. *gomphos,* a peg, Sansk. *gambhas,* a tooth)]

comb.[2], (*abbr.*) combined; combination.

combat, *v.i.* to contend, to fight, to struggle. *v.t.* to oppose, to contend against, to fight with. *n.* a fight, a battle; †a duel. **single combat,** *n.* a duel. **trial by combat,** (*Hist.*) a legal method of settling a dispute or testing the justice of a charge by a duel. **combat fatigue,** *n.* nervous disturbance occurring in a very stressful situation, such as on the battlefield. **combatable,** *a.* **combatant,** *a.* engaged in combat; bearing arms; antagonistic; (*Her.*) borne in the attitude of fighting. *n.* one who fights or contends with another. **combative,** *a.* inclined to combat; pugnacious. **combatively,** *adv.* **combativeness,** *n.* [OF *combatre* (COM-, *battre,* L *batuere,* to fight)]

combe, *n.* a valley on the side of hills or mountains; a valley running up from the sea. (The word often occurs as an element in place names, as in Ilfracombe.) [OE *cumb* (etym. doubtful; perh. from W *cwm, cumb;* or an application of OE *cumb,* a hollow vessel, of Teut. origin)]

comber[1] COMB[1].

comber[2], *n.* the wrasse, *Serranus cabrilla,* and the gaper, *Labrus maculatus,* var. *comber;* both British fish. [etym. doubtful]

combination, *n.* the act or process of combining; the state of being combined; a combined body or mass; a union, an association; combined action; chemical union; (*pl. Math.*) the different collections which may be made of certain given quantities in groups of a given number; (*Law*) an assembly of workers met to carry out a common purpose, formerly of an illegal nature; a motor-cycle and sidecar; (*pl.*) vest and knickers combined in one garment; a sequence of chess moves; the sequence of numbers that will open a combination lock. **Combination Laws,** *n.pl.* see separate article. **combination lock,** *n.* a lock which opens only when a set of dials is turned to show a particular combination of numbers. **combination-room,** *n.* the room in which the fellows of the colleges at Cambridge meet after dinner for dessert and conversation, elsewhere called the common-room. **combinative,** *a.* **combinatory,** *a.* [OF, from L *combīnātio -ōnem* (*combīnāre,* to COMBINE)]

Combination Laws, *n. pl.* laws passed in Britain 1799 and 1800 making trade unionism illegal, introduced after the French Revolution for fear that the unions would become centres of political agitation. The unions continued to exist, but claimed to be friendly societies or went underground, until the acts were repealed in 1824, largely owing to the radical Francis Place.

combine[1], *v.t.* to cause to unite or coalesce; to settle by agreement; to bring together; to have at the same time (properties or attributes usu. separate). *v.i.* to unite, to coalesce; to be joined or united in friendship or plans; (*Chem.*) to unite by chemical affinity. **combined operations,** operations in which sea, air and land forces work together under a single command. [L *combīnāre* (COM-, *bini,* two by two)]

combine[2], *n.* a combination, esp. of persons or companies to further their own commercial interests; a ring; (also **combine harvester**) a combined reaping and threshing machine.

combo[1], *n.* a white man living with an Aboriginal woman. [Austral.]

combo[2], *n.* a combination of instruments, a small band in jazz and popular music.

combust, *v.t.* to consume with fire. †*a.* burnt up, calcined; situated so near to the sun as to be obscured or eclipsed by its light. **combustible,** *a.* capable of being set on fire, flammable; irascible, hot-tempered. *n.* flammable material or thing. **combustibility,** *n.* **combustibleness,** *n.* **combustion,** *n.* the act of burning, the state of being on fire or destroyed by fire; (*Chem.*) the combination of a substance with oxygen or another element, accompanied by light and heat; oxidation of the tissue of organisms or of decomposing organic matter. **spontaneous combustion,** the ignition of a body by the development of heat within itself. †**combustious,** *a.* combustible, flammable; on fire; raging, tempestuous. **combustive,** *a.* [OF, from L *combustus,* p.p. of *combūrere* (COM-, *ūrere,* to burn)]

Comdr, (*abbr.*) commander.

Comdt, (*abbr.*) commandant.

come, *v.i.* (*past* **came**, p.p. **come**) to move from a distance to a place nearer to the speaker; to approach; to be brought to or towards; to move towards (opp. to *go*); to arrive; to advance to move into view; to travel (a certain distance) towards; to appear; to arrive at some state or condition; to happen; to befall; to result, to arise, to originate (from); to become, to get to be; to be descended (from); to bud, to shoot; (*sl.*) to experience orgasm. *v.t.* (*sl.*) to act the part of, to produce. *int.* used to excite attention or rouse to action (when repeated it expresses remonstrance or rebuke). **as it comes,** without additions or alterations. **come again,** say that again. **come along,** make haste. **come February** etc., when February etc. comes; from now until February. **come off it,** (*coll.*) stop behaving (or talking) so stupidly or pretentiously. **come to that,** in that case. **come up,** *imper.* go on; push on (to horse). **come what may,** whatever happens. **how come?** how does this happen? **to come,** in the future. **to come about,** to result, to come to pass; to recover; to change direction; to be perceived (as); to part (with money). **to come across,** to meet with acccidentally. **to come**

and go, to appear and disappear (as the colour in the cheeks); to pass to and fro; to pay a short call. **to come at,** to reach, to attain, to gain access to. **to come away,** to move away; to become parted or separated. **to come back,** to return; to recur to memory; to retort. **to come between,** to damage a relationship between (two people). **to come by,** to pass near; to obtain, to gain. **to come down,** to descend (to); to be humbled; to decide. **to come down handsome,** (*sl.*) to pay a handsome price, compensation or reward. **to come down to,** to amount to; to have as result. **to come down (up)on,** to reprimand; to chastise; to pay out. **to come down with,** to pay over (money); to contract (an ailment). **to come easy, expensive** etc. to prove easy, costly etc. **to come forward,** to make oneself known, to identify oneself (to the authorities etc.). **to come home,** to return home; to affect nearly; to be fully comprehended. **to come in,** to enter; to arrive at a destination; to become fashionable; to yield; to become (useful etc.); to enter (as an ingredient); to accrue; to assume power; (*coll.*) to secure an advantage or chance of benefit. **to come in for,** to arrive in time for; to obtain, to get (a share of). **to come into,** to join with; to comply with; to acquire, to inherit. **to come into the world,** to be born. **to come it over someone,** (*coll.*) to lord it over someone. **to come it strong,** (*sl.*) to exaggerate to affect. **to come near,** to approach; nearly to succeed. **to come of,** to be descended from; to proceed or result from. **to come off,** to part from; to fall off; to escape; to get off free; to take place; to appear; to be accomplished. **to come on,** to advance; to prosper; to happen, to arise; (*imper.*) approach; proceed; do what you propose. **to come out,** to come away; to be revealed, become public; to be introduced into society; to be published; to declare something openly, esp. one's homosexuality; to be covered (in); to emerge from; to turn out; (*N Am.*) to make profession of religion; to engage in a strike. **to come out of,** to issue forth, to proceed from. **to come out with,** to utter, to disclose. **to come over,** to cross over; to change sides; to prevail upon; (*coll.*) to become; to make a casual visit; to be perceived (as). **to come round,** to change; to cheat; to recover. **to come short,** to fail. **to come through,** to survive. **to come to,** to consent; to amount to; to recover from faintness; (*Naut.*) to cease moving; to sail close to the wind. **to come to an end,** to cease. **to come to a point,** to taper; to culminate; to reach a crisis. **to come to blows,** to begin fighting. **to come to harm,** to be injured. **to come to oneself,** to recover one's sense. **to come to pass,** to happen. **to come to stay,** to remain; to have qualities of a permanent nature. **to come under,** to be classed as; to be subjected to (authority, influence etc.). **to come up,** to ascend; to spring; to become public or fashionable; to arise; to be introduced as a topic; (*Naut.*) to slacken (as a rope). **to come up against,** to encounter or confront (some difficulty). **to come upon,** to attack; to befall; to find, discover; to meet with unexpectedly. **to come up to,** to amount to; to be equal to; to approach. **to come up smiling,** (*sl.*) to laugh at punishment, defeat or discomfiture. **to come up with,** to overtake to produce. **where one came in,** back at the beginning. **come-by-chance,** *n.* (*coll.*) a stray, a bastard. **come-back,** *n.* a retort; a return to popular favour. **come-down,** *n.* a fall or abasement. **come-hither,** *a.* sexually alluring. †**come-off,** *n.* a means of escape, an evasion. **come-on,** *n.* an invitation, encouragement, esp. sexual. [OE *cuman* (cp. Dut. *komen,* Icel. *koma,* G *kommen;* Sansk. *gam,* Gr. *bainein,* L *venīre*)]

comeatable, *a.* easy to come at, accessible. [COME, AT, -ABLE]

Comecon, *n.* an economic organization of E European states, founded in 1949. [*Co*uncil for *M*utual *Econ*omic Aid]

comedian, *n.* an actor or writer of comedy. [F *comédien*]

Comédie Française, *n.* the French national theatre (for both comedy and tragedy) in Paris, founded in 1680 by Louis XIV. Its base is the Salle Richelieu on the right bank of the Seine, and the Théatre de l'Odéon, on the left bank, is a testing ground for avant-garde ideas.

comedienne, *n.* a comedy actress. [F]

comedietta, *n.* a slight or brief comedy. [It., dim. of *comedia,* COMEDY]

comedo, *n.* (*pl.* **-dos, -dones**) a blackhead. [L glutton, from *comedere,* to eat]

comedy, *n.* a dramatic composition of a light and entertaining character depicting and often satirizing the incidents of ordinary life, and having a happy termination; an entertaining drama of ordinary life more serious and more realistic than farce; life or any incident or situation regarded as an amusing spectacle. **comedic,** *a.* **comedist,** *n.* a writer of comedies. [OF *comedie,* L *cōmaedia,* Gr. *kōmōidia,* from *kōmōidos,* a comic actor (*kōmos,* a revel, *aoidos,* a singer)]

comely, *a.* pleasing in person, or in behaviour; becoming, decent. **comeliness,** *n.* [OE *cymlic* (*cyme,* fine, beautiful, *lic,* like, -LY)]

comer, *n.* one who comes or arrives; a visitor. **all comers,** any one who accepts a challenge. **the first comer,** the one who arrives first.

comestible, *n.* (*usu. pl.*) food [F, from late L *comestibilis,* from *comest-,* stem of *comestus, comēsus,* p.p of *comedere* (COM-, *edere,* to eat)]

comet, *n.* a luminous heavenly body, consisting when perfect, of a nucleus or head, a coma, and a train or tail, revolving round the sun in a very eccentric orbit. **comet-finder, -seeker,** *n.* (*Astron.*) an equatorial telescope, with coarsely-divided circles and a large field, taking in at once a large part of the sky. **comet-wine,** *n.* wine made in the year of a comet, popularly supposed to be of superior quality. **cometary,** *a.* **cometic,** *a.* **cometography,** *n.* a discourse on or description of comets. **cometology,** *n.* the science dealing with comets. [L *comēta, comētēs,* Gr. *komētēs* (*komē,* the hair)]

comether, *n.* **to put the comether on,** to attract by persuasion or guile; to bring under one's influence. [*dial.,* COME HITHER]

comeuppance, *n.* retribution for past misdeeds. [COME, UP -ANCE]

comfit, *n.* a dry sweetmeat; a seed coated with sugar. [OF *confit,* L *confectum,* neut. p.p. of *conficere* (CON-, *facere,* to make)]

comfiture, *n.* a confection, a sweetmeat, a comfit. [F, from L *confectūra* (as prec.)]

comfort, *v.t.* to cheer, to encourage, to console; to make comfortable; †to make strong; †(*Law*) to abet. *n.* support or assistance in time of weakness; consolation; encouragement; that which affords consolation or encouragement; quiet enjoyment; ease, general well-being, absence of trouble or anxiety; (*pl.*) the material things that contribute to bodily satisfaction; a comforter. **cold comfort** COLD. **comfort station,** *n.* (*N Am.*) a public convenience. **comfortable,** *a.* at ease, in good circumstances, free from want, hardship, trouble or pain; quietly happy, contented; providing comfort or security. †comforting. **comfortableness,** *n.* **comfortably,** *adv.* **comforter,** *n.* one who or that which comforts; a long, narrow, woollen scarf; (*N Am.*) a quilted coverlet; (*Theol.*) the Holy Ghost. **Job's comforter,** one who makes a show of comforting but does exactly the opposite. **comfortless,** *a.* without comfort; cheerless. †**comfortlessly,** *adv.* †**comfortlessness,** *n.* [OF *conforter,* L *confortāre,* (CON-, *fortis,* strong)]

comfrey, *n.* a tall wild plant, *Symphytum officinale,* with rough leaves and yellowish or purplish flowers, formerly used for healing wounds. [OF *confirie,* med. L *cumfiria* (etym. doubtful)]

comfy, *a.* (*coll.*) short for COMFORTABLE under COMFORT.

comic, *a.* pertaining to comedy, laughable, absurd, provoking mirth; facetious, burlesque, intended to be laughable. *n.* a comedian; a droll; a children's magazine containing comic strips; the comic aspect of things. **to strike comical,** (*sl.*) to astonish. **comic**

opera, *n.* a type of opera with humorous episodes, a light, sentimental plot and usu. some spoken dialogue; a musical burlesque. **comic strip,** *n.* a usu. comic narrative told in a series of pictures. **comical,** *a.* ludicrous, laughable; exciting mirth. **comicality,** *n.* **comically,** *adv.* [L *cōmicus,* Gr. *kōmikos* (*kōmos,* a revel)]

comico-, *comb. form.* **comico-tragic,** *a.* **comico-didactic,** *a.*

Comines, *n.* **Philippe de** (*c.* 1445–1509), French diplomat in the service of Charles the Bold, Louis XI and Charles VIII; author of *Mémoires* (1489–98).

Cominform, *n.* the Information Bureau of the Communist Parties, founded in 1947, orig. including Yugoslavia. [Rus.]

coming, *a.* approaching; future, to come. *n.* the act of approaching or arriving, arrival; the act of sprouting, as malt; (*pl.*) sprouts or rootlets (of malted grain). **coming eleven,** nearly 11 years old. **to have it coming,** (*coll.*) to deserve what (unpleasant thing) is about to happen. **coming on,** *n.* approach, improvement, increase. *a.* affable, complaisant.

comingle, COMMINGLE.

Comintern, *n.* the Third Communist International, founded in Moscow in 1919, dissolved in June 1943. [Rus.]

comitatus, *n.* (*Hist.*) the retinue of a noble or chieftain; (*Law*) an English county. **posse comitatus** POSSE. [L, from *comes -item,* a companion]

comity, *n.* affability, friendliness, courtesy, civility. **comity of nations,** the courtesy by which a nation allows another's laws to be recognized within its territory, so far as is practicable. [L *cōmitās -tātem* (*cōmis,* courteous)]

Comm.[1], (*abbr.*) commodore.

comm.[2], (*abbr.*) commentary; commerce; commercial; commonwealth.

comma, *n.* a punctuation mark (,), denoting the shortest pause in reading; (*Mus.*) a minute difference of tone; a butterfly with a white comma-shaped mark beneath the hind-wing. **inverted commas,** raised or superior commas as thus: ' – '; " – " used to indicate quotations. **comma bacillus,** *n.* a comma-shaped species of *Spirillum* which causes cholera. [L, from Gr. *komma,* a stamp, a clause (*koptein,* to strike, cut)]

command, *v.t.* to order, to call for, to enforce, to govern, to hold in subjection, to exercise authority over; to dominate, to overlook; to control, to have at one's disposal; to master, to subjugate. *v.i.* to give orders; to exercise supreme authority. *n.* an order, a bidding, a mandate; power, authority; control, mastery, the power of dominating or overlooking; a naval or military force under the command of a particular officer; (*Comput.*) an instruction; a working knowledge (of). **at command,** ready for orders; at one's disposal. **command-in-chief,** *n.* the supreme command. **to command-in-chief,** to be commander-in-chief (of an army etc.). **command-night, performance,** *n.* a theatrical performance given by royal command. **command paper,** *n.* a government report presented to Parliament. **command post,** *n.* a place used as temporary headquarters by a military commander. **command sequence,** *n.* (*Comput.*) a series of commands for a specific task. **commandant** (komәndant'), *n.* the governor or commanding officer of a place. **commandantship,** *n.* **commanding,** *a.* giving or entitled to give commands; fitted to command; impressive; dominating, overlooking. **commandingly,** *adv.* [OF *comander,* late L *commandāre* (COM-, *mandāre,* to entrust)]

commandeer, *v.t.* to make use of for military purposes; to seize (goods), to impress (men); *v.i.* to exercise the right to seize and impress for military purposes. [Dut. *kommanderen,* from F *commander,* to command]

commander, *n.* one who commands or is in authority; a general or leader of a body of men; a member of one of the higher grades in some orders of knighthood; a naval officer between a lieutenant and a captain; a police officer in London in charge of a district; a large wooden mallet. **commander-in-chief,** *n.* the officer in supreme command of the British army, of the military forces in a colony or of a foreign expedition; (*Nav.*) the officer in supreme command of all the ships in a certain district. **commander-in-chiefship,** *n.* **commandership,** *n.* **commandery, -dry,** *n.* in military orders of knighthood, a district or manor, which, with its revenues, was administered by a commander; (*loosely*) a non-military priory.

commandment, *n.* an order, a command, esp. a Divine command; a precept; a law, esp. of the decalogue; †authority, power. **the Ten Commandments,** the decalogue. **the Eleventh Commandment,** (*coll.*) an additional precept, 'Thou shalt not be found out.'

commando, *n.* (*pl.* **-dos**) a body of men called out for military service; an expedition or raid by Boers or Portuguese in S Africa, esp. against natives; a body of men selected and trained to undertake a specially hazardous raid on or behind the enemy lines; a man thus selected; a mobile amphibious force. [Port., from *commandar,* to command]

commatic, *a.* in brief clauses; concise, terse; (*Mus.*) pertaining to or entailing the use of the comma. [COMMA]

commedia dell'arte, *n.* Italian comedy of the 16th–18th cents., using improvisation and stock characters. [It., comedy of art]

comme il faut, as it should be, correct, genteel. [F]

commemorate, *v.t.* to keep in remembrance by some solemn act; to celebrate the memory of; to be a memorial of. **commemorable,** *a.* **commemoration,** *n.* the act of commemorating; a service, ceremony or festival in memory of some person, deed or event; (*Oxford Univ.*) the annual festival commemorating benefactors to the University. **commemorative,** *a.* **commemoratively,** *adv.* [L *commemorātus,* p.p. of *commemorāre* (COM-, *memorāre,* to mention, from *memor,* mindful)]

commence, *v.i.* to start, to begin; to begin (to do something); to begin to be (something); to assume a character; (*Univ.*) to take a full degree. *v.t.* to enter upon; to perform the first act of. **commencement,** *n.* beginning, origin, rise; first instance, first existence; the day when the degrees of Master and Doctor are conferred, at Cambridge, Dublin and American universities; in N American schools, speech day. [OF *comencer* (cp. It. *cominciare*), from L COM-, *initiāre,* to begin (*initium,* a beginning, from IN-, *īre,* to go)]

commend, *v.t.* to commit to the charge of, to entrust; to recommend as worthy of notice, regard or favour; to praise, to approve. †*n.* commendation; (*pl.*) kind wishes, remembrances. **commend me to,** remember me to; give me as my choice. **commendable,** *a.* worthy of commendation; †bestowing commendation. **commendableness,** *n.* **commendably,** *adv.* **commendation,** *n.* the act of commending; recommendation of a person to the consideration or favour of another; †a greeting service, respects. **commendator,** *n.* one who holds a benefice *in commendam;* †the president of a commandery; a Spanish title corresponding to viceroy or lieutenant. **commendatory,** *a.* that serves to commend; holding a commendam; held as a commendam. *n.* commendation, eulogy. [L *commendāre* (COM-, *māndāre,* to entrust)]

commendam, *n.* (*Eccles.*) holding a vacant benefice in trust (abolished in 1836) till an incumbent was appointed; holding a benefice in the absence of the regular incumbent. [L, in trust]

commensal, *a.* eating at the same table, sharing the same food. *n.* an animal that lives in intimate association with, on the surface of or in the substance of another, without being parasitic. **commensalism,** *n.* **commensality,** *n.* [F, from med. L *commensālis* (COM-, *mensa,* table)]

commensurable, *a.* measurable by a common unit; (*Math.*) applied to two magnitudes which have a common measure; proportionate (to). **commensur-**

ability, **-ableness,** *n.* **commensurably,** *adv.* [L *commensūrābilis* (COM-, *mensūrābilis,* from *mensūrāre,* see foll.)]

commensurate, *a.* having the same measure or extent; proportional. **commensurately,** *adv.* **commensurateness,** *n.* [L *commensūrātus* (COM-, *mensūrātus,* p.p. of *mensūrāre,* to measure, from *mensūra,* a measure)]

comment, *n.* a remark; a criticism; a note interpreting or illustrating a work or portion of a work. *v.i.* to make explanatory or critical remarks or notes (on a book or writing); to criticize or make remarks (upon) unfavourably. *v.t.* †to expound; to remark. **no comment,** I refuse to answer or comment. **commentary,** *n.* a comment; a series of explanatory notes on a whole work; (*pl.*) a historical narrative; a broadcast description of an event as it takes place. **commentate,** *v.t.*, *v.i.* to act as commentator (of). **commentation,** *n.* **commentator,** *n.* the author of a commentary; an annotator, an expositor; the broadcaster of a commentary. [OF *comment,* L *commentum,* invention, comment, neut. p.p. of *comminisci* (COM-, *minisci,* from the root *men-,* cp. *mens,* mind, *memini,* I remember)]

commerce, *n.* trade, traffic; the interchange of commodities between nations or individuals; a card game; †intercourse, esp. sexual. †*v.i.* to trade; to have intercourse. **commerce-destroyer,** *n.* a cruiser employed to sink enemy merchant shipping on the high seas. [F, from L *commercium* (COM-, *merx, -cis,* wares, merchandise)]

commercial, *a.* pertaining to or connected with commerce; done for profit; of chemicals, of poor quality and produced in bulk for industry. *n.* †a commercial traveller; an advertisement broadcast on radio or television. **commercial art,** *n.* graphic art used in advertising etc. **commercial broadcasting,** *n.* broadcasting paid for by advertising or sponsorship. **commercial room,** *n.* a hotel room reserved for commercial travellers. **commercial traveller,** *n.* an agent sent out by a trader to solicit orders from retailers, a company representative. **commercial vehicle,** *n.* one used for the transport of goods or passengers. **commercialism,** *n.* a trading spirit; commercial practices. **commercialist,** *n.* **commerciality**, *n.* **commercialize, -ise,** *v.t.* **commercially,** *adv.*

commerge, *v.t.* to merge together.

commie, *n., a.* (*coll.* often *derog.*) short for COMMUNIST.

comminate, *v.t.* to threaten, to denounce. **commination,** *n.* a threat, a denunciation; in the Church of England, a service including a list of God's judgments on sinners, used on Ash Wednesday. **comminatory,** *a.* threatening, denunciatory. [L *comminātus,* p.p. of *comminārī* (*minārī,* to threaten)]

commingle, *v.t.* to mingle or mix together; to blend. [COM-, MINGLE]

comminute, *v.t.* to make smaller; to reduce to minute particles or to powder; to divide into small portions. **comminuted fracture,** *n.* a fracture in which the bone is broken into small pieces. **comminution**. [L *comminātus,* p.p. of *comminuere* (*minuere,* to make smaller)]

commis, *n.* an agent; an apprentice or assistant waiter or chef. [F, p.p. of *commettre,* COMMIT]

commiserate, *v.t.* to pity; to express pity or compassion for. **commiseration,** *n.* **commiserative,** *a.* **commiseratively,** *adv.* [L *commiserātus,* p.p. of *commiserārī* (*miserārī,* to pity)]

commissar, *n.* formerly, the head of a department of government in the USSR; a party official responsible for political education. [Rus., a commissioner]

commissariat, *n.* that department of the army charged with supplying provisions and stores; (*Sc. Law*) the jurisidiction of a commissary; formerly, a government department in the USSR. [F, as foll.]

commissary, *n.* a commissioner; a deputy; (*Mil.*) an officer in charge of the commissariat; the deputy who supplies a bishop's place in the remote parts of his diocese; (*Sc. Law*) the judge of a commissary court. **commissary court,** *n.* (*Law*) a court to try cases that in mediaeval times were under jurisdiction of the bishop's commissaries; (*Sc. Law*) a former supreme court dealing with probate and divorce cases. **commissary-general,** *n.* (*Mil.*) the head of the commissariat. **commissarial**, *a.* **commissaryship,** *n.* [late L *commissārius,* from *commissus,* p.p. of *committere* (*mittere,* to send)]

commission, *n.* the act of doing or committing; entrusting a duty to another; hence, trust, charge, command; delegation of authority; a number of persons entrusted with authority; the document conferring authority, esp. that of military and naval officers; a body of commissioners; an allowance made to a factor or agent; a percentage. *v.t.* to authorize, to empower, to appoint to an office; to put (a ship) in commission; to order (the painting of a picture, writing of a book etc.). **Commission of the Peace,** a warrant under the Great Seal empowering persons to serve as Justices of the Peace. **in commission,** entrusted with authority; (*Nav.*) prepared for active service; entrusted to a commission instead of the consitutional officer. **on commission,** a percentage of the proceeds of goods sold being paid to the agent or retailer. **Royal Commission,** a commission of enquiry ordered by Parliament. **commission agent, merchant,** *n.* one who acts as agent for others, and is paid by a percentage. **commission-day,** *n.* the opening day of assizes, when the judge's commission is read. **commissionaire,** *n.* one of a corps of time-expired soldiers and sailors, orig. enrolled in London in 1859, to carry messages, act as caretakers, timekeepers etc.; a uniformed doorman at a hotel, theatre etc. **commissional,** *a.* **commissioned,** *a.* holding a commission, esp. from the Crown. **commissioner,** *n.* one empowered to act by a commission or warrant; a member of a commission or government board; the head of some department of the public service. **commissioner for oaths,** (*Law*) in England, a person appointed by the Lord Chancellor with power to administer oaths or take affidavits. All practising solicitors have these powers. **commissioner of audit,** an officer appointed to check the public accounts. **High Commissioner,** *n.* the chief representative of a Commonwealth country in another Commonwealth country. **Lord High Commissioner,** *n.* the sovereign's representative in the Church of Scotland. **commissionership,** *n.* [F, from L *commissio -ōnem* (see prec.)]

commissure, *n.* a joint, a seam; the point of junction of two sides of anything separated, or of two similar organs, as the great commissure of the brain; a suture; a line of closure, as of eyelids, lips, mandibles; (*Arch.*) the joint of two stones; the application of one surface tò another; the line of junction of two opposite carpels. **commissural**, *a.* [L *commissūra,* from *commissus,* p.p. of *committere* (see foll.)]

commit, *v.t.* (*past, p.p.* **committed**) to entrust, to deposit; to consign, to perpetrate; to refer (as a Bill) to a Parliamentary committee; (*Law*) to send for trial or to prison; to assign, to pledge. **to commit oneself,** to pledge oneself; to make a mistake; to compromise oneself. **to commit to memory,** to learn by heart. **commitment,** *n.* the action of the verb TO COMMIT; the state of being committed; the delivery of a prisoner to the charge of the prison authorities; an engagement to carry out certain duties or meet certain expenses. **committable,** *a.* **committal,** *n.* a sending for trial, to prison or to the grave. **committer,** *n.* **committor,** *n.* (*Law*) one who commits someone mentally incompetent etc. to the care of a person or institution. [L *committere* (COM-, *mittere,* to send)]

committee, *n.* a board elected or deputed to examine, consider, and report on any business referred to them. (*Law*), the person to whom the care of a mentally incompetent person etc. is committed. **Committee of the Whole House,** the House of Commons sitting informally as a committee to discuss a bill. **committeeman, -woman,** *n.* a member of a committee. [late A-F F *commis*), p.p. of *commettre,* L *committere,* as prec.]

Committee of Imperial Defence, an informal group established 1902 to co-ordinate planning of the British Empire's defence forces. Initially meeting on a temporary basis, it was established permanently in 1904. Members were usually cabinet ministers concerned with defence, military leaders, and key civil servants.

commix, *v.t., v.i.* to mix together, to blend. **commixtion,** *n.* **commixture,** *n.*

commode, *n.* a head-dress worn by ladies in the time of William and Mary; a bureau; a night-stool. [F, from L *commodus,* convenient (*modus,* measure)]

commodious, *a.* roomy; convenient, suited to its purpose. **commodiously,** *adv.* **commodiousness,** *n.* [OF *commodieux,* late L *commodiōsus,* for L *commodus,* as prec.]

commodity, *n.* an article which yields accommodation or convenience; an article of commerce; †convenience, expediency; advantage, profit. [F *commodité,* L *commoditās* (*commodus,* see COMMODE)]

commodore, *n.* an officer ranking above captain or below rear-admiral; by courtesy, the senior captain when two or more ships of war are in company; the president of a yacht-club; a captain of pilots; the leading ship or the senior captain of a fleet of merchantmen. [formerly *commandore* (etym. obscure, from L *commandāre,* to COMMAND)]

Commodus, *n.* **Lucius Aelius Aurelius** (AD 161–192), Roman emperor from 180, son of Marcus Aurelius Antoninus. He was a tyrant, spending lavishly on gladiatorial combats, confiscating the property of the wealthy, persecuting the Senate, and renaming Rome 'Colonia Commodia'. There were many attempts against his life, and he was finally strangled at the instigation of his mistress and advisors, who had discovered themselves on the emperor's death list.

common, *a.* belonging equally to more than one; open or free to all; pertaining to or affecting the public; often met with, ordinary, usual; of low rank, position or birth; vulgar; inferior, mean; (*Math.*) belonging to several quantities; (*Gram.*) applicable to a whole class; (*Pros.*) variable in quantity. *n.* a tract of open ground, the common property of all members of a community; (*Law*) conjoint possession. *v.i.* †to participate in; †to confer, to discuss; to have a right in common ground; to board together. **above the common,** superior to most. **in common,** equally with another or others. **out of the common,** extra-ordinary, unusual. **right of common,** the right to pasture cattle, dig turf, cut wood, fish etc., on the property of another. **common carrier** CARRIER. **common chord,** a note accompanied by its third and fifth. **common cold,** *n.* a viral infection of the mucous membranes of the respiratory tract, accompanied by sneezing and coughing. **common council,** *n.* the governing body of a city or corporate town. **common councilman,** *n.* **common crier,** *n.* the public or town crier. **common era,** *n.* the Christian era. **common gender,** *n.* applied to a word used both for the masculine and the feminine. **common ground,** *n.* matter in a discussion accepted by both sides. †**common hackneyed,** *a.* hackneyed. **common jury,** *n.* (*Law*) a petty jury to try all cases. **common law,** *n.* the unwritten law, based on immemorial usage. **common-law husband, wife,** *n.* a person recognized as a husband or wife after long cohabitation. **common lawyer,** *n.* **common market,** *n.* the European Economic Community. **common measure,** *n.* (*Math.*) a number which will divide two or more numbers exactly; (*Mus.*) common time, two or four beats to the bar, esp. four crotchets to the bar. **common metre,** *n.* a metre for hymns, four lines of 8, 6, 8, 6 syllables. **common multiple,** *n.* any number containing two or more numbers an exact number of times without a remainder. **common noun,** *n.* the name of any one of a class of objects. **common or garden,** *a.* (*coll.*) ordinary. **Common Pleas,** *n.* a division of the High Court of Justice with a civil jurisdiction only (abolished 1875). **Common Prayer,** see separate entry. **common room,** *n.* a room in a college or school to which teachers or students resort for social purposes. **common sense,** *n.* sound practical judgment; the general feeling of mankind; the system of philosophy founded by Reid, based on general intuitions. **common-sense, -sensical,** *a.* marked by common sense. **Common Serjeant,** *n.* the judge of the City of London ranking next to the Recorder. **common time,** *n.* (*Mus.*) time with two beats, or any multiple of two beats, in a bar. **commonweal,** *n.* the welfare of the community. **commonish,** *a.* **commonly,** *adv.* usually, frequently; meanly, cheaply; in an ordinary manner; †jointly. **commonness,** *n.* [OF *comun,* L *commūnīs* (*-mūnis,* bound, earlier *moenis,* obliging, ready to serve)]

commonable, *a.* held in common; that may be pastured on common land. **commonage,** *n.* the right of using anything in common; the right of pasturing cattle on a common; common property in land; common land; commonalty.

Common Agricultural Policy, (CAP) a system that allows the member countries of the European Community (EC) jointly to organize and control agricultural production within their boundaries.

commonalty, *n.* the common people; mankind in general; a commonwealth; a corporation. [OF *comunalté,* from *comunal,* L *communālis*]

commoner, *n.* one of the commonalty, below the rank of a peer; a member of the House of Commons; a student at Oxford or Winchester not on the foundation; one having a joint right in common ground; †a prostitute.

commoney, *n.* a clay marble.

commonplace, *a.* common, trivial, trite, unoriginal. *n.* a general idea; a trite remark; anything occurring frequently or habitually. †*v.t.* to arrange under general heads; to enter in a commonplace-book. †*v.i.* to indulge in platitudes. **commonplace-book,** *n.* a book in which thoughts, extracts from books etc. are entered for future use. **commonplaceness,** *n.* [cp. L *locus communis,* a common topic]

Common Prayer, Book of, the service book of the Church of England, based largely on the Roman breviary. The first Book of Common Prayer in English was known as the First Prayer Book of Edward VI, published in 1549, and is the basis of the Book of Common Prayer still, although not exclusively, in use.

commons, *n.pl.* the common people; the House of Commons; food provided at a common table; a ration or allowance of food; fare. **Doctors' Commons,** a college near St Paul's Cathedral, London, for professors of civil law, where they used to common together; the buildings occupied by them, which included a court, registry of wills and office for marriage licences. **House of Commons,** the lower House of Parliament in the British and some other constitutions, the third estate of the realm. **short commons,** a scanty allowance of food.

commonty, *n.* (*Sc. Law*) Land belonging to two or more common proprietors; a common; †the commonalty, the commonwealth. [OF *communeté,* COMMUNITY]

commonweal COMMON.

commonwealth, *n.* the whole body of citizens; the body politic; a free state; a republic; (*Hist.*) the form of government in England from the death of Charles I (1649), to the abdication of Richard Cromwell (1659); the federation of Australian States; (*fig.*) a body of persons having common interests; the Commonwealth of Nations; †the commonweal. **commonwealthsman,** *n.* one who supported the English Commonwealth. [cp. L *res publica*]

Commonwealth conference, *n.* any consultation between the prime ministers (or defence, finance, foreign or other ministers) of the sovereign independent members of the Commonwealth. These are informal discussion meetings, and the implementation of policies is decided by individual governments.

Commonwealth Day, *n.* a public holiday in parts of the Commonwealth, celebrated on the second Monday in March (the official birthday of Elizabeth II). It was called **Empire Day** until 1958 and celebrated on 24 May (Queen Victoria's birthday) until 1966.

Commonwealth Development, Corporation an

organization founded as the Colonial Development Corporation in 1948 to aid the development of dependent Commonwealth territories; the change of name and extension of its activities to include those now independent were announced in 1962.

Commonwealth Games, *n. pl.* a multi-sport gathering of competitors from Commonwealth countries. Held every four years, the first meeting (known as the British Empire Games) was at Hamilton, Canada, Aug. 1930.

Commonwealth of Nations, the (British), a voluntary association of 48 states that have been or still are ruled by Britain. Independent states are full 'members of the Commonwealth', while dependent territories, such as colonies and protectorates, rank as 'Commonwealth countries'. Small self-governing countries, such as Nauru, may have special status. The Commonwealth is founded more on tradition and sentiment than political or economic factors. Queen Elizabeth II is the formal head, and its secretariat, headed from Oct. 1989 by Nigerian Emeka Anyaoko as secretary-general, is based in London.

commotion, *n.* violent motion; agitation, excitement; a popular tumult. [OF *comocion,* L *commōtio -ōnem* (*motio,* from *movēre,* to move)]

commove, *v.t.* to disturb, to agitate, to excite. [F *commovoir,* L *commovēre,* as prec.]

commune¹, *n.* a small territorial district in France and Belgium governed by a mayor and council; the inhabitants or members of the council of a commune; a group of people, not related, living together and sharing property and responsibilities; the house used by such a group. **the Paris Commune,** (*Hist.*) the revolutionary committee who replaced the municipality in 1789; the communistic body who took possession of Paris in 1871 after its evacuation by the Germans. **communal,** *a.* pertaining to a commune; for the common use or benefit; shared; pertaining to the Paris Commune; pertaining to the community or to the commons. **communalism,** *n.* the theory of government by communes of towns and districts; the theory or practice of living in communes. **communalist,** *n.* **communalistic,** *a.* **communalize, -ise,** *v.t.* **communally,** *adv.* **communard,**, *n.* an adherent of the Paris Commune; one who lives in a commune. [F, from late L *commūnia,* neut. pl. of *commūnis,* COMMON]

commune², *v.i.* to converse together familiarly, to hold converse with one's heart; (*N Am.*) to receive Holy Communion. *n.*, Communion; intimate converse. **communer,** *n.* [OF *comunier,* L *commūnicāre* (*commūnis,* COMMON)]

communicate, *v.t.* to impart, to give a share of, to transmit; to reveal; to give Holy Communion to. *v.i.* to share; to hold intercourse, to confer by speech or writing; to be connected, to open into; to partake of the Holy Communion; to establish mutual understanding (with someone). **communicable,** *a.* capable of being communicated or imparted. **communicability, -ableness,** *n.* **communicably,** *adv.* **communicant,** *a.* communicating; (*Anat.*) branching from or communicating with. *n.* one who communicates (information etc.); one who partakes of Holy Communion. **communication,** *n.* the act of communicating; that which is communicated; news; intercourse; means of passing from one place to another; a connecting link; (*pl.*) (the science of) means of communicating considered collectively (e.g. telecommunications, the press etc.); (*pl.*) (*Mil.*) a system of routes and vehicles for transport. **communication cord,** *n.* device whereby a passenger can stop a train in an emergency. **communication lines,** *n.pl.* the means of communication between an army and its base. **communications satellite,** *n.* an artificial satellite orbiting round the earth and relaying television, telephone etc. signals. **communicative,** *a.* inclined to communicate; not reserved. **communicatively,** *adv.* **communicativeness,** *n.* **communicator,** *n.* one who or that which imparts or informs; apparatus for sending a telegraphic message; apparatus on a train for communicating with the guard or driver; (*sl.*) a bell. **communicatory,** *a.* [L *commūnicāre* (*commūnis,* COMMON)]

communion, *n.* the act of communicating or communing; participation, sharing; fellowship, intercourse; union in religious faith; the act of partaking of the Eucharist; a religious body. **Holy Communion,** the administration of the Eucharist. **communion service,** *n.* the service used at the celebration of the Eucharist. **communion table,** *n.* the table (often called in the Church of England the altar) used in the celebration of the Eucharist. **communionist,** *n.* one having special views upon admission to Holy Communion. **close communionist,** *n.* one who would restrict partakers to those who are members of a particular church. **fellow-communionist,** *n.* a member of the same body of communicants. **open communionist,** one who believes in free and unrestricted admission to Holy Communion. [F, from L *commūnio -ōnem* (*commūnis,* COMMON)]

communiqué, *n.* an official announcement. [F]

communism, *n.* a theory of government based on common ownership of all property and means of production; the system of government, based on Marxist socialism, practised in the USSR etc. **communist,** *n., a.* an adherent of, or pertaining to, communism. **communistic,** *a.* **communize, -ise,** *v.t.* to make communal or communistic. [L *commūnis,* common]

Communism Peak, *n.* (Russian **Pik Kommunizma**) highest mountain in the USSR, in the Pamir range in Tadzhikistan; 7495 m/24,599 ft.

community, *n.* a body of people having common rights or interests; an organized body, municipal, national, social or political; society at large, the public; a body of individuals living in a common home; a body of individuals having common interests, occupation, religion, nationality etc.; common possession or enjoyment; fellowship; identity of nature or character; (*Ecol.*) a set of interdependent plants and animals inhabiting an area. **community centre,** *n.* a building open to all residents in the locality who can come there to enjoy social, recreative and educational activities. **community charge,** *n.* a flat-rate tax levied on all adults to raise money for local government, a poll tax. **community home,** *n.* a boarding school for young offenders. **community radio,** *n.* radio broadcasting to a smaller audience than local radio, to a town or part of a city. **community service order,** *n.* a form of sentence ordering a convicted person to work for a specified time for the benefit of the community. **community singing,** *n.* organized singing by the audience at a social gathering etc. [OF *communeté,* L *commūnitātem,* acc. of *commūnitās* (*commūnis,* COMMON]

commute, *v.t.* to put one for the other; to exchange, to substitute one (payment, punishment etc.) for another; to reduce the severity of (a punishment); to commutate. *v.i.* to travel (a considerable distance) daily to and from one's place of work. **commutable,** *a.* **commutability,** *n.* **commutate,** *v.t.* to reverse the direction of (an electric current); to convert (an alternating current) to a direct current. **commutation,** *n.* the act of commuting or commutating; change, exchange; a payment made in commuting; (*Law*) the substitution of a less penalty for a greater. **Commutation Act,** *n.* an enactment passed in 1836 substituting payment in money for tithes instead of payment in kind. **commutation ticket,** *n.* (*N Am.*) a season ticket. **commutative,** *a.* **commutatively,** *adv.* **commutator,** an instrument which reverses an electric current without changing the arrangement of the conductors. **commutator transformer,** *n.* a device for converting from low to high voltage direct current and vice versa. **commuter,** *n.* one who commutes to and from work. [L *commūtāre, mūtāre,* to change)]

Comoros, *n. pl.* Federal Islamic Republic of (*République fédérale islamique des Comores*), a group of islands situated in the Indian Ocean between Madagascar and the E coast of Africa. One island in the group, Mayotte, is a French dependency. **area** 1862 sq km/719 sq miles. **capital** Moroni. **physical** comprises the islands of Njazídja, Nzwani and Mwali (formerly Grand Comoro, Anjouan, Maheli); poor soil. **exports** copra, vanilla, cocoa, sisal, coffee, cloves, essential oils. **population** (1987) 423,000; annual growth rate 3.1%. **language** Comorian (Swahili and Arabic dialect), Makua, French, Arabic (official). **religion** Muslim (official).

comose COMATE.

comp.[1], *n.* short for COMPOSITOR, ACCOMPANIMENT.

comp.[2] (*abbr.*) company; comparative; comparison; competition.

compact[1], *n.* an agreement, a bargain, a covenant; (*N Am.*) a middle-sized motor car. [L *compactus,* p.p. of *compacīsci* (*pacīsci,* to covenant)]

compact[2], *a.* closely packed or joined together; solid, succinct. *n.* a small box with face-powder, puff and mirror. *v.t.* to consolidate; to join closely and firmly together; to compose. **compact disk,** *n.* a small audio disk, read by laser beam, on which sound is stored digitally as microscopic pits. **compacted,** *a.* **compactedly,** *adv.* **compactedness,** *n.* †**compactile**, *a.* **compaction,** *n.* **compactly,** *adv.* **compactness,** *n.* **compacture**, *n.* compact structure; close union of parts. [L *compactus,* p.p. of *compingere* (*pangere,* to fasten)]

compages, *n.* (*pl.* **compages**) a structure or system of many parts united. [L, joining together (*pag-,* root of *pangere,* as COMPACT[2])]

compaginate, *v.t.* to unite together in a structure or system. **compagination,** *n.* [L *compāginātus,* p.p. of *compāginare* (*compāgo -inem, compāges*)]

companion[1], *n.* one who associates or keeps company with another; a comrade; a partner; a member of the lowest grade in some orders of knighthood; a person employed to live with another; a handbook. *a.* accompanying; going along with or matching something. *v.t.* to accompany. *v.i.* to go or consort (with). **companionate marriage,** *n.* cohabitation with a view to marriage. **companionable,** *a.* fit to be a companion; sociable. **companionableness,** *n.* **companionably,** *adv.* †**companionage,** *n.* **companionless,** *a.* **companionship,** *n.* fellowship, association, company; (*Print.*) formerly, a body of compositors engaged on the same work. [OF *compaignon,* late L *compānio -ōnem* (*pānis,* bread)]

companion[2], *n.* (*Naut.*) the raised window-frame upon the quarter-deck through which light passes to the cabins and decks below. **companion-hatch,** *n.* in small ships, a porch over the entrance to the cabin. **companion-ladder,** *n.* the ladder leading from the cabin to the quarter-deck. **companion-stairs, -way,** *n.* the staircase or porch of the ladder-way from the cabin to the quarter-deck. [ult. from L *compānāticum,* provisions (cp. Dut. *kompanje,* OF *compagne,* It. *compagna, camera della compagna,* provision-room or pantry)]

Companion of Honour, British order of chivalry, founded by George V in 1917. It is of one class only, and carries no title, but Companions append 'CH' to their names. The number is limited to 65 and the award is made to both men and women.

company, *n.* society, companionship, fellowship; a number of persons associated together by interest or for carrying on business; a corporation; associates, guests, visitors; a body of actors engaged at a theatre; a subdivision of an infantry regiment under the command of a captain. †*v.t.* to accompany. †*v.i.* to associate (with), †to be a cheerful companion. **ship's company,** the crew of a ship. **to keep company (with),** to associate (with); to woo. [OF *compaignie,* from *compaignon,* see prec.]

comparative, *a.* involving comparison; estimated by comparison; grounded on comparison; expressing comparison, expressing a higher or lower degree of a quality. *n.* (*Gram.*) the comparative degree or the word or inflection expressing it. **comparative anatomy,** *n.* the general phenomena of organic structure derived from the anatomy of all organized bodies. **comparatively,** *adv.* **comparator,** *n.* an apparatus for comparing [as foll.]

compare, *v.i.* to show how one thing agrees with another; to liken one thing to another; to see how two things resemble each other or are mutually related; (*Gram.*) to inflect according to degrees of comparison. *v.i.* to bear comparison. *n.* comparison; an equal. **beyond compare,** peerless, unequalled. **to compare notes,** to exchange opinions. **comparable**, *a.* capable of being compared (with); worthy of being compared (to). **comparability**, *n.* [OF *comparer,* L *comparāre* (COM-, *par,* equal)]

comparison, *n.* the act of comparing; a comparative estimate; a simile, contrast, illustration; (*Gram.*) the inflection of an adjective or adverb. †*v.t.* to compare. [OF *comparaison,* L *comparātio -ōnem,* as prec.]

compart, *v.i.* to divide into compartments; to partition. †**compartition**, *n.* **compartment,** *n.* a division; a portion of a railway carriage, room etc., separated from the other parts; a portion of the hold of a ship shut off by a bulkhead and capable of being made watertight. **compartmental**, *a.* **compartmentalize, -ise,** *v.t.* to divide into separate units or categories. [OF *comparir,* late L *compartīre* (COM-, *partīre,* from *pars, -tis,* part)]

compass, *n.* a circle, circumference, area, extent; a circuit, a roundabout course; (*fig.*) reach, capacity; the range or power of the voice or a musical instrument; an instrument indicating the magnetic meridian, used to ascertain direction, and esp. to determine the course of a ship, aeroplane etc.; the mariner's compass; (*pl.*) an instrument with two legs connected by a joint for describing circles, measuring distances etc. *v.t.* to go round; to besiege, surround, invest; to comprehend; to accomplish, to contrive; to plot. **beam-compass** BEAM. **bow-compasses** BOW[2]. **gyro-compass** GYRO. **to box the compass** BOX[2]. **to fetch a compass,** to make a circuit. **compass-card,** *n.* the card or dial of a mariner's compass on which the points are drawn. **compass-needle,** *n.* the needle of the mariner's compass. **compass-plane,** *n.* (*Carp.*) a plane convex underneath for planing concave surfaces. **compass-saw,** *n.* a saw which cuts circularly. **compass-signal,** *n.* (*Naut.*) a flag indicating a point of the compass. **compass-timber,** *n.* curved timber used in shipbuilding. **compass-window,** *n.* a semicircular window. **compassable,** *a.* [F *compas,* a circle, a round, a pair of compasses, late L *compassus,* a circle, a circuit; later, a pair of compasses (cp. *compassāre,* to pace round, encompass; relation to *compassus* obscure)]

compassion, *n.* suffering with another; pity, sympathy for the sufferings and sorrows of others; an act of pity or mercy. †*v.i.* to compassionate. **compassion fatigue,** *n.* the state of being unwilling to contribute to charities because of the apathy etc. induced by the sheer number of charities and the promotion of these. **compassionable,** *a.* **compassionate**, *a.* merciful, inclined to pity; sympathetic. *v.t.*, to feel compassion for; to commiserate. **compassionate leave,** *n.* leave granted on account of domestic difficulties. **compassionately,** *adv.* **compassionateness,** *n.* †**compassive**, *a.* compassionate. [OF, from L *compassio -ōnem,* from *compatī* (COM-, *patī,* to suffer)]

compatible, *a.* that may coexist; congruous, consistent, harmonious; of electronic machinery of different types or by different manufacturers,, able to work together without modification. **compatibly,** *adv.* **compatibility**, *n.* [F, from late L *compatibilis,* from *compatī,* see prec.]

compatriot, *n.* a fellow-countryman. **compatriotic**, *a.* **compatriotism,** *n.* [F *compatriote*]

compear, *v.i.* (*Sc. Law*) to appear in court in person or by counsel. **compearance,** *n.* [F *comparoir,* L *compārēre* (*pārēre,* to appear)]

compeer, *n.* an equal, mate, peer. *v.t.* to equal, to be the peer of. [prob. from an OF *comper,* L *compar*]

compel, *v.t.* (*past, p.p.* **compelled**) to force, to oblige; to cause by force; to drive with force; †to take by force, to extort, exact; †to call, to gather together by force. **compellable,** *a.* **compelling,** *a.* very interesting. **compellingly,** *adv.* [OF *compeller,* L *compellere* (*pellere,* to drive)]

compellation, *n.* style of address; appellation. **compellative**, *n.* the name by which one is addressed. [L *compellātio -ōnem,* from *compellāre* (COM-, *pellāre,* freq. of *pellere,* see prec. and cp. *appellāre,* APPELLATION)]

compendium, *n.* (*pl.* **-diums**, **-dia**) an abridgment; a brief compilation; an epitome, a summary; a collection of board or card games in one box. **compend**, *n.* a compendium. **compendious,** *a.* abridged; summed up in a short compass; summary; succinct. **compendiously,** *adv.* **compendiousness,** *n.* [L, from *compendere* (*pendere,* to hang, weigh)]

compensate, *v.t.* to counterbalance; to make amends for; to recompense; (*Mech.*) to furnish with an equivalent weight or other device forming a compensation. *v.i.* to supply an equivalent; (*Psych.*) to make up for a perceived or imagined deficiency by developing another aspect of the personality. **compensation,** *n.* the act of compensating; payment, recompense, amends; that which balances or is an equivalent for something else; payment of a debt by an equal credit; a set-off. **compensation balance, pendulum,** *n.* a watch-balance or a pendulum constructed so as to make equal time-beats notwithstanding changes of temperature. **compensational,** *a.* **compensative**, *a.* compensating, *n.* an equivalent. **compensator,** *n.* **compensatory,** *a.* †**compense,** *v.t., v.i.* [L *compensātus,* p.p. of *compensāre* (*pensāre,* freq. of *pendere,* to weigh)]

compere, *n.* one who introduces the items in a (stage or broadcast) entertainment. *v.t., v.i.* to act as compere (of). [F]

compesce, *v.t.* to hold in check. [L *compescere*]

compete, *v.i.* to contend as a rival; to strive in emulation. [F *compéter,* L *competere* (*petere,* to fall upon, aim at)]

competent, *a.* qualified, sufficient; suitable, adequate; legally qualified; (*coll.*) admissible, permissible. **competence, -ency,** *n.* the state of being competent; sufficiency; adequate pecuniary support; the innate ability to acquire and understand language; legal capacity or qualification; admissibility (of evidence); ability (for or to do some task). **competently,** *adv.* [F from L *competens -entem,* pres.p. of *competere,* to COMPETE]

competition, *n.* the act of competing; rivalry; the struggle for existence or gain in industrial and mercantile pursuits; a competitive game or match; people or organizations competing against one. **competitioner,** *n.* a competitor; a person securing admission to a service by competition. **competitive,** *a.* pertaining to or involving competition; liking competition; of prices etc., such as to give one an advantage against competitors. **competitively,** *adv.* **competitiveness,** *n.* **competitor**, *n.* one who competes; a rival. **competitory**, *a.* [L *competitio,* from *competere,* COMPETE]

compile, *v.t.* to compose out of materials from various authors; to assemble various items as in an index or dictionary; to gather such materials into a volume; †to compose; †to comprise; (*Comput.*) to put (a program or instruction written in a high-level language) into machine code. **compilation**, †**compilement,** *n.* the act of compiling; that which is compiled; a book for which the materials have been drawn from various authors. **compiler,** *n.* one who compiles; (*Comput.*) a program which compiles. [OF *compiler,* L *compīlāre,* to plunder, to pillage (COM-, *pīlāre,* to thrust, from *pīlum,* a javelin)]

complacent, *a.* satisfied, gratified, self-satisfied. **complacently,** *adv.* **complacence, -ency,** *n.* a feeling of inward satisfaction; smugness; †the object which produces such satisfaction; †complaisance. [L *complacens -ntem,* pres.p. of *complacēre* (COM-, *placēre,* to please)]

complain, *v.i.* to express dissatisfaction or objection; to state a grievance; to make a charge; to murmur, to find fault; to express grief or pain, hence, to ail; to moan or wail. †*v.t.* to mourn over, bewail. **complainant,** *n.* one who complains or makes complaint; a plaintiff. **complaining,** *a.* that complains; querulous. *n.* a complaint. **complainingly,** *adv.* **complaint,** *n.* an expression of grief or pain, resentment or censure; the subject or ground of such expression; an accusation; a malady; (*Law*) a formal allegation or charge, an information. [OF *complaign-,* stem of *complaindre,* late L *complangere* (COM-, *plangere,* to bewail)]

complaisant, *a.* courteous, obsequious, obliging. **complaisantly,** *adv.* **complaisance,** *n.* [F]

compleat, COMPLETE (skilled).

complect, *v.t.* to knit together. **complected,** *a.* [L *complecti* (*plectere,* to twine)]

complement, *n.* full quantity; †completeness, perfection; the full number required to man a vessel; that which is necessary to make complete; a word or phrase required to complete the sense, the predicate; the interval necessary to complete an octave; (*Math.*) the difference between a given angle or arc and 90°; (*Math.*) the difference between a number and the next higher power of ten. *v.t.* to supply a deficiency; to complete. **complemental**, *a.* **complementally,** *adv.* **complementary**, *a.* that complements. **complementary colour,** *n.* a colour which produces white when mixed with another to which it is complementary. **complementary medicine,** *n.* alternative medicine. [L *complēmentum,* from *complēre* (*plēre,* to fill)]

complete, *a.* fulfilled, finished; free from deficiency; entire, absolute; skilled, highly accomplished. *v.t.* to bring to a state of perfection; to finish; to make whole, to make up the deficiencies of. **completely,** *adv.* **completeness,** *n.* **completion,** *n.* **completive,** *a.* [L *complētus,* p.p. of *complēre,* as prec.]

complex, *a.* composed of several parts; composite; complicated. *n.* a complicated whole; a collection; a complicated system; a group of emotions, ideas etc., partly or wholly repressed, which can influence personality or behaviour; (*loosely*) an obsession; a set of interconnected buildings for related purposes, forming a whole. **inferiority complex,** an intense conviction of inferiority, resulting either in a timid attitude or an assumed aggressiveness. **complex number,** *n.* one consisting of a real and an imaginary component. **complex sentence,** *n.* one consisting of a principal clause and at least one subordinate clause. †**complexed**, *a.* complex. **complexedness**, *n.* **complexity**, *n.* **complexly,** *adv.* **complexus**, *n.* a long, broad muscle lying along the back and side of the neck. [L *complexus,* p.p. of *complectere,* COMPLECT]

complexion, *n.* †the temperament or constitution; colour and appearance of the skin, esp. of the face; nature, character, aspect. **complexioned,** *a. usu. in comb.* **complexionless,** *a.* [F, from L *complexio -ōnem,* a comprehending; later, a bodily habit or combination of qualities (*complectere,* as prec.)]

complexity, complexus COMPLEX.

compliance, *n.* the act of complying; submission, agreement, consent. **compliable,** *a.* compliant. **compliant,** *a.* yielding; tending to comply. **compliantly,** *adv.* [COMPLY]

complicate, *v.t.* to make complex or intricate; to involve. **complicacy,** *n.* the state of being complicated. **complicated,** *a.* **complicatedly,** *adv.* **complication,** *n.* the act of complicating; the state of being complicated; a complicated or complicating matter or circumstance; a disease or morbid condition arising in the course of another disease. [L *complicātus,* p.p. of *complicāre* (*plicāre,* to fold)]

†**complice,** *n.* an accomplice. [F, from L *complex -icem,* confederate, lit. intertwined (see COMPLEX)]

complicity, *n.* participation, partnership, esp. in wrong-doing. [F *complicité,* from *complice,* as prec.]

complier COMPLY.

compliment, *n.* an expression or act of courtesy, approbation, respect or regard; delicate flattery; †a favour, a gift, a gratuity; (*pl.*) ceremonious greetings; courtesies, respects. *v.t.,* to pay compliments to; to congratulate, to praise, to flatter courteously. *v.i.,* to pay compliments. **compliments of the season,** greetings or remembrances appropriate to the season. **complimental**, *a.* **complimentary**, *a.* **complimentary ticket,** *n.* a free ticket. [F, from It. *complimento,* from L *complēmentum,* COMPLEMENT (perh. through Sp. *complimiento,* fulfilment of courtesies)]

compline, *n.* in the Roman Catholic Church, the last part of the divine office of the breviary, sung after vespers. [ME and OF *complie,* L *complēta* (*hōra*), fem. of *complētus,* COMPLETE, because it completed the hours of daily service]

complot, *n.* a conspiracy or plot. *v.t.*, *v.i.*, to plot together; to combine together. [F, a crowd, a struggle, a plot (etym. unknown)]

compluvium, *n.* the opening in the roof of a Roman atrium which collected the rainwater. [L, from *compluere* (*pluere,* to rain)]

comply, *v.i.* to assent, to agree; to act in accordance with the wishes of another; †to fulfil; †to fulfil courtesies. **complier,** *n.* [It. *complire,* from Sp. *complir* (now *cumplir*), to complete (cp. COMPLIMENT)]

compo[1], *n.* (*pl.* **-pos**), applied to different compounds in various trades, as the material of which printers' rollers are made, a kind of stucco etc. **compo rations,** *n.pl.* (*Mil.*) rations for several days for use in the field. [COMPOSITION]

compo[2], *n.* (*pl.* **-pos**) (*Austral.*) short for COMPENSATION (for injury etc.).

component, *a.* serving to make up a compound; a constituent. *n.* a constituent part. **componential**, *a.* [L *compōnens -ntem,* pres.p. of *compōnere* (*pōnere,* to put)]

comport, *v.t.* to conduct, to behave (oneself). *v.i.* to suit, to agree, to accord. *n.* manner of behaving. **comportment,** *n.* behaviour, conduct, bearing. [F *comporter,* late L *comportāre* (*portāre,* to carry)]

compose, *v.t.* to make, arrange or construct, by putting together several parts, so as to form one whole; to constitute, to make up by combination; to write, construct or produce (as a literary or musical work); to write music for given words; to calm, to soothe; to settle, to adjust; to arrange in proper order (as type for printing). *v.i.* to practise composition. **composed,** *a.* calm, tranquil, settled. **composedly**, *adv.* **composedness**, *n.* **composer,** *n.* one who composes, esp. the author of a musical composition. **composing,** *a.* that composes. *n.* the action of the verb TO COMPOSE. **composing-frame,** *n.* (*Print.*) an elevated frame on which the cases of type rest obliquely. **composing-machine,** *n.* a machine for setting type. **composing-room,** *n.* the room in a printing-office where the compositors work. **composing-stick,** *n.* an instrument in which the compositor sets the type from the cases, and adjusts the lines to the proper length. [F *composer* (*com-,* with, and *poser,* from late L *pausāre,* to cease, to place, to pose)]

Compositae, *n.* the daisy family; dicotyledonous flowering plants characterized by flowers borne in composite heads. It is the largest family of flowering plants, the majority being herbaceous. Birds seem to favour the family for use in nest 'decoration', possibly because many species either repel or kill insects. Species include the daisy and dandelion; food plants such as the artichoke, lettuce and safflower; and the garden chrysanthemum, dahlia, daisybush and zinnia.

composite, *a.* made up of distinct parts or elements; compound; pertaining to the Compositae, (see above). *n.* a composite substance, plant or thing; a compound; a composite term;, a composited motion. *v.t.*, to merge related motions from different branches of e.g. a trade union, political party, for presentation to e.g. a national conference. **composite candle,** *n.* a candle made of stearin or coconut oil and stearic acid. **composite carriage,** *n.* a railway carriage containing compartments of different classes. **composite number,** *n.* a number which is the product of two other numbers greater than unity. **composite order,** *n.* (*Arch.*) the last of the five orders, which partakes of the characters of the Corinthian and Ionic. **composite resolution,** *n.* one made up from related resolutions from local branches (of a trade union etc.) and containing the main points of each of them. **compositely,** *adv.* **compositeness,** *n.* **compositive**, *a.* [L *compositus,* p.p. of *compōnere* (COM-, *pōnere,* to put)]

composition, *n.* the act of composing or putting together to form a whole; the thing composed (esp. used of literary and musical productions); orderly disposition of parts, structural arrangement, style; an agreement to terms or conditions for putting an end to hostilities or any contest or disagreement; a combination of several parts or ingredients, a compound; compensation in lieu of that demanded; settlement by compromise; the amount so accepted; the process of setting type; the act of forming sentences; a piece written for the sake of practice in literary expression; the formation of compound words; the arrangement of columns, piers, doors etc. in a building; the arrangement of different figures in a picture. **composition of forces,** the combining of several forces or motions into a single (resultant) force. **composition-metal,** *n.* a kind of brass for sheathing ships. **compositional,** *a.* [F, from L *compositio, -ōnem,* as prec.]

compositor, *n.* one who sets type.

compos mentis, *a.* in one's right mind. **non compos**, (*coll.*) not in one's right mind. [L, master of or controlling the mind]

compossible, *a.* capable of coexisting. [OF, from med. L *compossibilis*]

compost, *n.* a fertilizing mixture of vegetable matter etc.; a kind of concrete used by plasterers; stucco. *v.t.* to make into or manure with compost; to plaster. **compost heap,** *n.* a heap of waste plant material decomposing into compost. [OF *composte,* L *compositus*]

composure, *n.* calmness, tranquillity, a calm frame of mind. [COMPOSE, -URE]

compotation, *n.* the act of drinking together. **compotator**, *n.* [*compōtātio -ōnem* (*pōtātio,* from *pōtāre,* to drink)]

compote, *n.* fruit stewed or preserved in syrup. [F *compote,* OF *composte,* L *composta, composita,* fem. of *compositus*]

compound[1], *v.t.* to make into one mass by the combination of several constituent parts; to mix, to make up, to form a composite; to combine; to settle amicably; to adjust by agreement; to compromise; to pay a lump sum instead of a periodical subscription. *v.i.* to settle with creditors by agreement; †to bargain; to come to terms by abating something of the first demand. **to compound a felony,** (*Law*) to forbear to prosecute a felony for some valuable consideration. **compoundable,** *a.* capable of being combined; capable of being compounded or commuted. **compounder,** *n.* one who compounds or mixes; one who effects a compromise; one who compounds a debt or a felony; (*Eng. Hist.*) a trimmer; one in favour of the restoration of James II under constitutional guarantees. †**grand compounder,** one who paid large fees for his degree at Cambridge. [ME *compounen,* OF *componre, compondre,* L *compōnere* (*pōnere,* to put)]

compound[2], *a.* composed of two or more ingredients or elements; composed of two or more parts; collective, combined, composite; (*Biol.*) formed by a combination of parts or of several individual organisms. *n.* a combination, a mixture; a compound word; a combination of two or more elements by chemical action. **compound addition, subtraction,** *n.* processes dealing with numbers of different denominations. **compound animal,** *n.* one consisting of a combination of organisms. **compound engine, locomotive** etc., *n.* an engine with one or more additional cylinders of larger diameter into which the steam passes and does further work after leaving the first cylinder. **compound eye,** *n.* one made up of many separate light sensitive units (as in insects). **compound flower,** *n.* an inflorescence consisting of numerous florets surrounded by an involucre; one of the flower-heads of any of the Compositae. **compound fracture,** *n.* a fracture in which the integuments are injured, usually by the protrusion of the bone. **compound fructification,** *n.* a fructification composed of confluent florets. **compound householder,** *n.* one who compounds with his or her landlord for the rates. **compound interest,** *n.* interest added to the principal and bearing interest; the method of computing such interest. **compound interval,** *n.* (*Mus.*) an interval greater than the octave. **compound leaf,** *n.* a leaf with branched petioles. **compound microscope,** *n.* a microscope with a combination of lenses. **compound quantity,** *n.* an arithmetical quantity of more than one denomination; an algebraic quantity, consisting of two or more terms connected by the signs + (plus), or – (minus), or expressed by more letters than one. **compound raceme,** *n.* a raceme composed of several small ones. **compound ratio,** *n.* (*Arith.*) the ratio which the product of the antecedents of two or more ratios has to the product of their consequents. **compound sentence,** *n.* one consisting of two or more principal clauses.

compound3**,** *n.* the yard or space surrounding a dwelling-house in India, China etc.; any similar walled or fenced space, as in a prison. **compound system,** *n.* a system of housing and feeding indentured and other labourers, as on the Rand. [Malayalam KAMPONG]

comprador, *n.* (*China and Japan*) a native employed in European houses of business as general factotum and intermediary with native customers. [Port., from late L *comparātor -tōrem,* from *comparāre,* to provide, to purchase]

comprehend, *v.t.* to grasp mentally; to understand; to comprise, to include; †(*erron.*) to apprehend. **comprehensible,** *a.* that may be comprehended; clear, intelligible; †that may be comprised. **comprehensibility,** *n.* **comprehensibly,** *adv.* [L *comprehendere* (*prae-,* beforehand, *hendere,* obs., to seize]

comprehension, *n.* the act or power of comprehending or comprising; the faculty by which ideas are comprehended by the intellect; (*Log.*) the sum of the attributes which a term implies; (*Eccles.*) inclusion of all Christians in one communion; also **comprehension test,** a school exercise to test a pupil's understanding of a given passage. **comprehensive,** *a.* extending widely; including much or many things; having the power of grasping many things at once with the intellect. **comprehensive school,** *n.* a secondary school serving all children of all abilities in an area. **comprehensively,** *adv.* **comprehensiveness,** *n.* [L *comprehensio -ōnem,* as prec.]

compress, *v.t.* to squeeze or press together; to bring into narrower limits; to condense; †to have carnal intercourse with. *n.,* (*Med.*) a soft pad used to preserve due pressure on an artery; a wet cloth for reducing inflammation. **compressible,** *a.* **compressibility,** *n.* **compression,** *n.* the act of compressing; the state of being compressed; condensation. **compression-spring,** *n.* a spring which opposes pressure. **compressive,** *a.* **compressor,** *n.* [OF *compresser,* L *compressāre*]

comprise, *v.t.* to contain, to include, to comprehend, to embrace; to bring (within certain limits). **comprisable,** *a.* [F *compris,* p.p. of *comprendre,* L *comprehendere,* COMPREHEND]

compromise, *n.* a settlement by mutual concession; adjustment of a controversy or of antagonistic opinions, principles or purposes by a partial surrender; a medium between conflicting purposes or courses of action. *v.t.* to settle by mutual concession; to place in a position of difficulty or danger; to expose to risk of disgrace. *v.i.* to make a compromise. **compromission,** *n.* compromise; submission to the decision of an arbitrator. [F *compromis,* p.p. of *compromettre,* L *comprōmittere* (COM-, *prōmittere,* PROMISE)]

Compromise of 1850, in US history, legislative proposals designed to resolve sectional conflict between north and south over the admission of California to the Union in 1850. Slavery was prohibited in California, but a new fugitive slave law was passed to pacify the slave states. The Senate debate on the compromise lasted nine months: acceptance temporarily revitalized the union.

†**compt** COUNT1.

†**compter** COUNTER1.

comptograph, *n.* a variety of calculating machine which sets down the results on paper. **Comptometer®,** *n.* a type of calculating machine. [F *compter*]

comptoir, *n.* a commercial agency or factory in a foreign country. [F, COUNTER1]

Compton, *n.* **Arthur Holly** (1892–1962), US physicist known for his work on X-rays. Working at Chicago 1923 he found that X-rays scattered by such light elements as carbon increased their wavelengths. Compton could only conclude from this unexpected result that the X-rays were displaying both wave-like and particle-like properties. For the discovery of the since named Compton effect, he shared the 1927 Nobel Physics prize with Charles Wilson.

Compton-Burnett, *n.* **Ivy** (1892–1969), English novelist. She used dialogue to show reactions of small groups of characters dominated by the tyranny of family relationships. Her novels set at the turn of the century include *Pastors and Masters* (1925), *More Women than Men* (1933), *Mother and Son* (1955).

comptroller CONTROLLER.

compulsion, *n.* the act of compelling by moral or physical force; constraint of the will; (*Psych.*) an irresistible impulse to perform actions against one's will. **compulsive,** †**compulsative,** *a.* involving compulsion; tending to compel. **compulsively,** †**compulsatively,** *adv.* **compulsiveness,** *n.* **compulsory,** *a.* **compulsory purchase,** *n.* purchase of a property against the owner's wishes, for a public development. **compulsatory,** *a.* exercising compulsion; enforced, necessitated. **compulsorily,** *adv.* [L *compulsio -ōnem* (*compellere,* COMPEL)]

compunction, *n.* pricking or reproach of conscience; remorse, contrition; regret. **compunctionless,** *a.* **compunctious,** *a.* **compunctiously,** *adv.* [OF from L *compunctio -ōnem,* from *compungere* (*pungere,* to prick)]

compurgation, *n.* vindication; evidence clearing one from a charge; (*Eng. Hist.*) a trial in which a number of persons declared the accused's innocence on oath. **compurgator,** *n.* **compurgatory,** *a.* [L *compurgātio -ōnem,* from *compurgāre* (*purgāre,* to purify)]

compute, *v.t.* to determine by calculation; to number, to estimate; to calculate using a computer. *v.i.* to calculate; to use a computer. **computable,** *a.* **computative,** *a.* **computation,** *n.* **computer,** *n.* an electronic device which does complex calculations or processes data according to the instructions contained in a program. **computer game,** *n.* a game of skill in which the player uses a computer keyboard to react to graphics on the screen. **computer graphics,** *n.pl.* visual images produced by a computer program on a screen, which can be manipulated and developed very rapidly, used in computer games and for simulators, etc.; (*sing. in constr.*) the design of programs to generate such images. **computer-language,** *n.* a programming language. **computer literacy,** *n.* ability to understand computers, their uses and working. **computer-literate,** *a.* **computer science,** *n.* the sciences connected with the construction and operation of computers. **computer system,** *n.* a self-contained unit consisting of items of hardware and the necessary software to carry out a particular range of tasks. **computer virus,** *n.* a self-replicating computer program which damages or destroys the memory or other programs of the host computer. **computerize, -ise,** *v.t.* to perform or control by means of computer; to install computers in (a business, etc.). *v.i.* to install computers. **computerization, -isation,** *n.* [F *computer,* L *computāre* (*putāre,* to think)]

comrade, *n.* a mate, a companion; an intimate associate. **comradeship,** *n.* [F *camarade,* Sp. *camarada,* a chamber-mate]

comsat, *n.* short for COMMUNICATIONS SATELLITE.

Comte, *n.* **Auguste** (1798–1857), French philosopher, regarded as the founder of sociology, a term he coined in 1830. He sought to establish sociology as an intellectual and 'scientific' discipline, using positivism as the basis of a new science of social order and social development. **Comtism**, *n.* the positivist philosophy of Auguste Comte. **Comtist,** *n.*

Comus, *n.* a Roman god of revelry; revelry; licentiousness. [L, from Gr. *kōmos,* a revel]

Con.[1], (*abbr.*) Conservative.

con.[2], (*abbr.*) conclusion; convenience; conversation.

con[3], *v.t.* (*past, p.p.* **conned**) to peruse carefully; to study over, to learn; to know. **to con thanks,** to be grateful. [OE *cunnian,* see CAN]

con[4], *v.t.* (*past, p.p.* **conned**) to direct the steering of (a ship). **conning-tower,** *n.* the armoured shelter in a warship or submarine from which the vessel is steered. **conner,** *n.* [prob. a form of *cond,* earlier *condue,* OF *conduire,* L *condūcere,* to CONDUCT]

con[5], *n., prep.* short for CONTRA. **pro** and **con,** for and against.

con[6], *n.* (*sl.*) a confidence trick; a fraud, swindle. *v.t.* to deceive; to swindle. **con-man,** *n.* **con trick,** *n.* [short for CONFIDENCE.]

con[7], *n.* (*sl.*) short for CONVICT[2].

con- COM-.

conacre, *n.* (*Ir.*) the practice of subletting land already prepared for cropping. [corr. of *cornacre*]

Conakry, *n.* the capital and chief port of the Republic of Guinea; population (1980) 763,000. It is on the island of Tumbo, linked with the mainland by a causeway and by rail with Kankan, 480 km/300 miles NE. Bauxite and iron ore are mined nearby.

conation, *n.* (*Phil.*) the faculty of desiring or willing. **conational,** *a.* **conative,** *a.* pertaining to conation. †**conatus,** *n.* an effort; an impulse in plants and animals analogous to human effort. [L *cōnātio -ōnem,* from *cōnārī,* to endeavour]

concamerate, *v.t.* to divide into chambers (as a shell); †to vault or arch. **concameration,** *n.* [L *concamerātus,* p.p. of *concamerāre* (*camera*)]

concatenate, *v.t.* to join or link together in a successive series. **concatenation,** *n.* [late L *concatēnātus,* p.p. of *concatēnāre* (*catēna,* a chain)]

concave, *a.* having a curve or surface hollow like the inner side of a circle or globe. *n.* a hollow curve; a hollow surface; an arch, a vault. *v.t.* (*poet.*) to make concave or hollow. **concavely,** *adv.* **concavity**, *n.* the state of being concave; the internal surface of a hollow spherical body. **concavous,** *a.*

concavo-, *comb. form.* (*Opt.*) concave; concavely. **concavo-concave**, *a.* concave on both sides. **concavo-convex,** *a.* concave on one side and convex on the other. [F, from L *concavus* (*cavus,* hollow)]

conceal, *v.t.* to hide or cover from sight or observation; to keep secret or hidden; to keep back from publicity or utterance. **concealable,** *a.* **concealment,** *n.* the act of concealing; the state of being concealed; a hiding-place; (*Law*) a suppression of material matters. [OF *conceler,* L *concēlāre* (*cēlāre,* to hide)]

concede, *v.t.* to yield, to give up, to surrender; to admit, to grant; to allow to pass unchallenged. *v.i.* to yield; to make concessions. [L *concēdere* (*cēdere,* to yield)]

conceit, *n.* a vain opinion of oneself, overweening self-esteem; a whim; a fanciful idea; in literature, an elaborate or far-fetched image; †a quaint or witty notion or turn of expression; †conception, opinion, judgment; †a thought, an idea. †*v.t.* to conceive; to imagine, to think; have a fancy for. †*v.i.* to form a notion; to conceive. **out of conceit with,** no longer fond of, or inclined to. **conceited,** *a.* full of conceit; inordinately vain; egotistical; †clever, witty. **conceitedly,** *adv.* **conceitedness,** *n.* †**conceitless,** *a.* dull, stupid, thoughtless. [L *concepta,* fem. p.p. of *concipere,* CONCEIVE (on anal. of DECEIT)]

conceive, *v.t.* to receive into and form in the womb; to form, as an idea or concept, in the mind; to imagine or suppose as possible; to think; to formulate clearly in the mind. *v.i.* to become pregnant; to form an idea or concept in the mind. **conceivable,** *a.* capable of being conceived in the mind. **conceivability**, *n.* **-ableness,** *n.* **conceivably,** *adv.* [OF *conceiv-,* stem of *concever,* L *concipere* (*capere,* to take)]

concelebrate, *v.i.* to celebrate (Mass or the Eucharist) along with another priest. **concelebrant,** *n.* **concelebration,** *n.* [L *concelebrātus* p.p. of *concelebrāre*]

†**concent,** *n.* a concord of voices; harmony. *v.t.* to harmonize. [L *concentus,* singing together, harmony, from *concinere* (CON-, *canere,* to sing)]

concentrate, *v.t.* to bring to a common focus, centre, or point; to reduce to a greater density by removing water, etc. *v.i.* to come to a common focus or centre; to direct all one's thoughts or efforts to one end. *a.* concentrated. *n.* a product of concentration; any concentrated substance, esp. a concentrated solution of a foodstuff. **concentration,** *n.* **concentration camp,** *n.* a camp for housing political prisoners and interned persons. **concentrative,** *a.* **concentrativeness,** *n.* the faculty of fixing the attention or thoughts on any one subject or point. **concentrator,** *n.* an apparatus for concentrating solutions; a pneumatic apparatus for separating dry comminuted ores. [CONCENTRE first in use, afterwards Latinized in form as if from a p.p. *concentrātus* (*concentrāre*)]

concentre, *v.t.* to draw or direct to a common centre. *v.i.* to have a common centre; to combine for a common object. **concentric,** *a.* having a common centre; (*Mil.*) concentrated. **concentric fire,** firing concentrated on the same point. **concentrically,** *adv.* **concentricity**, *n.* [F *concentrer*]

concentus, *n.* concordance, harmony; singing together or in harmony. [L]

concept, *n.* a general notion; (*Phil.*) a general notion or idea comprising all the attributes common to a class of things. **conception**, *n.* the act of conceiving; the impregnation of the ovum; (*Phil.*) the cognition of classes, as distinct from individuals; concept. **to have no conception of,** to be unable to imagine. **conceptional,** *a.* **conceptionist,** *n.* †**conceptious**, *a.* pregnant, fruitful. **conceptive**, *a.* [L *conceptum,* neut. p.p. of *concipere,* to CONCEIVE]

conceptacle, *n.* that in which anything is contained; (*Bot.*) a follicle; a surface cavity in fungi and algae in which reproductive bodies are produced; an analogous organ in animals of low organization. [L *conceptāculum,* dim. of *conceptum,* as prec.]

conceptual, *a.* (*Phil.*) belonging or relating to conception. **conceptualism,** *n.* the doctrine that universals exist only in the mind of the thinking subject (a doctrine intermediate between *nominalism* and *realism*). **conceptualist,** *n.* **conceptualize, -ise,** *v.t., v.i.* to form a concept (of). [med. L *conceptuālis,* from L *conceptus,* CONCEPT]

concern, *v.t.* to relate or belong to; to affect; to be of importance to; to interest; to disturb, to render uneasy. †*v.i.* to be of importance. *n.* that which affects or is of interest or importance to a person; interest, regard; anxiety, solicitude; a business, a firm, an establishment; a matter of personal importance; (*pl.*) affairs; (*coll.*) an affair, a thing. †**concernancy,** *n.* concern, business, import. **concerned,** *a.* interested, involved, engaged (with); anxious, solicitous (about); †muddled (with liquor). **concernedly**, *adv.* **concerning,** *prep.* with respect to. **concernment,** *n.* that which interests or concerns; an affair, a matter, business; importance. [F *concerner,* L *concernere* (*cernere,* to separate, sift), in med. L, to refer to, regard]

concert[1], *v.t.* to plan, to arrange mutually; to contrive, to adjust. **concerted,** *a.* mutually planned or devised; (*Mus.*) arranged in parts. [F *concerter,* It. *concertare,* to accord together (cp. Sp. *concertar,* to bargain), L *concertāre,* to dispute, contend (CON-, *certāre,* to vie)]

concert[2], *n.* harmony, accordance of plan or ideas; concord, harmonious union of sounds; a public musical entertainment. **in concert,** acting together; of musicians, performing live on stage. **concert grand,** *n.* a powerful grand piano for use at concerts. **concert party,** *n.* a group of companies or financiers engaged together in a (shady) project. **concert pitch,** *n.* (*Mus.*) the pitch used at concerts, slightly higher than the ordinary, for the sake of additional brilliancy; a high degree of readiness. [It. *concerto,* as prec.]

concertina, *n.* a portable instrument of the seraphine family, having a keyboard at each end, with bellows between. *v.i.* to collapse, fold up, like a concertina. [CONCERT[2]]

concertino, *n.* a short concerto. [It., dim. of CONCERTO]

concerto, *n.* a composition for a solo instrument or instruments with orchestral accompaniment. **concerto grosso**, *n.* a composition for an orchestra and a group of soloists playing together. [It.]

concession, *n.* the act of conceding; the thing conceded; esp. a privilege or right granted by a government for carrying out public works etc.; the (exclusive) right to market a particular product or service in a particular area; a subdivision of a township in Canada. **concessionnaire**, *n.* one who holds a concession from the government. **concessionary,** *a.* **concessive**, *a.* conceding; implying concession. [F, from L *concessio -ōnem,* from *concēdere,* to CONCEDE]

†**concetto,** *n.* (*pl.* **-ti**) affected wit. **concettism,** *n.* [It., from L *conceptum,* CONCEIT]

conch, *n.* a shellfish; a marine shell of a spiral form; a shell of this kind used as a trumpet; the domed roof of an apse, or the apse itself. **concha**, *n.* the largest and deepest concavity in the external ear; the concave ribless surface of a vault; the dome of an apse; an apse. **conchiferous**, *a.* shell-bearing. [L *concha,* Gr. *konche,* mussel, cockle]

conchie, conchy, *n.* (*coll. derog.*) short for CONSCIENTIOUS (objector).

conch(o)- *comb. form.* shell.

Conchobar, *n.* in Celtic mythology, king of Ulster whose intended bride, Deirdre, eloped with Noísi. She died of sorrow when Conchobar killed her husband and his brothers.

conchoid, *n.* (*Geom.*) a shell-like curve. **conchoidal**, *a.*

conchology, *n.* the branch of zoology that deals with shells and the animals inhabiting them. **conchological,** *a.* **conchologist,** *n.*

conchospiral, *n.* a spiral curve characteristic of certain shells.

concierge, *n.* a door-keeper, a porter, a janitor. [F]

conciliar, *a.* pertaining to a council, esp. an ecclesiastical council. [L *concilium,* COUNCIL]

conciliate, *v.t.* to win the regard or goodwill of; to gain over, to win; to reconcile (conflicting views or conflicting parties). **conciliation,** *n.* the act of conciliating; reconciliation of disputes, etc. **conciliative,** *a.* **conciliator,** *n.* **conciliatory,** *a.* **conciliatoriness,** *n.* [L *conciliātus,* p.p. of *conciliāre* (*concilium,* as prec.)]

concinnous, *a.* harmonious; elegant. **concinnity,** *n.* elegance, fitness, neatness, esp. of literary style. [L *concinnus,* well-adjusted]

concise, *a.* condensed, brief, terse. **concisely,** *adv.* **conciseness,** *n.* **concision**, *n.* conciseness; mutilation, a term applied by St Paul to the Judaizing teachers who insisted on the necessity of outward circumcision as distinct from change of heart; conciseness. [L *concīsus,* p.p. of *concīdere* (*caedere,* to cut)]

conclamation, *n.* a united or general outcry. [L *conclāmātio -ōnem,* from *conclāmāre* (*clāmāre,* to cry out)]

conclave, *n.* the assembly of cardinals met for the election of a pope; the apartment where they meet; a secret assembly. [F, from L *conclāve,* a room that may be locked (*clāvis,* key)]

conclude, *v.t.* to bring to an end, to finish; to determine, to settle; to gather as a consequence from reasoning, to infer. *v.i.* to make an end; to come to a decision; to draw an inference. **in conclusion,** to conclude. **to conclude,** in short, in fine. **to try conclusions,** to contest; to try which is superior. **concluding,** *a.* that concludes; final. **concludingly,** *adv.* **conclusion,** *n.* the end, the finish, the termination; the result; an inference; settlement (of terms etc.); a final decision; the inferential proposition of a syllogism; †experiment, an attempt. **conclusive,** *a.* that puts an end to argument, final. **conclusively,** *adv.* **conclusiveness,** *n.* **conclusory,** *a.* [L *conclūdere* (*claudere,* to shut)]

concoct, *v.t.* to prepare by mixing together; to plot, to devise; †to digest. **concoction,** *n.* the act of concocting; the thing concocted; a plan, plot, or design. **concoctive,** *a.* **concoctor,** *n.* [L *concoctus,* p.p. of *concoquere* (*coquere,* to cook)]

concolorous, *a.* (*Biol.*) uniform in colour. [L *concolor*]

concomitant, *a.* accompanying; existing in conjunction with. *n.* one who or that which accompanies. **concomitantly,** *adv.* **concomitance, -ancy,** *n.* the state of being concomitant; the doctrine of the presence in each element of the Eucharist of both the body and the blood of Christ. [L *concomitans -ntem,* pres.p. of *concomitārī* (*comitārī,* to accompany)]

concord, *n.* agreement; union in opinions, sentiments, or interests; the agreement of one word with another in number, gender etc.; a combination of notes satisfactory to the ear. **concordance**, *n.* the state of being concordant; agreement; a list of the words in a book (esp. in the Bible), with exact references to the places where they occur. **concordant**, *a.* in concord, harmony, or accord; agreeing, correspondent. **concordantly,** *adv.* [F *concorde,* L *concordia* (*cor cordis,* heart)]

concordat, *n.* a convention between a pope and a secular government. [F, from late L *concordātum,* p.p. of *concordāre,* to agree]

Concorde, *n.* the only successful supersonic airliner, which cruises at Mach 2, or twice the speed of sound, about 2170 kph/1350 mph. *Concorde,* the result of Anglo-French cooperation, made its first flight in 1969, and entered commercial service seven years later. It is 62 m/202 ft long and has a wing span of nearly 26 m/84 ft.

concorporate, *v.t.* to unite into one body or substance. *a.*, united into one body. [L *concorporātus,* p.p. of *concorporāre* (*corpus -oris,* body)]

concourse, *n.* a confluence, a gathering together; an assembly; †concurrence; a main hall or open space at an airport, railway station etc. [OF *concours,* L *concursus* (*concurrere,* see CONCUR)]

†**concreate,** *v.t.* to create at the same time. [L *concreātus,* p.p. of *concreāre* (*creāre,* to create)]

concremation, *n.* cremation at the same time; consumption by fire. [L *concremātio -ōnem,* from *concremāre* (*cremāre,* to burn)]

concrescence, *n.* a growing together, coalescence; union of parts, organs, or organisms. [L *concrēscentia,* from *concrēscere* (see foll.)]

concrete[1], *a.* formed by the union of many particles in one mass; (*Log., Gram.*) denoting a thing as distinct from a quality, a state, or an action; existing, real, not abstract; individual, not general; specific; made of concrete. *n.* a mass formed by concretion; cement, coarse gravel, and sand mixed with water. *v.t.* to treat with concrete. *v.i.* to apply concrete. **in the concrete,** in the sphere of reality, not of abstractions, or generalities. **reinforced concrete,** *n.* concrete work strengthened by having steel bars or webbing embedded in it. **concrete music,** *n.* music consisting of pieces of prerecorded music or other sound put together and electronically modified. **concrete poetry,** *n.* poetry which uses the visual shape of the poem to help convey meaning. **concretely,** *adv.* **concreteness,** *n.* **concretize, -ise,** *v.t.* to render concrete, solid, or specific. [L *concrētus,* p.p. of *concrēscere* (*crēscere,* to grow)]

concrete[2], *v.i.* to coalesce; to grow together. *v.t.* to form into a solid mass. **concreter,** *n.* an apparatus used in sugar-boiling for concentrating the syrup.

concretion, *n.* the act of concreting; the mass thus formed; (*Geol.*) an aggregation of particles into a more or less regular ball; a growth of solid matter in the body, a stone. **concretionary,** *a.* [L *concrētio -ōnem* (see CONCRETE[2])]

concubine, *n.* a woman who cohabits with a man without being married to him; a mistress; a lawful wife of inferior rank. **concubinage**, *n.* the act or state of living with one of the opposite sex without being legally married; the state of a concubine. **concubinary**, *a.* living in concubinage; pertaining to or sprung from concubinage. *n.* one living in concubinage. [F, from L *concubīna* (CON-, *cubāre,* to lie)]

concupiscence, *n.* unlawful or excessive (sexual) lust. **concupiscent,** *a.* †**concupiscible,** *a.* [L *concupiscentia,* desire, from *concupiscere,* incept. of *concupere* (*cupere,* to desire)]

concur, *v.i.* (*past., p.p.* **concurred**) to meet in one point, to converge, to coincide; to agree; to act in conjunction (with). **concurrence**, *n.* **concurrent**, *a.* that concurs; happening or existing at the same time; acting in union or conjunction; consistent, harmonious; contributing to the same effect or result. *n.* a concurrent person or thing; a concurrent circumstance; (*Sc. Law*) a sheriff's officer's assistant. **concurrently,** *adv.* [L *concurrere* (*currere,* to run)]

concuss, *v.t.* to shake or agitate violently; to force or intimidate. **concussion**, *n.* shaking by sudden impact; a shock; a state of unconsciousness suddenly produced by a blow to the skull, usu. followed by amnesia. **concussion-fuse,** *n.* a shell-fuse that ignites on impact. **concussive,** †**concutient**, *a.* [L *concussus,* p.p. of *concutere* (CON-, *quatere,* to shake)]

concyclic, *a.* of points, lying upon the circumference of one circle; of conoids showing circular sections when cut by the same system of parallel planes.

Condé1, *n.* **Louis de Bourbon, Prince of Condé** (1530–69), a prominent French Huguenot leader, founder of the house of Condé and uncle of Henry IV of France. He distinguished himself in the wars between Henry II and the Holy Roman emperor Charles V, particularly in the defence of Metz.

Condé2, *n.* **Louis II** (1621–86), prince of Condé, called the **Great Condé**. French commander, who won brilliant victories during the Thirty Years' War at Rocroi, 1643, and Lens, 1648, but rebelled in 1651 and entered the Spanish service. Pardoned in 1660, he commanded Louis XIV's armies against the Spanish and the Dutch.

condemn, *v.t.* to pronounce guilty; to give judgment against; to pass sentence on; to pronounce incurable or unfit for use; to adjudge to be forfeited; to censure, to blame. **condemned cell,** *n.* the cell in which prisoners condemned to death are confined before execution. **condemnable**, *a.* **condemnation**, *n.* the act of condemning; the state of being condemned; the ground for condemning. **condemnatory**, *a.* involving or expressing condemnation. [OF *condemner,* L *condemnāre* (*damnāre,* to condemn)]

condense, *v.t.* to make more dense or compact; to compress; to concentrate; to reduce into another and denser form (as a gas into a liquid). *v.i.* to become dense or compact; to be reduced into a denser form. †*a.* condensed, compact. **condensed milk,** *n.* a thickened and usu. sweetened form of preserved milk. **condensable,** *a.* **condensability**, *n.* **condensate**, *v.t.*, *v.i.* to condense. *n.* something made by condensation. **condensation,** *n.* the act of condensing; the state of being condensed; a condensed mass; conciseness, brevity. **condensation trail,** *n.* a vapour trail. [F *condenser,* L *condensāre* (*densāre,* to thicken, from *densus,* thick)]

condenser, *n.* one who or that which condenses; a lens for concentrating light on an object; a contrivance for accumulating or concentrating electricity; an apparatus for reducing steam to a liquid form; (*Elec.*) a capacitor. **condensity,** *n.*

condescend, *v.i.* to stoop, to yield; to stoop or lower oneself voluntarily to an inferior position; to deign. **to condescend upon,** (*Sc.*) to particularize. **condescendence,** *n.* condescension; (*Sc.*) particularization. **condescending,** *a.* marked by condescension; patronizing. **condescendingly,** *adv.* **condescension,** *n.* the act of condescending; gracious behaviour to imagined inferiors; patronizing behaviour. [F *condescendre,* late L *condēscendere* (*dēscendere,* to DESCEND)]

condign, *a.* worthy, adequate; of a punishment; well-deserved. **condignly,** *adv.* [F *condigne,* L *condignus* (*dignus,* worthy)]

condiment, *n.* a seasoning or sauce; anything used to give a relish to food. **condimental**, *a.* [F, from L *condimentum,* from *condīre,* to pickle, to spice, from *condere,* to put together, store up (*-dere, -dāre,* to put)]

condition, *n.* a stipulation, an agreement; a term of a contract; that on which anything depends; (*Gram.*) a clause expressing this; (*pl.*) circumstances or external characteristics; state or mode of existence; †character; †rank or position in life; high social position; a (good) state of health or fitness; a (long-standing) ailment. *v.t.* to stipulate, to agree on; to impose conditions on; to test, to examine; to make fit; to accustom; to establish a conditioned reflex in (a person or animal); to put in a certain condition; to put in a good or healthy condition. **in, out of, condition,** in good, or bad, condition. **conditional,** *a.* containing, implying, or depending on certain conditions; made with limitations or reservations; not absolute; (*Gram.*) expressing condition. *n.* a limitation; a reservation; (*Log.*) a conditional proposition; (*Gram.*) a conditional conjunction, the conditional mood. **conditionality**, *n.* **conditionally,** *adv.* †**conditionate**, *a.* arranged on or subject to certain conditions or terms. *v.t.* to condition; to regulate. **conditioned,** *a.* limited by certain conditions; (*usu. in comb.*) having a certain disposition, as **ill-conditioned, well-conditioned. conditioned by,** depending on; limited by. **conditioned reflex, response,** *n.* (*Psych.*) a natural response to a stimulus which, by much repetition, becomes attached to a different stimulus. **conditioner,** *n.* **conditioning,** *n.* [OF *condicion,* L *condicio -ōnem,* from *condīcere,* to talk over (*dīcere,* to speak)]

condo, *n.* (*N Am., coll.*) short for CONDOMINIUM.

condole, *v.i.* to sorrow, to mourn, to lament; to sympathize (with). †**condolement,** *n.* condolence. **condolence,** *n.* **condolatory,** *a.* expressing condolence. [L *condolēre* (CON-, *dolēre,* to grieve)]

condom, *n.* a contraceptive device, a rubber sheath worn over the penis during sexual intercourse. [name of inventor]

condominium, *n.* joint sovereignty over a state; (*N Am.*) a group of dwellings (e.g. a block of flats) of which each unit is separately owned; any such dwelling. [CON-, L *dominium,* ownership]

condone, *v.t.* to forgive, to remit (esp. breaches of marital duty). **condonation,** *n.* [L *condōnāre* (*dōnāre,* to give)]

condor, *n.* a large S American vulture, *Sarcorrhamphus gryphus;* a S American gold coin. [Sp., from Quechua *cuntur*]

Condorcet, *n.* **Marie Jean Antoine Nicolas Caritat, Marquis de Condorcet** (1743–94), French philosopher and politician, associated with the Encyclopédistes. One of the Girondins, he opposed the execution of Louis XVI, and was imprisoned and poisoned himself. His *Esquisse d'un tableau des progrès de l'esprit humain/Historical Survey of the Progress of Human Understanding* (1795) envisaged inevitable future progress, though not the perfectibility of human nature.

condottiere, *n.* (*pl.* **-ri**) an Italian soldier of fortune; a captain of mercenaries. [It.]

conduce, *v.i.* to contribute (to a result); to tend (to). **conducement,** *n.* **conducive,** *a.* **conduciveness,** *n.* [L *condūcere* (CON-, *dūcere,* to lead)]

conduct1, *n.* the act of leading or guiding; the way in which anyone acts or lives, behaviour; management, direction, control; (*Painting*) manner of treatment; †a safe conduct; †a guide, a guard, a conductor. [partly directly from L *conductus,* p.p. of *condūcere* (CON-, *dūcere,* to lead), partly through OF *conduit* (L *conductus*) or OF *conduite* (cp. Sp. *conducta,* It. *condotta*), defence, escort]

conduct2, *v.t.* to lead, to guide; to manage, to direct;

(*Phys.*) to transmit (as heat etc.); to direct (as an orchestra); (*reflex.*) to behave. *v.i.* to act as a conductor. **conductance,** *n.* the reciprocal of electrical resistance. **conductible,** *a.* capable of conducting or of being conducted. **conductibility,** *n.* **conduction,** *n.* transmission by a conductor; conveyance (of liquids, etc.). **conductive,** *a.* **conductively,** *adv.* **conductivity,** *n.* the ease with which a substance transmits electricity. **conductor,** *n.* a leader, a guide; a director, a manager; the director of an orchestra; (*N Am.*) the guard of a train; the person in charge of a bus or tramcar; a body capable of transmitting heat, electricity, etc.; †a general. **conductorship,** *n.* **conductress,** *n. fem.*

conduit, *n.* a channel, canal, or pipe, usu. underground, to convey water; †(*fig.*) a channel, a passage. **conduit system,** *n.* the enclosing of wiring in a steel conduit or pipe; in an electric tramway system, the arrangement of the conductor rail beneath the roadway. [as prec.]

conduplicate, *a.* (*Bot.*) having the sides folded in face to face (in aestivation). **conduplication,** *n.* [L *conduplicātus,* p.p. of *conduplīcāre*]

condyle, *n.* an eminence with a flattened articular surface on a bone. **condylar, -loid,** *a.* **condylar process,** *n.* the condyle at the extremities of the under jaw. [L *condylus,* Gr. *kondulos,* a knuckle]

cone, *n.* a solid figure described by the revolution of a right-angled triangle about the side containing the right-angle; a solid pointed figure with straight sides and circular or otherwise curved base; anything cone-shaped, as a wafer holder for ice-cream, a temporary marker for traffic on roads etc.; a strobilus or dry multiple fruit, such as that of the pines; a marine shell of the genus *Conus;* (*pl.*) fine white flour used by bakers for dusting loaves. *v.i.* to bear cones. *v.t.* to mark (off) with cones. **cone-flower,** *n.* any species of the genus *Rudbeckia,* belonging to the aster family. **conoid,** *n.* a cone-shaped object. *a.* cone-shaped. **conoidal,** *a.* conoid. [F *cône,* L *cōnus,* Gr. *kōnos*]

coney CONY.

conf., (*abbr.*) compare. [L *confer*]

confab, *n., v.i.* (*coll.*) short for CONFABULATION, CONFABULATE.

confabulate, *v.i.* to talk familiarly; to chat, to gossip. **confabulation,** *n.* **confabulatory,** *a.* [L *confābulātus,* p.p. of *confābulārī* (CON-, *fābulārī,* to converse, from *fābula,* a discourse)]

confarreation, *n.* the highest form of marriage among the Romans. [L *confārreātio ōnem,* from *confarreāre,* to join in marriage by the offering of bread (*farreus,* of grain or spelt, *far farris,* grain, spelt)]

confect, *v.t.* to make (by compounding); to construct, esp. in the imagination. **confection,** *n.* the act of compounding; a compound, esp. a sweet delicacy, a sweetmeat, a preserve; a drug made palatable by compounding with a sweetening agent; a ready-made dress or article of dress. *v.t.* to make confectionery; to make a confection. †**confectionary,** *a.* prepared as a confection. *n.* a confectioner; †a confection; †a store for confectionery. **confectioner,** *n.* one whose trade it is to prepare or sell confections, sweetmeats etc.; a pastrycook. **confectionery,** *n.* sweetmeats or preserves generally; confections, candies etc.; a confectioner's shop. [L *confectus,* p.p. of *conficere* (*facere,* to make)]

Confederacy, *n.* in US history, a popular name for the **Confederate States of America**, the government established by the Southern US states in Feb. 1861 when they seceded from the Union, precipitating the Civil War. Richmond, Virginia, was the capital, and Jefferson Davis the president. The Confederacy fell after its army was defeated in 1865 and Gen. Robert E. Lee surrendered.

confederate, *a.* united in a league; allied by treaty; (*Hist.*) applied to the Southerners in the American Civil War (1861–65). *n.* a member of a confederation; an ally, esp. an accomplice; (*Hist.*) a Southerner. *v.t., v.i.,* to unite in a league. **confederacy,** *n.* a league or compact by which several persons engage to support each other; a number of persons, parties, or states united for mutual aid and support; a league, a confederation; conspiracy, unlawful cooperation, collusion. **confederal,** *a.* **confederalist,** *n.* **confederation,** *n.* **confederatism,** *n.* **confederative,** *a.* [L *confoederātus,* p.p. of *confoederāre* (*foedus -eris,* a league)]

Confederation, Articles of, in US history, the means by which the 13 former British colonies created a form of national government. Ratified in 1781, the Articles established a unicameral legislature, Congress, with limited powers of raising revenue, regulating currency, and conducting foreign affairs, but the individual states retained significant autonomy. Superseded by the US Constitution in 1788.

Confederation of British Industry, UK organization of employers, established 1965, combining the former Federation of British Industries (founded 1916), British Employers' Confederation and National Association of British Manufacturers.

confer, *v.t.* (*past, p.p.* **conferred**) to bestow, to grant. *v.i.* to consult together; to compare views. **conferee,** *n.* one who is conferred with; one on whom something is conferred. **conference,** *n.* the act of conferring; a meeting for consultation or deliberation; a meeting of the representatives of various countries for deliberation; a meeting of two branches of a legislature to adjust differences; the annual meeting of the Wesleyan body to transact church business. **in conference,** at a meeting. **conferential,** *a.* **conferment,** *n.* **conferrable,** *a.* **conferrer,** *n.* [L *conferre* (*ferre,* to bring)]

Conferva, *n.* a genus of algae, consisting of plants with unbranched filaments. **confervaceous,** *a.* **conferval, -void,** *n., a.* [L]

confess, *v.t.* to own, to acknowledge, to admit; to declare one's adherence to or belief in; to manifest; to hear the confession of. *v.i.* to make confession, esp. to a priest. **confessant,** *n.* one who confesses to a priest. **confessedly,** *adv.* admittedly, avowedly. **confession,** *n.* the act of confessing; avowal, declaration; formal acknowledgment of sins to a priest in order to receive absolution. **confession of faith,** a formulary containing the creed of a Church. **confessional,** *n.* the place where a priest sits to hear confessions; the practice of confession. *a.* pertaining to confession. **confessionary,** *a.* **confessionist,** *n.* one who adopts a certain confession or creed, esp. the Augsburg Confession, a Lutheran. **confessor,** *n.* one who confesses; a title applied to canonized saints who are neither apostles nor martyrs; a priest who hears confessions. **The Confessor,** *n.* the Saxon king, Edward the Confessor. [OF *confesser,* late L *confessāre,* freq. of *confitērī* (p.p. *confessus*), *fatērī,* to acknowledge, cogn. with *fārī,* to speak, *fāma,* FAME]

confetti, *n.pl.* bonbons; bits of coloured paper thrown at weddings etc. **confetti money,** *n.* paper money made almost valueless by inflation. [It., pl. of *confetto,* from L *confectum,* COMFIT]

confidant, *n.* one entrusted with secrets, esp. with love affairs; a bosom friend. **confidante,** *n. fem.* [F *confident, -e* (see foll.)]

confide, *v.i.* to have trust or confidence (in); to talk confidentially (to). *v.t.* to entrust (to); to reveal in confidence (to). **confidence,** *n.* trust, belief; self-reliance, boldness, assurance; revelation of private matters to a friend; the matter revealed; †trustworthiness. **confidence man,** *n.* one who practises confidence tricks. **confidence trick,** *n.* a trick by which one is induced to part with valuable property for something worthless, to show the confidence the parties have in each other. **confident,** *a.* full of confidence; assured; self-reliant, bold. *n.* a confidant. **confidential,** *a.* trustworthy; entrusted with the private concerns of another; told or carried on in confidence. **confidentiality,** *n.* **confidentially,** *adv.* **confidentialness,** *n.* **confidently,** *adv.* **confider,** *n.* **confiding,** *a.* trusting. [L *confīdere* (*fīdere,* to trust; cp. *fides,* faith)]

configure, *v.t.* to give shape or form to. **configuration,** *n.* form; structural arrangement; contour or outline; (*Astron.*) the relative position of the planets at any given time; (*Psych.*) a gestalt; (the layout of) the several items of hardware making up a computing or word-processing system. [L *configūrāre* (*figūrāre,* from *figūra,* form)]

confine[1], *n.* (*usu. pl.*) boundaries, limits, frontier; (*usu. pl.*) a borderland of thought or opinion; (*usu. pl.*) †region, territory; †a place of confinement; (*sing.*) confinement. [OF *confines* (pl.), L *confines* (pl. a.), bordering upon (*fīnis,* a boundary)]

confine[2], *v.i.* †to have a common boundary (with or on). *v.t.* to shut up, to imprison, to keep within bounds; to limit in application. **to be confined,** to be in child-bed; to be delivered of a child. †**confineless,** *a.* unbounded, unlimited. **confinement,** *n.* the act of confining; the state of being confined, esp. in child-bed; restraint, restriction, seclusion. **confiner,** *n.* one who confines; †, one who lives on the borders or confines. **confinity,** *n.* nearness, contiguity. [see prec.]

confirm, *v.t.* to give firmness to; to establish; to ratify; to make valid; to bear witness to; to strengthen (in a course or opinion); to administer confirmation to. **confirmand,** *n.* one being prepared for the rite of confirmation. **confirmation,** *n.* the act of confirming; corroborative testimony; the rite of admitting into full communion with an episcopal church by the laying on of hands. **confirmative,** *a.* **confirmatively,** *adv.* **confirmatory,** *a.* **confirmed,** *a.* established, settled, perfect; beyond hope of recovery or help; having received confirmation. **confirmedly,** *adv.* **confirmedness,** *n.* **confirmee,** *n.* one who has received confirmation. [OF *confermer,* L *confirmāre* (*firmāre,* to make firm, from *firmus,* firm)]

confiscate[1], *v.t.* to adjudge to be forfeited, or to seize as forfeited, to the public treasury. **confiscation,** *n.* the act of confiscating; (*coll.*) robbery, plunder (usu. with the sense of *legalized*). **confiscable, confiscatable,** *a.* **confiscator,** *n.* **confiscatory,** *a.* [L *confiscātus,* p.p. of *confiscāre* (*fiscus,* the treasury)]

confiscate[2], *a.* confiscated.

confiteor, *n.* a Roman Catholic formula of confession. [L, I confess]

confiture COMFITURE.

confix, *v.t.* to fix firmly. [L *confixus,* p.p. of *configere* (*fīgere,* to fix)]

conflagration, *n.* a general burning; a large and destructive fire. †**conflagrate,** *v.t.* [L *conflagrātio,* from *conflagrāre* (*flagrāre,* to burn)]

conflate, *v.t.* to blow or fuse together; to blend (two variant readings) into one. **conflation,** *n.* [L *conflāre* (*flāre,* to blow)]

conflict[1], *n.* a fight, a collision; a struggle, a contest; opposition of interest, opinions, or purposes; mental strife, agony. [L *conflictus,* from *conflīgere* (*flīgere,* to strike)]

conflict[2], *v.i.* to come into collision; to strive or struggle; to differ, to disagree; to be discrepant. **conflicting,** *a.* contradictory, irreconcilable. **confliction,** *n.* **conflictive,** *a.* [as prec.]

confluent, *a.* flowing together; uniting in a single stream; (*Bot.*) cohering; running together as pustules. *n.* a stream which unites with another; (*loosely*) a tributary stream; †the place where two or more streams unite. **confluence,** *n.* a flowing together; the point of junction of two or more streams; a multitude, an assembly. [L *confluens -ntem,* pres.p. of *confluere* (*fluere,* to flow)]

conflux, *n.* confluence. [L *confluxus,* as prec.]

confocal, *a.* having common focus or foci.

conform, *v.t.* to make like in form, to make similar to; to accommodate, to adapt. *v.i.* to comply, to assent; to be in harmony or agreement. **conformable,** *a.* having the same shape or form; corresponding, similar; compliant, conforming; (*Geol.*) arranged (as strata) in parallel planes. **conformability,** *n.* **conformably,** *adv.* **conformal,** *a.* of maps, showing small areas in their true shape. **conformance,** *n.* **conformation,** *n.* the manner in which a body is formed; form, shape, structure; adaptation. **conformator,** *n.* a device for determining the conformation of anything that has to be fitted. **conformer,** *n.* **conformism,** *n.* **conformist,** *n.* one who conforms to the worship of the Church of England; one who accepts the prevailing orthodoxy in matters of dress, opinion etc. **conformist,** *a.* **conformity,** *n.* resemblance, similitude; agreement, compliance, congruity; the act of conforming to the worship of the Established Church. [F *conformer,* L *conformāre* (*formāre,* to form, fashion)]

confound, *v.t.* to throw into confusion; to perplex, to terrify; to put to shame; to destroy; to defeat, to overthrow; to mix up, confuse; to bring to shame or to perdition (used as a mild curse). **confounded,** *a.* **confoundedly,** *adv.* exceedingly, greatly (with strong disapprobation). [OF *confondre,* L *confundere* (*fundere,* to pour)]

confraternity, *n.* a brotherhood associated esp. for religious or charitable purposes; brotherhood.

confrère, *n.* a fellow-member of a profession, religion or association. [F]

confront, *v.t.* to face; to stand facing; to bring face to face; to be opposite to; to face defiantly; to oppose, to meet in hostility; to compare (with). **confrontation,** *n.* [F *confronter,* late L *confrontāre,* L *confrontāri* (*frons -ntis,* forehead)]

Confucian, *a.* pertaining to *Confucius* (see below), the Chinese philosopher, or his philosophical system. *n.* a follower of Confucius. **Confucianism,** *n.* the body of beliefs and practices that are based on the Chinese classics and supported by the authority of the philosopher Confucius (Kong Zi). For some 2500 years most of the Chinese people have derived from Confucianism their ideas of cosmology, political government, social organization, and individual conduct. Human relationships follow the patriarchal pattern. The origin of things is seen in the union of **yin** and **yang**, the passive and active principles.

Confucius, *n.* (latinized form of **Kong Zi**, 'Kong the master') (551–479 BC.), Chinese philosopher whose name is given to Confucianism. He devoted his life to relieving suffering of the poor through governmental and administrative reform. His emphasis on tradition and ethics attracted a growing number of pupils during his lifetime; *The Analects of Confucius*, a compilation of his teachings, was published after his death.

confuse, *v.t.* to mix or mingle so as to render indistinguishable; to jumble up; to confound, to perplex; to disconcert. **confusedly,** *adv.* **confusedness,** *n.* **confusible,** *a.* **confusion,** *n.* the act of confusing; the state of being confused; disorder, tumult; perplexity; †ruin, destruction; disturbance of consciousness characterized by impaired capacity to think or to respond in any way to current stimuli. [L *confūsus,* p.p. of *confundere,* to CONFOUND]

confute, *v.t.* to overcome in argument; to prove to be false. **confutable,** *a.* †**confutant,** *n.* one who confutes or disproves. **confutation,** *n.* the act or process of confuting; refutation, disproof. [L *confūtāre* (*fūt-,* stem of *fūtis,* a water-vessel, cogn. with *fundere,* to pour)]

cong., (*abbr.*) congregation(al); Congregationalist; congress; congressional.

conga, *n.* a Latin American dance performed by several people in single file; music for this dance. *v.i.* (*pres. p.* **congaing,** *past, p.p.* **congaed**) to perform this dance. **conga drum,** *n.* a narrow bass drum beaten by the hand. [Amer. Sp.]

congé, †**congee,** *n.* a bow; a courtesy before taking leave; leave, departure, farewell; dismissal. †*v.i.* to bow; to take leave with the usual civilities. **congé d'elire,** a writ giving the Crown's permission to a dean and chapter to elect a bishop, and naming the person to be elected. [OF *congiez,* late L *comiātus,* corr. of L *commeātus,* from *commeāre* (*meāre,* to go)]

congeal, *v.t.* to freeze; to convert from the liquid to the solid state by cold; to coagulate. *v.i.* to become hard with cold; to coagulate. **congealable,** *a.* **congealment,** *n.* [OF *congeler,* L *congelāre* (*gelāre,* from *gelu,* frost)]

†**congee** CONGÉ.

congelation, *n.* the act of congealing; the state of being congealed; a congealed mass. [CONGEAL]

congener, *n.* one of the same kind or class; an organism of the same stock or family. *a.* akin, closely allied (to). **congeneric**, *a.* of the same race or genus. **congenerous**, *a.* congeneric; (*Physiol.*) concurring in the same action, as muscles. [L *congener* (*genus -eris,* kind)]

congenetic, *a.* of natural phenomena; having the same cause, origin or place or time of origin.

congenial, *a.* partaking of the same natural characteristics; sympathetic; suitable; pleasant. **congeniality**, *n.* **congenially,** *adv.*

congenital, *a.* existing from birth; constitutional. **congenitally,** *adv.* [L *congenitus* (*genitus,* p.p. of *gignere,* to produce)]

conger, *n.* one of a genus (*Conger*) of marine eels; the conger-eel, *C. conger.* **congeroid, congroid,** *a.* [OF *congre,* L *conger,* Gr. *gongros*]

congeries, *n.* (*pl.* **congeries**) a collection or heap of particles or bodies. [L]

congest, *v.i.* to become congested. *v.t.* to overcharge (with blood). **congested,** *a.* closely crowded; unduly distended with an accumulation of blood. **congestion**, *n.* an abnormal accumulation of blood in the capillaries; abnormal accumulation (of inhabitants, traffic etc.). **congestive,** *a.* inducing or caused by congestion. [L *congestus,* p.p. of *congerere* (*gerere,* to carry, bring)]

conglobate, *v.t.* to form into a ball. *v.i.* to assume a globular form. *a.*, formed into a ball. **conglobation,** *n.* †**conglobe,** *v.t.*, *v.i.* to conglobate. [L *conglobātus,* p.p. of *conglobāre* (*globus,* a GLOBE, a round mass)]

conglomerate, *a.* gathered into a round body. *n.* a rock composed of water-worn pieces of rock cemented together; pudding-stone; a large firm formed by the merger of several smaller firms with diverse interests. *v.t.*, *v.i.*, to gather into a ball; to collect into a mass. **conglomeration,** *n.* a gathering into a ball or heap; a miscellaneous collection. [L *conglomerātus,* p.p. of *conglomerāre* (*glomus -eris,* a ball)]

conglutinate, *v.t.* to glue together; to unite the edges of a wound together with a glutinous substance. *v.i.* to stick together, to adhere. **conglutination,** *n.* [L *conglūtinātus,* p.p. of *conglūtināre* (*glūten -inis,* glue)]

Congo, *n.* People's Republic of the (*République Populaire du Congo*), a country in W central Africa, bounded to the north by Cameroon and the Central African Republic, to the east and south by Zaïre, to the west by the Atlantic Ocean, and to the north west by Gabon. **area** 342,000 sq km/132,012 sq miles. **capital** Brazzaville. **towns** chief port Pointe Noire. **physical** Zaïre (Congo) river on the border; half the country is rainforest. **exports** timber, potash, petroleum. **population** (1987) 2,270,000 (chiefly Bantu); annual growth rate 2.6%. **language** French (official). **religion** animist 50%, Christian 48%.

Congolese, *n.*, *a.* a native of, or pertaining to, the Congo.

congou, *n.* a kind of Chinese black tea. [Chin. *kong hu,* labour]

congratulate, *v.t.* to express pleasure or joy to, on account of some event; to compliment upon, rejoice with, felicitate. *v.i.* to express congratulations. **congratulant,** *a.* congratulating. **congratulation,** (*often pl.*) *n.* **congratulative,** *a.* **congratulator,** *n.* **congratulatory,** *a.* expressing congratulations. [L *congrātulātus,* p.p. of *congrātulārī,* to wish joy, from *grātus,* pleasing]

congregate, *v.t.* to gather or collect together into a crowd. *v.i.* to come together, to assemble. †*a.*, assembled, collective. **congregant,** *n.* one who congregates (with); a member of a congregation, esp. of a particular place of worship. **congregation,** *n.* the act of gathering together; the body gathered together; an assembly of persons for religious worship; such an assembly habitually meeting in the same place; a board of ecclesiastics meeting as commissioners at Rome; the assembly of qualified members of a university. **congregational**, *a.* pertaining to a congregation, or to Congregationalism. **Congregationalism,** *n.* that form of church government adopted by those Protestant Christians known as Congregationalists, who let each congregation manage its own affairs. The first Congregationalists were the Brownists. **Congregationalist,** *n.*, *a.* **congregationalize, -ise,** *v.t.* [L *congregātus,* p.p. of *congregare* (*gregāre,* to collect, from *grex gregis,* flock)]

congress, *n.* a discussion, a conference; a formal meeting of delegates or of envoys for the settlement of international affairs; the legislature of the US, consisting of a Senate and a House of Representatives; the body of senators and representatives during the two years for which the latter have been elected; the lower house of the Spanish Cortes and of the legislature of a S American republic. **Congressman, -woman,** *n.* a member of the US Congress. **congressional,** *a.* [L *congressus,* p.p. of *congredī,* to meet together (CON-, *gradī,* to walk, from *gradus,* step)]

Congress of Industrial Organizations, a branch of the American Federation of Labor and Congress of Industrial Organizations, the federation of US trade unions.

Congress of Racial Equality, (CORE) US nonviolent civil-rights organization, founded in Chicago in 1942.

Congress Party, *n.* an Indian political party, founded in 1885 as a nationalist movement. It played an important part in throwing off British rule and was the governing party from independence in 1947 until 1977, when Indira Gandhi lost the leadership she had held since 1966. Heading a splinter group, known as **Congress (I)**, she achieved an overwhelming victory in the elections of 1980, and reduced the main Congress Party in turn to a minority.

Congreve, *n.* **William** (1670–1729), English dramatist and poet. His first success was the comedy *The Old Bachelor* (1693), followed by *The Double Dealer* (1694), *Love for Love* (1695), the tragedy *The Mourning Bride* (1697), and *The Way of the World* (1700). His plays, which satirize the social affectations of the time, are noted for their elegant wit and wordplay.

Congreve match, *n.* a kind of friction match. **Congreve rocket,** *n.* a war rocket, now disused. [inventor, Sir William *Congreve,* 1772–1828]

congroid CONGER.

congrue, *v.t.* to agree, to suit, to correspond. **congruence, -ency**, *n.* **congruent**, *a.* agreeing, suitable, correspondent; of geometrical figures, having the same shape. **congruism**, *n.* the Roman Catholic doctrine that the efficacy of divine grace depends upon its adaptation to the character, disposition and circumstances of the recipient. **congruist,** *n.* **congruous**, *a.* suitable, conformable, appropriate, fitting. **congruously,** *adv.* **congruousness, congruity,** *n.* [L *congruere,* to agree (CON-, *-gruere,* cp. *ingruere*)]

conic, *a.* pertaining to or having the form of a cone. **conic sections,** *n.pl.* curves formed by the intersection of a cone and a plane – the parabola, the hyperbola, and the ellipse. **conical,** *a.* **conically,** *adv.* **conicalness,** *n.* **conics,** *n. sing.* the branch of mathematics dealing with conic sections.

conico-, *comb. form.* conical, or tending to be conical. **conicocylindrical**, *a.* nearly cylindrical, but tapering at one end.

conidium, *n.* (*pl.* **-dia**) an asexual reproductive cell or spore in certain fungi. **conidial, -ioid,** *a.* **conidiiferous, -diophorous**, *a.* **conidiophore**, *n.* a branch of the mycelium bearing conidia. [mod. L from Gr. *konis,* dust]

conifer, *n.* a cone-bearing plant or tree; any tree or shrub of the Coniferae. **Coniferae**, *n.pl.* (*Bot.*) an order of resinous trees, as the fir, pine and cedar, bearing a cone-shaped fruit. **coniferous**, *a.* **coniform**, *a.* [L]

coniine, *n.* an alkaloid constituting the poisonous principle in hemlock. **Conium**, *n.* the genus of Umbelliferae containing the hemlock; the fruit of the hemlock or the drug extracted therefrom. [L *conīum,*

Gr. *kōneion,* hemlock]

conj., (*abbr.*) conjugation; conjunction.

conjecture, *n.* a guess, surmise, or doubtful inference; opinion based on inadequate evidence; ill suspicion. *v.t., v.i.* to guess, to surmise. **conjecturable,** *a.* that may be conjectured. **conjecturably,** *adv.* **conjectural,** *a.* depending on conjecture. **conjecturally,** *adv.* **conjectured,** *a.* surmised, based on guesswork. †**conjecturer,** *n.* [F, from L *conjectūra*]

conjoin, *v.t.* to cause to unite, *v.i.* to unite, to come together. **conjoint,** *a.* united, associated, cooperating. **conjointly,** *adv.* [OF *conjoign-,* stem of *conjoindre,* L *conjungere* (*jungere,* to join)]

conjugal, *a.* of or pertaining to matrimony or to married life. **conjugality,** *n.* **conjugally,** *adv.* **conjugial,** *a.* pertaining to marriage as a spiritual union (word used by Swedenborg). [L *conjugālis,* from *conjugem,* acc. of *conjunx,* spouse (*jug-,* root of *jungere,* to join, *jugum,* a yoke)]

conjugate, *v.t.* to inflect (a verb) by going through the voices, moods, tenses etc.; (*Biol.*) to combine, to become united. *v.i.* of a verb, to be inflected; (*Biol.*) to unite sexually; to become fused. *a.,* joined in pairs, coupled; agreeing in grammatical derivation; (*Math.*) reciprocally related so as to be interchangeable; (*Bot.*) paired; of a word, agreeing in derivation with another word. *n.* a conjugate thing, substance, quantity etc. **conjugation,** *n.* the act or process of conjugating; the inflection of a verb; a class of verbs conjugated alike; the fusion of two or more cells or distinct organisms into a single mass. **conjugational,** *a.* **conjugative,** *a.* [L *conjugātus,* p.p. of *conjugāre* (*jug-,* as prec.)]

conjugial CONJUGAL.

conjunct, *a.* conjoined; closely connected; in union; conjoint. *n.* a person or thing joined with another. **conjunction,** *n.* union, association, connection; combination; a word connecting sentences or clauses or coordinating words in the same clause; of two heavenly bodies, the state of being in apparent union. **conjunctional,** *a.* **conjunctionally,** *adv.* **conjunctive,** *a.* serving to unite; (*Gram.*) connective, conjunctional, copulative; connective in sense as well as in construction, as opposed to *disjunctive;* †closely united. *n.* a conjunctive word or mood. **conjunctive mood,** *n.* a mood expressing condition or contingency, of a verb used in conjunction with another verb. **conjunctively,** *adv.* **conjunctly,** *adv.* **conjuncture,** *n.* a combination of circumstances or events; a crisis. [L *conjunctus, p.p.* of *conjungere,* see CONJOIN]

conjunctiva, *n.* (*pl.* **-vas, -vae**) the mucous membrane lining the inner surface of the eyelids and the front of the eyeball. **conjunctival,** *a.* **conjunctivitis,** *n.* inflammation of the conjunctiva. [see prec.]

conjure[1], *v.t.* to appeal to by a sacred name, or in a solemn manner; to bind by an oath; †to conspire, to plot. †*v.i.* to conspire. **conjuration,** *n.* †a conspiracy; the act of conjuring or invoking; a magic spell, a charm; a solemn adjuration. **conjurator,** *n.* a conspirator. **conjurement,** *n.* a solemn adjuration. **conjuror,** *n.* one bound with others by a common oath. [OF *conjurer,* L *conjūrāre* (*jūrāre,* to swear)]

conjure[2], *v.t.* to effect by magical influence; to raise up by or as by magic; to effect by jugglery. *v.i.* to practise the arts of a conjurer; to use anything as a charm. **a name to conjure with,** a person of great influence. **to conjure up,** to arouse the imagination about. **conjurer, -or,** *n.* a juggler; one who performs tricks by sleight of hand. [as prec.]

conk, *n.* (*sl.*) the head; (*sl.*) the nose; (*sl.*) a punch on the nose. *v.t.* (*sl.*) to hit (someone) on the nose. **to conk out,** (*sl.*) to give out, to fail; to die. [perh. from CONCH].

conker, *n.* a horse-chestnut; (*pl.*) a game played with conkers threaded on strings. [E dial. *conker,* a snail shell].

Conn., (*abbr.*) Connecticut.

Connacht, *n.* a province of the Republic of Ireland, comprising the counties of Galway, Leitrim, Mayo, Roscommon and Sligo; area 17,130 sq km/6612 sq miles; population (1986) 431,000. The chief towns are Galway, Roscommon, Castlebar, Sligo and Carrick-on-Shannon. Mainly lowland, it is agricultural and stock-raising country, with poor land in the west.

connate, *a.* innate, born with one, congenital; (*Biol.*) united, though originally distinct; united at the base, as two opposite leaves. [L *connātus,* p.p. of *connāscī* (*nāscī,* to be born)]

connatural, *a.* inborn; naturally belonging (to); of the same nature. **connaturally,** *adv.*

Connaught CONNACHT.

connect, *v.t.* to join, link, or fasten together; to conjoin, to unite, to correlate; to associate (in one's mind); to associate (with) as a cause or a result; to establish telephone communication between. *v.i.* to be or become connected; (*coll.*) to manage to hit something (with a punch, kick etc.); of a train etc., to have its arrival and departure times arranged to be convenient for those of other trains etc. **connecting rod,** *n.* one that transmits power from one part of a machine to another, esp. from the piston to the crankshaft in an internal-combustion engine. **connected,** *a.* united, esp. by marriage; closely related; coherent; associated (with). **well connected,** related to rich or socially powerful people. **connectedly,** *adv.* **connectedness,** *n.* **connecter, -or,** *n.* **connectible, -able,** *a.* **connective,** *a.* having the power of connecting; that connects. *n.* a connecting word; (*Bot.*) the part between the lobes of an anther, which holds them together. **connective tissue,** *n.* the fibrous tissue supporting and connecting the various parts throughout the body. **connectively,** *adv.* [L *connectere* (*nectere,* to bind)]

Connecticut, *n.* a state in New England, US; nickname Constitution State/Nutmeg State. **area** 13,000 sq km/5018 sq miles. **capital** Hartford. **towns** Bridgeport, New Haven, Waterbury. **physical** highlands in the NW; Connecticut River. **products** dairy, poultry and market garden products; tobacco, watches, clocks, silverware, helicopters, jet engines, nuclear submarines. **population** (1983) 3,138,000.

connection, connexion, *n.* the act of connecting; the state of being connected; relationship (esp. by marriage); one so connected; sexual intercourse; a connecting part; acquaintanceship; a party, a religious body; a body of customers or clients; the fitting of the departure and arrival of trains, aeroplanes etc., in a cross-country journey; a train, aeroplane etc., whose timetable is so fitted; (*Elec.*) the apparatus used in linking up electric current by contact; a telephone link; (*sl.*) a supplier of illegal drugs. **in connection with,** connected with (esp. of trains, steam-packets etc.). **in this connection,** in relation to this matter. **connectional,** *a.* of or pertaining to a (religious) connection; connective.

Connell, *n.* **James,** Irish socialist who wrote the British Labour Party anthem 'The Red Flag' during the 1889 London strike.

Connery, *n.* **Sean** (1930–), Scottish film actor, the most famous interpreter of James Bond in several films based on the novels of Ian Fleming. His films include include *Dr No* (1962), *From Russia with Love* (1963), *Marnie* (1964), *Goldfinger* (1964), *Diamonds are Forever* (1971), *A Bridge too Far* (1977), and *The Untouchables* (1987).

conniption, *n.* (*N Am., sl.*) (a fit of) rage or hysteria. [etym. unknown]

connive, *v.i.* to wink (at); voluntarily to omit or neglect to see or prevent any wrong or fault; †*v.t.* to wink at. **connivance,** *n.* passive cooperation in a fault or crime; tacit consent. **connivent,** *a.* †that connives; (*Biol.*) convergent. **conniver,** *n.* [L *connīvēre* (and a form conn. with *nicere,* to make a sign, *nictāre,* to wink)]

connoisseur, *n.* one skilled in judging of the fine arts; a critic, a person of taste. **connoisseurship,** *n.* [F]

Connolly, *n.* **Cyril** (1903–74), English writer. As founder-editor of the literary magazine *Horizon* (1930–50), he had considerable critical influence. His books include *The Rock Pool* (1935), a novel of artists on the Riviera, and *The Unquiet Grave* (1945).

Connors, *n.* **Jimmy** (1952–), US lawn tennis player. A popular and entertaining player, he became well known for his 'grunting' during play. He won the Wimbledon title in 1974, and has since won ten Grand Slam events. He was one of the first players to popularize the two-handed backhand.

connote, *v.t.* to imply, to betoken indirectly; to signify, to mean, to involve; (*Log.*) to include in the meaning (said of a term denoting a subject and implying attributes). **connotation,** *n.* **connotative,** *a.* **connotatively,** *adv.* [late L *connotāre* (L *notāre,* to mark, from *nota,* a mark)]

connubial, *a.* relating to marriage or the marriage state. **connubiality,** *n.* matrimony; (*pl.*) endearments. **connubially,** *adv.* [L *connūbiālis* (*nūbere,* to veil, to marry)]

conoid, conoidal CONE.

conquer, *v.t.* to win or gain by conquest; to vanquish, to overcome; to gain dominion, sovereignty, or mastery over; to subdue, to surmount. *v.i.* to be victorious. **conquerable,** *a.* †**conqueress,** *n. fem.* **conqueringly,** *adv.* **conqueror,** *n.* one who conquers; a victor. **The Conqueror,** William of Normandy, who conquered England in 1066. [OF *conquerre,* L *conquīrere* (*quaerere,* to seek)]

conquest, *n.* the act of conquering; that which is conquered; (*coll.*) a person whose affection has been gained; the acquisition of sovereignty by force of arms; victory, subjugation. **The (Norman) Conquest,** the conquest of England by William of Normandy in 1066. **to make a conquest of,** to win the love or admiration of. [OF *conquest* (F *conquêt*), anything acquired by conquest, *conqueste* (F *conquête*), the act of conquering, late L *conquīsīta,* fem. p.p. of *conquīrere,* as prec.]

conquistador, *n.* (*pl.* **-res**) one of the Spanish conquerors of America in the 16th cent. [Sp.]

Conrad, *n.* several kings of the Germans and Holy Roman Emperors, including:

Conrad I, *n.* king of the Germans from 911, when he succeeded Louis the Child, the last of the German Carolingians. During his reign the realm was harassed by Magyar invaders.

Conrad II, *n.* king of the Germans from 1024, Holy Roman Emperor from 1027. He ceded the march Sleswick (Schleswig), south of the Jutland peninsula, to King Canute, but extended his rule into Lombardy and Burgundy.

Conrad III *n.* (1093–1152), Holy Roman Emperor from 1138, the first king of the Hohenstaufen dynasty. Throughout his reign there was a fierce struggle between his followers, the **Ghibellines**, and the **Guelphs**, the followers of Henry the Proud, duke of Saxony and Bavaria (1108–39), and later of his son Henry the Lion (1129–95).

Conrad IV *n.* (1228–1254), elected king of the Germans 1237. Son of the Holy Roman Emperor Frederick II, he had to defend his right of succession against Henry Raspe of Thuringia (d. 1247) and William of Holland (1227–56).

Conrad V, *n.* **(Conradin)** (1252–68), son of Conrad IV, recognized as king of the Germans, Sicily and Jerusalem by German supporters of the Hohenstaufens 1254. He led Ghibelline forces against Charles of Anjou at the battle of Tagliacozzo, N Italy (1266), and was captured and executed.

Conrad, *n.* **Joseph** (1857–1924), British novelist, of Polish parentage, born Teodor Jozef Konrad Korzeniowski in the Ukraine. His novels include *Almayer's Folly* (1895), *Lord Jim* (1900), *Heart of Darkness* (1902), *Nostromo* (1904), *The Secret Agent* (1907), and *Under Western Eyes* (1911). His works vividly evoked for English readers the mysteries of sea life and exotic foreign settings, and explored the psychological isolation of the 'outsider'.

Conran, *n.* **Terence** (1931–), British designer and retailer of furnishings, fashion and household goods. He is chairman of the Habitat and Conran companies, with retail outlets in the UK, US and elsewhere.

cons., (*abbr.*) consecrated; consignment; consolidated; consonant; construction; consultant.

consanguine, -guineous, *a.* of the same blood; related by birth. **consanguinity,** *n.* [F *consanguin -e,* L *consanguineus* (*sanguis -inis,* blood)]

conscience, *n.* moral sense; the sense of right and wrong; consciousness; †inmost thought; †sense, understanding. **for conscience' sake,** for the sake of one's conscientious scruples; for the sake of one's religion. **in conscience,** in truth; assuredly. **in all conscience,** (*coll.*) in all reason or fairness. **on my conscience,** most assuredly (a strong asseveration). **to have on one's conscience,** to feel guilt or remorse about. **to have the conscience to,** to have the assurance or impudence to. **conscience clause,** *n.* a clause in an Act of Parliament to relieve persons with conscientious scruples from certain requirements. **conscience investment** ETHICAL INVESTMENT. **conscience money,** *n.* money paid voluntarily (and often anonymously), as compensation for evasion of commitments, esp. evaded income-tax. **conscience-proof,** *a.* proof against the monitions of conscience. **conscience-smitten, -stricken,** *a.* stung by conscience on account of some misdeed. **conscienceless,** *a.* [F, from L *conscientia,* from *conscīre* (*scīre,* to know)]

conscientious, *a.* actuated by strict regard to the dictates of conscience; scrupulous. **conscientious objector,** *n.* one who takes advantage of the conscience clause; one who refuses on principle to take part, or help in any way in war or in activities connected with it. **conscientiously,** *adv.* **conscientiousness,** *n.*

conscionable, *a.* regulated by conscience; scrupulous, just. **conscionableness,** *n.* **conscionably,** *adv.*

conscious, *a.* aware of one's own existence; self-conscious; having immediate knowledge, cognizant, aware; fully aware, with consciousness awake; present to consciousness, felt, sensible. *n.* the conscious mind. **-conscious,** *comb. form.* very aware of; attaching importance to. **consciously,** *adv.* **consciousness,** *n.* the state of being conscious; immediate knowledge, sense, perception; (*Psych.*) the faculty by which one knows one's own existence, acts, affections etc.; the intellectual faculties collectively or any class of them. [L *conscius,* aware, from *conscīre* (see CONSCIENCE)]

conscribe, *v.t.* to conscript. [L *conscrībere* (*scrībere,* to write)]

conscript[1], *a.* enrolled, registered, enlisted by conscription. *n.* one compelled to serve as a soldier. **conscription,** *n.* compulsory enrolment for military, naval or air service. [L *conscriptus,* p.p. of *conscrībere* (as prec.)]

conscript[2], *v.t.* to enlist compulsorily. **conscript fathers,** *n.pl.* the senators of ancient Rome; (*coll.*) the members of a town council.

consecrate, *v.t.* to set apart as sacred; to devote to the service of; to dedicate, to hallow; †to canonize. *a.* consecrated. **consecration,** *n.* the act of consecrating; dedication to a divine object; the state of being consecrated; †canonization; dedication to a sacred office, esp. that of bishop; the benediction of the elements in the Eucharist. **consecrator,** *n.* **consecratory,** *a.* [L *consecrātus,* p.p. of *consecrāre* (*sacrāre,* to consecrate, from *sacer,* holy)]

consectary, *n.* a corollary; a necessary deduction. [L *consectārium,* n. from *consectārius,* a. (*consectāri,* freq. of *consequī,* see foll.)]

consecution, *n.* the state of being consecutive; a succession or series; logical or grammatical sequence. [L *consecutio,* from *consequī* (CON-, *sequī,* to follow)]

consecutive, *a.* following without interval or break; expressing logical or grammatical consequence. **consecutive intervals,** *n.pl.* (*Mus.*) a succession of similar intervals in harmony, esp. consecutive fifths and octaves. **consecutively,** *adv.* **consecutiveness,** *n.*

conseil d'état, *n.* a council of state. [F]

consenescence, *n.* a growing old together; general decay with age. [L *consenēscere* (*senēscere,* to grow old, from *senex,* an old man)]

consensus, *n.* a general agreement, unanimity;

(*Physiol.*) the sympathetic agreement of the different organs for a particular purpose. **consensual,** *a.* (*Physiol.*) happening by sympathetic action, as opp. to volition; (*Law*) existing by consent. [L p.p. of *consentīre,* as foll.]

consent, *v.i.* to concur, to assent, to agree, to yield. †*v.t.* to agree to. *n.* acquiescence in feeling, thought, or action; compliance; permission; agreement, concurrence; †feeling, opinion. **with one consent,** unanimously. **consentable,** *a.* (*Pennsylvania Law*) agreed to by consent. **consenter,** *n.* **consenting,** *a.* **consenting adult,** *n.* a person over the age of consent, esp. legally able to enter into a homosexual relationship. **consentingly,** *adv.* [OF *consentir,* L *consentīre* (*sentīre,* to feel)]

consentaneous, *a.* mutually consenting, unanimous; accordant; simultaneous, concurrent. **consentaneously,** *adv.* **consentaneity,** *n.* **consentaneousness,** *n.* [L *consentāneus* (as prec.)]

consentient, *a.* of one mind, unanimous; consenting. [L *consentiens -ntem,* pres.p. of *consentīre,* to CONSENT]

consequent, *a.* following as a natural or logical result; consistent. *n.* the correlative to an antecedent; that which follows as a natural and logical result; (*Math.*) the second term in a ratio. **consequence,** *n.* a result or effect; inference; importance; social importance, distinction, note; (*pl.*) a parlour game. †*v.t.* to draw inferences. **in consequence,** as a result. **consequential,** *a.* following as a result or a necessary deduction; resulting indirectly; self-important, pompous, conceited; †important. **consequentiality,** *n.* **consequentially,** *adv.* **consequently,** *adv.* as a consequence; accordingly, therefore. [F *conséquent,* L *consequens -ntem,* pres.p. of *consequī* (*sequī,* to follow)]

conservancy, *n.* official preservation of forests, fisheries etc.; a commission or court with jurisdiction over a particular river, port etc. **conservant,** *a.* [L *conservans -ntem,* pres.p. of *conservāre*]

conservation, *n.* the act of conserving; preservation from waste or decay; protection of natural resources and the environment, esp. from destruction by human activity. **conservation of energy,** the theory that no energy is destroyed, but that the sum of energy in the universe remains the same although particular forces are continually being transformed. **conservation of mass,** the theory that the total mass in an isolated system is constant. **conservational,** *a.* **conservationist,** *n.* [L *conservātio* (as prec.)]

conservative, *a.* tending or inclined to conserve what is established; disposed to maintain existing institutions; pertaining to the Conservative Party; moderate, not extreme, as in a *conservative estimate;* relating to conservatism; conventional. *n.* a person inclined to preserve established things; a conventional person; a member or supporter of the Conservative Party. **conservatively,** *adv.* **conservatism,** *n.* conservative character; dislike of change; the political principles of the Conservative Party. [F *conservatif -ve,* L *conservātīvus* (as prec.)]

Conservative Party, *n.* a British political party, one of the two historic British parties; the name replaced **Tory** in general use from 1830 onwards. Traditionally the party of landed interests, it broadened its political base under Disraeli's leadership in the 19th cent. The modern Conservative Party's free-market capitalism is supported by the world of finance and the management of industry;

conservatoire, *n.* a public school of music or other fine art. [F, from L *conservātōrium,* see CONSERVATORY]

conservator, *n.* one who preserves from violence or injury; a member of a conservancy; a custodian, keeper, curator; an officer charged with maintaining the public peace. [F *conservateur,* L *conservātor -em,* as foll.]

conservatorium, *n.* (*Austral.*) a conservatoire.

conservatory, *n.* a greenhouse for exotics; a glasshouse for plants; a conservatoire. [L *conservātōrius,* a., from *conservāre,* to CONSERVE]

conserve, *v.t.* to preserve from injury, decay, or loss; to preserve (as fruit), to candy. *n.* a preserve; a confection; preserved or candied fruit. **conserver,** *n.* one who protects from loss or injury; one who makes conserves. [F *conserver,* L *conservāre* (CON-, *servāre,* to keep, serve)]

consider, *v.t.* to think on, to contemplate; to ponder; to observe and examine; to look upon as of importance; to estimate, to regard; to have regard for; to bear in mind; to discuss. *v.i.* to reflect, to deliberate. **all things considered,** taking everything into account. **in consideration of,** as a payment for; because of. **to take into consideration,** to consider, to bear in mind. **under consideration,** being considered; under discussion. **considerable,** *a.* worth consideration or regard; important; moderately large or great. **considerably,** *adv.* †**considerance,** *n.* reflection, deliberation. **considerate,** *a.* characterized by consideration for others; †careful, deliberate, prudent. **considerately,** *adv.* **considerateness,** *n.* **consideration,** *n.* the act of considering; reflection, thought; regard for others; a motive or ground for action; importance, worth; a recompense, a reward; an equivalent; (*Law*) the material equivalent given in exchange for something and forming the basis of a contract. **considered,** *a.* carefully thought out. **considering,** *prep.* taking into consideration; in view of. [F *considérer,* L *consīderāre* (*sīdus -eris,* a star), orig. to examine the stars]

consign, *v.t.* to commit to the care, keeping or trust of another; to send (as goods); to relegate; to devote, to set apart; †to mark with a sign. †*v.i.* to consent, to submit. **consignable,** *a.* **consignation,** *n.* the act of consigning; the formal paying over of money to an authorized person (*Sc. Law*) as a deposit during a trial or arbitration; the act of consecrating or blessing with the sign of the cross. **consignee,** *n.* one to whom goods are consigned; an agent, a factor. **consignment,** *n.* the act of consigning; goods consigned; the document by which anything is consigned. **consignor,** *n.* one who consigns goods to another. [F *consigner,* L *consignāre* (*signāre,* to mark, to sign, from *signum,* a mark)]

consilient, *a.* concurring, agreeing. **consilience,** *n.* [L *consiliens -ntem,* pres.p. (*salīre,* to leap)]

consist, *v.i.* to be composed (of); to be founded or constituted (in); to be compatible (with); to subsist, to continue to exist; †to stand together, to remain fixed. **consistence, -ency,** *n.* degree of density; cohesion, coherence; firmness, solidity; accord, harmony, congruity, compatibility. **consistent,** *a.* congruous, harmonious; uniform in opinion or conduct, not self-contradictory; compatible; †solid, not fluid. **consistently,** *adv.* [L *consistere* (*sistere,* to make to stand, causal of *stāre,* to stand)]

consistory, *n.* the court of a bishop for dealing with ecclesiastical causes arising in his diocese; the college of cardinals at Rome; an assembly of ministers and elders in the Lutheran and Calvinist Churches. **consistorial,** *a.* [ONorth. F *consistorie* (F *consistoire*), late L *consistōrium* (see CONSIST)]

consociate[1], *a.* associated together. *n.* an associate; a confederate, an accomplice. [L *consociātus,* p.p. of *consociāre* (*socius,* a partner, a fellow)]

consociate[2], *v.t.* to unite; (*N Am.*) to unite in a Congregational convention. *v.i.* to associate; (*N Am.*) to meet in convention. **consociation,** *n.* association, fellowship; (*N Am. Hist.*) a union of Congregational churches by means of pastors and delegates.

console[1], *v.t.* to comfort or cheer in trouble or distress. **consolable,** *a.* †**consolate,** *v.t.* to console, **consolation,** *n.* that which consoles, cheers or comforts; alleviation of misery or mental distress; a fact or circumstance that consoles. **consolation prize,** *n.* one awarded to a runner-up, **consolatory,** *a.* **consolatorily,** *adv.* [F *consoler,* L *consōlārī* (*sōlārī,* to solace)]

console[2], *n.* a bracket or corbel to support a cornice etc.; the carrier on which the breech-screw of a gun hinges; the frame enclosing the claviers, draw-knobs etc., of an organ when separate from the instrument; a free-standing cabinet for a television set etc.; (the desk or cabinet holding) the control panel of an electric or electronic system. **console table,** *n.* a table supported by a console or consoles. [F, etym. doubtful]

consolidate, *v.t.* to form into a solid and compact mass; to strengthen, to bring into close union; to combine. *v.i.* to become solid. *a.*, solidified, combined, hardened. **consolidated annuities, consols,** *n.pl.* the British Government securities, consolidated into a single stock in 1751, originally bearing interest at 3%. **consolidated fund,** *n.* a national fund for the payment of certain public charges, first formed in 1786 by consolidating the aggregate, general, and South Sea funds, to which the Irish exchequer was added in 1816. **consolidation,** *n.* **consolidator,** *n.* **consolidatory,** *a.* [L *consolidātus,* from *consolidāre* (*solidāre,* to make solid)]

consols CONSOLIDATE.

consommé, *n.* a soup made by boiling meat and vegetables to a jelly. [F]

consonant, *a.* agreeing or according, esp. in sound; congruous, in harmony; producing harmony. *n.* a letter of the alphabet which cannot be sounded by itself, as *b* or *p;* a sound that is combined with a vowel in order to make a syllable. **consonance, -ancy,** *n.* accord or agreement of sound; agreement, harmony; recurrence of sounds; assonance; pleasing agreement of sounds, concord. **consonantal,** *a.* **consonantly,** *adv.* **consonous,** *a.* agreeing in sound; harmonious. [F, from L, pres.p. of *consonāre* (*sonāre,* to sound)]

consort¹, *n.* a companion, an associate; a mate, a partner; a husband, a wife; a vessel accompanying another. **queen consort,** the wife of a king. **king, prince consort,** the husband of a queen. **consortism,** *n.* (*Biol.*) the vital union of two organisms for mutual support, symbiosis. **consortship,** *n.* [F *consort, -e,* L *consors -rtem,* sharer (*sors,* lot)]

consort², *v.i.* to associate, to keep company with; to agree, to be in harmony (with). *v.t.* to associate; to unite in harmony; to attend, to escort.

consort³, *n.* †an assembly, a company; a group of musical instruments of the same type playing together; †agreement, accord; harmony, harmonious music. [F *concert*]

consortium, *n.* (*pl.* **-tia**) fellowship, coalition, union; temporary association of states or of companies or financial interests. [L, fellowship]

conspecific, *a.* of or relating to the same species.

conspectus, *n.* a general sketch or survey; a synopsis. †**conspectuity,** *n.* the faculty of sight; vision. [L, from *conspicere* (*specere,* to look)]

conspicuous, *a.* obvious to the sight; attracting the eye; prominent, extraordinary. **conspicuous consumption,** *n.* lavish spending as a display of wealth. **conspicuously,** *adv.* **conspicuousness, conspicuity,** *n.* [L *conspicuus* (*conspicere,* as prec.)]

conspire, *v.i.* to combine secretly to do any unlawful act, esp. to commit treason, sedition, murder, or fraud; to concur, to unite. *v.t.* to plot, to concert. **conspiracy,** *n.* the act of conspiring; †harmonious concurrence; (*Law*) a secret agreement or combination between two or more persons to commit an unlawful act that may prejudice any third person. **conspiracy of silence,** an agreement not to talk about a particular subject. †**conspirant,** *n., a.* †**conspiration,** *n.* a conspiracy; concurrence, agreement. **conspirator,** *n.* one who conspires. **conspiratorial,** *a.* **conspiratress,** *n.fem.* **conspiringly,** *adv.* [F *conspirer,* L *conspīrāre* (*spīrāre,* to breathe)]

conspue, *v.t.* to spit upon; to abuse, denounce. [F *conspuer,* L *conspuere* (*spuere,* spit)]

constable, *n.* a policeman; an officer charged with the preservation of the peace; a warden, a governor, an officer; (*Hist.*) a high officer of state in the Roman Empire, in France, and in England. **chief constable,** an officer in charge of a police force in an area (as a county). †**high constable** HIGH. †**petty constable,** a constable appointed in parishes by the justices in petty sessions. **police constable,** a policeman or policewoman. **special constable,** a citizen sworn in to aid the police force in times of war, civil commotion etc. **to outrun the constable,** to get into debt. **constableship,** *n.* †**constablewick,** *n.* the district over which a (high or petty) constable's power extended. **constabulary,**, *n.* a body of police under one authority; †the district under a constable. *a.* pertaining to the police. [OF *conestable* (F *connétable*), L *comes stabulī,* count of the stable]

Constable, *n.* **John** (1776–1837), English landscape painter. The scenes of his native Suffolk are well loved and include *The Haywain* (1821) (National Gallery, London), but he travelled widely in Britain, depicting castles, cathedrals, landscapes and coastal scenes. His many sketches, worked in the open air, are often considered among his best work. The paintings are remarkable for their freshness and were influential in France as well as the UK.

Constance, Council of, a council held by the Roman Catholic church (1414–17) in Constance, Germany. It elected Pope Martin V, which ended the Great Schism (1378–1417) when there were rival popes in Rome and Avignon.

constant, *a.* firm, unshaken; unmoved in purpose or opinion; unchanging, steadfast; faithful in love or friendship; continuous, unceasing; (*Math.*) unvarying. *n.* anything unchanging or unvarying; any property or relation, expressed by a number, that remains unchanged under the same conditions; a quantity not varying or assumed not to vary, in value throughout a series of calculations. **constancy,** *n.* fixedness; firmness of mind; faithful attachment; permanence; †certainty; †perseverance; (*Math.*) that which remains invariable. **constantly,** *adv.* in a constant manner; invariably, regularly; continually, always. [F, from L *constans -ntem,* pres.p. of *constāre* (*stāre,* to stand)]

Constanţa, *n.* the chief Romanian port on the Black Sea, capital of Constanţa region, and third largest city of Romania; population (1985) 323,000. It has refineries, shipbuilding yards and food factories.

constantan, *n.* an alloy of copper and nickel used for electrical components because of its high electrical resistance at any temperature. [CONSTANT]

Constant de Rebecque, *n.* **(Henri) Benjamin** (1767–1830), French writer and politician. An advocate of the Revolution, he opposed Napoleon and in 1803 went into exile. Returning to Paris after the fall of Napoleon in 1814 he proposed a constitutional monarchy. He published the autobiographical novel *Adolphe* (1816), which reflects his affair with Madame de Stael, and later wrote the monumental study *De la Religion* (1825–31).

Constantia, *n.* a S African wine from Constantia, near Cape Town.

Constantine II, *n.* (1940–), king of the Hellenes (Greece). In 1964 he succeeded his father Paul I, went into exile 1967, and was formally deposed 1973.

Constantine the Great, *n.* (AD 274–337), first Christian emperor of Rome and founder of Constantinople. He defeated Maxentius, joint-emperor of Rome (312), and in 313 formally recognized Christianity. As sole emperor of the West of the Empire, he defeated Licinius, emperor of the East, to become ruler of the Roman world in 324. He presided over the Church's first council at Nicaea (325). In 330 Constantine moved his capital to Byzantium, renaming it Constantinople.

Constantinople, *n.* the former name of Istanbul, Turkey, (330–1453). It was founded by the Roman emperor Constantine the Great by the enlargement of the Greek city of Byzantium in 328, and became capital of the Byzantine Empire in 330. Its elaborate fortifications enabled it to resist a succession of sieges, but it was captured by crusaders in 1204, and was the seat of a Latin (W European) kingdom until recaptured by the Greeks in 1261. An attack by the Turks in 1422 proved unsuccessful, but it was taken by another Turkish army, 29 May 1453 after nearly a year's siege, and became the capital of the Ottoman Empire.

constellate, *v.i.* to shine with combined radiance. *v.t.* to set or adorn with or as with stars; to combine into a constellation; †to predestine (by the stars one is born under). **constellation,** *n.* a number of fixed stars grouped within the outlines of an imaginary figure in the sky; †(*Astrol.*) the star or planet one is born under; an assemblage of splendid or brilliant people or things; a grouping of related ideas etc. **constellatory,** *a.* [L *stellātus,* p.p. of *stellāre,* to set with stars (*stella,* a star)]

consternate, *v.t.* to affright, to dismay. **consternation,** *n.* [L *consternātus,* p.p. of *consternāre,* to affright, collateral with *consternere* (*sternere,* to strew)]

constipate, *v.t.* to confine; prevent the free movement of; to make costive. **constipation,** *n.* an undue retention or imperfect evacuation of the faeces. [L *constīpātus,* p.p. of *constīpāre* (*stīpāre,* to cram, to pack)]

constituent, *a.* constituting, making, composing; having power to elect or appoint, or to construct or modify a political constitution. *n.* one who or that which constitutes; a component part; one of a body which elects a representative; one who appoints another as his agent, a client. **Constituent Assembly,** *n.* the name assumed by the National Assembly of France shortly after that body had dropped the name of the Third Estate (17 June 1789); since revived in France and elsewhere as the name of an assembly entrusted with framing or voting a constitution. **constituency,** *n.* the whole body of constituents; a body of electors; the place or body of persons represented by a member of Parliament; (*coll.*) a body of clients, customers etc. [L *constituens -ntem,* pres.p. of *constituere,* as foll.]

constitute, *v.t.* to establish; to enact; to give legal form to; to give a definite nature or character to; to make up or compose; to elect or appoint to an office or employment. **constituted authorities,** *n.pl.* the magistrates or governors of a country, district, municipality etc. **constitutor,** *n.* [L *constitūtus,* p.p. of *constituere* (CON-, *statuere,* to place, to set)]

constitution, *n.* the act of constituting; the nature, form, or structure of a system or body; natural strength of the body; mental qualities; the established form of government in a kingdom or state; a system of fundamental rules or principles for the government of a kingdom or state; a law or ordinance made by civil or ecclesiastical authority. **constitutions of Clarendon,** statutes defining civil and ecclesiastical jurisdiction enacted at Clarendon, near Salisbury, in 1164. **constitutional,** *a.* inherent in the bodily or mental constitution; pertaining to or in accordance with an established form of government; legal. *n.* a walk or other exercise for the benefit of one's health. **constitutional government, monarchy,** *n.* a government or monarchy in which the head of the state is, in his or her sovereign capacity, subject to a written or unwritten constitution. **constitutionalism,** *n.* government based on a constitution; adherence to constitutional government. **constitutionalist,** *n.* an upholder of constitutional government; a writer or authority on the political constitution. **constitutionality,** *n.* **constitutionalize, -ise,** *v.t.* to render constitutional. *v.i.* to take a constitutional. **constitutionally,** *adv.* [F, from L *constitūtio -ōnem,* as prec.]

constitutive, *a.* that constitutes or composes, component, essential; that enacts or establishes. **constitutively,** *adv.*

constr., (*abbr.*) construction.

constrain, *v.t.* to compel, to oblige (to do or not to do); to restrain; to keep down by force; to confine, to repress; †to force; †to strain; †to bind. **constrained,** *a.* acting under compulsion; forced; embarrassed. **constrainedly,** *adv.* **constraint,** *n.* the act of constraining; restraint, compulsion, necessity; a compelling force; a constrained manner; reserve, self-control. [OF *constreign-,* stem of *constreindre,* L *constringere* (*stringere,* to draw tight)]

constrict, *v.t.* to draw together; to compress; to cause to contract; to keep within limits; to restrain. **constriction,** *n.* **constrictive,** *a.* that constricts. **constrictor,** *n.* that which constricts; a muscle which serves to contract or draw together; (*Surg.*) an instrument for constricting, a compressor; BOA-CONSTRICTOR. [L *constrictus,* p.p. of *constringere,* as prec.]

constringe, *v.t.* to draw together; to cause to contract; to constrict. **constringent,** *a.* **constringency,** *n.* [as prec.]

construct¹, *v.t.* to build up, to frame; to put together in proper order; to combine words in clauses and sentences; to form by drawing; to form mentally. **constructor,** *n.* **constructorship,** *n.* **constructure,** *n.* †construction, structure; (*Sc. Law*) the right to materials used in the repair of one's house on payment of compensation to their owner. [L *constructus,* p.p. of *construere* (CON-, *struere,* to pile, to build)]

construct², *n.* something constructed; (*Psych.*) a concept or idea built up from sense-impressions etc. [as prec.]

construction, *n.* the act or art of constructing; the thing constructed; style, mode, or form of structure; the syntactical arrangement and connection of words in a sentence; explanation, interpretation (of words, conduct etc.); construing. **constructional,** *a.* pertaining to construction; structural; pertaining to interpretation of language. **constructionist,** *n.* one who puts a certain kind of construction upon the law, legal documents etc. **constructive,** *a.* having ability or power to construct; tending to construct, as opposed to *destructive;* structural; inferential, virtual, implied by construction or interpretation. **constructively,** *adv.* [L *constructio -ōnem* (see CONSTRUCT¹)]

constructivism, *n.* a revolutionary art movement founded in Moscow in 1917 by the Russians Naum Gabo, Antoine Pevsner (1886–1962), and Vladimir Tatlin (1885–1953). Tatlin's abstract sculptures, using wood, metal and clear plastic, were hung on walls or suspended from ceilings. The brothers Gabo and Pevsner soon left the USSR and joined the European avant-garde.

construe, *v.t.* to combine syntactically; to arrange (as words) in order, so as to show the meaning; to translate; to explain, to interpret. *v.i.* to apply the rules of syntax; to translate. [as prec.]

consubstantial, *a.* having the same substance or essence, esp. of the three persons of the Trinity. **consubstantiality,** *n.* [L *consubstantiālis* (CON-, SUBSTANTIAL)]

consubstantiate, *v.t.* to unite in one substance. *v.i.* to join into one substance. **consubstantiation,** *n.* the Lutheran doctrine that the body and blood of Christ are present along with the eucharistic elements after consecration, as distinct from *transubstantiation.* [L *consubstantiāre,* as prec.]

consuetude, *n.* custom, usage, habit; familiarity. **consuetudinary,** *a.* customary. *n.* a ritual of monastic and ecclesiastical forms and customs. [OF, from L *consuētūdo -inem,* from *consuētus,* accustomed, p.p. of *consuēscere* (*suēscere,* to become used, accustomed)]

consul, *n.* one of the two supreme magistrates of ancient Rome, invested with regal authority for one year; one of the three supreme magistrates of the French Republic (1799–1804); an officer appointed by a state to reside in a foreign country to promote its mercantile interests and protect merchants, seamen and other subjects. **First Consul,** Napoleon Bonaparte. **consul general,** *n.* the chief consul of a state, having jurisdiction over ordinary consuls. **consular,** *a.* pertaining to a consul; (*Rom. Hist.*) of the rank of a consul. **consulate,** *n.* the official residence, jurisdiction, office, or term of office, of a consul; in France, the period of consular government (1799–1804). **consulship,** *n.* [L]

consult, *v.i.* to take counsel together; to deliberate. *v.t.* to ask advice or counsel from; to refer to (a book) for information; to have regard to; †to plot, to contrive. †*n.* the act of consulting; a deliberation; a meeting, esp. a secret cabal; (*Rom. Hist.*) a decree of the senate. **consultable,** *a.* **consultancy,** *n.* **consultant,** *n.* a person who consults; a person who is consulted, esp. an expert who is called on for advice and information; a doctor holding the most senior appointment in a branch of medicine in a hospital. **consultation,** *n.* the act of consulting; deliberation of two or more persons;

a meeting of experts to consider a point or case. **consultative, consultatory, consultive,** *a.* **consultee,** *n.* a person consulted. **consulter,** *n.* one who consults. **consulting,** *a.* giving advice; called in for consultation; used for consultation. **consultor,** *n.* a member of a consultative body. [L *consultāre,* freq. of *consulere,* to consult, consider (prob. as CONSUL)]

consume, *v.t.* to destroy by fire, waste, or decomposition; to use up; to eat or drink; to dissipate, to squander; †to exterminate. *v.i.* to waste away; to be burned. **consumable,** *a.* that may be consumed. *n.* something that may be consumed, esp. (*pl.*) food. †**consumedly,** *adv.* unrestrainedly, excessively. **consumer,** *n.* one who or that which consumes; a person who purchases goods and services for his or her own use. **consumer goods,** *n.pl.* manufactured goods destined for purchase by consumers. **consumerism,** *n.* protection of the interests of consumers; the economic theory that increased consumption of goods and services is desirable. **consumerist,** *n.* [L *consūmere* (*sūmere,* to take)]

consummate[1], *a.* complete, perfect; of the highest quality or degree. **consummately,** *adv.* [L *consummātus,* p.p. of *consummāre* (*summa,* a sum)]

consummate[2], *v.t.* to bring to completion, to perfect, to finish; to complete (a marriage) by sexual union. **consummation,** *n.* the act of consummating; the end or completion of something already begun; perfection, perfect development. **consummative,** *a.* **consummator,** *n.* [as prec.]

consumption, *n.* the act of consuming; the state or process of being consumed; the purchase and use by individuals of goods and services; a wasting disease, esp. pulmonary tuberculosis. **consumptive,** *a.* consuming, destructive; disposed to or affected with tuberculosis. *n.* a person suffering from tuberculosis. **consumptively,** *adv.* **consumptiveness,** *n.* [L *consumptio* (see CONSUME)]

cont., (*abbr.*) contents; continent(al); continued.

contabescent, *a.* wasting away; (*Bot.*) affected with contabescence. **contabescence,** *n.* (*Bot.*) an atrophied condition of the stamens and pollen; (*Med.*) wasting away. [L *contābēscens, -ntem,* pres.p. of *contābēscere* (*tābēscere,* to waste, from *tābes,* consumption)]

contact, *n.* touch, meeting, the relation of touching; a person who has been exposed to an illness and is likely to carry contagion; the touching of two lines or surfaces; a business or other acquaintance who can provide one with introductions etc.; the touching of conductors, allowing electric current to flow; the parts of the conductors which touch each other. *v.t.* to establish contact or communication with. **point of contact,** the point at which two lines, planes or bodies touch each other. **to be in contact with,** to be in touch, close proximity, or association with. **to come into contact with,** to meet, to come across. **to make contact,** to complete an electric circuit; to get in touch with. **contact-breaker,** *n.* a device for interrupting an electric circuit at regular intervals in order to produce a spark and explode gases in a cylinder in an internal combustion engine. **contact lens,** *n.* a lens worn in contact with the eyeball in place of spectacles. **contact man,** *n.* an intermediary. **contact print,** *n.* a photographic print made by placing a negative directly on to photographic paper. **contactable,** *a.* **contactual,** *a.* [L *contactus,* p.p. of *contingere* (*tangere,* to touch)]

contadino, *n.* (*pl.* **-ni**) an Italian peasant. **contadina,** *n.fem.* (*pl.* **-ne**). [It., from *contado,* a county, the country, L *comitātus,* COUNTY]

Contadora, *n.* a Panamanian island of the Pearl Island group in the Gulf of Panama. It was the first meeting place (1983) of the foreign ministers of Colombia, Mexico, Panama and Venezuela (now known as the **Contadora Group**) who came together to discuss the problems of Central America.

contagion, *n.* communication of disease by contact with a person suffering from it; contagious disease; transmission of social or moral qualities; deleterious influence; †venom, poison, poisonous exhalation. **contagionist,** *n.* one who believes in the contagious character of certain diseases. **contagious,** *a.* communicable by contact, communicating disease by contact; (*loosely*) infectious. **Contagious Diseases Acts,** acts passed to prevent the spread of certain contagious diseases. **contagious abortion,** *n.* brucellosis in cattle. **contagiously,** *adv.* **contagiousness,** *n.* **contagium,** *n.* (*pl.* **-gia**) the organism or substance that carries contagion. [F, from L *contāgio -ōnem* (*tāg-,* root of *tangere,* to touch)]

contain, *v.t.* to hold within fixed limits, as a vessel; to be capable of holding; to comprise, to include; (*Geom.*) to enclose; to be exactly divisible by; (*Mil.*) to hem in, to put out of action by investing; to restrain; to keep, retain. *v.i.* to restrain oneself; to be continent. **containable,** *a.* **container,** *n.* that which contains or encloses; a large rigid box of standard size and shape used for bulk transport and storage of goods. **container lorry, ship,** *n.* one designed for the transport of containers. **containerize, -ise,** *v.t.* to put into containers; to convert (e.g. a transportation system) to the use of containers. **containerization, -isation,** *n.* **containment,** *n.* the act of containing or restraining, esp. hostilities to a small area, or radioactive emission to a permitted zone in a nuclear reactor; **(Containment)** US policy dating from 1947 designed to prevent the spread of communism beyond the borders of the USSR. [OF *contenir,* L *continēre* (*tenēre,* to hold)]

contaminate, *v.t.* to defile, to sully, to pollute, esp. with radioactivity, to corrupt, to tarnish. †*a.,* contaminated. **contaminable,** *a.* **contaminant,** *n.* a substance that contaminates. **contamination,** *n.* **contaminative,** *a.* [L *contaminātus,* p.p. of *contāmināre*]

contango, *n.* the commission paid by a buyer for the postponement of transactions on the Stock Exchange. [etym. unknown]

contd., (*abbr.*) continued.

conte, *n.* a tale, esp. a short amusing story in prose. [F]

conteck, *n.* strife, dissension. [A-F *contek, contec* (etym. doubtful)]

contemn, *v.t.* to despise, to scorn; to slight, to neglect. **contemner,** *n.* [OF *contemner,* L *contemnere* (*temnere,* to despise)]

contemper, *v.t.* to temper by admixture; to adapt by tempering. **contemperation,** *n.* **contemperature,** *n.* [L *contemperāre* (*temperāre*)]

contemplate, *v.t.* to look at, to study; to meditate and reflect on; to purpose, to intend; to regard as possible or likely. *v.i.* to meditate. **contemplation,** *n.* **contemplative,** *a.* given to contemplation; thoughtful, studious. *n.* a member of a contemplative order. **contemplative life,** *n.* a life passed in prayer and meditation. **contemplative order,** *n.* a religious order, e.g. Carthusian, whose members are engaged wholly in worship and meditation. **contemplatively,** *adv.* **contemplativeness,** *n.* **contemplator,** *n.* [L *contemplātus,* p.p. of *contemplāre,* to observe (*templum,* a space of the sky for observation)]

contemporaneous, *a.* existing, living or happening at the same time; lasting, or of, the same period. **contemporaneously,** *adv.* **contemporaneousness,** *n.* **contemporaneity,** *n.* [L *contemporāneus* (*tempus, -poris,* time)]

contemporary, *a.* living at the same time; of the same age; belonging to the same period; up-to-date, modern. *n.* a contemporary person or thing. **contemporize, -ise,** *v.t.* to make contemporary. **contemporization, -isation,** *n.*

contempt, *n.* the act of contemning; scorn, disdain; the state of being contemned; shame, disgrace; (*Law*) an act of disobedience to the rules, orders or regulations of a sovereign, a court or a legislative body. **contempt of court,** disobedience or resistance to the orders or proceedings of a court of justice. **contemptible,** *a.* worthy of contempt, despicable, mean; †contemptuous. **(Old) Contemptibles,** troops of the British Expeditionary Force in 1914, so named from the Kaiser's allusion to them as 'a contemptible little army'. **contemptibility,** *n.* **contemptibleness,** *n.* **contempt-**

ibly, *adv.* **contemptuous**, *a.* expressive of contempt; disdainful, scornful. **contemptuously,** *adv.* **contemptuousness,** *n.* [L *contemptus,* scorn]

contend, *v.i.* to strive in opposition; to exert oneself in defence or support of anything; to strive to obtain or keep; to compete; to dispute. *v.t.* to maintain by argument. **contender,** †**contendent,** *n.* one who contends; an antagonist; an opponent. [OF *contendre,* L *contendere* (*tendere,* to stretch, strive)]

content[1], *a.* satisfied, pleased, willing; the term used to express an affirmative vote in the House of Lords; hence (*n.pl.*) those who vote in the affirmative. *v.t.* to satisfy, to appease; to make easy in any situation; to gratify. *n.* satisfaction, ease of mind; a condition or ground of satisfaction; †acquiescence. †**contentation**, *n.* contentment; satisfaction. **contented,** *a.* satisfied with what one has. **contentedly,** *adv.* **contentedness,** *n.* **contentless,** *a.* without any content or meaning; †discontented. **contentment,** *n.* the state of being contented or satisfied; gratification, satisfaction. [F, from L *contentus,* p.p. of *continēre,* to CONTAIN]

content[2], *n.* capacity or power of containing; volume; capacity; the meaning (of an utterance etc.) as opposed to the form; (*pl.*) that which is contained in a vessel, writing or book; the amount (of one substance) contained in a mixture, alloy etc. (*pl.*) a table or summary of subject-matter; (*pl.*) (*Math.*) the area or quantity contained within certain limits.

contention, *n.* the act of contending; quarrel, strife, controversy; emulation; a point contended for. **contentious,** *a.* disposed to or characterized by contention; quarrelsome. **contentiously,** *adv.* **contentiousness,** *n.* [F, from L *contentio -ōnem,* from *contendere,* to CONTEND]

conterminous, *a.* having a common boundary-line; having the same limits, coextensive (in line, range or meaning). **conterminal,** *a.* bordering, neighbouring, contiguous. **conterminously,** *adv.* [L *terminus,* a boundary]

contest[1], *v.t.* to contend for or about, to strive earnestly for; to dispute, to call in question, to oppose. *v.i.* to strive, to contend, to vie. **contestable,** *a.* **contestant,** *n.* one who contests. **contestation**, *n.* the act of contesting; disputation, controversy; something contended for, a contention; †contention; †attestation. **contester,** *n.* [F *contester,* L *contestārī* (*testārī,* to bear witness, from *testis,* a witness)]

contest[2], *n.* a struggle for victory or superiority; a dispute, a controversy; competition, rivalry. [as prec.]

context, *n.* the parts of a discourse or book immediately connected with a sentence or passage quoted; the setting, surroundings. **contextual**, *a.* **contextually,** *adv.* [L *contextus,* p.p. of *contexere* (*texere,* to weave)]

contexture, *n.* a weaving together; the disposition and relation of parts in a compound body or a literary composition; structure; †context. *v.t.* to give contexture to.

Conti, *n.* **Tom** (1945–), British stage and film actor specializing in character roles. His films include *The Duellists* (1976); *Merry Christmas Mr Lawrence* (1983); *Reuben, Reuben* (1983); *Beyond Therapy* (1987); *Shirley Valentine* (1989).

contiguous, *a.* meeting so as to touch; adjoining, neighbouring. **contiguity**, *n.* contact; proximity in time or space; (*Psych.*) the immediate relation of two impressions, a principle of association. **contiguously,** *adv.* [L *contiguus,* from *contingere* (*tangere,* to touch)]

continent[1], *a.* abstaining from indulgence in unlawful (or undue indulgence in lawful) pleasures; chaste; temperate; †restraining; †retentive; †continuous. **continence, -ency,** *n.* **continently,** *adv.* [OF, from L *continēre,* to CONTAIN]

continent[2], *n.* a large tract of land not disjoined or interrupted by a sea; one of the great geographical divisions of land; the mainland of Europe; †that which contains anything; the summary, the sum total; †mainland; †(*fig.*) a large and continuous extent of anything. **continental**, *a.* pertaining to a continent; European; (*US Hist.*) belonging to the Union forces in the Civil War. **continental breakfast,** *n.* a light breakfast of rolls and coffee. **continental climate,** *n.* one characteristic of the interior of a continent, with hot summers, cold winters and low rainfall. **continental drift,** *n.* the theory that the continents were orig. one landmass and have drifted apart slowly to their present positions. **continental quilt,** *n.* a duvet. **continental shelf,** *n.* an area of shallow water round a landmass before the ground begins to slope sharply down to the ocean depths. **continentalism**, *n.* **continentalist,** *n.* **continentalize, -ise,**, *v.t.* **continentally,** *adv.* [as prec.]

Continental Congress, in US history, the federal legislature of the original 13 states, acting as a provisional revolutionary government during the War of American Independence. It was convened in Philadelphia (1774–89), when the constitution was adopted. The second Continental Congress, convened May 1775, was responsible for drawing up the Declaration of Independence.

Continental System, *n.* the system of economic preference and protection within Europe created by the French emperor Napoleon in order to exclude British trade. Apart from its function of economic warfare, the system also reinforced the French economy at the expense of other European states. It lasted from 1806 to 1813, but failed due to British naval superiority.

contingent, *a.* dependent on an uncertain issue; of doubtful occurrence; accidental, not essential, conditional; (*Log.*) that may or may not be true. *n.* a fortuitous event; that which falls to one in a division or apportionment; a naval or military force furnished by a state for a joint enterprise; a quota of fighting men. **contingent liability,** *n.* a liability that will arise only in a certain event. **contingency,** *n.* the state of being contingent; a chance or possible occurrence; an accident; something dependent on an uncertain issue; (*pl.*) incidental expenses; money provided for these in an estimate. **contingency fund, plan,** *n.* a sum of money or plan of action kept in reserve in case some situation should arise. **contingently,** *adv.* [L *contingens -ntem,* pres.p. of *contingere* (*tangere,* to touch)]

continual, *a.* unbroken, incessant; without interruption or cessation; (*coll.*) very frequent. **continually,** *adv.* [OF *continuel,* L *continuālis*]

continuance, *n.* the act of continuing; duration; stay; (*Law*) adjournment. **continuant,** *a.* continuing; prolonged. *n.* a consonant whose sound can be prolonged, as *f, v, s, r.* [OF, from *continuer,* to CONTINUE]

continuate, *a.* continuous, uninterrupted; long-continued. **continuation,** *n.* the act of continuing; that by which anything is continued or carried on; extension or prolongation in a series or line; in the Stock Exchange, the carrying over of accounts for stock (see CONTANGO); (*pl.*) gaiters or bands of box-cloth continuous with knee-breeches; (*sl.*) trousers. **continuation class,** *n.* (*formerly*) one for teaching those who had left school. **continuation school,** *n.* (*formerly*) one for those who had left elementary school but were continuing their studies after work. **continuative,** *a.* causing or tending to continuation. **continuator,** *n.* one who continues a (literary) work begun by another. [L *continuātus,* p.p. of *continuāre,* to CONTINUE]

continue, *v.t.* to carry on without interruption; to keep up; to take up, to extend, to complete; (*Law*) to adjourn; †to suffer to remain. *v.i.* to remain, to stay; to last, to abide; to remain in existence; to persevere. **continued fraction,** *n.* one in which the denominator is a whole number plus a fraction, the denominator of which is a whole number plus a fraction etc. **continued proportion,** *n.* a series of quantities in which the ratio is the same between each two adjacent terms. **continuable,** *a.* [F *continuer,* L *continuāre* (*continuus,* CONTINUOUS)]

continuo, *n.* (*pl.* **-nuos**) thoroughbass.

continuous, *a.* connected without a break in space or time; uninterrupted, unceasing; (*Bot.*) without joints; (*Arch.*) having the mullions carried on into the tracery. **continuous assessment,** *n.* assessment of the progress of a pupil by means of checks carried out at intervals throughout the course of study. **continuous creation,** *n.* the theory that the creation of the universe is a continuous process, as opposed to the *big bang* theory. **continuous stationery,** *n.* (*Comput.*) paper in a long strip with regular perforations, which can be fed through a printer. **continuity,** *n.* uninterrupted connection; union without a break or interval; the detailed description of a film in accordance with which the production is carried out. **law of continuity,** the principle that nothing passes from one state into another without passing through all the intermediate states. **continuity girl, man,** *n.* the person responsible for seeing that there are no discrepancies between the scenes of a film. **continuously,** *adv.* **continuousness,** *n.* [L *continuus,* from *continuāre* (*tenēre,* to hold)]

continuum, *n.* (*pl.* **-nua**) (*Phys.*) an unbroken mass, series or course of events; a continuous series of component parts that pass into each other. **four-dimensional continuum,** the three space dimensions and the time dimension. [as prec.]

cont-line, *n.* (*Naut.*) the space between casks stowed side by side; the external space between the strands in a rope. [etym. doubtful]

conto, *n.* a Portuguese or Brazilian monetary unit, 1000 escudos or cruzeiros. [Port., from late L *computum,* COUNT[1]]

contorniate, *a.* of a coin, bordered by a deep furrow round the inside of the edge. *n.* a coin distinguished by this furrow. [F, from It. *contorno*]

contorno, *n.* contour, outline. [It.]

contort, *v.t.* to twist with violence, to wrench; to distort. **contorted,** *a.* (*Geol.*) twisted obliquely so as to form folds, used of strata curved or twisted as if by lateral pressure when soft. **contortion,** *n.* the act of twisting; a writhing movement; (*Surg.*) partial dislocation, the wresting of a member out of its natural situation. **contortionist,** *n.* an acrobat who bends his or her body into various shapes; one who twists the sense of words; an artist who paints contorted figures. **contortive,** *a.* [L *contortus,* p.p. of *contorquēre* (*torquēre,* to turn, to twist)]

contour, *n.* the defining line of any figure or body; outline; outline of coast or other geographical feature. *v.t.* to make an outline of; to mark with contour lines; to carry (a road) round a valley or hill. **contour line,** *n.* a line on a map marking a particular level. **contour map,** *n.* one exhibiting the elevations and depressions of the earth's surface by means of contour lines. **contour ploughing,** *n.* ploughing round sloping ground on a level instead of up and down. [F, from *contourner,* to turn (cp. CONTORNO)]

contr., (*abbr.*) contracted; contraction.

contra, *prep.* against, opposite. *n.* the opposite (usu. the credit) side of an account. **pro and contra,** for and against. [L, against]

Contra, *n.* a member of a Central American right-wing guerrilla force attempting to overthrow the democratically elected Nicaraguan Sandinista government from 1979. The Contras, many of them mercenaries or former members of the deposed Somoza's guard, have operated mainly from bases outside Nicaragua, especially in Honduras, with covert US funding as revealed by the Irangate hearings (1986–87). In 1989 US president Bush announced an agreement with Congress to provide $41 million in aid to the Contras until Feb. 1990. The Sandinista government was defeated by the National Opposition Union, a US-backed coalition, in the Feb. 1990 elections.

contra-, *pref.* against; denoting opposition, resistance, or contrariety; in music, signifying extreme.

contraband, *a.* prohibited, unlawful; forbidden by proclamation or law. †*v.t.* to declare contraband. *v.i.* to deal in contraband goods. *n.* prohibited traffic; articles forbidden to be exported or imported; smuggled articles; (also **contraband of war**) goods not allowed to be supplied to a belligerent nation by a neutral one. **contrabandist,** *n.* a dealer in contraband goods; a smuggler. [Sp. *contrabanda,* It. *contrabbando*]

contra-bass, *n.* double-bass.

contrabassoon, *n.* a double-reeded woodwind instrument with a range an octave lower than a bassoon.

contraception, *n.* birth-control, the taking of measures to prevent conception. **contraceptive,** *n., a.* (a device or drug) for preventing conception.

contract[1], *v.t.* to draw together; to bring into smaller compass; (*Gram.*) to abbreviate, shorten, draw together; to acquire, to incur; to become liable for; to be attacked by (disease); to agree to or settle by covenant; to settle, to establish. *v.i.* to shrink; to agree (to do any act or supply certain articles for a settled price). **to contract in, out,** to agree (not) to participate in some scheme, esp. a pension scheme. **contractable,** *a.* of a disease, capable of being contracted. **contracted,** *a.* drawn together; betrothed; mean, narrow, selfish. †**contractedly,** *adv.* †**contractedness,** *n.* **contractible,** *a.* capable of being drawn together. **contractibility,** *n.* **contractile,** *a.* tending to contract; having the power to shorten itself. **contractility,** *n.* **contraction,** *n.* the act of shrinking, the state of being drawn together, confined or shortened; an abbreviation; the shortening of a word by the omission of a letter or syllable; the act of contracting (a habit, a disease etc.). **contractive,** *a.* tending or serving to contract. [L *contractus,* p.p. of *contrahere* (CON-, *trahere,* to draw)]

contract[2], *n.* an agreement; a compact; the writing by which an agreement is entered into; a formal betrothal; an undertaking to do certain work or supply certain articles for a specified consideration; (*Law*) an agreement recognized as a legal obligation; an offer or promise which has been formally accepted. **contract bridge,** *n.* a form of auction bridge in which points are gained only for tricks made as well as bid. **contractual,** *a.* implying or relating to a contract.

contractor, *n.* one who undertakes a contract, esp. to do or supply anything for a stipulated consideration; an employer of labour who contracts to do building work, usu. on a large scale; a muscle that serves to contract an organ or other part of the body. [as prec.]

contra-dance, COUNTRY-DANCE.

contradict, *v.t.* to oppose in words; to deny the truth of; to assert the opposite of; to oppose. *v.i.* to deny the truth of a statement. **contradictable,** *a.* **contradiction,** *n.* the act of opposing in words; denial; contrary statement; repugnancy, inconsistency; that which is inconsistent with itself. **contradiction in terms,** a statement that is obviously self-contradictory or inconsistent. **contradictious,** *a.* inclined to contradiction; cavilling, disputatious. **contradictiously,** *adv.* **contradictiousness,** *n.* **contradictive,** *a.* contradictory. **contradictively,** *adv.* **contradictiveness,** *n.* **contradictor,** *n.* **contradictory,** *a.* affirming the contrary; inconsistent; mutually opposed, logically incompatible; disputatious. *n.* (*Log.*) a contradictory proposition; the contrary. **contradictorily,** *adv.* **contradictoriness,** *n.* [L *contrādictus,* p.p. of *contrādīcere* (*dīcere,* to speak)]

contradistinguish, *v.t.* to distinguish by contrasting opposite qualities. **contradistinction,** *n.*

contraflow, *n.* a form of motorway traffic regulation, two-way traffic being instituted on one carriageway so that the other may be closed.

contrahent, *a.* contracting; entering into a contract. [L *contrahens -ntem,* pres.p. of *contrahere,* to CONTRACT]

contrail, *n.* a condensation trail.

contraindicant, *n.* (*Med.*) a symptom which indicates that a particular treatment or drug would be unsuitable. **contraindicate,** *v.t.* **contraindication,** *n.*

contralto, *n.* the lowest of the three principal varieties of the female voice, and that to which in choral music the part next above the alto is assigned; one who sings this part; music written for this part. *a.* singing or arranged for contralto. [It.]

contraplex, *a.* of or pertaining to the sending of messages in opposite directions over the same wire. [L *-plex* (as in SIMPLEX, DUPLEX)]

contraposition, *n.* a placing opposite to, or in contrast; (*Log.*) a kind of conversion by means of negation. **contrapositive,** *a.*

contraption, *n.* a contrivance. [etym. doubtful; perh. CONTRIVANCE and TRAP[1]]

contrapuntal, *a.* (*Mus.*) pertaining or according to counterpoint. **contrapuntist,** *n.* one skilled in counterpoint. [It. *contrapuntal* (now *contrappuntal*), see COUNTERPOINT[1]]

contrary, *a.* opposite; opposed, diametrically different; contradictory, repugnant; (*Log.*) opposed as regards affirmation and negation; different from the right one; (*coll.*), antagonistic, wayward, perverse. *n.* a thing of opposite qualities; the opposite; a thing that contradicts; the opposite of a motion put from the chair. *adv.* contrarily; adversely; in an opposite manner or direction. †*v.t.* to contradict; to oppose. **by contraries,** by way of contrast; by negation instead of affirmation, and vice versa. **on the contrary,** on the other hand; quite the reverse. **to the contrary,** to the opposite effect. **contrariant,** *a.* opposed, antagonistic, contrary. **contrariety,** *n.* the state of being contrary; opposition; disagreement; inconsistency. **contrarily,** *adv.* in a contrary manner. **contrariness,** *n.* the state or quality of being contrary. †**contrarious,** *a.* inclined to oppose, perverse; adverse. †**contrariously,** *adv.* †**contrariousness,** *n.* **contrariwise,** *adv.* on the other hand, conversely; perversely. [OF *contrarie,* L *contrārius*]

contrast[1], *v.t.* to set in opposition, so as to show the difference between, or the superior excellence of one to another. *v.i.* to stand in contrast or opposition. [OF *contraster,* late L *contrāstāre* (CONTRA-, L *stāre,* to stand)]

contrast[2], *n.* opposition or unlikeness of things or qualities; the presentation of opposite things with a view to comparison; the degree of difference in tone between the light and dark parts of a photograph or TV picture. **contrastive,** *a.* **contrasty,** *a.* showing great contrast between light and dark tones. [as prec.]

contrasuggestible, *a.* reacting to a suggestion by doing the opposite.

contrate, *a.* (*Watch- and clock-making*) having teeth or cogs at right angles to the plane of the wheel.

contra-tenor, COUNTERTENOR.

contrat social, *n.* a social contract. [F]

contravallation, *n.* a chain of fortifications constructed by besiegers as a protection against sallies. [F *contrevallation* (L *vallatio -ōnem;* cp. CIRCUMVALLATION)]

contravene, *v.t.* to violate, to transgress; to be in conflict with, to obstruct; to oppose, to be inconsistent with. **contravention,** *n.* violation. [F *contrevenir,* L *contrāvenīre* (*venīre,* to come)]

contretemps, *n.* an unexpected event which throws everything into confusion; a disagreement, a confrontation. [F, bad or adverse time]

contribute, *v.t.* to give for a common purpose; to pay as one's share; to write (an article or chapter) for a publication. *v.i.* to give a part; to have a share in any act or effect; to write for a newspaper etc. **contributable,** *a.* liable to be contributed. **contribution,** *n.* the act of contributing; that which is contributed; a subscription; a levy or tax. **contributive,** *a.* contributing, assisting, promoting. **contributiveness,** *n.* **contributor,** *n.* one who contributes. **contributory,** *a.* contributing to the same fund, stock or result; promoting the same end. **contributory negligence,** *n.* partial responsibility for injury etc., by reason of failure to take adequate precautions. [L *contribūtus,* p.p. of *contribuere* (*tribuere,* to pay)]

contrite, *a.* deeply sorry for sin; thoroughly penitent; characterized by penitence. **contritely,** *adv.* **contrition,** *n.* heartfelt sorrow for sin; penitence. [F *contrit,* L *contrītus,* p.p. of *conterere* (*terere,* to rub, to grind)]

†**contriturate,** *v.t.* to grind thoroughly.

contrive[1], *v.t.* to devise, to invent; to bring to pass, to effect, to manage. *v.i.* to form designs, to scheme (against); to manage (successfully). **contrivable,** *a.* **contrivance,** *n.* the act of contriving; the thing contrived; device, plan; a trick, an artifice, a plot; invention, apparatus; inventiveness. **contrived,** *a.* forced, artificial. **contriver,** *n.* [ME *contreve, controve,* OF *controver* (*trover,* to find, from late L *tropāre*]

†**contrive[2],** *v.t.* to wear away; to pass, to spend (the time). [prob. from L *contrīvī,* past of *conterere* (cp. CONTRITE)]

control, *n.* check, restraint; restraining, directing and regulating power; authority, command; a person who controls, esp. a spirit controlling a medium; a standard of comparison for checking the results of experiment; (*pl.*) the mechanisms which govern the operation of a vehicle or machine, e.g. the gear-lever, clutch, brake-lever etc. of a car; *v.t.* (*past, p.p.* **controlled**) to exercise power over, to govern, to command; to restrain, to regulate, to hold in check; to verify or check, orig. to check by a duplicate register. **control board, panel,** *n.* one containing the switches etc. for operating an electrical or mechanical system. **control character,** *n.* (*Comput.*) one which functions as a signal to control some operation, e.g. start, print etc. **control column,** *n.* the lever by which the elevators and ailerons of an aircraft are operated, the joy-stick. **control experiment,** *n.* one carried out on two objects so as to have a means of checking and confirming the inferences deduced. **controlling interest,** *n.* a shareholding sufficiently large to ensure some control over the running of a company. **control panel** CONTROL BOARD. **control room,** *n.* a room from which a large electric or other installation is controlled. **control surface,** *n.* a movable surface, e.g. the elevators, rudder etc., by which the movements of an aeroplane are controlled. **control tower,** *n.* a tower at an airport from which traffic in and out is controlled. **control unit,** *n.* (*Comput.*) the part of a central processor which controls the execution of a program. **controllable,** *a.* **controller,** *n.* one who exercises control; a ruler, a director; an officer appointed to verify the accounts of other officers by means of a duplicate register; (*N Am.*) one who keeps the public accounts. **controllership,** *n.* **controlment,** *n.* control, regulation; the power or act of controlling. [OF *contre-rolle,* a duplicate roll or register]

controversy, *n.* disputation, esp. a dispute carried on in writing; †resolute resistance; †variance, contention. **controversial,** *a.* inclined, pertaining to or arousing controversy. **controversialism,** *n.* **controversialist,** *n.* one who carries on a controversy; a disputant. **controversially,** *adv.* [L *contrōversia,* a quarrel, from *contrōversus,* opposed (*versus,* p.p. of *vertere,* to turn)]

controvert, *v.t.* to dispute; to call in question; to oppose or refute by argument. †**controverter,** *n.* **controvertist,** *n.* [see prec.]

contumacious, *a.* perverse, obstinate, stubborn; stubbornly opposing lawful authority; (*Law*) wilfully disobedient to the orders of a court. **contumaciously,** *adv.* **contumaciousness,** *n.* **contumacy,** *n.* [L *contumāx -ācis* (*tumēre,* to swell with pride)]

contumely, *n.* rude, scornful abuse or reproach; insolence, contempt; disgrace, ignominy. **contumelious,** *a.* contemptuous, insolent, abusive; †dishonouring, disgraceful. **contumeliously,** *adv.* **contumeliousness,** *n.* [OF *contumelie,* L *contumēlia* (cogn. with *contumāx,* see CONTUMACIOUS)]

contund, *v.t.* to bruise, to knock about. [see foll.]

contuse, *v.t.* to bruise without breaking the skin. **contusion,** *n.* the act of contusing; the state of being contused; a bruise. [L *contūsus,* p.p. of *contundere* (CON-, *tundere,* to beat)]

conundrum, *n.* a riddle; a puzzling question. [etym. doubtful]

conurbation, *n.* the aggregation of urban districts. [L *urbs,* a city]

conv., (*abbr.*) convent; convention(al); conversation.

convalesce, *v.i.* to recover health. **convalescence,** *n.* **convalescent,** *a.* recovering from illness. *n.* one who is recovering health. **convalescent hospital, home,** *n.* a hospital for convalescent patients. [L *convalēscere* (*valēscere,* incept. of *valēre,* to grow)]

convallaria, *n.* a genus of Liliaceae, containing only one species, the lily of the valley. [L *convallis* (*vallis,* valley), *-āria,* neut. pl. of *ārius,* -ARY]

convection, *n.* the act of conveying; the propagation of heat or electricity through liquids and gases by the movement of the heated particles. **convectional,** *a.* **convective,** *a.* **convector,** *n.* a heater which works by the circulation of currents of heated air. [L *convectio,* from *convehere* (*vehere,* to carry)]

convenance, *n.* (*usu. pl.*) conventional usages, the proprieties. [F]

convene, *v.t.* to call together; to convoke; to summon to appear. *v.i.* to meet together, to assemble. **convenable,** *a.* **convener,** *n.* one who calls a committee etc. together; (*Sc.*) the chairman of a public body or committee. [F *convenir,* L *convenīre* (*venīre,* to come)]

convenient, *a.* suitable; commodious; useful, handy; opportune, at hand, close by. **convenience, -ency,** *n.* the quality or state of being convenient; comfort, accommodation; a cause or source of comfort or accommodation; advantage; a thing that is useful; a water-closet or urinal; (*pl.*) things or arrangements that promote ease and comfort or save trouble. **convenience food,** *n.* food bought already prepared so as to need very little further work before eating. **convenience store,** *n.* a shop which sells a wide range of useful articles as well as food, and is open at times convenient to the public. **conveniently,** *adv.* [L *conveniens -ntem,* pres.p. of *convenīre* (as prec.)]

convent[1], *n.* a community of religious persons of either sex (now usu. for women); the building occupied by such a community. **conventual,** *a.* belonging to a convent. *n.* a member of a convent; one of a branch of the Franciscans who follow a mitigated rule. **conventually,** *adv.* [ME and A-F *covent,* OF *convent,* L *conventus,* p.p. of *convenīre,* as prec.]

convent[2], †*v.t.* to convene, to summon. *v.i.* to meet. [see prec.]

conventicle, *n.* a clandestine gathering; a meeting or place of worship of dissenters in the 16th and 17th cents. [L *conventiculum,* dim. of *conventus,* as prec.]

convention, *n.* the act of coming together; a meeting; the persons assembled; a union of representatives; an agreement, a treaty; an accepted usage. **conventional,** *a.* agreed on by compact; founded on custom or use; slavishly observant of the customs of society; of painting, following tradition and accepted models; of energy sources, warfare etc., not nuclear. **conventionalism,** *n.* **conventionalist,** *n.* **conventionality,** *n.* **conventionalize, -ise,** *v.t.* **conventionally,** *adv.* **conventionary,** *a.* (*Law*) acting or holding under convention as distinguished from custom. *n.* a conventionary tenant. [F, from L *conventio -ōnem* (*convenīre,* to CONVENE)]

converge, *v.i.* to tend towards one point; (*Math.*) to approach a definite limit by an indefinite number of steps. *v.t.* to cause to converge. **convergence, -ency,** *n.* **convergent,** *a.* tending to meet in one point; used of rays of light which being continued will meet in a focus; used of a lens which will cause rays to meet in a focus; (*Biol.*) developing similar characteristics in a similar environment; (*Psych.*) referring to thinking which produces a logical or conventional result. [L *convergere* (*vergere,* to turn, incline)]

conversant, *a.* having knowledge acquired by study, use or familiarity; well acquainted, proficient; closely connected, familiar. **conversance, -ancy,** *n.* [CONVERSE[1]]

conversation, *n.* the act of conversing; familiar talk; intimate fellowship or intercourse; †sexual intercourse. **conversation piece,** *n.* representation of figures in familiar groupings; something that provides a topic of conversation. **conversational,** *a.* **conversationalist,** *n.* **conversationally,** *adv.* [CONVERSE[1]]

conversazione, *n.* (*pl.* **-nes, -ni**) a social meeting devoted to literary, artistic or scientific subjects. [It., from L *conversātio -ōnem,* conversation]

converse[1], *v.i.* to discourse easily and familiarly (with); †to hold intercourse, to have dealings (with). **conversable,** *a.* inclined to conversation; free, sociable, agreeable. **conversableness,** *n.* **conversably,** *adv.* [F *converser,* L *conversārī,* to be conversant or keep company with, pass. of *convertere,* to CONVERT]

converse[2], *n.* close and intimate connection, familiarity; conversation; opposite, counterpart or complement; (*Math.*) an inverted proposition; (*Log.*) a converted proposition. *a.* opposite, reciprocal, complemental. **conversely,** *adv.* in a contrary order; reciprocally. [see prec.]

conversion, *n.* change from one state to another; transmutation; the act of changing to a new mode of life, religion, morals or politics; (*Theol.*) the turning from sin to godliness; (*Math.*) the clearing of an equation of fractions; (*Log.*) transposition of the terms of a proposition; (*Stock Exch.*) change of one kind of securities into another kind; a change in the structure or use of a building; a building so changed, esp. a modernized dwellinghouse; the transformation of fertile to fissile material in a nuclear reactor. [F, from L *conversio -ōnem,* from *convertere,* to CONVERT]

convert[1], *v.t.* to change from one physical state to another, to transmute; to cause to turn from one religion or party to another; to change (one kind of securities) into another kind; (*Log.*) to transpose the terms of; in Rugby football, to complete (a try) by kicking a goal. †*v.i.* to be converted or changed; to undergo a change. **convertend,** *n.* (*Log.*) a proposition to be converted. **converter,** *n.* one who converts; an iron retort used in making Bessemer steel; a device for changing alternating current to direct current or vice versa; (*Comput.*) a device that converts data from one format to another; a reactor that converts fertile to fissile nuclear material. **convertible,** *a.* that may be converted or changed; transmutable; exchangeable for another kind of thing (as paper money for coin); of a car, having a roof that folds back. *n.* such a car. **convertible husbandry,** *n.* that which is based on rotation of crops. **convertible terms,** *n.pl.* (*Log.*) such as can be changed for equivalents. **convertibility,** *n.* **convertibly,** *adv.* [L *convertere* (CON-, *vertere,* to turn)]

convert[2], *n.* one who is converted from one religion or party to another, esp. one who is converted to Christianity, or from a worldly to a spiritual state of mind. [as prec.]

convex, *a.* having a rounded form on the exterior surface. *n.* a convex body. **convexity,** *n.* curvature. **convexly,** *adv.* **convexo-,** *comb. form.* convex. **convexo-concave,** *a.* convex on one side and concave on the other. **convexo-convex,** *a.* convex on both sides. **convexo-plane,** *a.* convex on one side and plane on the other. [L *convexus,* arched]

convey, *v.t.* to carry, to transport, to transmit; to impart; (*Law*) to transfer (property); (*sl.*) to remove secretly, to steal. *v.i.* to play the thief. **conveyable,** *a.* that may be conveyed. **conveyance,** *n.* the act, means or instrument of conveying; a vehicle; (*Law*) the act of transferring real property from one person to another; the document by which it is transferred; †communication of meaning, style; †stealing, plagiarism; †trickery. **conveyancer,** *n.* (*Law*) one who draws up conveyances. **conveyancing,** *n.* †**conveyer, -or,** *n.* one who or that which conveys; †a thief; †a juggler; (also **conveyor belt**) an endless mechanical belt or moving platform which carries work along a line of workers. [OF *conveier, convoier,* late L *conviāre* (CON-, *via,* way)]

convict[1], *v.t.* to prove guilty; to return a verdict of guilty against; to convince of sin; †to prove, to demonstrate; †to confute. †*a.* convicted. **conviction,** *n.* the act of convicting; the state of being convicted; the state of being convinced; strong belief, persuasion. **to carry conviction,** to be convincing. **convictive,** *a.* [L *convictus,* p.p. of *convincere* (CON-, *vincere,* to conquer)]

convict[2], *n.* a criminal sentenced to a term in prison. [as prec.]

convince, *v.t.* to satisfy the mind of; to persuade to conviction; to overcome by proof; †to convict; †to conquer; †to confute. **convincement,** *n.* conviction. **con-**

vincible, *a.* capable of conviction or refutation. **convincing,** *a.* persuasive, dispelling doubt. **convincingly,** *adv.* **convincingness,** *n.* [L *convincere,* as prec.]

convive, *n.* a guest at a banquet. **convivial,** *a.* festive, social, jovial. **convivialist,** *n.* **conviviality,** *n.* **convivially,** *adv.* [L *convīva,* from *convīvere* (later use from F *convive,* L *convīva*)]

†**convocate,** *v.t.* to convoke. [L *convocātus,* p.p. of *convocāre,* see CONVOKE]

convocation, *n.* the act of calling together; an assembly, a meeting, a gathering; an assembly of qualified graduates of certain universities; an assembly of the clergy of a province.

convoke, *v.t.* to call or summon together; to convene. [F *convoquer,* L *convocāre* (CON-, *vocāre,* to call)]

convolute, -luted, *a.* rolled together; of petals, leaves etc., rolled up in another of the same kind; intricate, complex. **convolution,** *n.* the act of convolving; the state of being convolved; a fold, esp. of brain matter; a winding; a winding motion; intricacy. **convolve,** *v.t.* to roll or wind together; to wind one part over another. **convolvulus,** *n.* a genus of climbing plants, containing the bindweed. [L *convolūtus,* p.p. of *convolvere* (CON-, *volvere,* to roll)]

convoy, *v.t.* to accompany on the way, by land or sea, for the sake of protection, esp. with a warship; †to escort (a lady). *n.* the act of convoying or escorting; a protecting force accompanying persons, goods, ships etc. for purposes of defence; an escort, a guard; that which is convoyed, esp. a company of merchant ships. [F *convoier,* CONVEY]

convulse, *v.t.* to agitate violently; to affect with convulsions; to excite spasms of laughter in. **convulsant,** *n.* a drug that induces convulsions. **convulsion,** *n.* (*usu. pl.*) a diseased action of the muscular tissues of the body characterized by violent contractions and alternate relaxations; hence, a violent agitation, disturbance or commotion. **convulsionary,** *a.* **convulsive,** *a.* producing or attended with convulsions. **convulsively,** *adv.* **convulsiveness,** *n.* [L *convulsus,* p.p. of *convellere* (*vellere,* to pluck)]

cony, coney, *n.* a rabbit; rabbit fur; (*Bibl.*) a small pachydermatous animal, *Hyrax syriacus,* living in holes among rocks. †**cony-catch,** *v.t., v.i.* to steal, to cheat, to gull. †**cony-catcher,** *n.* a thief, a cheat, a trickster. †**cony-fish,** *n.* the burbot. [OF *conil, connil;* the sing. *cony* from the pl. *conys* or *conies,* from the OF pl. *coniz,* L *cuniculus,* a rabbit (etym. doubtful)]

coo, *v.i.* to make a soft low sound, like a dove; to speak lovingly. *v.t.* to say in cooing fashion. *n.* the characteristic note of a dove. *int.* expressing astonishment. **to bill and coo** BILL[1]. [imit.]

cooboo, *n.* (*Austral.*) an Aboriginal child. [Abor.]

cooee, *n.* a call used to attract attention. *v.i.* to make this call. **within a cooee (of),** (*Austral.*) within calling distance (of). [Abor.]

cook[1], *n.* one who dresses or prepares food for the table. *v.t.* to prepare (as food) for the table by boiling, roasting etc.; to garble, falsify; to concoct (often with *up*). *v.i.* to act as a cook; to undergo the process of cooking. **to cook one's goose,** (*sl.*) to settle one; to stop one's game. **to cook the books,** (*coll.*) to falsify the accounts. **what's cooking?** (*coll.*) what's afoot? what's being done? **cook book,** *n.* one containing recipes and advice on preparing food. **cook-chill,** *v.t.* to cook and chill (convenience foods). *a.* of foods prepared in this way. **cook general,** *n.* a person employed to do cooking and housework. **cookhouse,** *n.* (*Naut.*) a galley; also a detached kitchen in warm countries. **cookout,** *n.* (*N Am.*) a party at which food is cooked out of doors. †**cook-room,** *n.* a kitchen; (*Naut.*) a galley; a cookhouse. **cook shop,** *n.* an eating-house. **cookable,** *a.* **cooker,** *n.* a stove or other apparatus for cooking; food that undergoes cooking well; one who garbles or concocts. **cookery,** *n.* the act or art of cooking; the occupation of a cook; (*N Am.*) a place for cooking. **cookery book,** *n.* a cook book. **cooking,** *a.* used in cooking; suitable for cooking rather than eating raw. **cooky,** *n.* (*coll.*) a cook. [OE *cōc,* L *coquus,* a cook (*coquere,* to cook; cogn. with Gr. *pessein,* Sansk. *pach*)]

cook[2], *v.i.* (*Sc.*) to appear and disappear. [etym. doubtful]

Cook, Mount, *n.* the highest point, 3764 m/12,353 ft, of the Southern Alps, range of mountains running through New Zealand.

Cook[1], *n.* **James** (1728–79), English naval explorer. After surveying the St Lawrence (1759), he made three voyages: 1769–71 to Tahiti, New Zealand and Australia; 1772–75 to the South Pacific; and 1776–79 to the South and North Pacific, attempting to find the Northwest Passage and charting the Siberian coast. He was killed in Hawaii.

Cook[2], *n.* **Robin Finlayson** (1946–), English Labour politician. A member of the moderate-left Tribune Group, he entered Parliament in 1974 and became a leading member of Labour's shadow cabinet.

Cook[3], *n.* **Thomas** (1808–92), pioneer British travel agent and founder of Thomas Cook & Son. He introduced traveller's cheques (then called 'circular notes'), in the early 1870s.

Cooke, *n.* **Sam** (1931–64), US soul singer and songwriter, who began his career as a gospel singer and turned to pop music in 1956. His hits include 'You Send Me' (1957) and 'Wonderful World' (1960) (re-released 1986).

cookie, *n.* (*Sc.*) a baker's plain bun; (*N Am.*) a small sweet cake, a biscuit; (*coll.*) a person. **the way the cookie crumbles,** the way things are, an unalterable state of affairs. [prob. from Dut. *koekje*]

Cook Islands, *n. pl.* a group of six large and a number of smaller Polynesian islands 2600 km/1600 miles NE of Auckland, New Zealand; area 290 sq km/112 sq miles; population (1986) 17,000. Their main products include fruit, copra and crafts. They became a self-governing overseas territory of New Zealand in 1965.

Cook Strait, *n.* a strait dividing North and South Island, New Zealand. A submarine cable carries electricity from South to North Island.

cool, *a.* slightly or moderately cold; not retaining or causing heat; not ardent or zealous, apathetic; chilling, frigid, aloof; calm, dispassionate; deliberate; indifferent; impudent, audacious; in hunting, faint (of scent); (*coll.*) sophisticated; (*coll.*) relaxed; (*coll.*) without exaggeration. *n.* coolness, moderate temperature; a cool place. *v.t.* to make cool; to quiet, to calm, to allay. *v.i.* to become cool. **to cool one's heels,** (*coll.*) to be kept waiting. **to keep, lose one's cool,** (*coll.*) to remain (stop being) calm. **cool bag, box,** *n.* an insulated bag or box in which food is kept cold. **cool cupboard,** *n.* a refrigerated storage cupboard for food or drink, esp. in a shop. **cool-headed,** *a.* dispassionate, self-possessed. **cooling tower,** *n.* a tower in which water is cooled by trickling over wooden slats, for industrial reuse. **cool tankard,** *n.* an old-fashioned drink, usu. made of wine and water mixed with lemon-juice etc. **coolant,** *n.* a liquid used for cooling or lubricating. **cooler,** *n.* that which cools; a vessel in which liquors are set to cool; (*sl.*) prison; a drink consisting of wine and fruit juice. **coolish,** *a.* **coolly,** *adv.* **coolness,** *n.* [OE *cōl,* from Teut. *kōl-, kal-* (cp. Dan. *köl,* G *kühl,* L *gelu*)]

coolabah, *n.* (*Austral.*) name given to several species of eucalyptus trees. [Abor.]

coolah, *n.* (*Austral.*) a bear. [Abor.]

coolamon, *n.* (*Austral.*) a wooden water-vessel or bowl for seeds. [Abor.]

Coolidge, *n.* **(John) Calvin** (1872–1933), 30th president of the US (1923–29), a Republican. As governor of Massachusetts (1919), he was responsible for crushing a Boston police strike. He became vice-president in 1921 and president on the death of Warren Harding. He was re-elected in 1924, and his period of office was marked by economic prosperity.

coolie, *n.* a hired labourer in or from any part of the East. [Hind. *qūli*]

coom[1], *n.* refuse matter, as soot, coal-dust, mould; the drip from journal boxes, wheels etc. [CULM[2]]

coom[2], *n.* (*Sc.*) the timber centering for an arch; perh. a dome-shaped hill or ridge (spelt also *comb, combe, coomb,* and sometimes identified with COMBE). [etym. doubtful]

coomb[1], COMBE.

coomb[2], *n.* a measure for corn, containing four bushels (0·15 cu. m). [OE *cumb,* cp. COMBE]

coon, *n.* (*coll.*) short for RACOON; (*offensive*) a Negro. **gone coon,** (*N Am., sl.*) one hopelessly ruined. **coonskin,** *n.* the fur of a racoon; a hat made of the skin and tail of a racoon. [short for RACOON]

coon-can, *n.* a card game like rummy. [Sp. *con quién,* with whom]

co-op, *n., a.* short for COOPERATIVE (society or shop).

coop, *n.* a box of boards, barred or wired on one side, for confining domestic birds; a cage for small animals; †a wickerwork trap for catching eels etc.; a confined space. *v.t.* to confine in or as in a coop. [ME *cupe,* a basket, perh. from L *cupa,* a lute, a cask]

cooper[1], *n.* one whose trade is to make barrels, tubs etc.; a mender of casks etc. on a ship; †a bottle-basket for wine; a mixture of stout and porter (orig. prepared for the coopers in breweries). *v.t.* to make or repair (casks etc.); (*coll.*) to furnish, to rig (up). **cooperage,** *n.* the trade or workshop of a cooper; the price paid for cooper's work. **coopery,** *n.* [prob. from WG (cp. MDut. *cuper,* MLG *küper*), med. L *cupārius,* from *cupa,* a cask]

cooper[2], COPER under COPE[3].

Cooper[1], *n.* a grand prix motor racing team formed by John Cooper. They built Formula Two and Formula Three cars before building their revolutionary rear-engined Cooper T45 in 1958.

Cooper[2], *n.* **Gary** (1901–62), US actor. He epitomized the lean, true-hearted Yankee, slow of speech but capable of outdoing the 'badmen' in *Lives of a Bengal Lancer* (1935), *Mr Deeds Goes to Town* (1936), *Sergeant York* (1940) (Academy Award 1941), and *High Noon* (1952).

Cooper[3], *n.* **James Fenimore** (1789–1851), US writer of 50 novels, becoming popular with *The Spy* (1821). He wrote volumes of *Leatherstocking Tales* about the frontier hero Leatherstocking and American Indians before and after the American Revolution, including *The Last of the Mohicans* (1826).

Cooper[4], *n.* **Leon** (1930–), UK physicist who in 1955 began work on the puzzling phenomena of superconductivity. He proposed that at low temperatures electrons would be bound in pairs (since known as Cooper pairs) and in this state electrical resistance to their flow through solids would disappear. He shared the 1972 Nobel physics prize with Bardeen and Schrieffer.

Cooper[5], *n.* **Susie** (married name Susan Vera Barker) (1902–), English pottery designer. Her style has varied from colourful Art Deco to softer, pastel decoration on more classical shapes. She started her own company in 1929. It became part of the Wedgwood factory, where she was senior designer from 1966.

cooperate, *v.i.* to work or act with another or others for a common end; to contribute to an effect. **cooperant,** *a.* **cooperation,** *n.* the act of cooperating; a form of partnership or association for the production or distribution of goods. **cooperative,** *a.* working with others for a common end or the common good; helpful; of a business venture etc., owned jointly by the workers etc., for the economic benefit of them all. *n.* a cooperative business, shop etc. **cooperative shop, store,** *n.* the shop of a **cooperative society** for the production or distribution of goods and the division of profits among the members. **cooperatively,** *adv.* **cooperator,** *n.* one who cooperates; a member of a cooperative society. [late L *coöperātus,* p.p. of *coöperārī* (co-, *operārī,* to work, from *opus operis,* work)]

Cooperative Party, *n.* a political party founded in Britain (1917) by the cooperative movement, to maintain its principles in parliamentary and local government. A written constitution was adopted in 1938. The party had strong links with the Labour Party; from 1946 Co-operative Party candidates stood in elections as Co-operative and Labour Candidates and, after the 1959 general election, agreement was reached to limit the party's candidates to 30.

Cooperative Wholesale Society, (CWS) a British concern, the largest cooperative organization in the world, owned and controlled by the numerous co-operative retail societies, which are also its customers. Founded in 1863, it acts as wholesaler, manufacturer and banker, and owns factories, farms and estates, in addition to offices and warehouses.

co-opt, *v.t.* to elect into a body by the votes of the members. **co-optation, co-option,** *n.* [L *cooptāre* (co-, *optāre,* to choose)]

coordinate, *a.* of the same order, rank or authority; of terms or clauses in a sentence, of equal order, as distinct from *subordinate. n.pl.* (*Math.*) lines used as elements of reference to determine the position of any point; clothes in harmonizing colours and patterns, designed to be worn together. *v.t.*, to make coordinate; to correlate, to bring into orderly relation of parts and whole. **coordinately,** *adv.* **coordination,** *n.* **coordinative,** *a.* [L *ordinātus,* p.p. of *ordināre,* to arrange (*ordo -dinis,* ORDER)]

coot, *n.* a small black British aquatic bird, *Fulica atra;* a stupid person. **bald as a coot,** (alluding to the broad base of the bill across the coot's forehead) quite bald. [Dut. *koet,* the sea-coot]

Coote, *n.* **Eyre** (1726–83), Irish general in British India. His victory (1760) at Wandiwash, followed by the capture of Pondicherry, ended French hopes of supremacy. He returned to India as commander in chief in 1779, and several times defeated Hyder Ali, sultan of Mysore.

cootie, *n.* (*N Am., sl.*) a body louse. [etym. doubtful; perh. from Malay *kutu,* a louse]

cop[1], *n.* the top; a hill; a bird's crest; a conical roll or thread on the spindle of a spinning-machine. [OE]

cop[2], *v.t.* (*past, p.p.* **copped**) (*sl.*) to seize; (*sl.*) to arrest; (*sl.*) to catch or get (something unpleasant). *n.* (*coll.*) a policeman; (*sl.*) an arrest. **a fair cop,** (*sl.*) a justified arrest. **not much cop,** (*sl.*) worthless. **to cop it,** (*sl.*) to be caught or punished. **to cop out,** (*sl.*) to refuse responsibility, or to do something. **cop-out,** *n.* **cop-shop,** *n.* (*sl.*) a police station. **copper,** *n.* (*coll.*) one who cops or seizes; (*coll.*) a policeman. [perh. F *caper,* to seize, from L *capere,* to take]

copaiba, copaiva, *n.* the balsam or gum-resin obtained from the **copaiba-plant,** *Copaifera officinalis,* or allied species. [Sp., from Tupí *cupauba*]

copal, *n.* a resin from a Mexican plant; a varnish made from this. [Sp., from Nahuatl *copalli,* resin, incense]

coparcener, *n.* a coheir or coheiress. **coparcenary,** *n.* joint heirship; joint ownership. *a.* relating to coparceners.

copartner, *n.* a partner, an associate; a partaker. **copartnership, -nery,** *n.*

copatriot, COMPATRIOT.

cope[1], *n.* an ecclesiastical sleeveless vestment worn in processions and at solemn ceremonies; anything spread overhead, a cloud, the sky. *v.t.* to cover with or as with a cope or coping. *v.i.* to form an overhang. **copestone** COPING-STONE. **coping,** *n.* the course projecting horizontally on the top of a wall. **coping-stone,** *n.* the topmost stone of a building; a stone forming part of the coping; the sloping course on a wall or buttress to throw off the water. [late L *cāpa*]

cope[2], *v.i.* to encounter, to contend successfully (with); to deal (with), manage successfully. [OF *couper,* to strike (see COUP[1])]

cope[3], *v.t.* to buy; to barter. *v.i.* to make a bargain, to deal. **coper,** *n.* a dealer, esp. in horses; (sometimes **cooper**) a floating grog-shop for North Sea fishermen. **horse-coper,** *n.* a horse-dealer. [from LG (cp. Dut. *koopen,* cogn. with OE *cēapian, cēap,* see CHEAP)]

copeck, KOPECK.

Copenhagen, *n.* (Danish **København**) capital of Denmark, on the islands of Zealand and Amager; population (1988) 1,344,000 (including suburbs).

Copenhagen, Battle of, naval victory, 2 Apr. 1801, by a British fleet under Sir Hyde Parker (1739–1807) and Nelson over the Danish fleet. Nelson put his telescope to his blind eye and refused to see Parker's signal for withdrawal.

copepod, *n.* one of the **Copepoda**, a class of very small marine crustaceans, found in plankton. [Gr. *kōpē,* an oar, *pous podos,* foot]

coper COPE[3].

Coperario, *n.* **John** (*c.* 1570–1626), English composer of songs with lute or viol accompaniment.

Copernicus, *n.* **Nicolaus** (1473–1543), Polish astronomer, who believed that the Sun, not Earth, is at the centre of the solar system, thus defying established doctrine. For 30 years he worked on the hypothesis that the the rotation and the orbital motion of Earth were responsible for the apparent movement of the heavenly bodies. His great work *De Revolutionibus Orbium Coelestium* was not published until the year of his death. **Copernican,** *a.* pertaining to his system. [*Copernicus,* L form of G *Kopernik*]

copia verborum, *n.* a plentiful supply of words, flow of language. [L]

copier COPY.

copilot, *n.* a second or assistant pilot of an aircraft.

copious, *a.* plentiful, abundant, ample; profuse, prolific, rich in vocabulary. **copiously,** *adv.* **copiousness,** *n.* [L *cōpiōsus,* from *cōpia,* plenty]

copita, *n.* a tulip-shaped sherry glass. [Sp., dim. of *copa,* cup]

Copland, *n.* **Aaron** (1900–), US composer. Copland's early works, such as the piano concerto of 1926, were in the jazz idiom but he gradually developed a gentler style with a regional flavour drawn from American folk music.

Copley, *n.* **John Singleton** (1738–1815), American painter. He was the leading portraitist of the colonial period, but from 1775 he lived mainly in London, where he painted lively historical scenes such as *The Death of Major Pierson* (1783) (Tate Gallery, London).

copper[1], *n.* a red malleable, ductile, tenacious metallic element, at. no. 29; chem. symbol Cu; a vessel, esp. a cooking or laundry boiler (formerly of copper); a copper (or bronze) coin. *a.* made of or resembling copper. *v.t.* to sheath with copper; to deposit a coating of copper on. **hot coppers,** a parched feeling in the throat and mouth. **copper beech,** *n.* a variety of beech with copper-coloured leaves. **copper-bit,** *n.* a soldering-iron with a copper point. **copper-bottomed,** *a.* (*Naut.*) sheathed with copper; (financially) reliable. **copper-butterfly,** *n.* the popular name for the genus *Lycaena*. **copper-faced,** *a.* faced with copper, as type. **copper-fastened,** *a.* (*Naut.*) fastened with copper bolts. **copperhead,** *n.* a highly venomous N American snake, *Trigonocephalus contortrix,* allied to the rattlesnake; its counterpart in Tasmania; (*Hist.*) a Northern sympathizer with the Confederates during the American Civil War. **copper-Indian,** *n.* a N American Indian. **copper-nose,** *n.* a red nose. **copperplate,** *n.* a polished plate of copper on which something is engraved for printing; an impression from such a plate. *a.* pertaining to the art of engraving on copper; of handwriting, neat and elegant. **copper pyrites,** *n.* (*Min.*) a compound of copper and sulphur. **coppersmith,** *n.* a worker in copper. **copper-work,** *n.* articles of copper. **coppery,** *a.* made of, containing or resembling copper. [OE *copor,* L*cuprum Cyprium,* Gr. *Kuprios,* Cyprian]

copper[2] COP[2].

copperas, *n.* a green sulphate of iron; green vitriol. [ME and OF *coperose,* L *cuprōsa,* from *cuprum,* copper]

coppice, *n.* a small wood of small trees and underwood, cut periodically for firewood. *v.t.* to cut (trees and bushes) to make a coppice. **coppicewood,** *n.* [OF *copeiz,* cut wood, from a late L *colpātīcium* (*colpāre,* to strike, to cut)]

Coppola, *n.* **Francis Ford** (1939–), US film director and screenwriter. He directed *The Godfather* (1972), which became one of the biggest money-makers of all time. Other successes include *Apocalypse Now* (1979), and *The Cotton Club* (1984).

copra, *n.* the dried kernel of the coconut, yielding coconut oil. [Port. and Sp., prob. from Malay *koppara,* coconut]

copresent, *a.* present at the same time. **copresence,** *n.*

copro-, *comb. form.* pertaining to or living on or among dung. [Gr. *kopros,* dung]

coprolite, *n.* the fossil dung of various extinct animals, chiefly saurians, largely used as fertilizer. **coprolitic,** *a.*

coprology, *n.* lubricity; filth in literature or art.

coprophagan, *n.* any individual of the Coprophagi, a section of lamellicorn beetles feeding on or living in dung. **coprophagous,** *a.* **coprophagy,** *n.* [Gr. *koprophagos* (*phagein,* to eat)]

coprophilia, *n.* morbid, esp. sexual, interest in excrement. **coprophiliac,** *n.* **coprophilous,** *a.* growing in dung.

copse, *n.* a coppice. *v.t.* to plant or preserve for copsewood; to clothe with copses. **copsewood,** *n.* underwood, brushwood. **copsy,** *a.* [COPPICE]

Copt, *n.* a descendant of those ancient Egyptians who accepted Christianity in the 1st cent. and refused to adopt Islam after the Arab conquest. They now form a small minority (about 5%) of Egypt's population. The head of the Coptic Church is the Patriarch of Alexandria, currently Shenonda III (1923–), 117th pope of Alexandria. Imprisoned by President Sadat in 1981, he is opposed by Muslim fundamentalists. **Coptic,** *a.* pertaining to the Copts, or to the old Egyptian Church. *n.* the language of the Copts. [F *Copt,* Arab. *quft,* Copt. *gyptios, kyptaios,* Gr. *Aiguptios,* Egyptian]

Coptic language, *n.* a member of the Hamito-Semitic language family and a minority language of Egypt. It is descended from the language of the ancient Egyptians and is the ritual language of the Coptic Christian Church. It is written in the Greek alphabet with some additional characters derived from Demotic script.

copula, *n.* (*pl.* **-lae**) that which couples; the word in a sentence or proposition which links the subject and predicate together; (*Mus.*) a brief connecting passage. **copular,** *a.* [L *cōpula* (co-, *apere,* to fasten, with dim. suf.)]

copulate, *v.t.* to couple together. *v.i.* to have sexual intercourse. **copulate,** *a.* joined, connected. **copulation,** *n.* the act of coupling; sexual intercourse; (*Log., Gram.*) connection. **copulative,** *a.* serving to unite; having two or more words, phrases or predicates connected by a copulative conjunction; pertaining to sexual conjunction. *n.* a copulative conjunction. **copulatively,** *adv.* **copulatory,** *a.* [L *cōpulātus,* p.p. of *cōpulāre,* as prec.]

copy, *n.* a transcript or imitation of an original; a thing made in imitation of or exactly like another; an original, a model, a pattern; manuscript ready for setting; in journalism, material for reporting, writing articles etc.; something that will make a good (newspaper) story; a writing exercise; an example of a particular work or book; the words, as opposed to the pictures or graphic material, in an advertisement etc. *v.t.* to transcribe, to imitate, to make a copy of; (*fig.*) to follow as pattern or model. *v.i.* to make a copy. **clean, fair copy,** matter transcribed from a rough copy or a first draft. **to set copies,** to write a headline in a copybook for imitation. **copybook,** *n.* a book in which proverbs, maxims etc. are written clearly to be copied by children learning to write. *a.* correct, conventional. **copycat,** *n.* (*coll.*) one who imitates someone else. **copyhold,** *n.* (*Law*) a tenure for which the tenant has nothing to show but the copy of the rolls made by the steward of the lord's court; property held by such tenure. *a.* held by such tenure. **copyholder,** *n.* **copyright,** *n.* the exclusive right for the author of a literary or artistic production, or the author's heirs, to publish or sell copies of his or her work. *a.* protected by copyright. *v.t.*

to secure copyright for (a book, music, picture etc.). **copy typist,** *n.* one who types from written copy, rather than from shorthand or tape. **copy-writer,** *n.* one who writes advertisements. **copier,** *n.* one who copies; an imitator, a plagiarist; a transcriber; a photocopier. **copying,** *a.* pertaining to or used for copying. **copying-ink,** *n.* a viscid ink allowing copies to be taken from documents written with it. **copying-press,** *n.* a machine for taking a copy by pressure of a document written with copying-ink. **copyist,** *n.* [F *copie,* L *cōpia,* abundance, med. L a transcript]

coq au vin, *n.* a stew of chicken in wine. [F]

coquelicot, *n.* a reddish-orange colour. [F, the poppy, orig. the cock's comb (*coq,* cock; termination onomat. from the cock's crowing)]

coquet, *a.* coquettish. *n.* a male flirt, a lady-killer. **coquet, -ette,** *v.i.* (*past, p.p.* **coquetted**) to flirt (with); to make love; to trifle; to take up a task or a subject without serious intentions of carrying it on. **coquetry,** *n.* the practices of a coquette; affectation of encouragement to an admirer; flirtation. **coquette,** *n.* a female flirt; a jilt. *v.i.* to coquet. **coquettish,** *a.* **coquettishly,** *adv.* [F, dim. of *coq,* cock]

coquilla, *n.* the nut of *Attaka funifera,* a Brazilian palm, used in turnery. [Sp., dim. of *coca,* a shell]

coquito, *n.* (*pl.* **-tos**) a Chilean nut-bearing palm-tree. [Sp., dim of *coco,* COCONUT]

cor[1], *n.* a Hebrew measure; a homer. [Heb. *kor*]

cor[2], *n.* (*Mus.*) a horn. **cor anglais**, *n.* the English horn, the tenor oboe. [F, from L *cornū*]

cor[3], *int.* (*sl.*) expressing surprise. **cor blimey,** *int.* [corr. of *God (blind me)*]

Cor., (*abbr.*) (*Bibl.*) Corinthians; coroner.

cor., (*abbr.*) (*Mus.*) cornet; correction; corrective; correlative.

cor- COM- (used before *r*).

coracle, *n.* a light boat used in Wales and Ireland, made of wickerwork covered with leather or oiled cloth. [W *cwrwgl,* dim. of *cwrwg,* a trunk (cp. OIr. *curach,* boat)]

coracoid, *n.* a hook-like process of the scapula in mammals; a separate bone in the pectoral arch in birds, reptiles and monotremes. *a.* hook-shaped; resembling a crow's beak. [mod. L *coracoīdes,* Gr. *korakoeidēs* (*korax -akos,* a raven)]

coradicate, *a.* derived from the same root. [L *rādīcātus,* from *radix,* root]

coraggio, *int.* courage! bravo! [It.]

coral, *n.* the calcareous polypary or structure secreted by certain polyps or zoophytes, esp. those of the genus *Corallium,* and deposited in masses on the bottom of the sea; the animal or colony of animals forming these structures; a deep orange-pink colour; an infant's toy made of coral; the unimpregnated eggs of a lobster (from their colour). *a.* made of or resembling coral. **red coral,** *Corallium rubrum,* the red polypary, much used for ornaments. **coral island,** *n.* an island formed by the growth and accumulation of coral. **coral rag,** *n.* a coralliferous limestone of the Middle Oolite. **coral reef,** *n.* a ridge or series of ridges of coral, tending to form a coral island. **coral snake,** *n.* any of the genus *Elaps.* **coral tree,** *n.* a tropical tree of the genus *Erythrina,* bearing blood-red flowers. **coralliferous**, *a.* **coralliform**, *a.* (*Bot.*) branching, like coral. **coralligenous**, *a.* producing coral. **coralline**, *a.* of the nature of coral; containing or resembling coral. *n.* a seaweed with calcareous fronds; popular name for the Polyzoa. **coralline-crag,** *n.* the white portion of the Suffolk crag. **coralline ware,** *n.* red Italian pottery of the 17th and 18th cents. **coralline zone,** *n.* the stratum in the ocean-depths, where corallines abound. **corallite**, *n.* a coral-shaped petrifaction; the skeleton or case of a polyp; coralline marble. **corallitic**, *a.* **coralloid,** *a.* resembling coral; coralliform. *n.* an organism akin to or resembling coral. [OF, from L *corallum,* Gr. *korallion*]

Coralli, *n.* **Jean** (1779–1854), French dancer and choreographer of Italian descent. He made his debut as a dancer in 1802. He choreographed *Le Diable boîteux* (1836) for the Austrian ballerina Fanny Elssler, *Giselle* (1841) and *La Péri* (1843) for the Italian ballerina Grisi; and many other well-known ballets.

Coral Sea, *n.* (or **Solomon Sea**) part of the Pacific Ocean lying between NE Australia, New Guinea, the Solomon Islands, Vanuatu and New Caledonia. It contains numerous coral islands and reefs. The Coral Sea Islands are a Territory of Australia; they comprise scattered reefs and islands over an area of about 1,000,000 sq km. They are uninhabited except for a meteorological station on Willis Island.

coram populo, *adv.* in public. [L]

coranto, *n.* a rapid kind of dance. [from F *courante* or It. *coranta*]

corb, *n.* a basket used in collieries; a basket. [L *corbis*]

corban, *n.* among the ancient Jews, a thing consecrated to God. [Heb. *qorbān,* an offering]

†**corbe,** CORBEL.

corbeil, *n.* a sculptured basket, esp. such as forms the ornamental summit of a pillar etc.; (*Fort.*) a small basket filled with earth, and set upon parapets as a protection from the besiegers' fire. [F *corbeille,* as foll.]

corbel, *n.* a bracket or projection of stone, wood or iron projecting from a wall to support some superincumbent weight. *v.t.* to support by means of corbels. **to corbel out,** to cause to project by constructing on corbels. **corbel-block,** *n.* a short timber helping to support a beam at either end. **corbel-table,** *n.* a projecting course, parapet etc. supported by corbels. [OF, from low L *corbellum,* from *corvellus,* dim. of *corvus,* a raven]

corbie, *n.* (*Sc.*) a raven, a crow. **corbie-steps,** *n.pl.* the stepped slopes of gables (common in Sc. and Flemish architecture). [OF *corbin,* dim. of *corb,* a raven]

Corbière, *n.* **Tristan** (1845–75), French poet. His *Les Amours jaunes/Yellow Loves* (1873) went unrecognized until Verlaine called attention to it in 1884. Many of his poems, such as *La Rhapsodie Foraine/Wandering Rhapsody*, deal with life in his native Brittany.

corchorus, *n.* a tropical genus of the lime-tree family, Tiliaceae, some yielding jute; the Japan globe-flower, *Kerria japonica*. [Gr. *korchoros*]

cord, *n.* thick string or thin rope composed of several strands; an electric flex; a raised rib in woven cloth; ribbed cloth, esp. corduroy; (*pl.*) corduroy trousers; a measure for cut wood, 128 cu. ft. (approx. 3·6 m^3); (*Anat.*) a cord-like structure; anything which binds or draws. *v.t.* to bind with a cord. **cord-wood,** *n.* wood piled up to be sold by the cord. **cordage,** *n.* a quantity or store of ropes; the ropes or rigging of a ship collectively; a quantity of wood measured in cords. **corded,** *a.* bound or fastened with cords; made with cords; ribbed or twilled (like corduroy). **cordless,** *a.* of an electrical appliance, operated by stored electricity, e.g. batteries, as in *cordless telephone*. [F *corde,* L *chorda,* Gr. *chordē*]

cordate, *a.* heart-shaped. [L *cor cordis,* heart]

Corday, *n.* **Charlotte** (1768–93), French Girondin (right-wing republican during the French Revolution). After the overthrow of the Girondins by the more extreme Jacobins in May 1793, she stabbed to death the Jacobin leader, Marat, with a bread knife as he sat in his bath in July of the same year. She was guillotined.

cordelier, *n.* a Franciscan friar of the strictest rule (from the knotted rope worn round the waist); a member of a revolutionary club founded in Paris in 1790, which met in an old convent of the Cordeliers. [F, from *cordelle,* dim. of *corde,* CORD]

cordial, *a.* proceeding from the heart; sincere, hearty, warm-hearted; cheering or comforting the heart. *n.* anything which cheers or comforts; a sweetened drink made with fruit juice; a medicine to increase the circulation or to raise the spirits. **cordiality**, *n.* **cordialize, -ise,** *v.t.* to render cordial. *v.i.* to become cordial; to have the warmest relations (with). **cordially,** *adv.* [F, from med. L *cordiālis* (*cor cordis,* the heart)]

cordiform, *a.* heart-shaped. [L *cor cordis,* the heart,

FORM]

cordillera, *n.* a ridge or chain of mountains. [Sp., from *cordilla,* a string or rope, dim. of *cuerda,* L *chorda,* cord]

Cordilleras, the, *n. pl.* the mountainous western section of North America, with the Rocky Mountains and the coastal ranges parallel to the contact between the North American and the Pacific plates.

cordite, *n.* a smokeless explosive, prepared in string-like grains. [CORD]

cordon, *n.* a ribbon or cord worn as an ornament, a mark of rank or the badge of an order; a line or series of persons, posts or ships placed so as to guard or blockade a place; a projecting band of stones in a wall, a string-course; a fruit-tree trained and closely pruned to grow as a single stem. **sanitary cordon,** (F) **cordon sanitaire,** a line of military posts on the borders of an infected district to cut off communication. **to cordon off,** to protect by surrounding with a cordon. **cordon bleu,** *n. (F)* a trained cook of the highest calibre. *a.* of food or cookery, of the highest standard. [F]

cordovan, *n.* fine leather, esp. horsehide, orig. made at Cordova in Spain; cordwain.

corduroy, *n.* a stout-ribbed cotton cloth made with a pile; (*pl.*) corduroy trousers. *a.* made of this material. **corduroy road,** *n.* a causeway of logs laid over a swamp. [prob. from F *corde du roi,* king's cord]

cordwain, *n.* a kind of leather, finished as a black morocco, orig. from Cordova, Spain. †**cordwainer,** *n.* a worker in cordwain; a shoemaker. [OF *cordoan,* late L *cordōanum,* from *Cordoa,* Cordova (see CORDOVAN)]

core[1], *n.* the heart or inner part of anything; the hard middle of an apple, pear or similar fruit, containing the seeds; the central strand of a rope; the insulated conducting wires of a cable; the round mass of rock brought up by an annular drill; a disease of sheep, or the tumour typical of this; the pith, the gist, the essence; the central part of the earth; (*Archaeol.*) the central portion of a flint left after flakes have been struck off; the essential part of a school curriculum, studied by all pupils; a piece of magnetic material, such as soft iron, inside an induction coil; the part of a nuclear reactor containing the fissile material; a small ring of magnetic material formerly used in a computer memory to store one bit; (also **core memory**) a computer memory which uses cores. *v.t.* to remove the core from. **core time,** *n.* in a flexitime system, the central part of the day when everyone is at work. **coreless,** *a.* **corer,** *n.* [etym. doubtful (L *cor,* the heart, and OF *cor,* horn, have been suggested)]

core[2], *n.* (*Sc.*) a company, a party; (*Sc.*) a crowd. [prob. for CORPS]

coregent, *n.* a joint ruler or governor.

corelation, CORRELATION.

coreless CORE[1].

coreligionist, *n.* one of the same religion.

Corelli, *n.* **Arcangelo** (1653–1713), Italian composer and violinist. He was one of the first virtuoso violinists and his music, marked by graceful melody, includes a set of *concerti grossi* and five sets of chamber sonatas.

coreopsis, *n.* a genus of yellow garden plants. [Gr. *koris,* a bug; *opsis,* appearance]

co-respondent, *n.* a joint respondent in a suit, esp. a divorce suit.

corf, *n.* (*pl.* **corves**) a basket for carrying ore or coal in mines; a large basket or perforated box for keeping lobsters or fish alive in the water. [prob. from LG (cp. Dut. *korf,* G *Korb*)]

Corfu, *n.* (Greek **Kérkira**) most northerly, second largest of the Ionian islands, off the coast of Epirus in the Ionian Sea; area 1072 sq km/414 sq miles; population (1981) 96,500. Its businesses include tourism, fruit, olive oil and textiles. Its largest town is the port of Corfu (Kérkira), population (1981) 33,560. Corfu was colonized by Corinthians about 700 BC, Venice held it (1386–1797), Britain from 1815–64.

corgi, *n.* a small, smooth-haired, short-legged, Welsh dog. [W]

coriaceous, *a.* made of or resembling leather; (*Bot.*) stiff like leather, as the leaves of the box. [L *coriāceus,* from *corium,* skin, leather]

coriander, *n.* an umbellifer, *Coriandrum sativum,* with aromatic and carminative seeds used as a spice in cooking. [F *coriandre,* L *coriandrum,* Gr. *koriannon*]

Corinna, *n.* a Greek lyric poet of 6th cent. BC, said to have instructed Pindar. Only fragments of her poetry survive.

Corinth, *n.* (Greek **Kórinthos**) port in Greece, on the isthmus connecting the Peloponnesos with the mainland; population (1981) 22,650. The rocky isthmus is dissected by the 6.5km/4 mile Corinth canal, opened in 1893. The site of the ancient city-state of Corinth lies 7km/4.5 miles SW.

Corinthian, *a.* of or pertaining to Corinth; licentious, dissipated. *n.* a native of Corinth; a debauchee; a dandy. **Corinthian order,** *n.* (*Arch.*) the most elaborate and ornate of the three Grecian orders, the capital being enriched with graceful foliated forms added to the volutes of the Ionic capital. **Corinthianesque,** *a.* (*Arch.*).

Coriolis effect, *n.* a result of the deflective force of the Earth's W to E rotation. Winds, ocean currents and aircraft are deflected to the right of their direction of travel in the Northern hemisphere and to the left in the Southern hemisphere.

corium, *n.* a kind of body-armour, composed of scales or small plates of leather, worn by Roman soldiers; the innermost layer of the skin in mammals. [L, skin, leather]

cork, *n.* the very light outer layer of bark of the cork-tree, from which stoppers for bottles, floats for fishing etc. are made; a stopper for a bottle or cask. *a.* made of cork. *v.t.* to stop with a cork; to blacken with burnt cork. **cork-jacket,** *n.* a jacket lined with cork, to sustain the wearer in the water. **cork-oak** CORK-TREE. **corkscrew,** *n.* a screw for drawing corks. *v.t.* to direct or push forward in a wriggling fashion. *a.* twisted to resemble a corkscrew, spiral. **cork-tree,** *n.* an oak, *Quercus suber,* much cultivated in Spain, Portugal and France for the sake of its bark. **corkwood,** *n.* cork in quantity; a light porous wood. **corkage,** *n.* the corking or uncorking of bottles; a charge levied at hotels on wines consumed by guests but not supplied by the hotel. **corked,** *a.* stopped with cork; blackened with burnt cork; of wine, tasting of the cork. **corker,** *n.* (*coll.*) something or somebody astounding; a statement that puts an end to the discussion. **corky,** *a.* resembling cork in nature or appearance; (*coll.*) sprightly, lively. [etym. doubtful (cp. OSp. *alcorque,* a cork shoe, and Sp. *corcho*)]

Cork, *n.* the largest county of the Republic of Ireland, in the province of Munster; county town Cork; area 7460 sq km/2880 sq miles; population (1986) 413,000. It is agricultural but there is also some copper and manganese mining, marble quarrying, and river and sea fishing. Natural gas and oil fields are found off the S coast at Kinsale.

†**corking-pin,** *n.* a large pin formerly used to fasten dresses etc. [prob. corr. of CALKIN]

corm, *n.* a bulb-like, fleshy subterranean stem, sometimes called a solid bulb. **cormo-,** *comb. form* the trunk, the stem. **cormophyte,** *n.* a name formerly used for a division of plants, those with roots, stems and leaves. [Gr. *kormos,* the trimmed trunk of a tree]

Corman, *n.* **Roger** (1926–), US film director and producer. He directed a stylish series of Edgar Allan Poe films starring Vincent Price that began with *House of Usher* (1960). After 1970 Corman confined himself to production and distribution.

cormophyte CORM.

cormorant, *n.* any species of the genus *Phalacrocorax,* esp. *P. carbo,* a voracious British sea-bird; a glutton. [OF *cormerant,* L *corvus marīnus,* sea-crow]

Corn., (*abbr.*) Cornish; Cornwall.

corn[1], *n.* grain; the seed of cereals; wheat; (*Sc.*) oats; (*chiefly N Am.*) maize, sweet corn; something corny, as a song, joke etc.; a single seed or grain of certain plants. *v.t.* to preserve and season with salt; †to granulate; †to feed with corn. **corn on the cob,** maize boiled and eaten direct from the cob. **corn-ball,** *n.* (*N Am.*) a sweetmeat composed of popped corn and white of egg; (*N Am., coll.*) a rustic person. **corn-brash,** *n.* a calcareous sandstone belonging to the Inferior Oolite. **corn-bread,** *n.* (*N Am.*) bread made from maize meal. **corn-chandler,** *n.* a retail dealer in corn etc. **corn-cob,** *n.* a spike of maize. **corn-cob pipe,** *n.* a tobacco-pipe with a bowl made from this. **corn-cockle,** *n.* a purple flower of the campion tribe, *Lychnis githago*. **corn-crake,** *n.* the landrail, *Crex pratensis*. **corn dolly,** *n.* a decorative figure made of plaited straw. **corned beef,** *n.* tinned seasoned and cooked beef. **corn exchange,** *n.* a market where corn is sold from samples. **corn-factor,** *n.* a dealer in corn. **cornfield,** *n.* a field in which corn is growing; corn land. **corn-flag,** *n.* a plant of the genus *Gladiolus*. **cornflakes,** *n.pl.* a breakfast cereal made from toasted flakes of maize. **cornflour,** *n.* finely-ground meal of maize or rice, used in cooking to sweeten sauces etc. **cornflower,** *n.* a popular name for several plants that grow amongst corn, esp. the common bluebottle, *Centaurea cyanus*. **corn land,** *n.* land suitable for or devoted to growing corn. **Corn Laws,** *n.pl.* laws designed to regulate the price of corn (abolished in England, 1846). **corn-loft,** *n.* a store for corn. **corn-marigold,** *n.* a yellow-flowered composite plant, *Chrysanthemum segetum*. **corn meal,** *n.* (*N Am.*) meal of maize. **cornmill,** *n.* (*N Am.*) a mill for grinding the cob of maize. **corn pone,** *n.* (*N Am.*) corn-bread baked or fried. **corn-rent,** *n.* rent paid in corn at the market-price. **corn-sheller,** *n.* (*N Am.*) an instrument for rubbing the grains from the cob of maize. **corn-shuck,** *n.* (*N Am.*) the husk of maize. **corn-stalk,** *n.* (*Austral.*) a European born in Australia. **cornstarch,** *n.* (*N Am.*) cornflour. **cornstone,** *n.* an earthy concretionary limestone forming a lower series in the Old Red Sandstone. **corny,** *a.* trite; old-fashioned and sentimental; unsophisticated. [OE from Teut. *korno-* (cp. Dut. *koren,* Dan. and Swed. *korn,* Goth. *kaurn,* G *Korn*), Aryan *grnòm* (L *grānum,* GRAIN[1])]

corn[2], *n.* a horny excrescence on the foot or hand, produced by pressure over a bone. **to tread on someone's corns,** to upset or offend a person's feelings. **corn-plaster,** *n.* a plaster for corns. **corny,** *a.* [OF *corn,* L *cornū,* horn]

cornea, *n.* (*pl.* **-neas, -neae**) the transparent forepart of the external coat of the eye, through which the rays of light pass. **corneal,** *a.* [L, fem. of *corneus,* horny (*cornū,* horn)]

Corneille, *n.* **Pierre** (1606–84), French dramatist. His many tragedies, such as *Oedipe* (1659), glorify the strength of will governed by reason, and established the French classical dramatic tradition for the next two centuries. His first play, *Mélite,* was performed in 1629, followed by others that gained him a brief period of favour with Cardinal Richelieu. *Le Cid* (1636) was attacked by the Academicians although it achieved huge public success. Later plays were based on Aristotle's unities.

cornel, *n.* the English name of the genus *Cornus,* which includes the cornelian cherry-tree, *C. mascula,* and the dogwood, *C. sanguinea*. [ult. from L *cornus;* derivation obscure]

cornelian[1], *n.* a variety of semi-transparent chalcedony. [F *cornaline;* etym. doubtful]

cornelian[2], *n.* the wild cornel or dogwood, or the cherry-tree, *Cornus mascula,* or its fruit. [CORNEL]

corneous, *a.* horny; hard, like horn. [L *corneus* (*cornū,* horn)]

corner, *n.* the place where two converging lines or surfaces meet; the space included between such lines or surfaces; an angle; a place enclosed by converging walls or other boundaries; a place where two streets meet; either of two opposite angles of a boxing ring; a region, a quarter, esp. a remote place; a nook; a position of difficulty or embarrassment; a combination to buy up the available supply of any commodity, in order to raise the price, a ring; in football, a free kick from a corner. *v.t.* to drive into a corner, or into a position of difficulty; to furnish with corners; to buy up (a commodity) so as to raise the price. *v.i.* to form a corner (in a commodity); esp. of vehicles, to turn a corner. **to cut (off) a corner,** to take a short cut; to sacrifice quality to speed. **to turn the corner,** to go round it into the next street; to pass the crisis of an illness; to get past a difficulty. **corner boy,** *n.* a street loafer. †**corner-cap,** *n.* a three- or four-cornered cap; (*fig.*) the chief embellishment. **corner-chisel, -punch,** *n.* one of an angular shape for cutting corners of mortises etc. **cornerman,** *n.* a cornerer; the performer at the end of the line in a minstrel show; a lounger at street corners. **corner shop,** *n.* a small neighbourhood shop, often on a street corner, selling a variety of goods. **cornerstone,** *n.* the stone which unites two walls of a building; the principal stone; the foundation; something of the first importance. **cornerwise,** *adv.* diagonally, with the corner in front. **cornered,** *a.* having corners or angles (*usu. in comb.*); (*fig.*) placed in a difficult position. **cornerer,** *n.* a member of a corner or ring. [OF *cornier,* late L *cornēria,* from L *cornū,* horn]

cornet[1], *n.* a wind instrument; a cornet-à-piston; †a square cap formerly worn by doctors of divinity; †a lady's head-dress, with two horn-like projections; a conical paper bag; a piece of paper twisted into a conical receptacle for small wares; the lower part of a horse's pastern; an ice-cream cone. **cornet-à -piston, -s,** *n.* (*Mus.*) a metallic wind-instrument of the trumpet class, but furnished with valves and stoppers. **cornetist, cornettist,** *n.* [OF from late L *cornetum,* L *cornū*]

cornet[2], *n.* (*formerly*) the lowest commissioned officer in a cavalry regiment; †the standard of a cavalry troop; †a troop of cavalry. **cornetcy,** *n.* [F *cornette,* dim. of *corne,* as prec.]

cornflower CORN[1].

Cornforth, *n.* **John** (1917–), Australian chemist who settled in England in 1941. In 1975 he shared a Nobel prize with Vladimir Prelog for work utilizing radioisotopes as 'markers' to find out how enzymes synthesize chemicals that are mirror images of one another (stereo isomers).

cornice, *n.* a moulded horizontal projection crowning a wall, entablature, pillar or other part of a building; an ornamental band of plaster between a wall and ceiling; a projecting mass of snow along the top of a precipice. **cornice-pole,** *n.* a pole carried along the tops of windows to support curtains. **corniced,** *a.* [F *cornice* (now *corniche*), It. *cornice* (etym. doubtful)]

corniche, *n.* a coast road, esp. one along the face of a cliff. [see prec.]

corniferous, *n.* containing hornstone, a term applied to a palaeozoic limestone of N America containing hornstone. **cornific,** *a.* producing horns or horny matter. **corniform,** *a.* horn-shaped. **cornigerous,** *a.* bearing horns; horned. [L *cornifer* (*cornū,* horn, -FEROUS)]

Cornish, *a.* of or pertaining to Cornwall. *n.* the ancient Celtic language of Cornwall. **Cornish chough,** *n.* the chough. **Cornish engine,** *n.* a single-acting steam pumping-engine. **Cornish granite,** *n.* a coarse-grained, whitish granite quarried in Cornwall. **Cornish pasty,** *n.* a half-moon shaped pasty filled with seasoned meat and vegetables.

Cornish language, *n.* an extinct member of the Celtic language, branch of the Indo-European language family, spoken in Cornwall until 1777. Written Cornish first appeared in 10th-cent. documents, some religious plays were written in Cornish in the 15th and 16th cents., but later literature is scanty, mainly folk-tales and verses.

Corn Laws CORN[1].

corno, *n.* (*Mus.*) a horn. **corno inglese,** *n.* cor anglais. [It., from L *cornū*]

cornopean, *n.* (*Mus.*) a cornet-à-piston.

cornu, *n.* (*pl.* **-nua**) (*Anat.*) a horn-like process. **cornual,** *a.* **cornuate,** *a.* [L]

cornucopia, *n.* (*pl.* **-pias**) the horn of plenty; a goat's horn wreathed and filled to overflowing with flowers, fruit, corn etc., the symbol of plenty and peace; a representation of a cornucopia; an abundant stock. **cornucopian,** *a.* [L *cornū copiae*]

cornute, †*v.t.* to cuckold. **cornuted,** *a.* horned or having horn-like projections; horn-shaped; cuckolded. [L *cornūtus,* horned, from *cornū,* horn]

†**cornuto,** *n.* (*pl.* **-tos**) a cuckold. [It., as prec.]

Cornwall, *n.* county in SW England including Scilly Islands (Scillies). **area** (excluding Scillies) 3550 sq km/ 1370 sq miles. **towns** administrative headquarters Truro; Camborne, Launceston; resorts of Bude, Falmouth, Newquay, Penzance, St Ives. **physical** Bodmin Moor (including Brown Willy, 419 m/1375 ft), Land's End peninsula, St Michael's Mount, rivers Tamar, Fowey, Fal, and Camel. **products** electronics; spring flowers; tin (mined since Bronze Age, some workings renewed in 1960s, though the industry has all but disappeared), kaolin (St Austell); fish. **population** (1987) 453,000.

Cornwallis, *n.* **Charles, 1st Marquess Cornwallis** (1738–1805), British soldier, eldest son of the 1st Earl Cornwallis. He led the British forces in the War of American Independence until 1781, when his surrender at Yorktown ended the war. Subsequently he was twice governor-general of India, and viceroy of Ireland, and was made a marquess in 1793.

corolla, *n.* the inner whorl of two series of floral envelopes occurring in the more highly developed plants, the petals. **corollaceous,** *a.* **corollate, -lated,** *a.* like a corolla; having a corolla. **corolline,** *a.* pertaining to a corolla. [L, dim. of *corōna,* a crown]

corollary, *n.* (*Log.*) an additional inference from a proposition; a natural consequence; something appended. [L *corollārium,* the price of a garland, a gratuity, a corollary, from *corollārius,* pertaining to a garland, as prec.]

corona, *n.* (*pl.* **-nas, -nae**) a broad projecting face forming the principal member of a cornice; a circular chandelier hanging from the roof, esp. in churches; the circumference or margin of a compound radiated flower; a disc or halo round the sun or the moon; an anthelion or disc of light opposite the sun; the zone of radiance round the moon in a total eclipse of the sun; (*Anat.*) any structure like a crown in shape; a glowing electrical discharge round a charged conductor; a kind of long cigar with straight sides. **Corona Australis,** *n.* a constellation of the southern hemisphere, located to the south of the constellation Sagittarius. **Corona Borealis,** *n.* a constellation of the northern hemisphere, representing the headband of Ariadne that was cast into the sky by Bacchus. Its brightest star is Gemma, which is 75 light years away. **coronal¹,** *a.* [L, a crown]

coronach, *n.* a dirge, a funeral lamentation, in the Scottish Highlands and in Ireland. [Ir. (cp. Gael. *corranach*), from *comh-,* together, *rànach,* an outcry, from *ràn,* to howl]

Coronado, *n.* **Francisco de** (*c.* 1500–54), Spanish explorer who sailed to the New World in 1535 in search of gold. In 1540 he set out with several hundred men from the Gulf of California on an exploration of what are today the Southern states. Although he failed to discover any gold, his expedition came across the impressive Grand Canyon of the Colorado and introduced the use of the horse to the indigenous Indians.

coronal¹ CORONA.

coronal², *a.* pertaining to a crown or the crown of the head; (*Bot.*) pertaining to a corona. *n.*, a circlet or coronet; a wreath, a garland. **coronal suture,** *n.* the suture extending over the crown of the skull and separating the frontal and parietal bones. **coronally,** *adv.* [F, from L CORONA]

coronary, *a.* resembling a crown; placed as a crown. *n.* a small bone in a horse's foot; a coronary thrombosis. **coronary arteries,** *n.pl.* two arteries springing from the aorta before it leaves the pericardium. **coronary thrombosis,** *n.* the formation of a clot in one of the arteries of the heart. **coronary vessels,** *n.pl.* certain vessels which furnish the substance of the heart with blood. [L *corōnārius,* as prec.]

coronate, -nated, *a.* (*Bot., Zool.*) having a crown, or arranged like a crown; of mollusc shells, having the whorls surrounded by a row of spines or tubercles. [L *coronātus,* p.p. of *coronāre,* as prec.]

coronation, *n.* the act or ceremony of solemnly crowning a sovereign. **coronation oath,** *n.* the oath taken by a sovereign at the coronation. **coronation stone,** *n.* the stone in the seat of the chair in Westminster Abbey in which British sovereigns are crowned, taken from the Scots in 1296. [as prec.]

coroner, *n.* an officer of the Crown whose duty it is to inquire into cases of sudden or suspicious death, and to determine the ownership of treasure-trove; formerly an officer in charge of the private property of the Crown. **coroner's inquest,** *n.* an inquiry held by a coroner and jury. **coronership,** *n.* [A-F *coruner,* from *coruna,* L *corona,* CROWN]

coronet, *n.* a little crown; an ornamental fillet worn as part of a woman's head-dress; an inferior crown worn by princes and noblemen, varying according to the rank of the wearer; nobility; the part of a horse's pastern where the skin turns to horn. **coroneted,** *a.* entitled to wear a coronet; of noble birth. [OF, dim. of *corone,* as prec.]

coronoid, *a.* (*Anat.*) resembling a crow's beak; hooked at the tip. [Gr. *korōnē,* a crow]

Corot, *n.* **Jean-Baptiste-Camille** (1796–1875), French painter, creator of a distinctive landscape style with cool colours and soft focus. His early work, particularly Italian scenes in the 1820s, influenced the Barbizon school of painters. Like them, Corot worked out of doors, but he also continued a conventional academic tradition with more romanticized paintings.

corozo, *n.* (*pl.* **-zos**) a S American ivory-nut tree, *Phytelephas macrocarpa,* the source of vegetable ivory. **corozo nut,** *n.* the fruit of this, used by turners for making ornaments etc. [native name]

corp., (*abbr.*) corporal; corporation.

corpora CORPUS.

corporal¹, *n.* an army non-commissioned officer of the lowest grade. **ship's corporal,** a sailor who attends to police matters under the master-at-arms. **corporalship,** *n.* [F (var. *caporal,* It. *caporale,* perh. from confusion with *capo,* head), as foll.]

corporal², *a.* relating to the body; material, corporeal. *n.* the fine linen cloth on which the elements are consecrated in the Eucharist. †**corporal oath,** *n.* a solemn oath, taken with the hand on the corporal. **corporal punishment,** *n.* punishment inflicted on the body. **corporality,** *n.* materiality; †a corporation; (*pl.*) material things; (*pl.*) bodily matters. **corporally,** *adv.* [OF *corporel,* L *corporālis* (*corpus -oris,* the body)]

corporate, *a.* united in a body and acting as an individual; collectively one; pertaining to a corporation; †united. **body corporate,** the State; the nation considered as a corporation. **corporate body,** *n.* a corporation. **corporate hospitality,** *n.* (lavish) entertainment by a company of (potential) clients or customers. **corporate raider,** *n.* one who clandestinely builds up a shareholding in a company in order to gain some control over it. **corporate state,** *n.* a system of government based on trade and professional corporations. **corporate town,** *n.* one having municipal rights and privileges. **corporately,** *adv.* [L *corporātus,* p.p. of *corporāre* (as prec.)]

corporation, *n.* a united body; (*Law*) a corporate body empowered to act as an individual; (*loosely*) a company or association for commercial or other purposes; an elected body charged with the conduct of civic business; (*coll.*) a prominent abdomen. **corporation aggregate,** *n.* one consisting of many persons, as a corporation of a town. **corporation sole,** *n.* one consisting of a single individual and his or her successors, as a king, a bishop etc. **corporation tax,** *n.* a tax levied on the profits of companies. **corporatism,** CORPORATE STATE. **corporative,** *a.* **corporator,** *n.* a member of a corporation. [L *corporātio,* as prec.]

corporeal, *a.* having a body; pertaining to the body; material, physical, as opp. to mental; (*Law*) tangible, visible. **corporeality**, *n.* **corporeally,** *adv.* [L *corporeus* (*corpus -oris*)]

corporeity, *n.* material existence; corporeality. [med. L *corporeitās,* from *corporeus,* as prec.]

corposant, *n.* a sailor's name for a luminous electric body often seen on the masts and rigging on dark stormy nights; also called St Elmo's fire. [Port. *corpo santo,* L *corpus sanctum,* sacred body]

corps, *n.* (*pl.* **corps**) a body of troops having a specific function. **army corps,** a grouping of two or more divisions. **corps de ballet**, *n.* a body of dancers in a ballet. **corps diplomatique**, *n.* the body of ambassadors, attachés etc. accredited to a court. [F]

corpse, *n.* a dead body, esp. of a human being; the body. **corpse-candle, -light,** *n.* an ignis fatuus seen in churchyards and regarded as an omen of death. [OF *cors* (F *corps*), L *corpus,* the body]

corpulent, *a.* excessively fat or fleshy; †corporeal, carnal. **corpulence, -ency,** *n.* **corpulently,** *adv.* [F, from L *corpulentus* (*corpus,* body)]

corpus, *n.* (*pl.* **corpora**) a body; the mass of anything; a collection of writings or of literature; (*Physiol.*) the body of an organ or any part of an organism. **Corpus Christi**, *n.* the festival of the body of Christ, celebrated in the Roman Catholic and Orthodox Churches, in honour of the real presence in the Eucharist, on the Thursday after Trinity Sunday. **corpus delicti**, *n.* (*Law*) the aggregation of facts which constitute a breach of the law. **corpus luteum**, *n.* (*pl.* **corpora lutea**) a mass of tissue which develops in the ovary after the discharge of an ovum. [L]

corpuscle, corpuscule, *n.* a minute particle of matter; (*Physiol.*) a minute body or cell forming part of an organism; a cell, esp. a *white* or *red corpuscle,* suspended in the blood. **corpuscular**, *a.* pertaining to corpuscles; atomic. **corpuscular forces,** *n.pl.* forces acting on corpuscles, and determining the forms and relations of matter. **corpuscular theory,** *n.* the obsolete theory that light is due to the rapid projection of corpuscles from a luminous body. [L *corpusculum,* dim. of *corpus,* body]

corr., (*abbr.*) correspond(ing); correspondence.

corrade, *v.t.* to wear down (rocks etc.), as a river by mechanical force and solution. **corrasion**, *n.* **corrasive,** *a.* [L *corrādere* (COR-, *rādere,* to scrape)]

corradiate, *v.i.* to radiate together.

corral, *n.* an enclosure (orig. of emigrants' wagons in Red Indian territory) for cattle or for defence; an enclosure for capturing elephants and other animals. *v.t.* (*past, p.p.* **corralled**) to pen up; to form into a corral. [Sp., from *corro,* a ring of people (*correr* (*toros*), to hold a bull-fight, L *currere,* to run)]

correct, *v.t.* to set right; to remove faults or errors from; to mark errors for rectification; to admonish, to punish, to chastise; to obviate, to counteract; to eliminate an aberration. *a.* free from fault or imperfection; conforming to a fixed standard or rule; right, proper, decorous; true, exact, accurate. **to stand corrected,** to acknowledge a mistake. **correctly,** *adv.* **correctness,** *n.* **corrector,** *n.* one who or that which corrects; a censor; a critic. **corrector of the press,** a proofreader. **correction,** *n.* the act of correcting; that which is substituted for what is wrong; amendment, improvement; punishment, chastisement; animadversion, criticism. **house of correction,** a gaol, a penitentiary. **under correction,** as liable to correction; perhaps in error. **correctional,** *a.* †**correctioner,** *n.* one who administers chastisement. **corrective,** *a.* having power to correct; tending to correct. *n.* that which tends to correct or counteract; an antidote. [L *correctus,* p.p. of *corrigere* (*regere,* to rule, to order)]

Correggio, *n.* **Antonio Allegri da** (*c.* 1494–1534), Italian painter of the High Renaissance, whose style followed the classical grandeur of Leonardo and Titian but anticipated the Baroque in its emphasis on movement, softer forms and contrasts of light and shade.

corregidor, *n.* the chief magistrate of a Spanish town. [Sp. (*corregir,* L *corrigere,* to CORRECT)]

correlate, *v.i.* to be reciprocally related. *v.t.* to bring into mutual relation. *a.* mutually related. *n.* a correlative. **correlation,** *n.* reciprocal relation; the act of bringing into correspondence or interaction; (*Phys.*) interdependence of forces and phenomena; the mutual relation of structure, functions etc. in an organism. **correlational**, *a.* **correlationist**, *n.* a believer in the doctrine of universal correlation of powers and forces as the outcome of one primary force. **correlative**, *a.* reciprocally connected or related; (*Gram.*) corresponding to each other, as *either* and *or, neither* and *nor*. *n.* one who or that which is correlated with another. **correlatively,** *adv.* **correlativity**, *n.*

correspond, *v.i.* to be congruous; to fit; to suit, to agree; to communicate by letters sent and received. **correspondence,** *n.* mutual adaptation; congruity; intercourse by means of letters; the letters which pass between correspondents. **correspondence college, school,** *n.* one whose students do not attend directly, but whose courses (**correspondence courses**) are conducted by post. **correspondent,** *a.* agreeing or congruous with; answering; †obedient. *n.* a person with whom intercourse is kept up by letters; a person or firm having business relations with another; one who sends news from a particular place or on a particular subject, to a newspaper, radio or TV station etc. **correspondently,** *adv.* **corresponding,** *a.* suiting; communicating by correspondence. **correspondingly,** *adv.* †**corresponsive,** *a.* corresponding, conformable. [F *correspondre,* med. L *correspondēre* (COR-, *respondēre,* to RESPOND)]

corrida, *n.* a bull-fight. [Sp.; cp. CORRAL]

corridor, *n.* a gallery or passage communicating with the apartments of a building; (*N Am.*) an aisle; a covered way encircling a place; a narrow strip of territory belonging to one state, which passes through the territory of another state (e.g. to reach the sea); a passageway along the side of a railway carriage (**corridor carriage**) with openings into the different compartments. **corridors of power,** the higher ranks in any organization, seen as the seat of power and influence. **corridor train,** *n.* one with corridors, allowing passage between carriages. [F, from It. *corridore* (*correre,* to run, L *currere*)]

corrie, *n.* a semi-circular hollow or cirque in a mountain side, usu. surrounded in part by crags. [Gael. *coire,* cauldron]

corrigendum, *n.* (*pl.* **-da**) an error needing correction, esp. in a book. **corrigent,** *a.* (*Med.*) corrective. *n.* a corrective ingredient (in a prescription etc.). [L, ger. of *corrigere,* to CORRECT]

corrigible, *a.* capable of being corrected; punishable; submissive, docile. **corrigibly,** *adv.* [F, from L *corrigere,* as prec.]

corrival, *n.* a rival, a competitor; a comrade, a compeer. *a.* emulous. [F, from L *corrīvālis* (*rīvālis*)]

corroborate, *v.t.* to strengthen, to confirm, to establish; to bear additional witness to. †*a.*, strengthened. **corroborant,** *a.* strengthening; confirming. *n.* a tonic. **corroboration,** *n.* the act of strengthening or confirming; confirmation by additional evidence. **corroborative,** *a.* corroborating. *n.* a corroborant. **corroborator,** *n.* **corroboratory,** *a.* [L *corrōborātus,* p.p. of *corrōborāre* (COR-, *rōborāre,* to strengthen, from *rōbur -boris,* strength)]

corroboree, *n.* a festive or warlike dance of the Australian Aborigines; any noisy party. [Abor.]

corrode, *v.t.* to wear away by degrees; to consume gradually; to prey upon. *v.i.* to be eaten away gradually. **corrodible,** *a.* **corrosion,** *n.* the act or process of corroding; a corroded state. **corrosive,** *a.* tending to corrode; fretting, biting, vexing, virulent. *n.* anything which corrodes. **corrosive sublimate,** *n.* mercuric chloride, a powerful irritant poison; any corrosive substance. **corrosively,** *adv.* **corrosiveness,** *n.* [L *corrōdere* (*rōdere,* to gnaw)]

corrugate, *v.t.* to contract or bend into wrinkles or folds. *v.i.* to become wrinkled. *a.*, wrinkled; (*Biol.*)

marked with more or less acute parallel angles. **corrugated iron,** *n.* sheet iron pressed into folds and galvanized. **corrugation,** *n.* the act of corrugating; a wrinkle, a fold. **corrugator,** *n.* a muscle which contracts the brow. [L *corrūgātus,* p.p. of *corrūgāre* (*rūgāre,* to wrinkle, from *rūga,* a wrinkle)]

corrupt, *a.* putrid, decomposed; spoiled, tainted; unsound; depraved; perverted by bribery; vitiated by additions or alterations; not genuine. *v.t.* to change from a sound to an unsound state; to infect, to make impure or unwholesome; to vitiate or defile; to debauch, to seduce; to bribe; to falsify. *v.i.* to become corrupt. **corrupt practices,** *n.pl.* (*Law*) direct or indirect bribery in connection with an election. **corrupter,** *n.* **corruptful,** *a.* corrupting; corrupt. **corruptibility**, *n.* **corruptible,** *a.* liable to corruption. **corruptibly,** *adv.* **corruption,** *n.* the act of corrupting; the state of being corrupt; decomposition, putrefaction; putrid matter; moral deterioration; misrepresentation; bribery; a corrupt reading or version. **corruption of blood,** (*Hist.*) the effect of attainder on one's heirs, depriving them of the right to inherit one's rank. **corruptive,** *a.* **corruptless,** *a.* free from or not liable to corruption; undecaying. **corruptly,** *adv.* **corruptness,** *n.* [L *corruptus,* p.p. of *corrumpere* (*rumpere,* to break)]

corsac, *n.* a small yellowish Asiatic fox, the Tartar fox. [Turk.]

corsage, *n.* the bodice of a woman's dress; a flower worn therein. [OF]

corsair, *n.* a pirate or a privateer, esp. on the Barbary coast; a pirate authorized by the government of his country; a pirate ship. [F *corsaire,* MIt. *corsaro,* late L *cursārius* (*cursus,* a course, from *currere,* to run)]

corse, *n.* (*poet.*) a corpse; †a human body. [OF *cors,* CORPSE]

corselet[1] CORSLET.

corselette, corselet[2]**,** *n.* a woman's one-piece supporting undergarment.

corset, *n.* a close-fitting stiffened or elasticated undergarment worn by women to give a desired shape to the body; a similar undergarment worn by either sex to support a weakened or injured part of the body. *v.t.* to restrain or support with a corset. **corsetry,** *n.* [F, dim. of OF *cors,* body]

Corsica, *n.* (French **Corse**) an island region of France, in the Mediterranean off the W coast of Italy, north of Sardinia; it comprises the *départements* of Haute Corse and Corse du Sud. **area** 8700 sq km/3358 sq miles. **capital and port** Ajaccio. **exports** wine, olive oil. **population** (1986) 249,000, of whom just under 50% are native Corsicans; there are about 400,000 *émigrés,* mostly in Mexico and Central America, who return to retire. **language** French (official); the majority speak Corsican, an Italian dialect.

corslet, corselet, *n.* body armour; a light cuirass; the thorax of insects. [F *corselet*]

†**corsned,** *n.* the bread of choosing; a piece of bread consecrated by exorcism, swallowed by a suspected person as a test of innocence, in early English times. [OE *cor-snæd* (*cor,* choice, trial, *snæd,* a bit, from *snīthan,* to cut)]

cortege, cortège, *n.* a train of attendants, a procession, esp. at a funeral. [F, from It. *corteggio* (*corte,* a court)]

Cortes, *n.* the legislative assemblies of Spain and (formerly) Portugal. [Sp. and Port., pl. of *corte,* court]

Cortés, *n.* **Hernando** (Ferdinand) (1485–1547), Spanish conquistador. He overthrew the Aztec empire (1519–21) and secured Mexico for Spain.

cortex, *n.* (*pl.* **-tices**) the layer of plant tissue between the vascular bundles and epidermis; the outer layer of an organ, as the kidney or brain. **cortical**, *a.* belonging to the outer part of a plant or animal; pertaining to the bark or rind. **corticata,** *n.pl.* a group of protozoa in which the fleshy portions project from a fixed axis. **corticate, -cated,** *a.* coated with bark; resembling bark. [L *cortex -icem,* bark]

corticin, *n.* (*Chem.*) an alkaloid obtained from the bark of the aspen.

corticosteroid, corticoid, *n.* a steroid (e.g. cortisone) produced by the adrenal cortex, or a synthetic drug with the same actions.

cortisone, *n.* a corticosteroid, natural or synthetic, used to treat rheumatoid arthritis, allergies and skin diseases. [abbr. of *corticosterone* (hormone)]

corundum, *n.* a rhombohedral mineral of great hardness, allied to the ruby and sapphire; a class of minerals including these, consisting of crystallized alumina. [Tamil *kurundam*]

coruscate, *v.i.* to sparkle, to glitter in flashes. **coruscant**, *a.* **coruscation,** *n.* [L *coruscātus,* p.p. of *coruscāre*]

corvee, *n.* an obligation to perform a day's unpaid labour for a feudal lord, as the repair of roads etc.; hence, forced labour. [F, from late L *corrogāta* (*opera*), requisitioned work (COR-, *rogāre,* to ask)]

corves CORF.

corvette, *n.* a small, fast escort vessel armed with anti-submarine devices; a flush-decked, full-rigged ship of war, with one tier of guns. [F, from Port. *corveta,* Sp. *corbeta,* prob. from L *corbīta* (*navis*), a ship of burden (*corbis,* basket)]

corvine, *a.* pertaining to the crows. [L *corvīnus* from CORVUS]

Corvus, *n.* a genus of conirostral birds, including the raven, jackdaw, rook and crow; a name for several ancient Roman war-engines (from the supposed resemblance to a crow's beak). [L, a raven]

corybant, *n.* (*pl.* **-tes**) a priest of Cybele, whose rites were accompanied with wild music and dancing. **corybantian**, *a.* **corybantic**, *a.* **corybantine,** *a.* **corybantism,** *n.* [F *Corybante,* L *Corybās -ntem,* Gr. *Korubas -anta*]

Corydon, *n.* a shepherd, a rustic (in pastoral literature), from the name of characters in the eclogues of Theocritus and Virgil. [L, from Gr. *Korudōn*]

corylus, *n.* a genus of shrubs including the hazel. [L]

corymb, *n.* a raceme or panicle in which the stalks of the lower flowers are longer than those of the upper. **corymbiate**, *a.* with clusters of berries or blossoms in the form of corymbs. **corymbiferous**, *a.* **corymbiform**, *a.* **corymbose**, *a.* [F *corymbe,* L *corymbus,* Gr. *korumbos,* a cluster]

coryphaeus, *n.* the leader of a chorus in a classic play; a chief, a leader; the assistant of the choragus at Oxford. [L, from Gr. *koruphaios* (*koruphē,* the head)]

coryphee, *n.* a ballerina, esp. the chief dancer in the corps de ballet. [F, from prec.]

coryza, *n.* nasal catarrh; a cold. [L, from Gr. *koruza,* running at the nose]

COS, (*abbr.*) Chief of Staff.

cos[1]**,** *n.* a curly variety of lettuce introduced from the island of Cos (now Stanchio) in the Aegean. [Gr. *Kōs*]

cos[2]**,** (*abbr.*) cosine.

'cos, *conj.* (*coll.*) short for BECAUSE.

Cosa Nostra, *n.* the branch of the Mafia operating in the US. [It., our thing]

cosaque, *n.* a Cossack dance; a cracker bon-bon. [F *cosaque,* a Cossack]

cosec, (*abbr.*) cosecant.

cosecant, *n.* (*Math.*) the secant of the complement of an arc or angle.

cosech, (*abbr.*) hyperbolic cosecant.

coseismal, *a.* relating to the points simultaneously affected by an earthquake. *n.* a coseismal line. **coseismal line, curve,** *n.* a line drawn on a map through all the points simultaneously affected by an earthquake. **coseismic,** *a.*

†**cosentient,** *a.* perceiving together. **cosentiency,** *n.*

coset, *n.* (*Math.*) a set which forms a given larger set when added to another one.

cosh[1]**,** *n.* a bludgeon, a life-preserver. *v.t.* to hit with a cosh. [perh. from Romany *kosh,* stick]

cosh[2]**,** (*abbr.*) hyperbolic cosine.

cosher, KOSHER.

†**coshering,** *n.* an Irish custom whereby the lord was entitled to exact from his tenant food and lodging for

himself and his followers; rack-rent. †**cosherer,** *n.* one who practised coshering. [Ir. *coisir,* a feast, feasting]

cosignatory, *n.* one who signs jointly with others.

cosin, cosinage, COUSIN.

cosine, *n.* (*Math.*) the sine of the complement of an arc or angle.

cosmetic, *a.* beautifying; used for dressing the hair or skin. *n.* an external application for rendering the skin soft, clear and white, or for improving the complexion. **cosmetic surgery,** *n.* surgery to improve the appearance rather than to treat illness or injury. †**cosmetical,** *a.* **cosmetically,** *adv.* **cosmetician**, *n.* one professionally skilled in the use of cosmetics. [F *cosmetique,* Gr. *kosmētikos* (*kosmein,* to adorn, from *kosmos,* order)]

cosmic, *a.* pertaining to the universe, esp. as distinguished from the earth; derived from some part of the solar system other than the earth; pertaining to cosmism; of inconceivably long duration; of world-wide importance. **cosmic dust,** *n.* minute particles of matter distributed throughout space. **cosmic radiation, rays,** *n.* very energetic radiation falling on the earth from outer space, consisting chiefly of charged particles. **cosmical,** *a.* cosmic. **cosmically,** *adv.* in a cosmic way. **cosmism**, *n.* the evolutionary philosophy of Herbert Spencer (1820–1903), who conceived of the universe as a self-acting whole, the laws of which were explicable by positive science. **cosmist,** *n.* [Gr. *kosmikos,* from *kosmos,* order, the world]

cosmo-, *comb. form* pertaining to the universe. [Gr. *kosmos,* the universe]

cosmogony, *n.* a theory, investigation or dissertation respecting the origin of the world. **cosmogonic, -ical**, *a.* **cosmogonist,** *n.* [Gr. *kosmogonia*]

cosmography, *n.* a description or delineation of the features of the universe, or of the earth as part of the universe. **cosmographer,** *n.* **cosmographic, -ical**, *a.* [Gr. *kosmographia*]

cosmology, *n.* the science which investigates the laws of the universe as an ordered whole; the branch of metaphysics dealing with the universe and its relation to the mind. **cosmological**, *a.* **cosmologist,** *n.*

cosmonaut, *n.* a (Soviet) astronaut. [Gr. *nautēs,* sailor]

cosmopolitan, *a.* common to all the world; at home in any part of the world; free from national prejudices and limitations. *n.* a cosmopolite. **cosmopolitanism,** *n.* **cosmopolitanize, -ise,** *v.t., v.i.* **cosmopolite**, *n.* a citizen of the world; one who is at home in any part of the world. *a.* world-wide in sympathy or experience; devoid of national prejudice. **cosmopolitical**, *a.* relating to world-wide polity. [Gr. *kosmopolitēs* (*kosmos,* the world, *politēs,* a citizen)]

cosmorama, *n.* an exhibition of pictures from all over the world, shown through lenses. [Gr. *horama,* a spectacle, from *horaein,* to see]

Cosmos, *n.* the name used since the early 1960s for nearly all Soviet artificial satellites. Nearly 2000 Cosmos satellites have been launched.

cosmos, *n.* the universe regarded as an ordered system; an ordered system of knowledge; order, as opp. to chaos; a genus (*Cosmos*) of tropical American plants, grown as garden plants for their showy flowers. [Gr., order, ornament]

cosmosphere, *n.* an apparatus for showing the relative position of the earth and the fixed stars.

cosmotheism, *n.* pantheism, the identification of God with the universe.

cosmothetic, *a.* believing in the existence of matter, but at the same time denying that we have any immediate knowledge of it. **cosmothetical,** *a.* [Gr. *thetikos,* putting, positing, from *tithēnai,* to put]

cosmotron, *n.* an electrical apparatus for accelerating protons to high energies.

Cossack, *n.* one of a race, probably of mixed Turkish origin, living on the southern steppes of Russia, and formerly furnishing light cavalry to the Russian army. [Rus. *Kazak,* Turk. *quzzaq,* a vagabond, an adventurer]

cosset, *v.t.* to pet, to pamper. *n.* a pet lamb; a pet. [etym. doubtful (perh. from OE *cot-sǣta,* cot-sitter, brought up within doors)]

cost, *v.i.* (*past, p.p.* **cost**) to require as the price of possession or enjoyment; to cause the expenditure of; to result in the loss of or the infliction of; (*past, p.p.* **costed**) to fix prices (of commodities). *n.* the price charged or paid for a thing; expense, charge; expenditure of any kind; penalty, loss, detriment; pain, trouble; †a costly thing; (*pl.*) expenses of a lawsuit, esp. those awarded to the successful against the losing party. **at all costs,** regardless of the cost. **at cost,** at cost price. **cost of living,** the cost of those goods and services considered necessary to a reasonable standard of living. **prime cost,** the cost of production. **cost-effective,** *a.* giving a satisfactory return on the initial outlay. **cost-plus,** *a.* used of a contract where work is paid for at actual cost, with an agreed percentage addition as profit. **cost price,** *n.* the price paid by the dealer. **costing,** *n.* the system of calculating the exact cost of production, so as to ascertain the profit or loss entailed. **costless,** *a.* costing nothing. **costly,** *a.* of high price; valuable; †extravagant; †gorgeous; †*adv.* in a costly manner. **costliness,** *n.* [OF *coster* (F *coûter*), L *constāre* (CON-, *stāre,* to stand)]

costa, *n.* (*pl.* **-tae**) a rib; any process resembling a rib in appearance or function; the midrib of a leaf. **costal,** *a.* **costate**, *a.* [L]

co-star, *n.* a star appearing (in a film) with another star. *v.i.* (*past, p.p.* **co-starred**) to be a co-star.

costard, *n.* a large, round apple; †(*sl.*) the head. †**costard-monger** COSTERMONGER. [perh. from OF *coste,* a rib (L *costa*), referring to apples with prominent ribs]

Costa Rica, *n.* Republic of (*República de Costa Rica*), a country in central America, bounded to the N by Nicaragua, to the S by Panama, to the E by the Caribbean, and to the W by the Pacific Ocean. **area** 51,100 sq km/19,725 sq miles. **capital** San José. **towns** ports Limón, Puntarenas. **physical** high central plateau and tropical coast. **exports** coffee, bananas, cocoa, sugar. **population** (1988) 2,810,000 (including 1200 Guaymi Indians); annual growth rate 2.6%. **language** Spanish. **religion** Roman Catholic.

costean, *v.i.* to sink mine-shafts down to the rock in search of a lode. **costean-pit,** *n.* a shaft sunk to find tin. [Corn. *cothas,* dropped, *stean,* tin]

coster, costermonger, *n.* a seller of fruit, vegetables etc., esp. from a street barrow. †*a.* mean, petty, mercenary. **costering, costermongering,** *n.* **costermongerdom**, *n.* **costermongery,** *n.* [COSTARD, MONGER]

costive, *a.* having the motion of the bowels too slow, constipated; reserved, reticent; niggardly. **costiveness,** *n.* [OF *costivé, costevé,* L *constīpātus,* CONSTIPATED]

costly COST.

costmary, *n.* an aromatic plant of the aster family, cultivated for use in flavouring. [OE *cost,* L *costum,* Gr. *kostos,* Arab. *qust; Mary* (St Mary)]

costo-, *comb. form* (*Anat., Physiol.*) pertaining to the ribs. [L *costa,* a rib]

†**costrel,** *n.* a vessel used by labourers for drink during harvest time. [OF *costerel*]

costume, *n.* dress; the customary mode of dressing; the dress of a particular time or country; fancy dress; the attire of an actor or actress; a set of outer garments; (*dated*) a woman's coat and skirt, usu. tailor-made, a suit. *v.t.* to furnish or dress with costume. **costume jewellery,** *n.* cheap and showy jewellery worn to set off one's clothes. **costume piece, play,** *n.* a play in which the actors wear historical or foreign costume. **costumer, costumier**, *n.* a maker or dealer in costumes. [F, from It. *costume,* late L *costūma,* L *consuētūdinem,* acc. of *consuētūdo,* CUSTOM]

cosy, *a.* comfortable; snug; complacent. *n.* a padded covering for keeping something warm, esp. a teapot (**tea-cosy**), or a boiled egg (**egg-cosy**); a canopied seat or corner for two people. **cosily,** *adv.* **cosiness,** *n.* [etym. doubtful]

cot[1], *n.* a small house, a hut; a shelter for beasts. **cot-folk,** *n.* (*Sc.*) cottar-folk. **cot-house,** *n.* a small cottage; (*Sc.*) the house of a cottar. **cotland,** *n.* land held by a cottar. †**cotquean**, *n.* a man who busies himself with household affairs. [OE *cot, cote* (cp. Dut. and Icel. *kot,* G *Koth*)]

cot[2], *n.* a light or portable bedstead; a small bedstead with high barred sides for a young child; (*Naut.*) a swinging bed like a hammock. **cot death,** *n.* the sudden and inexplicable death of a baby while sleeping. [from Hind. *khāt*]

cot[3], (*abbr.*) cotangent.

cotangent, *n.* (*Math.*) the tangent of the complement of an arc or angle.

cote[1], *n.* a sheepfold; a small house or shelter. [COT[1]]

†**cote**[2], *v.t.* in coursing, to outstrip; to pass by. [etym. doubtful]

Côte d'Ivoire, *n.* (English **Ivory Coast**) a country in W Africa, bounded to the N by Mali and Burkina Faso, E by Ghana, S by the Gulf of Guinea, and W by Liberia and Guinea.

cotemporary, CONTEMPORARY.

cotenant, *n.* a joint tenant.

coterie, *n.* a set of people associated together for friendly intercourse; an exclusive circle of people in society; a clique. [F, from low L *coteria,* an association of cottars for holding land, from *cota,* a COT[1] (of Teut. orig.)]

coterminous, CONTERMINOUS.

coth, (*abbr.*) hyperbolic cotangent.

cothurnus, *n.* the buskin worn by actors in Greek and Roman tragedy; tragedy; the tragic style. [L, from Gr. *kothornos*]

cotidal, *a.* having the tides at the same time as some other place.

cotillion, cotillon, *n.* an 18th-cent. French ballroom dance for four or eight persons; the music for this. [F *cotillon,* lit. a petticoat, dim. of *cotte,* coat]

Cotman, *n.* **John Sell** (1782–1842), British landscape painter, with Crome a founder of the Norwich school, a group of realistic landscape painters influenced by Dutch examples. He painted bold designs in simple flat washes of colour, such as *Greta Bridge, Yorkshire* (1805, British Museum, London).

cotoneaster, *n.* a genus of ornamental shrubs belonging to the order Rosaceae. [L *cotonea,* quince, -ASTER]

Cotonou, *n.* the chief part and largest city of Benin; population (1982) 487,000. Palm products and timber are exported.

Cotswold, *n.* a breed of sheep, formerly peculiar to the counties of Gloucester, Worcester and Hereford. [a range of hills in the west of England]

cotta, *n.* a short surplice. [med. L (see COAT)]

cottage, *n.* a small house, esp. for labourers; a cot; a small country or suburban residence. **cottage cheese,** *n.* a soft white cheese made from skimmed milk curds. **cottage hospital,** *n.* a small hospital without a resident medical staff. **cottage industry,** *n.* a small-scale industry in which the workers, usu. self-employed, work at home. **cottage loaf,** *n.* a loaf of bread made with two rounded masses of dough stuck one above the other. **cottage piano,** *n.* a small upright piano. **cottage pie,** *n.* shepherd's pie made with beef. **cottager,** *n.* one who lives in a cottage; (*N Am.*) a person living in a country or seaside residence; (*Hist.*) a cottar. **cottagey, -gy,** *a.* [COTE[1], -AGE]

cottar, *n.* a Scottish farm labourer living in a cottage belonging to a farm and paying rent in the form of labour; one holding a cottage and a plot of land on similar terms to Irish cottier-tenure. [COT[1] or COTE[1], perh. through med. L *cotārius* (*cota,* COTE[1])]

cotter, *n.* a key, wedge or bolt for holding part of a machine in place. **cotter pin,** *n.* [etym. doubtful]

cottier, *n.* a peasant living in a cottage; (*Ir.*) a peasant holding a piece of ground under cottier-tenure (cp. COTTAR). **cottier-tenure,** *n.* the system, now illegal, of letting portions of land at a rent fixed yearly by public competition. [OF *cotier,* med. L *cotārius* (*cota,* COTE[1])]

cotton, *n.* a downy substance, resembling wool, growing in the fruit of the cotton plant, used for making thread, cloth etc.; thread made from this; cloth made of cotton; cotton plants collectively, as a crop. *v.t.* to wrap up. *v.i.* to get on, to agree well (with); †to succeed, to prosper. **to cotton on,** to be attracted (to); to begin to understand. **cotton-cake,** *n.* cottonseed pressed into cakes as food for cattle. **cotton candy,** *n.* (*N Am.*) candy floss. **cotton-gin,** *n.* a device for separating the seeds from cotton. **cotton-grass,** *n.* plants with downy heads belonging to the genus *Eriophorum,* growing in marshy ground. **cotton-lord,** *n.* a rich cotton manufacturer. **cotton-picking,** *a.* (*chiefly N Am., sl.*) despicable. **cotton-seed,** *n.* the seed of the cotton plant, yielding oil, and when crushed made into cotton-cake. **cotton-spinner,** *n.* an operative employed in a cotton mill; an owner of a cotton mill. **cottontail,** *n.* any of several common American rabbits. **cotton waste,** *n.* refuse cotton used for cleaning machinery. **cotton-weed,** *n.* cudweed. **cottonwood,** *n.* (*N Am.*) several kinds of poplar, esp. *Populus monilifera* and *P. angulata;* (*Austral.*) the dogwood of Tasmania. **cotton wool,** *n.* cotton in its raw state, used for surgical purposes etc. **in cotton wool,** pampered, protected from hard reality. **cotton-yarn,** *n.* spun cotton ready for weaving. **cottonocracy**, *n.* the cotton lords, the great employers in the cotton industry. **cottony,** *a.* [F *coton,* from Sp. *coton,* Arab. *qutun*]

cotyle, *n.* (*Gr. Ant.*) a deep cup, a measure of capacity; the cavity of a bone which receives the end of another in articulation; the sucker of a cuttle-fish. **cotyliform,** *a.* **cotyloid,** *a.* cup-shaped. [Gr. *kotulē*]

cotyledon, *n.* the rudimentary leaf of an embryo in the higher plants, the seed-leaf; a genus of plants, chiefly greenhouse evergreens, including *Cotyledon umbilicus,* the navelwort. **cotyledonal,** *a.* resembling a cotyledon. **cotyledonous,** *a.* possessing cotyledons. [Gr. *kotulēdōn,* a cup-shaped hollow, from prec.]

couch[1], *v.t.* (*in p.p.*) to cause to lie; to lay (oneself) down; to deposit in a layer or bed; (*Malting*) to spread out (barley) on the floor for germination; to express in words; to imply, to veil or conceal; to set (a spear) in rest; to operate upon for a cataract; to treat (a cataract) by displacement of the lens of the eye. *v.i.* to lie down, to rest; to crouch; to stoop, to bend; to lie in concealment; to be laid or spread out. *n.* a bed, or any place of rest; an upholstered seat with a back for more than one person; a similar piece of furniture with a headrest for a doctor's or psychiatrist's patient to lie on; a layer of steeped barley germinating for malting; the frame or floor for this; a preliminary coat of paint, size etc. **couch-fellow,** *n.* a bedfellow; an intimate companion. **couch-mate,** *n.* a bedfellow. **couch potato,** *n.* (*sl.*) an inactive person who watches an excessive amount of television instead of taking part in other forms of entertainment or exercise. [F *coucher,* L *collocāre* (COL-, *locāre,* to place, from *locus,* place)]

couch[2], *n.* couch-grass. *v.t.* to clear of couch-grass. **couch-grass,** *n.* *Triticum repens,* whose long, creeping root renders it difficult of extirpation. [QUITCH]

couchant, *a.* lying in repose; lying hid; (*Her.*) lying down with the head raised. [F, pres.p. of *coucher,* to lie (see COUCH[1])]

†**couchée,** *n.* a reception in the evening, orig. at the king's retirement for the night. [F *couché,* var. of *coucher*]

couchette, *n.* a seat in a continental train which converts into a sleeping berth. [F, dim. of *couche,* couch]

Couéism, *n.* a therapeutic system based on autosuggestion. [Emil *Coué,* 1857–1926, F psychologist]

cougar, *n.* the puma or American lion. [F *couguar,* adapted from Guarani name]

cough, *n.* a convulsive effort, attended with noise, to expel foreign or irritating matter from the lungs; an irritated condition of the organs of breathing that excites coughing. *v.t.* to drive from the lungs by a cough. *v.i.* to expel air from the lungs in a convulsive and noisy manner, with a cough; of an engine, to make a similar noise when malfunctioning. **to cough down,**

to silence (a speaker) by a noise of or as of coughing. **to cough out,** to say with a cough. **to cough up,** to eject; (*sl.*) to produce (money or information), esp. under duress. **cough-drop,** *n.* a lozenge taken to cure or relieve a cough; (*sl.*) a sour or disagreeable person. [OE *cohhetan,* prob. representing an unrecorded *cohhian* (cp. Dut. *kuchen,* to cough, G *keuchen,* to pant); imit. in orig.]

could, *past* CAN[2].

coulee, coulée, *n.* a solidified lava-flow; (*N Am.*) a ravine or gully [F, fem. p.p. of *couler,* to flow]

coulisse, *n.* a grooved timber in which a sluice-gate or a partition slides; a side-scene in a theatre; (*pl.*) the space between the side-scenes. [F, from *couler,* to flow]

couloir, *n.* a steep gully or long, narrow gorge on a precipitous mountain-side. [F, from *couler,* to flow]

coulomb, *n.* a unit of electrical charge. [C.A. de *Coulomb* 1736–1806, F physicist]

coulter, *n.* the iron blade fixed in front of the share in a plough. [OE *culter,* L *culter*]

coumarin, *n.* an aromatic crystalline substance extracted from the Tonka bean, used in flavourings and as an anticoagulant. [F *coumarine;* Tupí *cumarú,* the Tonka bean]

council, *n.* a number of persons met together for deliberation or advice; persons acting as advisers to a sovereign, governor or chief magistrate; the higher branch of the legislature in some of the states of America and English colonies; an ecclesiastical assembly attended by the representatives of various churches; the governing body of a university; (*NT*) the Jewish Sanhedrin; an elected body in charge of local government in a county, parish, borough etc.; (*loosely*) a local bureaucracy. *a.* used by a council; provided or maintained by a council. **British Council,** an official organization for dissemination of British culture abroad. **Council of Ministers,** an EEC decision-making body consisting of ministers from member states. **Council of State,** a deliberative assembly advising the sovereign in Britain and other countries. **council of war,** a council of officers called together in time of difficulty or danger; a meeting to decide on future action. **Great Council,** (*Hist.*) the assembly of tenants-in-chief and great ecclesiastics which corresponded to the Saxon *witena gemot,* and was superseded by the House of Lords. **Privy Council,** a select council for advising the sovereign in administrative matters. **council-board,** *n.* the table round which a council deliberates; a council; the council in session. **council-chamber,** *n.* the room where a council meets. **council-fire,** *n.* the sacred fire kept burning by the Red Indians during their councils. **councilman, -woman,** *n.* (*N Am.*) a councillor. **councillor,** *n.* a member of a council. **councillorship,** *n.* [F *concile,* L *concilium* (CON-, *calāre,* to summon)]

Council for Mutual Economic Aid, full name for COMECON.

Council of Europe, a body constituted in 1949 to secure 'a greater measure of unity between the European countries'. The first session of the *Consultative Assembly* opened at Strasbourg (still its headquarters) in Aug. 1949, the members then being the UK, France, Italy, Belgium, the Netherlands, Sweden, Denmark, Norway, the Republic of Ireland, Luxembourg, Greece and Turkey. Iceland, West Germany, Austria, Cyprus, Switzerland, Malta, Portugal, Spain and Liechtenstein joined later. The widest association of European states, it has a *Committee* of foreign ministers, a *Parliamentary Assembly* (with members from National Parliaments) and a *European Commission* investigating violations of human rights.

counsel, *n.* a consultation; advice; opinion given after deliberation; (*Law*) a barrister; (*collect.*) the advocates engaged on either side in a law-suit. *v.t.* (*past, p.p.* **counselled**) to give advice or counsel to; to advise. **counsel of perfection,** a precept aiming at a superhuman standard of righteousness (ref. to Matt. xix.21). **Queen's, King's Counsel,** counsel to the Crown, who take precedence of ordinary barristers. **to keep one's counsel,** to keep a matter secret. †**counsel-keeper,** *n.* a confidant. †**counsel-keeping,** *a.* keeping secret. **counselling,** *n.* advice and information given in (difficult) personal situations by a qualified adviser. **counsellor,** *n.* one who gives counsel or advice; an adviser; (*N Am.*) a lawyer, esp. one who conducts a case in court; †a member of a council. **Counsellor-at-Law,** *n.* in Ireland, an advocate, a counsel, a barrister. **counsellorship,** *n.* [OF *conseil,* L *consilium,* from *consulere,* to consult (see CONSUL)]

count[1], *v.t.* to reckon up in numbers, to compute; to call the numerals in order; to keep up a reckoning, to esteem. *v.i.* to possess a certain value; to depend or rely (upon); †to take account (of). *n.* a reckoning or numbering; the sum (of); (*Law*) a statement of the plaintiff's case; one of several changes in an indictment; †an object of interest. **not counting,** excluding. **out for the count,** unconscious. **to count down,** to count in reverse order, towards zero, in preparing for a particular event. **to count for** or **against,** to be a factor in favour of, or against. **to count on,** to rely on; to consider as certain. **to count out,** to reckon one by one from a number of units; to adjourn a meeting, esp. of Parliament, after counting those present and finding they are not sufficient to form a quorum; to declare a boxer defeated upon his failure to stand up within 10 seconds of the referee beginning to count. **to count up,** to calculate the sum of. **to keep, lose count,** to keep or be unable to keep an accurate record of a numerical series. **to take the count,** in boxing, to be counted out. **count-down,** *n.* **counting house,** *n.* the house, room or office appropriated to the business of keeping accounts etc. **count-wheel,** *n.* a toothed wheel which regulates the striking of a clock. **countable[1],** *a.* **countless,** *a.* innumerable; beyond calculation. [OF *conter,* L *computāre,* to COMPUTE]

count[2], *n.* a foreign title of rank corresponding to an English earl. **count cardinal,** *n.* a count who is also a cardinal. **count palatine,** *n.* a high judicial officer under the Merovingian kings; the ruler of either of the Rhenish Palatinates. **countship,** *n.* [OF *conte,* L *comes -item,* companion]

countable[1] COUNT[1].

countable[2], ACCOUNTABLE.

countenance, *n.* the face; the features; air, look or expression; composure of look; favour, support, corroboration; †credit, estimation. *v.t.* to sanction, to approve, to permit; to abet, to encourage; †to favour; †to pretend, to make a show of. **in countenance,** in favour; confident, assured. **out of countenance,** out of favour; abashed, dismayed. **to keep one's countenance,** to continue composed in look; to refrain from laughter. **to put out of countenance,** to abash; to cause to feel ashamed. **countenancer,** *n.* [OF *contenance,* aspect, demeanour, L *continentia* (*continēre,* to contain)]

counter[1], *n.* one who or that which counts; a calculator; a piece of metal, ivory etc., used for reckoning, as in games; an imitation coin or token; a table or desk over which business is conducted (in a shop, bank, library, cafe etc.). **over the counter,** of medicines, not on prescription. **under the counter,** referring to trade in black market goods; secret(ly); surreptitious(ly). **counter-jumper,** *n.* (*dated; coll.*) a salesman, a shop assistant. [A-F *counteour,* OF *countour,* L *computātōrium,* from *computāre,* to COMPUTE]

counter[2], *n.* the opposite, the contrary; a horse's breast; the curved part of a ship's stern; in fencing, a circular parry; in boxing, a blow dealt just as the opponent is striking; the part of a boot or shoe enclosing the wearer's heel. *a.* contrary, adverse, opposed; opposing; duplicate. *adv.* in the opposite direction; wrongly; contrarily. *v.t.* to oppose, to return a blow by dealing another one. *v.i.* in boxing, to give a return blow. [F *contre,* L *contra,* against]

†**counter[3]** ENCOUNTER.

counter-, *comb. form* in return; in answer; in opposition; in an opposite direction. [COUNTER[2]]

counteract, *v.t.* to act in opposition to, so as to hinder or defeat; to neutralize. **counteraction,** *n.* **counteractive,** *a.*

counteragent, *n.* that which counteracts.

counterapproaches, *n.pl.* a line of trenches made by the besieged outside the permanent fortifications to hinder the approach of besiegers.

counterattack, *v.t., v.i.* to make an attack after an attack by the enemy. *n.* such an attack.

counterattraction, *n.* attraction in an opposite direction; a rival attraction. **counterattractive,** *a.*

counterbalance, *v.t.* to weigh against or oppose with an equal weight or effect; to countervail. *n.*, an equal weight or force acting in opposition.

counterblast, *n.* an argument or statement in opposition.

counterbrace, *n.* the lee brace of the foretopsail yard. *v.t.* to brace in opposite directions.

counterbrand, *v.t.* (*N Am.*) to brand (cattle when sold) on the opposite side to the original brand.

counterbuff, *n.* a blow in return. *v.t.* to strike back, or in an opposite direction.

†**counter-caster,** *n.* a merchant, a book-keeper.

counterceiling, *n.* pugging, dry material packed between the joists of a floor to deaden sound.

counterchange, *n.* exchange, reciprocation. *v.t.* to exchange, to alternate; to interchange, to chequer.

countercharge, *n.* a charge in opposition to another; a counterclaim. *v.t.* to make a charge against in return; to charge in opposition to (a charge of troops).

countercheck, *n.* a check brought against another; an opposing check.

counterclaim, *n.* a claim brought forward by a defendant against a plaintiff.

counterclockwise, *adv.* in a direction contrary to that of the hands of a clock.

counterculture, *n.* a way of life deliberately contrary to accepted social usages.

counterespionage, *n.* work of an intelligence service directed against the agents and networks of another service.

counterfeit, *v.t.* to imitate, to mimic; to imitate or copy without right and pass off as genuine; to put on a semblance of; (*Law*) to coin, to imitate in base metal; to pretend, to simulate. †*v.i.* to make pretences, to feign. *a.* made in imitation with intent to be passed off as genuine; forged. *n.* one who pretends to be what he is not, an impostor; a counterfeit thing. **counterfeiter,** *n.* one who counterfeits. [OF *contrefait,* p.p. of *contrefaire* (L *contra,* against, *facere,* to make)]

counterfoil, *n.* that portion of the tally formerly struck in the exchequer which was kept by an officer of that court, the other part being given to the person who had lent the king money; the counterpart of a cheque, receipt or other document, retained by the giver.

counterfort, *n.* a buttress, arch or oblique wall built against a wall or terrace to retain, support or strengthen it. [F *contrefort*]

countergauge, *n.* (*Carp.*) an adjustable double-pointed gauge for transferring the measurement of a mortise to the end of a stick where a tenon is to be made.

counterintelligence, *n.* work of an intelligence service designed to prevent or damage intelligence gathering by an enemy service.

counterirritant, *n.* an irritant applied to the body to remove some other irritation. *a.* acting as a counterirritant. **counterirritate,** *v.t.* **counterirritation,** *n.*

countermand, *v.t.* to revoke, to annul; to recall; to cancel; †to contradict, to oppose. *n.* an order contrary to or revoking a previous order. [OF *contremander* (L *contra,* against, *mandāre,* to command)]

countermarch, *v.i.* to march in an opposite direction; to perform a countermarch. *v.t.* to cause to countermarch. *n.* the action of countermarching; a change in the position of the wings or front and rear of a battalion; a change of measures or conduct.

countermark, *n.* an additional mark for identification or certification; an additional mark put upon goods belonging to several persons that they may not be opened except in the presence of all; the mark of the Goldsmiths' Company to show the standard of the metal.

countermine, *n.* a gallery or mine to intercept or frustrate a mine made by the enemy; a submarine mine employed to explode the mines sunk by the enemy; a stratagem to frustrate any project. *v.t.* to oppose by a countermine. *v.i.* to make or place countermines.

countermove, -movement, *n.* a movement in an opposite or contrary direction.

countermure, *n.* a wall raised before or behind another as an additional or reserve defence. [F *contremur* (COUNTER-, *mur,* L *murus,* wall)]

counteroffensive, *n.* a counterattack.

counteropening, *n.* (*Surg.*) an opening on the opposite side.

counterpane, *n.* a coverlet for a bed; a quilt. [earlier *counterpoint,* OF *contrepointe,* corr. of *coultepointe,* L *culcita puncta,* stitched QUILT (*puncta,* p.p. of *pungere,* to prick)]

counterpart, *n.* a correspondent part; a duplicate or copy; anything which exactly fits another, as a seal and the impression; one who is exactly like another in person or character; (*Law*) one of two corresponding copies of an instrument; (*Mus.*) a part written to accompany another. [OF *contrepartie* (COUNTER-, *partie,* part)]

counterplot, *v.t.* to oppose or frustrate by another plot. *n.* a plot to defeat another plot.

counterpoint[1], *n.* a melodious part or combination of parts written to accompany a melody; the art of constructing harmonious parts; the art of harmonious composition. **double, triple,** or **quadruple counterpoint,** counterpoint so arranged that the parts can be transposed in any way without impairing the harmony. [F *contrepoint,* med. L *contrapunctum,* point against point (*contra,* against, *punctum,* p.p. of *pungere,* to prick)]

†**counterpoint**[2] COUNTERPANE.

counterpoise, *n.* a weight in opposition and equal to another; a counterbalancing force, power or influence; equilibrium. *v.t.* to oppose with an equal weight so as to balance; to oppose, check or correct with an equal force, power or influence; to bring into or maintain in equilibrium. [F *contrepois* (now *poids*)]

counterpoison, *n.* a poison administered as an antidote.

counterproductive, *a.* producing an opposite, or undesired, result.

counterproof, *n.* a reversed impression taken from another just printed.

counterproposal, *n.* one made as an alternative to a previous proposal.

counter-reformation, *n.* a reformation of an opposite nature to another; (*Hist.*) the attempt of the Roman Church to counteract the results of the Protestant Reformation. Extending into the 17th cent., its dominant forces included the rise of the Jesuits as an educating and missionary group and the deployment of the Spanish Inquisition in other countries.

counter-revolution, *n.* a revolution opposed to a former one, and designed to restore a former state of things. **counter-revolutionary,** *n.* instigator or supporter of such a revolution; *a.* pertaining to such a revolution.

counterscarp, *n.* the exterior wall or slope of the ditch in a fortification; the whole covered way with the parapet and glacis. [F *contrescarpe,* It. *contrascarpa* (*contra,* against, *scarpa,* SCARP[1])]

counterseal, *v.t.* to seal with another seal.

countersecurity, *n.* security given to cover a person's risk as a surety.

countershaft, *n.* an intermediate shaft driven by the main shaft and transmitting motion.

countersign, *v.t.* to attest the correctness of by an additional signature; to ratify. *n.* a password, a secret word or sign by which one may pass a sentry, or by which the members of a secret association may recognize each other. **countersignature,** *n.* the signature of an official to a document certifying that of another person. [F *contresigner*]

countersink, *v.t.* to chamfer a hole for a screw or bolt head; to sink (the head of a screw etc.) into such a hole. *n.* a chamfered hole; a tool for making such a hole.

countertenor, *n.* (a singer with) a voice higher than tenor, an alto; a part written for such a voice.

countervail, *v.t.* to act against with equal effect or power; to counterbalance. *v.i.* to be of equal weight, power or influence on the opposite side. [OF *contrevail,* stem of *contrevaloir* (*contre,* against, *valoir,* L *valēre,* to avail)]

counterview, *n.* a position opposite to or facing another; an opposite view of a question.

counterweigh, *v.t.* to counterbalance. **counterweight,** *n.*

counterwork, *v.t.* to work against; to counteract. *n.* an opposing work or effort; (*Mil.*) a work constructed to oppose those of the enemy.

countess, *n.* the wife of a count or of an earl; a woman holding this rank in her own right. [OF *cuntesse,* late L *comitissa,* fem. of *comes,* COUNT]

counting house, countless COUNT[1].

countrified, *a.* rustic in manners or appearance. [p.p. of *countrify*]

country, *n.* a region or state; the inhabitants of any region or state; one's native land; the rural part as distinct from cities and towns; the rest of a land as distinguished from the capital. **across country,** not using roads etc. **in the country,** (*Cricket*) far from the wickets, at deep-long-off or long-on. **to appeal to the country,** to hold a general election, to appeal to the electors. **up country,** away from the coast or from the capital city. **country-and-western,** *n., a.* (pertaining to) country music. **country club,** *n.* a sporting or social club in country surroundings. **country cousin,** *n.* a relation of countrified ways or appearance. **country-dance** (altered to *contre-danse* in French, this being often mistaken for the orig. form), *n.* a dance in which the partners are ranged in lines opposite to each other; any rural English dance. **countryman, -woman,** *n.* one who lives in a rural district; an inhabitant of any particular region; a native of the same country as another. **country music,** *n.* a style of popular music based on the folk music of rural areas of the US. **country note,** *n.* a bank-note issued by a provincial bank. **country party,** *n.* a political party that professes to maintain the interests of the nation as a whole, or the agricultural interests as against the industrial; an Austral. party (official name National Country Party) representing the interests of the farmers and people of the smaller towns. **country-seat, -house,** *n.* a gentleman's country mansion. **countryside,** *n.* a rural district; the inhabitants of this. **countrywide,** *a.* extending right across a country. [OF *cuntrée, contrée,* late L *contrāta,* a region over against, from *contrā,* against]

Countryside Commission, *n.* an official conservation body, created for England and Wales under the Countryside Act 1968. It replaced the National Parks Commission, and had by 1980 created over 160 Country Parks.

county, *n.* a shire; †the country or district ruled by a count; a division of land for administrative, judicial and political purposes; in the British Isles, the chief civil unit, the chief administrative division; in the US, the civil division next below a state; county families collectively; †a count, an earl. *a.* pertaining to a county; characteristic of county families. **county borough,** *n.* (before 1974) a large borough ranking administratively as a county. **county corporate,** *n.* (*Hist.*) a city or town having sheriffs and other magistrates of its own, and ranking as a county. **county council,** *n.* the elected council administering the civil affairs of a county. **County court,** *n.* a local court dealing with civil cases. **county-court,** *v.t.* to sue in a County court. **county cricket,** *n.* cricket played between sides representing counties. **county family,** *n.* a family belonging to the nobility or gentry with an ancestral seat in the county. **county palatine,** *n.* a county of which the count or earl palatine was formerly invested with royal privileges, as Cheshire and Lancashire. **county road,** *n.* a main road maintained by a county council. **county town,** *n.* the chief town of any county. [OF *cunté, conté,* L *comitātus* (see COUNT[2])]

coup[1], *n.* a stroke, a telling or decisive blow; a victory; a successful move, piece of strategy or revolution; in billiards, a stroke putting a ball into a pocket without its touching another. **coup d'état,** a sudden and violent change of government, esp. of an illegal and revolutionary nature. **coup de foudre,** a flash of lightning; a sudden and overwhelming event. **coup de grâce,** a finishing stroke. **coup de main,** a sudden and energetic attack. **coup de soleil,** sunburn. **coup de théâtre,** a sensational stroke, a notable hit. **coup d'oeil,** a quick comprehensive glance; a general view. [F, from OF *colp* (It. *colpo*), late L *colpus, colapus,* L *colaphus,* Gr. *kolaphos,* a blow]

coup[2], *v.t.* (*Sc.*) to upset, to overturn. *v.i.* to be overturned. [Sc. for COPE[2]]

coup[3], *v.t.* (*Sc.*) to exchange, to barter. **couper,** *n.* [perh. from Icel. *kaupa,* to buy, to bargain, or a var. of COPE[3]]

coupe, *n.* a dessert made of fruit or ice-cream; the shallow glass dish in which it is served. [F, cup]

coupé, *n.* a four-wheeled closed carriage; a half compartment with glazed front at the end of a railway carriage; a two-doored car with an enclosed body. [F, p.p. of *couper,* to cut (as COUP[1])]

couped, *a.* (*Her.*) cut clean, as a head, hand etc. on a shield, opp. to *erased.* [p.p. of obs. *coop,* to cut (as prec.)]

Couperin, *n.* **François** (1668–1733), French composer, called *le Grand,* as the most famous of a distinguished musical family. Born in Paris, he held various court appointments and wrote vocal, chamber and harpsichord music.

couple, *n.* that which joins two things together; two of the same kind considered together; (*loosely*) two; a leash; a pair or brace; a betrothed or married pair; a pair of dancers; (*Carp.*) a pair of rafters connected by a tie; a pair of equal forces acting in parallel and opposite directions so as to impart a circular movement. *v.t.* to connect or fasten together; to unite persons together, esp. in marriage; to associate. *v.i.* to copulate. †**couplement,** *n.* the act of coupling; the state of being coupled; a couple. **coupler,** *n.* one who or that which couples; a connection between two or more organ manuals or keys, or manuals and pedals. **couplet,** *n.* two lines of running verse; †a couple. **coupling,** *n.* the action of the verb TO COUPLE; a device for connecting railway carriages etc. together; a device for connecting parts of machinery and transmitting motion. **coupling-box,** *n.* a contrivance for connecting the ends of two shafts and causing them to rotate together. **coupling-pin,** *n.* a bolt for fastening together parts of machinery; a part of a railway coupling. [OF *cople,* L COPULA]

coupon, *n.* a detachable certificate for the payment of interest on bonds; a detachable ticket or certificate entitling to food ration etc.; a voucher; the official recognition of a candidate as a genuine supporter of a particular party etc.; a detachable slip of paper to be used as an order form or as an entry form for a competition; a piece of paper which can be exchanged for goods in a shop. [F, a piece cut off, from *couper,* to cut]

coupure, *n.* a passage, esp. one cut through the glacis to facilitate sallies by the besieged. [as prec.]

courage, *n.* bravery, boldness, intrepidity. **Dutch courage,** valour inspired by drinking. **the courage of one's convictions,** the courage to act in accordance with one's beliefs. **to pluck up courage, heart,** to summon up boldness or bravery. **courageous,** *a.* **courageously,** *adv.* **courageousness,** *n.* [OF *corage, courage,* from L *cor,* the heart, -AGE]

courant, *a.* (*Heraldry*) in a running attitude. *n.* (also **courante**) an old dance with a running or a gliding step; the music for this. [F, pres.p. of *courir,* L *currere,* to run]

†**courb,** *v.i., v.t.* to bend, bow. *a.* bent, crooked. [F *courber,* L *curvāre*]

Courbet, *n.* **Gustave** (1819–77), French artist, a portrait, genre and landscape painter. His *Burial at Ornaus* (1850, Louvre, Paris) showing ordinary working people gathered round a village grave, shocked the public and the critics with its 'vulgarity'.

courbette, CURVET.

courgette, *n.* a small kind of vegetable marrow. [F, dim. of *courge,* gourd]

courier, *n.* a messenger sent in great haste, an express; a travelling servant who makes all necessary arrangements beforehand; a person employed by a travel agency to accompany a party of tourists or to assist them at a resort; an employee of a private postal company offering a fast collection and delivery service usu. within a city or internationally; a person who conveys secret information for purposes of espionage, or contraband for e.g. a drug-smuggling ring; a title of a newspaper. [ME *corour,* OF *coreor* (F *coureur*), late L *curritor -ōrem,* from L *currere,* to run (coalescing later with F *courier,* It. *corriere,* med. L *currerius,* from It. *corre,* L *currere,* to run)]

course, *n.* the act of moving or running, a race; the act of passing from one place to another; the track passed over, the route; the bed or the direction of a stream; the ground on which a race is run or a game (as golf) is played; a chase after a hare by one or a brace of greyhounds; continued progress; career; a series; one of a series of dishes served at one meal; mode of procedure; a planned programme of study; method of life or conduct; a row or tier of bricks or stones in a building; (*pl.*) behaviour; †(*pl.*) the menses; (*Hist.*) the charge of two mounted knights in the lists; (*pl., Naut.*) the sails set on a ship's lower yards. *v.t.* to run after, to pursue; to traverse. *v.i.* to chase hares with greyhounds; to run or move quickly; to circulate, as the blood. **in due course,** in due, regular or anticipated order. **in (the) course of,** in the process of; during. **matter of course,** a natural event. **of course,** by consequence, naturally. **courser,** *n.* a swift horse, a war-horse; one who practises coursing; a dog used in coursing; a bird of the genus *Cursorius,* noted for swiftness in running. **coursing,** *a.* that courses. *n.* the sport of hunting hares with greyhounds. **coursing-joint,** *n.* the mortar-joint between two courses of bricks or stones. [OF *cours,* L *cursum,* acc. of *cursus,* a running, from *currere,* to run]

Court, *n.* **Margaret** (born Smith) (1942–), Australian tennis player. The most prolific winner in the women's game, she won a record 66 Grand Slam titles, including a record 24 at singles.

court, *n.* a place enclosed by buildings, or enclosing a house; a narrow street; a quadrangle; a subdivision of a large building; an enclosed piece of ground used for games; a subdivision of a piece so enclosed or merely marked out; the residence of a sovereign; the retinue of a sovereign; the body of courtiers; the sovereign and advisers regarded as the ruling power; a State reception by a sovereign; any meeting or body having jurisdiction; the chamber in which justice is administered; the judges or persons assembled to hear any cause; deferential attention paid in order to secure favour or regard. *v.t.* to seek the favour of; to pay court to; to seek the affections of, to woo; (*coll.*) to county-court. *v.i.* to try to gain the affections of a woman; †to act the courtier. **Court of Arches,** ARCHES-COURT under ARCH[1]. **Court of St James's,** the court of the British Crown. **Court of Session,** the Supreme Court in Scotland, established in 1532, sitting in Edinburgh. **General Court,** (*N Am.*) the state legislature in Massachusetts and New Hampshire. **out of court,** not worth considering; without the case being heard in a civil court. **court-baron,** *n.* (*Law*) the court of a manor. **court-card,** *n.* any king, queen or knave in a pack of cards. **court circular,** *n.* an official daily report in a newspaper, of the activities and engagements of the royal family. **court-cupboard,** *n.* a kind of sideboard on which silver etc. could be displayed. **court-day,** *n.* a day on which a court of justice sits. **court-dress,** *n.* the costume proper for a royal levee. †**court-dresser,** *n.* a flatterer. **court-guide,** *n.* a directory of private residents (orig. of those entitled to be presented at court). **court hand,** *n.* (*Hist.*) the style of handwriting (based on Norman handwriting) used in records and judicial proceedings. **court-house,** *n.* a house or building containing rooms used by any court. †**court leet,** *n.* a court of record held once a year by the steward of a hundred, lordship or manor. **court-like,** *a.* elegant, polished. **court-martial,** *n.* a court for the trial of service offenders, composed of officers, none of whom must be of inferior rank to the prisoner. *v.t.* to try by court-martial. **drumhead court-martial,** a court held (orig.) round the drumhead in war-time. **court-plaster,** *n.* silk surfaced with a solution of balsam of benzoin (used in the 18th cent. by fashionable ladies for patches, and since for cuts or slight wounds). †**court-roll,** *n.* the record of a manorial court. **court shoe,** *n.* a woman's low-cut shoe without straps etc. **court tennis,** *n.* real tennis. **courtyard,** *n.* an open area round or within a large building. **courtship,** *n.* the act of soliciting in marriage; the act of seeking after anything; †good breeding, courtliness; courtly state; courteous attention. [OF *cort,* L *cōrtem, cohortem,* acc. of *cohors,* an enclosure, a cohort (cp. Gr. *chortos,* a courtyard, L *hortus,* a garden)]

Court of the Lord Lyon, Scottish heraldic authority, composed of one King of Arms, three Heralds and three Pursuivants who specialize in genealogical work. It embodies the High Sennachie of Scotland's Celtic kings.

Courtauld, *n.* **Samuel** (1876–1947), British industrialist, who developed the production of viscose rayon and other synthetic fibres from 1904.

Courtelle®, *n.* a synthetic acrylic fibre.

courteous, *a.* having court-like manners, polite, affable, considerate. **courteously,** *adv.* **courteousness,** *n.* [OF *cortois, curteis*]

courtesan, -zan, *n.* a prostitute; a woman of loose virtue. [F *courtisane,* It. *cortigiana*]

courtesy, *n.* courteousness, politeness; graciousness; gracious disposition; favour, as opposed to right; an act of civility; a bow, a curtsy. **by courtesy,** as a matter of courtesy, not of right. **courtesy of England,** (*Law*) a tenure by which a man having issue by a woman seized of land, after her death holds the estate for life. **courtesy title,** *n.* a title to which a person has no legal right (used esp. of the hereditary titles assumed by the children of peers). [OF *cortesie,* from *corteis,* COURTEOUS]

courtier, *n.* one who is in attendance or a frequenter at the court of a prince; one of polished or distinguished manners; one who courts. †**courtierism,** *n.* [from OF *cortoier,* to live at court (*cort,* COURT)]

courtly, *a.* of or pertaining to a court; polished, elegant, polite; flattering, obsequious. †*adv.* as befits a court or courtier. **courtliness,** *n.*

couscous, *n.* a N African dish of pounded wheat steamed over meat or broth. [F, from Arab. *kuskus,* from *kaskasa,* to pound]

cousin, *n.* the son or daughter of an uncle or aunt; a title used by a sovereign in addressing another sovereign or a nobleman; †a kinsman; a familiar form of address. †*a.* allied, related, kindred. **cousin once removed,** the child of one's first cousin. **first cousins,** the children of brothers or sisters. **second cousins,** the children of cousins. **to call cousins,** to profess kinship with. **cousin-german,** *n.* a first cousin. **cousinhood,** *n.* **cousinly,** *a.* †**cousinry,** *n.* kindred, relatives. **cousinship,** *n.* [F, from late L *cosīnus,* L *consobrīnus,* a cousin-german on the mother's side, from *soror,* a sister]

Cousteau, *n.* **Jacques-Yves** (1910–), French oceanographer, celebrated for his researches in command of the *Calypso* from 1951. He pioneered the invention of the aqualung in 1943 and techniques in underwater filming.

couthie, -thy, *a.* (*Sc.*) friendly, kindly, genial. *adv.* in a friendly or genial way. [prob. from OE *cūth*, known]

couture, *n.* dressmaking; dress-designing. **couturier,** *n.* a dress-designer or dress-maker. **couturière,** *n.fem.* [F]

couvade, *n.* a custom among primitive races, by which the father on the birth of a child performs certain acts and abstains from certain foods etc. [F, from *couver,* to hatch, L *cubāre,* to lie]

covalent, *n.* having atoms linked by a shared pair of electrons. **covalence, -ency,** *n.* [VALENCE]

covariant, *n.* (*Math.*) a function standing in the same relation to another from which it is derived as any of its linear transforms do to a transform similarly derived from the latter function. **covariance,** *n.*

cove[1], *n.* a small creek, inlet or bay; a nook or sheltered recess; (*N Am.*) a strip of prairie extending into woodland; (also **coving**) a hollow in a cornice-moulding; the cavity of an arch or ceiling. *v.t.* to arch over; to cause to slope inwards. **coved ceiling,** *n.* one with a hollow curve at the junction with the wall. **cove-let,** *n.* a small cove. [OE *cofa,* a chamber (cp. Icel. *kofi,* G *Koben,* a hut or cabin)]

cove[2], *n.* (*dated, sl.*) a man, a fellow, a chap. [prob. from Romany *kova,* thing, person]

coven, *n.* an assembly of witches. [CONVENT[1]]

covenant, *n.* an agreement on certain terms; a compact; a document containing the terms of agreement; (*Law*) a formal agreement under seal; a clause in an agreement; the name given to certain formal agreements in favour of the Reformation, and later (esp. in 1638 and 1643) in favour of Presbyterianism; (*Bibl.*) a covenant between the Israelites and Jehovah. *v.t.* to grant or promise by covenant. *v.i.* to enter into a covenant. **Ark of the Covenant** ARK. **Covenant of the League of Nations,** a series of articles embodying the principles of the League. **New Covenant,** the Christian relation to God. **Old Covenant,** the Jewish dispensation. **Solemn League and Covenant,** the Presbyterian compact of 1643. **covenantal, -anted,** *a.* secured by or held under a covenant; bound by a covenant. **Covenanted Service,** *n.* the former Indian Civil Service (in reference to the covenant entered into by members with the East India Company and later with the Secretary of State). **covenanter, -tor,** *n.* one who enters into a covenant; an adherent of the Scottish National Covenant of 1638 or the Solemn League and Covenant of 1643. [OF, pres.p. of *convenir* (see CONVENE)]

Coventry, *n.* an industrial city in West Midlands, England; population (1981) 313,800. Manufacturing includes cars, electronic equipment, machine tools and agricultural machinery. **to send to Coventry,** to refuse to have communication or dealings with. [town in Warwickshire]

cover, *v.t.* to overlay; to overspread with something; to overspread with something so as to protect or conceal; to clothe; to hide, cloak or screen; (*Cricket*) to stand behind so as to stop balls that are missed; to lie over so as to shelter or conceal; (*Bibl.*) to pardon, to put out of remembrance; to save from punishment, to shelter; to incubate; of the lower animals, to copulate with (a female); to include; to be enough to defray; to have range or command over; to extend over; to hold under aim with a fire-arm; to protect by insurance; to report on for a newspaper, broadcasting station etc.; (*Mil.*) to protect with troops. *v.i.* to be spread over so as to conceal; to put one's hat on. *n.* anything which covers or hides; a lid; (*often pl.*) the outside covering of a book; one side or board of this; anything which serves to conceal, screen, disguise; pretence, pretext; shelter, protection; a shelter; a thicket, woods which conceal game; (*Comm.*) sufficient funds to meet a liability or ensure against loss; the coverage of an insurance policy; a bed-covering, blanket; an envelope or other wrapping for a packet in the post; a place setting in a restaurant. **to cover for,** to substitute for or replace (an absent fellow worker). **to cover in,** to fill in; to finish covering. **to cover up,** to cover completely; to conceal (esp. something illegal). **under cover,** enclosed in an envelope addressed to another person; concealed; protected. **coverall,** *a.* covering everything. *n.* a one-piece garment covering limbs and body, e.g. a boiler-suit. **cover-charge,** *n.* the amount added to a restaurant bill to cover service. **cover crop,** *n.* one grown between main crops to provide protective cover for the soil. **cover-girl,** *n.* a pretty girl whose photograph is used to illustrate a magazine cover. **cover note,** *n.* a note given to an insured person to certify that he or she has cover. **cover-point,** *n.* (*Cricket*) a fielder or the position behind point. **cover-up,** *n.* **cover version,** *n.* a version of a song, etc., similar to the original, recorded by a different artist. **coverage,** *n.* the act of covering; the extent to which anything is covered; the area or the people reached by a broadcasting or advertising medium; the amount of protection provided by an insurance policy. **covered,** *a.* sheltered, protected; concealed. **covered wagon,** *n.* a type of large wagon with a tent roof used by American settlers to transport their families and belongings. **covered-way, covert-way,** *n.* a sunken area round a fortification between the counterscarp and glacis. **covering,** *n.* that which covers; a cover. **covering letter,** *n.* a letter explaining an enclosure. [OF *cuvrir, covrir,* L *coöperīre* (co-, *operīre,* to shut)]

†**coverchief,** *n.* a head-dress; a kerchief. [F *couvrechef* (*couvrir,* to cover, *chef,* head)]

Coverdale, *n.* **Miles** (1488–1569), English protestant priest whose translation of the Bible was the first to be printed in English (1535). His translation of the psalms is that retained in the Book of Common Prayer.

coverlet, coverlid, *n.* an outer covering for a bed; a counterpane. [A-F *coverlit* (COVER-, *lit,* bed)]

covert, *a.* (*esp. Amer.*), covered; disguised, secret, private; (*Law*) under protection. *n.* a place which covers and shelters; a cover for game. **feme-covert, femme-couvert,** (*Law*) a married woman. **covert-coat,** *n.* a short overcoat. **covert-way** COVERED-WAY. **covertly,** *adv.* **coverture,** *n.* covering, shelter, a hiding-place; secrecy; (*Law*) the state of a married woman, as being under the authority of her husband. [OF, p.p. of *covrir,* to COVER]

covertical, *a.* (*Geom.*) having common vertices.

covet, *v.t.* to desire (something unlawful) inordinately; to long for. *v.i.* to have an inordinate desire. **covetable,** *a.* †**covetise,** *n.* covetousness. **covetous,** *a.* eagerly desirous; eager to obtain and possess; avaricious; †aspiring. **covetously,** *adv.* **covetousness,** *n.* [A-F and OF *coveiter* (L *cupere,* to desire)]

covey, *n.* a brood or small flock of birds (prop. of partridges); †a small company, a party. [OF *covée* (F *couvée*), fem. p.p. of *couver,* to hatch, L *cubāre,* to lie down]

covin, *n.* (*Law*) an agreement between two or more persons to injure or defraud another. [OF, from late L *covenium,* a convention (*convenīre,* to CONVENE)]

coving COVE[1].

cow[1], *n.* (*pl.* **cows,** †**kine**) the female of any bovine species, esp. of the domesticated species *Bos taurus;* a female elephant or cetacean; (*sl., derog.*) a woman; (*Austral., sl.*) a difficult or unpleasant situation. **till the cows come home,** (*coll.*) forever. **cow-bane,** *n.* the water-hemlock, *Cicuta virosa.* **cow-berry,** *n.* the red whortleberry, *Vaccinium vitisdaea; V. myrtillus,* the bilberry or whortleberry. **cow-bird,** *n.* (*N Am.*) applied to several species of the genus *Molothrus,* from their accompanying cattle. **cowboy,** *n.* a boy who tends cattle; a man in charge of cattle on a ranch; (*sl.*) an unqualified or unscrupulous businessman or workman. **cow-catcher,** *n.* (*N Am.*) an inclined frame attached to the front of a locomotive etc., to throw obstructions from the track. **cow-fish,** *n.* the sea-cow or manatee; a fish, *Ostracion quadricorne,* with horn-like protuberances over the eyes. **cowgirl,** *n. fem.* **cow-grass,** *n.* a wild trefoil, *Trifolium medium.* **cow-heel,** *n.* the foot of a cow or ox used to make jelly. **cowherd,** *n.* one who tends cattle. **cowhide,** *n.* the hide of a cow; a whip made of cowhide; *v.t.* to thrash with a cowhide. **cow-house,** *n.* a house or shed in which cows are kept. †**cow-leech,** *n.* a cow-doctor. **cowlick,** *n.* a tuft of hair that grows up over the forehead. **cow-parsley,** *n.* the wild chervil, *Anthriscus sylvestris.* **cow-parsnip,** *n.* name of various umbelliferous plants of the genus *Heracleum,* esp. *H. sphondylium.* **cow-pat,** *n.* a small pile of cow dung. **cow-pock,** *n.* a pustule or pock of cowpox. **cowpoke,** *n.* (*N Am., sl.*) a cowboy. **cow-pony,** *n.* (*N Am.*) the mustang of a cowboy. **cowpox,** *n.* a vaccine disease affecting the udders of cows, capable of being transferred to human beings, and conferring immunity from smallpox. **cow-puncher,** *n.* (*N Am.*) a cowboy. **cow-tree,** *n.* various milky trees, esp. *Galactodendron utile.* **cow-weed** COW-PARSLEY. **cow-wheat,** *n.* the melampyre, *M. pratense,* and other plants of the genus *Melampyrum.* **cowish,** *a.* [OE *cū,* from Teut. *kō-* (cp. Dut. *koe,* G *Kuh,* Gael. *bo,* L *bos,* Gr. *bous*)]

cow[2], *v.t.* to intimidate, to deprive of spirit or courage, to terrify, to daunt. **cowed,** *a.* [prob. from Icel. *kūga*]

cowage, cowhage, *n.* (the sharp, stinging hairs of) a tropical climbing plant, *Macuna pruriens,* used as an anthelmintic. [Hind. *kawāñch*]

Coward, *n.* **Noel** (1899–1973), English playwright, actor, producer, director and composer, who epitomized the witty and sophisticated man of the theatre. From his first success with *The Young Idea* (1923), he wrote and appeared in plays and comedies such as *Hay Fever* (1925), *Private Lives* (1930) with Gertrude Lawrence, *Design for Living* (1933) and *Blithe Spirit* (1941).

coward, *n.* a poltroon; one without courage. *a.* timid, pusillanimous; (*Her.*) represented with the tail between the legs. **cowardice,** *n.* extreme timidity; want of courage. **cowardlike,** *a.* **cowardliness,** *n.* the quality of being cowardly. **cowardly,** *adv.* in the manner of a coward. *a.* craven, faint-hearted, spiritless. **cowardry,** *n.* cowardice. [OF *coart* (It. *codardo*), from *coe* (It. *coda*), a tail, L *cauda;* see -ARD]

cowboy cow[1].

cower, *v.i.* to stoop, to bend, to crouch; to shrink or quail through fear. [etym. doubtful (cp. Icel. *kūra,* to doze, to be quiet, Dan. *kure,* G *kauern*)]

cowl[1], *n.* a hooded garment, esp. one worn by a monk; a hood-like chimney-top, usu. movable by the wind, to facilitate the exit of smoke. *v.t.* to cover with a cowl. **cowled,** *a.* **cowling,** *n.* a removable metal casing for an aircraft engine. [ME *cowle, cule,* OE *cugele,* late L *cucalla,* a frock, L *cucullus,* a hood (blended with ME *covel, cuuel,* OE *cufle,* cp. Dut. *keuvel*)]

†**cowl**[2], *n.* a water-vessel borne on a pole between two men. †**cowl-staff,** *n.* the staff on which a cowl is carried. [OF *cuvele* (later *cuveau*), a small tub, L *cūpella,* dim. of *cūpa,* a vat, a large cask]

Cowley, *n.* **Abraham** (1618–67), British poet. He introduced the Pindaric ode (based on the Gr. poet Pindar) to English poetry, and published metaphysical verse with elaborate imagery, as well as essays.

cowlick, cowpox cow[1].

co-worker, *n.* a fellow worker.

Cowper, *n.* **William** (1731–1800), English poet, who trained as a lawyer, but suffered a mental breakdown in 1763 and entered an asylum, where he underwent an evangelical conversion. He later wrote hymns (e.g. 'God moves in a mysterious way'). His verse includes the six books of *The Task* (1785) and the comic poem 'John Gilpin'.

cowry, cowrie, *n.* a gasteropod of the genus *Cypraea,* esp. *C. moneta,* a small shell used as money in many parts of southern Asia and Africa. [Hind. *kaurī,* Sansk. *kaparda*]

cowslip, *n.* a wild plant with fragrant flowers, *Primula veris,* growing in pastures in England. **cowslip-tea, -wine,** *n.* beverages made from the flowers. [OE *cūslyppe,* cow-dung]

cox COXSWAIN.

coxa, *n.* (*pl.* **coxae**) the hip; the articulation of the leg to the body in arthropoda. **coxal,** *a.* **coxalgia,** *n.* pain in the hip; hip disease. **coxitis,** *n.* inflammation of the hip-joint. [L]

coxcomb, *n.* †the comb resembling that of a cock formerly worn by jesters; a conceited person, a fop, a dandy; †the head. **coxcombical,** *a.* **coxcombically,** *adv.* **coxcombly,** *adv.* **coxcombry,** *n.*

coxitis COXA.

coxswain, *n.* one who steers a boat, esp. in a race; the petty officer on board ship in charge of a boat and its crew. [COCK[2], SWAIN]

coy, *a.* shrinking from familiarity; modest, shy, reserved; disdainful; simulating reserve, coquettish; sequestered, secluded. †*v.t.* to caress. *v.i.* to be shy or reserved; †to disdain; to withdraw, to recede. **coyly,** *adv.* **coyness,** *n.* [F *coi* (fem. *coite*), L *quiētus,* QUIET]

coy., (*abbr.*) company.

coyote, *n.* the N American prairie wolf. [Sp., from Nahuatl *coyotl*]

coypu, *n.* a S American aquatic rodent, *Myopotamus,* naturalized in Europe; its fur. [Indian name]

coz, *n.* short for COUSIN.

cozen, *v.t.* to deceive, to cheat. **cozenage,** *n.* **cozener,** *n.* [perh. from COUSIN (cp. F *cousiner,* to claim kindred)]

Cozens, *n.* **John Robert** (1752–97), British landscape painter, a watercolourist whose Romantic views of Europe painted on tours in the 1770s and 1780s influenced Girtin and Turner.

†**cozier,** *n.* a cobbler. [OF *cousere,* from *couder,* to sew]

cozy, COSY.

CP, (*abbr.*) Common Prayer; Communist Party; (*Austral.*) Country Party.

cp, (*abbr.*) candlepower.

cp., (*abbr.*) compare.

CPAG, (*abbr.*) Child Poverty Action Group.

cpl, (*abbr.*) corporal.

CPO, (*abbr.*) chief petty officer.

CPR, (*abbr.*) Canadian Pacific Railway.

CPRE, (*abbr.*) Council for the Preservation of Rural England.

cps, (*abbr.*) characters per second; cycles per second.

CPSA, (*abbr.*) Civil and Public Services Association.

CPU, (*abbr.*) central processing unit.

CPVE, (*abbr.*) Certificate of Pre-Vocational Education, an educational qualification introduced in the UK in 1986 for students over 16 in schools and colleges who want a one year course of preparation for work or further vocational study.

CR, (*abbr.*) King Charles [L *Carolus Rex*]; Roman citizen [L *cīvis romanus*]; Keeper of the Rolls [L *custos rotulorum*].

Cr, (*chem. symbol*) chromium.

cr, (*abbr.*) created; credit(or); crown.

crab[1], *n.* a decapod crustacean of the group Brachyura, esp. the common crab, *Cancer pagurus,* and other edible species; the zodiacal constellation Cancer; a kind of crane; a kind of windlass for hauling ships into dock; a portable capstan; (*pl.*) deuceace or two aces, the lowest throw at dice; a crab-louse. **a case of crabs,** a disagreeable conclusion; failure. **to catch a crab,** in rowing, to sink an oar too deep and be pushed backwards by the resistance of the water; to miss a stroke. **crab-louse,** *n.* an insect, *Phthirius inguinalis,* found on the human body. **crab-pot,** *n.* a basket or wicker trap for catching lobsters. **crab's-eyes,** *n.pl.* concretions formed in the stomach of the crayfish. **crabwise,** *adv.* sideways. [OE *crabba* (cp. Icel. *krabbi,* Dut. *kreeft,* G *Krebs;* also Dut. and LG *krabben,* to scratch)]

crab[2], *v.t.* (*past, p.p.* **crabbed**) (*Falconry*) to claw, to scratch; (*coll.*) to criticize savagely, to pull to pieces; to hinder. *v.i.* (*Falconry*) to scratch and claw. [cogn. with prec. (cp. Dut. and LG *krabben*)]

crab[3], *n.* a crab-apple; a peevish, morose person. *a.* sour, rough, austere. *v.i.* (*past, p.p.* **crabbed**) (*coll.*) to complain, grumble. **crab-apple,** *n.* a wild apple, the fruit of *Pyrus malus;* (*N Am.*) wild apples of other species. **crab-tree,** *n.* [etym. doubtful]

Crabbe, *n.* **George** (1754–1832), British poet. Orig. a doctor, he became a clergyman in 1781, and wrote grimly realistic verse of the poor of his own time: *The Village* (1783), *The Parish Register* (1807) and *The Borough* (1810), which includes the story used in the Britten opera *Peter Grimes*.

crabbed, *a.* peevish, morose; sour-tempered; harsh, sour; intricate, perplexing, abstruse; cramped, undecipherable. **crabbedly,** *adv.* **crabbedness,** *n.* **crabby,** *a.* (*coll.*) bad-tempered. [CRAB[1] (influenced later in sense by CRAB[3])]

Crab Nebula, *n.* a cloud of gas 6000 light years away, in the constellation of Taurus, the remains of a supernova (observed on Earth in 1054). At its centre is a pulsar that flashes 30 times a second. The name comes from its crab-like appearance.

crack, *v.t.* to break without entire separation of the parts; to cause to give a sharp, sudden noise; to say smartly or sententiously; to open and drink (as a bottle of wine); †to utter boastfully; to break (molecules of a compound) down into simpler molecules by the application of heat. *v.i.* to break partially asunder; to be ruined; to fail; to utter a loud sharp sound; to boast, to brag; to change (applied to the changing of voices at puberty); to chat. *n.* a sudden and partial separation of parts; the chink, fissure or opening so made; a sharp sudden sound or report; a smart blow; the change of voice at puberty; (*dial.*) gossip, news; chat; boasting; a boast; (*sl.*) a burglar; (*sl.*) a burglary; something first-rate; (*coll.*) a sarcastic joke; (*sl.*) a relatively pure and highly addictive form of cocaine for smoking. *a.* having qualities to be boasted of; excellent, superior, brilliant. **a (fair) crack of the whip,** a fair opportunity or chance. **crack of dawn,** the first light of dawn. **crack of doom,** the end of the world. **to crack a crib,** (*sl.*) to break into a house. **to crack down (on),** (*coll.*) to take very strict measures (against). **to crack up,** to extol highly, to puff; to suffer a mental or physical breakdown. **to get cracking,** to start moving quickly. **to have a crack at,** (*coll.*) to have a try, to attempt. **crack-brained,** *a.* crazy, cracked. **crackdown,** *n.* **†crack-hemp, †-rope,** *n.* one who deserves hanging. **crack-jaw,** *a.* applied to long or unpronounceable words. **crackpot,** *n.* (*coll.*) a crazy person. *a.* of persons, ideas etc., crazy, eccentric. **cracksman,** *n.* (*sl.*) a burglar. **crackup,** *n.* **crackable,** *a.* **cracked,** *a.* (*coll.*) insane, crazy. **cracker,** *n.* one who or that which cracks; a form of explosive firework; a thin, brittle, hard-baked (savoury) biscuit; a paper tube containing a toy etc., that gives a sharp report in being torn open; an implement for cracking; (*N Am.*) a biscuit; †a boaster; (*sl.*) one who or that which is exceptional or excellent; a rattling pace; a lie. **crackerjack,** *n.* (*sl.*) an excellent person or thing. **crackers,** *a.* (*sl.*) crazy. **cracking,** *a.* (*coll.*) vigorous; very good. [OE *cracian* (cp. Dut. *kraken* and *krakken*, G *krachen*, imit. in orig.)]

crackle, *v.i.* to make short, sharp cracking noises; to be energetic. *n.* a rapid succession of slight, sharp noises like cracks; a small crack; a series of such cracks. **crackle-china, -glass, -ware,** *n.* porcelain or glass covered with a delicate network of cracks. **cracklin,** *n.* crackle-china. **crackling,** *a.* making short, sharp, frequent cracks. *n.* the browned scored skin of roast pork. [from prec.]

cracknel, *n.* a hard, brittle biscuit. [corr. of F *craquelin* (cp. dial. *crackling*)]

†Cracovienne, *n.* a light Polish dance. [F, fem. adj., from *Cracovie,* Cracow]

Cracow, alternative form of KRAKÓW.

-cracy, *suf.* government, rule of; influence or dominance by means of; as in *aristocracy, democracy, plutocracy, theocracy*. [F *-cratie,* Gr. *-kratia,* from *kratos,* power]

cradle, *n.* a baby's bed or cot, usu. rocking or swinging; place of birth or early nurture; infancy; a frame to protect a broken or wounded limb in bed; a bed or framework of timbers to support a vessel out of water; the apparatus in which sailors are brought to land along a line fastened to a ship in distress; a tool resembling a chisel used for scraping and preparing the plate for mezzotints; a set of fingers in a light frame mortised into a scythe to lay the corn more evenly; (*Mining*) a gold-washing machine; the centering for an arch, culvert etc.; a platform or trolley in which workers are suspended to work on the side of a building or boat. *v.t.* to lay or place in a cradle; to rock to sleep; to nurture or rear from infancy; to receive or hold in or as in a cradle; †to cut and lay (corn) with a cradle. †*v.i.* to lie or lodge as in a cradle. **from the cradle to the grave,** throughout one's life. **cradle-clothes,** *n.pl.* swaddling-clothes. **cradle-scythe,** *n.* a broad scythe fitted with a cradle. **cradlesong,** *n.* a lullaby. **†cradle-walk,** *n.* a walk under an avenue of trees. **cradling,** *n.* the act of laying or rocking in a cradle; (*Build.*) a framework of wood or iron; the framework in arched or coved ceilings to which the laths are nailed. [OE *cradol* (etym. doubtful)]

craft, *n.* dexterity, skill; cunning, deceit; an art, esp. one applied to useful purposes, a handicraft, occupation or trade; the members of a particular trade; (*pl.* **craft**) a vessel. *v.t.* to make with skill or by hand. **small craft,** small vessels of all kinds. **the craft,** the brotherhood of Freemasons; Freemasonry. **the gentle craft,** angling. **craft-brother,** *n.* one of the same craft or guild. **craft-guild,** *n.* an association of workers in the same occupation or trade. **craftsman,** *n.* a skilled artisan. **craftsmanship,** *n.* **-woman,** *n.* [OE *cræft* (cp. Dut. *kràcht,* Swed., Dan. and G *Kraft,* power)]

crafty, *a.* artful, sly, cunning, wily. **craftily,** *adv.* **craftiness,** *n.* [see prec.]

crag[1], *n.* a rugged or precipitous rock. **crag-and-tail,** *n.* a rock or hill with a precipitous face on one side and a gradually sloping descent on the other. **cragsman,** *n.* a skilful rock-climber. **cragged,** *a.* **craggedness,** *n.* **craggy,** *a.* full of crags, rugged, rough; †knotty. **cragginess,** *n.* [cp. W *craig,* Gael. and Ir. *creag*]

crag[2], *n.* the neck; (*dial.*) the crop of a fowl. [cp. Dut. *kraag,* G *Kragen*]

crag[3], *n.* shelly deposits, esp. in Norfolk, Suffolk and Essex, of Pliocene age. [perh. from CRAG[1]]

Craig[1], *n.* **Edward Gordon** (1872–1966), British director and stage designer. His innovations and theories on stage design and lighting effects, expounded in *On the Art of the Theatre* (1911), had a huge influence on stage production in Europe and the US.

Craig[2], *n.* **James** (1871–1940), Ulster Unionist politician, the first prime minister of Northern Ireland (1921–40). He became an MP in 1906 and was a highly effective organizer of Unionist resistance to Home Rule. As prime minister he carried out systematic discrimination against the Catholic minority.

crake, *n.* the corncrake; other birds of the same family; their cry. *v.i.* to cry like the corncrake. **crakeberry,** *n.* the black crowberry, *Empetrum nigrum.* [imit.; cp. CROAK, CROW]

cram, *v.t.* (*past, p.p.* **crammed**) to stuff, push or press in so as to fill to overflowing; to thrust in by force; to coach for examination by storing the pupil's mind with formulas and answers to probable questions. *v.i.* to eat greedily; to stuff oneself; to get up a subject hastily and superficially, esp. to undergo cramming for examination. *n.* the system of cramming for an examination; information acquired by cramming; a crush, a crowd; (*sl.*) a lie. **crammer,** *n.* one who crams; a coach who crams; a school which specializes in cramming; (*sl.*) a lie. [OE *crammian,* from *crimman,* to insert (cp. OHG *chrimman,* G *krimmen*)]

crambo, *n.* (*pl.* **-boes**) a game in which one selects a word to which another finds a rhyme. **dumb crambo,** a similar game in which the rhymes are expressed in dumb show. [L *crambē,* in ref. to Juvenal's *crambe repetīta,* cabbage served up again, Sat. vii.154]

cramoisy, cramesy, *a.* crimson. *n.* crimson cloth. [early It. *cremesí,* and OF *crameisi* (later *cramoisi*), Sp. *carmesi,* see CRIMSON]

cramp[1], *n.* a spasmodic contraction of some limb or muscle, attended with pain and numbness. *v.t.* to affect with cramp. **to cramp one's style,** to spoil the effect one is trying to make; to impede a person's actions or self-expression. **cramped,** *a.* contracted; difficult to read; knotty. **cramp-fish,** *n.* the torpedo fish. †**cramp-ring,** †**-stone,** *n.* a ring or stone worn or carried as a preservative against cramp. **crampedness,** *n.* [OF *crampe* (cp. Dut. *kramp;* also OHG *krimphan,* G *krampfen,* to cramp)]

cramp[2], *n.* a cramp-iron; a clamp; restraint, a hindrance. *v.t.* to confine closely; to hinder, to restrain; to fasten with a cramp-iron. **cramp-iron,** *n.* an iron with bent ends binding two stones together in a masonry course. [Dut. *kramp,* see prec.]

crampon, *n.* a hooked bar of iron; a grappling-iron; a plate with iron spikes worn on climbing boots to assist in climbing ice-slopes. [F, from late L *crampo -ōnem,* from LG (cp. CRAMP ([1] and [2]))]

cran, *n.* (*Sc.*) a measure of 37½ gall (170 l) by which herrings are sold. [Gael. *crann*]

Cranach, *n.* **Lucas** (1472–1553), German painter, etcher and woodcut artist, a leading light in the German Renaissance. He is best known for full-length nudes and precise and polished portraits, such as *Martin Luther* (1521, Uffizi, Florence).

cranage, *n.* the right to use a crane on a wharf; money paid for the use of the crane. [CRANE[2]]

cranberry, *n.* the American cranberry, *Vaccinium macrocarpon;* the British marsh whortleberry *V. oxycoccos,* both with a small, red, acid fruit used in sauces etc. [LG *kraanbere* (G *Kranbeere*), introd. by N Amer. colonists]

crance, *n.* (*Naut.*) a boom-iron, esp. one forming a cap to the bowsprit. [cp. Dut. *krans,* G *Kranz*]

Crane[1], *n.* **(Harold) Hart** (1899–1932), US poet. His long mystical poem *The Bridge* (1930) uses the Brooklyn Bridge as a symbol. He drowned after jumping overboard from a steamer bringing him back to the US after a visit to Mexico.

Crane[2], *n.* **Stephen** (1871–1900), US writer, who introduced grim realism into the US novel. Born in New Jersey, he became a journalist and wrote *Red Badge of Courage* (1895), dealing vividly with the US Civil War.

crane[1], *n.* a bird of the genus *Grus,* esp. *G. cinerea,* a migratory wading bird. *v.t.* to stretch out (the neck) like a crane, esp. to see over or round an object. *v.i.* to stretch out the neck thus. **crane-fly,** *n.* the daddy-long-legs, any fly of the genus *Tipula.* **crane's-bill,** *n.* various species of wild geranium; (*Surg.*) a pair of long-nosed forceps. **craner,** *n.* one who cranes. [OE *cran* (cp. Dut. *kraan,* G *Kranich,* Gr. *geranos,* L *grus*)]

crane[2], *n.* a machine for hoisting and lowering heavy weights; anything similar, as an iron arm turning on a vertical axis, fixed to the back of the fireplace, on which to support a kettle etc.; a siphon used for drawing liquors from a cask; a pipe for supplying a locomotive with water; (*Naut.*) a projecting pair of brackets in which to stow spare spars; a moving platform for a film camera. *v.t.* to raise by a crane. [as prec.]

cranio-, *comb. form* (*Anat., Ethn.*) pertaining to the skull. **craniognomy,** *n.* the study of the peculiarities of the cranium in different races or individuals. **craniology,** *n.* the scientific study of crania. **craniological,** *a.* **craniologist,** *n.* **craniometer,** *n.* an instrument for measuring the cubic capacity of skulls. **craniometrical,** *a.* **craniometry,** *n.* **cranioscopy,** *n.* the examination of the skull for scientific purposes. **craniotomy,** *n.* surgical incision into the skull. [L *crānium,* Gr. *kranion,* the skull]

cranium, *n.* (*pl.* **-niums, -nia**) the skull, esp. the part enclosing the brain. **cranial,** *a.* **cranial index,** *n.* the ratio of width to length of the skull, expressed as a percentage. **craniate,** *a.* having a cranium. [L, from Gr. *kranion*]

crank[1], *n.* an arm at right angles to an axis for converting rotary into reciprocating motion, or the converse; an iron elbow-shaped brace for various purposes; a machine formerly used in prisons for inflicting hard labour; a handle which turns the shaft of a motor until the pistons reach the maximum of compression. **to crank up,** to start an engine with the crank-handle. **crank-axle,** *n.* a shaft that turns or is turned by a crank. **crankcase,** *n.* a metal casing for the crankshaft, connecting-rods etc. in an engine. **crankpin,** *n.* a cylindrical pin parallel to a shaft and fixed at the outer end of a crank. **crankshaft,** *n.* a shaft that bears one or more cranks. [OE *cranc,* orig. past of *crincan,* a form of *cringan,* to be bent up]

crank[2], *n.* a whimsical turn of speech; a caprice, a whim, a crotchet; a crotchety person; an eccentric. [etym. doubtful; perh. conn. with prec.]

crank[3], *a.* infirm, shaky; (*Mach.*) shaky, liable to break down; (*Naut.*) liable to capsize; (*Sc.*) crooked, misshapen. [conn. with CRANK[1] and CRANKY]

crank[4], *a.* brisk, lively. *adv.* briskly, vigorously. [etym. doubtful]

crankle, *v.i.* to bend, to twist. *n.* a bend, a twist. [CRANK[1]]

cranky, *a.* irritable, fidgety; whimsical; eccentric; full of twists; shaky, sickly; (*Naut.*) liable to capsize. [formed from CRANK[1–4] in the various senses]

Cranmer, *n.* **Thomas** (1489–1556), English priest, archbishop of Canterbury from 1533. A Protestant convert, under Edward VI he helped to shape the doctrines of the Church of England. He was responsible for the issue of the Prayer Books of 1549 and 1552, and supported the succession of Lady Jane Grey.

crannog, *n.* a lake-dwelling, common in Scotland and Ireland, built up from the lake bottom on brushwood and piles, and often surrounded by palisades. [Ir., from *crann,* a tree, a beam]

cranny, *n.* a crevice, a chink; a corner, a hole. **crannied,** *a.* [prob. from F *cran,* a notch, a chink]

crap[1], CROP.

crap[2], *n.* (*taboo*) excrement; (*sl.*) rubbish, nonsense. *v.i.* (*past, p.p.* **crapped**) (*taboo*) to defecate. **crappy,** *a.* (*sl.*) rubbishy, worthless. [ME *crappe,* chaff, from MDut., from *crappen,* to break off]

crap[3], *n.* a losing throw in the game of craps. **crap-shooting** CRAPS. **crap-shooter,** *n.* [see CRAPS]

crape, *n.* a gauzy fabric of silk or other material, with a crisped, frizzly surface, formerly usu. dyed black, used for mourning; a band of this material worn round the hat as mourning. *v.t.* to cover, dress or drape with crape; †to curl, to frizzle. **crape-cloth,** *n.* a woollen fabric made in imitation of silk crape. **crape fern,** *n.* (*N Zealand*) a handsome, large-fronded fern. **crapy,** *a.* [F, CRÊPE]

crappit-head, *n.* (*Sc.*) a haddock's head stuffed with the roe, oatmeal, suet, onions etc. [p.p. of a v. *crap,* not extant (cp. Dut. *krappen,* to cram)]

crappy CRAP[2].

craps, *n.sing.* a game of dice. [poss. from *crabs,* lowest throw at dice; see CRAB[1]]

crapulent, *a.* surfeited, drunken; given to intemperance. **crapulence,** *n.* **crapulous,** *a.* [L *crāpulentus,* from *crāpula,* drunkenness, Gr. *kraipalē,* nausea, the effect of a debauch]

crash[1], *v.t.* to break to pieces with violence; to dash together violently; (*coll.*) to go to (a party) uninvited, to intrude. *v.i.* to make a loud smashing noise; (*Aviat.*) to crash in landing; to fail, be ruined; to be defeated; of a computer or its program, to cease operating suddenly. *n.* an act or instance of crashing; a loud sudden noise, as of many things broken at once; a violent smash; a sudden failure, collapse, bankruptcy. **to crash-land,** to make a crash-landing. **crash barrier,** *n.* a metal barrier along the edge of a motorway etc. to prevent crashes. **crash course,** *n.* a very rapid and intensive course of study. **crash dive,** *n.* (*Naut.*) a submarine's sudden and rapid dive, usu. to avoid an enemy. **crash helmet,** *n.* a helmet padded with resilient cushions, to protect the head in the event of an accident. **crash-landing,** *n.* an emergency landing of an aircraft, resulting in damage. **crashing,** *a.* (*coll.*) extreme. [imit. (cp. CRACK, CRAZE)]

crash[2], *n.* a coarse linen cloth used for towelling. [Rus. *krashenina,* coloured linen]

crasis, *n.* (*pl.* **crases**) the contracting of the vowels of two syllables into one long vowel or diphthong; the mixture of the constituents of the blood. **crasial,** *a.* [Gr., a mixture, a blending, from *kerannunai,* to mix]

crass, *a.* thick, coarse, gross, stupid; obtuse. **crassitude,** *n.* crassness. **crassly,** *adv.* **crassness,** *n.* [L *crassus*]

Crassus, *n.* **Marcus Licinius** (*c.* 108–53 BC), Roman general who crushed the Spartacus rising in 71 BC. In 60 BC he joined with Caesar and Pompey in the first Triumvirate and in 55 BC obtained command in the East. Invading Mesopotamia, he was defeated by the Parthians at the Battle of Carrhae, captured and put to death.

-crat, *suf.* a partisan, a supporter, a member, as *autocrat, democrat, plutocrat.* **-cratic,** *a.* **-cratically,** *adv.* [F *-crate,* Gr. *-kratēs* (cp. *-kratia,* -CRACY)]

Crataegus, *n.* a genus of thorny trees containing the hawthorns. [L, from Gr. *krataigos*]

cratch, *n.* a manger, a hay-rack, esp. for feeding animals out of doors. [OF *creche* (F *crèche*), OHG *chrippa*]

crate, *n.* a large wicker case for packing crockery; an open framework of wood for packing; (*dated, sl.*) an old and unreliable car, aircraft etc. *v.t.* to pack in a crate. **crateful,** *n.* [L *crātes,* or Dut. *krat*]

crater, *n.* the mouth of a volcano; a funnel-shaped cavity; a large cavity formed in the ground by the explosion of a shell or bomb. **crateriform,** *a.* [L, from Gr. *kratēr,* a bowl for mixing wine (*kerannunai,* to mix)]

cravat, *n.* a neckcloth for men (introduced into France by the Croats); a tie. [F *cravate,* orig. a Croat, G *krabate,* Croatian]

crave, *v.t.* to ask for earnestly and submissively; to beg, to beseech, to entreat; to long for; to require. *v.i.* to beg; to long (for). **craver,** *n.* **craving,** *n.* an intense desire or longing. **cravingly,** *adv.* [OE *crafian*]

craven, *n.* †one who is overcome; a word cried by the vanquished one in the ancient trial by battle; a coward, a recreant, a dastard. *v.t.* to make craven. *a.* cowardly, faint-hearted. **to cry craven,** to surrender. **cravenly,** *adv.* [ME *crauant,* prob. from OF *cravant,* pres.p. of *craver* (*crever*), to burst, break, overcome]

craw, *n.* the crop or first stomach of fowls or insects. [cogn. with Dut. *kraag,* the neck]

crawfish CRAYFISH.

Crawford, *n.* **Joan** (1908–77), US actress, who made her name from 1925 in dramatic films such as *Mildred Pierce* (1945) and *Whatever Happened to Baby Jane?* (1962).

crawl[1]**,** *v.i.* to move slowly along the ground; to creep; to move slowly; to assume an abject posture or manner; to get on by meanness and servility; to have a sensation as though insects were creeping over the flesh; to be covered with crawling things. *n.* the act of crawling; a racing stroke in swimming. **crawler,** *n.* one that crawls, a reptile. **crawlingly,** *adv.* **crawly,** *a.* [prob. from Scand. (cp. Icel. and Swed. *krafla,* to grope, Dan. *kravle,* to crawl)]

crawl[2]**,** *n.* an enclosure in shallow water for keeping fish, turtles etc. alive. [Dut. *kraal*]

Craxi, *n.* **Bettino** (1934–), Italian socialist politician, leader of the Italian Socialist Party (PSI) from 1976, prime minister (1983–87).

†**crayer, crare,** *n.* a kind of trading ship. [OF *craier,* low L *craiera, creyera* (etym. unknown)]

crayfish, crawfish, *n.* (*pl.* **crayfish**) the freshwater lobster, *Astacus fluviatilis;* the spiny lobster, *Palinurus vulgaris;* †any kind of crab. [ME *crevice,* OF *crevisse, crevice* (F *écrevisse*), OHG *crebiz* (cp. CRAB[1])]

crayon, *n.* a pencil of coloured chalk or similar material; a drawing made with crayons; the carbon pencil of an electric arc-lamp. *v.t.* to draw with crayons; to sketch. **crayon-drawing,** *n.* the act, art or result of drawing in crayons. [F, from *craie,* L *crēta,* chalk]

craze, *v.t.* to derange the intellect; to make cracks or flaws in (china etc.); †to break, to shatter. †*v.i.* to become weakened or impaired; to become cracked, as the glaze on pottery; to go mad. *n.* a mania, an extravagant idea or enthusiasm, a rage; madness; a flaw, impaired condition. **crazing-mill,** *n.* one for crushing tin-ore. **crazed,** *a.* deranged in intellect. **crazy,** *a.* broken down, feeble; unsound, shaky; broken-witted, deranged; ridiculous; (*coll.*) very enthusiastic. **like crazy,** (*sl.*) extremely. **crazy bone,** *n.* (*N Am.*) the funny-bone. **crazy paving,** *n.* a pavement of irregularly-shaped flat stones. **crazily,** *adv.* **craziness,** *n.* [perh. from Swed. *krasa* (cp. F *écraser*)]

Crazy Horse, *n.* (1849–87), Sioux Indian chief, one of the Indian leaders at the massacre of Little Bighorn. He was killed when captured.

CRE, (*abbr.*) Commission for Racial Equality.

creagh, creach, *n.* a Highland raid; (*chiefly Sc.*) booty. *v.t.* (*chiefly Sc.*) to plunder. [Gael. and Ir. *creach,* plunder]

creak, *v.i.* to make a continued sharp grating noise. †*v.t.* to cause to make such a noise. *n.* a creaking sound. **creaky,** *a.* [imit. (cp. CRAKE, CRACK)]

cream, *n.* the oily part of milk which rises and collects on the surface; a sweetmeat or dish prepared from cream; a cream-coloured horse; the best part of anything; essence or quintessence; a group of the best things or people; a pale yellowish-white colour; a cosmetic preparation with a thick consistency like cream. *v.t.* to skim cream from; to add cream to; to remove the best part from; to make creamy, as by beating. *v.i.* to gather cream; to mantle or froth. *a.* cream-coloured; of sherry, sweet. **cream of lime,** a creamy mixture of slaked lime and water. **cream of tartar,** purified potassium bitartrate. **cream-bun, -cake,** *n.* a cake with a cream filling. **cream-cheese,** *n.* a soft cheese made of unskimmed milk and cream. **cream cracker,** *n.* an unsweetened crisp biscuit. †**cream-faced,** *a.* pale or colourless. **cream-fruit,** *n.* a juicy fruit from Sierra Leone. **cream-laid,** *a.* applied to laid paper of a creamy colour. **cream-separator,** *n.* a machine for separating cream from milk. **cream soda,** *n.* a soft drink flavoured with vanilla. **cream-wove,** *a.* applied to woven paper of a cream colour. **creamer,** *n.* a flat dish used for skimming the cream off milk; a cream-separator; (*N Am.*) a small jug for cream. **creamery,** *n.* a shop for the sale of dairy produce and light refreshments; an establishment where cream is bought and made into butter. **creamy,** *a.* **creaminess,** *n.* [F *crème,* OF *cresme* (see CHRISM)]

†**creance,** *n.* faith, credit; a fine line fastened to a hawk's leash when she is first lured. [OF, from L (as CREDENCE)]

crease[1]**,** *n.* a line or mark made by folding or doubling; (*Cricket*) a line on the ground marking the position of bowler and batsman at each wicket. *v.t.* to make a crease or mark in; (*N Am.*) to graze the skin of with a bullet; (*sl.*) to exhaust; (*sl.*) to crease up. *v.i.* to become creased or wrinkled. **to crease up,** (*coll.*) to double up with laughter. **crease-resistant,** *a.* of a fabric, not creasing when in use. **creaser,** *n.* **creasy,** *a.* [etym. doubtful]

crease[2]**,** CREESE.

create, *v.t.* to cause to exist; to produce, to bring into existence; to be the occasion of; to originate; to invest with a new character, office or dignity; (*coll.*) to make a fuss; to cause a disturbance. †*a.* brought into existence; composed. **creative,** *a.* having the ability to create; imaginative; original. **creatively,** *adv.* **creativeness,** *n.* **creativity,** *n.* [L *creātus,* p.p. of *creāre*]

creatine, *n.* an organic compound found in muscular fibre. [Gr. *kreas -atos,* meat]

creation, *n.* the act of creating, esp. creating the world; that which is created or produced; the universe, the world, all created things; the act of appointing, constituting or investing with a new character or position; a production of art, craft, or intellect. **creational,** *a.* **creationism,** *n.* the doctrine that a human soul is created for each human being at birth; the theory that the universe was brought into existence out of nothing by God, and that new forms and species are the results of special creations. **creationist,** *n.* **creator,** *n.* one who or that which creates; a maker; the Maker of the Universe. [F, from L *creātio -ōnem* (*creāre,* to CREATE)]

creature, *n.* that which is created; a living being; an animal, esp. as distinct from a human being; a person (as an epithet of pity, or endearment); one who owes his or her rise or fortune to another; an instrument. *a.* of or pertaining to the body. **the creature,** (*esp. Ir., coll.*) drink, liquor, esp. whisky. **creature comforts,** *n.* those pertaining to the body, esp. food and drink. **creaturely,** *a.* of or pertaining to the creature; having the nature or qualities of a creature. [F *créature,* L *creatūra,* as prec.]

crèche, *n.* a day nursery in which young children are taken care of. [F, see CRATCH]

Crécy, Battle of, the first important battle of the Hundred Years' War (1346). Philip VI of France was defeated by Edward III of England at the village of Crécy-en-Ponthieu, now in Somme *département,* France, 18 km/11 miles NE of Abbeville.

credal CREED.

credence, *n.* belief, credit; reliance, confidence; that which gives a claim to credit or confidence; a credence table. **credence table,** *n.* a small table or shelf near the (south) side of the altar (or communion table) to receive the eucharistic elements before consecration; a small sideboard. **credent,** *a.* giving credence; bearing credit. **credently,** *adv.* **credential,** *a.* giving a title to credit; accredited. *n.* anything which gives a title to confidence; (*pl.*) certificates or letters accrediting any person or persons. [F, from med. L *crēdentia* (*crēdere,* to believe)]

credible, *a.* deserving of or entitled to belief. **credibility,** *n.* **credibility gap,** *n.* the discrepancy between the facts and a version of them presented as true. **credibly,** *adv.*

credit, *n.* belief, trust, faith; a reputation inspiring trust or confidence, esp. a reputation for solvency; anything due to any person; trust reposed with regard to property handed over on the promise of payment at a future time; the time given for payment of goods sold on trust; a source or cause of honour, esteem or reputation; the side of an account in which payment is entered, opposed to debit; an entry on this side of a payment received; (*pl.*) (also **credit titles**) a list of acknowledgments of contributors at the beginning or end of a film; an acknowledgment that a student has completed a course of study; the passing of an examination at a mark well above the minimum required. *v.t.* to believe; to set to the credit of (*to* the person); to give credit for (*with* the amount); to believe (a person) to possess something; to ascribe to. **letter of credit,** an order authorizing a person to draw money from an agent. **public credit,** the faith in the honesty and financial ability of a government seeking to borrow money. **credit account,** *n.* a type of account in which goods and services are charged to be paid for later. **credit card,** *n.* a card issued by a bank or credit company which allows the holder to buy goods and services on credit. **crédit foncier,** *n.* (*F*) a company for promoting improvements by means of loans on real estate. **crédit mobilier,** *n.* (*F*) a company for banking purposes, and for the promotion of public works by means of loans on personal estate. **credit rating,** *n.* a level of credit-worthiness. **credit squeeze,** *n.* government restrictions imposed on banks to limit their loans to clients. **credit-worthy,** *a.* deserving credit because of income-level, past record of debt-repayment etc. **credit-worthiness,** *n.* **creditable,** *a.* bringing credit or honour. **creditability,** *n.* **creditableness,** *n.* **creditably,** *adv.* **creditor,** *n.* one to whom a debt is due; the side of an account on which receipts are entered. [F *crédit,* It. *credito,* L *crēditus,* p.p. of *crēdere,* as prec.]

credo, *n.* (*pl.* **-dos**) the first word of the Apostles' and the Nicene Creed; hence either of these creeds; the Nicene Creed, said in the Mass; a musical setting of the Nicene Creed; the statement of a belief. [L, I believe]

credulous, *a.* disposed to believe, esp. without sufficient evidence; characterized by or due to such disposition. **credulity,** *n.* **credulously,** *adv.* **credulousness,** *n.* [L *crēdulus* (*crēdere,* to believe)]

Cree, *n.* an indigenous N Amer. people whose language belongs to the Algonquian family. The Cree are distributed over a vast area: in Canada from Québec to Alberta. In the US, the majority of Cree live in the Rocky Boys reservation in Montana.

Creed, *n.* **Frederick George** (1871–1957), Canadian inventor, who developed the teleprinter. He perfected the Creed telegraphy system (teleprinter) first used in Fleet Street in 1912, and now, usu. known as Telex, in offices throughout the world.

creed, *n.* a brief summary of the articles of religious belief; any system or solemn profession of religious or other belief or opinions. †*v.t.* to believe. **credal, creedal,** *a.* [OE *crēda,* L *crēdo*]

creek, *n.* a small inlet, bay or harbour, on the coast; a backwater or arm of a river; (*N Am., Austral.*) a small river, esp. a tributary; a narrow strip of land between mountains; a narrow winding passage. **up the creek,** (*sl.*) in trouble or difficulty. †**creeky,** *a.* [ME *crīke,* cp. OF *crique,* Dut. *krēke, kreek,* Swed. *krik,* Icel. *kriki*]

creel, *n.* an osier basket; a fisherman's basket. [etym. doubtful; orig. Sc.]

creep, *v.i.* (*past, p.p.* **crept**) to crawl along the ground as a serpent; to grow along, as a creeping plant; to move slowly and insensibly, stealthily, or with timidity; to gain admission unobserved; to behave with servility; to fawn; to have a sensation of shivering or shrinking as from fear or repugnance; (*Naut.*) to drag with a creeper at the bottom of the water. *n.* creeping; a slow, almost imperceptible movement; a place for creeping through; a low arch or passage for animals; (*pl.*) a feeling of shrinking horror; (*sl.*) an unpleasant or servile person. **to make someone's flesh creep** FLESH. **creep-hole,** *n.* a hole into which an animal may creep to escape danger; a subterfuge, an excuse. **creep-mouse,** *a.* shy, timid; sly, furtive. *n.* a childish game. **creeper,** *n.* one who or that which creeps or crawls; any animal that creeps; a reptile; a parasitic insect; a kind of patten worn by women; a small spike attached to a boot to prevent slipping on ice; a plant with a creeping stem; a four-clawed grapnel used in dragging a harbour, pond or well; (*sl.*) a soft-soled shoe. **creeping,** *n., a.* **creeping jenny** MONEYWORT. **creeping Jesus,** *n.* (*sl.*) a sly or sanctimonious person. **creepingly,** *adv.* **creepy,** *a.* having the sensation of creeping of the flesh; causing this sensation; characterized by creeping. **creepy-crawly,** *a.* creepy. *n.* a creeping insect. [OE *crēopan,* from Teut. *creup-* (cp. Dut. *kruipen,* Swed. *krypa*)]

creese KRIS.

†**creesh,** *n.* (*Sc.*) grease, fat; a stroke, a smack. *v.t.* (*Sc.*) to grease. **creeshy,** *a.* [OF *craisse,* grease]

cremate, *v.t.* to burn; to dispose of a corpse by burning. **cremation,** *n.* **cremationist,** *n.* **cremator,** *n.* one who cremates a dead body; a furnace for consuming corpses or rubbish. **crematorium,** *n.* a place where bodies are cremated. **crematory,** *a.* employed in or connected with cremation. *n.* a crematorium. [L *cremātus,* p.p. of *cremāre,* to burn]

crème, *n.* cream. **crème de la crème,**, the pick, the most select, the élite. **crème de menthe,** a liqueur made with peppermint. [F, CREAM]

Cremona, *n.* a violin made at *Cremona,* N Italy, by the Stradivarii, the Amatis, or their pupils.

cremona CROMORNE.

crenate, -nated, *a.* notched; (*Biol.*) having the edge notched. **crenation,** *n.* **crenato-,** *comb. form* (*Biol.*) notched. **crenature,** *n.* a scallop; a crenel; a small rounded tooth on the edge of a leaf. [late L *crēna,* a notch]

crenel, crenelle, *n.* a loophole through which to discharge musketry; a battlement; (*Bot.*) a crenature. **crenellate,** *v.t.* to furnish with battlements or loopholes. **crenellation,** *n.* [OF *crenel* (F *créneau*), dim. of *cren, crena* (as prec.)]

crenic, *a.* applied to an acid found in humus and in spirits from ferruginous springs. **crenitic,** *a.* (*Geol.*) formed by or pertaining to the action of springs. [Gr. *krēnē,* spring]

crenulate, *a.* of the edges of leaves, shells etc. finely crenate, notched or scalloped. **crenulated**, *a.* **crenulation,** *n.* [late L *crēnula,* dim. of *crēna,* notch, -ATE]

creole, *n.* one born of European parentage in the W Indies or Spanish America; in Louisiana, a native descended from French or Spanish ancestors; a native born of mixed European and Negro parentage; the native language of a region, formed from prolonged contact between the original native language and that of European settlers. *a.* relating to the Creoles or a creole language. **creolize, -ise,** *v.t.* **creolization, -isation,** *n.* [F *créole,* Sp. *criollo,* prob. from Port. *crioulo,* a nursling, from *criar,* from L *creāre,* to CREATE]

creophagous, *a.* carnivorous, flesh-eating. **creophagist**, *n.* **creophagy,** *n.* [Gr. *kreas -atos,* -PHAGOUS]

creosote, *n.* a liquid distilled from coal-tar, used for preserving wood etc. *v.t.* to saturate (as woodwork) with creosote. **creosote-bush, -plant,** *n.* a Mexican shrub, *Larrea mexicana,* smelling of creosote. [Gr. *kreas -atos,* flesh, *sōtēr,* saviour, from *sōzein,* to save, preserve]

crepe, crêpe, *n.* crape; a crapy fabric other than mourning crape; a thin pancake. **crepe de Chine**, *n.* crape manufactured from raw silk. **crepe paper,** *n.* thin crinkly paper, used in making decorations. **crepe rubber,** *n.* rubber with a rough surface used for shoe soles etc. **crepé**, *a.* frizzled. **creperie**, *n.* a restaurant or cafe specializing in crepes. **crepey, crepy,** *a.* like crepe, crinkled, as dry skin. [F, from L *crispa,* curled]

crepitate, *v.i.* to crackle; to burst with a series of short, sharp reports, as salt in fire; to rattle. **crepitant,** *a.* crackling. **crepitation,** *n.* **crepitus**, *n.* crepitation; a rattling sound heard in the lungs during pneumonia etc.; the sound of the ends of a broken bone scraping against each other. [L *crepitātus,* p.p. of *crepitāre,* freq. of *crepāre,* to creak]

crepon, crêpon, *n.* a mixed stuff of silk and wool or nylon, resembling crape. [F, as CREPE]

crept, *past, p.p.* of CREEP.

crepuscle, -cule, *n.* morning or evening twilight. **crepuscular**, *a.* pertaining to or connected with twilight; glimmering, indistinct, obscure; appearing or flying about at twilight. [F *crépuscule,* L *crepusculum*]

Cres., (*abbr.*) crescent (of buildings).

crescendo, *n.* (*pl.* **-dos**, **-di**) (a musical passage performed with) a gradual increase in the force of sound; a gradual increase in force or effect. *adv.* with an increasing volume of sound. [It., pres.p. of *crescere,* to grow (see foll.)]

crescent, *a.* increasing, growing; shaped like a new moon. *n.* the increasing moon in its first quarter; a figure like the new moon; the Turkish power; Islam; a row of buildings in crescent form; (*Her.*) a bearing in the form of a half-moon; a military order with a half-moon for a symbol. **Red Crescent,** the equivalent institution in Muslim countries to the Red Cross. [L *crēscens -ntem,* pres.p. of *crēscere,* to grow (incept. of *creāre,* to CREATE)]

cresol, *n.* a compound found in coal-tar and creosote, used in antiseptics and as a raw material for plastics. [*creos*ote, alcoh*ol*]

cress, *n.* a name for various cruciferous plants with a pungent taste (see WATER-CRESS). [OE *cærse,* from Teut. *kras-* (cp. Dut. *kers,* G *kresse,* OHG *chreson,* to creep)]

cresset, *n.* (*Hist.*) a metal cup or vessel, usu. on a pole, for holding oil for a light; a frame of open ironwork to contain a fire for a beacon; a torch; a brilliant light. [OF *cresset, craisset,* from *craisse,* CREESH]

crest, *n.* a plume or comb on the head of a bird; any tuft on the head of an animal; a plume or tuft of feathers, esp. affixed to the top of a helmet; the apex of a helmet; (*Her.*) any figure placed above the shield in a coat-of-arms; the same printed on paper or painted on a building etc.; the summit of a mountain or hill; the top of a ridge; the line of the top of the neck in animals; the ridge of a wave; a ridge on a bone; spirit, courage. *v.t.* to ornament or furnish with a crest; to serve as a crest to; to attain the crest of (a hill); †to mark with lines or streaks. *v.i.* to rise into a crest or ridge. **crestfallen,** *a.* dispirited, abashed. **crestfallenly,** *adv.* **crestfallenness,** *n.* **crested,** *a.* adorned with or wearing a crest. **crestless,** *a.* not entitled to a crest; not of gentle family. **crestlet,** *n.* [OF *criste,* L *crista*]

cretaceous, *a.* of the nature of or abounding in chalk. **Cretaceous,** *a., n.* (of or formed in) the last period of the Mesozoic era, during which seed-bearing plants evolved and dinosaurs and other reptiles reached a peak before almost complete extinction at the end of the period. **cretaceous formation,** *n.* (*Geol.*) the uppermost member of the Mesozoic rocks. [L *crētāceus,* from *crēta,* chalk]

Crete, *n.* (Greek **Kriti**), the largest Greek island, in the E Mediterranean Sea, 100 km/62 miles SE of Greece. **area** 8378 sq km/3234 sq miles. **capital** Iráklion. **towns** Khaniá (Canea), Rethymnon, Aghios Nikolaos. **products** citrus fruit, olives, wine. **population** (1981) 502,000. **language** Cretan dialect of Greek.

cretic, *n.* a metrical foot consisting of a short syllable preceded and followed by a long syllable, also called an amphimacer. [L *crēticus,* from *Crēta,* Crete]

cretin, *n.* a person mentally and physically deficient because of a (congenital) thyroid malfunction; (*coll.*) a very stupid person. **cretinism,** *n.* **cretinize, -ise,** *v.t.* **cretinous,** *a.* [F *crétin,* Swiss F *crestin, creitin,* L *Christiānus,* Christian]

cretonne, *n.* a cotton fabric with pictorial patterns, used for upholstering, frocks etc. [F, from *Creton,* a village in Normandy]

crevasse, *n.* a deep fissure in a glacier; (*N Am.*) a break in an embankment or levee of a river. [F, see foll.]

crevice, *n.* a crack, a cleft, a fissure. **creviced,** *a.* [ME and OF *crevace* (F *crevasse*), late L *crepātia,* from *crepāre,* to crackle, to burst]

crew¹, *n.* the company of seamen manning a ship or boat; the personnel on board an aircraft, train or bus; a number of persons associated for any purpose; a gang, a mob. *v.t., v.i.* to act as, or serve in, a crew (of). **crew cut,** *n.* a very short style of haircut. **crewman,** *n.* **crew neck,** *n.* a close-fitting round neckline on a jersey. [from OF *creue,* p.p. of *croistre* (F *croître*), to grow; or from OF *acreue,* ACCRUE (*acrewe,* eventually becoming *a crew*)]

crew², *past of* CROW².

crewel, *n.* fine two-threaded worsted; embroidery worked with such thread. **crewel-work,** *n.* [etym. unknown]

†**crewels,** *n.pl.* (*Sc.*) the king's-evil. [F *écrouelles,* scrofula]

crib, *n.* a rack or manger; a stall for cattle; a child's cot; a small cottage, a hut, a hovel; a wicker salmon-trap; a model of the Nativity scene (placed in churches at Christmas); a timber framework lining a mine shaft; (*N Am.*) a bin for grain; a salt-box; cribbage; a hand at cribbage made up of two cards thrown out by each player; (*coll.*) anything stolen; a plagiarism; a translation of or key to an author, used by students; something (as a hidden list of dates, formulae etc.) used to cheat in an examination; a situation, place, berth. *v.t.* (*past, p.p.* **cribbed**) to shut up in a crib; †to confine; (*coll.*) to steal, to appropriate; to plagiarize; to copy from a translation. *v.i.* of horses, to bite the crib; to cheat using a crib. **crib-biting,** *n.* a bad habit in some horses of biting the crib. **cribbing,** *n.* the act of enclosing in a crib or narrow place; stealing, plagiarizing; cheating; internal lining of a mine shaft to prevent caving in. [OE (cp. Dut. *krib,* OHG *krippha,* G *Krippe,* Icel. and Swed. *krubba*)]

cribbage, *n.* a game at cards for two, three or four players. **cribbage-board,** *n.* a board on which the progress of the game is marked. [CRIB]

cribriform, *a.* (*Anat., Bot.*) resembling a sieve; perforated like a sieve. **cribrate**, **cribrose**, *a.* [L *cribrum,* a sieve]

crick, *n.* a spasmodic affection from stiffness, esp. of the neck or back. *v.t.* to cause a crick to. [prob. onomat.]

Crick, *n.* **Francis** (1916–), British molecular biologist. From 1949 he researched into DNA's molecular structure, and the means whereby characteristics are transmitted from one generation to another. For this work he was awarded a Nobel prize (with Maurice Wilkins (1916–) and James D. Watson).

cricket¹, *n.* any insect of the genus *Acheta;* the house-cricket, well known from its chirp, is *A. domestica,* and the field-cricket *A. campestris.* [OF *criquet,* from *criquer,* to creak (imit.)]

cricket², *n.* an open-air game played by two sides of 11 each, consisting of an attempt to strike, with a ball, wickets defended by the opponents with bats. *v.i.* to play cricket. **not cricket,** unfair, not straightforward. **cricketer,** *n.* [etym. doubtful (perh. from OF *criquet,* a stick serving as a mark in some game with a ball)]

cricket³, *n.* a low, wooden stool. [etym. unknown]

cricoid, *a.* (*Anat.*) ring-like. **cricoid cartilage,** *n.* the cartilage at the top of the trachea. [Gr. *krikoeidēs* (*krikos, kirkos,* a ring, -OID)]

cri de coeur, *n.* a heartfelt appeal or protest. [F]

crier, *n.* one who cries or proclaims. **town crier,** an officer who makes public proclamation of sales, lost articles etc. [OF *criere, crieur,* from *crier,* to CRY]

crikey, *int.* (*coll.*) an expression of astonishment. [perh. euphem. for L *Christe,* O Christ]

crim. con., *n.* short for CRIMINAL CONVERSATION under CRIMINAL.

crime, *n.* a ground of accusation; a charge; an act contrary to law, human or divine; any act of wickedness or sin; wrong-doing, sin; (*Mil.*) any offence or breach of regulations. **capital crime,** a crime punishable with death. **crimeful,** *a.* criminal, wicked. **crimeless,** *a.* [F, from L *crīmen* (*cernere,* to decide, cp. Gr. *krinein,* to separate, *krîma,* a decision)]

Crimea, *n.* N peninsula on the Black Sea, a region of Ukraine Republic, USSR, from 1954. **area** 27,000 sq km/10,425 sq miles. **capital** Simferopol. **towns** Sevastopol, Yalta. **products** iron, oil.

Crime and Punishment, a novel by Dostoievsky, published in 1866. It analyses the motives of a murderer and his reactions to the crime he has committed.

Crimean War, *n.* a war (1853–56) between Russia and the allied powers of England, France, Turkey and Sardinia. The war arose from British and French mistrust of Russia's ambitions in the Balkans. It began with an allied Anglo-French expedition to the Crimea to attack the Russian Black Sea city of Sevastopol. The battles of the River Alma, Balaclava (including the charge of the Light Brigade) and Inkerman (1854) led to a siege which, due to military mismanagement, lasted for a year until Sept. 1855. The war was ended by the Treaty of Paris (1856). The scandal surrounding French and British losses through disease led to the organization of proper military nursing services by Florence Nightingale.

criminal, *a.* of the nature of a crime; contrary to duty, law or right; guilty of a crime; tainted with crime. *n.* one guilty of a crime; a convict. **Criminal Investigation Department,** see separate entry. **criminal conversation,** *n.* (*Law*) adultery. **criminality,** *n.* **criminalize, -ise,** *v.t.* **criminally,** *adv.* [late L *crimināls,* from L *crīmen;* see CRIME]

Criminal Injuries Compensation Board, a UK board established in 1964 to administer financial compensation by the state for victims of crimes of violence. Victims can claim compensation for their injuries, but not for damage to property. The compensation awarded is similar to the amount which would be obtained for a court in damages for personal injury.

Criminal Investigation Department, detective branch of the London Metropolitan Police, established in 1878, and comprising a force of about 4000 men and women, recruited entirely from the uniformed police and controlled by an Assistant Commissioner. Such branches are now also found in the regional police forces.

criminate, *v.t.* to accuse of a crime; to prove guilty of a crime; to blame, to condemn. **crimination,** *n.* **criminative,** *a.* **criminatory,** *a.* [L *crimināri -ātus;* see CRIME]

criminology, *n.* the scientific study of crime and criminals. [L *crīmen -inem,* crime, -LOGY]

criminous, *a.* guilty of a crime, criminal. **criminousness,** *n.* [OF *crimineux,* from L *criminōsus;* see CRIME]

crimp¹, *v.t.* to curl; to compress into ridges or folds, to frill; to corrugate, to flute, to crease; to cause to contract and become crisp and firm, as the flesh of live fish, by gashing it with a knife; to compress so as to shape or mould. **crimping-iron, -machine,** *n.* an instrument or machine for fluting cap fronts, frills etc. **crimpy,** *a.* [cp. CRAMP]

crimp², *n.* (*formerly*) one who decoyed men for military, naval or maritime service; a decoy, a disreputable agent. *v.t.* (*formerly*) to decoy into the military or naval service. [etym. doubtful]

Crimplene®, *n.* a kind of crease-resistant synthetic fabric.

crimson, *n.* a deep red colour. *a.* of this colour. *v.t.* to dye with this colour. *v.i.* to turn crimson; to blush. [Sp. *cremesin, carmesi,* Arab. *qirmazī,* see also CRAMOISY]

crinal, *a.* of or pertaining to the hair. [L *crīnālis,* from *crīnis,* hair]

cringe, *v.i.* to bend humbly; to crouch, to fawn; to pay servile court; to wince in embarrassment; to feel embarrassment or distaste. †*v.t.* to contract, to draw together, to distort. *n.* servile court or flattery; an obsequious action. **cringer,** †**cringeling,** *n.* one who cringes. [ME *crengen,* causal from *cringan,* to sink, to fall]

cringle, *n.* an iron ring on the bolt-rope of a sail, for the attachment of a bridle. [cp. LG *kringel,* dim. of *kring,* a circle, a ring; cogn. with CRANK, CRINKLE]

crinite, *a.* hairy; resembling a tuft of hair; (*Bot., Zool.*) covered with hair in small tufts. **crinitory,** *a.* relating to or consisting of hair. [L *crīnītus,* from *crīnis,* hair]

crinkle, *v.i.* to wind in and out; to make short frequent bends and turns. *v.t.* to wrinkle; to form with frequent bends or turns; to mould into inequalities. *n.* a wrinkle, a twist; a short bend or turn. **crinkle-crankle,** *n.* a twisting, a wavy line, a zigzag. *a., adv.* zigzag; (twisting) in and out. **crinkly,** *a.* **crinkum-crankum,** *n.* a crooked, twisted figure; a zigzag. *a.* full of twists and turns. [OE *crinkan,* cp. CRANK, CRINGE]

crinoid, *a.* (*Zool.*) lily-shaped. *n.* any individual of the Crinoidea. **crinoidal,** *a.* pertaining to or containing crinoids. **crinoidal limestone,** *n.* carboniferous limestone studded with the broken joints of encrinites. **Crinoidea,** *n.* a class of echinoderms, containing the sea-lilies and hair-stars. [Gr. *krinoeidēs* (*krinon,* a lily, -OID)]

crinolette, *n.* a kind of bustle for a woman's skirts. **crinoletted,** *a.* [F, dim. of foll.]

crinoline, *n.* a stiff fabric of horsehair formerly used for petticoats; a petticoat of this material; any stiff petticoat used to expand the skirts of a dress; a large hooped skirt, orig. worn in the mid-19th cent.; the whalebone hoops for such a skirt; a series of nets extended round a warship to keep off torpedoes. [F (*crin,* L *crīnis,* hair; *lin,* L *līnum,* flax)]

criosphinx, *n.* a sphinx with a ram's head. [Gr. *krios,* ram, SPHINX]

cripes, *int.* (*coll.*) expressing surprise. [euphem. for CHRIST]

cripple, *n.* a lame person; one who creeps, halts or limps; a rough staging such as is used for window-cleaning; (*Carp.*) a makeshift contrivance. *v.t.* to make lame; to deprive of the use of the limbs; to deprive of the power of action. †*v.i.* to walk like a cripple. **crippledom,** *n.* **cripplehood,** *n.* [OE *crypel,* conn. with *crēopan,* to creep, from OTeut. *kruipan*]

Cripps, *n.* **(Richard) Stafford** (1889–1952), British Labour politician, expelled from the Labour party (1939–45) for supporting a 'Popular Front' against Chamberlain's appeasement policy. He was ambassador to Moscow (1940–42), minister of aircraft production (1942–45), and chancellor of the Exchequer (1947–50).

crisis, *n.* (*pl.* **crises**) the turning-point, esp. that of a disease indicating recovery or death; a momentous juncture in war, politics, commerce, domestic affairs etc. [L, from Gr. *krisis,* a separating, a decision, from *krinein,* to decide]

crisp, *a.* firm but brittle, fragile; fresh-looking, cheerful, brisk; curt, sharp, decisive; curled; †twisting, rippling. *v.t.* to curl, to wrinkle, to ripple; to interlace. *v.i.* to become curly; to become crisp. **crispbread,** *n.* a thin, dry unsweetened biscuit of rye or wheat flour. †**crisping-iron,** †**-pin,** *n.* an iron or pin for crisping or crimping the hair. **crisped,** *a.* **crisper,** *n.* one who or that which curls or crisps; an instrument for crisping the nap of cloth; a crisping-iron; a compartment in a refrigerator for vegetables to keep them crisp. **crisply,** *adv.* **crispness,** *n.* **crisps,** *n.pl.* very thin slices of potato deep-fried and eaten cold. **crispy,** *a.* curled, curling; wavy; crisp. [OE, from L *crispus,* curled]

crispate, *a.* (*Biol.*) curled or wrinkled at the edges. †**crispation,** *n.* [L *crispātus,* p.p. of *crispāre,* as prec.]

Crispi, *n.* **Francesco** (1819–1907), Italian prime minister (1887–91) and (1893–96). He advocated the Triple Alliance of Italy with Germany and Austria, but was deposed in 1896.

crispin, *n.* a shoemaker, from the patron saint of the craft. [L *Crispinus*]

criss-cross, *n., a.* (a network of lines) crossing one another; repeated(ly) crossing to and fro. *v.t., v.i.* to move in, or mark with, a criss-cross pattern. [CHRIST-CROSS-ROW under CHRIST]

cristate, *a.* having a crest; tufted with hairs. [L *cristātus,* from *crista,* a crest]

crit., (*abbr.*) critical; criticism; critique; critical mass.

criterion, *n.* (*pl.* **-ria**) a principle or standard by which anything is or can be judged. [Gr., as foll.]

critic, *n.* a judge, an examiner; a censurer, a caviller; one skilled in judging of literary or artistic merit; a reviewer. **critical,** *a.* pertaining to criticism; competent to criticize; fastidious, exacting, captious; indicating a crisis; decisive, hazardous; attended with danger or risk; (*Math.*) relating to points of coincidence or transition. **critical mass,** *n.* the smallest amount of fissile material that can sustain a chain reaction. **critical temperature,** *n.* the temperature below which a gas cannot be liquefied. **critically,** *adv.* †**criticalness,** *n.* **criticaster,** *n.* a petty or contemptible critic. **criticism,** *n.* the act of judging, esp. literary or artistic works; a critical essay or opinion; the work of criticizing; an unfavourable judgment. **higher criticism,** a critical study of authenticity and the literary and historical aspects of the Scriptures. **textual criticism,** a critical study of the words to test their correctness and meaning. **criticize, -ise,** *v.t.* to examine critically and deliver an opinion upon; to censure. *v.i.* to play the critic. **criticizable, -isable,** *a.* [L *criticus,* Gr. *kritikos* (*kritēs,* a judge, from *krinein,* to judge)]

critico-, *comb. form* critically; with criticism.

critique, *n.* a critical essay or judgment; the art of criticism; the analysis of the basis of knowledge.

critter, *n.* (*N Am., coll.*) a creature.

Crivelli, *n.* **Carlo** (1435/40–1495/1500), Italian painter in the early Renaissance style, active in Venice. He painted extremely detailed, decorated religious works, sometimes festooned with garlands of fruit. His figure style is strongly N Italian, reflecting the influence of Mantegna.

CRO, (*abbr.*) cathode ray oscilloscope; criminal records office.

croak, *v.i.* to make a hoarse low sound in the throat, as a frog or a raven; to grumble, to forbode evil; (*sl.*) to die. *v.t.* to utter in a low hoarse voice; (*sl.*) to kill. *n.* the low harsh sound made by a frog or a raven. **croaker,** *n.* one who croaks; a querulous person; (*sl.*) a dying person. **croaky,** *a.* croaking, hoarse. [prob. imit.]

Croat, *n.* a native of Croatia; one of the irregular cavalry in the Austrian service which were largely recruited from Croats. **Croatian,** *a., n.* [OSlav. *Khruvat*]

Croatia, *n.* (Serbo-Croat **Hrvatska**) constituent republic of Yugoslavia. **area** 56,500 sq km/21,809 sq miles. **capital** Zagreb. **physical** Adriatic coastline with large islands; very mountainous, with part of the Karst region and the Julian and Styrian Alps; some marshland. **population** (1985) 4,660,000 including 3,500,000 Croats, 530,000 Serbs, and 25,000 Hungarians. **language** the Croatian variant of Serbo-Croat.

croc, *n.* (*coll.*) short for CROCODILE.

Croce, *n.* **Benedetto** (1866–1952), Italian philosopher and literary critic, an opponent of fascism. Like Hegel, he held that ideas do not represent reality but *are* reality; but unlike Hegel, he rejected every kind of transcendence.

croceate, croceous, *a.* of or like saffron; (*Bot.*) saffron-coloured. [L *croceus,* saffron]

crochet, *n.* a kind of knitting performed with a hooked needle. *v.t.* to knit or make in crochet. *v.i.* to knit in this manner. [F, dim. of *croche,* a hook]

crocidolite, *n.* a silky fibrous silicate of iron and sodium, also called blue asbestos; a yellow form of this used as a gem or ornament. [Gr. *krokis -idos,* the nap of cloth, -LITE]

crock[1]**,** *n.* an earthenware vessel; a pot, a pitcher, a jar; a potsherd; soot or black collected from combustion on pots or kettles etc. *v.t.* to blacken with soot from a pot. **crockery,** *n.* earthenware; earthenware vessels. [OE *crocca* (cp. OIr. *crocan,* Gael. *crog,* Icel. *krukka,* Dut. *kruik,* G *Krug*)]

crock[2]**,** *n.* †an old ewe; a broken-down horse; a broken-down machine or implement; (*coll.*) a sick person; a fool, a worthless person. *v.i.* to break down (often with **up**). [etym. doubtful; prob. cogn. with CRACK (cp. Norw. *krake,* a weakly or sickly animal; MDut. *kraecke,* EFris. *krakke,* a broken-down horse, house or man)]

crocket, *n.* (*Arch.*) a carved foliated ornament on a pinnacle, the side of a canopy etc. [A-F *crocket,* var. of F CROCHET]

Crockett, *n.* **Davy** (1786–1836), US folk hero, a Democrat Congressman (1827–31) and (1833–35). A series of books, of which he may have been part-author, made him into a mythical hero of the frontier, but their Whig associations cost him his office.

crocodile, *n.* a large amphibian reptile having the back and tail covered with large, square scales; (leather made from) the skin of the crocodile; a string of school children walking two by two; (*Rhet.*) a captious sophism to ensnare an enemy. **crocodile bird,** *n.* an African plover-like bird which feeds on the insect parasites of the crocodile. **crocodile tears,** *n.pl.* hypocritical tears like those with which the crocodile is fabled to attract its victims. **crocodilian,** *a.* [F, from L *crocodīlus,* Gr. *krokodeilos*]

crocus, *n.* (*pl.* **-cuses**) one of a genus (**Crocus**) of small bulbous plants belonging to the Iridaceae, with yellow, white or purple flowers, extensively cultivated in gardens; metal calcined to a deep red or yellow powder and used for polishing. [L, from Gr. *krokos*]

Croesus, *n.* last king of Lydia, famed for his wealth. His court included Solon, who warned him that no man could be called happy until his life had ended happily. When Croesus was overthrown by Cyrus the Great (546 BC) and condemned to be burned to death, he called out Solon's name. Cyrus, having learned the reason, spared his life.

croft, *n.* a piece of enclosed ground, esp. adjoining a house; a small farm in the Highlands and islands of Scotland. **crofter,** *n.* one who farms a croft, esp. one of the joint tenants of a farm in Scotland. [OE]

Crohn's disease, *n.* inflammation of the bowel, also known as regional ileitis or regional enteritis. It is characterized by ulceration, abscess formation, small perforations, and the development of adhesions binding the loops of the small intestine. It tends to flare up for a few days at a time, causing diarrhoea, abdominal cramps, loss of appetite and mild fever.

croissant, *n.* a crescent-shaped roll of rich flaky pastry. [F; see CRESCENT]

Croker, *n.* **Richard** (1841–1922), US politician, 'boss' of Tammany Hall, the Democratic party political machine in New York (1886–1902).

Cro-magnon, *n.* a type of prehistoric human, the first skeletons of which were found 1868 in the Cro-magnon cave near Les Eyzies, in the Dordogne region of France. They are thought to have superseded the Neanderthals, and lived between 40,000 and 35,000 years ago. Although biologically modern, they were larger in build than modern humans. Their culture produced flint and bone tools, jewellery, and cave paintings.

crome, *n.* a hook or crook. *v.t.* to hook; to drag with a hook. [from a non-extant OE *cramb* or *cromb* (cp. MDut. and LG *kramme,* Dut. *kram*)]

Crome, *n.* **John** (1768–1821), British landscape painter, founder of the Norwich school with Cotman (1803). His works include *The Poringland Oak* (*c.* 1818, Tate Gallery, London), showing Dutch influence.

cromlech, *n.* a prehistoric structure in which a large flat stone rests horizontally on upright ones. [W, from *crom,* bent, *llech,* stone, slab]

cromorne, cremona[2], *n.* one of the reed stops of an organ. [F, corr. of G *Krummhorn,* crooked horn]

Crompton[1], *n.* **Richmal** (pen name of British writer R. C. Lamburn) (1890–1969), remembered for her stories about the mischievous schoolboy 'William'.

Crompton[2], *n.* **Samuel** (1753–1827), British inventor at the time of the Industrial Revolution. He invented the 'spinning mule' (1779), combining the ideas of Arkwright and Hargreaves. Though widely adopted, his invention brought him little financial return.

Cromwell[1], *n.* **Oliver** (1599–1658), English general and politician, Puritan leader of the Parliamentary side in the Civil War. He raised cavalry forces (later called Ironsides) which aided the victories at Edgehill (1642) and Marston Moor (1644), and organized the New Model Army, which he led (with Gen. Fairfax) to victory at Naseby (1645). As Lord Protector (ruler) from 1653, he established religious toleration, and Britain's prestige in Europe on the basis of an alliance with France against Spain.

Cromwell[2], *n.* **Richard** (1626–1712), son of Oliver Cromwell, he succeeded his father as Protector, but resigned in May 1659, living in exile after the Restoration until 1680, when he returned to England.

Cromwell[3], *n.* **Thomas, Earl of Essex** (*c.* 1485–1540), English politician. Originally in Lord Chancellor Wolsey's service, he became secretary to Henry VIII (1534) and the real director of government policy. He had Henry proclaimed head of the church, suppressed the monasteries, ruthlessly crushed all opposition, and favoured Protestantism, which denied the divine right of the pope. His mistake in arranging Henry's marriage to Anne of Cleves (to cement an alliance with the German Protestant princes against France and the Holy Roman Empire) led to his being accused of treason and beheaded.

crone, *n.* an old woman; an old ewe. [ONorth.F *carogne,* an old woman (L *caro carnis,* see CARRION)]

cronk, *a.* (*Austral., coll.*) unwell; unsound. **to cronk up,** to go sick, to be ill. [CRANK[3]]

Cronkite, *n.* **Walter** (1916–), US broadcast journalist, who became a household name and face throughout the US as anchorman of the national evening news programme for CBS, a US television network, from 1962 to 1981.

crony, *n.* an intimate friend. [Gr. *chronios,* long-continued, from *chronos,* time]

crood, *v.i.* (*Sc.*) to coo, like a dove. [imit.]

crook, *n.* a bent or curved instrument; a shepherd's or bishop's hooked staff; a curve, a bend, a meander; †a bending, a genuflection; †a trick, a wile; (*sl.*) a thief, a swindler; a short tube for altering the key on a brass wind instrument. *a.* (*Austral., coll.*) sick; (*Austral., coll.*) unpleasant, dishonest. *v.t.* to make crooked or curved; to pervert, to misapply. *v.i.* to be bent or crooked; †to go astray. **by hook or by crook** HOOK. **to go crook (on),** (*Austral., coll.*) to become annoyed (with). **crook-back,** *n.* one who has a deformed back. **crook-backed,** *a.* †**crook-kneed,** *a.* with crooked or bent knees. **crook-neck,** *n.* (*N Am.*) a curved species of squash. **crooked,** *a.* bent, curved; turning, twisting, winding; deformed; not straightforward; perverse. **crookedly,** *adv.* **crookedness,** *n.* [prob. from Icel. *krōkr* (cp. Swed. *krok,* Dan. *krog,* OHG *kracho*)]

Crookes, *n.* **William** (1832–1919), English scientist, whose many chemical and physical discoveries included the metal thallium (1861), the radiometer (1875), and Crooke's high vacuum tube used in X-ray techniques.

crool, *v.i.* to make a low inarticulate sound like a baby. [imit.]

croon, *v.i.* to sing in a low voice. *v.t.* to mutter. *n.* a hollow, continued moan; a low hum. **crooner,** *n.* one who sings sentimental songs in low tones. [imit. (cp. Dut. *kreunen,* to groan)]

crop, *n.* the craw of a fowl, constituting a kind of first stomach; an analogous receptacle in masticating insects; the top or highest part; the upper part of a whip, a fishing-rod etc.; a short whipstock with a loop instead of a lash; that which is cut or gathered; the harvest yield; an entire hide; a short haircut; a piece chopped off; a name for various cuts of meat; the outcrop of a lode, a seam or a stratum of rock. *v.t.* (*past, p.p.* **cropped**) to cut off the ends of; to mow, to reap; to pluck, to gather; to cut off, to cut short; to sow; to plant and raise crops on; to reduce the margin of (a book) unduly, in binding. *v.i.* to yield a harvest, to bear fruit. **neck and crop,** altogether. **to crop out,** to come to light; (*Geol.*) to come out at the surface by the edges, as an underlying stratum of rock. **to crop up,** to come up unexpectedly. **crop-dusting,** *n.* the spreading of crops with powdered insecticide etc., from an aeroplane. **crop-ear,** *n.* a horse with cropped ears. **crop-eared,** *a.* having the hair or ears cut short. †**crop-sick,** *a.* sick from excess. †**cropful,** *a.* having a full crop; satiated. **cropper,** *n.* one who or that which crops; a grain or plant which yields a good crop; †a pigeon with a long crop, a pouter; (*coll.*) a heavy fall; a collapse, as in **to come a cropper. croppy,** *n.* one with hair cropped short; a Roundhead; an Irish rebel of 1798. [OE, a bird's crop, a swelling, a head or bunch sticking out (cp. LG and Dut. *krop,* G *Kropf,* W *cropa*)]

croquet, *n.* an open-air game played on a lawn with balls and mallets; the act of croqueting an opponent's ball. *v.t.* to drive an opponent's ball away in this game by placing one's own ball against it and striking. *v.i.* to play croquet. [ONorth.F *croket,* var. of F CROCHET, dim. of *croche,* a hook]

croquette, *n.* a savoury ball made with meat, potato etc. fried in breadcrumbs. [F, from *croquer,* to crunch]

crore, *n.* ten millions, a hundred lakhs (of rupees, people etc.). [Hind. *kror*]

Crosby, *n.* **'Bing' (Harry Lillis)** (1904–77), US film actor and singer, who achieved world success with his distinctive style of crooning in such songs as 'Pennies from Heaven', and 'White Christmas'. He won an acting Oscar for *Going My Way* (1944), and made a series of 'road' film comedies with Dorothy Lamour and Bob Hope, the last being *Road to Hong Kong* (1962).

crosier, *n.* the pastoral staff of a bishop or abbot; (*erron.*) an archbishop's staff, which bears a cross instead of a crook. [OF *crossier, crocier,* from *croce,* a bishop's staff, late L *crocia* (cp. OF *croc,* a crook, a hook); confused with F *crosier,* from *crois,* L *crux crucis,* CROSS[1]]

croslet CROSSLET.

cross[1], *n.* an ancient instrument of torture made of two pieces of timber set transversely at various angles; a monument, emblem, staff or ornament in this form; a sign or mark in the form of a cross; a market-place; a cross-shaped monument erected there; the mixture of two distinct stocks in breeding animals; the animal resulting from such a mixture; a mixture; a compromise; †money (from the cross formerly on the reverse); †the reverse of a coin; anything that thwarts or obstructs; trouble, affliction; the Christian religion, Christianity;

(*sl.*) a swindle, a preconcerted fraud; in football, a pass across the field, esp. towards the opposing goal. *a.* transverse, oblique, lateral; intersecting; adverse, contrary, perverse; peevish; (*sl.*) dishonest; ill-gotten. **cross as two sticks,** very peevish; in very bad humour. **cross of St Anthony,** one shaped like a **T**. **fiery cross,** two sticks dipped in blood sent out as a signal to rouse the inhabitants of a district. **Greek cross,** an upright beam with a transverse beam of the same length. **Latin cross,** one with a long upright below the cross-piece. **Maltese cross,** one with limbs of equal size widening from the point of junction towards the extremities. **on the cross,** diagonally; (*sl.*) unfairly, fraudulently. **St Andrew's cross,** one formed by two slanting pieces like an **X**. **St George's cross,** a Greek cross used on the British flag. **Southern Cross,** a cross-shaped constellation visible in the southern hemisphere. **to take up the cross,** to sacrifice self for some pious object. **Victoria Cross,** a decoration in the form of a Maltese cross awarded for military valour. **cross-action,** *n.* a case in which the defendant in an action brings another action against the plaintiff on points arising out of the same transaction. †**cross-arrow,** *n.* the arrow of a cross-bow. **cross-banded,** *a.* a term used of veneer when its grain is contrary to the general surface. **cross-bar,** *n.* a transverse bar. †**cross-barred,** *a.* secured by cross-bars. **cross-beam,** *n.* a large beam running from wall to wall. **cross-bearer,** *n.* one who bears a processional cross, esp. before an archbishop. **cross-bench,** *n.* (*Parl.*) one of the benches for those independent of the recognized parties; hence **cross-bench,** *a.* impartial. **cross-bencher,** *n.* **cross-bill,** *n.* a bird of the genus *Loxia,* the mandibles of the bill of which cross each other when closed; esp. *L. curvirostra,* an irregular British visitor. †**cross-bite,** *n.* a cheat. *v.i.* to swindle, to gull. **cross-bond,** *n.* bricklaying in which points of one course fall in the middle of those above and below. **cross-bones,** *n.pl.* the representation of two thigh-bones crossed as an emblem of mortality. **cross-bow,** *n.* a weapon for shooting, formed by placing a bow across a stock. **cross-bowman,** *n.* **cross-bred,** *a.* of a cross-breed, hybrid. **cross-breed,** *n.* a breed produced from a male and female of different strains or varieties; a hybrid. *v.t.* to produce a cross-breed; to cross-fertilize. **cross-bun,** *n.* a bun marked with a cross (eaten on Good Friday). **cross-buttock,** *n.* a wrestling throw over the hip. **cross-check,** *v.t.* to check (a fact etc.) by referring to other sources of information. **cross-country,** *a., adv.* across fields etc. instead of along the roads. *n.* a cross-country race. **cross-cultural,** *a.* concerning the differences between two cultures. **crosscut,** *n.* a cut across; a step in dancing; a figure in skating; (*Mining*) a drift from a shaft. *v.t.* to cut across. **crosscut saw,** *n.* a saw for cutting timber across the grain. **cross-dresser,** *n.* a transvestite. **cross-dressing,** *n.* **cross-entry,** *n.* (*Book-keeping*) an entry to another account; a cancelling of a former entry. **cross-examine,** *v.t.* to examine systematically for the purpose of eliciting facts not brought out in direct examination, or for confirming or contradicting the direct evidence. **cross-examination,** *n.* **cross-examiner,** *n.* **cross-eye,** *n.* a squinting eye. **cross-eyed,** *a.* with both eyes squinting inwards. **cross-fade,** *v.t.* in TV or radio, to fade out (one signal) while introducing another. **cross-fertilize, -ise,** *v.t., v.i.* to apply the pollen of one flower to the pistil of a flower of another species. **cross-fertilization, -isation,** *n.* **crossfire,** *n.* firing in directions which cross each other; a rapid or lively argument. **cross-grain,** *n.* the grain or fibres of wood running across the regular grain. **cross-grained,** *a.* having the grain or fibres running across or irregular; perverse, peevish; intractable. **cross-hatch,** *v.t.* to shade with parallel lines crossing regularly in drawing or engraving. **cross-head,** *n.* the block at the head of a piston-rod communicating motion to the connecting rod; a heading printed across the page or a column. **cross-infection,** *n.* infection of a hospital patient with an unrelated illness from another patient. **cross-jack**, **cross-jack yard,** *n.* (*Naut.*) the yard of a square-sail occasionally carried by a cutter in running before the wind; the lower yard on the mizzen-mast. **cross-legged,** *a.* having one leg over the other. **cross-light,** *n.* a light falling at an angle or crossing another; a view of a subject under a different aspect. **cross-match,** *v.t.* to test (as blood samples from two people) for compatibility. **crosspatch,** *n.* (*coll.*) a cross, ill-tempered person. **crosspiece,** *n.* a transverse piece; (*Shipbuilding*) the flooring-piece resting upon the keel; a bar connecting the bitt-heads. **cross-ply,** *a.* of motor-vehicle tyres, having the cords crossing each other diagonally to strengthen the tread. **cross-pollination,** *n.* the transfer of pollen from one flower to the stigma of another. **cross-pollinate,** *v.t.* **cross-purpose,** *n.* a contrary purpose; contradiction, inconsistency, misunderstanding; (*pl.*) a game carried on by question and answer. **to be at cross-purposes,** to misunderstand or act unintentionally counter to each other. **cross-question,** *n.* one put in cross-examination. *v.t.* to cross-examine. **cross-questions and crooked answers,** a game in which questions and answers are connected at random with ludicrous effect. **cross-reference,** *n.* a reference from one part of a book to another. **cross-refer,** *v.t., v.i.* **cross-road,** *n.* a road that crosses another or connects two others; a by-way; (*pl.*) the crossing of two roads. **cross-row** CHRIST-CROSS-ROW under CHRIST. **cross-ruff,** *n.* (*Whist*) the play in which partners trump different suits and lead accordingly. **cross-sea,** *n.* waves setting in contrary directions. **cross-section,** *n.* a cutting across the grain, or at right angles to the length; a cutting which shows all the strata; a comprehensive representation, a representative example. **cross-sectional,** *a.* **cross-springer,** *n.* (*Arch.*) a rib which extends from one pier to another in groined vaulting. **cross-staff,** *n.* an archbishop's staff; †an instrument for taking altitudes or offsets in surveying. **cross-stitch,** *n.* a kind of stitch crossing others in series; needlework done thus. **cross-stone** HARMOTOME. **cross-talk,** *n.* unwanted signals in a telephone, radio etc. channel, coming in from another channel; repartee. **cross-tie,** *n.* (*Arch.*) a connecting band. **cross-trees,** *n.pl.* timbers on the top of masts to support the rigging of the mast above. **cross-trump** CROSS-RUFF. **cross-vaulting,** *n.* the intersecting of two or more simple vaults of arch-work. †**cross-way,** *n.* a cross-road. **cross-wind,** *n.* an unfavourable wind; a side-wind. **crossword (puzzle),** *n.* a puzzle in which a square divided into blank chequered spaces is filled with words corresponding to clues provided. **crossly,** *adv.* in an ill-humoured manner. **crossness,** *n.* **crossways, -wise,** *adv.* across; in the form of a cross. [OE *cros,* L *crux crucis*]

cross[2], *v.t.* to draw a line across; to erase by cross lines, to cancel; to make the sign of the cross on or over; to pass across, to traverse; to intersect; to pass over or in front of; to meet and pass; to bestride; to cause to interbreed; to cross-fertilize; to write across the face of (a cheque) in order to render payable through another bank; to thwart, to counteract; to be inconsistent with. *v.i.* to lie or be across or over something; to pass across something; to move in a zigzag; to be inconsistent; to interbreed. **to cross** (a fortune-teller's) **hand,** to give money to. **to cross off, out,** to strike out; to cancel. **to cross one's mind,** to occur to one's memory or attention. **to cross the floor,** used of a member of Parliament leaving one political party to join another. **to cross the path of,** to meet with; to thwart. **crossed,** *a.* of a telephone line, connected in error to more than one telephone. **crossing,** *n.* the action of the verb TO CROSS; a place of crossing; the intersection of two roads, railways etc.; a place where a road etc. may be crossed; contradiction, opposition. **crossing-over,** *n.* the interchange of segments of homologous chromosomes during meiotic cell division. **crossing-sweeper,** *n.* (*Hist.*) a person who sweeps a street-crossing. [from prec.]

crosse, *n.* the long, hooked, racket-like stick used in the game of lacrosse. [F, from OF *croce,* a crook or

hook]
crossing CROSS[2].
crosslet, *n.* a small cross. **crossleted,** *a.*
Crossman, *n.* **Richard (Howard Stafford)** (1907–74), British Labour politician. He was minister of housing and local government (1964–66) and of health and social security (1968–70). His posthumous *Crossman Papers* (1975) revealed confidential cabinet discussion.
crossways, crosswise CROSS[1].
crotch, *n.* a forking; the parting of two branches; the angle between the thighs where the legs meet the body; a hook or crook; †a curved weeding tool; a small space in the corner of a billiard-table; (*Naut.*) CRUTCH. **crotched,** *a.* having a crotch; forked. [etym. doubtful (cp. CRUTCH)]
crotchet, *n.* a peculiar turn of mind; a whimsical fancy, a conceit; (*Printing*) a square bracket; (*Mus.*) a note, equal in length to one beat of a bar of 4/4 time. **crotchet-monger,** *n.* a crotcheteer. **crotcheteer,** *n.* a crotchety person; a faddist. **crotchety,** *a.* having crotchets; whimsical. **crotchetiness,** *n.* [F *crochet,* dim. of *croc,* a hook]
croton, *n.* a genus of euphorbiaceous medicinal plants from the warmer parts of both hemispheres. **croton-oil,** *n.* a drastic purgative oil expressed from *Croton tiglium*. [Gr. *krotōn,* a tick]
crottle, *n.* a name for several species of lichens used for dyeing. [Gael. *crotal,* a lichen]
crouch, *v.i.* to stoop, to bend low; to lie close to the ground; to cringe, to fawn. *n.* the action of crouching. [etym. doubtful]
crouchware, *n.* a collector's name for old salt-glazed Staffordshire pottery. [etym. doubtful]
croup[1], *n.* the rump, the buttocks (esp. of a horse); the part behind the saddle. [F *croupe* (cp. CROP)]
croup[2], *n.* inflammation of the larynx and trachea, characterized by hoarse coughing and difficulty in breathing, common in infancy. **croupy,** *a.* [imit.]
croupier, *n.* a vice-chairman; one who superintends a gaming-table and collects the money won by the bank. [F, orig. one who rides on the CROUP[1]]
crouse, *a.* (*Sc.*) bold, forward; lively, pert. *adv.* boldly, with plenty of confidence. **crousely,** *adv.* [ME *crūs* (cp. G *kraus,* Dut. *kroes*)]
croûton, *n.* a small cube of fried or toasted bread, served with soup or salads. [F, dim. of *croûte,* CRUST]
crow[1], *n.* a large black bird of the genus *Corvus,* esp. *C. cornix,* the hooded crow, and *C. corone,* the carrion crow; a crowbar; †a grappling-iron; (*sl.*) a confederate who keeps watch while another steals. **as the crow flies,** in a direct line. **stone the crows,** *int.* (*sl.*) an expression of amazement. **to eat crow,** (*coll.*) to (be made to) humiliate or abase oneself. **to have a crow to pluck with anyone,** to have some fault to find with or an explanation to demand from one. **to pluck, pull a crow,** to contend for trifles. **crowbar,** *n.* a bar of iron bent at one end (like a crow's beak) and used as a lever. **crowberry,** *n.* a heathlike plant, *Empetrum nigrum,* with black berries. **crow-bill,** *n.* (*Surg.*) a forceps for extracting bullets etc. from wounds. **croweater,** *n.* (*Austral., coll.*) a native of S Australia, a resident there. **crow-flower** CROWFOOT. **crowfoot,** *n.* name for several species of buttercup, *Ranunculus bulbosus, R. acris* and *R. repens;* (*Mil.*) a caltrop; (*Naut.*) a contrivance for suspending the ridge of an awning. **crow-keeper,** *n.* a boy employed to scare away crows; a scarecrow. **crow-quill,** *n.* a fine pen for sketching (orig. made from the quill of a crow). **crow's-foot,** *n.* a wrinkle at the corner of the eye in old age; (*Mil.*) a caltrop. **crow's nest,** *n.* a tub or box for the look-out man on a ship's mast. **crow-steps** CORBIE-STEPS. **crow-stone,** *n.* the top stone of a gable; (*Geol.*) a local name for sandstone in Yorkshire and Derbyshire. [OE *crāwe,* from *crawan* (see foll.)]
crow[2], *v.i.* (*past* **crew, crowed**) to make a loud cry like a cock; to make a cry of delight like an infant; to exult; to brag, to boast. *v.t.* to proclaim by crowing. *n.* the cry of a cock; the cry of delight of an infant. [OE *crāwan* (cp. Dut. *kraaijen,* G *krähen*), imit.]
crowd[1], *v.t.* †to drive, to push; to press or squeeze closely together; to fill by pressing; to throng or press upon; to press (into or through). *v.i.* to press, to throng, to swarm; to collect in crowds. *n.* a number of persons or things collected closely and confusedly together; the mass, the mob, the populace; (*coll.*) a set, a party, a lot; a large number (of things); any group of persons photographed in a film but not playing definite parts. **a crowd of sail,** (*Naut.*) a press of sail. **to crowd out,** to force (a person or thing) out by leaving no room; to fill to absolute capacity. **to crowd sail,** (*Naut.*) to carry an extraordinary force or press of sail. **crowd-puller,** *n.* an event that attracts a large audience. **crowded,** *a.* [OE *crūdan*]
crowd[2], *n.* an old instrument somewhat like a violin, but with six strings (in early times three), four played with a bow and two with the thumb. *v.i.* to play a crowd or fiddle. †**crowder,** *n.* one who plays upon a crowd; a fiddler. [W *crwth*]
crowdy, -die, *n.* (*Sc.*) meal and water (or milk) stirred together cold, to form a thick gruel; a kind of soft unripened cheese made from soured milk. [etym. unknown]
Crowley, *n.* **John** (1942–), US writer of science fiction and fantasy, notably *Little, Big* (1980) and *Aegypt* (1987), which contain esoteric knowledge and theoretical puzzles.
crown, *n.* a garland of honour worn on the head; the ornamental circlet worn on the head by emperors, kings or princes as a badge of sovereignty; an ornament of this shape; royal power; the sovereign; (*Hist.*) a five-shilling piece; a foreign coin of certain values; a size of paper, 15 in. × 20 in. (381 × 508 mm) (formerly with a crown for a watermark); the top of anything, as a hat, a mountain etc.; the head; the top of the head; the vertex of an arch; the upper member of a cornice; the highest part of a road, bridge or causeway; the portion of a tooth above the gum; an artificial crown for a broken or discoloured tooth; (*Naut.*) the part of an anchor where the arms join the shank; the culmination, glory; reward, distinction. *a.* belonging to the Crown or the sovereign. *v.t.* to invest with a crown, or regal or imperial dignity; (*fig.*) to surround, or top, as with a crown; to form a crown, ornament or top to; to dignify, to adorn; to consummate; to put a crown or cap on (a tooth); (*Draughts*) to make a king; †to fill so as to brim over. **Crown agent,** *n.* (*Sc. Law*) the solicitor who under the Lord Advocate takes charge of criminal prosecutions. **crown-antler,** *n.* the topmost antler of a stag's horn. **Crown Colony,** *n.* a colony administered by the home Government. **crown court,** see separate entry. **crown-glass,** *n.* the finest kind of window glass, made in circular sheets without lead or iron; glass used in optical instruments, containing potassium and barium in place of sodium. **crown green,** *n.* a type of bowling green which slopes slightly from the sides up to the centre. **crown imperial,** *n.* a garden flower from the Levant, *Fritillaria imperialis,* with a whorl of florets round the head. **crown jewels,** *n.pl.* the regalia and other jewels belonging to the sovereign. **Crown lands,** *n.pl.* lands belonging to the Crown as the head of the government. **crown law,** *n.* common law, as applicable to criminal matters. **crown lawyer,** *n.* a lawyer in the service of the Crown. **Crown Office,** *n.* a section of the Court of King's (or Queen's) Bench which takes cognizance of criminal cases; the office which now transacts the common law business of the Chancery. **crown-post,** *n.* a king-post. **crown prince,** *n.* the name given in some countries to the heir apparent to the Crown; **crown princess,** *n.fem.* **crown-side,** *n.* the Crown Office. **crown-solicitor,** *n.* the solicitor who prepares the cases when the Crown prosecutes. **crown-wheel,** *n.* a contrate wheel. **crown-witness,** *n.* a witness for the Crown in a criminal prosecution. **crown-work,** *n.* (*Fort.*) an extension of the main work, consisting of a bastion between two curtains. **crowned,** *a.* having a crown; invested with a crown. **high-crowned, low-crowned,** *a.* of hats, high or low in the crown. **crownless,** *a.* destitute or deprived of a crown. [A-F *cor-*

oune, OF *corone,* L *corōna,* a garland, a crown (cogn. with Gr. *korōnē,* the curved end of a bow)]

Crown Courts, *n. pl.* in England and Wales, courts at particular centres, which hear more serious criminal cases referred from magistrates' courts after committal proceedings. They replaced quarter sessions and assizes, which were abolished in 1971. Appeals against conviction or sentence at magistrates' courts may be heard in Crown Courts. Appeal from a Crown Court is to the Court of Appeal.

Crown Estate, *n.* a title (from 1956) of land in the UK formerly owned by the monarch but handed to Parliament (by George III in 1760) in exchange for an annual payment (called the civil list). It owns valuable sites in central London, and 268,400 acres in England and Scotland.

Crown Proceedings Act, an act of Parliament which provided that the Crown (as represented by, for example, government departments) could from 1948 be sued like a private individual.

croydon, *n.* a light two-wheeled gig. [town in Surrey]

croze, *n.* the groove in barrel staves near the end to receive the head; a cooper's tool for making this. *v.t.* to make this groove in. [perh. from F *creux,* OF *croz,* a hollow]

crozier, CROSIER.

CRT, (*abbr.*) cathode ray tube.

crucial, *a.* decisive; searching; (*Anat.*) in the form of a cross; intersecting; (*loosely*) very important; (*sl.*) excellent. **crucially,** *adv.* [F, from L *crux crucis,* a cross]

crucian, *n.* the German or Prussian carp, a small fish without barbels. [LG *karusse,* perh. from L *coracīnus,* Gr. *karakînos*]

cruciate, *a.* (*Biol.*) cruciform. [med. L *cruciātus* (L *crux crucis,* cross)]

crucible, *n.* a melting-pot of earthenware, porcelain, or of refractory metal, adapted to withstand high temperatures without softening, and sudden and great alterations of temperature without cracking; a basin at the bottom of a furnace to collect the molten metal; a searching test or trial. [late L *crucibulum,* perh. from *crux,* see prec.]

crucifer, *n.* a cross-bearer; one of the Cruciferae. **Cruciferae**, *n.pl.* a natural order of plants, the flowers of which have four petals disposed crosswise. **cruciferous,** *a.* bearing a cross; belonging to the Cruciferae. [L *crucifer* (*crux crucis,* a cross, *-fer,* a bearer)]

crucifix, *n.* a cross bearing a figure of Christ. **crucifixion,** *n.* the act of crucifying; punishment by crucifying; the death of Christ on the cross; a picture of this; torture; mortification. **cruciform,** *a.* cross-shaped; arranged in the form of a cross. [OF *crucefix,* L *cruci fixus,* fixed to a cross]

crucify, *v.t.* to inflict capital punishment by affixing to a cross; to torture; to mortify, to destroy the influence of; to subject to scathing criticism, obloquy or ridicule; to defeat utterly. [OF *crucifier,* late L *cruci fīgere* (L *cruci fīgere,* to fix to a cross)]

crud, *n.* (*sl.*) any dirty, sticky or slimy substance; (*sl.*) a contemptible person. **cruddy,** *a.* [var. of CURD]

crude, *a.* raw; in a natural state, not cooked; unripe; not digested; imperfectly developed, immature, inexperienced, rude; coarse, rough, unfinished; (*Gram.*) uninflected; of statistics, not classified or analysed. **crude form,** *n.* the original form of an inflected substantive divested of its case ending. **crude oil,** *n.* unrefined petroleum. **crudely,** *adv.* **crudeness,** *n.* **crudity,** *n.* [L *crūdus,* raw]

cruel, *a.* disposed to give pain to others; inhuman, unfeeling, hard-hearted; causing pain to others, painful. **cruel-hearted,** *a.* delighting in cruelty. **cruelly,** *adv.* †**cruelness,** *n.* **cruelty,** *n.* cruel disposition or temper; a barbarous or inhuman act. [F, from L *crūdēlis* (cogn. with *crūdus,* CRUDE)]

cruelty, theatre of, THEATRE.

cruet, *n.* a small container for pepper, salt etc. at table; a small bottle for holding the wine or water in the Eucharist. **cruet-stand,** *n.* a frame or stand for holding cruets. [A-F, dim. of OF *crue, cruie,* rob. from OLG *crûca* (cp. OHG *kruog*), a pot]

Cruft, *n.* **Charles** (1852–1938), British dog expert. He organized his first dog show in 1886, and from that year annual shows bearing his name were held in Islington, London.

Cruikshank, *n.* **George** (1792–1878), British painter and illustrator, remembered especially for his political cartoons and illustrations to Dickens's *Oliver Twist* and Defoe's *Robinson Crusoe*.

cruise, *v.i.* to sail to and fro for pleasure or in search of plunder or an enemy; of a motor vehicle or aircraft, to travel at a moderate but sustained speed. *n.* the act or an instance of cruising, esp. a pleasure-trip on a boat. **cruise missile,** *n.* a low-flying subsonic guided missile. **cruiser,** *n.* a person or ship that cruises; a warship designed primarily for speed, faster and lighter than a battleship. **armoured cruiser,** *n.* such a vessel armed like (usu. not so heavily as) a battleship. **cruiserweight,** *n.* in boxing, a light heavyweight. [Dut. *kruisen,* to cross, from *kruis,* L *crux crucis,* a cross]

cruisie CRUSIE.

cruiskeen, *n.* (*Ir.*) a small vessel for liquor; a measure of whisky.

cruive, *n.* (*Sc.*) †a cabin; a sty; a wickerwork enclosure on a tidal flat for catching fish. [etym. doubtful]

cruller, *n.* (*N Am.*) a light, sweet, often ring-shaped cake, deep-fried in fat. [Dut. *cruller,* from *crullen,* to curl]

crumb, *n.* a small piece, esp. of bread; the soft inner part of bread; a tiny portion, a particle; (*sl.*) an unpleasant or contemptible person. *v.t.* to break into crumbs; to cover with crumbs (for cooking). †*v.i.* to crumble. **crumb-brush,** *n.* a curved brush for sweeping crumbs from the table. **crumb-cloth,** *n.* a cloth laid over a carpet to receive the crumbs that fall from the table. **crumby,** *a.* covered with crumbs; (*sl.*) crummy. [OE *crūma* (cp. Dut. *kruim,* G *Krume*)]

crumble, *v.t.* to break into small particles. *v.i.* to fall into small pieces; to fall into ruin. *n.* a pudding topped with a crumbly mixture of flour, sugar and butter, as *apple crumble*. **crumbly,** *a.* apt to crumble. *n.* (*coll.*) a very old person. [as prec.]

crummy, *a.* (*sl.*) unpleasant, worthless; (*sl.*) unwell.

crump, *n.* the sound of the explosion of a heavy shell or bomb. *v.i.* to make such a sound. [onomat.]

crumpet, *n.* a thin, light, spongy tea-cake; (*sl.*) the head; (*sl.*) a girl or girls collectively. [etym. doubtful]

crumple, *v.t.* to draw or press into wrinkles. *v.i.* to become wrinkled, to shrink, as cloth, paper etc.; to collapse, give way. **crumplet,** *n.* **crumpling,** *n.* the action of the verb TO CRUMPLE; †a small apple with a wrinkled skin. [from obs. *crump,* to bend or curl up]

crunch, *v.t.* to crush noisily with the teeth; to grind with the foot. *v.i.* to make a noise, as of crunching; to advance with crunching. *n.* a noise of or as of crunching. **when it comes to the crunch,** (*coll.*) at the decisive moment. **crunchy,** *a.* [imit.]

cruor, *n.* coagulated blood. [L, blood, gore]

crupper, *n.* a strap with a loop which passes under a horse's tail to keep the saddle from slipping forward; the croup or hindquarters of a horse. *v.t.* to put a crupper on. [OF *cropiere* (as CROUP[1])]

crural, *a.* belonging to the leg; shaped like a human leg. [L *crūrālis* (*crūs crūris,* the leg)]

crusade, *n.* one of several expeditions undertaken in the Middle Ages under the banner of the Cross to recover possession of the Holy Land, then in Muslim hands; any hostile enterprise conducted in an enthusiastic or fanatical spirit. *v.i.* to engage in a crusade. **crusader,** *n.* [F *croisade* (OF *croisée* and Sp. *cruzada,* med. L *cruciāta,* p.p. of *cruciāre,* to mark with a CROSS)]

†**crusado,** *n.* (*pl.* **-does, -dos**) a Portuguese coin (stamped with a cross). [Port. *crusado,* as prec.]

cruse, *n.* a small pot, cup or bottle. [cp. Icel. *krūs,* Dut. *kroes,* G *Krause*]

crush, *v.t.* to press or squeeze together between two harder bodies so as to break or bruise; to crumple; to overwhelm by superior power; to oppress, to ruin. *v.i.* to be pressed into a smaller compass by external force or weight; to make one's way by crushing. *n.* the act of crushing; a crowd; (*coll.*) a crowded meeting or social gathering; (*Austral.*) the funnel of a stockyard where the cattle are got in hand; (*coll.*) an infatuation or the object of this; a drink made by or as by crushing fruit. **to crush a cup, pot,** to crack a bottle, to drink it. **to crush out,** to extinguish. **crush bar,** *n.* a bar in a theatre which patrons may use in the intervals of a play. **crush barrier,** *n.* a temporary barrier to keep back, or to separate, a crowd. **crush-hat,** *n.* a soft hat collapsing with a spring, so as to be carried under the arm without injury; an opera-hat. **crusher,** *n.* one who or that which crushes. [OF *cruisir, croissir,* from Teut. (cp. Dan. *kryste,* Swed. *krossa*)]

crusie, *n.* (*Sc.*) a small iron lamp burning oil or tallow. [prob. from F *creuset,* a crucible]

crust, *n.* the hard outer part of bread; the crusty end of a loaf; any hard rind, coating, layer, deposit or surface covering; a hard piece of bread; the pastry covering a pie; a scab; a deposit from wine as it ripens; (*Geol.*) the solid outer portion of the earth; a film deposited on the inside of a bottle of wine; a (meagre) living; (*sl.*) impertinence. *v.t.* to cover with a crust; to make into crust. *v.i.* to become encrusted. **crustal,** *a.* pertaining to the earth's crust. **crusted,** *a.* having a crust; antiquated, hoary, venerable; describing port or other wine from a bottle with a crust. **crusty,** *a.* resembling or of the nature of crust; harsh, peevish, morose. **crustily,** *adv.* **crustiness,** *n.* [OF *crouste,* L *crusta*]

Crustacea, *n.pl.* a class of Articulata, containing lobsters, crabs, shrimps etc., named from their shelly covering, cast periodically. **crustacean,** *n., a.* **crustaceology,** *n.* the branch of science dealing with the Crustacea. **crustaceologist,** *n.* **crustaceous,** *a.* of the nature of shell; crustacean. **crustation,** *n.* an incrustation. [mod. L neut. pl. of *crustāceus,* a. (L *crusta,* see prec.)]

crutch, *n.* a staff, with a crosspiece to fit under the arm-pit, to support a lame person; a support; (*Naut.*) various appliances for spars, timbers etc.; the crotch of a person; the corresponding part of a garment. †*v.t.* to support on or as on crutches. *v.i.* to go on crutches. [OE *cryce,* from Teut. *kruk-* (cp. Dut. *kruk,* Dan. *krukke,* G *Krücke*)]

†**crutched,** *a.* wearing a cross as a badge. **Crutched Friars,** *n.pl.* a minor order of friars who wore a cross as badge; the site of their convent in London. [ME *crouch,* to cross]

Crux, *n.* a constellation of the southern hemisphere, popularly known as the Southern Cross, the smallest of the 88 constellations. Its brightest star, Alpha Crucis, is a double star. Near Beta Crucis lies a glittering star cluster known as the Jewel Box. The constellation also contains the Coalsack, a dark cloud of dust silhouetted against the bright starry background of the Milky Way.

crux, *n.* (*pl.* **cruxes, cruces**) the real essential; anything exceedingly puzzling. [L, CROSS]

cruzeiro, *n.* (*pl.* **-ros**) the monetary unit of Brazil, equal to 100 centavos. [Port., from *cruz,* CROSS]

crwth CROWD[2].

cry, *v.i.* to call loudly, vehemently or importunately; to make utterance in a loud voice; to make proclamation; to exclaim; to lament loudly; to weep; to squall; of animals, to call; to utter inarticulate sounds; to yelp. *v.t.* to utter loudly; to proclaim, to declare publicly; to announce for sale; †to demand. *n.* a loud utterance, usu. inarticulate, expressive of intense joy, pain, suffering, astonishment or other emotion; an importunate call or prayer; proclamation, public notification; a catchword or phrase; a bitter complaint of injustice or oppression; weeping; lamentation; inarticulate noise; yelping; †a pack of dogs; †a pack of people, a company. **a far cry,** a long way off. **for crying out loud,** (*coll.*) interjection expressing impatience, annoyance. **to cry against,** to exclaim loudly by way of threatening or censure. **to cry down,** to decry, to depreciate; †to overbear. **to cry halves,** to demand a share of something. **to cry in church,** to publish the banns of marriage. **to cry mercy,** to beg pardon. **to cry off,** to withdraw from a bargain. **to cry out,** to vociferate, to clamour. **to cry out against,** to exclaim loudly, by way of censure or reproach. **to cry quits,** to declare matters equal. **to cry shame upon,** to protest against. **to cry stinking fish,** to decry or condemn, esp. one's own wares. **to cry up,** to extol, to praise highly. **crybaby,** *n.* (*coll.*) a child or person easily provoked to tears. **crying,** *a.* that cries; calling for notice or vengeance, flagrant. [F *crier,* L *quīrītāre,* lit. to cry for the help of the *Quīrītes,* or Roman citizens]

cryo-, *comb. form* very cold. [Gr. *kruos,* frost]

cryogen, *n.* (*Chem.*) a freezing mixture. **cryogenics,** *n.sing.* the branch of physics which studies very low temperatures and the phenomena associated with them. **cryogenic,** *a.*

cryolite, *n.* a brittle fluoride of sodium and aluminium from Greenland.

cryophorus, *n.* an instrument for freezing water by its own evaporation.

crypt, *n.* a vault, esp. one beneath a church, used for religious services or for burial. **cryptic,** *a.* hidden, secret, occult; of animal coloration, serving as camouflage. **cryptically,** *adv.* [L *crypta,* Gr. *kruptē,* fem. of *kruptos,* hidden (*kruptein,* to hide)]

crypt(o)-, *comb. form* secret; inconspicuous; not apparent or prominent.

cryptocrystalline, *a.* (*Min.*) having a crystalline structure which cannot be resolved under the microscope.

cryptogam, *n.* a plant destitute of pistils and stamens. **Cryptogamia,** *n.pl.* a Linnaean order of plants in which the reproductive organs are concealed or not distinctly visible, containing ferns, lichens, mosses and seaweeds, fungi etc. **cryptogamic, -mous,** *a.* **cryptogamist,** *n.* **cryptogamy,** *n.* concealed or obscure fructification. [Gr. *-gamos,* married (*gamein,* to marry)]

cryptogram, *n.* a cipher; cipher-writing. **cryptograph,** *n.* a system of writing in cipher; secret writing. **cryptographer, -phist,** *n.* **cryptographic,** *a.* **cryptography,** *n.*

cryptonym, *n.* a secret name; the name one bears in a secret society or brotherhood. [Gr. *onuma,* a name]

crystal, *n.* a clear transparent mineral; transparent quartz, also called rock crystal; an aggregation of atoms arranged in a definite pattern which often assumes the form of a regular solid terminated by a certain number of smooth plane surfaces; anything clear as crystal; a very pellucid kind of glass; a crystalline component in various electronic devices, used as an oscillator etc. *a.* clear, transparent, as bright as crystal; made of crystal. **crystal ball,** *n.* one made of glass, used in crystal gazing. **crystal detector,** *n.* a crystal arranged in a circuit so that the modulation on a radio carrier wave becomes audible in earphones etc. **crystal gazing,** *n.* looking into a crystal ball in order to foresee the future. **crystal set,** *n.* an early form of radio receiver using a crystal detector. **crystalline,** *a.* consisting of crystal; resembling crystal; clear, pellucid. **crystalline heavens, spheres,** *n.pl.* two transparent spheres which, according to the Ptolemaic cosmogony, were situated between the *primum mobile,* which carried with it in its revolution all that lay within it, and the firmament in which were the fixed stars. **crystalline lens,** *n.* a lenticular, white, transparent solid body enclosed in a capsule behind the iris of the eye, the lens of the eye. **crystallinity,** *n.* **crystallite,** *n.* one of the particles of definite form observed in thin sections of igneous rock cooled slowly after fusion. **crystallize, -ise,** *v.t.* to cause to form crystals; to coat (fruit) with sugar crystals. *v.i.* to assume a crystalline form; of views, thoughts etc., to assume a definite form. **crystallizable, -isable,** *a.* **crystallization, -isation,** *n.* [OF *cristal,* L *crystallum,* Gr. *krustallos,* ice, rock-crystal, from *krustainein,* to freeze (*kruos,* frost)]

crystallo-, *comb. form* forming, formed of, pertaining to crystal, crystalline structure or the science of crystals. [Gr. *krustallos,* CRYSTAL]

crystallogeny, *n.* that branch of science which treats of the formation of crystals. **crystallogenic,** *a.*

crystallographer, *n.* one who describes or investigates crystals and their formation. **crystallography,** *n.* the science which deals with the forms of crystals. **crystallographic,** *a.* **crystallographically,** *adv.*

crystalloid, *a.* like a crystal. *n.* a body with a crystalline structure.

†**crystallomancy,** *n.* divination by means of a crystal or other transparent body.

crystallometry, *n.* the art or process of measuring the forms of crystals.

Crystal Palace, *n.* a glass and iron building designed by Paxton, housing the Great Exhibition of 1851 in Hyde Park, London; later rebuilt in modified form at Sydenham Hill in 1854 (burned down 1936).

crystoleum, *n.* the process of transferring photographs to glass and painting with oil colours. [L *oleum,* oil]

CS, (*abbr.*) chartered surveyor; civil service; Court of Session.

Cs, (*chem. symbol*) caesium.

c/s, (*abbr.*) cycles per second.

csardas CZARDAS.

CSC, (*abbr.*) Civil Service Commission; Conspicuous Service Cross.

CSCE, (*abbr.*) Conference on Security and Cooperation in Europe, popularly known as the Helsinki Conference.

CSE, (*abbr.*) certificate of secondary education in the UK, the examinations taken by the majority of secondary school pupils who were not regarded as academically capable of GCE O Level, until the introduction of the common secondary examination system, GCSE, 1988.

CS gas, *n.* an irritant gas, causing tears, painful breathing etc., used in riot control. [from the initials of its US inventors Corson and Stoughton]

CSI, (*abbr.*) Companion of (the Order of) the Star of India.

CSIRO, (*abbr.*) Commonwealth Scientific and Industrial Research Organization.

CSM, (*abbr.*) Company Sergeant-Major.

CSO, (*abbr.*) Central Statistical Office; community service order.

CST, (*abbr.*) central standard time.

Ct, (*abbr.*) Connecticut; court.

ct, (*abbr.*) carat; cent.

CTC, (*abbr.*) city technology college; Cyclists' Touring Club.

ctenoid, *a.* comb-shaped; pectinated; having ctenoid scales, belonging to the Ctenoidei. **ctenoid scales,** *n.pl.* scales pectinated on the lower edge. *n.* a ctenoid fish. **Ctenoidei,** *n.pl.* one of Agassiz's artificial orders of fishes, founded on scales, now merged in the Teleostei, though the name is retained in palaeontology. [Gr. *ktenoeides* (*kteis ktenos,* a comb)]

Ctenophora, *n.pl.* (*Zool.*) a division of the Coelenterata, characterized by fringed or comb-like locomotive organs. **ctenophoral,** *a.* **ctenophore,** *n.* a member of the Ctenophora. [Gr. *kteis ktenos,* a comb, *-phoros,* bearing, a bearer]

Ctesiphon, *n.* a ruined royal city of the Parthians, and later capital of the Sassanian Empire, 19 km/12 miles SE of Baghdad, Iraq. A palace of the 4th cent. still has its throne room standing, spanned by a single vault of unreinforced brickwork some 24 m/80 ft across.

CT scanner CAT SCANNER.

CTT, (*abbr.*) capital transfer tax.

CU, (*abbr.*) Cambridge University; control unit.

Cu, (*chem. symbol*) copper. [L *cuprum*]

cub, *n.* the young of certain animals, as of a lion, bear, fox; a whelp; (*coll.*) an uncouth, mannerless youth; (also **Cub Scout**) a young Boy Scout. *v.i.* (*past, p.p.* **cubbed**) to bring forth cubs; to hunt young foxes. †**cub-drawn,** *a.* sucked by cubs. **cub-hunting,** *n.* **cub reporter,** *n.* an inexperienced newspaper reporter. **cubbing,** *n.* **cubbish,** *a.* **cubhood,** *n.* [etym. doubtful]

Cuba, *n.* Republic of (*República de Cuba*), an island in the Caribbean, the largest of the West Indies, off the South Coast of Florida. **area** 114,524 sq km/44,206 sq miles. **capital** Havana. **physical** comprises Cuba, the largest and westernmost of the West Indian islands, and smaller islands including Isle of Youth; low hills; Sierra Maestra mountains in E. **exports** sugar (largest producer after USSR), tobacco, coffee, iron, copper, nickel. **population** (1987) 10,240,000 (plus 125,000 refugees from the Cuban port of Mariel – *marielitos* – in US); 66% are of Spanish descent, and a large number are of African origin; annual growth rate 0.6%. **language** Spanish. **religion** Roman Catholic 45%.

cubage, cubature, *n.* the process of finding the solid contents of any body. [CUBE]

Cubango, *n.* Portuguese name for the Okavango river in Africa.

cuban heel, *n.* a straight heel of medium height on a boot or shoe. [*Cuba,* island in the Caribbean Sea]

Cuban missile crisis, a crisis in international relations (1962) when Soviet rockets were installed in Cuba and US President Kennedy compelled Khrushchev, by an ultimatum, to remove them. The drive by the USSR to match the US in nuclear weaponry dates from this event.

cubby, *n.* a cubby-hole; (*Orkney, Shetland*) a straw basket. **cubby-hole,** *n.* a narrow or confined space; a cosy place. [cp. obs. *cub,* a stall or pen, LG *kübbung, kübje,* a shed]

cube, *n.* a solid figure contained by six equal squares, a regular hexahedron; the third power of a number (as 8 is the cube of 2). *v.t.* to raise to the third power; to find the cube of a number or the cubic content of a solid figure. **cube estimate,** *n.* a builder's or architect's estimate based on the cubic dimensions of a building. **cube-powder,** *n.* gunpowder made in coarse cubical grains. **cube root,** *n.* the number which, multiplied into itself, and then into the product, produces the cube; thus $3 \times 3 \times 3 = 27$, 3 being the cube root of 27, which is the cube of 3; the rule for the extraction of the cube root. **cube sugar,** *n.* lump sugar. **cubic, -ical,** *a.* having the properties or form of a cube; being or equalling a cube, the edge of which is a given unit; (*Math.*) of the third degree. **cubic equation,** *n.* an equation involving calculation to the third degree. **cubic foot,** *n.* a volume equal to a cube every edge of which measures a foot. **cubically,** *adv.* **cubiform,** *a.* cube-shaped. [F, from late L *cubum,* acc. of *cubus,* Gr. *kubos*]

cubeb, *n.* the small spicy berry of *Cubeba officinalis,* a Javanese shrub used in medicine and cookery. **cubebic,** *a.* **cubebin,** *n.* a vegetable principle found in the seeds of the cubeb. [F *cubèbe* (Sp. and It. *cubeba*), Arab. *kabābah*]

cubebin CUBEB.

cubic CUBE.

cubicle, cubicule, *n.* a portion of a bedroom partitioned off as a separate sleeping apartment; a compartment. [L *cubiculum* (*cubāre,* to lie)]

cubiform CUBE.

cubism, *n.* a revolutionary movement in early 20th-cent. painting, pioneering abstract art. Its founders Braque and Picasso were admirers of Cézanne and were inspired by his attempt to create a structure on the surface of the canvas. About 1907–10 the cubists began to 'abstract' images from nature, gradually releasing themselves from the imitation of reality. Cubism announced that a work of art exists in its own right rather than as a representation of the real world, and it attracted such artists as Juan Gris, Fernand Léger, and Robert Delaunay. **cubist,** *n.*

cubit, *n.* an old measure of length, from the elbow to the tip of the middle finger, but varying in practice at different times from 18 to 22 in. (0·46 to 0·5 m). **cubit-arm,** *n.* an arm cut off at the elbow. **cubital,** *a.* †containing or of the length of a cubit; pertaining to the forearm or corresponding part of the leg in animals. [L *cubitus,* a hand, an elbow]

cuboid, *a.* resembling a cube. *n.* (*Geom.*) a solid like a cube but with the sides not all equal, a rectangular parallelepiped; (*Anat.*) a bone on the outer side of the foot. **cuboidal,** *a.* [Gr. *kuboeidēs*]

Cuchulain, *n.* in Celtic mythology, a legendary hero, the chief figure in a cycle of Irish legends. He is associated with his uncle Conchobar, king of Ulster; his most famous exploits are described in Taín Bó Cuailnge/The Cattle-Raid of Cuchullain.

cucking-stool, *n.* a kind of chair, formerly used for ducking scolds, dishonest tradesmen etc. [prob. from obs. *cuck,* to void excrement (cp. Icel. *kúka*)]

cuckold, *n.* one whose wife is unfaithful. *v.t.* to make (a man) a cuckold. †**cuckoldly,** *a.* like a cuckold; mean, sneaking. †**cuckoldom,** *n.* **cuckoldry,** *n.* [OF *cucualt,* from *cucu,* CUCKOO (cp. F. *coucou,* cuckoo, *cocu,* cuckold)]

cuckoo, *n.* a migratory bird, *Cuculus canorus,* which visits Britain in the spring and summer and lays its eggs in the nests of other birds; a foolish fellow; a fool. *a.* (*sl.*) crazy. **cuckoo in the nest,** an unwanted and alien person, an intruder. **cuckoo clock,** *n.* a clock which announces the hours by emitting a sound like the note of the cuckoo. **cuckoo-flower,** *n.* a local name for many plants, esp. for the lady's smock, *Cardamine pratensis.* **cuckoo-pint,** *n.* the common arum. **cuckoo-spit,** *n.* an exudation on plants from the frog-hopper. [F *coucou,* imit. (cp. L *cuculus,* Gr. *kokkuks*)]

cucullate, -ated, *a.* (*Bot., Zool.*) hooded; resembling a hood; formed like a hood. **cuculliform,** *a.* [late L *cucullātus,* p.p. of *cucullāre* (L *cucullus,* a hood)]

cucumber, *n.* a trailing plant, *Cucumis sativus;* its elongated fruit, extensively used as a salad and pickle. **cool as a cucumber,** very unemotional, imperturbable. **cucumber fish,** *n.* (*Austral.*) a variety of grayling. **cucumber tree,** *n.* any of several American magnolias with fruit like small cucumbers. **cucumiform,** *a.* [orig. *cucumer,* L *cucumis -merem* (later influenced by F *cocombre,* now *concombre*)]

cucurbit, *n.* a gourd; a gourd-shaped vessel used in distillation. **cucurbitaceous,** *a.* [F *cucurbite,* L *cucurbita*]

cud, *n.* food deposited by ruminating animals in the first stomach, thence drawn and chewed over again. **to chew the cud,** to ruminate; to reflect. [OE *cudu, cwidu* (cp. Icel. *kwatha,* resin, OHG *chuti, quiti,* glue)]

cudbear, *n.* a crimson dye obtained from *Lecanora tartarea* and other lichens. [named by the inventor, Dr *Cuthbert* Gordon, 18th-cent. British chemist]

cuddle, *v.i.* to lie close or snug together; to join in an embrace. *v.t.* to embrace, to hug, to fondle. *n.* a hug, an embrace. **cuddlesome, cuddly,** *a.* attractive to cuddle. [etym. doubtful]

cuddy[1], *n.* (*chiefly Sc.*) a donkey, an ass; a blockhead, a lout; a young coal-fish; a jack or lever for hoisting. [etym. doubtful (perh. an abbreviation of *Cuthbert*)]

cuddy[2], *n.* a cabin in a ship where officers and passengers take their meals; a small cabin in a boat; a closet or cupboard. [etym. doubtful]

cudgel, *n.* a short club or thick stick, a bludgeon. *v.t.* (*past, p.p.* **cudgelled**) to beat with a cudgel. **to cudgel one's brains,** to try to recollect or find out something. **to take up (the) cudgels,** to strike in and fight; to defend vigorously. **cudgel-play,** *n.* fighting with cudgels. **cudgel-proof,** *a.* able to resist a blow with a cudgel. [OE *cycgel;* etym. doubtful]

cudweed, *n.* popular name for the genus *Gnaphalium,* esp. *G. sylvaticum,* a plant formerly administered to cattle that had lost their cud.

cue[1], *n.* the last words of a speech, a signal to another actor that he or she should begin; any similar signal, e.g. in a piece of music; a hint, reminder. *v.t.* (*pres. p.* **cuing, cueing**) to give a cue to. **on cue,** at the right time. **to cue in,** to give a cue to, to inform. [etym. doubtful]

cue[2], *n.* a long straight rod used by billiard-players. *v.t., v.i.* (*pres. p.* **cuing, cueing**) to strike (a ball) with a cue. **cue ball,** *n.* the ball which is struck with a cue. **cueist,** *n.* [OF *cue* (F *queue*), L *cauda,* a tail]

cuff[1], *v.t.* to strike with the open hand. *n.* a blow of this kind. [cp. Swed. *kuffa,* to thrust, to push]

cuff[2], *n.* the fold or band at the end of a sleeve; a linen band worn round the wrist; (*pl.*) (*coll.*) handcuffs. **off the cuff,** extempore. **cufflink,** *n.* a usu. ornamental device consisting of a button-like disc attached to a short bar with a pivoting endpiece or a pair of buttons linked by a short chain, used to fasten a shirt cuff. [etym. doubtful]

Cugnot, *n.* **Nicolas** (1728–1804), French engineer who produced the first high pressure steam engine. While serving in the French army, he was asked to design a steam-operated gun-carriage. After several years labour, he produced a three-wheeled, high pressure carriage capable of carrying 400 gallons of water and four passengers at a speed of 3 mph. Although he worked further on the carriage, political conditions militated against much progress being made and his invention was ignored.

Cui, *n.* **Casar Antonovich** (1853–1918), Russian composer of operas and chamber music. A professional soldier, he joined Balakirev's Group of Five and promoted a Russian national style.

cui bono?, for whose advantage? [L]

cuirass, *n.* armour for the body, consisting of a breastplate and a backplate strapped or buckled together; a woman's close-fitting, sleeveless bodice; (*Nat. Hist.*) any analogous protective covering; a sheathing of iron plates on ironclads. **cuirassier,** *n.* a soldier wearing a cuirass. [F *cuirasse,* It. *corazza,* late L *corācium,* L *coriācea,* fem. of *coriāceus,* leathern (*corium,* leather)]

cuisine, *n.* the kitchen; style of cooking; cookery. [F]

Cukor, *n.* **George** (1899–1983), US film director. He moved to the cinema from the theatre, and was praised for his skilled handling of stars such as Greta Garbo (in *Camille,* 1937) and Katherine Hepburn (in *The Philadelphia Story,* 1940, among others). His films were usually civilized dramas or light comedies.

Culdee, *n.* one of an ancient Scoto-Irish Christian fraternity, founded about the 8th cent. [OIr. *céle dé,* a servant of God]

cul-de-sac, *n.* (*pl.* **culs-de-sac**) a street or lane open only at one end; (*Mil.*) a situation with no exit except in front; (*Anat.*) a vessel, tube or gut open only at one end. [F, bottom of a bag]

-cule, *dim. suf.,* as in *animalcule, corpuscule.* [F *-cule,* L *-culus -cula -culum* (which is fully anglicized in *-cle*)]

Culex, *n.* (*Zool.*) a genus of dipterous insects, containing the gnat and the mosquito. **culiciform,** *a.* [L, a gnat]

culinary, *a.* relating to the kitchen or cooking; used in kitchens or in cooking. [L *culīnārius* (*culīna,* a kitchen)]

cull, *v.t.* to pick; to select, to choose (the best); to select (an animal) from a group, esp. a weak or superfluous one, to kill it; to reduce the size of (a group) in this way. *n.* an instance of culling; (*pl.*) (*N Am.*) defective logs or planks picked out from lumber. **culler,** *n.* **culling,** *n.* the act of picking or choosing; that which is rejected; an undersized oyster. [OF *cuillir,* L *colligere,* to COLLECT]

cullender COLANDER.

cullet, *n.* broken glass for remelting. [COLLET]

cullion, *n.* a testicle; a mean, base wretch. **cullionly,** *a.* mean, cowardly, base. [F *couillon,* ult. from L *cōleus,* bag, Gr. *koleos,* sheath]

cullis, *n.* a gutter; a groove or channel. [F COULISSE]

Culloden, Battle of, defeat (1746) of the Jacobite rebel army of the British Prince Charles Edward Stuart by the Duke of Cumberland on a stretch of moorland in Inverness-shire, Scotland.

cully, *n.* (*sl.*) a dupe; one easily imposed upon. [etym. doubtful]

culm[1], *n.* a stem, esp. of grass or sedge. **culmiferous,** *a.* [L *culmus*]

culm[2], *n.* stone-coal; anthracite coal, esp. if in small pieces; coal-dust; soot, smut. **culmiferous,** *a.* abounding in anthracite. [prob. cogn. with COAL]

culmen, *n.* the ridge on the top of a bird's bill. [L, the top]

culminate, *v.i.* to reach the highest point; (*Astron.*) to come to the meridian. **culminant,** *a.* at the highest point; (*Astron.*) on the meridian; supreme, predominant. **culmination,** *n.* the highest point; the end of a series of events etc. [late L *culminātus,* p.p. of *culmināre* (see prec.)]

culotte(s), *n.* a divided skirt. [F]

culpable, *a.* blamable; blameworthy; guilty. **culpability,** *n.* **culpableness,** *n.* **culpably,** *adv.* **culpatory,** *a.* involving or expressing blame. [OF *culpable* (F *coupable*), L *culpābilis* (*culpa,* a fault)]

culprit, *n.* an offender; one who is at fault; one who is arraigned before a judge on a charge [from the A-F legal abbrev. *cul. prit* or *prist* (prob. in full *culpable*: *prist* or *prest d'averrer,* guilty: I am ready to confess)]

cult, *n.* a system of religious belief; the rites and ceremonies of any system of belief; a sect regarded as unorthodox or harmful to its adherents; an intense devotion to a person, idea etc.; the object of such devotion; an intense fad or fashion. *a.* pertaining to a pagan cult; very fashionable. **cultic,** *a.* **cultish,** *a.* **cultism,** *n.* adherence to a cult; Gongorism. **cultist,** *n.* **cultus,** *n.* a cult. [L *cultus,* from *colere,* to till, to worship]

culter COULTER.

cultivar, *n.* a variety of a naturally-occurring species, produced and maintained by cultivation. [*culti*vated *var*iety]

cultivate, *v.t.* to till; to prepare for crops; to raise or develop by tilling; to improve by labour or study, to civilize; to cherish, to foster, to seek the friendship of. **cultivable,** *a.* **cultivation,** *n.* the art or practice of cultivating; the state of being cultivated; a state of refinement or culture. **cultivation paddock,** *n.* (*Austral.*) a cultivated field. **cultivator,** *n.* one who cultivates; an implement to break up the soil and remove weeds. [late L *cultīvātus,* p.p. of *cultīvāre* (cp. *cultus,* CULT)]

cultrate, cultriform, *a.* (*Nat. Hist.*) shaped like a knife; having a sharp edge. [L *cultrātus* (*culter,* knife)]

cultrirostral, *a.* of birds, having a knife-shaped bill. [L *rōstrum,* a beak]

Cultural Revolution, *n.* a movement begun by Chinese communist party chairman Mao Zedong (1966) and directed against bureaucracy and university intellectuals. Intended to 'purify' Chinese communism, it was also an attempt by Mao to restore his political and ideological pre-eminence inside China.

culture, *n.* the act of tilling; husbandry, farming; breeding and rearing; the experimental growing of bacteria or other microorganisms in a laboratory; the group of microorganisms so grown; intellectual or moral discipline and training; a state of intellectual and artistic development. *v.t.* to cultivate; to grow (microorganisms) in a laboratory. **culture shock,** *n.* feelings of disorientation caused by the transition from one culture or environment to another. **cultural,** *a.* **cultured,** *a.* in a state of intellectual development; grown artificially, as pearls or microorganisms. †**cultureless,** *a.* **culturist,** *n.* [F, from L *cultūra* (cp. *cultus,* CULT)]

cultus CULT.

culver, *n.* a wood-pigeon; a pigeon, a dove. **culver-house,** *n.* a dove-cot. **culver-keys,** *n.pl.* a bunch of ash-keys; a dialect name for the columbine, squill, cowslip and male orchis. [OE *culfre*]

culverin, *n.* a long cannon or hand-gun, so called because like a serpent. [OF *coulevrine,* fem. of *coulevrin,* adder-like (*couleuvre,* L *colubra,* snake)]

culvert, *n.* a drain or covered channel for water beneath a road, railway etc.; an underground channel for electric wires or cables. [etym. unknown]

cum, *prep.* combined with; together with. [L]

Cumae, *n.* an ancient city in Italy, on the coast about 16 km/10 miles W of Naples. It was the seat of the oracle of the Cumaean Sibyl.

Cuman, *n.* a member of a powerful Turki federation of the Middle Ages, which dominated the steppes in the 11th and 12th cents. and built an empire reaching from the Volga to the Danube.

Cumb., (*abbr.*) Cumberland; Cumbria.

cumber, *v.t.* to hamper, to clog; to hinder, to impede; to perplex; to embarrass. *n.* a hindrance; an impediment. **cumberless,** *a.* free from care or encumbrance. **cumbersome,** *a.* unwieldy, unmanageable; burdensome, troublesome. **cumbersomely,** *adv.* **cumbersomeness,** *n.* **cumbrance,** *n.* an encumbrance. **cumbrous,** *a.* **cumbrously,** *adv.* [OF *combrer,* to hinder, late L *cumbrus,* a heap (cp. G *Kummer,* trouble, prov. rubbish)]

Cumberland¹, *n.* former county of NW England, merged in 1974 with Cumbria.

Cumberland², *n.* **Ernest Augustus, Duke of Cumberland** (1771–1851), king of Hanover from 1837, the fifth son of George III of Britain. A high Tory and an opponent of all reforms, his attempts to suppress the constitution met with open resistance that had to be put down by force.

Cumberland³, *n.* **William Augustus, Duke of Cumberland** (1721–65), British general, who ended the Jacobite rising in Scotland with the Battle of Culloden (1746); his brutal repression of the Highlanders earned him the nickname of 'Butcher'. Third son of George II, he was created Duke of Cumberland (1726). He fought in the War of the Austrian Succession at Dettingen (1743) and Fontenoy (1745). In the Seven Years' War he surrendered with his army at Kloster-Zeven (1757).

Cumbria, *n.* county in NW England. **area** 6810 sq km/2629 sq miles. **towns** administrative headquarters Carlisle; Barrow, Kendal, Whitehaven, Workington, Penrith. **physical** Lake District National Park, including Scafell Pike 978 m/3210 ft, highest mountain in England; Helvellyn 950 m/3118 ft; Lake Windermere, the largest lake in England, 17 km/10.5 miles long, 1.6 km/1 mile wide. **products** the traditional coal, iron and steel of the coast towns has been replaced by newer industries including chemicals, plastics and electronics; in the N and E there is dairying, and West Cumberland Farmers is the country's largest agricultural cooperative. **population** (1987) 487,000.

Cumbrian, *a.* belonging to Cumberland or Cumbria. *n.* a native of Cumberland or Cumbria. **Cumbrian system, group,** *n.* the slate or greywacke system, remarkably developed in Cumbria. [L *Cumbria,* Celt. *Cymry,* Welsh, or *Cymru,* Wales]

cumene, *n.* an aromatic hydrocarbon obtained from cumin oil.

cumin, *n.* a plant of the parsley family, the Umbelliferae, with aromatic and carminative seeds; the name of a genus containing this, together with the caraway and other plants. **cumin-oil,** *n.* a volatile extract from the seeds of cumin. **cumic,** *a.* [OE *cymen,* L *cuminum,* Gr. *kuminon*]

cummer, kimmer, *n.* (*Sc.*) a godmother; (*Sc.*) a close woman friend; (*Sc.*) a gossip. [F *commère,* late L *commāter* (COM-, *mater,* mother)]

cummerbund, *n.* a waistband or sash, worn esp. by men with evening dress. [Hind. *kamarband* (Pers. *kamar,* the waist, *band,* a band)]

cummin, CUMIN.

Cumming, *n.* **Mansfield** (1859–1923), British naval officer, first head of the British Secret Intelligence Service. The head of the service has always since been known by the initial letter 'C'.

Cummings, *n.* **E(dward) E(stlin)** (1894–1962), US poet. His poems initially gained notoriety for their idiosyncratic punctuation and typography (he always wrote his name 'e.e. cummings', for example), but their lyric power has gradually been recognized.

cumquat, *n.* a small orange, fruit of *Citrus aurantium,* var. *japonica.* [Chin. *kin keu,* golden orange]

cumshaw, *n.* a present, a tip, a douceur. *v.t.* to make a present. [Chin. pidgin English]

cumulate, *v.t., v.i.* to accumulate. *a.,* heaped up, accumulated. **cumulation,** *n.* **cumulative,** *a.* increasing by additions; tending to accumulate; (*Law*) enforcing a point by accumulated proof; used of drugs which, after remaining quiescent, exert their influence suddenly. **cumulative preference shares,** shares on which arrears of interest are paid before ordinary shareholders are paid any on the current year. **cumulative**

voting, *n.* a method of voting by which the votes of the elector can be all given to a single candidate instead of being given singly to several candidates. **cumulatively,** *adv.* **cumulativeness,** *n.* [L *cumulātus,* p.p. of *cumulāre,* to heap up (*cumulus,* a heap)]
cumulo-, *comb. form* (*Meteor.*) cumulus.
cumulocirrostratus, *n.* a combination of cirrus and stratus with or into cumulus, a common form of rain-cloud.
cumulonimbus, *n.* a very thick, dark cumulus cloud, usu. a sign of thunder or hail.
cumulostratus, *n.* a mass of cumulus cloud with a horizontal base.
cumulus, *n.* (*pl.* **-li**) a heap, a pile; a round billowing mass of cloud, with a flattish base; the thickened portion of a cellular layer containing the ovum. **cumulous,** *a.* [L, see prec.]
Cunarder, *n.* one of a line of steamers between England and America, and other countries. [Sir Samuel *Cunard,* 1787–1865, founder of the line]
cunctation, *n.* cautious delaying; delay, dilatoriness. **cunctative**, *a.* **cunctator,** *n.* [L *cunctātio* (*cunctārī,* to delay)]
cuneate, *a.* wedge-shaped. †**cuneal,** *a.* **cuneatic**, *a.* **cuneiform**, *a.* wedge-shaped. **cuneiform writing,** *n.* writing in characters resembling wedges or arrowheads, used in Babylonian, Hittite, Ninevite and Persian inscriptions. [L *cuneus,* a wedge, -ATE]
Cunene, Kunene, *n.* river rising near Nova Lisboa in W central Angola. It flows S to the frontier with Namibia then W to the Atlantic. Length 250 km/156 miles.
Cunha, *n.* **Euclydes da** (1866–1909), Brazilian writer. His novel *Os Sertoes/Rebellion in the Backlands* (1902) describes the Brazilian *sertao* (backlands), and how a small group of rebels resisted government troops.
cunjevoi, *n.* an Australian plant grown for its edible rhizome; (*Austral.*) a sea-squirt. [Abor.]
cunnilingus, cunnilinctus, *n.* stimulation of the female genitals by the lips and tongue. [L *cunnus,* vulva, *lingere, linctum,* to lick]
cunning, *a.* knowing, skilful; ingenious; artful, crafty; (*N Am.*) amusingly interesting, piquant. *n.* skill, knowledge acquired by experience; artfulness, subtlety. **cunning-man, -woman,** *n.* one who pretends to tell fortunes, or how to recover stolen goods etc. **cunningly,** *adv.* **cunningness,** *n.* [pres.p. of ME *cunnen,* OE *cunnan,* to know]
Cunningham, *n.* **Merce** (1919–), US dancer and choreographer. Influenced by Martha Graham, with whose company he was soloist from 1939–45, he formed his own dance company and school in New York in 1953. His works include *The Seasons* (1947), *Antic Meet* (1958), *Squaregame* (1976), and *Arcade* (1985).
Cuno, *n.* **Wilhelm** (1876–1933), German industrialist and politician who was briefly chancellor of the Weimar Republic in 1923.
cunt, *n.* (*taboo*) the female genitalia; (*taboo*) a contemptible person; (*taboo*) a woman regarded as a sexual object. [ME *cunte*]
CUP, (*abbr.*) Cambridge University Press.
cup, *n.* a vessel to drink from, usu. small and with one handle; the liquor contained in it; an ornamental drinking-vessel, usu. of gold or silver, awarded as a prize or trophy; anything shaped like a cup, as an acorn, the socket for a bone; one of two cup-shaped supports for the breasts in a brassière; in golf, the hole or its metal lining; the lot one has to endure; a cupping-glass; (*Naut.*) the step of the capstan; the chalice used in the Holy Communion; an alcoholic mixed drink, usu. with wine or cider as a base; in cooking, a measure of capacity equal to 8 fl oz (0·23 l). *v.t.* (*past, p.p.* **cupped**) (*Med.*) to bleed by means of a cupping-glass; (*Golf*) to strike the ground when hitting the ball; †to supply with liquor; to hold as if in a cup. *v.i.* (*Bot.*) to form a cup or cups. **a bitter cup,** a hard fate; a heavy retribution. **cup-and-ball,** *n.* a child's game consisting in throwing up a ball and catching it in a socket. **cup-and-ball joint,** a ball-and-socket joint. **in one's cups,** intoxicated. **one's cup of tea,** one's preferred occupation, company etc. **cupbearer,** *n.* a person who serves wine, esp. in royal or noble households. **cupcake,** *n.* a small sponge cake baked in a paper or foil case. **cup final,** *n.* the final match of a competition to decide who wins a cup. **cup-gall,** *n.* a cup-like gall on oak leaves. **cup-lichen, -moss,** *n.* a lichen, *Scyphophorus pyxidatus,* with cup-shaped processes rising from the thallus. **cup tie,** *n.* a match in a knock-out competition for a cup. **cupful,** *n.* **cupper,** *n.* one who uses a cupping-glass. **cupping,** *n.* the act of bleeding with a cupping-glass. **cupping-glass,** *n.* a partially evacuated glass vessel placed over a (usu.) scarified place to excite the flow of blood. [OE *cuppe,* late L *cuppa,* a cup, L *cūpa,* a vat, a cask]
cupboard, *n.* †a shelf on which cups were placed; a sideboard; an enclosed case with shelves to receive plates, dishes, food etc.; a wardrobe. †*v.t.* to keep in or as in a cupboard; to hoard. **cupboard-love,** *n.* greedy or self-interested love.
cupel, *n.* a small shallow vessel used in assaying precious metals. *v.t.* (*past, p.p.* **cupelled**) to assay in a cupel. **cupellation,** *n.* [late L *cūpella,* dim. of *cūpa,* a cask]
Cupid, *n.* the Roman god of Love; a picture or statue of Cupid; a beautiful boy. [L *Cupīdo* (*cupere,* to desire)]
cupidity, *n.* an inordinate desire to possess; covetousness, avarice. [F *cupidité,* L *cupiditās -tātem,* from *cupidus,* desirous, as prec.]
cupola, *n.* a little dome; a lantern or small apartment on the summit of a dome; a spherical covering to a building, or any part of it; a cupola furnace; a revolving dome or turret on a warship; (*Biol.*) a dome-like organ or part, esp. the extremity of the canal of the cochlea. **cupola furnace,** *n.* a furnace for melting metals. [It., from L *cūpula,* CUPEL]
cuppa, cupper[1], *n.* (*coll.*) a cup of tea.
cupper[2]**, cupping** CUP.
cupreous, *a.* of, like or composed of copper. **cupric,** *a.* having bivalent copper in its composition. **cupriferous,** *a.* copper-bearing. **cuprite,** *n.* red oxide of copper, a mineral with cubic crystal structure. **cuproid,** *a.* resembling copper. *n.* a crystal of the tetrahedral type, with twelve equal angles. **cupro-nickel,** *n.* an alloy of copper and nickel. **cuprous,** *a.* having monovalent copper in its composition. [L *cupreus,* copper]
Cupressus, *n.* a genus of conifers, containing the cypress. [L]
cupule, *n.* an inflorescence consisting of a cup, as in the oak or hazel; (*Zool.*) a cup-like organ. **cupular, -late**, *a.* **cupuliferous**, *a.* [L, CUPOLA]
cur, *n.* a mongrel, worthless dog; an ill-conditioned, surly fellow. **currish,** *a.* **currishly,** *adv.* **currishness,** *n.* [imit. (cp. Icel. *kurra,* to murmur, grumble, LG *kurren,* to snarl)]
curable CURE[1].
Curaçao, *n.* an island in the West Indies, one of the Netherlands Antilles; area 444 sq km/171 sq miles; population (1981) 147,000. The principal industry, dating from 1918, is the refining of Venezuelan petroleum. Curaçao was colonized by Spain (1527), annexed by the Dutch West India Company in 1634, and gave its name from 1924 to the group of islands renamed Netherlands Antilles in 1948. Its capital is the port of Willemstad.
curaçao, *n.* a liqueur flavoured with bitter orange peel, sugar and cinnamon, orig. from Curaçao.
curacy CURATE.
curare, *n.* the dried extract of the vine *Strychnos toxifera* used by the Indians of S America for poisoning arrows, and employed in physiological investigations as a muscle relaxant; it paralyses the motor nerves and ultimately causes death by suffocation. **curarine,** *n.* an alkaloid from curare. **curarize, -ise**, *v.t.* [Sp. and Port., from Carib *kurari*]
curassow, *n.* name of a tribe of turkey-like birds found in S and Central America. [CURAÇAO]

curate, *n.* one with a cure of souls; a clergyman of the Church of England who assists the incumbent. **perpetual curate** PERPETUAL. **curate's egg,** *n.* something of which (optimistically) parts are excellent. **curacy,** *n.* the office of a curate; the benefice of a perpetual curate. [med. L *cūrātus* (L *cūra,* a care, charge, cure)]

curative, *a.* tending to cure. *n.* anything that tends to cure. [F *curatif;* see CURE]

curator, *n.* one who has charge of a library, museum or similar establishment; (*Sc. Law*), a trustee for the carrying out of any purpose, a guardian; a member of a governing body in some British and foreign universities. **curatorial**, *a.* **curatorship,** *n.* **curatrix**, *n. fem.* [L, from *cūrāre,* to CURE]

curb[1], *n.* a chain or strap passing behind the jaw of a horse in a curb-bit; a kerb-stone; an injury to the hock-joint of a horse; a check, a restraint. *v.t.* to put a curb on; to restrain, to keep in check. **curb-bit,** *n.* a stiff bit forming a leverage upon the jaws of a horse. **curb-roof,** *n.* a mansard roof. **curbless,** *a.* without any curb or restraint. **curby,** *a.* [F *courbe,* from L *curvus,* bent, curved]

†**curb**[2], *v.i.* to bow, to cringe. [F *courber,* to bend]

curb[3], (*N Am.*) KERB.

curch, *n.* (*Sc.*) a piece of linen formerly worn by women; (*Sc.*) a kerchief. [cp. KERCHIEF]

curculio, *n.* a weevil, esp. of the genus *Curculio*. [L]

curcuma, *n.* a plant of a genus (*Curcuma*) of tuberous plants of the ginger family; turmeric, which is obtained from its root, and used as an ingredient in curry-powder, and for chemical, medicinal and other purposes. [Arab. *kurkum,* saffron (cp. CROCUS)]

curd, *n.* the coagulated part of milk, used to make cheese; the coagulated part of any liquid; the fatty matter found in the flesh of boiled salmon. *v.t.* to curdle. *v.i.* to congeal. **curd-breaker,** *n.* an instrument used to break the cheese-curd into small pieces. **curd-cutter, -mill,** *n.* an instrument with knives to cut the curd. **curd-soap,** *n.* a white soap manufactured of tallow and soda. **curdy,** *a.* full of curds; curdled, congealed. [perh. from OE stem *crud-, crūdan,* to CROWD[1]]

curdle, *v.t.* to break into curds; to coagulate; to congeal. *v.i.* to become curdled. **to curdle the blood,** to terrify, as with a ghost-story or the like.

cure[1], *n.* the act of healing or curing; a remedy; anything which acts as a remedy or restorative; the state of being cured or healed; the care or spiritual charge of souls. *v.t.* to heal, to restore to health, to make sound or whole; to preserve or pickle; to correct a habit or practice. *v.i.* to effect a cure; to be cured or healed. **cure of souls,** a benefice to which parochial duties are annexed. †**to do no cure,** to take no care. **cure-all,** *n.* a panacea, a universal remedy; a name for the plant *Geum rivale,* water avens. **curable,** *a.* **curability**, *n.* **cureless,** *a.* without cure or remedy. **curer,** *n.* one who cures or heals; one who prepares preserved food (*often in comb.*, as *fish-curer*). **curing,** *n.* the act of curing or healing; the act or process of preparing articles of food for preservation. **curing-house,** *n.* a building in which sugar is drained and dried; a house in which articles of food are cured. [OF, from L *cūra,* care, whence *cūrāre,* to take care of]

cure[2], *n.* (*coll.*) an odd or funny person, an eccentric. [perh. abbrev. of CURIOUS]

curé, *n.* a parish priest, a French rector or vicar. [F]

curette, *n.* an instrument used for scraping a body cavity. *v.t.* to scrape or clean with a curette. **curettage**, *n.* [F]

curfew, *n.* a regulation in the Middle Ages to extinguish fires at a stated hour; the bell announcing or the hour for this; a military or civil regulation to be within doors between stated hours. **curfew-bell,** *n.* the bell announcing curfew; a bell rung at a stated hour in the evening, still customary in certain places in France and the US. **curfew-time,** *n.* [A-F *coeverfu,* OF *couvrefeu* (*couvrir,* to COVER, *feu,* L *focus,* fire)]

curia, *n.* (*pl.* **curiae**) one of the ten subdivisions of the three Roman tribes, as instituted by Romulus; the building in which they met; the Roman senate-house; the senate of an ancient Italian town; a mediaeval court of justice; the Roman See, including Pope, cardinals etc. in their temporal capacity. **curial,** *a.* pertaining to a curia, esp. the Papal curia. **curialism,** *n.* [L]

Curia Romana, *n.* the judicial and administrative bodies through which the pope carries on the government of the Roman Catholic Church. It includes certain tribunals; the chancellery, which issues papal bulls; various offices including that of the cardinal secretary of state; and the Congregations, or councils of cardinals, each with a particular department of work.

Curie, *n.* **Marie** (born **Sklodovska**) (1867–1934), Polish scientist, who investigated radioactivity, and with her husband Pierre (1859–1906) discovered radium.

curie, *n.* the standard unit of radioactivity, $3{\cdot}7 \times 10^{10}$ disintegrations per second. [Pierre *Curie,* 1859–1906, and MARIE CURIE]

Curie temperature, *n.* the temperature above which a magnetic material cannot be strongly magnetized. Above the Curie temperature, the energy of the atoms is too great for them to join together to form the small areas of magnetized material, or domains, which combine to produce the strength of the overall magnetization.

curio, *n.* (*pl.* **curios**) a curiosity, esp. a curious piece of art; a bit of bric-a-brac. [short for CURIOSITY]

curiosa, *n.pl.* unusual (collectable) objects; erotic or pornographic books. [L, neut. pl. of *cūriōsus* (see foll.)]

curious, *a.* inquisitive, desirous to know; given to research; extraordinary, surprising, odd; †careful; †anxious, solicitous; †fastidious. **curiosity**, *n.* a desire to know; inquisitiveness; a rarity, an object of curiosity; (*coll.*) a strange personage. **curiously,** *adv.* **curiousness,** *n.* [OF *curios,* L *cūriōsus* (*cūra,* care)]

curium, *n.* an artificially-produced transuranic metallic element, at.no.96; chem. symbol Cm. [see CURIE]

curl, *n.* a ringlet or twisted lock of hair; anything coiled, twisted or spiral; the state of being curled; a contemptuous curving of the lip; a disease in potatoes of which curled shoots and leaves are a symptom. *v.t.* to twine; to twist into curls; to dress with ringlets; to curve up (the lip) in contempt. *v.i.* to twist, to curve up; to rise in curves or undulations; to play at the game of curling. **out of curl,** limp, out of condition. **to curl up,** to go into a curled position; (*coll.*) to be embarrassed or disgusted. **to make someone's hair curl,** to horrify or scandalize someone. **curl-cloud,** *n.* cirrus. **curl-paper,** *n.* paper round which hair is wound to form a curl. †**curled pate,** *a.* having curly hair. **curler,** *n.* one who or that which curls; a device for curling the hair; one who plays at curling. **curling,** *n.* the act of the verb TO CURL; a game on the ice in which contending parties slide smooth stones towards a mark. **curling-stone,** *n.* the stone used in the game. **curling-irons, -tongs,** *n.pl.* an instrument for curling the hair. **curlingly,** *adv.* in curls or waves. **curly,** *a.* having curls; wavy, undulated; (*Bot.*) having curled or wavy margins. **curliness,** *n.* [earlier *crul, crulle* (cp. Dut. *krul,* G *Krolle*)]

curlew, *n.* a migratory wading bird, esp. the European *Numenius arquatus*. [OF *courlieus* (imit. of the cry)]

curlicue, *n.* a fantastic curl; a flourish in writing. [CURLY, CUE (from either F *queue,* a tail, or the letter Q)]

curmudgeon, *n.* a miserly or churlish person. **curmudgeonly,** *adv.* [etym. unknown]

curmurring, *n.* (*Sc.*) a low rumbling, esp. a sound in the bowels from flatulence. [verbal noun of *curmur* (imit.), to make a low purring sound]

curr, *v.i.* to make a low murmuring or whirring sound like that made by an owl. *n.* a curring sound. [imit.]

currach, curragh, *n.* a skiff made of wickerwork and hides, a coracle. [Ir. *curach*]

Curragh, The, *n.* a horse-racing course in County Kildare where all five Irish Classic races are run. At one time used for hurdle races, it is now used for flat racing only.

Curragh 'Mutiny', *n.* a demand Mar. 1914 by the British Gen. Hubert Gough and his officers, stationed at Curragh, Ireland, that they should not be asked to take part in forcing Protestant Ulster to participate in Home Rule. They were subsequently allowed to return to duty, and after World War I the solution of partition was adopted.

currant, *n.* the dried fruit of a dwarf seedless grape from the Levant; the fruit of shrubs of the genus *Ribes,* containing the black, red and white currants. [formerly *raisins of corauns,* F *raisins de Corinthe* (L *Corinthus,* Gr. *Korinthos,* Corinth)]

currawong, *n.* an Australian crowlike songbird of the genus *Strepera.* [Abor.]

currency, *n.* a continual passing from hand to hand, as of money; the circulating monetary medium of a country, whether in coin or paper; the period during which anything is current; the state of being current; †running, rapid motion. **currency note,** *n.* paper money of the value of 10 shillings or £1 (issued from 1914 to 1928). [L *currere,* to run]

current, *a.* passing at the present time; belonging to the present week, month, year; in circulation, as money; generally received or acknowledged; in general circulation among the public; †running, flowing, fluent. *n.* a flowing stream, a body of water, air etc., moving in a certain direction; general drift or tendency; electrical activity regarded as the rate of flow of electrical charge along a conductor; the fall or slope of a platform or roof to carry off the water. **current account,** *n.* a bank account which usu. does not pay interest and on which one may draw cheques. **currentless,** *a.* **currently,** *adv.* with a constant progressive motion; generally; at present. [OF *curant,* pres.p. of *courre,* from L *currere,* to run (as prec.)]

curricle, *n.* a two-wheeled chaise for a pair of horses. †*v.i.* to drive in a curricle. [from foll.]

curriculum, *n.* (*pl.* **-la, -lums**) a fixed course of study at a school etc. **curriculum vitae,** *n.* a brief outline of one's education, previous employment, and other achievements. **curricular,** *a.* [L, a race-course, dim. from *currere,* to run]

currier, *n.* one who curries, dresses and colours leather after it has been tanned. **curriery,** *n.* the trade of a currier; the place where the trade is carried on. [OF *corier,* L *coriārius* (*corium,* hide, leather)]

currish etc. CUR.

curry[1], *v.i.* to dress a horse with a comb; to dress leather; to thrash; to flatter. *v.i.* to use flattery. **to curry favour,** to seek favour by officiousness or flattery. **curry-comb,** *n.* a comb used for grooming horses. [OF *correier, conreder* (CON-, *reder,* cp. ARRAY)]

curry[2], *n.* a highly-spiced Indian dish of stewed meat, fish etc., seasoned with turmeric etc.; a hash or stew flavoured with curry-powder. *v.t.* to season or dress with curry. **curry-paste, -powder,** *n.* a mixture of ginger, turmeric and other strong spices used in curries etc. [Tamil *kari*]

curse, *v.t.* to invoke harm or evil upon; to blast, to injure, vex or torment; to excommunicate. *v.i.* to swear, to utter imprecations. *n.* a solemn invocation of divine vengeance (upon); a sentence of divine vengeance; an oath; an imprecation (upon); the evil imprecated; anything which causes evil, trouble or great vexation; a sentence of excommunication; (*coll.*) menstruation (with *the*). **don't care a curse,** regard it as worthless or as too contemptible to trouble about. **cursed, curst,** *a.* execrable, accursed, deserving of a curse; blasted by a curse, execrated; vexatious, troublesome; †shrewish. **cursedly,** *adv.* **cursedness,** *n.* the state of being under a curse; †shrewishness. **curser,** *n.* one who curses; a blasphemer. [OE *cursian;* etym. unknown]

†**cursitor,** *n.* a clerk of Chancery, whose office was to make out original writs; †a courier; a vagrant. [med. L (cp. *cursitāre,* freq. of *currere,* to run)]

cursive, *a.* written in a running hand. *n.* cursive writing; manuscript written in a running hand, as opp. to uncial. [late L *cursīvus* (from *cursus,* p.p. of *currere,* to run)]

cursor, *n.* the moving part of a measuring instrument, e.g. the slide with the reference line in a slide rule; on a VDU screen, a movable point of light showing the position of the next action, e.g. the beginning of an addition or correction. [L, a runner; see prec.]

cursores, *n.pl.* an order of birds with rudimentary wings and strong feet well adapted for running, containing the ostrich, the emu, cassowary and apteryx. **cursorial,** *a.* [L, pl. of *cursor,* as prec.]

cursory, *a.* hasty, superficial, careless. **cursorily,** *adv.* **cursoriness,** *n.* [L *cursōrius,* as prec.]

curst CURSE.

curt, *a.* short, concise, abrupt; esp. rudely terse and abrupt. †**curt-hose,** *n.* short hose or short boot, a nickname of Robert, eldest son of William the Conqueror. **curtly,** *adv.* **curtness,** *n.* [L *curtus,* docked]

curtail, *v.t.* to shorten; to cut off the end or tail of; to lessen; to reduce. **curtailer,** *n.* **curtailment,** *n.* [CURTAL]

curtail-step, *n.* the bottom step of a flight of stairs, finished at its outer extremity in a scroll. [connection with CURTAIL doubtful]

curtain, *n.* a cloth hanging beside a window or door, or round a bed, which can be drawn across at pleasure; a screen, a cover, a protection; the screen in a theatre separating the stage from the spectators; the end of a scene or play, marked by the closing of the curtains; a curtain wall; a partition or cover of various kinds; a shifting plate in a lock; (*pl.*) (*sl.*) death, the end. *v.t.* to enclose with or as with curtains; to furnish or decorate with curtains. **curtain call,** *n.* applause for an actor which calls for a reappearance before the curtain falls. **curtain fire,** *n.* a form of artillery barrage. **curtain-lecture,** *n.* a reproof or lecture from a wife to a husband after they have retired. **curtain-pole,** *n.* a pole for hanging curtains on. **curtain-raiser,** *n.* a short piece given before the main play; any short preliminary event. **curtain-rings,** *n.pl.* rings running along the curtain-pole, by which the curtains can be drawn backwards or forwards. **curtain wall,** *n.* a wall that is not load-bearing; a wall between two bastions. **curtain-less,** *a.* **curtainless,** *a.* [OF *cortine,* L *cortīna* (etym. doubtful)]

†**curtal,** *n.* a horse with a cropped tail; anything docked or cut short. *a.* having a cropped tail; concise; niggardly. **curtal friar,** *n.* a friar with a short frock. [OF *cortald, courtault* (*court,* short, L *curtus,* CURT; with suf. *-ald, -ault,* from Teut.)]

†**curtal-ax, -axe,** *n.* a heavy sort of cutting sword. [corr. of CUTLASS]

curtana, *n.* the unpointed Sword of Mercy carried before the English sovereigns at their coronation. [Ang.-Lat. *curtana* (prob. *curtana spada,* curtailed sword), cp. CURTAL]

curtilage, *n.* a piece of ground lying near and belonging to a dwelling-house and included within the same fence. [OF *courtillage,* dim. of *courtil,* a little court (*cort,* a COURT)]

Curtin, *n.* **John** (1885–1945), Australian Labour politician, prime minister and minister of defence (1941–45). He was elected leader of the Labour Party 1935. As prime minister, he organized the mobilization of Australia's resources to meet the danger of Japanese invasion during World War II.

Curtis, *n.* **Tony** (stage name of Bernard Schwartz) (1925–), US actor, who starred in the 1950s and 1960s in such films as *The Vikings* (1959) and *Some Like it Hot* (1959), with Jack Lemmon and Marilyn Monroe.

Curtiz, *n.* **Michael (Mihaly Kersesz)** (1888–1962), Hungarian-born film director who worked in Austria, Germany and France before moving to the US where he made several Errol Flynn films and *Casablanca* (1942).

curtsy, -sey, *n.* a bow; an act of respect or salutation, performed by women by slightly bending the body and knees at the same time. *v.i.* to make a curtsy. [COURTESY]

curule, *a.* having the right to a curule chair; of high civic dignity. **curule chair,** *n.* the chair of honour of the old Roman kings, and of the higher magistrates of senatorial rank under the republic, originally ornamented with ivory, and in shape like a camp-stool with crooked legs. [L *curūlis* (perh. from *currus,* a chariot)]

curvaceous, *a.* (*coll.*) of a woman's body, generously curved. [CURVE, -ACEOUS]

curvate, *a.* curved, bent. **curvative,** *a.* (*Bot.*) having the margins slightly curved. **curvature,** *n.* deflection from a straight line; a curved form; (*Geom.*) the continual bending of a line from a rectilinear direction. [L *curvātus,* p.p. of *curvāre* (from foll.)]

curve, *n.* a bending without angles; that which is bent; a flexure; a line of which no three consecutive points are in a straight line. *v.t.* to cause to bend without angles. *v.i.* to form or be formed into a curve. [L *curvus,* bent]

curvet, *n.* a particular leap of a horse raising the forelegs at once, and, as the forelegs are falling, raising the hindlegs, so that all four are off the ground at once. *v.i.* to make a curvet; to frolic, to frisk. [It. *corvetta,* dim. of *corvo,* a curve, as prec.]

curvi-, *comb. form* curved. **curvicaudate,** *a.* having the tail curved. **curvicostate,** *a.* (*Bot.*) marked with small bent ribs. **curvifoliate,** *a.* having revolute leaves. **curviform,** *a.* of a curved form. **curvilinear,** *a.* bounded by curved lines; consisting of curved lines. **curvilinearity,** *n.* **curvilinearly,** *adv.* **curvirostral,** *a.* having a curved beak. [L *curvus,* bent]

Curwen, *n.* **John** (1816–80), English musician. Around 1840 he established the **tonic sol-fa** system of music notation (originated in the 11th cent. by Guido d'Arezzo) in which the notes of a scale are named by syllables (doh, ray, me, fah, soh, lah, te, with the key indicated) to simplify singing by sight.

Curzon, *n.* **George Nathaniel, 1st Marquess Curzon of Kedleston** (1859–1925), British Conservative politician. Viceroy of India from 1899, he resigned in 1905 following a controversy with Kitchener. He was foreign secretary (1919–22).

Curzon Line, *n.* Polish-Russian frontier proposed after World War I by the territorial commission of the Versailles conference (1919), based on the eastward limit of areas with a predominantly Polish population. It acquired its name after Lord Curzon suggested in 1920 that the Poles, who had invaded Russia, should retire to this line pending a Russo-Polish peace conference. The frontier established in 1945 in general follows the Curzon Line.

Cusack, *n.* **Cyril** (1910–), Irish actor who joined the Abbey Theatre, Dublin, 1932 and appeared in many of its productions, including Synge's *The Playboy of the Western World.* In Paris he won an award for his solo performance in Beckett's *Krapp's Last Tape.* In the UK he has played many roles as a member of the Royal Shakespeare Company and the National Theatre Company.

cuscus¹, *n.* the fibrous, aromatic root of an Indian grass, used for making fans, baskets etc. [Hind. *khas khas*]

cuscus², *n.* any of several tree-dwelling phalangers of N Australia, New Guinea etc. [native name in New Guinea]

cusec, cu.-sec., *n.* unit of rate of flow of water, 1 cu. ft. (0·0283 m^3) per second. [abbr. of *cu*bic feet per *sec*ond]

cushat, *n.* (*Sc., North.*) the woodpigeon or ringdove. [OE *cūsceote*]

Cushing¹, *n.* **Harvey Williams** (1869–1939), US neurologist who pioneered neurosurgery. He developed a range of techniques for the surgical treatment of brain tumours, and also studied the link between the pituitary gland and conditions such as dwarfism.

Cushing², *n.* **Peter** (1913–), British actor who specialized in horror roles in films made at Hammer studios 1957-73, including *Dracula* (1958); *Cash on Demand* (1963); *Frankenstein Must be Destroyed* (1969). Other films include *Star Wars* (1977) and *Top Secret* (1984).

Cushing's syndrome, *n.* a condition in which the body chemistry is upset by excessive production of steroid hormones from the adrenal cortex.

cushion, *n.* a kind of pillow or pad for sitting, kneeling or leaning on, stuffed with feathers, wool, hair or other soft material; anything padded, as the lining at the side of a billiard-table which causes the balls to rebound; a flat leather bag filled with sand, used by engravers to support the plate or block; a pad on which gilders and binders spread gold-leaf; a cushion-like organ, part or growth; the elastic body of steam left in the cylinder of a steam engine and acting as a buffer to the piston. *v.t.* to seat or support on a cushion; to protect or pad with cushions; to furnish with cushions; to place or leave (a billiard ball) close up to the cushion; to suppress or quietly ignore. **lady's cushion** LADY. **pin-cushion** PIN. **sea cushion** SEA. **cushion-capital,** *n.* (*Arch.*) a capital shaped like a cushion pressed down by a weight. **cushion-tyre,** *n.* a cycle tyre made of rubber stuffed with rubber shreds. **cushiony,** *a.* [F *coussin,* prob. OF *coissin* (prob. from L *coxa,* hip)]

cushy, *a.* (*sl.*) soft, easy, comfortable; well paid and little to do. **cushily,** *adv.* [Hind. *khushi,* pleasant; also CUSHIONY]

cusp, *n.* a point, an apex, a summit; (*Arch.*) a Gothic ornament consisting of a projecting point formed by the meeting of curves; the point in a curve at which its two branches have a common tangent; the pointed end of a leaf or other part; a projection on a molar tooth; either of the two points of a crescent moon; (*Astrol.*) a division between signs of the zodiac. **cusped,** *a.* **cuspid,** *a.* **cuspidal,** *a.* (*Geom.*) ending in a point. **cuspidate, -dated,** *a.* (*Nat. Hist.*) furnished with small eminences; (*Bot.*) tapering to a rigid point; abruptly acuminate. **cuspidate teeth,** *n.pl.* canine teeth. [L *cuspis -idem,* a point]

cuspidor, *n.* a spittoon. [Port., a spitter, from *cuspir,* to spit, L *conspuere,* CONSPUE]

cuss, *n.* (*coll.*) a curse; (*coll.*) a worthless fellow. *v.t.* (*coll.*) to curse. **cussedness,** *n.* perverseness; obstinacy, resolution. [CURSE]

custard, *n.* a composition of milk and eggs, sweetened and flavoured; a sweet sauce made of milk, sugar and custard powder; orig., an open pie. **custard-apple,** *n.* a W Indian fruit, *Anona reticulata,* with a soft pulp. †**custard-coffin,** *n.* the raised crust of a pie. **custard pie,** *n.* an open pie filled with custard, thrown in slapstick comedy. **custard powder,** *n.* a composition of cornflour, colouring and flavouring, used in the making of custard. [prob. from ME *crustade,* a pie with crust, OF *croustade,* L *crustāta,* fem. p.p. of *crustāre* (see CRUST)]

Custer, *n.* **George A(rmstrong)** (1839–76), US Civil War general. He campaigned against the Sioux from 1874, and was killed with a detachment of his troops by the forces of Sioux chief Sitting Bull in the Battle of Little Big Horn, Montana, known as Custer's Last Stand, 25 June 1876.

custodian, *n.* one who has the custody or guardianship of anything. **custodial,** *a.* pertaining to custody or guardianship. *n.* (*Hist.*) a portable shrine or relic-case.

custody, *n.* guardianship, security; imprisonment, confinement. **to take into custody,** to arrest. [L *custōdia* (*custos -todem,* a guardian)]

custom, *n.* a habitual use or practice; established usage; familiarity, use; buying of goods, business; frequenting a shop to purchase; (*pl.*) custom-duties; (*Law*) long established practice constituting common law. *a.* (*chiefly N Am.*) made to a customer's specifications. †*v.t.* to accustom; to give custom to; to pay duty on. †*v.i.* to be accustomed. **custom-duties,** *n.pl.* duties imposed on goods imported or exported. **custom(s)-house,** *n.* the office where vessels enter and clear, and where custom-duties are paid. **custom-made, -built,** *a.* (*chiefly N Am.*) made to measure, custom. †**customable,** *a.* customary; liable to duty. **customed,** *a.* usual, accustomed. **customize, -ise,** *v.t.* to make to a customer's specifications. [OF *costume,* L *consuētūdo -dinem,* custom, from *consuētus,* p.p. of *consuescere* (CON-, *suescere,* inceptive of *suēre,* to be accustomed)]

customary, *a.* habitual, usual, wonted; (*Law*) holding or held by custom, liable under custom. *n.* a written or printed record of customs. **customarily,** *adv.* **customariness,** *n.*

customer, *n.* one who deals regularly at a particular shop; a purchaser; (*coll.*) a person one has to do with, a fellow.

Customs and Excise, a government department responsible for taxes levied on certain imports, for example, tobacco, wine and spirits, perfumery, and jewellery. Excise duties are levied on certain goods produced (such as beer) and include VAT, or on licences to carry on certain trades (such as sale of wines and spirits) or other activities (theatrical entertainments, betting, and so on) within a country.

custos, *n.* a keeper, a custodian. **custos rotulorum,** *n.* the chief civil officer or Lord Lieutenant of a county and keeper of its records. [L]

cut[1], *v.t.* (*past, p.p.* **cut**) to penetrate or wound with a sharp instrument; to divide or separate with a sharp-edged instrument; to sever, to detach, to hew, to fell, to mow or reap; to carve, to trim or clip; to form by cutting; to reduce by cutting; to mutilate or shorten (a play, article or book); to edit (a film); to intersect, to cross; to divide (as a pack of cards); to hit (a cricket ball) with a downward stroke and make it glance to one side; to wound deeply; to leave, to give up; to renounce the acquaintance of; to reduce as low as possible; (*sl.*) to dilute (a drink or drug); to record e.g. a song on (a gramophone record). *v.i.* to make a wound or incision with or as with a sharp-edged instrument; to have a good edge; to come through the gums; to divide a pack of cards; (*sl.*) to move away quickly, to run; (*Med.*) to perform an operation by cutting, esp. in lithotomy; to intersect; to be cut; to be able to be cut or divided; to change abruptly from one scene to another in a film. *int.* ordering movie cameras to stop. **cut-and-cover,** *n.* a tunnel made by excavating an open cutting and covering it in. **cut and dry, dried,** prepared for use; ready-made; unoriginal, trite. †**cut and long tail,** all kinds of dogs; hence, everybody. **(not) cut out for,** (not) naturally fitted for. **to cut a caper,** to frisk about. **to cut across,** to pass by a shorter course so as to cut off an angle; to go contrary to (usual procedure etc.). **to cut a dash,** to make a show or display. **to cut a figure, a flourish,** etc., to look, appear or perform (usu. qualified by an adjective, and perhaps derived from the practice of cutting figures on ice in skating). **to cut and come again,** to help oneself and take more if one will. **to cut and run,** to depart rapidly. **to cut away,** to detach by cutting; to reduce by cutting. **to cut back,** to prune; to reduce. **to cut both ways,** to have both good and bad consequences. **to cut corners,** to take short cuts. **to cut dead,** to refuse to acknowledge. **to cut down,** to fell; to compress, to reduce. **to cut in,** to drive in front of another person's car so as to affect his driving; to take a lady away from her dancing partner; to interrupt, to intrude; (*coll.*) to allow to have a share in. **to cut it fine,** to reduce to the minimum; to take a risk by allowing little margin. **to cut it out,** to desist from doing something annoying. **to cut no ice** ICE. **to cut off,** to remove by cutting, to eradicate; to intercept; to prevent from access; to sever; to discontinue; to bring to an untimely end, to kill, to disinherit. **to cut one's losses,** to write off as lost, to abandon a speculation. **to cut one's stick,** (*coll.*) to go away; to run; to escape. **to cut one's teeth,** to have the teeth come through the gums. **to cut out,** to shape by cutting; to remove or separate by cutting; to excel, to outdo; to supplant; to cease doing, taking or indulging in something unpleasant or harmful; to cease operating suddenly and unexpectedly or by the automatic intervention of a cut-out device; (*Naut.*) to enter a harbour and seize and carry off (as a ship) by sudden attack; to relinquish a game as the result of cutting the cards. **to cut short,** to hinder by interruption; to abridge. **to cut to pieces,** to exterminate, to massacre. **to cut under,** to undersell. **to cut up,** to cut in pieces; to criticize severely; to distress deeply. **to cut up rough,** (*sl.*) to become quarrelsome or savage. **to cut up well,** (*coll.*) to leave plenty of money. **cutaway,** *a.* having the skirts rounded off; denoting a drawing of an engine etc. in which part of the casing is omitted to show the workings. *n.* a coat with the skirts rounded off. **cutback,** *n.* an instance of cutting back; a reduction. **cut-glass,** *n.* flint glass in which a pattern is formed by cutting or grinding. **cut-grass,** *n. Leersia oryzoides,* the leaves of which are so rough as to cut the hands. **cut-line,** *n.* a caption. **cut-off,** *n.* a passage cut by a river, affording a new channel; a mode of using steam by which it is admitted to the cylinder only during a portion of the piston-stroke; a valve to stop discharge. **cut-off road,** *n.* (*N Am.*) a by-pass. **cut-out,** *n.* a device for disconnecting the exhaust from the silencer in a racing car, to gain extra power; (*Motor.*) a device which automatically disconnects the battery from the dynamo; a device for automatic severance of an electric circuit in case the tension becomes too high for the wiring. *n.* a switch for shutting off a light or a group of lights from an electric circuit. **cut-price,** *a.* at the lowest price possible; at a reduced price. **cutpurse,** *n.* one who stole purses by cutting them from the girdle to which they were fastened; a highwayman, a thief. **cut-rate** CUT-PRICE. **cut-throat,** *n.* a murderer, an assassin. *a.* murderous, barbarous; of competition etc., fierce, merciless. **cutwater,** *n.* (*Naut.*) the fore-part of a ship's prow which cuts the water. **cutworm,** *n.* a caterpillar, esp. (*N Am.*) the larva of the genus of moths *Agrotis,* which cuts off plants near the roots. **cutter,** *n.* one who or that which cuts; one who cuts out men's clothes to measure; a cutting tool; (*Cinema*) a film editor; (*N Am.*) a light sledge; a soft brick adapted to be rubbed down for ornamental work or arching; †a cut-throat; (*Naut.*) a man-of-war's boat smaller than a barge, with from four to eight oars; a one-masted vessel with fore-and-aft sails. **cutter-bar,** *n.* the bar of a cutting-machine in which the cutters are fixed. **cutting,** *a.* dividing by a sharp-edged instrument; sharp-edged; wounding the feelings deeply; sarcastic, biting. *n.* the action of the verb TO CUT; underselling, keen competition by means of reduced prices; a piece cut off or out (of a newspaper etc.); (*Hort.*) a slip; an excavation for a road, railway or canal; lithotomy; the selection of those portions of a film that are finally to be shown. **cutting-bench,** *n.* the table on which a cutter assembles and edits a film. **cuttingly,** *adv.* in a cutting manner. [origin doubtful]

cut[2], *n.* the action of cutting; a stroke or blow with a sharp-edged instrument; an opening, gash or wound made by cutting; anything done or said that hurts the feelings; the omission of a part of a play; a slit, a channel, a groove, a trench; a part cut off; a gelding; a stroke with a whip; a particular stroke in various games with balls; the act of dividing a pack of cards; the shape in which a thing is cut, style; the act of ignoring a former acquaintance; †a dupe; a degree (from count being formerly kept by notches); an engraved wood block or an electrotype therefrom; an impression from such block or electrotype; the place where one strip of film ends in a picture and another begins. *a.* subjected to the act or process of cutting; severed; shaped by cutting; castrated. **a cut above,** (*fig.*) superior to. **cut and thrust,** cutting and thrusting; a hand-to-hand struggle. **short cut,** a near way; readiest means to an end.

cutaneous, *a.* belonging to or affecting the skin. [L *cutāneus,* from *cutis,* skin]

cutch, *n.* catechu, used in tanning. [Malay *cachu*]

cute, *a.* cunning, sharp, clever; (*chiefly N Am.*) piquant, delightful, attractive, amusing; pretty. **cutely,** *adv.* **cuteness,** *n.* **cutie**, *n.* (*sl.*) a bright, attractive girl. [ACUTE]

Cuthbert, St, *n.* (d. 687), Christian saint. He travelled widely as a missionary, became prior of Lindisfarne

(664), and retired (676) to Farne Island. In 684 he became bishop of Hexham and later of Lindisfarne. Feast day 20 Mar.

Cuthbert's duck, *n.* the eider duck, so called because it breeds on the Farne Islands, and is connected with the legend of St Cuthbert, the apostle of Northumbria. [St *Cuthbert*]

cuticle, *n.* the epidermis or scarf-skin; the outer layer of the integument in the lower animals; the thin external covering of the bark of a plant. **cuticular,** *a.* **cuticularize, -ise,** *v.t.* [L *cutīcula,* dim. of *cutis,* skin]

cutikin, *n.* (*Sc.*) a long gaiter, a spatterdash. [obs. *coot,* the ankle-joint]

cutin, *n.* a form of cellulose existing in the cuticle of plants.

cutis, *n.* the true skin beneath the epidermis; the peridium of certain fungi. [CUTICLE]

cutlass, *n.* (*Hist.*) a broad curved sword, esp. that used by sailors. [F *coutelas,* augm. of OF *coutel* (F *couteau*), a knife, L *cultellum,* acc. of *cultellus,* COULTER]

cutler, *n.* one who makes or deals in cutting instruments. **cutlery,** *n.* the business of a cutler; knives and other edged instruments or tools; knives, spoons and forks used for eating. [OF *coutelier, cotelier,* from *coutel* (see prec.)]

cutlet, *n.* a small slice of meat, usu. from the loin or neck, for cooking; minced meat or meat-substitute shaped to look like a cutlet. [F *côtelette,* dim. of *côte,* OF *coste,* L *costa,* rib]

cutter, cutting CUT[1].

cuttle[1], *n.* a cuttlefish. **cuttlebone,** *n.* the internal skeleton of the cuttlefish, used as a polishing agent and as a dietary supplement for cagebirds. **cuttlefish,** *n.* a 10-armed cephalopod, *Sepia officinalis;* other members of the genus *Sepia.* [OE *cudele;* etym. doubtful]

†**cuttle[2],** *n.* (*Shak.*) a knife, or one too ready to use a knife; a bravo. [prob. from OF *coutel* (F *couteau*), L *cultellum*]

cutty, *a.* (*Sc., North.*) short, cut short; hasty, quick. *n.* a cutty pipe; a short girl; a hare. **cutty pipe,** *n.* a short clay tobacco-pipe. **cutty-stool,** *n.* a bench in old Scottish churches on which women guilty of unchastity were compelled to sit and undergo public rebuke. [CUT[1]]

Cutty Sark, *n.* British sailing ship, built 1869, one of the tea clippers that used to compete in the 19th cent. to bring their cargoes fastest from China to Britain.

cuvée, *n.* a batch of blended wine. [F, p.p. of *cuver,* to ferment (wine) in a vat]

cuvette, *n.* a little scoop; a clay crucible. [F, dim. of *cuve,* L *cūpa,* a cask, a vat]

Cuvier, *n.* **Georges, Baron Cuvier** (1769–1832), French comparative anatomist. In 1799 he proved extinction (the phenomenon that some species have ceased to exist) by reconstructing extinct giant animals that he believed were destroyed in a series of giant deluges. These ideas are expressed in *Recherches sur les ossamens fossiles/Essay on the Theory of the Earth* (1817).

Cuyp, *n.* **Aelbert** (1620–91), Dutch painter of countryside scenes, seascapes and portraits. His idyllically peaceful landscapes are bathed in golden light, for example *A Herdsman with Cows by a River* (*c.* 1650, National Gallery, London). His father was **Jacob Gerritsz Cuyp** (1594–1652), also a landscape and portrait painter.

Cuzco, *n.* a city in S Peru, capital of Cuzco department, in the Andes, over 3350 m/11,000 ft above sea level and 560 km/350 miles SE of Lima; population (1988) 255,000. It was founded in the 11th cent. as the ancient capital of the Inca empire, and was captured by Pizarro in 1533.

CV, (*abbr.*) Common Version; curriculum vitae.

CVO, (*abbr.*) Commander of the (Royal) Victorian Order.

Cwlth, (*abbr.*) Commonwealth.

cwm, *n.* a valley in Wales; a cirque. [W]

cwo, (*abbr.*) cash with order.

CWS, (*abbr.*) Cooperative Wholesale Society.

cwt, (*abbr.*) hundredweight.

-cy, *suf.* forming nouns of quality from adjectives, and nouns of office (cp. -SHIP) from nouns. [L *-cia, -tia;* Gr. *-keia, -kia, -teia, -tia* (cp. -ACY)]

cyan, *n.* a bluish-green colour. *a.* of this colour. **cyan-,** *comb. form.* CYANO-. [Gr. *kuanos,* dark blue]

cyanate, *n.* a salt of cyanic acid.

cyanic, *a.* derived from cyanogen; blue. **cyanic acid,** *n.* a compound of cyanogen and hydrogen.

cyanide, *n.* a compound of cyanogen with a metallic element. [CYANOGEN]

cyanine, *n.* a blue colouring matter used for dyeing calico.

cyanite, *n.* a hard, translucent mineral, often blue, occurring in flattened prisms in gneiss and mica-schist. **cyanitic,** *a.*

cyan(o)-, *comb. form* of a blue colour; pertaining to or containing cyanogen. [Gr. *kuanos,* a dark-blue mineral]

cyanogen, *n.* a colourless, poisonous gas composed of carbon and nitrogen, burning with a peach-blossom flame, and smelling like almond.

cyanometer, *n.* an instrument for determining the depth of the tint of the atmosphere.

cyanosis, *n.* (*pl.* **-ses**) a condition in which the skin becomes blue or leaden-coloured owing to the circulation of oxygen-deficient blood.

cyanotype, *n.* a photographic process in which a cyanide is employed.

cyathiform, *a.* (*Bot.*) cup-shaped; resembling a drinking cup. [Gr. *kuathos,* cup]

Cybele, *n.* in Phrygian mythology, an earth goddess, identified by the Greeks with Rhea and honoured in Rome.

cybernetics, *n. sing.* the comparative study of control and communication mechanisms in machines and living creatures. **cybernetic,** *a.* **cybernate,** *v.t.* to control automatically, e.g. by means of a computer. **cybernation,** *n.* [Gr. *kubernetes,* a steersman]

cycad, *n.* a cycadaceous plant. **cycadaceous,** *a.* belonging to the Cycadaceae, an order of gymnosperms, allied to the conifers. [mod. L *cycas -adem* (from a supposed Gr. *kukas,* now recognized as an error for *koïkas,* acc. pl. of *koïx,* the Egyptian doum-palm)]

cyclamate, *n.* any of several compounds derived from petrochemicals, formerly used as sweetening agents. [*cyclo*hexylsulph*amate*]

cyclamen, *n.* the sowbread, a genus of tuberous plants with beautiful flowers. [late L, from Gr. *kuklamīnos* (perh. from *kuklos,* a circle, with reference to the bulbous root)]

cycle, *n.* a series of years, events or phenomena recurring in the same order; a series that repeats itself; a complete series or succession; the period in which a series of events is completed; a long period, an age; a body of legend connected with some myth; a bicycle or tricycle; †(*Astron.*) an imaginary circle in the heavens; one complete series of changes in a periodically varying quantity, e.g. an electric current. *v.i.* to revolve in a circle; to ride a bicycle or tricycle. **cycle of the moon, lunar cycle, Metonic cycle,** a period of 19 years, after which the new and full moon recur on the same days of the month. **cycle of the sun, solar cycle,** a period of 28 years, after which the days of the month recur on the same days of the week. **cycle-track, -way,** *n.* a path, often beside a road, reserved for cyclists. **cyclic, -ical,** *a.* pertaining to, or moving or recurring in, a cycle; (*Bot.*) arranged in whorls; of an organic chemical compound, containing a ring of atoms. **cyclic chorus,** *n.* the chorus which performed the songs and dithyrambs round the altar of Bacchus. **cyclic poets,** *n.pl.* poets dealing with the subject of the Trojan war, or with the cycle of legend that has grown up round any myth, e.g. King Arthur. **cyclically,** *adv.* **cyclist,** *n.* one who rides a bicycle or tricycle. [L *cyclus,* Gr. *kuklos,* a circle]

cyclo-, *comb. form* circular; pertaining to a circle or circles. [Gr. *kuklos,* a circle]

cyclo-cross, *n.* the sport of cross-country racing on a bicycle. [CYCLE, CROSS[1]]

cyclograph, *n.* an instrument for describing the arcs of large circles.

cycloid, *n.* the figure described by a point in the plane of a circle as it rolls along a straight line till it has completed a revolution (**common cycloid,** *n.* when the point is on the circumference; **curtate cycloid,** *n.* when the point is the circumference; **protate cycloid,** when the point is within the circumference). **cycloidal**, *a.* resembling a circle; (*Zool.*) having concentric striations; pertaining to the Cycloidei. **Cycloidei,** *n.pl.* an artificial order of fishes, founded by Agassiz, consisting of those with cycloid scales. [Gr. *kukloeides,* circular, from *kuklos,* circle]

cyclometer, *n.* an instrument for recording the revolutions of a wheel, esp. that of a bicycle, and hence the distance travelled. **cyclometry,** *n.* the art or process of measuring circles.

cyclone, *n.* a disturbance in the atmosphere caused by a system of winds blowing spirally towards a central region of low barometric pressure; a violent hurricane. **cyclonic**, *a.* [Gr. *kuklos,* a circle]

cyclopaedia, etc. ENCYCLOPAEDIA.

cyclopean, *a.* of or pertaining to the Cyclops; immense, gigantic. **cyclopean masonry,** *n.* a style of architecture of great antiquity, in which massive blocks are accurately fitted together, or rough blocks laid one on another, and the interstices filled up with small stones, no mortar being used in either form. [L *Cyclōpēus, Cyclōpius,* Gr. *Kuklōpeios, Kuklōpios*]

cyclopropane, *n.* a colourless hydrocarbon gas used as an anaesthetic.

Cyclops, *n.* (*pl.* **Cyclopes**) mythical one-eyed giants supposed to have dwelt in Sicily; (*fig.*) a one-eyed person; (*Zool.*) a genus of Entomostraca with a single eye. [L, from Gr. *Kuklōps* (*kuklos,* a circle, *ōps,* an eye)]

cyclorama, *n.* a panorama painted on the inside of a large cylinder and viewed by the spectator from the middle. [Gr. *horama,* a view]

cyclosis, *n.* circulation, as of blood, the latex in plants, or protoplasm in certain cells; (*Math.*) the occurrence of cycles. [Gr. *kuklōsis,* an encircling (*kukloein,* to move in a circle)]

Cyclostomata, *n.* a subclass of fishes, with a circular suctorial mouth, containing the lampreys and hags. **cyclostomatous**, **cyclostomous**, *a.* **cyclostome**, *n.* [Gr. *stomata,* pl. of *stoma,* mouth]

cyclostyle, *n.* a machine for printing copies of handwriting or typewriting by means of a sheet perforated like a stencil. *v.t.* to print using this machine.

cyclothymia, *n.* a psychological condition characterized by swings between elation and depression. [Gr. *thumos,* spirit]

cyclotron, *n.* a particle accelerator designed to accelerate protons to high energies.

cyder, CIDER.

cygnet, *n.* a young swan. [dim. of OF *cygne* or L *cygnus,* a swan]

Cygnus, *n.* large prominent constellation of the northern hemisphere, representing a swan. Its brightest star is first-magnitude Deneb.

cylinder, *n.* a straight roller-shaped body, solid or hollow, and of uniform circumference; (*Geom.*) a solid figure described by the revolution of a right-angled parallelogram about one of its sides which remains fixed; a cylindrical member of various machines, esp. the chamber in a steam-engine in which the piston is acted upon by the steam; the roller used in machine-printing. **cylinder-press,** *n.* a printing-press in which the type is secured on a cylinder, or in which the impression is given by a cylinder. **cylindrical**, *a.* having the form of a cylinder. **cylindriform**, *a.* [L *cylindrus,* Gr. *kulindros* (*kulindein,* to roll)]

cylindroid, *n.* (*Geom.*) a solid body differing from a cylinder in having the bases elliptical instead of circular. [Gr. *kulindroeidēs* (-OID)]

cyma, *n.* (*Arch.*) a convex and a concave curve forming the topmost member of a cornice; (*Bot.*) a cyme. **cymagraph**, *n.* an apparatus for tracing the outline of mouldings. **cyma recta**, *n.* a curve convex above and concave below. **cyma reversa**, *n.* a curve concave above and convex below, ogee. [Gr. *kûma,* anything swollen, a wave, an ogee moulding, a sprout]

cymar, *n.* a woman's light loose robe or undergarment. [F *simarre,* OF *chamarre* (see CHIMER)]

cymatium, *n.* a cyma. [L, from Gr. *kumation,* dim. of *kûma*]

cymbal, *n.* one of a pair of disks of brass or bronze more or less basin-shaped, clashed together to produce a sharp, clashing sound. **cymbalist,** *n.* [L *cymbalum,* Gr. *kûmbalon* (*kumbē,* hollow)]

cymbalo, *n.* (*pl.* **-los**) the dulcimer, a stringed instrument played by means of small hammers held in the hands. [It. *cembalo,* from L *cymbalum,* as prec.]

Cymbeline[1], *n.* a play by Shakespeare, first acted about 1610 and printed in 1623. It combines various sources to tell the story of Imogen (derived from Ginevra in Boccaccio's *Decameron*), the daughter of the legendary British king Cymbeline, who proves her virtue and constancy after several ordeals.

Cymbeline[2], *n.* another name for **Cunobelin**, king of the Catuvellauni (AD 5–40), who fought unsuccessfully against the Roman invasion of Britain. His capital was at Colchester.

cymbiform, *a.* of certain bones and grasses, boat-shaped, navicular. [L *cymba,* a boat, -FORM]

cyme, *n.* an inflorescence in which the central terminal flower comes to perfection first, as in the guelder-rose. **cymoid,** *a.* resembling a cyme. **cymose**, *a.* [F, from L *cŷma,* Gr. *kûma,* see CYMA]

cymophane, *n.* a variety of chrysoberyl. **cymophanous**, *a.* [Gr. *kûma,* a wave, *-phanēs,* appearing (*phainein,* to appear)]

Cymric, *a.* pertaining to the Welsh. *n.* the Welsh language. [W *Cymru,* Wales]

Cymru, *n.* Celtic name for Wales.

cynanthropy, *n.* madness in which a person fancies he is changed into a dog, and imitates the habits of that animal. [Gr. *kunanthropos* (*kun-,* stem of *kuōn,* a dog, *anthrōpos,* a man)]

Cynewulf, *n.* lived early 8th cent. Anglo-Saxon poet. He is thought to have been a Northumbrian monk, and is the undoubted author of 'Juliana' and part of the 'Christ' in the Exeter Book (a collection of poems now in Exeter Cathedral), and of the 'Fates of the Apostles' and 'Elene' in the Vercelli Book (a collection of Old English manuscripts housed at Vercelli, Italy), in all of which he inserted his name in the form of runic acrostics.

cynic, *n.* (*Hist.*) one of a rigid sect of Greek philosophers (of which Diogenes was the most distinguished member) founded at Athens by Antisthenes, a pupil of Socrates, who insisted on the complete renunciation of all luxury and the subjugation of sensual desires; one who is habitually morose and sarcastic; one who is pessimistic about human nature. **cynical,** *a.* bitter, sarcastic, misanthropical; (*Hist.*) of or belonging to the cynics. **cynically,** *adv.* **cynicism**, *n.* [L *cynicus,* Gr. *kunikos* (*kun-,* stem of *kuōn,* a dog)]

cynocephalus, *n.* a dog-headed man in ancient mythology; the dog-faced baboon. [L, from Gr. *kunokephalos* (Gr. *kuōn kunos,* dog, *kephalē,* head)]

cynophobia, *n.* a morbid fear of dogs; a neurosis resembling rabies. [Gr. *kuōn kunos,* dog]

cynosure, *n.* the constellation of the Lesser Bear (*Ursa Minor*), containing the north star; a centre of interest or attraction. [F, from L *cynosūra,* Gr. *kúnosoura,* the dog's tail, the Lesser Bear (*kuōn kunos,* dog, *oura,* tail)]

cypher CIPHER.

cy près, *adv., a.* (*Law*) as near as practicable (referring to the principle of applying a bequest to some object as near as may be to the testator's aim when that is impracticable). *n.* an approximation. [A-F (F *si près,* so near)]

cypress[1], *n.* a tree of the coniferous genus *Cupressus,* esp. *C. sempervirens,* valued for the durability of its wood; a branch of this as emblem of mourning. [OF *cyprès,* late L *cypressus,* Gr. *kupressos*]

†**cypress**2, *n.* (also **satin of Cypres**) a kind of satin that was highly valued; a piece of this worn as a token of mourning. †**cypress-lawn,** *n.* a thin, transparent black fabric, a kind of lawn or crape, worn as mourning. [prob. from OF *Cipré, Cypre,* Cyprus]

Cyprian, *a.* of or belonging to Cyprus, where the worship of Venus especially flourished. *n.* a Cypriot; a prostitute. **Cypriot, -ote**, *n.* an inhabitant of Cyprus.

Cyprian, St *n.* (*c.* 210–58), Christian martyr, one of the earliest Christian writers, and bishop of Carthage about 249. He wrote a treatise on the unity of the church. Feast day 16 Sept.

cyprine, *n.* of or belonging to the fish genus *Cyprinus,* containing the carp. [L *cyprīnus,* Gr. *kuprînos,* carp]

cypripedium, *n.* lady's slipper, an orchid (genus *Cypripedium*) possessing two fertile stamens, the central stamen (fertile in other orchids) being represented by a shield-like plate. [Gr. *Kupris,* Venus, and *podion,* a slipper]

Cyprus, *n.* a Mediterranean island, divided between the southern Republic of Cyprus (Greek *Kypriaki Dimokratia*), and the Turkish Republic of Northern Cyprus (Turkish *Kibris Cumhuriyeti*). **area** 9251 sq km/ 3571 sq miles, 37% in Turkish hands. **capital** Nicosia (divided between the Greeks and Turks). **towns** ports Paphos, Limassol and Larnaca (Greek); and Morphou, and ports Kyrenia and Famagusta (Turkish). **physical** central plain between two E–W mountain ranges. **exports** citrus, grapes, Cyprus sherry, potatoes, copper, pyrites. **population** (1987) 680,400 (Greek Cypriot 81%, Turkish Cypriot 19%); annual growth rate 1.2%. **language** Greek and Turkish (official); English. **religion** Greek Orthodox, Sunni Muslim.

Cyrano de Bergerac, *n.* **Savinien de** (1619–55), French writer. He joined a corps of guards at 19, and performed heroic feats which made him famous. He is the hero of a classic play by Rostand, in which his notoriously long nose is used as a counterpoint to his chivalrous character.

Cyrenaic, *a.* of or pertaining to Cyrene, an ancient Greek colony in the north of Africa, or to the hedonistic or eudaemonistic philosophy founded at that place about 400 BC by Aristippus. *n.* a philosopher of the Cyrenaic school.

Cyrenaica, *n.* an area of E Libya, colonized by the Greeks in the 7th cent. BC; later held by the Egyptians, Romans, Arabs, Turks and Italians. Present cities in the region are Benghazi, Derna and Tobruk.

Cyril and Methodius, two brothers, both Christian saints: Cyril (826–69) and Methodius (815–85). Born in Thessalonica, they were sent as missionaries to what is today Moravia. They invented a Slavonic alphabet, and translated the Bible and the liturgy from Greek to Slavonic.

Cyrillic, *a.* a term applied to the alphabet of the Slavonic nations who belong to the Orthodox Church, from the fact that it was introduced by Clement, a disciple of St Cyril.

Cyril of Alexandria, St (376–444), bishop of Alexandria from 412, persecutor of Jews and other non-Christians, and suspected of ordering the murder of Hypatia (*c.* 370–*c.* 415), a philosopher whose influence was increasing at the expense of his. He was violently opposed to Nestorianism.

cyrto-, *comb. form* curving; bent. **cyrtometer**, *n.* an apparatus used to measure and record the curves of a chart. [Gr. *kurtos,* curved]

Cyrus the Great, (d. 529 BC), founder of the Persian Empire. As king of Persia, originally subject to the Medes, whose empire he overthrew in 550 BC. He captured Croesus in 546 BC, and conquered all Asia Minor, adding Babylonia (including Syria and Palestine) to his empire in 539 BC, allowing exiled Jews to return to Jerusalem. He died fighting in Afghanistan.

cyst, *n.* a bladder, vesicle or hollow organ; a cell; a receptacle; a sac containing morbid matter. **cystic,** *a.* pertaining to or enclosed in a cyst, esp. the gall or urinary bladder; having cysts, or of the nature of a cyst. **cystic fibrosis,** *n.* a hereditary disease appearing in early childhood, marked by overproduction of mucus and fibrous tissue, with consequent breathing and digestive difficulties. **cystic worms,** *n.pl.* immature tapeworms, encysted in the tissues of their host. **cystiform,** *a.* **cystose**, **cystous,** *a.* containing cysts. [L *cystis,* from Gr. *kustis,* a bladder]

cyst(i)-, cysto-, *comb. forms* pertaining to the bladder; bladder-shaped. [Gr. *kustē, kustis,* a bladder]

cystine, *n.* a sulphur-containing amino acid discovered in a rare kind of urinary calculus.

cystitis, *n.* inflammation of the urinary bladder.

cysto- CYST(I)-.

cystocele, *n.* hernia caused by protrusion of the bladder.

cystopteris, *n.* a genus of ferns containing the bladder-ferns. [Gr. *pteris,* a fern]

cystoscope, *n.* an instrument or apparatus for the exploration of the bladder.

cystose CYST.

cystotomy, *n.* the act or practice of opening cysts; the operation of cutting into the bladder to remove calculi.

-cyte, *suf.* (*Biol.*) a mature cell, as in *leucocyte.* [Gr. *kutos,* a hollow, a receptacle]

cytherean, *a.* pertaining to Venus, the goddess of love, who was connected with Cythera (the modern Kithira, an island off the Peloponnese).

cyto-, *comb. form* (*Biol.*) cellular; pertaining to or composed of cells. **cytoblast**, *n.* a cell-nucleus. **cytology**, *n.* the study of cells. **cytological**, *a.* **cytologist**, *n.* **cytolysis**, *n.* the dissolution of cells. **cytoplasm**, *n.* the protoplasm of a cell apart from the nucleus. **cytoplasmic**, *a.* **cytotoxin**, *n.* a substance which is poisonous to cells. [Gr. *kutos,* a hollow]

czar, tsar, *n.* the title of the former emperors of Russia. **czarevich, -vitch**, *n.* the son of a czar. **czarevna**, *n.* the daughter of a czar. **czarina**, **czaritza**, *n.* an empress of Russia; the wife of a czar. [Pol. spelling of Rus. *tsar',* L *caesar*]

czardas, csardas, *n.* a Hungarian national dance. [Hung.]

Czech, *n.* a native or inhabitant of Bohemia or Moravia in W Czechoslovakia; the slavonic language of the Czechs; loosely, a Czechoslovak. *a.* of or pertaining to the Czechs, their language or (loosely) Czechoslovakia. **Czechoslovak**, **-vakian**, *n.* a native of Czechoslovakia (republic in Central Europe); a Czech or Slovak. *a.* of Czechoslovakia; of the Czechs or Slovaks, or their languages. [Pol. spelling of Czech *Čech*]

Czechoslovakia, *n.* the Czech and Slovak Federative Republic, a landlocked country in E central Europe, bounded to the NE by Poland, E by the USSR, S by Hungary and Austria, W by West Germany and NW by East Germany. **area** 127,903 sq km/49,371 sq miles. **capital** Prague. **towns** Brno, Bratislava, Ostrava. **physical** Carpathian Mountains, rivers Morava, Labe (Elbe), Vltava (Moldau); hills and plateau; Danube plain in S. **exports** machinery, timber, ceramics, glass, textiles. **population** (1986) 15,521,000 (63% Czech, 31% Slovak, with Hungarian, Polish, German, Russian and other minorities); annual growth rate 0.4%. **language** Czech and Slovak (official). **religion** 75% Roman Catholic, 15% Protestant.

Czerny, *n.* **Carl** (1791–1857), Austrian composer and pianist. He wrote an enormous quantity of religious and concert music, but is chiefly remembered for his books of graded studies and technical exercises used in piano teaching.

D

D, d, the fourth letter in the English alphabet, represents a dental sound formed by placing the tip of the tongue against the roots of the upper teeth, and then passing up vocalized breath into the mouth. After a non-vocal or surd consonant it takes a sharper sound, nearly approaching that of *t,* especially in the past tenses and past participles of verbs in *-ed.* D is a symbol for the second note of the musical scale of C, corresponding to the Italian *re;* the fourth in numerical series; (*Roman numeral*) 500. **D region, layer,** *n.* the lowest part of the ionosphere, between 25 and 40 miles (40 and 65 km) above the earth's surface.

D., (*abbr.*) democrat; department; God (L *deus*); Lord (L *dominus*).

d., (*abbr.*) date; daughter; day; dead; depart(s); penny (before decimalization, L *denarius*); diameter.

-d, *suf.* forming past tense and p.p. of weak verbs, as in *died, heard, loved, proved.* [OE *-de* (see -ED)]

da DAD[1].

DA, (*abbr.*) district attorney.

dab[1], *v.t.* (*past, p.p.* **dabbed**) to strike gently with some moist or soft substance; to pat; to rub with a dabber; to press with a soft substance. *n.* a gentle blow; a light stroke or wipe with a soft substance; a lump; (*often pl., sl.*) fingerprints; †a rap, a blow; (*sl.*) a dabster. **a dab hand at,** (*coll.*) an expert at. **dabber,** *n.* one who or that which dabs. [etym. doubtful; prob. imit. (cp. TAP)]

dab[2], *n.* a small flatfish, *Pleuronectes limanda.* [perh. from DAB[1]]

dabble, *v.t.* to keep on dabbing; to wet by little dips; to besprinkle, to moisten, to splash. *v.i.* to play or splash about in water; to do or practise anything in a superficial manner; to dip into a subject. **dabbler,** *n.* one who dabbles with or in any subject. **dabblingly,** *adv.* superficially, shallowly. [freq. of DAB[1] (cp. Norw. *dabla,* Dut. *dabbelen*)]

dabchick, *n.* the little grebe, *Podiceps minor.* [earlier *dap-chick, dop-chick (dap,* cogn. with DIP)]

dabster, *n.* (*coll.*) one who is expert at anything. [DAB[1]]

da capo, (*Mus. direction*) the player is to begin again. [It., from the beginning]

Dacca, *n.* former spelling of Dhaka.

dace, *n.* a small river fish, *Leuciscus vulgaris.* [ME *darse,* OF *darz,* DART]

dacha, datcha, *n.* a country house or cottage in Russia. [Rus., gift]

Dachau, *n.* site of a Nazi concentration camp during World War II in Bavaria, West Germany.

dachshund, *n.* a short-legged long-bodied breed of dog. [G, badgerhound]

Dacia, *n.* ancient region forming much of modern Romania. The various Dacian tribes were united around 60 BC, and for many years posed a threat to the Roman empire; they were finally conquered by the Roman emperor Trajan 101–106 AD, and the region became a province of the same name. It was abandoned to the invading Goths in about 275.

dacker, daiker, *v.i.* (*Sc.*) to toddle, to saunter; to vacillate. [cp. MFlem. *daeckeren*]

dacoit, *n.* one of an Indian or Burmese band of armed robbers. **dacoity,** *n.* robbery by armed gang. [Hind. *dakait* (*dākā,* robbery by a gang)]

dacryops, *n.* a cyst of the lachrymal gland; watery eye. [Gr. *dakru,* a tear; *opsis,* face]

dactyl, *n.* a metrical foot consisting of one long followed by two short syllables. **dactylic,** *a.* [L *dactylus,* as foll.]

dactyl-, dactylio-, dactylo-, *comb. form* having fingers or digits; pertaining to fingers or digits. [Gr. *daktulos,* a finger]

dactylioglyph, *n.* an engraver of rings or gems; the engraver's name on rings or gems. **dactylioglyphy,** *n.* [Gr. *daktulioglyphos* (*gluphos,* carver, from *gluphein,* to carve)]

dactyliography, *n.* the art of engraving gems.

dactyliology, *n.* the study of finger-rings.

†dactyliomancy, *n.* divination by finger-rings.

dactylogram, *n.* a fingerprint. **dactylography,** *n.* the study of fingerprints.

Dada, *n.* artistic and literary movement founded 1915 in Zürich, Switzerland, by the Romanian poet Tristan Tzara (1896–1963) and others in a spirit of rebellion and disillusion during World War I. Other Dadaist groups were soon formed by the artists Duchamp and Man Ray in New York and Picabia in Barcelona. Dada had a considerable impact on early 20th-cent. art, questioning established artistic rules and values.

Dadd, *n.* **Richard** (1817–87), British painter. In 1843 he murdered his father and was committed to an insane asylum, but continued to paint minutely detailed pictures of fantasies and fairy tales, such as *The Fairy Feller's Master-Stroke* (1855–64) (Tate Gallery, London).

Dadra and Nagar Haveli, *n.* since 1961 a Union Territory of W India; capital Silvassa; area 490 sq km/189 sq miles; population (1981) 104,000. Formerly part of Portuguese Daman. It produces rice, wheat, millet, and timber.

Daedalus[1], *n.* in Greek mythology, an Athenian artisan supposed to have constructed the labyrinth for King Minos in which the Minotaur was imprisoned. He fled from Crete with his son Icarus using wings made from feathers fastened with wax.

Daedalus[2], *n.* in space travel, a futuristic project proposed by the British Interplanetary Society to send a robot probe to nearby stars. The probe, 20 times the size of the Saturn V moon rocket, would be propelled by thermonuclear fusion, in effect, a series of small hydrogen-bomb explosions. Interstellar cruise speed would be about 40,000 km/25,000 miles per second.

Dafydd ap Gwilym (*c.* 1340–*c.* 1400), Welsh poet. His work is notable for its complex but graceful style, its concern with nature and love rather than with heroic martial deeds, and for its references to classical and Italian poetry. He was born into an influential Cardiganshire gentry family, and is traditionally believed to have led a life packed with amorous adventures.

Dagestan, *n.* autonomous republic of western USSR, situated E of the Caucasus, bordering the Caspian Sea. Capital Makhachkala; area 50,300 sq km/14,700 sq miles; population (1982) 1,700,000. It is mountainous, with deep valleys, and its numerous ethnic groups speak a variety of distinct languages. Annexed from Iran in 1723, which strongly resisted Russian conquest, it became an autonomous republic in 1921.

dagga, *n.* a type of hemp used as a narcotic. [Hottentot *dachab*]

dagger, *n.* a short two-edged weapon adapted for stabbing; (*Print.*) a reference mark (†). **at daggers drawn,** on hostile terms; ready to fight. **to look daggers,** to look with fierceness or animosity. **dagger-plant,** *n.* the yucca. [F *dague,* influenced by ME *daggen,* to pierce]

daggle, *v.t.* to trail through mud or wet; to bemire, as the bottom of a garment. *v.i.* to run through wet or mire. **daggle-tailed,** *a.* slatternly, sluttish. [freq. of obs. verb *dag,* etym. doubtful]

daglock, *n.* the dirt-covered clumps of wool around the hindquarters of sheep. [etym. doubtful]

dago, *n.* (*sl., offensive*) a contemptuous term for a Spaniard, Italian or Portuguese. [Sp. *Diego,* James]

dagoba, *n.* a dome-shaped Buddhist shrine containing relics. [Sinhalese *dāgaba*]

daguerreotype, *n.* the process of photographing on copper plates coated with silver iodide, developed by exposure to mercury vapour, used by Louis Daguerre (1789–1851), of Paris; a photograph by this process. *v.t.* to photograph by this process; (*fig.*) to picture exactly. **daguerreotyper, -pist,** *n.* one who produced daguerreotypes. **daguerreotypic, -ical,** *a.* pertaining to daguerreotype. **daguerreotypism,** *n.*

dahabeeyah, *n.* a native sailing-boat on the Nile. [Arab. *dhahabīyah,* the golden (*dhahab,* gold)]

dahl DAL.

Dahl[1], *n.* **Johann Christian** (1788–1857), Norwegian landscape painter in the Romantic style. He trained in Copenhagen but was active chiefly in Dresden from 1818. He was the first great painter of the Norwegian landscape, in a style that recalls the Dutch artist Ruisdael.

Dahl[2], *n.* **Roald** (1916–), British writer, celebrated for short stories with a twist, for example, *Tales of the Unexpected* (1979), and for children's books including *Charlie and the Chocolate Factory* (1964).

Dahlia, *n.* a genus of composite plants from Mexico, cultivated for their beautiful flowers. [*Dahl,* a pupil of Linnaeus]

Dahomey, *n.* former name (until 1975) of the People's Republic of Benin.

Dáil Eireann, *n.* the lower house of the legislature of the Republic of Ireland. It consists of 148 members elected by adult suffrage on a basis of proportional representation.

daily, *a.* happening, done or recurring every day; published every week-day; necessary for every day; ordinary, usual. *adv.* day by day; often; continually, always. *n.* a newspaper published every week-day; a woman employed daily for house-work. **daily dozen,** *n.* (*coll.*) daily physical exercises. [OE *dæglic* (found only in comb.)]

daimio, *n.* the official title of a former class of feudal lords in Japan. [Jap. (Chin. *dai,* great, *myo,* name)]

Daimler, *n.* **Gottlieb** (1834–1900), German engineer who pioneered the modern motorcar. In 1886 he produced his first motor vehicle and a motor-bicycle. He later joined forces with Karl Benz and was one of the pioneers of the high-speed 4-stroke petrol engine.

dainty, *n.* a delicacy; a choice morsel; a choice dish; †fastidiousness. *a.* pleasing to the taste, choice; pretty, delicate, elegant; fastidious, nice; luxurious; over-nice. †**daint,** *a.* dainty. **daintily,** *adv.* **daintiness,** *n.* [OF *dainté,* L *dignitās -tātem* (*dignus,* worthy)]

daiquiri, *n.* a cocktail made of rum and lime-juice. [town in Cuba]

dairy, *n.* the place or building or department of a farm where milk is kept and converted into butter or cheese; a place where milk, cream and butter are sold; a dairy-farm; a herd of milch cattle. *a.* belonging to a dairy or its business. **dairy-farm,** *n.* **dairy-maid,** *n. fem.* **dairy-man,** *n.* **dairy products,** *n.pl.* **dairying,** *n.* dairy-farming. [OE *dæge,* a maid-servant -ERY]

dais, *n.* the raised floor at the upper end of a mediaeval dining-hall; the principal table on such a raised floor; the chief seat at the high table; a chair of state; a platform. [A-F *deis,* OF *dois,* L *discus -um,* a quoit, late L, a table]

daisy, *n.* a small composite flower, *Bellis perennis;* other flowers resembling this; (*sl.*) a first-rate person or thing. **daisy-chain,** *n.* a string of daisies made by children. **daisy-cutter,** *n.* a trotting horse; a ball at cricket bowled so low that it rolls along the ground. **daisy-wheel,** *n.* a wheel-shaped printer with characters on spikes round the circumference. **daisied,** *a.* covered or adorned with daisies. [OE *dæges ēage,* day's eye]

dak DAWK.

Dakar, *n.* capital and chief port (with artificial harbour) of Senegal; population (1984) 1,000,000.

dakoit DACOIT.

dal, *n.* a split grain, pulse; a soup or purée made from this, eaten in the Indian subcontinent. [Hind. *dal,* to split, from Sansk.]

Daladier, *n.* **Edouard** (1884–1970), French Radical politician. As prime minister (Apr. 1938–Mar. 1940), he was largely responsible both for the Munich Agreement and France's declaration of war on Germany. Arrested on the fall of France, he was a prisoner in Germany (1943–45). He was re-elected to the Chamber of Deputies (1946–58).

Dalai Lama, *n.* (14th incarnation 1935–), spiritual and temporal head of the Tibetan state until 1959, when he went into exile in protest against Chinese annexation and oppression. Tibetan Buddhists believe that each Dalai Lama is a reincarnation of his predecessor and also of Avalokiteśvara. He was awarded the Nobel Peace Prize (1989) in recognition of his commitment to the nonviolent liberation of his homeland.

Dalbergia, *n.* a genus of tropical leguminous trees and climbing shrubs yielding valuable timber. [Nicholas *Dalberg*]

dale, *n.* a valley, esp. from the English midlands to the Scottish lowlands. **dalesman,** *n.* a native or inhabitant of a dale, esp. in the northern counties of England. **daleswoman,** *n.fem.* [OE *dæl,* a valley (cp. Icel. *dalr,* Dan. *dal,* Goth. *dal,* G *Thal*)]

Dalen, *n.* **Nils** (1869–1937), Swedish industrial engineer who invented the light-controlled valve. This allowed lighthouses to operate automatically and won him the 1912 Nobel Physics prize.

Dalgarno, *n.* **George** (1626–87), Scottish schoolteacher and inventor of the first sign-language alphabet 1680.

Dalhousie, *n.* **James Andrew Broun Ramsay, 1st Marquess and 10th Earl of Dalhousie** (1812–60), British administrator, governor general of India (1848–56). In the second Sikh War he annexed the Punjab (1849), and, after the second Burmese War, Lower Burma (1853). He reformed the Indian army and civil service and furthered social and economic progress.

Dali, *n.* **Salvador** (1904–89), Spanish painter. In 1928 he collaborated with Buñuel on the film *Un Chien Andalou.* In 1929 he joined the Surrealists and became notorious for his flamboyant eccentricity. Influenced by the psychiatric theories of Freud, he developed a repertoire of dramatic images, such as the distorted human body, limp watches, and burning giraffes. These are painted with a meticulous, polished clarity. He also painted religious themes and many portraits of his wife Gala.

Dallapiccola, *n.* **Luigi** (1904–75), Italian composer. In his early years he was a neo-classicist in the manner of Stravinsky, but he soon turned to serialism, which he adapted to his own style. His works include the operas *Il Prigioniero/The Prisoner* (1949) and *Ulisse/Ulysses* (1968), as well as many vocal and instrumental compositions.

Dallas, *n.* commercial city in Texas, US; population (1980) 904,000, metropolitan area (with Fort Worth) 2,964,000. Industries include banking, insurance, oil, aviation, aerospace and electronics. Dallas-Fort Worth Regional Airport (opened 1973) is one of the world's largest. John F. Kennedy was assassinated here in 1963.

dalles, *n.pl.* rapids where a river flows through a steep-sided gorge. [Can. F, trough, from F *dalle,* tile]

dally, *v.i.* to trifle, toy; to exchange caresses; to sport coquettishly (with); to idle, to delay, to waste time. *v.t.* to consume or waste (away). **dalliance,** *n.* [OF *dalier,* to chat]

Dalmatian, *a.* belonging to Dalmatia, in Yugoslavia. *n.* a Dalmatian dog; a native or inhabitant of Dalmatia. **Dalmatian dog,** *n.* a variety of hound, white with numerous black or brown spots, formerly kept chiefly as a carriage dog.

dalmatic, *n.* an ecclesiastical vestment worn by bishops and deacons in the Roman and Greek Churches at High Mass; a similar robe worn by monarchs at coronation and other ceremonies. [F *dalmatique,* L *dalmatica,* orig. a., of Dalmatia]

dal segno, *adv.* (*Mus.*) repeat from point indicated. [It., from the sign]

dalt, *n.* (*Sc.*) a foster-child. [Gael. *dalta*]

Dalton¹, *n.* **Hugh, Baron Dalton** (1887–1962), British Labour politician and economist. Chancellor of the Exchequer from 1945, he oversaw nationalization of the Bank of England, but resigned in 1947 after making a disclosure to a lobby correspondent before a budget speech.

Dalton², *n.* **John** (1766–1844), British chemist, the first to propose the existence of atoms, which he considered to be the smallest parts of matter. Extending the range of compounds, he produced the first list of relative atomic masses, *Absorption of Gases* (1805).

daltonism, *n.* colour-blindness, esp. inability to distinguish between red and green. [John DALTON, who suffered from this]

dam¹, *n.* a female parent (chiefly of quadrupeds); used of a human mother in contempt; (*Sc.*) a crowned man in the game of draughts (see DAMBROD). [DAME]

dam², *n.* a bank or mound raised to keep back water; the water so kept back; a causeway. *v.t.* (*past, p.p.* **dammed**) to keep back or confine by a dam; to obstruct, to hinder. [cp. OFris. *dam, dom,* Dut. *dam,* MHG *dam,* G *Damm,* Swed. and Dan. *dam;* also OE *fordemman,* to stop up]

Dam, *n.* **Carl** (1895–1976), Danish biochemist who discovered vitamin K. For his success in this field he shared the 1943 Nobel physiology or medicine prize with Edward Doisy.

damage, *n.* hurt, injury, mischief or detriment to any person or thing; loss or harm incurred; (*pl.*) value of injury done; (*sl.*) cost; (*Law, pl.*) reparation in money for injury sustained. *v.t.* to cause damage to. *v.i.* to receive damage. †**damage feasant,** *n.* (*Law*) the injury sustained by the cattle of another coming upon a man's land and damaging the crops. **damageable,** *a.* susceptible of damage; causing damage. [F, from *dam,* L *damnum,* cost, loss]

damascene, *v.t.* to ornament by inlaying or incrustation, or (as a steel blade) with a wavy pattern in welding. *a.* pertaining to Damascus. *n.* a native of Damascus; a damson. **Damascus blade,** *n.* a sword of fine quality the blade of which is variegated with streaks or veins. [F *damasquiner* (from L *Damascēnus,* Gr. *Damaskēnos,* of Damascus)]

Damascus, *n.* (Arabic **Dimashq**) capital of Syria, on the river Barada, SE of Beirut; population (1981) 1,251,000. It produces silk, wood products, and brass and copper ware. Said to be the oldest continuously inhabited city in the world, Damascus was an ancient city even in Old Testament times; most notable of the old buildings is the Great Mosque, completed as a Christian church in the 5th century.

damask, *n.* a rich silk stuff with raised figures woven in the pattern, orig. made at Damascus; a linen fabric, with similar figures in the pattern, used for tablecloths, dinner-napkins etc.; the colour of the damask rose; steel made with a wavy pattern by forging iron and steel together. *a.* made of damask; red, like the damask rose; of or resembling damask steel. *v.t.* to work flowers on; to damascene, to give a wavy appearance to (as steel work); to variegate. **damask plum,** *n.* the damson. **damask rose,** *n.* an old-fashioned rose, *Rosa gallica,* var. *damascena.* **damask steel,** *n.* a laminated metal of pure iron and steel, used for Damascus blades. [It. *damasco,* as prec.]

Dame, *n.* in the UK honours system, title of a woman who has been awarded the Order of the Bath, Order of St Michael and St George, Royal Victorian Order, or Order of the British Empire. Legal title of the wife or widow of a knight or baronet, placed before her name.

Damocles, *n.* (lived 4th cent. BC), in Classical legend, a courtier of the elder Dionysius, ruler of Syracuse, Sicily. Having extolled the happiness of his sovereign, Damocles was invited by him to a feast, during which he saw above his head a sword suspended by a single hair. He recognized this as a symbol of the insecurity of the great.

Dampier, *n.* **William** (1652–1715), English explorer and hydrographic surveyor who circumnavigated the world three times.

Danby, *n.* **Thomas Osborne, Earl of Danby** (1631–1712), British Tory politician. He entered Parliament in 1665, acted (1673–78) as Charles II's chief minister and in 1674 was created earl of Danby, but was imprisoned in the Tower of London (1678–84). In 1688 he signed the invitation to William of Orange to take the throne. Danby was again chief minister (1690–95), and in 1694 was created duke of Leeds.

Dance, *n.* **Charles** (1946–), British film and television actor who achieved fame in *The Jewel in the Crown* (1984). He has also appeared in *Plenty* (1986), *Good Morning Babylon, The Golden Child* (1987), *White Mischief* (1988).

dander¹, *v.i.* (*Sc., dial.*) to wander about idly; to maunder. [perh. conn. with DANDLE]

dander², *n.* (*coll.*) temper, anger. **to get one's dander up, to have one's dander raised,** to get into a passion. [etym. doubtful]

dander³, *n.* (*Sc.*) a cinder, a piece of slag. [etym. unknown]

Dandie Dinmont, *n.* a type of short-legged, rough-coated terrier. [*Dandie Dinmont,* in Walter Scott's *Guy Mannering*]

dandify, *v.t.* to make smart, or like a dandy. **dandification,** *n.* [DANDY¹]

dandle, *v.t.* to dance up and down on the knees or toss in the arms (as a child); to pet; †to trifle or toy with. *v.i.* to trifle or toy (with). **dandler,** *n.* [cp. LG *dand-* (WFlem. *danderen,* to bounce up and down); and It. *dandolare,* from *dandola, dondola,* a doll or puppet]

Dandolo, *n.* Venetian family that produced four doges (rulers), of whom the most outstanding, **Enrico Dandolo** (c. 1120–1205), became doge in 1193. He greatly increased the dominions of the Venetian republic and accompanied the crusading army that took Constantinople in 1203.

dandruff, *n.* scaly scurf on the head. [prob. a comb. of Yorks. *dander,* scurf on the skin, and *hurf* (cp. Icel. *hrufa,* scab)]

dandy¹, *n.* a man extravagantly fond of dress; a fop, a coxcomb; (*Ir.*) a small jug or glass of whisky; a sloop or cutter with a jigger-mast aft, on which a lug-sail is set. *a.* fond of dress, foppish; neat, spruce, smart; (*esp. N Am.*) very good, superior. **dandy-brush,** *n.* a hard whalebone brush for cleaning horses. **dandy-cart,** *n.* a spring-cart. **dandy-cock, -hen,** *n.* a bantam cock or hen. **dandy-roll,** *n.* a roller used to produce watermarks on paper. **dandiacal,** *a.* **dandyish,** *a.* **dandyism,** *n.* [Sc. var. of *Andrew*]

dandy², dandy-fever, *n.* dengue. [corr. of DENGUE]

dandy³, *n.* a Ganges boatman; a kind of hammock slung on a staff and carried by two or more bearers, used in the Himalayas. [Hind. *dāndī,* from *dānd,* an oar]

Dane, *n.* a native of Denmark; (*Hist.*) one of the Northmen who invaded Britain in the Middle Ages. **Great Dane,** a Danish breed of large, short-haired dogs. [Dan. *Daner,* OTeut. *Daniz,* pl.]

danegeld, *n.* an annual tax formerly levied on every hide of land in England to maintain forces against or furnish tribute to the Danes (finally abolished by Stephen). [ODan. *Danegjeld* (*gjeld,* payment, tribute, cogn. with OE *gield*)]

dane-hole DENE-HOLE.

Danelaw, *n.* 11th-century name for the area of N and E England settled by the Vikings in the 9th cent. It stretched from the river Tees to the river Thames, and occupied about half of England. Within its bounds, Danish law, customs, and language prevailed. Its linguistic influence is still apparent.

danewort, *n.* the dwarf elder, *Sambucus ebulus,* the flowers, bark and berries of which are used medicinally.

danger, *n.* risk, peril, hazard; exposure to injury or loss; anything that causes peril; (*Railway*) risk in going on owing to obstruction; the signal indicating this; †servitude, power, jurisdiction. **in danger (of),** liable (to). **on the danger list,** dangerously ill (in hospital). **danger-money,** *n.* money paid in compensation for the risks involved in any unusually dangerous job. **danger-signal,** *n.* a signal on railways directing stoppage or cautious progress. **dangerous,** *a.* **dangerously,** *adv.* [OF *dangier, dongier,* ult. from L *dominium,* from *dominus,* lord]

dangle, *v.i.* to hang loosely; to swing or wave about, to hang about, esp. to obtain some favour; to hover. *v.t.* to cause to dangle; to hold out (as a temptation, bait etc.). **dangler,** *n.* something which dangles; one who dangles after anything, esp. after women. [etym. doubtful; cp. DING, also Dan. *dangle*]

Daniel[1], *n.* an upright judge; an infallible judge. [from Daniel. i.-vi. and *Merchant of Venice,* IV. sc. I]

Daniel[2], *n.* (6th cent. BC), Jewish folk hero and prophet at the court of Nebuchadnezzar; also the name of a book of the Old Testament or Jewish Bible, probably compiled in the 2nd cent. BC. It includes stories about Daniel and his companions Shadrach, Meshach, and Abednego, set during the Babylonian captivity of the Jews.

Daniel[3], *n.* **Glyn** (1914–), British archaeologist. Prominent in the development of the subject, he was Disney professor of archaeology, Cambridge (1974–81). His books include *Megaliths in History* (1973) and *A Short History of Archaeology* (1981).

Daniell, *n.* **John Frederic** (1790–1845), British chemist and meteorologist who invented a primary electrical cell in 1836. In its original form, the **Daniell cell** consists of a central zinc cathode dipping into a porous pot containing zinc sulphate solution. The porous pot is, in turn, immersed in a solution of copper sulphate contained in a copper can, which acts as the cell's anode. The use of a porous barrier prevents polarization (the covering of the anode with small bubbles of hydrogen gas) and allows the cell to generate a continuous current of electricity.

Danish, *a.* pertaining to Denmark or the Danes. *n.* the Danish language, a member of the North Germanic group of the Indo-European language family, spoken in Denmark and Greenland. **Danish blue,** *n.* a strong-tasting, blue-veined cheese. **Danish pastry,** *n.* a flaky pastry usu. filled with jam, almonds or apples and often iced. [OE *Denisc*]

dank, *a.* damp, moist; chilly with moisture; soaked with cold moisture. *n.* a wet or marshy place; dampness. **dankish,** *a.* **dankly,** *adv.* **dankness,** *n.* [cp. Swed. dial. *dank,* a marshy place, Dan. dial. *dunkel,* moist]

danse macabre DANCE OF DEATH under DEATH.

danseuse, *n.* a female professional dancer. [F, fem. of *danseur*]

Dante Alighieri, *n.* (1265–1321), Italian poet. His masterpiece is *Divina Commedia/The Divine Comedy* (1300–21). Other works include the prose philosophical treatise *Convivio* (1306–08); *Monarchia* (1310–13), expounding his political theories; *De vulgari eloquentia/Concerning the Vulgar Tongue* (1304–06), an original Latin work on Italian, its dialects, and kindred languages; and *Canzoniere/Lyrics*, containing his scattered lyrics.

Dantean, *a.* relating to Dante; in the style of Dante, esp. of his *Inferno;* sombre, sublime. *n.* a student of Dante. **Dantesque**, *a.* Dantean.

Danton, *n.* **Georges Jacques** (1759–94), French revolutionary. Originally a lawyer, during the early years of the Revolution he was one of the most influential people in Paris. He organized the rising of 10 Aug. 1792 that overthrew the monarchy, roused the country to expel the Prussian invaders, and in Apr. 1793 formed the revolutionary tribunal and the Committee of Public Safety, of which he was the real leader until July. Thereafter he lost power, and when he attempted to recover it, he was arrested and guillotined.

Danube, *n.* (German **Donau**) second longest of European rivers, rising on the east slopes of the Black Forest, and flowing 2858 km/1776 miles across Europe to enter the Black Sea in Romania by a swampy delta.

Danzig, *n.* German name for Gdańsk.

dap, *v.t.* (*past, p.p.* **dapped**) to fish by letting the bait fall gently into the water. *v.t.* to let fall lightly; to cause to bounce on the ground. *n.* a bounce (of a ball etc.). [cp. DIP, DAB[1]]

Daphne, *n.* one of Diana's nymphs, fabled to have been changed into a laurel tree to escape Apollo's amorous pursuit; (**Daphne**) a genus of shrubs, partly evergreen, allied to the laurel; (**daphne**) a plant of this genus. **daphnin,** *n.* the bitter principle obtained from species of Daphne. [Gr.]

dapper, *a.* spruce, smart, brisk, active. †**dapperling,** *n.* **dapperly,** *adv.* **dapperness,** *n.* [cp. Dut. *dapper,* G *tapfer,* brave]

dapple, *n.* a spot on an animal; a mottled marking; a horse or other animal with a mottled coat. *a.* spotted; variegated with streaks or spots. *v.t.* to spot, to streak, to variegate. *v.i.* to become dappled. **dapple-grey,** *n.* a horse with a mottled grey coat. [cp. Icel. *depill,* a spot, dim. of *dapi,* pool]

darbies, *n.pl.* (*sl.*) handcuffs. [etym. doubtful]

Darby, *n.* **Abraham** (1677–1717), English iron manufacturer who developed a process for smelting iron ore using coke instead of the more expensive charcoal.

Darby and Joan, an elderly married couple living in domestic bliss. **Darby and Joan club,** a club for elderly people. [from an 18th-cent. English song]

Darbyites, *n.pl.* name given to the stricter adherents of the sect of Plymouth Brethren. [J.N. *Darby,* 1800–82]

Dardanelles, *n.* Turkish strait connecting the Sea of Marmara with the Aegean Sea (ancient name Hellespont, Turkish name *Canakkale Boğazi*); its shores are formed by the Gallipoli peninsula on the NW and the mainland of Turkey-in-Asia on the SE. It is 75 km/47 miles long and 5–6 km/3–4 miles wide.

dare[1], *v.i.* (*past, conditional* **durst**, **dared**) to venture; to have the courage or impudence; to be able, willing or ready; to be bold or adventurous. *v.t.* to attempt, to venture on; to challenge, to defy. *n.* daring, defiance; a challenge. **I dare say,** I suppose. **dare-devil,** *n.* a fearless, reckless fellow. **dare-devilry,** *n.* **daring,** *a.* courageous, bold; fearless, presumptuous. *n.* boldness, bravery; presumption. **daringly,** *adv.* [OE *durran,* to dare, pres. *dearr, durron,* past *dorste* (cp. Gr. *tharsein,* to be bold); the present is an old past tense, and consequently *dare* survives as 3rd sing. along with *dares*]

dare[2], *v.t.* to frighten, to terrify; to daze (birds) so as to catch them. *n.* a contrivance made with mirrors or bits of glass for daring and catching larks. **daring,** *n.* the act or process of catching birds by means of a mirror or a hawk. †**daring-glass,** *n.* a mirror used to dare larks; hence, any fascination. †**daring-net,** *n.* a net thrown over birds which have been dared. [etym. doubtful]

Dar es Salaam, *n.* (Arabic 'haven of peace'); chief seaport in Tanzania, on the Indian Ocean, and capital of Tanzania until its replacement by Dodoma in 1974; population (1985) 1,394,000.

darg, *n.* (*Sc.*) the quantity of work done in a day; a task. [corr. of *day work*]

daric, *n.* a gold coin of Darius I of Persia. [Gr. *Dareikos,* a.]

Darius I, *n.* **the Great** (*c.* 558–486 BC), king of Persia 521–485 BC. A member of a younger branch of the Achaemenid dynasty, he won the throne from the usurper Gaumata (died 522 BC), reorganized the government, and in 512 BC marched against the Scythians, a people north of the Black Sea, and subjugated Thrace and Macedonia.

dark, *a.* destitute of light; approaching black; shaded; swarthy, brown-complexioned; opaque; gloomy, sombre; (*fig.*) blind, ignorant; obscure, ambiguous; hidden, concealed; without spiritual or intellectual enlightenment; wicked, evil; cheerless; sad, sullen, frowning; unknown, untried (esp. used of a horse that has never run in public). †*v.i.* to become dark, to be eclipsed. *v.t.* to make dark; to obscure. *n.* darkness; absence of light; night, nightfall; shadow, shade; dark tint, the dark part of a picture; lack of knowledge; doubt, uncertainty. **to keep dark,** to keep silent about. **Dark Ages,** *n.pl.* the Middle Ages, esp. the period from the 5th to the 10th cent. (from an incorrect view of the ignorance then prevailing). **Dark Blues,** *n.pl.* the representatives of Oxford University in sporting events. **dark-browed,** *a.* stern of aspect. **Dark Continent,** *n.* Africa, esp. in the period before it was explored. **dark-eyed,** *a.* having dark-coloured eyes. **dark horse,** *n.* (*fig.*) one who keeps his/her own counsel; a person of unknown capabilities. **dark lantern,** *n.* a lantern that can be obscured at pleasure. †**dark-minded,** *a.* treacherous, revengeful. **dark room,** *n.* a room from which actinic light is shut out for photographic work. **dark star,** *n.* one emitting no light, whose existence is known only from its radio waves, infrared spectrum or gravitational effect. **darken,** *v.i.* to become dark or darker; to become obscure; to become darker in colour; to become gloomy or displeased. *v.t.* to make dark or darker; to deprive of vision; to render gloomy, ignorant or stupid; to perplex, to obscure; to sully. **not to darken one's door,** not to appear as a visitor; not to be welcome. **darkish,** *a.* **darkly,** *adv.* **darkness,** *n.* the state or quality of being dark; (*fig.*) blindness; obscurity; ignorance; wickedness; the powers of hell. **Prince of Darkness,** Satan. **darksome,** *a.* dark, gloomy. [OE *deorc*]

darkle, *v.i.* to lie in the dark, to lie hid; to grow dark; to become gloomy or dark with anger. *v.t.* to obscure. **darkling,** *adv.* in the dark. *a.* gloomy, dark; in the dark; obscure.

darky, *n.* (*coll. offensive*) a Negro; a dark lantern.

darling, *n.* one who is dearly beloved; a favourite, a pet. *a.* dearly beloved; (*coll.*) charming, delightful. [OE *dēorling* (*dēor*, DEAR, -LING[1])]

Darling, *n.* **Grace** (1815–42), British heroine. She was the daughter of a lighthouse keeper on the Farne Islands, off Northumberland. On 7 Sept. 1838 the *Forfarshire* was wrecked, and Grace Darling and her father rowed through a storm to the wreck, saving nine lives. She was awarded a medal for her bravery.

Darling pea, *n.* (*Austral.*) popular name of a poisonous plant and bush. **Darling shower,** *n.* (*Austral.*) a cyclone and dust storm. [Darling Downs]

darn[1], *v.t.* to mend by imitating the texture of the material of the garment etc. *n.* a place mended by darning. **darner,** *n.* one who darns; a needle for darning. **darning,** *n., a.* **darning-needle,** *n.* a needle used in darning. [cp. OE *gedyrnan,* to hide, to stop up a hole]

darn[2], *v.t.* a mild form of imprecation. [DAMN]

darnel, *n.* a kind of grass, *Lolium temulentum,* formerly believed to be poisonous, which grows among corn; the genus *Lolium.* [etym. doubtful (cp. Walloon *darnelle*)]

Darnley, *n.* **Henry Stewart** or **Stuart, Lord Darnley** (1545–67), British aristocrat, second husband of Mary Queen of Scots from 1565, and father of James I of England (James VI of Scotland). On the advice of her secretary, David Rizzio, Mary refused Darnley the crown matrimonial; in revenge Darnley led a band of nobles who murdered Rizzio in Mary's presence. Darnley was assassinated in 1567.

Darrow, *n.* **Clarence (Seward)** (1857–1938), US lawyer, born in Ohio, a champion of liberal causes and defender of the underdog. He defended many trade-union leaders, including Eugene Debs (1894). He was counsel for the defence in the Nathan Leopold and Richard Loeb murder trial in Chicago (1924), and in the Scopes monkey trial. He was an opponent of capital punishment.

dart, *n.* a short-pointed missile weapon thrown by the hand; a small pointed missile used in the game of darts; a javelin; the act of throwing; a sudden leap or rapid movement; a sting; a needle-like object which one snail fires at another during mating for sexual stimulation; (*Dressmaking*) a V-shaped tuck; (*Austral., coll.*) a plan, a project. *v.t.* to throw; to shoot or send forth suddenly; †to pierce with a dart. *v.i.* to run or move swiftly; to throw darts or other missiles. **dart-board,** *n.* a marked target used in the game of darts. **darter,** *n.* one who throws or hurls; one who moves with great rapidity; any species of *Plotus,* a genus of long-necked swimming birds; (*pl.*) the order Jaculatores, comprising the kingfishers and bee-eaters; the archer-fish. **darts,** *n.pl.* an indoor game of throwing small darts at a marked target. [OF *dart* (F *dard*), prob. from LG (cp. OE *daroth,* a javelin, OHG *tart,* a dart)]

Dart, *n.* **Raymond** (1893–1988), Australian anthropologist. He discovered the fossil remains of the 'southern African ape', *Australopithecus africanus* in 1924, near Taungs in Botswana.

dartre, *n.* a name for several skin diseases, esp. herpes; the scab characterizing these. [etym. doubtful]

Darwin[1], *n.* capital and port in Northern Territory, Australia, in NW Arnhem Land; population (1986) 69,000. It serves the uranium mining site at Rum Jungle to the south. Destroyed in 1974 by a cyclone, the city was rebuilt on the same site.

Darwin[2], *n.* **Charles Robert** (1809–82), English scientist who developed the modern theory of evolution and proposed the principle of natural selection. After much research in South America and the Galápagos Islands as naturalist on HMS *Beagle* (1831–36), Darwin published *On the Origin of Species by Means of Natural Selection or the Preservation of Favoured Races in the Struggle for Life* (1859). This explained the evolutionary process through the principles of natural and sexual selection, refuting earlier theories. It aroused bitter controversy because it disagreed with the literal interpretation of the Book of Genesis in the Bible.

Darwinian, *a.* pertaining to Charles Darwin, or to Darwinism. *n.* a believer in Darwinism. **Darwinianism, Darwinism,** *n.* the teaching of Charles Darwin, esp. the doctrine of the origin of species by natural selection. **Darwinist,** *n.* **Darwinistic,** *a.* **Darwinite,** *n.* **Darwinize, -ise,** *v.t., v.i.*

Darwinism, social, *n.* in US history, an influential social theory, drawing on the work of Charles Darwin and Herbert Spencer, which claimed to offer a scientific justification for late 19th-cent. *laissez-faire* capitalism (the principle of unrestricted freedom in commerce).

Dasam Granth, *n.* a collection of the writings of the tenth Sikh guru (teacher), Gobind Singh, and of poems by a number of other writers. It is written in a script called Gurmukhi, the written form of Punjabi popularized by Guru Angad. It contains a retelling of the Krishna legends, devotional verse and diverting anecdotes.

dash, *v.t.* (usu. with *to pieces*) to break by collision; (usu. with *out, down, away* etc.) to smite, to strike, to knock; to cause to come into collision; to throw violently or suddenly; to throw away suddenly; to bespatter, to besprinkle; to cause to rise; to dilute or adulterate by throwing in some other substance; (with *off*) to compose or sketch hastily; to obliterate with a stroke; to destroy; to frustrate; to confound, to abash, to discourage, to daunt; (*sl.*) to confound (as a mild imprecation). *v.i.* to rush, fall or throw oneself violently; to strike against something and break; (usu. with *up, off* or *away*) to run, ride or drive smartly; to move or behave showily or spiritedly. *n.* a sharp collision of two bodies; the sound of this, the sound of water in commotion; a rapid movement; a rush, an onset; a slight admixture; a sudden stroke; a blow; activity, daring; brilliancy, display, ostentation; a sudden check; a mark (–) denoting a break in a sentence, a parenthesis or omission; a hasty stroke with a pen etc.; (*Mus.*) a line drawn through a figure in thoroughbass, to raise the interval a semitone; a short stroke placed above notes or chords, directing that they are to be played staccato; the long element in Morse code; (*Athletics*) a sprint. **to cut a dash,** to make an impression. **dashboard,** *n.* a splashboard; the float of a paddle-wheel; a fascia in front of the driver of a car. **dash-light,** *n.* a light illuminating the dashboard of a car. **dasher,** *n.* one who or that which dashes; a float, a plunger; a contrivance for agitating the contents of a churn; (*fig.*) a dashing person. **dashing,** *a.* daring, spirited; showy, smart. **dashingly,** *adv.* **dashy,** *a.* ostentatious, showy, smart. [cp. Dan. *daske,* to slap, Swed. *daska,* to beat, LG *daschen,* to thrash]

Das Kapital, *n.* an exposition of Karl Marx's theories of economic production, published in three volumes (1867–95). It focuses on the exploitation of the worker and appeals for a classless society where the production process is shared equally.

dassie, *n.* (*S Afr.*) a hyrax.

dastard, *n.* a coward, a poltroon; a cowardly villain. *a.* cowardly; basely shrinking from danger. †**dastardize, -ise,** *v.t.* **dastardly,** *a.* **dastardliness,** *n.* [prob. from DAZE, -ARD]

dasymeter, *n.* an instrument for measuring the density of gases. [Gr. *dasus,* dense]

Dasypodidae, *n.* the South American family of armadillos. [Gr. *dasypous,* hairy-footed]

Dasyure, *n.* a genus of small marsupials found in Australia, Tasmania and New Guinea. [Gr. *dasus,* hairy, rough; *oura,* a tail]

data, *n.pl.* (*often sing. in constr.; pl. of* DATUM) facts or information from which other things may be deduced; the information operated on by a computer program. **data-bank, -base,** *n.* a large amount of information, usu. stored in a computer for easy access. **data-capture,** *n.* the conversion of information into a form which can be processed by a computer. **data-processing,** *n.* the handling and processing of data in computer files. [L *dăta,* things given, from *dăre,* to give]

datable DATE[1].

dataria, *n.* the papal chancery at Rome whence all bulls are issued. **datary,** *n.* an officer of the papal chancery who affixes *datum Romae* (given at Rome) to the papal bulls. [L *datārius,* that can be given]

date[1], *n.* a fixed point of time; the time at which anything happened or is appointed to take place; the specification of this in a book, inscription, document or letter; (*coll.*) a social or other engagement (usu. with one of the opposite sex); the person thus concerned; period, age, duration; conclusion. *v.t.* to affix the date to; to note or fix the date of. *v.i.* to reckon; to begin; to be dated. **out of date,** dated; obsolete. **to make, have, a date,** (*coll.*) to make or have an appointment. **up to date,** (*coll.*) recent, modern. †**date-broke,** *a.* not provided for on the appointed day. **date-line,** *n.* the line on either side of which the date differs, running meridionally across the western hemisphere from the poles and theoretically 180° from Greenwich; line with date and place of sending printed above a newspaper dispatch. **date-mark, -stamp,** *n.* a stamp on perishable goods showing the date before which they are best used or consumed. *v.t.* to mark (goods) in this way. **datable,** *a.* **dateless,** *a.* **dater,** *n.* one who dates; a stamp for marking dates. [F, from late L *dăta,* given, fem. p.p. of *dăre,* to give (referring to the time and place at which a letter was given)]

date[2], *n.* the fruit of the date-palm, an oblong fruit with a hard seed or stone; (*Bot.*) any species of the genus *Phoenix.* **date-palm, -tree,** *n. Phoenix dactylifera,* the palm-tree of Scripture, common in N Africa and Asia Minor. [OF, from L *dactylus,* Gr. *daktulos,* a finger, a date]

dative, *a.* denoting the grammatical case used to represent the remoter object, or the person or thing interested in the action of the verb; (*Law*) that may be parted with at pleasure; removable (from an office); appointed by a court. *n.* the dative case. **datival,** *a.* **datively,** *adv.* [L *datīvus,* pertaining to giving (*dăre,* to give)]

datum, *n.* (*pl.* **data**) a quantity, condition, fact or other premise, given or admitted, from which other things or results may be found (cp. DATA). **datum-line, -level, -plane,** *n.* the horizontal line, such as sea-level, from which calculations are made in surveying etc. [L, neut. p.p. of *dăre,* to give]

Datura, *n.* a genus of solanaceous plants, containing the thorn-apple, *D. stramonium,* which yields a powerful narcotic. **daturine,** *n.* an alkaloid obtained from the thorn-apple. [Hind. *dhatūra*]

daub, *v.t.* to smear or coat with a soft adhesive substance; to paint coarsely; to stain, to soil; to whitewash, to cloak, to disguise; †to flatter grossly. *v.i.* to paint in a crude or inartistic style; to indulge in gross flattery; to play the hypocrite. *n.* a smear; a coarse painting; a plaster or mud wall-covering. **dauber,** *n.* †**daubery,** *n.* daubing; (*fig.*) specious colouring; false pretence. **daubing,** *n.* coarse painting; gross flattery. **daubster,** *n.* [OF *dauber,* to plaster, L *dealbāre,* to whitewash (DE-, *albāre,* from *albus,* white)]

daughter, *n.* a female child with relation to its parents; a female descendant; a female member of a family, race, city etc.; a female in a child-like relation, as a penitent to her confessor; (*Biol.*) a cell formed from another of the same type; a nuclide formed from another by radioactive decay. **daughter-in-law,** *n.* a son's wife; (*loosely*) a step-daughter. **daughterhood,** *n.* **daughterly,** *a.* **daughterliness,** *n.* [OE *dohtor* (cp. Dut. *dochter,* G *Tochter,* Gr. *thugatēr,* Sansk. *duhitā*)]

Daumier, *n.* **Honoré** (1808–79), French artist. His sharply dramatic and satirical cartoons dissected Parisian society. His output was enormous and included 4000 lithographs and, mainly after 1860, powerful satirical oil paintings that were little appreciated in his lifetime.

daunt, *v.t.* to intimidate, to dishearten; to check by frightening; to discourage; †to daze. **dauntless,** *a.* fearless, intrepid. **dauntlessly,** *adv.* **dauntlessness,** *n.* [OF *danter* (F *dompter*), L *domitāre* (freq. of *domāre,* to tame)]

dauphin, *n.* the title of the heir-apparent to the French throne, from the fact that the principality of Dauphiné was an appanage of his. **dauphiness,** *n. fem.* **dauphine,** *n.* the wife of the dauphin. [OF *daulphin,* L *delphīnus,* DOLPHIN]

daur, (*Sc.*) DARE[1].

daut, dawt, *v.t.* (*Sc.*) to caress; to cherish. **dautie, dawtie,** *n.* a darling, a pet. [etym. unknown]

davenport, *n.* a small writing-desk with drawers on both sides; (*esp. N Am.*) a large sofa, a couch. [prob. from the first maker]

David[1], *n.* (*c.* 1060–970 BC), second king of Israel. According to the Bible he played the harp before King Saul to banish his melancholy, and later slew the Philistine giant Goliath with a sling and stone. After Saul's death David was anointed king at Hebron, took Jerusalem and made it his capital.

David[2], *n.* **Elizabeth** (1914–), British cookery writer. Her *Mediterranean Food* (1950) and *French Country Cooking* (1951) helped to spark an interest in foreign cuisine in Britain, and also inspired a growing school of informed, highly literate writing on food and wine.

David[3], *n.* **Félicien César** (1810–76), French composer. His symphonic fantasy *Desert* (1844) was inspired by travels in Palestine. He was one of the first Western composers to introduce oriental scales and melodies into his music.

David[4], *n.* **Jacques Louis** (1748–1825), French painter in the neo-classical style. He was an active supporter of and unofficial painter to the republic during the French Revolution, for which he was imprisoned (1794–95). He was later appointed court painter to the emperor Napoleon, of whom he created well-known images such as the horseback figure of *Napoleon Crossing the Alps* (1800, Louvre, Paris).

David Copperfield, *n.* a novel by Charles Dickens, published 1849–50. The story follows the orphan David Copperfield from his schooldays and early poverty to eventual fame as an author. Among the characters he encounters are Mr Micawber, Mr Peggotty, and Uriah Heep.

David I, *n.* (1084–1153), king of Scotland from 1124. The youngest son of Malcolm III Canmore and St

Margaret, he was brought up in the English court of Henry I, and in 1113 married Matilda, widow of the 1st earl of Northampton. He invaded England (1138) in support of Queen Matilda, but was defeated at Northallerton in the Battle of the Standard, and again in 1141.

David II, *n.* (1324–71), king of Scotland from 1329, son of Robert I (the Bruce). David was married at the age of four to Joanna, daughter of Edward II of England. In 1346 David invaded England, was captured at the battle of Neville's Cross and imprisoned for 11 years.

David, St, *n.* or **Dewi** (5th–6th cent.), patron saint of Wales, Christian abbot and bishop. According to legend he was the son of a prince of Cardiganshire and uncle of King Arthur, and responsible for the adoption of the leek as the national emblem of Wales, but his own emblem is a dove. Feast day 1 Mar.

Davies[1], *n.* **Peter Maxwell** (1934–), English composer and conductor. His music combines medieval and serial codes of practice with a heightened expressionism as in his opera *Taverner* (1962–68).

Davies[2], *n.* **Robertson** (1913–), Canadian novelist. He gained an international reputation with *Fifth Business* (1970), the first novel of his Deptford trilogy, a panoramic work blending philosophy, humour, the occult, and ordinary life. Other works include *A Mixture of Frailties* (1958), *The Rebel Angels* (1981), and *What's Bred in the Bone* (1986).

Da Vinci LEONARDO DA VINCI.

Davis[1], *n.* **Angela** (1944–), US left-wing activist for black rights, prominent in the student movement of the 1960s. In 1970 she went into hiding after being accused of supplying guns used in the murder of a judge who had been seized as a hostage in an attempt to secure the release of three black convicts (known as the Soledad brothers from the name of their prison). She was captured, tried, and acquitted. In 1980 she stood as the Communist vice-presidential candidate.

Davis[2], *n.* **Bette** (1908–89), US actress. She entered films in 1930, and established a reputation with *Of Human Bondage* (1934) as a forceful dramatic actress. Later films included *Dangerous* (1935) and *Jezebel* (1938), both winning her Academy Awards, and *Whatever Happened to Baby Jane?* (1962).

Davis[3], *n.* **Jefferson** (1808–89), US politician, president of the short-lived Confederate States of America 1861–65. He was a leader of the Southern Democrats in the US Senate from 1857, and a defender of 'humane' slavery; in 1860 he issued a declaration in favour of secession from the US. During the Civil War he assumed strong political leadership, but often disagreed with military policy. He was imprisoned for two years after the war, one of the very few cases of judicial retribution against Confederate leaders.

Davis[4], *n.* **Miles (Dewey Jr)** (1926–), US jazz trumpeter, composer, and band leader. He recorded bebop with Charlie Parker in 1945, pioneered cool jazz in the 1950s and jazz-rock fusion from the late 1960s. His influential albums include *Birth of the Cool* (1949), *Sketches of Spain* (1959), and *Bitches' Brew* (1970).

Davis[5], *n.* **Steve** (1957–), English snooker player. He has won every major honour in the game since turning professional in 1978. He has been world champion six times, including 1989. He has won as many major titles as all the other professionals between them.

Davis[6], *n.* **Stuart** (1894–1964), US abstract painter. He used hard-edged geometric shapes in primary colours and experimented with collage. In the 1920s he produced paintings of commercial packaging, such as *Lucky Strike* (1921) (Museum of Modern Art, New York), which foreshadow Pop art.

Davis Cup, *n.* annual lawn-tennis tournament for men's international teams, first held 1900 after Dwight Filley Davis (1879–1945) donated the trophy.

Davison, *n.* **Emily** (1872–1913), English militant suffragette, who died while trying to stop the King's horse at the Derby at Epsom (she was trampled by the horse). She joined the Women's Social and Political Union in 1906 and served several prison sentences for militant action such as stone throwing, setting fire to pillar boxes, and bombing Lloyd George's country house.

davit, *n.* a spar used as a crane for hoisting the anchor; one of a pair of beams projecting over a ship's side, with tackles to hoist or lower a boat. [formerly *david,* prob. from the personal name]

Davitt, *n.* **Michael** (1846–1906), Irish Fenian revolutionary. He joined the Fenians (forerunners of the Irish Republican Army) in 1865, and was imprisoned for treason during 1870–77. After his release, he and Charles Parnell founded the Land League (1879). Davitt was jailed several times for his share in the land-reform agitation. He was a Member of Parliament during 1895–99.

Davy, *n.* **Humphry** (1778–1829), English chemist. As a laboratory assistant in Bristol in 1799, he discovered the respiratory effects of laughing gas (nitrous oxide). He discovered, by electrolysis, the elements sodium, potassium, calcium, magnesium, strontium, and barium. He invented the 'safety lamp' for use in mines where methane was present, in effect enabling the miners to work in previously unsafe conditions.

Davy Jones, *n.* an imaginary malign spirit with power over the sea. **Davy Jones's locker,** a sailor's name for the sea as the tomb of the drowned. [etym. unknown]

daw[1], *n.* a jackdaw; an empty-headed fellow. [cp. OLG *dāha,* OHG *tāha,* G *Dohle* (imit. in origin)]

daw[2], *v.i.* (*obs. exc. in Sc.*) to dawn. *v.t.* to awaken. [OE *dagian*]

dawdle, *v.i.* to trifle; to idle about; to waste time. *n.* a dawdler; the act of dawdling. **dawdler,** *n.* [prob. a recent var. of DADDLE[1]]

Dawes, *n.* **Charles Gates** (1865–1951), US Republican politician. In 1923 he was appointed by the Allied Reparations Commission president of the committee that produced the Dawes Plan, a $200 million loan that enabled Germany to pay enormous war debts after World War I. It was superseded by the Young Plan (which reduced the total reparations bill) in 1929. Dawes was elected vice president of the US in 1924, received the Nobel Peace Prize (1925), and was ambassador to Britain during 1929–32.

dawk, dâk, *n.* the Indian post or transport by relays of runners, horses etc. **dawk-bungalow,** *n.* an inn or house for travellers at a dawk station. [Hind. *dāk* (prob. conn. with Sansk. *drāk,* quickly, from *drā,* to run)]

dawn, *v.i.* to grow light, to break (as day); to begin to open, expand or appear. *n.* the break of day; the first rise or appearance. **to dawn upon,** to be realized gradually by. **dawn-chorus,** *n.* the singing of birds at dawn. **dawning,** *n.* dawn; the time of dawn; (*fig.*) the east; the first beginning or unfolding. [ME *dawnen,* earlier *dawen,* DAW[2]]

dawt DAUT.

day, *n.* the time the sun is above the horizon; daylight; the space of twenty-four hours, commencing at midnight, a practice borrowed from the ancient Romans, and called the *civil day,* as distinguished from a *mean solar day* which begins at noon; the average time interval between two successive returns of the sun to the meridian. An *astronomical day* is the time in which the earth rotates on its axis relative to the stars (about four minutes less than the mean solar day), also called the *sidereal* or *natural day;* daylight, light, dawn, day-time; any specified time; the day in the week or month for receiving visitors; an age; (*often pl.*) life, lifetime, period of vigour, activity or prosperity; a day appointed to commemorate any event; a contest, a battle, the victory; today. **all day, all the day,** throughout the day. **better days, evil days,** a period of prosperity or of misfortune. **day and night,** throughout both day and night; always; by or in both day and night. **day by day,** daily. **day of doom,** the Last Judgment as described in Rev. xx.11–15. **Day of Judgment,** the end of the world, the Last Day. **days of grace,** (*Law*) days granted by a court for delay at the prayer of a plaintiff or defendant; a customary number of days (in England three) allowed for the payment of a note, or bill of exchange, after it becomes due. **every day,** daily. **let's call it a day,** that's all we can do today. **one day, one of these days,** shortly; in the near future; at some unspecified time in the future. **present day,** modern times; modern. **some day,** in the future. **the other day** OTHER. **this day week,** a week forward from today. **today,** this day, now. **to gain, win, the day,** to come off victor. **to name the day,** to settle the marriage date. **day-bed,** *n.* a couch, a sofa. **day-blindness,** *n.* indistinct vision by day. **day-boarder** *n.* a pupil who has meals but does not sleep at a school. **daybook,** *n.* one in which the business transactions of the day are recorded. **day-boy, -girl,** *n.* a boy or girl attending a day-school, but differing from a day-boarder in not taking dinner there. **day-break,** *n.* the first appearance of daylight. **day-care,** *n.* the daytime supervision by trained staff of pre-school children or elderly or handicapped people. **day-centre,** *n.* one providing social amenities for the elderly, handicapped etc. **day-dream,** *n.* a reverie, a castle in the air. **day-dreamer,** *n.* one who indulges in day-dreams. **day-dreaming,** *n.* **day-fly,** *n.* an insect of the genus *Ephemera.* **day-labour,** *n.* work done by the day. **day-labourer,** *n.* one who is hired by the day. **day-lily,** *n.* a liliaceous plant of the genus *Hemerocallis,* the flowers of which last one day. **day-long,** *a.* lasting all day. *adv.* the whole day. **day-nursery,** *n.* a children's playroom in the daytime; a crèche. **day-owl,** *n.* the hawk-owl which hunts by day. †**day-peep,** *n.* the break of day. **day-release,** *n.* a system which frees people from work for some hours each week to follow part-time education relevant to their employment. **day-return,** *n.* a special cheap ticket for travel to a place, returning the same day. **day-room,** *n.* a room used in daylight only; a common living-room in a school; a ward where prisoners are confined during the day. †**day-rule, †-writ,** *n.* a rule or order of court allowing a prisoner of the King's Bench to leave prison for one day. **day-school,** *n.* a school held in the daytime, distinguished from evening-school, Sunday school or boarding-school. **day-shift,** *n.* work during the day; the group of workers undertaking such work. **day-sight,** *n.* vision clear by day, but indistinct at night. †**days-man,** *n.* an umpire, a mediator (from appointing a day for arbitration); a day-labourer. **day-spring,** *n.* the dawn; day-break. **day-star,** *n.* the morning star; †the sun. **day's-work,** *n.* the work of one day; the reckoning of a ship's course for 24 hours, from noon till noon. **daytime,** *n.* day as opposed to night. **day-trip,** *n.* an excursion made to and from a place in a single day. †**day-wearied,** *a.* wearied with the occupation of the day. **day-work,** *n.* work done by the day. [OE *dæg* (cp. Dut., Dan. and Swed. *dag,* G *Tag*)]

Day, *n.* **Doris** (stage name of Doris von Kappelhoff) (1924–), US film actress and singing star of the 1950s and early 1960s, mostly in musicals and, later, rather coy sex comedies. Her films include *Tea for Two* (1950), *Calamity Jane* (1953), and *Lover Come Back* (1962).

Dayak, *n.pl.* several indigenous peoples of Indonesian Borneo and Sarawak, including the Bahau of central and E Borneo, the Land Dayak of SW Borneo, and the Iban of Sarawak. Their language belongs to the Austronesian family.

Dayan, *n.* **Moshe** (1915–81), Israeli general and politician. As minister of defence in 1967 and 1969–74, he was largely responsible for the victory in the 1967 Six-Day War, but was criticized for Israel's alleged unpreparedness in the 1973 October War, and resigned with Golda Meir. Foreign minister from 1977, he resigned in 1979 in protest over the refusal of the Begin government to negotiate with the Palestinians.

Day-glo®, *n.* a type of fluorescent paint. *a.* being or resembling this type of paint; (*loosely*) of a glowingly bright colour (usu. pink, orange or green).

Day Lewis, *n.* **Cecil** (1904–72), Irish poet, British poet laureate 1968–72. With Auden and Spender, he was one of the influential left-wing poets of the 1930s. He also wrote detective novels under the pseudonym Nicholas Blake.

daylight, *n.* the light of day as opposed to that of the moon or artificial light; dawn; light visible through an opening; hence, an interval, a gap; a visible space; openness, publicity. **to see daylight,** to begin to understand; to draw near to the end of a task. **daylight reflector,** *n.* a reflector placed near a window to throw in more light. **daylight robbery** ROBBERY under ROB. **daylight saving,** *n.* a system of advancing the clock by one hour in spring and setting back the hands by one hour in autumn. Summer time was introduced into Great Britain in 1919. **daylights,** *n.pl.* wits, as in *the living daylights.*

daze, *v.t.* to stupefy, to confuse, to dazzle, to overpower with light. *n.* the state of being dazed; mica (from its glitter). **dazed,** *a.* **dazedly,** *adv.* [ME *dasen,* v.t., v.i. (cp. Icel. *dasask,* to become weary, refl. of *dasa*)]

dazzle, *v.t.* to overpower with a glare of light; to daze or bewilder with rapidity of motion, brilliant display, stupendous number etc. *v.i.* to be dazzled; to be excessively bright. *n.* anything which dazzles; a method of painting ships for purposes of camouflage. **dazzlement,** *n.* **dazzling,** *a.* that dazzles; brilliant, splendid. **dazzlingly,** *adv.* [freq. of prec.]

dB, (*abbr.*) decibel(s).

dBASE, *n.* a family of microcomputer programs for manipulating large quantities of data; also, a related fourth-generation language. The first version, dBASE II, appeared in the early 1980s, since when it has become very widely used.

DBE, (*abbr.*) Dame Commander of the (Order of the) British Empire.

DBS, (*abbr.*) direct broadcasting by satellite.

DC, (*abbr.*) (*Mus.*) da capo; direct current; (*N Am.*) District of Columbia.

DCM, (*abbr.*) Distinguished Conduct Medal.

DD, (*abbr.*) Doctor of Divinity; direct debit.

D-day, *n.* 6 June 1944, the day the Allied invasion of Europe took place during World War II. The landings took place on the Normandy coast of France and began the campaign to liberate Europe. D-day was originally fixed for 5 June, but because of unfavourable weather the invasion was postponed for 24 hours.

DDR, (*abbr.*) German Democratic Republic (East Germany, G *Deutsche Demokratische Republik*).

DDS, (*abbr.*) Doctor of Dental Surgery.

DDT, (*abbr.*) dichlorodiphenyltrichloroethane, an insecticide discovered in 1939 by Swiss chemist Paul Müller. It is useful in the control of insects that spread malaria, but resistant strains develop. DDT is highly toxic, and persists in the environment and in living tissue. Its use is now banned in most countries.

de-, *pref.* from; down; away; out; (*intens.*) completely, thoroughly; (*priv.*) expressing undoing, deprivation, reversal or separation. [L *de,* prep., and *de-,* pref.; or from F *dé-* (L *dis-, de-*)]

deacon, *n.* one of a class entrusted with the care of the sick and the distribution of alms to the poor in the early Church; a cleric in orders next below a priest; one who superintends the secular affairs of a Presbyterian church; one who admits persons to membership, and assists at communion in the Congregational Church; (*Sc.*) the master of an incorporated guild of craftsmen. **deaconess,** *n.* a female deacon; a member of a Lutheran sisterhood. **deaconship, -ry,** *n.* [OE, from L *diāconus,* Gr. *diakonos,* a servant]

deactivate, *v.t.* to render harmless or less radioactive. **deactivation,** *n.* **deactivator,** *n.*

dead, *a.* having ceased to live; having no life, lifeless; benumbed, insensible, temporarily deprived of the power of action; resembling death; unconscious or unappreciative; without spiritual feeling; cooled, abated; obsolete, effete, useless; inanimate or inorganic as distinct from organic; extinct; lustreless, motionless, inactive, soundless; flat, vapid, dull, opaque; certain, unerring. *adv.* absolutely, quite, completely; profoundly.

n. a dead person; the time when things are still, stillness; (*pl.*) non-metalliferous rock excavated round a vein, or in forming levels, shafts etc. †*v.i.* to die. †*v.t.* to kill. **dead against,** immediately against or opposite (also **dead on end**); absolutely opposed to. **dead of night,** the middle of the night. **dead on the mark,** absolutely straight. **dead to the world,** (*coll.*) fast asleep. **the dead,** dead persons. **dead-alive, dead and alive,** *a.* spiritless. **dead-beat,** *a.* quite exhausted. *n.* (*coll.*) a worthless, lazy fellow; (*Austral.*) a ruined man, one down on his luck. **dead-beat escapement,** (*Horol.*) an escapement which gives no recoil to the escape wheel. **dead-born,** *a.* still-born; falling flat or spiritless. **dead-broke,** *a.* (*coll.*) penniless, ruined. **dead centre** DEAD POINT. **dead certainty,** *n.* something sure to occur; also (*coll.*) **dead cert. dead colouring,** *n.* the first layer of colour in a picture, usually of some shade of grey. †**dead-doing,** *a.* death-dealing. **dead-drunk,** *a.* helpless from drink. **dead duck,** *n.* (*coll.*) a person or idea doomed to failure. **dead-end,** *n.* a cul-de-sac. *a.* (*Radio*) describing the portion of a coil not connected into circuit. **dead-eye,** *n.* (*Naut.*) one of the flat, round blocks having eyes for the lanyards, by which the rigging is set up. **dead-fall,** *n.* a trap with a heavy weight which falls to crush the prey. **dead-fire,** *n.* St Elmo's fire, an augury of death. **dead-freight,** *n.* a sum paid for space reserved in a vessel but not made use of for cargo. **deadhead,** *n.* (*coll.*) one who has a free pass; a stupid, unimaginative person. *v.t.* to remove withered blooms (from flowers) to encourage future growth. **Dead Heart,** *n.* (*Austral.*) the land of the Central Australian Desert. **dead heat,** *n.* a race resulting in a draw. **dead-hedge, fence,** *n.* a hedge of dead wood. **dead horse,** *n.* something in which there is no longer any life or interest. **to flog a dead horse** FLOG. **dead-house,** *n.* a mortuary. **dead language,** *n.* a language no longer spoken, as classical Latin. †**dead latch,** *n.* a kind of latch the bolt of which may be so locked that it cannot be opened from within by the handle, or from without by the key. **dead letter,** *n.* a letter which cannot be delivered by the post office, and is sent to the Returned Office to be opened and returned to the sender; a law or anything that has become inoperative. **dead level,** *n.* a perfect level; flat country that offers no difficulty to making a railway or road. **dead lift, pull,** *n.* a lift or pull at a dead weight; a thankless effort. **dead-lights,** *n.pl.* shutters placed over port-holes or cabin windows in rough weather; the luminous appearance sometimes seen over rotting animal bodies; corpse candles. **deadline,** *n.* the time of newspapers, books etc. going to press; a fixed time or date terminating something. **deadlock,** *n.* a lock worked on one side by a handle, and on the other by a key; a complete standstill, a position whence there is no exit. **dead loss,** *n.* a loss with no compensation whatever; a useless person, thing or situation. **dead man,** *n.* (*sl.*) an empty wine bottle; a loaf charged for but not delivered. **dead man's, men's, fingers,** various species of orchis, the wild arum and other flowers; the zoophyte *Alcyonium digitatum,* also called **dead man's hand** or **dead man's toes. dead man's handle,** device for automatically cutting off the current of an electrically driven vehicle if the driver releases his pressure on the handle. **dead men's shoes,** inheritances, legacies. **dead march,** *n.* a piece of solemn music played at funerals (esp. of soldiers). **dead-nettle,** *n.* a non-stinging labiate plant, like a nettle, of several species belonging to the genus *Lamium.* **dead-pan,** *a.* (of the face) expressionless. †**dead pay,** *n.* pay drawn and appropriated by officials for subordinates who are dead or discharged. **dead point,** *n.* either of the two points at which a crank assumes a position in line with the rod which impels it. **dead reckoning,** *n.* the calculation of a ship's position from the log and compass, when observations cannot be taken. **dead ringer,** *n.* (*coll.*) a person or thing exactly resembling someone or something else. **dead-ropes,** *n.pl.* (*Naut.*) ropes which do not run in any blocks. **dead set,** *n.* a determined attack. **dead set on,** determined (to). **dead set against,** utterly opposed to. **dead shot,** *n.* a marksman who never misses. **dead stand,** *n.* determined opposition; a complete standstill. **dead stock,** *n.* farm equipment. **dead wall,** *n.* a blank wall. **dead-water,** *n.* water that is absolutely still; the eddy under the stern of a ship or boat. **dead weight,** *n.* a mass of inert matter, a burden that exerts no relieving force; any very heavy weight or load. **dead window,** *n.* a sham window. **dead-wood,** *n.* the built-up timbers fore and aft above the keel; a useless person etc. **deadness,** *n.* [OE *dēad,* from Teut. stem *dau-,* to die (cp. Dut. *dood,* Dan. and Swed. *död,* G *tot*)]

deaden, *v.t.* to diminish the vitality, brightness, force or power of; to make insensible, to dull; to blunt. *v.i.* to lose vitality, strength, feeling, spirit etc. [from prec.]

deadly, *a.* causing or procuring death; fatal; like death; implacable, irreconcilable; intense; very excessive. *adv.* as if dead; extremely, excessively, intensively; to death, mortally. **deadly-carrot,** *n.* southern European plants of the genus *Thapsia.* **deadly nightshade,** *n.* a poisonous shrub with dark purple berries, *Atropa belladonna;* wrongly applied to the woody nightshade, *Solanum dulcamara.* **deadly sin,** *n.* one of the seven mortal sins. †**deadly-standing,** *a.* with a dull, fixed stare. **deadliness,** *n.* [OE *dēadlic*]

Dead Sea, *n.* large lake, partly in Israel and partly in Jordan; area 1020 sq km/394 sq miles; lying 394 m/1293 ft below sea-level. The chief river entering it is the Jordan; it has no outlet to the sea, and the water is very salty.

Dead Sea Scrolls, collection of ancient scrolls (some intact in their jars) and fragments of scrolls found 1947–56 in caves on the W side of the Jordan 12 km/7 miles S of Jericho and 2 km/l miles from the N end of the Dead Sea, at Qumran. They date mainly from about 150 BC–68 AD, when the monastic community that owned them was destroyed by the Romans because of its support for a revolt against their rule. They include copies of Old Testament books a thousand years earlier than those previously known to be extant.

deaf, *a.* incapable or dull of hearing, unwilling to hear; disregarding, refusing to listen, refusing to comply; insensible (to). †*v.t.* to deafen. **deaf-and-dumb alphabet, language,** a system of signs for holding communication with deaf people. **to turn a deaf ear to,** to ignore. **deaf-aid,** *n.* a hearing-aid. **deaf-mute,** *n.* one who is deaf and dumb. **deaf-mutism,** *n.* **deafen,** *v.t.* to make wholly or partially deaf; to stun with noise; to render impervious to sound by pugging (as a floor, partition etc.). **deafening,** *a.* **deafly,** *adv.* **deafness,** *n.* [OE *dēaf* (cp. Dut. *doof,* Dan. *döv,* G *taub;* also Gr. *tuphlos,* blind)]

Deakin, *n.* **Alfred** (1856–1919), Australian Liberal politician, prime minister in 1903–04, 1905–08, and 1909–10. In his second administration, he enacted legislation on defence and pensions.

deal[1], *n.* an indefinite quantity; the distribution of cards to the players; a share, a part, a portion; a bargain, a piece of business; an underhand transaction. *v.t.* (*past, p.p.* **dealt** (delt)) to distribute; to award as his/her proper share to someone; to distribute or give in succession (as cards). *v.i.* to have business or traffic (with); to associate, occupy oneself, take measures (with); to distribute cards to the players. **a deal,** (*coll.*) a good amount. **a great, good, deal,** a large quantity; to a large extent; by much, considerably. **a raw deal,** harsh, unfair treatment. **to deal by,** to act towards. **to deal in,** to be engaged in; to trade in. **to deal with,** to have to do with; to consider judicially; to behave towards; to take action in respect of, to handle. **dealer,** *n.* a trader, a merchant; a drug-pusher; one who deals the cards. **dealership,** *n.* a dealer's premises. **dealing,** *n.* conduct towards others; intercourse in matters of business; traffic. [OE *dǣl,* a share, a portion (cp. Dut. and Dan. *deel,* OHG *teil,* G *Teil*), whence *dǣlan,* to divide]

deal[2], *n.* a plank of fir or pine not more than 3 in. (7·6 cm) thick, 7 in. (17·8 cm) wide, and 6 ft. (1·8 m) long; fir or pine wood. [cp. OE *thille,* THILL (prob. through

LG *dele* or Dut. *deel*)]

deambulation, *n.* walking about. **deambulatory,** *n.* a place for walking about in; a cloister; the passage round the screen enclosing the choir in a cathedral or other large church. [L *deambulātio,* from *deambulāre* (DE-, *ambulāre,* to walk)]

dean[1], *n.* an ecclesiastical dignitary presiding over the chapter of a cathedral or collegiate church; a rural dean, a clergyman charged with jurisdiction over a part of an archdeaconry; a title applied to the head of the establishment of a chapel royal, and to the Bishop of London (as Dean of the Province of Canterbury); a resident fellow in a university with disciplinary and other functions; the head of a faculty. **Dean of Faculty,** (*Sc.*) the president of the Faculty of Advocates. **Dean of Guild,** (*Sc.*) a magistrate with jurisdiction over buildings, weights and measures etc. **deanery,** *n.* the office, district or official residence of a dean. **deanship,** *n.* the office or personality of a dean. [OF *deien,* L *decānus -um,* one set over ten (*decem,* ten)]

dean[2], **dene**[1], *n.* a valley; a deep and narrow valley (chiefly in place-names). [OE *denu*]

Dean[1], *n.* **Basil** (1888–1978), British founder and director-general of ENSA (1939), which provided entertainment for the Allied forces in World War II.

Dean[2], *n.* **James (Byron)** (1931–55), US actor. Killed in a road accident after only his first film, *East of Eden* (1955), had been shown, he posthumously became a cult hero with *Rebel Without a Cause* and *Giant* (both 1956). He became a symbol of teenage rebellion against American middle-class values.

deaner, deener, *n.* (*Austral., coll.*) a shilling. [etym. doubtful]

dear, *a.* beloved, cherished; precious, valuable; costly, of a high price; characterized by high prices; †characterized by scarcity; †grievous, dire; a conventional form of address used in letter-writing. *n.* a darling, a loved one; a cherished person, a favourite; a term of endearment. *adv.* dearly, at a high price. *v.t.* to address as dear. *int.* expressing distress, sympathy or mild astonishment and protest. **Dear John letter,** (*esp. N Am., coll.*) a letter, esp. from a woman to a man, ending a relationship. **dearly,** *adv.* **dearness,** *n.* **deary, dearie,** *n.* (*dial., coll.*) a term of endearment. [OE *dēore* (cp. Dut. *dier,* OHG *tiuri,* G *teuer*)]

dearborn, *n.* (*N Am.*) a light four-wheeled family carriage. [name of inventor]

dearth, *n.* scarcity, causing high price; dearness, lack; want, privation. [ME *derthe,* from OE *dēore,* DEAR]

deasil, DEISEAL.

deaspirate, *v.t.* to remove the aspirate from.

death, *n.* extinction of life; the act of dying; the state of being dead; decay, destruction; a cause or instrument of death; a skull or skeleton as the emblem of mortality; spiritual destruction, annihilation; capital punishment; †an imprecation. **Black Death,** an epidemic of bubonic plague which spread through Europe and Asia in the 14th cent. **civil death,** extinction of one's civil rights and privileges. **death on,** deadly or ruinous to; skilful at killing; skilful at anything. **like grim death,** tenaciously. **to be at death's door,** to be close to death. **to be in at the death,** to be present at the finish. **to be the death of,** (*coll.*) to make (someone) 'die of laughing'; to be a source of great worry to. **to catch one's death of cold,** to catch a very bad cold. **to do to death,** to kill. **to look like death warmed up,** (*coll.*) to look very ill. **to put to death,** to execute. **unto death,** to the last, forever. **death-adder,** *n.* a genus of venomous snakes. **death-angel, -cap, -cup,** *n.* a poisonous fungus. **death-bed,** *n.* the bed on which a person dies; a last illness. *a.* of or pertaining to a death-bed. **death-bell,** *n.* a passing-bell; a ringing in the ears supposed to forebode death. **death-blow,** *n.* a mortal blow; utter ruin, destruction. **death certificate,** *n.* a document issued by a doctor certifying death and giving the cause, if known. **death duties,** *n.pl.* a tax levied on property when it passes to the next heir. **death-feud,** *n.* a feud that is brought to an end only by the death of one of the parties. **death-mask,** *n.* a plaster cast of the face after death. **death-rate,** *n.* the proportion of deaths in a given period in a given district. **death-rattle,** *n.* a gurgling sound in the throat of a person just before death. **death's-door,** *n.* a near approach to death. **death's-head,** *n.* a human skull, or a representation of one, as an emblem of mortality. **death's-head moth,** *Acherontia atropos,* the largest European moth, with markings on the back of the thorax faintly resembling a human skull. **death-struggle, -throe,** *n.* the agony of death. **death-trap,** *n.* a place unsuspectedly dangerous to life through insanitary or other conditions. **death-warrant,** *n.* an order for the execution of a criminal; an act or measure putting an end to something. **death-watch-beetle,** *n.* any species of *Anobium,* a genus of wood-boring beetles that make a clicking sound formerly thought to presage death. **death wish,** *n.* a desire for one's own death. **deathful,** *a.* fraught with death; mortal. **deathfully,** *adv.* **deathfulness,** *n.* a resemblance to death. **deathless,** *a.* immortal, imperishable. **deathlessly,** *adv.* **deathlessness,** *n.* **deathlike,** *a.* resembling death. **deathly,** *a.* like death; deadly; pertaining to death. *adv.* so as to resemble death. **deathsman,** *n.* an executioner. **deathwards,** *adv.* towards death. [OE *dēath,* from Teut. stem *dau-,* to die (cp. Dut. *dood,* G *Tod*)]

Death Valley, *n.* depression 225 km/140 miles long and 6–26 km/4–16 miles wide, in SE California, US. At 85 m/280 ft below sea level, it is the lowest point in North America. Bordering mountains rise to 3000 m/10,000 ft. It is one of the world's hottest places, with an average annual rainfall of 35 mm/1.4 in.

deave, *v.t.* (*Sc., North.*) to deafen; to stun with noise. [OE *-dēafian* (in *ādēafian*), from *dēaf,* DEAF]

deb, short for DEBUTANTE, DEBENTURE.

debacle, *n.* a breaking up of ice in a river; breaking up and transport of rocks and gravel by a sudden outburst of water; a rout, a complete overthrow; a stampede. [F *débâcle,* n., from *débâcler,* to unbar (DE-, *bâcler,* to bar)]

debag, *v.t.* (*coll.*) to remove (someone's) trousers by force.

debar, *v.i.* (*past, p.p.* **debarred**) to hinder or exclude from approach, enjoyment or action; to prohibit, to forbid.

debark, *v.t., v.i.* to disembark. **debarkation,** *n.* [F *débarquer*]

debarrass, *v.t.* to disembarrass. [F *débarrasser* (DE-, *barrasser,* from *barrer,* to BAR[1])]

debase, *v.t.* to lower in condition, quality or value; to adulterate; to degrade. **debasement,** *n.* **debasingly,** *adv.* so as to debase.

debate, *v.t.* to contend about by words or arguments; to contend for; to discuss; to consider. *v.i.* to discuss or argue a point; to engage in argument; to fight. *n.* a discussion of a question; an argumentative contest; contention; battle, strife. **debatable,** *a.* open to discussion or argument; contentious. **debatement,** *n.* **debating,** *n., a.* **debater,** *n.* one who takes part in a debate. **debating society,** *n.* a society established for holding debates, and to improve the extempore speaking of the members. [OF *debatre* (DE-, low L *battere,* from L *batuere,* to beat)]

debauch, *v.t.* to corrupt, to pervert; to lead into sensuality or intemperance; to seduce from virtue; to vitiate, to deprave. †*v.i.* to revel; to engage in riotous living. *n.* an act of debauchery; a carouse. **debauchee,** *n.* a profligate. **debaucher,** *n.* a corrupter, a seducer. **debauchery,** *n.* indulgence of the sensual appetites. [F *débaucher,* OF *desbaucher* (DE-, perh. *bauche,* a workshop)]

debenture, *n.* a written acknowledgment of a debt; a deed or instrument issued by a company or a public body as a security for a loan of money on which interest is payable till it is redeemed; a certificate issued by a custom-house to an importer entitling him to a drawback or bounty. **debenture-stock,** *n.* debentures consolidated or created in the form of stock, the interest on which constitutes the first charge on the dividend.

debentured, *a.* secured by debenture, entitled to drawback. [L *dēbentur,* they are due (*dēbēre,* to be due)]

debilitate, *v.t.* to weaken, to enfeeble; to enervate, to impair. **debilitating, debilitative,** *a.* **debilitation,** *n.* **debility,** *n.* weakness, feebleness. [L *dēbilitātus,* p.p. of *dēbilitāre,* to weaken, from *dēbilis,* weak]

debit, *n.* an amount set down as a debt; the left-hand side of an account, in which debits are entered. *v.t.* to charge to as a debt; to enter on the debit side. **debit card,** *n.* one issued by a bank which enables the holder to debit a purchase to his/her account at the point of purchase. †**debitor,** *n.* a debtor. [L *dēbitum,* DEBT]

debonair, debonnaire, *a.* courteous, genial, pleasing in manner and bearing. **debonairly,** *adv.* **debonairness,** *n.* [OF *debonaire* (*de bon aire,* of good disposition)]

de Bono, *n.* **Edward** (1933–), British medical doctor and psychologist, best known for his concept of lateral thinking, first expounded in *The Use of Lateral Thinking* (1967); it involves thinking round a problem rather than tackling it head on.

Deborah, *n.* in the Old Testament or Jewish Bible, a prophet and judge (leader). She helped lead an Israelite army against the Canaanite general Sisera, who was killed trying to flee; her song of triumph at his death is regarded as an excellent example of early Hebrew poetry.

debouch, *v.i.* to march out from a confined place into open ground; to flow out from a narrow ravine. **debouchment,** *n.* **debouchure,** *n.* the mouth of a river or channel. [F *déboucher,* lit. to unstop (DE-, *bouche,* the mouth)]

Debray, *n.* **Régis** (1941–), French Marxist theorist. He was associated with Che Guevara in the revolutionary movement in Latin America in the 1960s, and in 1967 was sentenced to 30 years' imprisonment in Bolivia, but was released after three years. His writings on Latin American politics include *Strategy for Revolution* (1970). He became a specialist adviser to President Mitterrand of France on Latin American affairs.

Debrecen, *n.* third largest city in Hungary, 193 km/120 miles E of Budapest, in the Great Plain (*Alföld*) region; population (1988) 217,000. It produces tobacco, agricultural machinery and pharmaceuticals. Kossuth declared Hungary independent of the Habsburgs here in 1849.

Debrett, *n.* **John** (1753–1822), London publisher of a directory of the peerage from 1802, baronetage in 1808, and knightage (1866–73/4); the books are still called by his name.

debrief, *v.t.* to gather information from (someone, e.g. a soldier, diplomat or spy) after a mission.

debris, *n.* broken rubbish, fragments; (*Geol.*) fragmentary matter detached by a rush of water. [F *débris,* fragments, from *débriser* (DE-, *briser,* to break)]

de Broglie[1], *n.* **Louis, 7th Duc de Broglie** (1892–1987), French theoretical physicist. He established that all subatomic particles can be described either by particle equations or by wave equations, thus laying the foundations of wave mechanics. Nobel prize 1929.

de Broglie[2], *n.* **Maurice, 6th Duc de Broglie** (1875–1960), French physicist, He worked on X-rays and gamma rays, and helped to establish the Einsteinian description of light in terms of photons. He was the brother of Louis de Broglie.

debruise, *v.t.* (*Her.*) to cross so as to hide. **debruised,** *a.* crossed or folded so as to be partly covered. [ONorth.F *debruisier,* OF *debrisier* (DE-, *brisier,* to break)]

Debs, *n.* **Eugene V(ictor)** (1855–1926), US labour leader and socialist, who organized the Social Democratic Party in 1897. He was the founder and first president of the American Railway Union in 1893, and was imprisoned for six months in 1894 for defying a federal injunction to end the Pullman strike in Chicago. He was socialist candidate for the presidency in every election from 1900 to 1920, except that of 1916.

debt, *n.* that which is owing from one person to another, esp. a sum of money that is owing; obligation, liability. **action of debt,** (*Law*) an action to recover a sum of money. **bad debt,** an irrecoverable debt. **debt of honour,** one which is morally but not legally binding; a gambling debt. **debt of nature,** death. **in debt,** under obligation to pay something due. **National Debt,** the debt of a nation in its corporate capacity (**funded debt,** the portion of this converted into bonds and annuities; **floating debt,** the portion repayable at a stated time or on demand). †**debted,** *a.* indebted; under obligation. **debtless,** *a.* **debtor,** *n.* one who is indebted to another; the left-hand or debit side of an account. [ME and OF *dette,* L *dēbitum,* neut. p.p. of *dēbēre,* to owe (*b* the result of acquaintance with the L word)]

debug, *v.t.* to find and remove hidden microphones from; to find and remove the faults in (a system); to remove insects from.

debunk, *v.t.* to dispel false sentiment, to destroy pleasing legends or illusions.

debus, *v.t., v.i.* (*Mil.*) to (cause to) alight from a motor vehicle.

Debussy, *n.* **(Achille-) Claude** (1862–1918), French composer. He broke with the dominant tradition of German Romanticism and introduced new qualities of melody and harmony based on the whole-tone scale, evoking oriental music. His work includes *Prélude à l'après-midi d'un faune* (1894) and the opera *Pelléas et Mélisande* (1902).

debut, *n.* a first appearance before the public; a first attempt. *v.i.* to make a first appearance. **debutant,** *n.* one who makes a debut at court. **debutante,** *n. fem.* [F, from *débuter,* to make a first stroke (DE-, *buter,* to throw at, from *but,* BUTT)]

Dec., (*abbr.*) December.

dec., (*abbr.*) declaration; declension; declination; decoration; decorative; deceased; (*Mus.*) decrescendo.

dec(a)-, *comb. form* ten. [Gr. *deka,* ten]

decachord, *n.* a Greek instrument with ten strings. [L *decachordus,* Gr. *dekachordos* (*chordē,* string)]

decade, *n.* a group of ten; a period of ten years. **decadal,** *a.* **decadic,** *a.* [F, from L *decas -adem,* Gr. *dekasa dos,* from *deka,* ten]

decadence, *n.* decay, deterioration; a falling-off from a high standard of excellence. **decadent,** *a.* in a state of decay. *n.* a decadent writer or artist, esp. one having weaknesses, vices and affectations indicating lack of strength and originality. [F *décadence,* late L *dēcadentia* (DE-, *cadere,* to fall)]

decaffeinate, *v.t.* to remove the caffeine from e.g. coffee. **decaffeinated,** *a.*

decagon, *n.* a plane figure with ten sides and ten angles. [Gr. *gōnos,* angled]

decagram, *n.* a weight of 10 grams, 0·353 oz.

Decagynia, *n.pl.* a Linnaean order of plants, containing those with ten pistils. **decagynian, decagynous,** *a.* [Gr. *gunē,* a female]

decahedron, *n.* a solid figure with ten sides. **decahedral,** *a.*

decal, *n.* a transfer. *v.t.* to transfer (a design). [short for DECALCOMANIA]

decalcify, *v.t.* to clear (bone etc.) of calcareous matter. **decalcification,** *n.*

decalcomania, *n.* the process of transferring a design; a design so transferred. [F *décalcomanie,* from *décalquer,* to copy, trace]

decalitre, *n.* a liquid measure of capacity containing 10 litres, nearly $2\frac{1}{2}$ gallons.

decalogue, *n.* the Ten Commandments. **decalogist,** *n.* one who treats of the decalogue. [F *décalogue,* L *decalogus,* Gr. *dekalogos* (DEC(A)-, -LOGUE)]

Decameron, The, *n.* a collection of tales by the Italian writer Boccaccio, brought together in 1348–53. Each of ten young people, fleeing plague-stricken Florence, amuse their fellow travellers by telling a story on each of the ten days they spend together. The work had a great influence on English literature, particularly Chaucer's *Canterbury Tales.*

decametre, *n.* a measure of length, containing 10 metres or 393·7 in.

decamp, *v.i.* to break camp; to depart quickly; to take oneself off. †**decampment,** *n.* [F *décamper* (DE-, CAMP)]
decanal, *a.* pertaining to a dean or a deanery, or to the south side of the choir, where the dean has his seat. **decani**, *a.* of the dean or the dean's side; of the side to the right of one facing the altar. [L *decānus,* DEAN [1]]
Decandria, *n.pl.* a Linnaean class of plants characterized by ten stamens. **decandrian, -drous,** *a.* having ten stamens. [Gr. *anēr andros,* a male]
decangular, *a.* having ten angles.
decant, *v.t.* to pour off by gently inclining, so as not to disturb the sediment; to pour from one vessel into another (as wine); to move (people) from one area to another to provide better housing etc. **decantation**, *n.* the act of decanting. **decanter,** *n.* a vessel for decanted liquors; an ornamental glass bottle for holding wine or spirits. [F *décanter,* med. L *décanthāre* (DE-, *canthus,* Gr. *kanthos,* corner of the eye, lip of a cup, CANT)[2]]
decaphyllous, *a.* having ten leaves in the perianth. [Gr. *phullon,* a leaf]
decapitate, *v.t.* to behead. **decapitable,** *a.* **decapitation,** *n.* [late L *dēcapitātus,* p.p. of *dēcapitāre* (DE-, *caput,* head)]
decapod, *n.* any individual of the Decapoda; a locomotive having ten driving-wheels. *a.* pertaining to the Decapoda; having ten limbs. **Decapoda**, *n.pl.* a section of cephalopods, with two tentacles and four pairs of arms, containing the cuttle-fishes, squids etc.; an order of crustaceans with five pairs of ambulatory limbs, the first pair chelate, comprising crabs, lobsters etc. **decapodal, -dous,** *a.* [F *décapode,* Gr. *dekapous* (DEC(A)-, *pous podos,* a foot)]
decarbonate, *v.t.* to decarbonize.
decarbonize, -ise, decarburize, -ise, (*coll.*) **decarb**, *v.t.* to clear of carbon or carbonic acid (as in the process of converting cast-iron into malleable iron or steel); to remove the solid carbon deposited in the combustion chamber and on the piston crown of an internal-combustion engine. **decarbonization, -isation,** *n.*
decastich, *n.* a poem consisting of ten lines. [Gr. *stichos,* a verse]
decastyle, *a.* (*Arch.*) having ten columns. *n.* a portico with ten columns in front. [med. L *decastylus,* Gr. *dekastulos* (DEC(A)-, *stulos,* column)]
decasyllabic, *a.* having ten syllables. *n.* a line of ten syllables. **decasyllable**, *n., a.*
decathlon, *n.* an athletic contest consisting of ten events. **decathlete,** *n.* [Gr. *athlon,* contest]
decay, *v.i.* to fall away, to deteriorate; to decline in excellence; to waste away; of radioactive matter, to disintegrate. *v.t.* to impair, to cause to fall away. *n.* gradual failure or decline; deterioration; a state of ruin; wasting away, consumption, gradual dissolution; decomposition of dead tissue, rot; decayed matter; disintegration of radioactive matter. [OF *decair,* folk L *decadēre* (DE-, *cadēre,* L *cadere,* to fall)]
decease, *n.* death; departure from this life. †*v.i.* to die. **deceased,** *a.* dead. *n.* one lately dead. [OF *deces,* L *dēcessus,* p.p. of *dēcēdere* (DE-, *cēdere,* to go)]
deceit, *n.* the act of deceiving; propensity to deceive; trickery, deception, duplicity; delusive appearance; a stratagem; (*Law*) any trick or craft to defraud another. **deceitful,** *a.* **deceitfully,** *adv.* **deceitfulness,** *n.* [OF *deceite,* orig. fem. p.p. of *deceveir,* to deceive, L *dēcipere* (DE-, *capere,* to take)]
deceive, *v.t.* to mislead; to impose upon; to cheat, to delude; to disappoint; to be unfaithful (of husband or wife). *v.i.* to act deceitfully. **deceivable,** *a.* **deceiver,** *n.* [OF *deceveir,* as prec.]
decelerate, *v.t.* to reduce speed, to slow down. **deceleration,** *n.* the rate of diminution of speed, measured, for example, in feet per second per second. [L *celer,* swift]
decem-, *comb. form* ten; in or having ten parts. [L *decem,* ten]
December, *n.* the twelfth and last month of the year; orig. the tenth and afterwards the twelfth month of the Roman year. **Decemberly,** *a.* **Decembrish,** *a.* **Decembrist,** *n.* one of the conspirators against the Czar Nicholas, at his accession in Dec. 1825. [L *decem,* ten]
decemfid, *a.* (*Bot.*) ten-cleft (applied to perianths with ten divisions). [L *fid-,* stem of *findere,* to cut]
decemlocular, *a.* having ten receptacles for seeds.
decemvir, *n.* (*pl.* **-viri, -virs**) one of the various bodies of ten magistrates appointed by the Romans to legislate or rule, esp. the body appointed in 451 BC to codify the laws in the Twelve Tables; a member of any governing council of ten. **decemviral,** *a.* **decemvirate,** *n.* the (term of) office of the decemviri; a governing body of ten persons. [L *decem viri,* ten men]
decency DECENT.
decennary, *n.* a period of ten years. *a.* pertaining to a period of ten years. **decenniad**, **decennium**, *n.* (*pl.* **-nniads, -nnia**) a period of ten years. **decennial,** *a.* lasting ten years; occurring every ten years. **decennially,** *adv.* [L *decennis* (*decem,* ten, *annus,* year)]
decent, *a.* becoming, seemly; modest; decorous; respectable; passable, tolerable. **to be decent,** (*coll.*) to be sufficiently clothed to be seen in public. **decentish,** *a.* (*coll.*) moderately good; passable. **decently,** *adv.* **decency**, *n.* propriety; that which is becoming in words or behaviour; freedom from immodesty or obscenity; decorum. [L *decens -entem,* pres.p. of *decēre,* to be becoming]
decentralize, -ise, *v.t.* to break up (as a centralized administration); to organize on the principle of local management rather than central government. **decentralization, -isation,** *n.*
deception, *n.* the act of deceiving; the state of being deceived; that which deceives; a deceit, a fraud. †**deceptible,** *a.* liable to be deceived. †**deceptibility**, *n.* †**deceptious,** *a.* deceitful, deceiving. **deceptive,** *a.* tending or apt to deceive, easy to mistake. **deceptively,** *adv.* †**deceptiveness,** *n.* †**deceptivity**, *n.* [F *déception,* L *dēceptio -ōnem* (*dēcipere,* DECEIVE)]
decern, *v.t.* (*Sc. Law*) to decree; †to discern. [F *décerner,* L *dēcernere* (DE-, *cernere,* to separate, to distinguish)]
dechristianize, -ise, *v.t.* to pervert from Christianity; to divest of Christian sentiments and principles.
deci-, *pref.* a tenth part of. [L *decimus,* tenth]
decibel, *n.* a unit to compare levels of intensity, esp. of sound.
decide, *v.t.* to determine; to adjudge; to settle by adjudging (victory or superiority); to bring to a decision. *v.i.* to come to a decision. **decidable,** *a.* **decided,** *a.* settled; clear, evident, unmistakable; determined, resolute, unwavering, firm. **decidedly,** *adv.* **decider,** *n.* one who or that which decides; a deciding heat or game. [F *décider,* L *dēcīdere* (DE-, *caedere,* to cut)]
deciduous, *a.* falling off, not permanent; having only a temporary existence; shed (as wings) during the lifetime of an animal; falling, not perennial (applied to leaves etc. which fall in autumn, and to trees which lose their leaves annually). **deciduous teeth,** *n.pl.* milk teeth. **decidua**, *n.* the membrane lining the internal surface of the uterus, coming away after parturition. **deciduate**, *a.* having a decidua; thrown off after birth. **deciduousness,** *n.* [L *dēciduus,* from *dēcidere* (DE-, *cadere,* to fall)]
decigram, *n.* a weight equal to one-tenth of a gram, 1·54 grain.
decilitre, *n.* a fluid measure of capacity of one-tenth of a litre, 0·176 pint.
decillion, *n.* a million raised to the tenth power, represented by 1 followed by 60 ciphers. **decillionth,** *a.* [F, from L *decem,* ten, comb. with million, cp. BILLION]
decimal, *a.* of or pertaining to ten or tenths; counting by tens. *n.* a decimal fraction. **decimal arithmetic,** *n.* arithmetic in which quantities are expressed by tens or tenths; arithmetic based on decimal notation. **decimal coinage, currency,** *n.* a monetary system in which the coins represent the value of a given unit in multiples of ten. **decimal fraction,** *n.* a fraction having some

power of 10 for its denominator, esp. when it is expressed by figures representing the numerator of tenths, hundredths etc. following a dot (the **decimal point**) to the right of the unit figure. **decimal notation,** *n.* the Arabic system of numerals. **decimal system,** *n.* a system of weights and measures in which the values increase by multiples of ten. **decimalist,** *n.* **decimalize, -ise,** *v.t.* to reduce or adapt to the decimal system. **decimalization, -isation,** *n.* **decimally,** *adv.* [late L *decimālis,* from L *decima,* tithe, fem. of *decimus,* tenth (*decem,* ten)]

decimate, *v.t.* to take the tenth part of; to destroy a tenth or a large proportion of; (*Mil.*) to punish every tenth man with death. **decimation,** *n.* [L *decimātus,* p.p. of *decimāre* (*decimus,* tenth)]

decimetre, *n.* the tenth part of a metre, 3·937 in.

decipher, *v.t.* to turn from cipher into ordinary language; to discover the meaning of (something written in cipher); to discover, to detect; to read or explain (as bad or indistinct writing). *n.* a translation of a cipher. **decipherable,** *a.* **decipherment,** *n.*

decision, *n.* the act or result of deciding; the determination of a trial, contest or question; resolution, firmness of character. **decisive,** *a.* having the power of deciding; conclusive, final; characterized by decision. **decisively,** *adv.* **decisiveness,** *n.* [F *décision,* L *dēcisio -ōnem* (*dēcīdere,* DECIDE)]

deciso, *adv.* (*Mus.*) energetically, decidedly. [It.]

decivilize, -ise, *v.t.* to render less civilized; to divest of civilization.

deck, *v.t.* to adorn, to beautify; to cover, to put a deck to. *n.* the plank or iron flooring of a ship; a pack (of cards), a heap, a pile (of cards); the floor of an omnibus or tramcar. **hurricane deck,** a partial deck over the saloon, or above the central part of some warships. **lower deck,** naval ratings and petty officers. **lower** and **middle decks,** below the main deck. **main deck** MAIN. **orlop deck,** below the lower deck. **poop** and **forecastle decks,** short decks at the ends of a vessel. **upper, spar, deck,** above the main deck. **to clear the decks,** (*Naut.*) to prepare for action; (*fig.*) to make tidy. **to hit the deck,** (*coll.*) to fall down quickly or suddenly. **to sweep the decks,** to clear the decks of boarders by a raking fire; to win all the stakes. **deck-chair,** *n.* a collapsible chair, camp-stool or long chair for reclining in. **deck-hand,** *n.* a seaman who works on deck, but is allowed to go aloft. **deck-house,** *n.* a room erected on deck. **deck-passenger,** *n.* a steerage passenger; one who has no right in the cabins. **decked,** *a.* adorned; furnished with a deck or decks; (*Her.*) edged with another colour, as the feathers of a bird. **-decker,** *comb. form.* having a specified number of decks, as in *double-decker,* a bus, etc. with two decks. [cp. Dut. *decken,* to cover, OTeut. *thakjan* (cp. OE *theccan,* to THATCH)]

deckle, *n.* a frame used in paper-making to keep the pulp within the desired limits. **deckle-edge,** *n.* the rough, untrimmed edge of paper. **deckle-edged,** *a.* of paper or books, uncut. [G *Deckel,* dim. of *Decke,* a cover]

declaim, *v.t.* to utter rhetorically. *v.i.* to speak a set oration in public; to inveigh; to speak rhetorically or passionately. **declaimer,** *n.* **declamation,** *n.* the act or art of declaiming according to rhetorical rules; practice in declaiming; a formal oration; impassioned oratory. **declamatory,** *a.* [L *dēclāmāre* (DE-, *clāmāre,* to cry out)]

declaration, *n.* the act of declaring or proclaiming; that which is declared or proclaimed; the document in which anything is declared or proclaimed; a manifesto, an official announcement, esp. of constitutional or diplomatic principles, laws or intentions; (*Law*) a statement reduced to writing; an affirmation in lieu of oath; (*Cricket*) a voluntary close of innings before all the wickets have fallen. [as foll.]

Declaration of Independence, historic US document stating the theory of government on which the US was founded, based on the right 'to life, liberty, and the pursuit of happiness'. The statement was issued by the American Continental Congress on 4 July 1776, renouncing all allegiance to the British crown and ending the political connection with Britain.

Declaration of Rights, in Britain, the statement issued by the Convention Parliament in Feb. 1689, laying down the conditions under which the crown was to be offered to William III and Mary. Its clauses were later incorporated in the Bill of Rights.

declare, *v.t.* to make known; to announce publicly, to proclaim formally; to pronounce, to assert or affirm positively. *v.i.* to make a declaration, to avow; to state the possession of (dutiable articles); (*Law*) to make an affirmation in lieu of oath; to recite the cause of action; (*Cards*) to name the trump suit; (*Cricket*) to announce an innings as closed. **to declare against, for,** to side against or with. **to declare an interest,** often of a Member of Parliament, to admit to a usu. financial interest in a company about which there is (parliamentary) discussion. **to declare off,** to refuse to proceed with any engagement or contract. **to declare oneself,** to avow one's intentions; to disclose one's character or attitude. **declarant,** *n.* (*Law*) one who makes a declaration. **declarative,** *a.* explanatory, declaratory. **declaratively,** *adv.* **declaratory,** *a.* making declaration; expressive, affirmatory. **declaredly,** *adv.* [F *déclarer,* L *dēclārāre* (DE-, *clārus,* clear)]

déclassé, *a.* (*fem.* **-ssée**) having lost social position or estimation. [F, p.p. of *déclasser* (DE-, *classe,* L *classis,* CLASS)]

declassify, *v.t.* to remove from the security list. **declassification,** *n.*

declension, *n.* declining, descent, deterioration, falling-off; a state of inferiority; (*Gram.*) the case-inflection of nouns, adjectives and pronouns; the act of declining a noun etc.; a number of nouns declined in the same way. [OF *declinaison,* DECLINATION]

declinable DECLINE.

declinate, *a.* bending or bent downwards in a curve, as the stamens of amaryllis. [L *dēclīnātus,* p.p. of *dēclīnāre,* to DECLINE]

declination, *n.* the act of bending or moving downwards; deviation from a straight line or fixed point; deviation from moral rectitude; the angular distance of a heavenly body north or south of the celestial equator. **declination of the needle, compass,** the angle between the geographic and the magnetic meridians, also called **magneticdeclination. declination-compass,** *n.* a declinometer. **declinational,** *a.* **declinator,** *n.* an instrument for taking the declination and inclination of a plane. **declinature,** *n.* (*Sc. Law*) refusal to acknowledge the jurisdiction of a court. [OF, from L *dēclīnātio -ōnem,* from *dēclīnāre,* to DECLINE]

decline, *v.i.* to incline from a right line; to slope downwards; to droop, to stoop; to deviate from rectitude; to sink, to fall off, to deteriorate, to decay; to approach the close. *v.t.* to depress, to lower; to direct to one side; to refuse, to turn away from; to reject; (*Gram.*) to inflect (as a noun); to recite the cases of a noun in order. *n.* a falling-off; deterioration, decay, diminution; fall in prices; gradual failure of strength or health; setting; gradual approach to extinction or death. **to go into a decline,** to deteriorate gradually in health. **declinable,** *a.* [F *décliner,* L *dēclīnāre* (DE-, *clīnāre,* to lean, cp. Gr. *klīnein,* to bend)]

Decline and Fall of the Roman Empire, The History of the, a historical work by Edward Gibbon, published in Britain in 1776–88. Arranged in three parts, the work spans 13 centuries and covers the history of the empire from Trajan and the Antonines through to the Turkish seizure of Constantinople in 1453.

declinometer, *n.* an apparatus for measuring the declination of the needle of the compass; (*Astron.*) an instrument for registering declinations. [L *dēclīno,* I decline]

declivity, *n.* an inclination, a slope or gradual descent of the surface of the ground; an inclination downward. **declivitous,** *a.* **declivous,** *a.* [L *dēclīvitās,* from *dēclīvis* (DE-, *clīvus,* a slope)]

declutch, *v.t.* to release the clutch (of a vehicle); to disconnect the drive.

decoct, *v.t.* to boil down or digest in hot water; to extract the virtue of by boiling; †to heat, to cook. **decoction,** *n.* the act of boiling or digesting a substance to extract its virtues; the liquor or substance obtained by boiling. [L *dēcoctus,* p.p. of *dēcoquere* (DE-, *coquere,* to COOK[1])]

decode, *v.t.* to translate from code symbols into ordinary language. **decoder,** *n.*

decoherer, *n.* a mechanical device for restoring a coherer to a condition of high resistance. **decohesion,** *n.*

decoke, *v.t.* to remove carbon from, to decarbonize.

decollate, *v.t.* to behead. **decollated,** *a.* beheaded; of spiral shells, having lost the apex. **decollation,** *n.* the act of beheading, esp. the beheading of St John the Baptist. [L *dēcollātus,* p.p. of *dēcollāre* (DE-, *collum,* the neck)]

décolleté, *a.* (*fem.* **-tée**) wearing a low-necked dress; low-necked (of a dress). **décolletage,** *n.* the low-cut neckline of a dress. [F, p.p. of *décolleter* (DE-, *collet,* a collar)]

decolonize, -ise, *v.t.* to grant independence to (a colonial state).

decolour, *v.t.* to deprive of colour. **decolorant,** *a.* bleaching, blanching. *n.* a bleaching substance. **decolorate,** *v.t.* **decoloration,** *n.* **decolorize, -ise,** *v.t.* **decolorization, -isation,** *n.* **decolorizer, -iser,** *n.*

decomplex, *a.* of complex constituents; doubly complex.

decompose, *v.t.* to resolve into constituent elements; to separate the elementary parts of, to analyse; to cause to rot. *v.i.* to become decomposed; to putrefy. **decomposable,** *a.* **decomposer,** *n.* **decomposition,** *n.* **decomposite,** *a.* doubly compound; compounded of compounds. *n.* a substance or word compounded of compound parts. [F *décomposer* (DE-, COMPOSE)]

decompound, *a.* decomposite. **decompound flower,** *n.* one composed of compound flowers. **decompound leaf,** *n.* one which is twice or thrice pinnated.

decompress, *v.t.* gradually to relieve pressure, to return to normal atmospheric pressure conditions. **decompression,** *n.* **decompression chamber,** *n.* one in which a person (e.g. a diver) is gradually returned to normal pressure conditions. **decompression sickness,** *n.* severe pain and breathing problems caused by sudden change in atmospheric pressure. **decompressor,** *n.* a contrivance for relieving pressure on an engine.

decongestant, *a.* relieving congestion. *n.* a drug or medicine relieving nasal or chest congestion.

deconsecrate, *v.t.* to deprive of consecration; to secularize. **deconsecration,** *n.*

decontaminate, *v.t.* to clear of a poisonous substance or radioactivity. **decontamination,** *n.*

decontrol, *v.t.* to terminate government control of (a trade etc.).

decor, *n.* the setting, arrangement and decoration of a scene on the stage, or of a room. [F]

decorate, *v.t.* to adorn, to beautify; to be an embellishment to; to confer a badge of honour on; to paint, paper etc. (a house). **decorated,** *a.* adorned, ornamented, embellished; possessing a medal or other badge of honour; an epithet applied to the middle pointed architecture in England (*c.* 1300–1400). **decoration,** *n.* the act of decorating; ornamentation, ornament; a badge of honour; (*pl.*) flags, flowers and other adornments put up at a church festival or on an occasion of public rejoicing. **Decoration Day,** *n.* (*US Hist.*) 30 May, appointed for the decoration of the graves of those who fell in the Civil War (1861–65). **decorative,** *a.* **decorativeness,** *n.* **decorator,** *n.* one who adorns or embellishes; one whose business it is to paint and paper rooms or houses. [L *decorātus,* p.p. of *decorāre* (*decor-,* stem of *decus,* an ornament)]

decorous, *a.* becoming, seemly; befitting, decent. **decorously,** *adv.* †**decorousness,** *n.* **decorum,** *n.* decency and propriety of words and conduct; etiquette, polite usage. [L *decōrus* (*decor,* seemliness, from *decēre,* to befit)]

decorticate, *v.t.* to strip the bark, skin or husk from. **decortication,** *n.* **decorticator,** *n.* a machine for stripping the hull from grain. [L *dēcorticātus,* p.p. of *dēcorticāre* (DE-, *cortex -icem,* bark)]

découpage, *n.* the art of decorating furniture with cut-out patterns. [F *découper,* to cut out]

decoy, *v.t.* to lure into a trap or snare; (*fig.*) to entrap, to allure, to entice. *n.* a pond or enclosed water into which wild-fowl are decoyed; a place for entrapping wild-fowl; a decoy-duck; a person employed to lure or entrap; a tempter; a bait, an attraction. **decoy-duck,** *n.* a tame duck or an imitation of one; a duck used to lure wild-fowl into the decoy. [formerly *coy,* Dut. *kooi,* MDut. *koye, kouwe,* late L *cavea,* CAGE]

decrease, *v.i.* to become less, to wane, to fail. *v.t.* to make less; to reduce in size gradually. *n.*, lessening, diminution; the waning of the moon. **decreasingly,** *adv.* [A-F *decreiss-,* stem of *decreistre* (OF *descreiss-, descreistre*), L *dēcrēscere* (DE-, *crēscere,* to grow)]

decree, *n.* an edict, law or ordinance made by superior authority; (*Law*) the decision in Admiralty cases; the predetermined purpose of God; a law of nature, the will of Providence; (*Eccles.*) an edict, law or ordinance of a council; the award of an umpire. *v.t.* to command by a decree; to ordain or determine; to decide by law or authoritatively; †to resolve. *v.i.* to make an edict; to resolve, to determine. **decree absolute,** *n.* the final decree in divorce proceedings. **decree nisi,** *n.* a provisional decree in divorce proceedings. [OF *decret,* L *dēcrētum,* neut. of *dēcrētus,* p.p. of *dēcernere* (DE-, *cernere,* to sift, to decide)]

decrement, *n.* decrease, diminution; the quantity lost by diminution; the wane of the moon; (*Radio*) a measure of the speed of damping out of damped waves. **decremeter,** *n.* an instrument for measuring this. [L *dēcrēmentum* (*dēcrē-,* stem of *dēcrēscere*)]

decrepit, *a.* broken down by age and infirmities; feeble, decayed. **decrepitude,** *n.* [L *dēcrepitus* (DE-, *crepitus,* p.p. of *crepāre,* to crackle)]

decrepitate, *v.t.* to calcine in a strong heat, so as to cause a continual crackling of the substance. *v.i.* to crackle, as salt in a strong heat. **decrepitation,** *n.*

decrescendo, *n., a., adv.* (*Mus.*) diminuendo. [It., decreasing]

decrescent, *a.* waning; (*Bot.*) decreasing gradually from base to summit. [L *decrēscens -entem,* pres.p. of *dēcrēscere* (see DECREASE)]

decretal, *a.* pertaining to a decree. *n.* a decree, esp. of the Pope; (*pl.*) a collection or body of papal decrees on points of ecclesiastical law or discipline. **decretalist,** *n.* **decretist,** *n.* one versed in decretals. **decretive,** *a.* having the force of a decree. **decretory,** *a.* judicial, deciding; determining. [F *décrétal,* late L *dēcrētāle,* neut. of *dēcrētālis* (L *dēcrētum,* DECREE)]

†**decrew,** *v.i.* to decrease. [OF *décreu,* p.p. of *décreistre,* to DECREASE]

decrial, decrier DECRY.

decriminalize, -ise, *v.t.* to make (an action) no longer illegal.

decrown, *v.t.* to discrown.

decry, *v.t.* to cry down; to clamour against; to depreciate. **decrial,** *n.* **decrier,** *n.* [F *décrier,* OF *descrier*]

decuman, *a.* the epithet of the principal gate of a Roman camp, near which the tenth cohorts were stationed; huge, applied to waves, the tenth being said to be much larger than the other nine. [L *decumānus,* var. of *decimānus* (*decimus,* tenth)]

decumbent, *a.* lying down, reclining; prostrate; (*Bot.*) lying flat by its own weight. **decumbence, -ncy,** *n.* [L *decumbens -entem,* pres.p. of *dēcumbere* (DE-, *cumbere,* to lie)]

decuple, *a.* tenfold. *n.* a tenfold number. *v.t., v.i.* to increase tenfold. [F *décuple,* L *decuplus* (*decem,* ten, *-plus,* as in *duplus,* double)]

decurion, *n.* (*Hist.*) a Roman officer commanding ten men; a member of a colony or municipal town; a member of the council of a town in Fascist Italy. **decurionate,** *n.* [L *decurio,* from *decem,* ten (cp. *centur-*

io)]

decurrent, *a.* attached along the side of a stem below the point of insertion (as the leaves of the thistle). **decurrence,** *n.* **decurrently,** *adv.* **decursive,** *a.* running down; decurrent. **decursively,** *adv.* [L *dēcurrens -entem,* pres.p. of *dēcurrere* (DE-, *currere,* to run)]

decussate, *v.t., v.i.* to intersect (as nerves, lines or rays) at acute angles, i.e. in the form of an X. *a.*, having this form; (*Bot.*) arranged in this manner. **decussated,** *a.* crossed, intersected; of leaves, crossing each other in pairs at right angles; (*Rhet.*) in the form of chiasmus. **decussately,** *adv.* **decussation,** *n.* [L *decussātus,* p.p. of *decussāre* (*decussis,* figure 10, X)]

dedal, dedalian DAEDAL, DAEDALIAN.

dedicate, *v.t.* to apply or give up wholly to some purpose, person or thing; to inscribe or address (as a literary work to a friend or patron); to set apart and consecrate solemnly to God or to some sacred purpose. *a.*, dedicated, consecrated. **dedicated,** *a.* devoting one's time to one pursuit or cause; of computers etc., designed to perform a specific function. **dedicatee,** *n.* the person to whom a thing is dedicated. **dedication,** *n.* the act of dedicating; the words in which a book, building etc. is dedicated. **dedicative,** *a.* **dedicator,** *n.* **dedicatory,** *a.* of the nature of or containing a dedication. †*n.* a dedication. [L *dēdicātus,* p.p. of *dēdicāre* (DE-; *dicāre,* to proclaim, to devote)]

deduce, *v.t.* to draw as a conclusion by reasoning, to infer; to trace down step by step; to trace the descent (from); †to derive. †**deducement,** *n.* **deducible,** *a.* **deduction,** *n.* the act of deducing; an inference, a consequence. **deductive,** *a.* deduced, or capable of being deduced, from premises. **deductive reasoning,** *n.* (*Log.*) the process of reasoning by which we arrive at the necessary consequences, starting from admitted or established premises. **deductively,** *adv.* a priori. [L *dēdūcere* (DE-, *dūcere,* to lead)]

deduct, *v.t.* to take away, to subtract; †to reduce. **deduction,** *n.* the act of deducting; that which is deducted; abatement. [L *dēductus,* p.p. of *dēdūcere,* as prec.]

dee, *n.* the fourth letter of the alphabet, D, d; anything shaped like the capital form of this letter, as a D-shaped loop or link in harness.

Dee[1], *n.* river in Grampian region, Scotland; length 139 km/87 miles. From its source in the Cairngorms, it flows E into the North Sea at Aberdeen (by an artificial channel). It is noted for salmon fishing. Also a river in Wales and England; length 112 km/70 miles. Rising in Lake Bala, Gwynnedd, it flows into the Irish Sea W of Chester. There is another Scottish river Dee (61 km/38 miles) in Kirkcudbright.

Dee[2], *n.* **John** (1527–1608), English alchemist and mathematician, who claimed to have transmuted metals into gold, although he died in poverty. He long enjoyed the favour of Elizabeth I and was employed as a secret, diplomatic agent.

deed[1], *n.* an action, a thing done with intention; an illustrious exploit, an achievement; fact, reality (see INDEED); (*Law*) an instrument comprehending the terms of a contract, and the evidence of its due execution. *v.t.* (*N Am.*) to transfer or convey by deed. **deed-poll,** *n.* (*Law*) a deed made by one person only, so called because the paper is cut or polled evenly, and not indented. **deedful,** *a.* **deedless,** *a.* **deedy,** *a.* (*dial.*) industrious, active. [OE *dǣd* (cp. Dut. *daad,* Icel. *dāth,* OHG *tat,* G *Tat*)]

deed[2], *adv.* (*chiefly Sc.*) indeed. [short for INDEED]

deejay, *n.* a written form of the abbreviation **DJ** (disk jockey).

deem, *v.t.* to suppose, to think; to judge, to consider; †to sit in judgment; †to estimate; †to distinguish between. *v.i.* to come to a decision; to think; to think (of). †*n.* judgment, sentence; idea. **deemster,** *n.* †a judge, an umpire; one of two officers who officiate as judges, one in the north and the other in the south part of the Isle of Man. [OE *dēman,* from Teut. *dōm-,* DOOM (cp. Dut. *doemen,* OHG *tuomian*)]

de-emphasize, -ise, *v.t.* to remove the emphasis from.

deener DEANER.

deep, *a.* extending far down; extending far in from the surface or away from the outside; having a thickness or measurement back or down; dark-coloured, intensely dark; profound, penetrating, abstruse; heartfelt, grave, earnest; intense, extreme, heinous; from far down, sonorous, low in pitch, full in tone; well-versed, sagacious; (*coll.*) artful, scheming, secretive; †weighty. *adv.* deeply, far down; far on; profoundly, intensely. *n.* anything deep; the sea; (*usu. pl.*) the deep parts of the sea; a deep place, an abyss, a gulf, a cavity; the abyss of space; the lower regions; the bottom of the heart, the mysterious region of personality; (*Naut., pl.*) the estimated fathoms between the marks on the hand lead-line. **deep litter egg,** one produced by hens living in sheds whose floors are thickly covered in straw or peat. **to be in deep water,** to be in trouble. **to go off the deep end,** to give way to one's anger. †**deep-contemplative,** *a.* given up to meditation. †**deep-drawing,** *a.* (*Naut.*) requiring great depth of water. **deep-drawn,** *a.* drawn from the depths. **deep-freeze,** *n.* the storage of foods and perishable goods at a very low temperature. **deep-fry,** *v.t.* to fry (food) submerged in fat or oil. **deep-laid,** *a.* profoundly, secretly or elaborately schemed. **deep-mouthed,** *a.* having a sonorous note. **deep-read,** *a.* deeply versed. **deep-rooted,** *a.* firmly established. **deep-sea,** *a.* pertaining to the open sea. **deep-sea fauna,** fauna living at a depth below 200 fathoms. **deep-sea line,** (*Naut.*) a line of 200 fathoms used for soundings. **deep-seated,** *a.* profound; situated far in; firmly seated. **deep-set,** *a.* of eyes, deeply set in the face. **deep space,** *n.* that area of space beyond the earth and the moon. **deep structure,** *n.* in generative grammar, the underlying structure of a sentence in which logical and grammatical relationships become clear. **deep therapy,** *n.* the method of treating disease by gamma rays. **deep-toned,** *a.* emitting a low, full sound. **deepen,** *v.t.* to make deeper. *v.i.* to become deeper. **deeply,** *adv.* **deepmost,** *a.* **deepness,** *n.* [OE *dēop,* from Teut. *deup-*, cogn. with DIP (cp. Dut. *diep,* OHG *tiuf,* G *tief*)]

deeping, *n.* one of the strips of twine-netting, a fathom deep, of which a fishing-net is constructed.

Deep-Sea Drilling Project, a research project initiated by the US in 1968 to sample the rocks of the ocean crust. The operation became international in 1975, when Britain, France, Germany, Japan, and the USSR also became involved.

deer, *n.* any of the Cervidae, ruminant quadrupeds, only the males horned, except in the one domesticated species, the reindeer. †**small deer,** (*Shak.*) small, insignificant animals. **deer-forest,** *n.* a tract of wild land on which red deer are bred or allowed to breed for stalking. **deer-hound,** *n.* a large greyhound with rough coat, formerly used for hunting deer. **deer-lick,** *n.* a wet or marshy spot impregnated with salt where deer come to lick. **deer-neck,** *n.* a thin, ill-formed neck in a horse. **deerskin,** *n.* the skin of a deer; leather made therefrom. *a.* of this material. **deer-stalker,** *n.* one who hunts deer by stalking; a cap peaked in front and behind. [OE *dēor* (cp. Dut. *dier,* Icel. *dȳr,* OHG *tior,* G *Tier*)]

de-escalate, *v.t.* to reduce the intensity of. **de-escalation,** *n.*

deeve DEAVE.

def, *a.* (*sl.*) very good; brilliant. [DEFINITIVE]

def., (*abbr.*) defendant; defined; definite; definition.

deface, *v.t.* to disfigure; to spoil the appearance or beauty of; to erase, to obliterate; †to defeat. **defaceable,** *a.* **defacement,** *n.* **defacer,** *n.*

de facto, in reality, actually, although not necessarily legally. [L]

defaecation DEFECATION.

defalcate, *v.t.* to take away fraudulently; to misappropriate (money etc.) held in trust, to embezzle; †to curtail, to reduce. *v.i.* to commit embezzlement. **defalcation,** *n.* **defalcator,** *n.* [late L *dēfalcātus,* p.p. of *dēfalcāre* (DE-, *falcāre,* to cut with a sickle, from *falx falcis,* sickle)]

de Falla FALLA.
defame, *v.t.* to speak evil of maliciously; to slander, to libel; †to disgrace; †to accuse. †*n.* infamy. **defamation**, *n.* **defamatory** , *a.* [OF *defamer, diffamer,* L *diffāmāre* (*dif-*, DIS-, *fāma,* report)]
default, *n.* want, lack, absence; omission or failure to do any act; neglect; (*Law*) failure to appear in court on the day assigned; failure to meet liabilities; †a fault, a defect; an assumption made by a computer if no alternative instructions are given. *v.i.* to fail in duty; to fail to meet liabilities, to break; (*Law*) to fail to appear in court. *v.t.* (*Law*) to enter as a defaulter and give judgment against, in case of non-appearance; †to omit, to neglect. **in default of,** instead of (something wanting). **judgment by default,** (*Law*) decree against a defendant who does not appear. **to make default,** to fail to appear in court, or to keep any engagement. **defaulter,** *n.* one who defaults; one who fails to account for moneys entrusted to him; one who is unable to meet his engagements (esp. on the Stock Exchange or turf); (*Law*) one who makes default; (*Mil.*) a soldier guilty of a military offence. [OF *defaute* (DE-, late L *fallita,* fem. p.p. of L *fallere,* to fail)]
defeasance, *n.* the act of annulling a contract; (*Law*) a condition relating to a deed which being performed renders the deed void; †defeat. **defeasible,** *a.* that may be annulled or forfeited. **defeasibility**, *n.* [OF *defesance,* from *defaire, desfaire* (*des-*, DE-, L *facere,* to do)]
defeat, *v.t.* to overthrow, to discomfit; to resist successfully, to frustrate; to render null; to baffle; †to disappoint; †to disfigure. *n.* overthrow, discomfiture, esp. of an army; a rendering null; disappointment; †ruin. **defeatism,** *n.* persistent belief in defeat in a war, and a consequent advocacy of a policy of surrender. **defeatist,** *n.* one who contemplates or desires defeat in a war, or advocates measures that would bring about defeat. [OF *defait,* p.p. of *defaire, desfaire* (as prec.)]
defeature, *v.t.* to disfigure; to disguise.
defecate, *v.t.* to purify from lees, dregs or other impurities; to purify, to clarify. *v.i.* to become clear by depositing impurities, excrement etc.; to eject faeces from the body. **defecation,** *n.* the ejection of faeces from the body. **defecator,** *n.* one who or that which defecates; an apparatus to remove feculent matter from a saccharine liquid such as sugar. [L *dēfaecātus,* p.p. of *dēfaecāre* (DE-, *faex faecis,* dregs)]
defect[1], *n.* absence of something essential to perfection or completeness; blemish, failing; moral imperfection; the degree to which one falls short; †default, faultiness. **defects of one's qualities,** (*coll.*) shortcomings that usually correspond to the particular abilities or good points one possesses. **defective**, *a.* imperfect, incomplete, faulty; wanting in something physical or moral; (*Gram.*) lacking some of the forms or inflections. **defectively,** *adv.* **defectiveness,** *n.* [L *dēfectus,* a want, p.p. of *dēficere,* to fail (DE-, *facere,* to do)]
defect[2], *v.i.* to desert one's country or cause for the other side. **defection,** *n.* a falling away from allegiance; desertion, apostasy. **defector,** *n.* one who defects. [as prec.]
defence, (*esp. N Am.*) **defense**, *n.* the state or act of defending; that which defends; fortifications, fortified posts; (*Cricket*) batting as opp. to bowling; justification, vindication; excuse, apology; (*Law*) defendant's reply to the plaintiff's declaration, demands or charges; †prohibition, a decree forbidding something. †*v.t.* to fortify. **Defence of the Realm Act,** an Act of Parliament in force from 1914 to 1921 giving the Government wide powers over most forms of national activity. **line of defence,** a succession of fortified places, forming a continuous line. **science, art, of self-defence,** boxing or fencing. **self-defence,** the defence of one's person against attack. **defence mechanism,** *n.* (*Psych.*) a usually unconscious mental adjustment for excluding from the consciousness matters the subject does not wish to receive. **defenceless,** *a.* **defencelessly,** *adv.* **defencelessness,** *n.* the state of being undefended. [ME and OF *defens,* L *defensum,* forbidden, neut. p.p. of *dēfendere,* to defend; ME and OF *defense,* defence, L *dēfensa,* fem. p.p. of *dēfendere*]
Defence, Ministry of, British government department created in 1964 from a temporary Ministry of Defence established after World War II together with the Admiralty, Air Ministry, and War Office. It is headed by the secretary of state for defence with undersecretaries for the Royal Navy, Army, and Royal Air Force. This centralization was influenced by the example of the US Department of Defense.
defend, *v.t.* to protect, to guard; to shield from harm; to keep safe against attack; to support, to maintain by argument, to vindicate; (*Law*) to plead in justification of; †to forbid, to prohibit. *v.i.* to plead on behalf of the defendant; to contest a suit. **defendable,** *a.* **defendant,** *n.* (*Law*) one summoned into court to answer some charge; one sued in a law-suit. *a.* holding this relationship. **defender,** *n.* one who defends; one of a society formed in Ireland late in the 18th century to defend Roman Catholic interests against the Orangemen; (*Law*) a lawyer who appears for the defence; (*Sc. Law*) a defendant. **defensible,** *a.* **defensibility**, *n.* **defensibly,** *adv.* **defensive,** *a.* serving to defend; entered into or carried on in self-defence; protective, not aggressive. *n.* an attitude or condition of defence; †a safeguard, a protection. **to be, act, stand, on the defensive,** to be, act or stand in a position to repel attack. **defensive medicine,** *n.* diagnostic procedures carried out by doctors whether absolutely necessary or not in order to avoid any future legal indictment. **defensively,** *adv.* **defensor,** *n.* (*Rom. Law*) an advocate for a defendant; (*Rom. Hist.*) a magistrate in a provincial city appointed to keep watch against acts of oppression by the governor. [OF *defender,* L *dēfendere* (DE-, *fendere,* to strike)]
Defender of the Faith, one of the titles of the English sovereign, conferred on Henry VIII in 1521 by Pope Leo X in recognition of the king's treatise against the Protestant Luther. It appears on British coins in the abbreviated form **F.D.** (Latin *Fidei Defensor*).
Defense, Department of, US government department presided over by a secretary of defence with a seat in the president's cabinet; each of the three services has a civilian secretary, not of cabinet rank, at its head. It was established when the army, navy, and air force were unified by the National Security Act of 1947.
defer[1], *v.t.* to put off; to postpone. *v.i.* to delay; to procrastinate. **deferred pay,** *n.* wages or salary, esp. of a soldier, held over to be paid at his discharge or death. **deferment,** *n.* [OF *differer,* L *differre* (*dif-*, DIS-, *ferre,* to bear)]
defer[2], †*v.t.* (*past, p.p.* **deferred**) to offer, to refer; to submit. *v.i.* to yield to the opinion of another. **deference,** *n.* submission to the views or opinions of another; compliance; respect, regard; courteous submissiveness. **deferent**[1], *a.* deferential. **deferential,** *a.* **deferentially,** *adv.* [F *déférer,* L *dēferre* (DE-, *ferre,* to bring)]
deferent[2], *n.* that which carries or conveys; (*Physiol.*) a vessel or duct conveying fluids. *a.* (*Physiol.*) conveying fluids. [F *déférent,* or directly from L *dēferens -entem,* pres.p. of *dēferre,* as prec.]
defervescence, *n.* (*Med.*) a cooling down; an abatement of symptoms of fever. **defervesce,** *v.i.* **defervescent,** *a.* [L *dēfervēscens -entem,* pres.p. of *dēfervēscere* (DE-, *fervēscere,* incept. of *fervēre,* to be hot)]
defeudalize, -ise, *v.t.* to deprive of feudal character or form.
defiance DEFY.
defibrillator, *n.* a machine used to apply an electric current to the chest and heart area to stop fibrillation of the heart.
deficiency, *n.* a falling short; deficit, lack, want, insufficiency; the amount lacking to make complete or sufficient. **deficiency bills,** *n.pl.* a monetary advance made by the Bank of England to the Government to meet a temporary deficiency. **deficiency disease,** *n.*

one due to lack or insufficiency of one or more of the essential food constituents. **deficient,** *a.* wanting, defective; falling short; not fully supplied; mentally defective. **deficiently,** *adv.* **deficit,** *n.* a falling short of revenue as compared with expenditure; the amount of this deficiency; the amount required to make assets balance liabilities. **deficit spending,** *n.* a remedy for economic depression whereby the government's expenditure exceeds its revenue, the resulting budget deficit being financed by loans. [late L *dēficientia,* from L *dēficiens -entem,* pres.p. of *dēficere* (see DEFECT[1])]

defier DEFY.

defilade, *v.t.* (*Mil.*) to arrange the defences so as to shelter the interior works when they are in danger of being enfiladed. *n.* defilading. **defilement,** *n.*

defile[1], *v.t.* to make foul or dirty; to soil, to stain; to corrupt the chastity of, to violate; to pollute, to desecrate, to make ceremonially unclean. **defilement,** *n.* [ME *defoulen,* OF *defouler,* to trample on (DE-, late L *fullāre,* to full cloth), afterwards assimilated to BEFOUL and the obs. *befile,* OE *fȳlan,* from *fūl,* FOUL]

defile[2], *v.i.* to march in a file or by files. *n.* a long, narrow pass or passage, as between hills, along which men can march only in file; a gorge. [F *défiler* (DE-, *filer,* to FILE[3])]

define, *v.t.* to determine the limits of; to mark out, to fix with precision (as duties etc.); to give a definition of, to describe a thing by its qualities and circumstances. *v.i.* to give a definition. **definable,** *a.* **definably,** *adv.* †**definement,** *n.* definition, description. **definite,** *a.* limited, determinate, fixed precisely; exact, distinct, clear; positive; (*Gram.*) indicating exactly, limiting, defining. **past, preterite, definite,** (*French Gram.*) the tense corresponding to the Greek aorist and the English past. **definite article,** *n.* the. **definitely,** *adv.* **definiteness,** *n.* **definition,** *n.* the act of defining; an exact description of a thing by its qualities and circumstances; (*Log.*) an expression which explains a term so as to distinguish it from everything else; an enumeration of the constituents making up the logical essence; distinctness, clearness of form, esp. of an image transmitted by a lens or a television image. **definitive,** *a.* decisive; conclusive; positive; †peremptory. *n.* a word used to limit the application of a common noun, as an adjective or pronoun. **definitively,** *adv.* [OF *definer* (superseded by F *définir*) for *definir,* L *dēfīnīre* (DE-, *fīnīre,* to set a bound, from *fīnis,* bound)]

deflagrate, *v.t.* to consume by means of rapid combustion. *v.i.* to be consumed by means of rapid combustion. **deflagration,** *n.* **deflagrator,** *n.* an instrument for producing rapid combustion, usu. a form of the voltaic battery. [L *dēflāgrātus,* p.p. of *dēflāgrāre* (DE-, *flāgrāre,* to burn)]

deflate, *v.t.* to let down (a pneumatic tyre, balloon etc.) by allowing the air to escape; to reduce the inflation of currency. **deflater, deflator,** *n.* **deflation,** *n.* reduction of size by allowing air to escape; the reduction and control of the issue of paper money, causing prices to fall. **deflationary,** *a.* [L *dēflātus,* p.p. of *dēflāre* (DE-, *flāre,* to blow)]

deflect, *v.i.* to turn or move to one side, to deviate. *v.t.* to cause to turn or bend. **deflector,** *n.* **deflection,** *n.* **deflexed,** *a.* (*Bot., Zool.*) deflected, bent downwards. **deflexion, deflexure,** *n.* [L *dēflectere* (DE-, *flectere,* to bend), p.p. *dēflexus*]

deflorate , *a.* (*Bot.*) having shed its pollen; having the flowers fallen. *v.t.* to deflower. **defloration,** *n.* [L *dēflōrātus,* p.p. of *dēflōrāre,* as foll.]

deflower, *v.t.* to deprive of virginity, to ravish; to cull the best parts from; to ravage, to despoil; to strip of its bloom. **deflowerer,** *n.* [OF *desfleurer* (F *défleurer*), L *dēflōrāre* (DE-, *flōs flōris,* flower)]

defluent, *a.* flowing down. *n.* that which flows down (as the lower part of a glacier). [L *dēfluens -entem,* pres.p. of *dēfluere* (DE-, *fluere,* to flow)]

defluxion, *n.* a flowing or running down; a flowing down of fluids, esp. from the inflamed mucous membrane of the air-passages, in catarrh. [L *dēfluxio,* from *dēfluxus,* p.p. of *dēfluere,* as prec.]

Defoe, *n.* **Daniel** (1660–1731), English novelist and journalist, who wrote *Robinson Crusoe* (1719), which was greatly influential in the development of the novel. An active pamphleteer and political critic, he was imprisoned during 1702–04 following publication of the ironic *The Shortest Way With Dissenters.* Fictional works include *Moll Flanders* (1722) and *A Journal of the Plague Year* (1724). Altogether he produced over 500 books, pamphlets, and journals.

defoliate, *v.t.* to deprive of leaves. **defoliant,** *n.* a chemical used to remove leaves. **defoliation,** *n.* the fall or shedding of leaves. [L *folium,* a leaf]

deforce, *v.t.* to withhold with violence; (*Law*) to withhold the possession of from its rightful owner (as an estate); (*Sc. Law*) to oppose (an officer of the law) in the execution of his duty. **deforcement,** *n.* **deforcer,** *n.* [OF *deforcier,* late L *difforciāre* (*dif-,* DIS-, *fortia,* power, L *fortis,* strong)]

deforest, *v.t.* to clear of forest. **deforestation,** *n.* [OF *desforester,* DISFOREST]

De Forest, *n.* **Lee** (1873–1961), US physicist who was able to exploit the commercial value of radio. Ambrose Fleming invented the diode valve in 1904. De Forest saw that if a third electrode was added, the triode valve could serve as an amplifier and radio communications could become a practical possibility. He patented his discovery 1906.

deform, *v.t.* to render ugly or unshapely; to disfigure, to distort; to mar, to spoil. †*a.* disfigured, distorted, unshapely. **deformation,** *n.* the act or process of deforming; a disfigurement, perversion or distortion; a change for the worse as opp. to reformation; alteration in the structure and external configuration of the earth's crust through the action of internal forces. **deformed,** *a.* disfigured, ugly, misshapen; †causing deformity. **deformer,** *n.* **deformity,** *n.* the state of being deformed; a disfigurement, a malformation; that which mars or spoils the beauty of a thing. [OF *deformer,* L *dēformāre* (DE-, *forma,* beauty, form)]

defraud, *v.t.* to deprive of what is right by deception; to cheat. **defrauder,** *n.* [OF *defrauder*]

defray, *v.t.* to pay; to bear the charge of; to settle. **defrayable,** *a.* †**defrayal,** *n.* **defrayment,** *n.* [OF *défrayer* (DE-, *frai,* sing. of *frais,* cost, expense, prob. from low L *fredum,* a fine, OHG *fridu,* peace)]

defrock, *v.t.* to unfrock (a priest etc.).

defrost, *v.t.* to remove frost from; to thaw. **defroster,** *n.* a device for defrosting a windscreen or a refrigerator.

deft, *a.* neat in handling; dexterous, clever. †*adv.* deftly. **deftly,** *adv.* **deftness,** *n.* [OE *gedæfte,* see DAFT]

defunct, *a.* dead, deceased; †no longer in operation. *n.* a dead person. †**defunction,** *n.* death, decease. †**defunctive,** *a.* funereal. [L *dēfunctus,* p.p. of *dēfungī* (DE-, *fungī,* to perform)]

defuse, *v.t.* to render (a bomb) harmless by removing the fuse; to dispel the tension of (a situation).

defy, *v.t.* to challenge to a contest of any kind; to dare, to brave; to challenge to do or substantiate; to disregard openly, to make light of; to resist, to baffle. †*n.* a defiance. **defiance,** *n.* challenge to battle, single combat or any contest; contemptuous disregard; opposition; open disobedience; †declaration of hostilities. **defiant,** *a.* challenging; openly disobedient; hostile in attitude; suspicious, distrustful. **defiantly,** *adv.* **defier,** *n.* [OF *defier,* late L *diffidāre* (*dif-,* DIS-, *fīdus,* faithful)]

deg., (*abbr.*) degree (of temperature).

dégagé, fem. -gée, *a.* easy, unembarrassed, unconstrained. [F, p.p. of *dégager,* to disengage (DE-, GAGE)]

Degas, *n.* **(Hilaire Germain) Edgar** (1834–1917), French impressionist painter and sculptor. He devoted himself to lively, informal studies of ballet, horse racing, and young women working, often using pastels. From the 1890s he turned increasingly to sculpture, modelling figures in wax in a fluent, naturalistic style.

de Gaulle, *n.* **Charles** (1890–1970), French conservative politician and general. He organized the Free French troops fighting the Nazis (1940–44), was head of the provisional French government (1944–46), and leader of his own Gaullist party. In 1958 the national assembly asked him to form a government during France's economic recovery, and to solve the crisis in Algeria. He was president during 1959–69, having changed the constitution.

de-gauss, *v.t.* (*Elec.*) to neutralize the magnetization of, e.g. a ship, by the installation of a current-carrying conductor.

degenerate, *a.* fallen off from a better to a worse state; sunk below the normal standard; declined in natural or moral growth. *n.* a person or animal that has sunk below the normal type. *v.i.*, to fall off in quality from a better to a worse physical or moral state; to deteriorate; (*Biol.*) to revert to a lower type; to become wild. **degeneracy,** *n.* **degenerately,** *adv.* **degeneration,** *n.* the act or process of degenerating; the state of being degenerated; the return of a cultivated plant to the wild state; (*Bot.*) transition to an abnormal state; gradual deterioration of any organ or class of organisms. **degenerative,** *a.* [L *dēgenerātus,* p.p. of *dēgenerāre,* from *dēgener,* base (DE-, *genus -neris,* race)]

degerm, *v.t.* to remove the germ from (wheat). **degerminator,** *n.*

deglutition, *n.* the act or power of swallowing. [F *déglutition* (DE-, down, L *glūtītus,* p.p. of *glūtīre,* to swallow)]

degradation, *n.* the act of degrading; the state of being degraded; debasement, degeneracy; diminution or loss of strength, efficacy or value; a lessening and obscuring of the appearance of objects in a picture to convey the idea of distance; the wearing away of higher lands, rocks etc.

degrade, *v.t.* to reduce in rank; to remove from any rank, office or dignity; to debase, to lower; to bring into contempt; (*Biol.*) to reduce from a higher to a lower type; to wear away; to disintegrate. *v.i.* to degenerate; to postpone entering for the honours degree at Cambridge University to a year later than the normal time. **degradable,** *a.* capable of decomposing biologically or chemically. **degraded,** *a.* reduced in rank, position, value or estimation; low, mean, base; (*Her.*) furnished with steps. †**degradement,** *n.* deprivation of rank. **degrading,** *a.* lowering the level or character; humiliating, debasing. **degradingly,** *adv.* [OF *degrader,* late L *dēgradāre* (DE-, *gradus,* a step)]

degree, *n.* †a step, a stair; a step or stage in progression, elevation, quality, dignity or rank; relative position or rank; a certain distance or remove in the line of descent determining proximity of blood; social, official or Masonic rank; a rank or grade of academic proficiency conferred by universities after examination, or as a compliment to distinguished persons; relative condition, relative quantity, quality or intensity; (*Geom.*) the 90th part of a right angle; the 360th part of the circumference of the earth; the unit of measurement of temperature; one of the three grades of comparison of adjectives and adverbs (POSITIVE, COMPARATIVE, SUPERLATIVE). **by degrees,** gradually, step by step. **degree of freedom,** an independent component of motion of a molecule or atom; (*Chem.*) any of the independent variables which define the state of a system. **honorary degrees,** those conferred by a university without examination. **third degree,** a long and gruelling cross-examination. **to a degree,** (*coll.*) exceedingly. **degree-day,** *n.* the day on which degrees are conferred at a university. **degreeless,** *a.* [OF *degre* (DE-, L *gradus,* a step)]

degust, *v.t.* to taste so as to relish. *v.i.* to relish. **degustate,** *v.t.* to degust. **degustation**, *n.* [L *dēgustāre* (DE-, *gustāre,* to taste)]

de Havilland, *n.* **Geoffrey** (1882–1965), British aircraft designer who designed the Moth, the Mosquito fighter-bomber of World War II, and the postwar Comet – the world's first jet-driven airliner to enter commercial service.

De Havilland, *n.* **Olivia** (1916–), US actress, a star in Hollywood from the age of 19, when she appeared in *A Midsummer Night's Dream* (1935). She later successfully played more challenging dramatic roles in films such as *Gone with the Wind* (1939), *Dark Mirror* (1946) and *The Snake Pit* (1948).

dehisce, *v.i.* to gape, to burst open (of the capsules or anthers of plants). **dehiscence,** *n.* **dehiscent,** *a.* [L *dēhiscere* (DE-, *hiscere,* to yawn)]

dehort, *v.t.* to dissuade from anything; to advise to the contrary. **dehortation**, *n.* **dehortative,** *a.* **dehortatory,** *a.* [L *dēhortārī* (DE-, *hortārī,* to exhort)]

dehumanize, -ise, *v.t.* to divest of human character, esp. of feeling or tenderness; to brutalize.

dehumidify, *v.t.* to remove humidity from. **dehumidifier,** *n.*

dehydrate, *v.t.* to release or remove water or its elements from e.g. the body or tissues. **dehydration,** *n.*

dehypnotize, -ise, *v.t.* to awaken from a hypnotic condition.

de-ice, *v.t.* to disperse ice which has formed on the wings and control surfaces of an aircraft or on the windows of a car. **de-icer,** *n.* an apparatus or liquid used to effect this.

deicide, *n.* the killing of a god; one concerned in this. [L *deus,* god, -CIDE]

deictic, *a.* (*Gram., Log.*) proving directly; demonstrative, as distinguished from indirect or refutative. [Gr. *deiktikos,* from *deiktos* (*deiknunai,* to show)]

deid, (*Sc.*) DEAD, DEATH.

deify, *v.t.* to make a god of; to make godlike; to adore as a god; to idolize. **deific** , *a.* making divine. **deification,** *n.* **deifier,** *n.* **deiform**, *a.* of godlike form; conformable to the will of God. [OF *deifier,* late L *deificāre* (*deus,* god, *facere,* to make)]

Deighton, *n.* **Len** (1929–), British author of spy fiction, including *The Ipcress File* (1963), and the trilogy *Berlin Game*, *Mexico Set*, *London Match* (1983–85), featuring the spy Bernard Samson.

deign, *v.i.* to condescend, to vouchsafe. *v.t.* to condescend to allow or grant. [OF *degnier,* L *dignārī,* to deem worthy]

dei gratia, by the grace of God. [L]

deil, *n.* (*Sc.*) the devil; a devil or evil sprite. [DEVIL]

Deimos, *n.* one of the two moons of Mars. It is irregularly shaped, 15 '3 12 '3 11 km/9 '3 7.5 '3 7 miles, orbits at a height of 24,000 km/15,000 miles every 1.26 days, and is not as roughly featured as the other moon, Phobos. Deimos was discovered by US astronomer Asaph Hall in 1877, and is thought to be an asteroid captured by Mars' gravity.

deindustrialize, -ise, *v.t.* to make (a country etc.) less industrial. **deindustrialization, -isation,** *n.*

deinstitutionalize, -ise, *v.t.* to remove from an institution, esp. from a mental hospital. **deinstitutionalization, -isation,** *n.*

deiparous, *a.* bringing forth a god (an epithet applied to the Virgin Mary). [L *deus,* god, *parus,* bearing, from *parere,* to bear]

deipnosophist, *n.* a table philosopher; a philosopher of eating and drinking, after the title of a work by Athenaeus in which a company of ancient Greek philosophers discourse learnedly at meals. [Gr. *deipnosophistēs* (*deipnon,* dinner, SOPHIST)]

Deirdre, *n.* in Celtic mythology, beautiful intended bride of Conchobar.

deiseal, deasil, *n.* motion towards the right, in the direction of the hands of a clock or of the apparent motion of the sun. [Gael. *deiseil,* righthandwise, cogn. with L *dexter,* Gr. *dexios*]

deism, *n.* the belief in the being of a god as the governor of the universe, on purely rational grounds, without accepting divine revelation. **deist,** *n.* **deistic, -ical**, *a.* **deistically,** *adv.* [F *déisme* (L *deus,* god, -ISM)]

deity, *n.* divine nature, character or attributes; the Supreme Being; a fabulous god or goddess; the divinity ascribed to such beings. [F *déité,* L *deitās -tātem,* from *deus,* god]

déjà vu, *n.* an illusion of already having experienced something one is experiencing for the first time. [F, already seen]

deject, *v.t.* to cast down; to depress in spirit; to dishearten. †*a.* dejected. **dejecta**, *n.pl.* excrement of man or animal. **dejected,** *a.* **dejectedly,** *adv.* **dejection,** *n.* the act of casting down; the state of being dejected; lowness of spirits; (*Med.*) evacuation of the bowels, excrement. [L *dejectus,* p.p. of *dējicere* (DE-, *jacere,* to throw)]

déjeuner, *n.* breakfast, luncheon. [F *jeun,* L *jejūnus,* fasting]

de jure, by right. [L]

dekad, *n.* an interval of 10 days. [Gr. *deka,* ten]

Dekker, *n.* **Thomas** (*c.* 1572–*c.* 1632), English dramatist and pamphleteer, who wrote mainly in collaboration with others. His plays include *The Shoemaker's Holiday* (1600), and *The Witch of Edmonton* (with Ford and Rowley).

dekko , *n.* (*pl.* **dekkos**) (*coll.*) a (quick) look at. *v.i.* to look. [Hind. *dekho,* imper. of *dekhna,* a look]

De Klerk, *n.* **F(rederik) W(illem)** (1936–), South African National Party politician, president from 1989. Trained as a lawyer, he entered the South African parliament in 1972. He served in the cabinets of B. J. Vorster and P. W. Botha (1978–89), and in Feb. and Aug. 1989 successively replaced Botha as National Party leader and state president. Projecting himself as a pragmatic conservative who sought gradual reform of the apartheid system, he won the Sept. 1989 elections for his party, but with a reduced majority. In Feb. 1990 he ended the ban on the African National Congress opposition movement and released its effective leader, Nelson Mandela.

Del., (*abbr.*) Delaware (US).

del., (*abbr.*) delegate.

Delacroix, *n.* **Eugène** (1798–1863), French painter in the Romantic style. His prolific output included religious and historical subjects and portraits of friends, among them the musicians Paganini and Chopin. Against French academic tradition, he evolved a highly coloured, fluid style, as in *The Death of Sardanapalus* (1827) (Louvre, Paris).

delaine, *n.* a kind of untwilled wool muslin; a fabric of wool and cotton. [F *mousseline de laine,* woollen muslin]

de la Mare, *n.* **Walter** (1873–1956), English poet, best known for his verse for children, such as *Songs of Childhood* (1902), and the novels *The Three Royal Monkeys* (1910) for children and, for adults, *The Memoirs of a Midget* (1921).

delapse, *v.i.* to descend, to sink. [L *dēlāpsus,* p.p. of *dēlābī* (DE-, *lābī,* to slip, to fall)]

de la Roche, *n.* **Mazo** (1885–1961), Canadian novelist, author of the 'Whiteoaks' family saga.

delate, *v.t.* to accuse, to inform against; to cite before an ecclesiastical court. **delation,** *n.* **delator,** *n.* [late L *dēlātāre,* to accuse (DE-, *lātus,* p.p. of *ferre,* to bring)]

Delaunay, *n.* **Robert** (1885–1941), French painter, a pioneer in abstract art. With his wife Sonia Delaunay-Terk he invented Orphism, an early variation on cubism, focusing on the effects of pure colour.

Delauney-Terk, *n.* **Sonia** (1885–1979), French painter and textile designer born in Russia, active in Paris from 1905. With her husband Robert Delaunay she was a pioneer of abstract art.

De Laurentis, *n.* **Dino** (1919–), Italian producer. His earlier efforts, including Fellini's *La Strada/The Street* (1954), brought more acclaim than later epics such as *Waterloo* (1970). He then produced a series of Hollywood films: *Death Wish* (1974), *King Kong* (remake) (1976), *Dune* (1984).

Delaware, *n.* state of NE US; nickname The First State or Diamond State. **area** 5300 sq km/2046 sq miles. **capital** Dover. **towns** Wilmington, Newark. **physical** divided into two physical areas, one hilly and wooded, and the other gently undulating. **population** (1987) 644,000. **products** dairy, poultry, and market garden produce; chemicals, motor vehicles, textiles.

de la Warr, Thomas West, Baron de la Warr (1577–1618), US colonial administrator, known as Delaware. Appointed governor of Virginia in 1609, he arrived in 1610 just in time to prevent the desertion of the Jamestown colonists, and by 1611 had reorganized the settlement. Both the river and state are named after him.

delay[1], *v.t.* to postpone, to put off; to hinder, to retard. *v.i.* to put off action; to linger. *n.* a stay or stopping; postponement, retardation; detention; hindrance. **delayed-action bomb,** a bomb timed to explode some time after striking its objective. **delayer,** *n.* **delayingly,** *adv.* [OF *delaier,* prob. from L *dīlātāre,* freq. of *differre* (*dif-*, DIS-, *ferre,* cp. prec.)]

†**delay**[2], *v.t.* to temper, to mitigate. [OF *desleier,* to unbind, to disunite (DIS-, L *ligāre,* to bind)]

Delbruck, *n.* **Max** (1906–81), German-born US biologist who pioneered techniques in molecular biology, studying genetic changes occurring when viruses invade bacteria. Nobel prize for medicine 1969.

Delcassé, *n.* **Théophile** (1852–1923), French politician. He became foreign minister in 1898, but had to resign in 1905 because of German hostility; he held that post again during 1914–15. To a large extent he was responsible for the *Entente Cordiale* with Britain.

dele, *v.t.* (*Print.*) take out, omit, expunge. **deleble, delible,** *a.* that can be deleted. [L, 2nd pers. sing. imper. of *dēlēre,* to DELETE]

delectable, *a.* delightful, highly pleasing. **delectability, delectableness,** *n.* **delectation,** *n.* delight, pleasure, enjoyment. [OF, from L *dēlectābilis* (*dēlectāre,* to DELIGHT)]

delectus, *n.* a textbook containing select passages for translation. [L, selection, from *dēligere* (DE-, *legere,* to gather, to choose)]

delegate, *n.* one authorized to transact business as a representative; a deputy, an agent; (*US*) a deputy from a territory in Congress. *v.t.*, to depute as delegate, agent or representative, with authority to transact business. **delegation,** *n.* the act of delegating; a body of delegates; (*Law*) the assignment of a debt; a share certificate; a deputation. [OF *delegat,* L *dēlēgātus,* p.p. of *dēlēgāre* (DE-, *lēgāre,* to send, to depute)]

De Lesseps, *n.* **Ferdinand, Vicomte** (1805–94), French engineer, who constructed the Suez Canal between 1859–69. He reluctantly began the Panama Canal in 1881, but failed when he tried to construct it without locks.

delete, *v.t.* to strike out, to erase. **delenda**, *n.pl.* things to be deleted. **deletion,** *n.* **deletitious**, *a.* such that anything may be erased (of paper etc.). **deletory,** *n.* that which deletes. [L *dēlētus,* p.p. of *dēlēre* (DE-, *lēre,* conn. with *linere,* to smear)]

deleterious, *a.* harmful; injurious to health or mind. [late L *dēlētērius,* Gr. *dēlētērios,* from *dēlētēr,* a destroyer (*dēleesthai,* to destroy)]

delf, *n.* glazed earthenware, orig. made at Delft, Holland.

Delhi, *n.* Union Territory of the Republic of India from 1956; capital New Delhi; area 1500 sq km/579 sq miles; population (1981) 6,196,000. It produces grains, sugar cane, fruits, and vegetables.

deli, *n.* short for DELICATESSEN.

Delian, *a.* of or pertaining to Delos. **Delian problem,** *n.* (*Gr. Ant.*) the duplication of the cube. [L *Dēlius,* Gr. *Dēlios,* from *Dēlos*]

deliberate, *a.* weighing matters or reasons carefully; circumspect, cool, cautious; done or carried out intentionally; leisurely, not hasty. *v.i.* to weigh matters in the mind, to ponder; to estimate the weight of reasons or arguments; to consider, to discuss, to take counsel. *v.t.* to weigh in the mind. **deliberately,** *adv.* **deliberateness,** *n.* **deliberation,** *n.* calm and careful consideration; discussion of reasons for and against; freedom from haste or rashness; leisurely, not hasty, movement. **deliberative,** *a.* pertaining to, proceeding from, or acting with, deliberation. **deliberatively,** *adv.* [L *dēlīberātus,* p.p. of *dēlīberāre* (DE-, *lībrāre,* to weigh, from *lībra,* a balance)]

Delibes, *n.* **(Clément Philibert) Léo** (1836–91), French composer. His works include the ballet *Coppélia* and the opera *Lakmé*.

delible DELEBLE under DELE.

delicacy, *n.* the quality of being delicate; anything that is subtly pleasing to the senses, the taste or the feelings; a luxury, a dainty; fineness of texture, design, tint or workmanship; subtlety and sensitiveness of construction and action; weakness, fragility, susceptibility to injury; nicety of perception; fineness, sensitiveness, shrinking from coarseness and immodesty; gentleness, consideration for others.

delicate, *a.* highly pleasing to the taste; dainty, palatable; fine, smooth, not coarse; exquisite in form or texture; fastidious, tender, soft, effeminate; sensitive, subtly perceptive or appreciative; subtle in colour, form or style; requiring acuteness of sense to distinguish; easily injured, fragile, constitutionally weak or feeble; requiring careful treatment; critical, ticklish; refined, chaste, pure; gentle, considerate; †luxurious, voluptuous, sumptuous; skilful, ingenious, dexterous. *n.* anything choice, esp. food, a dainty; a dainty or fastidious person. **delicately,** *adv.* **delicateness,** *n.* [L *dēlicātus* (cp. *deliciae,* delight)]

delicatessen, *n.pl.* cooked meats and preserves; (*sing. in constr.*) a shop or part of a shop selling such products. [G]

†**delice,** *n.* pleasure, delight. [OF *delices,* L *dēliciae,* see foll.]

delicious, *a.* yielding exquisite pleasure to the senses, to taste or to the sense of humour. **deliciously,** *adv.* **deliciousness,** *n.* [OF, from late L *dēliciōsus,* from L *dēliciae,* delight, from *dēlicere* (DE-, *lacere,* to entice)]

delict, *n.* an offence, a delinquency; the actual commission of an offence. **delictum,** *n.* (*pl.* **-ta**). [L *dēlictum,* a fault, a crime, from *dēlinquere* (DE-, *linquere,* to omit)]

deligation, *n.* (*Surg.*) a binding; tying up with a ligature. [L *dēligāre*]

delight, *v.t.* to please greatly, to charm. *v.i.* to be highly pleased; to receive great pleasure (in). *n.* a state of great pleasure and satisfaction; a source of great pleasure or satisfaction. **delightedly,** *adv.* **delightful,** *a.* **delightfully,** *adv.* **delightfulness,** *n.* †**delightless,** *a.* †**delightsome,** *a.* †**delightsomely,** *adv.* †**delightsomeness,** *n.* [OF *deliter,* L *dēlectāre,* freq. of *dēlicere*]

Delilah, *n.* a temptress; a loose woman. [the Philistine woman who betrayed Samson (Judges xvi)]

delimit, *v.t.* to fix the boundaries or limits of. **delimitate,** *v.t.* to delimit. **delimitation,** *n.* [F *délimiter,* L *dēlīmitāre* (DE-, *līmitāre,* to bound, from *līmes līmitem,* a boundary)]

delineate, *v.t.* to draw in outline; to sketch out; to describe, to depict, to portray. **delineation,** *n.* **delineative,** *a.* **delineator,** *n.* **delineatory,** *a.* [L *dēlīneātus,* p.p. of *dēlīneāre* (DE-, *līneāre,* to mark out, from *līnea,* a LINE[1])]

delinquent, *a.* offending, failing, neglecting. *n.* one who fails in his duty; an offender, a culprit. **juvenile delinquent,** in Britain, an offender under 17 years of age. **delinquency,** *n.* a failure or omission of duty; a fault, an offence; guilt. [L *dēlinquens -entem,* pres.p. of *dēlinquere* (DE-, *linquere,* to omit)]

deliquesce, *v.i.* to liquefy, to melt away gradually by absorbing moisture from the atmosphere; to melt away (as money). **deliquescence,** *n.* **deliquescent,** *a.* [L *dēliquēscere* (DE-, *liquēscere,* incept. of *liquēre,* to be liquid)]

deliquium, *n.* a failure of the sun's light without an eclipse; faintness, a swoon; a maudlin mood. [L, from *dēlinquere* (see DELINQUENT)]

†**deliration,** *n.* delirium, dotage. **deliriant,** *a.* producing or tending to produce delirium. *n.* a drug or poison that has this effect. **delirifacient,** *n., a.* [L *dēlīrātio,* see DELIRIUM]

delirious, *a.* suffering from delirium, wandering in mind; raving, madly excited; frantic with delight or other excitement. **deliriously,** *adv.*

delirium, *n.* a wandering of the mind; frantic excitement or enthusiasm, rapture, ecstasy; perversion of the mental processes, the results of cerebral activity bearing no true relation to reality, characterized by delusions, illusions or hallucinations. **delirium tremens,** *n.* an acute phase in chronic alcoholism. [L, from *dēlīrāre* (DE-, *līra,* a furrow)]

delitescent, *a.* concealed, latent; (*Surg.*) disappearing, subsiding. **delitescence,** *n.* [L *dēlitēscens -entem,* pres.p. of *dēlitēscere* (DE-, *litēscere,* incept. of *latēre,* to lie hid)]

Delius, *n.* **Frederick (Theodore Albert)** (1862–1934), English composer. His works include the the opera *A Village Romeo and Juliet* (1901); the choral pieces *Appalachia* (1903), *Sea Drift* (1904), *A Mass of Life* (1905); orchestral works such as *In a Summer Garden* (1908), *A Song of the High Hills* (1911); chamber music and songs.

deliver, *v.t.* to free from danger or restraint; to save, to rescue; to assist at the birth of a child; to discharge, to send forth; to utter, or pronounce formally or officially; to surrender, to give up; to give over, to hand over or on; to distribute, to present; (*Law*) to hand over to the grantee. *v.i.* (*coll.*) deliver the goods; †to speak, to deliver oneself. **to deliver out,** to distribute. **to deliver over,** to put into the hands of; to transmit. **to deliver the goods,** to fulfil a promise, to carry out an undertaking, to live up to expectations. **to deliver up,** to surrender possession of. **deliverable,** *a.* **deliverance,** *n.* the act of delivering; the state of being delivered; (*Law*) the acquittal of a prisoner; (*Sc.*) the decision of a judge or arbitrator. **deliverer,** *n.* one who delivers; one who releases or rescues; a saviour, a preserver. **delivery,** *n.* the act of delivering; setting free; rescue, transfer, surrender; a distribution of letters from the post-office; the utterance of a speech; style or manner of speaking; childbirth; discharge of a blow or missile; (*Cricket*) the act or style of delivering a ball, style of bowling; (*Law*) the act of putting another in formal possession of property; the handing over of a deed to the grantee. **delivery room,** *n.* a room in a hospital, where babies are delivered. [F *délivrer,* late L *dēlīberāre* (DE-, L *līberāre,* to set free)]

dell, *n.* a hollow or small valley, usually wooded. [OE, cp. DALE]

Della Cruscan, *a.* pertaining to the Accademia della Crusca, at Florence, which was established to purify the Italian language and published an authoritative dictionary; pertaining to the Della Cruscan school; hence, artificial, affected in style. **Della Cruscan school,** a name applied to some English writers residing at Florence about 1785.

Della Robbia ware, a kind of earthenware founded on terra-cotta. [Luca *della Robbia,* It. sculptor, *c.* 1400–82]

Delon, *n.* **Alain** (1935–), French actor, who appeared in the films *Rocco e i suoi Fratelli/Rocco and his Brothers* (1960), *Il Gattopardi/The Leopard* (1963), *Texas across the River* (1966), *Scorpio* (1972), *Swann in Love* (1984).

Delors, *n.* **Jacques** (1925–), French socialist politician, finance minister (1981–84). As president of the European Commission from 1984 he has overseen significant budgetary reform and the move towards a free European Community market in 1992, with increased powers residing in Brussels.

delouse, *v.t.* to rid a person or place of vermin, esp. lice.

delph DELF.

Delphi, *n.* city of ancient Greece, situated in a rocky valley N of the gulf of Corinth, on the southern slopes of Mount Parnassus, site of a famous oracle in the temple of Apollo noted for its ambiguous answers. **Delphian, Delphic,** *a.*

Delphin[1], *a.* a title given to an annotated edition of the Latin classics, prepared for the Dauphin, son of Louis XIV. [L, from Gr., dolphin, see DAUPHIN]

delphin[2], *n.* a natural fat found in the oil of the dolphin.

delphinine, *n.* a vegetable alkaloid obtained from stavesacre, *Delphinium staphysagria.* **delphinium,** *n.* the genus comprising the larkspurs. [L *Delphīnium,* Gr.

delphīnion, the larkspur, dim. of *delphis*, DOLPHIN]

Delphinus, *n.* a genus of cetaceans containing the dolphins. **delphinoid**, *n.*, *a.* [L, as prec.]

del Sarto ANDREA DEL SARTO.

delta, *n.* the fourth letter of the Greek alphabet (δ, Δ), corresponding to the English *d;* the delta-shaped alluvial deposit at the mouth of the Nile; any similar alluvial deposit at the mouth of a river. **delta-leaved,** *a.* having leaves resembling a delta. **delta rays,** *n.pl.* electrons moving at relatively low speeds. **delta rhythm, wave,** *n.* the normal activity of the brain during deep sleep. **delta wing,** *n.* a triangular-shaped wing on an aeroplane. **deltaic**, *a.* **deltoid,** *a.* shaped like a delta; triangular. *n.* a triangular muscle of the shoulder which moves the arm. [Gr.]

Delta Force, *n.* US antiguerrilla force, based at Fort Bragg, North Carolina, and modelled on the British Special Air Service.

deltiology, *n.* the study and collecting of postcards. **deltiologist,** *n.* [Gr. *deltion*, dim. of *deltos*, a writing-tablet]

delude, *v.t.* to deceive, to impose upon. **deluded,** *a.* under a false impression. **deluder,** *n.* [L *dēlūdere* (DE-, *lūdere*, to play)]

deluge, *n.* a general flood or inundation, esp. the general flood in the days of Noah; a heavy downpour of rain; a torrent of words; a torrent or flood of anything liquid, as lava; an overwhelming calamity. *v.t.* to flood, to inundate; to overflow with water. [F *déluge*, L *dīluvium*, from *dīluere*, DILUTE]

delusion, *n.* the act of deluding; a cheat, an imposition; the state of being deluded; an error, a fallacy; an erroneous idea in which the subject's belief is unshaken by facts. **delusional,** *a.* **delusive**, *a.* deceptive, misleading, unreal. **delusively,** *adv.* **delusiveness,** *n.* **delusory**, *a.* [L *dēlūsio*, from *dēlūdere*, to DELUDE]

de luxe, *a.* luxurious, of superior quality. [F, of luxury]

delve, *v.t.* to dig, to open up with a spade; (*fig.*) to fathom, to get to the bottom of. *v.i.* to work with a spade; to carry on laborious research; to dip, to descend suddenly. *n.* †a pit, a cavity, a depression; work with a spade; a cave, a den. †**delver,** *n.* [OE *delfan* (cp. Dut. *delven*, MHG *telben*]

demagnetize, -ise, *v.t.* to deprive of magnetism; to free from mesmeric influence. **demagnetization, -isation,** *n.*

demagogue, *n.* a leader of the people; an agitator who appeals to the passions and prejudices of the people; a facetious orator; an unprincipled politician. **demagogic**, *a.* **demagogism,** *n.* †**demagoguery,** *n.* **demagogy,** *n.* [Gr. *dēmagōgos* (DEMOS, *agōgos*, leading, from *agein*, to lead)]

†**demain** DEMESNE.

demand, *n.* an authoritative claim or request; the thing demanded, esp. price; a claim; a peremptory question; desire to purchase or possess; a legal claim. *v.t.* to ask or claim with authority or as a right; to question, to interrogate; to seek to ascertain by questioning; to need, to require; to ask in a peremptory or insistent manner. *v.i.* to ask something as a right; to ask. **demand and supply,** a phrase used to denote the relations between consumption and production: if demand exceeds supply, the price rises; if supply exceeds demand, the price falls. **in demand,** much sought after. **on demand,** whenever requested. **demand note,** *n.* the final notice served for payment of rates, taxes etc. **demandable,** *a.* **demandant,** *n.* (*Law*) a plaintiff in a real action; a plaintiff generally; one who demands. **demander,** *n.* [F *demande*, from *demander*, L *dēmandāre* (DE-, *mandāre*, to entrust, to order)]

demarcate, *v.t.* to fix the limits of. **demarcation,** *n.* the fixing of a boundary or dividing line; the division between different branches of work done by members of trade unions on a single job. [Sp. *demarcacion*, from *demarcar*, to demarcate]

demarche, *n.* a diplomatic approach; method of procedure; announcement of policy. [F]

dematerialize, -ise, *v.t.* to deprive of material qualities or characteristics; to spiritualize. *v.i.* to lose material form; to vanish. **dematerialization, -isation,** *n.*

deme, *n.* a subdivision or township in Greece; (*Biol.*) an undifferentiated aggregate of cells. [Gr. *dēmos*]

demean, *v.t.* to manage, to treat; to conduct (oneself), to behave; to debase, to lower (in this sense the meaning has been altered to suit an erroneous popular etymology). *n.* behaviour, demeanour. **demeanour,** *n.* conduct, carriage, behaviour, deportment; †management. [OF *demener* (DE-, *mener*, to lead, late L *mināre*, to drive cattle, L, to threaten)]

dement, *v.t.* to madden; to deprive of reason. **demented,** *a.* insane. **dementedly,** *adv.* **dementedness,** *n.* [L *dēmentāre* (DE-, *mens mentis*, mind)]

dementi, *n.* an official contradiction (of a rumour etc.). [F]

dementia, *n.* loss or feebleness of the mental faculties; idiocy; infatuation. **dementia praecox,** *n.* a mental disorder resulting from a turning inwards into self away from reality, schizophrenia.

demerara, *n.* a kind of brown sugar. [river in Guyana]

demerge, *v.t.* to split, to separate (of companies formerly acting as one). **demerger,** *n.*

demerit, *n.* ill-desert, that which merits punishment; †merit, desert. [L *dēmeritum*, neut. p.p. of *dēmerēre*, to deserve (DE-, *merēre*, to deserve)]

demersal, *a.* (*Zool.*) found in deep water or on the ocean bed. [L *dēmersus*, submerged, plunged into]

demesne, *n.* an estate in land; the manor-house and the lands near it, which a lord keeps in his own hands; (*Law*) possession as one's own; the territory of the Crown or State; a region, territory. [OF *demeine*, as DOMAIN]

Demeter, *n.* in Greek mythology, goddess of agriculture (identified with Roman Ceres), daughter of Kronos and Rhea, and mother of Persephone by Zeus. She is identified with the Egyptian goddess Isis and had a temple dedicated to her at Eleusis where mystery religions were celebrated.

Demetrius, *n.* **Donskoi** ('of the Don') (1350–89), grand prince of Moscow from 1363. He achieved the first Russian victory over the Tatars on the plain of Kulikovo, next to the Don (hence his nickname) 1380.

demi-, *pref.* half, semi-, partial, partially. **demi-bastion,** *n.* (*Fort.*) a single face and flank, resembling the half of a bastion. **demi-cadence,** *n.* (*Mus.*) a half-cadence ending on the dominant. †**demi-cannon,** *n.* a cannon carrying a ball of from 30 to 36 lb. (13·6 to 16·3 kg). †**demi-culverin,** *n.* a cannon carrying a ball of 9 or 10 lb. (4·1 or 4·5 kg). †**demi-deify,** *v.t.* to deify in part. †**demi-ditone,** *n.* (*Mus.*) a minor third. **demi-god,** *n.* one who is half a god; an inferior deity; the offspring of a god and a human being. **demi-gorge,** *n.* (*Fort.*) the line formed by the prolongation of the curtain to the centre of a bastion. †**demi-lance,** *n.* a light lance; a half-pike; a light horseman armed with a lance. **demi-monde,** *n.* persons not recognized in society, women of dubious character; the section of a profession etc. which is not wholly legal or above board. **demi-mondaine,** *n.* a prostitute. **demi-puppet,** *n.* a diminutive puppet. **demi-relief,** *a.* a term applied to sculpture projecting moderately from the face of a wall; between high and low relief. **demi-rep,** *n.* a woman of doubtful chastity. **demi-semiquaver,** *n.* a note of the value of half a semiquaver or one-fourth of a quaver. **demi-tint,** *n.* a half-tint, or medium shade. **demi-tone** SEMITONE. **demivolte,** *n.* an artificial motion of a horse in which he raises his legs in a particular manner. †**demi-wolf,** *n.* a cross between a wolf and a dog. [F, from L *dimidius*, half]

demijohn, *n.* a glass vessel or bottle with a large body and small neck, enclosed in wickerwork. [corr. of F *damejeanne*, Dame Jane]

demilitarize, -ise, *v.t.* to end military involvement (in) and control (of).

De Mille, *n.* **Agnes** (1909–), US dancer and choreographer. One of the most significant contributors to the American Ballet Theater with dramatic ballets like *Fall River Legend* (1948), she also led the change on Broadway to new-style musicals with her choreography of *Oklahoma!* (1943), *Carousel* (1945), and others.

de Mille, *n.* **Cecil B(lount)** (1881–1959), US film director. He entered films in 1913 with Jesse L. Lasky (with whom he later established Paramount), and was one of the founders of Hollywood. He specialized in biblical epics, such as *The Sign of the Cross* (1932) and *The Ten Commandments* (1956).

Demirel, *n.* **Suleyman** (1924–), Turkish politician. Leader from 1964 of the Justice Party, he was prime minister in 1965–71, 1975–77 and 1979–80. He favoured links with the West, full membership of the EEC, and foreign investment in Turkish industry.

demise, *n.* death, decease, esp. of the sovereign or a nobleman; (*Law*) a transfer or conveyance by lease or will for a term of years or in fee simple. *v.t.* to bequeath; (*Law*) to transfer or convey by lease or will. **demise of the Crown,** transference of sovereignty upon the death or abdication of the monarch. **demisable,** *a.* [OF, p.p. of *desmettre,* to DISMISS]

†**demiss,** *a.* submissive; abject. †**demission,** *n.* degradation; diminution of dignity; resignation. [L *dēmissus,* p.p. of *dēmittere* (DE-, *mittere,* to send)]

demist, *v.t.* to make clear of condensation. **demister,** *n.*

demit, *v.t., v.i.* to resign. **demission,** *n.* the act of resigning or abdicating. [F *démettre* (DIS-, *mettre,* L *mittere,* to send)]

De Mita, *n.* **Luigi Ciriaco** (1928–), Italian conservative politician, leader of the Christian Democratic Party (DC) from 1982, prime minister from 1988. He entered the Chamber of Deputies in 1963 and held a number of ministerial posts in the 1970s before becoming DC secretary- general.

demiurge, *n.* (*Gr. Hist.*) the name of a magistrate in some of the Peloponnesian states; a name given by the Platonists to the creator of the universe; the Logos of the Platonizing Christians. **demiurgic,** *a.* [L *dēmiūrgus,* Gr. *dēmiourgos* (*dēmios,* public, from DEMOS, *ergos,* worker)]

demi-veg, *a.* not completely vegetarian, but including white meat and fish in the diet. *n.* one who follows this diet.

demivolte DEMI-.

demo-, *comb. form* pertaining to the people or the population generally. [Gr. *dēmos*]

demo, *n.* short for DEMONSTRATION.

demob, *v.t.* (*past, p.p.* **demobbed**) (*coll.*) to demobilize. *n.* demobilization.

demobilize, -ise, *v.t.* to disband, to dismiss (as troops) from a war footing. **demobilization, -isation,** *n.*

democracy, *n.* the form of government in which the sovereign power is in the hands of the people, and exercised by them directly or indirectly; a democratic state; the people, esp. the unprivileged classes. **democrat,** *n.* one in favour of democracy; (*US*) a member of the Democratic party. **democratic,** *a.* pertaining to a democracy; governed by or maintaining the principles of democracy. **democratically,** *adv.* **democratism,** *n.* **democratize, -ise,** *v.t., v.i.* **democratization, -isation,** *n.* the inculcation of democratic views and principles. [F *démocratie,* L *dēmocratia,* Gr. *dēmokratia*]

Democratic Party, *n.* one of the two main political parties of the US. It tends to be the party of the working person, as opposed to the Republicans, the party of big business, but the divisions between the two are not clear-cut. Its stronghold has traditionally been the Southern states. In the 1960s the Northern Democrats ('Presidential wing') pressed for civil-rights reform, while Southern Democrats ('Congressional wing') voted against the president on social issues.

Democrats, *n.* in UK politics, common name for the Social and Liberal Democrats.

démodé, *a.* out of fashion. [F]

demodernization, -isation, *n.* the making less modern of, e.g. modern housing estates, to make them more habitable and less prone to social problems.

demodulate, *v.t.* to extract the original audio signal from (the modulated carrier wave by which it is transmitted). **demodulation,** *n.* **demodulator,** *n.*

demogorgon, *n.* a mysterious divinity, first mentioned by a scholiast on the *Thebaid* of Statius as one of the infernal gods; a personage of mysterious origin and attributes in poems by Ariosto, Spenser, Shelley etc. [late L, from Gr. (DEMOS, GORGON)]

demography, *n.* the study of population statistics dealing with size, density and distribution. **demographer,** *n.* **demographic,** *a.* **demographically,** *adv.*

demoiselle, *n.* the Numidian crane, *Anthropoides virgo,* from its graceful form and bearing; an unmarried woman. [F]

demolish, *v.t.* to pull or throw down; to raze; to ruin, to destroy; (*coll.*) to eat up. **demolition,** *n.* the act of demolishing; (*Mil.*) destruction using explosives. **demolitions expert,** *n.* one skilled in demolition using explosives. [F *démoliss-,* stem of *démolir,* L *dēmōlīrī* (DE-, *mōlīrī,* to construct, from *mōlēs,* mass)]

demon, daemon, *n.* (*Gr. Myth.*) a supernatural being, lesser divinity, genius or attendant spirit supposed to exercise guardianship over a particular individual, in many respects corresponding to the later idea of a guardian angel; an evil spirit having the power of taking possession of human beings; a fallen angel, a devil; a very cruel or malignant person; (*sl., usu. in comb.*) an extremely clever person, as *demon-bowler.* **demoness,** *n. fem.* **demoniac,** *a.* pertaining to or produced by demons; possessed by a demon; devilish; frantic, frenzied. *n.* one possessed by a demon. **demoniacal,** *a.* devilish; pertaining to possession by a devil. **demoniacally,** *adv.* †**demonian,** *a.* pertaining to a demon; possessed by a demon; devilish. **demonic, daemonic,** *a.* **demonism,** *n.* belief in demons or false gods. **demonist,** *n.* **demonize, -ise,** *v.t.* to make into a demon; to make devilish; to bring under demonic influence. **demonry,** *n.* demonic influence. [L *daemōn,* Gr. *daimōn,* a deity, a genius]

demonetize, -ise, *v.t.* to deprive of its character as money; to withdraw (a metal) from currency. **demonetization, -isation,** *n.*

demoniac, demonism etc. DEMON.

demono-, *comb. form* the power or government of demons.

demonolatry, *n.* the worship of demons or evil spirits.

demonology, *n.* the study of demons or of evil spirits.

demonomania, *n.* a kind of mania in which the sufferer believes himself possessed by devils. [Gr. *daimonomania*]

demonstrate, *v.t.* to show by logical reasoning; to prove beyond the possibility of doubt; to exhibit, describe and prove by means of specimens and experiments; to display, to indicate. *v.i.* to organize or take part in a military or public demonstration. **demonstrant,** *n.* **demonstrable,** *a.* that may be proved beyond doubt; †apparent, evident. **demonstrability,** *n.* **demonstrably,** *adv.* **demonstration,** *n.* the act of demonstrating; clear, indubitable proof; an outward manifestation of feeling etc.; a public exhibition or declaration of principles, feelings etc. by any party; exhibition and description of objects for the purpose of teaching; a series of syllogisms the premises of which are definitions, self-evident truths or propositions already established; (*Mil.*) a movement of troops as if to attack. **demonstrative,** *a.* having the power of exhibiting and proving; proving; conclusive; pertaining to proof; serving to show and make clear; manifesting the feelings strongly and openly. *n.* (*Gram.*) a class of determiners used to highlight the referent(s), as *this, that.* **demonstratively,** *adv.* **demonstrativeness,** *n.* **demonstrator,** *n.* one who demonstrates; one who teaches by means of exhibition and experiment; one who takes part in a public demonstration of political, religious or other opinions. **demonstratorship,** *n.* [L *dēmonstrātus,* p.p. of *dēmonstrāre* (DE-, *monstrāre,* to show)]

demoralize, -ise, *v.t.* to subvert and corrupt the morals and principles of; to corrupt the discipline or morale of; to discourage; to throw into confusion. **demoralization, -isation,** *n.* [F *démoraliser* (DE-, MORAL,

-IZE)]

de Morgan, *n.* **William Frend** (1839–1917), English pottery designer. He set up his own factory in 1888 in Fulham, London, producing tiles and pottery painted with flora and fauna in a style typical of the Arts and Crafts Movement.

Demos, *n.* the people, as distinguished from the upper classes; the mob; democracy. [Gr., the people]

Demosthenes, *n.* (*c.* 384–322 BC), Athenian orator and politician. From 351 BC he led the party that advocated resistance to the growing power of Philip of Macedon, and in his *Philippics* incited the Athenians to war. This policy resulted in the defeat of Chaeronea in 338, and the establishment of Macedonian supremacy. After the death of Alexander he organized a revolt; when it failed, he took poison to avoid capture by the Macedonians.

demote, *v.t.* to reduce in status or rank. **demotion,** *n.* [L *movēre,* to move]

demotic, *a.* of or belonging to the people; popular, common, vulgar; (**Demotic**) the spoken form of modern Greek. **demotic alphabet,** *n.* that used by the laity and people of Egypt as distinguished from the hieratic on which it was based. [Gr. *dēmotikos,* from *dēmotēs,* one of the people (see DEMOS)]

Demotic Greek, *n.* the common or vernacular variety of the modern Greek language.

Dempsey, *n.* **Jack** ('the Manassa Mauler') (1895–1983), US heavyweight boxing champion. He beat Jess Willard in 1919 to win the title and held it until losing to Gene Tunney in 1926. He engaged in the 'Battle of the Long Count' with Tunney in 1927.

dempster DEEMSTER.

†**dempt,** *past, p.p.* of DEEM.

†**demulce,** *v.t.* to soothe, to pacify, to soften. **demulcent,** *a.* softening, mollifying, lenitive. *n.* a medicine which allays irritation. [L *dēmulcēre* (DE-, *mulcēre,* to stroke)]

demur, *v.i.* (*past, p.p.* **demurred**) †to tarry; †to delay, to loiter, to hesitate; to have or express scruples, objections or reluctance; (*Law*) to take exception to any point in the pleading as insufficient. †*v.t.* to hesitate about; to take exception to; to put off. *n.* †hesitation, pause, delay; the act of demurring; scruple, objection. **demurrable,** *a.* liable to exception, esp. legal objection. **demurral,** *n.* **demurrant,** *n.* **demurrer,** *n.* (*Law*) an objection made to a point submitted by the opposing party on the score of irrelevance or legal insufficiency; an objection. [OF *demeurer,* L *dēmorārī* (DE-, *morārī,* to delay, from *mora,* delay)]

demure, *a.* staid; modest; affectedly modest. [OF *de* (*bons*) *murs,* of (good) manners]

demurrage, *n.* an allowance by the freighter of a vessel to the owners for delay in loading or unloading beyond the time named in the charter-party; the period of such delay; a charge for the detention by one company of trucks etc. belonging to another; a fee charged by the Bank of England for exchanging notes or coin for bullion.

demy, *n.* (*pl.* **demies**) a particular size of paper, $22\frac{1}{2} \times 17\frac{1}{2}$ in. (444·5 × 571·5 mm) for printing, $20 \times 15\frac{1}{2}$ in. (508 × 393·7 mm) for drawing or writing (*N Am.* 21 × 16 in.); a scholar of Magdalen College, Oxford. **demyship,** *n.*

demystify, *v.t.* to remove the mystery from, to clarify. **demystification,** *n.*

demythologize, -ise, *v.t.* to remove the mythological elements from, e.g. the Bible, to highlight the basic meaning. **demythologization, -isation,** *n.*

den, *n.* the lair of a wild beast; a retreat, a lurking-place; a hovel; a miserable room; (*coll.*) a study, a sanctum, a snuggery; (*Sc.*) a small valley. †*v.i.* (*also reflexive*) to live in a den. [OE *denn,* cp. *denu,* a valley, DEAN[2] (Dut. *denne,* G *Tenne*)]

denarius, *n.* (*pl.* **-rii**) a Roman silver coin, worth 10 asses; a penny. [L *dēnārius,* containing ten (*dēnī,* pl., ten by ten, from *decem,* ten)]

denary, *a.* containing 10; based on the number 10, decimal. [from prec.]

denationalize, -ise, *v.t.* to deprive of the rights, rank or characteristics of a nation; to make cosmopolitan; to transfer to another state; to deprive of citizenship; to transfer from public to private ownership. **denationalization, -isation,** *n.*

denaturalize, -ise, *v.t.* to render unnatural; to alter the nature of; to deprive of naturalization or citizenship. **denaturalization, -isation,** *n.*

denature, denaturize, -ise, *v.t.* to change the essential nature or character of (by adulteration etc.); to modify (e.g. a protein) by heat or acid; to render (alcohol) unfit for human consumption; to add non-radioactive material to radioactive material, to prevent the latter being used in nuclear weapons. **denatured alcohol,** *n.* alcohol which has been rendered unfit according to law for human consumption; (*N Am.*) methylated spirit. [F *dénaturer,* OF *desnaturer*]

denazify, *v.t.* to purge of Nazism and its evil influence on the mind.

Denbighshire, *n.* former county of Wales, largely merged in 1974, together with Flint and part of Merioneth, in Clwyd; a small area along the W border was included in Gwynedd. Denbigh, in the Clwyd valley (population about 9000), was the county town.

Dench, *n.* **Judi** (1934–), British actress who made her debut as Ophelia in *Hamlet* in 1957 with the Old Vic Company. Her Shakespearean roles include Portia in *Twelfth Night*, Lady Macbeth, and Cleopatra. She is also a versatile comedy actress and has appeared in films, for example *A Room with a View*, and on television.

dendr(i)-, dendro-, *comb. form.* resembling a tree; branching. [Gr. *dendron,* a tree]

dendriform, *a.* arborescent.

dendrite, *n.* a stone or mineral with arborescent markings; one of the branched extensions of a nerve cell which conduct impulses to the body of the cell. **dendritic, -ical,** *a.* like a tree; arborescent; with tree-like markings.

dendrochronology, *n.* the study of the annual growth rings in trees, used to date historical events.

dendrodentine, *n.* a modification of the fundamental tissue of the teeth, produced by the blending of several teeth into one mass, the whole presenting a dendritic appearance.

dendrodont, *a.* applied to a group of ganoid fishes from the Devonian, from the labyrinthine microscopic structure of their teeth.

dendrograph, *n.* an instrument for measuring the swelling of tree-trunks.

dendroid, *a.* tree-like, arborescent.

dendrolite, *n.* a fossil plant, or part of a plant; fossilized wood.

dendrology, *n.* the natural history of trees. **dendrologist,** *n.*

dendrometer, *n.* an instrument for measuring the height and diameter of trees.

dene[1] DEAN[2].

dene[2], *n.* a sandy down or low hill, a tract of sand by the sea. [etym. doubtful; cp. LG and G *Düne,* Dut. *duin,* F *dune*]

Dene, *n.* term applied to distinct but related indigenous people. In Canada, it has been used to describe the Native Americans in the Northwest Territories since the 1970s. The official body representing them is called the Dene nation.

Deneb, *n.* brightest star in the constellation Cygnus, and the 19th-brightest star in the sky. It is one of the greatest supergiant stars known, with a true luminosity of about 60,000 times that of the Sun. Deneb is 1600 light years away.

denegation, *n.* contradiction, denial. [F *dénégation,* L *dēnegātio -ōnem,* from *dēnegāre,* to DENY]

dene-hole, *n.* an excavation consisting of a shaft, from 2 ft. 6 in. to 3 ft. (about 75 cm to 1 m) in diameter and 20 ft. to 90 ft. (about 6 to 27 m) in depth, ending below in a cavern in the chalk; made originally to obtain chalk (in Essex called DANE-HOLE). [etym. doubtful; perh. DANE or OE *denu,* DEAN[2]]

Deneuve, *n.* **Catherine** (1943–), French actress acclaimed for her performance in Polanski's film *Repulsion* (1965). She also appeared in *Les Parapluies de Cherbourg/Umbrellas of Cherbourg* (1964), *Belle de Jour* (1967), *Hustle* (1975), *The Hunger* (1983).

dengue, *n.* an acute fever common in the E and W Indies, Africa and America, characterized by severe pains, an eruption like erysipelas and swellings. [W Indian Sp., prob. from Swahili]

Deng Xiaoping, *n.* (formerly **Teng Hsiao-ping**) (1904–), Chinese political leader. A member of the Chinese Communist Party (CCP) from the 1920s, he took part in the Long March (1934–36). He was in the Politburo from 1955 until ousted in the Cultural Revolution (1966–69). Reinstated in the 1970s, he gradually took power and introduced a radical economic modernization programme. He retired from the Politburo in 1987 and from his last official position (as chair of Central Military Commission) in Nov. 1989, but remained influential behind the scenes.

Den Haag, *n.* Dutch form of The Hague.

deniable, denial, denier[2] DENY.

denier[1], *n.* a small French coin, the 12th part of a sou; a coin of insignificant value; the unit for weighing and grading silk, nylon and rayon yarn, used for women's tights and stockings. [OF, from DENARIUS]

denigrate, *v.t.* to blacken; to defame. **denigration,** *n.* **denigrator,** *n.* [L *dēnigrātus,* p.p. of *dēnigrāre* (DE-, *niger,* black)]

Denikin, *n.* **Anton Ivanovich** (1872–1946), Russian general. He distinguished himself in the Russo-Japanese War (1904–05) and World War I. After the outbreak of the Bolshevik Revolution (1917) he organized a volunteer army of 60,000 Whites (counter-revolutionaries), but in 1919 was routed and escaped to France. He wrote a history of the Revolution and the Civil War.

denim, *n.* a coarse, twilled cotton fabric used for overalls, jeans etc.; (*pl.*) jeans made of denim. [short for F *serge de Nîmes,* serge of Nîmes]

De Niro, *n.* **Robert** (1943–), US actor. He won Oscars for *The Godfather Part II* (1974) and *Raging Bull* (1979). Other films include *Taxi Driver* (1976), *The Deer Hunter* (1978), and *The Untouchables* (1987).

denitrate, *v.t.* to set free nitric or nitrous acid or nitrate from. **denitrify,** *v.t.* to denitrate. **denitrification,** *n.* the liberation of nitrogen from the soil by the agency of bacteria.

denizen, *n.* a citizen, an inhabitant, a dweller, a resident; (*Eng. Law*) an alien who has obtained letters patent to make him an English subject; a foreign word, plant or animal, that has become naturalized. *v.t.* to naturalize; to make a denizen of. **denizenship,** *n.* [A-F *deinzein,* from *deinz* (F *dans*), within (L DE-, *intus,* within), -AN]

Denktash, *n.* **Rauf** (1924–), Turkish-Cypriot politician. In 1975 the Turkish Federated State of Cyprus (TFSC) was formed in the northern third of the island, with Denktash as its head, and in 1983 he became president of the breakaway Turkish Republic of Northern Cyprus (TRNC).

Denmark, *n.* Kingdom of (*Kongeriget Danmark*), country in N Europe. **area** 43,075 sq km/16,627 sq miles. **capital** Copenhagen. **towns** Aarhus, Odense, Aalborg, Esbjerg, all ports. **physical** the land is flat and cultivated; sand dunes and lagoons on the W coast and long inlets on the E. **territories** Faeroe Islands and Greenland; head of government Poul Schlüter from 1982. **population** (1988) 5,129,000; annual growth rate 0%. **exports** bacon, dairy produce, eggs, fish, mink pelts, car and aircraft parts, electrical equipment, textiles. **language** Danish (official). **religion** Lutheran.

†**dennet,** *n.* an open two-wheeled vehicle like a gig. [prob. a personal name]

Denning, *n.* **Alfred Thompson, Baron Denning of Whitchurch** (1899–), British judge, Master of the Rolls (1962–82). In 1963 he conducted the inquiry into the Profumo scandal. A vigorous and highly innovative civil lawyer, he was controversial in his defence of the rights of the individual against the state, the unions, and big business.

denominate, *v.t.* to name; to give a name, epithet or title to; to designate. **denomination,** *n.* the act of naming; a designation, title or appellation; a class, a kind, esp. of particular units (as coins, weights etc.); a particular body or sect. **denominational,** *a.* pertaining to a particular denomination, sectarian. **denominational education,** *n.* a system of education recognizing the principles of a religious denomination. **denominationalism,** *n.* **denominationalist,** *n.* **denominationalize, -ise,** *v.t.* **denominationally,** *adv.* [L *dēnōminātus,* p.p. of *dēnōmināre*]

denominative, *a.* that gives or constitutes a distinctive name. **denominator,** *n.* one who or that which denominates; (*Arith.*) the number below the line in a fraction which shows into how many parts the integer is divided, while the numerator, above the line, shows how many of these parts are taken. [L *dēnōminātīvus,* as prec.]

denote, *v.t.* to mark, to indicate, to signify; to mark out, to distinguish; (*Log.*) to be a name of, to be predicable of (distinguished from CONNOTE). **denotable,** *a.* **denotation,** *n.* the act of denoting; separation or distinction by means of a name or names; meaning, signification; a system of marks or symbols. **denotation of a term,** (*Log.*) the extent of its application. **denotative,** *a.* signifying, pointing out; designating, without implying attributes. **denotatively,** *adv.* **denotement,** *n.* a sign, an indication. [F *dénoter,* L *dēnotāre* (DE-, *notāre,* to mark, from *nota,* a mark)]

dénouement, *n.* the unravelling of a plot or story; the catastrophe or final solution of a plot; an outcome. [F, from *dénouer* (DIS-, L *nodāre,* to knot, from *nodus,* knot)]

denounce, *v.t.* to accuse publicly; to charge, to inform against; to declare in a solemn or threatening manner; to declare (war); to give formal notice of termination of (a treaty or convention). **denouncement,** *n.* denunciation. **denouncer,** *n.* [OF *denoncer,* L *dēnuntiāre* (DE-, *nuntiāre,* to announce, from *nuntius,* a messenger)]

de novo, *adv.* anew. [L]

Denpasar, *n.* capital town of Bali in the Lesser Sunda Islands of Indonesia. Population (1980) 88,100.

dense, *a.* thick, compact; having its particles closely united; (*fig.*) stupid, obtuse; (*Phot.*) opaque, strong in contrast. **densely,** *adv.* **denseness,** *n.* **densimeter,** *n.* an apparatus for measuring density or specific gravity. **densimetry,** *n.* **density,** *n.* denseness; (*Phys.*) the mass per unit volume of a substance measured, for example, in grams per cubic centimetre; a crowded condition; a measure of the reflection or absorption of light by a surface; (*fig.*) stupidity. [L *densus*]

dent[1], *n.* a depression such as is caused by a blow with a blunt instrument; an indentation; †a stroke or blow; (*fig.*) a lessening or diminution. *v.t.* to make a dent in; to indent. [DINT]

dent[2], *n.* a tooth of a wheel, a cog; (*Carding*) the wire staple that forms the tooth of a card; a wire of the reed-frame of a loom. [F, tooth, from L *dens dentis*]

dental, *a.* pertaining to or formed by the teeth; pertaining to dentistry. *n.* a letter or articulation formed by placing the end of the tongue against the upper teeth. **dental floss,** *n.* thread used to clean between the teeth. **dental formula,** *n.* a formula used to describe the dentition of a mammal. **dental plaque,** *n.* a deposit of bacteria and food on the teeth. **dental surgeon** DENTIST. **dentalize, -ise,** *v.t.* to pronounce as a dental; to alter to a dental sound. **dentary,** *a.* pertaining to the teeth. *n.* the bone in the lower jaw of fishes and reptiles carrying the teeth. [L *dens dentis,* as prec.]

dentate, dentated, *a.* (*Bot., Zool.*) toothed; indented. **dentately,** *adv.* **dentation,** *n.*

dentato-, *comb. form* toothed; having tooth-like processes. [L *dentātus*]

dentato-sinuate, *a.* (*Bot.*) having the margin scalloped and slightly toothed.

dentelle, *n.* a style of angular decoration like saw-teeth; a lace edging resembling a series of small teeth. [F, lace]

denti-, *comb. form.* of or pertaining to the teeth. [L *dens dentis,* a tooth]

denticle, *n.* a small tooth; a projecting point, a dentil. **denticular**, *a.* **denticulate**, **-lated**, *a.* finely toothed; formed into dentils. **denticulately,** *adv.* **denticulation,** *n.* [L *denticulus,* dim. of *dens dentis,* tooth]

dentiform, *a.* having the form of a tooth or teeth.

dentifrice, *n.* powder, paste or other material for cleansing the teeth. [F, from L *dentifricium* (DENTI-, *fricāre,* to rub)]

dentil, *n.* one of the small square blocks or projections under the bed-moulding of cornices. [obs. F *dentille,* from *dent,* a tooth]

dentilingual, *a.* formed by the teeth and the tongue. *n.* a consonant so formed.

dentine, *n.* the ivory tissue forming the body of a tooth.

dentiroster, *n.* one of a tribe of passerine birds, Dentirostres, having a tooth or notch near the top of the upper mandible. **dentirostral,** *a.*

dentist, *n.* one skilled in and qualified in treating disorders of the teeth. **dentistry,** *n.* **dentition**, *n.* teething; the time of teething; the arrangement of the teeth in any animal. **denture**, *n.* (*often pl.*) set of teeth, esp. artificial. [F *dentiste,* from *dent,* tooth]

denuclearize, -ise, *v.t.* to deprive of nuclear arms; to prohibit the presence of any nuclear material or any installation using nuclear power. **denuclearization, -isation,** *n.*

denude, *v.t.* to make bare or naked; to strip of clothing, attributes, possessions, rank or any covering; (*Geol.*) to lay bare by removing whatever lies above. **denudate**, *v.t.* to denude. *a.*, made naked, stripped; (*Bot.*) appearing naked. **denudation**, *n.* [L *dēnūdāre* (DE-, *nūdāre,* to strip, from *nūdus,* bare)]

denumerable, *a.* able to be put into a one-to-one correspondence with the positive integers; countable. **denumerably,** *adv.*

denunciate, *v.t.* to denounce. **denunciation,** *n.* **denunciative,** *a.* **denunciator,** *n.* **denunciatory,** *a.* [L *dēnuntiātus,* p.p. of *dēnuntiāre,* DENOUNCE]

Denver, *n.* city in Colorado, US, on the South Platte river, near the foothills of the Rocky Mountains; population (1980) 492,365, Denver-Boulder metropolitan area 1,850,000. It is a processing and distribution centre for a large agricultural area, and for natural resources (minerals, oil, gas). It was the centre of a gold and silver boom in the 1870s and 1880s, and for oil in the 1970s.

deny, *v.t.* to assert to be untrue or non-existent; to disown, to reject, to repudiate; to refuse to grant, to withhold from; to refuse admittance to; to refuse access to; †to contradict; to say 'no' to. *v.i.* to say 'no'; to contradict. **to deny oneself,** to refrain or abstain from; to practise self-denial. **deniable,** *a.* that may be denied. **denial,** *n.* the act of denying, contradicting or refusing; a negation; abjuration, disavowal; self-denial. **denier**[2], *n.* one who denies. [F *dénier,* L *dēnegāre* (DE-, *negāre,* to deny)]

deobstruent, *a.* (*Med.*) removing obstructions; aperient; having the quality of opening and clearing the ducts of the body. *n.* a deobstruent medicine. [L *obstruere,* to OBSTRUCT]

deodand, *n.* (*Hist.*) a personal chattel which had been the immediate cause of the death of any person, and on that account forfeited to be sold for some pious use. [A-F *deodande,* L *Deo dandum,* to be given to God (*dandum,* from *dare,* to give)]

deodar, *n.* a large Himalayan tree, *Cedrus deodara,* allied to the cedars of Lebanon. [Hind. *dē'odar, dēwdār,* Sansk. *deva-dāru,* timber of the gods (*deva-,* a deity, *dāru,* a kind of pine)]

deodorize, -ise, *v.t.* to deprive of odour; to disinfect. **deodorant,** *n.* an agent which counteracts unpleasant smells; a substance used to mask the odour of perspiration. **deodorization, -isation,** *n.* the act of deodorizing. **deodorizer, -iser,** *n.*

Deo favente, with the favour of God. [L]

Deo gratias, thanks be to God. [L]

deontology, *n.* the science of duty, the Benthamite doctrine of ethics. **deontic**, *a.* †**deontological**, *a.* †**deontologist,** *n.* [Gr. *deon deontos,* duty, neut. pres.p. of *deî,* it is binding]

Deo volente, God willing. [L]

deoxidize, -ise, *v.t.* to deprive of oxygen; to extract oxygen from. **deoxidization, -isation,** *n.* **deoxidizer, -iser,** *n.* **deoxygenate**, *v.t.* to deoxidize. **deoxygenation,** *n.* **deoxygenize, -ise,** *v.t.* to deoxidize.

deoxycorticosterone, deoxycortone, *n.* a hormone which maintains the sodium and water balance in the body.

deoxyribonucleic acid, desoxyribonucleic acid, *n.* the full name for DNA.

dep., (*abbr.*) depart(s); department; deposed; deputy.

De Palma, *n.* **Brian** (1941–), US film director, especially of thrillers. His technical mastery and enthusiasm for spilling blood are shown in films such as *Sisters* (1973), *Carrie* (1976), and *The Untouchables* (1987).

Depardieu, *n.* **Gerard** (1948–), versatile French actor who has appeared in the films *Deux Hommes dans la Ville* (1973), *Le Camion* (1977), *Mon Oncle d'Amérique* (1980), *The Moon in the Gutter* (1983), and *Jean de Florette* (1985).

depart, *v.i.* to go away, to leave; to diverge, to deviate, to pass away; to die. *v.t.* to go away from, to quit; †to divide, to distribute; †to separate. †**departal,** *n.* **departed,** *a.* past, bygone; dead. **the departed,** the dead. [OF *departir* (DE-, L *partīre,* to PART, to divide)]

department, *n.* a separate part or branch of business, administration or duty; a branch of study or science; one of the administrative divisions of a country, as in France; a ministry, e.g. War Department. **department store,** *n.* a shop selling a great variety of goods. **departmental**, *a.* **departmentalism**, *n.* a too-rigid adherence to regulations, red tape. **departmentalize, -ise**, *v.t.* **departmentally,** *adv.* [F *département* (as prec., -MENT)]

departure, *n.* the act of departing; leaving; starting; quitting; death; divergence, deviation; (*Law*) a deviation from ground previously taken in pleading; (*Naut.*) distance of a ship east or west of the meridian she sailed from; the position of an object from which a vessel commences her dead reckoning; †separation, severance. **new departure,** a new course of thought or ideas; a new enterprise. [OF *departeure*]

depasture, *v.t.* to graze upon; to put to graze. *v.i.* to graze. **depasturage,** *n.*

depauperate, *v.t.* to make poor; to deprive of fertility or vigour; to impoverish, stunt. *a.*, impoverished; (*Bot.*) imperfectly developed. **depauperation,** *n.* **depauperize, -ise,** *v.t.* to raise from pauperism, to dispauperize; †to make poor, to depauperate. [med. L *dēpauperātus,* p.p. of *dēpauperāre* (DE-, *pauperāre,* to make poor)]

dépêche, *n.* (*F*) a message; a dispatch.

depend, *v.i.* to hang down; to be contingent, as to the issue or result, on something else; to rely, to trust, to reckon (upon); to rely for support or maintenance; to be pending. **depend upon it,** you may rely upon it, you may be certain. **that depends,** that is conditional; perhaps. **dependable,** *a.* that may be depended upon. **dependableness,** *n.* **dependably,** *adv.* **dependant, -ent,** *n.* one depending upon another for support or favour; that which depends upon something else; a retainer. **dependence,** *n.* the state of being dependent; that on which one depends; connection, concatenation; reliance, trust, confidence; a dependency; (*Law*) pendency, waiting for settlement; †a subject of dispute or quarrel. **dependency,** *n.* something dependent, esp. a country or state subject to another; an accident, a quality. **dependent,** *a.* hanging down; depending on another; subject to, contingent (upon), relying on for support, benefit or favour; †impending. **dependent variable,** *n.* one in a mathematical equation whose value depends on that of the independent variable. **dependently,** *adv.* [OF *dépendre,* L *dēpendēre* (DE-, *pendēre,* to hang)]

depersonalize, -ise, *v.t.* to divest of personality; to regard as without individuality. **depersonalization, -isation,** *n.* the divesting of personality; (*Psych.*) the experience of unreality feelings in relation to oneself.

†**dephlogisticate,** *v.t.* to deprive of phlogiston; to relieve of inflammation. †**dephlogisticated air,** *n.* Joseph Priestley's name for oxygen.

depict, *v.t.* to paint, to portray; to describe or represent in words. **depicter,** *n.* **depiction,** *n.* **depictive,** *a.* **depicture**, *v.t.* to depict, to represent, to paint. [L *dēpictus,* p.p. of *dēpingere* (DE-, *pingere,* to paint)]

depilate, *v.t.* to pull out, or strip off (hair). **depilation,** *n.* **depilator,** *n.* **depilatory**, *a.* having the power of stripping off hair. *n.* an application for removing superfluous hair without injuring the skin. [L *dēpilātus,* p.p. of *dēpilāre* (DE-; *pilāre,* to pluck away, from *pilus,* a hair)]

deplane, *v.i.* (*N Am.*) to disembark from an aeroplane.

deplenish, *v.t.* to deprive of stock, furniture etc.; to empty of contents.

deplete, *v.t.* to empty, to exhaust; to empty or relieve (as in blood-letting). **depletion,** *n.* **depletive,** *a.* causing depletion. *n.* a depleting agent. **depletory,** *a.* [L *dēplētus,* p.p. of *dēplēre* (DE-, *plēre,* to fill)]

deplore, *v.t.* to lament over; to grieve; to regret; to regard with concern and resentment; †to complain of; to express disapproval (of), to censure. **deplorable,** *a.* **deplorableness, deplorability**, *n.* **deplorably,** *adv.* **deploration**, *n.* †**deploring,** *a.* **deploringly,** *adv.* [L *dēplōrāre* (DE-, *plōrāre,* to wail)]

deploy, *v.t.* (*Mil.*) to open out; to extend from column into line. *v.i.* to form a more extended front. **deployment,** *n.* use, esp. of troops or weapons. [F *déployer,* OF *desployer,* L *displicāre,* to unfold (DIS-, *plicāre,* to fold)]

deplume, *v.t.* to strip of plumage; to strip (of honour, money, ornaments etc.). **deplumation**, *n.* [F *déplumer* (DE-, L *plūma,* feather)]

depolarize, -ise, *v.t.* to free from polarization (as the gas-filmed plates of a voltaic battery); to deprive of polarity; (*fig.*) to divest of ambiguity; to remove the polarization of (a ray of light). **depolarization, -isation,** *n.* **depolarizer, -iser,** *n.*

depoliticize, -ise, *v.t.* to make non-political.

depone, *v.t.* to give evidence upon oath; to testify; †to lay down, to deposit; *v.i.* to testify, esp. on oath. **deponent,** *a.* †laying down; deposing. *n.* a deponent verb; (*Law*) a witness; one who makes an affidavit to any statement of fact. **deponent verb,** *n.* a Latin verb with a passive form and active meaning. [L *dēpōnere* (DE-, *pōnere,* to put)]

depopulate, *v.t.* to clear of inhabitants; to reduce the inhabitants of. *v.i.* to become less populous. **depopulation,** *n.* [L *dēpopulātus,* p.p. of *dēpopulāre,* to lay waste, late L, to divest of inhabitants (DE-, *populus,* people)]

deport, *v.t.* to carry away, esp. from one country to another; to conduct, to demean, to behave (oneself etc.). †*n.* deportment. **deportation**, *n.* the act of transporting to a foreign land; the state of being banished. **deportee,** *n.* one who is deported. [OF *deporter,* L *dēportāre* (DE-, *portāre,* to carry)]

deportment, *n.* conduct, demeanour, carriage, manners; the behaviour of a substance (as in an experiment).

depose, *v.t.* to remove from a throne or other high office; to bear witness, to testify on oath; †to lay down, to deposit; †to take away; †to examine on oath. *v.i.* to bear witness. **deposable,** *a.* **deposal,** *n.* [F *déposer* (DE-, *poser,* L *pausāre,* to PAUSE, late L, to place, by confusion with *pōnere,* to DEPONE)]

deposit, *v.t.* to lay down, to place; to let fall or throw down; to entrust; to lodge for safety or as a pledge; to lay (as eggs); to leave behind as precipitation; to bury. *n.* anything deposited or laid down; that which is entrusted to another; a pledge, an earnest or first instalment, a trust, a security; money lodged in a bank; matter accumulated or precipitated and left behind. **on deposit,** when buying on hire-purchase, payable as a first instalment. **deposit account,** *n.* a bank account earning interest, usu. requiring notice for withdrawals. **depositary,** *n.* one with whom anything is deposited for safety; a trustee. **deposition**, *n.* the act of depositing; the act of deposing, esp. from a throne; a statement, a declaration; an affidavit; the act of bearing witness on oath; the evidence of a witness reduced to writing. **the Deposition,** the taking down of Christ from the Cross; a picture of this. **depositor,** *n.* one who makes a deposit, esp. of money; an apparatus for depositing anything. **depository,** *n.* a depositary; a place where anything, esp. furniture, is placed for safety. [MF *depositer,* L *dēpositum,* neut. p.p. of *dēpōnere,* to DEPONE]

depot, *n.* a place of deposit, a magazine, a storehouse; a building for the storage and servicing of buses and trains; (*N Am.*) a railway station; (*Mil.*) a magazine for stores; a station for recruits; the headquarters of a regiment; that portion of the battalion at headquarters while the rest are abroad; a particular place at the end of the trenches out of reach of fire from the besieged place. [F *dépôt,* L *dēpositum,* DEPOSIT]

deprave, *v.t.* to make bad or corrupt; to vitiate; to deteriorate; †to defame. †*v.i.* to utter calumnies. **depravation,** *n.* the act of depraving; the state of being depraved; deterioration; †censure, detraction. **depraved,** *a.* corrupt. **depravity,** *n.* a state of corruption; viciousness, profligacy; perversion, degeneracy. [OF *depraver,* L *dēprāvāre* (DE-, *prāvus,* crooked, depraved)]

deprecate, *v.t.* to endeavour to avert by prayer; to argue or plead earnestly against; to express regret or reluctance about; to express disapproval of or regret for; †to implore mercy of. **deprecatingly,** *adv.* **deprecation,** *n.* **deprecative,** *a.* **deprecatory,** *a.* [L *dēprecātus,* p.p. of *dēprecārī* (DE-, *precārī,* to pray)]

depreciate, *v.t.* to lower the value of; to disparage, to undervalue, to decry; to reduce the price of; to lower the exchange value of (money etc.). *v.i.* to fall in value. **depreciatingly,** *adv.* **depreciation,** *n.* the act of depreciating; the state of becoming depreciated; fall in value; allowance for wear and tear. **depreciatory,** *a.* [L *dēpretiātus,* p.p. of *dēpretiāre* (DE-, *pretium,* price, value)]

depredation, *n.* plundering, spoliation. **depredator,** *n.* a pillager, a plunderer. [F *déprédation,* L *dēpraedātio -ōnem,* from *dēpraedārī* (DE-, *praedārī,* to rob, from *praeda,* booty)]

depress, *v.t.* to press down; to lower; to bring down; to humble, to abase; to reduce or keep down the energy or activity of; to cast down; to dispirit. **depressant,** *a.* lowering the spirits. *n.* a sedative. **depressed,** *a.* **depressed area,** *n.* an area of very serious unemployment. **depressed classes** UNTOUCHABLES. **depressible,** *a.* **depressing,** *a.* **depressingly,** *adv.* **depression**, *n.* the act of depressing; the state of being depressed; lowering of the spirits, dejection; lowering of energy or activity; a mental disorder characterized by low spirits, reduction of self-esteem and lowering of energy; slackness of business; an economic crisis; reduced vitality; operation for cataract; the reduction of an obtruding part; a hollow place on a surface; the angular distance of a heavenly body below the horizon; a low state of the barometer indicative of bad weather; the centre of low pressure in a cyclone; the lowering of the muzzle of a gun; (*Mus.*) lowering in pitch; flattening. **depressive,** *a.* causing depression; characterized by depression. *n.* one subject to periods of depression. **manic depressive,** one subject to periods of euphoria followed by periods of deep depression. **depressor,** *n.* one who or that which depresses; a muscle which depresses the part to which it is attached; an instrument for reducing or pushing back an obtruding part. [L *dēpressus,* p.p. of *dēprimere* (DE-, *premere,* to PRESS)]

Depression, *n.* in economics, a period of low output and investment, with high unemployment. Specifically, the term describes two periods of crisis in the world economies: 1873–96 and 1929–mid-1930s.

depressurize, -ise, *v.t.* to reduce the atmospheric pressure in (a pressure-controlled area, such as an aircraft cabin). **depressurization, -isation,** *n.*

deprive, *v.t.* to take from; to debar; to dispossess, to bereave; to divest of an ecclesiastical dignity or preferment. **deprivable,** *a.* **deprival,** *n.* **deprivation,** *n.* the act of depriving; the state of being deprived; loss, dispossession, bereavement; the act of divesting a clergyman of his spiritual promotion or dignity. **deprived,** *a.* lacking acceptable social, educational and medical facilities. [OF *depriver,* late L *dēprīvāre* (DE-, *prīvāre,* to deprive, from *prīvus,* single, peculiar)]

de profundis, *n.* a cry from the depths of penitence or affliction; the title of the 130th Psalm. [L, 'Out of the depths']

deprogram, *v.t.* to remove a program from (a computer); **(deprogramme)** to persuade (someone) to reject obsessive beliefs, ideas and fears.

dept., (*abbr.*) department.

depth, *n.* deepness; measurement from the top or surface downwards or from the front backwards; a deep place, an abyss; the deepest, innermost part; the middle or height of a season; (*pl.*) the sea, the deep part of the ocean, deep water; abstruseness, profundity, mental penetration; intensity of colour, shade, darkness or obscurity; profundity of thought or feeling; (*pl.*) the extremity, the extreme or inmost part; (*Mil.*) the number of men in a file. **depth of a sail,** the extent (of a square sail) from the head-rope to the foot-rope. **depth of field,** the distance in front of and behind an object focused on by a lens (such as a camera or microscope) which will be acceptably sharp. **out of one's depth,** in deep water; (*fig.*) puzzled beyond one's knowledge or ability. **depth-bomb, depth-charge,** *n.* a mine or bomb exploded under water, used for attacking submarines. **depth-psychology,** *n.* the study of the unconscious. **depthless,** *a.* without depth; unfathomable.

depurate, *v.t.* to purify. *v.i.* to become pure. **depuration,** *n.* **depurative,** *a.* **depurator,** *n.* one who or that which purifies; an apparatus to assist the expulsion of abnormal matter by the excretory ducts of the skin. [med. L *dēpūrātus,* p.p. of *dēpūrāre* (DE-, L *pūrus,* PURE)]

depute, *v.t.* to appoint or send as a substitute or agent; to give as a charge, to commit. *n.* (*Sc.*) a deputy. **deputation,** *n.* the act of deputing; an authority or commission to act; the person or persons deputed to act as representatives for others, (*N Am.*) a delegation. **deputational,** *a.* **deputationist,** *n.* **deputize, -ise,** *v.t.* to appoint or send as deputy. *v.i.* to act as deputy. **deputy,** *n.* one who is appointed or sent to act for another or others; a delegate, a member of a deputation; a member of the French and other legislative chambers; (*Law*) one who exercises an office in another's right; (*in comb.*) acting for, vice-; acting. **deputy-governor,** *n.* **deputy-speaker,** *n.* [F *députer,* L *dēputāre* (DE-, *putāre,* to think, to consider, to allot)]

de Quincey, *n.* **Thomas** (1785–1859), English author, whose works include *Confessions of an English Opium-Eater* (1821) and the essays 'On the Knocking at the Gate in Macbeth' (1823) and 'On Murder Considered as One of the Fine Arts' (1827). He was a friend of the poets Wordsworth and Coleridge.

der., deriv., (*abbr.*) derivation; derivative; derived.

deracinate, *v.t.* to tear up by the roots; (*fig.*) to destroy. **deracination,** *n.* [F *déraciner* (DE-, *racine,* ult. from L *rādix -īcem,* root)]

deraign, *v.t.* to prove, to vindicate; to set (a battle) in array; to array. [OF *desraisnier,* prob. from a late L *dērationāre* (DE-, *ratio rationem,* reckoning, account)]

derail, *v.t.* to cause to leave the rails. *v.i.* to run off the rails. **derailer,** *n.* **derailment,** *n.* [F *dérailler*]

Derain, *n.* **André** (1880–1954), French painter, who experimented with strong, almost primary colours and exhibited with the Fauves, but later developed a more sombre landscape style. His work includes costumes and scenery for Diaghilev's Ballets Russes.

derange, *v.t.* to put out of line or order; to disorganize; to disturb, to unsettle, to disorder (esp. the intellect). **deranged,** *a.* insane; slightly insane. **derangement,** *n.* [F *déranger*]

deration, *v.t.* to remove from the rationed category.

Derby[1], *n.* a race for three-year-old horses, held at Epsom in May or June, founded by the 12th Earl of Derby in 1780; any horse or donkey race; **(derby)** a match between two teams from the same area; a stout kind of boot; (*N Am.*) a bowler hat. **Derby day,** *n.* the day on which the Derby is run. **Derby Scheme,** *n.* a form of voluntary military conscription devised by the Earl of Derby in 1915.

Derby[2], *n.* industrial city in Derbyshire, England; population (1981) 216,000. Rail locomotives, Rolls-Royce cars and aero-engines, chemicals, paper, electrical, mining and engineering equipment are manufactured here.

Derby[3], *n.* **Edward Geoffrey Smith Stanley, 14th Earl of Derby** (1799–1869), British politician, prime minister 1852, 1858–59, and 1866–68. Originally a Whig, he became secretary for the colonies 1830, and introduced the bill for the abolition of slavery. He joined the Tories 1834, and the split in the Tory Party over Robert Peel's free-trade policy gave Derby the leadership for 20 years.

Derbyshire, *n.* county in N central England. **area** 2630 sq km/1015 sq miles. **towns** administrative headquarters Matlock; Derby, Chesterfield, Ilkeston. **population** (1987) 919,000. **products** cereals; dairy and sheep farming. There have been pit and factory closures, but the area is being redeveloped, and there are large reserves of fluorspar.

Derbyshire neck, *n.* goitre, so called because of its prevalence in parts of Derbyshire. **Derbyshire spar,** *n.* fluor-spar.

deregulate, *v.t.* to remove legal or other regulations from, often so as to open up to general competition, e.g. transport services.

derelict, *a.* left, forsaken, abandoned. *n.* anything abandoned (esp. a vessel at sea), relinquished or thrown away; land left dry by the sea; a down-and-out. **dereliction,** *n.* abandonment; the state of being abandoned; omission or neglect (as of a duty); the abandonment of land by the sea; land left dry by the sea. **dereliction of duty,** reprehensible neglect or shortcoming. [L *dērelictus,* p.p. of *dērelinquere* (DE-, *relinquere,* to RELINQUISH)]

derequisition, *v.t.* to free (requisitioned property).

derestrict, *v.t.* to free from restriction, e.g. a road from speed limits. **derestriction,** *n.*

deride, *v.t.* to laugh at, to mock. *v.i.* to indulge in mockery or ridicule. **deridingly,** *adv.* **derision,** *n.* the act of deriding; the state of being derided; ridicule, mockery, contempt. **in derision,** in contempt, made a laughing-stock. **derisive, -sory,** *a.* scoffing, deriding, ridiculing; ridiculous. **derisively,** *adv.* **derisiveness,** *n.* [L *dērīdēre* (DE-, *rīdēre,* to laugh)]

de rigueur, prescribed (by etiquette or fashion). [F]

derision, derisive etc. DERIDE.

derive, *v.t.* to obtain as by logical sequence; to deduce; to draw, as from a source, root or principle; to trace (an etymology); to deduce or determine from data; †to conduct, convey, transmit. *v.i.* to come, to proceed, to be descended; to originate. **derivable,** *a.* that may be derived; deducible. **derivation,** *n.* the act of deriving; deduction, extraction; the etymology of a word, the process of tracing a word to its root; (*Math.*) the process of deducing a function from another; the drawing off of inflammation or congestion; the theory of evolution as an explanation of the descent of organisms from other forms of life; †a drawing off or turning aside of anything from its natural course. **derivationist,** *n.* **derivative,** *a.* derived; taken from something else; secondary, not original. *n.* anything derived from a source; a word derived from or taking its origin in another; (*Math.*) a differential coefficient. **derivatively,** *adv.* **derived,** *a.* **derived unit,** *n.* a unit of measurement derived from the basic units of a system. [F *dériver,* L *dērīvāre,* to draw off water (DE-, *rivus,* a stream)]

derm, dermis, *n.* skin; true skin or corium lying beneath the epidermis. **dermal,** *a.* **dermic,** *a.* [Gr. *derma,* from *derein,* to flay]

derm-, dermo-, dermato-, *comb. form.* pertaining to the skin. [Gr. *derma dermatos,* the skin]

-derm, *comb. form.* skin.

dermalgia, dermatalgia, *n.* neuralgia of the skin. [Gr. *algos,* pain]

dermatic, *a.* of or pertaining to the skin.

dermatitis, *n.* inflammation of the skin.

dermatoid, *a.* skin-like.

dermatology, *n.* the science of the skin and its diseases. **dermatological,** *a.* **dermatologist,** *n.*

dermatosis, *n.* any disease of the skin.

dermophyte, *n.* any parasitic plant infesting the cuticle and causing various skin diseases.

dermoskeleton, *n.* the exoskeleton; the external bony shell of crabs, tortoises and other animals, both vertebrates and invertebrates.

†**dern,** *a.* secret, reserved; dark, sombre; gloomy, dire, dreadful. *n.* secrecy. †**dernful,** *a.* solitary, sad, mournful. †**dernly,** *adv.* [OE *derne* (cp. OS *derni,* OFris. *dern,* OHG *tarni*)]

dernier, *a.* last. **dernier cri**, *n.* the last word, the latest fashion. **dernier ressort**, *n.* the last resort. [F]

De Roburt, *n.* **Hammer** (1923–), President of Nauru from 1968, out of office during 1976–78 and briefly in 1986. During the country's occupation (1942–45), he was deported to Japan. He became head chief of Nauru in 1956 and was elected the country's first president in 1968.

derogate, *v.i.* to detract, to withdraw a part (from); to become inferior, to lower oneself, to degenerate; †to withdraw a part. *v.t.* to lessen the effect of; to detract from, to disparage; †to repeal or annul partially. †*a.*, debased, degenerate. **derogation,** *n.* the act of derogating; the act of detracting from worth, name or character; disparagement; deterioration. **derogative**, *a.* **derogatively,** *adv.* **derogatory**, *a.* tending to detract from honour, worth or character; disparaging, depreciatory. **derogatorily,** *adv.* [L *dērogātus,* p.p. of *dērogāre* (DE-, *rogāre,* to ask, to propose a law)]

derrick, *n.* a hoisting machine with a boom stayed from a central post, wall, floor, deck etc., for raising heavy weights; the framework over an oil-well. **derrick-crane,** *n.* [the name of a Tyburn hangman in the 17th cent.]

derrière, *n.* (*euphem.*) the buttocks, the behind. [F]

derring-do, *n.* courageous deeds; bravery. [Chaucer, *dorring don,* daring to do, mistaken by Spenser]

derringer, *n.* a short-barrelled pistol carrying a large ball. [Henry *Derringer,* the 19th-cent. inventor]

derris, *n.* an extract of the root of tropical trees of the genus *Derris,* which forms an effective insecticide.

Derry, *n.* county of Northern Ireland. **area** 2070 sq km/799 sq miles. **towns** Derry (county town, formerly Londonderry), Coleraine, Portstewart. **population** (1981) 187,000. **products** mainly agricultural, but farming is hindered by the very heavy rainfall; flax, cattle, sheep, food processing, textiles, light engineering.

derv, *n.* diesel engine fuel oil. [acronym for *d*iesel *e*ngine *r*oad *v*ehicle]

dervish, *n.* a member of one of the various Muslim ascetic orders, whose devotional exercises include meditation and often frenzied physical exercises; one of the Sudanese followers of the Mahdi or Khalifa. **whirling dervish,** a member of a Muslim ascetic order whose physical exercises take the form of wild, ecstatic, whirling dances. [Pers. *darvish,* poor]

DES, (*abbr.*) Department of Education and Science.

Desai, *n.* Morarji (1896–), Indian politician. An early follower of Mahatma Gandhi, he was prime minister, as leader of the Janata Party (1977–79), after toppling Indira Gandhi. Party infighting led to his resignation of both the premiership and the party leadership.

desalinate, *v.t.* to remove salt from, usu. sea water. **desalination,** *n.* **desalinator,** *n.*

de Savary, *n.* **Peter** (1944–), British entrepreneur. He acquired Land's End, Cornwall, England, in 1987 and built a theme park there. He revived Falmouth dock and the port of Hayle in N Cornwall. A yachting enthusiast, he sponsored the Blue Arrow America's Cup challenge team.

descant[1], *n.* a song, a melody; †a song or tune with modulations or in parts; a variation; a counterpoint above the plainsong, an accompaniment; the upper part, esp. the soprano, in part music; †a discourse branching into parts; a series of comments. [ONorth.F *descant,* OF *deschant,* med. L *discantus* (DIS-, L *cantus,* singing, song)]

descant[2], *v.i.* to comment or discourse at large, to dilate (on); to sing in parts; to compose music in parts; to add a part or parts to a melody or subject. [as prec.]

Descartes, *n.* **Rene** (1596–1650), French mathematician and philosopher. He believed that commonly accepted knowledge was doubtful because of the subjective nature of the senses, and attempted to rebuild human knowledge, using as foundation '*cogito ergo sum*' ('I think therefore I am'). He is also regarded as the discoverer of analytical geometry and the founder of the science of optics.

descend, *v.i.* to come or go down, to sink, to fall, to slope downwards; to make an attack, to fall upon suddenly; to have birth, origin or descent; to be derived; to be transmitted in order of succession; to pass on, as from more to less important matters, from general to particular, or from more remote to nearer times; to stoop; to condescend; to lower or abase oneself morally or socially; †to retire. *v.t.* to walk, move or pass along downwards. **descendable, -dible,** *a.* that may be transmitted from ancestor to heir. **descendant,** *n.* one who descends from an ancestor; offspring, issue. **descended,** *a.* derived, sprung (from a race or ancestor). **descender,** *n.* that part of a letter (e.g. j, p, y) which is below the level of the line of type. †**descension**, *n.* the act of falling, moving or sinking downwards; descent. †**descensional,** *a.* of or pertaining to descent. †**descensive,** *a.* tending downwards. [F *descendre,* L *dēscendere* (DE-, *scandere,* to climb)]

descent, *n.* the act of descending; a declivity, a slope downwards; a way of descending; downward motion; decline in rank or prosperity; a sudden attack, esp. from the sea; a fall; pedigree, lineage, origin, evolution; issue of one generation; transmission by succession or inheritance; (*Mus.*) a passing to a lower pitch; †the lowest part; †offspring, issue. **descent theory,** *n.* the theory of evolution. [F *descente,* as prec.]

describe, *v.t.* to draw, to trace out; to form or trace out by motion; to set forth the qualities, features or properties of in words; †to descry. *v.i.* to give a description. **describable,** *a.* **description**, *n.* the act of describing; an account of anything in words; a kind, a sort, a species; (*Log.*) an enumeration of properties or accidental attributes. **descriptive**, *a.* containing description; capable of describing; given to description; (*Gram.*) applied to a modifier which describes the noun modified, but is not limiting or demonstrative, e.g. 'red'. **descriptively,** *adv.* [OF *descrire,* L *dēscrībere* (DE-, *scrībere,* to write)]

†**descrive,** *v.t.* to describe. [OF *descrivre,* F *décrire,* see prec.]

descry, *v.t.* (*past, p.p.* **descried**) to make out, to espy; †to reveal; †to explore, to spy out. [OF *descrire,* see DESCRIBE]

desecrate, *v.t.* to divert from any sacred purpose; to profane; to divert from a sacred to a profane purpose. †*a.* desecrated. **desecration,** *n.* **desecrator,** *n.* [L *dēsecrātus,* p.p. of *dēsecrāre* (DE-, *sacrāre,* to make sacred, *sacer,* SACRED)]

desegregate, *v.t.* to end racial segregation in (an institution, e.g. a school). **desegregation,** *n.*

deselect, *v.t.* to drop from a group or team; to refuse to readopt as a candidate, esp. as a prospective parliamentary candidate.

desensitize, -ise, *v.t.* to render insensitive to e.g. a chemical agent. **desensitization, -isation,** *n.* **desensitizer, -iser,** *n.*

desert[1], *a.* uninhabited, waste; untilled, barren. *n.* a waste, uninhabited, uncultivated place, esp. a waterless and treeless region; solitude, dreariness. **cultural desert,** a place completely lacking in cultural activities. **desert-bird,** *n.* the pelican. **desert boots,** *n.pl.* suede ankle-boots with laces. **desert oak,** *n.* (*Austral.*) a variety of casuarina. **Desert Rat,** *n.* (*coll.*) a soldier of the 7th Armoured Division in N Africa (1941–2). [OF, from L *dēsertus,* p.p. of *dēserere* (DE-, *serere,* to bind, to join)]

desert[2], *v.t.* to forsake, to abandon; to quit, to leave; to fail to help; to fail. *v.i.* (*Mil. etc.*) to abandon the service without leave. **deserter,** *n.* **desertion,** *n.* [F *déserter,* late L *dēsertāre,* as prec.]

desert[3], *n.* what one deserves, either as reward or punishment; merit or demerit, meritoriousness; state of deserving; (*pl.*) deserved reward or punishment. **to get one's (just) deserts,** to receive what one's behaviour merits. **desertless,** *a.* without merit. [OF *deserte,* p.p. of *deservir,* see foll.]

deserve, *v.t.* to be worthy of, to merit by conduct or qualities, good or bad, esp. to merit by excellence, good conduct or useful deeds; †to earn. *v.i.* to be worthy or deserving. **deservedly,** *adv.* **deserver,** *n.* **deserving,** *a.* merited, worthy, having deserved. *n.* the act or state of meriting. **deservingly,** *adv.* [OF *deservir,* L *dēservīre* (DE-, *servīre,* to serve)]

desex, *v.t.* to desexualize. **desexualize, -ise,** *v.t.* to deprive of sexuality; to castrate or spay.

deshabille, *n.* undress, state of being partly or carelessly attired; a loose morning dress. [F *déshabillé,* p.p. of *déshabiller* (DIS-, *habiller,* to dress)]

de Sica, *n.* **Vittorio** (1902–74), Italian director and actor. He won his first Oscar with *Bicycle Thieves* (1948), a film of subtle realism. Later films included *Umberto D* (1952), *Two Women* (1960), and *The Garden of the Finzi-Continis* (1971).

desiccate, *v.t.* to dry, to exhaust of moisture. *a.*, dried up. **desiccant,** *a.* drying up. *n.* a drying agent. **desiccated,** *a.* **desiccation,** *n.* **desiccative,** *a.* **desiccator,** *n.* (*Chem.*) an apparatus for drying substances liable to be decomposed by moisture; an apparatus for drying food and other commercial substances. [L *dēsiccātus,* p.p. of *dēsiccāre* (DE-, *siccāre,* to dry, from *siccus,* dry)]

desiderate, *v.t.* to feel the loss of; to want, to miss. †**desideration,** *n.* **desiderative,** *a.* expressing desire. *n.* (*Gram.*) a verb formed from another, and expressive of a desire to do the action implied in the primitive verb. [L *dēsiderātus,* p.p. of *dēsiderāre,* to DESIRE]

desideratum, *n.* (*pl.* **-rata**) anything desired, esp. anything to fill a gap; a state of things to be desired.

design, *v.t.* to contrive, to formulate, to project; to draw, to plan, to sketch out; to purpose, to intend; to appropriate, to devote or apply to a particular purpose; †to point out, to specify, to appoint. *v.i.* to draw, esp. decorative figures. *n.* a plan, a scheme; a purpose, an object, an intention; thought and intention as revealed in the correlation of parts or adaptation of means to an end; an arrangement of forms and colours intended to be executed in durable material; a preliminary sketch, a study; a working plan; the art of designing; artistic structure, proportion, balance etc.; plot, construction, general idea; artistic invention. **designed,** *a.* intentional. **designedly,** *adv.* **designer,** *n.* one who designs; one who produces detailed plans for a manufacturer; one who makes designs for clothing, stage or film sets etc. *a.* of clothes, produced by a famous designer; applied generally to anything considered extremely fashionable, unusual or expensive. **designer drugs,** *n.pl.* illegal drugs made up from a mixture of existing narcotics. **designer stubble,** *n.* (*coll.*) two or three days' growth of beard, considered fashionable among young men. **designing,** *a.* crafty, scheming. **designingly,** *adv.* [F *désigner,* to denote, to signify, L *dēsignāre* (DE-, *signāre,* to mark, from *signum,* a sign)]

designate, *v.t.* to point out, to specify by a distinctive mark or name; to cause to be known; to indicate, to mark; to describe (as); to select, to nominate, to appoint. *a.* (*often placed after the noun*) nominated (to an office), as *president designate.* **designation,** *n.* the act of designating; appointment, nomination; name, appellation, title, description. **designative, -tory,** *a.* [L *dēsignātus,* p.p. of *dēsignāre,* as prec.]

desilverize, -ise, *v.t.* to extract the silver from (as lead).

desipient, *a.* foolish, childish, nonsensical. **desipience,** *n.* [L *dēsipiens -entem,* pres.p. of *dēsipere* (DE-, *sapere,* to be wise)]

desire, *v.t.* to wish (to do); to wish for the attainment or possession of; to express a wish to have, to request, to beseech, to command; †to need, to require; †to invite. *v.i.* to have desire. *n.* an eagerness of the mind to obtain or enjoy some object; a request, an entreaty; the object of desire; sensual appetite, lust. **desirable,** *a.* worthy of being desired; agreeable; attractive. **desirability,** *n.* **desirableness,** *n.* **desirably,** *adv.* **desireless,** *a.* **desirous,** *a.* desiring, wishful; characterized by desire, covetous. **desirously,** *adv.* [OF *desirer,* L *dēsiderāre,* to long for]

desist, *v.i.* to cease, to forbear; to leave off. **desistance,** *n.* [OF *desister,* L *dēsistere* (DE-, *sistere,* to put, to stop)]

desk, *n.* a table, frame or case for a writer or reader, often with a sloping top; the place from which prayers are read; a pulpit; a counter for information or registration in a public place, e.g. a hotel; a newspaper department, as *news desk;* the occupation of a clerk. **desk-top computer,** *n.* one small enough to use on a desk. **desk-top publishing,** *n.* the production of text at a desk equipped with a computer and printer capable of producing high-quality printed copy. **deskwork,** *n.* writing, copying. **deskful,** *n.* [med. L *desca,* L *discus,* a DISK]

desman, *n.* (*pl.* **-mans**) either of two mole-like aquatic mammals, the Russian or the Pyrenean desman. [short for Swed. *desmansråtta,* from *desman,* musk, *råtta,* rat]

desmid, *n.* a member of the Desmidiaceae, a group of microscopic conjugate freshwater algae differing from the diatoms in their green colour, and the absence of a siliceous covering. [mod. L *desmidium,* Gr. *desmos,* a bond, a chain, *eidos,* form]

desmine, *n.* stilbite, a zeolitic mineral occurring in bundles of crystals. [Gr. *desmē,* a bundle]

desmography, *n.* a description of the ligaments of the body. **desmoid,** *n.* morbid tissue of a fibrous character. **desmology,** *n.* a branch of anatomy which treats of the ligaments and sinews. **desmotomy,** *n.* the anatomy or dissection of the ligaments and sinews. [Gr. *desmos,* a bond]

Desmoulins, *n.* **Camille** (1760–94), French revolutionary, who summoned the mob to arms on 12 Jul. 1789, so precipitating the revolt that culminated in the storming of the Bastille. A prominent Jacobin, he was elected to the National Convention in 1792. His *Histoire des Brissotins* was largely responsible for the overthrow of the Girondins, but shortly after he was sent to the guillotine as too moderate.

desolate, *a.* forsaken, solitary, lonely; uninhabited, deserted, neglected, ruined; barren, forlorn, comfortless; upset; †destitute. *v.t.*, to deprive of inhabitants; to lay waste; to make wretched. **desolately,** *adv.* **desolateness,** *n.* **desolating,** *a.* wasting, ruining, ravaging. **desolation,** *n.* the act of desolating; the state of being desolated; neglect, ruin; loneliness; bitter grief, affliction. **desolator,** *n.* [L *dēsōlātus,* p.p. of *dēsōlāre* (DE-, *sōlāre,* to make lonely, from *sōlus,* alone)]

de Soto, *n.* **Hernando** (*c.* 1496–1542), Spanish explorer who sailed with d'Avila (1577–1658) to Darien, Central America, 1519, explored the Yucatan Peninsula (1528), and travelled with Pizarro in Peru (1530–35). In 1538 he was made governor of Cuba and Florida. In his expedition of 1539, he explored Florida, Georgia, and the Mississippi River.

despair, *v.i.* to be without hope; to give up all hope. †*v.t.* to lose all hope of. *n.* hopelessness; that which causes hopelessness. **despairer,** *n.* **despairful,** *a.* **despairfully,** *adv.* **despairing,** *a.* hopeless, desperate. **despairingly,** *adv.* [OF *despeir-,* stem of *desperer,* L *dēspērāre* (DE-, *spērāre,* to hope)]

despatch DISPATCH.

desperado, *n.* a desperate or reckless ruffian. [OSp., desperate, L *dēspērātus,* as foll.]

desperate, *a.* hopeless, reckless, lawless, regardless of danger or consequences; fearless; affording little hope of success, recovery or escape; tried as a last resource; extremely dangerous; very bad, awful. *adv.* (*coll.*) extremely, awfully; feeling despair; extremely desirous of. **desperately,** *adv.* in a desperate manner; awfully, extremely. **desperateness,** *n.* **desperation,** *n.* [L *dēspērātus,* p.p. of *dēspērāre,* to DESPAIR]

despicable, *a.* meriting contempt; vile, worthless, mean. **despicably,** *adv.* [L *dēspicābilis,* from *dēspicārī* (DE-, *specārī,* cogn. with *specere,* see DESPISE)]

despise, *v.t.* to look down upon; to regard with contempt; to scorn. †**despisedness,** *n.* **despisingly,** *adv.* [OF *despis-,* stem of *despire,* L *dēspicere* (DE-, *specere,* to look at)]

despite, *n.* spite, malice; aversion, vexation; contemptuous treatment, outrage, contumely; †an act of contempt or malice. *prep.* notwithstanding; in spite of. †*v.t.* to vex, to spite; to treat with despite. **despite,** †**despite of,** †**in despite of,** in spite of. †**to do despite to,** to dishonour. **despiteful,** *a.* spiteful, malicious, malignant. **despitefully,** *adv.* †**despiteous,** *a.* despiteful. †**despiteously,** *adv.* [OF *despit,* L *dēspectus,* contempt, p.p. of *dēspicere,* to DESPISE]

despoil, *v.t.* to strip or take away from by force; to plunder; to deprive. †*n.* plundering, robbery. **despoiler,** *n.* †**despoilment, despoliation,** *n.* plunder; the state of being despoiled. [OF *despoiller* (F *dépouiller*), L *dēspoliāre*]

despond, *v.i.* to be cast down in spririts; to lose hope. *n.* despondency. **despondency,** *n.* **despondent,** *a.* disheartened. **despondently,** *adv.* **despondingly,** *adv.* [L *dēspondēre* (DE-, *spondēre,* to promise)]

despot, *n.* an absolute ruler or sovereign; a tyrant, an oppressor. **despotic,** *a.* absolute, irresponsible, uncontrolled; arbitrary, tyrannical. **despotically,** *adv.* **despotism,** *n.* absolute authority; arbitrary government, autocracy; tyranny. **despotist,** *n.* an advocate of autocracy. **despotize, -ise,** *v.i.* [OF, from late L *despotus*]

Desprez JOSQUIN DESPREZ.

desquamate, *v.t.* (*Surg.*) to scale, to peel. *v.i.* to scale or peel off, to exfoliate. **desquamation,** *n.* the separation of the skin in scales. **desquamative, -tory,** *a.* [L *dēsquāmātus,* p.p. of *dēsquāmāre* (DE-, *squāma,* a scale)]

des res, (*estate agent's jargon or facet.*) a *des*irable *res*idence.

Dessalines, *n.* **Jean Jacques** (1758–1806), emperor of Haiti from 1804–06. Born in Guinea, he was taken to Haiti as a slave, where he succeeded Toussaint L'Ouverture as leader of a revolt against the French, and made himself emperor. He was killed when trying to suppress a revolt provoked by his cruelty.

dessert, *n.* the last course at dinner, consisting of fruit and sweetmeats; the sweet course. **dessert-spoon,** *n.* a medium-sized spoon holding half as much as a tablespoon and twice as much as a teaspoon. [F from *desservir,* to clear the table (*des-,* L DIS-, *servir,* to SERVE)]

destemper DISTEMPER [1].

destinate, *a.* fixed by destiny or fate. *v.t.* to destine, to appoint. [L *dēstinātus,* p.p. of *dēstināre,* to DESTINE]

destination, *n.* the act of destining; the purpose for which a thing is appointed or intended; the place to which one is bound or to which a thing is sent.

destine, *v.t.* to appoint, fix or determine to a use, purpose, duty or position. **destined,** *a.* foreordained. **destinism,** *n.* fatalism. [F *destiner,* L *dēstināre,* (root of *stāre,* to stand)]

destiny, *n.* the purpose or end to which any person or thing is appointed; fate, fortune, lot, events as the fulfilment of fate; invincible necessity; the power which presides over the fortunes of men. **the Destinies,** the three Fates.

destitute, *a.* in want, devoid of the necessities of life; forsaken, forlorn; bereft (of). †*n.* a destitute person. †*v.t.* to forsake; to deprive; to make destitute. **destitution,** *n.* [L *dēstitūtus,* p.p. of *dēstituere* (DE-, *statuere,* to place, from *status,* p.p. of *stāre,* to stand)]

†**destrier,** *n.* a war-horse, a charger. [ME and A-F *destrer* (OF *destrier*), late L *dextrārius,* from *dextra,* right hand]

destroy, *v.t.* to pull down or demolish; to pull to pieces; to undo, to nullify; to annihilate; to lay waste; to kill; to extirpate; to sweep away; to consume; to overthrow; to disprove; to put an end to. †**destroyable,** *a.* **destroyer,** *n.* one who destroys; a fast warship armed with torpedoes. [OF *destruire* (F *détruire*), late L *dēstruere* (DE-, *struere,* to build)]

destruction, *n.* the act of destroying; the state of being destroyed; demolition, ruin; death, slaughter; that which destroys. **destruct,** *v.t.* to destroy deliberately, e.g. a rocket or missile in flight. **destructible,** *a.* **destructibility,** *n.* **destructionist,** *n.* a believer in the annihilation of the wicked. **destructive,** *a.* causing or tending to destruction; ruinous, mischievous, wasteful; serving or tending to subvert or confute (arguments or opinions); negative, not constructive. *n.* a destroyer, esp. of existing institutions; a radical reformer. **destructive distillation** DISTILLATION. **destructively,** *adv.* **destructiveness,** *n.* **destructor,** *n.* a furnace for burning up refuse. [L *dēstructus,* p.p. of *dēstruere,* to DESTROY]

desuetude, *n.* disuse; cessation of practice or habit. [F *désuétude,* L *dēsuētūdo,* from *dēsuētus,* p.p. of *dēsuēscere* (DE-, *suēscere,* incept. of *suēre,* to be used)]

desulphurize, -ise, *v.t.* to free ores from sulphur. **desulphurization, -isation,** *n.*

desultory, *a.* passing quickly from one subject to another; following no regular plan; loose, disjointed, discursive. **desultorily,** *adv.* **desultoriness,** *n.* [L *dēsultōrius,* from *dēsultor,* a circus horse-leaper, from *dēsilīre* (DE-, *salīre,* to jump)]

desynonymize, -ise, *v.t.* to differentiate; to make distinctions between synonymous terms.

Det., (*abbr.*) Detective.

detach, *v.t.* to disconnect, to separate; to disengage; (*Mil., Nav.*) to separate from the main body for a special service; (*usu. pass.*) to free from prejudice, personal considerations etc. †*v.i.* to become disconnected. **detachable,** *a.* **detached,** *a.* separated; a term applied to figures standing out from one another or from the background; free from prejudice; disinterested. **detachedly,** *adv.* **detachedness,** *n.* **detachment,** *n.* the act of detaching; the state of being detached; a body of troops or a number of ships detached from the main body and sent on a special service or expedition; freedom from prejudice, self-interest or worldly influence; independence, isolation. [F *détacher*]

detail, *v.t.* to set forth the particular items of; to relate minutely; (*Mil.*) to appoint for a particular service. *n.* an item; a minute and particular account; (*pl.*) a number of particulars; (*Mil.*) a list of names detailed for particular duties; a body of men selected for a special duty; a minor matter; (*pl.*) minute parts of a picture, statue etc., as distinct from the work as a whole. **beaten in detail,** (*Mil., Nav.*) defeated by detachments or in a series of partial engagements. **in detail,** minutely; item by item. **detailed,** *a.* related in detail; minute, complete. [F *détailler*]

detain, *v.t.* to keep back or from; to withhold; to delay, to hinder; to restrain; to keep in custody. †*n.* detention. **detainee,** *n.* a person held in custody. **detainer,** *n.* one who detains; the holding possession of what belongs to another; the holding of a person in custody; a writ of detainer. **forcible detainer,** (*Law*) a violent taking or keeping possession of lands without legal authority. †**writ of detainer,** a writ commanding a governor of a prison to detain a prisoner on another suit. †**detainment,** *n.* [OF *detenir,* L *dētinēre* (DE-, *tenēre,* to hold)]

detant, *n.* an attachment on a pivot for preventing the sear from catching in the half-cock notch. [var. of DETENT]

detect, *v.t.* to discover or find out; to bring to light; †to expose. †*a.* detected, exposed. **detectable,** *a.* **detection,** *n.* the act of detecting; the discovery of crime, guilt etc., or of minute particles. **detective,** *a.* employed in or suitable for detecting. *n.* a police officer employed to investigate special cases of crime etc. (*in full,* **detective officer**). **amateur detective,** a person with theories supposed to explain police problems. **private detective,** a private person or an agent of a detective bureau employed privately to investigate cases. **detectophone,** *n.* an instrument for tapping and listening in on telephone wires. **detector,** *n.* one who detects; the part of a radio receiver which demodulates the radio waves. [L *dētectus,* p.p. of *dētegere* (DE-, *tegere,* to cover)]

detent, *n.* a pin, catch or lever forming a check to the mechanism in a watch, clock, lock etc. [F *détente,* from *détendre,* L *dētinēre* (DE-, *tenēre,* to hold)]

détente, *n.* relaxation of tension, esp. between nations, or other warring forces. [F, as prec.]

detention, *n.* the act of detaining; the state of being detained; hindrance; arrest; confinement, compulsory restraint; keeping in school after hours as a punishment. **house of detention,** a place where offenders are kept while under remand. **detention camp,** *n.* an internment camp. **detention centre,** *n.* a place where young offenders are detained. [DETAIN]

détenu, *n.* one kept in custody, a prisoner. **détenue,** *n.fem.* [F, p.p. of *détenir,* to DETAIN]

deter, *v.t.* to discourage or frighten (from); to hinder or prevent. **determent, deterrence,** *n.* the act of deterring; a deterrent. **deterrent,** *a.* tending to deter. *n.* that which deters; (*coll.*) a nuclear weapon the possession of which is supposed to deter the use of a similar weapon by another power. [L *dēterrēre* (DE-, *terrēre,* to frighten)]

detergent, *a.* cleansing, purging. *n.* a medicine or application which has the property of cleansing; a chemical cleansing agent for washing clothes etc. [L *dētergens -entem,* pres.p. of *dētergere* (DE-, *tergere,* to wipe)]

deteriorate, *v.t.* to make inferior; to reduce in value. *v.i.* to become worse; to degenerate. **deterioration,** *n.* **deteriorative,** *a.* [L *dēteriorātus,* p.p. of *dēteriorāre* (*dēterior,* worse, from *dē,* away, down)]

determinant, *a.* determinative, decisive. *n.* one who or that which determines or causes to fix or decide; the sum of a series of products of several numbers, the products being formed according to certain laws, used in the solution of equations and other processes; a conditioning element or unit of germ plasm in the development of cells.

determinate, *a.* limited, definite; specific, distinct, predetermined, positive; determined, resolute. *v.t.*, to determine. **determinate equation,** *n.* one which admits of a finite number of solutions. **determinate inflorescence,** *n.* centrifugal flowering beginning with the terminal bud. **determinate problem,** *n.* (*Math.*) one which admits of a finite number of solutions. **determinately,** *adv.* **determinateness,** *n.* **determination,** *n.* the act of determining or settling; that which is determined on; a conclusion; fixed intention, resolution, strength of mind; direction to a certain end, a fixed tendency; ascertainment of amount etc.; (*Law*) settlement by a judicial decision; final conclusion; (*Log.*) definition, delimitation; reference of an object to its proper genus and species. **determinative,** *a.* that limits or defines; directive, decisive; defining, serving to limit; tending to determine the genus etc. to which a thing belongs. *n.* that which decides, defines or specifies; a demonstrative pronoun; (*Hieroglyphics*) a sign indicating the exact signification. **determinator,** *n.* one who or that which determines. [DETERMINE]

determine, *v.t.* to terminate, to conclude; (*Law*) to bring to an end; to fix the limits of, to define; to fix, to settle finally, to decide; to direct, to condition, to shape; to ascertain exactly; to cause to decide; †to put an end to; †to destroy, to kill. *v.i.* to end, to reach a termination; to decide, to resolve. **determinable,** *a.* that may be determined. **determinable freehold,** *n.* (*Law*) an estate for life which may expire upon future contingencies before the life for which it was created ends. **determinability,** *n.* **determined,** *a.* resolute; having a fixed purpose; ended; limited, conditioned. **determinedly,** *adv.* **determiner,** *n.* one who or that which determines; (*Gram.*) a word that limits or modifies a noun, as *that, my, his.* **determinism,** *n.* the doctrine that the will is not free, but is determined by antecedent causes, whether in the form of internal motives or external necessity, the latter being the postulate of fatalism. **determinist,** *a.* pertaining to determinism. *n.* one who believes in determinism. **deterministic,** *a.* [OF *determiner,* L *dētermināre* (DE-, *termināre,* to bound, from *terminus,* a boundary)]

deterrent DETER.

detersive, *a.* cleansing. *n.* a cleansing agent or substance. [F *détersif -sive,* from *dētersus,* p.p. of *dētergēre* (DE-, *tergēre,* to wipe)]

detest, *v.t.* to hate exceedingly, to abhor. **detestable,** *a.* **detestableness,** *n.* **detestability,** *n.* **detestably,** *adv.* **detestation,** *n.* extreme hatred; abhorrence, loathing; a person or thing detested. [F *détester,* L *dētestārī* (DE-, *testārī,* to testify, from *testis,* a witness)]

dethrone, *v.t.* to remove or depose from a throne; to drive from power or pre-eminence. **dethronement,** *n.* **dethroner,** *n.*

detinue, *n.* (*Law*) unlawful detention. **action of detinue,** an action to recover property illegally detained. [OF *detenue,* p.p. of *detenir,* to DETAIN]

de Tocqueville TOCQUEVILLE.

detonate, *v.t.* to cause to explode with a report. *v.i.* to explode with a report. **detonating,** *n., a.* **detonating bulb,** *n.* a Prince Rupert's drop. **detonating powder,** *n.* a compound powder which explodes by a blow or when heated. **detonating tube,** *n.* a graduated glass tube used for the detonation of gases by means of electricity, a eudiometer. **detonation,** *n.* the act or process of detonating; an explosion with a loud report; a noise resembling this; a violent, noisy outburst of anger; the spontaneous combustion in a petrol engine of part of the compressed charge after sparking; the knock that accompanies this. **detonator,** *n.* one who or that which detonates; a device for causing detonation, a fog signal. [L *dētonātus,* p.p. of *dētonāre* (*tonāre,* to thunder)]

detour, *n.* a roundabout way; a deviation, a digression; (*N Am.*) a road-diversion. *v.t.* to send by an indirect route. *v.i.* to make a deviation from a direct route. [F *détour,* from *détourner,* to turn aside]

detoxicate, *v.t.* to detoxify. **detoxicant,** *n.* a detoxifying substance. **detoxication,** *n.*

detoxify, *v.t.* to remove poison or toxin from. **detoxification,** *n.*

detract, *v.t.* to take (something) away from; to take (a part) away from; to take away from the reputation or credit of. †*v.i.* to speak disparagingly. †**detractingly,** *adv.* **detraction,** *n.* the act of detracting; depreciation, slander. **detractive,** *a.* **detractor,** *n.* one who detracts; a defamer, a slanderer; a muscle which draws one part from another. [L *dētractus,* p.p. of *dētrahere* (DE-, *trahere,* to draw)]

detrain, *v.t.* to cause to alight from a train. *v.i.* to alight from a train. **detrainment,** *n.*

detriment, *n.* loss; harm, injury, damage; (*Her.*) the decrement of the moon in her wane or eclipse. †*v.t.* to damage. **detrimental,** *a.* causing detriment. **detrimentally,** *adv.* [F *détriment,* L *dētrīmentum,* from *dētrī-* (*dētritus,* p.p.), from *dēterere* (DE-, *terere,* to rub)]

detrited, *a.* (*Geol.*) worn away; disintegrated. **detrital,** *a.* **detrition,** *n.* a wearing down or away by rubbing. **detritus,** *n.* (*Geol.*) accumulated matter produced by the disintegration of rock; debris, gravel, sand etc. [L *dētrītus,* p.p. of *dēterere,* as prec.]

Detroit, *n.* city of Michigan, US, situated on Detroit river; population (1980) 1,203,339, metropolitan aea 4,353,000. It is an industrial centre with the headquarters of Ford, Chrysler, and General Motors, hence its nickname, Motown from 'motor town'.

de trop, in the way. [F]

detrude, *v.t.* to thrust or force down; to expel from. [L *dētrūdere* (DE-, *trūdere,* to thrust)]

detruncate, *v.t.* to lop or cut off; to shorten by cutting. †**detruncation,** *n.* [L *dētruncātus,* p.p. of *dētruncāre* (*truncāre,* to cut off)]

Dettingen, Battle of, battle in the Bavarian village of that name where on 27 Jun. 1743, in the War of the Austrian Succession, an army of British, Hanoverians, and Austrians under George II defeated the French under Adrien-Maurice, duc de Noailles (1678–1766).

detumescence, *n.* the diminution of swelling. [L *tumēscere,* to swell up]

deuce[1], *n.* two; a card or die with two spots; (*Tennis*) a score of 40 all, requiring two successive points to be scored by either party to win. **deuce-ace,** *n.* the one and two thrown at dice. [F *deux,* L *duos,* acc. of *duo*]

deuce[2], *n.* mischief, trouble, ruin, confusion; the devil, invoked as a mild oath. **the deuce to pay,** the consequences will be serious. **to play the deuce with,** to spoil completely, to ruin. **deuced,** *a.* confounded, devilish; very great. **deucedly,** *adv.* [prob. from prec. (G *Daus,* LG *duus* is used similarly)]

deus, *n.* god. **deus ex machina**, in Greek and Roman drama, a god brought on to resolve a seemingly irresolvable plot; a contrived dénouement. **Deus vobiscum**, God be with you. **Deus vult**, God wills it. [L]

Deut., (*abbr.*) Deuteronomy.

deuteragonist, *n.* the second actor in a classical Greek play; the next actor in importance to the protagonist. [Gr. *deuteragōnistēs* (*deuteros,* second, *agōnistēs,* actor)]

deuterium, *n.* heavy hydrogen, an isotope of hydrogen with double mass. [Gr. *deuteros,* second]

deutero-, deuto-, *comb. form.* second, secondary. [Gr. *deuteros*]

deuterocanonical, *a.* belonging to a second and inferior canon (of certain books of the Bible).

deuteron, *n.* a heavy hydrogen nucleus.

Deuteronomy, *n.* the fifth book of the Pentateuch, named from its containing a recapitulation of the Mosaic law. **Deuteronomic, -ical,** *a.* **Deuteronomist,** *n.* the supposed writer or one of the supposed writers of Deuteronomy. [L *Deuteronomium,* Gr. *Deuteronomion* (DEUTERO-, *nomos,* law)]

deuteroscopy, *n.* second sight.

deuto- DEUTERO-.

deutoplasm, *n.* that portion of the yolk that nourishes the embryo, the food yolk of an ovum or egg-cell.

Deutsche Mark, Deutschmark, *n.* the standard monetary unit in West Germany. [G]

deutzia, *n.* a genus of Chinese or Japanese shrubs of the saxifrage family, with clusters of pink or white flowers. [J. *Deutz,* 18th-cent. Dutch botanist]

de Valera, *n.* **Eamon** (1882–1975), Irish nationalist politician, prime minister of the Irish Free State/Eire/Republic of Ireland (1932–48, 1951–54 and 1957–59), and president (1959–73). Repeatedly imprisoned, he participated in the Easter Rising of 1916 and was leader of Sinn Féin (1917–26), when he formed the Fianna Fáil party; he directed negotiations with Britain in 1921 but refused to accept the partition of Ireland until 1937.

devall, *v.i.* †to sink; (*Sc.*) to ease, to leave off. [F *dévaler* (DE-, L *vallis,* a VALLEY)]

de Valois, *n.* **Ninette** (stage name of Edris Stannus) (1898–), Irish dancer, choreographer, and teacher. A pioneer of British national ballet, she worked with Diaghilev in Paris before opening a dance academy in London in 1926. Collaborating with Lilian Baylis at the Old Vic, she founded the Vic-Wells Ballet (1931), which later became the Royal Ballet and Royal Ballet School. Among her works are *Job* (1931) and *Checkmate* (1937).

devalue, devaluate, *v.t.* to reduce the value of currency; to stabilize currency at a lower level. **devaluation,** *n.*

Devanagari, *n.* the formal alphabet in which Sanskrit and certain vernaculars are usually written, also called simply Nagari. [Sansk., Hind., Marathi (Sansk. *deva,* god, *nāgarī,* alphabet, script)]

devastate, *v.t.* to lay waste, to ravage; to overwhelm. **devastation,** *n.* **devastating,** *a.* (*coll.*) overwhelming. **devastator,** *n.* [L *dēvastātus,* p.p. of *dēvastāre* (DE-, *vastāre,* to waste)]

develop, *v.t.* to unfold or uncover, to bring to light gradually; to work out; to bring from a simple to a complex state, to bring to completion; to evolve; to bring to completion or maturity by natural growth; (*Mil.*) to carry out the successive stages of an attack; to render visible (as the picture latent in sensitized film); to build on or change the use of (land); to elaborate upon (a musical theme). *v.i.* to expand; to progress; to be evolved; to come to light; to come to maturity. **developable,** *a.* **developer,** *n.* one who or that which develops, esp. one who develops land; a chemical agent used to expose the latent image on film or light-sensitive paper. **development,** *n.* the act of developing; the state of being developed; growth and advancement; the gradual advance of organized bodies from the embryonic to the perfect state; evolution; maturity, completion; the process of bringing into distinctness the picture latent in sensitized film. **development area,** *n.* a region where new industries are being encouraged by Government to combat unemployment. **development theory,** *n.* the theory of evolution. **developmental,** *a.* pertaining to development or growth; evolutionary. **developmentally,** *adv.* [F *développer;* etym. doubtful (cp. It. *viluppare,* to enwrap, *viluppo,* a wrapping, a bundle)]

devest, *v.t.* to undress; to strip; to denude, deprive; (*Law*) to alienate (as a right or title). [DIVEST]

deviate, *v.i.* to turn aside; to stray or swerve from the path of duty; to err. *v.t.* to cause to stray or err. *n.*, (*Psych.*) one who deviates from the norm. **deviant,** *n.* one whose behaviour deviates from what is socially acceptable. **deviance,** *n.* **deviation,** *n.* the act of deviating; error; the deflection of a compass from the true magnetic meridian; the divergence of a plumb-line or a falling body from the true vertical, caused by surface inequalities or differences of density in the earth's crust, or by the rotation of the earth; the divergence of one of the optic axes from the normal position. **deviationist,** *n.* one who departs from orthodox Communist doctrine. **deviator,** *n.* **deviatory,** *a.* [L *dēviātus,* p.p. of *deviāre,* from *dēvius,* out of the way (DE-, *via,* way)]

device, *n.* a plan, a scheme, a contrivance; a stratagem, a trick; an invention; inventive skill; a design, a figure, a pattern; (*Her.*) an emblem or fanciful design, a motto; a fanciful idea, a conceit; †a dramatic entertainment, a masque; †an opinion, a suggestion. **to leave (someone) to his/her own devices,** to leave (someone) to do as he/she wishes. †**deviceful,** *a.* full of devices; ingenious. †**deviceless,** *a.* [OF *devis,* fem. *devise,* late L *dīvīsa,* a division, mark, device, fem. of L *dīvīsum,* neut. p.p. of *dīvīdere,* to DIVIDE (cp. DEVISE)]

devil, *n.* Satan, the chief of the fallen angels, the spirit of evil, the tempter; any evil spirit; an idol or false god; the spirit possessing a demoniac; a wicked person; a malignant or cruel person; a person of extraordinary energy, ingenuity and self-will directed to selfish or mischievous ends; an unfortunate person, a wretch; a personification of evil; energy, dash, unconquerable spirit; an expletive expressing surprise or vexation; a printer's errand-boy; a hot grilled dish, highly seasoned; a kind of firework; a tackle for catching a number of fish at once; a device for tearing fishing-nets; one who does literary work for which another takes the credit; a barrister who prepares a case for another, or who takes the case of another without fee in order to gain reputation; a spiked mill for tearing rags; a Tasmanian marsupial, *Dasyurus ursinis;* various other animals, fish etc. *v.i.* to make devilish; to prepare (food) with highly spiced condiments; to tear up rags with a devil. *v.i.* to act as a literary or legal devil; to do the hard spade-work. **between the devil and the deep blue sea,** torn between two equally undesirable alternatives. **devil a bit,** not any. **devil a one,** not a single one. **devil's food cake,** (*N Am.*) rich chocolate cake. **speak of the devil!** said when the person who is the subject of conversation arrives. **the devil,** a nuisance; a dilemma, an awkward fix; (*int.*) an expression of surprise or annoyance. **the devil on two sticks,** an early kind of diabolo. **the devil take the hindmost,** one must look after one's own interests. **the devil to pay,** the consequences will be serious. **to give the devil his due,** to allow the worst man credit for his good qualities. **to go to the devil,** to go to ruin; (*imper.)* be off! **to play the devil,** to worry, to ruin. **you little, young, devil,** a playful, semi-ironical address. **devil-fish,** *n.* the octopus; various other fish, as (*N Am.*) *Lophius piscatorius* and *Cephalopterus vampyrus.* **devil-may-care,** *a.* reckless. **devil-may-careness,** *n.* **devil-may-carish,** *a.* **devil-may-carishness,** *n.* **Devil's advocate** ADVOCATE. **devil's bit,** *n.* a small dark-blue scabious, *Scabiosa succisa.* **devil's bones,** *n.pl.* dice. **devil's coach-horse,** *n.* a large cocktail beetle, *Ocypus olens.* **devil's darning-needle,** *n.* various species of dragon-fly; Venus's comb, *Scandix pecten-veneris.* †**devil's dirt,** †**devil's dung,** *n.* asafoetida. **devil's dust,** *n.* flock torn out of wool and made into cheap cloth, shoddy. **Devil's Own,** *n.* the 88th Regiment of the line; the Inns of Court Officers' Training Corps. **devil's playthings,** *n.pl.* playing-cards. **devil's tattoo,** *n.* a drumming with the fingers upon a table etc. by persons when unthinking or impatient. **devil-worship,** *n.* homage paid by primitive tribes to conciliate the spirit of evil. †**devildom,** *n.* †**devilet,** †**-kin,** *n.* a little devil; the deviling or swift. **devilhood,** *n.* **deviling,** *n.* †a young devil, an imp; a local name for the swift. **devilish,** *a.* befitting a devil; diabolical; damnable. *adv.* extraordinarily, damnably, infernally, awfully. **devilishly,** *adv.* **devilishness,** *n.* †**devilism** *n.* devilry; devil-worship. **devilment,** *n.* mischief, roguery, devilry. **devilry, -iltry,** *n.* diabolical wickedness, esp. cruelty; dealings with the devil; diabolism, black magic, demonology; devils collectively; wild and reckless mischief, revelry or high spirits. †**devilship,** *n.* **devilward, -wards,** *adv.* [OE *dēoful,* L *diabolus,* Gr. *diabolos,* from *diaballein,* to slander (*dia,* through, *ballein,* to throw)]

Devil's Island, *n.* smallest (Ile du Diable) of the Iles du Salut, off French Guiana, 43 km/27 miles NW of Cayenne. The group of islands was collectively and popularly known by the name Devil's Island, and formed a penal colony notorious for its terrible conditions.

devious, *a.* out of the way, sequestered; wandering out of the way; circuitous; erring, rambling; insincere; deceitful. **deviously,** *adv.* **deviousness,** *n.* [L *dēvius*; see DEVIATE]

devise, *v.t.* to invent, to contrive; to form in the mind, to scheme, to plot; (*Law*) to give or assign (real property) by will; †to guess; †to emblazon. †*v.i.* to consider, to plan. *n.* the act of bequeathing landed property by will; a will or clause of a will bequeathing real estate. **devisable,** *a.* **devisee,** *n.* (*Law*) one to whom anything is devised by will. **deviser,** *n.* one who devises. **devisor,** *n.* (*Law*) one who bequeaths by will. [OF *deviser,* late L *dīvīsāre,* to divide, to devise, to think, freq. of L *dīvīdere* (p.p. *dīvīsus*), to DIVIDE]

devitalize, -ise, *v.t.* to deprive of vitality or of vital power. **devitalization, -isation,** *n.*

devitrify, *v.t.* to deprive of vitreous quality; to deprive (glass or vitreous rock) of transparency by making it crystalline. **devitrification,** *n.*

devocalize, -ise, *v.t.* to make voiceless or non-sonant. **devocalization, -isation,** *n.*

devoice, *v.t.* to pronounce without vibrating the vocal chords. **devoiced,** *a.*

devoid, *a.* vacant, destitute, empty (of). †*v.t.* to avoid; to make devoid. [short for *devoided,* p.p. of obs. *devoid,* to empty, OF *devuidier,* from *vuide,* empty, VOID]

devoir, *n.* a service, a duty; (*usu. pl.*) politeness, courtesy. [ME *dever,* OF *deveir,* L *debēre,* to owe]

devolute, *v.t.* to transfer power or authority; to depute. **devolution,** *n.* transference or delegation of authority (as by Parliament to its committees); transference of authority from central to regional government, thus a modified form of Home Rule; passage from one person to another; descent by inheritance; descent in natural succession; degeneration of species; lapse of a right, privilege, or authority through desuetude. [L *dēvolūtus,* p.p. of *dēvolvere* (DE-, *volvere,* to roll)]

Devolution, War of, war waged 1667–68 by Louis XIV of France to gain Spanish territory in the Netherlands, of which ownership had allegedly 'devolved' on his wife Maria Theresa.

devolve, *v.t.* to cause to pass to another, to transfer, e.g. duties, power; †to cause to roll down. *v.i.* to be transferred, delegated or deputed (to); to fall by succession, to descend. †**devolvement,** *n.* [L *dēvolvere,* as prec.]

Devon or **Devonshire,** *n.* county in SW England. **area** 6720 sq km/2594 sq miles. **towns** administrative headquarters Exeter; Plymouth and the resorts Paignton, Torquay, Teignmouth, and Ilfracombe. **population** (1987) 1,010,000. **products** mainly agricultural, with sheep and dairy farming; cider and clotted cream; kaolin in the south; Honiton lace; Dartington glass.

Devonian, *a.* pertaining to Devonshire; relating to the fourth period of the Palaeozoic era, between the Silurian and Carboniferous periods. *n.* a native or inhabitant of Devon; (*Geol.*) the Old Red Sandstone formation, well displayed in Devonshire. **Devonshire cream,** *n.* clotted cream. **Devonshire split,** *n.* a yeast bun with jam and cream.

devonport DAVENPORT.

Devonshire, *n.* **Spencer Compton Cavendish, 8th Duke of Devonshire** (1833–1908), British Liberal politician, known as Lord Hartington (1858–91), and leader of the Liberal party (1874–80). He broke with Gladstone over Irish Home Rule (1885), and was president of the council (1895–1903) under Salisbury and Balfour. As a free-trader, he resigned from Balfour's cabinet.

devote, *v.t.* to consecrate, to dedicate; to apply; to give wholly up (to); to doom, to consign (to ruin etc.); †to curse. **devoted,** *a.* dedicated, consecrated, doomed; wholly given up, zealous, ardently attached. **devotedly,** *adv.* **devotedness,** *n.* **devotee,** *n.* a votary, a person devoted (to); a bigot, an enthusiast. †**devotement, devotion,** *n.* the act of devoting; the state of being devoted; (*pl.*) prayer, religious worship; deep, self-sacrificing attachment, intense loyalty; †purpose, object; †disposal. **devotional,** *a.* pertaining to or befitting religious devotion. **devotionalism,** *n.* **devotionalist,** *n.* **devotionality,** *n.* **devotionally,** *adv.* [L *dēvōtus,* p.p. of *dēvovēre* (DE-, *vovēre,* to vow)]

devour, *v.t.* to eat up ravenously or swiftly; to consume as a beast consumes its prey; to destroy wantonly, to waste; to swallow up, to engulf; to take in eagerly with the senses; to absorb, to overwhelm. **to devour the way,** (*poet.*) to move with extreme swiftness. **devourer,** *n.* **devouring,** *a.* that devours; consuming, wasting. **devouringly,** *adv.* [OF *devorer,* L *dēvorāre* (DE-, *vorāre,* to swallow)]

devout, *a.* deeply religious; pious, filled with devotion; expressing devotion; heartfelt, earnest, genuine. **devoutly,** *adv.* **devoutness,** *n.*

dew, *n.* moisture condensed from the atmosphere upon the surface of bodies at evening and during the night; (*fig.*) anything falling cool and light, so as to refresh; an emblem of freshness; dewy moisture, tears, sweat. *v.t.* to wet with dew. *v.i.* to form as dew; to fall as dew. **mountain-dew,** whisky distilled illicitly. **dewberry,** *n.* a kind of blackberry, *Rubus caesius.* †**dew-besprent,**, *a.* sprinkled with dew. †**dew-burning,** *a.* glistening like dew in the sun. **dew-claw,** *n.* one of the bones behind a deer's foot; the rudimentary upper toe often found in a dog's foot. **dewdrop,** *n.* a drop of dew; a drop at the end of one's nose. **dew-dropping,** *a.* wetting, rainy. **dewfall,** *n.* the falling of dew; the time when dew falls. **dewpoint,** *n.* the temperature at which dew begins to form. **dew pond,** *n.* a shallow, artificial pond formed on high land where water collects at night through condensation. **dew-rake,** *n.* a rake used for the surface of grass or stubble. **dew-retting,** *n.* the softening of flax by exposure to dew and rain. **dew-worm,** *n.* a large earth-worm. **dewless,** *a.* **dewy,** *a.* **dewy-eyed,** *a.* naive, innocent. **dewily,** *adv.* **dewiness,** *n.* [OE *dēaw* (cp. Dut. *daaw,* Icel. *dögg,* Dan. *dug,* G *Tau*)]

dewan, *n.* chief financial minister of an Indian state; prime minister of such a state. **dewani**, *n.* the office of a dewan. [Arab., Pers. *dīwān* (cp. DIVAN)]

Dewey Decimal System, a library book classification system based on ten main subject classes. [Melvil *Dewey,* 1851–1931, US educator]

dewlap, *n.* the flesh that hangs loosely from the throat of an ox or cow; the flesh of the throat become flaccid through age; the wattle of a turkey etc. **dewlapped,** *a.* [etym. of *dew* uncertain; *lap* from OE *læppa,* a skirt, a LAP[1] (cp. Dan. *doglœb,* Norw. *doglæp*)]

DEW line, *n.* the radar network in the Arctic regions of N America. [*d*istant *e*arly *w*arning]

dexter, *a.* pertaining to or situated on the right-hand side; situated on the right of the shield (to the spectator's left) etc. [L, a comparative from the root *dex-* (cp. Gr. *dexios, dexiteros,* Goth. *taihswa,* Sansk. *daksha*)]

dexterity, *n.* physical or mental skill, expertness; readiness and ease; cleverness, quickness, tact; †right-handedness. **dexterous**, *a.* expert in any manual employment; quick mentally; skilful, able; done with dexterity; †right-handed. **dexterously,** *adv.*

dextral, *a.* inclined to the right; having the whorls (of a spiral shell) turning towards the right, dextrorse. **dextrality**, *n.* **dextrally,** *adv.*

dextran, *n.* a carbohydrate produced by the action of bacteria in sugar solutions, used as a substitute for blood plasma in transfusions.

dextrin, *n.* a gummy substance obtained from starch, so called from its dextro-rotatory action on polarized light. [F *dextrine,* from L *dextra,* fem. of DEXTER]

dextro-, *comb. form* (*Chem.*) turning the plane of a ray of polarized light to the right, or in a clockwise direction (as seen looking against the oncoming light). [L *dexter,* the right hand]

dextrocardia, *n.* a condition in which the heart lies on the right side of the chest instead of the left. **dextrocardiac**, *n., a.*

dextro-glucose, *n.* dextrose.

dextro-gyrate, *a.* causing to turn towards the right hand. *v.t.* to cause to rotate clockwise.

dextro-rotary, dextro-rotatory, *a.* causing to rotate clockwise. **dextro-rotation,** *n.*

dextrorse, *a.* rising from left to right in a spiral line. **dextrorsely,** *adv.* [L *dextrorsum, -sus* (DEXTRO-, *-vorsum, -versum,* turned)]

dextrose, *n.* a form of glucose which rotates polarized light clockwise; grape-sugar.

dextrous DEXTEROUS.

dey, *n.* the title of the old sovereigns of Algiers, Tripoli and Tunis. **deyship,** *n.* [F, from Turk. *dāī,* lit. a maternal uncle, a title in the janizaries]

dey-woman, *n.* a dairywoman. †**dey-girl,** *n.* [OE *dæge,* a maid-servant, later, a dairywoman or dairyman]

DF, (*abbr.*) Defender of the Faith; Dean of Faculty; direction-finding.

DFC, (*abbr.*) Distinguished Flying Cross.

DG, (*abbr.*) by the grace of God (L *Dei gratia*); Director-General.

dg, (*abbr.*) decigram(me).

Dhaka, *n.* capital of Bangladesh since 1971, in Dhaka region, W of the river Meghna; population (1984) 3,600,000. It trades in jute, oilseed, sugar and tea, and produces textiles, chemicals, glass and metal products.

dhal DAL.

dharma, *n.* in Hinduism and Buddhism, the fundamental concept of both natural and moral law, by which everything in the universe acts according to its essential nature or proper station. [Sansk., habit, law]

dhobi, *n.* an Indian washerman. [Hind. *dhōbī,* from *dhōb,* washing, Sansk. *dhāv-,* to wash]

dhole, *n.* the wild dog of India, *Canis dukhunensis.* [etym. unknown]

dhoti, *n.* a loin-cloth worn by male Hindus. [Hind.]

dhow, *n.* a native vessel with one mast, a very long yard, and a lateen sail, used on the Arabian Sea; an Arab vessel, esp. one used in the slave-trade. [etym. unknown]

DHSS, (*abbr.*) Department of Health and Social Security.

dhurrie, *n.* a coarse cotton fabric, made in squares, and used in India for carpets, curtains, coverings for furniture etc. [Hind. *darī*]

di-[1], *pref.* form of DIS- used before *b, d, g, l, m, n, r, s, v* and sometimes *j.*

di-[2], *pref.* twice, two, dis-, double. [Gr. *di-,* double, two]

di-[3], *pref.* form of DIA- used before a vowel.

dia-, *pref.* through; thorough, thoroughly; apart, across. [Gr. *dia,* through]

diabase, *n.* an igneous rock which is an altered form of basalt; it includes most greenstone and trap. **diabasic,** *a.*

diabetes, *n.* a disease marked by excessive discharge of urine containing glucose, insatiable thirst and great emaciation. **diabetes insipidus**, *n.* diabetes caused by a disorder of the pituitary gland. **diabetes mellitus**, *n.* diabetes characterized by a disorder of carbohydrate metabolism, caused by insulin deficiency. **diabetic**, *a.* pertaining to diabetes. *n.* a person suffering from diabetes. [L, from Gr., from *diabainein* (DIA-, *bainein,* to go)]

diablerie, *n.* dealings with the devil; diabolism, magic or sorcery; rascality, devilry. [F, from *diable,* L *diabolus,* DEVIL]

diabolic, -ical, *a.* pertaining to, proceeding from, or like the devil; outrageously wicked or cruel; fiendish, devilish, satanic, infernal. **diabolically,** *adv.* **diabolism**, *n.* devil-worship; belief in the Devil or in devils; black magic; devilish conduct or character, devilry. **diabolist,** *n.* **diabolize, -ise,** *v.t.* to make diabolical; to represent as a devil. [F *diabolique,* L *diabolicus,* Gr. *diabolikos,* from *diabolos,* DEVIL]

diabolo, *n.* a game with a double cone spun in the air by a cord on two sticks; an adaptation of the old game of the devil on two sticks. [a recent formation from L *diabolus,* devil]

diacaustic, *a.* formed by refracted rays. **diacaustic curve,** *n.* [Gr. *kaustikos,* burning, from *kaiein,* to burn]

diachronic, *a.* applied to the study of the historical development of a subject, e.g. language. **diachronically,** *adv.* **diachronism**, *n.* **diachronistic**, *a.* **diachronous**, *a.* [Gr. *chronos,* time]

diachylon, diaculum, *n.* a plaster made by boiling hydrated oxide of lead with olive oil; sticking-plaster. [late L *diachylōn,* Gr. *dia chūlōn,* lit. by means of juices (*chūlōn,* gen. pl. of *chūlos,* juice)]

diachyma, *n.* parenchyma of leaves. [Gr. *chūma,* liquid, juice]

diacid, diacidic, *a.* having two replaceable hydrogen atoms; capable of neutralizing two protons with one molecule.

diaconal, *a.* pertaining to a deacon. **diaconate**, *n.* the office, dignity or tenure of the office of a deacon; deacons collectively. [F, from late L]

diacoustic, *a.* pertaining to diacoustics. **diacoustics,** *n. sing.* the science of refracted sounds.

diacritic, -ical, *a.* distinguishing, distinctive; discerning, able to perceive distinctions. **diacritical mark, diacritic,** *n.* a mark (e.g. accent, cedilla, umlaut) attached to letters to show modified phonetic value or stress. [Gr. *diakritikos*]

diactinic, *a.* transparent to or capable of transmitting actinic rays.

diaculum DIACHYLON.

diadelph, *n.* a plant of the Linnaean order Diadelphia, in which the stamens are united into two bodies or bundles by their filaments. **diadelphous**, *a.* [Gr. *adelphos,* brother]

diadem, *n.* a fillet or band for the head, worn as an emblem of sovereignty; a crown, a wreath, a reward; a crown of glory or victory; supreme power, sovereignty. *v.t.* to adorn with a diadem. **diadem-spider,** *n.* the garden spider, *Epeira diadema,* so called from its markings. [OF *dyademe,* L, Gr. *diadēma* (DIA-, Gr. *deein,* to bind)]

diaeresis, *n.* (*pl.* **diaereses**) the resolution of one syllable into two; a mark placed over the second of two vowels to show that it must be pronounced separately, as *Laïs*. **diaeretic**, *a.* [L, from Gr. *diairesis,* from *diaireein,* to divide (DI-², *haireein,* to take)]

Diaghilev, *n.* **Sergei Pavlovich** (1872–1929), Russian ballet impressario, who in 1909 founded the *Ballets Russes* (headquarters Monte Carlo), which he directed for 20 years. Through the company he brought Russian ballet to the West, introducing and encouraging a dazzling array of dancers, choreographers and composers, such as Pavlova, Nijinsky, Fokine, Massine, Balanchine, Stravinsky and Prokofiev.

diaglyph, *n.* a piece of sculpture in which the figures are sunk into the general surface; an intaglio. **diaglphic**, *a.* [from Gr. *diagluphein* (DIA-, *gluphein,* to carve)]

diagnosis, *n.* (*pl.* **-noses**), determination of diseases by their symptoms; a summary of these; a summary of the characteristics by which one species is distinguished from another; differentiation of character, style etc. by means of distinctive marks; an analysis of phenomena or problems in order to gain an understanding. **diagnose**, *v.t.* to distinguish, to determine; to ascertain the nature and seat (of a disease) from symptoms. *v.i.* to make a diagnosis of a disease. **diagnosable,** *a.* **diagnostic**, *a.* that serves to distinguish; that serves to determine a disease etc.; characteristic. *n.* a sign or symptom by which anything is distinguished from anything else; a characteristic; (*pl.*) diagnosis. **diagnostically,** *adv.* **diagnostician**, *n.* one who diagnoses, esp. a doctor. [L, from Gr. *diagnōsis* (DIA-, *gnōsis,* inquiry, knowledge, from *gignōskein,* to learn, to recognize)]

diagometer, *n.* an instrument for measuring the relative conductivity of substances, orig. used to detect adulteration in olive oil. [F *diagomètre* (Gr. *diagein,* to carry across)]

diagonal, *a.* extending from one angle of a quadrilateral or multilateral figure to a non-adjacent angle, or from one edge of a solid to a non-adjacent edge; oblique, crossing obliquely; marked by oblique lines, ridges etc. *n.* a right line or plane extending from one angle or edge to a non-adjacent one; a diagonal row, line, beam, tie etc.; a fabric with diagonal twills or ridges. **diagonal scale,** *n.* (*Math.*) a scale in which small divisions are marked by oblique lines, so as to make minute measurements. **diagonally,** *adv.* [L *diagōnālis,* Gr. *diagōnios* (DIA-, *gōnia,* an angle)]

diagram, *n.* (*Geom.*) a drawing made to demonstrate or illustrate some proposition, statement or definition; an illustrative figure drawn roughly or in outline; a series of marks or lines representing graphically the results of meteorological, statistical or other observations, or symbolizing abstract statements. **diagrammatic**, *a.* **diagrammatically,** *adv.* **diagrammatize, -ise,** *v.t.* [F *diagramme,* L and Gr. *diagramma,* from Gr. *diagraphein* (DIA-, *graphein,* to write)]

diagraph, *n.* an instrument used for drawing mechanically outline sketches, enlargements of maps etc. [F *diagraphe*]

diaheliotropic, *a.* (*Bot.*) growing or turning transversely to the light. **diaheliotropism**, *n.* tendency to grow transversely to the light.

dial., (*abbr.*) dialect.

dial, *n.* an instrument for showing the time of day by the sun's shadow; the graduated and numbered face of a timepiece; a similar plate on which an index finger marks revolutions, indicates steam-pressure etc.; an instrument used by lapidaries; the panel or face on a radio showing wavelength and frequency; †a timepiece, a watch; the rotating, numbered disk on a telephone; (*sl.*) the human face. *v.t.* (*past, p.p.* **dialled**) to measure or indicate with or as with a dial; to survey with a dial; to indicate on the dial of a telephone the number one wishes to call up. **dialling code,** *n.* a group of numbers dialled to obtain an exchange in an automatic dialling system. **dialling tone,** *n.* the sound given by a telephone to show that the line is clear. **dial-plate,** *n.* the face of a timepiece or other instrument with a dial. [med. L *diālis,* daily, from *diēs,* day]

dialect, *n.* a form of speech or language peculiar to a limited district or people. **dialectal**, *a.* **dialectally,** *adv.* **dialectology**, *n.* the study of dialects. **dialectologist,** *n.* [L *dialectus,* Gr. *dialektos,* from *dialegesthai,* to discourse (DIA-, *legein,* to speak)]

dialectic, -ical, *a.* dialectal; pertaining to logic; logical, argumentative. *n.* (*often pl.*) logic in general; the rules and methods of reasoning; discussion by dialogue; the investigation of truth by analysis; the logic of probabilities; (*Kant*) critical analysis of knowledge based on science; (*Hegel*) the philosophic process of reconciling the contradictions of experience in a higher synthesis, the world-process which is the objective realization of this synthesis; a person skilled in logical reasoning and analysis. **dialectical materialism,** *n.* the economic, political and philosophical system developed by Marx and Engels, based on the idea of constant change through a dialectical process of thesis, antithesis and synthesis. **dialectically,** *adv.* in a logical manner; dialectally. **dialectician**, *n.* one skilled in dialectics; a logician; a reasoner. [OF *dialectique,* L *dialectica,* Gr. *dialektikē* (*technē*), the dialectic (art), as prec.]

diallage¹, *n.* a rhetorical figure by which arguments, having been considered from various points of view, are brought to bear on one point. [Gr. *diallagē,* from *diallassein* (DIA-, *allassein,* to change)]

diallage², *n.* a dark to bright-green non-aluminous variety of pyroxene, common in serpentine rock. **diallagic**, *a.* [F, from prec.]

dialogue, *n.* a conversation or discourse between two or more persons; a literary composition in conversational form; the conversational part of a novel etc.; a political discussion between two groups or nations. *v.i.* to hold a dialogue. *v.t.* to put into theform of dialogue. **dialogic**, *a.* of the nature of a dialogue. **dialogically,** *adv.* **dialogist**, *n.* one who takes part in a dialogue; a writer of dialogues. †**dialogistic**, *a.* †**dialogize, -ise**, *v.i.* to discourse in dialogue. **dialogue-wise,** *adv.*

dialysis, *n.* (*Rhet.*) a figure by which connectives are omitted; a diaeresis mark; the process of separating the crystalloid from the colloid ingredients in soluble substances by passing through moist membranes; a method of detecting poisons most of which are crystalloids; the filtering of blood to remove waste products, either by semipermeable membranes in the body, or by a kidney machine in the case of kidney failure. **dialyse,** (*esp. N Am.*) **dialyze**, *v.t.* **dialyser, -yzer**, *n.* the apparatus in which the process of dialysis is performed. **dialytic**, *a.* [Gr. *dialusis* (DIA-, *luein,* to loose)]

diam., (*abbr.*) diameter.

diamagnetic, *a.* pertaining to or exhibiting diamagnetism. *n.* a diamagnetic body or substance. **diamagnetically,** *adv.* **diamagnetism**, *n.* the force which causes certain bodies, when suspended freely and magnetized, to assume a position at right angles to the magnetic meridian, and point due east and west; the branch of magnetism treating of diamagnetic substances and phenomena. **diamagnetize, -ise**, *v.t.*

diamanté, *n.* material covered with glittering particles, such as sequins. *a.* decorated with glittering particles. **diamantine**, *a.* diamond-like. **diamantiferous**, *a.* yielding diamonds. [F *diamanter,* to adorn with diamonds, from *diamant,* DIAMOND]

diameter, *n.* a straight line passing through the centre of any object from one side to the other; a straight line passing through the centre of a circle or other curvilinear figure, and terminating each way in the circumference; the length of such a line; the length of a straight line extending from side to side of anything; transverse measurement, width, thickness; (*Opt.*) the unit of measurement of magnifying power. **diametral,** *a.* **diametrally,** *adv.* **diametrical**, *a.* pertaining to a diameter, diametral; along a diameter, direct; directly opposed; as far removed as possible. **diametrically,** *adv.* [OF *diametre,* L and Gr. *diametros* (DIA-, *metrein,* to measure, cp. METER[1])]

diamond, *n.* the hardest, most brilliant and most valuable of the precious stones, a transparent crystal of pure carbon, colourless or tinted; a facet of this when cut; a figure resembling this, a rhomb; a playing-card with figures of this shape; a glazier's cutting tool with a diamond at the point; a very small type for printing; a small rhomboid sheet of glass used in old-fashioned windows; a glittering point or particle; †adamant, a hard and impenetrable substance. *a.* made of, or set with, diamonds; resembling a diamond or lozenge. *v.t.* to adorn with or as with diamonds. **black diamonds,** dark-coloured diamonds; coal. **rough diamond,** a diamond in the native state, not yet cut; (*coll.*) a worthy, good-hearted, but uncouth person. **diamondback,** *n.* the salt-marsh turtle or terrapin; a kind of moth; a deadly N American rattlesnake with diamond-shaped markings. **diamond-cement,** *n.* cement used for setting diamonds. **diamond-drill,** *n.* an annular drill the cutting edge of which is set with diamonds for boring very hard substances. **diamond-field,** *n.* a region yielding diamonds. **diamond jubilee,** *n.* the 60th anniversary of a sovereign's accession. **diamond-point**, *n.* a stylus or cutting tool with a point tipped with a diamond, used by etchers, engravers, lapidaries etc.; (*pl.*) an oblique crossing of railway lines. **diamond-snake,** *n.* a diamond-marked snake of southern Australia and Tasmania. **diamond wedding,** *n.* the 60th anniversary of a marriage. **diamondiferous**, *a.* yielding diamonds. **diamond-wise,** *adv.* [OF *diamant,* late L *diamas -antem,* L *adamas -antem,* Gr. *adamas,* ADAMANT]

Diana[1], *n.* a fine horsewoman; a woman who hunts; the 78th asteroid. **diana-monkey,** *n.* a large African monkey, *Cercopithecus diana,* named from the white crescent-shaped band on its forehead. [Latin name of the Greek Artemis, the goddess of hunting]

Diana[2], *n.* **Princess of Wales** (1961–), popularly known as Princess Di. The daughter of the 8th Earl Spencer, she married Prince Charles at St Paul's Cathedral in 1981, the first English bride of a royal heir since 1659. She is descended from the only sovereigns from whom Prince Charles is not descended, Charles II and James II.

Diandria, *n.pl.* a Linnaean order of plants the flowers of which have only two stamens. **diandrous,** *a.* [mod. L (DI-[2], Gr. *andr-,* stem of *anēr,* man, male)]

dianoetic, *a.* pertaining to the rational or discursive faculty; intellectual. *n.* logic as treating of reasoning; the science that deals with the laws of conception, judgment and reasoning. [Gr. *dianoētikos,* from *dianoētos,* conceived in the mind, from *dianoeesthai* (DIA-, *noeein,* to think)]

dianthus, *n.* a genus of caryophyllaceous plants, including the pinks and carnations. [Gr. *Dios,* of Zeus, *anthos,* flower]

diapason, †**diapase**, *n.* a harmonious combination of notes; a melodious succession of notes; the foundation stops of an organ; a harmonious burst of music; a recognized standard of pitch amongst musicians; harmony, concord; range, pitch. [L *diapāsōn,* Gr. *diapasōn* (short for *dia pasōn chordōn,* through all the chords)]

diapause, *n.* a period of suspended growth in insects. [Gr. *diapausis,* pause]

diaper, *n.* a silk or linen cloth woven with geometric patterns; a towel or napkin made of this; (*esp. N Am.*) a baby's napkin, a nappy; a surface decoration consisting of square or diamond reticulations. *v.t.* to decorate or embroider with this. **diaper-work,** *n.* [OF *diapre,* *diasper,* Byz. Gr. *diaspros* (DIA-, *aspros,* white)]

diaphanometer, *n.* an instrument for measuring the transparency of the atmosphere. [see DIAPHANOUS]

diaphanoscope, *n.* a dark box for exhibiting transparent positive photographs. [see foll.]

diaphanous, *a.* transparent, pellucid; having the power of transmitting light. **diaphanously,** *adv.* †**diaphane**, *n.* a transparent substance; a transparency. †**diaphaneity**, *n.* transparency; perviousness to light. **diaphanie**, *n.* a process for imitating stained glass by transparencies. [med. L *diaphanus,* Gr. *diaphanēs* (DIA-, *phan-,* stem of *phainein,* to show)]

diaphoretic, *a.* having the power of promoting perspiration. *n.* a medicine having this property. [L *diaphorēticus,* Gr. *diaphorētikos,* from *diaphorēsis,* sweat, from *diaphoreein* (DIA-, *pherein,* to carry)]

diaphragm, *n.* the large muscular partition separating the thorax from the abdomen; the straight calcareous plate dividing the cavity of certain shells into two parts; the vibrating disk in the mouthpiece and earpiece of a telephone, or in the loudspeaker of a radio receiver; a dividing membrane or partition; an annular disk excluding marginal rays of light; a thin rubber or plastic cap placed over the mouth of the cervix as a contraceptive. **diaphragmatic**, *a.* **diaphragmatitis**, *n.* inflammation of the diaphragm. [L, from Gr. *diaphragma,* from *diaphrēgnunai* (DIA-, *phrassein,* to fence)]

diaphysis, *n.* the shaft of a bone as distinct from the ends; (*Bot.*) an abnormal elongation of the inflorescence. [Gr. *diaphusis* (DIA-, *phuein,* to bring forth)]

diapositive, *n.* a positive photographic transparency; a slide.

†**diarchy,** *n.* a government by two rulers. [Gr. *archia,* rule]

diarist etc. DIARY.

diarrhoea, *n.* the excessive discharge of faecal matter from the intestines. **diarrhoeal, diarrhoeic,** *a.* [L, from Gr. *diarrhoia* (DIA-, *rheein,* to flow)]

diarthrosis, *n.* an articulation of the bones permitting them to act upon each other; free arthrosis.

diary, *n.* an account of the occurrences of each day; the book in which these are registered; a daily calendar with blank spaces for notes; (*Sc.*) a railway time-table. **diarial**, *a.* **diarian**, *n.* **diarist,** *n.* one who keeps a diary. **diaristic**, *a.* **diarize, -ise**, *v.t., v.i.* [L *diārium,* from *diēs,* a day]

diaskeuast, *n.* a reviser, esp. one of those who brought the old Greek epics into their present shape. **diaskeuasis**, *n.* [Gr. *diaskeuastēs,* a reviser, from *diaskeuazein* (DIA-, *skeuazein,* to make ready)]

Diaspora, *n.* (*Hist.*) the dispersion of the Jews after the Babylonian captivity; Jews living outside Palestine, or now, outside Israel; a dispersion or migration of peoples. [Gr. *spora,* scatter]

diastaltic, *a.* (*Physiol.*) a term applied to reflex action and the nerves governing this. [Gr. *diastaltikos,* from *diastellein,* to separate (DIA-, *stellein,* to set, to send)]

diastase, *n.* a nitrogenous substance produced during the germination of all seeds, and having the power of converting starch into dextrine, and then into sugar. **diastasic**, *a.* [F, from Gr. *diastasis,* separation (DIA-, *stasis,* a placing, from the root *sta-,* to stand)]

diastasis, *n.* (*Path.*) separation of bones without fracture, or of the pieces of a fractured bone. [as prec.]

diastema, *n.* (*pl.* **-mata**) a space between two adjacent teeth, as in most mammals except man. [L, from Gr. *diastēma* (as DIASTASE)]

diastole, *n.* dilatation of the heart and arteries alternating with systole. **systole and diastole,** the pulse; (*fig.*) regular reaction; fluctuation. **diastolic,** *a.* [med. L, from Gr. *diastolē,* from *diastellein* (DIA-, *stellein,* to send)]

diastrophism, *n.* deformation of the earth's crust, giving rise to mountains etc. [Gr. *diastrophē,* a twisting]

diastyle, *n.* an arrangement of columns in which the space between them is equal to three or four diameters of the shaft. *a.* arranged on this plan. [L *diastylos,* Gr. *diastulus* (DIA-, *stulos,* a pillar)]

diatessaron, *n.* a harmony of the four Gospels; †(*Mus.*) the interval of a fourth, composed of a greater and lesser tone and a greater semitone. [OF, from L *diatessarōn,* Gr. *dia tessarōn,* by four]
diathermancy, *n.* the property of being freely pervious to heat. †**diathermal,** *a.* **diathermaneity**, *n.* **diathermanous, diathermous,** *a.* **diathermometer**, *n.* [F *diathermansie* (DIA-, Gr. *thermansis,* heating, from *thermainein,* to heat)]
diathermy, *n.* (*Med.*) the employment of high-frequency currents for the production of localized heat in the tissues.
diathesis, *n.* (*pl* **-theses**) a constitution of body predisposing to certain diseases. **diathetic**, *a.* [Gr., from *diatithenai* (DIA-, *tithenai,* to put)]
diatom, *n.* an individual of the genus *Diatoma* or of the order Diatomaceae, a group of microscopic algae with siliceous coverings which exist in immense numbers at the bottom of the sea, multiplying by division or conjugation, and occurring as fossils in such abundance as to form strata of vast area and considerable thickness. **diatomaceous**, *a.* **diatomic**, *a.* (*Chem.*) containing only two atoms; containing two replaceable univalent atoms. **diatomist**, *n.* one who studies diatoms. **diatomite**, *n.* (*Geol.*) any diatomaceous deposit. **diatomous**, *a.* (*Min.*) having crystals with one distinct diagonal cleavage. [Gr. *diatomos,* cut through, from *diatemnein* (DIA-, *temnein,* to cut)]
diatonic, *a.* (*Mus.*) of the regular scale without chromatic alteration; applied to the major and minor scales, or to chords, intervals and melodic progressions. **diatonically,** *adv.* [F *diatonique,* L *diatonicus,* Gr. *diatonikos,* from *diatonos* (DIA-, *tonos,* TONE)]
diatribe, *n.* an invective discourse; a strain of harsh criticism or denunciation; abusive criticism. [F, from L *diatriba,* Gr. *diatribē,* a wearing away, a discussion, a discourse, from *diatribein* (DIA-, *tribein,* to rub)]
Diaz[1], *n.* **Bartolomeu** (*c.* 1450–1500), Portuguese explorer, the first European to reach the Cape of Good Hope (1488) and to establish a route around Africa.
Diaz[2], *n.* **Porfirio** (1830–1915), dictator of Mexico during 1877–80 and 1884–1911. He lost the 1876 election, revolted, and seized power. He was supported by conservative landowners and foreign capitalists, who invested especially in railways and mines. He centralized the state at the expense of the peasants and Indians, and dismantled all local and regional leadership. He faced mounting opposition in his final years and was forced into exile in 1911.
diazepam, *n.* a type of tranquillizer and muscle relaxant.
diazo, *a.* of a compound, having two nitrogen atoms and a hydrocarbon radical; of a photocopying technique using a diazo compound exposed to light. *n.* a copy made in this way.
dib[1], *v.i.* to tap; to dap; to dibble. **dibber,** *n.* a dibble. [var. of DAB]
dib[2], *n.* a sheep's knuckle-bone; (*pl.*) a children's game in which these are thrown into the air and caught on the back of the hand; a counter used with card games; (*pl.*) (*sl.*) money. [prob. from prec.]
dibasic, *a.* containing two bases or two replaceable atoms.
dibber DIB[1].
dibble, *n.* a pointed instrument used to make a hole in the ground to receive seed. *v.t.* to make holes with a dibble; to plant with a dibble. *v.i.* to use a dibble; to dap as in angling. **dibbler,** *n.* one who dibbles; a machine for dibbling. [perh. from DIB[1]]
Dibranchiata, *n.pl.* an order of cephalopods, having only two gills, the shell rarely external and never chambered. **dibranchiate** , *n., a.* [Gr. *branchia,* gills]
dicacity, *n.* talkativeness; fluency, pertness. [L *dicāx dicācem,* from *dīcere,* to speak]
dicast, dikast, *n.* one of 6000 Athenians chosen each year to act as judges. **dicastery**, *n.* their court. **dicastic**, *a.* [Gr. *dikastēs,* from *dikē,* justice]
dice, *v.i.* to play at dice. *v.t.* to gamble (away) at dice; to weave into a pattern with squares; to trim or ornament with such a pattern; (*Book-binding*) to ornament with squares or diamonds by pressure. **no dice,** an expression of refusal or lack of success. **to dice with death,** to take a great risk. **dice-box,** *n.* the case out of which dice are thrown. **dicer,** *n.* [pl. of DIE[2]]
dicephalous, *a.* having two heads on one body. [Gr. *dikephalos* (DI-[2], *kephalē,* head)]
dicey, *a.* (*coll.*) risky, difficult. [DICE]
dichlamydeous, *a.* having both corolla and calyx. [Gr. *chlamus -udos,* a cloak]
dichloride, *n.* a compound having two atoms of chlorine with another atom.
dichlorodiphenyltrichloroethane , *n.* the full name for DDT, an insecticide.
dichogamous, *a.* (*Bot.*) having stamens and pistils maturing at different times, so that self-fertilization is prevented. **dichogamy,** *n.* [Gr. *dicho-,* asunder, *gamos,* wedded]
dichotomy, *n.* a separation into two; (*Log.*) distribution of ideas into two mutually exclusive classes; (*Astron.*) the moon's phase when half the disk is illuminated; (*Bot., Zool.*) a continued bifurcation or division into two parts. **dichotomic**, *a.* **dichotomist,** *n.* **dichotomize, -ise,** *v.t., v.i.* **dichotomous,** *a.* [Gr. *dicho-,* as prec.]
dichroic, *a.* assuming two or more colours, according to the direction in which light is transmitted. **dichroism**, *n.* **dichroitic**, *a.* **dichroscope**, *n.* [Gr. *dichroos* (DI-[2], *chrōs,* colour, complexion)]
dichromate, *n.* a double chromate.
dichromatic, *a.* characterized by or producing two colours, esp. of animals. **dichromatism**, *n.* inability to distinguish more than two colours.
dichromic, *a.* having or perceiving only two colours. **dichromism** *n.* a form of colour-blindness in which only two of the three primary colours are distinguished. [Gr. *dichrōmos,* two-coloured, *chrōma,* colour]
dicht, *v.t.* (*Sc.*) to wipe, to clean up. *n.* an act of wiping. [DIGHT]
dick[1], *n.* a fellow or person; (*N Am. sl.*) a detective; (*sl., taboo*) the penis. **clever dick,** a know-all. **dickhead,** *n.* (*sl.*) a fool. [*Dick*, short for Richard]
dick[2], *n.* a declaration. **to take one's dick,** to make a solemn declaration; to swear. **up to dick,** up to the mark, quite satisfactory; artful, wide-awake. [prob. short for DECLARATION]
dickens[1], *n.* (*coll.*) the devil, the deuce. [perh. from *Dickon,* Richard]
Dickens[2], *n.* **Charles** (1812–70), English novelist, popular for his memorable characters and his portrayals of the social evils of Victorian England. In 1836 he published the first number of the *Pickwick Papers*, which established his position as a writer. This was followed by *Oliver Twist* (1838), the first of his 'reforming' novels; *Nicholas Nickleby* (1839); *Barnaby Rudge* (1840); *The Old Curiosity Shop* (1841); and *David Copperfield* (1849). Among his later books are *A Tale of Two Cities* (1859) and *Great Expectations* (1861).
Dickensian, *a.* pertaining to or in the style of Charles Dickens; applied to squalid conditions as described in his novels. *n.* an admirer of Dickens.
dicker, *n.* half-a-score, esp. of hides. *v.i.* to barter, to haggle; to carry on a petty trade. *v.t.* to barter or exchange. [ME *dyker,* late L *dicora,* L *decūria,* a set of ten, from *decem,* ten]
Dickinson, *n.* **Emily** (1830–86), US poet. Born in Amherst, Massachusetts, she lived in near seclusion there from 1862. Almost none of her many short, mystical poems were published during her lifetime. Her concentrated work has only become well known in the 20th cent.
dicky[1], *n.* (*coll.*) an ass, a donkey; a pinafore or bib; a front separate from the shirt; a seat behind the body of a carriage or a motor-car; a driver's seat; a bird. **dicky-bird,** *n.* (*coll.*) a little bird. **dicky-bow,** *n.* a bow-tie. [etym. doubtful]
dicky[2], *a.* doubtful, questionable; unsteady, unwell.

[etym. unknown]

diclinic, *a.* (*Cryst.*) having two of the axes obliquely inclined. [Gr. *klinē,* a bed]

diclinous, *a.* having the stamens and the pistils on separate flowers, on the same or different plants. **diclinism,** *n.* [as prec.]

dicotyledon, *n.* a plant with two cotyledons. **Dicotyledones,** *n.pl.* the largest and most important class of flowering plants containing all those with two cotyledons. **dicotyledonous,** *a.*

dicrotic, *a.* (*Physiol.*) double-beating (of a pulse in an abnormal state). [Gr. *dikrotos* (DI-[3], *krotos,* a beat)]

dict., (*abbr.*) dictionary.

dicta DICTUM.

Dictaphone®, *n.* an apparatus for recording sounds, used for taking down correspondence etc., to be afterwards transcribed.

dictate[1], *v.t.* to read or recite to another words to be written or repeated; to prescribe, to lay down with authority, to impose, as terms. *v.i.* to give orders; to utter words to be written or repeated by another. **dictation,** *n.* the dictating of material to be written down or recorded; the material dictated; a command. **dictator,** *n.* one who dictates; one invested with supreme and often tyrannical authority; a Roman magistrate created in time of emergency, and invested with absolute power; a ruler with similar authority appointed in a time of civil disorder or securing the supremacy after a revolution. **dictatorate, dictature,** *n.* **dictatorial,** *a.* pertaining to a dictator; imperious, overbearing. **dictatorially,** *adv.* **dictatorship,** *n.* †**dictatory,** *a.* dictatorial, dogmatical. **dictatress,** *n. fem.* [L *dictātus,* p.p. of *dictāre,* freq. of *dīcere,* to say]

dictate[2], *n.* an order, an injunction; a direction; a precept.

diction, *n.* the use of words; manner of expression; style; †verbal description. [L *dictio*]

dictionary, *n.* a book containing the words of any language in alphabetical order, with their definitions, pronunciations, parts of speech, etymologies and uses, or with their equivalents in another language; a work of information on any subject under words arranged alphabetically. [med. L *dictiōnārium,* from prec.]

dictum, *n.* (*pl.* **-ta**) a positive or dogmatic assertion; a judge's personal opinion on a point of law as distinguished from the decision of a court; a maxim, an adage. [L, neut. p.p. of *dīcere,* to say]

dictyogen, *n.* (*Bot.*) a sub-class (proposed by Lindley) of monocotyledonous plants with reticulated leaves often articulated with the stem. [Gr. *diktuon,* a net]

dicynodont, *n.* a large fossil reptile of a lizard-like form with turtle jaws. [Gr. *kun-* (stem of *kuōn*), dog, *odont-,* tooth]

did, past of DO[1].

Didache, *n.* a Christian manual written in the second century. **Didachist,** *n.* [Gr. *didachē,* teaching, first word of title, 'Teaching of the Twelve Apostles']

didactic, *a.* adapted or tending to teach, esp. morally; containing rules or precepts intended to instruct; in the manner of a teacher. *n.pl.* the science or art of teaching. **didactically,** *adv.* **didacticism,** *n.* [Gr. *didaktikos,* from *didaskein,* to teach]

didactyl, -tylous, *a.* having only two toes, fingers or claws. [Gr. *daktulos,* finger]

didapper, *n.* a small diving-bird, the dab-chick. [earlier *dive-dapper,* OE *dūfe-doppa* (*dūfan,* to dive, *doppa* dapper, dipper)]

diddicoy DIDICOI.

diddle, *v.t.* to cheat, to overreach; to swindle; to jog, to jerk to and fro. *v.i.* to fritter away, to waste time; to totter, to walk unsteadily. **diddler,** *n.* [etym. unknown]

diddums, *int.* expressing commiseration to a baby. [baby-talk, did you/he/she]

Didelphia, *n.pl.* a family of marsupials, including the opossums. **didelphian,** *a.* **didelphic,** *a.* **didelphoid,** *a.* [Gr. *delphus,* a womb]

Diderot, *n.* **Denis** (1713–84), French philosopher of the Enlightenment and editor of the *Encyclopédie* (1751–80). He exerted an enormous influence on contemporary social thinking with his materialism and anti-clericalism.

didgeridoo, *n.* an Austral. instrument, a long, hollow wooden tube that gives a deep booming sound when blown. [Abor.]

didicoi, did(d)icoy, *n.* an itinerant traveller or tinker, who is not a true Romany. [Romany]

dido, *n.* an extravagrant doing, an antic, a caper. **to cut up didoes,** to behave extravagantly; to behave rowdily. [sl., etym. doubtful]

Dido, *n.* Phoenician princess, legendary founder of Carthage, who committed suicide in order to avoid marrying a local prince. However Virgil records that it was because Aeneas deserted her.

didst, 2nd sing. past of DO[1].

didymium, *n.* a mixture of the two elements neodymium and praseodymium, orig. thought to be a single element. [Gr. *didumos,* twin]

didymous, *a.* (*Bot.*) twin, growing in pairs. [Gr. *didymos,* twin]

Didynamia, *n.pl.* (*Bot.*) a Linnaean class, containing plants with four stamens. **didynamian, didynamous,** *a.* [Gr. *dunamis,* power]

die[1], *v.i.* to lose life, to expire; to depart this life; to come to an end; to cease to exist; to wither, to lose vitality, to decay; to fail, to become useless; to go out, to disappear, to be forgotten; to cease or pass away gradually; to faint, to fade away, to languish with affection; to suffer spiritual death; to perish everlastingly. **to die away,** to become gradually less distinct. **to die down,** of plants, to die off above ground, with only the roots staying alive in winter; to become less loud, intense etc., to subside. **to die of laughing,** (*fig.*) to laugh at something immoderately. **to die for,** to sacrifice one's life for; to pine for. **to die off,** to die in large numbers; to languish. **to die out,** to become extinct. **to be dying to do,** (*fig.*) to be eager to do. **to die unto,** to cease to be affected by (sin). **die-away,** *a.* fainting or languishing. **die-hard,** *n.* one resistant to change, or holding an untenable position, esp. in politics; (*pl.*) the old 47th Foot (from the colonel's rallying cry at Albuera). [ME *degen, deghen,* Icel. *deyja* (cp. OS *dōian,* OHG *touwan,* from Teut. *tāu-*)]

die[2], *n.* (*pl.* **dice, dies**) a small cube marked with figures on the sides, used in gaming, being thrown from a box; hazard, chance, lot; (*pl.* **dice**) the game played with these; (*in foll. senses pl.* **dies**) (*Arch.*) the cube or plinth of a pedestal; a machine for cutting out, shaping or stamping; a stamp for coining money, or for impressing a device upon metal, paper etc. **straight as a die,** completely honest. **the die is cast,** an irrevocable decision has been taken. **die-cast,** *v.t.* to shape an object by forcing molten lead or plastic into a reusable mould. **die-casting,** *n.* **die-sinker,** *n.* one who cuts or engraves dies for coins, medals etc. **die-stock,** *n.* a handle or stock to hold the dies in screw-cutting. [OF *de, det,* late L *dătum,* neut. of *dătus,* p.p. of *dăre,* to give]

Diefenbaker, *n.* **John George** (1895–1979), Canadian Progressive Conservative politician, prime minister during 1957–63, when he was defeated after criticism of the proposed manufacture of nuclear weapons in Canada.

dieldrin, *n.* an insecticide containing chlorine. [Otto *Diels,* d.1954, and Kurt *Alder,* d.1958, G chemists]

dielectric, *n.* any medium, such as glass, through or across which electric force is transmitted by induction; a non-conductor; an insulator. *a.* non-conductive, insulating.

Dien Bien Phu, Battle of, decisive battle in the Indo-China War at a French fortress in North Vietnam, near the Laotian border, 320 km/200 miles from Hanoi. Some 10,000 French troops under Général de Castries were besieged during 13 Mar.–7 May 1954 by the communist Viet Minh. The fall of Dien Bien Phu resulted in the end of French control of Indo-China.

dieresis DIAERESIS.

dies, *n.* (*pl.* **dies**) day. **dies fausti, infausti,** *n.pl.* auspicious or inauspicious days. **dies irae,** *n.* a day of wrath, the Day of Judgment; a 13th-cent. Latin hymn describing the Last Judgment, used in the mass for the dead. **dies nefasti**, *n.pl.* days on which the courts could not be held in ancient Rome; unlucky days. **dies non**, *n.* a Sunday, holiday or other day on which the courts are not open; a day on which business cannot be transacted; a day that does not count. [L]

diesel, *n.* any vehicle driven by a diesel engine; diesel oil. **diesel-electric,** *a.* using power from a diesel-operated electric generator. *n.* a locomotive so powered. **diesel engine,** *n.* a type of reciprocating internal-combustion engine which burns heavy oil. **diesel oil, fuel,** *n.* a heavy fuel oil used in diesel engines, also called DERV. **diesel train,** *n.* one drawn by a diesel engine. **dieselize, -ise,** *v.t.* to adapt or convert (an engine) to diesel fuel. *v.t.* to be equipped with a diesel engine. **dieselization, -isation,** *n.* [R. *Diesel,* 1858–1913, G engineer]

diesis, *n.* (*pl.* **-eses**) the double dagger (‡); a reference mark; (*Mus.*) the difference between three true major thirds and one octave. [L, from Gr., from *diienai* (DIA-, *hienai,* to send)]

diet¹, *n.* a prescribed course of food, a regimen followed for health reasons, or to reduce or control weight; the food and drink usually taken; an allowance of food; †an allowance for board, or for living expenses. *v.t.* to feed according to the rules of medicine; to feed in a restricted way as a punishment; to feed. *v.i.* to take food, esp. according to a prescribed regimen or to reduce or control weight. **to be, go, on a diet,** to follow a strict plan of eating so as to lose weight. †**to take diet,** to be under regimen for a disease. **dietary,** *a.* pertaining to a rule of diet. *n.* a regimen; a prescribed course of diet; a fixed daily allowance of food (esp. in prisons, workhouses etc.). **dietary fibre** FIBRE. †**dieter,** *n.* one who prescribes or prepares food according to rules; one who follows a diet to lose weight. **dietetic, -ical**, *a.* pertaining to diet; prepared according to special dietary needs. **dietetically,** *adv.* **dietetics,** *n.pl.* the science of diet; rules of diet. **dietician, dietitian**, *n.* a professional adviser on dietetics. [OF *diete,* late L *diēta,* Gr. *diaita,* mode of life (prob. conn. with *zaein,* to live)]

diet², *n.* a legislative assembly or federal parliament holding its meetings from day to day (esp. as an English name for Continental parliaments); a conference or congress, esp. on international affairs; (*Sc.*) a session of a court or any assembly. **dietine,** *n.* a subordinate or local diet; a cantonal convention. [L *diēta* (as prec.), confused with *diēs,* a day]

dietetic, dietician DIET¹.

Dietrich, *n.* **Marlene** (stage-name of Magdalene von Losch) (1904–), German-American actress, born in Berlin. She first won fame by her appearance with Emil Jannings in *The Blue Angel* (1930), and went to Hollywood, becoming a US citizen in 1937. Later films include *Blonde Venus* (1932), and *Destry Rides Again* (1939). Her husky, sultry singing voice added to her appeal.

Dieu et mon droit, God and my right (motto of British sovereigns). [F]

dif-, *pref.* form of DIS- used before *f* in words from Latin.

differ, *v.i.* to be dissimilar; to disagree in opinion; to dissent; to be at variance; to quarrel. †*v.t.* to make different or distinct; to set at variance. *n.* (*Sc.*) difference. **to agree to differ,** to give up trying to convince each other. [F *différer,* L *differre* (DIF-, *ferre,* to bear)]

difference, *n.* the state of being unlike or distinct; the quality by which one thing differs from another; disproportion between two things; the remainder of a quantity after another quantity has been subtracted from it; the alteration in the price of stock from one date to another; a distinction, a differential mark, the specific characteristic or differentia; a point or question in dispute, a disagreement in opinion, a quarrel, a controversy; a figure on a coat-of-arms which distinguishes one family from another, or shows how distant a younger branch is from the elder. *v.t.* to distinguish between; to make different; (*Her.*) to mark with a difference. *v.i.* to serve as a distinguishing mark. **to make a difference,** to have an effect; to behave differently. **to split the difference,** to compromise; to divide the remainder in an equal way. **with a difference,** with something distinctive added; differently; (*Her.*) as a mark of distinction. [as prec.]

different, *a.* unlike, dissimilar, distinct, not the same. **differently,** *adv.*

differentia, *n.* (*pl.* **-tiae**) that which distinguishes one species from another of the same genus; an essential attribute, which when added to the name of the genus distinctly marks out the species. [L, difference, diversity; see DIFFER]

differential, *a.* differing; consisting of a difference; making or depending on a difference or distinction; relating to specific differences; pertaining to differentials; relating to the difference between sets of motions acting in the same direction, or between pressures etc. *n.* (*Math.*) an infinitesimal difference between two consecutive states of a variable quantity; a differential gear; the amount of difference within a wages structure between rates of pay for different classes of work. **differential car axle,** the driving axle of a car (usu. the rear axle) in which the motive power is transmitted through a differential gear. **differential calculus,** *n.* (*Math.*) the method of finding an infinitely small quantity, which, being taken infinite times, shall equal a given quantity. **differential coefficient,** *n.* (*Math.*) the measure of the rate of change of a function relative to its variable. **differential duties,** *n.pl.* duties levied unequally upon the productions of different countries. **differential gear,** *n.* a device of bevelled planetary and other wheels which permits of the relative rotation of two shafts driven by a third; applied to a motor-car it enables the rear (driving) wheels to rotate at different speeds when rounding a corner. **differential motion,** *n.* a mechanical movement in which a part moves with a velocity equal to the difference between the velocities of two other parts. **differential screw,** *n.* a screw with two threads of unequal pitch on the same shaft, one unwinding as the other winds up. **differential winding,** *n.* the combination of two insulated wires in an electric coil, through which currents pass in opposite directions, employed in telegraphy as a resistance coil. **differentially,** *adv.* [as prec.]

differentiate, *v.t.* to make different; to constitute difference between, of or in; to discriminate by the differentia, to mark off as different; (*Math.*) to obtain the differential coefficient of; (*Biol.*) to develop variation in; to specialize. *v.i.* to develop so as to become different, to acquire a distinct character. **differentiation,** *n.* **differentiator,** *n.* one who or that which differentiates. [mod. L *differentiātus,* p.p. of *differentiāre;* see DIFFER]

difficile, *a.* (*F*) awkward, hard to deal with; uncompliant, uncompromising. [L *difficilis* (DIF-, *facilis,* easy)]

difficult, *a.* hard to do or carry out; troublesome; hard to please; not easily managed; hard to understand; cantankerous. **difficultly,** *adv.* **difficulty,** *n.* the quality of being difficult; anything difficult; an obstacle; objection, reluctance, scruple; (*pl.*) pecuniary embarrassment. [OF *difficulté,* L *difficultās -tātem,* from *difficilis,* as prec.]

diffident, *a.* distrustful of oneself or of one's powers; bashful, modest, shy; †distrustful. **diffidence,** *n.* distrust of oneself; bashfulness, shyness; †distrust of others. **diffidently,** *adv.* [L *diffīdens -entem,* pres.p. of *diffīdere* (DIF-, *fīdere,* to trust, from *fīdēs,* faith)]

diffluent, *a.* flowing apart or away, dissolving; deliquescing, becoming fluid. **diffluence,** *n.* [L *diffluens -entem,* pres.p. of *diffluere* (DIF-, *fluere,* to flow)]

diffract, *v.t.* to break in parts; to bend or deflect a ray of light by passing it close to an opaque object. **diffraction,** *n.* **diffraction grating,** *n.* an array of fine, closely-spaced opaque lines on glass which disperses light into its component colours since the amount of diffraction differs for different-coloured rays of light. [L *diffractus,* p.p. of *diffringere* (DIF-, *frangere,* to break)]

diffuse[1], *v.t.* to pour forth; to spread abroad by pouring out; to circulate; to cause to intermingle; to dissipate; †to confuse. *v.i.* to be diffused; to intermingle by diffusion. **diffused,** *a.* **diffused lighting,** *n.* a form of illumination in which the light is softened and spread over an area instead of being concentrated in one spot. **diffusedly**, *adv.* **diffuser,** *n.* one who or that which diffuses or circulates. **diffusible,** *a.* **diffusibility**, *n.* [L *diffūsus,* p.p. of *diffundere* (DIF-, *fundere,* to pour)]

diffuse[2], *a.* diffused, scattered, spread out; copious, prolix, not concise; (*Bot.*) diverging or spreading widely. **diffusely,** *adv.* copiously, verbosely, fully. **diffuseness,** *n.* **diffusion**, *n.* the act of diffusing a liquid, fluid etc.; a spreading abroad of news etc.; the state of being widely dispersed; the mingling of liquids, gases or solids through contact; spread of cultural elements from one community to another. **diffusion-tube,** *n.* an instrument for determining the rate of diffusion of different gases. **diffusive,** *a.* diffusing; tending to diffuse; spreading, circulating, widely distributed. **diffusively,** *adv.* **diffusiveness,** *n.* [as prec.]

dig, *v.t.* (*past* **dug**, *p.p.* **dug**) to excavate or turn up with a spade or similar instrument, or with hands, claws etc.; to thrust or push into something; to obtain by digging; to make by digging; to poke, to pierce; (*dated sl.*) to approve of or like. *v.i.* to work with a spade; to excavate or turn up ground with a spade or other implement; to search, make one's way, thrust, pierce or make a hole by digging. *n.* a piece of digging (esp. archaeological); a thrust, a poke; a cutting remark; (*N Am., coll.*) a plodding student. **to dig oneself in,** (*fig.*) to take up permanent quarters; to refuse to budge; to make oneself indispensable. **to dig one's heels in** HEEL[1]. **to dig out,** to obtain by digging; to obtain by research. **to dig through,** to open a passage through. **to dig up,** to excavate; to extract or raise by digging; to break up (ground) by digging; to obtain by research. **to have a dig at,** to make a cutting or sarcastic remark. **digger,** *n.* one who digs, esp. a gold-miner; an implement, machine or part of a machine that digs; one of a tribe of N American Indians who live chiefly on roots; (*Austral.*) a fellow, a man. **digger-wasp,** *n.* any of several wasps that dig a hole in the ground for a nest. **digging,** *n.* the act of opening the ground with a spade; (*pl.*) a gold-mine or gold-field. **diggings, digs,** *n.pl.* (*coll.*) lodgings. [prob. from F *diguer,* to make a dike (*digue*)]

digamma, *n.* a letter in the oldest Greek alphabet (**F**) which had the sound of *w,* named from its resemblance to two gammas placed one above the other. [L, from Gr. (DI-[2], *gamma,* the letter g)]

digamy, *n.* marrying a second time. **digamist,** *n.* **digamous,** *a.* [L, Gr. *digamia,* from Gr. *digamos* (DI-[1], *gamos,* marriage)]

digastric, *a.* having a double belly or protuberance. **digastric muscle,** *n.* a double muscle which depresses the lower jaw. [Gr. *gastēr,* belly]

digest[1], *v.t.* to arrange under proper heads or titles, to classify; to reduce to system or order; to arrange methodically in the mind; to think over; to soften and prepare by heat; to break (food) down in the stomach into forms which can be assimilated by the body; to promote the digestion of; to assimilate; (*fig.*) to receive and enjoy; to put up with. *v.i.* to be digested; to be prepared by heat. **digester,** *n.* one who digests; anything which helps to promote digestion; an apparatus for cookingfood by exposure to heat above boiling point. **digestible,** *a.* **digestibility**, *n.* **digestibly,** *adv.* **digestion**, *n.* the act or process of assimilating food in the stomach; the conversion of food into chyme; the power of digesting; concoction for the purpose of extracting the essence from a substance, stewing; (*Bot.*) the absorption of carbonic acid by plants under the influence of light; mental reduction to order and method. **digestive,** *a.* pertaining to or promoting digestion. *n.* any substance which aids or promotes digestion; an application disposing to suppurate. **digestive biscuit,** *n.* a semi-sweet biscuit made of wholemeal flour. **digestively,** *adv.* [L *dīgestus,* p.p. of *dīgerere* (DI-[1], *gerere,* to carry)]

digest[2], *n.* a compendium or summary arranged under proper heads or titles; a magazine containing summaries of articles etc. in current literature; (*Law*) a collection of Roman laws arranged under proper heads, as the pandects of Justinian.

digger, digging DIG.

Diggers, *n.pl.* an English 17-cent. radical sect which became prominent in Apr. 1649 when, headed by Gerrard Winstanley (*c.* 1609–60), it set up communal colonies near Cobham, Surrey, and elsewhere. They were broken up by mobs and, being pacifists, made no resistance. Their ideas considerably influenced the early Quakers.

†**dight,** *v.t.* to dress, array, to adorn; (*usu. p.p.*) to equip, to prepare. *a.* dressed, adorned, embellished. [OE *dihtan,* L *dictāre* (cp. G *dichten,* to make poetry)]

digit, *n.* a finger or toe; the measure of a finger's breadth, or three-quarters of an inch; any integer under ten, so called from the primitive habit of counting on the fingers; the 12th part of the diameter of the sun or moon (used to express the quantity or magnitude of an eclipse). **digital,** *n., a.* **digital clock, watch,** *n.* one without a traditional face, the time being indicated by a display of numbers. **digital computer,** *n.* an electronic computer which uses binary or decimal notation. **digital disk, digital (audio) tape,** *n.* a record or tape which is recorded using a digital sound signal. **digitalize, -ise,** *v.t.* to digitize. **digitize, -ise,** *v.t.* to put into digital form for use in a computer. **digitization, -isation,** *n.* [L *digitus*]

digitalin, digitalia, *n.* an alkaloid obtained from the foxglove.

digitalis, *n.* a genus of scrophulariaceous plants, containing the foxglove (*Digitalis purpurea*); the dried leaves of the foxglove, which act as a cardiac sedative. [mod. L, pertaining to the fingers, alluding to G *Fingerhut,* thimble]

digitate, -tated, *a.* having finger-like processes; (*Bot.*) branching into distinct leaves or lobes like fingers. **digitately,** *adv.* **digitation,** *n.* [L *digitātus,* from *digitus,* DIGIT]

digitiform, *a.* finger-shaped (used of the corolla of digitalis).

digitigrade, *a.* belonging to the Digitigrada, a section of the Carnivora (according to Cuvier's classification) comprising the families of cats, dogs, hyenas and weasels, in which the heel is raised above the ground, so that these animals walk on their toes. *n.* a digitigrade animal. [F, from L *digitus,* DIGIT, *-gradus,* walking]

diglot, *a.* bilingual. *n.* a bilingual book or person.

diglyph, *n.* a projection like a triglyph, with only two channels instead of three. [Gr. *digluphos* (DI-[2], *gluphein,* to carve)]

dignify, *v.t.* to make worthy; to invest with dignity; to make illustrious; to exalt. **dignified,** *a.* invested with dignity; stately; gravely courteous. [OF *dignifier,* late L *dignificāre* (*dignus,* worthy)]

dignity, *n.* worth, nobility; estimation, rank; the importance due to rank or position; elevation of mien or manner, stateliness; a high office, a position of importance or honour. **to be beneath one's dignity,** to be degrading, in one's own opinion. **to stand on one's dignity,** to assume a manner showing one's sense of self-importance. **dignitary,** *n.* one who holds a position of dignity, esp. ecclesiastical. [OF *dignité,* L *dignitās -tātem* (*dignus,* worthy)]

digraph, *n.* a combination of two letters to represent one simple sound, as *ea* in *mead, th* in *thin*. **digraphic**, *a.* [Gr. *graphē,* a mark]

digress, *v.i.* to turn aside from the direct path; to deviate, to wander from the main topic. **digression**, *n.* a deviation from the direct course; a departure from the path of virtue; a part of a discourse etc. which wanders from the main subject. †**digressional,** *a.* **digressive,** *a.* **digressively,** *adv.* **digressiveness,** *n.* [L *dīgressus,* p.p. of *dīgredī* (DI-[1], *gradī,* to step, from *gradus,* a step)]

digs DIGGINGS under DIG.

Digynia, *n.pl.* a Linnaean order of plants with two free pistils, or a single style deeply cleft into two parts. **digynian, digynous,** *a.* [Gr. *gunē,* a female]

dihedral, *a.* (*Cryst.*) having two sides or faces; (*Math.*) of the nature of a dihedron. **dihedral angle,** *n.* that made by the wing of an aeroplane in relation to the horizontal axis. **dihedron,** *n.* (*Geom.*) a figure with two sides or surfaces. [Gr. *hedra,* seat]

dihexagonal, *a.* (*Cryst.*) twelve-sided; consisting of two hexagonal parts combined.

dihexahedron, *n.* (*Cryst.*) a six-sided prism with three planes at the extremities. **dihexahedral,** *a.*

dihybrid, *n.* the offspring of parents that differ in two pairs of genes.

dikast DICAST.

dik-dik, *n.* a name for several small E African antelopes. [native name]

dike, dyke, *n.* a ditch, a moat, a water-course or channel, natural or artificial; a mound or dam to protect low-lying lands from being flooded; (*Sc.*) a wall or fence of turf or stone without cement; a causeway; (*fig.*) a barrier, a defence; a wall-like mass of cooled and hardened volcanic or igneous rock, occupying rents and fissures in sedimentary strata; (*Mining*) a fissure filled with mineral matter; (*Austral., sl.*) a lavatory; (*sl., offensive*) a lesbian. *v.t.* to defend with dikes or embankments; †to dig. **dike-reeve,** *n.* an officer in charge of dikes, drains and sluices in fen districts. [OE *dīc* (cp. Dut. *dijk,* G *Teich*)]

diktat, *n.* a settlement imposed on the defeated; an order or statement allowing no opposition. [G, dictation, from L *dictāre,* to dictate]

dilacerate, *v.t.* to tear in pieces, to rend asunder. †**dilaceration,** *n.* [L *dīlacerātus,* p.p. of *dīlacerāre*]

dilapidate, *v.t.* to damage, to bring into decay or ruin. *v.i.* to fall into decay or ruin. **dilapidated,** *a.* ruined; shabby. **dilapidation,** *n.* decay for want of repair; a state of partial ruin, decay; the action of an incumbent in suffering ecclesiastical buildings etc. to fall into disrepair; charge for making this good; the falling down or wasting away of rocks, cliffs etc.; the debris resulting. **dilapidator,** *n.* [L *dīlapidātus,* p.p. of *dīlapidāre* (DI-[1], *lapid-,* stem of *lapis,* stone)]

dilate, *v.t.* to expand, to widen, to enlarge in all directions; †to spread abroad; to enlarge upon. *v.i.* to be extended or enlarged; to expand, to swell; (*fig.*) to expatiate, to speak fully and copiously (upon a subject). †*a.* extended, expanded. **dilatable,** *a.* capable of dilatation; elastic. **dilatability,** *n.* **dilatant,** *n., a.* **dilatancy,** *n.* **dilatation,** *n.* the act of dilating; the state of being dilated; a dilated or expanded form or part; amplification, diffuseness; †extension, expansion. **dilation** DILATATION. **dilatometer,** *n.* **dilator,** *n.* a muscle that dilates the parts on which it acts; (*Surg.*) an instrument for dilating the walls of a cavity. [F *dilater,* L *dīlātāre (lātus,* broad)]

dilatory, *a.* causing or tending to cause delay; addicted to or marked by procrastination; slow, tardy; wanting in diligence. **dilatorily,** *adv.* **dilatoriness,** *n.* [L *dīlātōrius,* from *dīlātōr -tōrem,* a delayer (from *dīlāt-,* p.p. stem of *differre,* to DEFER[1])]

dildo(e), *n.* an object serving as an erect penis. [etym. doubtful]

dilemma, *n.* (*Log.*) an argument in which a choice of alternatives is presented, each of which is unfavourable; (*fig.*) a position in which one is forced to choose between alternatives equally unfavourable. **the horns of a dilemma,** the alternatives presented to an adversary in a logical dilemma. **dilemmatic,** *a.* **dilemmist,** *n.* [L, from Gr. *dilēmma* (DI-[2], *lēmma,* an assumption, from *lambanein,* to take)]

dilettante, *n.* (*pl.* **-tantes, -tanti**) a lover or admirer of the fine arts; a superficial amateur, a would-be connoisseur, a dabbler. *a.* art-loving; amateurish, superficial. **dilettantish,** *a.* **dilettantism,** *n.* [It., from *dilettare,* L *dēlectāre,* to DELIGHT]

diligence[1], *n.* a public stage-coach, formerly used in France and adjoining countries. [F]

diligence[2], *n.* steady application or assiduity in business of any kind; †care, heedfulness; †officiousness; †a deligent person; †speed, dispatch. [see foll.]

diligent, *a.* assiduous in any business or task; persevering, industrious, painstaking. **diligently,** *adv.* [F, from L *dīligens -entem,* pres.p. of *dīligere (legere,* to choose)]

dill, *n.* an annual umbellifer, *Anethum graveolens,* cultivated for its carminative seeds, and for its flavour. **dill pickle,** *n.* a pickled cucumber flavoured with dill. **dill-water,** *n.* a popular remedy for flatulence in children, prepared from the seeds of dill. [OE *dile* (cp. Dut. *dille,* G *Dill*)]

dilly, *n.* (*N Am. coll.*) a remarkable person or thing. *a.* (*Austral. coll.*) silly.

dilly-bag, *n.* an Australian Aboriginal basket or bag made of rushes or bark. [Queensland native name *dilli*)

dilly-dally, *v.i.* to loiter about; to waste time; to hesitate. [redupl. of DALLY]

dilute, *v.t.* to make thin or weaken (as spirit, acid or colour) by the admixture of water; to reduce the strength or brilliance of; to water down. *a.* diluted; weakened, washed out, faded, colourless. **dilutedly,** *adv.* **diluent,** *a.* making thin or liquid; diluting. *n.* that which dilutes; a substance tending to increase the proportion of fluid in the blood. **dilution,** *n.* **dilution of industry,** the employment of unskilled workers in positions hitherto held by skilled workers. [L *dīlūtus,* p.p. of *dīluere* (DI-[1], *luere,* to wash)]

diluvial, -vian, *a.* pertaining to Noah's flood; (*Geol.*) produced by or resulting from a flood; pertaining to the diluvium or glacial drift. **diluvial clay,** *n.* the boulder clay. **diluvial theory,** *n.* the theory that explains many geological phenomena as the result of a catastrophic deluge. **diluvialist,** *n.* one who regards certain physical phenomena as the result of Noah's flood or a series of catastrophic floods. **diluvium,** *n.* (*pl.* **-via**) an accumulation of deposits apparently the result of water-action on a vast scale, formerly attributed to Noah's flood, now referred to the drift or boulder formation. [L *dīluviālis,* from *dīluvium,* a deluge, from *dīluere,* as prec.]

dim., (*abbr.*) dimension; diminuendo; diminutive.

dim, *a.* lacking in light or brightness; somewhat dark; obscure; not clear, not bright; faint, indistinct, misty; devoid of lustre, tarnished, dull; not clearly seen; imperfectly heard; not clearly understanding or understood; (*fig.*) mentally obtuse. *v.t.* (*past, p.p.* **dimmed**) to render dim. *v.i.* to become dim. **dim-dip headlights,** *n.pl.* low-powered dipped headlights which come on automatically when the engine is running, to make the vehicle more visible and to reduce headlight glare. **to take a dim view of,** (*coll.*) to regard pessimistically, to view with suspicion or disfavour. **dim-eyed,** *a.* having indistinct vision. **dim-out,** *n.* a less rigorous form of black-out. **dim-shining,** *a.* giving a dim light. **dim-sighted,** *a.* dull, obtuse. **dim-twinkling,** *a.* twinkling or shining feebly. **dimly,** *adv.* **dimmer,** *n.* (*Elec.*) a device whereby an electric lamp can be switched on and off gradually. **dimmish,** *a.* **dimness,** *n.* [OE (cp. Icel. *dimmr,* MHG *timmer, timbar*)]

dime, *n.* a silver coin of the US, worth 10 cents or one-tenth of a dollar. **a dime a dozen,** (*coll.*) cheap, ordinary. **dime novel,** *n.* a sensational story, the equivalent of the penny dreadful. [OF *dime, disme,* L *decima,* fem. of *decimus* (*decem,* ten)]

dimension, *n.* (*usu. pl.*) measurable extent or magnitude, length, breadth, height, thickness, depth, area, volume, size, scope, extent etc.; (*Alg.*) the number of unknown or variable quantities contained as factors in a given product (thus ab^2c^3 is a term of six dimensions); an aspect. **new dimension,** a new aspect. **of large dimensions,** very large. **three dimensions,** length, breadth and thickness; a line, a surface, a volume, constituting the three degrees of measurement. **fourth dimension,** the extra (time) coordinate needed to locate a point in space. **dimensional,** *a.* (*usu. in* *comb.*). **fourth-dimensional,** *a.* **dimensioned,** *a.* having dimensions; (*usu. in comb.*) proportional. **four-dimensioned,** *a.* **dimensionless,** *a.* [F, from L *dīmensio -ōnem,* from *dīmensus,* p.p. of *dīmetīrī* (DI-¹, *metīrī,* to measure)]

dimerous, *a.* (*Bot., Entom.*) having two parts, joints, divisions etc.; arranged in pairs. **dimeric,** *a.* bilaterally symmetrical. **dimerism,** *n.*

dimeter, *n.* a verse of two prosodial measures. [L *dimetrus,* Gr. *dimetros* (DI-², *metron,* measure)]

dimethyl, *n.* ethane, an organic compound in which two equivalents of methyl take the place of two of hydrogen. **dimethylaniline,** *n.* one of the aniline bases, an oily liquid from which various dyes are obtained.

dimidiate, *a.* divided into two halves; (*Bot.*) divided or split into parts; (*Zool.*) a term used when corresponding organs have different functions. **dimidiation,** *n.* [L *dīmidiātus,* p.p. of *dīmidiāre,* from *dīmidium,* half (*medius,* middle)]

diminish, *v.t.* to make smaller or less; to reduce in quantity, power, rank etc.; to disparage, to degrade; to take away or subtract from; (*Mus.*) to lessen by a semitone. *v.t.* to become less, to decrease; to taper. **diminishable,** *a.* **diminished,** *a.* made less or smaller; reduced in size or quality; (*Mus.*) lessened by a semitone. **diminished responsibility,** *n.* a plea in law in which criminal responsibility is denied on the grounds of mental derangement. **diminisher,** *n.* one who or that which diminishes. **diminishing returns,** *n.pl.* progressively smaller increases in output in spite of increased work or expenditure. **diminishingly,** *adv.* **diminution**, *n.* the act of diminishing; subtraction; amount subtracted; the state of becoming less or smaller; (*Arch.*) the gradual decrease in the diameter of the shaft of a column from the base to the capital. [MINISH (formed on anal. of obs. *diminue,* F *diminuer,* L *dīminuere,* to break into small pieces)]

diminuendo, *a., adv.* (*Mus.*) gradually decreasing in loudness. *n.* (*pl.* **-dos, does**) a gradual decrease in loudness; a passage characterized by this. [It., pres.p. of *diminuire,* L *dīminuere;* see prec.]

diminutive, *a.* small, tiny; (*Gram.*) expressing diminution. *n.* anything of a small size; a word formed from another to express diminution in size etc, or affection. **diminutival**, *a.* expressing diminution; pertaining to a diminutive word. **diminutively,** *adv.* **diminutiveness,** *n.*

dimissory, *a.* dismissing, discharging; giving leave to depart. **dimissory letter,** *n.* letter addressed by one bishop to another, giving leave for the bearer to be ordained by the latter. [L *dīmissōrius,* from *dīmittere* (DI-¹, *mittere,* to send)]

Dimitrov, *n.* **Georgi** (1882–1949), Bulgarian communist, prime minister from 1946. He was elected a deputy in 1913, and from 1919 was a member of the executive of the Comintern. In 1933 he was arrested in Berlin and tried with others in Leipzig for allegedly setting fire to the parliament building (see REICHSTAG FIRE). So forceful was his defence that he was acquitted, and he went to the USSR, where he became general secretary of the Comintern until its dissolution in 1943.

dimity, *n.* a stout cotton fabric with stripes or patterns, chiefly used for bed-hangings. [It., pl. of *dimito,* late L *dimitum,* Gr. *dimitos* (DI-², *mitos,* a thread)]

dimmer, dimming DIM.

dimorphic, *a.* having or occurring in two distinct forms. **dimorphism,** *n.* the power of assuming or crystallizing into two distinct forms; a difference of form between members of the same species; a state in which two forms of flower are produced by the same species; the existence of a word in more than one form. **sexual dimorphism,** difference in form between the two sexes of a species. **dimorphous,** *a.* [Gr. *dimorphos* (DI-², *morphē,* form)]

dimple, *n.* a little depression or hollow; a small natural depression on the cheek or chin; a ripple; a shallow dell or hollow in the ground. *v.t.* to mark with dimples. *v.i.* to form dimples; to sink in slight depressions. **dimply,** *a.* [ME *dympull;* etym. doubtful (cp. G *Tümpel,* a pool, OHG *dumphilo*)]

dim sum, *n.* a Chinese appetizer consisting of small steamed dumplings with various fillings. [Chin.]

dimwit, *n.* (*coll.*) a stupid person. **dimwitted,** *a.* **dimwittedness,** *n.*

Dimyaria, *n.pl.* a group of conchiferous bivalves having the shells closed with two distinct adductor muscles, as in the common mussel. **dimyarian,** *a.* [Gr. *mus,* a muscle]

DIN, *n.* a method of classifying the speed of photographic film by sensitivity to light (the greater the light sensitivity the higher the speed). [acronym for *D*eutsche *I*ndustrie *N*orm (G, German industry standard)]

din, *n.* a loud and continued noise; a rattling or clattering sound. *v.t.* (*past, p.p.* **dinned**) to harass with clamour; to stun with a loud continued noise; to repeat or impress with a loud continued noise. *v.i.* to make a din. **to din into,** (*fig.*) to teach by constant repetition. [OE *dyn, dyne* (whence *dynnan,* to make a loud noise)]

dinar, *n.* an Eastern coin; a Persian money of account; the monetary unit of Yugoslavia, Iraq, Jordan, Kuwait, Algeria, South Yemen and Tunisia. [Arab., Pers. *dīnār,* L *dēnārius*]

dinarchy DIARCHY.

dine, *v.i.* to take dinner. *v.t.* to give or provide a dinner for; to afford accommodation for dining. **to dine out on,** to be invited to dinner, to be popular socially, because of (something interesting to recount). **to dine with Duke Humphrey,** to go dinnerless (said to allude to *Duke Humphrey's Walk,* a part of old St Paul's where people were supposed to stroll whilst others were dining). **to wine and dine (someone),** to entertain (someone) to dinner. **diner,** *n.* one who dines; a railway dining-car. **diner-out,** *n.* one who habitually dines away from home; one who is frequently invited out to dinner. **dinette,** *n.* an alcove or a small part of a room set aside for eating. **dining-car,** *n.* a railway coach in which meals are cooked and served. **dining-chamber, -hall, -room, -table,** *n.* a place or table for taking dinner at. [F *dîner,* prob. from a late L *disjūnāre* or *disjējūnāre* (DIS-, L *jējūnus,* fasting)]

Dine, *n.* **Jim** (1935–), US Pop artist. He experimented with combinations of paintings and objects, such as a washbasin attached to a canvas.

Dinesen, *n.* **Isak** (1885–1962), pen name of writer Karen Blixen.

ding, *v.t.* to strike; to beat violently; to beat, to surpass; to knock or drive with violence; to damn or confound (as an imprecation). *v.i.* to knock or thump; to fall heavily; to be impressed or moved; to ring, keep sounding. [ME *dingen* (cp. Icel. *dengja,* Swed. *dänga*)]

Dingaan, *n.* Zulu chief from 1828. He obtained the throne by murdering his predecessor, Shaka, and was known for his cruelty. In warfare with the Boer immigrants into Natal he was defeated on 16 Dec. 1838 – 'Dingaan's Day'. He escaped to Swaziland, where he was deposed by his brother Mpande and subsequently murdered.

dingbat, *n.* (*Austral. sl.*) a stupid person; (*pl.*) an attack of nerves.

ding-dong, *n.* the sound of a bell; a jingle, a jingling rhyme or tune; (*coll.*) a violent argument. *a.* sounding like a bell; jingling. *adv.* in a hammering way; like the sound of a bell. *v.i.* to ring; to jingle; to read, speak or recite in a jingling or ding-dong fashion. **ding-dong race,** a neck-and-neck race. [onomat.]

dinges, *n.* (*S Afr. coll.*) a name for any person or thing whose name is forgotten or unknown. [Africkaans, thing]

dinghy, *n.* orig. a rowing-boat on the Ganges; a small ship's boat; any small boat. [Hind. *dēngī* or *dīngī*]

dingle, *n.* a dell, a wooded valley between hills. [etym. doubtful]

dingo, *n.* (*pl.* **-goes**) the Australian wild dog, *Canis dingo*. [Abor.]

dingy, *a.* soiled, grimy; of a dusky, soiled, or dun colour; faded. **dingily,** *adv.* **dinginess,** *n.* [perh. from

DUNG]

dink, *a.* (*Sc.*) fine, trim. *v.t.* to dress finely; to deck. **dinky,** *a.* (*fam.*) charming, dainty, pleasing. [etym. unknown]

Dinka, *n.* person of Dinka culture from southern Sudan. Numbering approximately 1,000,000, the Dinka are primarily cattle herders, and inhabit the lands around the river system that flows into the White Nile. Their language belongs to the Chari-Nile family.

dinkum, *a.* (*Austral. coll.*) good, genuine, satisfactory.

dinky, *n.* (*coll.*) a socially upwardly mobile couple with two incomes and no children. [acronym for *d*ual *i*ncome *n*o *k*ids]

dinmont, *n.* (*Sc., North.*) a wether between the first and the second shearing. [etym. doubtful]

dinner, *n.* the principal meal of the day; a feast, a banquet. **dinner dance,** *n.* a dinner followed by dancing. **dinner-hour,** *n.* the time set apart for dinner. **dinner-jacket,** *n.* a formal jacket, less formal than a dress coat, without tails and worn with black tie. **dinner party,** *n.* invitation of guests to dinner; the guests so invited. **dinner service, set,** *n.* the china plates etc., used for serving dinner. **dinner-table,** *n.* a dining-table. **dinner-time,** *n.* the hour for dinner. **dinner-wagon,** *n.* a tray or set of trays or shelves on castors. **dinnerless,** *a.* [F *dîner,* to DINE]

Dinoceras, *n.* an extinct genus of gigantic mammals found in Wyoming, apparently armed with three pairs of horns. [Gr. *deinos,* terrible, *keras,* horn]

Dinornis, *n.* a genus of gigantic fossil birds, with rudimentary wings, found in New Zealand. [Gr. *deinos,* terrible, *ornis,* bird]

Dinorwig, *n.* Europe's largest pumped-storage hydroelectric scheme, completed in 1984, in Gwynedd, North Wales. Six turbogenerators together produce a maximum output of some 1880 megawatts. The working head of water for the station is 530 m/1740 ft.

dinosaur, *n.* a gigantic Mesozoic reptile. **dinosaurian,** *a.* pertaining to the group Dinosauria. *n.* a dinosaur. [Gr. *deinos,* terrible, *sauros,* lizard]

Dinotherium, *n.* a genus of gigantic fossil pachyderms, having enormous tusks projecting from the lower jaw, and a trunk. [mod. L, from Gr. *deinos,* terrible, *thērion,* wild beast]

dint, *n.* a blow, a stroke; the mark or dent caused by a blow; †violence, force. *v.t.* to mark with a dint. *v.i.* to make a dint. **by dint of,** by force of; by means of. [OE *dynt* (cp. Icel. *dyntr*)]

dioc., (*abbr.*) diocese; diocesan.

diocese, *n.* the district under the jurisdiction of a bishop. **diocesan**, *a.* pertaining to a diocese. *n.* one who has ecclesiastical jurisdiction over a diocese; a bishop or archbishop; a member of a diocese. [OF, from L *dioecēsis,* Gr. *dioikēsis* (DI-[3], *oikeein,* to keep house, to inhabit)]

Diocletian, *n.* **(Gaius Valerius Diocletianus)** (245–313), Roman emperor 284–305, when he abdicated in favour of Galerius. He reorganized and subdivided the Empire, with two joint and two subordinate emperors, and in 303 initiated severe persecution of the Christians.

diode, *n.* a simple electron tube in which the current flows in one direction only between two electrodes; a semiconductor with two terminals. [Gr. *hodos,* way]

Diodon, *n.* (*Palaeont.*) a genus of teleostean fishes with inflatable bodies and undivided jaws which exhibit one piece of bony substance above and another below. [Gr. *odous odontos,* a tooth]

Dioecia, *n.pl.* a Linnaean class of plants, having the stamens on one individual and the pistils on another. **dioecious,** *a.* (*Bot.*) belonging to the Dioecia; (*Zool.*) having the sexes in separate individuals. [mod. L (DI-[2], Gr. *oikos,* house)]

Diogenes, *n.* (*c.* 412–323 BC), ascetic Greek Philosopher of the Cynic school. He believed in freedom and self-sufficiency for the individual, and did not believe in social mores.

Dion Cassius, *n.* (150–235), Roman historian. He wrote in Greek a Roman History in 80 books (of which 26 survive), covering the period from the foundation of the city to AD 229, including the only surviving account of Claudius' invasion of Britain.

Dionysius, *n.* name of two tyrants of the ancient Greek city of Syracuse in Sicily. **Dionysius the Elder** (432–367 BC) seized power in 405. His first two wars with Carthage further extended the power of Syracuse, but in a third (383–378 BC) he was defeated. He was succeeded by his son **Dionysius the Younger**. Driven out of Syracuse by Dion in 356, he was tyrant again in 353, but in 343 returned to Corinth.

Dionysus, *n.* in Greek mythology, god of wine (son of Semele and Zeus), and also of orgiastic excess; he was identified with Bacchus, whose rites were less savage. **dyonysian**, *a.* relating to Dionysus; wild.

Diophantine equation, *n.* (*Math.*) an indeterminate equation which needs an integral or rational solution. [*Diophantos, c.* AD 275, Alexandrian mathematician]

diopside, *n.* pyroxene, esp. the transparent variety. [F (DI-[2], Gr. *opsis,* appearance)]

dioptase, *n.* an emerald-green ore of copper. [F (DI-[3], Gr. *optos,* visible)]

dioptric, *a.* affording a medium for assisting the sight in the view of distant objects; refractive; pertaining to dioptrics. **dioptric light,** *n.* light produced in lighthouses by refraction through a series of lenses. **dioptric system,** *n.* illumination by this method. **dioptre,** *n.* the unit of refractive power, being the power of a lens with a focal distance of one metre. **dioptrically,** *adv.* **dioptrics,** *n.sing.* that part of optics which treats of the refraction of light in passing through different mediums, esp. through lenses. [Gr. *dioptrikos,* from *dioptra,* an optical instrument (DI-[3], *op-,* stem of verb, to see, *-tra,* instr. suf.)]

Dior, *n.* **Christian** (1905–57), French couturier. He established his own Paris salon in 1947, and made an impact with the 'New Look' – long and full-skirted – after war-time austerity.

diorama, *n.* a scenic representation viewed through an aperture by means of reflected and transmitted light, various alterations of colour and lighting imitating natural effects; a building in which dioramic views are shown. **dioramic**, *a.* [Gr. *horama* (*horaein,* to see)]

diorite, *n.* a granite-like rock, consisting principally of hornblende and feldspar. **dioritic,** *a.* [F, from Gr. *diorizein,* to distinguish (DI-[3], *horos,* a boundary)]

Dioscuri, *n.pl.* the twins Castor and Pollux. [Gr. *Dioskouroi* (*Dios,* gen. of *Zeus, kouroi koroi,* pl. of *koros,* a lad)]

diosmose, *n.* the gradual passage of a fluid through a permeable wall.

diothelism, etc. DYOTHELISM.

dioxide, *n.* one atom of a metal combined with two of oxygen.

dioxin, *n.* a highly toxic substance found in some weedkillers which causes birth defects, cancers and various other diseases.

dip, *v.t.* (*past, p.p.* **dipped**) to plunge into a liquid for a short time, to immerse; to baptize by immersion; to wash, to dye, to coat by plunging into a liquid; to lower for an instant; to put the hand or a ladle into liquid and scoop out; †to mortgage, to pledge, to implicate; to lower (the headlights); (*Naut.*) to salute by lowering (the flag) and hoisting it again. *v.i.* to plunge into liquid for a short time; to sink, as below the horizon; to bend downwards, to bow; to slope or extend downwards, to enter slightly into any business; to read a book cursorily; to choose by chance. *n.* the act of dipping in a liquid; bathing, esp. in a river, sea etc.; a candle made by dipping wicks in melted tallow; the quantity taken up at one dip or scoop; a preparation for washing sheep; sauce, gravy etc., into which anything is to be dipped; a savoury mixture into which biscuits or raw vegetables are dipped before being eaten; depth or degree of submergence; the angle at which strata slope downwards into the earth; a curtsy; (*sl.*) a pickpocket. **dip of the horizon,** the apparent angular depression of the visible horizon below the horizontal plane through the observer's eye, due to his elevation. **dip of the needle,** the angle which a magnetic needle makes with the horizontal, also called **magnetic dip. to dip deep,** to plunge far in; to investigate. **to dip into,** to draw upon (e.g. resources); to read in cursorily. **dip-chick,** *n.* the dabchick. **dip-net,** *n.* a small fishing-net with a long handle. **dip-pipe, -trap,** *n.* a pipe bent down from a gas-main with its end plunged into liquid to form a seal. **dipstick,** *n.* a rod for measuring the level of liquid in a container. **dip switch,** *n.* a device in a car for dipping headlights. **dipper,** *n.* one who dips; a vessel used for dipping; a contrivance for lifting negatives out of the developer; a contemptuous name for the Baptists or Anabaptists; (*N Am.*) the seven stars of the Great Bear; popular name for several birds, esp. the water-ousel; (*N Am.*) a pannikin, a ladle. **dipping compass, dipping-needle,** *n.* a magnetized needle which, when mounted on an axis passing at right angles through its centre of gravity, will point downwards indicating the inclination of the lines of magnetic force. **dipping-tube,** *n.* a tube for taking microscopic objects out of a liquid. [OE *dyppan,* cogn. with *dēop,* DEEP (cp. Dut. *doopen,* G *taufen*)]

Dip., (*abbr.*) Diploma.

Dip.Ed., (*abbr.*) Diploma in Education.

dipeptide, *n.* a peptide with two amino acid molecules in its structure.

dipetalous, *a.* having two petals.

diphase, diphasic, *a.* having two phases.

diphtheria, *n.* an infectious disease characterized by acute inflammation and the formation of a false membrane, chiefly on the pharynx, nostrils, tonsils and palate. **diphtherial, diphtheric,** *a.* **diphtheritis,** *n.* **diphtheritic,** *a.* **diphtheroid,** *a.* [F *diphthérie,* Gr. *diphthera,* leather, skin]

diphthong, *n.* the union of two vowels in one syllable; a digraph or combination of two vowel characters to represent a vowel sound; the vowel ligatures, *æ, œ.* **diphthongal, -gic,** *a.* **diphthongally,** *adv.* **diphthongize, -ise,** *v.t.* **diphthongization, -isation,** *n.* [F *diphthongue,* L *diphthongus,* Gr. *diphthongos* (DI-2, *phthongos,* voice)]

diphyllous, *a.* having two leaves or sepals. [Gr. *phullon,* a leaf]

diphyodont, *a.* a term applied to those mammals which have two sets of teeth, one deciduous, the other permanent. [Gr. *diphuēs,* of double nature, *odous odontos,* tooth]

diphysite, etc. DYOPHYSITE.

dipl., (*abbr.*) diploma; diplomat(ist); diplomatic.

dipleidoscope, *n.* an instrument for determining the moment of transit of a heavenly body over the meridian by the coincidence of two images produced by single and double refraction. [Gr. *eidos,* form]

dipl(o)-, *comb. form* double. [Gr. *diploos*]

diploblastic, *a.* (*Bot.*) having two germ-layers. [Gr. *blastos,* a sprout]

diplocardiac, *a.* having the heart double or the two sides separated.

Diplock court, *n.* in Northern Ireland, a type of court established in 1972 by the British government under Lord Diplock (1907–) to try offences linked with terrorist violence. The right to jury trial was suspended and the court consisted of a single judge, since it was alleged that potential jurors were being intimidated and were unwilling to serve. Despite widespread criticism, the Diplock courts have remained in operation.

Diplodocus, *n.* a genus of sauropod dinosaurs characterized by a large tail and a small head.

diploe, *n.* the spongy tissue between the plates of the skull; the tissue of a leaf between the two layers of epiderm. [Gr., double]

diploid, *a.* having the full number of paired homologous chromosomes; double, twofold. **diploidic,** *a.*

diploma, *n.* (*pl.* **-as,** rarely **-ata**) a document conveying some authority, privilege or honour; a charter, a state paper; a certificate of a degree, licence etc. **diplomaed,** *a.* **diplomaless,** *a.* **diplomate,** *n.* **diplomatics,** *n. sing.* the art or science of ascertaining the authenticity, date, genuineness etc. of ancient literary documents; †diplomacy. [L, from Gr. *diplōma* (*diploos,* double, folded)]

diplomacy, *n.* the art of conducting negotiations between nations; the act of negotiating with foreign nations; skill in conducting negotiations of any kind; adroitness, tact. **diplomat,** *n.* a professional diplomatist, one skilled or trained in diplomacy. **diplomatic,** *a.* pertaining to diplomacy or to ambassadors. **diplomatic bag,** *n.* one used for sending official mail, free of customs control, to and from embassies and consulates. **diplomatic corps,** *n.* the body of diplomatic representatives accredited to any government. **diplomatic immunity,** *n.* the immunity from taxation and local laws given to diplomats resident in a foreign country. **diplomatic relations,** *n.pl.* official relations between countries marked by the presence of diplomats in each other's country. **Diplomatic Service,** *n.* that part of the Civil Service which provides diplomats to represent Britain abroad. **diplomatically,** *adv.* **diplomatics** see DIPLOMA. **†diplomatism,** *n.* **diplomatist,** *n.* one skilled or engaged in diplomacy. **diplomatize, -ise,** *v.i.* to act as a diplomatist; to exert the arts of a diplomatist. [F *diplomatie,* from *diplomate,* from *diplomatique,* mod. L *diplōmaticus,* from prec.]

diplopia, *n.* a disease of the eyes in which the patient sees objects double. [Gr. *ōps,* an eye]

Diplozoon, *n.* (*pl.* **-zoa**) a trematode or flat-worm composed of two individual organisms fused together in the shape of a cross, parasitic on the gills of fishes.

Dipnoi, *n.pl.* an order of fishes, of very ancient type, breathing both by gills and true lungs, exhibiting a transition to the amphibia. **dipnoid,** *n., a.* **dipnoous,** *a.* [mod. L, from Gr. *dipnoos* (DI-2, *pnoē,* breathing)]

dipody, *n.* (*Pros.*) a double foot. [L, Gr. *dipodia* (DI-2, Gr. *pous podos,* foot)]

dipole, *n.* two equal and opposite electric charges or magnetic poles a small distance apart; a molecule in which the centres of positive and negative charge do not coincide; an aerial made of a single metal rod with the connecting wire attached half-way down. **dipolar,** *a.* (*Elec., Opt.*) having two poles. **dipolarize, -ise,** *v.t.* **dipolarization, -isation,** *n.*

dipper, dipping DIP.

dippy, *a.* (*sl.*) slightly mad.

dipsas, *n.* a serpent whose bite was said to produce unquenchable thirst; **(Dipsas)** a genus of non-venomous tree-snakes. [L, from Gr. *dipsas* (*dipsa,* thirst)]

dipsomania, *n.* alcoholism; a morbid, irresistible craving for stimulants. **dipsomaniac,** *n.* **dipsomaniacal,** *a.* **dipsopathy,** *n.* (*Med.*) treatment of dipsomania by enforced abstinence. **dipsosis,** *n.* morbid craving for drink. [as prec.]

Diptera, *n.pl.* an order of insects, such as flies and gnats, that have two wings and two small knobbed organs called poisers. **dipteran,** *a.* **dipterous,** *a.* two-winged; belonging to the Diptera; (*Bot.*) having two wing-like appendages. [mod. L, from Gr. *diptera* (DI-2, *pteron,* wing)]

dipteral, *a.* applied to a temple having a double row of columns all round. [as prec.]

diptych, *n.* an ancient writing-tablet of two hinged leaves, made of carved ivory waxed on the inner side; an altar-piece or other painting with hinged sides closing like a book. [late L *diptycha,* Gr. *diptucha,* neut. pl. of *diptuchos,* folding (DI-2, *ptuchē,* a fold)]

dire, *a.* dreadful, fearful, dismal, lamentable, sad. **direful,** *a.* **direfully,** *adv.* **direfulness,** *n.* **direly,** *adv.* [L *dīrus*]

direct, *a.* straight; in a straight line from one body or place to another; not curved or crooked; not reflected or refracted; nearest, shortest; tending immediately to an end or result; not circuitous; not collateral in the line of descent; diametrical; not contrary or retrograde; immediate; personal, not by proxy; honest, to the point; not inverted; (*Mus.*) (*Gram.*) as spoken, not in reported form; plain, to the point, straightforward, upright; from east to west, applied to the motion of a planet when in the same direction as the movement of the sun amidst the fixed stars. *v.t.* to point or turn in a direct line towards any place or object; to show the right road to; to inscribe with an address or direction; to address, to speak or write to; to guide, to prescribe a course to, to advise; to order, to command; to manage, to control, to act as leader or head of; (e.g. a group of musicians, a play or film); to compel (work-people) in time of emergency to engage in certain occupations. *v.i.* to give orders or instructions. *adv.* (*coll.*) directly; immediately; absolutely. **direct broadcasting by satellite,** a system of broadcasting television programmes direct to the consumer using satellites in orbit round the earth. **directed-energy weapon,** one that destroys its target by directing high-energy radiation or sub-atomic particles on to it. **direct grant school,** (before 1979) a school funded by fees and a state grant on condition that it accepted a specified number of non-fee-paying pupils. **direct access,** *n.* a way of reading data in a computer file without having to read through the whole file. **direct action,** *n.* the use of the strike as a weapon to force political or social measures on a government. **direct chord,** *n.* (*Mus.*) a chord in which the fundamental note is the lowest. **direct circuit,** *n.* a circuit going from one station to another without using relays. **direct current,** *n.* (*Elec.*) a current which flows in one direction only. **direct debit,** *n.* a method by which a creditor is paid directly from the payer's bank account. **direct interval,** *n.* (*Mus.*) an interval which forms any kind of harmony with the fundamental sound that produces it. **direct object,** *n.* the word or group of words which is acted upon by a transitive verb. **direct pick-up,** *n.* the transmission of television images directly, without photographic medium. **direct primary,** *n.* in the US, a primary election in which voters select the candidates who are to stand for office. **direct speech,** *n.* a report of actual words spoken. **direct tax,** *n.* one levied on the persons who ultimately bear the burden. †**directitude,** *n.* a ludicrous formation in Shakespeare (*Coriolanus,* iv. 5), perh. difficulties. **directive,** *n.* an authoritative instruction or direction. *a.* having the power of directing; capable of being directed; directory. **directly,** *adv.* in a direct or straight line; in a direct manner; as an immediate step; without any intervening space; at once; †openly, without ambiguity. *conj.* (*coll.*) as soon as, directly that. **directness,** *n.* [L *dīrectus,* p.p. of *dīrigere* (DI-[1], *regere,* to rule)]

direction, *n.* the act of directing; the end or object aimed at; the course taken; the point towards which one looks; the act of inscribing with an address; (*often pl.*) the superscription of a letter or parcel; an order or instruction; a directorate; sphere, subject. **direction finder,** *n.* an apparatus for finding the bearings of a transmitting station. **directional,** *a.* **directional aerial,** *n.* one that transmits or receives radio waves from one direction. **directional drilling,** *n.* non-vertical drilling of oil wells, esp. when several are drilled from the same platform.

directoire, *a.* term applied to the costume and furniture of the Directory period in France, 1795–99. [F]

director, *n.* one who directs or manages; an instructor, a counsellor; anything which controls or regulates; one appointed to direct the affairs of a company; a spirtual adviser, a confessor; a device for controlling the application of a knife, an electric current etc.; the person responsible for the acting etc. in a film or play; (*F Hist.*) a member of the Directory. **director general,** *n.* the head of a large, often non-commercial organization, such as the BBC. **directorate,** *n.* the position of a director; a body or board of directors. **directorial,** *a.* **directorship,** *n.* **directress, directrix**[1], *n.fem.* [F *directeur* (as prec.)]

Director of Public Prosecutions, the head of the Crown Prosecution Service (established in 1985), responsible for the conduct of all criminal prosecutions in England and Wales. The DPP was formerly responsible only for the prosecution of certain serious crimes, such as murder.

directory, *a.* directing, commanding advising; (*Law*) directive, not coercive. *n.* a board of directors; a book containing the names, addresses and telephone numbers of the inhabitants etc. of a district; a book of direction for public worship; a list of all the files on a computer disk; (*Hist.*) the executive council of the French Republic in 1795–99.

directrix[1] DIRECTOR.

directrix[2], *n.* (*pl.* **directrices**) (*Geom.*) a line determining the motion of a point or another line so that the latter describes a certain curve or surface.

Dire Straits, *n.* UK rock group formed in 1977 by the guitarist, singer, and songwriter Mark Knopfler (1949–). In the 1980s they sold a record number of compact discs, including *Brothers in Arms* (1985).

dirge, *n.* a funeral song or hymn; a mournful tune or song; a lament. [L *dīrige,* direct thou, imper. of *dīrigere,* to DIRECT (first word of antiphon in the office for the dead)]

dirham, dirhem, *n.* an eastern measure of weight; the standard monetary unit in Morocco; a coin (of different values) in the monetary systems of several N African and Middle Eastern countries. [Arab. *dirham, dirhim,* L *drachma,* Gr. *drachmē,* DRACHM]

dirigible, *a.* that may be directed or steered. *n.* a balloon or airship that can be steered. **dirigibility,** *n.* [L *dīrigere,* to DIRECT]

diriment, *a.* (*Law*) nullifying, rendering a marriage null and void. [L *dirimens -entem,* pres.p. of *dirimere* (*dir-* (for DIS-), *emere,* to take)]

dirk, *n.* a dagger, esp. that worn by a Highlander; the short sword of a midshipman. *v.t.* to stab with a dirk. [earlier *dork* (cp. Dut. *dolk,* G *Dolch*)]

dirl, *v.t.* (*Sc.*) to thrill; to cause to vibrate or ring. *v.i.* to vibrate. *n.* a thrill; a tingling sensation from a blow. [cp. THRILL (Sc. *thirl*), DRILL[1]]

dirndl, *n.* an Alpine peasant woman's dress with tight-fitting bodice and full gathered skirt; any full skirt like this. [G dial. *Dirndl,* little girl, dim. of *Dirne*]

dirt, *n.* foul or unclean matter, matter that soils; mud, mire, dust; a worthless thing, trash, refuse; dirtiness; earth, soil; (*derog.*) land; foul talk, scurrility; (*Mining*) the material put into the cradle to be washed; (*fig.*) meanness, sordidness. *v.t.* to make dirty or filthy. **to eat dirt,** to put up with insult and abuse. **to throw dirt at,** (*coll.*) to speak ill of, to vilify. **dirt-beds,** *n.pl.* loam-like beds occurring interstratified with the oolitic limestones and sandstones of Portland. **dirt-cheap,** *a.* very cheap. **dirt-eating,** *n.* a disease of the nutritive functions causing an irresistible craving to eat dirt. **dirt-road,** *n.* (*N Am.*) an unmade-up road. **dirt-track,** *n.* a racing-track with a soft, loose surface, for motorcycle racing; a speedway. **dirty,** *a.* full of, mixed, or soiled with dirt; foul, nasty, unclean; (*fig.*) base, obscene; sordid, mean; contemptible; of weather, sloppy, rough, gusty; of nuclear weapons, producing much radioactive fall-out. *v.t.* to make dirty, to soil; to sully, to tarnish. *v.i.* to become dirty. **dirty old man,** a lewd old man, or one with the sexual appetites thought proper to a younger man. **to do the dirty on,** (*coll.*) to play an underhand trick on. **Dirty Allan,** *n.* a seabird, *Stercorareus crepidatus,* that eats food which it has forced gulls etc. to disgorge. **dirty dog,** *n.* (*coll.*) a dishonest or untrustworthy person. **dirty look,** *n.* (*coll.*) a glance of disapproval or dislike. **dirty money,** *n.* extra pay for unpleasant or dirty work. **Dirty Shirts,** *n.pl.* the 101st Regiment of Foot, from their fighting in their shirtsleeves at Delhi in 1857. **dirty word,** *n.* (*coll.*) a swear word or taboo word; something currently out of favour or very much disliked. **dirty work,** *n.* work that involves dirtying the hands and clothes; (*coll.*) dishonesty, trickery, foul play. **dirtily,** *adv.* **dirtiness,** *n.* **dirtyish,** *a.* [ME *drit,* prob. from Icel *drit,* dirt, excrement (cp. OE *drītan,* to defecate]

dis DISS.

Dis, *n.* in Roman mythology, the god of the underworld (Greek **Pluto**); ruler of Hades.

dis-, *pref.* asunder, apart, away; between, separating, distinguishing; separately; (*intensively*) utterly, exceedingly; (*forming negative compounds*) not, the reverse of; undoing, depriving or expelling from. [direct from L *dis-* (conn. with *bis,* twice, orig. *duis,* Gr. *dis,* and *duo,* two; or F *dés-*, *dé-*, OF *des-*, L *dis-*, *di-*; or late L *dis-*, L *dé-*)]

disability, *n.* want of physical or intellectual power, or pecuniary means; weakness, incapacity, inability; handicap; legal disqualification. [from obs. *disable,* unable]

disable, *v.t.* to render unable; to deprive of adequate physical or intellectual power, to incapacitate; to disqualify legally; to injure so as to incapacitate, to cripple. **disabled,** *a.* **disablement,** *n.*

disabuse, *v.t.* to free from error or misapprehension, to undeceive.

disaccord, *v.i.* to disagree; to refuse assent. *n.* disagreement; lack of harmony, incongruity.

disaccustom, *v.t.* to do away with a habit; to free from the force of custom.

disacknowledge, *v.t.* to disown, to deny acquaintance with.

disadvance, *v.t.* to draw back, to lower (as a weapon). [OF *desavancer*]

disadvantage, *n.* injury, detriment, hurt; an unfavourable position or condition. *v.t.* to cause disadvantage to. **disadvantaged,** *a.* deprived of social or economic resources; discriminated against. **disadvantageous,** *a.* prejudicial, detrimental; unfavourable to one's interest; disparaging, depreciative. **disadvantageously,** *adv.* **disadvantageousness,** *n.*

disadventurous, *a.* unfortunate, unprosperous. **disadventure,** *n.* misadventure, misfortune.

disaffect, *v.t.* (*chiefly pass.*) to estrange, alienate the affection or loyalty of. **disaffected,** *a.* alienated in affection, estranged; disloyal. **disaffectedly,** *adv.* **disaffection,** *n.* alienation of feeling or affection, esp. from those in authority; disloyalty.

disaffiliate, *v.t.* to end an affiliation to; to detach. *v.t.* to separate oneself (from). **disaffiliation,** *n.*

disaffirm, *v.t.* to deny what has been affirmed; to reverse, to repudiate. †**disaffirmance,** *n.* **disaffirmation,** *n.*

disafforest, *v.t.* to reduce from the legal status of forest to that of ordinary land; to strip of forest. **disafforestation,** *n.* [med. L *afforestāre,* to AFFOREST]

disaggregate, *v.t., v.i.* to separate into components, parts or particles. **disaggregation,** *n.*

disagree, *v.i.* to differ; to be different or unlike; to differ in opinion; to quarrel, to fall out; to be unsuitable or injurious (to health, digestion etc.). **disagreeable,** *a.* not in agreement or accord; offensive, unpleasant, repugnant; ill-tempered. *n.* (*usu. pl.*) annoyances, troubles, worries. **disagreeableness,** *n.* **disagreeably,** *adv.* **disagreement,** *n.* want of agreement; unsuitableness, unfitness; difference of opinion; a quarrel, a falling out, dissension. [F *désagréer*]

disallow, *v.t.* to refuse to sanction or permit; to refuse assent to; to disavow, to reject; to prohibit. *v.i.* to refuse allowance (of). †**disallowance,** *n.* [OF *desalouer*]

disally, *v.t.* to cancel the alliance of; to separate.

disanchor, *v.t.* to weigh the anchor of. *v.i.* to weigh anchor, to depart.

disanimate, *v.t.* to deprive of vitality, to discourage, to depress. †**disanimation,** *n.*

disannul, *v.t.* to annul, to abrogate. **disannulment,** *n.*

disanoint, *v.t.* to annul the consecration of.

disapparel, *v.t.* to disrobe, to strip.

disappear, *v.i.* to go out of sight; to become invisible; to be lost; to cease to exist. **disappearance,** *n.*

disappoint, *v.t.* to defeat of expectation, wish, hope or desire; to frustrate, to hinder, to belie; to fail or neglect to keep an appointment with; †to annul the appointment of. **disappointed,** *a.* frustrated, thwarted, deceived or defeated in one's desires or expectations; †unfurnished, unprepared. **disappointedly,** *adv.* **disappointing,** *a.* **disappointingly,** *adv.* **disappointment,** *n.* the failure of one's hopes; that which disappoints. [F *désappointer*]

disapprobation, *n.* disapproval, condemnation. **disapprobative,** *a.* **disapprobatory,** *a.*

disappropriate, *v.t.* to remove from individual possession; to sever, as an appropriation.

disapprove, *v.t.* to condemn or censure as wrong; to reject, as not approved of. **disapproval,** *n.* **disapprovingly,** *adv.*

disarm, *v.t.* to take the weapons away from; to deprive of weapons; to disband; to reduce to a peace footing; to dismantle; (*fig.*) to render harmless; to subdue, to tame. *v.i.* to lay aside arms; to be reduced to a peace footing; to reduce or abandon military and naval establishments. **disarmament,** *n.* reduction of armaments by mutual agreement between nations. **disarmer,** *n.* **disarming,** *a.* tending to allay hostility or criticism; charming. **disarmingly,** *adv.* [F *désarmer*]

disarrange, *v.t.* to put out of order; to derange. **disarrangement,** *n.*

disarray, *v.t.* to throw into confusion, to rout; †to undress, disrobe. *n.* disorder, confusion; disorderly attire.

disarticulate, *v.t.* to separate the joints of, to disjoint. *v.i.* to become disjointed or separated at the joints. **disarticulation,** *n.*

disassemble, *v.t.* to take apart.

disassimilation, *n.* the conversion of assimilated substances into such as are less complex or waste substances; catabolism.

disassociate, *v.t.* to separate, to disjoin. **disassociation,** *n.* [F *désassocier* (DIS-, *associer,* ASSOCIATE)]

disaster, *n.* a sudden misfortune, a calamity; misfortune, ill luck; (*coll.*) fiasco, flop; †(*Astrol.*) the influence of an unfavourable planet; an evil omen. †*v.t.* to blast by the influence of an unfavourable planet; to injure, to disfigure. **disaster area,** *n.* one which has suffered a disaster and needs emergency aid; (*coll.*) one that is very untidy, or a situation that is very unfortunate. **disastrous,** *a.* occasioning or threatening disaster; ruinous, calamitous. **disastrously,** *adv.* [F *désastre* (DIS-, *astre,* L *astrum,* Gr. *astron,* a star)]

disavow, *v.t.* to deny the truth of, to disown; to disapprove; to disclaim; to repudiate. **disavowal,** *n.* [F *désavouer* (DIS-, *avouer,* to AVOW)]

disband, *v.t.* to break up (as a body of men in military service). *v.i.* to be disbanded; to separate, to disperse. **disbandment,** *n.* [F *desbander* (DIS-, OF, BAND[4])]

disbar, *v.t.* (*past, p.p.* **disbarred**) to deprive of status as a barrister; to expel from membership of the bar.

disbelieve, *v.t.* to refuse credit to, to refuse to believe in. *v.t.* to be a sceptic. **disbelief,** *n.* **disbeliever,** *n.*

disbench, *v.t.* to deprive of status as a bencher, to dismiss from senior membership of the Inns of Court; †to unseat.

disbody, *v.t.* to disembody.

disbosom, *v.t.* to unbosom, to confess.

disbowel, *v.t.* to disembowel.

disbranch, *v.t.* to strip of branches; to sever (as a branch).

disbud, *v.t.* to cut away (esp. the superfluous) buds from.

disburden, *v.t.* to remove a burden or encumbrance from; to relieve, to get rid of. *v.i.* to unload; to ease one's mind.

disburse, *v.t.* to pay out, to expend; to defray. **disbursement,** *n.* **disburser,** *n.* [OF *desbourser* (DIS-, BURSE)]

disc DISK.

disc., (*abbr.*) discovered; discoverer.

discalced, *a.* unshod, barefoot, wearing sandals (of friars, nuns etc.). *n.* a barefoot or sandalled friar or nun. **discalceated,** *a.* **discalced,** *a.* [L *discalceātus,* p.p. of *discalceāre* (DIS-, *calceāre,* to shoe, from *calceus,* a shoe)]

discandy, *v.t.* to melt away, to dissolve.

discant DESCANT[1, 2].

discapacitate, *v.t.* to incapacitate.

discard[1], *v.t.* to throw aside or away as useless; to get rid of, to reject; to cast aside; to dismiss; to play (a particular card) that does not follow suit. *v.t.* to play a non-trump card that does not follow suit.

discard[2], *n.* the playing of useless cards; the card or cards so played; rejection as useless; anything so rejected.

discarnate, *a.* having no flesh, disembodied. [DIS-, L *caro carnis,* flesh]

discern, *v.t.* †to discriminate, to perceive the difference between, to distinguish (from); to perceive distinctly with the senses, to make out; to recognize clearly or perceive mentally; to judge or decide between. *v.i.* to make distinction (between); to discriminate; to see. **discernible,** *a.* **discernibleness,** *n.* **discernibly,** *adv.* **discerning,** *a.* having power to discern; discriminating, acute, penetrating. *n.* discernment. **discerningly,** *adv.* **discernment,** *n.* the act, power or faculty of discerning; clear discrimination, accurate judgment. [F *discerner,* L *discernere* (DIS-, *cernere,* to separate)]

discerptible, *a.* separable, capable of being torn apart. **discerptibility**, *n.* **discerption,** *n.* severance, division into parts or pieces; a severed portion. [L *discerptus,* p.p. of *discerpere* (DIS-, *carpere,* to pick, to pluck)]

discharge[1], *v.t.* to unload from ship, vehicle etc.); to take out or away, as a load; to get rid of; to emit, to let fly; to dismiss, to release from confinement; to relieve of a load; to set free from something binding; to fire off; to empty (as a cistern); to pay off; to settle; to perform; to remove colour from by process of bleaching; †to cancel, to annul. *v.i.* to discharge a cargo; to unload or empty itself (as a river). **discharger,** *n.* one who or that which discharges; (*Elec.*) a discharging rod. **discharging,** *n., a.* **discharging arch,** *n.* an arch in a wall (e.g. over a window) to relieve the part below from undue pressure. **discharging rod,** *n.* an instrument to discharge an electrical jar or battery by opening a communication between the two surfaces. [OF *descharger*]

discharge[2], *n.* the act of discharging; unloading, release, emission, firing off; payment, satisfaction; dismissal, release, acquittal, liberation, performance; a paper certifying any of these; that which is discharged; (*Elec.*) neutralization or loss of electrical charge. **discharge in gases,** the passage of electricity through a tube containing gas at low pressure, used in fluorescent lighting. **discharge-valve,** *n.* a valve covering the top of the air-pump in marine engines, opening only to discharge.

discide, *v.t.* to cut in two or in pieces. [L *discīdere* (DIS-, *caedere,* to cut)]

disciple, *n.* a pupil or adherent of a philosopher, leader etc.; a follower of a particular cult, area of interest etc.; one of the early followers, esp. one of the twelve personal followers of Christ. †*v.t.* to teach; to make a disciple of; to discipline. **discipleship,** *n.* **discipular**, *a.* [OE *discipul* and OF *deciple* (L *discipulus,* from *discere,* to learn), both assim. to L spelling]

discipline, *n.* instruction, training, exercise, or practice of the mental, moral and physical powers to promote order, regularity and efficient obedience; correction, chastisement; training supplied by adversity; military training; order, systematic obedience, methodical action, the state of being under control; in the Roman Catholic Church, penitential chastisement, the instrument by which this is applied corporeally; control over the members of a church, the rules binding on the members of a church; penal or reformatory action against a transgressor of these; †a branch of instruction; †military skill, generalship. *v.t.* to bring into a state of discipline; to teach, to train, to drill, esp. in obedience, orderly habits and methodical action; to chastise, to chasten, to bring into a state of order and obedience. **disciplinable,** *a.* **disciplinal**, *a.* †**disciplinant,** *n.* one of a Spanish religious body of the Middle Ages who used to take discipline in public. **disciplinarian**, *a.* pertaining to discipline. *n.* one who rigidly enforces discipline; one skilled in maintaining discipline; †a Puritan, a Presbyterian, esp. one of those who in the Elizabethan period endeavoured to introduce the Genevan or Presbyterian ecclesiastical system. **disciplinary**, *a.* pertaining to or promoting discipline; tending to promote efficient mental action. **discipliner,** *n.* [F, from L *dīsciplīna,* as prec.]

disclaim, *v.t.* to deny, to repudiate; to refuse to acknowledge, to disown, to disavow; to reject; (*Law*) to renounce, to relinquish or to disavow; †to decline, refuse. †*v.i.* to deny all claim or participation. **disclaimer,** *n.* the act of disclaiming; renunciation, disavowal, repudiation. [A-F *desclamer*]

disclose, *v.t.* to uncover; to lay bare or open; to make known, to reveal, to divulge. †*n.* a discovery, a coming to light. **disclosure**, *n.* the act of disclosing; that which is disclosed, a revelation. [OF *desclore* (DIS-, L *claudere,* to shut, p.p. *clausus*)]

disco, *n.* (*pl.* **-cos**) short and more usual form of DISCOTHEQUE. *a.* suitable for or adapted for discotheques, as in *disco dancing.*

discobolus, *n.* (*pl.* **-li**) (*Class. Ant.*) a quoit-thrower; a statue by Myron of an athlete throwing the discus. [L, from Gr. *diskobolos* (*diskos,* quoit, *-bolos,* from *ballein,* to throw)]

discography, *n.* the literature and study of gramophone records; a list of gramophone records.

discoid, discoidal, *a.* having the shape of a disk. **discoid flowers,** *n.pl.* composite flowers not radiated by having the corollas tubular, as in the tansy. **discoidal shells,** *n.pl.* univalve shells in which the whorls lie in the same plane. [L *discoīdēs,* Gr. *diskoeidēs* (*diskos;* -OID)]

discolour, *v.t.* to alter the colour of; to give an unnatural colour to; to stain; to tarnish; to give a wrong colour to. *v.i.* to become stained or tarnished in colour; to fade, to become pale. **discoloration,** *n.* the act of discolouring; the state of being discoloured; a discoloured appearance, a spot, a stain. **discolourment,** *n.* [OF *descolorer,* med. L *discolōrāre* (DIS-, L *colōrāre,* in place of L *dēcolōrāre*)]

discombobulate, *v.t.* (*esp. N Am. coll.*) to confuse. [etym. doubtful]

discomfit, *v.t.* to defeat, to rout; to scatter in fight; to thwart, to frustrate; to disconcert, to confound. †*n.* discomfiture. **discomfiture,** *n.* defeat, overthrow; disappointment, frustration. [OF *desconfit,* p.p. of *desconfire,* late L *disconficere* (DIS-, *conficere,* to finish, to preserve),]

discomfort, *v.t.* to deprive of comfort; to cause pain or uneasiness to. *n.* deprivation of ease or comfort; uneasiness, disquietude, distress. †**discomfortable,** *a.* causing or suffering discomfort; causing disquiet or discouragement. [OF *desconforter*]

discommend, *v.t.* to blame, to censure; to disapprove; to disparage. †**discommendable,** *a.* †**discommendation,** *n.*

discommode, *v.t.* to incommode. †**discommodious,** *a.* inconvenient, troublesome. †**discommodity,** *n.* [obs. v. *commode,* L *commodāre,* to suit, from *commodus,* suitable]

discommon, *v.t.* to appropriate from being common land; to deprive of the use of a common; to deprive of a privilege (esp. tradesmen in an English university town who may be debarred from serving undergraduates). **discommons,** *v.t.* to deprive of commons; to deprive (a tradesman) of the right to serve undergraduates.

discommunity, *n.* lack of community; absence of common properties or relations.

discompose, *v.t.* to disturb, to destroy the composure of; to agitate, to vex, to disquiet; †to disarrange, to disorder. **discomposedly**, *adv.* **discomposingly,** *adv.* **discomposure**, *n.* want of composure; agitation, perturbation, disquiet; disorder.

disconcert, *v.t.* to derange, to disorder, to throw into confusion, to baffle, to foil, to defeat; to discompose, to disquiet. †**disconcertion,** *n.* **disconcertment,** *n.* [MF *disconcerter*]

disconformity, *n.* a want of conformity or agreement; inconsistency.

discongruity, *n.* a want of congruity.

disconnect, *v.t.* to separate; to disunite, to sever. *a.* separated; incoherent, ill-connected. **disconnectedly,** *adv.* **disconnectedness,** *n.* **disconnecting-pit,** *n.* a pit in which a house-drain is separated from direct discharge into a main sewer. **disconnection, disconnexion,** *n.* the act of disconnecting; the state of being separated, ill-connected or incoherent.

disconsolate, *a.* inconsolable, dejected, cheerless, forlorn; without hope or consolation; that cannot be consoled or comforted; not affording comfort or consolation. **disconsolately,** *adv.* **disconsolateness,** *n.* †**disconsolation,** *n.* [late L *disconsōlātus,* p.p. of *disconsōlārī* (DIS-, *consōlārī,* to CONSOLE)]

discontent, *n.* want of content; dissatisfaction; cause of dissatisfaction, a grievance; (*pl.*) a feeling of dissatisfaction or annoyance; †a discontented person. *a.* not content, dissatisfied. *v.t.* to make discontented, dissatisfied or uneasy. **discontented,** *a.* dissatisfied, uneasy, disquieted. **discontentedly,** *adv.* **discontentedness,** *n.* **discontentment,** *n.*

discontiguous, *a.* not contiguous; having the parts not in contact.

discontinue, *v.t.* to break off, to interrupt; to leave off, to cease to use; to give up. *v.i.* to cease; to lose continuity. **discontinuance,** *n.* interruption in continuance; a break in succession; cessation, interruption, intermission; (*Law*) an interruption or breaking-off of possession. **discontinuance of a suit,** failure on the part of a plaintiff to carry on a suit, by not continuing it as the law requires. †**discontinuation,** *n.* **discontinuous,** *a.* not continuous, disconnected; incoherent; intermittent, †gaping. **discontinuity**, *n.* **discontinuously,** *adv.* [F *discontinuer,* late L *discontinuāre* (DIS-, L *continuāre*)]

discophile, *n.* one who collects gramophone records. [Gr. *philos,* loving]

discord[1]**,** *n.* want of concord or agreement; disagreement, contention, strife; disagreement or opposition in quality, esp. in sounds; a lack of harmony in a combination of notes sounded together; the sounding together of two or more inharmonious or inconclusive notes; the interval or the chord so sounded; a note that is out of harmony with another. †**discordful,** *a.* quarrelsome, contentious. [OF *descord,* from *descorder,* L *discordāre* (DIS-, *cor cordis,* heart)]

discord[2]**,** *v.i.* to be out of harmony (with); to disagree; to be inconsistent, to clash (with). **discordance**, *n.* **discordant**, *a.* disagreeing, not in accord, unpleasing, esp. to the ear; opposite, contradictory; inconsistent; causing discord. **discordantly,** *adv.*

discorporate, *a.* not incorporated, disunited.

discotheque, *n.* a club or public place where people dance to recorded pop music; mobile apparatus for playing records at this. [F, a record library, from Gr. *diskos,* quoit, *thēkē,* case]

discounsel, *v.t.* to dissuade, disadvise.

discount[1]**,** *v.t.* to deduct a certain sum or rate per cent from (an account or price); to lend or advance the amount of; deducting interest at a certain rate per cent from the principal; to leave out of account; to anticipate, to enjoy beforehand; to make allowance for, to make little account of, to disregard. *v.i.* to advance money on bills and other documents due at some future date, deducting the interest at the time of the loan. **discountable**, *a.* [OF *desconter,* late L *discomputāre* (DIS-, L *computāre,* to COMPUTE)]

discount[2]**,** *n.* a deduction from the amount of a price or an account for early or immediate payment; a deduction at a certain rate from money advanced on a bill of exchange which is not yet due; the deduction of a sum for payment in advance; the act of discounting; the rate of discount; allowance for exaggeration. **at a discount,** depreciated; below par; not in much esteem. **discount-broker,** *n.* one who cashes bills of exchange; a bill-broker. **discount-day,** *n.* the day of the week on which the bank discounts bills and notes. **discount house,** *n.* a company engaged in discounting bills of exchange on a large scale. **discount store,** *n.* a shop which sells most of its merchandise at below the recommended price.

discountenance, *v.t.* to discourage; to set one's face against; to express disapprobation of; to put out of countenance, to abash. †*n.* discouragement, disfavour. [MF *descontenancer*]

discourage, *v.t.* to deprive of courage; to dishearten, to dispirit; to discountenance; to deter (from). **discouragement,** *n.* **discourager,** *n.* **discouraging,** *a.* **discouragingly,** *adv.* [OF *descoragier*]

discourse[1]**,** *n.* talk, conversation, exchange of ideas; a dissertation, a lecture or sermon; a formal treatise; †the process of reasoning; †familiar intercourse. †**discourse of reason,** use or exercise of the faculty of reason. [F *discours,* L *discursus,* p.p. of *discurrere* (DIS-, *currere,* to run)]

discourse[2]**,** *v.t.* to utter, to give forth; to pass (time) in conversation; to tell, to narrate; to discuss. *v.i.* to talk, to speak, to converse; to talk formally, to hold forth (upon).

discourteous, *a.* uncourteous, uncivil, rude. **discourteously,** *adv.* **discourteousness,** *n.* **discourtesy,** *n.*

discover, *v.t.* to disclose, to reveal, to make known, to betray; to gain the first sight of; to find out by exploration; to ascertain, to realize suddenly; to detect; †to explore; †to uncover. **discoverable,** *a.* **discoverer,** *n.* one who discovers; †an explorer, †a spy, a scout. [OF *descovrir,* med. L *discooperīre* (DIS-, L *cooperīre,* to COVER)]

discovert, *a.* uncovered, exposed, unprotected; not covert, not protected by a husband, unmarried or widowed. †**at discovert,** uncovered or exposed. **discoverture**, *n.* the state of an unmarried woman or a widow; freedom from coverture. [OF *descovert,* p.p. of prec.]

discovery, *n.* the act of discovering; that which is made known for the first time; something that is found out; revelation; disclosure, manifestation; the unravelling of the plot of a play; (*Law*) compulsory disclosure of facts and documents essential to the proper consideration of a case.

discredit, *n.* want or loss of credit; disrepute, disgrace; the cause of disrepute or disgrace; disbelief; lack of credibility; loss of commercial credit. *v.t.* to disbelieve; to bring into disrepute; to deprive of credibility. **discreditable,** *a.* tending to discredit; disreputable, disgraceful, **discreditably,** *adv.*

discreet, *a.* prudent, wary, cirumspect; judicious, careful in choosing the best means of action; (*Sc.*) polite, well-spoken, decently behaved; †discrete; †needing discretion. **discreetly,** *adv.* **discreetness,** *n.* [F *discret,* L *discrētus,* p.p. of *discernere,* to DISCERN (differentiated from DISCRETE by late L sense, discerning, distinguishing, judicious)]

discrepant, *a.* differing, disagreeing, inconsistent. **discrepancy,** *n.* a difference; a conflict, esp. between two figures or claims. [L *discrepans -antem,* pres.p. of *discrepāre* (DIS-, *crepāre,* to sound)]

discrete, *a.* distinct, discontinuous, detached, separate; (*Mus.*) applied to a movement in which the successive notes vary considerably in pitch; (*Phil.*) not concrete, abstract. **discrete proportion,** *n.* a proportion in which the ratio of the first term to the second=that of the third to the fourth, but does not=that of the second to the third, as, for example, 5:10::9:18. **discreteness,** *n.* **discretive,** *a.* disjunctive, separate. **discretive proposition,** *n.* a proposition in which some opposition or contrariety is noted by the use of a discretive particle. **discretively,** *adv.* [L *discrētus,* see DISCREET]

discretion, *n.* the power or faculty of distinguishing things that differ, or discriminating correctly between what is right and wrong, useful and injurious; discernment, judgment, circumspection; freedom of judgment and action; †separation, distinction. **at discretion,** at the judgment or pleasure (of). **to surrender at discretion,** to surrender unconditionally. **years of discretion,** the age when one is capable of exercising one's own judgment; (*Eng. Law*) the age of 14. †**discretional,** *a.* †**discretionally,** *adv.* **discretionary,** *a.*

discriminate, *v.t.* to distinguish; to mark or observe the difference or distinction between; to distinguish by marks of difference, to differentiate. *v.i.* to make a distinction or difference; to mark the difference between things. *a.*, distinctive; having the difference clearly marked. **to discriminate against,** to distinguish or deal with unfairly or unfavourably. **discriminately,**, *adv.* **discriminating,** *a.* distinguishing clearly, distinctive; exercising discrimination, discerning. **discriminating duties, rates** etc., *n.pl.* such as fall unequally on different parties according to their country, position etc.; differential duties etc. **discriminatingly,** *adv.* **discrimination,** *n.* power or faculty of discriminating; discernment, penetration, judgment; the act of discriminating; a distinguishing mark or feature; unfair treatment of an individual or group of people on the grounds of race, religion, sex or age. **positive discrimination,** discrimination in favour of an individual or group of people previously discriminated against or likely to be discriminated against in areas such as employment. **discriminative**, *a.* serving to distinguish; observing distinctions or differences. †**discriminatively**, *adv.* **discriminator,** *n.* **discriminatory**, *a.* [L *discrīminātus,* p.p. of *discrīmināre* (*discrīmen,* separation, distinction, from *discernere,* to DISCERN)]

discrown, *v.t.* to divest or deprive of a crown; to depose.

disculpate, *v.t.* to exculpate. [L *disculpātus,* p.p. of *disculpāre* (DIS-, *culpāre,* to blame)]

discumber, *v.t.* to disencumber.

discursive, *a.* passing from one subject to another; rambling, desultory; (*Psych., Log.*) rational, argumentative, ratiocinative as opp. to intuitive. **discursively,** *adv.* **discursiveness,** *n.* **discursory,** *a.* [L *discurs-,* p.p. stem of *discurrere,* see DISCOURSE[1]]

discus, *n.* (*pl.* **-cuses, -ci**) (*Class. Ant.*) a metal disk thrown in athletic sports, a quoit; a similar disk, with a thick, heavy middle, thrown in modern sporting contests. [L, from Gr. *diskos*]

discuss, *v.t.* to debate; to consider or examine by argument; (*fig.*) to try the flavour of (as a dish, wine etc.); (*Med.*) to break up, to disperse (as a tumour); (*Sc. Law*) to proceed against by discussion; to put aside, shake off; †to make known. **discussible, -able,** *a.* **discussion**, *n.* the act of discussing; consideration or investigation by argument for and against; the enjoyment of food; (*Med.*) scattering, dispersion; (*Sc. Law*) the proceeding against a principal debtor before proceeding against his surety or sureties, or against an heir for a debt due from his ancestor in respect of the subject inherited before proceeding against the other heirs. **discussion group,** *n.* a group (in school, club etc.) formed to discuss current political and other topics. [L *discussus,* p.p. of *discutere,* to shake asunder, late L, to discuss (DIS-, *quatere,* to shake)]

discutient, *a.* (*Med.*) having power to disperse morbid or abnormal matter. *n.* a discutient preparation.

disdain, *n.* scorn, a feeling of contempt combined with haughtiness and indignation; †shame, disgrace; †that which is worthy of disdain. *v.t.* to regard as unworthy of notice; to despise or repulse as unworthy of oneself; to scorn, to contemn. *v.i.* to feel or manifest scorn. **disdained,** *a.* treated with disdain; †disdainful. **disdainful,** *a.* **disdainfully,** *adv.* †**disdainfulness,** *n.* [OF *desdein,* from *desdaigner* (F *dédaigner*), to scorn, from L *dēdignārī* (DE- *dignārī,* to deem worthy, from *dignus,* worthy)]

dis-ease, *n.* lack of ease, discomfort. †*v.t.* to deprive of ease; †to disturb.

disease, *n.* any alteration of the normal vital processes of man, the lower animals or plants, under the influence of some unnatural or hurtful condition; any disorder or morbid condition, habit or function, mental, moral, social etc. **diseased,** *a.* affected with disease; morbid, unhealthy, deranged. †**diseaseful,** *a.* troublesome; affected with disease. [OF *desaise*]

diseconomy, *n.* something which is uneconomic or unprofitable.

disedify, *v.t.* to shock, to scandalize; to weaken the faith of. **disedification,** *n.*

disembark, *v.t.* to put on shore. *v.i.* to come on shore. **disembarkation,** *n.* [F *désembarquer*]

disembarrass, *v.t.* to free from embarrassment or perplexity; to disencumber (of); to liberate (from). **disembarrassment,** *n.*

disembellish, *v.t.* to divest of ornament.

disembody, *v.t.* to divest of body or the flesh; to free from the concrete; to disband. **disembodiment,** *n.*

disembogue, *v.t.* to pour out or discharge at the mouth, as a stream; to pour forth, to empty itself. †*v.i.* to flow out; to be discharged at an outlet, as at the mouth; †to pass out at the mouth of a river, bay, gulf etc. †**disemboguement**, *n.* [Sp. *desembocar* (*des-*, DIS-, *em-,* IN-, *boca,* the mouth, L *bucca,* cheek, mouth)]

disembosom, *v.t.* to unbosom (oneself); to reveal. *v.i.* to make confidences.

disembowel, *v.t.* to take out the bowels of, to eviscerate; to lacerate so as to let the bowels protrude; †to draw from the bowels (as a spider does its web). **disembowelment,** *n.*

disembroil, *v.t.* to free from confusion or perplexity.

disemburden, *v.t.* to disburden.

disemploy, *v.t.* to cease to employ, to remove from employment. **disemployed,** *a.* **disemployment,** *n.*

disenable, *v.t.* to disable, to incapacitate (from).

disenchain, *v.t.* to set free from restraint.

disenchant, *v.t.* to free from enchantment or glamour, to free from a spell; to disillusion. **disenchanted,** *a.* **disenchanter,** *n.* **disenchantment,** *n.* [F *désenchanter*]

disencumber, *v.t.* to free from encumbrance. **disencumberment,** *n.* **disencumbrance,** *n.* [F *désencombrer*]

disendow, *v.t.* to strip of endowments. **disendowment,** *n.*

disenfranchise, *v.t.* to disfranchise. **disenfranchisement,** *n.*

disengage, *v.t.* to separate; to loosen, to detach; to withdraw (oneself); to release; to disentangle; to set free from any engagement; to pass the point of one's foil to the other side of one's adversary's. *n.* (*Fencing*) the act of disengaging. **disengaged,** *a.* separated, disjoined; at leisure, having the attention unoccupied; free from any engagement. †**disengagedness**, *n.* **disengagement,** *n.* the act of disengaging; extrication; (*Chem.*) liberation of a component; the state of being disengaged; freedom from mental occupation or care; detachment; ease, freedom of manner; dissolution of a matrimonial engagement; (*Fencing*) a disengage.

disenrol, *v.t.* to remove from a roll.

disentail, *v.t.* to free from or break the entail of.

disentangle, *v.t.* to unravel, to free from entanglement; to disengage, to disembarrass. *v.i.* to come clear (from). **disentanglement,** *n.*

disenthral, *v.t.* to set free from thraldom, to emancipate. **disenthralment,** *n.*

disequilibrium, *n.* (*pl.* **-ria**) a lack of balance or equilibrium, esp. in economic affairs.

disestablish, *v.t.* to annul the establishment of, esp. to deprive a Church of its connection with the State; to depose from established use or position. **disestablishment,** *n.*

disesteem, *n.* a lack of esteem or regard. *v.t.* to look upon without esteem; to slight, despise.

diseur, *n.* a reciter. **diseuse**, *n. fem.* [F]

disfame, *n.* ill-fame, dishonour.

disfavour, *n.* a feeling of dislike or disapprobation; disesteem; displeasure, odium; †an ungracious or disobliging act. *v.t.* to treat or regard with disfavour, to discountenance.

disfeature, *v.t.* to deprive of a feature; to deface, disfigure.

disfellowship, *n.* lack of fellowship. *v.t.* (*N Am.*) to exclude from fellowship, esp. of a church.

disfigure, *v.t.* to injure the beauty or appearance of; to deform, to mar, to spoil, to sully. **disfigurement,** *n.* **disfiguration**, *n.* **disfigurer,** *n.* [OF *desfigurer* (*des-*, DIS-, *figurer,* L *figūrāre,* to fashion; from *figūra,* FIGURE]

disforest, *v.t.* to disafforest, to clear of forest. [OF *desforester*]

disform, *v.i.* to alter in form.
disfranchise, *v.t.* to deprive of electoral privileges; to withdraw the rights of citizenship from. **disfranchisement,** *n.*
disfrock, *v.t.* to strip of clerical attire; to depose from the clerical office.
disfurnish, *v.t.* to strip of equipment, apparatus or furniture; to strip, to deprive. [OF *desfourniss-*, stem of *desfournir* (DIS-, *fournir,* to FURNISH)]
disgarnish, *v.t.* to disfurnish, to despoil. [OF *desgarniss-, desgarnir* (DIS-, *garnir,* to GARNISH)]
disgorge, *v.t.* to eject from the mouth or stomach; to vomit; to empty (as a river); (*fig.*) to give up (esp. what has been unjustly acquired). *v.i.* to yield, give up, surrender; to disembogue, to discharge. **disgorgement,** *n.* [OF *desgorger* (DIS-, GORGE)]
disgrace, *n.* the state of being out of favour; disesteem, discredit, ignominy, shame, a fall from honour or favour; infamy; the cause or occasion of discredit or shame; †opprobrium, reprobation, †a loss or lack of grace or of decency. *v.t.* to dismiss from favour; to degrade; to dishonour; to bring disgrace on. **disgraceful,** *a.* shameful, dishonourable. *a.* **disgracefully,** *adv.* **disgracefulness,** *n.* †**disgracious**, *a.* ungracious; out of favour. [F *disgrâce,* It. *disgrazia,* med. L *disgrātia* (DIS-, L *grātia,* GRACE)]
disgruntled, *a.* (*coll.*) disgusted, offended, disappointed, discontented. **disgruntle,** *v.t.* to disappoint. [DIS-, *gruntle,* obs. freq. of GRUNT]
disguise, *v.t.* to conceal or alter the appearance of, with a mask or unusual dress; (*fig.*) to hide by a counterfeit appearance; to alter, to misrepresent; (*sl.*) to intoxicate. *n.* a dress, mask or manner put on to disguise or conceal; a pretence or show; †a masque, an interlude, a mummery; †the state of intoxication. **disguisedly**, *adv.* **disguisement,** *n.* **disguiser,** *n.* one who or that which disguises; a masquer, a mummer. **disguising,** *n.* the act of concealing with or wearing a disguise; †a masque; mummery. [OF *deguisier*]
disgust, *v.t.* to excite loathing or aversion in; to offend the taste of. *n.* a strong disrelish or distaste; aversion, loathing, repulsion. **disgustedly,** *adv.* †**disgustful,** *a.* causing disgust, disgusting; full of or inspired by disgust. **disgusting,** *a.* **disgustingly,** *adv.* [MF *desgouster* (DIS-, L *gustāre,* to taste)]
dish, *n.* a broad, shallow, open vessel for serving up food at table; the food so served; any particular kind of food; †a deep, hollow vessel for liquors; †a cup; any dish-like utensil, receptacle, or concavity; (*Mining*) a box, containing 672 cub. in. (1102 cm^3), for measuring ore; a dish-shaped concave reflector used as a directional aerial for radio or TV transmissions; (*sl.*) an attractive person. *v.t.* to put into or serve in a dish; (*fig.*) to prepare; to make concave; (*coll.*) to foil, to disappoint, to frustrate, *v.i.* to assume a concave form. †**dish of tea,** a tea-drinking; whence, **dish of gossip,** a chat; tittle tattle. **made dish,** a dish compounded of various ingredients. **side-dish,** an extra dish at a meal, such as a salad. **standing dish,** a dish that is brought in day after day; a familiar topic, grievance etc. **to dish out,** to distribute freely. **to dish up,** to serve up; to present in an attractive or new way. **dish-cloth, -clout,** *n.* one used for washing up dishes, plates etc. **dish-cover,** *n.* a cover of metal or earthenware for keeping food warm in a dish. **dish-mat,** *n.* a mat on which dishes are placed. **dish-pan,** *n.* (*N Am.*) a washing-up bowl. **dish-towel,** *n.* a tea-cloth. **dish-wash, -water,** *n.* water in which dishes have been washed. **dishwasher,** *n.* the pied wagtail, *Montacilla lugubris;* a machine for washing dishes and cutlery. **dished,** *a.* concave. **dished wheel,** *n.* one that has been made concave, the spokes slanting outward from the nave. **dishful,** *n.* the amount in a dish. **dishy,** *a.* (*sl.*) good-looking. [OE *disc,* L *discus,* DISK]
dishabille DESHABILLE.
dishabit, *v.t.* to move from its place; to expel from a habitation.
dishabituate, *v.t.* to make unaccustomed (to).
dishallow, *v.t.* to make unholy; to profane.
dishallucination, *n.* release from hallucination; disillusion.
disharmony, *n.* lack of harmony; discord, incongruity. **disharmonious**, *a.* **disharmonize, ise,** *v.t., v.i.*
dishearten, *v.t.* to discourage, to dispirit. **disheartening,** *a.* **dishearteningly,** *adv.* **disheartenment,** *n.*
disherit, *v.t.* to disinherit; to dispossess. †**disherison**, *n.* the act of disinheriting. [OF *desheriter* (*des-,* DIS-, *heriter,* L *hērēditāre,* to inherit, from *hērēditās,* heirship)]
dishevel, *v.t.* to disorder (the hair); to let (the hair) down. *v.i.* to be spread in disorder. **dishevelled,** *a.* flowing in disorder; hanging loosely and negligently; with disordered hair; untidy, unkempt. **dishevelment,** *n.* [OF *descheveler* (*des-,* DIS-, *chevel,* L *capillus,* hair)]
dishonest, *a.* destitute of honesty, probity or good faith; fraudulent, deceitful, insincere, untrustworthy; †dishonourable, disgraced; disgraceful; †unchaste, lewd. **dishonestly,** *adv.* **dishonesty,** *n.* want of honesty or uprightness; fraud, cheating, violation of duty or trust; †disgrace, dishonour; †unchastity, lewdness. [OF *deshoneste,* L *dehonestus* (DE-, *honestus,* HONEST)]
dishonour, *n.* lack of honour; disgrace, discredit, ignominy; reproach, disparagement; the cause of this; refusal to honour a cheque etc. *v.i.* to bring disgrace or shame on; to damage the reputation of; to treat with indignity; to violate the chastity of; to refuse to accept or pay (as a bill or draft). **dishonourable,** *a.* causing dishonour; disgraceful, ignominious; unprincipled, mean, base; destitute of honour. **dishonourableness,** *n.* **dishonourably,** *adv.* **dishonourer,** *n.* one who dishonours; a debaucher. [OF *deshonneur* (DIS-, L *honor -ōrem,* HONOUR)]
dishorn, *v.t.* to deprive of horns.
dishorse, *v.t.* to unhorse.
dishwasher, dishy DISH.
disilluminate, *v.t.* to deprive of light; to obscure.
disillusion, *v.t.* to free or deliver from an illusion; to undeceive. *n.* disenchantment; release from an illusion. **disillusioned,** *a.* freed from deception or illusion. **disillusionize, -ise,** *v.t.* **disillusionment,** *n.*
disimpassioned, *a.* dispassionate; tranquillized.
disimprison, *v.t.* to release from captivity; to liberate.
disincentive, *n.* that which discourages. *a.* discouraging.
disincline, *v.t.* to make averse or indisposed (to). **disinclination**, *n.* a want of inclination, desire or propensity; unwillingness.
disincorporate, *v.t.* to deprive of the rights, powers or privileges of a corporate body; to dissolve (such a body). **disincorporation,** *n.*
disindividualize, -ise, *v.t.* to take away the individuality of.
disinfect, *v.t.* to free or cleanse from infection, often by chemical means. **disinfectant,** *n.* that which removes infection by destroying its causes. **disinfection**, *n.* **disinfector,** *n.*
disinfest, *v.t.* to rid of vermin, rats and insects, esp. lice. **disinfestation,** *n.*
disinflation, *n.* a return to normal economic conditions after inflation, without a reduction in production. **disinflationary,** *a.*
disinformation, *n.* the deliberate propagation or leaking of misleading information.
disingenuous, *a.* not ingenuous; wanting in frankness, openness or candour; underhand, insincere. **disingenuously,** *adv.* **disingenuousness,** *n.*
disinherit, *v.i.* to cut off from a hereditary right; to deprive of an inheritance; (*fig.*) to dispossess. †**disinherison,** *n.* **disinheritance,** *n.*
disinhume, *v.t.* to exhume, to disinter.
disintegrate, *v.t.* to separate into component parts; to reduce to fragments or powder. *v.i.* to fall to pieces, to crumble, to lose cohesion. **disintegrable,** *a.* **disintegration,** *n.* the separation of a solid body into its component parts; the wearing down of rocks by the action of the weather. **disintegrator,** *n.* one who or that which causes disintegration; a machine for grinding bones etc.

disinter, *v.t.* to dig up, esp. from a grave; (*fig.*) to unearth. **disinterment,** *n.* [F *désenterrer*]

disinterest, *n.* impartiality, disinterestedness; †disadvantage, prejudice. *v.t.* †to divest of personal interest, to make disinterested. **disinterested,** *a.* without personal interest or prejudice; unbiased, impartial, unselfish; (*loosely*) uninterested. **disinterestedly,** *adv.* **disinterestedness,** *n.*

disinvestment, *n.* a reduction or cessation of investment, esp. in a country generally disapproved of, as a form of sanction.

disinvolve, *v.t.* to disentangle; to remove from involvement.

disjasked, *a.* (*Sc.*) broken-down, worn-out; jaded. [prob. corr. of DEJECTED]

disjoin, *v.t.* to separate, to put asunder. †*v.i.* to be separated, to part. **disjoinable,** *a.* [OF *desjoign-, desjoindre,* L *disjungere* (DIS-, *jungere,* to JOIN)]

disjoint, *v.t.* to put out of joint, to dislocate; to separate at the joints; (*fig.*) to derange, to put out of working order; to break the connection of. †*v.i.* to fall in pieces. *a.* disjointed, disconnected, out of order. **disjointed,** *a.* out of joint; broken up, incoherent. **disjointedly,** *adv.* **disjointedness,** *n.* [OF *desjoint,* p.p. of *desjoindre,* as prec.]

disjunction, *n.* the act of disjoining; separation; (*Log.*) a disjunctive proposition. **disjunct,** *a.* disjoined (in various technical applications). **disjunctive,** *a.* separating, disjoining; marking separation. *n.* (*Log.*) a disjunctive proposition. **disjunctive conjunction,** *n.* a conjunction (*as or, but, though* etc.), which unites sentences or clauses in composition, but divides them in sense. **disjunctive proposition,** *n.* (*Log.*) with alternate predicates united by the conj. *or.* **disjunctive syllogism,** *n.* (*Log.*) in which the major is a disjunctive proposition. **disjunctively,** *adv.* [L *disjunctio,* from *disjungere,* as prec.]

†**disjune,** *n.* (*Sc.*) breakfast. [OF *desjun,* F *déjeuner*]

disk, disc, *n.* a flat circular plate or surface; a gramophone record; (*Astron.*) the face of a celestial body, any round, luminous and apparently flat object; the central part of a radiate compound flower; a round flattish part of an animal organism; a layer of fibrocartilage between vertebrae; (*Comput.*) a small, circular piece of plastic in a rigid case, coated with a magnetic oxide substance, used for storing information and software. **floppy disk,** a computer disk made of flexible plastic, used in microcomputers. **parking disk,** one displayed in a parked vehicle to show the time of arrival or the latest time of departure. **slipped disk,** a displacement of one of the disks between the vertebrae. **disk brake,** *n.* one consisting of a metal disk attached to the axle, on the opposite surfaces of which the pads press. **disk drive,** *n.* the electromechanical device in a computer which reads information from, and writes it on to, the disk. **disk file, store,** *n.* a random-access device in which information is stored, in tracks, on magnetic disks. **disk flower, floret,** *n.* one of the tubular inner flowers in a composite flower. **disk harrow,** *n.* one consisting of sharpened saucer-shaped disks for cutting clods of soil. **disk jockey,** *n.* (*Radio*) the compere of a programme of popular recorded music. **disk scanner,** *n.* (*TV*) a rotating disk carrying the picture-scanning elements. **diskette**, *n.* another name for a computer disk. [L *discus,* Gr. *diskos*]

diskinesia, *n.* abnormal, involuntary nervous muscular movement.

disleal, *a.* disloyal. [prob. from It. *disleale* (DIS-, LEAL)]

dislike, *v.t.* to regard with repugnance or aversion; †to displease; †to express aversion towards. *n.* a feeling of repugnance; aversion. **dislikable, dislikeable,** *a.* †**dislikeful,** *a.* disagreeable, unpleasant. **disliker,** *n.* **disliking,** *n., a.*

disload, *v.t., v.i.* to unload.

dislocate, *v.t.* to put out of joint; to disturb, derange; to break the continuity of (strata), to displace. **dislocation,** *n.* [late L *dislocātus,* p.p. of *dislocāre* (*locāre,* to place, from *locus,* place)]

dislodge, *v.t.* to eject from a place of rest, retirement or defence; to drive out, to expel. *v.i.* to quit a place, to remove. **dislodgement,** *n.* [OF *desloger*]

disloyal, *a.* not true to allegiance; unfaithful to the sovereign, disaffected towards the government. **disloyally,** *adv.* **disloyalty,** *n.* [OF *desloial*]

dismal, *a.* dark, cheerless, depressing, doleful, dreary; †unlucky, unpropitious, sinister, bodeful, disastrous. *n.pl.* low spirits, the blues. **the dismal science,** political economy of the old-fashioned deductive kind. **dismally,** *adv.* **dismalness,** *n.* [OF *dis mal,* L *diēs mali,* evil days, unlucky days]

disman, *v.t.* to unman; to divest of men.

dismantle, *v.t.* to strip of covering, equipment or means of defence; to take to pieces; to unrig (as a ship); to remove the defences (of a fortress). **dismantlement,** *n.* [MF *desmanteller*]

dismask, *v.t.* to unmask. [OF *desmasquer*]

dismast, *v.t.* to deprive a ship of a mast or masts.

dismay, *v.t.* to deprive of courage; to dispirit; to terrify, to daunt; †to vanquish. †*v.i.* to be dismayed. *n.* utter loss of courage or resolution; a state of terror or affright; †ruin, destruction. **dismayful,** *a.* **dismayfully,** *adv.* [prob. OF *des-,* DIS-, *mayer,* OHG *magan,* to be able, to have power, cogn. with OE *magan,* MAY[1] (cp. *esmayer,* to lose power, to faint, also Sp. *desmayer,* to DISMAY)]

dismayd, *a.* misshapen, deformed (?). [perh. DIS-, MADE]

dismember, *v.t.* to separate limb from limb; to divide, to distribute, to partition; (*fig.*) to tear asunder. **dismemberment,** *n.* [OF *desmembrer*]

dismiss, *v.t.* to send away; to dissolve, disband; to allow to depart; to discharge from office or employment; to put aside, reject; to cast off, discard; to pass on to something else; (*Law*) to discharge from further consideration; (*Mil., imper.*) break ranks! disperse! **dismissal,** *n.* **dismissible,** *a.* †**dismission,** *n.* †**dismissive,** *a.* [L *dīmittere* (DI-, *mittere,* to send), *dis-*, due to influence of OF *desmettre* (p.p. *dismit*)]

dismount, *v.i.* to alight from a horse; †to descend. *v.t.* to throw down or remove from a carriage or support (as cannon); to unhorse; to take down or to pieces; †to get down from: †to bring down, to lower; †to withdraw a sheathed sword from its frog. *n.* the act of dismounting, the mode of dismounting. [prob. from OF *desmonter*]

disnature, *v.t.* to render unnatural; to divest of essential nature. **disnaturalize, -ise,** *v.t.* to denaturalize. [OF *desnaturer*]

Disney, *n.* **'Walt' (Walter Elias)** (1901–66), US film-maker, who became a pioneer of family entertainment. He established his own studio in Hollywood in 1923, and his first Mickey Mouse cartoon *Plane Crazy* appeared in 1928. He developed the 'Silly Symphony', a type of cartoon based on the close association of music with the visual image, such as *Fantasia* (1940). His many feature-length cartoons include *Snow White and the Seven Dwarfs* (1938), *Pinocchio* (1940) and *Dumbo* (1941).

Disneyesque, *a.* pertaining to the type of cartoon film or character created by Walt Disney; pertaining to fantasy, whimsical.

disobedience, *n.* refusal to obey; wilful neglect or violation of duty; non-compliance. **disobedient,** *a.* refusing or neglecting to obey; refractory. **disobediently,** *adv.* [OF *desobedience*]

disobey, *v.t.* to neglect or refuse to obey; to violate, transgress. *v.i.* to be disobedient. **disobeyer,** *n.* [F *désobéir*]

disoblige, *v.t.* to act in a way contrary to the wishes or convenience of; to inconvenience, to incommode; †to release from an obligation. †**disobligation**, *n.* a disobliging act; freedom from obligation. †**disobligement,** *n.* the act of disobliging; the state of being released from an obligation. **disobliging,** *a.* not obliging, not disposed to gratify the wishes of another; churlish, ungracious. **disobligingly,** *adv.* **disobligingness,** *n.* [F *désobliger*]

disorb, *v.t.* †to unsphere, to remove from its orbit; to deprive of the orb of sovereignty.

disorder, *n.* want of order; confusion, irregularity; tumult, commotion; neglect or infraction of laws or discipline; discomposure of mind; disease, illness. *v.t.* to throw into confusion; to derange the natural functions of. **disorderly,** *a.* confused, disarranged; unlawful, irregular; turbulent, causing disturbance, unruly. **disorderly conduct,** *n.* public misconduct leading to distress or harassment. **disorderly house,** *n.* (*Law*) a term including brothels, gaming-houses, betting-houses and certain unlicensed places of entertainment. **disorderliness,** *n.* †**disordinate**, *a.* inordinate, excessive; disorderly, irregular, vicious. †**disordinately,** *adv.* [F *désordre*]

disorganize, -ise, *v.t.* to throw into confusion; to destroy the systematic arrangement of. **disorganization, -isation,** *n.* **disorganized, -ised,** *a.* lacking order, confused. [F *désorganiser*]

disorient, *v.t.* to turn from the east; to throw out of one's reckoning; to confuse. **disorientate,** *v.t.* to disorient; to place (a church) with the chancel not pointing due east. **disorientation,** *n.* [F *désorienter* (DIS-, *orienter,* to ORIENT)]

disown, *v.t.* to refuse to own; to disclaim, to renounce, to repudiate. **disownment,** *n.*

disoxygenate DEOXYGENATE.

dispace, *v.i.* (*Spens.*) to wander to and fro. [etym. doubtful]

disparage, *v.t.* to think lightly of, to undervalue; to treat or speak of slightingly; to depreciate; to injure by unjust comparison. **disparagement,** *n.* the act of disparaging; depreciation, detraction; diminution of value or excellence; †an unequal marriage, the disgrace due to this. **disparagingly,** *adv.* [OF *desparagier* (*parage,* lineage, rank, late L *parāgium,* from *par,* equal)]

disparate, *a.* dissimilar, discordant; incommensurable; having nothing in common, not coordinate. *n.* (*usu. pl.*) things so unlike that they admit of no comparison with each other. **disparately,** *adv.* **disparateness,** *n.* [L *disparātus,* p.p. of *disparāre* (DIS-, *parāre,* to make ready), assimilated in sense to *dispar,* unequal]

disparity, *n.* inequality; difference in degree; unlikeness. [F *disparité*]

dispark, *v.t.* to throw open parkland; to employ it for other purposes.

dispart[1], *v.t.* to part; to separate, to dissolve; to divide, to distribute. *v.i.* to separate. [L *dispartīre,* to distribute]

dispart[2], *n.* the difference between the external semi-diameter of a gun at the muzzle and at the breech. **dispartsight,** *n.* a sight allowing for the dispart, and bringing the line of sight parallel to the axis. [etym. doubtful]

dispassionate, *a.* free from passion; calm, temperate; impartial. **dispassion,** *n.* **dispassionately,** *adv.*

dispatch, despatch, *v.t.* to send off to some destination, esp. to send with celerity and haste; to transact quickly; to settle, to finish; to put to death; †to deliver (from), to relieve (of); †to deprive; †to get rid of. *v.i.* †to conclude an affair with another; to go quickly, to hurry; to hasten. *n.* the act of dispatching or being dispatched; prompt execution; promptitude, celerity, quickness, expedition; a message or letter dispatched, esp. an official communication on state affairs; a putting to death; †dismissal, deliverance, riddance; †management, care; †transaction of business. **mentioned in dispatches,** cited for bravery or valuable services. **dispatch box,** *n.* one for carrying dispatches and other state papers. **dispatch case,** *n.* (*Mil.*) a leather case for carrying papers. **dispatch-rider,** *n.* a motor-cyclist who carries dispatches. **dispatcher,** *n.* **dispatchful,** *a.* [Sp. *despachar* (DIS-, late L *pactāre,* to make an agreement, from L *pactum,* an agreement, neut. p.p. of *pangere,* to fasten)]

dispauper, *v.t.* to deprive of public support as a pauper; to deprive of the privilege of suing *in forma pauperis*. **dispauperize, -ise,** *v.t.* to relieve (a community) of paupers; to free from pauperism.

dispel, *v.t.* to dissipate, to disperse; to drive away, to banish. **dispeller,** *n.* [L *dispellere* (DIS-, *pellere,* to drive)]

dispensable, *a.* (*Eccles.*) for which a dispensation may be granted, pardonable; that may be dispensed with, inessential. **dispensability**, *n.*

dispensary, *n.* a place where medicines are dispensed; an establishment where medicines and medical advice are given gratis to the poor. **dispensatory,** *a.* granting dispensation. *n.* a book listing medical prescriptions, their composition and use. [see DISPENSE]

dispensation, *n.* the act of dispensing; distribution; (*fig.*) scheme, plan, economy; the government of the universe; the management of the world by Providence; God's dealings with man, esp. the divine relation to man at a particular period (as the Mosaic dispensation); a system of principles, rights and privileges enjoined; in the Roman Catholic Church, a licence to omit or commit something enjoined or forbidden by canon law; the act of dispensing with or doing without; †management, administration. **dispensational,** *a.* [L *dispensātio,* as foll.]

dispense, *v.t.* to deal out, to distribute; to administer, to prepare and give out medicine; to grant a dispensation to; to grant exemption (from). *v.i.* to dispense medicines; †to make amends. **to dispense with,** to forgo, to do without; to render unnecessary; to suspend, to waive the observance of; †to set aside, disregard; to excuse, condone. †*n.* the act of dispensing or spending; a dispensation. **dispenser,** *n.* one who or that which dispenses; (*Med.*) one who dispenses medicines; †a steward. **dispensing optician** OPTICIAN. **dispensing-power,** *n.* the power claimed by the Stuart kings to dispense with or suspend the operation of any law. [OF *dispenser,* L *dispensāre,* freq. of *dispendere* (DIS- *pendere,* to weigh)]

dispeople, *v.t.* to depopulate.

dispermatous, dispermous, *a.* (*Bot.*) having only two seeds. [DI-[2], Gr. *sperma -atos,* seed]

disperse, *v.t.* to scatter; to send, drive or throw in different directions; to dissipate, to cause to vanish; to distribute, to diffuse; to disseminate; (*Opt.*) to distribute with its component colours; †to publish; to put (particles) into a colloidal state, to distribute evenly in a fluid. *v.i.* to be scattered abroad; to break up, to vanish; to become spread abroad. **dispersal,** *n.* dispersion; the spreading of animals or plants to new areas. **dispersedly**, *adv.* **dispersive,** *a.* **dispersively,** *adv.* **dispersiveness,** *n.* [F *disperser,* from L *dispersus,* p.p. of *dispergere* (DIS-, *spargere,* to scatter)]

dispersion, *n.* the act of dispersing; the state of being dispersed; the removal of inflammation from a part; (*Statistics*) the scattering of variables around the arithmetic mean or median. **the Dispersion,** (*Hist.*) the scattering of the tribes of Israel, esp. the Babylonian captivity. **dispersion of heat, light, etc.,** (*Opt.*) the separation produced by the refraction at different angles of rays of different wavelengths. [L *dispersio,* as prec.]

dispirit, *v.t.* to deprive of spirit or courage; to discourage, to dishearten, to deject. **dispirited,** *a.* **dispiritedly,** *adv.* in a dispirited manner. **dispiritedness,** *n.* **dispiriting,** *a.* **dispiritingly,** *adv.* †**dispiritment,** *n.*

dispiteous, *a.* pitiless. **dispiteously,** *adv.* **dispiteousness,** *n.*

displace, *v.t.* to remove from the usual or proper place; to remove from a position or dignity; to dismiss; to take the place of, to put something in the place of, to supersede; †to banish. **displaced persons,** *n.pl.* refugees who for any reason cannot be repatriated. **displacement,** *n.* the act of displacing; the state of being displaced; removal by supersession; change of position; supersession by something else; the water displaced by a floating body (as a ship), the weight of which equals that of the floating body at rest; (*Phys.*) the amount by which anything is displaced; (*Meteor.*) alteration of the zero in a thermometer; the movement of electricity in a dielectric acted upon by an electric force; (*Geol.*) a fault; (*Psych.*) the unconscious transferring of strong emotions from the original object to another.

displant, *v.t.* to pluck up; to remove (as plants, trees etc.); to displace; to strip of inhabitants. †**displantation,** *n.* [OF *desplanter*]

display, *v.t.* to exhibit, to expose, to show; to exhibit ostentatiously, to parade; to make known, to unfold, to reveal; to make prominent; †to discover. †*v.i.* to make a show, to parade. *n.* displaying, show, exhibition; ostentatious parade; setting in prominent type. [OF *despleier* (DIS-, *pleier,* L *plicāre,* to fold)]

displease, *v.t.* to dissatisfy, to offend; to vex, to annoy; to be disagreeable to. *v.i.* to cause displeasure or offence. **to be displeased at, with,** to be annoyed or vexed (at or with); to disapprove. †**displeaser,** *n.* one who displeases. **displeasing,** *a.* **displeasingly,** *adv.* †**displeasance,** *n.* displeasure, vexation. [OF *desplaisir*]

displeasure, *n.* a feeling of annoyance, vexation, irritation or anger; a state of disgrace or disfavour; †injury, offence. †*v.t.* to displease, to annoy. [OF *desplaisir,* as prec. (assim. to PLEASURE)]

displume, *v.t.* to strip of plumes, feathers or decorations.

dispone, *v.t.* †to dispose, or dispose of; (*Sc. Law*) to make over or convey (as property). **disponee,** *n.* (*Sc. Law*) one to whom property is disponed. **disponer,** *n.* (*Sc. Law*) one who dispones property. [L *dispōnere* (DIS-, *pōnere,* to place)]

disport, *v.t.* to amuse, to divert (one-self); to enjoy (oneself); to display, to sport; †to remove, to carry away. *v.i.* to play, to amuse or divert oneself; to gambol. *n.* sport, play, diversion, relaxation. [OF *desporter* (*des-,* DIS-, *porter,* L *portāre,* to carry)]

disposal, *n.* the act of disposing; distributing, bestowing, giving away or dealing with things in some particular way; disposition; sale or assignment; control, management, command; order or arrangement in which things are disposed. **at the disposal of,** in the power of, at the command of. [as foll.]

dispose, *v.t.* to arrange, to set in order; to place; to settle; to adjust, to direct, to incline; to regulate, to fix, to determine; †to control, to manage; †to hand over, to bestow. **to dispose of,** to apply to any purpose; to put into the hands of another; to get rid of; to sell, to alienate; to finish, to settle, to kill; to use up; to dismiss, to put away, to stow away. *v.i.* to determine or arrange affairs; †to come to terms. †*n.* disposal, control; disposition, turn of mind; inclination, behaviour. **disposable,** *a.* capable of being disposed of; applied to anything designed for disposal after use, as *disposable plates*. *n.* any item intended for disposal after use. **disposable income,** *n.* net income after payment of tax, available for use. **disposed,** *a.* inclined (towards). **well, ill, disposed towards,** viewing with favour, disfavour. **disposedness,** *n.* disposition, inclination. **disposer,** *n.* **disposure,** *n.* disposition; disposal. [OF *disposer* (DIS-, *poser,* L *pausāre,* to cease, to POSE[1], substituted for *pōnere,* to place)]

disposition, *n.* the act of disposing, ordering, arranging or bestowing; disposal; the state or manner of disposal; arrangement in general; fitness, aptitude; inclination, temperament, propensity, bent, natural tendency; a humour, caprice, fancy; (*Arch.*) the arrangement of the whole design of a building; (*Painting*) composition in regard to general effect; (*Sc. Law*) the disposal of property; any unilateral writing by which a person makes over to another a piece of heritable or movable property; (*usu. pl.*) arrangement, plan, preparation; the posting of troops in the most advantageous position. **dispositional,** *a.* **dispositioned,** *a.* [F, from L *dispositio -ōnem,* from *dispositus,* p.p. of *dispōnere* (DIS-, *pōnere,* to place)]

dispossess, *v.t.* to oust from possession, esp. of real estate; to disseize, to eject, to dislodge; to deprive; to rid; to exorcise. **dispossession,** *n.* †**dispossessor,** *n.* [OF *despossesser*]

dispraise, *v.t.* to censure, to express disapprobation of. *n.* blame, disapprobation, disparagement. †**dispraiser,** *n.* †**dispraisingly,** *adv.* [OF *despreisier,* L *dēpretiāre,* to DEPRECIATE]

†**dispread,** *v.t.* to spread in different directions. *v.i.* to be spread out. [DIS-, SPREAD]

disproof, *n.* refutation; proof of error or falsehood.

disproportion, *n.* want of proportion between things or parts; inadequacy, disparity; lack of symmetry. *v.t.* to make out of proportion; to spoil the symmetry of, disfigure, deform; †to make inconsistent. †**disproportionably,** *adv.* †**disproportional,** *a.* disproportionate. †**disproportionality,** *n.* †**disproportionally,** *adv.* **disproportionate,** *a.* not duly proportioned; unsymmetrical; too large or too small in relation to something. **disproportionately,** *adv.* †**disproportionateness,** *n.*

disprove, *v.t.* to prove to be erroneous or unfounded; to refute; †to disapprove. **disprovable,** *a.* **disproval,** *n.* [OF *desprover*]

†**dispurse,** *v.t.* to disburse, to pay.

dispute, *v.i.* to contend in argument; to argue in opposition to another; to quarrel, to wrangle; to strive against another, to compete; †to debate, to discuss. *v.t.* to contend about in argument; to oppose, to question, to challenge or deny the truth of; to reason upon, to discuss, to argue; to contend or strive for, to contest; †to strive against, to resist. *n.* contention or strife in argument; debate, controversy; a difference of opinion; a falling out, a quarrel; contest, strife, struggle; the possibility of being disputed. **disputable,** *a.* open to dispute, controvertible; questionable, uncertain; †given to argument or controversy; disputatious. **disputability,** *n.* **disputableness,** *n.* **disputably,** *adv.* **disputant,** *a.* engaged in disputation or controversy. *n.* one who disputes; one who engages in controversy. **disputation,** *n.* the act of disputing; controversy, discussion; an exercise in arguing both sides of a question for the sake of practice; †conversation. **disputatious,** *a.* given to dispute or controversy; cavilling, contentious. **disputatiously,** *adv.* **disputatiousness,** *n.* †**disputative,** *a.* inclined to argument. **disputer,** *n.* [OF *desputer,* L *disputāre* (DIS-, *putāre,* to think)]

disqualify, *v.t.* to render unfit, to disable, to debar; to render or declare legally incompetent for any act or post; to disbar from a sporting competition on account of an irregularity. **disqualification,** *n.* the act of disqualifying; that which disqualifies.

disquiet, *v.t.* to disturb, to make uneasy, to harass, to vex, to fret. *a.* †uneasy, disquieted, restless. *n.* want of quiet or peace; uneasiness, restlessness, anxiety. **disquieting,** *a.* **disquietingly,** *adv.* **disquietness,** *n.* **disquietous,** *a.* **disquietude,** *n.* the state of being disquieted; anxiety, uneasiness.

disquisition, *n.* a formal and systematic inquiry into, an investigation; a formal discourse or treatise. **disquisitional,** *a.* **disquisitive,** *a.* disquisitional; fond of inquiry; inquisitive. [L *disquīsītio,* from *disquīsitus,* p.p. of *disquīrere* (DIS-, *quaerere,* to seek)]

Disraeli, *n.* **Benjamin, Earl of Beaconsfield** (1804–81), British Conservative politician and novelist. He was chancellor of the Exchequer under Lord Derby (1852, 1858–59 and 1866–68), and prime minister (1868 and 1874–80). His imperialist policies brought India directly under the crown and he personally purchased control of the Suez Canal. The central Conservative Party organization is his creation. His popular, political novels reflect an interest in social reform and include *Coningsby* (1844) and *Sybil* (1845).

disrate, *v.t.* (*Naut.*) to degrade or reduce in rating or rank.

disregard, *n.* want or omission of attention or regard; slight, neglect. *v.t.* to take no notice of; to neglect; to ignore as unworthy of regard. **disregarder,** *n.* **disregardful,** *a.* negligent, careless, heedless, regardless. **disregardfully,** *adv.*

disrelish, *n.* a distaste or dislike; aversion, antipathy. *v.t.* to dislike the taste of; to make unpleasant or nauseous; to feel dislike of or aversion to.

disremember, *v.t.* (*dial., coll.*) to be unable to remember; to forget.

disrepair, *n.* a state of being out of repair; dilapidation.

disreputable, *a.* not reputable; of bad repute, not respectable; discreditable, mean. **disreputableness,** *n.* **disreputably,** *adv.* †**disreputation,** *n.* disgrace, dishonour, discredit. **disrepute,** *n.* a loss or want of reputation; discredit.

disrespect, *n.* want of respect or reverence; rudeness, incivility; an act of rudeness. †*v.t.* to treat with disrespect. †**disrespectable,** *a.* not respectable. **disrespectful,** *a.* wanting in respect; uncivil, rude. **disrespectfully,** *adv.* **disrespectfulness,** *n.*

disrobe, *v.t.* to strip of a robe or dress; to undress (oneself). *v.i.* to undress. **disrober,** *n.*

disroot, *v.t.* to tear up by the roots; to tear from the foundations.

disrupt, *v.t.* to tear asunder, to break in pieces; to interrupt. *a.* disrupted. **disruption,** *n.* the act of tearing or bursting asunder; the state of being torn asunder; breach, rent, split; (*Hist.*) the great secession from the Established Church of Scotland in 1843. **disruptive,** *a.* tending to cause disruption. **disrupture,** *v.t.* to tear or rend asunder. *n.* disruption. [L *disruptio,* from *disruptus,* p.p. of *disrumpere* (DIS-, *rumpere,* to break)]

diss, dis, *v.t.* (*sl.*) to dismiss or reject; to put down; to insult. [DIS-]

diss., (*abbr.*) dissertation.

dissatisfy, *v.t.* to fall short of the expectations of; to make discontented, to displease. **dissatisfaction,** *n.* **dissatisfactory,** *a.*

disseat, *v.t.* to remove from a seat.

dissect, *v.t.* to cut in pieces; to anatomize; to cut up (an organism) so as to examine the parts and structure; to analyse, to criticize in detail; to apportion the items of (an invoice etc.) to different departments. **dissected,** *a.* (*Bot.*) cut into narrow segments; (*Geol.*) applied to hills and valleys cut by erosion. **dissectible,** *a.* **dissecting-clerk,** *n.* a clerk employed to dissect invoices etc. **dissecting microscope,** *n.* one allowing dissection of the object being examined. **dissecting room, table,** *n.* a room or table where dissection is carried out. **dissection,** *n.* **dissector,** *n.* [L *dissectus,* p.p. of *dissecāre* (DIS-, *secāre,* to cut)]

disseise, *v.t.* to deprive of possession (of estates etc.); to dispossess wrongfully. **disseisee,** *n.* one who is deprived unlawfully of the possession of an estate. **disseisin,** *n.* unlawful dispossession. **disseisor,** *n.* [A-F *disseiser,* OF *dessaisir*]

dissemble, *v.t.* to hide under a false appearance; †to disguise; to pretend, to feign, to simulate; †to ignore, to shut the eyes. *v.i.* to give a false appearance to, to cloak, to conceal; to hide one's feelings, opinions or intentions; to play the hypocrite. †**dissemblance,** *n.* the act of dissembling; unlikeness, dissimilarity. **dissembler,** *n.* **dissemblingly,** *adv.* [OF *dissimuler,* L *dissimulāre* (DIS-, *simulāre,* to simulate), assim. to RESEMBLE]

disseminate, *v.t.* to scatter abroad, as seed, with a view to growth or propagation; to diffuse, to circulate. †*v.i.* to spread; to be dispersed. **disseminated,** *a.* **disseminated sclerosis,** *n.* another name for MULTIPLE SCLEROSIS. **dissemination,** *n.* **disseminator,** *n.* [L *dissēminātus,* p.p. of *dissēmināre* (DIS-, *sēmināre,* to sow, from *sēmen,* seed)]

dissension, *n.* disagreement of opinion; discord, contention, strife. †**dissensious,** †**-tious,** *a.* [F, from L *dissentio -ōnem,* as foll.]

dissent, *v.i.* to differ or disagree in opinion; to hold opposite views; to withhold assent or approval; to differ from an established Church, esp. from the Church of England. *n.* difference or disagreement of opinion; refusal of assent; a declaration of disagreement or nonconformity; the principles of Dissenters from the established Church; Dissenters collectively; a protest by a minority. †**dissentaneous,** *a.* disagreeing, discordant. **dissenter,** *n.* one who dissents or disagrees, esp. one who dissents from an established Church; (**Dissenter**) a member of a sect that has separated from the Church of England. †**dissenterism,** *n.* [L *dissentīre* (DIS-, *sentīre,* to feel)]

dissentient, *a.* disagreeing or differing in opinion; holding or expressing contrary views. *n.* one who holds or expresses contrary views; a dissenter from the views of a political or other party. **Dissentient Liberals,** *n.pl.* a name formerly applied to Liberal Unionists. **dissentience, -tiency,** *n.* [L *dissentiens -entem,* pres.p. of *dissentīre,* as prec.]

dissepiment, *n.* (*Bot., Zool.*) a division or partition in an organ or part. [L *dissaepīmentum, dissaepīre* (DIS-, *saepīre,* to hedge off, from *saepēs,* a hedge)]

dissert, †**dissertate,** *v.i.* to discourse in a formal manner; to write a dissertation. **dissertation,** *n.* a formal discourse on any subject; a disquisition, treatise or essay. †**dissertational,** *a.* †**dissertationist,** *n.* [L *dissertus,* p.p. and *dissertāre,* freq. of *disserere* (DIS-, *serere,* to join)]

disserve, *v.t.* to do a disservice to; to injure. **disservice,** *n.* an injury, detriment or ill service.

dissever, *v.t.* to sever, to separate. †**disseverance,** †**disseveration,** *n.* disseverment. **disseverment,** *n.*

dissident, *a.* not in agreement; disagreeing, dissenting. *n.* one who dissents from or votes against any motion; one who disagrees with the government; a dissenter. **dissidence,** *n.* [L *dissidens -entem,* pres.p. of *dissidēre* (DIS-, *sedēre,* to sit)]

dissilient, *a.* (*Bot.*) jerking apart; separating with force and elasticity. **dissilience,** *n.* [L *dissiliens -entem,* pres.p. of *dissilīre* (DIS-, *salīre,* to leap)]

dissimilar, *a.* not similar; unlike in nature, properties or appearances; discordant. **dissimilarity,** *n.* **dissimilarly,** *adv.*

dissimilate, *v.t.* (*Philol.*) to make unlike. **dissimilation,** *n.* (*Philol.*) the rendering two similar sounds unlike, or two dissimilar sounds identical, when such sounds come together. [L *similus,* after ASSIMILATE]

dissimilitude, *n.* unlikeness, dissimilarity.

dissimulate, *v.t.* to dissemble, to conceal, to disguise. **dissimulation,** *n.* the act of dissimulating; concealment under a false pretence; hypocrisy. **dissimulator,** *n.* [L *dissimulātus,* p.p. of *dissimulāre* (DIS-, *simulāre,* to SIMULATE)]

dissipate, *v.t.* to scatter; to drive in different directions; to disperse, to dispel; to squander, to waste, to fritter away. *v.i.* to be dispersed, to vanish; to indulge in dissolute or frivolous enjoyment. **dissipated,** *a.* scattered, dispersed; given to dissipation, dissolute; wasted in dissipation. **dissipation,** *n.* the act of dissipating or scattering; the state of being dispersed or scattered; distraction of energy; lack of concentration or perseverance; excessive indulgence in luxury, frivolity or vice; dissoluteness; wasteful expenditure, extravagance; (*Phys.*) insensible loss or waste; disintegration, dispersion, diffusion. [L *dissipātus,* p.p. of *dissipāre* (DIS-, obs. *sipāre,* to throw)]

†**dissociable,** *a.* incongruous, discordant; separable, unsociable. **dissociableness,** *n.* †**dissocial,** *a.* unfitted for society. †**dissocialize, -ise,** *v.t.* to make unsocial; to disunite.

dissociate, *v.t.* to separate, to disconnect; (*Chem.*) to decompose, esp. by the action of heat. **dissociation,** *n.* separation, disconnection; (*Psych.*) a loosening of control over consciousness in which the personality is temporarily taken control of by unconscious complexes. **dissociative,** *a.* [L *dissociātus,* p.p. of *dissociāre* (DIS-, *sociāre,* to associate, from *socius,* a comrade)]

dissoluble, *a.* that can be dissolved, decomposed or disconnected. **dissolubility,** *n.* [L *dissolūbilis,* from *dissolvere,* to DISSOLVE]

dissolute, *a.* given to dissipation, loose in conduct; licentious, debauched; †relaxed, negligent, remiss. †*n.* a dissolute person. **dissolutely,** *adv.* **dissoluteness,** *n.* [L *dissolūtus,* p.p. of *dissolvere,* to DISSOLVE]

dissolution, *n.* the act or process of dissolving, separating, disintegrating, decomposing; liquefaction; the destruction of any body by the separation of its parts; death, the separation of soul and body; separation of a meeting, assembly or body; (*Chem.*) resolution into the elements or components; †a solution; †dissoluteness, corruption, depravity; †melting by the action of heat. **dissolution of parliament,** the end of a parliament to be followed by a general election. **Dissolution of the Monasteries,** (*Hist.*) the suppression of the monasteries by Henry VIII. [L *dissolūtio,* as prec.]

dissolve, *v.t.* to diffuse the particles of (a substance) in a liquid; to convert from a solid to a liquid state by heat or moisture; to decompose; to separate; to break up; to put an end to (as a meeting etc.); to dismiss, to disperse; to relax; to rescind, to annul; †to part, to sunder. *v.i.* to become liquefied; to decompose, to disintegrate; to break up, to separate; to fade away, to melt away; †to become weak or powerless; to melt by the action of heat; to vanish; (*coll.*) to become emotionally weak; in films and TV, to fade out one scene and merge in the next. *n.* a scene in a film or TV programme which is dissolved. **dissolvable,** *a.* **dissolvent,** *a.* having power to melt or dissolve. *n.* anything which has the power of dissolving or melting, a solvent. **dissolver,** *n.* **dissolving views,** *n.pl.* pictures projected on a screen and made to fade one into another by a special magic-lantern apparatus. [L *dissolvere* (DIS-, *solvere,* to loosen)]

dissonant, *a.* discordant, inharmonious; harsh, incongruous. **dissonance, dissonancy,** *n.* discordant sounds; want of harmony; an unresolved chord in music. **dissonantly,** *adv.* [L *dissonans -antem,* pres.p. of *dissonāre,* to be unlike in sound, from *dissonus,* discordant]

dissuade, *v.t.* to seek to persuade not to do some act; to advise against; to divert from a purpose by argument; †to represent as unadvisable. **dissuader,** *n.* **dissuasion,** *n.* **dissuasive,** *a.* tending to dissuade; dehortatory. *n.* a dissuasive argument or reason. **dissuasively,** *adv.* [L *dissuādēre* (DIS-, *suādēre,* to persuade)]

dissyllable etc. DISYLLABLE.

dissymmetry, *n.* absence of symmetry between objects or parts. **dissymmetrical,** *a.* **dissymmetrically,** *adv.*

dist., (*abbr.*) distant; distinguished; district.

distaff, *n.* a cleft stick about 3 ft. (0·91 m) long, on which wool or carded cotton was wound for spinning; (*fig.*) an emblem of woman; women collectively. **distaff side,** *n.* the female side of a family or descent. †**distaff-woman,** *n.* a spinner. [OE *distæf* (cp. LG *diesse,* a bunch of flax)]

distal, *a.* applied to the extremity of a bone or organ farthest from the point of attachment or insertion; situated at the farthest point from the centre. **distally,** *adv.* [formed from DISTANCE]

distance, *n.* the space between two objects measured along the shortest line; extent of separation however measured; the quality of being distant, remoteness; a set interval; the length of a course run in a competition; reserve, coolness; avoidance of familiarity; constraint, unfriendliness, alienation; remoteness in time (past or future); separation in rank or relationship; ideal space or separation; the remoter parts of a view or the background of a picture; (*Mus.*) a tone interval; a point on a racecourse 204 yd. (219·5 m) from the winning post; †discord, dissension. *v.t.* to place far off; to leave behind in a race; to outstrip, to outdo; to cause to seem distant; to give an appearance of distance to. **angular distance,** the space included between the lines drawn from two objects to the eye. **line of distance,** a straight line drawn from the eye to the principal point in the plane. **middle distance,** the central portion of a picture between the foreground and the distance. **point of distance,** that point of a picture where the visual rays meet. **to go the distance,** to complete something one has started; to endure to the end of a game or bout in sport. **to keep at a distance,** not to become (too) friendly with. **to keep one's distance,** to behave respectfully; to behave with reserve or coldness. **distance-rod,** *n.* a rod for keeping different parts of a motor (as chains, axle-arms etc.) at a proper distance from each other. **distance-signal,** *n.* a railway signal reached before the home-signal and indicating whether that is at danger or not. [OF, from L *distantia* (see foll.)]

distant, *a.* separated by intervening space; remote in space, time (past or future), succession, consanguinity, resemblance, kind or nature; at a certain distance (specified numerically); not plain or obvious; faint, slight; reserved, cool. **distant-signal** DISTANCE-SIGNAL. **distantly,** *adv.* **distantness,** *n.* [F, from L *distans -ntem,* pres.p. of *distāre* (DIS-, *stāre,* to stand)]

distaste, *n.* disrelish, aversion of the taste; dislike or disinclination (for); †unpleasantness, discomfort. †*v.t.* to dislike the taste of; to make distasteful; to offend. †*v.i.* to be distasteful. **distasteful,** *a.* unpleasant to the taste; offensive, displeasing; †repulsive; †exhibiting dislike. **distastefully,** *adv.* **distastefulness,** *n.*

distemper[1], *v.t.* to derange (the mental or bodily functions of); to disturb, to vex. *n.* a derangement of the health; a catarrhal disorder affecting young dogs; mental derangement or perturbation; ill-humour; undue predominance of a passion or appetite; dissatisfaction, discontent; want of due balance or proportion of parts; political disturbance; †intoxication. **distempered,** *a.* disordered in mind or body; intemperate, immoderate. [L *temperāre,* to TEMPER, to mix in due proportions (cp. OF *destempré,* immoderate)]

distemper[2], *v.t.* to paint or colour with distemper; †to dilute, to weaken. *n.* a method of painting with colours soluble in water, mixed with chalk or clay, and diluted with size instead of oil; the coloured preparation used in this style of painting; a painting done by this method or with this preparation; tempera. [OF *destemprer,* as prec.]

distend, *v.t.* to spread or swell out; to inflate; to cause to open. *v.i.* to swell out. **distensible,** *a.* **distensibility** (-bil′-), *n.* **distension,** *n.* the act of distending; the state of being distended; breadth, expansion. **distent,** *a.* spread out, extended; expanded, swollen. [L *distendere* (DIS-, *tendere, tentum* or *tēnsum,* to stretch)]

disthrone, *v.t.* to dethrone.

distich, *n.* a couplet; two lines of poetry making complete sense. [L *distichus, distichon,* Gr. *distichon* (DI-[2], *stichos,* a row)]

distichous, *a.* (*Bot.*) having two rows (of leaves etc.); arranged in two rows. [as prec.]

distil, distill, *v.i.* (*past, p.p.* **distilled**) to fall in drops; to trickle; to flow forth gently, to exude; to undergo the process of distillation. *v.t.* to extract by means of vaporization and condensation; to extract the essence of; to make or obtain by this process; to purify by this process; to let fall in drops, to shed; †to melt. **distillable,** *a.* **distillate,** *n.* the product of distillation. **distillation,** *n.* the act of distilling; the act or process of heating a solid or liquid in a vessel so constructed that the vapours thrown off from the heated substance are collected and condensed; the product of this process, a distillate. **destructive distillation,** distillation at a temperature sufficiently high to decompose the substance, and evolve new products possessing different qualities. **dry distillation,** the distillation of a solid substance without the addition of water. **fractional distillation,** the separation of liquids having different boiling-points. **vacuum distillation,** distillation carried out under reduced pressure. **distillatory,** *a.* **distiller,** *n.* one who distils, esp. a manufacturer of spirits by distillation. **distillery,** *n.* a building where spirits are produced by distillation. [L *distillāre* (DI-[1], *stillāre,* to trickle, from *stilla,* a drop)]

distinct, *a.* clearly distinguished or distinguishable, different, separate; standing clearly apart, not identical; unmistakable, clear, plain, evident, definite; (*coll.*) decided, positive; †adorned, variegated; †marked off, specified. †*n.* a distinct or individual person. **distinction,** *n.* a mark or note of difference; a distinguishing quality, a characteristic difference; the act of distinguishing, discrimination; that which differentiates; honour, title, rank; eminence, superiority; (*Lit. crit.*) individuality; †variety of detail. **without distinction,** promiscuously, indiscriminately. **distinctive,** *a.* serving to mark distinction or difference; separate, distinct. **distinctively,** *adv.* **distinctiveness,** *n.* **distinctly,** *adv.* **distinctness,** *n.* †**distincture,** *n.* distinctness. [L *distinctus,* p.p. of *distinguere,* to DISTINGUISH]

distingué, *a.* (*fem.* **-guée**) having an air of distinction. [F, p.p. of *distinguer,* to DISTINGUISH]

distinguish, *v.t.* to discriminate, to differentiate; to indicate the difference of from others by some external mark; to classify; to tell apart, to discriminate between; to perceive the existence of by means of the senses; to recognize; to be a mark of distinction or characteristic property; to separate from others by some token of honour or preference; to make eminent, prominent, or well known. *v.i.* to differentiate; to draw distinctions. **distinguishable,** *a.* **distinguishably,** *adv.* **distinguished,** *a.* marked by some distinctive sign or property; eminent, celebrated, remarkable; conspicuous, specially marked. **Distinguished Conduct Medal,** medal awarded to warrant officers and other ranks for gallantry in the field. **Distinguished Flying Cross,** medal for gallantry awarded to officers and warrant officers of RAF. **Distinguished Service Cross, Medal,** medals awarded for gallantry to RN officers and warrant officers, and CPOs and other ratings. **Distinguished Service Order,** medal for meritorious service awarded to officers in the three Services. **distinguishedly,** *adv.* in a distinguished manner; eminently. **distinguisher,** *n.* one who distinguishes one thing from another by marks of difference; a critical observer. **distinguishing,** *a.* constituting a difference or distinction; peculiar. **distinguishingly,** *adv.* with some mark of distinction; markedly. †**distinguishment,** *n.* distinction; observation of difference. [L *distinguere* (DI-[1], *stinguere,* prob. cogn. with Gr. *stizein,* to prick)]

Distoma, *n.pl.* a genus of Trematoda, parasitic worms or flukes, typified by the liver-fluke, the cause of sheep-rot. [Gr. *distomos -on,* double-mouthed (DI-[2], *stoma,* mouth)]

distort, *v.t.* to twist or alter the natural shape or direction; to pervert from the true meaning. †*a.* distorted. **distortedly,** *adv.* **distortion,** *n.* the act of distorting; the state of being distorted; a writhing, a contortion; a distorted part of the body, a deformity; a perversion of meaning, a misrepresentation; (*Radio*) deviation from strict reproduction in a receiver or loud-speaker. **distortional,** *a.* **distortionist,** *n.* a caricaturist; one who distorts his/her body for public entertainment. **distortive,** *a.* [L *distortus,* p.p. of *distorquēre* (DIS-, *torquēre,* to twist)]

distract, *v.t.* to draw or turn aside, to divert the mind or attention (from); to draw in different directions, to confuse, bewilder, perplex; (*usu. p.p.*) to drive mad, to craze; †to tear asunder. †*a.* separated, divided; deranged, distracted. **distracted,** *a.* disturbed mentally, crazed, maddened; confounded, harassed, perplexed; †divided, separated. **distractedly,** *adv.* **distracting,** *a.* **distractingly,** *adv.* **distraction,** *n.* diversion of the mind or attention; the thing that diverts; an interruption, a diversion, relaxation, relief, amusement; confusion, perplexity, agitation, violent mental excitement arising from pain, care etc.; mental aberration, madness, frenzy; †separation, a division; †disorder, dissension, tumult. **distractive,** *a.* **distractively,** *adv.* [L *distractus,* p.p. of *distrahere* (DIS-, *trahere,* to draw)]

distrain, *v.t.* to seize for debt; to take the personal chattels of, in order to satisfy a demand or enforce the performance of an act; †to rend asunder; to oppress, to compel; †to take possession of, to seize. *v.i.* to levy a distress. **distrainable,** *a.* **distrainee,** *n.* one whose goods are distrained. **distrainer, -or,** *n.* **distrainment,** *n.* **distraint,** *n.* the act of seizing goods for debt. [OF *destreign-,* stem of *destreindre,* L *distringere* (DI-[1], *stringere,* to STRAIN, compress)]

distrait, *a.* absent-minded, abstracted, inattentive. [F, p.p. of *distraire,* to DISTRACT]

distraught, *a.* torn asunder, bewildered, agitated, distracted. [DISTRACT, *a.*, distracted, assim. to CAUGHT, TAUGHT etc.]

distress, *n.* extreme anguish or pain of mind or body; misery, poverty, destitution; exhaustion, fatigue; calamity, misfortune; a state of danger; (*Law*) the act of distraining; goods taken in distraint. *v.t.* to afflict with anxiety, unhappiness or anguish, to vex; to exhaust, to tire out; †to constrain, to compel by pain or suffering; (*Law*) to distrain. **in distress,** (*Naut.*) in a disabled or perilous condition (of a ship). **distress-gun, -rocket,** *n.* a signal for help from a ship in imminent danger. **distress sale,** *n.* a sale of goods under a distress warrant. **distress signal,** *n.* a radio or light signal, e.g. from a ship in need of prompt assistance. **distress warrant,** *n.* a writ authorizing the seizure and compulsory sale of household effects etc. in settlement of a debt. **distressed,** *a.* afflicted with pain or anxiety; destitute, exhausted; in a position of danger. **distressed areas,** *n.pl.* industrial areas where there is wide unemployment and poverty. †**distressedness,** *n.* **distressful,** *a.* painful, afflictive; attended by distress; †gained by toil. **distressfully,** *adv.* **distressing,** *a.* painful, afflicting; awakening pity or compassion. **distressingly,** *adv.* [OF *destrece,* from *destrecier,* late L *districtiāre,* from *districtus,* p.p. of *distringere,* to DISTRAIN]

distribute, *v.t.* to divide or deal out amongst a number; to spread abroad, to disperse; to give in charity; (*Print.*) to separate and return (as type) to the cases; to arrange, to allocate, to classify; (*Log.*) to employ (a term) in its fullest extent, so as to include every individual of the class. **distributable,** *a.* **distributary,** *a.* distributive. **distributing-machine,** *n.* a machine for distributing type. **distribution,** *n.* the act of distributing; apportionment, division; the apportionment of wealth among the various classes of the community; the dispersal of commodities among the consumers; dispersal, arrangement of a number of scattered units; an assigning to different positions, the act of dividing or arranging into classes etc.; (*Log.*) the application of a term to all the members of a class individually, as distinct from collective application; the manner, degree and extent in which the flora and fauna of the world are distributed over the surface of the earth. **distributional,** *a.* **distributive,** *a.* distributing or allotting the proper share to each; pertaining to distribution; (*Gram.*) expressing distribution, separation or division; (*Log.*) indicating distribution, as distinguished from collective terms. *n.* a distributive word as *each, every, either* and *neither*. **distributively,** *adv.* **distributiveness,** *n.* **distributor,** *n.* one who or that which distributes; a wholesaler or middleman who distributes goods to retailers; the device in a petrol engine which distributes current to the sparking plugs. [L *distribūtus,* p.p. of *distribuere* (DIS-, *tribuere,* to divide, allot)]

district, *n.* a portion of territory specially defined for judicial, administrative, fiscal or other purposes; a division having its own representative in a legislature, its own district council, a church or chapel of its own or a separate magistrate; a separate sphere of organization or operation; a region, tract of country. *v.t.* (*N Am.*) to divide into districts. **district attorney,** *n.* (*N Am.*) the prosecuting officer of a district. **district commissioner,** *n.* a magistrate or official exercising semi-judicial authority over a district in a Crown Colony. **district court,** *n.* (*N Am.*) a court having cognizance of cases arising within a defined district. **district judge,** *n.* (*N Am.*) the judge of a district court. **district nurse,** *n.* a nurse employed by a local authority to visit and tend patients in their own homes. **district surveyor,** *n.* a local officer, usually a civil engineer, appointed to examine buildings, roads etc., superintend repairs etc. **district visitor,** *n.* a church worker who visits the sick etc. in a section of a parish. [F, from late L *districtus,* p.p. of *distringere,* to DISTRAIN]

District of Columbia, federal district of the US.

distrust, *v.t.* to have no confidence in; to doubt, to suspect; to question the reality, truth or sincerity of; †to be anxious about. *n.* want of confidence, reliance or faith (in); suspicion, †discredit. †**distruster,** *n.* **distrustful,** *a.* inclined to distrust; suspicious, without confidence, diffident. **distrustfully,** *adv.* **distrustfulness,** *n.*

distune, *v.t.* to put out of tune.

disturb, *v.t.* to agitate, to disquiet; to move from any regular course; to discompose, unsettle; to make uneasy, to hinder, to interrupt, to interfere with; (*Law*) to put out of possession. †*n.* disturbance. **disturbance,** *n.* interruption of a settled state of things; agitation, public agitation or excitement, tumult, disorder, uproar, an outbreak; (*Law*) the interruption of a right; the hindering and disquieting of a person in the lawful and peaceable enjoyment of his/her right; (*Radio*) any interruption from unwanted stations, atmospherics etc. in the reception of a signal; a minor earthquake; a small atmospheric depression; a mental or emotional disorder. †**disturbant,** *a.* causing disturbance. **disturbed,** *a.* emotionally or mentally unstable. [OF *destourber,* L *disturbāre* (DIS-, *turbāre,* to trouble, from *turba,* a crowd, a tumult)]

distyle, *n.* a portico having two columns. [DI-[2], Gr. *stulos,* a pillar]

disulphate, *n.* a salt of sulphuric acid, containing two equivalents of the acid to one of the base. **disulphide,** *n.* a compound in which two atoms of sulphur are united to another element or radical.

disunion, *n.* the state of being disunited; disagreement, discord; in the US, secession from the Union. **disunionist,** *n.*

disunite, *v.t.* to disjoin, to divide, to put at variance. *v.i.* to become divided. **disunity,** *n.* disunion; a state of variance.

disuse, *n.* a cessation of use, practice or exercise: the state of being disused; desuetude. *v.t.*, to cease to use; †(*usu. p.p.*) to disaccustom. **disused,** *a.* no longer in use; obsolete; unaccustomed.

disvalue, *v.t.* to undervalue; to depreciate, to disparage.

disyllable, dissyllable, *n.* a word or metrical foot of two syllables. *a.* disyllabic. **disyllabic,** *a.* **disyllabically,** *adv.* **disyllabism,** *n.* **disyllabize, -ise,** *v.t.* [F *dissyllabe* (DI-[2], SYLLABLE)]

disyoke, *v.t.* to unyoke.

dit[1]**,** *n.* a word representing the dot in the Morse code when this is spoken.

dit[2]**,** *a.* (*F*) named; reputed.

dital, *n.* (*Mus.*) a thumb stop on a guitar or lute for raising the pitch of a string by a semitone. [It. *dito,* finger]

ditch, *n.* a trench made by digging to form a boundary or for drainage; (*Fort.*) a trench or fosse on the outside of a fortress, serving as an obstacle to assailants. *v.t.* to make a ditch, trench or drain in; to surround with a ditch. *v.i.* to dig or repair ditches. **last ditch,** a last resort. **to die in the last ditch,** to resist to the uttermost. †**ditch-delivered,** *a.* brought forth in a ditch. †**ditch-dog,** *n.* a dead dog thrown in a ditch or, perhaps, the water-vole. **ditch-water,** *n.* stagnant water in a ditch, whence **dull as ditch-water,** very uninteresting or unentertaining. **ditcher,** *n.* one employed in making ditches; a machine which makes or repairs ditches. [OE *dīc,* cp. DIKE]

dite DIGHT OR DITTY.

ditetragonal, *a.* (*Cryst.*) twice tetragonal.

ditetrahedral, *a.* (*Cryst.*) twice tetrahedral.

ditheism, *n.* the theory of two co-equal gods or opposing powers of good and evil, the basic principle of Zoroastrianism and Manichaeism. **ditheistic,** *a.*

dither, *v.t.* to be distracted or uncertain; to hesitate, to be indecisive; to quiver, thrill. **ditherer,** *n.* **dithery,** *a.* [rel. to DODDER[2]]

dithyramb, *n.* a choric hymn in honour of Bacchus, full of frantic enthusiasm; hence, any wild, impetuous poem or song. **dithyrambic,** *a.* of the nature of a dithyramb; wild, enthusiastic. *n.* a dithyramb. [L *dīthyrambus,* Gr *dīthurambos* (etym. unknown)]

ditriglyph, *n.* (*Arch.*) the interval between two triglyphs; an interval between Doric columns allowing the insertion of two triglyphs in the frieze between those over the columns. [F *ditriglyphe*]

ditrochee, *n.* a metrical foot of two trochees. [L *ditrochaeus,* Gr. *ditrochaios*]

dittany, *n.* a herb, *Origanum dictamnus,* which was prized by the ancients as a vulnerary; (*N Am.*) a small herb, *Cunila mariana,* growing in the Eastern US; *Dictamnus fraxinella,* the bastard dittany. [OF *ditain,* L *dictamnum,* Gr. *diktamnon,* from *Diktē,* in Crete]

dittay, *n.* (*Sc. Law*) an indictment, a charge. [OF *dité,* DITTY]

ditto, *n.* (*pl.* **-ttos**) that which has been said before; the same thing, a similar thing. *a.* similar. **suit of dittos,** a suit of clothes of the same stuff. **to say ditto,** to repeat, endorse a view; to coincide in opinion. **ditto marks,** *n.pl.* a mark consisting of two dots, placed under a word to show that it is to be repeated on the next line. **dittography,** *n.* repetition of words or letters in copying. **dittographic,** *a.* **dittology,** *n.* a twofold reading of a text. [It., from L *dictus,* p.p. of *dīcere,* to say]

ditty, *n.* a little poem, a song, an air; anything sung; †a saying, a refrain. *v.i.* to sing verses, to fit to music. [OF *dité,* L *dictātum,* a thing dictated, neut. p.p. of *dictāre,* to DICTATE]

ditty-bag, *n.* (*Naut.*) a sailor's bag for needles, thread and odds and ends. **ditty-box,** *n.* a box similarly used by fishermen. [etym. doubtful]

ditzy, ditsy, *a.* excessively refined, affected. **ditz,** *n.*

diuretic, *a.* (*Med.*) provoking the secretion of urine. *n.* a diuretic medicine. [L *diūrēticus,* Gr. *diourētikos,* from *diourein,* to void urine]

diurnal, *a.* of or pertaining to a day or the day-time; performed in a day; daily, of each day; of common occurrence; (*Zool.*) of the day, as distinct from *nocturnal*. *n.* †a journal, a day-book; in the Roman Catholic Church, a book containing the little hours of the divine office. **diurnal arc,** *n.* (*Astron.*) the arc described by a heavenly body from rising to setting. **diurnally,** *adv.* [L *diurnālis,* from *diurnus,* daily (*diēs,* day)]

†**diuturnal,** *a.* of long continuance. †**diuturnity,** *n.* lastingness, long duration. [L *diūturnus,* from *diū,* long]

div., (*abbr.*) divide(d); dividend; divine; division; divorced.

diva, *n.* (*pl.* **-vas, -ve**) a famous female singer, a prima donna. [It., from L *dīva,* a goddess, fem. of *dīvus,* divine, a deity]

divagate, *v.t.* to ramble, to diverge, to digress. **divagation,** *n.* [L *dīvagātus,* p.p. of *dīvagārī* (DI-[1], *vagārī,* to wander)]

divalent, *a.* (*Chem.*) with a valency of two. [DI-[2], L *valens -entem,* pres.p. of *valēre,* to be worth]

divan, *n.* in oriental countries, a court of justice, the highest council of state; a council, a council-chamber; a restaurant; a smoking-saloon; a thickly-cushioned backless seat or sofa against the wall of a room; †a collection of poems by one author. **divan bed,** *n.* a mattress bed that can be converted into a sofa by day. [Turk. *divān,* Pers. *dīvān,* a brochure, a collection of poems, a tribunal, a custom-house (cp. DOUANE)]

divaricate, *v.i.* to diverge into branches or forks; (*Bot.*) to branch off from the stem at a right or obtuse angle. †*v.t.* to divide into two branches. *a.*, spreading irregularly and widely asunder; branching off at a right or obtuse angle. **divarication,** *n.* [L *dīvāricātus,* p.p. of *dīvāricāre* (DI-[1], *vāricāre,* to spread apart, to straddle, from *vāricus,* straddling)]

dive, *v.i.* to plunge, esp. head first, under water; to descend quickly; to descend quickly and disappear; to thrust one's hand rapidly into something; (*fig.*) to enter deeply into any question, science or pursuit. *v.t.* to explore by diving; to dip, to duck. *n.* a sudden plunge head foremost into water; a sudden plunge or dart; a drinking-saloon of a low type; an underground room in a restaurant or bar; (*Aviat.*) a steep descent with the nose down. **dive-bomber,** *n.* a military aeroplane which releases its bombs while in a steep dive. **dive-bombing,** *n.* diving suddenly on a target to release bombs. **dive-dapper,** *n.* a didapper. **diver,** *n.* one who dives; esp. one who dives for pearls, or to work on sunken vessels etc.; (*Ornith.*) any member of the family Colymbidae, remarkable for their habit of diving.

diving-bell, *n.* a hollow vessel, orig. bell-shaped, in which persons may remain for a time under water, air being supplied through a flexible tube. **diving board,** *n.* a platform from which one may dive into a swimming pool. **diving-dress, -suit,** *n.* waterproof clothing and breathing-helmet for divers working at the bottom of the sea. [OE *dūfan,* to dive, to sink, and *dyfan,* to dip (eventually combined)]

diverge, *v.i.* to tend in different directions from a common point or from each other; to branch off; to vary from a normal form; to deviate, to differ. *v.t.* to cause to diverge. †**divergement,** *n.* **divergence, -gency,** *n.* **divergent,** *a.* **divergent series,** *n.* an infinite series the sum of which becomes indefinitely greater as more are taken. **divergent thinking,** *n.* thinking in which several different ideas emanate from a single idea or problem. **divergingly,** *adv.* [L *vergere,* to VERGE]

divers, *a.* several, sundry; †different. [OF, from L *dīversus,* various, p.p. of *dīvertere,* to DIVERT]

diverse, *a.* different, unlike, distinct; varying, changeable, multiform; †divers. †*v.t.* to diversify. †*v.i.* to turn aside, to diverge. **diversely,** *adv.* **diverseness,** *n.* **diversiform,** *a.* of divers or varied forms; (*Bot.*) applied to organs of the same nature but of different forms. **diversify,** *v.t.* to make different from others; to give variety to; to variegate; to invest in securities of different types; to be engaged in the production of several types of manufactured goods etc. **diversification**, *n.* [as prec.]

diversion, *n.* the act of diverting or turning aside; that which tends or serves to divert the mind or attention from care, business or study; a relaxation, distraction, amusement; a redirection of traffic owing to the temporary closing of a road; (*Mil.*) the act of diverting the attention of the enemy from any design by demonstration or feigned attack. **diversity,** *n.* difference, unlikeness; variance; variety, distinctness or non-identity; variegation; (*Law*) plea by a prisoner that he is not the person charged. [med. L *dīversio,* from *dīvertere,* to DIVERT]

divert, *v.t.* to turn from any course or direction, to turn aside, to deflect; to turn in another direction, to avert; to draw off, to distract; to entertain, to amuse; †to turn away. †*v.i.* to go out of the way, to go astray. †**diverter,** *n.* **divertible,** *a.* **divertimento**, *n.* (*pl.* **-ti**) a piece of entertaining music; a musical pot-pourri; a ballet-interlude. **diverting,** *a.* entertaining, amusing. **divertingly,** *adv.* **divertisement**, *n.* diversion; source of amusement. **divertissement**, *n.* an interlude, ballet, light entertainment. [MF *divertir,* L *dīvertere* (DI-[1], *vertere,* to turn), to turn aside, *dēvertere* (DE-, *vertere*), to turn away]

diverticulum, *n.* (*pl.* **-la**) an abnormal sac or pouch on the wall of a tubular organ, esp. the intestine. **diverticulitis**, *n.* inflammation of the diverticula. [L, by-path]

Dives, *n.* the popular name for a wealthy man (after the parable of Lazarus and the rich man in Luke xvi.19–31). **Dives costs,** *n.pl.* (*Law*) costs on a higher scale. [L, rich]

divest, *v.t.* to strip of clothing; to deprive, rid (of). **divestiture**, *n.* divestment; the state of being divested; (*Law*) deprivation or alienation of property. **divestment,** *n.* the act of divesting. [formerly *devest,* OF *devestir, desvestir,* late L *disvestīre, dīvestīre* (DI-[1], *vestīre,* from *vestis,* a garment)]

divide, *v.t.* to cut or part asunder; to sever, to partition; to cause to separate, to break into parts; to distribute, to deal out; to make an opening or passage through; to form the boundary between; to sunder; to part or to mark divisions on (as on mathematical instruments etc.); to distinguish the different kinds of, to classify; to distribute as a dividend; to share, to take a portion of with others; to separate (as Parliament, a meeting) by taking opinions on, for and against; to draw or attach to different sides; to destroy unity amongst, to disunite in feelings; (*Math.*) to separate into factors, to perform the operation of division on. *v.i.* to be parted or separated; to share; to diverge; to express decision by separating into two parts, as a legislative house; (*Math.*) to be an exact division of; (*fig.*) to be disunited in feelings, opinions etc. †**dividable,** *a.* †**dividant,** *a.* divided, separated. **dividedly,** *adv.* **divider,** *n.* one who or that which divides; one who causes division or disunion; (*pl.*) compasses used to divide lines into a given number of equal parts; (*N Am.*) a watershed. [L *dīvidere* (DI-[1], *-videre,* cp. *vidua,* WIDOW)]

dividend, *n.* the share of the interest or profit which belongs to each shareholder in a company, bearing the same proportion to the whole profit that the shareholder's capital bears to the whole capital; (*Law*) the fractional part of the assets of a bankrupt paid to a creditor, in proportion to the amount of his debt; (*Math.*) a number to be divided by a divisor; a bonus. **dividend-warrant,** *n.* the authority on which shareholders receive the amount of a dividend from the bankers of a company. [F *dividende,* L *dīvidendum,* gerund of *dīvidere,* as prec.]

dividivi, *n.* a tropical American tree, *Caesalpinia coriaria;* the seedpods of this, used for tanning and dyeing. [native Carib. name]

dividual, *a.* divided; shared with others; separate, distinct, particular. †**dividually,** *adv.* †**dividuous,** *a.* dividual; separable, accidental, not essential. [L *dividuus,* as DIVIDE]

divine[1], *v.t.* to find out by inspiration, intuition or magic; to foresee, to presage; to conjecture, to guess; to feel a presentiment of. *v.i.* to practise divination; to have a presentiment; to guess. **divination**, *n.* the act of predicting or foretelling events, or of discovering hidden or secret things by real or by alleged supernatural means; an omen, an augury; a prediction or conjecture as to the future. †**divinator**, *n.* **divinatory**, *a.* **diviner,** *n.* one who divines; a dowser. **divining-rod,** *n.* a forked twig or other staff used by dowsers to discover subterranean waters or minerals. [F *deviner,* L *dīvīnāre,* from *dīvīnus,* as foll.]

divine[2], *a.* pertaining to, proceeding from or of the nature of God, a god, or gods; appropriated to the service of the Deity, religious, sacred; above the nature of man, superhuman, god-like, celestial; pertaining to theology; †prescient; †(of the soul) beatified; †immortal; †holy, pious; divining, presaging. *n.* a clergyman, an ecclesiastic; a theologian; †a priest, a soothsayer. **divine office,** *n.* the office of the Roman breviary, consisting of matins with lauds, prime, tierce, sext, none, vespers and compline, the recitation of which is obligatory on all clerics holding a benefice, on all persons in Holy Orders, and on all monastics of both sexes professed for the service of the choir. **divine right,** *n.* the claim of kings to hold their office by divine appointment, and hence to govern absolutely without any interference on the part of their subjects. **divine service,** *n.* the worship of God according to established forms. **divinely,** *adv.* †**divineness,** *n.* the quality of being divine; perfection, excellence. **divinify**, *v.t.* to make divine deify. [OF *devin,* L *dīvīnus,* cogn. with *dīvus, deus,* god]

diving DIVE.

divinity, *n.* the quality of being divine, deity, godhead; the Divine Being; God; a deity, a god; a being who partakes of the divine nature; a supernatural power or influence; the science of divine things; theology; a university faculty of theology. **divinity-calf,** *n.* dark brown calf, ungilded and with blind stamping, used for binding theological works. **divinize, -ise**, *v.t.* to treat as divine; to deify. **divinization, -isation,** *n.*

divisible, *a.* capable of division; able to be divided into equal parts by a divisor without a remainder. **divisibility**, *n.* **divisibly,** *adv.* [L *dīvīsibilis,* from *dīvīsus,* p.p. of *dīvidere,* to DIVIDE]

division, *n.* the act of dividing; the state of being divided; separation; distribution; that which divides or separates; a boundary, a partition; a separate or distinct part; a district, an administrative unit; a separate body of men; a distinct sect or body; disunion, disagreement, variance; (*Nat. Hist.*) a separate class, kind, species or variety; a distinction; the part of a county or borough returning a Member of Parliament; the separation of Members of Parliament for the purpose of voting; a formal vote in Parliament; (*Math.*) the process of dividing one number by another; (*Log.*) the separation of a genus into its constituent species; classification; analysis of meaning; (*Mil.*) a body of men, usu. three brigades, under the command of a general officer, applied loosely to smaller bodies; (*Nav.*) a number of vessels under one command; †arrangement, disposition; (*Mus.*) variation. **division of labour,** distribution of parts of industrial and other work among different persons in order to secure specialization on particular processes and to save time. **long division,** (*Arith.*) the process of dividing a number by another number greater than 12, the stages being fully set forth. **short division,** (*Arith.*) division by a number less than 12, the successive steps being performed mentally. **division lobby,** *n.* either of the two corridors in Parliament in which the members vote. **division sign,** *n.* the sign ÷, indicating division. **divisional, -sionary,** *a.* **divisionally,** *adv.* **divisive,** *a.* forming or noting separation or division, analytical; tending to division or dissension. **divisively,** *adv.* **divisiveness,** *n.* **divisor,** *n.* (*Math.*) that number by which a dividend is divided; a number that divides another without a remainder. **divisural,** *a.* divisional (used of the dividing line in the peristome of mosses). [DIVIDE]

divorce, *n.* the dissolution of the marriage tie by competent authority; the separation of husband and wife by judicial sentence of a secular or ecclesiastical court; (*fig.*) a separation of things closely connected. *v.t.* to dissolve by legal process the bonds of marriage between; to separate (a married pair) by divorce; to obtain a divorce from; to put away (a spouse) by divorce; (*fig.*) to dissolve (a union); to disunite things closely connected; to remove, to separate. †**divorceable,** *a.* **divorcee,** *n.* one who has been divorced. †**divorcement,** *n.* a divorce; a dissolution of the marriage contract. **Bill of Divorcement,** an Act of Parliament as formerly required, setting forth the grounds for a divorce. **divorcer,** *n.* one who procures a divorce; one who or that which produces separation. †**divorcive,** *a.* [F, from L *dīvortium,* from *dīvortere,* old form of *dīvertere,* to DIVERT]

divot, *n.* (*Sc., North.*) a turf, a sod used for roofing or capping dry walls; a piece of turf torn up by the head of a golf club when driving. [etym. unknown]

†**divulgate,** *v.t.* to spread or publish abroad; to make public. **divulgation,** *n.* [L *dīvulgātus,* p.p. of *dīvulgāre,* as foll.]

divulge, *v.t.* to make known; to reveal, disclose; to publish; †to proclaim publicly. †*v.i.* to become known. **divulgence,** *n.* **divulger,** *n.* **divulgement,** *n.* [prob. from F *divulguer* or directly from L *dīvulgāre* (DI-[1], *vulgāre,* to publish, from *vulgus,* the people)]

†**divulsion,** *n.* the act of tearing away or asunder; a rending asunder; laceration. †**divulsive,** *a.* [F, from L *dīvulsio -ōnem,* from *dīvellere* (DI-[1], *vellere,* to pluck, pull)]

divvy, *n.* (*coll.*) a dividend; a share. *v.t.* to divide (up).

Diwali, *n.* Hindu festival in Oct./Nov. celebrating Lakshmi, goddess of light and wealth. It is marked by the lighting of lamps and candles, feasting, and exchange of gifts.

dixie, *n.* a field-service kettle, a pot for cooking over an outdoor fire. [Hind. *degshi,* a pot]

Dixieland, Dixie, *n.* an early type of jazz music played by small combinations of instruments. [*Dixie,* name given to the US southern states]

DIY, (*abbr.*) do-it-yourself.

dizen, *v.t.* to dress up; to deck out gaudily. [cp. LG *diesse,* OE *distæf,* DISTAFF]

dizzy, *a.* giddy, dazed, vertiginous; causing dizziness, confusing; high; whirling; reeling; †foolish, stupid. *v.t.* to make dizzy; to confuse, to confound. **dizzily,** *adv.* **dizziness,** *n.* [OE *dysig,* foolish, stupid, *dysigian,* to be foolish]

DJ, (*abbr.*) dinner jacket; disk jockey.

Djakarta JAKARTA.

djellaba, djellabah, *n.* a cloak with wide sleeves and a hood. [Arab. *jallabah*]

Djibouti, *n.* Republic of (*Jumhouriyya Djibouti*), country on the E coast of Africa. **area** 23,200 sq km/8955 sq miles. **capital** and chief port Djibouti. **physical** mountains divide an inland plateau from a coastal plain; hot and arid. **population** (1988) 484,000 (Issa 47%, Afar 37%, European 8%, Arab 6%); annual growth rate 3.4%. **exports** acts mainly as a transit port for Ethiopia. **language** Somali, Afar, French, Arabic. **religion** Sunni Muslim.

djinn JINN.

dl, (*abbr.*) decilitre.

DLit(t), (*abbr.*) Doctor of Literature, Doctor of Letters (L *Doctor Litterarum*).

DM, (*abbr.*) Deutschmark.

dm, (*abbr.*) decimetre.

DMA, (*abbr.*) (*Comput.*) direct memory access.

DMus, (*abbr.*) Doctor of Music.

DMZ, (*abbr.*) demilitarized zone.

DNA, (*abbr.*) deoxyribonucleic acid, the main constituent of chromosomes, in the form of a double helix, which is self-replicating and transmits hereditary characteristics. **DNA fingerprinting** GENETIC FINGERPRINTING.

Dnepropetrovsk, *n.* city in the Ukraine, USSR, on the right bank of the Dnieper; population (1985) 1,153,00. Centre of an important industrial region, with iron, steel, chemical and engineering industries. It is linked with the Dnieper Dam, 60 km/37 miles downstream.

Dnieper, Dnepr, *n.* Russian river rising in the Smolensk region and flowing S past Kiev, Dnepropetrovsk, and Zaporozhe, to enter the Black Sea E of Odessa. Total length 2250 km/1400 miles.

D-notice, *n.* in the UK, a censorship notice issued by the Department of Defence to the media to prohibit the publication of infomration of matters alleged to be of national security. The system dates from 1922.

do., (*abbr.*) ditto.

do[1], *v.t.* (*2nd sing.* **doest**, *aux.* **dost**, *3rd sing.* **does**, †**doth**, *past,* **did, didst**, ; *p.p.* **done**, ; **don't**, ; **didn't**, (*coll.*) for *do not, did not;* **doesn't**, for *does not*) to execute, perform, effect, transact, carry out (a work, thing, service, benefit, injury etc., or the action of any verb understood); to bring about as a result; to produce, to make; to bring to an end, to complete, finish, accomplish; to produce, to cause, to render (good, evil, honour, justice, injury etc.) to; to work, act, operate, deal with; hence, to translate, to prepare, to cook, to play the part of; (*coll.*) to cheat, to swindle, to humbug; (*coll.*) to injure, to kill; (*sl.*) to entertain, feed; (*coll.*) to undergo (as a punishment); to tire out, fatigue, exhaust; (*coll.*) to visit and see the sights of; to employ, exert, put forth (as effort). *v.i.* to act, behave, conduct oneself; to strive, to work or act vigorously; to perform deeds; to finish, make an end, to cease; to fare, to get on (in an undertaking or in health etc.); to serve, to suffice, to be enough (for), to answer the purpose. *aux.v.* (in neg. and in interrog. sentences), as *I do not play, do you not play*?; with inf. for special emphasis, as *I do believe, they do love him;* in the imper., as *do give it him, do but ask;* in inverted sentences, as *seldom did it occur;* also poetically, *it did appear;* substitute (for a verb expressing any action, usu. to avoid repetition), as *I walked there in the same time as he did; you play whist as well as he does; did he catch the train? I did; he often comes here, I seldom do. n.* a swindle, a fraud; a party, a jollification. **anything doing,** anything going on. **do's and don't's,** rules for action. **nothing doing,** (*Comm.*) no business; (*coll.*) no offers; no acceding to a request. **to-do,** bustle, confusion. **to do away with,** to put out of sight or mind; to abolish; to make away with, to kill. **to do by,** to treat, to deal with. **to do down,** to get the better of, to cheat; to humiliate. **to do for,** to suit; to put an end to; to ruin, to kill; (*coll.*) to do domestic work for. **to do in,** (*sl.*) to kill. **to do one's best** or **diligence,** to exert one's best efforts. **to do or die,** to make a last, desperate attempt. **to do over,** to perform a second time; to cover with a coating. **to do (someone) proud,** (*coll.*) to treat (someone) very well. **to do time,** (*sl.*) to serve a prison sentence. **to do to,** to do by. **to do to death,** to put, or cause to put, to death; to kill. **to do up,** to put in repair; to paint and paper (as a house); to pack in a parcel; to tire out. **to do well,** to prosper. **to do with,** to have business or connection with; to dispose of, to employ; to make shift with. **to do without,** to dispense with. **to have done with,** to have finished with. **to have to do with,** to have business or intercourse with; to deal with. **well-to-do,** well off; prosperous. †**do-all,** *n.* a factotum. **do-gooder,** *n.* one who tries to help others, often in a meddlesome or ineffectual way. **do-it-yourself,** *n.* decorating, household repairs and building as a hobby. **do-nothing,** *n.* an idler. *a.* lazy, idle. **doable,** *a.* **doer,** *n.* [OE *dōn,* past *dyde,* p.p. *gedōn,* from Teut. *dō-* (Dut. *doen, deed, gedaan,* G *tun, tat, taten, getan*)]

do², *n.* (*Mus.*) the first of the syllables used for the solfeggio of the scale; the note C. [arbitrary]

DOA, (*abbr.*) dead on arrival.

dob, *v.t.* (*Austral., sl.*) to betray.

dobbin, *n.* a draught horse. [familiar form of *Robert,* cp. ROBIN]

dobby, *n.* a brownie; an attachment to a loom for weaving small figures. [cp. prec.]

dobchick DABCHICK.

Dobermann pinscher, *n.* a large breed of dog with a smooth usu. black and tan coat, used as a guard dog. [L *Dobermann,* 19th-cent. German dog-breeder, G. *Pinscher,* terrier]

Döblin, *n.* **Alfred** (1878–1957), German novelist. *Berlin-Alexanderplatz* (1929) owes much to Joyce in its minutely detailed depiction of the inner lives of a city's inhabitants.

doc, *n.* short for DOCTOR.

Docetae, *n.pl.* a sect in the early Church who maintained that Christ had not a natural but only a phantasmal or celestial body. **Docetic,** *a.* **Docetism,** *n.* **Docetist,** *n.* [Gr. *Dokētai,* from *dokeein,* to seem]

doch-an-dorris, deoch-an-dorris, *n.* a stirrup cup; a farewell drink. [Gael.]

dochmius, *n.* (*pl.* **-mii**) a metrical foot of five syllables, one short, two long, one short, and one long: ◡––◡–. **dochmiac,** *a.* pertaining to or consisting of dochmii. *n.* (*usu. pl.*) a line composed of such feet. [L, from Gr. *dochmios,* pertaining to a *dochmē,* a hand's-breadth]

docile, *a.* teachable; willing or ready to learn; tractable; easily managed. **docility,** *n.* [F, from L *docilis,* from *docēre,* to teach]

docimasy, *n.* (*Min.*) the act or process of assaying metals; (*Chem., Med.*) act or process of testing, esp. in materia medica and forensic medicine. **docimastic,** *a.* **docimology,** *n.* a treatise on metallurgy, or the art of assaying metals etc. [Gr. *dokimasia,* from *dokimazein,* to examine]

dock¹, *n.* a common name for various species of the genus *Rumex,* perennial herbs, most of them troublesome weeds, esp. the common dock, *R. obtusifolius.* [OE *docce*]

dock², *n.* the solid fleshy part of an animal's tail; the tail after being cut short; †a leather case for a docked tail; the divided part of the crupper through which a horse's tail is put. *v.t.* to cut the tail off; to cut short; to abridge, to curtail; to deduct a part from; to deprive of a part of. [cp. Icel. *dockr,* a short, stumpy tail, LG *dokke,* a bunch, a stump, G *Docke,* a plug, a peg]

dock³, *n.* an artificial basin in which ships are built or repaired; (*often pl.*) an artificial basin for the reception of ships to load and unload; a dockyard; a wharf; an enclosure between platforms where lines terminate; (*N Am.*) a wharf. *v.t.* to bring into dock; to place in a dry dock; to equip with docks. **dry, graving dock,** a dock from which the water can be pumped out for building and repairing vessels. **floating dock,** a capacious iron or wooden structure into which a vessel can be floated, the internal water then being pumped out to result in a floating dry dock. **to be in, to put into, dock,** to be, to send, away for repairs. **wet dock,** a dock with the water kept at high-tide level, in which vessels load or unload. **dock-charges, -dues,** *n.pl.* dues payable by vessels using docks. **dock-glass,** *n.* a large glass, orig. used for sampling wine at the docks. **dockland,** *n.* the land around the docks. **dock-master,** *n.* the officer in charge of docks or of a dockyard. **dockside,** *n.* the area beside a dock. **dockyard,** *n.* a large enclosed area with wharves, docks etc. where vessels are built or repaired, usually in connection with the Navy. **dockage,** *n.* accommodation in docks; dock-dues. **docker,** *n.* a labourer at the docks. **dockize, -ise,** *v.t.* to convert a river into a floating harbour or range of docks. **dockization, -isation,** *n.* [cp. MDut. *docke, dokke* (mod. Dut. *dok*), also E dial. *doke,* a hollow]

dock⁴, *n.* the enclosure for prisoners in a criminal court. **in the dock,** charged with some offence. **dock brief,** *n.* (*Law*) a brief undertaken without a fee for a prisoner who would not otherwise be defended. [perh. through thieves' cant from *dok,* a hutch, a pen]

docket, *n.* a summary or digest; a register of judgments; an alphabetical list of cases for trial; a similar summary of business to be dealt with by a committee or assembly; an endorsement of a letter or document summarizing the contents; a warrant certifying payment of duty, issued by a custom-house; a certificate from the clearing house entitling to delivery of cotton goods; a ticket or label showing the address of a package etc.; a form of rationing coupon. *v.t.* (*Law*) to make an abstract, digest or summary of judgments and enter in a docket; to make an abstract or note of the contents of (a document) on the back. [etym. doubtful]

dockize, -ise DOCK³.

Doc Martens®, *n.pl.* heavy, strong, lace-up shoes or calf-length boots.

doctor, *n.* a qualified practitioner of medicine or surgery; †a teacher, a learned man; one who has taken the highest degree in a faculty at a university either for proficiency or as a compliment; a name for various mechanical devices; an artificial fly for salmon; (*sl.*) a loaded die; brown sherry, from its being doctored; a ship's cook; (*Austral.*) a camp cook. *v.t.* to administer medicines to; to treat medically; to confer the degree of doctor on; to patch up, to mend; to adulterate; to falsify; to castrate or spay (a dog or cat). *v.i.* to practise as a physician. **Doctors' Commons** COMMONS. **Doctors of the Church,** a name applied to certain early Fathers, esp. Ambrose, Augustine, Jerome and Gregory, in the Western Church, and Athanasius, Basil, Gregory of Nazianzus and Chrysostom, in the Eastern. **(just) what the doctor ordered,** something much needed or desired. **doctor's stuff,** *n.* physic. **doctoral,** *a.* **doctorate,** *n.* the degree, rank or title of a doctor; doctorship. **doctorhood,** *n.* **doctorial,** *a.* **doctoring,** *n.* medical treatment; adulteration, falsification. **doctorless,** *a.* **doctorship,** *n.* doctorate; the personality of a doctor. †**doctress,** *n. fem.* [OF *doctour,* L *doctor -ōrem,* from *docēre,* to teach]

Doctor Faustus, *n.* a tragedy by Christopher Marlowe, published (in two versions) in 1604 and 1616, first performed in 1594. The play, based upon the medieval Faust legend, tells how Faustus surrenders his soul to the Devil in return for 24 years of life and the services of Mephistopheles, who will grant his every wish.

doctrinaire, *n.* one who theorizes in politics without regard to practical considerations; a theorizer, an ideologist; (*Hist.*) one of a party of French politicians, who, under the Restoration (1814–30), advocated a limited monarchy with representative institutions. *a.* visionary, theoretical, impractical. **doctrinarian,** *n., a.* **doctrinairism, doctrinarianism,** *n.* [F, from L *doctrīna,* DOCTRINE]

doctrine, *n.* that which is taught; the principles, tenets or dogmas of any church, sect, literary or scientific school, or party; †a lesson; †learning, erudition. **Monroe doctrine,** the view that non-American powers should not intervene in American affairs, first set forth by President Monroe in 1823. **doctrinal,** *a.* †pertaining to the act, art or practice of teaching; pertaining to doctrine; of the nature of or containing a doctrine. **doctrinally,** *adv.* **doctrinism,** *n.* **doctrinist,** *n.* **doctrinize, -ise,** *v.i.* [F, from L *doctrīna,* from DOCTOR]

document, *n.* a written or printed paper containing information for the establishment of facts; (*loosely*) any mark, fact, deed or incident furnishing evidence or illustration of a statement or view; †a precept, a dogma; †an example, a warning; †a lesson. *v.i.* to furnish with documents necessary to establish any fact; to prove by means of documents; †to teach. **documental,** *a.* **documentary,** *a.* relating to documents; presenting facts or reality. **documentary (film),** *n.* one which represents real events or phases of life. **documentation,** *n.* the preparation or use of documents; the documents or references given. [F, from L *documentum,* from *docēre,* to teach]

dodder[1], *n.* a plant of the genus *Cuscuta,* which consists of slender, twining leafless parasites, enveloping and destroying the plants on which they grow. [ME *doder,* cp. Dan. *dodder,* G *Dotter*]

dodder[2], *v.i.* to shake, to tremble, to totter; to be feeble and worn out. **doddering-grass,** *n.* quaking-grass. **dodderer,** *n.* **doddery,** *a.* [etym. doubtful; cp. TOTTER]

doddered, *a.* having lost their top or branches (of aged oaks etc.); †(*erroneously*) overgrown with dodder. [prob. from obs. *dod,* to poll or top]

doddle, *n.* (*coll.*) something very easily accomplished.

Dodds, *n.* Charles (1899–1973), British biochemist. He was largely responsible for the discovery of stilboestrol, the powerful synthetic hormone used in treating prostate conditions and also for fattening cattle.

doddy, *a.* (*Sc.*) cross-grained, crabbed. [Gael. *dod,* peevishness]

dodec(a)-, *pref.* twelve. [Gr. *dōdeka*]

dodecagon, *n.* (*Geom.*) a plane figure of 12 equal angles and sides. [Gr. *dōdekagōnon*]

dodecagyn, *n.* a plant having 12 separate styles. **Dodecagynia,** *n.pl.* a Linnaean order of plants containing those having from 12 to 19 free styles. **dodecagynian, dodecagynous,** *a.* [Gr. *gunē,* a woman, a female]

dodecahedron, *n.* (*Geom.*) a solid figure of 12 equal sides, each of which is a regular pentagon. **dodecahedral,** *a.* [Gr. *dōdekaedron* (*hedra,* a seat)]

Dodecandria, *n.pl.* a Linnaean class of plants, comprising those having 12 to 19 free stamens. **dodecandrian, -drous,** *a.* [Gr. *anēr andros,* a male]

dodecapetalous, *a.* (*Bot.*) having 12 petals.

dodecaphonic, *a.* relating to a 12-tone musical system. **dodecaphonist,** *n.* a composer of 12-tone music.

dodecasyllable, *n.* (*Pros.*) a verse of 12 syllables; an alexandrine. **dodecasyllabic,** *a.*

dodge, *v.i.* to start aside suddenly; to change place by a sudden movement; to move rapidly from place to place so as to elude pursuit etc.; to act trickily, to prevaricate, to quibble. *v.t.* to escape from by starting aside; to evade by craft; to baffle by playing fast and loose with, to cheat; to dog. *n.* a sudden start or movement to one side; a trick, an artifice; an evasion; a skilful contrivance or expedient; a particular change or order in bell-ringing. **dodger,** *n.* one who dodges or evades; a trickster, a cheat; (*N Am.*) a hard-baked cake or biscuit. **dodgery,** *n.* **dodgy,** *a.* full of dodges; crafty, artful, tricky; uncertain, risky. [etym. doubtful]

Dodgem®, *n.* a bumper car in an amusement ground.

Dodgson, *n.* **Charles Lutwidge**, real name of Lewis Carroll.

dodo, *n.* (*pl.* **-does, -dos**) a large bird, *Didus ineptus,* allied to the pigeons, with rudimentary wings, found in Mauritius in great numbers when that island was colonized in 1644 by the Dutch, but soon totally exterminated, the last record of its occurrence being in the year 1681; an incorrigibly conservative person. **as dead as a dodo,** completely obsolete or defunct. [Port. *doudo,* silly, foolish]

Dodoma, *n.* capital (replacing Dar-es-Salaam in 1974) of Tanzania; 1132 m/3713 ft above sea level; population (1984) 180,000. Centre of communications, linked by rail with Dar-es-Salaam and Kigoma on Lake Tanganyika, and by road with Kenya to the N, and Zambia and Malawi to the S.

dodonaean, *a.* an epithet of Jupiter, worshipped in the temple of Dodona, in Epirus, where there was a famous oracle. [L *Dōdōnaeus,* Gr. *Dōdōnaios*]

DOE, (*abbr.*) Department of the Environment.

doe, *n.* the female of the fallow deer; the female of the rabbit, hare and sometimes of other animals. **doeskin,** *n.* the skin of a doe; an untwilled fine woollen cloth resembling this. [OE *dā,* cp. L *dāma*]

doer, does, doest DO[1].

doff, *v.t.* to take off (as clothes); to lay aside, to discard. *v.i.* to take off the hat as a mark of respect. **doffer,** *n.* a part of a carding-machine for stripping the cotton or wool from the cylinder; a person who removes the full bobbins or spindles. [contr. of DO OFF]

dog, *n.* a wild or domesticated quadruped of numerous breeds classed together as *Canis familiaris,* derived from crossing of various species living and extinct; the male of the wolf, fox and other animals; a surly fellow; a contemptible person; a gay young fellow; one of two southern constellations; a name given to various mechanical contrivances acting as holdfasts; a device with a tooth which penetrates or grips an object and detains it; an andiron or firedog; †the hammer of a firearm. *v.t.* to follow like a dog; to track the footsteps of; (*fig.*) to follow or attend closely; (*Naut.*) to fasten, to secure. †**dead dog,** a thing of no worth. **dog in the manger,** one who prevents other people from enjoying what he/she cannot enjoy; a churlish person. **dressed up like a dog's dinner,** dressed too flamboyantly. **give a dog a bad name,** if a person once gets a bad reputation it is difficult to regain people's good opinion. **hair of the dog** HAIR. **hot dog,** (*coll.*) a hot sausage sandwich. **lucky dog,** a lucky fellow. **sea-dog,** a jack-tar, an old sailor, esp. one of the Elizabethan adventurers; a luminous appearance on the horizon presaging storm. **sly dog,** an artful fellow. **sun-dog,** *n.* a parhelion. **the dogs,** *n.pl.* (*coll.*) greyhound races. **to die a dog's death,** to perish miserably or shamefully. **to go to the dogs,** to go to ruin. **to lead a dog's life,** to live a life of continual wretchedness; to be continually bickering. **to let sleeping dogs lie,** to leave well alone. **to rain cats and dogs,** to rain in torrents. **to throw, give, to the dogs,** to throw away. †**dog-ape,** *n.* a male ape. **dog-bane,** *n.* a plant with a bitter root, belonging to the genus *Apocynum,* supposed to be poisonous to dogs. **dog-belt,** *n.* a belt with a chain attached, worn by those who draw sledges in mines. **dog-biscuit,** *n.* coarse biscuit, often mixed with greaves for feeding dogs. †**dog-bolt,** *n.* a wretch, a villain. **dog-box,** *n.* a railway van for dogs. **dog-cart,** *n.* a light, two-wheeled, double-seated, one-horse vehicle. **dog-cheap,** *a.* extremely cheap, dirt-cheap. **dog-collar,** *n.* a leather or metal collar worn by dogs; (*fig.*) a high, straight shirt-collar; a stiff, white collar fastening at that back, as worn by clergymen. **dog-days,** *n.pl.* the period in July and August during which the dog-star rises and sets with the sun, a conjunction formerly supposed to account for the great heat usual at that season. **dog-eared,** *a.* dog's-eared. **dog-eat-dog,** *n.* ruthless pursuit of one's own interests. **dog-end,** *n.* (*sl.*) a cigarette-end. **dog-faced,** *a.* applied to a kind of baboon. **dog-fall,** *n.* a fall in which both wrestlers touch the ground together. **dog-fancier,** *n.* one who keeps and breeds dogs for sale. **dog-fennel,** *n.* the stinking camomile, *Anthemis cotula,* an acrid emetic. **dog-fight,** *n.* a fight between dogs; a wrangle; (*Aviat.*) a duel in the air between two aircraft. **dog-fish,** *n.* any species of the genus *Scyllium,* sometimes extended to the family Scylliidae, comprising small sharks which follow their prey in packs, whence their popular name. **dog-fox,** *n.* a male fox; †(*fig.*) a crafty fellow. **dog-grass,** *n.* couch-grass, *Triticum repens.* **dog-head,** *n.* the hammer of a gun-lock. **dog-hearted,** *a.* cruel, pitiless, malicious. **dog-hole,** *n.* a place fit only for dogs. **dog-house, -hutch,** *n.* a dog-kennel; (*fig.*) a miserable room. **in the dog-house,** in disfavour. **dog-kennel,** *n.* a house or hut for a dog. **dog-Latin,** *n.*

barbarous, ungrammatical Latin. **dog-lead,** *n.* a string or thin chain for leading a dog. †**dog-leech,** *n.* a dog doctor; used as a term of reproach or contempt. **dog-leg,** *a.* bent like a dog's hind leg, applied to a crook-shanked chisel; in golf, of a hole with a bent fairway. **dog-leg fence,** (*Austral.*) a fence made of logs laid horizontally on X-shaped supports. **dog-legged,** *a.* applied to staircases constructed in zigzags without a well-hole. **dog-, doggy-paddle,** *n.* a simple swimming stroke in which the arms imitate the front legs of a swimming dog. **dog-power,** *n.* a mechanical device worked by a dog; (*N Am.*) a churn worked by a dog. **dog-rose,** *n.* the wild brier, *Rosa canina.* **dogsbody,** *n.* (*coll.*) someone made use of by others; a useful person treated as a drudge. **dog's chance,** *n.* the slightest chance. **dog's-ear,** *n.* a corner of a leaf of a book turned down like a dog's ear. *v.t.* to turn the corners of (a book) by careless handling. **dog's-eared,** *a.* **dog's grass** DOG-GRASS. **dog-shore,** *n.* one of two struts that hold the cradle of a ship from sliding on the slipways when the keel-blocks are taken out. **dog-sick,** *a.* exceedingly sick; vomiting. **dog-skin,** *n.* the skin of a dog tanned for gloves; an imitation of this. *a.* made of dog-skin. **dog sled,** *n.* (*N Am.*) a sleigh pulled by a team of dogs. **dog-sleep,** *n.* a light, fitful sleep. **dog's letter,** *n.* the letter *r,* from its snarling sound. **dog's meat,** *n.* coarse meat, given as food to dogs; (*fig.*) refuse, rubbish. **dog's mercury,** *n.* *Mercurialis perennis,* a common poisonous plant. **dog's-nose,** *n.* a mixture of gin and beer. **dog's-tail,** *n.* a pasture-grass, *Cynosurus cristatus.* **dog-star,** *n.* Sirius, the principal star in the constellation *Canis major.* **dog's-tongue,** *n.* the hound's tongue, *Cynoglossum officinale.* **dog's-tooth,** *n.* a canine tooth; (*Arch.*) a kind of ornament used in Early English mouldings. **dog-tag,** *n.* (*N Am.*) an identification tag for military personnel. **dog-tired,** *a.* worn out. **dog-tooth,** *n.* dog's-tooth. **dog-tooth spar,** a kind of calcareous spar crystallizing in pointed rhombohedral forms. **dog-trot,** *n.* a gentle easy trot; a jog-trot. **dog-vane,** *n.* (*Naut.*) a small vane of cork and feathers, placed on the weather-rail as a guide to the man at the wheel. **dog-violet,** *n.* the scentless wild violet, *Viola canina.* **dog-watch,** *n.* (*Naut.*) one of two watches of two hours each between 4 and 8 p.m. **dog-wolf,** *n.* a male wolf. **doggish,** *a.* **doggishly,** *adv.* **doggishness,** *n.* **doggo,** *a.* hidden. **to lie doggo,** (*coll.*) to wait silently and motionlessly. **doggy, doggie,** *n.* pet term for a dog. *a.* pertaining to a dog; (*fig.*) smart, chic, with an air; flashy, raffish. **doggy bag,** *n.* (*coll.*) a bag for taking home uneaten food after a restaurant meal. **doghood,** *n.* **dogless,** *a.* **doglike,** *a.* like a dog; unquestioningly obedient. [OE *docga*]

Dogberry, *n.* an ignorant, conceited, but good-natured constable in *Much Ado about Nothing;* an officious constable or policeman; an incapable and overbearing magistrate. [Shakespeare]

dogberry, *n.* the fruit of the wild cornel or dogwood, *Cornus sanguinea;* also *Viburnum opulus, Arctostaphylos uva ursi,* and the fruit of *Rosa canina.* **dogberry tree** DOGWOOD.

doge, *n.* the title of the chief magistate of the republics of Venice and Genoa. **dogate,** *n.* the position, office or rank of a doge. [It. *doge* (dō′jā), L *ducem,* acc. of *dux,* leader (cp. DUKE)]

dogged, *a.* stubborn like a dog, obstinate, persistent, tenacious; †ill-conditioned, malignant. **doggedly,** *adv.* **doggedness,** *n.*

dogger, *n.* a Dutch fishing-vessel with bluff bows like a ketch, employed in the North Sea in the cod and herring fishery. [A-F *doggere;* etym. unknown]

doggerel, *n., a.* orig. applied to loose, irregular verses, such as those in Butler's *Hudibras;* now to verses written with little regard to rhythm or rhyme. [etym. unknown]

doggone, *int.* expressing annoyance. **doggoned,** *a.* (*euphem.*) god-damned. [GOD, DAMN]

dogma, *n.* (*pl.* **-mas, -mata**) an established principle, tenet or system of doctrines put forward to be received on authority, esp. that of a Church, as opposed to one deduced from experience or reasoning; a positive, magisterial or arrogant expression of opinion. **dogmatic,** †**-ical,** *a.* pertaining to dogma, doctrinal; based on theory not induction; asserted with authority, positive, authoritative; magisterial, arrogant, dictatorial. **dogmatically,** *adv.* **dogmaticalness,** *n.* **dogmatics,** *n. sing.* doctrinal theology, the science which deals with the statement and definition of Christian doctrine. **dogmatism,** *n.* dogmaticalness; arrogance or undue positiveness in assertion; the rule of dogma in the realm of thought. **dogmatist,** *n.* **dogmatize, -ise,** *v.i.* to make dogmatic assertions; to lay down principles with undue positiveness and confidence. *v.t.* to lay down as a dogma. **dogmato-,** *comb. form.* [L, from Gr. *dogma -matos,* from *dokeein,* to seem, to think, cogn. with L *docēre,* to teach]

dogwood, *n.* (*Bot.*) the genus *Cornus,* esp. *C. sanguinea,* the wild cornel; also applied to *Euonymus europaeus* and *Rhamnus frangula.*

doh DO².

Doha, *n.* capital and chief port of Qatar; population (1985) 150,000. Industries include oil refining, refrigeration plants, engineering and food processing. Centre of vocational training for all the Gulf states.

doiled, doilt, *a.* (*Sc., North.*) crazy, foolish.

doily, doyley, *n.* a small ornamental mat or napkin on which to place cakes, sandwiches, bottles, glasses etc. [*Doily,* an 18th-cent. London haberdasher]

doings, *n.pl.* (*coll.*) things done or performed; events, transactions, proceedings, affairs, goings-on; objects; behaviour, conduct; applied to any object whose name one has forgotten or does not want to say.

doit, *n.* a small Dutch copper coin worth about half a farthing; a small Scots copper coin; any small piece of money, a trifle. [Dut. *duit;* perh. conn. with OE *thwitan,* to cut]

doited, *a.* crazed; mentally affected, esp. by old age. [perh. a var. of DOTED, see DOTE]

dolabra, *n.* (*pl.* **-brae**) a kind of mattock or pickaxe used by Roman soldiers in making entrenchments and destroying fortifications. **dolabriform,** *a.* having the form of an axe; hatchet-shaped, as the leaves of *Mesembryanthemum dolabriforme;* (*Ent.*) applied to joints of the antennae. [L]

Dolby®, *n.* a system used to cut down interference on broadcast or recorded sound. [R. *Dolby,* b.1933, US engineer]

dolce, *a.* sweet, soft, usu. of music. *adv.* sweetly, softly. **dolce far niente,** *n.* sweet idleness. **dolce vita,** *n.* a life of luxury and self-indulgence. [It.]

doldrums, *n.pl.* low spirits, the dumps; that part of the ocean near the equator between the regions of the trade-winds where calms and variable winds prevail. **in the doldrums,** in low spirits, in the dumps; (*Naut.*) becalmed. [prob. a slang deriv. from DULL]

dole¹, *n.* sorrow, lamentation; a cause of grief. **doleful,** *a.* sorrowful, sad; afflicted, lamentable; dismal, gloomy. **dolefully,** *adv.* **dolefulness,** *n.* †**dolesome,** *a.* doleful, cheerless, dispiriting. †**dolesomely,** *adv.* **dolesomeness,** *n.* [OF *doel* (F *deuil*), late L *dolium,* L *dolor*]

dole², *n.* a share, a lot, a portion; distribution, esp. in charity; alms, money or food distributed in charity; †fortune, lot; †dealing, delivery (of blows, death etc.); unemployment benefit. *v.t.* to distribute. **on the dole,** in receipt of unemployment benefit. **to dole out,** to distribute in small quantities. **dole-bludger,** *n.* (*Austral. sl.*) one who draws unemployment benefit and makes no attempt to find work. **dolesman,** *n.* one who receives a small charitable gift. **doleswoman,** *n. fem.* [OE *dāl,* var. of *dæl,* DEAL¹]

dolerite, *n.* a variety of trap-rock consisting of feldspar and pyroxene. [F *dolérite,* Gr. *doleros,* deceptive, from the difficulty of discriminating the compounds]

dolichocephalic, -cephalous, *a.* long-headed; applied to skulls in which the width from side to side bears a less proportion to the width from front to back than 80%. **dolichocephalism,** *n.* [Gr. *dolichos,* long]

Dolichos, *n.* a genus of papilionaceous plants with long pods, allied to the kidney bean. [Gr., long]
dolichosaurus, *n.* (*Palaeont.*) a small snake-like lacertilian reptile from the chalk. [Gr. *dolichos,* as prec., *sauros,* a lizard]
dolichurus, *n.* (*Pros.*) a verse having a redundant foot. [Gr. *dolichoouros* (*dolichos,* long, *oura,* a tail)]
Dolium, *n.* a genus of gasteropodous molluscs from warm seas. [L, a cask, a jar]
doll, *n.* a child's toy representing a human figure; a pretty (but silly) woman; (*esp. N Am. coll.; sometimes derog.*) a term of endearment to a woman. **to doll up,** (*coll.*) to dress up, to make oneself look smart. **dollish,** *a.* **dollishly,** *adv.* **dollishness,** *n.* [pet name for *Dorothy*]
Doll, *n.* **William Richard** (1912–), British physician who proved the link between smoking and lung cancer.
dollar, *n.* the unit of currency (orig. a silver coin) in the US and Canada, also Australia, New Zealand etc., equivalent to 100 cents; applied to coins of different values; (*sl.*) five shillings (25p); a crown piece. **dollar area,** *n.* the area in which currency is linked to the US dollar. **dollar diplomacy,** *n.* diplomacy dictated by financial interests abroad; diplomacy which uses financial power as a weapon. **dollar gap,** *n.* the excess of imports over exports in trade with a dollar-area country. [LG *daler,* G *Thaler,* abbr. of *Joachimsthaler,* coins of silver from a mine in the *Joachimsthal*]
Dollfuss, *n.* **Engelbert** (1892–1934), Austrian Christian Socialist politician. He was appointed chancellor in 1932, and in 1933 suppressed parliament and ruled by decree. Negotiations for an alliance with the Austrian Nazis broke down. On 12 Feb. 1934 he crushed the Social Democrats by force, and in May Austria was declared a corporative state. The Nazis attempted a coup d'état on 25 Jul.; the Chancellery was seized and Dollfuss murdered. He was known as the 'pocket chancellor' because of his small stature.
dollop, *n.* (*coll.*) a shapeless lump; a heap, quantity. **all the dollop,** (*sl.*) the whole thing. [etym. doubtful]
dolly, *n.* a pet name for a doll; (*Mining*) a perforated board placed over a tub to wash ore in; the tub itself; a hoisting platform; a trolley; an appliance used in pile-driving; a stick or club with which dirty clothes are agitated in the wash-tub; †a mistress; a simple catch in cricket. *a.* dollish. **dolly camera,** *n.* a cine-camera moving on a type of trolley. **dolly mixture,** *n.* a mixture of tiny coloured sweets. **dolly-shop,** *n.* an unlicensed pawnshop; a marine-store (from a black doll being used as a sign). **dolly shot,** *n.* one taken with a dolly camera. **dolly switch,** *n.* one for an electric light etc. consisting of a lever to be pushed up and down. **dolly-tub,** *n.* a washing-tub.
Dolly Varden, *n.* a large-patterned print dress; a wide-brimmed woman's hat with one side bent down. [a character in Dickens's *Barnaby Rudge*]
dolman, *n.* a long Turkish robe, open in front, and with narrow sleeves; a woman's loose mantle with hanging sleeves; a hussar's jacket or cape with sleeves hanging loose. **dolman sleeve,** *n.* one which tapers from a wide armhole to a tightly-fitting wrist. [F, from G, from Hung. *dolmany,* Turk. *dōlān*]
dolmen, *n.* a cromlech; the megalithic framework of a chambered cairn, consisting usually of three or more upright stones supporting a roof-stone. [F, prob. from Corn. *dolmēn, tolmēn* (*doll, toll,* hole, *mēn,* stone)]
dolomite, *n.* a brittle, subtransparent or translucent mineral consisting of the carbonates of lime and magnesia. **dolomitic,** *a.* **dolomitize, -ise, dolomize, -ise,** *v.t.* **dolomitization, -isation,** *n.* [*Dolomieu,* 1750–1801, French geologist. Nothing to do with the Dolomite Mts in Tyrol]
dolorous, *a.* full of pain or grief; causing or expressing pain or grief, dismal, doleful. **doloroso,** *a., adv.* (*Mus.*) in a soft, dolorous manner. **dolorously,** *adv.* **dolorousness,** *n.* [OF *dolerus,* from DOLOUR]
dolose, *a.* (*Law*) with criminal intent. [L *dolōsus,* from *dolus,* deceit]
dolour, *n.* pain, suffering, distress; grief, sorrow, lamentation. **Feast of the Dolours,** a festival in commemoration of these on the Friday after Passion Sunday. **Our Lady of Dolours,** in the Roman Catholic Church, a title given to the Virgin Mary on account of her sorrows at the Passion. [OF, from L *dolor dolōrem,* from *dolēre,* to grieve]
dolphin, *n.* the cetacean genus *Delphinus,* esp. *D. delphis,* the common dolphin; the dorado, *Coryphaena hippuris,* which takes a series of brilliant colours in dying; (*Naut.*) a mooring-post; an anchored spar with rings, serving as a mooring-buoy; (*Her. etc.*) a conventional representation of a curved fish; †a ponderous mass of metal let fall suddenly from the yard-arm of a vessel upon an enemy's ship; †the Dauphin. **river dolphin,** any of several freshwater mammals found in rivers in N and S America and S Asia. **dolphin fly,** *n. Aphis fabae,* an insect infesting bean-plants. **†dolphin-like,** *a.* showing the back above the surface of the sea etc. **dolphinarium,** *n.* an aquarium for dolphins, often one for public displays. **†dolphinet,** *n. fem.* [ME *delfyn,* L *delphīnus,* see DAUPHIN, OF *daulphin,* which affected the later spelling]
dolt, *n.* a stupid fellow; a numskull. **doltish,** *a.* **doltishly,** *adv.* **doltishness,** *n.* [prob. *dult,* DULLED, see DULL]
DOM, (*abbr.*) to God the best and greatest (L *Deo optimo maximo*).
dom., (*abbr.*) domestic; dominion.
dom[1], *n.* in the Roman Catholic Church, a title given to members of the Benedictine and Carthusian orders; the Portuguese form of DON[1]. [abbr. of L *dominus,* lord]
dom[2], *n.* a Continental cathedral. [G, cathedral, L *domus,* DOME[1]]
-dom, *comb. form* noting power, jurisdiction, office or condition, a group of people, as in *earldom, kingdom, officialdom, freedom.* [OE *dōm,* judgment, cogn. with G *-tum*]
Domagk, *n.* **Gerhard** (1895–1964), German pathologist, discoverer of antibacterial drugs. He found that a dye substance called prontosil red contains chemicals with powerful antibacterial properties. This became the first of the sulphonamide drugs, used to treat a wide range of conditions, including pneumonia and septic wounds.
domain, *n.* territory, district or space over which authority, jurisdiction or control is or may be exercised; one's landed property, demesne, estate; (*fig.*) sphere, province, field of influence, thought or action; †lordship, authority; in physics, that part of a ferromagnetic solid where all the atoms are magnetically aligned; (*Math.*) the aggregate to which a variable belongs. **eminent domain,** (*N Am. and Internat. Law*) the sovereign power of the state to exercise control over private property for public purposes on payment of compensation to owners. **domainal, domanial,** *a.* [F *domaine,* late L *dominicum,* L *dominium,* from *dominus,* lord]
domboc DOOM-BOOK under DOOM.
domdaniel, *n.* a fabulous submarine hall in the continuation of the *Arabian Nights* by Chaves and Cazotte; an 'infernal cave', a 'den of iniquity' (Thomas Carlyle). [F, prob. from Gr. *dōma Daniēl,* the house or hall of Daniel]
dome[1], *n.* a roof, usually central, the base of which is a circle, an ellipse or a polygon, and its vertical section a curved line, concave towards the interior; a cupola; a natural vault, arching canopy or lofty covering; a rounded hill-top; a mansion, temple or other building of a stately kind; any dome-shaped object or structure; a termination of a prism by two planes meeting above in a horizontal edge; (*sl.*) the head. *v.t.* to cover with, shape into, a dome. *v.i.* to swell into a domelike shape. **domed,** *a.* furnished with a dome; dome-shaped. **domelike,** *a.* **domic, domical,** *a.* **domy,** *a.* [MF *dome,* It. *duomo,* L *domus,* a house]
dome[2] DOOM.
Domenico Veneziano, *n.* (*c.* 1400–61), Italian painter, active in Florence. His few surviving frescoes and

altarpieces show a remarkably delicate use of colour and light (which recurs in the work of Piero della Francesca, who trained under him).

Dome of the Rock, building in Jerusalem dating from the 7th century AD that enshrines the rock from which, in Muslim tradition, Mohammed ascended to heaven on his Night Journey. It stands on the site of the Jewish national Temple and is visited by pilgrims.

Domesday Book, *n.* a register of the lands of England compiled (1084–86) by order of William the Conqueror, from the results of a Great Inquisition or survey, forming a basis for all historical accounts of the economic state of the country at that epoch. [ME DOOMSDAY]

domestic, *a.* pertaining to the home or household; made, done or performed at home; employed or kept at home; fond of home; tame, not wild; relating to the internal affairs of a nation; not foreign; made in one's own country; (*N Am.*) inland (as for postage etc.), native grown (as for wine etc.). *n.* a household servant; †a fellow-countryman; (*pl.*) articles of home (as opp. to foreign) manufacture, esp. (*N Am.*) cotton cloth. **domestic architecture,** *n.* the architecture of dwelling-houses. **domestic economy,** *n.* the economical management of household affairs. **domestic science,** *n.* the study of household skills, inc. cookery, needlework etc. **domesticable,** *a.* **domestically,** *adv.* **domesticate,** *v.t.* to make domestic or familiar; to naturalize (foreigners etc.); to accustom to domestic life and the management of household affairs; to tame; to bring into cultivation from a wild state; to civilize. **domesticated,** *a.* tamed; content with home life; used to household chores. **domestication,** *n.* [F *domestique,* L *domesticus,* from *domus,* home]

domesticity, *n.* the state of being domestic; domestic character, homeliness; home life; the circumstances of home life; (*pl.*) domestic affairs, family matters.

domett, *n.* a plain cloth made of cotton and wool. [etym. unknown]

domicile, domicil, *n.* a house, a home, a place of abode; (*Law*) a place of permanent residence; length of residence (differing in various countries) necessary to establish jurisdiction in civil actions; the place at which a bill of exchange is made payable. *v.t.* to establish in a place of residence; to make payable at a certain place. *v.i.* to dwell. **domiciled,** *a.* **domiciliary**, *a.* pertaining to a domicile or residence. **domiciliary visit,** *n.* a visit under legal authority to a private house to search for suspected persons or things. **domiciliate**, *v.t.*, *v.i.* to establish, be established, in a residence. **domiciliation**, *n.* [F, from L *domicilium,* from *domus,* home]

dominant, *a.* ruling, governing; predominant, overshadowing, supereminent; pertaining to the fifth note of a scale. *n.* the fifth note of the scale of any key, counting upwards; the reciting note of Gregorian chants; a prevalent species in a plant community. **dominant chord,** *n.* a chord formed by grouping three tones rising from the dominant by intervals of a third. **dominance,** *n.* **dominancy,** *n.* **dominantly,** *adv.* [F, from L *dominans -antem,* pres.p. of *dominārī,* from *dominus,* lord]

dominate, *v.t.* to predominate over; to be the most influential or the chief or most conspicuous; to overlook (as a hill); to influence controllingly, to rule, govern. *v.i.* to predominate, to prevail. **domination,** *n.* the exercise of power or authority; rule, sway, control, dominion, ascendancy; (*pl.*) the fourth order of angels. †**dominative,** *a.* †**dominator,** *n.* [L *dominātus,* p.p. of *dominārī,* from *dominus,* lord]

dominee, *n.* a minister in any of the Afrikaner Churches in South Africa. [from Dut.]

domineer, *v.i.* to exercise authority arrogantly and tyrannically; to assume superiority over others; to hector, to bluster; †to roister, to revel. *v.t.* to tyrannize over. **domineering,** *a.* **domineeringly,** *adv.* [MDut. *domineren,* OF *dominer,* L *dominārī,* see DOMINANT]

Domingo, *n.* **Plácido** (1941–), Spanish tenor. One of a celebrated musical family, he emigrated with them to Mexico as a boy. He excels in romantic operatic roles.

Dominica, *n.* Commonwealth of, island in the West Indies. **area** 751 sq km/290 sq miles. **capital** Roseau, with a deepwater port. **physical** largest of the Windward Islands, mountainous, tropical. **population** (1987) 94,200 (mainly black African in origin, but with a small Carib reserve of some 500); annual growth rate 1.3%. **exports** bananas, coconuts, citrus, lime, bay oil. **language** English (official), but the Dominican *patois* still reflects earlier periods of French rule. **religion** Roman Catholic 80%.

dominical, *a.* pertaining to the Lord or the Lord's Day. *n.* the Lord's Day; one who observes the Lord's Day as distinguished from the Jewish Sabbath; a dominical letter. **dominical letter,** *n.* the letter (one of the seven A–G in the calendar) which denotes Sunday in any particular year. **dominical year,** *n.* the year of our Lord, AD. [med. L *dominicālis,* L *dominicus,* from *dominus,* lord]

Dominican, *n.* one of an order of preaching friars, founded in 1216 by Domingo de Guzman (canonized as St Dominic); a Black Friar; a nun in one of the orders founded by St Dominic. a native of the Dominican Republic. *a.* pertaining to the Dominicans. [med. L *Dominicānus,* from *Dominicus,* Domingo]

Dominican Republic, *n.* (*República Dominicana*), country in the West Indies. **area** 48,446 sq km/18,700 sq miles. **capital** Santo Domingo. **physical** comprises E part of island of Hispaniola; central mountain range; fertile valley in N. **population** (1987) 6,708,000; annual growth rate 2.3%. **exports** sugar, gold, coffee, ferro-nickel. **language** Spanish (official). **religion** Roman Catholic.

dominie, *n.* (*Sc.*) a pedagogue, a schoolmaster; a minister or clergyman. [L *domine,* sir, voc. of *dominus,* lord]

dominion, *n.* sovereign authority, lordship; control, rule, government; (*Law*) uncontrolled right of possession or use; the domain of a feudal lord; a district, region or country under one government; a self-governing country of the British Commonwealth, esp. Canada. **Dominion Day,** *n.* another name for Canada Day, which commemorates Canada receiving dominion status on 1 July 1867. [OF, from late L *dominio -ōnem,* L *dominium,* from *dominus,* lord]

domino, *n.* (*pl.* **-noes**) a masquerade dress worn for disguise by both sexes, consisting of a loose black cloak or mantle with a small mask; a kind of half mask; a person wearing a domino; one of 28 oblong dotted pieces, orig. of bone or ivory, used in playing dominoes; (*sl.*) an employee's check handed in to the timekeeper on entering the works or factory. **domino effect,** *n.* the fall of a long row of dominoes, all standing on end, caused by pushing the first domino in the row. **domino theory,** *n.* the theory that a single event leads to many similar events elsewhere as a chain reaction. **dominoed,** *a.* wearing a domino. **dominoes,** *n.pl.* any of various games played with dominoes, often involving pairing up matching values. [Sp. or F, from L *dominus,* lord (orig. perh. the hood worn by a master)]

Domitian, *n.* **(Titus Flavius Domitianus)** (AD 51-96), Roman emperor. Born in Rome, he became emperor in AD 81. He finalized the conquest of Britain, strengthened the Rhine-Danube frontier, and suppressed immorality as well as freedom of thought in philosophy, and religion (Christians were persecuted). His reign of terror led to his assassination.

don[1], *n.* a title formerly restricted to noblemen and gentlemen, now common to all classes in Spain, Sir, Mr; a Spanish gentleman; a Spaniard; a fellow or tutor of a college, esp. at Oxford or Cambridge; the head of a student dormitory in Canadian universities and colleges; a person of distinction; one who assumes airs of importance; (*sl.*) an adept, an expert. **Don Juan**, *n.* a lady-killer (from the hero of Byron's poem); a male flirt; a would-be rake. **Don Quixote**, *n.* one who is excessively idealistic or chivalrous, esp. one who goes to foolish extremes (from the hero of Cervantes' *Don Quixote de la Mancha*, 1605). **donnish,** *a.* **donnishness,** *n.* [Sp., from L *dominus,* lord]

don², *v.t.* (*past, p.p.* **donned**) to put on, to assume. [contr. of DO ON]

Don, *n.* river in Soviet Union, rising to the south of Moscow and entering the NE extremity of the Sea of Azov; length 1900km/1180 miles. In its lower reaches the Don is 1.5 km/1 mile wide, and for about four months of the year it is closed by ice. Its upper course is linked with the Volga by a canal.

doña, *n.* lady; madam; Mrs; (*sl.*) a woman; a sweetheart. [Sp. or Port., from L *domina,* lady]

Donald, *n.* **Ian** (1910–87), English obstetrician who introduced ultrasound scanning. He pioneered its use in obstetrics as a means of scanning the growing foetus without exposure to X-rays.

donate, *v.t.* to bestow as a gift, esp. on a considerable scale for public or religious purposes. **donator,** *n.* a donor. [L *dōnāre,* to give]

Donatello, *n.* **(Donato di Niccolo)** (1386–1466), Italian sculptor of the early Renaissance, born in Florence. He was instrumental in reviving the Classical style, as in his graceful bronze statue of the youthful *David* (Bargello, Florence) and his equestrian statue of the general *Gattamelata*, 1443 (Padua). The course of Florentine art in the 15th cent. was strongly influenced by his style.

donation, *n.* the act of giving; that which is given, a gift, a presentation, a contribution, esp. to a public institution; (*Law*) an act or contract by which any thing, or the use of and the right to it, is transferred as a free gift to any person or corporation. **donation-party,** *n.* (*N Am.*) a party or number of persons assembling at the house of one person (usu. a pastor), each bringing a present. [F, from L *dōnātio -ōnem,* from *dōnāre,* to give, from *dōnum,* a gift]

Donation of Constantine, the name given to the forged 8th-cent. document purporting to record Emperor Constantine's surrender of temporal sovereignty in W Europe to Pope Sylvester I (314–25).

Donatism, *n.* the doctrine of an Arian sect, founded in AD 311 by *Donatus,* a Numidian bishop who denied the infallibility of the Church and insisted on individual holiness as a condition of membership. **Donatist,** *n.* **Donatistic, -ical,** *a.* [med. L *Donatismus*]

donative, *n.* a gift, a present, a gratuity, esp. an official donation; a benefice directly given by a patron without presentation to or institution by the ordinary. *a.* vested or vesting by this form of presentation. **donatory,** *n.* the recipient of a donation. [L *dōnātivus,* from *dōnāre,* to give]

done, *p.p.* performed, executed; (*coll.*) cheated, baffled; cooked. *int.* accepted (used to express agreement to a proposal, as a wager, or a bargain). **to have done,** to have finished. **to have done with,** to have no further concern with. **done for,** *a.* ruined, killed, exhausted. **done up,** *a.* worn out or exhausted. [DO¹]

donee, *n.* the person to whom anything is given; (*Law*) the person to whom lands or tenements are given gratuitously or conveyed in fee-tail. [L *dōnum,* a gift, -EE]

Donegal, *n.* mountainous county in Ulster province in the NW of the Republic of Ireland, surrounded on three sides by the Atlantic; area 4830 sq km/1865 sq miles; population (1981) 125,112. The county town is Lifford; the market town and port of Donegal is at the head of Donegal Bay in the SW. Commercial activities include sheep and cattle raising, tweed and linen manufacture, and some deep-sea fishing.

doner kebab, *n.* a Turkish dish of lamb sliced from a block grilled on a spit, usu. served with salad in pitta bread. [Turk.]

Donetsk, *n.* city in the Ukraine, capital of Donetsk region, situated in the Donets Basin, a major coal mining area, 600 km/380 miles SE of Kiev, USSR; population (1983) 1,055,000. It has blast furnaces, rolling mills, and other heavy industries.

donga, *n.* a gully, a watercourse with steep sides. [Zulu]

Dönitz, *n.* **Karl** (1891–1980), German admiral, originator of the wolf-pack submarine technique which sank 15 million tonnes of Allied shipping in World War II. He succeeded Hitler in 1945, capitulated, and was imprisoned during 1946–56.

Donizetti, *n.* **Gaetano** (1797–1848), Italian composer, who composed more than 60 operas, including *Lucrezia Borgia* (1833), *Lucia di Lammermoor* (1835), *La Fille du régiment* (1840), *La Favorite* (1840) and *Don Pasquale* (1843). They show the influence of Rossini and Bellini, and their chief feature is their flow of expressive melodies.

donjon, *n.* the grand central tower or keep of esp. a mediaeval Norman castle, the lower storey generally used as a prison. [DUNGEON]

Don Juan, *n.* character of Spanish legend, Don Juan Tenorio, supposed to have lived in the 14th cent. and notorious for his debauchery. Tirso de Molina, Molière, Mozart, Byron and G. B. Shaw have featured the legend.

donkey, *n.* a member of the horse family, an ass; (*fig.*) a stupid person. **to talk the hindlegs off a donkey,** to talk with great persistence. **donkey-engine,** *n.* an auxiliary engine for light work on board steamships. **donkey jacket,** *n.* a short, thick workman's jacket. **donkey-pump,** *n.* a steam-pump, worked independently of the main engine, for supplying boilers with water and for other purposes. **donkey's years,** *n.pl.* (*facet.*) a long time. **donkey vote,** *n.* (*Austral.*) one where the voter's preference follows the order the candidates are listed in. **donkey-work,** *n.* drudgery, routine work. [perh. a double dim. of DUN¹, from the colour]

donna, *n.* a lady; madam; a prima donna. [It., from L *domina,* lady]

Donne, *n.* **John** (1571–1631), British metaphysical poet, whose work is characterized by subtle imagery and figurative language. In 1615 Donne took orders in the Church of England and as Dean of St Paul's was noted for his sermons. His poetry includes the sonnets 'No man is an island' and 'Death be not proud', elegies, satires and verse-letters.

donnered, donnard, *a.* (*Sc.*) stunned, stupefied. [Sc. *donner,* to stupefy, to din]

Donnerwetter, *n.* a thunderstorm. *int.* expressing annoyance. [G]

donnybrook, *n.* a rowdy brawl. [*Donnybrook* Fair, held annually near Dublin until 1855]

donor, *n.* a giver; (*Law*) one who grants an estate; one who gives blood for transfusion. **donor card,** *n.* one carried by a person willing to have parts of his/her body used for transplant. [OE *donour,* OF *doneur,* L *dōnātōr -ōrem,* from *dōnāre,* to give]

donsie, *a.* (*Sc.*) neat, trim; luckless, unfortunate; stupid, dull. [etym. unknown]

don't, *imper.* (*coll.*) do not. *n.* (*facet.*) a prohibition. **don't care,** *a.* careless), reckless. **don't know,** *n.* a person without a firm opinion on any matter; an answer given by one with such a lack of opinion.

donut DOUGHNUT under DOUGH.

donzel, *n.* a young gentleman following arms, but not yet knighted. [OF, cp. DAMOISEAU]

doodah, doodad, *n.* any small decorative article or gadget. **to be all of a doodah,** (*sl.*) to be flustered, in a state of confusion.

doodle¹, *v.t.* to draw pictures or designs semi-consciously while thinking or listening. *n.* a picture drawn in this way. **doodler,** *n.* [imit.]

doodle², *v.t.* (*Sc.*) to play (the bagpipes). *v.i.* to drone (as a bagpipe). **doodlebug,** *n.* (*coll.*) the earliest type of flying bomb used by the Germans in the war of 1939–45, the V-1; the larva of the ant-lion; a diviner's rod; any scientific or unscientific instrument for locating minerals. [G *dudeln* (*Dudelsack,* bagpipe)]

doolally, *a.* insane, eccentric. [*Deolali,* a town near Bombay, India]

doolie, *n.* a covered litter of bamboo. [Hind. *dōlī*]

Doolittle, *n.* **Hilda** (1886–1961), US poet. She went to Europe in 1911, and was associated with Ezra Pound and the British writer Richard Aldington (to whom she was married during 1913–37), in founding the Imagist school of poets. Her work includes the *Sea Garden* (1916) and *Helen in Egypt* (1916). She signed her work

'HD'.

doom, *n.* judgment; judicial decision or sentence; condemnation, penalty; †the Day of Judgment; fate or destiny (usu. in an evil sense); ruin, destruction, perdition; †an enactment, statute or law; †an opinion; †decision. *v.t.* †to judge, decide; to pass sentence upon; to condemn to punishment; to condemn (to do something); to predestine; to consign to ruin or calamity. **crack of doom,** the dissolution of all things at the universal Judgment. †**doom-book,** *n.* a book of laws, customs and usages, esp. one compiled under King Alfred. **doomsday,** *n.* the Day of Judgment; the end of the world; a day of judgment or dissolution. **till doomsday,** forever. **Doomsday Book** DOMESDAY BOOK. **doomwatch,** *n.* pessimism, esp. about the future of the environment; observation of the environment to prevent its destruction by pollution etc. **doomwatcher,** *n.* [OE *dōm,* from OTeut. *dōmo* (Dan., Swed. *dom,* OHG *tuom,* cp. Gr. *themis,* law)]

door, *n.* a frame of wood or metal, usually on hinges, closing the entrance to a building, room, safe etc.; an opening for entrance and exit; entrance, exit, access, means of approach; (*fig.*) a house, a room; the entrance or beginning; means of access. **door-to-door,** from one house to the next; of a journey, direct. **front door,** the principal entrance from the street. **in, within, doors,** inside the house. **next door,** in the next house or room. **next door to,** closely bordering on, nearly, almost. **out of door(s),** outside the house; in the open air; done away with. **to lie at one's door,** to be chargeable to. **to show the door,** to turn out; to send away unceremoniously. **to turn from the door,** to refuse to admit; to refuse a beggar or petitioner. **door-bell,** *n.* a bell inside a building actuated by a handle outside a door. **door-case, -frame,** *n.* the structure in which a door swings. **door-keeper,** *n.* a porter, a janitor. **door-knob,** *n.* a handle on a door. **door-knocker,** *n.* a hinged device attached to a door, for knocking. **doorman,** *n.* a porter, one employed to open doors. **doormat,** *n.* a mat for removing dirt from the boots, placed inside or outside a door; (*coll.*) a submissive person, often imposed on by others. **door-money,** *n.* payments taken at a place of entertainment. **door-nail,** *n.* a large nail formerly used for studding doors. **door-plate,** *n.* a metal plate on a door bearing the name of the occupant. **door-post,** *n.* side-piece or jamb of a doorway. **doorsill,** *n.* the wooden plank, or flat stone, forming the bottom of a door-frame. **doorstep,** *n.* a step leading up to an outer door; a thick slice of bread. *v.t.* to go from door to door to canvass during a political campaign, or to try to sell goods, often intrusively. **doorstepping,** *n.* **door-stone,** *n.* a slab in front of a door; the threshold. **doorstop,** *n.* a device which stops a door from moving. **doorway,** *n.* an opening in a wall fitted with a door; a means of access. **doored,** *a.* (*usu. with a. prefixed*). **doorless,** *a.* [OE *dor,* fem. *duru* (cp. Dan. *dor,* Icel. *dyrr,* G *Tür,* Gr. *thura,* L *fores*)]

dope, *n.* any thick liquid or semi-fluid used for food or as a lubricant; axle-grease; opium paste; (*coll.*) a drug given to a horse or greyhound to make it win a race; any drug; (*sl.*) a stupefying drink; an absorbent material used for holding liquid; the material used to hold nitroglycerine and other explosives; a varnish used for waterproofing, protecting and strengthening the fabric parts of an aircraft; (*sl.*) inside information, particulars. *v.t.* to add impurities to; to stupefy with drink, to drug. **dope-fiend,** *n.* a drug addict. **dopey,** *a.* (*coll.*) stupid; drugged; sluggish. **doping,** *n.* the adding of impurities to a semiconductor to produce a modification of its properties. [Dut. *doop,* dipping, sauce, from *doopen,* to dip]

doppelganger, *n.* the apparition of a living person; a wraith. [G *Doppelgänger,* double-goer]

Dopper, *n.* a member of the Reformed Church of South Africa, a religious sect characterized by extreme simplicity of manners and dress. [Dut. *Dooper,* Baptist]

dopplerite, *n.* a black substance found in peat beds.

Doppler's principle, *n.* (*Phys.*) when the source of any wave motion is approached the frequency appears greater than it would to an observer moving away. **Doppler sound effect,** the apparent change of pitch of sound produced by a body when approaching and passing with considerable velocity. **Doppler effect, shift,** *n.* an observed shift in the frequency of light according to Doppler's principle. [Austrian physicist C. *Doppler,* 1803–53]

dor, *n.* name of several insects that make a loud humming noise in flying, esp. the black dung-beetle, *Geotrupes stercorarius;* the cockchafer; the rose-beetle. **dorhawk,** *n.* the goat- sucker or night-jar. [OE *dora,* bumble-bee, prob. onomat.]

dorado, *n.* (*pl.* **-dos**) a fish, *Coryphaena hippuris,* of brilliant colouring, sometimes called a dolphin; (*Astron.*) a southern constellation, the Swordfish. [Sp., gilded, from L *deaurātus,* p.p. of *deaurāre* (DE-, *aurum,* gold)]

Dorcas, *n.* a meeting of women for making clothes for the poor. **Dorcas Society,** *n.* a charitable association for providing clothes for the poor. [Gr., gazelle, transl. of Aram. *Tabitha* (Acts ix.36)]

Dordogne, *n.* river in SW France, rising in Puy-de-Dôme *département* and flowing 490 km/300 miles to join the Garonne, 23 km/14 miles N of Bordeaux. It gives its name to a *département* and is an important source of hydroelectric power.

Doré, *n.* **Gustave** (1832–83), French artist, a prolific illustrator, and also active as a painter, etcher and sculptor. He produced closely worked engravings of scenes from, for example, Rabelais, Dante, Cervantes, the Bible, Milton and Poe.

doree DORY[1].

Dorian, *a.* of or relating to *Doris,* in ancient Greece, or its inhabitants. *n.* an inhabitant of Doris; a member of a people of ancient Greece, which entered the country from the N sometime before 1000 BC and conquered most of the Peloponnese from the Achaeans and destroyed the Mycenaean civilization. **Dorian mode,** *n.* (*Mus.*) a simple, solemn form of music, the first of the authentic Church modes. **Doric,** *a.* Dorian. *n.* (*Arch.*) the Doric order; a broad rustic dialect. **Doric dialect,** *n.* the broad, hard dialect of the natives of Doris; any broad, hard dialect, esp. the Scottish. **Doric order,** *n.* the earliest, strongest and most simple of the three Grecian orders of architecture.

Dorking, *n.* name of a breed of domestic fowls, orig. from Dorking. [town in Surrey]

dorlach, *n.* a bundle carried by Scottish Highlanders instead of a knapsack. [Gael.]

dorm, *n.* short for DORMITORY.

dormant, *a.* in a state resembling sleep, torpid, inactive (of animals hibernating); undeveloped, inoperative, not asserted or claimed; in abeyance; †fixed, stationary. **dormant partner,** *n.* a sleeping partner. **dormancy,** *n.* [F, pres.p. of *dormir,* L *dormīre,* to sleep]

dormer, *n.* †a sleeping chamber; a dormer-window. **dormer-window,** *n.* a window piercing a sloping roof and having a vertical frame and a gable (orig. used in sleeping chambers, whence the name). [OF *dormeor,* L *dormītōrium,* as prec.]

dormie DORMY.

dormitive, *a.* promoting sleep; narcotic, soporific. *n.* an opiate, a soporific. [L *dormit,* p.p. stem of *dormīre,* to sleep]

dormitory, *n.* a sleeping-chamber, esp. in a school or public institution, containing a number of beds; (*fig.*) a resting-place; †a burial-place. **dormitory suburb, town,** *n.* one whose inhabitants work elsewhere, often in a nearby city. [L *dormītōrium,* DORMER]

Dormobile®, *n.* a van equipped for living in while travelling.

dormouse, *n.* (*pl.* **-mice**) a small British hibernating rodent, *Myoxus avellanarius;* others of the genus *Myoxus,* animals between the mouse and the squirrel. †*a.* dormant. [dial. Eng. *dorm,* to sleep, F *dormir* (see DORMANT)]

dormy, dormie, *a.* (*Golf*) applied to a player when he is as many holes ahead of his opponent as there remains holes to play. [etym. doubtful, perh. F *dormi,* p.p. of *dormir,* to sleep]

dornic, *n.* a stout damask linen cloth, orig. made at Tournai. [Flem. *Doornik,* Tournai, in Flanders]

dorp, *n.* a S African small town. [Dut.]

dorsabdominal, *a.* relating to the back of the abdomen.

dorsal, *a.* of or pertaining to the back; situated on the back; shaped like a ridge. **dorsal fin,** *n.* the fin on the back of a fish which aids balance. **dorsally,** *adv.* [F, from late L *dorsālis,* from *dorsum,* the back]

Dorset, *n.* county in SW England. **area** 2654 sq km/ 1024 sq miles. **towns** administrative headquarters Dorchester; Poole, Shaftesbury, Sherborne; resorts Bournemouth, Lyme Regis, Weymouth. **population** (1986) 627,000. **products** Wytch Farm is the largest onshore oilfield in the UK.

dors(i)-, dorso-, *comb. form* belonging to, situated on, the back. [L *dorsum,* back]

dorsibranchiate, *a.* belonging to the Dorsibranchiata, a group of annelids in Cuvier's classification.

dorsiferous, -siparous, *a.* (*Bot.*) an epithet applied to ferns which have the seeds at the back of the frond. [-FEROUS; L *-parus,* bringing forth]

dorsiflexion, *n.* a bending backwards.

dorsigrade, *a.* walking on the back of the toes.

dorsispinal, *a.* belonging to the spine and the back.

dorsum, *n.* (*Zool., Anat.*) the back; (*Bot.*) the part of a carpel farthest from the axis; the surface of the body of a shell opposite the opening. [L, the back]

dorter, dortour, *n.* a dormitory. [OF, L *dormītōrium,* DORMITORY]

Dortmund, *n.* industrial centre in the Ruhr, West Germany, 58 km/36 miles NE of Düsseldorf; population (1984) 584,800. Largest mining town of the Westphalian coalfield and the S terminus of the Dortmund-Ems canal. Industries include iron, steel, construction machinery, engineering and brewing.

dory¹, *n.* a golden-yellow sea-fish, *Zeus faber,* called also John Dory. [F *dorée,* fem. p.p. of *dorer,* to gild (cp. DORADO)]

dory², *n.* a small, flat-bottomed boat. [etym. unknown]

dos-à-dos, dosi-do, *a.* back-to-back. *n.* a seat designed for sitting back-to-back; a square-dance step in which dancers pass each other back-to-back. [F]

dose, *n.* so much of any medicine as is taken or prescribed to be taken at one time; (*fig.*) a quantity or amount of anything offered or given; anything nauseous or unpleasant which one has to take; a share. *v.t.* to administer doses to; to give anything unpleasant to; to adulterate, to mix (as spirits with wine). **like a dose of salts,** very quickly (and thoroughly). **dosage,** *n.* the process or method of dosing; the application of doses (as of spirits to wine). **dosimeter,** *n.* an instrument which measures radiation. **dosimetric,** *a.* [F, from med. L and Gr. *dosis,* a giving, from *didonai,* to give]

dosh, *n.* (*sl.*) money; loot. [etym. doubtful]

dosi-do DOS-À-DOS.

Dos Passos, *n.* **John** (1896–1970), US author, born in Chicago. He made a reputation with the war novels *One Man's Initiation* (1919) and *Three Soldiers* (1921). His greatest work is the *USA* trilogy (1930–36), which gives a panoramic view of US life through the device of placing fictitious characters against the real setting of newspaper headlines and contemporary events.

doss, *n.* (*sl.*) a bed or a sleeping-place in a common lodging-house. *v.i.* to sleep in this; to sleep; to go to bed. **dosser,** *n.* one who sleeps in cheap lodging-houses or hostels; (*sl.*) a lazy, idle person. **to doss down,** (*sl.*) to go to sleep in a makeshift bed. **doss-house,** *n.* a cheap lodging-house. [prob. from F *dos,* back, L *dorsum*]

dossal, *n.* an ornamental hanging at the back of an altar or a stall, or round the sides of a chancel. [med. L *dossāle,* L *dorsum*]

dossier, *n.* a collection of papers and other documents relating to a person, a thing or an event. [F, from *dos,* L *dorsum,* back (from its bulging shape)]

dossil, *n.* a plug for stopping a wound; a cloth for wiping the face of a copper-plate. [OF *dosil,* late L *duciculus,* dim. of *dux ducis,* leader]

dost, DO¹.

Dostoievsky, *n.* **Fyodor Mihailovich** (1821–81), Russian novelist. Remarkable for their profound psychological insight, Dostoievsky's novels have greatly influenced Russian writers, and since the beginning of the 20th cent. have been increasingly influential abroad. In 1849 he was sentenced to four years hard labour in Siberia followed by army service, for printing socialist propaganda. *The House of the Dead* (1861) recalls his prison experiences, followed by his major works *Crime and Punishment* (1866), *The Idiot* (1868–69) and *The Brothers Karamazov* (1880).

dot¹, *n.* a little mark, spot or speck made with a pen or pointed instrument; a period mark, a full point, a point over *i* or *j,* or used as a diacritic; (*Mus.*) a point used as a direction, in various senses; a tiny thing, a little child; (*coll.*) a lame person. *v.i.* (*past, p.p.* **dotted**) to make dots or spots. *v.t.* to mark with dots; to mark or diversify with small detached objects like dots. **dot and carry one,** a school-child's phrase for putting down the units and transferring the tens to the next column. **dot and dash,** the system of symbols in Morse telegraphy. **on the dot (of),** (*coll.*) precisely (at). **the year dot,** (*coll.*) as far back as memory reaches. **to dot one's i's and cross one's t's,** to be precisely exact. **dot-, dotting-wheel,** *n.* a wheel used for making dotted lines. **dotter,** *n.* [OE *dott,* the head of a boil (cp. Dut. *dot,* a little bundle, LG *dutte,* a plug)]

dot², *n.* a dowry. *v.i.* to dower. †**dotal,** *a.* pertaining to a dowry; constituting or comprised in a dowry. †**dotation,** *n.* [F, from L *dōtem,* acc. of *dōs*]

dotage, *n.* impairment of the intellect by age; silliness, infatuation. **dotard,** *n.* a man in his dotage; one who is foolishly and excessively fond. **dotardly,** *a.* [F *radoter,* to talk nonsense]

dote, *v.i.* to be silly or deranged, infatuated or feeble-minded. **to dote on,** to be foolishly fond of. **doter,** *n.*

doth, DO¹.

dotterel, *n.* a small migratory plover, *Endromias morinellus,* said to be so foolishly fond of imitation that it mimics the actions of the fowler, and so suffers itself to be taken; a dupe, a gull, a dotard. [from DOTE]

dottle, *n.* a plug of tobacco left unsmoked in a pipe. [prob. from DOT¹]

dotty, *a.* marked with dots, dot-like; (*sl.*) unsteady of gait; shaky, imbecile. [DOT¹]

douane, *n.* a continental custom-house. **douanier,** *n.* a custom-house officer. [F, from Arab. *dīwān,* DIVAN]

Dou, *n.* **Gerard** (1613–75), Dutch genre painter, a pupil of Rembrandt. He is known for small domestic interiors, minutely observed.

Douay, *n.* an ancient town in N France. **Douay Bible,** *n.* an English version of the Vulgate, made by the students of the Roman Catholic college at Douai and published 1582–1609, still in general use. [*Douai*]

double¹, *a.* composed of two, in a pair or in pairs; forming a pair, twofold; folded, bent back or forward; twice as much, as great or as many; of twice the strength or value; of two kinds, aspects or relations; ambiguous; (*fig.*) hypocritical, treacherous, deceitful; an octave lower in pitch; applied to flowers when the stamens become more or less petaloid. *adv.* twice; in two ways; in twice the number, quantity, amount, strength etc.; two together. **double summer time,** the time indicated by clocks advanced one hour more than summer time or two hours in front of Greenwich mean time. **double-acting,** *a.* exerting power in two directions. **double-action,** *n.* in a pianoforte movement, an arrangement of a jointed upright piece at the back end of the key, used to lift the hammer. **double agent,** *n.* a spy working for two opposing sides at the same time. **double ale,** *n.* ale of double strength. **double-axe,** *n.* a double-headed axe, a religious symbol in Minoan Crete. **double-back,** *v.i.* to go back in the direction one has come from. **double-banked,** *a.* used of a boat or galley which has two men to work the same oar, or two tiers of oars. **double bar,** *n.* (*Mus.*) two single bars put together, to denote the end of a part. **double-barrel,** *a.* double-barrelled. *n.* a double-barrelled gun. **double-barrelled,** *a.* having two barrels, as a gun; producing a double effect, serving a double purpose; (of a surname) having two parts. **double-bass,** *n.* the largest and lowest-toned of the stringed instruments played with a bow, a contra-basso. **double bassoon,** *n.* the largest instrument in the oboe class, with the lowest pitch. **double-bearing,** *a.* producing twice in one season. **double-bedded,** *a.* having two beds or a double bed. **double-bitt,** *v.t.* (*Naut.*) to pass twice round a bitt or round two bitts (of ropes). **double boiler,** *n.* (*N Am.*) a double saucepan. **double bottom,** *n.* an articulated lorry with a second trailer. **double-breasted,** *a.* lapping over and buttoning on either side, as a coat or waistcoat. †**double-charge,** *v.t.* to entrust with a double share; to charge (a gun) with a double quantity. **double-check,** *v.t.* to check a second time. **double chin,** *n.* two chins, due to obesity etc. **double concerto,** *n.* one for two solo instruments. **double cream,** *n.* thick cream, with a higher fat content than single cream. **double-cross,** *v.t.* (*coll.*) to betray to both sides. **double-crosser,** *n.* **double-crown,** *n.* a size of printing paper, 20 × 30 in. (50·8 × 76·2 cm). **double-dagger,** *n.* a reference mark (‡). **double-dealer,** *n.* one who acts two parts at the same time or in the same business. **double-dealing,** *a.* deceitful, tricky. *n.* the conduct of a double-dealer. **double-decker,** *n.* a passenger vehicle with two decks; a novel etc. in two volumes. **double-declutch,** *v.i.* to change to a different gear by moving into neutral and then into the desired gear. **double-decomposition,** *n.* a reaction in which two chemical compounds exchange some of their constituents. **double diapason,** *n.* an organ stop of 16-foot tone. **double-dotted,** *a.* **double-dotted note,** one increased in length by three-quarters, as shown by two dots placed after it. **double-dotted rhythm,** one characterized by double-dotted notes. **double-drummer,** *n.* (*Austral.*) a large cicada with swollen drums. **double-Dutch,** *n.* gibberish, jargon; a language not understood by the hearer. †**double-dye,** *v.t.* to dye with double intensity. **double-dyed,** *a.* stained or tainted with infamy; doubly infamous. **double-eagle,** *n.* an American gold coin worth 20 dollars; a representation, as in the imperial arms of Russia and Austria, of an eagle with two heads. **double-edged,** *a.* having two edges; (*fig.*) telling for and against; cutting both ways. **double-ender,** *n.* a kind of gunboat, round at both ends, used in the American Civil War (1861–65). **double-entendre,** *n.* a word or phrase with two interpretations, one of which is usually indelicate. **double entry,** *n.* a method of book-keeping in which every transaction is entered twice, once on the credit side of the account that gives, and once on the debit side of the account that receives. **double event,** *n.* the winning of two races or matches by a horse or a team in the same race or season. **double exposure,** *n.* the recording of two superimposed images on a single piece of film; the picture resulting from this. **double-face,** *n.* a double-dealer. **double-faced,** *a.* double-dealing; insincere. †**double-fatal,** *a.* fatal in two ways. **double-fault,** *n.* in tennis, two faults in succession, resulting in the loss of a point. **double feature,** *n.* two full-length feature films shown in a single programme. **double figures,** *n.pl.* a number greater than 9 but less than 100. **double first,** *n.* one who comes out first in two subjects in an examination for a degree. **double flat,** *n.* (*Mus.*) a sign indicating a drop of two semitones. **double-ganger,** DOPPELGANGER. †**double-gild,** *v.t.* to gild with a double coating; (*fig.*) to excuse. **double-glazing,** *n.* the fitting of a double layer of glass in a window to act as a form of insulation. **double-glaze,** *v.t.* **double Gloucester,** *n.* a rich hard cheese orig. made in Gloucestershire. **double-handed,** *a.* deceitful, treacherous. **double-headed,** *a.* having two heads; (*Bot.*) having the flowers growing one to another. **double header,** *n.* a train drawn by two locomotives; (*N Am.*) two games played consecutively; (*Austral.*) a coin with a head on each side. **double-hearted,** *a.* false-hearted, deceitful, treacherous. **double helix,** *n.* two helices coiled round the same axis, the molecular structure of DNA. **double-hung,** *a.* a term applied to the sashes of a window when both are movable and fitted with lines and weights. **double jeopardy,** *n.* a second trial for the same offence. **double-jointedness,** *n.* abnormal mobility of joints not associated with injury or disease, nor causing symptoms. **double knit,** *n.* a fabric knitted on a double set of needles to give a double thickness. **double-leaded,** *a.* (*Print.*) having spaces of double width between the lines for the sake of display. **double-lock,** *v.t.* to fasten by shooting the lock twice; to fasten with extra security. **double-manned,** *a.* furnished or equipped with twice the number of men. †**double-meaning,** *a.* saying one thing and meaning another; speaking equivocally. **double-minded,** *a.* unsettled, wavering; fickle, undetermined. †**double-mouthed,** *a.* deceitful, untrustworthy in statement. **double-natured,** *a.* having a double or twofold nature. **double negative,** *n.* (*Gram.*) a construction with two negatives where only one is needed, as in, *I don't need nothing.* **double-octave,** *n.* (*Mus.*) an interval of two octaves or fifteen notes. **double park,** *v.t.* to park (a vehicle) outside one already parked at the kerb. **double pneumonia,** *n.* pneumonia in both lungs. **double-quick,** *n.* (*Mil.*) the quickest pace next to a run; (*US*) a marching step at the rate of 165 steps a minute. *adv.* at the rate of this marching step. **double-reed,** *n.* a set of two reeds in the mouthpiece of a wind instrument, which vibrate against each other. **double-reef,** *v.t.* (*Naut.*) to reduce (the spread of sail) by two reefs. **double-refine,** *v.t.* to refine twice over. **double refraction,** *n.* birefringence. **double salt,** *n.* one which, when dissolved, gives two different salts in solution. **double saucepan,** *n.* two saucepans, one fitting into the other, food being cooked gently in the inner pan by the heat of boiling water in the outer one. †**double-shade,** *v.t.* to make doubly dark or shady. **double sharp,** *n.* (*Mus.*) a sign indicating a rise of two semitones. **double-shuffle,** *n.* a kind of clog-dance, jig or hornpipe. **double space,** *v.t.* to type with a line-space between the lines. **double-speak,** *n.* double-talk. **double standard,** *n.* a single moral principle applied in different ways to different groups of people and allowing different behaviour, esp. that of allowing young men but not young women to have sexual experience before marriage. **double-stars,** *n.pl.* stars so near each other that they appear to be one when seen with the naked eye. **double-stop,** *v.i.* (*Mus.*) to play chords on a violin on two stopped strings. **double-take,** *n.* a delayed reaction. **double-talk,** *n.* talk that sounds sensible though it is actually a compound of sense and gibberish. **double-think,** *n.* the holding of two contradictory beliefs at the same time. **double-time,** *n.* a marching step at the rate of 165 steps (of 33 in. (83·8 cm)) to the minute, or (*US*) of 180 steps (of 36 in. (91·4 cm)) to the minute. **double-tongue,** *v.i.* (*Mus.*) to apply the tongue rapidly to the teeth and the palate alternately, as in staccato passages played on the flute or cornet; to play with double-tonguing. **double-tongued,** *a.* giving contrary accounts of the same thing at different times; deceitful, double-dealing. **double twill,** *n.* twill woven with intersecting diagonal lines. **double-u,** *n.* W, the 23rd letter of the alphabet. **double-vantage,** *v.t.* to benefit doubly. **double vision,** *n.* diplopia. **doubleness,** *n.* **doubly,** *adv.* [OF from L *duplus* (*duo*, two, *-plus*, cogn. with Gr. *-plos*, -fold)]

double[2], *n.* twice as much or as many, a double quantity; a fold, a plait; a bend or twist (in a road or river); a wraith, a doppelganger; a person exactly resembling someone else; (*Theat.*) an understudy; (*Mil.*) running, the pace for charging; a turn in running to escape pursuit; (*fig.*) †a trick, an artifice; (*Lawn Tennis etc., pl.*) a game between two pairs; (*Whist*) the score when one side has scored five before the other scores three; a bet on two races, the stake and winnings on the first being applied to the second race; (*Darts*) a throw between the two outer circles. *v.t.* to increase by an equal quantity, amount, number, value etc.; to multiply by two; to make twice as thick; to fold down or over, to bend, to turn upon itself; to be twice as much as; (*Mus.*) to add the upper or lower octave to; to act two (parts) in the same play; (*Naut.*) to sail round or by; †to copy, to make a duplicate of. *v.i.* to become twice as much or as great; to enlarge a wager to twice the previous amount; (*Bridge*) on the strength of one's own hand to double the number of points an opponent may gain or lose; to turn or wind to escape pursuit; (*fig.*) to use tricks or artifices; to run. **at, on, the double,** at twice the normal speed; very fast. **double or quits,** a game such as pitch and toss to decide whether the person owing shall pay twice his debt or nothing. **to double and twist,** to add one thread to another and twist them together. **to double up,** to bend one's body into a stooping or folded posture; to collapse; to make another person to do this; to clench; of paper etc., to become folded or crumpled. **to double upon,** (*Mil.*) to shut in between two fires; to turn back on a parallel course so as to elude (pursuers). **doubler,** *n.* [as prec.]

doublet, *n.* one of a pair; one of two words from the same root, but differing in meaning; (*Print.*) a word or passage printed twice by mistake; (*Opt.*) a combination of two lenses; a pair of birds brought down at once with a double-barrelled gun; (*pl.*) a pair of thrown dice showing the same number; (*Hist.*) a close-fitting garment covering the body from the neck to a little below the waist, introduced from France in the 14th cent., and worn by all ranks until the time of Charles II; a counterfeit gem made of two pieces of crystal with a coloured substance between them. **doublet and hose,** regular masculine attire in the Tudor period; an undress attire suitable for active exertion (implying the absence of a cloak). [F, dim. of prec.]

doubletree, *n.* the horizontal bar on a vehicle to which the swingletree for harnessing horses is attached.

doubloon, *n.* a Spanish and S American gold coin, orig. the double of a pistole (whence the name). [F *doublon,* or Sp. *doblon* (*doble,* DOUBLE)]

doublure, *n.* an ornamental lining for a book cover. [F, lining, from *doubler,* to DOUBLE, to line]

doubt, *v.i.* to be in uncertainty about the truth, probability or propriety of anything; to hesitate, to waver; †to be afraid, to be apprehensive; †to suspect. *v.t.* to hold or think questionable; to hestitate to believe or assent to; †to be undecided about; †to distrust, suspect or fear. *n.* uncertainty of mind upon any point, action or statement; an unsettled state of opinion; indecision, hesitation, suspense; distrust, inclination to disbelieve; a question, a problem, an objection; †fear, dread, apprehension, suspicion. **beyond a doubt, no doubt, without doubt,** certainly, admittedly, unquestionably. **to give the benefit of the doubt,** to presume innocent, esp. when proof of guilt is lacking or dubious. **doubtable,** *a.* **doubter,** *n.* **doubtful,** *a.* liable to doubt; uncertain, admitting of doubt; ambiguous, not clear in meaning; uncertain, undecided, hesitating; suspicious; characterized by fear or apprehension. **doubtfully,** *adv.* **doubtfulness,** *n.* **doubting,** *n., a.* **doubting Thomas,** *n.* one who persists in doubt until he/she has tangible evidence (from Thomas the apostle who would not believe in the Resurrection until he had seen Jesus, John, xx.24–25). **doubtingly,** *adv.* **doubtless,** †*a.* free from fear; sure, confident, certain. *adv.* assuredly, certainly, admittedly. **doubtlessly,** *adv.* **doubtlessness,** *n.* [OF *douter,* L *dubitāre,* from *dubius,* doubtful]

douce, *a.* (*Sc.*) sober, sedate, peaceable, †sweet, pleasant. **doucely,** *adv.* **douceness,** *n.* [OF *doux,* fem. *douce, dolz,* L *dulcis,* sweet]

douceur, *n.* a small present; a gift, a bribe; †mildness, gentleness; †a courtesy, a compliment. [F, as prec.]

douche, *n.* a jet of water or vapour directed upon some part of the body; an instrument for applying this. *v.t.* to apply a douche, esp. to flush out the vagina or other cavity. *v.i.* to take a douche. [F, from It. *doccia,* a conduit, from L *ductus,* p.p. of *ducere,* to lead]

dough, *n.* the paste of bread etc. yet unbaked; a mass of flour or meal moistened and kneaded; anything resembling this in appearance or consistency; (*sl.*) money. †**dough-baked,** *a.* not perfectly baked; hence imperfect, unfinished; deficient in intellect. **dough-boy,** *n.* a flour dumpling boiled in salt water (see also DUFF[1]); (*N Am.*) a private soldier in the US army. **dough-faced,** *a.* (*N Am.*) cowardly, weak, pliable. **dough-kneaded,** *a.* soft like dough. **dough-nut, do-nut,** *n.* a cake made of sweetened dough and fried in fat. **doughy,** *a.* like dough; soft, half-baked; (*fig.*) soft, unsound. **doughiness,** *n.* [OE *dāh* (cp. Dut. *deeg,* Dan. *deig,* G *Teig,* also Sansk. *dih-,* to smear, L *fingere,* to shape, Gr. *teichos,* an (earth) wall]

doughty, *a.* brave, valiant, stout, redoubtable. †**doughty-handed,** *a.* strong-handed, mighty. **doughtily,** *adv.* **doughtiness,** *n.* [OE *dohtig* (cp. *dugan,* to be strong, G *taugen,* to be worth, whence *tüchtig,* able)]

Douglas[1], *n.* capital of the Isle of Man in the Irish Sea; population (1981) 20,000. A holiday resort and terminus of shipping routes to and from Fleetwood and Liverpool.

Douglas[2], *n.* **Gavin** (or **Gawain**) (1475–1522), Scottish poet. A son of the Earl of Angus, he became bishop of Dunkeld in 1515, and was active in Scottish politics. He wrote two allegories, *The Palace of Honour* and *King Hart,* but is best known for his translation of Virgil's *Aeneid,* the first English versions.

Douglas fir, pine, spruce, *n.* a tall American conifer, grown for ornament and timber. [D. *Douglas,* 1798–1834, British botanist]

Douglass, *n.* **Frederick** (*c.* 1817–95), US anti-slavery campaigner. Born a slave in Maryland, he escaped in 1838. His autobiographical *Narrative of the Life of Frederick Douglass* (1845) aroused support in northern states for the abolition of slavery. After the Civil War, he held several US government posts, including minister to Haiti.

Doukhobor DUKHOBOR.

douleia DULIA.

Doulton, *n.* **Henry** (1820–97), British ceramicist. He developed special wares for the chemical, electrical and building industries and in 1846 established the world's first stoneware drainpipe factory. From 1870 he created at Lambeth, in London, and Burslem, near Stoke-on-Trent, a reputation for art pottery and domestic tablewares.

Doumergue, *n.* **Gaston** (1863–1937), French prime minister during the time leading up to World War I and again after the fall of Léon Blum's Popular Front government in 1937.

doum-palm, *n.* an Egyptian palm, *Hyphaene thebaïca,* remarkable for the dichotomous division of the trunk and branches. [Arab. *daum, dūm*]

doup, *n.* (*Sc.*) the bottom, the posterior; the bottom of an eggshell; the end (as of a candle). [cp. Icel. *daup,* a hollow]

dour, *a.* (*Sc., North.*) hard, bold, sullen; stern, severe, obstinate, pertinacious. **dourly,** *adv.* **dourness,** *n.* [L *dūrus*]

doura DURRA.

Douro, *n.* (Spanish **Duero**) river rising in N central Spain and flowing through N Portugal to the Atlantic at Oporto; length 800 km/500 miles.

douroucouli, *n.* a nocturnal ape of Central and South America.

douse[1], dowse, *v.t.* to plunge into water, to dip; to throw water over, to drench; (*Naut.*) to strike or slacken suddenly (as sails); to extinguish. *v.i.* to be plunged into water. **to douse the glim,** (*sl., dated*) to put out the light. [etym. doubtful]

douse[2] DOWSE[1].

dout, *v.t.* to extinguish. **douter,** *n.* one who or that which extinguishes; (*Gas-making*) a man employed to throw water over flaming coke from the retorts. [contr. of DO OUT]

dove, *n.* one of several kinds of pigeon, a bird of the genus *Columbia;* an emblem of gentleness and innocence; the symbol of the Holy Ghost; a messenger of peace or deliverance (in allusion to the dove sent by Noah, Gen. viii.8–12); advocate of peaceable and conciliatory policies towards opponents; a term of endearment. **dove-coloured,** *a.* grey with a tinge of pink. **dove-cot, -cote,** *n.* a small house or box for domestic pigeons. **to flutter the dove-cots,** to throw peaceful people into alarm; to scandalize conventional circles. **dove-eyed,** *a.* having eyes like a dove; meek, gentle-looking. **dove-feathered,** *a.* disguised in feathers like those of the dove. **dove-hawk,** *n.* the dove-coloured falcon, *Circus cyaneus,* also called the hen-harrier. **dovekie,** *n.* an Arctic bird, *Uria grylle,* the black guillemot. **dove's-foot,** *n.* one of the crane's-bills, *Geranium molle,* and some other plants. **dovelet,** *n.* a young dove. **dovelike,** *a.* [OE *dūfe* (only in *dūfe-doppa*), from *dūfan,* to dive (cp. G *Taube,* and for sense L *columba,* dove, Gr. *kolumbos,* diver)]

dover, *v.i.* (*Sc., North.*) to slumber lightly, to doze. *v.t.* to stupefy. *n.* a light slumber.

Dover's powder, *n.* a sweat-inducing compound, with opium, potassium sulphate and ipecacuanha. [Dr T. *Dover,* 1660–1742]

Dover, Strait of, (French **Pas-de-Calais**) stretch of water separating England from France, and connecting the English Channel with the North Sea. It is about 35 km/22 miles long and 34 km/21 miles wide at its narrowest part. It is one of the world's busiest sea lanes, and by 1972 increasing traffic, collisions, and shipwrecks had become so frequent that traffic-routeing schemes were enforced.

dovetail, *n.* a mode of fastening boards together by fitting tenons, shaped like a dove's tail spread out, into corresponding cavities; a tenon or a joint of this kind. *v.t.* to fit together by means of dovetails; to fit exactly. *v.i.* to fit into exactly. **dovetail joint,** *n.* one fastened by such tenons. **dovetail-moulding,** *n.* (*Arch.*) one consisting of a series of projections somewhat like doves' tails.

dowager, *n.* a widow in possession of a dower or jointure; a title given to a widow to distinguish her from the wife of her husband's heir; (*sl.*) an old lady. [OF *douagere,* from *douage,* dowry, *douer,* to DOWER]

dowdy, *n.* an awkward, shabby, badly or vulgarly dressed woman. *a.* awkward, shabby, unfashionable. **dowdily,** *adv.* **dowdiness,** *n.* **dowdyish,** *a.* **dowdyism,** *n.* [ME *dowd,* a shabby or untidily dressed person, etym. doubtful]

dowel, *n.* a pin or peg for connecting two stones or pieces of wood, being sunk into the side of each; a thin wooden rod for hanging light curtains. *v.t.* to fasten by dowels. **dowel-joint,** *n.* a junction by means of a dowel: **dowel-pin,** *n.* a dowel. [perh. from F *douille,* a socket (but cp. LG *dovel,* G *Döbel,* plug or tap, OF *douelle,* a barrel-stave)]

Dowell, *n.* **Anthony** (1943–), British ballet dancer, who was principal dancer with the Royal Ballet during 1966–86, and director from 1986.

dower, *n.* the property which a wife brings to her husband in marriage; that part of the husband's property which his widow enjoys during her life; dowry, endowment, natural gifts, talents. *v.t.* to endow; to give a dower or portion to. **dower house,** *n.* a house on an estate reserved for the widow of the late owner. **dowerless,** *a.* [OF *doaire,* late L *dōtārium,* from *dōtāre,* to endow (*dōs dōtis,* cp. Gr. *dōs,* a gift)]

dowf, *a.* (*Sc., North.*) dull, flat, spiritless. *n.* a stupid or spiritless fellow. [cp. Icel. *daufr,* deaf]

dowie, *a.* (*Sc.*) dull, low-spirited, dreary. [prob. from OE *dol,* DULL]

dowitcher, *n.* either of two snipelike birds, found on the shores of arctic and subarctic N America. [Am. Ind.]

Dow-Jones average, index, *n.* an index of the prices of stocks and shares on the New York Stock Exchange. [Charles *Dow,* 1851–1902, and Edward *Jones,* 1856–1920, US economists]

Dowland, *n.* **John** (1563–1626), English composer. He failed to establish himself at the court of Queen Elizabeth – he was a Roman Catholic convert – but later reverted to Protestantism and from 1612 was patronized by the Stuart royal family. He is remembered for his songs to lute accompaniment.

dowlas, *n.* a kind of coarse linen or calico. [*Daoulas,* near Brest, in Brittany]

dowle, *n.* one of the filaments of a feather; wool-like down. [etym. doubtful (Skeat suggests OF *doulle, douille,* soft, L *ductilis,* DUCTILE)]

down¹, *n.* a tract of upland, esp. the chalk uplands of southern England, used for pasturing sheep; a bank of sand etc. cast up by the sea. **the Downs,** the downs in the south of England; a roadstead between the North and South Forelands. **downland,** *n.* [OE *dūn* (cp. ODut. *dúna,* whence Dut. *duin,* LG *düne,* F *dune*)]

down², *n.* the fine soft plumage of young birds or that found under the feathers; fine soft hair, esp. the first hair on the human face; the pubescence of plants; the feather-like substance by which seeds are transported to a distance; any soft, fluffy substance. **Downie®,** *n.* a duvet. **downy,** *a.* covered with down; made of down; resembling down; (*fig.*) soft, placid, soothing; (*sl.*) cunning, knowing, artful. **downily,** *adv.* **downiness,** *n.* [Icel. *dúnn* (cp. LG *dûne,* G *Daune*)]

down³, *adv.* (*superl.* **downmost**) towards the ground; from a higher to a lower position; on the ground; from the sky upon the earth; below the horizon; (*fig.*) from former to later times; from north to south; away from the capital or a university; with a stream or current; (*Naut.*) to leeward; into less bulk; to finer consistency; to quiescence; to or in a state of subjection, disgrace or depression; at a low level, prostrate, in a fallen posture or condition; downstairs, out of bed; reduced in price. *prep.* along, through, or into, in a descending direction; from the top or the upper part to the bottom or a lower part of; at a lower part of; along (a river) towards the mouth. *a.* moving, sloping or directed towards a lower part or position; downcast. *v.t.* (*coll.*) to put, strike or throw down, to overcome. *v.i.* to descend. *n.* (*esp. pl.*) a reverse; (*coll.*) a grudge, dislike; (*sl.*) suspicion, alarm. **down!** *imper.* (*ellipt.*) get, lie, put or throw down. **down and out,** utterly destitute and without resources. **down at heel,** shabby, disreputably dressed. **down in the mouth,** discouraged. **down on one's luck,** (*sl.*) hard-up. **down to earth,** realistic, practical, sensible. **down with!** (*imper.*) swallow; abolish. **to be down on,** to be severe towards; to pounce upon. **to bear, bear down,** (*Naut.*) to sail from windward. **to down tools,** to stop work; to strike. **to down with,** to pull or throw down. **to get down,** to alight; to swallow (something). **to go down,** to sink; to leave the university for the vacation, or at the end of one's term; to prove acceptable. **to have a down on,** (*coll.*) to have a grudge against. **to put a down on,** (*sl.*) to peach, to give information about. **to put, set, take** or **write down,** to write on paper etc.; hence **down for Tuesday,** announced to take place on Tuesday. **to ride, hunt down,** to overtake by pursuit; to bring to bay. **to send down,** (*Univ.*) to expel or suspend an undergraduate. **to shout down,** to silence with noise. **up and down,** here and there; altogether; throughout. **ups and downs,** vicissitudes (of fortune, life etc.). **downbeat,** *n.* a downward movement of a conductor's baton; an accented beat marked in this way. **downcast,** *a.* cast downward; dejected, sad. *n.* a ventilating shaft; (*Geol.*) a downthrow. **downcome,** *n.* a sudden fall, ruin; an overthrow. **down-draught,** *n.* a downward current of air. **down-easter,** *n.* (*N Am.*) a person from New England. **downfall,** *n.* a fall of rain, snow etc.; a sudden loss of prosperity, rank, reputation; ruin, overthrow; †that which falls suddenly downwards; †a precipice. **downfallen,** *a.* ruined, fallen, fallen down. **downgrade,** *n.* a downward gradient on a railway; (*fig.*) decadence. *v.t.* to lower in status. **downgrowth,** *n.*

growth in a downward direction. **down-haul,** *n.* (*Naut.*) a rope for hauling down a sail. *v.t.* to pull down (a sail). **down-hearted,** *a.* dispirited, dejected. **downhill**, *a.* descending, sloping downwards, declining. *n.* a declivity, a downward slope; a decline. *adv.*, on a descending slope; (*fig.*) towards ruin or disgrace. **to go downhill,** to deteriorate physically or morally. **downhole,** *a.* pertaining to any equipment in the oil industry which is used in the well itself. **down line,** *n.* a railway line for trains going away from a main terminus. **download,** *v.t.* to transfer data directly from one computer to another. **down-looked,** *a.* having a downcast face; gloomy. **down-lying,** *n.* (*dial.*) lying down or going to bed; (*Sc.*) childbed, confinement. **down-market,** *a.* applied to cheaply produced goods of poor quality. **down payment,** *n.* a deposit paid on an article bought on hire purchase. **downpipe,** *n.* a drainpipe which carries water from a roof to the ground. **down platform,** *n.* the platform adjoining a down line. **downpour,** *n.* a heavy persistent fall of rain. **downrange,** *a., adv.* in the flight path of a rocket or missile. **downright,** *a.* directed straight downwards; directly to the point; plain, unequivocal; outspoken, artless, blunt. *adv.* straight downwards; thoroughly, absolutely; †plainly, definitely. **downrightness,** *n.* †**down-roping,** *a.* hanging down in filaments. **downside,** *n.* that side of a coin which faces downwards when a coin has been tossed; a negative aspect of any situation; the negative side, adverse aspect; disadvantage. **down-sitting,** *n.* the act of sitting down, repose, rest. **downsize,** *v.t.* to reduce in size. **downstage,** *a., adv.* at the front of the stage in a theatre. **downstairs,** *adv.* down the stairs; on or to a lower floor. *n.* the lower part of a building; the servant's quarters. **downstair, -stairs,** *a.* pertaining to a lower floor. **downstream,** *a.* in the direction of the current of a river. **downswing,** *n.* a downward trend in trade etc. statistics; that part of a swing in golf when the club is moving downward towards the ground. **downthrow,** *n.* (*Geol.*) the casting down, by earthquake or other action, of the strata on one side of a fault to a lower level. **downtime,** *n.* the time during a normal working day when a computer, or other machinery, is inoperative. **downtown,** *n.* the business and commercial centre of a city. *a.* situated in, belonging to, this area. *adv.* towards this area. **down train,** *n.* one travelling away from a main terminus. **downtrodden,** *a.* trodden under foot; oppressed; tyrannized over. **downturn,** *n.* a downward trend, esp. in business. **down under,** *n., a., adv.* (*coll.*) (in or to) Australia and New Zealand. **downward, -wards,** *adv.* from a higher to a lower position, level, condition or character; from earlier to later; from superior to inferior etc. **downward,** *a.* moving, directed or tending from higher, superior or earlier to lower, inferior or later. **downwind,** *a., adv.* in the direction in which the wind is blowing. [ME *adown,* OE *of- dūne,* ADOWN]

Down, *n.* county in the SE of Northern Ireland, facing the Irish Sea on the E; area 2465 sq km/952 sq miles; population (1981) 53,193. In the S are the Mourne mountains, in the E Strangford sea lough. The county town is Downpatrick; the main industry is dairying.

Downing Street, *n.* street in Westminster, London, leading from Whitehall to St James's Park, named after Sir George Downing (died 1684), a diplomat under Cromwell and Charles II. Number 10 is the official residence of the prime minister, number 11 is the residence of the chancellor of the Exchequer, and number 12 is the office of the government whips.

Down's syndrome, *n.* chromosomal abnormality (the presence of an additional chromosome) which produces a rather flattened face, coarse, straight hair, and a fold of skin at the inner edge of the eye (hence the former name 'mongolism'). There is often mental retardation. [J. Longdon-Down, 1828–96, British physician]

downy DOWN².

dowry, *n.* the property which a wife brings to her husband; an endowment, gift or talent. [A-F *dowarie,* as DOWER]

dowse¹, *v.t.* to use the divining rod for the discovery of subterranean waters or minerals. **dowser,** *n.* **dowsing-rod,** *n.* [etym. unknown]

dowse² DOUSE¹.

-dox, *comb. form* pertaining to doctrines or opinions. [Gr. *doxa,* opinion]

Doxiadis, *n.* **Constantinos** (1913–75), Greek architect and town planner; designer of Islamabad.

doxology, *n.* a brief formula or hymn of praise to God. **doxological**, *a.* [late L, Gr. *doxologia* (*doxa,* glory, -LOGY)]

doxy¹, *n.* a jade, a trull, a paramour; a loose woman. [etym. doubtful]

doxy², *n.* (*facet.*) opinion, esp. in religious matters. [from ORTHODOXY etc.]

doyen, *n.* the senior member of a body. [F, from L *decānus,* DEAN]

Doyle, *n.* **Arthur Conan** (1859–1930), British writer, creator of the detective Sherlock Holmes and his assistant Dr Watson, who feaured in a number of stories, including *The Hound of the Baskervilles* (1902). Conan Doyle is also known for adventure novels, for example *The Lost World* (1912).

doyley DOILY.

D'Oyly Carte, *n.* **Richard** (1844–1901), British producer of the Gilbert and Sullivan operas at the Savoy Theatre, London, which he built. The old D'Oyly Carte Opera Company founded in 1876 was disbanded in 1982, but a new one opened its first season in 1988.

doz., (*abbr.*) dozen.

doze, *v.i.* to sleep lightly; to be drowsy. *v.t.* to spend in drowsy inaction; †to stupefy, to muddle. *n.* a light sleep; a nap. **dozer,** *n.* **dozily,** *adv.* †**doziness,** *n.* **dozy,** *a.* [cp. Dan. *döse,* Icel. *dūsa,* LG *dussen*]

dozen, *n.* an aggregate of 12 things; an indefinite number. *a.* 12. **baker's, devil's dozen,** 13. **daily dozen,** daily physical exercises. **to talk nineteen to the dozen,** to talk incessantly. **dozenth,** *a.* [OF *dozaine* (*doze,* L *duodecim,* twelve, *-aine,* L *-ēna,* as in *centēna*)]

DP, (*abbr.*) data processing; displaced person(s).

DPhil, (*abbr.*) Doctor of Philosophy.

DPP, (*abbr.*) Director of Public Prosecutions.

dpt, (*abbr.*) department.

Dr, (*abbr.*) Doctor; Drive.

dr., (*abbr.*) debit; debitor; drachma; drain.

drab¹, *n.* a prostitute, a slut, a slattern. *v.i.* to associate with loose women. **drabber,** *n.* **drabbish,** *a.* [cp. Irish *drabog,* Gael. *drabach*]

drab², *a.* of a dull brown or dun colour; (*fig.*) dull, commonplace, monotonous, *n.* drab colour; a group of moths. **drabet**, *n.* a coarse drab linen used for smock-frocks. **drably,** *adv.* **drabness,** *n.* [F *drap,* cloth]

Draba, *n.* a genus of low cruciferous herbs, the whitlow-grasses. [Gr. *drabē*]

drabble, *v.t.* to draggle; to make wet and dirty, as by dragging through filth. **drabble-tail,** *n.* a slattern. [ME *drabelen,* cp. LG *drabeln*]

Drabble, *n.* **Margaret** (1939–), British writer. Her novels include *The Millstone* (1966), filmed as *The Touch of Love, The Middle Ground* (1980), and *The Radiant Way* (1987).

Dracaena, *n.* a genus of tropical plants of the lily family, including the dragon tree, *Dracaena draco,* of the Canaries. [mod. L, from Gr. *drakaina,* fem. of *drakōn,* dragon]

drachm, *n.* a drachma, a dram; (*Apothecary's weight*) 60 grains ($\frac{1}{8}$ ounce, 3·542 g); (*Avoirdupois*) 27$\frac{1}{3}$ grains ($\frac{1}{16}$ ounce, 1·771 g). **drachma**, *n.* an Attic weight, about 60 gr. avoirdupois (3·542 g); the principal silver coin of the ancient Greeks, worth six obols; the standard coin of modern Greece. [F *drachme,* L *drachma,* Gr. *drachmē* (*drassesthai,* to grasp), cp. *dragma,* a grasp, handful]

drac(k), *a.* (*Austral., sl.*) unattractive. [etym. doubtful]

Draco, *n.* a large but faint constellation, representing a dragon coiled around the north celestial pole. The star Alpha Draconis (Thuban) was the pole star 4800 years ago.

draconian, draconic, *a.* inflexible, severe, cruel. [*Dracōn,* an Athenian legislator (about 621 BC), whose laws were extremely severe]

Dracula, *n.* in the novel *Dracula* (1897), by Bram Stoker, the caped count who, as a vampire, drinks the blood of beautiful women.

draff, *n.* refuse, lees, esp. of malt after brewing or distilling; hog's-wash; (*fig.*) anything vile and worthless. †**draffish,** *a.* [ME *draf* (cp. Dut., Icel., Swed. *draf*)]

draft, *n.* the first outline of any writing or document; a rough copy; a rough sketch of work to be executed; a written order for the payment of money; a cheque or bill drawn, esp. by a department or a branch of a bank upon another; a number of men selected for some special purpose, a detachment, a contingent; (*N Am.*) conscription for army etc. *v.t.* to draw up an outline of, to compose the first form, or make a rough copy of; to draw off (a portion of a larger body of men) for some special purpose; (*Austral.*) to separate and sort out (cattle). **draftee,** *n.* (*N Am.*) a conscript. **drafter, draughter,** *n.* one who drafts; (*Austral.*) a man engaged in drafting cattle; a draught-horse. **drafting-gate,** *n.* (*Austral.*) a gate whereby cattle are sorted out. **drafting-yard,** *n.* a yard where cattle or sheep are herded into separate groups. **draftsman,** *n.* one who draws up documents; a draughtsman. [DRAUGHT]

drag, *v.t.* (*past, p.p.* **dragged**) to pull along the ground by main force; to draw by force; to haul; to draw along with difficulty; to break the surface with a harrow; to search (a river etc.) with a grapnel; to search or rack (as the brains); to put a drag on (a wheel); to perform too slowly; (*coll.*) to draw on (a cigarette). *v.i.* to trail along the ground (as a dress); to search a river etc. with a grapnel, nets etc.; (*Mus.*) to move slowly or heavily; to keep behind in singing. *n.* anything which retards movement; an iron shoe or skid fastened on a wheel of a vehicle to check the speed; a rough, heavy sledge; a kind of open four-horse coach; a dredge; a low cart; a four-clawed grapnel for dragging or dredging under water; a drag-net; a heavy kind of harrow; an implement to spread manure; the total resistance of an aeroplane along its line of flight; (*Hunting*) an artificial scent; the trail of a fox; a drag-hunt; the action of dragging; laborious movement, slow progress; a clog; an impediment; a drawback; (*sl.*) clothes appropriate to the opposite sex, esp. women's clothes worn by men. **to drag in,** to introduce (a subject) gratuitously or out of season. **to drag one's feet,** (*coll.*) to go slow deliberately. **to drag out,** to protract. **to drag (something) out of (someone),** to get (information) from (someone) with difficulty. **to drag the anchor,** to trail it along the bottom when it will not take firm hold (said of a ship). **to drag up,** to bring up or rear in a careless fashion; to pull along contemptuously, as unworthy to be carried. **drag-anchor,** *n.* a sail stretched by spars and thrown overboard to lessen the leeway of a drifting vessel. **drag-chain,** *n.* a chain for clogging a wheel in descending steep roads. **drag-hunt,** *n.* a hunt in which a drag is used; a club devoted to this kind of hunting. **dragman,** *n.* a fisherman who uses a drag-net. **drag-net,** *n.* a net dragged along the bottom of a river etc. for catching fish; a net drawn over a field to enclose game. **drag race,** *n.* one in which specially modified cars race over a timed course. **drag racing,** *n.* **drag-sheet,** *n.* (*Naut.*) a drag-anchor. **dragger,** *n.* one who or that which drags; a street hawker. **dragsman,** *n.* the driver of a drag or coach. **dragster,** *n.* a car modified for drag racing. **dragstrip,** *n.* a track for drag racing. [prob. a var. of DRAW]

dragée, *n.* a sweetmeat consisting of a nut, fruit etc. with a hard sugar coating; a small (silver-coloured) sugar ball for decorating cakes; a pill with a hard sugar coating. [F]

draggle, *v.t.* to make wet and dirty by dragging on the ground; to wet, to drabble. *v.i.* to become dirty by being trailed along the ground; to trail along the ground; (*fig.*) to lag, to straggle. **draggletail,** *n.* a slut. **draggle-tailed,** *a.* sluttish; draggling. **draggling,** *a.*

dragoman, *n.* (*pl.* **-mans**) one who acts as guide, interpreter and agent for travellers in the East. [F, from It. *dragomanno,* med. Gr. *dragoumanos,* OArab. *targumān,* interpreter]

dragon, *n.* a fabulous monster found in the mythology of nearly all nations, generally as an enormous winged serpent with formidable claws etc.; (*Astron.*) a constellation in the northern hemisphere; any species of the lacertilian genus *Draco,* comprising the flying lizard; a kind of pigeon; a violent, spiteful person; a guardian, a duenna; (*Bibl.*) various formidable animals, such as the crocodile, serpent, whale and shark; †a musket of large bore with a figure of a dragon on the muzzle. **the Old Dragon,** Satan. **to chase the dragon,** (*sl.*) to smoke heroin. **dragon-fly,** *n.* an anisopterous insect belonging to the Libellulidae, having a long brilliant body and two pairs of large wings. **dragon's-blood,** *n.* a red resin exuding from various trees, much used for staining and colouring. **dragon's-tail,** *n.* (*Astron.*) the descending node of the moon's orbit with the ecliptic. **dragon's teeth,** (*fig.*) seeds or causes from which wars and disputes spring. **dragon tree,** *n.* a liliaceous tree, *Dracaena draco* of W Africa and the adjacent islands. **dragonet,** *n.* †a little dragon; a fish of the genus *Callionymus.* **dragonish,** *a.* shaped, or otherwise like, a dragon. [F, from L *draco -ōnem,* Gr. *drakōn,* serpent (*drak-,* stem of *derkesthai,* to see)]

dragonnade, *n.* (*usu. pl.*) the persecutions of Protestants in France during the reign of Louis XIV by means of dragoons who were quartered upon them; a persecution by means of troops. *v.i.* to persecute by this means. [F, from *dragon,* DRAGOON]

dragoon, *n.* a cavalry soldier, orig. a mounted infantryman armed with a short musket or carbine called a dragon; in the British army the name is applied to certain regiments that were formerly mounted infantry; a kind of pigeon. *v.t.* to abandon to the mercies of soldiers; to subdue by military force; to compel to submit by violent measures. [F *dragon,* orig. a kind of musket, DRAGON]

dragsman DRAG.

drail, *n.* a piece of lead on the shank of the hook of a fishing-rod. *v.i.* to draggle. [perh. *draggle, tail*]

drain, *v.t.* to draw off gradually; to cause to run off by tapping etc.; to empty by drawing away moisture from, to exhaust; to drink up; to deprive (of vitality, resources etc.). *v.i.* to flow off gradually; to be emptied of moisture. *n.* the act of draining; a strain, heavy demand, exhaustion; a channel for conveying water, sewage etc.; (*Surg.*) a tube for drawing off pus etc.; (*sl.*) a drink. **down the drain,** wasted. **drain-cock,** *n.* a tap for emptying a tank or other vessel. **drain-pipe,** *n.* a pipe for draining superfluous or waste water, particularly from a roof or gutter. *n., a.* (*coll.*) (of) trousers with very tight legs. **drain-trap,** *n.* a device for preventing the escape of foul gases from drains. **drainable,** *a.* **drainage,** *n.* the act, practice or science of draining; the natural or artificial system by which land or a town is drained; that which is carried away through drains; the surface drained. **drainage-area, basin,** *n.* the region drained by a river and its tributaries. **drainage-tube,** *n.* a tube introduced into a suppurating wound or chronic abscess to allow free discharge of putrid accumulations. **drainer,** *n.* one who or that which drains; one who constructs drains; a vessel in which wet things are put to drain. **draining,** *n., a.* **draining-board,** *n.* a board beside a sink on which washed-up crockery is put to dry. **draining-engine,** *n.* a pumping-engine for removing water from mines etc. **draining-plough,** *n.* a plough for cutting drains. [OE *dreahnian,* cogn. with *drȳge,* DRY]

drake[1], *n.* the male of the duck. **drake-fly,** *n.* an artificial fly made with drake's feathers. **drake-stone,** *n.* a flat stone thrown so as to skim over water (cp. DUCKS AND DRAKES). [etym. doubtful (cp. G dial. *draak,* OHG *antrahho,* G *Enterich,* dial. *endedrach,* from *Ente, Ende,* duck)]

drake[2], *n.* the may-fly, an ephemeral insect common in meadows in early summer; †a dragon; †a kind of small cannon. [OE *drāca,* L *draco,* DRAGON]

Drake, *n.* **Francis** (*c.* 1545–96), English sea captain. Having enriched himself as a pirate against Spanish interests in the Caribbean (1567–72), he was sponsored by Elizabeth I for an expedition to the Pacific, sailing around the world (1577–80) in the *Golden Hind.* He was mayor of Plymouth (1582) and Member of Parliament (1584–85). In 1587 he raided the Spanish port of Cadiz. Against the Spanish Armada (1588) he was vice-admiral.

Dralon®; *n.* an acrylic fibre usu. used in upholstery.

dram, *n.* a drachm in apothecaries' weight and in avoirdupois weight; (*fig.*) a small quantity; as much spirit as is drunk at once. *v.i.* to drink drams. *v.t.* to ply with stimulants. **dram-drinker,** *n.* one who habitually drinks spirits. **dram-shop,** *n.* a tavern where spirits are sold. [DRACHM]

drama, *n.* a poem or composition representing life and action, usually intended for performance by living actors on the stage; a series of events invested with the unity and interest of a play; dramatic art, the composition and presentation of plays; the dramatic literature or theatrical art of a particular country or period. **drama documentary,** *n.* a film, play etc. composed of a mixture of fact and fiction. **dramatic, -ical,** *a.* pertaining to or of the nature of drama; pertaining to the stage, theatrical; intended or suitable for representation on the stage; striking, catastrophic, impressive; meant for effect; expressing the personalities of different characters. **dramatic irony,** *n.* a situation in a film or play where the irony is clear to the audience but not to the characters. **dramatics,** *n.pl.* (*coll.*) a display of exaggerated behaviour; (*usu. sing. in constr.*) the producing or study of plays. **dramatically,** *adv.* **dramaticism,** *n.* [late L *drāma,* Gr. *drāma -atos* (*draein* to do, to act)]

dramatis personae, *n.pl.* the set of characters in a play; a list of these. [L, characters of the play]

dramatist, *n.* a writer of plays.

dramatize, -ise, *v.t.* to set forth in the form of a drama; to describe dramatically; to exaggerate; to convert (a story, novel etc.) into a play. **dramatizable, -isable,** *a.* **dramatization, -isation,** *n.*

dramaturge, *n.* a dramatist, a playwright. **dramaturgic, -ical,** *a.* **dramaturgist,** *n.* **dramaturgy,** *n.* the technique of writing or producing plays. [F, from Gr. *dramatourgos* (*drāma -atos,* DRAMA, *ergein,* to work)]

drammock, *n.* (*Sc.*) oatmeal and water mixed without cooking. [prob. from Gael. *dramag*]

drank, past tense of DRINK.

drant, draunt, *v.t., v.i.* (*Sc.*) to drawl; to drone. *n.* a droning tone. [prob. onomat., cp. DRAWL, RANT]

drape, *v.t.* to cover, clothe or decorate with cloth etc.; to adjust or arrange the folds of (a dress, curtains etc.). *n.pl.* (*esp. N Am.*) hangings which drape, curtains. **draper,** *n.* one who deals in cloth and other fabrics. **Drapers' Company,** *n.* the third of the 12 great London livery companies, whose charter was granted by Edward III. **drapery,** *n.* the trade of a draper; cloth and other fabrics; (*N Am.*) dry-goods; items of dress etc. made of these materials; that with which an object is draped, hangings, tapestry etc.; (*esp. N Am.*) (*pl.*) curtains; the arrangement of dress in sculpture, painting etc. **draperied,** *a.* †**drapet,** *n.* a cloth, a coverlet. [F *draper,* from *drap,* cloth]

drastic, *a.* acting vigorously; effective, efficacious; (*Med.*) strongly purgative. **drastically,** *adv.* [Gr. *drastikos,* from *drasteos,* to be done (*draein,* to do)]

drat, *v.t.* (*sl.*) confound, bother, dash (as a mild form of imprecation). **dratted,** *a.* [said to be a corr. of GOD ROT]

draught, (*esp. N Am.*) **draft,** *n.* the act of drawing; the capacity of being drawn; the act of dragging with a net; the quantity of fish taken in one sweep of a net; the act of drinking; the quantity of liquor drunk at once; a dose; a current of air; the depth to which a ship sinks in water; a draft, a preliminary drawing, design or plan for a work to be executed; the drawing of liquor from a vessel; †a privy, a cess-pool; (*pl.*) a game played by two persons on a chess-board with twelve round pieces of different colours on each side. *v.t.* to draw out or off; to sketch; to draft. **beast of draught,** an animal for drawing loads. **black draught,** a purgative medicine. **forced draught,** a strong current of air in a furnace, maintained by means of an exhaust or an apparatus for driving. **on draught,** able to be obtained by drawing off (from a cask etc.). **to feel the draught,** (*coll.*) to be aware of, or affected by, adverse (economic) conditions. **draught beer,** *n.* beer drawn from the cask, as distinguished from bottled or canned beer. **draught-board,** *n.* a board on which draughts are played. **draught-engine,** *n.* an engine for raising ore, water etc. **draught-hole,** *n.* a hole for supplying a furnace with air. **draught-hook,** *n.* an iron hook on the cheeks of a gun-carriage to manoeuvre it. **draught-horse,** *n.* a horse for drawing heavy loads. †**draught-house,** *n.* a house where filth is deposited; a privy. [ME *drahte,* as if from OE *dragan,* to DRAW (cp. Dut. *dragt,* G *Tracht*)]

draughtsman, (*esp. N Am.*) **draftsman,** *n.* one who draws, designs or plans; one skilled in drawing; a piece used in the game of draughts. **draughtsmanship,** *n.* **draughtswoman,** *n.fem.*

draughty, (*esp. N Am.*) **drafty,** *a.* full of draughts or currents of air; (*Sc.*) artful, crafty. **draughtiness,** *n.*

draunt DRANT.

†**drave,** past tense of DRIVE.

Dravidian, *a.* of or pertaining to Dravida, an old province of southern India. *n.* one of the dark-skinned non-Aryan peoples of India, comprising the peoples speaking Tamil, Telugu, Canarese and Malayalam.

draw, *v.t.* (*past* **drew,** *p.p.* **drawn**) to drag or pull; to pull after one; to haul; to pull out or up from; to extract or remove by pulling; to cause to flow or come forth, to elicit; to take, to receive, to derive; to infer, deduce; to take in, to inhale; to draft, to picture, to portray; to lengthen, to pull out, to stretch, to protract; to extract, to disembowel; to take out of a box or wheel (as tickets); to unsheathe (as a sword); to allure, attract, to cause to follow one; to cause to come out; (*Hunting*) to search for game; to write (a cheque, draft, order) on a banker etc.; (*Naut.*) to need a specified depth of water to float; †to withdraw; †to draw aside (as a curtain); †to muster; †to track; to leave undecided, as a match. *v.i.* to pull, to haul; to attract; to allow a free motion, current etc. (as a chimney, pipe etc.); to unsheathe a sword or take a pistol from its holster; to draw lots; to extract the essence, to extract humour etc. (as a poultice); to move, to approach (as if drawn towards); to come together, to contract; to come out or away (as if pulled); to practise the art of delineation; to write out a draft for payment; (*Naut.*) to require a certain depth of water. *n.* the act or power of drawing; a pull, a strain; an attraction, a lure; the act of drawing lots; a lot or chance drawn; the act of drawing a covert; a drawn game or contest; a feeler, a device to elicit information. **draw and quarter,** (*Hist.*) penalty of disembowelling and dismemberment after hanging. **to draw a bead** BEAD. **to draw away,** to get further in front. **to draw back,** to move back; to withdraw; to be unwilling to fulfil a promise. **to draw (a) blank,** to find nothing. **to draw in,** to collect, to contract; to entice, to inveigle; of days, to close in, to shorten. **to draw it mild,** to draw beer from the cask of mild; (*coll.*) to state, describe or ask moderately, not to exaggerate or be exorbitant. **to draw lots,** to choose (a person, course of action etc.) by the random selection of objects, usu. straws of different lengths. **to draw near, nigh,** to approach. **to draw off,** to withdraw, retire, retreat; to rack wine etc. **to draw on,** to lead to as a consequence; to allure, attract, entice; to approach. **to draw out,** to lengthen; to set in order for battle; to induce to talk, to elicit; to write out; to protract; of days, to become longer. **to draw over,** to bring over; to induce to change parties. **to draw rein,** to slow down; to stop. **to draw stumps,** (*Cricket*) to stop playing for the day. **to draw the line at,** to refuse to go any further. **to draw the long bow,** to tell incredible stories. **to draw the shots,** in bowls, to bowl close to the jack. **to draw the teeth of,** to render harmless. **to draw trumps,** to play trumps at cards until the opponents have none left. **to draw up,** to range in order, or in line of battle; to compose, to put into proper form; to put (oneself) into a stiff erect attitude. **to draw up with,** to overtake. **drawback,** *n.* money paid back, esp. excise or import duty remitted or refunded on goods exported; a deduction, a rebate; a disadvantage; an inconvenience; an obstacle. **drawback lock,** *n.* one having a spring-bolt that can be drawn back by a knob inside the door. **draw-bar,** *n.* a bar to connect a locomotive with a tender. **drawbridge,** *n.* one that may be raised on hinges at one or both ends to allow vessels to pass or to prevent passage across; a game of bridge for two. **drawgate,** *n.* the valve or door of a sluice or lock. **draw-gear,** *n.* harness for horses drawing wagons etc.; railway-carriage couplings. **draw-head,** *n.* a device in spinning, by which the slivers are lengthened and receive an additional twist; the projecting part of a draw-bar in which the coupling-pin connects with the link. **draw knife, drawshave,** *n.* a cutting blade with a handle at each end, for shaving wood. †**draw-latch,** *n.* a thief. **draw-link,** *n.* a connecting link for railway carriages. **draw-net,** *n.* one with wide meshes for catching large birds; a seine. **draw-plate,** *n.* a drilled steel plate through which wire is drawn to reduce and equalize its thickness. **draw-sheet,** *n.* (*Med.*) an extra sheet doubled lengthwise and placed across the bed so that it may be pulled beneath the patient as required. **drawstring,** *n.* a cord or thread, threaded through or otherwise attached to fabric, which can be pulled together in the fabric. **draw-well,** *n.* a deep well from which water is drawn by means of a rope and bucket. [OE *dragan,* cp. Dut. *dragen,* G *tragen*]

drawee, *n.* the person on whom a bill of exchange or order for payment in money is drawn.

drawer, *n.* one who draws; a tapster, a barman;, a sliding receptacle in a table etc.; one who draws a bill or order for the payment of money; one who or that which has the quality of attracting. **chest of drawers** CHEST. **out of the top drawer,** belonging to the upper social class. **drawerful,** *n.* **drawers,** *n.pl.* an undergarment covering the lower body and part of the legs.

drawing, *n.* the action of the verb to draw; the art of representing objects on a flat surface by means of lines drawn with a pencil, crayon etc.; a delineation of this kind; a sketch in black and white, or monochrome; the distribution or prizes in a lottery. **out of drawing,** incorrectly drawn. **drawing-block,** *n.* a number of sheets of drawing-paper adhering at the edges so that the uppermost sheet can be detached. **drawing-board,** *n.* a rectangular frame for holding a sheet of paper while drawing. **drawing-compass, -passes,** *n.pl.* a pair of compasses with a pencil or pen at one of the points. **drawing-knife,** *n.* a blade having a handle at each end, used by coopers etc.; a tool used for cutting a groove as a starting-point for a saw. **drawing office,** *n.* the department in an engineering works where designs and plans are set out. **drawing-pin,** *n.* a flat-headed tack for securing drawing-paper to a board. **drawing-room,** *n.* a room for the reception of company; a formal reception by a sovereign or person of high official rank; the company assembled in a drawing-room; (*N Am.*) a private compartment in a railway coach. *a.* suitable for a drawing-room. **drawings,** *n.pl.* takings; receipts.

drawl, *v.t.* to utter in a slow, lengthened tone; to protract, drag (out). *v.i.* to speak with a slow, prolonged utterance; †to dawdle. *n.* a slow, lengthened manner of speaking. **drawler,** *n.* **drawling,** *a.* **drawlingly,** *adv.* [prob. from DRAW (cp. Dut. *dralen*)]

drawn, past participle of DRAW. *a.* pulled out (as a sword); depicted, sketched, composed; pulled to one side, distorted; haggard; eviscerated (as a fowl). **at daggers drawn,** hostile, on the point of fighting each other. **drawn-thread work,** fancy work in which the threads of a fabric are some pulled out and some fastened so as to form a pattern. **drawn game, battle,** *n.* a game or battle in which neither side can claim any decided advantage.

dray, *n.* a low cart, generally of strong and heavy construction, used by brewers etc. **dray-horse,** *n.* a strong, heavy horse for drawing a dray. **drayman,** *n.* a driver in charge of a dray. **drayage,** *n.* the use of a dray or the charge for its use. [from OE *dragan,* to DRAW (cp. *dræge,* a draw-net)]

dread, *v.t.* to fear greatly; to anticipate with terror and shrinking; †to be apprehensive or anxious about, to doubt. *v.i.* to be in great fear. *n.* great fear or terror; apprehension of evil; awe, reverence; the person or thing dreaded. *a.* exciting great fear or terror, frightful; awe-inspiring, to be reverenced. **dreadlocks,** *n.pl.* long hair worn in many tight plaits by Rastafarians. **dreadnought,** *n.* one totally devoid of fear; a heavy, woollen, felted cloth; a heavy overcoat made of this material; a type of battleship, first built 1905–06, with its main armament composed of big guns. **dreadful,** *a.* inspiring dread; terrible; awe-inspiring; †full of dread; (*coll.*) annoying, disagreeable, troublesome, frightful, horrid; (*coll.*) very, exceedingly. **penny dreadful,** a journal or story-book dealing with crude sentiment and horrors. **dreadfully,** *adv.* **dreadfulness,** *n.* **dreadless,** *a.* free from dread; undaunted; secure. **dreadlessly,** *adv.* [OE *drǣdan* (in *on-drǣdan, of-drǣdan* etc.)]

dream, *n.* a vision; thoughts and images that pass through the mind of a sleeping person; the state of mind in which these occur; a visionary idea, a fancy, reverie; something beautiful or enticing; a chimerical scheme, a castle in the air. *v.i.* (*past* **dreamt,** or **dreamed**) to have visions; to think, to imagine as in a dream; to conceive as possible; to waste time in idle thoughts. *v.t.* to see, hear, feel etc. in dream; to imagine or conceive in a visionary fashion, to picture in hope or imagination. **day-dream,** a romantic scheme or vain fancy voluntarily indulged in. **waking-dream,** a waking experience of involuntary vision; a hallucination. **to dream away,** to spend (time) idly or vainly. **to dream up,** (*coll.*) to invent, esp. an idea or excuse. **to go like a dream,** to work very smoothly; to be very successful. **dreamboat,** *n.* (*coll.*) a very desirable member of the opposite sex. **dreamland,** *n.* the region of fancy or imagination. **dream-reader,** *n.* a person who professes to reveal the meanings of dreams. **dreamtime,** *n.* in Austral. aboriginal mythology, a Golden Age after the Creation of the world. **dream-world,** *n.* a world of illusions. **dreamer,** *n.* †**dreamery,** *n.* **dreamful,** *a.* **dreamingly,** *adv.* **dreamless,** *a.* **dreamlessly,** *adv.* **dreamlike,** *a.* **dreamy,** *a.* full or or causing dreams; visionary; addicted to dreaming. **dreamily,** *adv.* **dreaminess,** *n.* [ME *dream,* OE *drēam,* music, joy, mirth, appear to be distinct and to have caused a non-extant *drēam,* vision, to be avoided in favour of *swefn,* to sleep (cp. OS *drōm,* a dream, G *Traum*)]

dream-hole, *n.* a hole in the wall of a steeple (perh. one of the holes in belfries through which the sound passes out). [perh. from OE *drēam,* music, mirth]

dreary, drear, *a.* dismal, gloomy; cheerless, tiresome, dull. *n.* dreariness. **drearily, drearly,** *adv.* **dreariment,** *n.* **dreariness,** *n.* **drearisome,** *a.* †**drearihead,** *n.* dreariness. **drearness,** *n.* [OE *drēorig,* from *drēor,* gore]

dredge[1], *n.* a drag-net for taking oysters; an apparatus for dragging under water to bring up objects from the bottom for scientific purposes; a bucket or scoop for scraping mud etc. from the bed of a pond etc. *v.t.* to gather or bring up with a dredge; to remove or clear away by means of a dredge; to clean or deepen (as a river) with a dredging machine. *v.i.* to use a dredge. **to dredge up,** to lift with a dredge; to find (something) previously obscure or well hidden. **dredger,** *n.* one who fishes with a dredge; a ballast-lighter; a ship for dredging; a dredging-machine. **dredging-machine,** *n.* a floating machine for raising silt etc. from the bottom of a river, harbour, channel etc. to deepen it or obtain ballast. [Sc. *dreg,* ME *drege,* prob. from OE *dragan,* to DRAW, DRAG]

dredge², *v.t.* to sprinkle (flour etc.) upon or over; to sprinkle with flour etc. **dredger,** *n.* a box with perforated lid for sprinkling. **dredging-box,** *n.* [ME *dragie,* later *dredge,* a comfit, from OF *dragee,* late L and Gr. *tragēmata,* spices, condiments]

Dred Scott Case, The, in US history, a Supreme Court case brought by a Missouri black slave, Dred Scott (*c.* 1800–58), seeking to obtain his freedom on the grounds that his owner had taken him to reside temporarily in the free state of Illinois. The decision of the Supreme Court against Scott in 1857 intensified sectional discord before the Civil War.

dree, *v.t.* to suffer, to endure. **to dree one's weird,** to abide by one's lot. [A-S *drēogan,* to perform, to endure]

dreg, *n.* (*usu. pl.*) the sediment or lees of liquor; feculence; the end, the bottom; worthless refuse; vile matter; the lowest class; the most undesirable part. **not a dreg,** not a drop, not the least part (left). **dreggy,** *a.* [cp. Icel. *dregg,* pl. *dreggjar,* Swed. *dragg*]

dreich, *a.* (*Sc.*) tedious, wearisome, long; bleak. [DREE]

Dreikaiserbund, *n.* an informal alliance from 1872 between the emperors of Russia, Germany, and Austria-Hungary. It was effectively at an end by 1879.

Dreiser, *n.* **Theodore** (1871–1945), US novelist, formerly a Chicago journalist. He wrote the Naturalist novel *Sister Carrie* (1900) and *An American Tragedy* (1925), based on the real-life crime of a young man who in 'making good' kills a shop assistant he has made pregnant.

drench, *v.t.* to wet thoroughly; to soak, to saturate; to cause to swallow (a medicinal draught); (*Tanning*) to bate; †to submerge, to drown; †to overwhelm; to purge violently. †*v.i.* to be drowned. *n.* a liquid medicine for horses or cattle; a soaking, a flood; (*Tanning*) a solution for bating etc.; †a large draught, a potion. **drencher,** *n.* one who or that which drenches; an apparatus for drenching cattle; (*coll.*) a heavy downpour. [OE *drencan,* causal of *drincan,* to drink]

Dresden, *n.* city of E Germany, capital of Dresden district, formerly capital of Saxony; population (1982) 521,000. Manufactures include chemicals, machinery, glassware, and musical instruments. One of the most beautiful German cities prior to its devastation by Allied bombing in 1945; subsequently rebuilt.

Dresden china, porcelain, ware, *n.* fine, delicately decorated china made at Meissen, near Dresden from 1710.

dress, *v.t.* to make straight; (*Mil.*) to form (ranks) into a straight line; to order, arrange, array; to clothe, to attire; to adorn, to deck; (*Naut.*) to decorate with flags etc.; to furnish with costumes; to cleanse, trim, brush, comb etc.; to curry or rub down (as a horse); to cleanse and apply remedies to; to prepare for use, to cook; to cover with dressing (as a salad); to prune, to cut; to manure; to square and give a smooth surface to (as stone); of a shop window, to arrange goods attractively in; to size (as yarn); to smooth and give a nap to (as cloth); †to address, to apply; †to put right, to adjust; †to train, to break in; †to direct one's course. *v.i.* to clothe onself; to put on evening cloths; to attire oneself elaborately; to pay great attention to dress; (*Mil.*) to arrange oneself in proper position in a line; †to direct one's course. *n.* that which is worn as clothes, esp. outer garments; garments, apparel; a lady's gown, a frock; the art of adjusting dress; an external covering, as plumage; external appearance, outward form. **evening dress,** clothes worn at dinners, evening receptions etc. **full dress,** that worn on state or important occasions. **morning dress,** formal clothes worn during the day. **to dress down,** to chastise, to thrash; to reprimand severely. **to dress to death,** to overdress. **to dress up, out,** to clothe elaborately; to deck, to adorn; to invest with a fictitious appearance. **dress-circle,** *n.* the first tier of seats above the pit in a theatre. **dress-coat,** *n.* a man's coat with narrow pointed tails, worn as evening dress. **dress-goods,** *n.pl.* fabrics for women's and children's outer garments. **dress-guard,** *n.* a guard made of wire or thread over a bicycle wheel to keep the rider's clothing from becoming entangled. **dress-improver,** *n.* a bustle. **dress length,** *n.* enough fabric to make a dress. **dressmaker,** *n.* one who makes women's dresses. **dressmaking,** *n.* **dress parade,** *n.* a formal military parade in full uniform. **dress-preserver, -shield,** *n.* a protector, usu. of waterproof materials, fitted under the armpits of a woman's dress to prevent staining of this by perspiration. **dress rehearsal,** *n.* the final rehearsal, with costumes and effects. **dress sense,** *n.* a knowledge of style in dress and the ability to pick clothes which suit one. **dress shirt,** *n.* a man's shirt worn with formal evening dress. **dress tie,** *n.* a tie for wearing with formal evening dress. **dress uniform,** *n.* a full ceremonial military uniform. **dressy,** *a.* fond of showy dress; wearing rich or showy dress; showy; stylish, smart. **dressiness,** *n.* [OF *dresser,* ult. from L *directus,* DIRECT]

dressage, *n.* the training of a horse in deportment, obedience and response to signals given by the rider's body. [F]

dresser¹, *n.* one who dresses another, esp. an actor for the stage; a surgeon's assistant in operations etc. who dresses wounds etc. **window dresser,** one who arranges the window displays in a shop.

dresser², *n.* a kitchen sideboard; a set of shelves or an open cupboard for plates etc.; (*N Am.*) a chest of drawers; †a bench or table on which meat was prepared or dressed for use. [OF *dresseur,* from *dresser,* as prec.]

dressing, *n.* the action of the verb to DRESS; gum, starch etc. used in sizing or stiffening fabrics; stuffing, sauce, salad-dressing; manure applied to a soil; ointment, liniment, bandages etc. applied to a wound or sore; a thrashing, a scolding; any stuff used for stiffening fabrics; (*pl.*) the mouldings and sculptured decorations on a wall or ceiling. **French dressing** FRENCH. **dressing-bag, -case,** *n.* a small bag or case for toilet requisites. **dressing-bell,** *n.* a bell rung as a signal to dress for dinner. **dressing-down,** *n.* a severe telling-off. **dressing-gown,** *n.* a loose robe worn over night- or underclothes. **dressing-room,** *n.* a room appropriated to dressing; the room where actors put on costumes and stage make-up. **dressing-station,** *n.* (*Mil. etc.*) a first-aid post. **dressing-table,** *n.* a table fitted with drawers and a mirror, used by women while dressing, making-up etc.

dressmaker etc. DRESS.

drew, past tense of DRAW.

drey, dray, *n.* a squirrel's nest. [etym. unknown]

Dreyfus, *n.* **Alfred** (1859–1935), French army officer, victim of miscarriage of justice, and anti-semitism. Employed in the War Ministry, in 1894 he was accused of betraying military secrets to Germany, court-martialled, and sent to Devil's Island. When his innocence was discovered in 1896 the military establishment tried to conceal it, and the implications of the Dreyfus affair were passionately discussed in the press until in 1906 he was exonerated.

drib, *v.t.* to cut off by bits; to cheat by petty tricks; to entice by degrees. *v.i.* to dribble; to shoot at short distances. *n.* a driblet, a petty amount or quantity. **in dribs and drabs**, little bits at a time. [prob. onomat., or from OE *drepan,* to hit]

dribble, *v.i.* to fall in a quick succession of small drops; to drip, to trickle; to fall or run slowly; to slaver, to drivel; to fall weakly, like a drop; †to want energy or vigour; to manoeuvre a football in a forward direction by slight kicks from alternate sides; (*Billiards*) to cause the ball just to roll into a pocket; †to fly (as an arrow) so as to fall short. *v.t.* to allow to drip; to give out slowly by drops. *n.* drivelling; drizzle; (*Football etc.*) a piece of dribbling. **dribbler,** *n.* **dribbly,** *a.* **driblet**, *n.* a small or petty portion or sum. [freq. of prec.]

drier DRY.

drift, *n.* that which is driven along by a wind or current; a driving; a current, a driving or compelling force; the course of drifting or movement; tendency, purpose, aim, tenor; a mass (of snow, leaves, sand etc.) driven together; a loose accumulation of sand and debris deposited over the surface by the action of water or ice; (*Naut.*) deviation from a direct course caused by currents, the tendency of a current; (*Mining*) a horizontal passage following a lode or vein; a drive of cattle, esp. (*Forest Law*) to a particular place on a given day for determination of ownership etc.; a drift-net; (*S Afr.*) a ford; (*Arch.*) the horizontal thrust of an arch upon its abutments; †a shower, a storm; †a scheme; a tool for enlarging or aligning holes; a controlled skid for taking bends at high speed; a gradual change in a supposedly constant piece of equipment. *v.i.* to be driven into heaps; to float or be carried along by or as by a current; to be carried along by circumstances; (*Mining*) to make a drift. *v.t.* to drive along or into heaps; to carry along (of a current); to cover with drifts or driftage; to shape or enlarge (a hole). **drift-anchor,** *n.* a drag-anchor. **drift-bolt,** *n.* a steel rod used to drive out a bolt. **drift-ice,** *n.* floating masses of ice drifting on the sea. **drift-land,** *n.* a yearly rent paid by some tenants for driving cattle through a manor. **drift-net,** *n.* a large fishing net. **drift-way,** *n.* (*Mining*) a drift; (*dial.*) a common way for driving cattle; the course of a ship drifting. **drift-wood,** *n.* wood carried by water to a distance from its native locality. **driftage,** *n.* drifting or drifted substances; the distance to which a ship drifts in bearing up against wind and currents. **drifter,** *n.* a trawler or fishing-boat using a drift-net to fish, esp. for enemy mines; one who wanders aimlessly from place to place. **driftless,** *a.* without clear meaning or aim. **drifty,** *a.* forming snow-drift. [from OE *drīfan,* DRIVE (cp. Dut., Icel., Swed. *drift,* G *Trift*)]

drill[1], *v.t.* to bore or pierce with a pointed tool, to perforate; to make holes by this means; to train by repeated exercise, to train to the use of arms, to exercise in military exercises; †to draw on, to decoy. *v.i.* to go through a course of military exercise. *n.* a metal tool for boring holes in hard material; a boring shellfish; constant practice or exercise in any art or business; the act of drilling soldiers or sailors, the series of exercises by which they are rendered efficient; rigorous training or discipline; (*coll.*) correct procedure, the right way to do something. **drill-bow,** *n.* a bow by the string of which a drill is rotated. **drill hall,** *n.* a hall for physical exercises or social functions. **drillmaster,** *n.* a military drill instructor; one who instructs in a strict, militaristic manner. **drill-press,** *n.* an upright drilling-machine. **drill-serjeant,** *n.* a non-commissioned officer who drills soldiers or schoolboys; a martinet, a narrow-minded devotee of routine. **drill-stock,** *n.* a handle or holder for a metal drill. **drilling fluid,** *n.* a mixture of clay and water pumped down during the drilling of an oil-well. **drilling-machine,** *n.* a machine for drilling holes in metal. **drilling platform,** *n.* one which is either mobile or attached to the sea bed, used as a base for equipment during the drilling of an oil-well. **drilling rig,** *n.* the machinery needed to drill an oil-well; an offshore mobile drilling platform. [cp. MDut. *drillen,* to bore, to turn round, to form to arms, to exercise]

drill[2], *v.t.* to sow (seed) or plant in rows. *v.i.* to sow or plant in this manner. *n.* a small trench or furrow, or a ridge with a trench along the top, for seeds or small plants; a row of plants in such a furrow; a machine for sowing grain in rows. **drill-barrow,** *n.* a manual machine for drilling and sowing. **drill-harrow,** *n.* one for crushing the earth and removing weeds between the rows of plants. **drill-husbandry,** *n.* the practice of sowing in drills by a machine. **drill-plough,** *n.* one for sowing grain in drills. **driller,** *n.* [etym. doubtful; perh. from prec.]

drill[3], *n.* a heavy cotton twilled cloth used for trousers etc. [earlier *drilling,* corr. of G *Drillich,* corr. of L *trilix trilīcem* (*tri-,* three, *līcium,* a thread)]

drill[4], *n.* a baboon from the coast of Guinea, *Cynocephalus leucophaeus.* [perh. from local name]

drily DRY.

drink, *v.t.* (*past* **drank**, *p.p.* **drunk**) to swallow (a liquid); to imbibe, absorb, suck in; to swallow up, to empty; to take in by the senses; to pledge, to toast; to waste (money, wages, property) on indulgence in liquor; †to inhale. *v.i.* to swallow a liquid; to take intoxicating liquors to excess. *n.* something to be drunk; a draught, a potion; intoxicating liquor; excessive indulgence in intoxicating liquors, intemperance. **in drink,** intoxicated. **strong drink,** alcoholic liquor. **the drink,** the sea. **to drink deep,** to take a long draught; to drink to excess. **to drink down,** to destroy the memory of by drinking; to beat another in drinking. **to drink in,** to absorb readily; to receive greedily, as with the senses; to gaze upon, listen to etc. with delight. **to drink like a fish,** to be a habitual heavy drinker. **to drink off,** to swallow at a single draught. **to drink (someone) under the table,** to drink and remain comparatively sober while one's drinking companion gets completely drunk. **to drink the health of,** to wish health to one in drinking; to toast. **to drink to,** to salute in drinking; to drink the health of. **to drink up,** to swallow completely. **drink-money,** *n.* money given to buy liquor; a tip. **drink-offering,** *n.* a Jewish offering of wine; a libation. **drinkable,** *a.* that may be drunk; fit for drinking. *n.* a liquor that may be drunk; (*pl.*) the beverages provided at a meal. **drinkableness,** *n.* **drinkably,** *adv.* **drinker,** *n.* one who drinks; a tippler, a drunkard. **drinking,** *n., a.* **drinking-up time,** the time between the call for last orders and closing time, in which to finish drinks. **drinking-bout,** *n.* a set-to at drinking; a revel. **drinking-fountain,** *n.* a fountain erected in a public place to supply water. **drinking-horn,** *n.* a drinking-vessel make of horn. **drinking-house,** *n.* an ale-house, a tavern. †**drinking-money,** *n.* drink-money. **drinking-song,** *n.* a song in praise of drinking parties. **drinking water,** *n.* water suitable for drinking. **drinkless,** *a.* [OE *drincan,* from Teut. *drenk-* (cp. Dut. *drinken,* G *trinken*)]

drip, *v.i.* (*past, p.p.* **dripped**) to fall in drops; to throw off moisture in drops. *v.t.* to let fall in drops. *n.* the act of dripping, a falling in drops; that which falls in drops; the projecting edge of a moulding or corona over a door or window; an apparatus for the intravenous administration of some liquid, drop by drop; (*coll.*) a stupid or insipid person. **drip-drop,** *n.* a persistent dripping. **drip dry,** *a.* of clothing, made of such a material that it dries quickly without wringing and needs no ironing. **drip-feed,** *v.t.* to feed nutrients to (a patient etc.) in liquid form, using a drip. *n.* nutrients thus administered. **drip-moulding, -stone,** *n.* a corona or projecting tablet or moulding over the heads of doorways, windows etc. to throw off rain; a filtering-stone. **drip-tray,** *n.* the tray in a refrigerator for catching the drops of water and ice during defrosting. **dripless,** *a.* **dripper,** *n.* **dripping,** *n.* the act of falling in drops; the fat which falls from roasting meat; (*pl.*) water, grease etc. falling or trickling from anything. **dripping-pan,** *n.* a pan for receiving the fat which drips from roasting meat. **drippy,** *a.* inclined to drip; insipid, inane. [OE *dryppan* (cp. OS *driopan,* G *triefen*)]

drive, *v.t.* (*past* **drove**, *p.p.* **driven**) to push or urge by force; to urge in a particular direction, to guide, to direct (as a horse, an engine, a ship); to convey in a carriage; to constrain, to compel; to prosecute, to carry on; to chase, hunt, esp. to frighten into an enclosure or towards guns; to distress, straiten, overwork; to throw, to propel; (*Golf*) to propel (the ball) with the driver; (*Cricket*) to hit (the ball) to or past the bowler with a swift free stroke; to force (a nail etc.) with blows; to propel (machinery etc.); to bore (a tunnel etc.); to delay, defer; to press (as an argument); †to distrain (cattle). *v.i.* to be urged forward by violence; to dash, to rush violently, to hasten; to drift, to be carried; to travel in a carriage, esp. under one's own direction or control; to control or direct a vehicle, engine etc.; to aim a blow, to strike furiously; to tend, to aim, to intend; (*Golf*) to hit the ball with the driver; †to distrain goods. *n.* a ride in a vehicle; the distance one is driven; a road for driving on, esp. a private carriageway to a house; a forward stroke at cricket etc.; a driving of game, cattle, or of an enemy; (*N Am.*) an annual gathering of cattle for branding; push, energy; (*sl.*) a blow, a violent stroke; energy, motivation; a device for writing information on to, and reading it from, magnetic tape; a series of competitive games of whist or bridge. **to drive a coach and horses through,** (*coll.*) to demolish (an argument or idea) by pointing out the obvious faults. **to drive a good bargain,** to make a good bargain. **to drive a hard bargain,** to be hard in making a bargain. **to drive at,** (*fig.*) to hint at. **what are you driving at?** what exactly do you mean? **to drive away,** to force to a distance; to scatter; to go away in a carriage etc. **to drive home,** to force (something) completely in; to explain (something) emphatically and make sure it is understood. **to drive in,** to hammer in; (*Mil.*) to force to retreat on their supports. **to drive off,** to compel to move away; †to put off, to defer. **to drive out,** to expel; to oust; to take the place of; in printing, to space widely. **to drive up the wall,** (*coll.*) to madden. **to let drive,** to strike furiously, to aim a blow (at). **drive-in,** *n.* a café or cinema where customers are served or can watch a film without leaving their cars. **driveway,** *n.* a path large enough for a car, from a road to a house. **driver,** *n.* one who or that which drives; one who drives a vehicle or an engine; one who conducts a team; a tool used by coopers in driving on the hoops of casks; an overseer on a plantation; that which communicates motion to something else, as a wheel; the piece of wood which impels the shuttle in weaving through the shed of the loom; (*Golf*) a wooden-headed club used to propel the ball from the tee. **driver-ant,** *n.* a W African ant, *Anomma arcens*. **driverless,** *a.* **driving,** *a.* having great force. **driving-band, -belt,** *n.* the strap or belt for connecting and communicating motion to parts of machinery. **driving-band,** *n.* a soft metal band at the end of a projectile which engages with the rifling of the gun and causes the fired shell to rotate. **driving licence,** *n.* a permit to drive, granted to one who has passed a **driving test,** or examination in the driving and handling of a motor-car. **driving mirror,** *n.* the small mirror inside a car which enables a driver to see what is behind his car. **driving seat,** *n.* the seat for the driver in a vehicle; a position of authority or control. **driving-shaft,** *n.* a shaft transmitting motion from the driving-wheel. **driving-wheel,** *n.* the wheel which communicates motion to other parts of the machinery; a large wheel of a locomotive, a cycle-wheel or motor-wheel to which motive force is applied directly. [OE *drīfan* (cp. Dut. *drijven,* Goth. *dreiban,* G *treiben*)]

drivel, *v.i.* (*past, p.p.* **drivelled**) to slaver; to allow spittle to flow from the mouth, as a child, idiot or dotard; to be weak or silly; to dote. *v.t.* to utter childishly or foolishly; to fritter (away). *n.* slaver; spittle flowing from the mouth; silly, nonsensical talk, twaddle. **driveller,** *n.* a slaverer, an idiot, a dotard, a fool. [OE *dreflian,* from same stem as DRAFF]

driver DRIVE.

drizzle, *v.i.* to fall, as rain, in fine drops; to rain slightly. *v.t.* to shed in small fine drops; to wet with fine drops. *n.* fine small rain **drizzly,** *a.* [freq. of ME *dresen,* OE *drēosan,* to fall in drops]

drogher, *n.* a slow W Indian coasting-vessel for carrying heavy burdens, as timber etc. [obs. F *droguer,* Dut. *drogher,* from *droogen,* to dry (herrings etc.)]

drogman, -oman DRAGOMAN.

drogue, *n.* a bag drawn behind a boat to prevent her broaching to; a drag attached to a harpoon line to check the progress of a whale when struck; a windsock; a parachute which reduces the speed of a falling object or landing aircraft; a target for firing practice, pulled along by an aircraft; cone-shaped device on the end of the refuelling hose of a tanker aircraft into which the probe of the receiving aircraft fits. [prob. var. of DRAG]

droguet, *n.* a kind of rep. [F, DRUGGET]

droil, *n.* a drudge, a slave; drudgery. *v.i.* to drudge, to toil, to moil. [etym. doubtful]

droit, *n.* a right, a due; a legal right; †(*Law*) a writ of right; (*pl.*) legal perquisites. **droits of Admiralty,** rights to the property of enemies, proceeds of wrecks etc. which go into the public treasury. [F, from late L *drictum,* L *dīrēctum,* DIRECT, late L, a right, a law]

droll, *a.* odd, merry, facetious, ludicrous, comical, laughable. *n.* a merry fellow, a jester, a buffoon. *v.i.* to play the wag or buffoon; to jest, to joke, to trifle. **drollery,** *n.* idle sportive jocularity, buffoonery; †a puppet; †a puppet-show; †a lively or comical sketch. **drollness,** *n.* **drolly,** *adv.* [F *drôle,* etym. doubtful]

-drome, *comb. form* a large area specially prepared for some specific purpose, as in *aerodrome* for aircraft, *hippodrome,* for races.

dromedary, *n.* the Arabian camel, *Camelus dromedarius,* distinguished from the Bactrian camel by its single hump; a swift variety of the species used for riding on. †**dromedarian,** *n.* the rider or driver of a dromedary. [OF *dromedaire,* late L *dromedārius,* L *dromas -adem,* Gr. *dromas -ada,* running, runner, from *dramein,* to run]

dromond, *n.* a large mediaeval ship. [A-F *dromund,* OF *dromon,* late L *dromō -ōnem,* Gr. *dromōn,* from *dromos,* racing, a course]

-dromous, *comb. form* running, as in *anadromous*. [Gr. *dromos,* race, race-course]

drone, *n.* the male of the bee, larger than the worker by which the honey is made; an idler, a lazy person who lives on the industry of others; a deep humming sound; the humming sound made by a bee; the unchanging bass produced from the three lower pipes of the bagpipe; any of these lower pipes; one with a low, monotonous speaking voice; a monotonous speech; a radio-controlled aircraft. *v.i.* to make a monotonous humming noise, as a bee or a bagpipe; to talk in a monotonous tone; to live in idleness. *v.t.* to read or speak in a monotonous tone. **drone-pipe,** *n.* the drone of a bagpipe. **droner,** *n.* **droning,** *a.* **droningly,** *adv.* [OE *drān, dræn,* a bee, cogn. with ME *drounen,* Sansk. *dhran,* to sound]

drongo, *n.* a member of the Dicruridae family, glossy, black, insect-eating birds of tropical Africa and Asia; (*Austral., sl.*) a slow-witted person. [Malagasy]

drool, *v.i.* to drivel, to slaver; to show excessive or lascivious pleasure in something. [contr. of DRIVEL]

droop, *v.i.* to hang, lean or bend down; to sink as if languishing; to fail, to flag, to languish, to decline; to be dejected, to despond, to lose heart. *v.t.* to let (the head, eyes, face) fall or hang down. *n.* the act of drooping; a drooping attitude. **droop snoot,** *n.* (*coll.*) an adjustable nose (of an aircraft). **droopily,** *adv.* **droopiness,** *n.* **droopingly,** *adv.* **droopy,** *a.* [cp. Icel. *drūpa,* see foll.]

drop, *n.* a globule or small portion of liquid in a spherical form, which is falling, hanging or adhering to a surface; a very small quantity of a fluid; (*Med.*) the smallest quantity separable of a liquid; (*pl.*) a dose or doses measured by such units; (*fig.*) a minute quantity, an infinitesimal particle; (*coll.*) a glass or drink of liquor; anything resembling a drop, or hanging as a drop, as an earring, or other pendent ornament; a sugar plum; (*pl.*) various sweetmeats; the act of dropping, a fall, a descent, a collapse; a thing that drops or is dropped; the unloading of troops by parachute; a drop-curtain; a falling trap-door; the part of a gallows contrived so as to fall from under the feet of persons to be hanged; the distance they are allowed to fall; a machine for lowering anything heavy into the hold of a vessel; an abrupt fall in a surface; the amount of this; (*N Am.*) a slot in a receptacle through which things can be dropped; a drop-kick. *v.t.* (*past, p.p.* **dropped**) to allow or cause to fall in drops, as a liquid; to cause to fall, to fell; to lower, to let down; to dismiss, to give up; to set down from a passenger vehicle; to let fall, to utter casually; to write to in an informal manner; to mention casually; to bear a foal, calf etc.; to omit; to stop (doing something), to have done with; to let go; to sprinkle with drops; (*coll.*) to bring down, to kill; (*coll.*) to lose; to score (a goal) with a drop-kick; to stop seeing or associating with (someone). *v.i.* to fall in drops; to drip, to discharge itself in drops; to fall; to collapse suddenly, to sink as if exhausted, to faint; to kneel; to disappear; to die; to die suddenly; to be uttered; to cease, to lapse, to come to an end; to fall (behind); †to submerge. **a drop in the ocean,** a proportionately tiny amount. **a drop too much,** slightly too much to drink. **at the drop of a hat,** immediately. **to drop a curtsy,** to curtsy. **to drop anchor,** to let down the anchor. **to drop across,** to meet with accidentally; to reprimand. **to drop astern,** to move or pass towards the stern; to reduce speed so as to allow another to pass ahead. **to drop away,** to depart; to desert a cause. **to drop down,** to sail down a river towards the sea. **to drop in,** to make an informal visit; to call unexpectedly. **to drop out,** (*coll.*) to refuse to follow a conventional life style, esp. to leave school or college early. **to let drop,** to disclose, seemingly without any intention of so doing. **to drop off,** (*fig.*) to fall gently asleep. **drop-curtain,** *n.* (*Theat.*) a drop-scene. **drop-drill,** *n.* a contrivance for simultaneously manuring and sowing in drills. **drop forge,** *a.* a forge for metal with two dies, one of them fixed, the other acting by force or gravity. **drop goal,** *n.* one scored in rugby with a drop-kick. **drop-hammer,** *n.* a drop forge. **drop-handle,** *n.* a handle or knob of a drawer, door etc. that hangs down when not in use. **drop handlebars,** *n.pl.* curving, lowered handlebars on a racing bicycle. **drop-kick,** *n.* a kick made by letting the ball drop and kicking it on the rise; whence **drop-off, drop-out. drop leaf,** *n.* a hinged flap on a table which can be lowered or raised. **drop-letter,** *n.* a letter posted for delivery in the same district. **dropout,** *n.* (*coll.*) one who rejects conventional society. **drop-press,** *n.* a machine for embossing, punching etc. by means of a weight made to drop on an anvil. **drop-scene,** *n.* (*Theat.*) a painted curtain suspended on pulleys which is let down to conceal the stage. **drop scone,** *n.* one cooked on a hot griddle. **drop shot,** *n.* a shot in tennis, squash or badminton which falls to the ground immediately after crossing the net or hitting the wall. **drop-shutter,** *n.* a shutter in a camera for making instantaneous exposures. **drop-sulphur, -tin,** *n.* sulphur or tin granulated by being dropped in a molten state into water. **drop-wort,** *n.* a plant with tuberous root-fibres, *Spiraea filipendula;* other species of spiraea; various species of *Oenanthe,* esp. *O. fistulosa.* **droplet,** *n.* a tiny drop. **dropper,** *n.* one who or that which drops; a small glass tube with a rubber bulb at one end, for administering medicinal drops; (*Angling*) an artificial fly set at some distance from the end of a cast. **dropping,** *n.* **dropping-bottle,** *n.* an apparatus for supplying small quantities to test-tubes etc. **dropping fire,** *n.* an irregular discharge of small arms. **dropping-tube,** *n.* a tube for allowing liquid to exude in drops. †**droppingly,** *adv.* **droppings,** *n.pl.* that which falls or has fallen in drops; the dung of beasts or birds. [OE *dropa,* whence *dropian,* to drop (cogn. with DRIP, DROOP)]

dropsy, *n.* an accumulation of watery fluid in the areolar tissues or serous cavities; a disease in plants caused by an excess of water; any swollen or bloated condition. **dropsical,** *a.* **dropsically,** *adv.* **dropsied,** *a.* suffering from dropsy; †inflated. [ME *dropesie, ydropesie,* MF *hydropisie,* L *hydrōpisis,* Gr. *hudrōps -ōpos* (*hudōr,* water)]

drosera, *n.* a genus of insectivorous plants comprising the sundew. [Gr. *droseros,* fem. *-ra,* dewy, from *drosos,* dew]

droshky, drosky, *n.* a Russian open four-wheeled vehicle in which the passengers ride astride a bench, their feet resting on bars near the ground; a public cab in Berlin and other German towns. [Russ. *drozhki,* dim. of *drozi,* a wagon]

drosometer, *n.* an instrument for measuring the quantity of dew collected on the surface of a body during the night. [Gr. *drosos,* dew]

drosophila, *n.* (*pl.* **-las, -lae**) any of the small fruit flies used in laboratory genetic experiments. [Gr. *drosos,* dew, *-phila,* -PHILE]

dross, *n.* the scum or useless matter left from the melting of metals; anything utterly useless, refuse, rubbish; anything impure. **drossy,** *a.* **drossiness,** *n.* [OE *drōs* (cp. MDut. *droes,* G *Drusen,* lees, dregs)]

drought, †**drouth,** *n.* dryness, dry weather; an absence of rain or moisture; long-continued rainless weather; thirst. **droughty,** *a.* †**drouthy,** *a.*

drouk, *v.t.* (*Sc., North.*) to drench; to duck. **droukit,** *p.p., a.* [etym. doubtful (cp. Icel. *drukna,* to be drowned, DRUNK)]

drove[1], *n.* a collection of animals driven in a body; a road for driving cattle on; a shoal, a crowd, a mass of people, esp. as moving together; a narrow channel in the Fens for draining or irrigation; a stone-mason's broad chisel. *v.t.* to dress (stone) with a drove. *v.i.* to drive cattle in droves. **drove-road,** *n.* an old grassy track used by droves of cattle. **drover,** *n.* one who drives cattle or sheep to market; a cattle-dealer; a boat used for fishing with a drift-net. [OE *drāf,* from *drīfan,* to DRIVE]

drove[2], past tense of DRIVE.

drow, *n.* (*Sc.*) a drizzling mist. [etym. doubtful]

drown, *v.i.* to be suffocated in water or other liquid; to perish in this manner. *v.t.* to suffocate by submersion in water or other liquid; to submerge, to drench, to overwhelm with water, to overflow, to deluge; (*fig.*) to overpower (as by a volume of sound); to overwhelm, to quench, to put an end to. **to drown one's sorrows,** to drink alcohol in order to forget one's problems and sorrows. **to drown out,** to drive out by a flood. **drowner,** *n.* one who is drowning. [OE *druncnian,* to become intoxicated, to drown, from *druncen,* p.p. of *drincan,* to DRINK]

drowse, *v.i.* to be sleepy or half-asleep; to be heavy and dull; to doze. *v.t.* to make drowsy; to spend (time) in an idle or sluggish way. *n.* the state of being half-asleep; a nap, a doze; drowsiness, heaviness. **drowsy,** *a.* inclined to sleep, sleepy; disposing to sleep; sluggish, stupid. **drowsy-head,** *n.* a sleepy person. **drowsy-headed,** *a.* sleepy, sluggish in disposition; dull. †**drowsihead, drowsiness,** *n.* **drowsily,** *adv.* [OE *drūsian,* to become languid]

drub, *v.t.* to beat with a stick; to cudgel; to beat thoroughly in a fight or contest. **drubber,** *n.* **drubbing,** *n.* a cudgelling, a heavy beating. [prob. from Arab. *darb,* a beating]

drudge, *v.i.* to perform menial work; to work hard with little reward; to slave. *v.t.* to spend or pass laboriously. *n.* one employed in menial work; one who toils at uncongenial work and is ill-paid; a slave; a hack. **drudger[1],** *n.* a drudge. **drudgery,** *n.* hard menial or tedious work. †**drudgingly,** *adv.* [prob. cogn. with OE *drēogan,* to DREE]

drudger[1] DRUDGE.

drudger[2] DREDGER.

drug, *n.* any substance, mineral, vegetable or animal, used as the basis or as an ingredient in medical preparations, a poison, a potion; a narcotic causing addiction. *v.t.* (*past, p.p.* **drugged**) to mix drugs with, esp. to make narcotic; to administer drugs to, esp. narcotics; to render insensible with drugs; (*fig.*) to deaden; to surfeit, to cloy. **drug in the market,** so common as to be unsaleable. **drug addict, fiend,** *n.* one addicted to the use of narcotics. **drug-pusher,** *n.* one who sells narcotic drugs illegally. **drugstore,** *n.* (*N Am.*) a chemist's shop where pharmaceuticals and other small articles are sold including refreshments. **drug traffic,** *n.* illicit trading in narcotic drugs. **druggist,** *n.* one who deals in drugs; a pharmaceutical chemist; (*N Am.*) a chemist. [F *drogue,* etym. doubtful]

drugget, *n.* a coarse woollen fabric, felted or woven, used as a covering or as a substitute for carpet. [F *droguet,* etym. doubtful]

druid, *n.* the name commonly given to the priests and teachers of the early Gauls and Britons or perh. of pre-Celtic peoples, who taught the transmigrating of souls, frequently celebrated their rites in oak-groves, and are stated by Caesar to have offered human sacrifices; a member of the Ancient Order of Druids, a benefit society, established in 1781; an officer of the Welsh Gorsedd; a member of any of several movements trying to revive druidic practices. **druidess,** *n. fem.* **druidic, -ical,** *a.* **druidism,** *n.* [F *druide,* L *druidae, -des,* pl., from OCelt. (cp. OIr. *druid-,* Gael *draoi, draoidh, druidh,* a magician, a sorcerer)]

drum[1], *n.* a musical instrument made by stretching parchment over the head of a hollow cylinder or hemisphere; the tympanum or hollow part of the middle-ear; the membrane across this; the hollow hyoid bone of a howling monkey; applied to certain resonant organs in birds, fishes and insects; the drum-like cry of the bittern and other animals; anything drum-shaped, esp. a small cylindrical box for holding fruit, fish etc.; the quantity contained in such a box; (*Austral., coll.*) a swag, a bundle, a tramp's roll, a bluey; the solid part of the Corinthian and composite capitals; the upright part of a cupola, either above or below a dome; a cylindrical block forming part of a column; (*Mach.*) a revolving cylinder over which a belt or band passes; the drum-fish; †an evening or afternoon party at which card-playing was carried on; a cylindrical instrument on which computer data can be stored; (*Austral., sl.*) a brothel. *v.i.* (*past, p.p.* **drummed**) to beat or play a tune on a drum; to beat rapidly or thump, as on a table, the floor or a piano; to make a sound like the beating of a drum (as certain insects, birds etc.); (*N Am.*) to tout for customers. *v.t.* to perform on a drum; to summon; to beat (up) recruits by the sound of a drum; to din (into) a person, to drive a lesson (into) by persistence. **to beat the drum for,** to try to raise interest in. **to drum out,** to expel from a regiment with disgrace; to cashier. **to drum up,** to canvass (aid or support). **to drum upon,** to beat or thump repeatedly. **drum beat,** *n.* the sound made by a beating drum. **drum brake,** *n.* a type of brake with shoes which rub against a brake drum. **drum-fish,** *n.* the American genus *Pogonias,* the two species of which emit a drumming or grunting noise. **drum-head,** *n.* the membrane stretched at the top of a drum; the membrane across the drum of the ear; the top of the capstan. **drum-head court-martial** COURT. **drum-major,** *n.* a non-commissioned officer in charge of the drums of a regiment, or who leads the band on the march. **drum majorette,** *n.* a girl who marches in a procession dressed in a uniform and twirling a baton. **drum scanner,** *n.* (*TV*) a rotating drum carrying the picture-scanning elements. **drumstick,** *n.* the stick with which a drum is beaten; anything resembling such a stick, as the leg of a fowl. **drummer,** *n.* one who performs on a drum, esp. a soldier whose office is to beat the various calls etc. on his drum; the member of an orchestra in charge of the percussion instruments; a commercial traveller. [cp. MDut. *tromme* and Dut. *trom,* MHG *trumme,* orig. a trumpet]

drum[2], *n.* a narrow hill or ridge; (*Geol.*) a long narrow ridge of drift or alluvial formation; also called a **drumlin**. [Gael. and Ir. *druim*]

drumble, *v.i.* to be sluggish; to move sluggishly. **drumble-dore,** *n.* a dor-beetle; a stupid, heavy fellow. [etym. doubtful (cp. Swed. and Norw. *drumla,* to be half asleep)]

drumlin DRUM[2].

drumly, *a.* (*Sc.*) muddy, turbid; troubled, cloudy, overcast. [prob. var. of obs. *drubly*]

Drummond light, *n.* the limelight or oxy-hydrogen light. [Capt. *Drummond,* 1797–1840, the inventor]

drunk, *a.* intoxicated, stupefied or overcome with alcoholic liquors; inebriated, highly excited (with joy etc.) *n.* (*sl.*) a drunken person; a fit of drunkenness. **drunkard,** *n.* one addicted to the excessive use of alcoholic liquors; one who is habitually or frequently drunk. **drunken,** *p.p., a.* intoxicated; given to drunkenness; caused by drunkenness; characterized by intoxication. **drunkenly,** *adv.* **drunkenness,** *n.* [p.p. of DRINK]

Drupaceae, *n.pl.* a sub-order of *Rosaceae,* including the plum, cherry, peach, olive, and other trees bearing stone-fruit. **drupaceous,** *a.* belonging to the Drupaceae; bearing drupes; pertaining to or of the nature of drupes. [L *drūpa,* Gr. *druppa,* an over-ripe olive]

drupe, *n.* a fleshy fruit containing a stone with a kernel, as the peach, plum etc. **drupel**, **drupelet**, *n.* a succulent fruit formed by an aggregation of small drupes, as the raspberry.

Druse[1], **Druz(e)**, *n.* a member of a politico-religious sect of Islamic origin, inhabiting the region of Mt Lebanon in Syria; Druse militia groups have been heavily involved in the Lebanese civil war. [Arab. *Durūz,* said to be from Ismail al-*Darazi,* or the Tailor, founder of the sect in 1040]

druse[2], *n.* a cavity in a rock lined or studded with crystals; the crystalline lining of this. **drusy,** *a.* [G, from Czech *druza*]

dry, *a.* devoid of moisture; arid; without sap or juice, not succulent; lacking rain, having an insufficient rainfall; thirsty; dried up, removed by evaporation, draining or wiping; not giving milk, not yielding juice; not under water (of land, a shore etc.); not sweet (of wines etc.); without butter (as bread); prohibited by law for sale of alcoholic liquors; without mortar, as a *dry stone wall;* (*fig.*) lifeless, insipid, lacking interest, dull; meagre, bare, plain; sarcastic, cynical, ironical, sly; without sympathy or cordiality, cold, discouraging, harsh; exhibiting a sharp, frigid preciseness in execution or the want of a delicate contour in form. *n.* (*Austral.*) the rainless season. *v.t.* to free from or deprive of water or moisture; to deprive of juice, sap or succulence; to drain, to wipe; to cause to cease yielding milk; to exhaust. *v.i.* to lose or be deprived of moisture; to grow dry; to cease to yield moisture; †to become withered; †to be thirsty. **dry-bulb thermometer,** one of a pair of thermometers the other of which is always kept moist, the two together indicating the degree of humidity of the air. **the Dry,** *n.* (*Austral.*) the dry season; the inland desert. **to dry out,** to make or become dry; to undergo treatment for alcohol or drug abuse. **to dry up,** to deprive totally of moisture; to deprive of energy; to lose all moisture; to cease to flow, to cease to yield water; to become withered; (*Theat.*) to forget one's lines; (*sl.*) to leave off talking or doing something. **to go dry,** to prohibit the sale of alcoholic liquors. **dry-battery,** *n.* one made up of dry cells. **dry-beat,** *v.t.* to beat severely. **dry-bob,** *n.* (*School sl.*) one who plays cricket and football, as distinguished from a boy who rows. **dry canteen,** *n.* a canteen where no alcoholic drinks are served. **dry cell,** *n.* a battery cell in which the electrolyte is a paste and not a fluid. **dry-clean,** *v.t.* to clean with a petrol-based solvent or other detergent. **dry-cooper,** *n.* a maker of casks for dry goods. **dry-cure,** *v.t.* to cure by drying and salting, as distinguished from pickling. **dry dock,** *n.* one which can be emptied of water for ship repairs. *v.t.* to put in dry dock. **dry-eyed,** *a.* without tears. **dry farming,** *n.* a method of growing crops in semi-arid regions by reducing the moisture lost through evaporation. **dry-fly,** *n.* an angler's fly that floats on the surface, as distinguished from one that is allowed to sink. **dry-foot,** *adv.* dry-shod, without wetting the feet; †following game by the scent of the foot. **dry-footed,** *a.* dry-shod. **dry-goods,** *n.pl.* cloths, silks, drapery, haberdashery etc., as distinguished from grocery; sometimes extended to include any non-liquid goods. **dry-goods store,** (*N Am.*) a draper's shop. **dry-hole,** *n.* an oil-well which does not produce a viable amount of oil. **dry ice,** *n.* solid carbon dioxide used in refrigeration. **dry lodging,** *n.* (*sl.*) accommodation without board. **dry-measure,** *n.* a measure for dry-goods, as a bushel. **dry-nurse,** *n.* a nurse who rears a child without the breast; (*coll.*) one who looks after and instructs another; (*Mil. sl.*) a subordinate officer who coaches a superior. *v.t.* to rear without the breast; (*Mil.*) to act as instructor to (a superior officer). **dry-pile,** *n.* a voltaic battery in which the plates are separated by layers of dry substance. **dry-plate,** *n.* a photographic plate with a hard, dry, sensitized film, adapted for storing and carrying about. **dry-point,** *n.* a needle for engraving on a copper plate without acid; an engraving so produced. *v.i.* to engrave by this process.

dry riser, *n.* a vertical, empty pipe with connections on every floor of a building, to which a fireman's hose can be attached. **dry-rot,** *n.* decay in timber caused by fungi which reduce it to a dry brittle mass. **dry-run,** *n.* shooting practice without live ammunition; a practice run, a rehearsal. **dry-salt,** *v.t.* to dry-cure. **drysalter,** *n.* a dealer in dried and salted meat, pickles etc.; a dealer in dye-stuffs, chemical products etc. **drysaltery,** *n.* the goods sold by a drysalter; the shop or business of a drysalter. **dry shaver,** *n.* an electric razor. **dry ship,** *n.* a ship in which no alcoholic liquor is permitted. **dry-shod,** *a., adv.* without wetting the feet. **dry ski,** *n.* a specially adapted ski for use on a dry surface. **dry skiing,** *n.* **dry-stone,** *a.* of a wall, built without mortar. **dry waller,** *n.* one who builds walls without mortar. **dryish,** *a.* **drily, dryly,** *adv.* **dryness,** *n.* **drier, dryer,** *n.* a desiccative; a material added to oil paints and printers' ink to make them dry quickly; an apparatus for drying the hair after shampoo, clothes after washing etc. [OE *drȳge* (cp. Dut. *droog,* G *trocken*)]

dryad, *n.* (*pl.* **-ades**) a nymph of the woods. [L *dryas,* pl. *-ades,* Gr. *druas -ades* (*drūs,* a tree)]

dry-as-dust, *n.* a dull, prosy, plodding historian; an antiquary who carried on his researches in a mechanical spirit (from the name of the imaginary person to whom Scott dedicated some of his novels). *a.* dull, prosy; dry, uninteresting.

Dryden, *n.* **John** (1631–1700), English poet and dramatist, noted for his satirical verse and for his use of the heroic couplet. His poetry includes the verse-satire *Absalom and Achitophel* (1681), 'Annus Mirabilis', and 'St Cecilia's Day' (1687); plays include the comedy *Marriage à la Mode* (1671) and *All for Love* (1678), a reworking of Shakespeare's *Antony and Cleopatra.* Critical works include *Essay on Dramatic Poesy* (1668).

dryopithecine, *n.* a member of a genus of extinct apes, thought to be the ancestors of modern apes. [Gr. *drūs,* tree, *pithēkos,* ape]

Drysdale, *n.* **George Russell** (1912–69), Australian artist, who depicted the Australian outback, its drought, desolation and poverty, and Aboriginal life.

DSc, (*abbr.*) Doctor of Science.

DSC, (*abbr.*) Distinguished Service Cross.

DSM, (*abbr.*) Distinguished Service Medal.

DSO, (*abbr.*) Distinguished Service Order.

DST, (*abbr.*) daylight saving time; double summer time.

DTI, (*abbr.*) Department of Trade and Industry.

DTs, DT's, (*abbr.*) (*coll.*) delirium tremens.

duad DYAD.

dual, *a.* consisting of two; twofold, binary, double; expressing two; applied to an inflection of a verb, adjective, pronoun or noun, which, in certain languages, expresses two persons or things, as distinct from the plural which expresses more than two. *n.* the dual number. **dual carriageway,** *n.* a road which has at least two lanes in each direction, with traffic travelling in opposite directions separated by a central reservation. **dual control,** *a.* that can be operated by either of two people. **Dual Monarchy,** *n.* the former union of Austria-Hungary. **dual personality,** *n.* a psychological condition in which a single person has two distinct characters. **dual purpose,** *a.* having, or intended for, two separate purposes. **dualism,** *n.* duality, the state of being twofold; a system or theory based on a radical duality of nature or animating principle, as mind and matter, good and evil in the universe, divine and human personalities in Christ, independence of the cerebral hemispheres. **dualist,** *n.* **dualistic,** *a.* **duality,** *n.* **dualize, -ise,** *v.t.* **dually,** *adv.* [L *duālis,* from *duo,* two]

Dual Entente, *n.* an alliance between France and Russia which lasted from 1893 until the Bolshevik Revolution of 1917.

dualin, *n.* an explosive compound, composed of nitroglycerine, fine sawdust, and nitre.

duan, *n.* a song; a canto. [Gael.]

dub¹, *v.t.* (*past, p.p.* **dubbed**) to confer knighthood upon by a blow of a sword on the shoulder; to confer any dignity, rank, character or nickname upon; to dress or trim; to smear with grease so as to soften, e.g. leather; †to invest, to clothe. **to dub a cock,** to trim the hackles, and cut off the comb and gills for cockfighting. **to dub a fly,** to dress an artificial fly for fishing. **to dub cloth,** to raise a nap on by striking it with teasels. [late OE *dubbian,* perh. from OF (cp. *adober, adouber,* It. *addobare*), etym. unknown]

dub², *v.i.* to strike, to poke (at); to make a noise of beating (as a drum). **dub-a-dub,** *adv.* with the sound of or as of a beaten drum. [prob. onomat.]

dub³, *n.* (*Sc., North.*) a deep pool in a stream; a puddle. [etym. doubtful]

dub⁴, *v.t.* to give a new sound-track (esp. in a different language) to a film.

Dubai, *n.* one of the United Arab Emirates.

dubbin, dubbing, *n.* a preparation of grease for preserving and softening leather.

Dubček, *n.* **Alexander** (1921–), Czech politician. As first secretary of the Communist Party (1967–69), he launched a liberalization campaign (the Prague Spring). He was arrested by invading Soviet troops, and expelled from the party in 1970. He returned to public life in 1990 after the restoration of democracy.

dubious, *a.* undetermined; doubtful; wavering in mind; of uncertain result or issue; obscure, vague, not clear; questionable; open to suspicion. **dubiety,** *n.* **†dubiosity,** *n.* **dubiously,** *adv.* **dubiousness,** *n.* [L *dubiōsus,* from *dubius,* doubtful (*duo,* two)]

dubitation, *n.* the act of doubting; doubt, hesitation, uncertainty. **dubitative,** *a.* tending to doubt; expressing doubt. **dubitatively,** *adv.* [F, from L *dubitātio -ōnem,* from *dubitāre,* to DOUBT]

Dublin¹, *n.* county in Leinster province, Republic of Ireland, facing the Irish Sea; area 922 sq km/356 sq miles; population (1981) 1,003,164. Mostly level and low-lying, but rising in the south to 753 m/2473 ft in Kippure, part of the Wicklow mountains.

Dublin², *n.* (Gaelic **Baile Atha Cliath**) capital and port on the E coast of the Republic of Ireland, at the mouth of the Liffey, facing the Irish Sea; population (1981) 525,500; Greater Dublin (including Dublin Laoghaire) 915,000. It is the site of one of the world's largest breweries (Guinness); other industries include textiles, pharmaceuticals, electrical goods, and machine tools. It was the centre of English rule from 1171 (exercised from Dublin Castle from 1220) until 1922.

Dublin Bay prawn, a large prawn usu. cooked as scampi.

Dubuffet, *n.* **Jean** (1901–85), French artist. He originated *l'art brut,* raw or brutal art, in the 1940s. He used a variety of materials in his paintings and sculptures – plaster, steel wool, straw, and so on – and was inspired by graffiti and children's drawings. L'art brut emerged in 1945 with an exhibition of his own work and of paintings by psychiatric patients and naive or untrained artists.

ducal, *a.* of or pertaining to a duke or duchy. **ducally,** *adv.* [F, from late L *ducalis,* from *dux ducis,* DUKE]

ducat, *n.* a coin, of gold or silver, first minted in the Duchy of Apulia in about 1140, afterwards current in several European countries; (*sl., pl.*) money, cash. **ducatoon,** *n.* an old silver coin, originally Venetian, formerly circulating in the Netherlands. [F, from It. *ducato,* late L *ducātus,* a DUCHY]

Duccio di Buoninsegna (*c.* 1255–1319), Italian painter, a major figure in the Sienese school. His greatest work is his altarpiece for Siena Cathedral, the *Maestà* (1308–11); the figure of the Virgin is Byzantine in style, with much gold detail, but Duccio also created a graceful linear harmony in drapery hems, for example, and this proved a lasting characteristic of Sienese style.

Duce, *n.* (Italian 'leader') title bestowed on the Fascist dictator Mussolini by his followers, and later adopted as his official title.

Duchamp, *n.* **Marcel** (1887–1968), US artist, born in France. He achieved notoriety with his *Nude Descending a Staircase* (1912, Philadelphia Museum of Art), influenced by cubism and futurism. An active member of Dada, he invented *ready-mades,* everyday items like a bicycle wheel on a kitchen stool, which he displayed as works of art.

duchess, *n.* the wife or widow of a duke; a lady who holds a duchy in her own right; (*coll.*) a woman of imposing appearance; a size of roofing slate; a kind of fancy blind with ornamental edging. **duchesse,** *n.* a table cover or centre-piece. **duchesse lace,** *n.* Flemish lace with designs in cord outline. **duchesse potatoes,** *n.pl.* mashed potatoes mixed with butter, milk and egg-yolk, piped on to a dish and baked. **duchy,** *n.* the territory, jurisdiction or dominions of a duke; the royal dukedom of Cornwall or Lancaster. **duchy-court,** *n.* the court of a duchy, esp. that of Lancaster in England. [F *duchesse*]

duck¹, *n.* a kind of untwilled linen or cotton fabric lighter and finer than canvas, used for jackets, aprons etc.; (*pl.*) trousers or a suit made of this. [prob. from Dut. *dock* (cp. Dan. *dug,* Swed. *duk,* G *Tuch*)]

duck², *n.* a web-footed bird of the genus *Anas,* esp. the domestic duck, a variety of *A. boschas,* the wild duck or mallard; the female of this species (as distinguished from a drake); a stone made to skip along the surface of water; (*coll.*) darling; (*Cricket*) a duck's egg, a score of nothing; (*Mil.*) popular name for an amphibious motor vehicle. **Bombay-duck** BUMMALO. **ducks and drakes,** a game of making a flat stone skip along the surface of water. **lame duck,** a crippled person; a defaulter on the Stock Exchange. **like water off a duck's back,** quite without effect. **sitting duck,** an easy target. **to break one's duck,** to score one's first (cricket) run. **to make ducks and drakes of,** to squander. **duck-billed,** *a.* having a bill like a duck, esp. applied to the duck-billed platypus or ornithorhynchus. **duck-board,** *n.* planking used to cover muddy roads or paths. **duck-hawk,** *n.* the marsh-harrier, *Circus aeruginosus.* **duck-meat,** *n.* **duck pond,** *n.* **duck's arse,** *n.* hair at the back of the neck cut to look like a duck's tail. **duck's-egg,** *n.* (*Cricket*) no score. **duck-shot,** *n.* small shot for shooting wild duck. **duck soup,** *n.* (*N Am.*) anything easy to do. **duck-weed,** *n.* a popular name for several floating water-weeds of the genus *Lemna,* esp. *L. minor,* which is eaten by duck and geese. **ducker,** *n.* a breeder of ducks. **duckling,** *n.* a young duck. **ducky, ducks,** *n.* (*coll.*) a term of familiarity or endearment. [OE *dūce,* cogn. with foll.]

duck³, *v.i.* to dive, dip or plunge under water; to bob the head; to bow, to cringe. *v.t.* to dip under water and suddenly withdraw; to throw into water; to wet thoroughly. *n.* a quick plunge or dip under water; a bob or sudden lowering of the head. **ducker,** *n.* a diving-bird, esp. the dabchick or little grebe, and the water ouzel. **ducking,** *n.* immersion in water; a thorough wetting. **ducking-pond,** *n.* a pond wherein petty offenders were ducked. **ducking-stool,** *n.* a kind of stool or chair on which scolds were tied and ducked. [ME *duken, douken,* as from an OE *dūcan* (cp. Dut. *duiken,* Dan. *dukke,* G *tauchen*)]

duct, *n.* a tube, canal or passage by which a fluid is conveyed; (*Anat.*) a tubular passage for conveying chyle, lymph and other fluids; (*Bot.*) a canal or elongated cell holding water, air etc. **ductless,** *a.* **ductless glands,** *n.pl.* endocrine glands. [L *ductus,* p.p. of *ducere,* to lead]

ductile, *a.* that may be drawn out into threads or wire; malleable, not brittle; capable of being moulded, plastic; (*fig.*) pliant, tractable, yielding to persuasion or advice. **ductileness, ductility,** *n.* [F, from L *ductilis,* as prec.]

dud, *n.* (*coll.*) a useless thing; a bad coin; a valueless cheque; a forgery; a shell that has failed to explode. *a.* useless, worthless. **duds,** *n.pl.* clothes; old clothes, rags. [etym. doubtful]

dude, *n.* a fop, an exquisite, an affected person; a swell, a masher; an aesthete; (*N Am.*) a city-bred person. **dude ranch,** *n.* (*N Am.*) a ranch run as a pleasure resort by city people. **dudette, dudine,** *n.fem.* **dudish,** *a.* **dudishly,** *adv.* **dudism,** *n.* [LG *duden-dop, dudenkop,* a lazy fellow]

dudeen, *n.* (*Ir.*) a short clay tobacco pipe. [etym. unknown]

dudgeon¹, *n.* the root of the box-tree; the handle of a dagger formerly made of this wood; a small dagger. [etym. unknown]

dudgeon², *n.* anger, sullen resentment, indignation. [etym. doubtful]

due¹, *a.* owed, owing, that ought to be paid, rendered or done to another; claimable, proper, suitable, appropriate; expected, appointed to arrive, calculated to happen; ascribable, that may be attributed (to); †punctual, exact. *adv.* exactly directly; †punctually; †duly. *n.* that which is owned or owing to one; that which one owes; a debt, an obligation, tribute, toll, fee or other legal exaction; †a debt; †just right or title; (*N Am., pl.*) a club subscription. **dock-, harbour-dues,** charges levied by corporate bodies for the use of docks or harbours. **in due course,** when the right time comes. **to fall due,** to become payable; to mature (as a bill). **to give someone his/her due,** to be fair to someone. **to give the devil his due** DEVIL. †**dueful,** *a.* due, bounden, suitable. **dueness,** *n.* [OF *deū,* p.p. of *devoir,* to owe, L *debēre*]

due², *v.t.* to endow; to endue, invest. [var. of obs. *dow,* F *douer,* L *dōtāre,* to endow (*dōs dōtis,* a gift)]

duel, *n.* a combat between two persons with deadly weapons to decide a private quarrel, usu. an affair of honour; any contest or struggle between two persons, parties, causes, animals etc. *v.i.* (*pres.p.* **duelling,** *past, p.p.* **duelled**) to fight in a duel; to contest. **duellist,** *n.* **duello,** *n.* (*It.*) a duel; the rules of duelling. [F, from It. *duello,* L *duellum,* archaic form of *bellum,* war (cp. *duo,* two)]

duenna, *n.* an elderly female employed as companion and governess to young women, a chaperon. [Sp. *dueña,* L *domina,* lady]

duet, duetto, *n.* a composition for two performers, vocal or instrumental; a dialogue; any performance by two persons. **duettino,** *n.* a short duet. **duettist,** *n.* [It. *duetto,* dim. of *duo* (L *duo,* two)]

Dufay, *n.* **Guillaume** (1400–74), French composer. He is recognized as the foremost composer of his time, both of secular songs and sacred music, including 84 songs, eight masses, motets, and antiphons. His work marks a transition between the music of the Middle Ages and that of the Renaissance, and is characterized by expressive melodies and rich harmonies.

Dufaycolor, *n.* (*Phot.*) a colour process using a specially designed colour screen separate from the sensitive plate. [name of inventor]

duff¹, *n.* (*dial., coll.*) a stiff, flour pudding boiled in a bag. **plum duff,** such a pudding made with raisins. **up the duff,** (*Austral., sl.*) pregnant. [DOUGH]

duff², *v.t.* (*sl.*) to fake up (rubbishy articles) for sale; (*Austral.*) to steal (cattle) by altering the brands; to cheat; to beat (someone) up. *a.* useless, not working. **duffing,** *a.* counterfeit, rubbishy; faked up for sale. [perh. from DUFFER]

duffel, *n.* a thick, coarse kind of woollen cloth, having a thick nap or frieze; (*N Am.*) a camper-out's change of clothes, outfit, kit. **duffel bag,** *n.* (*Nav.*) a sort of kit-bag. **duffel coat,** *n.* a three-quarter-length coat usu. made from duffel, hooded and fastened with toggles. [*Duffel,* town in Brabant]

duffer, *n.* a pedlar, a hawker of women's dress, or of cheap and flash jewellery, sham smuggled goods etc.; a stupid, awkward or useless person; one who steals cattle; (*Austral., sl.*) an unproductive mine. [etym. doubtful (cp. DUFF²)]

Dufy, *n.* **Raoul** (1877–1953), French painter and designer. He originated a fluent, brightly coloured style in watercolour and oils, painting scenes of gaiety and leisure, such as horse racing, yachting and life on the beach.

dug¹, *n.* a teat, a nipple (now used only of the lower animals). [etym. obscure (cp. Sansk. *duh,* to milk)]

dug², past and p.p. of DIG. **dug-out,** *n.* a canoe made of a single log hollowed out, or of parts of two logs thus hollowed out and afterwards joined together; a rough cabin cut in the side of a bank or hill; a cellar, cave or shelter used as a protection against enemy shelling; (*sl.*) a retired officer recalled for service; (*N Am.*) the enclosure at baseball occupied by the trainer and men waiting to bat; in Canada, a reservoir dug on a farm to collect rain and snow for irrigation.

dugong, *n.* a large herbivorous aquatic mammal, *Halicore dugong,* with two forelimbs only, belonging to the Sirenia, and inhabiting the Indian seas. [Malay *dūyōng*]

duiker, duyker, *n.* one of several small African antelopes; any of various southern African cormorants. [Dut. *duiker,* diver]

Dukas, *n.* **Paul (Abraham)** (1865–1935), French composer. He was professor of composition at the Paris Conservatoire, and composed the opera *Ariane et Barbe-Bleue* (1907) and the ballet *La Péri* (1912). His orchestral scherzo *L'Apprenti Sorcier/The Sorcerer's Apprentice* (1897) is full of the colour and energy which characterizes much of his work.

duke, *n.* a noble holding the highest hereditary rank outside the royal family; the sovereign prince of a duchy; a provincial military commander under the later Roman emperors; †a commander, a leader, a chieftain; (*pl.*) (*sl.*) fists; hands. **dukedom**, *n.* the territory, title, rank or quality of a duke. **dukeling**, *n.* a petty duke; a little duke. **dukeship,** *n.* [F *duc,* L *dux ducis,* a leader]

Dukeries, *n.pl.* a district in Nottinghamshire formerly comprising five ducal seats. [from prec.]

Dukhobor, *n.* a member of a Russian mystical sect who were oppressed for their passive resistance to militarism, and migrated in large numbers from their homes in the Caucasus to Canada. [Rus. *dukhoborets,* spirit-wrestler, *dukh,* spirit, soul, *borets,* fighter]

dulcamara, *n.* the bittersweet *Solanum dulcamara.* [med. L (*dulcis,* sweet, *amāra,* fem. of *amārus,* bitter)]

dulcet, *a.* sweet to the ear; sweet to the senses; †luscious. **dulcetly,** *adv.* [OF *doucet,* dim. of *doux,* L *dulcis,* sweet; assim. to L]

dulcify, *v.t.* to sweeten; to free from acidity, acrimony or saltness. **dulcification**, *n.* [L *dulcificāre,* as prec.]

dulcimer, *n.* a musical instrument with strings of wire, which are struck with rods. [OF *doulcemer,* Sp. *dulcemele,* perh. from L *dulce melos,* a sweet song]

Dulcinea, *n.* a sweetheart; an idealized mistress. [a character in Cervantes' *Don Quixote*]

dule-tree, *n.* (*Sc.*) the gallows. [DOLE[2]]

dulia, *n.* the lowest of the three degrees of adoration recognized in the Roman Catholic Church, the reverence paid to angels, saints etc. [med L, from Gr. *douleia,* slavery, servitude, from *doulos,* slave]

dull, *a.* slow of understanding; stupid, not quick in perception; without sensibility; blunt, obtuse, not sharp or acute; wanting keenness in any of the senses; sluggish, inert, slow of movement; stagnant; not brisk or active (as trade); not bright, dim, tarnished; cloudy, overcast, gloomy, depressing; uninteresting, tedious, wearisome; hard of hearing, deaf; not loud or clear. *v.t.* to make dull or stupid; to stupefy; to make blunt of edge, to render less acute, sensitive, interesting or effective; to make heavy or sluggish, to deaden; to tarnish, to dim. *v.i.* to become dull, blunt, stupid or inert. **dull-brained,** *a.* stupid; of dull intellect. **dull-eyed,** *a.* having a listless or gloomy look. †**dull-head,** *n.* a stupid, silly fellow. **dull-sighted,** *a.* not sharp-sighted; having dim vision. **dull-witted,** *a.* stupid. **dullard**, *n.* a blockhead; a dunce. *a.* stupid, doltish, inert. **dullish,** *a.* **dully,** *adv.* **dullness, dulness,** *n.* [ME *dul* (cp. OE *dol,* stupid, Dut. *dol,* G *toll,* mad)]

Dulles[1], *n.* **Alan** (1893–1969), US lawyer, brother of John Foster Dulles, and director of the Central Intelligence Agency (CIA) during 1953–61.

Dulles[2], *n.* **John Foster** (1888–1959), US politician. Senior US adviser at the founding of the United Nations, he largely drafted the Japanese peace treaty of 1951, and as secretary of state (1952–59), was critical of Britain in the Suez Crisis. He was the architect of US Cold War foreign policy, securing US intervention in support of South Vietnam following the expulsion of the French in 1954.

dulse, *n.* an edible kind of seaweed, *Rhodymenia palmata.* [Ir., Gael. *duileasg*]

duly, *adv.* in suitable manner; properly; becomingly; regularly; punctually; sufficiently. [DUE[1]]

Duma, *n.* in Russia, before 1917, an elected assembly which met four times following the abortive 1905 revolution. With progressive demands the government could not accept, the Duma was largely powerless. After the abdication of Nicholas II the Duma directed the formation of a provisional government.

Dumas[1], *n.* **Alexandre** (1802–70), French author, known as Dumas *père* (the father). His play *Henri III et sa cour/Henry III and his Court* (1829) established French romantic historical drama, but today he is remembered for his romances, the reworked output of a 'fiction-factory' of collaborators. They include *Les Trois Mousquetaires/The Three Musketeers* (1844) and its sequels. Dumas *fils* was his illegitimate son.

Dumas[2], *n.* **Alexandre** (1824–95), French author, known as Dumas *fils* (the son), son of Dumas *père* and remembered for the play *La Dame aux camélias/The Lady of the Camellias* (1952), based on his own novel, and source of Verdi's opera *La traviata.*

Du Maurier, *n.* **Daphne** (1907–89), British novelist, whose romantic fiction includes *Jamaica Inn* (1936), *Rebecca* (1938) and *My Cousin Rachel* (1951).

dumb, *a.* unable to utter articulate sounds; unable to speak; mute, silent, speechless, refraining from speaking, reticent, taciturn; soundless; (*coll.*) stupid, unintelligent. *v.t.* to make dumb; to silence; †to confound. **to strike dumb,** to confound; to astonish; to render speechless by astonishment. **dumb-barge, -craft,** *n.* a heavy boat or hopper without means of propulsion, used for lifting matter from the bottom of the water, and similar purposes. **dumb-bells,** *n.pl.* pairs of weights connected by short bars or handles, swung in the hands for exercise. *v.i.* to perform exercises with these. **dumb cluck,** *n.* (*coll.*) a fool. **dumb crambo** CRAMBO. **dumb-iron,** *n.* a carriage-spring consisting of two half-elliptical springs joined at the ends; (*Motor*) the curved forward end of the frame to which a front spring is made fast. **dumb-piano,** *n.* a keyboard for exercising the fingers. **dumb-show,** *n.* gestures without speech; pantomime. **dumbstruck,** *a.* temporarily shocked into silence. **dumb terminal,** *n.* a computer terminal which can only receive data and has no processing power. **dumb-waiter,** *n.* a dining-room apparatus with (usu. revolving) shelves for holding dishes etc.; a movable framework for conveying food etc. from one room to another, a service-lift. **dumb-well,** *n.* a well for carrying off drainage. **dumbly,** *adv.* **dumbness,** *n.* [OE; cp. Dut. *dom,* Swed. *dumb,* Dan. *dum,* OHG *tump,* G *dumm,* mute, stupid]

Dumbarton Oaks, *n.* an 18th-cent. mansion near Washington DC, US, used as a centre for conferences and seminars. It was the scene of a conference held in 1944 which led to the foundation of the United Nations.

dumbfound, *v.t.* to strike dumb; to confound, confuse, perplex, to astound.

dumbledore, *n.* (*dial.*) the bumble bee; the brown cockchafer. [*dumble,* prob. conn. with DUMB, DOR]

dumdum bullet, *n.* a soft-nosed expanding bullet that lacerates the flesh. [*Dumdum,* town and military station near Calcutta]

Dumfries and Galloway, region of Scotland. **area** 6369 sq km/2458 sq miles. **towns** administrative headquarters Dumfries. **population** (1981) 145,000. **products** horses and cattle, for which the Galloway area was especially famous; sheep; timber.

Dumfriesshire, *n.* former county of S Scotland, merged in 1975 in the region of Dumfries and Galloway.

dummy, *n.* one who is dumb; any sham article; a sham package displayed in a shop; a lay-figure, for showing off dress etc.; the fourth exposed hand when three persons are playing at whist etc.; a game so played; a person who appears on the stage without speaking; a mere tool; a doll; a stupid fellow; a mallet; a rubber teat for a baby to suck; a prototype of a book; the design for a page. **double dummy,** a game at whist etc., with only two players, the two other hands being exposed. **to sell the dummy,** to feign a pass or move in a football game. **dummy run,** *n.* a trial run, a rehearsal.

Dumouriez, *n.* **Charles François du Périer** (1739–1823), French general during the Revolution. In 1792 he was appointed foreign minister, supported the declaration of war against Austria, and after the fall of the monarchy was given command of the army defending Paris; later he won the battle of Jemappes, but was defeated at Neerwinden (Austrian Netherlands) in 1793. After intriguing with the royalists he had to flee for his life, and from 1804 he lived in England.

dump[1], *v.t.* to throw into a heap; to unload (as dirt) from wagons by tilting them up; to shoot, to deposit; to send surplus produce, esp. manufactured goods that are unsaleable at home, to a foreign market for sale at a low price; to get rid of superfluous or objectionable things or people (e.g. emigrants) by sending elsewhere; to record (the data on an internal computer memory) on an external storage device during a computer run. *v.i.* to sit down heavily and suddenly. *n.* a pile of refuse; a place for shooting rubbish; a mean house or room; an army storage depot; (*N Am.*) a refuse-tip; the act of dumping computer data. **dump bin,** *n.* a container in a shop for e.g. sale and bargain items. **dump-car, -cart, -truck, -wagon,** *n.* a vehicle that tips up in front and so dumps its load. **dumpage,** *n.* (*N Am.*) the right of shooting loads of earth, rubbish etc. in a certain spot; money paid for such right. **dumper,** *n.* (*Austral.*) a heavy wave dangerous to swimmers. **dumping-ground,** *n.* [ME *dumpen,* to fall flat, prob. from Scand. (cp. Norw. *dumpa,* to thump, Swed. dial. *dompa,* Dan. *dumpe,* to fall plump)]

dump[2], *n.* a leaden counter used in playing chuck-farthing; a small coin formerly current in Australia; (*sl.*) a small coin; a short, thick and heavy object of various kinds; a kind of nail or bolt; a kind of sweetmeat; a stocky person. [etym. doubtful; perh. from DUMPY]

dumpling, *n.* a mass of dough or pudding, boiled or baked, often enclosing fruit etc. [prob. dim. of DUMP[2]]

dumps, *n.pl.* sadness, depression, melancholy. **in the dumps,** low-spirited, depressed. †**dumpish,** *a.* sad, gloomy, melancholy; depressed in spirits. [etym. doubtful; cp. DAMP]

dumpy, *a.* short and thick; plump; depressed. *n.* a short-legged Scottish breed of domestic fowls; (*pl.*) the 19th Hussars. **dumpy level,** *n.* a spirit level with a short telescope and a compass attached, used in surveying. **dumpily,** *adv.* **dumpiness,** *n.* [etym. doubtful; cp. DUMP[2]]

dun[1], *a.* of a dull brown or brownish-grey colour; (*poet.*) dark, gloomy. *n.* a dun-fly; a dun horse. *v.t.* †to darken; (*N Am.*) to preserve or cure (as codfish), so as to impart a dark colour to. **dun-bird,** *n.* the pochard. **dun-diver,** *n.* the female and young male of the goosander or merganser. **dun-fish,** *n.* (*N Am.*) codfish cured by dunning. **dun-fly,** *n.* a kind of artificial fly used by anglers; a local name for a horse-fly. [OE *dunn,* cp. Ir., Gael. *donn,* W *dwn*]

dun[2], *v.t.* (*past, p.p.* **dunned**) to demand payment from with persistence; to press, to plague, to pester. *n.* a creditor who presses persistently for payment; a debt-collector; an importunate demand for the payment of a debt. [perh. a var. of DIN]

dun[3], *n.* a hill, a mound, an earthwork (largely used in place-names). [Ir., Gael.]

Dunbar, *n.* **William** (*c.* 1460–*c.* 1520), Scottish poet at the court of James IV. His poems include a political allegory "The Thrissel and the Rose' and the elegy 'Timor mortis conturbat me'.

Dunbartonshire, *n.* former county of Scotland, bordering the N bank of the Clyde estuary, on which stand Dumbarton (the former county town), Clydebank and Helensburgh. It was merged in 1975 in the region of Strathclyde.

Duncan, *n.* **Isadora** (1878–1927), American dancer and teacher. An influential pioneer of American modern dance, she adopted an expressive, free form, dancing barefoot and wearing a loose tunic, inspired by the ideal of Hellenic beauty. She toured extensively, often returning to Russia after her initial success there in 1905, but died in an accident when her long scarf was caught in the wheel of a car.

dunce, *n.* a dullard; one slow in learning; †a sophist, a hairsplitter. **dunce's cap,** *n.* a conical paper cap formerly worn by a school pupil to indicate slowness of learning. †**duncedom,** *n.* the realm of dunces; dunces collectively. **duncehood,** *n.* †**duncery,** *n.* stupidity; dullness of intellect. **Dunciad,** *n.* the epic of dunces, title of a satire (1728) by Alexander Pope. [a word introduced by the Thomists or disciples of Thomas Aquinas, in ridicule of the followers of John *Duns* Scotus, d. 1308]

dunch, *v.t.* (*Sc., North.*) to push with the elbow; to gore. *n.* a jog, a smart push or blow. [etym. unknown]

Dundee, *n.* city and fishing port, administrative headquarters of Tayside, Scotland, on the north side of the Firth of Tay; population (1981) 175,000. Important shipping and rail centre with jute, marine engineering, watch and clock and textile industries.

Dundee cake, *n.* a fruit cake usu. decorated with almonds. [*Dundee,* city in Scotland]

dunder, *n.* the dregs from sugar-cane juice. [Sp. *redundar,* to overflow]

dunderhead, *n.* a blockhead, a numskull, a dolt, a dunce. **dunderheaded,** *a.* **dunderpate,** *n.* [etym. doubtful]

dundreary whiskers, *n.pl.* long side-whiskers worn without a beard. [Lord *Dundreary,* character in a play]

dune, *n.* a hill, mound or ridge of sand on the seashore. **dune-buggy,** *n.* (*N Am.*) a small open car with wide tyres for driving on beaches. **duny,** *a.* [F, from MDut. *dûne,* cogn. with OE *dūn*]

Dunedin, *n.* port on Otago harbour, South Island, New Zealand; population (1986) 106,864. Also a road, rail and air centre, with engineering and textile industries. The city was founded in 1848 by members of the free Church of Scotland and the university established in 1869.

Dunfermline, *n.* industrial town near Firth of Forth in Fife region, Scotland; population (1981) 52,000. Site of the naval base of Rosyth; industries include engineering, shipbuilding, electronics and textiles. Many Scottish kings, including Robert the Bruce, are buried in Dunfermline Abbey.

dung, *n.* the excrement of animals; manure; anything filthy. *v.t.* to manure or dress with dung; to immerse (as printed calico) in a dung-bath to fix the colour. *v.i.* to void excrement. **dung-bath,** *n.* a bath used in calico-printing works. **dung-beetle,** *n.* a beetle, *Geotrypes stercorarius,* and other species the larvae of which develop in dung. **dung-fly,** *n.* a two-winged fly of the genus *Scatophaga* that feeds upon dung. **dung-fork,** *n.* a fork for spreading manure. **dungheap, dunghill,** *n.* a heap of dung; an accumulation of dung and refuse in a farmyard; (*fig.*) a mean, filthy abode; any vile or contemptible situation, position or condition; †one meanly born. *a.* of low, mean or vile extraction; mean, poor. **dung-hill cock,** the common barn-door cock as distinguished from the spirited game-cock. **dung-worm,** *n.* a worm or larva found in dung and used as bait for fish. **dungy,** *a.* full of dung; filthy, base, mean, vile. [OE (cp. G *Dung,* Swed. *dynga,* Dan. *dynge*)]

dungaree, *n.* a coarse kind of calico used for overalls; (*pl.*) overalls made of this. [Hind. *dungrī*]

dungeon, *n.* †a donjon or keep of a mediaeval castle; a close prison or place of confinement, esp. one that is dark and underground. †*v.t.* to confine in or as in a dungeon. [F *donjon,* late L *domnio, -ōnem,* L *dominio,* from *dominus,* lord (cp. DOMINION)]

dunghill etc. DUNG.

Dunham, *n.* **Katherine** (1912–), US dancer, born in Chicago, noted for a free, strongly emotional method. She founded her own school and company in 1945.

dunite, *n.* a rock consisting essentially of olivine, frequently accompanied by chromite. [Mt Dun, New Zealand]

duniwassal, *n.* a Highland gentleman of inferior rank, a yeoman. [Gael. *duine vasal* (*duine,* a man, *vasal,* noble, cp. W *uchel*)]

dunk, *v.t., v.i.* to dip (cake, biscuits etc.) in what one is drinking, e.g. tea or coffee. [G *tunken,* to dip]

Dunker, *n.* a member of a sect of German–American Baptists, more properly called Tunkers. [G *Tunker,* from *tunken,* to dip]

Dun Laoghaire, *n.* port and suburb of Dublin, Republic of Ireland. It is a terminal for ferries to England and there are fishing industries.

dunlin, *n.* the redbacked sand-piper, *Tringa alpina,* a common shore-bird. [DUN[1], -LING]

Dunlop[1], *n.* a kind of rich, white cheese made in Scotland of unskimmed milk. [*Dunlop* in Ayrshire]

Dunlop[2], *n.* **John Boyd** (1840–1921), Scottish inventor, who founded the rubber company that bears his name. In 1887, to help his child win a tricycle race, he bound on inflated rubber hose to the wheels. The same year he developed commercially practical pneumatic tyres (first patented by R. W. Thompson in 1846) for bicycles and cars.

dunnage, *n.* (*Naut.*) loose wood, faggots, boughs etc., laid in the hold to raise the cargo above the bilge-water, or wedged between the cargo to keep it from rolling when stowed. [formerly *dinnage;* etym. doubtful]

dunning[1], *n.* the process of curing codfish, so as to give them a dun colour. [DUN[1]]

dunning[2], *n.* (*Cinema*) a process for superimposing action on a separately-taken picture.

dunno, (*coll.*) contr. form of (I) DON'T KNOW.

dunnock, *n.* the hedge-sparrow, from its colour.

dunny[1], *a.* hard of hearing. [etym. doubtful (perh. conn. with DIN)]

dunny[2], *n.* (*esp. Austral.*) a lavatory; (*esp. Sc.*) an outside lavatory; (*Sc.*) a basement.

Dunstable, *n.* **John** (*c.* 1385–1453), English composer. Little is known of his life, though he may have had some connection with St. Albans Cathedral, and seems to have travelled widely in Europe, achieving a reputation also as a mathematician and astrologer. He wrote songs and anthems and is generally considered one of the founders of Renaissance music.

dunt[1], *n.* (*dial.*) staggers, a disease of yearling lambs. [etym. doubtful]

dunt[2], *n.* (*Sc.*) a blow or stroke; a dint or wound; a bump, a jolt. *v.t.* to knock. *v.i.* to heal (of the heart). [perh. a var. of DINT]

duo, *n.* a duet. [It., DUET]

duo-, *pref.* two. [L, two]

duodecagon DODECAGON.

duodecahedron DODECAHEDRON.

duodecennial, *a.* occurring once every twelve years. [L *duodecim,* twelve, *annus,* year]

duodecimal, *a.* proceeding in computation by twelves; applied to a scale of notation in which the local value of the digits increases twelvefold as they proceed from right to left. *n.pl.* a method of cross-multiplying units of feet, inches etc. without reduction to a common denominator, so as to find areas or cubic contents. **duodecimally,** *adv.* **duodecimo,** *a.* consisting of 12 leaves to the sheet. *n.* a book consisting of sheets of 12 leaves or 24 pages; the size of such a book (written 12mo and called 'twelve-mo'). [L *duodecimus,* twelfth, *duodecim,* twelve (DUO-, *decem,* ten)]

duodenary, *a.* pertaining to the number twelve; proceeding by twelves. **duodene,** *n.* (*Mus.*) a group of 12 notes having fixed relations of pitch, taken as a base for determining exact intonation and exhibiting harmonic relations. [L *duodenarius,* from *duodēnī,* twelve apiece, as prec.]

duodenum, *n.* (*pl.* **-na, -nums**) the first portion of the small intestine, so called from being about the length of twelve fingers' breadths. **duodenal,** *a.* **duodenectomy,** *n.* excision of the duodenum. **duodenitis,** *n.* inflammation of the duodenum. [med. L, as prec.]

duologue, *n.* a dialogue for two persons; a dramatic composition for two actors.

duomo, *n.* a Italian cathedral. [It. (see DOME)]

duopoly, *n.* an exclusive trading right enjoyed by two companies. [L *duo,* two, Gr. *pōleein,* to sell]

duotone, *n.* a picture in two tones or colours. *a.* in two tones or colours. [L *duo,* two]

dupe, *n.* one who is easily deceived; a credulous person; a gull. *v.t.* to trick, to cheat, to make a dupe of, to gull. **dupable,** *a.* **dupability,** *n.* †**duper,** *n.* †**dupery,** *n.* [F, etym. unknown]

dupion, *n.* a double cocoon formed by two or more silkworms; silk made from such cocoons. [F *doupion,* from It. *doppione,* from *doppio,* L *duplus,* DOUBLE]

duple, *a.* double, twofold; duplicate; (*Mus.*) having two beats to the bar. **duple-ratio,** *n.* the ratio of 2 to 1, 6 to 3 etc.; (*Mus.*) duple measure. [L *duplus,* double (*duo,* two, *-plus,* -fold)]

duplex, *a.* double, twofold; compounded of two. *n.* (*N Am.*) a duplex apartment or house. *v.t.* (*Teleg.*) to make (a wire, cable or system) duplex, so that two messages can be sent at once in opposite directions. **duplex apartment,** *n.* (*N Am.*) a two-storey apartment. **duplex escapement,** *n.* so called from the double character of its scape-wheel, which has spur and crown teeth. **duplex gas-burner,** *n.* one with two jets that coalesce into a single flame. **duplex house,** *n.* (*N Am.*) a semi-detached house. **duplex-lamp,** *n.* a lamp with two wicks. [L (*duo,* two, *plic-,* see foll.)]

duplicate, *a.* double, twofold, existing in two parts exactly corresponding; corresponding exactly with another. *n.* one of two things exactly similar in material and form; a reproduction, replica, copy; a copy of an original legal document having equal binding force; a copy made in lieu of a document lost or destroyed; the second copy of a bill drawn in two parts; a pawn-ticket; complete similarity between two things. *v.t.,* to make a reproduction of; to double; to make in duplicate; to make copies of on a machine; to divide and form two parts or organisms. **in duplicate,** in the original plus a copy. **duplicate ratio, proportion,** *n.* the ratio or proportion of squares. **duplication,** *n.* **duplication of the cube,** the impossible problem of finding a cube whose volume shall be double that of a given cube. **duplicative,** *a.* **duplicator,** *n.* a machine for duplicating typescript. [L *duplicātus,* p.p. of *duplicāre* (*duo,* two, *plicāre,* to fold)]

duplicity, *n.* doubleness of speech or action; double-dealing, dissimulation. **duplicitous,** *a.* [F *duplicité,* L *duplicitās -tātem,* from DUPLEX]

dupondius, *n.* a coin in ancient Rome, worth two asses. [L]

duppy, *n.* a malevolent ghost in W Indian folklore. [prob. from an African language]

Du Pré, *n.* **Jacqueline** (1945–87), British cellist. Noted for her extraordinary technique and powerful interpretations of the classic cello repertory, particularly of Elgar. She had an international concert career while still in her teens and made many recordings.

durable, *a.* having the quality of endurance or continuance; lasting, permanent, firm, stable. **durability,** *n.* **durableness,** *n.* **durably,** *adv.* [F, from L *dūrābilis,* from *dūrāre,* to last, from *dūrus,* hard]

Duralumin®, *n.* an alloy of aluminium, copper and other metals, having great strength and lightness. [L *dūrus,* hard]

dura mater, *n.* the first of three lining membranes of the brain and spinal cord. [med. L, the hard mother, a trans. of an Arabic phrase]

duramen, *n.* the heart-wood or central wood in the trunk of exogenous trees. [L, hardness, from *dūrāre,* to harden]

durance, *n.* imprisonment; endurance, durability. [F, from *durer,* to last, as prec.]

Duras, *n.* **Marguerite** (1914–), French writer. Her

works include short stories, plays, film scripts (*Hiroshima Mon Amour*, 1960) and novels such as *Le Vice-Consul* (1966), evoking an existential world from the actual setting of Calcutta. Her autobiographical novel, *La Douleur*, is set in Paris in 1945.

duration, *n.* continuance; length of time of continuance; power of continuance. **for the duration,** (*sl.*) so long as the war or situation lasts. **durative,** *a.* denoting the aspect of a verb which implies continuance of action in time, as the imperfect and progressive tenses. *n.* a verb in this aspect. [OF, from late L *dūrātio -ōnem,* from L *dūrāre,* to last]

Durban, *n.* principal port of Natal, South Africa, and second port of the republic; population (1985) 634,300. Exports coal, maize, and wool; imports heavy machinery and mining equipment; also an important holiday resort.

durbar, *n.* an Indian ruler's court; a state-reception by an Indian ruler or formerly by a British governor; a hall of audience. [Pers., Hind. *darbār,* a court]

dure, *v.i.* to last, to endure, to continue. **dureful,** *a.* [F, *durer,* from L *dūrāre,* to endure, from *dūrus,* hard]

Dürer, *n.* **Albrecht** (1471–1528), German artist, the leading figure of the northern Renaissance. He was born in Nuremberg and travelled widely in Europe. Highly skilled in drawing and a keen student of nature, he perfected the technique of woodcut and engraving, producing woodcut series such as the *Apocalypse* (1498) and copperplate engravings such as *The Knight, Death and the Devil* (1513) and *Melancholia* (1514), he may also have invented etching. His paintings are relatively few; the altarpieces are inferior to the meticulously observed portraits (including many self-portraits).

duress, *n.* constraint, compulsion, restraint of liberty, imprisonment; (*Law*) restraint of liberty or threat of violence to compel a person to do some act of exculpation by one who has been so restrained or threatened. [OF *duresce,* L *dūritia,* from *dūrus,* hard]

Durex®, *n.* a make of condom; (**durex**; *coll.*) any condom.

Durham¹, *n.* county in NE England. **area** 2436 sq km/6309 sq miles. **towns** administrative headquarters Durham; Darlington, and the new towns of Peterlee and Newton Aycliffe. **population** (1986) 603,700. **products** sheep and dairy produce; the county lies on one of Britain's richest coalfields.

Durham², *n.* **John George Lambton, 1st Earl of Durham** (1792–1840), British politician. Appointed Lord Privy Seal in 1830, he drew up the first Reform Bill of 1832, and as governor general of Canada briefly in 1837 drafted the Durham Report which led to the union of Upper and Lower Canada.

durian, *n.* the globular pulpy fruit of a tree, *Durio zibethinus,* cultivated in the Malay Archipelago. [Malay *durian,* from *durī,* prickle]

during, *prep.* in or within the time of; throughout the course or existence of. [orig. pres.p. of DURE]

Durkheim, *n.* **Emile** (1858–1917), French sociologist, one of the founders of modern sociology, who also influenced social anthropology.

durmast (oak), *n.* a European oak, *Quercus sessiliflora.* [etym. doubtful]

durra, doura, dhurra, dura, dari, *n.* Indian millet, *Sorghum vulgare,* cultivated for grain and fodder. [Arab. *durah, durrah*]

Durrell¹, *n.* **Gerald (Malcolm)** (1925–), British naturalist. Director of Jersey Zoological Park, he is the author of travel and natural history books, and the humorous memoir *My Family and Other Animals* (1956). He is the brother of Lawrence Durrell.

Durrell², *n.* **Lawrence (George)** (1912–), British novelist and poet. Born in India, he joined the foreign service, and has lived mainly in the E Mediterranean, the setting of his novels, including the Alexandria Quartet: *Justine*, *Balthazar*, *Mountolive*, and *Clea* (1957–60); he has also written travel books.

Dürrenmatt, *n.* **Friedrich** (1921–), Swiss dramatist, author of grotesquely farcical tragi-comedies, for example *The Visit* (1956) and *The Physicists* (1962).

Durrës, *n.* chief port of Albania; population (1983) 72,000. It is an important commercial and communications centre, with flour mills, soap and cigarette factories, distilleries, and an electronics plant. It was the capital of Albania during 1912–21.

durst, past tense of DARE¹.

durum (wheat), *n.* a variety of spring wheat with a high gluten content, used mainly for the manufacture of pasta. [L *dūrum,* neut. of *dūrus,* hard]

Dushanbe, *n.* (formerly [1929–69] **Stalinabad**), capital of Tadzhik Republic, USSR, 160 km/100 miles north of the Afghan frontier; population (1987) 582,000. It is an important road, rail, and air centre. Industries include cotton mills, tanneries, meat-packing factories, and printing works. It is the seat of Tadzhik state university.

dusk, *a.* tending to darkness or blackness; darkish, shadowy, dim, obscure; swarthy. *n.* a tendency to darkness; shade, gloom; partial darkness, twilight. †*v.t.* to make somewhat dark; to obscure. *v.i.* to grow or to appear dark. **duskish,** *a.* **dusky,** *a.* swarthy. **duskily,** *adv.* **duskiness,** *n.* [ME *dose,* dark, dim, OE *dox* (cp. Swed. *dusk,* a shower, Norw. *dusk,* mist)]

Düsseldorf, *n.* industrial city of W Germany, on the right bank of the Rhine, 26 km/16 miles NW of Cologne, capital of North Rhine-Westphalia; population (1983) 579,800. A river port and the commercial and financial centre of the Ruhr area, with food processing, brewing, agricultural machinery, textile, and chemical industries.

dust, *n.* earth or other matter reduced to such small particles as to be easily raised and carried about by the air; a stirring of such fine particles; household refuse; pollen; the decomposed bodies of the dead; the human body; the grave; a low or despised condition; turmoil, excitement, confusion, commotion, a row; (*sl.*) money. *v.t.* to brush or sweep away the dust from; to sprinkle or cover with or as with dust; to make dusty; to clean by brushing or beating, hence **to dust one's jacket,** to give one a drubbing. **dust and ashes,** extreme penitence and humility. **to bite the dust,** (*fig.*) to be beaten; to be humiliated; to die. **to raise, make, kick up a dust,** to make a disturbance. **to shake the dust of from one's feet,** to leave (a place) angrily. **to throw dust in someone's eyes,** to mislead, to deceive, to delude. **to turn to dust and ashes,** to become utterly worthless. **dust bath,** *n.* the rubbing of dust into their feathers by birds, prob. to get rid of parasites. **dustbin, -hole,** *n.* a receptacle for household refuse. **dust-bowl,** *n.* an area reduced to aridity by drought and over-cropping. **dust-brand,** *n.* smut, a disease of corn. **dust-cart,** *n.* a cart for removing refuse from houses, streets etc. **dust-cloth,** *n.* a dusting sheet. **dust-coat,** *n.* a light overcoat. **dust-colour,** *n.* a light greyish brown. **dust-cover, -jacket,** *n.* a paper book-jacket. **dust devil,** *n.* a small whirlwind which whips up dust, leaves and litter. **dust-guard,** *n.* a fitting on a machine to protect a worker, rider etc. from dust. **dustman,** *n.* one whose occupation is to remove refuse from dust-bins. **dust-pan,** *n.* a domestic utensil into which dust is swept. **dust-sheet,** *n.* one thrown over furniture while a room is being dusted or while it is unused. **dust-shot,** *n.* shot of the smallest size, also called mustard seed. **dust storm,** *n.* a windstorm which whips up clouds of dust as it travels through arid areas. **dust-up,** *n.* a row, a heated quarrel. **duster,** *n.* a cloth or brush used to remove dust; a person who dusts; a machine to remove particles of flour from bran; (*Naut. coll.*) a flag; (*N Am.*) a dust-coat. **dusting,** *n., a.* **dusting-down,** *n.* a scolding, a severe reprimand. **dusting powder,** *n.* very fine powder, esp. talcum powder. **dustward,** *a., adv.* **dusty,** *a.* covered with or full of dust; like dust; dull, uninteresting. **not so dusty,** (*sl.*) pretty good. **dusty answer,** *n.* an unsatisfactory response. **dusty miller,** *n.* the auricula, from the dusty appearance of the leaves and flowers; (*Angling*) an artificial fly. **dustily,** *adv.* **dustiness,** *n.* [OE *dūst* (cp. Dut. *duist,* G *Dunst*)]

Dutch[1], *a.* pertaining to the Netherlands, its people or language; (*Hist.*) pertaining to the Low Germans, or to the German or Teutonic race; from the Netherlands; made or invented by the Dutch; (*N Am.*) of German extraction. *n.* (*pl.* **Dutch**), a member of the Germanic branch of the Indo-European family, taken to include the standard language and dialects of the Netherlands (excluding Frisian) and also Flemish (in Belgium and N France) and, more remotely, its offshoot Afrikaans in South Africa, †the German language, esp. Low German; (*pl.*) the Low Germans, esp. the Hollanders. **double Dutch** DOUBLE. **Dutch elm disease,** a fungal disease of elms carried by beetles, causing withering and defoliation, and often fatal. **Dutch Reformed Church,** the Afrikaans-speaking branch of the Calvinist church in South Africa. **High Dutch,** the southern Germans; their language. **Low Dutch,** the Germans of the coast, esp. of the Netherlands; their language. **to go Dutch,** to pay for oneself. **Dutch auction** AUCTION. **Dutch barn,** *n.* one for storage, with open sides and a steel frame supporting a curved roof. **Dutch cap,** *n.* a moulded rubber cap fitting over the cervix to act as a contraceptive barrier. **Dutch cheese,** *n.* a small round cheese manufactured in Holland from skim milk. **Dutch clinker,** *n.* a yellow hard brick made in Holland. **Dutch-clover,** *n.* white clover, *Trifolium repens.* **Dutch courage,** *n.* false or fictitious courage, esp. inspired by stimulants. **Dutch doll,** *n.* a wooden doll. **Dutch door,** *n.* (*N Am.*) a stable door. **Dutch foil, gold, leaf, metal,** *n.* a highly malleable copper alloy with zinc, used instead of gold-leaf. **Dutch hoe,** *n.* a garden hoe with a blade. **Dutchman,** *n.* **if so, I'm a Dutchman,** an emphatic negative. **the Flying Dutchman,** a legendary mariner condemned to sail against the wind till the Day of Judgment; his spectral ship. **Dutch medicine,** *n.* (*S Afr.*) patent medicine, esp. that made from herbs. **Dutch oven,** *n.* a cooking-chamber suspended in front of a fire so as to cook by radiation. **Dutch-rush,** *n.* the scouring rush, *Equisetum hyemale,* used for cleaning and polishing wood. **Dutch School,** *n.* a school of painters distinguished for minute realism and for the artistic treatment of commonplace subjects. **Dutch tile,** *n.* a variegated or painted glazed tile made in Holland, formerly used for lining their capacious fireplaces. **Dutch treat,** *n.* (*coll.*) each paying his own score. **Dutch uncle,** *n.* one who criticizes in a stern, blunt manner. **Dutchwoman,** *n. fem.* [MDut. *Dutsch,* Hollandish, or G *Deutsch,* German]

dutch[2], *n.* (*Cockney sl.*) a wife. [perh. short for DUCHESS]

Dutch East India Company, a trading company established in the Northern Netherlands in 1602 and given a trading monopoly in the Indonesian archipelago, with certain sovereign rights such as the creation of an army and a fleet. During the 17th and 18th cent. the company used its monopoly of East Indian trade to pay out high dividends, but wars with England and widespread corruption led to a suspension of payments in 1781 and an eventual takeover of the company by the Dutch government in 1798.

Dutch East Indies, former Dutch colony which in 1945 became independent as Indonesia.

Dutch Guiana, *n.* former Dutch colony which in 1984 became independent as Suriname.

Dutilleux, *n.* **Henri** (1916–), French composer of instrumental music in elegant neo-romantic style. His works include *Mataboles* (1962–65) for orchestra and *Ainsi la Nuit* (1975–76) for string quartet.

duty, *n.* that which is bound or ought to be paid, done or performed; that which a particular person is bound morally or legally to do; moral or legal obligation; the course of conduct prescribed by ethics or religion, the binding force of the obligation to follow this course; obedience or submission due to parents, superiors; an act of reverence, respect or deference; any service, business or office; toll, tax, impost or custom charged by a government upon the importation, exportation, manufacture or sale of goods; office, function, occupation, work; the various acts entailed in these; the obligations and responsibilities implied in one's engagement to perform these; the useful work actually done by an engine or motor, measured in units against units of fuel. **off duty,** not engaged in one's appointed duties. **on duty,** engaged in performing one's appointed duties. **to do duty for,** to serve in lieu of someone or something else; to serve as makeshift. **duty bound,** *a.* obliged by one's sense of duty (to do something). **duty-free,** *a.* not liable to duty, tax or custom. **duty-free shop,** one, usu. on a ship or at an airport, where duty-free goods are on sale. **duty officer,** *n.* the officer on duty at any particular time. **duty-paid,** *a.* on which duty has been paid. **duteous,** *a.* obedient, obsequious, dutiful. **duteously,** *adv.* **duteousness,** *n.* **dutiable,** *a.* liable to the imposition of a duty or custom. **dutied,** *a.* charged with duty. **dutiful,** *a.* careful in performing the duties required by law, justice or propriety; reverential, deferential. **dutifully,** *adv.* **dutifulness,** *n.* [A-F *dueté*]

duumvir, *n.* (*pl.* **-viri, -virs**) one of two officers or magistrates in ancient Rome appointed to carry out jointly the duties of any public office. **duumviral,** *a.* **duumvirate,** *n.* the association of two officers or magistrates in the carrying out of any public duties; a government of two; their term of office. [L (*duo,* two, *viri,* men)]

Duvalier[1], *n.* **François** (1907–71), right-wing president of Haiti (1957–71). Known as Papa Doc, he ruled as a dictator, organizing the Tontons Macoutes ('bogeymen') as a private security force to intimidate and assassinate opponents of his regime. He rigged the 1961 elections in order to have his term of office extended until 1967, and in 1964 declared himself president for life. He was excommunicated by the Vatican for harassing the church, and was succeeded on his death by his son Jean-Claude Duvalier.

Duvalier[2], *n.* **Jean-Claude** (1951–), right-wing president of Haiti (1971–86). Known as Baby Doc, he succeeded his father François Duvalier, becoming, at the age of 19, the youngest president in the world. He was forced by the US to moderate his father's tyrannical regime, yet he tolerated no opposition. In 1986, with Haiti's economy stagnating and with increasing civil disorder, Duvalier fled to France.

duvet, *n.* a quilt stuffed with down or man-made fibres, used as a bed-covering instead of blankets. [F, down, earlier *dumet,* dim. of OF *dum* (cp. Icel. *dūnn*)]

Duwez, *n.* **Pol** (1907–), US scientist, born in Belgium, who in 1959 developed metallic glass with his team at the California Institute of Technology.

dux, *n.* (*Sc.*) the top pupil of a school. [L, leader]

duyker DUIKER.

DV, (*abbr.*) God willing (L *Deo volente*).

Dvořák, *n.* **Antonin (Leopold)** (1841–1904), Czech composer. International recognition came with his series of Slavonic Dances (1877–86), and he was director of the National Conservatory, New York, during 1892–95. Works such as his *New World Symphony* (1893) reflects his interest in American folk themes, including black and Native American. He wrote nine symphonies, tone poems, and operas, including *Rusalka* (1901); large-scale choral works; the *Carnival* and other overtures; violin and cello concertos; chamber music; piano pieces; and songs. His Romantic music extends the classical tradition of Beethoven and Brahms and displays the influence of Czech folk music.

dwaal, *n.* (*S Afr.*) a state of bewilderment. [Afrikaans, wander]

dwale, *n.* the deadly nightshade, *Atropa belladonna.* [ME *dwale* (cp. Dan. *dvale,* Swed. *dwala,* a trance, OE *dwala,* an error, stupe-faction)]

dwalm, dwam, *n.* (*Sc., North.*) a swoon; a daydream, absentmindedness. *v.i.* to faint; to sicken. **dwaminess,** *n.* [cp. OE *dwolma,* confusion]

dwarf, *n.* (*pl.* **dwarfs, dwarves**) a human being, animal or plant much below the natural or ordinary size; a supernatural being of small stature. *a.* below the ordinary or natural size; stunted, puny, tiny. *v.t.* to stunt;

to cause to look small by comparison; to check the physical or mental development of. *v.i.* to become stunted. **dwarf star,** *n.* any relatively small star with high density and ordinary luminosity, e.g. the sun. **dwarf tree,** *n.* a tree whose branches have been made to shoot near the root. **dwarf wall,** *n.* a low wall serving to surround an enclosure; such a wall as that on which iron railing is commonly set. **dwarfed,** *a.* **dwarfish,** *a.* **dwarfishly,** *adv.* **dwarfishness,** *n.* **dwarfism,** *n.* the condition of being a dwarf. **dwarflike,** *a.* [OE *dweorg, dweorh,* from OTeut. *dwerg-* (Dut. *dwerg,* Swed., Dan. *dverg,* G *Zwerg*)]

dwell, *v.i.* (*past, p.p.* **dwelt**) to reside, to abide (in a place); to live, spend one's time; to linger, pause, tarry; †to delay; †to continue in any state. †*v.t.* to inhabit. *n.* (*Mech.*) a pause; a slight regular stoppage of a movement whilst a certain operation is effected. **to dwell on, upon,** to occupy a long time with; to fix the attention upon; to be absorbed with; to expatiate. **dweller,** *n.* a resident, an inhabitant. **dwelling,** *n.* the action of the verb to DWELL; residence, abode, habitation. **dwelling-house,** *n.* a house for residence in contradistinction to a house of business, office, warehouse etc. **dwelling-place,** *n.* a place of residence. [OE *dwellan,* to lead astray (later, *dwelian,* to lead astray, to err, to be delayed, to tarry)]

dwindle, *v.i.* to shrink, to diminish, to become smaller; to waste or fall away; to degenerate, to decline. [OE *dwinan*]

dwt, (*abbr.*) pennyweight.

DX, *n.* long-range radio transmissions. **DXer,** *n.* one whose hobby is listening to such transmissions. **DXing,** *n.*

Dy, (*chem. symbol*) dysprosium.

dyad, *n.* two units treated as one; a group of two, a pair, a couple; a diatomic element, atom or radical. **dyadic,** *a.* [L *dyas dyadis,* Gr *duas duados* (*duo,* two)]

Dyak, Dayak, *n.* an individual of the aboriginal race inhabiting Borneo, probably related to the Malays. [native name]

dybbuk, *n.* (*pl.* **-buks, -bukkim**) in Jewish folklore, the soul of a dead sinner that enters the body of a living person and takes control of his/her actions. [Heb. *dibbūq,* devil]

Dyck, *n.* **Anthony van** (1599–1641), Flemish painter. Born in Antwerp, he was an assistant to Rubens (1618–20), then briefly worked in England at the court of James I, and moved to Italy in 1622. In 1626 he returned to Antwerp, where he continued to paint religious works and portraits. He painted his best-known portraits during his second period in England from 1632, for example, *Charles I on Horseback* (*c.* 1638, National Gallery, London).

dye, *v.t.* (*pres.p.* **dyeing,** *past* **dyed**) to stain, to colour; to impregnate with colouring-matter; to cause (a material) to take a certain colour. *v.i.* to follow the business of a dyer; to take a colour (of a material that is being dyed). *n.* a fluid used for dyeing, colouring-matter; colour, tinge, hue, produced by or as by dyeing; (*fig.*) stain. **to dye in the wool,** to dye the wool before spinning to give a more permanent result. **dye-house, -works,** *n.* a building where dyeing is carried on. **dye-stuffs,** *n.pl.* the materials used in dyeing. **dye-wood,** *n.* any wood from which a dye is extracted. **dyed,** *a.* **dyed-in-the-wool,** *a.* fixed in one's opinions, uncompromising. **dyeing,** *n.* **dyer,** *n.* one whose business is dyeing. **dyer's-weed,** *n.* name of various plants yielding dye-stuff, as dyer's green-weed or dyer's broom, *Genista tinctoria,* dyer's rocket, *Reseda luteola,* which yields a yellow dye, and dyer's woad, *Isatis tinctoria*. **dyster**, *n.* (*Sc.*) a dyer. [OE *dēagian,* from *dēag,* a dye]

Dyfed, *n.* county in SW Wales. **area** 5770 sq km/2227 sq miles. **towns** administrative headquarters Carmarthen; Aberystwyth, Cardigan, Lampeter. **population** (1987) 343,000. **language** 46% Welsh, English.

dying, *a.* about to die; mortal, perishable; done, given or uttered just before death; associated with death; drawing to an end, fading away; perishing. *n.* the act of expiring, death. **dying declaration,** *n.* a legal declaration made by a person on the point of death. **dyingly,** *adv.* [DIE[1]]

dyke DIKE.

Dylan, *n.* **Bob** (adopted name of Robert Allen Zimmerman) (1941–), US singer and songwriter, whose work in the 1960s, first in the folk-music tradition and from 1965 in an individualistic rock style, was highly influential on later pop music.

dynam, *n.* a foot-pound, as a unit of measurement. [short for Gr. *dunamis,* see DYNAMIC]

dynameter, *n.* an instrument for measuring the magnifying powers of a telescope. **dynametric, -ical,** *a.*

dynamic, *a.* of or pertaining to forces not in equilibrium, as distinct from *static;* motive, active, energetic, as distinct from *potential;* pertaining to dynamics; involving or dependent upon mechanical activity, as the dynamic theory of Kant; (*Med.*) functional, as distinct from *organic*. *n.* the motive force of any action. **dynamical,** *a.* dynamic; pertaining to dynamism; (*Theol.*) inspiring or animating, not impelling mechanically. **dynamically,** *adv.* **dynamics,** *n.sing.* the branch of mechanics which deals with the behaviour of bodies under the action of forces which produce changes of motion in them; in music, signs indicating levels of loudness. [F *dynamique,* Gr. *dunamikos,* from *dunamis,* power, *dunamai,* I am strong]

dynamism, *n.sing.* a system or theory explaining phenomena as the ultimate result of some immanent force, as the doctrine of Leibnitz that all substance involves force; the restless energy of a forceful personality. **dynamist,** *n.* **dynamistic,** *a.*

dynamite, *n.* a powerful explosive compound, extremely local in its action, consisting of nitroglycerine mixed with an absorbent material. *v.t.* to smash or destroy with dynamite. **dynamite-gun,** *n.* a pneumatic gun for hurling shells filled with dynamite. **dynamiter, -mitard**, *n.* a revolutionary or criminal employing dynamite. **dynamitic**, *a.* **dynamitism,** *n.* **dynamitist,** *n.* [Gr. *dunamis,* see DYNAMIC]

dynamize, -ise, *v.t.* to increase the power of medicines by trituration etc. **dynamization, -isation,** *n.*

dynamo-, *comb. form* pertaining to force or power. [Gr. *dunamis,* power]

dynamo, *n.* (*pl.* **-mos**) a dynamoelectric machine. **dynamoelectric,** *a.* pertaining to current electricity; pertaining to the conversion of mechanical into electric energy or the reverse. **dynamoelectric machine,** *n.* a machine for converting mechanical energy into electric by means of electromagnetic induction (usu. applied only to d.c. generators). **dynamoelectrical,** *a.*

dynamograph, *n.* a dynamometer used for recording speed, power, adhesion etc. on electric railways; a recording telegraphic instrument; an instrument for testing muscular strength, esp. by means of gripping.

dynamometer, *n.* an instrument for the measurement of power, force or electricity.

dynamotor, *n.* an electrical machine capable of acting as a motor and a generator which converts direct current into alternating current.

dynast, *n.* a ruler, a monarch; a member or founder of a dynasty. **dynastic**, *a.* **dynastically,** *adv.* **dynasty**, *n.* a line, race or succession of sovereigns of the same family. [late L *dynastēs,* Gr. *dunastēs,* a lord, from *dunatos,* able (*dunamai,* I am strong)]

dynatron, *n.* a four-electrode thermionic valve which generates continuous oscillation.

dyne, *n.* a unit for measuring force, the amount that, acting upon a gram for a second, generates a velocity of one centimetre per second. [F, from stem of Gr. *dunamai,* see prec.]

dyophysite, *n.* one who held that two natures were combined in the personality of Christ, a divine and a human. **dyophysitic**, *a.* **dyophysitism**, *n.* [late Gr. *diophusitai,* pl. (*duo,* two, *phusis,* nature)]

dyothelete, *a.* holding that Christ had two wills, a human and a divine. *n.* an adherent of this creed. **dyothelism, dyotheletism,** *n.* [Gr. *duo,* two, *thelētēs,* willer, from *thelein,* to will]

dys-, *pref.* bad, badly, depraved; difficult, working badly, painful. [Gr. *dus-*, badly, with difficulty]

dysaesthesia, *n.* (*Path.*) insensibility; derangement of sensation or the senses.

dyscrasia, *n.* a morbid condition of the blood or fluids of the body. [Gr. *duskrasia* (*krasis,* mixing)]

dysentery, *n.* an infectious tropical febrile disease, seated in the large intestines, accompanied by mucous and bloody evacuations. **dysenteric**, *a.* [OF *dissenterie,* L *dysenteria,* Gr. *dusenteria* (*entera,* bowels)]

dysfunction, *n.* impaired or abnormal functioning of any organ or part of the body. **dysfunctional,** *a.*

dysgenic, *a.* unfavourable to the hereditary qualities of any stock or race. **dysgenics,** *n.sing.* the study of racial degeneration.

dysgraphia, *n.* inability to write; impaired ability in writing. **dysgraphic,** *a.* [Gr. *graphein,* to write]

dyslexia, *n.* word-blindness, impaired ability in reading and spelling caused by a neurological disorder. **dyslexis,** *a.* [Gr. *lexis,* word]

dyslogistic, *a.* disparaging, disapproving, censuring. **dyslogistically,** *adv.*

dysmenorrhoea, *n.* difficult or painful menstruation. **dysmenorrhoeal, -rrhoeic,** *a.*

dysorexia, *n.* want of appetite; a bad or depressed appetite. [Gr. *dusorexia* (*orexis,* a longing, from *oregein,* to long, yearn)]

dyspepsia, dyspepsy, *n.* indigestion arising from functional derangement of the stomach. **dyspeptic**, *a.* pertaining to, of the nature of, or suffering from dyspepsia. *n.* one subject to dyspepsia. [L, from Gr. *duspepsia,* from *duspeptos,* hard to digest (*peptein,* to cook)]

dysphagia, *n.* (*Path.*) difficulty of swallowing. **dysphagic,** *a.* [Gr. *phagein,* to eat]

dysphasia, *n.* difficulty in speaking or understanding speech, caused by injury to or disease of the brain. **dysphasic,** *a.* [Gr. *phasis,* speech]

dysphemism, *n.* the use of an offensive word or phrase in place of an inoffensive or mild one; the offensive word or phrase used. **dysphemistic**, *a.* [eu*phemism*]

dysphonia, *n.* a difficulty in speaking arising from disease or malformation of the organs. [Gr. *dusphōnia,* harshness of sound (*phōnē,* sound)]

dysphoria, *n.* a morbid uneasiness; feeling unwell. **dysphoric,** *a.* [Gr. *pherein,* to bear]

dyspnoea, (*esp. N Am.*) **dyspnea**, *n.* difficulty of breathing. **dyspnoeal, dyspneal,** *a.* **dyspnoic**, *a.* [L, from Gr. *duspnoia* (*pnoē,* breathing)]

dysprosium, *n.* a rare metallic element, at. no. 66; chem. symbol Dy, of the rare earth group. [Gr. *dysprositos,* difficult of access]

dysthymic, *a.* morbidly depressed in spirits; dejected. **dysthymia**, *n.* **dysthymiac,** *n.* one who suffers from depression of spirits. [Gr. *dusthumos,* desponding (*thumos,* spirit)]

dystopia, *n.* an imaginary wretched place, the opposite of *Utopia*. **dystopian,** *a.*

dystrophy, *n.* any of various disorders characterized by the wasting away of muscle tissue; the condition of lake water when it is too acidic to support life. **dystrophic**, *a.* [Gr. *trophē,* nourishment]

dysuria, dysury, *n.* difficulty and pain in passing urine; morbid condition of the urine. **dysuric,** *a.* [OF *dissurie,* L *dysūria,* Gr. *dusouria* (*ouron,* urine)]

dyvour, *n.* (*Sc.*) a debtor; a bankrupt who has made a cessio bonorum to his creditors. [etym. unknown]

dziggetai, *n.* a species of wild ass, *Equus hemionus,* somewhat resembling the mule, native to Central Asia. [Mongol.]

Dzungarian Gates, *n.* ancient route in central Asia on the border of Kazakhstan, USSR, and Xinjiang Uygur region of China, 470 km/290 miles NW of Urümqi. The route was used by the Mongol hordes on their way to Europe.

E

E, e, the fifth letter and second vowel of the alphabet, has three principal sounds, long as in *me* (marked ē), short as in *men, set* (left unmarked), and short with a modification caused by a subsequent *r*, as in *her* (marked œ). There is also the indeterminate *e* in *camel, garment* (marked ə), and in many words, as *there,* it is pronounced as long **a** (marked eə). At the end of words it is usually silent as in *mane, cave,* where it also indicates that the preceding syllable is long. It is employed after *c* and *g* to denote that those letters are to be sounded as *s* and *j* respectively. (*Mus.*) the third note of the diatonic scale; (*Naut.*) a second-class ship in Lloyd's register; (*Math.*) symbol for the base of Napierian logarithms, approximately equalling 2·718. **E-boat,** *n.* a small, fast motor-boat of the German navy armed with guns and torpedoes. **E number,** *n.* a number preceded by the letter E denoting a certain food additive in accordance with EEC regulations.

e-, *pref.* a form of EX-, as in *elocution, emend, evade, evolve.*

each, *a., pron.* every one (of a number) considered separately. †**eachwhere,** *adv.* everywhere. [OE *ælc* (*ā, ge-, līc,* aye-like or everlike)]

eager, *a.* excited by an ardent desire to attain, obtain or succeed in anything; keen, ardent, vehement, impatient; †sharp, acrid. **eagerly,** *adv.* **eagerness,** *n.* [A-F *egre,* OF *aigre,* L *ācer ācrem,* keen]

eagle, *n.* a large bird of prey, the larger species of the Falconidae; any bird of the genus *Aquila,* esp. the golden eagle; a figure representing this, a lectern in the form of an eagle with expanded wings, a Roman or French military ensign bearing such a device; one of the nobler armorial bearings, emblematic of fortitude and magnanimity, and adopted as a national emblem by the US, Prussia, Austria, Russia and France; hence, used as the name of various coins stamped with an eagle, esp. for a gold coin of the US; worth 10 dollars; the constellation Aquila in the northern hemisphere. **eagle-eyed,** *a.* sharp-sighted as an eagle; quick to discern. **eagle-flighted,** *a.* mounting to a great height. **eagle-hawk,** *n.* a S American hawk of the genus *Morphuus.* **eagle-owl,** *n.* name of large European and American owls, esp. the European *Buvo maximus.* **eagle-stone,** *n.* an argillaceous oxide of iron occurring in nodules of various sizes, which often contain a loose kernel or nucleus, from the ancient belief that the eagle carried such a nodule to her nest to facilitate the laying of her eggs. **eagle-winged,** *a.* having wings like those of the eagle; soaring high like an eagle. **eaglet,** *n.* a young eagle. [A-F *egle,* OF *aigle,* L *aquila*]

eagre, *n.* a tidal wave or bore in an estuary. [etym. unknown]

ealdorman, ALDERMAN.

†**ean,** *v.i.* to bring forth lambs, to yean. **eaning-time,** *n.* the time or season of bearing young. †**eanling,** *n.* a lamb just brought forth. [OE *ēanian* (prob. cogn. with OE *eown,* EWE)]

-ean, -aean, -eian, *suf.* belonging to; like. [-AN, embodying the end of the stem in L words in *-aeus, -eius;* Gr. words in *-aios, -eios;* and Eng. words in *-ey* and *-y*]

ear[1], *n.* the organ of hearing; the external part of this organ; the sense of hearing; a delicate perception of the differences of sounds, and judgment of harmony; notice or attention (esp. favourable consideration); a small ear-like projection from a larger body, usually for support or attachment; judgment, opinion, taste. **middle ear,** the ear-drum. **over head and ears, up to the ears,** completely, so as to be overwhelmed. **to be all ears,** (*coll.*) to listen carefully. **to bring (down) about one's ears,** to involve oneself in (trouble etc.). **to give, lend, an ear,** to listen. **to go in one ear and out the other,** to make no lasting impression. **to have, keep, one's ear to the ground,** to be well informed about what is happening. **to prick up one's ears,** to begin to listen attentively. **to send away with a flea in one's ear,** to dismiss (someone) angrily or contemptuously. **to set by the ears,** to incite or cause strife between. **to turn a deaf ear** TURN. **earache,** *n.* pain in the ear-drum. **ear-cap,** *n.* a cover to protect the ears against cold. †**ear-drop,** *n.* a jewel hanging from the ear, an ear-ring. **ear-drum,** *n.* the tympanum; the membrane of the tympanum. **ear-lap,** *n.* the lobe of the ear. †**ear-lock,** *n.* a curl worn near the ear by dandies early in the 17th cent. **ear-mark,** *n.* a mark on the ear by which a sheep can be identified; any distinctive mark or feature. *v.t.* to mark (as sheep) by cutting or slitting the ear; to set a distinctive mark upon; to allocate (funds etc.) for a particular purpose. **ear-muffs,** *n.pl.* a pair of pads joined on a band and used to keep the ears warm. **earphone,** *n.* an instrument which is held close to the ear and converts electrical signals into audible speech, music etc. **ear-pick,** *n.* a small scoop to extract hardened wax from the ear. **ear-piercing,** *a.* loud and shrill. **ear-plug,** *n.* soft material put in the ear to block sound or water. **ear-ring,** *n.* a pendant or ornamental ring worn in the lobe of the ear. **earshot,** *n.* hearing distance. **ear-splitting,** *a.* ear-piercing. **ear-trumpet,** *n.* a tube to aid the sense of hearing by the collection and conduction of sounds. **ear-wax,** *n.* a wax-like substance found in the ear, cerumen. †**ear-witness,** *n.* one who can attest anything as heard with his own ears. **eared,** *a.* having ears; (*Bot.*) auriculate. **earless,** *a.* **earlet,** *n.* a little ear. [OE *ēare* (cp. Dut. *oor,* Icel. *eyra,* G *Ohr,* L *auris,* Gr. *ous*)]

ear[2], *n.* a spike or head of corn. *v.i.* to form ears, as corn. **ear-cockle,** *n.* a disease of wheat and other corn. [OE *ēar,* pl. (cp. Dut. *aar,* Icel., Dan. and Swed. *ax,* G *Ähre;* cogn. with L *acus, aceris,* husk of corn)]

†**ear[3],** *v.t.* to plough, to till. [OE *erian* (cp. Icel. *erja,* Goth. *arjan,* L *arāre,* Gr. *aroein*)]

earache EAR.

earing, *n.* (*Naut.*) a small line for fastening a reef or the corner of a sail to the yard, gaff etc. [see also EAR-RING under EAR[1]]

earl, *n.* an English nobleman ranking next below a marquess and next above a viscount. cp. COUNT[2]. **Earl Marshal,** *n.* an English officer of state, head of the College of Arms, with whom lies the determination of all questions relating to arms and grants of arms. **earldom,** *n.* the rank, title or position of an earl. [OE *eorl,* a warrior (cp. Icel. *jarl, earl,* OS *erl,* a man)]

early, *adv.* (*comp.* **earlier,** *superl.* **earliest**) in good time; soon; towards, in or near the beginning. *a.* soon; in advance, as compared with something else; coming before or in advance of the usual time; situated in or near the beginning. **early warning system,** a system of advance notice, esp. of danger such as a nuclear attack. **early days,** (*coll.*) *adv.* too soon to take effect, have results etc. **early door,** *n.* admission to a theatre before the official time for opening on payment of an extra charge. **Early English,** *n, a.* (of) the first of the pointed or Gothic styles of architecture employed in England, characterized by lancet windows, clustered pillars and vaulted roofs with moulded groins on the ribs only. **earliness,** *n.* [OE *ǣrlīce* (*ǣr,* sooner, *līc,* like, *līce,* -LY)]

earn[1], *v.t.* to gain as the reward of labour; to merit, deserve or become entitled to as the result of any action or course of conduct. **earned income,** *n.* income from paid employment. **earnings,** *n.pl.* that which is earned, gained or merited; wages, reward. [OE *earnian* (cp. OHG *arnōn,* also G *ernten,* to reap, from *Ernte,* harvest)]

earn[2], *v.i.* to long; to grieve. [YEARN [1]]

earnest[1], *a.* serious, important, grave; ardent, eager or zealous in the performance of any act or the pursuit of any object; heartfelt, sincere. *n.* seriousness; reality, not a pretence; a serious object or business, not a jest. **in earnest,** seriously; with sincerity. **earnestly,** *adv.* **earnestness,** *n.* [OE *eornost,* whence *eorneste,* a., adv. (cp. Dut. and G *ernst*)]

earnest[2], *n.* a pledge, an assurance of something to come; earnest-money. **earnest-money,** *n.* an instalment paid to seal a bargain. [ME *ernes,* prob. a corr. of *erles,* ARLES]

earphone EAR.

earth, *n.* the ground, the visible surface of the globe; the globe, the planet on which we live; dry land, as opposed to the sea; this world, as opposed to other possible worlds; soil, mould, as distinguished from rock; dead, inert matter; clay, dust, the body; the hole of a fox, badger etc.; the part of the ground completing an electrical circuit; a connection to ground; (*Radio*) plates or wires buried in the earth which provide a path to ground for currents flowing in the aerial; an earth-like metallic oxide, such as alumina. *v.t.* (*usu. with up*) to cover with earth; to drive (fox etc.) to his earth; †to hide or place under the earth; to complete a circuit by connecting with the earth. *v.i.* to retire to an earth (as a fox). **rare earth metals** RARE. **earth-bath,** *n.* a kind of bath in which one is partially covered with loose earth. **earth-board,** *n.* a mould-board of a plough. **earth-born,** *a.* born from or on the earth, terrigenous; relating to or arising from earthly things; human, mortal; of mean birth. **earth-bound,** *a.* fixed or fastened in or to the earth; (*fig.*) fixed on earthly objects. †**earth-bred,** *a.* low-born, abject, grovelling. **earth circuit,** *n.* that portion of a radio receiver or transmitter which includes the earth lead. **earth-closet,** *n.* a lavatory in which earth is used instead of water. **earth-fall,** *n.* a landslide. **earth-hunger,** *n.* an inordinate desire to possess land. **earth-light,** *n.* light reflected from the earth upon the dark part of the moon, when the latter is either very young or has waned considerably. **earth-nut,** *n.* the pig-nut or ground-nut; the truffle, the heath-pea and other plants. **earth-plate,** *n.* (*Elec.*) a plate buried in the earth connected with a terminal or return wire, so as to utilize the earth itself as a part of the circuit. **earthquake,** *n.* a movement of a portion of the earth's crust produced by volcanic forces; (*fig.*) a social, political or other disturbance. **earth science,** *n.* any science dealing with the earth, e.g. geography or geology. **earth-shine** EARTH-LIGHT. **earth-wolf** AARDWULF under AARDVARK. **earthwork,** *n.* mounds, ramparts etc. used for defensive purposes; embankments, cuttings etc. **earth-worm,** *n.* a burrowing worm, esp. belonging to the genus *Lumbricus;* (*fig.*) a grovelling or sordid person. **earthen,** *a.* made of earth, baked clay or similar substance. **earthenware,** *n.* ware made of baked clay; pottery, esp. the coarser forms of ceramic work. **earthling,** *n.* an inhabitant of the earth; an earthly-minded person. **earthly,** *a.* of or pertaining to this world; mortal, human; carnal, as opposed to spiritual; pertaining to this life, as opposed to a future life; corporeal, not mental; (*coll.*) possible, conceivable; †in the earth. **not an earthly,** (*coll.*) not a chance. **earthly-minded,** *a.* having a mind fixed on this earth; destitute of spirituality. **earthly-mindedness,** *n.* **earthliness,** *n.* **earthward, -wards,** *adv.* **earthy,** *a.* consisting or composed of earth or soil; resembling earth; cold and lifeless as earth; gross, carnal, material; dull, lustreless. **earthiness,** *n.* [OE *eorthe* (cp. Dut. *aarde,* Icel. *jörth,* Goth. *airtha,* G *Erde*)]

earwig, *n.* an insect, *Forficula auricularia,* having curved forceps at its tail; a prying, insinuating informer or tale-bearer. [OE *ēar-wicga,* ear-runner (*wicga,* from *wegan,* to move, allied to L *vehere, vec-,* to carry), from the erroneous belief that it crept into the ear]

ease, *n.* a state of freedom from labour, trouble or pain; freedom from constraint or formality; facility, readiness; absence of effort. *v.t.* to free from pain, anxiety, labour or trouble; to relieve or free from a burden; to make easier or lighter; to assuage, to mitigate; to render less difficult; to make looser, to relax, to adjust; (*Naut.*) to slacken (a rope, sail, speed etc.). *v.i.* to relax one's efforts or exertions. **at ease,** in a state free from anything likely to disturb, annoy or cause anxiety. **ease her,** (*Naut.*) the command to reduce the speed of the engines of a steamer. **ill at ease,** in a state of mental or bodily disquiet, trouble or pain. **stand at ease,** (*Mil.*) a command to stand with the legs apart and hands behind the back. **to ease away** or **off,** (*Naut.*) to slacken gradually (as a rope); to become less oppressive. **to ease oneself,** to empty the bowels; to urinate. **easeful,** *a.* promoting ease, quiet or repose; comfortable; indolent. **easement,** *n.* the act of easing; alleviation, mitigation; a convenience; (*Law*) a liberty, right or privilege, without profit, which one proprietor has in or through the estate of another, as a right of way, light, air etc. [OF *aise,* etym. doubtful (cp. It. *agio*)]

easel, *n.* a wooden frame used to support a picture, blackboard, open book etc. [Dut. *ezel,* a little ass (cp. G *esel*)]

easily EASY.

east, *a.* situated towards the point where the sun rises when in the equinoctial; coming from this direction. *n.* the point of the compass where the sun rises at the equinox; 90° to the right of north; the eastern part of a country; the countries to the east of Europe; the east wind. *adv.* towards, at or near the quarter of the rising sun. *v.i.* to move towards the east; to veer from the north or south towards the east; (*reflex.*) to find one's east, to orientate oneself. **Far East,** the regions east of India. **Middle East,** Iraq, Iran, Mesopotamia etc. **Near East,** Turkey, the Levant, etc. **East End,** *n.* the east and unfashionable end of London. **East-Ender,** *n.* **East Indiaman,** *n.* (*Naut. hist.*) a ship sailing to and from the E Indies. **east wind,** *n.* a wind coming from an easterly direction. **easterly,** *a.* situated or in the direction of the east; looking towards the east; coming from the east, or parts lying towards the east. *adv.* in the direction of the east; in or from the east. *n.* a wind from the east. **easting,** *n.* (*Naut.*) distance traversed on an easterly course; distance east of a given meridian; movement to the east. **eastward,** *a, n.* **eastwards,** *adv.* [OE *ēast,* adv., in the east, eastwards, *ēastan,* from the east (cp. Dut. *oost,* Icel. *austr,* G *osten*)]

East Anglia, *n.* region of E England, formerly a Saxon kingdom, including Norfolk, Suffolk, and parts of Essex and Cambridgeshire. The University of East Anglia was founded at Norwich in 1962, and the Sainsbury Centre for the Visual Arts, opened in 1978, has a collection of ethnographic art and sculpture.

Easter[1], *n.* the festival in commemoration of the resurrection of Christ, taking place on the Sunday after the full moon that falls on or next after 21 Mar. **Easter Day,** *n.* Easter Sunday. **Easter-dues, -offerings,** *n.pl.* payments or offerings to the parson of a parish at Easter. **Easter-eggs,** *n.pl.* eggs boiled hard and stained or gilded, to symbolize the resurrection; egg-shaped presents given at Easter. **Easter-eve,** *n.* the day before Easter Day. **Easter sepulchre,** *n.* a canopied recess in a choir or chancel for the reception of the elements of the Eucharist consecrated on Maundy Thursday. **Easter week,** *n.* the week beginning with Easter Day. [*ēastre, Ēastre, Ēostre* (Teutonic dawn-goddess)]

†**easter**[2], *a.* eastern. [perh. comp. of EAST]

Easter Island, (or **Rapa Nui**) *n.* Chilean island in the S Pacific Ocean, part of the Polynesian group, about 3500 km/2200 miles W of Chile. **area** about 166 sq km/

64 sq miles. **population** (1985) 2000. It was first reached by Europeans on Easter Sunday in 1722. It is famous for its huge carved statues and stone houses, the work of neolithic peoples of unknown origin. The chief centre is Hanga-Roa.

†**easterling,** *n.* a native of eastern Germany or the Baltic, esp. a citizen of the Hanse towns; a native or inhabitant of the east; an inhabitant of the eastern part of a country. [prob. from prec., after Dut. *oosterling*]

eastern, *a.* situated in the east; pertaining to the east; blowing from the east. *n.* an inhabitant of the East, an Oriental; a member of the Eastern or Greek Church. **Eastern Church,** *n.* term for the Greek, as distinguished from the Latin or Western, Church. **Eastern question,** *n.* the political question in the late 19th and early 20th cents. as to the distribution of political power in Eastern Europe, esp. those parts under the actual or nominal rule of Turkey. **Easterner,** *n.* in the US, an inhabitant of the eastern or New England States. **easternmost,** *a.* [OE *ēasterne*]

Easter Rising, *n.* traditionally known as the Easter Rebellion. In Irish history, a republican insurrection that began on Easter Monday, Apr. 1916 in Dublin. It was inspired by the Irish Republican Brotherhood (IRB) in an attempt to overthrow British rule in Ireland.

East Germany, *n.* see GERMANY, EAST.

East India Company, an English commercial company (1600–1858) that was chartered by Queen Elizabeth I and given a monopoly of trade between England and the Far East. In the 18th cent. it became in effect the ruler of a large part of India, and a form of dual control by the company and a committee responsible to Parliament in London was introduced by Pitt's India Act of 1784. The end of the monopoly of China trade came in 1834, and after the Indian Mutiny of 1857 the crown took complete control of the government of British India; the India Act of 1858 abolished the company.

East India Company, Dutch (*VOC*, or *Vereenigde Oost-Indische Compagnie*), a trading company chartered by the States General (parliament) of the Netherlands, and established in N Netherlands in 1602. It was given a monopoly on Dutch trade in the Indonesian archipelago, and certain sovereign rights such as the creation of an army and a fleet. In the 17th century some 100 ships were regularly trading between the Netherlands and the East Indies. The company's main base was Batavia in Java (Indonesia); ships sailed there via the Cape of Good Hope, a colony founded by the company in 1652 as a staging post. During the 17th and 18th centuries the company used its monopoly of East Indian trade to pay out high dividends, but wars with England and widespread corruption led to a suspension of payments in 1781 and a takeover of the company by the Dutch government in 1798.

easting EAST.

East Lothian, *n.* former county of SE Scotland, merged with West Lothian and Midlothian in 1975 in the new region of Lothian. Haddington was the county town.

Eastman, *n.* **George** (1854–1932), US entrepreneur and inventor who founded the Kodak photographic company. From 1888 he marketed daylight-loading flexible roll films (to replace the glass plates used previously) and portable cameras. By 1900 his company was selling a pocket camera for as little as $1.

East Sussex, *n.* county in SE England. **area** 1800 sq km/695 sq miles. **towns** administrative headquarters Lewes; cross-channel port of Newhaven; Brighton, Eastbourne, Hastings, Bexhill, Winchelsea, Rye. **population** (1987) 698,000. **products** electronics, gypsum, timber.

East Timor, *n.* disputed territory on the island of Timor in the Malay Archipelago; prior to 1975, a Portuguese colony for almost 460 years. **area** 14,874 sq km/5706 sq miles. **capital** Dili. **population** (1980) 555,000. **products** coffee.

Eastwood, *n.* **Clint** (1930–), US film actor and director. As the 'man with no name' caught up in Wild West lawlessness in *A Fistful of Dollars* (1964), he started the vogue for 'spaghetti westerns'. Later westerns include *The Good, the Bad, and the Ugly* (1966) and *High Plains Drifter* (1973). He also starred in the 'Dirty Harry' series, and directed *Bird* (1988).

easy, *a.* at ease; free from pain, trouble, care or discomfort; in comfortable circumstances, well-to-do; not strict; free from embarrassment, constraint or affectation; smooth, flowing, fluent; not difficult, not requiring great labour, exertion or effort; easily persuaded, compliant; indulgent, not exacting; (*Comm.*) not straitened, not hard to get (as distinct from *tight*); fitting loosely; slight, trivial. *adv.* in an easy manner. *n.* a relaxation of effort or a pause in rowing. **easy!** move or go gently. **easy ahead!** move or steam at a moderate speed. **easy all!** stop rowing. **honours easy,** (*Cards.*, *coll.*) honours equally divided. **in easy circumstances,** well-to-do, affluent. **take it easy!** take your time! **easy chair,** *n.* an arm-chair stuffed and padded for resting or reclining in. **easy-going,** *a.* moving easily; taking things in an easy manner; indolent. **easy mark,** *n.* (*coll.*) a gullible fellow. **easy money,** *n.* (*coll.*) money acquired without much effort. **easy-osy,** *a.* indolent, easy-going. **easy street,** *n.* (*coll.*) a position of financial good fortune or security. **easily,** *adv.* **easiness,** *n.* [OF *aisié* (F *aisé*), p.p. of *aiser,* to EASE]

eat, *v.t.* (*past* **ate**, *p.p.* **eaten**) to chew and swallow as food; to devour; to destroy by eating; (*fig.*) to corrode; to consume; to wear away, to waste. *v.i.* to take food; to be eaten; to taste, to relish. **eaten up with pride,** absorbed with self-conceit. **to eat away,** to destroy, to rust, to corrode. **to eat crow, dirt,** to retract or acquiesce humbly. **to eat into,** to corrode. **to eat one's heart out,** to pine away. **to eat one's terms,** to study for the English bar (from the fact that the student has to eat so many dinners each term in the public hall of the Inn to which he/she belongs). **to eat one's words,** to retract what one has said. **to eat out,** to eat in a restaurant, cafe or hotel. **to eat out of house and home,** to ruin (someone) by consuming all he/she has. **eatable,** *a.* fit to be eaten. *n.* anything fit or proper for food; (*pl.*) the solid materials of a meal. **eater,** *n.* one who eats; fruit suitable for eating uncooked. **eatery,** *n.* (*coll.*) a restaurant, cafe etc. **eating-house,** *n.* a shop where provisions are sold ready for eating; a restaurant. [OE *etan* (cp. Dut. *eten,* G *essen;* also L *edere,* Gr. *edein*)]

eau, *n.* water (used in compounds to designate various spirituous waters and perfumes). **eau-de-Cologne**, *n.* a scent consisting of a solution of volatile oils in alcohol, orig. made in Cologne. **eau-de-Nil**, *n.* a pale greenish colour, said to be like Nile water. **eau de vie**, *n.* brandy. [F]

eaves, *n.pl.* the lower edge of the roof which projects beyond the wall, and serves to throw off the water which falls on the roof. **eavesdrop,** *n.* the water which drops from the eaves of a house. *v.i.* to listen under the eaves of a house in order to catch what may be said indoors; to listen secretly so as to overhear confidences. **eavesdropper,** *n.* [OE *efes,* sing., prob. cogn. with OVER (now taken as pl. and *eave* sometimes used as sing.)]

Eban, *n.* **Abba** (1915–), Israeli diplomat and politician, Israeli ambassador in Washington (1950–59) and foreign minister (1966–74).

ebb, *n.* the reflux of the tide; (*fig.*) decline, failure, decay. *v.i.* to flow back; (*fig.*) to recede, to decline, to decay. **at a low ebb,** weak or in a state of decline. **to ebb and flow,** to rise and fall; (*fig.*) to increase and decrease. **ebb-tide,** *n.* the retiring tide. [OE *ebba,* the ebb, whence *ebbian,* to ebb (cp. Dut. *ebbe, eb*)]

ebenezer, *n.* a chapel or meeting-house. [Heb. *eben hā' ēzer,* the stone of help, a memorial set up by Samuel after the victory of Mizpah (I Sam. vii.12)]

Ebionite, *n.* a Christian sect of the 1st and 2nd cents. consisting of those Jewish converts who considered the Mosaic law as still binding, and sought to Judaize Christianity. **Ebionitic,** *a.* **Ebionitism,** *n.* [L *Ebionita* (Heb. *ebiōnīm,* the poor)]

Eblis, *n.* (*pl.* **Iblees**) the chief of the jinn who were cast out of heaven. **hall of Eblis,** Pandemonium. [Arab. *Iblis*]

ebony, *n.* the wood of various species of *Diospyros,* noted for its solidity and black colour, capable of a high polish, and largely used for mosaic work and inlaying. *a.* made of ebony; intensely black. †**ebon,** *a.* consisting of or like ebony; black. *n.* ebony. †**ebon-coloured,** *a.* black, dark. **ebonist,** *n.* a worker in ebony. **ebonite,** *n.* vulcanite. **ebonize, -ise,** *v.t.* to make the colour of ebony. [OF and L *ebenus,* Gr. *ebenos* (prob. of Oriental origin)]

Eboracum, *n.* Roman name for York. The archbishop of York signs himself 'Ebor'.

éboulement, *n.* (*Fort.*) the crumbling of a wall; (*Geol.*) a sudden fall of rock in a mountainous district. [F, from *ébouler,* to crumble]

ebracteate, *a.* (*Bot.*) without bracts. [E-, BRACT, -ATE]

ebriety, *n.* drunkenness, intoxication. [F *ébriété,* L *ēbrietās -tātem,* from *ēbrius,* drunk] **ebriate,** *v.t.* to intoxicate. **ebriosity,** *n.* habitual drunkenness; (*fig.*) exhilaration. **ebriose, ebrious,** *a.* drunk; addicted to drink; characteristic of drunkenness. [L *ēbriātus,* p.p. of *ēbriāre,* to intoxicate]

ebullient, *a.* boiling over; (*fig.*) overflowing (with high spirits or enthusiasm). **ebullience, -ency,** *n.* **ebullition,** *n.* the boiling or bubbling of a liquid; effervescence; (*fig.*) sudden outburst (of feeling). [L *ēbulliens -entem,* pres.p. of *ēbullīre (bullīre,* to boil)]

eburnation, eburnification, *n.* an excessive deposition of bony matter, sometimes found in a diseased state of the joints. [L *eburnus,* ivory, -ATION]

eburnean, -ian, eburnine, *a.* of ivory; ivory-like. [as prec.]

EC, (*abbr.*) European Community.

écarté, *n.* a game of cards played by two persons with 32 cards. [F, from *écarter,* to discard]

ecaudate, *a.* without a tail; without a stem. [E-, L *cauda,* a tail]

ecbasis, *n.* (*Rhet.*) an argument dealing with probable consequences. **ecbatic,** *a.* [Gr. *ekbasis* (*ekbainein,* to go out)]

ecbole, *n.* (*Rhet.*) a digression. **ecbolic,** *n.* a drug which stimulates uterine contractions and promotes the expulsion of the foetus. [Gr. *ekbolē,* a throwing-out]

ecce homo, *n.* a name given to paintings representing Christ crowned with thorns, as He appeared before Pilate (John xix.5). [L, behold the man]

eccentric, *a.* deviating from the centre; departing from the usual practice or established forms or laws; erratic, irregular, anomalous; peculiar or odd in manner or character; (*Geom.*) not having the same centre, a term applied to circles and spheres which are not concentric. *n.* a person of odd or peculiar habits; an oddity; a mechanical contrivance for converting circular into reciprocating rectilinear motion, esp. that operating the slide-valve of a steam-engine. **eccentric-rod,** *n.* a rod transmitting the motion of an eccentric-wheel. **eccentric-strap,** *n.* the iron band within which an eccentric-wheel revolves. **eccentric-wheel,** *n.* a wheel whose axis of revolution is different from its centre. **eccentrically,** *adv.* **eccentricity,** *n.* the state of not being concentric; deviation from the centre; departure from what is usual, regular or established; whimsical conduct or character; oddity, peculiarity; (*Astron.*) a measure of the departure from circularity of the orbit of a planet. [late L *eccentricus,* Gr. *ekkentros* (*ek,* out, *kentron,* CENTRE)]

ecce signum, behold the proof. [L]

ecchymosis, *n.* a bruise; a discoloration of the skin due to the effusion of blood from blood-vessels ruptured by a blow. [Gr. *ek,* out; *chumos,* CHYME]

Eccles cake, *n.* a cake like a Banbury cake. [from *Eccles* in Lancashire]

ecclesia, *n.* an assembly of free citizens, esp. the legislative assembly of ancient Athens; a church; a religious assembly, a congregation. †**ecclesiarch,** *n.* a ruler of the church. †**ecclesiast,** *n.* a member of a Greek ecclesia; Solomon regarded as preacher or author of the Book of Ecclesiastes. **ecclesiastic,** *a.* ecclesiastical. *n.* a person in holy orders, a clergyman. **ecclesiastical,** *a.* pertaining to the Church or the clergy. **Ecclesiastical Commissioners,** *n.pl.* members of a permanent commission (1836–1948), established to administer the revenues of the Church of England. **ecclesiastical courts,** *n.pl.* courts for administering ecclesiastical law and for maintaining the discipline of the Established Church; courts in the Presbyterian Church for deciding matters of doctrine and discipline. **ecclesiastical modes,** *n.pl.* (*Mus.*) the Ambrosian and Gregorian scales in which plain song and plain chant are composed. **ecclesiastical states,** *n.pl.* the territory formerly under the temporal rule of the Pope. **ecclesiastically,** *adv.* **ecclesiasticism,** *n.* [med. L, from Gr. *ekklēsia,* from *ekkalein* (*ek,* out, *kalein,* to call)]

Ecclesiastes, *n.* also known as 'The Preacher', a book of the Old Testament or Hebrew Bible, traditionally attributed to Solomon, on the theme of the vanity of human life.

ecclesi(o)-, *comb. form.* pertaining to the Church or Churches or to ecclesiastic matters. [see prec.]

ecclesiography, *n.* descriptive history of the Church or of Churches.

ecclesiolatry, *n.* excessive reverence for ecclesiastical forms and traditions. **ecclesiolater,** *n.*

ecclesiology, *n.* the science which treats of all matters connected with churches, esp. church architecture, decoration and antiquities. **ecclesiological,** *a.* **ecclesiologist,** *n.*

eccrine, *a.* denoting a gland that secretes externally, esp. the sweat glands. **eccrinology,** *n.* the branch of physiology relating to secretions. [Gr. *ek,* out of, *krīnein,* to separate, secrete]

ecdysis, *n.* the casting of the skin, as by snakes, insects and crustaceans. [Gr. *ekdusis,* from *ekduein* (*ek,* off, *duein,* to put)]

ECG, (*abbr.*) electrocardiogram; electrocardiograph.

†**eche,** *v.t.* to increase, to augment; to eke (out). [OE *ēcan, īecan,* to increase, to add, cogn. with L *augēre,* Gr. *auxanein*]

echelon, *n.* the arrangement of troops as in the form of steps, with parallel divisions one in advance of another; (a group of persons in) a level, stage or grade of an organization etc. *v.t.* to form in echelon. [F, from *échelle,* L *scāla,* a ladder]

Echidna, *n.* a genus of mammals from Australia, Tasmania and New Guinea, popularly known as porcupine ant-eaters, which lay eggs instead of bringing forth their young alive like other mammals. [Gr., viper]

echinoderm, *a.* (*Zool.*) having a prickly skin; pertaining to the Echinodermata. *n.* any individual of the Echinodermata. **Echinodermata,** *n.pl.* a class of animals containing the sea-urchins, starfish and sea-cucumbers. **echinodermatous,** *a.* [Gr. *echīnus,* as foll., *derma,* skin, pl. *dermata*]

echinus, *n.* a sea-urchin; the convex projecting moulding below the abacus of an Ionic column and in the cornices of Roman architecture. **echinate, -nated,** *a.* furnished with numerous rigid hairs or straight prickles; bristly or spiny like a hedgehog or sea-urchin. **echinid, -nidan,** *n.* a sea-urchin. **echinite,** *n.* (*Geol.*) a fossil echinoderm or sea-urchin. **echinoid,** *a.* [L, from *echīnus,* a hedgehog]

echo, *n.* the repetition of a sound caused by its being reflected from some obstacle; the personification of this phenomenon or its cause; (*fig.*) close imitation in words or sentiment; a hearty response; (*Mus.*) repetition of a phrase in a softer tone; repetition of the last syllables of a verse in the next line, so as to give a continuous sense; in whist, a response to a partner's call for trumps. *v.i.* to give an echo; to resound; to be sounded back. *v.t.* to return or send back (as a sound); (*fig.*) to repeat with approval; to imitate closely. **echo chamber,** *n.* a room whose walls echo sound for recording or radio effects or for measuring acoustics. **echogram,** *n.* a recording made by an echo sounder.

echometer, *n.* an instrument for measuring the duration of sounds. **echo sounder,** *n.* (*Naut.*) an apparatus for sounding the depth of water beneath the keel of a ship. **echoer,** *n.* **echoism,** *n.* onomatopoeia. **echoless,** *a.* [L, from Gr. *ēchō* (cp. *ēchos, ēchē,* sound); in Greek mythology, a nymph who pined away until only her voice remained, after being rejected by Narcissus]

Eckert, *n.* **John Presper Jr** (1919–), US mathematician who collaborated with John Mauchly on the development of the ENIAC and Univac 1 computers.

eclair, *n.* an iced, finger-shaped cream cake. [F, lightning]

éclaircissement, *n.* an explanation or clearing up of a subject of dispute or misunderstanding. [F, from *éclaircir,* to clear up]

eclampsia, *n.* (*Path.*) convulsions or fits, particularly the type that occurs with acute toxaemia in pregnancy. [Gr. *ek,* out, *lampein,* to shine]

eclat, *n.* brilliant success; acclamation, applause; splendour, striking effect. [F, from *éclater,* OHG *skleizan,* to burst into fragments]

eclectic, *a.* selecting, choosing, picking out at will from the (best of) doctrines, teachings etc. of others; broad, not exclusive; containing or consisting of selections from the works of others. *n.* a philosopher who borrows doctrines from various schools; one who derives opinions, tastes or practical methods from various sources. **eclectically,** *adv.* **eclecticism**, *n.* [Gr. *eklektikos* (*eklegein,* see ECLOGUE)]

eclipse, *n.* the total or partial obscuration of the light from a heavenly body by the passage of another body between it and the eye or between it and the source of its light; a temporary failure or obscuration; loss of brightness, glory, honour or reputation. *v.t.* to cause an eclipse of (a heavenly body) by passing between it and the spectator or between it and its source of light; to intercept the light of, to obscure; to outshine, surpass, excel. *v.i.* to suffer an eclipse; to be eclipsed. **ecliptic**, *a.* constituting or pertaining to the sun's apparent path in the sky; pertaining to an eclipse. *n.* the apparent path of the sun round the earth; the plane passing through the sun's centre which contains the orbit of the earth; a great circle on the terrestrial globe answering to, and falling within, the plane of the celestial ecliptic. [OF, from L *eclipsis,* Gr. *ekleipsis,* from *ekleipein* (*ek,* out of, *leipein,* to leave)]

eclogue, *n.* an idyll or pastoral poem, esp. one containing dialogue. [L *ecloga,* Gr. *eklogē,* from *eklegein* (*ek,* out of, *legein,* to pick)]

Eco, *n.* **Umberto** (1932–), Italian cultural and literary critic *The Role of the Reader* (1979), and author of the 'philosophical thriller' *The Name of the Rose* (1983).

eco-, *comb. form.* concerned with ecology, habitat or the environment. [see foll.]

ecology, *n.* the branch of biology dealing with the relations between organisms and their environment. **ecological**, *a.* **ecologist,** *n.* [Gr. *oikos,* house; -LOGY]

econometrics, *n. sing.* statistical and mathematical analysis of economic theories. [see METRE[1]]

economic, *a.* relating to the science of economics; pertaining to industrial concerns or commerce; maintained for the sake of profit or for the production of wealth; capable of yielding a profit, financially viable; economical. **economic zone,** *n.* a coastal area which a country claims as its own territory for purposes of fishing etc. **economical,** *a.* characterized by economic management; careful, frugal, thrifty; economic. **economically,** *adv.* **economics,** *n. sing.* the science of the production and distribution of wealth, political economy; the condition of a country, community, or individual, with regard to material prosperity. **economist,** *n.* one who manages with economy; one skilled in the science of economics. **economize, -ise,** *v.i.* to manage domestic or financial affairs with economy. *v.t.* to use, administer or expend with economy; to use sparingly, to turn to the best account. **economization, -isation,** *n.* [L *oeconomicus,* Gr. *oikonomikos,* see foll.]

economy, *n.* the management, regulation, and government of a household or household affairs; a frugal and judicious use or expenditure of money; carefulness, frugality; (*usu. pl.*) a saving or reduction of expense; cheapness of operation; a careful and judicious use of anything, as of time; the disposition, arrangement or plan of any work; the operations of nature in the generation, nutrition and preservation of animals and plants; the administration of the internal affairs of a state, nation or department; organization, system; an organized body or system; a system of laws, principles, doctrines, rights etc. **political economy,** the science of the production and distribution of wealth. [L *oeconomia,* Gr. *oikonomia,* from *oikonomein,* to manage a household (*oikos,* house, *nemein,* to deal out)]

écorché, *n.* an anatomical figure with the muscular system exposed for the purpose of study. [F, p.p. of *écorcher,* to flay]

ecospecies, *n.* a taxonomic species regarded as an ecological unit.

ecosphere, *n.* the parts of the universe, esp. the earth, where life can exist.

écossaise, *n.* a Scottish dance or the music to it. [F, fem. of *écossais,* Scottish]

ecostate, *a.* having no central rib (as some leaves). [E-, L *costa,* a rib]

ecosystem, *n.* a system consisting of a community of organisms and its environment.

écraseur, *n.* an instrument for removing tumours etc. without effusion of blood. [F, crusher, from *écraser,* to crush]

ecru, *n, a.* the colour of unbleached linen. [F, raw, unbleached]

ecstasy, *n.* a state of mental exaltation; excessive emotion, rapture, excessive delight, or excessive grief, distress or pain; prophetic or poetic frenzy; a trance; a morbid state of the nervous system in which the mind is completely absorbed by one idea; †madness, distraction; (*sl.*) a stimulant drug related to amphetamines. **ecstasize, -ise,** *v.t.* to fill with ecstasy, to enrapture. *v.i.* to go into ecstasies. **ecstatic,** *a.* pertaining to or producing ecstasy; ravishing, entrancing, rapturous; subject to ecstasy; ravished, entranced. **ecstatically,** *adv.* [OF *extasie,* med. L *ecstasis,* Gr. *ekstasis* (*ek,* out, *stasis,* a standing, from *histanai,* to place)]

ECT, (*abbr.*) electroconvulsive therapy.

ecthyma, *n.* a skin disease characterized by an eruption of pimples. [Gr. *ekthuma,* from *ekthuein* (*ek,* out, *thuein,* to boil)]

ecto-, *comb. form.* (*Biol., Zool.*) pertaining to the outside of something. [Gr. *ektos,* outside]

ectoblast, *n.* the membrane composing the walls of a cell. [Gr. *blastos,* a sprout]

ectocyst, *n.* the external investment of a polyzoon.

ectoderm, *n.* the outer layer of the ectoblast; the external integument of the Coelenterata.

ectomorph, *n.* a person of slight or thin build. [Gr. *morphē,* form]

ectopia, *n.* congenital displacement of an organ or part. **ectopic**, *a.* out of place. **ectopic pregnancy,** *n.* the abnormal development of a foetus outside the womb, usu. in a Fallopian tube. [Gr. *ek,* out of, *topos,* place]

ectoplasm, *n.* the outer layer of protoplasm or sarcode of a cell.

ectosarc, *n.* the outer transparent sarcode-layer of certain protozoa, as the amoeba.

ectozoon, *n.* (*pl.* **-zoa**) an animal parasitic on the outside of other animals.

ectropium, -pion, *n.* an everted eyelid, so that the red inner surface becomes external. **ectropic**, *a.* [Gr. *ektropion* (*ek,* out, *trepein,* to turn)]

ECTU, (*abbr.*) European Confederation of Trade Unions.

ectype, *n.* a copy as distinguished from an original. **ectypal**, *a.* **ectypography**, *n.* a mode of etching which leaves the design in relief. [Gr. *ektupon* (*ek,* out, *tupos,* figure)]

ECU, (*abbr.*) European Currency Unit, official monetary unit of the EEC. It is based on the value of the different currencies used in the European Monetary System.

écu, *n.* a French silver coin of varying value, usu. considered as equivalent to the English crown; the old 5-franc piece. [F, from L *scutum,* a shield]

Ecuador, *n.* Republic of (*República del Ecuador*) country in South America, bounded to the north by Colombia, to the east and south by Peru, and to the west by the Pacific Ocean. **area** 270,670 sq km/104,479 sq miles. **capital** Quito. **towns** Cuenca; chief port Guayaquil. **physical** Andes mountains, divided by a central plateau, or Valley of the Volcanoes, including Chimborazo and Cotopaxi, which has a large share of the cultivable land and is the site of the capital. **population** (1986) 9,640,000; annual growth rate 2.9%. **exports** bananas, cocoa, coffee, sugar, rice, balsa wood, fish. **language** Spanish (official); Quechua, Jivaroan. **religion** Roman Catholic.

ecumenical, *a.* general, universal, world-wide; belonging to the Christian church or Christian world as a whole; pertaining to the ecumenical movement. **ecumenical movement,** *n.* a movement in the Christian church encouraging and promoting unity on issues of belief, worship etc. **ecumenically,** *adv.* **ecumenicism, ecumenism,** *n.* **ecumenics,** *n.sing.* the study of the ecumenical movement. [L *oecumenicus,* from Gr. *oikoumenikos* (*oikoumenē* (*gē*), the inhabited (world)]

eczema, *n.* an inflammatory disease of the skin; a skin disease. **eczematous,** *a.* [Gr., a pustule, from *ekzeein* (*ek,* out, *zeein,* to boil)]

ed., (*abbr.*) edited; edition; editor.

-ed, *suf.* forming the past tense and p.p. of regular verbs; used also (representing OE *-ede*) to form adjectives, as in *cultured, moneyed, talented.* [OE *-ed, -ad, -od*]

edacious, *a.* greedy, voracious, ravenous. **edacity,** *n.* [L *edax edācis,* from *edere,* to eat]

Edam, *n.* a kind of pressed, yellow cheese with a red outer skin. [town in Holland]

edaphic, *a.* relating to the soil. [Gr. *edaphos,* ground]

Edda, *n.* the title of two Icelandic books, the *Elder* or *Poetic Edda* (*c.* 1200), ascribed to Saemund, a collection of ancient poems dealing with the Norse mythology and heroic traditions, and the *Younger* or *Prose Edda,* partly written by Snorri Sturluson (*c.* 1230), a handbook of prosody, grammar and rhetoric for the training of young poets. [Icel.]

Eddery, *n.* **Patrick (Pat)** (1952–), Irish-born flat racing jockey who has won the jockey's championship seven times including four in succession.

eddish, *n.* aftermath, or the crop of grass which grows after mowing; a stubble field. [etym. doubtful]

eddy, *n.* a small whirlpool; a current of air, fog, smoke etc. moving in a circle, whirling. *v.i., v.t.* to whirl in an eddy. **eddy current,** *n.* electrical current circulating in the mass of a conductor caused by a change in the magnetic field. [etym. doubtful]

Eddy, *n.* **Mary Baker** (1821–1910), US founder of the Christian Science movement. Her faith in divine healing was confirmed by her recovery from injuries caused by a fall in 1866, and she based a religious sect on this belief, set out in her pamphlet *Science and Health with Key to the Scriptures* (1875).

Edelman, *n.* **Gerald** (1929–), US biochemist. The structure of the antibody gamma globulin (IgG) was worked out by Rodney Porter by 1962. Edelman tackled the related problem of working out the sequence of 1330 amino acids which composed the antibody. The task was completed by 1969 and won for Edelman a share of the 1972 Nobel Physiology or Medicine Prize with Porter.

edelweiss, *n.* a small white composite plant, *Gnaphalium leontopodium,* growing in rocky places in the Alps. [G *edel,* noble, *weiss,* white]

edema, etc. OEDEMA.

Eden¹, *n.* the region in which Adam and Eve were placed at their creation; a region or abode of perfect bliss; a state of complete happiness. **Edenic,** *a.* [Heb. *'ēden,* pleasure, delight]

Eden², *n.* **Anthony, 1st Earl of Avon** (1897–1977), British Conservative politician, foreign secretary (1935–38, 1940–45, and 1951–55); prime minister (1955–57), when he resigned after the failure of the Anglo-French military intervention in the Suez Crisis.

Eden³, *n.* river in Cumbria, NW England; length 104 km/65 miles. From its source in the Pennines, it flows NW to enter the Solway Firth NW of Carlisle.

edentate, *a.* having no incisor teeth; belonging to the Edentata. **edental,** *a.* edentate. *n.* an edentate animal. **Edentata,** *n.pl.* an order of mammals with no front teeth or no teeth whatsoever, containing the armadillos, sloths and ant-eaters. **edentulous,** *a.* edentate. [L *ēdentātus,* p.p. of *ēdentāre,* to render toothless (E-, *dens dentem,* a tooth)]

edge, *n.* the sharp or cutting part of an instrument, as a sword; the sharpness of this; anything edge-shaped, the crest of a ridge, the line where two surfaces of a solid meet; a boundary-line; the brink, border, margin or extremity of anything; sharpness, keenness, of mind or appetite; acrimony, bitterness. *v.t.* to sharpen, to put an edge on; to make an edge or border to; to be a border to; to incite, to egg on, to instigate; to move or put forward by little and little. *v.i.* to move forward or away by little and little; to move sideways, to sidle (up). **to be on edge,** to be irritable. **to edge out,** to get rid of gradually. **to have the edge on,** to have an advantage over. **to set the teeth on edge,** to cause a tingling or grating sensation in the teeth; to cause a feeling of irritation or revulsion. **edge-bone** AITCH-BONE. **edge-rail,** *n.* a form of rail which bears the rolling stock on its edge; a rail placed by the side of the main rail at a switch. **edge-, edged-tool,** *n.* a general name which includes the heavier varieties of cutting-tools; (*fig.*) anything dangerous to deal or play with. **edgeless,** *a.* **edgeways, -wise,** *adv.* with the edge turned up, or forward in the direction of the edge; sideways. **to get a word in edgeways,** to say something with difficulty because of someone else talking. **edging,** *n.* that which forms the border or edge of anything, as lace, trimming etc. on a dress; a border or row of small plants set along the edge of a bed. **edgy,** *a.* having or showing an edge; (*Art*) too sharply defined; sharp in temper; irritable, nervy. [OE *ecg,* cp. Dut. *egge,* G. *Ecke;* also L *aciēs,* Gr. *akis,* a point)]

Edgehill, Battle of, the first battle of the English Civil War. It took place in 1642, on a ridge in S Warwickshire, between Royalists under Charles I and Parliamentarians under the Earl of Essex. The result was indecisive.

Edgeworth, *n.* **Maria** (1767–1849), Irish novelist. Her first novel, *Castle Rackrent* (1800), dealt with Anglo-Irish country society, and was followed by the similar *The Absentee* (1812) and *Ormond* (1817).

edible, *a.* fit for food, eatable. *n.* anything fit for food; an eatable. **edibility,** *n.* [late L *edibilis,* from *edere,* to eat]

edict, *n.* a proclamation or decree issued by authority. **edictal,** *a.* [L *ēdictum,* neut. p.p. of *ēdīcere (E-, dīcere,* to speak)]

edifice, *n.* a building, esp. one of some size and pretension. †**edificial,** *a.* [F *édifice,* L *aedificium* (*aedes,* a building, *-ficium,* from *facere,* to make)]

edify, *v.t.* †to build, to construct; †to organize, to establish; to build up spiritually; to improve, to instruct; to enlighten. **edification,** *n.* **edificatory,**, *a.* [F *édifier,* L *aedificāre* (as prec.)]

edile AEDILE.

Edinburgh, *n.* capital of Scotland and administrative centre of the region of Lothian, near the S shores of the Firth of Forth; population (1985) 440,000. A cultural centre, it is known for its annual festival of music and the arts; the university was established in 1583. Industries include printing, publishing, banking, insurance, chemical manufactures, distilling, brewing, and some shipbuilding.

Edison, *n.* **Thomas Alva** (1847–1931), US scientist and inventor. Born in Ohio, of Dutch-Scottish parentage, he became first a newsboy and then a telegraph operator. His first invention was an automatic repeater for telegraphic messages. Later came the carbon transmitter (used as a microphone in the production of the Bell telephone); the phonograph; the electric filament lamp; a new type of storage battery; and the kinetoscopic camera, an early film camera. He also anticipated the Fleming thermionic valve. He supported direct current (DC) transmission, but alternating current (AC) was eventually found to be more efficient and economical.

edit, *v.t.* to prepare for publication by compiling, selecting, revising etc.; (*fig.*) to censor, to alter; to conduct or manage, as a periodical, by selecting and revising the literary matter. **edition**, *n.* the form in which a literary work is published; the whole number of copies published at one time. **editio princeps**, *n.* the first printed edition of a book. **edition de luxe**, *n.* a handsomely printed and bound edition of a book. **editor,** *n.* one who prepares the work of others for publication; one who conducts or manages a newspaper or periodical; one who cuts and makes up the shots for the final sequence of a film. **editorial**, *a.* of or pertaining to an editor. *n.* an article written by or proceeding from an editor; a leading article. **editorialize, -ise,** *v.t.*, *v.i.* to introduce personal opinions into reporting. **editorially,** *adv.* **editorship,** *n.* **editress**, *n. fem.* [L *ēditus,* p.p. of *ēdere* (E-, *dare,* to give)]

Edmonton, *n.* capital of Alberta, Canada, on the North Saskatchewan river; population (1986) 785,000. It is the centre of an oil and mining area to the north, and also an agricultural and dairying region. Petroleum pipelines link Edmonton with Superior, Wisconsin, US, and Vancouver, British Columbia.

Edmund, St, *n.* (*c.* 840–870), king of East Anglia from 855. In 870 he was defeated and captured by the Danes at Hoxne, Suffolk, and martyred on refusing to renounce Christianity. He was canonized and his shrine at Bury St Edmunds became a place of pilgrimage.

Edmund Ironside *n.* (*c.* 989–1016), king of England, the son of Ethelred the Unready. He led the resistance to Canute's invasion in 1015, and on Ethelred's death in 1016 was chosen as king by the citizens of London, while the Witan (the king's council) elected Canute. Edmund was defeated by Canute at Assandun (Ashington), Essex, and they divided the kingdom between them.

Edom, *n.* in the Old Testament, a mountainous area of S Palestine, which stretched from the Dead Sea to the Gulf of Aqaba. Its people, supposedly descendants of Esau, were enemies of the Israelites.

educate, *v.t.* to bring up (a child or children); to train and develop the intellectual and moral powers of; to provide with schooling; to train or develop (an organ or a faculty); to train (an animal). **educable**, *a.* **educability**, *n.* **education,** *n.* the process of educating, systematic training and development of the intellectual and moral faculties; instruction; a course of instruction; the result of a systematic course of training and instruction. **educational**, *a.* **educationalist, educationist,** *n.* an advocate of education; one who is versed in educational methods. **educationally,** *adv.* **educative**, *a.* **educator,** *n.* [L *ēducātus,* p.p. of *ēducāre,* rel. to *ēdūcere,* to EDUCE]

educe, *v.t.* to bring out, evolve, develop; to deduce, infer; (*Chem.*) to extract. **educible,** *a.* **educt**, *n.* that which is educed; an inference, a deduction; (*Chem.*) a body separated by the decomposition of another body in which it had previously existed. **eduction**, *n.* the act of educing. **eduction pipe,** *n.* the pipe which carries off the exhaust steam from the cylinder. [L *ēdūcere* (E-, *dūcere,* to lead)]

edulcorate, *v.t.* to sweeten; to remove acidity from; to free from acids, salts or impurities, by washing. **edulcoration,** *n.* **edulcorator,** *n.* one who or that which sweetens or removes acidity; a dropping-tube for applying small quantities of water to test-tubes, watch-glasses etc. [L *ēdulcorātus,* p.p. of *ēdulcorāre* (E-, *dulcor,* sweetness)]

Edward, *n.* **the Black Prince** (1330–76), prince of Wales, eldest son of Edward III of England. The epithet supposedly derived from his black armour. During the Hundred Years' War he fought at the Battle of Crécy in 1346 and captured the French king at Poitiers in 1356. In 1367 he invaded Castile and restored to the throne the deposed king, Pedro the Cruel (1334–69).

Edward, *n.* (full name Edward Antony Richard Louis) (1964–), prince of the UK, third son of Queen Elizabeth II. He is seventh in line to the throne after Charles, Charles' two sons, Andrew, and Andrew's two daughters.

Edward the Elder (*c.* 870–924), king of the West Saxons. He succeeded his father Alfred the Great in 899. He reconquered SE England and the Midlands from the Danes, uniting Wessex and Mercia with the help of his sister, Athelflad. By the time Edward died, his kingdom was the most powerful in the British Isles. He was succeeded by his son Athelstan.

Edward, *n.* ten kings of England or the UK:

Edward the Martyr (*c.* 963–78), king of England from 975. Son of King Edgar, he was murdered at Corfe Castle, Dorset, probably at his stepmother Aelfthryth's instigation (she wished to secure the crown for her son, Ethelred). He was canonized in 1001.

Edward the Confessor (*c.* 1003–66), king of England from 1042, the son of Ethelred II. He lived in Normandy until shortly before his accession. During his reign power was held by Earl Godwin and his son Harold, while the king devoted himself to religion. He was buried in Westminster Abbey, which he had rebuilt. He was canonized in 1161.

Edward I, *n.* (1239–1307), king of England from 1272, son of Henry III. Edward led the royal forces in the Barons' War (1264–67), and was on a crusade when he succeeded to the throne. He established English rule over all Wales (1282–84), and secured recognition of his overlordship from the Scottish king, though the Scots (under Wallace and Bruce) fiercely resisted actual conquest. In his reign Parliament took its approximate modern form with the Model Parliament of 1295. He was succeeded by his son, Edward II.

Edward II, *n.* (1284–1327), king of England from 1307. Son of Edward I and born at Caernarvon Castle, he was created the first prince of Wales in 1301. His invasion of Scotland in 1314 to suppress revolt resulted in defeat at Bannockburn. He was deposed in 1327 by his wife Isabella (1292–1358), daughter of Philip IV of France, and her lover Roger de Mortimer, and murdered in Berkeley Castle, Gloucestershire. He was succeeded by his son, Edward III.

Edward III, *n.* (1312–77), king of England from 1327, son of Edward II. He assumed the government in 1330 from his mother, through whom in 1337 he laid claim to the French throne and thus began the Hundred Years' War. He was succeeded by Richard II.

Edward IV, *n.* (1442–1483), king of England (1461–70) and from 1471. He was the son of Richard, Duke of York, and succeeded Henry VI in the Wars of the Roses, temporarily losing the throne to Henry when Edward fell out with his adviser Warwick but regaining it at the Battle of Barnet. He was succeeded by his son Edward V.

Edward V, *n.* (1470–83), king of England in 1483. Son of Edward IV, he was deposed three months after his accession in favour of his uncle (Richard III), and is traditionally believed to have been murdered (with his brother) in the Tower of London on Richard's orders.

Edward VI, *n.* (1537–53), king of England from 1547, son of Henry VIII and Jane Seymour. The government was entrusted to his uncle the Duke of Somerset (who fell in 1549), and then to the Earl of Warwick, later created Duke of Northumberland. He was succeeded by his sister, Mary I.

Edward VII, *n.* (1841–1910), king of Great Britain and Ireland from 1901. As Prince of Wales he was a prominent social figure, but his mother Queen Victoria considered him too frivolous to take part in political life. In 1860 he made the first tour of Canada and the US ever undertaken by a British prince.

Edward VIII, *n.* (1894–1972), king of Great Britain and Northern Ireland Jan.–Dec. 1936, when he abdicated to marry Wallis Warfield Simpson. He was created duke of Windsor and was governor of the Bahamas (1940–45), subsequently settling in France.

Edwardian, *a.* referring to the periods of any of the kings of England named Edward, but usu. to that of Edward VII (1901–10). **Edwardian prayer-book,** the prayer-book authorized by Edward VI in 1549.

Edwards, *n.* **Blake** (adopted name of William Blake McEdwards) (1922–), US film director and writer, formerly an actor. Specializing in physical comedies, he directed the series of *Pink Panther* films (1963-1978), starring Peter Sellers. His other work includes *Breakfast at Tiffany's* (1961) and *Blind Date* (1986).

ee, *n.* (*pl.* **een**) Scots form of EYE.

-ee, *suf.* denoting the recipient, as in *grantee, legatee, payee, vendee;* or [F *-é,* fem. *-ée*] the direct or indirect object, as in *addressee, employee;* also used arbitrarily, as in *bargee, devotee.* [A-F *-é,* p.p. used as noun (e.g. *apelé,* summoned, corr. to *apelour,* summoner)]

EEC, (*abbr.*) European Economic Community.

EEG, (*abbr.*) electroencephalogram; electroencephalograph.

eel, *n.* a snake-like fish, the genus *Anguilla,* esp. the common European species, *A. anguilla;* an eel-like fish; a slippery person; an eel-worm, as the vinegar-eel. **eel-buck, -pot,** *n.* a basket trap for catching eels. **eel-fare,** *n.* the passage of young eels up streams; a brood of young eels. **eel-fork, -spear,** *n.* a pronged instrument or fork for spearing eels. **eel-grass** GRASS-WRACK. **eel-pout,** *n.* a burbot; a blenny. **eel-worm,** *n.* a minute eel-like worm found in vinegar, sour paste etc. **eely,** *a.* [OE *ael* (cp. Dut. *aal,* G *Aal,* Icel. *āll*)]

een EE.

e'en EVEN[1].

-eer, *suf.* denoting an agent or person concerned with or who deals in, as *charioteer, musketeer, pamphleteer, sonneteer.* [F *-ier,* L *-iārius,* or F *-air,* L *-ārius*]

e'er EVER.

eerie, *a.* causing fear; strange, weird; (*chiefly Sc.*) superstitiously frightened. **eerily,** *adv.* **eeriness,** *n.* [ME *eri,* prob. from OE *earg, earh,* timid, cowardly]

ef-, *pref.* form of EX- used before *f,* as in *efface, effigy.*

efface, *v.t.* to rub out, to wipe out, obliterate; to cast into the shade; make not noticeable; to render negligible. **effaceable,** *a.* **effacement,** *n.* [F *effacer* (EF-, L *facies,* face)]

effect, *n.* the result or product of a cause or operation, the consequence; efficacy, power of producing a required result; accomplishment, fulfilment; purport, aim, purpose; the impression created by a work of art; a combination of colours, forms, sounds, rhythm etc., calculated to produce a definite impression; (*pl.*) goods, movables, personal estate. *v.t.* to produce as a consequence or result; to bring about, to accomplish; †to give effect to. **for effect,** in order to produce a striking impression. **in effect,** in reality, substantially; practically. **of no effect,** without validity or force; without result. **special effects,** the creation of lighting, sounds and other effects for a film, play, TV or radio. **to give effect to,** to carry out; to make operative. **to no effect,** in vain, uselessly. **to take effect,** to operate, to produce its effect. **without effect,** invalid, without result. **effective,** *a.* producing its proper effect; producing a striking impression; fit for duty or service; real, actual. *n.* one who is fit for duty. **effectively,** *adv.* **effectiveness,** *n.* **effectless,** *a.* **effector,** *n.* an organ that effects response to stimulus, e.g. muscle, gland. **effectual,** *a.* productive of an intended effect; adequate, efficacious. **effectuality,** *n.* **effectually,** *adv.* **effectualness,** *n.* **effectuate,** *v.t.* to effect, to bring to pass, to accomplish. **effectuation,** *n.* [OF *effect,* L *effectus,* p.p. of *efficere* (EF-, *facere,* to make)]

effeminate, *a.* womanish; unmanly, weak. **effeminacy,** *n.* **effeminately,** *adv.* [L *effēminātus, p.p.* of *effēmināre* (EF-, *fēmina,* woman)]

Effendi, *n.* (*formerly*) master, as a title of respect, bestowed on civil dignitaries and learned men. [Turk. *efendī,* sir, lord (corr. of Gr. *authentēs*)]

efferent, *a.* (*Physiol.*) conveying outwards; discharging. *n.* an efferent vessel or nerve; a stream carrying off water from a lake etc. [L *efferens -ntem,* pres.p. of *efferre* (EF-, *ferre,* to carry)]

effervesce, *v.i.* to bubble up, from the escape of gas, as fermenting liquors; to escape in bubbles; to boil over with excitement. **effervescence,** *n.* **effervescent,** *a.* [L *effervescere* (EF-, *fervescere,* incept. of *fervēre,* to boil)]

effete, *a.* worn out or exhausted; having lost all vigour and efficiency; decadent; sterile, barren. **effeteness,** *n.* [L *effētus,* weakened by bringing forth young (EF-, *fētus,* FOETUS)]

efficacious, *a.* producing or having power to produce the effect intended. **efficaciously,** *adv.* **efficaciousness,** *n.* **efficacy,** *n.* [L *efficax -ācis,* from *efficere,* to EFFECT]

efficient, *a.* causing or producing effects or results; competent, capable. *n.* †an efficient agent or cause. **efficiency,** *n.* adequate fitness; power to produce a desired result; (*Eng.*) the ratio of the output of energy to the input of energy. **efficiently,** *adv.* [F, from L *efficiens -ntem,* pres.p. of *efficere,* to EFFECT]

effigy, †effigies, *n.* the representation or likeness of a person, as on coins, medals etc. **to burn** or **hang in effigy,** to burn or hang an image of, to show hatred, dislike or contempt. [L *effigiēs* (EF-, *fingere,* to fashion)]

effloresce, *v.i.* to burst into flower, to blossom; (*Chem.*) to crumble to powder through loss of water or crystallization on exposure to the air; of salts, to form crystals on the surface; of a surface, to become covered with saline particles; (*fig.*) to blossom forth. **efflorescence,** *n.* **efflorescent,** *a.* [L *efflōrescere,* incept. of *efflōrēre,* to blossom (EF-, *flōrēre,* to blossom, from *flōs flōris,* a flower)]

effluent, *a.* flowing or issuing out; emanating. *n.* a river or stream which flows out of another or out of a lake; the liquid that is discharged from a sewage tank. **effluence,** *n.* the act or state of flowing out; that which flows out, an emanation. [L *effluens -ntem,* pres.p. of *effluere* (EF-, *fluere,* to FLOW)]

effluvium, *n.* (*pl.* **-via**) an emanation affecting the sense of smell, esp. a disagreeable smell and vapour as from putrefying substances etc. [late L, as prec.]

efflux, *n.* the act of flowing out or issuing; outflow, effusion; an emanation, that which flows out; a passing away, lapse, expiry. **effluxion,** *n.* [L *effluxus,* as prec.]

effort, *n.* an exertion of physical or mental power, a strenuous attempt, an endeavour; a display of power, an achievement. **effortful,** *a.* **effortless,** *a.* **effortlessness,** *n.* [F, from OF *esforcier,* to force, from L *ex,* out, *fortis,* strong]

effrontery, *n.* impudence, shamelessness, insolence. [F *effronterie,* from *effronté,* shameless (EF-, *frons, -ntis,* forehead)]

effulge, *v.i.* (*poet.*) to shine forth; to become famous or illustrious. **effulgence,** *n.* **effulgent,** *a.* shining brightly; diffusing radiance. **effulgently,** *adv.* [L *effulgēre* (EF-, *fulgēre,* to shine)]

effuse, *v.t.* to pour out, to emit; to diffuse. *a.,* (*Bot.*) spreading loosely (of an inflorescence); of a shell, having the lips separated by a groove. †*n.* effusion, outpouring. **effusion,** *n.* the act of pouring out; that which is poured out; a shedding, as of blood; (*contemptuously*) an outpouring of genius or emotion; frank expression of feeling, effusiveness; the escape of any fluid out of the proper part of the body into another. **effusive,** *a.* gushing, exuberant, demonstrative. **effusively,** *adv.* **effusiveness,** *n.* [L *effūsus,* p.p. of *effundere* (EF-, *fundere,* to pour)]

E-fit, *n.* (*acronym*) *e*lectronic *f*acial *i*dentification *t*echnique, a computerized form of photofit with a wide range of possible facial features, usu. used in helping police and witnesses build up a picture of suspects.

EFL, (*abbr.*) English as a foreign language.

eft, *n.* the common newt. [OE *efete* (etym. doubtful)]

EFTA, (*acronym*) European Free Trade Association.

EFTPOS, eftpos, (*acronym*) electronic funds transfer at point of sale, debiting of a bank account directly at the time of purchase. For example, a bank customer inserts a plastic card in a point-of-sale computer terminal in a supermarket, and telephone lines are used to make an automatic debit from the customer's bank account to settle the bill. See also CREDIT CARD under CREDIT.

EFTS, (*abbr.*) electronic funds transfer system.

eftsoon, -s, *adv.* soon after, speedily, forthwith; †presently, by and by. [OE *eftsōna,* again (AFT, SOON)]

e.g., (*abbr.*) for example. [L *exempli gratia*]

egad, *int.* by God (a minced oath). [prob. *a,* AH, GOD]

egalitarian, *a.* believing in the principle of human equality. *n.* **egality,** *n.*

egence, *n.* the state of being needy. [L *egens -ntem,* pres.p. of *egēre,* to be in need]

†eger EAGRE.

Egerton, *n.* family name of Dukes of Sutherland; seated at Mertoun, Roxburghshire, Scotland.

egest, *v.t.* to eject; to void as excrement. **egesta,** *n.* thrown out; excreta. **egestion,** *n.* waste matter. [L *ēgestus,* p.p. of *ēgerere* (E-, *gerere,* to carry)]

egg[1], *n.* the ovum of birds, reptiles, fishes and many of the invertebrates, usually enclosed in a spheroidal shell, and containing the embryo of a new individual; the egg of a bird, esp. of domestic poultry, largely used as food; an ovum or germ-cell; the early stage of anything; the germ, the origin. *v.t.* (*N Am.*) to pelt with rotten eggs. *v.i.* to collect eggs. **bad egg,** (*coll.*) a worthless person; a bad or risky speculation. **egg and anchor, dart, tongue,** (*Arch.*) various kinds of moulding carved alternately with egg-shapes and anchors etc. **egg and spoon race,** a race in which the runners carry eggs in spoons. **good egg!** *int.* (*sl.*) excellent! **egg-bird,** *n.* a sea-bird, the eggs of which are collected for food etc., esp. a W Indian tern, *Hydrochelidon fuliginosum.* **egg-bound,** *a.* term applied to the oviduct of birds when obstructed by an egg. **egg-cleavage,** *n.* the first process of germination, in which the fertilized cell of the ovum becomes divided. **egg-cosy** COSY. **egg-cup,** *n.* a cup-shaped vessel used to hold an egg at table. **egg-dance,** *n.* a dance by a blindfold person among eggs; (*fig.*) a task of extreme intricacy. **egg-flip, -nog,** *n.* a drink compounded of eggs beaten up, sugar, and beer, cider, wine or spirits. **egg-head,** *n.* (*coll.*) an intellectual. **egg-plant,** *n.* popular name for the *Solanum esculentum,* or aubergine, an edible plant of the nightshade family. **egg-shape,** *n.* an egg-shaped object. **egg-shaped,** *a.* having the form of an egg, oval, esp. with one end smaller than the other. **egg-shell,** *n.* the calcareous envelope in which an egg is enclosed. **egg-shell china,** very thin porcelain. **egg-shell paint,** paint with a slightly glossy finish. **egg-slice,** *n.* a kitchen utensil for removing eggs, omelets etc. from the pan. **egg-spoon,** *n.* a small spoon used for eating eggs. **egg-tooth,** *n.* a hard point or knob on the bill-sheath or snout of an embryo bird or reptile, for cracking the containing shell. **egg-whisk,** *n.* a kind of wire utensil used for beating up eggs. **egger,** *n.* one who gathers eggs. **egger-, eggar-moth,** *n.* various British moths of the genera *Lasiocampa* and *Ereogaster.* [ON *egg* (cp. OE *æg,* Dan. *oeg,* Dut. *ei,* G. *Ei*)]

egg[2], *v.t.* (*usu. with* **on**) to incite, to urge. [Icel. *eggja,* to EDGE]

egis AEGIS.

eglandulose, eglandular, *a.* (*Bot.*) without glands.

eglantine, *n.* the sweet brier. [F *églantine,* from OF *aiglant,* prob. from L *acus,* needle, *-lentus,* -LENT]

Egmont, *n.* **Lamoral, Count of Egmont** (1522–68), Flemish nobleman, born in Hainault. As a servant of the Spanish crown, he defeated the French at St Quentin in 1557 and Gravelines in 1558, and became stadholder (chief magistrate) of Flanders and Artois. From 1561 he helped to lead the movement against Spanish misrule, but in 1567 the Duke of Alva was sent to crush the Resistance, and Egmont was beheaded.

ego, *n.* individuality, personality; the self-conscious subject, as contrasted with the non-ego, or object; (*Psych.*) the conscious self, which resists on the one hand the threats of the super-ego, and on the other the impulses of the id. **ego-altruistic,** *a.* (*Phil.*) a term introduced by Herbert Spencer to denote sentiments which, while they imply self-gratification, also imply gratification in others. **egocentric,** *a.* self-centred. **egocentricity,** *n.* **egomania,** *n.* excessive or pathological egotism. **ego trip,** *n.* (*coll.*) an action or experience which adds to a person's self-important feelings. **egoism,** *n.* the theory that man's chief good is the complete development and happiness of self, and that this is the proper basis of morality; pure self-interest, systematic selfishness; the doctrine that man can be absolutely certain of nothing but his own existence and the operations of his own mind; egotism. **egoist,** *n.* **egoistic, -ical,** *a.* **egoistically,** *adv.* **egotism,** *n.* the habit of too frequently using the word I in writing or speaking; hence a too frequent mention of oneself in writing or conversation; self-glorification, self-conceit. **egotist,** *n.* **egotistic, -ical,** *a.* **egotistically,** *adv.* **egotize, -tise,** *v.i.* [L, I]

egregious, *a.* extraordinary, out of the common, remarkable, exceptional; notable, notorious; conspicuously bad, flagrant. **egregiously,** *adv.* **egregiousness,** *n.* [L *ēgregius* (E-, *grex gregis,* flock)]

egress, *n.* the act or power of going out; departure; a means or place of exit; (*Astron.*) the end of a transit or eclipse. **egression,** *n.* [L *ēgressus,* p.p. of *ēgredī* (E-, *gradī,* to go)]

egret, *n.* a heron, esp. the lesser white heron, of those species that have long and loose plumage over the back; the feathery or hairy down of seeds; an aigrette. [OF *egrette, aigrette,* AIGRETTE]

Egypt, *n.* Arab Republic of (*Jumhuriyat Misr al-Arabiya*), country in NE Africa, bounded to the north by the Mediterranean, to the east by the Suez Canal and Red Sea, to the south by Sudan, and to the west by Libya. **area** 1,002,000 sq km/386,772 sq miles. **capital** Cairo. **towns** Gîza; ports Alexandria, Port Said. **physical** mostly desert; hills in E; fertile land along river Nile; the cultivated and settled area is about 35,500 sq km/13,700 sq miles. **population** (1987) 49,280,000; annual growth rate 2.4%. **exports** cotton and textiles. **language** Arabic (ancient Egyptian survives to some extent in Coptic). **religion** Sunni Muslim 95%, Coptic Christian 5%.

Egyptian, *a.* of or pertaining to Egypt or the Egyptians. *n.* a native of Egypt; †a gipsy; (*Print.*) type with thick stems. **Egyptian lotus,** *n. Nymphaea lotus.* **Egyptian pebble, jasper,** *n.* a variety of jasper with zones of brown and yellow, found between Cairo and Suez. **Egyptian thorn,** *n.* the tree *Acacia vera,* which yields gum-arabic. **Egyptology,** *n.* see separate entry. **Egyptological,** *a.* **Egyptologist,** *n.*

Egyptian religion, *n.* the worship of totemic animals believed to be the ancestors of the clan. Totems later developed into gods, represented as having animal heads. The cult of Osiris was important. Immortality, conferred by the magical rite of mummification, was originally the sole prerogative of the king, but was extended under the New Kingdom to all who could afford it; they were buried with the Book of the Dead.

Egyptology, *n.* the study of ancient Egypt. Interest in the subject was aroused by the discovery of the Rosetta Stone in 1799. Excavations continued throughout the 19th century, and gradually assumed a more scientific character, largely as a result of the work of Sir Flinders Petrie from 1880 onwards and the formation of the Egyptian Exploration Fund in 1892. In 1922 the British archaeologist Howard Carter discovered the tomb of Tutankhamen, the only royal tomb with all its treasures intact.

eh, *int.* an exclamation expressive of doubt, inquiry, surprise etc. [ME *ey,* OE *ēa*]

Ehrlich, *n.* **Paul** (1854–1915), German bacteriologist and immunologist, who developed the first cure for syphilis. He developed the arsenic compounds, in particular salvarsan, used in the treatment of syphilis before the discovery of antibiotics. He shared the

Nobel prize in 1908.

Eichendorff, *n.* **Joseph Freiherr von** (1788–1857), German lyric poet and romantic novelist, born in Upper Silesia. His work was set to music by Schumann, Mendelssohn, and Wolf. He held various judicial posts.

Eichmann, *n.* **(Karl) Adolf** (1906–62), Austrian Nazi. As an SS official during Hitler's regime he was responsible for atrocities against Jews and others, including the implementation of genocide. He managed to escape at the fall of Germany in 1945, but was discovered in Argentina in 1960, abducted by Israeli agents, tried in Israel in 1961, and executed.

eident, *a.* (*Sc.*) diligent, attentive. [prob. from ME *ithen,* cp. Icel. *ithinn*]

eider, *n.* a large Arctic sea-duck, *Somateria mollissima.* **eiderdown,** *n.* the soft and elastic down from the breast of this bird; a quilt filled with eiderdown. [Icel. *æthar,* gen. of *æthr,* an eider duck (as in *æthar-dūn,* eiderdown)]

eidetic, *a.* able to reproduce a vivid image of something previously seen or imagined. [Gr. *eidētikos,* belonging to an image, from *eidos,* form]

eidograph, *n.* an instrument for copying plans or drawings on an enlarged or reduced scale. [Gr. *eidos,* form]

eidolon, *n.* an image, likeness or representation; an apparition, a spectre. [Gr., see IDOL]

Eiffel, *n.* **Gustave Alexandre** (1832–1923), French engineer who constructed the Eiffel Tower for the 1889 Paris exhibition.

Eiffel Tower, *n.* iron tower 320 m/1050 ft high, designed by Gustave Eiffel for the Paris Exhibition of 1889. It stands in the Champ de Mars, Paris.

eight, *n.* the number or figure 8 or VIII; the age of eight; a set of eight things or people; (*Rowing*) a crew of eight in a boat; (*Skating*) a curved outline resembling the figure 8; articles of attire such as shoes etc. denoted by the number 8; a card with eight pips; a score of eight points; the eighth hour after midday or midnight. *a.* consisting of one more than seven. **one over the eight,** (*coll.*) slightly drunk. **eight-day,** *a.* (of clocks) going for eight days. **eight-fold,** *a.* **eighth,**, *n.* one of eight equal parts; (*Mus.*) the interval of an octave. *n., a.* (the) last of eight (people, things etc.); the next after the seventh. **eighthly,** *adv.* **eightsome,** *n.* a form of Scottish reel for eight dancers. [OE *eahta* (cp. Dut. and G *acht,* L *octo,* Gr. *oktō,* Gael. *ochd,* Sansk. *ashtau*)]

eighteen, *n.* the number or figure 18 or XVIII; the age of 18. *a.* 18 in number; aged 18. **eighteen-mo,** *n.* (*coll.*) an octodecimo, a book whose sheets are folded to form 18 leaves, written 18mo. **eighteenth,** *n.* one of 18 equal parts. *n., a.* (the) last of 18 (people, things etc.); (the) next after the 17th. [OE *eahtatȳne*]

eighty, *n.* the number or figure 80 or LXXX; the age of 80. *a.* 80 in number; aged 80. **eighties,** *n.pl.* the period of time between one's 80th and 90th birthdays; the range of temperature between 80 and 90 degrees; the period of time between the 80th and 90th years of a century. **eightieth,** *n.* one of 80 equal parts. *n., a.* (the) last of 80 equal parts; the next after the 79th. [OE *eahtatig*]

eikon ICON.

eild, *a.* (*Sc.*) not yielding milk. [prob. a var. of YELD]

†**eine** *pl.* EYE.

Einstein, *n.* **Albert** (1879–1955), German-Swiss physicist, who formulated the theories of relativity, and did important work in radiation physics and thermodynamics. In 1905 he published the special theory of relativity, and in 1915 issued his general theory of relativity. His latest conception of the basic laws governing the universe was outlined in his unified field theory, made public in 1953; and of the 'relativistic theory of the non-symmetric field', completed by 1955. Einstein wrote that this simplified the derivations as well as the form of the field equations and made the whole theory thereby more transparent, without changing its content.

einsteinium, *n.* a radioactive element, at. no. 99; chem. symbol Es; artificially produced from plutonium and named after Albert *Einstein.*

Einthoven, *n.* **Willem** (1860–1927), Dutch physiologist and inventor of the electrocardiograph. He was able to show that particular disorders of the heart alter its electrical activity in characteristic ways.

Eire, *n.* Gaelic name for the Republic of Ireland.

eirenicon, *n.* a measure or proposal intended to make or restore peace. [Gr. *eirēnikon,* neut. of *eirēnikos,* from *eirēnē,* peace]

Eisai, *n.* (1141–1215), Japanese Buddhist monk who introduced Zen and tea from China to Japan and founded the Rinzai school.

Eisenhower, *n.* **Dwight D(avid) ('Ike')** (1890–1969), 34th president of the US (1953–60), a Republican. A general in World War II, he commanded the Allied forces in Italy in 1943, then the Allied invasion of Europe, and from Oct. 1944 all the Allied armies in the West. As president he promoted business interests at home and conducted the Cold War abroad. His vice president was Richard Nixon.

Eisenstein, *n.* **Sergei Mikhailovich** (1898–1948), Latvian film director. He pioneered the use of montage (a technique of deliberately juxtaposing shots to create a particular meaning) as a means of propaganda, as in *The Battleship Potemkin* (1925). His *Alexander Nevsky* (1938) was the first part of an uncompleted trilogy, the second part, *Ivan the Terrible* (1944), being banned in Russia.

eisteddfod, *n.* (*Welsh*) a competitive congress of bards and musicians held annually to encourage native poetry and music. [W, a sitting, from *eistedd,* to sit]

either, *a., pron.* one or the other of two; each of two. *a., adv.* or *conj.* in one or the other case (as a disjunctive correlative); any more than the other (with neg. or interrog., as *If you don't I don't either*). [OE *ægther,* contr. of *æghwæther* (*ā,* aye, *ge-,* pref., *hwæther,* WHETHER)]

ejaculate, *v.t.* to utter suddenly and briefly; to exclaim; to eject. *v.i.* to utter ejaculations; to emit semen. **ejaculation,** *n.* an abrupt exclamation; emission of seminal fluid. **ejaculative,** *a.* **ejaculatory,** *a.* [L *ējaculātus,* p.p. of *ējaculārī* (E-, *jaculārī,* to cast, from *jaculum,* a dart, as foll.)]

eject[1], *v.t.* to discharge, to emit; to drive away, to expel; (*Law*) to oust or dispossess. **ejection,** *n.* **ejective,** *a.* tending to eject; pertaining to an eject. **ejectment,** *n.* the act of casting out or expelling; ejection, expulsion; dispossession; (*Law*) an action to recover possession. **ejector,** *n.* one who ejects, drives out, or dispossesses; an appliance by which a jet of elastic fluid, such as steam or air, is made to exhaust a fluid of the same or a different kind; a contrivance for removing a spent cartridge from a breech-loading gun. **ejector seat,** *n.* a seat that can be shot clear of the vehicle in an emergency. [L *ējectus,* p.p. of *ējicere* (E-, *jacere,* to throw)]

eject[2], *n.* (*Psych.*) something that is not an object of our own consciousness but inferred to have actual existence. [as prec.]

eke[1], *v.t.* to make up for or supply deficiencies in (with *out*); (*coll.*) to produce, support or maintain with difficulty. [OE *īecan* (cp. Goth. *aukan,* L *augēre*)]

†**eke**[2], *adv.* also, besides, likewise. [OE *ēac,* cogn. with prec.]

el[1], *n.* the 12th letter of the alphabet, L, l; anything shaped like the capital form of this letter.

el[2], *n.* (*US*) an *E*levated railway.

-el -LE.

El Aaiún, *n.* Arabic name of La'Youn.

elaborate, *a.* carefully or highly wrought; highly finished. *v.t.,* to produce by labour; to develop in detail; to work up and produce from its orig. material (as the food of animals or plants, so to adapt it for nutrition). **elaborately,** *adv.* **elaborateness,** *n.* **elaboration,** *n.* **elaborative,** *a.* [L *ēlabōrātus,* p.p. of *ēlabōrāre* (E-, *labōrāre,* to work (*labor,* LABOUR))]

elaeo-, *comb. form.* relating to oil. **elaeometer,** *n.* an instrument for determining the specific gravity and hence the purity of oils. [Gr. *elaion,* olive-oil]

élan, *n.* ardour; dash. [F, prob. from foll.]

eland, *n.* a large ox-like antelope, *Oreas canna,* from S Africa. [Dut., an elk (cp. W *elain,* a hind)]

elapse, *v.i.* to glide or pass away. [L *ēlapsus,* p.p. of *ēlābī* (E-, *lābī,* to glide)]

elasmobranch, *n.* one of a class of fishes, the Elasmobranchii, having plate-like gills, containing the sharks, rays and chimeras. **elasmobranchiate,** *a.* [Gr. *elasmos,* a metal plate, *branchia,* gills]

elastic, *a.* having the quality of returning to that form or volume from which it has been compressed, expanded or distorted; springy, rebounding; flexible, adaptable; admitting of extension; readily recovering from depression or exhaustion, buoyant. *n.* a strip of elastic substance, a string or cord woven with india-rubber threads. **elastic band,** *n.* a rubber band for holding things together. **elastic bitumen, pitch,** *n.* elaterite. **elastic tissue,** *n.* yellow fibrous tissue occurring in the ligaments of the vertebrae, the jaw etc. **elastically,** *adv.* **elasticin, elastin,** *n.* (*Chem.*) the substance forming the fibres of elastic tissue. **elasticity,** *n.* **elasticize, -ise,** *v.t.* to make elastic. [Gr. *elastikos,* propulsive, from *ela-,* stem of *elaunein,* to drive]

Elastoplast®, *n.* gauze surgical dressing on a backing of adhesive tape, suitable for small wounds, cuts and abrasions; (**elastoplast;** *fig.*) a temporary measure used in an emergency etc.

elate, *v.t.* to raise the spirits of, to stimulate; to make exultant; †to raise, to elevate. *a.* lifted up, in high spirits, exultant. **elation,** *n.* [L *ēlātus* (E-, *lātus,* p.p. of *ferre,* to bear, to raise)]

Elater, *n.* a genus of coleopterous insects, called click-beetles or skip-jacks, from their ability to spring up and alight on their feet; (*Bot.*) an elastic spiral filament attached to spores. [ELASTIC]

elaterin ELATERIUM.

elaterite, *n.* a soft elastic mineral, elastic bitumen.

elaterium, *n.* a powerful purgative obtained from the fruit of the squirting cucumber. **elaterin,** *n.* the active principle of elaterium. [L, from Gr. *elatērios,* driving away; see ELASTIC]

Elbe, *n.* one of the principal rivers of Germany, 1166 km/725 miles long, rising on the S slopes of the Riesengebirge, Czechoslovakia, and flowing NW across the German plain to the North Sea.

elbow, *n.* the joint uniting the forearm with the upper arm; an elbow-shaped (usu. obtuse) angle, bend or corner. *v.t.* to push or thrust with the elbows, to jostle; to force (a way or oneself into, out of etc.) by pushing with the elbows. *v.i.* to make one's way by pushing with the elbows; to jostle; to go out of one's way; to zig-zag. **at one's elbow,** near at hand. **more power to your elbow** POWER. **out at elbows,** shabby in dress; in needy circumstances. **to crook** or **lift the elbow,** to drink. **to jog the elbow,** to give a reminder. **up to the elbows,** deeply engaged in business. **elbow-chair,** *n.* an armchair. **elbow-grease,** *n.* hard and continued manual exercise. **elbow-pipe,** *n.* a pipe with an end resembling an elbow. **elbow-room,** *n.* ample room for action. [OE *elboga, elnboga* (*eln,* ELL, *boga,* BOW[1])]

Elbruz, Elbrus *n.* highest mountain, 5642 m/18,517 ft, on the continent of Europe, in the Caucasus, Georgian Republic, USSR.

†eld, *n.* old age; an old man; people of old times; former ages; antiquity. *a.* old; former. *v.t.* to make old or aged. [OE *ield, ieldo,* from *eald,* OLD]

elder[1], *a.* older; senior in position; pertaining to former times; in card-playing, having the right to play first. *n.* a senior in years; one whose age entitles him to respect; (*pl.*) persons of greater age; a member of a senate, a counsellor; an officer in the Jewish synagogue, in the early Christian, and in the Presbyterian and other churches. **Elder Brethren,** *n.pl.* the masters of Trinity House, London. **Elder Statesman,** *n.* one of the confidential advisers of the Emperor of Japan, *genro;* a retired and respected politician or administrator. **elderly,** *a.* bordering on old age. **eldership,** *n.*

eldest, *a.* oldest; first born of those surviving; †of earliest date, of longest standing. [OE *ieldra,* comp. of *eald,* OLD]

elder[2], *n.* a tree of the genus *Sambucus,* esp. *S. nigra,* the common elder, a small tree bearing white flowers and dark purple berries. **elderberry,** *n.* another name for the elder tree; the fruit of the elder tree. **elder-gun,** *n.* a pop-gun made of the hollow stem of the elder. **elder-wine,** *n.* a wine made from elderberries and elder-flowers. [OE *ellen, ellern*]

Eldon, *n.* **John Scott, 1st Earl of Eldon** (1751–1838), English politician, born in Newcastle. He became a Member of Parliament in 1782, solicitor-general in 1788, attorney-general in 1793, and Lord Chancellor from 1801–05 and 1807–27. During his period the rules of the Lord Chancellor's court on the use of the injunction and precedent in equity finally became fixed.

El Dorado, Eldorado, *n.* an imaginary land of gold in S America, between the Orinoco and Amazon; any place where money or profit is easily obtained; an inexhaustible mine. [Sp., the gilded]

eldritch, *n.* (*Sc.*) strange, weird, ghastly, frightful. [etym. doubtful]

Eleanor of Aquitaine, *n.* (*c.* 1122–1204), queen of France (1137–51) and of England from 1154. She was the daughter of William X, Duke of Aquitaine, and was married (1137–52) to Louis VII of France, but the marriage was annulled. The same year she married Henry of Anjou, king of England from 1154. Henry imprisoned her (1174–89) for supporting their sons, the future Richard I and King John, against him.

Eleanor of Castile, *n.* (*c.* 1245–90), queen of Edward I of England, the daughter of Ferdinand III of Castile. She married Prince Edward in 1254, and accompanied him on his crusade of 1270. She died at Harby, Nottinghamshire, and Edward erected stone crosses in towns where her body rested on the funeral journey to London. Several Eleanor Crosses are still standing.

Eleatic, *a.* pertaining to Elea, a town of Magna Graecia; relating to the school of philosophy founded by Xenophanes at Elea. *n.* a follower of the philosophy of Xenophanes, Parmenides and Zeno. **Eleaticism,** *n.* [L *Eleāticus*]

elecampane, *n.* a composite plant, *Inula helenium;* the candied root-sticks of this used as a sweetmeat. [F *enule-campane,* L *inula campāna* (*enule,* assim. to OE *eolone, elene,* a perversion of L *inula, elecampane; campāna,* either growing in the fields or Campanian)]

elect, *a.* chosen, picked out; (*placed after the noun*) designated to an office, but not yet in possession of it, as in *president elect;* chosen by God for everlasting life. *v.t.* to choose for any office or employment; to choose to vote; to choose to everlasting life; to determine on any particular course of action; †to pick out. **the elect,** those chosen by God etc.; highly select or self-satisfied people. **election,** *n.* the act of choosing out of a number, esp. by vote; the ceremony or process of electing; power of choosing or selection; (*Theol.*) the selection of certain individuals from mankind to be eternally saved (the characteristic doctrine of Calvinism). **by-election** BY. **general election,** an election of members of Parliament in all constituencies in the United Kingdom. **electioneer,** *v.i.* to work at an election in the interests of some particular candidate. **elective,** *a.* appointed, filled up or bestowed by election; pertaining to election or choice; having or exercising the power of choice. **electively,** *adv.* **elector,** *n.* one who has the right, power or privilege of electing; (*Hist.*) one of the princes of Germany who were entitled to vote in the election of the Emperor. **electoral,** *a.* **electoral college,** *n.* in the US the body of people who elect the President and the Vice-President, having been themselves elected by vote. **electorate,** *n.* electorship; the whole body of electors; (*Hist.*) the dignity or territory of an elector of the German Empire. **electorship,** *n.* **electress,** *n. fem.* a female elector; (*Hist.*) the wife of a German elector. [L *ēlectus,* p.p. of *ēligere* (E-, *legere,* to choose)]

Electra, *n.* in ancient Greek legend, the daughter of

Clytemnestra and Agamemnon, king of Mycenae, and sister of Iphigenia and Orestes. Her story is the subject of two plays of the 5th century BC by Sophocles and Euripides.

Electra complex, *n.* (*Psych.*) attraction of a daughter for her father accompanied by hostility to her mother.

electric, *a.* containing, generating or operated by electricity; resembling electricity, magnetic, spirited. *n.* a non-conductor, in which electricity can be excited by means of friction. **electric battery** BATTERY. **electric bell,** *n.* a bell in which the hammer is operated electrically by means of a solenoid. **electric blanket,** *n.* a blanket containing an electrically-heated element. **electric blue,** *n.* a steely blue. **electric cable,** *n.* an insulated wire or flexible conductor for conveying a current. **electric chair,** *n.* a chair in which persons condemned to death are electrocuted. **electric charge,** *n.* the accumulation of electric energy in an electric battery. **electric circuit,** *n.* the passage of electricity from a body in one electric state to a body in another by means of a conductor; the conductor. **electric clock,** *n.* a clock worked by electricity, esp. one operated by a synchronous motor working off AC mains. **electric cooker,** *n.* an assembly of electrically-heated boiling-plates, grill and oven for commercial or domestic cooking. **electric current,** *n.* continuous transition of electricity from one place to another. **electric eel,** *n.* a large S American eel, *Gymnotus electricus,* able to give an electric shock. **electric eye,** *n.* a photocell; a miniature cathode-ray tube. **electric fence,** *n.* a wire fence charged with electricity, used for purposes of security. **electric field,** *n.* a region in which forces are exerted on any electric charge present in the region. **electric fire, heater, radiator,** *n.* apparatus which uses electricity to heat a room. **electric furnace,** *n.* a furnace used for industrial purposes heated by electricity. **electric guitar,** *n.* an electrically amplified guitar. **electric hare,** *n.* an artificial hare made to run by electricity, used in greyhound racing. **electric jar,** *n.* a Leyden jar. **electric light,** *n.* a light produced by the passage of an electric current. **electric locomotive,** *n.* a locomotive in which the power is derived from a battery, a generator or a contact wire or rail. **electric railway,** *n.* a system employing electricity to drive trains. **electric ray,** *n.* a flat-fish of the genus *Torpedo.* **electric razor, shaver,** *n.* an appliance for removing bristles, hair etc. by the rapid movement of a protected blade actuated by electricity. **electric shock,** *n.* the sudden pain felt from the passing of an electric current through the body. **electric storm,** *n.* a disturbance of electric conditions of the atmosphere. **electric strength,** *n.* the maximum electric field strength that can be applied to an insulator without causing breakdown. **electrical,** *a.* relating to electricity; electric. **electrically,** *adv.* **electrician,** *n.* one skilled in the science and application of electricity. **electricity,** *n.* a powerful physical agent which makes its existence manifest by attractions and repulsions, by producing light and heat, chemical decomposition and other phenomena; the science of the laws and phenomena of this physical agent. **electrify,** *v.t.* to charge with electricity; to give an electric shock to; (*fig.*) to thrill with joy, surprise or other exciting emotion. **electrification,** *n.* the act or process of electrifying; the state of being electrified; conversion of a steam or other mechanical system into one worked by electricity. **electrize, -ise,** *v.t.* to electrify. **electrization, -isation,** *n.* [L *ēlectrum,* Gr. *ēlektron,* amber, conn. with *ēlektōr,* shining]

electro, *n.* an electrotype; electroplate.

electro-, *comb. form.* having electricity for its motive power; resulting from, or pertaining to, electricity. **electrobath,** *n.* a solution of a metallic salt used in electrotyping and electroplating. **electrobiology,** *n.* electrophysiology, the science of the electric phenomena of living organisms. **electrobiologist,** *n.* **electrocardiograph,** *n.* an instrument which indicates and records the manner in which the heart muscle is contracting. **electrocardiogram,** *n.* a record so produced. **electrochemistry,** *n.* the science of the chemical effects produced by electricity. **electrochemical,** *a.* **electroconvulsive therapy,** *n.* the treatment of mental or nervous disorders by the use of electric shocks. **electrocopper,** *v.t.* to give copper coating by electrolysis. **electroculture,** *n.* the application of electricity to tillage. **electrodynamics,** *n.* the science of electricity in motion. **electrodynamic,** *a.* **electrodynamometer,** *n.* an instrument for measuring the strength of an electric current. **electroencephalograph,** *n.* an instrument recording small electrical impulses produced by the brain. **electroencephalography,** *n.* **electroengraving,** *n.* engraving by means of electricity. **electrokinetics,** *n.* electrodynamics. **electromagnet,** *n.* a bar of soft iron rendered magnetic by the passage of a current of electricity through a coil of wire surrounding it. **electromagnetic,** *a.* **electromagnetism,** *n.* magnetism produced by an electric current; the science which treats of the production of magnetism by electricity, and the relations between magnetism and electricity. **electrometallurgy,** *n.* the act of separating metals from their alloys by means of electrolysis. **electromotion,** *n.* the passage of an electric current in a circuit; mechanical motion produced by means of electricity. **electromotive,** *a.* **electromotor,** *n.* a machine for converting electric into mechanical energy. **electromuscular,** *a.* pertaining to the action of the muscles under electric influence. **electronegative,** *a.* passing to the positive pole in electrolysis; pertaining to or producing negative electricity. *n.* an electronegative element. **electroplate,** *v.t.* to cover with a coating of silver or other metal by exposure in a solution of a metallic salt, which is decomposed by electrolysis. *n.* articles so produced. **electropolar,** *a.* denoting a conductor positively electrified at one end and negatively at the other. **electropositive,** *a.* having a tendency to pass to the negative pole in electricity; pertaining to or producing positive electricity. *n.* an electropositive element. **electrostatics,** *n.* the science of static electricity. **electrostatic,** *a.* pertaining to electrostatics; produced by electricity at rest. **electrotherapeutics,** *n.* electropathy, also called **electrotherapy**. **electrothermancy,** *n.* the science of the relations of electric currents and the temperature of bodies. **electrothermic,** *a.* [Gr. *ēlektron,* amber]

electrocute, *v.t.* to kill by an electric shock; to carry out a judicial sentence of death by administering a powerful electric shock. **electrocution,** *n.*

electrode, *n.* one of the poles of a galvanic battery, or of an electrical device; an anode, cathode, grid, collector, base etc.

electrograph, *n.* the record of an electrometer.

electrolier, *n.* a pendant or bracket for supporting an electric lamp in a building.

electrology, *n.* the science of electricity.

electrolyse, -yze, *v.t.* to decompose by direct action of electricity; to subject to electrolysis; to remove (hair) by electrolysis.

electrolysis, *n.* the decomposition of chemical compounds by the passage of an electric current through them; the science dealing with this process and its phenomena; the removal of unwanted body hair by applying an electrically charged needle to the hair follicles.

electrolyte, *n.* a compound which may be decomposed by an electric current.

electrometer, *n.* an instrument for measuring the amount of electrical force, or for indicating the presence of electricity. **electrometrical,** *a.*

electron, *n.* (*Phys.*) a particle bearing a negative electric charge, the most numerous constituent of matter and probably the cause of all electrical phenomena. **electron camera,** *n.* a device which converts an optical image into an electric current by electronic means. **electron microscope,** *n.* a thermionic tube in which a stream of electrons is focused on to a cathode and thence casts a magnified image of the cathode on to a screen, capable of very high magnification. **electron volt,** *n.* a unit of energy in atomic physics, the increase in energy of an electron when its potential is raised by 1 volt. **electronics**, *n. sing.* the science of applied physics that deals with the conduction of electricity in a vacuum, or a semiconductor, and with other devices in which the movement of electrons is controlled. **electronic,** *a.* pertaining to electronics; operated or produced by means of electronics. **electronic brain,** *n.* an electronic computer. **electronic data interchange,** a process whereby information is transferred by linked computer terminals, telephones, fax machines etc. **electronic funds transfer at point of sale** EFTPOS. **electronic mail,** *n.* messages sent from one computer or fax machine to another by means of linked terminals. [ELECTRO-]

electropathy, *n.* the treatment of disease by electricity.

electrophorus, *n.* an instrument for generating static electricity by induction.

electroscope, *n.* an instrument for detecting the presence and the quality of electricity.

electrotonus, *n.* the alteration in the activity of a nerve or muscle under the action of a galvanic current. **electrotonic**, *a.*

electrotype, *n.* the process of producing copies of medals, woodcuts, type etc., by the electric deposition of copper upon a mould; the facsimile so produced. *v.t.* to copy by this process. **electrotyper,** *n.* **electrotypist,** *n.*

electrum, *n.* an alloy of gold and silver in use among the ancients; native gold containing silver; an alloy of copper, zinc and nickel, also called German silver. [L *ēlectrum,* Gr. *ēlektron,* amber, conn. with *ēlektōr,* shining]

electuary, *n.* a purgative medicine mixed with some sweet confection. [late L *ēlectuārium,* prob. from Gr. *ekleikton* (*ekleichein,* to lick away, cp. LICK)]

eleemosynary, *a.* given or done by way of alms; devoted to charitable purposes; supported by or dependent on charity. †*n.* one who subsists on charity. [med. L *eleēmosynārius,* Gr. *eleēmosunē,* ALMS]

elegant, *a.* pleasing to good taste; graceful, well-proportioned, delicately finished, refined; †having a fine sense of beauty or propriety; excellent, first-rate. **elegance,** *n.* **elegantly,** *adv.* [F *élégant,* L *ēlegans,* acc. *ēlegantem,* conn. with *ēligere,* to choose, see ELECT]

elegy, *n.* a lyrical poem or a song of lamentation; a poem of a plaintive, meditative kind; a poem written in elegiac verse. **elegiac**, *a.* pertaining to or of the nature of elegies; suited to elegy; mournful. *n.pl.* verse consisting of alternate hexameters and pentameters, in which the elegies of the Greeks and Romans were commonly written. **elegize, -ise,** *v.t.* to compose an elegy upon. *v.i.* to compose an elegy; to write in a plaintive strain. **elegist,** *n.* [F *élégie,* L *elegīa,* Gr. *elegeia* (*elegos,* a lament)]

eleme, *a.* applied to a superior kind of dried fig from Turkey. [Turk.]

element, *n.* one of the fundamental parts of which anything is composed; a substance which cannot be resolved by chemical analysis; (*pl.*) earth, air, fire and water, formerly considered as simple elements; the natural habitat of any creature, as water of fish; the proper or natural sphere of any person or thing; anything necessary to be taken into account in coming to a conclusion; (*pl.*) the rudiments of any science or art; (*pl.*) the bread and wine used in the Eucharist; the resistance wire of an electric heater; one of the electrodes of a primary or secondary cell. **elemental**, *a.* pertaining to or arising from first principles; pertaining to the four elements of which the world was supposed to be formed; hence, pertaining to the primitive forces of nature; ultimate, simple, uncompounded. **elemental spirits,** *n.pl.* those identified with natural forces, as salamanders, sylphs, gnomes and undines, said to inhabit respectively fire, air, earth and water. **elementalism,** *n.* the theory which resolves the gods of antiquity into the forces and aspects of nature. **elementally,** *adv.* in an elemental manner; literally. **elementary**, *a.* consisting of one element; primary, uncompounded; rudimentary, treating of first principles, introductory. **elementary particle,** *n.* any of several particles, such as electrons, protons or neutrons, which are less complex than atoms, so called because believed to be incapable of subdivision. **elementary-school** *n.* (*esp. formerly*), a primary school; (*N Am.*) one attended by children for the first six to eight years of education. **elementary substance,** *n.* an element. **elementarily,** *adv.* **elementariness,** *n.* [OF, from L *elementum* (etym. doubtful)]

elemi, *n.* a gum resin obtained from the Manila pitch-tree, *Canarium commune,* used in pharmacy. **elemin**, *n.* (*Chem.*) [etym. unknown]

elenchus, *n.* (*pl.* **-chi** (-ī)) an argument by which an opponent is made to contradict himself; a refutation. **elenctic**, *a.* [L, from Gr. *elenchos,* cross-examination]

elephant, *n.* a large pachydermatous animal, four-footed, with flexible proboscis and long curved tusks, of which two species now exist, *Elephas indicus* and *E. africanus,* the former partially domesticated and used as a beast of draught and burden; a size of paper (28×23 in.; double, 40×26¾ in.) (71·1×58·4 cm; 101·6×67·9 cm). **white elephant,** a useless and expensive possession (alluding to the cost of an elephant's keep). **elephant-beetle,** *n.* a large W African beetle, *Goliathus giganteus* or *G. cacicus.* **elephant fish,** *n.* the southern chimera, *Callorhyncus antarcticus,* found off New Zealand, S Australia and Tasmania, so called from its prehensile snout. **elephantiasis**, *n.* a cutaneous disease occurring in tropical countries, in which the skin of the patient becomes hardened and the part affected greatly enlarged. **elephantine**, *a.* pertaining to or resembling an elephant; huge, immense; unwieldy, clumsy. **elephantine epoch,** *n.* that period during which the large pachyderms abounded. **elephantoid**, *n., a.* [ME *olifaunt,* OF *olifant,* L *-antem elephas,* Gr. *elephas* (etym. doubtful)]

Eleusinian, *a.* relating to Eleusis, in ancient Attica, or to the mysteries annually celebrated there; (*fig.*) darkly mysterious. [L *Eleusīnius,* Gr. *Eleusinios*]

Eleusinian Mysteries, *n.pl.* ceremonies in honour of the Greek deities Demeter, Persephone, and Dionysus, celebrated in the remains of the temple of Demeter at Eleusis, Greece. Worshippers saw visions in the darkened temple, supposedly connected with the underworld.

eleuthero-, *comb. form.* free; not adherent. †**eleutheromania**, *n.* a mad passion or enthusiasm for freedom. †**eleutheromaniac**, *n., a.* **eleutheropetalous**, *a.* (*Bot.*) composed of distinct or separate petals. [Gr. *eleutheros,* free]

elevate, *v.t.* to lift up; to raise aloft; to raise from a lower to a higher place; to exalt in position or dignity; to make louder or higher; to raise in character or intellectual capacity; to refine, to improve; to elate, to animate, to exhilarate. **elevated,** *a.* raised; at or on a higher level; (*coll.*) slightly intoxicated. **elevated railway,** *n.* a city railway raised on pillars above the street-level. **elevation,** *n.* the act of elevating; the state of being elevated; an elevated position or ground; height above sea-level; the height of a building; a side or end view of an object or building drawn with or without reference to perspective; (*Astron.*) the angular altitude of a heavenly body above the horizon; (*Gunnery*) the angle of the line of fire with the plane of the horizon; (*fig.*) exaltation, grandeur, dignity. **elevation of the Host,** in the Roman Catholic Church, the part of the Mass in which the celebrant raises the Host above his head, to be adored. **elevator,** *n.* one who or that which elevates; a muscle whose function it is to raise any part of the body; a machine to raise grain from a car or ship to a high level, whence it can be discharged into any other receptacle; a lift; a hinged flap on the tailplane to provide vertical control. **elevatory,** *a.* [L *ēlevātus,* p.p. of *ēlevāre* (E-, *levāre,* to lift, from *levis,* light)]

eleven, *n.* the number or figure 11 or XI; the age of 11; a set of eleven things or people; an article of attire, such as a shoe etc., denoted by the number 11; a score of 11 points; the 11th hour after midday or midnight; (*Cricket, Assoc. Football*) the eleven people selected to play for a particular side. *a.* 11 in number; aged 11. **the eleven,** the disciples of Christ without Judas. **eleven plus exam,** (*formerly*) a school examination taken by children of about 11 to determine the particular type of secondary education they were suited for. **eleven year period,** (*Astron.*) the cycle of periodic changes in the occurrence of sun-spots. **elevenses**, *n.pl.* (*coll.*) a snack taken in the middle of the morning. **eleventh,** *n.* one of 11 equal parts; (*Mus.*) the interval of an octave and a fourth. *n., a.* (the) last of 11 (people, things etc.); (the) next after the 10th. **at the eleventh hour,** at the last moment (in allusion to the parable of the labourers, Matt. xx). [OE *endlufon, endleofan,* from OTeut. *ainlif-* (cp. Dut. and G *Elf,* Goth. *ainlif,* Icel. *ellifu*)]

elf, *n.* (*pl.* **elves**, elvz) a tiny supernatural being supposed to inhabit groves and wild and desolate places and to exercise a mysterious power over man; a fairy; a mischievous person; an imp; a tiny creature, a dwarf; a pet name for a child. †*v.t.* to twist or tangle (the hair) in an intricate manner. **elf-arrow, -bolt, -dart,** *n.* a flint arrow-head used in the Stone Age, popularly thought to be shot by fairies. **elf-child,** *n.* a child supposed to be left by fairies in exchange for one taken away by them. **elf-lock,** *n.* hair twisted in a knot, as if done by elves. **elf-struck,** *a.* bewitched by elves. **elfin,** *a.* elfish. *n.* a little elf; a sprite, an urchin. **elfish, elvish,** *a.* like an elf; of the nature of an elf; proceeding from or caused by elves; mischievous. [OE *ælf* (cp. Icel. *ālfr,* G *Elf,* also *Alp,* a nightmare)]

Elgar, *n.* **Edward (William)** (1857–1934), English composer. His *Enigma Variations* appeared in 1899, and although his celebrated choral work, the oratorio setting of Newman's *The Dream of Gerontius*, was initially a failure, it was well received at Düsseldorf in 1902. Many of his earlier works were then performed, including the *Pomp and Circumstance* marches.

Elgin marbles, *n.pl.* a collection of ancient Greek sculptures mainly from the Parthenon at Athens, assembled by the 7th Earl of Elgin. Sent to England in 1812, and bought for the nation in 1816 for £35,000, they are now in the British Museum. Greece has asked for them to be returned to Athens.

elicit, *v.t.* to draw out, evoke; to educe, extract. [L *ēlicitus,* p.p. of *ēlicere* (E-, *lacere,* to entice)]

elide, *v.t.* to strike out, omit, delete; (*esp. in Gram.*) to cut off (as the last syllable); to annul; †to destroy. **elision**, *n.* the suppression of a letter or syllable for the sake of euphony, metre etc.; the suppression of a passage in a book or a discourse. [L *ēlīdere* (E-, *laedere,* to dash)]

eligible, *a.* fit or deserving to be chosen; desirable, suitable; fit or qualified to be chosen to any office or position; (*coll.*) desirable for marriage. **eligibility**, *n.* **eligibly,** *adv.* [F *éligible,* L *ēligibilis,* from *ēligere,* see ELECT]

Elijah, *n.* (*c.* mid-9th cent. BC), in the Old Testament or Jewish Bible, a Hebrew prophet during the reigns of the Israelite kings Ahab and Ahaziah. He came from Gilead. He defeated the prophets of Baal, and was said to have been carried up to heaven in a fiery chariot in a whirlwind. In Jewish belief, Elijah will return to Earth to herald the coming of the messiah.

eliminate, *v.t.* to cast out, expel; to cast aside, remove, get rid of; to exclude, to ignore (certain considerations); (*Math.*) to cause to disappear from an equation; (*incorrectly*) to disengage, to isolate. **eliminable,** *a.* **elimination,** *n.* the act of eliminating; expulsion, ejection; leaving out or passing over; (*Math.*) removal of a quantity from an equation. **eliminator,** *n.* (*Radio.*) a device for supplying a battery receiving-set with electricity from the mains. [L *ēlimınātus,* p.p. of *ēlimināre* (E-, *līmin-* stem of *līmen,* threshold)]

Eliot[1], *n.* **George** (pen name of Mary Ann Evans) (1819–80), English novelist, who portrayed Victorian society, particularly its intellectual hypocrisy, with realism and irony. In 1857 she published the story 'Amos Barton', the first of the *Scenes of Clerical Life*. This was followed by the novels *Adam Bede* (1859), *The Mill on the Floss* (1860), and *Silas Marner* (1861). *Middlemarch* (1872) is now considered one of the greatest novels of the 19th century. Her final book *Daniel Deronda* (1876) was concerned with anti-Semitism. She also wrote poetry.

Eliot[2], *n.* **T(homas) S(tearns)** (1888–1965), US poet, playwright, and critic, who lived in London from 1915. His first volume of poetry, *Prufrock and Other Observations* (1917), introduced new verse forms and rhythms; further collections include *The Waste Land* (1922), *The Hollow Men* (1925), and *Old Possum's Book of Practical Cats* (1939). *Four Quartets* (1943) revealed his religious vision. His plays include *Murder in the Cathedral* (1935) and *The Cocktail Party* (1949). His critical works include *The Sacred Wood* (1920). He won the Nobel prize in 1948.

eliquation, *n.* liquefaction; (*Metal.*) the separation of a fusible substance from another less fusible by heating to a degree sufficient to melt the former but not the latter. [L *ēliquatio -ōnem*]

Elisabethville, *n.* former name of Lubumbashi, a town in Zaïre.

elision ELIDE.

elisor, *n.* (*Law*) a sheriff's substitute for selecting a jury.

elite, *n.* the pick, the flower, the best part; a type size for type-writers of 12 characters per in. (2.54 cm). **elitism,** *n.* (*often derog.*) the favouring of the creation of an elite. [F, from L *ēlecta,* fem. of *ēlectus,* ELECT]

elixir, *n.* the alchemists' liquor for transmuting metal into gold; a potion for prolonging life, usu. called **elixir vitae** or **elixir of life;** a cordial, a sovereign remedy; †the essential principle or quintessence; †a distillation or concentrated tincture. [med. L, from Arab. *al-iksīr* (*al,* the, Gr. *xērion,* dry powder for wounds)]

Elizabeth[1], *n.* in the New Testament, mother of John the Baptist. She was a cousin of Jesus Christ's mother Mary, who came to see her shortly after the Annunciation; on this visit (called the Visitation), Mary sang the hymn of praise later to be known as the Magnificat.

Elizabeth[2], *n.* **the Queen Mother** (1900–), wife of King George VI of England. She was born Lady Elizabeth Angela Marguerite Bowes-Lyon, and on 26 Apr. 1923, she married Albert, Duke of York. Their children are Queen Elizabeth II and Princess Margaret.

Elizabeth[3], *n.* (1709–62), empress of Russia from 1741, daughter of Peter the Great. She carried through a palace revolution and supplanted her cousin, the infant Ivan VI (1730–64), on the throne. She continued the policy of westernization begun by Peter, and allied herself with Austria against Prussia.

Elizabeth, *n.* two queens of England or the UK:

Elizabeth I, *n.* (1533–1603), queen of England (1558–1603), the daughter of Henry VIII and Anne Boleyn. Through her Religious Settlement of 1559 she enforced the Protestant religion by law and she had Mary, Queen of Scots, executed in 1587. Her conflict with Catholic Spain led to the defeat of the Spanish Armada in 1588. The Elizabethan age was expansionist in commerce and geographical exploration, and arts and literature flourished. The rulers of many European states made unsuccessful bids to marry Elizabeth, and she used these bids to strengthen her power. She was succeeded by James I.

Elizabeth II, *n.* (1926–), queen of Great Britain and Northern Ireland from 1952, the elder daughter of George VI. She married her third cousin, Philip, the Duke of Edinburgh in 1947. They have four children: Charles, Anne, Andrew, and Edward.

Elizabethan, *a.* pertaining esp. to Queen Elizabeth I or her time; in the style characterizing the architecture, dress etc., of her time. *n.* a personage or writer of that time.

Elizabethan literature, *n.* literature produced during the reign of Elizabeth I of England (1558–1603). Her reign was remarkable for the development of the arts in England. The literature of her age is pre-eminent in energy, richness and confidence. Renaissance humanism, Protestant zeal and geographical discovery all contributed to this upsurge of creative power. Drama was the dominant form of the age, and Shakespeare and Marlowe were popular with all levels of society. Other writers of the period included Edmund Spenser, Philip Sidney, Frances Bacon, Thomas Lodge, Robert Greene and John Lyly.

elk, *n.* the largest animal of the deer family, *Alces malchis,* a native of northern Europe and of N America, where it is called the moose; applied also to the wapiti, *Cervus canadensis,* and the eland. **Irish elk,** an extinct animal, *Cervus megaceros.* **elk-nut,** *n.* the buffalo nut, *Hamiltonia oleifera.* **Elks,** *n.pl.* a US fraternal society. [OE *elh, elch* (cp. Icel. *elgr,* OHG *elaho,* L *alces,* Gr. *alkē*)]

ell, *n.* a measure of length, varying in different countries, for measuring cloth; the (obsolete) English ell is 45 in. (114·3 cm). **give him/her an inch he'll/she'll take an ell,** he/she will take liberties if possible. **ell-wand,** *n.* a measuring rod an ell long; (*Sc.*) the belt of Orion. [OE *eln* (cp. Dut. *el,* G *Elle,* Goth. *aleina,* Swed. *aln,* Gr. *ōlenē,* L *ulna,* whence F *aune*)]

ellagic, *a.* pertaining to gall-nuts or to gallic acid. **ellagic acid,** *n.* an acid obtained from gallic acid, bezoars, certain barks etc. [F *ellagique,* from *ellag,* anagram of *galle,* gall-nut]

elleborin HELLEBORE.

Ellice Islands, *n.pl.* former name of Tuvalu, a group of islands in the W Pacific Ocean.

Ellington, *n.* **'Duke'** (Edward Kennedy) (1899–1974), US pianist, who had an outstanding career as a composer and arranger of jazz. He wrote numerous pieces for his own jazz orchestra, and became one of the most important figures in jazz over a 55-year span. Compositions include 'Mood Indigo', 'Sophisticated Lady', 'Solitude', and 'Black and Tan Fantasy'.

ellipse, *n.* a regular oval, a plane curve of such a form that the sum of two straight lines, drawn from any point in it to two given fixed points called the foci, will always be the same; a conic section formed by a plane intersecting a cone obliquely. **ellipsograph,** *n.* an instrument for describing ellipses. **ellipsis, ellipse,** *n.* (*pl.* **-ses**) omission of one or more words necessary to the complete construction of a sentence; †a mark denoting the omission of one or more words or letters, as in *d——d* for 'damned'. **ellipsoid,** *n.* a solid figure of which every plane section through one axis is an ellipse and every other section an ellipse or a circle; †a solid figure produced by the revolution of an ellipse about its axis. *a.* ellipsoidal. **ellipsoidal,** *a.* pertaining to an ellipsoid. **elliptic, -ical,** *a.* pertaining to an ellipse; (*Gram., Rhet.*) pertaining to ellipsis. **elliptically,** *adv.* **ellipticity,** *n.* the quality of being elliptic; the extent to which any ellipse differs from a circle, or any ellipsoid from a sphere. [L *ellipsis,* Gr. *elleipsis,* from *elleipein* (*el-, en,* in, *leipein,* to leave)]

Ellis Island, *n.* island off the shore of New Jersey, US, former reception centre for steerage-class immigrants on arrival in New York (1892–1943). No longer used, it was declared a National Historic Site in 1964 by President Johnson.

Ellison, *n.* **Ralph** (1914–), US novelist. His *Invisible Man* (1952) portrays with humour and energy the plight of a black man whom society cannot acknowledge; it is regarded as one of the most impressive novels published in the US in the 1950s.

elm, *n.* a tree of the genus *Ulmus;* the common English elm, *U. campestris.* †**elmen,** *a.* pertaining to the elm. **elmy,** *a.* [OE (cp. Icel. *ālmr,* Swed. and Dan. *alm,* G *Ulm,* L *ulmus*)]

Elmo's, St Elmo's fire, *n.* the corposant. [perh. corr. of *Helena,* sister of Castor and Pollux, or after It. *Elmo* or *Ermo, St Erasmus,* a Syrian martyr of the 3rd cent.]

elocution, *n.* the art, style or manner of speaking or reading; effective oral delivery; †eloquence, oratory; †rhetoric, literary expression; appropriate language in speaking or writing. **elocutionary,** *a.* **elocutionist,** *n.* [L *ēlocūtio -ōnem,* from *ēloquī* (E-, *loquī,* to speak)]

eloge, *n.* an encomium, a panegyric, esp. a discourse in honour of a deceased person. [F *éloge,* L *ēlogium,* a short saying (Gr. *logos,* a saying, a word), confused with *eulogium,* EULOGY]

Elohim, *n.* ordinary name of God in the Hebrew Scriptures. **Elohist,** *n.* a Biblical writer or one of the writers of parts of the Hexateuch, where the word *Elohim* is habitually used for *Yahveh,* Jehovah. **Elohistic,** *a.* [Heb. *elōhim,* pl. used in sing. sense, God]

†**eloin,** *v.t.* to remove; to remove or seclude (oneself); to carry off; (*Law.*) to remove beyond the jurisdiction of a court or sheriff. [OF *esloignier* (F *éloigner*), late L *exlongāre, ēlongāre,* as foll.]

elongate, *v.t.* to extend; to make longer; †to remove to a distance. *v.i.* to grow longer; (*Bot.*) to increase in length, to taper; †to depart; to recede. *a.* lengthened, extended; (*Bot., Zool.*) very slender in proportion to length. **elongation,** *n.* the act of lengthening or extending; the state of being elongated; a prolongation, an extension; (*Astron.*) the angular distance of a planet from the sun or of a satellite from its primary. [late L *ēlongātus,* p.p. of *ēlongāre,* to remove (E-, *longus,* long)]

elope, *v.i.* to run away with a lover, with a view to clandestine marriage, or with a paramour in defiance of social or moral restraint; to run away in a clandestine manner, to abscond. **elopement,** *n.* [*aloper,* perh. from a ME *alope* or *ilope,* p.p. of *aleapen* or *leapen,* to LEAP (cp. the later MDut. *ontlōpen* and G *entlaufen*)]

eloquence, *n.* fluent, powerful and appropriate verbal expression, esp. of emotional ideas; eloquent language; rhetoric. **eloquent,** *a.* having the power of expression in fluent, vivid and appropriate language; full of expression, feeling or interest. **eloquently,** *adv.* [F *éloquence,* L *ēloquentia, ēloquens -ntem,* pres.p. of *ēloquī* (E-, *loquī,* to speak)]

El Paso, *n.* city in Texas, US, situated at the base of the Franklin Mountains, on the Rio Grande, opposite the Mexican city of Ciudad Juárez; population (1980) 425,200. It is the centre of an agricultural and cattle-raising area, and there are electronics, food processing and packing, and leather industries, as well as oil refineries and industries based on local iron and copper mines.

El Salvador, *n.* Republic of (*República de El Salvador*), country in central America, bounded N and E by Honduras, S and SW by the Pacific Ocean, and NW by Guatemala. **area** 21,393 sq km/8258 sq miles. **capital** San Salvador. **physical** flat in S, rising to mountains in N. **population** (1985) 5,480,000 (mainly of Spanish-Indian extraction, including some 500,000 illegally in the US); annual growth rate 2.9%. **exports** coffee, cotton. **language** Spanish. **religion** Roman Catholic.

Elsan®, *n.* a type of chemical lavatory.

else, *adv.* besides, in addition, other; instead; otherwise, in the other case, if not. **elsewhere,** *adv.* in or to some other place. [OE *elles,* gen. sing. used as adv. (cp. OHG *elles, alles,* also L *alius,* other)]

Elsheimer, *n.* **Adam** (1578–1610), German painter and etcher, active in Rome from 1600. His small paintings, nearly all on copper, depict landscapes darkened by storm or night, with figures picked out by beams of light, as in *The Rest on the Flight into Egypt* (1609) (Alte Pinakothek, Munich).

elsin, *n.* (*Sc., North*) an awl. [perh. from MDut. *elssene* (Dut. *els*), cp. AWL]

ELT, (*abbr.*) English Language Teaching.

Elton, *n.* **Charles** (1900–), British ecologist, a pioneer of the study of animal and plant forms in their natural environments, and of animal behaviour as part of the complex pattern of life. Elton published *Animal Ecology and Evolution* (1930) and *The Pattern of Animal Communities* (1966).

Eluard, *n.* **Paul** (pen name of Eugène Grindel) (1895–1952), French poet, born in Paris. He expressed the suffering of poverty in his verse, and was a leader of the surrealists. He fought in World War I, the inspiration for *Poèmes pour la paix/Poems for Peace* (1918), and was a member of the Resistance in World

War II. His books include *Poésie et vérité/Poetry and Truth* (1942) and *Au Rendezvous allemand/To the German Rendezvous* (1944).

elucidate, *v.t.* to make lucid, throw light on; to render intelligible; to explain. **elucidation,** *n.* **elucidative,** *a.* **elucidator,** *n.* **elucidatory,** *a.* [late L *ēlūcidātus,* p.p. of *ēlūcidāre* (E-, *lūcidus,* bright)]

†**elucubration** LUCUBRATION.

elude, *v.t.* to escape from by artifice or dexterity; to evade, to dodge, to shirk; to remain undiscovered or unexplained by; to baffle (search or inquiry); †to delude. †**eludible,** *a.* **elusion,** *n.* **elusive,** *a.* **elusively,** *adv.* **elusiveness,** *n.* **elusory,** *a.* [L *ēlūdere* (E-, *lūdere,* to play, p.p. *lūsus*)]

Elul, *n.* the sixth month of the Jewish ecclesiastical, and the 12th of their civil year, beginning with the new moon of our September. [Heb. *âlal,* to reap]

elute, *v.t.* to wash out by the action of a solvent. **elution,** *n.* purification or separation by washing. **eluant,** *n.* a liquid used for elution. [L *ēlūtio -ōnis,* washing]

†**elutriate,** *v.t.* to purify by straining or washing so as to separate the lighter and the heavier particles; to decant liquid from. †**elutriation,** *n.* [L *ēlutriātus,* p.p. of *ēlutriāre,* to wash out]

elvan, *n.* intrusive igneous rock penetrating sedimentary strata in Cornwall, Devon and Ireland; a vein or dike of this. **elvanite,** *n.* **elvanitic,** *a.* [etym. doubtful (perh. Corn. *elven*)]

elver, *n.* a young eel, especially a young conger. [EELFARE]

elvish, *a.* pertaining to elves; elfish; mischievous. †**elvish-marked,** *a.* marked by the fairies. **elvishly,** *adv.* [ELF]

Elysée Palace, *n.* (French **Palais de l'Elysée**) building in Paris erected in 1718 for Louis d'Auvergne, Count of Evreux. It was later the home of Mme de Pompadour, Napoleon I, and Napoleon III, and became the official residence of the presidents of France in 1870.

Elysium, *n.* (or **Elysian Fields**), in classical mythology, an afterworld or paradise (sometimes called the Islands of the Blessed) for the souls of those who found favour with the gods; it was situated near the river Oceanus; (*fig.*) a place or state of perfect happiness. [L, from Gr. *Elusion* (*pedion*), (the plain) of the blessed]

elytron, *n.* (*pl.* **-tra,** -ə) one of the horny sheaths which constitute the anterior wings of beetles; (*Anat.*) the vagina. **elytriform,** *a.* [Gr. *elutron,* a sheath, from *eluein,* to roll round]

Elzevir[1], *n.* a book printed by the Elzevirs. *a.* printed by the Elzevirs; pertaining to or resembling the type used by them.

Elzevir[2], *n.* **Louis** (1540–1617), founder of the Dutch printing house of Elzevir in the 17th century. Among the firm's publications were editions of Latin, Greek, and Hebrew works, and French and Italian classics.

em, *n.* the 13th letter of the alphabet, M, m; (*Print.*) the square of the body of any size of type, used as the unit of measurement for printed matter; a printers' general measure of 12 points or 1/6 in. (0·42 cm).

'em, *pron.* (*coll.*) short for THEM. [ME *hem*]

em-, *pref.* a form of EN- used before *b, p* and sometimes *m,* as in *embank, empanoply, emmarble.*

emaciate, *v.t.* to cause to lose flesh or become lean; to reduce to leanness, to impoverish (soil etc.). †*v.i.* to waste or pine away. **emaciation,** *n.* [L *ēmaciātus,* p.p. of *ēmaciāre* (E-, *maciēs,* leanness, from *macer,* lean)]

emanate, *v.i.* to issue or flow as from a source, to originate; to proceed (from). **emanation,** *n.* the act of emanating from something, as from a source; that which emanates, an efflux, an effluence; the theory that all things are outflowings from the essence of God; any product of this process. **emanative,** *a.* [L *ēmānātus,* p.p. of *ēmānāre*]

emancipate, *v.t.* to release from bondage, slavery, oppression, or legal, social or moral restraint; to set free, to liberate; (*Roman Law*) to liberate from parental authority. **emancipation,** *n.* the releasing from slavery, oppression, restraint or legal disabilities; the state of being freed from any bond or restraint. **emancipationist,** *n.* an advocate of emancipation of slaves. **emancipator,** *n.* **emancipatory,** *a.* **emancipist,** *n.* (*Austral. Hist.*) a convict who had served his/her term. [L *ēmancipātus,* p.p. of *ēmancipāre* (E-, *mancipāre,* to transfer property, from *manceps,* from *manus,* hand, *capere,* to take)]

Emancipation Proclamation, The, in US history, President Lincoln's Civil War announcement on 22 Sept. 1862, stating that from the beginning of 1863 all black slaves in states still engaged in rebellion against the federal government would be emancipated. Slaves in border states still remaining loyal to the union were excluded.

emarginate, *v.t.* to take away the edge or margin of; to emphasize the contour lines of (a microscopic object embedded in jelly) through unequal refraction. **emarginate, -nated,** *a.* with the margin notched; (*Bot.*) notched at the apex. **emargination,** *n.* [L *ēmarginātus,* p.p. of *ēmargināre* (E-, *margināre,* to furnish with a border, from *margo -ginis,* MARGIN]

emasculate, *v.t.* to castrate; to deprive of masculine strength or vigour; to make effeminate, to weaken; to deprive (as language) of force or energy; to enfeeble (a literary work) by undue expurgation or excision; to remove coarse expressions from a literary production. *a.*, castrated; enfeebled, effeminate, weak. **emasculation,** *n.* **emasculative,** *a.* **emasculatory,** *a.* [L *ēmasculātus,* p.p. of *ēmasculāre* (E-, *masculus,* male)]

embalm, *v.t.* to preserve (as a body) from putrefaction by means of spices and aromatic drugs; to imbue with sweet scents; (*fig.*) to preserve from oblivion. **embalmer,** *n.* **embalmment,** *n.* [F *embaumer*]

embank, *v.t.* to confine or defend with a bank or banks, dikes, masonry etc. **embankment,** *n.* the act or process of embanking; a bank or stone structure for confining a river etc.; a raised mound or bank for carrying a road etc.

†**embar,** *v.t.* to shut in, confine, imprison; to hinder, to stop; (*Law*) to forbid, to bar; to put under embargo. [F *embarrer* (EM-, *barre,* BAR[1])]

†**embarcation** EMBARKATION.

embargo, *n.* (*pl.* **-goes**) a prohibition by authority upon the departure of vessels from ports under its jurisdiction; a complete suspension of foreign commerce or of a particular branch of foreign trade; a hindrance, check, impediment; a prohibition or restraint, as on publication. *v.t.* to lay an embargo upon; to seize for purposes of State; to requisition, seize, confiscate; to prohibit, to forbid. [Sp., from *embargar,* to arrest, hinder, prob. from late L *imbarricāre* (*im-,* IN-, *barra,* BAR[1])]

embark, *v.t.* to put on board ship; to invest (as money) in any business. *v.i.* to go on board ship; (*fig.*) to engage or enter (upon any undertaking). **embarkation,** *n.* the act of putting or going on board a ship or vessel; †a cargo, anything that is embarked; †a vessel, a craft. †**embarkment,** *n.* [F *embarquer,* late L *imbarcāre*]

embarras de, a perplexing amount or number of, as *embarras de richesse,* a perplexing abundance of wealth, too much of anything; *embarras de choix,* a perplexing number of things to choose from. [F]

embarrass, *v.t.* to encumber, hamper, entangle, impede, hinder; to confuse, perplex, disconcert; to complicate, render difficult; to involve in pecuniary difficulties. *n.* (*N Am.*) a place where navigation is rendered difficult by accumulations of drift-wood etc. **embarrassing,** *a.* causing embarrassment. **embarrassingly,** *adv.* **embarrassment,** *n.* perplexity of mind, discomposure, uneasiness, perturbation arising from bashfulness; confusion or intricacy of affairs; pecuniary difficulties; an impediment, a hindrance. [F *embarrasser,* from *embarras,* conn. with *embarrer,* to EMBAR]

†**embase,** *v.t.* to lower; (*fig.*) to degrade, humiliate; to impair, to corrupt. †**embasement,** *n.*

embassy, *n.* the function, office or mission of an ambassador; the body of persons sent as ambassadors; an ambassador and his suite; the official residence of an ambassador; †the message sent by an ambassador. †**embassade**, *n.* embassy. †**embassador**, *n.* an ambassador. †**embassadorial**, *a.* †**embassadress**, *n.fem.* †**embassage**, *n.* embassy. [OF *ambassée,* late L *ambactiāta, ambasciāta,* orig. fem. p.p. of *ambactiāre,* to go on a mission (see AMBASSADOR)]

†**embathe,** *v.t.* to imbathe, immerse, suffuse.

embattle[1], *v.t.* to array in order of battle; to prepare for battle; to fortify. *v.i.* to be drawn up in battle array. [OF *embataillier*]

embattle[2], *v.t.* to furnish with battlements. [BATTLEMENT]

embay, *v.t.* to enclose (a vessel) in a bay, to landlock; to force (a vessel) into a bay; to shut in, confine, enclose, surround. **embayment,** *n.*

embed, *v.t.* (*past, p.p.* **embedded**) to lay as in a bed; to set firmly in surrounding matter; to enclose firmly (said of the surrounding matter). †**embedment,** *n.*

embellish, *v.t.* to beautify, to adorn; to add incidents or imaginary accompaniments so as to heighten a narrative. **embellishment,** *n.* [OF *embellir* (EM-, *bel,* L *bellus,* handsome)]

ember[1], *n.* a smouldering piece of coal or wood; (*pl.*) smouldering remnants of a fire or (*fig.*) of passion, love etc. [OE, *aemerge* (cp. Dan. *emmer,* OHG *eimurja*)]

ember[2], *n.* an anniversary, a recurring time or season. **Ember days,** *n.pl.* certain days set apart for fasting and prayer; the Wednesday, Friday and Saturday next following the first Sunday in Lent, Whit-Sunday, Holy Cross Day (14 Sept.), and St Lucy's Day (13 Dec.). **Ember-tide,** *n.* the season at which Ember days occur. **Ember weeks,** *n.pl.* the weeks in which the Ember days fall. †**emberings,** *n.pl.* the Ember days; called also **embering days**. [OE *ymbren,* prob. corr. of *ymbryne,* a period, revolution (*ymb,* about, *ryne,* running)]

ember-goose, *n.* the northern diver or loon, *Colymbus glacialis,* also called **ember-diver**. [Norw. *emmer-gaas*]

embezzle, *v.t.* to appropriate fraudulently what is committed to one's care; †to squander, waste, dissipate. *v.i.* to commit embezzlement. **embezzlement,** *n.* **embezzler,** *n.* [A-F *enbeseler,* OF *besillier,* to maltreat, to ravage, prob. from *bes-,* late L *bis-,* a pejorative pref. (cp. OF *besil,* ill-treatment, torture), influenced by L *imbecillāre,* to weaken]

embitter, *v.t.* to make bitter, or more bitter; to render harder or more distressing, to aggravate; to add poignancy or sharpness to; to exasperate. **embitterment,** *n.*

†**emblaze,** *v.t.* to set in a blaze, to kindle; (*fig.*) to light up, to cause to glitter; to emblazon, to set forth by heraldic devices; to glorify.

emblazon, *v.t.* to blazon; to adorn with heraldic figures or armorial designs; to decorate; to make brilliant; to celebrate, to render illustrious. **emblazoner,** *n.* **emblazoning,** *n.* emblazonment. **emblazonment,** *n.* the act or art of blazoning; blazonry. **emblazonry** BLAZONRY.

emblem, *n.* †inlaid or mosaic work; a symbolic figure; a picture, object or representation of an object symbolizing some other thing, class, action, or quality, as a crown for royalty or a balance for justice; a symbol, a type, a personification; a heraldic device. *v.t.* to symbolize, to represent or show forth by an emblem. **emblema**, *n.* (*usu. in pl.* **-mata** -mətə) figures with which the ancients decorated gold, silver and copper vessels, and which could be fixed on or taken off at pleasure, **emblematic, -ical**, *a.* **emblematically,** *adv.* **emblematist**, *n.* a writer of allegories or inventor of emblems. **emblematize, -ise,** *v.t.* to represent by or as an emblem; to symbolize. **emblematology**, *n.* [L and Gr. *emblēma,* from *emballein* (EM-, *ballein,* to throw)]

emblement, *n.* (*usu. in pl.*) (*Law*) the produce of land sown or planted; growing crops annually produced by the cultivator's labour, which belong to the tenant, though his lease may terminate before harvest, and in the event of his death fall to his executors; sometimes extended to the natural products of the soil. [OF *emblaement,* from *emblaer* (F *emblaver*), to sow with corn, med. L *imbladāre* (IN-, *bladum,* L *ablatum,* the gathered-in harvest, hence corn)]

emblossom, *v.t.* to cover with blossoms.

embody, *v.t.* to incarnate or invest with a material body; to express in a concrete form; to be a concrete expression of, to form into a united whole; to incorporate, include. †*v.i.* to unite, coalesce, come into a body. **embodier,** *n.* **embodiment,** *n.*

embog, *v.t.* to plunge into a bog; to encumber in or as in a bog.

embogue, *v.i.* to disembogue, to discharge (as a river into the sea). [Sp. *embocar* (EM-, *boca,* mouth)]

embolden, *v.t.* to give boldness to; to encourage.

embolism, *n.* an intercalation; the insertion of days, months or years in the calendar in order to produce regularity; anything intercalated, such as a period of time, a prayer in the order of public worship etc.; partial or total blocking-up of a blood-vessel by a clot of blood. †**embolismic**, *a.* **embolus**, *n.* a thing inserted in another and moving therein, as a piston; the clot which causes embolism. [L *embolismus,* late Gr. *embolismos,* from *embolē,* a throwing in (EM-, *ballein,* to throw)]

embonpoint, *n.* plumpness of person or figure. *a.* plump, well-nourished; stout; (*euphem.*) fat. [F, orig. *en bon point,* in good condition]

emborder, *v.t.* to adorn or furnish with a border.

embosom, *v.t.* to place or hold in or as in the bosom of anything; to enclose, surround; to embrace, to cherish.

emboss, *v.t.* to engrave or mould in relief; to decorate with bosses or raised figures; to cause to stand out in relief. **embossment,** *n.* [OF *embosser* (EM-, *bosse,* BOSS[1])]

embouchure, *n.* the mouth of a river etc.; (*Mus.*) the mouthpiece of a wind instrument; the shaping of the lips to the mouthpiece. [F, from *emboucher,* to put in the mouth, to discharge by a mouth (EM-, *bouche,* mouth)]

†**embound,** *v.t.* to hem or shut in, to enclose.

†**embow,** *v.t.* to bend, to curve like a bow; to arch, to vault.

embowel, *v.t.* to disembowel; †to put or convey into, to enclose, to embed. **embowelment,** *n.* the act of disembowelling; the inward parts of anything. [OF *enboweler* (EM-, *bouel,* BOWEL)]

embower, *v.t.* to enclose in or as in a bower; to shelter, to surround (as with trees or shrubs).

embox, *v.t.* to set or shut in or as in a box.

embrace[1], *v.t.* to enfold in the arms; to clasp and hold fondly; to clasp or twine round (as a creeping plant); to enclose, encircle, surround; to include, contain, comprise; to receive, adopt, accept eagerly; to take in with the eye, to comprehend; †to have sexual intercourse with. *v.i.* to join in an embrace; †to join in sexual intercourse. *n.* a clasping in the arms; sexual intercourse; a hostile struggle or grapple. **embraceable,** *a.* **embracement,** *n.* **embracer**[1], *n.* **embracingly,** *adv.* **embracingness,** *n.* **embracive,** *a.* [OF *embracer,* (EM-, *brace,* L *bracchia,* pl., the arms)]

†**embrace**[2], *v.t.* to fasten or fix with a brace.

embracer[2], *n.* (*Law*) one who endeavours to corrupt a jury by embracery. **embracery,** *n.* (*Law*) an attempt to influence a jury by threats etc. [OF *embraceor,* from *embraser,* to set on fire (EM-, *braise,* hot charcoal)]

embranchment, *n.* a branching out; that part of the tree where the branches diverge; a ramification.

embrangle, *v.t.* to entangle, to complicate; to confuse, perplex. **embranglement,** *n.*

embrasure, *n.* an opening in a parapet or wall to fire guns through; the inward enlargement, bevelling or splaying of the sides of a window or door. [MF, from *embraser* (F *ébraser*), to splay or chamfer (EM-, *braser,* to splay or chamfer)]

embrave, *v.t.* to inspire with courage, to embolden; to adorn, beautify, embellish.

embreathe, *v.t.* to breathe into, inspire; to breathe in, inhale.

embrocate, *v.t.* to moisten, bathe or forment (as a diseased part of the body). **embrocation,** *n.* a preparation for application by rubbing or painting; the act of bathing or fomenting; the liquid used. [med. L *embrocātus,* p.p. of *embrocāre,* from *embrocha,* Gr. *embrochē,* from *embrechein* (EM-, *brechein,* to wet)]

embroglio IMBROGLIO.

embroider, *v.t.* to ornament with figures or designs in needlework; to variegate, to diversify; to embellish with additions, esp. a narrative with exaggerations or fiction. **embroiderer,** *n.* **embroidery,** *n.* the act, process or art of embroidering; ornamentation done with the needle; the fabric ornamented; additional embellishment; exaggeration or fiction added to a narrative. [A-F *enbroyder* (OF EM-, *broder,* prob. rel. to *bord,* edge, border)]

embroil, *v.t.* to throw into confusion; to entangle, to confuse; to involve (someone) in a quarrel or contention (with another). **embroilment,** *n.* [F *embrouiller* (EM-, *brouiller,* see BROIL 1)]

embrown, *v.t.* to make brown; to darken, obscure.

embrue IMBRUE.

embryectomy, *n.* the operation of removing the foetus through an incision in the abdomen.

embryo, *n.* (*pl.* **-bryos**) the unborn offspring; the germ, the undeveloped foetus; the vitalized germ; the rudimentary plant in the seed after fertilization; the beginning or first stage of anything. *a.* in the germ, undeveloped; rudimentary. **in embryo,** in the first or earliest stage; in a rudimentary or undeveloped state. **embryonic,** *a.* [med. L *embryo -ōnis,* Gr. *embruon* (EM-, *bruon,* neut. of *bruōn,* pres.p. of *bruein,* to be full of a thing, to swell with it)]

embry(o)-, *comb. form.* of or pertaining to the embryo or embryos. [as prec.]

embryoctony, *n.* the destruction of the foetus in the womb. [Gr. *embruoktonos* (*ktenein,* to kill)]

embryogenesis , embryogeny, *n.* **embryogony,** *n.* the formation of an embryo. [Gr. *-gonia,* production]

embryology, *n.* the science of the embryo and the formation and development of organisms. **embryological,** *a.* **embryologist,** *n.*

embryotomy, *n.* a cutting up of an embryo or foetus in the uterus.

embus, *v.t.* (*past, p.p.* **embussed**) (*Mil.*) to put troops into omnibuses for transport. *v.i.* of troops, to mount an omnibus or lorry.

†**eme,** *n.* an uncle; a neighbour, friend, gossip. [OE *ēam* (? maternal) uncle (cp. Dut. *oom,* OHG *ôheim,* G. *Oheim, Ohm*)]

emend, *v.t.* to correct, remove faults; to improve (as the result of criticism). **emendable,** *a.* **emendals,** *n.pl.* (*formerly*) a term signifying the sum total in the bank or in stock (orig. prob. set aside for making up losses), still used in the books of the Society of the Inner Temple. **emendation,** *n.* **emendator,** *n.* **emendatory,** *a.* [L *ēmendāre* (E-, *menda,* a fault)]

emerald, *n.* a variety of beryl, distinguished by its beautiful green colour; the colour of this; (*Her.*) the green colour in coat armour, vert; (*Print.*) old name for a small type, between nonpareil and minion. *a.* of a bright green colour. **emerald-copper,** *n.* dioptase, an emerald green crystallized mineral. **emerald green,** *n.* a bright green pigment, produced from arsenate of copper. **the Emerald Isle,** Ireland. [OF *emeraude, esmeralde,* L *smaragdum -dus,* Gr. *smaragdos* (Sansk. *asmā,* a stone, *marakata,* emerald)]

emerge, *v.i.* to rise up out of anything in which a thing has been immersed or sunk; to appear in sight (from below the horizon or from a place of concealment); to appear, to come out (as facts on an enquiry); to crop up, become apparent; to issue from a state of depression, suffering or obscurity. **emergence,** *n.* **emergent,** *a.* coming into being, evolving; arising or appearing unexpectedly; of a country etc., having recently acquired independence. **emergent year,** *n.* the epoch or date from which any people begin to compute their time. [L *ēmergere* (E-, *mergere,* to dip)]

emergency, *n.* a sudden occurrence or situation demanding immediate action; a crisis. **emergency exit,** *n.* (*Theat. etc.*) a door specially provided for exit in case of fire or other contingency. **emergency landing,** *n.* a forced descent by a plane due to engine trouble etc. **emergency man,** *n.* one employed in a pressing necessity; a bailiff's officer temporarily employed on land in Ireland from which tenants had been evicted. [late L *ēmergentia,* as prec.]

emeritus, *a.* a term applied in ancient Rome to one who had served his time and retired from the public service; (*placed after the noun*) having served one's term of office, as *professor emeritus. n.* (*pl.* **-ti**) one who has served his time and retired from any office. [L, p.p. of *ēmerērī* (E-, *merērī,* to earn)]

emerods, *n.pl.* (I Sam. v.6–7) haemorrhoids. [HAEMORRHOIDS]

emersion, *n.* the action of emerging; the reappearance of a heavenly body from behind another at the end of an eclipse or occultation.

Emerson, *n.* **Ralph Waldo** (1803–82), US philosopher, essayist, and poet. He settled in Concord, Massachusetts, which he made a centre of transcendentalism, and wrote *Nature* (1836), which states the movement's main principles emphasizing the value of self-reliance and the God-like nature of human souls. His two volumes of *Essays* (1841, 1844) made his reputation.

emery, *n.* a coarse variety of corundum, of extreme hardness, and black or greyish-black colour, used for polishing hard substances. **emery board,** *n.* a strip of card or wood, coated with crushed emery and used to file fingernails. **emery-cloth, -paper,** *n.* cloth or paper brushed with liquid glue and dusted with powdered emery. **emery-wheel,** *n.* one faced with emery, used for grinding and polishing metal articles. [F *émeri,* MF *emeril, esmeril,* It. *smeriglio* (or late L *smericulum*), Gr. *smēris*]

emesis EMETIC.

emetic, *a.* inducing vomiting. *n.* a preparation for causing vomiting. **emetically,** *adv.* **emesis,** *n.* the action of vomiting. **emetine,** *n.* an alkaloid obtained from ipecacuanha, of which it forms the chief active principle. **emetocathartic,** *a.* producing vomiting and purging. **emetology,** *n.* [L *emeticus,* Gr. *emetikos,* from *emeein,* to vomit]

émeute, *n.* a seditious or revolutionary outbreak; a riot or popular disturbance. [F, from *émouvoir,* L *ēmovēre* (E-, *movēre,* to move)]

emiction, *n.* the discharge of urine; urine. **emictory,** *n., a.* [L *ēmictio,* from *ēmict-,* p.p. stem of *ēmingere* (E-, *mingere,* to make water)]

emigrate, *v.i.* to leave one's country in order to settle in another; (*coll.*) to leave one's place of abode for another. *v.t.* to send emigrants out of the country. **emigrant,** *a.* emigrating; pertaining to emigration. *n.* one who emigrates. **emigration,** *n.* **emigrationist,** *n.* an advocate for or promoter of emigration. **emigratory,** *a.* [L *ēmigrātus,* p.p. of *ēmigrāre* (E-, *migrāre,* to MIGRATE)]

émigré, *n.* an emigrant, esp. one of the royalists who left France at the time of the French Revolution.

Emi Koussi, *n.* highest point of the Tibesti massif in N Chad, rising to 3425m/11,204 ft.

Emilia-Romagna, *n.* region of N central Italy including much of the Po valley. **area** 22,100 sq km/8531 sq miles. **capital** Bologna; other towns include Reggio, Rimini, Parma, Ferrara, and Ravenna. **population** (1988) 3,924,000. **products** fruit, wine, sugar beet, beef, and dairy products; oil and natural gas resources have been developed in the Po valley.

eminent, *a.* rising above others; high, lofty, prominent; distinguished; of services, qualities etc., remarkable. **eminent domain,** *n.* the right of the State to confiscate private property for public use, payment usually being made in compensation. **eminence, -nency,** *n.* loftiness, height; a part rising above the rest, or projecting above the surface; high rank, superiority; distinction, celebrity; †supreme degree; a title of honour applied to cardinals. †**to have the eminence of,** to be better than. **eminence grise,** *n.* (*F*) a man in the background exercising power unofficially. **eminently,** *adv.* [L *ēminens -ntem,* pres.p. of *ēminēre,* to stand out, project

(E-, *minae,* threats, projections)]

Emin Pasha, *n.* **Mehmed,** born Eduard Schnitzer (1849–92), German explorer, doctor and linguist. Appointed by General Gordon as chief medical officer and then governor of the Equatorial Province, he carried out extensive research in anthropology, botany, zoology, and meteorology.

emir, *n.* in the Middle East and N Africa, a prince, chieftain, governor or commander; a title given to the descendants of Mohammed through Fatima, his daughter. [Arab. *amīr,* AMEER (*amara,* he commanded)]

emissary, *n.* a messenger or agent, esp. one sent on a secret, dangerous or unpleasant mission; †an outlet for water; (*Physiol.*) an excretory vessel. *a.* of or pertaining to a messenger or agent; serving as an outlet. [L *ēmissārius,* from *ēmiss-,* p.p. stem of *ēmittere,* to EMIT]

emission, *n.* the act or process of emitting or being emitted; the thing given off or out; the act of issuing bank-notes etc.; the number and value of the notes etc.; sent out; (*Radio.*) a stream of electrons radiated from the filament of a thermionic valve; radiating power. **theory of emission,** the theory of Newton that light consists of particles emitted by luminous bodies. **emissive, emissory,** *a.* **emissivity**, *n.* [L *ēmissio,* as prec.]

emit, *v.t.* to give out, to give vent to, to issue, to discharge; to print and send into circulation (as banknotes). **emitter,** *n.* an electrode of a transistor. [L *ēmittere* (E-, *mittere,* to send)]

emmarble, *v.t.* to turn into marble; to decorate with marble.

emmenagogue, *n.* (*Med.*) a medicine that induces or restores the menses. **emmenology**, *n.* [Gr. *emmēna,* menses, *agōgos,* drawing forth]

Emmental, -thal, *n.* a Swiss cheese with holes in it, made in the Emmenthal valley.

emmet, *n.* an ant. [OE *æmete,* see ANT]

Emmy, *n.* (*pl.* **Emmys**, **Emmies**) the television equivalent of an Oscar, awarded by the American Academy of Television Arts and Sciences. [etym. doubtful]

emollient, *a.* softening, relaxing; making soft or supple. *n.* a substance which softens the part to which it is applied, and diminishes irritation; (*fig.*) anything intended to soothe or comfort. [L *ēmolliens -ntem,* pres.p. of *ēmollīre,* to soften (E-, *mollis,* soft)]

emolument, *n.* the profit arising from any office or employment; remuneration; †gain, profit. **emolumentary**, *a.* [OF, from L *ēmolumentum,* profit, from *ēmolere* (E-, *molere,* to grind) or *ēmōlīrī* (E-, *mōlīrī,* to work)]

emotion, *n.* agitation of the mind; a state of excited feeling of any kind, whether of pain or pleasure; excitement. **emote,** *v.i.* to show or express exaggerated emotion as in acting. **emotional,** *a.* pertaining to emotion; easily affected with emotion. **emotionalism,** *n.* **emotionalist,** *n.* **emotionality**, *n.* **emotionally,** *adv.* **emotionless,** *a.* **emotive,** *a.* emotional; tending to produce emotion. **emotively,** *adv.* [L *ēmōtio -ōnem,* from *ēmovēre* (E-, *movēre,* to move)]

emove, *v.t.* to affect with emotion.

Emp., (*abbr.*) Emperor; Empire; Empress.

empacket, *v.t.* to pack up. [F *empaqueter*]

empanel, *v.t.* to enter on the list of jurors; to enrol as a jury.

†**empanoply,** *v.t.* to invest in complete armour.

empathy, *n.* the capacity for reacting to the experience of, or appreciating things or emotions outside, ourselves; the losing of one's identity in, e.g. a work of art. **empathetic**, *a.* **empathize, -ise,** *v.t.* [Gr. *empathēs,* in a state of emotion]

Empedocles, *n.* (*c.* 490–430 BC), Greek philosopher and scientist. He lived at Acragas (Agrigentum) in Sicily, and is known for his analysis of the universe into four elements – fire, air, earth, and water – which through the action of love and discord are eternally constructed, destroyed, and constructed anew. According to tradition, he committed suicide by throwing himself into the crater of Mount Etna.

†**empeople,** *v.t.* to populate; to establish as inhabitants.

emperor, *n.* the sovereign of an empire; the sovereign of the Holy Roman Empire; the highest dignity (superior to king). **purple emperor,** *Apatura iris,* a large and handsome British butterfly. **emperor moth,** *n. Saturnia pavonia,* a large and beautiful British moth. **emperor penguin,** *n.* the large penguin, *Aptenodytes forsteri.* **emperorship,** *n.* †**empery,** *n.* sovereignty, empire; the territory of an emperor. [OF *empereor,* nom. *emperere,* L *imperātor -ōrem,* from *imperāre,* to command (IM-, *parāre,* to prepare, order)]

emphasis, *n.* (*pl.* **-ses**) a particular stress laid upon a word or words, to indicate special significance; force or intensity of expression, language, feeling, gesture etc.; accent, stress, prominence, sharp definition. **emphasize, -ise,** *v.t.* to pronounce with emphasis; to lay stress upon; to make more distinct, prominent or impressive. **emphatic, -ical,** *a.* bearing emphasis or special stress; accentuated, forcible, striking; positive, earnest. **emphatically,** *adv.* [L, from Gr. (EM-, *phasis,* from *phainein,* to show)]

emphractic, *a.* having the quality of closing the pores of the skin. *n.* an emphractic medicine. [Gr. *emphraktikos,* from *emphrattein* (EM-, *phrattein,* to block)]

emphysema, *n.* the pressure of air causing distension in the cellular tissue; such distension in the tissue of the lung, causing breathing difficulties. **emphysematous,** *a.* [Gr. *emphusēma,* from *emphusaein* (EM-, *phusaein,* to blow, puff)]

empire, *n.* supreme and extensive dominion; absolute power; the region over which an emperor rules; a State in which the sovereign is an emperor; supreme control, rule, sway. *a.* indicating the style of costume and furniture of the First or Second French Empire. **British Empire,** former name of the British Commonwealth of Nations, the association of self-governing dominions, colonies, dependencies etc. acknowledging the sovereignty of the King or Queen of Great Britain, Ireland and the Dominions. **Eastern Empire,** the Greek or Byzantine Empire formed by the division of the Roman Empire at the death of Theodosius the Great (AD 395). **Empire Marketing Board,** (*Hist.*) a body set up to foster the employment in the Mother Country of the produce of the Dominions. **the Empire,** the British Empire, the first Napoleonic Empire (1804–15); the Holy Roman Empire. **the Second Empire,** the empire of Napoleon III (1852–70). **Western Empire,** the Latin Empire, the part of the Roman Empire which fell to Honorius at the death of his father Theodosius. **empire-builder,** *n.* a person who seeks added power and authority, esp. by increasing the number of his/her staff. **Empire Day, Commonwealth Day,** *n.* (*formerly*) a British celebration held annually on 24 May, Queen Victoria's birthday. **empire gown,** *n.* a high-waisted gown after the style of those worn during the First French Empire. **empire preference,** *n.* (*Hist.*) the policy of granting favourable tariffs to countries within the British Empire. **Empire State,** *n.* the state of New York. [OF, from L *imperium,* conn. with *imperāre* (see EMPEROR)]

empiric, *a.* founded on experience or observation, not theory; acting on this; of the nature of a quack, charlatanic; pertaining to quackery. *n.* one who relies solely on experience or observation, esp. a medical practitioner without scientific training; a quack, a charlatan; †one of an ancient medical sect who considered observation and experiment the only true method of obtaining knowledge. **empirical,** *a.* **empirically,** *adv.* **empiricism**, *n.* **empiricist**, *n.* †**empiricutic**, *a.* (*Shak.*) empiric (assim. to PHARMACEUTIC). **empirism**, *n.* a conclusion attained on empirical grounds; empiricism. **empiristic**, *a.* [F *empirique,* L *empīricus,* Gr. *empeirikos,* from *empeiros,* experienced (EM-, *peira,* trial)]

emplacement, *n.* location, situation, position; a setting in position; (*Fort.*) a platform for guns.

emplane, *v.i.* to go on board an aeroplane. *v.t.* to place in an aeroplane.

employ, *v.t.* to use, to exercise; to set at work; to keep in one's service; to spend or pass (time, oneself etc.) in any occupation. *n.* occupation, business, profession. **in the employ of,** employed by. **employable,** *a.* **employee,** *n.* one who is employed regularly in some task or occupation for salary or wages. **employer,** *n.* one who employs people for salary or wages. **employment,** *n.* the act of employing; the state of being employed; regular occupation, trade or profession. **employment agency,** *n.* one used by people looking for work and employers seeking employees. [OF *employer,* L *implicāre* (IM-, *plicāre,* to fold)]

emplume, *v.t.* to adorn with or as with plumes; †to tar and feather. [F *emplumer* (EM-, PLUME)]

empoison, *v.t.* to mix poison with; to envenom; to taint, vitiate, corrupt; to render hostile; †to administer poison to; †to kill with or as with poison. †**empoisonment,** *n.* [F *empoisonner* (EM-, POISON)]

emporium, *n.* (*pl.* **-ria** -iə) a commercial centre; a mart; (*coll., often facet.*) a large shop where many kinds of goods are sold. [L, from Gr. *emporion,* neut. of *emporios,* commercial, from *emporos,* a passenger, a merchant (EM-, *poros,* a way)]

empoverish, IMPOVERISH.

empower, *v.t.* to authorize; to enable. [EM-, POWER]

empress, *n. fem.* the consort of an emperor; a female ruler of an empire. [OF *emperesse,* fem. of *empereor,* EMPEROR]

empressement, *n.* cordiality, goodwill, eagerness. [F, from *empresser,* to urge, *s'empresser,* to be eager]

†**emprise,** *n.* an adventurous or chivalrous undertaking. *v.t.* to undertake. [OF, orig. fem. of *empris,* p.p. of *emprendre* (EM-, *prendre,* L *prehendere,* to take)]

†**emption,** *n.* the act of buying; a purchase. **emptor,** *n.* a purchaser. [L *emptio -ōnem,* from *emere,* to buy]

empty, *a.* void, containing nothing; devoid (of); vacant, unoccupied; unloaded; destitute, desolate; meaningless, unsubstantial, shadowy; senseless, inane; without intelligence, ignorant; hungry, unsatisfied. *n.* an empty packing-case, trunk, barrel, crate, bottle etc. *v.t.* to remove the contents from, to make vacant; to remove from a receptacle (to another); to pour out, discharge. *v.i.* to become empty; to discharge (as a river). **empty-handed,** *a.* bringing nothing; carrying away nothing. **empty-headed,** *a.* silly, witless. **empty-hearted,** *a.* heartless. **emptyings,** *n.pl.* (*N Am.*) the lees of beer, cider etc. used as yeast. **emptier,** *n.* **emptiness,** *n.* [OE *æmtig,* from *æmetta,* leisure]

†**empurple,** *v.t.* to tinge or colour with purple.

empyema, *n.* a collection of pus consequent on pleurisy. [Gr. *empuēma,* from *empueein* (EM-, *pueein,* to suppurate)]

empyrean, *n.* the highest and purest region of heaven, where the element of fire was supposed by the ancients to exist without any admixture of grosser matter; the upper sky. *a.* pertaining to the highest heaven or to the upper sky. **empyreal,** *a.* [med. L *empyraeus,* Gr. *empuros,* fiery (EM-, *pur,* fire)]

empyreuma, *n.* (*pl.* **-mata**) the disagreeable smell and taste produced when animal or vegetable substances in closed vessels are submitted to considerable heat. **empyreumatic, -ical,** *a.* **empyreumatize, -ise,** *v.t.* [Gr. *empureuma,* from *empureuein,* to set on fire (EM-, *pur,* fire)]

EMS, (*abbr.*) European Monetary System.

EMU, (*abbr.*) economic and monetary union; the proposed European Community policy for a single currency and common economic policies.

emu, *n.* a large Australian cursorial bird of the genus *Dromaeus,* esp. *D Novae-Hollandiae,* resembling the cassowary but different in having no casque. **emu-wren,** *n.* a small Australian bird, *Stipiturus malachurus,* having the tail feathers loose-webbed, and somewhat resembling those of the emu. [Port. *ema,* ostrich]

emulate, *v.t.* to try to equal or excel; to rival; to imitate with intent to equal or excel. †*a.*, ambitious, emulous.

emulation, *n.* the act of emulating; ambition to equal or excel the action of others; rivalry, envy, jealousy. **emulative,** *a.* **emulatively,** *adv.* **emulator,** *n.* one who emulates; a rival; †a disparager. †**emulatress,** *n. fem.* †**emule,** *v.t.* to emulate. [L *aemulātus,* p.p. of *aemulārī,* from *aemulus,* EMULOUS]

emulgent, *a.* milking or draining out; (*Physiol.*) applied to the renal arteries and veins, the ancients assuming that they milked out the serum by means of the kidneys. [L *ēmulgens -ntem,* pres.p. of *ēmulgēre* (E-, *mulgēre,* to milk)]

emulous, *a.* desirous of equalling or excelling others; engaged in rivalry or competition; desirous of fame or honour; envious, factious, contentious. **emulously,** *adv.* **emulousness,** *n.* [L *aemulus*]

emulsifier, *n.* a food additive used to keep oils dispersed and in suspension, in products such as mayonnaise and peanut butter. Egg yolk is a naturally occurring emulsifier, but most of the emulsifiers in commercial use today are synthetic chemicals. **emulsify,** *v.t.* to convert into emulsion. **emulsification,** *n.*

emulsion, *n.* a colloidal suspension of one liquid in another; a light-sensitive substance held in suspension in collodion or gelatine, used for coating plates or films. *v.t.* to apply emulsion paint. **emulsion paint,** *n.* a water-thinnable paint made from an emulsion of a resin in water. **emulsin,** *n.* a neutral fermenting substance found in almonds. **emulsionize, -ise,** *v.t.* **emulsive,** *a.* [L *ēmūls-,* p.p. stem of *ēmulgēre,* to drain out (see EMULGENT)]

emunctory, *a.* serving to wipe the nose; serving to carry noxious or useless particles out of the body. *n.* an excretory duct. [L *ēmunct-,* p.p. stem of *ēmungere,* to wipe the nose]

emys, *n.* (*pl.* **emydes**) (*Zool.*) the freshwater tortoise. [Gr. *emus*]

en, *n.* the 14th letter of the alphabet, N, n; (*Print.*) the unit of measurement for casting-off copy, an en being the average width of a letter.

en-, *pref.* in, on, into, upon; as in *enambush, encamp, encourage, engulf, enjewel, enslave, enlighten, encomium, energy, enthusiasm.* [F *en-, em-,* L *in-, im-,* in; also Gr. *en-, em-*]

-en, 1 [OE, from OTeut. *-înom*] diminutive; as in *chicken, maiden.* 2 [OE, from OTeut. *-inî* (G *-in*)] noting the feminine; as in *vixen.* 3 [OE, from OTeut. *-īno-* (cp. Gr. and L *-ino-*)] pertaining to, made of, of the nature of; as in *earthen, flaxen, golden, woollen.* 4 [OE *-an,* pl. of weak decl.] forming pl.; as in *oxen.* 5 [OE *-nan, -nian*] forming verbs from adjectives; as *deepen, fatten, heighten, moisten, sweeten.* 6 [OE *-en*] forming p.p. of strong verbs; as *bounden, spoken.*

enable, *v.t.* to make able; to authorize, empower (to); to supply with means (to do any act). **enabling act,** *n.* legislation conferring specified powers on a person or organization.

enact, *v.t.* to decree; to pass, as a bill into a law; to represent, act, play; †to accomplish, perform. †*n.* that which is enacted; (*fig.*) a purpose, a resolution. **enacting clauses,** *n.pl.* clauses in a bill which contain new enactments. **enaction,** *n.* **enactive,** *a.* **enactment,** *n.* **enactory,** *a.* †**enacture,** *n.* (*Shak.*) action, fulfilment.

enallage, *n.* a change of words, or a substitution of one mood, tense, number, case or gender of the same word for another. [L, from Gr., conn. with *enallassein* (EN-, *allassein,* to change)]

enamel, *n.* a vitreous, opaque or semitransparent material with which metal, porcelain and other vessels, ornaments etc. are coated by fusion, for decorative or preservative purposes; any smooth, hard, glossy coating; a lacquer, a varnish, a paint, a cosmetic; the ivory-like substance which covers the surface of the teeth; a bright smooth surface; †gloss, polish. *v.t.* (*past, p.p.* **enamelled**) to coat with enamel; to paint, encrust or inlay with enamel; to form a smooth glossy surface upon; to decorate with various colours. *v.i.* to practise the art of enamelling. **enameller,** *n.* **enamel-**

list, *n.* [ME *enamayl,* OF *esmail,* med. L *smaltum,* from Teut. (cp. OHG *smalzjan,* Dut. *smelten,* to SMELT)]

enamour, *v.t.* to captivate, to charm; to inflame with love. **to be enamoured,** to be in love; to be fond (of). [OF *enamorer*]

enantiosis, *n.* a figure of speech by which one says (usually ironically) the reverse of what one means. [Gr., from *enantioesthai,* from *enantios,* contrary]

enarch, *v.t.* to arch over; (*Her.*) to arch with a chevron; (*Hort.*) to inarch.

†**enarration,** *n.* a narration or description. [L *ēnārrātio -ōnem, īnārrāre* (E-, *nārrāre,* to NARRATE)]

enarthrosis, *n.* a ball-and-socket joint. **enarthrodial,** *a.* [Gr., from *enarthros,* jointed (EN-, *arthron,* a joint)]

enation, *n.* (*Bot.*) the production of outgrowths upon the surface of an organ. [L *ēnātus,* born]

en avant, forward. [F]

en bloc, as a unit, all together. [F]

encaenia, *n.pl.* a festival to commemorate the dedication of a church, the founding of a city etc.; the annual commemoration of founders and benefactors of Oxford Univ. [L, from Gr. *enkainia* (EN-, *kainos,* new)]

encage, *v.t.* to shut in or as in a cage; to confine.

encamp, *v.i.* to form an encampment; to settle down temporarily in tents. *v.t.* to settle (troops) in an encampment; to lodge (troops) in tents. **encampment,** *n.* the act of encamping; a camp; the place where troops are encamped.

encapsulate, *v.t.* to enclose in a capsule; to capture the essence of; to put in a shortened form.

encarnalize, -ise, *v.t.* to make carnal; to make fleshly; to embody in the flesh.

encase, *v.t.* to put into a case; to enclose in a case; to protect with a case. **encasement,** *n.* [F *encaisser* EN-, *caisse,* CASE[1])]

encash, *v.t.* to cash, to convert (bills etc.) into cash; to realize, to obtain in the form of cash. **encashable,** *a.* **encashment,** *n.*

encaustic, *n.* a mode of painting in which the colours are fixed by heat (now chiefly of painting on vitreous or ceramic ware in which the colours are burnt in). *a.* pertaining to or executed by this method. **encaustic brick, tile,** *n.* one which is inlaid with clay patterns burnt in. [F *encaustique,* L *encausticus,* Gr. *enkaustikos,* from *enkaiein* (EN-, *kaiein,* to burn)]

encave, *v.t.* to hide in a cellar. [OF *encaver,* to put in a cellar]

-ence, *suf.* forming abstract nouns, as *existence, corpulence.* [F *-ence,* or directly from L *-entia,* from pres.p. in *-ens -entis* (rarely from neut. pl. of adjectives)]

enceinte, *a.* pregnant; with child. *n.* the space within the ramparts of a fortification. [F, fem. of *enceint,* L *incinctus,* p.p. of *incingere* (IN-[1], *cingere,* to girdle)]

encephalitis, *n.* inflammation of the brain. **encephalitis lethargica,** *n.* acute inflammation of the brain, commonly called sleepy sickness.

encephalocele, *n.* hernia of the brain. [-CELE, a tumour]

encephalography, *n.* radiography of the brain. **encephalograph, -gram,** *n.* an X-ray of the brain.

encephalon, *n.* (*pl.* **-la** -ə) the brain; the contents of the skull. **encephalic,** *a.* **encephaloid,** *a.* pertaining to or resembling brain matter. *n.* a kind of cancer in which the parts affected resemble the medullary parts of the brain. **encephalous,** *a.* having a distinct brain or head, used of certain molluscs called the Encephala. [Gr. *enkephalon* (EN-, *kephalē,* the head)]

encephalopathy, *n.* disease referable to a disorder of brain. **encephalopathic,** *a.*

encephalotomy, *n.* the operation of cutting into the brain; dissection of the brain.

enchafe, *v.t.* to make hot; to excite, to irritate. [ME *enchaufe,* OF *eschaufer*]

enchain, *v.t.* to bind with chains; to chain up; to hold fast, to rivet (attention etc.). **enchainment,** *n.* [OF *enchainer*]

enchant, *v.t.* to influence by magic, to bewitch; to endow with magical powers; to fascinate, to charm; to delight in the highest degree. **enchanter,** *n.* one who practises enchantment; a magician; one who delights or fascinates. **enchanter's nightshade,** *n.* a woodland plant of the genus *Circaea,* esp. *C. lutetiana.* **enchantingly,** *adv.* **enchantment,** *n.* **enchantress,** *n. fem.* [F *enchanter,* L *incantāre* (IN-[1]), *cantāre,* to sing)]

encharge, *v.t.* to enjoin, to give (something) in charge; to commission (with). [OF *encharger*]

†**enchase,** *v.t.* to set or encase within any other material, as a gem in precious metal; to serve as a setting, to encircle; to adorn with embossed work; to decorate with figures; to enshrine, to enclose. [F *enchâsser* (EN-, *châsse,* shrine, L *capsa,* CASE[1])]

enchilada, *n.* a Mexican dish of a meat-filled tortilla served with chilli sauce.

enchiridion, *n.* a handbook or manual, a small guide or book of reference. [Gr. *encheiridion* (EN-, *cheir,* hand, *-idion,* dim. suf.)]

enchorial, *a.* belonging to or used in a country; popular, common; applied to the demotic characters formed from Egyptian hieroglyphics. **enchoric,** *a.* [Gr. *enchorios* (EN-, *chora,* country)]

encincture, *v.t.* to surround with or as with a ring or girdle. *n.* a girdle; a surrounding or enclosing.

encircle, *v.t.* to enclose or surround (with); to take up a position round; to embrace, to encompass. **encirclement,** *n.* a German phrase to describe the formation of an alliance between her neighbouring countries to prevent her expansion.

Encke's comet, *n.* a comet with the shortest known orbital period, 3.3 years. It is named after German mathematician and astronomer, Johann Franz Encke (1791–1865) who in 1819 calculated the orbit from earlier sightings.

en clair, *a.* of telegrams etc., not in code or cipher. [F]

enclasp, *v.t.* to enfold in a clasp, to embrace.

enclave, *n.* a territory completely surrounded by that of another power; an enclosure. *a.* (*Her.*) shaped like a dovetail; dovetailed. **enclavement,** *n.* [F, from *enclaver,* late L *inclāvāre* (IN-[1], *clāvus,* nail, or *clāvis,* key)]

enclitic, *a.* (*Gr. Gram.*) applied to a word which cannot, as it were, stand by itself, but is pronounced as part of the preceding word, on which it throws its accent, e.g. *thee* in *prithee. n.* an enclitic word or particle. **enclitically,** *adv.* [L *encliticus,* Gr. *enklitikos* (EN-, *klīnein,* to lean)]

†**encloister,** *v.t.* to shut up in a cloister; to immure.

enclose, *v.t.* to shut in; to surround or hem in on all sides; to surround by a fence; to put one thing inside another for transmission or carriage; to contain. **enclosed order,** *n.* a Christian contemplative order which does not allow its members to go into the outside world. **encloser,** *n.* **enclosure,** *n.* the act of enclosing, esp. the act of enclosing common land so as to make it private property; that which is enclosed; a space of ground enclosed or fenced in; that which encloses, as a fence; anything enclosed in an envelope, wrapper etc.

encode, *v.t.* to translate a message into code.

encolure, *n.* (*Browning*) a horse's mane. [F (EN-, *col* (L *collum*), neck, -URE)]

encomiast, *n.* one who composes an encomium, a panegyrist; a flatterer. **encomiastic,** *a.* bestowing praise; laudatory, panegyrical. †*n.* an encomium. †**encomiastical,** *a.* **encomiastically,** *adv.* [Gr. *enkōmiastēs,* from *enkōmiazein,* to praise, as foll.]

encomium, *n.* (*pl.* **-miums, -mia**) a formal eulogy or panegyric; high commendation; high-flown praise. [L, from Gr. *enkōmion,* neut. of *enkōmios,* laudatory (EN-, *kōmos,* revelry)]

encompass, *v.t.* to surround, to invest; to go round, to encircle; to include, contain; †to get in one's power, circumvent. **encompassment,** *n.*

encore, *adv.* again, once more; used as a call for a repetition at a concert, theatre etc. *n.* a demand for a repetition of a song etc.; the repetition itself. *v.t.* to call for a repetition of. *v.i.* to call for an encore. [F, again, L (*in*) *hanc horam,* to this hour]

encounter, *v.t.* to meet face to face; to meet in a hostile manner; to confront resolutely; to attack and endeavour to refute; to meet with, come across. *n.* a meeting face to face; a hostile meeting, a skirmish, a battle; an unplanned or unexpected meeting; †address, manner of accosting. **encounter group,** *n.* a group of people who meet to develop self-awareness and understanding of others by frank exchange of feelings, opinions and contact. **encounterer,** *n.* an adversary, an opponent; †one who is quick to accost another. [OF *encontrer,* late L *incontrāre* (IN-[1], *contra,* against)]

encourage, *v.t.* to give courage or confidence to; to animate, embolden; to urge, to incite (to do); to stimulate, to promote, to foster (trade, opinion etc.). **encouragement,** *n.* **encourager,** *n.* **encouragingly,** *adv.* [OF *encoragier* (EN-, COURAGE)]

encradle, *v.t.* to place in a cradle.

encraty, *n.* mastery over the senses, self-control. [Gr. *egkrateia,* mastery]

encrimson, *v.t.* to make crimson, redden.

encrinite, *n.* a fossil crinoid. **encrinal, encrinic, encrinital,** *a.* pertaining to or containing encrinites. [Gr. EN-, *krinon,* lily; -ITE]

encroach, *v.i.* to intrude (upon) what belongs to another; to infringe (upon); to get possession of anything gradually or by stealth. **encroacher,** *n.* **encroachingly,** *adv.* **encroachment,** *n.* the act of encroaching; that which is taken by encroaching; (*Law*) the act of unlawfully trespassing upon or interfering with the rights, property or privileges of another. [OF *encrochier* (EN-, *croc,* hook, cp. MDut. *kroke,* Icel. *krōkr,* crook)]

encrust, *v.t.* to cover with a crust or hard coating; to form a crust upon the surface of; to apply a decorated layer or lining to the surface of. **encrustation, encrustment** INCRUSTATION. [prob. through F *incruster,* from L *incrustāre* (IN-, *crusta,* CRUST)]

encumber, *v.t.* to hamper, impede or embarrass by a weight, burden or difficulty; to burden; to weigh down with debt; to perplex; †to fold (the arms). **encumberment,** *n.* **encumbrance,** *n.* a hindrance to freedom of action or motion; a burden, a hindrance, a clog; (*Law*) a liability upon an estate, such as a mortgage, a claim etc. **encumbrancer,** *n.* (*Law*) one who holds an encumbrance upon another person's estate. [OF *encombrer,* late L *incumbrāre* (IN-, *cumbrus,* an obstacle, see CUMBER)]

encurtain, *v.t.* to enwrap or veil with or as with a curtain.

-ency, *suf.* forming nouns of state or quality. [-ENCE]

encyclic, -ical, *a.* sent about to many persons or places. *n.* a circular letter, esp. a letter from the Pope to the bishops or to the Church at large. [late L *encyclicus,* Gr. *enkuklios* (EN-, *kuklos,* a ring, a circle)]

encyclopaedia, (*esp. N Am.* **-pedia**), *n.* a book containing information on all branches of knowledge, or on a particular branch, usually arranged alphabetically, esp. the great French Encyclopaedia (see below); a general system of knowledge or instruction. **encyclopaedian, encyclopaedic, -ical,** *a.* **encyclopaedism,** *n.* the compilation of an encyclopaedia; the possession of a large range of knowledge and information; the doctrines of the French Encyclopaedists. **encyclopaedist,** *n.* a compiler of an encyclopaedia; one who has acquired an extensive range of knowledge or information; (*pl.*) Diderot, D'Alembert, and their associates, who produced the great French Encyclopaedia between 1751 and 1772. [late L, from pseudo-Gr. *enkuklopaideia,* a false reading for *enkuklios paideia,* general instruction (as prec., and *paideia,* from *paideuein,* to educate, from *pais paidos,* a child)]

encyst, *v.t.* to enclose in a cyst, bladder or vesicle. **encystation,** *n.* **encystis,** *n.* (*Path.*) an encysted tumour. **encystment,** *n.*

end, *n.* the extreme point or boundary of a line or of anything that has length; the termination, limit or last portion; the last part of a period; the conclusion of a state or action; a ceasing to exist; the final lot or doom; abolition; death; the cause of death; a result, a natural consequence, a necessary outcome; a purpose, an object, a designed result; a reason for (a thing's) existence, a final cause; (*usu. in pl.*) a remnant. *a.* final; farthest; last. *v.i.* to come to an end, to cease; to result (in). *v.t.* to bring to an end; to put to an end, to destroy; †(*fig.*) to harvest, to get in (corn). **at a loose end,** (*coll.*) temporarily disengaged. **at one's wits' end,** bewildered, utterly perplexed, nonplussed. **at the end of one's tether,** unable to do anything more. **end on,** with the end pointing towards one. **end to end,** with the ends touching, lengthwise. **in the end,** finally; after all. **no end,** plenty, much, many. **odds and ends,** odd remnants. **on end,** upright, erect. **rope's end,** the end of a rope whipped with cord; such a piece cut off and used for flogging. **shoe-maker's end,** a waxed thread armed with a bristle. **the be all and end all,** the sole aim, ambition. **the end of the road,** the point beyond which a person or thing can no longer go on or survive. **the ends of the earth,** the remotest parts of the earth. **to come to an end,** to end, to be finished, to be exhausted. **to go off the deep end,** to lose one's temper. **to keep one's end up,** (*coll.*) to stand one's ground. **to make both ends meet,** to keep expenditure within income. **to put an end to,** to terminate, to stop; to abolish. **to that end,** for that purpose. **without end,** everlasting; very long; inexhaustible. **wrong end of the stick,** the contrary to what is meant. **end-game,** *n.* the last part of a game of chess etc., when only a few pieces remain in play. **end-iron,** *n.* a movable plate in a kitchen range for enlarging or contracting the fire space. **end-paper,** *n.* one of the blank pages placed between the cover and the body of a book. **end product,** *n.* the final product obtained after a series of processes. **end result,** *n.* the final outcome. **end-stopped,** *a.* (*Pros.*) having a pause in sense at the end of a line of poetry. **end-user,** *n.* the person, firm etc. in receipt of a manufactured product being sold. **end-zone,** *n.* part of the pitch markings in a game of American football. **ending,** *n.* a conclusion, a termination; the latter part of a story, an occurrence etc.; the terminating syllable of a word in grammar. **endless,** *a.* having no end; infinite, unlimited, perpetual; incessant. **endless band, cable** or **chain,** *n.* a band with ends fastened together for conveying mechanical motion. **endless screw,** *n.* a screw conveying motion to a wheel in the teeth of which the threads engage. **endlessly,** *adv.* **endlessness,** *n.* **endlong,** *adv.* lengthwise as distinguished from crosswise; straight along; †continuously. †*a.* standing on end, vertical. **endmost,** *a.* the nearest to the end, the furthest. **endways,** *adv.* on end; with the end foremost or uppermost; end to end; lengthwise. **endwise,** *adv.* [OE *ende* (cp. Dut. *einde,* Icel. *endi,* Dan. *ende,* G *Ende*)]

end- END(O)-.

endamage, *v.t.* to damage; to prejudice.

endanger, *v.t.* to expose to danger, to put in hazard. †**endangerment,** *n.*

endear, *v.t.* to make dear (to); to cause to be loved; †to secure the affections of; †to bind (to) by gratitude etc.; †to make dear or costly. **endearing,** *a.* **endearingly,** *adv.* **endearment,** *n.*

endeavour, *v.i.* to strive (after) a certain end; to try, to make an effort (to). †*v.t.* to attempt or essay. *n.* an effort, an attempt; exertion for the attainment of some object. †**endeavourment,** *n.*

endeictic, *a.* showing, exhibiting. **endeixis,** *n.* a symptom. [Gr. *endeiktikos,* from *endeiknunai* (EN-, *deiknunai,* to show)]

endemic, *a.* peculiar to a particular locality or people. *n.* an endemic disease. **endemic disease,** *n.* one common from local causes in a particular district or among a particular people or class, beyond which it shows no tendency to spread. **endemically,** *adv.* **endemicity,** *n.* **endemiology,** *n.* the study of endemic diseases. [EN-, Gr. *dēmos,* people (cp. *endēmios*)]

endermic, *a.* acting upon or through the skin, as an unguent applied after blistering. **endermically,** *adv.*

enderon, *n.* (*Physiol.*) the inner derm or true skin. [EN-, Gr. *deros, derma,* skin]

en déshabille, in a state of undress. [F].
endive, *n.* a kind of chicory, *Cichorium endivia,* much cultivated for use in salads, or *C. intybus,* the wild endive. [F, from L *intibus*]
end(o)-, *comb. form.* pertaining to the inside of anything. [Gr. *endon,* within]
endocardium, *n.* a membrane lining the interior of the human heart. **endocardiac**, *a.* **endocarditis**, *n.* inflammation of the endocardium. [Gr. *kardia,* heart]
endocarp, *n.* (*Bot.*) the inner layer of a pericarp.
endochrome, *n.* a colouring matter found in the cells of plants.
endocrane, *n.* the inner surface of the cranium.
endocrine, *n.* the internal secretion of a gland. **endocrine gland,** *n.* an organ of a glandular structure possessing no duct but yielding an internal secretion which is poured into the blood-stream. **endocrinology**, *n.* the study of the secretions of the endocrine glands.
endoderm, *n.* the inner layer of the blastoderm; the membrane lining the internal cavity of certain organisms, esp. the Coelenterata; (*Bot.*) an inner layer of cells beneath the liber; the inner layer of the wall of a cell.
endogamous, *a.* necessarily marrying within the tribe. **endogamy,** *n.* the custom of taking a wife only within the tribe; pollination between two flowers on the same plant. [Gr. *gamos,* marriage]
endogen, *n.* an endogenous plant; (*pl.*) one of the divisions of the vegetable kingdom, in which the plants increase by internal layers and elongation at the summit, instead of externally, and have no distinction of bark and pith, as in the palm, the sugar-cane etc. **endogenous**, *a.* growing from within.
endolymph, *n.* the serous fluid in the membranous labyrinth of the ear.
endometrium, *n.* the membrane lining the cavity of the womb. **endometritis**, *n.* inflammation of this. [Gr. *metra,* womb]
endomorph, *n.* a mineral enclosed inside another; a person of plump, thick-set build.
endoparasite, *n.* (*Zool.*) a parasite living in the interior of its host. **endoparasitic**, *a.*
endophyllous, *a.* denoting leaves evolved from a sheath.
endoplasm, *n.* the partially fluid inner layer of protoplasm. **endoplast**, *n.* the nucleus in the protoplasm of some of the Protozoa.
endopleura, *n.* the internal tegument of a seed.
endorhiza, *n.* (*Bot.*) the sheath-enclosed radical of the embryo in many monocotyledonous plants. **endorhizal, -rhizous,** *a.* [Gr. *rhiza,* root]
endorphin, *n.* any of a group of chemicals occurring in the brain which have a similar effect to morphine.
endorse, *v.t.* to write (one's name, a note of contents etc.) on the back of (a document); (*fig.*) to assign by indorsement; to ratify, confirm, approve; †to load the back (with); †to take upon one's back; to record a conviction on (an offender's driving licence). **to endorse over,** to transfer one's rights in (a bill etc.) to another person. **endorsee**, *n.* the person to whom a bill etc. is assigned by indorsement. **endorsement,** *n.* **endorser,** *n.* [ME *endosse,* OF *endosser,* med. L *indorsāre* (IN-, L *dorsum,* the back)]
endosarc, *n.* endoplasm.
endoscope, *n.* an instrument for inspecting internal parts of the body. **endoscopy**, *n.*
endoskeleton, *n.* the internal bony and cartilaginous framework of the vertebrates.
endosmose, endosmosis, *n.* the passage of a fluid from outside inwards through a porous diaphragm. **endosmotic**, **endosmic**, **endosmosmic**, *a.*
endosperm, *n.* the albumen of a seed. **endospermic**, *a.*
endospore, *n.* the inner layer of the wall of a spore.
endostome, *n.* the aperture in the inner integument of an ovule.
endothelium, *n.* a membrane lining blood-vessels, tubes, cavities etc.
endow, *v.t.* to invest with goods, estate, privileges etc.; to invest (with qualities etc.); to bestow a permanent income upon; to give a dowry to. **endowment,** *n.* the act of settling a dower or portion upon a woman; the act of making permanent provision for the support of any person, institution etc.; the fund or property so appropriated; (*pl.*) natural gifts, qualities or ability. **endowment assurance,** *n.* an assurance to provide a fixed sum at a specified age or on death before that age. [EN-, F *douer,* L *dōtāre,* to DOWER]
endozoic, *a.* living inside an animal, a term applied to the method of seed-dispersal by being swallowed by an animal and then passed out in its excreta.
endue, *v.t.* to put on (as clothes); to clothe, to invest (with); (*usu. in p.p.*) to endow, to furnish. [OF *enduire,* L *indūcere* (IN-, *dūcere,* to lead, draw)]
endure, *v.t.* to bear, to stand (a test or strain); to undergo, to suffer; to submit to. *v.i.* to last; to abide in the same state; to bear sufferings with patience and fortitude. **endurability**, *n.* **endurable,** *a.* **endurableness,** *n.* **endurance,** *n.* the act or state of enduring or suffering; the capacity of bearing or suffering with patience; continuance, duration. **endurer,** *n.* **enduring,** *a.* bearing; durable, permanent. **enduringly,** *adv.* **enduringness,** *n.* [OF *endurer,* L *indūrāre* (*dūrus*, hard)]
endways, endwise END.
Endymion, *n.* in Greek mythology, a beautiful young man loved by Selene, the moon goddess. He was granted eternal sleep in order to remain for ever young. The English poet Keats's poem *Endymion* (1818) is an allegory of searching for perfection.
ENE, (*abbr.*) East North East.
†ene, *adv.* once. [OE *æne,* instrumental of *ān*, one]
-ene, *suf.* (*Chem.*) denoting a hydrocarbon, such as *benzene, naphthalene*. [L *-ēnus,* adj. suf.]
en effet, in effect. [F]
enema, *n.* an injection; a liquid or gaseous substance injected into the rectum; the apparatus with which an injection is made. [Gr. *enēma,* from *enienai* (EN-, *hienai,* to send)]
enemy, *n.* one hostile to another; an adversary, one opposed to any subject or cause; a hostile army, military force or ship; a member of a hostile force or nation. **the Enemy,** the Devil. **how goes the enemy?** (*coll.*) what is the time? [OF *enemi,* L *inimīcus* (*in,* UN-, *amīcus,* friend)]
energetic ENERGY.
energumen, *n.* one possessed by a spirit, esp. an evil spirit, a demoniac; an enthusiast, a fanatic. [late L *energūmenus,* Gr. *energoumenos,* p.p. *energeein,* to work in or upon, as foll.]
energy, *n.* internal or inherent power; force, vigour; capability of action or performing work; active operation; emphasis; (*Phys.*) a body's power of performing mechanical work. **actual, kinetic** or **motive energy,** the energy of a body in actual motion (measured by the product of half the mass and the square of the velocity). **conservation of energy,** (*Phys.*) the doctrine that no energy is destroyed but that it is transformed into some equivalent capable of doing the same amount of work that it could have done if unchanged. **latent, potential** or **static energy,** the energy possessed by virtue of the relative condition of parts of a body or of bodies to each other. **energetic**, *a.* forcible, powerful; active, vigorously operative. **energetically,** *adv.* **energetics,** *n.* physical, as distinct from vital, dynamics. **†energic**, *a.* energetic. **energize, -ise**, *v.i.* to act energetically and vigorously. *v.t.* to give energy to. [late L *energīa,* Gr. *energeia* (EN-, *ergon,* work)]
enervate, *v.t.* to deprive of force or strength; to weaken; to render effeminate. *a.*, weakened; wanting in spirit, strength or vigour. **enervation**, *n.* [L *ēnervātus,* p.p. of *ēnervāre* (E-, *nervus,* sinew)]
enface, *v.t.* to write, print, stamp the face of.
en famille, at home with the family. [F]
enfant terrible, *n.* a child who makes embarrassing remarks; a person who embarrasses people by behaving indiscreetly, unconventionally etc. [F, terrible child]

enfeeble, *v.t.* to make feeble. **enfeeblement,** *n.*

enfeoff, *v.t.* (*Law*) to invest with a fief; to bestow or convey an estate in fee simple or fee tail; (*fig.*) to surrender, to give (oneself) up. **enfeoffment,** *n.* (*Law*) the act of enfeoffing; the deed by which the fee simple is conveyed. [A-F *enfeoffer,* OF *enfeffer* (EN-, FIEF)]

en fête, dressed for and/or celebrating a holiday. [F]

enfetter, *v.t.* to fetter; to enslave (to).

enfilade, *n.* †a straight passage or suite of apartments; a position liable to a raking fire; a fire that may rake a position, line of works or body of troops, from end to end. *v.t.* to pierce or rake with shot from end to end. [F, from *enfiler,* to thread (EN-, *fil,* L *fīlum,* a thread)]

enfold, *v.t.* to wrap up, to enwrap, to enclose; to clasp, to embrace; to arrange or shape in folds. †**enfoldment,** *n.*

enforce, *v.t.* to carry out vigorously, to execute strictly; to compel obedience to; to give force to; to press or urge forcibly; †to force, to compel; †to ravish; †to prove; to strengthen, to fortify. †*v.i.* to strive, to endeavour, to struggle. †*n.* power, strength; effort. **enforceable,** *a.* **enforced,** *a.* forced, not voluntary. **enforcedly**, *adv.* **enforcement,** *n.* **enforcement officer,** *n.* a government official employed to report on infringements of regulations. [OF *enforcer,* late L *infortiāre* (IN-, L *fortis,* strong)]

enframe, *v.t.* to set in or as in a frame; to be a frame to.

enfranchise, *v.t.* to set free; †to release from custody; †to release from anything which exercises power or influence; to give (a town, constituency etc.) full municipal or parliamentary rights and privileges; to give (someone) the right to vote. †**enfranch,** *v.t.* **enfranchisement**, *n.* the act of enfranchising; the state of being enfranchised; admission to the municipal or the parliamentary franchise. **enfranchisement of copyhold lands,** (*Law*) the conversion of such lands into freeholds. **enfranchiser,** *n.* [OF *enfranchiss-,* stem of *enfranchir* (EN-, *franc,* FRANK[2])]

ENG, (*abbr.*) electronic newsgathering.

Eng., (*abbr.*) England; English.

eng., (*abbr.*) engineer; engineering; engraver; engraving.

engage, *v.t.* to bind by a promise or contract, esp. by promise of marriage; to hire, order, bespeak; to employ, to occupy the time or attention of; to attack, to come into conflict with. *v.i.* to pledge oneself (to do something); to undertake; to enter into, embark (on); to begin to fight, to enter into conflict (with); to interlock (with). *n.* †an engagement, pledge or bargain; (*Fencing*) the order to interlock (swords or foils). **engaged,** *a.* **engaged column,** *n.* (*Arch.*) a column fastened into a wall so that it is partly concealed. **engaged couple,** *n.* two persons who have exchanged promises of marriage. **engaged wheels,** *n.pl.* wheels interlocking with each other by means of cogs etc. **engagement,** *n.* the act of engaging; an obligation, a contract; a mutual promise of marriage; employment or occupation of time or attention; an appointment; a hiring, a contract to employ; the state of being hired; an enterprise embarked on; an action or battle between armies or fleets; (*pl.*) the contracts entered into by a trader. **engagement ring,** *n.* a ring worn by a woman on the third finger of the left hand to show that she is engaged to be married. **engaging,** *a.* winning, pleasing, attractive (used of manners or address). **engagingly,** *adv.* [F *engager* (EN-, *gage,* a pledge)]

en garde, in fencing, a warning to be ready to receive attack; the stance taken at the start of a fencing bout. [F]

engarland, *v.t.* to invest with a garland, to wreathe (with).

Engel, *n.* **Carl Ludwig** (1778–1840), German architect, who from 1815 worked in Finland. His great neoclassical achievement is the Senate Square in Helsinki, which is defined by his Senate House (1818–22) and University Building (1828–32), and crowned by the domed Lutheran cathedral (1830–40).

Engels, *n.* **Friedrich** (1820–95), German social and political philosopher, a friend of, and collaborator with, Karl Marx on *The Communist Manifesto* (1848) and other key works. His later interpretations of Marxism, and his own philosophical and historical studies such as *Origins of the Family, Private Property, and the State* (1884) (which linked patriarchy with the development of private property), developed such concepts as historical materialism. His use of positivism and Darwinian ideas gave Marxism a scientific and deterministic flavour which was to influence Soviet thinking.

engender, *v.t.* to beget; (*now usu. fig.*) to give birth to; to be the cause of, to bring about. †*v.i.* to come into existence. [F *engendrer,* L *ingenerāre* (IN-, *genus,* a race, a brood)]

engine, *n.* an apparatus consisting of a number of parts for applying mechanical power, esp. one that converts energy into motion; a machine or instrument used in war; an instrument, a tool; means to effect a purpose; †native wit; understanding. *v.t.* †to torture by means of an engine; to furnish (a ship) with engines. **engine-driver, -man,** *n.* one who drives or manages a locomotive. **engine-lathe,** *n.* one driven by machinery. **engine plane,** *n.* (*Mining*) an underground passage along which an endless chain or rope worked by an engine hauls tubs and trucks. **engine-sized,** *a.* of paper, sized by machinery. **engine-turning,** *n.* complex ornamental turning, as on the outside of watch-cases, done by machinery. †**enginery**, *n.* engines; apparatus, mechanism, machinery; (*fig.*) artful contrivances; †engines of war, artillery. [OF *engin,* L *ingenium,* genius (see INGENIOUS)]

engineer, *n.* one who designs or carries out construction work of mechanical, electrical or civic nature; (*N Am.*) one who manages or attends to an engine, an engine-driver; a member of that part of an army which attends to engineering work; (*fig.*) one who carries through any undertaking. *v.t.* to direct or carry out, as an engineer, the formation or execution of (as railways, canals etc.); (*coll.*) to contrive, to manage by tact or ingenuity. **engineering,** *n.* **civil engineering,** construction of works of public utility, esp. bridges, canals, railways etc. **electrical engineering,** *n.* construction of electrical engines and equipment. **electronic engineering,** construction of electronic equipment and apparatus. **hydraulic engineering,** construction of waterworks, the application of water-power, the construction of dams, docks etc. **mechanical engineering,** the construction of engines and machinery. **military engineering,** the construction of fortifications, and of roads, bridges etc., used for military purposes. [OF *engigneor,* late L *ingeniātor -ōrem,* from *ingeniāre,* as prec.]

†**enginery** ENGINE.

†**engird,** *v.t.* (*past, p.p.* **engirt**) to encircle, to encompass, as with a girdle.

engirdle, *v.t.* to surround with or as with a girdle.

England, *n.* largest division of the United Kingdom. **area** 130,357 sq km/50,318 sq miles. **capital** London. **towns** Birmingham, Cambridge, Coventry, Leeds, Leicester, Manchester, Newcastle-upon-Tyne, Nottingham, Oxford, Sheffield, York; ports Bristol, Dover, Felixstowe, Harwich, Liverpool, Portsmouth, Southampton. **population** (1986) 47,255,000. **exports** agricultural (cereals, rape, sugar beet, potatoes); meat and meat products; electronic (esp. software), and telecommunications equipment (main centres Berkshire and Cambridge); scientific instruments; textiles and fashion goods; North Sea oil and gas, petrochemicals, pharmaceuticals, fertilizers; beer; china clay, pottery, porcelain, and glass; film and television programmes, and sound recordings. Tourism is important. There are worldwide banking and insurance interests. **language** English, with more than 100 minority languages. **religion** Christian, with the Anglican Communion as the established church, 31,500,000; and various Protestant sects, of which the largest is the Methodist 1,400,000; Roman Catholic about 5,000,000; Jewish 410,000; Muslim 900,000; Sikh 175,000; Hindu 140,000.

English, *a.* pertaining to England or its inhabitants; spoken or written in the English language; characteristic of or becoming an Englishman. *n.* the language of the British Isles, N America, Australasia, parts of Southern Africa, and other parts of the British Commonwealth; in printing, a size of type between great primer and pica; the people of England (sometimes of Britain); the soldiers fighting on the English side. *v.t.* to translate into the English language; to express in plain English. **Basic English** BASIC. **Middle English,** the English language in use from about 1150 to 1500. **Old English,** the English language in use before 1150, also called Anglo-Saxon; (*Print.*) BLACK-LETTER. **plain English,** plain, unambiguous terms. **Queen's, King's English,** correct English as spoken by educated people. **English bond,** *n.* (*Bricklaying*) bonding by means of alternate courses of headers and stretchers. **Englishism,** *n.* **Englishman,** *n.* a native or a naturalized inhabitant of England; one of English blood. **Englishness,** *n.* †**Englishry,** *n.* the quality or state of being an Englishman; the part of the population of a country that is of English blood, esp. the English settlers in Ireland and their descendants; the English population, the English quarter. **Englishwoman,** *n. fem.* [OE *Englisc, Ænglisc,* from *Engle,* the Angles]

English architecture, *n.* the main styles in English architecture are: Saxon, Norman, Early English (of which Westminster Abbey is an example), Decorated, Perpendicular (15th century), Tudor (a name chiefly applied to domestic buildings of about 1485–1558), Jacobean, Stuart (incl. the Renaissance and Queen Anne styles), Georgian, the Gothic revival of the 19th century, Modern, and Post-Modern. Notable architects include Christopher Wren, Inigo Jones, Vanbrugh, Hawksmoor, Charles Barry, Edwin Lutyens, Hugh Casson, Basil Spence, Frederick Gibberd, Denys Lasdun and Richard Rogers.

English horn, *n.* alternative name for cor anglais, musical instrument of the oboe family.

English language, *n.* a member of the Germanic branch of the Indo-European language family. It developed through four major stages over about 1500 years: *Old English* or *Anglo-Saxon* (*c.* 500–1050), rooted in the dialects of settling invaders (Jutes, Saxons, Angles, Danes); *Middle English* (*c.* 1050–1550), influenced by Norman French after the Conquest (1066) and by ecclesiastical Latin; *Early Modern English* (*c.* 1550–1700), standardization of the diverse influences of Middle English, and *Late Modern English* (*c.* 1700 onwards), the development and spread of current Standard English. Through extensive exploration, colonization, and trade, English spread worldwide from the 17th century onwards and remains the most important international language of trade and technology. It is used in many variations, for example, British, US, Canadian, Indian, Singaporean, and Nigerian English, and many pidgins and creoles.

English law, *n.* one of the major European legal systems, Roman law being the other. English law has spread to many other countries, particularly former English colonies such as the US, Canada, Australia, and New Zealand.

englut, *v.t.* to swallow; to gulp down, to glut, to satiate. [OF *englotir,* L *inglutīre* (IN-, *gluttire,* to swallow); and in later senses formed from EN-, GLUT]

engorge, *v.t.* to swallow up, to devour; (*in p.p.*) to fill to excess; (*Path.*) to congest (with blood). **engorgement,** *n.* [F *engorger* (EN-, *gorge,* GORGE)]

engraft, *v.t.* to graft upon, to insert (a scion of one tree) upon or into another; to incorporate; to implant, instil; to superadd.

engrail, *v.t.* (*chiefly Her.*) to indent in curved lines, to make ragged at the edges as if broken with hail; (*poet.*) to adorn. **engrailment,** *n.* [OF *engresler,* perh. from *gresle* (F *grêle*), hail]

engrain, *v.t.* †to dye in fast colours; to dye deeply; (*fig.*) to implant (qualities, esp. vices) ineradicably.

en grande tenue, in full evening dress. [F]

en grand seigneur, like a great lord. [F]

engrave, *v.t.* to cut figures, letters etc. on, with a chisel or graver; to represent on wood, metal etc., by carving with a graver; to inscribe or decorate (a surface) with figures etc.; to imprint; to impress deeply. *v.i.* to practise the art of engraving. **engraver,** *n.* **engraving,** *n.* the act, process or art of cutting figures, letters etc. on wood, stone or metal; that which is engraved; an impression from an engraved plate, a print.

engroove, *v.t.* to make a groove in; to set in a groove.

engross, *v.t.* to write in large, bold letters; to write out in legal form; to buy up the whole or large quantities of in order to enhance the price; to monopolize, to occupy entirely, to absorb; †to make gross or fat. **to be engrossed in,** to be absorbed in (as in reading a book). **engrosser,** *n.* **engrossment,** *n.* exorbitant appropriation or acquisition; the act of engrossing documents; the state of having one's attention wholly taken up. [A-F *engrosser* (EN-, *grosse,* late L *grossa,* large writing)]

enguard, *v.t.* to guard or defend.

engulf, (*esp. formerly*) **-gulph**, *v.t.* to swallow up, as in a gulf or whirlpool; to cast, as into a gulf. **engulfment,** *n.*

engyscope, *n.* (*Opt.*) a reflecting microscope; †any kind of compound microscope. [Gr. *engus,* close at hand]

enhalo, *v.t.* to encircle with or as with a halo.

enhance, *v.t.* to raise in importance, degree etc.; to augment, to intensify; to heighten (in price); to exaggerate; †to advance, to exalt. *v.i.* to be raised; to grow larger, to increase. **enhanced radiation weapon,** a neutron bomb. **enhancement,** *n.* **enhancive,** *a.* [A-F *enhauncer,* OF *enhaucer* (IN-, late L *altiāre,* to heighten, from *altus,* high)]

enharmonic, *a.* (*Mus.*) having intervals less than a semitone, as between G sharp and A flat. *n.* enharmonic music. **enharmonic modulation,** *n.* change as to notation, but not as to sound. **enharmonically,** *adv.* [L *enharmonicus,* Gr. *enarmonikos* (EN-, *harmonia,* HARMONY)]

enhearten, *v.t.* to encourage, cheer, strengthen.

Eniac, (*acronym*) electronic *n*umeral *i*ntegrator *a*nd *c*alculator, the first electronic computer (1946).

enigma, *n.* a saying in which the meaning is concealed under obscure language, a riddle; any inexplicable or mysterious proceeding, person or thing. **enigmatic, -ical,** *a.* **enigmatically,** *adv.* **enigmatist,** *n.* a maker of or dealer in enigmas or riddles. **enigmatize, -ise,** *v.i.* to speak or write enigmatically; to deal in enigmas. [L *aenigma,* Gr. *ainigma -atos,* from *ainissesthai,* to speak obscurely or allusively, from *ainos,* fable]

enjamb(e)ment, *n.* the continuation of a sentence or clause, without a pause in sense, from one verse or couplet into the next. [F *enjambement,* from *enjamber* (EN-, *jambe,* leg)]

enjoin, *v.t.* to direct, prescribe, impose (an act or conduct); to direct or command (a person to do something); to instruct (that); †to prohibit or restrain. †**enjoinment,** *n.* [OF *enjoindre,* L *injungere* (IN-, *jungere,* to join)]

enjoy, *v.t.* to take pleasure or delight in; to have the use or benefit of; to experience or have; to have sexual intercourse with. **to enjoy oneself,** (*coll.*) to experience pleasure or happiness. **enjoyable,** *a.* **enjoyableness,** *n.* **enjoyably,** *adv.* **enjoyment,** *n.* [OF *enjoier*]

enkephalin, *n.* a chemical found in the brain, having an effect similar to that of morphine. [Gr. *en,* in, *kephalē,* head]

enkindle, *v.t.* to kindle, to set on fire; (*fig.*) to inflame, to rouse into passion, action etc.

enlace, *v.t.* to encircle tightly, to surround; to embrace, enfold, entwine; to entangle. **enlacement,** *n.* [F *enlacer* (EN-, *lacer,* ult. from L *laqueāre,* to ensnare, from *laqueus,* a noose)]

†**enlard,** *v.t.* to dress with lard or grease; to baste; to fatten.

enlarge, *v.t.* to make greater; to extend in dimensions, quantity or number; to expand, to widen; to make more comprehensive; to set free from confinement.

v.i. to become bigger; to expatiate (upon). **to enlarge the heart,** to expand or extend the affections. **enlargement,** *n.* the act or process of extending or increasing; increase in size or bulk; something added on, an addition; release from confinement; diffuseness of speech or writing; (*Phot.*) a print or negative of a larger size taken from another. **enlarger,** *n.* [OF *enlarger*]

enlevement, *n.* (*esp. Scots law*) the abduction of a woman or child.

enlighten, *v.t.* to give mental or spiritual light to, to instruct; to give (someone) information (on); to supply with light; (*poet.*) to shed light upon; to release from ignorance, prejudice or superstition. **enlightener,** *n.* **enlightenment,** *n.*

Enlightenment, *n.* a European intellectual movement, reaching its high point in the 18th century. Enlightenment thinkers were believers in social progress and in the liberating possibilities of rational and scientific knowledge. They were often critical of existing society and were hostile to religion, which they saw as keeping the human mind chained down by superstition.

enlink, *v.t.* to join together as with a link, to connect closely.

enlist, *v.t.* to enrol, esp. to engage for military service; to gain the interest, assistance, participation or support of. *v.i.* to engage oneself for military service. **enlisted man,** *n.* (*US*) a private soldier, not a conscript. **enlistment,** *n.*

enliven, *v.t.* to give spirit or animation to; to impart life to, to stimulate; to brighten, render cheerful in appearance. **enlivener,** *n.*

enlumine, *v.t.* to light up, to illuminate. [OF *enluminer,* late L *inlūmināre* (L *illūmināre*) (IN-, *lūmen -inis,* light)]

en masse, in a group, all together. [F]

enmesh, *v.t.* to entangle or catch in or as in a net; to entrap. **enmeshment,** *n.*

enmity, *n.* the quality of being an enemy; hatred, hostility. [A-F *enemité,* OF *enemistié,* late L *inimīcitas -tātem,* from L *inimīcus,* enemy]

ennea-, *comb. form.* nine. [Gr.]

ennead, *n.* a set of nine, esp. of nine books or discourses. [Gr. *enneas -ados*]

enneagynous, *a.* (*Bot.*) having nine pistils. [Gr. *gunē,* woman]

enneahedral, *a.* having nine sides.

Enneandria, *n.pl.* (*Bot.*) a Linnaean class of plants distinguished by the nine stamens of the flowers. **enneandrian, -drous,** *a.* [Gr. *anēr andros,* man]

enneapetalous, *a.* (*Bot.*) having nine petals.

enneaphyllous, *a.* (*Bot.*) having nine leaflets composing a compound leaf.

ennoble, *v.t.* to make noble; to make a noble of; to elevate in character or dignity; to make famous or illustrious. **ennoblement,** *n.* [OF *ennoblir* (EN-, NOBLE)]

ennui, *n.* listlessness; want of interest in things; boredom. **ennuyé,** (*fem.* **ennuyée**), **ennuied,** *a.* affected with ennui. [F, from OF *enui,* L *in odio* (cp. ANNOY)]

enormous, *a.* †out of all rule; exceedingly great in size, number or quantity; huge, immense; †extraordinary, extravagant. **enormity,** *n.* the state or quality of being enormous, inordinate, outrageous, esp. of being excessively wicked; a monstrous crime, an outrage, an atrocity. **enormously,** *adv.* **enormousness,** *n.* [earlier *enorm,* MF *enorme,* L *enormis* (E-, *norma,* pattern, NORM)]

Enosis, *n.* the proposed political union of Cyprus with Greece. [Gr.]

enough, *a.* (*usu. placed after the noun*) sufficient for or adequate to need or demand. *n.* a sufficiency; a quantity or amount which satisfies requirement or desire; that which is equal to the powers or abilities. *int.* an exclamation denoting sufficiency or satisfaction. *adv.* sufficiently, tolerably, passably. **well enough,** tolerably well. [OE *genōh, genōg,* allied to impers. *geneah,* it suffices (cp. Goth. *ganohs,* enough, *ganah,* it suffices, also Icel. *gnogr,* Dan. *nok,* G. *genug,* enough, Sansk. *naç,* to attain, L *nancisci,* to obtain, p.p. *nactus*)]

enounce, *v.t.* to enunciate, state definitely; to pronounce. **enouncement,** *n.* [F *énoncer,* L *ēnuntiāre,* to ENUNCIATE]

†**enow**[1] ENOUGH.

enow[2], *adv.* (*Sc.*) just now; soon. [prob. short for *e'en now*]

en passant, by the way; applied to the taking of a pawn in chess that has moved two squares as if it has moved only one. [F]

en pension, (*F*) on boarding-house terms.

enplane, *v.i.* to board an aeroplane.

enprint, *n.* an enlarged photographic print.

enquire INQUIRE.

enrage, *v.t.* to put in a rage; to exasperate; to provoke to fury. †**enragement,** *n.* [OF *enrager*]

†**enrange,** *v.t.* to arrange; to set in place or order; to range, or wander over.

en rapport, (*F*) in sympathy with.

enrapture, *v.t.* to fill with rapture; to transport with delight.

†**enravish,** *v.t.* to throw into ecstasy; to enrapture.

enregiment, *v.t.* to form into a regiment; to organize and discipline. [F *enrégimenter*]

†**enregister,** *v.t.* to enrol; to enter in a register. [F *enregistrer*]

enrich, *v.t.* to make rich or wealthy; to fertilize; to add to the contents of; to make richer. **enrichment,** *n.* [F *enrichir*]

enring, *v.t.* to encircle, to surround (with); to put a ring upon, to adorn with a ring.

enrobe, *v.t.* to put a robe upon, to attire.

enrol, *v.t.* (*past, p.p.* **enrolled**) to write down on or enter in a roll; to record, to register, to celebrate; to include as a member, to record the admission of. **enroller,** *n.* one who enrols or registers. **enrolment,** *n.* [OF *enroller*]

enroot, *v.t.* to fix by the root; to implant deeply; to entangle by or as by the roots.

en route, on the way; on the road. [F]

ens, *n.* (*pl.* **entia**, enʹshiə) (*Phil.*) entity, being, existence; any existing being or thing. [late L *ēns,* pres.p of *esse,* to be]

Ens., (*abbr.*) Ensign.

Ensa, *n.* an official organization for entertaining men and women in the armed services during World War II. Directed by Basil Dean (1888–1978) from headquarters in the Drury Lane Theatre, it provided a variety of entertainment throughout the UK and also in all war zones abroad. [acronym for *e*ntertainments *n*ational *s*ervices *a*ssociation]

ensample, *n.* an example, a pattern, a model. *v.t.* to exemplify; to show by example. [A-F, corr. of OF *essample,* EXAMPLE]

ensanguine, *v.t.* (*now only in p.p.*) to smear or cover with blood; to make crimson. [EN-, L *sanguis -inis,* blood]

ensate, *a.* (*Bot.*) shaped like a sword with a straight blade. [L *ensis,* a sword, -ATE]

ensconce, *v.t.* to hide; to settle (oneself) comfortably or securely as in a sconce or fort.

enseam, *v.t.* to bring together, to contain. [etym. doubtful; cp. ME *in same, inseme,* together]

ensemble, *n.* all the parts of anything taken together; (*Mus.*) the joint effort of all the performers; a combination of two or more performers or players; a group of supporting players or performers; an outfit consisting of several (matching) garments. **tout ensemble,** the general effect. [F, from late L *insimul* (*in simul,* at the same time)]

ensepulchre, *v.t.* to place in a sepulchre.

†**ensew** ENSUE.

enshield, *v.t.* to shield, guard, protect. †*a.* protected, covered.

enshrine, *v.t.* to place in or as in a shrine; to enclose and cherish as if it is sacred. **enshrinement,** *n.*

enshroud, *v.t.* to cover with or as with a shroud; to conceal.

ensiform, *a.* sword-shaped, as the leaf of an iris. **ensi-**

form cartilage, process, *n.* the cartilaginous part at the end of the sternum or breast-bone. [L *ensis,* a sword, -FORM]

ensign, *n.* a national banner, a standard, a regimental flag, the flag with distinguishing colours carried by ships; a badge of rank or office; a sign or symbol; formerly, the lowest rank of commissioned officers in an infantry regiment, by the senior of whom the colours were carried; the lowest ranking commissioned officer in the US navy. *v.t.* to distinguish by a badge; to be the distinguishing mark of; (*Her.*) to distinguish by any mark or ornament, borne on or over a charge. **naval ensign,** a flag with a field of white, blue or red, with the union in the upper corner next the staff (white ensign carried by Royal Navy and Royal Yacht Squadron, blue by naval reserve and red by merchant service). †**ensign-bearer,** *n.* the soldier who carries the colours; an ensign. **ensigncy, ensignship,** *n.* [OF *enseigne,* late L *insignia,* orig. neut. pl. of *insignis,* remarkable, from *signum,* a SIGN]

ensilage, *n.* a method of preserving forage crops whilst moist and succulent, without previously drying, by storing them en masse in pits or trenches; fodder so preserved. *v.t.* to preserve by the process of ensilage. **ensile,** *v.t.* to put into a silo for this purpose; to ensilage. [F, from *ensiler,* Sp. *ensilar,* to preserve grain in a pit, see SILO]

enslave, *v.t.* to make a slave of, to reduce to bondage; to bring under the domination of some influence, habit, vice etc. **enslavement,** *n.* servitude. **enslaver,** *n.* one who or that which enslaves.

ensnare, *v.t.* to entrap; to overcome by treachery.

Ensor, *n.* **James** (1860–1949), Belgian painter and printmaker. His bold style uses strong colours to explore themes of human cruelty and the macabre, as in the *Entry of Christ into Brussels in 1889* (1888) (Musée Royale des Beaux-Arts, Brussels), and anticipated German expressionism.

ensorcell, *v.t.* to bewitch, to fascinate. [OF *ensorceler* (EN-, *sorceler,* from *sorcier,* SORCERER)]

ensphere, *v.t.* to place in or as in a sphere; to form into a round body.

enstamp, *v.t.* to mark as with a stamp.

enstatite, *n.* a rock-forming mineral, magnesium silicate. [Gr. *enstatēs,* adversary]

ensue, *v.i.* to follow in course of time, to succeed; to result (from). †*v.t.* to pursue, to practise. **ensuing,** *a.* coming next after. [OF *ensu-,* stem of *ensuivre,* late L *insequere,* L *insequī* (IN-, *sequī,* to follow)]

en suite, in succession; in a set or series; forming a unit, as a *bathroom en suite*. [F]

ensure, *v.t.* to make certain (that); to make safe (against or from any risk); to assure or guarantee (something to or for); †to insure. [A-F *enseurer,* from OF *seur,* SURE]

enswathe, *v.t.* to enwrap or swathe, to bandage. **enswathement,** *n.*

ENT, (*abbr.*) Ear, Nose and Throat.

-ent, *suf.* forming adjectives, e.g. *consistent, frequent;* noting an agent, e.g. *student*. [L *-entem,* acc. of *-ens,* pres.p. ending]

entablature, *n.* (*Arch.*) that part of an order supported upon the columns, consisting in upward succession of the architrave, frieze and cornice. [ult. from late L *intabulāre,* to form an *intabulātum* or flooring (cp. It. *intavolatura*)]

entablement, *n.* the platform or series of platforms supporting a statue, above the dado and base; an entablature. [F, from *entabler*]

entail, *v.t.* to bestow or settle a possession inalienably on a certain person and his heirs; to restrict an inheritance to a particular class of heirs; to impose (certain duties, expenses etc. upon someone); to involve, to necessitate. *n.* an estate in fee limited in descent to a particular heir or heirs; the limitation of inheritance in this way; (*fig.*) anything that is inherited as an inalienable possession; †carved or inlaid work; †shape, form. **to cut off the entail,** to put an end to the limitation of an inheritance to a particular class of heirs. **entailment,** *n.* [EN-, F *taille,* TAIL²]

entamoeba, *n.* any amoeba of the *Entamoeba* genus, which causes amoebic dysentery in humans.

entangle, *v.t.* to twist together so that unravelling is difficult; to ensnare, as in a net; to involve in difficulties, obstacles, contradictions etc.; to perplex, to embarrass. **entanglement,** *n.*

entasis, *n.* (*Arch.*) the almost imperceptible convex curvature given to a shaft or a column. [Gr., from *enteinein* (EN-, *teinein,* to strain)]

Entebbe, *n.* town in Uganda, on the NW shore of Lake Victoria, 20 km/12 miles SW of Kampala, the capital; 1136 m/3728 ft above sea level; population (1983) 21,000. Founded in 1893, it was the administrative centre of Uganda from 1894–1962.

entelechy, *n.* (*Phil.*) Aristotle's term for complete realization or full expression of a function or potentiality; a monad in the system of Leibnitz. [Gr. *entelecheia* (EN-, *telei,* dat. of *telos,* the end, perfection, *echein,* to have)]

entellus, *n.* (*Zool.*) an East Indian monkey. [name of a person in Virgil's *Aeneid* v.437–72]

†**entender,** *v.t.* to make tender, to soften (as the heart).

entente, *n.* a friendly understanding. **Little Entente,** that between Czechoslovakia, Yugoslavia and Romania. **Triple Entente,** that between Britain, France and Russia, 1907. [F]

Entente Cordiale, *n.* the agreement reached by Britain and France in 1904 recognizing British interests in Egypt and French interests in Morocco. It formed the basis for Anglo-French cooperation before the outbreak of World War I in 1914.

enter, *v.t.* to go or come into; to pierce, to penetrate; to associate oneself with, become a member of; to insert, to set down in a writing, list, book etc.; to put down the name of as a competitor for a race etc.; to initiate into a business etc.; to admit into the regular pack (said of a young dog); to cause to be inscribed upon the records of a court or legislative body; to admit as a pupil or member, to procure admission as such; (*Law*) to take possession of; to report a vessel's arrival at the custom-house; †to initiate, to introduce. *v.i.* to go or come in; to become a competitor; (*Theat.*) to appear on the scene. **to enter an appearance,** to show oneself. **to enter a protest,** to make a protest. **to enter into,** to form a part of; to join; to engage or take an interest in, to sympathize with; to become a party to (an agreement, treaty, recognizances etc.). **to enter up,** to set down in a regular series; to complete a series of entries. **to enter upon,** to begin, set out upon; to begin to treat of (a subject etc.); to take legal possession of. **enterable,** *a.* See ENTRANCE¹, ENTRY. [F *entrer,* L *intrāre,* from *intrā,* within]

enterectomy, *n.* surgical removal of part of the small intestine.

enteric, *a.* pertaining to the intestines. **enteric fever,** *n.* typhoid fever. [Gr. *enterikos,* from *enteron,* intestine]

enteritis, *n.* inflammation of the bowels, esp. of the small intestine.

enter(o)-, *comb. form.* pertaining to the intestines. [Gr. *enteron,* from *entos,* within]

enterocele, *n.* a hernia containing part of the intestines.

enterolite, *n.* a stony calculus.

enterology, *n.* a treatise or discourse on the intestines, often extended to all the internal parts of the human body.

enteropathy, *n.* disease of the intestines.

enterotomy, *n.* dissection of the intestines.

enterovirus, *n.* one which infects the intestinal tract.

enterprise, *n.* an undertaking, esp. a bold or difficult one; spirit of adventure, boldness, readiness to attempt. *v.t.* to undertake, to venture on. †*v.i.* to attempt a difficult undertaking. **enterprise scheme,** *n.* a government scheme to encourage the setting up of small firms with state financial support. **enterprise zone,** *n.* a depressed area given special government financial etc. backing to encourage commercial etc. improvement. †**enterpriser,** *n.* **enterprising,** *a.* ready to undertake schemes involving difficulty or hazard; energetic, adventurous; full of enterprise. **enterprisingly,** *adv.* [OF *entreprise,* from *entrepris,* p.p. of *entreprendre,* late L *interprendere,* to undertake (L *inter,* among, *prendere, prehendere,* to take in hand)]

entertain, *v.t.* to receive and treat as a guest; to occupy agreeably; to divert, to amuse; to harbour; to hold in mind, cherish; to consider favourably; †to keep or maintain in one's service; †to maintain, to keep up; †to take into one's service, to hire, to retain; †to while away time; †to engage (as an enemy's forces). *v.i.* to exercise hospitality; to receive company. **entertainer,** *n.* one who entertains, esp. one who performs amusingly at an entertainment. **entertaining,** *a.* amusing. **entertainingly,** *adv.* **entertainment,** *n.* the act of entertaining; receiving guests with hospitality; accommodation for a traveller or guest; a banquet; the art of entertaining, amusing or diverting; the pleasure afforded to the mind by anything interesting; amusement; a dramatic or other performance intended to amuse; †hospitality. [F *entretenir,* late L *intertenēre* (*inter,* among, *tenēre,* to hold)]

†**entertake,** *v.t.* to receive, to entertain.

enthalpy, *n.* (*Phys.*) heat content of a substance per unit mass. [Gr. *thalpos,* heat]

enthral, *v.t.* (*past, p.p.* **enthralled**) to reduce to the condition of a thrall; to enslave, to captivate. **enthralment,** *n.*

enthrone, *v.t.* to place on a throne or place of dignity; to invest with sovereign power; to induct or instal (as an archbishop or bishop) into the powers or privileges of a see. **enthronement,** *n.*

enthronize, -ise, *v.t.* to enthrone, to induct. **enthronization, -isation,** *n.* [OF *intronizer,* late L *inthronīzāre,* Gr. *enthronizein* (EN-, *thronos,* THRONE)]

enthusiasm, *n.* intense and passionate zeal; ardent admiration; fervour; †ecstatic feeling arising from supposed inspiration or possession by a divinity. **enthusiast,** *n.* one filled with or prone to enthusiasm; one whose mind is completely possessed by any subject; a visionary; †one who believes himself possessed or inspired. **enthusiastic,** †*n, a.* **enthusiastically,** *adv.* **enthuse,** *v.i.* (*coll.*) to manifest enthusiasm; to gush. [late L *enthūsiasmus,* Gr. *enthousiasmos,* from *enthousiazein,* to be inspired, from *enthousia,* from *entheos,* possessed by a god (EN-, *theos,* god)]

enthymeme, *n.* (*Log.*) a syllogism of which one premise is suppressed, and only an antecedent and a consequent expressed in words. **enthymematic,** *a.* [L *enthȳmēma,* Gr. *enthumēma -atos,* from *enthumeesthai,* to think (EN-, *thumos,* mind)]

entice, *v.t.* to allure, esp. into evil or to do evil; to tempt, seduce (from). **enticement,** *n.* **enticer,** *n.* **enticing,** *a.* alluring, seductive. **enticingly,** *adv.* [OF *enticier,* prob. from a late L *intitiāre,* to kindle, set on fire (EN-, L *titio,* a firebrand)]

entire, *a.* whole, complete, perfect; unbroken, undivided; unmixed, pure; unqualified, unreserved; not castrated (of a horse); (*Bot.*) having the edges (as of a leaf) unbroken or unserrated; †honest, sincere; unfeigned, earnest; †unimpaired, fresh. *n.* a kind of porter or stout. **entirely,** *adv.* wholly, in every part; fully, completely; exclusively. **entireness,** *n.* **entirety,** *n.* entireness, completeness; the entire amount, quantity or extent. **in its entirety,** completely, as a whole. **possession by entireties,** joint possession by two persons, neither of whom can alienate without the other's consent. [OF *entier,* L *integrum,* acc. of *integer* (*in-,* not, *tāg-,* root of *tangere,* to touch)]

entitle, *v.t.* to give a certain name or title to, to designate; to dignify (someone) by a title; to give a right, title or claim to anything. **entitlement,** *n.* [OF *entiteler,* L *intitulāre* (IN-[1], *titulus,* TITLE)]

entity, *n.* essence, existence, as distinguished from qualities or relations; anything that has real existence, a being; the essential nature of a thing, that which constitutes its being. **entitative,** *a.* [late L *entitās -tātem,* from ENS]

ent(o)-, *comb. form.* pertaining to the inside of anything. [Gr. *entos,* within]

entoblast, *n.* (*Biol.*) the nucleus of a cell. [Gr. *blastos,* a sprout]

entoil, *v.t.* to entrap. **entoilment,** *n.*

entomb, *v.t.* to place in a tomb, to bury; to be a grave or tomb for. **entombment,** *n.* [F *entomber* (EN-, *tombe,* TOMB)]

entom(o)-, *comb. form.* pertaining to insects. **entomic,** *a.* relating to insects. **entomoid,** *a.* resembling an insect. *n.* anything resembling an insect. [Gr. *entomon,* an insect, neut. of *entomos,* cut into, from *entemnein* (EN-, *temnein,* to cut)]

entomolite, *n.* a fossil insect.

entomology, *n.* the science which treats of insects. **entomologic, -ical,** *a.* **entomologically,** *adv.* **entomologist,** *n.*

entomophagous, *a.* feeding on insects.

entomophilous, *a.* attractive to insects. **entomophilous flowers,** *n.pl.*. those in which the pollen is carried by insects from the male to the female flowers.

entomostracous, *a.* belonging to the Entomostraca, a division of crustaceans, small in size, with the body segments usually distinct, and gills attached to the feet or organs of the mouth. [Gr. *ostrakon,* shell]

entonic, *a.* (*Path.*) exhibiting abnormal tension. [Gr. *entonos* (EN-, *tonos,* a straining)]

entoparasite, *n.* (*Zool.*) an internal parasite.

entophyte, *n.* any parasitic plant growing in the interior of animal or vegetable structures.

entourage, *n.* surroundings, environment; retinue, attendant company. [F, from *entourer,* to surround, from *entour* (EN-, *tour,* circuit)]

entozoon, *n.* (*pl.* **-zoa**) (*Zool.*) an animal living within the body of another animal. **entozoal, entozoic,** *a.* **entozoology,** *n.* the study of the entozoa. **entozoologist,** *n.* [Gr. *zōon,* animal]

entr'acte, *n.* the interval between the acts of a play; music, dancing or other performance between the acts of a play. [F *entre,* between, *acte,* act]

entrails, *n.pl.* the internal parts of animals; the intestines; the internal parts (as of the earth). [OF *entraile,* late L *intrālia,* from *inter,* among]

entrain[1], *v.t.* to draw after, to bring as a consequence. [F *entraîner* (*en-,* L *inde,* away, *traîner,* to drag, see TRAIN)]

entrain[2], *v.t.* to put into a railway train. *v.i.* to get into a train.

en train, in progress, under way. [F]

entrammel, *v.t.* to entangle, hamper, fetter.

entrance[1], *n.* the act of entering; the power, right or liberty of entering; the passage or doorway by which a place is entered; the means of entering into; the act of coming on to the stage; entering into or upon; the right of admission; entrance-fee, or fee paid for admission, as to an entertainment, club, race etc.; the entering of a ship or goods at the custom-house; (*Naut.*) the bow of a vessel. **entrance-fee, -money,** *n.* money paid for entrance or admission. **entrant,** *n.* one who enters; one entering upon or into a new profession, sphere, competition etc. [ENTER]

entrance[2], *v.t.* to throw into a state of ecstasy; to carry away, transport, enrapture; to overwhelm (with some strong emotion). **entrancement,** *n.* [EN-, TRANCE]

entrant ENTRANCE[1].

entrap, *v.t.* to catch in or as in a trap; to lure into making a compromising statement or into committing a (criminal) offence; to entangle in contradictions, difficulties etc. **entrapment,** *n.* [OF *entraper* (EN-, *trape,* a trap)]

entreasure, *v.t.* to lay up in or as in a treasury.

entreat, *v.t.* to beseech, to ask earnestly; †to obtain by solicitation; to treat, to act towards; to treat of, to discuss. *v.i.* to make entreaties; †to discourse; †to negotiate. **entreatingly,** *adv.* †**entreative,** *a.* of the nature of an entreaty; entreating. †**entreatment,** *n.* conversation, interview; treatment; entreaty. **entreaty,** *n.* an urgent solicitation; importunity; †treatment, usage; †handling, discussion, †negotiation. [OF *entraiter* (EN-, *traiter,* to TREAT)]

entrechat, *n.* a leap in dancing, esp. a striking of the heels together several times in a leap from the ground. [F]

entrée, *n.* freedom or right of entrance; a made dish served between the fish and the joint; (*orig. N Am.*) the main course of a meal. [F, entry]

entremets, *n.pl.* side dishes. [F, from OF *entremès* (*entre,* between, *mès,* viands)]

entrench, *v.t.* to surround with trenches; to defend (oneself) as if with trenches; to trespass, encroach (upon); to make furrows in. **entrenchment,** *n.*

entre nous, between ourselves, in confidence. [F]

entrepot, *n.* a warehouse for the temporary deposit of goods; a free port where foreign merchandise is kept in bond till re-exported; a commercial centre to which goods are sent for distribution. [F, from L *interpositum,* neut. p.p. of *interpōnere* (*inter,* between, *pōnere,* to put)]

entrepreneur, *n.* one who undertakes a (financial) enterprise, esp. one with an element of risk; a contractor; an organizer of entertainments for the public. [F, from *entreprendre,* to undertake (see ENTERPRISE)]

entresol, *n.* a low storey between two higher ones, usually between the first and the ground floor. [F (*entre,* between, *sol,* the ground)]

entrochite, *n.* (*Palaeont.*) a wheel-like joint or segment of an encrinite. **entrochal,** *a.* pertaining to or containing entrochites. [L *entrochus* (EN-, Gr. *trochos,* wheel), -ITE]

entropion, *n.* introversion of the eyelids. [Gr. *entropē,* rel. to *entrepein* (EN-, *trepein,* to turn)]

entropy, *n.* (*Phys.*) the property of a substance, expressed quantitatively, which remains constant when the substance changes its volume or does work with no heat passing into or from it, thus forming an index of the availability of the thermal energy of a system for mechanical work. [Gr. *tropē,* a transformation or turning, from *trepein,* to turn]

entrust, *v.t.* to commit or confide to a person's care; to charge with (a duty, care etc.).

entry, *n.* the act of entering; a ceremonial entrance into a place; the passage, gate, opening or other way by which anything is entered; the act of entering or inscribing in a book etc.; an item so entered; the exhibiting of a ship's papers at the custom-house to procure leave to land goods; (*Law*) the act of taking possession by setting foot upon land or tenements; the depositing of a document in the proper office; the formal putting upon record; unauthorized entrance into premises, thus one of the acts necessary to constitute burglary or trespass; (*pl.*) a list of competitors etc. **double entry, single entry,** systems of accounts in which each item is entered twice or once in the ledger etc. **entryism,** *n.* the policy of joining a political party etc., in order to influence policy from within. [F *entrée,* late L *intrāta,* from *intrāre,* to ENTER]

Entry phone®, *n.* a telephonic device at the entrance to a block of flats etc., which allows visitors to communicate with the flat occupier.

entwine, *v.t.* to twine or twist together; (*fig.*) to interlace, to mingle together; to embrace, clasp, enfold. *v.i.* to become twined or twisted together. **entwinement,** *n.*

entwist, *v.t.* to twist around; to form into a twist; to twist (with something else).

enucleate, *v.t.* to bring to light, elucidate, solve; (*Surg.*) to extract (a tumour) from its covering. **enucleation,** *n.* [L *ēnucleātus,* p.p. of *ēnucleāre*]

E number E.

enumerate, *v.t.* to reckon up one by one, to count; to specify the items of. **enumeration,** *n.* **enumerative,** *a.* **enumerator,** *n.* [L *ēnumerātus,* p.p. of *ēnumerāre*]

enunciate, *v.t.* to pronounce distinctly, articulate clearly; to express definitely, state or announce with formal precision. *v.i.* to pronounce words or syllables; to speak. **enunciable,** *a.* **enunciation,** *n.* a declaring or announcing; the manner of pronunciation or utterance; statement, formal expression; the statement of a proposition; a proposition, esp. one that has not been proved or disproved. **enunciative,** *a.* **enunciatively,** *adv.* **enunciator,** *n.* [L *ēnuntiātus,* p.p. of *ēnuntiāre* (E-, *nuntius,* a messenger)]

enure INURE.

enuresis, *n.* involuntary urinating, incontinence of urine. [Gr. *en,* in, *ouron,* urine]

enveigle INVEIGLE.

envelop, *v.t.* to enwrap, to enclose, to surround so as to hide, to enshroud; to wrap in or as in an envelope or covering; to surround with troops or offensive works. **envelopment,** *n.* [OF *enveloper* (etym. doubtful; cp. DEVELOP)]

envelope , *n.* a wrapper, a covering, esp. a paper case to contain a letter; (*Astron.*) the nebulous covering of the head of a comet; a whorl of altered leaves surrounding the organs of fructification; the gas-bag of a balloon. **window envelope** WINDOW. [F *enveloppe,* as prec.]

envenom, *v.t.* to make poisonous, to impregnate with poison; (*fig.*) to make bitter or spiteful; †to poison; †(*fig.*) to corrupt. [OF *envenimer*]

envermeil, *v.t.* to tinge with vermilion. [OF *envermeiller* (EN-, VERMEIL)]

Enver Pasha, *n.* (1881–1922), Turkish politician and soldier. He led the military revolt in 1908 that resulted in the Young Turk revolution. He was killed fighting the Bolsheviks in Turkestan.

enviable etc. ENVY.

environ, *v.t.* to surround, to be or extend round, to encompass; to surround so as to attend or protect, to beset; to surround (with persons or things); †to travel round. **environage,** *n.* environment. **environment,** *n.* the act of surrounding; that which encompasses, surrounding objects, scenery, circumstances etc.; the sum of external influences affecting an organism; (*loosely*) living conditions. **environmental,** *a.* pertaining to the environment. **environmental health officer,** an official employed to investigate and prevent potential public health hazards, such as lack of hygiene. **environmentalism,** *n.* the belief that the environment is the main influence on people's behaviour and development; concern for the environment and its preservation from pollution etc. **environmentalist,** *n.* one who believes in environmentalism; one who is concerned with or involved in the protection and preservation of the environment. **environs,** *n. pl.* the parts or districts round any place. [F *environner,* from *environ,* round about (EN-, *virer,* to veer, to turn)]

Environmentally Sensitive Area (ESA), scheme introduced by the UK Ministry of Agriculture in 1984 to protect the most beautiful areas of the British countryside from the loss and damage caused by agricultural change. The areas are in the Pennine Dales, the North Peak District, the Norfolk Broads, the Breckland, the Suffolk River Valleys, the Test Valley, the South Downs, the Somerset Levels and Moors, West Penwith, Cornwall, the Shropshire Borders, the Cambrian Mountains, and the Lleyn Peninsula.

Environmental Protection Agency, a US agency set up in 1970 to control water and air quality, industrial and commercial wastes, pesticides, noise, and radiation. In its own words, it aims to protect 'the country from being degraded, and its health threatened, by a multitude of human activities initiated without regard to long-ranging effects upon the life-supporting properties, the economic uses, and the recreational value of air, land, and water'.

envisage, *v.t.* to look into the face of, to look directly at; to face, confront; to contemplate, esp. a particular aspect of; (*Phil.*) to perceive by intuition. **envisagement,** *n.* [F *envisager*]

envoy[1], *n.* a postscript to a collection of poems, or a concluding stanza to a poem. [OF *envoié,* properly, a message, p.p. of *envoyer,* to send (*en voie,* L *in via,* on the way)]

envoy[2], *n.* a diplomatic agent, next in rank below an ambassador, sent by one government to another on some special occasion; a messenger, a representative. **envoyship,** *n.* [as prec.]

envy, *n.* ill-will at the superiority, success or good fortune of others, a grudging sense of another's superiority to oneself; the object of this feeling; †odium, hatred, malice. *v.t.* to regard with envy; to feel jealous of; to covet. *v.i.* to have envious feelings. **enviable,** *a.* capable of exciting envy; of a nature to be envied; greatly to be desired. **enviably,** *adv.* **envious,** *a.* infected with envy; instigated by envy; †enviable. **enviously,** *adv.* [OF *envie,* L *invidia,* from *invidus,* rel. to *invidēre,* to envy (IN-, *vidēre,* to see)]

enwind, *v.t.* to wind or coil around.

enwrap, *v.t.* to wrap or enfold; to envelop; to engross, to absorb; to involve, implicate.

enwreathe, *v.t.* to encircle with or as with a wreath.

enzootic, *a.* pertaining to a disease which affects animals in a certain district either constantly or periodically, endemic among animals. *n.* an enzootic disease. [EN-, Gr. *zōon,* animal]

enzyme, *n.* a catalyst produced by living cells, esp. in the digestive system. **enzymic, enzymotic,** *a.* **enzymosis, enzymation,** *n.* **enzymology,** *n.* [Gr. *enzumos,* unfermented (cp. AZYME)]

eoan, *a.* pertaining to the dawn; eastern. [L *ēōus,* Gr. *ēōos,* from *ēōs,* dawn]

EOC, (*abbr.*) Equal Opportunities Commission.

Eocene, *n.* second epoch of the Tertiary period of geological time, 55–38 million years ago. Originally considered the earliest division of the Tertiary, the name means 'early recent', referring to the early forms of mammals evolving at the time, following the extinction of the dinosaurs.

eod, (*abbr.*) every other day.

eohippus, *n.* an extinct forerunner of the horse, the earliest known form of horse-like mammal. [Gr. *ēōs,* dawn, *hippos,* horse]

EOKA, *n.* (Greek **Ethnikí Organósis Kipriakóu Agónos**/National Organization of Cypriot Struggle), an underground organization formed by Gen. George Grivas in 1955 to fight for the independence of Cyprus from Britain and ultimately its union (*enosis*) with Greece. In 1971, 11 years after the independence of Cyprus, Grivas returned to the island to form EOKA B, to resume the fight for *enosis* which had not been achieved by the Cypriot government.

Eolian, etc. AEOLIAN.

eolipyle AEOLIPYLE.

eolith, *n.* (*Palaeont.*) a supposed stone implement of rude construction anterior in date to the Palaeolithic age, found abundantly in parts of the North Downs, but not accepted as artificial by many archaeologists. **eolithic,** *a.* [Gr. *ēōs,* dawn]

eon AEON.

Eos, *n.* in Greek mythology, the goddess of the dawn, equivalent to the Roman Aurora.

eosin, *n.* a red fluorescent dye, sometimes used in biology. [Gr. *ēōs,* dawn]

-eous, *suf.* forming adjectives, as *arboreous, ligneous, righteous.* [L *-eus,* pertaining to, of the nature of]

Eozoon, *n.* a hypothetical genus of Protozoa found in the Laurentian strata in Canada, the supposed remains of which are now believed to be inorganic. **eozoic,** *a.* [Gr. *ēōs,* dawn, *zōon,* animal]

EP, (*abbr.*) extended play (record); electroplated.

ep-, *pref.* a form of EPI used before a vowel, as in *epact, epoch.*

epact, *n.* the moon's age at the beginning of the year; the excess of the solar year above the lunar year. [MF *epacte,* late L *epacta,* Gr. *epaktē,* from *epagein,* to intercalate (EP-, *agein,* to bring)]

epagoge, *n.* (*Log.*) the bringing forward of particular examples to prove a universal conclusion; argument by induction. [Gr. *epagōgē,* from *epagein* (EP-, *agein,* to bring)]

Epaminondas, *n.* (*c.* 420–362 BC), Theban general and politician who won a decisive victory over the Spartans at Leuctra in 371. He was killed at the moment of victory at Mantinea.

epan(a)-, *comb. form* (*Rhet.*) denoting repetition, doubling. [Gr. EP-, *ana,* up, again]

epanadiplosis, *n.* a figure by which a sentence ends with the same word with which it begins. [Gr. *diplōsis,* a doubling]

epanalepsis, *n.* a figure of speech by which the same word or clause is repeated after other words intervening. [Gr. *lēpsis,* from *lambanein,* to take]

epanastrophe, *n.* a figure of speech by which the end word of one sentence becomes the first word of the following sentence.

epanodos, *n.* a figure in which the second member of a sentence is an inversion of the first; resumption after a digression. [Gr. *hodos,* way]

epanorthosis, *n.* a figure by which a person recalls what he has said for the purpose of putting it more forcibly. [Gr. *orthōsis,* a setting straight, from *orthos,* straight]

epanthous, *a.* growing upon a flower, as certain fungi. [EP-, Gr. *anthos,* flower]

eparch, *n.* a governor or prefect of an eparchy; in the Russian Church, the bishop of an eparchy; a governor of a province in modern Greece. **eparchy,** *n.* a province of modern Greece; (*Hist.*) a prefecture; a diocese in the Russian Church. [Gr. *eparchos* (EP-, *archos,* a ruler)]

epaulement, *n.* (*Fort.*) a breastwork, short parapet or bank of earth, to defend the flank of a battery etc. [F, *épaulement,* from *épauler,* to protect by an *épaule,* shoulder]

epaulet, *n.* an ornamental badge worn on the shoulder in military, naval and certain civil full dress uniforms; (*fig., pl*). the rank of officer. **epauletted,** *a.* [F *épaulette,* from *épaule,* shoulder]

épée, *n.* a duelling sword; fencing foil. [F, a sword]

epeirogenesis, *n.* (*Geol.*) the making of a continent. [Gr. *epeiros,* mainland, GENESIS]

epencephalon, *n.* the hindmost division of the brain.

epenthesis, *n.* (*Gram.*) the addition of a letter or letters in the middle of a word, as in *alitium* for *alitum;* (*Philol.*) the phonetic change resulting from the transference of a semi-vowel to the preceding syllable. **epenthetic,** *a.* [late L, from Gr. (EP-, *en-,* in, *thesis,* a placing, from *tithenai,* to place)]

epergne, *n.* an ornamental stand, usu. branched, for the centre of a table etc. [poss. F *épargne,* a saving]

epexegesis, *n.* further elucidation of something which has gone before; further statement. **epexegetical,** *a.* [Gr. *epexēgēsis* (EP-, EXEGESIS)]

eph-, *pref.* a form of EPI- used before *h,* as in *ephemera, ephor.*

ephah, *n.* a Jewish measure of capacity for dry goods. [Heb. *ēyphāh,* said to be of Egyptian origin]

ephebe, *n.* (*Gr. Ant.*) a freeborn youth between the ages of 18 and 20, qualified for citizenship. **ephebic,** *a.* (*Zool.*) adult, mature, at the maximum of development. [L *ephēbus,* Gr. *ephēbos* (EPI-, *hēbē,* early manhood)]

Ephemera, *n.* (*pl.* **-rae**) a genus of ephemeropterous insects, containing the may-fly; the may-fly; (**ephemera**) a fever of only one day's continuance; anything short-lived. **ephemeral,** *a.* beginning and ending in a day; short-lived, transient. **ephemerality,** *n.* **ephemeric,** *a.* ephemeral. **ephemeris,** *n.* a journal, an account of daily transactions; (*Astron.*) a collection of tables or data showing the daily position of the planets; an astronomical almanac; ephemera. **ephemeron,** *n.* (*pl.* **-ra**) an insect of the Ephemera; (*usu. in pl.*) anything short-lived. [Gr. *ephēmeros* (EPI-, *hēmera,* day)]

Ephesian, *a.* of or pertaining to Ephesus. *n.* an inhabitant of Ephesus; †a jolly companion. [L *Ephesius,* Gr. *Ephesios*]

Ephesus, *n.* ancient Greek seaport in Asia Minor, a centre of the Ionian Greeks, with a temple of Artemis destroyed by the Goths in AD 262.

ephod, *n.* an emblematic short coat covering the shoulders and breast of the Jewish High Priest; a similar but less splendid garment worn by the ordinary priests. [Heb. *āphad,* to put on]

ephor, *n.* (*pl.* **ephori**) one of the five magistrates chosen at Sparta and invested with the highest power, controlling even the kings. **ephoralty,** *n.* [Gr. *ephoros* (EPI-, *horaein,* to see)]

epi-, *pref.* upon, at, to, besides, in addition, as in *epigram, episode.* [Gr. *epi*]

epi, *n.* a tuft of hair, esp. on a horse's forehead; a cowlick. [F]

epiblast, *n.* (*Biol.*) the outermost of the layers in the blastoderm. [EPI-, Gr. *blastos,* sprout]

epic, *a.* narrating some heroic event in a lofty style; large-scale; impressive; (*coll.*) very good. *n.* a long poem narrating the history, real or fictitious, of some notable action or series of actions, accomplished by a hero or heroes; a work of art associated with some aspect of the epic poem, such as a long adventure novel, a long historical film. **national epic,** a heroic poem embodying a nation's traditional history. **epic dialect,** *n.* the Greek dialect in which the *Iliad* and the *Odyssey* were composed. **epical,** *a.* **epically,** *adv.* [L *epicus,* Gr. *epikos,* from *epos,* a word]

epicalyx, *n.* a whorl of leaves forming an additional calyx outside the true calyx.

epicarp, *n.* (*Bot.*) the integument of fruits; peel, rind, skin. [EPI-, Gr. *karpos,* fruit]

epicedium, epicede, *n.* (*pl.* **-dia, -diums**) a dirge; a funeral ode. **epicedial,** *a.* [L *epicēdīum,* Gr. *epikēdeion* (EPI-, *kēdos,* care)]

epicene, *a.* (*Gram.*) of common gender, having only one form for both sexes; pertaining to both sexes; hermaphrodite; sexless; effeminate. *n.* a noun common to both genders, as *sheep;* a person having the characteristics of both sexes. [L *epicoenus,* Gr. *epikoinos* (EPI-, *koinos,* common)]

epicentre, epicentrum, *n.* the point over the focus of an earthquake. [Gr. *epikentron,* nom. *-ros* (EPI-, *kentron,* centre)]

epichirema, *n.* (*Log.*) a syllogism in which the proof of the premises is introduced with the premises themselves. [Gr. *epicheirēma,* from *epicheireein,* to undertake (EPI-, *cheir,* hand)]

Epictetus, *n.* (*c.* AD 55–135), Greek Stoic philosopher, who encouraged people to refrain from self-interest, and to promote the common good of humanity. He believed that people were in the hands of an all-wise providence, and that they should endeavour to do their duty in the position to which they were called.

epicure, *n.* one devoted to sensual pleasures, esp. those of the table; †an Epicurean. **epicurism,** *n.* **Epicurean,** *a.* pertaining to Epicurus or his system of philosophy, which taught that pleasure is the supreme good and the basis of morality; devoted to pleasure, esp. the more refined varieties of sensuous enjoyment. *n.* a follower of Epicurus; a person devoted to pleasure; a sensualist, a gourmet. **epicureanism,** *n.* [*Epicūrus,* Gr. *Epikouros*]

Epicurus, *n.* (341–270 BC), Greek philosopher, founder of Epicureanism, who taught at Athens from 306 BC.

epicycle, *n.* a small circle the centre of which is carried round upon another circle. **epicyclic,** *a.* **epicycloid,** *n.* a curve generated by the revolution of a point in the circumference of a circle rolling along the exterior of another circle. **epicycloidal,** *a.* [L *epicyclus,* Gr. *epikuklos* (EPI-, *kuklos,* circle)]

Epidaurus, *n.* ancient Greek city and port on the E coast of Argolis, in the NE Peloponnese. The site contains a well-preserved amphitheatre of the 4th cent. BC; nearby are the ruins of the temple of Aesculapius, the god of healing.

epideictic, *a.* showing off; displaying (applied to set orations). [Gr. *epideiktikos,* from *epideiknunai* (EPI-, *deiknunai,* to show)]

epidemic, *a.* affecting at once a large number in a community. *n.* a disease attacking many persons at the same time, and spreading with great rapidity. **epidemical,** *a.* **epidemically,** *adv.* **epidemiology,** *n.* the study and treatment of epidemic diseases. **epidemiologist,** *n.* [F *épidémique,* from *épidémie,* late L and Gr. *epidēmia,* from *epidēmios* (EPI-, *dēmos,* people)]

epidermis, *n.* the cuticle or skin constituting the external layer in animals; (*Bot.*) the exterior cellular coating of the leaf or stem of a plant. **epidermal, -mic,** *a.* pertaining to the epidermis. **epidermoid, -moidal,** *a.*

epidiascope, *n.* a magic lantern which may be used for opaque objects or transparencies. [Gr. *epi,* upon; *dia,* through; *skopeein,* to view]

epididymis, *n.* a mass of sperm-carrying tubes at the back of the testes.

epidote, *n.* a brittle mineral, a silicate of alumina and lime, of vitreous lustre and of various colours, mostly found in crystalline rocks. **epidotic,** *a.* [F *épidote,* formed from Gr. *epididonai* (EPI-, *didonai,* to give)]

epidural, *a.* situated on, or administered outside, the lower portion of the spinal canal. *n.* (also **epidural anaesthetic**) the epidural injection of an anaesthetic, e.g. in childbirth. **epidurally,** *adv.* [EPI- and DURA (MATER)]

epigastrium, *n.* the upper part of the abdomen, esp. that part above the stomach. **epigastric,** *a.* [Gr. *epigastrion* (EPI-, *gastēr,* stomach)]

epigene, *a.* (*Geol.*) originating on the surface of the earth; of a crystal, having undergone an alteration in its chemical character while retaining the same crystalline form as before; pseudomorphous. [F *épigène,* Gr. *epigenēs* (EPI-, *genēs,* born)]

epigenesis, *n.* (*Biol.*) the theory that in reproduction the organism is brought into being by the union of the male and female elements. **epigenesist,** *n.* **epigenetic,** *a.* **epigenous,** *a.* (*Bot.*) growing upon the surface of a part, as do many fungi.

epiglottis, *n.* a leaf-like cartilage at the base of the tongue which covers the glottis during the act of swallowing. **epiglottic,** *a.* [Gr. *epiglōttis* (EPI-, *glōssa,* tongue)]

epigone, *n.* one belonging to a later and less noteworthy generation. [Gr.]

epigram, *n.* a short poem or composition of a pointed or antithetical character; a pithy or antithetical saying or phrase. **epigrammatic, -ical,** *a.* **epigrammatically,** *adv.* **epigrammatist,** *n.* **epigrammatize, -ise,** *v.t.* to write or express by way of epigrams. [F *épigramme,* L and Gr. *epigramma* (EPI-, -GRAM)]

epigraph, *n.* a sentence placed at the beginning of a work, or of divisions in a work, as a motto; an inscription placed on buildings, statues, tombs and the like, denoting their use and appropriation. **epigraphic, -ical,** *a.* **epigraphically,** *adv.* **epigraphist, -grapher,** *n.* **epigraphy,** *n.* the deciphering and explanation of inscriptions; inscriptions taken collectively. [Gr. *epigraphē* (EPI-, *graphein,* to write)]

epigynous, *a.* (*Bot.*) of the stamens or corolla, growing on the top of the ovary, with only the upper portions free. [EPI-, Gr. *gunē,* woman]

epilate, *v.t.* to remove hair by the roots, by any method. **epilation,** *n.* [F *épiler,* from L *ex,* from, out, *pilus,* hair]

epilepsy, *n.* a functional disorder of the brain which involves convulsions of varying intensity, with or without loss of consciousness. **epileptic,** *a.* suffering from epilepsy; pertaining to or indicating the presence of epilepsy. *n.* one who has epilepsy. **epileptical,** *a.* **epileptoid,** *a.* [MF *epilepsie,* L and Gr. *epilēpsia,* from *epilambanein* (EPI-, *lambanein,* to take)]

epilogue, *n.* a short speech or poem addressed to the spectators at the end of a play; the concluding part of a book, essay or speech, a peroration. **epilogist,** *n.* **epilogize,** †**-guize, -g(u)ise,** *v.i.* to pronounce or deliver an epilogue. *v.t.* to put an epilogue to. [F, from L *epilogus,* Gr. *epilogos* (EPI-, *logos,* speech)]

epinasty, *n.* (*Bot.*) curving of an organ through more rapid growth of the upper surface. [EPI-, Gr. *nastos,* from *nassein,* to squeeze close]

epiperipheral, *a.* originating at the periphery.

epipetalous, *a.* (*Bot.*) of stamens, growing separately on the corolla.

Epiphany, *n.* the manifestation of Christ to the Magi at Bethlehem; the annual festival, held on 6 Jan., the 12th day after Christmas, to commemorate this; the appearance or manifestation of a divinity. [F *épipha-*

nie, from late L, from Gr. *epiphania,* neut. pl., from *epiphainein* (EPI-, *phainein,* to show), used as equivalent to *epiphaneia,* appearance, manifestation, from *epiphanēs,* manifest]

epiphenomenon, *n.* a phenomenon that is secondary and incidental, a mere concomitant of some effect.

epiphragm, *n.* (*Zool.*) the disk-like secretion with which snails and other molluscs close their shells during hibernation; (*Bot.*) a membrane closing the aperture of the sperm-case in urn-mosses and fungi. [Gr. *epiphragma,* a lid, from *epiphrassein* (EPI-, *phrassein,* to fence)]

epiphyllous, *a.* (*Bot.*) growing on a leaf; (of stamens) growing on the perianth.

epiphysis, *n.* (*pl.* **-physes**) (*Anat.*) a process formed by a separate centre of ossification. [EPI-, Gr. *phusis,* growth]

epiphyte, *n.* a plant growing upon another, usu. not deriving its nourishment from this; a fungus parasitic on an animal body. **epiphytal**, **epiphytic**, *a.*

epiploon, *n.* the fatty membrane enwrapping the entrails; the omentum. **epiploic,** *a.* [Gr., from *epipleein* (EPI-, *pleein,* to sail or float)]

epirhizous, *a.* growing on a root. [EPI-, Gr. *rhiza,* root]

Epirus[1], *n.* country of ancient Greece; the N part was in Albania; the remainder, in NW Greece, was divided into four provinces – Arta, Thesprotia, Yannina, and Preveza.

Epirus[2], *n.* (Greek **Ipiros**) region of NW Greece; area 9200 sq km/3551 sq miles; population (1981) 325,000. Its capital is Yannina, and it consists of the nomes of Arta, Thesprotia, Yannina, and Preveza. There is livestock farming.

episcopacy, *n.* government of a Church by bishops, the accepted form in the Latin and Greek communions and the Church of England, prelacy; the bishops taken collectively. **episcopal,** *a.* appertaining to a bishop; constituted on the episcopal form of government. **episcopal church,** *n.* a Church, like the Anglican, constituted on this basis. **episcopalian,** *n.* a member of an episcopal Church; a supporter of episcopal Church government and discipline. *a.* episcopal. **episcopalism,** *n.* **episcopally,** *adv.* **episcopate,** *n.* the office or see of a bishop; the term during which any bishop holds office; bishops collectively. †*v.i.* to fill the office of a bishop; to discharge episcopal functions. †**episcopy,** *n.* oversight, superintendence; **episcopacy;** episcopate. [late L *episcopātus, episcopus,* bishop, -ACY]

Episcopalianism, *n.* US term for the Anglican Communion.

episcope, *n.* (*Opt.*) a projection lantern used for throwing on a screen an enlarged image of an opaque object. [Gr. *skopeein,* to look]

episiotomy, *n.* cutting of the perineum during childbirth in order to prevent its tearing. [Gr. *epision,* pubic region, -TOMY]

episode, *n.* orig., the parts in dialogue between the choric parts in Greek tragedy, which were primarily interpolations; an incident or series of events in a story, separable though arising out of it; an incident or closely connected series of events in real life; (*Mus.*) a portion of a fugue deviating from the main theme; one part of a series on radio or television. **episodic, -ical**, *a.* **episodically,** *adv.* [Gr. *epeisodion,* addition, episode (EPI-, *eisodos,* entering)]

epispastic, *a.* drawing, exciting action in the skin; blistering. *n.* any preparation for producing counter-irritation, a blister. [Gr. *epispastikos* (EPI-, *spaein,* to draw)]

episperm, *n.* the outer integument of a seed. **epispermic**, *a.*

epistaxis, *n.* a nose-bleed. [Gr. *epistazein,* to shed in drops]

epistemology, *n.* the science which deals with the origin and method of knowledge. [Gr. *epistēmē,* knowledge]

episternum, *n.* the upper part of the sternum or breast-bone in mammals, or that portion of an articulate animal immediately adjoining the sternum. **episternal,** *a.*

epistle, *n.* a written communication, a letter (now only in a formal or facetious sense); a literary work (usu. in verse) in the form of a letter; (*pl.*) letters written by Apostles to the Churches, now forming part of the New Testament; a lesson in the Church service, so called as being taken from the apostolic epistles. †*v.t.* to write or communicate by a letter; to write an introduction or preface. **epistle-side,** *n.* the (right facing) side of the altar at which the epistle is read. **epistler, -toler**, *n.* a writer of letters; the person who reads the epistle in a church service. **epistolary**, *a.* pertaining to or suitable for letters; contained in or carried on by means of letters. *n.* a book containing the epistles. †**epistolet**, *n.* a short letter or epistle. †**epistolist**, *n.* †**epistolize, -ise**, *v.i.* †**epistolizer, -iser**, *n.* †**epistolographic**, *a.* pertaining to the writing of letters, demotic. †**epistolography**, *n.* [OF, from L *epistola,* Gr. *epistolē,* from *epistellein* (EPI-, *stellein,* to send)]

epistrophe, *n.* (*Rhet.*) a figure in which several sentences or clauses end with the same word; (*Bot.*) the return of a variegated form to the normal condition.

epistyle, *n.* (*Arch.*) the architrave. [L *epistylium* (Gr. *stulos,* pillar)]

epitaph, *n.* an inscription on a tomb; an inscription in prose or verse, as for a tomb or monument. *v.t.* †to commemorate in an epitaph. **epitaphial**, *a.* †**epitaphian, -taphic**, *a.* **epitaphist,** *n.* [L *epitaphium* (directly or through F *épitaphe*), Gr. *epitaphion,* neut. of *epitaphios,* a., over a tomb (EPI-, *taphos,* tomb)]

epitasis, *n.* the portion of a play in which the plot is developed, between the protasis or introduction and the catastrophe. [Gr., from *epiteinein* (EPI-, *teinein,* to stretch)]

epitaxy, *n.* the growth of one layer of crystals on another so that they have the same structure. [Gr. *taxis,* arrangement]

epithalamium, *n.* (*pl.* **-mia**) a nuptial song or poem. **epithalamial,** *a.* **epithalamic,** *a.* [L, from Gr. *epithalamion,* neut. of *epithalamios,* a. (EPI-, *thalamos,* bridal chamber)]

epithelium, *n.* (*pl.* **-lia**) the cell-tissues lining the alimentary canal; the outer layer of the mucous membranes; (*Bot.*) the thin epidermis lining inner cavities, the stigma etc. of plants. [mod. L (EPI-, Gr. *thēlē,* teat)]

epithem, *n.* (*Med.*) any external application, except ointment or plasters. [Gr. *epithema,* from *epitithenai* (EPI-, *tithenai,* to place)]

epithet, *n.* an adjective or phrase denoting any quality or attribute; a descriptive term; (*coll.*) an abusive expression; a nickname; †a term, phrase or expression. †*v.t.* to describe by epithets; to entitle. **epithetic, -ical**, *a.* **epithetically,** *adv.* †**epitheton**, *n.* epithet. [L and Gr. *epitheton,* from *epitithenai* (as prec.)]

epithymetic, *a.* pertaining to desire. [Gr. *epithumētikos,* from *epithumeein,* to desire (EPI-, *thumos,* soul, appetite)]

epitome, *n.* a brief summary of a book, document etc.; a condensation, abridgment, abstract; (*fig.*) a representation in little. **epitomist,** *n.* **epitomize, -ise,** *v.t.* to make an abstract, summary or abridgment of; to represent in miniature; †to cut down, curtail. *v.i.* to make epitomes. [L, from Gr. *epitomē* (EPI-, *temnein,* to cut)]

epitonic, *a.* overstrained. [Gr. *epitonos,* from *epiteinein* (EPI-, *teinein,* to stretch)]

epitrite, *n.* a metrical foot consisting of three long syllables and a short one, in any order. [L and Gr. *epitritos* (EPI-, *tritos,* third)]

epizoon, *n.* (*pl.* **-zoa**) an animal parasitic upon the exterior surface of another. **epizootic**, *a.* pertaining to diseases epidemic among animals; (*Geol.*) containing fossil remains, and therefore posterior to the advent of organic life. *n.* an epizootic disease; an epidemic among cattle. [EPI-, Gr. *zōon,* animal]

EPLF, (*abbr.*) Eritrean People's Liberation Front.

e pluribus unum, (*L*) one out of many (motto of the

United States).

EPNS, (*abbr.*) electroplated nickel silver; see ELECTROPLATE under ELECTRO-.

epoch, *n.* a fixed point from which succeeding years are numbered, a memorable date; a period characterized by momentous events, an era; a subdivision of geological time; (*Astron.*) the moment when a certain event takes place or a certain position is reached; the longitude of a planet at any given time. **epoch-making,** *a.* of such importance as to mark an epoch. **epochal,** *a.* [late L *epocha,* Gr. *epochē,* a stop, check, pause, from *epechein* (EP-, *echein,* to have, to hold)]

epode, *n.* in lyric poetry, the part after the strophe and antistrophe; a chorus; lyric poetry in which a shorter line follows a longer one. **epodic,** *a.* [OF, from L *epōdos,* Gr. *epōdos,* from *epadein* (EP-, *adein, aeidein,* to sing)]

eponym, *n.* a name given to a people, place or institution, after some person; the name of a mythical person made to account for the name of a country or people; a character whose name is the title of a play or book. **eponymic, eponymous,** *a.* [Gr. *epōnumos* (EP-, *onoma,* Aeolic *onuma,* name)]

epopee, epopoeia, *n.* an epic or heroic poem; epic poetry, the series of events forming the material for an epic. [F *épopée,* Gr. *epopoiia,* from *epopoios* (*epos,* word, song, *poios,* maker, from *poieein,* to make)]

epos, *n.* an epopee; epic poetry; unwritten narrative poetry embodying heroic traditions.

epoxy, *a.* containing oxygen plus two other atoms, frequently carbon, themselves already attached. **epoxy** or **epoxide resin,** *n.* any of a group of synthetic resins containing epoxy groups and used for coatings and adhesives. **epoxide,** *n.* an epoxy compound. [EPI-, OXY-]

EPROM, (*acronym*) (*e*rasable *p*rogrammable *r*ead-*o*nly *m*emory); a computer memory device in the form of a chip that can record data and retain it indefinitely. The data can be erased by exposure to ultraviolet light and new data added. Other kinds of memory are ROM, PROM, and RAM.

eprouvette, *n.* an apparatus for determining the strength of gunpowder; a spoon used in assaying. [F, from *éprouver,* to try, test]

epsilon, *n.* the fifth letter of the Greek alphabet. [Gr. *e psilon,* bare or mere e]

Epsom salts, *n.* hydrated magnesium sulphate, $MgSO_4.7H_20$, known as a saline purgative. The name is derived from a bitter saline spring at Epsom, Surrey, England, which contains the salt in solution. **epsomite,** *n.* native sulphate of magnesia.

Epstein, *n.* **Jacob** (1880–1959), British sculptor, born in New York. He experimented with abstract forms, but is better known for muscular nude figures such as *Genesis* (1931) (Whitworth Art Gallery, Manchester).

equable, *a.* characterized by evenness or uniformity; smooth, level, even; not varying, not irregular; not subject to irregularities or disturbance. **equability,** *n.* **equableness,** *n.* **equably,** *adv.* [L *aequābilis,* from *aequāre,* to make level, from *aequus,* equal]

equal, *a.* the same in magnitude, number, quality, degree etc.; even, uniform, not variable; impartial, unbiased, fair, just; having adequate power, ability or means (to). *n.* one not inferior or superior to another; one of the same or similar age, rank, office, talents or the like; a match; (*pl.*) equal things; †equality. *v.t.* (*past, p.p.* **equalled**) to be equal (to); †to make equal; †to make level or even; †to become equal to, to match; †to return a full equivalent for; †to compare. **equality,** *n.* the state of being equal; †evenness; †equability. **on an equality with,** on equal terms with. **equalize, -ise,** *v.t.* to make equal (to, with). **equalization, -isation,** *n.* **equally,** *adv.* **equalness,** *n.* [L *aequālis,* as prec.]

Equal Opportunities Commission, *n.* commission established by the UK government in 1975 to implement the Sex Discrimination Act of 1975. Its aim is to prevent discrimination, particularly on sexual or marital grounds.

equanimity, *n.* evenness or composure of mind; temper not easily disturbed; resignation. †**equanimous,** *a.* of an even frame of mind; not easily elated or depressed. †**equanimously,** *adv.* †**equanimousness,** *n.* [F *équanimité,* L *aequanimitās -tātem,* from *aequanimis* (*aequus,* equal, *animus,* mind)]

equate, *v.t.* to equalize; to reduce to an average or common standard. [L *aequatus,* p.p. of *aequāre,* from *aequus,* equal]

equation, *n.* the act of making equal; equality; (*Math.*) two algebraic expressions equal to one another, and connected by the sign =; (*Astron.*) a sum added or subtracted to allow for any special circumstance affecting the exactness of a calculation. **equation of light,** (*Astron.*) the allowance made in determining the position of a heavenly body for the time occupied in the transmission of its light to the eye of the observer. **equation of payments,** a rule for ascertaining at what time a person should pay the whole of a debt contracted in different portions to be repaid at different times. **equation of time,** the difference between mean and apparent time. **personal equation,** (*Astron.*) the quantity of time by which a person is in the habit of noting a phenomenon wrongly; (*fig.*) aberration from strict accuracy, logical reasoning or absolute fairness, due to personal characteristics. **equational,** *a.* **equationally,** *adv.* [L *aequātio -ōnem,* from *aequāre,* as prec.]

equator, *n.* a great circle on the earth's surface, equidistant from its poles, and dividing it into the northern and southern hemispheres; (*Astron.*) a great circle of the heavens, dividing it into a northern and a southern hemisphere, constituted by the production of the plane of the earth's equator. **equatorial,** *a.* pertaining to the equator; situated on or near the equator. **equatorial telescope,** *n.* a telescope mounted on an axis parallel to that of the earth, used for noting the course of the stars as they move through the sky. **equatorially,** *adv.* [late L, as prec.]

Equatorial Guinea, *n.* Republic of (*República de Guinea Ecuatorial*), country in W central Africa, bounded N by Cameroon, E and S by Gabon, and W by the Atlantic Ocean; also several small islands off the coast and the larger island of Bioko off the coast of Cameroon. **area** 28,051 sq km/10,828 sq miles. **capital** Malabo. **physical** comprises mainland Rio Muni, plus the small islands of Corisco, Elobey Grande and Elobey Chico, and Bioko (formerly Fernando Po) together with Annobón (formerly Pagalu). **population** (1988 est.) 336,000 (plus 110,000 estimated to live in exile abroad); annual growth rate 2.2%. **exports** cocoa, coffee, bananas, timber. **language** Spanish (official); pidgin English is widely spoken, and on Pagalu (whose people were formerly slaves of the Portuguese) a Portuguese dialect. **religion** nominally Christian, mainly Catholic, but in 1978 Roman Catholicism was banned.

equerry, *n.* an officer having the care of the horses of nobles or princes; an officer of a royal household. [F *écurie,* med. L *scūria,* a stable, OHG *scûr, sciura,* a shed (G *Scheuer,* barn), confused with L *equus,* horse]

equestrian, *a.* pertaining to horses or horsemanship; mounted on horseback; †given to or skilled in horsemanship; (*Rom. Ant.*) pertaining to the Equites or Knights. *n.* a rider on horseback; one who performs feats of horsemanship; a circus-rider. **equestrianism,** *n.* **equestrienne,** *n. fem.* [L *equestris,* from *eques,* horseman, from *equus,* horse]

equi-, *comb. form.* equal. [L *aequus,* equal]

equiangular, *a.* (*Math.*) having or consisting of equal angles.

Equiano, *n.* **Olaudah** (1745–97), African anti-slavery campaigner and writer. He travelled widely both as a slave and a free man. His autobiography, *The Interesting Narrative of the Life of Olaudah Equiano or Gustavus Vassa the African* (1789), is one of the earliest significant works by an African written in English.

equidifferent, *a.* having equal differences; arithmetically proportional.

equidistant, *a.* equally distant from some point or

place; separated from each other by equal distances. **equidistance,** *n.* **equidistantly,** *adv.*

equilateral, *a.* having all the sides equal. *n.* a figure having all its sides equal. **equilaterally,** *adv.*

equilibrate, *v.t.* to balance (two things) exactly; to counterpoise. *v.i.* to balance (each other) exactly; to be a counterpoise (to). **equilibration,** *n.*

equilibrium, *n.* a state of equal balance, equipoise; equality of weight or force; the equal balancing of the mind between conflicting motives or reasons; due proportion between parts; (*Mech.*) a state of rest or balance due to the action of forces which counteract each other. **equilibrist,** *n.* one who balances in unnatural positions, a rope-dancer, an acrobat. [L *aequilībrium* (EQUI-, *lībrāre,* to balance, from *lībra,* a balance)]

equimultiple, *a.* multiplied by the same number. *n.pl.* the products obtained by multiplying quantities by the same quantity; numbers having a common factor.

equine, *a.* pertaining to a horse or horses; resembling a horse. **equinia,** *n.* a contagious disease to which equine animals are subject, horse-pox, glanders. [L *equīnus,* from *equus,* a horse (cp. Gr. *hippos, hikkos,* OE *eoh*)]

equinox, *n.* the moment at which the sun crosses the equator and renders day and night equal throughout the world, now occurring (vernal equinox) on 21 Mar. and (autumnal equinox) on 23 Sept.; (*Astron.*) one of two points at which the sun in its annual course crosses the celestial equator; †an equinoctial gale. **equinoctial,** *a.* of or pertaining to the equinoxes, or the regions or climates near the terrestrial equator; designating an equal length of day and night; happening at or about the time of the equinoxes. *n.* the equinoctial line; (*pl.*) equinoctial gales. **equinoctial gales,** *n.pl.* gales happening at or near either equinox. **equinoctial line,** *n.* (*Astron.*) the celestial equator, a circle the plane of which is perpendicular to the axis of the earth and passes through the terrestrial equator. **equinoctial points,** *n.pl.* the two points wherein the equator and ecliptic intersect each other. **equinoctial time,** *n.* time reckoned from the moment when the sun passes the vernal equinox. **equinoctially,** *adv.* in the direction of the equinoctial line. [F *équinoxe,* L *aequinoctium* (EQUI-, *nox noctis,* night)]

equip, *v.t.* (*past, p.p.* **equipped**) to furnish, accoutre, esp. to supply with arms and military apparatus; to fit out (as a ship), to prepare for any particular duty; to qualify. **equipage,** *n.* that with which one is equipped; arms and general outfit of a body of troops, including baggage, provisions etc.; the outfit of a ship for a voyage; a carriage with horses and attendants; †retinue, attendance, train of followers. **camp-equipage,** (*Mil.*) tents, cooking-utensils etc. **field-equipage,** †(*Mil.*) saddle-horses, bat-horses, baggage-wagons and other things for the movements of an army. **siege-equipage,** the train of siege-guns, ammunition etc. **equipaged,** *a.* **equipment,** *n.* the act of equipping; the state of being equipped; that which is used in equipping or fitting out; outfit, furniture, apparatus required for work, intellectual and other qualifications. [F *équiper, esquiper* (A-F *eskiper*), prob. from Icel. *skipa,* to arrange, to man (a ship), from *skip,* ship]

equipedal, *a.* (*Zool.*) having the pairs of feet equal. [L *aequipedus* (EQUI-, *pes pedis,* foot)]

equipoise, *n.* a state of equality of weight or force, equilibrium; that which counterbalances. *v.t.* to counterbalance; to hold in equilibrium; (*fig.*) to hold (a person) in mental suspense.

equipollent, *a.* having equal force, power, significance etc.; equivalent. **equipollence, -lency,** *n.* equality of force etc.; (*Log.*) equivalence between two or more propositions. **equipollently,** *adv.* [OF *equipolent,* L. *aequipollens -ntem* (EQUI-, *pollens,* pres.p. of *pollēre,* to be strong)]

equiponderate, *v.t.* to counterpoise; to put into equipoise. †**equiponderance,** *n.* **equiponderant,** *a.* [med. L *aequiponderātus,* p.p. of *aequiponderāre* (EQUI-, *ponderāre,* to weigh, from *pondus,* weight)]

equipotential, *a.* (*Phys.*) having the same, or at the same, potential at all points (of a line, surface or region).

Equisetum, *n.* (*pl.* **-ta, -tums**) (*Bot.*) a genus of cryptogams containing the horse-tails and constituting the order Equisetaceae. **equisetaceous,** *a.* **equisetic,** *a.* pertaining to or derived from any species of *Equisetum.* **equisetic acid,** *n.* an acid obtained from some species of *Equisetum,* identical with aconitic acid. **equisetiform,** *a.* [L (*equus,* horse, *saeta,* bristle)]

equisonance, *n.* (*Mus.*) the concord between octaves.

equitable, *a.* acting or done with equity; fair, just; (*Law*) pertaining to a court or the rules of equity. **equitableness,** *n.* **equitably,** *adv.* [F *équitable*]

equitant, *a.* riding on horseback; overlapping, astride or overriding (of leaves etc.). [L *equitans -ntem,* pres.p. of *equitāre,* as foll.]

equitation, *n.* the act or art of riding on horseback; horsemanship. **equitative,** *a.* [L *equitātio -ōnem,* from *equitāre,* from *eques -itis,* horseman, from *equus,* horse]

Equites, *n.pl.* (*Rom. Ant.*) the Knights, the equestrian order of nobility. [L, pl. of *eques,* see prec.]

Equity, *n.* in the UK theatre, a shortened term for the British Actors' Equity Association, the trade union for professional actors in theatre, film and television, founded in 1929. In the US, its counterpart is the American Actors' Equity Association which, however, deals only with performers in the theatre.

equity, *n.* justice, fairness; the application of principles of justice to correct the deficiencies of law; (*Law*) the system of law, collateral and supplemental to statute law, administered by courts of equity; the net value of mortgaged property. **equity of redemption,** (*Law*) the right allowed to a mortgagor to a reasonable time within which to redeem his estate when mortgaged for a sum less than it is worth. **equities,** *n.pl.* stocks and shares not bearing a fixed rate of interest. [OF *equité,* L *aequitās -tātem,* from *aequus,* fair]

equivalent, *a.* of equal value, force or weight; alike in meaning, significance or effect; interchangeable, corresponding; having the same result; (*Geom.*) having equal areas or dimensions; (*Chem.*) having the same combining power; (*Geol.*) corresponding in position, and, within certain limits, in age. *n.* anything which is equal to something else in amount, weight, value, force etc. **equivalently,** *adv.* **equivalence, -lency,** *n.* [MF, from late L *aequivalens -ntem* (EQUI-, *valēre,* to be worth)]

equivocal, *a.* doubtful of meaning, ambiguous, capable of a twofold interpretation; of uncertain origin, character etc.; open to doubt or suspicion; †equivocating. **equivocality,** *n.* **equivocally,** *adv.* **equivocalness,** *n.* [late L *aequivocus* (EQUI-, *voc-,* root of *vocāre,* to call)]

equivocate, *v.i.* to use words in an ambiguous manner; to speak ambiguously so as to deceive; to prevaricate. †*v.t.* to render equivocal. **equivocation,** *n.* **equivocator,** *n.* **equivocatory,** *a.* [late L *aequivocātus,* p.p. of *aequivocāre,* as prec.]

equivoque, *n.* an ambiguous term or phrase, an equivocation; a pun or other play upon words. [ME, from late L *aequivocus,* EQUIVOCAL]

ER, (*abbr.*) Elizabeth Regina. [L, Queen Elizabeth]

Er, (*chem. symbol*) erbium.

er, *int.* a sound made when hesitating in speech.

-er, *suf.* [1] denoting an agent or doer, as *hatter, player, singer;* sometimes doubled, as in *caterer, poulterer;* denoting residence etc., as *Lowlander, Londoner* [OE *-ere,* from OTeut. *-ârjoz* (cp. L *-arius*)]; [2] denoting a person or thing connected with, as *butler, draper, officer, sampler* [OF *-er,* L *-ar -ārem;* A-F *-er,* OF *-ier,* L *-arius;* or OF *-eüre,* L *-ātūram*]; [3] denoting the comparative, as *richer, taller* [ME *-er, -ere, -re,* OE *-ra*]; [4] denoting an action, as *disclaimer, user* [F *-er, -re,* indicating the infinitive]; [5] frequentative, as *chatter, slumber, twitter.* [OE *-rian,* OTeut. *-rôjan*]

era, *n.* a historical period or system of chronology running from a fixed point of time marked by an important event such as the birth of Christ, the Hegira etc.; the date from which this is reckoned. [late L *aera,* a number, orig. pl. of *aes,* money]

eradiate, *v.i.* to shoot out, as rays of light. *v.t.* to emit (as rays). **eradiation,** *n.*

eradicate, *v.t.* to root up; to extirpate. **eradicable,** *a.* **eradication,** *n.* [L *ērādīcātus,* p.p. of *ērādīcāre* (E-, *rādix,* root)]

erase, *v.t.* to rub out; to obliterate, to expunge; (*fig.*) to raze. **erasable,** *a.* †**erasement,** *n.* **eraser,** *n.* †**erasion**, *n.* **erasure**, *n.* [L *ērāsus,* p.p. of *ērādere* (E-, *rādere,* to scrape)]

Erasmian, *a.* pertaining to Desiderius Erasmus or his teaching, esp. with regard to the pronunciation of Greek. *n.* a follower of Erasmus; one who pronounces Greek in the manner taught by Erasmus.

Erasmus, *n.* **Desiderius** (*c.* 1466–1536), Dutch scholar and humanist. Born at Rotterdam, the illegitimate son of Rogerius Gerardus (whose story is told in Charles Reade's novel *The Cloister and the Hearth* (1861), he adopted the Latin-Greek name which means 'beloved'. As a youth he was a monk in an Augustinian monastery near Gouda. After becoming a priest, he went to study in Paris in 1495 and paid the first of a number of visits to England in 1499. Here he met Linacre, More, and Colet, and for a time he was professor of Divinity and Greek at Cambridge University. His pioneer edition of the Greek New Testament was published in 1516, and an edition of the writings of St Jerome, and his own *Colloquia* (dialogues on contemporary subjects) in 1519. He went to Basle in 1521, where he edited the writings of the early Christian leaders.

Erastian, *n.* one holding the opinions on ecclesiastical matters attributed to Erastus; see ERASTIANISM. *a.* pertaining to Erastus or holding his doctrines. **Erastianize, -ise,** *v.t.* to imbue with Erastian doctrines; to organize (a Church system) on these principles. *v.i.* to hold Erastian views.

Erastianism, *n.* the belief that the church should be subordinated to the state. The name is derived from Thomas Erastus (1534–83), a German-Swiss theologian and opponent of Calvinism, who maintained in his writings that the church should not have the power of excluding people as a punishment for sin.

Erato, *n.* (*Gr. Myth.*) the Muse of love poetry. [Gr. *Eratō*]

Eratosthenes, *n.* (*c.* 276–194 BC), Greek geographer and mathematician, whose map of the world was the first to contain lines of latitude and longitude, and who calculated the earth's circumference with an error of less than 322 km/200 miles. His mathematical achievements include a method for duplicating the cube, and for finding prime numbers (Eratosthenes' 'sieve').

erbium, *n.* (*Chem.*) a rare metallic element, at.no.68; chem. symbol Er, forming a rose-coloured oxide, one of three formerly known together as Yttria. [*Ytterby,* in Sweden]

ere, *prep.* before, sooner than. *conj.* before that, sooner than. **ere long,** before long; soon. **erewhile,** *adv.* some time ago, formerly. [OE *aer* (cp. Dut. *eer,* OHG *ēr,* G *eher,* sooner) from OTeut. *airiz,* orig. comparative of *air,* early]

Erebus[1]**,** *n.* (*Class. Myth.*) a deity of hell, the son of Chaos and Night; the lower world; the region between earth and Hades. [L, from Gr. *Erebos*]

Erebus[2]**, Mount,** *n.* the world's southernmost active volcano, 3794 m/12,452 ft high, on Ross Island, Antarctica.

erect, *a.* upright; standing up straight; not bending or stooping; vertical; (*Bot.*) pointing straight up (as leaves); (*fig.*) uplifted, undismayed, firm; attentive, alert. *v.t.* to set upright; to raise; to construct, to build; (*fig.*) to elevate, to exalt; to set up; †to establish, to found; †to animate, to cheer. †*v.i.* to rise upright; to become erect. **to erect a perpendicular,** (*Geom.*) to draw a line at right angles to another line or plane. **erectile**, *a.* susceptible of erection. **erectile tissue,** *n.* tissue formed of blood-vessels intermixed with nervous filaments, and capable of dilatation under excitement. **erection,** *n.* the act of setting upright, building, constructing, establishing etc.; the state of being erected; a building, a structure; the distension of a part consisting of erectile tissue, esp. the penis. **erectly,** *adv.* **erectness,** *n.* **erector,** *n.* [L *ērectus,* p.p. of *ērigere* (E-, *regere,* to rule, to set)]

eremite, *n.* a hermit or anchorite. **eremetic, -ical,** *a.* [late L *erēmīta,* HERMIT]

Eremurus, *n.* a genus of liliaceous plants flowering in tall scapes, natives of Central Asia. [Gr. *erēmos,* solitary; *oura,* tail]

erethism, *n.* undue excitation of an organ or tissue. [F *éréthisme,* Gr. *erethismos,* from *erethizein,* to irritate]

erewhile ERE.

Erewhon, *n.* the imaginary country of Samuel Butler's satirical utopia in *Erewhon* (1872) and *Erewhon Revisited* (1901). [NOWHERE spelt backwards, modified]

Erfurt, *n.* city in East Germany on the river Gera, capital of Erfurt county; population (1986) 217,000. It is a rich horticultural area, and its industries include textiles, typewriters, and electrical goods. Erfurt county has an area of 7350 sq km/2837 sq miles, and a population of 1,235,000.

erg, ergon, *n.* the unit of work done in moving a body through 1 cm of space against the resistance of 1 dyne. **ergograph**, *n.* **ergometer**, *n.* [Gr. *ergon,* work]

ergal, *n.* a function expressing potential energy.

ergo, *adv.* therefore; consequently. [L]

ergonomics, *n. sing.* the science concerned with the relationship between workers, their environment and machinery. [Gr. *ergon,* work, and (eco)*nomics*]

ergot, *n.* a disease in various grains and grasses, esp. in rye, caused by the presence of a fungus; the dried fungus, used medicinally; a preparation of ergot of rye used in midwifery to produce contraction of the uterus. **ergotine,** *n.* a slightly bitter substance, forming the active principle of ergot of rye. **ergotism**[1]**,** *n.* the disease of ergot in grasses; an epidemic disease produced by eating grain affected with ergot. [F, from OF *argot,* a cock's spur, hence spurred rye; etym. doubtful]

ergotism[2]**,** *n.* arguing, wrangling. [ERGO]

Erhard, *n.* **Ludwig** (1897–1977), West German Christian Democrat politician, chancellor of the Federal Republic (1963–66). The 'economic miracle' of West Germany's recovery after World War II is largely attributed to Erhard's policy of social free enterprise (German *Marktwirtschaft*).

Erica, *n.* a genus of shrubby plants forming the heath family. **ericaceous**, *a.* [L, from Gr. *ereikē*]

Ericsson[1]**,** *n.* **John** (1803–89), Swedish born, US. engineer who took out a patent to produce screw-propeller powered paddle-wheel ships in 1836. He built a number of such ships, including the *Monitor*, which was successfully deployed during the Civil War.

Ericsson[2]**,** *n.* **Leif,** lived about AD 1000. Norse explorer, son of Eric 'the Red', who sailed west from Greenland about 1000 to find a country first sighted by Norsemen in 986. Landing with 35 companions in North America, he called it Vinland, because he discovered grape vines growing there.

Eric, *n.* **'the Red'** (940–1010 AD), allegedly the first European to find Greenland. According to a 13th-century saga, he was the son of a Norwegian chieftain, who was banished from Iceland in about 982 for murder and then sailed westward and discovered a land that he called Greenland.

Eridu, *n.* ancient city of Mesopotamia about 5000 BC, according to tradition the cradle of Sumerian civilization. On its site is now the village of Tell Abu Shahrain, Iraq.

Erie, Lake, *n.* fourth largest of the Great Lakes of North America, connected to Lake Ontario by the Niagara River, and bypassed by the Welland Canal; area 25,720 sq km/9930 sq miles.

Erigeron, *n.* a genus of plants resembling the aster, and including the flea-bane. [Gr. *ērigerōn* (*ēri,* early, *gerōn,* old man)]

Erin, *n.* poetic name for Ireland derived from the dative case Érinn of the Gaelic name Ériu, possibly derived from Sanskrit 'western'.

eringo, *n.* sea holly, a species of the umbelliferous genus *Eryngium.* [mod. L *Eryngium*]

erinite, *n.* a native emerald-green arsenate of copper from Cornwall, Giant's Causeway etc. [*Erin,* old name of Ireland]

eriometer, *n.* an optical instrument for measuring the diameters of small fibres, such as wool etc. [Gr. *erion,* wool]

eristic, *a.* controversial. *n.* a controversialist; the art of disputation. [Gr. *eristikos,* from *erizein,* to contend, from *eris,* strife]

Eritrea, *n.* province of N Ethiopia. **area** 117,600 sq km/ 45,394 sq miles. **capital** Asmara. **towns** ports Assab and Massawa are Ethiopia's outlets to the sea. **physical** coastline on the Red Sea 1000 km/620 miles; narrow coastal plain which rises to an inland plateau. **population** (1984) 2,615,000. **products** coffee, salt, citrus fruits, grains, cotton. **language** Amharic (official). **religion** Islam.

erk, *n.* (*sl.*) an aircraftsman. [*air*craftsman]

Erl-King, *n.* in Germanic folklore, the king of the elves. He inhabited the Black Forest and lured children to their death. The Romantic writer J. W. Goethe's poem 'Erlkönig' was set to music by Franz Schubert in 1816.

†ermelin, *n.* ermine. [conn. with ERMINE; etym. doubtful]

ermine, *n.* an animal of the weasel tribe, *Mustela erminea,* the stoat, hunted in winter for its fur, which then becomes snowy white, with the exception of the tip of the tail which is always black; the fur of this used for the robes of judges, peers etc.; (*fig.*) the office of judge; an emblem of purity; (*Her.*) a fur represented by triangular black spots on white. **ermined,** *a.* clothed with or wearing ermine. [OF (F *hermine,* cp. Prov. *ermini*), prob. from L (*mūs*) *armenius,* lit. (mouse) of Armenia]

-ern, *suf.* forming adjectives, as in *northern, southern.* [OE, from OTeut. *-rônjo-* (*-ro-, -ônjo-,* cp. L *-āneus*)]

erne, *n.* an eagle, esp. the golden eagle or the sea-eagle. [OE *earn* (cp. Dut. *arend,* Icel. *orn;* also Gr. *ornis,* bird)]

ERNIE, *n.* (*acronym*) *E*lectronic *R*andom *N*umber *I*ndicator *E*quipment. In the UK, machine designed and produced by the Post Office Research Station to select a series of random 9-figure numbers to indicate prizewinners in the government's national lottery.

Ernst, *n.* **Max** (1891–1976), German artist, who worked in France (1922–38) and in the US from 1941. He was an active Dadaist, experimenting with collage, photomontage, and surreal images, and helped found the Surrealist movement in 1924. His paintings are highly diverse.

erode, *v.t.* to eat into or away; to corrode; (*Geol.*) to wear away; to eat out a channel etc. **erose,** *a.* gnawed; (*Bot.*) irregularly indented, as if bitten away. **erosion,** *n.* **erosionist,** *n.* (*Geol.*) one who holds that geological changes are due to denudation rather than to subterranean agencies. **erosive,** *a.* [F *éroder,* L *ērōdere* (E-, *rōdere,* to gnaw, p.p. *rōsus*)]

erogenous, *a.* sensitive to sexual stimulation; producing sexual desire. [Gr. *erōs,* love]

Eros[1], *n.* in Greek mythology, boy-god of love, traditionally armed with bow and arrows. He was the son of Aphrodite, and fell in love with Psyche. He is identified with the Roman Cupid.

Eros[2], *n.* in astronomy, an asteroid, discovered in 1898, 22 million km/14 million miles from the Earth at its nearest point. Eros was the first asteroid whose orbit comes within that of Mars to be discovered. It is elongated, measures about 36 ′3 12 km/22 ′3 7 miles, rotates around its shortest axis every 5.3 hours, and orbits the Sun every 1.8 years.

erotic, *a.* pertaining to or caused by sexual love; amatory. *n.* an amatory poem. **eroticism,** *n.* sexual excitement; an exaggerated display of sexual feelings. **erotomania** , *n.* melancholia or insanity caused by sexual love or desire. [Gr. *erōtikos,* from *erōs erōtos,* love]

err, *v.i.* to blunder, to miss the truth, right or accuracy; to be incorrect; to deviate from duty; to sin. †*v.t.* to miss, to mistake. †**errable,** *a.* liable to error; fallible. [OF *errer,* L *errāre* (cogn. with Goth. *airzjan,* whence G *irren*)]

errand, *n.* a short journey to carry a message or perform some other commission for a superior; the object or purpose of such a journey; †a message. **a fool's errand,** a useless or foolish undertaking. **errand-boy, -girl,** *n.* a boy/girl employed to run on errands. [OE *ærende* (cp. OS *ārundi,* Icel. *eyrindi, ōrindi, erindi,* OHG *ārunti*); etym. doubtful]

errant, *a.* wandering, roving, rambling, esp. roaming in quest of adventure as a knight errant; erring; †complete, unmitigated, arrant. **knight errant** KNIGHT. **errancy, errantry,** *n.* [OF, wandering, pres.p. of *errer,* low L *iterāre,* L *iter,* a journey; or L *errans -antem,* pres.p. of *errāre,* see ERR]

erratic, *a.* irregular in movement, eccentric; wandering, straying (formerly applied to the planets in contradistinction to the fixed stars); (*Path.*) shifting from one place to another; (*Geol.*) of boulders, transported from their original situation. *n.* †a rogue, a vagabond; (*Geol.*) an erratic block, a transported boulder. **erratically,** *adv.* [L *errāticus,* from *errāre,* see ERR]

erratum, *n.* (*pl.* **-ta**) an error or mistake in printing or writing; (*pl.*) a list of corrections appended to a book. [L, neut. p.p. of *errāre,* as prec.]

erroneous, *a.* mistaken, incorrect; †straying from the right course, faulty, criminal. **erroneously,** *adv.* **erroneousness,** *n.* [L *errōneus,* from *erro -ōnis,* a vagabond (see ERR)]

error, *n.* a mistake in writing, printing etc.; deviation from truth or accuracy; wrong opinion; false doctrine or teaching; a transgression, a sin of a venial kind; (*Astron.*) the difference between the positions of the heavenly bodies as determined by calculation and by observation; in statistics, a measure of the difference between some quantity and an approximation of it, usu. expressed as a percentage. †a wandering or roving course. **writ of error,** (*Law*) a writ or order for reviewing the proceedings of an inferior court on the ground of error. †**errorist,** *n.* one who is in error, or who encourages or promotes error. **errorless,** *a.* [OF *errour,* L *errōrem,* acc. of *error,* a wandering, from *errāre* (see ERR)]

ersatz, *n.* a substitute in a pejorative sense. *a.* imitation; artificial. [G]

Erse, *n.* the Gaelic dialect of the Scottish Highlands. *a.* Gaelic; (*erroneously*) Irish. [early Sc. var. of *Irish*]

Ershad, *n.* **Hussain Mohammad** (1930–), military ruler of Bangladesh from 1982. He became chief of staff of the Bangladeshi army in 1979 and assumed power in a military coup in 1982. As president from 1983, Ershad introduced a successful rural-orientated economic programme. He was re-elected in 1986 and lifted martial law, but faced continuing political opposition.

erst, *adv.* once, formerly, of yore. †**at erst,** at earliest, at once. **erstwhile,** *adv.* some while ago. [OE *ærest,* superl. of *ær,* soon]

erubescent, *a.* reddening, blushing; reddish. **erubescence,** *n.* [L *ērubescens -entem,* pres.p. of *ērubescere* (E-, *rubescere,* incept. of *rubēre,* to be red)]

Eruca, *n.* a genus of herbs of the family Cruciferae. **erucic acid,** *n.* a crystalline fatty acid found in rape-seed, wallflower-seed and mustard-seed. [L *ērūca,* rocket[1]]

eruciform, *a.* resembling a caterpillar; applied to certain larvae, such as the sawfly, with fleshy, cylindrical body. [L *ērūca,* a caterpillar]

eructation, *n.* the act of belching; that which is ejected by belching; any sudden ejection of gases or solid matter from the earth. [L *ēructātio -ōnem,* from *ēructāre* (E-, *ructāre,* to belch)]

erudite, *a.* learned; well-read, well-informed. **eruditely,** *adv.* **eruditeness,** *n.* **erudition,** *n.* learning, extensive knowledge gained by study; scholarship. [L *ērudītus,* p.p. of *ērudīre* (E-, *rudis,* rude)]

erupt, *v.t.* to emit violently, as a volcano, geyser etc.; to force through (as teeth through the gums). *v.i.* to burst out; to break through. **eruption,** *n.* the act of bursting forth; a sudden emission; that which breaks out; (*Path.*) the breaking out of vesicles, pimples, rash etc. upon the skin; the breaking through of teeth; an outburst of lava etc. from a volcano or other vent. **eruptive,** *a.* [L *ēruptus,* p.p. of *ērumpere* (E-, *rumpere,* to break)]

-ery, -ry, *suf.* used with nouns and adjectives, and sometimes with verbs, to form nouns, generally abstract or collective, meaning a business, place of business, cultivation etc., conduct, things connected with or of the nature of etc.; originally confined to Romance words, but now used with those of Teutonic origin, e.g., *foolery, grocery, pinery, rockery, tannery, witchery*. [F *-erie* (L *-ārio-, -ia;* or L *-ātor -ōrem*)]

eryngo, *n.* †a sweetmeat prepared from eryngo-root; (*Bot.*) any plant of the genus *Eryngium*. **eryngo-root,** *n.* the root of *E. maritimum,* a reputed aphrodisiac, prepared as a sweetmeat. **Eryngium**, *n.* a genus of umbelliferous plants, including the sea-holly. [L *ēryngion,* Gr. *ērungion,* dim. of *ērungos,* goat's beard]

erysipelas, *n.* an inflammation of the skin in which the affected parts are of a deep red colour, with a diffused swelling of the underlying cutaneous tissue and cellular membrane; popularly called the rose, or St Anthony's fire. [L, from Gr. *erusipelas* (*erusi-,* rel. to *eruthros,* red, *pella,* skin)]

erythema, *n.* a superficial skin-disease characterized by redness in patches. **erythematic**, **erythematous,** *a.* [Gr. *eruthēma,* from *eruthainein,* to be red, from *eruthros,* red]

erythism ERETHISM.

erythrite, *n.* a red or greenish-grey variety of feldspar. [Gr. *eruthros,* red, -ITE]

erythr(o)-, *comb. form.* red. [Gr. *eruthros,* red]

erythrocyte, *n.* a red blood-cell in vertebrates.

erythromycin, *n.* an antibiotic used to treat bacterial infections. [Gr. *mukēs,* fungus]

erythrophobia, *n.* (*Path.*) a morbid fear of blushing.

erythropoiesis, *n.* the formation of red blood-cells. [Gr. *poiēsis,* a making, production, from *poieein,* to make]

Es, (*chem. symbol*) einsteinium.

-es, *suf.* [1]used to form the pl. of most nouns that end in *-s;* [2]used to form the 3rd pers. sing. pres. of most verbs that end in *-s*.

Esaki, *n.* **Leo** (1925–), Japanese physicist who in 1957 noticed that electrons could sometimes 'tunnel' through the barrier formed at the junctions of certain semiconductors. The effect is now widely used in the electronics industry and for this early success Esaki shared the 1973 Nobel physics prize with Josephson and Giaver.

Esarhaddon, *n.* (*d.* 669 BC), King of Assyria from 680, when he succeeded his father Sennacherib. He conquered Egypt (671–74).

Esau, *n.* in the Old Testament or Jewish Bible, the son of Isaac and Rebekah, and the elder twin brother of Jacob, who tricked Isaac into giving him the blessing intended for Esau by putting on goatskins. Earlier Esau had sold his birthright to Jacob for a 'mess of red pottage'. He was the ancestor of the Edomites.

escalade, *n.* an attack on a fortified place in which scaling-ladders are used to mount the ramparts etc. *v.t.* to storm by means of scaling-ladders. [F, from Sp. *escalada,* fem. p.p. of *escalar,* med. L *scalāre,* to scale, from *scāla,* ladder]

escalate, *vi, v.t.* to increase in extent, intensity or magnitude. **escalation,** *n.* [see foll.]

escalator, *n.* a conveyor for passengers consisting of a continuous series of steps on an endless chain, ascending or descending and arranged to give facilities for mounting or leaving at either end; a moving staircase. [F *escalader,* to scale, to climb]

Escallonia, *n.* a genus of S American flowering trees or shrubs of the saxifrage family. [*Escallon,* a Spanish traveller]

escallop SCALLOP.

escalope, *n.* a thin boneless slice of meat, esp. veal or pork.

escapade, *n.* a wild freak or prank; an escape from restraint; a wild fling of a horse. [F, from Sp. or Prov. *escapada,* from *escapar,* to escape (as foll.)]

escape, *v.t.* to get safely away from; to flee so as to be free from; to evade, to avoid (a thing or act); to slip away from, elude attention or recollection of; to find an issue from; to slip from unawares or unintentionally. *v.i.* to get free; to get safely away; to find an issue, to leak; to evade punishment, capture, danger, annoyance etc. *n.* the act of escaping; the state of having escaped, a means of escaping; evasion, flight, deliverance; a leakage (from a gas or water pipe, electric main etc.); a plant from a garden apparently growing wild; (*Law*) violent or privy evasion out of lawful restraint. **fire-escape** FIRE. **escape-pipe, -valve,** *n.* an outlet for steam, water etc. in case of necessity. **escape-shaft,** *n.* a shaft provided in case of emergency for the escape of miners. **escape warrant,** *n.* (*Law*) a warrant addressed to sheriffs etc. to retake an escaped prisoner. **escapee,** *n.* one who has escaped, esp. an escaped prisoner. **escapement,** *n.* a device in a clock or watch for checking and regulating the movement of the wheels; a vent, an escape. **escapism,** *n.* (*Psych.*) shirking unpleasant facts and realities by filling the mind with pleas- ing irrelevancies. **escapist,** *n., a.* **escapologist**, *n.* a performer whose stage turn is escaping from locked handcuffs, chains, boxes etc. [A-F *escaper,* OF *eschaper* (F *échapper*), prob. from a late L *excappāre* (EX-, *cappa,* cloak)]

escargot, *n.* an edible snail. [F]

escarp, *v.t.* (*Fort.*) to cut or form into a slope; to scarp. *n.* the slope on the inner side of a ditch, below a rampart, opposite the counterscarp; a scarp. **escarpment,** *n.* the precipitous face of a hill or ridge; (*Fort.*) ground cut away precipitously so as to render a position inaccessible. [F *escarper,* from *escarpe,* SCARP]

-esce, *suf.* forming inceptive verbs, as *acquiesce, coalesce, effervesce*. **-escent**, *suf.* forming adjectives from inceptive verbs, as *acquiescent, coalescent, iridescent, opalescent*. **-escence**, *suf.* forming abstract nouns from inceptive verbs, as *acquiescence, coalescence, opalescence*. [L *-escere,* infin. ending, *-escens -entem,* pres.p. ending, of inceptive verbs]

eschalot SHALLOT.

eschatology, *n.* the doctrine of the final issue of things, death, the last judgment, the future state etc. **eschatological**, *a.* [Gr. *eschatos,* last]

escheat, *n.* the reverting of property to the lord of the fee, or to the Crown or the state, on the death of the owner intestate without heirs; property so reverting; †a plunder, booty. *v.t.* to confiscate; to forfeit (to). *v.i.* to revert by escheat. **escheator,** *n.* an officer formerly appointed in every county to register the escheats of the Crown. [OF *eschete,* fem. p.p. of *escheoir* (F *échoir*), late L *excadere* (EX-, L *cadere,* to fall)]

Escher, *n.* **Maurits Cornelis** (1902–72), Dutch graphic artist. His prints are often based on mathematical concepts and contain paradoxes and illusions. The lithograph *Ascending and Descending* (1960), with interlocking staircases creating a perspective puzzle, is typical.

eschew, *v.t.* to flee from; to avoid; to shun; to abstain from. **eschewal,** *n.* †**eschewance,** *n.* **eschewer,** *n.* [OF *eschiver,* OHG *sciuhan* (G *scheuen*), cogn. with OE *sceoh,* SHY]

Eschscholtzia, *n.* a genus of flowering herbs comprising the California poppy. [J. F. von *Eschscholtz,* 1793–1831, German naturalist]

escort[1]**,** *n.* an armed guard attending a person or persons, baggage, munitions etc. which are being conveyed from one place to another, as a protection against attack or for compulsion or surveillance; a guard of honour; a person or persons accompanying another for protection, guidance or company; guidance, protection, guardianship. **escort agency,** *n.* a company which provides people, usu. of the opposite sex, to act as hired escorts on social occasions. [F *escorte,* It. *scorta,* fem. p.p. of *scorgere,* to guide, conduct (EX-, L *corrigere,* to CORRECT)]

escort², *v.t.* to act as escort to; to attend upon. [as prec.]

escribe, *v.t.* to draw (a circle) so as to touch one side of a triangle exteriorly and the other two produced. [E-, L *scrībere,* to write]

escritoire, *n.* a writing-desk, with drawers etc. for papers and stationery, a bureau. [F, now *écritoire,* L *scriptōrium,* from *scriptus,* p.p. of *scrībere,* to write]

escrow, *n.* (*Law*) a fully-executed deed or engagement to do or pay something, put into the custody of a third party until some condition is fulfilled. [OF *escroue,* a scroll]

Esculapian AESCULAPIAN.

esculent, *a.* fit or good for food; edible. *n.* a thing suitable for food. [L *esculentus,* from *esca,* food]

escutcheon, *n.* a shield or shield-shaped surface charged with armorial bearings; any similar surface or device; an ornamental name-plate on a coffin; a perforated plate to finish an opening, as a keyhole etc.; part of a ship's stern bearing her name; (*Zool.*) a depression behind the beak of a bivalve. **a blot on the escutcheon,** a stain on the reputation of a person, family etc. [A-F and ONorth.F *escuchon,* OF *escusson,* prob. from a late L *scūtiō -ōnem,* from L *scūtum,* a shield]

ESE, (*abbr.*) East South East.

-ese, *suf.* belonging to a country etc. as inhabitant(s) or language, as *Maltese, Chinese;* pertaining to a particular writer, writing etc. with regard to style, language, theme etc., as *Johnsonese, journalese.* [OF *-eis,* L *ensis,* pl. *-enses*]

esemplastic, *a.* moulding, shaping or fashioning into one, unifying. [Gr. *es,* into, *hen,* neut. of *heis,* one, *plastikos,* from *plassein,* to mould]

Esenin, *n.* **Sergey** (1895–1925), Soviet poet, born in Konstantinovo (renamed Esenino in his honour). He went to Petrograd in 1915, attached himself to the Symbolists, welcomed the Russian Revolution, revived peasant traditions and folklore, and initiated the Imaginist group of poets in 1919. A selection of his poetry was translated in *Confessions of a Hooligan* (1973). He was married briefly to the US dancer Isadora Duncan from 1922–23.

eskar, *n.* a bank or long mound of glacial drift such as are found abundantly in Irish river-valleys. [Ir. *eiscir*]

Eskimo, *n.* member (or language) of a people of the Arctic. The Eskimos of Greenland and Canada are Inuit and their language Inuktitut; the Eskimos of South Alaska and Siberia are Yupik and their language Yuk. **Eskimo-dog,** *n.* a wolf-like variety of the domestic dog, used by the Eskimos to draw sledges. [NAmer.Indian, eaters of raw flesh]

Eskişehir, *n.* city in Turkey, 200 km/125 miles west of Ankara; population (1985) 367,000. Products include meerschaum, chromium, magnesite, cotton goods, tiles, and aircraft.

Esky®, *n.* in Australia, a portable container or chest for cooled drinks. [ESKIMO]

esophagus OESOPHAGUS.

esoteric, -ical, *a.* of philosophical doctrines, religious rites etc., meant for or intelligible only to the initiated; recondite, secret, confidential; of disciples etc., initiated; arising from internal causes. **esoterically,** *adv.* **esoterism,** *n.* †**esotery,** *n.* [Gr. *esōterikos,* from *esōteros,* inner, compar. from *esō,* within, from *eis,* into]

ESP, (*abbr.*) extrasensory perception.

espadrille, *n.* a rope-soled shoe with a cloth upper. [F, from Prov. *espardilho,* from *espart,* esparto]

espagnolette, *n.* a bolt used for fastening a french window, one turn of the knob securing the sash both at top and bottom. [F, from *espagnol,* Spanish]

espalier, *n.* lattice-work on which to train shrubs or fruit-trees; a tree so trained. *v.t.* to train a tree or shrub in this way. [F, from It. *spalliera,* from *spalla,* a shoulder, L *spatula,* a blade]

esparto, *n.* a kind of coarse grass or rush, *Macrochloa tenacissima,* growing in the sandy regions of northern Africa and Spain, largely used for making paper, mats etc. [Sp., from L *spartum,* Gr. *sparton,* a rope made of a plant called *spartos*]

especial, *a.* distinguished in a certain class or kind; pre-eminent, exceptional, particular; pertaining to a particular case, not general or indefinite. **especially,** *adv.* [OF, from L *speciālis,* SPECIAL]

†**esperance,** *n.* hope. [F, ult. from L *sperans -antis,* pres.p. of *sperāre,* to hope]

Esperanto, *n.* language devised 1887 by Dr Ludwig L. Zamenhof (1859–1917) as an international auxiliary language. For its structure and vocabulary it draws on various European languages. Esperantists refer to Esperanto as a 'planned language' and to the natural languages of the world as 'ethnic languages'. Its spelling is phonetic, but the accent varies according to the regional backgrounds of its users. **Esperantist,** *n.* [Esperanto, hopeful]

espial ESPY.

espiègle, *a.* roguish, frolicsome. **espièglerie,** *n.* [F, corr. of G *Eulenspiegel,* a German peasant with a traditionary reputation for impish practices]

espionage, *n.* the act or practice of spying; the employment of spies. [F, from *espionner,* from *espion,* spy]

esplanade, *n.* a level space, esp. a level walk or drive by the seaside etc.; a clear space between the citadel and the houses of a fortified town. [MF, from *esplaner,* to level (as Sp. *esplanada* and It. *spianata*), L *explānāre* (EX-, *plānus,* level)]

espouse, *v.t.* to marry; to give in marriage (to); (*fig.*) to adopt, to support, defend (a cause etc.). **espousal,** *n.* (*usu. in pl.*) the act or ceremony of contracting a man and woman to each other; betrothal, marriage; (*fig.*) adoption (of a cause etc.). [OF *espouser,* from *espouse,* SPOUSE, wife, L *sponsa,* fem. p.p. of *spondēre,* to promise]

espressivo, *a.* (*Mus.*) with expression. [It.]

espresso, *n.* a coffee-making machine using pressure for high extraction; coffee made in this way. **espresso (bar),** *n.* a coffee-bar where such coffee is served. [It.]

esprit, *n.* with sprightliness. **esprit de corps**, the spirit of comradeship, loyalty and devotion to the body or association to which one belongs. **esprit fort**, *n.* (*pl.* **esprits forts**) a strong-minded person, esp. a determined free-thinker in religious matters. [F, from L *spīritus,* SPIRIT]

espy, *v.t.* to catch sight of; to detect, to discern; †to watch, to spy upon. *v.i.* to watch or look narrowly. **espial**, *n.* spying, observation; †a spy, a scout. [OF *espier,* OHG *spehōn* (G *spähen*), to SPY]

Esq., (*abbr.*) Esquire.

-esque, *suf.* like, in the manner or style of, as *arabesque, burlesque, Dantesque, picturesque*. [F, from It. *-esco,* med. L *-iscus* (cp. OHG *-isc,* G *-isch,* -ISH)]

Esquimau (*pl,* **-maux**) ESKIMO.

Esquipulas, *n.* a pilgrimage town in Chiquimula department, SE Guatemala. Seat of the 'Black Christ' which is a symbol of peace throughout Central America. In May 1986 five Central American presidents met here to discuss a plan for peace in the region.

esquire, *n.* the armour-bearer or attendant on a knight, a squire; a title of dignity next in degree below a knight; a title properly belonging to the eldest sons of baronets and the younger sons of noblemen, and to officers of the king's courts, barristers, justices of the peace etc., but commonly given to all professional men, and used as a complimentary adjunct to a person's name in the addresses of letters. *v.t.* to attend upon as an escort; to dignify with the title of esquire. [OF *escuyer,* L *scūtārius,* from *scūtum,* shield]

ess, *n.* the 19th letter of the alphabet, S, s; anything shaped like this. **collar of esses,** a chain or collar composed of S-shaped links. [OE]

-ess, *suf.* noting the feminine; as *empress, murderess, seamstress, songstress* (the last two are double feminines formed on the OE fem. *-ster,* as in *spinster*). [F *-esse,* L *-issa*]

ESS, *n.* (evolutionary stable strategy) in sociobiology, an assemblage of behavioural or physical characters (collectively termed a 'strategy') that is resistant to replacement by any forms bearing new traits, because these new traits will not be capable of successful reproduction.

essay[1], *n.* an attempt; an informal literary composition or disquisition, usu. in prose. **essayist,** *n.* a writer of essays. [OF *essai,* ASSAY]

essay[2], *v.t.* to try, to attempt; to test; to test the quality or nature of. *v.i.* to make an endeavour. [as prec.]

Essen, *n.* city in North Rhine-Westphalia, West Germany; population (1988) 615,000. It is the administrative centre of the Ruhr, with textile, chemical, and electrical industries.

essence, *n.* that which constitutes the nature of a thing; that which makes a thing what it is; that which differentiates a thing from all other things, or one thing of a kind from others of the same kind; being, existence; an ethereal or immaterial being, a solution or extract obtained by distillation; the essential oil or characteristic constituent of a volatile substance; perfume, scent. *v.t.* to perfume, to scent. [F, from L *essentia,* from *essens -entis,* pres.p. of *esse,* to be]

Essene, *n.* member of a Jewish religious order that existed in the area near the Dead Sea *c.* 200 BC–AD 200, whose members lived an extremely simple life bound by strict rules; they believed the day of judgment was imminent. **Essenism,** *n.* [L *Essēni,* pl., Gr. *Essēnoi* (etym. doubtful)]

essential, *a.* of or pertaining to the essence of a thing; necessary to the existence of a thing, indispensable (to); important in the highest degree; real, actual, distinguished from accidental; containing the essence or principle of a plant etc.; (*Path.*) idiopathic, not connected with another disease; of an amino or fatty acid, necessary for the normal growth of the body, but not synthesized by the body. *n.* that which is fundamental or characteristic; an indispensable element; a point of the highest importance; †essence, being. **essential character,** *n.* the quality which serves to distinguish one genus, species etc. from another. **essential harmony,** *n.* (*Mus.*) one belonging to one particular key. **essential oil,** *n.* a volatile oil containing the characteristic constituent or principle, usually obtained by distillation with water. **essential proposition,** *n.* one that predicates of a subject something entailed in its definition. **essentiality,** *n.* **essentially,** *adv.* [late L *essentiālis,* see ESSENCE]

Essequibo, *n.* the longest river in Guyana, South America, rising in the Guiana Highlands of S Guyana; length 1014 km/630 miles. Part of the district of Essequibo, which lies to the west of the river, is claimed by Venezuela.

Essex[1], *n.* county in SE England. **area** 3670 sq km/1417 sq miles. **towns** administrative headquarters Chelmsford; Colchester; ports Harwich, Tilbury; resorts Southend, Clacton. **products** dairy, cereals, fruit. **population** (1987) 1,522,000.

Essex[2], *n.* **Robert Devereux, 2nd Earl of Essex** (1566–1601), English soldier and politician. He fought in the Netherlands in 1585–86 and distinguished himself at the Battle of Zutphen. In 1596 he jointly commanded a force that seized and sacked Cadiz. He became a favourite with Elizabeth I from 1587, but was executed because of his policies in Ireland.

Essex board®, *n.* a building-board made of layers of wood-fibre cemented together with fire-resisting material.

†**essoign, essoin,** *n.* an excuse; an exemption; an excuse offered for non-appearance in a court of law. *v.t.* to make an excuse or to excuse for non-appearance in a court of law. †**essoiner,** *n.* one who makes an excuse for the non-appearance of another in a court of law. [A-F *essoigne,* OF *essoine,* from *essoignier, essoinier,* to excuse, from *essoyne,* med. L *exsoniāre* (EX-, *sonia,* OHG *sunna,* excuse, cogn. with Goth. *sunja,* truth, cp. OE *soth,* true)]

EST, (*abbr.*) Eastern Standard Time; electric shock treatment.

est., (*abbr.*) established; estimated.

-est, *suf.* forming the superlative degree of adjectives and adverbs, as *richest, tallest, liveliest.* [OE *-est, -ast, -ost, -st,* OTeut. *-isto-* (cp. Gr. *-isto-*)]

establish, *v.t.* to set upon a firm foundation, to found, institute; to settle or secure firmly (in office, opinion etc.); to make firm or lasting (as a belief, custom, one's health etc.); to substantiate, verify, put beyond dispute; to ordain officially and settle on a permanent basis (as a Church). **to establish a suit,** to exhaust all higher cards of a particular suit that are in the hands of opponents. **established Church,** *n.* the church established by law, the State Church. **establishment,** *n.* the act of establishing; the state of being established; a permanent organization such as the army, navy or civil service, staff of servants etc.; a public institution, business organization or large private household with the body of persons engaged in it; (*iron.*) a phrase of journalistic use to suggest the unconscious association of the respectable and conventional leaders in education and public affairs. **peace, war, establishment,** the reduced (augmented) military and naval forces in time of peace or of war. **separate establishment,** a household maintained for a lover. **establishmentarian,** *n.* an advocate or supporter of an established Church. *a.* advocating or supporting an established Church. [OF *establiss-,* stem of *establir,* L *stabilīre* (*stabilis,* firm)]

estafette, *n.* a military courier; an express, a messenger. [F, from It. *staffetta,* dim. of *staffa,* stirrup, OHG *stapho,* step]

estaminet, *n.* a cafe in which wine etc. is sold; a wineshop. [F, etym. doubtful]

estancia, *n.* in Spanish America, a cattle-farm, ranch or country estate; the residence on this. **estanciero,** *n.* a Spanish-American cattle-farmer. [Sp., from med. L *stantia,* from *stare,* to stand]

estate, *n.* property, esp. a landed property; (*Law*) a person's interest in lands and tenements (**real estate**) or movable property (**personal estate**); a person's assets and liabilities taken collectively; land built on either privately or by a local authority for housing (**housing estate**) or for factories and businesses (**industrial estate**); state, condition, circumstances, standing, rank; a class or order invested with political rights (in Great Britain the Three Estates are the Lords Spiritual, the Lords Temporal and the Commons). **fourth estate,** the newspaper press. **third estate,** the bourgeoisie of France before the Revolution, as distinguished from the nobles and the clergy. **estate agent,** *n.* the manager of a landed property; an agent concerned with the renting or sale of real estate. **estate car,** *n.* one with a large open space behind the passenger seats, and a rear door. **estate duty,** *n.* death duty. [OF *estat,* L *statum,* acc. of *status,* STATE]

esteem, *v.t.* to hold in high estimation, to regard with respect; to prize; to consider, to reckon. *n.* opinion or judgment as to merit or demerit, esp. a favourable opinion; respect, regard. **estimable,** *a.* worthy of esteem or regard. **estimably,** *adv.* [OF *estimer,* L *aestimāre,* to ESTIMATE]

ester, *n.* (*Chem.*) an organic compound deived by the replacement of hydrogen in an acid by an organic radical. [coined word]

Esther, *n.* in the Old Testament or Jewish Bible, the wife of the Persian King Ahasuerus, who prevented the extermination of her people by the vizier Haman, a deliverance celebrated in the Jewish festival of Purim. Her story is told in the Old Testament book Esther.

esthete, etc. AESTHETE.

estimable ESTEEM.

estimate, *v.t.* to compute the value of, to appraise; to form an opinion about; †to esteem. *n.* (-mət) an approximate calculation of the value, number, extent etc. of anything; the result of this; a contractor's statement of the sum for which he would undertake a piece of work; (*pl.*) statement of probable expenditure submitted to Parliament or other authoritative body; a judgment respecting character, circumstances etc.; †repute, reputation. **estimation,** *n.* the act of estimating; opinion or judgment; esteem; †conjecture. **estimative,** *a.* **estimator,** *n.* [L *aestimātus,* p.p. of *aestimāre,* to value]

estival etc. AESTIVAL.

Estonia (Russian **Estonskaya**) *n.* constituent republic of the USSR from 1940. **area** 45,100 sq km/17,413 sq miles. **capital** Tallinn. **population** (1987) 1,556,000; 65% Estonian, 28% Russian, 3% Ukrainian, 2% Byelorussian. **products** oil from shale, wood products, flax, dairy and pig products. **language** Estonian, allied to Finnish. **religion** traditionally Lutheran.

estop, *v.t.* (*past, p.p.* **estopped**) (*Law*) to bar, preclude, prevent. **estoppage,** *n.* **estoppel,** *n.* (*Law*) an act or statement that cannot legally be denied; a plea alleging such an act or statement. [A-F *estopper,* OF *estouper* (late L *stuppāre,* to stuff with tow, from L *stuppa,* tow)]

Estoril, *n.* fashionable resort on the coast 20 km/13 miles W of Lisbon, Portugal. There is a Grand Prix motor racing circuit. Population (1981) 16,000.

estovers, *n.pl.* (*Law*) necessaries or supplies allowed by law, esp. wood which a tenant can take from a landlord's estate for repairs etc.; allowance to a person out of an estate for support. [OF *estover, estovoir,* to be necessary]

estrade, *n.* a slightly raised platform, a dais. [F, from Sp. *estrado,* L *strātum,* neut. p.p. of *sternere,* to spread]

estrange, *v.t.* to alienate, to make indifferent or distant in feeling; to cut off from friendship; to make (oneself) a stranger to. **estranged,** *a.* having been estranged; of a man and wife, no longer living together. **estrangement,** *n.* [OF *estranger,* L *extrāneāre,* from *extrāneus,* STRANGE]

estray, *n.* a domestic animal, as a horse, ox etc. found straying or without an owner. †*v.i.* to stray. [A-F, from *estraier,* to stray, see ASTRAY]

estreat, *n.* (*Law*) a true copy of an original writing, esp. of penalties set down in the rolls of a court. *v.t.* (*Law*) to extract or copy from the records of a court; to levy a fine under estreat. [A-F *estrete,* OF *estraite,* fem. p.p. of *estraire,* L *extrahere,* to EXTRACT]

estuary, *n.* the mouth of a river etc. in which the tide meets the current; a firth. **estuarine,** *a.* [L *aestuārium,* from *aestuāre,* to surge, from *aestus,* heat, surge, tide]

esurient, *a.* hungry; needy. **esurience,** *n.* **esuritis,** *n.* (*Path.*) ulceration of the stomach from want of food. [L *ēsuriens -entem,* pres p. of *ēsurīre,* desiderative from *ēsus,* p.p. of *edere,* to eat]

-et, *suf.* diminutive, as *chaplet, circlet, coronet, dulcet, russet, violet.* [OF *-et, -ette,* etym. doubtful (cp. It. *-etto, -etta*)]

ETA, (*abbr.*) estimated time of arrival.

eta, *n.* the seventh letter of the Greek alphabet. **etacism,** *n.* the Erasmian pronunciation of eta as ā. [Gr. *ēta*]

et al., (*abbr.*) and others. [L *et alii, aliae* or *alia*]

eta patch, *n.* (*Aviat.*) a fan-shaped patch of fabric whereby the rigging is secured to the envelope of a balloon.

etcetera, and the rest; and others of like kind; and so forth, and so on, usually written *etc.* or *&c.* **etceteras,** *n.pl.* sundries, extras; things unspecified. [L, and the rest]

etch, *v.t.* to produce or reproduce (figures or designs) on metallic plates, for printing copies, by biting with an acid through the lines previously drawn with a needle on a coated surface. *v.i.* to practise this art. **etcher,** *n.* **etching,** *n.* the act of etching; an impression taken from an etched plate. **etching-ground,** *n.* the coating of the plate for etching. **etching-needle,** *n.* a sharp-pointed instrument for making lines in the etching-ground. [Dut. *etsen,* G *ätzen,* OHG *ezjan,* OTeut. *atjan* (causal), to make eat]

ETD, (*abbr.*) estimated time of departure.

eternal, *a.* without beginning or end; everlasting, perpetual; (*coll.*) incessant, unintermittent. **the Eternal,** the everlasting God; the Deity. **Eternal City,** *n.* Rome. **eternal triangle,** *n.* a sexual or emotional relationship involving three people, usu. two of one sex and one of the other, often resulting in tension or conflict. †**eternalize, -ise, eternize, -ise,** *v.t.* to make eternal; to prolong indefinitely; to immortalize. **eternally,** *adv.* †**eterne,** *a.* [OF *eternel,* late L *aeternālis,* from *aeternus* (*aeviternus,* from *aevum,* age)]

eternity, *n.* eternal duration; endless past or future time; unchangeableness of being; the future life; immortality of fame; (*pl.*) the eternal realities. **eternity ring,** *n.* a ring set all round with stones, signifying continuity. [OF *eternité,* L *aeternitas -tātem,* from *aeternus* (see prec.)]

etesian, *a.* annual; blowing periodically. **etesian winds,** *n.pl.* periodical winds, esp. north-westerly winds blowing for about six weeks in summer in the Mediterranean. [L *etēsius,* Gr. *etēsios,* from *etos,* year]

-eth, *suf.* forming ordinal numbers, as *fortieth.* [OE]

ethane, *n.* (*Chem.*) a colourless and odourless gaseous compound of the paraffin series. [*eth*er, -ANE]

Ethelred II, *n.* **the Unready** (*c.* 968–1016), king of England from 978. The son of King Edgar, he became king after the murder of his half-brother, Edward the Martyr. He tried to buy off the Danish raiders by paying Danegeld, and in 1002 ordered the massacre of the Danish settlers, provoking an invasion by Sweyn I of Denmark. War with Sweyn and Sweyn's son, Canute, occupied the rest of Ethelred's reign. He was nicknamed the 'Unready' because of his apparent lack of foresight.

ether, *n.* a fluid of extreme subtlety and elasticity (formerly) assumed to exist throughout space and between the particles of all substances, forming the medium of transmission of light and heat; the upper air, the higher regions of the sky, the clear sky; (*Chem.*) a light, volatile and inflammable fluid, produced by the distillation of alcohol with an acid, esp. sulphuric acid, and used as an anaesthetic. †**ether waves,** *n.pl.* (*Radio.*) electromagnetic waves. **ethereal,** *a.* of the nature of ether; resembling celestial ether, light, airy, tenuous, subtle, exquisite, impalpable, spiritual; (*Phys.*) pertaining to the ether; (*Chem.*) pertaining to the liquid known as ether. **ethereal oil,** *n.* (*Chem.*) an essential oil produced by distillation. **ethereality,** *n.* **etherealize, -ise,** *v.t.* to convert into ether; to render spiritual. **etherealization, -isation,** *n.* **ethereally,** *adv.* †**ethereous,** *a.* ethereal. **etheric,** *a.* **etherify,** *v.t.* (*Chem.*) to make or convert into an ether. **etherification,** *n.* **etheriform,** *a.* **etherism,** *n.* (*Med.*) the effects produced by the administration of ether as an anaesthetic. **etherize, -ise,** *v.t.* (*Chem.*) to convert into ether; (*Med.*) to subject to the influence of ether. **etherization, -isation,** *n.* **etheromania,** *n.* an uncontrolled desire for and use of ether. [L *aether,* Gr. *aithēr,* from root of *aithein,* to burn]

Etherege, *n.* **George** (*c.* 1635–*c.* 1691), English Restoration dramatist whose play *Love in a Tub* (1664) was the first attempt at the **comedy of manners** (a genre further developed by Congreve and Sheridan). Later plays include *She Would if She Could* (1668) and *The Man of Mode, or Sir Fopling Flutter* (1676).

ethic, ethical, *a.* treating of or relating to morals; dealing with moral questions or theory; conforming to a recognized standard. **ethic dative,** *n.* (*Gram.*) the dative of a personal pronoun indicating indirect interest in the fact stated, e.g. 'I will buy *me* a hat.' **ethical investment,** *n.* the practice of investing money only in those companies which are not involved in racial discrimination or in products causing potential harm to health, life or the environment, as cigarettes, nuclear weapons. **ethically,** *adv.* **ethicize, -ise,** *v.t.* to make ethical; to treat ethically. **ethicism,** *n.* **ethics,** *n.pl.* the science of morals; a treatise on this subject; a system of principles and rules of conduct; the whole field of moral science, including political and social science, law, jurisprudence etc. [L *ēthicus,* Gr. *ēthikos,* from ETHOS]

ethine, *n.* (*Chem.*) acetylene. [*eth*er, -INE]

Ethiopia, *n.* People's Democratic Republic of (*Hebretesebawit Ityopia,* formerly also known as Abyssinia), country in E Africa, bounded NE by the Red Sea, E and SE by Somalia, S by Kenya, and W and NW by Sudan. **area** 1,221,900 sq km/471,653 sq miles. **capital**

Addis Ababa. **towns** Asmara (capital of Eritrea), Dire Dawa; ports are Massawa, Assab. **physical** a high plateau with mountains; plains in east; Blue Nile river. **population** (1986) 46,000,000 (Oromo 40%, Amhara 25%, Tigré 12%, Sidama 9%); annual growth rate 2.5%. **exports** coffee, pulses, oilseeds, hides, skins. **language** Amharic (official); Tigré, Galla, Arabic. **religion** Christian (Ethiopian Orthodox church) 50%, Sunni Muslim 50%.

Ethiopian, *a.* pertaining to Ethiopia or Abyssinia or its inhabitants; *n.* an inhabitant of Ethiopia or Abyssinia; †a Negro. †**Ethiop**, *n.* **Ethiopic**, *a.* Ethiopian. *n.* the language of Ethiopia. [L *Aethiops -pis,* Gr. *Aithiops -pos* (etym. doubtful)]

ethmoid, -moidal, *a.* resembling a sieve. *n.* the ethmoid bone. **ethmoid bone,** *n.* a cellular bone situated between the orbital processes at the root of the nose, through which the olfactory nerves pass. **ethmoiditis**, *n.* (*Path.*) inflammation of this. [Gr. *ēthmoeidēs* (*ēthmos,* sieve, -OID)]

ethnarch, *n.* the governor of a people or district. [Gr. *ethnos,* nation, *archos,* ruler]

ethnic, *a.* pertaining to or characteristic of a race, people or cult; pertaining to the culture or traditions of a particular race or cult; (*coll.*) out of the ordinary; racial, ethnological; †not Jewish nor Christian. †*n.* a Gentile, a heathen or pagan. **ethnical,** *a.* **ethnically,** *adv.* †**ethnicism**, *n.* heathenism, paganism; a non-Jewish and non-Christian religion. **ethnicity,** *n.* [L *ethnicus,* Gr. *ethnikos,* from *ethnos,* nation]

ethn(o)- *comb. form.* pertaining to race. [Gr. *ethnos,* nation]

ethnocentrism, *n.* the mental habit of viewing the world solely from the perspective of one's own culture.

ethnography, *n.* the science which describes different human societies. **ethnographer,** *n.* **ethnographic, -ical**, *a.* **ethnographically,** *adv.*

ethnology, *n.* the science which treats of the varieties of the human race, and attempts to trace them to their origin. **ethnologic, -ical**, *a.* **ethnologically,** *adv.* **ethnologist,** *n.* a student of ethnology.

ethnomusicology, *n.* the study of the music of different societies. **ethnomusicologist,** *n.*

ethology, *n.* the science of animal behaviour. **ethologic, -ical**, *a.* [L and Gr. *ēthologia*]

ethos, *n.* the characteristic spirit, character, disposition or genius of a people, community, institution, system etc. [Gr., character, disposition]

ethyl, *n.* a monovalent fatty hydrocarbon radicle of the paraffin series, forming the base of common alcohol and ether, acetic acid etc. **ethyl alcohol,** *n.* the ordinary alcohol of commerce. [*ether*, -YL]

etiolate, *v.t.* to blanch (a plant kept in the dark); to render (persons) pale and unhealthy. *v.i.* to become blanched by deprivation of light. **etiolation,** *n.* [F *étioler,* Norm. *s'étieuler,* to grow into haulm, from *éteule,* OF *esteule,* L *stipula,* straw]

etiology AETIOLOGY.

etiquette, *n.* the conventional rules of behaviour in polite society; the established rules of precedence and ceremonial in a court, or a professional or other body; †a rule of etiquette; †a label. [F *étiquette,* a TICKET]

Etna, *n.* volcano on the E coast of Sicily, 3323 m/10,906 ft, the highest in Europe; its most recent eruptions were Dec. 1985. **Etnean**, *a.*

etna, *n.* an apparatus which is used for heating small quantities of liquid by means of burning spirit.

Etonian, *n.* a person educated at Eton College. **Old Etonian,** an Etonian. **Eton collar,** *n.* a wide, starched collar worn outside the jacket. **Eton crop,** *n.* a fashion of cutting a woman's hair short like a man's. **Eton jacket,** *n.* a boy's untailed dress-coat.

étrier, *n.* a small rope ladder used in mountaineering. [F, a stirrup]

Etrurian, *a.* pertaining to Etruria, an ancient country in central Italy. *n.* a native of Etruria. **Etruscan,** *a.* Etrurian.

Etruscan art, *n.* sculpture, painting, and design of the first known Italian civilization. Etruscan terracotta coffins (*sarcophagi*), carved with reliefs and topped with portraits of the dead, reclining on one elbow, were to influence the later Romans and early Christians. **Etruscan vases,** *n.pl.* vases found in Etruscan tombs, but which are of Grecian design. [L *Etrūria, Etruscus*]

et seq., (*abbr.*) and the following (passage). [L *et sequentes, et sequentia*]

-ette, *suf.* meaning [1]diminutive, as *palette, cigarette;* [2]female, as *brunette,* often offensive, as *jockette;* [3]imitation, as *flannelette, leatherette*. [OF *-ette,* fem. of *-et* (diminutive suf.)]

ettle, *v.t.* †to purpose, intend; (*Sc.*) to design, intend (for). *v.i.* (*Sc.*) to aim at. *n.* (*Sc.*) aim, object. [Icel. *ætla, etla,* to think, intend (cogn. with OE *eaht,* council, *eahtian,* to watch over)]

étude, *n.* (*Mus.*) a short composition written mainly to test a player's technical skill. [Fr, a study]

etui, *n.* a pocket-case for pins, needles etc. [F, a case]

etymology, *n.* the science that treats of the origin and history of words; the history of the origin and modification of a particular word; derivation; that part of grammar which relates to individual words, their formation, inflection etc. **etymologer, etymologist,** *n.* **etymologic, -ical, etymologically,** *adv.* †**etymologicon**, *n.* a book on etymologies; an etymological dictionary. **etymologize, -ise,** *v.t.* to give or trace the etymology of. *v.i.* to study etymology; to search into the source of words; to propose etymologies for words. [OF *ethimologie,* L *etymologia,* Gr. *etumologia* (*etumos,* real, rel. to *eteos,* true, -LOGY)]

etymon, *n.* the primitive or root form of a word. [L from Gr., neut. of *etumos* as prec.]

eu-, *comb. form.* good, well, pleasant, as in *eulogy, euphony*. [Gr., well]

Euboea, *n.* (Greek **Evvoia**) mountainous island off the E coast of Greece, in the Aegean Sea; area 3755 sq km/1450 sq miles; about 177 km/110 miles long; population (1981) 188,410. Mount Delphi reaches 1743 m/5721 ft. The chief town, Chalcis, is connected by a bridge to the mainland.

eucaine, *n.* a form of local anaesthetic. [*cocaine*]

Eucalyptus, *n.* (*pl.* **-ti**) an Australasian genus of evergreen myrtaceous trees comprising the gum-trees. [Gr. *kaluptos,* covered, from *kaluptein,* to cover (the flower being protected by a cap)]

eucharis, *n.* a bulbous plant from S America, cultivated in hot-houses for the sake of its pure white bell-shaped flowers. [Gr. *eucharis* (EU-, *charis,* grace)]

Eucharist, *n.* the sacrament of the Lord's Supper; the elements, bread and wine, given in this sacrament. **eucharistic, -ical,** *a.* [OF *eucariste*, late L and Gr. *eucharistia*, from *eucharistos*, grateful (EU-, *charizesthai*, to show favour to, from *charis*, grace)]

euchlorine, *n.* a yellow explosive gas with bleaching properties, obtained from a mixture of chlorate of potash and dilute hydrochloric acid. [Gr. *chlōros,* green, -INE (on analogy of CHLORINE)]

euchology, *n.* the liturgy of the Greek Church; a formulary of prayers. [Gr. (*euchē,* prayer; see LOGOS)]

euchre, *n.* an American card game for several persons, usu. four, with a pack from which the cards from the twos to the nines have been excluded. *v.t.* to beat by taking three of the five tricks at euchre; (*coll.*) to beat thoroughly, to ruin; to outwit. [etym. doubtful]

euclase, *n.* a monoclinic green, blue or white transparent silicate of aluminium and beryllium. [F (EU-, Gr. *klasis,* breaking, from *klaein,* to break)]

Euclid, *n.* (*c.* 330–*c.* 260 BC), Greek mathematician, who lived at Alexandria and wrote the *Stoicheia*/*Elements* in 13 books, of which nine deal with plane and solid geometry, and four with number theory. His main work lay in the systematic arrangement of previous discoveries, based on axioms, definitions, and theorems.

Euclidean, *a.* of or pertaining to Euclid, Alexandrian mathematician (fl. 300 BC); according to the axioms and postulates of Euclid's geometry.

eudemonism, *n.* the system of ethics which makes the

pursuit of happiness the basis and criterion of moral conduct. **eudemonic**, *a.* **eudemonics,** *n.pl.* **eudemonist,** *n.* **eudemonistic**, *a.* [Gr. *eudaimōn,* happy]

eudiometer, *n.* an instrument for ascertaining the quantity of oxygen in a given bulk of air. **eudiometric, -ical**, *a.* **eudiometrically,** *adv.* **eudiometry,** *n.* the measurement of the purity of the air, or the composition of a gaseous mixture, by means of the eudiometer. [Gr. *eudios* (EU-, *Di-,* stem of *Zeus,* gen. *Dios,* the God of the sky), -METER]

Eugène, *n.* **Prince of Savoy** (1663–1736), Austrian general, who had many victories against the Turkish invaders (whom he expelled from Hungary in 1697 in the Battle of Zenta) and against France, especially in the War of the Spanish Succession (battles of Blenheim, Oudenaarde, and Malplaquet).

Eugene Onegin, *n.* a novel in verse by Aleksandr Pushkin, published from 1823–31. Eugene Onegin, bored with life but sensitive, rejects the love of Tatyana, a humble country girl, but she rises in society and in turn rejects him. Onegin was the model for a number of Russian literary heroes.

eugenic, *a.* pertaining to the development and improvement of offspring, esp. human offspring, through selective breeding. **eugenics,** *n. sing.* the science or political beliefs relating to this. **eugenicist,** *n.* **eugenism**, *n.*

Eugénie, *n.* **Marie Ignace Augustine de Montijo** (1826–1920), empress of France, daughter of the Spanish count of Montijo. In 1853 she married Louis Napoleon, who had become emperor as Napoleon III. She encouraged court extravagance, Napoleon III's intervention in Mexico, and urged him to fight the Prussians. After his surrender to the Germans at Sedan, NE France, in 1870 she fled to England.

eugenin, *n.* clove camphor; a crystallized substance deposited from water distilled from cloves. [*Eugeno,* a genus of trees named in honour of *Eugene,* Prince of Savoy, -IN]

euharmonic, *a.* (*Mus.*) producing perfect harmony.

euhemerism, *n.* the theory formulated by Euhemerus of Messenia in Sicily (about 300 BC), that the classic gods are merely deified national kings and heroes, and their miraculous feats exaggerated traditions of actual events. **euhemerist,** *n.* **euhemeristic**, *a.* **euhemerize, -ise,** *v.i.* to follow euhemerism. *v.t.* to treat or explain (myths) rationalistically.

eukaryon, *n.* a highly organized cell nucleus, surrounded by membrane, characteristic of higher organisms. **eukaryote**, *n.* an organism which has such cell nuclei. [Gr. *karuon,* kernel]

eulogy, *n.* praise, encomium, panegyric; a writing or speech in praise of a person. **eulogist,** *n.* **eulogistic, -ical**, *a.* **eulogistically,** *adv.* †**eulogium**, *n.* (*pl.* **-ums**) eulogy. **eulogize, -ise,** *v.t.* to speak or write of in praise; to commend, to extol. [late L *eulogium,* Gr. *eulogia* (EU-, -LOGY)]

Eumenides, *n.* ('kindly ones') in Greek mythology, appeasing name for the Furies.

eunuch, *n.* a castrated man, esp. an attendant in a harem, or a state functionary in Oriental palaces and under the Roman emperors; (*loosely*) an ineffectual or powerless person. *a.* castrated; emasculate; unproductive. †*v.t.* To make into a eunuch. **eunuchal,** *a.* **eunuchize, -ise,** *v.t.* [L *eunūchus,* Gr. *eunouchos,* one in charge of a bed-chamber (*eunē,* bed, *och-,* stem of *echein,* to hold)]

Euonymus, *n.* a genus of shrubs containing the spindle-tree. [L, from Gr. *euonumos,* of good name, luck (EU-, *onoma,* Aeolic *onuma,* name)]

eupatrid, *n.* (*pl.* **-ids, -idae**) a member of the hereditary aristocracy of Attica, a patrician. [Gr. *eupatridēs* (EU-, *patēr,* father)]

eupeptic, *a.* having a good digestion; pertaining to or characteristic of good digestion. **eupepsia**, *n.* **eupepticity**, *n.* [Gr. *eupeptos* (EU-, *peptein,* to digest)]

euphemism, *n.* the use of a soft or pleasing term or phrase for one that is harsh or offensive; such a term or phrase. **euphemistic**, *a.* **euphemistically,** *adv.* **euphemize, -ise,** *v.t.* to speak of euphemistically; to express in euphemism. *v.i.* to speak in euphemism. [Gr. *euphēmismos,* from *euphēmos* (EU-, *phēmē,* speaking, fame)]

euphobia, *n.* a fear of good news. [Gr. *eu,* well, *phobos,* fear]

euphonium, *n.* (*Mus.*) a brass instrument related to the tuba. [as foll.]

euphony, *n.* an agreeable sound; smoothness or agreeableness of sound in words and phrases; a pleasing pronunciation; (*Philol.*) the tendency towards greater ease of pronunciation shown in phonetic changes. **euphonic, -ical**, *a.* **euphonically,** *adv.* **euphonious**, *a.* **euphoniously,** *adv.* **euphonize, -ise,** *v.t.* [F *euphonie,* Gr. *euphōnia* (EU-, *phōnē,* voice)]

Euphorbia, *n.* a genus of plants known as the spurges, comprising about 700 species, many of which are poisonous while others have medicinal qualities. **euphorbiaceous**, *a.* **euphorbium**, *n.* an acrid poisonous, inflammable resin flowing from some African species of *Euphorbia.* [L *euphorbea,* from *Euphorbus,* Greek physician]

euphoria, *n.* a feeling of well-being, supreme content. [Gr.]

euphrasy, *n.* the eye-bright; (*fig.*) something that cheers. [med. L and Gr. *euphrasia,* cheerfulness]

Euphrates, *n.* (Arabic **Furat**), river, rising in E Turkey, flowing through Syria and Iraq and joining the Tigris above Basra to form the Shatt-al-Arab, at the head of the Persian/Arabian Gulf; 3600 km/2240 miles in length. The ancient cities of Babylon, Eridu, and Ur were situated along its course.

euphuism, *n.* a pedantic affectation of elegant and high-flown language (from *Euphues* (1578–80), a work by John Lyly, which brought the style into vogue). **euphuist,** *n.* **euphuistic**, *a.* **euphuistically,** *adv.* †**euphuize, -ise,** *v.i.* [Gr. *euphuēs,* well-grown or well-endowed (EU-, *phuein,* to produce)]

Eurasian, *a.* of mixed European and Asian blood; a term formerly applied in British India etc. to those born of a European father and an Asian mother; pertaining to both Europe and Asia. *n.* one of European and Asian blood.

Euratom, *n.* the European Atomic Energy Community of 1958 in which France, Belgium, West Germany, Italy, the Netherlands and Luxemburg united for the peaceful development of nuclear energy.

eureka, *n.* a discovery, an invention; exultation over a discovery (Archimedes' exclamation on discovering a test for the purity of the gold in Hiero's crown, involving the displacement of water). [Gr. *heurēka,* I have found]

Eureka Stockade, *n.* incident at Ballarat, Australia, when about 150 goldminers, or 'diggers', rebelled against authority. They took refuge behind a wooden stockade, which was taken in a few minutes by the military on 3 Dec. 1854. Some 30 diggers were killed, and a few soldiers killed or wounded, but the majority of the rebels were taken prisoner. Among those who escaped was Peter Lalor, their leader. Of the 13 tried for treason, all were acquitted, thus marking the emergence of Australian democracy.

eurhythmics, *n. sing.* the science or art of rhythmical movement, esp. as applied to dancing and gymnastic exercises. **eurhythmic, -ical,** *a.* **eurhythmy**, *n.*

Euripides, *n.* (*c.* 484–407 BC), Greek dramatist whose plays deal with ordinary people and social issues rather than the more grandiose themes used by his contemporaries. He wrote more than 80 plays, of which 18 survive, including *Alcestis* (438), *Medea* (431), *Andromache* (426), *Trojan Women* (415), *Electra* (417), *Iphigenia in Tauris* (413), *Iphigenia in Aulis* (405), and *Bacchae* (405).

Euro-, *comb. form* pertaining to Europe to Europeans.

euro, *n.* (*Austral.*) a kangaroo, the wallaby of S and Central Australia. [Abor.]

Eurobond, *n.* a bond underwritten by an international syndicate and sold in countries other than the country of the currency in which the issue is denominated.

They provide longer-term financing than is possible with loans in Eurodollars.

Eurocheque, *n.* a type of cheque able to draw on certain international banks on receipt of the appropriate card.

†**euroclydon,** *n.* a stormy north-east wind in the Mediterranean in the early spring. [Gr. (in Acts xxvii.14), *eurokludōn* (*euros,* east wind, *kludōn,* surge)]

Eurocodes, *n.* a series of codes giving design rules for all types of engineering structures, except certain very specialized forms, such as nuclear reactors. The codes will be given the status of ENs (European standards) and will be administered by CEN (European Committee for Standardization). ENs will eventually replace national codes, in Britain currently maintained by BSI (British Standards Institute), and will include parameters to reflect local requirements.

Eurocommunism, *n.* policy followed by communist parties in Western Europe to seek power within the framework of national political initiative rather than by revolutionary means. In addition, Eurocommunism has enabled these parties to free themselves from total reliance on the Soviet Union. **Eurocommunist,** *n.*

Eurocrat, *n.* an official involved in the administration of any part of the EEC.

Eurodollar, *n.* US currency deposited outside the US and held by individuals and institutions, not necessarily in Europe. They originated in the 1960s when E European countries deposited their US dollars in W European banks. Banks holding Eurodollar deposits may lend in dollars, usually to finance trade, and often redeposit with other foreign banks. The practice is a means of avoiding credit controls and exploiting interest rate differentials.

Euroformat, *a.* of a passport, issued to a citizen of member countries of the European Community to replace national passports.

Euromart, *n.* European Common Market.

Europa[1], *n.* in astronomy, the fourth-largest moon of the planet Jupiter, diameter 3100 km/1900 miles, orbiting 671,000 km/417,000 miles from the planet every 3.55 days. It is covered by ice and criss-crossed by thousands of thin cracks, each some 50,000 km/30,000 miles long.

Europa[2], *n.* in Greek mythology, the daughter of the king of Tyre, carried off by Zeus (in the form of a bull); she personifies the continent of Europe.

Europe, *n.* second smallest continent, comprising the land west of the Ural mountains; it has 8% of the Earth's surface, with 14.5% of world population. **area** 10,400,000 sq km/4,000,000 sq miles. **largest cities** (over 1.5 million inhabitants) Athens, Barcelona, Berlin, Birmingham, Budapest, Hamburg, Istanbul, Kiev, Leningrad, London, Madrid, Manchester, Milan, Moscow, Paris, Rome, Vienna, Warsaw. **population** (1985) 492,000,000 (excluding Turkey and USSR). **languages** mostly of Indo-European origin, with a few exceptions, including Finno-Ugrian (Finnish and Hungarian) and Basque. **religion** Christianity (Protestantism, Roman Catholicism, Greek Orthodox), Islam, Judaism.

European, *a.* of, pertaining to, happening in, or extending over, Europe; native to Europe. *n.* a native or inhabitant of Europe; one of European race. **European plan,** *n.* (*N Am.*) the system of charging for a hotel room without including meals. **Europeanism,** *n.* **Europeanize, -ise,** *v.t.* **Europeanization, -isation,** *n.*

European Atomic Energy Commission (EURATOM), organization established by the second Treaty of Rome in 1957, which seeks the cooperation of member states of the European Community in nuclear research and the rapid and large-scale development of non-military nuclear energy.

European Coal and Steel Community (ECSC), former organization established by the treaty of Paris in 1951 (ratified 1952) as a single authority for the coal and steel industries of France, West Germany, Italy, Belgium, Holland, and Luxembourg, eliminating tariffs and other restrictions; in 1967 it became part of the European Community.

European Community *n.* (EC), political and economic alliance consisting of the European Coal and Steel Community (1952), European Economic Community (EEC, popularly called the Common Market, 1957), and the European Atomic Energy Commission (Euratom, 1957). The original six members – Belgium, France, West Germany, Italy, Luxembourg, and the Netherlands – were joined by the UK, Denmark, and the Republic of Ireland (1974), Greece (1981), Spain and Portugal (1985).

European Court of Justice, the court of the European Community (EC) which is responsible for interpreting Community law and ruling on breaches by member states and others of such law. It sits in Luxembourg with judges from the member states.

European Democratic Group, the group of British Conservative Party members of the European Parliament.

European Economic Community (EEC), one of the organizations of the European Community (EC).

European Free Trade Association (EFTA), an organization established in 1960 and as of 1988 consisting of Austria, Finland, Iceland, Norway, Sweden, and Switzerland. There are no import duties between members. Of the original members, Britain and Denmark left (end 1972) to join the European Community, as subsequently did Portugal (end 1985).

European Monetary System (EMS), an attempt by the European Community to bring financial cooperation and monetary stability to Europe. It was established in 1979 in the wake of the 1974 oil crisis which brought growing economic disruption to European economies because of floating exchange rates. Central to the EMS is the Exchange Rate Mechanism (ERM), a voluntary system of semi-fixed exchange rates based on the European Currency Unit (ECU).

European Monetary Union (EMU), the proposed European Community policy for a single currency and common economic policies. The proposal was announced by a European Community committee headed by EC Commission president Jacques Delors in Apr. 1989.

European Parliament, *n.* the parliament of the European Community, which meets in Strasbourg to comment on the legislative proposals of the Commission of the European Communities. Members are elected for a five-year term. The European Parliament has 518 seats, of which the UK, France, West Germany, and Italy have 81 each, Spain 60, the Netherlands 25, Belgium, Greece, and Portugal 24 each, Denmark 16, the Republic of Ireland 15, and Luxembourg 6.

European Space Agency (ESA), an organization of European countries (Belgium, Denmark, France, Ireland, Italy, Netherlands, Spain, Sweden, Switzerland, the UK, and West Germany) which engages in space research and technology. It was founded in 1975, with headquarters in Paris.

europium, *n.* an extremely rare metallic element, at.no.63; chem. symbol Eu, discovered in 1901.

Eurovision, *n.* the network of European television.

Eurus, *n.* the east wind; the god of the east wind. [L, from Gr. *Euros*]

Eurydice, *n.* in Greek mythology, the wife of Orpheus. She was a dryad, or forest nymph, and died of snake bite. Orpheus attempted unsuccessfully to fetch her back from the realm of the dead.

Eusebian, *a.* pertaining to Eusebius; (*Bibl.*) pertaining to Eusebius of Caesarea (whence Eusebian Canons, a classified arrangement of the four Gospels). *n.* a member of a semi-Arian sect, named after Eusebius of Nicomedia, a bishop of the 4th cent., who held that there was a subordination among the persons of the Godhead.

Eusebio, *n.* **(Eusebio Ferreira da Silva)** (1942–), Portuguese footballer, born in Lourenco Marques. He made his international debut in 1961 and played for his country 77 times. He spent most of his league career with Benfica, and also played in the US.

Euskadi, *n.* the Basque name for the Basque country.

Euskarian, *a.* Basque. *n.* the Basque language; a Basque. [*Euskara,* the name applied by the Basques to their own language]

Eustachian, *a.* of or pertaining to Eustachius, an Italian physician of the 16th cent. **Eustachian tube,** *n.* a duct leading to the cavity of the tympanum of the ear from the upper part of the pharynx.

eustasy, *n.* changes in the world shore-line level or sea-level. **eustatic,** *a.* [Gr. *stasis,* a standing]

Euston Road School, British art school in Euston Road, London (1937–39). William Coldstream (1908–87) and Victor Pasmore were teachers there. Despite its brief existence, the school influenced many British painters with its emphasis on careful, subdued naturalism.

eutectic, *a.* (*Chem.*) applying to the mixture of two or more substances with a minimum melting-point. [Gr. *eu,* well, *tektos,* molten]

Eutelsat, (*abbr.*) European Telecommunications Satellite Organization.

Euterpe, *n.* (*Gr. Myth.*) the Muse of music, figured with a flute; (*Bot.*) a genus of graceful palms, all S American; (*Astron.*) the 27th asteroid. **Euterpean,** *a.* pertaining to music. [Gr. (EU-, *terpein,* to please)]

euthanasia, *n.* easy, painless death; a method of producing this; putting to death in this manner, esp. in cases of extreme or terminal suffering. **euthanase,** *v.t., v.i.* [Gr., from *euthanatos* (EU-, *thanatos,* death)]

euthenics, *n. sing.* the study of the improvement of human living standards. **euthenist,** *n.* [Gr. *euthēneein,* to flourish]

Eutheria, *n.pl.* the subclass of mammals which have a placenta. **eutherian,** *n., a.* [Gr. *thēr,* a beast]

eutrophic, *a.* of a body of water, rich in dissolved nutrients and supporting an abundance of plant life. [Gr. *eutrophos,* well-fed]

evacuate, *v.t.* to make empty, esp. to eject from or to empty the excretory passages; to form a vacuum; to withdraw from (esp. of troops); to remove inhabitants from a danger zone; (*fig.*) to divest of its meaning; †to nullify. **evacuant,** *a.* producing evacuation; purgative. *n.* a medicine producing this effect. **evacuation,** *n.* the act of evacuating; also, the transfer of people from a danger zone. **evacuee,** *n.* a person, esp. a child, thus evacuated. [L *ēvacuātus,* p.p. of *ēvacuāre* (E-, *vacuus,* empty)]

evade, *v.t.* to avoid or elude by artifice, stratagem or sophistry; to avoid (doing something), to shirk; to defeat, baffle, foil. †*v.i.* to escape; to practise sophistry; to act evasively. **evadable,** *a.* [F *évader,* L *ēvādere* (E-, *vādere,* to go)]

evaginate, *v.t.* to turn inside out, to unsheathe (as a tubular organ). **evagination,** *n.* [L *ēvaginātus,* p.p. of *ēvagināre* (E-, *vagina,* sheath)]

evaluate, *v.t.* to determine the value or worth of, to appraise; (*Math.*) to find a numerical expression for. **evaluation,** *n.* [F *évalure*]

evanesce, *v.i.* to disappear; to be dissipated in vapour; to vanish. **evanescence,** *n.* **evanescent,** *a.* disappearing gradually; fading, fleeting; (*Math.*) approaching zero, infinitesimal; imperceptibly minute. **evanescently,** *adv.* [L *ēvānescere* (E-, *vānescere,* from *vānus,* vain)]

†**evangel,** *n.* the Gospel; one of the four Gospels; (*pl.*) the Gospels; (*fig.*) a gospel, a doctrine of political or social reform. **evangelical,** *a.* pertaining to the Gospel; according to the doctrine of the Gospel; proclaiming or maintaining the truth taught in the Gospel; accepting for gospel only what Protestants consider the fundamental teaching of Scripture, the doctrines of the Fall, Christ's atonement, and salvation by faith not works; firmly believing in and actively promoting a cause. *n.* a member of this party in the Church, esp. in the Church of England, where it corresponds to the Low Church Party. **evangelicalism,** *n.* **evangelically,** *adv.* **evangelicity,** *n.* **evangelist,** *n.* one of the four writers of the Gospels (Matthew, Mark, Luke and John); a preacher of the Gospel; a lay preacher; one who evangelizes or believes in evangelism; an enthusiastic and active supporter of a cause. **evangelism,** *n.* preaching of the Gospel; evangelicalism. †**evangelistary,** *n.* a book containing a selection of passages from the Gospels, as for lessons in divine service. **evangelistic,** *a.* pertaining to the four Evangelists; pertaining to preaching of the Gospel; evangelical. **evangelize, -ise,** *v.t.* to preach the Gospel to; to convert to Christianity; to try to persuade (people) to join or support a cause. **evangelization, -isation,** *n.* [OF *evangile,* eccles. L *ēvangelium,* Gr. *euangelion* (EU-, *angellein,* to announce)]

Evangelical Movement, *n.* in Britain, a 19th-century party which stressed basic protestant beliefs and the message of the four gospels. The movement was associated with Rev. Charles Simeon (1783–1836). It aimed to raise moral enthusiasm and ethical standards among Church of England clergy.

evanish, *v.i.* to vanish, to disappear. **evanishment,** *n.* [OF *evaniss-,* stem of *evanir,* L *ēvānescere,* to EVANESCE]

Evans[1], *n.* **Arthur John** (1851–1941), English archaeologist. His excavation of Knossos on Crete resulted in the discovery of pre-Phoenician Minoan script and proved the existence of the legendary Minoan civilization.

Evans[2], *n.* **Edith** (1888–1976), English character actress, who performed on the London stage and on Broadway. She is particularly remembered for the film role of Lady Bracknell in Oscar Wilde's comedy *The Importance of Being Earnest* (1952).

Evans[3], *n.* **Walker** (1903–75), US photographer, known for his documentary photographs of the people in the rural US south during the Great Depression of the 1930s. Many of his photographs appeared in James Agee's book *Let Us Now Praise Famous Men* (1941).

evaporate, *v.t.* to convert into vapour; to vaporize; to drive off the moisture from by heating or drying. *v.i.* to become vapour; to pass away in vapour; to exhale moisture; (*coll.*) to disappear, to vanish. **evaporated milk,** *n.* unsweetened tinned milk from which some of the water has been evaporated. **evaporable,** *a.* **evaporation,** *n.* **evaporative,** *a.* **evaporator,** *n.* **evaporimeter,** *n.* [L *ēvaporātus,* p.p. of *ēvaporāre*]

evasion, *n.* the act of evading or escaping (as from a question, argument or charge), a subterfuge, an equivocation. **evasive,** *a.* **evasively,** *adv.* **evasiveness,** *n.* [F *évasion,* late L *ēvāsio -ōnem,* from *ēvādere,* to EVADE]

Eve, *n.* (*Bibl.*) the wife of Adam and mother of mankind; who was tempted by Satan in the form of a snake to eat the fruit of the Tree of Knowledge of Good and Evil, and thus brought about the expulsion from the Garden of Eden; the personification of womankind. **daughter of Eve,** (*often derog.*) a woman, usu. with an implication of curiosity, vanity etc. [OE *Efe,* L *Eva, Heva,* from Heb. *Hawwah*]

eve, *n.* the evening before a holiday or other event or date; the period immediately preceding some important event; †evening. [OE *æfen, ēfen* (cp. OHG *ābant,* G *Abend*)]

evection, *n.* an inequality in the longitude of the moon, due to the action of the sun. [L *ēvectio,* from *ēvehere* (E-, *vehere,* to carry, p.p. *vectus*)]

Evelyn, *n.* **John** (1620–1706), English diarist and author. He was a friend of Pepys, and like him remained in London during the Plague and the Great Fire. He wrote 300-odd books, most noted of which is his diary, first published in 1818, which covers the period 1640–1706.

even[1], *n.* evening. **evenfall,** n. (*Poet.*) early evening. **evensong,** *n.* a form of worship for the evening; the time for evening prayer. **eventide,** *n.* evening. **eventide home,** *n.* a home for elderly people.

even[2], *a.* level, smooth, uniform; on the same level, in the same plane (with); parallel; capable of being divided by the number 2 without any remainder;

opposed to odd; equal; equally balanced, fair, impartial; unvarying, equable, unruffled; †plain, clear; †without blemish, pure; †equal in rank. **odd or even,** a game of chance. **on an even keel,** (*Naut.*) said of a ship when she draws the same water fore and aft; well-balanced, emotionally, mentally or financially. **to be even with,** to revenge oneself on; to be quits with. **to even out,** to become even or equal. **to even up,** to balance, to make equal. **to make even,** †to square accounts with; (*Print.*) to space out the lines, so that a given passage may end with a full line. **even chance,** *n.* an equal likelihood of success or failure. **even date,** *n.* (*Comm.*) today. **even-handed,** *a.* impartial, equitable, fair. **even-handedly,** *adv.* **even-handedness,** *n.* **even-minded,** *a.* **even-mindedly,** *adv.* **even money,** *n.* an equal amount placed on each side of a bet. †**even-pleached,** *a.* smoothly or evenly intertwined. **even-tempered,** *a.* **evenly,** *adv.* **evenness,** *n.* **evens,** *n.* odds quoted on a racehorse etc. such that if it wins the person betting gains an amount equal to the stake. [OE *efen, efn* (cp. Dut. *even,* OHG *eban,* G *eben*)]

even[3], *v.t.* to make smooth or level; to place on a level; †to treat as equal, to compare; †to make quits (with); to act up to, to satisfy. †*v.i.* to be equal. **evener,** *n.* [OE *efnan,* as prec.]

even[4], *adv.* to a like degree, equally; as much as, so much as (expressing unexpectedness, surprise, concession or emphasis, a comparison being implied); evenly; exactly, just, simply, neither more nor less than. **even so,** exactly; yes. [OE *efne,* as prec.]

evening, *n.* the close or latter part of the day; the period from sunset to dark, or from sunset to bed-time; (*fig.*) the close or decline, as of life; the latter part. **evening dress,** *n.* the dress prescribed by convention for wearing for a formal occasion in the evening. **evening primrose,** *n.* a plant belonging to the genus *Oenothera,* the yellow flowers of which usually open in the evening. **evening star,** *n.* (also called Hesperus or Vesper) Jupiter, Mercury or Venus when visible in the west in the evening. [OE *æfnung,* from *æfnian,* to grow towards evening, from *æfen,* EVEN[1]]

event, *n.* anything that happens, as distinguished from a thing that exists; an occurrence, esp. one of great importance; the contingency or possibility of an occurrence; the consequence of any action; the issue or conclusion; any of several possible occurrences regarded as having a probability of its own; any item in a programme of games, contests etc., esp. one on which money is wagered; †fate. **at all events,** in any case, at any rate. **double event,** the coincidence of two occurrences. **in the event of,** if so, if it so happens. **one-day event, three-day event,** an equestrian competition taking place over one or three days and including dressage, show-jumping and cross-country riding. **eventer,** *n.* a horse that takes part in one- or three-day events. **eventful,** *a.* full of events; attended by important changes. **eventing,** *n.* taking part in one- or three-day events. **eventless,** *a.* [OF, from L *ēventus,* p.p. of *ēvenīre,* to happen (E-, *venīre,* to come)]

eventide, EVEN[1].

eventual, *a.* happening as a consequence of something else; finally resulting, ultimate, final. **eventuality,** *n.* **eventually,** *adv.* **eventuate,** *v.i.* to happen, to come to pass, to result; to turn out (well or ill). [EVENT]

ever, *adv.* at all times; always; continually; at any time; in any degree. **ever after,** *adv.* or **since,** continually after a certain time. **ever and anon,** now and then; at one time and another. **ever so,** *adv.* to any degree or extent conceivable. **ever such a,** (*coll. or dial.*) a very. **for ever,** for all future time, eternally; incessantly. **or ever** OR[2]. †**ever-during,** *a.* everlasting. **everglade,** *n.* (*US*) a low, marshy, tract of country, interspersed with patches covered with high grass; (*pl.*) the region of this character in Florida. **evergreen,** *a.* always green; retaining its verdure throughout the year; (*fig.*) always young or fresh. *n.* a plant which retains its verdure through the year. **everlasting,** *a.* lasting for ever, eternal, perpetual; continual, unintermittent; (*fig.*) interminable, tiresome; of flowers, not changing colour when dried. *n.* eternity; a plant whose flowers retain their colour when dried. **the Everlasting,** the Deity, the Eternal Being. **everlastingly,** *adv.* **everlastingness,** *n.* **ever-living,** *a.* living without end; immortal; unceasing. **evermore,** *adv.* always, eternally, continually. [OE *æfre* (etym. doubtful, perh. rel. to OE *ā, āwa,* AYE[2], cp. Gr. *aiōn,* L *aevum*)]

Everest, Mount, *n.* the world's highest mountain, in the Himalayas, on the China-Nepál frontier; height 8872 m/29,118 ft. It was first climbed by Edmund Hillary and Norghay Tenzing in 1953.

evert, *v.i.* to turn outwards, to turn inside out; †to overthrow. **eversion,** *n.* [L *ēvertere* (E-, *vertere,* to turn)]

Evert, *n.* **Chris** (1954–), US lawn tennis player. She won her first Wimbledon title in 1974, and has since won 21 Grand Slam titles. She became the first woman tennis player to win $1 million in prize money.

every, *a.* each of a number, all separately; each. **every bit,** quite; the whole. **every now and then, every now and again, every so often,** from time to time; at brief intervals. **every one,** each one. **every other** OTHER. **everybody,** *n.* every person. **everybody else,** (*collect.*) all other persons. **everyday,** *a.* met with or happening daily; worn or used on ordinary occasions; common, usual; commonplace. *adv.* on each or every day; continually. **Everyman,** *n.* a figure in a mediaeval morality play who represents everyone or mankind; **(everyman)** the person in the street, everyone. **everyone,** *n.* everybody. **everything,** *n.* (*collect.*) all things; all of the things making up a whole; (*fig.*) something of the highest importance. **everyway,** *adv.* in every way; in every respect. **everywhere,** *adv.* in every place. [ME *everi, everich* (OE *æfre,* ever, *ælc,* each)]

evict, *v.t.* to dispossess by legal process; to eject from lands, tenements or property by law; †to prove, to evince. **eviction,** *n.* **evictor,** *n.* [L *ēvictus,* p.p. of *ēvincere* (E-, *vincere,* to conquer)]

evidence, *n.* anything that makes clear or obvious; ground for knowledge, indication, testimony; that which makes truth evident, or renders evident to the mind that it is truth; (*Law*) information by which a fact is proved or sought to be proved, or an allegation proved or disproved; such statements, proofs etc. as are legally admissible as testimony in a court of law. *v.t.* to make evident, to attest. **in evidence,** received or offered as tending to establish a fact or allegation in a court of law; (*coll.*) plainly visible, conspicuous. **to turn King's, Queen's, evidence,** to bear witness against one's accomplice in return for a free pardon. **evident,** *a.* open or plain to the sight; manifest, obvious; †conclusive. **evidential,** *a.* affording evidence; proving conclusively. **evidentially,** *adv.* **evidentiary,** *a.* of, pertaining to, or of the nature of evidence. **evidently,** *adv.* [F *évidence,* L *ēvidentia,* from *ēvidens -entem,* pres.p. of *ēvidēre* (E-, *vidēre,* to see)]

evil, *a.* bad, injurious, mischievous, worthless, morally bad, wicked; calamitous, agitated, sorrowful; unlucky, producing disastrous results; malicious, slanderous. *adv.* in an evil manner; maliciously, abusively, harmfully, injuriously; unfortunately, cruelly. *n.* an evil thing; that which injures or displeases, calamity, harm; sin, depravity, malignity; †a malady, a disease. **King's evil,** scrofula. **the Evil One,** the Devil. **evil-disposed, -affected, -minded,** *a.* unkindly and injuriously disposed. **evil-doer,** *n.* one who does evil, a wrong-doer, a malefactor. **evil eye,** *n.* a supposed power of fascinating, bewitching or materially injuring by the look. **evil-eyed,** *a.* malicious; looking malicious; having the power of the evil eye. **evil-speaking,** *n.* slander, calumny, defamation. **evil-tempered,** *a.* having a bad temper, unpleasant. **evilly,** *adv.* [OE *yfel* (cp. Dut. *euvel,* OHG *upil,* G *Übel*)]

evince, *v.t.* to show clearly; to indicate, to make evident; to demonstrate. †*v.i.* to furnish proof. **evincive,** *a.* [L *ēvincere* (E-, *vincere,* to conquer)]

evirate, *v.t.* to emasculate; to divest of strength or virility. [L *ēvirātus,* p.p. of *ēvirāre* (E-, *vir,* man)]

eviscerate, *v.t.* to disembowel; (*fig.*) to empty of all that is vital; to empty, to gut. **evisceration,** *n.* [L *ēviscerātus,* p.p. of *ēviscerāre* (E-, *viscera,* bowels)]

evite, *v.t.* (*chiefly Sc.*) to avoid, to shun. [F *éviter,* L *ēvītāre* (E-, *vītāre,* to shun)]

evoke, *v.t.* to call up, to summon forth (a memory etc.) esp. from the past; to elicit or provoke; to cause (spirits) to appear; (*Law*) to remove from one tribunal to another. †**evocate,** *v.t.* **evocation,** *n.* **evocative,** *a.* **evocator,** *n.* [F *évoquer,* L *ēvocāre* (*vocāre,* to call)]

evolute, *n.* (*Geom.*) a curve from which another is described by the end of a thread gradually wound upon or unwound from the former, thus forming the locus of the centres of curvature of the other, which is called the INVOLUTE. **evolutility,** *n.* (*Biol.*) capability of manifesting change as the result of nutrition. [L *ēvolūtus,* p.p. of *ēvolvere,* to EVOLVE]

evolution, *n.* the act of unrolling, unfolding, opening or growing; a series of things unrolled or unfolded; development, as of an argument, plot, design, organism or political, social or planetary system etc.; the process by which a germ develops into a complex organism; the derivation of all forms of life from early forms of a simpler character or from a single rudimentary form; the theory based on this principle, opp. to that of special creation (see CREATIONISM); the theory that the germ is not produced by fecundation, but pre-exists in the parent, having all the characters of the mature species in embryo; development of this germ, opp. to epigenesis; (*Math.*) the opening or unfolding of a curve; the extraction of roots from any given power, the reverse of involution; the evolving of gas, heat etc.; (*Mil., Nav.*) doubling of ranks or files, countermarching or other changes of position, by which the disposition of troops or ships is changed; (*pl., fig*). movements, changes of position etc. in dancing etc. **evolutional, -tionary,** *a.* produced by or pertaining to evolution. **evolutionism,** *n.* the theory or doctrine of evolution. **evolutionist,** *n.* one who holds the doctrine of evolution; one skilled in evolutions. **evolutionistic,** *a.* **evolutive,** *a.* tending to or promoting evolution; evolutionary. [L *ēvolūtio -ōnem,* as prec.]

evolve, *v.t.* to unfold, to expand; to develop, to bring to maturity; to give off (gas, heat etc.); to bring forth, work out, set forth (an argument etc.) in an orderly manner. *v.i.* to open; to develop. **evolvable,** *a.* **evolvement,** *n.* **evolver,** *n.* [L *ēvolvere* (E-, *volvere,* to roll)]

evulsion, *n.* the act of forcibly plucking or extracting. [L *ēvulsio -ōnem,* from *ēvulsus,* p.p. of *ēvellere* (E-, *vellere,* to pluck)]

Evvoia, *n.* Greek name for the island of Euboea.

ewe, *n.* a female sheep. **ewe lamb,** *n.* (*fig.*) a dearest possession. [OE *eowu* (cp. Dut. *ooi,* OIr. *oi,* Gr. *ois,* L *ovis,* Sansk. *avi*)]

ewer, *n.* a kind of pitcher or large jug for water; a toilet-jug with a wide mouth. [A-F, from OF *aiguier,* L *aquārium,* from *aqua,* water]

ex¹, *n.* the 24th letter of the alphabet, X, x; anything shaped like this.

ex², *prep.* (*Comm.*) from, out of, sold from; without. **ex dividend,** not including the next dividend. [L, out of]

ex³, *n.* (*coll.*) a former spouse, boyfriend or girlfriend.

ex-, *pref.* out, forth, out of; thoroughly; without, -less; formerly, previously occupying the position of; as *exceed, exclude, exit, extend, extol; exacerbate, excruciate; exonerate, expatriate; exalbuminous, exstipulate; ex-chancellor, ex-president.* [L *ex-, ex,* out of, from, or Gr. *ex, ek*]

exacerbate, *v.t.* to irritate, to exasperate, to embitter; to aggravate, to increase the violence of (as a disease). **exacerbation, exacerbescence,** *n.* [L *exacerbātus,* p.p. of *exacerbāre* (EX-, *acerbus,* bitter)]

exact¹, *a.* precisely agreeing in amount, number or degree; accurate, strictly correct; precise, strict, punctilious; consummate, perfect. **not exactly,** (*iron.*) not at all. **exact sciences,** *n.pl.* those in which mathematical accuracy is attainable. **exactitude,** *n.* exactness, precision. **exactly,** *adv.* in an exact manner; quite so; precisely, just so (in answer to a question or affirmation); in express terms. **exactness,** *n.* the quality of being exact. [L *exactus,* p.p. of *exigere* (EX-, *agere,* to drive)]

exact², *v.t.* to compel to be paid or surrendered; to demand as of right, to insist on, to require authoritatively. *v.i.* to practise extortion. **exactable,** *a.* **exacting,** *a.* severe or excessive in demanding; urgently requiring. **exactingly,** *adv.* **exaction,** *n.* the act of exacting; a forcible, illegal or exorbitant demand; extortion; that which is exacted; a compulsory or oppressive impost or service. **exactor,** *n.* [as prec.]

exaggerate, *v.t.* to heighten, to overstate, to represent as greater than truth warrants; to increase, intensify, aggravate; to represent (features, colours etc.) in a heightened manner; †to accumulate, heap up. *v.i.* to use or be given to exaggeration. **exaggeratedly,** *adv.* **exaggeration,** *n.* **exaggerative,** *a.* **exaggeratively,** *adv.* **exaggerator,** *n.* [L *exaggerātus,* p.p. of *exaggerāre* (EX-, *agger,* a heap)]

exalbuminous, *a.* (*Bot.*) of seeds, destitute of albumen.

exalt, *v.t.* to raise in dignity, rank, power or position; to elevate in character, spirits, diction or sentiment, to ennoble, to dignify; to elate; to praise, extol, glorify; to increase in force, to intensify. **exaltation,** *n.* the act of exalting; elevation in power, rank, dignity or position; elation, rapture, ecstasy; intensification, augmentation; †the position of a planet in the zodiac where it exerts the maximum of influence. **exaltedly,** *a.* **exaltedness,** *n.* †**exalter,** *n.* [L *exaltāre* (EX-, *altus,* high)]

examine, *v.t.* to inquire into, to investigate, scrutinize; to consider critically, to weigh and sift (as arguments for and against); to inspect, to explore; to question (as a witness); to test the capabilities, qualifications, knowledge of etc., by questions and problems; to inspect ((a part of) a patient's body) with a view to diagnosing possible illness. *v.i.* to make inquiry or research. **examinable,** *a.* that may be examined. **examinant,** *n.* an examiner; †an examinee. †**examinate,** *n.* **examination,** *n.* the act of examining; careful inspection, scrutiny or inquiry; the process of testing the capabilities or qualifications of a candidate for a post, or the progress, attainments or knowledge of a student; the act of inspecting a patient's body to diagnose possible illness; (*Law*) a careful inquiry into facts by taking evidence. **examination paper,** *n.* a paper containing questions for candidates, pupils etc.; a series of answers to such questions by an examinee. †**examinational,** *a.* †**examen,** *n.* **examinee,** *n.* **examiner,** *n.* **examinator,** *n.* (*Sc.*). **examinatorial,** *a.* [F *examiner,* L *exāmināre,* from *exāmen* (*exagmen,* the tongue of a balance, conn. with *exigere,* to weigh out (EX-, *agere,* to drive))]

example, *n.* a sample, a specimen; a copy, model or pattern; any person, fact or thing illustrating a general rule; a warning; a precedent, an instance; a problem or exercise (in mathematics etc.) for the instruction of students. *v.t.* to exemplify; to serve as an example to; to give a precedent for. [OF, from L *exemplum* (EX-, *emere,* to take, to buy, see EXEMPT)]

exanimate, *a.* lifeless, dead; without animation, depressed, spiritless. [L *exanimātus,* p.p. of *exanimāre* (EX-, *anima,* life)]

exanthema, *n.* any disease which is accompanied by a skin rash, e.g. measles. [Gr. *antheein,* to blossom]

exarch, *n.* a governor of a province under the Byzantine Empire; in the Greek Church, a grade in the ecclesiastical hierarchy instituted by Constantine the Great, formerly equivalent to patriarch or metropolitan, later a bishop in charge of a province, and also a legate of a patriarch. **exarchate,** *n.* [L *exarchus,* Gr. *exarchos* from *archein,* to rule (EX-, *archein,* to begin)]

exasperate, *v.t.* to aggravate, to embitter; to irritate to a high degree; to provoke; †to incite. **exasperation,** *n.* [L *exasperātus,* p.p. of *exasperāre* EX-, *asper,* rough)]

Excalibur, *n.* the magic sword of King Arthur, which only he could wield. [OF *Escalibor,* prob. corr. of *Cali-*

burn, med. L *Caliburnus* (in Geoffrey of Monmouth)]

ex cathedra, from the chair, with authority. [L]

excavate, *v.t.* to hollow out; to form by digging or hollowing out; to remove by digging; to uncover by digging, to dig out, esp. for archaeological research. **excavation,** *n.* **excavator,** *n.* [L *excavātus,* p.p. of *excavāre* (EX-, *cavus,* hollow)]

exceed, *v.t.* to go or pass beyond; to be more or greater than; to do more than is warranted by; to surpass, to outdo, to excel. *v.i.* to go too far, to go beyond bounds; to be greater; to excel, to be pre-eminent. **exceeding,** *a.* very great in amount, duration, extent or degree. †*adv.* exceedingly. †*n.* excess; superfluity. **exceedingly,** *adv.* very much. [F *excéder,* L *excēdere* (EX-, *cēdere,* to go)]

excel, *v.t.* (*past, p.p.* **excelled**) to surpass in qualities; to exceed, to outdo; †to be too much or too great for. *v.i.* to be superior, distinguished or pre-eminent (in or at). **excellence,** *n.* the state of excelling; superiority, pre-eminence; surpassing virtue, goodness or merit; that in which any person or thing excels; an excellent quality, feature or trait. **excellency,** *n.* excellence; a title of honour given to a governor, an ambassador, a commander-in-chief and certain other officers. **excellent,** *a.* surpassing others in some good quality; of great virtue, worth etc.; †exceeding, remarkable; superior or pre-eminent in bad or neutral qualities. **excellently,** *adv.* [F, from L *excellere* (EX-, *-cellere,* in *antecellere,* rel. to *celsus,* high)]

excelsior, *a.* higher, loftier. **Excelsior®,** *n.* (*N Am.*) packing material composed of thin wood-shavings. **Excelsior State,** *n.* New York (from use of the word as a motto on the State seal). [L, comp. of *excelsus,* lofty (EX-, *celsus,* high)]

except, *v.t.* to leave out, to omit, to exclude. *v.i.* to make objection (to or against). *prep.* not including, exclusive of, omitting, but. *conj.* unless. **excepter,** *n.* an objector, a caviller. **excepting,** *prep.* (*usu. after* not) omitting, with the exception of. **exception,** *n.* the act of excepting; that which is excepted; an instance of that which is excluded from or is at variance with a rule, class or other generalization; an objection, disapproval. **to take exception,** to object, to find fault; to express disapproval. **exceptionable,** *a.* liable to objection; objectionable; unusual. †**exceptionableness,** *n.* **exceptional,** *a.* forming an exception; unusual, extraordinary, unprecedented. **exceptionality,** *n.* **exceptionally,** *adv.* **exceptionary,** *a.* indicating an exception. †**exceptioner,** *n.* one who takes exception, an objector. †**exceptious,** *a.* peevish; given to cavilling or taking exception; censorious. †**exceptiousness,** *n.* **exceptive,** *a.* forming an exception; excepting. †**exceptless,** *a.* extending to all; with no exception. [OF *excepter,* L *exceptāre,* freq. of *excipere* (EX-, *capere,* to take)]

excerpt[1], *v.t.* to make an extract of or from; to cite, to quote. **excerptible,** *a.* **excerption,** *n.* [L *excerptus,* p.p. of *excerpere,* to select (EX-, *carpere,* to pluck)]

excerpt[2], *n.* (*pl.* **excerpts, -pta**) an extract or selection from a book, play, film etc., esp. an article printed off separately from the proceedings of a learned society. [see prec.]

excess, *n.* that which exceeds what is usual or necessary; the quality, state or fact of exceeding the ordinary measure, proportion or limit; the amount by which one number or quantity exceeds another; (*usu. pl.*) transgression of due limits; intemperance, overindulgence, extravagance; outrage. **Excess Profits Tax,** a tax levied in wartime upon the excess of net profits earned in any trade or business over a specified pre-war standard. **excess fare,** *n.* the amount paid for travelling beyond the point for which a ticket has been taken or in a higher class. **excess luggage,** *n.* a quantity above the weight allowed free carriage. **excess postage,** *n.* payment due when not enough stamps have been put on a letter or package. **excessive,** *a.* **excessively,** *adv.* [OF *exces,* L *excessus -cessum,* a going out, from *excēdere,* to EXCEED]

exchange, *v.t.* to give or receive in return for something else; to hand over for an equivalent in kind; to give and receive in turn, to interchange; to give, resign or abandon (as one state or condition for another). *v.i.* to be given or received in exchange; to be received as of equal value; to pass from one regiment to another by taking the place of another officer. *n.* the act of exchanging; a parting with one article or commodity for an equivalent in kind; the act of giving and receiving reciprocally, interchange; the act of resigning one state for another; that which is given or received in exchange; exchanging of coin for its value in coins of the same or another country; the system by which goods or property are exchanged and debts settled, esp. in different countries, without the transfer of money; the place where merchants, brokers etc. meet to transact business; the central office where telephone connexions are made; (*coll.*) an exchange student or teacher. **bill of exchange** BILL[3]. **course, rate, exchange,** the rate at which bills drawn upon drawees in a foreign country may be sold where they were drawn. **par of exchange,** the value of a given amount of the currency of one country in terms of another currency. **to exchange words, blows,** to quarrel verbally or physically. **exchange-cap,** *n.* a fine quality of paper used for printing bills of exchange. **exchange rate,** *n.* the ratio at which the currency of one country can be exchanged for that of another. **exchange student, teacher,** *n.* one who exchanges posts with a corresponding person from another country. **exchangeable,** *a.* that may be exchanged (for); rateable by what can be procured in exchange. **exchangeability,** *n.* **exchanger,** *n.* [OF *eschangier,* late L *excambiāre* (EX-, *cambiāre,* L *cambīre,* to CHANGE)]

exchequer, *n.* the State treasury; the Government department dealing with the public revenue; finances or pecuniary resources; the Court of Exchequer; †a chess-board. †*v.t.* to institute a process against a person in the Court of Exchequer. **Chancellor of the Exchequer** CHANCELLOR. **Court of Exchequer,** a court originally intended for the recovery of debts due to the king and to vindicate his proprietary rights etc., but afterwards developed into an ordinary law-court with a jurisdiction in equity, which was transferred to the Court of Chancery, the Court itself being made in 1873 one of the divisions of the High Court of Justice, and this in 1881 merged into the Queen's (King's) Bench Division. **exchequer bill,** *n.* a bill for money, or a promissory bill, issued from the Exchequer by authority of Parliament. **exchequer bond** TREASURY BOND. [ME *eschekere,* OF *eschequier,* med. L *scaccārium,* a chess-board]

excide, *v.t.* to cut out; to extirpate. [L *excīdere* (EX-, *caedere,* to cut)]

excise[1], *n.* a tax or duty on certain articles produced and consumed in a country (in the United Kingdom on spirits, beer and tobacco); the branch of the Civil Service which collects and manages the excise duties, usually called the Inland Revenue; †a tax of any kind. *v.t.*, to impose an excise duty on; (*fig.*) to impose upon, to overcharge. **excise laws,** (*n.pl.*) (*N Am.*) licensing laws. **excise-officer, exciseman,** *n.* an officer who collects excise duties, and prevents any evasion of the excise laws. **excisable,** *a.* subject or liable to excise duty. [prob. from MDut. *excijs,* OF *acceis,* late L *accēnsum,* from *accensāre,* to tax (*ac-,* AD-, *census,* tax)]

excise[2], *v.t.* to cut out (part of a book or of the body). **excision,** *n.* [L *excīsus,* p.p. of *excīdere,* to EXCIDE]

excite, *v.t.* to rouse, to stir into action, energy or agitation; to stimulate, to bring into activity; to inflame the spirits of; to provoke, to bring about by stimulating; to set up electric activity in; to magnetize the poles of (an electric machine). **excitable,** *a.* susceptible of excitement; characterized by excitability. **excitability,** *n.* **excitant,** †*a.* stimulating; tending to excite. *n.* that which excites increased action in an organism; a stimulant. **excitation,** *n.* †**excitative,** *a.* †**excitatory,** *a.* **excitedly,** *adv.* **excitement,** *n.* **exciter,** *n.* one who or that which excites; a stimulant. **exciting,** *a.* stimulating; producing excitement. **excitingly,** *adv.* **excitive,** *a.* **excitor,** *n.* an afferent nerve belonging to the spinal group. **excitomotory**, *a.* causing muscular contraction or movement independently of volition (applied to the spinal group of nerves). [OF *exciter,* L *excitāre,* freq. of *exciēre* (EX-, *ciēre,* to summon)]

exclaim, *v.i.* to cry out abruptly or passionately; †to inveigh (against). *v.t.* to utter in an abrupt or passionate manner. †*n.* exclamation; clamour. [F *exclamer,* L *exclāmāre* (EX-, *clāmāre,* to cry aloud)]

exclamation, *n.* the act of exclaiming; an expression of surprise, pain etc. **exclamation mark,** a sign (!) indicating emotion etc. **exclamatory**, *a.* containing or expressing exclamation; using exclamation. [L *exclāmātio -ōnem;* see prec.]

exclave, *n.* part of a country disjoined from the main part and surrounded by foreign territory, where it is considered an enclave. [L *ex,* out, *clavis,* a key]

exclosure, *n.* an area shut off from entry or intrusion.

exclude, *v.t.* to shut out, to prevent from coming in; to prevent from participating; to debar; to expel and keep out; to reject, to except, to leave out. **exclusion**, *n.* **exclusion order,** *n.* one preventing the entry into Britain of anyone known to be involved in terrorism. †**exclusionary,** *a.* tending to exclude. †**exclusionism,** *n.* **exclusionist,** *n.* one who would exclude another from any privilege, position etc.; one who supported the Bill, introduced in the reign of Charles II, to exclude the Duke of York (afterwards James II) from the throne; the free settlers of Australia who opposed the granting of the franchise to ex-convicts. **exclusive**, *a.* shutting out or tending to shut out; desiring to shut out; fastidious in the choice of associates, snobbish; not inclusive (of); excluding all else; excluding all that is not specified. *adv.* not taking into account or not inclusively (of). *n.* one who is exclusive in his manners or tastes; one who excludes all but a very few from his society, a snob; (*Log.*) an exclusive proposition. **exclusive zone,** *n.* an area of a country's territorial waters in which exploitation by other countries is officially banned. **exclusively,** *adv.* **exclusiveness,** *n.* **exclusivism,** *n.* the act or practice of excluding; systematic exclusiveness. [L *exclūdere,* p.p. *exclūsus* (EX-, *claudere,* to shut)]

excogitate, *v.t.* to think out; to devise by thinking. **excogitation,** *n.* [L *excōgitātus,* p.p. of *excōgitāre* (EX-, *cōgitāre,* to COGITATE)]

excommunicate, *v.t.* to exclude from the communion and privileges of the Church; to expel. **excommunication,** *n.* **greater excommunication,** total exclusion from the Church. **lesser excommunication,** a debarring from the sacraments. **excommunicative,** *a.* **excommunicatory,** *a.* [late L *excommūnicātus,* p.p. of *excommūnicāre* (EX-, *commūnis,* COMMON]

excoriate, *v.t.* to strip the skin from; to gall or tear off the skin by abrasion. **excoriation,** *n.* the act of excoriating; an abrasion; †(*fig.*) robbery, spoliation. [L *excoriātus,* p.p. of *excoriāre* (EX-, *corium,* skin, hide)]

excrement¹, *n.* refuse matter discharged from the body after digestion, faeces; excretion. **excremental**, *a.* **excrementitious**, *a.* [F *excrément,* L *excrēmentum,* from *excernere,* as EXCRETE]

excrement², *n.* an out-growth, such as hair, feathers, nails etc. [L *excrēmentum,* from *excrescere* (EX-, *crescere,* to grow)]

excrescence, *n.* an unnatural, useless or disfiguring outgrowth. †a natural outgrowth. **excrescent,** *a.* growing abnormally or redundantly, superfluous, redundant. [L *excrescentia,* as prec.]

excrete, *v.t.* to separate and discharge superfluous matter from the organism.

excruciate, *v.t.* to torture; to inflict severe pain or mental agony upon. **excruciating,** *a.* **excruciatingly,** *adv.* **excruciation,** *n.* [L *excruciātus,* p.p. of *excruciāre* (EX-, *crux, crucis,* cross)]

exculpate, *v.t.* to clear from a charge; to free from blame, exonerate; to vindicate. **exculpation**, *n.* **exculpatory**, *a.* [L *exculpātus* (EX-, *culpa,* fault)]

excurrent, *a.* running or passing out; flowing out (as blood from the heart); forming a passage outward; (*Bot.*) projecting beyond the edge or point. [L *excurrens -entem,* pres.p. of *excurrere* (see foll.)]

excurse, *v.i.* to make a digression; to make an excursion. **excursive,** *a.* rambling, deviating, exploring. **excursively,** *adv.* **excursiveness,** *n.* [L *excurs-,* p.p. stem of *excurrere* (EX-, *currere,* to run)]

excursion, *n.* a journey or ramble for health or pleasure; a short tour, a trip by an individual or a body of persons; a wandering from the subject, a digression; (*Astron.*) a deviation from the fixed course; †a sally, a sortie, an expedition. **excursion fare,** *n.* a special cheap fare allowed on some journeys on public transport. **excursion train,** *n.* a train carrying excursionists at a reduced fare. **excursional, -ary,** *a.* of or pertaining to an excursion. **excursionist,** *n.* one who goes on an excursion; one who organizes excursions. [as prec.]

excursus, *n.* a dissertation appended to a work, containing an exposition of some point raised or referred to in the text. [L, verbal n. of *excurrere,* as prec.]

excuse¹, *v.t.* to free from blame or guilt; to pardon, to acquit; to ask pardon or indulgence for; to serve as a vindication or apology for, to justify; to relieve of or exempt from an obligation or duty; to remit, not to exact (as a debt); to dispense with. †*v.i.* to make excuses. **excuse me,** *int.* expressing apology or disagreement. **to be excused,** (*euphem.*) to go to the lavatory. **excuse-me,** *n.* a dance during which partners may be changed on request. **excusable,** *a.* **excusableness,** *n.* **excusably,** *adv.* †**excusator,** *n.* **excusatory,** *a.* **excuser,** *n.* [OF *excuser,* L *excūsāre* (EX-, *causa,* CAUSE]

excuse², *n.* a plea offered in extenuation of a fault or for release from an obligation, duty etc.; an apology, a justification; the ground or reason for excusing; a pretended reason; the act of excusing, an exculpation.

ex-directory, *a.* of a telephone number, not listed in a telephone directory and not revealed to inquirers; of a person, having such a telephone number.

exeat, *n.* leave of absence, as to a student at university; permission granted by a bishop to a priest to go out of his diocese; permission by a Roman Catholic bishop to one of his subjects to take orders in another diocese. **exeant,** *n.* leave of absence to several persons. [L *exeat,* let him go out, *exeant,* let them go out, 3rd pers. subj. of *exīre,* to go out]

execrate, *v.t.* to curse, to imprecate evil upon; to detest; †to denounce as accursed. *v.i.* to utter curses. **execrable,** *a.* detestable, accursed; abominable; very bad; †lamentable. **execrably,** *adv.* **execration,** *n.* **execrative,** *a.* **execratory,** *a.* [L *execrātus,* p.p. of *execrārī, exsecrārī* (EX-, *sacrāre,* to consecrate, from *sacer,* sacred, accursed)]

execute, *v.t.* to carry into effect, to put in force; to perform, to accomplish, complete; to perform what is required to give validity to any legal instrument, as by signing and sealing; to discharge (a duty, function, office etc.); to play or perform (a piece of music, a part in a play); to inflict capital punishment on. *v.i.* to perform, accomplish or discharge (a piece of music, one's part etc.). **executable** *a.* **executant**, *n.* one who performs; (*Mus.*) a performer on any instrument. **execution,** *n.* the act of executing; performance, accomplishment; the act of carrying into effect; the infliction of capital punishment; destruction, destructive effect, slaughter; the mode of performing a work of art, skill, dexterity; the act of giving validity to a legal instrument, as by signing; the carrying into effect of the judgment of a court; the warrant empowering an officer to carry a judgment into effect, esp. one authorizing the seizure of a debtor's goods in default of payment. **executioner,** *n.* one who inflicts capital punishment; one who kills; one who tortures; †one who performs or carries into effect. **executive**, *a.* having the function or power of executing; pertaining to performance or carrying into effect; carrying laws, decrees etc. into effect. *n.* the person or body of persons carrying laws, ordinances, sentences etc. into effect; the administrative branch of a government. **executive order,** *n.* (*US*) the equivalent to an Order in Council. [OF *executer,* med. L *executāre,* L *executus, exsecūtus,* p.p. of *exsequī* (EX-, *sequī,* to follow)]

executor, *n.* one who executes, esp. a person appointed by a testator to carry out the provisions of his will; †an executioner. **literary executor,** *n.* a person appointed to deal with the copyrights and unpublished works of a deceased author. **executorial,** *a.* **executorship,** *n.* **executrix,** *n. fem.* (*pl.* **-trices**) [A-F *executous,* L *exsecūtor -ōrem,* as prec., -OR]

exedra , *n.* the portico of the Grecian palaestra in which disputations were held; a hall for conversation; an elevated seat, a bishop's throne, a porch, a projecting chapel; a recess. [L, from Gr. (EX-, *hedra,* a seat)]

exegesis, *n.* (*pl.* **-geses**) exposition, interpretation, esp. of the Scriptures. **exegete,** *n.* one who is skilled in the exegesis of the Scriptures. **exegetic,** *a.* pertaining to exegesis, expository. **exegetics,** *n.pl.* scientific interpretation, esp. of Scripture; hermeneutics. **exegetical,** *a.* **exegetically,** *adv.* **exegetist,** *n.* [Gr. *exēgēsis,* from *exēgeisthai* (EX-, *hēgeisthai,* to lead)]

†exeme, *v.t.* (*Sc. Law*) to release, exempt. [L *eximere* (EX-, *emere,* to take)]

exemplar, *n.* a pattern or model to be copied; a noted example; a typical example; an instance, a parallel; a copy, as of a book. †*a.* exemplary. **exemplary,** *a.* serving as a pattern or model; worthy of imitation; typical, serving to exemplify, illustrative; serving as a warning. **exemplary damages,** *n.* damages given in excess of the loss suffered by the plaintiff, in order to act also as punishment to the defendant. **exemplarily,** *adv.* **exemplariness,** *n.* [OF *exemplaire,* L *exemplārium,* from *exemplāris,* from *exemplum,* an EXAMPLE]

exemplify, *v.t.* to illustrate by example; to be an example of, to prove by an attested copy; to make an authenticated copy of. **exemplifiable,** *a.* **exemplification,** *n.* [med. L *exemplificāre*]

exemplum, *n.* an example; a short story or anecdote which illustrates a moral. [L, example]

exempt, *a.* free (from); not liable or subject to; †cut off, removed. *n.* one who is exempted or freed (from); one of four officers of the Yeomen of the Guard, ranking as corporals, now usu. called exons. *v.t.* to free or allow to be free; to grant immunity (from); †to take away (from or out of); †to single out. **exemption,** *n.* the state of being exempt; immunity; freedom from the obligation of doing compulsory military service. [OF, from L *exemptus,* p.p. of *eximere* (EX-, *emere,* to take)]

exenterate, *v.t.* (*now only fig.*) to disembowel, eviscerate. **exenteritis,** *n.* inflammation of the outer coating of the intestines. [L *exenterātus,* p.p. of *exenterāre* (EX-, Gr. *enteron,* intestine)]

exequatur, *n.* a written recognition of a consul or commercial agent, given by the government to which he is accredited; official authority or permission to execute some act; an authorization by a sovereign or government for the exercise of episcopal functions under papal authority or the promulgation of a papal bull. [L, he may perform, 3rd sing. subj. of *exequī,* see EXECUTE]

exequies, *n.pl.* funeral rites; the ceremony of burial; obsequies. **exequial,** *a.* [OF *exeques,* L *exequias,* acc. of *exequiae* (EX-, *sequī,* to follow)]

exercise, *n.* the act of using, employing or exerting; practice (of a function, virtue, occupation, art etc.); systematic exertion of the body for the sake of health; exertion for the training of the body or mind; a task set for this purpose; a composition for the improvement of a player or singer; (*pl.*) drill, athletics; a devotional observance, an act of public or private worship; †a discourse; (*Sc.*) a meeting of the Presbytery for holding a discussion on a passage of Scripture; the Presbytery itself; †exertion, action. *v.t.* to employ, to exert, to put in practice or operation; to perform the duties of, to fulfil; to train; to keep employed or busy; to make anxious or solicitous, to perplex, worry; to exert (muscles, brain, memory etc.) so as to develop their power. †*v.i.* to use action or exertion (upon). **I am greatly exercised about,** I am deeply anxious regarding. **the object of the exercise,** the purpose of a particular action or activity. **exercisable,** *a.* **exerciser,** *n.* [OF *exercice,* L *exercitium,* from *exercitus,* p.p. of *exercēre,* to keep at work (EX-, *arcēre,* to shut up)]

exercitation, *n.* exercise, practice; a dissertation, a literary or rhetorical display of skill. [L *exercitātio -ōnem,* from *exercitāre,* freq. of *exercēre* (as prec.)]

exergue, *n.* the small space beneath the base line of a subject engraved on a coin or medal; the name, date or inscription placed there. [F, prob. from Gr. EX-, *ergon,* work]

exert, *v.t.* to put forth (as strength, power, or ability); to put in action or operation. **to exert oneself,** to strive, to use effort. **exertion,** *n.* [L *exsertus,* p.p. of *exserere,* to put forth (EX-, *serere,* to bind, to put)]

exeunt, *v.i.* (*stage direction*) they go off the stage, they retire. **exeunt omnes**, they all go off the stage. [L, they go out]

exfoliate, *v.i.* of skin, bark, rocks etc., to shed or come off in flakes or scales; to separate into flakes. *v.t.* to remove in flakes; to cause to come off in flakes. **exfoliation,** *n.* **exfoliator, exfoliant,** *n.* a substance or device used to remove dead skin cells. [L *exfoliātus,* p.p. of *exfoliāre* (EX-, *folium,* a leaf)]

ex gratia, *a., adv.* as an act of favour, and with no acceptance of liabilty. [L]

exhalation, *n.* the act or process of exhaling; evaporation; that which is exhaled; a breathing out; vapour, mist; effluvium, an emanation; †a meteor.

exhale, *v.t.* to breathe forth; to emit, or cause to be emitted, in vapour; to draw up in vapour; to breathe out; †to draw (as a sword). *v.i.* to be given off as vapour; (*fig.*) to pass off as an emanation; to make an expiration, as distinct from inhaling. **†exhalant,** *a.* having the quality of exhaling or evaporating. [F *exhaler,* L *exhālāre* (EX-, *hālāre,* to breathe)]

exhaust, *v.t.* to draw off; to empty by drawing out the contents; to use up the whole of, to consume; to wear out by exertion; to drain of resources, strength or essential properties; to study, discuss, treat the whole of a subject. *n.* the discharge or escape of steam, gas, vapour etc. from an engine after it has performed its work; apparatus for withdrawing vitiated air by means of a partial vacuum. **exhausted receiver,** *n.* the receiver of an air-pump after the air has been pumped out. **exhaust-pipe,** *n.* a pipe conducting spent steam etc. from the cylinder. **exhaust silencer,** *n.* a chamber fitted in the exhaust-pipe where the noise of the exhaust is reduced by baffles. **exhaust-steam,** *n.* steam which passes out of the cylinder after having performed its function in moving the piston. **exhauster,** *n.* **exhaustible,** *a.* **exhaustibility**, *n.* **exhausting,** *a.* tending to exhaust or tire out completely. **exhaustion**, *n.* the act of exhausting; the state of being exhausted; a complete loss of strength; a method of proving a point by showing that all alternatives are absurd or impossible. **exhaustive,** *a.* tending to exhaust (esp. a subject), comprehensive. **exhaustively,** *adv.* so as to exhaust; by the process of exhaustion. **exhaustiveness,** *n.* [L *exhaustus,* p.p. of *exhaurīre* (EX-, *haurīre,* to draw)]

exhibit, *v.t.* to offer to public view; to present for inspection; to show, to display, to manifest; to furnish an instance of; to bring forward officially; to administer. *n.* anything exhibited; an article or collection of articles sent to an exhibition; a document or other voucher produced in court and used as evidence. **†exhibiter, exhibitor,** *n.* **exhibition**, *n.* the act of exhibiting; a display; the act of allowing to be seen, as temper; the production of documents etc. before any tribunal in proof of facts; a public display of works of art or manufacture, natural products etc.; an allowance to a student in college, school etc., originally maintenance, support, pecuniary assistance; (*Sc. Law*) an action for compelling delivery of documents; †a gift, present. **to make an exhibition of oneself,** to behave so as to appear contemptible. **exhibitioner,** *n.* one who has obtained an exhibition at a college or school. **exhibition-**

ism, *n.* a tendency to show off, to attract attention to oneself; a tendency to indecent exposure in public. **exhibitionist,** *n.* **exhibitory,** *a.* [L *exhibitus,* p.p. of *exhibēre* (EX- *habēre,* to have)]

exhilarate, *v.t.* to gladden, to enliven, to animate. **exhilarant,** *a.* **exhilarating,** *a.* **exhilaratingly,** *adv.* **exhilaration,** *n.* **exhilarative,** *a.* [L *exhilarātus,* p.p. of *exhilarāre* (EX-, *hilaris,* glad, cheerful)]

exhort, *v.t.* to incite by words (to good deeds); to admonish; to urge, to stimulate; to advise or encourage by argument; †to recommend. *v.i.* to deliver an exhortation. †*n.* an exhortation. **exhortation,** *n.* the act or practice of exhorting; an admonition, earnest advice; a formal address. **exhortative,** *a.* **exhortatory,** *a.* [OF *exhorter,* L *exhortārī* (EX-, *hortārī,* to urge)]

exhume, *v.t.* to disinter; (*fig.*) to unearth, to discover. **exhumation,** *n.* [F *exhumer,* late L *exhumāre* (EX-, *humus,* the ground)]

exigeant, *a.* (*fem.* **-ante**) exacting. [F, p.p. of *exiger,* L *exigere,* as foll.]

exigence, -gency, *n.* urgent need, demand, necessity; a state of affairs demanding immediate action or remedy, an emergency. [F *exigence,* L *exigentia,* from *exigere* (EX-, *agere,* to drive)]

exigent, *a.* urgent, pressing, demanding more than is reasonable, exacting. †*n.* a pressing need; an emergency, a crisis, †the extremity, the end. **exigible,** *a.* that may be exacted (from or against). [L *exigens -entem,* pres. p. of *exigere* (see prec.)]

exiguous, *a.* small, slender, scanty. **exiguity,** *n.* exiguousness, *n.* [L *exiguus,* small, as prec.]

exile, *n.* banishment, expatriation; long absence from one's native country, whether voluntary or enforced; one who is banished, or has been long absent from his native country. *v.t.* to banish from one's native country. †**exilement,** *n.* **exilian, exilic,** *a.* pertaining to exile or banishment, esp. to that of the Jews in Babylon. [OF *exil,* L *exilium, exsilium* (EX-, *salīre,* to leap)]

exility, *n.* thinness, scantiness, (*fig.*) tenuity, subtlety. [L *exīlitās,* from *exīlis,* thin]

eximious, *a.* excellent, illustrious. [L *eximius,* select, from *eximere,* to EXEMPT]

exist, *v.i.* to be, to have actual being; to live; to continue to be; to live or have being under specified conditions. **existence,** *n.* the state of being or existing; continuance of being; life; mode of existing; a thing that exists; all that exists; †a being, an entity; †reality. **existent,** *a.* having being or existence, existing, actual. **existential,** *a.* pertaining to or consisting in existence. **existentialism,** *n.* a philosophy largely deriving from Kierkegaard, implying a special conception of the idea of existence, in effect substituting 'Sentio ergo sum' for Descartes' 'Cogito ergo sum'. 'It considers self as a unity of finiteness and freedom, of involvement in natural process and transcendence over process' (R. Niebuhr). **existentialist,** *n.* †**existentially,** *adv.* **existible,** *a.* **existibility,** *n.* [F *exister,* L *existere, esistere* (EX-, *sistere,* causal of *stare,* to stand)]

exit[1], *n.* the departure of an actor from the stage; departure, esp. from this life; death, decease; a going out; freedom to go out; a passage, a way out. **exit poll,** *n.* an unofficial poll taken by asking people leaving a polling station how they have voted. [L *exitus,* a going out, from *exīre* (EX-, *īre,* to go)]

exit[2], *v.i.* (*stage direction*) goes off the stage. [L, he goes out, 3rd sing. of *exīre*]

ex-libris, *n.* (*often as pl.*) a book-plate, a label bearing an owner's name, crest, device etc. [L *ex librīs,* out of books, from the library (of)]

exo- *comb. form.* pertaining to the outside of anything. [Gr. *exō,* without, outside]

Exocet®, *n.* a French-built surface-skimming missile that can be launched from surface or air; (*fig.*) an exceptionally effective weapon.

exocrine, *a.* producing secretions that are released through a duct. *n.* an exocrine gland. [Gr. *krīnein,* to separate]

exoderm, *n.* (*Anat.*) the epidermis, the outer layer of the blastoderm.

Exodus, *n.* in the Old Testament, the departure of the Israelites from slavery in Egypt, under the leadership of Moses, for the Promised Land of Canaan. The journey included the miraculous parting of the Red Sea, Pharaoh's pursuing forces being drowned as the waters returned. Exodus is also the name of the second book of the Old Testament, narrating this event.

exodus, *n.* a departure, esp. of a large body of persons; (*coll.*) the departure of many people at once. [Gr. *exodos*]

ex officio, *adv.* by virtue of one's office. *a.* official. [L *ex,* out of, *officiō,* abl. of *officium,* duty, OFFICE]

exogamy, *n.* the custom prevalent among some tribes forbidding a man to marry a woman of his own tribe. **exogamic, exogamous,** *a.* [Gr. *gamos,* marriage]

exogen, *n.* a plant whose stem increases by an annual layer growing on the outside of the wood, as opposed to *endogen;* a dicotyledon. **exogenous,** *a.* pertaining to an exogen; developing externally; having external origins, as *exogenous depression.* [Gr. *gen-,* root of *gignes-thai,* to be born or produced]

exon, *n.* one of four officers of the Yeomen of the Guard. [prob. representing F pron. of EXEMPT]

exonerate, *v.t.* to free from a charge or blame; to exculpate; to relieve from a duty, obligation or liability; †to relieve of a weight or burden. **exoneration,** *n.* **exonerative,** *a.* [L *exonerātus,* p.p. of *exonerāre* (EX-, *onus oneris,* a burden)]

exopathic, *a.* of diseases, originating from causes outside the organism.

exophagy, *n.* cannibalism in which only persons of a different tribe are eaten. **exophagous,** *a.*

exophthalmia, exophthalmos, *n.* protrusion of the eyeball. **exophthalmic,** *a.*

exoplasm, *n.* the denser outer layer of the cuticular protoplasm of certain protozoans.

exorbitant, *a.* out of all bounds, grossly excessive, inordinate, extravagant. **exorbitance,** *n.* **exorbitantly,** *adv.* [L *exorbitans -antem,* pres.p. of *exorbitāre,* to fly out of the track (EX-, *orbita,* a track]

exorcize, -ise, *v.t.* to expel (as an evil spirit) by adjurations, prayers and ceremonies; to free or purify from unclean spirits; †to call upon, to conjure up. **exorcizer, -iser,** *n.* **exorcism,** *n.* **exorcist,** *n.* one who exorcizes; one of the minor orders in the Roman Catholic Church, to the members of which the function of exorcism (now restricted to priests) was formerly committed. [late L *exorcizāre,* Gr. *exorkizein* (EX-, *horkos,* oath)]

exordium, *n.* (*pl.* **-iums, -ia**) the beginning of anything, esp. the introductory part of a literary work or discourse. **exordial,** *a.* [L, from *exordīrī* (EX-, *ordīrī,* to begin)]

exoskeleton, *n.* an external skeleton formed by a hardening of the integument.

exosmose, exosmosis, *n.* passage of a liquid through a porous membrane from within outwards to mix with an external fluid. **exosmotic,** *a.* [Gr. *ōsmos,* a pushing]

exosphere, *n.* the outermost layer of the earth's atmosphere. [Gr. *sphaira,* sphere]

exostome, *n.* the aperture in the outer integument of an ovule.

exostosis, *n.* (*pl.* **-stoses**), *n.* a tumour of a bony nature growing upon and arising from a bone or cartilage; a morbid growth of hard wood projecting like warts or tumours from the stem or roots of a plant.

exoteric, -ical, *a.* external, public, fit to be imparted to outsiders; comprehensible to the vulgar, as opposed to *esoteric;* of disciples, not admitted to esoteric doctrines; ordinary, popular. *n.* one of the uninitiated; (*pl.*) truths or doctrines suitable for popular instruction. **exoterically,** *adv.* [Gr. *exōterikos,* from *exōterō,* comp. of *exō,* outward, from *ex,* out]

exothermal, exothermic, *a.* (*Chem.*) involving the evolution of heat. [Gr. *thermē,* heat]

exotic, *a.* foreign; introduced from a foreign country; (*coll.*) rare, unusual. *n.* anything foreign; anything introduced from a foreign country, as a plant. **exotica,**

n.pl. rare or unusual objects, esp. when forming a collection. **exotic dancer,** *n.* a striptease or belly dancer. **exoticism**, *n.* [L *exōticus,* Gr. *exōtikos,* from *exō,* as prec.]

expand, *v.t.* to open or spread out; to distend, to cause to increase in bulk; to widen, to extend, to enlarge; to write out in full (what is condensed or abbreviated); (*Math.*) to develop into a series, to state in a fuller form. *v.i.* to become opened or spread out, distended, or enlarged in bulk, not mass. **expanded metal,** *n.* sheet metal cut and formed into a lattice, used for reinforcing concrete etc. **expanded plastic,** *n.* foam plastic. **expanding universe,** *n.* the theory that the universe is ever expanding, based on the Doppler effect in the light from stars and galaxies. **expansible**, *a.* **expansibility**, *n.* **expansile,**, *a.* capable of expanding; expansible. [L *expandere* (EX-, *pandere,* to spread (p.p. *expansus*), rel. to *patēre,* see PATENT]

expanse, *n.* that which is expanded; a wide, open extent or area; expansion. [EX-, *pans-,* p.p. stem of *pandere,* see prec.]

expansion, *n.* the act of expanding; the state of being expanded; enlargement, extension, distension; extension of business, increase of liabilities, extension of the currency; increase of volume, as of steam in a cylinder. **expansion-engine,** *n.* a steam-engine in which the latter part of the stroke of the piston is performed by expansion of the steam already admitted. **double-, triple-expansion engine,** a steam-engine in which the steam passes into a second and third cylinder so that its expansive force is utilized in two or three stages. **expansion-gear,** *n.* the apparatus by which access of steam to the cylinder is cut off at a given part of the stroke. **expansionism,** *n.* **expansionist,** *n.* one who advocates territorial expansion; (*N Am.*) one who advocates extension of the national domain. [late L *expansio -ōnem,* as prec.]

expansive, *a.* having the power of expanding; able or tending to expand; extending widely, comprehensive; frank, effusive. **expansively,** *adv.* **expansiveness,** *n.* [as prec., -IVE]

ex parte, *adv.* (*Law*) proceeding from one side only; in the interests of one side. **ex-parte,** *a.* one-sided. [L, from one side]

expat EXPATRIATE.

expatiate, *v.i.* to dilate; to speak or write copiously on a subject; (*fig.*) to wander at large. **expatiation,** *n.* **expatiatory,** *a.* [L *expatiātus,* p.p. of *expatiārī* (EX-, *spatiārī,* to roam, from *spatium,* space)]

expatriate, *v.t.* to exile; to drive into banishment; to expatriate oneself. *v.i.* to emigrate; to renounce one's citizenship in one's country. *n.*, (*coll. abbr.* **expat**) one living away from his/her own country. **expatriation,** *n.* [L *expatriātus,* p.p. of *expatriāre* (EX-, *patria,* one's native land)]

expect, *v.t.* to look forward to; to regard as certain or likely to happen, to anticipate; to require as due; (*coll.*) to think, to suppose; †to await. *v.i.* to wait. †*n.* expectation. **expectancy, -ance,** *n.* the act or state of expecting, expectation; the state of being expected; (*Law*) abeyance, suspense; prospect of possessing, enjoying etc.; that which is expected. **expectant,** *a.* expecting, waiting in expectation (of); anticipating, presumptive; (*Law*) existing in expectancy, reversionary; relying on the efforts of nature, without using active medicines. *n.* one who waits in expectation of something, as a candidate for an office, a pregnant woman etc. **expectantly,** *adv.* **expectation**, *n.* the act or state of expecting, anticipation, a confident awaiting (of); (*pl.*) prospects (of); the ground for confident anticipation (of); the probability of a future event; something expected; the treatment of a disease by leaving it to the efforts of nature. **expectation of life,** the number of years which a person of a given age may, on the average of chances, expect to live. **expectative,** *a.* of, pertaining to, or giving rise to expectation; (*Eccles. Law*) reversionary, pertaining to the reversion of benefices. *n.* the object of expectation; (*Eccles. Hist.*) a mandate nominating to a benefice. **expecter,** *n.* one who expects; an expectant. **expecting,** *a.* pregnant. **expectingly,** *adv.* [L *expectāre* (EX-, *spectāre,* freq. of *specere,* to see)]

expectorate, *v.t.* to discharge from the lungs or air-passages by coughing, hawking or spitting. *v.i.* to discharge matter from the lungs or air-passages by coughing etc.; to spit. **expectorant,** *a.* having the quality of promoting expectoration. *n.* a medicine promoting expectoration. **expectoration,** *n.* **expectorative,** *a.* [L *expectorātus,* p.p. of expectorāre (EX-, *pectus -oris,* the breast)]

expedient, *a.* promoting the object in view; advantageous, convenient; conducive to personal advantage; politic as opposed to just; †speedy, expeditious. *n.* that which promotes an object; an advantageous way or means; a shift, a contrivance. **expedience, -ency,** *n.* **expediential**, *a.* **expediently,** *adv.* [F *expédient,* L *expediens -entem* (pres.p. of *expedīre,* as foll.)]

expedite, *v.t.* to facilitate, to assist or accelerate the progress of; to dispatch. †*a.* easy, disencumbered; speedy, ready, expeditious, active, light-armed. **expeditious,** *a.* speedy, ready, active; done with dispatch. **expeditiously,** *adv.* [L *expedītus,* p.p. of *expedīre* (EX-, *pēs pedis,* the foot)]

expedition, *n.* speed, promptness, dispatch; a march or voyage of an army or fleet to a distance with hostile intentions; any journey or voyage by an organized body for some definite object; the persons with their equipment engaged in this. **expeditionary,** *a.* relating to or constituting an expedition. [as prec.]

expel, *v.t.* (*past, p.p.* **expelled**) to drive or force out; to eject, to banish; to turn out formally (as from a school, college, or society); †to discharge; †to reject, to refuse. **expellable,** *a.* **expellent,** *a.* [L *expellere* (EX-, *pellere,* to drive, p.p. *pulsus*)]

expend, *v.t.* to spend, to lay out; to consume, to use up; †to consider. **expendable,** *a.* likely to be or intended to be wasted. **expenditure**, *n.* the act of expending; disbursement, consumption; the amount expended. [L *expendere* (EX-, *pendere,* to weigh, p.p. *pensus*)]

expense, *n.* a laying out or expending; cost, charge, outlay, price paid; (*pl.*) outlay in performance of a duty or commission; (*coll.*) money reimbursed for this. **at the expense of,** at the cost of; (*fig.*) to the discredit or detriment of. **expense account,** *n.* an account of expenses refunded to an employee by an employer. **expenseless,** *a.* **expensive,** *a.* costly, requiring a large expenditure; extravagant, lavish. **expensively,** *adv.* **expensiveness,** *n.* [A-F, from late L *expensa,* fem. of *expensus,* p.p. of *expendere,* see prec.]

experience, *n.* practical acquaintance with any matter; knowledge gained by observation or trial; a particular instance of such knowledge; something undergone of an affecting or impressive nature; (*usu. pl.*) a phase of religious emotion; †experiment. *v.t.* to make trial or proof of; to gain a practical knowledge of by trial or observation; to train; to undergo, to feel, to meet with; to practise; to train (oneself in). **to experience religion,** (*N Am.*) to be converted. **experienced,** *a.* taught by experience; practised, skilled; known from personal trial or observation. [OF, from L *experientia,* from *experīrī,* to go through, to try, as in p.p. *perītus,* skilled)]

experiential, *a.* pertaining to or derived from experience. **experientialism,** *n.* the doctrine that all our ideas are derived from experience, and that there are no intuitions. **experientialist,** *a.* **experientially,** *adv.* [L *experientia*]

experiment, *n.* a trial, proof or test of anything; an act, operation or process designed to discover some unknown truth, principle or effect, or to test a hypothesis; †experience. *v.i.* to make an experiment or trial (on or with); to investigate by this means; to search by trial. †*v.t.* to make trial or proof of. **experimental,** *a.* pertaining to, derived from, or founded upon experiment; practising experiments; empirical. **experimental philosophy,** *n.* philosophy based on induction and insisting on experiment and observation as indispensable to reasoned knowledge. **experimentalism,** *n.* **experimentalist,** *n.* **experimentalize, -ise,** *v.i.* **experimentally,** *adv.* **experimentation,** *n.* the act or practice of making experiments. **experimentative,** *a.* **experimenter, experimentist,** *n.* [OF, from L *experīmentum,* from *experīrī,* to EXPERIENCE]

expert, *a.* experienced, dexterous from use and experience; practised, skilful (at or in). *n.* one who has special skill or knowledge; a scientific or professional witness. †*v.t.* to make trial of; to experience. **expert system,** *n.* a computer system designed to mimic human thought processes so that apparently intelligent dialogue with the machine is possible. **expertise,** *n.* expert skill, opinion or knowledge. **expertly,** *adv.* **expertness,** *n.* [OF, from L *expertus,* p.p. of *experīrī,* as prec.]

expiate, *v.t.* to atone for; to make reparation or amends for; to pay the penalty of; †to avert. **expiable,** *a.* **expiation,** *n.* **expiator,** *n.* **expiatory,** *a.* [L *expiātus,* p.p. of *expiāre* (EX-, *piāre,* to propitiate, from *pius,* devout)]

expire, *v.t.* to breathe out from the lungs; to send forth, to emit, to exhale; †to bring to an end. *v.i.* to breathe out; to emit the last breath; to die; to die out (as a fire); to come to an end; (*Law*) to cease, to come to an end, to become extinct; †to be shot out. **expiration,** *n.* the act of breathing out; cessation, termination; †exhalation, evaporation. **expiratory,** *a.* pertaining to the emission of breath from the lungs. **expiree,** *n.* (*Austral., Hist.*) a time-expired convict. **expiry,** *n.* expiration, termination. [F *expirer,* L *expīrāre* (EX-, *spīrāre,* to breathe)]

expiscate, *v.t.* (*Sc.*) to fish out, to discover as if by fishing. **expiscation,** *n.* **expiscator,** *n.* **expiscatory,** *a.* [L *expiscātus,* p.p. of *expiscārī* (EX-, *piscis,* fish)]

explain, *v.t.* to make clear, plain, or intelligible; to expound and illustrate the meaning of; to account for; †to make plane, to flatten. *v.i.* to give explanations. **to explain away,** to get rid of (difficulties) by explanation; to modify or do away with (a charge etc.) by explanation. **to explain oneself,** to make one's meaning clear; to give an account of one's motives, intentions, conduct etc. **explainable,** *a.* **explainer,** *n.* [MF *explaner,* L *explānāre* (EX-, *plānāre,* to flatten, from *plānus,* flat)]

explanate, *a.* (*Zool.*) spread out flat.

explanation, *n.* the act of explaining; the sense or definition given by an interpreter or expounder; the process of arriving at a mutual understanding or reconciliation; that which accounts for anything. **explanatory,** *a.* containing an explanation; serving to explain. **explanatorily,** *adv.*

explant , *v.t.* to remove (living tissue) to a medium for tissue culture. *n.* a piece of living tissue removed for that purpose. **explantation,** *n.* [L *explantāre,* to plant out]

expletive, *a.* serving to fill out or complete; introduced merely to fill a gap or vacancy. *n.* a word not necessary to the sense introduced to fill up; an interjection or word added for emphasis, esp. a profane exclamation. **expletory,** *a.* [L *explētīvus,* from *explētus,* p.p. of *explēre* (EX-, *plēre,* to fill)]

explicate, *v.t.* to unfold the meaning of; to free from obscurity or difficulty; to develop (the contents of an idea, proposition, etc.). **explicable,** *a.* **explication,** *n.* **explicative, -plicatory** *a.* serving to explain or interpret. [L *explicātus,* p.p. of *explicāre* (EX-, *plica,* a fold)]

explicit[1]**,** *a.* plainly expressed, distinctly stated, opposed to implied; definite; unreserved, outspoken. **explicitly,** *adv.* **explicitness,** *n.* [F *explicite,* L *explicitus,* old form of *explicātus,* as prec.]

†**explicit**[2]**,** *n.* a word formerly written at the end of manuscript books and equivalent to 'finis,' 'the end'. [med. L, here ends, orig. abbr. of *explicitus,* see prec.]

explode, *v.t.* to cause to burst with a loud report; to refute, expose, discredit (a theory, fallacy etc.); †to drive off the stage; †to cry down, to hoot or hiss away. *v.i.* to burst with a loud report; to break forth with violence; (*fig.*) to come to an end as if by bursting, to collapse. **explodent,** *n.* an explosive consonant. **exploder,** *n.* one who explodes or rejects. **exploding,** *n., a.* **exploding star,** *n.* (*Astron.*) a nova or supernova. [MF *exploder,* L *explōdere,* p.p. *explōsus* (EX-, *plaudere,* to clap)]

exploit[1]**,** *n.* a feat, a great or noble achievement; an adventure. [OF *esploit,* profit, achievement, L *explicitum,* neut. p.p. of *explicere,* see EXPLICATE]

exploit[2] **,** *v.t.* to turn to account; to utilize, esp. to make use of for one's own profit; †to perform, to achieve. **exploitable,** *a.* **exploitage,** *n.* **exploitation,** *n.*

explore, *v.t.* to search or inquire into; to investigate, to examine; to travel over in order to examine; to travel into unknown country; to probe a wound. **exploration,** *n.* **explorative,** *a.* **explorator,** *n.* an explorer. **exploratory,** *a.* **exploratory operation,** *n.* one carried out for purposes of diagnosis. **explorer,** *n.* one who explores; a traveller into unknown or little-known parts. [F *explorer,* L *explōrāre,* to search out (prob. EX-, *plōrāre,* to make to flow, from *pluere,* to flow)]

Explorer, *n.* one of a series of US scientific satellites. Explorer 1, launched in Jan. 1958, was the first US satellite in orbit and discovered the Van Allen belts around the Earth.

explosion, *n.* a bursting or exploding with a loud report; a sudden and violent noise; a sudden and violent outbreak, as of physical forces, anger etc. **explosion welding,** *n.* welding metals with different melting points using the pressure created by an explosion. **explosive,** *a.* bursting or driving forth with great force and noise; liable to explode or cause explosion; (of consonants) produced by a sudden expulsion of breath, as *p, b, t, d, k, g,* discontinuous, forming a complete vocal stop. *n.* an explosive agent or substance, as gunpowder, dynamite etc.; a mute or non-continuous consonant. **explosively,** *adv.* **explosiveness,** *n.* [L *explōsio -ōnem,* from *explōdere,* EXPLODE]

expo, *n.* a public exhibition. [*expo*sition]

exponent, *a.* setting forth or explaining; exemplifying. *n.* one who sets forth or explains; one who or that which represents a party, principle or character; a type, a representative; a number or quantity written to the right of and above another number or quantity, to show how many times the latter is to be taken as a factor (thus, in the expression a^3, ^{3} is an exponent, and shows that a is to be taken three times as a factor thus, $a \times a \times a$). **exponential,** *a.* pertaining to an exponent or exponents; involving variable exponents. **exponential curve,** *n.* a relationship between two quantities such that as one quantity increases by equal steps the other increases by equal percentages of its previous value. **exponential equation,** *n.* an equation into which the unknown quantity enters as an exponent. **exponential horn,** *n.* a horn-shaped loud-speaker in which the sides of the horn follow an exponential curve. **exponential quantity,** *n.* a quantity with a variable exponent. [L *expōnens entem,* pres.p. of *expōnere* (EX-, *pōnere,* to put, p.p. *positus*)]

exponible, *a.* capable of or requiring explanation; (*Log.*) requiring restatement in regular logical form. *n.* an exponible proposition.

export[1]**,** *v.t.* to carry or send (goods) to foreign countries. *v.i.* to send out commodities to foreign countries. **exportable,** *a.* **exportation,** *n.* the act or practice of exporting goods. **exporter,** *n.* [L *exportāre* (EX-, *portāre,* to carry)]

export[2]**,** *n.* the act of exporting, exportation; a commodity sent to a foreign country; (*pl.*) the quantity or value of goods exported. **invisible exports,** items on a national trade balance such as money spent by tourists from abroad. **export duty,** *n.* a duty paid on goods exported. [as prec.]

expose, *v.t.* to lay bare or open; to leave unprotected; to subject (to any influence or action); to turn out and abandon (as a child); to exhibit, to display, esp. for sale; to disclose, lay bare, reveal; to unmask. **to expose oneself,** to lay bare one's genitals in public to shock or embarrass others; to reveal one's faults, weaknesses etc. **exposé**, (F) *n.* a formal declaration or recital of facts; a disclosure, an exposure. **exposition**, *n.* the act of exposing; an explanation or interpretation of the meaning of an author or a work, a commentary; exposure; a public exhibition. **expositive**, *a.* **expositor**, *n.* one who expounds or explains; a commentator. **expository,** *a.* **exposure**, *n.* the act of exposing; the state of being exposed to view, inconvenience, danger etc.; the state of being unsheltered from cold, heat, sun etc.; abandonment (of a child, aged person etc.); display, esp. of goods for sale; a disclosure, revelation, unmasking; situation with respect to the points of the compass, or free access of light and air; outlook, aspect; (*Phot.*) the act of allowing light from an object to fall upon a sensitized plate; the duration of this exposure. **indecent exposure,** public uncovering of the sexual organs. [F *exposer* (EX-, *poser,* L *pausāre,* to rest, to lay down)]

expostulate, *v.i.* to reason earnestly (with a person), to remonstrate. †*v.t.* to demand, to claim; to argue, to discuss; to call in question. **expostulation,** *n.* **expostulative,** *a.* **expostulator,** *n.* **expostulatory,** *a.* [L *expostulātus,* p.p. of *expostulāre* (EX-, *postulāre,* to demand)]

expound, *v.t.* to set forth the meaning of; to explain, to interpret. **expounder,** *n.* [ME *expounen,* OF *espondre,* L *expōnere* (see EXPONENT)]

express[1], *a.* set forth or expressed distinctly; direct, explicit, definitely shown or stated, not merely implied; intended, prepared, done, made, sent for a special purpose. *adv.* with speed; by express messenger; †specially, on purpose. *n.* an express train; an express messenger; an express rifle. **express bullet,** *n.* a bullet with hollow point causing it to spread on striking. **express delivery,** *n.* delivery by special messenger. **express rifle,** *n.* a sporting rifle with a high muzzle-velocity and low trajectory. **express train,** *n.* a fast train with a few intermediate stops. **expressly,** *adv.* [OF *expres,* L *expressus,* p.p. of *exprimere* (EX-*primere,* to press)]

express[2], *v.t.* to squeeze or press out; to emit, to exude; to set forth, to make manifest to the understanding, to put into words; to reveal, to exhibit; (*Alg.*) to represent (by symbols, in terms etc.); to send by express post; †to denote, to betoken; to resemble, to be like. **to express oneself,** to declare one's opinions or feelings in words (*usu. with* well, strongly etc.). **expressible,** *a.* **expression**, *n.* the act of expressing; that which is expressed, an utterance, saying, statement of a thought; a word, a phrase; (*Alg.*) a combination of symbols representing a quantity or meaning; mode of expression; the aspect of the face as indicative of feeling and character, purpose etc.; intonation of voice; the exhibition of character and feeling (in a picture, statue etc.); (*Mus.*) the mode of execution that expresses the spirit and feeling of a passage; expressiveness. **expression mark,** *n.* (*Mus.*) a word or sign indicating the way in which a passage is to be expressed. **expression stop,** *n.* a harmonium stop regulating the wind-pressure and force of the notes. **expressional,** *a.* of or pertaining to expression; having the power of expression, esp. in language, painting etc. **expressionist,** *n.* an artist who devotes himself to the expression of feeling, character etc. **expressionless,** *a.* **expressive,** *a.* serving to express; significant; vividly indicating any expression or emotion. **expressively,** *adv.* **expressiveness,** *n.* **expressure**, *n.* the act of expressing; expression; a mark, impression; an image, a picture. [OF *expresser* (as prec.)]

expressionism, *n.* a style of painting, sculpture, and literature that expresses inner emotions; in particular, a movement in early-20th-century art in N and central Europe. Expressionists tended to distort or exaggerate natural appearance in order to create a reflection of an inner world, as in the Norwegian painter Munch's *Skriket/The Scream* (1893) (National Gallery, Oslo). Expressionist writers include Strindberg and Wedekind.

exprobration, *n.* reproachful language; upbraiding, censure. [L *exprobrātio -ōnem,* from *exprobrāre* (EX-, *probrum,* a shameful deed)]

expropriate, *v.t.* to take from an owner, esp. for public use; to dispossess. **expropriation,** *n.* [late L *expropriātus,* p.p. of *expropriāre* (EX-, *proprium,* property, neut. of *proprius,* own)]

expulsion, *n.* the act of expelling; the state of being expelled; ejection. †**expulse,** *v.t.* to expel. **expulsive,** *a.* serving or tending to expel. *n.* an expulsive drug. [L *expulsio -ōnem,* from *expellere,* to EXPEL]

expunge, *v.t.* to blot or rub out; to efface, to erase. **expunction**, *n.* [L *expungere* (EX-, *pungere,* to prick, p.p. *punctus*)]

expurgate, *v.t.* to free from anything offensive, obscene or noxious (used esp. of books); to remove such parts; †to purge, to clear (as of guilt). **expurgation,** *n.* **expurgator,** *n.* **expurgatorial**, *a.* **expurgatory**, *a.* serving to expurgate. **expurgatory index** INDEX EXPURGATORIUS. [L *expurgātus,* p.p. of *expurgāre* (EX-, *purgāre,* to cleanse)]

exquisite, *a.* fine, delicate, dainty; delicately beautiful; very beautiful; delicate or refined in perception, keenly sensitive, nice, fastidious; acute; poignant; intensely pleasurable or painful; †far-fetched, abstruse. *n.* a fop; one who dresses or behaves finically. **exquisitely,** *adv.* **exquisiteness,** *n.* [L *exquīsītus,* choice, p.p. of *exquīrere* (EX-, *quaerere,* to seek)]

exsanguinate, *v.t.* to drain off blood. **exsanguine,** *a.* bloodless; suffering from poorness of blood. **exsanguinity**, *n.* destitution of blood. **exsanguinous,** *a.* [L *exsanguinātus,* p.p. of *exsanguināre* (EX-, *sanguis -inis,* blood)]

exscind, *v.t.* to cut off or out, to sever, to excise. [L *exscindere* (EX-, *scindere,* to cut)]

exsect, *v.t.* to cut out. [L *exsectus,* p.p. of *exsecāre* (EX-, *secāre,* to cut)]

exsequies, EXEQUIES.

exsert, *v.t.* to thrust out, protrude. **exserted,** *a.* (*Biol.*) protruding, thrust out, unsheathed; applied to stamens longer than the corolla. **exsertile**, *a.* that may be thrust out. [L *exsertus,* p.p. of *exserere,* to put forth]

exsiccate, *v.t.* to dry up; to evaporate; to drain dry. **exsiccation,** *n.* **exsiccator,** *n.* an apparatus for drying moist substances. [L *exsiccātus,* p.p. of *exsiccāre* (EX-, *siccus,* dry)]

exstipulate, *a.* devoid of stipules. [EX-, L *stipula,* a stalk]

extant, *a.* still existing; surviving; †publicly known; †standing out, protruding. [L *extans, -antem,* pres.p. of *exstāre* (EX-, *stāre,* to stand)]

extasy, ECSTASY.

extemporal, *a.* extemporaneous, unpremeditated. **extemporally,** *adv.*

extemporaneous, extemporary, *a.* uttered, made, composed or done without preparation. **extemporaneously,** *adv.* **extemporaneousness,** *n.* **extemporarily,** *adv.*

extempore, *adv.* without premeditation or preparation. *a.* unstudied, delivered without preparation. **extemporize, -ise,** *v.t.* to compose or produce without preparation. *v.i.* to speak without notes or previous study. **extemporization, -isation,** *n.* [L *ex tempore,* from the time]

extend, *v.t.* to stretch out; to make larger in space, time or scope; to prolong (as a line, a period etc.); to amplify, to expand, to write out in full; to cause to reach (to, over or across); to enlarge; to put forth; to hold out, offer, grant; to value, to assess, to seize under a writ of extent; to stretch out, to unbend (of muscles); †to praise, to magnify, to exaggerate; †to seize. *v.i.* to stretch, to reach (in space, time or scope). **to extend a welcome (to),** to welcome cordially. **extended,** *a.* spread out; of type, having a broad face. **extended family,** *n.* social unit comprising more than a couple and their children, e.g. grandparents, aunts, uncles etc. **extendedly,** *adv.* **extendible, extensible,** *a.* **extensibility** (-bil'-), *n.* **extensile,** *a.* capable of being stretched out or protruded. [L *extendere,* p.p. *extensus*

(EX-, *tendere,* to stretch)]

extension, *n.* the act or process of extending; the state of being extended; extent, range, space; prolongation, enlargement; an increase of dimension, an addition, an additional part; words amplifying the subject or predicate of a sentence; the property by virtue of which every body occupies a limited portion of space in three dimensions; the pulling of the broken part of a limb in a direction away from the trunk, to bring the ends of the bone into their proper position; (*Log.*) the extent of the application of a general term, as opposed to *intension;* an additional wing or annexe of a house; an additional telephone using the same line as the main one. **university extension,** a system by which university instruction is extended to non-members of universities by means of lectures, classes and examinations. **extensionist,** *n.* a promoter of university extension; a student connected with this. [L *extentio -ōnem, -sio -ōnem,* as prec.]

extensive, *a.* widely spread or extended; large; comprehensive; (*Agric.*) depending on amplitude of area, as opposed to *intensive*. **extensively,** *adv.* **extensiveness,** *n.* [late L *extensīvus,* as prec.]

extensor, *n.* a muscle which serves to extend or straighten any part of the body. [late L, as prec.]

extent, *n.* the space, dimension or degree to which anything is extended; size, width, compass, scope, comprehension, distribution, degree; a large space; a writ of execution against the body, lands and goods of a debtor; seizure of lands etc., execution; (*Log.*) extension; †fact of extending, offering or granting. **extent-in-aid,** *n.* a writ issued at the suit of a Crown debtor against a person indebted to him. [A-F *extente, estente,* p.p. of *estendre,* L *extendere*]

extenuate, *v.t.* to lessen, to diminish the gravity of, to palliate; to offer excuses for; †to make thin, meagre or lean; †to make less dense; †to disparage, to degrade; †to underrate, to belittle; (erroneously) to diminish the apparent guilt or impropriety of. **extenuating,** *a.* **extenuating circumstances,** *n.pl.* those which make an act seem less wrong or less criminal. †**extenuatingly,** *adv.* **extenuation,** *n.* **extenuator,** *n.* **extenuatory,** *a.* extenuating, palliating. [L *extenuātus,* p.p. of *extenuāre* (EX-, *tennuis,* thin)]

exterior, *a.* external, outer; situated on the outside; coming from without, extrinsic; outward, visible. *n.* the outer surface; the external features; the outward or visible aspect, dress, conduct, deportment etc. **exterior angle,** *n.* an angle between any side of a rectilinear figure and the adjacent side produced. **exteriority,** *n.* **exteriorize, -ise,** *v.t.* to realize in outward form; to externalize. **exteriorization, -isation,** *n.* **exteriorly,** *adv.* [L comp. of *exter* or *exterus,* outer]

exterminate, *v.t.* to extirpate, to eradicate, to destroy utterly; †to put an end to. **extermination,** *n.* **exterminator,** *n.* **exterminatory,** *a.* **extermine,** *v.t.* to exterminate. [L *exterminātus,* p.p. of *extermināre* (EX-, *terminus,* a boundary)]

extern, *a.* external. *n.* a student or pupil who does not reside in a college or seminary; the outward appearance.

external, *a.* situated on the outside; pertaining to the outside, superficial; derived from outside; belonging to the world of phenomena as distinguished from the conscious mind, objective; (*Theol.*) consisting in outward acts; applied to the outside of the body; pertaining to foreign countries; extraneous, extrinsic. *n.* an exterior or outer part; (*pl.*) outward features, symbols, rites, circumstances; non-essentials. **external degree,** *n.* a degree taken without actually attending the university that awards it, studying being done elsewhere. **external examiner,** *n.* one from another educational institution who ensures examinations are fairly conducted. **externalism,** *n.* **externality,** *n.* **externalize, -ise,** *v.t.* to give external shape or objective existence to; to treat as consisting of externals. **externalization, -isation,** *n.* **externally,** *adv.* [L *externus,* from *exter,* see EXTERIOR]

exteroceptor, *n.* a sensory organ which receives impressions from outside the body, e.g. the eye.

exterrestrial, *a.* of or from outside the earth.

exterritorial, *a.* beyond the jurisdiction of the laws of the country in which one resides. **exterritoriality,** *n.* immunity from the laws of a country, such as that enjoyed by diplomats.

extinct, *a.* extinguished, put out; that has ceased eruption; worn out, ended, finished; come to an end, that has died out (as a family, species etc.); obsolete. †*v.t.* to extinguish. [L *extinctus,* p.p. of *extinguere*]

extincteur, *n.* a fire-extinguisher. [F, from L *extinctor* (as prec.)]

extinction, *n.* (*Bot.*) the act of extinguishing; the state of being extinguished; extermination, destruction, annihilation. **extinctive,** *a.* †**extincture,** *n.* extinction. [L *extinctio -ōnem,* as prec.]

extine, *n.* (*Bot.*) the outer coat of a grain of pollen. [L *exterus,* outer, -INE]

extinguish, *v.t.* to put out, to quench (as a light, hope, passion, life etc.); to eclipse, to cloud, to obscure, to throw into the shade; to destroy, to annihilate; to suppress; to pay off (a debt, mortgage etc.). **extinguishable,** *a.* **extinguisher,** *n.* one who or that which extinguishes; a conical cap for extinguishing a candle (or, formerly, a link); a device for putting out a fire. **extinguishment,** *n.* [L *extinguere* (EX-, *stinguere,* to quench)]

extirpate, *v.t.* to root out, to destroy utterly, to exterminate; to cut out or off. †**extirp,** *v.t.* to extirpate. **extirpation,** *n.* **extirpator,** *n.* [L *extirpātus,* p.p. of *extirpāre, exstirpāre* (EX-, *stirps, -pis,* a stem)]

extol, *v.t.* to praise in the highest terms, to glorify. [L *extollere* (EX-, *tollere,* to raise)]

extort, *v.t.* to wrest or wring (from) by force, threats, importunity etc.; (*Law*) to exact illegally under colour of a public office; (*fig.*) to extract (a meaning, esp. an arbitrary one, from a passage, data etc.). **extorter,** *n.* an extortioner. **extortion,** *n.* the act of extorting; oppressive or illegal exaction; that which is extorted; a gross overcharge. †**extortionary,** *a.* **extortionate,** *a.* characterized by extortion; oppressive; of prices, exorbitant. **extortioner,** *n.* **extortive,** *a.* [L *extortus,* p.p. of *extorquēre,* to twist)]

extra, *a.* beyond what is absolutely necessary; larger or better than is usual; supplementary, additional; of superior quality. *adv.* over and above what is usual; more than usually; additionally. *n.* something beyond what is absolutely necessary or usual, esp. something not covered by the ordinary fee; an addition; (*cricket*) a run scored otherwise than off the bat; an actor temporarily engaged as one of a crowd etc. **extra-special,** *a.* latest (edition of an evening paper). **extra time,** *n.* additional time allowed at the end of a sports match to compensate for time lost through injury etc. [L *extrā,* beyond, from outside, or short for EXTRAORDINARY]

extra-, *comb. form.* on the outside, without. **extra-atmospheric,** *a.* of or pertaining to the space beyond the atmosphere. **extracorporeal,** *a.* outside the body. **extra-cosmical,** *a.* acting outside the universe. **extracranial,** *a.* lying outside the skull. **extra-curricular,** *a.* of an activity, outside or in addition to the normal course of study. **extra-essential,** *a.* not included in the essence of a thing. **extra-essentially,** *adv.* **extragalactic,** *a.* outside the Milky Way. **extrajudicial,** *a.* taking place outside the court, not legally authorized; outside the ordinary course of law or justice. **extrajudicially,** *adv.* **extramarital,** *a.* (esp. of sexual relations) outside marriage. **extramundane,** *a.* existing in or pertaining to a region outside our world or outside the universe. **extra-mural,** *a.* situated beyond or outside the walls or boundaries of a place. **extra-official,** *a.* outside the proper duties of an office. **extra-parochial,** *a.* beyond, outside of, or not reckoned within the limits of, any parish. **extra-physical,** *a.* not subject to or bound by physical laws or processes. **extra-professional,** *a.* not coming within the ordinary duties of a profession. **extra-sensory,** *a.* beyond the ordinary senses, e.g.

telepathic perception. **extra-spectral,** *a.* lying outside the visible spectrum. **extra-terrestrial** EXTERRESTRIAL. **extraterritorial** EXTERRITORIAL. **extra-tropical,** *a.* beyond or outside of the tropics, north or south. **extravascular,** *a.* outside the vascular system. **extravehicular,** *a.* taking place outside a spacecraft. [L]

extract[1], *v.t.* to draw or pull out; to draw out by mechanical or chemical means; to select a part from, to copy out or quote (as a passage from a book etc.); to derive (from); to deduce (from). **to extract the root of,** to find the root of (a number or quantity). **extractable,** *a.* **extraction,** *n.* the act of extracting; descent, family, lineage, derivation; the act of drawing anything from a substance by chemical or mechanical process. **extractive,** *a.* tending or serving to extract; capable of extraction. *n.* an extract; (*Chem.*) the principle forming the basis in extracts. **extractive industries,** *n.pl.* those (e.g. mining, agriculture, fishing) concerned with obtaining natural productions. **extracter, extractor,** *n.* **extractor fan,** *n.* an electric fan which extracts air, gas etc. from a room. [L *extractus,* p.p. of *extrahere* (EX-, *trahere,* to draw)]

extract[2], *n.* that which is extracted by distillation, solution etc.; a passage quoted from a book or writing; an essential obtained from a substance; a preparation containing the essence of a substance. [as prec.]

extradition, *n.* the surrender of fugitives from justice by a government to the authorities of the country where the crime was committed; (*Psych.*) in perception, the localizing of sensations at a distance from the centre of sensation. **extraditable,** *a.* subject to extradition, rendering one liable to extradition. **extradite,** *v.t.* to surrender under a treaty of extradition; to secure the extradition of. [F (EX-, L *traditio -ōnem,* TRADITION)]

extrados, *n.* the exterior curve of an arch, esp. measured on the top of the voussoirs (cp. INTRADOS). [F (EXTRA-, *dos,* L *dorsum,* the back)]

extraforaneous, *a.* out-door. [med. L *forāneus*]

extraneous, *a.* foreign, not belonging to a class, subject etc.; not intrinsic, external; not essential. **extraneously,** *adv.* **extraneousness, extraneity,** *n.* [L *extrāneus,* from *extrā,* outside]

extraordinary , *a.* beyond or out of the ordinary course, unusual; of an uncommon degree or kind, remarkable, rare, exceptional, surprising; additional, extra; sent or appointed for a special purpose or occasion. *n.* an extraordinary thing; †(*pl.*) extra allowances or receipts, esp. to troops. **envoy extraordinary,** formerly a minister sent on a special mission, now one of the second class of diplomatic ministers ranking next below ambassadors. **extraordinarily,** *adv.* **extraordinariness,** *n.* [L *extraordinārius* (*extrā ordinem,* outside the usual order)]

extrapolate, *v.t.* to estimate (the value of a function etc.) beyond the known values by the extension of a curve; to infer, conjecture from what is known. **extrapolation,** *n.* **extrapolative, extrapolatory,** *a.* [L *extrā,* and inter*polate*]

extravagant, *a.* exceeding due bounds, unrestrained by reason, immoderate; visionary, fantastic; prodigal in expenditure, wasteful; (of prices etc.) exorbitant; †wandering out of bounds, straying, vagrant. **extravagance,** *n.* the state or quality of being extravagant; an extravagant act, statement or conduct; excessive expenditure, prodigality; †a digression, a vagary. **extravagantly,** *adv.* **extravagate,** *v.i.* to wander or roam at will; to go beyond reasonable bounds; to go to extremes. [L *extrāvagans -antem,* pres.p. of *extrāvagārī* (EXTRA-, *vagārī,* to wander)]

extravaganza, *n.* a fantastic composition in drama, fiction, poetry, music or other literary form; a fantastic piece of conduct, sentiment or imagination. **extravaganzist,** *n.* [It. *estravaganza*]

extravasate, *v.t.* to force or let out of the proper vessels (as blood). *v.i.* to flow out of the proper vessels. **extravasation,** *n.* [EXTRA; L *vās,* a vessel, -ATE]

†extreat, *n.* (*Spens.*) extraction. [var. of ESTREAT]

Extremadura, *n.* autonomous region of W Spain including the provinces of Badajoz and Cáceres; area 41,600 sq km/16,058 sq miles; population (1986) 1,089,000. Irrigated land is used for growing wheat; the remainder is either oak forest or used for pig or sheep grazing.

extreme, *a.* outermost, farthest; at the utmost limit, at either end; last, final; of the highest degree, most intense; very strict or rigorous; going to great lengths, immoderate; (*Mus.*) the highest and lowest (parts), augmented (of intervals). *n.* the utmost or farthest point or limit, the extremity; the utmost or highest degree; the first or the last term of a ratio or series; the subject or the predicate of a proposition as distinguished from the copula, the major or the minor term in a syllogism as distinguished from the middle; (*pl.*) things or qualities as different or as far removed from each other as possible; (*Mus.*) the highest and lowest parts; †an excessive degree, extremity. **extreme and mean ratio,** the ratio of a line to its two parts when the whole is to the greater part as the greater to the less. **in the extreme,** in the highest degree; extremely. **to extremes,** (resorting) to the most severe or drastic measures. **extreme unction,** *n.* in the Roman Catholic Church, a sacrament in which those believed to be dying are anointed with holy oil. **extremely,** *adv.* very, greatly, to a great degree. **extremeness,** *n.* **extremism,** *n.* **extremist,** *n.* one ready to go to extremes; one holding extreme opinions and ready to undertake extreme actions. **extremity,** *n.* the utmost point, side or limit; the greatest degree; the remotest part, the end; a condition of the greatest difficulty, danger or distress; (*pl.*) the limbs; extreme measures. [OF, from L *extrēmus,* superl. of *exterus,* outward]

extricate, *v.t.* to disentangle, to set free from any perplexity, difficulty or embarrassment; to cause to be given off (as a gas from a state of combination). **extricable,** *a.* **extrication,** *n.* [L *extrīcātus,* p.p. of *extrīcāre* (EX-, *tricae,* impediments)]

extrinsic, *a.* being outside or external; proceeding or operating from without; not inherent or contained in a body; not essential. **extrinsicality,** *n.* **extrinsically,** *adv.* [F *extrinsèque,* L *extrinsecus,* adv., from without (*extrin,* from *exter,* outward, *secus,* beside)]

extrorse, *a.* of anthers, turned outwards from the axis of growth. [F, from L *extrorsus* (EXTRA-, *versus,* towards)]

extrovert, *n.* a term to denote a type of temperament which is predominantly engaged with the external world; a person more interested in other people and his/her surroundings etc. than in his/her own thoughts etc. *a.* pertaining to (the personality of) such a person. [L *extrā,* outside; *vertere,* to turn]

extrude, *v.t.* to thrust or push out or away; to expel. **extrusion,** *n.* **extrusive,** *a.* thrusting out or tending to thrust out; poured out on the surface (as volcanic rocks). [L *extrūdere,* p.p. *extrūsus* (EX-, *trūdere,* to thrust)]

exuberant, *a.* exceedingly fruitful; luxuriant in growth; characterized by abundance or richness; overflowing, copious, superabundant; effusive, overflowing with vitality, spirits or imagination. **exuberance,** *n.* **exuberantly,** *adv.* **exuberate,** *v.i.* to abound, to overflow; to indulge freely (in). [L *exūberans -antem,* pres.p. of *exūberāre* (EX-, *ūber,* fertile, cp. *ūber,* an udder)]

exude, *v.t.* to emit or discharge through pores, as sweat, moisture, or other liquid matter; to give out slowly. *v.i.* to ooze or flow out slowly through pores etc. **exudation,** *n.* **exudative,** *a.* [L *exūdāre* (EX-, *sūdāre* to sweat)]

†exulcerate, *v.t.* to cause or raise sores or ulcers on; (*fig.*) to afflict, to vex, to exasperate. **exulceration,** *n.* [L *exulcerātus,* p.p. of *exulcerāre* (EX-, *ulcerāre,* to ULCERATE)]

exult, *v.i.* to rejoice exceedingly; to triumph (over). **exultant,** *a.* rejoicing, triumphing; feeling or displaying exultation. **exultantly,** *adv.* **exultancy, exultation,** *n.* **exultingly,** *adv.* [F *exulter,* L *exultāre, exsultāre,* freq. of *exsilere* (EX-, *salīre,* to leap)]

exurbia, *n.* residential areas outside the suburbs of a town or city. **exurb,** *n.* one such area. **exurban,** *a.*

exuviae, *n.pl.* the cast or shed skin, shells, teeth etc. of animals; fossil remains of animals in a fragmentary state; things cast off or relinquished. **exuvial,** *a.* **exuviate,** *v.t.* to cast off, to shed. *v.i.* to cast the old shell, skin etc. **exuviation,** *n.* [L, cast skins of animals, spoils of an enemy, from *exuere,* to put off]

ex-voto, *adv.* in pursuance of a vow. *n.* anything offered to a divinity in gratitude for an exemplary favour. **ex-votive,** *a.* [L *ex vōtō,* out of a vow]

eyas, *n.* an unfledged hawk; (*Falconry*) one taken from the nest for training or whose training is not complete. †*a.* unfledged. †**eyas-musket,** *n.* an unfledged sparrow-hawk; (*fig.*) a pet name for a young boy. [earlier *nyas,* F, *niais,* a nestling, ult. from L *nīdus,* nest]

Eyck, *n.* **Jan van** (*c.* 1390–1441), Flemish painter of the early northern Renaissance, one of the first to work in oil. His paintings are technically brilliant and sumptuously rich in detail and colour. Little is known of his brother Hubert van Eyck (died 1426), who is supposed to have begun the huge and complex altarpiece in St Bavo's cathedral, Ghent, *The Adoration of the Mystical Lamb*, completed by Jan. 1432.

eye¹, *n.* the organ of vision; the eyeball, iris or pupil; the socket or part of the face containing this organ; sight, ocular perception, view, public observation; the power of seeing, discernment, acuteness of vision; careful observation, oversight, care, attention; look, mien, expression; mental perception, way of regarding; (*pl.*) estimation, judgment (of conduct etc.); anything more or less eye-shaped; the bud of a plant; a spot on some feathers, as those of the peacock and argus pheasant; the centre of a target, a bull's-eye; a small opening or perforation; the thread-hole of a needle; the loop or catch in which the hook of a dress is fastened; the hole in the head of an eye-bolt; a circular or oval window; the circular aperture at the summit of a dome, the central point or circle in an Ionic volute; the face (of the wind), direct opposition; †a slight tinge, a shade. **all my eye and Betty Martin,** all humbug, rubbish. **eye for an eye,** strict retaliation. **eye of day,** the sun. **eyes front, right, left,** turn your head and eyes in front, to right or to left. **if you had half an eye,** if you were not blind or stupid. **in the eye** or **eyes of,** in the regard, estimation or judgment of; from the point of view of. **in the wind's eye,** in the face of the wind, directly against the wind. **mind's eye,** mental view or perception. **mind your eye,** take care, look out. **my eye,** (*sl.*) expressing astonishment. **to be all eyes,** to watch intently. **to catch the Speaker's eye,** to succeed in being called on to speak in the House of Commons. **to find favour in the eyes of,** to be graciously received and treated by. **to give the glad eye,** (*sl.*) to ogle. **to have an eye for,** to pay due regard to; to appreciate; to be on the look-out for. **to have an eye to,** to regard, to have designs on. **to keep an eye on,** to watch carefully or narrowly. **to make eyes at,** to regard amorously. **to open one's eyes,** to be greatly astonished. **to pipe the eye,** (*sl.*) to weep. **to pull the wool over someone's eyes** WOOL. **to see eye to eye,** to be in complete agreement (with). **to see with half an eye,** to see at a glance. **to set, lay** or **clap eyes on,** to have sight of. **to turn a blind eye to** TURN. **to view with a friendly, jealous, eye,** to regard with these feelings. **to wipe the eye of,** to show up the foolishness of; to shoot what someone has missed. **up to the eyes,** deeply (immersed, engaged, in debt etc.). **eyeball,** *n.* the pupil or globe of the eye. *v.t.* (*esp. N Am., sl.*) to stare at. **eyeball to eyeball,** of discussions etc., at close quarters, face to face. **eye-bath,** *n.* a small utensil for bathing the eyes. **eye-bolt,** *n.* (*Naut.*) a bolt having an eye or loop at one end for the reception of a ring, hook etc. **eyebright,** *n.* the euphrasy, *Euphrasia officinalis,* formerly much used as a remedy for diseases of the eye. **eye-brightening,** *a.* clearing the sight. **eyebrow,** *n.* the fringe of hair above the orbit of the eyes. **eyebrow pencil,** *n.* a pencil applied to the eyebrows to alter their shape or colour. **eye-catching,** *a.* striking. **eye contact,** *n.* a direct look between people. **eye-drop,** *n.* a tear. **eyeglass,** *n.* a lens to aid the sight; (*pl.*) a pair of these fastened over the nose or held in the hand; the lens nearest the eye in an optical instrument; a glass for applying lotion to the eyes; †the lens of the eye. **eyehole,** *n.* a hole to look through; the cavity containing the eye. **eyelash,** *n.* the row of hairs edging the eyelids; a single hair from the edge of the eyelid. **eyelid,** *n.* a fold of skin covering the eye that can be moved to open or close the eye. **eye-liner,** *n.* a cosmetic used to draw a line along the edge of the eyelid. **eye-offending,** *a.* offending to the sight. **eye-opener,** *n.* something that furnishes enlightenment or astonishment. **eyepiece,** *n.* the lens or combination of lenses at the end nearest the eye in an optical instrument. **eye-pit,** *n.* the pit or socket of the eye. **eye-salve,** *n.* salve or ointment for the eyes. **eye-servant,** *n.* one who works or attends to his duty only while watched. **eye-service,** *n.* service performed only while under supervision. **eye shadow,** *n.* a coloured cosmetic for the eyelids. **eyeshot,** *n.* sight, range of vision, view. **eyesight,** *n.* vision; view, observation. **eyesore,** *n.* anything offensive to the sight; an object of disgust or dislike. **eye-splice,** *n.* (*Naut.*) a splice made by turning the end of a rope back on itself, and interlacing the strands of this with those of the standing part, leaving a loop. **eyestrings,** *n.pl.* the tendons by which the eye is moved. **eye-teeth,** *n.pl.* the upper canine teeth of man. **eye-wash,** *n.* (*coll.*) deception, humbug, a fraudulent pretence, a covering up of unpleasant facts. **eye-water,** *n.* a medicated bath or water for the eyes; tears; humour of the eye. **eye-wink,** *n.* a wink of the eye given as a hint; (*fig.*) an instant. **eyewitness,** *n.* one who sees a transaction with his own eyes and is able to bear witness. **eyeful,** *n.* as much as the eye can take in at a look; (*sl.*) an attractive woman. **eyeless,** *a.* destitute of eyes; blind; sightless. [OE *ēage* (cp. Dut. *oog,* Icel. *auga,* Goth. *augō,* G *Auge,* also L *oculus*)]

eye², *v.t.* to watch, to observe (fixedly, suspiciously, jealously etc.). †*v.i.* to appear (in a particular aspect). **to eye askance,** to look at with suspicion or distrust. [from prec.]

eyelet, *n.* a small hole or opening, an aperture like an eye; a loophole; a small eye. **eyelet-hole,** *n.* a hole made as an eyelet for looking or shooting through or for fastening a hook etc. [ME *oilet,* OF *oeillte,* dim. of *oeil,* L *oculus,* eye]

†**eyne,** *pl.* EYE¹.

eyot AIT.

eyre, *n.* a journey or circuit; a court of itinerant justices. †**justices in eyre,** judges who travelled in circuit to hold courts in the different counties; judges of assize. [OF *eire, erre,* from *errer,* late L *iterāre,* to journey, *ire itum,* to go]

Eyre¹, Lake, *n.* Australia's largest lake, in central South Australia, which frequently runs dry, becoming a salt marsh in dry seasons; area up to 9000 sq km/3500 sq miles. It is the continent's lowest point, 12 m/39 ft below sea level.

Eyre², *n.* **Richard** (Charles Hastings) (1943–), English stage and film director. He succeeded Peter Hall as artistic director of the National Theatre, London in 1988. His films include *The Ploughman's Lunch* (1983).

eyrie AERIE.

Eysenck, *n.* **Hans Jurgen** (1916–), English psychologist. He concentrated on personality theory and testing by developing behaviour therapy. He is an outspoken critic of psychoanalysis as therapeutic method.

Ezekiel, *n.* (*c.* 600 BC), in the Old Testament, a Hebrew prophet. Carried into captivity in Babylon by Nebuchadnezzar (597), he preached that Jerusalem's fall was due to the sins of Israel.

Ezra, *n.* in the Old Testament, a Jewish scribe who was allowed by Artaxerxes, king of Persia (probably Artaxerxes I, 464–423 BC), to lead his people back to Jerusalem from Babylon 458 BC. He re-established the Mosaic law and eradicated intermarriage.

F

F¹, f, the sixth letter, is a labiodental spirant, formed by the emission of breath between the lower lip and the upper teeth; (*Mus.*) the fourth note of the diatonic scale of C major. **F clef,** *n.* the bass clef. **f number,** *n.* the ratio of the focal length to the true diameter of a lens; a number expressing the size of the aperture of a camera lens.

F², (*abbr.*) Fahrenheit; fail, failure; farad; filial generation; force; France. **F_1, F_2,** (*abbr.*) first and second filial generations.

F³, (*chem. symbol*) fluorine.

f, (*abbr.*) fathom; feminine; folio; following; forte; franc(s).

FA, (*abbr.*) Fanny Adams (*euphem.* for *fuck all*); Football Association; (*euphem.*) fuck all.

fa, *n.* the fourth note in the sol-fa notation. [It.]

fab, *a.* (*coll.*) wonderful, very good. [short for *fabulous*]

fabaceous, *a.* leguminous, bean-like. [late L *fabāceus,* from L *faba,* a bean]

Fabergé, *n.* **Peter Carl** (1846–1920), Russian goldsmith and jeweller. His workshops in St Petersburg and Moscow were celebrated for the exquisite delicacy of their products, especially the use of gold in various shades. Among his masterpieces was a series of jewelled Easter eggs, the first of which was commissioned by Alexander III for the tsarina in 1884. Fabergé died in exile in Switzerland.

Fabian, *a.* of or pertaining to Fabius Maximus Cunctator, who harassed Hannibal in the second Punic war by his cautious and dilatory strategy; hence, cautious, avoiding open conflict. *n.* a member of the Fabian Society. **Fabianism,** *n.* **Fabianist,** *n.* [L *Fabiānus*]

Fabian Society, *n.* UK socialist organization for research, discussion, and publication, founded in London in 1884. Its name is derived from the Roman commander Fabius Maximus, and refers to the evolutionary methods by which it hopes to attain socialism by a succession of gradual reforms. Early members included George Bernard Shaw, and Beatrice and Sidney Webb.

Fabius, *n.* **Laurent** (1946–), French socialist politician, prime minister (1984–86). He introduced a liberal, free-market economic programme, but his career was damaged by the 1985 Greenpeace sabotage scandal.

fable, *n.* a story, esp. one in which lower animals are represented as endowed with speech in order to convey some moral lesson; a legend, a myth; the plot of a drama or epic poem; a fabrication, a falsehood; gossip. *v.i.* to write fables or fictitious tales; to romance; to tell falsehoods. *v.t.* to feign, to invent; to describe or narrate fictitiously or falsely. **fabled,** *a.* mythic, legendary, fictitious; celebrated in fable. **fabler,** *n.* one who composes fables. [F, from L *fābula,* from *fārī,* to speak]

fabliau, *n.* (*pl.* **-liaux**) a metrical tale, dealing usually with ordinary life, composed by the trouvères in the 12th and 13th cents., and intended for recitation. [F, from OF *fablel,* through the pl. *fabliaux* (dim. of FABLE)]

Fabre, *n.* **Jean Henri Casimir** (1823–1915), French entomologist, noted for his vivid and intimate descriptions and paintings of the life of wasps, bees, and other insects.

fabric, *n.* something put together, a system of correlated parts; a building, an edifice; the basic structure of a building, stonework, timbers etc.; woven, felted or knitted material; mode of construction or manufacture, workmanship, texture. **fabricant,** *n.* a manufacturer. [F *fabrique,* L *fabrica,* rel. to *faber,* artificer]

fabricate, *v.t.* to build, to construct; to form by art or manufacture; to forge, to invent, to trump up. **fabrication,** *n.* forgery, a forgery, a falsehood; manufacture, construction. **fabricator,** *n.* [as prec.]

Fabricius, *n.* **Geronimo** (1537–1619), Italian anatomist and embryologist. He made a detailed study of the veins, and discovered the valves which direct the bloodflow towards the heart. He also studied the development of chick embryos.

Fabritius, *n.* **Carel** (1622–54), Dutch painter, a pupil of Rembrandt. His own style, lighter and with more precise detail than his master's, is evident for example in *The Goldfinch* (1654). He painted religious scenes and portraits.

fabulist, *n.* a writer or inventor of fables; a liar. **fabulize, -ise,** *v.i.* to write or speak in fables. **fabulous,** *a.* feigned, fictitious, invented; given to fabling; related or described in fables; mythical, legendary, unhistorical; exaggerated, absurd; beyond belief, incredible; (*coll.*) wonderful, very good, very enjoyable. **fabulous age,** *n.* the age of myths and legends preceding the dawn of authentic history. **fabulously,** *adv.* **fabulosity, fabulousness,** *n.* [F *fabuliste* (see FABLE, -IST)]

facade, façade, *n.* the front of a building, the principal face; outward appearance, esp. one put on for show or to deceive, a front. [F, from *face,* after It. *facciata,* from *faccia,* FACE]

face, *n.* the front part of the head, the visage, the countenance; that part of anything which presents itself to the view, the front, the upper or main surface; the plane surface of a solid; an exposed surface of rock on a cliff or mountain, or in a mine or quarry; the dial of a watch, clock etc.; the working side of a tool or instrument; the printed surface of a playing card; the printing surface of type; a design or style of type; the striking surface of a bat, racket or golf-club; the visible state of things, the appearance, aspect; a facial expression, a look; a grimace; dignity, reputation; (*coll.*) impudence, effrontery, cheek; (*coll.*) make-up. *v.t.* to turn the face towards; to meet in front; to confront boldly, to stand up to; to acknowledge without evasion; to bring face to face with; to stand opposite to; to put a coating or covering on; to put facings on (a garment); to mix (as tea) with colouring matter, so as to make it appear of better quality; to cause to turn in any direction; (*Golf*) to strike (the ball) with the face of the club full in the middle, in driving from the tee. *v.i.* to look in a certain direction; to be situated with a certain aspect; to turn the face in a certain direction; †to present a false appearance, to play the hypocrite. **about face, left face, right face,** (*Mil., order*) turn right-about, left or right, without moving from the same spot. **face to face (with),** in someone's or each other's actual presence; in confrontation; opposite; clearly, without anything interposed. **face-to-face,** *a.* **in the face of,** in spite of. **loss of face,** humiliation, loss of personal prestige. **on the face of it,** to judge by appearances. **to face down,** to confront sternly or defiantly; to force to give way. **to face out,** to carry off by boldness or effrontery. **to face the enemy,** to meet the enemy with determination. **to face the music,** to meet an emergency without quailing; to meet consequences boldly. **to face up to,** to meet courageously. **to fly in the face of,** to defy openly; to act in direct opposition to. **to have the face,** to be impudent, cool or composed enough (to). **to look in the face,** to confront steadily and unflinchingly. **to lose face,** to be humiliated; to suffer loss of personal prestige. **to make, pull a face,** to distort the features; to grimace. **to (some)one's face,** openly; in plain words. **to put a bold, brave, or good face on,** to adopt a confident air; to maintain that all is well with something; to make the best of. **to put one's face on,** (*coll.*) to put on make-up. **to save (one's) face,** to save oneself from manifest disgrace or discomfiture. **to set one's face against,** to oppose, to withstand firmly. **to show one's face,** to appear. **until one is blue in the face,** for ever without success. **face-ache,** *n.* neuralgia. **face-card,** *n.* a court-card. **face-cloth, -flannel,** *n.* a cloth used to wash the face. **face-guard,** *n.* a guard to protect the face in fencing, welding etc. **face-harden,** *v.t.* to harden the surface of (as steel). **face-lift,** *n.* an operation to remove wrinkles and make the face look younger and smoother; (*coll.*) renovations, repairs carried out to improve or modernize the appearance of something. **face-lifting** *n.* FACE-LIFT. **face-off,** *n.* the dropping of the puck or ball between two opposing players to start or restart a game of ice-hockey or lacrosse; (*coll.*) a confrontation. **face pack,** *n.* a creamy cosmetic mixture applied to the face. **face powder,** *n.* cosmetic powder for the face. **face-saving,** *a.* intended to prevent humiliation or loss of prestige. **face-value,** *n.* the nominal value shown on coin, bank-notes etc.; the apparent value of anything. **face-worker,** *n.* a miner who works at the face. **faced,** *a.* dressed, as tea; smoothed on the surface, as stone; having a face of a certain kind. **-faced,** *comb. form* having a face of a certain kind; having a certain number of faces. **faceless,** *a.* destitute of a face; anonymous; of bureaucrats etc., remote from and unmoved by the concerns of ordinary citizens. **facer,** *n.* a blow in the face; a sudden check; a dilemma. [F, from pop. L *facia,* L *facies*]

facet, *n.* a small face or surface; one of the small planes which form the sides of a crystal, a cut diamond or other gem; a flat surface with a definite boundary as a segment of a compound eye; (*Arch.*) a flat projection between the flutings of a column; an aspect. *v.t.* to cut a facet or facets on. [F *facette,* dim. of *face,* FACE]

facetiae, *n.pl.* humorous or witty sayings; (*Bibliog.*) curious, comic, esp. indecent books. [L, pl. of *facētia,* wit, from *facētus,* elegant, urbane]

facetious, *a.* given to or characterized by levity, flippant; waggish, jocular; intended to be amusing. **facetiously,** *adv.* **facetiousness,** *n.* [F *facétieux,* from *facétie,* L *facētia,* see prec.]

facia, FASCIA.

facial, *a.* of or pertaining to the face. *n.* a beauty treatment for the face. **facial angle,** *n.* the angle formed by lines drawn from the nostrils to the ear and to the forehead. [F, from med. L *faciālis*]

-facient *comb. form* added to L infinitive and Eng. words to give sense of producing the action expressed in the verb, as *calefacient, liquefacient.* [L *faciens -ntem,* pres.p. of *facere,* to make]

facies, *n.* the general aspect of an assembly of organisms characteristic of a particular locality or period of the earth's history. [L, face]

facile, *a.* easily done; easily surmountable; easily led, pliant, yielding; dexterous, skilful, handy; ready, fluent; easy-tempered, gentle; glib, superficial. [F, from L *facilis,* from *facere,* to do]

facilis descensus Averno, the descent to hell is easy, getting into trouble is easy (getting out less so). [L]

facilitate, *v.t.* to make easy or less difficult; to further, to help forward. **facilitation,** *n.* **facility,** *n.* easiness in performing or in being performed; freedom from difficulty; ease, readiness, fluency (of speech etc.); quickness, dexterity, aptitude; readiness to be persuaded or led, pliability; (*usu. pl.*) means or equipment provided to facilitate any activity; a service; (*chiefly N Am.*) a building or plant serving a particular purpose; a sum made available for borrowing. [as prec.]

facing, *n.* the action of the verb TO FACE; a covering in front for ornament or other purposes; a coating of a different material, on a wall etc.; (*pl.*) the trimmings on the collar, cuffs etc. of a uniform, serving to distinguish one regiment from another; the process of adulterating inferior tea, coffee etc. by mixing it with colouring matter and other substances; (*pl.*) the movements of a soldier in turning or wheeling in the course of drill.

†**facinorous,** *a.* criminal, atrocious. [L *facinorōsus,* from *facinus -oris,* a deed, a crime]

façon de parler, manner of speaking; phrase, phrasing. [F]

facsimile, *n.* an exact copy of handwriting, printing, a picture etc.; the transmission by wire or radio and reproduction of written or pictorial material. *v.t.* to make a facsimile of. **in facsimile,** exactly like. **facsimilist,** *n.* [L (*fac,* imper. of *facere,* to make, *simile,* neut. of *similis,* like)]

fact, *n.* an act or deed; something that has really occurred or been done; something known to be true or existing, as distinct from an inference or conjecture; reality, actuality, the concrete basis of experience; the occurrence of an event, the actual doing of a deed. **as a matter of fact,** actually, in fact. **before, after the fact,** before or after the actual event. **facts of life,** the details of esp. human reproduction; the (often unpleasant) realities of a situation. **in (point of) fact,** in reality, actually, independently of theory or argument. **fact-finding,** *a.* investigative, appointed to establish the facts of a situation. **factual,** *a.* **factually,** *adv.* [L *factum,* a thing done, orig. neut. p.p. of *facere,* to do]

faction[1], *n.* a body of persons combined or acting in union, esp. a party within a party combined to promote their own views or purposes at the expense of order and the public good; party spirit, discord, dissension; one of the companies who supplied horses, charioteers etc. form the chariot-races in the ancient Roman circus. **faction fight,** *n.* (*Ir.*) a fight between factions or parties of different religions, politics or family connections; (*S Afr.*) a fight between blacks of different tribes. **factional,** *a.* †**factionary,** *a.* adhering to a faction; active as a partisan. †**factionist,** *n.* one who promotes or supports factions. **factious,** *a.* given to faction or party; opposed to the established government; seditious, turbulent. **factiously,** *adv.* **factiousness,** *n.* [F, from L *factio -ōnem,* a doing, a way of making (cp. FASHION), a class, a party, from *facere,* to do, p.p. *factus*]

faction[2], *n.* literary etc. work which blends factual events and characters with fiction. [from *fact* and *fiction*]

-faction *comb. form* denoting making, turning or converting, as in *rarefaction, satisfaction, tumefaction.* [L *-factio -ōnem,* n. of action of verbs in *-facere;* or, occasionally, from verbs in *-ficāre,* as in *petrifaction*]

factitious, *a.* made by art, artificial; unnatural, conventional, affected; unreal, bogus. **factitiously,** *adv.* **factitiousness,** *n.* [L *facticius,* from *factus,* p.p. of *facere,* to make]

factitive, *a.* causing, effecting; (*Gram.*) applied to that relation existing between two words, as between an active verb and its object, when the action expressed by the verb causes a new state or condition in the object, as in *The people made him a king.* [L *factus,* as prec.]

factoid, *n.* a piece of information accepted as true simply on the basis of its repetition or appearance in print, but not proved.

factor, *n.* an agent, a deputy; (*Sc.*) a steward or agent of an estate; an agent employed to sell goods on commission; one of the quantities that multiplied together make up a given number or expression; any circumstance, fact or influence which contributes to a result. *v.t.* to act as factor for or to look after (property); to manage. **factor of safety,** the ratio of the breaking stress to the greatest stress likely to be applied. **Factor 8,** *n.* a blood-clotting agent used in the treatment of haemophiliacs. **factorage,** *n.* the commission given to a factor by his or her employer. **factorial,** *a.* pertaining to a series of mathematical factors; pertaining to a factor or land agent; (*rare*) of or pertaining to a factory. *n.* the product of a series of factors in arithmetical progression, as $(x+2)$ $(x+4)$ $(x+6)$; the product of an integer multiplied into all its lower integers, e.g. the factorial of $4 = 4 \times 3 \times 2 = 24$. **factoring,** *n.* the work of a factor; the buying up of trade debts or lending money on the security of them. **factorize, -ise,** *v.t.* to express a number in terms of its factors. **factorization, -isation,** *n.* **factorship,** *n.* [F *facteur,* L *factōr -em,* as prec.]

factory, *n.* a trading station established in a foreign place by a company of merchants; a building in which any manufacture is carried out; a works, a workshop, a mill; †manufacture. **Factory Acts,** *n.pl.* acts to provide for the health and safety of those employed in factories. **factory-cotton,** *n.* (*N Am.*) unbleached cotton goods. **factory farm,** *n.* a farm practising factory farming. **factory farming,** *n.* the intensive rearing of animals for milk, egg or meat production in a largely man-made environment. **factory-hand,** *n.* a person employed in a factory. **factory ship,** *n.* a vessel in a fishing fleet which processes the catches. [med. L *factōria,* as prec.]

factotum, *n.* a person employed to do all sorts of work, a handyman; a servant who manages all his or her employer's concerns. [med. L (L *fac,* imper. of *facere,* to do, *totum,* neut. a., all)]

factual FACT.

factum, *n.* (*pl.* **-ta**) a thing done; an act or deed; (*Law*) a deed, a sealed instrument; a memorial reciting facts or points in a controversy. [L, FACT]

†**facture,** *n.* making, manufacture; manner of making, construction, workmanship. [F, from L *factūra,* as prec.]

facula, *n.* (*pl.* **-lae**) (*Astron.*) a luminous spot or streak upon the sun's disc. [L, dim. of *fax facis,* a torch]

faculty, *n.* power or ability of any special kind; (*Psych.*) a natural power of the mind, as the will, reason, sense etc.; capacity for any natural action, as seeing, feeling, speaking; (*N Am.*) the ability to do or manage; the members collectively of any of the learned professions; one of the departments of instruction in a university; the professors and lecturers in such a department; an authorization or licence to perform certain functions, esp. ecclesiastical; †personal quality or disposition; †efficacy, active quality; †an art, trade, profession. **Court of Faculties,** a court under an archbishop, having power to grant faculties or dispensations in certain cases. **Faculty of Advocates,** the college or incorporated body of barristers in Scotland. **the Faculty,** the medical profession and its members. **the Four Faculties,** Theology, Law, Medicine, Arts. **facultative,** *a.* imparting a faculty or power; empowering, permissive, as opposed to compulsory; optional; pertaining to a faculty; able to live under more than one set of environmental conditions. **facultize, -ise,** *v.t.* [F *faculté,* L *facultās -tātem,* contr. from *facilitās,* see FACILE]

fad, *n.* a crotchet, a whim, a passing fancy, taste or fashion, a craze; a hobby; a favourite theory or idea; an idiosyncratic taste or distaste for something. **faddish,** *a.* **faddishness,** *n.* **faddism,** *n.* **faddist,** *n.* **faddy,** *a.* **faddiness,** *n.* [etym. doubtful]

Fadden, *n.* **Arthur 'Artie'** (1895–1973), Australian politician, born in Queensland. He was leader of the Country Party (1941–58) and prime minister Aug.–Oct. 1941.

fade, *v.i.* to wither, as a plant, to lose freshness, brightness, vigour or beauty; to languish; to grow lighter in colour, pale, dim or indistinct; to disappear gradually; of a person, to grow weaker, to decline; of electronic signals, to decrease in strength or volume; of brakes, to lose their effectiveness gradually; of an athlete, team etc., to perform less well, to cease to mount a serious challenge; to perform a fade-in or fade-out. *v.t.* to cause to wither or decay; to cause to grow lighter in colour; to cause to decrease in strength or volume; (*Golf*) to slice a shot slightly. *n.* an instance of fading in or out or both simultaneously; a dimming of stage lighting; (*Golf*) a slight (often deliberate) slice. **to fade away,** to fade; (*coll.*) to grow very thin. **to fade in, up,** to cause sound or a picture to appear gradually. **to fade out, down,** to cause sound or a picture to disappear gradually. **fade-in, -up,** *n.* **fade-out, -down,** *n.* **fadeless,** *a.* unfading. **fadelessly,** *adv.* **fadingly,** *adv.* [OF *fader,* from *fade,* dull, tasteless, L *vapidum,* acc. of *vapidus*]

†**fadge,** *v.i.* to suit, to fit; to agree; to get on, to prosper. [etym. unknown]

faeces, (*esp. N Am.*) **feces,** *n.pl.* sediment, lees, dregs; excrement from the bowels. **faecal,** *a.* **faecula,** FECULA. [L, pl. of *faex,* etym. unknown]

†**faerie,** †**faery,** *n.* fairyland, esp. the imaginary realm depicted in Spenser's *Faerie Queene*. *a.* visionary, beautiful but unsubstantial. [var. of FAIRY]

Faerie Queene, The, a poem by Edmund Spenser, published from 1590–96, dedicated to Elizabeth I. The poem, in six books, describes the adventures of six knights. Spenser used a new stanza form, later adopted by Keats, Shelley, and Byron.

Faeroe Islands, Faeroes see FAROE ISLANDS.

faff, *v.i.* (*coll.*) to dither, to fuss (often with *about*).

fag, *v.i.* (*past, p.p.* **fagged**) to toil wearily; to work till one is weary; to act as a fag in a public school. *v.t.* to tire, to exhaust, to weary (often with *out*); to use as a fag or drudge in a public school. *n.* laborious drudgery, toil; fatigue, exhaustion; a tiresome or unwelcome task; a junior at a public school who has to perform certain duties for some senior boy; (*coll.*) a cigarette; (*coll.*) a boring task; (*chiefly N Am., offensive*) a male homosexual. **fag-end,** *n.* the loose end of a web of cloth, generally of coarser texture; the latter or meaner part of anything; the fringed or untwisted end of a rope; (*coll.*) a cigarette butt. [etym. doubtful (perh. corr. of FLAG[1])]

Fagatogo, *n.* capital of American Samoa. Situated on Pago Pago Harbour, Tutuila Island.

faggot, *n.* a bundle of sticks or small branches of trees, used for fuel, filling ditches, road-making etc.; a bundle of steel or wrought-iron rods; as a definite quantity of this, 120 lb (54 kg); a cake or ball of chopped liver, herbs etc.; (*chiefly N Am., offensive*) a male homosexual. †a bundle of any material; †a person hired to take the place of another at the muster of a military company. *v.t.* to bind or tie up in a faggot or bundle; †to collect together. *v.i.* to make faggots. **faggot-vote,** *n.* a vote manufactured by the transfer of property to an unqualified person. **faggot-voter,** *n.* **faggoting,** *n.* a type of embroidery in which some horizontal threads are tied together in hourglass shapes. [F *fagot,* etym. doubtful (perh. from Norw. *fagg,* a bundle)]

fagotto, *n.* (*pl.* **-tti**) the bassoon. [It.]

fah, FA.

Fahd, *n.* (1921–), king of Saudi Arabia from 1982, when he succeeded his half-brother Khalid. As head of government he has been active in trying to bring about a solution to the Middle East conflicts.

Fahrenheit[1], *a.* pertaining to the temperature scale on which the freezing-point of water is marked at 32° and the boiling-point at 212°.

Fahrenheit[2], *n.* **Gabriel Daniel** (1686–1736), German physicist who lived mainly in England and Holland. He devised the Fahrenheit temperature scale.

faience, *n.* glazed blocks of terracotta used as facings; tin-glazed earthenware of a particular kind. [F *faience;* It. Faenza, town in Romagna]

fail[1], *n.* (*Sc.*) a turf, sod. **fail-dyke,** *n.* (*Sc.*) a wall of sods. [prob. from Gael, *fàl,* a sod]

fail[2], *v.i.* to be or become deficient or wanting; to run short; to come short of the due amount or measure; not to succeed (in); not to succeed in the attainment (of); to lose strength or spirit, to sink, to decline; to die away; to be or become ineffective or inoperative; to become bankrupt or insolvent; not to pass an examination. *v.t.* to be insufficient for; to come short of; to deceive, to disappoint, to desert; to neglect or omit (to do something); not to pass (an examination); to cause not to pass. *n.* failure, default; a failure grade in an examination; one who fails an examination; †death, extinction. **without fail,** assuredly, certainly, in spite of all hindrances. **failsafe,** *a.* of a mechanism, incorporated in a system to render it safe in the event of failure or malfunction. **failing,** *n.* deficiency, failure; the act of becoming insolvent or bankrupt; an imperfection, a weakness, a foible. *prep., pres.p.* in default of. **failing this,** if this does not happen. **failure,** *n.* a failing or coming short; an omission, non-performance, non-occurrence; decay, breaking down; insolvency, bankruptcy; want of success; an unsuccessful person or thing. [OF *faillir,* to miss, pop. L *fallīre,* to be wanting, to disappoint, L *fallere,* to deceive]

faineant, *a.* do-nothing; idle, sluggish; an epithet applied to the later Merovingian kings of France, who were puppets in the hands of the Maires du Palais. *n.* a do-nothing, an idler. [F, as if formed of *fait-néant,* do nothing; actually from OF *faignant,* sluggard, pres.p. of *faindre,* to skulk, see FAINT]

fains, fens, *int.* (*dated*) a children's formula for claiming exemption, for whoever says it first, from a task, e.g. 'Fains I batting'. [etym. doubtful]

faint, *a.* weak, feeble; languid, giddy, inclined to swoon; timid, fearful; of sound or brightness, dim, indistinct, slight, feeble; of smells, sickly, oppressive. *v.i.* to swoon; †to lose courage, to give way. *n.* a swoon, a fainting fit; (*pl.*) crude spirit that distils over at the beginning and end in the manufacture of whisky, sold as spirit of an inferior grade. †**faint-heart, faint-hearted,** *a.* cowardly, timid, spiritless. **faint-heartedly,** *adv.* **faint- heartedness,** *n.* **faint-ruled,** *a.* of paper, ruled with faint lines to guide writing. **faintish,** *a.* **faintly,** *adv.* **faintness,** *n.* [OF *feint,* p.p. of *feindre, faindre,* to FEIGN]

fair¹, *a.* beautiful, comely, pleasing to the eye; pleasing to the mind; satisfactory, specious; just, equitable, legitimate; not effected by unlawful or underhand means, above-board; passably good, not bad, of moderate quality; clear, pure, clean; free from spot, blemish or cloud, serene; favourable, auspicious, promising; open, unobstructed; civil, obliging, polite; legible, plain; light in colour or complexion; blond; †orderly, neat; †liberal, mild. *adv.* courteously, civilly, plausibly; openly, honestly, justly; on equal terms; according to the rules, straight, clean. *n.* a beautiful woman; beauty. †*v.t.* to make fair or beautiful. *v.i.* of the weather, to become fair. **by fair means or foul** MEAN². **fair and square,** honourable, straightforward, without finesse, above-board. **fair dos,** (*coll.*) (a phrase used when asking for, or consenting to, fair play, equal shares etc.) fair treatment. **fair enough,** *int.* (*coll.*) (indicating at least partial assent to a proposition, terms etc.) all right, OK. **fair to middling,** (*coll.*) not bad, about average. **to be in a fair way,** to stand a good chance. **to bid fair** BID. **to hit fair,** to hit straight or clean. †**fair-boding,** *a.* auspicious. **fair copy,** *n.* a copy (of a document etc.) not defaced by corrections. †**fair-faced,** *a.* having a fair or handsome face; of bright complexion; fair to the eye, specious. **fair game,** *n.* a legitimate target for attack, criticism or ridicule. **fair-haired,** *a.* having hair of a light colour, blond. †**fair-head,** *n.* beauty. **fair-minded,** *a.* honest-minded, impartial, just. **fair play,** *n.* equitable conduct; just or equal conditions for all. **fair-seeming,** *a.* superficially favourable or equitable; plausible, specious. **fair sex,** *n.* women. **fair-spoken,** *a.* using courteous language; bland, polite, plausible. **fair trade,** *n.* reciprocity, the granting of free trade only to such nations as allow it in return; †open and legal trade; †(*euphem.*) contraband trade, smuggling. **fairway,** *n.* the navigable part of a river, channel or harbour; (*Golf*) the smooth passage of turf between holes. **fair-weather,** *a.* appearing only in times of prosperity; not good at need. **fairing,** *n.* a structure to provide streamlining of an aircraft, car etc. **fairish,** *a.* pretty fair; tolerably large. **fairly,** *adv.* in a fair manner; completely, absolutely, utterly; moderately, passably; †softly, gently. **fairness,** *n.* **in all fairness,** it is only right or just that, in justice, being strictly honest. [OE *fæger* (cp. Icel. *fagr,* OHG *fagar*)]

fair², *n.* a market or gathering for trade in a particular town or place, usu. held annually, with shows and entertainments; a funfair; a charity bazaar; a trade show. **fancy fair,** a sale of fancy goods for the benefit of a religious or philanthropic institution, a bazaar. **fairground,** *n.* open space where fairs, exhibitions etc. are held. **fairing,** *n.* a present bought at a fair. [OF *feire* (F *foire*), L *fēria* or pl. *fēriae,* a holiday]

Fairbanks¹, *n.* **Douglas** (stage name of Douglas Elton Ulman) (1883–1939), US actor. He played swashbuckling heroes in silent films such as *The Mark of Zorro* (1920), *The Three Musketeers* (1921), *Robin Hood* (1922), *The Thief of Baghdad* (1924), and *Don Quixote* (1925). He often produced and wrote his own films under a pseudonym. He was married to the film star Mary Pickford from 1920–33.

Fairbanks², *n.* **Douglas, Jr** (1909–), US actor who appeared in the same type of swashbuckling film roles as his father, Douglas Fairbanks; for example in *Catherine the Great* (1934) and *The Prisoner of Zenda* (1937).

Fairfax, *n.* **Thomas, 3rd Baron Fairfax of Cameron** (1612–71), English general, commander in chief of the Parliamentary army in the English Civil War. With Cromwell he formed the New Model Army, defeated Charles I at Naseby, and suppressed the Royalist and Presbyterian risings in 1648.

Fair Isle, *a.* applied to woollen articles knitted in coloured patterns typical of *Fair Isle* (one of the Shetland Islands).

Fair Trading, Office of, UK government department established (1973) to keep commercial activities under review. It covers the areas of consumer affairs and credit, monopolies and mergers, and anti-competitive and restrictive trade practices. The US has a Bureau of Consumer Protection with similar scope.

fairy, *n.* a small supernatural being having magical powers, supposed to assume human form and to meddle for good or for evil in human affairs; (*offensive*) an effeminate man or homosexual; †an enchantress; †enchantment, magic; †fairyland; fairies taken collectively. *a.* pertaining to or connected with fairies; fairy-like; fanciful, imaginary. **fairy cycle,** *n.* a child's bicycle. **fairy godmother,** *n.* an (often unexpected) benefactor. **fairyland,** *n.* the imaginary abode of the fairies; a region of enchantment. **fairy lights,** *n.pl.* small lights of many colours used for decoration. **fairy-ring,** *n.* a circular band of turf greener than the rest caused by the growth of fungi, but formerly supposed to be caused by the dancing of fairies. **fairy-stones,** *n.pl.* the fossil remains of sea-urchins; recent concretions of hardened clay occurring near the source of some chalybeate springs. **fairy story,** *n.* a fairy-tale. **fairy-tale,** *n.* a tale about fairies; a fanciful or highly improbable story. *a.* as in a fairy-tale; extremely beautiful; extremely fortunate. **fairily,** *adv.* **fairydom,** *n.* **fairyhood,** *n.* **fairyism,** *n.* [OF *faerie,* enchantment (F *féerie*), from *fée,* a fairy]

Faisal, *n.* **Ibn Abdul Aziz** (1905–75), king of Saudi Arabia from 1964. The younger brother of King Saud, on whose accession in 1953 he was declared crown prince. He was prime minister (1953–60) and from 1962 until his assassination by a nephew. In 1964 he emerged victorious from a lengthy conflict with his brother and adopted a policy of steady modernization of his country.

Faisalabad, *n.* city in Punjab province, Pakistan; population (1981) 1,092,000. It trades in grain, cotton, and textiles.

fait accompli, *n.* (F) an accomplished fact.

faith, *n.* the assent of the mind to what is stated or put forward by another; firm and earnest belief, conviction, complete reliance, trust; spiritual apprehension or voluntary acceptance of divine revelation apart from absolute proof; operative belief in the doctrines and moral principles forming a system of religion; a system of religious belief; a philosophical, scientific or political creed or system of doctrines; fidelity, constancy, loyalty; a promise, pledge or engagement; credibility, reliability, trustworthiness. *int.* in faith, verily, indeed. †*v.t.* to give faith or credence to; to believe, to credit. **bad faith,** intent to deceive. **in faith,** in deed, in truth. **in good faith,** with honest intentions. **on the faith of,** in reliance on; on the warrant of. **Punic faith,** bad faith, faithlessness, treachery. **the faith,** the Christian religion; the true religion. **to keep faith with,** to be loyal to. †**faithbreach,** *n.* a breach of faith or honour. **faith-cure, -healing,** *n.* curing of disease by means of prayer and faith, without the use of drugs etc. **faith-curer, -doctor, -healer,** *n.* **faithful,** *a.* loyal to one's promises, duty or engagements; conscientious, trustworthy; upright, honest; truthful, worthy of belief; exact, accurate. **the faithful,** true believers in a particular creed or religious system. **faithfully,** *adv.* in a faithful manner. **to deal faithfully with, by,** to treat frankly, conscientiously, uncompromisingly; to tell the truth to without shirking. **to promise faithfully,** with the most emphatic assurances. **yours faithfully,** a conventional mode of subscribing a letter. **faithfulness,** *n.* **faithless,** *a.* destitute of faith, unbelieving; disloyal, unfaithful, not true to promises or duty, unreliable; perfidious, treacherous. **faithlessly,** *adv.* **faithlessness,** *n.* [OF *fei, feid,* L *fides fidem* (cp. Gr. *pistis,* faith, *peithein,* to persuade)]

†**faitour,** *n.* a lazy, disreputable fellow; an impostor; a vagabond. [A-F, from OF *faitor,* L *factōr -em,* FACTOR]

faix, *int.* (*Ir., dial.*) in faith, verily. [corr. of FAITH]

fake[1], *v.t.* to do up, to cover up defects and faults, so as to give a presentable appearance to, to doctor; to contrive, to fabricate, to make up from defective material; to cheat, to defraud, to deceive; to pretend, to simulate. *n.* a thing thus prepared for deception, esp. a manufactured antique (furniture etc.), a sham; a swindle, a dodge. *a.* bogus, sham, counterfeit. **fakement,** *n.* **faker,** *n.* [etym. doubtful]

fake[2], *n.* (*Naut.*) one of the coils in a rope or cable when laid up. *v.t.* to coil (a rope). [etym. doubtful]

fakir, *n.* a Muslim religious mendicant; often used for a mendicant, ascetic or wonder-worker of other faiths, esp. in India; a very holy man. [Arab. *faqīr* orig. poor, indigent]

Falange Española, *n.* former Spanish Fascist Party, founded in 1933 by José Antonio de Rivera, son of the military ruler Miguel Primo de Rivera. It was closely modelled in programme and organization on the Italian fascists and on the Nazis. In 1937, when Franco assumed leadership, it was declared the only legal party, and altered its name to Traditionalist Spanish Phalanx.

Falangist, *n.* name adopted by General Franco and his supporters in the revolution against the republican government of Spain (1936–39). [L *falanga,* a band of persons, from Gr. *phalanx*]

Falasha, *n.* a member of a small community of black Jews in Ethiopia. They suffered discrimination, and began a gradual process of resettlement in Israel after being accorded Jewish status by Israel in 1975. Only about 30,000 Falashas remain in Ethiopia.

falbala, *n.* a trimming, a flounce; a furbelow. [etym. unknown, cp. FURBELOW]

falcate, *a.* (*Nat. Hist.*) hooked; bent or curved like a sickle or scythe. **falcated,** *a.* (*Astron.*) sickle-shaped, applied to the moon in the first and fourth quarters. [L *falcātus,* from *falx falcis,* sickle]

falchion, *n.* a short, broad sword with a slightly curved blade. [OF *fauchon,* late L *falcio -ōnem,* L *falx falcis,* a sickle]

falciform, *a.* having the form of a sickle. [L *falx falcis,* sickle]

falcon, *n.* a small diurnal bird of prey, esp. the peregrine falcon and others trained to hawk game; a female falcon, esp. the peregrine (cp. TIERCEL); †a small cannon. **falconer,** *n.* one who keeps and trains hawks for hawking; one who hunts with hawks. **falconet,** *n.* a species of shrike; †a small cannon. **falconry,** *n.* the art of training falcons to pursue and attack game; the sport of hawking. [OF *faucon,* late L *falco -ōnem,* perh. as prec.]

Falconet, *n.* **Etienne-Maurice** (1716–91), French sculptor whose works range from formal baroque to gentle rococo in style. He directed sculpture at the Sèvres porcelain factory (1757–66). His bronze equestrian statue of *Peter the Great* in Leningrad was commissioned in 1766 by Catherine II.

falderal, *n.* a trifle, a gewgaw. [refrain to a song]

faldstool, *n.* a portable folding seat, stool or chair, used by a bishop officiating out of his own cathedral; a desk at which the Litany is said; a desk or stool to kneel at during one's devotions. [OF *faldestoel,* med. L *faldistolium,* OHG *faldstuol* (*faldan,* to fold, *stuol,* cp. G *Stuhl,* a chair)]

Falernian, *n.* wine made in ancient times from grapes grown on Mount *Falernus,* in Campania. [L (*vīnum*) *Falernum*]

Falkender, *n.* **Marcia, Baroness Falkender** (Marcia Williams) (1932–), British political secretary to Labour prime minister Harold Wilson from 1956, she was influential in the 'kitchen cabinet' of the 1964–70 government, as described in her book *Inside No 10* (1972).

Falkland, *n.* **Lucius Cary, 2nd Viscount Falkland** (*c.* 1610–43), English soldier and politician. He was elected to the Long Parliament of 1640. Falkland was opposed to absolute monarchy but alienated by Puritan extremism, and tried hard to secure a compromise peace between Royalists and Parliamentarians. He was killed at the Battle of Newbury in the Civil War.

Falkland Islands, *n.pl.* British Crown Colony in the S Atlantic. **area** 12,173 sq km/4700 sq miles, made up of two main islands: E Falkland 6760 sq km/2610 sq miles, and W Falkland 5413 sq km/2090 sq miles. **capital** Stanley; new port facilities were opened 1984, and Mount Pleasant airport in 1985. **population** (1986) 1916. **exports** wool, alginates (used as dyes and as a food additive) from seaweed beds.

Falkland Islands, Battle of the, British naval victory (under Admiral Sturdee) on 8 Dec. 1914 over the German admiral von Spee.

fall, *v.i.* (*past,* **fell,** *p.p.* **fallen**) to descend from a higher to a lower place or position by the force of gravity; to descend suddenly, to drop; to sink, to flow down, to be poured down, to become lower in level of surface; to come down, to become prostrate; to be hit or wounded; to be killed (esp. in battle); to be overthrown, to lose power; to be taken by the enemy; (*Cricket*) to be taken by the bowling side; to decrease in number, amount, value, weight, loudness etc.; to become lower in pitch; to subside, to abate, to ebb, to languish, to die away; to fail, to be degraded or disgraced; to sink into sin, vice, error, to give away to temptation; to lose one's virginity; of the face, to assume a despondent expression; to become, to pass into a specified state, as in *fall asleep, fall ill;* to be transferred by chance, lot, inheritance, or otherwise; to turn out, to result, to happen; to be uttered or dropped, as a chance remark; to be born (said of some of the lower animals); to hang down, to droop. *v.t.* to cut down, to fell, †to let fall, to drop; †to lower, to depress; †to bring forth, to drop. *n.* the act of falling; a bout at wrestling or a throw in this; a cataract, a cascade, a waterfall; the degree of inclination, the gradient or slope; a declivity; the amount of descent, the distance through which anything falls; the disemboguing of a river; the fall of the leaf, (*chiefly N Am.*) autumn; the act of felling or cutting down; the amount of timber cut down; the amount of rain, snow etc. in a district; the number of lambs born; downfall, degradation, declension from greatness or prosperity, ruin, disgrace; death, destruction, overthrow; the surrender or capture of a town; a lapse from virtue; a yielding to temptation; a veil; that part of the rope in hoisting-tackle to which the power is applied; (*Mus.*) a cadence. **the Fall,** the lapse of Adam and, through him, of his posterity from a state of primeval innocence; see FALL OF MAN. **to fall about,** to laugh hysterically. **to fall among,** to come among accidentally. **to fall apart,** to collapse, to become unstitched, unstuck etc., to go to pieces. **to fall astern,** (*Naut.*) to drop behind. **to fall away,** to desert; to revolt; to apostatize; to fall into wickedness; to decay, to languish; to pine, to become thin; to extend or slope downwards. **to fall back,** to recede, to give way, to retreat. **to fall back (up)on,** to have recourse to. **to fall behind,** to be passed by, to lag behind; to become in arrears with. **to fall between two stools,** to fail through being unable to choose between two alternatives; to be neither one thing nor the other. **to fall by the ears,** to quarrel. **to fall down,** to be thrown down, to drop; to prostrate oneself; to fail, to be inadequate. **to fall down on,** to fail to carry out. **to fall flat,** to be a failure; to fail to arouse interest. **to fall for,** (*coll.*) to be impressed by, to fall in love with; to be fooled by. **to fall foul of** FOUL. **to fall from,** to drop away from, to desert, to forsake. **to fall from grace,** to fall into sin. **to fall home,** (*Naut.*) to curve inwards, as timbers or sides of a ship. **to fall in,** to give way inwards; to become due; to become the property of a person by expiration of time; to run out, to lapse; (*Mil.*) to take one's place in line. **to fall in with,** to meet with accidentally; to agree to, to concur in; to coincide with. **to fall off,** to withdraw, to recede; to prove faithless; to become depreciated, to decrease in quality, quantity or amount; to revolt; of a ship, to fail to keep her head to the wind. **to fall on,** to make an attack, to join battle; to set to, to begin eagerly. **to fall out,** to happen, befall, to turn out, to result; to quarrel; (*Mil.*) to leave the ranks. **to fall over,** to tumble or be knocked down; to trip or stumble over. **to fall over backwards** BACKWARD. **to fall over oneself,** to be eager, or over-eager (to do something). **to fall short,** to be deficient; to drop before reaching the mark. **to fall short of,** to fail to attain. **to fall through,** to fail, to miscarry, to come to nothing. **to fall to,** to begin hastily or eagerly, to set to; to begin eating. **to fall under,** to be subject to; to come within the range of; to be classed with or reckoned with or under. **to fall (up)on,** to come across; to attack; of eyes, to take the direction of. **to fall within,** to be included in. **to try a fall,** to have a bout at wrestling; (*fig.*) to engage in a contest of any kind. **fall-back,** *a.* which one can retreat to; alternative (and usu. less ambitious). **fall guy,** *n.* a scapegoat, cat's paw; one who is easily duped. **fall-out,** *n.* the deposit of radioactive dust after a nuclear explosion; secondary consequences, by-products. **fall-trap,** *n.* a trap with a door which falls and imprisons. **fallen,** *a.* killed, esp. in battle; seduced; morally degraded; overthrown. **faller,** *n.* a racehorse which falls during a race. **falling,** *n.* **falling away,** *n.* apostasy. **falling off,** *n.* declension. †**falling-sickness,** *n.* epilepsy. **falling star,** *n.* a meteor appearing to fall rapidly to the earth. [OE *feallan,* cp. Dut. *vallen,* Icel. *falla,* G *fallen,* also L *fallere,* to deceive]

Falla, *n.* **Manuel de** (1876–1946), Spanish composer. His opera *La vida breve/Brief Life* (1905) (performed 1913) was followed by the ballets *El amor brujo/Love the Magician* (1915) and *El sombrero de tres picos/The Three-Cornered Hat* (1919), and his most ambitious concert work, *Noches en los jardines de España/Nights in the Gardens of Spain* (1916). The folk idiom of southern Spain is an integral part of his compositions. He also wrote songs and pieces for piano and guitar.

fallacy, *n.* an unsound argument or mode of arguing, anything, that misleads or deceives the mind; (*Log.*) a delusive mode of reasoning, an example of such; an error, a sophism; sophistry, delusiveness, unsoundness of reasoning or of belief. **fallacious,** *a.* **fallaciously,** *adv.* **fallaciousness,** *n.* [L *fallăcia,* from *fallax,* deceptive, from *fallere,* to deceive]

fal-lal, *n.* a gaudy ornament or trinket, a gewgaw. [cp. KNICK-KNACK, GEWGAW; perh. conn. with FALBALA]

fallible, *a.* liable to err or to be mistaken. **fallibility,** *n.* [late L *fallibilis,* from *fallere,* to deceive]

Fall of Man, the, a myth that explains the existence of evil as the result of some primeval wrongdoing by humanity. It occurs independently in many cultures, but in the Bible it is recorded in the Old Testament in Genesis iii. This was the source for the epic poem of John Milton *Paradise Lost* (1667).

Fallopian tubes, *n.pl.* (*Physiol.*) two ducts or canals by which ova are conveyed to the uterus. An egg is fertilized by sperm in the Fallopian tubes, which are lined with cells whose cilia move the egg towards the ovary. [from *Fallopius,* 1523–62, Italian anatomist, incorrectly credited with their discovery]

fallow[1], *a.* of a pale brownish or reddish-yellow colour. **fallow deer,** *n.* a small species of deer, *Dama vulgaris,* preserved in a semi-domesticated state in many English parks. [OE *fealu* (cp. Dut. *vaal,* G *fahl,* also L *pallidus,* pale, Gr. *polios,* grey)]

fallow[2], *n.* land ploughed and harrowed but left unsown; land left uncultivated for a period. *a.* ploughed and tilled but not sown; uncultivated, unused, neglected. *v.t.* to plough and harrow and leave unsown. [ME *falwe,* ploughed land, OE *fælging; fealga,* harrows for breaking crops]

false, *a.* not true, contrary to truth, not conformable to fact; deceptive, misleading; erroneous, wrong, incorrect; uttering untruth, lying, deceiving; deceitful, treacherous, faithless (to); feigned, sham, spurious, counterfeit, not genuine; forced, unconvincing; artificial, man-made; fitting over or replacing a main part; esp. of plants, resembling a different species; (*Mus.*) out of tune. *adv.* falsely; wrongly; (*Mus.*) out of tune. †*n.* falsehood; untruth. †*v.t.* to deceive, to mislead; to feign, to counterfeit; to betray. **to play one false,** to deceive. **false alarm,** *n.* a needless warning, a cause of unnecessary anxiety or excitement. **false bedding,** *n.* (*Geol.*) strata in which the layers are not parallel through disturbance by currents whilst they were being laid down. **false-boding,** *a.* prophesying amiss. **false bottom,** *n.* a partition inserted above the true bottom often concealing a secret compartment. **false colours,** *n.pl.* flags to which a ship has no right, hoisted to deceive an enemy. **to sail under false colours,** to assume a false character. **false concord,** *n.* (*Gram.*) a breach of the rules of agreement in number, gender, tense etc. **false-creeping,** *a.* moving insidiously and imperceptibly. **false dawn,** *n.* light appearing just before sunrise; delusive signs of change, progress etc. **false face,** *n.* a mask. †**false-faced,** *a.* hypocritical. †**false-hearted,** *a.* treacherous, perfidious. †**false-heartedness,** *n.* **false imprisonment,** *n.* illegal imprisonment. **false move,** *n.* unwise movement or action. **false position,** *n.* an awkward position that may lead to misrepresentation or misunderstanding. **false pregnancy,** *n.* a psychosomatic condition producing symptoms of pregnancy, pseudocyesis. **false pretences,** *n.pl.* (*Law*) misrepresentations made with intent to deceive or defraud. **false quantity,** *n.* incorrect length of syllable in pronunciation, scansion etc. **false rib,** *n.* a rib not directly attached to the breastbone. **false roof,** *n.* a roof-shaped ceiling below the actual roof. **false start,** *n.* a disallowed start to a race, usu. caused by a competitor getting away too early; an abortive beginning to any activity. **false step,** *n.* a stumble; an imprudent action. **false teeth,** *n. pl.* artificial teeth, dentures. **falsework,** *n.* a temporary structure supporting actual construction work. **falsehood,** *n.* untruthfulness, falseness; a lie, an untruth; lying, lies; deceitfulness, unfaithfulness; a counterfeit, an imposture. **falsely,** *adv.* **falseness,** *n.* †**falser,** *n.* one who falsifies; a deceiver, a liar. **falsies,** *n.pl.* (*coll.*) pads used to improve the shape of the breasts. **falsity,** *n.* [OE and OF *fals*, L *falsus*, p.p. of *fallere*, to deceive]

falsetto, *n.* a pitch or range of (usu. the male) voice higher than the natural register; a singer using this range. *a.* pertaining to or produced by such a voice; artificial, affected. [It., dim. of *falso,* FALSE]

falsify, *v.t.* to make false; to give a false or spurious appearance to (a document, statement etc.); to misrepresent; to counterfeit, to forge; to disappoint (expectations), to confute, to disprove. **falsification,**

n. [F *falsifier,* late L *falsificāre,* from *falsificus* (*falsus,* FALSE, *ficus,* rel. to *facere,* to make)]

Falstaffian, *a.* fat, coarsely humorous, convivial; ragged and nondescript, like Falstaff's troops. [*Falstaff,* a character in Shakespeare's *Henry IV* and *V* and *Merry Wives of Windsor*]

falter, *v.i.* to stumble, to totter, to waver, to be unsteady; to stammer, to stutter; to hesitate in action; to act with irresolution; to tremble, to flinch. *v.t.* to utter with hesitation or stammering. **falteringly,** *adv.* [etym. unknown]

fam., (*abbr.*) familiar, familiarly; family.

Famagusta, *n.* seaport on the E coast of Cyprus, in the Turkish Republic of Northern Cyprus; population (1985) 19,500. It was the chief port of the island prior to the Turkish invasion of 1974.

fame, *n.* public report or rumour; reputation, esp. good reputation, renown, celebrity. *v.t.* to make famous or renowned; to celebrate. **house of ill fame,** a brothel. **ill fame,** evil reputation. **famed,** *a.* much talked of; renowned, celebrated. †**fameless,** *a.* [F, from L *fāma* (*fārī,* to speak), cp. Gr. *phēmē*]

familial FAMILY.

familiar, *a.* of one's own acquaintance, well-known, intimate; closely acquainted, intimate (with); unduly or unlawfully intimate; usual, common, ordinary, not novel; easily understood, not abstruse; unconstrained, free, unceremonious; †pertaining to one's family. *n.* an intimate or close friend or companion; a demon or spirit supposed to attend at call; a confidential servant in the household of the Pope or a bishop; †the assistant of a magician or witch. **familiarity,** *n.* use, habitude; close friendship, intimacy; freedom from constraint, unceremonious behaviour, esp. towards superiors or inferiors; a liberty. **familiarize, -ise,** *v.t.* to make familiar; to habituate, to accustom; to make well acquainted (with). **familiarization, -isation,** *n.* **familiarly,** *adv.* †**familiary,** *a.* of or pertaining to a household or family; domestic. [OF *familier,* L *familiāris* from *familia,* FAMILY]

family, *n.* those that live in the same house, including parents, children and servants; father and mother and children; such a group including other relations; children, as distinguished from their parents; those who can trace their descent from a common ancestor, a house, kindred, lineage; a race, a group of peoples from a common stock; a brotherhood of persons or peoples connected by bonds of civilization, religion etc.; genealogy, lineage; honourable descent, noble lineage; a group of genera; (*Zool.*) a subdivision of an order; (*Bot.*) an order; (*Chem.*) a group of compounds having a common basic radical. *a.* esp. of entertainment, deemed suitable for the family with young children, not containing bad language or scenes of sex or violence. **family income supplement,** (*formerly*) in Britain, a social security benefit paid to families with earnings below a set level. **Holy Family** HOLY. **in a family way,** in a domestic way; without ceremony. **in the family way,** pregnant. **to keep something in the family,** to ensure that something, e.g. possession or piece of information, does not pass outside the family or a select group. **family allowance,** *n.* the former name for child benefit. **family Bible,** *n.* a large Bible in which the names and dates of birth of members of a family are entered. **family butcher, grocer,** *n.* tradesmen who supply families, as distinct from those who supply ships, the army etc. **family coach,** *n.* a large closed carriage; a game of forfeits. **family credit,** *n.* in Britain, a social security benefit paid to low-income people in work who have at least one child. **Family Division,** *n.* a division of the High Court dealing with divorce, custody of children etc. **family doctor,** *n.* a general practitioner who treats a family. **family likeness,** *n.* physical or other resemblance between near relations. **family living,** *n.* a benefice in the gift of the head of a family. **family man,** *n.* one who has a (large) family; one who is fond of home life. **family name,** *n.* (*esp. N Am.*) surname. **family planning,** *n.* regulating the number of, and intervals between, children, usu. by means of contraception; (*coll.*) an agency or clinic giving advice on, or help with, the above. **family tree,** *n.* a genealogical chart. **familial,** *a.* characteristic of a family. [L *familia* from *famulus* a servant]

famine, *n.* distressing scarcity of food; extreme scarcity of anything; hunger, starvation. [F, from late L *famīna,* L *famēs,* hunger, whence F *faim*]

famish, *v.i.* to suffer extreme hunger; to die of hunger; †to faint. *v.t.* to starve; to reduce to extreme hunger. **to be famished,** (*coll.*) to be very hungry. **famishing,** *a.* feeling extremely hungry. [obs. v. *fame,* L *famēs,* as prec., -ISH]

famous, *a.* renowned, celebrated; illustrious; noted; (*coll.*) first-rate, very good, excellent; †defamatory. **famously,** *adv.* **famousness,** *n.* [A-F, from OF *fameus,* L *fāmōsus,* from *fāma,* FAME]

Famous Five, *n.* a series of 21 stories for children by Enid Blyton, published in the UK from 1942–63, which describe the adventures of the 'Five' (four children and a dog) who spend their holidays together. The same author's *Secret Seven* series (1949–63) has a similar theme.

famulus, (*pl.* **-li**) an assistant or servant, esp. of a magician. **famulary,** *a.* [L, a servant]

fan¹, *n.* an instrument, usu. flat, with radiating sections opening out in a wedge-shape for agitating the air and cooling the face; an implement shaped like an open fan; a winnowing implement or machine; a small sail or vane for keeping the sails of a windmill to the wind; (*Naut.*) the blade of a screw-propeller; a bird's tail, a wing, a leaf shaped like a fan; a rotatory apparatus for causing a current of air for ventilation; a fan-shaped talus; †a quintain. *v.t.* (*past, p.p.* **fanned**) to agitate the air with a fan; to stir up; to spread like a fan; to cool with a fan; to move or stimulate with or as with a fan; to stir up; to spread like a fan; to winnow; to winnow or sweep away (as chaff). *v.i.* to move or blow gently; to spread out like a fan. **to fan out,** to radiate outwards in a fan-shape, to move off in divergent directions. **fanbelt,** *n.* a belt which drives the radiator fan and generator in a car engine. **fan-blast,** *n.* the blast produced by a rotatory fan in a furnace etc. **fan-blower,** *n.* an apparatus in which a series of vanes fixed on a rotating shaft create a blast of air. **fan dance,** *n.* a titillating dance by a nude solo performer manipulating a large fan or fans. **fan heater,** *n.* an electric heater in which the heat from the element is dispersed by a fan. **fan-jet,** *n.* (an aircraft with) a jet engine with rotating fans in which some of the air sucked in bypasses the combustion chamber. **fanlight,** *n.* a window with divisions in the shape of an open fan; the light placed over a doorway. **fanning-machine, -mill,** *n.* a winnowing-machine. **fan-palm,** *n.* a name applied to all palms having fan-shaped leaves, as *Chamaerops humilis,* esp. the genus *Corypha* typified by the talipot, *C. umbraculifera,* from Sri Lanka and Malabar. **fantail,** *n.* a variety of the domestic pigeon; an Australian flycatcher of the genus *Rhidipura;* a form of gas-burner giving a broad, flat flame; a fan-shaped joint or mortise; a coal-heaver's hat with a large flap behind, a sort of sou'wester. **fan-tailed,** *a.* **fan-vaulting,** *n.* (*Arch.*) vaulting in which the tracery spreads out like a fan from springers or corbels. **fanner,** *n.* one who or that which fans; a winnowing-machine. [OE *fann,* L *vannus,* a winnowing-fan]

fan², *n.* an enthusiastic admirer; a devotee. **fan club,** *n.* an organized group of devotees. **fan mail,** *n.* adulatory letters to a celebrity from admirers. [abbr. of FANATIC]

†**fanal,** *n.* a small lighthouse; a beacon; a ship's lantern. [F, from It. *fanale,* med. L *fanāle,* Gr. *phanos,* a lantern (*phainein,* to shine)]

fanatic, *a.* wild or extravagant in opinions, esp. on religious matters; enthusiastic in the extreme; extravagant, bigoted. *n.* a person affected with fanaticism. **fanatical,** *a.* **fanatically,** *adv.* **fanaticism,** *n.* **fanaticize, -ise,** *v.t.* to render fanatical. *v.i.* to become a fanatic. [F *fanatique,* L *fānāticus,* from *fānum,* a temple]

fancy, *n.* the faculty or the act of forming images, esp. those of a playful, frivolous or capricious kind; imagination as an inventive and comparative power, distinguished from creative imagination; a mental image; a visionary idea or supposition; a delusion, a baseless impression, a caprice, a whim; a personal inclination, liking or attachment; a fad, a hobby; †artistic invention, fantasy; †taste, aesthetic feeling; †fantasticalness; †love; †a short piece of music, esp. of an impromptu kind. *v.t.* to form as a conception in the mind, to picture to oneself; to be inclined to think, to suppose; to imagine or believe erroneously; to think a good deal of (oneself etc.); to like, to take a fancy to, to be attracted to; to breed as a hobby or sport. †*v.i.* to love. *a.* adapted to please the fancy rather than for use; ornamental, decorative; not plain. **fancy!, just fancy!** an expression of surprise. **the fancy,** sporting characters generally, esp. pugilists, pugilism, dog-fanciers etc. **to fancy oneself,** to have a good opinion of oneself. **to take a fancy to,** to conceive a liking or an affection for, to desire. **to tickle one's fancy,** to attract. **fancy dress,** *n.* masquerade costume. **fancy-dress ball,** *n.* **fancy fair** FAIR. **fancy-free,** *a.* not in love, not involved in a relationship, hence able to do as one likes. **fancy-goods,** *n.pl.* articles of a showy rather than a useful kind; ornamental fabrics such as ribbons, coloured silks etc. **fancy man,** *n.* (*derog.*) a woman's lover; a prostitute's pimp, a ponce. **fancy price,** *n.* a capricious or extravagant price. †**fancy-sick,** *a.* distempered in mind; love-sick. **fancy stocks,** *n.pl.* (*N Am.*) stocks having no intrinsic or determinate value, and therefore affording an opportunity for stock-gambling. **fancystore,** *n.* (*N Am.*) a store or shop where fancygoods are sold. **fancy-woman,** *n.* (*derog.*) a kept mistress. **fancy work,** *n.* ornamental knitting, embroidery, crocheting etc. **fancier,** *n.* one who breeds or sells birds, dogs, rabbits etc. for their special points; a connoisseur, an amateur (*usu. in comb.*, as *bird-fancier*). **fanciful,** *a.* dictated by or arising in the fancy; baseless, unreal, imaginary; indulging in fancies; whimsical, fantastical. **fancifully,** *adv.* **fancifulness,** *n.* †**fanciless,** *a.* without fancy; unimaginative. [corr. of FANTASY]

fandangle, *n.* a gaudy trinket, a gewgaw; a nonsensical idea or behaviour. [prob. coined from foll.]

fandango, *n.* a lively Spanish dance in triple time, for two persons who beat time with castanets; the accompaniment of such a dance. [Sp., prob. from native African]

fane, *n.* (*poet.*) a temple, a place of worship, a sanctuary. [L *fānum*]

fanfare, *n.* a flourish of trumpets or bugles; †ostentation, parade; (*Mus.*) a certain flourish in opera; any short, prominent passage of the brass. [F, prob. onomat.]

fanfaronade, *n.* swaggering, blustering or boasting; ostentation; †a fanfare. *v.i.* to make a flourish or noisy display. †**fanfaron,** *n.* a boaster, a bully. [F *fanfaronnade,* from *fanfaron,* as prec.]

fang, *n.* a tusk or long pointed tooth: the canine tooth of a dog, wolf or boar; the long, hollow or grooved tooth through which a poisonous snake injects its venom; a curved spike, the point of any device for seizing or holding; the part of a tooth embedded in the gum; †a grip, a clutch. *v.t.* †to catch, to snare; †to seize; to strike the fangs into; (*Sc.*) to put water into (a pump) to make it work. **fanged,** *a.* furnished with fangs. **fangless,** *a.* [OE, a taking or seizing (cp. Dut. *vangen,* G *fangen,* to catch)]

†**fangle,** *n.* a trifle, a fancy, a gewgaw; a fashion, a crotchet. *v.t.* to trick out fancifully. †**fangled,** *a.* crotchety, fantastical. **fanglement,** *n.* [NEWFANGLE under NEW]

fanlight FAN[1].

fanny, *n.* (*taboo*) the female genitals; (*sl.*) the buttocks. [*Fanny,* nickname for *Frances*]

Fanny Adams, *n.* (*Naut., sl.*) tinned mutton; (*usu.* **sweet Fanny Adams**) (*sl.*) nothing at all, euphem. for *fuck-all.* [from the name of a young murder victim whose body was cut up into small pieces]

fanon, *n.* in the Roman Catholic Church, a maniple or napkin used by the officiating priest at Mass; later, an embroidered band attached to the wrist of the celebrant. [F, from med. L *fanō fanōnem,* a napkin, OHG *fano*]

fan-tan, *n.* a Chinese gambling game. [Chin.]

fantasia, *n.* (*Mus.*) a composition in which form is subservient to fancy. [It., FANTASY]

†**fantasm,** PHANTASM.

fantastic, *a.* fanciful, whimsical, capricious; odd, grotesque; uncertain, fickle, capricious, arbitrary; extravagant; wonderful, very good, very enjoyable; †illusory, imaginary. *n.* a fanciful, extravagant or absurd person; a fop. **fantastical,** *a.* **fantasticality,** *n.* **fantastically,** *adv.* **fantasticalness,** *n.* **fantasticism,** *n.* †**fantastico,** *n.* (*pl.* **-coes**) a fantastic. [as foll.]

fantasy, (*esp. formerly*) **phantasy,** *n.* an extravagant, whimsical or bizarre fancy, image or idea; the faculty of inventing or forming fanciful images; a mental image or daydream which gratifies a psychological need; a fanciful or whimsical invention or design; a novel, drama, film etc. characterized by strange, unrealistic, alien or grotesque characters and settings; such works collectively; (*Mus.*) a fantasia; a visionary idea or speculation; †a hallucination, a delusive vision; a caprice, whim. **fantasize, -ise,** *v.i.* to conjure up and indulge in gratifying mental images; to dream up fantastic (and usu. impracticable) schemes, ideas etc. **fantasist,** *n.* [OF *fantasie,* L, from Gr. *phantasia,* from *phantazein,* to make visible, from *phainein,* to show]

Fanti, Fante, *n.* (*pl.* **Fantis, Fantes,** *collectively* **Fanti, Fante**) (the language of) a member of a Ghanaian tribe.

fantoccini, *n.pl.* puppets or marionettes made to perform by concealed wires or strings; dramatic representations at which such puppets are made to perform. [It., pl. of *fantoccino,* dim. of *fantoccio,* a puppet, from *fante,* a lad]

fantom, PHANTOM.

fanzine, *n.* a magazine for fans of a celebrity. [FAN[2], maga*zine*]

FAO (*abbr.*) Food and Agriculture Organization (of the United Nations).

Fao, Faw *n.* an oil port on a peninsula at the mouth of the Shatt al-Arab in Iraq. Iran launched a major offensive against Iraq in 1986, capturing Fao for two years.

faquir, FAKIR.

far, *a.* (*comp.* **farther, further,** *superl.* **farthest, furthest**) distant, a long way off; separated by a wide space; extending or reaching a long way; more distant of two, other, opposite; remote from or contrary to one's purpose, intention or wishes; †remote in affection; alienated. *adv.* at or to a great distance in space, time or proportion; to a great degree, very greatly, by a great deal; by a great interval, widely. *n.* a long distance, a distant place; a large amount, a great degree. **a far cry** CRY. **as far as,** up to (a certain point); to the extent that. **by far,** in a very great measure; very greatly; exceedingly. **far and away** AWAY. **far and wide,** everywhere. **far be it from me,** I would not even consider; I repudiate the intention (of doing something). **far from,** anything but, not at all; (*followed by pres.p.*) indicates that the speaker's actions or intentions are the opposite of those stated. **far from it,** on the contrary. **so far,** up to a specified point; up to now, hitherto. **so far as** AS FAR AS. **to go far,** to be successful (esp. in one's career); (*esp. in neg.*) to be sufficient for. **to go too far,** to exceed reasonable limits. **far-away,** *a.* remote in time, place or relationship, distant; dreamy, absent-minded. **far between,** *a.* at long intervals, infrequent. **Far East** EAST. **far-famed,** *a.* widely celebrated, renowned. †**far-fet,** *a.* subtle, deep. **far-fetched,** *a.* of reasons or arguments forced, unnatural, fanciful, fantastic. **far-flung,** *a.* extending to far-off places. **far-forth,** *adv.* to a great degree; to a (specified) extent. **far-gone,** *a.* in an advanced state (of exhaustion, illness, wear etc.). **far left,** *n.* the extreme left wing of a political party etc. *a.* holding very left-wing views. **Far North,** *n.* the Arctic regions. **far-off,**

a. distant, remote. *adv.* at or to a great distance. **far-out,** *a.* (*sl.*) unconventional, eccentric, weird; (*also int.*) wonderful, great. **far-reaching,** *a.* having broad scope, influence or implications, extensive, thorough-going. **far right,** *n.* the extreme right wing of a political party etc. *a.* holding very right-wing views. **far-seeing, -sighted,** *a.* seeing to a great distance; (*fig.*) looking far ahead; provident for remote issues. **far-sightedly,** *adv.* **far-sightedness,** *n.* **Far South,** *n.* the Antarctic regions. **Far West,** *n.* that part of the United States lying west of the Mississippi. *a.* lying to the west of the Mississippi; pertaining to the Far West. **farness,** *n.* [OE *feor* (cp. Dut. *ver,* Icel. *fjarri,* G *fern,* also Gr. *peran,* beyond)]

farad, *n.* the practical unit of capacitance, the capacity of a condenser in which the electrical potential is raised 1 volt by the addition of 1 coulomb. **faradic,** *a.* of an electric current, inductive. **faradize, -ise,** *v.t.* to stimulate (the muscles) with faradic currents. **faradization, -isation,** *n.* [Michael *Faraday,*]

Faraday, *n.* **Michael** (1791–1867), English chemist and physicist. In 1821 he began experimenting with electromagnetism, and ten years later discovered the induction of electric currents and made the first dynamo. He subsequently found that a magnetic field will rotate the plane of polarization of light. Faraday also investigated electrolysis.

Faraday's laws, *n.pl.* three laws of electromagnetic induction, and two laws of electrolysis, all proposed originally by Michael Faraday. **induction** (1) a changing magnetic field induces an electromagnetic force in a conductor; (2) the electromagnetic force is proportional to the rate of change of the field; (3) the direction of the induced electromagnetic force depends on the orientation of the field. **electrolysis** (1) the amount of chemical change during electrolysis is proportional to the charge passing through the liquid; (2) the amount of chemical change produced in a substance by a given amount of electricity is proportional to the electrochemical equivalent of that substance.

farandine, FERRANDINE.

farandole, *n.* a lively Provençal dance. [Prov. *farandoulo*]

farce[1]**,** *n.* a short dramatic work in which the action is trivial and the sole purpose to excite mirth; drama of this kind; an absurd proceeding; a pretence, mockery, hollow formality. **farcical,** *a.* of or pertaining to farce; ludicrous, droll, comical; ridiculous, absurd, contemptible. **farcicality,** *n.* **farcically,** *adv.* [F, orig. stuffing, hence, an interlude or an inserted jest, from *farcer,* L *farcīre,* to stuff]

farce[2] *v.t.* to stuff (poultry etc.) with forcemeat; †to cram, to stuff; †to season (a literary composition). **farcing,** *n.* stuffing; forcemeat. [OF *farcir,* as prec.]

farceur, *n.* a joker, a jester, a wag. **farceuse,** *n.fem.* [F, as prec.]

farcy, -cin, *n.* a disease in horses, closely allied to glanders. **farcy-bud, -button,** *n.* a little tumour on the face, neck or inside of the thigh in horses, generally the first indication of farcy. [F *farcin,* L *farcīminum,* from *farcīre,* to stuff]

fard, *n.* paint or rouge for the face, esp. white paint. *v.t.* to paint (the face) with this; to beautify; to hide the blemishes of. [F, prob. from or rel. to OHG *gifarwit,* p.p. of *farwjan,* to paint]

†**fardel,** *n.* a bundle, a pack, a burden. [OF, dim. of *farde,* a burden (F *fardeau*), perh. from Arab. *fardah,* a package]

†**fardingale,** FARTHINGALE.

fare, *v.i.* to go, to travel; to get on, to be in any state, to happen, to turn out (well or ill); to be entertained; to live as regards food and drink; to feed or be fed (well etc.). *n.* the sum paid for conveyance on a journey, passage-money; the person or persons conveyed in a vehicle for hire; food provided; †a going, a journey; †condition, hap, welfare; the quantity of fish taken in a fishing-boat. [OE *faran* (cp. Dut. *varen,* OHG *faran,* G *fahren,* also Gr. *poros,* a way, L *portāre,* to carry)]

farewell, *int.* adieu, good-bye; orig. and properly addressed to one about to start on a journey, now a common formula of leave-taking; used also as expression of simple separation, and in the sense of 'no more of', 'good-bye to'. *n.* a good-bye, an adieu. *a.* valedictory. [as prec.]

Fargo, *n.* **William George** (1818–81), US transport pioneer. In 1844 he established with Henry Wells (1805–78) and Daniel Dunning the first express company to carry freight west of Buffalo. Its success led to his appointment in 1850 as secretary of the newly established American Express Company, of which he was president (1868–81). He also established Wells Fargo & Company in 1851, carrying goods express between New York and San Francisco via Panama.

farina, *n.* flour or meal; the powder obtained by grinding the seeds of gramineous and leguminous plants, nuts, roots etc.; any powdery substance; pollen; starch. **farinaceous,** *a.* **farinaceously,** *adv.* **farinose,** *a.* producing farina; (*Nat. Hist.*) covered with a meal-like dust, floury, meally. [L, from *far,* corn, spelt]

farl, *n.* (*Sc.*) orig. the quarter of a cake of oatmeal or flour; a cake of this kind and size. [corr. of obs. *fardel,* OE *fēortha,* FOURTH]

farm, *n.* a tract of land used under one management for cultivating crops or rearing livestock (orig. used only of land under lease); a farmhouse; a place where children are lodged or looked after; an area of land or water where a particular kind of animal or fish is bred; †the system of letting out revenues or taxes; †an annual sum paid as composition by a collector or by a town or district in respect of taxes; †a district farmed out for the collection of revenue; †a lease. *v.t.* to till, to cultivate, to take (land) on lease for cultivating; to lease or let out (as taxes, offices etc.) at a fixed sum or rate per cent; to take the proceeds of (taxes, offices etc.) for such a fixed sum or rate; to let out (labourers) on hire; to contract for the feeding, lodging etc. of (as children) at so much per head. *v.i.* to be a farmer. **home-farm,** a farm occupied and cultivated by the owner of a larger estate. **to farm out,** to delegate, to contract out; to board out, to put into someone's care. **farm hand, labourer,** *n.* an agricultural labourer employed on a farm. **farmhouse,** *n.* a dwelling-house attached to a farm. **farmstead,** *n.* a farm with the dwelling and other buildings on it. **farmyard,** *n.* a yard or open area surrounded by or adjacent to farm buildings. **farmer,** *n.* one who farms or cultivates land; one who contracts to collect taxes, imposts etc. at a certain rate per cent. **farmer-general,** *n.* one of a company who, under the French monarchy, contracted for the right of levying certain taxes in a particular district. **farming,** *n.* the business of cultivating land. [A-F and OF *ferme* (*à ferme,* on lease), med. L *firma,* orig. a fixed payment (cp. FIRM[1]), L *firmus,* firm, durable]

Farmer, *n.* **Frances** (1913–70), US actress who starred in such films as *Come and Get It* (1936), *The Toast of New York* (1937), and *Son of Fury* (1942), before her career was ended by alcoholism and mental illness.

Farnese, *n.* an Italian family who held the duchy of Parma from 1545–1731.

faro, *n.* a game at cards in which persons play against the dealer. [PHARAOH]

Faroe Islands, Faroes (Danish **Færøerne**), or **Faeroe Islands, Faeroes,** *n.pl.* island group (18 out of 22 inhabited) in the N Atlantic, between the Shetland Islands and Iceland, forming an outlying part of Denmark. **area** 1399 sq km/540 sq miles; largest islands are Strømø, Østerø, Vagø, Suderø, Sandø, and Bordø. **capital** Thorshavn on Strømø, population (1986) 15,287. **population** (1986) 46,000. **exports** fish, crafted goods. **language** Færøese, Danish.

farouche, *a.* wild, untamed; (*coll.*) unsociable, unmannerly, brutal. [F, from L *ferox,* ferocious]

Farouk, *n.* (1920–65), king of Egypt from 1936–52. He succeeded his father Fuad I. In 1952 he was compelled to abdicate, his son Fuad II being temporarily proclaimed in his stead.

Farquhar, *n.* **George** (1677–1707), Irish dramatist. His most famous plays, *The Recruiting Officer* (1706), and

The Beaux' Stratagem (1707), are in the tradition of the Restoration comedy of manners, although less robust.

farrago, *n.* (*pl.* **-goes**) a confused mixture, a medley. **farraginous**, *a.* [L, mixed fodder, a medley, from *far*, spelt]

far-reaching FAR.

Farrell, *n.* **James T(homas)** (1904–79), US novelist. His naturalistic 'Studs Lonigan' trilogy (1932–35), comprising *Young Lonigan, The Young Manhood of Studs Lonigan*, and *Judgement Day*, describes the growing up of a young Catholic man in Chicago after World War I.

farrier, *n.* one who shoes horses; a shoeing smith who is also a horse-doctor; a non-commissioned officer in charge of the horses in a cavalry regiment. *v.i.* to practise as a farrier. **farriery,** *n.* the occupation of a farrier; a farrier's shop, a smithy. [OF *ferrier,* L *ferrārius,* from *ferrum,* iron]

farrow, *n.* a litter of pigs; the act of bringing forth a litter of pigs. *v.t.* to bring forth (as pigs). *v.i.* to bring forth pigs. [OE *fearh,* a pig (cp. Dut. *varken,* OHG *farah,* also L. *porcus*)]

†**farse,** *n.* (*Eccles. Ant.*) the explanation in the vernacular inserted between the Latin sentences of the epistle. *v.t.* to furnish (an epistle etc.) with such passages; to insert (such a passage). [FARCE[2]]

far-sighted FAR.

fart, *v.i.* (*sl., sometimes considered taboo*) to break wind through the anus. *n.* (*sl., sometimes considered taboo*) a discharge of wind from the anus; (*sl.*) an unpleasant, stupid or boring person. **to fart about,** (*sl.*) to behave foolishly, to waste time. [OE *feortan,* cp. OHG *verzen,* G *farzen,* also Gr. *perdein*]

farther, *a.* more distant or remote; more extended; additional. *adv.* at or to a greater distance, extent or degree; (now usu. **further**) in addition, moreover, besides, also. *v.t.* to further. **farthest,** *a.* the most distant. *n.* the greatest distance, the latest, the most. *adv.* at or to the greatest distance. [var. of FURTHER]

farthing, *n.* the fourth part of an old penny, the smallest British copper coin (withdrawn in 1961); the smallest possible amount; †an old division of land. **farthingsworth,** *n.* as much as was sold for a farthing; a matter of trifling moment. [OE *fēorthing, fēortha,* FOURTH]

farthingale, *n.* a hooped skirt used to extend the wide gown and petticoat of the 16th cent. [OF *verdugale,* corr. of Sp. *verdugado,* from *verdugo,* a rod]

fasc., (*abbr.*) fasciculus.

fasces, *n.pl.* the ancient insignia of the Roman lictors, consisting of a bundle of elm or birch rods, in the middle of which was an axe; an emblem of authority. [L, pl. of *fascis,* a bundle (see foll.)]

fascia, *n.* (*pl.* **fasciae**) a thin, tendon-like sheath surrounding the muscles and binding them in their places; a band, belt, sash, fillet; the nameboard above a shop; (*Arch.*) a flat surface in an entablature or elsewhere, a facia; the belt of a planet; a bandage or ligature; the instrument board of a car. **fasciated,** *a.* (*Bot.*) flattened by the growing together of several parts; striped. **fasciation,** *n.* union of stems or branches in a ribbon-like form; binding up of diseased or injured parts; a bandage. [L, a band, conn. with *fas,* that which is binding]

fascicle, fascicule, *n.* a small bundle, cluster or group; a cluster of leaves, flowers etc., a tuft; (*Anat.*) a bundle of fibres; a serial division of a book sold separately. **fascicled,** *a.* clustered together in a fascicle. **fascicular**, *a.* **fasciculate, -lated**, *a.* (*Nat. Hist.*) collected in clusters, small bundles or bunches. **fasciculation,** *n.* [FASCICULUS]

fasciculus, *n.* (*pl.* **-li**) a bundle or package; a division of a book sold separately. [L, dim. of *fascis,* see FASCES]

fascinate, *v.t.* to exercise an irresistible influence over; of snakes etc., to deprive of volitional power by magic or by means of look or presence; to captivate, to attract irresistibly, to enchant, to charm. **fascinating,** *a.* irresistibly attractive, charming, bewitching. **fascinatingly,** *adv.* **fascination,** *n.* **fascinator,** *n.* one who or that which fascinates; a light covering for the head worn by women. [L *fascinātus,* p.p. of *fascināre,* from *fascinum,* a spell]

fascine, *n.* a cylindrical faggot of brushwood bound with withes, and used in building earthworks, for filling trenches, protecting riverbanks etc. [F, from L *fascīna,* a bundle of sticks, from *fascis*]

Fascism, *n.* a theory of government introduced into Italy by Benito Mussolini in 1922. Its object was to oppose socialism and communism by controlling every form of national activity. It was anti-democratic in principle, permitting no other party to exist and tolerating no opposition; (usu. **fascism**) any ideology or system regarded as brutal, repressive, excessively nationalistic or militaristic. **fascist, -istic,** *a.* **Fascist,** *n.* a member of a fascist party; (usu. **fascist**) one who advocates brutal or repressive policies, or (*loosely*) is regarded as holding very right-wing, illiberal views. [It. *Fascismo,* from *fascio,* L *fascis,* a bundle]

fash, *v.t.* (*chiefly Sc.*) to vex, to annoy; to trouble, to bother. *v.i.* to take trouble; to be vexed. *n.* trouble, pains, inconvenience, vexation. [OF *fascher* (F *fâcher*), ult. from L *fastidium,* from *fastus,* arrogance]

fashion, *n.* the form, make, style or external appearance of any thing; mode, manner, way, pattern; the prevailing style or mode of dress; custom, usage, prevailing practice, esp. in dress; the conventional usages of polite society; the usages prevailing at a given period; genteel or fashionable society; †kind, sort. *v.t.* to give shape and form to; to frame, to mould; to fit, to adapt; †to make or form according to the rules prescribed by custom; †to counterfeit, to pervert; †to contrive. **after, in a fashion,** in a way; middling, rather badly; somehow or other. **after the fashion of,** in the same way as; like. **in, out of fashion,** conforming or not conforming to the prevailing mode. **to set the fashion,** to set the example in a new style of dress or behaviour. †**fashion-monger,** *n.* one who affects the fashion; a fop, a dandy. **fashion-plate,** *n.* a picture illustrating a style in dress; an ultra-fashionably dressed woman. **fashionable,** *a.* conforming to or observant of the fashion or established mode; made according to the fashion; characteristic of, approved by, or patronized by people of fashion. †*n.* a person of fashion. **fashionableness,** *n.* **fashionably,** *adv.* **-fashioned,** *comb. form* made or shaped (in a certain way). †**fashioner,** *n.* one who fashions or gives shape to anything. †**fashionist,** *n.* **fashionless,** *a.* without shape or fashion. [OF *faceon,* L *factiōnem,* nom. *-tio,* a making, from *facere,* to make (cp. FACTION)]

-fashion, *comb. form* in the manner of, like.

Fashoda Incident, *n.* dispute in 1898 in a town in the Sudan, now known as Kodok, then called Fashoda, in which French forces under Colonel Marchand clashed with British, under Lord Kitchener. Although originally a disagreement over local territorial claims, it almost led the two countries into war.

Fassbinder, *n.* **Rainer Werner** (1946–82), West German film director, who began his career as a fringe actor and founded his own 'anti-theatre' before moving into films. His works are mainly stylized indictments of contemporary German society. He made over 30 films, including *Die bitteren Tränen der Petra von Kant/The Bitter Tears of Petra von Kant* (1972) and *Die Ehe von Maria Braun/The Marriage of Maria Braun* (1979).

fast[1], *a.* firmly fixed, firm, tight; firmly adhering, faithful, steady, close; lasting, durable, permanent, unfading, not washing out; swift, rapid, moving quickly; taking a short time; promoting quick motion, as a billiard-table, cricket-pitch etc.; imparting quick motion, as a bowler, pitcher etc.; of a clock etc., showing a time ahead of the true time; of photographic film, requiring a short exposure time; of a camera shutter, permitting short exposure times; dissipated, rakish, pleasure-seeking, promiscuous; acquired with little effort or by shady means. *adv.* firmly, tightly, securely; quickly, swiftly, in rapid succession; in a dissipated manner, so as to expend one's energies quickly. *n.* anything which fastens or holds; (*Naut.*) a hawser securing a vessel to the shore. **fast and furious,** vigorous and eventful, noisy or heated. **fast asleep,** sound or firmly asleep. †**fast beside, by,** close, very near. **fast-breeder reactor,** a nuclear reactor which produces at least as much fissionable material as it consumes. **to make fast,** to fasten securely, to tie. **to play fast and loose** PLAY. **to pull a fast one,** (*coll.*) to trick, to use underhand methods. **fastback,** *n.* (a car with) a back which forms a continuous slope from roof to bumper. **fast food,** *n.* food, e.g. burgers and chicken pieces, which can be prepared and served very quickly. **fast-food,** *a.* serving fast food. **fast-forward,** *n., a.* (a switch) enabling video or recording tape to be wound on very rapidly. †**fast-handed,** *a.* close-fisted, avaricious. **fast lane,** *n.* a part of the carriageway used by fast-moving traffic, esp. the outer lane of a motorway. **in the fast lane,** (*coll.*) pace of life particularly fast, exciting, risky. **fast neutron,** *n.* a neutron with high kinetic energy. **fast-talk,** *n., v.t.* (*chiefly N Am., coll.*) (to persuade by) fluent, forceful (and often facile) speech. **fast train,** *n.* an express train. **fast worker,** *n.* a person who gets things done quickly; (*coll.*) one who makes rapid progress in relations with the opposite sex. **fastish,** *a.* rather fast or dissipated. **fastness,** *n.* the quality or state of being fast or secure; a fortress, a stronghold, esp. in a remote and inaccessible place. [OE *fæst*]

fast[2], *v.i.* to abstain from food; to abstain entirely or partially from food voluntarily for a certain time for the mortification of the body or as a token of grief, affliction or penitence. *n.* a (period of) total or partial abstinence from or deprivation of food, esp. from religious motives; a time set apart for fasting; any holy time or season. **fast day,** *n.* a day appointed as a fast; (*Sc.*) a day of humiliation and prayer in preparation for Holy Communion. **fasting,** *n.* [OE *fæstan* (cp, Dut. *vasten,* Icel. *fasta,* G *fasten,* from Goth. *fastan,* in the sense of to be firm, strict)]

fasten, *v.t.* to fix firmly to make fast, to attach; to secure, as by a bolt, a lock, a tie, knot etc.; to fix or set firmly or earnestly. *v.i.* to become fast; to seize, to lay hold (upon). **to fasten on,** to lay hold on; to become aware of and concentrate one's attention on; to attach (blame, responsibility, nickname etc.) to. **fastener,** *n.* one who or that which fastens, makes fast or secures. **fastening,** *n.* the act of making fast or secure; anything which makes fast or secure, as a bolt, bar, strap, catch etc. [OE *fæstnian* (prec., -EN)]

Fastext®, *n.* a page-searching system used with teletext that facilitates rapid access to the desired information.

fasti, *n.pl.* (*Rom. Ant.*) the calendar of days when legal business might be transacted; the register of events during the official year; hence, annals, chronological records of events. [L, pl. of *fastus* (*dies*), lawful (day)]

fastidious, *a.* difficult to please; extremely careful, delicate, refined, esp. in matters of taste; squeamish, easily disgusted; †disgusting, loathsome. **fastidiously,** *adv.* **fastidiousness,** *n.* [L *fastīdiōsus,* from *fastīdium,* loathing]

fastigiate, *a.* (*Bot.*) tapering to a point like a pyramid. **fastigium,** *n.* (*pl.* **-gia**) the pediment of a portico; the ridge of a roof; (*Path.*) the period of highest temperature in a fever or illness. [L *fastīgium,* the apex of a gable]

fat[1], *a.* (*comp.* **fatter,** *superl.* **fattest**) plump, fleshy, corpulent, full-fed; of animals, fed up for killing; oily, greasy, unctuous; resinous; of coal, bituminous; of clay etc., sticky, plastic; of printing type, thick, broad-faced; prosperous, thriving, rich, affluent; producing a large income; fertile, fruitful, rich; substantial, rewarding; (*Print.*) applied to a page having many blank spaces or lines, hence to any work that pays well; dull, stupid, lazy, sluggish; †of a room, close. *n.* an animal substance of a more or less oily character, deposited in vesicles in adipose tissue; the fat part of anything; the best or choicest part of anything; that part of anything which is deemed redundant or excessive; (*Print.*) matter profitable to the compositor; a part that gives an actor opportunity to display his or her powers; an organic compound of glycerine with one of a group of acids. *v.t.* to make fat or plump; to fatten. *v.i.* to become fat, to gain flesh. **a fat lot,** (*coll., iron.*) very little. **the fat is in the fire,** (*coll.*) there's going to be trouble. **to live off the fat of the land,** to have the best of everything, esp. in terms of food. **fat-brained,** *a.* dull of apprehension. **fat cat,** *n.* (*chiefly N Am., coll.*) a wealthy person, esp. one who contributes to political campaigns. **fat chance,** *n., int.* (*iron.*) very little or no chance. **fat-faced,** *a.* having a plump round face. **fat-head,** *n.* dull, stupid fellow. **fat-hen,** *n.* kinds of goose-foot or *Chenopodium,* esp. Australian varieties used for food. †**fat-kidneyed,** *a.* gross, corpulent, obese. **fat-witted,** *a.* stupid, dull, slow. **fatling,** *n.* a young animal fattened for slaughter; a fattened animal. †*a.* fat, plump. **fatness,** *n.* **fatten,** *v.t.* to make fat, to feed for the table; to make (ground) fruitful, to fertilize. *v.i.* to grow or become fat, to gain flesh. **fattish,** *a.* somewhat fat. **fatty,** *a.* consisting of or having the qualities of fat; greasy, unctuous; adipose. *n.* (*coll.*) a fat person. **fatty acid,** *n.* any of a class of aliphatic, carboxylic acids, e.g. palmitic acid, acetic acid. **fatty degeneration,** *n.* the abnormal conversion of the protein elements into a granular fatty matter. [OE *fæt, fætt,* OFris. *fat,* Dut. *vet,* G *fett*]

fat[2], *n.* a vat, tub, barrel; a measure of capacity differing for different commodities. [VAT]

fatal, fatalism etc. FATE.

fata Morgana, *n.* a mirage observed from the harbour of Messina and adjacent places, and supposed by the Sicilians to be the work of the fairy Morgana; objects reflected in the sea, and sometimes in a kind of aerial screen high above it. [It., *fata,* a fairy, *Morgana,* the legendary sister of King Arthur, famed for her magical powers]

fate, *n.* the power by which the course of events is unalterably predetermined; destiny, lot, fortune; one's ultimate condition as brought about by circumstances and events; what is destined to happen; death, destruction; (*pl.* **the Fates**) the Parcae or Destinies, three Greek goddesses supposed to preside over the birth, life and fortunes of men Clotho held the spindle, Atropos drew out the thread of man's destiny, and Lachesis cut it off. *v.t.* (*usu. pl.*) to decree by fate or destiny; to destine to destruction. **fatal,** *a.* decreed by fate, inevitable; fateful, decisive; foreboding ruin or destruction; causing death or ruin, mortal; having unwelcome consequences. **fatalism,** *n.* the doctrine that events are predetermined and beyond human control; submission to fate. **fatalist,** *n.* **fatalistic,** *a.* **fatalistically,** *adv.* **fatality,** *n.* a fixed, unalterable course of things; predetermination by fate esp. to death or disaster; deadliness; a (person who suffers) death by accident or violence. **fated,** *a.* decreed by fate, predetermined; doomed to destruction; fatal, fateful; †exempted by fate; †invested with the power of determining fate or destiny. **fateful,** *a.* having momentous or catastrophic consequences; bringing death or destruction. **fatefully,** *adv.* †**fatefulness,** *n.* [L *fātum,* orig. neut. p.p. of *fārī,* to speak]

father, *n.* a male parent; he who begets a child; a male ancestor, a patriarch; the first to practise any art; an originator, author, contriver, an early leader; a respectful mode of address to an old man or any man deserving great reverence; the title of the senators of ancient Rome; one who exercises paternal care; a stepfather; a father-in-law; the senior member of any profession or body; the First Person of the Trinity; a priest, a confessor, the superior of a convent, a religious teacher etc.; (*pl.*) elders, senators, the leading men (of a city etc.). *v.t.* to beget; to be or act as father of; to adopt as a child; to originate; to adopt or assume as one's own child, work etc.; to accept responsibility for. **Conscript Fathers,** the Roman senators. **father-in-law,** *n.* the father of one's husband or wife. **father of lies,** Satan. **father of the chapel** CHAPEL. **Fathers of the Church,** the ecclesiastical writers of the early church. **how's your father,** (*coll., facet.*) illicit goings-on, esp. of a sexual nature. **Right, Most Rever-**

end Father in God, the formal title of a bishop or archbishop. **the Holy Father,** the Pope. **to father (up)on,** to suggest that someone is responsible for. **Father Christmas** SANTA CLAUS. **father confessor,** *n.* a priest who hears confessions; a person to whom one confides intimate matters. **father figure,** *n.* an older man whom one looks to for advice and support. **fatherland,** *n.* one's native country. **Father's day,** *n.* the third Sunday in June. **father superior,** *n.* the head of a religious house. **fatherhood,** *n.* the condition of being a father; the character or authority of a father. **fatherless,** *a.* having no living father; without any known author. **fatherlessness,** *n.* **fatherly,** *a.* like a father; proper to or becoming a father; kind, tender, loving. *adv.* in the manner of a father. **fatherliness,** *n.* **fathership,** *n.* [OE *fæder* (cp. Dut. *vader,* G *Vater,* L *pater,* Gr. *patēr*)]

fathom, *n.* a measure of length, 6 ft. (1·8 m) used principally in nautical and mining measurements; 6 ft. (1·8 m) square, as a measure of wood in section independently of length; †depth; penetration. *v.t.* †to embrace, to encompass with the extended arms; to ascertain the depth of; (often with *out*) to get to the bottom of, to penetrate, to comprehend. **fathom-line,** *n.* (*Naut.*) a sounding-line. **fathom-wood,** *n.* waste timber sold by fathom lots. †**fathomable,** *a.* **fathomless,** *a.* not to be fathomed. **fathomlessly,** *adv.* **fathometer,** *n.* an instrument for measuring the depth of the sea by sound waves. [OE *fæthm,* the space enclosed by the arms outstretched (cp. Dut. *vadem,* G *Faden,* also L *patēre,* to extend, Gr. *petannunai*)]

†**fatidic, -ical,** *a.* having the power to foretell future events; prophetic. **fatidically,** *adv.* [L *fātidicus* (*fātum,* FATE, *dic-,* root of *dīcere,* to speak)]

fatigue, *n.* weariness, exhaustion from bodily or mental exertion; toil or exertion causing weariness or exhaustion; labour not of a military nature performed by soldiers; a weakening in metals due to prolonged strain or repeated blows; (*pl.*) military overalls, fatigue-dress. *v.t.* to tire, to weary; to exhaust the strength of by bodily or mental exertion; to harass, to importune. **fatigue-dress,** *n.* the dress worn by soldiers on fatigue-duty. †**fatigate,** *v.t.* to weary, to tire out, to exhaust. *a.*, tired out, wearied, exhausted. **fatigueless,** *a.* **fatiguing,** *a.* [OF *fatiguer,* L *fatīgāre*]

Fatimid, *n.* dynasty of Muslim Shi'ite caliphs founded in 909 by Obaidallah, who claimed to be a descendant of Fatima, the prophet Mohammed's daughter, and her husband Ali, in N Africa. In 969 the Fatimids conquered Egypt, and the dynasty continued until overthrown by Saladin in 1171.

fatness, fatten etc. FAT[1].

fatuous, *a.* stupid, imbecile, foolish; meaningless, inane, silly. **fatuity,** *n.* **fatuitous,** *a.* **fatuously,** *adv.* **fatuousness,** *n.* [L *fatuus*]

fatwa FETWA.

faubourg, *n.* a suburb of a town; a part now within a city, but formerly outside the walls. [F]

fauces, *n.pl.* the hinder part of the mouth, terminated by the pharynx and larynx; the orifice or opening of a monopetalous flower; the opening into the first chamber of a shell. **faucal,** *a.* pertaining to the fauces or gullet; deeply guttural. [L]

faucet, *n.* (*chiefly N Am.*) a tap; a beer-tap. [F *fausset;* etym. doubtful]

faugh, *int.* an exclamation of disgust or abhorrence. [onomat.]

Faulkner[1], *n.* **Brian** (1921–77), Northern Ireland Unionist politician. He was the last prime minister of Northern Ireland (1971–72) before the Stormont Parliament was suspended.

Faulkner[2], *n.* **William** (1897–1962), US novelist. His works include *The Sound and the Fury* (1929), dealing with a Southern US family in decline, *As I Lay Dying* (1930), *Light in August* (1932), a study of segregation, *The Unvanquished* (1938), stories of the Civil War, and *The Hamlet* (1940), *The Town* (1957), and *The Mansion* (1959), a trilogy covering the rise of the materialist Snopes family. He wrote in an experimental stream-of-consciousness style, and was awarded the Nobel Prize for literature in 1949.

fault, *n.* a defect, blemish, imperfection; an error, failing, mistake or blunder; a slight offence or deviation from right or propriety; responsibility for a mistake or mishap, blame; loss of the scent in hunting; an improper service at tennis; a penalty point in showjumping; (*Teleg.*) a leak through broken insulation etc.; the sudden interruption of the continuity of strata till then upon the same plane, this being accompanied by a crack or fissure, usually filled with broken stone, clay or similar material. *v.i.* to commit a fault, to blunder; (*Geol.*) to undergo a break in continuity. *v.t.* (*Geol.*) to break the continuity of; to find a fault in, criticize. **at fault,** at a loss, puzzled, embarrassed; in error, to blame. **in fault,** to blame. **to find fault with,** to complain of, to blame, to censure, esp. in a carping manner. **fault-finder,** *n.* one given to fault-finding. **fault-finding,** *a.* censorious. *n.* censoriousness. †**faulter,** *n.* an offender; one who is in fault. †**faultful,** *a.* faulty, guilty, criminal. **faultless,** *a.* **faultlessly,** *adv.* **faultlessness,** *n.* **faulty,** *a.* **faultily,** *adv.* **faultiness,** *n.* [ME and OF *faute,* pop. L *fallita,* a defect, fem. p.p. of *fallere,* to FAIL[2]]

faun, *n.* one of a kind of demigods, or rural deities, bearing a strong resemblance in appearance and character to the satyrs, with whom they are generally identified. [L *Faunus,* a Latin rural deity whose attributes bear a strong analogy to those of Pan, with whom he is sometimes identified]

fauna, *n.* (*pl.* **-nas, -nae**) the animals found in or peculiar to a certain region or epoch; a treatise upon these. **faunal,** *a.* **faunist,** *n.* **faunistic,** *a.* [L, a Roman goddess, sister of Faunus]

Faunus, *n.* in Roman mythology, god of fertility and prophecy, with goat's ears, horns, tail and hind legs, identified with the Greek Pan.

Faust, *n.* a legendary magician. The historical Georg Faust appears to have been a wandering scholar and conjuror in Germany during the opening decade of the 16th century, but earlier figures such as Simon Magus (1st century AD, Middle Eastern practitioner of magic arts) contributed to the Faust legend.

faute de mieux, for lack of anything better. [F]

fauteuil, *n.* an easy, upholstered armchair; the chair or seat of a president; membership of the French Academy; an upholstered stall in a theatre etc. [F, from MF *fauldeteuil,* low L *faldistolium,* see FALDSTOOL]

fauvette, *n.* Bewick's generic name for the warbler family, adopted from the French. [F, from *fauve,* fallow]

Fauvism, *n.* a 20th-cent. art movement, characterized by vivid use of colour and a free treatment of form. **Fauvist,** *n.* [F *fauvisme,* from *fauve,* a wild beast]

faux pas, *n.* a blunder, a slip. [F]

faveolate, *a.* (*Bot.*) honeycombed, cellular. [from FAVUS, on anal. with F *faveole*]

favonian, *a.* of or pertaining to the west wind; hence, mild, auspicious. [L *favōniānus,* from *Favōnius,* the west wind]

favour, (*esp. N Am.*) **favor,** *n.* friendly regard, kindness, goodwill; countenance, approval; partiality, preference, excessive kindness or indulgence; a kind or indulgent act; aid, support, furtherance, facility, convenience for doing something; behalf, advantage (of); leave, consent; (*Comm.*) a letter, a communication; a token of love or affection, esp. something given by a lady to her lover; a knot of ribbons worn on any festive occasion; a small gift given to a guest at a party; (*pl.*) a woman's consent to sexual activity; †aspect, appearance, looks. *v.t.* to regard or behave toward with kindness; to befriend, to support; to facilitate; to promote; to oblige (with); to be propitious or fortunate for; to approve, to countenance, to show partiality to; to resemble in features; to avoid using, to treat with special care (as an injured limb). **in favour,** approved; approving. **in favour of,** approving, on the side of; to the account of; to the advantage of; in preference for. **out of favour,** disapproved. **to curry favour** CURRY[1]. **favourable,** *a.* friendly, well-disposed, encouraging;

propitious; approving, commending, consenting; tending to promote or encourage; convenient, advantageous; †well-favoured. **favourableness,** *n.* **favourably,** *adv.* **favoured,** *a.* **-favoured,** *comb. form* having a certain look or appearance, as in *ill-favoured, well-favoured.* **favouredly,** *adv.* **favouredness,** *n.* **favouring,** *a.* countenancing, supporting; resembling in features. **favouringly,** *adv.* †**favourless,** *a.* not regarded with favour; unfavourable; not propitious. [OF, from L *favor-ōrem,* from *favēre,* to show goodwill to]

favourite, *n.* a person or thing regarded with special affection, predilection or partiality; one chosen as a companion and intimate by a superior and unduly favoured; (*Sport*) the competitor considered to have the best chance, and against whom or which the shortest odds are offered. *a.* regarded with special favour; beloved; preferred before all others. **favouritism,** *n.* showing a special preference for a person or group, partiality. [OF *favorite,* fem. p.p. of *favorir,* to FAVOUR]

favus, *n.* (*Path.*) a disease of the scalp, characterized by pustules succeeded by cellular crusts bearing some resemblance to a honeycomb. [L, honeycomb]

Fawcett, *n.* **Millicent Garrett** (1847–1929), English suffragette, younger sister of Elizabeth Garrett (see ANDERSON). A non-militant, she rejected the violent acts of some of her contemporaries in the suffrage movement. She joined the first Women's Suffrage Committee in 1867 and became president of the Women's Unionist Association in 1889.

Fawkes, *n.* **Guy** (1570–1606), English conspirator, born in York. He converted to Roman Catholicism as a youth, and joined in the Gunpowder Plot to blow up King James I and the members of both Houses of Parliament. He was arrested in the cellar underneath the House on 4 Nov. 1605, tortured, and executed. The event is still commemorated in Britain with bonfires and fireworks on 5 Nov.

fawn[1], *n.* a young deer; a buck or doe in its first year; the colour of a young deer. *a.* like a fawn in colour, yellowish-brown. *v.t.* of deer, to bring forth. *v.i.* to bring forth a fawn. **fawn-colour,** *n.* **fawn-coloured,** *a.* [OF *fan, faon,* through low L from L *foetus,* FOETUS]

fawn[2], *v.i.* of animals, esp. dogs, to show affection by cringing, licking the hand etc.; (*usu. with upon*) to court in a servile manner, to grovel, to cringe. †*n.* a cringe, a bow; servile flattery. †**fawner,** *n.* **fawning,** *a.* courting servilely; flattering by cringing or meanness. *n.* servile flattery. **fawningly,** *adv.* [OE *fahnian,* from *fægen,* see FAIN]

fax, *n.* a system for electronically scanning, transmitting and reproducing documents etc. via a telephone line; a document etc. sent in this way. **fax machine,** *n.* [abbr. of *facsimile*]

fay[1], *n.* a fairy. [OF *fae* (F *fée*), L *fata,* the FATES]

†**fay[2],** *n.* faith; religious belief; allegiance. **by my fay,** a kind of oath or asseveration. [OF *fei, feid,* FAITH]

fay[3], *v.i.* (*N Am.*) to fit; (*dial.*) to suit, to get on well; (*Naut.*) to fit closely. *v.t.* (*Naut.*) to fit accurately. [OE *fēgan,* to join, unite (cp. Dut. *voegen,* G *fügen*)]

fayence, FAIENCE.

faze, *v.t.* (*chiefly N Am.*) to disconcert, to put off one's stroke.

FBA, (*abbr.*) Fellow of the British Academy.

FBI, (*abbr.*) Federal Bureau of Investigation (in US).

FC, (*abbr.*) Football Club; Forestry Commission.

FCA, (*abbr.*) Fellow of the Institute of Chartered Accountants.

FD, (*abbr.*) Defender of the Faith. [L *Fidei Defensor*]

Fe, (*chem. symbol*) iron. [L *ferrum*]

feague, *v.t.* to whip; (*fig.*) to confound, to settle the hash of. **to feague it away,** to work at high pressure. [cp. G *fegen,* Dut. *vogen*]

fealty, *n.* fidelity of a vassal or feudal tenant to his lord; fidelity, loyalty, allegiance. [OF *fealte,* L *fidēlitās -tātem,* FIDELITY]

fear[1], *n.* a painful apprehension of danger or of some impending evil; dread, a state of alarm; anxiety, solicitude; awe, reverence; an object of fear. *v.t.* to be afraid of, to dread; to shrink from, to hesitate (to do); to reverence, to venerate; to suspect, to doubt; †to terrify. *v.i.* to be afraid; to feel anxiety or solicitude; to doubt, to mistrust. **for fear,** in dread (that or lest); lest. **no fear,** (*coll.*) not likely; certainly not. **fear-naught,** *n.* a heavy, shaggy, woollen fabric, used for seamen's coats, for lining port-holes, doors of powder magazines etc. **fear-palsied, -shaken, -struck,** *a.* overwhelmed with fear †**fear-surprised,** *a.* suddenly overcome by fear. **feared,** *a.* regarded with fear; †afraid. **fearful,** *a.* timid, timorous; apprehensive, afraid (lest); †anxious, solicitous; †produced by or indicating fear; †full of fear (or reverence); terrible, awful, frightful; (*coll.*) extraordinary, unusual, annoying. **fearfully,** *adv.* **fearfulness,** *n.* **fearless,** *a.* **fearlessly,** *adv.* **fearlessness,** *n.* **fearsome,** *a.* fearful, terrible, alarming. **fearsomely,** *adv.* **fearsomeness,** *n.* [OE *fǣr,* danger, calamity (cp. G *Gefahr,* also L *perīculum*)]

†**fear[2],** FERE[1].

feasible, *a.* that may or can be done, practicable, possible; (*coll.*) manageable; likely, plausible. **feasibility,** *n.* †**feasibleness,** *n.* **feasibly,** *adv.* [OF *faisable,* from *fais,* stem of *faire,* L *facere,* to do]

feast, *n.* a sumptuous meal or entertainment of which a large number of persons partake, esp. a public banquet; an anniversary or periodical celebration of some great event or personage, esp. a religious anniversary; anything giving great enjoyment to body or mind. *v.t.* to entertain sumptuously; to gratify or please greatly, as with something delicious or luscious. *v.i.* to feed sumptuously; to be highly gratified or pleased. **immovable, movable feasts,** festivals or anniversaries occurring on a fixed date, as Christmas, or on varying dates, as Easter. **feast-day,** *n.* a day of feasting; a festival. †**feast-rites,** *n.pl.* the rites or customs observed at a feast. †**feast-won,** *a.* gained or bribed by feasting. **feaster,** *n.* one who fares sumptuously; a guest, a partaker of a feast; †the giver of a feast. [OF *feste* (F *fête*), late L *festa,* orig. neut. pl. of L *festus,* joyful]

feat[1], *n.* a notable act or performance, esp. one displaying great strength, skill or daring; an exploit, achievement; a surprising trick. [OF *fait,* L *factum,* FACT]

†**feat[2],** *a.* dexterous, skilful; nimble; smart, neat, trim. †**featly,** *adv.* †**featliness,** *n.* †**featness,** *n.* †**featous,** *a.* neat, comely, handsome. †**featously,** *adv.* [OF *fait,* made, L *factus,* p.p. of *facere,* to make]

feather, *n.* a plume or quill, one of the dermal appendages forming collectively the covering of a bird; such a plume worn as an ornament, esp. in the hat; a strip of a feather attached to an arrow-shaft; (*usu. pl.*) a hairy fringe on a dog's tail or legs, a tuft of long hair on a horse's leg; a tongue on the edge of a board fitting into a groove on the edge of another board; (*Rowing*) the act of feathering; something extremely light. *v.t.* to dress, cover or furnish with feathers; to adorn with or as with feathers; to turn (an oar) so that the blade passes horizontally through the air; to change the angle or allow free rotation of (a propeller blade) to minimize wind resistance; †to adorn; †to tread (as a cock). *v.i.* to move as feathers; to have a feathery appearance; (*Rowing*) to turn the oar and carry through the air edgeways; to change the angle of a propeller blade; (*Hunting*) to set hounds directly on the trail; of hounds, to make a quivering movement with the tail when searching for traces of deer etc. **a feather in one's cap,** an honour, a distinction. **birds of a feather,** people of the same sort, taste, disposition etc. **to be in high feather,** to be in high spirits, to be elated. **to cut a feather,** (*Naut.*) to leave a foamy ripple, as a ship moving rapidly; (*fig.*) to move briskly; to make oneself conspicuous; to cut a dash. **to feather one's nest,** to accumulate wealth; to make provision for oneself. **to show the white feather,** to show signs of cowardice or timidity (said to be derived from the belief that a white feather in the tail of a game-cock was a sign of cowardice). **feather-bed,** *n.* a mattress stuffed with feathers. **to feather-bed,** to pamper, to spoil; to give financial assistance to (an industry). **feather-bedding,** *n.* the practice of protecting jobs by allowing overmanning. **feather-boarding,** *n.* a roof or other covering of boards that thin off at the top and overlap like a bird's feathers. **feather duster,** *n.* a long-handled brush of feathers. **feather-edge,** *n.* an edge like a feather; the thinner edge of a wedge-shaped board or plank. **feather-edged,** *a.* of boards, having one edge thinner than the other. **feather-fern,** *n.* a branching plant, *Astilbe japonica,* of the saxifrage family. **feather-few** corr. of FEVERFEW. **feather grass,** *n.* a perennial grass, *Stipa pennata,* with graceful, feathered awns. **feather-head, -brain, -pate,** *n.* a silly, frivolous person. **feather-headed, -brained, -pated,** *a.* **feather-stitch,** *n.* an embroidery stitch producing a zigzag line somewhat like feathers. **featherweight,** *n.* something as light as a feather; a jockey of the lightest weight allowed to be carried by a horse in a handicap, 4 st. 7 lb. (28 kg); a boxer not above 9 st. (57 kg). **feathered,** *a.* covered with feathers (*also in comb.,* as *well-feathered*); winged; fitted, fringed or adorned with a feather or feathers; having feather appendages; feathery, feather-like; swift, rapid. **feathered game,** *n.* game birds. **feathering,** *n.* the action of the verb to FEATHER; plumage; feathers on an arrow; a feathery fringe or coat (of setters etc.); (*Arch.*) an arrangement of small arcs or foils separated by projecting points or cusps. **featherless,** *a.* destitute or deprived of feathers; unfledged. **featherlet,** *n.* **feathery,** *a.* covered, fringed or adorned with or as with feathers; feather-like, resembling feathers; (*fig.*) light, flimsy, fickle; (*Bot.*) plumose. **featheriness,** *n.* [OE *fether* (cp. Dut. *veder,* G *Feder,* L *penna,* Gr. *pteron,* wing, *petesthai,* to fly)]

feature, *n.* (*usu. pl.*) a part of the face, esp. such as gives individual expression and character; a prominent or distinctive part of anything, a salient point, a striking incident, a mark of individuality; a full-length film, esp. the main film in a programme; a prominent article in a newspaper or magazine on a particular topic; a radio or television documentary; †shape, form, figure; †general appearance; †handsomeness of form or figure. *v.t.* (*coll.*) to resemble in features, to favour; to have as a characteristic; to give prominence to, to make a feature of; (*Cinema*) to present in a role less important than that of a star. *v.i.* to be a characteristic, to figure prominently. **featured,** *a.* **-featured,** *comb. form* having a certain kind of features or cast of face. **featureless,** *a.* without any distinct or distinctive features; shapeless. †**featurely,** *a.* handsome, shapely; having distinctive features. [OF *faiture,* L *factūra,* from *facere,* to make]

Feb, (*abbr.*) February.

febricula, febricule, *n.* (*Path.*) a slight fever of no specific type and of short duration. **febriculose,** *a.* slightly feverish. †**febriculosity,** *n.* [L *febrĭcula,* dim. of *febris,* FEVER]

febrifacient, *a.* causing fever. *n.* anything which causes fever. †**febriferous,** *a.* inducing fever. **febrific,** *a.* productive of fever; feverish. [as prec., -FACIENT]

febrifuge, *n.* a medicine which has the property of dispelling or mitigating fever. **febrifugal,** *a.* [F *fébrifuge* (L *febris,* FEVER, *fugāre,* to drive away)]

febrile, *a.* pertaining to, proceeding from, or indicating fever. [F, from L *febrīlis,* as prec.]

Febronian, *a.* of or pertaining to Febronius or his doctrines (pubd. 1763), which maintained the independence of national churches against the claims of the Pope. **Febronianism,** *n.* [Justinus *Febronius,* pseud. of J. N. von Hontheim, coadjutor bishop of Trèves]

February, *n.* the second month of the year, containing in ordinary years 28 days, and in the bissextile or leap-year 29. [L *Februārius,* from *februa,* pl., a festival of purification, sing. *februum,* purification]

February Revolution, RUSSIAN REVOLUTION.

fec. (*abbr.*) he/she made it. [L *fecit*]

feces, fecal, etc. FAECES.

fecial, FETIAL.

feck, *n.* (*Sc.*) efficacy, strength, vigour; (*Sc.*) space, value, quantity, number; (*Sc.*) the bulk, the greatest part. **feckless,** *a.* puny, weak, feeble in mind; improvident, irresponsible. **fecklessly,** *adv.* **fecklessness,** *n.* **feckly,** *adv.* (*chiefly Sc.*) mostly, chiefly; almost. [etym. doubtful; perh. corr. of EFFECT]

†**fecks,** †**fegs,** FAY[2].

fecula, *n.* lees, sediment, from vegetable infusions, esp. starch. [as foll.]

feculent, *a.* full of dregs, lees or sediment; muddy, turbid; filthy, fetid. **feculence,** †**-lency,** *n.* [F *féculent,* L *faeculentus,* from *faex, faeces,* FAECES]

fecund, *a.* fruitful, prolific, fertile. **fecundate,** *v.t.* to make fruitful or prolific; to impregnate. **fecundation,** *n.* **fecundity,** *n.* the quality of being fruitful or prolific; the power or property of producing young or germinating; power of production or creation; richness of invention. **fecundize, -ise,** *v.t.* [F *fécond,* L *fēcundus*]

Fed.[1], **fed**[1], (*abbr.*) Federal; Federation.

fed[2], *past, p.p.* FEED[1]. **fed up,** *a.* (*coll.*) sick or tired (of). **to be fed up (to the back teeth) with,** to have had more than enough of, to be sick of.

fed[3], *n.* (*coll.*) a federal agent (in the US).

†**fedarie,** *n.* (*Shak.*) a confederate. [var. of *feodary,* FEUDARY]

fedayee, *n.* (*pl.* **-yeen**) a member of an Arab commando group, esp. against Israel. [Arab. *fidāī,* one who sacrifices himself]

federal, *a.* pertaining to or based upon a treaty, league or contract; (*Theol.*) arising from or based on the doctrine of a covenant between God and man; relating to, arising from or supporting a polity formed by the union of several states; relating to such a government as distinguished from the separate states; supporting the cause of the Union in the American Civil War. *n.* a supporter of the principle of federation, esp. a supporter of the American Union in the Civil War. **Federal Bureau of Investigation,** a branch of the US Department of Justice concerned with internal security, espionage and sabotage. **Federal Reserve Bank,** one of 12 US banks holding reserves and performing functions similar to those of the Bank of England. **Federal Party,** *n.* (*US Hist.*) a party existing from 1787 to *c.* 1830, orig. under the leadership of Alexander Hamilton, supporting the Federal constitution and centralization of government. **federacy,** *n.* a federation of states. **federalism,** *n.* **federalist,** *n.* **federalize, -ise,** *v.t.* to bring together in a political confederacy. *v.i.* to combine into a political confederacy. **federally,** *adv.* **federate,** *v.t.* to organize as a federal group of states; to federalize; to bring together for a common object. *v.i.* to combine and form a federal group; to league together for a common object. *a.*, united under a federal government; leagued together. **federation,** *n.* the act of uniting in a confederacy; a confederated body; a federal government. **Imperial Federation,** the doctrine that the colonies in the British Empire should combine to share the control and expense of the whole Empire. **Social Democratic Federation,** the earliest British socialist party, intended esp. for the promotion of a reform movement among the middle classes. **federationist,** *n.* **federative,** *a.* **federatively,** *adv.* [F *fédéral,* from L *faedus -eris,* a treaty, covenant, cogn. with *fidēs,* FAITH]

Federal Deposit Insurance Corporation (FDIC), US government authority established in 1933 to regulate US banks and insure them against loss.

fedora, *n.* (*N Am., coll.*) a soft felt hat with a curled brim.

fee, *n.* (*Feudal Law*) land and estate held of a superior; a freehold estate of inheritance; †ownership, property; payment or remuneration to a public officer or a professional person for the execution of official functions or for the performance of a professional service; a charge paid for a privilege, such as admission to an examination, society, public building etc.; charge, payment; gratuity; †perquisite; (*Sc.*) wages; †property, estate, esp. cattle. *v.t.* (*past, p.p.* **feed**) to pay a fee or reward to; to engage for a fee, to hire; †to bribe; (*Sc.*) to hire oneself out. **retaining fee,** a payment made to a lawyer, doctor or other professional engaging his or her services for a case etc. **to hold in fee,** (*Law*) to own absolutely. †**fee-grief,** *n.* a private sorrow. **fee-simple,** *n.* (*Law*) an estate held by a person in his or her own right, without limitation to any particular class of heirs. **fee-tail,** *n.* (*Law*) an estate entailed to the possessor's heirs. **feeless,** *a.* [A-F *fee,* OF *fé, fieu, fief,* prob. through med. L *feodum, feudum* or *fevum,* from OHG *fehu,* payment, wages, money, property, cattle (cp. OE *feoh,* Dut. *vee,* L *pecus,* cattle, *pecunia,* money)]

feeble, *a.* weak, destitute of physical strength; infirm, debilitated; lacking in force, vigour or energy; lacking in moral or intellectual power; ineffective, pointless, insipid; dim, faint; unconvincing, lame. †*n.* a feeble person; weakness; the foible of a sword. *v.t.* to weaken. **feeble-minded,** *a.* intellectually deficient, imbecile; wanting in resolution. **feebleness,** †**feebless,** *n.* **feeblish,** *a.* **feebly,** *adv.* [A-F *feble,* OF *foible* (F *faible*), L *flēbilis,* mournful, from *flēre,* to weep]

feed[1], *v.t.* (*past, p.p.* **fed**) to give food to; to put food into the mouth of; to supply with that which is necessary to existence, continuance or development; to cause (cattle) to graze; to serve as food or nourishment for; to nourish, to cause to grow or develop; to cause (land) to be grazed; to cause to pass (as a rope or tape) through or into something; to supply (as a machine) with material; to supply (a signal, power) to an electric circuit; to cue in a response from (another performer); to pass the ball or puck to (another player); to gratify; †to entertain, to edify. *v.i.* to take food; to eat; to subsist (on or upon); to grow fat; to support oneself; to indulge or gratify oneself mentally. *n.* food, fodder, pasturage; the act of feeding or giving food; amount of food or provender given to horses, cattle etc. at a time; (*coll.*) a meal, a feast; the operation of supplying a machine with material, or of bringing a tool into operation; the machinery for this; the amount supplied; the charge for a gun; a performer who supplies cues, esp. a straight man. **at feed,** eating, grazing. **off one's feed,** without appetite. **on the feed,** feeding, eating; of fish, taking or looking out for food. **to feed down,** to supply (material) continuously; to bring down (a tool) into continuous operation; of cattle etc., to eat away by pasturing. **to feed up,** to give plenty to eat, to fatten. **feedback,** *n.* the return of part of the output of a system, circuit or mechanical process to the input; the return of part of the sound output of a loud-speaker to the microphone, producing a high-pitched whistle; reactions and comments from customers, consumers, audience etc. **feed-pipe,** *n.* the pipe carrying water to the boilers of steam-engines. **feed-pump,** *n.* a force-pump for supplying water to boilers. **feed-tank, -trough,** *n.* a cistern or trough holding a water-supply for locomotives. **feeder,** *n.* one who supplies food or nourishment; one who fattens cattle; one who eats, esp. one who eats in a certain manner, as a *quick feeder;* a feeding-bottle; a child's bib; a tributary stream; an artificial channel supplying a canal etc.; a branch railway; (*Elec.*) a wire, usu. in pairs, carrying electricity to various points in a system; the apparatus feeding a machine; a theatrical feed; one who nourishes, encourages or supports; †a dependant, a parasite. **feeding,** *n.* eating; that which is eaten; food. **feeding-bottle,** *n.* a bottle for supplying liquid nutriment to infants. **feeding-cup,** *n.* a specially shaped cup for feeding a patient in bed. **feeding-ground,** *n.* a place where animals or fish resort for food. [OE *fēdan* (cp. Dut. *voeden,* Goth. *fōdjan,* OHG *fuotan,* see also FOOD]

feed[2], *past, p.p.* FEE.

fee-faw-fum, *int.* a sham bloodthirsty exclamation. *n.* nonsense or mummery to frighten the ignorant or childish. [spoken by the Giant in *Jack the Giant-Killer*]

feel, *v.t.* to perceive by the touch; to have the sense of touch; to have a sensation of, otherwise than by the senses of sight, hearing, taste or smell; to be conscious of; to have the emotions stirred by; to experience, to undergo; to be affected by; to know in one's inner consciousness, to be convinced (that); to examine or explore by the touch; to touch, to handle, to try or find out by handling or groping. *v.i.* to have perception by the sense or act of touching; to be conscious of a certain sensation (as cold, wet, hungry or tired); (*reflex.*) to be conscious of (oneself) as in a certain state (as afraid, anxious, busy etc.); to be stirred in one's emotions; to seem to the sense of touch, to produce a certain sensation, as *the air feels damp or cold. n.* the sense of touch; characteristic sensation of something, esp. one related to that of touch; perception, esp. of an emotional kind. **to feel after,** to try to find out by the sense of touch, to search for as by groping. **to feel for,** to feel after; to have sympathy or compassion for. **to feel like,** to wish to, to be in the mood for. **to feel up,** (*sl.*) to touch someone in such a way as to arouse oneself or the other person sexually. **to feel up to,** (*coll.*) to feel able or strong enough to. **feeler,** *n.* one who feels; (*fig.*) any device to ascertain the designs, wishes or opinions of others; a scout; a generic term for various organs of touch in invertebrate animals. **to put out feelers,** to make tentative enquiries. **feeler gauge,** *n.* a thin metal strip of a known thickness used to measure a gap. **feeling,** *n.* the sense of touch; the sensation produced when a material body is touched; a physical sensation of any kind; emotion; an emotional state or reaction; (*pl.*) susceptibilities, sympathies; an impression, a sense, an intuition; a sentiment, belief or conviction (usu. non-rational); the emotional content or mood of a work of art. *a.* perceiving by the touch; easily affected or moved, sensitive, of great sensibility; expressive of or manifesting great sensibility; affecting. **feelingly,** *adv.* [OE *fēlan* (cp. Dut. *voelen,* OHG *fuolan,* G *fühlen,* also OE *folm,* L *palma,* Gr. *palamē,* palm of the hand)]

feet FOOT.

fegs, FAY[2].

feign, *v.t.* to invent, to pretend, to simulate, to counterfeit; †to imagine, to represent in fiction; †to dissemble, to hide. *v.i.* to dissimulate; to make pretences. **feigned issue,** *n.* (*Law*) an action arranged so as to try a question of right. **feignedly,** *adv.* **feignedness,** *n.* [OF *feindre,* L *fingere*]

Feininger, *n.* **Lyonel** (1871–1956), US abstract artist, an early Cubist. He worked at the Bauhaus, Germany (a key centre of modern design), from 1919–33, and later helped to found the Bauhaus in Chicago.

feint[1], *n.* a feigned or sham attack; a pretence of aiming at one point while another is the real object; a pretence. *v.i.* to make a feint or pretended attack (upon, against or at). †*a.* feigned, counterfeit. [F *feinte,* from *feindre,* see prec.]

feint[2], *a.* of ruled lines on paper, faint. [alt. of FAINT]

feisty, *a.* (*chiefly N Am.*) plucky, full of fight. [from N Am. dial. *feist,* a small dog]

felafel, falafel, *n.* a thick paste of ground chick peas with spices, onion etc. formed into balls and deep-fried. [Arab.]

feldspar, *n.* (*Min.*) a name including several minerals found abundantly in igneous rocks, varying in colour, crystalline form and chemical composition, but chiefly silicates of alumina combined with some other mineral. **feldsparization, -isation,** *n.* (*Geol.*) alteration of other material into feldspar. **feldspathic, -thoid, -those,** *a.* pertaining to feldspar; having feldspar in the composition. [G *Feldspath* (*Feld,* field, *Spath,* spar)]

felicide, *n.* killing of a cat. [L *fēlis,* cat, -CIDE]

felicity, *n.* happiness, blissfulness, a source of happiness, a blessing; appropriateness, neatness; a happy turn or expression; a happy way or faculty of expressing, behaving etc. **felicific,** *a.* producing happiness. **felicitate,** *v.t.* †to confer happiness upon; to congratulate. †*a.* made happy. **felicitation,** *n.* congratulation. **felicitous,** *a.* happy, delightful, prosperous; well-suited, apt, well-expressed; charming in manner, operation etc. **felicitously,** *adv.* **felicitousness,** *n.* [L *fēlīcitās -tātem,* good fortune, *fēlīcitātus,* p.p. of *fēlīcitāre,* from *fēlix -līcis,* happy]

felid, *n.* one of the Felidae, a family of fissiped carnivores, containing lions, tigers, leopards, pumas and cats. [L *fēlis,* a cat]

feline, *a.* belonging to the Felidae; of or pertaining to cats, cat-like; sly, stealthy; graceful, sinuous. *n.* one of the Felidae. **felinity,** *n.*

fell[1], *v.t.* to knock down; to bring to the ground; to hew or cut down; (*Sewing*) to finish with a fell. *n.* a quantity of timber felled; a seam or hem in which one edge is folded over another and sewed down. **feller**[1], *n.* one who fells or cuts down trees. [OE *fiellan,* causal, from *feallan,* to FALL]

fell[2], *n.* the hide or skin of an animal, esp. if covered with hair; a fleece; a thick woolly or hairy covering; a dense, matted growth (of hair etc.). **fell-monger,** *n.* a dealer in hides and skins. [OE *fel,* skin (cp. Dut. *vel,* G *Fell,* also L *pellis,* Gr. *pella*)]

fell[3], *n.* a rocky hill; a lofty tract of barren moorland. [Icel. *fjall*]

fell[4], *a.* cruel, savage, fierce; terrible, deadly, dire; (*Sc.*) huge; †keen, spirited, eager, angry, enraged. †*adv.* cruelly; (*Sc.*) hugely, greatly. **felly**[1], *adv.* [OF *fel,* late L *fello, felo,* FELON]

†**fell**[5], *n.* bitterness, anger, resentment, rancour. [L *fel,* gall]

fell[6], *past* FALL.

fella, *n.* (*coll.*) fellow, man; (*dial.*) a male sweetheart. [alteration of FELLOW]

fellah, *n.* (*pl.* **fellaheen**) an Egyptian agricultural labourer or peasant. [Arab. *fellāh*]

fellatio, *n.* oral stimulation of the penis. [L *fellātus,* p.p. of *fellāre,* to suck]

feller[1] FELL[1].

feller[2], *n.* (*coll.*) fellow, man; (*dial.*) a male sweetheart. [alteration of FELLOW]

fellic, fellinic, *a.* of or pertaining to gall. [L *fel,* gall, see -IN, -IC]

Fellini, *n.* **Federico** (1920–), Italian film director, noted for his strongly subjective poetic imagery. His films include *I vitelloni/The Young and the Passionate* (1953), *La dolce vita/The Sweet Life* (1960), and *La città delle donne/City of Women* (1981).

felloe, *n.* one of the curved segments of a wheel, joined together by dowels to form the rim; the whole rim of a wheel. [OE *felg* (cp. Dut. *velg,* G *Felge*)]

fellow, *n.* an associate, a comrade; a partner; a companion; a contemporary; one of the same kind or species; an equal in rank, a peer, a compeer; one of a pair; a person or thing like or equal to another, a counterpart, a match; a member of an incorporated society; an incorporated member of a college; the holder of a fellowship or stipendiary position endowed for purposes of research; (*N Am.*) one of the trustees of a college; a man, a boy; a person of little estimation; †a partaker, a sharer; (*in comb.*) one associated with oneself or of the same class or relationship. *v.t.* to match, to pair with, to suit; †to partake with, share (in); †to accompany. **fellow-commoner,** *n.* (*Univ.*) one who has the right to dine with the fellows. **fellow-craft,** *n.* a Freemason of the second degree. **fellow-creature,** *n.* one of the same race, the work of the same Creator. **fellow-feeling,** *n.* sympathy; joint interest. **fellow traveller,** *n.* (*usu. derog.*) one who without declaring himor herself a member sympathizes with the aims of the Communist Party or other similar organization. **fellowship,** *n.* the condition or state of being a fellow; companionship, association, close intercourse, friendliness, cordiality of feeling, community of interest, participation; a body of associates; a brotherhood, a fraternity; a company, a corporation; the dignity of fellow in a college or learned society; an endowment for maintaining a graduate engaged in research; (*Relig.*) membership of a community partaking of Holy Communion together; the rule by which profit or loss is divided among partners in proportion to the capital invested. *v.t.* (*Relig.*) to admit to fellowship. *v.i.* (*chiefly N Am., Relig.*) to associate with, to unite with. [Icel. *fēlagi,* a partner, one who lays down fee or goods in partnership, from *fē,* property, cogn. with OE *feoh,* cattle, see FEE]

felly[1] FELL[4].

felly[2], alternative spelling of FELLOE.

felo-de-se, *n.* (*pl.* **felos-**) orig., one who commits felony by self-murder; self-murder, suicide. [A-L, felon upon himself (see foll.)]

felon, *n.* one who has committed a felony; †a villain; a whitlow or abscess close to the nail. *a.* cruel, malignant, malicious; wicked, murderous. **felonious,** *a.* of the nature of a felony; (*Law*) done with deliberate purpose to commit a crime; that has committed felony; villainous, malignant, malicious; (*coll.*) thievish. **feloniously,** *adv.* **feloniousness,** *n.* †**felonry,** *n.* a body of felons; (*Austral. Hist.*) British convicts. **felony,** *n.* an offence of a heinous character, conviction for which formerly involved loss of lands and goods; in US law and in Eng. law until 1967, an offence of graver character than a misdemeanour; †crime, wickedness, sin. [OF from late L *fellōnem,* nom. *fello, felo* (perh. from L *fel,* gall)]

felsite, *n.* (*Min.*) felstone. **felsitic,** *a.* [from *fels-,* corr. form, see FELDSPAR]

felspar, etc. FELDSPAR.

felstone, *n.* (*Min.*) feldspar occurring in compact masses. [G *Felsstein* (*Fels,* rock, *Stein,* stone)]

felt[1], *n.* a kind of cloth made of wool or wool and cotton compacted together by rolling, beating and pressure, with lees or size; a piece of this stuff; an article made of it, a felt hat. *v.t.* to make into felt; to cover with felt; to press into a compact mass. *v.i.* to become matted together. **felt-tip pen,** a pen with a writing point made of pressed felt or similar fibres. **felt-grain,** *n.* the grain of wood whose direction is from the pith to the bark. **felt hat,** *n.* a hat made of felt. †**felt-lock,** *n.* a matted and unkempt lock of hair. **felt-maker,** *n.* **felter,** *n.* a maker of or worker in felt; a bird that makes its nest with or as with felt. †*v.t., v.i.* to mat or clot together like felt. **felting,** *n.* the act or process of making felt. **felty,** *a.* [OE, cp. Dut. *vilt,* G *Filz*]

felt[2], *past, p.p.* FEEL.

felucca, *n.* a small vessel used in the Mediterranean, propelled by oars or lateen sails or both. [It., prob. from Arab.]

fem., (*abbr.*) feminine.

female, *a.* denoting the sex which brings forth young or lays eggs from which new individuals are developed; (*Bot.*) having a pistil, but no stamens, capable of being fertilized and producing fruit; of, pertaining to or characteristic of woman or womanhood; womanly, feminine; (*Mech.*) fitted to receive the corresponding male part as a *female screw. n.* (*sometimes derog.*) a woman or girl; (*Zool.*) an individual of the female sex. **female die,** *n.* the concave die, into which the male or convex die is struck. **female impersonator,** *n.* a male performer who dresses as and imitates a woman for the purposes of his act. **female rhymes,** *n.pl.* rhymes in which two syllables, one accented and the other unaccented, correspond at the end of each line, as *fable, table; notion, motion.* **female screw,** *n.* the spiral-threaded cavity into which another (male) screw works. [OF *femelle,* L *fēmella,* dim. of *fēmina,* a woman]

feme covert, *n.* (*Law*) a married woman. **feme sole,** *n.* (*Law*) an unmarried woman, spinster or widow; a married woman having rights of property or trade independent of her husband. [A-F and OF]

feminine, *a.* of, pertaining to or characteristic of women or the female sex; womanly; effeminate; soft, tender, delicate; of the female sex; womanish; (*Gram.*) belonging to the gender denoting females; of rhymes, having two syllables, the first accented. **feminine caesura,** *n.* a caesura following an unstressed syllable, as in 'And eat our pot of honey on the grave'. **feminality,** *n.* the quality of being female; the characteristic nature of woman or the female sex; something characteristic of female nature. **femineity,** *n.* womanliness; womanishness. **femininely,** *adv.* **feminineness,** *n.* **femininity, feminity,** *n.* the qualities or manners becoming a woman. **feminism,** *n.* advocacy of the claims of women to political, economic and social equality with men. **feminist,** *n., a.* **feministic,** *a.* **feminize, -ise,** *v.t.* to make feminine. *v.i.* to become feminine. [OF *femi-*

nin, L *fēminīnus,* from *fēmina,* woman]

femme de chambre, *n.* (*pl.* **femmes,**) a chambermaid; a lady's-maid. [F, bedroom woman]

femme fatale, *n.* (*pl.* **femmes fatales**) a seductive woman, esp. one who lures men into ruin. [F, fatal woman]

femto-, *pref.* a thousand million millionth (10^{-15}). [Dan. or Norw. *femten,* fifteen]

femur, *n.* (*pl.* **femurs, femora**) the thigh-bone; the third joint of the leg in insects. **femoral,** *a.* of or belonging to the thigh. *n.* the femoral artery. [L *femur -oris,* the thigh]

fen, *n.* low, flat and marshy land, esp. the low-lying districts in the east of England, partially drained and abounding in broads or lakes; a marsh, a bog. **fen-berry,** *n.* the cranberry, *Vaccinium oxycoccos.* **fen-duck,** *n.* the shoveller. **fen-fire,** *n.* the will-o'-the-wisp. **fenland,** *n.* a fen; the fens. **fenlander, -man,** *n.* an inhabitant of the fens. **fen-pole,** *n.* a pole used in the fens for jumping ditches. **fen-reeve,** *n.* an officer in charge of the common lands in the fens. **fen-runners,** *n.pl.* a long kind of skates suitable for high speed. **fenny,** *a.* [OE *fenn* (cp. Dut. *ven, veen,* G *Fenne*)]

fence, *n.* a structure serving to enclose and protect a piece of ground, or to keep cattle from straying, as a wall, a hedge, a paling, a bank, a line of rails or posts etc.; a guardplate, guide or gauge of various kinds in machinery etc.; the art of fencing or swordplay; skill in debate; repartee; equivocation; (*sl.*) a purchaser or receiver of stolen goods, or a place where such are purchased or deposited. *v.t.* to defend, shield or protect; to ward (off); to enclose, encircle or protect with or as with a fence; to parry. *v.i.* to practise the art of swordplay; to use a sword skilfully; to defend oneself or repel attack skilfully; to parry enquiries adroitly, to equivocate; (*sl.*) to deal in stolen goods. **dog-leg fence** DOG. **master of fence,** a skilled fencer or swordsman; an expert debater or dialectician. **over the fence,** (*Austral., coll.*) unreasonable, utterly indecent. **ring-fence,** a fence encircling a whole estate. **sunk fence,** a fence set along the bottom of a ditch; a ditch forming a fence. **to mend one's fences,** to restore good relations, to make up differences. **to sit on the fence,** to remain neutral in respect to opposing policies. **Virginia fence, worm fence,** (*N Am.*) a zigzag fence of split rails without posts. **fence-month, -season, -time,** *n.* the fawning month (*c.* 9 June to 9 July), during which deer-hunting is forbidden; a close time for fish. **fenced,** *a.* enclosed with a fence; fortified. **fenceless,** *a.* unenclosed; undefended, defenceless. **fencer,** *n.* one skilled in fencing; a builder of fences; a horse good at leaping fences. **fencing,** *n.* the act of making fences; (*collect.*) fences, a railing or railings; materials for fences; the act or art of using a sword or foil in attack or defence; a protection or guard round any dangerous piece of machinery; equivocation, parrying of argument. **fencing-cully,** *n.* (*sl.*) a receiver of stolen goods. **fencing-crib, -ken, -repository,** *n.* (*sl.*) a place for receiving stolen goods. [short for DEFENCE]

fencible, *n.* a soldier enlisted for home defence. *a.* (*chiefly Sc.*) capable of defence or of being defended; belonging to the fencibles. [short for DEFENSIBLE]

fend, *v.t.* †to defend; (*Sc.*) to provide for, to support. *v.i.* (*Sc.*) to strive, to resist, to offer opposition. **to fend for,** to provide or to get a living for. **to fend off,** to keep off, ward off. [short for DEFEND]

Fender, *n.* pioneering series of electric guitars and bass guitars. The first solid-body electric guitar on the market was the 1948 Fender Broadcaster (renamed the Telecaster in 1950), and the first electric bass guitar was the Fender Precision of 1951. The Fender Stratocaster guitar dates from 1954. Their designer, Leo Fender, began manufacturing amplifiers in the US in the 1940s.

fender, *n.* one who or that which serves to defend, protect or ward off anything hurtful or dangerous; a piece of furniture, usu. of iron or brass, placed on the hearth to confine the ashes; a piece of timber or plastic or mass of rope to protect the side of a vessel from injury by collision; (*N Am.*) the wing or mudguard of a motor vehicle. **fender-beam,** *n.* a beam hung over the side of a vessel to protect her from injury by ice. **fender-pile,** *n.* a piece of timber placed in front of dock walls and similar structures to protect against blows from vessels. **fender-stool,** *n.* a long stool placed close to the fender before a fire. **fenderless,** *a.* [from prec.]

fenestella, *n.* (*Arch.*) a niche on the south side of the altar containing the piscina, and often the credence. [L, dim. of *fenestra,* see foll.]

fenestra, *n.* (*pl.* **-trae**) a window-like aperture in a bone; a transparent spot or aperture in a wing, leaf etc. **fenestral,** *a.* †of or pertaining to a window; (*Biol.*) having small transparent spots or fenestrae. **fenestral bandage,** *n.* one having openings through which matter can discharge. **fenestrate,** *a.* applied to leaves in which there is only a network of filamentous cells formed; applied to the naked hyaline transparent spots on the wings of butterflies. **fenestrated,** *a.* furnished with windows; (*Anat.*) fenestral. **fenestration,** *n.* (*Arch.*) the construction, arrangement or mode of design of windows; (*Nat. Hist.*) the formation of fenestrae; the condition of having fenestrae. [L, a window]

Fenian, *n.* a member of an Irish secret society which was formed in America about 1858 having for its object the overthrow of the British Government in Ireland, and the establishment of an independent republic; (*offensive*) an (esp. Irish) Roman Catholic. *a.* pertaining to this society or to Fenianism; (*offensive*) (Irish) Roman Catholic. **Fenianism,** *n.* [OIr. *Fēne,* a name of the ancient Irish, confused with *Fīann,* the warriors who defended Ireland in the time of Finn]

fenks, *n.pl.* refuse of whale-blubber, used for manure. [etym. unknown]

fennec, *n.* a small fox-like animal, *Canis zerda,* common in Africa. [Arab. *fenek*]

fennel, *n.* a fragrant umbelliferous plant with yellow flowers, *Foeniculum vulgare.* **fennel-flower,** *n.* a herb of the genus *Nigella,* such as ragged lady, *N. damascena,* or the nutmeg-flower, *N. sativa.* [OE *finol, finugl,* L *faeniculum,* dim. of *faenum,* hay]

Fens, *n.pl.* level, low-lying tracts of land in E England, west and south of the Wash, about 115 km/70 miles N–S and about 55 km/34 miles E–W. They fall within the counties of Lincolnshire, Cambridgeshire, and Norfolk, consisting of a huge area, formerly a bay of the North Sea, but now crossed by numerous drainage canals and forming some of the most productive agricultural land in Britain.

fens FAINS.

fent, *n.* the opening left in a garment (as in a shirt-sleeve) for convenience of putting it on; a crack, a rift; a remnant. [F *fente,* from *fendre,* L *findere,* to cleave]

Fenton, *n.* **Roger** (1819–69), British photographer. The world's first war photographer, he went to the Crimea in 1855; he also founded the Royal Photographic Society in London.

fenugreek, *n.* a leguminous plant, *Trigonella faenum-Graecum,* the seeds of which are used in animal condiments. [F *fenugrec,* L *faenugræcum* (*faenum,* hay, *Graecum,* neut. a., Greek)]

†feod, FEUD².

feoff, *v.t.* (*Law*) to grant possession, to enfeoff; †to endow. *n.* a fief. **feoffee,** *n.* one who is invested with an estate by feoffment. **feoffment,** *n.* the conveyance of any corporeal hereditament to another, accompanied by actual delivery of possession; the mode of such conveyance. **feoffor,** *n.* one who grants a fief. [OF *feoffer, fieffer,* from *fief,* FEE]

feracious, *a.* fruitful, fertile. **feracity,** *n.* [L *fērāx -ācis,* fruitful, from *ferre,* to bear]

ferae naturae, *a.* of a wild nature or state, applied to deer, hares, pheasants etc., as distinguished from domesticated animals. [L, of a wild nature]

feral, *a.* wild, savage; lapsed from a domesticated into a wild state; uncultivated; (*fig.*) brutal, savage. [L *fera,* a wild beast]

fer-de-lance, *n.* the yellow viper of Martinique, *Both-*

rops lanceolatus. [F, lance-head (*fer,* iron)]

Ferdinand[1], *n.* (1861–1948), king of Bulgaria from 1908–18. Son of Prince Augustus of Saxe-Coburg-Gotha, he was elected prince of Bulgaria in 1887, and in 1908 proclaimed Bulgaria's independence of Turkey and assumed the title of tsar. In 1915 he entered World War I as Germany's ally, and in 1918 abdicated and retired to Coburg.

Ferdinand[2], *n.* (1865–1927), king of Romania from 1914, when he succeeded his uncle Charles I. In 1916 he declared war on Austria. After the Allied victory in World War I, Ferdinand acquired Transylvania and Bukovina from Austria-Hungary, and Bessarabia from Russia. In 1922 he became king of Greater Romania.

Ferdinand, *n.* five kings of Castile, including:

Ferdinand I, *n.* **the Great** (*c.* 1016–65), king of Castile from 1035. He began the reconquest of Spain from the Moors and united all NW Spain under his and his brothers' rule.

Ferdinand V, *n.* (1452–1516), king of Castile from 1474, **Ferdinand II** of Aragon from 1479, and **Ferdinand III** of Naples from 1504; first king of all Spain. In 1469 he married his cousin Isabella I, who succeeded to the throne of Castile in 1474. They introduced the Inquisition in 1480, expelled the Jews, forced the surrender of the Moors at Granada in 1492, and financed Columbus' expedition to the Americas.

Ferdinand, *n.* three Holy Roman emperors, including:

Ferdinand II, *n.* (1578–1637), king of Bohemia from 1617 and Hungary from 1618, Holy Roman emperor from 1619, when he succeeded his uncle Matthias. He was a zealous Catholic who provoked the Bohemian revolt that led to the Thirty Years' War.

Ferdinand III, *n.* (1608–57), Holy Roman emperor from 1637 when he succeeded his father Ferdinand II; king of Hungary from 1625. Although anxious to conclude the Thirty Years' War, he did not give religious liberty to Protestants.

†**fere**[1], *n.* a mate, a companion; a consort, a spouse. [ME *fere,* OE *gefēra,* cogn. with *faran,* to go, to FARE]

†**fere**[2], *a.* able, strong, whole. [Icel. *færr,* or prec.]

feretory, *n.* the bier or shrine in which relics of saints were borne in procession, a reliquary, a chapel or place in a church in which shrines were kept. [OF *fiertre,* L *feretrum,* Gr. *pheretron,* from *pherein,* to bear]

Ferguson, *n.* **Harry** (1884–1960), Irish engineer, who pioneered the development of the tractor, joining forces with Henry Ford in 1938 to manufacture it in the US.

ferial, *a.* (*Eccles.*) pertaining to ordinary week-days, such as are not festival or fast days; pertaining to holidays; formerly used in Scotland of days on which the courts did not sit. [F *férial,* L *fēriālis,* from *fēria,* a holiday, see FAIR[1]]

ferine, *a.* wild, savage, untamed; bestial, brutish. †**ferinely,** *adv.* [L *ferīnus,* from *fera,* wild animal]

Feringhee, *n.* the name given by the Hindus to the English and other Europeans, formerly more especially to Portuguese settlers and their descendants. [corr. of FRANK[1]]

†**ferly,** *a.* sudden; strange; marvellous. *n.* a marvel, a wonder. *v.i.* (*Sc.*) to wonder, to be amazed (at). [OE *fǣrlic,* sudden, from *fǣr,* see FEAR[1]]

Fermanagh, *n.* county in the southern part of Northern Island. **area** 1680 sq km/648 sq miles. **towns** Enniskillen (county town), Lisnaskea, Irvinestown. **physical** in the centre is a broad trough of low-lying land, in which lie Upper and Lower Lough Erne. **population** (1981) 52,000. **products** mainly agricultural; livestock, tweeds, clothing.

Fermat, *n.* **Pierre de** (1601–65), French mathematician, who with Pascal founded the theory of probability and the modern theory of numbers, and made contributions to analytical geometry.

fermata, *n.* (*Mus.*) a continuation of a note or rest beyond its usual length. [It. *fermare,* to stop]

ferment[1], *n.* any substance, organic or inorganic, which causes fermentation; leaven; fermentation; internal motion of the constituent parts of a fluid; commotion, tumult, agitation. [as foll.]

ferment[2], *v.t.* to excite fermentation in; to rouse, to agitate, to excite. *v.i.* to be in a state of fermentation, to effervesce; to be agitated, as by violent emotions. **fermentable,** *a.* †**fermentability,** *n.* **fermentation,** *n.* a process excited in certain substances or liquids by living organisms or chemical agents, with evolution of heat, effervescence and chemical decomposition; commotion, agitation, excitement. **fermentative,** *a.* causing, produced by or of the nature of fermentation. **fermentescible,** *a.* able to cause fermentation; capable of fermentation. [F, from L *fermentum,* from root of *fervēre,* to boil]

fermeture, *n.* the mechanism for closing the breech of a gun or other firearm. [F, from *fermer,* to shut]

fermi, *n.* a unit of length equal to 10^{-15} metre. **fermion,** *n.* any of a group of subatomic particles which obeys the exclusion principle. **fermium,** *n.* an element, at. no 100; chem. symbol Fm, artificially produced from plutonium. [after Enrico *Fermi*]

Fermi, *n.* **Enrico** (1901–1954), Italian physicist, who proved the existence of new radioactive elements produced by bombardment with neutrons, and discovered nuclear reactions produced by slow neutrons. Won the Nobel prize of 1938.

Fermilab, *n.* US centre for particle physics in Chicago, named after Fermi.

Fermor, *n.* **Patrick (Michael) Leigh** (1915–), English travel writer who joined the Irish Guards in 1939 after four years' travel in central Europe and the Balkans. His books include *The Traveller's Tree* (1950), *Mani* (1958), *Roumeli* (1966), *A Time of Gifts* (1977), and *Between the Woods and the Water* (1986).

fern, *n.* a cryptogamic plant springing from a rhizome, and having the reproductive organs on the lower surface of fronds or leaves, which are often divided in a graceful, feathery form. **fern bird,** *n.* the grass-bird or New Zealand pipit. **fern-owl,** *n.* the goat-sucker or nightjar, *Caprimulgus europaeus.* **fern-seed,** *n.* the seeds or spores of ferns, formerly supposed to render a person invisible. **fernshaw,** *n.* a thicket of fern. **fern-tree** (*Austral.*) TREE-FERN. **fernery,** *n.* a place where ferns are cultivated. **fernless,** *a.* **ferny,** *a.* [OE *fearn* (cp. Dut. *varen,* G *Farn,* also Sansk. *parna* and Gr. *pteron,* wing, feather)]

Fernandez de Quirós, Pedro (1565–1614), Spanish navigator, one of the first Europeans to search for the great southern continent that Magellan believed lay to the south of the Magellan Strait. Despite a series of disastrous expeditions, he took part in the discovery of the Marquesas Islands and the main island of Espíritu Santo in the New Hebrides.

ferocious, *a.* fierce, savage, cruel, barbarous. **ferociously,** *adv.* †**ferociousness,** *n.* **ferocity,** *n.* the state or quality of being ferocious, savageness, fierceness, wildness, fury; a ferocious act. [L *ferōci-,* stem of *ferox,* cogn. with *ferus,* wild]

-ferous, *suf.* bearing, producing, having, as in *auriferous, fossiliferous.* [L *fer-,* stem of *ferre,* to bear, -OUS]

ferox, *n.* the great lake-trout. [mod. L *Salmo ferox,* the fierce salmon]

†**ferrandine,** †**farandine,** *n.* a mixed stuff of silk and other materials. [prob. from F. *Ferrand,* name of inventor]

Ferranti, *n.* **Sebastian de** (1864–1930), British electrical engineer who electrified central London. He made and sold his first alternator in 1881. Soon after he became chief engineer with the London Electric Supply Company. He worked on the design of a large power station at Deptford but legislation permitting low-powered stations to operate killed the scheme. He resigned in 1892, moved to Oldham in Lancashire, and in 1896 opened his business to develop high-voltage systems for long-distance transmission.

ferrara, *n.* a broadsword of special excellence, often called an *Andrew Ferrara* after Andrea Ferrara, one of a famous family of swordsmiths in the 16th cent. [perh. from native of It. town *Ferrara,* or from It. *ferrajo,* cutter, L. *ferrārius,* from *ferrum,* iron]

Ferrari, *n.* **Enzo** (1898–1988), Italian founder of the Ferrari car empire, which specializes in Grand Prix racing cars and high-quality sports cars. He was a racing driver for Alfa Romeo in the 1920s, went on to become one of their designers and in 1929 took over their racing division. In 1947 the first 'true' Ferrari was seen. The Ferrari car has won more world championship Grands Prix than any other car.

Ferraro, *n.* **Geraldine** (1935–), US Democrat politician, vice-presidential candidate in the 1984 election.

ferrate, *n.* (*Chem.*) a salt of ferric acid. **ferreous,** *a.* of or pertaining to iron; of the nature of iron; made of iron. [L *ferrum,* iron]

ferret¹, *n.* a partially tamed variety of polecat, *Putorius foetidus,* used for killing rats and driving rabbits out of their holes; a sharp-eyed searcher or detective. *v.t.* to drive out of a hole or clear (ground) with ferrets; to hunt or take with ferrets; to search (out) by persevering means; †to worry. *v.i.* to hunt rabbits etc. with a ferret; to search or rummage about (for). **ferreter,** *n.* one who ferrets. **ferrety,** *a.* [OF *furet,* late L *fūrētus,* identified with *fūrō -ōnem,* L *fūr,* robber]

ferret², *n.* a tape made of silk or cotton. †**ferret-silk,** *n.* floss-silk. [prob. from It. *fioretti,* a kind of silk, pl. of *fioretto,* dim of *fiore,* flower, L *flōrem,* nom. *flōs*]

ferri-, *comb. form* (*Chem.*) denoting a compound of iron in the ferric state (cp. FERRO-). [L *ferrum,* iron]

ferriage, *n.* the fare paid for conveyance by a ferry.

ferric, *a.* of, pertaining to, or extracted from iron; containing trivalent iron. [L *ferrum,* iron]

ferricyanic, *a.* of or pertaining to a compound of iron in its ferric state with cyanogen.

Ferrier, *n.* **Kathleen (Mary)** (1912–53), English contralto who sang oratorio and opera. In Britten's *The Rape of Lucretia* (1946) she created the role of Lucretia, and she appeared in Mahler's *Das Lied von der Erde* (1947).

ferriferous, *a.* yielding iron.

Ferris wheel, *n.* a big, upright fairground wheel with seats suspended from its rim. [after G.W.G. *Ferris,* US engineer, 1859–96]

ferrite, *n.* a sintered ceramic consisting of a mixture of ferric oxide and other metallic oxides, which possesses magnetic properties.

ferro-, *comb. form* (*Min.*) denoting a substance containing iron; (*Chem.*) denoting a compound of iron in the ferrous state (cp. FERRI-). [L *ferrum,* iron]

ferrocalcite, *n.* calcite containing carbonate of iron and turning brown on exposure.

ferroconcrete, *n.* concrete strengthened by incorporation of iron bars, strips etc.; reinforced concrete.

ferrocyanic, *a.* (*Chem.*) of or pertaining to iron in the ferrous state and cyanogen. **ferrocyanic acid, ferrocyanhydric acid,** *n.* a white crystalline powder derived from iron and cyanogen. **ferrocyanide,** *n.* a salt of ferrocyanic acid. **ferrocyanogen,** *n.* a radical supposed to be contained in ferrocyanides.

ferromagnetic, *a.* acting magnetically like iron. *n.* a substance acting thus.

ferrosilicon, *n.* (*Chem.*) a compound of silicon and iron added to molten iron to give it a larger proportion of silicon.

ferrotype, *n.* a positive photograph on a sensitized film laid on a thin iron plate; the iron plate used in this process.

ferrous, *a.* (*Chem.*) of, pertaining to or containing divalent iron. [L *ferrum,* iron]

ferruginous, *a.* containing iron or iron-rust; of the colour of iron-rust. **ferruginous deposits,** *n. pl.* rocks containing sufficient iron ore to make it worth mining. **ferruginate,** *v.t.* †**ferrugo,** *n.* the rust, a disease of plants. [L *ferrūginus,* from *ferrūgo -inis,* from *ferrum,* iron]

ferrule, *n.* a metallic ring or cap on the handle of a tool, the end of a stick, the joint of a fishing rod, a post etc. to strengthen it; a short piece of pipe screwed into a main to form a connection with a service-pipe. **ferruled,** *a.* [formerly *verrel,* OF *virelle* (F *virole*), late L *virola,* L *viriola,* dim. of *viriae,* bracelets]

ferry, *v.t.* to transport over a river, strait or other narrow water, in a boat, barge etc. *v.i.* to pass across narrow water in a boat etc. *n.* the passage where a ferry-boat plies to carry passengers and goods across a river etc.; the provision of such a method of transport; the right of ferrying and charging toll for so doing; a ferry-boat. **ferry-boat,** *n.* a boat used at a ferry. **ferry-bridge,** *n.* a large vessel used for carrying trains across a ferry; (*N Am.*) the landing-stage at a ferry, esp. on a tidal river where it rises and falls with the tide. **ferryman,** *n.* [OE *ferian,* from *faran,* to FARE]

fertile, *a.* able to sustain abundant growth; able to bear offspring, fruit; capable of growing or developing; productive, fruitful; inventive, resourceful; able to be transformed into fissionable material. **fertility,** *n.* **fertility drug,** *n.* a drug given to apparently infertile women to stimulate ovulation. **fertility rite,** *n.* a pagan religious ceremony intended to ensure the fertility of the soil, beasts or human population. **fertility symbol,** *n.* **fertilize, -ise,** *v.t.* to make fertile or productive; to make rich (as soil); (*Bot. etc.*) to impregnate, fecundate. **fertilizable, -isable,** *a.* **fertilization, -isation,** *n.* **fertilizer, -iser,** *n.* a fertilizing agent; a chemical applied to the soil to improve its growth-promoting qualities and modify its acidity or alkalinity. [OF *fertil,* L *fertilis,* from *ferre,* to bear]

Fertö tó, *n.* Hungarian name for the Neusiedler See.

ferula, *n.* (*pl.* **-lae**) the sceptre of the emperors of the Eastern Empire; a genus of umbelliferous plants, from the shores of the Mediterranean and Persia, yielding gum-resin, typified by the giant fennel; a ferule. **ferulaceous,** *a.* of or pertaining to canes or reeds; having a reed-like stem. [L, a rod, orig. giant fennel]

ferule, *n.* a rod or cane used to punish children in school. *v.t.* to punish with a ferule. [see prec.]

fervent, *a.* hot, boiling, glowing; ardent, earnest, zealous, vehement. **fervently,** *adv.* **fervency,** *n.* **fervid,** *a.* burning, very hot, fervent; impassioned. **fervidly,** *adv.* **fervidness,** *n.* **fervour,** *n.* heat, warmth; ardour, intensity of feeling, vehemence; zeal. [OF, from L *fervens, -ntem,* pres.p. of *fervēre,* to boil]

†**fervescent,** *a.* growing hot. [L *fervescens, -ntem,* pres.p. of *fervescere,* incept. of *fervēre*]

fescennine, *a.* of or pertaining to the ancient festivals of *Fescennia,* a town of Etruria; hence scurrilous, licentious. **fescennine verses,** *n.pl.* extempore dialogues in verses, characterized by broad and licentious satire. [L *Fescennīnus*]

fescue, *n.* a twig, a branch; a small rod or pin with which a teacher pointed out the letters to a child learning to read; a genus of grasses, *Festuca.* **fescue-grass,** *n. Festuca ovina,* an important pasture grass. [ME, OF *festu,* L *festūca,* a stalk, a stem]

fesse, *n.* (*Her.*) a broad band of metal or colour crossing the shield horizontally, and occupying one-third of it; one of the nine honourable ordinaries, representing a knight's girdle. **fesse-point,** *n.* the centre of an escutcheon. [OF, from L *fascia,* see FASCIA]

Fessenden, *n.* **Reginald Aubrey** (1866–1932), Canadian physicist who worked in the US, first for Thomas Edison and then for Westinghouse. He patented the modulation of radio waves (transmission of a signal using a carrier wave), an essential technique for voice transmission. At the time of his death, he held 500 patents.

-fest, *comb. form,* an event or gathering for a particular activity, as *songfest.* [G *Fest,* a celebration]

festal, *a.* pertaining to a feast or holiday; festive, joyous, gay, merry. **festally,** *adv.* [OF, from L *festum,* FEAST]

fester, *v.i.* to ulcerate or suppurate; to form purulent matter; to rankle; to become corrupted or rotten. *v.t.* to cause to fester or rankle. *n.* a purulent tumour or sore; the act or state of festering or rankling. [OF *festre* (whence *festrir,* to fester), L *fistula,* see FISTULA]

festina lente, *v.i.* (*imper.*) make haste slowly, do not be impetuous. [L]

†**festinate,** *a.* hasty, hurried. *v.i.*, to hasten. *v.t.* to

hurry, accelerate. †**festinately,** *adv.* **festination,** *n.* [L *festīnātus,* p.p. of *festīnāre,* to hasten]

festino, *n.* (*Log.*) a mnemonic name for the third mode of the second figure of syllogisms, where the middle term is the predicate of both premises.

festival, *a.* pertaining to or characterizing a feast; festal. *n.* a festal day or time, a joyous celebration or anniversary; a merry-making; a musical entertainment on a large scale, usually periodical; (*N Am.*) an entertainment or fair where fruit and other eatables are sold. **festive,** *a.* of or befitting or used for a feast or festival; joyous, gay, mirthful; (*N Am.*) fast, loud. **festively,** *adv.* **festivity,** *n.* a feast, a festival, a joyous celebration or entertainment; gaiety, mirth, joyfulness; (*pl.*) merry-making. [OF, from late L *festīvālis,* L *festīvus,* from *festum,* FEAST]

festoon, *n.* a chain or garland of flowers, foliage, drapery etc. suspended by the ends so as to form a depending curve; a carved ornament in the form of a garland or wreath. *v.t.* to form into or adorn with or as with festoons. [F *feston,* It. *festone,* prob. from *festum,* see prec.]

festschrift, *n.* a collection of learned writings by various authors, published in honour of some person, usu. a scholar. [G *Fest,* a celebration and *Schrift,* writing]

feta, fetta, *n.* a firm white Greek cheese made from sheep's or goat's milk. [mod. Gr. (*tyri*) *pheta,* from *tyri,* cheese, *pheta,* It. *fetta,* slice]

fetal, fetus, FOETUS.

fetch[1], *v.t.* to go for and bring; to cause to come; to draw forth, to heave (as a sigh); to derive, to elicit; to bring in, to sell for (a price); to bring to any state, condition or position; to reach, to arrive at, to accomplish; (*coll.*) to delight, to charm; (*coll.*) to strike. *v.i.* (*Naut.*) to reach a place, to bring up. *n.* a stratagem, a trick, a dodge, a striving after, a powerful effort; a deep breath, a sigh. **to fetch about, to fetch a compass,** to take a circuitous route or method. **to fetch and carry,** to go to and fro with things; to perform menial tasks. **to fetch a pump,** to pour water into it to make it draw. †**to fetch off,** to get the better of. **to fetch out,** to bring out, to cause to appear. **to fetch to,** to revive, as from a faint. **to fetch up,** to recall, to bring to mind; to vomit; to come to a stand; (*coll.*) to end up; to recover, to make up (lost time etc.); †to overtake; †to bring up, raise, elevate. **to fetch up all standing,** to stop suddenly with sails set. **fetcher,** *n.* **fetching,** *a.* (*coll.*) fascinating, charming, taking. [OE *feccan, fetian,* prob. rel. to *fæt,* step, journey]

fetch[2], *n.* a wraith or double. **fetch-candle,** †**-light,** *n.* a light appearing at night, believed by the superstitious to portend the death of some person. [etym. unknown]

fete, fête, *n.* a festival, an entertainment; in Roman Catholic countries, the festival of the saint after whom a person is named; an outdoor event with stalls and sideshows, usu. locally organized to raise money for charity. *v.t.* to entertain, to feast; to honour with festivities. **fête champêtre,** *n.* an open-air festival. **fête-day,** *n.* a festival day. [F *fête,* OF *feste,* L *festum,* FEAST]

fetial, *a.* of or pertaining to the Fetials; ambassadorial, heraldic. *n.* one of a college of priests in ancient Rome, who presided over the ceremonies connected with the ratification of peace or the formal declaration of war. [L *fetiālis* (etym. unknown)]

feticide, FOETUS.

fetid, foetid, *a,* having an offensive smell; stinking. **fetidly,** *adv.* **fetidness,** *n.* **fetor,** *n.* a strong or offensive smell; a stench. [L *fētidus,* from *fētēre,* to stink]

fetish, *n.* any material object supposed to be the vessel, vehicle or instrument of a supernatural being, the possession of which gives to the possessor or joint possessors power over that being; an object of devotion, an idol; (*Psych.*) an object providing sexual gratification. **fetisheer,** *n.* a sorcerer, a medicine-man. **fetishism,** *n.* belief in fetishes; worship of them; (*Psych.*) a form of perversion in which sexual gratification is obtained from other than the genital parts of the body. **fetishist,** *n.* **fetishistic,** *a.* [F *fétiche,* Port. *feitiço,* sorcery, L *factītius,* artificial]

fetlock, *n.* a tuft of hair behind the pastern joint of a horse; the pastern joint; a fetterlock. [etym. obscure (cp. LG *fitlock,* G *Fissloch*)]

fetor, FETID.

fetta FETA.

fetter, *n.* a chain for the feet; (*usu. pl.*) a shackle, a bond; anything which restrains or confines. *v.t.* to put fetters upon, to bind with fetters; to confine, restrain; to hamper, impede. **fetterlock,** *n.* a shackle for a horse when turned out to grass; (*Her.*) a figure of a shackle and padlock. **fettered,** *a.* chained, bound; hampered, impeded; a term applied to the feet of animals when they stretch backwards so as to be unfit for walking, as in the seals. **fetterless,** *a.* [OE *fetor* (cp. Dut. *veter,* race, G *Fesser,* from OTeut. *fet-,* rel. to *fōt-,* foot, also L *pedica,* Gr. *pedē,* fetter)]

fettle, *v.t.* to clean or put right; to work with activity or zeal. *v.i.* to fuss about, to be busy. *n.* condition, order, trim. **in fine, good fettle,** in good form or trim. [perh. from OE *fetel,* a girdle, belt]

fettuccine, *n.* tagliatelle. [It., pl. of *fettuccina,* dim. of *fettuccia,* a small slice]

fetus, FOETUS.

fetwa, fatwa, *n.* a declaration, interpretation or decision by a mufti on a point of Muslim law. [Arab.]

feu, *n.* (*Sc. Law*) orig., tenure on condition of the performance of certain services or certain returns in money or kind; now, a perpetual lease at a fixed rent; the land, houses or other real estate so held. *v.t.* (*Sc. Law*) to give or take in feu. **feu-duty,** *n.* the annual rent for such a holding. **feu-holding,** *n.* **feu-right,** *n.* **feuar,** *n.* one who holds real estate on feu. [var. of FEE]

feud[1], *n.* hostility between two tribes or families in revenge for an injury, often carried on for several generations; enmity, quarrel, contention, animosity. [ME *fede,* OF *faide,* OHG *fēhida,* cogn. with OE *fæhth,* enmity]

feud[2], *n.* a fief; the right to lands or hereditaments held in trust, or on condition of performing certain services. **feudal,** *a.* pertaining to, consisting of or founded upon a feud or fief; according to or resembling the feudal system. **feudal system,** *n.* a system of social polity prevailing in Europe during the Middle Ages, by which the ownership of land inhered in the lord, possession or tenancy being granted to the vassal in return for military service. **feudalism,** *n.* **feudalist,** *n.* a supporter of feudalism; one versed in feudal law. **feudalistic,** *a.* **feudality,** *n.* the quality or state of being feudal; feudal principles; a fief, a feudal holding. **feudalize, -ise,** *v.t.* to reduce to feudal tenure. **feudalization, -isation,** *n.* **feudally,** *adv.* **feudary,** *a.* held by or pertaining to feudal tenure. *n.* a feudatory; a retainer, a servant; †an officer in the ancient Court of Wards. **feudatory,** *a.* holding or held by feudal tenure; subject; under foreign overlordship. *n.* one who holds lands of another by feudal tenure; a vassal; a fief, a dependent lordship. [med. L *feudum,* see FEE]

feu de joie, *n.* (*pl.* **feux**) the firing of guns in token of public rejoicing. [F, fire of joy]

feuilleton, *n.* that part of a French newspaper which is devoted to light literature, criticism or fiction; a light article or a serial story in a newspaper. [F, from *feuillet,* dim. of *feuille,* L *folia,* pl. of *folium,* leaf]

feuter, FEWTER.

fever, *n.* a disease or group of diseases usu. characterized by high temperature, quickened pulse, nervous and muscular prostration and destruction of tissues; a body temperature above normal; a state of nervous excitement; agitation. *v.t.* to put or throw into a fever. *v.i.* to become feverish. **fever-heat,** *n.* the abnormally high temperature of the body characteristic of fever. **fever-trap,** *n.* a place where fever germs are supposed to abound. **fever-tree,** *n.* the blue-gum tree, *Eucalyptus globulus;* also other trees with febrifugal properties. **fevered,** *a.* **feverish,** *a.* suffering from or affected with fever; indicating fever; resembling a fever; infested with fever; excited, restless, inconstant. **feverishly,** *adv.* **feverishness,** *n.* **feverous,** *a.* [OE *fēfor,* L *febris*]

feverfew, *n.* a common British plant, *Pyrethrum parthenium,* supposed to act as a febrifuge. [corr. of OE *fēferfuge,* L *febrifuga* (*febris, fugāre,* to put to flight)]

few, *a.* not many; small, limited or restricted in number. *n.* a small number (of). **a good few,** (*coll.*) a considerable number. **every few days, hours,** once in every series of a few days or hours. **few and far between,** rare, occurring very infrequently. **in few,** shortly, briefly. **not a few,** a good many. **some few,** not a great number. **the few,** the minority; the elect. **fewness,** *n.* [OE *fēa, fēawe* (cp. OHG *fao,* L *paucus,* Gr. *pauros*)]

fewter, feuter, *n.* a rest for the lance attached to the saddle (orig. lined with felt). [OF *feutre,* med. L *filtrum,* cogn. with FELT, see FILTER]

fewtrils, *n.pl.* (*dial.*) trifles, odds and ends. [OF *fatraille,* trumpery]

fey, *a.* (*chiefly Sc.*) fated, doomed, on the verge of death (implying both the proximity of this event and the impossibility of avoiding it); (*chiefly Sc.*) in unnaturally high spirits; (*chiefly Sc.*) clairvoyant, psychic; eccentric, odd in a whimsical, other-worldly way. [OE *fæge* (cp. Icel. *feigr,* Dut. *veeg,* about to die, G *feige,* cowardly)]

Feynman, *n.* **Richard** (1918–88), US physicist whose work provided foundations for quantum electrodynamics. For this work he was awarded the Nobel physics prize. As a member of the committee investigating the *Challenger* space-shuttle disaster of 1986, he demonstrated the lethal faults in the rubber seals on the shuttle's booster rocket.

fez, *n.* (*pl.* **fezes**) a red cap without a brim, fitting close to the head, with a tassel of silk, wool etc., worn in the Near East. [F, prob. from *Fez,* the chief town of Morocco, where they are manufactured]

Fezzan, *n.* former province of Libya, a desert region, with many oases, and with rock paintings from about 3000 BC. It was captured from Italy in 1942, and placed under French control until 1951 when it became a province of the newly-independent United Kingdom of Libya. It was split into smaller divisions in 1963.

ff, (*abbr.*) folios; (and those e.g. pages) following fortissimo.

fiacre, *n.* a French hackney-coach invented about 1640. [F, said to be named after an innkeeper at the Hotel de St *Fiacre*]

fiancé, *n.* one who is betrothed. **fiancée,** *n. fem.* [F, p.p. of *fiancer,* to betroth]

Fianna Fail, *n.* Republic of Ireland political party, founded by the Irish nationalist de Valera in 1926. It has been the governing party in the Republic of Ireland from 1932–48, 1951–54, 1957–73, 1977–81, 1982, and 1987 to date. It aims at the establishment of a united and completely independent all-Ireland republic.

†**fiant** *n.* a warrant to the Irish Chancery. [L, 3rd pers., pl., let (documents or letters patent) be made out]

fiar, *n.* (*Sc. Law*) one who has the fee-simple or reversion of property. [perh. from FEE, -ER]

fiars, *n.pl.* the prices of grain legally fixed by the sheriff of a Scottish county for the current year, as a basis for certain rates. [ME and OF *feor,* L *forum,* market]

fiasco, *n.* (*pl.* **-cos, -coes**), a failure in a public performance; a ridiculous breakdown, an ignominious sequel. [It., a flask, a bottle (sense obscure)]

fiat, *n.* an order, command, decree, usu. a peremptory one; (*Law*) the order or warrant of a judge or other constituted authority sanctioning or allowing certain processes. [L, let it be done]

fib[1], *n.* a harmless or venial lie; a white lie. *v.i.* (*past, p.p* **fibbed**) to tell fibs. **fibber, fibster,** *n.* one who tells fibs. [perh. from FABLE or obs. redupl. *fible-fable,* nonsense]

fib[2], *n.* a blow. *v.t.* (*past, p.p.* **fibbed**) to pummel. *v.i.* to deal short, smart blows. [etym. unknown]

Fibonacci, *n.* **Leonardo** (*c.* 1175–*c.* 1250), Italian mathematician. He published *Liber abaci* in Pisa (1202), which led to the introduction of Arabic notation into Europe. From 1960, interest increased in Fibonacci numbers, in their simplest form a series in which each number is the sum of its two predecessors (1, 1, 2, 3, 5, 8, 13,...). They have unusual characteristics with possible applications in botany, psychology, and astronomy (for example, a more exact correspondence than is given by Bode's law to the distances between the planets and the Sun).

fibre, (*esp. N Am.*) **fiber,** *n.* a slender filament; a thread, string or filament, of which the tissues of animals and plants are constituted; the substances composed of animal or vegetable tissue forming the raw material in textile manufactures; a structure composed of filaments; foodstuffs with a high fibre content, roughage; essence, nature, material, character, nerve, strength. **fibreboard,** *n.* a building-board composed of fibrous material. **fibreglass,** *n.* very fine filaments of molten glass worked into a synthetic fibre. **fibre-optics,** *n. sing.* a technology based on the transmission of light along bundles of very thin glass or plastic fibres, used esp. in telecommunications and exploratory medicine. **fibrescope,** *n.* a flexible instrument using fibre-optics which enables the operator to see into otherwise inaccessible areas. **fibred,** *a.* composed of or having fibres (*esp. in comb.,* as *finely-fibred*). **fibreless,** *a.* **fibriform,** *a.* **fibrous,** *a.* **fibrously,** *adv.* **fibrousness,** *n.* [F, from L *fibra*]

fibril, fibrilla, *n.* (*pl.* **fibrillae**) a little fibre; (*Bot.*) one of the minute subdivisions in which a branching root terminates; a minute subdivision of a fibre in a nerve, muscle etc. **fibrillar, -lary, fibrillate, -ated,** *a.* **fibrillate,** *v.i.* **fibrillation,** *n.* **fibrilliform,** *a.* **fibrillose,** *a.* [dim. of L *fibra,* as prec.]

fibrin, *n.* a protein contained in the blood, causing it to clot. **vegetable fibrin,** a similar substance left as a residue when gluten is boiled with alcohol. **fibrination,** *n.* the production of an excess of fibrin in the blood, as in inflammatory diseases. **fibrin(o)-,** *comb. form.* **fibrinogen,** *n.* a protein entering into the formation of fibrin and into coagulation. **fibrinolysin,** *n.* an enzyme that promotes the breakdown of blood clots. **fibrinous,** *a.* composed of or of the nature of fibrin. [as prec., -IN]

fibr(o)- *comb. form* denoting a substance consisting of or characterized by fibres. [FIBRE]

fibroid, *a.* of the nature or form of fibre. *n.* a benign tumour.

fibroin, *n.* (*Chem.*) the chief constituent of silk, cobweb, the horny skeleton of sponges etc.

fibroline, *n.* a yarn spun from waste in hemp, flax and jute work, for backing carpets, rugs etc.

fibroma, *n.* (*Path.*) (*pl.* **-mas, -mata**) a benign fibrous tumour.

fibrosis, fibrositis, *n.* muscular rheumatism. [mod. L, as FIBRE]

fibrous etc. FIBRE.

fibula, *n.* (*pl.* **-lae, -las**) the outer and smaller bone of the leg; a clasp, buckle or brooch. **fibular,** *a.* [L, a brooch, from *fīvere,* var. of *fīgere,* to fix]

-fic, *suf.* forming adjectives from nouns, verbs etc., as *honorific, horrific, malefic.* [L *-ficus,* from weakened root of *facere,* to make]

-fication, *suf.* forming nouns from verbs in -FY, as *purification.* [L *-ficātio -ōnem,* from *-ficāre,* see -FY]

ficelle, *a.* of the colour of packthread. [F, packthread]

fiche MICROFICHE.

fichu, *n.* a light covering worn by women over the neck, throat and shoulders. [F, from *ficher,* to fix, to put on]

fickle, *a.* changeable, inconstant. **fickleness,** *n.* †**fickly,** *adv.* [OE *ficol,* rel. to *befician,* to deceive]

†**fico,** *n.* (*pl.* **-coes**) a fig; a gesture of contempt shown by a snap of the fingers. [It., from L *fīcus,* FIG]

fictile, *a.* capable of being moulded; moulded by art; made of earth or clay; manufactured by or suitable for the potter. [L *fictilis,* from *fingere,* to fashion]

fiction, *n.* the act or art of feigning or inventing; that which is feigned, imagined or invented; an invented statement or narrative; a story, a romance; literature, esp. in prose, consisting of invented narrative; a falsehood; any point or thing assumed for the purposes of justice or convenience. **legal fiction,** an accepted falsehood which averts the raising of an awkward issue. **fictional,** *a.* **fictionalize, -ise,** *v.t.* to introduce fictional elements into (a narrative of real events). **fictionist,** *n.* a writer of fiction; a novelist. **fictitious,** *a.* feigned, imaginary, counterfeit, false, assumed; of or pertaining to novels; having no real existence; accepted by a conventional or legal fiction. **fictitiously,** *adv.* **fictitiousness,** *n.* **fictive,** *a.* imaginative, creative; imaginary, fictitious, feigned, counterfeit. [F, from L *fictio -ōnem,* from *fingere,* see prec.]

fid, *n.* (*Naut.*) a bar of wood or iron to support a topmast; a pointed wooden pin used to open the strands of a rope in splicing; a wooden or metal bar used as a support etc.; a plug of oakum for the vent of a cannon. [etym. doubtful]

-fid *comb. form* divided into parts. [L *-fidus,* from *findere,* to split]

fiddle, *n.* a violin; (*Naut.*) a frame of bars and strings, to keep things from rolling off the cabin table in bad weather; (*coll.*) a swindle, a dishonest practice; (*coll.*) an awkward or tricky operation. *v.i.* to play on a fiddle; to make restless movements with the hands or fingers; to waste time in aimless activity. *v.t.* to play (as a tune) on a fiddle; to falsify (accounts etc.); to contrive to do or obtain something by underhand means. **fit as a fiddle,** in good condition, ready for anything. **on the fiddle,** (*coll.*) cheating, being dishonest, falsifying accounts etc. for one's own advantage. **to fiddle (about, around) with,** to tinker, to fuss with; to interfere or tamper with. **to play first, second fiddle,** to take a leading or a subordinate part or position. **fiddle-block,** *n.* (*Naut.*) a block with two sheaves. **fiddle-bow,** *n.* the bow with which a fiddle is played. **fiddle-case,** *n.* a case for holding a fiddle. **fiddlededee,** *n., int.* nonsense. **fiddle-faddle,** *n.* trifling talk; nonsense. *a.* trifling; making a fuss about trifles. *v.i.* to trifle; to make a fuss about trifles. **fiddle-faddler,** *n.* **fiddle-head,** *n.* ornamental carving at the bows of a ship, in the form of a volute. **fiddle-pattern,** *n.* a fiddle-shaped pattern for the heads of spoons and forks. **fiddlestick,** *n.* a fiddle-bow; (*pl.*) rubbish, something absurd. *int.* (*pl.*) fiddlededee. **fiddle-wood,** *n.* one of several tropical American trees yielding hard wood. **fiddler,** *n.* one who plays the fiddle; a small crab, *Gelasimus vocans,* having one large claw and one very small one; (*Austral.*) a variety of ray; one who makes a fuss about trifles; †(*sl.*) a sixpence. **fiddler-fish,** *n.* a W Indian ray, *Rhinobatus percellens,* also called the guitar fish. **fiddling,** *a.* trifling, fussy; petty, contemptible. **fiddly,** *a.* tricky, awkward; small, difficult to manipulate; fiddling. [OE *fithele,* etym. doubtful (cp. Dut. *vedel,* G *Fiedel*)]

fiddley, *n.* (*Naut.*) the iron framework enclosing the deck-hatch leading to the stoke-hole of a steamer; the space below this. [etym. unknown]

fidei-commissum, fidei-commiss, *n.* a testator's bequest to trustees; a trust or trust estate. **fidei-commissary,** *n.* a beneficiary by such a bequest or trust. **fidei-commissor,** *n.* one who creates a fidei-commissum. [L, neut. p.p. of *fidei-committere* (*fidei* dat. of *fidēs,* faith, *committere,* to entrust, COMMIT)]

Fidei Defensor, *n.* title of 'Defender of the Faith' (still retained by British sovereigns) conferred by Pope Leo X on Henry VIII of England to reward his writing of a treatise against the Protestant Martin Luther. [L]

fidelity, *n.* careful and loyal observance of duty; faithful adherence to a bond, covenant, engagement or connection; loyalty, faithfulness, esp. to husband or wife; honesty, veracity, reliability; accurate correspondence (of a copy, description, picture etc.) to the original. [F *fidélité,* L *fidēlitās -tātem,* from *fidēlis,* from *fidēs,* faith]

fidget, *n.* a state of nervous restlessness; one who fidgets; one who worries or makes (others) uncomfortable; (*pl.*) restless movements. *v.i.* to move about restlessly; to worry, to be uneasy. *v.t.* to worry or make (others) uncomfortable. **fidgety,** *a.* **fidgetiness,** *n.* [from prec.]

fidibus, *n.* a paper match or spill for lighting pipes, candles etc. [etym. unknown]

fiducial, *a.* confident, sure, firm; of the nature of a trust; (*Phys., Surv.* etc.) denoting a fixed point or line used as a basis for measurement or comparison. **fiducially,** *adv.* **fiduciary,** *a.* pertaining to or of the nature of a trust or a trusteeship; held in trust; confident, trustful, unwavering. *n.* a trustee. [L *fidūciālis,* from *fidūcia,* trust, from *fidēre,* to trust, *fidēs,* faith]

fidus Achates, *n.* a trusty friend, a faithful henchman. [L, the faithful Achates, the devoted follower of Aeneas in Virgil's *Aeneid*]

fie, *int.* an exclamation indicating contempt, irony, disgust, shame or impatience. [ME and OF *fi,* L *fī*]

fief, *n.* an estate held of a superior under feudal tenure; feudal tenure. [OF, from L *fevum,* see FEE]

Field, *n.* **Sally** (1946–), US film and television actress. She won an Academy Award for *Norma Rae* (1979) and again for *Places in the Heart* (1984). Her other films include *Hooper* (1978), *Absence of Malice* (1981), and *Murphy's Romance* (1985).

field, *n.* a piece of land, esp. one enclosed for tillage or pasture; a region yielding some natural product abundantly (as an oil- or coal-field); the place where a battle is fought; the battle itself; the scene of military operations; the ground on which cricket, football or other games are played; the fielders or players taken collectively; all the competitors in a race, or all except the favourite; the participants in a hunt; a sphere of activity or knowledge; an interest or speciality; the sphere of practical operations away from the office, laboratory etc.; the open country; a wide expanse, as of sea or sky; the surface on which the figures in a picture are drawn; (*Her.*) the surface of a shield or one of its divisions; a field of force; (*Math.*) a set of mathematical elements subject to two binary operations, addition and multiplication, such that the set is a commutative group under addition and also under multiplication if zero is excluded; (*Comput.*) a set of characters comprising a unit of information; (*TV*) one of two interlaced sets of scanning lines. *v.t.* (*Cricket etc.*) to catch or stop (the ball) and return it; to retrieve (something or someone liable to go astray); to deal with (as questions), esp. off the cuff; to assemble ready for action (as a team, an army). *v.i.* to act as fielder in cricket and other games; (*Sporting*) to back the field against the favourite. **field of force,** (*Phys.*) an agency acting in a region of space by which an object exerts a force on another non-touching object because of certain properties they both possess. **field of view, vision,** the space visible in an optical instrument at one view. **to bet, lay against the field,** to bet on one or more horses, dogs etc. against all the others in a race. **to hold the field,** to maintain one's ground against all comers; to surpass all competitors. **to play the field,** to diversify one's interests or activities, esp. not to commit oneself to a steady boy or girl friend. **to take the field,** to commence active military operations; to begin a campaign; to go on to the field of play. **field-allowance,** *n.* an extra payment to officers on a campaign to meet the increased cost of living etc. **field-artillery,** *n.* light ordnance suitable for use in the field. **field-bed,** *n.* a folding bed; a camp-bed; †a bed in the open air. **field-book,** *n.* a book used by surveyors, engineers etc., in which the memoranda of surveys are set down. **field-botanist, -geologist, -naturalist,** *n.* one who observes, tests and demonstrates the principles of his or her science by means of practical study of outdoor nature. †**field-colours,** *n.pl.* (*Mil.*) camp colours, small flags for marking out the ground for squadrons and battalions; the colours used by troops on a campaign. **field-cricket,** *n.* a large cricket, *Acheta (Gryllus) campestris,* found in hot sandy localities. **field-day,** *n.* a day on which troops are exercised in field evolutions; (*fig.*) a day of unusual importance, excitement or display. **to have a field day,** to take gleeful advantage of. **field-dressing,** *n.* medical appliances for use on the battlefield. **field-duck,** *n.* the little bustard, *Otis tetrax*. **field-equipage,** *n.* (*Mil.*) equipage, accoutrements etc. for service in the field. **field events,** *n.pl.* athletic events other than racing, e.g. running, jumping etc. **field-glass(es),** *n.* (*pl.*) a binocular telescope in compact form. **field goal,** *n.* in American football, a score made by kicking the ball over the crossbar from ordinary play; in basketball, a score made while the ball is in play. **field-gun,** *n.* a light artillery piece for service in the field. **field hockey,** *n.* (*N Am.*) hockey played on grass. **field-hospital,** *n.* an ambulance or temporary hospital near a battlefield. **field-ice,** *n.* ice formed in the polar regions in fields or floes, as distinct from icebergs. **field-marshal,** *n.* an officer of highest rank in the British Army. **field-meeting,** *n.* an open-air meeting for worship or preaching, a conventicle. **fieldmouse,** *n.* one of several species of mice living in fields etc. **field-night,** *n.* an evening or night marked by some important meeting, business or event. **field-notes,** *n.pl.* notes made on the spot during fieldwork. **field-officer,** *n.* (*Mil.*) an officer above the rank of captain, but below that of general (as a major, a colonel etc.). **field-piece** FIELD-GUN. **field-preacher,** *n.* one who preaches at religious meetings in the open air. **field-sports,** *n.pl.* outdoor sports, such as hunting, shooting, coursing etc. **field-strength,** *n.* the power of an electric (magnetic) field at some precise point. **field-telegraph,** *n.* a movable telegraph system for use on campaign, manoeuvres etc. **field-train,** *n.* a department of the Royal Artillery for the supply of ammunition to the army at the front. **field trial,** *n.* (*often pl.*) a test on a new invention, design etc. carried out under actual operating conditions. **field trip,** *n.* a visit undertaken by schoolchildren or students to study phenomena or collect information in situ. **field-winding,** *n.* a coil of wire wound on iron in order to make a strong electromagnetic field when the current is passing. **fieldwork,** *n.* observations or operations carried out in situ by students, researchers, anthropologists, surveyors etc.; (*pl.*) temporary fortifications thrown up by besiegers or besieged. **fieldworker,** *n.* †**fielded,** *a.* engaged in the field or in action; encamped. **fielder, fieldsman,** *n.* one who fields at cricket etc. **fieldwards,** *adv.* [OE *feld* (cp. Dut. *veld,* G *Feld*)]

fieldfare, *n.* a species of thrush, *Turdus pilaris,* a winter visitant in England. [OE *feldefare;* prob. fieldgoer]

Fielding, *n.* **Henry** (1707–54), English novelist, whose narrative power influenced the form and technique of the novel and helped to make it the most popular form of literature in England. In 1742 he parodied Richardson's novel *Pamela* in his *Joseph Andrews,* which was followed by *Jonathan Wild the Great* (1743); his masterpiece *Tom Jones* (1749), which he described as a 'comic epic in prose'; and *Amelia* (1751).

Fields[1], *n.* **Gracie** (stage name of Grace Stansfield) (1898–1979), English comedian and singer. Her humorously sentimental films include *Sally in our Alley* (1931) and *Sing as We Go* (1934).

Fields[2], *n.* **W. C.** (stage name of William Claude Dukenfield) (1879–1946), US actor and screenwriter. His distinctive speech and professed attitudes such as hatred of children and dogs gained him enormous popularity in films such as *David Copperfield* (1935), *My Little Chickadee* (co-written with Mae West) and *The Bank Dick* both (1940), and *Never Give a Sucker an Even Break* (1941).

fiend, *n.* †an enemy; a demon, a devil, an infernal being; a person of diabolical wickedness or cruelty. **the fiend,** Satan. **fiendish,** *a.* **fiendishly,** *adv.* **fiendishness,** *n.* **fiendlike,** *a.* [OE, *fēond,* from *fēogan,* to hate (cp. G *Feind*)]

Fiennes, *n.* **Ranulph Twisleton-Wykeham** (1944–), British explorer who made the first surface journey around the world's polar axis (1979–82). Earlier expeditions included explorations of the White Nile (1969), Jostedalsbre Glacier, Norway (1970), and the Headless Valley, Canada (1971). Accounts of his adventures include *A Talent for Trouble* (1970), *Hell on Ice* (1979), and the autobiographical *Living Dangerously* (1987).

fierce, *a.* savage, furiously hostile or combative; raging, violent; vehement, ardent, eager, impetuous; intense, strong; †great. **fiercely,** *adv.* **fierceness,** *n.* [OF *fers, fiers,* nom. of *fer, fier,* L *ferus,* wild]

fieri-facias, *n.* (*Law*) a writ to the sheriff to levy of the goods and chattels of the defendant the sum or debt to be recovered. [L, cause it to be done]

fiery, *a.* consisting of fire, on fire, flaming with fire; hot, like fire; glowing or red, like fire; flashing, ardent, inflaming, inflamed; highly inflammable, liable to explosions, as a mine; of curry etc., hot-tasting; vehement, ardent, eager; passionate, hot-tempered, irascible; pugnacious, mettlesome, untamed. **fiery cross,** *n.* a wooden cross, the ends of which had been set on fire, and extinguished in the blood of an animal slain for the purpose, formerly sent round in the Highlands to summon a clan to war; a flaming cross used as a means of intimidation by the Ku Klux Klan. **fiery-footed,** *a.* swift, rapid, impetuous. †**fiery-new,** *a.* brand-new. †**fiery-pointed,** *a.* emitting rays pointed with fire. **fiery-red,** *a.* red as fire. **fiery-wheeled,** *a.* having wheels of or like fire. **fierily,** *adv.* **fieriness,** *n.*

fiesta, *n.* a saint's day; a holiday or festivity. [Sp.]

Fife, *n.* region of E Scotland (formerly the county of Fife), facing the North Sea and Firth of Forth. **area** 1300 sq km/502 sq miles. **towns** administrative headquarters Glenrothes; Dunfermline, St Andrews, Kirkcaldy, Cupar. **physical** the only high land is the Lomond Hills, in the NW; chief rivers Eden and Leven. **population** (1987) 345,000. **products** potatoes, cereals, electronics, petrochemicals (Mossmorran), light engineering.

fife, *n.* a small flute-like pipe, chiefly used in martial music. *v.i.* to play upon a fife. *v.t.* to play (tunes) on the fife. †**fife-major,** *n.* a non-commissioned officer who formerly superintended the fifers of a regiment. **fife-rail,** *n.* (*Naut.*) a rail on the quarter-deck and poop or around the mast of a vessel, said to be so called because a fifer sat on this whilst the anchor was being weighed. **fifer,** *n.* [either from F *fifre* or through G *Pfeife,* pipe, from OHG *pfīfa,* a PIPE, from *pfīfan,* to PIPE]

fifish, *a.* queer, cranky, not quite right mentally. [county of *Fife*]

fifteen, *n.* the number or figure 15 or XV; the age of 15; a set of fifteen players, pips on a card, or other things; a Rugby football team; (a shirt with) a neck measuring 15 inches. *a.* 15 in number; aged 15. **the Fifteen,** see separate entry. **fifteenth,** *n.* one of 15 equal parts; (*Mus.*) the interval of a double octave; an organ-stop sounding two octaves above the open diapason. *n., a.* (the) last of 15 (people, things etc.); (the) next after the 14th. [OE *fīftȳne*]

Fifteen, the, Jacobite rebellion of 1715, led by the 'Old Pretender' James Francis Edward Stuart and the Earl of Mar, in order to place the former on the English throne. Mar was checked at Sheriffmuir, Scotland, and the revolt collapsed.

fifth, *n.* one of five equal parts; (*Mus.*) a diatonic interval of five notes, equal to three tones and a semitone; two notes separated by this interval sounded together; the resulting concord. *n., a.* (the) last of five (people, things etc.); (the) next after the fourth. **the Fifth Amendment,** an amendment to the US constitution allowing a defendant the right to refuse to testify against him- or herself and prohibiting a second trial for an offence of which a person has been acquitted. **fifth column,** *n.* persons in a country who, whether as individuals or as members of an organization, are ready to give help to an enemy. Origin of the phrase is attributed to General Mola who, in the Spanish Civil War, said that he had four columns encircling Madrid and a fifth column in the city, being sympathizers ready to assist the attacking party. **fifth columnist,** *n.* **Fifth Monarchy,** *n.* the last of the five great empires referred to in Dan. ii.44, identified with the millennial reign of Christ prophesied in the Apocalypse. **Fifth-monarchy man,** one of a sect of enthusiasts in the time of Cromwell, who declared themselves 'subjects only of King Jesus', and believed that a fifth universal monarchy (after those of Assyria, Persia, Greece and Rome) would be established shortly on earth under the personal reign of Christ, and that no government ought to rule mankind until His coming. **fifth wheel,** *n.* (*chiefly N Am.*) a spare wheel; a superfluous person or thing. **fifthly,** *adv.* in the fifth place. [OE *fifta* (cp. G *fünfte,* Gr. *pemptos,* L *quinctus*)]

fifty, *n.* the number or figure 50 or L; the age of 50. *a.* 50 in number; aged 50. **fifty-fifty,** *adv.* in equal shares, half each. *a.* even, as likely to be unfavourable as favourable. **fifties,** *n.pl.* the period of time between one's 50th and 60th birthdays; the range of temperatures between 50 and 60 degrees; the period of time between the 50th and 60th years of a century. **fiftieth,** *n.* one of 50 equal parts. *n., a.* (the) last of 50 (people, things etc.); (the) next after the 49th. **fifty-fold,**, *a., adv.* [OE *fiftig* (cp. G *fünfzig*)]

fig[1], *n.* the pear-shaped fleshy fruit of the genus *Ficus,* esp. *F. carica;* the tree bearing this, noted for its broad and handsome leaves; other trees bearing similar fruit; the fruit of these; anything valueless, a trifle; a spongy excrescence on a horse's frog, consequent on a bruise; (*N Am. sl.*) a small piece of tobacco; †a fico; †(*pl.*) the piles. †*v.t.* (*past, p.p.* **figged**) to insult with ficoes or contemptuous motions of the fingers. **fig-leaf,** *n.* the leaf of a fig-tree; a flimsy covering, from the use made of the fig-leaf in statuary to conceal nakedness. **fig-tree,** *n. Ficus carica,* a native of W Asia, which produces the edible fig; other trees bearing similar fruit. **figwort,** *n.* plants of the genus *Scrophularia,* esp. *S. aquatica* and *S. nodosa* (from their being popular remedies for piles); the pilewort, *Ranunculus ficaria*. [F *figue,* L *ficus*]

fig[2], *v.t.* (*past, p.p.* **figged**) to dress, deck, rig (up or out). *n.* dress, array, outfit, equipment. **in full fig,** in full dress. **in good fig,** in good form or condition. **to fig out** (a horse), to make lively. **figgery,** *n.* elaborate ornament. [var. of FEAGUE]

fig[3], (*abbr.*) figure; figurative(ly).

fight, *v.i.* (*past, p.p.* **fought**) to contend in arms or in battle, or in single combat (with, against); to strive for victory or superiority, to war; to oppose, to offer resistance; (*chiefly N Am.*) to quarrel, to disagree. *v.t.* to contend with, to struggle against; to maintain by conflict; to contend over; to engage in, to carry on or wage (a contest, battle, lawsuit, campaign etc.); to gain or win by conflict; to manage, lead or manoeuvre in battle; to take part in (a boxing match); to set on or cause (as cocks) to fight. *n.* a struggle between individuals or armies, to injure each other or obtain the mastery; a battle, a combat; a contest of any kind, contention; a boxing match; a quarrel, a row; power of or inclination for fighting; †(*usu. pl.*) a kind of screen or bulwark for protecting the crew on shipboard. **running fight,** a fight in which one party flees and the other pursues, the contest being continued during the chase; a protracted battle, esp. one that is continually broken off and renewed. **sham fight,** a series of manoeuvres carried out for practice or display. **stand-up fight,** an open encounter. **to fight back,** to resist; to counter-attack. **fightback,** *n.* **to fight (it) out,** to decide (a contest or wager) by fighting. **to fight off,** to repel. **to fight shy of,** to avoid from a feeling of mistrust, dislike or fear. **fighter,** *n.* one who fights; a boxer; a combative person, one who does not give in easily; an aircraft equipped to attack other aircraft. **fighter-bomber,** *n.* **fighting,** *n.* **fighting chance,** *n.* a chance of success if every effort is made. **fighting-cock,** *n.* a game-cock. **to live like fighting-cocks,** to get the best of food and drink. **fighting-fish,** *n.* an artificial variety of *Betta pugnax,* a small Thai freshwater fish, kept for fighting. **fighting fit,** *a.* in peak condition. **fighting-man,** *n.* [OE *feohtan* (cp. Dut. *vechten,* OHG *fehtan,* G *fechten*)]

figment, *n.* a fiction, an invented statement, something that exists only in the imagination, a fabrication, a fable. [L *figmentum* (*fig-,* base of *fingere,* to feign, -MENT)]

†**figo,** FICO.

figuline, *a.* produced by or suitable for the potter; fictile. *n.* pottery; potter's clay. [L *figulīnus,* from *figulus,* a potter]

figure, *n.* the external form or shape of a person or thing; bodily shape, esp. from the point of view of its attractiveness; the representation of any form, as by carving, modelling, painting, drawing, embroidery, weaving or any other process; a statue, an image; a combination of lines or surfaces enclosing a space, as a triangle, sphere etc.; a diagram, an illustrative drawing, a pattern; an emblem, a type, a simile; a fancy, a creation of the imagination, an idea; a personage, a character; the sensible or mental impression that a person makes, appearance, distinction; a symbol representing a number, esp. one of the 10 Arabic numerals; the several steps or movements which a dancer makes in accord with the music; a certain movement or division in a set dance; (*Skating*) a movement or combination of movements beginning and ending at a fixed point; (*Rhet.*) any mode of speaking or writing in which words are deflected from their literal or ordinary sense, such as metaphor, ellipsis, hyperbole; (*Gram.*) a recognized deviation from the ordinary form or construction; (*Mus.*) a phrase, a short series of notes producing a single impression; (*Log.*) the form of a syllogism with respect to the position of the middle term; (*Astrol.*) a horoscope; a sum, an amount; value, a price. *v.t.* to form an image, likeness or representation of; to represent, to picture, to imagine; to symbolize, to typify; to cover, adorn or ornament with figures; to work out in figures, to cipher, to reckon; to mark with numbers or prices; to express by a metaphor or image; (*Mus.*) to mark with figures indicating the harmony; (*chiefly N Am.*) to believe, to consider, to conclude. *v.i.* to cipher; to appear, to be conspicuous; to make or cut a figure; to seem rational, to accord with expectation. **a high, low figure,** high or low price. **double, three, four figures,** number, price or income between 9 and 100, 99 and 1000, or 999 and 10,000. **figure of eight,** (*esp. N Am.*) **figure eight,** a shape or movement resembling the Arabic numeral eight (8). **figure of speech,** a figurative use of language. **to cut a figure** CUT[1]. **to figure on,** (*chiefly N Am.*) to plan to; to base one's plans or calculations on. **to figure out,** to ascertain by computation, to work out; to understand, to fathom. **to figure up,** to add up, reckon. **to keep, lose one's figure,** to remain or cease to be shapely and attractive. **to put a figure on,** (*coll.*) to state the exact number or amount of. †**figure-caster,** *n.* an astrologer, a fortune-teller. **figure-dance,** *n.* a dance or dancing with elaborate figures. **figure-dancer,** *n.* **figure eight** FIGURE OF EIGHT. **figurehead,** *n.* the ornamental bust or full-length carving on the prow of a ship above the cutwater, and immediately below the bowsprit; a nominal leader or chief personage without real authority. **figure skating,** *n.* skating in prescribed patterns. **figure-weaving,** *n.* the process of weaving figured fabrics. †**figurable,** *a.* that may be brought to a definite figure or shape; that may be represented figuratively. †**figural,** *a.* represented by a figure or delineation; (*Mus.*) figurate. **figurant,** *n.* a ballet-dancer who merely appears as one of a group. **figurante,** *n. fem.* †**figurate,** *a.* of a fixed and determinate form; resembling anything of a distinctive form; (*Mus.*) florid, figured; figurative, metaphorical. **figuration,** *n.* the act of giving a certain determinate form to; determination to a certain form; form, shape, conformation, outline; a figurative representation; ornamentation; (*Mus.*) florid or figured counterpoint. **figurative,** *a.* representing something by a figure or type, typical; emblematic, symbolic, metaphorical, not literal; full of figures of speech; flowery, ornate; pictorial or plastic. **figuratively,** *adv.* **figurativeness,** *n.* **figured,** *a.* adorned with figures or devices; represented by figures, pictured; of wood, with variegated or ornamental grain; shaped in a (certain) fashion; †figurative; †figurate. **-figured**, *comb. form* having a certain or specified kind of figure. **figured bass,** *n.* (*Mus.*) a bass having the accompanying chords indicated by numbers above or below the notes. **figured muslin,** *n.* muslin in which a pattern is worked. **figureless,** *a.* shapeless. †**figurial**, *a.* represented by a figure. **figurine**, *n.* a statuette in clay or metal. †**figurist,** *n.* one who makes use of or interprets figures. [F, from L *figūra,* from *fig-*, stem of *fingere,* see FEIGN]

figwort FIG[1].

Fiji, *n.* group of islands in the SW Pacific. **area** 18,337 sq km/7078 sq miles. **capital** Suva on Viti Levu. **physical** comprises some 800 Melanesian islands (about 100 inhabited), the largest being Viti Levu (10,386 sq km/ 400 sq miles) and Vanua Levu (5535 sq km/2137 sq miles); mountainous, with tropical forest. **population** (1986) 714,000 (46% Fijian, holding 80% of the land communally, and 49% Indian, introduced in the 19th century to work the sugar crop); annual growth rate 1.9%. **exports** sugar, coconut oil, ginger, timber, canned fish; tourism is important. **language** English (official); Fijian, Hindi. **religion** Hindu 50%, Methodist 44%.

Fijian, *n.* a member of the Melanesian population of the Fiji islands; the language of this people; a citizen of Fiji. **Fijian,** *a.*

fike, *v.i.* (*chiefly Sc.*) to fidget, to be fussy or restless. *v.t.* to trouble, to worry. *n.* (*chiefly Sc.*) fuss, trouble. **the fikes,** the fidgets. **fikey,** *a.* [etym. doubtful]

†**filaceous,** *a.* consisting of threads. [L *fīlum,* a thread, -ACEOUS]

filacer, -zer, *n.* an officer who filed original writs, and issued processes, attachments etc. in connection with the Court of Common Pleas, the King's Bench and the Court of Exchequer. [from. A-F *filaz,* med. L *filacium,* prob. from L *fīlum,* thread]

filament, *n.* a slender, thread-like process, a fibre or fibril, such as those of which animal and vegetable tissues are composed; the thread of carbon or metal in an incandescent electric lamp; the heater wire of a thermionic valve; that part of the stamen which supports the anther. **filamentary**, *a.* of the nature of or formed by a filament or filaments. **filamented,** *a.* furnished with filaments. **filamentose, -tous**, *a.* like a filament; composed of filaments; bearing filaments. [F, from late L *fīlāmentum,* from *fīlāre,* to spin, L *fīlum,* a thread]

filar, *a.* of or pertaining to a thread; furnished with threads. **filatory,** *n.* a machine for forming or spinning threads. [L *fīlum,* a thread]

Filaria, *n.* a genus of parasitic nematode worms producing live embryos which find their way into the bloodstream of the human host. **filarial,** *a.* **filariasis,** *n.* elephantiasis and other manifestations of filarial infection. [L *fīlum,* a thread]

filasse, *n.* prepared fibre as distinguished from the raw material. [F, as prec.]

filature, *n.* the reeling of silk from cocoons; the apparatus used; floss-silk; an establishment for reeling silk. [F, from L *fīlāre,* to spin, as prec.]

filazer FILACER.

filbert, *n.* the nut of the cultivated hazel, *Corylus avellana.* [F *noix de filbert,* from St *Philibert,* whose feast is on 22 Aug. (o.s.), when they are ripe]

filch, *v.t.* to steal, to pilfer. *n.* that which is filched; a filcher; the act of filching. **filcher,** *n.* a petty thief, a pilferer. [etym. doubtful]

Filchner, *n.* **Wilhelm** (1877–1957), German explorer who travelled extensively in Central Asia, but is remembered for his expedition into the Weddell Sea of Antarctica, where his ship became ice-bound for a whole winter. He landed a party and built a hut on the floating ice shelf, which eventually broke up and floated northwards.

file[1], *n.* a box or folder, a string or wire, or similar devices in or on which documents are kept in order, for preservation and convenience of reference; the papers so preserved; a collection of papers arranged in order of date or subject for ready reference, esp. in a court of law in connection with a case; a set of periodicals arranged in order of publication; (*Comput.*) a block of data with a unique name by means of which it can be accessed; a row of soldiers ranged one behind the other from front to rear; a row of persons or things arranged in this way; (*Chess*) a line of squares extending from player to player; †a roll, list, catalogue; †a rank, series or class. *v.t.* to place in or on a file; to arrange in order and endorse; (*Law*) to place on the records of a court, to initiate (charges, a lawsuit); to send in (a story) to a newspaper. *v.i.* to place in file; to initiate a lawsuit; to march in file or line, as soldiers. **a file of men,** a small body, now usu. two, told off for a specific duty. **Indian, single file,** a single line of people drawn up or marching thus. **in file,** drawn up or marching in a line or lines of people one behind another. **on file,** preserved and catalogued for reference. **rank and file,** RANK. **to file away,** to preserve or catalogue in a file. **to file off,** to wheel off by files and march at right angles to the former direction. †**to file with,** to keep pace with. **file-leader,** *n.* the soldier placed in front of a file; †a captain of a troop. **filing cabinet,** *n.* a cabinet with drawers for storing files. [F *fil,* L *fīlum,* a thread]

file[2], *n.* a steel instrument with ridged surface, used for cutting and smoothing metals, ivory, wood etc.; anything used to polish or refine; (*sl.*) a sly, cunning or artful person; a cove. *v.t.* to smooth or polish; to cut (the surface) away with a file; to polish, to elaborate. **close file,** a miser. **to gnaw a file,** to attempt obstinately a task that ends only in vexation. **file-cutter,** *n.* a maker of files. **file-fish,** *n.* any fish of the family *Balistidae* from the toothed character of the dorsal spine; (*New Zealand*) an edible, thick-skinned fish. [OE *fēol* (cp. Dut. *vijl,* G *Feile*)]

†**file[3],** *v.t.* to defile, to taint, to pollute. [OE *-fȳlan* (in *gefȳlan*), to make foul, from *fūl,* FOUL]

†**filemot,** *a.* coloured like a dead leaf; russet-yellow. *n.* this colour. [corr. of F *feuille morte,* dead leaf]

filet, FILLET. **filet mignon** , *n.* a small, very tender steak cut from tail end of a fillet of beef. [F]

filial, *a.* pertaining to a son or daughter; befitting a child in relation to parents; †bearing the relation of a son or daughter. **filial generation,** *n.* (*Genetics*) a generation following a parental generation. **filiality**, *n.* **filially,** *adv.* †**filiate,** *v.t.* to affiliate. **filiation,** *n.* the relation of a child to its father, the correlative of paternity; descent, transmission (from); genealogical relation; (*Law*) affiliation. [late L *fīliālis,* from *fīlius,* son, *fīlia,* daughter]

filibeg, *n.* a kilt of the modern kind, dist. from the great kilt of olden times, which covered the body. [Sc., from Gael. *feileadh-beag* (*feileadh,* fold, *beag,* little)]

filibuster, *n.* a lawless military adventurer, esp. one in quest of plunder, a freebooter, a buccaneer; one who takes part in an unauthorized military expedition into a foreign state; a parliamentary obstructionist, one who seeks to hinder legislation by prolonged speeches. *v.i.* to act as a filibuster. **filibusterism,** *n.* **filibusterous,** *a.* [Sp., corr. from Dut. *vrijbuiter,* a freebooter (*vrij,* free, *buit,* booty)]

Filices, *n.pl.* the order or group containing the ferns, more recently called **Filicales**, **filical**, *a.* pertaining to the ferns or Filicales. **filiciform**, *a.* having the shape of a fern. **filicite**, *a.* a fossil fern or fern-like plant. **filicoid**, *a.* filiciform. *n.* a fern-like plant. [L, pl. of *filix,* fern]

filiform, *a.* having the form of a thread; long, slender, round and equally thick throughout. [L *fīlum,* a thread]

filigree, †**filigrane**, *n.* ornamental work, executed in fine gold or silver wire, plaited, and formed into delicate openwork or tracery; any ornamental tracery or openwork; anything delicate and fantastic, showy and fragile. *a.* pertaining to filigree; composed of or resembling filigree. **filigreed,** *a.* ornamented with filigree. [F *filigrane,* It. *filigrana* (*filo,* L *fīlum,* a thread, *grano,* L *grānum,* GRAIN)]

filings, *n.pl.* the fine particles cut or rubbed off with a file.

Filioque, *n.* the clause in the Nicene Creed asserting the procession of the Holy Ghost from the Son as well as from the Father, which is rejected by the Eastern Church. *a.* pertaining to this. [L, and from the Son]

Filipino, *n.* (*pl.* **-nos**) an inhabitant of the Philippine Islands. *a.* pertaining to the Philippines or their inhabitants. [Sp., from *Felipe, Philip II,* of Spain]

fill¹, *v.t.* to put or pour into till no more can be admitted; to make full (with); to occupy the whole capacity or space of, to pervade, to spread over or throughout; to block up (cracks with putty, hollow tooth with stopping etc.); to satisfy, to glut; to fulfil, to meet; to stock or store abundantly; to cause to be filled or crowded; to appoint an incumbent or person to discharge the duties of; to hold; to discharge the duties of; to occupy (time); to distend (as sails); to trim (a sail) to catch the wind; (*N Am.*) to make up (a prescription). *v.i.* to become or grow full; to be distended; to be satisfied; to pour out liquor, to give to drink; †to become satisfied or replete. *n.* as much as will satisfy; a full supply; as much as will fill. **to fill an order,** to execute a trade order. **to fill in,** to insert, so as to fill a vacancy; to complete (anything that is unfinished, as an outline or a form); (*coll.*) to provide with necessary or up-to-date information; to occupy (time); to act as a temporary substitute (for). **to fill out,** to become bigger or fatter, to become distended; to enlarge; (*chiefly N Am.*) to complete (a form etc.). **to fill the bill,** (*coll.*) to do or be all that is required. **to fill up,** to fill or occupy completely; to make up the deficiencies in, to supply what is wanting in; to supply, to discharge; to fulfil, to satisfy; to stop up by filling; to become full. **to have one's fill of,** to have rather too much of. †**fill-belly,** *n.* a glutton. **filler,** *n.* one who or that which fills; a funnel used in filling casks, bottles etc.; material used to fill cracks and holes in plaster, woodwork etc.; an item used to fill a space between more important items (as in a newspaper, a TV programme, a schedule etc.); the filling orifice of a petrol tank, gearbox, crankcase etc. **filler cap,** *n.* **filling,** *a.* occupying the whole space or capacity; satisfying. *n.* anything serving to fill up; gold or other material used to fill up a cavity in a tooth; substances used to fill up holes, cavities or defects; inferior material used to fill up space in goods of better quality; rubble and other rough material filling up the interior of a stone- or brick-faced wall; (*chiefly N Am.*) the woof of a woven fabric; a food mixture filling sandwiches, cakes etc. **filling-in pieces,** timbers occurring in partitions, groins and roofs, of less length than those with which they range. **filling-station,** *n.* a roadside establishment supplying petrol, oil etc. [OE *fyllan,* OS *fullian,* cogn. with FULL¹]

†**fill²,** *n.* (*pl.*) thills or shafts. †**fill-horse,** *n.* a shaft-horse. [var. of THILL]

fillet, *n.* a band of metal, a string or ribbon for binding the hair or worn round the head; a ribbon, a narrow band or strip; a bandage; a fleshy portion or slice of meat; the fleshy part of the thigh of an animal used for meat; portions of meat or fish removed from the bone and served either flat or rolled together and tied round; a raised rim or moulding; a plain liner band on the back of a book; (*pl.*) the loins of a horse; a narrow, flat band between mouldings; the projection between the flutes of a column; any small scantling less than a batten; a small horizontal division of a shield. *v.t.* to bind with a fillet or bandage; to adorn with a fillet or fillets; to make into fillets (as meat or fish). [ME and OF *filet,* dim. of *fil,* L *filum,* a thread]

fillibeg, FILIBEG.

fillip, *v.t.* to strike with the nail of the finger by a sudden jerk from under the thumb; to propel with such a blow; to stimulate, incite, encourage. *n.* a sharp, sudden blow with the finger jerked from under the thumb; a stimulus, an incentive; anything of small moment, a trifle. [prob. var. of FLIP]

fillister, *n.* the rabbet on the outer edge of a sash-bar; a plane for making a rabbet. [etym. unknown]

Fillmore, *n.* **Millard** (1800–74), 13th president of the US (1850–53), a Whig. He was Zachary Taylor's vice president from 1849, and succeeded him on Taylor's death. Fillmore supported a compromise on slavery in 1850 to reconcile North and South, and failed to be renominated.

filly, *n.* a female foal; (*dated*) a young, lively girl. **filly-foal,** *n.* [cogn. with FOAL]

film, *n.* a thin pellicle, skin, coating or layer; a fine thread or filament; a thin, slight covering or veil; a thin sheet of plastic or similar material used for packaging; a series of connected cinematographic images projected on a screen; (*often pl.*) the cinematographic industry generally; (*Phot.*) a thin coating of sensitized material spread over a plate for receiving a negative or positive image; a thin plate or strip of celluloid or other material supporting such a coating. *v.t.* to cover with a film; to record on a cinematographic film. *v.i.* to become covered with or as with a film. **filmgoer** CINEMAGOER. **film recorder,** *n.* the apparatus which records sound on film. **film recording,** *n.* the process whereby sound is recorded on the edge of a film for synchronous reproduction. **filmset,** *v.t.* to expose type characters on to photographic film from which printing plates are made. **filmsetter,** *n.* **filmsetting,** *n.* **film star,** *n.* a leading cinema actor or actress. **filmstrip,** *n.* a sequence of images on a strip of photographic film, projected as stills. **filmic,** *a.* pertaining to motion pictures. **filmography**, *n.* a list of films by a particular artist or director or on a particular subject. **filmy,** *a.* gauzy, transparent; misted, blurred. **filmy fern,** *n.* the widely-distributed genus *Hymenophyllum.* **filmily,** *adv.* **filminess,** *n.* [OE *filmen,* membrane, prepuce, cogn. with *fel,* FELL²]

Filofax®, *n.* a small ring-binder with a leather or similar cover into which the owner can insert sheets at will to make up e.g. a diary, an address-list etc., intended as a personal, portable compendium of information.

filoplume, *n.* a thread feather, one having an almost invisible stem. **filoplumaceous,** *a.* [mod. L *filoplūma* (L *fīlum,* a thread, *plūma,* a feather)]

filose, *a.* (*Biol.*) ending in a thread-like process. [L *fīlum,* a thread]

filoselle, *n.* floss-silk. [F, from It. *filosello* (L *follis,* a bag, or *fīlum,* a thread)]

filter, *n.* an apparatus for straining liquids and freeing them from impurities, usu. by means of layers of sand, charcoal or other material through which they are passed; the layer of porous material through which the liquids are passed; the material so used; an apparatus for purifying air by a similar process; a filter-tip; a device for altering the relative intensity of the wavelengths in a beam of light; a circuit for altering the relative intensity of different frequencies of an alternating current; an auxiliary traffic light at a road junction in the form of a green arrow, which permits a stream of traffic to turn left or right while the main stream is held up. *v.t.* to pass (liquid) through a filter; to strain, to purify by passing through a filter. *v.i.* to pass through a filter; to percolate. **to filter out,** to remove by filtering. **to filter through,** to pass through in diffused or diluted form; to become known by degrees. **filter-bed,** *n.* a reservoir with a layer of sand or other filtering material at the bottom through which water is allowed to flow. **filter-paper,** *n.* paper used for filtering liquids. **filter-tip,** *n.* (a cigarette with) an attached tip made of a porous substance to trap impurities. [OF *filtre,* med. L *filtrum,* OLG *filt,* FELT¹]

filth, *n.* anything dirty or foul; foulness, corruption, pollution; anything that defiles morally; foul language, obscenity. **the filth,** (*sl., offensive*) the police. **filthy,** *a.* dirty, foul, unclean; morally impure. **filthy lucre,** *n.* gain obtained by base methods; (*facet.*) money. **filthily,** *adv.* **filthiness,** *n.* [OE *fȳlth,* from *fūl,* FOUL]

filtrate, *n.* any liquid that has passed through a filter. *v.t., v.i.* to filter. **filtration,** *n.* the act or result of filtering; the absorption of traffic from a secondary road into the traffic of a main road; the holding-up of main-road traffic while this is done.

fimbria, *n.* (*pl.* **fimbriae**) the radiated fringe of the Fallopian tube; an elastic-toothed membrane situated beneath the operculum of the urn mosses. **fimbriate,** *a.* fringed. **fimbriated,** *a.* fringed; (*Biol.*) having fimbriae or fringes; (*Her.*) ornamented, as an ordinary, with a narrow border or hem of another tincture. **fimbricate, -cated,** *a.* fimbriate. [L, a thread, fibre or fringe]

fin, *n.* the organ by which fishes propel and steer themselves, consisting of a membrane supported by rays, named according to position on the body, as *anal, caudal, dorsal, pectoral,* or *ventral fin;* anything resembling a fin, the flipper of a seal, whale etc.; a ridge left in casting; (*Aviat.*) a fixed aerofoil, usu. inserted in or parallel to the plane of symmetry, generally constituting part of the tail structure; (*sl.*) the hand. *v.t.* (*past, p.p.* **finned**) to carve or cut up (used of serving a chub). *v.i.* to beat the water with the fins, as a whale. **fin-back** FINNER. **fin-footed,** *a.* web-footed. **fin-keel,** *n.* a fin-shaped keel; a vessel with such a keel. **fin-ray, -spine,** *n.* a spinous ray in the fin of a fish. **fin-toed,** *a.* web-footed. **finless,** *a.* **finlike,** *a.* **finned,** *a.* having fins; having broad edges on either side. **-finned,** *comb. form* having a certain kind of fins, as *prickly-finned, red-finned.* **finner, finner-whale,** *n.* a whale with an adipose fin on its back, as those of the genus *Balaenoptera,* esp. the rorqual. **finny,** *a.* having fins; like a fin; abounding in fish. [OE *finn* (cp. Dut. *vin,* also L *pinna*)]

Fin., (*abbr.*) Finland; Finnish.

fin., (*abbr.*) finance; financial.

finable FINE[1].

final, *a.* pertaining to the end or conclusion; ultimate, last; finishing, conclusive, decisive; concerned with the end or purpose. *n.* the deciding heat of an athletic contest; (*usu. pl.*) the last of a series of public examinations. **final cause,** *n.* (*Phil.*) the end or aim contemplated in the creation of the universe. **final clause,** *n.* (*Gram.*) a clause expressing the object or purpose. **finalist,** *n.* a competitor in the finals of exams, sports etc. **finality,** *n.* the state or quality of being final; the state of being finally and completely settled; the end of everything, completeness; the final and decisive act or event; (*Phil.*) the doctrine that everything exists or was created for a determinate cause. **finalize, -ise,** *v.t.* to put in final form; to settle; to give final approval to. **finally,** *adv.* [OF, from L *fīnālis,* from *fīnis,* the end]

finale, *n.* the last part, piece, scene or action in any performance or exhibition; the last piece in a programme; (*Mus.*) the last movement of a musical composition; (*fig.*) the close, end, the final catastrophe. [It., as prec.]

finality, finalize FINAL.

finance, *n.* the science or system of management of revenue and expenditure, esp. public revenue and expenditure; (*pl.*) monetary affairs, the income of a state, sovereign, firm, or individual; obtaining money, esp. to fund purchases etc.; money. *v.t.* to manage the financial arrangements of; to provide with capital. *v.i.* to manage financial operations; to obtain capital by borrowing. **finance company,** *n.* a company that specializes in making loans, esp. for hire purchase. **financial,** *a.* pertaining to finance or revenue; monetary, fiscal. **Financial Times Index,** see separate entry. **financial year,** *n.* the period for which public or official accounts are made up. **financialist,** *n.* a financier. **financially,** *adv.* **financier,** *n.* one who is skilled in finance, esp. the management of public revenues; one engaged in large-scale monetary dealings; a capitalist; †a receiver or farmer of the public revenues. *v.i.* to manage financial affairs; to raise money by negotiation. *v.t.* to manage the financial affairs of; to finance; (*chiefly N Am.*) to get rid of or swindle (away or out of) by financial operations. [OF, from late L *fīnancia,* from *fīnāre,* to pay a fine or tax, from *fīnis,* a final payment, L, the end]

Financial Times Index (FT Index), an indicator measuring the daily movement of 30 major industrial share prices on the London Stock Exchange (1935 = 100), issued by the UK *Financial Times* newspaper. Other FT indices cover government securities, fixed-interest securities, goldmine shares, and Stock Exchange activity.

Finch, *n.* **Peter** (1916–77), British cinema actor who began his career in Australia before becoming internationally known for his roles in *A Town Like Alice* (1956); *The Trials of Oscar Wilde* (1960); *Sunday, Bloody Sunday* (1971); *Network* (1976).

finch, *n.* a popular name for various small birds, many of them of the family Fringillidae; the genus *Fringilla* see also BULLFINCH, CHAFFINCH, GOLDFINCH. **finch-backed, finched,** *a.* of cattle, striped or spotted on the back. [OE *finc* (cp. Dut. *vink,* G *Fink*)]

find, *v.t.* (*past, p.p.* **found**) to chance on, to meet with, to come across; to discover, learn or acquire by search study or other effort; to rediscover (something lost); to ascertain by experience or experiment; to perceive, to recognize; to consider, to be of the opinion that; to reach, to arrive at; to succeed in obtaining; to reach the feelings of, to come home to; to gain or regain the use of; to supply; to furnish, to provide; to maintain, to support; (*Law*) to decide, to determine; to declare by verdict; to invent. *v.i.* to discover anything by searching or seeking; to arrive at a decision in a cause; to start a fox. *n.* the discovery of anything valuable; the thing so found; the finding of a fox. **to find a bill,** of a grand jury, to remit a case for trial by judge and ordinary jury. **to find a ship's trim,** (*Naut.*) to ascertain how she will sail best. **to find fault with,** FAULT. **to find in,** to provide with. **to find oneself,** to be or perceive oneself to be (in a certain situation); to be or feel as regards health; to provide oneself (with) the necessaries of life; to realize one's own capabilities or vocation. **to find one's feet,** FEET. **to find out,** to discover; to unravel, to solve; to invent; to detect, to catch tripping. **†find-fault,** *n.* a censorious, cavilling person. **findable,** *a.* **finder,** *n.* one who finds; a discoverer, an inventor; a small telescope fixed to the tube and parallel to the axis of a larger one, for finding objects to be examined by the larger telescope; a contrivance for the same purpose attached to a microscope or to a camera. **finders keepers,** (*coll.*) whoever finds something has the right to keep it. **†finder-out,** *n.* **finding,** *n.* the action of the verb TO FIND; a discovery; the act of returning a verdict; a verdict; (*pl.*) the results of an investigation; (*pl.*) tools and materials which some workers have to furnish at their own expense; (*N Am.*) shoemaker's tools and other requisites; (*coll.*) things found. **finding-store,** *n.* (*N Am.*) a shop where shoemaker's tools are sold. [OE *findan* (cp. Dut. *vinden,* Swed. and Icel. *finna,* G *finden*)]

fin de siècle, *a.* pertaining to or characteristic of the close of the 19th cent.; decadent. [F, end of the age]

findon, FINNAN.

fine[1], *n.* a sum of money imposed as a penalty for an offence; a fee paid by an incoming tenant to the landlord; (*Feud. Law*) a fee paid by a tenant or vassal on the transfer or alienation of the tenant-right; any sort of penalty; †an end, cessation, conclusion; †decrease, death; †(*pl.*) borders, boundaries, extreme limits. *v.t.* to impose a pecuniary penalty upon; to punish by fine; †to pay as a fine or composition; †to bring to an end, to finish. *v.i.* to pay a fine or monetary consideration; †to pay a penalty or ransom. **in fine,** in conclusion, in short, finally; to sum up. **to fine down, off,** to pay a fine to secure a reduction of rent. **finable,** *a.* deserving or liable to a fine. **†fineless,** *a.* endless, boundless, limitless. [OF *fin,* L *fīnis,* end]

fine[2], *a.* excellent in quality, form or appearance; refined, pure, free from dross or extraneous matter; of feelings, taste etc., also of differences, distinctions etc., delicate, subtle, nice, fastidious, dainty; in small grains or particles; thin, small, slender, tenuous; keen, sharp; of delicate texture or material; finished, consummate, accomplished, brilliant; handsome, beautiful; showy, smart, pretentious; good, satisfactory, enjoyable, pleasant; well, in good health; free from clouds or rain, sunshiny; complimentary, euphemistic; (*iron.*) anything but pleasant or satisfactory; (*Cricket*) at or through a position close to the line of the stumps. *adv.* (*coll.*) finely. *v.t.* to refine, purify, clear from impurities; to make finer, to sharpen, taper; to make less coarse. *v.i.* to become finer, purer, clarified; to taper, to dwindle (away). *int.* Good! all right! Well done! **fine-tooth(ed) comb,** a comb with thin teeth set very close together. **to go over, through with a fine-tooth(ed) comb,** to examine minutely, to investigate very thoroughly. **one of these fine days,** at some unspecified date in the future. **to cut it fine** CUT. **to fine down,** to clear or to become clear of grossness, opacity or impurities; to reduce and improve by the removal of superfluous matter. **fine arts,** *n.pl.* the arts, such as poetry, music, painting, sculpture and architecture, that appeal to our sense of the beautiful. **fine-draw,** *v.t.* to draw together the edges of and mend a rent so that no trace remains visible. **fine-drawn,** *a.* drawn out finely, as wire; excessively subtle; (*Athletics*) reduced by training. †**fine-fingered,** *a.* skilful, dexterous; delicate, fastidious. **fines herbes,** , *n.pl.* a mixture of finely chopped herbs used as flavouring. **fine-spoken,** *a.* using fine phrases. **fine-spun,** *a.* drawn or spun out to minuteness; hence, over-refined or elaborate; unpractical; delicate, flimsy. **fine- stuff,** *n.* slaked lime for the second coat of plaster. **fine-tune,** *v.t.* to make delicate adjustments to. **fine-tuning,** *n.* **finely,** *adv.* **fineness,** *n.* quality or state of being fine; the quantity of pure metal in an alloy expressed in fractions or in carats. †**finer,** *n.* a refiner of metals. **finery,** *n.* fine clothes, showy decorations; †the quality of being fine or showy; a furnace in which cast-iron is made malleable; the art of refining iron. **fines,** *n.pl.* ores that are too fine or powdery for smelting in the ordinary way. **fining,** *n.* the process of refining metals, esp. of making cast-iron malleable; the clarifying of wines, malt liquors etc.; the preparation, generally a solution of gelatine or isinglass, used to fine or clarify liquors. **fining-pot,** *n.* a crucible in which metals are refined. [OF *fin,* late L *fīnus,* prob. from L *fīnītus,* well-rounded, finished, from *fīnīre,* to end, *fīnis,* as prec.]

Fine Gael, *n.* Republic of Ireland political party founded by W.J. Cosgrave and led by Alan Dukes from 1987. It is socially liberal but fiscally conservative.

finesse, *n.* artifice, stratagem or artful manipulation; a subtle contrivance to gain an end; skill, dexterity, adroitness, esp. in handling difficult situations; elegance, refinement; (*Whist etc.*) an attempt to take a trick with a lower card, so as to retain a higher one for later tricks. *v.i.* to use artifice to gain an end; to try to win a trick with a lower card than one possibly in your opponent's hand, while you have a higher card in your own. *v.t.* to play (a card) in this manner; to manipulate, to manage by means of trickery or stratagem. [F, as prec.]

finger, *n.* one of the five digits or terminal members of the hand; one of the four longer digits as distinguished from the thumb; anything resembling or serving the purpose of a finger, an index, a gripper, a catch, a guide shaped like a finger; the part of a glove that covers a finger; the width of a finger, a measure of length or of the quantity of liquid in a glass; (*pl.*) the hand, the instrument of work or art; skill in using the fingers, as in playing on a keyed instrument. *v.t.* to touch with or turn about in the fingers; to meddle or interfere with; to touch thievishly, to pilfer; to perform with the fingers; to play with the fingers (as a musical instrument); to mark (a piece of music) so as to indicate which fingers should be used; (*sl.*) to identify (to the police). *v.i.* to use the fingers esp. skilfully in playing an instrument. **fingers and toes** ANBURY. **not to lift a finger,** to do nothing, to stand idly by. **to get, pull one's finger out,** (*sl.*) to start making an effort, to get cracking. **to have a finger in,** to be concerned in or mixed up with. **to have a finger in every pie,** to be involved in everything. **to have at one's finger-tips** or **-ends,** to know familiarly, to be well versed in. **to lay, put a finger (up)on,** to touch, to interfere with in the slightest. **to lay one's finger (up)on,** to detect or point out precisely (the cause, meaning etc.). **to point the finger (at),** to accuse; to censure. **to put the finger on,** (*sl.*) to identify or inform against. **to the finger-tips,** completely. **to twist, wrap around one's little finger,** to have someone in thrall, to be able to do as one likes with someone. **finger-alphabet, -language,** *n.* signs made on the fingers for talking to the deaf. **finger-board,** *n.* the board at the neck of a stringed instrument, where the fingers act on the strings; a keyboard, a manual. **finger-bowl, -glass,** *n.* a bowl or glass in which to rinse the fingers after dessert. **finger-fern,** *n.* one of the spleenworts, *Asplenium ceterach.* **finger-fish,** *n.* the starfish. **finger-grass,** *n.* a genus of grasses, *Digitaria,* two of which, cock's-foot finger-grass and smooth finger-grass, are British. **fingermark,** *n.* a dirty mark left by fingers. **fingernail,** *n.* **finger paint,** *n.* thickish paint for applying with the fingers, hand etc., used esp. by children. **finger painting,** *n.* **finger-plate,** *n.* a plate on the side of a door, near the handle, to preserve the paint from finger-marks. **finger-post,** *n.* a sign-post where roads cross or divide, pointing out direction. **fingerprint,** *n.* an impression of the whorls of lines on fingers, used for purposes of identification. *v.t.* to take the fingerprints of. **finger-stall,** *n.* a cover for protecting a finger during dissections, or when injured or diseased. **fingered,** *a.* having fingers; (*Bot.*) digitate. **-fingered,** *comb. form* having a certain kind of fingers. **fingerer,** *n.* one who fingers; a pilferer. **fingering,** *n.* the act of touching with the fingers; delicate work done with the fingers; a thick, loose, woollen yarn used for knitting stockings and the like; (*Mus.*) the management of the fingers in playing upon a keyed, stringed or holed instrument; marks upon a piece of music to guide the fingers in playing. **fingerless,** *a.* **fingerling,** *n.* the young of the salmon or trout when no longer than a finger; †the finger of a glove. [OE (cp. Dut. *vinger,* Icel. *fingr,* Dan., Swed. *finger,* G *Finger*)]

finial, *n.* a terminal ornament surmounting the apex of a gable, pediment, roof, canopy etc. [var. of FINAL]

finical, *a.* affecting great nicety, precision or delicacy; over-nice, fastidious; particular about trifles; crotchety. **finicality,** *n.* **finically,** *adv.* **finicalness,** *n.* **finicking,** *a.* (*coll.*) **finicky,** *a.* finical. [prob. from FINE[2]]

fining FINE[2].

finis, *n.* (*printed at end of book*) the end, finish, conclusion; the end of all things, death. [L]

finish[1], *v.t.* to bring to an end; to complete; to arrive at the end of; to perfect; to give the final touches to, to trim, to polish; to consume, to get through; to kill, to defeat, to render powerless; to complete the education of. *v.i.* to come to the end, to cease, to expire; to leave off. *n.* the act of finishing; the termination, the final stage, the end of a race, when the competitors are close to the winning-post; the last touches, that which gives the effect of perfect completeness; the final stage of any work, as the last raw coat of plaster on a wall; grace, elegance, polish, refinement. **to finish off,** to complete; to consume or use up the remainder of; to kill or destroy someone or something already wounded or facing defeat or ruin. **to finish up,** to consume or use up entirely; to arrive, come to rest or end up. **finisher,** *n.* one who or that which finishes; a workman or a machine that performs the final operation in a process of manufacture; a blow that settles a contest. **finishing-coat,** *n.* the last coat in painting or plastering. **finishing school,** *n.* a private school where girls are taught social graces. [OF *finiss-,* base of *finir,* L *fīnīre,* to end, see FINIS]

finish[2], *a.* rather fine, fairly fine. [FINE[2]]

finite, *a.* having limits or bounds, opposed to infinite; applied to those moods of a verb which are limited by number and person, as the indicative, subjunctive, imperative. **finitely,** *adv.* in a finite manner. **finiteness, finitude,** *n.* [L *fīnītus,* p.p. of *fīnīre*]

fink, *n.* (*chiefly, N Am., coll.*) an informer; a strikebreaker; a contemptible person. [etym. unknown]

Finland, *n.* Republic of (*Suomen Tasavalta*), country in Scandinavia, bounded N by Norway, E by the USSR, S and W by the Baltic Sea, and NW by Sweden. **area** 352,752 sq km/136,162 sq miles. **capital** Helsinki. **towns** Tampere, the port of Turku, Espoo, Vantaa. **physical** archipelago in south; most of the country is forest, with about 60,000 lakes; one third is within the Arctic Circle; mountains in the north. **population** (1987) 4,938,600; annual growth rate 0.5%. **exports** metal, chemical and engineering products (icebreakers and oil rigs), paper, timber, textiles, fine ceramics, glass, furniture. **language** Finnish 94%, Swedish (official), Lapp. **religion** Lutheran 90%, Eastern Orthodox.

Finland, Gulf of, eastern arm of the Baltic Sea, separating Finland from Estonia.

Finn, *n.* the Teutonic name for the Finlanders, or as they call themselves Suomi, who inhabit parts of NW Russia and NE Scandinavia; a native or naturalized inhabitant of Finland. **Finlander,** *n.* **Finlandization, -isation,** *n.* being under the necessity of accommodating the wishes of a powerful neighbour, esp. the USSR. **Finnic,** *a.* belonging to the Finnish group of peoples. **Finnish,** *a.* pertaining to Finland, the Finns or their language. *n.* the language of the Finns; see separate entry. **Finno-Ugrian, Finno-Ugric,** *n.* a family of languages spoken by some 22 million people in Hungary, Lapland, Finland, Estonia, and NW USSR. *a.* pertaining to these languages. [OE *Finnas,* pl. (Icel. *Finnr,* Swed., Dan. and G *Finne*)]

finnan, *n.* a kind of smoke-dried haddock, also called **finnan-haddock**. [etym. doubtful; perh. corr. of *Findhorn,* a fishing-village near Forres]

finned, finner etc. FIN.

Finney, *n.* **Albert** (1936–), English stage and film actor. He created the title roles in Keith Waterhouse's *Billy Liar* (1960) and John Osborne's *Luther* (1961), and was artistic director of the Royal Court Theatre from 1972–75. His films include *Saturday Night and Sunday Morning* (1960), *Tom Jones* (1963), *Murder on the Orient Express* (1974), and *The Dresser* (1984).

finnicking etc. FINICAL.

Finnish language, *n.* a member of the Finno-Ugric language family, the national language of Finland and closely related to neighbouring Estonian, Livonian, Karelian, and Ingrian languages. At the beginning of the 19th century Finnish had no official status, Swedish being the language of education, government, and literature in Finland. The publication of the *Kalevala*, a national epic poem, in 1835, contributed greatly to the arousal of Finnish national and linguistic feeling.

Finsen Rays, *n.pl.* ultraviolet rays used in the treatment of skin diseases such as lupus. [N. R. *Finsen,* 1860–1904, Danish physician]

fiord, fjord, *n.* a long, narrow inlet of the sea, bounded by high cliffs, as on the coast of Norway. [Norw.]

fiorin, *n.* white bent-grass, *Agrostis alba.* [Ir. *fiorthan*]

fiorite, *n.* a siliceous incrustation formed by the decomposition of volcanic rocks. [from Santa *Fiora* in Tuscany, where it is found]

fioritura, *n.* (*pl.* **fioriture**) a decorative phrase or turn, a flourish. [It., FLOURISH]

fipple, *n.* an arrangement of a block and a sharp edge, the sound-producing mechanism in e.g. a recorder. **fipple-flute,** *n.*

fir, *n.* the popular name for many coniferous timber trees of the genus *Abies* or allied genera; the wood of these. **Scotch fir,** SCOTS PINE under SCOTS. **silver fir,** a European mountain fir, *Abies pectinata;* the silver fir of Canada, *A. balsamea,* which yields Canada balsam. **spruce fir,** the Norway spruce, *Picea excelsa.* **fir-apple, -ball, -cone,** *n.* the cone-shaped fruit of the fir. **fir-needle,** *n.* the spine-like leaf of the fir. **firry,** *a.* consisting of or containing firs. [ME *firre,* prob. from Scand. (cp. Icel. *fyri-,* Dan. *fyr*), perh. cogn. with OE *furh,* OHG *forha,* G *föhre,* and also L *quercus,* oak]

Firdausi, *n.* **Abdul Qasim Mansur,** (*c.* 935–*c.* 1020), Persian poet, whose epic *Shahnama/The Book of Kings* relates the history of Persia in 60,000 verses.

fire, *n.* the production of heat and light by combustion; combustion, flame, incandescence; fuel in a state of combustion, as in a furnace, grate etc.; a radiant gas or electric heater; anything burning; a conflagration; a light, glow or luminosity resembling fire; a spark or sparks emitted when certain substances are struck violently; intense heat, fever; the discharge of firearms; ardent emotion, fervour; liveliness of imagination, vigour of fancy, poetic inspiration; a severe affliction, torture, persecution. *v.t.* to set on fire, to kindle, to ignite; to discharge, to cause to explode; to bake (as pottery); (*Vet.*) to cauterize; to supply with fuel (as a furnace); to inflame, to irritate; to excite, to animate, to inspire; to dismiss, to discharge from employment. *v.i.* to take fire, to be kindled; of an internal-combustion engine, to be in operation; to discharge firearms; to shoot (at) with firearms; to ring (as a peal of bells) simultaneously. *int.* a word of command for soldiers to discharge their firearms. **ball of fire,** an unusually energetic or enthusiastic person. **cross-fire** CROSS. **Greek fire,** an artificial combustible used by the Greeks in their wars with the Saracens for setting hostile ships on fire. **on fire,** burning, in flames; excited, ardent, eager. **running fire,** a discharge of firearms in rapid succession by a line of troops. **St Anthony's fire,** erysipelas. **St Elmo's fire,** the corposant. **to catch, take fire,** to ignite. **to fire away,** to begin, to proceed. **to fire off,** to discharge (a firearm); to shoot (a round, a shell); to utter in rapid succession. **to fire out,** to expel forcibly, to chuck out. **to fire up,** to kindle a fire; to be inflamed with passion, to be irritated. **to play with fire,** to expose oneself to risk. **to set fire to, on fire, a-fire,** to kindle; to excite, to inflame. **to set the Thames on fire,** to do something clever or remarkable. **under fire,** exposed to the enemy's firearms. **fire-alarm,** *n.* an automatic apparatus for communicating warning of a fire. **firearm,** *n.* a weapon that projects a missile by the explosive force of gunpowder, esp. a rifle or pistol. **fire away!** begin! **fireback,** *n.* the rear wall of a furnace or fireplace; a pheasant of the genus *Euplocamus* found in Sumatra. **fireball,** *n.* a ball or sack filled with combustible composition, a grenade; globular lightning; a large meteor or shooting star; the luminous cloud of hot gases at the centre of a nuclear explosion. **fire-bar,** *n.* one of the bars in a furnace on which the fuel rests. **fire-basket,** *n.* a small portable grate. **firebird,** *n.* the Baltimore oriole. **fire-blast, -blight,** *n.* a disease in plants, esp. in hops. **fire-board,** *n.* a chimney-board used to close up a fireplace in summer. **fire bomb,** *n.* an incendiary bomb. **firebox,** *n.* the chamber in which the fuel is burned in a locomotive etc. **firebrand,** *n.* a piece of wood kindled or on fire; an arsonist; one who inflames passions or kindles strife. **firebreak,** *n.* a strip of land kept clear of trees or vegetation to stop the spread of fire. **fire-brick,** *n.* a brick capable of withstanding fire used for fireplaces, furnaces and all kinds of work exposed to intense heat. **fire-brigade,** *n.* a body of people organized by a public authority etc. for the extinction of fires. **fire-bucket,** *n.* a bucket (usu. filled with water) kept in readiness in case of fire. **fire-bug,** *n.* (*coll.*) an arsonist. **fire-clay,** *n.* a kind of clay consisting of nearly pure silicate of alumina, capable of standing intense heat, used in the manufacture of fire-bricks. **fire-cock,** *n.* a street plug for attachment of hose for extinguishing fire etc. **fire-company,** *n.* (*N Am.*) a fire-brigade; a fire insurance company. **fire-control,** *n.* (*Nav., Mil.*) the system of controlling gunfire from one spot. **fire-cross** FIERY-CROSS. **firedamp,** *n.* the explosive carburetted hydrogen which accumulates in coal-mines. **fire department,** *n.* (*N Am.*) the fire-brigade. **fire-dog,** *n.* an and-iron. **fire-drake,** *n.* a fiery dragon or serpent; an ignis fatuus; a firework. **fire-drill,** *n.* an instrument used by the Australians and Tasmanians for producing fire, consisting of two pieces of soft dry wood, one of which is made to revolve quickly upon the other till they ignite; practice in the routine to be observed in case of fire. **fire-eater,** *n.* a juggler who pretends to swallow fire; a belligerent person, a lover of fighting. **fire-engine,** *n.* a vehicle equipped with fire-fighting equipment. **fire-escape,** *n.* an apparatus for enabling persons to escape from the upper parts of buildings that are on fire. **fire-extinguisher,** *n.* a portable apparatus for extinguishing fires by spraying them with water or chemicals. **firefight,** *n.* an exchange of fire between military units. **fire-fighter,** *n.* a fireman. **fire-fighting,** *n., a.* **fire-flair,** *n.* the sting-ray, *Trygon pastinaca.* **firefly,** *n.* a small luminous winged insect, chiefly of the families Elateridae and Lampyridae. **fireguard,** *n.* a wire frame placed before an open fire as a safeguard against accidental fire or injury to children etc. **fire-hose,** *n.* a hosepipe employed for extinguishing fires. **fire-insurance,** *n.* insurance against loss by fire. **fire-irons,** *n.pl.* the implements for tending a fire – poker, tongs and shovel. **fire-light,** *n.* the light from a fire. **fire-lighter,** *n.* an inflammable substance for kindling fuel. **fire-lock,** *n.* an old-fashioned musket or other gun having a lock with a flint and steel, by means of which the priming was ignited. **fireman,** *n.* one who is employed to extinguish fires; a member of a fire-brigade; a stoker; (*Coal-min.*) a man employed to examine the workings to see that no firedamp is present. **fire-master,** *n.* the chief of a fire-brigade; †an officer who directed the making of fireworks. †**fire-new,** *a.* brand-new. **fire-office,** *n.* a fire-insurance office. **fire-opal** GIRASOL. **fire-pan,** *n.* a pan for holding fire, a brazier; †the receptacle for the priming in a fire-lock. **fire-place,** *n.* a grate; a hearth. **fire-plug,** *n.* a hydrant for connecting a fire-hose with a water-main. **fire-policy,** *n.* a policy or certificate guaranteeing compensation up to a stated limit in case of damage by fire. **fire-pot,** *n.* the pot or receptacle in a stove for holding the fuel; a crucible; †(*Mil.*) a small earthen pot filled with combustibles. **firepower,** *n.* the effective capability of weaponry, missiles etc. **fire-proof,** *a.* proof against fire; incombustible. *v.i.* to render proof against fire. **fire-proof curtain** SAFETY CURTAIN. **fire-proofing,** *n.* the process of rendering fire-proof; material used for this purpose. **fire-raising,** *n.* the act of setting on fire; incendiarism, arson. **fire-resistant,** *a.* tending not to catch fire and resistant to the effects of fire to a required degree. **fire risk,** *n.* risk of accidental damage by fire. **fire-screen,** *n.* a fireguard; a screen placed between a person and the fire to intercept the direct rays. **fire-ship,** *n.* a vessel freighted with combustibles and explosives, and sent among an enemy's ships in order to set them on fire. **fire-shovel,** *n.* a shovel for putting coals on a fire. **fireside,** *n.* the space around a fire-place, the hearth; hence home, home life. *a.* home, domestic. **fire station,** *n.* a building from which fire-engines and fire-fighters operate. **fire-step, firing-step,** *n.* a raised ledge inside a trench on which soldiers stand to fire. **fire-stick,** *n.* (*Austral.*) an Aboriginal torch. **firestone,** *n.* a stone capable of bearing a high degree of heat, used in furnaces etc.; a stone used for striking fire, as a flint or iron pyrites. **fire storm,** *n.* a huge fire, esp. one started by bombing, which causes and is kept ablaze by violent inrushing winds. **fire-trap,** *n.* (*coll.*) a building without adequate means of exit in case of fire. **fire-tree,** *n.* the Queensland tulip-tree. **fire watcher,** *n.* a person who watches for the outbreak of fires, esp. during an air raid. **fire-water,** *n.* the name given by the native Indians of N America to ardent spirit. **fireweed,** *n.* (*Austral.*) any weed springing up after a forest fire. **firewood,** *n.* wood for burning; fuel. **firework,** *n.* a preparation of various kinds of combustibles and explosives for producing a brilliant display at times of public rejoicing etc.; similar preparations used for illumination, signalling, incendiary purposes or in war; (*pl.*) a display of bad temper; (*pl.*) a spectacular display of virtuosity. **fire-worship,** *n.* worship of fire as a living being or deity. **fire-worshipper,** *n.* one who worships fire, a Parsee. **fireless,** *a.* destitute of or without fire (a term applied to races said to be ignorant of any method of producing fire). **firer,** *n.* one who or that which fires; (*in comb.*) a gun with one or more barrels, as a *single-firer.* **firing,** *n.* the adding of fuel to a boiler furnace; the ignition of an explosive mixture in an internal-combustion cylinder; the act of discharging firearms; fuel; the baking of ceramic products in a kiln; the act of cauterizing; the application of a cautery to a horse. **firing-charge,** *n.* the explosive used for detonating the charge in a torpedo, mine etc. **firing-iron,** *n.* a veterinary's cautery. **firing-line,** *n.* a line of troops engaging the enemy with firearms. **to be in the firing-line,** to be at the forefront of any activity and hence exposed to greatest risk. **firing-party,** *n.* a detachment told off to fire over a grave at a military funeral, or to shoot a condemned man. **firing-pin,** *n.* a sliding pin in firearms that strikes upon the detonator and explodes the charge. **firing-point** FLASH POINT. **firing-squad,** *n.* a detachment which carries out executions by shooting. [OE *fȳr* (cp. Dut. *vuur,* Dan. and Swed. *fyr,* G *Feuer,* also Gr. *pūr*)]

Firenze, FLORENCE.

firk, *v.t.* to drive or rouse (up, out or off); †to whip, to beat. [OE *fercian,* prob. from *fær,* journey, see FARE]

firkin, *n.* a measure of capacity; the fourth part of a barrel or 9 gallons (41 l); a small wooden cask used for butter, tallow etc., of no fixed capacity. [formerly *ferdekyn,* prob. from MDut. (*vierde,* fourth, *ken,* -KIN)]

†**firlot,** *n.* (*Sc.*) a dry measure; the fourth part of a boll. [perh. corr. of FOUR or FOURTH and LOT]

firm[1], *a.* fixed, stable, steady; difficult to move or disturb; solid, compact, unyielding; securely established, immutable; steadfast; staunch, enduring, resolute; constant, unwavering, not changing in level of prices etc. *adv.* firmly. *v.t.* to fix firmly; to make firm, to consolidate; †to confirm. *v.i.* to become firm; to solidify. **firm offer,** *n.* a definite offer. **firmware,** *n.* a computer program or data stored in a read-only memory. **firmly,** *adv.* **firmness,** *n.* [OF *ferme,* L *firmus*]

firm[2], *n.* a partnership or association of two or more persons for carrying on a business; the business itself. **long firm,** a gang of swindlers who get hold of goods for which they do not pay. [late L *firma,* a signature, L *firmāre,* to confirm, as prec. (cp. FARM)]

firmament, *n.* the sky regarded as a solid expanse, the vault of heaven; †a foundation, a basis. **firmamental,** *a.* of or pertaining to the firmament; celestial; of the upper regions. [OF, from L *firmāmentum*]

firman, *n.* a decree, mandate or order of an Eastern monarch, issued for any purpose, as a passport, grant, licence etc. [Pers. *fermān*]

firn, *n.* névé, snow on the higher slopes of lofty mountains, not yet consolidated into ice. [G, last year's snow (*firne,* of last year)]

first, *a.* foremost in order, time, place, rank, importance or excellence; earliest in occurrence; nearest, coming next (to something specified); chief, highest, noblest. *adv.* before all others in order, time, place, rank, importance or excellence; before some time, act or event (specified or implied); sooner, rather, in preference, for the first time. *n.* that which or the person who comes first; the first mentioned; the beginning; a place in the first class of an examination list, a candidate winning this; the first place in a race, the winner of this; (*pl.*) the best quality of a commodity (such as flour); the upper part in a duet, trio etc.; first gear. **at first,** at the beginning; originally. **at first blush** BLUSH. **first and last,** essentially. **first of exchange,** the first of a set of bills of exchange of even date. **first off,** (*coll.*) firstly, first of all. **first-past-the-post,** *a.* of an electoral system in which each voter casts a single vote and only the candidate who polls highest is returned. **first thing,** early, as the first action of the day. **from first to last,** throughout; altogether. **not to know the first thing about,** to be entirely ignorant of. **first aid,** *n.* assistance rendered to an injured person before a doctor comes. **first-aider,** *n.* **first-begot, -begotten,** *a.* first-born among offspring (applied esp. to Christ as the offspring of the Father). *n.* the eldest child. **first-**

born, *a.* born first, eldest. *n.* the first in order of birth. **first-class,** *a.* first-rate; of the highest quality or degree; in the first class; of postage, charged at higher rate for quicker delivery. *n.* the highest division in an examination list; a place in this; the first or best class of railway carriage or other accommodation. **first costs,** *n.pl.* the original costs, as dist. from the price which includes profit. **first day,** *n.* Sunday, as being the first day of the week. **first-day cover,** an envelope postmarked on the first day of issue of new stamps. **First Fleet,** *n.* (*Austral. Hist.*) the ships that brought the original convicts to Australia in 1788. **First Fleeter,** *n.* one of these convicts. **first floor,** *n.* the floor or storey of a building next above the ground floor; (*N Am.*) the ground floor (the first floor in Eng. is N Am. second floor). **first-foot,** *n.* (*Sc.*) the first caller at a house on New Year's Day; the first person met in setting out on some important business. *v.t.* to enter as first-foot. **first form,** *n.* the lowest class in schools. **first-fruits,** *n.pl.* the fruit or produce first gathered in any season and offered to God by the Jews; the first effects or results; the first profits of any office, paid to a superior; (*Feud. Law*) a year's profit on land after the death of a tenant, payable to the king; (*Eccles. Law*) the first year's income of a spiritual benefice, orig. paid to the Pope, but appropriated by Henry VIII, and afterwards transferred to Queen Anne's Bounty. **first gear,** *n.* the lowest forward gear on a motor vehicle. **first-hand,** *a.* obtained directly from the first or original source; direct. **at first hand** HAND. **first lady,** *n.* the wife of or official hostess for the US president or a state governor; any woman pre-eminent in her field. **first mate,** *n.* the chief officer of a merchant-vessel, next in rank to the captain. **first name,** *n.* christian name or first forename. **first-nighter,** *n.* one who makes a point of attending first performances of plays. **first offender,** *n.* one not previously convicted. **first-rate,** *a.* of the first or highest class or quality; of the highest excellence. *adv.* excellently, very well. *n.* a warship of the most powerful class. **first school,** *n.* a primary school for children aged 5 to 8. **first strike,** *n.* an initial, unprovoked or preemptive attack with nuclear missiles. **first-strike** *a.* **first string,** *a.* of regular team members as opposed to substitutes. **first-time,** *a.* doing something for the first time. **first time,** *adv.* immediately. **first water,** *n.* the purest quality (of diamonds etc.). **firstling,** *a.* †that is first produced or brought forth. *n.* the first-born, the first-born in a season; (*pl.*) the first-fruits. **firstly,** *adv.* in the first place, to begin with. [OE *fyrst* (cp. Icel. *fyrstr,* Dan. *förste,* also G *fürst,* prince), superl. from stem *fur-, for-,* see FORE, FORMER]

First World War, WORLD WAR I.

firth, *n.* (*Sc.*) an estuary, an arm of the sea. [prob. from Icel. (cp. Norw. FIORD)]

fisc, *n.* the treasury of the State, the public purse or exchequer; the Crown Treasury of Scotland; (*facet.*) one's purse. **fiscal,** *a.* pertaining to the public revenue or exchequer, financial. *n.* a public functionary with legal or financial duties in various foreign countries; †a treasurer; a procurator-fiscal. **fiscally,** *adv.* [L *fiscus,* a basket, a purse, the treasury]

Fischer[1], *n.* **Emil Hermann** (1852–1919), German chemist who produced synthetic sugars and from these the various enzymes. His descriptions of the chemistry of the carbohydrates and peptides laid the foundations for the science of biochemistry. He won the Nobel Prize in 1902.

Fischer[2], *n.* **Hans** (1881–1945), German chemist awarded the Nobel Prize in 1930 for his discovery of haemoglobin in blood.

Fischer-Dieskau, *n.* **Dietrich** (1925–), German baritone, renowned for his interpretation of Schubert's songs.

fisgig, FIZGIG.

fish[1], *n.* (*pl.* in general **fish**; in particular **fishes**) an aquatic, oviparous, cold-blooded vertebrate animal, provided with permanent gills, usu. covered with scales, and progressing by means of fins, the homologues of the limbs of higher vertebrates; the flesh of fish used as food; one who is being angled for; (*Naut.*) a strip of wood for mending or strengthening a spar; (*coll.*) a certain kind of person, as an *odd fish. v.i.* to try to catch fish, by angling, netting etc.; to search for something under water; to grope or feel around for; to seek to learn or obtain anything by indirect means or finesse. *v.t.* to attempt to catch fish in; to lay hold of and drag up from under water or from inside something; to search (water etc.) by sweeping, dragging etc.; to strengthen (as a piece of timber or a sprung mast or yard) by securing a piece of timber or a spar on each side of the weak part. **a fish out of water,** anyone out of his or her element, in a strange or bewildering situation. **fish and chips,** fried fish and fried potato chips. **neither fish, flesh nor fowl,** or **nor good red herring,** nondescript; of a vague indefinite character. **other fish to fry,** more important matters to attend to. **to drink like a fish,** to drink to excess. **to feed the fishes,** to be drowned. **to fish for compliments,** to lead people to pay compliments. **to fish out,** to find and draw out; to ascertain by cunning inquiry. **to fish the anchor,** to draw up the flukes to the bulwarks after the anchor has been catted. **fish-ball, -cake,** *n.* a fried cake of chopped fish and mashed potatoes. **fish-basket,** *n.* a basket for serving fish. **fish-carver,** *n.* a large flat knife for serving fish. **fish-curer,** *n.* one who salts or smokes fish. **fish-day,** *n.* a day on which fish is eaten instead of meat. **fish-eye,** *a.* of a wide-angle photographic lens with a convex front which covers almost 180°. **fish farm,** *n.* an installation for the rearing of fish, usu. in ponds or tanks. **fish farmer,** *n.* **fish farming,** *n.* **fish finger,** *n.* a small bar-shaped portion of fish coated in breadcrumbs or batter. **fish-garth,** *n.* a staked or dammed enclosure on a river for taking or preserving fish. **fish-gig,** *n.* a spear with several barbed prongs used in taking fish. **fish-globe,** *n.* a small globular aquarium for goldfish etc. **fish-glue,** *n.* a glue made of the entrails and skin of fish; isinglass. **fish-hawk,** *n.* the osprey. **fish-hook,** *n.* a barbed hook for catching fish; (*Naut.*) the hook in tackle for raising an anchor. **fish-joint,** *n.* a joint made with fish-plates on a railway-line. **fish-kettle,** *n.* a long oval pan for boiling fish. **fish-knife,** *n.* a silver or silver-plated knife for eating fish. **fish ladder,** *n.* a series of pools arranged in step to enable fish swimming upstream to bypass dams etc. **fish-louse,** *n.* a small crustacean parasitic upon fishes and other aquatic animals. **fishmonger,** *n.* a retail dealer in fish. **fishnet,** *n.* open mesh fabric resembling netting. **fish-oil,** *n.* oil obtained from fish and other marine animals, as whales etc. **fish-plate,** *n.* a plate used to fasten rails end to end. **fish-pond,** *n.* a pond in which fish are kept; (*facet.*) the sea. †**fish-room,** *n.* a room or compartment in a ship, between the after-hold and the spirit-room. **fish-slice,** *n.* a broad-bladed knife, usually of silver, for serving fish at table; a similar instrument used by cooks for turning or taking fish out of the pan etc. **fish-sound,** *n.* the swimming-bladder of a fish. **fish-spear,** *n.* a spear or dart, usu. with barbs, for striking fish. **fish stick,** *n.* (*N Am.*) a fish finger. **fish-strainer,** *n.* a metal colander with handles, used for taking fish out of the fish-kettle; a perforated slab at the bottom of a dish to drain cooked fish. **fish-tackle,** *n.* a tackle used for raising an anchor to the gunwale for stowage after being catted. **fish-tail,** *a.* shaped like the tail of a fish. **fish-tail burner,** a gas-burner producing a jet like a fish's tail. **fish-tail wind,** a variable wind blowing down a rifle range from behind the firers. **fish-torpedo,** *n.* a fish-shaped, self-propelled torpedo. **fishway** FISH LADDER. **fish-wife,** *n.* a woman that sells fish; a coarse, foul-mouthed woman. **fisher,** *n.* one who is employed in fishing; a fisherman; an animal that fishes; a fishing-boat. **fisherman,** *n.* one whose employment is to catch fish; an angler; a boat or vessel employed in catching fish. **fisherman's bend,** *n.* a kind of knot. **fishery,** *n.* the business of catching fish; any place where fishing is carried on; (*Law*) permission to fish in reserved water. **fish-**

ing, *n.* the action of the verb TO FISH; the sport of angling; a place where angling is carried on; a fishery. **fishing-boat,** *n.* a boat employed in catching fish. **fishing-frog,** *n.* the angler-fish. **fishing-line,** *n.* a line with hook attached for catching fish. **fishing-net,** *n.* a net for catching fish. **fishing-rod,** *n.* a long, slender, tapering rod, usu. in sections jointed together, for angling. **fishing-tackle,** *n.* all the apparatus required by a fisherman. **fishy,** *a.* like, consisting of, pertaining to, or suggestive of fish; inhabited by or abounding in fish; of a doubtful character, questionable, dubious. **fishily,** *adv.* **fishiness,** *n.* [OE *fisc* (cp. Dut. *visch,* Icel. *fiskr,* G *Fisch,* also L *piscis*)]

fish[2], *n.* a counter used in various games. [F *fiche,* a peg, from *ficher,* prob. L *figere,* to fix]

Fisher[1], *n.* **Andrew** (1862–1928), Australian Labor politician. Born in Scotland, he went to Australia in 1885, and entered the Australian parliament in 1901. He was prime minister (1908–09, 1910–13, and 1914–15), and Australian high commissioner to the UK (1916–21).

Fisher[2], *n.* **John, St** (*c.* 1469–1535), English bishop, created bishop of Rochester in 1504. He was an enthusiastic supporter of the revival in the study of Greek, and a friend of the humanists More and Erasmus. In 1535 he was tried on a charge of denying the royal supremacy and beheaded.

Fisher[3], *n.* **Ronald Aylmer** (1890–1962), English statistician and geneticist. He modernized Darwin's theory of evolution, thus securing the key biological concept of genetic change by natural selection. Fisher developed several new statistical techniques and, applying his methods to genetics, published *The Genetical Theory of Natural Selection* in 1930.

†**fisk,** *v.i.* to bustle; to frisk (about). [perh. from OE *fȳsan,* to hurry]

†**fisnomy,** PHYSIOGNOMY.

fissi, fisso-, *comb. form* (*Anat., Biol. etc.*) divided; dividing; by division. [L *fissus,* p.p. of *findere,* to split, cleave]

fissidactyl, *a.* having the digits divided. [Gr. *daktulos,* finger]

fissile, *a.* that may be cleft or split, esp. in the direction of the grain, as wood, or along natural planes of cleavage, as rock. †**fissility,** *n.* [L *fissilis,* from *findere,* to cleave]

fission, *n.* the act or process of cleaving, splitting or breaking up into parts, particularly of uranium or plutonium to liberate nuclear energy; a form of asexual reproduction in certain simple organisms, the individual cell dividing into new cells.

fissiparous, *a.* propagating by fission. **fissiparously,** *adv.* **fissiparity,** *n.*

fissiped, *a.* having the toes separate. *n.* an individual of the carnivorous group Fissipedia.

fissirostral, *a.* having a deeply cleft beak; belonging to the tribe of insessorial birds Fissirostres.

fissure, *n.* a cleft or opening made by the splitting or parting of any substance; a slit or narrow opening, as the deep narrow depression between the anterior and middle lobes of the cerebrum on each side. *v.t.* to cleave, to split. *v.i.* to become split or cleft. [F, from L *fissūra,* as FISSILE]

fist, *n.* the clenched hand, esp. in readiness to strike a blow; (*coll.*) the hand; (*facet.*) handwriting; (*Typography*) a hand pointing, as fist; †the talons of a bird of prey. *v.t.* to strike or grip with the fist; (*Naut.*) to handle (ropes, sails etc.). **-fisted,** *comb. form* having a certain kind of fist. **fistic, -ical,** *a.* pertaining or relating to pugilism. **fisticuffs,** *n.pl.* a fight in which the fists are used; a boxing-match. [OE *fyst* (cp. Dut. *vuist,* G *Faust*)]

fistula, *n.* (*pl.* **-las, -lae**) a kind of ulcer or suppurating swelling, in form like a pipe; a narrow pipe-like passage, duct or spout, in insects, whales etc.; (*Rom. Ant.*) a kind of flute made of reeds. **fistular, -ulate,** *a.* hollow like a reed; pertaining to a fistula. **fistuliform,** *a.* of a fistular form; in round hollow columns, as minerals. **fistulose, -ulous,** *a.* hollow like a pipe or reed; of the form or nature of a fistula. [L, a pipe, a flute]

fit[1], *n.* a violent seizure or paroxysm; a sudden transitory attack of illness; a sudden attack of epilepsy or other disease characterized by convulsions; a spasm, a seizure; a transient state of impulsive action, a mood, a caprice. **by fits and starts,** intermittently. **to have a fit,** (*coll.*) to be very angry or upset. **fitful,** *a.* spasmodic, capricious, wavering; acting by fits and starts. **fitfully,** *adv.* **fitfulness,** *n.* [OE *fitt,* etym. and sense doubtful (perh. as foll.)]

†**fit**[2], †**fytte,** *n.* a short canto or division of a poem. [OE *fitt,* a song, part of a poem]

fit[3], *a.* (*comp.* **fitter,** *superl.* **fittest**) adapted, suitable, appropriate; becoming, proper, meet; qualified, competent; ready, prepared, in a suitable condition (to do or for); in good physical condition; (*coll.*) as if, in such a mood or condition as (to cry, to do something violent etc.). *v.t.* (*past, p.p.* **fitted**) to adapt to any shape, size or measure; to make suitable, to accommodate; to try on (a garment); to supply, to furnish, to equip; to qualify, to prepare; to be adapted, suitable or proper for; to be of the right size, measure and shape for; to correspond to exactly. *v.i.* to be adjusted or adapted to the right shape, measure, form etc.; to be proper, suitable, convenient or becoming. *n.* exact adjustment, as of a dress to the body; the manner in which anything fits, the style in which a garment fits. **to fit in,** to find room or time for; to prove accommodating or suitable. **to fit out,** to equip, to furnish with the necessary outfit, stores, armament etc. **to fit up,** to furnish with the things suitable or necessary; (*sl.*) to frame. **to think fit to,** to decide to (do something). **fitly,** *adv.* **fitment,** *n.* a piece of furniture; (*usu. pl.*) fittings; an accessory part of a machine. **fitness,** *n.* suitability; good physical condition or health. **fitted,** *a.* adapted, suitable (for); cut or sewn or constructed to fit exactly over or into a certain space, and usu. permanently attached; furnished with fitted, matching cupboards etc. **fitter,** *n.* one who or that which fits; one who puts together the several parts of machinery; one who fits or repairs certain kinds of apparatus, as in *gas-fitter*. **fitting,** *a.* suitable, appropriate, right, proper. *n.* the act of making fit; a small, removable part or attachment, as electric *light fitting;* (*pl.*) apparatus, furniture employed in fitting up a house, shop etc.; preliminary trying on of a garment. **fitting-shop,** *n.* a workshop in which machinery is fitted up. **fitting-up,** *n.* the act or process of furnishing with the necessary fittings or fixtures. **fittingly,** *adv.* [ME *fyt,* etym. doubtful]

fitch, *n.* the fur of the polecat; a brush made of this. **fitch-brush,** *n.* [cp. MDut. *fisse,* a polecat]

fitchew, *n.* a polecat. [as prec.]

Fitzalan-Howard, *n.* family name of dukes of Norfolk; seated at Arundel Castle, Sussex.

FitzGerald, *n.* **Garret** (1926–), Irish politician. As *Taoiseach* (prime minister) in 1981–82 and again from 1982–86, he was noted for his attempts to solve the Northern Ireland dispute, ultimately by participating in the Anglo-Irish agreement of 1985. He tried to remove some of the overtly Catholic features of the constitution to make the Republic more attractive to Northern Protestants. He retired as leader of the Fine Gael Party in 1987.

Fitzgerald[1], *n.* family name of the dukes of Leinster.

Fitzgerald[2], *n.* **Edward** (1809–83), English poet and translator. In 1859 he published his poetic version of the *Rubaiyat of Omar Khayyam*, which is generally considered more an original creation than a translation.

Fitzgerald[3], *n.* **Ella** (1918–), US jazz singer, recognized as one of the greatest voices of jazz, both in solo work and with big bands. She is particularly noted for her interpretations of Gershwin and Cole Porter songs.

Fitzgerald[4], *n.* **F(rancis) Scott (Key)** (1896–1940), US novelist. His autobiographical novel *This Side of Paradise* (1920) made him known in the postwar society of the East Coast, and *The Great Gatsby* (1925) epitomizes the Jazz Age. His wife Zelda's descent into mental illness forms the subject of *Tender is the Night* (1934).

Fitzgerald[5], *n.* **George** (1851–1901), Irish physicist known for his work on electromagnetics. He was professor of physics at Trinity College, Dublin. He explained the anomalous results of previous experiments by supposing that bodies moving through the ether contracted, an effect since known as the Fitzgerald-Lorenz contraction.

Fitzherbert, *n.* **Maria Anne** (1756–1837), wife of the Prince of Wales, later George IV. She became Mrs Fitzherbert by her second marriage in 1778 and, after her husband's death in 1781, entered London society. She secretly married the Prince of Wales in 1785, and finally parted from him in 1803.

Fitzroy, *n.* family name of dukes of Grafton; descended from King Charles II by his mistress Barbara Villiers; seated at Euston Hall, Norfolk.

five, *n.* the number or figure 5 or V; the age of five; the fifth hour after midnight or midday; a card, counter etc. with five pips; (*pl.*) articles of attire, such as boots, gloves etc. of the fifth size. *a.* five in number, aged five. **a bunch of fives,** the fist. **five-figure tables,** tables of five-figure logarithms. **five-o'clock shadow,** beard growth which becomes visible on a man's shaven face late in the day. **five-per-cents,** *n.pl.* stocks or shares paying 5%. **Five Power Treaty,** treaty adopted at the Washington Conference in 1922, whereby the British Empire, US, France, Italy and Japan agreed upon definite limitations of naval armaments. **Five Year Plan,** see separate entry. **five-eighth,** *n.* (*Austral.*) a player in rugby football posted between the half-backs and three-quarter backs. **five-finger,** *n.* a name for various plants, esp. *Potentilla reptans, Lotus corniculatus;* species of starfish, *Uraster rubens* and *Solaster papposus*. **five-finger exercises,** exercises to improve the touch in playing the piano. †**five-finger tied,** tied by the whole hand; securely or strongly tied. **five-leaf,** *n.* cinquefoil. **five-penny**, *a.* priced at five pence. **five-star,** *a.* of the highest class, esp. of hotels. **fivefold,** *a., adv.* five times as much or as great. **fiver,** *n.* (*coll.*) a five-pound note; anything that counts as five, as a stroke for five at cricket etc. **fives**[1], *n.* a game in which a ball is struck against a wall by the open hand or a small wooden bat. **fives-court,** *n.* a court with two, three or four walls where the game of fives is played. [OE *fīf* (cp. Dut. *vijf,* G *fünf,* Gr. *pente,* L *quinque*)]

five pillars of Islam, *n.* the five duties required of every Muslim: repeating the creed, which affirms that Allah is the one God and Mohammed is his prophet; daily prayer or salat; giving alms; fasting during the month of Ramadan; and, if not prevented by ill health or poverty, the hajj, or pilgrimage to Mecca, once in a lifetime.

†**fives**[2], *n.pl.* a disease in horses, the strangles. [F *vives, avives,* Sp. *avivas, adivas,* Arab. *ad-dībah* (*al-,* the, *dībah,* she-wolf)]

Five-Year Plan, *n.* a long-term strategic plan for the development of a country's economy. Five-year plans were from 1928 the basis of economic planning in the USSR, aimed particularly at developing heavy and light industry in a primarily agricultural country. They have since been adopted by many other countries.

fix, *v.t.* to make fast, firm or stable; to fasten, attach, secure firmly; to establish; to deprive of volatility, to make permanent or stable (as colours, a photographic picture etc.); to solidify; to arrest and hold (as eyes, attention etc.); to direct steadily; to settle, to determine, to decide (on); to adjust, to appoint a definite position for; (*coll.*) to adjust, to arrange properly, to set to rights, to repair; (*chiefly N Am.*) to prepare; (*usu. pass. coll.*) to be provided with; (*euphem.*) to spay or castrate (an animal); (*sl.*) to punish, to get even with; (*sl.*) to influence illicitly. *v.i.* to become fixed; to settle down permanently; to lose volatility; to become congealed; (*chiefly N Am., coll.*) to be about to, to be set to. *n.* an awkward predicament, a dilemma; the position of a ship, aircraft etc. as determined by radar etc.; the determination of such a position; (*sl.*) an injection of heroin or a similar drug. **to fix on, upon,** to determine on; to choose, to select. **to fix up,** (*coll.*) to arrange, to organize; to settle; to assemble or construct; to provide. **fixable,** *a.* **fixed,** *a.* fast, firm; established, settled, unalterable. †**fixed air,** carbon dioxide. **fixed alkalis, oils,** *n.pl.* alkalis or oils not easily volatilized. **fixed assets,** *n.pl.* business assets of a relatively permanent nature, as buildings, plant etc. **fixed idea,** *n.* a rooted idea, one tending to become a monomania. **fixed link,** *n.* a permanent means of crossing a stretch of water, e.g. a bridge or tunnel, as opposed to e.g. a ferry. **fixed-penalty,** *a.* involving the payment of a predetermined and invariable fine. **fixed property,** *n.* landed estate, houses etc. **fixed stars,** *n.pl.* stars which apparently maintain the same relative positions to each other in the sky, as distinct from planets. **fixed-wing,** *a.* having permanently attached wings, as opposed to e.g. a helicopter. **fixedly,** *adv.* steadfastly, firmly; intently. **fixedness**, *n.* the quality or state of being fixed; immobility, steadfastness; absence of volatility. **fixer,** *n.* a person adept at finding, esp. crafty or illicit solutions to problems. **fixings,** *n.pl.* (*N Am.*) trimmings. [orig. an adj., from OF *fixe,* L *fixus,* p.p. of *figere,* to fix]

fixate, *v.t.* to render fixed; to fix the gaze upon; (*Psych.*) to arrest the psychological development of at an immature stage; (*usu. pass.*) to be obsessed. **fixation,** *n.* the act of fixing; the process of making nonvolatile, as causing a gas to combine with a solid; the process of ceasing to be fluid and becoming firm; (*Psych.*) an emotional arrest of development of the personality; an obsession. **fixative,** *a.* serving to fix. *n.* a substance used to make colours permanent or prevent crayon or pastel drawings from becoming blurred; a substance used for holding e.g. hair or false teeth in place.

fixer, fixings FIX.

fixity, *n.* coherence of parts; fixedness, stability, permanence; the quality of being able to resist the tendency to lose weight or become volatilized through heat.

fixture, *n.* anything fixed in a permanent position; (*Law*) articles of a personal nature fitted in a house; a person or thing regarded as permanently established and immovable; a sporting event arranged for a particular date.

fizgig, *n.* a gadding, flirting girl; a firework of damp powder that fizzes. [etym. obscure (perh. foll. and GIG[1])]

fizz, *v.i.* to make a hissing or sputtering sound. *n.* a hissing, sputtering sound; (*coll.*) champagne, from its effervescence; (*coll.*) ginger-beer, lemonade. **fizzy,** *a.* [imit.]

fizzle, *v.i.* to fizz; (*N Am., sl.*) to fail ignominiously (at an examination). *v.t.* (*N Am., sl.*) to cause to fail (at an examination). *n.* the sound or action of fizzing or fizzling; (*sl.*) a lame ending, a fiasco. **to fizzle out,** to come to a lame conclusion, to make a fiasco. [freq. of prec.]

fjord, FIORD.

FL, (*abbr.*) Florida.

fl., (*abbr.*) florin; flourished.

Fla, (*abbr.*) Florida.

flab FLABBY.

flabbergast, *v.t.* to strike with wonder and amazement; to astound, to stagger with surprise. [etym. doubtful]

flabby, *a.* hanging loosely, limp, flaccid; lacking in fibre or nerve, languid, feeble. **flab,** *n.* (*coll.*) flaccid body tissue, a sign of being overweight or out of condition. **flabbily,** *adv.* **flabbiness,** *n.* [var. of obs. *flappy,* a., see FLAP]

flabellate, *a.* fan-shaped. **flabellation,** *n.* (*Med.*) cooling with a fan or similar contrivance. **flabelliform,** *a.*

flabellum, *n.* (*pl.* **-lla**) a fan, esp. one used in the Greek Church to drive away flies from the chalice or in the Roman Catholic Church to carry in religious processions; (*Biol.*) a fan-shaped part or organ. [L, a fan]

flaccid, *a.* lacking firmness or vigour; limp, flabby,

drooping; relaxed, feeble. **flaccidity,** *n.* **flaccidly,** *adv.* **flaccidness,** *n.* [F *flaccide,* L *flaccidus,* from *flaccus,* flabby]

flack, *v.t.* to flap, flick or flourish (as a whip); to flap or flick (with). [ME *flacken,* onomat. (cp. FLAP, FLIC[1])]

†**flacket,** *n.* a little flask or flagon. [ONF *flaquet,* OF *flaschet,* dim. of *flasque,* see FLASK]

flacon, *n.* a small bottle, esp. a scent-bottle. [F, see FLAGON]

flag[1], *v.i.* (*past, p.p.* **flagged**) to hang loosely, to droop; to become limp; to lose strength or vigour; to become spiritless or dejected; to lose interest. †*v.t.* to allow to droop; †to tire out, to enfeeble; †to slacken, to cease to move vigorously (as wings). [prob. imit. in origin (cp. ME *flakken,* to waver, flutter, OF *flaquir,* to hang down, become flaccid, L *flaccus,* limp; also FLABBY, FLICKER)]

flag[2], *n.* a piece of bunting or other cloth, usu. square or oblong, and plain or bearing a device, attached by one edge to a staff or halyard by which it can be hoisted on a pole or mast, and displayed as a banner, ensign or signal; (*Naut.*) a flag carried by a flagship to show that the admiral is in command; the flagship itself; the bushy part of a dog's tail, as of a setter; the uncut tuft of hair on a brush; the long quill-feathers of a bird's wing; †a bird's wing. *v.t.* (*past, p.p.* **flagged**) to put a flag over; to decorate with flags; to mark out with flags; to signal by means of a flag or flags. **black flag,** BLACK. **flag of convenience,** a foreign flag under which a vessel is registered to escape taxation etc. in its real country of origin. **flag of truce,** a white flag indicating that the enemy has some pacific communication to make; an offer of peace. **red flag** RED. **to dip the flag,** (*Naut.*) to lower and then raise it as a salute. **to flag down,** to signal to (a vehicle) to stop. **to hang the flag half-mast high,** to fly it halfway up the staff as a token of mourning. **to hoist one's flag:** of an admiral, to take up the command of a squadron. **to keep the flag flying,** to continue to represent or stand up for e.g. a country or principles. **to show the flag,** to send an official representative or military unit to a place as a courtesy or a means of asserting a claim etc.; (*coll.*) to put in an appearance. **to strike, lower the flag,** to pull the flag down in token of surrender or submission; of an admiral, to relinquish the command. **white flag** FLAG OF TRUCE. **yellow-flag** YELLOW. **flag-captain,** *n.* the commanding officer of a flagship. **flag day,** *n.* a day on which street collections are made for a specific charity, a small flag being worn as a token of having given money. **flag-lieutenant,** *n.* an officer in immediate attendance upon a flag-officer. **flag-list,** *n.* the roll or register of flag-officers. **flag-man,** *n.* one who makes signals with flags; †a flag-officer. **flag-officer,** *n.* a commander of a squadron; a commodore, admiral, vice-admiral or rear-admiral; **flagpole** FLAGSTAFF. **to run (something) up the flagpole,** to sound out an idea etc., to test reactions to something. **flagship,** *n.* the ship which carries the admiral, and on which his flag is displayed; the largest and most important of a set, esp. something regarded as embodying e.g. a company's prestige. **flagstaff,** *n.* (*pl.* **-staffs, -staves**) the pole or staff on which a flag is displayed. **flag-station,** *n.* a railway station at which trains stop only when signalled. **flag-wagging,** *n.* (*Mil. sl.*) signalling or signalling-drill. [perh. imit. (cp. prec., also Dut. *vlag,* Dan. *flag,* Norw. and Swed. *flagg,* G *Flagge*)]

flag[3], *n.* one of various herbaceous plants with long blade-like leaves growing in moist places, chiefly belonging to the genus *Iris;* (*pl.* or *collect.*) a coarse, reedy kind of grass. **flag-basket,** *n.* a basket made of reeds for carrying tools. **flag-worm,** *n.* a worm or grub found in the roots of flags and used as bait by anglers. **flaggy,** *a.* [prob. rel. to prec., from its waving or fluttering (cp. Dut. *flag,* mod. Dan. *flaeg*)]

flag[4], flagstone, *n.* a broad flat stone used for paving; (*pl.*) a pavement made of such stones; a fine-grained rock which can be split into slabs for paving. *v.t.* (*past, p.p.* **flagged**) to pave with flags. **flagging,** *n.* the act of paving with flagstones; flagstones; a pavement of flagstones. [prob. a form of FLAKE[1]]

flagellate, *v.t.* to whip, to beat, to scourge. *a.*, (*Zool., Bot. etc.*) having whip-like processes or flagella. **flagellant,** *n.* one of a sect of fanatics which arose in Italy about 1260 who sought to avert the divine wrath by scourging themselves till the blood came; (*Psych.*) one who thrashes (himself or others) for sexual gratification. *a.* given to scourging. **flagellation,** *n.* a scourging or flogging. **flagellator,** *n.* **flagellatory,** *a.* **flagelliform,** *a.* **flagellum,** *n.* (*pl.* **-lla**) (*Zool., Biol.*) a minute whip-like appendage; a trailing shoot; a runner. [L *flagellātus,* p.p. of *flagellāre,* to scourge, from *flagellum,* dim. of *flagrum,* a scourge]

flageolet[1], *n.* a small wind instrument blown from a mouthpiece at the end, and producing a shrill sound similar to but softer than that of the piccolo; a tin-whistle. **flageolet-tones,** *n.pl.* the natural harmonics of stringed instruments. [F, dim. of OF *flageol,* etym. doubtful]

flageolet[2], *n.* the green pod of the haricot bean, *Phaseolus vulgaris.* [F, corr. of *fageolet,* dim. of *fageol,* L *faseolus*]

flagitate, *v.t.* to demand with importunity. †**flagitation,** *n.* [L *flāgitātus,* p.p. of *flāgitāre*]

flagitious, *a.* heinous, flagrant, villainous; deeply criminal. **flagitiously,** *adv.* **flagitiousness,** *n.* [L *flāgitiōsus,* from *flāgitium,* a disgraceful act (rel. to prec.)]

flagon, *n.* a vessel with a narrow mouth or spout, used for holding liquors; a flat bottle holding the contents of nearly two bottles, used in the wine-trade. [OF *flacon,* late L *flasco -ōnem, flasca,* FLASK]

flagrant, *a.* glaring, notorious, outrageous, scandalous; †burning, blazing; †eager. **flagrancy,** *n.* **flagrantly,** *adv.* [L *flagrans -ntem,* pres.p. of *flagrāre,* to blaze]

flagrante delicto, (L) in the very act, red-handed.

Flagstad, *n.* **Kirsten (Malfrid)** (1895–1962), Norwegian soprano who specialized in Wagnerian opera.

flagstone FLAG4.

flail, *n.* a wooden instrument consisting of a staff or swingle hinged to a longer staff or handle, used for threshing grain by hand. *v.t.* to swing or beat wildly; to strike (as) with a flail. *v.i.* to thresh around. [OE *fligel,* prob. from L FLAGELLUM (form influenced by the cognate OF *flael,* whence F *fléau*)]

flair, *n.* a keen sense of smell; keen perception, discernment; a natural aptitude or gift; stylishness. [F, from *flairer,* to smell, pop. L *flāgrāre,* L *frāgrāre*]

flak, *n.* fire from anti-aircraft guns; adverse criticism, dissent. **flak-catcher,** *n.* (*chiefly N Am., sl.*) a subordinate who deals with adverse criticism on a superior's behalf. **flak jacket,** *n.* a reinforced jacket worn by soldiers, police etc. as protection against gunshot etc. [initials of G *Flug abwehr kanone,* anti-aircraft gun]

flake[1], *n.* a thin scale-like fragment; a thin piece peeled off; a chip (as of flint); a loosely cohering mass, a fleecy particle (as of snow); a carnation with petals striped on a white ground; (*N Am., sl.*) a flaky person; †a flash, a gleam of light. *v.t.* to form into flakes or loose particles; to chip flakes off or in flakes; to sprinkle with flakes, to fleck. *v.i.* to peel or scale off in flakes. **flake-white,** *n.* English white lead in the form of scales, used as a pigment. **flaky,** *a.* consisting of flakes; liable to flake; (*N Am., sl.*) unstable, unreliable; (*N Am., sl.*) unattractively unconventional; not with-it. **flakiness,** *n.* [etym. obscure]

flake[2], *n.* a light platform or rack; a frame for storing provisions, esp. oatcake; a rack for drying fish; a stage hung over a ship's side, for the use of painters etc.; (*dial.*) a hurdle, esp. one used for a fence. [perh. from Icel. *flake, fleke,* a hurdle, rel. to L *plectere,* and Gr. *plekein,* to plait]

flam, *n.* a false pretext, a sham, a deception, a lie. †*a.* lying, false, deceitful. *v.t.* to deceive, to impose upon. [etym. doubtful]

flambé, *v.t.* (*past, p.p.* **flambéed**) to sprinkle with brandy and ignite. *a.* served as above. [from F *flamber,* to flame]

flambeau, *n.* a torch, esp. one made of thick wicks

covered with wax or pitch. [F, dim. of OF *flambe*]

flamboyant, *a.* a term applied to the decorated French Gothic (contemporary with the Perpendicular style in England), from the flame-like tracery; florid, highly decorated; gorgeously coloured; of hair etc., wavy or flame-like; exuberant, extravagant, showy. [F, pres.p. of *flamboier,* as prec.]

flame, *n.* a mass or stream of vapour or gas in a state of combustion; a blaze; fire; a glow, a bright light; a blaze of colour; ardour, excitement, passion; the object of one's affection, a sweetheart. †*v.t.* to burn; to inflame, to excite; to send with or as with flame. *v.i.* to burn with a flame; to send out flame, to blaze, to burst into flames; (*fig.*) to break (out) or blaze (up) in violent passion; to shine, to glow, to flash. **flame-colour,** *n.* a bright yellow colour. **flame-coloured,** *a.* †**flame-eyed,** *a.* having eyes burning like fire. **flame-flower,** *n.* a plant of the genus *Tritoma* or *Kniphofia,* pop. called the red-hot poker. **flame-thrower,** *n.* a weapon that projects a stream of burning liquid. **flame-tree,** *n.* the Australian fire-tree. **flameless,** *a.* **flamelet,** *a.* **flaming,** *a.* burning, blazing; (*fig.*) intensely hot; intensely bright; inflaming, exciting; vehement, violent; exaggerated, florid, extravagant; (*sl.*) bloody. **flaming onion,** *n.* an anti-aircraft projectile having the appearance of a string of yellow fire-balls. **flamingly,** *adv.* **flamy,** *a.* [OF *flambe,* L *flamma,* prob. from the base *flag-,* to burn (*flagrāre,* to blaze), or *flāre,* to blow]

flamen, *n.* an ancient Roman priest devoted to some special deity. **flaminical**, *a.* [L, prob. as prec.]

flamenco, *n.* (*pl.* **-cos**) a Gipsy song or dance from Andalusia.

flamingo, *n.* (*pl.* **-gos, -goes**) a long-necked bird, with small body and very long legs, its feathers rose or scarlet in colour, belonging to the genus *Phaenicopterus.* [Port. *flamengo,* Sp. *flamenco*]

Flaminius, *n.* **Gaius** (d. 217 BC); Roman consul and general. He constructed the Flaminian Way northward from Rome to Rimini in 220 BC, and was killed at the battle of Lake Trasimene fighting Hannibal.

flan, *n.* an open pastry or sponge tart with a fruit or savoury filling. **flan-case,** *n.* [F]

Flanagan, *n.* **Bud** (stage name of Robert Winthrop) (1896–1968), British comedian, leader of the 'Crazy Gang' (1931–62). He played in variety theatre all over the world and, with his partner Chesney Allen, popularized such songs as 'Underneath the Arches'.

flanch, *n.* a flange; (*Her.*) a sub-ordinary or part of a shield enclosed by an arc from the upper corners to the base, and always borne in pairs. [perh. a var. of FLANGE or FLANK]

flanconnade, *n.* (*Fencing*) a thrust in the flank. [F, from *flanc*]

Flanders[1], *n.* a region of the Low Countries which in the 8th and 9th centuries extended from Calais to the Scheldt, and is now covered by the Belgian provinces of Oost Vlaanderen and West Vlaanderen (East and West Flanders), the French *département* of Nord, and part of the Dutch province of Zeeland. The language is Flemish. East Flanders, capital Ghent, has an area of 3000 sq km/1158 sq miles, and a population (1987) of 1,329,000. West Flanders, capital Bruges, has an area of 3100 sq km/1197 sq miles, and a population (1987) of 1,035,000.

Flanders[2], *n.* lace from Flanders. **Flanders brick,** *n.* a soft brick used for cleaning knives, the same as Bath brick. **Flanders horse**, *n.* a carriage horse formerly imported from Flanders. [Dut. *Vlaanderen,* pl., a district of the Netherlands]

flaneur, *n.* a lounger, an idler. **flanerie**, *n.* the practice or habit of sauntering or idling. [F, from *flâner,* to saunter]

flange, *n.* a projecting rib or rim affixed to a wheel, tool, pipe etc., for strength, as a guide, or for attachment to something else. *v.t.* to supply with a flange. **flange-rail,** *n.* a rail having a bent-up flange to keep the wheel on the metals. **flanged,** *a.* [prob. from OF *flanche*]

flank, *n.* the fleshy or muscular part of the side between the hips and the ribs; either side of a building, mountain etc.; the side of an army or body of troops; (*Fort.*) the portion of a bastion reaching from the curtain to the face; (*Mech.*) the acting surface of a cog within the pitch-line. *v.t.* to stand or be at the flank or side of, to border; to attack, turn or threaten the flank of; to secure or guard the flank of. *v.i.* to border, to touch; to be posted on the flank or side. **flank-company,** *n.* the company posted on the extreme right or left of a body of troops. **flank-files,** *n.pl.* the first two men on the right and the last two men on the left. **flank-movement,** *n.* a manoeuvre directed at turning the enemy's flank. **flanker,** *n.* one who or that which flanks, or is posted, stationed or placed on the flanks; (*pl.*) skirmishers thrown out on the flanks of an army when marching; (*Fort.*) a work projecting so as to command the flank of an assailing body; (*Rugby*) a wing forward. [F *flanc;* perh. from Teut. (cp. OHG *hlanca,* the loin, the side, also OE *hlanc,* slender)]

flannel, *n.* a soft woollen stuff of open texture, with a light nap; (*pl.*) garments made of this material, esp. underclothing, also trousers for cricketers etc.; a piece of flannel used for washing the face etc.; (*coll.*) flattery, soft-soap; (*coll.*) evasive waffling, nonsense; †(*Shak.*) a Welshman. *v.t.* (*past, p.p.* **flannelled**) to wrap in or rub with flannel or a flannel; (*coll.*) to flatter. *v.i.* (*coll.*) to waffle on evasively. **flannel-flower,** *n.* the mullein. **flannel-weed,** *n.* a water plant that covers stones and the surface of water with woolly fibres, esp. in time of drought. **flannelette,** *n.* a cotton fabric made to imitate flannel. **flannelled,** *a.* covered with or wrapped up in flannel. **flannelly,** *a.* [from W *gwlanen,* from *gwlan,* wool (Skeat), or from OF *flaine,* blanket, coverlet]

flap, *v.t.* (*past, p.p.* **flapped**) to beat, strike or drive away with anything broad and flexible; to move rapidly up and down or to and fro (as wings); to let fall (as the brim of a hat). *v.i.* to move the wings rapidly up and down or to and fro; to be moved loosely to and fro, to flutter, swing about or oscillate; to hang down, as the brim of a hat; to strike a loose blow or blows, to beat (as with the wings). *n.* anything broad and flexible, hanging loosely, or attached by one side only, usu. used to cover an opening; the hinged leaf of a table or shutter; a movable control surface on the wing of an aircraft to increase lift on take-off and drag on landing; the motion or act of flapping; a light stroke or blow with something broad and loose; a slap; an implement for driving flies away; (*coll.*) a state of anxiety or confusion; (*pl.*) a disease in the lips of horses. **flapdoodle,** *n.* rubbish, nonsense, bunkum. †**flap-eared,** *a.* having broad, pendulous ears. **flapjack,** *n.* a kind of pancake; a biscuit made of oat flakes and syrup; a flattish circular case for holding a powder-puff and a mirror. **flapper,** *n.* one who or that which flaps; a partridge or wild duck not yet able to fly; a flap, a part or organ loosely attached or hanging; (*sl.*) in the 1920s, a flighty young woman. [prob. imit.]

flare, *v.i.* to blaze, to flame up, or to glow, esp. with an unsteady light; to be gaudy, glaring, or too showy in dress; (*sl.*) to bounce, to swagger; to open or spread outwards. *v.t.* to cause to flare up; to burn off excess gas or oil; to provide with a flare or flares (as a skirt or trousers). *n.* a large unsteady light, a glare; a sudden outburst; (*Dressmaking*) material cut on the cross to give additional fullness; a widening or spreading out; (a thing with) a flared shape; (a device producing) a blaze of light used for illumination, signalling, or to attract attention. **to flare up,** to blaze out; to fly into a passion. **flare-up,** *n.* a sudden outbreak into flame; a showy but transient display; an outburst of anger, violence, hostilities etc. **flared,** *a.* having a flare or flares, flare-shaped. **flaring,** *a.* flaming, dazzling; gaudy, too showy or ostentatious. **flaringly,** *adv.* **flary,** *a.* gaudy, showy. [cp. Norw. *flara;* also G *flattern,* to flicker]

flash, *v.i.* to appear with a sudden and transient gleam; to burst suddenly into flame or light; to send out a rapid gleam; to reflect light, to glitter, to burst forth, appear or occur suddenly; to rush swiftly, to dash, break or splash, as water or waves; to signal using e.g. a torch or the headlights of a car; (*sl.*) to expose oneself indecently. *v.t.* to emit or send forth in flashes or like flashes; to cause to gleam; to convey or transmit instantaneously (as news by telegraph); to signal (a message) to (someone) using light; to display or expose suddenly and briefly; to display ostentatiously; (*Glass-making*) to expand into a dish or sheet, to cover (plain glass) with a thin coating of coloured glass; to send swiftly along; to send a rush of water down (a river, weir etc.); †to strike or throw up in glittering spray. *n.* a sudden and transitory blaze or gleam of bright light; the space of time taken by this, an instant; a sudden occurrence or display; a body of water driven along with violence; a sluice or lock just above a shoal, to raise the water while boats are passing; a preparation of capsicum, burnt sugar etc., used for colouring and giving a fictitious strength to rum and brandy; a label with regimental name etc. sewn on the uniform shoulder; a sticker on goods etc. advertising e.g. a reduction in price; (*Phot.*) flashlight, an apparatus for producing flashlight; a newsflash; a sudden outburst, as of anger, wit, merriment etc.; show, ostentation; thieves' jargon, cant, slang; †a showy person, a fop. *a.* occurring or carried out very quickly; gaudy, vulgarly showy; counterfeit, forged; slang, cant; pertaining to thieves or vagabonds. **a flash in the pan,** a flash produced by the hammer of a gun upon a flint which fails to explode the powder; hence, an abortive attempt. **flashback,** *n.* an interruption in the narrative of e.g. a film or novel to show past events. **flash-board,** *n.* a hatch for releasing water in a mill-leat. **flashbulb,** *n.* (*Phot.*) a (usu. disposable) bulb used to produce flashlight. **flash burn,** *n.* a burn suffered as the result of momentary exposure to intense heat. **flash card,** *n.* a card with e.g. words or numbers printed on it for children to look at briefly as an aid to learning. **flash cube,** *n.* (*Phot.*) a plastic cube containing four flashbulbs. **flash flood,** *n.* a sudden flood, caused by heavy local rainfall. **flash gun,** *n.* (*Phot.*) a device which holds and fires a flashbulb. **flash-house,** *n.* a house frequented by thieves, and in which stolen goods were received. **flashlight,** *n.* (*Phot.*) a brilliant light for taking (usu. indoor) photographs; an electric battery torch; a flashing-light. †**flashman,** *n.* a rogue; a fancy man; a sporting character. **flash-notes, -money,** *n.* (*pl.*) counterfeit notes or coin. †**flash-pipe,** *n.* a perforated gas-pipe for lighting burners. **flashpoint,** *n.* the degree of temperature at which the vapour from oil or spirit ignites; the point at which tension erupts into violence; a place or region where such eruptions are likely to occur. **flasher,** *n.* one who or that which flashes; a device that causes a light to flash; a vehicle indicator light; (*sl.*) one who exposes himself indecently. **flashing,** *n.* a lap-joint used in roofing with sheet metal, a strip of lead carrying the drip of a wall into a gutter. **flashing-light,** *n.* a light exhibited from some lighthouses in which brilliant flashes alternate with periods of entire obscuration. **flashing point** FLASHPOINT. **flashy,** *a.* showy but empty, brilliant but shallow; gaudy, tawdry, cheap and showy; †insipid, vapid; †impulsive, fickle. **flashily,** *adv.* **flashiness,** *n.* [prob. onomat. in sense of dashing or flapping like water]

flask, *n.* a small bottle or similar vessel; (usu. **powder-flask**) a leather or metal case for powder or shot; a flat bottle, usu. mounted in metal, for carrying spirits in the pocket; a thin, long-necked bottle, encased in wicker, for wine or oil; a vacuum flask; a large reinforced metal container for transporting nuclear waste. [F *flasque* or It. *flasco* (cp. G *Flasche,* OHG *flasca,* OE *flasce, flaxe*), ult. perh. from L *vasculum,* dim. of *vas,* a vessel]

flasket, *n.* a long shallow basket with two handles; a small flask. [OF *flasquet,* dim. of *flasque,* as prec.]

flat[1]**,** *a.* having a level and even surface; horizontal, level; even, smooth, having few or no elevations or depressions; having little depth or thickness; level with the ground, lying prone, prostrate; having a surface or side in continuous contact with another surface; of feet, having little or no arch; of shoes, not having a raised heel; of a battery, having little or no charge; of a tyre, deflated; depressed, dejected; monotonous, dull, uninteresting, vapid, insipid, pointless, spiritless; having lost sparkle or freshness; plain, positive, absolute, downright; neither more nor less, as in *ten seconds flat;* dull; of prices, low; (*Painting*) wanting relief or prominence of the figures; uniform, without variety of tint or shading; (*Mus.*) below the true pitch; minor (applied to intervals); having only a small rise, as some arches. *adv.* flatly, positively; prostrate, level with the ground; below the true pitch. *n.* a flat, plain surface; a level plain or low tract of land; a plot of ground laid down level; a shoal, a shallow, a low tract flooded at high tide; a flat part of anything; anything that is flat; a broad, flat-bottomed boat; (*N Am.*) a broad-brimmed straw hat; the palm of the hand; (*Theat.*) scenery on a wooden frame pushed on to the stage from the sides; a note a semitone lower than the one from which it is named, the sign indicating this lowering of pitch; a punctured tyre. *v.i.* (*past, p.p.* **flatted**) to flatten, to make flat and smooth. **flat broke,** (*coll.*) having no money, skint. **flat out,** at full speed, with maximum effort; completely exhausted. **that's flat!** that is final, irrevocable. **the flat,** the flat-racing season. **to fall flat** FALL. **flat-boat,** *n.* a large boat with a flat bottom, used for transport on rivers in the US. **flat cap,** *n.* a size of writing paper, 14×17 in. (35·6×43·2 cm); a cap with a low, flat crown. **flat fish,** *n.* any fish (such as the sole, plaice, turbot etc.) of the Pleuronectidae, distinguished by their laterally compressed body, absence of coloration on the under side, and the position of both eyes on the upper side. **flatfoot,** *n.* (*derog.*) a policeman. **flat-footed,** *a.* with the feet not arched; awkward; ponderous, unimaginative; (*coll.*) off guard; (*chiefly N Am., sl.*) downright, resolute, determined. **flat-head,** *n.* (*Austral.*) an edible fish with flattened head and body. **flat-iron,** *n.* an instrument for smoothing clothes etc. **flat-race,** *n.* a race on level ground without obstacles. **flat rate,** *n.* a rate of payment not varying in proportion with the amount supplied. **flat spin,** *n.* a spin in which the aircraft is almost horizontal; a confused and frantic state. **flatly,** *adv.* **flatness,** *n.* **flatten,** *v.t.* to make flat, to level; to lay flat; to make vapid, dull or insipid; to deject, to dispirit; (*Mus.*) to depress or lower in pitch; to knock down or out; to defeat resoundingly. *v.i.* to become flat or level; to lose force or interest, to pall; to depress the voice, to fall in pitch. **to flatten a sail,** to extend it fore and aft so as to catch the side wind. **to flatten out,** of a plane, to change from the gliding approach to the position to alight, when approaching to land. **flatting,** *n.* the act or process of flattening; a covering of size over gilding; the process of rolling out metal into sheets; a style of inside house-painting in which the colours are not glossy. **flatting-mill,** *n.* a mill for rolling out metal by cylindrical pressure. **flattish,** *a.* [Icel. *flatr,* etym. doubtful]

flat[2]**,** *n.* a floor or storey of a house; a suite of rooms on one floor forming a separate residence. **flatmate,** *n.* a person with whom one shares a flat. **flatlet,** *n.* a small flat. [OE *flet,* a floor, cogn. with prec.]

flatter, *v.t.* to court, cajole or gratify by compliment, adulation or blandishment; to praise falsely or unduly; to raise false hopes in; to persuade (usu. oneself of some favourable contingency); to represent too favourably; to display to advantage. *v.i.* to use flattery. **flatterer,** *n.* **flatteringly,** *adv.* **flattery,** *n.* the act or practice of flattering; false or venal praise; adulation, cajolery. [etym. obscure; prob. from OF *flater,* to flatten, smooth, caress, cogn. with FLAT[1] (*-er* not from OF infin., but from the derivative *flaterie,* or from assim. to or substitution for the obs. v. *flatter,* to flutter or float)]

flatulent, *a.* affected with or troubled by wind or gases generated in the alimentary canal; generating or likely to generate wind in the stomach; inflated, empty, vain; pretentious, turgid. **flatulence, -lency,** *n.* **flatulently,** *adv.* **flatus,** *n.* wind in the stomach or bowels; flatulence. [F, from late L *flātulens -ntem,* from *flātus,* a blowing, from *flāre,* to blow]

Flaubert, *n.* **Gustave** (1821–80), French novelist, author of *Madame Bovary* (1857). *Salammbô* (1862) earned him the Legion of Honour (1866), and was followed by *L'Education sentimentale/Sentimental Education* (1869), and *La Tentation de Saint Antoine/The Temptation of St Anthony* (1874). Flaubert also wrote the short stories *Trois contes/Three Tales* (1877).

flaught, *n.* (*Sc.*) a flapping, a commotion; a flight (as of birds); a flash (as of lightning). [var. of FLIGHT[1]]

flaunt, *v.i.* to make an ostentatious or gaudy show; to behave pertly or saucily. *v.t.* to display ostentatiously or impudently; to parade, to show off; to wave or flutter in the wind. *n.* the act of flaunting; impudent parade; finery; a boasting or vaunting; (*pl.*) finery. **flauntingly,** *adv.* **flaunty,** *a.* flaunting, ostentatious. [etym. doubtful]

flautist, *n.* a player on the flute. [It. *flautista,* from *flauto,* a flute]

flavescent, *a.* yellowish; turning yellow. [L *flāvescens -ntem,* pres.p. of *flāvescere,* to become yellow, from *flāvus,* yellow]

flavour, (*esp. N Am.*) **flavor,** *n.* that quality in any substance which affects the taste, or the taste and smell; a characteristic or distinctive quality. *v.t.* to impart a flavour to; to render pleasing to the palate; to season. **flavour of the month,** (*often iron.*) a person or thing much in favour at a particular time. **flavorous, flavoursome,** *a.* pleasing to taste or smell. **flavoured,** *a.* having a distinct flavour; (*in comb.*) having a particular flavour, as *full-flavoured.* **flavouring,** *n.* an (artificial) substance that gives flavour. **flavourless,** *a.* [ME *flauor, flavoure,* prob. from OF *flaur, fraar,* smell (L *frāgrāre,* to smell sweet, or *flāre,* to blow)]

flaw[1], *n.* a crack, a slight fissure; a defect, an imperfection; (*Law*) a defect in an instrument, evidence etc., rendering it invalid; †a flake; †a fragment. *v.t.* to break, to crack; to mar; to render invalid. *v.i.* to crack; †to flake (off). **flawless,** *a.* **flawlessly,** *adv.* **flawlessness,** *n.* **flawy,** *a.* full of flaws; defective. [perh. from Icel. *flaga,* a slab (cp. Swed. *flaga,* flake, flaw)]

flaw[2], *n.* a sudden puff or gust; a squall, a violent but transient storm; †a tumult; †a mental commotion. **flawy,** *a.* gusty. [perh. cogn. with prec. or with FLAY (cp. Dut. *vlaag*)]

†flawn, *n.* a kind of custard. [OF *flaon* (F *flan*), med. L *fladō -ōnem,* OHG *flado,* a broad flat cake]

flax, *n.* a plant of the genus *Linum,* esp. *L. usitatissimum,* the common flax, the fibre of which is made into yarn, and woven into linen cloth; the fibrous part of the plant prepared for manufacture; one of various kinds of similar plants, as white flax, false flax or toad-flax. **New Zealand flax,** a textile fibre obtained from the flax-bush, *Phormium tenax,* a native of New Zealand. **flax-comb,** *n.* a comb or hackle for dressing flax. **flax-dresser,** *n.* one who prepares flax for the spinner. **flax-mill,** *n.* a mill or place where flax is spun. **flax-seed,** *n.* linseed. **flax-weed,** *n.* the toad-flax, *Linaria vulgaris.* **†flax-wench,** *n.* a woman who dresses flax. **flaxen,** *a.* made of flax; like flax in softness, silkiness or colour; light yellow or straw-coloured. **flaxen-haired, -headed,** *a.* **flaxy,** *a.* [OE *fleax* (cp. Dut. *vlas,* G *Flachs;* perh. cogn. with Gr. *plekein,* and L *plectere,* to weave)]

Flaxman, *n.* **John** (1755–1826), English sculptor and illustrator in the neo-classical style. From 1775 he worked for the Wedgwood pottery as a designer. His public works include the monuments of Nelson (1808–10) in St Paul's Cathedral, London, and of Burns and Kemble in Westminster Abbey.

flay, *v.t.* to strip the skin from; to peel; to pare; to strip; to plunder; to criticize savagely. **flay-flint,** *n.* a skinflint, a miser. [OE *flēan* (cp. Icel. *flā,* MDut. *vlaen;* cogn. with Gr. *plēssein,* to strike)]

flea, *n.* a blood-sucking insect belonging to the genus *Pulex,* parasitic on mammals and birds, and remarkable for its leaping powers. **sand-flea,** (*N Am.*) **beach-flea, water-flea,** small crustaceans with similar leaping powers. **with a flea in one's ear** EAR. **flea-bag,** *n.* (*sl.*) a sleeping bag; (*sl.*) a dirty or neglected person; (*chiefly N Am., sl.*) an inferior lodging house. **flea-bane, -wort,** *n.* compositous plants of the genus *Pulicaria, erigeron* or *Conyza,* from their supposed efficacy in driving away fleas. **flea-beetle,** *n.* a small leaping beetle of the family Halticidae, very destructive to hops and other plants. **flea-bite,** *n.* the bite of a flea; the red spot caused by the bite; a tiny amount; the smallest trifle; a trifling inconvenience. **flea-bitten,** *a.* bitten by a flea; full of fleas; coloured, as some horses, with small red spots on a lighter ground. **flea-dock,** *n.* the burdock, *Petasites vulgaris.* **flea-louse,** *n.* a jumping plant-louse of the family Psythidae. **flea market,** *n.* an open-air market selling usu. second-hand goods. **fleapit,** *n.* (*coll., facet.*) a shabby cinema or theatre. [OE *flēah* (cp. Dut. *vloo,* G *Floh;* prob. cogn. with FLEE)]

fleam, *n.* a lancet for bleeding horses and cattle. [OF *flieme,* med. L *flētoma,* abbr. of L *phlebotomum,* Gr. *phlebotomon,* see PHLEBOTOMY]

flèche, *n.* a spire, esp. a slender one, usu. of wood covered with lead, over the intersection of nave and transepts; (*Fort.*) a simple kind of redan, usu. constructed at the foot of the glacis, consisting of a parapet with faces. [F, orig. an arrow]

fleck, *n.* a spot, a freckle, a stain a speck; a dot, stain or patch of colour or light. *v.t.* to spot, to streak, to dapple, to variegate with spots or flecks. **fleckless,** *a.* spotless, stainless, blameless. **flecker,** *v.t.* to fleck, to spot, to dapple; to scatter (light) in flakes or patches. [cp. Icel. *flekkr,* Dut. *vlek,* G *Fleck*]

flection, FLEXION under FLEXIBLE.

fled, *past, p.p.* FLEE.

fledge, *v.t.* to furnish with feathers or plumage; to wing for flight; to feather (an arrow); to deck or cover with anything resembling feathers. *v.i.* to acquire feathers or plumage for flight. **fledged,** *a.* feathered; able to fly. **fledgeless,** *a.* **fledgeling,** *n.* a young bird just fledged; a raw and inexperienced person. *a.* newly fledged. [OE *flycge* (found in *unflycge,* unfledged), cp. Dut. *vlug,* G *flügge* (cogn. with FLY[2])]

flee, *v.i.* (*past, p.p.* **fled**) to run away, as from danger; to vanish, to disappear; to pass away. *v.t.* to run away from; to shun. [OE *flēon,* cp. G *fliehen,* Goth. *thliuhan*]

fleece, *n.* the woolly covering of a sheep or similar animal; the quantity of wool shorn from a sheep at one time; anything resembling a fleece, as a woolly head of hair, a fleecy cloud or fall of snow; a web of carded fibres of cotton or wool; †a snatch. *v.t.* to shear the wool from; to furnish with a fleece; to cover with anything fleecy; to rob, to plunder, to overcharge. **fleeceable,** *a.* **fleeceless,** *a.* **fleecer,** *n.* one who fleeces or plunders. **fleecy,** *a.* woolly, wool-bearing; resembling a fleece in appearance or qualities. [OE *flēos* (cp. Dut. *vlies,* G *Fliess*)]

fleech, *v.t.* (*Sc.*) to flatter; (*Sc.*) to beg, to entreat. [etym. doubtful]

fleer, *v.i.* to grin or laugh in contempt or scorn; to gibe, to sneer; †to leer, to smirk. *v.t.* to laugh or sneer at. *n.* mockery or scorn expressed by words or looks; †a leer, a smirk. **fleeringly,** *adv.* [cp. Norw. *flira,* Swed. *flissa,* to titter]

fleet[1], *n.* a number of ships or smaller vessels in company with a common object or destination, esp. a body of warships under one command; the entire body of warships belonging to one government, a navy; a collection of road vehicles used for a common purpose and usu. under one ownership. **First Fleet** FIRST. [OE *flēot,* a ship, from *flēotan,* to float]

fleet[2], *n.* a creek, an inlet. **the Fleet,** a stream or ditch, now a sewer, emptying into the Thames east of Fleet St; the prison that stood near this. **fleet-dike,** *n.* an embankment to prevent inundation. **Fleet marriage,** *n.* a clandestine marriage performed by disreputable clergymen in the Fleet Prison and recorded in the Fleet Books (prohibited 1753). **Fleet-Street,** *n.* (*esp. formerly*) the centre of newspaper offices in London;

journalism. **Fleet-Streeter,** *n.* a journalist. [OE *flēot* (cp. Dut. *vliet,* G *Fliess,* Icel. *fljōt;* cogn. with prec.)]

fleet[3], *v.i.* to move swiftly; to pass swiftly; (*fig.*) to glide away, to vanish; †to flow away. *v.t.* (*Naut.*) to change the position of, to shift; †to pass (the time) quickly or pleasantly. *a.* swift of pace, nimble, rapid, speedy. **fleet-footed,** *a.* able to run with great speed. **fleeting,** *a.* passing quickly, transient. **fleetingly,** *adv.* **fleetly,** *adv.* **fleetness,** *n.* [OE *flēotan* (cp. Dut. *vlieten,* G *Fliessen,* Icel. *fljōta,* also Gr. *pleein,* to sail)]

fleet[4], *a.* (*prov.*) shallow. *adv.* at no great depth. **fleetly,** *adv.* [prob. cogn. with prec. (cp. Dut. *vloot*)]

Fleming[1], *n.* a native of Flanders; one of Belgian or Dutch descent. **Flemish,** *a.* pertaining to Flanders. *n.* the Flemish language; see separate entry. **Flemish bond** BOND[1]. **Flemish bricks,** *n.pl.* a kind of brick used for paving, of a yellowish colour, and harder than ordinary bricks. [MDut. *Vlâming,* whence *Vlaemisch,* from *Flân-,* whence FLANDERS]

Fleming[2], *n.* **Alexander** (1881–1955), Scottish bacteriologist who discovered lysozyme (a nasal enzyme with antibacterial properties) in 1922, and in 1928 the antibiotic drug penicillin. With H.W. Florey and E.B. Chain, he won the Nobel Prize for Medicine in 1945.

Fleming[3], *n.* **Ian** (1908–64), English author of suspense novels featuring the ruthless, laconic James Bond, UK Secret Service agent No. 007.

Fleming[4], *n.* **John Ambrose** (1849–1945), English electrical physicist and engineer, who invented the thermionic valve in 1904.

Fleming's rules, *n.pl.* memory aids for the directions of the magnetic field, current, and motion in an electric generator or motor, using one's fingers. The three directions are represented by the thu*m*b (for *m*otion), *f*orefinger (for *f*ield) and se*c*ond finger (*c*urrent), all held at right angles to each other. The right hand is used for generators, such as a dynamo, and the left for motors.]John *Fleming*, English physicist]

Flemish, *n.* a member of the W Germanic branch of the Indo-European language family, spoken in N Belgium and the Nord *département* of France. It is closely related to Dutch.

Flemish art, *n.* the style of painting developed and practised in Flanders (a county in the Lowlands of NW Europe, largely coinciding with modern Belgium). A Flemish style emerged in the early 15th century. Paintings are distinguished by keen observation, minute attention to detail, bright colours, and superb technique – oil painting was a Flemish invention. Apart from portraits, they depict religious scenes, often placed in contemporary Flemish landscapes, townscapes, and interiors. Flemish sculpture shows German and French influence.

flense, flench, flinch[2], *v.t.* to strip the blubber or the skin from (a whale or seal). [Dan. *flense*]

flesh, *n.* the soft part of an animal body, esp. the muscular tissue, investing the bones and covered by the skin; animal tissue used as food, as distinct from vegetable, fish, and sometimes from poultry; the body, as distinguished from the soul; animal nature; the human race; carnal appetites; the present state of existence; kindred; the soft pulpy part of a fruit or plant; that which is carnal; a carnal, unrenewed state. *v.t.* to encourage by giving flesh to, to make eager (from the sportsman's practice of giving hawks, dogs etc. the flesh of the first game they take); to initiate; to exercise or use for the first time; to harden, to inure or accustom to any practice or habit. **an arm of flesh,** human strength or aid. **flesh and blood,** the body; human nature, esp. as alive not imaginary, or as liable to infirmities; one's children or near relations. **flesh and fell,** the entire body; completely. **in the flesh,** in bodily form. **proud flesh,** a granular growth resembling flesh growing over a wound. **to be made flesh,** to become incarnate. **to be one flesh,** to be closely united as in marriage. **to flesh out,** to elaborate, to give more substance or detail to. **to lose flesh,** to lose plumpness, to become thin. **to make someone's flesh creep,** to arouse (a physical sense of) horror in someone. **flesh-brush, -glove,** *n.* a brush or glove for stimulating the action of the skin by friction. **flesh-colour,** *n.* the colour of flesh; yellowish pink. **flesh-coloured,** *a.* **flesh-fly,** *n.* a carnivorous insect of the genus *Sarcophaga,* esp. *S. carnaria,* the larvae of which feed on decaying flesh. **flesh-hook,** *n.* a hook to take meat out of a pot. **flesh-meat,** *n.* the flesh of animals used or prepared for food. †**flesh-monger,** *n.* one who deals in meat; a sensualist, a profligate. **flesh-pot,** *n.* a pot in which flesh is cooked; (*usu. pl.*) sumptuous living; (*often pl.*) a night-club etc. offering lavish or sexually titillating entertainment. **the flesh-pots of Egypt,** material welfare, sordid considerations (ref. to Exodus xvi.3). **flesh-pottery,** *n.* **flesh-tints,** *n.pl.* the colours which best represent the human skin. **flesh-worm,** *n.* the flesh-eating larva of an insect. **flesh-wound,** *n.* a wound not reaching the bone or any vital organ. **flesher,** *n.* (*Sc.*) a butcher. **fleshhood,** *n.* corporeal existence. **fleshless,** *a.* destitute of flesh, lean, scraggy. **fleshling,** *n.* one devoted to carnal pleasures; (*pl.*) light flesh-coloured tights to represent the skin, worn by actors, dancers etc. **fleshly,** *a.* pertaining to the flesh, corporeal, sensual, lascivious; human, as distinct from spiritual; mortal, material; wordly. **fleshly-minded,** *a.* addicted to sensual pleasures. **fleshliness,** *n.* †**fleshment,** *n.* eagerness consequent on an initial success. **fleshy,** *a.* like flesh; fat, plump, corpulent; of fruit etc., pulpy. **fleshiness,** *n.* [OE *flǣsc* (cp. Dut. *vleesch,* G *Fleisch;* also Icel. and Dan. *flesk,* pork, bacon)]

†**fletch,** *v.t.* to feather (as an arrow). **fletcher,** *n.* one who feathered arrows, a maker of bows and arrows. [CORR. of FLEDGE]

Fletcher, *n.* **John** (1579–1625), English dramatist. He collaborated with Beaumont, producing, most notably, *Philaster* (1609) and *The Maid's Tragedy* (1610–11). He is alleged to have collaborated with Shakespeare on *The Two Noble Kinsmen* and *Henry VIII* in 1612.

fleur de lis, *n.* (*pl.* **fleurs de lis**) various species of iris; the heraldic lily, a charge borne in the French royal arms. **fleury, flory,** *a.* adorned with fleurs de lis. [F, lily flower]

fleuret, *n.* an ornament like a small flower; †a fencing-foil. [F *fleurette,* dim. of *fleur*]

fleuron, *n.* a flower-shaped ornament, used for a tail-piece, in architecture, on coins etc. [F, from *fleur*]

fleury FLEUR DE LIS.

Flevoland, *n.* (formerly **IJsselmeerpolders**) a low-lying province of the Netherlands established in 1986; area 1410 sq km/544 sq miles; population (1988) 194,000. Chief town is Dronten. The polder land of the Ijsselmeer was reclaimed during 1950–57.

flew, *past* FLY[2].

flews, *n.pl.* the large chaps of a deep-mouthed hound. [etym. doubtful]

flex[1], *v.t.* to bend or cause to bend; (*Geol.*) to subject (strata) to fracture or distortion. **to flex one's muscles,** to contract the muscles, esp. of the arm in order to display them or as a preliminary to a trial of strength; (*fig.*) to put on a show of power or strength. [L *flexus,* p.p. of *flectere*]

flex[2], *n.* flexible insulated wire, or a piece of this. [short for FLEXIBLE]

flexible, *a.* pliant, easily bent; tractable, easily persuaded; manageable, plastic, supple, versatile. **flexibility,** *n.* **flexibly,** *adv.* in a flexible manner. **flexile,** *a.* easily bent; pliant, tractable; supple, versatile. **flexility,** *n.* **flexion,** *n.* the act or process of bending; a bend, a curve; (*Gram.*) inflection; bending movement of a joint or limb; (*Math.*) flexure. **flexional,** *a.* **flexionless,** *a.* **flexor,** *n.* a muscle that causes a limb or part to bend. **flexuose,** *a.* winding, serpentine; crooked, zigzag. **flexuosity,** *n.* **flexuos(o)-** *comb. form* **flexuous,** *a.* full of bends or turns, winding; wavering, unsteady; (*Bot., Zool. etc.*) presenting alternating curvatures in opposite directions. **flexuously,** *adv.* **flexure,** *n.* the act, process or manner of bending; the state of being bent; a bend, curve, turn, curvature; curving of a line, surface or solid; (*Geol.*) bending or folding of strata under pressure. **flexure of a curve,** the bending of a curve towards or from a straight line.

flexitime, *n.* a system of working which allows the worker some freedom to choose when to arrive for and leave work, usu. so long as he or she is present during a stipulated period (core time) [*flexi*ble *time*]

fley, *v.t.* (*Sc., North.*) to frighten; to affright. [OE *flȳgan* (found in *a-flȳgan*), causative of *flēogan,* to FLY[2]]

flibbertigibbet, *n.* a chatterer; a flighty, thoughtless person; an impish knave (in allusion to Scott's *Kenilworth*); a fiend. [onomat., or meaningless jargon]

flick[1], *n.* a smart, light blow or flip, as with a whip. *v.t.* to strike with such a stroke; to jerk or flip (dust etc. away). **to flick through,** to read through quickly or inattentively. **flick-knife,** *n.* a knife with a blade that springs out when a button in the handle is pressed. [onomat.]

flick[2], *n.* (*coll.*) a film, a movie. **the flicks,** the cinema.

flicker, *v.i.* to flutter, to flap the wings; to quiver, to burn unsteadily, to waver. *n.* the act of flickering; an unsteady or dying light; (*Cinema*) discontinuity of projection caused by too few flashes of the pictures per second. **flickeringly,** *adv.* [OE flicerian, onomat.]

flickermouse, FLITTERMOUSE.

flier, FLYER under FLY[2].

flight[1], *n.* the act or power of flying through the air; an air or space journey, esp. a scheduled trip made by a commercial air service; swift movement or passage, as the motion of a projectile, the passing away of time; a trajectory; a soaring, a sally, an excursion, a sustained effort; the distance to which anything can fly; a number of birds or insects moving together; a migration; a volley (of arrows, spears etc.); a series of steps mounting in one direction; the basic tactical unit of an airforce; (*Racing*) a line of hurdles on a course; (*Angling*) a device for causing the bait to spin rapidly; a feather or vane attached to the tail of an arrow or dart. *v.t.* to shoot at wild-fowl flying overhead; to give a high, slow trajectory to (a ball etc.); to put a feather or vane on (an arrow or dart); †to put to flight. **flight-arrow,** *n.* a light, blunt, well-feathered arrow for long-distance shooting. **flight-deck,** *n.* an aircraft-carrier's deck from which planes take off and land; the compartment at the front of a large aircraft housing the controls, navigation equipment etc. **flight-engineer,** *n.* a member of the crew of an aeroplane in charge of the motors. **flight-feather,** *n.* one of the large wing-quills used in flying. **Flight Lieutenant,** *n.* a commissioned rank in the RAF equivalent to captain in the Army. **flight-muscle,** *n.* one of the muscles working the wings of a bird. **flight-path,** *n.* the path of the centre of gravity of an aeroplane relative to the air. **flight plan,** *n.* the proposed route and schedule of an aircraft flight. **flight recorder,** *n.* an instrument which records details of an aircraft's (performance in) flight. **Flight Sergeant,** *n.* a non-commissioned rank in the RAF. **flight-shooting,** *n.* shooting with flight-arrows; shooting at flocks of wild-fowl on the wing. †**flight-shot,** *n.* the distance to which a flight-arrow can be shot. **flightless,** *a.* unable to fly. **flighty,** *a.* capricious, volatile; wild, fickle; †fleeting, swift. **flightily,** *adv.* **flightiness,** *n.* [OE *flyht,* from OTeut. *fleugan,* to FLY[2]]

flight[2], *n.* the act of fleeing or running away; a hasty departure, retreat or evasion. **to put to flight,** to cause to run away or disappear. **to take (to) flight,** to run away, to flee. [ME *fliht, fluhte,* OHG *flucht,* from OTeut. *thliuhan,* to FLEE]

flighty FLIGHT[1].

flimflam, *n.* nonsense, bosh; humbug, deception; a piece of deception. [prob. onomat.]

flimsy, *a.* thin, slight, frail; without strength or solidity; unsubstantial; easily torn; ineffective, unconvincing; frivolous, trivial, paltry. *n.* thin paper used for manifolding; copy for the press written on this; (*sl.*) an old-style £5 bank-note. **flimsily,** *adv.* **flimsiness,** *n.* [etym. doubtful, prob. onomat.]

flinch[1], *v.i.* to shrink from (an undertaking, suffering etc.); to wince, to give way, to fail. **flincher,** *n.* **flinchingly,** *adv.* [OF *flenchir,* etym. doubtful]

flinch[2] FLENSE.

flinder, *n.* (*usu. pl.*) a fragment, a piece, a splinter. [Norw. *flindra,* a chip, a splinter, Dut. *flenter*]

Flinders, *n.* **Matthew** (1774–1814), English navigator who explored the Australian coasts from 1795–99 and from 1801–03. **Flinders grass,** *n.* native pasture grass, chiefly in E Australia.

fling, *v.i.* (*past, p.p.* **flung**) to rush violently, to flounce; of horses, to kick, struggle, plunge (out); to flout, sneer, to throw invective or aspersions (at); †to dash, to rush, to fly. *v.t.* to cast or throw with sudden force; to hurl; to send or put suddenly and unceremoniously; to send forth, to emit; to throw to the ground, to defeat. *n.* a cast or throw from the hand; a gibe, a sneer; a period of unrestrained enjoyment; a lively Highland dance; a kick, plunge, jump or flounce. **to fling away,** to discard, to reject. **to fling down,** to cast or throw to the ground, to demolish, to ruin. **to fling off,** to abandon, discard, disown; to baffle in the chase. **to fling open,** to throw open suddenly or violently. **to fling out,** to be violent or unruly; to make violent or insulting remarks; to utter hastily or violently. **to fling to,** to shut violently. **to fling up,** to abandon. **to have a fling at,** to make a passing attempt at; to gibe or scoff at. **to have one's fling,** to give oneself up to unrestrained enjoyment; to have one's own way. [cp. Icel. *flengja,* Swed. *flänga*]

flint, *n.* a variety of quartz, usu. grey, smoke-brown or brownish-black and encrusted with white, easily chipped into a sharp cutting edge; a nodule of flint, a flint pebble; a piece of flint shaped for use in a gun, a tinder-box, lighter, or as an implement used by savages or prehistoric man; a piece of iron alloy used to make a spark in a modern lighter; anything extremely hard; extreme hardness. **flint and stone work,** architectural decoration with stone on a ground of flints, frequent in East Anglian churches. **flint age** STONE AGE. **flint-glass,** *n.* a very pure and lustrous kind of glass, orig. made with calcined flints. †**flint-heart, -hearted,** *a.* hard-hearted, unfeeling. **flint implements,** *n.pl.* a generic name for flint tools or weapons etc. made by prehistoric man. **flint-knapper,** *n.* one who makes flints for guns or strike-a-lights. **flint-lock,** *n.* a lock for firearms, in which the cock holds a piece of flint, and comes down upon the steel cap of the pan containing the priming, which is ignited by the spark thus caused; a firearm having such a lock. **flintwood,** *n.* (*Austral.*) the black-butt tree. **flinty,** *a.* composed of flint; of the nature of or resembling flint; cruel, pitiless, hard-hearted. **flintiness,** *n.* [OE (cp. Dan. *flint,* Swed. *flinta*); perh. Gr. *plinthos,* brick]

flip, *v.t.* (*past, p.p.* **flipped**) to fillip, flick or jerk; to strike lightly; to move (about or away) with a light blow. *v.i.* to strike lightly, to flap or flick (at); (*sl.*) to lose control of oneself, to become very angry; (*sl.*) to become wildly enthusiastic. *n.* a quick, light blow; a mixed alcoholic drink containing beaten egg; a somersault; a short trip in an aeroplane. *a.* (*coll.*) flippant; (*coll.*) impertinent. **to flip one's lid,** (*coll.*) to lose self-control. **to flip over,** to (cause to) turn over. **to flip through,** to read through quickly or carelessly. **flip-flap, flip-flop,** *adv.* with (a noise as of) repeated flapping. **flip-flop,** *n.* a backward handspring; an electronic device or circuit capable of assuming either of two stable states; (*N Am.*) a complete reversal (of opinion etc.); a kind of sandal consisting simply of a sole and a strap held between the toes. *v.i.* to move about with a flapping noise. **flipside,** *n.* the B side of a popular single record on which material additional to the title number is recorded. **flipper,** *n.* the broad fin of a fish; the limb or paddle of a turtle, penguin etc.; a paddle-shaped shoe worn for esp. underwater swimming; (*dated, sl.*) the hand. **flipping,** *a., adv.* (*coll., euphem.*) bloody. [prob. onomat.]

flippant, *a.* pert, trifling, lacking in seriousness; impertinent, disrespectful. **flippancy,** *n.* **flippantly,** *adv.* [perh. from FLIP]

flipper FLIP.

flirt, *v.t.* to jerk (away); to wave or jerk to and fro rapidly (as a fan); †to jeer or gibe at. *v.i.* to make sexual advances for amusement or self-gratification; to play at love-making, to coquet; to move with jerks, short flights or springs; †to flit about. *n.* a flirting motion, a jerk, a fling; a person, esp. a woman, who plays at courtship. **to flirt with,** to treat lightly, to risk carelessly; to entertain thoughts of, to toy with. †**flirtgill,** *n.* a light woman. **flirtation,** *n.* coquetry; a playing at courtship; a casual involvement or interest. **flirtatious,** *a.* **flirtingly,** *adv.* **flirtish,** *a.* **flirty,** *a.* [prob. imit.]

†**flisk,** *v.i.* to frisk; to be restive. *n.* a whim, a freak. [onomat., cp. WHISK]

flit, *v.i.* (*past, p.p.* **flitted**) to move, to pass from place to place; to fly about lightly and rapidly; to depart; to leave one's house, usu. secretly; (*Sc.*) to move from one place of abode to another; †to flutter. *n.* a stealthy departure. [cogn. with FLEET[4], cp. Icel. *flytja,* Swed. *flitta*]

flitch, *n.* the side of a pig salted and cured; a steak from a fish, esp. halibut; a board or plank from a tree-trunk, usu. from the outside. *v.t.* to cut into flitches. **Dunmow flitch**, a flitch of bacon formerly given at Dunmow, in Essex, to any married couple proving that they lived in harmony for a year and a day. [OE *flicce* (cp. Icel. *flikki,* Dan. *flik*)]

flite, *v.i.* †to contend; to wrangle; (*Sc.*) to brawl, to scold. *n.* (*Sc.*) a scolding, a heated dispute. †**flyting,** *n.* (*Sc.*) a poetical dispute or abusive dialogue in alternate tirades of verse. [OE *flītan*]

flitter, *v.i.* to flit about; to flutter. **flittermouse,** *n.* a bat.

†**flittern,** *n.* a young oak; the wood or the bark of young oak-trees, as distinguished from that of old ones. [etym. doubtful]

flivver, *n.* (*N Am., dated, sl.*) a cheap small motor-car; (*Naval sl.*) a small destroyer.

flix, *n.* fur, esp. the down of the beaver. [etym. unknown]

float, *v.i.* to be supported on the surface of or in a fluid; to swim on water; to hover in the air; to move or glide without effort; to move with a fluid, to drift; to move aimlessly; of a currency, to be free to find its own level on foreign exchange markets. *v.t.* to support on the surface of or in a fluid; of water, to bear up or bear along; to convey, to carry on or as on water; to set afloat, to launch; to flood with a liquid; to waft through the air; to put into circulation; (*Finance*) to be or become current; to form a limited company with a view to making a public issue of shares; to offer for sale on the Stock Exchange. *n.* anything buoyed up on the surface of a liquid; a buoyant device designed to keep a person afloat; the cork or quill on a fishing-line; a cork on a fishing-net; the bladder supporting fish, animals etc. in the water; the wall of a ballcock regulating a supply-tap; a timber-raft, a floating wharf; the gear of an aircraft for alighting on water; a small delivery vehicle with a flat platform for goods; (a vehicle carrying) a tableau or exhibit in a parade; (*usu. pl.*) the footlights of a theatre; a kind of trowel for smoothing the plastering on walls; a float-board; a drink with a lump of ice-cream floating in it; a small sum of money used to provide change at the start of business; an act of floating. **float roll calender,** an ironing machine in which articles with buttons can be ironed and pressed without damage. **float-board,** *n.* one of the boards of an undershot waterwheel or a paddle-wheel. **float-bridge,** *n.* a bridge of boats or rafts. **float-carburettor,** *n.* a carburettor in which the feed is controlled by a float. **float-feed,** *n.* (*Mech.*) a feed regulated by a float. **float seaplane,** *n.* an aeroplane equipped with floats instead of wheels, for alighting on water. **float-stone,** *n.* a spongy variety of opal light enough to float on the surface of water. **floatable,** *a.* able to float; navigable. **floatage,** *n.* anything found floating, flotsam, floating power, buoyancy. **floatation** FLOTATION. **floater,** *n.* one who or that which floats; a Government stock certificate, bond etc. accepted as a recognized security. **floating,** *a.* resting on the surface of a fluid; at sea; unattached, free, disconnected; circulating, not fixed or invested; fluctuating, variable, of uncertain amount. **floating assets,** *n.pl.* assets held for the purpose of being subsequently converted into money. **floating axle,** *n.* a live axle in which the revolving part turns the wheels, while the weight of the vehicle is supported on the ends of a fixed axle-housing. **floating battery,** *n.* an armoured vessel employed to defend harbours etc. **floating bridge,** *n.* a bridge of rafts and timber floating on the surface of the water; a kind of double bridge for enabling troops to pass narrow moats; a large steam-ferry. **floating capital** CAPITAL[2]. **floating debt** DEBT. **floating dock** DOCK[3]. **floating harbour,** *n.* a breakwater of heavy timbers, fastened together and anchored, so as to form a protection for shipping. **floating kidney,** *n.* a malformation in which the kidney is entirely surrounded by peritoneum; a condition in which the kidney is displaced. **floating-light,** *n.* a lightship; a life-buoy to which a light is attached, to attract the attention of a person in the water, and to direct the boat's crew coming to the rescue. **floating pier,** *n.* a landing-stage which rises and falls with the tide. **floating ribs,** *n.pl.* the lowest two pairs of ribs, which are not attached to the sternum. **floating voter,** *n.* a person of no fixed party-political allegiance. **floatingly,** *adv.* [OE *flotian,* cogn. with FLEET[4]; influenced by OF *floter* (F *flotter*)]

floccus, *n.* (*pl.* **-cci**) a long tuft of hair terminating the tail in some mammals; the down of unfledged birds. **floccillation,** *n.* a picking of the bedclothes by a delirious patient, a very unfavourable symptom. **floccose,** *a.* covered with little woolly tufts. **floccosely,** *adv.* **floccule,** *n.* a loose tuft; a small woolly or tuft-like portion. **flocculent,** *a.* in small flakes, woolly, tufted. **flocculose, flocculous,** *a.* **flocculus,** *n.* (*pl.* **-li**) a lobe on the under surface of the human cerebellum; a cloudy marking on the surface of the sun. [L *floccus,* a lock of wool, dim. *flocculus*]

flock[1], *n.* a company or collection of animals, esp. sheep, goats or birds; a crowd, a large body; a congregation, considered in relation to their minister. *v.i.* to come together in a flock; to congregate, to assemble, to move in crowds. *v.t.* to crowd; to press by crowding. **flock-master,** *n.* a sheep-farmer. [OE *flocc* (cp. Icel. *flokkr*)]

flock[2], *n.* a lock or tuft of wool, cotton, hair etc.; (*usu.pl.*) wool-dust used in coating certain portions of the patterns in some wallpapers (FLOCK-PAPER); fibrous material, made by tearing up woollen rags by machinery, used to stuff upholstery, mattresses etc.; (*Chem.*) matter in woolly or loose floating masses precipitated in a solution. **flock-bed,** *n.* a bed stuffed with flocks of wool, hair or torn-up rags. **flock-paper,** *n.* wallpaper, to which flock is attached with size. **flocky,** *a.* [prob. from OF *floc,* L *floccus*]

Flodden, Battle of, the defeat of the Scots by the English under the Earl of Surrey on 9 Sept. 1513 on a site 5 km/3 miles SE of Coldstream, Northumberland, England; many Scots, including King James IV, were killed.

floe, *n.* a large sheet of floating ice. [prob. from Norse *flo,* a layer]

flog, *v.t.* (*past, p.p.* **flogged**) to thrash, esp. with a whip or birch rod; to whip, to lash (as the water in fly-fishing); to urge or drive by beating; to repeat or labour to the point of tedium; (*sl.*) to sell. **to flog a dead horse,** to try to revive interest in something stale; to pursue a hopeless task. **flogger, flogster,** *n.* **flogging,** *n.* punishment by whipping. [perh. corr. of L *flagellāre,* see FLAGELLATE]

flong, *n.* (*Print.*) prepared paper used for the matrices in stereotyping. [F *flan,* FLAWN]

flood, *n.* an abundant flow of water; a body of water rising and overflowing land not usually covered with water, an inundation; the inflow of the tide; a downpour, a torrent; (*poet.*) a river, the sea; an overflowing abundance; excessive menstrual discharge. *v.t.* to overflow, to inundate, to deluge; to supply copiously (with). *v.i.* to be at the flood (of the sea); to rise and overflow; to have uterine haemorrhage, to have excessive menstrual discharge. **flood-gate,** *n.* a gate in a waterway arranged to open when the water attains a certain height, and so allow it to escape freely to prevent floods, a sluice; the lower gate of a lock; a restraint against an emotional outburst. **floodlight,** *n.* a powerful beam of artificial light used esp. in the theatre, in sports stadiums or to illuminate buildings; a lamp producing such light. *v.t.* to illuminate with floodlight. **floodlighting,** *n.* **flood-mark,** *n.* high-water mark. **floodometer,** *n.* an instrument for registering the height of floods. **flood plain,** *n.* an area of flat land near a river, formed by sediment deposited during floods. **flood-tide,** *n.* the rising tide. **flooding,** *n.* the act of inundating; the state of being flooded, an inundation; an abnormal discharge of blood from the uterus. [OE *flōd* (cp. Icel. *flōd,* Dut. *vloed,* G *Flut*), cogn. with FLOW]

Flood, the, *n.* in the Old Testament or Hebrew Bible and the Koran, disaster alleged to have obliterated all humanity except a chosen few (the family of Noah).

floor, *n.* the bottom surface of a room, on which the inmates walk and which supports the furniture; the boards or other material of which this is made; a storey in a building; a suite of rooms on the same level; the part of the house assigned to members of a legislative assembly; the (area occupied by) people attending a meeting or debate as audience; any level area corresponding to the floor of a room; the flat portion of a vessel's hold; the bottom of a coal seam; the lowest limit of prices. *v.t.* to furnish with a floor; to be or serve as a floor (to); to knock down; to put to silence (as in argument); to pose (a difficult question); to get the better of, to defeat. **to cross the floor,** of an MP etc., to change one's party-political allegiance. **to have the floor,** to be given the right to address a meeting, assembly etc. **to take the floor,** to rise to speak, to take part in a debate; (*Ir.*) to get up to dance; **to wipe, mop the floor with,** to defeat completely. **floorboard,** *n.* one of the planks making up a floor. **floorcloth,** *n.* a piece of soft fabric used for washing floors; a substitute for a carpet. **floor-lamp,** *n.* a lamp, usu. portable, that stands on the floor. **floor manager,** *n.* the stage manager of a television programme; the manager of a floor in a large store. **floorshow,** *n.* a performance on the floor of a restaurant etc. **floor-timbers,** *n.pl.* the main timbers on which a floor is laid. **floorwalker,** *n.* a shopwalker. **floorer,** *n.* (*coll.*) that which floors or defeats; a knockdown blow; a poser, a baffling question; a decisive report. **flooring,** *n.* material for floors; a floor, a platform; the process of spreading and turning grain to restrict germination. **floorless,** *a.* [OE *flōr* (cp. Dut. *vloer,* G *Flur*)]

floozy, floozie, floosie, *n.* (*derog.*) a woman who is attractive in a common sort of way and thought to be free with her company and favours. [etym. doubtful]

flop, *v.i.* (*past, p.p.* **flopped**) to tumble about or fall loosely and heavily; to sway about heavily, to flap; to make a dull sound as of a soft body flapping; to move or walk about (in an ungainly manner); to fail dismally; (*chiefly N Am.*) to go to bed. *v.t.* to let fall negligently or noisily; to cause to strike with a heavy dull sound. *n.* the act or motion of flopping; the noise of a soft outspread body falling suddenly to the ground; a complete failure. *adv.* with a flop; suddenly. **flop-house,** *n.* (*N Am.*) a doss-house, a cheap lodging-house. **floppily,** *adv.* **floppiness,** *n.* **floppy,** *a.* soft and flexible, limp. **floppy disc,** *n.* (*Comput.*) a flexible magnetic disc for data storage. [var. of FLAP]

flor., (*abbr.*) floruit.

flora, *n.* (*pl.* **-ras, -rae**) the whole vegetation of a country or geological period; a book dealing with the vegetation of a country or district. **floral,** *a.* of or pertaining to floras; of or pertaining to flowers; consisting of, or decorated with, flowers. **floral envelope,** *n.* the perianth or parts surrounding the stamens and pistils, generally consisting of calyx and corolla. **florally,** *adv.* [L, Flora, the Roman goddess of flowers and gardens, from *flōs flōris,* FLOWER]

floreat, (L) may it flourish.

Florence[1], *n.* (Italian **Firenze**), capital of Tuscany, N Italy, 88 km/55 miles from the mouth of the river Arno; population (1988) 421,000. It has printing, engineering, and optical industries, many crafts, including leather, gold and silver work, and embroidery, and its art and architecture attract large numbers of tourists.

Florence[2], *n.* a kind of red wine from Florence. **Florence flask,** *n.* a thin glass flask, with large globular body and long narrow neck. **Florence oil,** *n.* a superior olive oil. [F, from L *Flōrentia* (It. *Firenze*)]

Florentine, *a.* of or pertaining to Florence. *n.* a native or inhabitant of Florence; a kind of silk stuff; a kind of pie or tart, esp. a meat pie without under-crust; †a Florentine ship. **Florentine iris,** *n.* a white or pale-blue iris, *I. florentina,* also called the Florentine flower de luce. [L *Flōrentīnus,* from *Flōrentia,* see prec.]

florescence, *n.* the flowering of a plant; the season when a plant flowers. **florescent,** *a.* [L *flōrescens -ntem,* pres.p. of *flōrescere,* incept. of *flōrēre,* see FLOURISH, -ENCE]

floret, *n.* a small flower; a small flower forming part of a composite one. [OF *florete,* dim. of *fleur*]

Florey, *n.* **Howard Walter, Baron Florey** (1898–1968), Australian pathologist whose research into lysozyme, an antibacterial enzyme discovered by Fleming, led him to study penicillin, which he and Chain isolated and prepared for widespread use. With Fleming, they were awarded the Nobel Prize for Physiology or Medicine in 1945.

floriate, -ated, *a.* adorned with floral ornaments or designs. **floriation,** *n.* [L *flōs flōris*]

floricomous, *a.* having the head or top adorned with flowers; (*Zool.*) applied to sponges having a terminal bunch of curved branches. [late L *flōricomus,* as prec., *coma,* hair]

floriculture, *n.* the cultivation of flowers or flowering plants. **floricultural,** *a.* **floriculturist,** *n.*

florid, *a.* covered with or abounding in flowers; bright in colour; flushed with red, ruddy; flowery, highly embellished, elaborately ornate; showy; applied to the richly ornamented architecture of the latest stages of the pointed style in England about 1400-1537. **floridity, floridness,** *n.* **floridly,** *adv.* [L *flōridus*]

Florida, *n.* most southeasterly state of the US; mainly a peninsula jutting into the Atlantic, which it separates from the Gulf of Mexico; nickname Sunshine State. **area** 152,000 sq km/58,672 sq miles. **capital** Tallahassee. **towns** Miami, Tampa, Jacksonville. **physical** 50% forested; lakes (including Okeechobee 1800 sq km/695 sq miles); Everglades National Park (5000 sq km/1930 sq miles, with birdlife, cypresses, alligators). **products** citrus fruit, melons, vegetables, fish, shellfish, phosphates (one third of world supply), chemicals, uranium (largest US producer), space research. **population** (1989) 13,000,000; the fastest-growing state. [Sp. *Florida,* orig. *Pascua florida,* or flowery Easter, because, it is said, Ponce de Leon discovered the country on Easter Day, 1513]

Florida water, *n.* a perfume like eau-de-Cologne, much used in the US. **Florida wood,** *n.* a hard, close-grained wood used for inlaying.

floriferous, *a.* bearing flowers. [L *flōrifer*]

floriform, *a.* having the shape of a flower.

florilegium, *n.* an anthology. [L *flōs flōris, legere,* to cull]

florin, *n.* a British coin, orig. silver, worth the equivalent of 10p, a two-shilling piece; a foreign gold or silver coin, of various values according to country and period; †an English gold coin of Edward III, worth 6s. 8d. (33p); orig. a Florentine coin, stamped with the lily flower, the national badge of Florence. [OF, from It. *fiorino,* dim. of *fiore,* L *flōrem,* as prec.]

florist, *n.* a cultivator of flowers; one who sells flowers; one skilled in flowers.

floruit, *n.* the period of a person's eminence; the date at which he or she was known to be alive (in the absence of exact dates of birth and death). [L, he flourished, 3rd sing. perf. of *flōrēre,* see FLOURISH]

flory FLEURY.

floscular, -ulous, *a.* having little flowers; bearing many florets (as the composites). **floscule,** *n.* a floret. [L *flōsculus,* dim. of *flōs,* FLOWER]

flos ferri, *n.* (*Min.*) a spicular variety of aragonite. [L, flower of iron]

floss, *n.* the exterior soft envelope of a silkworm's cocoon; the downy substance on the husks of certain plants, as the bean; dental floss. *v.t., v.i.* to use dental floss. **floss-silk,** *n.* untwisted filaments of the finest silk, used in embroidery etc. **floss-thread,** *n.* soft flaxen yarn or thread for embroidery. **flossy,** *a.* [perh. from OF *flosche,* down, cp. FLOCK[2]]

flotage, FLOATAGE.

flotant, *a.* (*Her.*) floating, as a flag, bird, or anything swimming. [F *flottant,* pres.p. of *flotter,* see foll.]

flotation, *n.* the act or state of floating; the science of floating bodies; (*Finance*) the floating of a company. **centre of flotation,** the centre of gravity in a floating body. **flotative,** *a.* capable of floating; tending to float.

flotel, *n.* a boat or platform providing accommodation for off-shore oil-rig workers. [*flo*ating-hot*el*]

flotilla, *n.* a small fleet; a fleet of small vessels. [Sp., dim. of *flota,* a fleet]

flotsam, *n.* goods lost in shipwreck and found floating. **flotsam and jetsam,** wreckage or any property found floating or washed ashore. [A-F *floteson,* OF *flotaison,* from *floter,* to FLOAT]

flounce[1], *v.i.* to move abruptly or violently; to exaggerate one's movements as a means of calling attention to oneself or one's impatience etc. *n.* an abrupt or impatient movement. [prob. cogn. with Norw. *flunsa,* to hurry, Swed. dial. *flunsa,* to plunge]

flounce[2], *n.* a gathered or pleated strip of cloth sewed to a petticoat, dress etc., with the lower border hanging loose. *v.t.* to attach flounces to; to deck or trim with flounces. [ME *frounce,* OF *fronce,* from *froncer,* to wrinkle, L *frons,* the forehead]

flounder[1], *n.* a flatfish, *Pleuronectes flesus,* resembling the plaice, but with paler spots; a tool to stretch leather for a boot-front. [OF *flondre* (cp. Norw. *flundra,* Dan. *flynder*)]

flounder[2], *v.i.* to struggle or stumble about violently, as when stuck in mire; to struggle along with difficulty; to blunder along, to do things badly. *n.* a stumbling or blundering effort; the motion or act of floundering. [prob. cogn. with Norw. *flundra,* Dut. *flodderen*]

flour, *n.* the finer part of meal, esp. of wheatmeal; fine soft powder of any substance. *v.t.* to sprinkle flour upon; (*N Am.*) to grind and bolt flour. **flour-bolt, -dresser,** *n.* a machine for bolting or bolting and dressing flour. **flour-dredge, -dredger,** *n.* a perforated tin for sprinkling flour. **flour-mill,** *n.* a mill for grinding and sifting flour. **floury,** *a.* covered with flour; like flour. [var. of FLOWER (ME *flour of whete,* the finest meal)]

†flouret, †flourette, FLOWERET.

flourish, *v.i.* to grow luxuriantly; to thrive, to prosper, to increase in wealth, honour or happiness; to be in a state of complete development; to be alive or at work (at or about a certain date); to use florid language; to make bold and fanciful strokes in writing; to move about fantastically; (*Mus.*) to play in a bold, dashing style, with ornamental notes; to sound a fanfare; †to brag; †to blossom. *v.t.* to brandish, fling or wave about; to flaunt, to show ostentatiously; to embellish with ornamental or fantastic figures; †to cause to thrive or bloom; †to varnish over. *n.* a flourishing condition, prosperity; a figure formed by strokes or lines fancifully drawn; rhetorical display, florid diction, a florid expression; a brandishing or waving of a weapon or other thing; (*Mus.*) a passage played for display, a fanfare of trumpets etc, an improvised prelude or other addition. **flourish of trumpets,** the sounding of trumpets when receiving any person of distinction; an ostentatious announcement. **flourished,** *a.* adorned with flourishes; (*Her.*) fleury. **flourishing,** *a.* thriving, prosperous; making a show. **flourishingly,** *adv.* **flourishy,** *a.* [OF *floriss-,* stem of *florir,* L *flōrēre,* from *flōs* *flōris,* FLOWER]

flouse, floush, *v.i.* to splash. [prob. onomat.; cp. FLUSH[2]]

flout, *v.t.* to mock, to insult; to treat with contempt, to disregard, to defy. *v.i.* to sneer; to behave with contempt or mockery. *n.* a word or act of contempt; a sneer, an insult. **flouter,** *n.* **floutingly,** *adv.* [prob. var. of FLUTE (cp. MDut. *fluyten,* to play the flute, to jeer)]

flow, *v.i.* to move, run or spread, as a fluid; to circulate, as the blood; to rise, as the tide; to issue, to spring, to gush out; to sway, glide or float, to move easily or freely, to undulate; to be poured out abundantly, to abound, to come or go in abundance or great numbers; to issue, to be descended (from); to discharge blood in excess from the uterus; †to melt, to become liquid; to overflow. †*v.t.* to overflow, to flood; to cover with varnish. *n.* the act, state or motion of flowing; the quantity that flows; a flowing liquid, a stream; a copious stream, abundance, a plentiful supply; the rise of the tide; an overflowing; undulation (of drapery etc.); a wet or marshy tract; a quicksand. **flowchart, flowsheet,** *n.* a diagram showing the sequence of operations in an industrial process or computer program. **flow-lines,** *n.pl.* lines in igneous rocks resulting from the flow of the material before consolidation. **†flowage,** *n.* the act or state of flowing. **flowing,** *a.* moving as a stream; copious, fluent, easy; smooth, unbroken, not abrupt or stiff; hanging loose and waving; of a fore-and-aft sail, slackened, with the wind across the vessel's course. **flowingly,** *adv.* **flowingness,** *n.* [OE *flōwan* (cp. Dut. *vloeijen,* Icel. *flōa*), cogn. with Gr. *pleein,* to sail, L *pluere,* to rain (not *fluere,* to flow)]

flower, *n.* the organ or growth comprising the organs of reproduction in a plant; a flowering plant; the blossom, the bloom; the finest, choicest or best individual, part, period etc., an embellishment; a figure of speech; the prime; the period of youthful vigour; (*pl.*) (*Chem.*) substances of a powdery consistency or form, esp. if produced by sublimation; †(*pl.*) the menstrual discharge. *v.i.* to produce flowers, to bloom, to blossom; †to flourish; to be in the prime; †to froth, to ferment gently. *v.t.* to embellish with flowers; to cause to blossom. **flowers of sulphur,** a form of sulphur obtained by distillation from other forms. **flower-bearing,** *a.* producing flowers. **flower-bed,** *n.* a plot of ground in which flowering-plants are grown. **flower-bud,** *n.* a bud which develops into a flower. **flower-de-luce,** FLEUR-DE-LIS. **flower-garden,** *n.* a garden devoted to the cultivation of flowers. **flower-girl,** *n.* a girl or woman selling flowers. **flower-head** CAPITULUM. **flower-piece,** *n.* a picture of flowers. **flowerpot,** *n.* an earthenware pot to hold plants. **flower-show,** *n.* a horticultural exhibition, usu. competitive. **flower-stalk,** *n.* the peduncle supporting the flowers of a plant. **flowerage,** *n.* the state of being in flower; flowers in general. **flowered,** *a.* having or embellished with flowers or figures of flowers; (*in comb.*) bearing flowers, as *blue-flowered, six-flowered.* **flowerer,** *n.* a plant that flowers (at a particular time or in a particular way), as *spring-flowerer.* **floweret,** *n.* a little flower. **flowering,** *a.* that flowers; flowery. **flowering-fern,** *n.* the king-fern, *Osmunda regalis.* **flowering-rush,** *n.* a water-plant, *Butomus umbellatus,* with an umbel of pink flowers. **flowerless,** *a.* **flowerlessness,** *n.* **flowery,** *a.* abounding in flowers or blossoms; highly figurative, florid. **flowery-kirtled,** *a.* adorned with garlands of flowers. [OF *flour,* L *flōrem,* nom. *flōs,* cogn. with BLOW[2]]

Flowers of Evil, (French *Les Fleurs du mal*), a collection of poems by Baudelaire, published in France in 1857, which deal with the conflict between good and evil. The work was condemned by the censor as endangering public morals, but paved the way for Rimbaud, Verlaine, and the Symbolist school.

flowing FLOW.

flown *p.p.* FLY[2].

fl.oz., (*abbr.*) fluid ounce.

flu, *n.* short for INFLUENZA.

fluctuate, *v.i.* to rise and fall like waves; to vary, to change irregularly in degree, to be unsettled; to hesitate, to waver. †*v.t.* to cause to move or roll about like waves. †**fluctuant,** *a.* †undulating, moving like a wave; unsteady, wavering. **fluctuating,** *a.* unsteady, wavering. **fluctuation,** *n.* [L *fluctuātus, p.p.* of *fluctuāre,* from *fluctus,* a wave]

Fludd, *n.* **Robert** (1574–1637), British physician who attempted to present a comprehensive account of the universe based on Hermetic principles (see HERMES TRISMEGISTUS under HERMES), *The History of the Macrocosm and the Microcosm* (1617).

flue[1], *n.* a passage or tube by which smoke can escape or hot air be conveyed; †a chimney. **flue-pipe,** *n.* an organ pipe in which the sound is produced by air passing through a fissure and striking an edge above. **flue-work,** *n.* the flue-stops of an organ as distinct from the reed-stops. [etym. doubtful, perh. from obs. *flue,* shallow, or from FLUE[4]]

flue[2], *n.* light down or fur; fluff. **fluey,** *a.* [etym. unknown, perh. cogn. with FLY[2] (cp. Norw. *flu,* G *flug,* flight)]

flue[3], *n.* a fishing-net, of various kinds. [etym. doubtful, cp. Dut. *flouw*]

flue[4], *v.i.* to widen or spread out; to splay. *v.t.* to cause (a window, jambs etc.) to splay. [prob. from obs. a. *flue,* see FLUE[1]]

fluent, *a.* †flowing, liquid; fluid, mobile, changeable; moving or curving smoothly, graceful; ready in the use of words; eloquent, copious, voluble. *n.* (*Math.*) the variable quantity in fluxions. **fluency,** *n.* the quality of being fluent; readiness and easy flow (of words or ideas). **fluently,** *adv.* [L *fluens -entem,* pres.p. of *fluere,* to flow]

fluff, *n.* light down or fur; flocculent matter; the nap of anything; a mistake made esp. in delivering lines, reading a text or playing a piece of music. *v.t.* to cover with fluff or give a fluffy surface to; to shake or spread (feathers out, as a bird); (*coll.*) to bungle. *v.i.* (*coll.*) to make a mistake in performing. **a bit of fluff,** (*sl.*) a girl. **fluffy,** *a.* **fluffiness,** *n.* [prob. from FLUE[2]]

flugelhorn, *n.* a valued brass instrument resembling, but slightly larger than, a cornet. [G *Flügel,* wing, *Horn,* horn]

fluid, *a.* composed of particles that move freely in relation to each other; capable of flowing, as water; liquid, gaseous; not rigid or stable; smooth, graceful. *n.* a liquid or gas, not a solid; a substance whose particles readily move and change their relative positions. **fluid drive,** *n.* (*Eng.*) a system of transmitting power through a change in the momentum of oil. **fluid measure,** *n.* apothecaries' measure of capacity of the British Pharmacopoeia. **fluid ounce,** *n.* a British unit of liquid capacity equal to 1/20th of an imperial pint (28·4 ml); a unit equal to 1/16th of a US pint (29·5 ml). **fluidify, fluidize, -ise,** *v.t.* **fluidity,** *n.* [OF *fluide,* L *fluidus,* from *fluere,* to flow]

fluke[1], *n.* a flounder; applied, with distinctive epithet, to other flatfish; a parasitic worm belonging to the Trematoda, found chiefly in the livers of sheep; a kind of potato. **fluky,** *a.* infested with flukes, as sheep. [OE *flōc;* cogn. with G *flach,* flat]

fluke[2], *n.* the broad holding portion of an anchor; one of the flat lobes of a whale's tail; a barb of a lance, harpoon etc.; a tool for cleansing a hole previous to blasting. [prob. from prec.]

fluke[3], *n.* an accidentally successful stroke, esp. in billiards; any lucky chance. *v.i.* to score by luck, esp. in billiards. *v.t.* to hit or obtain in this way. **fluky,** *a.* obtained by chance, not skill; unsteady, variable. **flukily,** *adv.* **flukiness,** *n.* [etym. doubtful]

flume, *n.* †a river; an artificial channel for conveying water to a mill or for some other industrial use; a chute; (*N Am.*) a deep ravine traversed by a torrent. *v.t.* to carry down a flume; to drain by means of a flume. *v.i.* to make flumes. **to go, be up the flume,** (*N Am., sl.*) to come to grief; to be done for. [OF *flum,* L *flumen,* a river, from *fluere,* to flow]

flummery, *n.* a food made of oatmeal or bran boiled to a jelly; a kind of blancmange; anything insipid or out of place; nonsense, humbug; empty compliment. [W *llymru*]

flummox, *v.t.* (*sl.*) to perplex, confound; to abash, to silence; to best, to cheat. [prob. onomat.]

flump, *v.i.* to fall down heavily; to flop; to sit down with a flop. *v.t.* to throw down with a dull, heavy noise. *n.* a dull, heavy noise, as of something let fall. [imit.]

flung, *past, p.p.* FLING.

flunk, *v.t.* (*chiefly N Am., coll.*) to (cause to) fail a subject, course etc. *v.i.* to fail, esp. in an examination or course. **to flunk out,** (*chiefly N Am., coll.*) to be expelled for failure.

flunkey, *n.* a servant in livery, a footman; a lackey; a toady; a snob. **flunkeydom,** *n.* **flunkeyish,** *a.* **flunkeyism,** *n.* [Sc., prob. from FLANKER (cp. F *flanquer,* to run at the side of)]

fluor- FLUOR(O)-.

fluor, *n.* (also **fluorspar,, fluorite**) an isometric, transparent or subtranslucent, brittle mineral, having many shades of colour, composed of fluoride of calcium; formerly applied to any mineral containing fluorine; †a fluid state; †a menstrual flux. [L, flow, from *fluere,* to flow]

fluorate FLUORINE.

fluorescence, *n.* a quality existing in certain substances of giving out light of a different colour from their own or that of the light falling upon them; the coloured luminosity thus produced, esp. the visible light produced by the action of ultraviolet rays. **fluoresce,** *v.i.* to exhibit fluorescence. **fluorescein,** *n.* a colouring matter or dye used only for certain purposes because the colours produced are not fast. **fluorescent,** *a.* having the quality of fluorescence. **fluorescent lamp,** *n.* a lamp consisting of a glass tube with a fluorescent coating inside, which emits light on the passage through the tube of an electric discharge.

fluorhydric, HYDROFLUORIC.

fluorine, *n.* a non-metallic gaseous element, at. no. 9; chem. symbol F, forming with chlorine, bromine and iodine the halogen group. **fluorate,** *n.* a salt of fluoric acid. **fluoric,** *a.* containing fluorine. **fluoric acid,** *n.* **fluoridate,** *v.t.* to add fluoride to. **fluoridation,** *n.* **fluoride,** *n.* a compound of fluorine with an element or radical.

fluorite, FLUOR.

fluor(o)-, *comb. form* fluorine; fluorescence. [FLUOR]

fluorocarbon, *n.* any of a series of compounds of fluorine and carbon, which are chemically inert and highly resistant to heat.

fluoroscope, *n.* an apparatus consisting of a light-proof box with a fluorescent screen, for observing the effects of röntgen rays. **fluoroscopy,** *n.*

fluorotype, *n.* a photographic process in which sodium fluorate is used.

fluorspar FLUOR.

fluosilicic, *a.* obtained from fluorine and silica.

flurry, *n.* a squall; a sudden and violent shower of rain, snow etc.; commotion, agitation, bustle, confusion; nervous excitement; the death-struggle of a harpooned whale. *v.t.* to agitate, to fluster, to upset, to bewilder with noise or excitement. [onomat.; cp. HURRY]

flush[1], *v.i.* to take wing; of game birds, to start up suddenly. *v.t.* to cause to take wing; to put up. *n.* the flushing of a bird; a flock of birds put up at once. [prob. imit.; cp. *flisk,* var. of FRISK, RUSH]

flush[2], *v.i.* to flow swiftly; to rush; to become filled (as pipes) with a sudden rush of water; to become suffused. *v.t.* to cleanse by a rush of water; to flood. *n.* a sudden flow of water; the run or race from a mill-wheel; the cleansing of a drain with a rush of water; a morass, a bog. **flusher,** *n.* one who flushes drains etc. **flushing-box, -cistern, -tank,** *n.* a cistern for supplying water-closets or urinals with a rush of water. [perh. from prec., or a form of FLASH]

flush[3], *v.i.* to colour as with a rush of blood, to redden up, to blush, to glow. *v.t.* to cause to colour or become red; to redden; to inflame; to encourage, to excite, as with passion. *n.* a sudden flow or rush of blood to the face causing a redness; any warm colouring or glow; a sudden access of emotion, elation, excitement; a hot fit in fever; vigour; bloom, blossoming. [perh. the same as prec., influenced by BLUSH (but cp. Swed. dial. *flossa,* to blaze, to flare)]

flush⁴, *a.* full to overflowing; copious, abounding; plentifully supplied, esp. with money; abundant; filled up even; level, even, on the same plane (with). *v.t.* to make even; to level (up); to fill in (a joint) so as to make even with the surface. **flush-deck,** *n.* a deck with a level floor from stem to stern. **flushness,** *n.* fullness; abundance. [prob. from FLUSH²]

flush⁵, *n.* a hand of cards all of one suit. **royal flush,** cards in a sequence headed by the ace. **straight flush,** cards in a sequence. [perh. from F *flux,* L *fluxus,* from *fluere,* to flow]

Flushing Meadow, *n.* lawn-tennis centre in the US, officially the national tennis centre. It is situated in the Queens district, New York, and replaced the West Side Club as the home of the US Open championships in 1978. The main court is the Stadium Court, one of the largest in the world.

fluster, *v.t.* to flurry or confuse; to agitate, to make nervous; to befuddle, to make tipsy. *v.i.* to be in an agitated or confused state. *n.* flurry, confusion of mind, agitation. [conn. with Icel. *flaustra,* to be flustered (cp. EFris. *flostern, flustern,* to rustle)]

flustra, *n.* (*pl.* **-trae**) (*Zool.*) a sea-mat, an individual of the genus of Polyzoa called *Flustridae.* [mod. L, substituted by Linnaeus for *eschara*]

flute, *n.* a tubular wind-instrument with a blow-hole near the end and holes stopped by the fingers or with keys for producing variations of tone, esp. a transverse flute; an organ-stop with a similar tone; a long vertical groove semicircular in section, esp. in the shaft of a column; a similar groove or corrugation in a dress etc.; a long thin French roll of bread; a tall, narrow wine glass. *v.i.* to play a flute; to whistle or sing with a flute-like sound. *v.t.* to play, sing or utter with flute-like tones; to play (an air) on a flute; to form flutes or grooves in. **fluted,** *a.* (*Arch.*) channelled, furrowed; of the upper notes of a soprano, clear and mellow. **flutina,** *n.* a kind of accordion resembling the concertina. **fluting,** *n.* a groove, a channel; fluted work in pillars etc. **flutist,** *n.* one who plays upon the flute, a flautist. **fluty,** *a.* resembling a flute in tone. [OF *fleute, flaute, flahute* (prob. imit.; perh. conn. with L *flāre,* to blow)]

flutter, *v.i.* to flap the wings rapidly; to hover, flit or move about in a fitful, restless way; to move with quick, irregular motions; to quiver, to vibrate; to beat spasmodically, as the pulse; to be agitated or uncertain; to wander; to act frivolously. *v.t.* to cause to move about with quick vibrations; to vibrate, to cause to quiver or flap about rapidly; to agitate or alarm. *n.* the act of fluttering; quick, short and irregular vibration; a variation or distortion in pitch occurring at higher frequencies in sound reproduction; potentially dangerous oscillation set up in something, e.g. part of an aircraft, by natural forces; a state of excitement, anxiety, or agitation; disorder, stir; (*coll.*) a gamble, a bet; a toss or spin (as of a coin); a venture or speculation. **flutteringly,** *adv.* [OE *flotorian,* from *flēotan,* to FLEET⁴]

fluvial, fluviatic, fluviatile, *a.* of or belonging to a river; (*Geol.*) caused by a river; living in rivers. [F *fluvial,* L *fluvialis,* F *fluviatile,* L *fluviātilis;* from *fluvium,* river]

fluvio-, *comb.form* relating to a river or rivers.

fluvio-marine, *a.* pertaining to or produced by the joint action of a river and the sea (as deposits at a river-mouth).

fluviometer, *n.* an apparatus for measuring the rise and fall in a river.

flux, *n.* the act or state of flowing; the motion of a fluid; a state of movement or continual change; an issue or flowing out, a discharge; the flow of the tide, as opposed to the ebb; an abnormal discharge of fluid matter from the body; †dysentery; any substance which assists the fusion of minerals or metals; fusion; the quantity of light falling on an area; the strength of a magnetic field; (*Math.*) continuous motion (as a line considered as the flux of a point). *v.t.* to melt, to fuse; to facilitate fusion with a flux; (*Med.*) to purge; †to overflow or cause to overflow. *v.i.* to flow; of the tide etc., to rise; to issue in a flux; to melt. **flux-spoon,** *n.* a small ladle for dipping out molten metal. †**fluxation,** *n.* a flowing or passing away, and giving place to others. †**fluxible,** *a.* **fluxibility,** *n.* **fluxion,** *n.* the act or state of flowing; that which flows; fusion of metals; continuous variation; (*Path.*) an unnatural flow of blood or humour towards any organ; (*Math.*) the rate of variation of a fluent quantity; (*pl.*) the Newtonian method now known as the differential calculus. **fluxional, -nary,** *a.* pertaining to fluxions. †**fluxionist,** *n.* one skilled in fluxions. [OF, from L *fluxus,* from *fluere,* to flow]

fly¹, *n.* (*pl.* **flies**) a two-winged insect, esp. of the genus *Musca,* of which the house-fly, *M. domestica,* is the type; (*loosely*) any winged insect; a disease in turnips, hops etc. caused by various flies; an artificial fly for fishing; †a familiar spirit, orig. in the shape of a fly or louse; †an unimportant or valueless thing. **a fly in the ointment,** a slight flaw, or minor disadvantage, that spoils the quality of something. **a fly on the wall,** an intimate, but unnoticed, observer of events. **like flies,** in vast numbers and offering no resistance. **there are no flies on him/her,** etc., he/she is no fool. **fly-agaric,** *n.* a scarlet mushroom, *Agaricus muscarius,* growing in woods. **fly-bane,** *n.* a popular name for the catch-fly and other plants. **fly-bitten,** *a.* marked by the bites of flies. **fly-blister,** *n.* (*Med.*) a blister prepared from cantharides. **fly-block,** *n.* (*Naut.*) a block which moves with the tackle from one position to another. **fly-blow,** *v.t.* to deposit eggs in, as the blow-fly in meat; to corrupt, to taint. *n.* the egg of a blow-fly. **fly-blown,** *a.* tainted by maggots; impure, corrupt, tainted. **fly-book,** *n.* a book or case for anglers' flies. **fly-case,** *n.* an elytron. **fly-catcher,** *n.* a fly-trap; a bird of the genus *Muscicapa.* **fly-fish,** *v.i.* to angle with natural or artificial flies for bait. **fly-fisher,** *n.* **fly-flap,** *n.* an instrument to drive away flies. **fly-net,** *n.* a net to protect (a horse etc.) from flies. **fly-paper,** *n.* paper prepared to catch or poison flies. **fly-powder,** *n.* a powder usu. consisting of arsenic mixed with sugar, used to kill flies. **fly-rod,** *n.* a flexible resilient rod used in fly-fishing. **fly-speck,** *n.* the small speck of a fly's excrement; any small speck. **flyspecked,** *a.* **flyspray,** *n.* (an aerosol containing) insecticide. **fly-trap,** *n.* a trap for catching flies; the spreading dog-bane, *Apocynum androsaemifolium,* a sensitive plant; also Venus's fly-trap, *Dionaea muscipula.* **fly-tying,** *n.* preparing angler's flies. **fly-water,** *n.* a solution of arsenic etc. for killing flies. **flyweight,** *n.* a professional boxer weighing not more than 112 lb. (50·4 kg); an amateur boxer weighing between 106 and 112 lb. (47·7–50·4 kg); a wrestler weighing not more than 115 lb. (51·7 kg). **fly-whisk,** *n.* a whisk for driving away flies. [OE *flēoge,* from foll.]

fly², *v.i.* (*past* **flew,** *p.p.* **flown,**) to move through the air with wings; to pilot or ride in an aircraft; to flutter or wave in the air; to pass or be driven through the air with great speed or violence; to pass, as time, very swiftly; to depart in haste; (*with p.p.* **fled,** fled) to flee, to run away, to try to escape; to burst or break violently (in pieces); to start, to pass suddenly or violently, to spring, to hasten, to burst (as to arms or into a rage). *v.t.* to cause to fly or float in the air; to pilot (an aircraft); to travel over by air; to transport by air; to use for air travel (as an airline); to flee from, to avoid, to quit by flight; to hunt with a hawk; to make (a hawk, pigeon etc.) fly; to set or keep (a flag) flying. *n.* (*pl.* **flies**) the act or state of flying; the distance that something flies; a one-horse carriage, a hackney coach; a fly-wheel or a regulating device acting on the same principle; the portion of a vane that shows the direction of the wind; the length of a flag from the staff to the outer edge; the part of a flag farthest from the staff; a flap covering button-holes; a loose flap for covering the entrance to a tent; (*pl.*) a gallery over the proscenium in a theatre where the curtains or scenes are controlled. **fly-by-night,** *n.* one given to nocturnal excursions; a runaway debtor; †a kind of sedan-chair on wheels, introduced at Brighton in 1816. *a.* unreliable, untrustworthy. **on the fly,** (*Baseball*) in the air, without bouncing. **to fly a kite** KITE. **to fly at,** to attack suddenly, to rush at with violence or fierceness; (*Hawking*) to soar at and attack. **to fly high,** to be ambitious. **to fly in the face of** FACE. **to fly off,** to become suddenly detached; †to revolt, to desert. **to fly off the handle,** HANDLE. **to fly open,** to open suddenly and violently. **to fly out,** to burst into a passion; to break out into licence or extravagance. **to let fly,** to shoot or throw out; to direct a violent blow (at); to use violent language; (*Naut.*) to let go suddenly and entirely. **fly-away,** *a.* streaming, loose; of hair, tending not to stay in place; flighty, volatile. *n.* a runaway. **fly-ball,** *n.* a baseball hit high into the air. **flyby,** *n.* an observation flight, esp. by a spacecraft, past a target at close range. **fly-cutter,** *n.* a machine for shaping the ends of metal rods, cutting the teeth of wheels etc. **fly-drill,** *n.* a hand drill with a fly-wheel on its shank which gives it the requisite momentum to rewind the cord that gives its reciprocating motion. **fly-front,** *n.* a concealed closing on the front of a garment. **fly-half,** *n.* (*Rugby*) the player who acts as a link between the scrum-half and the three-quarter line. **fly-kick,** *n.* a kick made while running. **fly-leaf,** *n.* a blank leaf at the beginning or end of a book. **flyman,** *n.* the driver of a fly; the person who works the ropes of scenes etc. in a theatre. **flyover,** *n.* an intersection, esp. of two roads at which the one is carried over the other on a bridge; (*N Am.*) a flypast. **flypast,** *n.* a ceremonial flight by aircraft over a certain point. **fly-posting,** *n.* unauthorized affixing of posters. **fly-sheet,** *n.* a handbill; a prospectus; a two- or four-page tract; an extra sheet of canvas that can be fitted over the roof of a tent. **fly-wheel,** *n.* a heavy-rimmed wheel attached to a machine for regulating the speed by its inertia. **flyer,** *n.* one who flies or flees; (*in comb.*) one who or that which flies in a particular way as a *high-flyer;* a flying jump; (*coll.*) a flying start; (*coll.*) a horse, vehicle, train etc. that goes with exceptional speed; a fly-wheel; (*Print.*) a vibratory rod with fingers to carry the sheet from the tapes to the delivery table; (*pl.*) a straight flight of stairs; (*Austral.*) the kangaroo; a speculative attempt or venture. [OE *flēogan* (cp. Dut. *vliegen,* Icel. *fljūga,* G *fliegen*), not conn. with FLEE]

fly[3]**,** *a.* (*sl.*) sharp, wide-awake. [etym. doubtful]

flyer FLY[2].

flying, *a.* moving with or as with wings; moving or adapted to move swiftly; brief, hurried. **flying jib-boom,** an extension of the jib-boom. **flying army, column, squadron,** *n.* a body of troops kept moving from one place to another, either to protect its own garrisons and posts, or to harass the enemy. **flying bedstead,** *n.* a framework resembling a bedstead raised vertically from the ground by jet-propulsion. **flying boat,** *n.* a large seaplane with a buoyant fuselage. **flying bomb,** *n.* a jet-propelled, pilotless aeroplane with a charge of explosive in the head which is detonated when the plane falls with the failure of the propelling jet. **flying bridge,** *n.* a temporary bridge for military purposes. **flying buttress,** *n.* an arched or slanting structure springing from solid masonry and serving to support another part of a structure. **flying colours** COLOUR[1]. **flying doctor,** *n.* a doctor in remote areas who uses an aircraft to answer calls. **flying dog,** *n.* a variety of vampire-bat. **Flying Dutchman** DUTCHMAN. **flying fish,** *n.* a fish which has the power of sustaining itself in the air for a time by means of its fins. **flying fox,** *n.* an E Indian frugivorous bat belonging to the genus *Pteropus;* (*Austral.*) a conveyor on a suspended wire. **flying-gurnard,** *n.* a fish with large pectoral fins, *Dactylopterus volitans.* **flying jib,** *n.* a sail extending beyond the standing jib. **flying jump,** *n.* a jump taken with a running start. **flying-lemur,** *n.* any individual of the genus *Galeopithecus,* esp. *G volans,* whose fore and hind limbs are connected by a fold of skin enabling the animal to take flying leaps from tree to tree. **flying machine,** *n.* a machine for flying through the air. **Flying Officer,** *n.* a junior commissioned rank in the RAF equivalent to lieutenant in the Army. **flying party,** *n.* a detachment of men employed in skirmishing round an enemy. **flying-phalanger,** *n.* a popular name for the marsupial genus *Petaurus.* **flying picket,** *n.* (a member of) a mobile band of pickets who reinforce local pickets during a strike. **flying saucer,** *n.* a UFO, esp. in the shape of a large disc. **flying squad,** *n.* (*Police*) a mobile detachment of police. **flying-squadron,** *n.* (*Mil., Nav.*) a squadron kept distinct from a main force to carry out a special manoeuvre. **flying-squirrel,** *n.* a squirrel with a patagium or fold of skin like that of the flying-lemurs, by which it makes flying leaps.

Flynn, *n.* **Errol** (1909–59), Australian actor. He is renowned for his portrayal of swashbuckling heroes in such films as *Captain Blood* (1935), *The Sea Hawk* (1940), and *The Master of Ballantrae* (1953).

FM[1]**,** (*abbr.*) Field Marshal.

FM[2]**,** *n.* (*abbr.*) frequency modulation. Used in radio, FM is constant in amplitude and varies the frequency of the carrier wave. Its advantage over AM is its better signal-to-noise ratio.

Fm, (*chem. symbol*) fermium.

fm, (*abbr.*) fathom.

FNLA, *n.* (*abbr.*) Front National de Libération de l'Angola (French 'National Front for the Liberation of Angola').

FO, (*abbr.*) Field Officer; Flying Officer; Foreign Office.

fo., (*abbr.*) folio.

Fo, *n.* **Dario** (1926–), Italian playwright. His plays are predominantly political satires combining black humour with slapstick. They include *Morte accidentale di un anarchico/Accidental Death of an Anarchist* (1970), and *Non si paga non si paga/Can't Pay? Won't Pay!* (1975/1981).

foal, *n.* the young of an equine animal, as of the horse, ass etc.; a colt, a filly. *v.i.* to bring forth young, as a mare or she-ass. *v.t.* to bring forth (a foal). **foal-foot,** *n.* the coltsfoot, *Tussilago farfara.* [OE *fola* (cp. Dut. *veulen,* G *Fohlen*), cogn. with L *pullus,* Gr. *pōlos*]

foam, *n.* the aggregation of bubbles produced in liquids by violent agitation or fermentation; the similar formation produced by saliva in an animal's mouth; froth, spume; chemical froth used in fire-fighting; a light, cellular solid, produced by aerating and then solidifying a liquid; (*poet.*) the sea. *v.i.* to gather, produce or emit foam; to be covered or filled with foam; to move (along, against etc.) with production of foam; to pass (away) in foam. †*v.t.* to cause to foam; to throw out or express with violence. †**foam-crested,** *a.* crested with foam. **foam-rubber,** *n.* rubber of foamlike consistency largely used in upholstery etc. **foamingly,** *adv.* **foamless,** *a.* **foamy,** *a.* [OE *fām* (cp. G *Feim*); prob. cogn. with L *spūma*]

fob[1]**,** *n.* a watch-pocket, formerly in the waistband of breeches. *v.t.* to put into one's pocket. [etym. doubtful (cp. G dial. *Fuppe*)]

fob[2]**,** *v.t.* (*past, p.p.* **fobbed**) to cheat, to impose upon; †to beat, to ill-treat. **to fob off,** to put off with lies or excuses. **to fob off with,** to delude into accepting by a trick. [prob. from LG *foppen* (cp. G *foppen,* to befool)]

f.o.b., (*abbr.*) free on board.

focal FOCUS.

Foch, *n.* **Ferdinand** (1851–1929), Marshal of France during World War I. He was largely responsible for the first Allied victory of the Marne, and commanded on the NW front from Oct. 1914–Sep. 1916. He was appointed commander in chief of the Allied armies in the spring of 1918, and launched the Allied counter-offensive in July that brought about the negotiation of an armistice to end the war.

fo'c'sle FORECASTLE.

focus, *n.* (*pl.* **-ci, -cuses**) a point at which rays of light, heat, electrons etc. meet after reflection, deflection or refraction, or from which they appear to diverge; the relation between the eye or lens and the object necessary to produce a clear image; the point from which any activity (as a disease or an earthquake wave) originates; the point on which attention or activity is concentrated; (*Geom.*) one of two points having a definite relation to an ellipse or other curve. *v.t.* (*past, p.p.* **focused, focussed**) to bring (rays) to a focus or point; to adjust (eye or instrument) so as to be at the right focus; to bring into focus; to concentrate. **in focus,** adjusted so as to obtain a clear image; clearly perceived or defined. **focal,** *a.* of, pertaining to or situated at a focus. **focal distance, length,** *n.* the distance between the centre of a lens and the point where initially parallel rays converge. **focal plane,** *n.* a plane containing the foci of the systems of parallel rays passing through a lens. **focalize, -ise,** *v.t.* to focus. **focalization, -isation,** *n.* **focimetry,** *n.* the measurement of focal distances. [L, hearth]

fodder, *n.* food served to cattle, as hay etc., distinguished from pasture; (*facet.*) food. *v.t.* to feed or supply with fodder; †to feed. **fodderer,** *n.* one who fodders cattle. **fodderless,** *a.* [OE *fōdor,* from *fōda,* FOOD (cp. Dut. *voeder,* G *Futter*)]

foe, *n.* a personal enemy; an opponent, an adversary; an enemy in war; an ill-wisher. †*v.t.* to treat as a foe. **foe-like,** *a.* like a foe. *adv.* as a foe. **foeman,** *n.* an enemy in war. [OE *fāh, fāg,* hostile (*gefā,* an enemy, *fēon, fēogan,* to hate)]

foetid, FETID.

foetus, (*esp. N Am.*) **fetus,** *n.* the young of viviparous animals in the womb, and of oviparous vertebrates in the egg, after the parts are distinctly formed. **foetal,** *a.* pertaining to a foetus. **foetation,** *n.* the formation of a foetus. **foeticide,** *n.* the destruction of a foetus; abortion. [L *fētus,* offspring, rel. to *fu-, fuī,* I was, *futurus,* to be, Gr. *phuein,* to beget]

fog[1], *n.* coarse, rank grass which has not been eaten off in summer, aftermath; coarse grass remaining through the winter; (*Sc.*) moss. *v.t.* (*past, p.p.* **fogged**) to feed (cattle) with fog. †*v.i.* to grow mossy. **foggy,** *a.* full of coarse, rank grass; consisting of or resembling rank grass; (*Sc.*) covered with moss, mossy. [etym. doubtful]

fog[2], *n.* a dense watery vapour rising from land or water and suspended near the surface of land or sea; (*Phot.*) a cloudiness on a negative; a state of confusion or perplexity. *v.t.* (*past, p.p.* **fogged**) to surround with or as with a fog; to becloud, to perplex, to bewilder; to make (a negative) cloudy. *v.i.* to become foggy; (*Phot.*) to become cloudy; to lay fog-signals on a railway line. **fog-bank,** *n.* a dense mass of fog at sea resembling land at a distance. **fog-bell,** *n.* a bell rung by waves as a warning to mariners. **fog-bound,** *a.* immobilized by fog; covered in fog. **fog-bow,** *n.* a faint bow, resembling a rainbow, produced by light on a fog. **fog-horn,** *n.* an instrument to give warning to ships in a fog. **foglamp,** *n.* a strong light fitted to a vehicle to facilitate driving in fog. **fog-signal,** *n.* a detonator placed on a railway for the guidance of engine-drivers. **fogger,** *n.* one who lays fog-signals on railway lines. **foggy,** *a.* thick, murky; full of or subject to fog; beclouded, obscure, perplexed, indistinct. **not the foggiest,** (*coll.*) not the slightest notion. **foggily,** *adv.* **fogginess,** *n.* [etym. doubtful]

fogle, *n.* a pocket-handkerchief. [thieves' slang]

fogy, fogey, *n.* an old-fashioned eccentric person. **fogydom,** *n.* **fogyish,** *a.* **fogyism,** *n.*

föhn, *n.* the warm south wind in the Alps. [G, perh. ult. from L *Favōnius*]

foible, *n.* a weak point in one's character; the part of a sword-blade between the middle and point. [F, now *faible,* FEEBLE]

foie gras, *n.* (F) the fatted liver of an animal, used esp. in the making of pâté.

foil[1], *n.* an amalgam of quicksilver and tin at the back of a mirror; very thin sheet metal; a thin leaf of metal put under gems to increase their lustre or brighten or alter their colour; that which serves to set off something else to advantage; a rounded leaf-like space or arc in window tracery. *v.t.* to back (glass, crystal etc.) with foil; to set off by contrast; (*Arch.*) to decorate or design with foils. **foiling,** *n.* decoration with or consisting of foils. [OF *foil* (F *Feuille*), L *folium* a leaf (cp. Gr. *phullion*)]

foil[2], *v.t.* to baffle, to frustrate; to throw off the scent; to defeat, to repulse, to parry; †to foul, to dishonour. *n.* the trail of hunted game; †a defeat, a frustration, a failure when success seems certain. **foilable,** *a.* **foiling,** *n.* the track of a deer on the grass. [OF *fouler,* to tread, to stamp or full (cloth), late L *fullāre,* from L *fullo,* a fuller (perh. influenced by ME *fylen,* to make foul)]

foil[3], *n.* a straight thin sword, blunted by means of a button on the point, used in fencing. [etym. doubtful, perh. from foll., or from FOIL[1,2]]

†**foin,** *v.t.* to thrust at. *v.i.* to lunge or thrust. *n.* a thrust or lunge; a stroke, as in fencing. †**foiningly,** *adv.* [OF *foine, foisne,* L *fusana,* a fish-spear]

†**foison,** *n.* plenty, abundance; power, strength; (*pl.*) resources. [OF, from L *fūsio -ōnem,* from *fundere,* to pour]

foist, *v.t.* to introduce surreptitiously or wrongfully; to insert fraudulently; to palm off (on or upon) as genuine; †to cheat. †*n.* a swindle, an imposition; a foister, a cheat, a sharper. †**foister,** *n.* one who foists. [orig. to palm or conceal in the hand, prob. from Dut. prov. *vuisten,* from *vuist,* fist]

Fokine, *n.* **Mikhail** (1880–1942), Russian dancer and choreographer, born in St Petersburg. He was chief choreographer to the *Ballets Russes* (1909–14), and with Diaghilev revitalized and reformed the art of ballet, promoting the idea of artistic unity among dramatic, musical, and stylistic elements.

fol., (*abbr.*) following.

fold[1], *n.* a pen or enclosure for sheep; a flock of sheep; (*fig.*) the Church, the flock of Christ; †a boundary. *v.t.* to put or enclose in or as in a fold. **foldless,** *a.* [OE *fald* (cp. Dut. *vaalt,* Dan. *fold*)]

fold[2], *v.t.* to double or lay one part of (a flexible thing) over another; to bring together and entwine (as arms, legs); to close (as wings, petals); to clasp (arms etc.) round; to embrace; to enfold, to envelop; †to enswathe, to conceal. *v.i.* to become folded or doubled; to shut in folds; (*Geol.*) to be doubled up; to fail, to cease operations. *n.* a part doubled or laid on another; a bend or doubling, a pleat; a hollow between two parts (as of a fabric); a coil, a folding, an embrace; (*Geol.*) a flexure in strata. **to fold in,** (*Cookery*) to mix in gradually and carefully. **folding-chair,** *n.* a collapsible chair. **folding-doors,** *n.pl.* two doors hung on opposite side-posts, and meeting in the middle. **folding-machine,** *n.* a machine for folding printed sheets for newspapers or books; a machine which shapes pans and tinware by pressure. **folding-stool,** *n.* a portable collapsible stool. **foldless,** *a.* [OE *fealdan* (cp. Icel. *falda,* G *falten,* also Gr. *plassein, plekein,* L *plicāre*)]

-fold, *suf.* forming adjectives and adverbs denoting multiplication, as *fourfold, manifold.* [OE *feald,* cogn. with prec. (cp. Gr. *-plasios,* L *-plex*)]

folder, *n.* one who or that which folds; a holder for loose papers; a bone or ivory blade used in folding papers.

foldstool, FALDSTOOL.

foliaceous, *a.* having the texture, structure or organs of or as of leaves; leaf-shaped; furnished with leaves; (*Cryst.*) consisting of thin laminae; splitting into thin laminae; (*Zool.*) †shaped or arranged like leaves. [L *foliāceus,* from *folium,* a leaf]

foliage, *n.* leaves in the aggregate; (*Art, esp. Arch.*) the representation of leaves or clusters of leaves, as ornament. *v.t.* to work or ornament with representation of foliage. **foliar,** *a.* consisting of or pertaining to leaves; of the nature of leaf. **foliferous,,** *a.* bearing leaves. **foliose, -ous,** *a.* leafy, abounding in or of the nature of leaves. [MF, *fueillage, foillage* (F *feuillage*), from *fueille,* L *folia,* leaves]

foliate, *v.i.* to split or disintegrate into thin laminae. *v.t.* to decorate with leaf-patterns, foils, leaf-like tracery etc.; †to beat into a leaf or thin plate; †to cover over with a thin coat or sheet of tin, quicksilver etc. (as a mirror). *a.*, leaf-shaped; furnished with leaves. **foliation,** *n.* foliating; (*Arch.*) ornamentation by trefoil, quatrefoil, cinquefoil, and similar tracery based on the form of a leaf. †**foliature,** *n.* foliage; the state of being beaten into foil.

folic acid, *n.* a vitamin of the vitamin B complex found esp. in green vegetables and liver and used in the treatment of anaemia.

folie, *n.* (F) madness; folly. **folie à deux**, the presence of similar delusions in the minds of two closely associated people. **folie de grandeur**, delusions of grandeur.

Folies-Bergère, *n.* music hall in Paris, France, built in 1869, named after its original proprietor and featuring lavish productions and striptease acts.

foliferous FOLIATE.

folio, *n.* (*pl.* **-lios**) a sheet of paper folded once; a book of the largest size, whose sheets are folded once, hence, any large volume or work; a page of manuscript; a leaf of paper or other material for writing etc., numbered on the front; a page in an account book, or two opposite pages numbered as one; the number of a page; 72 words of manuscript in legal documents, 90 words in Parliamentary proceedings. [abbr. of L *in foliō,* in the form of a sheet folded once]

foliole, *n.* a leaflet; one of the separate parts of a compound leaf. **foliolate,** *a.* [F, from L *foliolum,* dim. of *folium,* a leaf]

foliose, -ous FOLIAGE.

folk, *n.* (*pl. in constr.*) people, people collectively; (*pl. in constr.*) a particular class of people, as old folk; (*pl. in constr.*) members of one's own family; a people, nation or race; folk music; (*in comb.*) people of a specified kind, as *menfolk, kinsfolk. a.* originating among the common people; based on or employing traditional motifs. **folk-custom,** *n.* a custom of the people. **folk dance,** *n.* a traditional dance of countryfolk. **folk etymology,** *n.* a popular but often erroneous derivation of a word. †**folkland,** *n.* (*Feud. Law*) the land of the people as distinguished from land held by deed. **folklore,** *n.* popular superstitions, tales, traditions or legends; the systematic study of such superstitions etc. **folklorism,** *n.* **folklorist,** *n.* one versed in the study of folklore. **folkloristic,** *a.* **folk memory,** *n.* a memory of a distant event passed down through several generations of a community. †**folkmoot,** *n.* an assembly of the people of a shire, city or town; a courtleet or local court. **folk music,** *n.* the traditional popular music of the common people; modern popular music in the style of this. **folk-right,** *n.* common law, the right of the people. **folk-singer,** *n.* **folk-song,** *n.* a song or ballad, supposed to have originated among the people and to have been handed down by tradition. **folk-tale,** *n.* a popular myth. **folkways,** *n.pl.* traditional social customs. **folks,** *n.pl.* people, folk; family members. **folksy,** *a.* (*chiefly N Am., coll.*) informal, casual; sociable, friendly; (affectedly) traditional in style. [OE *folc* (cp. Icel. *fōlk,* Dan. and Swed. *folk,* Dut. *volk,* G *Volk*)]

foll., (*abbr.*) following.

follicle, *n.* a small cavity, sac or gland; a fruit formed by a single carpel dehiscing by one suture, usu. the ventral; a cocoon; (*pl.*) roots of the hair. **follicular, folliculated,** *a.* **folliculous,** *a.* abounding in follicles; having or producing follicles. [F, from L *folliculus,* a little bag, dim. of *follis,* bellows]

follow, *v.t.* to go or come after; to move behind; to pursue, as an enemy; to accompany, to attend upon, to serve; to adhere to, to side with, to espouse the cause of; to imitate, to pattern oneself upon; to go after as an admirer or disciple; to go along (a path, road etc.); to engage in, to practise (as a profession); to conform to, act upon (a rule, policy etc.); to come or happen after in point of time, order, rank or importance; to watch the course of; to keep the mind or attention fixed on; to understand, to grasp the meaning of; to result, to be the consequence of; to seek after, to try to attain; †to follow up, to prosecute (an affair). *v.i.* to come or go after another person or thing; to pursue; to be the next thing to be done or said; to be a natural consequence, to ensue; to be the logical consequence, to be deducible. **as follows,** a prefatory formula to a statement, enumeration etc. **follow-my-leader,** (*chiefly N Am.*) **-the-leader,** *n.* a game in which those behind must follow the steps and imitate the actions of the leader. **to follow on,** to continue without break; to continue from where somebody else left off; (*Cricket*) to bat again immediately after completing one's first innings because one is more than a predetermined number of runs behind. **to follow suit** SUIT. **to follow through,** (*Golf, Cricket etc.*) to continue the swing after hitting the ball; to take further action consequent upon an initial act; to follow to a conclusion. **to follow up,** to pursue closely and steadily; to prosecute an advantage; to make further efforts to the same end; to take appropriate action about; (*Med.*) to re-examine a patient, or check progress, at intervals after treatment. **follow-on,** *n.* an act of following on. **follow-up,** *n.* a reminding circular sent by an advertiser; (*Med.*) a check or checks on a patient's progress; (a) further or consequent action. **follower,** *n.* one who follows; a disciple, an imitator or adherent, an attendant; a companion; a subordinate, a servant; one of the same party; an admirer; a Victorian maidservant's sweetheart. **following,** *a.* coming next after, succeeding, now to be mentioned; of wind, blowing in the direction one is travelling. *n.* a body of followers or adherents. *prep.* after. [ME *folwan,* OE *folgian* (cp. Dut. *volgen,* G *folgen*)]

folly, *n.* foolishness, want of understanding or judgment, senselessness; a foolish act, idea or conduct; an object of foolish attention or imitation; a structure built for picturesque effect or to gratify the builder's whim; (*derog.*) any building which seems more grand, elaborate or expensive than its purpose warrants; †wantonness, immorality, depravity. [OF *folie,* from *fol,* FOOL[1]]

Fomalhaut, *n.* brightest star in the southern constellation Pisces Austrinus, and the 18th-brightest star in the sky; known as 'the Solitary One' because it lies in a rather barren region of sky. It is a dwarf star 23 light years away, with a true luminosity 14 times that of the Sun. Fomalhaut is one of a number of stars around which the Infra-Red Astronomy Satellite detected excess infrared radiation, presumably from a region of solid particles around the star. This material may be a planetary system in the process of formation.

foment, *v.t.* to apply warm or medicated lotions to; to warm; to poultice; to nourish, to foster, to encourage, to promote. **fomentation**, *n.* the act of fomenting; the lotion, poultice, warm cloths etc. applied. **fomenter,** *n.* [F *fomenter,* L *fōmentāre,* from *fōmentum* (for *fovimentum*), from *fovēre,* to warm, cherish]

fomes, *n.* (*pl.* **fomites**) a substance of a porous kind liable to absorb and retain contagious effluvia and thus propagate disease. [L, touchwood]

†**fon,** *n.* a fool, an idiot. *a.* foolish. *v.i.* to play the fool, to be foolish. †**fonly,** *adv.* [etym. doubtful]

fond[1], *a.* tender or loving; doting on, delighting in; †trivial; †foolish, silly, simple. †*v.t.* to fondle, to caress. †*v.i.* to be fond or doting. **to be fond of,** to like very much, to love. **fondly,** *adv.* affectionately; foolishly, credulously. **fondness,** *n.* [ME *fonned,* p.p. of prec. v.]

†**fond[2]** FOUND[2].

Fonda[1], *n.* **Henry** (1905–82), US actor whose engaging acting style made him ideal in the role of the American pioneer and honourable man. His many films include *The Grapes of Wrath* (1940), *My Darling Clementine* (1946), and *On Golden Pond* (1981). He was the father of the actress Jane Fonda and the actor and director Peter Fonda (1939–).

Fonda[2], *n.* **Jane** (1937–), US film actress. Her early films include *Cat Ballou* (1965) and *Barbarella* (1968), and she won Academy Awards for *Klute* (1971) and *Coming Home* (1979). She is also active in left-wing politics and in promoting physical fitness. She is the daughter of Henry Fonda.

fondant, *n.* a soft kind of sweetmeat. [F, from *fondre,* to melt, L *fundere,* to pour]

fondle, *v.t.* to caress; †to treat with great kindness or indulgence. *v.i.* to indulge in caresses (with). **fondler,** *n.* **fondling,** *n.* a person or thing fondled; †a fool, an idiot. [freq. of FOND[1]]

fondue, *n.* a dish consisting of a hot sauce (usu. of cheese and white wine) into which pieces of bread etc. are dipped, or of cubes of meat which are cooked by dipping into hot oil at table and eaten with a variety of spicy sauces. [F fem. of *fondu,* p.p. of *fondre,* to melt]

fons et origo, (*L*) the source and origin.

font[1], *n.* the vessel or basin to contain water for baptism; the oil-reservoir for a lamp; †a spring; †a fountain. **†font-stone,** *n.* a baptismal font. **fontal,** *a.* of or pertaining to a fount or source, to a baptismal font, or to baptism. [OE *fant, font,* L *fontem,* nom. *fons,* a FOUNT[1]]

font[2], FOUNT[2].

Fontainebleau school, *n.* French school of mannerist painting and sculpture, established at the court of Francis I. He brought Italian artists to Fontainebleau near Paris to decorate his hunting lodge: Rosso Fiorentino (1494–1540) arrived in 1530, Francesco Primaticcio (1504/5–1570) came in 1532. They soon evolved a distinctive decorative style using a combination of stucco sculpture and painting.

Fontana, *n.* **Lucio** (1899–1968), Italian painter and sculptor. He developed a unique abstract style, presenting bare canvases with straight parallel slashes.

fontanel, -nelle, *n.* an interval between the bones of the infant cranium; an issue for the discharge of humours from the body. [F *fontanelle,* dim. of *fontaine,* FOUNTAIN]

Fontanne, *n.* **Lynn** (1887–1983), US actress, one half of the husband-and-wife acting partnership known as the 'Lunts' with her husband Alfred Lunt.

Fontenoy, Battle of, battle in the War of the Austrian Succession in 1745. Marshal Saxe and the French defeated the British, Dutch, and Hanoverians under the Duke of Cumberland at a village in Hainaut province, Belgium, SE of Tournai.

Fonteyn, *n.* **Margot** (stage name of Margaret Hookham) (1919–), English ballet dancer. She made her debut with the Vic-Wells Ballet in *Nutcracker* (1934) and first appeared as Giselle in 1937, eventually becoming prima ballerina of the Royal Ballet, London. Renowned for her perfect physique, musicality, and interpretive powers, she created several roles in Ashton's ballets and formed a successful partnership with Nureyev.

fonticulus, *n.* a small ulcer produced artificially; (*Anat.*) the depression just above the breastbone. [L, dim. of *fons,* see FONT[1]]

food, *n.* any substance which, taken into the body, is capable of sustaining or nourishing, or which assists in sustaining or nourishing the living being; aliment, nutriment; victuals, provisions, esp. edibles as distinguished from drink; nutriment for plants; that which nourishes, sustains or is material for; †feeding, eating. **food chain,** *n.* a community of organisms thought of as a hierarchy in which each eats the one below and is eaten by the one above. **food poisoning,** *n.* a severe gastrointestinal condition caused by eating food which is naturally poisonous or has been contaminated. **food processor,** *n.* an electrical appliance which chops, shreds or blends etc. food. **foodstuff,** *n.* any thing or material used for food. **food-yolk,** *n.* the part of the yolk of an egg which nourishes the embryo. **†foodful,** *a.* furnishing food; fruitful, fertile. **foodie,** *n.* (*coll.*) a person with an intense interest in (esp. more exotic kinds of) food. **foodism,** *n.* **foodless,** *a.* **foodster,** *n.* a foodie. [OE *foda,* from root *fōd-, fad,* cp. Gr. *pateesthai,* L *pāscere,* to feed, *pānis,* bread]

Food and Agriculture Organization, (FAO) United Nations agency that coordinates activities to improve food and timber production and levels of nutrition throughout the world. It is also concerned with investment in agriculture, and dispersal of emergency food supplies. It has headquarters in Rome and was founded in 1945.

fool[1], *n.* a person without common sense or judgment; a silly person; a dupe; †a jester, a buffoon; †an idiot, an imbecile; †a wicked person. *a.* (*coll.*) foolish, silly. *v.i.* to play the fool; to trifle, to idle. *v.t.* to make a fool of; to dupe, to cheat, to impose upon, to play tricks upon; to disappoint; to waste (time away); †to make foolish. **to fool around, about,** to behave foolishly or irresponsibly; to waste time; to trifle (with). **to fool with,** to meddle with in a careless and risky manner. **to make a fool of,** to cause to appear ridiculous; to deceive, to disappoint. **to play, act the fool,** to act like a fool; to act the buffoon. **†fool-begged,** *a.* foolish, idiotic. **†fool-born,** *a.* born of or sprung from folly. **†fool-happy,** *a.* fortunate; lucky by chance. **foolproof,** *a., adv.* secure against any ignorant mishandling. **fool's-errand,** *n.* an absurd or fruitless errand or quest; the pursuit of what cannot be found. **fool's gold,** *n.* iron pyrites. **fool's mate,** *n.* the simplest mate in chess. **fool's paradise,** *n.* a state of unreal or deceptive joy or good fortune. **fool's-parsley,** *n.* a poisonous umbelliferous herb, *Aethusa cynapium.* **foolery,** *n.* habitual folly; the act of playing the fool; folly; absurdity. **fooling,** *n.* buffoonery. **foolish,** *a.* **foolishly,** *adv.* **foolishness,** *n.* [OF *fol* (F *fou*), L *follem,* acc. of *follis,* bellows, wind-bag, late L fool]

fool[2], *n.* a dish made of fruit, esp. gooseberries, stewed and crushed with cream etc. [prob. from prec.]

foolhardy, *a.* daring without sense or judgment, foolishly bold; rash, reckless. **foolhardily,** *adv.* **foolhardihood, foolhardiness,** *n.* [OF *folhardi* (*fol,* fool, *hardi,* bold)]

foolscap, *n.* a pointed cap with bells, formerly worn by professional jesters; a size of writing-paper $17\times13\frac{1}{2}$ in. ($43{\cdot}2\times34{\cdot}3$ cm) or of printing paper, folio, $13\frac{1}{2}\times8\frac{1}{2}$ in. ($34{\cdot}3\times21{\cdot}6$ cm), quarto, $8\frac{1}{2}\times6\frac{3}{4}$ in. ($21{\cdot}6\times17{\cdot}1$ cm), octavo, $6\frac{3}{4}\times4\frac{1}{4}$ in. ($17{\cdot}1\times10{\cdot}8$ cm), named from its original watermark of a fool's cap and bells.

Foot[1], *n.* **Isaac** (1880–1960), British Liberal politician. A staunch Nonconformist, he was minister of mines (1931–32). He was the father of Dingle, Hugh, and Michael Foot.

Foot[2], *n.* **Michael** (1913–), British Labour politician. A leader of the left-wing Tribune Group; he was secretary of state for employment (1974–76), Lord President of the Council and leader of the House (1976–79), and succeeded Callaghan as Labour Party leader (1980–83).

foot, *n.* (*pl.* **feet**) the part of the leg which treads on the ground in standing or walking, and on which the body is supported; the part below the ankle; (*Zool.*) the locomotive organ of invertebrate animals, the tube-foot of an echinoderm; that which serves to support a body; that part of an article of dress which receives the foot; a measure containing 12 in. (30·5 cm), named as being roughly the length of a man's foot; the lowest part, the base, the lower end; the bottom; foot-soldiers, infantry; (*Pros.*) a set of syllables forming the rhythmical unit in verse; (*pl.* **foots**) sediment, dregs, oil refuse etc.; †basis, footing, status. *v.i.* to walk, to dance; to pace; to go or travel on foot. *v.t.* to travel over by walking; to add a new foot to (as to stockings); to add up figures and set the total at the foot; †to kick, spurn with the foot. **a foot in both camps,** connections with two mutually antagonistic groups. **a foot in the door,** a first step towards a desired end; a favourable position from which to advance. **at the feet of,** humbly adoring or supplicating; submissive to; as a disciple or student of. **feet of clay,** initially unsuspected weaknesses. **foot-and-mouth disease,** a contagious eczematous disease chiefly affecting cattle. **my foot!** an exclamation of disbelief. **on foot,** walking; in motion, action or process of execution. **on one's feet,** standing up; in good health; thriving, getting on well. **to catch on the**

wrong foot, to take unprepared or at a disadvantage. **to fall on one's feet,** to emerge safely or successfully. **to find one's feet,** to become accustomed to, and able to function effectively in, new circumstances. **to foot a bill,** (*coll.*) to pay a bill, to acknowledge payment. **to foot it,** to go on foot; to dance. **to foot up to,** of items in an account, to mount or total up to. **to get off on the wrong foot,** to make a bad start, esp. in personal relations with someone. **to have one foot in the grave,** to be near death, very old or moribund. **to have one's feet on the ground,** to be realistic, sensible or practical. **to keep one's feet, footing,** not to fall. **to put a foot wrong,** to make a mistake. **to put one's best foot forward,** to step out briskly; to try to show oneself at one's best. **to put one's foot down,** to be firm, determined. **to put one's foot in it,** to blunder, to get into a scrape. **to set on foot,** to put in motion; to originate. **to sweep off one's feet,** to enrapture, to make a complete and sudden conquest of. **to think on one's feet,** to react to situations as they arise. **under foot,** on the ground. **foot-barracks,** *n.* barracks for infantry. **foot-bath,** *n.* a vessel in which to wash the feet; the act of washing the feet. **footboard,** *n.* a platform for a footman behind a carriage; a step for getting into or out of a vehicle; a foot-plate; a treadle; a board at the foot of a bed. **foot-boy,** *n.* a page, a boy in livery. **foot-bridge,** *n.* a narrow bridge for foot-passengers. †**foot-cloth,** *n.* the housings of a horse, reaching down to the ground. **foot-drill,** *n.* a drill worked by a treadle. **footfall,** *n.* the sound of a footstep. **foot-fault,** *n.* (*Lawn tennis*) the act of overstepping the baseline when serving. **foot-guards,** *n.pl.* regiments of infantry, the Grenadier, Coldstream, Scots, Welsh and Irish Guards. **foothill,** *n.* a hill lying at the base of a range of mountains. **foothold,** *n.* that which sustains the foot; support at the foot; a position of stability or security; a basis of operations. †**foot-hot,** *adv.* in hot haste; immediately. †**foot landraker,** *n.* a footpad. **foot-licker,** *n.* a sycophant, a mean flatterer. **footlights,** *n.pl.* a row of lights, screened from the audience, in front of the stage of a theatre. **footloose,** *a.* free, unbound by ties. **footman,** *n.* a male domestic servant in livery; a foot-soldier; a stand for holding a kettle before the fire. **footmark,** *n.* a footprint. **footmuff,** *n.* a covering lined with fur, to keep the feet warm. **footnote,** *n.* a note at the bottom of the page of a book. **foot-pace,** *n.* a pace no faster than a walk. **footpad,** *n.* a highwayman who robs on foot. **footpage,** *n.* a foot-boy. **foot-pan,** *n.* a vessel for washing feet. **foot-passenger,** *n.* one who travels on foot. **footpath, -road, -way,** *n.* a narrow path or way for foot-passengers only. **footplate,** *n.* a platform for the driver and fireman on a locomotive. **foot-pound,** *n.* a unit of energy, the amount that will raise one pound avoirdupois one foot. **footprint,** *n.* the mark or print of a foot; any sign of the presence of a person. **foot-race,** *n.* a running-match on foot. **foot-rope,** *n.* a rope beneath a yard upon which seamen stand in reefing and furling sails; a rope at the foot of a sail. **foot-rot,** *n.* a disease in the feet of sheep and cattle, characterized by an abnormal growth. **foot-rule,** *n.* a measure 12 in. (30·5 cm) long. **foot-slogger,** *n.* (*sl.*) an infantryman, a foot-soldier. **foot-soldier,** *n.* an infantry soldier. **footsore,** *a.* having the feet sore or tender. **foot-stalk,** *n.* the petiole of a leaf; the peduncle of a flower; (*Zool.*) the attachment of a crinoid etc.; the lower portion of a mill spindle. **foot-stall,** *n.* a stirrup on a side-saddle. **footstep,** *n.* the act of stepping or treading with the feet; tread; a footprint; the sound of the step of a foot; (*pl.*) traces of a course pursued or actions done. **foot-stick,** *n.* a bevelled piece of wood or iron placed against the foot of a page to lock up the type. **foot-stone,** *n.* a stone placed at the foot of a grave, distinguished from the headstone. **footstool,** *n.* a stool for the feet. **foot-warmer,** *n.* a metal vessel containing hot water for warming the feet; a hot-water bottle. **footwork,** *n.* skilful use of the feet in boxing, dancing etc.; clever manoeuvring, esp. of an evasive kind. **foot-worn,** *a.* footsore. **footage,** *n.* payment of miners by the running foot of work; the length of a film (in feet). **footed,** *a.* having feet; (*usu. in comb.*) having a particular kind of feet (as *swift-footed*). **footer,** *n.* (*coll.*) the game of football. **footsie,** *n.* (*coll.*) erotic or flirtatious touching with the feet. [OE *fōt* (cp. Dut. *voet,* Icel. *fōtr,* G *Fuss,* also Gr. *pous podos,* L *pes pedis*)]

football, *n.* an inflated bladder encased in leather used in the game of football: a game between two teams in which a football is kicked, or handled and kicked, to score goals or points, there being many different varieties of the game; a contentious issue, esp. one which is bandied about between opposing groups. **Football Association,** *n.* the body founded in 1863 to make rules, supervise and preside over Association football in Britain. **Football League,** *n.* an organized collection of Association Football clubs founded in 1888 to arrange matches and supervise the business arrangements of its constituents. **football pools,** (*n.pl.*) a form of gambling based on forecasting the results of football matches. **footballer,** *n.*

footing, *n.* a place for standing or putting the feet on; foothold; a firm or secure position; relative position, status or condition; relationship; entrance into a new sphere, society, profession, trade etc.; the adding up of a column of figures and putting the total at the foot; (*Arch.*) a course at the base or foundation of a wall; (*pl.*) foundations, bases; †a footprint, a track. **to pay one's footing,** to pay a sum of money on doing anything for the first time, as on being admitted to a trade etc.

footie, *v.i.* (*sl.*) to trifle; to potter about aimlessly. *n.* rubbish, twaddle; nonsense, foolery. **footling,** *n., a.* [etym. doubtful]

†**footy,** *a.* musty; paltry, contemptible, worthless. [earlier *foughty*, prob. from OE *fūht*, damp]

foozle, *v.i.* to waste time, to fool about. *v.t.* to make a mess of; (*Golf*) to boggle. *n.* a fogy; (*Golf*) a bungled stroke. **foozler,** *n.* **foozling,** *n.* [cp. G prov. *fuseln*, to work slowly]

fop, *n.* a man over-fond of dress; a dandy, a coscomb. †**fopling,** *n.* a petty fop. **foppery,** *n.* **foppish,** *a.* **foppishly,** *adv.* **foppishness,** *n.* [ME *foppe* (cp. Dut. and G *foppen*, to cheat, to hoax)]

for-, *pref.* away, off, as in *forget, forgive*; negative, prohibitive or privative, as in *forbear, forbid, forfend, forsake*; amiss, badly, as in *fordo, forshapen*; intensive, as in *forlorn, forspent, forwearied*. [OE *for-* (cp. Icel. and Dan. *for-*, Dut. and G *ver-*), cogn. with Gr. *peri-, pro-, para-*, L *per-, pro-*]

for, *prep.* in the place of, instead of; in exchange against, as the equivalent of; as the price or requital of payment of; in consideration of, by reason of; because of, on account of, in favour of, on the side of; in order to, with a view to; appropriate or suitable to; toward, tending toward, conductive to; to fetch, to get, to save; to attain, to reach, to arrive at; (*sl.*) against; on behalf of, for the sake of; with regard to, in relation to; as regards; so far as; as, as being, in the character of; to the amount or extent of; at the cost of; in spite of, notwithstanding; in comparison of, contrast with; during; to prevent; because of. *conj.* since, because; seeing that; in view of the reason that; †on this account that; †in order that. **as for** AS. **to be for it,** (*coll.*) to be marked for reprimand or punishment. **for all that,** nevertheless; in spite of all that. **for all the world,** exactly, completely. **for as much as** FORASMUCH. **for good,** for ever, once and for all, permanently. **for short,** as an abbreviation or contraction. **once (and) for all,** finally. [OE, prob. abbr. from *fore* (cp. Dut. *voor*, G *vor*, also L *prō*, Gr. *pro*)]

forage, *n.* food for horses and cattle, esp. for the horses of an army; the act of foraging. *v.i.* to seek for or to collect forage; to hunt for supplies; to rummage (about); †to raven. *v.t.* to overrun in order to collect forage; to ravage, to plunder; to obtain for forage; to supply with forage or food. **forage-crop,** *n.* a military undress cap. **forager,** *n.* [OF *fourrage*, from *forre* (F *feurre*), low L *fōdrum*, from Teut., cogn. with FODDER]

foramen, *n.* (*pl.* **foramina**) a small natural opening, passage or perforation in parts of plants and animals. **foraminate, -nated,** *a.* **foraminifer,** *n.* one of the Foraminifera. **Foraminifera,** *n.pl.* (*Zool.*) a large group of Protozoa, esp. an order of Rhizopoda, the body of which is contained within a calcareous shell, many-chambered, the outer surface presenting a punctate appearance, produced by numerous foramina. **foraminiferal, -iferous,** *a.* **foraminous,** *n.* [L, from *forāre*, to bore]

forane, *a.* (*Eccles.*) pertaining to things remote. **vicar forane** VICAR. [F *forain*, L *foraneus*, out of doors]

forasmuch, *conj.* (*foll.* by as) seeing that; since; in consideration that.

foray, *v.t.* to pillage, to ravage; to make a raid on. *v.i.* to make a raid; to go foraging or pillaging. *n.* a predatory expedition, a raid. [Sc., prob. from ME *forreyer*, a forager, OF *forrier*, from *forre*, FORAGE]

forbear[1], *v.t.* (*past* **-bore,** *p.p.* **-borne**) to refrain or abstrain from; to bear with, to treat with patience. *v.i.* to refrain or abstain (from); to be patient, to refrain from feelings of resentment. **forbearance,** *n.* **forbearingly,** *adv.* [OE *forberan*]

forbear[2], FORBEAR.

Forbes, *n.* **Bryan** (John Clarke) (1926–), British film producer, director, and screenwriter. After acting in films like *An Inspector Calls* (1954), he made his directorial debut with *Whistle Down the Wind* (1961); among his other films is *The L-Shaped Room* (1962).

forbid, *v.t.* (*past* **-bad, -bade,** *p.p.* **-bidden**) to order not to do; to interdict, to prohibit; to exclude, to oppose; †to defy. **forbiddance,** *n.* the act of forbidding. **forbidden,** *a.* prohibited, interdicted. **forbidden fruit,** *n.* the fruit of the tree of the knowledge of good and evil, which Adam was commanded not to eat (Gen. ii.17); anything desired but pronounced unlawful; the Adam's apple, a name applied to various species of *Citrus*, esp. *C. paradisi* and *C. decumana*. †**forbiddenly,** *adv.* **forbidder,** *n.* **forbidding,** *a.* repulsive, disagreeable; giving rise to aversion or dislike; threatening, formidable. **forbiddingly,** *adv.* **forbiddingness,** *n.* [OE *forbēodan*]

forbore, *past,* **-borne,** *p.p.* FORBEAR[1].

forby, *prep.* (*Sc., dial.*) besides, in addition to; †near, past. *adv.* besides, moreover.

force[1], *n.* strength, energy, active power; military or naval strength; an organized body, esp. an army or part of an army; (*pl.*) troops; power exerted on a person or object; violence, coercion, compulsion; unlawful violence; efficacy, validity; significance, weight, import, full meaning; persuasive or convincing power; energy, vigour, animation, vividness; that which produces or tends to produce a change of velocity in a body at rest or in motion. *v.t.* to constrain by force (to do or to forbear from); to compel, to constrain; to use violence to, to ravish; to strain, to distort; to impose or impress (upon) with force; to bring about, to accomplish, or to make a way by force; to stimulate artificially, to cause to grow or ripen by artificial heat; to cause to ripen prematurely; (*Cards*) to compel (a player) to play in a certain way, to compel (a certain card) to be played; †to enforce; †to care for. **by force,** by compulsion. **in force,** in operation, valid, enforced; (*Mil.*) in large numbers. †**of force,** of necessity. **the Force,** the police. **to come into force,** to become valid; to be enforced or carried out. **to force from,** to elicit by force; to wrest from. **to force one's way,** to push through obstacles by force. **to force out,** to drive out. **to force someone's hand** HAND. **to force the pace** PACE[1]. **force-feed,** *v.t.* (*past, p.p.* **force-fed**) to feed forcibly. **force-land,** *v.i.* to make a forced landing. **force-pump, forcing-pump,** *n.* a pump which delivers water under pressure, so as to raise it to an elevation above that attainable by atmospheric pressure. **forcing-house,** *n.* a hot-house. **forcing-pit,** *n.* a sunk hot-bed containing fermenting materials to produce bottom heat for forcing plants. **forced,** *a.* constrained, affected; unnatural. **forced draught** DRAUGHT. **forced landing,** *n.* a landing, due to mechanical failure or other mishap, elsewhere than at one's destination. **forced march,** *n.* a march in which the physical capacity of troops is exerted to the utmost. **forcedly,** *adv.* **forceful,** *a.* full of or possessing force, forcible; impelled with force; violent, impetuous. **forcefully,** *adv.* **forcefulness,** *n.* **forceless,** *a.* **forcible,** *a.* done or brought about by force; having force, powerful, efficacious, impressive; †valid, binding. **forcible detainer,** *n.* (*Law*) the keeping of houses, land etc., from the owner by force. **forcible entry,** *n.* (*Law*) a violent taking possession of or entering into or upon houses or lands. †**forcible-feeble,** *a.* feeble but making a show of vigour. *n.* one who tries to appear vigorous. **forcibleness,** *n.* **forcibly,** *adv.* [OF, from late L *fortia,* from L *fortis,* strong]

force[2], *n.* (*North.*) a waterfall. [Icel. and Norw. *foss*]

†**force**[3], *v.t.* to stuff. **forcemeat,** *n.* meat chopped fine and highly seasoned, used as stuffing or served up alone. [FARCE[2]]

force majeure, *n.* superior power; circumstances not under one's control. [F]

forceps, *n.* a pair of tongs, pincers or pliers for holding or extracting anything; (*Anat., Zool.*) an organ shaped like a pair of forceps. **forcipate, -pated,** *a.* formed like a forceps, to open and enclose, as the chelae of a lobster etc. [L *forceps -cipis*]

forcible FORCE.

forcite, *n.* a kind of dynamite. [FORCE[1], -ITE]

forclose, FORECLOSE.

Ford[1], *n.* **Ford Madox** (adopted name of Ford Madox Hueffer) (1873–1939), English writer of the novel *The Good Soldier* (1915), and editor of the *English Review* of 1908, to which Thomas Hardy, D. H. Lawrence, and Joseph Conrad contributed. He was a grandson of the painter Ford Madox Brown.

Ford[2], *n.* **Gerald R(udolph)** (1913–), 38th president of the US (1974–77), a Republican. He was elected to the House of Representatives in 1949, was nominated to the vice-presidency by Richard Nixon in 1973 following the resignation of Spiro Agnew, and in 1974, when Nixon resigned, became president. He pardoned Nixon, and gave amnesty to those who had resisted the draft for the Vietnam War.

Ford[3], *n.* **Glenn** (Gwyllym Samuel Newton) (1916–), Canadian actor, active in Hollywood during the 1940s–1960s. Usually cast as the tough but good-natured hero, he was equally at home in westerns, thrillers, and comedies. His films include *Gilda* (1946), *The Big Heat* (1953), and *Dear Heart* (1965).

Ford[4], *n.* **Henry** (1863–1947), US automobile manufacturer, who built his first car in 1893 and founded the Ford Motor Company in 1903. His Model T (1908–27) was the first car to be constructed by purely mass-production methods, and 15 million of these cars were made.

Ford[5], *n.* **John** (1586–*c.* 1640), English poet and dramatist. His play *'Tis Pity She's a Whore* (performed about 1626, printed in 1633) is a study of incest between brother and sister.

Ford[6], *n.* **John,** (assumed name of Sean O'Fearn) (1895–1973), US film director. His films, especially his westerns, were of great influence, and include *Stagecoach* (1939), *The Grapes of Wrath* (1940), and *The Man who Shot Liberty Valance* (1962).

ford, *n.* a shallow part of a river where it may be crossed by wading. *v.t.* to cross (as water) by wading. *v.i.* to cross water by wading. **fordable,** *a.* **fordless,** *a.* [OE, cogn. with FARE (cp. G *Furt,* also L *portus,* a harbour)]

fordo, *v.t.* (*past* **-did,** *p.p.* **-done**) to destroy, to ruin; to kill, to put an end to; (*usu. in p.p.*) to wear out, to exhaust. [OE *fordōn*]

fore, *prep.* before; (*chiefly now in asseverations*) for, in the presence of, as *fore God;* †in preference to. *adv.* †previously; in the front part; (*Naut.*) in or towards the bows. *a.* being in front; being in front of some other thing; being the front part; front; anterior, prior, former, first. *n.* the front part; (*Naut.*) the bow; the foremast. *int.* (*Golf*) before, beware in front (warning to persons standing in the direction of a drive). **at the**

fore, (*Naut.*) displayed on the foremast. **fore-and-aft,** at, along or over the whole length of a ship from stem to stern. **fore-and-aft rigged,** having sails set lengthwise to the ship, as opposed to square sails set on yards. **to the fore,** to the front, prominent, conspicuous; ready, available, forthcoming; (*Sc.*) still surviving. [OE, for, before, prep., beforehand, adv. (see FOR, with which it is radically identical)]

fore-, *pref.* (*chiefly with verbs*) before, in front, beforehand, as *foreconceive, foreordain;* in front, the front or front part of; (*Naut.*) of, near or at the bow or the foremast; (*with nouns*) as *forecourt, forearm, forecastle, forepeak, forerunner*.

fore-advise, *v.t.* to advise beforehand.

forearm[1], *v.t.* to prepare beforehand for attack or defence.

forearm[2], *n.* the anterior part of the arm, between the wrist and elbow.

forebear, *n.* a forefather, an ancestor.

forebode, *v.t.* to foretell, predict; to prognosticate, to portend; to feel a presentiment of. *v.i.* to prognosticate, esp. evil. †**forebodement,** *n.* **foreboder,** *n.* **foreboding,** *n.* prophecy, presage or anticipation, esp. of evil. **forebodingly,** *adv.*

fore-body, *n.* that part of a vessel's hull forward of midship.

forebrace, *n.* a rope on the fore yard-arm for shifting the sail.

forebrain, *n.* the front part of the brain.

forecabin, *n.* a forward cabin, usu. for second-class passengers.

fore-carriage, *n.* a carriage in front; a seat in front of a motor-cycle.

forecast[1], *v.t.* (*past, p.p.* **forecast,** *erron.* **forecasted**) to calculate beforehand; to foresee, to predict; to be an early sign of. *v.i.* to form a scheme beforehand. **forecaster,** *n.*

forecast[2], *n.* a previous contrivance; provision against the future, or calculation of probable events, esp. regarding future weather; foresight, prevision.

forecastle, fo'c'sle, *n.* the part of the upper deck forward of the after-shroud; a short upper deck forward, formerly raised to command the enemy's decks; in merchant-ships, a forward space below deck where the crew live. [FORE-, CASTLE]

fore-cited, *a.* cited before or above.

foreclose, *v.t.* to shut out, exclude or bar; to preclude; to put an end to or settle beforehand (as an arguable matter). *v.i.* to foreclose a mortgage. **to foreclose a mortgage,** to deprive the mortgagor of his or her equity of redemption on failure to pay money due on a mortgage. **foreclosure,** *n.* the act of foreclosing. [OF *forclos,* p.p. of *forclore* (*for-,* L *foris,* outside, *clore,* to CLOSE[1])]

forecourt, *n.* the first or outer court, that immediately inside the entrance to the precincts of a building; an open or paved area in front of a building, esp. a filling station.

foredeck, *n.* the forepart of a deck; the deck in the forepart of a ship.

foredoom[1], *v.t.* to doom beforehand; to predestinate.

foredoom[2], *n.* doom or judgment previously delivered; destiny.

fore-edge, *n.* the front or outer edge of a book or of a leaf in a book.

forefather, *n.* an ancestor.

forefeel, *v.t.* to feel beforehand; to have premonition of. **forefeelingly,** *adv.*

forefend, FORFEND.

forefinger, *n.* the finger next to the thumb, also called the first or index finger.

forefoot, *n.* (*pl.* **-feet**) a front foot of a quadruped; the forward end of a vessel's keel.

forefront, *n.* the extreme front, the foremost part or position.

foregather, FORGATHER.

foregift, *n.* (*Law*) a premium paid by a tenant for the renewal of a lease.

forego[1], *v.t., v.i.* (*past* **-went,**, *p.p.* **-gone**) to go before, to precede in time, order or place. **foregoer,** *n.* one who goes before another, a predecessor; †an ancestor; †a royal purveyor. **foregoing,** *a.* preceding, previously mentioned. **foregone,** *a.* past; preceding; determined before. **foregone conclusion,** *n.* a conclusion determined on beforehand or arrived at in advance of evidence or reasoning; a result that might be foreseen.

forego[2], FORGO.

foreground, *n.* the nearest part of a view; the part of a picture which seems to lie nearest the spectator; a prominent position.

fore-hammer, *n.* (*Sc.*) a sledge-hammer.

forehand, *n.* a forehand stroke; the side on which such strokes are made; that part of a horse before the rider; the chief part, the mainstay; the upper hand, superiority, advantage. *a.* (*Tennis etc.*) with the palm of the hand facing in the direction of the stroke; foremost, leading; †anticipative, in advance; †(*Archery*) for a point-blank shot (of an arrow). **forehanded,** *a.* (*N Am.*) done in good time; timely; thrifty, well-off; formed in the forehand or foreparts (of horses).

forehead, *n.* that part of the face which reaches from the eyebrows upwards to the hair; the front part, the brow; assurance, impudence. [OE *forhēafod* (FORE-, HEAD[1])]

forehold, *n.* the forepart of a ship's hold.

forehorse, *n.* the foremost horse in a team.

foreign, *a.* belonging to, connected with, or derived from another country or nation; alien, strange, extraneous, dissimilar, not belonging (to); having no connection with, irrelevant, impertinent, inappropriate. †*adv.* (*Naut.*) to foreign parts. **foreign body,** *n.* a substance occurring in an organism or tissue where it is not normally found. **foreign-built,** *a.* built in a foreign country. **foreign correspondent,** *n.* a representative of a newspaper sent to a foreign country to report on its politics etc. **foreign exchange,** *n.* (trading in) foreign currencies. **foreign legion,** see separate entry. **foreign minister, secretary,** *n.* a government minister in charge of relations with foreign countries. **Foreign Office,** *n.* the government department for foreign affairs; the building occupied by this. **foreigner,** *n.* a person born or belonging to a foreign country or speaking a foreign language, an alien; a foreign ship, an import or production from a foreign country; a stranger, an outsider. **foreignism,** *n.* **foreignness,** *n.* **foreignize, -ise,** *v.t., v.i.* [OF *forain,* late L *forāneus,* from L *forās,* out of doors, conn. with *foris,* a door]

Foreign Legion, *n.* a volunteer corps of foreigners within a country's army. The French Légion Etrangère, formed in 1831, is one of a number of such forces. Enlisted volunteers are of any nationality (about half are now French), but the officers are usually French. Headquarters until 1962 was in Sidi Bel Abbés, Algeria; the main base is now Corsica, with reception headquarters at Aubagne, near Marseille, France.

forejudge, *v.t.* to judge before trial or decide before hearing the evidence. **forejudgment,** *n.*

foreknow, *v.t.* (*past* **-knew,**, *p.p.* **-known**) to know beforehand. †**foreknowable,** *a.* **foreknower,** *n.* †**foreknowingly,** *adv.* **foreknowledge,** *n.* prescience; knowledge of a thing before it happens.

forel, forrel, *n.* a kind of parchment used for book-covers. [OF *forrel* (F *fourreau*), dim. of *forre,* a sheath]

foreland, *n.* a point of land extending into the sea, a promontory; a strip of land outside of or in front of an embankment etc.; a space between a fortified wall and the moat.

forelay, *v.t.* to contrive beforehand.

foreleg, *n.* a front leg of an animal, chair etc.

†**forelie,** *v.t.* to lie before.

forelock[1], *n.* a lock of hair growing over the forehead. **to take by the forelock,** to seize at the earliest opportunity.

forelock[2], *n.* a pin or wedge passing through the end of a bolt to prevent this from being withdrawn. *v.t.* to secure by a forelock.

foreman, *n.* a head or chief man; the person who acts as chairman and spokesman for a jury; a worker supervising others. **forewoman,** *n. fem.*

foremast, *n.* the mast nearest the bow of a vessel. **foremastman, -hand, -seaman,** *n.* a common sailor.

†**fore-mean,** *v.t.* (*past, p.p.* **-meant**) to intend beforehand.

forementioned, *a.* already mentioned.

foremost, *a.* first in time, place, order, rank or importance; chief, most notable. *adv.* in the first place; first, before anything else. [OE *foremost, fyrmest,* double superlative from *forma,* first, old superlative of *fore,* before, above; assim. to MOST]

forename, *n.* a name preceding the surname; a Christian name. **forenamed,** *a.* named or mentioned before.

forenight, *n.* (*Sc.*) the evening.

forenoon, *n.* (*Sc.*) the early part of the day, from morning to noon.

forensic, *a.* pertaining to courts of judicature, or to public debate; used in debates or legal proceedings. *n.* (*N Am.*) an argumentative thesis at a college. **forensic medicine,** *n.* the science of medicine in its relation to law, medical jurisprudence. **forensically,** *adv.* [L *forensis,* pertaining to the forum, see FORUM]

foreordain, *v.t.* to ordain beforehand, to predestinate. **foreordination,** *n.*

forepart, *n.* the first or most advanced part; the earlier part.

forepast, *a.* of time, already past.

forepeak, *n.* the part of a vessel's hold in the angle of the bow.

foreplane, *n.* a plane intermediate between the jack-plane and the smoothing-plane; sometimes applied to the jack-plane, the first used after saw or axe.

foreplay, *n.* sexual stimulation preceding intercourse.

†**fore-point,** *v.t.* to appoint beforehand; to foreshadow. *v.i.* to point beforehand.

forequarter, *n.* the front half of the side of a carcass, as of beef; (*pl.*) the forelegs, shoulders and chest of a horse.

forerank, *n.* the foremost rank; the front.

forereach, *v.t.* (*Naut.*) to gain upon; to get ahead of. *v.i.* to shoot ahead (on), esp. on a ship going in stays.

foreread, *v.t.* to tell beforehand; to signify by tokens. **forereading,** *n.* a previous perusal.

forerun, *v.t.* (*past* **-ran,**, *p.p.* **-run**) to precede; to betoken, to usher in. **forerunner,** *n.* a messenger sent before; a precursor, herald, harbinger; a predecessor, an ancestor; †an omen, a prognostic.

foresail, *n.* the principal sail on the foremast.

†**foresay,** *v.t.* to say beforehand; to predict; to prognosticate. [OE *fore-secgan*]

foresee, *v.t.* (*past* **-saw,**, *p.p.* **-seen**) to see beforehand; to know beforehand, to have prescience of. **foreseeing,** *a.* exercising foresight. **foreseeingly,** *adv.* †**foreseer,** *n.*

foreshadow, *v.t.* to shadow beforehand; to typify beforehand, to prefigure. *n.* a foreshadowing or prefiguration of something.

foresheet, *n.* the rope holding the lee corner of a foresail; (*pl.*) the space in a boat forward of the foremost thwart, usu. covered with a grating.

foreship, *n.* the forepart of a ship; the prow. [OE *forscip* (as FORE-, SHIP)]

foreshore, *n.* the part of the shore lying between high- and low-water marks; the ground between the sea and land that is cultivated or built upon; the slightly inclined portion of a breakwater, projecting seaward.

foreshorten, *v.t.* in drawing or painting, to represent (figures or parts of figures that project towards the spectator) so as to give a correct impression of form and proportions. **foreshortened,** *a.*

foreshow, *v.t.* (*p.p.* **-shown**) to predict, to represent beforehand; to foreshadow. [OE *fore-scēawian*]

†**foreside,** *n.* the front side; a specious outside.

foresight, *n.* prescience, forethought; provident care for the future, prudence, precaution; the muzzle-sight of a gun. †**foresighted,** *a.* †**foresightful,** *a.*

foresignify, *v.t.* to betoken beforehand; to typify; to foreshow.

foreskin, *n.* the prepuce, the loose skin covering the end of the penis.

foreskirt, *n.* the loose hanging portion of a coat in front.

foresleeve, *n.* that part of a sleeve between the wrist and elbow.

†**forespeak,** *v.t.* (*past,* **-spoke,**, *p.p.* **-spoken**) to predict, to foretell; (*Sc.*) to bespeak.

forespur, *n.* a foreleg of bacon or pork.

forest, *n.* an extensive wood or tract of wooded country; a wild uncultivated tract of ground partly covered with trees and underwood; a large tract of country set apart for game and hunting, in many cases orig. a royal hunting-ground; something resembling a forest. *v.t.* to plant with trees; to convert into a forest. †**forest-born,** *a.* born in a forest; wild. **forest-fly,** *n.* a fly frequenting woodlands, *Hippobosca equina,* troublesome to horses. **forest-laws,** *n.pl.* laws for the regulation of forests and preserving game, instituted by William I. **forest-marble,** *n.* a stratum of Lower Oolitic age abounding in marine fossils, named from Wychwood Forest, Oxfordshire, where it is quarried. **forest-oak,** *n.* the she-oak or *Casuarina,* an Australian genus of timber-trees. †**forestage,** *n.* a tribute payable to the king's foresters; an ancient service paid by foresters to the king; the right to take estovers from a forest. †**forestal,** *a.* **forester,** *n.* one who has charge of a forest; an inhabitant of a forest; one who looks after the trees on an estate; a bird, beast or tree of a forest; a member of the Forester's Benefit Society; (*Austral.*) the largest variety of kangaroo. **forestry,** *n.* the act or art of cultivating trees and forests; the management of growing timber; (*poet.*) woodland, a multitude of trees; (*Sc. Law*) the privileges of a royal forest. [OF (F *forêt*), from late L *foresta,* a wood, *forestis* (*silva*), the outside or open (wood), from L *foris,* outside]

forestall, *v.t.* to hinder by preoccupation or anticipation; to anticipate; to be beforehand with; to buy up (commodities) beforehand so as to control the sale; †to deprive (of); †to obstruct or stop up (as a road). **to forestall the market,** to engross or buy up commodities, so as to obtain the control of the market. **forestaller,** *n.* [OE *forsteall,* interference, interception]

forestay, *n.* (*Naut.*) a strong rope, reaching from the foremast head to the bowsprit end, to support the mast.

forester, forestry FOREST.

Forester, *n.* **C(ecil) S(cott)** (1899–1966), English novelist, born in Egypt. He wrote a series of historical novels set in the Napoleonic era which, beginning with *The Happy Return* (1937), cover the career – from midshipman to admiral – of Horatio Hornblower.

foretaste[1], *n.* experience or enjoyment (of) beforehand; anticipation.

foretaste[2], *v.t.* to taste beforehand; to anticipate enjoyment (of).

foretell, *v.t.* (*past, p.p.* **-told**) to predict, to prophesy; to foreshadow. **foreteller,** *n.*

forethought, *n.* consideration beforehand; premeditation; foresight, provident care. **forethoughtful,** *a.*

foretime, *n.* time past; early times.

foretoken[1], *v.t.* to foreshadow, to prognosticate.

foretoken[2], *n.* a token beforehand, an omen.

foretooth, *n.* (*pl.* **-teeth**) a front tooth.

foretop, *n.* (*Naut.*) the top or platform at the head of the foremast; the fore-topgallant-masthead; (*fig.*) †the top of a periwig; †the forehead; †an erect tuft of hair, esp. a horse's forelock. **foretopman,** *n.* a man stationed in the foretop. **fore-topmast,** *n.* the mast at the head of the foremast, and surmounted by the **fore-topgallant-mast. fore-topsail, fore-topgallant-sail,** *n.*

foretype[1], *n.* an antitype.

foretype[2], *v.t.* to prefigure.

forever, *adv.* for ever. *n.* (*poet.*) eternity; (*coll.*) a very long time. **forevermore,** *adv.*

†**foreward,** *n.* the vanguard; the front.
forewarn, *v.t.* to warn or caution beforehand; to give notice to beforehand.
†**forewind,** *n.* a favourable wind.
forewoman FOREMAN.
foreword, *n.* a preface, a short introduction.
foreyard, *n.* the lowest yard on a foremast.
†**forfairn,** *a.* (*Sc.*) worn out, exhausted with travail, age etc. [p.p. of obs. v. *forfare,* OE *forfaran* (FOR-, FARE)]
forfeit, *n.* that which is lost through fault, crime, omission or neglect; a penalty, a fine, esp. a stipulated sum to be paid in case of breach of contract; (*pl.*) a game in which for every breach of the rules the players have to deposit some article, which is subsequently redeemed by the performance of a playful task or ceremony; the article so deposited; †a misdeed, a crime; one condemned to capital punishment. *a.* lost or alienated through fault or crime; †subject, liable. *v.t.* to lose the right to or possession of by fault, crime, omission or neglect; to lose; to cause to lose, to confiscate; †to subject to loss of property etc. †**forfeitable,** *a.* that may be forfeited; subject to forfeiture. **forfeiter,** *n.* one who incurs a penalty. **forfeiture,** *n.* the act of forfeiting; that which is forfeited; a penalty or amercement. [OF *forfait,* orig. p.p. of *forfaire,* late L *foris facere,* to transgress, lit. to act beyond or outside]
forfend, *v.t.* to avert, to ward off.
forfex, *n.* a pair of scissor-like anal appendages in earwigs; a pair of scissors. **forficate, -cated,** *a.* [L, scissors]
forfoughten, *a.* (*Sc.*) worn out with fighting, war-worn; exhausted, tired out.
forgather, *v.i.* to meet or associate (with); to meet together, to assemble; to unite (with) in marriage. *v.t.* to be friendly or intimate with.
forgave, *past* FORGIVE.
forge[1], *n.* the workshop of a smith; a blacksmith's open fireplace or hearth where iron is heated by forced draught; a furnace or hearth for making wrought iron; a place where anything is made; a workshop; †the working of iron or steel; †workmanship. *v.t.* to form or fabricate by heating and hammering; to make or construct; to make, invent, or imitate fraudulently, to counterfeit; to fabricate, esp. to counterfeit or alter a signature or document with intent to defraud. *v.i.* to commit forgery. **forgeman,** *n.* a forger or smith, esp. one with a hammer-man under him. **forgeable,** *a.* **forger,** *n.* one who commits forgery; a smith, one who forges metal. **forgery,** *n.* the act of forging, counterfeiting or falsifying; a fraudulent imitation; a deception. **forging,** *n.* that which is forged; a piece of forged metal work. [OF, ult. from L *fabrica,* FABRIC]
forge[2], *v.i.* to move steadily (forward or ahead); to move at an increased speed (forward or ahead). [etym. doubtful]
forget, *v.t., v.i.* (*past* **-got,**, *p.p.* **-gotten,** *poet.* **-got**) to lose remembrance of; to put out of mind purposely; to fail to remember through inadvertence; to neglect (to do something). **to forget oneself,** to lose one's self-control, to behave unbecomingly; to become unconscious; to act unselfishly. **forgetful,** *a.* **forgetfully,** *adv.* **forgetfulness,** *n.* **forgettable,** *a.* **forgetter,** *n.* †**forgettingly,** *adv.* [OE *forgitan* (FOR-, GET[1])]
forget-me-not, *n.* a small plant of the genus *Myosotis,* esp. *M. palustris,* with bright blue flowers.
forgive, *v.t.* (*past* **-gave,**, *p.p.* **-given**) to pardon or remit, as an offence or debt; not to exact the penalty for; to pardon, not to punish (a person or offence, or a person his or her offence); to cease to feel resentment towards. *v.i.* to show forgiveness. **forgivable,** *a.* **forgiveness,** *n.* the act of forgiving; a disposition to forgive; remission, pardon. **forgiver,** *n.* **forgiving,** *a.* disposed to forgive; merciful, gracious. **forgivingly,** *adv.* **forgivingness,** *n.* [OE *forgifan* (FOR- GIVE)]
forgo, *v.t.* (*past* **forwent,** *p.p.* **forgone**) to go without, to refrain from; to give up, deny oneself, renounce, relinquish; to quit. [OE *forgān*]
forgotten, †**forgot,** *p.p.* FORGET.
forint, *n.* the monetary unit of Hungary since 1946, equivalent to 100 fillér. [Hung.]
†**forisfamiliate,** *v.t.* (*Law*) to emancipate from parental authority; to bestow a portion of lands on (a son in his father's lifetime, and thus discharge him from the family). *v.i.* to renounce all further claim on the parental estate. *a.*, having possession of property during the father's lifetime. [med. L *forisfamiliātus,* p.p. (of *forisfamiliāre foris,* outside, *familia,* FAMILY)]
forjudge, *v.t.* (*Law*) to deprive, dispossess or exclude by a judgment. **forjudger,** *n.* †**forjudgment,** *n.* [OF *forjuger*]
fork, *n.* an agricultural implement terminating in two or more prongs, used for digging, impaling, lifting, carrying or throwing; a pronged implement used in cooking or at table; anything of a similar form; a forking or bifurcation; a diverging branch; a confluent, a tributary; a point where a road divides into two; the crutch, the bifurcation of the human body; a forked support into which a bicycle wheel fits; (*Chess, Draughts*) a simultaneous attack on two pieces; †a barbed point, as of an arrow; †a point; †a gibbet. *v.t.* to raise or pitch with a fork; to dig or break up with a fork, as ground; to make sharp or pointed; (*Chess, Draughts*) to attack two pieces so that only one can escape. *v.i.* to divide into two; to send out branches. **to fork out, over,** (*sl.*) to hand or deliver over; to produce the cash for. **fork-chuck,** *n.* a piece of steel in a turning-lathe carrying points which enter the wood and cause it to rotate. **fork-head,** *n.* the double head of a rod which divides to form a connection by means of a pin; †the barbed head of an arrow. **forklift (truck),** *n.* a vehicle which raises and transports objects on mobile steel prongs. **forktail,** *a.* having a forked tail. *n.* a salmon in its fourth year's growth. **forked,** *a.* dividing into branches, branching, cleft, bifurcated; terminating in points or prongs. †**forkedly,** *adv.* †**forkedness,** *n.* †**forkless,** *a.* **forky,** *n.* forked, fork-like. [OE *forc,* L *furca*]
forlorn, *a.* deserted, abandoned; helpless, wretched, hopeless; †deprived, bereft (of); †lost. †**forlornly,** *adv.* **forlornness,** *n.* [OE *forloren,* p.p. of *forlēosan* (FOR-, LOSE[1])]
forlorn hope, *n.* a detachment of people selected for some service of uncommon danger; a bold, desperate enterprise. [after Dut. *verloren hoop,* lit. lost troop (from *hoop,* heap, see HEAP), cp. F *enfans perdus*]
form, *n.* the shape or external appearance of anything apart from colour; configuration, figure, esp. of the human body; particular arrangement, disposition, organization or constitution; established practice or method; a rule of procedure, ceremony or ritual; the mode in which anything is perceptible to the senses or intellect; kind, specific state, species, variety, variation; a specific shape of a word as regards inflection, spelling or pronunciation; a shape, mould or model upon which a thing is fashioned; a customary method or formula, a fixed order of words; a document with blanks to be filled in; (*Art*) style or mode of expression, as opposed to content or subject-matter, orderly arrangement of parts, order, symmetry; behaviour according to accepted rules or conventions; good physical condition or fitness, a good state of health or training; a long seat without a back; a class in a public or secondary school considered as an administrative unit, all the pupils in a particular year or a subdivision of a year group; the seat or bed of a hare; a body of type composed and locked in a chase ready for printing; literary nature of a book etc., as distinct from the subject; the structure of a mathematical expression; that which differentiates matter and generates species; that which the mind contributes, the mode of knowing, the subjective element in perception; (*Kant*) the categories or subjective elements by which the mind apprehends objects. *v.t.* to give form or shape to; to arrange in any particular manner; to make, construct or create; to model or mould to a pattern; to train, to instruct, to mould or shape by discipline; to conceive, devise, construct (ideas etc.); to articulate; to become; to be the

material for; to be or constitute (a part or one of); (*Mil.*) to combine into (a certain order); (*Gram.*) to make by derivation or by affixes or prefixes. †*v.i.* to assume a form; (*Mil.*) to combine (into a certain order). **bad, good form,** bad, good manners; ill, good breeding. **in, on form,** showing one's talent to advantage, playing or performing well. **off form,** playing or performing below one's usual standard. **form letter,** *n.* (a copy of) a standard letter sent to many different people, often with relevant individual details added. **form-master, -mistress, -teacher,** *n.* the teacher with general administrative and tutelary responsibility for a form. [OF *forme,* L *forma*]

form-, *comb.form* (*Chem.*) containing formyl as a radical. [FORMYL]

-form, *suf.* like, having the shape of, as *cruciform, dendriform;* having a certain number of forms, as *multiform, uniform.* [F *-forme,* L *-formis,* from *forma,* FORM]

formal, *a.* in a set form; made, performed or done according to established forms; orderly, regular; explicit, definite; observant of established form, ceremonious, punctilious, precise; conventional, perfunctory; of or pertaining to the outward form as opposed to reality, outward; (*Log.*) pertaining to form as opposed to matter; (*Phil.*) pertaining to the formative essence that makes a thing what it is, essential, not material. **formalism,** *n.* the quality of being formal; formality, esp. in religion. **formalist,** *n.* **formalistic,** *a.* **formality,** *n.* the condition or quality of being formal; conformity to custom, rule or established method; conventionality, mere form; an established order or method, an observance required by custom or etiquette; (*Art*) precision, observance of rule as opposed to originality. **formalize, -ise,** *v.t.* to render formal; to formulate. **formalization, -isation,** *n.* **formally,** *adv.* [L *formālis,* from *forma,* FORM]

formaldehyde, *n.* formic aldehyde, a colourless gas generated by the partial oxidation of methyl alcohol, and used as an antiseptic and disinfectant.

formalin, *n.* a solution of formaldehyde used as an antiseptic, for the destruction of disease germs, and as a food preservative.

formant, *n.* a component of a sound which gives it its particular tone colour or quality. [G, from L *formans,* pres.p. of *formare,* to shape, fashion]

format, *n.* the external form and size of a book; the general plan, arrangement and style of e.g. a television programme; (*Comput.*) the arrangement of data on a disc etc. *v.t.* (*past, p.p.* **formatted**) to arrange in a specific format; (*Comput.*) to prepare a disc etc. for the reception of data. [F, from L *formātus,* from *forma,* FORM]

formate FORMIC.

formation, *n.* the act or process of forming or creating; the state of being formed or created; the manner in which anything is formed; conformation, arrangement, disposition of parts, structure; a thing formed, regarded in relation to form or structure; a group of rocks or strata of common origin, structure or physical character; an arrangement of troops; aircraft, ships etc. **formative,** *a.* having the power of giving form, shaping; plastic; pertaining to formation, growth or development; of combining forms, prefixes etc., serving to form words, inflectional, not radical. *n.* (*Philol.*) that which serves to form, and is no part of the root; a word formed in accordance with some rule or usage. [L *formātio -ōnem,* from *forma,* FORM]

Formby, *n.* **George** (1904–61), English comedian. He established a stage and screen reputation as an apparently simple Lancashire working lad, and sang such songs as 'Mr Wu' and 'Cleaning Windows', accompanying himself on the ukulele. His father was a music-hall star of the same name.

forme, (*Print.*) FORM.

former, *a.* preceding in time; mentioned before something else, the first-mentioned (of two); past, earlier, ancient, bygone. **formerly,** *adv.* in former times; of the past or earlier times; †first, beforehand; †just now. [formed from ME *formest,* FOREMOST, double superl. from OE *forma,* first]

formic, *a.* (*Chem.*) pertaining to or produced by ants. **formic acid,** *n.* an acid found in the fluid emitted by ants, in stinging-nettles etc., and now obtained from oxalic acid distilled with glycerin. **formate,** *n.* a salt of formic acid. **formene,** *n.* methane. **formicant,** *a.* of the pulse, weak, almost imperceptible, creeping like an ant. **formicary,** *n.* an ant-hill. **formicate,** *a.* resembling an ant. **formication,** *n.* irritation of the skin like the crawling of ants. **formyl,** *n.* (*Chem.*) the radical theoretically constituting the base of formic acid. [short for *formicic,* from L *formīca,* an ant]

Formica®, *n.* a heat-proof plastic laminate, widely used for wipe-down kitchen surfaces. It is made from formaldehyde resins akin to Bakelite.

formidable, *a.* tending to excite fear; to be feared; dangerous to encounter; difficult to resist, overcome or accomplish. **formidableness, formidability,** *n.* **formidably,** *adv.* [F, from L *formīdābilis,* from *formīdāre*), to dread]

formin, *n.* a white crystalline powder produced from formaldehyde and ammonia, used as an antiseptic and diuretic.

formless, *a.* without form, shapeless; having no regular form. **formlessly,** *adv.* **formlessness,** *n.*

formula, *n.* (*pl.,* **-lae, -las**) a prescribed form of words; a formal enunciation of faith, doctrine, principle etc.; a compromise solution to a dispute, an agreed form of words; a fixed rule, a set form, a conventional usage; a prescription, a recipe; a milk mixture or substitute used as baby food; (*Chem.*) an expression by means of symbols of the elements of a compound; the expression of a rule or principle in algebraic symbols; a technical specification which determines the class in which a racing car competes. **formularize, -ise,** *v.t.* to formulate. **formularization, -isation,** *n.* **formulary,** *a.* stated, prescribed; of the nature of a formula; formal, ritual. *n.* a collection of formulas; a book containing stated and prescribed forms, esp. relating to religious belief or ritual; a formula. **formulate,** *v.t.* to express in a formula; to set forth in a precise and systematic form. **formulation,** *n.* **formulism,** *n.* strict observance of or dependence upon formulas. **formulist,** *n.* **formulistic,** *a.* **formulize, -ise,** *v.t.* to formulate. **formulization, -isation,** *n.* [L, dim. of *forma,* FORM]

formyl FORMIC.

fornent, -nenst, *prep.* (*Sc.*) right opposite to. *adv.* (*Sc.*) opposite. [FORE, ANENT]

fornicate, *v.i.* to commit fornication. **fornication,** *n.* sexual intercourse of unmarried persons or of a married with an unmarried person; (*Bibl.*) applied to idolatry, incest or adultery. **fornicator,** *n.* †**fornicatress,** *n. fem.* [L *fornicātus,* p.p. of *fornicārī,* from *fornix -icis,* an arch, a brothel]

fornix, *n.* (*pl.* **fornices**) (*Anat.*) the arch of the vagina; the roof of the pharynx; an arch-shaped formation in the brain; a similar part or organ in a plant or shell. [L, an arch]

forpit, *n.* (*Sc., North.*) the fourth part of a measure (as a peck). [corr. of FOURTH PART]

forrel, FOREL.

Forrest, *n.* **John, 1st Baron Forrest** (1847–1918), Australian explorer and politician. He crossed Western Australia W–E in 1870, when he went along the southern coast route, and in 1874, when he crossed much further N, exploring the Musgrave Ranges. He was born in Western Australia, and was its first premier (1890–1901).

forrit, *adv.* (*Sc.*) forward. [prob. corr. of FORWARD]

forsake, *v.t.* (*past* **-sook,**, *p.p.* **-saken**) to leave, to abandon, to withdraw from; to renounce, to cast off, to reject; †to refuse; †to deny. **forsaker,** *n.* [OE *forsacan* (FOR-, *sacan,* to quarrel, see SAKE)]

†**forsay,** *v.t.* to renounce, to forsake; to deny, to forbid.

†**forshapen,** *a.* misshaped, deformed; transformed. [p.p. of obs. *forshape,* OE *forscieppan,* (FOR-, SHAPE)]

†**forslow,** *v.t.* to delay, to put off; to neglect, to omit; to render slow, to obstruct. *v.i.* to be slow. [OE *for-*

slāwian (as FOR-, *slāwian,* from *slāw,* SLOW)]

forsooth, *adv.* (*chiefly iron.*) in truth, certainly, doubtless.

†**forspeak,** *v.t.* to forbid, to speak against; to bewitch, to charm.

forspend, *v.t.* (*past, p.p.* **-spent**) (*usu. p.p.*) to wear out, to exhaust with toil.

Forster, *n.* **E(dward) M(organ)** (1879–1970), English novelist, concerned with the interplay of personality and the conflict between convention and instinct. His novels include *A Room with a View* (1908), *Howards End* (1910), and *A Passage to India* (1924). He also wrote short stories, for example 'The Eternal Omnibus' (1914); criticism, including *Aspects of the Novel* (1927), and essays, including *Abinger Harvest* (1936).

forswear, *v.t.* (*past* **-swore,** *p.p.* **-sworn**) to abjure; to renounce upon oath or with protestations; †to break (an oath, allegiance, etc.). *v.i.* to swear falsely. **to forswear oneself,** to perjure oneself. †**forswearer,** *n.* a perjurer. †**forswornness,** *n.* the state of being forsworn; perjury. [OE *forswerian*]

Forsyth, *n.* **Frederick** (1938–), English thriller writer. His books include *The Day of the Jackal* (1970), *The Dogs of War* (1974), and *The Fourth Protocol* (1984).

forsythia, *n.* a genus of oleaceous shrubs bearing numerous yellow flowers in early spring before the leaves. [W. *Forsyth,* 1737–1804]

fort, *n.* a fortified place, esp. a detached outwork or an independent fortified work of moderate extent; (*N Am., Hist.*) a trading-post. †**forted,** *a.* guarded by forts, fortified. [OF, from L *fortis* (*domus,* strong (house)]

fortalice, *n.* an outwork of a fortification; a small fort. [med. L *fortalitia,* as prec.]

Fort-de-France, *n.* capital, chief commercial centre, and port of Martinique, West Indies; population (1982) 99,844.

forte[1], *n.* the strong part of a sword blade, i.e. from the hilt to the middle;, a person's strong point;, that in which one excels. [F fem. a., strong, as prec. (fem. unmeaningly adopted instead of masc.)]

forte[2], *adv.* (*Mus.*) with loudness or force. **forte forte,** *adv.* very loud. **forte piano,** *adv.* loudly, then softly. **fortepiano,** *n.* an early form of pianoforte. [It., strong, as prec.]

forth, *adv.* forward; out; out into view; out from home; out of doors; forward in place, time or order; indefinitely forward, in time. †*prep.* out of, away from. **and so forth,** and the rest, and so on, and the like. **back and forth,** to and fro. **forthcoming,** *a.* coming forth, ready to appear, or to be brought forward; approaching, soon to take place; available; of people, communicative, responsive. *n.* a coming forth; (*Sc. Law*) an action by which an assessment is made effectual. **forth-going,** *a.* going forth; proceeding; affable, encouraging. *n.* a going out or proceeding from; that which goes forth; an utterance. **forth-issuing,** *a.* issuing forth. **forth-putting,** *a.* putting forth or forward; (*N Am.*) forward, pushing, obtrusive. **forthright,** *a.* going straight forward, direct; outspoken; to the point. *adv.* straight forward; at once, straightway. *n.* a direct course. **forthwith,** *adv.* immediately; without delay. [OE, from *fore,* see FORE[1] (cp. Dut. *voort,* G *fort*)]

†**forthink,** *v.t.* to repent of; to be sorry for. [OE *forthencan* (FOR-, THINK)]

Forth, *n.* river in SE Scotland, with its headstreams rising on the NE slopes of Ben Lomond. It flows approximately 72 km/45 miles to Kincardine where the Firth of Forth begins. The Firth is approximately 80 km/50 miles long, and is 26 km/16 miles wide where it joins the North Sea.

forties, *n.pl.* the period of time between one's 40th and 50th birthdays; the range of temperature between 40 and 50 degrees; the period of time between the 40th and 50th years of a century. **the roaring forties,** the stormy part of the Atlantic between 39° and 50° S lat.

fortieth, *n.* one of 40 equal parts. *n., a.* (the) last of 40 (people, things etc.); the next after the 39th.

fortify, *v.t.* to make strong; to give power or strength to; to invigorate; to encourage; to add alcoholic strength to; to enrich (a food) by adding vitamins etc.; to confirm, to corroborate; (*Fort.*) to strengthen or secure by forts, ramparts etc.; to make defensible against the attack of an enemy. *v.i.* to raise fortifications. **fortifiable,** *a.* **fortification,** *n.* the act, art or science of fortifying a place or position against the attacks of an enemy; a defensive work, a fort; (*pl.*) works erected to defend a place against attack; increasing the strength of wine with alcohol; †an accession of strength, a strengthening. **fortifier,** *n.* [OF *fortifier,* L *fortificāre* (*fortis,* strong, *-ficāre,* from *facere,* to make)]

fortissimo, *adv.* (*Mus.*) very loud. [It., superl. of *forte,* see FORTE[2]]

fortition, *n.* trusting to chance; selection by chance. [erroneously formed from L *fors fortis,* chance]

fortitude, *n.* strength, esp. that strength of mind which enables one to meet danger or endure pain with calmness. **fortitudinous,** *a.* [F, from L *fortitūdo,* from *fortis,* strong]

Fort Knox, *n.* US army post and gold depository in Kentucky, established in 1917 as a training camp. The US Treasury gold-bullion vaults were built in 1937.

fortlet, *n.* a small fort.

fortnight, *n.* a period of two weeks or 14 days. **fortnightly,** *a.* happening once a fortnight. *adv.* once a fortnight; every fortnight. *n.* a fortnightly publication. [ME *fourtenight,* OE *fēowertȳne niht,* 14 nights]

Fortran, FORTRAN, *n.* a high-level computer language used esp. for mathematical and scientific purposes. Developed in the mid-1950s, and one of the earliest languages, it is still widely used today.

fortress, *n.* a fortified place, esp. a strongly fortified town accommodating a large garrison and forming a permanent stronghold. *v.t.* (*poet.*) to furnish with or serve as a fortress, to defend. [OF *forteresse,* var. of *fortalesce, fortalice*]

Fort Sumter, *n.* fort in Charleston, South Carolina, US, 6.5 km/4 miles SE of Charleston. The first shots of the US Civil War were fired here on 12 Apr. 1861, after its commander had refused the call to surrender made by the Confederate general Beauregard.

Fort Ticonderoga, *n.* fort in New York State, US, on a route to Canada near Lake Champlain. It was the site (1758–59) of battles between the British and the French, and was captured from the British on 10 May 1775 by Benedict Arnold and Ethan Allen (leading the Green Mountain Boys).

fortuitous, *a.* happening by chance; casual, accidental. **fortuitously,** *adv.* **fortuitousness,** *n.* **fortuitism,** *n.* (*Phil.*) the doctrine that mere chance, not design, is the principle governing the operation of natural causes. **fortuitist,** *n.* **fortuity,** *n.* a chance occurrence; an accident; fortuitousness. [L *fortuitus,* from *fors fortis,* chance]

fortunate, *a.* happening by good luck; bringing or presaging good fortune; auspicious; lucky, prosperous. **fortunately,** *adv.* †**fortunateness,** *n.* [L *fortūnātus,* p.p. of *fortūnāre,* from *fortūna,* see foll.]

fortune, *n.* chance, luck, that which happens as if by chance; that which brings good or ill, a personification of this, a supernatural power supposed to control one's lot and to bestow good or evil; one's future lot; (*pl.*) the progress or history of a person or thing; good luck, prosperity; wealth; a large property or sum of money. †*v.t.* to control the fortunes of; to provide with a fortune. *v.i.* to happen, to chance. **a small fortune,** a large sum of money. **fortune cookie,** *n.* (*N Am.*) a biscuit with a slip of paper inside it, which has a prediction, proverb, joke etc. written on it. **fortune-hunter,** *n.* one who seeks to marry a wealthy woman. **fortune-hunting,** *n., a.* **fortune-teller,** *n.* one who claims to reveal future events. **fortune-telling,** *n.* **fortuneless,** *a.* †luckless; without a dowry. †**fortunize, -ise,** *v.t.* to regulate the fortunes of; to make fortunate. [F, from L *fortūna,* cogn. with *fors fortis,* chance, and *ferre,* to bring]

forty, *n.* the number or figure 40 or XL; the age of 40. *a.*

40 in number; aged 40. **forty-five,** *n.* a record played at 45 r.p.m. **the Forty-five,** see separate entry. **forty-niner,** *n.* one of the adventurers who went to California at the time of the gold-rush in 1849. **forty winks,** *n.* a nap. [OE *fēowertig* (FOUR, -TY), cp. Dut. *veertig,* G *vierzig*]

Forty-five, the, Jacobite rebellion of 1745, led by Prince Charles Edward Stuart. With his army of Highlanders 'Bonnie Prince Charlie' occupied Edinburgh and advanced into England as far as Derby, but then turned back. The rising was crushed by the Duke of Cumberland at Culloden in 1746.

forum, *n.* (*Rom. Ant.*) the public place in Rome in which were the courts of law, public offices etc. and where orations were delivered; a market-place; a place of assembly for public discussion or judicial purposes; a meeting to discuss matters of public interest; a medium for open discussion; a tribunal, a court of law; in the Roman Catholic Church, the sphere in which the Church exercises jurisdiction. [L]

forward, *a.* at or near the forepart of anything; in front; towards the front; onward; in advance, advancing or advanced; well advanced, progressing, early, premature, precocious; eager, prompt; pert, presumptuous. *n.* a mainly attacking player at football etc. stationed at the front of a formation. *v.t.* to help onward, to promote; to hasten the growth of; to send on or ahead, to send to a further destination; to send. *adv.* (*Naut.*) towards, at or in the fore part of a vessel. **forward, -wards,** *adv.* towards the front; onward in place or time; towards the future; to an earlier time; ahead, in advance; to the front, to a prominent position. **forward-looking,** *a.* progressive; looking to, or planning for, the future. **forwarder,** *n.* one who helps forward; a promoter; one who transmits goods; a person or firm whose business is to facilitate the onward shipment of goods to their destination; (*Bookbinding*) one who prepares a sewed book for the finisher by plain covering. **forwardly,** *adv.* **forwardness,** *n.* the quality or state of being forward; assurance; pertness. [OE *foreweard* (FORE[1], -WARD)]

†**forweary,** *v.t.* (*p.p.* **-wearied, -worn**) to tire out.

forwent *past* FORGO.

Foss, *n.* **Lukas** (1922–), US composer and conductor. He wrote the cantata *The Prairie* (1942) and *Time Cycle* for soprano and orchestra in 1960.

fossa, *n.* (*pl.* **-ssae**) (*Anat.*) a shallow depression, pit or cavity. **fossiform,** *a.* [L, a ditch, orig. fem. p.p. of *fodere,* to dig]

fosse, *n.* a ditch, a trench, esp. around a fortification, commonly filled with water; a canal; a fossa. **fossette,** *n.* a dimple, a small fossa. [F, from L FOSSA]

Fosse, *n.* **Robert ('Bob')** (1927–87), US film director who entered films as a dancer and choreographer from Broadway, making his directorial debut with *Sweet Charity* (1968). He gained an Academy Award for his second film as director, *Cabaret* (1972). His other work includes *All That Jazz* (1979).

†**fosset,** *n.* a faucet. [FAUCET]

fossick, *v.i.* (*Mining*) to search for gold or precious stones, esp. in abandoned workings; to rummage about. **fossicker,** *n.* [Austral., from E dial. *fussock,* to bustle about]

fossiform FOSSA.

fossil, *a.* found underground; dug up; preserved in the strata of the earth's crust, esp. if mineralized; antiquated. *n.* an organic body preserved in the strata of the earth's crust; an antiquated, out-of-date or inflexible person or thing; a form once current but now found only in a few special contexts. **fossil fuel,** *n.* a naturally-occurring fuel formed by the decomposition of prehistoric organisms. **fossilate,** *v.t.*, *v.i.* to fossilize. **fossilation,** *n.* **fossiliferous,** *a.* **fossilify,** *v.t.* to fossilize. †**fossilism,** *n.* the study of fossils. †**fossilist,** *n.* **fossilize, -ise,** *v.t.* to convert into a fossil; to render antiquated or inflexible. *v.i.* to be converted into a fossil; to become antiquated or inflexible. **fossilization, -isation,** *n.* †**fossilogy, fossilology,** *n.* †**fossilogist, fossilologist,** *n.* [OF, from L *fossilis,* from *fossus,* p.p. of *fodere,* to dig]

fossor, *n.* (*Eccles. Ant.*) one of an order of inferior clergy charged with the burial of the dead. **Fossores,** *n.pl.* (*Zool.*) burrowing Hymenoptera, insects with legs formed for burrowing; a group of mammals containing the burrowing moles. **fossorial,** *a.* adapted for digging; (*Zool.*) pertaining or relating to the Fossores. [late L, grave-digger, as prec.]

Foster[1], *n.* **Jodie** (1962–), US film actress, who began as a child in a great variety of roles. Her work includes Scorsese's *Taxi Driver* (1976), *Bugsy Malone* (1976), and *The Accused* (1988).

Foster[2], *n.* **Norman** (1935–), British architect of the high-tech school. His works include the Willis Faber office, Ipswich (1978), the Sainsbury Centre for Visual Arts at the University of East Anglia (1979), and the headquarters of the Hongkong and Shanghai Bank, Hong Kong (1986).

Foster[3], *n.* **Stephen Collins** (1826–64), US songwriter. He wrote sentimental popular songs including 'My Old Kentucky Home' (1853) and 'Beautiful Dreamer' (1864), and rhythmic minstrel songs such as 'Oh! Susannna' (1848) and 'Camptown Races' (1850).

foster, *v.t.* to bring up or nurse (esp. a child not one's own); to place in the charge of foster parents; to nourish, to support, to encourage, to promote the growth of; to harbour (as an ill feeling). †*v.i.* to be brought up together. †*n.* a fosterer. **foster-brother, -sister,** *n.* a brother or sister by fostering, but not by birth. **foster-child, -daughter, -son,** *n.* a child brought up or nursed by someone other than its natural parent(s). †**foster-dam,** *n.* a nurse, a foster-mother. **foster-father, -mother, -parent,** *n.* one who takes the place of a parent in rearing a child. **foster-land,** *n.* †land allotted for the support of monks; one's adopted country. †**foster-nurse,** *n.* a nurse. **fosterage,** *n.* the act of fostering; the state of being a foster-child; the custom of fostering; the care of a foster-child; fostering or encouraging. **fosterer, fostress,** *n.* one who fosters; a nurse, a foster-parent. **fosterling,** *n.* a foster-child. [OE *fōstrian,* from *fōstor,* nourishment, cogn. with *fōda,* FOOD]

fother[1], *v.t.* to stop (a leak) at sea by letting down a sail and putting oakum, yarn etc. between it and the ship's sides or bottom; to use (a sail) thus. [perh. from Dut. *voederen* (now *voeren*) or LG *fodern,* to line (cp. Icel. *fōthra*)]

fother[2], *n.* †a load, a cartload; †a large quantity; a load of lead, 19½ cwt. (983 kg); a large quantity, load or weight; a heavy weight. [OE *fōther* (cp. MDut. *voeder,* Dut. *voer,* G *Fuder*)]

fou, *a.* (*Sc.*) drunk. †*n.* a bushel. [FULL[1]]

Foucault[1], *n.* **Jean Bernard Léon** (1819–1868), French physicist who used a pendulum to demonstrate the rotation of the Earth on its axis, and invented the gyroscope.

Foucault[2], *n.* **Michel** (1926–84), French philosopher, who rejected phenomenology and existentialism. His work was concerned with how forms of knowledge and forms of human subjectivity are constructed by specific institutions and practices.

Fouché, *n.* **Joseph, Duke of Otranto** (1759–1820), French politician. He was elected to the National Convention (the post-Revolutionary legislature), and organized the conspiracy which overthrew the Jacobin leader Robespierre. Napoleon employed him as police minister.

foudroyant, *a.* overwhelming, thundering or flashing, like lightning; (*Path.*) beginning in a sudden and intense form. [F, pres.p. of *foudroyer,* to strike with lightning, from *foudre,* ult. from L *fulgur,* lightning]

fougade, fougasse, *n.* (*Mil.*) a small mine for blowing up assailants or abandoned works. [F]

fought, *past, p.p.;* †**foughten,** *p.p.* FIGHT.

foul, *a.* dirty, filthy, unclean; loathsome, offensive to the senses; covered or filled with noxious matter, overgrown with weeds, clogged, choked; morally offensive, obscene, disgusting; polluted; unfair, unlawful, dishonest, against the rules; stormy, cloudy, rainy; of a proof, full of printer's errors, dirty, inaccurate; †unlucky, unfavourable; †coarse, gross; †unsightly, ugly. *adv.* irregularly, against the rules. *n.* foul weather or fortune; (*Sport*) a foul stroke; a wilful collision, an interference, any breach of the rules of a game or contest. *v.t.* to make foul; to defile, to soil, to pollute; to dishonour; to come into collision with, to impede, block or entangle; to commit a foul against. *v.i.* to become foul or dirty; to come into collision; to become clogged or entangled; to commit a foul. **to fall, run foul of,** to come or run against with force; to come into collision with; to quarrel with. **to foul up,** to make dirty, to pollute; to block, to entangle; to become blocked or entangled; (*coll.*) to blunder; (*coll.*) to spoil or cause to break down by making mistakes etc. **to hit, play foul,** to hit or deal with an opponent or competitor in a manner forbidden by the rules. †**foul-faced,** *a.* having a repulsive face. †**foul-feeding,** *a.* feeding on filthy food. **foul fish,** *n.* a fish in or just after the spawning season. **foul-mouthed, -spoken, -tongued,** *a.* addicted to profane, scurrilous or obscene language. **foul play,** *n.* unfair behaviour in a game or contest, a breach of the rules; dishonest or treacherous conduct; violence, murder. **foully,** *adv.* in a foul manner; abominably, treacherously, wickedly. **foulness,** *n.* [OE *fūl* (cp. Dut. *vuil,* Icel. *fūll,* G *faul,* also Gr. *puon,* stinking, L *pus,* see PUS) whence *fūlian,* to decay]

foulard, *n.* a soft, thin material of silk or silk mixed with cotton; a silk handkerchief. [F, etym. unknown]

†**foulder,** *v.i.* to flash or flame as lightning. [OF *fouldrer,* from *fouldre* (F *foudre*), ult. from L *fulgur,* lightning]

foumart, *n.* the polecat. [ME *fulmart, folmard,* OE *fūl,* FOUL, *mearth,* a marten]

found[1], *v.t.* to cast by melting (metal) or fusing (material for glass) and pouring it into a mould; to make of molten metal or glass. **founder**[1], *n.* one who casts metal. **founders'-dust,** *n.* charcoal powder and coal or coke dust ground fine for casting purposes. **founders'-sand,** *n.* a fine sand for making founding-moulds. **foundry,** *n.* a building where metals are cast; the act or art of casting metals. [F *fondre,* L *fundere,* to pour]

found[2], *v.t.* to lay the foundation or basis of; to fix firmly; to begin to erect or build; to set up, to establish; to endow; to originate; to give origin to; to conduct or base (on). *v.i.* to rest (on) as a foundation. **founder**[2], *n.* one who founds or originates anything, esp. one who endows a permanent fund for the support of an institution. **founder-member,** *n.* one of the original members who combined to establish a society etc. **founder's share,** *n.* a share of stock allotted to a promoter of a corporation as part payment for goodwill, plant etc. **foundership,** *n.* **founding,** *n., a.* **Founding Father,** *n.* a member of the American Constitutional Convention of 1787; one who establishes or institutes something. **foundress,** *n. fem.* [F *fonder,* L *fundāre,* from *fundus,* bottom, base]

found[3], *past, p.p.* FIND. **all found,** *adv.* with complete board and lodging.

foundation, *n.* the act of founding or establishing; that on which anything is established or by which it is sustained; permanent basis; the fund or endowment which supports an institution; the natural or artificial basis of a structure; (*pl.*) the part of a structure below the surface of the ground; the first set of stitches in crochet or knitting; the stiff fabric forming the basis of various articles of attire; a cosmetic used as a base for other facial make-up; the grounds, principles or basis on which anything stands; the reasons on which an opinion etc. is founded; that which is founded or endowed; an endowed institution. **foundation course,** *n.* a basic, general course, taught e.g. in the first year at some universities and colleges. **foundation garment,** *n.* a woman's undergarment that supports the figure, e.g. a corset. **foundation-muslin, -net,** *n.* openwork, gummed fabrics for stiffening dresses and bonnets. **foundation-school,** *n.* an endowed school. **foundation stone,** *n.* a stone laid with ceremony to commemorate the founding of a building. **foundationer,** *n.* one who derives support from the endowment of a college or school. **foundationless,** *a.* without foundation. [L *fundātio* (FOUND[2])]

founder[1,2] FOUND[1,2].

founder[3], *v.i.* (*Naut.*) to fill with water and sink, as a ship; of a horse, to fall lame; to fall in, to give way; to fail, to break down; to be ruined. *v.t.* to lame by causing soreness or inflammation in the feet of (a horse); to sink (a ship) by making her fill with water. *n.* inflammation of the sensitive parts of a horse's foot from overwork. †**founderous,** *a.* causing to founder; full of ruts and holes; puzzling, perplexing. [OF *fondrer,* to sink in, from *fond,* L *fundus,* the bottom]

foundling, *n.* a deserted child of unknown parents. **foundling hospital,** *n.* a charitable institution where deserted children are reared. [FOUND[3], -LING]

foundry FOUND[1].

fount[1], *n.* a spring, a fountain, a well; a source. †**fountful,** *a.* [F *font,* L *fons fontis*]

fount[2], *n.* a set of type of one face and size. [F *fonte,* from *fondre,* to FOUND[1]]

fountain, *n.* a spring of water, natural or artificial; the source of a river or stream; an ornamental jet of water driven high into the air by pressure; the structure for producing such a jet; a public structure with a drinking-supply; a reservoir to contain a liquid, as in a lamp, printing-press, fountain-pen etc.; a source, a first principle; (*Her.*) a roundel divided into six spaces by waved lines across the shield. **fountain-head,** *n.* an original source or spring. **fountain-pen,** *n.* a pen with an ink reservoir. **fountained,** *a.* (*esp. in comb.*) having fountains, as *many-fountained.* †**fountainless,** *a.* [OF *fontaine,* late L *fontāna,* L *fons fontis*]

Fountains Abbey, *n.* Cistercian abbey in North Yorkshire, England. It was founded in about 1132, and suppressed in 1540. The ruins were incorporated into a Romantic landscape garden (1720–40) with lake, formal water garden, temples, and a deer park.

Fouquet[1], *n.* **Jean** (*c.* 1420–81), French painter. He became court painter to Charles VIII in 1448 and to Louis XI in 1475. His *Melun diptych* (about 1450, Musées Royaux, Antwerp, and Staatliche Museen, Berlin), shows Italian Renaissance influence.

Fouquet[2], *n.* **Nicolas** (1615–80), French politician, a rival to Louis XIV's minister Colbert. Fouquet became *procureur général* of the Paris parliament in 1650 and *surintendant des finances* in 1651, responsible for raising funds for the long war against Spain, a post he held until arrested and imprisoned for embezzlement (at the instigation of Colbert, who succeeded him) from 1661 until his death.

four, *n.* the number or figure 4 or IV; the age of four; the fourth hour after midnight or midday; a set of four persons or things, a team of four horses, a four-oared boat or its crew; a card or domino with four spots; (*Cricket*) (a score of four runs from) a shot which crosses the boundary after hitting the ground; (*pl.*) (*Mil.*) a marching column four men wide. *a.* four in number; aged four. **carriage and four,** a carriage drawn by four horses. **four-foot way,** the space between the metals (actually 4ft 8½in., 1·435 m) on a railway. **four-in-hand,** *a.* drawn by four horses. *adv.* with four horses driven by one driver. *n.* a vehicle so drawn and driven. **four-letter word,** any of a number of short English words referring to the body, sex or excrement and considered vulgar or obscene. **the four seas,** those surrounding Great Britain on N, S, E and W. **to be, go, run on all fours,** to crawl on the hands and feet or knees; to agree precisely (with). **four-ale,** *n.* small ale, once sold at fourpence a quart. **four-ball** FOURSOME. **four-centred,** *a.* of an arch, having the curve described from four centres. **four-coupled,** *a.* of a locomotive, with two pairs of wheels coupled together. **four-course,** *n.* a four years' series of crops in rotation. **four-eyes,** *n.* (*sl.*) a person in spectacles. **four flush,** *n.* a worthless poker hand in which only four of the five cards are of the same suit. **four-**

flusher, *n.* (*N Am., sl.*) a bluffer. **four-footed,** *a.* having four feet; quadruped. **four-handed,** *a.* quadrumanous; of games, for four players; of music, for two performers. **four-horse,** *a.* drawn by four horses. †**four-inched,** *a.* four inches wide. **four-leaf, four-leaved,** *a.* applied to a clover leaf with four leaflets instead of three, supposed to bring good luck. **four-oar,** *a.* propelled by four oars. **four o'clock,** *n.* the Marvel of Peru, *Mirabilis dichotoma,* so named from its flowers opening at four o'clock in the afternoon. **fourpence,** *n.* the sum of four pennies. **fourpenny,** *n.* a old silver coin worth 4d. *a.*, worth fourpence; costing fourpence. **fourpenny one,** *n.* (*dated sl.*) a blow, a cuff. **four-post,** *a.* having four high posts at the corners to support a canopy and curtains. **four-poster,** *n.* a (usu. large) bedstead with these. **four-pounder,** *n.* a gun throwing a four-pound shot. **fourscore,** *n., a.* 4 times 20, 80; 80 years old. *n.* the number of 4 times 20. **four-square,** *a.* having four sides and angles equal; square-shaped; firmly established; immovable. **four-stroke,** *a.* (*Mach.*) term applied to an internal-combustion engine which fires once every four strokes of movement of the piston. **four-way,** *a.* allowing passage in any one of four directions. **four-wheel, -wheeled,** *a.* having four wheels. **four-wheel drive,** a system whereby power is transmitted to all four wheels of a motor vehicle. **four-wheeler,** *n.* a vehicle having four wheels, esp. a horse-drawn cab. **fourfold,** *a.* four times as many or as much, quadruple. *adv.* in fourfold measure. **foursome,** *a.* done by four persons. *n.* (*Golf*) a game between two pairs, the partners playing their ball alternately. [OE *fēower* (cp. Dan. *fire,* Dut. and G *vier,* W *pedwar,* L *quatuor,* Gr. *tessares*)]

fourchette, *n.* a fork-shaped piece between the fingers of gloves; (*Surg.*) a forked instrument formerly used for cutting the fraenum in tongue-tied infants. [F, dim. of *fourche,* L *furca,* FORK]

Fourdrinier machine, *n.* a papermaking machine, patented by the Fourdrinier brothers Henry and Sealy in England (1803). On the machine, liquid pulp flows onto a moving wire-mesh belt, and water drains and is sucked away, leaving a damp paper web. This is passed first through a series of steam-heated rollers, which dry it, and then between heavy calendar rollers, which give it a smooth finish. The machine can measure up to 90 m/300 ft in length, and is still in use.

fourgon, *n.* a French baggage-wagon. [F, etym. unknown]

Fourier[1], *n.* **François Charles Marie** (1772–1837), French socialist. In *Le Nouveau monde industriel/The New Industrial World* (1829–30), he advocated that society should be organized in self-sufficient cooperative units of about 1500 people. Conventional marriage was to be abandoned. **Fourierism,** *n.* a system of social reorganization advocated by Fourier, based on the principle of natural affinities. **Fourierist, -ite,** *n.*

Fourier[2], *n.* **Jean Baptiste Joseph** (1768–1830), French applied mathematician whose formulation of heat flow in 1807 contains the proposal that, with certain constraints, any mathematical function can be represented by trigonometrical series. This principle forms the basis of Fourier analysis, used today in many different fields of physics. His idea, not immediately well received, gained currency and is embodied in his *Théorie analytique de la chaleur/The Analytical Theory of Heat* (1822).

Four Noble Truths, in Buddhism, a summary of the basic concepts: life is suffering (Sanskrit *duhkha,* sour); suffering has its roots in desire (*trishna,* clinging or grasping); the cessation of desire is the end of suffering, *nirvana*; and this can be reached by the Noble Eightfold Path of *dharma* (truth).

fourteen, *n.* the number or figure 14 or XIV; the age of 14. *a.* 14 in number; aged 14. **fourteenth,** *n.* one of 14 equal parts; an interval of an octave and a seventh; a note separated from another by this interval, two such notes sounded together. *n., a.* (the) last of 14 (people, things etc.); (the) next after the 13th.

Fourteen Points, *n.pl.* the terms proposed by President Wilson of the US in his address to Congress 8 Jan. 1918, as a basis for the settlement of World War I that was about to reach its climax. The creation of the League of Nations was one of the points.

fourth, *n.* one of four equal parts, a quarter; the person or thing in fourth position; the fourth forward gear of a motor vehicle; (*Mus.*) an interval of four diatonic notes, comprising two whole tones and a semitone; two notes separated by this interval sounded together; (*pl.*) goods of fourth-rate quality. *n., a.* (the) last of four (people, things etc.); (the) next after the third. **Fourth of July,** see separate entry. **fourth estate,** *n.* the press. **fourth-rate,** *n.* formerly a 50- to 70-gun vessel, later a gunboat carrying from one to four guns. *a.* fourth best, as a grade of quality in various commodities; (*coll.*) mediocre, poor, inferior. **fourthly,** *adv.* in the fourth place.

Fourth of July, *n.* in the US, the anniversary of the day in 1776 when the Declaration of Independence was adopted by the Continental Congress. It is a public holiday, officially called Independence Day.

Fourth Republic, *n.* the French constitutional regime that was established between 1944 and 1946, and lasted until 4 Oct. 1958: from liberation after Nazi occupation during World War II to the introduction of a new constitution by Gen. de Gaulle.

†**fouter, -tre,** *n.* a coarse term of contempt, as in *a fouter for, not to care a fouter.* [OF *foutre,* L *futuere,* to have sexual intercourse]

fouth, *n.* (*Sc.*) fullness, plenty. [form of obs. *fulth* (cp. LENGTH)]

fovea, *n.* (*pl.* **-veae**) (*Anat. etc.*) a small pit or depression. **foveate,** *a.* [L]

foveola, *n.* (*Anat.*) a small depression. **foveolate, -lated,** *a.* [L, dim. of prec.]

fovilla, *n.* the matter contained in the pollen grain, the immediate agent in fertilization. [from *fov-,* root of L *fovēre,* to cherish, after *favilla*]

fowl, *n.* a bird; birds collectively; a cock or hen of the domestic or poultry kind; their flesh used as food. *v.i.* to hunt, catch or kill wild birds for sport. **barn-door fowl** BARN-DOOR. **fowling-piece,** *n.* a light smooth-bore gun adapted for shooting wild-fowl. **fowl-pest,** *n.* a contagious virus disease of birds. **fowl-run,** *n.* an enclosure in which domestic fowls can run about; a breeding-establishment for fowls. **fowler,** *n.* one who pursues wild-fowl for sport. [OE *fugol* (cp. Dut. *vogel,* G *Vogel,* Icel. and Dan. *fugl*), from Teut. *flug-,* to FLY]

Fowler[1], *n.* **Henry Watson** (1858–1933) and his brother **Francis George** (1870–1918), English scholars and authors of a number of English dictionaries. *Modern English Usage* (1926), the work of Henry Fowler, has become a classic reference work for advice on matters of style and disputed usage.

Fowler[2], *n.* **(Peter) Norman** (1938–), British Conservative politician. He was a junior minister in the Heath government, transport secretary in the first Thatcher administration in 1979, social services secretary in 1981, and was employment secretary (1987–89).

Fox[1], *n.* **Charles James** (1749–1806), English Whig politician. He entered Parliament in 1769 as a supporter of the court, but went over to the opposition in 1774. As secretary of state (1782), leader of the opposition to Pitt, and foreign secretary (1806), he welcomed the French Revolution and brought about the abolition of the slave trade.

Fox[2], *n.* **George** (1624–91), English founder of the Society of Friends. He became a travelling preacher in 1647, and in 1650 was imprisoned for blasphemy at Derby, where the name Quakers was first applied derogatorily to him and his followers, supposedly because he enjoined Judge Bennet to 'quake at the word of the Lord'.

fox, *n.* a quadruped, *Canis vulpes,* with a straight bushy tail, reddish-brown hair, and erect ears, notorious for its cunning, hunted in England for sport; a sly, cunning person. *v.t.* to baffle, to perplex; to trick, to outwit; to make sour, in fermenting; (*chiefly p.p.*) to discolour (pages of a book etc.); (*N Am.*) to repair (boots) by adding an outer covering over the upper; to intoxicate. *v.i.* to become sour, in fermenting; of paper etc., to become discoloured, esp. to turn reddish; †to be crafty. **fox-brush,** *n.* the tail of a fox. **fox-case,** *n.* the skin of a fox. **fox-earth, fox's earth,** *n.* the burrow of a fox. **fox-evil, fox's-evil,** *n.* a disease in which the hair falls off. **foxglove,** *n.* the genus *Digitalis,* esp. *D. purpurea,* with purple flowers resembling the fingers of a glove, the leaves of which are used as a sedative. **fox-hole,** *n.* (*Mil.*) a small trench. **foxhound,** *n.* a hound trained to hunt foxes. **foxhunt,** *n.* the chase of a fox. *v.i.* to hunt foxes with hounds. **foxhunter,** *n.* one who hunts foxes. **foxhunting,** *a.* pertaining to, or fond of hunting foxes. *n.* the act or practice of hunting foxes with a pack of hounds. **fox-shark,** *n.* the thresher, *Alopias vulpes,* a shark about 15 ft (4·5 m) long, with a long rough tail. **foxtail,** *n.* the tail of a fox; kinds of grasses, esp. *Alopercurus pratensis;* a club-moss, *Lycopodium clavatum;* the cinder obtained in the last stage of the charcoal process of refining iron. **fox-terrier,** *n.* a short-haired dog, orig. employed to unearth foxes, now chiefly as a pet. **fox-trap,** *n.* a snare to catch foxes. **fox-trot,** *n.* a kind of ballroom dance; short steps taken by a horse when changing its pace. **foxed,** *a.* stained with spots, as a book or print; (*sl.*) drunk. **fox-like,** *a.* †**fox-ship,** *n.* the character of a fox; artfulness. **foxy,** *a.* fox-like, tricky, crafty; foxed; (*chiefly N Am.*) physically attractive; reddish-brown in colour; (*Painting*) having too much of this colour, hot-coloured. **foxiness,** *n.* [OE (cp. Dut. *vos,* G *Fuchs*)]

Foxe, *n.* **John** (1516–87), English Protestant propagandist. He became a canon of Salisbury in 1563. His *Book of Martyrs* (1563) luridly described persecutions under Queen Mary, reinforcing popular hatred of Roman Catholicism.

foy, *n.* (*chiefly Sc.*) a parting entertainment given by one setting out on a journey. [MDut. (Dut. *fooi*), prob. from F *voie,* way, journey]

foyer, *n.* a large public room in a theatre; the entrance hall of a hotel; the crucible in a furnace to receive the molten metal. [F, from low L *focārum,* from *focus,* see FOCUS]

fozy, *a.* (*Sc.*) spongy, soft; (*fig.*) without backbone. **foziness,** *n.* [cp. LG *fussig*]

fp, (*abbr.*) fortepiano; freezing point.

FPA, (*abbr.*) Family Planning Association.

fps, (*abbr.*) feet per second; foot-pound-second; frames per second.

Fr[1], (*chem. symbol*) francium.

Fr.[2], (*abbr.*) Father; Franc; France; French; Friar.

Fr.[3], (*abbr.*) franc; from.

Fra, *n.* brother, a title given to an Italian monk or friar. [It., short for *frate,* from L *frater,* brother]

frab, *v.t.* (*dial.*) to worry. [onomat.]

fracas, *n.* (*pl.* **fracas**) a disturbance, a row; an uproar; a noisy quarrel. [F, from *fracasser,* It. *fracassare,* to break in pieces]

Fracastoro, *n.* **Girolamo** (*c.* 1478–1553), Italian physician known for his two medical books. He was born and worked mainly in Verona. His first book was written in verse, *Syphilis sive morbus gallicus/Syphilis or the French disease* (1530). It was one of the earliest texts on syphilis, a disease Fracastaro named. In a second work, *De contagione/On contagion* (1546), he wrote, far ahead of his time, about 'seeds of contagion'.

frack FRECK.

fractal, *n.* an irregular or fragmented figure or surface of a type unsuitable for conventional geometric representation. **fracted,** *a.* broken. **fractile,** *a.* liable to break; (*Geol.*) indicating breakage or cleavage. [L *fractus,* as foll.]

fraction, *n.* the act of breaking, esp. by violence; the state of being broken; a fragment, a small piece; (*Math.*) the expression of one or more parts of a unit; †dissension, a rupture; the rite of breaking the bread in the Eucharist. **fractional, -nary,** *a.* of or pertaining to fractions; constituting a fraction; forming but a small part, insignificant. **fractionally,** *adv.* **fractionate,** *v.t.* to separate (a mixture) into portions having different properties, by distillation or analogous process. **fractionation,** *n.* **fractionize, -ise,** *v.t.* to break up into fractions or divisions. [OF *fraccion,* from eccles. L *fractio -ōnem,* from *fractus,* p.p. of *frangere,* to break]

fractious, *a.* apt to quarrel; snappish, cross, fretful, peevish. **fractiously,** *adv.* **fractiousness,** *n.* [from prec., in the sense of dissension]

fracture, *n.* the act of breaking by violence; a break, a breakage; (*Min.*) the irregularity of surface produced by breaking a mineral across, as distinguished from splitting it along the planes of cleavage; the breakage of a bone (when only the bone is broken the fracture is called **simple,** when there is also a wound of the surrounding tissue it is termed **compound**). *v.t.* to break across; to separate the continuity of the parts of. *v.i.* to break or crack. [OF, from L *fractūra,* as FRACTION]

fraenum, frenum, *n.* (*pl.* **-na**) a band or ligament restraining the action of an organ, as that of the tongue. **fraenulum,** *n.* a small fraenum. [L, a bridle]

fragaria, *n.pl.* (*Bot.*) a genus of Rosaceae, consisting of the cultivated and wild strawberries. [L *frāga,* pl., strawberries]

fragile, *a.* brittle, easily broken; weak, frail, delicate. **fragility,** *n.* [F, from L *fragilis,* from *frag-,* root of *frangere,* to break]

fragment[1], *n.* a piece broken off; a small detached portion; an incomplete or unfinished portion; the surviving portion of a whole that has been destroyed; †a term of extreme contempt. **fragmental, -tary,** *a.* pertaining to or consisting of fragments; disconnected. **fragmentary rocks,** *n.pl.* (*Geol.*) rocks made up of fragments, as breccias, conglomerates etc. **fragmentally, fragmentarily,** *adv.* **fragmentariness,** *n.* [F, or directly from L *fragmentum,* as prec.]

fragment[2], *v.t.; v.i.* to (cause to) break into fragments.

fragmentation *n.* the breaking into fragments; (*Biol.*) the breaking-up of a chromosome. **fragmentation bomb,** *n.* a bomb whose casing is designed to shatter in small, deadly fragments on explosion. **fragmented,** *a.*

Fragonard, *n.* **Jean Honoré** (1732–1806), French painter, the leading exponent of the rococo style (along with his master Boucher). His light-hearted subjects include *The Swing* (about 1766, Wallace Collection, London).

fragrant, *a.* emitting a pleasant perfume, sweet-smelling, odorous. **fragrance,** *n.* a sweet smell; the particular scent of a perfume, toilet water etc. **fragrantly,** *adv.* [F, from L *frāgrans -ntem,* pres.p. of *frāgrāre,* to emit a perfume]

frail[1], *a.* fragile, delicate; infirm, in weak health; perishable; weak in character or resolution, liable to be led astray; (*euphem.*) unchaste. **frailish,** *a.* †**frailly,** *adv.* **frailness,** *n.* **frailty,** *n.* [OF *fraile,* L *fragilis,* FRAGILE]

frail[2], *n.* a rush basket used for packing figs etc.; a certain quantity of figs or raisins, about 75 lb (34 kg), contained in a frail. [OF *frayel, freël,* acc. to Skeat from earlier *fleël,* L *flagellum,* a whip, a vine-shoot]

fraise[1], *n.* a ruff; a horizontal or sloping palisade round a rampart; a tool for enlarging a drill-hole etc. [F, a ruff]

fraise[2], *n.* (*Sc., North.*) a commotion. [etym. doubtful]

framboesia, *n.* (*Path.*) the yaws, a contagious eruption characterized by swellings like raspberries. [F *framboise,* a raspberry]

Frame, *n.* **Janet** (pen name of Janet Paterson Frame Clutha) (1924–), New Zealand novelist. After being wrongly diagnosed as schizophrenic, she reflected her experiences (1945–54) in the novel *Faces in the Water* (1961) and the autobiographical *An Angel at My Table* (1984).

frame, *v.t.* to form or construct by fitting parts together; to fit, adapt or adjust; to contrive; to devise, to invent; to compose, to express; to plan, to arrange; to form in the mind, to conceive, imagine; to articulate, to form with the lips; to surround with a frame, to serve as a frame to; to (conspire to) incriminate; †to shape; †to direct (one's course); †to cause, bring about. *n.* a fabric or structure composed of parts fitted together; a structure or fabric of any kind; the skeleton of a structure; the rigid part of a bicycle; the construction, constitution or build of anything; the established order or system (of society or the body politic); disposition of mind; a case or border to enclose or surround a picture, a pane of glass etc.; (*Hort.*) a glazed portable structure for protecting plants from frost; various machines in the form of framework used in manufacturing, mining, building, printing etc.; a structure on which embroidery is worked; a single exposure on a film; a single, complete television picture; a wooden triangle used to set up the balls for a break in snooker etc.; the balls so arranged; a single round of a game of snooker etc.; a frame-up. **frame of reference,** a set of axes used to describe the location of a point; a set or system of standards, derived from an individual's experience, to which he or she refers when making judgments etc. **frame-aerial,** *n.* (*Radio*) an aerial consisting of wire wound on a frame. **frame-bridge,** *n.* a bridge constructed of timbers so as to combine the greatest strength with the least material. **frame-house,** *n.* a house with a wooden framework covered with boards. **frame-saw,** *n.* a flexible saw-blade stretched in a frame to stiffen it. **frame-up,** *n.* (*sl.*) an attempt to incriminate, a false criminal charge. **framework,** *n.* the frame of a structure; the fabric for enclosing or supporting anything, or forming the substructure to a more complete fabric; (*fig.*) structure, arrangement (of society etc.). **framer,** *n.* one who frames; a maker, a contriver. **frameless,** *a.* **framing,** *n.* a frame, framework; setting. **framing-chisel,** *n.* a heavy chisel used for making mortises. [OE *framian,* to avail, to further, from *fram,* adv., forward]

franc, *n.* the standard unit of currency in France, Belgium, Switzerland and various other countries; †a French gold coin of the 14th cent.; †a French silver coin first issued in 1575. [F, said to be from *Francorum Rex,* King of the Franks, the inscription on the earliest coins]

France, *n.* French Republic (*République Française*), country in W Europe, bounded NE by Belgium and West Germany, E by Switzerland and Italy, S by the Mediterranean, SW by Spain and Andorra, and W by the Atlantic ocean. **area** (including Corsica) 543,965 sq km/209,970 sq miles. **capital** Paris. **towns** Lyon, Lille, Bordeaux, Toulouse, Nantes, Strasbourg; ports Marseille, Nice. **physical** rivers Seine, Loire, Garonne, Rhône, Rhine; mountain ranges Alps, Massif Central, Pyrenees, Jura, Vosges, Cévennes. **territories** Guadeloupe, French Guiana, Martinique, Réunion, St Pierre and Miquelon, Southern and Antarctic Territories, New Caledonia, French Polynesia, Wallis and Futuna. **population** (1988 est.) 55,854,000 (including 4,500,000 immigrants, chiefly from Portugal, Algeria, Morocco, and Tunisia); annual growth rate 0.3%. **exports** fruit (especially apples), wine, cheese, cars, aircraft, chemicals, jewellery, silk, lace; tourism is very important. **language** French (regional languages include Breton). **religion** mainly Roman Catholic; Muslim 3 million, Protestant 750,000.

Franche-Comté, *n.* region of E France; area 16,200 sq km/6253 sq miles; population (1987) 1,086,000. Its capital is Besançon, and includes the *départements* of Doubs, Jura, Haute Saône, and Territoire de Belfort. In the mountainous Jura, there is farming and forestry, and elsewhere there are engineering and plastics industries.

franchise, *n.* a right, privilege, immunity or exemption granted to an individual or to a body; a licence to market a company's goods or services in a specified area; the district or territory to which a certain privilege or licence extends; citizenship; the right to vote; the qualification for this; †a sanctuary for persons liable to be arrested; †liberty. *v.t.* to grant a franchise to. **franchisee,** *n.* the holder of a franchise. †**franchisement,** *n.* **franchiser,** *n.* one having the elective franchise; one who grants a franchise. [OF, from *franchiss-,* stem of *franchir,* to free oneself, from *franc,* FRANK[2]]

Francis, François, two kings of France:

Francis I, *n.* (1494–1547), king of France from 1515. He succeeded his cousin Louis XII, and from 1519 European politics turned on the rivalry between him and the Holy Roman emperor Charles V, which led to war (1521–29, 1536–38, and 1542–44). In 1525 Francis was defeated and captured at Pavia, and released only after signing a humiliating treaty. At home, he developed absolute monarchy.

Francis II, *n.* (1544–60), king of France from 1559 when he succeeded his father, Henry II. He married Mary Queen of Scots in 1558. He was completely under the influence of his mother, Catherine de' Medici.

Francis II, *n.* (1768–1835), Holy Roman emperor (1792–1806). He became Francis I, Emperor of Austria in 1804, and abandoned the title of Holy Roman emperor in 1806. During his reign Austria was five times involved in war with France (1792–97, 1798–1801, 1805, 1809, and 1813–14). He succeeded his father Leopold II.

Franciscan, *a.* of or pertaining to St *Francis* of Assisi (1182–1226), or the order of mendicant friars founded by him in 1209. *n.* a member of the Franciscan order, a grey friar. [med. L *Franciscus,* Francis]

Francis Ferdinand, FRANZ FERDINAND.

Francis Joseph, FRANZ JOSEPH.

Francis of Assisi, St (1182–1226), Italian founder of the Roman Catholic Franciscan order of friars in 1209 and, with St Clare, of the Poor Clares in 1212. In 1224 he is said to have undergone a mystical experience during which he received the *stigmata* (five wounds of Jesus). Many stories are told of his ability to charm wild animals, and he is the patron saint of ecologists. His feast day is 4 Oct.

Francis of Sales, St (1567–1622), French bishop and theologian. He became bishop of Geneva in 1602, and in 1610 founded the order of the Visitation, an order of nuns. He is the patron saint of journalists and other writers. Feast day 24 Jan.

francium, *n.* a radioactive chemical element of the alkali metal group, at. no. 87; chem. symbol Fr. [mod. L, from *France*]

Franck[1], *n.* **César Auguste** (1822–90), Belgian composer. His music, mainly religious and Romantic in style, includes the Symphony in D minor (1866–68), *Symphonic Variations* (1885) for piano and orchestra, the Violin Sonata (1886), the oratorio *Les Béatitudes/The Beatitudes* (1879), and many organ pieces.

Franck[2], *n.* **James** (1882–1964), US physicist influential in atom technology. He was awarded the 1925 Nobel prize for his 1914 experiments on the energy transferred by colliding electrons to mercury atoms, showing that the transfer was governed by the rules of quantum theory.

Franco-, *comb. form* pertaining to the French. **Franco-German, -Prussian War,** see separate entry. **Franco-Chinese,** *a.* applied to a method of decorating pottery adopted by the French from the Chinese. **Francophile,** *n.* **Francophobe,** *n.* **Francophone,** *a.* French-speaking, having French as the native or an official language. [med. L *Francus,* FRANK[1]]

Franco (Bahamonde), *n.* **Francisco** (Paulino Hermenegildo Teódulo) (1892–1975), Spanish dictator from 1939. As a general, he led the insurgent Nationalists to victory in the Spanish Civil War (1936–39), supported by Fascist Italy and Nazi Germany, and established a dictatorship. In 1942 Franco reinstated the Cortes (Spanish parliament), which in 1947 passed an act by which he became head of state for life.

Franco-German entente, *n.* resumption of friendly relations between France and Germany, designed to erase the enmities of successive wars. It was initiated by the French president de Gaulle's visit to West Germany in 1962, followed by the Franco-German Treaty of Friendship and Cooperation of 1963.

François, FRANCIS.

francolin, *n.* a bird of the genus *Francolinus,* allied to the partridges, esp. *F. vulgaris,* a richly-coloured species common in India. [F, from It. *franco-lino*]

Franco-Prussian War, (1870–71), the Prussian chancellor Bismarck put forward a German candidate for the vacant Spanish throne with the deliberate, and successful, intention of provoking the French emperor Napoleon III into declaring war. The Prussians defeated the French at Sedan, then besieged Paris. The Treaty of Frankfurt in May 1871 gave Alsace, Lorraine, and a large French indemnity to Prussia. The war established Prussia, at the head of a unified Germany, as Europe's leading power.

franc-tireur, *n.* (*pl.* **francs-tireurs**) a French light-infantry soldier belonging to an irregular corps. [F, free-shooter (*franc,* FRANK[2], *tirer,* to shoot)]

frangible, *a.* that may be easily broken. **frangibleness, frangibility**, *n.* [late L *frangibilis,* from *frangere,* to break]

frangipane, frangipani, *n.* a kind of pastry made with cream, almonds and sugar; a perfume prepared from the flowers of *Plumiera rubra,* a W Indian tree. [prob. from the inventor of the perfume, the Marquis *Frangipani*]

Franglais, *n.* the French language when mixed with (usually unwelcome) elements of modern, especially American, English (for example a mineral water described as *le fast drink des Alpes*). [F Français, French and an*glais,* English]

†**franion,** *n.* a boon companion; a woman of loose character. [etym. doubtful]

Frank[1], *n.* a member of a Germanic people influential in Europe in the 3rd–8th centuries. Believed to have originated in Pomerania on the Baltic Sea, they had settled on the Rhine by the 3rd century, spread into the Roman Empire by the 4th century, and gradually conquered most of Gaul and Germany under the Merovingian and Carolingian dynasties. The kingdom of the W Franks became France, the kingdom of the E Franks became Germany. **Frankish,** *a.* [L *Francus,* OHG *Franko,* prob. from the name of a weapon (cp. OE *franca,* a javelin)]

Frank[2], *n.* **Anne** (1929–45), German diarist who fled to the Netherlands with her family in 1933 to escape Nazi anti-semitism. During the German occupation of Amsterdam, they remained in a sealed-off room (1942–44). Betrayal resulted in Anne's deportation and death in Belsen concentration camp. Her diary of her time in hiding was published in 1947.

Frank[3], *n.* **Ilya** (1908–), Russian physicist known for his work on radiation. In 1934, Cherenkov had noted a peculiar blue radiation sometimes emitted as electrons passed through water. It was left to Frank and his colleague at Moscow University, Igor Tamm, to realize that this form of radiation was produced by charged particles travelling faster through the medium than the speed of light in the same medium. Franck shared the 1958 Nobel physics prize with Cherenkov and Tamm.

frank[1], *a.* open, ingenuous, sincere, candid; generous, liberal, profuse, free, unrestrained; †licentious; (*Law*) free, privileged, exempt. *v.t.* to mark (a letter etc.) in such a way as to indicate that postage has been paid; to send or cause to be sent under an official privilege, such as, formerly, the signature of a member of Parliament, so as to pass free; to secure the free passage of (a person or thing). *n.* a signature authorizing a letter to go through the post free of charge; the right to send letters etc. in this manner; the letter or package thus sent. †**frankfee,** *n.* (*Law*) a tenure of land in fee-simple. †**frankfold,** *n.* liberty to fold sheep. **franking machine,** *n.* a machine that franks letters etc. †**frank-pledge,** *n.* the system by which freemen in a tithing were pledged for each other's good behaviour. †**frank-service,** *n.* service performed by freemen. †**frank-tenement,** *n.* (*Law*) an estate in freehold; freehold property. **frankly,** *adv.* **frankness,** *n.* [OF *franc,* low L *francus,* free, from prec.]

frank[2], *n.* a pigsty; an enclosure in which animals are fattened. *v.t.* to shut up in a frank; to fatten up; to feed high. [OF *franc*]

frankalmoign, *n.* (*Law*) a tenure by which a religious body holds lands with no obligations except such as prayers, almsgiving etc. [OF *franc,* FRANK[2], A-F *almoine,* OF *almosne* (F *aumône*), alms]

Frankenstein, *n.* (or, The Modern Prometheus) a Gothic horror story by Mary Shelley, published in England in 1818. Frankenstein, a scientist, discovers how to bring inanimate matter to life, and creates a man-monster. When Frankenstein fails to provide a mate to satisfy its human emotions, the monster seeks revenge by killing Frankenstein's brother and bride. Frankenstein dies in an attempt to destroy his creation.

Frankenthaler, *n.* **Helen** (1928–), US abstract expressionist painter, inventor of the colour-staining technique whereby the unprimed, absorbent canvas is stained or soaked with thinned-out paint, creating deep, soft veils of translucent colour.

Frankfurt-am-Main, *n.* city in Hessen, West Germany, 72 km/45 miles NE of Mannheim; population (1988) 592,000. It is a commercial and banking centre, with electrical and machine industries, and an inland port on the river Main. An international book fair is held annually.

Frankfurter, *n.* a small, smoked sausage of beef and pork. [short for G *Frankfurter Wurst,* a sausage made in Frankfurt am Main]

Frankfurt Parliament, *n.* an assembly of liberal politicians and intellectuals that met for a few months in 1848 in the aftermath of the revolutions of 1848 and the overthrow of monarchies in most of the German states. They discussed a constitution for a united Germany, but the restoration of the old order and the suppression of the revolutions ended the parliament.

frankincense, *n.* a gum or resin burning with a fragrant smell, used as incense; in the East, olibanum, an exudation from trees of the genus *Boswellia,* is used. [OF *franc encens*]

franking, *n.* (*Carp.*) the notching out a portion of a sash-bar for the passage of the transverse bar, to make a mitre-joint. **franking machine** FRANK[2]. [prob. from FRANK[2]]

franklin, *n.* in the 14th and 15th cents., an English freeholder, not liable to feudal service. [A-F *fraunclein,* low L *francus,* free, -LING]

Franklin[1], *n.* **Benjamin** (1706–90), US scientist and politician. He proved that lightning is a form of electricity by the experiment of flying a kite in a storm, distinguished between positive and negative electricity, and invented the lightning conductor. He helped to draft the Declaration of Independence and the US constitution, and was ambassador to France (1776–85).

Franklin[2], *n.* **John** (1786–1847), English naval explorer who took part in expeditions to Australia, the Arctic, and N Canada, and in 1845 commanded an expedition to look for the Northwest Passage, during which he and his crew perished.

Franklin[3], *n.* **Rosalind** (1920–58), English biophysicist whose research on X-ray diffraction of DNA crystals helped Francis Crick and James D. Watson to deduce the chemical structure of DNA.

frantic, *a.* raving, outrageously excited or demented; suffering from frenzy; marked by extreme haste or agitation. †*n.* one who is frantic; a lunatic. **frantically, -ticly,** *adv.* †**franticness,** *n.* [OF *frenetique,* late L *phrenēticus,* Gr. *phrenitikos,* from *phrenitis,* inflammation of the brain, from *phrēn,* brain]

Franz Ferdinand, Francis Ferdinand (1863–1914), archduke of Austria. He became heir to his uncle, Emperor Franz Joseph, from 1884 but while visiting Sarajevo on 28 June 1914, he and his wife were assassinated by Serbian nationalists. Austria used the episode to make unreasonable demands on Serbia that ultimately precipitated World War I.

Franz Joseph, Francis Joseph (1830–1916), emperor of Austria-Hungary from 1848, when his uncle, Ferdinand I, abdicated. After the suppression of the 1848 revolution, Franz Joseph tried to establish an absolute monarchy, but had to grant Austria a parliamentary constitution in 1861, and Hungary equality with Austria in 1867. He was defeated in the Italian War of 1859 and the Prussian War of 1866. In 1914 he made the assassination of his nephew, Franz Ferdinand, the excuse for attacking Serbia, precipitating World War I.

frap, *v.t.* (*past, p.p.* **frapped**) (*Naut.*) to draw together by ropes crossing each other, to secure and strengthen, to bind the end of a rope with string. [OF *fraper,* to strike]

frappé, *a.* iced. [F, p.p. of *frapper,* to strike, to ice]

Frasch process, *n.* a process used to extract underground deposits of sulphur. Superheated steam is piped to the sulphur deposit and melts it. Compressed air is then pumped down to force the molten sulphur to the surface. It was developed in the US in 1891 by German-born Herman Frasch (1851–1914).

Fraser¹, *n.* **Antonia** (1932–), English author of biographies, including *Mary Queen of Scots* (1969); historical works, such as *The Weaker Vessel* (1984); and a series of detective novels featuring investigator Jemima Shore.

Fraser², *n.* **(John) Malcolm** (1930–), Australian Liberal politician, prime minister (1975–83); nicknamed 'the Prefect' because of a supposed disregard of subordinates.

Fraser³, *n.* **Peter** (1884–1950), New Zealand Labour politician, born in Scotland. He held various cabinet posts (1935–40), and was prime minister (1940–49).

frass, *n.* excrement of larvae; refuse left by a wood-boring insect. [G *Frasz,* cogn. with *fressen,* to devour]

fratch, *v.i.* (*chiefly North.*) to quarrel; to worry. *n.* a quarrel. **fratchety, fratching, fratchy,** *a.* quarrelsome; irritable. [prob. onomat.]

frate, *n.* (*pl.* **frati**) a friar. [It., brother]

frater, *n.* a refectory in a monastery. [OF *fraitur,* short for *refreitor,* from low L *refectorium*]

fraternal, *a.* brotherly; pertaining to or becoming brethren; existing between brothers; of twins, from two separate ova. **fraternally,** *adv.* **fraternity,** *n.* the state of being a brother; brotherliness; a brotherhood, a body of men associated for a common interest or for religious purposes; a body of men associated or linked together by similarity of rank, profession, interests etc.; (*N Am.*) a college association of students. **fraternize, -ise,** *v.i.* to associate or hold fellowship with others of like occupation or tastes; to associate (with) on friendly terms. **fraternization, -isation,** *n.* **fraternizer, -iser,** *n.* [OF *fraternel,* late L *frāternālis,* L *frāternus,* from *frāter,* brother]

fratricide, *n.* the murder of a brother; one who murders a brother. **fratricidal,** *a.* [OF, from L *frātricīda* (*frāter,* brother, -CIDE)]

fratry, fratery, FRATER.

Frau, *n.* (*pl.* **Frauen**) a German woman, wife or widow; Mrs. **Fräulein,** *n.* (*pl.* **Fräulein**) a young lady, a German spinster; Miss; a German governess. [G]

fraud, *n.* an act or course of deception deliberately practised to gain unlawful or unfair advantage; (*Law*) such deception directed to the detriment of another; a deception, a trick, trickery; (*coll.*) a deceitful person, a humbug; †a plot, a snare. †*v.t.* to defraud. †**fraudful,** *a.* †**fraudfully,** *adv.* **fraudulence,** *n.* **fraudulent,** *a.* practising fraud; characterized by or containing fraud; intended to defraud, deceitful. **fraudulently,** *adv.* [OF *fraude,* L *fraudem,* nom. *fraus*]

fraught, *a.* freighted, laden, stored (with); involving, entailing, attended by, charged (with); tense, characterized by or inducing anxiety. †*n.* a cargo, a burden; (*Sc.*) a load, two pails (of water). [p.p. of obs. v. *fraught,* to load, from obs. n. *fraught,* cargo, from LG (see EFris. *fracht,* G *Fracht,* MDut. and MLG *vracht*), cp. FREIGHT]

Fraunhofer, *n.* **Joseph von** (1787–1826), German physicist who did important work in optics. The dark lines in the solar spectrum (Fraunhofer lines), which revealed the chemical composition of the sun's atmosphere, were accurately mapped by him.

fraxinella, *n.* kinds of rue or dittany, esp. *Dictamnus fraxinella* and *D. albus,* cultivated for their leaves and flowers. **Fraxinus,** *n.* a genus of deciduous trees containing the common ash etc. [dim. of L *fraxinus,* ash]

fray¹, *n.* an affray; a noisy quarrel, a brawl, a riot; a combat, a contest; †anxiety, fear. †*v.t.* to frighten; to drive away; to fight against. †*v.i.* to fight.

fray², *v.t.* to wear away by rubbing; to fret, to chafe; to make strained or irritated; †to rub. *v.i.* of a garment, cloth etc., to become rubbed or worn, esp. so as to become unravelled or ragged at the edges. †*n.* a fret or chafe in cloth; a sore place caused by rubbing. **fraying,** *n.* the velvet off a deer's horns. [OF *freier,* L *fricāre,* to rub]

Frazer, *n.* **James George** (1854–1941), Scottish anthropologist, author of *The Golden Bough* (1890), a pioneer study of the origins of religion and sociology on a comparative basis. It exerted considerable influence on writers such as T.S. Eliot and D.H. Lawrence, but by the standards of modern anthropology many of its methods and findings are unsound.

frazil, *n.* anchor-ice. [French-Canadian, perh. from F *fraisil,* cinders]

frazzle, *v.t.* to fray at the edge, to unravel; to reduce to a state of physical or nervous exhaustion. *v.i.* to be worn out, nervous. *n.* an exhausted state. **to beat, burn** etc. **to a frazzle,** to beat, burn etc. thoroughly. [from E dial. *fazle,* to fray]

freak, *n.* a sudden wanton whim or caprice; a humour, a vagary; an abnormal or deformed person or thing; an unconventional or eccentric person; an unrestrained enthusiast for something. *a.* highly unusual, abnormal, esp. in magnitude or intensity. *v.t.* (*usu. p.p.*) to variegate, to streak. **to freak (out),** (*coll.*) to (cause to) hallucinate; to (cause to) be in a highly emotional or excited state. **freakful,** *a.* **freakish,** *a.* whimsical; eccentric, unconventional; abnormal. **freakishly,** *adv.* **freakishness,** *n.* **freaky,** *a.* (*coll.*) freakish. [etym. doubtful (perh. conn. with OE *frec,* bold, rash, or *frīcian,* to dance)]

freck, frack, *a.* (*Sc.*) eager, ready, prompt, lusty. [OE *frec,* greedy, bold (cp. Icel. *frekr,* Swed. *frach,* G *frech*)]

freckle, *n.* a yellowish or light-brown spot on the skin, due to sunburn or other causes; any small spot or discoloration. *v.t.* to mark with freckles. *v.i.* to become marked with freckles. **freckling,** *n.* marking with freckles; a mark like a freckle. **freckly,** *a.* [earlier *frecken*]

Frederick IX, *n.* (1899–1972), king of Denmark from 1947. He was succeeded by his daughter who became Queen Margrethe II.

Frederick V, *n.* (known as **the Winter King**) (1596–1632), elector palatine of the Rhine (1610–23) and king of Bohemia from 1619–20 (for one winter, hence the name 'winter king'), having been chosen by the Protestant Bohemians as ruler after the deposition of Catholic emperor Ferdinand II. His selection was the cause of the Thirty Years' War. Frederick was defeated at the Battle of the White Mountain, near Prague, in Nov. 1620 by the army of the Catholic League, and fled to Holland. He was the son-in-law of James I of England.

Frederick, *n.pl.* two Holy Roman emperors:

Frederick I, *n.* (*c.* 1123–90), Holy Roman emperor from 1152, known as *Barbarossa* 'red-beard'. Originally duke of Swabia, he was elected emperor in 1152, and was engaged in a struggle with Pope Alexander III (1159–77), which ended in his submission; the Lombard cities, headed by Milan, took advantage of this to establish their independence of imperial control. Frederick joined the Third Crusade, and was drowned in Anatolia.

Frederick II, *n.* (1194–1250), Holy Roman emperor from his election in 1212, called 'the Wonder of the World'. He led a crusade (1228–29) that recovered Jerusalem by treaty without fighting. He quarrelled with the pope, who excommunicated him three times, and a feud began which lasted at intervals until the end of his reign. Frederick, who was a complete sceptic in religion, is often considered the most cultured man of his age.

Frederick, *n.pl.* three kings of Prussia, including:

Frederick II, *n.* **the Great** (1712–86), king of Prussia from 1740, when he succeeded his father Frederick William I. In that year he started the War of the Austrian Succession by his attack on Austria. In the peace of 1745 he secured Silesia. The struggle was renewed in the Seven Years' War (1756–63). He acquired West Prussia in the first partition of Poland in 1772, and left Prussia as Germany's foremost state. He was an efficient and just ruler in the spirit of the Enlightenment, and a patron of the arts.

Frederick III, *n.* (1831–88), king of Prussia and emperor of Germany in 1888. The son of Wilhelm I, he married the eldest daughter (Victoria) of Queen Victoria of the UK in 1858, and, as a liberal, frequently opposed Chancellor Bismarck. He died three months after his accession.

Frederick William, *n.* (1620–88), elector of Brandenburg from 1640, 'the Great Elector'. By successful wars against Sweden and Poland, he prepared the way for Prussian power in the 18th century.

Frederick William, *n.* four kings of Prussia:

Frederick William I, *n.* (1688–1740), king of Prussia from 1713, who developed Prussia's military might and commerce.

Frederick William II, *n.* (1744–97), king of Prussia from 1786. He was a nephew of Frederick II, but had little of his relative's military skill. He was unsuccessful in waging war on the French (1792–95), and lost all Prussia west of the Rhine.

Frederick William III, *n.* (1770–1840), king of Prussia from 1797. He was defeated by Napoleon (1806), but contributed to his final overthrow (1813–15), and profited in territory allotted at the Congress of Vienna.

Frederick William IV, *n.* (1795–1861), king of Prussia from 1840. He upheld the principle of the divine right of kings, but was forced to grant a constitution in 1850 after the Prussian revolution of 1848. He suffered two strokes in 1857, and became mentally debilitated.

Fredericton, *n.* capital of New Brunswick, Canada, on the St John river; population (1986) 44,000. It was formerly known as St Anne's Point, and in 1785 was named after Prince Frederick, second son of George III.

free[1], *a.* (*comp.* **freer**, *superl.* **freest**) at liberty; not in bondage or under restraint; living under a government based on the consent of the citizens; of a government, not arbitrary or despotic; of a State, not under foreign domination; released from authority or control; not confined, restricted, checked or impeded; at liberty to choose or act, permitted (to do); independent, unattached, unconnected with the State; released, clear, exempt (from); unconstrained, not bound or limited (by rules, conventions etc.); of a translation, not literal; unconventional, unceremonious, careless, reckless; forward, impudent; indelicate, broad; unreserved, frank, ingenuous; admitted to or invested with certain privileges (of); not subject to (charges, duties, fees etc.); without restriction, open, gratuitous; liberal, generous; spontaneous, unforced; unoccupied, vacant; clear, unobstructed; not busy, having no obligations or commitments; not fixed or joined; (*Chem.*) not combined with another body; (*Zool.*) unattached; (*Bot.*) not adhering, not adnate. *adv.* freely; without cost or charge; (*Naut.*) not close-hauled. **for free,** (*coll.*) gratis, for nothing. **free alongside ship,** delivered free on the dock or wharf. **free-and-easy,** *a.* unconstrained, unceremonious; careless. *n.* an unceremonious kind of social gathering or other entertainment. **free collective bargaining,** negotiations between trade unions and employers unhampered by government guidelines or legal restraints. **free-for-all,** *n.* a free fight, a disorganized brawl or argument. **free on board,** of goods, delivered on board or into conveyance free of charge. **to make free,** to take liberties (with). **free agency,** *n.* the state of acting freely, or without constraint upon the will. **free agent,** *n.* one who is free to act according to his/her own opinions and wishes. **free alms** FRANKALMOIGN. **free arts** LIBERAL ARTS under LIBERAL. **free association,** *n.* (*Psych.*) the bringing to consciousness of unconscious processes through words and ideas which the subject spontaneously associates with key words provided by a psychoanalyst. **free-base,** *v.t., v.i.* (*sl.*) to purify (cocaine); to smoke (cocaine) so purified. **free bench,** *n.* (*Law*) a widow's dower in a copyhold. **free-board,** *n.* the space between the water-line on a vessel and the upper side of the deck, or the uppermost full deck. **free-born,** *a.* born free; inheriting the right and liberty of a citizen. **Free Church,** *n.* see separate entry. **Free Churchism,** *n.* **free city, town,** *n.* a city or town of the German Empire, independent in its government and franchise, and virtually forming an independent State. **freedman** FREE[2]. **free enterprise,** *n.* the conduct of business without state interference or control. **free fall,** *n.* the motion of an unrestrained or unpropelled body in a gravitational field; the part of a parachute jump before the parachute opens; a rapid and sudden fall in share prices etc. **free fight,** *n.* a fight in which anyone can join. **free flight,** *n.* the flight of a rocket etc. when its motor has ceased to produce thrust. **free-floating,** *a.* unattached, having no specific object, uncommitted. †**free-footed,** *a.* unrestrained. **free hand,** *n.* (to be given) complete freedom to do. **free-hand,** *a.* (*Drawing*) executed by the hand without the aid of instruments. **free-handed,** *a.* open-handed, liberal. **free-hearted,** *a.* frank, open, unreserved; liberal. **free-heartedly,** *adv.* **free-heartedness,** *n.* **free house,** *n.* a public-house free to buy its goods from any supplier. **free kick,** *n.* (*Football*) a kick with which an opponent may not interfere, awarded for a foul or infringement by the other side. **free labour,** *n.* labour performed by freemen, not slaves; workers not belonging to trade unions. **free-labourer,** *n.* **freelance,** *n.* (*Hist.*) a member of one of the free companies of mercenaries in the Middle Ages; (also **freelancer**) a self-employed person hired by others for specific (usu. short-term) assignments. *a., adv.* not bound to a particular employer. *v.i.* to work freelance. **free-liver,** *n.* one who indulges his or her appetites, esp. at table; (*Biol.*) an organism which is neither parasitic nor symbiotic. **free-living,** *n., a.* **freeload,** *v.i.* (*coll.*) to sponge, to live at another's expense. **freeloader,** *n.* **free love,** *n.* sexual intercourse without marriage; the doctrine that the affections should be free to fix on any object to which they are drawn, without restraint of marriage obligation. **free lover,** *n.* one who advocates or practises free love. **free man** FREEMAN (below). **free market,** *n.* an economic market in which there is free competition. †**free-minded,** *a.* having the mind free from care, trouble or perplexity. **free pass,** *n.* a ticket that has not been paid for, entitling the holder to travel or to enter an exhibition, theatre etc. **free port,** *n.* a port where ships of all nations may load or unload free of duty. **free radical,** *n.* an atom, or group of atoms, containing at least one unpaired electron. **free-range,** *a.* kept or produced in natural conditions. **free school,** *n.* a school where no fees are charged. **free selection,** *n.* (*Austral.*) the legal right to select Crown lands, those who did so being termed 'selectors'. **free-sheet,** *n.* a newspaper distributed free. **free ship,** *n.* a neutral ship, free from liability to capture. **free skating,** *n.* that part of a figure-skating competition in which the competitors have partial or complete freedom to organize their programmes. **free soil,** *a.* (*Hist.*) applied to the principles of a party in the US who advocated the non-extension of slavery. **free-soiler,** *n.* **free-soilism,** *n.* **free-spoken,** *a.* speaking without reserve; blunt, candid, frank. **free-spokenness,** *n.* **free-standing,** *a.* not attached to, supported by or integrated with other objects. **Free States,** *n.pl.* those States of the American Union in which slavery never existed, or was abolished before the Civil War. **free-stone,** *n.* a stone which can be cut freely in any direction. **free-stone,** *n.* a kind of peach easily freed from its stone when ripe. **freestyle,** *n.* a (swimming) race in which each competitor can choose which style to use; all-in wrestling. **free-thinker,** *n.* a rationalist, sceptic or agnostic; one who rejects authority in religious belief. **free-thinking,** *n., a.* **free-thought,** *n.* **free-tongued,** *a.* free-spoken. **free town** FREE CITY. **free trade,** *n.* the liberty of unrestricted trade with other countries; free interchange of commodities without protection by customs duties. **free-trader,** *n.* one who advocates free trade; †a smuggler. **free verse,** *n.* unrhymed verse with no set metrical pattern. **free vote,** *n.* a vote left to the individual's choice, free from party discipline. **free-warren,** *n.* a royal franchise or exclusive right of killing beasts and fowls of warren within certain limits. **freeway,** *n.* (*N Am.*) a motorway; a toll-free highway. **free-wheel,** *n.* a driving wheel on a cycle that can be disconnected from the driving gear and allowed to revolve while the pedals are at rest; a cycle with such a wheel. *v.i.* to run down a hill (on a cycle or motor-car) without employing locomotive power or brakes; to move or live in an unconstrained or irresponsible fashion. **freewheeling,** *n. a.* **free will,** *n.* the power of directing one's own actions without constraint by any external influence; voluntariness, spontaneity. **free-will,** *a.* given freely, voluntary. **free-wind,** *n.* (*Naut.*) a fair wind. **Free World,** *n.* the non-Communist countries collectively. **freely,** *adv.* **freeness,** *n.* [OE *frēo* (cp. Dut. *vrij,* G *frei,* cogn. with Sansk. *priya,* beloved)]

free[2], *v.t.* to set at liberty, to emancipate; to rid or relieve (of or from); to extricate, to clear, to disentangle; †to remove; †to acquit; †to frank. **freedman,** *n.* a manumitted slave. [from prec.]

-free, *comb. form* free from, not containing.

freebie, *n.* (*coll.*) something for which one does not have to pay. [from *freeby,* obs. sl., gratis]

freebooter, *n.* a pirate or buccaneer, an adventurer who makes a business of plundering. **freeboot,** *v.i.* **freebootery,** *n.* **freebooting,** *a.* [Dut. *vrijbuiter,* from *vrijbuit* (FREE[1], BOOTY)]

Free Church, *n.* the Protestant denominations in England and Wales that are not part of the Church of England; for example, the Methodist Church, Baptist Union, and United Reformed Church (Congregational and Presbyterian). These churches joined for common action in the Free Church Federal Council in 1940.

Free Church of Scotland, *n.* the body of Scottish Presbyterians who seceded from the Established Church of Scotland in the Disruption of 1843. In 1900 all but a small section that retains the old name, and is known as the Wee Frees, combined with the United Presbyterian Church to form the United Free Church, which reunited with the Church of Scotland in 1929.

freedom, *n.* the state of being free, liberty, independence; personal liberty, non-slavery, civil liberty; liberty of action, free will; exemption, immunity (from); lack of conventionality, frankness, excessive familiarity; violation of the rules of good breeding, a liberty; ease or facility in doing anything; participation in certain privileges, exemptions, and immunities pertaining to citizenship of a city or membership of a company; free use (of); †a free, unconditional grant; †liberality, generosity. **freedom fighter,** *n.* one who fights (esp. as an irregular soldier) for the liberation of a nation etc. from foreign rule or a tyrannical regime. †**freedomless,** *a.* [OE *frēodōm* (as FREE[1], -DOM)]

Freedom, Presidential Medal of, the highest peacetime civilian honour in the US. Instituted by President Kennedy in 1963, it is awarded to those 'who contribute significantly to the quality of American life'. A list of recipients is published each Independence Day and often includes unknown individuals as well as artists, performers, and statesmen.

Free French, *n.* in World War II, movement formed by Gen. de Gaulle in the UK in June 1940, consisting of French soldiers who continued to fight against the Axis after the Franco-German armistice. They took part in campaigns in Africa, the Middle East, Italy, France, and Germany. Their emblem was the Cross of Lorraine, a cross with two bars.

freehold, *n.* an estate held in fee-simple or fee-tail; the tenure by which such an estate is held; also applied to an office held for life. *a.* held in fee-simple or fee-tail; of the nature of a freehold. **freeholder,** *n.* the possessor of a freehold.

freeman, *n.* one not a slave or serf; one who holds the franchise of a citizen or a particular privilege, esp. the freedom of a city, company etc. **freewoman,** *n. fem.*

freemartin, *n.* a sexually imperfect cow, usu. born as twin with a bull-calf. [etym. unknown]

Freemason, *n.* a member of an association of 'Free and Accepted Masons', a secret order or fraternity, stated to have been traced back to the building of Solomon's Temple, but probably originating as a fraternity of skilled masons, with right of free movement, about the 14th cent. **Freemasonry,** *n.* the beliefs and practices of a group of linked national organizations open to men over the age of 21, united by the possession of a common code of morals and certain traditional 'secrets'. Modern Freemasonry began in 18th-century Europe. Freemasons do much charitable work, but have been criticized in recent years for their secrecy, their male exclusivity, and particularly their alleged use of influence within and between organizations (for example, the police or local government) to further each other's interests. There are approximately 6 million members.

freesia, *n.* any of a S African genus of bulbous flowering plants allied to the iris. [etym. unknown]

Freetown, *n.* capital of Sierra Leone, W Africa; population (1988) 470,000. It has a naval station and a harbour. Industries include cement, plastics, footwear, and oil refining. Platinum, chromite, diamonds, and gold are traded.

freeze, *v.i.* (*past,* **froze,** *p.p.* **frozen**) to be turned from a fluid to a solid state by cold; (*impers.*) to be at that degree of cold at which water turns to ice or becomes covered with ice; to become clogged by ice; to become attached (to) or fastened (together) by frost; to feel very cold; to die of cold; to be chilled (by fear); to become motionless or paralysed. *v.t.* to congeal by cold; to form ice upon or convert into ice; to injure, overpower or kill with cold; to preserve (food) by freezing and storing at a temperature below 32° F or 0° C; to chill with fear; to anaesthetize (as if) by cold; to render motionless or paralysed; to stop at a particular stage or state; to stop (a moving film) at a particular frame; (*Finance*) to prohibit the use of or dealings in; to fix or stabilize (prices etc.). *n.* the act or state of freezing; a frost. **to freeze on to,** (*sl.*) to seize or hold tightly. **to freeze out,** (*coll.*) to compel the retirement of from business, competition, society etc., by boycotting, contemptuous treatment or similar methods. **freeze-dry,** *v.t.* to dehydrate while in a frozen state in a vacuum, esp. for preservation. **freeze-frame,** *n.* a single frame of a film repeated to give the effect of a still photograph; a single frame of a video recording viewed as a still. **freezer,** *n.* an apparatus for freezing (meat etc.), a room or cabinet, or a compartment in a refrigerator for the long-term storage of perishable foodstuffs; (*Austral.*) a sheep bred for export as frozen lamb or mutton. **freezing,** *a.* very cold; distant, chilling. **freezing-mixture,** *n.* a mixture of salt and snow, or pounded ice, or a combination of chemicals with or without ice, for producing intense cold. **freezing-point,** *n.* the point at which water freezes, marked 32° on the Fahrenheit scale, and 0° on the Centigrade (Celsius) and Réaumur scales; the temperature at which a substance freezes. **freezingly,** *adv.* **frozenly,** *adv.* **frozenness,** *n.* [OE *frēosan* (cp. Dut. *vriezen,* G *frieren,* also L *pruīna,* hoar-frost)]

Frege, *n.* **Gottlob** (1848–1925), German philosopher. The founder of modern mathematical logic, he published *Die Grundlagen der Arithmetik/The Foundations of Arithmetic* (1884), which was to influence Russell and Wittgenstein.

freight, *n.* the money due or paid for the transportation of goods, esp. by water; that with which a ship is loaded; a cargo; ordinary transportation, as distinct from express; a goods train. *v.t.* to load (a ship) with goods for transportation; to hire or charter for this purpose; to load, †to fill. **freight-car,** *n.* (*N Am.*) a railway car for goods, distinguished from a *passenger-car.* **freightliner,** *n.* a train designed for the rapid transportation of containerized cargo. **freight-note,** *n.* a statement supplied to ship-owners by dock authorities giving weights, measurements etc. of cargo. **freight train,** *n.* (*N Am.*) a goods train. **freightage,** *n.* money paid for the hire of a ship or the transportation of goods; the transporting of goods; freight. **freighter,** *n.* one who hires or loads a ship; a cargo-boat; one who sends goods by railway; one who contracts to receive and forward goods. **freightless,** *a.* [cp. MDut. *vrecht, vracht,* OF *fret,* OHG *frēht,* see also FRAUGHT]

freit, *n.* (*Sc.*) an omen, a charm; superstition. **freity,** *a.* [cp. Icel. *frett,* news, OE *freht,* an oracle]

Frelimo, *n.* (*Fr*ont for th*e Li*beration of *Mo*zambique) nationalist group aimed at gaining independence for Mozambique from the occupying Portuguese. It began operating out of S Tanzania in 1963, and continued until victory in 1975.

fremescent, *a.* noisy, tumultuous, riotous. **fremescence,** *n.* [L *fremere,* to roar (as if from pres.p. of a freq. form)]

fremitus, *n.* (*Path.*) a movement or vibration perceptible externally, as on the walls of the chest when a patient speaks. [L, a roaring from *fremere,* to roar]

Frémont, *n.* **John Charles** (1813–90), US explorer and politician who travelled extensively throughout the western US. He surveyed much of the territory between the Mississippi River and the coast of California with the aim of establishing an overland route E–W across the continent. In 1842 he crossed the Rocky Mountains, climbing a peak that is named after him.

French, *a.* pertaining to France or its inhabitants; belonging to or native to France. *n.* the language spoken by the people of France, see separate entry; (*collect.*) the people of France. **excuse, pardon, my French,** excuse my bad language. **to take French leave,** to go away or do a thing without permission. **French-bean,** *n.* the kidney or haricot bean, *Phaseolus vulgaris.* **French bread,** *n.* crusty white bread in thin, long loaves. **French Canadian,** *n.* a French-speaking Canadian. *a.* of the French-speaking part of Canada or its people. **French chalk,** *n.* a variety of talc, steatite, or soapstone used for marking cloth, and in powder as a dry lubricant for tight boots, etc. **French curve,** *n.* an instrument designed to assist in drawing curved lines. **French dressing,** *n.* a salad dressing made of oil and vinegar or lemon juice with seasoning. **French fries,** (*orig. esp. N Am.*) (potato) chips. **French grey,** *n.* a tint composed of white with ivory-black, Indian red and Chinese blue. **French horn,** *n.* a metal wind instrument of circular shape with a gradual taper from the mouthpiece to a large everted bell. **French kiss,** *n.* a kiss in which the tongue is inserted into the partner's mouth. **French knickers,** *n.pl.* wide-legged knickers. **French letter,** *n.* (*coll.*) a contraceptive sheath, a condom. **Frenchman,** *n.* a native or naturalized inhabitant of France; a French ship. **French mustard,** *n.* a type of mustard mixed with vinegar etc. **French polish,** *n.* a solution of resin or gum-resin in alcohol or wood naphtha, for polishing cabinet-work etc.; the polish produced. *v.t.* to polish with this. **French polisher,** *n.* **French-roll,** *n.* a light kind of fancy bread. **French roof,** *n.* a mansard roof or one having portions of two different pitches. **French seam,** *n.* a double seam, stitched first on the wrong, then on the right side, so that the edges are invisible. **French white,** *n.* finely pulverized talc. **French window,** *n.* (*often pl.*) a pair of doors with full-length glazing. **Frenchwoman,** *n.* a woman native of or naturalized in France. **Frenchify,** *v.t.* to make French; to influence with French tastes or manners. **Frenchification,** *n.* **Frenchless,** *a.* not knowing French. **Frenchlike,** *a.* [OE *Frencisc* (FRANK[1], -ISH)]

French art, *n.* painting and sculpture of France. A number of influential styles have emerged in France over the centuries, from gothic in the Middle Ages to impressionism, cubism, surrealism, and others.

French Community, *n.* former association consisting of France and those overseas territories joined with it by the constitution of the Fifth Republic, following the 1958 referendum. Many of the constituent states withdrew during the 1960s, and it no longer formally exists, but in practice all former French colonies have close economic and cultural as well as linguistic links with France.

French Guiana, *n.* (French **Guyane Française**), French overseas department from 1946, and administrative region from 1974, on the N coast of South America, bounded to the W by Suriname and to the E and S by Brazil. **area** 83,500 sq km/32,230 sq miles. **capital** Cayenne. **towns** St Laurent. **population** (1987) 89,000. **exports** timber, shrimps, gold. **language** 90% Creole, French, Amerindian.

French horn, *n.* musical instrument. See under FRENCH.

French India, *n.* former French possessions in India: Pondicherry, Chandernagore, Karaikal, Mahé, and Yanaon (Yanam). They were all transferred to India by 1954.

French language, *n.* a member of the Romance branch of the Indo-European language family, spoken in France, Belgium, Luxembourg, and Switzerland in Europe, Canada (especially the province of Québec) in North America, and various Caribbean and Pacific Islands (overseas territories such as Martinique and French Guiana), as well as certain N and W African countries (for example, Mali and Senegal).

French Polynesia, *n.* French Overseas Territory in the S Pacific, consisting of five archipelagoes: Windward Islands, Leeward Islands (the two island groups comprising the Society Islands), Tuamotu Archipelago (including Gambier Islands), Tubuai Islands, and Marquesas Islands. **total area** 3940 sq km/1521 sq miles. **capital** Papeete on Tahiti. **exports** cultivated pearls, coconut oil, vanilla; tourism is important. **population** (1987) 185,000. **languages** Tahitian (official), French.

French Revolution, *n.* the period from 1789–1795 which saw the end of the monarchy and its claim to absolute rule. On 5 May 1789, after the monarchy had attempted to increase taxation and control of affairs, the States General (three 'estates' of nobles, clergy, and commons) met at Versailles to try to establish some constitutional controls. Divisions within the States General led to the formation of a National Assembly by the third (commons) estate on 17 June. Repressive measures by Louis XVI led to the storming of the Bastille by the Paris mob on 14 July 1789. On 20 June 1791 the royal family attempted to escape from the control of the Assembly, but Louis XVI was brought back a prisoner from Varennes and forced to accept a new constitution. War with Austria after 20 Apr. 1792 threatened to undermine the revolution, but on 10 Aug. the mob stormed the royal palace, and on 21 Sept. the First French Republic was proclaimed. On 21 Jan. 1793 Louis XVI was executed. The moderate Girondins were overthrown on 2 June by the Jacobins, and control of the country was passed to the infamous Committee of Public Safety, and Robespierre. The mass executions of the Reign of Terror began on 5 Sept., and the excesses led to the overthrow of the Committee and Robespierre on 27 July 1794 (9 Thermidor under the Revolutionary calendar). The Directory was established to hold a middle course between royalism and Jacobinism. It ruled until Napoleon seized power in 1799.

French revolutionary calendar, in the French Revolution 1789 became initially known as the 1st Year of Liberty. When monarchy was abolished on 21 Sept. 1792, the 4th year became 1st Year of the Republic. This calendar was formally adopted in Oct. 1793 but its usage was backdated to 22 Sept. 1793 which became 1 Vendémiaire. The calendar was discarded as from 1 Jan. 1806.

French Sudan, MALI.

French West Africa, *n.* group of French colonies administered from Dakar (1895–1958). They have become the modern Senegal, Mauritania, Sudan, Burkina Faso, Guinea, Niger, Ivory Coast, and Benin.

frenetic (*esp. formerly*) **phrenetic**, *a.* frantic, frenzied. **frenetically,** *adv.* [ME and OF *frenetike,* L *freneticus,* Gr. *phrenitikos,* see FRANTIC]

†**frenne,** †**fren**, *a.* strange. *n.* a foreigner; an enemy. [corr. of FREMD]

frenum FRAENUM.

frenzy, *n.* delirium, madness; temporary mental derangement; a violent access of mania, delirium or unnatural excitement; extravagant folly. †*a.* mad, frantic. *v.t.* (*usu. p.p.*) to drive to madness; to infuriate. †**frenzical,** *a.* **frenzied,** *a.* **frenziedly,** *adv.* [OF *frenesie,* late L and late Gr. *phrenēsis,* Gr. *phrenitis,* inflammation of the brain (cp. FRANTIC)]

freq., (*abbr.*) frequent, frequently, frequentative.

frequence, -ency, *n.* the quality of occurring frequently; common occurrence; repetition at short intervals; rate of occurrence; the comparative number of occurrences in a given time; (*Statistics*) the number or proportion of individuals in a single class; (*Elec.*) a term referring to the speed of variations of alternating currents, alternating electromotive forces, and electromagnetic waves; (*Phys.*) rate of repetition or recurrence; †a throng. **high frequency** HIGH. **frequency distortion,** *n.* (*Radio*) the phenomenon when amplitude of modulation varies with frequency. **frequency distribution,** *n.* (*Statistics*) an arrangement of data which shows the frequency of occurrence of the different values of a variable. **frequency modulation,** *n.* (*Radio*) the varying of the frequency of the carrier wave in accordance with the frequency of speech or music, for example; the broadcasting system using this. [as foll.]

frequent[1], *a.* occurring often, common; repeated at short intervals; occurring near together, abundant; †crowded, thronging; †currently reported. **frequentative,** *n., a.* (*Gram.*) (a verb) expressing frequent repetition of an action. **frequently,** *adv.* often, commonly, at frequent intervals; †populously. **frequentness,** *n.* [L *frequens, -ntem,* pres.p. of lost v. *frequēre,* allied to *farcīre,* to cram, see FARCE[1]]

frequent[2], *v.t.* to visit or resort to often or habitually. **frequentage, frequentation**, *n.* **frequenter,** *n.*

Frere, *n.* **John** (1740–1807), English archaeologist, high sheriff of Suffolk and Member of Parliament for Norwich. He discovered Palaeolithic tools at Hoxne, Suffolk, in 1790 and suggested that they predated the conventional biblical timescale.

fresco, *n.* (*pl.* **-cos, -coes**) a kind of water-colour painting on fresh plaster or on a wall covered with mortar not quite dry. *v.t.* to paint (a picture) or decorate (a wall etc.) in fresco. [It., orig. a FRESH]

Frescobaldi, *n.* **Girolamo** (1583–1643), Italian composer of virtuoso pieces for the organ and harpsichord.

fresh, *a.* new; not known, met with or used previously, recent; other, different, additional; newly produced, not withered or faded, not stale, decayed or tainted; pure, not salt, drinkable; not preserved with salt, or by pickling, tinning etc.; raw, inexperienced; just arrived (from); looking young or healthy; vividly and distinctly retained in the mind; refreshed, reinvigorated; of a horse, frisky; brisk, active, vigorous, fit; of air, a breeze etc., refreshing, reviving, cool; cheeky, impertinent, amorously impudent; quarrelsome. *adv.* (*esp. in comb.*) freshly, as *fresh-blown;* recently; coolly, refreshingly; with fresh vigour. *n.* a freshet; a day of open weather; a freshwater river or spring; (*ellipt.*) the fresh part (of the day, season etc.); (*Sc.*) a thaw, open weather; (*pl.*) the mingling of fresh and salt water in bays or rivers; the increased current of an ebbtide caused by a flood of fresh water flowing into the sea. †*v.t.* to refresh. †*v.i.* to become fresher. **fresh out of,** (*chiefly N Am.*) having recently (completely) run out of. **to get fresh,** (*coll.*) to take undesired liberties with someone of the opposite sex. **to have, gather fresh way,** (*Naut.*) to go at increased speed. **fresh-blown,** *a.* newly flowering. **fresh-coloured,** *a.* having a young-looking or ruddy complexion. **fresh fish,** *n.* (*coll.*) a novice. **fresh-looking,** *a.* appearing fresh. **freshman,** *n.* a novice, a beginner, esp. a student in the first year at a university. **freshmanship,** *n.* †**fresh-new,** *a.* unpractised. **fresh-run,** *a.* of salmon, sea-trout etc., newly come up from the sea. **freshwater,** *a.* pertaining to, found in or produced by fresh water; used to river or coasting trade, as a sailor; †raw, †unskilled. **fresh-watered,** *a.* supplied with fresh water; newly watered. **freshen,** *v.t.* to make fresh; to enliven, to revive; to make less salty; (*Naut.*) to relieve (as a rope) by altering the position of a part subject to friction. *v.i.* to become fresh; to lose saltness; to become brisk, to gain strength; of cattle, to come into milk. **to freshen up,** to refresh oneself, to have a wash or shower, change one's clothes etc.; to revive, to give a fresher, more attractive appearance to; to replenish (a drink). **fresher,** *n.* (*coll.*) a freshman. **freshet**, *n.* a sudden flood caused by heavy rains or melted snow; a freshwater stream. †**freshish,** *a.* **freshly,** *adv.* **freshness,** *n.* [OE *fersc* (cp. Dut. *versch,* G *frisch,* OHG *frisc,* assim. to the cognate OF *fresche,* fem. of *freis*)]

Fresnel, *n.* **Augustin** (1788–1827), French physicist who refined the theory of the polarized light. In the early 19th century, physicists found it difficult to describe the manner in which light travelled. Fresnel realized in 1821 that light waves did not vibrate like sound waves longitudinally in the direction of their motion, but transversely, at right angles to the direction of the propagated wave.

fret[1], *v.t.* (*past, p.p.* **fretted**) to eat away, to corrode; to wear away, to rub or chafe; to make (a way or passage) by rubbing; to grieve, to repine; to be uneasy; to irritate, vex, annoy; to make rough or disturb (as water); †to devour. *v.i.* to be worn or eaten away; to be irritated, vexed, or troubled, to chafe; to be in a state of agitation or commotion; to flow in little waves or ripples; to make way by attrition or corrosion. *n.* the act or process of fretting or rubbing away; a spot abraded or corroded; an agitation of the surface of a fluid; a state of chafing or vexation; a chafing of the skin; herpes. **fretful,** *a.* angry, peevish, irritable; captious. **fretfully,** *adv.* **fretfulness,** *n.* **fretty,** *a.* [OE *fretan* (cp. Dut. *vreten,* G *fressen*), from *ētan,* to EAT, with pref. *fra-,* FOR-]

fret[2], *v.t.* to ornament, to decorate; to ornament (esp. a ceiling) with carved work; to variegate. *n.* fretwork; ornamental work; an ornament formed by small bands or fillets intersecting each other at right angles, used in classical architecture; (*Her.*) a figure composed of bars crossed and interlaced. **fretsaw,** *n.* a small ribbon-saw used in cutting fretwork. **fretwork,** *n.* carved or open woodwork in ornamental patterns and devices; a variegated pattern composed of interlacing lines of various patterns. **fretted,** *a.* ornamented with fretwork; having raised or sunken ornamentation in rectangular forms; (*Her.*) applied to charges or ordinaries interlaced with each other. **fretty,** *a.* (*Her.*) fretted. [prob. from OF *freter,* found in p.p. *frete,* adorned with interlaced work]

fret[3], *n.* a small piece of wood or ivory placed upon the fingerboard of certain stringed instruments to regulate the pitch of the notes. †*v.t.* to put such a fret on (a musical instrument). **fretted,** *a.* [etym. doubtful; perh. from OF *frete,* a ferrule]

Freud[1], *n.* **Clement** (1924–), British journalist, television personality, and until 1987 Liberal Member of Parliament; a grandson of Sigmund Freud.

Freud[2], *n.* **Lucian** (1922–), British painter, known for realist portraits with the subject staring intently from an almost masklike face, for example *Francis Bacon* (1952) (Tate Gallery, London). He is a grandson of Sigmund Freud.

Freud[3], *n.* **Sigmund** (1865–1939), Austrian psychiatrist who pioneered study of the unconscious mind. He developed the methods of free association and interpretation of dreams that are still techniques of psychoanalysis. His books include *Die Traumdeutung/The Interpre-*

tation of Dreams (1900), *Totem and Taboo* (1913), and *Das Unbehagen in der Kultur/Civilization and its Discontents* (1930). **Freudian**, *a.* of or pertaining to the psychological theories of Freud. *n.* a follower of Freud. **Freudian slip,** *n.* an unintentional action, such as a slip of the tongue, held to betray an unconscious thought.

Freya, Frigg, *n.* in Scandinavian mythology, wife of Odin and mother of Thor, goddess of married love and the hearth. See FRIDAY.

Freyberg, *n.* **Bernard Cyril, Baron Freyberg** (1889–1963), New Zealand soldier and administrator. He fought in World War I, and during World War II he commanded the New Zealand expeditionary force. He was governor-general of New Zealand (1946–52).

friable, *a.* capable of being easily reduced to powder; readily crumbled. **friability, friableness,** *n.* [F, from L *friābilis,* from *friāre,* to rub, to crumble]

friar, *n.* one belonging to a monastic order, esp. one of the four mendicant orders, Augustinians or Austin Friars, Franciscans or Grey Friars, Dominicans or Black Friars, and Carmelites or White Friars; a patch in a printed sheet that has not received the ink. **friar bird,** *n.* (*Austral.*) a honey-eater with bald head and neck. **friar's balsam,** *n.* a tincture of benzoin for application to ulcers and wounds. **friar's cowl,** *n.* the wake-robin, *Arum arisarum* or *A. maculatum.* **friar's lantern,** *n.* the ignis fatuus. **friarlike, -ly,** *a.* **friary,** *n.* a monastery of a mendicant order. [ME and OF *frere,* L *frātrem,* nom. *frāter,* brother]

fribble, *v.i.* to act frivolously; †to totter. *v.t.* to waste or trifle (away); (*Sc.*) to frizzle. *a.* frivolous, silly. *n.* a trifler; a frivolous, contemptible fellow. **fribbledom,** *n.* **fribbler,** *n.* **fribbling,** *a.* **fribblish,** *a.* [prob. onomat.]

fricandeau, *n.* (*pl.* **-deaus, -deaux**) a larded veal cutlet, braised or roasted and glazed. *v.t.* to make into a fricandeau. [F, etym. unknown]

fricassee, *n.* small pieces of meat, esp. chicken or veal, fried, stewed and served in a usu. white sauce. *v.t.* to cook as a fricassee. [F *fricassée,* orig. fem. p.p. of *fricasser,* etym. unknown]

fricative, *n.* a consonant, such as *f, sh, th,* produced by the friction of the breath issuing through a narrow opening. *a.* produced by this friction. [L *fricāre,* to rub, -ATIVE]

friction, *n.* the act of rubbing two bodies together; (*Phys.*) resistance which any body meets with in moving over another body; conflict, disagreement, lack of harmony; chafing or rubbing a part of the body to promote circulation. **friction-balls,** *n.pl.* balls placed in bearings to relieve friction. **friction-clutch, -cone, -coupling, -gear, -gearing,** *n.* contrivances for applying or disconnecting parts of machinery by the use of friction. **friction-rollers,** *n.pl.* a bearing formed of two rollers. **friction-wheel,** *n.* one whose motion is caused by the friction of a moving body, or which communicates motion by frictional contact. **frictional,** *a.* **frictionally,** *adv.* **frictionless,** *a.* [F, from L *frictiōnem,* nom. *frictio,* from *fricāre,* to rub]

Friday, *n.* the sixth day of the week, dedicated by Teutonic peoples to Frigg, the wife of Odin, as a translation of the late L *dies Veneris,* day of the planet Venus. **Black Friday** BLACK. **Good Friday** GOOD. [OE *frīgedæg* (cp. OHG *Frīatag,* G *Freitag*)]

fridge, *n.* short for REFRIGERATOR.

fried, *past, p.p.* FRY[1].

Friedan, *n.* **Betty** (1921–), US liberal feminist. Her book *The Feminine Mystique* (1963) was one of the most influential books for the women's movement in both the US and the UK. She founded the National Organization for Women (NOW) in 1966, the National Women's Political Caucus in 1971, the First Women's Bank in 1973, and called the First International Feminist Congress in 1973.

Friedman, *n.* **Milton** (1912–), US economist. The foremost exponent of monetarism, he argues that a country's economy, and hence inflation, can be controlled through its money supply, although most governments lack the 'political will' to control inflation by cutting government spending and thereby increasing unemployment.

Friedrich, *n.* **Caspar David** (1774–1840), German landscape painter in the romantic style, active mainly in Dresden. He imbued his subjects – mountain scenes and moonlit seas – with great poetic melancholy, and was later admired by symbolist painters.

friend, *n.* one attached to another by intimacy and affection, as distinguished from sexual love or family relationship; an acquaintance; one of the same nation or party, one who is not an enemy; one on the same side, an adherent, a sympathizer, a patron or promoter (of a cause, institution etc.); a member of the Society of Friends; anything that helps one, esp. in an emergency; a term of salutation; (*pl.*) one's near relations; (*euphem.*) a lover. †*v.t.* to befriend. **a friend at court,** one who has influence to help another. **Society of Friends,** see separate entry. **to make friends,** to become intimate or reconciled (with). †**friended,** *a.* (*esp. in comb.*) having friends, as *well-friended.* †**friending,** *n.* friendliness. **friendless,** *a.* **friendlessness,** *n.* †**friendlike,** *a.* **friendly,** *a.* having the disposition of a friend, good-natured; acting as a friend; characteristic of friends or of kindly feeling; amicable, not hostile; favourable, propitious; played for amusement or entertainment, not as part of a competition. *adv.* in the manner of a friend. *n.* a game played for entertainment, not a league or competition fixture; (*pl.*) natives belonging to a friendly tribe. **-friendly,** *comb.form* helpful to; favouring, protecting. **friendly society,** *n.* a society for the purpose of mutual assurance against sickness, distress or old age. **friendly suit,** *n.* a suit instituted between two parties not at variance to obtain a judicial decision upon a certain point. **friendlily,** *adv.* **friendliness,** *n.* **friendship,** *n.* mutual attachment between persons, as distinguished from sexual and family affection; the state of being friends; an act of personal kindness or goodwill; †aptness to unite or combine. [OE *frēond,* cp. Dut. *vriend,* G *Freund,* Goth. *frijōnds,* pres.p. of *frijōn,* to love (cp. OE *frēon, frēogan,* see FREE [1,2])]

Friendly Islands, TONGA.

Friends, Society of, Christian Protestant sect popularly known as Quakers, founded by George Fox in England in the 17th century. They were persecuted for their nonviolent activism, and many emigrated to form communities abroad, for example in Pennsylvania and New England, US. They now form a worldwide movement of about 200,000. Their worship stresses meditation and the freedom of all to take an active part in the service (called a meeting, held in a meeting house). They have no priests or ministers.

Friends of the Earth (FoE, FOE), environmental pressure group, established in the UK in 1971, that aims to protect the environment and to promote rational and sustainable use of the Earth's resources. It campaigns on issues such as acid rain; air, sea, river, and land pollution; recycling; disposal of toxic wastes; nuclear power and renewable energy; the destruction of rainforests; pesticides; and agriculture. FoE has branches in 30 countries.

Friesian, *n.* any of a breed of large black and white dairy cattle from N Holland and Friesland; FRISIAN. [var. of FRISIAN]

Friesland, *n.* maritime province of the N Netherlands, which includes the Frisian Islands and land which is still being reclaimed from the former Zuyder Zee; area 3400 sq km/1312 sq miles; population (1988) 599,000. Its capital is Leeuwarden.

frieze[1], *n.* the middle division of an entablature, between the architrave and the cornice, usu. enriched by sculpture; the band of sculpture occupying this; a horizontal band or strip, either plain or decorated, elsewhere in a wall. **frieze-panel,** *n.* one of the upper panels of a six-panel door. [F *frise* (cp. Sp. *friso*), perh. from It. *fregio,* a fringe, L *Phrygium* (*opus*), Phrygian (work)]

frieze[2], *n.* a coarse woollen cloth, with a rough nap on one side. **friezed,** *a.* made rough like the nap of frieze. [F *frise* (in *drap de frise,* cloth of Friesland, from Dut. *Vries,* a Frieslander)]

frig, *v.t., v.i.* (*past, p.p.* **frigged**) (*taboo*) to masturbate; (*taboo*) to have sexual intercourse (with). **to frig about,** (*sl.*) to potter or mess about. **frigging,** *a., adv.* (*taboo*) bloody, fucking. [E dial. *frig,* to rub]

frigate, *n.* a warship of the period *c.* 1650–1840, next in size and strength to a line-of-battle ship, having a main deck usu. carrying from 28 to 44 guns, and a raised quarter-deck and forecastle; a steam warship of considerably larger size and strength which preceded the ironclad; (*loosely*) a cruiser, a general-purpose escort vessel smaller than a destroyer; a frigate bird; †a light, swift vessel, propelled by oars and sails, also a larger sailing vessel. **frigate-bird,** *n.* a large tropical raptorial bird, *Tachypetes aquilus,* of great swiftness, usu. found at sea near land. **frigate-built,** *a.* with a quarter-deck and forecastle above the main-deck. [MF *fregate,* It. *fregata,* etym. doubtful]

frigatoon, *n.* a Venetian vessel with a square stern, and only a main- and mizzen-mast. [It. *fregatone,* as prec.]

fright, *n.* sudden and violent fear or alarm; a state of terror; one who presents a ridiculous appearance in person or dress. †*v.t.* to frighten. **frighten,** *v.t.* to throw into a state of fright; to alarm, terrify, scare; to drive (away, out of, or into) by fright. **frighteners,** *n.pl.* (*sl.*) something intended to frighten a person, esp. for criminal purposes. **to put the frighteners on,** (*sl.*) to (attempt to) coerce or deter someone with threats (of violence). **frightful,** *a.* dreadful, fearful, shocking; horrible, hideous, very disagreeable; causing fright; (*coll.*) awful, extraordinary. **frightfully,** *adv.* **frightfulness,** *n.* [OE *fyrhto,* cogn. with *forht,* afraid, cp. OS *foroht, forht,* G *Furcht*]

frigid, *a.* cold; wanting heat or warmth; lacking warmth or feeling or ardour; stiff, formal, forbidding; without animation or spirit, dull, flat; sexually unresponsive. **frigid zones,** *n.pl.* the parts of the earth between the Arctic Circle and the North Pole and the Antarctic Circle and the South Pole. **frigidarium,** *n.* (*pl.* **-aria**) the cooling-room in a Roman bath; the cold bath itself. **frigidity,** *n.* the state of being frigid; (*Psych.*) the decrease or absence in a woman of sexual response. **frigidly,** *adv.* **frigidness,** *n.* [L *frīgidus,* from *frīgēre,* to be cold, from *frīgus,* cold]

frigorific, *a.* (*Phys.*) producing cold, from an old theory that cold is due to an imponderable substance called *frigoric* (cp. CALORIC). [F *frigorifique,* L *frīgorificus,* from L *frīgus -oris,* cold]

frijole, *n.* a Mexican bean, resembling the kidney-bean. [Mex. Sp.]

frill, *n.* a pleated or fluted edging, as of linen on the front of a shirt; a ruffle, a flounce; a ruff or frill-like fringe of hair, feather etc. on an animal, bird or plant; (*pl.*) (*coll.*) airs, affectations, finery, frippery, decorative non-essentials; the puckering of a film at the edge of a negative. *v.t.* (*past, p.p.* **frilled**) to furnish with a frill; to serve as a frill to. *v.i.* (*Phot.*) to pucker at the edge of a plate. **with no frills, without frills,** plain, unornamented, no-nonsense. **frilled,** *a.* furnished with a frill or frills. **frilled lizard,** *n.* a large Australian lizard with an erectile fold of skin around its neck. **frillery,** *n.* a quantity or mass of frills; frills taken collectively. **frilling,** *n.* **frilly,** *a.* [etym. doubtful; acc. to Skeat prob. from LG (cp. WFlem. *frul, frulle,* Swed. dial. *fräll, fröll*)]

fringe, *n.* an ornamental border to dress or furniture, consisting of loose threads or tassels; a border, an edging; the front hair cut short with a straight edge along the forehead; (*Bot.*) a row of long filiform processes; (*Zool.*) a border of hairs or other processes; (*Opt.*) one of the coloured bands seen when a beam of light is transmitted through a slit; something marginal or additional; a group with marginal or extreme views. *v.t.* to border with or as with a fringe. *a.* existing alongside mainstream or conventional forms, institutions etc.; marginal, secondary. **The Fringe,** that part of an arts festival, the London theatre etc. which presents new, experimental or avant-garde works away from the main venues. **fringe benefit,** *n.* something additional to wages or salary regularly received as part of one's remuneration from one's employer. **fringe-flower,** *n.* the genus *Schizanthus,* cultivated plants from Chile with beautiful fringed and coloured flowers. **fringe-net,** *n.* a net, usu. made of hair, for confining a woman's hair. **fringeless,** *a.* **fringe-like,** *a.* **fringing,** *n.* **fringy,** *a.* [OF *frenge* (F *frange*), L *fimbria*]

fringilla, *n.* a genus of small singing birds, containing the finches. **fringillaceous,** *a.* [L]

Frink, *n.* **Elisabeth** (1930–), British sculptor of rugged, naturalistic bronzes, mainly based on animal forms.

frippery, *n.* worthless, needless or trumpery adornments; tawdry finery; mere display; knick-knacks, gewgaws; old clothes; second-hand furniture; a shop or mart for old clothes; trade in old clothes. *a.* tawdry, trifling. **fripper, -perer,** *n.* a dealer in old clothes. [OF *freperie,* from *frepe,* a rag, prob. from L *fibra,* FIBRE]

Frisbee®, *n.* a plastic disc, used in throwing and catching games.

Frisch¹, *n.* **Karl von** (1886–1982), German zoologist, founder with Konrad Lorenz of ethology, the study of animal behaviour. He specialized in bees, discovering how they communicate the location of sources of nectar by 'dances'. Nobel prize of 1973 shared with Lorenz and Nikolaas Tinbergen.

Frisch², *n.* **Max** (1911–), Swiss dramatist. Influenced by Brecht, his early plays such as *Als der Krieg zu Ende war/When the War Is Over* (1949) are more romantic in tone than his later symbolic dramas, such as *Andorra* (1962), dealing with questions of identity. His best-known play is *Biedermann und die Brandstifter/The Fire Raisers* (1958).

Frisch–Peierls memorandum, *n.* a document revealing, for the first time, how small the critical mass (the minimum quantity of substance required for a nuclear chain reaction to begin) of uranium needed to be if the isotope Uranium-235 was separated from naturally occurring uranium; the memo thus implied the feasibility of using this isotope to make an atomic bomb. It was written by Otto Frisch and Rudolf Peierls (1907–) at the University of Birmingham in 1940.

frisette, *n.* a front or band of artificial curls worn on the forehead. [F, from *friser,* to FRIZZ]

friseur, *n.* a hairdresser. †**frisure,** *n.* hairdressing. [F, as prec.]

Frisian, Friesian, *a.* of, pertaining to or native of Friesland. *n.* the language of Friesland; a member of a Germanic people of NW Europe. In Roman times they occupied the coast of Holland, and may have taken part in the Anglo-Saxon invasions of Britain. Their language was closely akin to Anglo-Saxon, with which it formed the Anglo-Frisian branch of the West Germanic languages. [L *Frisii,* pl., OFris. *Frise*]

frisk, *v.i.* to leap, skip or gambol about; to frolic. *v.t.* (*coll.*) to search (a person) for firearms etc. *n.* a gambol, a frolic. **frisker,** *n.* one who frisks; (*sl.*) a pilferer. **friskful,** *a.* **frisky,** *a.* **friskily,** *adv.* **friskiness,** *n.* [from obs. a. *frisk,* OF *frisque,* lively, OHG *frisc,* FRESH]

frisket, *n.* the light frame by which a sheet of paper to be printed is held in place. [F *frisquette*]

frisson, *n.* a shudder, a thrill. [F]

frit, *n.* a calcined mixture of sand and fluxes ready to be melted in a crucible to form glass; applied to other vitreous compositions used in manufactures. *v.t.* (*past, p.p.* **fritted**) to expose to dull red heat so as to decompose and fuse. [F *fritte,* It. *fritta,* fem. p.p. of *friggere,* to FRY]

frit-fly, *n.* a small fly that arrests the growth of wheat by boring into the bud. [etym. unknown]

frith¹, FIRTH.

†**frith²,** *n.* peace. **frith-stool,** *n.* (*Eccles. Ant.*) a seat near the altar which was the most sacred refuge for those claiming sanctuary. [OE *frith, frithu* (cp. Dut. *vrede,* OHG *fridu,* G *Friede*)]

frith³, *n.* a forest for game; ground covered with underwood; a small field taken out of a common. [ME, from OE *gefyrhthe,* etym. doubtful]

fritillary, *n.* the liliaceous genus *Fritillaria,* esp. *F. meleagris,* with flowers speckled with dull purple; a butterfly of the genus *Argynnis,* from their wings being marked like this flower. [late L *fritillāria,* from L *fritillus,* a dice-box]

fritter¹, *n.* a piece of fruit, meat etc. dipped in a light batter and fried; (*pl.*) fenks. [OF *friture,* L *frictus,* p.p. of *frīgere,* to FRY]

fritter², *n.* (*pl.*) fragments, bits, shreds. *v.t.* to break into small pieces. **to fritter away,** to waste in trifles. [etym. doubtful; perh. from obs. *fitters,* n.pl., cogn. with G *Fetzen,* a rag, a scrap; or from OF *fretura,* L *fractūra,* FRACTURE; or from prec.]

Friuli-Venezia Giulia, *n.* autonomous agricultural and wine-growing region of NE Italy, bordered on the east by Yugoslavia; area 7800 sq km/3011 sq miles; population (1988) 1,210,000. It includes the capital Udine, Gorizia, Pordenone, and Trieste.

frivolous, *a.* trifling, trumpery, of little or no moment; inclined to unbecoming levity or trifling, silly. **frivol,** *v.i.* (*past, p.p.* **frivolled**) to trifle. *v.t.* to trifle (away). **frivolity,** *n.* **frivolously,** *adv.* **frivolousness,** *n.* [L *frīvolus,* prob. cogn. with *friāre, fricāre,* to rub]

†**frize,** FRIEZE².

frizz, *v.t.* to curl, to crisp; to form (the hair) into a curly, crinkled mass; to raise a nap on (cloth). *n.* frizzed hair, a mass or row of curls. **frizzy,** *a.* [F *friser,* from *frise,* FRIEZE²]

frizzle¹, *v.t., v.i.* to form (into) crisp, tight curls. *n.* a curled or crisped lock of hair; frizzed hair. **frizzly,** *a.* [etym. doubtful, older than but prob. conn. with prec.]

frizzle², *v.t.* to fry (bacon etc.) with a hissing noise. *v.i.* to make a hissing noise while being fried. [prob. from earlier *frizz,* imit. adaptation of FRY¹]

fro, *adv.* away, backwards. **to and fro,** forwards and backwards. [Icel. *frā,* FROM; cp. OE *fram*]

Frobisher, *n.* **Martin** (1535–94), English navigator. He made his first voyage to Guinea, West Africa, in 1554. In 1576 he set out in search of the Northwest Passage, and visited Labrador, and Frobisher Bay, Baffin Island. Second and third expeditions sailed in 1577 and 1578.

frock, *n.* the long upper garment worn by monks; a loose garment, formerly a loose over-garment worn by men, now a gown worn by women or children; a woman's dress; a frock-coat; a military coat of similar shape; a smock-frock; a woven woollen tunic worn by sailors. **frock-coat,** *n.* a close-fitting body-coat, with broad skirts of the same length before and behind. **frocked,** *a.* **frocking,** *n.* material for smock-frocks. †**frockless,** *a.* [F *froc,* prob. from late L *frocus, floccus,* FLOCK²]

Froebel, *n.* **Friedrich August Wilhelm** (1782–1852), German educationist. He evolved a new system of education using instructive play, described in *Education of Man* (1826) and other works. In 1836 he founded the first kindergarten in Blankenburg. He was influenced by Pestalozzi. *a.* applied to the Froebel System.

frog¹, *n.* a squat, smooth-skinned, tailless amphibian of any species of the genus *Rana;* (*often* **Frog**) (*derog.*) a French person; an iron or steel plate to guide train wheels over an intersection in the track; the hollow in one or both faces of a brick; the block by which the hair is attached to the heel of a violin etc. bow. **a frog in one's throat,** phlegm on the vocal cords impeding speech. **frog-bit,** *n.* a small aquatic plant, *Hydrocharis morsusranae.* **frog-fish,** *n.* the angler, *Lophius piscatorius,* and other fish. **froghopper,** *n.* a genus of small insects, remarkable for their leaping powers, living on plants. **frogman,** *n.* an underwater swimmer equipped with rubber suit, flippers, face mask etc. **frogmarch,** *v.t.* to carry face downwards between four people each holding a limb; to move (a person) by force, usu. by seizing from behind and propelling forwards while the arms are pinioned, or by dragging backwards between two people each grasping an arm. **frog-mouth,** *n.* (*Austral.*) a bird of the mopoke family, a variety of goat-sucker. **frog-spawn,** *n.* a gelatinous mass of frog's eggs; certain freshwater algae. **froggery,** *n.* a place where frogs are kept or abound. **froggy,** *a.* abounding with frogs. [OE *frogga, frox* (cp. Icel. *froskr,* G *Frosch*)]

frog², *n.* a spindle-shaped button or toggle used for fastening military cloaks and undress coats, ladies' mantles etc.; the loop of a scabbard. **frogged,** *a.* [Port. *froco,* L *floccus* FLOCK²]

frog³, *n.* a tender horny substance in the middle of the sole of a horse's foot. [etym. unknown; perh. corr. of FORK]

frolic, *a.* gay, merry, sportive; full of pranks. *n.* a wild prank; an outburst of gaiety and mirth; a merry-making; a light-hearted entertainment. *v.i.* (*past, p.p.* **frolicked**) to play pranks; to frisk; to indulge in merry-making. †**frolicful,** *a.* †**frolicky,** *a.* **frolicsome,** *a.* **frolicsomely,** *adv.* **frolicsomeness,** *n.* [prob. from MDut. *vrolick* (Dut. *vrolijk*), cp. G *fröhlich* (*vrō-* or *froh-,* merry, joyous, -LIKE)]

from, *prep.* away, out of (expressing separation, departure, point of view, distinction or variation); beginning with, after (expressing the starting-point or lower limit in time or space); arriving, coming, deriving (indicating the original location, source or model); by means of, because of, by reason of (expressing instrumentality, cause, reason or motive). **from out,** out from, forth from. **from time to time,** at intervals, now and then. †**fromward,** *prep.* from, away from. [OE *from, fram* (cp. Icel. *frā,* FRO, OS and OHG *fram,* Goth. *framis*), orig. forward]

fromage frais, *n.* a soft curd cheese. [F]

Fromm, *n.* **Erich** (1900–80), German psychoanalyst who moved to the US in 1933 to escape the Nazis. His *The Fear of Freedom* (1941) and *The Sane Society* (1955) were source books for modern alternative life-styles.

frond, *n.* (*Bot.*) a leaf-like expansion in which the functions of stem and foliage are not entirely differentiated, often bearing the organs of fructification, as in many cryptogams, esp. the ferns; (*Zool.*) a leaf-like expansion, as in many zoophytes. **frondage,** *n.* †**frondesce,** *v.i.* to come into leaf. **frondescence,** *n.* **frondescent,** *a.* **frondiferous,** *a.* **frondlet,** *n.* **frondose, frondous,** *a.* [L *frons -ndis,* a leaf]

Fronde, *n.* (*Fr. Hist.*) the name given to a party (1648–57) who attacked Mazarin and the Court during the minority of Louis XIV; any party of malcontents. **Frondeur,** *n.* a member of the Fronde; an opponent of the government, an irreconcilable. [F, lit. a sling]

front, *n.* the forward part or side of anything; the most conspicuous part; the begining, the first part; the part of a garment covering the chest; a face of a building, esp. the principal face; a frontage; a seaside promenade; a position directly ahead, or in the foremost part of something; the position of leadership; the vanguard; the main forward positions of an army; the lateral space occupied by a military unit; the direction in which a line of troops faces; a particular sphere of activity; a group of people or organizations who make common cause together; the line of separation between air masses of different density and temperature; outward appearance or bearing; impudence, boldness; something which serves as a cover or disguise for secret or nefarious activities; a front man; a set of false hair or curls worn over the forehead; a dicky; (*poet.*) the forehead; †the face. *a.* relating to or situated in or at the front; articulated at or towards the front of the mouth. *v.t.* to stand or be situated opposite to; to face, to look (to or towards); to confront, to meet face to face, to oppose; to furnish with a front; to be the leader or head of; to be the presenter of (a TV programme etc.). *v.i.* to face, to look, to be situated with the front (towards); to act as a front or cover for; †to be foremost; †to be opposed. **front!** (*Mil.*) word of command for persons to turn to the front. **front of house,** (*Theat.*) those activities which involve direct contact with the public in a theatre, e.g. box office, selling programmes. **front-of-house,** *a.* **in front of,**

before; in advance of; in the presence of. **out front,** (*Theat.*) in the audience or auditorium. **to come to the front,** to take a prominent position. **to front up,** (*Austral.*) to turn up. **two-pair front,** a second-floor room in the front of a house. **front bench,** *n.* the foremost bench in either house of Parliament, assigned to ministers or ex-ministers. **front bencher,** *n.* **front door,** *n.* the principal entrance to a building. **front line,** *n.* the positions closest to the enemy in a battle; the most advanced and active and/or most exposed and dangerous positions in any field of activity. **frontline,** *a.* pertaining to or suitable for the front line in battle; neighbouring a hostile state or a scene of (armed) conflict. **front man,** *n.* a nominal leader or figurehead; the presenter of a TV programme. **front-page,** *a.* (worthy of) figuring on the front page of a newspaper. **front piece,** *n.* (*Theat.*) a small play acted in front of the curtain. **front room,** *n.* a room in the front of a house, esp. a living room. **front-runner,** *n.* the leader or most favoured contestant in a race, election etc.; a person who runs or performs best when in the lead. **frontage,** *n.* the front part of a building; the extent of this; land between this and a road; land facing a road or water; the direction in which anything faces. **frontager,** *n.* the owner of a frontage, one who lives on the frontier. **frontal,** *a.* situated on or pertaining to the front; belonging to the forehead. *n.* a small pediment over a door or window; an ornamental hanging or panel in front of an altar; a bandage or application for the forehead. **frontal attack,** *n.* an attack on the front of an army, distinguished from a flank attack. **frontal lobe,** *n.* the front lobe of either side of the brain. **frontate, -ated,** *a.* (*Bot.*) increasing in breadth. **fronted,** *a.* formed with a front, as troops; changed into or towards a front sound. **-fronted,** *comb. form* having a front of a specified type. **frontless,** *a.* without a front; †full of effrontery, shameless. **frontward,** *a.*, *adv.* **frontwards,** *adv.* [OF, from L *frontem,* nom. *frons,* the forehead]

Frontenac et Palluau, Louis de Buade, Comte de Frontenac et Palluau (1622–98), French colonial governor. He began his military career in 1635, and was appointed governor of the French possessions in North America in 1672. Although efficient, he quarrelled with the local bishop and his followers and was recalled in 1682. After the Iroquois, supported by the English, won several military victories, Frontenac was reinstated in 1689. He defended Quebec against the English in 1690 and defeated the Iroquois in 1696.

frontier, *n.* that part of a country which fronts or borders upon another; (*chiefly N Am.*) the margins of settled or developed territory; (*often pl.*) the current limit of knowledge or attainment in a particular sphere; †an outwork. *a.* pertaining to or situated on the frontier. †*v.i.* to lie on the frontier. †*v.t.* to surround as a frontier; to oppose, to bar the advance of. **frontiersman,** *n.* [OF, late L *frontēria, -tāria,* as prec.]

Frontignac, *n.* a muscat wine made at Frontignan, in the department of Hérault, France. [erroneously for *Frontignan*]

frontispiece, *n.* a picture fronting the title-page of a book; a façade, a decorated front or chief entrance. *v.t.* to furnish with, to serve or put as, or to supply a frontispiece (to a book). [F *frontispice,* late L *frontispicium* (*frons -ntis,* the forehead, *specere,* to look), assim. to PIECE]

frontlet, *n.* a small band or fillet worn on the forehead, a phylactery; the forehead in birds.

fronto- *comb. form* pertaining to the forehead, the frontal bone of the forehead, or the frontal region. [L *frons -ntis,* the forehead]

fronton, *n.* a pediment; a frontal. [F, from It. *frontone,* as prec.]

†**frore,** *a.* frozen, frosty. *adv.* frostily, keenly. †**frory,** *a.* [OE *froren,* p.p. of *frēosan,* to FREEZE]

Frost, *n.* **Robert (Lee)** (1874–1963), US poet whose verse, in traditional form, is written with an individual voice and penetrating vision; his best-known poems include 'Mending Wall' ('Something there is that does not love a wall'), 'The Road Not Taken', and 'Stopping by Woods on a Snowy Evening'.

frost, *n.* the act or state of freezing, the congelation of fluids by the abstraction of heat; temperature below freezing-point; the state of the atmosphere that produces freezing; frosty weather; minute crystals of frozen dew or vapour, rime or hoar frost; coldness of manner or attitude; (*sl.*) a disappointment, a fiasco, a 'fraud'. *v.t.* to injure by frost; to cover with or as with rime; to whiten (as the hair); to sharpen (as the nails of a horse's shoes) in frosty weather; to give a fine-grained, slightly roughened appearance to (glass, metal etc.); to dredge with fine sugar; (*chiefly Am.*) to ice (a cake). **black frost,** frost without rime. **degrees of frost,** (*with number*) degrees below freezing-point. **Jack Frost,** frost personified. **white frost,** frost with rime. **frost-bite,** *n.* inflammation often resulting in gangrene, usu. of the extremities, caused by exposure to extreme cold. **frost-bitten,** *a.* **frost-bound,** *a.* confined by frost. **frost-fish,** *n.* (*Austral. New Zealand*) a variety of thin, edible scabbard fish. **frost-nail,** *n.* a projecting nail driven into a horse's shoe to prevent slipping in frosty weather. **frost-work,** *n.* the figures formed by frost on glass etc. **frosted,** *a.* covered with frost or any substance resembling frost; damaged by frost; having a rough, granulated surface; (*chiefly N Am.*) iced. **frosting,** *n.* (*chiefly N Am.*) icing; a rough, granulated surface produced on glass, metal etc. in imitation of frost. **frostless,** *a.* **frosty,** *a.* producing frost; excessively cold; attended with frost; affected or injured by frost; covered with or as with rime; cool, unenthusiastic. †**frosty-spirited,** *a.* tame, spiritless. **frostily,** *adv.* **frostiness,** *n.* [OE *forst*]

froth, *n.* foam, spume, the mass of small bubbles caused in liquors by agitation or fermentation; foamy excretion, scum; empty display of wit or rhetoric; light, unsubstantial matter. *v.t.* to cause to foam; to cover with froth. *v.i.* to form or emit froth. **frothless,** *a.* **frothsome,** *a.* **frothy,** *a.* **frothily,** *adv.* **frothiness,** *n.* [cogn. with Icel. *frotha* (cp. OE *āfrēothan,* to froth)]

frottage, *n.* the technique of producing images or textures by rubbing with e.g. a pencil on a sheet of paper placed on top of an object. [F, from *frotter,* to rub]

frou-frou, *n.* a rustling, as of a silk dress. [F, imit.]

†**frounce,** *v.t.* to form into folds or wrinkles; to curl, to crisp; to trim with flounces. *v.i.* to frown. *n.* a wrinkle, a plait, a fold, a flounce; a disease in hawks. [OF *froncir,* see FLOUNCE[2]]

frow, *n.* a Dutchwoman. [Dut. *vrouw,* cp. FRAU]

froward, *a.* not willing to comply, refractory, perverse, mutinous; †adverse, untoward. †*prep.* (also **frowards**) away from. †*adv.* away. **frowardly,** *adv.* **frowardness,** *n.* [ME *fraward*]

frown, *v.i.* to express displeasure or seriousness by contracting the brows; to look gloomy, threatening or with disfavour; to scowl, to lower; to manifest displeasure (at or upon). *v.t.* to repress, repel or rebuke with a frown; to express with a frown. *n.* a knitting of the brows in displeasure or mental absorption; any sign of displeasure. **frowningly,** *adv.* [OF *frongnier* (cp. F *renfrogner, refrogner*), from Teut. (cp. Swed. dial. *fryna,* to make a wry face)]

frowst, *n.* stuffiness; an unwholesome smell (in a room). **frowsty,** *a.* [etym. unknown]

frowzy, *a.* musty, fusty, close; slovenly, unkempt, dirty. **frowziness,** *n.* [etym. doubtful]

froze, *past* FREEZE.

frozen, *p.p.* FREEZE. *a.* preserved by freezing; very cold; fixed, immobilized; of prices etc., pegged at a certain level; of assets etc., not convertible; frigid, aloof, disdainful. **the frozen mitt,** (*sl.*) hostility, rejection. **frozen shoulder,** *n.* painful stiffness in the shoulder joint.

FRS, (*abbr.*) Fellow of the Royal Society.

Fructidor, *n.* the name given in the French revolutionary calendar to the 12th month of the republican year (18 Aug. to 16 Sept.); the coup d'état that occurred in Fructidor in 1797. [F, from L *frūctus,* fruit, Gr. *dōron,* gift]

fructify, *v.t.* to make fruitful or productive; to fertilize.

v.i. to bear fruit. **fructiferous**, *a.* bearing fruit. **fructification**, *n.* the act or process of fructifying; (*Bot.*) the organs of reproduction; the fruit and its parts. **fructiform**, *a.* **fructose**, *n.* fruit-sugar. †**fructuary**, *a.* (*Rom. Law*) of or pertaining to usufruct. *n.* one who enjoys the produce, fruits or profits of anything. **fructuate** *v.i.* to bear fruit, to come to fruit. **fructuation**, *n.* coming to fruit; fruition. **fructule**, *n.* a drupel, or part of a compound fruit. **fructuous**, *a.* fruitful, fertile. [F *fructifier,* L *frūctificāre* (*frūctus,* FRUIT, *-ficāre, facere,* to make)]

frugal, *a.* thrifty, sparing; not profuse or lavish; economical in the use or expenditure of food, money etc. **frugality**, *n.* economy, thrift; a sparing use of anything. **frugally,** *adv.* [L *frūgālis,* from *frūgi,* dat. of *frūx,* fruit, profit]

†**frugiferous,** *a.* bearing fruit, fruitful. **frugivorous**, *a.* feeding on fruit. [L *frūgifer*]

fruit, *n.* the edible succulent product of a plant or tree in which the seeds are enclosed; (*Bot.*) the matured ovary or seed-vessel with other parts adhering thereto; the spores of cryptogams; (*pl.*) the vegetable products yielded by the earth, serving for food to humans and animals; (*Bibl.*) offspring; product, result or consequence; benefit, profit; (*chiefly N Am., sl., offensive*) a male homosexual. *v.i.* to bear fruit. *v.t.* to cause to produce fruit. **fruit bat,** *n.* a large Old World fruit-eating bat found in tropical and subtropical regions. **fruit-bearer,** *n.* a tree or plant which produces fruit. **fruit-bearing,** *a.* **fruit-bud,** *n.* a bud which produces fruit. **fruit-cake,** *n.* a cake containing currants etc. **fruit-clipper,** *n.* a swift sailing-vessel carrying fruit. **fruit-fly,** *n.* a small insect of the genus *Drosophila.* **fruit-knife,** *n.* a knife with a silver blade for paring and cutting fruit. **fruit machine,** *n.* a coin-in-the-slot gambling machine which spins symbols (as of fruit) past little windows in its front and pays out if certain combinations are visible when it stops. **fruit-piece,** *n.* a picture of fruit. **fruit salad,** *n.* a mixture of fruits cut up and sweetened. **fruit-spur,** *n.* a small branch the growth of which is arrested for the development of fruit-buds. **fruit-sugar,** *n.* laevulose, fructose or glucose, obtained from fruit or honey. **fruit-tree,** *n.* a tree cultivated for its fruit. **fruitage,** *n.* **fruitarian**, *n.* one that feeds on fruit. **fruiter,** *n.* a tree that bears; a fruit-ship; (*N Am.*) a fruit-grower. **fruiterer,** *n.* one who deals in fruits. †**fruitery,** *n.* fruit; a fruit crop; a fruit-loft. **fruitful,** *a.* producing fruit in abundance; productive, fertile; bearing children, prolific. **fruitfully,** *adv.* **fruitfulness,** *n.* **fruiting,** *a.* bearing fruit. **fruitless,** *a.* not bearing fruit; unsuccessful, unprofitable, useless, vain, idle. **fruitlessly,** *adv.* **fruitlessness,** *n.* **fruitlet**, *n.* a drupel. **fruity,** *a.* like fruit, in taste etc.; of wine, tasting of the grape; rich, full-flavoured; of the voice, round, mellow and rich; salacious, risque; (*N Am., sl.*) crazy; (*chiefly N Am., sl.*) homosexual. **fruitiness,** *n.* [OF, from L *frūctum,* nom. *-us,* from *fruī,* to enjoy]

fruition, *n.* attainment, fulfilment; pleasure or satisfaction derived from attainment of a desire. **fruitive**, *a.* pertaining to fruition; able to enjoy. [OF, from *fruitiōnem,* nom. *-tio,* from *fruī,* to enjoy (cp. FRUIT)]

frumentaceous, *a.* of the nature of, resembling or composed of wheat or other cereal. †**frumentarious**, *a.* of or pertaining to corn. †**frumentation,** *n.* (*Rom. Ant.*) a gift or largess of corn to the Roman people. [L *frūmentāceus,* from *frūmentum,* corn]

frumenty, *n.* a dish made of wheat boiled in milk and flavoured with spices. [OF *frumentée,* from *frument,* L *frūmentum,* as prec.]

frump, *n.* an old-fashioned, prim or dowdy-looking woman; †a sneer, a flout; †a lie. †*v.t.* to mock, to jeer, to snub. **frumpish,** *a.* **frumpy,** *a.* [etym. doubtful]

†**frush**[1], *v.t.* to batter, to smash; to knock down. *v.i.* to rush. *n.* a rush, an onset, an encounter; a noise, as of violent collision; splinters, fragments. *a.* (*Sc.*) easily broken, brittle. [OF *fruissier* (F *froisser*), to break in pieces, from L *frustum,* a fragment]

†**frush**[2], *n.* a frog in a horse's foot; a discharge of fetid matter therefrom. [prob. from OE *frosc,* frog]

frustrate[1], *v.t.* to make of no avail; to defeat, to thwart, to balk; to nullify, to disappoint; to cause feelings of dissatisfaction or discouragement.

frustrate[2], *a.* vain; of no effect. **frustrated,** *a.* thwarted; dissatisfied, discouraged. **frustration,** *n.* †**frustrative**, *a.* †**frustratory**, *a.* [L *frustrātus,* p.p. of *frustrārī,* from *frustrā,* in vain]

frustule, *n.* the covering or shell, usu. in two valves, of a diatom. [F, from late L *frustulum,* dim. of foll.]

frustum, *n.* (*pl.* **-tums, -ta**) the part of a regular solid next to the base, formed by cutting off the top; the part of a solid between two planes. [L, a fragment]

frutex, *n.* (*pl.* **frutices**) a woody plant smaller than a tree, a shrub. **frutescent**, *a.* shrubby. **frutescence,** *n.* **fruticetum**, *n.* an arboretum for fruit-trees and shrubs. **fruticose**, *a.* of the nature of a shrub, shrubby; (*Zool.*) shrub-like in appearance (as certain zoophytes). **fruticulose**, *a.* resembling or branching like a small shrub. [L]

†**frutify,** *v.i.* to notify. [Shak., humorous word, *Merchant of Venice,* II. ii. 147]

Fry, *n.* **Elizabeth** (born Gurney) (1780–1845), English Quaker philanthropist. She formed an association for the improvement of female prisoners in 1817, and worked with her brother, Joseph Gurney (1788–1847), on an influential report in 1819 on prison reform.

fry[1], *v.t.* to cook with fat in a pan over the fire. *v.i.* to be cooked in a frying-pan; †to boil; †to ferment. *n.* (*pl.* **fries**) a dish of anything fried; the liver, lights, heart etc. of pigs, sheep, calves and oxen; (*pl.*) French fries; a state of worry, agitation or excitement. **fryer, frier,** *n.* a vessel for frying. **frying-pan,** *n.* a shallow metal pan with a long handle, in which food is fried. **out of the frying-pan into the fire,** out of one trouble into a worse. [OF *frire,* L *frīgere,* cp. Gr. *phrugein,* to parch]

fry[2], *n.* young fish, esp. those fresh from the spawn, also yearling salmon; a swarm of children, a quantity of trifling objects. **small fry,** unimportant, insignificant people or things. [cp. Icel. *friō,* Dan. and Swed. *frō*]

FSH, (*abbr.*) follicle-stimulating hormone.

FT, (*abbr.*) the Financial Times.

ft., (*abbr.*) foot, feet; fort.

fth, fthm, (*abbr.*) fathom.

ft lb, (*abbr.*) foot-pound.

Fuad, *n.pl.* two kings of Egypt:

Fuad I, *n.* (1868–1936), king of Egypt from 1922. Son of the Khedive Ismail, he succeeded his elder brother, Hussein Kiamil, as sultan of Egypt in 1917, and when Egypt was declared independent in 1922 he assumed the title of king.

Fuad II, *n.* (1952–), grandson of Fuad I, he was king of Egypt from 1952–53 between the abdication of his father Farouk and the establishment of the republic.

fub, FOB.

fubby, fubsy, *a.* fat, squat. [from obs. *fub,* chubby, onomat.]

Fuchs, *n.* **Klaus (Emil Julius)** (1911–88), German spy who worked on atom-bomb research in the UK in World War II. He was imprisoned (1950–59) for passing information to the USSR and resettled in East Germany.

fuchsia, *n.* any of a genus of garden plants with pendulous funnel-shaped flowers. [L *Fuchs,* German botanist, 1501–66]

fuchsine, *n.* a magenta dye of the rosaniline series. [from prec., owing to resemblance to flower]

fuck, *v.i., v.t.* (*taboo*) to have sexual intercourse (with). *n.* an act of sexual intercourse; a partner in sexual intercourse. *int.* used to express violent displeasure or (with an object, as *fuck you*) one's disregard or defiance of someone. **fuck all,** nothing at all. **not to give a fuck,** not to care in the least. **to fuck about, around,** to waste time, to mess around; to treat inconsiderately. **to fuck off,** to go away. **to fuck up,** to botch, to damage; to make a mess of. **fuck-up,** *n.* **fucked,** *a.* (*taboo*) broken, damaged, kaput; exhausted. **fucker,** *n.* (*taboo*) a (stupid) person, fellow. **fucking,** *n.* (*taboo*) sexual intercourse. *a.* used to express one's annoyance with something, often a virtually meaningless expletive. *adv.* very, extremely. [etym. doubtful; perh. G *ficken,* to strike, to fuck]

fucus, *n.* (*pl.* **-ci**) a genus of algae, containing some of the commonest seaweeds; any species of this genus; †a paint, a dye; (*fig.*) deceptive show. **fucivorous,** *a.* feeding on seaweed, as the sirenians. **fucoid,** *a.* resembling a fucus. *n.* a fossil plant, like a fucus. **fucoidal,** *a.* [L, rock-lichen, red dye, rouge]

fud, *n.* (*Sc., North.*) a hare's scut; the buttocks; woollen waste. [etym. obscure]

fuddle, *v.t.* to make stupid with drink, to intoxicate; to confuse. *v.i.* to tipple, to get drunk. *n.* a drinking bout; the state of being muddled; †drink. **fuddler,** *n.* a drunkard, a sot. [cp. LG *fuddeln,* to work lazily]

fuddy-duddy, *n.* (*coll.*) an old fogy; a carper. *a.* old-fogyish, old-fashioned; stuffy, pompous; prim, censorious.

fudge[1], *int.* nonsense, stuff, humbug. *n.* nonsense; a made-up or nonsensical story; a soft confection of chocolate, candy etc. [onomat.]

fudge[2], *v.t.* to patch or make up, to fake; to contrive in a makeshift, careless way; to falsify, to make imprecise, esp. as a means of covering up unpalatable facts; to dodge, to evade. *v.i.* to contrive in a makeshift way; to be evasive and imprecise; to cheat. *n.* (*Print.*) an attachment on rotary machines for the insertion of a small form giving an item of late news; a makeshift compromise; an evasion. **fudgy,** *a.* [etym. doubtful; perh. var. of FADGE]

fuel, *n.* combustible matter, such as wood, coal, peat etc., for fires; fissile material for use in a nuclear reactor; anything which serves to feed or increase passion or excitement. *v.t.* (*past, p.p.* **fuelled**) to supply or store with fuel. *v.i.* to get fuel. **fuel cell,** *n.* a cell in which chemical energy is continuously converted into electrical energy. **fuel injection,** *n.* a system whereby fuel is introduced directly into the combustion chamber of an internal-combustion engine, obviating the need for a carburettor. †**fueller,** *n.* **fuelless,** *a.* **fuelling,** *n.* fuel, firing. [A-F *fewaile,* OF *fouaille,* low L *focālia,* neut. pl. of *focālis,* from *focus,* a hearth]

Fuentes, *n.* **Carlos** (1928–), Mexican novelist, whose first novel *La región más transparente/Where the Air is Clear* (1958) encompasses the history of the country from the Aztecs to the present day.

fuero, *n.* (*Sp. Hist.*) a code, charter, grant of privileges or custom having the force of law; a tribunal or a place where justice is administered. [Sp., L *forum,* see FORUM]

fuff, *n.* (*Sc.*) a puff, a whiff; a huff, an ebullition of temper; the spitting of a cat. *v.t.* to puff, to whiff. **fuffy,** *a.* puffy, light. [onomat.]

fug, *n.* the close atmosphere of an unventilated room. **fuggy,** *a.*

fugacious, *a.* fleeting, lasting but a short time, transitory, ephemeral; (*Bot.*) falling off early. †**fugaciousness,** *n.* **fugacity,** *n.* fleetingness, transience; (*Chem.*) the tendency to expand or escape. [L *fugax -ācis,* from *fugere,* to flee]

fugal, fugato FUGUE.

-fuge, *suf.* (*Med.*) expelling, driving out, as in *febrifuge.* [L *-fugus,* from *fugere,* to flee, but altered in meaning to *fugāre,* to put to flight]

fugitive, *a.* fleeing, running away, having taken flight, runaway; transient, not stable or durable, volatile, easily wafted or carried away; fleeting, evanescent, ephemeral, of only passing interest; †wandering, vagabond. *n.* one who flees from danger, pursuit, justice, bondage or duty; a runaway, a deserter, a refugee; a person or thing hard to be caught or detained. **fugitive compositions,** *n.pl.* (*Lit., Mus.*) occasional pieces written for the moment or for a special purpose, and not intended to be permanent. †**fugitively,** *adv.* **fugitiveness,** *n.* [F *fugitif -tive,* L *fugitīvus,* from *fugere,* to flee]

fugleman, *n.* (*pl.* **-men**) a soldier who takes up a position in front of a company as a guide to the others in their drill; one who sets an example for others to follow, a leader, a ringleader; a spokesman. [G *Flügelmann* (*Flügel,* wing, *Mann,* man)]

fugue, *n.* a polyphonic composition on one or more short subjects, which are repeated by successively entering voices and developed contrapuntally; (*Psych.*) an attempt to escape from reality; (*Psych.*) loss of memory coupled with disappearance from one's usual resorts. **fugal,** *a.* (*Mus.*) in the style of a fugue. **fugally,** *adv.* **fugato,** *adv.* in the fugue style but not in strict fugal form. **fuguist,** *n.* a writer or performer of fugues. [F, from It. *fuga,* L *fuga,* flight, cogn. with *fugere,* to flee]

Führer, *n.* the head of the National-Socialist German government, Adolf Hitler (1889–1945). **Führer Prinzip,** *n.* the principle of subordination to a leader. [G, leader]

Fujairah, Fujayrah, *n.* one of the seven constituent member states of the United Arab Emirates; area 1150 sq km/450 sq miles; population (1985) 54,000.

Fujian, *n.* (formerly **Fukien**), province of SE China, bordering Taiwan Strait, opposite Taiwan. **area** 123,100 sq km/47,517 sq miles. **capital** Fuzhou. **physical** dramatic mountainous coastline. **population** (1986) 27,490,000. **products** sugar, rice, special aromatic teas, tobacco, timber, fruit.

Fujiyama, Mount Fuji, *n.* Japanese volcano and highest peak, on Honshu Island; height 3778 m/12,400 ft.

Fukuoka, *n.* (formerly **Najime**), Japanese industrial port on the NW coast of Kyushu island; population (1987) 1,142,000. It produces chemicals, textiles, paper, and metal goods.

-ful, *suf.* full of, abounding in, having, as in *artful, beautiful, sinful, wilful;* the quantity or number required to fill, as in *cupful, handful, houseful.* [OE *full,* see FULL[1]]

Fulah, *n.* a member of one of the dominant races in the Sudan; the language of this race. [African native]

Fulani, *n.* person of Fulani culture from the southern Sahara and Sahel. Traditionally pastoralists and traders, Fulani groups are found in Senegal, Guinea, Mali, Burkina Faso, Niger, Nigeria, Chad, and Cameroon. The Fulani language is divided into four dialects, and belongs to the West Atlantic branch of the Niger-Congo family.

Fulbright, *n.* **William** (1905–), US Democratic politician. He was responsible for the Fulbright Act of 1946 which provided grants for thousands of Americans to study overseas and for overseas students to enter the US; he had studied at Oxford, UK, on a Rhodes scholarship. He chaired the Senate Foreign Relations Committee (1959–74), and was a strong internationalist and supporter of the United Nations.

fulcrum, *n.* (*pl.* **-crums, -cra**) the fixed point on which the bar of a lever rests or about which it turns; a means of making any kind of force or influence effective; (*Bot., Zool.*) an additional organ, as a stipule, scale, spine etc. **fulcraceous, fulcral, fulcrant,** *a.* **fulcrate,** *a.* (*Bot.*) furnished with or supported by fulcrums. [L, a support, from *fulcīre,* to prop]

fulfil, (*esp. N Am.*) **fulfill,** *v.t.* to accomplish, to carry out, to execute, perform; to satisfy, to correspond to, to comply with; to fill out; to finish, to complete (a term of office etc.); to realize the potential of. **fulfiller,** *n.* **fulfilment, fulfilling,** *n.* [OE *fullfyllan* (as FULL[1], FILL)]

fulgent, *a.* shining, dazzling, exceedingly bright. **fulgency,** *n.* **fulgently,** *adv.* **fulgid,** *a.* **fulgor,** *n.* splendour, dazzling, brightness. **fulgorous,** *a.* **fulguration,** *n.* (*usu. pl.*) flashing of lightning; †(*Assaying*) the sudden brightening of gold or silver in the crucible as the last traces of dross leave the surface. **fulgurite,** *n.* (*Geol.*) a vitrified tube in sand, supposed to be produced by the action of lightning; an explosive made from nitroglycerine. [L *fulgens -ntem,* pres.p. of *fulgēre,* to shine]

†**fulham,** *n.* (*sl.*) a loaded die. [perh. from *Fulham,* the place-name]

fuliginous, *a.* sooty, smoky, soot-coloured; dusky, gloomy. **fuliginously,** *adv.* **fuliginosity,** *n.* [L *fūlīgi-*

nōsus, from *fūlīgo -inis,* soot]

full[1], *a.* filled up, replete; having no space empty, containing as much as the limits will allow; well supplied, having abundance (of); filled to repletion, satisfied with; charged or overflowing (with feeling etc.); preoccupied or engrossed with; plentiful, copious, ample; complete, perfect, at the height of development; visible in its entire dimensions; of the moon, having the whole disc illuminated; ample in volume or extent, swelling, plump; strong, sonorous; pregnant; high, as the tide. *adv.* quite, equally; completely, exactly, directly; very. *n.* complete measure or degree; the utmost or fullest extent; the highest state or point; a state of satiety. *v.t.* to fill (out), to give fullness to, to make full; †to fulfil. *v.i.* to become full. **at the full,** at the height or the highest condition; of the moon, with the whole disc illuminated. **in full,** completely, without abridgment, abatement or deduction. **keep her full,** (*Naut.*) keep the sails filled (order to the steersman). **to be full of oneself,** to have an exaggerated view of one's own importance. **to the full,** to the utmost extent. **full back,** *n.* (*Football etc.*) a defensive player, usu. the rearmost in any on-field formation. **full-blooded,** *a.* vigorous; sensual; of pure blood. **full-blown,** *a.* fully expanded, as a flower; mature, perfect, fully developed; fully qualified. **full-bodied,** *a.* having a full, rich flavour or quality. **full-bottomed,** *a.* having a large bottom, as distinguished from a bob-wig. **full-bound,** *a.* of books, bound entirely in leather. **full brother, sister,** *n.* one having both parents in common. **full-butt,** *adv.* (*sl.*) with sudden violent collision. **full-cream,** *a.* of milk, not skimmed. **full-cry,** *a.* giving tongue in chorus, as a pack of hounds. **full dress,** *n.* dress worn on ceremonious occasions; evening dress. *a.* at which full dress is to be worn. **full-dress debate,** one previously arranged on some important question, opp. to one arising casually. **full-drive,** *adv.* (*coll.*) with great force or speed. **full-eyed,** *a.* having prominent eyes. **full-faced,** *a.* having a broad chubby face; facing directly towards the spectator; of type, having the heavy lines very thick. **full-flavoured,** *a.* strongly flavoured, highly spiced; (*sl.*) of a story, indecent. **full-fledged** FULLY FLEDGED. †**full-fraught,** *a.* fully laden. **full-frontal,** *a.* of a nude, with the genitals fully revealed; unrestrained, omitting no detail. †**full-hearted,** *a.* brave, confident, courageous; deeply stirred. **full-hot,** *a.* heated to the utmost degree. **full house,** *n.* in poker, three of a kind and a pair; in bingo etc., the set of numbers needed to win; an auditorium filled to capacity. **full-length,** *a.* of the entire figure; of the standard length. *n.* a full-length portrait. *adv.* stretched to the full extent. **full-manned,** *a.* having a complete crew. †**full-orbed,** *a.* showing a complete disc. **full-out,** *adv.* at full power. **full-page,** *a.* taking up a whole page. **full pitch,** *n., adv.* (a delivery which reaches the batsman) without touching the ground. **full-pitched,** *a.* **full-scale,** *a.* of the same size as the original; using all available resources; all-out. **full stop,** *n.* a period (.), the longest pause in reading; an abrupt finish. **full term,** *n.* the normal or expected end date for a pregnancy. **full-term,** *a.* **full-throated,** *a.* with the full power of the voice. **full time,** *n.* the end of play in e.g. a football match. *adv.* for the whole of the (standard) working week. **full-time,** *a.* **full-timer,** *n.* **full-toss** FULL PITCH. **full up,** *adv.* quite full; with no room for more. **full-winged,** *a.* having powerful or complete wings. **fullish,** *a.* **fully,** *adv.* completely, entirely, quite. **fully-fashioned,** *a.* shaped to the lines of the body. **fully-fledged,** *a.* of a bird, having all its feathers; fully qualified, having full status as. **fullness, fulness,** *n.* the state or quality of being full; completeness, satiety; largeness, richness, volume, force. **in the fullness of time,** at the destined time. [OE *full* (cp. Dut. *vol,* Icel. *fullr,* Goth. *fullo,* G *voll,* Sansk. *pūrna,* L *plēnus,* Gr. *plērēs*)]

full[2], *v.t.* to cleanse and thicken (as cloth). **fuller**[1], *n.* one whose occupation is to full cloth. **fuller's earth,** *n.* an argillaceous earth which absorbs grease, much used in fulling cloth. **fullery,** *n.* a place where cloth is fulled. **fulling-mill,** *n.* [OF *fouler,* late L *fullāre,* from L *fullo,* a fuller]

fuller[2], *n.* a blacksmith's tool for making grooves; a groove made by this. *v.t.* to form a groove or channel in with this. [etym. unknown]

Fuller[1], *n.* **(Richard) Buckminster** (1895–1983), US architect and engineer. In 1947 he invented the lightweight geodesic dome, a half-sphere of triangular components independent of buttress or vault. It combined the maximum strength with the minimum structure. Within 30 years over 50,000 had been built.

Fuller[2], *n.* **Roy** (1912–), English poet and novelist. His collections of poetry include *Poems* (1939), *Epitaphs and Occasions* (1951), *Brutus's Orchard* (1957), *Collected Poems* (1962), and *The Reign of Sparrows* (1980). Novels include *My Child, My Sister* (1965) and *The Carnal Island* (1970).

fullness, fully FULL[1].

fulmar, *n.* a sea-bird, *Fulmaris glacialis,* allied to the petrels, abundant in the Arctic seas. [prob. Scand. (cp. Icel. *fūll,* FOUL, *mar,* a MEW[1])]

fulminate[1], *v.i.* to lighten or thunder; to explode with a loud noise or report, to detonate; to thunder out denunciations. *v.t.* to cause to explode; to utter (threats, denunciations or censures). **fulminant,** *a.* fulminating; of diseases, developing suddenly; †thundering. *n.* something that fulminates or explodes. **fulminating,** *a.* thundering, explosive. **fulminating powder,** *n.* an explosive compound. **fulmination,** *n.* **fulminatory,** *a.* †**fulmine,** *v.i.* to flash and thunder like lightning; to fulminate. *v.t.* to send forth (thunder and lightning); to thunder forth. **fulmineous,** *a.* [L *fulminātus,* p.p. of *fulmināre,* from *fulmen,* lightning]

fulminate[2], *n.* a salt of fulminic acid; an explosive containing this. **fulminic,** *a.* pertaining to or capable of detonation. **fulminic acid,** *n.* an unisolated acid that unites with certain metals to form explosive fulminates.

fulness, FULLNESS under FULL[1].

fulsome, *a.* esp. of compliments, flattery etc., disgusting by excess or grossness, coarse, excessive, satiating. **fulsomely,** *adv.* **fulsomeness,** *n.*

Fulton, *n.* **Robert** (1765–1815), US engineer and inventor who designed the first successful steamships. He produced a submarine, the *Nautilus,* in Paris, France, in 1797, and experimented with steam navigation on the Seine, then returned to the US. The first steam vessel of note, the *Clermont,* appeared on the Hudson in 1807, sailing between New York and Albany. The first steam warship was the *Fulton,* of 38 tonnes, built from 1814–15.

fulvous, *a.* (*chiefly Bot. Zool.*) tawny, reddish-yellow; fox-coloured. **fulvescent,** *a.* †**fulvid,** *a.* fulvous. [L *fulvus*]

fum, fung, *n.* a fabulous bird, sometimes called the Chinese phoenix, a symbol of imperial dignity, much used in Chinese and Japanese decoration. [Chin. *fung* (in *fung-whang*)]

fumacious, *a.* smoky; addicted to tobacco or smoking. [L *fūmāre,* to smoke]

fumade, †**fumado,** *n.* a smoked pilchard. [Sp. *fumado,* smoked, as prec.]

†**fumage,** *n.* hearth-money. [med. L *fūmāgium,* L *fūmus,* smoke]

fumarium, *n.* (*pl.* **-riums, -ria**) a smoke-chamber in an ancient Roman house, for drying wood, seasoning meat etc. [late L, from *fūmāre,* to smoke]

fumarole, *n.* a hole in the ground in a volcanic region forming an exit for subterranean vapours; a smoke-vent. **fumarolic,** *a.* [It. *fumaruolo,* L *fūmāriolum,* dim. of *fūmārium,* as prec.]

fumatorium, *n.* (*pl.* **-riums, -ria**) a room or apparatus for fumigating; a chamber in a conservatory etc. for destroying insects by chemical fumes. [L *fūmāre,* to smoke]

fumatory, *n.* a place for smoking or fumigation.

fumble, *v.i.* to grope about; to act, esp. to use one's hands, in an uncertain aimless, or awkward manner; to bungle in any business; †to stammer, to be confused. *v.t.* to handle or manage awkwardly; to fail to catch or hold; to deal with in an uncertain or hesitating manner. **fumbler,** *n.* one who acts awkwardly; a fumbling attempt. **fumblingly,** *adv.* [perh. from Dut. *fommelen* (cogn. with OE *folm,* L *palma,* the palm of the hand)]

fume, *n.* (*usu. pl.*) a smoke, vapour or gas, esp. a malodorous or toxic one; (*usu. pl.*) a narcotic vapour, esp. such as is supposed to rise from alcoholic liquors and to affect the brain; mental agitation, esp. an angry mood; anything empty, fleeting or unsubstantial; †vanity, emptiness; †flattery; †incense; †smoke. *v.i.* to emit smoke or vapour; to pass off in smoke or vapour; to show irritation, to fret, to chafe. *v.t.* to dry, perfume, stain or cure with smoke, esp. to darken (oak, photographic plates etc.) with chemical fumes, as of ammonia; to dissipate in vapour; to flatter; to perfume. †**fumeless,** *a.* †**fumid**, *a.* smoky. †**fumingly,** *adv.* angrily; with passion. †**fumish,** *a.* smoky; passionate, irascible. **fumishness,** *n.* heat of temper; passion. †**fumous, fumose,** *a.* producing fumes or vapours; fumy; (*Bot.*) smoke-coloured. **fumosity**, *n.* tendency to emit fumes; fumes arising from excessive drinking. **fumy,** *a.* full or composed of fumes; causing fumes; smoky, vaporous. [OF *fum,* L *fūmus,* smoke]

†**fumet, fumette**, *n.* the smell of game or meat when high. [F, from *fumer,* L *fūmāre,* to FUME]

fumigate, *v.t.* to subject to the action of smoke or vapour, esp. for the purpose of disinfection; †to perfume. **fumigation,** *n.* **fumigator,** *n.* one who or that which fumigates, esp. an apparatus for applying smoke, gas etc. for the purpose of cleansing, disinfecting, or perfuming. †**fumigatory,** *a.* [L *fūmigātus,* p.p. of *fūmigāre* (*fūmus,* smoke, *-ig-, ag-,* base of *agere,* to drive)]

fumitory, *n.* a herb belonging to the genus *Fumaria,* esp. *F. officinalis,* formerly used for skin diseases. [ME and OF *fumeterre* (*fume de terre*), late L *fūmus terræ,* smoke of the earth]

fumosity, fumy FUME.

fun, *n.* (a source of) amusement, merriment, jollity; hectic activity or argument. *a.* enjoyable; amusing, entertaining. **a figure of fun,** a butt of ridicule. **for fun, for the fun of it,** for pleasure simply. **fun and games,** (*iron.*) hectic activity, trouble. **in fun,** as a joke. **like fun,** (*coll.*) energetically; thoroughly. **to make fun of, to poke fun at,** to hold up to or turn into ridicule; to banter. **funfair,** *n.* a usu. outdoor show with rides, sideshows, games of skill and other amusements. **fun fur,** *n.* inexpensive, artificial fur (often dyed) for clothes, seat covers etc. [prob. corr. of FON]

funambulist, *n.* a performer on the tight or slack rope; a rope-walker or rope-dancer. †**funambulate,** *v.i.* to walk or dance on a rope. **funambulation,** *n.* †**funambulatory,** *a.* performing like a rope-dancer; narrow, like the walk of a rope-dancer. [earlier *funambule,* L *fūnambulus* (*fūnis,* rope, *ambūlare,* to walk)]

function, *n.* the specific activity, operation or power belonging to an agent; duty, occupation, office; a public or official ceremony, esp. a religious service of an elaborate kind; hence (*coll.*) a social entertainment of some importance; (*Physiol.*) the specific office of any animal or plant organ; (*Math.*) a quantity dependent for its value on another or other quantities so that a change in the second correspondingly affects the first. *v.i.* to perform a function or duty; to operate. **functional,** *a.* pertaining to some office or function; official; formal; practical, utilitarian, eschewing ornament; able to perform (its function), working; (*Physiol.*) pertaining to or affecting the action or functions of an organ, not its substance or structure; (*Math.*) relating to or depending on a function. **functional disease,** *n.* derangement of some function of the body, as distinguished from organic or structural disease. **functionalism,** *n.* **functionally,** *adv.* **functionary,** *n.* one who holds any office or trust; an official. *a.* pertaining to a function or functions; official. **functionate,** *v.i.* to function. **functionless,** *a.* [OF (F *fonction*), L *functiōnem,* nom. *functio,* from *fungī,* to perform]

functionalism, *n.* in architecture and design, a 20th-century school, also called modernism or international style, characterized by a desire to exclude everything that serves no practical purpose. It was a reaction against the 19th-century practice of imitating earlier styles, and its finest achievements are in the realm of industrial building.

fund, *n.* a sum of money or stock of anything available for use or enjoyment; assets, capital; a sum of money set apart for a specific object, permanent or temporary; (*pl.*) money lent to a government and constituting a national debt; the stock of a national debt regarded as an investment; (*pl.*) (*coll.*) money, finances, pecuniary resources; †the bottom. *v.t.* to convert into a single fund or debt, esp. to consolidate into stock or securities bearing interest at a fixed rate; to amass, collect, store; to place in a fund; to provide money for. **in funds,** provided with cash, flush of money. **fundholder,** *n.* one who has property invested in the public funds. **fund-raiser,** *n.* one who raises money for an (often charitable) organization, project etc. **fundraising,** *n.*, *a.* **fundable,** *a.* **funded,** *a.* invested in public funds; forming part of the national debt of a country, existing in the form of bonds bearing regular interest. **funded debt,** *n.* **funding,** *n.* financial provision, support. **fundless,** *a.* [F *fond,* L *fundus,* the bottom; later assim. to L]

fundament, *n.* †a foundation; the lower part of the body, the buttocks; the anus. [ME and OF *fondement,* L *fundāmentum,* from *fundāre,* to found (later form directly from L)]

fundamental, *a.* pertaining to or serving as a foundation or base; basal, essential, primary, original, indispensable. *n.* a principle, rule or article forming the basis or groundwork; the lowest note or 'root' of a chord. **fundamental bass,** *n.* (*Mus.*) a bass consisting of a succession of fundamental notes. **fundamentalism,** *n.* (*Christianity*) belief in the literal truth of the Bible; (*Islam*) strict observance of the teachings of the Koran and of Islamic law. **fundamentalist,** *n.*, *a.* **fundamentality**, *n.* **fundamentally,** *adv.* [as prec.]

funeral, *a.* pertaining to or connected with the committal of the dead. *n.* the solemn and ceremonious committal of the dead; a funeral service; a procession of persons at a funeral; †a death; †a funeral sermon. **it's your** etc. **funeral,** it's your affair. **funeral director,** *n.* an undertaker. **funeral home,** (*esp. N Am.*) **parlour,** *n.* a place where the dead are prepared for burial or cremation and funerals may be held. **funebrial**, **funerary,** *a.* pertaining to funerals. **funereal**, *a.* pertaining to or suitable for a funeral; dismal, sad, mournful; gloomy, dark. **funereally,** *adv.* [OF, from late L *fūnerālis,* from *fūnus fūneris,* a funeral procession]

†**funest,** *a.* portending or causing death or disaster; sad, lamentable, mournful. [F *funeste,* L *fūnestus,* from *fūnus,* see prec.]

funfair FUN.

fung FUM.

fungible, *a.* (*Law*) of such a nature that it may be replaced by another thing of the same class. *n.* (*pl.*) movable goods which may be valued by weight or measure. [med. L *fungibilis,* from *fungī,* to perform, operate, see FUNCTION]

fungus, *n.* (*pl.* **-gi**) a mushroom, toadstool, mould, mildew, or other cryptogamous plant, destitute of chlorophyll and deriving its nourishment from organic matter; (*Path.*) a morbid growth or excrescence of a spongy nature; something of rapid or parasitic growth. **fungaceous**, *a.* **fungal,** *a.* of, pertaining to or of the nature of a fungus. *n.* a fungus. **fungic**, *a.* obtained from fungi. **fungic acid,** *n.* an acid contained in the juice of most fungi. **fungicide**, *n.* anything that destroys fungi or their spores. **fungiform**, **fungiliform**, *a.* having a termination like the head of a fungus. **fungin**, *n.* the cellulose of fungi and lichens. **fungivorous**, *a.* feeding on fungi. **fungoid**, *a.* of the nature of or like a fungus. **fungology**, *n.* the science of fungi. **fungological**, *a.* **fungologist**, *n.* **fungous,** *a.* like or of the nature of a fungus; excrescent, springing up suddenly, ephemeral; spongy, unsubstantial. **fungosity**, *n.* **fungusy,** *a.* [L, prob. cogn. with Gr. *sphongos,* a SPONGE]

funicular, *a.* pertaining to, consisting of, or depending on a rope or cable. *n.* a railway worked by means of a cable, usu. a mountain railway. **funicle**, *n.* (*Bot.*) a funiculus. **funiculus**, *n.* (*pl.* **-culi**) the umbilical cord; a number of nerve-fibres enclosed in a tubular sheath; (*Bot.*) a cord connecting the seed with the placenta. **funiliform**, *a.* (*Bot.*) formed of cord-like fibres. **funis**, *n.* the umbilical cord. [L *fūniculus,* dim. of *fūnis,* a rope, -AR]

Funk, *n.* **Casimir** (1884–1967), US biochemist, born in Poland, who did pioneering research into vitamins.

funk[1], *n.* (*coll.*) a state of fear or panic; a coward. *v.i.* (*coll.*) to be in a state of terror; to flinch, to shrink in fear or cowardice. *v.t.* to be afraid of; to shirk, to try to evade through fear or cowardice; (*usu. p.p.*) to frighten, to scare. **blue funk,** (*coll.*) abject terror. **funkhole,** *n.* a dugout; any refuge one can retreat to. **funker,** *n.* **funky,** *a.* [etym. doubtful]

funk[2], *v.t.* †to blow smoke upon so as to stifle or annoy. *v.i.* †to smoke; to stink. *n.* †a stink; (*sl.*) funky music. **funky,** *a.* (*sl.*) smelly, stinking; of jazz, pop etc., earthy, unsophisticated, soulful, like early blues; (*sl.*) with it; (*sl.*) kinky, odd, quaint. [etym. doubtful (perh. from OF *funkier,* ult. from L *fūmigāre,* see FUMIGATE)]

funk[3], *v.i., v.t.* (*Sc.*) of a horse, to kick. **funky,** *a.* [perh. onomat.]

funkia, *n.* a genus of liliaceous plants, comprising the plantain-lilies, from China and Japan. [H.C. *Funck,* 1771–1839, German botanist]

funnel, *n.* a conical vessel usu. terminating below in a tube, for conducting liquids etc. into vessels with a small opening; a tube or shaft for ventilation, lighting etc.; the chimney of a steamship or steam-engine; the inside of a chimney, a flue. *v.t.* (*past, p.p.* **funnelled**) to pour or pass (as if) through a funnel. *v.i.* to move (as if) through a funnel. **funnel-web spider,** (*Austral.*) a large venomous spider found in New South Wales. **funnel-form, -shaped,** *a.* (*Bot.*) of a calyx, corolla etc., having the tube gradually enlarging upwards so as to constitute a funnel. **funnel-net,** *n.* a tapering, funnel-shaped net. **funnelled,** *a.* having a funnel or funnels; funnel-shaped. [ME *fonel,* prob. through OF (cp. Prov. *founil,* Sp. *fonil,* Port. *funil*), from late L *fundibulum* (L *infundibulum*), from *fundere,* to pour]

funny[1], *a.* droll, comical, laughable; causing mirth or laughter; strange, curious, queer, puzzling; suspicious; underhand, involving trickery; (*coll.*) slightly unwell. *n.* (*coll.*) a joke; (*pl.*) comic strips or the comics section of a newspaper. **funny-bone,** *n.* the lower part of the elbow over which the ulnar nerve passes, a blow on which causes a curious tingling sensation. **funny business,** *n.* trickery; dubious or suspicious goings on; jokes, drollery. **funny farm,** *n.* (*coll.*) a mental hospital. **funny man,** *n.* a clown; a buffoon or wag. **funnily,** *adv.* **funniment,** *n.* (*facet.*). **funniness,** *n.* **funnyism,** *n.* [see FUN]

funny[2], *n.* a narrow, clinker-built pleasure-boat, for a pair of sculls. [etym. doubtful, perh. from prec.]

fur., (*abbr.*) furlong.

†**furacious,** *a.* inclined to steal; thievish. †**furacity,** *n.* [L *fūrax -cis*]

fur, *n.* the soft fine hair growing thick upon certain animals, distinct from ordinary hair; (*pl.*) the skins, esp. dressed skins, of such animals; the skin of such animals used for lining or trimming garments; a garment made of fur; the downy covering on the skin of a peach; a coat or crust deposited by a liquid; a deposit from wine; a coat of morbid matter collected on the tongue; a crust deposited on the interior of kettles etc. by hard water. *v.t.* (*past, p.p.* **furred**) to cover, line or trim with fur; to cover or coat with morbid matter; to nail pieces of timber to (as joists or rafters) in order to bring them into a level. *v.i.* to become encrusted with fur or scale, as the inside of a boiler. **fur and feather,** fur-bearing animals and game birds. **to make the fur fly,** to create a scene, to start a row. **fur-seal,** *n.* a seal or sea-bear yielding a fur valuable commercially. **furred,** *a.* lined or ornamented with fur; coated with fur or scale. **furrier**, *n.* a dealer in furs; one who prepares and sells furs. **furring,** *n.* trimming or lining with furs; a deposit of scale (on the inside of boilers etc.); thin pieces fixed on the edge of timber to make the surface even; a lining on a brick wall to prevent dampness; double planking on the sides of a ship. **furry,** *a.* covered or clad in fur; made of fur; resembling fur; coated with a scale or deposit. [OF *forrer,* to line, to sheathe (F *fourrer*), from Teut. (cp. OE *fōdor,* G *Futter,* Icel. *fōthr*)]

furbelow, *n.* a piece of stuff, plaited and puckered, used as trimming on skirts and petticoats, a flounce; (*pl.*) finery; a seaweed, *Laminaria bulbosa,* with wrinkled fronds. *v.t.* to furnish or trim with furbelows. [var. of FALBALA]

furbish, *v.t.* to rub so as to brighten, to polish up; to renovate, to restore the newness or brightness of; to clean or brighten (up). **furbisher,** *n.* [OF *forbiss-*, stem of *forbir,* OHG *furban*]

furcate, *a.* forked, dividing into branches like the prongs of a fork. *v.i.* to fork, to divide into branches. **furcation**, *n.* **furcato-,** *comb. form.* **furciferous**, *a.* having a forked process, as the larvae of some butterflies; †scoundrelly, rascally. **furcula**, *n.* (*pl.* **-lae**) the two clavicles of birds anchylosed together so as to form one V-shaped bone, the merrythought or wishbone. **furcular,** *a.* [L *furcātus,* from *furca,* a FORK]

furfur, *n.* scurf or dandruff; (*pl.* **-fures**) particles of scurf, bran-like scales of skin. **furfuraceous**, *a.* **furfuration,** *n.* **furfurous,** *a.* [L]

furfurol, *n.* (*Chem.*) an oil formed in the dry distillation of sugar, or by distilling bran with dilute sulphuric acid. [as prec., -OL]

†**furibund,** *a.* raging, furious. [L *furibundus,* from *furere,* to rage]

Furies, *n.pl.* in Greek mythology, the Erinyes, appeasingly called the Eumenides, ('kindly ones'). They were the daughters of Earth or of Night, represented as winged maidens with serpents twisted in their hair. They punished such crimes as filial disobedience, murder, and inhospitality.

furioso, *adv.* (*Mus.*) with fury or vehemence. †*n.* a furious or impetuous person. [It., as foll.]

furious, *a.* full of fury, raging, violent, frantic; rushing with vehemence or impetuosity, tempestuous; vehement, eager. **furiosity,** *n.* **furiously,** *adv.* **furiousness,** *n.* [OF *furieus* (F *furieux*), L *furiōsus,* from *furia,* FURY]

furl, *v.t.* to roll up (a sail) and wrap about a yard, mast or stay; to roll, wrap, fold or close (up). *v.i.* to become rolled or folded up. [acc. to Skeat, prob. contr. from earlier *furdle,* corr. of *fardle,* to pack up, see FARDEL]

furlong, *n.* a measure of length, the eighth part of a mile, 40 rods or 220 yd. (201 m); a group of strips of land in the open-field system of agriculture. [OE *furlang* (*furh,* FURROW, *lang,* LONG)]

furlough, *n.* leave of absence, esp. to a soldier. *v.t.* to grant leave of absence to. [Dut. *verlof* (cp. Dan. *forlov,* G *Verlaub*), as FOR-, LEAVE[1]]

furmenty, furmety, FRUMENTY.

furnace, *n.* a chamber or structure containing a chamber in which fuel is burned for the production of intense heat, esp. for melting ores, metals etc.; a closed fireplace for heating a boiler, hot-water or hot-air pipes etc.; a time, place or occasion of severe trial or torture. *v.t.* to cast into or heat in a furnace; †to exhale like a furnace. [OF *fornais* (F *fournaise*) L *fornācem,* nom. *-nax, for-, furnus,* oven]

†**furniment,** *n.* furniture, equipment. [OF *fourniment,* as foll.]

furnish, *v.t.* to provide or supply (with); to equip, to fit up, esp. (a house or room) with movable furniture; to supply, to afford, to yield; †to provide with what is necessary; †to decorate. *v.i.* (*Racing sl.*) of a horse, to fill out, to improve in strength and appearance. **furnisher,** *n.* **furnishings,** *n.pl.* furniture, upholstery, apparatus; †mere externals or incidentals. †**furnishment,** *n.* [OF *fourniss-,* stem of *fournir,* ult. from OHG *frumjan,* to perform, provide (cogn. with *fruma,* profit, advantage, G *fromm,* good, Eng. FORMER)]

furniture, *n.* equipment, equipage, outfit; movable articles, esp. chairs, tables etc. with which a house or room is furnished; an ornamental addition; (*Print.*) the material, of wood, metal or plastic, which keeps the pages firmly fixed in the chase, and separates them so as to allow a uniform margin when printed; accessories; locks, door and window trimmings etc.; the mountings of a gun; the masts and rigging of a ship; the trappings of a horse. [F *fourniture,* as prec.]

furor, *n.* †rage, fury, madness; (*N Am.*) furore. [L, from *furere,* to rage]

furore, *n.* great excitement or enthusiasm; a craze, a rage; an uproar, an outburst of public indignation. [It., as prec.]

furphy, *n.* (*Austral.*) a groundless rumour, a false report, orig. circulated by the drivers of Furphy's military water- and sanitary-carts. **furphy merchant,** *n.* one who circulates groundless rumours. [J. *Furphy,* maker of the cart]

furrier, furring FUR.

furrow, *n.* a trench in the earth made by a plough; a narrow trench, groove or hollow; a rut; the track of a ship; a wrinkle on the face. *v.t.* to plough; to make grooves, furrows or wrinkles in; to mark (the face) with deep wrinkles. **furrow-drain,** *n.* a deep open channel made by a plough, to carry off water. *v.t.* to make furrow-drains in. †**furrow-faced,** *a.* having a wrinkled face or surface. **furrow-slice,** *n.* the strip of earth thrown up from a furrow by the plough. †**furrow-weed,** *n.* a weed growing on ploughed land. **furrowless,** *a.* **furrowy,** *a.* [OE *furh* (cp. Dut. *voor,* Icel. *for,* G *Furche*)]

furry FUR.

furry dance, *n.* a festival dance through the streets of Helston and certain other Cornish towns on 8 May, called Flora's day. [perh. *Flora*]

further, *a.* more remote; more advanced; going or extended beyond that already existing or stated, additional (chiefly used when distance in space is not implied, cp. FARTHER). *adv.* to a greater distance, degree or extent; moreover, in addition, also. *v.t.* to help forward, to advance, to promote. **further education,** *n.* formal, post-school education other than at a university or polytechnic. **furtherance,** *n.* promotion, help, assistance. **furtherer,** *n.* **furthermore,** *adv.* moreover, besides. **furthermost,** *a.* furthest, most remote. †**furthersome,** *a.* advantageous. **furthest,** *a.* most remote in time or place. *adv.* at or to the greatest distance or extent. [OE *furthra,* adv. *furthor* (cogn. with FORE, *-ther* is the comp. suf.), cp. Dut. *vorders,* G *vorder,* Gr. *proteros,* comp. of *pro*]

furtive, *a.* stealthy, sly; secret, surreptitious, designed to escape attention; obtained by or as by theft; †thievish. **furtively,** *adv.* **furtiveness,** *n.* [F *furtif,* fem. *furtive,* L *furtīvus,* from *furtum,* theft (*fūr,* a thief, cp. Gr. *phōr*)]

Furtwängler, *n.* **(Gustav Heinrich Ernst Martin) Wilhelm** (1886–1954), German conductor; leader of the Berlin Philharmonic Orchestra (1922–54). His interpretations of the German Romantic composers, especially Wagner, were regarded as classically definitive. He remained in Germany during the Nazi regime.

furuncle, *n.* a superficial inflammatory tumour, with a central core; a boil. **furuncular, -culoid, -culous,** *a.* [L *fūrunculus,* orig. dim. of *fūr,* thief]

fury, *n.* vehement, uncontrollable anger, rage; a fit of raving passion; impetuosity, violence; intense, ecstatic passion, inspiration, enthusiasm; (**Fury**) one of the three avenging goddesses of classical mythology; hence, a furious woman, a virago. **like fury,** (*coll.*) with furious energy. †**fury-like,** *a.* raging, frenzied. [OF *furie,* L *furia,* from *furere,* to rage]

furze, *n.* the gorse or whin, *Ulex europaeus,* a spinous evergreen shrub with bright yellow flowers, common on waste, stony land. **furze-chat,** *n.* the whinchat. **furzeling, furze-wren,** *n.* the Dartford warbler. **furzy,** *a.* [OE *fyrs*]

fusarole, *n.* a moulding placed immediately under the echinus in Doric, Ionic and composite capitals. [F *fusarolle,* It. *fusaruola,* L *fūsus,* a spindle]

fuscous, *a.* brown tinged with grey or black; dingy. [L *fuscus*]

fuse¹, *v.t.* to melt; to reduce to a liquid or fluid state by heat, to unite by or as by melting together; to cause to fail by blowing a fuse. *v.i.* to melt; to become fluid; to become united by or as by melting together; to fail because of a blown fuse. *n.* (a device containing) a strip of fusible wire or metal which melts if the current in an electric circuit exceeds a certain value; the melting of wire etc. caused by a short circuit. **fuse box,** *n.* a box containing one or more fuses. **fusing-point,** *n.* the temperature at which a given substance melts. **fusible,** *a.* capable of being fused or melted. **fusible alloy, metal,** *n.* an alloy, usually of lead, tin and bismuth, compounded in definite proportions to melt at a given temperature. **fusible plug,** *n.* a plug of fusible metal used in a steam-boiler or an electric circuit to obviate an excessive increase of temperature. **fusibility,** *n.* †**fusile,** *a.* fusible; fluid through heat; produced by melting or casting. **fusion,** *n.* the act of melting or rendering liquid by heat; the state of being so melted or liquefied; union by or as by melting together, blending; a product of such melting or blending; the combination at very high temperature of atomic nuclei of hydrogen or deuterium to form helium nuclei and liberate nuclear energy; coalescence or coalition (as of political parties). **fusion bomb,** *n.* a bomb, e.g. the hydrogen bomb, whose energy results from nuclear fusion. **fusion reactor,** *n.* a nuclear reactor operating on the fusion principle. **fusionism,** *n.* **fusionist,** *n.* one who advocates political fusion. [L *fūsus,* p.p. of *fundere,* to pour]

fuse², *n.* a tube, cord or casing filled or saturated with combustible material, and used for igniting a charge in a mine or projectile; (*esp. N Am.* **fuze**) a detonating device in a bomb or shell. *v.t.* (*esp. N Am.* **fuze**) to furnish with a fuse or fuses. [It. *fuso,* L *fūsus,* a spindle]

fusee¹, fuzee, *n.* the cone round which the chain is wound in a clock or watch; a fuse; a match with a mass of inflammable material at its head, used for lighting pipes etc. in a wind. **fusiform,** *a.* shaped like a spindle; tapering at both ends. [F *fusée,* L *fūsāta,* spindleful, orig. fem. p.p. of *fūsāre,* from *fūsus,* a spindle]

†**fusee²** FUSIL¹.

fuselage, *n.* the main body of an aeroplane. [F *fuselé,* spindle-shaped, -AGE]

Fuseli, *n.* **Henry** (1741–1825), British artist born in Switzerland, working in the romantic style. He painted macabre and dreamlike images such as *The Nightmare* (1781) (Detroit Institute of Arts).

fusel oil, *n.* a poisonous oily product, composed chiefly of amyl alcohol, formed during the manufacture of corn, potato or grape spirits. [G *Fusel,* spirits of inferior quality]

fusil¹, †**fusee,** *n.* an obsolete firelock, lighter than a musket. **fusilier,** *n.* orig. a soldier armed with a fusil, as distinguished from a pikeman or archer, still applied in the British army to certain regiments of the line. **fusillade,** *n.* a continuous, rapid discharge of firearms; a rapid succession of blows, critical comments etc. *v.t.* to shoot down or storm by fusillade. [F *fusil,* It. *focile,* a fire-steel, ult. from L *focus,* a hearth]

fusil², *n.* (*Her.*) a bearing resembling a lozenge, longer in proportion to breadth. [OF *fusel* (F *fuseau*), from L *fūsus,* a spindle]

fusion FUSE¹.

fuss, *n.* excessive activity, labour or trouble, taken or exhibited; unnecessary bustle or commotion, too much ado; undue importance given to trifles or petty details. *v.i.* to make much ado about nothing; to worry, to be nervous or restless. *v.t.* to worry, to agitate. **to make,**

kick up a fuss, to cause a commotion, esp. by complaining. **to make a fuss of,** to lavish attention on as a sign of affection. **fussbudget, fusspot,** *n.* (*coll.*) one who fusses. **fussy,** *a.* nervous, excitable, esp. over small details; finicky, fastidious; overelaborate, overornate. **fussily,** *adv.* **fussiness,** *n.* [prob. onomat.]

fust, *n.* †a wine-cask; a strong, musty smell, as of a cask; (*Arch.*) the shaft of a column. *v.i.* to grow mouldy; of wine, to taste of the cask. **fusty,** *a.* mouldy, musty; rank, ill-smelling. **fustiness,** *n.* [OF (F *fût*), L *fūstem,* nom. *fūstis,* a stick, a log]

fustanella, *n.* the short white skirt worn by men in Greece and Albania. [It., dim. of mod. Gr. *phoustani,* It. *fustagno,* FUSTIAN]

fustet, *n.* the wood of the Venetian sumach, *Rhus cotinus,* fustic. [F, Sp. *fustete,* corr. of *fustoc,* FUSTIC]

fustian, *n.* a coarse twilled cotton or cotton and linen cloth, with short velvety pile; applied as an old tradename to velveteen, corduroy etc.; inflated or pompous writing or speaking; bombast; clap-trap, mere verbiage; †a kind of egg flip. *a.* bombastic; pompous, pretentious, inflated; using bombastic language. **fustianed,** *a.* **fustianist,** *n.* one who uses bombastic language in writing or speaking. **fustianize, -ise,** *v.i.* [ME *fustane,* OF *fustaigne,* It. *fustagno,* low L *fustāneum,* neut. a. masc. *fustāneus,* prob. from Arab. *Fustāt,* a suburb of Cairo]

fustic, *n.* a yellow wood used in dyeing, that of *Maclura tinctoria,* a large W Indian tree, sometimes called in distinction **old fustic**, and that of *Rhus cotinus,* a bushy shrub of southern Europe, now usu. called **young fustic**. [F and Sp. *fustoc,* Arab. *fustuq,* Gr. *pistakē,* PISTACHIO (acc. to OED, earlier traced to L *fūstis,* a cudgel)]

†fustigate, *v.t.* to beat with a cudgel; to cane. **†fustigation,** *n.* [late L *fūstīgātus,* p.p. of *fūstīgāre,* from *fūstis,* a cudgel]

†fustilarian, *n.* a low fellow. [Shak., 2 *Henry IV,* II. i, prob. coined from FUSTY]

fusty FUST.

fut., (*abbr.*) future.

futchel, *n.* one of the timbers set lengthwise in the framework of a carriage, to support the splinter-bar and the shafts or pole. [etym. unknown]

futhark, futhorc, futhork, *n.* the Runic alphabet. [from the first six letters *f u þ o r k*]

futile, *a.* useless; of no effect; trifling, worthless, frivolous. **futilely,** *adv.* **futility,** *n.* [L *fūtilis, futtilis,* leaky, easily poured out, prob. from root of *fundere,* to pour]

futon, *n.* a Japanese floor-mattress used as a bed. [Jap.]

futtock, *n.* (*Naut.*) one of the timbers in the compound rib of a vessel. **futtock-plate,** *n.* an iron plate at the head of a lower mast, to which the futtock-shrouds and the dead-eyes of the topmast shrouds are secured. **futtock-shrouds,** *n.pl.* the short shrouds from this to a band on the mast below. [prob. corr. of FOOT HOOK]

future, *a.* that will be; that is to come or happen hereafter; (*Gram.*) expressing action yet to happen; that will be something specified, as *our future king*. *n.* time to come; that which will be or will happen hereafter; prospective condition, state, career, etc.; likelihood of success; (*Gram.*) the future tense; (*pl.*) goods, stocks etc.; bought or sold for future delivery. **to deal in futures,** to speculate for a rise or fall. **future perfect,** *n., a.* (the tense) expressing an action as completed in the future, as *it will have been*. **futureless,** *a.* **†futurely,** *adv.* **futureness,** *n.* **futurism,** *n.* see separate entry. **futurist,** *n.* one who holds that a great part of Scripture prophecy (esp. of the Apocalypse) is still to be fulfilled; (*often* **Futurist**) a follower of futurism. **futuristic**, *a.* of the future or futurism; of design, architecture etc., ultramodern, apparently anticipating styles of the future. **†futurition**, *n.* the state of being future; existence or accomplishment in the future. **futurity**, *n.* the state of being future; future time, esp. eternity; (*often pl.*) future events, things to come. **futurology**, *n.* the prediction of future developments from current, esp. sociological and technological, trends. **futurological**, *a.* **futurologist**, *n.* [OF *futur,* fem. *future,* L *futurus,* fut.p. of *esse,* to be]

futurism, *n.* a literary and artistic movement (1909–14), originating in Paris. The Italian poet Marinetti published the Futurist Manifesto in 1909 urging Italian artists to join him in futurism. They eulogized the modern world and the 'beauty of speed and energy' in their works, trying to capture the dynamism of a speeding car or train by combining the shifting geometric planes of Cubism with vibrant colours. As a movement it died out during World War I, but futurists' exultation in war and violence was seen as an early manifestation of fascism.

fuze FUSE[2].

fuzee FUSEE[1].

Fuzhou, *n.* (formerly **Foochow**), industrial port and capital of Fujian province, SE China; population (1986) 1,190,000. It is a centre for shipbuilding and steel production, and rice, sugar, tea, and fruit pass through the port. There are joint foreign and Chinese factories.

fuzz, *v.i.* to fly off in minute particles. *n.* minute light particles of down or similar matter, fluff; fuzziness. **the fuzz,** (*sl.*) the police. **fuzz-ball,** *n.* a puff-ball. **fuzzwig,** *n.* a wig of frizzed curls. **fuzzy,** *a.* covered with fuzz; having many small, tight curls; blurred, indistinct. **fuzzy-wuzzy,** *n.* (*Austral. offensive*) a native of new Guinea; (*Kipling*) a Sudanese, a Sudanese fighter; (*loosely, derog.*) any black (African) person. **fuzzily,** *adv.* **fuzziness,** *n.* [prob. echoic of blowing]

FWD, (*abbr.*) four-wheel drive.

fwd., (*abbr.*) forward.

fy, FIE.

-fy, *suf.* to make, to produce; forming verbs, to bring into a certain state, as in *beautify, deify, horrify, petrify, sanctify, terrify;* (*coll.*) as in *argufy, Frenchify, speechify*. [F *-fier,* L *-ficāre, facere,* to make]

fyke, *n.* (*N Am.*) a bag-net, open at one end so as to allow fish to enter but opposing their exit. [Dut. *fuik*]

fylfot, *n.* an ancient figure consisting of a great cross with arms continued at right angles, used heraldically, as a mystic symbol, or for decoration; called also gammadion and swastika. [borrowed by mod. antiquaries from a MS. (*c.* 1500) where it prob. means *fill-foot*]

Fylingdales, *n.* site in the North Yorkshire Moors National Park, England, of an early-warning radar station, linked with similar stations in Greenland and Alaska, to give a four-minute warning of nuclear attack.

fyrd, *n.* an array, at the command of the king in Anglo-Saxon times, of all able to bear arms. [OE, cogn. with FARE]

fytte FIT[2].

fz, (*abbr.*) sforzando.

G

G, g, gee, *n.* the seventh letter, and fifth consonant, of the Roman and English alphabets, **G, g,** has two sounds in modern English; one hard, a guttural stop, before *a, o, u,* as in *gate, god, gun* (except in *gaol*), and when initial, always before *e* and *i* in words of English origin, as in *get, give,* and when final as in *bag;* as also before the consonants *l* and *r,* as in *glove, grove;* the other soft, like that of *j,* in words of Gr. or L origin before *e* or *i; (pl.* **Gs, G's, Gees**); (*Mus.*) the fifth note of the diatonic scale of C major; the key or scale corresponding to this; the fourth string of a violin, the third of the viola and violoncello, the first of the double-bass; the mark of the treble clef; German **g,** (*Phys.*) a symbol of the acceleration on the surface of the earth due to gravity, about 32 ft (9.8 m) per second; (*chiefly N Am., sl.*) a symbol for *grand* (1000 dollars or pounds). **G-clef,** *n.* (*Mus.*) a sign indicating the position of G above middle C; a treble clef. **G-forces,** *n. pl.* the forces pilots and astronauts experience when their craft accelerate or decelerate rapidly. One G is the ordinary pull of gravity. Early astronauts were subjected to launch and re-entry forces up to six Gs or more. Pilots and astronauts wear G-suits that prevent their blood 'pooling' too much under severe G-forces, which can lead to unconsciousness. **G-man,** *n.* US police term for a member of the Federal Bureau of Investigation specially selected for his intrepidity as a criminal-hunter. [initials of *G*overnment *man*] **G-string,** *n.* a loincloth; a garment consisting of a small piece of cloth covering the pubic area and attached front and back to a waistband that is worn e.g. by an entertainer when performing striptease.

Ga, (*chem. symbol*) gallium.

gab, *n.* idle talk, chatter; (*Sc.*) the mouth. *v.i.* to talk glibly, to chatter, to prate. **the gift of the gab,** (*coll.*) a talent for speaking, fluency. **gabfest,** *n.* (*chiefly N Am., coll.*) a prolonged session of speeches, discussion or gossip; a gathering for this. **gabby,** *a.* talkative, loquacious. **gabster,** *n.* [prob. onomat.]

gabarage, *n.* a coarse kind of packing-cloth. [etym. uncertain]

gabardine, GABERDINE.

†**gabbart,** *n.* (*Sc.*) a flat river-vessel, a lighter. [F *gabarre* (now *gabare*), It. *gabara*]

gabble, *v.i.* to utter inarticulate sounds rapidly; to talk rapidly and incoherently. *v.t.* to utter noisily or inarticulately. *n.* rapid, incoherent or inarticulate talk; cackle, chatter. †**gabblement,** *n.* **gabbler,** *n.* [prob. imit. (cp. BABBLE)]

gabbro , *n.* rock composed of feldspar and diallage, sometimes with serpentine or mica. **gabbronite,** *n.* a bluish-green or grey variety of scapolite somewhat resembling gabbro. [It.]

gabelle, *n.* a tax or duty, esp. the tax on salt in France before the Revolution (1789). [F, from med. L *gabella, gablum,* from Teut. (cp. GAVEL)]

gaberdine, gabardine, *n.* a long coarse gown or cloak, worn in the Middle Ages by Jews and others; a cloth with a corded effect, used largely for rain-coats; a rain-proof coat made of this. [from Sp. *gabardina* or OF *gauvardine,* prob. a pilgrim's frock]

gaberlunzie, *n.* (*Sc.*) a strolling beggar; a beadsman; (*erroneously*) a beggar's wallet. **gaberlunzie man** or **beggar,** *n.* [etym. unknown]

gabion, *n.* a cylindrical basket of wicker- or iron-work, filled with earth, used for foundations etc. in engineering work and (*esp. formerly*) for shelter against an enemy's fire while trenches are being dug. **gabionade,** *n.* a work formed of gabions. **gabionage,** *n.* gabions collectively. **gabioned,** *a.* furnished with, formed of or protected with gabions. [F, from It. *gabbione,* augm. form of *gabbia,* cage]

gable, *n.* the triangular portion of the end of a building, bounded by the sides of the roof and a line joining the eaves; a wall with upper part shaped like this; a canopy or other architectural member with this shape. **gable-end,** *n.* the end wall of a building with such an upper part. **gable-roof,** *n.* a ridge roof ending in a gable. **gable-window,** *n.* a window in a gable or with a gable over it. **gabled,** *a.* having gables. **gablet,** *n.* a small gable, esp. forming an ornamental canopy over a tabernacle or niche. [OF, from Teut. (cp. Icel. *gafl,* Dut. *gevel,* pinnacle, Gr. *kephalē,* head; also OHG *gabala,* G *Gabel,* fork)]

Gable, *n.* **Clark** (1901–60), US film actor. He was a star for more than 30 years in 90 films, including *It Happened One Night* (1934), *Gone with the Wind* (1939), and *The Misfits* (1961). He was nicknamed the 'King' of Hollywood.

Gabo, *n.* **Naum.** adopted name of Naum Neemia Pevsner (1890–1977), US abstract sculptor, born in Russia. One of the leading exponents of CONSTRUCTIVISM (see under CONSTRUCTION), he left the USSR in 1922 for Germany and taught at the Bauhaus (a key centre of modern design). He lived in the UK in the 1930s, then in the US from 1946. He often used transparent coloured plastics in his sculptures.

Gabon, *n.* Gabonese Republic (*République Gabonaise*), country in central Africa, bounded N by Cameroon, E and S by the Congo, W by the Atlantic Ocean, and NW by Equatorial Guinea. **area** 267,667 sq km/103,319 sq miles. **capital** Libreville. **physical** virtually the whole country is tropical rainforest; mountains alternate with lowlands; Ogooué River flows S–W. **exports** petroleum, manganese, iron, uranium, timber. **population** (1988) 1,226,000; annual growth rate 1.6%. **language** French (official), Bantu. **religion** animist 60%, Roman Catholic 35%, small Muslim minority

Gaborone, *n.* capital of Botswana from 1965, mainly an administrative centre; population (1988) 111,000. Light industry includes textiles.

Gabriel, *n.* in the New Testament, the archangel who foretold the birth of John the Baptist to Zacharias and of Jesus to the Virgin Mary. He is also mentioned in the Old Testament in the book of Daniel. In Muslim belief, Gabriel revealed the Koran to Mohammed and escorted him on his Night Journey.

Gabrieli, *n.* **Giovanni** (*c.* 1555–1612), Italian composer and organist. Although he composed secular music, and madrigals, he is best known for his motets, which are frequently dramatic and often use several choirs and groups of instruments. In 1585 he became organist at St Mark's, Venice,

gaby, *n.* a fool, a simpleton. [perh. cogn. with GAPE]

gad¹, *n.* (*Mining*) a pointed tool of iron or steel, also an iron punch with a wooden handle; an iron wedge sharply pointed for splitting stone etc.; †a pointed bar or rod, a spike, a goad, a stylus. †**gadling,** *n.* a boss or small spike of steel on the knuckles of gauntlets. †**gadman,** †**gadsman,** *n.* (*Sc.*) a goadsman. [Icel. *gaddr,* cogn. with L *hasta,* a spear]

gad², *v.i.* (*past, p.p.* **gadded**) to rove or wander idly (about, out etc.); to ramble or straggle (as a plant). *n.* gadding or roaming about. **gadabout,** *n.* one who gads about habitually. **gadder,** *n.* **gaddingly,** *adv.*

†**gaddish,** *a.* inclined to gad about. †**gaddishness,** *n.* [etym. doubtful (perh. from gad-fly, or from obs. *gadling,* OE *gædling,* a companion, from *gæd,* fellowship)]

gad[3], *int.* an exclamation of surprise etc. **begad** or **by gad, gadzooks**, minced oaths. [minced pron. of GOD]

Gaddafi, *n.* alternative form of Khaddhafi, Libyan leader.

Gaddi, *n.* family of Italian painters in Florence: **Gaddo Gaddi** (*c.* 1250–*c.* 1330); his son **Taddeo Gaddi** (*c.* 1300–*c.* 1366), who was influenced by Giotto and painted the fresco cycle *Life of the Virgin* in Santa Croce, Florence; and grandson **Agnolo Gaddi** (active 1369–96), who also painted frescoes in Santa Croce, *The Story of the Cross*, 1380s, and produced panel paintings in characteristic pale pastel colours.

gadfly, *n.* an insect of the genus *Tobanidae* or *Oestrus,* which bites cattle and other animals, a breeze-fly; a person, thing or impulse that irritates or torments; †a gadabout. [etym. doubtful; perh. GAD[1] or OE gād, GOAD]

gadge, *n.* an instrument of torture. [used by Browning, etym. unknown]

gadget, *n.* a tool, an appliance; a contrivance for making a job easier; a trick of the trade. [etym. doubtful]

Gadhelic, *a.* of or pertaining to the branch of the Celtic race that includes the Gaels of Scotland, the Irish and the people of the Isle of Man, as dist. from the Cymri. *n.* the language spoken by this branch of the Celtic race. [Ir. *Gaedheal,* pl. *Gaedhil,* Gael]

gadoid, *a.* of or belonging to the family *Gadidae,* which comprises the cod-fishes. *n.* any fish of the family *Gadidae*. [Gr. *gados,* -OID]

gadolinite, *n.* a black, vitreous silicate of yttrium, formed in crystals. **gadolinium,** *n.* a soft metallic element, at. no. 64; chem. symbol Gd, of the rare-earth group. [J.*Gadolin,* 1760–1852, Finnish mineralogist]

gadroon, *n.* (*usu. pl.*) an ornament consisting of a series of convex curves, used in architecture and metalwork for edgings, mouldings etc. **gadrooned,** *a.* [F *godron*]

Gadsden Purchase, The, in US history, the purchase of approximately 77,720 sq km/30,000 sq miles in what is now New Mexico and Arizona by the US in 1853. The land was bought from Mexico for $10,000,000 in a treaty negotiated by James Gadsden (1788–1858) of South Carolina in order to construct a transcontinental railroad route, the Southern Pacific, completed in the 1880s.

gaduin, *n.* a brown substance contained in cod-liver oil, and one of its essential constituents. [GADOID]

gadwall, *n.* a large freshwater duck, *Anas strepera,* of N Europe and America. [perh. corr. of *gadwell* (GAD[2], WELL[2])]

gae, (*Sc.* var. of GO)

Gael, *n.* a Scottish Celt; (*less commonly*) an Irish Celt. **Gaelic,** *a.* of or pertaining to the Gaels or their language. *n.* a member of the Celtic branch of the Indo-European language family, spoken in Ireland, Scotland, and (until 1974) the Isle of Man. **Gaelic coffee,** *n.* IRISH. **Gaelic football,** *n.* a game involving two teams of 15 players, the object of which is to kick, bounce or punch a ball into a net stretched between two posts or over a crossbar above the net. The game was first played in 1712 and is now one of the sports under the auspices of the Gaelic Athletic Association. The leading tournament is the All-Ireland Championship culminating in the final which is played in Dublin on the third Sunday in September each year, the winners receiving the Sam Maguire Trophy. **Gaelic League,** *n.* an association formed to further the revival of the Irish language and ancient culture. [Gael. *Gaidheal*]

gaff[1], *n.* a stick with a metal hook at the end, used by anglers to land heavy fish; the spar which extends the upper edge of fore-and-aft sails not set on stays. *v.t.* to seize or land with a gaff. **gaff-topsail,** *n.* a sail spread by a gaff above the mainsail of a fore-and-aft rigged vessel. [OF *gaffe* (cp. LG *gaffel,* G *Gabel,* a fork)]

gaff[2], *n.* a theatre, music-hall or other place of entertainment of the lowest class; †a fair. [etym. doubtful]

gaff[3], *n.* outcry. **to blow the gaff,** (*sl.*) to let out the secret; to give information. [etym. doubtful]

gaff[4], *v.i.* (*sl.*) to gamble; to toss, esp. for liquor. [etym. unknown]

gaffe, *n.* a social solecism. **to make a gaffe,** to put one's foot in it. [F]

gaffer, *n.* an old fellow, esp. an aged rustic (formerly a term of respect, now of familiarity); a foreman, an overseer; a schoolmaster; (*coll.*) the chief lighting electrician on a television or film set. [corr. of GRANDFATHER]

gag, *v.t.* (*past, p.p.* **gagged**) to stop the mouth (of a person) by thrusting something into it, so as to prevent speech; to silence; to deprive of freedom of speech; to apply the gag-bit to a horse; (*Theat.*) to put interpolations into; (*sl.*) to deceive. *v.i.* (*Theat.*) to introduce interpolations into a part; (*sl.*) to practise imposture; to choke, retch. *n.* something thrust into the mouth to prevent one from speaking; (*Surg.*) an instrument for holding the mouth open; in Parliament, the closure; (*Theat.*) interpolation introduced by an actor into his part; (*sl.*) an imposture, a lie; a joke. **gag-bit,** *n.* a very powerful bit used in horse-breaking. **gag-rein,** *n.* a rein used for pulling the bit upward or backward. **gagger,** *n.* one who gags; (*Metal.*) a light T-shaped lifter used in iron-founding. [prob. imit.]

gaga, *a.* foolish, senile, fatuous. [F sl.]

Gagarin, *n.* **Yuri (Alexeyevich)** (1934–68), Soviet cosmonaut, who in 1961 became the first human in space in VOSTOK 1.

gage[1], *n.* a pledge, a pawn; something laid down as security, to be forfeited in case of non-performance of some act; a glove or other symbol thrown down as a challenge to combat; hence, a challenge. *v.t.* to deposit as a pledge or security for some act; to stake, to risk, to wager; to guarantee; †to engage; †to bind or entangle. †**gagelike,** *adv.* [OF *gage, gauge, wage,* from Teut. (cp. WED, also WAGE)]

gage[2], *n.* a greengage. [Sir William *Gage, c.* 1725, the introducer]

gage[3] GAUGE.

gaggle, *v.i.* to make a noise like a goose; to cackle, to chatter. *n.* a collection of geese. [imit.; cp. GUGGLE, also CACKLE]

gagliarda, *n.* a dance in 3/4 time. [It.]

Gaia, *n.* (or **Ge.**) in Greek mythology, the goddess of the Earth. She sprang from primordial Chaos and herself produced Uranus, by whom she was the mother of the Cyclopes and Titans.

Gaia hypothesis, *n.* theory that the Earth's living and nonliving systems form an inseparable whole that is regulated and kept adapted for life by living organisms themselves. Since life and environment are so closely linked, there is a need for humans to understand and maintain the physical environment and living things around them. The Gaia hypothesis was elaborated by James Lovelock in the 1970s.

gaiety, *n.* the state of being gay; mirth, merriment; *pl.* amusements, festivities; gay appearance, brave show. [OF *gayeté*]

Gaikwar, *n.* the ruler of Baroda, India; formerly monarch of the Mahrattas. [Marathi, cowherd]

†**gaillard,** GALLIARD.

gaily GAY.

gain[1], *n.* anything obtained as an advantage or in return for labour; profit; increase, growth, accession; amount of this; (*pl.*) profits, emoluments; the acquisition of wealth; the ratio of the output power of an amplifier to the input power usu. measured in decibels, volume. *v.t.* to obtain by or as by effort; to earn, to win, to acquire; to progress, to advance, to get more of; to reach, to attain to; to win (over); to obtain as a result, to incur. *v.i.* to advance in interest, possessions or happiness; to gain ground, to encroach (upon); to get the advantage (on or upon). **to gain ground,** to advance in any undertaking; to make progress. **to gain on** or upon, to get nearer to (an object of pursuit); to encroach upon. **to gain ground upon,** to get nearer (to one pursued). **to gain over,** to win over to any side, party or view. **to gain the ear of,** to secure favourable consideration from. **to gain the upper hand,**to be victorious. **to gain the wind,** to get to the windward side (of another ship). **to gain time,** to obtain delay for any purpose. **gain-control,** *n.* the volume control in an amplifier or receiving set. **gainable,** *a.* †**gainage,** *n.* in law, the gain or profit of tilled or planted land. **gainer,** *n.* one who gains profit, return or advantage. **gainful,** *a.* profitable, advantageous, remunerative; devoted to gain. **gainfully,** *adv.* **gainfulness,** *n.* **gainings,** *n.pl.* profits, gains. **gainless,** *a.* unprofitable. **gainlessness,** *n.* [OF, from *gaigner, gaaignier* (cp. F *gagne, gagner*), OHG *weidenēn,* to pasture, to graze, from *weida,* pasturage]

†**gain**2, *a.* near, straight; kindly favourable. *prep.* against, contrary to. *adv.* back, again. **the gainest way,** the shortest way. [Icel. *gegn,* straight, direct]

gaine, *n.* a metal tube containing explosive which is screwed to a fuse. [F *guine,* a sheath]

gainly, *a.* suitable, gracious; comely, shapely. [Icel. *gegn,* straight, ready, serviceable, -LY]

gainsay, *v.t.* (*past, p.p.* **-said**) to contradict, to deny; to controvert, to dispute, †to hinder. †*n.* contradiction. **gainsayer,** *n.* **gainsaying,** *n.*

Gainsborough, *n.* **Thomas** (1727–88), English landscape and portrait painter. He was born in Sudbury, Suffolk; in 1759 he settled in Bath, gaining fame as a painter of high society. In 1774 he went to London and became one of the original members of the Royal Academy. He was one of the first British artists to follow the Dutch in painting realistic landscapes rather than imaginative Italianate scenery.

gainst, 'gainst, AGAINST.

gair, *n.* a strip, as of grass. [Sc., from Icel. *geire,* cogn. with GORE2]

gairfowl, GAREFOWL.

gait1, *n.* a manner of walking or going, carriage. **(-)gaited,** *a.* (*usu. in comb.*) having a particular gait. [Icel. *gata,* GATE2]

gait2, *n.* a sheaf of grain tied up; charge for pasturage etc. *v.t.* to set up in sheaves for drying. [prov., etym. doubtful]

gaiter, *n.* a covering for the ankle or the leg below the knee, usu. fitting down upon the shoe; (*N Am.*) a half-boot with a cloth top or elastic sides. *v.t.* to dress with gaiters. **gaiterless,** *a.* [F *guétre,* etym. unknown]

Gaitskell, *n.* **Hugh Todd Naylor** (1906–63), British Labour politician. In 1950 he became minister of economic affairs, and then chancellor of the Exchequer until Oct. 1951. In 1955 he defeated Aneurin Bevan for the succession to Attlee as party leader, and tried to reconcile internal differences on nationalization and disarmament. He was re-elected leader in 1960.

gal1, GIRL.

gal2, *n.* in physics, a unit of acceleration equal to 1 cm per second per second. [*Gal*ileo see GALILEAN].

gal., (*abbr.*) GALLON.

gala, *n.* a festivity, a fête; †festivity, gaiety; †festive attire. **gala day,** *n.* a holiday with sports or festivities. **gala dress,** *n.* festive attire. [F, from It., conn. with *galante,* gay]

galact GALACT(O)-.

galactic, *a.* pertaining to milk or the secretion of milk, lactic; in astronomy, pertaining to a galaxy, esp. the Milky Way. **galactic circle** or **equator,** *n.* the great circle of the celestial sphere which contains the galactic plane. **galactic plane,** *n.* the plane of the galactic circle. **galactic poles,** *n. pl.* the two opposite points on the celestial sphere that are the furthest N and S and which can be joined by an imaginary line perpendicular to the galactic plane. **galactia,** *n.* morbid flow of milk. **galactin,** *n.* a nitrogenous substance obtained from milk, and existing in the juices or the seeds of certain plants. **galactonic,** *a.* [Gr. *galaktikos,* from *gala galaktos,* milk]

galact(o)-, *comb. form* milk or milky. [Gr. *gala galaktos,* milk]

galactogogue, *a.* promoting the flow of milk. *n.* a medicine which promotes the secretion of milk. [Gr. *agōgos,* leading, from *agein,* to lead]

galactometer, *n.* a lactometer.

galactophagist, *n.* one who subsists on milk. [Gr. *galaktophagos* (*-phagos,* eating, from *phagein,* to eat)]

galactophagous, *a.* subsisting on milk.

galactophorous, *a.* producing milk.

galactopoietic, *a.* increasing the flow of milk. *n.* a substance which increases the flow of milk. [Gr. *poētikos,* from *poiein,* make]

galactorrhoea, *n.* an excessive secretion of milk. [Gr. *rhoia,* a flowing]

galactose, *n.* a sweet crystalline glucose obtained from milk-sugar by treatment with dilute acid.

galago, *n.* (*pl.* **-gos**) an African genus of lemurs. [from African name]

galah, *n.* the grey, rose-breasted cockatoo; (*coll.*) a silly person, a simpleton. [Austral. Abor.]

Galahad, Sir, *n.* in Arthurian legend, one of the knights of the Round Table. Galahad succeeded in the quest for the Grail because of his virtue. He was the son of Lancelot of the Lake.

Galanthus, *n.* a genus of bulbous plants, containing the snowdrop. [Gr. *gala,* milk, *anthos,* flower]

galantine, *n.* a dish of white meat, freed from bone, tied up, sliced, boiled, covered with jelly, and served cold. [F, from low L *galatina,* corr. of *gelatina,* GELATINE (n. due to conf. with *galant,* GALLANT)]

galanty show, *n.* a miniature shadow pantomime. [probably from It. *galanti,* pl. of *galante,* GALLANT]

Galápagos Islands, *n.pl.* group of 15 islands (official name Archipeliégo de Colón) in the Pacific, belonging to Ecuador; area 7800 sq km/3000 sq miles; population (1982) 6120. The capital is San Cristóbal on the island of the same name. The islands are a nature reserve. Their unique fauna (including giant tortoises, iguanas, penguins, flightless cormorants, and Darwin's finches), are under threat from introduced species.

galatea, *n.* a blue-and-white striped cotton fabric. [L *Galatea,* a sea-nymph]

Galatia, *n.* ancient province of Asia Minor occupying part of the inland plateau; it was occupied in the 3rd cent. BC by the GAULS, and was a Roman province from 25 BC. **Galatian,** *a.* belonging to Galatia. *n.* a native or inhabitant of Galatia.

galaxy, *n.* the Milky Way, a luminous band, consisting of innumerable stars indistinguishable to the naked eye, stretching across the sky; any similar nebula or large cluster of stars beyond the Milky Way; a brilliant assemblage of persons or things. [OF *galaxie,* L *galaxiam,* nom. *-ias,* Gr. *galaxias,* from *gala,* milk]

galbanum, *n.* a bitter, odorous gum resin obtained from Persian species of *Ferula,* esp. *F. galbaniflua,* an ingredient in the anointing-oil used by Jewish people. †**galbanean,** *a.* derived from or resembling galbanum. [L, from Gr. *chalbanē,* prob. from an Oriental word]

Galbraith, *n.* **John Kenneth** (1908–), Canadian economist of the Keynesian school whose major works include *The Affluent Society* (1958) and *Economics and the Public Purpose* (1974). In the former he argued that industrialized societies like the US were suffering from private affluence accompanied by public squalor.

gale1, *n.* a wind stronger than a breeze but less violent than a tempest; a wind with a velocity of 40 mph (64 km) or over, registering force eight on the Beaufort scale; at sea, a storm; (*fig.*) a quarrel, a disturbance. [cp. Dan. *gal,* Norw. *galen,* mad, furious, Icel. *gola,* a breeze]

gale2, *n.* a periodic payment of rent. **gale-day,** *n.* rent-day. [prob. from OE *gafol,* GAVEL]

gale3, *n.* the bog-myrtle, *Myrica gale,* a twiggy shrub growing on marshy ground, also called **sweet-gale.** [OE *gagel* (cp. Dut. and G *gagel*)]

galea, *n.* (*pl.* **-leae**) a helmet-like organ or part; (*Anat.*) the amnion; a bandage for the head; in botany, the arched upper lip in some labiates. **galeate, galeated,** *a.* [L, a helmet]

galeeny, *n.* (*prov.*) a guinea-fowl. [Sp. *gallina Morisca,* a Moorish fowl]

Galega, *n.* the goat's rue, a genus of leguminous herbs. [etym. doubtful]

Galen *n.* (*c.* 130–*c.* 200 AD), Greek physician whose ideas dominated Western medicine for almost 1500 years. Born at Pergamum in Asia Minor, he personally attended the Roman emperor Marcus Aurelius. Central to his thinking were the theories of humours and the threefold circulation of the blood. **Galenic, -ical,** *a.* of or according to Galen, esp. applied to medicines prepared from vegetable substances by infusion or decoction, as opp. to chemical remedies. **Galenism,** *n.* **Galenist,** *n.*

galena, *n.* native sulphide of lead or lead-ore. **galenic, -ical,** *a.* **galenite,** *n.* Galena. **galenoid,** *n., a.* [L]

galeopithecus, *n.* a genus of flying lemurs. **galeopithecine, -coid,** *a.* [Gr. *galeē,* weasel, *pithēkos,* an ape]

galette, *n.* a flat, round cake. [F, from *galet,* a pebble, Bret. *kalet,* hard as a stone]

Galicia, *n.* mountainous but fertile autonomous region of NW Spain, formerly an independent kingdom; area 29,400 sq km/11,348 sq miles; population (1986) 2,785,000. It includes La Coruña, Lugo, Orense, and Pontevedra. Industries include fishing and the mining of tungsten and tin. The language is similar to Portuguese. **Galician,** *a.* of or pertaining to Galicia. *n.* a native or inhabitant of Galicia.

Galilean¹ GALILEE².

Galilean², *a.* of or according to Galileo, esp. applied to the simple telescope developed and used by him.

Galilee¹, *n.* region of N Israel (once a Roman province) which includes Nazareth and Tiberias, frequently mentioned in the Gospels of the New Testament.

Galilee², *n.* a porch or chapel at the entrance of a church; prob. so called because, like Galilee in respect to Judea, it was less sacred than the body of the church, or in allusion to Matt. iv.15, 'Galilee of the Gentiles'. **Galilean¹,** *a.* pertaining to Galilee. *n.* a native or inhabitant of Galilee; (*Eccles. Hist.*) (applied contemptuously by pagans) a Christian. **the Galilean,** (*derog.*) Jesus Christ.

Galilee³, Sea of, alternative name for Lake Tiberias in N Israel.

Galileo¹, *n.* spacecraft launched from the Space Shuttle Atlantis in Oct. 1989, on a six-year journey to Jupiter.

Galileo², *n.* **(Galileo Galilei)** (1564–1642), Italian mathematician, astronomer, and physicist. He developed the astronomical telescope and was the first to see sunspots, the four main satellites of Jupiter, mountains and craters on the Moon, and Venus' appearance of going through 'phases', thus proving it was orbiting the Sun. In mechanics, Galileo discovered that freely falling bodies, heavy or light, had the same, constant acceleration (though the story of his dropping cannonballs from the Leaning Tower of Pisa is questionable), and that a body moving on a perfectly smooth horizontal surface would neither speed up nor slow down.

galimatias, *n.* nonsense; an absurd jumble or rigmarole. [F, etym. unknown]

galingale, *n.* the aromatic root-stock of certain E Indian plants of the ginger family and of the genus *Alpinia* and *Kaempferia,* formerly used for culinary purposes; applied to a rare English sedge, *Cyperus longus.* [OF *galingal,* Arab. *khalanjān,* acc. to OED through Pers. from Chin. *Ko-liang-Kiang,* mild ginger]

galiongee, *n.* a Turkish sailor, esp. on a man-of-war. [Turk. *qālūnjī,* from It. *galeone,* GALLEON]

galipot¹, *n.* a yellowish-white, viscid resin exuding from *Pinus maritimus* and hardening into a kind of turpentine, called, after refining, white, yellow or Burgundy pitch. **galipot varnish,** *n.* [F, etym. doubtful]

galipot², GALLIPOT.

galium, *n.* bedstraw, a genus of slender herbaceous plants, containing goose-grass, lady's bedstraw etc. [Gr. *galion*]

gall¹, *n.* a bitter, yellowish fluid secreted by the liver, bile; the gall-bladder; anything exceedingly bitter; rancour, malignity, bitterness of mind; †spirit, courage; self-assurance, cheek. **gall and wormwood,** a symbol for all that is hateful, exasperating and unwelcome. **gall-bladder,** *n.* a pear-shaped membraneous sac, lodged on the under surface of the liver, which receives the bile. **gall-duct, -passage, -pipe,** *n.* a duct which conveys the bile. **gall-stone,** *n.* an abnormal calcareous concretion formed in the gall-bladder. **gall-less,** *a.* [OE *gealla* (cp. Dut. *gal,* Icel. *gall,* G *Galle,* also L *fel,* Gr. *cholē*), cogn. with YELLOW]

gall², *n.* an abnormal excrescence on plants, esp. the oak, caused by the action of some insect. *v.t.* to impregnate with a decoction of galls. **oak-gall, gall-apple** GALL-NUT. **gall-fly, -insect, -louse,** *n.* an insect, chiefly belonging to the genus *Cynips,* that causes the production of galls. **gall-nut, -apple,** *n.* a gall produced on the oak, esp. by the puncture by *C. gallae tinctoria* of the leaf-buds of the gall-oak, used (*esp. formerly*) in the making of ink and for other purposes. **gall-oak,** *n.* the oak, *Quercus infectoria.* [OF *galle,* L *galla*]

gall³, *n.* a sore, swelling, or blister, esp. one produced by friction or chafing on a horse; soreness, irritation; one who or that which causes this; a bare place in a field or a crop; †a blemish, a defect; (*US*) a marshy lowland (in the southern States). *v.t.* to chafe, hurt or injure by rubbing; to make sore by friction; to annoy, to harass, to vex. *v.i.* to fret; †to act in an irritating manner. **galling,** *a.* vexing, irritating, chafing. **gallingly,** *adv.* [OE *gealla,* perh. cogn. with GALL²]

gall., gal., (*abbr.*) GALLON.

Gall, *n.* **Franz Joseph** (1758–1828), Austrian anatomist, instigator of the discredited theory of phrenology.

gallant¹, *a.* showy, well-dressed; fine, stately; brave, high-spirited, courageous, chivalrous. **gallantry,** *n.* bold, dashing, magnanimous courage. [OF *gallant, galant,* pres.p. of *galer,* to make merry, from G]

gallant², *n.* a man of fashion, a beau; †a bold and dashing fellow;, a man attentive and polite to women; a lover, a wooer; a paramour., *a.* specially attentive to women; pertaining to love. *v.t.*, to attend as a gallant or cavalier, to escort; to pay court to; to flirt with; †to handle (a fan) in a fashionable manner. *v.i.* to play the gallant; to flirt (with). **gallantly,** *adv.* **gallantry,** *n.* politeness and deference to women, with or without evil intent; amorous intrigue; †showy appearance, a brave show; †gallants collectively.

Gallé, *n.* **Emile** (1846–1904), French Art Nouveau glassmaker. He produced glass in sinuous forms or rounded, solid-looking shapes almost as heavy as stone, typically decorated with flowers or leaves in colour on colour.

Galle, *n.* **Johann Gottfried** (1812–1910), German astronomer who located the planet Neptune in 1846, close to the position predicted by French mathematician Urbail Leverrier.

galleass, *n.* a heavy, low-built vessel propelled both by sails and oars, usu. with three masts and about 20 guns. [OF *galeace,* It. *galeazza,* late L *galea,* GALLEY¹]

galleon, *n.* a large ship, with three or four decks, much used in 15th–17th cents., esp. by the Spaniards in their commerce with their American possessions. [Sp. *galeon,* late L *galeo -ōnem,* from *galea,* GALLEY¹]

gallery, *n.* an elevated floor or platform projecting from the wall toward the interior of a church, hall, theatre, or other large building, commonly used for musicians, singers or part of the congregation or audience; (*Theat.*) the highest and cheapest tier of seats; the persons occupying these, hence (*fig.*) the most unrefined of the auditors; a passage open at one side, usu. projecting from the wall of a building and supported on corbels or pillars; a corridor, a passage, a long and narrow room; such a room used for the exhibition of pictures, hence, a collection of pictures; a portico or colonnade, a balcony, a veranda; (*Fort.*) a covered passage in a fortification, either for defence or communication; (*Mining*) an adit, drift, or heading. *v.t.* to furnish or pierce with a gallery or galleries. **to play to the gallery,** to court popular applause. **gallery forest,** *n.* a stretch of forest, esp. beside a river, in open country. **galleried,** *a.* **galleryful,** *n.* [OF *galerie,* late L *galeria,* etym. doubtful]

gallet, garret[2], *n.* a chip or splinter of a stone. *v.t.* to insert bits of stone in the joints of coarse masonry. **galleting, garreting,** *n.* [prob. from F *galet,* a pebble, dim. of OF *gal,* a stone]

galley[1], *n.* a low, flat vessel, with one deck, navigated with sails and oars, which were usu. worked by slaves or convicts; an ancient Greek or Roman war-vessel of this type with one or more tiers of oars; a row-boat of large size, esp. one, larger than the gig, used by the captain of a man-of-war; a state barge; the cook-house on board ship. **galley-slave,** *n.* a criminal condemned to the galleys; a drudge. [OF *galie,* late L *galea,* a galley]

galley[2], *n.* (*Print.*) in hot-metal composition, an oblong tray on which compositors place matter as it is set up; a galley-proof. **galley-press,** *n.* a press at which galley-proofs are pulled. **galley-proof,** *n.* a proof taken from type in a galley, usu. in one column on a long strip of paper as dist. from that arranged in pages. [F *galée*]

galley-west, *adv.* (*N Am., coll.*) **to knock galley-west,** to put somebody or something into a state of confusion, unconsciousness or inaction. [Eng. dial. *colly-west,* awry]

galliambic, *n.* (*Pros.*) a tetrameter catalectic composed of Ionics, a minore (˘ ˘) with variations and substitutions – the metre of the *Attis* of Catullus and of Tennyson's *Boadicea;* (*pl.*) verses in this metre. *a.* in this metre. [L *galliambus,* the metre used by the Galli or priests of Cybele in their chants]

†**Gallian,** GALLIC[2].

galliard, *a.* merry, jaunty. *n.* a merry or lively person; a lively dance; the music to this. **galliardise,** *n.* merriment, liveliness. [F *gaillard* (fem. *gaillarde,* whence the n.)]

gallic[1], *a.* **gallic acid,** *n.* (*Chem.*) an acid derived from oak-galls and other vegetable sources. [GALL[1]]

Gallic[2], *a.* of or pertaining to ancient Gaul; (*loosely*) French. **Gallice,** *adv.* in French. **Gallicism,** *n.* a French expression or idiom. **Gallicize, -ise,** *v.t.* [L *Gallicus,* from *Gallus,* a GAUL]

Gallican, *a.* pertaining to the ancient Church of Gaul or France; ultramontane, claiming autonomy for the Church in France and repudiating papal control. *n.* a member of the French Church who holds these views. **Gallicanism,** *n.* **Gallicanist,** *n.* [L *Gallicānus,* as prec.]

galligaskins, *n.pl.* loose breeches; gaiters worn by sportsmen; orig. loose hose or breeches such as were worn in the 16th and 17th cents. [corr. of F *garguesques,* corr. of *greguesques,* It. *Grechesca,* orig. fem. of *Grechesco,* Greekish]

gallimaufry, *n.* a hash, a hodge-podge; an inconsistent or ridiculous medley. [F *gallimafrée,* etym. unknown]

gallinaceous, *a.* of or pertaining to the Gallinae, a group of birds containing pheasants, partridges, grouse, turkeys, domestic fowls, and allied forms. **gallinacean,** *a.* gallinaceous. *n.* one of the Gallinae. [L *gallīnāceus,* from *gallīna,* a hen]

gallinazo, *n.* (*pl.* **-azos**) an American vulture. [Sp. *gallinaza,* from *gallina,* as prec.]

galling GALL[3].

gallinule, *n.* any bird of the genus *Gallinula,* esp. *G. chloropus,* the moor-hen. [late L *gallīnula,* dim. of L *gallina,* hen]

Gallio, *n.* one who pays no attention to matters, however grave or sacred, that do not directly concern him. [Junius Annaeus *Gallio,* pro-consul of Achaia, AD 53, who refused to attend to the Jewish agitation against Paul, Acts xviii.12–17]

galliot, *n.* a small, swift galley propelled by sails and oars; a one- or two-masted Dutch or Flemish merchant vessel. [OF *galiote,* late L *galeota,* from *galea,* GALLEY[1]]

Gallipoli, *n.* port in European Turkey, where in World War I, at the instigation of Winston Churchill, an unsuccessful attempt was made Feb. 1915– Jan. 1916 by Allied troops to force their way through the Dardanelles and link up with Russia. The campaign was fought mainly by Australian and New Zealand (ANZAC) forces who suffered heavy losses.

gallipot, *n.* a small glazed earthenware pot used to contain ointments, medicines, preserves etc. [prob. GALLEY[1], POT]

gallium, *n.* a soft, grey metallic element of extreme fusibility, at. no. 31; chem. symbol Ga, used in semiconductors. [from L *gallus,* a cock, alluding to the name of its discoverer M. *Lecoq* de Boisbaudren]

gallivant, *v.i.* to gad about, to go pleasure-seeking. [prob. from GALLANT]

gallivat, *n.* a large swift-sailing boat used in the E Indies. [corr. of Port. *galeota,* GALLIOT]

galliwasp, *n.* a small harmless W Indian lizard, *Celestus occiduus,* erroneously reputed to be venomous. [etym. doubtful]

gallize, -ise, *v.t.* to treat (unfermented grape-juice) with water and sugar, so as to produce a larger quantity of wine. [the inventor, Dr L. *Gall,* of Treves]

gallo-[1], *comb. form* pertaining to gallic acid, gallic.

Gallo-[2], *comb. form* French. [L *Gallus,* a Gaul]

gallo-bromol, *n.* a grey crystalline powder obtained from gallic acid and bromine, used as a sedative, astringent, antiseptic etc. [BROMINE, -OL]

galloglass, *n.* an armed soldier or retainer of an ancient Irish chieftain. [Ir. *gallóglách* (*gall,* a foreigner, *óglách,* a youth, a warrior)]

Gallomania, *n.* a mania for French fashions, habits, or practices, literature etc. **Gallomaniac** (-ak), *n.*

gallon, *n.* an English measure of capacity; a dry measure equal to one-eighth of a bushel (4·55 l). **imperial gallon,** *n.* a British measure for liquids, containing 277¼ cu. in. (4·55 l). **Winchester gallon,** *n.* a measure for wine forming the standard in the US, containing 231 cu. in. (3·78 l). [OF *galon, jalon,* prob. cogn. with F *jale;* etym. unknown]

galloon, *n.* a narrow braid of silk, worsted, or cotton, with gold or silver thread interwoven, for binding uniforms, dresses etc.; other materials used for binding or edging. [F *galon,* prob. from OF *gall,* see GALA]

gallop, *v.i.* to run in a series of springs, as a horse at its fastest pace; to ride at a gallop; to go or do anything at a very rapid pace. *v.t.* to make (a horse) gallop. *n.* the motion of a horse at its fastest speed, with all the feet off the ground at one point in the progressive movement of the four limbs; the act of riding or a ride at this pace; a galop. **the gallops,** horseracing over flat ground. **gallopade,** *n.* a sidelong or curvetting kind of gallop; a brisk dance, of Hungarian origin. *v.i.* to dance this. **galloper,** *n.* a horse that gallops; a person who gallops on a horse, or who makes great haste; an aide-de-camp; a light field-gun attached to cavalry. **galloping consumption,** *n.* a rapid consumption or phthisis. [OF *galoper,* prob. from Teut. (cp. Flem. *walop,* gallop, OS *hlōpan,* to LEAP]

Gallophil, *n.* a devotee of French customs etc.

Gallophobe, *n.* one who hates French ways or fears the French. **Gallophobia,** *n.*

Gallovidian, *a.* of or belonging to Galloway. *n.* a native of Galloway. [med. L *Gallovidia,* W *Gallwyddel,* Galloway]

†**gallow,** GALLY.

Galloway, *n.* a small, hardy variety of horse, or black breed of cattle, orig. bred in Galloway. [*Galloway,* in SW Scotland]

gallows, *n. sing.* a framework, usu. consisting of timber uprights and a crosspiece, on which criminals are executed by hanging; execution by hanging; a similar framework used for gymnastics, for hanging things on, in printing, cookery etc.; †a wretch who deserves the gallows; (*N Am., Sc., coll., pl.* **gallowses**) braces, suspenders. **gallows-bird,** *n.* one who deserves hanging. **gallows-bitts,** *n.pl.* (*Naut.*) a strong frame erected amidships on the deck to hold spare spars. **gallows-free,** *a.* saved from hanging. **gallows hu-**

mour, *n.* macabre, ironic humour. **gallowsripe,** *a.* ready to be hanged. **gallows-top,** *n.* (*Naut.*) a cross-piece of timber placed at the top of the gallows-bitts. **gallows-tree,** *n.* the gallows. [OE *galga* (cp. Icel. *gālgi,* Dut. *galg,* G. *Galgen*)]

Gallup, *n.* **George Horace** (1901–84), US journalist and statistician, founder in 1935 of the American Institute of Public Opinion and deviser of the **Gallup Poll®**, protected name of a method of ascertaining the trend of public opinion by questioning a representative cross-section of the population.

†**gally,** *v.t.* to frighten, to scare. **gally-beggar, -crow,** *n.* a scarecrow. [OE *gælwan* (in the form *agælwan*) to astonish, to alarm]

galoche, GALOSH.

Galois, *n.* **Évariste** (1811–32), French mathematician, who originated the theory of groups. His attempts to gain recognition for his work were largely thwarted by the French mathematical establishment, who saw not his genius but his lack of formal qualifications. Galois was killed in a duel before he was 21. The night before he had hurriedly written out his unpublished discoveries on group theory, the importance of which would come to be appreciated more and more as the 19th century progressed.

galoot, *n.* a clumsy soldier; an awkward, uncouth person. [sl; etym. doubtful]

galop, *n.* a lively dance in 2/4 time; the music to the dance. *v.i.* to dance this. [F, see GALLOP]

galore, *n.* plenty, abundance. *adv.* in plenty, abundantly. [Ir. *go leor* (*go,* to, *leor,* sufficient)]

galosh, *n.* (*usu. pl.*) an overshoe, usu. of vulcanized rubber, for protecting one's boots or shoes in wet weather; in boot-making, a piece of leather or other material sewn round the lower part of uppers. *v.t.* to furnish (boots or shoes) with this. [F *galoche,* prob. through L from Gr. *kalopodion,* dim. of *kalopous,* a shoemaker's last (*kalon,* wood, *pous podos,* foot)]

Galsworthy, *n.* **John** (1867–1933), British novelist and dramatist, whose work examines the social issues of the Victorian period. He is famous for *The Forsyte Saga* (1922), and its sequel *A Modern Comedy* (1929). Other novels include *The Country House* (1907) and *Fraternity* (1909); plays include *The Silver Box* (1906).

galt, GAULT.

Galtieri, *n.* **Leopoldo** (1926–), Argentinian general. Leading member of the right-wing military junta that ordered the 1982 seizure of the Falkland Islands (Malvinas), a UK colony in the SW Atlantic claimed by Argentina. He and his fellow junta members were tried for abuse of human rights and court-martialled for their conduct of the war; he was sentenced to 12 years in prison in 1986.

Galton, *n.* **Francis** (1822–1911), English scientist, noted for his study of the inheritance of physical and mental attributes in humans which he called EUGENICS.

galumph, *v.i.* to prance exultantly. **galumphing,** *a.* [coined by Lewis Carroll, prob. from GALLOP and TRIUMPH]

galvan- GALVAN(O)-.

galvanic, *a.* of, pertaining to or produced by galvanism; forced and spasmodic (of movements, expression etc.) as if caused by the action of an electric current. **galvanic battery** or **pile,** *n.* a number of connected galvanic cells for producing an electric current. **galvanic belt,** *n.* a galvanic apparatus in the form of a belt for applying electricity to the body. **galvanic electricity,** *n.* **galvanically,** *adv.* **galvanism,** *n.* electricity produced by chemical action, esp. that of acids on metals; the branch of science dealing with this; its application for medical purposes. **galvanist,** *n.*

galvanize, -ise, *v.t.* to apply galvanism to, esp. to stimulate muscular action etc. by galvanism; to plate with gold or other metal by galvanism; to rouse into life or activity as by a galvanic shock. **galvanization,** *n.* **galvanizer, -iser,** *n.* **galvanized, -ised, iron,** *n.* iron coated with zinc (orig. by galvanic deposition), to protect it from moisture. [L. *Galvani,* 1737–98, Italian physician and its discoverer]

galvan(o)-, *comb. form.* galvanic current.

galvanography, *n.* the production of a printing-plate by electrotype from a drawing in viscid ink on a silvered plate. **galvanograph,** *n.* a plate so produced; the resulting impression, which resembles that from copper-plate. **galvanographic,** *a.*

galvanology, *n.* the science of galvanism; a treatise on its phenomena. **galvanologist,** *n.*

galvanometer, *n.* a delicate apparatus for determining the existence, direction, and intensity of electric currents. **galvanometric, -ical,** *a.* **galvanometry,** *n.*

galvanoplasty, *n.* the coating of objects with a metal deposit by galvanism, electrotype. **galvanoplastic,** *a.* **galvanoplastically,** *adv.* [Gr. *-plastos,* moulded, from *plassein,* to mould]

galvanoscope, *n.* an instrument for detecting the presence and showing the direction of electric currents.

galvanotropism, *n.* the directional movement in a growing plant induced by an electric stimulus.

Galway[1], *n.* county on the W coast of the Republic of Ireland, in the province of Connacht; area 5940 sq km/2293 sq miles; population (1986) 178,000. Towns include Galway (county town), Ballinasloe, Tuam, Clifden, and Loughrea (near which deposits of lead, zinc, and copper were found 1959).

Galway[2], *n.* **James** (1939–), Irish flautist, born in Belfast. He was a member of the Berlin Philharmonic Orchestra (1969–75), before taking up a solo career.

Galwegian, *a., n.* Gallovidian; of or belonging to Galway, Ireland. [*Galloway,* assim. to NORWEGIAN]

gam, *n.* a herd of whales; a keeping company or exchange of visits among whalers at sea. *v.i.* to congregate or form a school (as whales); to exchange courtesies (of whalers and their crews). *v.t.* to forgather with or exchange visits with (another whaler and its crew at sea). [etym. doubtful]

gam- GAM(O)-.

Gama, *n.* **Vasco da** (1460–1524), Portuguese navigator who commanded an expedition in 1497 to discover the route to India around the Cape of Good Hope in modern South Africa. He reached land on Christmas Day 1497, which he named Natal. He then crossed the Indian Ocean, arriving at Calicut, May 1498, and returning to Portugal, Sept. 1499.

gama grass, *n.* a fodder grass, *Tripsacum dactyloides,* with culms from 4 to 7 ft (1-2 m) high, growing in the south of the US [perh. var. of GRAMA GRASS]

gamash, *n.* (*usu. pl.*) a kind of leggings, spatter-dashes or high-boots. [F *gamache,* perh. ult. from Arab *ghadāmasī,* from *Ghadāmas,* in Tripoli, a place where leather was made]

gamb, *n.* in heraldry, a figure of an animal's leg on a coat-of-arms. [OF *gambe* (F *jambe*)]

gamba[1], *n.* the metacarpus or metatarsus. [L]

gamba[2], *n.* a *viola da gamba,* an organ stop with a tone like that of the violin or violoncello. [for VIOLA DA GAMBA]

gambade, gambado[1], *n.* (*pl.* **-bades, -bados, -badoes**), a bound or spring of a horse; a caper, a fantastic movement, a freak, a frolic. [F *gambade* or Sp. *gambada,* GAMBOL]

gambado[2], *n.* (*pl.* **-dos, -does**) a leather legging or large boot for equestrians. [It. *gamba,* the leg]

†**gambeson,** *n.* a body-covering or tunic extending over the thighs, quilted and stuffed with wool, and usu. worn under armour, chiefly in the 14th cent. [OF *gambison, wambison,* prob. from Teut. (cp. OHG *wamba,* WOMB)]

gambet, *n.* the redshank. [It. *gambetta,* from *gamba,* leg]

Gambia, *n.* Republic of The, country in W Africa, surrounded to the N, E, and S by Senegal, and bordered to the W by the Atlantic Ocean. **area** 10,689 sq km/4126 sq miles. **capital** Banjul. **physical** banks of the river Gambia. **population** 788,200 (1988); annual growth rate 1.9%. **exports** groundnuts, palm oil, fish. **language** English (official). **religion** Muslim 70%, with animist and Christian minorities

gambier, *n.* an extract from the leaves of *Uncaria*

gambir, used in medicine as an astringent, and also for dyeing and tanning. [*gambir,* Malay]

Gambier Islands, *n.pl.* island group, part of French Polynesia, administered with the Tuamotu Archipelago; area 36 sq km/14 sq miles; population (1983) 582. It includes four coral islands and many small islets. The main island is Mangareva, with its town Rikitea.

gambit, *n.* an opening in chess, in which a pawn is sacrificed in order to obtain a favourable position for attack [most of the gambits have distinctive names, as *King's gambit, Queen's gambit, Steinitz gambit*]; the opening move in a concerted plan. **gambit-pawn,** *n.* a pawn so sacrificed. [derivation obscure, ult. from It. *gambetto,* a tripping up, from *gamba,* leg]

gamble, *v.i.* to play, esp. a game of chance, for money; to risk large sums or other possessions on some contingency; to speculate financially. *n.* gambling; a gambling venture or speculation. **to gamble away,** to squander or lose in gambling. **gambler,** *n.* **gamblesome,** *a.* [prob. from OE *gamenian,* to play, from *gamen,* a GAME, with freq. suf. -LE]

gamboge, *n.* a gum-resin, from Kampuchea, Sri Lanka etc., used as a yellow pigment, and in medicine. [mod. L *Gambogium, Cambodia* (the former name of Kampuchea), in Annam]

gambol, *v.i.* to frisk or skip about; to frolic. *n.* a frolic; a skipping or playing about. [earlier *gambold, gambalde,* OF *gambade,* It. *gambata,* from *gamba,* leg]

gambrel, *n.* a horse's hock; a bent piece of wood used for suspending carcases; (*N Am.*) a gambrel-roof. **gambrel-roof,** *n.* a curved or double-pitched roof. [etym. doubtful (cp. CAMBREL)]

gambroon, *n.* a twilled linen fabric for linings; a twilled cloth for trousers. [prob. from seaport of *Gambroon,* on the Persian Gulf]

game¹, *n.* sport, merriment, diversion; jest, as opp. to earnest; an exercise for diversion, usu. in concert with other players, a pastime; a contest played according to specified rules and decided by chance, strength, skill or combination of these; (*pl.*) athletic contests, esp. such as are held at periodical dates, as the Olympic Games etc.; (*N Am.*) a match, e.g. football; a single round in a sporting contest; the number of points required to win a game; a project, plan, or scheme designed to defeat others; success in a game or contest; (*coll., pl.*) tricks, dodges, subterfuges; wild animals or birds pursued in the chase, as hares, grouse, partridges, pheasants; the flesh of these; an object of pursuit; (*coll.*) a lark, an amusing incident; †field sports, as hunting, coursing, falconry etc.; †gallantry. *a.* pertaining to game; having the spirit of a game-cock; plucky, spirited; ready, willing (to do etc.). *v.i.* to play at games of chance; to play for a stake; to gamble. *v.t.* to gamble (away). **game, set and match,** (*coll.*) a final and convincing victory. **the game,** (*coll.*) prostitution. **the game is up,** everything has failed; the game (bird or animal) has started up. **to be off one's game,** to be playing poorly, not giving one's best performance. **to be on the game,** (*coll.*) to be earning a living as a prostitute. **to die game,** to maintain a resolute attitude to the last. **to give the game away,** to reveal a secret or strategy; (*coll.*) to reject or abandon (a competition etc.). **to have the game in one's hands,** to be sure of winning; to have success (in any contest, undertaking etc.) at one's command. **to make game of,** to turn into ridicule. **to play the game,** to abide by the rules; to act in an honourable way. **game-bag,** *n.* a bag to hold the game killed or taken by a sportsman. **game ball,** *n.* GAME POINT. **game-bird,** *n.* a bird hunted for sport. **game-book,** *n.* a book for recording game killed. **game-cock,** *n.* a cock bred and trained for fighting. **game-egg,** *n.* an egg from which game-fowls are bred. **game fish,** *n.* a large fish that is caught for sport. **game-fowl,** *n.* GAME-BIRD. **gamekeeper,** *n.* one who is employed to look after game, coverts etc., and to prevent poaching on a private estate or game reserve. **game laws,** *n.pl.* laws for the preservation of game; the regulation of the seasons for killing it etc. **game licence,** *n.* one giving the right to kill or deal in game. **game plan,** *n.* the tactics etc. of a football team, prearranged before a match; any carefully planned strategy. **game point,** *n.* a situation in a game of tennis when one point is enough to determine the game. **game reserve,** *n.* an area of privately-owned land stocked with game preserved for sport. **game-preserver,** *n.* a landowner who strictly preserves game, and rigidly insists on his legal rights in that respect. **game reserve,** *n.* an area of land set aside for the protection of wild animals. **gameshow, games show,** *n.* a television programme, esp. a quiz show, in which selected contestants compete for prizes. **gamesmanship,** *n.* the art or practice of winning games by disconcerting the opponent (by talking etc.) but without actually cheating. **game tenant,** *n.* a person renting an estate or piece of land for shooting or fishing. **game theory, games theory,** *n.* the analysis of all choices and strategies available in a game or military, social etc. conflict in order to choose the best possible course of action. **game warden,** *n.* one who is employed to look after game, esp. on a game reserve. **gameful,** *a.* full of sport or mirth; sportive. **gamely,** *adv.* **gameness,** *n.* **gamesome,** *a.* inclined to play; merry, gay. **gamesomely,** *adv.* **gamesomeness,** *n.* **gamester,** *n.* one who is addicted to gaming, a gambler; †a frolicsome person, †a prostitute. **gaming,** *n.* gambling. **gaming-house,** *n.* a house where gambling is carried on; a house of ill-repute. **gaming-table,** *n.* a table for gambling games. **gamy,** *a.* having the flavour or odour of game, high; abounding in game; plucky, spirited, game. **gaminess,** *n.* **gamer,** *n.* one who plays a game, esp. a role-playing game or a computer one. [OE *gamen* (cp. Icel. and OHG *gaman,* Dut. *gammen*)]

game², *a.* (*coll.*) lame, crippled; (of the arm or leg) crooked. **gammy,** *a.* wrong, spurious; crippled, crooked. *n.* a lame person. [etym. doubtful]

gamelan, *n.* a SE Asian percussion instrument; an orchestra made up of a number of gamelans. [Javanese]

gamet- GAMET(O)-.

gametangium, *n.* (*pl.* **-gia**) a cell or organ in which gametes are formed.

gamete, *n.* a sexual reproductive cell, either of the two germ cells that unite to form a new organism – in the male, a spermatozoon, in the female an ovum. **gamete intra-fallopian transfer,** (GIFT), *n.* a treatment for infertile women in which eggs and sperm (the gametes) are injected directly into the fallopian tubes via a catheter. **gametal, gametic,** *a.* [Gr. *gametes,* husband]

gamet(o)-, *comb. form* gamete.

gametocyte, *n.* a cell that breaks up into gametes.

gametogenesis, *n.* the formation of gametes.

gametophyte, *n.* a plant of the generation that produces gametes in plant species which show alternation of generations.

gamic, *a.* (*Biol.*) of or pertaining to sex, sexual; capable of development after sexual fertilization (of ova). [Gr. *gamikos,* from *gamos,* marriage]

gamin, *n.* a street arab, an urchin. [F, perh. from G *Gemein,* a common soldier]

gamine, *n.* a small boy-like girl or woman. [F]

gamma, *n.* the third letter of the Greek alphabet, Γ, γ, G, g, representing 3 in enumerations; a moth *Flusia gamma,* also called the gamma moth; an instrument for cauterizing a hernia (from its resemblance to the Greek gamma); †(*Mus.*) the gamut. **gamma globulin,** *n.* any of a group of proteins that are carried in blood and serum and include most known antibodies. **gamma-rays,** *n.pl.* (*Phys.*) short-wavelength, penetrating electromagnetic rays emitted by radioactive substances; used in treatment of cancer and in radiography of metals. [Gr.]

gammadion, gammation, *n.* (*pl.* **-tia**) an ornament composed of the gamma singly or in combination, formerly used in sacerdotal vestments in the Greek Church; a cruciform ornament composed of four gammas, placed back to back, forming a voided Greek cross; a fylfot, swastika. [late Gr., from prec.]

gammer, *n.* (*esp. dial.*) an old woman. [prob. a corr. of GRANDMOTHER]

gammon[1], *n.* the buttock or thigh of a hog salted and dried; a cured ham. *v.t.* to make into bacon; to salt and dry in smoke. [OF *gambon* (F *jambon*), from *gambe,* a leg]

gammon[2], *n.* nonsense, humbug; a fraud, a hoax. *int.* nonsense, humbug. *v.t.* to hoax, to impose upon. *v.i.* to make pretences; to talk deceptively, to chaff. [orig. thieves' slang, prob. from ME and OE *gamen,* GAME[1]]

gammon[3], *n.* a defeat at backgammon in which the winner's score is equivalent to two games; †backgammon. *v.t.* to win a gammon against (an opponent in backgammon). [prob. from OE *gamen,* GAME[1]]

gammon[4], *v.t.* (*Naut.*) to make fast (the bowsprit) to the stem. *n.* the lashing so used. **gammoning,** *n.* **gammoning-hole, -plate,** *n.* the hole through which or the hole to which the gammoning is fastened. [etym. doubtful]

gammy GAME[2].

gam(o)-, *comb. form* (*Biol.*) sexual; having certain parts united. [Gr. *gamos,* marriage]

gamogenesis, *n.* (*Biol.*) sexual reproduction. **gamogenetic,** *a.* **gamogenetically,** *adv.*

gamopetalous, *a.* (*Bot.*) having the petals united.

gamophyllous, *a.* (*Bot.*) having the leaves united.

gamosepalous, *a.* (*Bot.*) having the sepals united.

Gamow, *n.* **George** (1904–68), Soviet cosmologist, nuclear physicist, and popularizer of science. His work in astrophysics included a study of the structure and evolution of stars and the creation of the elements. He also explained how the collision of nuclei in the solar interior could produce the nuclear reactions that power the Sun.

gamp, *n.* (*coll.*) an umbrella, esp. a large and clumsy one. [Mrs *Gamp,* the monthly nurse in Dickens's *Martin Chuzzlewit*]

gamut, *n.* †the first or lowest note in Guido's scale equivalent to G on the lowest line of the modern bass stave; the major diatonic scale; the whole series of notes recognized by musicians; the whole range, compass or extent. [med. L *gamma ut* (*gamma,* the third letter of the Greek alphabet, used by Guido of Arezzo to mark the first or lowest note in the mediaeval music scale, combined with *ut,* the first word in a mnemonic stanza from a hymn beginning *Ut queant laxis resonare fibris,* containing the six names of the hexachord *Ut re mi fa sol la*)]

gamy GAME[1].

-gamy, *comb. form.* marriage or kind of marriage, as in *bigamy, endogamy, misogamy.* [Gr. *gamos,* marriage]

Gance, *n.* **Abel** (1889–1981), French film director, whose *Napoléon* (1927) was one of the most ambitious silent epic films, including colour and triple-screen sequences, as well as multiple exposure shots.

ganch, *v.t.* to impale, esp. to execute by dropping on to hooks or stakes. [F *gancher,* from It. *gancio,* prob. from Turk. *ganja,* hook]

gander, *n.* the male of the goose; a simpleton, a noodle; (*coll.*) a quick look. **gander-party,** *n.* a gathering of men only. **ganderism,** *n.* [OE *gandra,* earlier *ganra* (*d* inserted as in Dut. *gander*), perh. cogn. with GOOSE]

Gandhi[1], *n.* **Indira** (1917–84), Indian politician. Prime minister of India (1966–77 and 1980–84), and leader of the Congress Party (1966–77) and subsequently of the Congress (I) Party. She was assassinated by members of her Sikh bodyguard, resentful of her use of troops to clear malcontents from the Sikh temple at Amritsar.

Gandhi[2], *n.* **Mohandas Karamchand,** called **Mahatma** ('Great Soul') (1869–1948), Indian nationalist leader. A pacifist, he led the struggle for Indian independence from the UK by nonviolent noncooperation (*satyagraha,* defence of and by truth) from 1915. He was imprisoned several times by the British authorities, and was influential in the nationalist Congress Party and in the independence negotiations of 1947. He was assassinated by a Hindu nationalist in the violence which followed the Partition of India and Pakistan.

Gandhi[3], *n.* **Rajiv** (1944–), Indian politician, prime minister from 1984, following his mother Indira Gandhi's assassination, to Nov. 1989. As prime minister he faced growing discontent with his party's elitism and lack of concern for social issues.

Ganesh, *n.* Hindu god, son of Siva and Parvati; he is represented as elephant-headed and worshipped as a remover of obstacles.

gang[1], *n.* a number of persons associated for a particular purpose (often in a bad sense); a number of workmen under a foreman, or of slaves or convicts; a set of tools operating in concert; (*Mining*) a course or vein; a gangue; (*Sc.*) a walk or pasturage (for cattle). *v.i.* to act in concert with. **Gang of Four,** *n.* the chief members of the radical faction that tried to seize power in China after the death of Mao Zedong 1976. It included his widow, Jiang Qing; the other members were Zhang Chunjao, Wang Hungwen, and Yao Wenyuan. The coup failed, and they were soon arrested. **to gang up,** to join with others (in doing something). **to gang up on,** to join with others to make an attack on somebody. **gang-bang,** *n.* (*sl.*) an occasion on which a number of males have successive sexual intercourse with one female. **gangland,** *n.* the world of organized crime. **gang mill,** *n.* a saw mill with gang saws. **gangsman,** *n.* a ganger. **gang saw,** *n.* a saw with several blades fitted in a frame, producing parallel cuts. **ganger,** *n.* the overseer or foreman of a gang of labourers. **gangster,** *n.* a member of a criminal gang. **gangsterland,** *n.* gangland.

gang[2], *v.i.* (*Sc., past, p.p.* **gaed**) to go. **gang-cask,** *n.* a small cask for bringing off water in boats. **gang-days,** *n.pl.* the three days preceding Ascension Day or Holy Thursday, Rogation-days. **gang-plank, gang-board,** *n.* a plank, usu. with cleats, used for boarding or landing from a vessel. **gangway,** *n.* a passage into or out of a building or between rows of seats; in the House of Commons, a narrow cross passage giving access to the back benches, and dividing the more independent members from the immediate supporters of the Government and the opposition; a temporary bridge affording means of passage from a ship to the shore; an opening in the bulwarks affording entrance to or exit from a vessel; a passage connecting different parts of a vessel; in a mine, a main level. *int.* clear the way! **to bring to the gangway,** (formerly) to punish (a sailor) by tying up and flogging. **to sit below the gangway,** to sit as a more or less independent member of the House of Commons. **gang-week,** *n.* Rogation-week. [OE *gangan* (cp. Icel. *ganga,* OHG *gangan*)]

gange, *v.t.* to cover (a fish-hook or part of fishing-line) with fine wire; to fasten (a fish-hook) to a ganging-line. **ganging, ganging line,** *n.* fastening a fish-hook to a line; the part of the line to which it is fastened. [etym. doubtful]

Ganges, *n.* (Hindi **Ganga**) major river of India and Bangladesh; length 2510 km/1560 miles. It is the most sacred river for Hindus.

Gangetic, *a.* pertaining to the river Ganges or the region in which it runs. [L *Gangēticus,* from *Ganges,* Gr. *Gangēs*]

gangling, *a.* loosely built, lanky, awkward. [OE *gangan,* to go]

ganglion, *n.* (*pl.* **-lia**) an enlargement in the course of a nerve forming a local centre for nervous action; an aggregation of nerve-cells forming a nucleus in the central nervous system; a glandiform organ such as the spleen or the thyroid body; in pathology, a globular growth in the sheath of a tendon. **gangliac, gangliar, ganglionic,** *a.* pertaining to a ganglion or ganglia. **gangliated, ganglionated,** *a.* **gangliform,** *a.* **ganglionary,** *a.* composed of ganglia. [Gr.]

†**gangrel,** *n.* a vagrant. [prob. from GANG ([1] or [2])]

gangrene, *n.* cessation of vitality in a part of the body, the first stage of mortification, usu. followed by decay; (*fig.*) corruption, decay. *v.t.* to cause this in; (*fig.*) to inject with decay or vice; to corrupt. *v.i.* to mortify. †**gangrenate,** *v.t.* **gangrenescent,** *a.* **gangrenous,**

a. [L *gangraena,* Gr. *gangraina*]

gangster GANG[1].

gangue, *n.* the earthy matter or matrix in which ores are embedded. [F, from G *Gang,* vein, lode, cogn. with GANG[1]]

ganister, *n.* a kind of grit or hard sandstone from the lower coal-measures; a mixture of ground quartz and fire-clay used for lining Bessemer converters. [etym. doubtful]

ganja, *n.* a dried preparation of *Cannabis sativa* or Indian hemp, smoked as an intoxicant and narcotic. [Hind. *gānjhā*]

gannet, *n.* a sea-bird, *Sula bassana,* also called *solan goose*. [OE *ganot* (cp. Dut. *gent,* MHG *ganze,* GANDER]

Gannet Peak, *n.* the highest peak in Wyoming state, US, rising to 4207 m/13,804 ft.

ganoid, *a.* bright, smooth, like enamel of fish-scales; of fish belonging to the Ganoidei. *n.* any fish of the Ganoidei. **ganoidal, ganoidean,** *a.* **Ganoidei,** *n. pl.* a division of fishes comprising the sturgeons and numerous extinct forms, so called from their shining scales. **ganoin,** *n.* a calcareous substance that forms a shiny, enamel-like coating on ganoid scales. [F *ganoïde* (Gr. *ganos,* brightness, -OID)]

Gansu, formerly **Kansu** *n.* province of NW China. **area** 530,000 sq km/204,580 sq miles. **capital** Lanzhou. **products** coal, oil, hydroelectric power from the Huang He (Yellow) River. **population** (1986) 20,710,000, including many Muslims.

gant, gaunt[1], *v.i.* (*Sc.*) to yawn. [from OE *gānian,* to yawn]

gantlet, GAUNTLET[1].

gantry, *n.* a wooden frame for standing a barrel upon; a structure for carrying a travelling crane. [etym. doubtful (perh. from OF *gantier,* also *chantier,* L *canterium*)]

Ganymede, *n.* in Greek mythology, a youth so beautiful he was chosen as cupbearer to Zeus; (*facet.*) a waiter; †a catamite; in astronomy, the largest moon of the planet Jupiter, and the largest moon in the solar system, 5300 km/3300 miles in diameter (larger than the planet Mercury). It orbits Jupiter every 7.2 days at a distance of 1.1 million km/700,000 miles. Its surface is a mixture of cratered and grooved terrain. [L *Ganymēdēs,* Gr. *Ganumēdēs*]

gaol JAIL.

gap, *n.* an opening, a breach, as in a hedge, a fence etc.; a chasm, a break in a mountain ridge; a breach of continuity, a blank, hiatus, interruption; a deficiency; a wide divergence. *v.t.* (*past, p.p.* **gapped**) to make a gap in. **to stand in the gap,** to expose oneself for the protection of others. **to stop, fill,** or **supply a gap,** to repair a defect or make up a deficiency. **gap-toothed,** *a.* having spaces between the teeth. **gapped,** *a.* **gappy,** *a.* [Icel., from *gapa,* see foll.]

gape, *v.i.* to open the mouth wide; to yawn; to stare with open mouth in wonder, surprise or perplexity; to open in a fissure or chasm, to split open; †to bawl, to shout. *n.* the act of gaping; a stare with open mouth, a yawn; the width of the mouth when opened, as of birds etc.; the part of a beak that opens; the opening between the shells of a bivalve that does not shut completely; (*pl.*) a disease in young poultry caused by the gapeworm and characterized by much gaping; a fit of yawning; (*Facet.*) a fit of staring. **to gape at,** to open the mouth and gaze at with astonishment. **to gape for** or **after,** to desire eagerly, to crave. **gapeworm,** *n.* a nematode worm, *Syngamus trachea,* that causes gapes in poultry. **gaper,** *n.* one who or that which gapes, esp. various kinds of birds, fish and molluscs. **gapingly,** *adv.* [Icel. *gapa* (cp. Dut. *gapen,* G *gaffen*)]

gar[1], **garfish,** *n.* a fish with a long pointed snout, esp. *Belone vulgaris,* a European fish called also greenbone, in allusion to the bones of its spine; (*N Am.*) species of the genus *Lepidosteus,* also called **garpike**. [OE *gār,* a spear, FISH]

gar[2], *v.i.* to make, to cause (to do). [Icel. *gerua* (cp. Swed. *göra,* cogn. with OE *gearwian*), to make ready, to make, do (cp. YARE)]

garage, *n.* a building for housing or repairing motor-cars; an establishment where this is done as a business and where motor fuels etc. are sold. *v.t* to put or keep in a garage. *a.* (*coll.*) rough-and-ready, amateurish, improvised. **garage sale,** *n.* a sale of second-hand goods held on the grounds of a private home, esp. in a garage. [F, from *garer,* to put into dock, from Teut. (cp. Goth. *warjan,* OE *werian,* to defend)]

garancin, *n.* a colouring matter produced by the action of sulphuric acid upon madder. [F, from *garance,* madder]

garb[1], *n.* dress, costume; distinctive style of dress; outward appearance; †appearance, demeanour. *v.t.* to put garments upon, esp. to put in a distinctive dress. [through F *garbe* (now *galbe*) or directly from It. *garbo,* grace, elegance, from Teut. (cp. OHG *garwī, garawī,* cogn. with GEAR)]

garb[2], *n.* in heraldry, a sheaf of grain. [AF *garbe* (F *gerbe*), from Teut. (cp. OHG *garba,* G. *Garbe*)]

garbage, *n.* animal refuse, esp. the entrails; offal; anything worthless or offensive, sordid rubbish; (*N Am.*) kitchen waste. **garbage can,** *n.* (*N Am.*) a dustbin. **garbage disposal unit,** *n.* (*N Am.*) a waste disposal unit. [etym. doubtful (Skeat suggests OF *garbage, gerbage,* a tax paid in sheaves, from *garbe,* see prec.)]

garble, *v.t.* to separate the fine or valuable parts of from the coarse and worthless; to mutilate, in such a way as to convey a false impression; to pervert, to falsify. **garbler,** *n.* [perh. through OF *garbeller,* from It. *garbellare,* to garble spices, from Arab. *gharbala,* to sift]

garbo, *n.* (*pl.* **-bos**) (*Austral., coll.*) a dustman. [GARBAGE]

Garbo, *n.* **Greta** (stage name of Greta Lovisa Gustafsson) (1905–90), Swedish film actress. She went to the US in 1925, and her leading role in *The Torrent* (1926) made her one of Hollywood's first stars. Her later films include *Queen Christina* (1933), *Anna Karenina* (1935), and *Ninotchka* (1939).

garboard, *n.* (*Naut.*) the first plank fastened on either side of a ship's keel. **garboard-strake,** *n.* the row of planks next to the keel on a ship's bottom; the row of plates corresponding to this in an iron ship. [obs. Dut. *gaarboord*]

†**garboil,** *n.* a tumult, an uproar, a broil. *v.t.* to disturb, to upset. [OF *garbouil,* It. *garbuglio* (etym. doubtful; second part conn. with L *bullīre,* to boil)]

García Lorca, Federico, LORCA, FEDERICO GARCÍA.

García Márquez, *n.* **Gabriel** (1928–), Colombian novelist, whose *Cien años de soledad* (*One Hundred Years of Solitude*, 1967), the story of six generations of a family, is an example of magic realism, a technique for heightening the intensity of realistic portrayal of social and political issues by introducing grotesque or fanciful material. Other books include *El amor en los tiempos del cólera* (*Love in the Time of Cholera*, 1985). Nobel Prize for Literature 1982.

Garcia Perez, *n.* **Alan** (1949–), Peruvian politician, president from 1985.

garçon, *n.* a waiter. [F, dim of *gars,* lad]

gardant, GUARDANT.

garden, *n.* an enclosed piece of ground appropriated to the cultivation of fruit, flowers or vegetables; a place or region particularly fertile, well-cultivated or delightful; (*pl.*) a public pleasure-ground adorned with trees, flower-beds etc. *a.* pertaining to a garden; cultivated, not wild. *v.i.* to cultivate a garden; (*coll.*) in cricket, to smooth out bumps etc. in the pitch with the bat, often as delaying tactic. **common or garden,** (*coll.*) the ordinary (sort). **everything in the garden is lovely,** everything appears to be well. **the Garden,** the philosophical school of Epicurus or their tenets. **garden centre,** *n.* a place where plants, fertilizers, and garden tools and equipment are sold. **garden city** or **suburb,** *n.* a planned township or suburb in rural surroundings. **garden-cress,** *n.* pepper-grass, *Lepidium sativum*. **garden-engine,** *n.* a pump and tank on wheels for watering plants. **garden flat,** *n.* a flat that opens onto a garden. **garden-frame,** *n.* a glazed frame for protecting plants during the winter or for forcing. **garden-**

glass, *n.* a bell-glass for protecting plants. **garden-party,** *n.* a social meeting or a company entertained on a lawn or in a garden. **garden-plot,** *n.* a piece of ground used as a garden. **garden-seat,** *n.* a seat, esp. a long one for several persons, for use in a garden. **garden-stuff,** *n.* vegetables, herbs, fruit etc. **garden-warbler,** *n.* a bird, *Sylvia hortensis*. **gardened,** *a.* cultivated like a garden; furnished with gardens. **gardener,** *n.* one who gardens, esp. one whose occupation is to attend to or to manage gardens. **gardenesque,** *a.* **gardening,** *n.* horticulture; work in a garden. [A-F *gardin* (F *jardin*), from Teut. (cp. OS *gardo,* OE *geard,* YARD, Icel. *garthr,* GARTH, G *Garten*)]

gardenia, *n.* a genus of tropical shrubs and trees cultivated in greenhouses for their large fragrant flowers. [Dr Alexander *Garden,* US botanist, *d.* 1791]

Gardner, *n.* **Ava** (1922–90), US actress, who starred in the 1940s and 1950s in such films as *The Killers* (1946), *Pandora and the Flying Dutchman* (1951) and *The Barefoot Contessa* (1954). She remained active in films until the 1980s.

†**gardyloo,** *int.* the warning cried in old Edinburgh when slops were emptied from windows into the streets. [incorrect F *gare de l'eau,* beware of the water (properly, *gare l'eau*)]

gare, *a.* covetous, miserly. [Sc., from Icel. *gorr,* cogn. with YARE]

garefowl, *n.* the great auk; the razor-billed auk. [Icel. *geir-fugl*]

Garfield, *n.* **James A(bram)** (1831–81), 20th president of the US (1881), a Republican. He was born in a log cabin in Ohio, and served in the American Civil War on the side of the Union. He was elected president but held office for only four months before being assassinated in a Washington station by a disappointed office-seeker.

garfish GAR[1].

gargantuan, *a.* immense, enormous, incredibly big. **gargantuism,** *n.* [*Gargantua,* the giant of Rabelais]

gargarism, *n.* a gargle. **gargarize, -ise,** *v.t.* to gargle. [L *gargarisma,* from Gr. *gargarizein,* gargle, of imit. orig.]

garget, *n.* a distemper affecting the throat in cattle; an affection of the udder of cows or ewes. [OF *gargate,* the throat (etym. doubtful; cp. GARGOYLE)]

gargle, *v.t.* to rinse (the mouth or throat) with some medicated liquid, which is prevented from passing down the throat by the breath; †to warble. *n.* a liquid used for washing the mouth or throat. [F *gargouiller*]

gargol, GARGLE.

gargoyle, *n.* a grotesque spout, usu. carved to represent a human or animal figure, projecting from a Gothic building to throw rain-water clear of the wall. [F *gargouille,* weasand (cp. F *gorge,* throat, Gr. *garg-,* base of *gargarizein,* GARGARIZE)]

Garibaldi, *n.* **Giuseppe** (1807–82), Italian soldier who played an important role in the unification of Italy by conquering Sicily and Naples in 1860. From 1834 a member of the nationalist Mazzini's Young Italy society, he was forced into exile until 1848 and again 1849–54. He fought against Austria (1848–49, 1859, and 1866), and led two unsuccessful expeditions to liberate Rome from papal rule in 1862 and 1867.

garibaldi, *n.* a loose kind of blouse worn by women or children, like the red shirts worn by Garibaldi and his men. **garibaldi biscuit,** *n.* a sandwich-type biscuit with a layer of currants.

garish, *a.* gaudy, showy, flashy; excessively or extravagantly decorated; dazzling, glaring. **garishly,** *adv.* **garishness,** *n.* [earlier *gaurish,* from obs. *gauren,* to stare, etym. doubtful]

garland, *n.* a wreath, chaplet or festoon of flowers, leaves etc., a similar festoon of metal, stone, ribbons or other material used for decoration etc.; the prize, the chief honour; a collection of choice pieces, esp. of poems; †the thing most prized. *v.t.* to deck with a garland. **garlandage,** (*poet.*), **garlandry,** *n.* **garlandless,** *a.* [OF *garlande,* etym. doubtful (F *guirlande,* from It. *ghirlanda*)]

Garland, *n.* **Judy** (1922–69), stage name of Frances Gumm, US singer and actress whose films include *The Wizard of Oz* (1939, including the song 'Over the Rainbow'), *Meet Me in St Louis* (1944), and *A Star is Born* (1954). Her unhappy personal life led to her early death from alcohol and drug addiction.

garlic, *n.* a bulbous-rooted plant, *Allium sativum,* with a strong odour and a pungent taste, used in cookery. **garlic bread,** *n.* a long thin bread roll sliced, spread with garlic butter and heated. **garlic butter,** *n.* butter flavoured with garlic. **garlic-eater,** *n.* **garlic mustard,** *n.* a plant, *Alliaria petiolara,* of the mustard family with small white flowers and a garlic smell. **garlicky,** *a.* [OE *gārlēac* (as GAR[1], LEEK)]

garment, *n.* an article of clothing, esp. one of the larger articles, as a coat or gown; apparel, dress; (*pl.*) clothes. *v.t.* (*poet., usu. in p.p.*) to attire with or as with a garment. **garmentless,** *a.* **garmenture,** *n.* dress, apparel, clothing. [ME and OF *garnement,* from *garnir,* see GARNISH]

garner, *n.* a place for storing grain, a granary; a store, a repository. *v.t.* to store in or as in a garner, to gather. [OF *gernier, grenier,* L *grānārium,* GRANARY]

garnet[1], *n.* a vitreous mineral of varying composition, colour and quality, the deep red, transparent kinds of which are prized as gems. [OF *grenat, granat,* late L *grānātus,* from (*mālum*) *grānātum,* POMEGRANATE, from the resemblance to its seeds]

garnet[2], All Sir Garnet, (*Army sl.*) all fit and proper, as it should be. [Sir *Garnet* Wolseley, 1883–1913]

garnish, *v.t.* to adorn; to embellish (as a dish) with something laid round it; to supply, to furnish; (*Law*) to warn, to give notice to. *n.* an ornament; a decoration, especially things put round a dish as embellishment; (*sl.*) a fee; †a fee paid by a prisoner to the jailer; †outfit. **maiden-garnish,** (*formerly*) a fee or imposition among workmen paid by a man getting a job. **garnish-money,** *n.* garnish paid to a jailer. **garnishee,** *n.* one who has received notice not to pay any money which he owes to a third person, who is indebted to the person giving notice. **garnisher,** *n.* one who garnishes. **garnishing,** *n.* the act of ornamenting; things used for decoration, esp. of dishes. **garnishment,** *n.* an ornament, an embellishment; in law a warning to a party to appear in court, or not to pay money etc. to a defendant. **garnishry,** *n.* embellishment. [OF *garniss-,* stem of *garnir, guarnir, warnir,* to defend, to fortify, from Teut. (cp. OHG *warnōn,* G *warnen,* to WARN)]

†**garnison,** *n.* a guard, a protection, a garrison. [as prec.]

garniture, *n.* furniture, appurtenances; ornamental appendages, trimmings, ornament, embellishment; costume, dress.

garotte, GARROTTE.

garpike GAR[1].

garret[1], *n.* an upper room or storey immediately under the roof; †a turret, a watch-tower; (*sl.*) the head. **garret-master,** *n.* a maker of household furniture who sells his work to dealers. **garreteer,** *n.* one who lives in a garret, esp. an impecunious writer. [OF *garite* (F *guérite*), from *garir, warir,* to defend, from Teut. (cp. OHG *warjan,* OE *werian*)]

garret[2] GALLET.

Garrick, *n.* **David** (1717–79), British actor and theatre manager. He was a pupil of Samuel Johnson. From 1747 he became joint licensee of the Drury Lane theatre with his own company, and instituted a number of significant theatrical conventions including concealed stage lighting and banishing spectators from the stage. He performed Shakespeare characters such as Richard III, King Lear, Hamlet, and Benedick. He collaborated with Colman in writing the play *The Clandestine Marriage* (1766). He retired from the stage in 1766, but continued as a manager.

garrison, *n.* a body of troops stationed in a fort or fortified place; a fortified place manned with soldiers, guns, etc., a stronghold. *v.t.* to furnish (a fortress) with soldiers; to occupy as a garrison. **garrison-town,** *n.* a town in which a garrison is stationed. [F *garison,* defence, safety, from *garir,* to defend (sense influ. by GARNISON)]

garron, *n.* a small horse bred in Galloway, the Highlands and Ireland. [Gael. *gearran,* a gelding]

garrot¹, *n.* a sea-duck, esp. the golden-eye. [F, etym. doubtful]

garrot², *n.* a tourniquet formed of a band and a stick, the former being twisted by turning the latter. [from foll.]

garrotte, *n.* a method of execution in which the victim is fastened by an iron collar to an upright post, and a knob operated by a screw or lever dislocates the spinal column, or a small blade severs the spinal cord at the base of the brain (orig. the method was strangulation by a cord twisted with a stick); hence, robbery by means of strangling. *v.t.* to execute by this means; to render helpless or insensible in order to rob. **garrotter,** *n.* [Sp. *garrote,* a stick, etym. doubtful]

garrulous, *a.* talkative, loquacious, wordy; chattering. **garrulity,** *n.* **garrulously,** *adv.* **garrulousness,** *n.* [L *garrulus,* from *garrīre,* to chatter]

garter, *n.* a band round the leg for holding the stocking up; (*N Am.*) a sock-suspender. *v.t.* to fasten (a stocking) with a garter; to put a garter upon; †to invest with the Order of the Garter, **Order of the Garter,** the badge of the highest order of British knighthood, instituted by Edward III, about 1348; the order itself; membership of this. **Garter Principal King-of-Arms,** *n.* the chief herald of this order. **garter-snake,** *n.* a harmless American snake belonging to the genus *Eutaenia.* [OF *gartier* (F *jarretiere*), from *garet* (F *jarret*), the leg. perh. from Celt. (cp. Bret. and W *gar,* the shank of the leg)]

garth, *n.* a close, a yard; a garden, croft or paddock; the grass-plot surrounded by the cloisters of a religious house; a fish-weir. [Icel. *garthr,* cogn. OE *geard,* YARD²]

Garvey, *n.* **Marcus (Moziah)** (1887–1940), Jamaican political thinker and activist, an early advocate of black nationalism. He founded the UNIA (Universal Negro Improvement Association) in 1914, and moved to the US in 1916, where he established branches in New York and other northern cities. Aiming to achieve human rights and dignity for black people through black pride and economic self-sufficiency, he led a BACK TO AFRICA movement for black Americans to establish a black-governed country in Africa. Rastafarianism is based largely on his ideas.

garvie, *n.* (*Sc.*) a sprat, also called **garvock**. [etym. unknown; Gael. *garbhag,* perh. cogn.]

gas, *n.* (*pl.* **gases**) a substance in the form of air, possessing the condition of perfect fluid elasticity; such a fluid used for lighting and heating, esp. that obtained from coal; (*esp. N Am., coll.*) gasolene, petrol; in coal-mining, an explosive mixture of fire-damp and air; (*coll.*) a gas-jet; empty talk, frothy eloquence; bouncing, brag; (*dated coll. or dial.*) something great or wonderful. *a.* great or wonderful. *v.i.* (*past, p.p.* **gassed**) to indulge in empty talk; to boast. *v.t.* to supply gas to; to subject to the action of burning gas (as lace) in order to free from loose fibres; to attack, to stupefy or kill by means of poison-gas. **to step on the gas,** to accelerate a motor-car; to hurry. **gasbag,** *n.* a bag for holding gas or stopping an escape from a gas-main; (*coll.*) a talkative person. **gas black,** *n.* the fine black powder produced by burning natural gas and used as a pigment in paints. **gas-bottle,** *n.* a steel cylinder for holding compressed gas. **gas-bracket,** *n.* a pipe projecting from a wall and fitted with a burner or burners. **gas-burner,** *n.* the tube or jet at which the gas issues and is ignited. **gas chamber** or **oven,** *n.* an airtight place designed for killing animals or humans by means of a poisonous gas. **gas chromatography,** *n.* a method of analysing a mixture of volatile substances which depends on the relative speeds at which the various components of the mixture pass through a long narrow tube that contains an inert gas and a solvent. **gas-coal,** *n.* bituminous coal from which gas for heating and illuminating purposes can be made. **gas-cooled,** *a.* cooled by a flow of gas. **gas-cooled reactor,** *n.* a nuclear reactor that uses a gas as the coolant. **gas coke,** *n.* coke left as a residuum after gas has been extracted from gas-coal. **gas-engine** or **-motor,** *n.* an engine in which the motive power is obtained from the explosion of gas. **gas escape,** *n.* a leakage of gas. **gasfield,** *n.* a region in which natural gas occurs. **gas-fire,** *n.* a device for burning gas for heating a room etc. **gas-fired,** *a.* fuelled by a gas or gases. **gas-fitter,** *n.* a person employed to lay pipes and put up fixtures for gas. **gas-fittings,** *n.pl.* gas-brackets, stoves, fires and other apparatus for lighting and heating by gas. **gas gangrene,** *n.* a gangrenous infection in deep wounds caused by bacteria which produce gases in the surrounding tissues. **gas-gauge,** *n.* an instrument for testing gas pressure. **gas-guzzler,** *n.* (*N Am., coll.*) a (usu. large) car that uses a lot of petrol. **gas-holder,** *n.* a structure for storing gas, a gasometer. **gas-jet,** *n.* a gas burner; a jet of flame from it. **gas-lamp,** *n.* a lamp that burns gas. **gaslight,** *n.* the light produced by the combustion of coal-gas; a gas-jet. **gas-main,** *n.* a principal pipe leading from a gas-works and having branches and distributing pipes. **gas-man,** *n.* a person employed at a gas-works; a collector of money due for the supply of gas; a gas-fitter; a person employed to read household gas-meters. **gas mantle,** *n.* a chemically-prepared incombustible gauze hood for a gas-lamp that becomes incandescent when heated. **gas-mask,** *n.* a mask with a chemical filter to protect the wearer against poisonous gases and fumes. **gas-meter,** *n.* a machine for measuring and recording the quantity of gas consumed. **gas-oil,** *n.* an oil distilled from crude petroleum used as a fuel for heating etc. **gas-ring,** *n.* a hollow pipe with perforations that serve as gas-jets, used for cooking. **gas-shell,** *n.* an artillery shell containing a chemical mixture that produces or diffuses poison-gas on explosion. **gas station,** *n.* (*N Am., coll.*) a filling-station, petrol station. **gas-tank,** *n.* a gasometer; (*N Am., coll.*) the petrol tank on a motor vehicle. **gas-tar,** *n.* coal-tar. **gas-tight,** *a.* of pipes etc., not allowing gas to escape, not leaky. **gas-trap,** *n.* in plumbing, a double curve or U-shaped section of a pipe in which water remains and forms a seal that blocks the escape of foul gases. **gas-well,** *n.* a well that yields natural gas. **gas-works,** *n.pl.* an industrial plant where gas, esp. coal-gas, is produced. **gaseous,** *a.* in the form of gas; like gas. **gaseity,** *n.* **gasiform,** *a.* of the nature or form of gas. **gasify,** *v.t.* to convert into gas. **gasifiable,** *a.* **gasification,** *n.* **gasless,** *a.* **gassy,** *a.* containing gas; like gas; gaseous; full of empty talk; (*coll.*) quick to flare up, touchy, irascible. **gassiness,** *n.* [Dut., invented by the chemist J.B. van Helmont, 1577–1644, from Gr. *chaos,* see CHAOS]

Gascon, *n.* a native of Gascony, France; a boaster. **gasconade,** *n.* boasting, bravado, bragging. *v.i.* to boast, to brag. **gasconader, gasconism,** *n.* [F]

Gascony, *n.* ancient province of SW France. With Guienne it formed the duchy of Aquitaine in the 12th century; Henry II of England gained possession of it through his marriage to Eleanor of Aquitaine in 1152, and it was often in English hands until 1451. It was ruled by the king of France until it was united with the French royal domain in 1607 under Henry IV.

gaselier, *n.* an ornamental metal-work pendant with branches carrying gas-burners for lighting a room etc. [GAS, (CHAND)ELIER]

gaseous GAS.

gash¹, *v.t.* to make a long, deep, gaping cut in. *n.* a deep, open cut, especially in flesh; a flesh-wound, a cleft. [earlier *garsh, garse,* OF *garser,* perh. from late L *caraxāre,* Gr. *charassein,* to scratch, incise]

gash², *a.* (*Sc.*) sagacious, shrewd; dignified, neat, trim; dignified-looking, pert. [etym. doubtful]

gash³, *v.i.* (*Sc.*) to gossip, to tattle. [etym. doubtful]

gash⁴, gashly, *a.* (*Sc.*) ghastly, dismal. **gashliness,** *n.* **gashful,** *a.* [corr. of GHASTLY, influ. by GASH¹]

gasiform etc. GAS.

Gaskell, *n.* **'Mrs' Elizabeth Cleghorn** (born Stevenson) (1810–65), British novelist. Her books include *Mary Barton* (set in industrial Manchester) (1848), *Cranford* (set in the town in which she was brought up, Knutsford, Cheshire) (1853), *North and South* (1855), *Sylvia's Lovers* (1863–64), the unfinished *Wives and Daughters* (1866), and a life of her friend Charlotte Brontë.

gasket, *n.* a plaited cord by which the sails, when furled, are bound close to the yards or gaffs; a strip of leather, tow, or other material for packing or caulking joints in pipes, engines etc. to make them air-tight or water-tight. **to blow a gasket,** (*coll.*) to lose one's temper. [etym. doubtful]

gaskin¹, *n.* the part of a horse's hind leg between the stifle and the hock, lower thigh.

gaskin², GASKET.

gaskins, *n.pl.* GALLIGASKINS.

gas(o)- *comb. form* pertaining to or using gas.

gasolene, gasoline, *n.* a volatile inflammable product of the distillation of petroleum, for heating and lighting; (*N Am.*) petrol.

gasolier, GASELIER.

gasometer, *n.* a large cylindrical reservoir used at gasworks for the storage of gas, a gas-holder; in chemistry, an apparatus for measuring, collecting, preserving or mixing different gases; an instrument for measuring the gases used in chemical experiments etc. **gasometric,** *a.* **gasometry,** *n.* the science, act or practice of measuring gases.

gasoscope, *n.* an instrument for detecting the presence of carburetted hydrogen in mines, buildings etc.

gasp, *v.i.* to breathe in a convulsive manner, as from exhaustion or astonishment. *v.t.* to emit or utter with gasps. *n.* a short painful catching of the breath. **at the last gasp,** at the last extremity; at the point of death. **to gasp out** or **away,** to breathe out (as one's life) convulsively. **gasper,** *n.* (*dated sl.*) a cigarette. **gaspingly,** *adv.* [prob. from Icel. *geispa,* to yawn (cp. Dut. *gijpen,* OE *gipian,* in *gipung,* a gaping)]

gaspacho, GAZPACHO.

Gasperi, *n.* **Alcide de** (1881–1954), Italian politician. A founder of the Christian Democrat Party, he was prime minister (1945–53), and worked for European unification.

†**gast,** *v.t.* to terrify. †**gastness,** *n.* terror, fright, fear. [OE *gǣstan*]

Gastarbeiter, *n.* a migrant worker in West Germany. [G]

gasteral GASTRIC.

gasteropod, *n.* an individual of the Gasteropoda. *a.* gasteropodous. **Gasteropoda,** *n.pl.* a class of molluscs, usu. inhabiting a univalve shell (as the snails), of which the general characteristic is a broad muscular ventral foot. **gasteropodous,** *a.* belonging to or characteristic of the Gasteropoda. [Gr. *gastēr -eros,* stomach, *pous podos,* foot]

gastraea, *n.* a primordial animal organism in the form of a gastrula, supposed by Haeckel to have been the germ of all later animal life. [mod. L, from Gr. *gastēr -eros,* as prec.]

gastral GASTRIC.

gastralgia, *n.* neuralgia in the stomach. **gastralgic,** *n., a.*

gastrectomy, *n.* the surgical removal of (part of) the stomach.

gastric, *a.* of or pertaining to the stomach. **gastric acid** GASTRIC JUICE. **gastric fever,** *n.* inflammation of the stomach; now usu. applied to enteric or typhoid fever. **gastric juice,** *n.* a colourless pellucid acid secreted by the stomach, one of the principal agents in digestion. **gastric ulcer,** *n.* an ulcer of the inner wall of the stomach. **gasteral, gastral,** *a.* **gastrin,** *n.* a hormone produced in the pyloric mucosa that stimulates the secretion of gastric juice. [late L *gastricus,* from Gr. *gastēr -eros,* stomach]

gastritis, *n.* inflammation of the stomach.

gastr(o)- *comb. form* stomach. [Gr. *gastēr -eros,* stomach]

gastrocnemius, *n.* (*pl.* **-ii**) the large muscle in the calf of the leg which helps to extend the foot. [Gr. *gastroknēmia* (as GASTRO-, *knēmē,* leg)]

gastrodynia, *n.* (*Path.*) pain in the stomach; gastralgia. [Gr. *odunē,* pain]

gastroenteric, *a.* pertaining to the stomach and the intestines. **gastroenteritis,** *n.* inflammation of the stomach and of the intestines.

gastroenterology, *n.* the study of diseases of the stomach and the intestines. **gastroenterologist,** *n.*

gastroenterostomy, *n.* the surgical formation of an opening between the stomach and the small intestine.

gastrograph, *n.* an instrument for recording the motions of the stomach and the food within it.

gastrointestinal, *n.* of or pertaining to the stomach or the intestines.

gastrology, *n.* the science of matters pertaining to the stomach; the science of cookery or of eating, gastronomy. **gastrologer, -logist,** *n.* **gastrological,** *a.*

gastromancy, *n.* divination by means of words seemingly spoken in the belly, that is, by ventriloquism; divination by means of large-bellied glasses in which magical figures were supposed to appear.

gastronomy, *n.* the art or science of good eating, epicurism. **gastronome, gastronomer, gastronomist,** *n.* one given to good living; an epicure; a judge of good eating. **gastronomic, -ical,** *a.* **gastronomically,** *adv.* [F *gastronomie,* Gr. *gastronomia* (from *gastēr -eros,* stomach, on anal. of *astronomia,* ASTRONOMY)]

gastrophile, *n.* a lover of his stomach or of good eating. **gastrophilism,** *n.* **gastrophilist,** *n.* **gastrophilite,** *n.*

gastropod, GASTEROPOD.

gastroscopy, *n.* an examination of the abdomen in order to discover disease.

gastrosoph, *n.* one skilled in the art of good eating. **gastrosopher,** *n.* **gastrosophy,** *n.* [Gr. *sophos,* wise]

gastrostomy, *n.* an operation to introduce food directly into the stomach, in the case of stricture of the gullet.

gastrotomy, *n.* the operation of cutting into or opening the abdomen. **gastrotomic,** *a.*

gastrovascular, *a.* pertaining both to the vascular system and to the stomach; serving both for circulation and the digestion of food.

gastrula, *n.* an embryonic form or stage in the development of a metazoon, consisting of a double-walled sac enclosing a cup-like cavity. **gastrular,** *a.* **gastrulation,** *n.* the formation of a gastrula. [mod. L, dim. from Gr. *gastēr -eros,* stomach]

gat¹, *n.* a narrow passage between sandbanks, a strait, a channel; an opening in cliffs. [prob. Icel.]

gat², *n.* (*N Am., sl.*) a revolver. [abbr. of GATLING]

gate¹, *n.* a movable barrier, consisting of a frame of wood or iron, usu. dist. from a door by open-work instead of solid panels, swinging on hinges or sliding, to close a passage or opening; an opening in a wall or fence affording entrance and exit to an enclosure, a gateway; an entrance, an opening, an opportunity; a natural opening, as a strait, a mountain pass etc.; a sluice admitting water to or shutting it off from a lock or dock; either of a pair of barriers that close a road at a level-crossing; in horseracing, a device to start racing usu. consisting of a set of stalls with barriers that are simultaneously removed at the moment of starting, starting gate; the number of people attending a race-meeting, football match etc.; the amount of money taken at the gates; an electronic circuit (in a computer) that controls the passage of information signals when permitted by another independent source of similar signals. *v.t.* to furnish with a gate; to confine (a student) to the grounds of a school or college. **to gate-crash,** to attend a function or entertainment without an invitation. **gate-bill,** *n.* the record of an undergraduate's lateness in returning to college; the account of fines imposed for late returns. **gate-change,** *n.* in motor vehicles, the mechanism on the gear lever in which the latter is held for change in an **H**-shaped rack. **gatefold,** *n.* a folded insert in a book or magazine that exceeds the size of the other pages; foldout. **gate-**

house, *n.* a lodge, house or defensive structure at or over a gate; a toll-gate cottage. **gate-keeper,** *n.* person in charge of a gate; the lessee or collector of tolls at a toll-gate; a variety of butterfly. **gate-leg, gate-legged,** *a.* descriptive of a folding table with legs that swing in to permit of the leaves being shut down. **gate-meeting,** *n.* a race-meeting or other gathering at which there is a charge for admission. **gate-money,** *n.* entrance money taken at a sports ground etc. **gate-post,** *n.* a post on which a gate is hung or against which it shuts. **gate-valve,** *n.* a valve which opens the full area of a pipe. **gateway,** *n.* an opening or passage that may be closed by a gate; an entrance, a means of ingress or egress; a location through which one has access to an area. **gateage,** *n.* the gates used in controlling a flow of water; area of a gate-opening, as in the case of a turbine gate. [OE *geat*]

gate[2], *n.* †a way, a road; (*Sc.*) one's way, manner of doing; course; (*usu. in comb.* as *Boargate, Friargate*) a street. **any gate, some gate, that gate,** (*dial.*) anywhere, somewhere etc. [Icel. *gata,* see GAIT[1]]

gate[3], *n.* (*Metal.*) †a hole or channel for pouring molten metal into a mould; a waste piece of metal formed in this, also called **gate-piece, -shutter**. [cp. OE *gyte,* a pouring out, from *gēotan,* to pour]

-gate, *comb. form* indicating events or actions associated with political scandal. [from *Watergate*]

gâteau, *n.* (*pl.* **-teaux**) a cake. **veal gateau,** *n.* minced veal boiled in a shape or mould, like a pudding. [F, OF *gastel* (cp. OHG *wastel*)]

gather, *v.t.* to bring together, to collect, to cause to assemble; to accumulate, to acquire; to cull, to pluck; to pick (up); to get in, as harvest; to deduce, to infer, to conclude; to draw together, to contract, to pucker, to draw into folds or pleats; to sum (up); in printing, to arrange (pages) in their proper sequence. *v.i.* to come together, to assemble, to congregate, to unite; to grow by addition, to increase; to concentrate, to generate pus or matter; (*fig.*) to ripen. *n.* a pleat or fold of cloth, made by drawing together. **to gather breath,** to recover one's wind, to have respite. **to gather head,** to gain strength; to ripen (as a fester etc.). **to gather oneself together,** to concentrate all one's strength or faculties, as on an effort. **to gather way,** of a vessel, to begin to move, to gain impetus, so as to answer to the helm. **gatherable,** *a.* **gathered,** *p.p.* (*euphem.*) dead. **gatherer,** *n.* **gathering,** *n.* the act of collecting or assembling together; an assembly, a meeting, a party; an abscess, a boil. **gathering-coal, -peat,** *n.* (*Sc.*) a large piece of coal or peat put on the fire at night to keep it alive. **gathering-cry,** *n.* a rallying-cry, a summons to war. **gathering-ground,** *n.* the region from which a river and its tributaries draw their supplies; the area feeding a reservoir. **gathers,** *n.* small pleats. [OE *gædrian, gaderian,* from *geador,* together (cp. Dut. *gaderen,* from *gader*)]

Gatling, *n.* **Richard Jordan** (1818–1903), US inventor of a rapid-fire gun. Patented in 1862, the **Gatling gun,** is a machine gun with a series of ten barrels arranged as a cylinder rotated by a hand crank. Cartridges from an overhead hopper or drum drop into the breech mechanism, which loads, fires and extracts them at a rate of 320 rounds per minute.

gator, (*abbr.*) alligator.

gauche, *a.* awkward, clumsy; tactless, uncouth, boorish. **gaucherie,** *n.* awkwardness; a blunder, esp. a social mistake or awkwardness; awkward manners. (cp. OHG *welk,* orig. awkward, weak)]

gaucho, *n.* (*pl.* **-chos**) an inhabitant of the pampas of Uruguay and Argentina, a race of Spanish or mixed descent, noted for their horseriding skills. [Sp., prob. from Quechuan]

gaud, *n.* a showy ornament or trinket, finery; (*pl.*) gewgaws, trumperies, pomps and shows; †a trick. **gaudery,** *n.* finery, showy ornament, show. **gaudy**[1], *a.* vulgarly and tastelessly brilliant and ornate, garish, flashy. **gaudily,** *adv.* **gaudiness,** *n.* [OF *gaudir,* L *gaudēre,* to rejoice]

gaudeamus, *n.* a students' feast or merry-making. [L, let us rejoice, as prec.]

Gaudí, *n.* **Antonio** (1852–1926), Spanish architect. His spectacular Church of the Holy Family, Barcelona, begun 1883, is still under construction.

Gaudier-Brzeska, *n.* **Henri** (1891–1915), French sculptor, active in London from 1911. He studied art in Bristol, Nuremberg, and Munich, and became a member of the English Vorticist movement. From 1913 his sculptures showed the influence of Brancusi and Epstein. He died in World War I.

gaudy[1] GAUD.

gaudy[2], *n.* a grand festival or entertainment, esp. one held annually at an English college in commemoration of some event. **gaudy-day,** *n.* the day on which this is held; a holiday. [L *gaudium,* joy]

gauffer, GOFFER.

gauge, (*Naut.*) **gage**, *v.t.* to ascertain the dimensions, quantity, content, capacity or power of; to test the content or capacity of (casks etc.) for excise purposes; to estimate or appraise (abilities, character etc.); to reduce to a standard size; in dressmaking, to gather into a uniform series of puckers. *n.* a standard of measurement; an instrument for regulating or determining dimensions, amount, capacity etc. according to a fixed standard; a graduated instrument showing the height of a stream, quantity of rainfall, force of the wind, steam-pressure in a boiler etc.; the diameter of the barrel of a gun; the thickness of a sheet of plastic, film, metal etc.; the diameter of wire, screws, needles etc.; the depth to which a vessel sinks in the water; the position of a ship with reference to another and the wind, the **weather-gauge** being to windward, and the **lee-gauge** to leeward; (*Print.*) a piece of hard wood, variously notched, used to adjust the dimensions, slopes etc. of the various sorts of letters in type-founding; a strip for regulating length of pages, width of margins etc; in carpentry, an instrument for striking a line parallel to the straight side of a board; the distance between the two rails of a railway track, the **standard gauge** being 4 ft. 8½ in. (1.43 m), and the **broad gauge,** now disused, 7 ft. (2.13 m). **gauge-glass,** *n.* a tube to indicate the height of water in a boiler. **gauge-able,** *a.* **gauger,** *n.* one who gauges; esp. one who gauges casks etc., a customs officer. **gauging-rod, -rule, -ruler, -stick,** *n.* a customs officer's measuring instrument. [OF *gauger* (F *jauger*), etym. unknown]

Gauguin, *n.* **Paul** (1848–1903), French post-impressionist painter. After a few years as a stock-broker, he took up full-time painting, exhibited with the impressionists, and spent two months with van Gogh in Arles 1888. On his return to Brittany he concentrated on his new style, synthetism, based on the use of powerful, expressive colours and boldly outlined areas of flat tone. He went to live in Tahiti (1891–93 and 1895–1901) and from 1901 in the Marquesas Islands. Influenced by symbolism, he chose subjects reflecting his interest in the beliefs of other cultures.

Gaul, *n.* a member of the Celtic-speaking peoples who inhabited France and Belgium in Roman times; (*loosely*) a Frenchman. **Gaulish,** *a.* pertaining to Gaul; hence, French. *n.* the language of ancient Gaul. [F *Gaule,* L *Gallus,* prob. conn. with OE *wealh,* a foreigner]

Gaulle, Charles de, see DE GAULLE, CHARLES. **Gaullist,** *n.* one who adheres to the policies and principles associated with General Charles de Gaulle, president of France 1959–69. [F]

gault, *n.* (*Geol.*) a series of geological beds of stiff dark-coloured clay and marl between the upper and lower Green-sand. *v.t.* to dress land with gault. **gaulter,** *n.* [prov., etym. doubtful]

gaultheria, *n.* a genus of evergreen aromatic shrubs of the heath family, containing the wintergreen, *Gaultheria procumbens*. [Dr *Gaultier,* 18th-cent. Canadian botanist]

gaum, *v.t.* to smear or bedaub; to put (some sticky substance) on anything. **gaumy,** *a.* [cp. COOM[1]]

gaumless, gormless, *a.* witless, clumsy, stupid. [ON *gaumr,* care, attention]

†gaunt[1] GANT.

gaunt[2], *a.* attenuated, thin, emaciated, haggard. **gauntly,** *adv.* **gauntness,** *n.* [etym. doubtful (cp. Norw. *gaud,* a thin stick, a tall, thin man)]

gauntlet[1], *n.* a long glove covered with plate-metal, worn with armour; a long stout glove covering the wrists. **to take up the gauntlet,** to accept a challenge. **to throw down the gauntlet,** to challenge, to defy. **gauntleted,** *a.* wearing gauntlets. [OF *gantelet,* dim. of *gant,* a glove, prob. from Scand. (cp. OSwed. *wante*)]

gauntlet[2], **†gantlope,** *n.* a military (and sometimes a naval) punishment, in which the prisoner had to run between two files of men armed with sticks, knotted cords or the like, with which they struck him as he passed. **to run the gauntlet,** to suffer this punishment; to undergo severe criticism etc. [Swed. *gatlopp* (*gata,* GATE[2], *lopp,* a course, from *löpa,* to run, cogn. with LEAP)]

gauntry, GANTRY.

gaup, gawp, *v.i.* to gape, esp. in astonishment. **gaupus, gawpus,** *n.* a simpleton. **gaupy,** *a.* [prov., cogn. with YELP]

gaur, *n.* a large fierce ox, *Bos gaurus,* found in the mountain jungles in India. [Hindustani]

gauss, *n.* the cgs unit of magnetic flux density. [K.F. *Gauss,* 1777–1855, German mathematician]

Gautama, *n.* family name of the historical Buddha.

Gautier, *n.* **Théophile** (1811–72), French Romantic poet, whose later work emphasized the perfection of form and the 'polished' beauty of language and imagery (for example, *Emaux et Camées/Enamels and Cameos,* 1852). He was also a novelist (*Mlle de Maupin,* 1835) and later in his life turned to journalism.

gauze, *n.* a light, transparent silk or cotton stuff; any perforated material resembling this, esp. a surgical dressing of muslin; a thin veil or haze. **wire-gauze,** *n.* a textile fabric made of wire, used for very fine sieves, respirators etc. **gauze-lamp,** *n.* a safety-lamp with gauze surrounding the flame. **gauzy,** *a.* **gauziness,** *n.* [F *gaze,* perh. from *Gaza,* in the Middle East]

gavage, *n.* the fattening of poultry by forced feeding; the feeding of a patient unable or unwilling to feed himself. [pop. F, from *gaver,* from *gave,* the crop of a bird]

Gavaskar, *n.* **Sunil Manohar** (1949–), Indian cricketer. Between 1971 and 1987 he scored a record 10,122 test runs in a record 125 matches (including 106 consecutive tests).

gave, *past* GIVE.

gavel[1], *n.* formerly, partition of land among the whole tribe or clan at the holder's death. **gavel-act, -law,** *n.* a statute of Queen Anne's time enacting that the estates of Irish Catholics should descend to males, according to English gavelkind. **gavelkind,** *n.* in law, formerly, a system of land tenure prevalent in Kent and Wales whereby the lands of a person dying intestate descend to all the sons in equal shares, or in default of sons, to all the daughters. **gavelman, †gavelkinder,** *n.* a tenant holding land by this tenure. [OE *gafol,* tribute, toll, cogn. with GIVE; or from the first part of *gavelkind*]

gavel[2], *n.* a mason's setting-maul; a small mallet, esp. one used by a chairman for demanding attention or by an auctioneer. [etym. doubtful]

gavel[3], (*Sc., North.*) GABLE.

gavial, *n.* the Gangetic crocodile, *Gavialis gangeticus.* [F, corr. of Hind. *ghariyāl*]

gavotte, *n.* a dance of a lively yet dignified character resembling the minuet; the music for this; a dance-tune in common time and in two parts, each repeated. [F, from Prov. *gavoto,* from *Gavot,* an inhabitant of *Gap,* in Dauphiné]

Gawain, Sir, *n.* in Arthurian legend, one of the knights of the Round Table who participated in the quest for the Grail. He is the hero of the 14th-century epic poem *Sir Gawayne and the Greene Knight.*

†gawd, GAUD.

gawk, *n.* a simpleton, a booby. *v.i.* to stare (at or about) stupidly. **gawky,** *a.* awkward, clownish, *n.* an awkward or clownish person; a simpleton. **gawkihood, gawkiness,** *n.* **gawkish,** *a.* [etym. doubtful]

gawp GAUP.

gawsy, *a.* (*Sc., North.*) jolly-looking, portly, handsome, smart. [etym. unknown]

gay, *a.* full of mirth; light-hearted, lively, cheerful, merry; given to pleasure; (*euphem.*) wanton, licentious; showy, brilliant in appearance, dressed in bright colours; (*coll.*) homosexual. *n.* (*coll.*) a homosexual. **gay liberation, gay lib,** *n.* (*coll.*) a movement whose aims are to secure rights for homosexuals. **gay-libber,** *n.* (*coll.*). **gaily,** *adv.* **†gayness,** *n.* **gaysome,** *a.* full of gaiety; merry. [OF *gai,* prob. from OHG *wāhi,* fine]

Gay, *n.* **John** (1685–1732), British poet and dramatist. He was the friend of Pope and Arbuthnot, and wrote *Trivia* (1716), a verse picture of 18th-cent. London. His *The Beggar's Opera* (1728), a 'Newgate pastoral' using traditional songs and telling of the love of Polly for highwayman Captain Macheath, was an extraordinarily popular success. Its satiric political touches led to the banning of *Polly,* a sequel.

gayal, *n.* an ox, *Bos frontalis,* with horns depressed at the base and extended outwards, widely domesticated in Asia. [Hind. *gayāl*]

Gaye, *n.* **Marvin** (1939–84), US soul singer and songwriter, whose hits, including 'Stubborn Kinda Fellow' (1962), 'I Heard It Through the Grapevine' (1968), and 'What's Going On' (1971), exemplified the Detroit Motown sound. He was killed by his father.

gaz., (*abbr.*) gazette, gazetteer.

Gazankulu, *n.* Black National State in Transvaal province, South Africa, with self-governing status from 1971; population (1985) 497,200.

Gaza Strip, *n.* strip of Palestine under Israeli administration; capital Gaza; area 363 sq km/140 sq miles; population (1988) 564,000. Clashes between the Israeli authorities and the Palestinian people escalated to intifada (uprising) in 1988.

gaze, *v.i.* to fix the eye intently (at or upon). *†v.t.* to view steadfastly. *n.* a fixed look; a look of curiosity, attention, admiration or anxiety; †that which is gazed at. **†at a gaze,** gaping in wonder. **at gaze,** in heraldry, represented full-faced, as a deer. **to stand at gaze,** to be an intent spectator. **gaze-hound,** *n.* a hound which hunts by sight, as a greyhound. **gazement,** *n.* **gazer,** *n.* **gazing,** *n.* **gazing-stock,** *n.* a person gazed at with scorn or abhorrence; an object of curiosity and contempt. **gazy,** *a.* [etym. unknown; cp. Swed. dial. *gasa*]

gazebo, *n.* an ornamental turret, lantern, or summer-house with a wide prospect, often erected in a garden; a belvedere; a balcony or projecting window. [prob. a facetious coinage from GAZE on anal. of LAVABO]

gazel, GHAZAL.

gazelle, *n.* a swift and very graceful antelope, esp. *Gazelle dorcas,* noted for its large, soft black eyes. [F *gazelle,* earlier *gazel,* Arab. *ghazāl*]

gazette, *n.* a newspaper; an official journal containing lists of appointments to any public office or commission, legal notices, lists of bankrupts etc. *v.t.* to publish in a gazette, esp. to announce the appointment or bankruptcy of (*usu. in p.p.*). **gazetteer,** *n.* †a writer for a gazette; a geographical dictionary. *v.t.* to describe in a geographical dictionary. **gazetteerage,** *n.* **gazetteerish,** *a.* [F, from It. *gazzetta,* prob. after Venetian coin, the price of the first newspaper or of the privilege of reading it]

†gazon, *n.* (*Fort.*) a sod used as a revetment for parapets and earthen banks. [F, grass]

gazpacho, *n.* a spicy iced soup made from uncooked ripe tomatoes, chopped onion, cucumber and green peppers etc. [Sp.]

gazump, *v.t., v.i.* esp. of a house vendor before entering into a binding contract, to force an intending purchaser to agree a higher price than that originally accepted. *n.* an act of gazumping. [prob. Yiddish *gezumph,* to swindle]

gazunder, *v.t., v.i.* to force an intending seller (of property) to accept a lower price than originally negotiated. ["goes under" – an analogy with gazump]

GB, (*abbr.*) Great Britain.
GBE, (*abbr.*) (Knight or Dame) Grand Cross of the British Empire (a British title).
GBH, gbh, (*abbr.*) grievous bodily harm.
GC, (*abbr.*) George Cross.
GCB, (*abbr.*) (Knight or Dame) Grand Cross of the Bath (a British title).
GCE, (*abbr.*) General Certificate of Education.
GCHQ, (*abbr.*) Government Communications Headquarters.
gcm, (*abbr.*) greatest common measure.
GCMG, (*abbr.*) (Knight or Dame) Grand Cross of the Order of St Michael and St George (a British title).
GCSE, (*abbr.*) General Certificate of Secondary Education.
GCVO, (*abbr.*) (Knight or Dame) Grand Cross of the Royal Victorian Order (a British title).
Gd, (*chem. symbol*) gadolinium.
Gdańsk, *n.* (German **Danzig**) Polish port; population (1985) 467,000. Oil is refined, and textiles, televisions, and fertilizers are produced. In the 1980s there were repeated strikes at the Lenin shipyards against the government.
Gdns, (*abbr.*) Gardens.
GDP, (*abbr.*) gross domestic product.
GDR, (*abbr.*) German Democratic Republic.
gds, (*abbr.*) goods; guards regiments.
Ge, (*chem. symbol*) germanium.
geal[1], *a.* pertaining to the earth as a planet. [Gr. *gē*, earth]
geal[2], *v.t., v.i.* to congeal. [F *geler,* L *gelāre,* to freeze]
gean, *n.* (*chiefly Sc.*) the wild cherry, *Prunus avium.* [F *guigne,* etym. unknown]
gear, *n.* apparatus, tools, mechanical appliances, harness, tackle, equipment, dress; combinations of cog-wheels, links, levers etc.; a connection by which an engine, motor etc. is brought into work; the arrangement by which the driving-wheel of a cycle, motor-car etc. performs more or fewer revolutions relatively to the pedals, piston etc.; the state of being engaged or connected up, or of being in working order; on a vessel, the ropes, blocks etc. belonging to any particular sail or spar; (*coll.*) clothes; goods, movables; (*coll.*) illegal drugs, esp. marijuana; (*Sc.*) property, wealth; †worthless matters, rubbish, stuff; †proceedings, doings, business. *v.t.* to harness, to put gear on; of a machine or motor vehicle, to put into gear; to furnish with gearing; in company finance, to borrow money in order to increase the amount of total liabilities in relation to the share capital. *v.i.* to come or be in gear (with); to fit (into) exactly (as a cog-wheel). **alighting gear, landing gear,** *n.* mechanism such as wheels or skids fixed beneath an aeroplane to absorb shock on landing. **change-speed-gear,** *n.* mechanism for changing the engine speed in relation to the speed of the vehicle. **conical gear,** *n.* a bevel gear; a gear with bevelled teeth for transmitting rotary motion at an angle. **crowning-gear,** *n.* a gear-wheel with teeth projecting at right-angles to the plane of the wheel. **differential gear,** DIFFERENTIAL. **equalizing gear,** *n.* a gear in the mechanism of traction engines to permit the driving wheels to turn independently of each other. **free gear,** *n.* a gear engaging in one direction only, as in a free-wheel. **high** or **low gear,** on cycles etc. apparatus for transmitting high or low speed to the driving-wheel relatively to the motion of pedals, etc. **in gear,** of a machine or motor vehicle, connected up and ready for work. **landing gear** ALIGHTING GEAR. **sliding gear,** *n.* a gear sliding along an axle or shaft, and thereby being capable of being instantly disconnected. **star-gear,** *n.* a variable-speed gear. **to throw out of gear,** to disconnect (gearing or couplings); to put out of working order; to disturb, to upset. **gear-box, -case,** *n.* the casing in which gears are enclosed in a motor vehicle or bicycle etc. **gear-cutter,** *n.* a machine for making cog-wheels; a manufacturer of cog-wheels. **gear lever, shift, stick,** *n.* in a motor vehicle, a device for selecting or connecting gears. **gear-wheel,** *n.* a wheel with cogs, esp. the wheel transmitting motion in a cycle. **gearing,** *n.* gear, working parts; a series of wheels etc. for transmitting motion; (*Naut.*) tackle; in company finance, the ratio of the amount a company has borrowed to its share capital, usu. expressed as a percentage. **gearing-chain,** *n.* an endless chain with rack-like projections, passing around cogged wheels and thereby transmitting motion. **gearless,** *a.* [ME *gere,* prob. from Icel. *gervi*]
gebbie, *n.* (*Sc.*) the crop of a fowl; a person's stomach. [etym. doubtful]
Geber, *n.* latinized form of **Jabir ibn Hayyan** (*c.* 721–*c.* 776), Arabian alchemist. His influence lasted for more than 600 years, and in the late 1300s his name was adopted by a Spanish alchemist whose writings spread the knowledge and practice of alchemy throughout Europe.
gebur, *n.* a tenant farmer, not fully free, in the Old English village-community. [OE, *gebūr,* cp. BOOR, NEIGHBOUR]
†**geck,** *n.* a dupe, a fool; (*Sc.*) a gesture of contempt or derision. *v.i.* (*Sc.*) to scoff (at); to toss the head. [cp. LG *geck,* Dut. *gek,* G *Geck*]
gecko, *n.* (*pl.* **-os, -oes**) a genus of lizards with adhesive toes, by which means they can walk on a wall or ceiling. [Malay *gēkoq,* from its cry]
ged, *n.* (*Sc.*) the pike. [Icel. *gedda*]
Geddes, *n.* **Patrick** (1854–1932), Scottish town planner, who established the importance of surveys, research work, and properly-planned 'diagnoses before treatment'. His major work is *City Development* (1904).
gee[1], **gee-up,** *int.* go on, move faster (command to horse). **gee-gee,** *n.* (*childish and coll.*) a horse.
gee[2], *n.* (*Sc.*) a fit of ill-temper. **to take the gee,** to take offence. [etym. doubtful]
gee[3], *int.* (*coll.*) an exclamation expressing surprise, delight etc., also **gee-whizz.** [euphem. var. of JESUS]
gee-bung, *n.* any shrub or tree of the proteaceous genus *Persoonia,* or its fruit. [Austral. Abor.]
geek, *n.* a sideshow performer who bites the heads off live animals; (*sl.*) a freak; (*sl.*) an unattractive or uninteresting person.
geep, *n.* a cross between a goat and a sheep.
geese, *n.pl.* GOOSE.
gee-string, G.
geezer, *n.* (*coll.*) an old man or woman. [sl. perh. from F *guiser,* masquerader]
gefilte, gefüllte fish, *n.* in Jewish cookery, cooked chopped fish mixed with matzo meal, egg and seasonings and then poached, either stuffed back into the skin of the fish or as dumplings. [Yiddish, filled fish]
gegenschein, *n.* a faint glow in the night sky at a position opposite to that of the sun. [G *gegen,* against, counter, *Schein,* shine]
gegg, *n.* (*Sc.*) a hoax, a trick. *v.t.* to hoax. **gegger,** *n.* **geggery,** *n.* [perh. conn. with GAG]
Gehenna, *n.* a valley near Jerusalem, where (Jer. xix.) men sacrificed their children to Baal or Moloch; whence, hell, a place of torment. [L, from Gr. *geenna,* late Heb. *gēhinnōm,* the valley of Hinnom]
gehlenite, *n.* a green mineral silicate of aluminium and calcium occurring in tetragonal crystalline form. [A.A. *Gehlen,* 1775–1815, German chemist]
Gehry, *n.* **Frank** (1929–), US architect, based in Los Angeles. His architecture approaches abstract art in its use of collage and montage techniques.
Geiger, *n.* **Hans** (1882–1945), German physicist who produced the Geiger counter. After studying in Germany, he spent the period 1907–12 in Manchester, working with Ernest Rutherford, where they developed the **Geiger counter,** a device for detecting and/or counting nuclear radiation and particles. It detects the momentary current that passes between electrodes in a suitable gas when a nuclear particle or a radiation pulse causes ionization in the gas. The electrodes are connected to electronic devices which enable the intensity of radiation or the number of particles passing to be measured.
geisha, *n.* (*pl.* **-sha, -shas**) a Japanese dancing-girl.

[Jap.]

Geissler tube, *n.* high-voltage discharge tube in which traces of gas ionize and conduct electricity. It was developed in 1858 by the German physicist Heinrich Geissler (1814–1879).

Geist, *n.* the spirit, principle or tendency of an age, time-spirit. [G, spirit]

gel, *n.* the jelly-like material formed when a colloidal solution is left standing. *v.* to become or cause to become a gel. [JELLY]

gelastic, *a.* causing laughter; risible. [Gr. *gelastikos,* from *gelān,* to laugh]

gelatine, *n.* a transparent substance forming a jelly in water, obtained from connective animal tissue, such as skin, tendons, bones, horns etc. **blasting** or **explosive gelatine,** *n.* an explosive compound of nitroglycerine. **vegetable gelatine,** *n.* gelatine extracted from gluten. **gelatine paper,** *n.* photographic paper coated with sensitized gelatine. **gelatine process,** *n.* a photographic or photo-engraving process in which gelatine is used. **gelatigenous,** *a.* producing gelatine. **gelatinate, -ize, -ise,** *v.i.* to be converted into jelly, or a substance like jelly. *v.t.* to convert into a substance like jelly. **gelatination, -ization, -isa'tion,** *n.* **gelatinizable, -isable,** *n.* **gelatinoid,** *n., a.* **gelatinous,** *a.* of the nature of or consisting of gelatine, jelly-like. **gelose,** *n.* a gelatinous substance obtained from Chinese and Japanese moss and seaweeds, used for finishing cotton goods, and in Asian cookery. [F *gélatine,* It. *gelatina,* L *gelata,* JELLY]

gelation, *n.* solidification by cooling or freezing. [L *gelātio,* from *gelāre,* to freeze]

geld¹, *v.t.* to castrate (esp. a horse), to emasculate; to deprive of any essential part; to expurgate excessively. †**geldable,** *a.* that may be gelded. **gelder,** *n.* one who gelds (*usu. in comb., a sow-gelder*). **gelding,** *n.* the act of castrating, castration; a castrated animal, esp. a castrated horse; †a eunuch. [Icel. *gelda,* from *geldr* (cp. G *Gelt*), barren]

†**geld²,** *n.* money, tribute, the tax paid by land-holders to the Crown under the Saxon and early Norman kings. **geldable,** *a.* [OE *gield,* from *gieldan,* see YIELD (cp. Icel. *giald,* OHG *gelt,* G *geld*)]

gelder, gelders rose, GUELDER ROSE.

Gelderland, Guelders, *n.* province of the E Netherlands; area 5020 sq km/1938 sq miles; population (1988) 1,784,000. Its capital is Arnhem. In the NW is the Veluwe, a favourite holiday resort.

Geldof, *n.* **Bob** (1954–), Irish fundraiser and rock singer, leader of the group Boomtown Rats (1975–86). He instigated the charity Band Aid, which raised large sums of money for famine relief, especially in Ethiopia, by recording a song, 'Do They Know It's Christmas?' (1984), and staging two simultaneous concerts (Live Aid) in 1985, one in London and one in Philadelphia, broadcast live worldwide.

gelid, *a.* extremely cold; icy. **gelidity,** *n.* **gelidly,** *adv.* [L *gelidus,* from *gelu,* frost]

gelignite, *n.* an explosive containing nitroglycerine. [GEL-ATINE, L *ign-is,* fire, -ITE]

Gell-Mann, *n.* **Murray** (1929–), US physicist. In 1964, he formulated the theory of the quark as the fundamental constituent of all matter, and smallest particle in the Universe.

gelose, GELATINE.

gelsemium, *n.* (*pl.* **-iums**) a genus of climbing shrubs containing three species, of which the best known is the American yellow jasmine, *Gelsemium sempervirens,* the poisonous root of which yields a medicinal substance. [mod. L, from It. *gelsomino,* JASMINE]

gelt¹, *p.p.* GELD¹.

†**gelt²,** *n.* money, pay. [G or Dut. *geld,* money, cogn, with GELD²]

†**gelt³,** GILT².

gem, *n.* a precious stone, as the diamond, ruby, emerald etc., esp. when cut and polished for ornamental purposes (**gemstone**); an object of great rarity, beauty or value; a treasure, the most prized or the choicest part; in zoology, a gemma; a geometrid moth; †a bud. *v.t.* (*past, p.p.* **gemmed**) to adorn with or as with gems; †to put forth in buds. *v.i.* to bud. **gemless,** *a.* **gemmeous, gemmy,** *a.* full of or set with gems; bright, glittering; (*sl.*) spruce, smart, neat. **gemmily,** *adv.* **gemminess,** *n.* [OF *gemme,* L *gemma,* a bud, a jewel]

Gemara, *n.* the second portion of the Talmud, consisting of a commentary on the Mishna, or text. **Gemaric,** *a.* of or pertaining to the Gemara. **Gemarist,** *n.* [Aram.]

gematria, *n.* a cabbalistic system of interpreting the Hebrew Scriptures by interchanging words whose letters have the same numerical value when added. [Rabbinical Heb. *gēmatriyā,* Gr. *geōmetria,* GEOMETRY]

Gemayel, *n.* **Amin** (1942–), Lebanese politician, a Maronite Christian; president (1982–88). He succeeded his brother, president-elect Bechir Gemayel, on his assassination on 14 Sept. 1982.

gemeinschaft, *n.* a social group united by kinship, common beliefs etc. [G, community]

gemel, *n.* †one of twins; in heraldry, a pair of parallel bars; a kind of finger-ring formed of two (or more) rings, also called a **gemel-ring. gemel-hinge,** *n.* a hinge formed of a hook and loop. **gemel-window,** *n.* a window with two bays. [OF (F *jumeau*), L *gemellus,* dim. of *geminus,* twin]

geminate, *a.* united or arranged in pairs. *v.t.,* to double, to arrange in pairs. *v.i.* to occur in pairs. **gemination,** *n.* **geminative,** *a.* [L *geminātus,* p.p. of *gemināre,* to double, from *geminus,* twin]

Gemini, *n.pl.* a constellation, the Twins, containing the two conspicuous stars, Castor and Pollux; the third sign of the zodiac; †a pair; a mild oath, **geminy,** (*coll.*), **jiminy**. **Gemini project,** *n.* US space programme (1965–66) in which astronauts practised rendezvous and docking of spacecraft, and working outside their spacecraft, in preparation for the Apollo Moon landings. **Geminids,** *n.pl.* meteoric bodies radiating, usu. in early December, from the constellation Gemini. †**geminous,** *a.* double, in pairs, twin. †**geminy,** *n.* a couple. [L, twins, pl. of *geminus,* see prec.]

gemma, *n.* (*Bot.*) (*pl.* **-mae**) a leaf-bud; (*pl.*) minute green cellular bodies in the fructification of Marchantia, and in some mosses and Hepaticae; (*Zool.*) a bud-like outgrowth in polyps, ascidians etc., which separates from the parent organism and develops into an individual. **gemmaceous,** *a.* pertaining to or of the nature of leaf-buds. [L, see GEM]

gemmate, *a.* (*Bot.*) having buds; (*Zool.*) reproducing by gemmation. *v.i.,* to bud; to reproduce by gemmation. **gemmation,** *n.* the act of budding; vernation, or the arrangement of the leaf in the bud; the time of budding; the disposition of buds on the plant; (*Zool.*) reproduction by the development of gemmae from the parent body. **gemmative,** *a.* [L *gemmātus,* p.p. of *gemmāre,* to bud, from *gemma,* see GEMMA]

gemmeous, gemmy GEM.

gemmiferous, *a.* producing gems; producing or propagating by buds or gemmae.

gemmiparous, *a.* (*Bot.*) producing buds; (*Zool.*) propagating by gemmation. **gemmiparity,** *n.* **gemmiparously,** *adv.*

gemmule, *n.* (*Biol.*) a small gemma or reproductive bud; (*Bot.*) the plumule or growing point of an embryo; a reproductive cell of a cryptogam; (*Zool.*) the ciliated embryo of many of the Coelenterata; one of the small reproductive bodies thrown off by sponges. **gemmuliferous,** *a.* [F, from L *gemmŭla,* dim. of GEMMA]

gemote, *n.* a public meeting or assembly, esp. the court held in Anglo-Saxon England in each shire or hundred before the Norman Conquest. [OE *gemōt* (*ge-,* together, MOOT)]

gemsbok, *n.* a large antelope of Southern Africa, *Oryx gazella,* about the size of a donkey, with long straight horns, also **gemsbuck**. [Dut., from G *Gemsbock* (*Gemse,* chamois, *Bock,* buck)]

gemstone GEM.

gen, *n.* (*coll.*) full particulars of, information about. **to**

gen up, to read up about. [*Gen*eral Information]

gen., (*abbr.*) gender; general; generally; generic; genitive; genus.

Gen., (*abbr.*) General; Genesis.

-gen, *suf.* producing; produced; growth; as in *hydrogen, nitrogen, oxygen; acrogen, endogen, exogen.* [F *-gène,* Gr. *genēs,* born of a certain kind, from *gen-*, root of *gignesthai,* to be born, *gennaein,* to beget etc.]

gendarme, *n.* an armed policeman, in France and some other Continental countries; †(*F. Hist.*) a mounted knight or man-at-arms, later a trooper, esp. in the royal bodyguard. **gendarmerie**, **gendarmery**, *n.* the armed police of France; a body of gendarmes. [F, from pl. *gens d'armes,* men of arms]

gender, *n.* (*Gram.*) one of the classes (MASCULINE, FEMININE and NEUTER) into which words are divided according to the sex, natural or grammatical, of the things they represent; classification of words into genders according to their forms etc.; (*facet.*) sex; †kind, sort, class. †*v.t.* to beget, to produce, to cause. †*v.i.* to breed, to copulate. **gender bender,** *n.* (*coll.*) one whose appearance and behaviour isof a kind usu. associated with members of the opposite sex. **gender bending,** *n.* sexually ambiguous appearance or behaviour, e.g. bisexuality or transvestism. **gender gap,** *n.* lack of communication, understanding etc. between the sexes. [ME *gendre,* OF *genre,* L *genere,* abl. of GENUS]

gene, *n.* the unit of heredity; the factor in a gamete which determines the appearance of an hereditary characteristic. **gene therapy,** *n.* the treatment of certain diseases by the insertion of new genes into non-reproductive cells in a patient, such new genes not being inherited by the patient's off-spring as distinct from *germ-line therapy*. **genetic**, **genic**, *a.* [Gr. *genos,* born of a certain kind]

genealogy, *n.* the history or investigation of the descent of families; a record or exhibition of a person's or family's descent in the natural order of succession; pedigree, lineage; the course of a plant's or an animal's development from earlier forms. **genealogical**, *a.* of or pertaining to genealogy; exhibiting the successive stages of family descent. **genealogical tree,** *n.* the genealogy of a family drawn out in the figure of a tree, with the root, stem, branches etc. **genealogically,** *adv.* **genealogize, -ise,** *v.i.* to investigate descent; to trace a pedigree; to prepare a genealogy. **genealogist,** *n.* [OF *genealogie,* late L *geneālogia,* Gr. *genealogia* (*genea,* race)]

Genée, *n.* **Adeline** (1878–1970), stage name of Anina Jensen, Danish-British dancer, president of the Royal Academy of Dancing (1920–54).

genera GENUS.

general, *a.* relating to a whole genus, kind, class or order; not special, particular, partial or local; common, universal; ordinary, usual, widespread, prevalent; not limited in scope or application; indefinite, vague; not specialized or restricted; taken or viewed as a whole; commonly affixed to words expressive of rank or office, with the force of chief or supreme within a certain sphere. *n.* †the public, the common people; in the Roman Catholic Church, the chief of a religious order, or of all the houses or congregations having the same rule; an officer ranking next below a field-marshal, usu. extended to lieutenant-generals and major-generals; the commander of an army; a strategist; (*coll.*) a general servant; †the whole; the chief part, the majority; (*pl.*) general facts or principles; in former times, a general drum-call beaten in the morning to give notice to the infantry to be ready to march (var. **generale**). **General Agreement on Tariffs and Trade (GATT),** *n.* an organization within the United Nations founded 1948 with the aim of encouraging free trade between nations through low tariffs, abolitions of quotas, and curbs on subsidies. **General Certificate of Education (GCE),** formerly, in England and Wales a certificate in secondary education obtainable in Ordinary, Advanced and Scholarship levels. **in general,** in the main, generally; in most cases or in all ordinary cases, for the most part. **general anaesthetic,** *n.* a drug which anaesthetizes the whole body, with loss of consciousness. **General Assembly,** *n.* the body of representatives that directs the affairs of the Church of Scotland. **general average** AVERAGE. **General Certificate of Secondary Education (GCSE),** *n.* a certificate of secondary education replacing the General Certificate of Education and the Certificate of Secondary Education. **general confession,** *n.* one in which the whole congregation joins. **general council,** *n.* a council called together by the authority of the Church at large. **General Court,** *n.* the State legislature in Massachusetts and New Hampshire. **general dealer,** *n.* one who deals in many articles of daily use. **general election,** *n.* an election for representatives for all constituencies in a state. **general hospital,** *n.* one taking patients whatever their disease. **general officer,** *n.* an officer above the rank of colonel. **general post,** *n.* a general postal delivery; a romping indoor game. **general post office,** (GPO) *n.* a chief or head post office. **general practitioner,** *n.* a physician or surgeon treating all kinds of cases. **general reader,** *n.* one who reads miscellaneous books etc., as dist. from one following a course of special study. **general servant,** *n.* (*dated*) a female servant whose duties are not special, a maid-of-all-work. **general staff,** *n.* in the army, officers assigned to advise senior officers on operations and policy. **general strike,** *n.* a strike by all or most workers in a city or in most parts of a province or country. **general term,** *n.* in logic, a term which is the sign of a general conception or notion. **general warrant,** *n.* in law, a warrant (now illegal) to apprehend all suspected persons, without naming any particular individual. **generale** GENERAL. **generalia,** *n.pl.* general principles. [L, neut. pl. of *generalis* GENERAL] **generalism,** *n.* a general conclusion, statement, or opinion. **generalissimo,** *n.* (*pl.* **-mos**) the chief commander of a force furnished by several powers, or military and naval in combination; a commander-in-chief; (*coll.*) any esp. autocratic leader. [It., superl. of *generale* GENERAL] **generalist,** *n.* a person knowledgeable in many fields as dist. from a specialist. **generality,** *n.* the state of being general, as opp. to specific; a general statement or principle; a vague statement, vagueness; the main body, the majority. [F *généralité,* L *generālitātem,* nom. *-tas*]. **generalize, -ise,** *v.t.* to reduce to a genus or genera; to deal with as a class not as an individual; to apply generally, to make of wider or of universal application; to deduce or infer (as a general principle) from many particulars. *v.i.* to form general ideas; to reason inductively; to draw general inferences; to speak vaguely, to employ generalities; in paintings, to represent typical not particular features. **generalizable, -isable,** *a.* **generalization, -isation,** *n.* the act or process of generalizing; the act of making general, or of bringing several objects, agreeing in some point, under one head or class; a general inference; an induction; **generalizer, -iser,** *n.* **generally,** *adv.* in general; for the most part, in most cases; ordinarily, commonly, usually; without minute detail, without specifying. †**generalness,** *n.* **generalship**, *n.* the office or rank of a general; skill in the management of troops and the conduct of war, strategy; skilful leadership, management or organization; tactful diplomacy. [OF, from L *generālis,* from GENUS]

generant GENERATE.

generate, *v.t.* to produce or bring into existence; to cause to be; to produce, to evolve, to originate; to beget, to procreate; (*Math.*) to trace out or form by the motion of a point or a magnitude of inferior order. **generable,** *a.* **generant,** *a.* generating, producing. *n.* that which generates; (*Math.*) a point, line or surface conceived of as, by its motion, generating a line, surface or solid. **generating plant,** *n.* all the equipment needed for generating electrical energy. **generation,** *n.* the act of generating; propagation of the species; reproduction, propagation; production, creation, bringing into existence; a single succession or step in natural descent; an age or period between one succession and another; the people of the same period or age; the average time in which the child takes the place of the parent (usu. estimated at about ⅓ of a century), progeny, offspring, issue; †a family, race; †pedigree, lineage. **generation gap,** *n.* the difference in opinions and understanding between members of different generations. **generative**, *a.* having the power of generating; pertaining to generation or production; productive, fruitful. **generator**, *n.* one who or that which begets, generates, or produces; any apparatus for the production of gas, steam, electricity etc.; (*Chem.*) a compound from which a more complex substance is moulded; (*Elec.*) a dynamo; (*Mus.*) the principal sound or fundamental tone of a chord etc. **asynchronous generator,** a generator without fixed alternation. **generator unit,** *n.* an independent generator in an electrical plant capable of working or stopping without affecting the rest of the machinery. **generatrix**, *n.* a female parent; (*Math.*) a generant. [L *generātus,* p.p. of *generāre,* from *genus generis,* kind]

generic, -al, *a.* pertaining to a genus, class or kind, opp. to specific; comprehensive, applied to large classes of goods or drugs, identified by the product itself and not by a brand name, not having a trademark. **generic name,** *n.* the name of a genus, as Saxifraga in *Saxifraga longifolia;* a general name for a product, not a brand name or trademark. **generically,** *adv.* [*genus generis,* see GENUS, -IC]

generous, *a.* liberal, munificent, open-handed, bountiful; overflowing, abundant, fertile; strong, stimulating (as wine); magnanimous, high-spirited; †nobly-born. **generosity**, *n.* **generously,** *adv.* †**generousness,** *n.* [F *généreux,* L *generōsus,* as prec.]

genesis, *n.* (*pl.* **-ses**) the act of begetting, producing, or giving origin to; creation, beginning, origination, mode of production or formation. **Genesis,** *n.* the first book of the Old Testament, in which the story of the Creation is told. [L, from Gr. *genesis,* from *gen-,* root of *gignesthai,* to become, to be born]

genet, *n.* a small mammal, *Genetta vulgaris,* allied to the civet; its fur, or cat-skin dressed in imitation of this fur. [OF *genete,* Sp. *jineta,* Arab. *jarnait*]

Genet, *n.* **Jean** (1910–86), French dramatist, novelist, and poet, an exponent of the Theatre of Cruelty. His turbulent life and early years spent in prison are reflected in his drama, characterized by ritual, role-play, and illusion, in which his characters come to act out their bizarre and violent fantasies. His plays include *Les Bonnes/The Maids* (1947), *Le Balcon/The Balcony* (1957), and two plays dealing with the Algerian situation: *Les Nègres/The Blacks* (1959), and *Les Paravents/The Screens* (1961).

†**genethliac,** *a.* of or pertaining to nativities as calculated by astrologers. *n.* one who is skilled in the calculation of nativities; (*pl.*) the science of this; a birthday poem or ode. †**genethliacal**, *a.* †**genethliacally,** *adv.* †**genethliacon**, *n.* a birthday poem. **genethlialogy**, *n.* [late L *genethliacus,* Gr. *genethliakos,* from *genethlē,* race, birth, from *gen-,* root of *gignesthai,* to be born]

genetic, *a.* of or relating to the origin, generation, or creation of a thing. *n.pl.* the study of heredity and variation. **genetic affinity,** *n.* affinity founded on resemblances existing from a very early age, and therefore presumed to imply a common origin. **genetic code,** *n.* the system, based on the molecular arrangement of the chromosomes, that ensures the transmission of hereditary characteristics. **genetic engineering,** *n.* the artificial alteration of the genes of an organism in order to control the transmission of certain hereditary characteristics. **genetic fingerprint,** *n.* the particular DNA pattern that is unique to an individual and can be used to identify that individual or his or her offspring. **genetic fingerprinting,** *n.* the act or process of taking a genetic fingerprint from an individual's saliva, blood or sperm, used in forensic science etc. **genetical,** *a.* **genetically,** *adv.* **geneticist**, *n.* one who studies genetics. [from GENESIS (cp. ANTITHETIC from ANTITHESIS)]

Geneva¹, *n.* (French **Genève**) Swiss city, capital of Geneva canton, on the shore of Lake Geneva; population (1987) 385,000. It is a point of convergence of natural routes, and is a cultural and commercial centre. Industries include the manufacture of watches, scientific and optical instruments, foodstuffs, jewellery, and musical boxes. *a.* of, originating from, or pertaining to Geneva. **Geneva bands,** *n.pl.* clerical bands such as those worn by Swiss Calvinist clergy. **Geneva Bible,** *n.* a translation of the Bible into English, made and published at Geneva in 1560. **Geneva Convention,** *n.* international agreement (1864) regulating the treatment of those wounded in war, and later extended to cover the types of weapons allowed, the treatment of prisoners and the sick, and the protection of civilians in wartime. The rules were revised at conventions held 1906, 1929, and 1949, and by the 1977 Additional Protocols. **Geneva cross,** *n.* a red Greek cross on a white ground, the distinguishing mark of military ambulances etc., and symbol of the Red Cross Society. **Geneva gown**, *n.* the black preaching gown worn by Presbyterian ministers and Low Church clergymen in England. **Geneva Protocol,** *n.* international agreement (1925), designed to prohibit the use of poisonous gases, chemical weapons, and bacteriological methods of warfare. It came into force in 1928, but was not ratified by the US until 1974. **Genevan,** *a.* of or pertaining to Geneva. *n.* a Genevese, a Calvinist. **Genevanism,** *n.* Calvinism, from the long residence of its founder and the establishment of his doctrines at Geneva. **Genevese**, *a.* Genevan. *n.* an inhabitant of Geneva. [town in Switzerland]

Geneva², Lake, *n.* (French **Lac Léman**) largest of the central European lakes, between Switzerland and France; area 580 sq km/225 sq miles.

geneva, *n.* a spirit distilled from grain flavoured with juniper-berries, also called Hollands. **genevrette**, *n.* a wine made on the Continent from wild fruits and flavoured with juniper-berries. [Dut. *genever,* OF *genèvre,* L *juniperus,* JUNIPER, assim. to foll.]

Genghis Khan, *n.* (*c.* 1160–1227), Mongol conqueror, ruler of all Mongol peoples from 1206. He began the conquest of N China 1213, overran the empire of the shah of Khiva (1219–25), and invaded N India, while his lieutenants advanced as far as the Crimea. When he died his empire ranged from the Yellow Sea to the Black Sea.

genial¹, *a.* of a cheerful and kindly disposition, cordial, sympathetic, enlivening; conducive to life and growth, soft, mild; pertaining to marriage or procreation, generative; †presiding over marriage; †native, inborn. **geniality**, *n.* **genialize, -ise,** *v.t.* to give geniality to; to render genial. **genially**, *adv.* †**genialness,** *n.* [from F or directly from L *geniālis*]

genial², *a.* of, pertaining to, or near the chin. [Gr. *geneion,* chin from *genus,* jaw]

genic GENE.

-genic, *comb. form* of or pertaining to generation, as in *antigenic;* suitable for, as in *photogenic.*

geniculate, -lated, *a.* kneed, knee-jointed; in botany, bent abruptly like a knee, as the stems of many grasses. *v.t.*, to form a knot or joint in. **geniculation**, *n.* the quality of having knots or joints; †the act of kneeling. [L *geniculātus,* from *geniculum,* dim. of *genu,* knee]

genie, *n.* (*pl.* **genii**), a jinnee. [F *génie,* L GENIUS]

genio-, *comb. form* chin. [Gr. *geneion,* chin, see GENIAL²]

genio-hyoid, *a.* a muscle from the hyoid bone to the chin.

genipap, *n.* the fruit of *Genipa americana,* about the size of an orange, with a vinous taste. [Port. *genipapo,* from Tupi]

genista, *n.* a genus of leguminous shrubs and small trees, with yellow flowers. [L]

genital, *a.* pertaining to generation or procreation. *n.pl.* also, **genitalia**, the external organs of reproduction. [OF, from L *genitālis,* from *genit-,* part. stem of *gignere,* to beget]

genitive, *a.* in grammar, indicating origin, possession, or the like (applied to a case in inflected languages roughly corresponding to the Eng. possessive). *n.* the genitive case. **genitival**, *a.* [L *genetīvus,* of generation, as prec. (a mistranslation of Gr. *genikē,* generic)]

genito- *comb. form.* genital.

genitor, *n.* one who begets; a sire, biological father. †**geniture**, *n.* procreation, birth; nativity, horoscope. [F *geniteur,* L *genitōrem,* nom. *-tor,* as GENITAL]

genito-urinary, *a.* pertaining to the genital and urinary organs.

genius, *n.* (*pl.* **genii**) a tutelary deity or spirit, supposed to preside over the destinies of an individual, place, nation etc.; also one of two spirits attendant on a person through life, one good, the other evil; (*fig.*) one who exercises a powerful influence over another for good or ill; a jinnee; (*pl.* **geniuses**) natural bent or inclination of the mind; the dominant character, spirit, or sentiment (of); an extraordinary endowment of intellectual, imaginative, expressive or inventive faculty; a person so endowed; a representative type or impersonation. [L, from *gen-,* root of *gignere,* to beget]

genius loci, *n.* the presiding deity of a place; hence, the spirit or associations predominant in a locality, community, or institution. [L]

Genoa, *n.* historic city in NW Italy, capital of Liguria; population (1988) 722,000. It is Italy's largest port; industries include oil-refining, chemicals, engineering, and textiles. **Genoa cake,** *n.* a rich fruit-cake with almonds on the top. **Genoese**, *a.* of or pertaining to Genoa. *n.* an inhabitant of Genoa; (as *pl.*) the people of Genoa. [L *Genua,* It. *Genova*]

genocide, *n.* the intentional and systematic destruction of a national, racial, ethnical or religious group, e.g. the Jews by the Nazi Germans during World War II. [Gr. *genos,* born of a certain kind, -CIDE]

†**genouillère,** *n.* a jointed metal cap for covering the knees of an armed man; in a fortification, the interior slope of the parapet below the sill of an embrasure. [F, from OF *genouil* (F. *genou*), L *genu,* the knee]

genome, *n.* the complete set of chromosomes that is contained in any single cell. **genomic**, *a.* [G. *Genom,* from *Gen,* gene + chromo*some*]

genotype, *n.* the basic genetic structure of an organism; a group of organisms with the same genetic structure. **genotypic, -typical**, *a.* **genotypically,** *adv.*

-genous, *comb. form* born; bearing, producing; as in *indigenous, polygenous.* [L *-genus,* born, from *gen-,* root of *gignere,* to beget]

Genova, *n.* Italian form of GENOA, Italy.

genre, *n.* kind, sort, class; style, manner; a painting the subject of which is some scene in everyday life; this style of painting, also called **genre-painting**. [F, kind, see GENDER]

genro, *n.pl.* elder statesmen in Japan who were on occasion consulted by the Emperor. [Jap.]

gens, *n.* (*pl.* **gentes**) a clan, house, or sept among the ancient Romans; a similar group of families among the ancient Greeks. [L, from *gen-,* stem of *gignere,* to beget]

Genscher, *n.* **Hans-Dietrich** (1927–), West German politician, chairman of the Free Democratic Party (FDP) 1974–85, foreign minister from 1974.

†**gent**[1], *n.* noble; gentle. [OF from L genitus, born]

gent[2], *n.* (*coll.*) a gentleman; a would-be gentleman. **gents**, **gents'**, a public lavatory for men.

genteel, *a.* (*now coll. or iron.*) gentlemanly or ladylike; elegant in mien, manners, or dress, stylish; well-bred, refined, free from vulgarity. †*n.* a genteel person. **genteelish,** *a.* **genteelly,** *adv.* [earlier *gentile,* F *gentil,* see GENTILE]

gentian, *n.* the English name of *Gentiana,* a genus of bitter herbs, usu. having blue flowers, common in mountain regions, one among which, the yellow gentian, *G. lutea,* yields gentian-root, used in medicine as a tonic. **gentian violet,** *n.* a greenish crystalline substance that forms a violet solution in water and is used in the treatment of burns and boils, as an antiseptic, and as a biological stain. **gentianaceous**, *a.* of or belonging to the Gentianaceae family of flowering plants that includes the felwort and the gentian. **gentianella**, *n.* a dwarf species, *G. acaulis,* with flowers of intense blue. **gentianic**, *a.* **gentianin**, *n.* a bitter compound extracted from gentian-root, also called **gentianic acid**. [L *gentiāna,* from *Gentius,* king of Illyria]

gentile, *a.* not a Jew; heathen, pagan; applied by the Mormons to all who are not of their faith; †pertaining to a race or tribe; (*Gram.*) denoting race, country, or locality. *n.* one who is not a Jew; a heathen, a pagan; one who is not a Mormon; (*Gram.*) a word denoting race, country, or locality. **gentiledom**, *n.* †**gentilic**, *a.* †**gentilish**, *a.* †**gentilism**, *n.* **gentilitial**, **gentilitious**, *a.* of or pertaining to a gens, tribe or nation. [OF *gentil,* L *gentīlis,* from *gens gentis,* see GENS]

Gentile, *n.* **da Fabriano** (*c.* 1370–1427), Italian painter of frescoes and altarpieces in the International Gothic style. *The Adoration of the Magi* (1423, Uffizi, Florence) is typically rich in detail and crammed with courtly figures.

Gentileschi[1], *n.* **Artemisia** (1593–*c.* 1652), Italian painter, born in Rome. She trained under her father Orazio Gentileschi, but her work is more melodramatic than his. She settled in Naples from about 1630, and focused on macabre and grisly subjects such as *Judith Decapitating Holofernes* (Museo di Capodimonte, Naples).

Gentileschi[2], *n.* **Orazio** (1563–1637), Italian painter, born in Pisa. From 1626 he lived in London, painting for King Charles I. Like most of his contemporaries, he was influenced by Caravaggio's dramatic treatment of light and shade, as in *The Annunciation* (1623, Turin).

†**gentilesse,** *n.* courtesy; gentle birth.

Gentili, *n.* **Alberico** (1552–1608), Italian jurist. He practised law in Italy, but having adopted Protestantism was compelled to flee to England, where he lectured on Roman Law in Oxford. His publications, such as *De Jure Belli libri tres/On The Law Of War, Book Three* (1598), made him the first true international law writer and scholar.

gentility, *n.* the quality of being genteel, assumed social superiority; manners and habits distinctive of good society; gentle birth; genteel people; †elegance of manners, politeness; the state of belonging to a gens or clan. [OF *gentilité*]

†**gentilize, -ise**, *v.t.* to render gentle or gentlemanly; to make gentile, to paganize. *v.i.* to act as a gentleman; to live like a gentile.

gentle, *a.* mild, tender, kindly; not rough, coarse, violent or stern; moderate, not severe, not energetic; not steep; in heraldry, having the right to bear arms. *n.* †one of good family; †(*pl.*) gentlefolk; the larva of the flesh-fly, used as bait in angling. *v.t.* to make gentle, amiable, or kind; to tame (as a colt); to handle gently but firmly, †to raise to gentle rank. of **gentle birth,** of honourable birth, belonging to the gentry, having good breeding. **the gentle craft,** angling, also called **the gentle art**; †the trade of shoemaking. **the gentle** or **gentler sex,** women. **gentlefolk,** *n.* (*earlier in pl.* **gentlefolks**) people of good position of gentle birth. **gentlehood**, *n.* gentle birth, rank, or breeding. **gentleness,** *n.* **gently,** *adv.* **gently born,** of gentle birth. [OF *gentil,* see GENTILE]

gentleman, *n.* †a man of gentle birth, a man above the rank of yeoman; a man belonging to the gentry, or following the profession of arms, the church, or the law; strictly, a man entitled to bear arms; a man of good breeding, kindly feelings and high principles, a man of honour; one who by education, occupation or income holds a good social position; used as a polite equivalent for man, esp. (*pl.*) in addressing the male members of an audience; a man of respectable position who follows no occupation; (*coll.*) the personal attendant of a man of rank. **Gentlemen-at-arms, Honourable Corps of,** in the British army, theoretically the main bodyguard of the sovereign; its functions are now ceremonial. Established 1509, the corps is, next to the Yeomen of the Guard, the oldest in the army; it was reconstituted 1862. It consists of army officers of distinction under a captain, a peer, whose appointment is political. **gentleman of fortune,** (*euphem.*) an adventurer. **gentleman-commoner,** *n.* (*formerly*) at Oxford and Cambridge Univ., one of a privileged class of commoners who enjoyed special privileges. **gentleman-farmer,** *n.* a man of property who occupies his own farm. †**gentleman-pensioner, gentleman-ranker,** *n.* a gentleman enlisting in the ranks, usu. with the object of working up for a commission. **gentleman's gentleman,** *n.* (*facet.*) a valet. **gentleman-usher,** *n.* a gentleman who officiates as usher to a sovereign or other person of high rank. **gentlemanhood, gentlemanship,** *n.* **gentlemanlike,** *a.* **gentlemanly,** *a.* like a gentleman in appearance, feeling or behaviour; pertaining to or becoming a gentleman. **gentlemanliness,** *n.* **gentlemen's agreement,** *n.* an agreement binding in honour but not legally.

gentlewoman, *n.* a woman of gentle birth or breeding; a lady; a woman who waits upon a lady of high rank. **gentlewomanhood,** *n.* **gentlewomanlike, -ly,** *a.* **gentlewomanliness,** *n.*

gentry, *n.* the social class below the nobility; †high birth; the rank of gentleman; politeness, good breeding; (*coll.*) people, folks. **gentrification,** *n.* the process by which the character of an esp. inner urban area formerly lived in by working-class people is changed by an influx of middle-class people, with a consequent increase in property values. **gentrify,** *v.t.* [probably corr. of prec.]

gents GENT.

genty, *a.* neat, graceful; genteel. [Sc., from F *gentil,* see GENTILE]

genu, *n.* the technical name for the knee; any knee-like part or bend. **genual,** *a.* of or pertaining to the knee. [L *genu,* knee]

genuflect, *v.i.* to bend the knee, esp. in worship. **genuflector,** *n.* **genuflectory,** *a.* **genuflexion, -ection,** *n.* [late L *genuflectere* (*genu,* the knee, *flectere,* to bend)]

genuine, *a.* belonging to or coming from the true stock; real, true; not counterfeit, false, spurious or adulterated; (*Zool.*) true to type, not aberrant. **genuinely,** *adv.* **genuineness,** *n.* [L *genuīnus,* from the root *gen-,* to beget]

genus, *n.* (*pl.* **genera**) a class or kind of objects containing several subordinate classes or species; (*Zool. and Bot.*) a group or class of plants or animals differentiated from all others by certain common characteristics and comprising one or more species; kind, group, class, order, family. **subaltern genus,** *n.* a genus which may be considered as a species of some higher genus. **summum genus, highest genus,** *n.* one which cannot be considered as a species of another genus. [L, as prec.; cogn. with KIN]

-geny, *comb. form* production or mode of production, as in *ontogeny, philogeny.* [F *génie,* from Gr. *geneia* or L *gen-,* stem of *genesis*]

geo, gio, *n.* (*Orkney and Shetland*) a narrow inlet, a creek. [Sc., from Icel. *gja*]

geo-, *comb. form* pertaining to the earth. [Gr. *geo-,* from *gē,* earth]

geo-botany, *n.* a branch of botany treating of plants as regards their geographical distribution.

geocentric, -al, *a.* as viewed from or having relation to the earth as centre; having reference to the centre of the earth, as distinguished from any spot on its surface. **geocentric system,** *n.* the obsolete doctrine that the earth is the centre of the planetary system. **geocentrically,** *adv.* **geocentricism,** *n.*

geochemistry, *n.* the study of the chemical composition of the crust of the earth.

geochronology, *n.* the measuring of geological time.

geocyclic, *a.* pertaining to the revolutions of the earth. **geocyclic machine,** *n.* a machine for exhibiting the processes by which day and night and the seasons are produced.

geod., (*abbr.*) geodesy.

geode, *n.* a hollow nodule of any mineral substance, often lined with crystals; the cavity in such a nodule. **geodic,** *a.* **geodiferous,** *a.* [F *géode,* from L *geōdes,* from Gr. *geōdēs,* earthy, from *gē,* earth]

geodesy, *n.* the science or art of measuring the earth's surface or large portions of it, as distinguished from surveying, which deals only with limited tracts. **geodesic, geodetic,** *a.* pertaining to geodesy; carried out or determined by means of geodesy. *n.pl.* geodesy. **geodesic dome,** *n.* a light, strong dome built from a lattice-work of polygons so that the pressure load is evenly distributed throughout the structure. **geodetic, geodesic line,** *n.* the shortest line between two points on the earth's surface or that of a geometrical solid. **geodetic surveying,** *n.* a method of surveying large areas which takes into account the curvature of the earth. **geodetically,** *adv.* **geodesist,** *n.* [F *géodésie,* from Gr. *geōdaisia* (as GEO-, *-daisia,* division, from *daiein,* to divide)]

geodynamic, -al, *a.* relating to the latent forces of the earth. **geodynamics,** *n.*

Geoffrey of Monmouth, *n.* (*c.* 1100–54), Welsh writer and chronicler. While a canon at Oxford, he wrote *Historia Regum Britanniae/History of the Kings of Britain* (*c.* 1139), which included accounts of the semi-legendary kings Lear, Cymbeline, and Arthur, and *Vita Merlini,* a life of the legendary wizard. He was bishop-elect of St Asaph, N Wales (1151) and ordained a priest in 1152.

geog., (*abbr.*) geographer; geographical; geography.

geogeny, *n.* the science or study of the formation of the crust of the earth.

geognosy, *n.* knowledge of the structure of the earth, structural geology; knowledge of the mineral and structural character of rocks; local geology. **geognostic, -al,** *a.* [F *géognosie* (GEO-, Gr. *gnōsis,* knowledge, from *gignōskein,* to know)]

geogony, *n.* the theory of the formation of the earth.

geography, *n.* the science of the surface of the earth, its physical features, natural productions, inhabitants, political divisions, commerce etc.; a book dealing with this. **mathematical geography,** *n.* those parts of the science involving mathematics, such as astronomical geography, geodesy and cartography. **physical geography,** *n.* geography treating of the physical features of the earth's surface, the distribution of land and water, climate, and the distribution of plants and animals. **political geography,** *n.* dealing with countries, states, political, social and economic conditions. **geographer,** *n.* **geographic, -al,** *a.* of or pertaining to geography; relating to or containing a description of the earth. **geographic latitude,** *n.* the angle between the plane of the equator and a perpendicular to the surface of the earth at a given point. **geographic variation,** *n.* the alteration in form, habits etc. of a species or variety of plant or animal due to a change of habitat. **geographical mile,** *n.* one minute of longitude measured at the equator, nautical mile. **geographically,** *adv.* [F *géographie,* L *geographia,* Gr. *geōgraphia*]

geoid, *n.* the surface the earth would have if all parts of it were the same height as the mean sea level of the oceans; the shape of this. **geoidal,** *a.* [G from Gr. *geoeidēs,* earthlike]

geol., (*abbr.*) geological; geologist; geology.

geology, *n.* the science of the earth's crust, its composition, its structure, and the history of its development; a treatise on this subject. **dynamical geology,** *n.* the study of the forces that have brought about geological changes. **economic geology,** *n.* the study of such rocks and minerals as are of use to mankind, and their geological relations. **stratigraphical geology,** *n.* the study of the stratification of the rock-masses forming the earth's crust, stratigraphy. **structural geology,** *n.* the study of the relations between these masses and of the physical causes to which they are due. **geologic,** *a.* forming part of the subject-matter of geology. **geological,** *a.* pertaining to geology. **geological time,** *n.* the time occupied by the development of the planet earth to the present. **geologically,** *adv.* **geologist,** †**-ger,** *n.*

geologize, -ise, *v.i.* to study geology; to make geological investigation, esp. in a particular district. [med. L *geōlogia*]

geom., (*abbr.*) geometer; geometrical; geometry.

geomagnetism, *n.* the magnetic field of the earth; the study of the earth's magnetism. **geomagnetic,** *a.* **geomagnetically,** *adv.* **geomagnetist,** *n.*

geomancy, *n.* divination by means of lines, figures or dots on the earth or on paper, or by particles of earth cast on the ground. **geomancer,** *n.* **geomantic,** *a.* [F *géomancie,* L *geōmantīa,* Gr. *geōmanteia*]

geometer, *n.* a geometrician; a moth or its caterpillar belonging to the tribe called Geometrae, on account of their seeming to measure the ground as they move along, looper. **geometrid,** *a.* [L and G *geōmetrēs* (GEO-, *metrēs,* measurer, from *metrein,* to measure)]

geometry, *n.* the science of magnitudes, whether linear, superficial or solid, with their properties and relations in space. **plane geometry,** *n.* the branch of geometry dealing with magnitudes and their relations in one plane. **solid geometry,** *n.* geometry dealing with all three dimensions of space. **geometric, -ical,** *a.* pertaining to geometry; done, determined or prescribed by geometry; disposed in mathematical figures. **geometrical pen,** *n.* an instrument for drawing geometrical curves. **geometrical progression,** *n.* a progression in which the terms increase or decrease by a common ratio, as 1, 3, 9, 27; 144, 72, 36, 18. **geometrical proportion,** *n.* one based on equal ratios in its two parts, as 2 : 4, 6 : 12. **geometrical stairs,** *n.* spiral stairs of which the steps are secured into the wall at one end only. **geometrical spider,** *n.* one that spins a web in a geometrical form. **geometrical tracery,** *n.* window tracery of which the openings are simple geometrical patterns. **geometrically,** *adv.* **geometrician, geometrist,** *n.* **geometrize, -ise,** *v.i.* to work or construct according to the rules or methods of geometry; to proceed geometrically. [OF *geometrie,* L and Gr. *geōmetria*]

geomorphic, *a.* of or relating to the form of the earth or the solid features of its surface.

geomorphology, *n.* the study of the origin, development and characteristics of land forms. **geomorphologist,** *n.* **geomorphologic, geomorphological,** *a.* **geomorphologically,** *adv.*

geonomy, *n.* the science of the physical laws relating to the structure and development of the earth.

geophagy, *n.* the act or habit of eating earth. **geophagist,** *n.*

geophysics, *n.* the science that deals with the physical characteristics of the earth.

geopolitics, *n.* the study of how the political views and aims of a nation are affected by its geographical position.

geoponics, geopony, *n.* the art and science of agriculture.

georama, *n.* a hollow globe on the inside of which the countries, oceans etc. of the earth are represented, the observer standing on a framework in the centre. [F *géorama* (Gr. *gē,* earth, *horama,* a view, from *horaein,* to see)]

Geordie, *n.* a guinea, which had the figure of St George on the reverse; a pitman; a safety-lamp invented by George Stephenson; a sailing collier-boat; (*coll.*) a native of Tyneside, NE England. [Sc. and North., dim of GEORGE]

George[1], *n.* a jewel bearing the figure of St George, the patron saint of England, worn by the knights of the Garter; †(*sl.*) a coin bearing the figure of St George, a half-crown or a guinea; †a kind of loaf; (*Aviat., coll.*) an automatic aircraft pilot. **brown George,** *n.* a coarse, earthenware water-jug. **by George,** a mild oath, *int.* **George Cross,** a decoration instituted in 1940, primarily for civilians in recognition of acts performed of the greatest heroism or most conspicuous courage in circumstances of extreme danger; **George Medal,** *n.* similarly awarded for acts of great bravery. **George noble,** *n.* a gold coin, with St George on the reverse, minted in the reign of Henry VIII. **St George's cross** CROSS[1]. [L *Georgius,* Gr. *Geōrgios,* a saint said to have been martyred under Diocletian]

George[2]**, St,** *n.* patron saint of England. The story of St George rescuing a woman by slaying a dragon, evidently derived from the Perseus legend, first appears in the 6th cent. The cult of St George was introduced into W Europe by the Crusaders. His feast day is 23 Apr.

George[3], *n.* **Stefan** (1868–1933), German poet. His early poetry was influenced by French Symbolism, but his concept of himself as regenerating the German spirit first appears in *Der Teppich des Lebens/The Tapestry of Life* (1899), and later in *Der siebente Ring/The Seventh Ring* (1907).

George, *n.* six kings of Great Britain:

George I, *n.* (1660–1727), king of Great Britain from 1714. He was the son of the first elector of Hanover, Ernest Augustus (1629–98), and his wife Sophia, and a great-grandson of James I. He succeeded to the electorate in 1698, and became king on the death of Queen Anne. He attached himself to the Whigs, and spent most of his reign in Hanover, never having learned English.

George II, *n.* (1683–1760), king of Great Britain from 1727, when he succeeded his father, George I. His victory at Dettingen, 1743, in the War of the Austrian Succession, was the last battle commanded by a British king. He married Caroline of Anspach in 1705. He was succeeded by his grandson George III.

George III, *n.* (1738–1820), king of Great Britain from 1760, when he succeeded his grandfather George II. He supported his ministers in a hard line towards the American colonies, and opposed Catholic emancipation and other reforms. Possibly suffering from porphyria, he had repeated attacks of insanity, permanent from 1811. He was succeeded by his son George IV.

George IV, *n.* (1762–1830), king of Great Britain from 1820, when he succeeded his father George III, for whom he had been regent during the king's insanity 1811–20. Strictly educated, he reacted by entering into a life of debauchery, and in 1785 married a Catholic widow, Mrs Fitzherbert, but in 1795 also married Princess Caroline of Brunswick, in return for payment of his debts. He attempted to divorce her on charges of adultery, but this was dropped after Parliament passed the bill with increasingly smaller majorities. He had one child, Charlotte, who died in childbirth 1817. He was succeeded by his brother, the duke of Clarence, who became William IV.

George V, *n.* (1865–1936), king of Great Britain from 1910, when he succeeded his father Edward VII. He was the second son, and became heir 1892 on the death of his elder brother Albert, Duke of Clarence. In 1893, he married Princess Victoria Mary of Teck (Queen Mary), formerly engaged to his brother. During World War I he made several visits to the front. In 1917, he abandoned all German titles for himself and his family.

George VI, *n.* (1895–1952), king of Great Britain from 1936, when he succeeded after the abdication of his brother Edward VIII. Created Duke of York 1920, he married in 1923 Lady Elizabeth Bowes-Lyon (1900–), and their children are Elizabeth II and Princess Margaret. During World War II, he visited the Normandy and Italian battlefields.

George I, *n.* (1845–1913), king of Greece, 1863–1913. The son of king Christian IX of Denmark, he was nominated to the Greek throne and, in spite of early unpopularity, became a highly successful constitutional monarch. He was assassinated by a Greek, Schinas, at Salonika.

George II, *n.* (1890–1947), king of Greece, 1922–23 and 1935–47. He became king on the expulsion of his father Constantine I, 1922, but was himself overthrown 1923. Restored by the military, 1935, he set up a dictatorship under Metaxas, and went into exile during the German occupation (1941–45).

Georgetown[1], *n.* capital and port of Guyana; population (1983) 188,000. **Declaration of Georgetown,** *n.* call in 1972, at a conference in Guyana of nonaligned countries, for a multipolar system to replace the two world power blocs, and for the Mediterranean Sea and Indian Ocean to be neutral.

Georgetown[2], *n.* or **Penang**, chief port of the Federation of Malaysia, and capital of Penang, on the Island of Penang; population (1980) 250,600. It produces textiles and toys.

georgette, *n.* a plain semi-transparent dress material. [Mme *Georgette,* a French modiste]

Georgia[1], *n.* state of the S US; nickname Empire State of the South/Peach State. **area** 152,600 sq km/58,904 sq miles. **capital** Atlanta. **towns** Columbus, Savannah, Macon. **products** poultry, livestock, tobacco, maize, peanuts, cotton, china clay, crushed granite, textiles, carpets, aircraft. **population** (1987) 6,222,000. **Georgian**[1], *a.* of or relating to Georgia. *n.* a native or inhabitant of Georgia.

Georgia[2], *n.* (Georgian **Sakartvelo** Russian **Gruzia**) constituent republic of the SW USSR from 1936. **area** 69,700 sq km/26,911 sq miles. **capital** Tbilisi. **products** tea, citrus, orchard fruits, tung oil, tobacco, vines, silk, hydroelectricity. **population** (1987) 5,266,000; 69% Georgian, 9% Armenian, 7% Russian, 5% Azerbaijani, 3% Ossetian, 2% Abkhazian. **language** Georgian. **religion** Georgian Church, independent of the Russian Orthodox Church since 1917.

Georgian[1] GEORGIA[1].

Georgian[2], *a.* of or relating to Georgia. *n.* a native or inhabitant of Georgia.

Georgian[3], *a.* relating to the period of George I–IV in Great Britain (1714–1830); relating to the reign of George V (1910–36). *n.* a period of English architecture, furniture making, and decorative art between 1714 and 1830. The architecture is mainly Classical in style, although external details and interiors were often rich in Rococo carving. Furniture was frequently made of mahogany and satinwood, and mass production became increasingly common; designers included Thomas Chippendale, George Hepplewhite, and Thomas Sheraton. The silver of this period is particularly fine, and ranges from the earlier, simple forms to the more ornate, and from the neo-classical style of Robert Adam to the later, more decorated pre-Victorian taste.

georgic, *a.* pertaining to agriculture; treating of rural affairs. *n.* a poem on husbandry or rural affairs; one book of Virgil's *Georgics,* a poem in four books on husbandry. [L *geōrgicus,* Gr. *geōrgikos,* from *geōrgos,* a husbandman (GEO-, *ergein,* to work)]

geoscience, *n.* any of the sciences that are concerned with the earth, e.g. geology, geophysics or geodesy; these sciences collectively.

geoscopy, *n.* knowledge of the ground or soil gained by inspection.

geoselenic, *a.* pertaining or relating to the earth and the moon.

geosphere, *n.* the solid part of the earth, as distinct from the *atmosphere* or *hydrosphere;* lithosphere.

geostatic, *a.* applied to an arch so constructed as to be in equilibrium under vertical pressure, as in an embankment. **geostatics,** *n. sing.* the study of the statics of rigid bodies.

geostationary, *a.* of a satellite, orbiting the earth at the same speed as the earth rotates so remaining above the same spot on the earth's surface.

geostrophic, *a.* of or caused by the force produced by the rotation of the earth. **geostrophic wind,** *n.* a wind the direction and force of which are influenced by the earth's rotation.

geosynchronous, *a.* of a satellite, geostationary.

geosyncline, *n.* a part of the earth's crust that has sunk inwards, resulting in a usu. long and broad depression containing deep thicknesses of rock or sediment.

geotaxis, *n.* the response of an organism or a plant to the stimulus of gravity.

geotectonic, *a.* pertaining to the structure of the earth.

geothermal, *a.* pertaining to the internal heat of the earth. **geothermal energy,** *n.* energy from the natural heat of the earth, e.g. hot springs. **geothermic,** *a.*

geothermometer, *n.* an instrument for measuring the earth's heat at different depths, as in mines or wells.

geotropism, *n.* the tendency exhibited by the organs of a plant to turn towards the centre of the earth. **geotropic,** *a.* **geotropically,** *adv.*

Ger., (*abbr.*) German; Germany.

ger., (*abbr.*) gerund, gerundive.

gerah, *n.* a unit of weight and of money equivalent to 1/20 of a shekel. [Heb.]

Gerald of Wales, *n.* English name of GIRALDUS CAMBRENSIS.

geranium, *n.* a genus, with about 100 species, of hardy herbaceous plants, rarely shrubs, natives of all temperate regions, typified by *Geranium maculatum,* the crane's-bill, so called from the shape of its seed-pod; a plant of this genus; a cultivated plant of the allied genus *Pelargonium.* [L, from Gr. *geranion,* from *geranos,* a crane]

gérant, *n.* a business-manager; an editor. [F, pres.p. of *gérer,* from L *gerere,* to manage]

geratology, *n.* the science dealing with the phenomena of deterioration and decay. **geratologic, geratologous,** *a.* [Gr. *gēras gēratos,* old age, -LOGY]

gerbe, *n.* a wheatsheaf; (*Her.*) a figure resembling this; a firework giving this effect. [F]

gerbil, gerbille, *n.* any of numerous small, burrowing, mouselike rodents of the subfamily gerbillinae, of desert regions of Asia and Africa. [F *gerbille,* from mod. L *gerbillus,* a little JERBOA]

gerent, *n.* a manager; a ruler or controller. [L *gerens -ntem,* pres.p. of *gerere,* to manage]

gerfalcon, *n.* a large and powerful falcon of northern regions, typified by the Iceland falcon, *Falco islandus;* †a large falcon used for hawking at herons etc. [OF *gerfaucon,* med. L *gēro- gīrefalco,* MHG *gīrvalke*]

Gerhard, *n.* **Roberto** (1896–1970), Spanish-British composer. He studied with Granados and Schoenberg and settled in England in 1939, where he composed twelve-tone works in Spanish style. He composed the *Symphony No 1* (1952-3), followed by 3 more symphonies and chamber music incorporating advanced techniques.

geriatrics, *n.sing.* the branch of medicine dealing with old age and its diseases. **geriatric,** *a.* **geriatrician,** *n.* [Gr. *geras,* old age; *iatros,* a physician]

Géricault, *n.* **(Jean Louis André) Théodore** (1791–1824), French Romantic painter. *The Raft of the Medusa* (1819, Louvre, Paris) was notorious for exposing a relatively recent scandal in which shipwrecked sailors had been cut adrift and left to drown.

germ, *n.* (*Biol.*) the portion of living matter from which an organism develops; the embryo of an animal or plant; a partially-developed organism; a microorganism, esp. such as is supposed to cause disease, a microbe; that from which anything springs; the origin, source or elementary principle. **in germ,** existing in an undeveloped state. **germ-cell,** *n.* the parent cell from which a new individual develops usu. dist. as the female element in reproduction from the sperm-cell or male element. *v.i.* to sprout, to germinate. **germ-line therapy,** *n.* in medicine, the treatment of certain diseases by the insertion of new genes into the reproductive cells of a patient, such genes then being passed on to all future generations, as distinct from *gene therapy.* **germ-plasm,** *n.* the part of the protoplasm in which the power of reproduction is supposed to reside and which is transmitted from one generation to its offspring. **germ theory,** *n.* the theory that certain diseases are caused by the development of microorganisms introduced into the body through germs or spores. **germ-tube,** *n.* the tube-like growth issuing from a germinating spore. **germ-warfare,** *n.* the use of bacterial weapons against enemy troops. **germless,** *a.* **germicide,** [-CIDE] *a.* destroying germs, esp. disease-germs. *n.* a substance used for this purpose. **germicidal,** *a.* [F *germe,* L *germen -inis*]

German[1], *a.* pertaining or relating to Germany. *n.* (*pl.* **Germans**) a native or inhabitant of Germany; the language of Germany, a member of the Germanic group of the Indo-European language family, the national language of West Germany, East Germany, and Austria, and an official language of Switzerland. There are many spoken varieties of German, the best known distinction being between High German (*Hochdeutsch*) and Low German (*Plattdeutsch*). **High German,** originally the form of German spoken in the south, but since Luther's translation of the Bible (1450) adopted as the literary language all over Germany. **Low German,** German of the Netherlands, including Dutch, Frisian, Flemish and Old Saxon. **German art,** *n.* painting and sculpture in the Germanic north of Europe from the early Middle Ages to the present. **German Empire,** *n.* the Western Empire; the empire established in 1871 by the union of the North German Confederation, Baden, Hesse, Bavaria and Württemberg. **German alloy,** *n.* an aluminium alloy comprising aluminium, copper and zinc. **German measles,** *n.pl.* rubella, a virus disease, usually caught by children, having an incubation period of two to three weeks. It is marked by a sore throat, pinkish rash, and slight fever. If a woman contracts it in the first three months of pregnancy, it may cause serious damage to the unborn child. **German millet,** *n.* an edible grain produced by a grass, *Setaria germanica*. **German Ocean,** *n.* the North Sea. **German-paste,** *n.* a paste made of hard-boiled eggs, pea-meal, almonds, lard, sugar etc., for feeding singing-birds. **German sausage,** *n.* a large kind of sausage stuffed with partly-cooked meat, highly spiced. **German silver,** *n.* a white alloy of nickel, copper and zinc, used for mathematical instruments, table-ware, etc. **German text,** *n.* a **black-letter** closely resembling old English and modern German. **Germanesque,** *a.* **Germanic,** *a.* of or pertaining to Germany; of or pertaining to the Teutonic race. *n.* the primitive Teutonic language. **East Germanic,** the group of Teutonic languages represented by Gothic, and some like Burgundian and Vandal of which mere vestiges survive. **North Germanic,** the Scandinavian group of languages. **West Germanic,** the group comprising High and Low German, Dutch, Frisian, English etc. **Germanish,** *a.* **Germanism,** *n.* **Germanist,** *n.* **Germanity,** *n.* **Germanize, -ise,** *v.t.* to assimilate or make to conform to German ideas, customs, idioms etc. *v.i.* to conform to these. **Germanization, -isation,** *n.* **Germanizer, -iser,** *n.* [L *Germānus,* perh. from Celt. (cp. OIr. *gair,* neighbour)]

german[2], *a.* sprung from the same parents (*usu. in comb.,* as *cousin-german*); closely connected, relevant, pertinent; †genuine, true; †closely related, akin. *n.* one sprung from the same stock. [OF *germain,* L *germānus,* having the same parents (cogn. with prec.)]

germander, *n.* a plant of the genus *Teucrium,* esp. the wall germander, *T. chamaedrys*. **germander speedwell,** *n.* an English wild plant with blue flowers, *Veronica chamaedrys*. [F *germandrée,* late L *germandra, gamandria,* late Gr. *chamandrua,* corr. of Gr. *chamaidrus* (*chamai,* on the ground, *drûs,* tree)]

germane, *a.* relevant to, pertaining to, relating to.

Germanicus Caesar, *n.* (15 BC–AD 19), Roman general. He was the adopted son of the emperor Tiberius and married the emperor Augustus' granddaughter Agrippina. Although he refused the suggestion of his troops that he claim the throne on the death of Augustus, his military victories in Germany made Tiberius jealous. Sent to the East, he died near Antioch, possibly murdered at the instigation of Tiberius. He was the father of Caligula, and of Agrippina, mother of Nero.

germanium, *n.* a metallic element of a greyish-white colour, at. no. 32; chem. symbol Ge, used in the construction of transistors because of its electrical properties. [L *Germānus,* GERMAN[2]]

Germano-, *comb. form* German.

Germanomania, *n.* enthusiasm for Germany or German things.

Germanophil, *n.* **Germanophilist,** *n.* a lover of Germany or Germans.

Germanophobe, *n.* one who hates Germany or Germans. **Germanophobia,** *n.* **Germanophobic,** *a.*

Germany, *n.* nation of central Europe, divided after World War II into East Germany, West Germany, with land to the east of the Oder and western Neisse rivers being divided between the USSR and Poland. Restoration of these 'lost territories' (Silesia, Pomerania, Sudetenland, and East Prussia), a third of the former area, is no longer a political issue. **East Germany,** *n.* German Democratic Republic (*Deutsche Demokratische Republik*). **area** 108,350 sq km/41,823 sq miles. **capital** East Berlin. **towns** Leipzig, Dresden, Chemnitz, Magdeburg Halle, Erfurt, Jena; chief port Rostock. **physical** flat in north, mountains in south; rivers Elbe, Oder, and Neisse; many lakes, including Müritz. **exports** lignite, uranium, cobalt, coal, iron, steel, fertilizers, plastics. **population** (1986) 16,640,000; annual growth rate –0.1%. **language** German. **religion** Protestant 80%, Roman Catholic 11%. **West Germany,** *n.* Federal Republic of Germany (*Bundesrepublik Deutschland*). **area** 248,706 sq km/96,001 sq miles. **capital** Bonn. **towns** West Berlin, Cologne, Munich, Essen, Frankfurt-am-Main, Dortmund, Düsseldorf; ports Hamburg, Kiel, Cuxhaven, Bremerhaven. **physical** flat in N, mountainous in S with Alps; rivers Rhine, Weser, Elbe flow N, Danube flows SE. **exports** machine tools (world's leading exporter), cars, commercial vehicles, electronics, industrial goods, textiles, chemicals, iron, steel, wine. **population** (1986) 61,170,000 (including 4,400,000 guest workers, *Gastarbeiter*, of whom 1,600,000 are Turks; the rest are Yugoslavs, Italians, Greeks, Spanish, and Portuguese); annual growth rate –0.2%. **language** German. **religion** Protestant 49%, Roman Catholic 47%.

germen, *n.* the ovary or rudimentary seed-vessel of a plant; †a shoot or sprout; †a germ. **germigenous,** *a.* **germiniparous,** *a.* **germinal,** *a.* pertaining to or of the nature of a germ; germinative; in the earliest stage of development. **germinal vesicle,** *n.* the large nucleus of an oocyte before it develops into an ovum. **germinally,** *adv.* [L, *see* GERM]

germicide GERM.

Germinal[1], *n.* the name given by the French Convention to the seventh month of the republican year, 21 Mar. to 19 Apr. [F]

germinal[2] GERMEN.

germinate, *v.t.* to sprout, to shoot, to bud; to develop. *v.i.* to cause to sprout or bud; to put forth; to produce. **germinable,** *a.* **germinant,** *a.* sprouting, growing, developing. **germination,** *n.* the first act of growth in an embryo plant, ovum etc.; the act or process of germinating. **germinator,** *n.* **germinative,** *a.* [L *germinātus,* p.p. of *germināre,* from *germen,* see GERM]

germon, *n.* the long-finned tunny. [F]

Geronimo, *n.* (1829–1909), chief of the Chiricahua Apache Indians and war leader. From 1875–1885, he fought US federal troops and settlers encroaching on tribal reservations in the Southwest, especially SE Arizona and New Mexico. After surrendering to Gen. George Crook Mar. 1886, and agreeing to go to Florida where their families were being held, Geronimo and his followers escaped. Captured again Aug. 1886, they were taken to Florida, then to Alabama. The climate proved unhealthy, and they were taken to Fort Sill, Oklahoma, where Geronimo became a farmer. He dictated *Geronimo's Story of His Life* (1906).

geront(o)-, *comb. form* pertaining to old age. **gerontic,** *a.* pertaining to old people, senile. [as foll.]

gerontocracy, *n.* government by old men; a government of old men. **gerontarchical,** *a.* pertaining to government by old men. [Gr. *gerōn gerontos,* an old man]

gerontogeous, *a.* indigenous to the Old World. [Gr. *gerōn gerontos,* an old man, *gē,* the earth]

gerontology, *n.* the science dealing with the phenomena of deterioration and decay in the aged.

geropigia, jerupigia, *n.* a mixture used to adulterate port wine, made of unfermented grape-juice with brandy, sugar and colouring-matter. [Port., corr. of

HIERAPICRA]

-gerous, *comb. form* bearing, having; as in *armigerous, florigerous*. [L *-ger* from *gerere,* to bear]

gerrymander, *v.t.* to tamper with (an electoral district or constituency) so as to secure unfair advantages for a particular candidate, party or class; to misconstrue or garble (a question, argument etc.) so as to arrive at unfair conclusions. *n.* an unfair rearrangement of a constituency in this manner. **gerrymanderer,** *n.* [Elbridge *Gerry,* governor of Massachusetts, *-mander* (SALAMANDER, which the map of one district was supposed to resemble)]

Gershwin, *n.* **George** (1898–1937), US composer, who wrote the tone poem *An American in Paris* (1928), *Rhapsody in Blue* (1924), and the opera *Porgy and Bess* (1935), in which he incorporated the essentials of jazz. He also wrote popular songs with his brother, the lyricist Ira Gershwin (1896–1983).

gerund, *n.* in Latin, a part of the verb used as a noun instead of the infinitive in cases other than the nominative; in English, a verbal noun ending in *-ing,* when used as a part of the verb. **gerund-grinder,** *n.* a pedantic schoolmaster. **gerundial**, *a.* **gerundive**, *a.* pertaining to or of the nature of a gerund. *n.* in Latin, a verbal adjective formed on the gerundial stem giving the sense of *must* and *should* (be done). **gerundival**, *a.* **gerundively**, *adv.* [L *gerundium,* from *gerundum,* neut. ger. of *gerere,* to do]

gesellschaft, *n.* a social group, held together by practical concerns and not by ties of kinship, as distinct from *gemeinschaft*. [G, society]

gesso, *n.* a prepared ground of plaster of Paris for painting, sometimes for sculpture. **gesso work,** *n.* [It., from L GYPSUM]

gest[1]**, geste**, *n.* a deed, an exploit, an achievement; a tale or history of the exploits of a hero or heroes, esp. a mediaeval ballad or metrical romance. *v.i.* to compose or recite gests or legendary tales. [OF *geste,* from L *gesta,* exploits, orig. neut. pl. of *gestus,* p.p. of *gerere,* to carry on, to perform]

†**gest**[2]**,** *n.* carriage, bearing; a gesture. [F *geste,* L *gestus,* bearing, gesture, as prec.]

gest[3]**,** *n.* (*in. pl.*) the successive stages of a journey or progress; the time allotted for a stay. [OF *giste* (cp. GIST), from *gêstr,* to lie]

gestalt, *n.* in psychology, an organized whole in which each part affects every other part. Its exponents have demonstrated that the mind tends to perceive events and situations as a pattern, or whole, rather than as a collection of separate and independent elements. [G, form, pattern]

Gestapo, *n.* the body of secret police formed in 1933 to secure strict obedience to the government of Nazi Germany, under the direction of Heinrich Himmler from 1936. [first letters of G *Geheime Staats Polizei,* secret state police]

gestation, *n.* the act of carrying; the state of being carried; the act of carrying or the process of being carried in the uterus from the time of conception to that of parturition; the period of this. †**gestant**, *a.* laden, burdened, pregnant. **gestate**, *v.t.* **gestatorial**, *a.* for carrying. **gestatorial chair,** *n.* the state chair in which the Pope is carried on special occasions. †**gestatory**, *a.* that may be carried or worn; pertaining to gestation or pregnancy. [through F, or directly from L *gestātiōnem,* nom. *gestātio,* from *gestāre,* freq. of *gerere,* to carry]

gesticulate, *v.i.* to make expressive gestures or motions, as in speaking or instead of speaking. *v.t.* to express or represent by gestures. **gesticulation,** *n.* the act or art of gesticulating to express emotion or illustrate an argument; a gesture. **gesticulator,** *n.* **gesticulative, gesticulatory,** *a.* pertaining to or represented by gesticulation. [L *gesticulātus,* p.p. of *gesticulārī,* from *gesticulus,* dim. of *gestus,* gesture, see GEST[2]]

gesture, *n.* a motion of the face, body or limbs, used to express emotion or to illustrate or enforce something that is said; the art of using such movements for rhetorical or dramatic purposes; †bearing, deportment; †posture; a significant move or act, usu. of a friendly nature. *v.i.* to gesticulate. *v.t.* to accompany or represent with gestures or action. **gestural,** *a.* **gestureless,** *a.* **gesturer,** *n.* [late L *gestūra,* from *gestus,* p.p. of *gerere,* to carry, to deport (oneself)]

gesundheit, *int.* your health (said after someone has sneezed). [G]

get[1]**,** *v.t.* (*p.* **got,** *p.p.* **got,** (*US*) **gotten**), to procure, to obtain, to gain possession of by any means, to acquire; to earn, to win; to receive, to obtain; to receive as one's portion or penalty, to suffer; to learn, to commit to memory; (*coll. in p.p.*) to have, to possess; (*coll.*) to be obliged (to); to beget, to procreate; to succeed in obtaining, bringing, putting etc.; to induce, to persuade (to); to betake (oneself); (*coll.*) to catch, to outwit, to nonplus. *v.i.* to arrive at any place, condition or posture; to go, to depart; (*coll.*) to succeed, to find the way or opportunity (to); to be a gainer, to profit. **get!** (*imper.*) be off! **get away,** an exclamation of mild disbelief; also, **get lost, get out,** (*imper.*) be off! **has got to be done,** must be done. **to get about,** to be able to move or walk about (after an illness); to become known, to be reported abroad; to travel from place to place. **to get ahead,** to prosper; to come in advance of. **to get along,** to proceed, to advance; to succeed, to fare, to manage (well or badly); (*coll.*) to go away. **to get among,** to become one of. **to get asleep,** to fall asleep. **to get at,** to be able to reach; to ascertain; (*sl.*) to banter, to tease; (*sl.*) to influence, corrupt, bribe (a jockey etc.); to drug or illegally tamper with (a racehorse). **to get away,** to quit; to escape; to disengage oneself (from). **to get away with,** to make off with; to escape discovery in connection with (something wrong or illegal). **to get back,** to receive back, to recover; to return, to come back. **to get before,** to arrive in front (of). **to get behind,** to fall into the rear; to lag; to fall into arrears; to penetrate, to unravel. **to get by,** to elude; to be good enough; to come off with impunity. **to get clear,** to disengage oneself; to be released. **to get cracking** CRACK. **to get done with,** to finish with. **to get down,** to dismount, to descend. **to get down to,** to concentrate upon; to start work on. **to get even with,** to revenge oneself on; to pay back. **to get forward,** to make progress, to advance. **to get going,** to begin; to make haste. **to get home,** to arrive at one's home; to arrive at the winning post. **to get in,** to be elected; to enter; to collect and place under cover (as crops); to make room for. **to get into,** (*coll.*) to put on (as clothes etc.); (*coll.*) to become involved in; to possess, dominate or take over (a person's mood, personality etc.). **to get into one's head,** to be convinced of. **to get it in the neck** NECK. **to get it together,** to achieve harmony or success. **to get loose** or **free,** to liberate or disengage oneself. **to get near,** to approach within a small distance. **to get off,** to dismount, to alight (from); to escape, to be released (from); to be acquitted, to be let off (with or for); to start; to take off, to remove; to procure the acquittal of. **to get off on,** (*coll.*) to be impressed by; to enjoy. **to get off one's bike,** (*esp. Austral.*) to become angry. **to get off with,** (*coll.*) to behave flirtatiously with; to have a sexual relationship with; to escape blame or punishment for. **to get on,** to put or pull on; to move on; to advance; to succeed or prosper; to grow late; to grow old; to have a friendly relationship; to do, fare or manage (with or without); to mount. **to get one's eye in** EYE. **to get one's goat** GOAT. **to get one's own back,** to revenge oneself. **to get onto,** to make contact with; to become aware of, discover. **to get out,** to pull out, to extract; to escape from any place of confinement or restraint; to be divulged. **to get out of,** to avoid (doing something). **to get over,** (*coll.*) to persuade; to surmount, overcome (a difficulty etc.); to recover from (illness, surprise, disappointment etc.); to make intelligible; to accept or appreciate. **to get quit** or **rid of,** to disengage oneself from. **to get round,** to evade, to circumvent. **to get set,** (a command at the start of a race) be ready; (*esp. Austral.*

coll.) to place a bet. **to get stuck in** or **into,** (*coll.*) to eat hungrily; to start doing a task vigorously; to attack (someone) physically or verbally. **to get the better** or **best of,** to overcome; to gain the advantage; to be victorious. **to get the hang of,** to come to understand; to acquire the knack of. **to get there,** (*coll.*) to succeed; to understand. **to get the worst of it,** to be defeated. **to get through,** to reach a point beyond, to reach one's destination; to pass (as a Bill); to succeed in doing, to complete, to finish (with); to pass (an examination); to use up. **to get through to,** to make a telephone connection with; (*coll.*) to make (someone) understand. **to get to,** to reach, to arrive at; to begin (a task etc.); (*coll.*) to annoy or irritate. **to get together,** to meet, to assemble; to bring together, to amass. **to get under one's skin** SKIN. **to get under way,** to start a ship, to start, to begin to move (of a ship). **to get up,** to prepare, to get ready; to learn, to work up; to dress up, to disguise; to invent, to devise; to rise (as from a bed etc.); to mount; to begin to rage or be violent (as the wind, waves etc.). **to get wind of** WIND. **to get with child,** to make pregnant. **get-at-able,** *n.* accessible. **getaway,** *n.*, *a.* (*coll.*) (of) an escape. **get-together,** *n.* (*coll.*) an informal gathering. **get-up,** *n.* dress and other accessories; the manner in which anything is presented, as on the stage; the style or format (of a book). **get-up-and-go,** *n.* energy and enthusiasm; ambition. **gettable,** *a.* obtainable. **getter,** *n.* **getting,** *n.pl.* gains, profits. [Icel. *geta* (cp. OE *-gietan,* in *forgietan, engietan* etc., also Goth. *-gitan,* G *vergessen,* cogn. with L *-hendere,* in *prehendere,* to seize, Gr. *chandanein,* to seize)]

get[2], *n.* the act of begetting; that which is begotten, offspring, progeny; (*Sc.*) a brat. [from prec.]

geta, *n.* (*pl.* **geta, getas**) a Japanese wooden sandal. [Jap.]

Gethsemane, *n.* site of the garden where Judas Iscariot, according to the New Testament, betrayed Jesus. It is on the Mount of Olives, east of Jerusalem. When Jerusalem was divided between Israel and Jordan in 1948, Gethsemane fell within Jordanian territory.

Getty, *n.* **J(ean) Paul** (1892–1976), US oil billionaire, president of the Getty Oil Company from 1947, and founder of the Getty Museum (housing the world's highest funded art gallery) in Malibu, California. In 1985 his son John Paul Getty Jr (1932–) established an endowment fund of £50 million for the National Gallery, London.

Gettysburg, *n.* site in Pennsylvania of a decisive battle of the American Civil War in 1863, won by the North. The site is now a national cemetery, at the dedication of which President Lincoln delivered the **Gettysburg Address**, 19 Nov. 1863, a speech in which he reiterated the principles of freedom, equality, and democracy embodied in the US constitution.

Getz, *n.* **Stan(ley)** (1927–), US tenor saxophonist of the 1950s 'cool jazz' school. He was the first US musician to be closely identified with the Latin American *bossa nova* sound.

geum, *n.* a hardy genus of rosaceous plants comprising the avens or herb-bennet. [L]

gewgaw, *n.* a showy trifle; a toy, a bauble. †*a.* showy without value, gaudy. **gewgawed,** *a.* tricked out with gewgaws. **gewgawish, gewgawy,** *a.* **gewgawry,** *n.* [perh. from ME *givegove,* a reduplication of GIVE]

gey, *a.* (*Sc.*) considerable, middling (in amount), *adv.* considerably, very. [var. of GAY]

geyser, *n.* a hot spring throwing up a column of water at intervals (in SW Iceland, the Yellowstone region in N America, and New Zealand); an apparatus for heating a stream of water supplying a bath, etc. **geyserite,** *n.* an opal-like silica deposited from the waters of geysers and hot springs, sinter. [Icel. *geysir,* 'gusher', name of a hot spring in Iceland, from *geysa,* to gush]

GG, (*abbr.*) Girl Guides; Governor-General; Grenadier Guards.

Ghana, *n.* Republic of, country in W Africa; bounded to the N by Burkina Faso, E by Togo, S by the Gulf of Guinea, and W by the Ivory Coast. **area** 238,305 sq km/91,986 sq miles. **capital** Accra. **towns** Kumasi, and ports Sekondi-Takoradi, Tema. **physical** mostly plains; bisected by river Volta. **exports** cocoa, coffee, timber, gold, diamonds, manganese, bauxite. **population** (1988) 13,812,000; annual growth rate 3.2%. **language** English (official). **religion** Christian 43%, animist 38%, Muslim 12%. **Ghanaian,** *n.* an inhabitant of Ghana. *a.* pertaining to Ghana.

Ghana, Ancient, *n.* a great trading empire that flourished in NW Africa during the 5th–13th cents. Founded by the Soninke people, the Ghana Empire was based, like the Mali Empire which superseded it, on the Saharan gold trade. At its peak in the 11th cent., it occupied an area that includes parts of present-day Mali, Senegal, and Mauritania. Wars with the Berber tribes of the Sahara led to its fragmentation and collapse in the 13th cent., when much of its territory was absorbed into Mali.

gharry, *n.* a variety of wheeled carriage in India. [Hind. *gārī*]

ghastly, *a.* pale, death-like, haggard; horrible, frightful, shocking; (*coll.*) awful, unpleasant. *adv.* in a ghastly manner. **ghastlily,** *adv.* **ghastliness,** *n.* †**ghastful,** *a.* frightful, horrible. †**ghastfully,** *adv.* [GAST, -LY]

Ghats, Eastern and **Western,** *n.pl.* twin mountain ranges in S India, to the E and W of the central plateau; a few peaks reach about 3000 m/9800 ft. The name is a European misnomer, the Indian word *ghat* meaning pass, not mountain.

ghaut, ghat, *n.* a mountain pass; a range of mountains; a flight of steps descending to a river, a landing-place. **Eastern** and **Western Ghauts,** two ranges of mountains parallel to the coasts of southern India. [Hind. *ghāt*]

ghazal, *n.* an Oriental lyric poem, usu. erotic, convivial or religious in subject, having a limited number of couplets, all with the same rhyme. [Arab., an ode]

Ghazi, *n.* one who has fought for Islam against infidels. **Ghazism,** *n.* [Arab. *ghāzi,* p.p. of *ghazā,* to fight]

Ghazzali, al-, *n.* (1058–1111), Muslim philosopher and one of the most famous Sufis (Muslim mystics). He was responsible for easing the conflict between the Sufi and the Ulema, a body of Muslim religious and legal scholars.

gheber, ghebre, GUEBRE.

ghee, ghi, *n.* butter, usu. prepared from buffalo-milk, clarified into an oil, which can be kept for a long time. [Hind. *ghī*]

Ghent, *n.* (Flemish **Gent**, French **Gand**) city and port in East Flanders, NW Belgium; population (1982) 237,500. Industries include textiles, chemicals, electronics, and metallurgy.

Gheorgiu-Dej, *n.* **Gheorge** (1901–65), Romanian communist politician. A member of the Romanian Communist Party (RCP) from 1930, he played a leading part in establishing a communist regime in 1945. He was prime minister (1952–55) and state president (1961–65). Although retaining the support of Moscow, he adopted an increasingly independent line during his final years.

gherkin, *n.* a young and green small variety of cucumber, used for pickling. [Dut. *agurkken* (now *agurkje*), ult. from late Gr. *angourion,* Pers. *angārah*]

ghetto, *n.* (*pl.* **-tos, -toes**) the quarter of a town formerly inhabited by Jews; a poor, densely populated area of a city, esp. inhabited by a racial minority. **ghetto-blaster,** *n.* a large portable stereo radio-cassette player. **ghettoize, -ise,** *v.t.* to make into a ghetto. **ghettoization, -isation,** *n.* [It., perh. abbr. of *borghetto,* dim. of *borgo,* BOROUGH]

ghi GHEE.

Ghibelline, *n.* one who sided with the Emperors in their contests with the Guelphs or partisans of the Popes, in Italy during the Middle Ages. **Ghibellinism,** *n.* [It. *ghibellino,* said to be a corr. of *Waiblingen,* an estate in Württemberg belonging to the Hohenstaufen family, from which sprang several Emperors during the 12th and 13th cents.]

Ghiberti, *n.* **Lorenzo** (1378–1455), Italian sculptor and goldsmith. In 1401 he won the commission for a pair of gilded bronze doors for Florence's baptistry. He produced a second pair (1425–52), the *Gates of Paradise*, one of the masterpieces of the Early Italian Renaissance. They show sophisticated composition and use of perspective.

ghilgai, gilgai, *n.* a saucer-shaped depression containing a pool of water. [Austral. Abor.]

ghillie GILLIE.

Ghirlandaio, *n.* **Domenico** (*c.* 1449–1494), Italian fresco painter, head of a large and prosperous workshop in Florence. His fresco cycle (1486–90) in S Maria Novella, Florence includes portraits of many Florentines and much contemporary domestic detail. He also worked in Pisa, Rome, and San Gimignano, and painted portraits.

ghost, *n.* the spirit or soul of a deceased person appearing to the living, an apparition; the soul of a dead person in the other world; the soul or spirit, the vital principle; a mere shadow or semblance; the remotest likelihood; one who does literary or artistic work for which another takes the credit; in optics, a spot, gleam or secondary image caused by a defect in a lens; in television reception, a duplicated image. *v.i.* to play the ghost, to prowl as a ghost; †to die. *v.t.* to haunt as a ghost; to ghost-write. **Holy Ghost,** the Third Person of the Trinity. **to give up the ghost,** to die, to expire. **ghost gum,** *n.* a species of eucalyptus of inland Australia having a smooth white trunk. **ghost-moth,** *n.* a nocturnal moth, *Hepialus humuli,* the caterpillars of which wreak havoc on the roots of hop-plants. **ghost-story,** *n.* a tale concerned with the supernatural, esp. one of a terrifying character. **ghost town,** *n.* a deserted or semi-deserted town, as a formerly flourishing mining town. **ghost-word,** *n.* a word having no right to existence, due to the errors of copyists, printers etc. **ghost write,** *v.t., v.i.* to write (a speech etc.) for another. **ghost writer,** *n.* one who writes (speeches etc.) for another who is presumed to be the author. **ghosthood,** *n.* **ghost-like,** *a.* **ghostly,** *a.* pertaining to the spirit or soul, spiritual; pertaining to religious matters; pertaining to ghosts or apparitions; dismal, gloomy. *adv.* spiritually. **ghostliness,** *n.* [OE *gāst* (cp. Dut. *geest,* G *Geist*), prob. cogn. with Icel. *geisa,* to rage, Goth. *usgaisjan,* to terrify]

Ghosts, *n.* a play by Henrik Ibsen, first produced 1881. Mrs Alving hides the profligacy of her late husband. The past catches up with her when her son inherits his father's syphilis and unwittingly plans to marry his half-sister.

ghoul, *n.* an evil spirit supposed, in Eastern tales, to devour human corpses; a person who robs graves; a person interested in morbid things. **ghoulish,** *a.* **ghoulishly,** *adv.* **ghoulishness,** *n.* [Arab. *ghūl*]

GHQ, (*abbr.*) General Headquarters.

ghyll, GILL[2].

GI, *n.* (*pl.* **GIs, GI's**) (*N Am., coll.*) a soldier in the US Army, esp. a private. *a.* (of equipment etc.) conforming to US Army regulations. [abbr. of *government issue*]

giallo antico, *n.* a yellow marble found among ruins of ancient buildings in Italy, used for decoration. [It., antique yellow]

giant, *n.* a mythical being of human form but superhuman size; (*pl.*) in Greek mythology, the offspring of Uranus and Gaea (heaven and earth) who rebelled against the gods; a man of extraordinary size; any person, animal, plant etc. of abnormal size; a person of extraordinary powers, ability etc. *a.* gigantic; like a giant; †enormous, monstrous. **giant-killer,** *n.* in folklore, one who overcomes giants. **giant panda** PANDA. **giant-powder,** *n.* a form of dynamite, consisting of infusorial earth saturated with nitroglycerine. †**giant-rude,** *a.* rough or rude as a giant. **giant star,** *n.* a star of great brightness and a very low mean density. **giantess,** *n. fem.* **gianthood,** *n.* **giantship,** *n.* †**giantish,** *a.* **giantism,** *n.* abnormal development in size esp. as caused by dysfunction of the pituitary gland. **giantlike,** *a.* **giantly,** *a., adv.* **giantry,** *n.* [OF *geant,* L *gigantem,* nom. *gigas,* from Gr. *gigas -antos,* etym. doubtful]

giaour, *n.* an infidel, a name given by the Turks to those who disbelieve in Mohammed, esp. Christians. [Pers. *gāwr*]

Gib., (*abbr.*) Gibraltar.

gib[1], *n.* a cat, esp. a tom-cat; a cat that has been castrated. †**gib-cat,** *n.* a tom-cat. [short for *Gilbert*]

gib[2], JIB[1].

gibber[1], *v.i.* to jabber, to talk rapidly and inarticulately. *n.* talk or noise of this kind. **gibberish,** *n.* inarticulate sounds; unmeaning or unintelligible language, jargon. *a.* unmeaning. [imit.]

gibber[2], *n.* (*Austral.*) a stone; boulder. [Abor.]

gibberellic acid, *n.* a product extracted from the fungus *Gibberella fujikuroi,* used to stimulate plant growth.

gibbet, *n.* an upright post with a crosspiece from which criminals were formerly hanged; a gallows; the gallows, death by hanging; †the projecting arm of a crane. *v.t.* to execute by hanging; to hang or expose on or as on a gibbet; to expose to public contempt and derision. [OF *gibet,* dim. of *gibe,* a staff or club; cp. JIB[1]]

gibbon, *n.* any individual of the genus *Hylobates,* long-armed anthropoid apes from E Asia. [F, prob. from Eng. GIB[1] (conferred by Buffon)]

gibbose GIBBOUS.

gibboso-, *comb. form* gibbous. [see foll.]

gibbous, gibbose, *a.* hunch-backed, humped, crook-backed; protuberant, convex, swelling into inequalities; a term used when the illuminated portion of the moon or of a planet exceeds a semicircle but falls short of a circle; very convex or tumid. **gibbosity,** *n.* **gibbously,** *adv.* [L *gibbōsus,* from *gibbus,* a hump]

gibe, *v.i.* to use sneering or taunting expressions; to rail, to flout, to jeer, to scoff (at). *v.t.* to use sneering or taunting expressions towards; to mock, to taunt, to sneer at. *n.* a sneer, a scoff, a taunt. **giber,** *n.* **gibingly,** *adv.* [etym. doubtful (cp. Icel. *geipa,* to talk nonsense, from *geip,* nonsense; also OF *giber,* to play rude pranks)]

Gibeonite, *n.* one of the inhabitants of Gibeon, condemned for their duplicity to be 'hewers of wood and drawers of water' (Joshua ix.23); a drudge, the lowest of servants. [*Gibeon,* a city in ancient Palestine]

giblets, *n.pl.* the feet, neck, and internal eatable parts of a fowl, such as the heart, liver, gizzard etc., which are removed before cooking. **giblet-pie, -soup,** *n.* pie or soup made with these. [OF *gibelet,* cogn. with *gibier,* game, and *gibelotte,* rabbit-stew]

Gibraltar, *n.* British dependency, situated on a rocky promontory in S Spain. **area** 6.5 sq km/2.5 sq miles. **exports** mainly a trading centre for the import and re-export of goods. **population** (1988) 30,000. **recent history** captured from Spain 1704 by English admiral George Rooke (1650–1709), it was ceded to Britain under the Treaty of Utrecht 1713. A referendum (1967) confirmed the wish of the people to remain in association with the UK, but Spain continues to claim sovereignty, and closed the border (1969–85). In 1989, the UK government announced it would reduce the military garrison by half.

Gibraltar[2], *n.* an impregnable stronghold; a very hard rock-candy. **Gibraltar monkey,** *n.* an African species of monkey, *Inuus ecaudatus,* a colony of which exists on the rock of Gibraltar.

Gibraltar[3], Strait of, strait between N Africa and Spain, with the Rock of Gibraltar on the north side and Jebel Musa on the south, the so-called Pillars of Hercules.

gibus, *n.* a crush-hat, an opera-hat. [name of orig. maker]

gid, *n.* a disease in sheep; sturdy. [short for GIDDY]

giddy, *a.* having a whirling, swimming or dizziness in the head; reeling, tending to stagger or fall; causing this sensation (as a precipice, a dance, success etc.); inconstant, changeable, fickle, flighty; elated, excited, rash. **to play the giddy goat,** to act the fool. **giddy-brained, -headed, -pated,** *a.* frivolous, flighty. †**giddy-head,** *n.* a thoughtless person. **giddy-go-round,** *n.* a round-about or merry-go-round. †**giddy-paced,** *a.* moving irregularly; reeling, wavering in gait. **giddy-up,** *imper.* a command to a horse to make it start moving or go faster. **giddily,** *adv.* **giddiness,** *n.* [OE *gydig,* prob. cogn. with GOD (cp. Gr. *entheos,* possessed by the god)]

Gide, *n.* **André** (1869–1951), French novelist, born in Paris. His work is largely autobiographical and concerned with the themes of self-fulfilment and renunciation. It includes *L'Immoraliste/The Immoralist* (1902), *La Porte étroite/Strait is the Gate* (1909), *Les Caves du Vatican/The Vatican Cellars* (1914), and *Les Faux-monnayeurs/The Counterfeiters* (1926); and an almost lifelong *Journal.* Nobel Prize for Literature (1947).

Gideon, *n.* in the Old Testament, one of the Judges of Israel, who led a small band of Israelite warriors which succeeded in routing an invading Midianite army of overwhelming number in a surprise night attack.

gidgee, *n.* a small Australian tree, *Acacia cambagei,* which gives off a foul smell at the approach of rain. Also, **stinking wattle**.

gie, (*Sc.*) GIVE.

Gielgud, *n.* **John** (1904–), English actor and director. He played many Shakespearean roles, including Hamlet (1929). Film roles include Clarence in *Richard III* (1955) and the butler in *Arthur* (1981, for which he won an Oscar).

gier-eagle, *n.* a bird mentioned in Lev.xi.18 and Deut.xiv.17, probably the Egyptian vulture. [Dut. *gier* (cp. G *Geier*) a vulture, EAGLE]

Gierek, *n.* **Edward** (1913–), Polish Communist politician. He entered the Politburo of the ruling Polish United Workers' Party (PUWP) in 1956 and was party leader (1970–80). His industrialization programme plunged the country heavily into debt and sparked a series of Solidarity-led strikes.

gif, *conj.* if. [Sc., from ME *zif,* IF]

Giffard, *n.* **Henri** (1825–82), French inventor of the first passenger-carrying steerable airship, called a dirigible, built 1852. The hydrogen-filled airship was 45 m/150 ft. long, had a 3 hp steam engine which drove a propeller, and was steered using a sail-like rudder. It flew at a speed of 8 kph/5 mph.

GIFT, (*acronym*) *g*amete *i*ntra-*f*allopian *t*ransfer.

gift, *n.* the act, right, or power of giving; that which is given, a present, a contribution; in law, the voluntary bestowal of property without consideration; a natural quality, talent or endowment; †**an oblation;** †**a bribe.** *v.t.* to bestow or confer; to endow with gifts; to present (with) as a gift. **must not look a gift-horse in the mouth,** must not criticize what one is given for nothing. **the gift of the gab** GAB. **gift-book,** *n.* a book given as a present, or suitable for so giving. **gift-wrap,** *v.t.* to wrap (a gift) in attractive paper. **gifted,** *a.* given, bestowed; largely endowed with intellect, talented. **giftling,** *n.* a gift of trifling value. [from OE or Icel. *Gift* (cp. Dut. and G *gift,* from the verb GIVE]

gig¹, *n.* a fish-spear. [from *fishgig,* earlier *fizgig,* Sp. *fisga,* harpoon]

gig², *n.* a light two-wheeled vehicle drawn by one horse; a light clinker-built boat, 20–28 ft (6–9 m) long, rowed by 4, 6 or 8 alternate oars, usu. reserved for the commanding officer; a somewhat similar boat used on the Thames for racing; a machine for raising a nap on cloth by passing it over rotary cylinders furnished with wire teeth; a frolic, a romp; (*coll.*) a fool, a freak; (*N Am.*) a queerly-dressed person; †fun, merriment; †a whipping-top. **gig-lamps,** *n.pl.* (*dated sl.*) spectacles. **gig-man,** *n.* one who keeps a gig. [orig. a whipping-top (cp. Norw. *giga,* to totter)]

gig³, *n.* (*coll.*) a job, esp. a booking for a musician to perform.

gig⁴, GIGLET.

giga-, *pref.* denoting ten to the ninth power (10^9) as in *gigavolt, gigahertz.*

gigantic, *a.* huge, enormous, giant-like; immense, extraordinary. **gigantean, gigantesque,** *a.* **gigantically,** *adv.* **giganticidal,** *a.* **giganticide,** *n.* **gigantify,** *v.t.* **gigantism,** *n.* GIANTISM under GIANT. [L *gigas -ntis,* GIANT]

giggle, *v.i.* to laugh in a silly or affected manner, to titter; to laugh in a nervous, catchy way, with attempts to restrain oneself. *n.* a laugh of such a kind. **giggler,** *n.* one who giggles. **gigglesome,** *a.* [imit., freq. in form (cp. Dut. *giggelen*)]

giglet, -lot, *n.* a light, giddy girl; a wanton. *a.* fickle, inconstant, wanton. [orig. a wanton woman, prob. cogn. with GIG²]

gig-mill, *n.* a gig or machine for putting a nap on cloth; a mill furnished with such machines.

gigolo, *n.* (*pl.* **-los**) a professional dance-partner or escort; a man who battens on women's favours; a man who is kept by a much older woman. [F sl., a low fellow]

gigot, *n.* a leg of mutton; †a piece, a fragment. **gigot-sleeve,** *n.* a sleeve shaped like a leg of mutton. [F, dim. of *gigue,* a leg]

gigue, *n.* a piece of dance music, usu. in 6/8 time.

Gila monster, *n.* a large poisonous lizard, *Heloderma suspectum,* found in Arizona and New Mexico. [from *Gila,* on Arizona River]

gilbert, *n.* the cgs unit for measuring magneto-motive force. [William *Gilbert,* 1544–1603, Eng. scientist]

Gilbert¹, *n.* **Cass** (1859–1934), US architect, born in Ohio, who became known for his skyscrapers, including the Woolworth Building in New York (1913).

Gilbert², *n.* **Humphrey** (*c.* 1539–83), English soldier and navigator who claimed Newfoundland (landing at St John's) for Elizabeth I in 1583. He died when his ship sank on the return voyage.

Gilbert³, *n.* **Walter** (1932–), US molecular biologist. Gilbert worked on the problem of genetic control, seeking the mechanisms which switch genes on and off. By 1966 he had established the existence of the lac repressor, the molecule which suppressed lactose production. Further work on the sequencing of DNA nucleotides won for Gilbert a share of the 1980 Nobel Chemistry Prize with Frederick Sanger and Paul Berg.

Gilbert⁴, *n.* **William** (1544–1603), scientist and physician to Elizabeth I and (briefly) James I. He studied magnetism and static electricity, deducing that the Earth's magnetic field behaves as if a huge bar magnet joined the North and South poles. His book on magnets, published 1600, is the first printed scientific book based wholly on experimentation and observation.

Gilbert⁵, *n.* **W(illiam) S(chwenk)** (1836–1911), British humorist and dramatist who collaborated with Arthur Sullivan, providing the libretti for their series of light comic operas from 1871; they include *HMS Pinafore* (1878), *The Pirates of Penzance* (1879), and *The Mikado* (1885). **Gilbertian,** *a.* absurdly topsy-turvy.

Gilbert and Ellice Islands, former British colony in the Pacific, known since independence (1978) as Tuvalu and Kiribati.

Gilbert and George, *n.* Gilbert Proesch (1943–) and George Passmore (1942–), English painters and performance artists. They became known in the 1960s for their presentation of themselves as works of art, living sculpture. Their art works make much use of photography.

gild¹, *v.t.* (*past, p.p.* **gilded** or **gilt**) to coat, overlay or wash thinly with gold; to impart a golden colour or appearance to; to make brilliant, to brighten; to give a specious or agreeable appearance to, to gloss over; †to enrich; †to flush or make red with drinking; †to besmear with blood. **Gilded Chamber,** the House of Lords. **gilded youth,** young people of wealth and fashion. **to gild** or **sugar a pill,** to make disagreeable necessity acceptable. **to gild the lily,** to spoil beauty by overembellishing. **gilder¹,** *n.* one whose occupation is to coat articles with gold. **gilding,** *n.* the act, process, or art of overlaying with gold; gilding-metal in leaf, powder, or liquid, for application to any surface; outward decoration, covering, or disguise designed to give a fair appearance to anything. **gilding-metal,** *n.* an alloy of copper, brass and tin. **gilding-size,** *n.* sizing used for cementing gold-leaf on a surface. [OE *gyldan,* in *begyldan,* see GOLD]

gild², GUILD.

Gilded Age, the, in US history, a derogatory term referring to the post-Civil War decades. It borrows the title of an 1873 political satire by Mark Twain and Charles Dudley Warner (1829–1900), which highlights the respectable veneer of public life covering the many scandals of graft and corruption.

gilder¹ GILD¹.

gilder², GUELDER ROSE.

Gilgamesh, *n.* hero of Sumerian, Hittite, Akkadian, and Assyrian legend. The 12 verse 'books' of the *Epic of Gilgamesh* were recorded in a standard version on 12 cuneiform tablets by the Assyrian king Ashurbanipal's scholars in the 7th cent. BC, and the epic itself is older than Homer's *Iliad* by at least 1500 years. One-third mortal and two-thirds divine, Gilgamesh is Lord of the Sumerian city of Uruk. Its incident of the Flood is similar to the Old Testament account.

Gill¹, *n.* a girl, a lass; a sweetheart; ground-ivy; malt liquor flavoured with ground-ivy; a female ferret. **Jack and Gill,** lad and lass. **gill-flirt,** *n.* a wanton girl, a flirt. [short for *Gillian,* F *Juliane,* L *Juliana,* from *Julius*]

Gill², *n.* **Eric** (1882–1940), English sculptor and engraver. He designed the typefaces Perpetua (1925) and Gill Sans (without serifs) (1927), and created monumental stone sculptures with clean, simplified outlines, such as *Prospero and Ariel* (1929–31, on Broadcasting House, London).

gill¹, *n.* (*usu. in pl.*) the organs of respiration or branchiae of fishes and some amphibia; a double row of long slender lamellae, extending, like the teeth of a comb, from the convex side of a branchial arch, and supported by a delicate membrane; hair or leaf-like respiratory processes projecting from the body of some aquatic insects; the vertical lamellae under the cap of fungi; the wattles of a fowl; (*facet.*) the flesh about a person's jaws and chin. **to be, go white** or **green at, around, about the gills,** to be pale in the face because of nausea, fear, exhaustion etc. **gill-cover,** *n.* the external bony covering of a fish's gills. **gill-net,** *n.* a net, usu. set vertically, for entangling fish by the gills. **gill-opening,** *n.* the opening by which the water passes into the gills. **gilled radiator,** *n.* on a motor vehicle, a radiator consisting of tubes with metal fins attached to dissipate heat. [cp. Dan. *giælle,* Swed. *gäl,* also Gr. *cheilos,* lip]

gill², *n.* a deep and narrow ravine, often wooded; a gully or stream-bed on a precipitous hillside. [Icel. *gil*]

gill³, *n.* a liquid-measure, usu. one-fourth of a pint (about 140 cl). [OF *gille, gelle,* low L *gillo, gella*]

gillaroo, *n.* an Irish variety of the common trout, *Salmo fario,* in which the coats of the stomach are said to be thickened by feeding on shellfish. [Ir. *giolla* (cp. GILLIE), *ruadh,* red]

Gillespie, *n.* **Dizzy** (stage name of John Birks Gillespie) (1917–), US jazz trumpeter, together with Charlie Parker the chief creator and exponent of the bebop style.

gillie, ghillie, *n.* (*Sc.*) a Highland man-servant, esp. one who attends a sportsman in fishing or hunting. [Gael. *gille*]

gillion, *n.* in Britain, one thousand million (equivalent to US billion).

gillyflower, *n.* the clove-pink *Dianthus caryophyllus;* also applied to the white stock, *Matthiola incana,* and the wallflower, *Cheiranthus cheiri.* †**gillyvor,** *n.* [earlier *gylofre,* OF *girofle,* late L *caryophyllum,* Gr. *karuophullon* (*karuon,* nut, *phullon,* leaf), ending assim. to FLOWER]

gilpy, *n.* (*Sc.*) a frolicsome young person, male or female. [etym. doubtful]

†**gilravage,** *v.i.* to frolic or gad about; to be riotous or extravagant. *n.* a noisy frolic or merry-making; disorder, confusion. [etym. unknown]

gilt¹, *a.* gilded; adorned with gold or something resembling gold. *n.* gold laid over the surface of a thing, gilding; money, gold; (*pl.*) gilt-edged securities. **gilt-edged,** *a.* having the edges gilded. **gilt-edged securities,** *n.pl.* investments of the most reliable character. **gilt-head,** *n.* a name given to several fishes with golden spots or lines on their heads, including the dorado, the striped tunny or bonito, and the golden wrasse. [GILD¹].

gilt², *n.* a young sow. [N *gyltr*]

gimbal, *n.* (*usu. in pl.*) a form of universal joint for securing free motion in suspension, or for suspending anything, as a lamp, a compass, a chronometer etc., so that it may always retain a horizontal or other required position, or be in equilibrium. [alt. form of GIMMAL, GEMEL]

gimblet, GIMLET.

gimcrack, jimcrack, *n.* †a showy person, a dandy, a fop; a pretty but useless or flimsy article, a gewgaw. *a.* showy but flimsy and worthless. **gimcrackery,** *n.* **gimcracky,** *a.* [etym. doubtful, perh. in first sense from obs. *gim,* JIMP, spruce, and *crack,* a lively boy]

gimlet, *n.* a small boring-tool with a worm or screw for penetrating wood, and a wooden crosspiece for handle. *v.t.* to bore or pierce with a gimlet; to turn round (as an anchor) with a motion like the turning of a gimlet. [OF *guimbelet,* dim.; see WIMBLE]

gimmal, *n.* (*pl.*) a pair or series of interlocking rings, as in machinery, a gimbal; a gemel-ring. **gimmal-bit,** *n.* the double bit of a bridle. [var. of GEMEL]

gimmer, *n.* (*Sc., North.*) a ewe between one and two years old. [Icel. *gymbr*]

gimmick, *n.* a trick, device or oddity of behaviour used to attract extra interest, attention or publicity. [etym. unknown]

gimp¹, *n.* silk, wool, or cotton twist interlaced with wire or coarse cord; a silk fishing-line whipped with thin wire to protect it against injury from the teeth of large fish. *v.t.* to trim or whip with gimp or with fine wire. [etym. doubtful, cp. Dut. *gimp,* F *guimpe*]

†**gimp²,** *v.t.* to jag, to indent, to denticulate. [etym. unknown]

gimp³, JIMP.

gin¹, *n.* an ardent spirit, Geneva. **gin-fizz,** *n.* a drink composed of gin, aerated water, and lemon. **gin-mill,** *n.* (*N Am. sl.*) a tippling shop. **gin-palace,** *n.* a gaudily-decorated public-house or drinking-saloon, esp. one in which spirits are largely sold. **gin rummy,** *n.* a card game. **gin-shop,** *n.* a tavern or drinking saloon where spirits are sold. **gin-sling,** *n.* a cold drink, composed of gin, soda-water, lemon, and sugar. [short for GENEVA²]

gin², *n.* a trap, a snare for small mammals and birds; a portable hoisting-machine usu. having a tripod frame, one leg being movable; a pump worked by a windmill; a machine for hoisting coal, a whin; a machine for separating cotton-fibre from the seeds; †any kind of machine; †an engine of torture. †artifice of any kind. *v.t.* to clean (as cotton) of the seeds by means of a gin; to snare, to entrap. **gin-horse,** *n.* a mill-horse. **gin-house,** *n.* a house where cotton is ginned. **ginning,** *n.* the operation by which cotton is cleared of its seeds. [contraction of OF *engin,* ENGINE]

†**gin³,** *v.i., v.t.* to begin, to commence. [ME *ginnen,* OE *-ginnan* in *onginnan,* to begin etc.]

gin⁴, *n.* (*Austral.*) an Aboriginal woman. [Abor.]

gin⁵, *prep.* (*Sc.*) against. [GAIN²]

gin⁶, *conj.* (*Sc., North.*) if. [prob. conn. with GIF]

gingal, jingall, *n.* an E Indian breech-loading firearm, carrying a ball of 4–8 oz. (110–220 g), and fired from a rest. [Hind. *janjāl*]

ginger, *n.* a plant, *Zingiber officinale,* with a pungent, spicy root-stock; the root-stock of this, either whole or powdered, used in cookery, as a sweetmeat, or in medicine; (*coll.*) a red-haired person; mettle, dash, go. *v.t.* to flavour with ginger; to spirit (up). **preserved ginger,** a conserve or sweetmeat made from the immature root. **gingerade,** *n.* ginger-beer. **ginger-ale,** *n.* an aerated beverage, prepared by dissolving sugar in water, flavouring with ginger or essence of ginger, and colouring with a solution of caramel. **ginger-beer, -pop,** *n.* an effervescing fermented beverage prepared from ginger, white sugar, water and yeast. **ginger-brandy,** *n.* a cordial prepared by steeping bruised ginger in brandy. **ginger-cordial,** *n.* a cordial or liqueur made with raisins, lemon-rind, and ginger and water strengthened with spirits. **ginger-nut,** *n.* a gingerbread-nut. **ginger-snap,** *n.* a crisp ginger-flavoured biscuit. **ginger-wine,** *n.* a wine made by the fermentation of sugar, water and ginger. **gingerous,** *a.* (*coll.*) sandy, carroty (of hair). **gingery,** *a.* spiced with ginger; (*coll.*) red-haired, carroty. [earlier *gingivere,* OE *gingifere,* late L *gingiber,* L *zingiber,* Gr. *zingiberis,* Sansk. *çṛngavera* (*çṛnga,* horn, *vera,* body)]

gingerbread, *n.* a dark-coloured cake made of flour, treacle or molasses, ground ginger and other spices. *a.* showy, tawdry; flimsy and fantastic (in allusion to the fanciful shapes, often gilded, in which gingerbread used to be moulded). **gingerbread-nut,** *n.* a small button-like cake of gingerbread. **gingerbread-tree, -palm,** *n.* the doum-palm; a W African tree, *Parinarium macrophyllum,* with a farinaceous stone-fruit called the **gingerbread-plum, gingerbreadwork,** *n.* work cut or carved in fanciful shapes.

gingerly, *adv.* daintily, fastidiously, cautiously, so as to move without noise or risk of hurting oneself or anything trodden upon. *a.* dainty, fastidious, cautious. **gingerliness,** *n.* [perh. from OF *gensor,* compar. of *gent,* see GENT[2]]

gingham, *n.* a kind of linen or cotton fabric woven of dyed yarn, usu. in stripes or checks. [F *guingan,* Malay *ginggang,* orig. striped]

gingili, *n.* an E Indian herb, *Sesamum indicum,* the seeds of which yield a sweet oil. [Hind. *jingalī,* ult. from Arab. *juljulān*]

ginging, *n.* the lining of a shaft with bricks or masonry. [etym. doubtful]

gingival, *a.* pertaining to the gums. [L *gingīva,* the gum]

gingko, ginkgo, *n.* (*pl.* **-koes, -goes**) a Japanese tree, *Gingko biloba,* with handsome fan-shaped leaves, also called the maidenhair-tree or, in modern Japanese, the i-cho. [Jap. *ginkyo,* from Chin. *yin-hing* (*yin,* silver, *hing,* apricot)]

†gingle, JINGLE.

ginglymus, *n.* a joint admitting only of flexion and extension in one plane, as the elbow. **ginglyform,** *a.* **ginglymate,** *v.i.* to form a hinge. **ginglymoid,** *a.* [Gr. *ginglumos,* hinge]

gink, *n.* (*coll.*) fellow, man, person.

†ginnet, JENNET.

ginning GIN[2].

ginny-, jenny-carriage, *n.* a strong railway car for conveying materials. [prob. from *Jenny,* a form of Janet, see JENNY]

Ginsberg, *n.* **Allen** (1926–), US poet. His *Howl* (1956) was an influential poem of the beat generation, criticizing the materialism of contemporary US society. In the 1960s Ginsberg travelled widely in Asia, and was a key figure in introducing Eastern thought to students of that decade.

ginseng, *n.* one of two herbs belonging to the genus *Arabia* or *Panax,* the root of which has a sharp, aromatic taste, and is highly esteemed as a medicine or tonic by the Chinese and others. [Chin. *jên shên* (*jên,* man, *shên,* meaning doubtful)]

Giolitti, *n.* **Giovanni** (1842–1928), Italian liberal politician, born in Mondovi. He was prime minister in 1892–93, 1903–05, 1906–09, 1911–14, and 1920–21. He opposed Italian intervention in World War I, and pursued a policy of broad coalitions, which proved ineffective in controlling Fascism after 1921.

Giordano, *n.* **Luca** (1632–1705), Italian baroque painter, born in Naples, active in Florence in the 1680s. In 1692 he was summoned to Spain by Charles II, and painted ceilings in the Escorial palace for the next ten years.

Giorgione, *n.* **del Castelfranco** (*c.* 1475–1510), Italian Renaissance painter, active in Venice, probably trained by Giovanni Bellini. His work influenced Titian and other Venetian painters. His subjects are imbued with a sense of mystery and treated with a soft technique reminiscent of Leonardo da Vinci's later works, as in *Tempest* (1504, Accademia, Venice).

Giotto[1], *n.* space probe built by the European Space Agency to study Halley's comet. Launched by an Ariane rocket in July 1985, Giotto passed within 600 km/375 miles of the comet's nucleus on 13 Mar. 1986.

Giotto[2], *n.* **di Bondone** (1267–1337), Italian painter and architect. He broke away from the conventional gothic style of the time, and had an enormous influence on subsequent Italian painting. The interior of the Arena Chapel, Padua, is covered in a fresco cycle (completed by 1306) illustrating the life of Mary and the life of Jesus. He is said to have designed the campanile (bell tower) in Florence. **Giottesque,** *a.* in the style of or after Giotto. *n.* the style established by Giotto and his school.

gip[1], GYP[1,3].

gip[2], *v.t.* to take out the entrails of (as herrings). [etym. unknown]

gippo, *n.* (*pl.* **-pos**) (*offensive*) Egyptian; gypsy. **gippy tummy,** diarrhoea, esp. as afflicting visitors to hot countries.

gipsy, *n.* one of a nomad race (calling themselves Romany), prob. of Hindu extraction, dark in complexion and hair, and speaking a corrupt Sanskrit dialect, who live largely by dealing, fortune-telling etc.; one resembling a gipsy, esp. in dark complexion; an itinerant traveller, wanderer. *v.i.* to picnic or camp out in the open air. **gipsy-bonnet, -hat,** *n.* a bonnet or hat with a large brim or side flaps, often tied down to the side of the head. **gipsy-cart, -van, wagon,** *n.* a large horse-drawn van such as gipsies formerly lived and travelled in from place to place. **gipsy-flower, -rose,** *n.* the scabious. **gipsy moth,** *n.* a moth whose hairy caterpillar is destructive of trees. **gipsy-table,** *n.* a light round table on a tripod made orig. of sticks roughly tied together. **gipsydom, gipsyhood, gipsyism,** *n.* the habits, practices or life of gipsies. **gipsify,** *v.t.* (*usu. in p.p.*). **gipsyish,** *a.* [earlier *gypcian, Egypcien,* OF *Egyptien,* late L *Aegyptiānus,* from L *Aegyptius,* an inhabitant of Egypt]

giraffe, *n.* an African ruminant, *Giraffa camelopardalis,* with an extremely long neck, and two bony excrescences on the head, light fawn in colour with darker spots, formerly called the camelopard. [F (now *girafe*), Sp. *girafa,* Arab. *zarāfah*]

Giraldus Cambrensis, *n.* (*c.* 1146–1220), Welsh historian, born in Pembrokeshire. He was elected bishop of St David's in 1198. He wrote a history of the conquest of Ireland by Henry II, and *Itinerarium Cambriae* (*Journey through Wales,* 1191).

girandole, *n.* a branching chandelier or candlestick; a revolving firework discharging rockets; a rotating jet of water; a pendent jewel, usu. for the ears, with a large set encircled by smaller ones. [F, from It. *girandola,* from *girare,* L *gȳrare,* to turn in a circle, from *gȳrus,* Gr. *guros,* circle]

Girardon, *n.* **François** (1628–1715), French academic sculptor. His *Apollo Tended by Nymphs,* commissioned 1666, is one of several marble groups sculpted for the gardens of Louis XIV's palace at Versailles.

girasol, *n.* a variety of opal with reddish refractions, also called fire-opal. [It. *girasole,* orig. sunflower; *girare,* as prec., *sole,* sun]

Giraudoux, *n.* **(Hippolyte) Jean** (1882–1944), French playwright and novelist, who wrote the plays *Amphitryon 38* (1929) and *La Folle de Chaillot/The Madwoman of Chaillot* (1945), and the novel *Suzanne et la Pacifique/Suzanne and the Pacific* (1921).

gird[1], *v.t.* (*past, p.p.* **girded, girt**) to bind round (usu. the waist) with some flexible band, esp. in order to secure or confine the clothes; to secure (one's clothes) with a girdle, belt etc.; to fasten (a sword on or to) with a girdle or belt; to invest or equip (with); to surround or encircle with or as with a girdle, to encompass, to besiege; †to dress, to clothe. **to gird up**

one's loins, to get ready to do something; to prepare oneself for (vigorous) action. [OE *gyrdan* (cp. Dut. *gorden,* G *gürten*), cogn. with GIRTH, GARDEN, YARD[2]]

gird[2], *v.i.* to sneer, to mock (at). *n.* a sarcasm, a sneer. [etym. unknown]

girder, *n.* a principal beam, esp. a compound structure of iron plates or lattice-work, wood or metal, spanning the distance from wall to wall, or pier to pier, used to support joints, walls, roof, roadway, or other superincumbent weight. **girder bridge,** *n.* a bridge consisting of girders. **girding,** *n.* that which girds; †a girdle; †a covering; (*Sc.*) a saddle-girth.

girdle[1], *n.* a belt, zone or cord for securing a loose garment round or encircling the waist; anything that encircles as a belt or zone; the bones by which the limbs are united to the trunk in vertebrate animals; a small circular band or fillet round the shaft of a column; the line of greatest marginal circumference of a brilliant, at which it is grasped by the setting; (*Bot.*) a zone-like ring on a stem, etc. *v.t.* to gird or surround with or as with a girdle, to surround, to environ; to make a cut round (the trunk of a tree) through the bark, so as to kill it or in some cases to make it fruit better. **girdler,** *n.* one who girdles; a maker of girdles. [OE *gyrdel,* from OE *gyrdan,* to GIRD[1]]

girdle[2], *n.* (*Sc., North.*) a round flat plate of iron hung over a fire for baking cakes. [var. of GRIDDLE]

girkin, GHERKIN.

girl, *n.* a female child, a young and unmarried woman; a maid-servant; a sweetheart; †a roebuck of two years old. **old girl,** a slighting or unceremonious term for an elderly woman, mare etc. **one's best girl,** (*dated coll.*) one's sweetheart. **the girls,** the daughters of a family; girls collectively. **the principal** or **leading girl,** in the theatre, the leading actress, esp. in pantomime and musical comedy. **girl Friday,** *n.* a female secretary and general assistant in an office. **girlfriend,** *n.* a female friend; a regular female companion, esp. one with whom there is a romantic relationship. **girl guide,** *n.* a member of the **Girl Guides,** a Scout organization founded 1910 in the UK by Baden-Powell and his sister Agnes. There are three branches: Brownie Guides (age 7–11); Guides (10–16); Ranger Guides (14–20); and adult leaders – Guiders. The World Association of Girl Guides and Girl Scouts (as they are known in the US) has over 6.5 million members. **girl scout,** *n.* (*N Am.*) GIRL GUIDE. **girlhood,** *n.* **girlie, girly,** *n.* **girlish,** *a.* **girlishly,** *adv.* **girlishness,** *n.* [ME *gerle,* a young person, cp. LG *gör,* a child]

†girlond, GARLAND.

girn, *v.i.* (*now chiefly Sc.*) to grin, to snarl; to be fretful. [var. of GRIN[1]]

girnel, *n.* (*Sc.*) a granary; a large meal-chest. [var. of *garnel,* GARNER]

giro, *n.* (*pl.* **-ros**) in the UK, a system operated by banks and post offices whereby, when the required instructions have been issued, payments can be made by transfers from one account to another. **giro cheque,** *n.* in the UK, a benefit cheque for people who are ill, unemployed etc. that can be cashed at a post office or bank.

Gironde, *n.* in French history, the name given to the right-wing republican party in the French Revolution, so called because a number of their leaders came from the Gironde *département.* They were driven from power by the Jacobins, 1793. **Girondin,** *n.* a member of the Gironde. **Girondist,** *n.* and *a.* [a maritime department in SW France, adjacent to the Bay of Biscay]

girouette, *n.* a weather-cock; a time-serving politician. [F, from *girer,* L *gȳrare,* to revolve, from *gȳrus,* Gr. *guros,* a circle]

girr, *n.* (*Sc.*) a child's hoop; a barrel-hoop. [var. of GIRTH]

girt[1], *a.* girded, bound; of a vessel, moored so taut by cables fixed in opposite directions as to prevent her swinging.

girth, †girt[2], *n.* the band by which a saddle or burden is made fast and kept secure on a horse's back by passing round its belly; a circular bandage or anything that encircles or girds; measure round anything, circumference, waist-measure; a small girder; one of two bands attached to the carriage of a printing press, to run it in and out. *v.t.* to measure the girth of; to measure (a certain amount) in girth; to surround, to encompass; to fit with a girth; to secure with a girth. **girt-line,** *n.* a rope through a block on a lower-mast head used to hoist the rigging. [Icel. *gjörth,* a girdle, cp. Goth. *gairda*]

Giscard d'Estaing, *n.* **Valéry** (1926–), French conservative politician, president (1974–81). He was finance minister to de Gaulle (1962–66) and Pompidou (1969–74). As leader of the Union pour la Démocratie Française, which he formed in 1978, Giscard has sought to project himself as leader of a 'new centre'.

Gish, *n.* **Lillian** (stage name of Lillian de Guiche), (1896–), US film actress, who began her career in silent films. Her most celebrated work was with the American director D.W. Griffith, including *Way Down East* (1920) and *Orphans of the Storm* (1922), playing virtuous heroines. She later made occasional appearances in character roles, as in *The Whales of August* (1987).

gismo, GIZMO.

Gissing, *n.* **George (Robert)** (1857–1903), English writer, dealing with social issues. Among his books are *New Grub Street* (1891) and the autobiographical *Private Papers of Henry Ryecroft* (1903).

gist, *n.* the essence or main point of a question. [OF (F *gît*), it lies, 3rd pers. sing. of *gésir,* L *jacēre,* to lie]

git, *n.* (*sl.*) a contemptible person; a bastard. [alteration of GET[2]]

gitano, *n.* (*fem.* **gitana**) a gipsy. [Sp., ult. from L *Aegyptiānus* (cp. GIPSY)]

gite, *n.* a sleeping-place, a lodging in France, a privately-owned, self-contained, self-catering apartment or cottage available for holiday lets. [F *gîte,* OF *giste,* as GIST]

†gittern, *n.* an instrument like a guitar, a cithern. †*v.i.* to play upon a gittern. [OF *guiterne,* as CITHERN]

giubiloso, *a.* of tempo in music, jubilant. [It.]

Giulini, *n.* **Carlo Maria** (1914–), Italian conductor. Principal conductor at La Scala in Milan, 1953–55, and musical director of the Los Angeles Philharmonic, 1978–84, he is renowned as an interpreter of Verdi.

Giulio, *n.* **Romano** (*c.* 1499–1546), Italian painter and architect. An assistant to Raphael, he soon developed mannerist tendencies, creating effects of exaggerated movement and using rich colours, for example in the Palazzo del Tè (1526, Mantua).

giusto, *a.* of tempo in music, regular; strict, accurate. [It., from L *justus,* JUST]

give[1], *v.t.* (*past* **gave,** *p.p.* **given**) to hand over or transfer the possession of or right to without price or compensation; to bestow, to confer, to present, to render without payment; to grant, to concede, to allow, to put in one's power; to hand over, to deliver; to commit, to consign, to put in one's keeping; to transfer as price or in exchange, to pay, to sell; to return, to render as due; to surrender, to relinquish; to yield up, to devote; to yield as product; to communicate, to impart; to be the source or author of; to occasion, to cause; to offer, to hold out, to show or exhibit; to assign, to suppose, to assume (as conditions or circumstances). *v.i.* to part with freely and gratuitously; to yield as to pressure, to collapse; to move back, to recede; to make way or room; to lead, to open (upon); †to make an attack; †to weep. **give me,** I prefer. **give you good day, even,** or **morrow,** (*ellipt.*) God give you good day etc. **to give and take,** to be fair; to play fair. **to give a dog a bad name** NAME. **to give a miss,** (*coll.*) to avoid. **to give away,** to make over, to transfer; to give in marriage; (*sl.*) to let out or divulge inadvertently. **to give birth to,** to bring forth. **to give back,** to restore; †to retire, to retreat. **to give chase to,** to pursue. **to give ear,** to listen, to pay attention (to). **to give forth,** to publish, to tell. **to give ground** GROUND. **to give in,** to yield. **to give it anyone,** (*coll.*) to punish. **to give it best,** (*Austral.*) to give up hope, to give in without trying further. **to give in marriage,** to permit the marriage of (a daughter). **to give into custody** or **in charge,** to hand over or consign to a police constable etc. **to give it to one,** (*coll.*) to scold, punish severely, beat. **to give of,** to contribute. **to give off,** to emit; †to forbear, to cease. **to give on,** †to rush or fall (on); to afford a prospect on or into, to face. **to give one his head** HEAD. **to give out,** to emit; to publish, to proclaim; to distribute; (*coll.*) to show, to profess; to break down; to run short. **to give over,** to hand over, to transfer; to abandon, to despair of; (*in p.p.*) to devote or addict; to cease (from), to desist; to yield. **to give place,** to give precedence; to yield; to be succeeded by. **to give one's hand,** to espouse, to accept in marriage. **to give place to,** to yield, to retire. **to give rise to,** to occasion, to cause. **to give the lie to** LIE. **to give the sack** or **boot,** (*coll.*) to dismiss, esp. in a summary fashion. **to give tongue,** to bark. **to give up,** to surrender; to resign; to commit; to despair of. **to give way,** to yield, to fail to resist; to make room; to break down; to abandon (oneself to); to be depreciated in value; to begin to row; to row with increased energy. **to give what for,** (*coll.*) WHAT. **give-away,** *n.* (*coll.*) an unintentional revelation; something given free. **given name,** *n.* a baptismal name. **giver,** *n.* [OE *giefan* (cp. Dut. *geven,* Icel. *gefa,* Goth. *giban,* G *geben*)]

give[2], *n.* the state of yielding or giving way; elasticity. **give and take,** mutual concession or forbearance; fair measure on either side. [from prec.]

give[3], GYVE.

gizmo, *n.* (*pl.* **-mos**) (*coll.*) a gadget. **gizmology,** *n.* (*sl.*) technological gadgetry.

gizz, *n.* (*Sc.*) a wig; the face. [etym. unknown]

gizzard, *n.* a strong muscular division of the stomach, esp. the second stomach in birds; a thickened muscular stomach in certain fish, insects and molluscs. **it sticks in one's gizzard,** (*coll.*) it is very disagreeable to one. [ME *giser,* OF *giser, gezier* (F *gésier*), L *gigeria,* pl. cooked entrails of poultry]

gizzen, *v.i.* to shrink and become leaky through dryness; to become dry and wizened. [Sc., from Icel. *gisna*]

Gk., (*abbr.*) Greek.

gl, (*chem. symbol*) glucinum.

gl., (*abbr.*) glass; gloss.

glabella, *n.* the smooth flat area of bone between the eyebrows.

glabrous, *a.* smooth; devoid of hair or pubescence. **glabrate,** *a.* **glabrescent,** *a.*

glacé, *a.* iced, or with a surface or covering like ice (as confectionery); polished, glossy (as leather goods). [F, p.p. of *glacer,* to ice, from *glace,* ice]

glacial, *a.* of or pertaining to ice; due to or like ice, icy; of geological formations, due to or characterized by glaciers, ice-sheets or floating ice; (*Chem.*) crystallizing at ordinary temperatures. **glacial drift,** *n.* gravel, sand, clay and other debris transported or deposited by ice. **glacial period, epoch, era,** *n.* a period during which a large part of the northern hemisphere was covered with an ice-sheet, called also the ice age. **glacialist,** *n.* one who considers that certain geological phenomena are due to the action of ice. **glacially,** *adv.* **glaciate,** *v.t.* (*Geol.*) to scratch, polish or wear down by means of ice; to cover with ice in the form of sheets or glaciers. *v.i.* to be converted into ice. **glaciation,** *n.* the subjection of an area to glacial conditions. [F, from L *glaciālis,* from *glacies,* ice]

glacier, *n.* a stream-like mass of ice, formed by consolidated accumulations of snow at high altitudes, slowly descending to lower regions. **glacier-lake,** *n.* a lake held back temporarily or permanently by a glacier or its deposits. **glacier-mud, -silt,** *n.* mud, sand or pulverized debris formed underneath glaciers and deposited by glacier streams. **glacier-table,** *n.* a block of stone left standing on a pillar of ice which it has sheltered from the sun's rays while all the ice around has melted away. [F, from *glace,* L *glacies,* ice]

glacière, *n.* a natural or artificial cavity in which ice remains unmelted during the summer, esp. an ice-cave, or natural cave containing a small glacier below the snow-line. [F, as prec.]

glacio-, *comb. form* glacial; glacier.

glaciology, *n.* the study of glacial action and its geological effects. **glaciologic, -cal,** *a.* **glaciologist,** *n.*

glaciometer, *n.* an apparatus or device for measuring the rate of movement of glaciers.

glacis, *n.* (*Fort.*) a sloping bank, such as the declivity in front of a rampart, where assailants would be exposed to fire. [F, orig. a slippery place, from OF *glacer,* from *glace,* ice]

glad, *a.* pleased, gratified; indicating pleasure or satisfaction; affording pleasure, joy or satisfaction; bright, gay. †*v.t.* to make glad. *v.i.* to be or become glad. **glad-eye,** *n.* (*coll.*) ogling. **glad hand,** *n.* (*coll.*) a welcome. *v.t.* to welcome, esp. by shaking hands. **gladhanding,** *n.* **gladhander,** *n.* **glad rags,** *n.* (*coll.*) best or smartest clothes; evening dress. **gladden,** *v.t.* to make glad or joyful; to cheer; †*v.i.* to rejoice. †**gladder,** *n.* †**gladful,** *a.* †**gladfully,** *adv.* †**gladfulness,** *n.* **gladly,** *adv.* **gladness,** *n.* **gladsome,** *a.* **gladsomely,** *adv.* **gladsomeness,** *n.*

glade, *n.* an open space in a wood or forest; (*N Am.*) an opening in the ice of rivers or a tract of smooth ice; an everglade. †**gladly,** *a.* [prob. from Scand. (cp. Icel. *glathr,* see prec.)]

gladiate, *a.* in botany, sword-shaped. [as foll.]

gladiator, *n.* in Roman times, a man employed to fight in the amphitheatre; a political combatant; a controversialist. **gladiatorial,** †**-an,** †**gladiatory,** *a.* **gladiatorism,** *n.* the act or practice of fighting as gladiators; prize-fighting. **gladiatorship,** *n.* [L, from *gladius,* a sword]

gladiolus, *n.* (*pl.* **-li**) an iridaceous genus of plants with a fleshy bulb, sword-shaped leaves, and spikes of bright-coloured flowers. Also called **sword lily.** [L, dim. of prec.]

gladius, *n.* the cuttlebone or pen of a cuttlefish. [L, see prec.]

Gladstone, *n.* **William Ewart** (1809–98), British Liberal politician. He entered Parliament as a Tory in 1833 and held ministerial office, but left the party, 1846, and after 1859 identified himself with the Liberals. He was chancellor of the Exchequer (1852–55 and 1859–66), and prime minister (1868–74, 1880–85, 1886, and 1892–94). He introduced elementary education (1870) and vote by secret ballot, 1872, and many reforms in Ireland, although he failed in his efforts to get a Home Rule Bill passed. **gladstone bag,** *n.* a light leather bag with flexible sides, opening along the middle and secured with a clasp and straps. **Gladstonian,** *a.* pertaining to, an adherent of W. E. Gladstone, esp. a supporter of his Home Rule policy.

Glagol, *n.* the earliest Slavonic alphabet, principally used in Istria and Dalmatia, in the offices of the Roman Catholic Church. **Glagolitic,** *a.*

glaik, *n.* (*Sc.*) (*usu. in. pl.*) a trick, a hoax; a childish toy; a flash, a glance of the eye. **glaikit,** *a.* foolish, giddy, flighty. [prob. conn. with GLEEK[2]]

glair, *n.* white of egg, or a preparation made with this, used as size or varnish; any similar viscous, transparent substance. *v.t.* to smear or overlay with glair. **glaireous, glairy,** *a.* **glairine,** *n.* a glairy substance on the surface of some thermal waters. [OF *glaire,* prob. from L *clāra,* fem. of *clārus,* clear, bright]

glaive, *n.* a broadsword, a sword, a falchion; a weapon for foot-soldiers, consisting of a cutting edge fixed to the end of a pole. [OF, from L *gladius,* a sword]

Glamorgan, *n.* three counties of S Wales – Mid, South, and West Glamorgan – created in 1974 from the former county of Glamorganshire.

glamour, (*esp. N Am.*) **glamor,** *n.* the influence of some charm on the vision, causing things to seem different from what they are; magic, enchantment; witching, delusive charm or illusion. **glamour-girl,** *n.* an esp. pretty girl or woman regarded as being particularly attractive to men; a girl or woman who has a job that is regarded as glamorous. **glamorize, -ise,** *v.t.* to make glamorous or seem glamorous. **glamorization, -isation,** *n.* **glamorous,** *a.* [corr. of GRAMMAR, introd. by Scott (cp. GRAMARYE)]

glance, *v.i.* to glide off or from (as a blow); to touch, to allude, to hint (at); to dart or flash a gleam of light or brightness; to give a quick or cursory look (at); to move about rapidly. *v.t.* to shoot or dart swiftly or suddenly; to direct (a look or the eye) rapidly or cursorily; †to hint at, to allude to. *n.* an oblique impact of an object on another causing it to be deflected; in cricket, a hit with the bat turned obliquely to the ball; a flash, a gleam; a quick or transient look, a hurried glimpse (at). **glance-coal,** *n.* anthracite. **glancingly,** *adv.* [prob. from OF *glacier,* to slip, to glide, from *glace,* ice (influenced by ME *glenten,* to glide, to glance, cogn. with OHG *glanz,* bright, clear)]

gland, *n.* an organ secreting certain constituents of the blood, either for extraction and specific use or for elimination as waste products; a cellular organ in plants, usu. secreting oil or aroma; a sleeve employed to press packing tight on or around a piston-rod. **glandule,** *n.* a small gland. **glandular,** *a.* characterized by the presence of a gland or glands; consisting or of the nature of a gland or glands; affecting the glands. **glandular fever,** *n.* an infectious disease characterized by the swelling of the lymph nodes. **glandularly,** *adv.* †**glandulation,** *n.* the arrangement and structure of the glandules in plants. **glanduliferous,** *a.* **glandulose,** (*Bot.*), **glandulous,** (*physiol.*) *a.* **glandless,** *a.* [F *glande,* OF *glandre,* L *glandula,* dim. of *glans -ndis,* acorn]

glanders, *n.pl.* a very dangerous and contagious disease in horses, attended with a running of corrupt matter from the nostrils, and enlargement and induration of the glands of the lower jaw. **glandered,** *a.* **glanderous,** *a.* [from OF *glandre,* as prec.]

glandiferous, *a.* bearing acorns or other nut-like fruits. **glandiform,** *a.* having the form of an acorn; in physiology, resembling a gland. [L *glandifer* (*glans -ndis,* see GLAND)]

glandule GLAND.

glans, *n.* the nut-like fruit of some forest trees; an acorn, a beech-nut, a chestnut etc.; a structure of somewhat similar form, as the extremity of the penis; a strumous swelling. [GLAND]

glar, glaur, *n.* (*Sc.*) slime, mud. *v.t.* to make muddy. [etym. doubtful]

glare, *v.i.* to shine with a dazzling or overpowering light; to look with fierce, piercing eyes, to stare; to be obtrusively overdressed or gaudy; to be very conspicuous. *v.t.* to shoot or dart forth in or as in intense lustre. *n.* a fierce overpowering light, disagreeable brightness; tawdry splendour; an intense, fierce look or stare. **glaring,** *a.* shining with dazzling brightness; staring; too conspicuous or overcoloured; notorious, barefaced, infamous. **glaringly,** *adv.* **glaringness,** *n.* **glary,** *a.* of dazzling brightness. [prob. cogn. with GLASS, cp. OE *gloer,* a transparent substance]

glareous GLAIR.

Glaser, *n.* **Donald Arthur** (1926–), US physicist, who invented the bubble chamber in 1952, for which he received the Nobel prize in 1960.

Glasgow, *n.* city and administrative headquarters of Strathclyde, Scotland; population (1985) 734,000. Industries include engineering, chemicals, printing, and distilling.

Glashow, *n.* **Sheldon** (1933–), US theoretical physicist. He shared the 1979 Nobel Prize for Physics with Abdus Salam and Steven Weinberg for their work demonstrating that weak nuclear force and the electromagnetic force are both aspects of a single force, now called electroweak force. He also introduced the idea of charm in particle physics.

glasnost, *n.* esp. of the USSR government under Mikhail Gorbachev, a willingness to be more open and accountable. [Rus., frankness]

glass, *n.* (*pl.* **-es**) a hard, brittle, transparent substance, formed by fusing together mixtures of the silicates of potash, soda, lime, magnesia, alumina and lead in various proportions, according to the quality or kind required; a substance of vitreous structure or composition; an article made of glass; a mirror, a looking-glass; a drinking-vessel of glass; the quantity which such vessel will hold; a lens; an optical instrument composed partly of glass, an eye-glass, a telescope; a sand-glass, an hour-glass; an instrument for indicating atmospheric changes, a barometer; a thermometer; a window-pane; a carriage window; (*pl.*) a pair of spectacles; (*collect.*) ornaments or utensils made of glass, greenhouses, windows. *v.t.* to mirror, to reflect (oneself or itself) in or as in a glass; to case in glass; to fit or cover with or as with glass, to glaze; to make (the eye) glassy. **glass-blower,** *n.* one whose business is to blow and mould glass. **glass-blowing,** *n.* the art or process of shaping molten or softened glass into vessels. **glass case,** *n.* a case or shallow box having a glass lid or sides to show the contents. **glasscloth,** *n.* a cloth for wiping and cleaning glasses; cloth covered with powdered glass, like sand-paper; a fabric woven of fine-spun glass threads. **glass-coach,** *n.* a kind of carriage with glass windows instead of curtains, a superior kind of hackney carriage. **glass-crab,** *n.* the flat, transparent larva of a shrimp, formerly regarded as a distinct genus. **glass-culture,** *n.* the cultivation of plants under glass. **glass-cutter,** *n.* a worker or a tool that cuts glass. **glass-cutting,** *n.* the art or process of cutting, grinding and polishing glass-ware. **glass-dust,** *n.* powdered glass used for grinding and polishing. **glass eye,** *n.* an artificial eye of glass; a species of blindness in horses; a Jamaican thrush, *Turdus jamaicensis;* (*pl.*) (*dated coll.*) a person wearing spectacles. †**glass-faced,** *a.* reflecting, like a mirror, the looks of another. **glass-furnace,** *n.* a furnace in which the materials of glass are fused. †**glass-gazing,** *a.* often contemplating oneself in a mirror. **glass-grinding,** *n.* glass-cutting. **glass-house,** *n.* a house or building where glass is made; a greenhouse or conservatory; a glass-roofed photographic studio; (*sl.*) a military prison. **to live in glass houses,** to be susceptible to criticism through one's pursuits or opinions. **glass jaw,** *n.* esp. in boxing, a jaw that is particularly susceptible to injury. †**glass-man,** *n.* one who deals in glass-ware; a glass-maker. **glass-metal,** *n.* glass in fusion in the pot. **glass-painting,** *n.* the art of painting designs on glass with colours which are burnt in. **glass-paper,** *n.* paper covered with finely-powdered glass used for rubbing down and smoothing rough surfaces of wood etc. **glass-pot,** *n.* the pot or crucible in which the material for glass-making is fused. **glass-reinforced plastic,** usu. known as fibreglass, but only strengthened by glass fibres, the rest being plastic. Now a favoured material for boat hulls and the bodies and some structural components of performance cars; it is also used in saloon car-body manufacture. **glass-snake,** *n.* an American lizard without limbs, *Ophisaurus ventralis.* **glass-soap,** *n.* oxide of manganese and other substances used in the manufacture of glass to remove colour due to ferrous salts etc. **glass-stainer,** *n.* **glass-staining,** *n.* the art or process of colouring glass during manufacture. **glass-ware,** *n.* (*collect.*) articles made of glass. **glass-work,** *n.* glass manufacture; glass-ware. **glass-worker,** *n.* **glass-works,** *n.* a place or building where glass is manufactured. **glasswort,** *n.* one of various maritime herbs containing alkali formerly used in glass-making. **glassful,** *n.* as much as a glass will hold. **glassless,** *a.* **glass-like,** *a.* **glassy,** *a.* like glass, vitreous; lustrous, smooth, mirror-like (of water); hard, dull, lacking fire, fixed (of the eye). **glassily,** *adv.* **glassiness,** *n.* [OE *glæs* (cp. Dut. *glas,* Icel. *gler,* G *glas,* perh. from Teut. root rel. to OE *glōwan,* to GLOW)]

Glass, *n.* **Philip** (1937–), US composer. As a student of Nadia Boulanger, he was strongly influenced by Indian music; his work is characterized by repeated rhythmic figures that are continually expanded and modified. His compositions include the operas *Einstein on the Beach* (1975), *Akhnaten* (1984), and *The Making of the Representative for Planet 8* (1988).

Glasse, *n.* **Hannah** (1708–70), British cookery writer whose *The Art of Cookery made Plain and Easy* (1747) is regarded as the first classic recipe book in Britain.

Glassite, *n.* a name sometimes given to the Sandemanians. [John *Glass,* 1695–1773, minister of the Church of Scotland, deposed for his 'Testimony of the King of the Martyrs' (1727), maintaining that a congregation is subject to no jurisdiction but that of Christ]

Glastonbury, *a.* pertaining to Glastonbury. **Glastonbury chair,** *n.* an 'antique' arm-chair modelled upon the former Abbot's chair preserved at Wells. **Glastonbury thorn,** *n.* a variety of *Crataegus* or hawthorn flowering on old Christmas Day, said to have sprung from the staff of Joseph of Arimathaea planted at Glastonbury. [town in Somerset, the seat of a celebrated abbey, now in ruins]

Glaswegian, *n.* a native or inhabitant of Glasgow in Scotland. [mod. L *Glaswegiānus,* from *Glasgow*]

Glauber, *n.* **Johann** (1604–68), German chemist. Glauber, who made his living selling patent medicines, is remembered for his discovery of the salt known variously as 'sal mirabile' and 'Glauber's salt'. **Glauber's salt,** *n.* in chemistry, crystalline sodium sulphate decahydrate $Na_2SO_4.10H_2O$, which melts at 31°C; the latent heat stored as it solidifies makes it a convenient thermal energy store. It is used in medicine. **glauberite,** *n.* a yellow, grey or brick-red mineral, composed of sulphate of soda and sulphate of lime.

glaucescent, *a.* tending to become or becoming glaucous. **glaucescence,** *n.* [L *glaucus*]

glaucoma, *n.* a disease of the eye, causing opacity in the crystalline humour, tension of the globe, dimness and ultimately loss of vision. **glaucomatous,** *a.* **glaucosis,** *n.* [Gr., from *glaukos*]

glauconite, *n.* an amorphous green hydrous silicate of iron, potassium etc. [G *Glauconit,* from Gr. *glaukon,* neut. of *glaukos,* as foll.]

glaucous, *a.* sea-green, pale greyish-blue; in botany, covered with a bloom or down of this tinge (as grapes). [L *glaucus,* Gr. *glaukos*]

glaucus, *n.* (*Zool.*) a genus of nudibranchiate gasteropods found floating on seaweed in the Atlantic and Pacific; the burgomaster gull, *Larus glaucus.* [L, some kind of fish, as prec.]

glaum, *v.i.* (*Sc.*) to grasp or snatch (at). [etym. doubtful]

glaur GLAR.

glaux, *n.* a genus of plants belonging to the Primulaceae, with one species, *Glaux maritima,* the sea-milkwort. [Gr., from *glax,* a milky plant]

glave, GLAIVE.

glaze, *v.t.* to furnish, fit or cover with glass; to fit with a sheet or panes of glass; to furnish with windows; to overlay (pottery) with a vitreous substance; to cover (a surface) with a thin glossy coating; to make smooth and glossy; †to cover (the eyes) with a film. *v.i.* to become glassy (as the eyes). *n.* a smooth, lustrous coating; such a coating, formed of various substances, used to glaze earthenware, pictures, paper, confectionery etc. **double-glazing** DOUBLE. **glaze-kiln,** *n.* a kiln in which glazed biscuit-ware is placed for firing. **glazed,** *a.* having been glazed; esp. of a person's expression, vacant, bored. **glazer,** *n.* one who glazes earthenware; a wheel for grinding or polishing cutlery; a calico-smoothing wheel; †a glazier. **glazier,** *n.* one whose business it is to set glass in windows etc. **glazier's diamond,** *n.* a small diamond fixed on a handle, used by glaziers for cutting glass. **glaziery,** *n.* **glazing,** *n.* the act or process of setting glass in window-sashes, picture-frames etc.; covering with a glaze, or giving a glazed or glossy surface to pottery and other articles; the material used for this; glass-work; glazed-windows; the process of applying semi-transparent colours thinly over other colours to tone down asperities. **glazy,** *a.* [ME *glasen,* from OE *glœs,* GLASS]

gld, (*abbr.*) guilder.

gleam, *n.* a flash, a beam, a ray, esp. one of a faint or transient kind. *v.i.* to send out rays of a quick and transient kind; to shine, to glitter. **gleamingly,** *adv.* **gleamy,** *a.*

glean, *v.t.* to gather (ears of corn which have been passed over on the cornfield); to gather ears of corn from; to collect bit by bit, to pick up here and there; †to strip, so as to leave nothing behind. *v.i.* to gather the ears of corn left on the ground. †*n.* a collection or sheaf, as of corn, obtained by gleaning. **gleaner,** *n.* **gleaning,** *n.* **gleanings,** *n.* [OF *glener* (F *glaner*), etym. doubtful]

glebe, *n.* †land, soil, ground; †a piece of cultivated ground; the land furnishing part of the revenue of an ecclesiastical benefice; (*Mining*) land containing ore; †a lump, mass or clod of earth, ore etc. **glebe-house,** *n.* a parsonage-house. **glebe-land,** *n.* **glebeless,** *a.* †**glebous,** †**gleby,** *a.* abounding in clods; fertile, rich. [OF, from L *glēba,* a clod of earth, the soil]

glede, *n.* (*Sc., North.*) the kite, *Milvus regalis.* [OE *glida,* cogn. with GLIDE]

gledge, *v.i.* (*Sc.*) to squint; to look slyly. *n.* a sly or cunning look. [cp. GLEE[2], GLEY]

glee[1], *n.* joy, mirth, gladness, delight; a musical composition for several voices in harmony, consisting usu. of two or more contrasted movements and without instrumental accompaniment; †music, minstrelsy. **glee-craft,** *n.* minstrelsy. †**glee-maiden, -woman,** *n.* a female singer. †**gleeman,** *n.* a minstrel or singer. **gleeful,** *a.* merry, gay, joyous. **gleefully,** *adv.* [OE *glēo, glīw* (cp. Icel. *glȳ*)]

glee[2], gley, *v.i.* (*Sc., North.*) to squint, to have a cast in the eye. *n.* a squint; a side-look. [etym. doubtful]

gleed, *n.* a burning coal, an ember; a fire. [OE *glēd,* cogn. with GLOW]

gleek[1], *n.* a game of cards played by three persons; a set of three court-cards of the same rank; hence, three of the same sort of thing. [OF *glic,* prob. from MDut. *ghelic* (Dut. *gelijk*), cogn. with LIKE]

†**gleek[2],** *n.* a scoff, a jest; an enticing glance. *v.i.* to mock, to scoff. *v.t.* to trick, to take in. [etym. doubtful]

gleet, *n.* a purulent discharge from the urethra, a morbid discharge from a sore, ulcer etc.; †slime, filth. *v.i.* to discharge humour; †to ooze, to flow slowly. **gleety,** *a.* [OF *glette,* slime, filth]

gleg, *a.* (*Sc.*) quick, sharp, alert, clever; lively; sharp-edged, keen. **glegly,** *adv.* **glegness,** *n.* [Icel. *glegger,* cogn. with OE *glēaw,* sagacious, wise]

glen, *n.* a narrow valley, a dale. [Gael. *gleann* (cp. W *glyn*)]

Glendoveer, *n.* a beautiful and beneficent spirit in Southey's poems dealing with Hindu myth. [altered from the F adaptation *grandouver,* prob. from Sansk. *gandharva*]

Glendower, *n.* **Owen** (*c.* 1359–1415), Welsh leader of a revolt against the English in N Wales, who defeated Henry IV in three campaigns (1400–02), although Wales was reconquered during 1405–13. **Sons of Glendower,** (Meibion Glyndwr) anonymous group, taking its name from Owen Glendower, active from 1979 against England's treatment of Wales as a colonial possession. Houses owned by English people in the Principality and offices of estate agents dealing in them are targets for arson or bombing. The Welsh language Society also campaigns openly and peaceably with the slogan Nid yw Cymru Ar Werth

glene, *n.* the ball or pupil of the eye; a small socket or cavity in a bone receiving a condyle to form a joint. **glenoid,** *a.* **glenoid cavity,** *n.* **glenoidal,** *a.* [Gr.]

glengarry, *n.* a woollen cap, high in front with ribbons hanging down behind, worn by some Highland regiments; also called **glengarry bonnet.** [valley in Scotland]

Glenn, *n.* **John (Herschel)** (1921–), US astronaut and politician. On 20 Feb. 1962, he became the first American to orbit the Earth, three times in the Mercury spacecraft Friendship 7, in a flight lasting 4 hr 55 min. After retiring from NASA, he became a senator for Ohio (1974 and 1980), and unsuccessfully sought the Democratic presidential nomination in 1984.

gliadin, *n.* gluten. [F *gliadine,* from Gr. *glia,* glue]

glib[1], *a.* smooth, slippery; moving easily; off-hand; voluble, fluent, not very weighty or sincere. †*adv.* glibly. **glibly,** *adv.* **glibness,** *n.* [prob. imit. (cp. Dut. *glibberig,* slippery)]

†**glib**[2], *n.* a long lock of hair; a thick mass of bushy hair hanging over the brows. [Ir.]

glide, *v.i.* to move smoothly and gently; to slip or slide along, as on a smooth surface; to pass rapidly, smoothly, and easily; to pass imperceptibly (away); (*Mus.*) to pass from tone to tone without a perceptible break; (*Aviat.*) to fly an engineless heavier-than-air aeroplane which is catapulted or launched from a height, and makes use of rising air currents. *n.* the act of gliding; (*Mus.*) a passage from one tone to another without a break; (*Phon.*) a continuous sound produced in passing from one position of the organs of speech to another. **glide path,** *n.* the path followed by an aircraft as it descends to a landing. **glider,** *n.* one who or that which glides; a heavier-than-air flying-machine with no motive power. **gliding,** *n.* the art or sport of piloting such an aircraft. **glidingly,** *adv.* [OE *glīdan* (cp. Dut. *glijden,* G *gleiten*)]

gliff, *n.* (*Sc.*) a glimpse; a moment; a fright, scare. [etym. doubtful]

glim, *n.* †brightness; (*sl.*) a light, a candle etc. **douse the glim** DOUSE[1]. [orig. obscure, cogn. with GLEAM and GLIMPSE]

glimmer, *v.i.* to emit a faint or feeble light; to shine faintly. *n.* a faint, uncertain or unsteady light; a faint gleam, an uncertain sign (as of intelligence etc.); a glimpse; (*sl., pl.*) the eyes. **glimmering,** *n.* a glimmer, a twinkle; a faint gleam (as of knowledge, sense etc.); an inkling, a glimpse. **glimmeringly,** *adv.* [as prec.]

glimpse, *n.* a momentary look, a rapid and imperfect view (of); a passing gleam, a faint and transient appearance; †a faint resemblance, a slight tinge. *v.t.* to catch a glimpse of; to see for an instant. *v.i.* to appear for an instant; to glance (at); to appear faintly, to glimmer. **glimpsing,** *n.* a glimpse. [ME *glimsen,* as prec.]

Glinka, *n.* **Mikhail Ivanovich** (1804–57), Russian composer. He broke away from the prevailing Italian influence and turned to Russian folk music as the inspiration for his opera *A Life for the Tsar* (originally *Ivan Susanin*) 1836. His later works include another opera, *Ruslan and Lyudmila* (1842), and the orchestral *Kamarinskaya* (1848).

glint, *v.i.* to gleam, to flash; to glitter, to sparkle; †to glance aside. *v.t.* to reflect, to flash back. *n.* a gleam, a flash, a sparkle; †a glimpse. [prob. from the earlier *glent,* ME *glenten,* cogn. with G *glänzen,* to make bright, from *Glanz,* brightness]

glisk, *n.* (*Sc.*) a glimpse, a gleam, a glint. [prob. cogn. with GLITTER]

glissade, *n.* a method of sliding down a steep snow-slope, usu. with an ice-axe or alpenstock held as rudder and support; a gliding step. *v.i.* to slide down a steep snow-slope in this manner. [F, from *glisser,* to slip or slide. OF *glier,* from Teut. (cp. G *gleiten,* GLIDE)]

glissando, *n., a.* (*pl.* **-dos**) (of) a rapid sliding of the finger(s) up and down the musical scale. [F from *glisser,* slide]

glist, *n.* a gleam or glitter; †mica. [shortened form of foll.]

glisten, *v.i.* to gleam, to sparkle, usu. by reflection. *n.* a glitter or sparkle, esp. by reflection; a gleam. **glistening,** *a.* **glisteningly,** *adv.* [ME *glistnen,* OE *glisnian,* from *glisian,* to shine]

†**glister,** *v.i.* to glitter, to sparkle. *n.* glitter, lustre, brightness. †**glisteringly,** *adv.* [ME *glisteren,* OE *glisian,* as prec.]

glitch, *n.* (*sl.*) an extraneous electric current or false signal, esp. one that disrupts the smooth operation of a system; malfunction. [prob. from G *glitschen,* to slip]

glitter, *v.i.* to gleam, sparkle; to shine with a succession of brilliant gleams or flashes; to be brilliant, showy or specious. *n.* a bright sparkling light; brilliancy, splendour; speciousness, attractiveness; tiny glittering particles used for decoration. **glitterati,** *n. pl.* (*sl.*) fashionable people, as media personalities, artists, jet-setters etc., as a social group. **glitteringly,** *adv.* **glittery,** *a.* [Icel. *glitra,* freq. of *glita* (cogn. with G *gleissen,* OE *glitenian*), from Teut. *glis,* to shine]

glitz, *n.* (*coll.*) ostentation, conspicuous showiness. *v.i.* to dress in a showy ostentatious way. **glitzy,** *a.* (*coll.*) [*gl*amour and R*itz* perh. influ. by G *Glitzern,* glitter]

gloaming, *n.* evening twilight. **gloam,** *v.i.* to begin to grow dark; to be sullen or threatening. *n.* gloaming. [OE *glōmung,* cogn. with GLOW]

gloat, *v.i.* to look or dwell (on or over) with exultant feelings of malignity, lust or avarice. **gloatingly,** *adv.* [cp. Icel. *glotta,* to grin, G *glotzen,* to stare]

glob, *n.* a rounded lump of something soft, dollop. [perh. blend of BLOB and GLOBE]

global, globate GLOBE.

globe, *n.* a ball, a sphere, a round or spherical body; the earth; a sphere on which are represented the heavenly bodies (called a **celestial globe**), or representing the land and sea, and usu. the political divisions of the world (called a **terrestrial globe**); anything of a globular or nearly globular shape; an orb borne as emblem of sovereignty; an almost spherical vessel, as an aquarium, lampshade etc.; the eyeball; (*Austral.*) an electric light bulb. †a body of men etc. drawn up in a circle. *v.t.* to form into a globe. *v.i.* to become globular. **globe-amaranth,** *n.* the tropical genus *Gomphrena* of the amaranth family, esp. *G. globosa.* **globe artichoke,** *n.* a type of artichoke *Cynara scolymus,* cultivated for food. **globe-fish,** *n.* a fish having the power of inflating the skin till it becomes nearly globular. **globe-flower,** *n.* the ranunculaceous genus *Trollius,* esp. the British *T. europaeus,* with yellow, almost spherical flowers. **globe-lightning,** *n.* a fire-ball. **globe-thistle,** *n.* various species of *Echinops,* a thistle-like genus of composite plants belonging to the aster family. **globe-trotter,** *n.* a traveller who hurries from place to place sight-seeing or who visits many foreign countries. **globe-trotting,** *n., a.* **globe-valve,** *n.* in plumbing, a ball-valve; one of spherical shape, usu. operated by a screw stem; a valve enclosed in a globular chamber. **global,** *a.* relating to the globe as an entirety; world-wide; taking in entire groups of classes; across-the-board. **global village,** *n.* the world viewed as an integrated system, esp. as linked by means of instant (mass) communication. **globate, -bated,** *a.* spherical, spheroidal. **globalism,** *n.* **globalize, -ise,** *v.t.* to make global in scope or application. **globalization, -isation,** *n.* **globally,** *adv.* **globigerina,** *n.* (*pl.* **-nae**) a genus of Foraminifera, with a many-chambered shell. **globigerina mud,** or **ooze,** *n.* a light-coloured calcareous mud or ooze in places in the ocean 3000 fathoms (5500 m) deep, consisting of shells of globigerinae. **globoid,** *a.* like a globe in shape. *n.* a globular granule or concretion of mineral matter found in aleuron. **globose,** *a.* spherical, globular. **globosity,** *n.* [L *globātus,* p.p. of *globāre,* to make into a ball; *globōsus,* spherical, (OF *globe*) from *globus*]

Globe Theatre, *n.* a London theatre, octagonal and open to the sky, near Bankside, Southwark, where many of Shakespeare's plays were performed by Richard Burbage and his company. Built 1599 by Cuthbert Burbage, it was burned down in 1613 after a cannon, fired during a performance of *Henry VIII,* set light to the thatch. It was rebuilt in 1614 but pulled down in 1644. The site was rediscovered Oct. 1989 near the remains of the contemporary Rose Theatre.

globin, *n.* a colourless protein of the blood. [L *globus,* a globe]

globoid GLOBE.

globose GLOBE.

globule, *n.* a particle of matter in the form of a small globe; a minute drop or pill; a blood-corpuscle. **globular,** *a.* having the shape of a small globe or sphere; composed of globules. **globular chart,** *n.* a chart on a globular projection. **globular projection,** *n.* a kind of projection in which the eye is supposed to look from the distance of half the chord of 90°.

globular sailing, *n.* the sailing from one point to another over an arc of a great circle, or the shortest distance between any two points. **globularity,** *n.* shaped like a globe or globule. **globularly,** *adv.* **globularness,** *n.* **globuliferous,** *a.* producing, containing or having globules. **globulin,** *n.* an albuminous protein or class of proteins obtained from animals and plants; such a compound obtained from the crystalline lens of the eye, the blood etc.; the amylaceous granules in the cells of plants. **globulism,** *n.* a contemptuous term sometimes applied to homoeopathy. **globulist,** *n.* **globulite,** *n.* a minute globular body representing the most rudimentary stage in the formation of crystals. **globulous,** *a.* [F, from L *globulus,* dim. of *globus,* GLOBE]

glochidiate, *a.* (*Bot.*) barbed (of hairs etc.). **glochidium,** *n.* (*pl.* **-dia**). [Gr. *glōchidion,* dim. of *glochis,* arrow-point]

glockenspiel, *n.* an instrument consisting of hanging metal bars or tubes, to be struck with a hammer. [G, play of bells]

glom, *v.t.* (*sl., esp. N Am.*) to snatch, seize; to steal. **to glom onto,** to take possession of; to grab hold of. [etym. doubtful; perh. Sc. *glaum,* to snatch]

glome, *n.* a roundish head of flowers, a glomerule. †**glomerous,** *a.* **glomerule,** *n.* in botany, a flower-cluster forming a compact head; in anatomy, a convoluted mass of blood-vessels, tissues etc. **glomerulate,** *a.* [L *glomus,* a ball]

glomerate, *v.t.* to gather into a ball or sphere. *v.i.* to gather or come together into a mass. *a.,* in anatomy, compactly clustered (as glands, vessels etc.); in botany, congregated into a head. **glomeration,** *n.* [L *glomerātus,* p.p. of *glomerāre,* from prec.]

glomerous, glomerule GLOME.

gloom, *v.i.* to appear obscurely or dimly; to look dismal, sullen or frowning; to lour, to be, become cloudy or dark. *v.t.* to fill or cover with darkness or obscurity; to render dark, sullen, or dismal. *n.* obscurity, partial darkness; depression, dejection, melancholy; circumstances that occasion melancholy or despondency; †a dark or dismal place. **gloomful,** *a.* **gloomfully,** *adv.* †**glooming,** *a.* dismal, gloomy, depressing. *n.* the gloaming. **gloomy,** *a.* dark, obscure; louring, sad, melancholy, dispiriting; sullen, morose, threatening. **gloomily,** *adv.* **gloominess,** *n.* [ME *gloumen,* to lour, cogn. with GLUM]

gloria[1], *n.* (*pl.* **-as**) a halo. [L]

gloria[2], *n.* (*pl.* **-as**) a song or versicle of praise, forming part of the English Church service or the Mass; a doxology; the music to which one of these, esp. the *Gloria in excelsis,* is sung. **Gloria in excelsis,** the Greater Doxology or hymn beginning 'Glory to God in the highest'. **Gloria Patri,** the Lesser Doxology or response beginning 'Glory be to the Father'. **Gloria Tibi,** the sentence 'Glory be to Thee, O Lord'. [L, glory]

glorify, *v.t.* to magnify, to make glorious, to pay honour and glory to in worship, to praise, to extol; to exalt to celestial glory; to make splendid, to beautify; to trick out with resplendent qualities. **glorifiable,** *a.* **glorification,** *n.* **glorifier,** *n.* [F *glorifier,* L *glōrificāre* (*gloria,* GLORY, *-ficāre,* to make)]

gloriole, *n.* a glory, halo or nimbus. [F, from L *glōriola,* dim. of *glōria,* GLORY]

glory, *n.* high honour, honourable distinction; fame, renown; an occasion of praise, a subject for pride or boasting; illustriousness, splendour of estate, magnificence, grandeur; brilliance, effulgence, splendour; a state of exaltation; adoration or praise ascribed in worship; the divine presence or its manifestations; the felicity of heaven; a combination of the nimbus and aureola; a halo; †arrogance, vainglory, †ambition. *v.i.* to boast, to feel pride, to exult. †*v.t.* to glorify. **crowning glory,** *n.* something that is esp. distinctive or worthy of praise. **in glory,** enjoying the felicity of heaven. **in (all) his glory,** (*coll.*) in full enjoyment of his doings, idiosyncrasies etc. **to glory in,** to be proud of. **morning glory** MORNING. **glory be!,** *int.* an exclamation expressing surprise. **glory box,** *n.* (*Austral.*) a box, chest etc. in which a young woman stores her trousseau etc., bottom drawer. **glory flower, glory pea,** *n.* an evergreen N Zealand tree of the papilionaceous genus *Clianthus,* also known as the parrot-bill or kaka-beak. **glory-hole,** *n.* (*coll.*) a room, cupboard etc. where rubbish and odds and ends have been stowed away anyhow; an opening through which one can look into the interior of a furnace. **gloryingly,** *adv.* †**gloryless,** *a.* **glorious,** *a.* full of glory, illustrious; worthy of admiration or praise; entitling one to fame or honour; splendid, magnificent; (*coll.*) hilarious, uproarious; very amusing; completely satisfactory. **gloriously,** *adv.* **gloriousness,** *n.* [OF *glorie* (F *gloire*), L *glōria*]

glose, GLOZE.

gloss[1], *n.* an explanatory word or note in the margin or between the lines of a book, as an explanation of a foreign or strange word; a comment, interpretation or explanation; a superficial or misleading interpretation etc.; a glossary, translation, or commentary. *v.t.* to explain by note or comment; to annotate; to comment upon, esp. in a censorious way. *v.i.* to make comments, to annotate, to write glosses. **glossator, glosser,** †**-ist,** *n.* a writer of glosses. [ME and OF *glose,* med. L *glosa,* L and Gr. *glōssa,* the tongue, a word requiring explanation]

gloss[2], *n.* the brightness or lustre from a polished surface; polish, sheen; a specious or deceptive outward appearance. *v.t.* to make glossy or lustrous; to render specious or plausible. **to gloss over,** to palliate, to excuse. **gloss paint,** *n.* paint containing a varnish that gives it a shiny finish. **glosser,** *n.* one who puts a gloss on. **glossing,** *n.* the steaming, drying and twisting of silk thread, so as to develop a gloss. **glossy,** *a.* having a smooth, lustrous surface. **glossy magazine,** *n.* magazine printed on glossy paper with many colour illustrations. **glossily,** *adv.* **glossiness,** *n.* [prob. from Scand. (cp. Icel. *glossi,* a blaze, Norw. *glosa,* to glow)]

gloss, (*abbr.*) glossary.

glossa, *n.* (*pl.* **-sae, -sas**) tongue. glossal, *a.* of or pertaining to the tongue, lingual. **glossic,** *a.* a phonetic system of writing English. **glossitis,** *n.* an inflammation of the tongue. [Gr. *glōssa,* tongue]

glossary, *n.* a list, vocabulary or dictionary of explanations of obsolete, rare, technical or dialectal words or forms; a collection of glosses or notes. **glossarial,** *a.* **glossarist,** *n.* [L *glōssārium,* from *glōssa,* GLOSS[1]]

glosso-, *comb. form* Pertaining to the tongue; linguistic. [Gr. *glōssa,* the tongue, language]

glossocele, *n.* a protrusion of the tongue caused by swelling or inflammation. [Gr. *kēlē,* tumour]

glosso-epiglottic, -tid, *a.* pertaining to the tongue and the epiglottis.

glossography, *n.* the writing of glosses or comments; a treatise on the tongue. **glossographer,** *n.* **glossographical,** *a.*

glossolalia, *n.* speech in an unknown tongue, occurring in religious ecstasy, trances etc.

glossology, *n.* the explanation of technical terms, as of a science; the science of language. **glossological,** *a.* **glossologist,** *n.*

glossy GLOSS[2].

glottis, *n.* (*pl.* **-tises, -tides**) the mouth of the windpipe forming a narrow aperture covered by the epiglottis when one holds the breath or swallows, contributing, by its dilatation and contraction, to the modulation of the voice. **glottal,** *a.* **glottal stop,** *n.* a speech sound in some languages, e.g. German, produced by closing and suddenly opening the glottis. **glottic,** *a.* **glottologic,** *n.* **glottologist,** *a.* **glottology,** *n.* [GLOSSOLOGY, see GLOSSO-]

Gloucester, Gloster, *n.* a rich cheese made in Gloucestershire. **double Gloucester,** a Gloucester cheese of extra thickness.

Gloucester, *n.* **Richard Alexander Walter George, Duke of Gloucester** (1944–), prince of the United Kingdom. Grandson of George V, he succeeded his father to the dukedom owing to the death of his elder brother Prince William (1941–72) in an air crash. He married in 1972 Birgitte van Deurs, daughter of a Danish lawyer. His heir is his son Alexander, Earl of Ulster (1974–).

Gloucestershire, *n.* county in SW England. **area** 2640 sq km/1019 sq miles. **towns** administrative headquarters Gloucester; Stroud, Cheltenham, Tewkesbury, Cirencester. **products** cereals, fruit, dairy products; engineering, coal in the Forest of Dean. **population** (1987) 522,000.

glove, *n.* a covering for the hand, usu. with a separate division for each finger; a padded glove for the hands in boxing, also called **boxing-glove**. *v.t.* to cover with or as with a glove. **hand in glove** HAND. **to fight with the gloves off,** to box without gloves; to fight or contend in earnest, to show no mercy. **to fit like a glove,** to fit perfectly in size and shape. **to throw down** or **take up the glove,** to make or accept a challenge. **glove-compartment, -box,** a small storage compartment in a car, usu. set into the dashboard. **glove-fight,** *n.* a pugilistic contest in which the men wear gloves. †**glove-money,** *n.* a gratuity (ostensibly to buy gloves), esp. money given by the sheriff to the clerk of assize and judge's officers when no offenders were left for execution. **glove-puppet,** *n.* a puppet that fits onto the hand. **glove-sponge,** *n.* a sponge shaped like a glove. **glove-stretcher,** *n.* an instrument for stretching the fingers of gloves so that they may be drawn on easily. **gloved,** *a.* **glover,** *n.* one who makes or sells gloves. **gloveress,** *n. fem.* **gloveless,** *a.* **gloving,** *n.* the occupation of making gloves. [OE *glōf,* prob. from Teut. *lōf-,* cogn. with LOOF[1], the hand]

glow, *v.i.* to radiate light and heat, esp. without flame; to be incandescent; to be bright or red with heat, to show a warm colour; to feel great bodily heat; to be warm or flushed with passion or fervour; to be ardent. †*v.t.* to cause to glow. *n.* incandescence, red or white heat; brightness, redness, warmth of colour; vehemence, ardour; heat produced by exercise. **glow-worm,** *n.* a beetle, *Lampyris noctiluca* or *L. splendidula,* the female of which is phosphorescent. **glowingly,** *adv.* [OE *glōwan* (cp. Icel. *glōa,* Dut. *gloeijen,* G *glüten*)]

glower, *v.i.* to scowl, to stare fiercely or angrily. *n.* a savage stare, a scowl. **gloweringly,** *adv.* [etym. doubtful, cp. LG *gluren*]

gloxinia, *n.* a genus of plants with large bell-shaped flowers, from tropical America. [B. P. *Gloxin,* 18th cent. German botanist]

gloze, *v.t.* to palliate, to extenuate; †to explain by note or comment; †to flatter, to wheedle. *v.i.* to comment; †to use flattery. *n.* flattery, wheedling; specious show; †a gloss, a comment; †(*pl.*) specious talk. †**to gloze over,** to palliate speciously or explain away. †**glozer,** *n.* a glosser; a flatterer. [F *gloser,* from *glose,* GLOSS[1]]

glucinum, *n.* (*formerly*) beryllium (the salts have a sweet taste, hence the name). **glucina**, *n.* oxide of glucinum. [F *glucine,* Gr. *glukus,* sweet]

Gluck, *n.* **Christoph Willibald von** (1714–87), German composer who settled in Vienna as Kapellmeister to Maria Theresa in 1754. In 1762 his *Orfeo ed Euridice/ Orpheus and Eurydice* revolutionized the 18th-cent. conception of opera by giving free scope to dramatic effect. *Orfeo* was followed by *Alceste/Alcestis* (1767) and *Paris ed Elena/Paris and Helen* (1770).

glucohaemia, GLUCOSURIA.

glucose, *n.* a fermentable sugar, less sweet than cane-sugar, obtained from dried grapes and other fruits, dextrin etc. and occurring in the urine of persons suffering from glucosuria; any of the group of sweet compounds including dextrose, laevulose etc. **glucic**, **glucosic**, *a.* derived from or pertaining to glucose. **glucic acid,** *n.* a colourless, honey-like compound obtained from glucose or cane-sugar by the action of acids or alkalis. **glucoside**, *n.* a vegetable substance yielding glucose when decomposed. [Gr. *glukus,* sweet]

glucosuria, *n.* one form of diabetes, the principal characteristic of which is the occurrence of sugar in the urine. **glucosuric,** *a.* [Gr. *ouron,* URINE]

glue, *n.* an impure gelatine made of the chippings of hides, horns and hoofs, boiled to a jelly, cooled in moulds, and used hot as a cement; an adhesive or sticky substance. *v.t.* to join or fasten with or as with glue; to unite, to attach firmly. †*v.i.* to stick together; to be firmly attached. **glue-pot,** *n.* a vessel for heating glue, with an outer vessel to hold water and prevent burning. **glue-sniffing,** *n.* the inhalation of the fumes of certain glues for their narcotic effects. **glue-sniffer,** *n.* **gluer,** *n.* **gluey,** *a.* **glueyness,** *n.* **gluing,** *pres.p.* †**gluish,** *a.* [OF *glu,* late L *glūtem,* nom. *glūs,* cogn. with GLUTEN]

glug, *n.* (*coll.*) the sound of liquid being poured, esp. out of or into a narrow opening. [imit.]

glum, †*v.i.* to look sullen or gloomy. *a.* sullen, moody, dejected, dissatisfied. **glumly,** *adv.* **glumness,** *n.* [var. of GLOOM]

glume, *n.* a chaff-like scale or bract forming part of the inflorescence in grasses; a husk. **glumaceous**, *a.* **glumiferous**, *a.* **glumose, -mous,** *a.* [L *glūma,* from *glūbere,* to peel, cp. Gr. *gluphein,* to hollow out]

glut, *v.t.* to fill to excess, to stuff, to gorge, to sate; to fill with an over-supply (as a market); to swallow, to swallow down. *n.* a surfeit; plenty even to loathing; a superabundance; an over-supply of a market. [OF *gloutir,* L *glūtīre,* to swallow, to devour]

glutaeus, gluteus, *n.* (*pl.* **-taei**, **-tei**) one of the three large muscles forming the buttock. **gluteal, -taeal, -tean,** *a.* [L, from Gr. *gloutos,* rump]

glutamate, *n.* a salt or ester of glutamic acid.

glutamic acid, *n.* an amino acid occurring in proteins which plays an important part in the nitrogen metabolism of plants and animals.

gluten, *n.* a yellowish-grey, elastic albuminous substance, left in wheat flour which has been washed in water; a sticky substance, glue. **animal gluten,** *n.* fibrin. **gluten-bread,** *n.* bread containing a large quantity of gluten, largely used in the diet of those suffering from diabetes. **glutin**, *n.* vegetable gelatine; gliadin. †**glutinate,** *v.t.* to cement with glue; to glue. †**glutination,** *n.* **glutinative,** *a.* **glutinize, -ise,** *v.t.* to render viscous or gluey. **glutinous,** *a.* viscous, gluey, tenacious; covered with a sticky exudation. **glutinously,** *adv.* **glutinosity**, *n.* [L *glūten -tinis*]

glutton, *n.* one who eats to excess; a gormandizer; one who indulges in anything to excess, as a voracious reader, worker etc.; a carnivorous animal of the weasel tribe, the wolverine, formerly supposed to be a voracious feeder. †*v.i.* to gluttonize. **glutton-like,** *a.* †**gluttonish,** *a.* **gluttonize, -ise,** *v.i.* to eat to excess, to gorge. **gluttonous,** *a.* **gluttonously,** *adv.* **gluttony,** *n.* [OF *glutun, glouton,* L *glūtōnem,* nom. *glūto,* from *glūtīre,* to swallow, see GLUT]

glycerine, glycerin, *n.* a viscid, sweet, colourless liquid obtained from animal and vegetable fats and oils, used in the manufacture of soaps, medicines, confectionery etc. **glyceral**, *n.* one of a series of compounds obtained by heating glycerine with aldehydes. **glyceric**, *a.* of or pertaining to glycerine. **glycerate**, *n.* a salt of glyceric acid; a solution in glycerine. **glyceride**, *n.* **glycerinate,** *v.t.* to treat (esp. vaccine lymph) with glycerine. **glyceroid,** *n.* **glycerol**, *n.* glycerine. **glyceryl**, *n.* the radical of glycerine and the glycerides. [F *glycérine,* Gr. *glukeros, glukus,* sweet]

glycero-, *comb. form* **glycerophosphate**, *n.* **glycerophosphoric**, *a.*

glyc(o)-, *comb. form* containing glycerol or compounds producing sugars. [Gr. *glukus,* sweet]

glycocoll, *n.* a crystalline sweetish compound found in bile.

glycogen, *n.* a white insoluble, starch-like compound occurring in animal tissues such as the liver and convertible into dextrose. **glycogenic**, *a.* **glycogenesis**, *n.*

glycol, *n.* a diatomic alcohol of the fatty group typified by ethyl glycol, used as an antifreeze in car engines and for de-icing aircraft wings. **glycolic, glycollic**, *a.* **glycollate**, *n.*

glyconic, *a.* (*Pros.*) applied to varieties of classic verse consisting of three trochees and a dactyl. [*Glukōn,* a Gr. poet]

glycoprotein, *n.* any of a group of complex proteins containing a carbohydrate mixed with a simple protein. Also, **glycopeptide**.

glycosuria, GLUCOSURIA.

Glyndebourne, *n.* site of an opera house in East Sussex, England, established in 1934 by John Christie (1882–1962). Operas are staged at an annual summer festival and a touring company is also based there.

glyph, *n.* (*Arch.*) a fluting or channel, usu. vertical; a hieroglyph. **glyphic,** *a.* carved, sculptured. *n.* a hieroglyph. [Gr. *gluphē,* from *gluphein,* to carve]

glyphograph, *n.* a plate prepared by glyphography; an impression from such a plate. *v.t., v.i.* to engrave by glyphography. **glyphographer**, *n.* **glyphographic**, *a.* **glyphography**, *n.* the process of making engravings for printing in which an electrotype with the design in relief is obtained from an intaglio etching.

glyptic, *a.* relating to carrying or engraving, esp. on gems. *n.* (*usu. pl.*) the art of engraving, esp. on gems. [Gr. *gluptikos,* from *gluptos,* carved, from *gluphein,* see GLYPH]

glyptodon, *n.* a huge fossil quadruped allied to the armadillo, from S America. [Gr. *gluptos,* carved, as prec., *odous, odontos,* tooth]

glyptography, *n.* the art of engraving on gems; a description of this. **glyptograph**, *n.* an engraving on a gem. **glyptographer**, *n.* **glyptographic**, *a.* [Gr. *gluptos,* see prec., -GRAPHY]

glyptotheca, *n.* a room or building for the preservation of sculpture. [Gr. *gluptos,* see GLYPTIC, *thēkē,* a repository]

GM, (*abbr.*) George Medal; General Manager; Grand Master.

G-man G.

Gmc., (*abbr.*) Germanic.

GMT, *n.* (*abbr.*) Greenwich Mean Time.

gnamma hole, NAMMA HOLE.

Gnaphalium, *n.* a genus of woolly plants, typified by the cudweed, having small sessile flower-heads. [Gr. *gnaphalion,* a downy plant]

gnar, KNAR.

gnarl, *v.t.* to twist or contort (*usu. in. p.p.*) *n.* a protuberance, a twisted growth, or contorted knot, in a tree. **gnarled,** *a.* rugged, lined, weather-beaten, twisted. **gnarly,** *a.* full of knots or gnarls; peevish, perverse. [var. of KNURL]

gnash, *v.t.* to strike or grind (the teeth) together; to grind or champ. *v.i.* to grind the teeth together, as in rage, despair etc.; to rage. **gnasher,** *n.* one who gnashes; (*sl.*) a tooth. **gnashingly,** *adv.* [ME *gnasten,* onomat. in orig. (cp. Icel. *gnastan,* a gnashing, G *knastern,* to gnash)]

gnat, *n.* a small two-winged fly, the female of which has a blood-sucking proboscis, esp. *Culex pipiens* and some other species of the genus *Culex.* **to strain at a gnat and swallow a camel,** (Matt. xxiii.24) to be scrupulous about trifles and lax in matters of great moment. [OE *gnœt*]

gnathic, *a.* of or pertaining to the jaw. **gnathal**, *a.* **gnathism,** *n.* classification of mankind according to measurements of the jaw. **gnathion**, *n.* the lowest point of the midline of the lower jaw, used as a reference point in craniometry. [Gr. *gnathos,* jaw]

gnathitis, *n.* inflammation of the upper jaw or cheek.

gnath(o)-, *comb. form* pertaining to the jaw or cheek.

Gnathonic, *a.* like or after the manner of Gnatho, parasitical, sycophantic. **Gnathonical,** *a.* **Gnathonism**, *n.* [L *Gnathōnicus,* from *Gnatho,* the chief character in *Terence's Gnatho,* from Gr. *gnathos,* jaw]

gnathoplasty, *n.* the formation of a cheek by plastic surgery.

gnathopod, *n.* (*pl.* **gnathopoda**) the foot-jaw of crustaceans.

-gnathous, *comb. form* having a jaw of a certain kind, as in *prognathous*.

gnaw, *v.t.* (*p.p.* **gnawed, gnawn**) to bite or eat away by degrees; to bite repeatedly or persistently; to bite in agony, rage or despair; to corrode; to consume or wear away by degrees. *v.i.* to use the teeth in biting repeatedly or persistently (at or into); to cause corrosion or wearing away. **gnawer,** *n.* **gnawing,** *n.* **gnawingly,** *adv.*

gneiss, *n.* a laminated metamorphic rock consisting of feldspar, quartz and mica. **gneissic,** *a.* **gneissoid,** *a.* **gneissose,** *a.* **gneissy,** *a.* [G, from OHG *gneistan,* to sparkle]

gnocchi, *n.* an Italian dish consisting of small potato or semolina dumplings, served with a sauce or used to garnish soup etc. [It., *lumps*]

gnome[1], *n.* an imaginary being, a kind of misshapen sprite, supposed to inhabit the interior of the earth, and to be the guardian of mines, quarries etc. **Gnomes of Zurich,** (*coll.*) international bankers thought to have great power and exercise a sinister and mysterious effect on world economics. **gnomish,** *a.* [F, from L *gnomus* (used by Paracelsus), perh. from foll., or *gēnomos* (Gr. *gē,* earth, *-nomos,* dweller)]

gnome[2], *n.* a maxim, an aphorism, a saw. **gnomic,** *a.* dealing in maxims, sententious, didactic. **gnomic aorist,** *n.* in Greek grammar, a use of the aorist tense to express, not the past, but a general truth, as in proverbs etc. [Gr. *gnōmē,* from *gignōskein,* to know]

gnomo-, *comb. form* pertaining to a maxim or saying.

gnomology, *n.* a collection of maxims or sententious reflections or sayings; the sententious element in writing and literature. **gnomologic, -al,** *a.* **gnomologist,** *n.*

gnomometry, *n.* a dividing or arranging according to subject.

gnomon, *n.* a rod, pillar, pin or plate on a sundial, indicating the time of day by its shadow; a vertical pillar used in an analogous way for determining the altitude of the sun; the index of the hour-circle of a globe; in geometry, the figure remaining when a parallelogram has been removed from the corner of a larger one of the same form. **gnomonic, -al,** *a.* pertaining to the art of making and using dials. **gnomonic projection,** the projection of the lines of a sphere from the centre. **gnomonically,** *adv.* **gnomonics,** *n.pl.* the art or science of making and using dials. †**gnomonology**, *n.* a treatise on dials. [Gr. *gnōmōn,* an inspector, gnomon of a dial, as prec.]

gnosiology, *n.* the philosophy dealing with cognition, the theory of knowledge, or the operation of the cognitive faculties. [Gr. *gnōsis,* see foll.]

gnosis, *n.* (*pl.* **-ses**) knowledge, esp. of mysteries; gnostic philosophy. [Gr., GNOME[2]]

-gnosis, *comb. form* esp. in medicine, recognition, as in *diagnosis*. [NL from Gr., knowledge]

gnostic, *a.* relating to knowledge or cognition, intellectual; (*facet.*) knowing, shrewd, worldly-wise; having esoteric knowledge; of or belonging to the Gnostics or Gnosticism. *n.* an adherent of Gnosticism. †**gnostically,** *adv.* **Gnosticism**, *n.* a system of religious philosophy flourishing in the first six centuries of the Church, that combined ideas from Greek and Oriental philosophy with Christianity, which it professed to expound as a mystical philosophy or gnosis. The mediaeval French Cathar and the modern *Mandean* sects (in S Iraq) descend from Gnosticism. **gnosticize, -ise**, *v.t., v.i.* **gnosticizer, -iser,** *n.* [Gr. *gnōstikos,* from *gnōstos,* known, as prec.]

GNP, (*abbr.*) Gross National Product.

gnu, *n.* a large-horned antelope, *Catoblepas gnu* of southern Africa. [Hottentot]

go[1], *v.i.* (*past* **went**, *p.p.* **gone**, *2nd sing.* **goest**, *3rd sing.* **goes**, †**goeth**) to move, to move from one place, condition, or station to another; to begin to move, to start to move from a place, to depart, to pass away (opp. to come); to keep up a movement, to be moving, to be acting, operating, or working; to travel; to proceed, to advance; to end, to come out, to succeed, to turn out (well or ill); to take a certain course (as for or against); to be habitually (as hungry, naked etc.); to be used, said etc., habitually, to pass, to be circulated or current; to average; to extend, to reach, to point in a certain direction; to tend, to conduce; to run, to have a certain tenor; to be applicable, to fit, to suit (with); to belong, to be harmonious (with a tune etc.); to be released, to get away; to be given up, to be abandoned, abolished, or lost; to fail, to give way, break down; (*usu. in. p.p.*) to die; to pass into a certain state, to become (as wild, mad etc.); to be sold; to be spent; (*as aux. verb*) to be about (to do), to intend, to purpose. **go ahead,** start, proceed without hesitation. **go on,** †**go to,** come now; (*iron., remonstr.*) come, come! **go to Jericho, Bath, Putney,** etc., be off! [cp. BLAZES]. **have gone and done it,** (*coll.*) have been foolish enough to do it. **to go,** (*esp. N Am. coll.*) of food, for taking away from the restaurant. **to go about,** to get to work at; to go from place to place; to take a circuitous course; of a vessel, to tack, to change course, to wear. **to go abroad,** to go to a foreign country; to go out of doors; †to be disclosed. **to go against,** to be in opposition to. **to go ahead,** to proceed in advance; to make rapid progress; to start. **to go aside,** to withdraw apart from others; to go wrong. **to go astray,** to wander from the right path. **to go at,** to attack; to work at vigorously. **to go away,** to depart. **to go back from** or **upon,** to fail to keep (one's word). **to go bail,** to act as bail for; (*coll.*) to vouch. **to go behind,** to call in question; to look beyond (the apparent facts etc.). **to go between,** to mediate between. †**to go beyond,** to cheat, to outdo. **to go bush,** (*Austral.*) to take to the bush, to go to a place where one cannot be contacted. **to go by,** to pass by or near to; to pass by; to pass unnoticed or disregarded; to take as a criterion. **to go down,** to descend; to set; to founder (as a ship); to fall (before a conqueror); to be set down in writing; esp. in the UK, to leave the university for the vacation or at the end of one's term; to be swallowed, to be palatable or acceptable. **to go dry,** (*coll.*) to adopt prohibition; to give up drinking or having alcoholic liquor on the premises. **to go for nothing,** to count for nothing. **to go far,** (*coll.*) to be very successful; to attain distinction. **to go for,** to go somewhere to obtain something; to attack; to be true for, include; to be attracted by; to be sold for. **to go forth,** to issue or depart from a place; to be published or spread abroad. **to go forward,** to advance. **to go hard with,** (*impers.*) to cause great trouble, danger or difficulty to. **to go ill** or **well with,** (*impers.*) to happen or fare evil or well with. **to go in,** to enter; to go behind clouds; in cricket, to have an innings. **to go in and out,** to be perfectly at liberty. **to go in for,** to be in favour of; to follow as a pursuit or occupation. **to go into,** to enter; to frequent; to take part in; to investigate or discuss. **to go in unto,** to enter the presence of; †to have sexual intercourse with. **to go it,** to carry on; to keep a thing up; to conduct oneself recklessly or outrageously. **to go native,** to adopt the ways and customs of a place. **to go off,** to depart; to fall away; to die; to be discharged (as a firearm); to cease to be perceptible; to become unconscious; to be sold off; to fare, to succeed (well or ill). **to go off one's head,** (*coll.*) to become insane. **to go on,** to proceed, to continue, to persevere; to become chargeable to (the parish etc.); (*coll.*) to behave (badly etc.); to grumble, to complain; (*coll., in imper.*) rubbish, nonsense; to appear on the stage. **to go one better,** to excel, to cap. **to go out,** to depart, to leave (a room etc.); to be extinguished; to vacate office; to leave home and enter employment; to go into society; to go on strike; to be drawn forth in sympathy etc. **to go over,** to cross, to pass over; to rat, to change one's party or opinions; to read, to examine; to rehearse; to retouch. **to go phut** PHUT. **to go round,** to pay a number of visits; to encompass or be enough to encompass, to be enough for (the whole party etc.). **to go steady,** to go about regularly with the same boyfriend or girlfriend. **to go the whole hog,** HOG. **to go through,** to pass through; to undergo; to suffer; to examine; (*coll.*) to overhaul, to ransack, to strip; to discuss thoroughly; to perform (a duty, ceremony etc.). **to go through with,** to perform thoroughly, to complete. **to go together,** to harmonize, to be suitable to or to match each other. **to go under,** to be known as (by a title or name); to sink; to be submerged or ruined; to perish. **to go up,** to climb, pass upwards; to rise, increase; to be constructed; to be destroyed, as by fire or explosion. **to go upon,** to act upon as a principle. **to go west,** (*sl.*) to die. **to go with,** to accompany; to follow the meaning of, to understand; to be with (child); to side or agree with; to suit, to match. **to go without,** to be or manage without, to put up with the want of. **go-ahead,** *a.* characterized by energy and enterprise. **go-as-you-please,** *a.* unceremonious, untroubled by rules etc. **go-between,** *n.* one who acts as an intermediary between two parties. **go-by,** *n.* the act of passing without notice; intentional failure to notice; evasion, deception. **to give the go-by to,** to evade; to cut, to slight; to pass or outstrip; to dismiss as of no moment. **go-cart,** *n.* a small framework without a bottom, running on casters, for teaching infants to walk; a small handcart; a child's toy wagon. **go-getter,** *n.* a bustling, pushing person. **go-kart,** a small light racing car with a low-powered engine. **go-off,** *n.* the start. **go-slow,** *n.* a deliberate curtailment of the rate of production by organized labour in an industrial dispute. **go-to-meeting,** *a.* suitable for church or chapel (of clothes). [OE *gān* (cp. Dut. *gaan,* G *gehen*)]

go[2], *n.* (*pl.* **goes**) the act of going; spirit, life, animation; rush, energy, enterprise; (*coll.*) a fix, a scrape, an awkward turn of affairs; a turn, a bout (of doing something); one's turn in a game; in cribbage, a player's turn at which he is unable to play, counting one to his opponent; (*coll.*) fashion, the mode; a spree; a drink of liquor, esp. of gin. **all** or **quite the go,** entirely in the fashion. **great go, little go,** in UK universities, the final and preliminary or previous examinations for degrees. **near go,** (*coll.*) a narrow squeak, a close shave. **no go,** of no use; not to be done; a complete failure. **on the go,** on the move; vigorously in motion. **pretty go,** (*sl.*) a startling affair. **to have a go,** (*coll.*) to make an attempt. **to have a go at somebody,** (*coll.*) to attack, physically or verbally. [from prec.]

Goa, *n.* Union Territory of India comprising the former Portugese coastal possessions of Goa and Daman, and the island of Diu, forcibly seized by India in 1961. **area** 3700 sq km/1428 sq miles. **capital** Panaji. **population** (1981) 1,003,000.

goad, *n.* a pointed instrument to urge oxen to move faster; (*fig.*) anything that stings, spurs or incites. *v.t.* to prick, drive or urge on with a goad; to stimulate, to incite; to drive (on, to, into etc.). **goadsman, goadster,** *n.* one who drives with a goad. [OE *gād* (cp. Lombardic *gaida,* arrowhead, OIr. *gai,* spear)]

goaf, *n.* a waste place in a colliery, a part from which the coal has been removed. [etym. doubtful]

goal, *n.* the winning-post or mark indicating the end of a race; the end or terminus of one's ambition; destination, purpose, aim; in football, hockey etc. the posts connected by a crossbar between which the ball must be driven to win a point; also the act of kicking the ball between such posts or over such bar. **goalie,** *n.* (*coll.*) goal-keeper. **goal-keeper,** *n.* a player stationed near to guard the goal. **goal kick,** *n.* in soccer, a free kick from the corner taken by the defending side after the ball has been put out of play by a member of the attacking side. **goal-line,** *n.* a line drawn through the goal-posts to form the boundary at each end of the field of play in football. **goal post,** *n.* in football etc. either of the two posts marking the goal. **to move the goalposts,** (*coll.*) to change the conditions, regulations, limits etc. applying to a particular matter or action. [etym. doubtful, perh. from an OE *gāl,* conn. with *gœlan,* to impede]

goanna, *n.* (*Austral.*) a large monitor lizard, esp. the **lace monitor**; (*N Zealand*) the tuatara. [corr. *iguana*]

goat, *n.* a hairy, horned and bearded domesticated ruminant belonging to the genus *Capra,* esp. *C. hircus,* of which there are many varieties; (*pl.*) the genus *Capra;* a bad or inferior person or thing; a fool; a lascivious person; †a lecher. **to get one's goat,** to make one angry. **to play the giddy goat,** to play the fool. **goat-**

god, *n.* pan. **goatherd,** *n.* one who tends goats. **goat-moth,** *n.* a large moth, *Cossus ligniperda,* brown and grey with black markings. **goat's-beard,** *n.* the meadow-sweet, *Spiraea ulmaria;* also *Tragopogon pratense,* and *T. porrifolius* or salsify. **goat's-rue,** *n.* a leguminous plant, *Galega officinalis.* **goatskin,** *n.* the skin of a goat. *a.* made of goatskin. **goat's-thorn,** *n.* names of plants, *Astragalus tragacantha,* the great, and *A. poterium,* the small goat's-thorn. **goatsucker,** *n.* any bird of the genus *Caprimulgus,* chiefly nocturnal and insectivorous, fabled to milk goats, esp. *C. europaeus,* a British summer visitant. **goatish,** *a.* resembling a goat; of a rank smell; lecherous. **goatishly,** *adv.* **goatishness,** *n.* **goatling,** *n.* **goaty,** *a.* [OE *gāt* (cp. Dut. *geit,* G *Geiss,* also L *hœdus*)]

goatee, *n.* a small beard like a goat's on the point of the chin.

gob, *n.* the mouth; a mouthful; a clot of something slimy, as saliva. *v.i.* (**gobbed**) to spit. **gob-stopper,** *n.* esp. in UK, a large boiled sweet. **gobbin, gobbins,** *n.* in coal-mining, waste material used to pack into spaces from which the coal has been removed. **gobsmacked, gobstruck,** *a.* (*sl.*) amazed, dumbfounded. [from OF *gobe,* mouthful (*gober,* to swallow), or perh. directly from Celt. (cp. Gael. and Ir. *gob,* beak, mouth)]

gobang, *n.* a game played on a chequer-board, with 50 coloured counters, the object being to get five into a row. [Jap. *goban,* chess-board]

gobbet, *n.* a mouthful, a lump, a piece, esp. of meat. [OF *gobet,* dim. of *gobe,* GOB]

Gobbi, *n.* **Tito** (1913–84), Italian baritone singer renowned for his opera characterizations of Figaro, Scarpia, and Iago.

gobbin, gobbins GOB.

gobble, *v.t.* to swallow down hastily and greedily or noisily. *v.i.* to swallow food in this manner; to make a noise in the throat as a turkey-cock; *n.* a noise made in the throat like that of a turkey-cock; in golf, a rapid stroke in putting which sends the ball straight into the hole. **gobble-stitch,** *n.* a stitch made too long through hurrying. **gobbler,** *n.* one who gobbles; a gormandizer; a turkey-cock. [perh. from GOB, later adapt. as imit. of turkey]

gobbledegook, gobbledygook, *n.* (*coll.*) pretentious language characterized by jargon and circumlocution. [perh. from GOBBLE]

gobelin, *a.* applied to a superior kind of French tapestry, or an imitation of this made at the Gobelins factory, originally founded as a dyeworks in Paris by Gilles and Jean Gobelin about 1450. The firm began to produce tapestries in the 16th century, and in 1662 the establishment was bought by Colbert for Louis XIV. With the support of the French government, it continues to make tapestries. **gobelin blue,** *n.* a blue such as appears a good deal in this tapestry. **gobelin tapestry,** *n.*

gobe-mouches, *n.* (*F*) a credulous person, one who swallows anything. [lit. fly-catcher (*gober,* to swallow, *mouches,* flies, L *muscæ*)]

go-between GO[1].

Gobi, *n.* Asian desert divided between the Mongolian People's Republic and Inner Mongolia, China; 800 km/500 miles N–S, and 1600 km/1000 miles E–W. It is rich in fossil remains of extinct species.

Gobind Singh, *n.* (*c.* 1666–1708), Indian religious leader, the tenth and last guru (teacher) of Sikhism, 1675–1708, and founder of the Sikh brotherhood known as the Khalsa. On his death the Sikh holy book, the *Guru Granth Sahib,* replaced the line of human gurus as the teacher and guide of the Sikh community.

gobioid, *a.* of or relating to the Gobiidae family of fishes that includes the goby.

goblet, *n.* a drinking-vessel, with a stem and without a handle, usu. bowl-shaped and of glass or metal; a drinking-cup. [OF *gobelet,* dim. of *gobel,* cup, etym. doubtful, but perh. from L *cūpellum,* nom. *-us,* dim. of *cūpa,* cask]

goblin, *n.* a mischievous spirit of ugly or grotesque shape; an elf, a gnome. **goblinism,** *n.* [F *gobeline,* low L *gobelīnus,* perh. from Gr. *kobālos,* a rogue, a goblin (but cp. KOBOLD)]

gobo, *n.* (*pl.* **-bos** or **-boes**) in television, film etc., a shield placed around a camera to exclude unwanted light; a device on a microphone to exclude unwanted sound.

goby, *n.* a small fish belonging to the genus *Gobius,* characterized by the union of the ventral fins into a disc or sucker. [L *gōbius, cōbius,* Gr. *kōbios*]

GOC, (*abbr.*) General Officer Commanding.

go-cart GO[1].

god[1], *n.* a superhuman or supernatural being regarded as controlling natural forces and human destinies and worshipped or propitiated by man; a deity, a divinity; a personification of any of the forces of nature; a person formally recognized as divine and entitled to worship; an image, animal etc., worshipped as an embodiment or symbol of supernatural power, an idol; (*fig.*) a person or thing greatly idolized; (*pl.*) the occupants of the upper gallery in a theatre; (in monotheist religions, **God**) the Supreme Being, the self-existent and eternal Creator and Ruler of the universe. **for God's sake** SAKE. **God almighty,** *int.* expressing surprise or anger. †**God-a-mercy,** God have mercy! **God knows,** God is my (etc.), witness that; a mild oath expressing apathy or annoyance. **God of war,** Mars. **God of wine,** Bacchus. **God Save the King/Queen,** *n.* British national anthem. The melody resembles a composition by John Bull (1563–1628) and similar words are found from the 16th century. In its present form it dates from the 1745 Rebellion, when it was used as an anti-Jacobite Party song. In the US the song 'America', with the first line, 'My country, 'tis of thee' is sung to the same tune. **God's (own) country,** (*sometimes iron.*) any country seen as being ideal. Also (*Austral., N Zealand coll.*) **Godzone**. **God willing,** if circumstances permit. **household gods,** in Roman times, the lares and penates or gods of the hearth; one's household treasures. **the blind god,** Cupid. **to play God** PLAY. **ye gods!** (*facet.*) **ye gods and little fishes,** grandiloquent exclamations of surprise, protest etc. **god-awful,** *a.* (*coll.*) terrible, dreadful. **goddam(n), goddamned,** *a.* damned; hateful; complete; *int.* (*esp. N Am. coll.*) expressing annoyance. **goddaughter** GODCHILD. **God-fearing,** *a.* worshipping or reverencing God, upright. **God forbid,** *int.* expressing the hope that a certain event etc. will not happen. **God-forsaken,** *n.* abandoned by God; wretched, miserable, forlorn, depraved. **godmother, -parent** GODFATHER. †**god-smith,** *n.* a maker of idols. **godson** GODCHILD. **Godman,** *n.* one both God and man, Jesus Christ. **God's acre,** *n.* a burial ground. **God's ape,** *n.* an imbecile; a natural fool. **God's image,** *n.* the human body. †**God's lid,** God's eyelid (an oath). **God-speed,** *n.* the wish 'God speed you' to a person starting on a journey, undertaking etc. **goddess,** *n.* a female deity; (*fig.*) a woman of pre-eminent beauty, goodness or charm. **goddess-like,** *a., adv.* **goddess-ship,** *n.* **Godhead,** *n.* divine nature or essence; a deity. **the Godhead,** God. **Godhood,** *n.* **godkin, godlet,** *n.* **godless,** *a.* acknowledging no god; without God; impious, irreligious; wicked. **godless,** *a.* **godlessly,** *adv.* **godlessness,** *n.* **godlike,** *a.* †**godlikeness,** *n.* †**godling,** *n.* a little god; a petty deity. **godly,** *a.* God-fearing, pious, devout. †*adv.* piously, religiously. **godliness,** *n.* **godsend,** *n.* an unlooked-for acquisition or gain, a piece of good fortune. **godship,** *n.* **godward,** *adv., a.* **godwards,** *adv.* [OE (cp. Dut. *god,* Dan. *gud,* G *Gott*), prob. from root *ghu-,* to worship (not conn. with GOOD)]

god[2], *v.t.* to deify. **to god it,** to play the god. [from prec.]

Godard, *n.* **Jean-Luc** (1930–), French film director, one of the leaders of new wave cinema. His works are often characterized by experimental editing techniques, and an unconventional dramatic form. His films include *À bout de souffle* (1960), *Weekend* (1968) and *Je vous salue, Marie* (1985).

godchild, *n.* one for whom a person stands sponsor at

baptism. **godson,** *n.* **goddaughter,** *n.*

Goddard, *n.* **Robert Hutchings** (1882–1945), US rocket pioneer. His first liquid-fuelled rocket was launched at Auburn, Massachusetts, US, Mar. 1926. By 1935 his rockets had gyroscopic control and carried cameras to record instrument readings. Two years later a Goddard rocket gained the world altitude record with an ascent of 3 km/1.9 miles.

goddess GOD.

godet, *n.* in dressmaking, a piece of cloth inserted in a skirt, so that it may hang in folds suggestive of a flare. [Fr.]

godetia, *n.* a genus of hardy annual flowering herbs allied to the evening primroses. [M. *Godet,* Swiss botanist]

godfather, godmother, *n.* one who is sponsor for a child at baptism; one who gives a name to any person or thing; the head of a Mafia family or other criminal organization. *v.t.* to act as sponsor to; to give one's name to; to be responsible for.

Godiva, *n.* **Lady** (*c.* 1040–80), wife of Leofric, Earl of Mercia (died 1057). Legend has it that her husband promised to reduce the heavy taxes on the people of Coventry if she rode naked through the streets at noon. Everyone remained indoors, but 'Peeping Tom' bored a hole in his shutters, and was struck blind. He founded a Benedictine monastery at Coventry, England, where she is buried.

godly GOD.

godown, *n.* an E Indian warehouse. [Malay *godong*]

godroon, GADROON.

Godthaab, *n.* (Greenlandic **Nuuk**) capital and largest town of Greenland; population (1982) 9700. It is a storage centre for oil and gas, and the chief industry is fish processing.

Godunov, *n.* **Boris** (1552–1605), Czar of Russia from 1598. He was assassinated by a pretender to the throne. The legend that has grown up around this forms the basis of Pushkin's play *Boris Godunov* (1831) and Mussorgsky's opera of the same name (1874).

Godwin¹, *n.* (died 1053), earl of Wessex from 1020. He secured the succession to the throne in 1042 of Edward the Confessor, to whom he married his daughter Edith, and whose chief minister he became. King Harold II was his son.

Godwin², *n.* **William** (1756–1836), English philosopher, novelist, and father of Mary Shelley. His *Enquiry concerning Political Justice* (1793) advocated an anarchic society based on a faith in people's essential rationality. At first a Nonconformist minister, he later became an atheist. His first wife was Mary Wollstonecraft.

godwit, *n.* a marsh or shore bird of the genus *Limosa,* resembling the curlew but having a slightly upturned bill. [etym. unknown]

Goebbels, *n.* **Paul Josef** (1897–1945), German Nazi leader. He was born in the Rhineland, became a journalist, joined the Nazi party in its early days, and was given control of its propaganda (1929). As minister of propaganda from 1933, he brought all cultural and educational activities under Nazi control, and built up sympathetic movements abroad to carry on the 'war of nerves' against Hitler's intended victims. On the capture of Berlin by the Allies he poisoned himself.

Goehr, *n.* **(Peter) Alexander** (1932–), British composer, born in Berlin. A lyrical but often hard-edged serialist, he nevertheless usually remained within the forms of the symphony and traditional chamber works, and more recently turned to tonal and even neo-baroque models.

goel, *n.* an avenger of blood, the next of kin of a murdered man whose duty it was to hunt down and slay the murderer. **goelism,** *n.* [Heb.]

goer, *n.* one who or that which goes (*usu. in comb.,* as a *fast-goer,* a fast horse; one who attends regularly (*usu. in comb.,* as in a *church-goer*); (*Austral., coll.*) one who or that which is likely to succeed, a proposal etc. that is acceptable. [GO¹, -ER]

Goering, Hermann Wilhelm, GÖRING.

Goes, *n.* **Hugo van der** (died 1482), Flemish painter, chiefly active in Ghent. His *Portinari altarpiece* (about 1475, Uffizi, Florence) is a huge oil painting of the Nativity, full of symbolism and naturalistic detail, and the *Death of the Virgin* (about 1480, Musée Communale des Beaux Arts, Bruges) is remarkable for the varied expressions on the faces of the apostles.

Goethe, *n.* **Johann Wolfgang von** (1749–1832), German poet, novelist, and dramatist, the founder of modern German literature, and leader of the Romantic *Sturm und Drang* movement. His works include the autobiographical *Die Leiden des Jungen Werthers/The Sorrows of the Young Werther* (1774) and *Faust* (1808), his masterpiece. A visit to Italy, 1786–88, inspired the classical dramas *Iphigenie auf Tauris/Iphigenia in Tauris* (1787) and *Tasso* (1790). **Goethian,** *a.* of, pertaining to or characteristic of Goethe. *n.* a follower or admirer of Goethe.

†**goety,** *n.* black magic. **goetic,** *a.* [Gr. *goēteia,* from *goēs goētos,* a wizard, lit. a howler, from *goaein,* to wail]

gofer¹, *n.* a thin butter-cake baked between two hinged plates that imprint a honeycomb pattern on both sides. [F *gaufre,* honeycomb, wafer, from Teut. (cp. WAFER)]

gofer², *n.* (*coll.*) a person employed to run errands, give general assistance etc. [*go for,* influ. by GOPHER¹]

goff, GOLF.

goffer, *v.t.* to plait, to crimp (edges of lace etc.) with a heated iron; to raise in relief, to emboss (edges of books). *n.* a plaiting, fluting, or ruffle; a tool for goffering. **goffering,** *n.* this process; a plait or ruffle so produced; an embossed design on the edge of a book. [F *gauffrer* (now *gaufrer*), to print with a pattern, as prec.]

Gog and Magog, the nations represented in the Apocalypse as the forces of Satan at Armageddon (Rev. xx.8); the last two survivors of a mythical race of giants in ancient Britain.

go-getter GO¹.

goggle, *v.i.* to strain or roll the eyes; to squint; to stare; to project (of the eyes). *v.t.* to roll (the eyes) about or turn (the eyes) sideways. *a.* prominent, staring, full; rolling from side to side. *n.* a strained or staring rolling of the eyes; a squint, a leer; (*pl.*) spectacles for protecting the eyes against dust or glare, usu. with tinted glasses; †spectacles to cure squinting; blinds for horses that are apt to take fright; (*sl.*) spectacles; (*sl.*) the eyes; a disease of sheep, staggers. **goggle-eyed,** *a.* **goggled,** *a.* staring, prominent (of the eyes). **goggly,** *a.* [etym. doubtful, perh. imit. (cp. Gael, *gog,* a nodding of the head)]

Gogh, *n.* **Vincent van** (1853–90), Dutch painter, a post-impressionist. He began painting in the 1880s. He met Gauguin in Paris, and when he settled in Arles, Provence, 1888, Gauguin joined him there. After a quarrel van Gogh cut off part of his own earlobe, and in 1889 he entered an asylum; the following year he committed suicide. The Arles paintings vividly testify to his intense emotional involvement in his art; among the best known are *The Yellow Chair* and several *Sunflowers.*

goglet, *n.* an earthenware vessel, a water-cooler used esp. in India. [Port. *gorgoleta* (cp. F *gargoulette*)]

go-go, gogo, *a.* (*coll.*) active, alert; lively. **go-go dancer,** *n.* a (scantily clad) dancer who performs gyrating, usu. erotic routines in nightclubs etc.

Gogol, *n.* **Nicolai Vasilyevich** (1809–52), Russian writer. His first success was a collection of stories, *Evenings on a Farm near Dikanka* (1831–32), followed by *Mirgorod* (1835). Later works include *Arabesques* (1835), the comedy play *The Inspector General* (1836), and the picaresque novel *Dead Souls* (1842), depicting Russian provincial society.

Goidel, *n.* one belonging to the Gadhelic branch of the Celts. **Goidelic,** *a.* [OIr., a Gael, see GADHELIC]

going, *n.* the act of moving or walking; departure; course of life; pregnancy, gestation; the condition of ground, roads, racecourse, track etc., as regards walking, riding, etc. (*also in comb.* as *slow-going, rough-*

going). *a.* working, in actual operation; (for AGOING) existing, to be had. **the best that are going,** the best to be had. **to be hard going,** to be difficult (to make progress); **a going concern,** a business etc., in actual operation. **to set the clock going,** (*properly*) **agoing, to go while the going's good,** seize the chance of getting away, put it into action. **going down,** setting, sunset. **going on,** esp. of the time, one's age etc. almost, nearly. **going order,** *n.* order or condition suitable for working. **going-over,** *n.* an examination, a check; (*coll.*) a beating. **goings-on,** *n.pl.* behaviour, conduct (usu. in a bad sense). **going-train,** *n.* the train of wheels turning the hands in a clock. **going-wheel,** *n.* a ratchet arrangement for keeping a clock going while it is being wound up.

goitre, *n.* a morbid enlargement of the thyroid gland, causing an unsightly deformity of the neck. **goitred,** *a.* affected with goitre. **goitrous,** *a.* pertaining to, affected with, or resembling goitre; characterized by cases of goitre (of places). [F *goître,* from *goitreux,* affected with goitre, ult. from L *guttur,* the throat]

go-kart GO[1].

Gokhale, *n.* **Gopal Krishna** (1866–1915), political adviser and friend of Mohandas Gandhi, leader of the moderate group in the Indian National Congress before World War I.

Golan Heights, *n.* (Arabic **Jawlan**) plateau on the Syrian border with Israel, bitterly contested in the Arab-Israeli Wars, and annexed by Israel on 14 Dec. 1981.

Golconda, *n.* an inexhaustible mine of wealth. [a ruined city NW of Hyderabad, India]

gold, *n.* a precious metallic element of a bright yellow colour, at. no. 79, chem. symbol Au; the most ductile, malleable, and one of the heaviest of metals, much used for coins, jewellery etc.; this metal in the form of coin, money; wealth, riches; anything very precious or valuable and genuine or pure; this metal used as a coating or wash, gilding; the colour of gold; the corn marigold. *a.* made of gold, consisting of gold; coloured like gold. **dead gold,** unburnished gold. **old gold,** a dull brownish-gold colour. **old-gold,** *a.* **as good as gold** GOOD. **gold-amalgam,** *n.* gold combined with mercury in a soft plastic state. **gold-beater,** *n.* one who beats out gold for gilding. **gold-beater's skin,** *n.* a prepared membrane of the caecum of the ox, used for separating the leaves of gold under the hammer; used also as an application to cuts. **gold-beating,** *n.* the act or trade of beating out gold for gilding. †**gold-bound,** *a.* surrounded with gold. **gold-brick,** *n.* something with a bogus display of value; a fraud. **gold-bug,** *n.* (*coll.*) a millionaire. **gold-cloth,** *n.* cloth interwoven with gold thread. **gold-digger,** *n.* one who mines for gold; someone who embarks upon a romantic association merely for gain. **gold-digging,** *n.* the act of digging for gold; (*usu. in pl.*) a place or district where gold is found. **gold-dust,** *n.* gold in very fine particles. **gold-fever,** *n.* a mania for gold-seeking, esp. the gold-rush to California in 1848–9. **gold-field,** *n.* a district where gold is found. **gold-filled,** *a.* more thickly plated with gold than ordinary gold-plated articles (of watch-covers, spectacles etc.). **goldfinch,** *n.* a yellow-marked singing bird, *Carduelis elegans*. **goldfish,** *n.* a golden-red carp, *Cyprims auratus,* kept in ponds, aquaria etc. **goldfish-bowl,** *n.* a fishbowl; (*coll.*) a state or situation of exposure to public curiosity; a place lacking privacy. **gold-foil,** *n.* a thicker kind of gold leaf. **gold-lace,** *n.* lace made of gold wire. **gold leaf,** *n.* gold beaten into a thin leaf. **gold medal,** *n.* an award for first place in a race or competition, esp. in the Olympic Games (as dist. from *silver medal* or *bronze medal*). **gold-mine,** *n.* a place where gold is mined; (*fig.*) a source of wealth or profit. **gold-plate,** *n.* vessels, dishes etc. of gold. **gold record,** *n.* a gold-plated record presented to a singer etc. by the recording company after a certain number of records have been sold, also, **gold disk**. **gold reserve,** *n.* the total amount of gold held by a central bank to make national and international payments and to protect the value of currency. **gold rush,** *n.* a rush to a place where gold has been discovered. **gold-size,** *n.* a size used in gilding. **goldsmith,** *n.* a worker in gold; a dealer in gold-plate; †a banker. **goldsmithy, -ery, -ry,** *n.* goldsmith's work. **gold standard,** *n.* a legal obligation on the part of a nation's central bank to sell gold at a fixed rate in terms of its own currency. **Gold Stick,** *n.* a court official (colonel of the Life Guards or captain of the Gentlemen-at-arms) carrying a gilt rod, attending the sovereign on state occasions. **gold thread,** *n.* a flattened silver-gilt wire, laid over a thread of silk. **gold-washer,** *n.* one who or that which washes the refuse dirt from gold ore. **gold wire,** *n.* gold drawn to the form of wire. **goldless,** *a.* [OE (cp. Dut. *goud,* Icel. *gull,* G *Gold*), cogn. with YELLOW]

golden, *a.* made or consisting of gold; of the colour or lustre of gold; bright, shining, resplendent; excellent, precious, most valuable; most favourable; rich in or yielding gold. **golden age,** *n.* a fabled primeval period of perfect human happiness and innocence, in which the earth yielded her fruits without toil, and all creatures lived in peace; the most illustrious period of a nation's literature or prosperity, esp. the first part of the Classical age of Latin literature. **golden balls,** *n.* the three balls, *n.pl.* displayed as the emblem of a pawnbroker. **Golden Bull,** *n.* an edict of Charles IV settling the law of imperial elections (1356). **golden calf,** *n.* (*fig.*, see Ex. xxxii.4) money as an aim in itself. **golden-cup,** *n.* various species of *Ranunculus* and other yellow-flowered plants. **Golden Delicious,** *n.* a variety of sweet, green-skinned apple. **golden eagle,** *n.* a large eagle, *Aquila chrysaëtos,* found in the mountainous parts of Britain, esp. Scotland. **golden-eye,** *n.* a sea-duck of the genus *Clangula*. **Golden Fleece,** *n.* the fleece of gold taken from the ram on which Phryxus was carried through the air to Colchis, and in quest of which the Argonauts sailed under Jason; an order of knighthood instituted in 1429 in Spain and Austria. **golden handcuff,** *n.* (*coll.*) a payment or benefit given to an employee as an inducement to continue working for the same company. **golden handshake,** *n.* (*coll.*) a payment or benefit given to an employee when leaving a job, esp. upon retirement. **golden hello,** *n.* (*coll.*) a payment or benefit given to an employee upon joining a company. **Golden Horde,** *n.* the invading Mongol-Tatar army that first terrorized Europe from 1237 under the leadership of Batu Khan, a grandson of Genghis Khan. Tamerlane broke their power 1395, and Ivan III ended Russia's payment of tribute to them 1480. **golden jubilee,** *n.* the 50th anniversary of an event of public importance. **golden knop,** *n.* a ladybird. **golden maidenhair,** *n.* a British moss, *Polytrichum commune*. **golden mean,** *n.* the principle of neither too much nor too little, moderation. **golden mouse- ear,** *n.* mouse-ear hawkweed, *Hieracium pilosella*. **golden-mouthed,** *a.* eloquent, musical. **golden number,** *n.* the number denoting the year's place in a Metonic lunar cycle of 19 years, used in calculating the movable feasts, as Easter. **golden oldie,** *n.* (*coll.*) an old recording or film that is still popular. **golden rain,** *n.* a kind of firework. **golden-rod,** *n.* a tall yellow-flowered plant of the genus *Solidago,* esp. *S. virgaurea*. **golden rule,** *n.* the rule that we should do as we would be done by (Matt. vii.12). **golden-samphire,** *n.* a herb, *Inula crithmoides,* of the aster family. **golden share,** *n.* a controlling share (block), esp. as held by the government in a privatized company, that can be used to prevent a take-over by an unacceptable party. **golden-syrup** SYRUP. **golden-tressed,** *a.* having fair or golden hair. **golden wedding,** the 50th anniversary of marriage. †**goldenly,** *adv.* splendidly, excellently. †**goldy,** *a.* golden.

goldfinch GOLD.

goldfish GOLD.

goldilocks, *n.* a buttercup, *Ranunculus auricomus;* other plants with bright yellow flowers.

Golding, *n.* **William** (1911–), English novelist. His first book, *Lord of the Flies* (1954), was about savagery taking over among a group of English schoolboys marooned on a Pacific island. Later novels include *The*

Spire (1964), *Rites of Passage* (1980), and *The Paper Men* (1984). Nobel prize 1983.

goldsmith GOLD.

Goldsmith[1], *n.* **Jerrald ('Jerry')** (1930–), US composer of film music who originally worked in radio and television. His prolific output includes *Planet of the Apes* (1968), *The Wind and the Lion* (1975), *The Omen* (1976), and *Gremlins* (1984).

Goldsmith[2], *n.* **Oliver** (1728–74), Irish writer, whose works include the novel *The Vicar of Wakefield* (1766), the poem *The Deserted Village* (1770), and the play *She Stoops to Conquer* (1773). He was a member of Johnson's Literary Club.

Goldwater, *n.* **Barry** (1909–), US Republican politician, presidential candidate in the 1964 election, when he was heavily defeated by Lyndon Johnson. Many of Goldwater's ideas were later adopted by the Republican right and the Reagan administration.

Goldwyn, *n.* **Samuel** (1882–1974), US film producer. Born in Warsaw, he emigrated to the US in 1896. He founded the Goldwyn Pictures Corporation, 1917, precursor of the Metro-Goldwyn-Mayer Company, 1925, later allied with United Artists. He was famed for his illogical aphorisms known as 'goldwynisms', for example 'Anyone who visits a psychiatrist should have his head examined'.

golem, *n.* in Jewish legend, a figure constructed in the form of a human being and brought to life by supernatural means.

golf, *n.* a game played by two persons or couples with club-headed sticks and small hard balls, on commons, moorlands, fields or links with short grass, consisting in driving the balls into a series of small holes in the ground in as few strokes as possible. *v.i.* to play golf. **golf-arm,** *n.* a nervous affection of the triceps due to exertion in playing golf. **golf-ball,** *n.* a small, hard, white ball used in playing golf; (an electric typewriter that has) a small metal ball bearing the type that moves to press them onto the paper (as dist. from daisy-wheel). **golf club,** *n.* the club used in playing golf; a golfing association. **golf-links,** *n.pl.* the course of 9 or 18 holes on which golf is played, also, **golf-course**. **golfer,** *n.* [perh. from Dut. *kolf* (cp. LG *kulf,* G *Kulbe,* club)]

Golgi, *n.* **Camillo** (1843–1926), Italian cell biologist who with Ramon Y Cajal produced the first detailed knowledge of the fine structure of the nervous system. **Golgi apparatus**, or **Golgi body,** *n.* a membranous structure found in the cells of eukaryotes. It produces the membranes that surround the cell vesicles or lysosomes.

Golgotha, *n.* a burial-place, a charnel-house. [Gr., a place near Jerusalem, where Christ was crucified, from Aram. *gulgalta,* Heb. *gulgōleth,* skull]

†**Goliard,** *n.* a name given to the authors of satirical and ribald Latin verses (12th–13th cents.), some of which were signed by a mythical *Golias;* a buffoon, a jester. **goliardic,** *a.* **goliardy, -ery,** *n.* [OF, a glutton, from *gole* (F *gueule*), L *gula,* gluttony]

Goliath, *n.* in the Old Testament, champion of the Philistines, who was said to have been slain with a stone from a sling by David in single combat in front of the opposing armies of Israelites and Philistines; a gigantic person or thing. **goliath beetle,** *n.* a huge tropical beetle, *Goliathus giganteus*. **goliath frog,** *n.* the largest living frog, *Rana goliath,* of Africa.

gollar, *v.i.* to make a guggling sound; to shout or scold. *n.* a noise or utterance of this kind. [Sc., imit.]

golliwog, gollywog, *n.* a black-faced doll. [*Golliwogg,* character in children's books first published by US writers Florence and Bertha Upton]

golly[1], *int.* God; by God. [minced form of GOD]

golly[2], *v.i.* (*Sc.*) to shout, esp. with a deep or husky voice. [imit.]

golosh, GALOSH.

GOM, (*abbr.*) Grand Old Man. [orig. applied to W.E. Gladstone, 1809–98, British statesman]

gombeen, *n.* usury. **gombeen-man, -woman,** *n.* a moneylender. **gombeenism,** *n.* [Ir. *gaimbin,* said to be from same OCelt. root as L *cambium,* CHANGE]

gombo, GUMBO.

gombroon, *n.* Persian semi-transparent white pottery imitated in Chelsea ware. [town on Persian Gulf, cp. GAMBROON]

gomerel, *n.* (*Sc., North.*) a simpleton. [etym. obscure]

Gómez[1], *n.* **Diego** (1440–82), Portuguese navigator who discovered the coast of Liberia during a voyage sponsored by Henry the Navigator (1458–60).

Gómez[2], *n.* **Juan Vicente** (1864–1935), Venezuelan dictator (1908–35). The discovery of oil during his rule attracted US, British, and Dutch oil interests and made Venezuela one of the wealthiest countries in Latin America. Gómez amassed a considerable personal fortune and used his well-equipped army to dominate the civilian population.

Gomorrah, *n.* a dissolute town. [Gr., from Heb. *'Amōrā,* one of the cities of the plain (Gen. xvii–xix)]

Gompers, *n.* **Samuel** (1850–1924), US labour leader. His early career in the Cigarmakers' Union led him to found and lead the American Federation of Labor in 1882. Gompers advocated non-political activity within the existing capitalist system to secure improved wages and conditions for members.

gomphiasis, *n.* looseness of the teeth, especially the molars. [Gr., from *gomphios,* a molar]

gomphosis, *n.* in anatomy, a kind of articulation by which the teeth are firmly implanted in their sockets. [Gr., from *gomphoein,* to bolt together, from *gomphos,* bolt]

Gomułka, *n.* **Władysław** (1905–82), Polish communist politician, party leader (1943–48 and 1956–70). He introduced moderate reforms, including private farming and tolerance for Roman Catholicism.

gomuti, *n.* a black hair-like fibre, not decaying in water, obtained from the sago-palm, and used for cordage, thatching etc. [Malay]

gon- GON(O)-.

-gon, *comb. form* angled, as in *hexagon, octagon, pentagon*. [Gr. *-gōnos,* angled]

gonads, *n.pl.* undifferentiated sex-glands, the embryonic sexual apparatus, with rudiments of both sexes which later develop into either ovaries or testes. **gonadic**, **gonadotrophic**, *a.* stimulating the gonads. **gonadotrophin**, *n., a.* hormone that does this. [Gr. *gonē,* cogn. with *gignesthai,* to become, to be born, -AD]

gonagra, *n.* gout in the knee. **gonalgia**, *n.* any painful affection of the knee. **gonarthritis**, *n.* inflammation of the knee-joint. [Gr. *gonu,* knee, *agra,* a catching]

Goncharov, *n.* **Ivan Alexandrovitch** (1812–1891). Russian novelist. His first novel, *A Common Story* 1847, was followed in 1858 by his humorous masterpiece, *Oblomov*, which satirized the indolent Russian landed gentry.

Goncourt, de, *n.* the brothers **Edmond** (1822–96) and **Jules** (1830–70), French writers. They collaborated in producing a compendium, *L'Art du XVIIIême siècle/ 18th-Century Art* (1859–75), historical studies, and a *Journal* (1887–96), which depicts French literary life of their day. Edmond de Goncourt founded the *Académie Goncourt*, opened 1903, which awards an annual prize, the PRIX GONCOURT, to the author of the best French novel of the year. Equivalent to the Booker Prize in prestige, the monetary value is only 50 francs.

gondola, *n.* a long, narrow Venetian boat with peaked ends, propelled by one oar; the car of an airship or balloon; (*N Am.*) a large, light, flat-bottomed freight-boat. **gondolier**, *n.* one who rows a gondola. [It.]

Gonds, *n.pl.* a non-homogenous people of Central India, about half of whom speak unwritten languages belonging to the Dravidian family. There are over 4,000,000 Gonds, most of whom live in Madhya Pradesh, E Maharashtra and N Andhra Pradesh, though some are found in Orissa.

Gondwanaland, *n.* land mass, including the continents of South America, Africa, Australia, and Antarctica, that formed the southern half of Pangaea, the 'super-continent' or world continent that existed between 250 and 200 million years ago. The northern half was Laurasia. The baobab tree of Africa and Australia is a relic of Gondwandaland.

gone, *a.* ruined, undone; lost, beyond hope; past, bygone. **gone on,** (*sl.*) infatuated with. **goneness,** *n.* a sensation of weakness, exhaustion or depression. **goner,** *n.* (*coll.*) one who is ruined or ill beyond recovery. [p.p. of GO[1]]

gonfalon, *n.* an ensign or bannerole, usu. displayed from a crossyard on a pole, with streamers, as the standard of certain Italian republics. **gonfalonier,** *n.* a gonfalon- or standard-bearer; title of the chief magistrate in certain Italian republics. **gonfanon,** *n.* a gonfalon. [It. *gonfalone,* OHG *gundfano* (*gund,* OTeut. *gunthja,* war, *fano,* banner)]

gong, *n.* a tambourine-shaped metal instrument which when struck with a padded stick emits a loud sonorous note, used as a signal for meals etc.; a flattish bell struck with a hammer; (*sl.*) a medal. *v.t.* (*coll.*) to stop a person or activity by sounding a gong. **gong metal,** *n.* a sonorous metal, 100 parts copper, 25 parts tin. [Malay]

Gongorism, *n.* a florid and affected style of writing somewhat analogous to euphuism, introduced by Góngora. **gongoresque,** *a.* **Gongorist,** *n.* [Luis de *Góngora* y Argote, 1561–1627, Spanish poet]

gongylus, *n.* a round deciduous reproductive body produced by certain seaweeds; a spore of certain fungi; a granule in the shields of some lichens. [Gr. *gongulos,* round]

goniatite, *n.* a Palaeozoic genus of ammonites. [mod. L *gōniatītēs,* from the Gr. *gōnia,* angle]

gonidium, *n.* (*pl.* **-dia**) a reproductive cell produced asexually in algae; one of the green algal cells or buds in the thallus of lichens. **gonidial, gonidic, gonidioid, gonidiose,** *a.* [from Gr. *gonē,* offspring, seed]

goniometer, *n.* an instrument for measuring angles, esp. of crystals. **goniometric, -al,** *a.* **goniometry,** *n.* [F *goniomètre*]

gonk, *n.* a soft round toy with arms and legs.

gon(o)-, *comb. form* sexual or reproductive, as in *gonochorism.*

gonochorism, *n.* in zoology, the determination of sex. [Gr. *gonos,* offspring, Gr. *choris,* separately]

gonococcus, *n.* (*pl.* **-cocci**) the organism that causes gonorrhoea. **gonococcal,** *a.*

gonocyte, *n.* a germ cell; oocyte; spermatocyte.

gonophore, *n.* in botany, a stalk holding the pistil and stamens above the floral envelope in certain plants; in zoology, one of the zooids containing the reproductive elements in Hydrozoa. [Gr. *gonos,* offspring, generation, cogn. with prec., -PHORE]

gonorrhoea, *n.* a venereal disease affecting the urethra and other mucous surfaces, accompanied by inflammation and mucopurulent discharge; clap. [med. L, from Gr. *gonorrhoia* (*gonos,* seed, *rhoia,* a flowing, from *rheein,* to flow)]

González Márquez, *n.* **Felipe** (1942–), Spanish socialist politician, leader of the Socialist Workers' Party (PSOE), prime minister from 1982.

goo, *n.* (*coll.*) sticky matter. **gooey,** *a.*

good, *a.* (*comp.* **better,** *superl.* **best**) having such qualities as are useful, proper, and satisfactory; fit, proper, suitable, expedient; conducive to the end desired, profitable, serviceable; adequate, satisfactory, competent; advantageous, beneficial; genuine, sound, valid, wholesome; perfect, complete, thorough; reliable, safe, sure; sound financially; ample, considerable; possessed of moral excellence, righteous, virtuous; kind, benevolent, friendly, amiable, courteous; pleasant, acceptable, palatable. *n.* that which contributes to happiness, advantage etc.; that which is right, useful etc.; welfare; prosperity; benefit, advantage; goodness, good qualities, virtuous and charitable deeds; (*pl.*) movable property, chattels, effects; wares, merchandise. **as good as,** not less than, the same as, practically, virtually. **as good as gold,** esp. of children, very well behaved. **as good as one's word,** fulfilling one's promises; trustworthy; not to be deterred. **for good, for good and all,** finally, definitely, completely. **a good one,** (*coll.*) a funny joke; an implausible or unbelievable statement or assertion. **goods and chattels,** personal property. **good on** or **for you!** an exclamation expressing approval, encouragement etc. **in good sooth,** in truth. **to be good for,** to be relied on to pay or bring in (a stated amount). **to be in someone's good books,** to be in favour with someone. **to come good,** (*esp. Austral., coll.*) esp. after a setback, to succeed or improve; to recover one's health after illness etc. **to make good,** to confirm; to perform, to fulfil; to supply a deficiency; to replace; to compensate (for). **to stand good,** to remain valid. **to the good,** as a balance or profit; extra, over and above. **to think good, to see good,** to consider good; to be pleased. **Good Book,** *n.* the bible. **good breeding,** *n.* courteous manners formed by nurture and education. †**good-conceited,** *a.* well-devised; fanciful. †**good-conditioned,** *a.* being in a good state. **good day,** *n., int.* a form of salutation at meeting or parting. †**good e'en, good even, good evening,** *n., int.* a form of salutation. **good-faced,** *a.* having a handsome face, pretty. **good fellow,** *n.* a person of a good easy nature; a genial, sociable person. **good-fellowship,** *n.* sociability; pleasant company; conviviality. **good folk** or **people,** (*euphem.*) the fairies. **good-for-nothing, -nought,** *a.* of no value, worthless. *n.* an idle person, a vagabond. **Good Friday,** *n.* the Friday of Holy Week, kept as a fast in memory of the Crucifixion. **good grace** GRACE. **good humour,** *n.* a cheerful temper, amiability. **good-humoured,** *a.* **good-humouredly,** *adv.* **Good King Henry,** *n.* perennial plant *Chenopodium bonus-henricus* growing to 50 cm/1.6 ft, with triangular leaves which are mealy when young. Spikes of tiny greenish-yellow flowers appear above the leaves in midsummer. **good-lack,** *int.* an exclamation of wonder. [see ALACK] **good lady,** *n.* wife. **good-looking,** *a.* handsome; appearing to be good or virtuous. **good-looker,** *n.* **good looks,** *n.* handsomeness. **good luck,** *n., int.* good-fortune, prosperity. **goodman,** *n.* (*dated*) a rustic term of respect; the head of a family; the master of a house; a husband. **good morning,** *n.* †good morrow, *n., int.* a wish or salutation. **good nature,** *n.* kindness of disposition; freedom from selfishness. **good-natured,** *a.* **good-naturedly,** *adv.* **good-neighbourhood, -ship, -liness,** *n.* friendliness, kindly conduct and intercourse, between neighbours. **good night,** *n., int.* a wish at parting. †**good now,** *int.* an exclamation of wonder, entreaty etc. **good offices,** *n. pl.* mediating influence. **good oil,** *n.* (*Austral. coll.*) reliable information, true report. **Good Samaritan,** *n.* a friend in need (alluding to Luke x.33 etc.). **good sense,** *n.* sound judgment. **good show!,** *n., int.* well done! **good temper,** *n.* freedom from irritability. **good-tempered,** *a.* good-humoured. **good-temperedly,** *adv.* **Good Templar,** *n.* a member of a society pledged to teetotalism. **good thing,** *n.* a witty remark or story; a favourable bargain or speculation; (*pl.*) delicacies, good fare. **good-time girl,** *n.* (*euphem.*) a prostitute. **good turn,** *n.* a kindly helpful act. **goodwife,** *n.* (*dated*) the mistress of a house. **goodwill,** *n.* kindly feeling or disposition; benevolence; favour; acquiescence; ready consent; the established popularity or custom of a business sold with the business itself. **goodies,** *n. pl.* objects, gifts etc. which are especially desirable. **goodish,** *a.* **goodly,** *a.* handsome, comely, graceful, kind; large, considerable; (*iron.*) poor, rubbishy. †*adv.* kindly. **goodliness,** *n.* **goodness,** *n.* the quality of being good; that which is good; moral excellence; virtue; kindness, good nature, generosity; the virtue or essence of anything; (*euphem.*) God. **goodness gracious!,** *int.* expressing surprise etc. **goodness knows!,** *int.* expressing lack of knowledge etc. **goods,** *n.* merchandise. **the goods,** (*sl.*) just what is wanted; (*esp. N Am. coll.*) evidence (against someone). **to deliver the goods,** to carry out one's promise, keep one's word. **goods train,** *n.* a train carrying merchandise only, a freight train. **goods truck,** *n.* a truck for goods only. **goody,** *int.* (*coll.*) esp. used by children, an exclamation expressing delight. **goody-**

goody, *n.* (*coll. usu. derog.*) esp. used by children, a priggishly good person. *a.* priggishly good. [OE *gōd* (cp. Dut. *goed,* Icel. *gōthr,* G *Gut*), cogn. with GATHER]

good-bye, *n., int.* farewell. [corr. of *God be with you!*]

goodletite, *n.* the matrix in which rubies are formed. [discoverer W. *Goodlet*]

Goodman[1], *n.* **'Benny' (Benjamin David)** (1909–86), US clarinetist, nicknamed 'the King of Swing' for the new jazz idiom he introduced. Leader of his own band from 1934, he is remembered for numbers such as 'Blue Skies' and 'King Porter Stomp'. Bartók's *Contrasts* (1939) and Copland's *Clarinet Concerto* (1950) were written for him.

Goodman[2], *n.* **Paul** (1911–), US writer and social critic, whose many writings (novels, plays, essays) express his anarchist, anti-authoritarian ideas. He studied youth offenders in *Growing up Absurd* (1960).

Goodyear, *n.* **Charles** (1800–60), US inventor, who developed vulcanized rubber in 1839, particularly important for motor-vehicle tyres.

goof, *n.* (*coll.*) a foolish mistake, a blunder; a stupid person. *v.i., v.t.* to blunder. **goof-ball,** *n.* (*sl.*) a barbiturate pill; a mentally abnormal person. **goofy,** *n.* (*coll.*) silly; infatuated. **goofiness,** *n.*

googly, *n.* in cricket, a ball bowled so as to break a different way from that expected from the apparent action of the bowler.

goon, *n.* a stupid person; a racketeer who terrorizes workers. [etym. unknown]

goonda, *n.* a desperado, a hooligan. [Hind.]

goondie, *n.* (*Austral.*) a hut, a gunyah. [Abor.]

Goonhilly, *n.* British Telecom satellite tracking station in Cornwall, England. It is equipped with a communications satellite transmitter–receiver in permanent contact with most parts of the world.

Goorkha, GURKHA.

goosander, *n.* a merganser, *Mergus merganser*. [etym. doubtful (perh. GOOSE, *-ander,* cp. Icel. *önd,* a duck, pl. *andir*)]

goose, *n.* (*pl.* **geese**) a web-footed bird intermediate in size between the duck and the swan, belonging to the genus *Anser,* esp. the domesticated variety *A. ferus;* the female of this, dist. from gander; a silly person, a simpleton; (*pl.* **gooses**) a tailor's smoothing iron; (*sl.*) a prod between the buttocks. *v.t.* (*sl.*) to prod between the buttocks. **to cook his goose,** COOK. **goose-bump** GOOSE-FLESH. **goose-cap,** *n.* a silly person. **gooseclub,** *n.* a society for providing subscribers with a Christmas goose paid for by instalments. **goose-corn,** *n.* a coarse rush, *Juncus squarrosus.* **goose-fish,** *n.* (*N Am.*) the angler-fish, *Lophius piscatorius.* **goose-flesh, -pimples, -skin,** *n.* a peculiar roughness of the human skin produced by cold, fear etc. **goose-foot,** *n.* herbs with leaves shaped like a goose's foot, as *Aspalathus chenopoda* and the genus *Chenopodium.* **goose-grass,** *n.* silverweed, *Potentilla anserina;* cleavers, *Galium aparine.* **goose-grease,** *n.* the melted fat of the goose, formerly used as remedy for various ailments. **gooseherd,** *n.* one who tends geese. **goose-pimples** GOOSE-FLESH. **goose-neck,** *n.* on a vessel, a bent iron fitted at the end of a yard or boom for various purposes; a piece of iron shaped like the neck of a goose. **goose-quill,** *n.* a quill-feather of a goose, esp. (formerly) used as a quill pen. **goose-skin** GOOSE-FLESH. **goose-step,** *n.* (*Mil.*) marking time by raising the feet alternately, as a balancing-drill for recruits; a marching step in which the legs are raised almost parallel with the ground without bending the knees. **goose-wing,** *n.* on a vessel, a lower corner of a square mainsail or foresail when the middle part is furled. **goose-winged,** *a.* **goosey**. [childish dim. of GOOSE], *n.* **goosy,** *a.* [OE *gōs* (cp. Dut. and G *Gans,* Icel. *gās,* L *anser,* Gr. *chēn,* perh. conn. with *chainein,* to gape)]

Goose Bay, *n.* a settlement at the head of Lake Melville on the Labrador coast of Newfoundland, Canada. In World War II it was used as a staging post by US and Canadian troops on their way to Europe. Until 1975 it was used by the US Air Force as a low-level-flying base.

gooseberry, *n.* the fruit of a thorny shrub, *Ribes grossularia.* **to play gooseberry,** to act as unwanted third to a pair of lovers. **gooseberry fool,** *n.* stewed gooseberries strained through a sieve and mixed with cream. [prob. GOOSE, BERRY]

gopak, *n.* a folkdance from the Ukraine characterized by high leaps, performed by men. [Rus.]

gopher[1], *n.* a name given to various American burrowing animals. [said to be from F *gaufre,* honeycomb]

gopher[2], *n.* the wood of which Noah's ark was made, so far unidentified. [Heb.]

gopher[3], GOFFER.

gopher[4], GOFER[2].

goral, *n.* a Himalayan goat-like antelope, *Naemorhedus goral.* [Hind. prob. from Sansk.]

goramy, *n.* a nest-building Oriental fish, *Osphromenus alfax,* much valued for food. [Javanese]

Gorbachev, *n.* **Mikhail Sergeyevich** (1931–), Soviet leader. He was a member of the Politburo from 1980 and, during the Chernenko administration (1984–85), was chairman of the Foreign Affairs Commission. As general secretary of the Communist Party (CPSU) from 1985, and president of the Supreme Soviet from 1988, he introduced liberal reforms at home (see PERESTROIKA, GLASNOST) and attempted to halt the arms race abroad. In 1990 he gained significantly increased powers for the presidency. **Gorbachevism,** *n.* adherence to or support for Gorbachev or his policies.

†**gorbellied,** *a.* big-bellied, corpulent. **gorbelly,** *n.* [obs. *gor,* filth]

gorcock, *n.* (*Sc., North.*) the moor-cock or male of the red grouse. [etym. doubtful]

gorcrow, *n.* the carrion crow. [*gor,* see GORE[1], -CROW[1]]

Gordian, *a.* intricate, complicated. **Gordian knot,** *n.* in Greek myth, a knot in the harness of Gordius, a king of Phrygia, which Alexander cut with his sword upon hearing the promise of the oracle that whoso could untie it should possess the empire of Asia; any apparently inextricable difficulty or deadlock. **to cut the Gordian knot,** to remove a difficulty by drastic measures.

Gordimer, *n.* **Nadine** (1923–), South African novelist, an opponent of apartheid. Her first novel, *The Lying Days*, appeared in 1953, and other works include *The Conservationist* (1974), the volume of short stories *A Soldier's Embrace* (1980), and *July's People* (1981). Her books are banned in South Africa.

gordius, *n.* a genus of threadlike worms, endoparasitic during part of their life. [as prec.]

Gordon[1], *n.* **Charles (George)** (1833–85), British general sent to Khartoum in the Sudan 1884 to rescue English garrisons that were under attack by the Mahdi; he was himself besieged by the Mahdi's army. A relief expedition arrived 28 Jan. 1885, to find that Khartoum, after a siege of ten months, had been captured, and Gordon killed, two days before.

Gordon[2], *n.* **George** (1751–93), British organizer of the so-called **Gordon Riots** of 1778, a protest against removal of penalties imposed on Roman Catholics in the Catholic Relief Act of 1778; he was acquitted on a treason charge. Gordon and the 'No Popery' riots figure in Dickens's novel *Barnaby Rudge*.

gore[1], *n.* blood from a wound, esp. thick, clotted blood. **gore-blood,** *n.* **gory,** *a.* covered with gore; bloody involving bloodshed and killing. **gory-dew,** *n.* a minute freshwater alga, *Palmella cruenta,* coating damp walls in shady places with rosy gelatinous patches. **goriness,** *n.* [OE *gor,* dirt, filth (cp. Icel. *gor,* Dut. *goor*)]

gore[2], *n.* a triangular piece sewed into a dress, a sail, balloon etc. to widen it out at any part; a triangular piece of land; (*Her.*) a curved abatement cut from a shield, orig. denoting cowardice. *v.t.* to make into or shape as a gore; to fit with a gore. [OE *gāra,* cogn. with foll.]

gore[3], *v.t.* to pierce, to stab; to pierce with or as with a horn or horn-like point. [OE *gār,* a spear (cp. Icel. *geirr,* and perh. OIr. *gár*)]

gorge, *n.* the throat; the gullet; that which is swallowed or gorged; the act of gorging; a heavy meal, a surfeit; a narrow pass between cliffs or hills; in a fortification, the narrow entrance into a bastion or other outwork; in angling, a bait to be swallowed by a fish. *v.t.* to swallow, to devour greedily; to glut, to satiate, to choke up. *v.i.* to feed greedily. **gorged,** *a.* having a gorge or throat; in heraldry, bearing a crown or the like round the neck. [OF, etym. doubtful]

gorgeous, *a.* splendid, richly decorated, magnificent; ornate; (*loosely*) very fine, beautiful etc. **gorgeously,** *adv.* **gorgeousness,** *n.* [OF *gorgias,*]

gorget[1], *n.* a piece of armour for defending the throat or neck; a metallic ornament formerly worn on the breast by officers on duty; a ruff or wimple formerly worn by women; a necklace. [OF *gorgete,* dim. of *gorge,* see GORGE]

gorget[2], *n.* a tabular lithotomic cutting instrument used in surgery. [F *gorgeret,* as prec.]

Gorgio, *n.* gipsy name for one not a gipsy. [Romany]

Gorgon, *n.* (*Gr. Myth.*) one of three snake-haired female monsters of an aspect so terrible that the sight of them was fabled to turn beholders into stone; a terrible or hideous creature, esp. a repulsive-looking woman. **gorgoneion,** *n.* (*pl.* **-neia**) a mask or other representation of the Gorgon's head, often used as a keystone. **gorgonesque,** *a.* **gorgonize, -ise,** *v.t.* to gaze at so as to paralyse or turn to stone. [L *Gorgō -ōnis,* Gr. *Gorgō*, pl. *-ones*, from *gorgos*, terrible]

gorgonia, *n.* (*pl.* **iae, -ias**) the sea-fan; a genus of flexible polyps growing in the form of shrubs, feathers etc. **gorgonian,** *a.* any coral of the order of Gorgonacea. [from prec., in allusion to their petrified character]

Gorgonzola, *n.* a blue-veined cheese somewhat like Stilton. [village near Milan]

Goria, *n.* **Giovanni** (1943–), Italian Christian Democrat (DC) politician, prime minister 1987–88. He entered the Chamber of Deputies 1976 and held a number of posts, including treasury minister, until he was asked to form a coalition government in 1987.

gorilla, *n.* a large vegetarian African anthropoid ape, *Gorilla gorilla,* about $5\frac{1}{2}$ ft (1·6 m) in height. [Gr. form of alleged African name for a wild man in account of Hanno the Carthaginian's travels in 5th or 6th cent. BC]

Göring, or **Goering,** *n.* **Hermann** (1893–1946), German field marshal from 1938 and Nazi leader. Göring was part of Hitler's 'inner circle', and with Hitler's rise to power in 1933, established the Gestapo and concentration camps. Appointed successor to Hitler 1939, he built a vast economic empire in occupied Europe, but later lost favour, and was expelled from the party 1945. Tried at Nuremberg, he poisoned himself before he could be executed.

Gorky[1], *n.* (Russian **Gor'kiy**) (former name **Nizhny-Novgorod** until 1932) city in central USSR; population (1987) 1,425,000. Cars, locomotives, and aircraft are manufactured here.

Gorky[2], *n.* **Arshile** (1904–48), US painter, born in Armenia, who settled in the US in 1920. He painted Cubist abstracts before developing a more surreal abstract expressionist style, using organic shapes and bold paint strokes.

Gorky[3], *n.* **Maxim** (1868–1936), pen name of Alexei Peshkov, Russian writer. Born in Nizhny-Novgorod (renamed Gorky 1932 in his honour), he was exiled 1906–13 for his revolutionary principles. His works, which include the play *The Lower Depths* (1902) and the recollections *My Childhood* (1913), combine realism with optimistic faith in the potential of the industrial proletariat.

gormandize, -ise, *n.* taste in the provision and appreciation of table delicacies; †indulgence in eating, gluttony. *v.t.* to eat greedily, to gorge. *v.i.* to eat food greedily. **gormandizer, -iser,** *n.* **gormandizing, -ising,** *n.* [OF *gourmandise,* gluttony, from GOURMAND]

gormless GAUMLESS.

gorse, *n.* a prickly shrub with yellow flowers, furze, whin. **gorsy,** *a.* [OE *gorst* (cogn. with G *Gerst,* L *hordeum,* barley, L *horridus,* bristly)]

Gorsedd, *n.* a meeting of bards and Druids. [W]

Gorton, *n.* **John Grey** (1911–), Australian Liberal politician. He was minister for education and science (1966–68), and prime minister (1968–71).

gory GORE[1].

gosh, *int.* a minced oath. [GOD]

goshawk, *n.* a large, short-winged hawk, *Astur palumbarius;* applied also to other species of *Astur.* [OE *gos-hafuc* (as GOOSE, HAWK[1])]

Goshen, *n.* a land of plenty. [the land in Egypt given by Pharaoh to the Israelites to dwell in (Gen. xlv)]

gosling, *n.* a young goose; a silly or inexperienced person; †a catkin.

go-slow GO[1].

gospel, *n.* the revelation of the grace of God through Jesus Christ; the doctrine preached by Christ and the Apostles; (*cap.*) one of the canonical books ascribed respectively to Matthew, Mark, Luke and John; a selection from these books read in the Church service; anything accepted as infallibly true; the principle that one adopts as a guide to life or action; the creed of a party etc. †*v.t.* to instruct in gospel precepts; to fill with sentiments of religion. **gospel-book,** *n.* a book containing the Gospels or one of them, or the New Testament for use at Holy Communion. **gospel oath,** *n.* an oath sworn on the Gospels. **gospel side,** *n.* the north side of the chancel where the Gospel is read. **gospel truth,** *n.* something as true as the Gospel. **gospel-wagon,** *n.* a vehicle used at open-air services. **gospeller,** *n.* one of the four Evangelists; the priest who reads the Gospel in the Communion service; a missionary; one who claims that his religious beliefs are based exclusively on the Gospels (often applied contemptuously to Protestants, Puritans etc.). †**gospellize, -ise,** *v.t.* to lay down as gospel; to evangelize. [OE *godspell,* good tidings]

†**goss,** GORSE.

Gossaert, *n.* **Jan.** (*c.* 1478–*c.* 1533), Flemish painter, known as MABUSE.

gossamer, *n.* the slender cobweb-like threads floating in the air in calm weather, produced by small spiders; thin, filmy gauze; anything exceedingly flimsy or unsubstantial. **gossamered,** *a.* **gossamery,** *a.* [ME *gossomer,* lit. goose-summer, i.e. St Martin's summer (early Nov.), when geese were eaten, the time of its prevalence]

Gossamer Albatross, *n.* the first human-powered aircraft to fly across the English Channel, in June 1979. It was designed by Paul MacCready and piloted and pedalled by Bryan Allen. The Channel crossing took 2 hours 49 minutes. The same team was behind the first successful human-powered aircraft (*Gossamer Condor*) two years earlier.

gossan, *n.* in mining, decomposed, ferruginous rock forming the upper part of a metallic vein. [Cornish dial., etym. doubtful]

Gosse, *n.* **Edmund William** (1849–1928), English author. Son of a marine biologist, who was a member of the Plymouth Brethren, Gosse's strict Victorian upbringing is reflected in his masterpiece of autobiographical work *Father and Son* (published anonymously in 1907).

gossip, *n.* †a sponsor; a friend, an acquaintance; one who runs about tattling; idle talk, tittle-tattle; mere rumour; informal chat or writing, esp. about persons or incidents of the day. †*v.t.* to stand sponsor to. *v.i.* to tattle, to chat; to talk or write in an informal easy-going way. **gossipmonger,** *n.* a spreader of gossip. **gossiper,** *n.* **gossipry,** *n.* **gossipy,** *a.* [OE *godsibb,* orig. related in God, a sponsor in baptism]

gossoon, *n.* (*Ang.-Ir.*) a boy, a lad. [corr. of F GARÇON]

gossypium, *n.* a tropical genus of herbs and shrubs belonging to the *Malvaceae* or mallow family, including three species whence the cotton of commerce is obtained. [L *gossypion*]

got, got-up, *a.* dressed up, disguised, or prepared for effect or to take in. [past, p.p. of GET[1]]

Göteborg, *n.* (German **Gothenburg**) port and industrial (ships, vehicles, chemicals) city on the west coast of Sweden, on the Göta Canal (built 1832), which links it with Stockholm; population (1988) 432,000.

Goth, *n.* E Germanic people who settled near the Black Sea around the 2nd cent. AD. There are two branches, the eastern Ostrogoths, and the western Visigoths. The **Ostrogoths** were conquered by the Huns 372. They regained their independence 454, and under Theodoric the Great conquered Italy 488–93; they disappeared as a nation after the Byzantine emperor Justinian I reconquered Italy 535–55. The **Visigoths** migrated to Thrace. Under Alaric they raided Greece and Italy 395–410, sacked Rome, and established a kingdom in S France. Expelled from there by the Franks, they established a Spanish kingdom which lasted until the Moorish conquest of 711. **Gothic,** *a.* pertaining to the Goths or their language **Gothish,** *a.* [late L *Gothī*, Gr. *Gothoi*, Goth. *Gutōs* or *Gutans*, pl.]

Goth., (*abbr.*) Gothic.

Gothamist, *n.* a foolish person, one easily taken in. **Gothamite,** *n.* a Gothamist; (*US, facet.*) a New Yorker. [*Gotham*, a village in Nottinghamshire, said to be noted for its foolish inhabitants]

gothic, *a.* in the style of architecture characterized by pointed arches, clustered columns etc.; rude, barbarous; (*Print.*) black-letter. *n.* the language of the Goths; the Gothic style of architecture; (*Print.*) black-letter. **gothic architecture,** *n.* style of architecture characterized by vertical lines of tall pillars, spires, greater height in interior spaces, the pointed arch, rib vaulting, and the flying buttress. **Gothic art,** *n.* painting and sculpture in the style that dominated European art from the late 12th cent. until the early Renaissance. The great gothic church façades held hundreds of sculpted figures and profuse ornament, and manuscripts were lavishly decorated. Stained glass replaced mural painting to some extent in N European churches. The International Gothic style in painting emerged in the 14th cent. characterized by delicate and complex ornament and increasing realism. **Gothic novel,** *n.* genre established by Horace Walpole's *The Castle of Otranto* (1765), and marked by mystery, violence, and horror; other exponents of the genre were Mrs Radcliffe, Matthew 'Monk' Lewis, Bram Stoker, and Edgar Allan Poe. **gothic revival,** *n.* the modern resurgence of interest in Gothic architecture, especially as displayed in 19th-cent. Britain and the US. Gothic revival buildings in England include the Houses of Parliament and St Pancras Station, London. **gothically,** *adv.* **Gothicism,** *n.* a Gothic idiom; conformity to the gothic style of architecture; rudeness of manners. **Gothicist,** *n.* **gothicize, -ise,** *v.t.* to make gothic; to bring back to barbarism. *v.i.* to go back to barbarism. [GOTH]

gotten, *p.p.* GET[1].

Götterdämmerung, *n.* in German mythology, the final destruction of the world. [G, twilight of the gods]

Gottfried von Strassburg (lived *c.* 1210), German poet, author of the unfinished epic *Tristan und Isolde* which inspired Wagner.

gouache, *n.* a method of painting with opaque colours mixed with water, honey and gum. [F, from It. *guazzo*]

Gouda, *n.* a round mild cheese made at Gouda, in Holland.

gouge, *n.* a chisel with a concave blade, used to cut holes or grooves; (*sl.*) a swindle, a fraud. *v.t.* to cut, force or scoop (out) with or as with a gouge; (*N Am.*) to cheat. **gouge-slip,** *n.* a hone used for sharpening gouges. [F, late L *guvia*, etym. doubtful]

goujon, *n.* a small strip of fish, chicken etc. coated in flour or breadcrumbs and fried. [F]

goulard, *n.* a lotion composed of subacetate of lead in solution. **goulard water,** *n.* [Thomas *Goulard*, d. *c.* 1790, French surgeon]

goulash, *n.* a stew of meat and vegetables highly seasoned with paprika. [Hung. *gulyas*, herdsman]

Gould [1], *n.* **Bryan Charles** (1939–), British Labour politician, member of the shadow cabinet from 1986.

Gould [2], *n.* **Elliott** (stage name of Elliot Goldstein) (1938–), US film actor. A successful child actor, his film debut, *The Night They Raided Minsky's* (1968), led rapidly to starring roles in such films as *M.A.S.H.* (1970), *The Long Goodbye* (1972), and *Capricorn One* (1978).

Gould [3], *n.* **Stephen Jay** (1941–), US palaeontologist and author. In 1972 he proposed the theory of punctuated equilibrium, suggesting that the evolution of species did not occur at a steady rate but could suddenly accelerate, with rapid change occurring over a few hundred thousand years.

Gounod, *n.* **Charles François** (1818–93), French composer. His operas include *Sappho* (1851), *Faust* (1859), *Philémon et Baucis* (1860), and *Roméo et Juliette* (1867). He also wrote sacred songs, masses, and an oratorio, *The Redemption* (1882). His music has great lyrical appeal and emotional power and it inspired many French composers of the later 19th cent.

goupen, GOWPEN.

goura, *n.* a genus of pigeons found on the island of New Guinea. [Papuan name]

gourami, GORAMY.

gourd, *n.* a large fleshy fruit of climbing or trailing plants belonging to the Cucurbitaceae, the outer coat of which serves for vessels to hold water; a bottle, cup etc. made of the hard rind of this; a vessel of a similar shape; (*pl.*) hollow dice employed for cheating. **gourd-worm,** *n.* a fluke-worm. **gourdful,** *n.* [F *gourde*, ult. from L *cucurbita*]

gourmand, *a.* gluttonous, fond of eating. *n.* one who loves delicate fare, a gourmet; a glutton. [F, etym. doubtful]

gourmet, *n.* a connoisseur in wines and meats; a dainty feeder, an epicure. [F, orig. a wine-taster]

gousty, *a.* (*Sc., North.*) dreary, desolate, forlorn; gusty. **goustrous,** *a.* violent, boisterous. [etym. doubtful]

gout, *n.* a disease affecting the joints, esp. the great toe, with inflammation, pain and irritability being the leading symptoms; †a drop, a clot; a disease of wheat caused by the **gout-fly**. **gouty,** *a.* affected with or pertaining to gout; swollen. **goutily,** *adv.* **goutiness,** *n.* [OF *goute*, L *gutta*, a drop]

goût, *n.* taste, relish; good taste, artistic discernment. [F, earlier *goust*, L *gustus*]

gov., (*abbr.*) Governor; Government.

govern, *v.t.* to direct and control; to rule with authority, esp. to administer the affairs of a state; to exercise military command over; to regulate, to sway, to influence, to determine; to conduct (oneself) in a specific way; to restrain, to curb; in grammar, to require a particular case in the word following it, to have a noun or case dependent upon it (said of a verb or preposition). *v.i.* to exercise authority; to administer the law; to have the control (over). **governable,** *a.* **governability,** *n.* **governably,** *adv.* **governance,** **†governall,** *n.* [OF *governer*, L *gubernāre*, to steer, guide, from Gr. *kubernân*, to steer]

governess, *n.* a woman who has the care and instruction of young children, esp. in a private household; an instructress. **governess-car, -cart,** *n.* a light two-wheeled vehicle with two seats only, facing each other. **†governante,** *n.* [earlier *governeress*, OF *gouverneresse*, fem. of *gouverneur*, GOVERNOR]

government, *n.* control, direction, regulation, exercise of authority, esp. authoritative administration of public affairs; the form or system of such administration; the body of persons in charge of the government of a state at any particular time, an administration, a ministry; self-control, manageableness; the power of controlling; the form of policy in a state; the right of governing; the executive power; (*N Am.*) state administration; the territory under a governor, a province; †deportment; (*Gram.*) the influence of a word in determining the case or mood of another. **Government Communications Headquarters,** the centre of the British government's electronic surveillance operations, in Cheltenham, Gloucestershire. It monitors broadcasts of various kinds from all over the world. It was established in World War I, and was successful in breaking the German Enigma code in 1940. **government issue,** *n.* (*esp.* US) supplied by the government. **government**

man, *n.* (*Austral.*) a convict, an assigned servant. **governmental**, *a.* **governmentally,** *adv.* **governmentalism**, *n.* **governmentalist,** *n.* [OF *governement*]

governor, *n.* one who governs, esp. one invested with authority to execute the laws and administer the affairs of a state, province etc.; a ruler, a head of the executive; the Crown representative in a colony or dependency; (*US*) the elective chief magistrate of a state; the commander in a fortress or garrison; (*sl.*), one's father, one's employer; an unceremonious mode of address; a contrivance for regulating the speed of an engine motor etc., or the flow or pressure of a fluid or gas; †a pilot; †a tutor. **governor-general,** *n.* a chief of the executive in a large dependency, having deputy-governors under him. **governor-generalship,** *n.* **governorship,** *n.* [OF *governeur*]

Gov.-Gen., (*abbr.*) Governor-General.

gowan, *n.* (*Sc., North.*) the daisy. [perh. conn. with Icel. *gulr,* YELLOW, or with OE *golde,* GOLD]

gowd, (*Sc.*) GOLD.

Gower[1], *n.* **David** (1957–), English cricketer. A left-hander, since his debut for Leicestershire 1975 he has scored over 20,000 first-class runs. He made his England debut in 1978, and was captain 1984 and 1989.

Gower[2], *n.* **John** (*c.* 1330–1408), English poet. He is remembered for his tales of love *Confessio Amantis* (1390), written in English, and other poems in French and Latin.

gowff, *v.t.* (*Sc.*) to strike, to cuff. [conn. with GOLF]

gowk, *n.* (*Sc., North.*) †the cuckoo; a fool, a simple or awkward person. [Icel. *gaukr* (cp. G *Gauch,* OE *gēak*)]

gowl, *v.i.* (*Sc., North.*) to howl, to cry. *n.* a howl, a yell. [from Icel. *gaula,* to YAWL]

gown, *n.* a woman's loose, long, outer garment, a dress, esp. a handsome or stylish one; a long, loose robe worn by clergymen, judges, lawyers, university graduates etc.; protective garment as worn by surgeons during an operation; a Roman toga. **town and gown,** the townspeople as opposed to or contrasted with the professors and students in a university town. **gown-boy,** *n.* a boy wearing a gown, as one belonging to an endowed school. †**gown-cloth,** *n.* a piece of cloth for making a gown. **gowned,** *a.* **gownsman,** *n.* one whose professional dress is a gown; a member of a university; a lawyer; †a clergyman; one wearing a gown as emblem of peace, a civilian. [OF *gaune, gonne,* late L *gunna,* a skin, a fur garment; etym. doubtful]

Gowon, *n.* **Yakubu** (1934–), Nigerian politician, head of state, 1966–75. Educated at Sandhurst, he became chief of staff, and in the military coup of 1966 seized power. After the Biafran civil war (1967–70), he reunited the country with his policy of 'no victor, no vanquished'. In 1975 he was overthrown by a military coup.

gowpen, *n.* a handful, a double handful; as much as can be held in the hollow of the two hands; a perquisite of meal allowed to a miller's man. [Sc., from Icel. *gaupn*]

Goy, *n.* Yiddish name for a non-Jewish person. [Heb., a nation]

Goya, *n.* **Francisco José de Goya y Lucientes** (1746–1828), Spanish painter and engraver. He painted portraits of four successive kings of Spain, and his etchings include *The Disasters of War*, depicting the French invasion of Spain (1810–14). Among his last works are the 'black paintings' (Prado, Madrid), with horrific images such as *Saturn Devouring One of his Sons* (about 1822).

Goyen, *n.* **Jan van** (1596–1656), Dutch landscape painter, active in Leiden, Haarlem, and from 1631 in The Hague. He was a pioneer of the realist style of landscape with Ruisdael, and sketched from nature and studied clouds and light effects.

Gozzoli, *n.* **Benozzo** (*c.* 1421–97), Florentine painter, a late exponent of the International gothic style. He painted frescoes 1459 in the chapel of the Palazzo Medici-Riccardi, Florence: the walls are crammed with figures, many of them portraits of the Medici family.

GP, (*abbr.*) General Practitioner; (*mus.*) general pause; Gallup Poll; Grand Prix.

gp., (*abbr.*) group.

GPO, (*abbr.*) General Post Office.

GPU, *n.* former name (1922–23) for KGB, the Soviet secret police.

Gr., (*abbr.*) Grand; Greece; Greek.

gr., (*abbr.*) grain, grains.

Graaf, *n.* **Regnier de** (1641–73), Dutch physician and anatomist who discovered the ovarian follicles, which were later named Graafian follicles. He gave exact descriptions of the testicles, and named the ovaries. He was also the first to isolate and collect the secretions of the pancreas and gall bladder. **Graafian**, *a.* named after de Graaf. **Graafian follicle** or **vesicle,** *n.* during the menstrual cycle, a fluid-filled capsule that surrounds and protects the developing egg cell inside the ovary. After the egg cell has been released, the follicle remains and is known as a corpus luteum.

graal, GRAIL[2].

grab, *v.t.* (*past, p.p.* **grabbed**) to seize, snatch or grasp suddenly; to take possession of violently or lawlessly; (*coll.*) to capture, to arrest; (*coll.*) to interest. *v.i.* to grasp, snatch, or clutch (at). *n.* a sudden snatch, grasping or seizing (at); an implement for clutching, a grip; rapacious or dishonest acquisition, esp. in commerce or the foreign policy of a government. **grab-bag,** *n.* (*N Am.*) a bag from which articles are grabbed for on payment, at fairs, sports etc., a lucky dip. **up for grabs,** (*coll.*) on offer; for sale; ready for the taking. **grabber,** *n.* **land-grabber,** *n.* (*chiefly Irish*) one who gets hold of land by underhand means. [prob. orig. Eng., perh. from GRIP (cp. Swed. *grabba,* MDut. and MLG *grabben*)]

grabble, *v.i.* to grope, to feel about (for); to sprawl on all fours (after, for etc.). [freq. of prec.]

Grable, *n.* **'Betty' (Elizabeth Ruth)** (1916–73), US actress, singer and dancer, who starred in, *Moon over Miami* (1941), *I Wake Up Screaming* (1941), and *How to Marry a Millionaire* (1953). As a publicity stunt, her legs were insured for a million dollars.

Gracchus, *n.* the brothers Tiberius Sempronius (163–133 BC) and Gaius Sempronius (153–121 BC). Roman agrarian reformers. As tribune 133 BC, Tiberius tried to prevent the ruin of small farmers by making large slave-labour farms illegal but was murdered. Gaius, tribune 123–122 BC, revived his brother's legislation, and introduced other reforms, but was outlawed by the Senate and committed suicide.

grace, *n.* that quality which makes form, movement, expression or manner elegant, harmonious, refined and charming; a natural gift or endowment; an acquired accomplishment, charm or attraction; a courteous or affable demeanour; free, unmerited favour or goodwill; clemency, mercy; a boon, a benefaction; (*Mus.*) an ornamental note or passage introduced as an embellishment; (*Theol.*) the free, unmerited favour of God; a divine, regenerating and invigorating influence; the state of being forgiven by and reconciled to God, with participation in the favours granted through the merits of Christ; a spiritual favour or excellence; a short prayer invoking a blessing before or returning thanks after a meal; a privilege or indulgence, esp. an extension of time legally allowed after a payment falls due; at a university, a vote, decree, a licence to take a degree, a dispensation from statutes etc.; †(*pl.*) thanks. **Act of grace,** a general pardon granted by Act of Parliament. **airs and graces,** affectation; assumed refinement. **days of grace,** DAY. **grace-and-favour,** *a.* of a house, flat etc., granted free of rent by the sovereign as a mark of gratitude. **her, his, your grace,** courteous phrases adopted in speaking to or of an archbishop, duke, duchess and formerly sovereigns. **the Graces,** *n.* in Greek mythology, three goddesses (Aglaia, Euphrosyne, Thalia), daughters of Zeus and Hera, the personification of grace and beauty and the inspirers of the arts and the sciences. **to be in the good graces of,** to enjoy the favour of. **to fall from grace** FALL. **with a good** or **bad grace,** to do a thing willingly or reluctantly. **year of grace** YEAR. **grace-**

cup, *n.* a cup, usu. of wine, passed round after a meal for drinking the concluding health or healths. **grace-note,** *n.* (*Mus.*) an extra note introduced for embellishment. **grace-stroke,** *n.* a finishing stroke. **graceful,** *a.* full of grace, elegance or beauty, esp. of form or movement. **gracefully,** *adv.* **gracefulness,** *n.* **graceless,** *a.* void of grace; lacking in propriety or decency, mannerless; depraved, abandoned; ungraceful; †out of favour, unfortunate. **gracelessly,** *adv.* **gracelessness,** *n.* [OF *grace* (F *grâce*), L *grātia,* from *grātus,* pleasing]

Grace, *n.* **W(illiam) G(ilbert)** (1848–1915), English cricketer. By profession a doctor, he became the best batsman in England. He began playing first class cricket at the age of 16, scored 152 runs in his first Test match, and scored the first triple century 1876.

gracile, *a.* slender, lean, thin. **gracility,** *n.*

gracious, *a.* exhibiting grace, favour or kindness; benevolent, kind; courteous, condescending, affable; graceful, pleasing, bland; proceeding from divine grace; benignant, merciful. **gracious me! gracious goodness!** *int.* exclamations of surprise or protest. **graciously,** *adv.* **graciousness,** *n.* [OF (F *gracieux*), L *gratiōsus,* as prec.]

grackle, *n.* any bird of the genus *Gracula,* allied to the starlings. [L *grāculus,* a jackdaw]

gradate GRADATION.

gradatim, *adv.* gradually, by degrees. [L, as foll.]

gradation, *n.* an orderly arrangement, succession or progression step by step; a step, stage or degree in order, rank, quality, merit etc. (*usu. in pl.*); (*Fine Art*) the gradual blending of one tint, tone etc. with another; (*Mus.*) an ascending or descending succession of chords; (*Philol.*) ablaut. **gradate,** *v.t.* to arrange or blend (colours etc.) by imperceptible gradation. *v.i.* to pass from one tint to another by such gradations. **gradational,** *a.* **gradationally,** *adv.* **gradationed,** *a.* formed by gradation. **gradatory,** *a.* proceeding by gradations. *n.* a flight of steps, as from a cloister into a church. [L *gradātio -ōnem,* from *gradus,* a step]

grade, *n.* a degree or step in rank, quality, value, order etc.; a class of people of similar rank, ability, proficiency etc.; class (at school); an animal or class of animals (as cattle or sheep) produced by crossing a common stock with some better breed; (*Zool.*) a group supposed to have branched off from a parent stem at a certain stage of development; degree of intensity (of a disease); gradient, the degree of slope in a road; a road, track etc., or part of such, inclined to the horizontal; (*Philol.*) the position of a vowel or root in an ablaut series. *v.t.* to arrange in grades; to gradate; to adjust the rate of slope in, as a road; of cattle, to cross (a stock) with a better breed. **at grade,** (*N Am.*) at the same level (as of a place where two roads cross each other). **down** or **up grade,** a descending or ascending road or part of a road. **on the down** or **the up grade,** descending or ascending a slope; falling or rising. **to grade up,** to improve (stock) by crossing with a better breed. **to make the grade,** to succeed. **grade cricket,** *n.* (*Austral.*) competitive cricket played between teams arranged in grades. **grade-crossing,** *n.* (*N Am. Rail.*) a level-crossing. **grade school,** *n.* (*N Am.*) elementary school. **gradable,** *a.* **grader,** *n.* one who or that which grades; a motor-driven vehicle with a blade for pushing earth, rubble etc., used in road construction etc. [F, from L *gradum,* nom. *-us,* see prec.]

-grade, *comb. form* of a kind or manner of movement or progression, as in *retrograde.*

gradely, *a.* (*dial.*) decent, respectable, worthy; well; proper, suitable; good-looking. *adv.* decently, properly, well, becomingly. [ME *graythly,* Icel. *greithliga* (cp. GRAITH, OE *gerœde,* G *gerade,* ready)]

gradient, *n.* the rate of ascent or descent in a railway or road; degree of slope, inclination; in civil engineering, grade; rate of variation or increase or decrease in height of thermometer or barometer over a large area; the diagrammatic line denoting such variation. [from GRADE, after L *gradiens -ntem,* p.p. of *gradi,* to walk]

gradin, gradine¹, *n.* one in a series of rising steps or a tier of seats; a shelf or step at the back of an altar. [F *gradin,* It. *gradino,* from *grado,* GRADE]

gradine², **gradino,** *n.* a toothed chisel used by sculptors. [as prec.]

gradual, *a.* proceeding by steps or degrees; regular and slow, opp. to abrupt, steep, rapid. *n.* an antiphon sung between the Epistle and the Gospel; a book containing such antiphons or the music for them. **gradualism,** *n.* esp. regarding political policy, the principle of making change slowly and gradually rather than quickly or by violent means. **gradualist,** *n.* **gradually,** *adv.* **gradualness,** *n.*

graduate, *v.t.* to mark with degrees; to divide into or arrange by gradations; to apportion (a tax etc.) according to a scale of grades; to temper or modify by degrees; (*N Am.*) to confer an academic degree upon; in chemistry, to bring a fluid to a certain degree of consistency, as by evaporation. *v.i.* to alter, change or pass by degrees; to take a degree in a university. *n.*, one who has received a degree in a university; in chemistry, a graduated vessel for measuring liquids. **graduand,** *n.* a person who is about to graduate from a university. **graduateship,** *n.* **graduation,** *n.* regular progression by successive degrees; a division into degrees or parts; the conferring or receiving of academical degrees; in chemistry, the reduction of a liquid to a certain consistency by evaporation. **graduation exercises,** (*N Am.*) prize-day at school etc. **graduator,** *n.* an instrument for dividing lines into minute equal parts. [late L *graduātus,* p.p. of *graduāre,* as prec.]

graduction, *n.* in astronomy, the division of circular arcs into degrees, minutes etc. [erroneously formed from *gradus,* as prec.]

gradus, *n.* a dictionary of Greek or Latin prosody formerly used in public schools. [short for *Gradus ad Parnassum,* steps to Parnassus]

Graecism, *n.* a Greek idiom, style or mode of expression; cultivation of the Greek spirit, style or mode of expression. **graecize, -ise,** *v.t.* to give a Greek form or character to. *v.i.* to cultivate or follow the Greek spirit, ideas, ways of expression etc. [F *grécisme,* med. L. *Graecismus,* from *Graecus,* GREEK]

graeco-, *comb. form* Greek. **Graeco-maniac,** *n.* **Graeco-phil,** *n.* **Graeco-Roman,** *a.* pertaining to both Greeks and Latins.

Graf, *n.* **Steffi** (1969–), West German lawn tennis player, who brought Martina Navratilova's long reign as the world's number one female player to an end. She reached the semi-final of the US Open in 1985 at the age of 16, and won five consecutive Grand Slam singles titles (1988–89).

†graff, *n.* a ditch or trench; a grave. [cp. MDut. *graft*]

graffito, *n.* (*pl.* **-ti**) a drawing or inscription scratched on a wall or other surface, as in ancient buildings at Pompeii or Rome; decoration by means of scratches through plaster, revealing a differently coloured ground. (*usu. pl.*) drawings or words, sometimes obscene, sometimes political, painted or written on walls etc. in public view. [It., from *graffio,* a scratch]

graft¹, *n.* a small shoot of a tree or plant inserted into another tree of a different stock which supplies the sap to nourish it; living tissue from a person or animal transplanted to another; incorporation with a foreign stock. *v.t.* to insert (a shoot or scion) in or upon another plant or tree; to insert as a graft; to insert grafts upon; to plant (a tree or stock) thus with another variety; to transplant (as living animal tissue); to incorporate with another stock; to insert or implant (upon) so as to form a vital union; on a vessel, to cover (a ring-bolt etc.) with spun yarn or a weaving of thin cord. *v.i.* to insert grafts or scions in or on other stocks. **grafter,** *n.* one who grafts; †a tree from which a graft was taken. **grafting clay** or **wax,** *n.* a plastic composition used for covering grafted parts and excluding air. **grafting scissors,** *n.* scissors used by surgeons in skin-grafting. [earlier *graff,* OF *grafe* (F *greffe*), low L *graphium,* Gr. *graphion,* a stylus, from *graphein,* to write]

graft², *n.* a spit of earth, the amount thrown up at one dig with the spade. [conn. with GRAVE²]

graft3, *n.* a swindle; acquisition of money etc. by taking advantage of an official position; bribery; manipulation of state or municipal business in order to secure illicit profits or influence; illicit gains so obtained. **grafter,** *n.* [etym. doubtful]

graft4, *n.* hard work, unremitting labour. *v.i.* (*coll.*) to work (hard).

Grafton, *n.* **Augustus Henry, 3rd Duke of Grafton** (1735–1811), British politician. Grandson of the first duke, who was the son of Charles II and Barbara Villiers (1641–1709), Duchess of Cleveland. He became First Lord of the Treasury in 1766 and an unsuccessful acting prime minister (1767–70).

Graham1, *n.* family name of Dukes of Montrose.

Graham2, *n.* **'Billy' (William Franklin)** (1918–), US Baptist evangelist. At 17 he was converted at an evangelistic meeting. His Evangelistic Association conducts worldwide 'crusades'.

Graham3, *n.* **Martha** (1894–), US dancer, choreographer, teacher and director. The leading exponent of modern dance in the US, she has created over 150 works and developed a unique vocabulary of movement, *The Graham Technique*, now taught worldwide.

Graham4, *n.* **Thomas** (1805–69), Scottish chemist who laid the foundations of physical chemistry (the branch of chemistry concerned with changes in energy during a chemical transformation) by his work on the diffusion of gases and liquids. **Graham's Law** states that the diffusion rate of two gases varies inversely as the square root of their densities.

Grahame, *n.* **Kenneth** (1859–1932), Scottish author. The early volumes of sketches of childhood, *The Golden Age* (1895) and *Dream Days* (1898), were followed by his masterpiece *The Wind in the Willows* (1908), an animal fantasy created for his young son, which was dramatized by A. A. Milne as *Toad of Toad Hall.*

grail1, *n.* a dish or cup said to have been used by Christ at the Last Supper, and employed by Joseph of Arimathea to collect His blood while on the Cross; also called the **Holy Grail, Saint Grail,** and **Sangreal**. [OF *graal, greal,* late L *gradālis,* etym. doubtful]

grail2, *n.* a coarse file formerly used in making combs by hand. [F *grêle,* see foll.]

†**grail**3, *n.* fine gravel or sand. [etym. doubtful, perh. from MF *graisle* (F *grêle*), L *gracilis,* slender, or a var. of GRAVEL]

grain1, *n.* a single seed of a plant, particularly of those kinds whose seeds are used for food; (*collect.*) corn in general or the fruit of cereal plants, as wheat, barley, rye etc.; (*N Am.*) wheat; (*pl.*) the husks or refuse of malt after brewing or of any grain after distillation; any small, hard particle; the smallest particle or amount; the unit of weight in the English system, 1/7000 lb. avoirdupois or 1/5760 lb. troy (65 mg); a unit of weight for pearls equal to 50 mg or $\frac{1}{4}$ of a carat, also called **metric grain** in photography, one of the particles in a photographic emulsion of a film or plate the size of which limit the extent to which the projected image can be enlarged; granular texture, degree of roughness or smoothness of surface; texture, arrangement of particles, esp. the arrangement of the fibres of wood or other fibrous substance; the body or substance of wood as modified by the fibres; the lines of fibre in wood or, in stone, of cleavage planes, forming a pattern; a red dye made from cochineal or kermes insects; any fast dye, esp. red, crimson or purple; temper, disposition, natural tendency. *v.t.* to form into grains, to granulate; to treat so as to bring out the natural grain; to paint or stain in imitation of this; to give a granular surface to; to scrape the hair off (hides) with a grainer. *v.i.* to form grains, to become granulated. **against the grain,** against one's natural inclination. **in grain,** downright, thorough, absolute, inveterate. **to dye in grain,** to dye in a fast colour, esp. in kermes; to dye deeply or into the fibre. **grain alcohol,** *n.* alcohol made by the fermentation of grain. **grain elevator,** *n.* a machine that raises grain to a higher floor, esp. one having an endless belt fitted with scoops. **grain leather,** *n.* leather dressed with the grain-side outwards. **grain-side,** *n.* the side (of leather) from which the hair has been removed. **grain-sick,** *n.* a disease in cattle caused by distension of the rumen with food. **grains of paradise** or **Guinea grains,** *n. pl.* the seeds of *Amomum melegueta,* a tropical W African spice, used in stimulants, diuretics and spirituous liquors. **grainage,** *n.* mangy tumours on the legs of horses. **grained,** *a.* (*esp. in comb.,* as *fine-grained*). **grainer,** *n.* one who paints or stains in imitation of the grain of wood; also the brush he uses; an infusion of pigeon's dung for giving flexibility to skins in tanning; a tanner's knife. **graining,** *n.* the act of producing a grain; milling on the edge of a coin; a process in tanning; painting in imitation of the grain of wood; *Leuciscus lancastriensis,* a fish allied to the dace. **grainless,** *a.* **grainy,** *a.* [OF, from L *grānum,* rel. to CORN]

grain2, *n.* a fork, a tine, a prong; (*pl., usu. construed as sing.*) a forked fish-spear, a kind of harpoon. [Icel. *grein,* division, branch]

Grainger, *n.* **Percy Aldridge** (1882–1961). Australian-born US composer and concert pianist. He is remembered for a number of songs and short instrumental pieces drawing on folk idioms, including *Country Gardens* (1925), and for his settings of folk songs, such as *Molly on the Shore* (1921).

graip, grape, *n.* (*Sc., North.*) a three- or four-pronged fork, used for lifting potatoes etc. [cp. Icel. *greip,* grasp, Dan. *greb,* fork, also GRIP, GROPE]

graith, *n.* (*now Sc.*) equipment, attire; apparatus, gear; armour; harness; goods, possessions. *a.* (*Sc.*) ready. *v.t.* (*Sc., North.*) to make ready; to array. [Icel. *greithe,* cogn. with OE *gerǣde,* trappings, gear]

grakle, GRACKLE.

grallae, grallatores, *n.pl.* waders, an order of birds with long bare legs and usu. long necks and bills, as the crane. **grallatorial**, **grallatory, grallic, gralline,** *a.* [L *grallātor,* one who walks on stilts, from *grallae,* stilts]

gralloch, *v.t.* to disembowel (a deer). *n.* the viscera of a deer. [Gael. *grealach,* the viscera]

gram1, *n.* the chick-pea, *Cicer arietinum,* or other kinds of pulse, used esp. in Asia as food. [perh. from Port. *grão,* L *grānum,* GRAIN1]

gram2, **gramme,** *n.* the standard unit of weight in the metric system, defined as the mass of one cubic centimetre of distilled water at its maximum density weight *in vacuo,* equalling a thousandth part of a standard kilogram (about 0.04 oz). **grammetre, gram-centimetre,** *n.* a unit of work, equalling the amount done in raising one gram vertically one centimetre. [F *gramme,* late L and Gr. *grammă,* a small weight, see -GRAM]

gram., (*abbr.*) grammar, grammarian, grammatical.

-gram, *comb. form* forming compounds with prepositional prefixes, numerals etc., as in *epigram, monogram, phonogram, telegram.* [Gr. *gramma -atos,* a letter, that which is written, from *graphein,* to write]

grama, gramma grass, *n.* various species of low pasture grass in W and S W US [Sp. *grama,* L *grāmen,* grass]

†**gramarye,** *n.* magic, necromancy. [OF, *gramaire,* GRAMMAR]

gramercy, *int.* thanks; an exclamation expressive of surprise. *n.* an expression of thanks. [OF *grant merci,* great thanks]

gramineae, *n.pl.* the botanical order of endogens, containing the grasses. **graminaceous**, **gramineous**, *a.* pertaining to grass or the tribe of grasses. **graminifolious**, *a.* having leaves like grass. **graminivorous**, *a.* subsisting on grass. [mod. L, from *grāmen -inis,* grass]

gramma grass GRAMA.

grammalogue, *n.* in phonography, a word represented by a single sign; a logogram, or letter or character standing for a word. [Gr. *gramma,* -GRAM, *logos,* word]

grammar, *n.* the principles or science of the correct use of language; dealing with phonology, the science of sounds, etymology, the grammar of words, accidence, the science of inflections, and syntax, the arrangement of words in sentences; a system of principles and rules for speaking and writing a language; a book containing these principles and rules; one's manner of applying these rules, or speech or writing considered with regard to its correctness according to these rules; the elements of an art or science, a treatise on these. **grammar-school,** *n.* a school originally established (mostly in the 16th cent.) for teaching Latin; esp. formerly, a secondary school with an academic course. **grammarian**, *n.* one versed in grammar; a philologist; one who writes upon or teaches grammar. **grammarless,** *a.* †**grammatic, -al**, *a.* pertaining to grammar; according to the rules of grammar. **grammatical gender,** *n.* gender based on grammar, not sex. **grammatical sense,** *n.* the literal sense. **grammatical subject,** *n.* the literal as dist. from the logical subject. **grammatically,** *adv.* **grammaticism**, *n.* a point in grammar. **grammaticize, -ise**, *v.t.* to render grammatical. [OF *gramaire,* L *grammatica,* Gr. *grammatikē -kos,* pertaining to letters, from *gramma,* a letter, from *graphein,* to write]

gramophone, *n.* a device for reproducing sounds stored on disk (invented by E. Berliner, 1887); (*N Am.*) a phonograph; a record-player. [Gr. *gramma,* a letter, *phonē,* sound (cp. PHONOGRAM)]

Grampian, *n.* region of Scotland. **area** 8600 sq km/3320 sq miles. **towns** administrative headquarters Aberdeen. **products** beef cattle (Aberdeen Angus and Beef Shorthorn), fishing, North Sea oil service industries, tourism (winter skiing). **population** (1987) 503,000.

grampus, *n.* a large delphinoid cetacean belonging to the genus *Orca,* esp. the voracious *O. gladiator;* also the inoffensive cetacean *Grampus griseus* or cow-fish. [AF *grampais,* OF *grapois,* L *crassum piscem,* nom. *crassus piscis,* fat fish]

Gramsci, *n.* **Antonio** (1891–1937), Italian Marxist, who attempted to unify social theory and political practice. He helped to found the Italian Communist party, 1921, and was elected to parliament in 1924, but was imprisoned by Mussolini from 1926; his *Quaderni di carcere/Prison Notebooks* (1947) were published after his death.

Granada, *n.* city in the Sierra Nevada in Andalucia, S Spain; population (1986) 281,000. It produces textiles, soap, and paper.

granadilla, *n.* various species of passion-flower, *Passiflora;* used also of their edible fruit. [Sp., dim. of *granada,* a pomegranate, L *grānātus,* from *grānum,* GRAIN [1]]

Granados, *n.* **Enrique** (1867–1916), Spanish composer-pianist. His piano-work *Goyescas* (1911), inspired by the art of Goya, was converted to an opera in 1916.

granam, GRANNOM.

granary, *n.* a storehouse for grain; a country or district producing and exporting abundance of corn. [L *grānārium,* as prec.]

Gran Chaco, *n.* large lowland plain in N Argentina, W Paraguay, and SE Bolivia; area 650,000 sq km/251,000 sq miles. It consists of swamps, forests (a source of quebracho timber), and grasslands, and there is cattle-raising.

grand, *a.* great or imposing in size, character or appearance; magnificent, fine, splendid; dignified, lofty, noble; morally impressive, inspiring; (*Mus.*) great, of full compass, for full orchestra, or with all accessory parts and movements; (*coll.*) distinguished, fashionable or aristocratic (society); (*coll.*) highly satisfactory, excellent; pre-eminent in rank etc., chief; (*Law*) principal, as opp. to petty, common etc.; main, comprehensive, complete, final; in the second degree (of relationships). *n.* (*sl.*) 1000 dollars, pounds. **grand air,** an air of distinction. **Grand Almoner, Chamberlain, Falconer** etc., titles of officers of state formerly denoting the highest in rank among several almoners etc. †**grandam,** *n.* a grandmother; an animal's dam's dam; an old woman. **grand assize** or **inquest,** *n.* (*Law*) an assize or inquest of great or chief importance, as opp. to petty or common. **grandaunt,** *n.* the sister of a grandfather or grandmother. **Grand Banks**, *n.* continental shelf in the N Atlantic off SE Newfoundland, where the shallow waters are rich fisheries, especially for cod. **Grand Canal**, *n.* (Chinese **Da Yune**) the world's longest canal. It is 1600 km/1000 miles long, and runs north from Hangzhou to Tianjin, China. The earliest section was completed 486 BC, and the northern section was built AD 1282–92, during the reign of Kublai Khan. **Grand Canyon**, *n.* vast gorge containing the Colorado River, Arizona, US. It is 350 km/217 miles long, 6–29 km/4–18 miles wide, and reaches depths of over 1.5 km/1 mile. **grand captain,** *n.* a chief captain, commander, or general. **grandchild**, *n.* the child of a son or daughter. **grand committee,** *n.* one of two standing committees of the House of Commons appointed every session to consider Bills relating to law or trade. **granddaughter**, *n.* the daughter of a son or daughter. **granddad**, **granddaddy,** *n.* (*coll.*) grandfather. **Grand Duke,** *n.* a sovereign of lower rank than a king, the ruler in certain European states; hence, **Grand Duchy; Grand Duchess. Grand Ducal,** *a.* **grandfather,** *n.* the father of a parent. **grandfather clock,** *n.* an old-fashioned clock worked by weights, in a tall wooden case. **grandfatherly,** *a.* **Grand Fleet,** *n.* formerly, the portion of the British Navy employed in British and northern seas. **grand juror,** *n.* a member of a grand jury. **grand jury,** *n.* a jury whose duty is to enquire if there is sufficient ground for a prisoner to be tried by a petty or ordinary jury. **grand larceny** LARCENY. **grandma**, **grandmamma,** *n.* (*coll.*) grandmother. **Grand Master,** *n.* the head of a military order of knighthood, the head of the Freemasons, Good Templars etc.; in chess or bridge, an outstanding player, winner of many international tournaments, competitions etc. **grandmother,** *n.* the mother of a parent. **grandmother clock,** *n.* a clock similar to but slightly smaller than a grandfather clock. **grandmotherly,** *a.* like a grandmother; fussy. **Grand National,** *n.* an annual steeplechase run at Aintree, Liverpool. **grandnephew,** *n.* the grandson of a brother or sister. **grandniece,** *n.* the granddaughter of a brother or sister. **grand opera,** *n.* an opera with a serious plot that is sung throughout, as opp. to comic opera. **grandpa**, **grandpapa,** *n.* (*coll.*) grandfather. **grandparent,** *n.* a grandfather or grandmother. **grand passion,** *n.* an overwhelming love affair. **grand piano,** *n.* a large piano with horizontal framing. **grandsire,** *n.* a grandfather; an animal's sire's sire; a male ancestor. **grand slam,** *n.* in auction bridge, the winning of 13 tricks by a side; in contract bridge, a fulfilled contract to take all 13 tricks; in tennis, golf etc., the winning of all the major competitions in a season. **grandson,** *n.* the son of a son or daughter. **grandstand,** *n.* the principal stand for spectators on a race-course etc. *v.i.* (*coll.*) to behave in an ostentatious way in order to impress. **grandstand finish,** *n.* a close and exciting finish in a sporting contest. **grand total,** *n.* the total of all subordinate sums. **grand tour,** *n.* a tour through the countries of continental Europe esp. as formerly undertaken as an essential part of the education of young people of good family; any extended esp. educational sightseeing tour. **Grand Turk,** *n.* formerly, the Sultan of Turkey. **Grand Vizier,** *n.* formerly, the prime minister of the Ottoman Empire, or of any eastern monarchy. **grandly,** *a.* **grandness,** *n.*

grand cru, *n.* of a wine, from a famous vineyard, top-ranking. [F, great growth]

granddaughter GRAND.

Grand Design, *n.* in the early 17th cent., a plan attributed by the French minister Sully to Henry IV of France (who was assassinated before he could carry it out) for a great Protestant union against the Holy Roman Empire; the term was also applied to President de Gaulle's vision of France's place in a united Europe.

Grande Dixence dam, the world's highest dam, in Switzerland, which measures 285 m/935 ft from base to crest. Completed in 1961, it contains 6 million cu m/8 million cu yds of concrete.

grandee, *n.* a Spanish or Portuguese nobleman of the highest rank; a person of high rank or power. **grand-**

eeship, *n.* [Sp. and Port. *grande,* as prec.]

grandeur, *n.* the quality of being grand; greatness, nobility, impressiveness, sublimity, majesty; splendour, magnificence, dignity, splendid or magnificent appearance or effect. [F, from *grand,* GRAND]

grandfather GRAND.

grand guignol, *n.* genre of short horror play produced at the Grand Guignol theatre in Montmartre, Paris [after the bloodthirsty character Guignol in late 18th-cent. marionette plays].

grandiloquent, †-loquous, *a.* using lofty or pompous language; bombastic. **grandiloquence,** *n.* **grandiloquently,** *adv.* [L *grandiloquus* (GRAND, L *-loquus,* speaking, from *loquī,* to speak), *assim.* to ELOQUENT]

grandiose, *a.* imposing, impressive, producing the effect of grandeur; intended to produce the effect of grandeur, affecting impressiveness, pompous; great in style or scale. **grandiosely,** *adv.* **grandioseness,** *n.* **grandiosity,** *n.* [F, from It. *grandioso,* L *grandis,* GRAND]

Grandisonian, *a.* elaborately and pompously courteous and chivalrous. [Sir Charles *Grandison,* the hero of Richardson's novel of that title]

grand mal, *n.* a major epileptic attack, as opp. to *petit mal.* [F, great illness]

grand marnier, *n.* a liqueur somewhat like curaçao. [F]

grand monarque, *n.* Louis XIV, King of France. [F]

grand monde, *n.* highest society. [F, the great world]

grandmother GRAND.

Grand Old Baby, Party, *n.* (GOB, GOP) popular name for US Republican Party.

grandparent GRAND.

Grand Prix, *n.* an international horse-race for 3-year-olds held annually at Longchamps, Paris; certain motor races. [F, great prize]

Grand Remonstrance, *n.* petition passed by the British Parliament in Nov. 1641 which listed all the alleged misdeeds of Charles I and demanded Parliamentary approval for the king's ministers and the reform of the church. Charles refused to accept the Grand Remonstrance and countered it by trying to arrest five leading members of the House of Commons (Pym, Hampden, Holles, Hesilrige, and Strode). The worsening of relations between king and Parliament led to the outbreak of the English Civil War in 1642.

grand seigneur, *n.* a person of high rank; a noble gentleman.

grandson GRAND.

Grand Teton, *n.* highest point of the spectacular Teton range, NW Wyoming, US, rising to 4197 m/13,770 ft. Grand Teton National park was established in 1929.

grange, *n.* a barn; a farmhouse with the out-buildings etc., esp. if occupied as a country residence; (*N Am.*) a farmers' union. **granger,** *n.* a farm-bailiff; (*N Am.*) a farmer; (*N Am.*) a member of a grange. [OF, from L *grānea, grānica,* from L *grānum,* GRAIN [1]]

Grange Movement, the, in US history, a farmers' protest in the southern and midwestern states against economic hardship and exploitation. The National Grange of the Patrons of Husbandry, formed 1867, was a network of local organizations, employing co-operative practices and advocating 'granger' laws. The movement petered out in the late 1870s, to be superseded by the Greenbackers.

Granger, *n.* **Stewart (James Stewart)** (1913–), British film actor. After several leading roles in British romantic films during World War II, he moved to Hollywood in 1950 and subsequently appeared in adventure films, for example, *Scaramouche* (1952); *The Prisoner of Zenda* (1952); *The Wild Geese* (1978).

grangerize, -ise, *v.i.* to extra-illustrate (a book etc.) with portraits etc. (usu. taken from other books). *v.t.* to illustrate (a book or pamphlet) with engravings bearing on the subject matter (from the practice of so illustrating Granger's *Biographical History of England*). **grangerism,** *n.* the act or practice of grangerizing books. **grangerization, -isation,** *n.* **grangerite,** **grangerizer, -iser,** *n.* one who grangerizes books. [James *Granger,* 1716–76, author of a *Biographical History of England* (1769) published with blank leaves for illustration]

graniferous, *a.* bearing grain or seed of grainlike form. **graniform,** *a.* **granivorous,** *a.* feeding on grain. [L *grānifer* (*as grānum*)]

granite, *n.* a granular, igneous rock consisting of feldspar, quartz and mica, confusedly crystallized. **granite ware,** *n.* an enamelled ironware or hard pottery with speckled surface resembling granite. **granitic, -al,** *a.* **granitification,** *n.* formation into granite. **granitiform,** *a.* **granitoid,** *a.* resembling granite. [It. *granito,* p.p. of *granire,* to speckle, from *grano,* L *grānum,* as prec.]

grannom, *n.* a four-winged fly frequenting streams; an imitation of this used in fly-fishing. [etym. doubtful]

granny, grannie, gran, *n.* a grandmother; an old woman. **granny flat,** *n.* a self-contained flat added to or part of a house, designed to accommodate an elderly relative. **granny-knot** or **granny's bend,** a badly-tied reef-knot having the tie crossed the wrong way. **Granny Smith,** *n.* a green-skinned apple.

granodizing, *n.* a process for preventing the corrosion of ferrous metals.

granolith, *n.* artificial stone consisting of crushed granite and cement. **granolithic,** *n., a.* [Gr. *lithikos,* from *lithos,* stone]

grant, *v.t.* to bestow, concede or give, esp. in answer to request; to allow as a favour or indulgence; (*Law*) to transfer the title to, to confer or bestow (a privilege, charter etc.); to admit as true, to concede or allow (as premises to an argument). †*v.i.* to agree, to consent. *n.* the act of granting; the thing granted; a gift, an assignment, a formal bestowal; a sum of money bestowed or allowed; a concession or admission of something as true; (*Law*) a conveyance in writing; the thing conveyed. **to be taken for granted,** to assume as admitted basis of an argument. **grant-in-aid,** *n.* a sum granted towards the maintenance of a school or other institution. **grantable** *a.* **grantee,** *n.* (*Law*) the person to whom a grant or conveyance is made. **granter,** *n.* one who grants. **grantor,** *n.* (*Law*) one who makes a conveyance. [OF *graunter, greanter, creanter,* late L *crēantāre* for *crēdentāre,* from *crēdent-,* part. stem. of *crēdere,* to trust, see CREED]

Grant [1], *n.* **Cary** (stage-name of Archibald Leach), (1904–86), US actor, born in England, he first travelled to the US with a troupe of acrobats. His witty, debonair screen personality made him a favourite for more than three decades. His films include *Bringing Up Baby* (1937), *The Philadelphia Story* (1940), *Arsenic and Old Lace* (1944), *Notorious* (1946), and *North by Northwest* (1959).

Grant [2], *n.* **Duncan** (1885–1978), British painter and designer, a member of the Bloomsbury group and a pioneer of abstract art in the UK. He lived with Vanessa Bell from about 1914 and worked with her on decorative projects. Later works, such as *Snow Scene* (1921), showed the influence of the post-impressionists.

Grant [3], *n.* **Ulysses S(impson)** (1822–85), 18th president of the US (1869–77). He was a Union general in the American Civil War and commander-in-chief from 1864. As a Republican president, he carried through a liberal Reconstruction policy in the South, although he failed to suppress extensive political corruption within his own party and cabinet, which tarnished the reputation of his presidency.

granule, *n.* a little grain; a small particle. **granular,** **†granulary,** *a.* composed of or resembling granules. **granularity,** *n.* **granularly,** *adv.* **granulate,** *v.t.* to form into granules or small particles; to make rough on the surface. *v.i.* to collect or be formed into grains. *a.*, granulated. **granulated sugar,** *n.* coarse-grained white sugar. **granulation,** *n.* the act of forming into granules; a granulated surface; the process of rendering a metal granular, as by pouring it in a melted state on to a rapidly rotating disk; healing by the formation of little grain-like bodies or projections, in sores or wounds; (*pl.*) the prominences thus formed. **granulative,** *n.* **granulator,** *n.* **granuliferous,** *a.* bearing or full of granules. **granuliform**, *a.* **granulitic**, *a.* **granulize, -ise,** *v.t.* [late L *grānulum,* dim. of *grānum,* grain]

granulo-, *comb. form.* pertaining to granules. **granulous,** *a.*

granulocyte, *n.* a white blood cell that ingests bacteria etc. and that has granular cytoplasm. **granulocytic**, *a.* [late L *grānulum,* as prec., Gr. *kutos,* a hollow]

grape[1], *n.* a berry constituting the fruit of the vine; grape-shot; (*pl.*) a mangy tumour on the legs of horses. **the grape,** (*coll.*) wine. **sour grapes,** some object of desire which one disparages because it is out of reach. **grape-brandy,** *n.* brandy distilled from grapes or wine. **grapefruit,** *n.* the shaddock, *Citrus decumana.* **grape-house,** *n.* a glass-house for growing vines. **grape-hyacinth,** *n.* a bulbous plant belonging to the genus *Muscari.* **grape-scissors,** *n.pl.* scissors for thinning out bunches of grapes on the vines, or for dividing bunches at the table. **grapeseed,** *n.* the seed of the vine. **grapeseed oil,** *n.* the oil expressed from this, used in cooking. **grapeshot,** *n.* shot arranged in three tiers between plates, so as to scatter when fired. **grape-stone,** *n.* a stone or seed of the grape. **grape sugar,** *n.* glucose or dextrose. **grape-vine,** *n.* any species of *Vitis,* esp. *V. vinifera;* in skating, a figure in which the feet, which are both on the ice simultaneously, cut interlacing lines; (*coll.*) news or a rumour, conveyed by underground sources of intelligence. **grape-wort,** *n.* the baneberry, *Actaea spicata.* **grapeless,** *a.* without grapes; wanting the strength and flavour of the grape. **grapery,** *n.* **grapy,** *a.*

grape[2], (*Sc.*) GROPE.

grape[3] GRAIP.

graph, *n.* a diagram representing mathematical or chemical relationship and based on two graduated scales. *v.t.* to plot on a graph. **graph paper,** *n.* squared paper used for drawing graphs, diagrams etc. [short for GRAPHIC]

-graph, *comb. form* -written, -writing, -writer, as in *autograph, lithograph, seismograph, telegraph.* **-grapher,** *comb. form* a person versed in the science denoted by the *comb. form* -GRAPHY. [Gr. *-graphos,* from *graphein,* to write]

graphic, -al, *a.* pertaining to the art of writing, delineating, engraving, painting etc.; well delineated; vividly or forcibly descriptive; having the faculty of vivid description; indicating by means of diagrams etc. instead of numbers, statistics etc. *n.* (*pl.*) the art of drawing, esp. in mathematics, engineering etc., (*pl.*) the production of designs and images by computer; the designs so produced. **graphic formula,** *n.* in chemistry, a formula representing the relations of the atoms of a molecule to each other. **graphic granite,** *n.* a compound of quartz and feldspar, in which the quartz is disposed through the matrix roughly like Hebrew characters. **-graphic, -ical,** *comb. form* **graphically, †-icly,** *adv.* **graphicalness, graphicness,** *n.* [L *graphicus,* Gr. *graphikos,* from *graphein,* to write]

graphite, *n.* blacklead, plumbago. **graphitic**, *a.* **graphitoid**, *a.* [G *Graphit,* as prec.]

graphium, *n.* (*pl.* **-phia**) a stylus, a pencil. [L, from Gr. *grapheion,* as prec.]

graphiure, *n.* a southern African rodent resembling the dormouse, with a tufted tail. [Gr. *grapheion,* as prec., *oura,* tail]

grapho-, *comb. form* of, pertaining to or for writing. [Gr., from *graphē,* writing, from *graphein,* to write]

grapholite, *n.* a kind of slate suitable for writing on.

graphology, *n.* the study of handwriting; the art of inferring character from handwriting; graphic formulae or notation. **graphologic, -ical**, *a.* **graphologist,** *n.*

graphomania, *n.* a psychological urge to write or scribble maybe senseless words.

graphometer, *n.* a surveying instrument for taking angles. **graphometric**, *a.* pertaining to a graphometer; of a class of functions pertaining equally to graphic and metric geometry. **graphometrics,** *n.pl.* the science of such functions.

-graphy, *comb. form* description; style of writing; as in *bibliography, geography, lithography, stenography.* [GRAPHO]

grapnel, *n.* an instrument with several flukes or claws for seizing, grasping or lifting; a grappling-iron; an anchor with flukes for mooring boats, balloons etc. [ME *grapenel,* dim., from OF *grapin* (F *grappin*), from *grape,* a hook]

grappa, *n.* a coarse brandy distilled from the residue of a wine press. [It., grape stalk]

grapple, *n.* a grappling-iron; a grapnel or similar clutching device; a close hold or grip in wrestling or other contest; a close struggle. *v.t.* to lay fast hold of, to seize, to clutch; to come to close quarters with. *v.i.* to contend or struggle (with or together) in close fight; to get to close quarters (with a task, subject etc.) and strive to accomplish etc. **†grapplement,** *n.* **grappling-iron, -hook,** *n.* an iron instrument with claws or hooks for seizing and holding fast. [MF *grappil,* a ship's grapnel, dim. of *grape,* see GRAPE[1]]

graptolite, *n.* a fossil zoophyte with a solid axis somewhat resembling a pencil or quill pen. **graptolitic**, *a.* [Gr. *graptos,* painted, marked, from *graphein,* to write, draw]

Grashow, *n.* **Sheldon Lee** (1932–), US physicist who as an elementary particle physicist at Harvard, has made major contributions to our understanding of quarks. In 1964 he proposed the existence of a fourth 'charmed' quark, and later argued that quarks must be coloured. Insights gained from these theoretical studies enabled Grashow to consider ways in which some of the fundamental forces of nature (the weak and the electromagnetic) could be unified. For this work he shared the Nobel physics prize with Salam and Weinberg.

grasp, *v.t.* to seize and hold fast; to lay hold of and keep possession of, esp. with eagerness or greed; to comprehend with the mind. *v.i.* to clutch (at); to attempt to lay hold. *n.* a fast grip, clutch or hold; ability to seize and hold; forcible possession, mastery; intellectual comprehension. **to grasp at,** to try to seize; to be eager to accept. **graspable,** *a.* **grasper,** *n.* **grasping,** *a.* greedy. **graspingly,** *adv.* **graspingness,** *n.* **grasping reflex,** *n.* the response by an infant's fingers or toes to grasp an object that touches them. [ME *grapsen,* cogn. with OE *grāpian* to GROPE]

grass, *n.* the green-bladed herbage on which cattle, sheep etc. feed; any plant of the Gramineae, distinguished by simple, sheathing leaves, a stem usu. jointed and tubular, and flowers enclosed in glumes, including the cereals, reeds and bamboos, as well as the plants pop. known as grasses; pasture, grazing; (*coll.*) marijuana; (*sl.*) an informer; (*Mining*) the surface of the ground; (*pl.*) heads or spires of grass-flowers gathered. *v.t.* to cover with grass or turf; to lay on the grass to bleach; to bring to grass, to land (as a fish); (*sl.*) to fall, to knock down; to discharge. *v.i.* (*sl.*) to inform against. **as green as grass** GREEN. **to bring to grass,** (*Mining*) to bring up to the pit-head. **to go** or **send to grass,** to be knocked or to knock down. **to go, put, send** or **turn out to grass,** to go or send out to pasture; to go or send out from work, on a holiday, into retirement etc. **to let the grass grow under one's feet,** to waste time and so lose an opportunity. **grass-blade,** *n.* a blade of grass. **grass-box,** *n.* a container attached to a lawn-mower to catch grass cuttings. **grass-cloth,** *n.* a fine soft Eastern fabric made from the fibres of the inner bark of the **grass-cloth plant,** *Boehmeria nivea.* **grass court,** a tennis court with a surface of closely mown grass. **grass-cutter,** *n.* one who or that which cuts grass. **grass-green,** *a.* verdant, dark green. *n.* the colour of grass. **grass-grown,** *a.* overgrown with grass. **grass hand,** *n.* in printing, a compositor who fills a temporary vacancy. **grassland,** *n.* land kept under grass. **grass of Parnassus,** *Parnassia palustris,* a white-flowered plant belonging to the saxifrage order, unrelated to grasses, growing in marshes and on wet moors in Europe and Asia. It is low-growing, with a rosette of heart-shaped stalked leaves and has five-petalled, white flowers with conspicuous veins growing singly on stem tips in late summer. **grass-oil,** *n.* a fragrant volatile oil distilled from various Indian grasses. **grass-plot,** *n.* a plot of ground covered with grass. **grass roots,** *n. pl.* (*coll.*) the ordinary people; the basic essentials, foundation, origin. **grass-snake,** *n.* a harmless snake, *Natrix natrix.* **grass-tree,** *n.* an Australasian tree belonging to the *Xanthorrhaea* or other genera, having spear-like stalks etc. **grass widow,** *n.* a wife temporarily separated from her husband; (*formerly*) a divorced woman; †a discarded mistress. **grass-widower,** *n.* **grass-widowhood,** *n.* **grass-wrack,** *n.* a seaweed belonging to the genus *Zostera,* also called eel-grass. **grassed,** *a.* of a golf-club, with the face slightly filed back. **grasser,** *n.* (*sl.*) (*formerly*) a jobbing printer. **grassless,** *a.* destitute of grass. **grasslike,** *a.* **grassy,** *a.* covered with grass; like grass; green. **grassiness,** *n.* [OE *gœrs, grœs* (cp. Dut., Icel., and G *Gras,* cogn. with GREEN, GROW and L *grāmen,* grass)]

Grass, *n.* **Günter** (1927–), German writer. Born in Danzig, he studied at the art academies of Düsseldorf and Berlin, worked as a writer and sculptor, first in Paris and later in Berlin, and in 1958 won the coveted 'Group 47' prize. The grotesque humour and socialist feeling of his novels *Die Blechtrommel/The Tin Drum* (1959) and *Der Butt/The Flounder* (1977) characterize many of his poems.

grasshopper, *n.* an orthopterous insect of various species, esp. *Locusta viridissima,* with hind legs formed for leaping. *a.* of a mind etc., constantly moving from subject to subject. **to be knee-high to a grasshopper,** to be young, small. **grasshopper-beam,** *n.* on a steam engine, a working-beam pivoted at the end instead of the centre, and acting on the principle of parallel motion. **grasshopper-warbler,** *n.* a small warbler, so called from its note, esp. *Locustella naevia.*

grate¹, *n.* a frame composed of parallel or cross bars, with interstices, a grating; a frame of iron bars for holding fuel for a fire. *v.t.* to furnish with a grate or grating. **grated,** *a.* **grateless,** *a.* [late L *grāta,* var. of *crāta,* L *crātes,* hurdle]

grate², *v.t.* to rub against a rough surface so as to reduce to small particles; to rub, as one thing against another, so as to cause a harsh sound; to grind down; to produce (as a hard, discordant sound) by the collision or friction of rough bodies; to irritate, to vex, to offend (one's nerves). *v.i.* to rub (upon) so as to emit a harsh, discordant noise; to have an irritating effect (upon). **grater,** *n.* a utensil with a rough surface for reducing a substance to small particles (*often in comb.,* as *nutmeg-grater*). **grating¹,** *a.* harsh, discordant, irritating. **gratingly,** *adv.* [OF *grater* (F *gratter*), from Teut. (cp. Dan. *kratte,* G *kratzen,* to scratch)]

grateful, *a.* pleasing, agreeable, acceptable, refreshing; thankful, marked by or indicative of gratitude. **gratefully,** *adv.* **gratefulness,** *n.* [obs. *grate,* agreeable, L *grātus,* -FUL]

graticulation, *n.* the division of a design or drawing into squares for the purpose of reducing or enlarging it; a surface divided up in this way. [F, from *graticuler,* to divide with squares, from *graticule,* L *grāticula,* var. of *crāticula,* dim. of *crātes,* see GRATE¹]

gratify, *v.t.* to please, to delight; to humour, to satisfy the desire of; to indulge, to give free rein to; to requite, to reward; (*coll.*) to give a present, gratuity or bribe to. **gratifying,** *a.* **gratifyingly,** *adv.* **gratification,** *n.* the act of gratifying; that which gratifies; an enjoyment, a satisfaction; a reward, a recompense, a gratuity. **gratifier,** *n.* [F *gratifier,* L *grātificārī* (as *grātus,* pleasing, -FY)]

gratility, (*Shak.*) facet. perversion of GRATUITY.

gratin, *n.* a dish prepared with bread-crumbs and grated cheese; a mode of preparing dishes with bread-crumbs and cheese, and cooking so as to make a light crust. [F, from *gratter,* to grate, see GRATE²]

grating¹ GRATE².

grating², *n.* an open framework or lattice of metal bars or wooden slats, parallel or crossed; a series of parallel wires or lines ruled on glass or the like for producing spectra by diffraction. GRATE¹.

gratis, *adv., a.* for nothing; without charge, free. [L, for *grātiis,* abl. of *grātia,* favour]

gratitude, *n.* grateful feeling towards a benefactor; thankfulness, appreciation of kindness. [F, from late L *grātitūdinem,* nom. *-tūdo,* from *grātus,* pleasing]

grattoir, *n.* (*Archaeol.*) a flint implement with a shaped edge, used as a scraper. [F]

gratuitous, *a.* granted without claim or charge; free, voluntary; without cause, motive or warrant; uncalled for, unnecessary. **gratuitously,** *adv.* **gratuitousness,** *n.* [L *grātuītus,* freely or spontaneously given, as prec.]

gratuity, *n.* a gift, a present voluntarily given in return for a service, a tip; a bonus or bounty paid to soldiers on retirement; discharge etc. [OF *gratuité,* late L *grātuitātem,* nom. *-tas,* cogn. with prec.]

gratulate, etc. CONGRATULATE.

gratulatory, *a.* congratulatory, complimentary, expressing joy. [from L *grātulārī,* to CONGRATULATE]

graupel, *n.* soft hail. [G]

gravamen, *n.* (*pl.* **-mina**) (*Law*) the substantial cause of an action; the most serious part of a charge; a memorial from the Lower to the Upper House of Convocation setting forth a grievance; a motion in Convocation. [late L, from *gravāre,* to load, from *gravis,* heavy]

grave¹, *v.t.* to clean by scraping or burning, and cover with pitch and tallow (as a ship's bottom). **graving-dock,** *n.* a dry dock into which vessels are floated for this purpose. [etym. doubtful, perh. from OF *grave* (F *grève),* a strand or shore]

grave², *v.t.* †to dig; †to bury; to form or shape by cutting or carving into a surface, to engrave; to carve, to sculpture; to produce (a figure, inscription etc.) by engraving or carving; to impress by or as by engraving or carving. *n.* a hole in the earth for burying a dead body in; a place of burial, a sepulchre; a monument over this, a tomb; mortality, death, destruction; a place of destruction, extinction, or abandonment. **to have one foot in the grave,** to be very ill, near death; old and ailing. **to turn in one's grave,** (of a dead person) to be (thought to be) shocked or distressed by some modern event. **grave-clothes,** *n.pl.* wrappings in which the dead are buried. **grave-digger,** *n.* one who digs graves; an insect that buries dead insects etc., to feed its larvae. **grave-maker,** *n.* a grave-digger. **grave-making,** *n.* **grave-mound,** *n.* a barrow, a tumulus. **gravestone,** *n.* a stone, usu. inscribed, set over or at the head or foot of a grave. **graveyard,** *n.* a burial ground. **graveless,** *a.* **graven,** *a.* carved or inscribed **graven image,** an idol. **graver,** *n.* an engraver; an engraving tool, a burin. [OE *grafan,* whence *grœf,* a grave (cp. Dut. *graven,* Icel. *grafa,* G *graben*), cogn. with GROOVE]

grave³, *a.* important, serious, momentous; sedate, solemn, dignified; sombre, plain, not gaudy; (*Mus.*) low in pitch; slow in movement; (*Gram.*) low-pitched, not acute (of accents); †heavy, ponderous. **gravely,** *adv.* †**graveness,** *n.* [F, from L *gravis,* heavy]

gravel, *n.* small water-worn stones or pebbles intermixed with sand etc.; fragments of water-worn rock larger than sand, a stratum of this; a bed of such material bearing gold; a disease characterized by the presence of minute concretions in the urine. *v.t.* to cover, lay or strew with gravel. †to run (a vessel) ashore on sand, gravel etc.; to embarrass, to confound, to perplex. **gravel-blind,** *a.* (*Shak.*) worse than sand-blind, almost blind. **gravel-pit,** *n.* a pit out of which gravel is dug. **gravel-walk,** *n.* a path laid with gravel. **gravelling,** *n.* the action of laying gravel; a covering of gravel. **gravelly,** *a.* [OF *gravele,* dim. of *grave,* strand, gravel, cp. GRAVE¹]

graven, etc. GRAVE².

†**graveolent,** *a.* smelling strongly and offensively. †**graveolence,** *n.* [L *graveolens -ntem* (*grave,* adv., from *gravis,* GRAVE³, *olens -ntem,* pres.p. of *olēre,* to smell)]

Graves¹, *n.* a light wine of the claret type, pressed in the Graves district. [F]

Graves², *n.* **Robert (Ranke)** (1895–1985), English poet and author. He was severely wounded on the Somme in World War I, and his frank autobiography *Goodbye to All That* (1929) is one of the outstanding war books. Other works include the poems *Over the Brazier* (1916); historical novels of Imperial Rome, *I Claudius* and *Claudius the God* (1934); and books on myth, for example *The White Goddess* (1948).

gravestone, graveyard GRAVE².

gravid, *a.* pregnant; containing a foetus. [L *gravidus,* from *gravis,* GRAVE³]

gravigrade, *a.* (*Zool.*) walking heavily. *n.* one of the heavy-walking animals, like the elephant or the megatherium; an animal of the group Gravigrada. [L *gravis,* GRAVE³, *gradī,* to walk]

gravimeter, *n.* an instrument for determining the specific gravities of bodies. **gravimetric,** *a.* **gravimetrically,** *adv.* **gravimetry** *n.*

gravitate, *v.i.* to be acted on by gravity; to be attracted, to tend (towards); to tend downwards, to sink, to settle down; to be powerfully drawn (towards). *v.t.* esp. in diamond digging, to treat (gravel) by hand or machinery so as to cause the heavy particles to sift to the bottom. **gravitater,** *n.* **gravitation,** *n.* the act or process of gravitating; the force of gravity. **gravitational,** *a.* **Gravitational Lens,** *n.* the gravitational field from a very large body, such as a star, which deflects light. It was predicted by Einstein's General Theory of Relativity and tested successfully during the solar eclipse of 1917 when the light from stars located beyond the sun was captured on photographs. **gravitative,** *a.* [mod. L *gravitāre,* from *gravis,* GRAVE³]

gravity, *n.* weight, heaviness; importance, seriousness, enormity; solemnity, sedateness, sobriety, grave demeanour; (*Phys.*) the force causing bodies to tend towards the centre of the earth; the degree of intensity of this force; the similar tendency towards the centre of other bodies. **specific gravity** SPECIFIC. **gravity feed,** *n.* a feed or supply in which the material (oil, grain etc.) runs downhill. [from *gravité,* or directly from L *gravitātem,* nom. *-tas,* from *gravis,* GRAVE³]

gravure, *n.* an engraving; (short for) photogravure. [F, from *graver,* to ENGRAVE]

gravy, *n.* the fat and juice from meat during and after cooking; a sauce made with this or other ingredients. **gravy beef,** *n.* a part of leg of beef cooked for its gravy. **gravy boat,** *n.* a boat-shaped bowl or dish for holding gravy. **gravy dish,** *n.* a meat-dish with a hollow for gravy; a dish in which gravy is served. **gravy train,** *n.* (*sl.*) a job, course of action etc. requiring little effort in return for easy money, benefits etc. [etym. doubtful, perh. OF *grané,* L *grānātus,* full of grains (*grānum,* GRAIN), misread *graué*]

gray, GREY.

Gray¹, *n.* **Eileen** (1879–1976), Irish-born architect and furniture designer. She set up her own workshop and became known for her Art Deco designs which, in furniture, explored the use of tubular metal, glass, and new materials such as aluminium.

Gray², *n.* **Thomas** (1716–61), English poet, whose 'Elegy Written in a Country Churchyard' (1750) is one of the most quoted poems in English. Other poems include 'Ode on a Distant Prospect of Eton College', 'The Progress of Poesy', and 'The Bard'; these poems are now seen as the precursors of Romanticism.

grayling, *n.* a freshwater fish with a large dorsal and an adipose fin, belonging to the genus *Thymallus,* esp. the European *T. vulgaris.* [GREY, -LING]

Graz, *n.* capital of Styria province, and second largest city in Austria; population (1981) 243,400. Industries include engineering, chemicals, iron, and steel.

graze¹, *v.i.* to eat growing grass; to supply grass for grazing (of land, fields etc.); to feed, to browse; to move along devouring; (*coll.*) to eat (snacks etc.) standing up or moving around (as at a party, gathering etc.) rather than sitting down to a meal; (*coll.*) to watch only short excerpts of television programmes whilst constantly changing channels. *v.t.* to feed (cattle, etc.) on growing grass; to supply with pasturage; to tend (cattle etc.) at pasture; to pasture; to feed on, to eat. **grazer,** *n.* an animal that grazes. **grazing,** *n.* the act of pasturing or feeding on grass; a pasture. [OE *grasian,* from *græs,* GRASS]

graze², *v.t.* to touch, rub or brush slightly in passing; to scrape or abrade in rubbing past. *v.i.* to touch some person or thing lightly in passing; to pass (along, by, past etc.) in light or momentary contact. *n.* a slight touch or rub in passing; a slight abrasion. [prob. from prec.]

grazier, *n.* one who pastures cattle, and rears and fattens them for market. **graziery,** *n.*

grazioso, *a.* (*Mus.*) graceful, elegant. **graziosamente,** *adv.* elegantly. [It.]

grease, *n.* animal fat in a melted or soft state; oily or fatty matter of any kind; inflammation of a horse's heels. *v.t.*, to smear, lubricate or soil with grease; to cause to go smoothly; to infect (horses) with grease. **like greased lightning,** (*coll.*) very quickly; **to grease someone's palm** or **hand,** (*coll.*) to bribe. **greasebox,** *n.* a holder on a wheel or axle for grease as a lubricant. **greasecup,** *n.* a cup-shaped vessel through which grease is driven into machinery. **greasegun,** *n.* a syringe for injecting grease or oil into machinery. **grease monkey,** *n.* (*coll.*) a mechanic. **greasepaint,** *n.* a paste used for painting the face in theatrical make-up. **greasetrap,** *n.* a contrivance fixed in drains for catching grease from sinks etc. **greaser,** *n.* one who or that which greases, a mechanic; (*N Am., offensive*) a Mexican or Spanish-American. [OF *graisse,* L *crassus,* adj., fat]

greasy, *a.* smeared, saturated or soiled with grease; made of or like grease; unctuous, oily, exuding grease; slimy or slippery with something having the effect of grease; (of horses) affected with the disease called grease; corpulent, fat; gross, unpleasantly unctuous; †indelicate, indecent. **greasy spoon,** *n.* (*coll.*) a cheap restaurant, esp. one selling mainly fried foods. **greasily,** *adv.* **greasiness,** *n.*

great, *a.* large in bulk, number, amount, extent or degree; very large, big, vast; beyond the ordinary, extreme; important, weighty, momentous, critical; of the highest importance, capital (of letters), pre-eminent, the chief; of exceptional ability, highly gifted, possessing genius; (*coll.*) very skilful, experienced or knowing (at); having lofty moral qualities, magnanimous, noble; grand, majestic, sublime; big with child, gravid; teeming, pregnant (with); excessive, grievous, burdensome; notorious; denoting a step of ascending or descending consanguinity (as **great-grandfather,** the father of a grandfather; **great-grandson,** the son of a grandson etc.). *n.* (*collect.*) great people; (*pl.*) GREATS; †the mass, the bulk, the gross. **to be great at,** to be skilful at. **great ape,** *n.* one of the larger apes, such as the gorilla, chimpanzee etc.; (*coll.*) a clumsy or foolish person. **Great Artesian Basin,** *n.* the largest area of artesian water in the world, it underlies much of Queensland, New South Wales and South Australia, and in prehistoric times formed a sea. It has an area of 1,750,000 sq km/676,250 sq miles **Great Australian Bight**, broad bay in S Australia, notorious for storms. It was discovered by a Dutch navigator, Captain Thyssen (1627). The coast was charted by the English explorer, Captain Matthew Flinders in 1802. **Great Assize Day** or **Inquest,** the Day of Judgment. **Great Barrier Reef**, a chain of coral reefs and islands about 2000 km/1250 miles long, off the E coast of Queensland, Australia at a distance of 15–45 km/10–30 miles. It forms an immense natural breakwater, and the coral rock forms a structure larger than all human-made structures on Earth combined. **†great-bellied,** *a.* far advanced in pregnancy. **Great Britain** BRITAIN. **great circle,** *n.* a circle on a sphere (such as the earth) formed by a plane passing through the centre of the sphere. **great-coat,** *n.* an overcoat. **greatcoated,** *a.* **greatcoatless,** *a.* **Great Dane,** *n.* large short-haired dog, usu. fawn in colour, standing up to 92 cm/36 in., and weighing up to 70 kg/154 lb. It has a long head, a large nose, and small ears. It was formerly used for hunting boar and stags. **Great Divide**, or **Great Dividing Range** *n.* E Australian mountain range, extending 3700 km/2300 m N–S from Cape York Peninsula, Queensland, to Victoria. **Great Exhibition**, *n.* an exhibition held in Hyde Park, London, UK in 1851, proclaimed by its originator Prince Albert as 'the Great Exhibition of the Industries of All Nations'. **great go,** *n.* the final examination for the degree of BA at Cambridge Univ. **great gross,** 144 dozen. †**great-grown,** *a.* increased in power or importance. **great-hearted,** *a.* high-spirited, magnanimous; brave. **great house,** *n.* the hall, mansion or principal residence in a country place. **Great Lakes**, *n.pl.* series of five freshwater lakes along the US–Canada border: Lakes Superior, Michigan, Huron, Erie, and Ontario; total area 245,000 sq km/94,600 sq miles. Interconnecting canals make them navigable by large ships, and they are drained by the St Lawrence River. They are said to contain 20% of the world's fresh water. **great organ** ORGAN. **Great Power**, *n.* the major European powers of the 19th cent.; Russia, Austria (Austria-Hungary), France, Britain and Prussia. **great primer,** *n.* 18-point type. **Great Schism**, *n.* in European history, the period 1378–1417 in which there were rival popes in Rome and Avignon; it was ended by the election of Martin V during the Council of Constance (1414–17). **Great Scot(t),** *int.* an exclamation expressing surprise etc. **Great Seal** SEAL[2]. **Great Spirit,** *n.* the name given by the N American Indians to their deity. **great toe,** *n.* the big toe. **Great Trek**, *n.* in South African history, the movement of 12,000–14,000 Boer (Dutch) settlers from Cape Colony in 1836 and 1837 to escape British rule. They established republics in Natal (1838–43) and the Transvaal. It is seen by many white South Africans as the main event in the founding of the present republic, and also as a justification for continuing whites-only rule. **Great Wall of China**, continuous defensive wall stretching from W Gansu to the Gulf of Liaodong (2250 km/1450 miles). It was once even longer. It was built under the Qin dynasty from 214 BC to prevent incursions by the Turkish and Mongol peoples. Some 8 m/25 ft high, it consists of a brick-faced wall of earth and stone, has a series of square watchtowers, and has been carefully restored. It can be seen from space, as is shown in satellite photos. **Great War**, *n.* another name for World War I. **greaten,** *v.t.* to make greater, to enlarge; to magnify. *v.i.* to become greater, to dilate; †to become pregnant. **greatly,** *adv.* in a great degree, much, exceedingly; nobly, magnanimously; †grandly, illustriously. **greatness,** *n.* **greats,** *n.pl.* the course of study in *Literae Humaniores* at Oxford Univ.; the final examination for this. [OE *grēat* (cp. Dut. *groot*, G *gross*)]

Great Awakening, the, a religious revival in the N American British colonies from the late 1730s to the 1760s, sparked off by George Whitefield (1714–70), an itinerant English Methodist preacher whose evangelical fervour and eloquence made many converts.

Great Bear Lake, a lake on the Arctic Circle, in the Northwest Territories, Canada; area 31,800 sq km/ 12,275 sq miles.

Greater London Council (GLC), *n.* in the UK, local authority that governed London (1965–86). When the GLC was abolished in 1986 (see LOCAL GOVERNMENT) its powers either devolved back to the borough councils or were transferred to certain nonelected bodies.

Great Expectations, *n.* a novel by Charles Dickens, published 1860–61.

Great Leap Forward, the change in Chinese economic policy introduced under the second five-year plan of 1958–62. The aim, instigated by Mao Zedong, was to convert China into an industrially based economy by transferring resources away from agriculture. This coincided with the creation of people's communes. The inefficient and poorly planned allocation of state resources led to the collapse of the strategy by 1960 and a return to more adequate support for agricultural production.

Great Plains, *n.pl.* a semiarid region to the E of the Rocky Mountains, US, stretching as far as the 100th meridian of longitude through Oklahoma, Kansas, Nebraska and the Dakotas. The plains, which cover one-fifth of the US, extend from Texas in the S over 2400 km/1500 miles N to Canada. Ranching and wheat farming have resulted in over-exploitation of the water resources to such an extent that available farmland has been reduced by erosion.

Great Red Spot, *n.* a prominent feature of Jupiter.

Great Rift Valley, the longest 'split' in the Earth's surface, 8000 km/5000 miles long, running south from the Dead Sea (Israel/Jordan) to Mozambique.

Great Slave Lake, a lake in the Northwest Territories, Canada; area 28,450 sq km/10,980 sq miles. It is the deepest lake (615 m/2020 ft) in North America.

Great Wall, *n.* an array of galaxies arranged almost in a perfect plane, discovered by US astronomers in Cambridge, Mass, in Nov. 1989. It consists of some 2000 galaxies (about 500 million × 200 million light years) and is thought to be the largest structure ever discovered.

greave, *n.* (*usu. pl.*) armour for the legs. [OF *greve*, shin; etym. doubtful]

greaves, *n.pl.* fibrous scraps or refuse of melted tallow, used for feeding dogs and by anglers as bait. [cp. LG *greven*]

grebe, *n.* a diving-bird of the genus *Podiceps*, with lobed feet and no tail. [F *grèbe*]

Grecian, *a.* of or pertaining to Greece. *n.* a Greek; one who adopted Greek manners or habits; a Greek scholar; a senior boy at Christ's Hospital. **Grecian bend,** *n.* an affected walk fashionable with women about 1870, in which the body was bent forward from the hips. **Grecian knot,** *n.* a mode of dressing women's hair with a knot at the back of the head. **Grecian nose,** *n.* a nose continuing the line of the forehead. **Grecianize, -ise,** *v.t.*, *v.i.* [L *Græcia*, Greece, -AN]

Grecism, Grecize, etc. GRAECISM.

Greco, El, *n.* **(Doménikos Theotokopoulos)** (1541–1614), Spanish painter called 'the Greek' because he was born in Crete. He studied in Italy, worked in Rome from about 1570, and by 1577 had settled in Toledo. He painted elegant portraits and intensely emotional religious scenes with increasingly distorted figures and flickering light, for example *The Burial of Count Orgaz* (1586, Toledo).

grecque, *n.* an ornamental Greek fret; a coffee-strainer or a coffee-pot fitted with a strainer. [F, fem. of *grec*, GREEK]

†**gree[1],** *n.* goodwill, favour, pleasure, satisfaction. *v.i.* to come into agreement; to be in agreement. *v.t.* to reconcile. [OF *gré*, L *grātum*, nom. *-tus*, pleasing]

†**gree[2],** *n.* (*pl.* **grees, grece, greece**, often used as sing. in the sense of a staircase or a flight of steps) a step; a degree; a stage or degree of rank; degree, rank; the prize, the pre-eminence. [OF *gré*, L *gradum*, step, see GRADE]

Greece, *n.* Hellenic Republic (*Elliniki Dimokratia*), country in SE Europe, comprising the S Balkan peninsula; bounded N by Yugoslavia and Bulgaria, NE by Turkey, E by the Aegean Sea, S by the Mediterranean Sea, W by the Ionian Sea, and NW by Albania, and numerous islands to the S and E. **area** 131,957 sq km/ 50,935 sq miles. **capital** Athens. **towns** ports Thessaloniki, Patras, Larisa, Iráklion. **physical** mountainous; a large number of islands, notably Crete, Corfu, and Rhodes. **population** (1987) 9,990,000; annual growth rate 0.5%. **exports** tobacco, fruit (including currants), vegetables, olives, olive oil, textiles. **language** Greek. **religion** Greek Orthodox, Christian 97%. **ancient Greece**, *n.* the first Greek civilization, known as Mycenaean (*c.* 1600–1200 BC) which owed much to the Minoan civilization of Crete and may have been produced by the intermarriage of Greek-speaking invaders with the original inhabitants.

greed, *n.* greediness; avarice, insatiable desire or covetousness. **greedy,** *a.* having an inordinate desire for food or drink, voracious, gluttonous; eager to obtain, covetous, desirous (of). **greedily,** *adv.* **greediness,** *n.* [OE *grǣdig* (cp. Dut. *gretig,* Dan. *graadig*)]

Greek, *n.* a native of Greece; one of the Greek race; the Greek language; something one does not understand. *a.* pertaining to Greece or its people or to the Hellenic race. **when Greek meets Greek,** describing an equal encounter of champions. **Greek art,** *n.* sculpture, mosaic, and crafts of ancient Greece (no large-scale painting survives). It is usually divided into three periods: Archaic (late 8th cent.–480 BC), showing Egyptian influence; Classical (480–323 BC), characterized by dignified realism; and Hellenistic (323–27 BC), more exuberant or dramatic. Sculptures of human figures dominate all periods, and vase painting was a focus for artistic development for many centuries. **Greek Church,** *n.* the Orthodox or Eastern Church, including most of the Christians in Greece, Russia, the Balkan States and the Turkish Empire, which separated from Rome in the 9th cent. **Greek cross** CROSS. **Greek fire** FIRE. **Greek gift,** *n.* a gift bestowed with some treacherous motive (in alln. to Virgil's *Aeneid* ii.49). **Greek language**, *n.* a member of the Indo-European language family. *Modern Greek*, which is principally divided into the general vernacular (*Demotic Greek*) and the language of education and literature (*Katharevousa*), has a long and well-documented history: *Ancient Greek* from 14th to 12th cent. BC; *Archaic Greek* including Homeric epic language, until 800 BC; *Classical Greek* until 400 BC; Hellenistic Greek, the common language of Greece, Asia Minor, W Asia, and Egypt to 4th cent. AD, and *Byzantine Greek* used until the 15th cent. and still the ecclesiastical language of the Greek Orthodox Church. †**Greekish,** *a.* [OE *Grēcas, Crēcas,* pl., L *Graecus,* from Gr. *Graikos,* ancient name for the Hellenes]

green, *a.* having a colour like growing herbage, of the colour in the spectrum between blue and yellow; unripe, immature; undeveloped, inexperienced, easily imposed on; fresh, not withered, not dried, seasoned, cured, dressed or tanned; (of a wound) not healed; pale, sickly. *n.* the colour of growing herbage; a colour composed of blue and yellow; a green pigment or dye; a grassy plot or piece of land (*esp. in comb.,* as *bowling-green*); (*coll.*) a person who is concerned about environmental issues; (*pl.*) fresh leaves or branches of trees; (*pl.*) the young leaves and stems of plants of the cabbage kind, used for food; vigour, youth, prime. *v.i.* to become or grow green. *v.t.* to make green; to make urban areas more attractive by the addition of trees, gardens and parks; (*sl.*) to hoax. **as green as grass,** naive, inexperienced, immature. **to get the green light,** (*coll.*) to get permission to go ahead with a project. **greenback,** *n.* (*coll.*) a legal-tender banknote first issued by the US in 1862, the back being printed in green; a note issued by any national bank in US. **green ban,** *n.* (*Austral.*) the refusal by trade unionists to work on a construction project that would necessitate the destruction of something of natural, historical or social significance. **green belt,** *n.* an area around a city in which building is restricted. **green cheese,** *n.* unripened cheese, whey cheese; cheese coloured with sage. **Green Cloth,** *n.* a Board in the royal household under the Master of the Household, chiefly concerned with the commissariat. **green cloth** or **table,** *n.* a gaming-table. **green-coloured,** *a.* pale, sickly. **green-crop,** *n.* a crop of food-stuff in the green state. **green drake,** *n.* the May-fly. **green-earth,** *n.* glauconite. **green eye,** *n.* jealousy. **green-eyed,** *a.* having green eyes; seeing things with jealous eyes. **the green-eyed monster,** jealousy. **green fat,** *n.* the green gelatinous part of the turtle, much esteemed by epicures. **greenfinch,** *n.* a common British singing-bird, *Chloris chloris,* with green and gold plumage. **green fingers,** *n.pl.* skill at growing plants. **greenfly,** *n.* any of several small green insects that are destructive to plants, esp. the green aphid. **greengrocer,** *n.* a retailer of green vegetables, fruit etc.; (*Austral.*) a large bright green common cicada. **greengrocery,** *n.* **green heart,** *n.* a hard-timbered W Indian tree, *Nectandra rodiaei,* which is used for dock-gates, ship-building, fishing-rods etc., and yields a febrifuge. **greenhide,** *n.* (*Austral.*) untanned raw hide as used for whips. **greenhorn,** *n.* a simpleton, a raw person. **greenhouse,** *n.* a glass-house for cultivating and preserving tender plants. **greenhouse effect,** *n.* the increased temperature of the earth caused by its atmosphere acting as the glass of a greenhouse does. **greenkeeper,** *n.* the person in charge of a golf-course. **green laver,** *n.* an edible seaweed, *Ulva lactuca* and *U. latissima*. **green light,** *n.* a signal to proceed. **greenmail,** *n.* a business tactic whereby a company buys a large number of shares in another company with the threat of a takeover, thereby forcing the threatened company to repurchase the shares at a higher price. *v.t.* to practise this tactic. **greenmailer,** *n.* **green manuring,** *n.* the cultivation and ploughing-in of a crop of vetch, rape etc. **Green Paper**, *n.* a publication issued by a British government department setting out various aspects of a matter on which legislation is contemplated, and inviting public discussion and suggestions. In due course it may be followed by a White Paper, giving details of proposed legislation. The first Green Paper was published in 1967. **Green Party**, *n.* political party aiming to 'preserve the planet and its people', based on the premise that incessant economic growth is unsustainable. The leaderless party structure reflects a general commitment to decentralization. Green parties sprang up in W Europe in the 1970s and spread in the 1980s. Parties in different countries are linked to one another but unaffiliated to any pressure group, and had a number of parliamentary seats in 1989. **green pepper,** *n.* the green unripe fruit of the sweet pepper eaten raw or cooked. **Green Paper,** *n.* a set of policy proposals issued by the government. **green-room,** *n.* a room in which actors or musicians wait during the intervals of their parts; a room in a warehouse where new or green cloth is received. **Green-sand,** *n.* two series of beds of sandstone (largely consisting of green-earth or glauconite) called the Upper and Lower Green-sand, in the Cretaceous series. **greenshank,** *n.* a large sandpiper, *Tringa nebularia*. **green-sickness,** *n.* chlorosis. **green snake,** *n.* the popular name of two harmless N American snakes. **green stick,** *n.* a form of fracture to which children are very liable in which one side of the bone is broken and the other merely bent. **green-stone,** *n.* a greenish eruptive rock consisting of a crystalline granular admixture of feldspar and hornblende; a fine-grained stone used for putting a very keen edge on surgical instruments; a kind of jade. **green stuff,** *n.* green vegetables for culinary use. **greensward,** *n.* turf covered with grass. **green tea,** *n.* tea prepared by drying with steam. **greentail,** *n.* the grannom. **greenthumb** GREEN FINGERS. †**green vitriol,** *n.* crystallized ferrous sulphate. **greenweed,** *n.* *Genista tinctoria* and *G. pilosa,* used in dyeing. **greenwood,** *n.* a wood in summer; wood which has become green in tint under the influence of the fungus *Chlorosplenium aeruginosum*. *a.* pertaining to a greenwood. **greener,** *n.* (*sl.*) a green or raw hand, a novice; a black-leg, a scab. **greenery,** *n.* **greenie**, *n.* (*coll.*) a conservationist. **greening,** *n.* the act of becoming green; greenness; a kind of apple which is green when ripe. **greenish,** *a.* **greenishness,** *n.* **greenly,** *adv.* **greenness,** *n.* †**greenth**, *n.* **greeny,** *a.* [OE *grēne* (cp. Dut. *groen,* G *grün,* cogn. with *grōwan,* to GROW)]

Green, *n.* **Henry** (pen name of Henry Vincent Yorke) (1905–74), British novelist, whose works (for example *Loving* (1945), and *Nothing* (1950)) are characterized by an experimental colloquial prose style and extensive use of dialogue.

Greenaway, *n.* **Kate** (1846–1901), British illustrator, known for her drawings of children. In 1877 she first exhibited at the Royal Academy, and began her collaboration with the colour-printer Edmund Evans, with whom she produced a number of children's books, including *Mother Goose*.

Greenbackers, the, in US history, supporters of an alliance of agrarian and industrial organizations, known as the Greenback Labor Party, which campaigned for currency inflation by increasing the paper dollars (greenbacks) in circulation. In 1880 the party's presidential nominee polled only 300,000 votes: the movement was later superseded by POPULISM.

Greene, *n.* **(Henry) Graham** (1904–), English writer, whose novels of guilt, despair, and penitance, include *The Man Within* (1929), *Brighton Rock* (1938), *The Power and the Glory* (1940), *The Heart of the Matter* (1948), *The Third Man* (1950), *Our Man in Havana* (1958), *The Honorary Consul* (1973), and *Monsignor Quixote* (1982).

greengage, *n.* a green, fine-flavoured variety of *Prunus domestica*. [Sir Wm. *Gage* who introduced it *c.* 1725]

Greenham Common, *n.* site of a continuous peace demonstration on common land near Newbury, Berkshire, UK, outside a US airbase. The women-only camp was established Sept. 1981 in protest against the siting of US cruise missiles in the UK. The demonstrations ended 1990 with the closure of the base. Greenham Common will revert to standby status and all missiles will be removed by 1991.

Greenland, *n.* (Greenlandic **Kalaalit Nunaat**) world's largest island. It lies between the North Atlantic and Arctic Oceans. **area** 2,175,600 sq km/840,000 sq miles. **capital** Godthaab (Greenlandic **Nuuk**) on the W coast. **population** (1983) 51,903; Inuit, Danish and other European. **language** Greenlandic. **economy** fishing and fish processing.

Green Mountain Boys, in US history, irregular troops who fought to keep Vermont free from New York interference, and in the War of American Independence captured Fort Ticonderoga. Their leader was Ethan Allen (1738–89), who was later captured by the British. Vermont is popularly called the Green Mountain State.

Greenpeace, *n.* international environmental pressure group, founded 1971, with a policy of nonviolent direct action backed by scientific research. During a protest against French atmospheric nuclear testing in the S Pacific (1985), its ship *Rainbow Warrior* was sunk by French intelligence agents, killing a crew member.

Greenstreet, *n.* **Sidney** (1879–1954), British character actor. He made an impressive film debut in *The Maltese Falcon* (1941) and became one of the cinema's best known villains. His other films included *Casablanca* (1943) and *The Mask of Dimitrios* (1944).

Greenwich, *a.* pertaining to Greenwich or its meridian. **Greenwich Mean Time,** *n.* mean time for the meridian of Greenwich, adopted as the standard time in Great Britain and several other countries. [borough in SE London, where an astronomical observatory was situated from 1646 to 1958]

Greenwich Village, *n.* section of New York's lower Manhattan. From the 1900s it became the bohemian and artistic quarter of the city and, despite rising rentals, remains so.

Greer, *n.* **Germaine** (1939–), Australian feminist, who became widely known on the publication of *The Female Eunuch* (1970). Later works include *The Obstacle Race* (1979), a study of contemporary women artists, and *Sex and Destiny: The Politics of Human Fertility* (1984).

greet[1], *v.t.* to address with a salutation at meeting; to accost, to hail; to receive at meeting or on arrival (with speech, gesture etc.); to meet; †to congratulate. *v.i.* to exchange greetings. **greeting,** *n.* the act of saluting or welcoming; a salutation, a welcome. [OE *grētan* (cp. Dut. *groeten,* G *grüssen*)]

greet[2], *v.i.* (*now chiefly Sc.*) to weep, to cry, to lament. *n.* weeping, lamentation. [OE *grǣtan* (cp. Icel. *grāta,* Goth. *grētan,* to weep) blended with *grēotan,* etym. doubtful]

greffier, *n.* a registrar, clerk or notary (chiefly in the Channel Isles and foreign countries). [F, from *greffe,* a style]

gregarious, †gregarian, *a.* living or going in flocks or herds; tending to associate, not solitary; growing in clusters or in association with others; sociable. **gregariously,** *adv.* **gregariousness,** *n.* [L *gregārius,* from *grex gregis,* flock, herd]

Gregorian, *a.* pertaining to or established or produced by Gregory. *n.* a Gregorian chant; a member of a secret brotherhood established in England in the 18th cent. **Gregorian calender,** *n.* the reformed calendar introduced by Pope Gregory XIII in 1582; hence **Gregorian epoch, style, year. Gregorian chant,** *n.* any of a body of plainsong choral chants associated with Pope Gregory the Great (540–604), which became standard in the Roman Catholic Church. **Gregorian telescope,** *n.* the first form of reflecting telescope, invented by James Gregory, *c.* 1663. [late L *Gregōrius,* Gr. *Grēgorios,* Gregory, -AN]

Gregory, *n.* **Isabella Augusta** (born Persse) (1852–1932), Irish playwright, associated with W. B. Yeats in creating the Abbey Theatre (1904). Her plays include the comedy *Spreading the News* (1904) and the tragedy *Gaol Gate* (1906). Her journals 1916–30 were published in 1946.

Gregory, *n.* 16 popes including:

Gregory I, *n.* **St, the Great** (*c.* 540–604), pope from AD 590, who asserted Rome's supremacy and exercised almost imperial powers. In AD 596 he sent St Augustine to England. He introduced Gregorian chant into the liturgy. Feast day 12 Mar.

Gregory VII, *n.* or **Hildebrand** (*c.* 1023–1085), chief minister to several popes before his election to the papacy (1073). In 1077 he forced the Holy Roman emperor Henry IV to wait in the snow at Canossa for four days, dressed as a penitent, before receiving pardon. He was driven from Rome and died in exile. His feast day is 25 May.

Gregory XIII, *n.* (1502–1585), pope from 1572, who introduced the reformed Gregorian calendar.

Gregory of Tours, St, *n.* (538–594), French Christian bishop of Tours from AD 573, author of a *History of the Franks*. Feast day 17 Nov.

Gregory powder, *n.* the compound powder of rhubarb, magnesium carbonate and ginger, used as an aperient, sometimes called **Gregory**. [James *Gregory,* 1758–1822, Scottish physician]

greige, *n., a.* (of) a greyish beige colour. [F]

gremial, *a.* of or pertaining to the lap or bosom; dwelling in the bosom of the university, resident; intimate, confined to members. *n.* in the Roman Catholic Church, an episcopal vestment covering the lap, orig. to prevent drops of chrism falling on the vestments during ordination etc. [late L *gremiālis,* from *gremium,* the lap]

gremlin, *n.* (*sl.*) a sprite that accompanies an aviator in the air, performing good or ill-natured tricks on him/her; any source of mischief. [etym. unknown]

Grenada, *n.* island in the Caribbean, the southernmost of the Windward Islands. **area** (including the Grenadines, notably Carriacou) 310 sq km/120 sq miles. **capital** St George's. **physical** southernmost of the Windward Islands; mountainous. **population** (1987) 92,000; annual growth rate 1.2%. **exports** cocoa, nutmeg, bananas, mace. **language** English. **religion** Roman Catholic.

grenade, *n.* a small explosive shell thrown by hand or fired from a rifle; a glass shell containing chemicals for extinguishing fires, discovering leakages in drains etc. [F, from Sp. *granada,* orig. POMEGRANATE]

grenadier, *n.* orig. a foot-soldier armed with grenades; a member of what used to be the first company of every battalion of foot, chosen for long service and approved courage; the title is now confined in the British Army to one regiment, the Grenadier Guards; a southern African weaver-bird, *Pyromelana oryx,* with vivid red and black plumage.

grenadine[1], *n.* a thin, gauzy, silk or woollen fabric for women's dresses etc. [F, perh. from *Granada,* city in Spain]

grenadine[2], *n.* a fancy dish, usu. of fillets of veal or poultry, larded and glazed; a pomegranate syrup. [F *grenadin,* etym. doubtful]

Grenadines, *n.* chain of about 600 small islands in the

Caribbean, part of the group known as the Windward Islands. They are divided between St Vincent and Grenada.

grenado, GRENADE.

Grenville¹, *n.* **George** (1712–70), British Whig politician, whose introduction of the the Stamp Act (1765) to raise revenue from the colonies was one of the causes of the American War of Independence. Prime minister and chancellor of the Exchequer (1763–65), Grenville's other measures to reduce the military and civil costs in N America included the Sugar Act and the Quartering Act. His inept management of the Regency Act (1765) damaged his relationship with George III. His government was also responsible for prosecuting the radical John Wilkes.

Grenville², *n.* **Richard** (1542–91), English naval commander and adventurer, renowned for his heroic death aboard his ship *The Revenge* when attacked by Spanish warships. Grenville fought in Hungary and Ireland, 1566–69, and was knighted about 1577. In 1585 he commanded the expedition that founded Virginia, US, for his cousin, Walter Raleigh. From 1586–88 he organized the defence of England against the Spanish Armada.

Grenville³, *n.* **William Wyndham, Baron** (1759–1834), British Whig politician, son of George Grenville. He was foreign secretary in 1791 and resigned along with Pitt in 1801 over King George III's refusal to assent to Catholic emancipation. He headed the 'All the Talents' coalition of 1806–07 that abolished the slave trade.

gressorial, *a.* adapted for walking, applied to the feet of birds having three toes in front (two of them connected) and one behind. [L *gressor,* walker, from *gradī,* to walk, -IAL]

Gretna Green, *n.* village in Dumfries and Galloway region, Scotland. It was famous for runaway marriages after they were banned in England in 1754; all that was necessary was the couple's declaration, before witnesses, of their willingness to marry.

greve, GREAVE.

Greville, *n.* **Fulke, 1st Baron Brooke** (1554–1628), poet and courtier, friend and biographer of Philip Sidney. Greville's works, none of them published during his lifetime, include *Caelica*, a sequence of poems in different metres; *Mustapha* and *Alaham*, tragedies modelled on the Latin Seneca, and the Life of Sir Philip Sidney (1652). He has been commended for his plain style and tough political thought.

grew, *past* GROW.

grewsome, GRUESOME.

grey, *a.* of a colour between white and black; ash-coloured; dull, clouded, dim; dark, dismal, depressing; hoary with age; old, aged, pertaining to old age; ancient; mature, experienced. *n.* a grey colour, grey pigment; grey light, twilight, cold, sunless light; grey clothes; a grey animal, esp. a horse; (*pl.*) GREYS. *v.t.* to make grey; (*Phot.*) to give a soft effect to by covering the negative in printing with ground glass. *v.i.* to become grey. **grey area,** *n.* the area midway between two extremes; an issue or situation that is not clear-cut. **greybeard,** *n.* an old man; a large earthen jar for spirit; a hydroid polyp *Sertularia argentea,* infesting oyster-beds. *a.* having a grey beard. **greybeard lichen,** *n. Usnea barbata*. **grey-bearded,** *a.* **greyhead,** *n.* a person with grey hair; an old male sperm whale. **grey-coated,** *a.* having a grey coat. **grey drake,** *n.* a species of *Ephemera*. **grey eminence** EMINENCE. **grey-eyed,** *a.* having grey eyes. **grey falcon,** *n.* the hen-harrier; also the peregrine falcon. **grey fly,** *n.* (*Milton*) probably a dor beetle. **Grey Friar,** *n.* a Franciscan friar. **grey goose,** *n.* the grey lag. **grey-haired, -headed,** *a.* having grey hair; old, time-worn; of long service (in). **grey-hen,** *n.* the female of the black grouse. †**grey-hooded,** *a.* grey; dusky. **grey lag,** the European wild goose, *Anser ferus,* the original of the domestic goose. †**grey malkin,** *n.* a grey cat. **grey market,** *n.* the unofficial, but not necessarily illegal, selling of products, alongside selling on the official market. **grey matter,** *n.* the greyish tissue of the brain and spinal cord containing the nerve cells; (*coll.*) intellect, intelligence. **grey nurse,** *n.* a shark found in E Australian waters. **grey squirrel,** *n.* a N American squirrel, *Sciurus carolinensis,* now established in Britain. **greystone,** a compact volcanic grey or greenish rock, composed of feldspar and augite. **grey tin,** *n.* the powder into which tin crumbles when cooled to a low temperature. **grey wether,** *n.* (*usu. pl.*) detached blocks of sarsen or sandstone occurring chiefly in SW England, often in the form of circles. **grey wolf,** *n.* the N American timber wolf. **greyish,** *a.* **greyly,** *adv.* **greyness,** *n.* **Greys,** *n.pl.* a British cavalry regiment, the 2nd Dragoons (orig. Scottish), so called from all the horses being greys. [OE *grǣg* (cp. Dut. *grauw,* Icel. *grār,* G *grau*)]

Grey¹, *n.* **Beryl** (1927–), British ballerina. Prima ballerina with the Sadler's Wells Company (1942–57), she then danced internationally, and was artistic director of the London Festival Ballet (1968–79).

Grey², *n.* **Charles, 2nd Earl Grey** (1764–1845), British Whig politician. He entered Parliament, 1786, and in 1806 became First Lord of the Admiralty, and foreign secretary soon afterwards. As prime minister, 1830–34, he carried the Great Reform Bill 1832, and the Act abolishing slavery throughout the British Empire 1833.

Grey³, *n.* **Edward, 1st Viscount Grey of Fallodon** (1862–1933), British Liberal politician, nephew of the 2nd Earl Grey. As foreign secretary (1905–16) he negotiated an entente with Russia in 1907, and backed France against Germany in the Agadir Incident of 1911. In 1914 he said: 'The lamps are going out all over Europe; we shall not see them lit again in our lifetime.'

Grey⁴, *n.* **Henry, 3rd Earl Grey** (1802–94), British politician, son of Charles Grey. He served under his father as undersecretary for the colonies (1830–33), resigning because the cabinet would not back the immediate emancipation of slaves; he was secretary of war (1835–39), and colonial secretary (1846–52).

Grey⁵, *n.* **Lady Jane** (1537–54), queen of England 9–19 July 1553, the great-granddaughter of Henry VII. She was married 1553 to Lord Guildford Dudley (died 1554), son of the Duke of Northumberland. Since she was a Protestant, Edward VI was persuaded by Northumberland to set aside the claims to the throne of his sisters Mary and Elizabeth. When Edward died 6 July, Jane reluctantly accepted the crown and was proclaimed queen four days later. Mary I, however, had the support of the populace and the Lord Mayor of London announced that she was queen 19 July. Grey was executed on Tower Green.

Grey⁶, *n.* **Zane** (1875–1939), US author of westerns, such as *Riders of the Purple Sage* (1912).

greyhound, *n.* a variety of dog used for coursing, characterized by slender form, keen sight, and swiftness. **ocean greyhound,** a swift ship. **greyhound racing,** *n.* racing greyhounds in pursuit of an electrically-propelled dummy hare. [OE *grīgund* (cf. ON *grey-hundr–grey,* dog, bitch, *hundr,* hound)]

greywacke, *n.* (*Geol.*) a gritstone or conglomerate, usu. consisting of small fragments of quartz, flinty slate etc. cemented together, occurring chiefly in Silurian strata. [G *Grauwacke* (*grau,* GREY, WACKE)]

grice, *n.* (*now chiefly Sc.*) a young or sucking-pig; (*Her.*) a wild boar. [Icel. *grīss*]

grid, *n.* a grating of parallel bars; a gridiron for cooking; a perforated or ridged plate used in a storage battery; a system of main transmission lines; (*Mining.*) a griddle; a gridiron for docking ships; an electrode placed in a thermionic tube between two other electrodes for the purpose of controlling the flow of current between them. **grid bias,** *n.* voltage applied to the grid of a valve. **grid circuit,** *n.* the circuit connected between grid and cathode. **grid current,** *n.* the current passing between grid and cathode. **grid leak,** *n.* a fixed resistance for the leakage of electrons from the grid circuit. **grid potentiometer,** *n.* a mechanism to facilitate critical adjustment of grid potential or grid-bias.

[short for GRIDIRON]

griddle, *n.* a circular iron plate for baking cakes; (*Mining*) a wire-bottomed sieve or screen. *v.t.* (*Mining*) to screen with a griddle. **griddle-cake,** *n.* a cake baked on a griddle. [AF *gridil,* OF *greil* (F *grille*), perh. from L *crātīcula,* dim. of *crātes,* a hurdle]

gride, *v.i.* to grind, scrape or jar (along, through etc.); to grate. †*v.t.* to pierce, to cut; to cause to grate. *n.* a grating sound. [metathesis of GIRD[2]]

gridelin, *n.* a colour of mixed white and red, a grey-violet or purple. [F (*gris-de-lin,* flax-grey)]

gridiron, *n.* a grated iron utensil for broiling fish, flesh etc.; a framework of parallel timbers or iron beams for supporting a ship in dry dock; (*Theat.*) a framework above the stage for supporting the apparatus for drop-scenes etc.; a series of parallel lines for shunting goods trains; wire network between cathode and anode; (*N Am.*) a football field. **gridiron manoeuvre,** *n.* a naval movement in which ships in two parallel columns cross each to the opposite column. **gridiron pendulum,** *n.* a compensation pendulum constructed with parallel bars of different metals. [ME *gredire,* as GRIDDLE (assim. to IRON)]

grief, *n.* deep sorrow or mental distress due to loss, disaster or disappointment; regret, sadness; that which causes sorrow or sadness; bodily pain. **to come to grief,** to meet with disaster; to fail; to come to ruin. **grief-stricken,** *a.* suffering great sorrow. **griefless,** *a.* **grieflessness,** *n.* [OF, from *grever,* to GRIEVE[1]]

Grieg, *n.* **Edvard Hagerup** (1843–1907), Norwegian composer. Much of his music is small scale, particularly his songs, dances, sonatas, and piano works. Among his orchestral works are the *Piano Concerto* (1869) and the incidental music for Ibsen's *Peer Gynt* (1876).

grievance, *n.* that which causes grief; a wrong, an injustice; a ground for complaint. **to air a grievance,** to state a cause of complaint. **grievance-monger,** *n.* a confirmed grumbler. [OF *grevance,* from foll.]

grieve[1], *v.t.* to annoy; to cause pain or sorrow to; to lament, to sorrow over. *v.i.* to feel grief, to mourn, to sorrow. **grievingly,** *adv.* **grievous,** *a.* causing grief or pain; hard to be borne, distressing, oppressive; hurtful, injurious; flagrant, atrocious, heinous. **grievous bodily harm (gbh),** *n.* in law, a serious injury to a person caused by another person. **grievously,** *adv.* **grievousness,** *n.* [OF *grever,* L *gravāre,* to burden, from *gravis,* GRAVE[3]]

grieve[2], *n.* an overseer, steward or bailiff; †a sheriff. [Sc., North., from O Northumbrian *græfa,* OE *gerēfa,* REEVE]

grievous GRIEVE[1].

griffin[1], -on[1], *n.* a fabulous creature, with the body and legs of a lion, the head and wings of an eagle and listening ears, emblematic of strength, agility and watchfulness; (*sl.*) a betting tip; a hint; a watchful guardian, a duenna. **griffin-like,** *a.* [F *griffon,* L *grȳphus, gryps,* Gr. *grups,* from *grupos,* hooked, hook-beaked]

griffin[2], *n.* (*dated Ang.-Ind.*) a newcomer from Europe, a greenhorn. **griffinage, griffinhood, griffinship,** *n.* **griffinish,** *a.* [etym. unknown]

Griffith, *n.* **D(avid) W(ark)** (1875–1948), US film director. He made hundreds of 'one reelers' (lasting 12 minutes), 1908–13, in which he pioneered the techniques of the flash-back, cross-cut, close-up, and long-shot. After much experimentation with photography and new techniques came *Birth of a Nation* (1915), followed by *Intolerance* (1916).

Griffith-Joyner, *n.* **Delorez Florence** (born Griffith) (1959–), US track athlete who won three gold medals at the 1988 Seoul Olympics, the 100 and 200 metres and the sprint relay. Her time in the 200 metres was a world record 21.34 seconds.

griffon[1] GRIFFIN[1].

griffon[2], griffon-vulture, *n.* a vulture, *Gyps fulvus*.

griffon[3], *n.* a variety of dog like a terrier, with short, coarse hair. [F, ident, by Littré with *griffon,* GRIFFIN[1]]

grig, *n.* a sand-eel or a young eel; a cricket or grass-hopper; a lively or merry person. [etym. doubtful (perh. the later senses distinct and onomat. in orig.)]

Grignard, *n.* **François Auguste-Victor** (1871–1935), French chemist. The so-called **Grignard re-agents** (compounds containing a hydrocarbon radical, magnesium and a halogen such as chlorine) found important applications as some of the most versatile in organic synthesis.

grill, *v.t.* to broil on a gridiron; to bake or torture as if by fire; (*coll.*) to interrogate severely. *n.* meat etc. broiled; a gridiron. **grill-room,** *n.* a room in a restaurant where meat etc. is grilled and served. †**grillade,** *n.* the act of grilling; grilled meat etc. **griller,** *n.* [F *griller,* from *gril,* OF *graïl,* prob. as GRIDDLE]

grillage, *n.* a structure of sleepers and cross-beams forming a foundation in marshy soil for a pier, wharf or the like. [foll., -AGE]

grille, *n.* an open grating, railing or screen of lattice-work, to enclose or shut a sacred or private place, or to fill an opening in a door etc.; (*Real Tennis*) a square opening in the end wall on the hazard side of the court; in fish culture, a frame with glass tubes for fish-eggs during incubation. [F, as GRIDDLE (cp. GRILL)]

Grillparzer, *n.* **Franz** (1791–1872), Austrian poet and dramatist. His plays include the tragedy *Die Ahnfrau/The Ancestress* (1817), the classical *Sappho* (1818) and the trilogy *Das goldene Vliess/The Golden Fleece* (1821).

grilse, *n.* a young salmon when it first returns from the sea, usu. in its second year. [etym. doubtful (perh. a corr. of OF *grisle,* grey)]

grim, *a.* stern, relentless, severe, unyielding; of a forbidding aspect; savage, cruel; hideous, ghastly. †**grim-looked,** *a.* **like grim death,** with determination, unyieldingly. **grimly,** *a.* grim, stern-looking. *adv.* in a grim manner. †**grimliness,** *n.* **grimness,** *n.* [OE (cp. G *grimm*), cogn. with obs. *grame,* angry]

grimace, *n.* a distortion of the features, a wry face, expressing disgust, contempt, affectation etc. *v.i.* to make grimaces. **grimaced,** *a.* distorted. **grimacer, grimacier,** *n.* [F, etym. doubtful]

Grimaldi, *n.* **Joseph** (1779–1837), British clown, born in London, the son of an Italian actor. He appeared on the stage at two years old. He gave his name 'Joey' to all later clowns, and excelled as 'Mother Goose' performed at Covent Garden in 1806.

grimalkin, *n.* an old cat, esp. a she-cat; a jealous or spiteful old woman. [GREY, *Malkin,* dim. of *Maud, Matilda*]

grime, *n.* dirt, smut; dirt deeply engrained. *v.t.* to dirty; to begrime. **grimy,** *a.* **grimily,** *adv.* **griminess,** *n.* [cp. W Flem. *grijm,* Dan. *grim,* Swed. dial. *grima,* a spot or smut]

Grimm, *n.* **Jakob Ludwig Karl** (1785–1863), German philologist and collaborator with his brother Wilhelm Karl (1786–1859) in the *Fairy Tales* (1812–14), based on collected folk tales. Jakob's main work was his *Deutsche Grammatik/German Grammar* (1819), which gave the first historical treatment of the Germanic languages. **Grimm's law,** *n.* a law formulated by Grimm respecting the modification of consonants in the most important of the Indo-European languages.

Grimond, *n.* **Jo(seph), Baron Grimond** (1913–), British Liberal politician. As leader of the party (1956–67), he aimed at making it 'a new radical party to take the place of the Socialist Party as an alternative to Conservatism'.

grin[1], *v.i.* to show the teeth as in laughter, derision or pain; to smile in a malicious, sickly or affected manner; to gape, to stand wide open (as a joint). *v.t.* to express by grinning. *n.* the act of grinning; a smile with the teeth showing. **grinningly,** *adv.* [OE *grennian,* cp. OHG *grînnan* to mutter (prob. the sense was influenced by the root seen in OHG *grînan,* to distort the face)]

†**grin[2],** *n.* a snare, a noose. [OE *grīn*]

grind, *v.t.* (*past, p.p.* **ground**) to reduce to powder or fine particles by crushing and friction; to produce (flour etc.) by this process; to wear down, sharpen, smooth or polish by friction, esp. on a grindstone; to grate; to oppress with exactions; to work (a mill); to turn the handle of (various appliances); to study laboriously; to teach (a pupil in a subject) laboriously. *v.i.* to perform the act of grinding; to be rubbed together; to be ground; to admit of being ground; to grate; to rub gratingly; to toil hard and distastefully, to drudge; to study laboriously. *n.* the act or process of grinding; hard and monotonous work; hard study, esp. for an examination; a turn at the handle of a machine or instrument. **grinder,** *n.* one who or that which grinds (*esp. in comb.* as *knife-grinder*); a grinding-machine; a molar tooth, a tooth generally; (*sl.*) a crammer; one who studies hard. **grindery,** *n.* a place where tools etc. are ground; materials and tools for leather-workers; a shop where these materials are sold. **grindingly,** *adv.* **grindstone,** *n.* a flat circular stone, used for grinding tools; †a millstone. **to keep one's nose to the grindstone,** to stick to one's work. [OE *grindan* (cp. Dut. *grendan,* and perh. L *frendere,* to gnash, grind)]

gringo, *n.* (*pl.* **-gos**) (*esp. N Am., offensive*) a contemptuous name for an English-speaking foreigner. [Mex. Sp.]

grip[1]**,** *n.* the act of seizing or holding firmly; a firm grasp, a clutch; the power of grasping; a particular mode of clasping hands; the part of a weapon, instrument etc. that is held in the hand; a grasping or clutching part of a machine, a clutch; a grappling-tool; on a film set or in the theatre, a person employed to carry equipment, shift scenery props, etc.; (*pl.*) close combat, hand-to-hand conflict; power of holding the attention; a suitcase, a hold-all, also called **handgrip**. *v.t.* (*past, p.p.* **gripped**) to seize hold of; to grasp or hold tightly; to hold the attention of. *v.i.* to take firm hold. **to come** or **get to grips with,** to deal with, tackle (a problem etc.). **grip-brake,** *n.* a brake that is worked by gripping with the hand. **grip-sack,** *n.* (*N Am.*) a travelling bag, suitcase. **gripper,** *n.* **gripping,** *a.* having the power of holding the attention. [OE *gripa,* a handful, and *gripe,* a clutch, both cogn. with GRIPE]

grip[2]**,** *n.* a small ditch or furrow. †*v.t.* to trench, to drain. [OE *grȳpe, grēpe,* a trench, a burrow]

gripe, *v.t.* to seize and hold firmly; to clutch, to pinch; to oppress; to affect the bowels of with colic pains. *v.i.* to lay fast hold of anything; to get money by extortion; of a vessel, to come up too close to the wind against the helm as in sailing close-hauled. *n.* a grasp, a firm hold with the hands; a pinch, a squeeze; the part by which anything is grasped; a handle or hilt; clutch, power, control, bondage; pinching distress; a mean, niggardly person; a clutch, a brake applied to the wheel of a crane or derrick; (*pl.*) pains in the abdomen; the fore-foot of a ship, the forward end of the keel; a series of ropes, dead-eyes and hooks, fastened to ring-bolts in the deck, for securing boats; one of a pair of bands passing round a boat when suspended from the davits. **gripe water,** *n.* a solution given to a baby to ease the pain of colic. **griper,** *n.* an extortioner, an oppressor. **griping,** *a.* grasping, greedy; pinching the bowels. **gripingly,** *adv.* †**gripple,** *a.* griping, exacting; niggardly. **grippy,** *a.* [OE *grīpan* (cp. Dut. *grȳpen,* Goth. *greipan,* G *greipen*)]

grippe, grip, *n.* a former name for influenza. [cp. F *la grippe*]

gripper GRIP[1].

Griqua, *n.* (*pl.* **-qua, quas**) one of a mixed ancestry people, descended from Dutch settlers and the Hottentot of southern Africa.

Gris, *n.* **Juan** (1887–1927), Spanish abstract painter, one of the earliest Cubists. He developed a distinctive geometrical style, often strongly coloured. He experimented with collage and made designs for Diaghilev's ballet (1922–23).

grisaille, *n.* a style of painting or staining in grey monochrome, esp. on stained glass, representing solid bodies in relief, such as ornament of cornices etc. [F, from *gris,* grey, OHG *grīs,* etym. unknown]

grisamber, *n.* (*Milton*) ambergris.

grise[1]**,** GREE[2]. **grise**[2]**,** GRICE.

Griselda, *n.* a woman of great meekness and patience. [from a character in Boccaccio, Chaucer and elsewhere]

griseofulvin, *n.* an antibiotic used to treat fungal infections. [L, from *Penicillium griseofulvin,* (the fungus from which it was obtained) from ML *griseus,* grey, and L *fulvus,* reddish-yellow]

griseous, *a.* bluish-grey. [med. L *griseus,* OHG *grīs,* see GRISAILLE]

grisette, *n.* †a grey woollen fabric, used for dresses by women of the working classes; a lively and attractive girl or young woman of the French working classes. [F, from *gris,* see GRISAILLE]

griskin, *n.* the lean part of the loin of a bacon pig. [GRICE, -KIN]

grisled, GRIZZLED under GRIZZLE[2].

grisly, *a.* horrible, terrible, fearful, grim. †*adv.* horribly, terribly, fearfully. [OE *grīslīc* (*grīs-* in *āgrīsan,* to shudder, *-līc,* -LY)]

Grisons, *n.* French name for the Swiss canton of Graubünden.

grist[1]**,** *n.* corn to be ground; corn which has been ground; malt for a brewing. **to bring grist to the mill,** to bring profitable business or gain. **grist-mill,** *n.* a mill for grinding corn. [OE *grīst,* cogn. with GRIND]

grist[2]**,** *n.* a size of rope as denoted by the number and thickness of the strands. [etym. doubtful; perh. conn. with GIRD[1]]

gristle, *n.* cartilage, esp. when found in meat. **gristly,** *a.* [OE, etym. doubtful (cp. OFris. and MLG *gristal*)]

grit[1]**,** *n.* coarse rough particles such as sand or gravel; gritstone, a compact sandstone of sharp siliceous grain; the character of a stone as regards texture or grain; (*coll.*) firmness, determination, pluck. *v.i.* (*past, p.p.* **gritted**) to be ground together; to give out a grating sound; to grate. *v.t.* to grind or grate (as the teeth). **gritstone,** *n.* a coarse-grained sandstone. **gritty,** *a.* **grittiness,** *n.* [OE *grēot* (cp. Icel. *grjōt,* G *Griess*), allied to GROUT[1]]

grit[2]**,** (*Sc.*) GREAT.

grits, *n.pl.* husked and granulated but unground meal, esp. coarse oatmeal. [OE *gryttan* (cp. MDut. *grutte,* barley, G *Grütze,* also GROATS)]

Grivas, *n.* **George** (1898–1974), Greek Cypriot general who led EOKA's attempts to secure the union (Greek *enosis*) of Cyprus with Greece.

grizzle[1]**,** *a.* grey. *n.* a grey-haired man; grey hair; a kind of wig; a grey colour; †roan-coloured. **grizzled,** *a.* grey, grey-haired; interspersed with grey. **grizzly,** *a.* grey, greyish. *n.* a grizzly-bear. **grizzly-bear,** *n.* a N American bear, *Ursus ferox,* of great size and strength. [OF *grisel,* from *gris,* grey, see GRISAILLE]

grizzle[2]**,** *v.i.* to worry, to fret; to whimper. *n.* one who grizzles. [prov., etym. doubtful]

gro., (*abbr.*) gross.

groan, *v.i.* to utter a deep moaning sound, as in pain or grief; to grieve; to suffer hardship; to be burdened; to long or strive with or as with groans. *v.t.* to silence or express disapprobation of by groans; to utter with groans. *n.* a low moaning sound, as of one in pain or sorrow; such a sound simulated in derision or disapprobation. †**groanful,** *a.* **groaningly,** *adv.* [OE *grānian* (cp. G *greinen,* to GRIN)]

groat, *n.* †a small silver coin, value 4d., coined 1357–1662; the silver fourpenny-piece coined 1836–56; any trifling sum. **not worth a groat,** worthless. **groatsworth,** *n.* as much as can be bought for a groat. [ME and LG *grote* (cp. MDut. *groot*), cogn. with GREAT]

groats, *n.pl.* husked oats or wheat. [cp. OE *grūt,* coarse meal, cogn. with GRITS]

grocer, *n.* a dealer in tea, sugar, coffee, spices and miscellaneous household supplies. **grocery,** *n.* (*usu. in pl.*) grocers' wares; a grocer's shop; (*N Am.*) a grog-shop. [OF *grossier,* one who sells in the gross, med. L *grossārius,* from *grossus,* GROSS]

grog, *n.* a mixture of spirit and cold water; spirituous liquor; (*Austral., coll.*) any esp. cheap alcoholic drink. †*v.t.* to make grog by adding water to (spirits); to extract spirits (from an emptied cask) by pouring in hot water. *v.i.* to drink grog. **to grog on,** (*Austral., coll.*) to take part in a session of heavy drinking. **grog-blossom,** *n.* a redness or eruption on the nose or face, due to excessive drinking. **grog on,** *n.* (*Austral., coll.*) a drinking party. **grog-shop,** *n.* a place where spirits are sold. **groggery,** *n.* (*N Am.*) a grog-shop. **groggy,** *a.* tipsy, drunk; staggering; acting like one stupefied with drink; moving uneasily, as with tender feet or forelegs (said of a horse); unwell. **grogginess,** *n.* [said to be from a nickname 'Old Grog' of Admiral Vernon, from his wearing a GROGRAM cloak; about 1745 he ordered his sailors to dilute their rum with water]

grogram, †**-ran**, *n.* a coarse stuff of silk and mohair or silk and wool. *a.* made of grogram. [F *gros grain,* coarse grain]

groin[1], *n.* the hollow in the human body where the thigh and the trunk unite; (*Arch.*) the edge formed by an intersection of vaults; the fillet or moulding covering this. *v.t.* to form (a roof) into groins; to furnish with groins. **groin-centring,** *n.* the centring of timber during construction. **groined,** *a.* **groining,** *n.* [earlier *grine, grynae* (supposed by Skeat to be from OE *grynde,* an abyss or depression, cogn. with G *Grund,* valley, GROUND[1])]

†**groin[2],** *v.i.* to groan, grunt or growl; to pout, to grumble. *n.* the snout of a swine. [OF *grognir* (F *grogner*), L *grunnīre*]

groin[3], GROYNE.

Grolier, *n.* a book or binding from Grolier's collection. **Grolier design,** *n.* in bookbinding, geometrical or arabesque ornament such as characterized Grolier's bindings. **Grolieresque**, *a.* [Jean *Grolier,* 1479–1565, French bibliophile]

gromel, grommel, GROMWELL.

grommet, GRUMMET.

gromwell, *n.* a genus of trailing herbs of the borage family, esp. *Lithospermum officinale,* the hard stony seeds of which were formerly used in medicine. [earlier *gromil,* OF (etym. doubtful)]

Gromyko, *n.* **Andrei** (1909–1989), president of the USSR (1985–88). As ambassador to the US from 1943, he took part in the Tehran, Yalta, and Potsdam conferences; as United Nations representative (1946–49), he exercised the Soviet veto 26 times. He was foreign minister 1957–85. It was Gromyko who formally nominated Mikhail Gorbachev as Communist Party leader in 1985.

Groningen, *n.* most northerly province of the Netherlands; area 2350 sq km/907 sq miles; population (1988) 557,000. Capital is Groningen; population (1988) 207,000. Industries include textiles, tobacco, and sugar refining.

groom, *n.* a person in charge of horses or a stable; one of several officers in the royal household, as *Groom in waiting, Groom of the privy* or *great Chamber, Groom of the stole* etc.; a bridegroom. *v.t.* to tend or care for, as a groom does a horse; to curry and brush. **well-groomed,** *a.* neatly or smartly got up, well tended, esp. as regards the hair and beard. **groomsman,** *n.* an unmarried friend who attends on the bridegroom. [perh. from OF *gromet, groumet* (F *gourmet,* see GOURMET), dim. of *groume,* a boy, a servant]

groove, *n.* a channel, furrow or long hollow, such as may be cut with a tool for something to fit into or work in; natural course or events of one's life, a rut; (*dated sl.*) an exalted state; (*dated sl.*) a satisfying experience. (*prov.*) a shaft or pit. *v.t.* to cut or form a groove or grooves in. *v.i.* (*dated sl.*) to be in an exalted state; (*dated sl.*) to be delighted, pleased, satisfied etc. **grooved,** *a.* **groover,** *n.* **groovy,** *a.* of a groove; up-to-date; excellent; very good; pleasant; **grooviness,** *n.* [Dut. *groeve,* cogn. with OE *grafan,* to GRAVE]

grope, *v.i.* to feel about with the hands; to search (after) something as in the dark, by feeling about with the hands; to feel one's way; to seek blindly. *v.t.* to seek out by feeling with the hands in the dark, or as a blind person; (*sl.*) to fondle for sexual gratification †to handle; †to seek into; †to inquire into. **groper[1],** *n.* **gropingly,** *adv.* [OE *grāpian* (cogn. with *grīpan,* to GRIPE)]

groper[2], GROUPER.

Gropius, *n.* **Walter Adolf** (1883–1969), German architect, who lived in the US from 1937. A founder-director of the BAUHAUS school in Weimar (1919–28), he was an advocate of team architecture and artistic standards in industrial production. His works include the Fagus-Werke (a shoe factory in Prussia), the Model Factory at the 1914 Werkbund exhibition in Cologne, and the Harvard Graduate Center (1949–50).

grosbeak, †**gross-beak,** *n.* a name given to several birds having thick bills, esp. the genus *Coccothraustes,* comprising the hawfinch. [F *grosbe* (GROSS, BEAK)]

groschen, *n.* an old German silver coin, an Austrian coin worth one-hundredth of a schilling; a German 10-pfennig piece. [G]

groset, grossart, *n.* (*Sc.*) a gooseberry. [earlier *groser,* F *groseille*]

grosgrain, *n.* a heavy ribbed silk or rayon fabric or ribbon. [F, large grain]

gros point, *n.* a stitch in embroidery covering two horizontal and two vertical threads (as dist. from *petit point*). [F, large point]

gross, *a.* big, rank; fat, bloated, overfed; coarse, uncleanly; lacking fineness, dense, thick, material; dull, unrefined; indelicate, obscene; flagrant, glaring; total, not net; general, not specific; †plain, palpable. *n.* 12 dozen; the main body, the mass; the sum total. **in the gross, in gross,** in the bulk, wholesale; in a general way, on the whole. **gross domestic product,** *n.* the total annual value of all goods and services produced domestically in a country. **gross-headed,** *a.* thick-headed; stupid. **gross national product,** *n.* the total annual value of all goods and services produced in a country, including net investment incomes from foreign nations. **gross up,** *v.t.* to convert a net figure to a gross figure (as net income to its pre-tax value). **gross weight,** *n.* the weight of goods with the cask or whatever contains them. **grossly,** *adv.* **grossness,** *n.* [OF *gros,* fem. *grosse,* late L *grossus,* thick, etym. doubtful]

Grossmith, *n.* **George** (1847–1912), British actor and singer. Turning from journalism to the stage, in 1877 he began a long association with the Gilbert and Sullivan operas, in which he created a number of parts. He collaborated with his brother Weedon Grossmith (1853–1919) in the comic novel *Diary of a Nobody* (1894).

grossulaceous, grossularious, *a.* of or belonging to the Grossulariaceae, an order of plants containing the gooseberry and currant. **grossular,** *a.* of or belonging to a gooseberry. *n.* a Siberian variety of garnet, sometimes called the gooseberry garnet. [mod. L *grossulāria,* from OF *groselle,* gooseberry]

Grosz[1], *n.* **Georg** (1893–1959), German expressionist painter and illustrator, a founder of the Berlin group of the Dada movement (1918). Grosz excelled in savage satirical drawings criticizing the government and the military establishment. After numerous prosecutions he emigrated to the US in 1932.

Grosz[2], *n.* **Károly** (1930–), Hungarian Communist politician, prime minister (1987–88). As leader of the ruling Hungarian Socialist Workers' Party (HSWP) (1988–89), he sought to establish a flexible system of 'socialist pluralism'.

grot[1], *n.* a grotto. [F *grotte,* GROTTO]

grot[2], *n.* (*coll.*) dirt, filth. [back-formation from GROTTY]

Grotefend, *n.* **George Frederick** (1775–1853), German scholar. Although a student of the classical rather than the oriental languages, he nevertheless solved the riddle of the cuneiform script as used in ancient Persia: decipherment of Babylonian cuneiform followed from his work.

grotesque, *a.* irregular, extravagant or fantastic in form; ludicrous through these qualities, absurd, bizarre. *n.* whimsically designed ornamentation consisting of figures of plants and animals of fanciful invention; (*pl.*) whimsical figures or scenery; (*Print.*) a square-cut type without serifs. **grotesquely,** *adv.* **grotesqueness,** *n.* **grotesquerie,** *n.* [OF, from It. *grottesca,* antique work (GROTTO, -ESQUE)]

Grotius, *n.* **Hugo** (1583–1645), Dutch jurist and politician, born in Delft. He became a lawyer, and later received political appointments. In 1618 he was arrested as a republican and sentenced to imprisonment for life: his wife contrived his escape in 1620, and he settled in France, where he composed the *De Jure Belli et Pacis/ On the Law of War and Peace* (1625), the foundation of international law. He was Swedish ambassador in Paris (1634–45).

grotto, *n.* (*pl.* **-oes, -os**) a small cave, esp. one that is picturesque; an artificial cave or cave-like room decorated with rocks, shells and the like. **grotto-work,** *n.* ornamental rock-work etc. in a garden to imitate a grotto. **grottoed,** *a.* [It. *grotta,* late L *crupta,* L *crypta,* Gr. *kruptē,* CRYPT]

grotty, *a.* (*coll.*) dirty, filthy; inferior, substandard; unattractive. **grottily,** *adv.* [by shortening and alteration from *grotesque*]

grouch, *v.i.* to grumble, to grouse. *n.* a discontented mood; an irritable and complaining person, a grumbler. **grouchy,** *a.*

ground[1], *n.* the surface of the earth as dist. from the air or the heavens; a floor, pavement or other supporting surface; a region or tract of land; land, landed estates; (*pl.*) private enclosed land attached to a house; the firm, solid earth; the bottom of the sea; the substratum, the base or foundation; the background, the surface on which a picture or design is laid, the prevailing colour or tone; the reason, motive, origin, cause; (*pl.*) basis, valid reason, pretext, the first or fundamental principles; the extent of an inquiry or survey, area, scope; (*pl.*) sediment, dregs, esp. of coffee; the position occupied by an army; an acid-resisting composition spread over the surface of the metal to be etched; strata containing a mineral lode or coal-seam; (*Painting*) the first layer of paint; the flat surface from which the figures rise; in sport, the area allotted to a single player or to a side; †the pit of a theatre. *v.t.* to set or place upon or in the ground; to base or establish (on); to instruct thoroughly (in) the elementary principles of; to run (a ship) aground; to prevent an aeroplane from taking to the air. *v.i.* of a vessel, to strike the ground. **above ground** ABOVE. **below ground** BELOW. **common ground** COMMON. **down to the ground,** (*coll.*) thoroughly; in every respect. **forbidden ground,** an area or subject that must be avoided. **home ground** HOME. **to break (new) ground,** to cut the first sod; to take the first step; to make a start. **to cut the ground from under someone** or **from under someone's feet,** (*coll.*) to anticipate someone's arguments or actions etc., and thereby render them meaningless or ineffective. **to fall to the ground,** to come to naught; to fail. **to get off the ground,** (*coll.*) to make a start, esp. one that is successful. **to gain ground,** to advance, to meet with success, to prevail. †**to gather ground,** †**to get ground,** to gain ground. **to give ground,** to give way, to retire, to yield. **to have one's feet on the ground** FOOT. **to lose ground,** to be driven back, to give way; to lose advantage or credit; to decline, to fall off. **to shift one's ground,** to change the basis or premises of one's reasoning; to try a different plan. **to stand one's ground,** not to yield or give way. **ground-angling,** *n.* angling without a float, with the weight placed close to the hook. **ground-ash,** *n.* an ash sapling. **ground-bait,** *n.* bait thrown into the water to attract fish. *v.t.* to put ground-bait into in preparation for angling. **ground-bass,** *n.* a bass passage of a few bars constantly repeated, with a varied melody and harmony. **ground-box,** *n.* small box shrubs for edging garden plots and paths. **ground-colour,** *n.* the first coat of paint; the general colour or tone on which a design is painted. **ground control,** *n.* control of landing an aircraft or spacecraft by information transmitted from the ground. **groundcover,** *n.* low-growing plants and shrubs, esp. as used to cover a whole area; air support for ground troops. **ground floor,** *n.* the storey or rooms level with the exterior ground, (in America called the first floor). **ground frost,** *n.* a ground temperature on grass of 32° F (0° C) or under. **ground game,** *n.* running game, as hares, rabbits etc., dist. from birds. **ground-gudgeon,** *n.* the loach. **ground-hog,** *n.* the aardvark, *Orycteropus capensis;* the American marmot, *Arctomys monax.* **ground-ice,** *n.* ice formed at the bottom of the water before the surface freezes, also called anchor-ice. **ground-ivy,** *n.* a labiate creeping plant, *Nepeta glechoma,* with purple-blue flowers. **ground-landlord,** *n.* the owner of land let on a building lease. **ground-note,** *n.* (*Mus.*) the note or fundamental bass on which a common chord is built. **ground-nut,** *n.* the pea-nut, *Arachis hypogaea;* the edible tuber of *Burnium flexuosum;* the American wild bean, *Apios tuberosa,* having an edible tuber. **ground-oak,** *n.* an oak sapling. **ground-pine,** *n.* a herb, *Ajuga chamaepitys,* with a resinous odour. **ground-plan,** *n.* a horizontal plan of a building at the ground level; an outline or general plan of anything. **ground plane,** *n.* the horizontal plane of projection in perspective drawing. **ground-plot,** *n.* the ground upon which a building is placed. **ground-rent,** *n.* rent paid to a ground-landlord for a building-site. **ground rule,** *n.* (*often pl.*) a basic rule of a game, procedure etc. **ground-sea,** *n.* a heavy sea or swell without apparent cause. **ground-sheet, -cover,** *n.* a waterproof sheet spread on the ground to give protection against dampness, esp. inside a tent. **groundsman,** *n.* a person employed to look after a cricket pitch. **ground speed,** *n.* the speed of an aircraft relative to a point on the earth's surface. **ground-squirrel,** *n.* any species of *Tamias,* a genus of American burrowing squirrels, esp. the chipmunk. **ground stroke,** *n.* a stroke (as in tennis) made by hitting a ball that has rebounded from the ground. **ground staff,** *n.* the non-flying staff of an aerodrome. **ground-swell,** *n.* a long, deep swell or rolling of the sea, occasioned by a past or distant storm or earthquake. **ground-tackle,** *n.* of a vessel, the ropes and tackle connected with the anchors and mooring apparatus. **ground-tier,** *n.* the lower range of boxes in a theatre. **ground-torpedo,** *n.* a torpedo laid at the bottom of the sea. **ground water,** *n.* underground water consisting mainly of surface water that has seeped down. **groundwork,** *n.* that which forms the foundation or basis; a fundamental principle; the original reason; the parts of any object not covered by decoration etc. **groundage,** *n.* dues paid for space occupied by a ship on a beach or in port. **groundedly,** *adv.* **grounding,** *n.* instruction in the elements of a subject. **groundless,** *a.* without foundation, reason or warrant, baseless; †without bottom. **groundlessly,** *adv.* **groundlessness,** *n.* **groundling,** *n.* a spectator who stood on the floor of a theatre, hence one of the vulgar; a fish that keeps at the bottom, esp. *Cobitis taenia,* the spined loach, and *Gobius niger,* the black goby; a creeping plant. **groundy,** *a.* full of sediment or dregs. [OE *grund* (cp. Dut. *grond,* G *Grund*)]

ground[2], *a.* having been ground. **ground glass,** *n.* glass with the surface ground to make it obscure. [p.p. of GRIND]

groundsel[1], *n.* a composite plant with pinnatifid leaves and small yellow flowers, esp. the common weed, *Senecio vulgaris,* which is used for feeding cage-birds. [OE *gund-* or *grun-deswylige* (perh. *gund,* pus, *swylige,* from *swelgan,* to SWALLOW, lit, pus-swallower, from use in poultices)]

groundsel[2], **-sill,** *n.* the timber of a building next to the ground; a threshold; a foundation. [GROUND[1], SILL]

groundwork GROUND[1].

groundy GROUND[1].

group, *n.* the combination of several figures or objects to form a single mass; a number of persons or things stationed near each other, a cluster, an assemblage; a number of persons or things classed together on account of certain resemblances; a grade in classification not corresponding precisely to any regular division or sub-division; a series of minerals agreeing essentially in chemical composition; a series of rocks or strata deposited about the same period; in the RAF the highest subdivision of a Command. *v.t.* to form into or place in a group; to put (an object) in close relation or contact (with); to bring together so as to produce a harmonious whole or effect. *v.i.* to form or fall into a group. **Group Captain,** *n.* commissioned rank in the RAF equivalent to that of Colonel in the Army. **group practice,** *n.* a medical practice run by a partnership of general practitioners. **group therapy,** *n.* in psychiatry, the treatment of a group of patients in regular sessions where problems are shared in group discussion. **groupage,** *n.* **Grouper,** *n.* a member of the Oxford Group. **groupy, -ie,** *n.* (*sl.*) a (usu. female) fan who travels with and is sexually available to the members of a pop group. [F *groupe,* It. *groppo,* prob. from Teut. (cp. CROP)]

grouper, *n.* name of certain Californian, Atlantic and Australian fish. [Port. *garupa,* perh. from S Am. word]

grouse[1], *n.* (*pl.* **grouse**) a gallinaceous game-bird with feet more or less feathered, esp. *Lagopus scoticus,* the red grouse, moor fowl or moor game, *Lyrurus tetrix,* the black game or heath fowl, *Tetrao urogallus,* the capercailzie, wood or great grouse, and *Lagopus mutus,* the ptarmigan or rock grouse; the flesh of these, esp. of the red grouse. *v.i.* to hunt or shoot grouse. **grousy,** *a.* [etym. doubtful]

grouse[2], *v.i.* to grumble. *n.* a grievance. **grouser,** *n.* [cp. GRUDGE]

grouse[3], *a.* (*Austral., coll.*) fine, very good.

grout[1], *n.* coarse meal; (*pl.*) dregs, grounds; a thin, coarse mortar to run into the joints of masonry and brickwork; a finishing coat of fine stuff for ceilings. *v.t.* to fill up with grout. **grouting,** *n.* the act or process of filling in or finishing with grout; the grout filled in; (*Build.*) the injection of cement grout into foundations etc. for strengthening. **grouty,** *a.* muddy, dirty. [OE *grūt,* cogn. with GRIT[1]]

grout[2], *v.t.* to turn (up) with the snout (of a pig). *v.i.* to turn up the ground with the snout. [perh. conn. with prec., or from ROOT]

grouter, *n.* (*Austral., coll.*) a bet in the game of two-up. **to come in** or **be on the grouter,** to get an unfair advantage; in a game of two-up, to bet on a change in the fall of the coins.

grove, *n.* a small wood; a cluster of trees shading an avenue or walk; a wood or forest sacred to a divinity; in the Bible, erron. translation of Heb. *Asherah,* a goddess, or her pillar or symbol. **groved,** *a.* **groveless,** *a.* **grovy,** *a.* [OE *grāf,* etym. unknown]

grovel, *v.i.* to lie or move with the body prostrate on the earth; to prostrate oneself, to be low, mean or abject. **groveller,** *n.* **grovellingly,** *adv.* [erron. formed from obs. adv. *grovelling* (obs. *groof* in *on groof* or *grufe,* face downwards, Icel. *āgrūfu,* -LING[2]]

grow, *v.i.* (*past* **grew,** *p.p.* **grown**) to increase in bulk by the assimilation of new matter into the living organism; to develop; to increase in number, degree, power etc.; to exist as a living thing; to spring up, to be produced, to arise; to pass into a certain state; to adhere; to become rooted; †to swell (as the sea). *v.t.* to cultivate; to raise by cultivation; to produce. **to grow downward,** to diminish. **to grow on one,** to increase in one's estimation; to impress one more and more. **to grow out of,** to issue from; to develop or result from; to become too big or mature for, outgrow. **to grow together,** to become closely united, to become incorporated in each other. **to grow up,** to arrive at manhood or womanhood; to advance to full maturity; to arise, to become prevalent or common. **grow-, growing-bag,** *n.* a large plastic bag, containing a growing medium (as compost) in which seeds can be germinated and plants grown to full size. **growable,** *a.* **grower,** *n.* one who or that which grows (*usu. in comb.,* as *free-grower*); a producer of corn, vegetables etc.; a cultivator. **growing,** *n., a.* **growing pains,** *n.pl.* incorrect term for rheumatic pains in the limbs felt by young children. **growingly,** *adv.* **grown,** *a.* **grown-up,** *a.* adult. *n.* an adult. **grownie,** *n.* (*usu. pl.*) (*sl.*) a grown-up, esp. one's parent (ref. to GROAN). **growth,** *n.* the act or process of growing; increase, development, in number, extent, bulk, stature etc.; cultivation of vegetable produce; that which grows or is grown; (*Path.*) an abnormal formation, as a tumour; a product, a result. [OE *grōwan* (cp. Dut. *groeijen,* Icel. *grōa*), cogn. with GRASS, GREEN]

growl, *v.i.* to make a deep guttural sound as of anger; to murmur; to grumble; to speak angrily or gruffly; to rumble. *v.t.* to utter or express by a growl. *n.* a deep guttural sound like that made by an angry dog; a grumbling; a complaint. **growler,** *n.* one who growls; a grumbler; an American fish, *Grystis salmonides,* from the sound it emits when landed; other fishes; a small iceberg; (*coll.*) a four-wheeled horse-drawn cab. **growlery,** *n.* growling, grumbling; a place to grumble in, one's private room or 'den'. **growlingly,** *adv.* [prob. onomat.]

grown, etc. GROW.

groyne, *n.* a structure of piles, concrete etc., acting as a breakwater on a foreshore, and causing sand and shingle to be retained. *v.t.* to furnish with groynes. [etym. doubtful, perh. from GROIN[1]; but cp. F *groin,* snout, from *grogner,* L *grunnīre,* to grunt]

GRP, (*abbr.*) glass-reinforced plastic.

grub, *v.i.* (*past, p.p.* **grubbed**) to dig by scratching or tearing up the ground superficially; to search, to rummage; to drudge, to toil, to do manual work; (*sl.*) to take one's food. *v.t.* to dig (up or out); to clear (ground) of roots etc.; to find by searching; (*sl.*) to provide with food. *n.* the larva of an insect, esp. of bees and wasps, with a distinct head but no legs; a drudge, a hack; in cricket, a ball bowled along the ground; (*sl.*) food; †a short thick-set person, a dwarf. **to grub along,** (*coll.*) to plod or drudge along. **to grub up,** to dig up by the roots. **grub-axe, -hoe, -hook** etc. GRUBBING-AXE etc. **grub-screw,** *n.* a small headless screw. **grub-stake,** *n.* provisions etc., given to a prospector in return for a share of the finds. **to grub-stake,** (*sl.*) to supply food etc. in return for a share of profit. **grubber,** *n.* one who or that which grubs; an instrument for stirring up the soil and clearing out weeds; a machine to pull up stumps and roots; (*Austral., coll.*) in football, a kick that sends the ball along the ground, also **grub-, grubber-kick**. **grubbing,** *n., a.* **grubbing-axe, -hoe, -hook, -machine, -tool** etc., *n.* implements for grubbing up roots, stumps etc. **grubby,** *a.* full of grubs; dirty, grimy. **grubbiness,** *n.* [prob. cogn. with OE *grafan,* to GRAVE[1]]

Grub Street, *n.* (*collect.*) poor, mean or needy authors, or the region they live in. *a.* of or pertaining to this kind of writer. [a street (now Milton Street near Moorfields, London, once much inhabited by literary hacks]

grudge, *v.i.* †to murmur, to complain, to grumble, †to grieve, to repine; to be unwilling or reluctant; to be envious, to cherish ill-will. *v.t.* to feel discontent or envy at; to give or take unwillingly or reluctantly; †to cherish an envious and discontented spirit towards. *n.* ill-will, a feeling of malice or malevolence; unwillingness, reluctance; †remorse; †a slight symptom of disease. **grudgeful,** *a.* **grudger,** *n.* **grudgingly,** *adv.* [ME *grachen,* OF *groucier* (low L *groussāre*), etym. doubtful]

grue, *v.i.* (*Sc., North.*) to shudder; to feel horror or dread. [cogn. with Dan. *grue,* Dut. *gruwen,* G *grauen*]

gruel, *n.* semi-liquid food made by boiling oatmeal or other meal in water or milk; any food of like consistency. **to give one his gruel,** (*coll.*) to defeat, punish severely, or kill one. **gruelling,** *n.* severe or harsh treatment. *a.* exacting, requiring fortitude. [OF, from late L *grūtellum,* dim. of *grūtum,* from Teut. (cp. OLG and OE *grūt,* GROATS)]

gruesome, *a.* frightful, horrible, repulsive. **gruesomely,** *adv.* **gruesomeness,** *n.* [GRUE, -SOME[1]]

gruff, *a.* of a rough, surly or harsh aspect; sour, rough, harsh, hoarse-voiced. **gruffish,** *a.* **gruffly,** *adv.* **gruffness,** *n.* [cp. Dut. *grof,* G *grov*]

grumble, *v.i.* to murmur with discontent; to complain in a surly or muttering tone; to growl, to mutter, to rumble. *v.t.* to express or utter in a complaining manner. *n.* the act of grumbling; a complaint; (*pl.*) a discontented disposition. **grumbler,** *n.* one who grumbles; a discontented person; various species of gurnard, from the sound uttered when caught. **grumbling,** *n., a.* causing intermittent discomfort or discontent. **grumblingly,** *adv.* [history doubtful (cp. F *grommeler,* Dut. *grommelen,* freq. of *grommen,* and G *grummelen*)]

grume, *n.* a fluid of a thick, viscid consistence; a clot, as of blood. **grumous,** *a.* thick; concreted; clotted, coagulated (of blood); (*Bot.*) divided into little clustered grains. **grumousness,** *n.* [OF, from late L *grūmus,* a small heap]

grummet, *n.* (*Naut.*) a ring formed of rope laid round and spliced, used as a rowlock etc.; a ring or eyelet of metal, rubber or plastic designed to strengthen or protect the opening of a hole; †a wad made of rope, rammed between the ball and the charge in a muzzle-loading gun. [OF *gromette* (F *gourmette*), a curb, from *gourmer,* to curb, etym. unknown]

grumous GRUME.

grump, *n.* a bad-tempered person; (*pl.*) a fit of bad-temper or sulkiness. **grumpy,** *a.* surly, cross, peevish, ill-tempered. **grumpily,** *adv.* **grumpiness,** *n.* **grumpish,** *a.* [obs. n. *grump* (imit., cp. GRUNT)]

grumph, *v.i.* to grunt. *n.* a grunt. **Grumphie,** *n.* a name for the pig. [Sc., imit.]

Grundyism, *n.* prudishness; a slavish respect for conventions in matters of sex. **Grundified,** *a.* **Grundyish,** *a.* **Grundyist, Grundyite,** *n.* [Mrs *Grundy,* a character in Morton's *Speed the Plough,* (1798), adopted as the type of conventional respectability]

Grünewald, *n.* **(Mathias Gothardt-Neithardt)** (*c.* 1475–1528), German painter, active in Mainz, Frankfurt, and Halle. He was court painter, architect, and engineer to the prince bishop elector of Mainz (1508–14). His few surviving paintings show an intense involvement with religious subjects.

grungy, *a.* (*esp. N Am., sl.*) squalid, seedy.

grunsel, GROUNDSEL[1 and 2].

grunt, *v.i.* to make a deep guttural noise like a pig; to grumble, to growl, to complain. *v.t.* to express or utter in a grunting manner. *n.* a deep guttural sound, as of a hog. **grunter,** *n.* one who grunts; a hog; the drum-fish and other fishes. **gruntingly,** *adv.* **gruntle,** *n.* (*Sc.*) a snout, esp. of a pig; a face or muzzle. **gruntling,** *n.* a young pig or hog. [OE *grunnettan,* freq. of *grunian*]

Gruyère, *n.* a Swiss or French cheese made from cows' milk, pale-coloured, firm and full of cavities. [town in Switzerland]

gr. wt., (*abbr.*) gross weight.

grype, GRIPE.

†**gryphon,** GRIFFIN[1].

gryposis, -phosis, *n.* the abnormal incurvation or growing inward of the nails. [Gr., from *gruphos,* hooked]

grysbok, *n.* a speckled, reddish-brown southern African antelope, *Antilope melanotis.* [Dut. *grijsbok* (*grijs,* GREY, BUCK)]

GS, (*abbr.*) General Secretary; General Staff.

G-string, G-suit G.

GT., (*abbr.*) (*It.*) grand turismo, a touring car, usu. a fast sports car.

GU, (*abbr.*) genitourinary.

guacamole, *n.* a Mexican dish of mashed avocado, citrus juice and seasonings. [Sp., from S Am. Indian *ahuaca,* avocado, *molli,* sauce]

guacharo, *n.* (*pl.* **-ros**) the oil-bird, *Steatornis caripensis,* a S American goatsucker, feeding on fruit. [Sp., from S Am. native]

guacho, GAUCHO.

guaco, *n.* (*pl.* **-cos**) a tropical American plant, *Aristolochia guaco,* and others, said to cure snake-bites. [Sp., from S Am. Indian language]

Guadalajara, *n.* industrial (textiles, glass, soap, pottery) capital of Jalisco state, W Mexico; population (1986) 2,587,000. It is a key communications centre.

Guadalcanal, *n.* largest of the Solomon Islands; area 6500 sq km/2510 sq miles; population (1987) 71,000. Gold, copra, and rubber are produced. During World War II it was the scene of a battle which was won by US forces after six months of fighting.

Guadeloupe, *n.* an island group in the Leeward Islands, West Indies, an overseas department of France; area 1705 sq km/658 sq miles; population (1982) 328,400. The main islands are Basse-Terre, on which is the chief town of the same name, and Grande-Terre. Sugar refining and rum distilling are the main industries.

guaiac, *n.* wood of the guaiacum; the resin or drug.

guaiacol, *n.* a phenol obtained by distillation from guaiacum resin and found in wood tar.

guaiacum, *n.* a genus of W Indian and tropical N American trees and shrubs, one of which, *Guaiacum officinale,* furnishes *lignum vitae,* while its bark, wood and resin, with those of *G. sanctum,* are used in medicine; the wood of this genus; a drug made from the resin used as a stimulant and alterative. [Sp. *guayaco,* from Haytian]

Guam, *n.* largest of the Mariana Islands in the W Pacific, an unincorporated territory of the US. **area** 540 sq km/208 sq miles. **capital** Agaña. **towns** port Apra. **population** (1984) 116,000. **products** sweet potatoes, fish; tourism is important. **language** English, Chamorro (basically Malay-Polynesian). **religion** Roman Catholic 96%.

guan, *n.* any species of the S American genus *Penelope,* gallinaceous birds allied to the curassou. [native name]

guana, IGUANA; †(*Austral.*) GOANNA.

guanaco, *n.* (*pl.* **-cos**) a wild llama, *Auchenia huanaco,* inhabiting the chain of the Andes to their most southerly point. [S Am. native *huanaco*]

Guangdong, *n.* (formerly **Kwantung**) province of S China. **area** 231,400 sq km/89,320 sq miles. **capital** Guangzhou. **population** (1986) 63,640,000. **products** rice, sugar, tobacco, minerals, fish.

Guangxi, *n.* (formerly **Kwangsi Chuang**) autonomous region in S China. **area** 220,400 sq km/85,074 sq miles. **capital** Nanning. **population** (1986) 39,460,000, including the Zhuang people, allied to the Thai, who form China's largest ethnic minority. **products** rice, sugar, fruit.

Guangzhou, *n.* (formerly **Kwangchow/Canton**) capital of Guangdong province, S China; population (1986) 3,290,000. Its industries include shipbuilding, engineering, chemicals, and textiles.

guano, *n.* (*pl.* **-nos**) a valuable manure, composed chiefly of the excrement of sea-fowl, brought from S America and the Pacific; an artificial manure, esp. fish-manure or fish-guano. *v.t.* to manure or fertilize with guano. **guaniferous,** *a.* producing guano. **guanine,** *n.* a white amorphous substance found in guano and in the liver and pancreas of animals. [Sp., from Quichua *huanu,* dung]

Guanyin, *n.* in Chinese Buddhism, the goddess of mercy. In Japan she is Kwannon or Kannon, an attendant of the Amida Buddha (Amitābha). Her origins were in India as the male bodhisattva Avalokiteśvara.

guarana, *n.* the powdered seeds of *Paullinia sorbilis,* a Brazilian shrub. **guarana-bread, -paste,** *n.* bread or paste made from guarana by the Brazilian Indians for food and medicinal purposes. [S Am. Indian language]

guarantee, *n.* an engagement to see an agreement, duty or liability fulfilled; guaranty; the act of guaranteeing; any security, warranty or surety given; the person to whom the guarantee is given; (*incorrectly*) one who becomes surety for the performance of certain acts by another. *v.t.* to become guarantor or surety for; to undertake responsibility for the fulfilment of a promise, contract etc.; to pledge oneself or engage (that); to assure the continuance or permanence of; to undertake to secure (to another); to assure or secure against or from risk or damage. **guarantee fund,** a sum subscribed to provide an indemnity in case of loss. **guar-**

anteed, *a.* warranted. **guarantor,** *n.* one who guarantees. [GUARANTY (perh. the orig. sense, one who guarantees, from Sp. *garante*]

guaranty, *n.* the act of guaranteeing, esp. an undertaking to be responsible for a debt or obligation of another person; that which guarantees, that on which a guarantee or security is based. [A-F *guarantie,* from OF *garantir,* to WARRANT]

guard, *v.t.* to secure the safety of; to watch over, to protect, to defend (from or against); to stand guard over, to prevent the escape of; to secure (against criticism etc.); †to trim, to deck; †to gird. *v.i.* to be cautious or take precautions (against). *n.* defence, protection, a state of vigilance, watch against attack, surprise etc.; a state, posture or act of defence, esp. in boxing, fencing, cricket etc.; a protector; a man or body of men on guard; a sentry, an escort; (*N Am.*) prison warder; a contrivance to prevent injury, accident or loss; a man in charge of a railway train or a coach; the part of a sword-hilt which protects the hand; a watch-chain; an ornamental edging or border; a screen to prevent accident placed in front of a fire-place etc. **to be on** or **off one's guard,** to be prepared or unprepared for attack, surprise etc. **to guard against (something),** to take precautionary action to try to prevent something happening. **to mount guard,** to go on duty as a guard or sentinel. **to stand guard,** of a sentry, to keep watch. **guard-boat,** *n.* a boat patrolling a fleet in harbour; an official harbour boat for preventing infringement of customs or quarantine regulations. **guard cell,** *n.* in botany, either of the two cells that border the pore of a stoma and cause it to open and close. **guard-chain,** *n.* a chain for securing a watch, brooch etc. †**guard-chamber,** *n.* a guard-room. **guard-house, -room,** *n.* a house or room for those on guard or for prisoners. **guard-rail,** *n.* a rail to protect against falling off a deck etc.; a rail fixed inside the inner rail at curves, points etc., to prevent derailment. **guard-ring,** *n.* a keeper for a wedding-ring etc. **guardship,** *n.* a vessel stationed in a port or harbour for defence. **guard's van,** *n.* a carriage usu. at the rear of a train for the use of the guard. †**guardage,** *n.* guardianship, wardship. **guardant,** *a.* †guarding, protecting; (*Her.*) presenting the full face to the spectator. †*n.* a guardian, protector. **guardedly,** *adv.* **guardedness,** *n.* **guarder,** *n.* †**guardful,** *a.* wary, cautious. **guardfully,** *adv.* **guardless,** *a.* [OF *garder,* from Teut., see WARD]

Guardi, *n.* **Francesco** (1712–1793), Italian painter. He produced souvenir views of his native Venice, which were commercially less successful than Canaletto's but are now considered more atmospheric, with subtler use of reflected light.

guardian, *n.* one who has the charge, care or custody of any person or thing; a protector; a guardian of the poor; the superior of a Franciscan convent; in law, one who has the charge, custody and supervision of a person not legally capable of managing his own affairs. *a.* guarding; acting as a guardian or protector. **guardians of the poor,** formerly members of a board elected by the ratepayers to administer the Poor Laws in a particular parish or district. **guardian angel,** *n.* an angel or spirit supposed to be assigned to a person as guardian and protector; (*pl.*; **Guardian Angels**) an orig. US group which organizes vigilante patrols, esp. on underground trains. **guardianship,** *n.* the office of a guardian; care, protection, esp. legal tutelage. [OF *gardien,* from *garde,* as prec.]

Guards, *n.pl.* British household troops consisting of the Coldstream, Grenadier, Irish, Welsh and Scots Guards. **Guardsman,** *n.* an officer or private in the Guards. [GUARD]

Guarneri, *n.* celebrated family of stringed-instrument makers of Cremona, Italy. The one known as Giuseppe 'del Gesù' (1698–1744) produced the finest models.

Guatemala, *n.* Republic of (*República de Guatemala*) country in central America, bounded N and NW by Mexico, E by Belize and the Caribbean Sea, SE by Honduras and El Salvador, and SW by the Pacific Ocean. **area** 108,889 sq km/42,031 sq miles. **capital** Guatemala City. **towns** Quezaltenango, Puerto Barrios (naval base). **physical** mountainous, tropical. **population** (1988) 8,990,000 (Mayaquiche Indians 54%, mestizos 42%); annual growth rate 2.8%. **exports** coffee, bananas, cotton. **language** Spanish. **religion** Roman Catholic. **Guatemala City,** *n.* capital of Guatemala; population (1983) 1,300,000. It produces textiles, tyres, footwear, and cement.

guava, *n.* the luscious fruit of various species of the tropical American myrtaceous genus *Psidium,* esp. *P. pyriferum* and *P. pomiferum;* the trees on which they grow. [Sp. *guayaba,* from S Am. Indian]

Guayaquil, *n.* city and chief Pacific port of Ecuador, at the mouth of the Guayas River; population (1982) 1,300,868.

†**gubernation,** *n.* government or guiding control. **gubernatorial,** *a.* pertaining to a governor, esp. of a US state. [F, from L *gubernātio -ōnem,* from *gubernāre,* to steer, to GOVERN]

guddle, *v.i.* (*Sc.*) to grope for fish with the hands. *v.t.* to catch (fish) by groping and tickling. *n.* (*coll.*) a muddle, confusion. [etym. doubtful]

gude, (*Sc.*) GOOD.

Guderian, *n.* **Heinz** (1888–1954), German general in World War II. He created the Panzer armoured divisions of the German army that formed the ground spearhead of Hitler's *Blitzkrieg* strategy, and achieved an important breakthrough at Sedan in Ardennes, France 1940 and the advance to Moscow in 1941.

gudgeon[1], *n.* a small freshwater fish, *Gobio fluviatilis,* easily caught and largely used as bait; one easily taken in. [F *goujon,* L *gōbiōnem,* nom. *gōbio,* GOBY]

gudgeon[2], *n.* the metallic journal-piece let into the end of a wooden shaft; the bearing of a shaft; an eye or socket in which a rudder turns. **gudgeon pin,** *n.* a metal pin that links the piston of an internal combustion engine to the little-end bearing of the connecting rod. [OF *gougeon,* perh. as prec.]

gue, gu, gju, *n.* a rude kind of musical instrument, apparently like a violin, formerly used in Shetland. [perh. from Icel. *gīgja*]

Guebre, *n.* a fire-worshipper, a Zoroastrian. [F *guèbre,* from Pers. *gabr*]

guelder rose, *n.* a shrubby plant, of the family Caprifoliaceae, *Viburnum opulus,* bearing ball-shaped bunches of white flowers, also called the snowball-tree. [*Guelders,* town in Prussia, or *Guelderland,* province of Holland, formerly a German duchy with Guelders for capital]

Guelph, Guelf, *n.* a member of the popular party in mediaeval Italy which aimed at national independence, and supported the Pope against the Ghibellines. **Guelphic,** *a.* of or belonging to the Guelphs. **Guelphic order,** an order of knighthood instituted for Hanover in 1815. [It. *Guelfo,* MHG *Welf,* name of the Dukes of Bavaria, a distinguished princely family now represented by the ducal house of Brunswick and the royal family of Great Britain, used as a war-cry in 1140 at the battle of Weinsberg against the Emperor Conrad III]

guenon, *n.* any of various long-tailed African monkeys of the genus *Cercopithecus.* [F]

Guercino, *n.* (1590–1666) (adopted name of Giovanni Francesco Barbieri) Italian baroque painter active chiefly in Rome. In his ceiling painting of *Aurora* (1621–23, Villa Ludovisi, Rome), the chariot-borne figure of dawn rides across the heavens, and the architectural framework is imitated in the painting, giving the illusion that the ceiling opens into the sky.

guerdon, *n.* (*poet.*) a reward, a recompense. †*v.t.* to reward. **guerdonless,** *a.* [OF, from med. L *widerdōnum,* OHG *widarlōn* (*wider,* against, *lōn,* LOAN, assim. to L *dōnum,* gift)]

guereza, *n.* a black Abyssinian monkey, *Colobus guereza,* with a fringe of white hair and a bushy tail. [African]

guerilla GUERRILLA.

Guérin, *n.* **Camille** (1872–1961), French bacteriologist who, with Calmette, developed the Bacille Calmette-Guérin (BCG) vaccine for tuberculosis.

guerite, *n.* (*Mil.*) a small loopholed tower, usu. on the point of a bastion, to hold a sentinel. [F, GARRET]

Guernsey[1], *n.* second largest of the Channel Islands; area 63 sq km/24.5 sq miles; population (1986) 55,500. The capital is St Peter Port. From 1975 it has been a major financial centre.

Guernsey[2], *n.* a close-fitting knitted or woven woollen shirt, usu. blue, worn by seamen (*Austral.*) a similar garment, sometimes sleeveless, worn by football players. **to get a guernsey,** (*Austral.*) to be selected for a football team; (*coll.*) to win approval, succeed. **Guernsey cow,** *n.* one of a breed of dairy cattle originating from Guernsey. **Guernsey lily,** *n.* a southern African or Japanese amaryllis, *Nerine sarniensis,* pink in colour, cultivated in Guernsey for the market. [one of the Channel Islands]

guerrilla, guerilla, *n.* an irregular warfare carried on by small independent bands; a member of such a band; an irregular, petty war. *a.* belonging to or consisting of guerrillas; carried on in an irregular manner (of a war). **guerrilla strike,** *n.* a sudden industrial strike. [Sp., dim. of *guerra*]

Guesdes, *n.* **Jules** (1845–1922), French socialist leader from the 1880s who espoused Marxism and revolutionary change. His movement, the *Partie Ouvrier Français* (French Workers' Party), was eventually incorporated in the foundation of the SFIO (*Section Française de l'International Ouvrière* – French Section of International Labour) in 1905.

guess, *v.t.* to judge or estimate on imperfect grounds, to conjecture; to imagine, to suppose on probable grounds, to divine (one to be); to conjecture rightly; (*N Am., coll.*) to suppose; to believe. *v.i.* to form a conjecture, to judge at random; to hazard a supposition (that). *n.* a conjecture; an opinion, estimate or supposition based on imperfect grounds. **by guess,** at haphazard. **guesstimate,** *n.* (*coll.*) an estimate made by guessing. *v.t.*, to estimate in this way. **guess-rope** GUEST-ROPE. **guess-work,** *n.* action or calculation based on guess; procedure by guessing. **guessable,** *a.* **guesser,** *n.* **guessingly,** *adv.* [ME gessen (cogn. with Dut. *gissen,* Dan. *gisse,* prob. from OE *gitan,* to GET)]

guest, *n.* a person received and entertained in the house or at the table of another; one who resides temporarily at a hotel or boarding-house; a parasitic animal or vegetable. †*v.t.* to entertain; to treat hospitably. *v.i.* to be a guest; to appear as a guest on a television or radio show etc. **paying guest,** a boarder. **guest-chamber,** *n.* a room appropriated to the entertainment of guests. **guest house,** *n.* a boarding-house, a small hotel. **guest-night,** *n.* a night when visitors are entertained by a club etc. †**guest-rite,** *n.* the offices due towards a guest. **guest-room,** *n.* a room for the accommodation of a guest. **guesten** *v.i.* to stay as a guest. [assim. to obs. *gesten*], †**guester,** *n.* †**guestling,** *n.* an assembly, formerly annual, of representatives of the Cinque Ports; a young guest. **guestship,** *n.* †**guestwise,** *adv.* like a guest. [OE *gœst, giest* (cp. Icel. *gestr,* Dut. and G *Gast,* also L *hostis,* foe, orig. stranger)]

guest-, guess-rope, *n.* a hawser carried by a boat to a distant object for warping a vessel towards this; a rope for making fast a boat to a ship; also called **guest-, guess-warp.** [etym. unknown]

Guevara, *n.* **Ernesto 'Che'** (1928–1967), Latin American revolutionary. He was born in Argentina and trained there as a doctor, but in 1953 left his homeland because of his opposition to the right-wing president Perón. In effecting the Cuban revolution of 1959, he was second only to Castro and Castro's brother Raúl. In 1965 he went to the Congo to fight against white mercenaries, and then to Bolivia, where he was killed in an unsuccessful attempt to lead a peasant rising. He was an orthodox Marxist, and renowned for his guerrilla techniques.

guff, *n.* (*coll.*) nonsense, humbug. [prob. imit.]

guffaw, *n.* a burst of loud or coarse laughter. *v.i.* to laugh loudly or coarsely. *v.t.* to say with such a laugh. [imit.]

guggle, GURGLE.

Guiana, *n.* the NE part of South America, which includes FRENCH GUIANA, GUYANA, and SURINAME.

guide, *v.t.* to direct, lead or conduct; to rule, to regulate, to govern; to direct the course of; to be the object, motive or criterion of (action, opinion etc.). *n.* one who leads another or points the way; a leader, a conductor, esp. a person employed to conduct a party of tourists etc.; an adviser; a girl guide; anything adopted as a sign or mark of direction or criterion of accuracy; a guide-book; a subaltern acting as a pivot to regulate an evolution or alignment; (*pl.*) a company formed for reconnoitring etc.; a ship by which a squadron or fleet regulate their movements; a bar, rod, bearing-surface or other device acting as indicator or regulating motion. **guide-bars, -block,** *n.pl.* pieces of metal on which the cross-head of a steam-engine slides, keeping it parallel to the cylinder. **guide-book,** *n.* a book for tourists, describing places of interest, means of transit etc. **guide-dog,** *n.* a dog trained to lead a blind person. **guideline,** *n.* a line drawn as a guide for further drawing or writing; a statement setting out future policy, courses of action etc. **guide-post,** *n.* a finger-post to show the way. **guide-rope** GUY[1]. **guide-way,** *n.* on a machine, a groove, track or frame directing the motion of a part. **guidable,** *a.* **guidage,** *n.* guidance; in law, pay for safe-conduct through a strange country. **guidance,** *n.* the act of guiding; direction; government. **guideless,** *a.* **guider,** *n.* †**guideship,** *n.* **guided missile,** *n.* a rocket- or jet-propelled projectile with a war-head, electronically guided to its target by remote control. **guiding light, star,** *n.* person or thing used as a guide or model. [OF *guider,* earlier *guier,* prob. from Teut. (cogn. with OE *wītan,* to know, whence *wīsian,* to guide)]

Guido Reni, RENI.

guidon, *n.* the forked or pointed flag of a troop of light cavalry; the flag of a guild or fraternity; a standard-bearer. [F, from It. *guidone,* prob. from *guida,* GUIDE]

Guienne, *n.* ancient province of SW France which formed the duchy of Aquitaine with Gascony in the 12th cent. Its capital was Bordeaux. It became English (1154) and passed to France in 1453.

guignol GRAND GUIGNOL.

guild, *n.* a society or corporation belonging to the same class, trade or pursuit, combined for mutual aid and protection of interests. **guild-brother,** *n.* a fellow-member of a guild. **guild-hall,** *n.* a hall where a guild or corporation meets; a town-hall; the hall where the corporation of a city meets. **guildsman, guildswoman,** *n.* **Guild Socialism,** *n.* a form of socialism under which every industry would be organized as an autonomous guild, holding the factories etc. from the central government, but managing its own affairs through representatives of the workers. **guildry,** *n.* (*Sc.*) a guild, the corporation of a burgh royal. [OE *gild,* a payment from *gildan,* to YIELD (cp. Dut. and G *Geld,* money)]

guilder, *n.* a coin formerly current in the Netherlands; GULDEN. [corr. of Dut. GULDEN]

guile, *n.* deceit, craft, cunning. †*v.t.* to deceive, to beguile. **guileful,** *a.* **guilefully,** *adv.* **guilefulness,** *n.* **guileless,** *a.* **guilelessly,** *adv.* **guilelessness,** *n.* †**guiler,** *n.* [OF, from Teut., cp. WILE]

Guilin, *n.* (formerly **Kweilin**) principal tourist city of S China, on the Li river, Guangxi province. The dramatic limestone mountains are a major attraction.

Guillaume, *n.* **Charles** (1861–1938), Swiss physicist who studied measurement and alloy development. He discovered a nickel-steel alloy, invar, which showed negligible expansion with rising temperatures. Nobel physics prize 1920.

guillemot, *n.* any swimming bird of the genus *Alca* or *Uria,* with a short tail and pointed wings. [F, dim. of *Guillaume,* OHG *Wilhelm,* William]

guilloche, *n.* an ornament of intertwisted or interlaced bands. [F]

guillotine, *n.* an apparatus for beheading persons at a stroke, consisting of an upright frame, down which a weighted blade slides in grooves; a machine for cutting thicknesses of paper etc.; (*Surg.*) an instrument for cutting tonsils, uvula etc.; in Parliament, the curtailment of debate by fixing beforehand the hours when parts of a Bill must be voted on. *v.t.* to execute by guillotine; to cut with a guillotine. [F, after Dr J. I. *Guillotin,* 1738–1814, who introduced it (1792) during the French Revolution]

guilt[1], *n.* the state of having committed a crime or offence; criminality, culpability; †an offence. **guiltless,** *a.* free from guilt; innocent; having no knowledge (of), inexperienced; clear (of). **guilt complex,** *n.* (real or imagined) obsessive feeling of guilt or responsibility. **guiltlessly,** *adv.* **guiltlessness,** *n.* **guilty,** *a.* having committed a crime; criminal, culpable (of); characterized by guilt. **guilty-like,** *a.* like one guilty. **guiltily,** *adv.* **guiltiness,** *n.* [OE *gylt*]

†**guilt**[2], GILT[1].

guimp GIMP[1].

guinea, *n.* a gold coin formerly current in Great Britain, coined 1663–1813, orig. of gold from Guinea, with the nominal value of 20s. (£1) until 1717, when this was fixed at 21s.; a sum of money equivalent to a guinea £1.05p. **Guinea corn,** *n.* Indian millet *Sorghum vulgare,* called also durra. **guinea-fowl, -hen,** *n.* a gallinaceous bird of the genus *Numida,* esp. *N. meleagris,* something like the turkey, of a dark-grey colour with white spots, orig. from Africa. **Guinea grains** GRAIN[1]. †**guinea pepper,** *n.* cayenne pepper, *Capsicum;* also two species of *Amomum, A. grana paradisi* and *A. grandiflorum.* **guinea-pig,** *n.* a small domesticated cavy, *Cavia cobaya,* native to Brazil; (*sl.*) a person rendering services more or less nominal for a guinea fee, such as a company director, a juryman, an officer on special duty or a deputy clergyman; a person used as a subject for a medical or other experiment. **guinea-pigging,** *n.* **Guinea worm,** *n.* a whitish or dark-brown nematode worm *Filaria medinensis,* parasitic in the skin of the human feet etc. [*Gnea,* Port. *Guiné,* country on W coast of Africa]

Guinea, *n.* Republic of (*République de Guinée*) country in W Africa, bounded to the N by Senegal, NE by Mali, SE by the Ivory Coast, SW by Liberia and Sierra Leone, W by the Atlantic, and NW by Guinea-Bissau. **area** 245,857 sq km/94,901 sq miles. **capital** Conakry. **towns** Labe, N'Zerekore, KanKan. **physical** mainly mountainous; sources of rivers Niger, Gambia, and Senegal; forest in SE. **population** (1988) 6,533,000 (chief peoples are Fulani 40%, Mandingo 25%); annual growth rate 2.3%. **exports** coffee, rice, palm kernels, alumina, bauxite, diamonds. **language** French (official). **religion** Muslim 62%, Christian 15%, local 35%.

Guinea-Bissau, *n.* (*Republica da Guiné-Bissau*) country in W Africa, bounded to the N by Senegal, E and SE by Guinea, and SW by the Atlantic. **area** 36,125 sq km/13,944 sq miles. **capital** and chief port Bissau. **physical** flat lowlands. **population** (1988 est.) 932,000; annual growth rate 1.9%. **exports** rice, coconuts, peanuts, fish, salt. **language** Crioulo, Cape Verdean dialect of Portuguese. **religion** Muslim 40%, Christian 4%.

Guinevere, *n.* (Welsh **Gwenhwyfar**) in British legend, the wife of King Arthur. Her adulterous love affair with the knight Lancelot led ultimately to Arthur's death.

Guinness, *n.* **Alec** (1914–), English actor. His many stage roles include Shakespeare's Hamlet (1938) and Lawrence of Arabia (in *Ross,* 1960). In 1979 he gained a 'lifetime achievement' Oscar (films include *Kind Hearts and Coronets* (1949), *The Bridge on the River Kwai* (1957), and *Star Wars* (1977)).

Guinness affair, *n.* a case of alleged financial fraud during the attempted takeover by the brewing company, Guinness PLC, of Distillers Co. in 1986. Those accused of acting illegally to sustain Guinness share prices include Ernest Saunders, former chief executive. The trial, which opened Feb. 1990, was widely seen as the first major test of the UK government's legislation increasing control of financial dealings on London's Stock Exchange.

guipure, *n.* a lace without a ground or mesh, the pattern being held in place by threads; a kind of gimp. [F, from OF *guiper,* from Teut. (cp. Goth. *weipan,* to crown, G *weifen,* to wind)]

guise, *n.* external appearance; semblance, pretence; manner, way, fashion; habit, dress. *v.t.* to dress up. *v.i.* to play the mummer. **guiser,** *n.* (*chiefly Sc.*) a person in disguise; a masker, a mummer, esp. at Halloween. [OF, from Teut. (cp. OHG *wīsa,* WISE[2]]

Guise, *n.* **Francis, 2nd Duke of** (1519–63), French soldier and politician. He led the French victory over Germany at Metz (1552) and captured Calais from the English (1558). Along with his brother Charles (1527–74) he was powerful in the government of France during the reign of Francis II. He was assassinated attempting to crush the Huguenots.

guitar, *n.* a (usu. six-) stringed instrument, somewhat like the violin in shape, but larger, with frets stopped by one hand, the strings being plucked with the fingers of the other or with a plectrum. **guitar-fish,** *n.* a tropical sea-fish, one of the rays. **guitarist,** *n.* [Sp. *guitarra,* ult. from Gr. *kithara* (cp. CITHERN, GITTERN)]

Guiyang, *n.* (formerly **Kweiyang**) capital and industrial city of Guizhou province, S China; population (1986) 1,380,000. Industries include metals and machinery.

Guizhou, *n.* (formerly **Kweichow**) province of S China. **area** 174,000 sq km/67,164 sq miles. **capital** Guiyang. **population** (1986) 30,080,000. **products** rice, maize, nonferrous minerals.

Guizot, *n.* **François Pierre Guillaume** (1787–1874), French politician and historian, professor of modern history at the Sorbonne, Paris, 1812–30. He wrote a history of civilization, and became prime minister in 1847. His resistance to all reforms led to the revolution of 1848.

Gujarat, *n.* state of W India. **area** 196,000 sq km/75,656 sq miles. **capital** Ahmedabad. **population** (1984) 33,961,000. **products** cotton, petrochemicals, oil, gas, rice, textiles. **languages** Gujarati, Hindi. **Gujarati,** *n.* inhabitant of Gujarat on the NW seaboard of India. The Gujaratis number approximately 27 million, and speak their own language, Gujurati. They are predominantly Hindu (90%), with Muslim (8%) and Jain (2%) minorities. **Gujarati, Gujerati language,** *n.* a member of the Indo-Iranian branch of the Indo-European language family, spoken in and around the state of Gujarat in India. It is written in its own script, a variant of the Devanagari script used for Sanskrit and Hindi.

Gujranwala, *n.* city in Punjab province, Pakistan; population (1981) 597,000. It is a centre of grain trading. It is a former Sikh capital, and the birthplace of Sikh leader Ranjit Singh (1780–1839).

gula, *n.* †the throat; a large plate supporting the submentum in some insects. **gular,** *a.* [L]

gulag, *n.* the system of forced labour camps in the USSR, esp. as used to correct dissidents. [Rus. *G(lavnoye) U(pravleniye Ispravitelno-Trudovykh) Lag(erei),* Main Administration for Corrective Labour Camps, described by Rus. writer A. Solzhenitsyn, 1918– , in *The Gulag Archipelago*]

gulch, *n.* a deep ravine caused by the action of water. †*v.t.* to swallow greedily. [etym. doubtful (n. prob. from v., the latter imit.)]

gulden, *n.* one of various gold coins of Germany or the Netherlands; a silver coin, the florin of Austria and Hungary, and the guilder of Holland. [Dut. and G]

gules, *n.* (*Her.*) a red colour, represented on an engraved escutcheon by vertical lines. *a.* red. **guly,** *a.* [ME and OF *goules* (F *gueules*), med. L *gulæ* ermine, dyed red, etym. doubtful]

gulf, *n.* an inlet of the sea, deeper and narrower proportionately than a bay; a deep hollow, chasm or abyss; a whirlpool, anything that swallows or engulfs; a profound depth, as of the ocean; an impassable chasm, interval or difference; (*sl.*) in Oxford and Cambridge Univs., the pass or ordinary degree permitted to candidates who fail to get honours; (*Mining*) a large deposit of ore in a lode. †*v.t.* to swallow up, to engulf; to form gulfs in; (*sl.*) in universities to award the gulf to. *v.i.* to flow like a gulf or eddy. **Gulf States**, *n.pl.* oil-rich countries sharing the coastline of the Persian Gulf (Bahrain, Iran, Iraq, Kuwait, Oman, Qatar, Saudi Arabia, and the United Arab Emirates). In the US, the term refers to those states bordering the Gulf of Mexico (Alabama, Florida, Louisiana, Mississippi, and Texas). **Gulf Stream,** *n.* an ocean current carrying warm water from the Gulf of Mexico across the Atlantic to the British Isles and Scandinavia. **Gulf War,** *n.* another name for the Iran-Iraq War. **gulf-weed,** *n.* a seaweed with berry-like air-vessels, *Sargassum bacciferum,* found in the Gulf Stream, the Sargasso Sea etc. **gulfy,** *a.* full of whirlpools; deep as a gulf. [F *golfe,* ult. from late Gr. *kolphos,* Gr. *kolpos*]

gull, *n.* a long-winged, web-footed bird of the genus *Larus,* mostly marine in habitat; a simpleton, a dupe. *v.t.* to fool, to trick; to impose upon. **gull wing,** *a.* of an aircraft wing, having a short inner section that slopes up from the fuselage and a long horizontal outer section; of a car door, opening upwards. **gullery,** *n.* a breeding-place for gulls. **gullish,** *a.* [prob. Corn. *gullan,* cp. W *gwylan,* Bret. *gwelan,* prob. from root, to wail]

gullet, *n.* the throat; the oesophagus; a water-channel; a gore or gusset. [OF, dim. of *gole,* L GULA]

gullible, *a.* credulous, easily deceived. **gullibility,** *n.*

Gullit, *n.* **Ruud** (1962–), Dutch international footballer born of a Surinamese father. Famous for his dreadlock hairstyle. He played an important role in Holland's capture of the European Championship in 1988.

Gulliver's Travels, *n.* satirical novel by the Irish writer Jonathan Swift, published (1726). The four countries visited by the narrator Gulliver ridicule different aspects of human nature, customs, and politics.

gully¹, *n.* a channel or ravine worn by water; a ditch, drain or gutter; a gully-hole; a tram-plate or rail; in cricket, (a fielder in) the position between slips and point. *v.t.* to wear a gully or gullies in, to furrow or channel by water action. **gully-drain,** *n.* a drain connecting a gully-hole with a sewer. **gully-hole,** *n.* an opening into a drain at the side of a street; a man-hole. **gully-hunter,** *n.* (*sl.*) one who hunts for lost things in gutters. **gully-raker,** *n.* (*Austral.*) a long stock whip; (*coll.*) one who steals stock. **gully-trap,** *n.* a grated trap to receive the discharge from rainwater pipes etc. [var. of prec., or from F *goulet,* GULLET]

gully², *n.* (*Sc., North.*) a large knife. [perh. orig. a knife for the GULLET]

gulosity, *n.* gluttony, greediness. [late L *gūlōsitās,* from L *gūlōsus,* gluttonous, from GULA]

gulp, *v.t.* to swallow (down) eagerly or in large draughts. *v.i.* to make a noise in swallowing or trying to swallow, to gasp or choke. *n.* the act of gulping; a large mouthful; an effort to swallow, a catching or choking in the throat. **to gulp back,** esp. of tears, to keep back or suppress. **gulpingly,** *adv.* [imit. (cp. Dut. *gulpen,* Norw. *glupa*)]

gum¹, *n.* the fleshy tissue investing the necks of the teeth; †arrogant talk. **gumboil,** *n.* a boil or small abscess on the gums. **gum-rash,** *n.* a teething rash frequent in children. **gumshield,** *n.* a pad worn by boxers etc. to protect the gum and teeth. **gummy,** *a.* toothless. *n.* (*Austral.*) a sheep that has lost its teeth; a shark found off coasts of Tasmania and Victoria. [OE *gōma* (cp. Icel. *gomr,* G *Gaumen,* palate)]

gum², *n.* a viscid substance which exudes from certain trees, and hardens, but is more or less soluble in water, used for sticking things together; a gum-tree or other plant or tree exuding this; (*coll.*) chewing-gum. *v.t.* (*past, p.p.* **gummed**) to cover or stiffen with gum; to fasten or stick (down, in, together, up) with or as with gum. *v.i.* to exude gum; to become sticky or clogged with disuse, dirt etc. (as an axle). **gum ammoniac** AMMONIAC under AMMONIA. **gum arabic,** *n.* a gum that exudes from certain species of acacia. **gum-boots,** *n.pl.* knee-high rubber boots, Wellingtons. **gum-digger,** *n.* (*NZ*) one who digs for fossilized gum. **gum-dragon** TRAGACANTH. **gum-drop,** *n.* a hard gelatinous sweet containing gum arabic. **gum-elastic,** *n.* caoutchouc, indiarubber; (sometimes) gutta-percha. **gum-juniper,** *n.* sandarac. **gumnut,** *n.* (*Austral.*) the woody seed capsule of the eucalyptus. **gum-resin,** *n.* a vegetable secretion consisting of a gum and a resin, e.g. gamboge. **gum-senegal,** *n.* a variety of gum arabic. **gum shoe,** *n.* (*esp. N Am.*) a rubber overshoe, one of a pair of galoshes; (*N Am., coll.*) a policeman or detective. *v.i.* (*N Am., coll.*) to go about silently; to move or act stealthily. **gum-tree,** *n.* (*Austral.*) one of several species of eucalyptus; the name of various trees. **to be up a gum-tree,** to be cornered, in a fix, brought to bay. **to gum up the works,** (*coll.*) to interfere with, spoil or delay (something). **gummiferous,** *a.* producing gum. **gumming,** *n.* a disease in trees bearing stone-fruit, characterized by a morbid exudation of gum. **gummous,** *a.* of the nature of gum. **gummosity,** *n.* **gummy,** *a.* sticky, viscous, adhesive; productive of or covered with gum; puffy, swollen (of legs, ankles etc.). **gumminess,** *n.* [ME and OF *gomme,* L *gommi,* Gr. *kommi,* prob. from Egypt.]

gum³, by gum, a mild oath or expletive. [minced form of GOD]

gumbo, *n.* (*pl.* **-bos**) the okra, *Hibiscus esculentus;* a soup or a dish made of young capsules of this, seasoned, stewed and served with melted butter; a Negro patois in Louisiana and the W Indies; a silty soil of the W and S US prairies that becomes very sticky when wet. [Am., F, from Bantu]

gumma, *n.* (*pl.* **-as, -ata**), a tumour with gummy contents, usu. due to syphilis. **gummatous,** *a.* [mod. L, from GUM²]

Gummer, *n.* **John Selwyn** (1939–), British Conservative politician. He was minister of state for employment (1983–84), paymaster general (1984–85), minister for agriculture (1985–), chairman of the party (1983–85), and minister for agriculture from 1989.

gummiferous etc. GUM².

gumption, *n.* common sense, practical shrewdness, acuteness, tact, capacity for getting on; in painting, the art of preparing colours; a medium for mixing colours. **gumptious,** *a.* [Sc., etym. doubtful]

gun, *n.* a tubular weapon from which projectiles are shot by means of gunpowder or other explosive force, a cannon, musket, rifle or carbine; a person with a gun, a member of a shooting party. †*v.i.* to use a gun, esp. to go fowling. *a.* (*Austral., coll.*) of a person, skilled, expert. **as sure as a gun,** undoubtedly; absolutely certain. **great gun,** a cannon; a distinguished person. **son of a gun,** a rascal. **to beat** or **jump the gun,** to begin (a race) before the starting pistol has fired, make a false start; (*coll.*) to begin prematurely. **to blow great guns,** to blow tempestuously. **to give (something) the gun,** (*coll.*) to increase the speed of (a car etc.); to give (a task etc.) one's maximum effort. **to go great guns,** (*coll.*) to make vigorous and successful progress. **to gun for,** (*coll.*) to seek to kill, harm or destroy; to strive to obtain. **to spike someone's guns,** to frustrate someone's aims, spoil someone's chances. **to stick to one's guns,** to maintain an opinion in face of opposition. **gun-barrel,** *n.* the barrel or tube of a gun. **gunboat,** *n.* a warship of small size carrying heavy guns; formerly armed with a single heavy gun. **gunboat diplomacy,** *n.* the use of naval or military threats as part of international negotiations. **gun-carriage,** *n.* the apparatus upon which a cannon is mounted for service. **gun-case,** *n.* a case for a sporting-gun. **gun-cotton,** *n.* a highly explosive substance made by soaking cotton in nitric and sulphuric acids, and then carefully drying. **gun dog,** *n.* a dog which accompanies a shooting party and is trained to locate and retrieve game. **gunfight,** *n.* a fight using firearms. **gunfighter,** *n.* (*N Am.*) esp. formerly, person known for his skill in fighting with firearms. **gun-fire,** *n.* the hour at which the morning or evening gun is fired; discharge of guns. **gun-flint,** *n.* a flint used for firing an old-fashioned flint-lock gun. **gun-harpoon,** *n.* a harpoon shot from a gun, not thrown by hand. **gun-house,** *n.* a shelter for a gun and the gunners against the enemy's fire. **gun-layer,** *n.* the gunner whose duty it is to sight and elevate a gun or howitzer. **gun-lock,** *n.* the mechanism by which the charge in a gun is exploded. **gunman,** *n.* an armed gangster; one engaged in the manufacture of arms. **gun-metal,** *n.* an alloy of copper and tin or zinc from which cannon were formerly cast. **gun-pit,** *n.* a pit in which a gun-mould is fixed for casting, or where a built-up gun is welded together; an excavation for sheltering a gun and gunners. **gun play,** *n.* the use of guns. **gunpoint,** *n.* the muzzle of a gun. **at gunpoint,** being under the threat of being shot. **gunpowder,** *n.* a mixture of saltpetre, carbon and sulphur, reduced to a fine powder, then granulated and dried, used as an explosive; gunpowder-tea. **Gunpowder Plot,** *n.* a plot to blow up the Houses of Parliament by gunpowder on 5 Nov. 1605, and at one blow destroy King James I, the Lords and the Commons. **gunpowder-tea,** *n.* a fine kind of green tea, each leaf of which is rolled up. **gun-reach,** *n.* (*N Am.*) gunshot. **gun-room,** *n.* a room on one of the lower decks of a war vessel to accommodate junior officers; a room where guns are stored. **gun-runner,** *n.* one who smuggles any kind of firearms into a country. **gun-running,** *n.* **gunshot,** *n.* the range of a gun. **gun-shy,** *a.* frightened at the report of firearms (of a dog, horse etc.). **gunslinger** GUNFIGHTER. **gunsmith,** *n.* one who makes or repairs small firearms. **gunstock,** *n.* the shaped block of wood to which the barrel of a gun is fixed. †**gunstone,** *n.* a shot for a cannon, round stones having been originally so used. **guntackle,** *n.* the ropes, pulleys etc. attached to the sides of the ports, and to the gun-carriage on an old-fashioned war-ship. **gunner,** *n.* in the navy, a warrant officer in charge of ordnance or ordnance stores; in the army, an artilleryman, esp. a private; a person shooting game. **to kiss** or **marry the gunner's daughter,** (*dated Nav. sl.*) to be lashed to a gun and flogged. **gunnery,** *n.* the art of managing heavy guns; the science of artillery; practice with heavy guns. **gunnery-lieutenant,** *n.* an officer trained on a gunnery-ship and qualified to supervise gunnery. **gunnery-ship,** *n.* a vessel for training officers and men in gunnery. **gunless,** *a.* **gunning,** *n.* shooting game with a gun. [short for Icel. *Gunnhildr* (*gunn-*, war, *hildr*, battle), a woman's name given to a war-engine (Skeat)]

gunge, *n.* (*coll.*) an unpleasant sticky substance, a dirty encrustation. **gungy,** *a.*

gung ho, excessively enthusiastic, over-zealous. [Chin. *kung,* to work *ho,* together adopted as a motto by certain World War II US marines]

gunk, *n.* (*sl.*) an unpleasant sticky or slimy substance, gunge. [Orig. trademark of a grease solvent]

gunnel[1], *n.* the butter-fish, *Centronotus gunnellus,* a blenny common on the British coasts and on the N American shores of the Atlantic. [etym. unknown]

gunnel[2] GUNWALE.

gunny, *n.* a heavy coarse sackcloth, usu. of jute or hemp, of which bags etc. are made. [Hind. *gōnī,* Sansk. *gōnī*]

Gunter, *n.* a Gunter's scale; on a vessel, an arrangement of topmast and rigging, in which the former slides up and down the lower mast on rings or hoops, so called from the resemblance to a sliding Gunter. **according to Gunter,** a phrase like '**according to Cocker**.' **Gunter's chain,** *n.* an ordinary surveyor's chain, 22 yd. (approx. 20 m) in length. **Gunter's line,** *n.* (*N Am.*) a logarithmic line on Gunter's scale, used for performing the multiplication or division of numbers. **Gunter's scale,** *n.* a flat, 2-ft. (60-cm) rule having scales of chords, tangents etc. and logarithmic lines, engraved on it, by which questions in navigation and surveying were solved mechanically. [Edmund *Gunter,* 1581–1626, English mathematician and astronomer]

gunwale, gunnel[2], *n.* the upper edge of a ship's side next to the bulwarks; a strip forming the upper edge of a boat. [GUN-, WALE[2]]

gunyah, *n.* a native hut, usu. built of twigs and bark. [Austral. Abor.]

Guomindang, *n.* Chinese National People's Party, founded 1894 by Sun Yat-sen (Sun Zhong Shan), which overthrew the Manchu Empire 1912. By 1927 the right wing, led by CHIANG KAI-SHEK (Jiang Jie Shi), was in conflict with the left, led by Mao Zedong until the Communist victory 1949 (except for the period of the Japanese invasion, 1937–45). It survives as the sole political party of Taiwan, where it is still spelled Kuomintang.

Guppie, *n.* (*coll.*) an environmentally-conscious young professional person. [*G*reen and *Y*uppie]

guppy, *n.* a small brightly-coloured W Indian freshwater fish, now a common aquarium fish. [R.J.L. *Guppy,* naturalist who first presented specimens to the British Museum]

†**gurge,** *n.* a whirlpool, an eddy. *v.t.* to swallow up, to overwhelm. **gurgitation,** *n.* the movement of a liquid in a whirlpool or in boiling. [L *gurges*]

gurgle, *v.i.* to make a purling or bubbling sound, as water poured from a bottle or running over a stony bottom; to run or flow with such a sound. *v.t.* to utter with such a sound. *n.* a gurgling sound; a purling noise. [prob. after It. *gorgogliare,* from L *gurgulio,* the gullet]

gurgoyle, GARGOYLE.

Gurkha, *n.* a member of the dominant ethnic group in Nepal, of Hindu descent, expelled from Rajputana by the Muslim invasion; (*pl.*) soldiers of Nepalese origin, who have been recruited since 1815 for the British army. The Brigade of Gurkhas has its headquarters in Hong Kong. In 1989 the UK government proposed to reduce the Gurkha force in Hong Kong by 50% to 4,000 men by 1992. [Hind.]

gurly, *a.* (*Sc.*) rough, stormy. [obs. n. *gurl,* imit. of sound]

gurnard, -net, *n.* the popular name of any fish of the genus *Trigla,* characterized by a large angular head, covered with bony plates, and three free pectoral rays. [prob. from F *grognard,* from *grogner,* to grunt]

gurrah, *n.* a plain, coarse Indian muslin. [Hind. *gārhā*]

gurry, *n.* in whale-fishing, fish-offal. [etym. unknown]

guru, *n.* a Hindu spiritual teacher or guide; a mentor. [Sansk., heavy, weighty]

gush, *v.i.* to flow or rush out copiously or with violence; to be uttered rapidly and copiously; to be filled with water, tears etc.; to be effusive or affectedly sentimental. *v.t.* to pour (out) rapidly or copiously. *n.* a violent and copious issue of a fluid; the fluid thus emitted; an outburst; extravagant affectation of sentiment. **gusher,** *n.* one who or that which gushes; an oil-well that discharges with great force or without requiring pumps. **gushing,** *n., a.* **gushingly,** *adv.* **gushy,** *a.* [cp. EFris. *gūsen,* LG *gusen,* Icel. *gusa,* G *giessen*]

Gush Emunim, *n.* Israeli fundamentalist group, founded 1973, who claim divine right to the West Bank, Gaza Strip, and Golan Heights as part of Israel through settlement, sometimes extending the claim to the Euphrates.

gusset, *n.* a small triangular piece of cloth inserted in a dress to enlarge or strengthen some part; an angle-iron or bracket for stiffening an angle in construction work; in heraldry, a gore. **gusseted,** *a.* [OF *gousset,* a flexible piece of armour filling up a joint, dim. of *gousse,* a nutshell]

gust[1], *n.* a short but violent rush of wind; a squall; an outburst of passion. *v.i.* of wind, to blow in gusts. †**gustful,** *a.* **gusty,** *a.* **gustily,** *adv.* [Icel. *gustr,* cogn. with GUSH]

gust[2], *n.* the sense or pleasure of tasting; relish, taste. †*v.t.* to have a relish for. †**gustable,** *a.* that may be tasted; pleasant to the taste. *n.* anything agreeable to the taste. †**gustation,** *n.* **gustative, gustatory,** *a.* of or pertaining to gustation. **gustatory nerve,** *n.* the lingual nerve upon which taste depends. [L *gustus,* taste, whence *gustāre,* to taste, *gustātio,* tasting]

Gustavus Adolphus, Gustavus II *n.* (1594–1632), king of Sweden from 1611, when he succeeded his father Charles IX. He waged successful wars with Denmark, Russia, and Poland, and in the Thirty Years' War became a champion of the Protestant cause. Landing in Germany in 1630, he defeated the German general Wallenstein at Lützen, SW of Leipzig, on 6 Nov. 1632, but was killed in the battle. He was known as the 'Lion of the North'.

Gustavus Vasa, Gustavus I, *n.* (1496–1560), king of Sweden from 1523, when he was elected after leading the Swedish revolt against Danish rule. He united and pacified the country and established Lutheranism as the state religion.

gusto, *n.* zest, enjoyment, pleasure; flavour, relish. [see prec.]

gusty etc. GUST[1].

gut, *n.* the intestinal canal; (*pl.*) the intestines; an intestine or a part of the alimentary canal; (*pl.*) the belly or the stomach as symbol of gluttony; (*pl.*) the core or essential part of something; courage; catgut, the prepared intestines of animals used for the strings of musical instruments; fibre drawn from a silkworm before it spins its cocoon, used for fishing-lines; a narrow passage, esp. a sound or strait; (*pl.*) (*coll.*) stamina, courage, persistence. *v.t.* (*past, p.p.* **gutted**) to eviscerate; to draw the entrails out of; to plunder, to remove or destroy the contents of (as by fire). *a.* of or pertaining to instinctive feelings, intuition; of or pertaining to that which involves or engenders emotions etc. **to have guts,** (*coll.*) to be courageous. **to hate someone's guts,** (*coll.*) to dislike someone intensely. **to work** or **slog** etc., **one's guts out,** to work etc. extremely hard. **gutful,** *n.* (*Austral., coll.*) more than enough of an unacceptable situation etc. **gutless,** *a.* cowardly. **guts,** (*coll.*) *n.* a glutton. *v.i.* to gormandize. **gut-scraper,** *n.* (*coll.*) a fiddler. **gutsy,** *a.* greedy; plucky. **gutsiness,** *n.* **gutser,** *n.* (*coll.*) a glutton. **to come a gutser,** (*Austral., coll.*) to fall over; to fail. **gutted,** *a.* (*sl.*) fed up, disappointed. **gutty,** *a.* corpulent. [OE *gutt,* in pl. *guttas* (cp. G *Gosse*), prob. cogn. with *gēotan,* to pour]

Gutenberg, *n.* **Johann** (*c.* 1400–68), German printer, the inventor of printing from moveable metal type. Gutenberg set up a printing business in Mainz with Johann Fust (*c.* 1400–66) as a partner in 1440. The partnership was dissolved through monetary difficulties, but Gutenberg set up another printing press. He is believed to have printed the Mazarin and the Bamberg Bibles.

Guthrie, *n.* **Woody** (1912–67) (stage name of Woodrow Wilson Guthrie) US folk singer and songwriter, whose left-wing protest songs, 'dustbowl ballads', and talking blues were an influence on, among others, Bob Dylan; they include 'Deportees', 'Hard Travelin', and 'This Land Is Your Land'.

gutta, *n.* (*pl.* **-tae**) a drop; an ornament resembling a drop, used in the Doric entablature. **gutta rosacea, rosea**, or **rubea**, *n.* inflammation of the face, with redness and pimples. **gutta serena**, *n.* amaurosis. **guttate**, *a.* (*Bot.*) besprinkled or speckled. **gutté**, **guttee**, *a.* (*Her.*) sprinkled with drops. **guttiferous**, *a.* (*Bot.*) yielding gum or resinous sap. **guttiform**, *a.* drop-shaped. [L]

gutta-percha, *n.* the inspissated juice of *Isonandra gutta,* the Malayan gutta-percha tree, forming a horny substance used for insulators etc. **gutty**, *n.* a gutta-percha golf-ball. [Malay *gatah,* gum, *percha,* name of the tree]

gutté GUTTA.

gutter, *n.* a channel at the side of a street or a trough below eaves for carrying away water; a channel worn by water; a trench, conduit etc. for the passage of water or other fluid; (*Sc., usu. in pl.*) dirt, mire; †a receptacle for filth; in printing, the space between the printed matter in two adjacent pages. *v.t.* to form channels or gutters in; to provide with gutters. *v.i.* to become channelled or worn with hollows, as a burning candle; to stream (down). **gutter-bird, -child,** *n.* a street urchin. †**gutter-blood,** *n.* one of base birth. **gutter-man,** *n.* a street vendor of cheap articles. **gutter press,** *n.* cheap and sensational newspapers. **guttersnipe,** *n.* a street urchin; **guttering,** *n.* the act of forming gutters; a gutter or arrangement of gutters; material for gutters; the act of falling in drops. [OF *gutiere,* from *goute,* see GOUT]

guttiform etc. GUTTA.

guttle, *v.i.* to eat voraciously, to gobble. *v.t.* to devour gluttonously, to gobble up. **guttler,** *n.* [from GUT, after GUZZLE]

guttural, *a.* pertaining to the throat; produced or formed in the throat. *n.* a sound or combination of sounds produced in the throat or the back part of the mouth, as *k, q,* hard *c* and *g, ng* and the G *ch.* **gutturalize, -ise,** †**gutturize, -ise,** *v.t.* to form in the throat. **gutturalism,** *n.* **gutturally,** *adv.* [F, from L *guttur,* throat]

gutturo- *comb. form* of the throat. **gutturo-nasal**, *a.* pertaining to or produced by the throat and the nose. **gutturo-maxillary,** *a.*

gutty GUT, GUTTA-PERCHA.

guv, *n.* (*coll., esp. dial.*) used as a term of address to a man (in authority). [contr. of *guv*nor=governor]

guy[1], *n.* a rope, chain etc., to steady a load in hoisting or to act as a stay. *v.t.* to guide or steady by means of a guy or guys. **guy-rope,** *n.* [OF *guie,* from *guier,* see GUIDE]

guy[2], *n.* an effigy of Guy Fawkes burnt on 5 Nov. in memory of GUNPOWDER PLOT; a fright, a dowdy, a fantastic figure. (*coll.*) a man, a fellow, a person. **a regular guy,** (*N Am., coll.*) a good fellow. *v.t.* to display in effigy; to quiz, to chaff, to ridicule. *v.i.* to carry a guy round on 5 Nov. **to do a guy,** to run away, decamp. [*Guy* Fawkes, the conspirator who attempted to blow up Parliament in 1605]

Guyana, *n.* Cooperative Republic of, country in South America, bounded to the N by the Atlantic Ocean, E by Suriname, S and SW by Brazil, and NW by Venezuela. **area** 214,969 sq km/82,978 sq miles. **capital** and port Georgetown. **physical** mostly tropical rainforest. **population** (1987) 812,000 (51% E Indians, introduced to work the sugar plantations after the abolition of slavery, 30% black, 5% Amerindian); annual growth rate 2%. **exports** sugar, rice, rum, timber, diamonds. **language** English (official), Hindi. **religion** Christian 57%, Hindu 33%, Sunni Muslim 9%.

Guzmán Blanco, *n.* **Antonio** (1829–99), Venezuelan dictator and military leader (*caudillo*). He seized power in 1870 and remained absolute ruler until 1889. He modernized Caracas to become the political capital; committed resources to education, communications, and agriculture; and encouraged foreign trade.

guzzle, *v.i.* to drink liquor greedily; to eat greedily. *v.t.* to drink or eat greedily; to waste (one's income) in guzzling. *n.* a debauch; †drink. **guzzler,** *n.* [perh. from OF *gosiller,* to vomit, cogn. with *gosier,* the throat]

Gwalior, *n.* city in Madhya Pradesh, India; population (1981) 543,862. It was formerly a small princely state, and has Jain and Hindu monuments.

Gwent, *n.* county in S Wales. **area** 1380 sq km/533 sq miles. **towns** administrative headquarters Cwmbran; Abergavenny, Newport, Tredegar. **population** (1987) 443,000. **products** salmon and trout on the Wye and Usk; iron and steel at Llanwern. **language** 2.5% Welsh, English.

Gwyn, *n.* **'Nell' (Eleanor)** (1651–87), English comedy actress from 1665, formerly an orange-seller at Drury Lane Theatre, London. The poet Dryden wrote parts for her, and from 1669 she was the mistress of Charles II.

Gwynedd, *n.* county in NW Wales. **area** 3870 sq km/1494 sq miles. **towns** administrative headquarters Caernarvon; Bangor, resorts Pwllheli, Barmouth. **products** cattle, sheep, gold (at Dolgellau), textiles, electronics, slate. **population** (1987) 236,000. **language** 61% Welsh, English.

gwyniad, *n.* a salmonoid fish, *Coregonus pennantii,* found in Bala Lake and the English Lakes. [W, from *gwyn,* white]

gybe, *v.i.* to swing from one side of the mast to the other (of a fore-and-aft sail); to take the wind on the other quarter (of a vessel). *v.t.* to shift (a sail) in this way; to make (a vessel) take the wind on the opposite quarter. *n.* the act or process of gybing. [Naut., prob. from Dut *gijben* (now *gijpen*)]

gym, *n.* short for GYMNASIUM; short for GYMNASTICS under GYMNAST. **gym shoe,** *n.* a plimsoll. **gymslip,** *n.* a tunic worn by schoolgirls as part of a school uniform. *a.* (*coll.*) of or pertaining to a school-age girl.

gymkhana, *n.* a meeting for equestrian sports and games; orig. a place for athletic sports. [Hind. *gend-khāna,* ball-house, racket-court, assim. to GYMNASTICS]

gymnasium, *n.* (*pl.* **-ia, -ums**) a building or room where athletic exercises are performed;, in Germany, a school of the highest grade preparatory to the universities. **gymnasial,** *a.* **gymnasiarch,** *n.* in ancient Greece, a public official who superintended athletes; a leading athlete; a head instructor in an academy. **gymnasiast,** *n.* [L, from Gr. *gumnasion,* from *gumnazein,* to exercise naked, from *gumnos,* naked]

gymnast, *n.* an expert in gymnastic exercises. **gymnastic,** *a.* of or pertaining to exercises for the development of the body; involving athletic effort; involving great mental effort or discipline. *n.* (*usu. in pl.*) a course of instruction, discipline or exercise for the development of body or mind; exercises for the development of bodily strength and agility; the gymnastic art. **gymnastically,** *adv.* †**gymnic,** *a.* gymnastic. [Gr. *gymnastēs,* as prec.]

gymno-, *comb. form* naked; destitute of protective covering. [Gr. *gumnos,* naked]

gymnocarpous, *a.* of plants, having the fruit or spore-bearing parts bare. [Gr. *karpos,* fruit]

gymnogenous, GYMNOSPERMOUS.

gymnogynous, *a.* of plants, having the ovary naked.

gymnorhinal, *a.* of birds, having the nostrils naked or unfeathered.

gymnosophist, *n.* one of an ancient Hindu sect of philosophic hermits who went nearly naked and used contemplation and asceticism. **gymnosophy,** *n.* [*gymnosophistae, pl.,* Gr. *gumnosophistai* (GYMNO-, SOPHIST)]

gymnosperm, *n.* one of a class of plants having naked seeds, as the pine. **gymnospermous,** *a.*

gymnospore, *n.* of plants, a naked spore. **gymnosporous,** *a.* having naked spores.

gymnotus, *n.* (*pl.* **-ti**) an electric eel. [Gr. *nōtos,* the back]

gymp, JIMP.

gymslip GYM.

gynaeceum, *n.* in Classical Antiquity, the part of a house reserved for the women; (*Bot.*) the female organs in a plant. **gynaecian,** *a.* relating to women. [L, from Gr. *gunaikeion,* from *gunē gunaikos,* woman]

gynaeco- *comb. form* pertaining to women. [Gr. *gunē gunaikos,* woman]

gynaecocracy, *n.* government by women. **gynaecocrat,** *n.* **gynaecocratic,** *a.*

gynaecology, *n.* the science dealing with the functions and diseases peculiar to women. **gynaecological,** *a.* **gynaecologist,** *n.*

gynander, *n.* a plant of the class Gynandria; a masculine woman. **Gynandria,** *n.pl.* a Linnaean class of plants, in which the stamens and pistils are united, as in orchids. **gynandrian, -drous,** *a.* of a plant, having the stamens and pistil connate. **gynandromorph,** *n.* an animal with both male and female characteristics. **gynandromorphically,** *adv.* **gynandromorphism,** *n.* **gynandromorphous,** *a.* **gynandry,** *n.* a tendency in the female towards a male body. [Gr. *gunandros* (*gunē,* woman, *anēr andros,* man)]

†**gynarchy,** *n.* gynaecocracy. [Gr. *gunē,* woman, *archia,* rule, from *archein,* to reign]

gyneco- GYNAECO-.

gyniolatry, *n.* excessive devotion to women. [Gr. *gunē,* woman, -LATRY]

gyn(o)-, *comb. form* distinctively feminine; pertaining to the female organs of plants. [Gr. *gunē,* woman]

gynobase, *n.* enlargement of the receptacle of a flower, bearing the gynaeceum.

gynoecium, GYNAECEUM.

gynophobia, *n.* a morbid fear of women.

gynophore, *n.* (*Bot.*) the pedicel or stalk of the ovary, as in the passion-flower; (*Zool.*) one of the branches in hydrozoa bearing female gonophores.

-gynous, *comb. form* pertaining to women; of a plant, having female organs or pistils; as *androgynous, misogynous.* [Gr. *-gunos,* from *gunē,* woman]

gyp[1]**,** *n.* a male servant in college at Cambridge and Durham Univs. **gyp-room,** *n.* a room used by a gyp as pantry etc. [perh. short for GIPSY (or for obs. *gippo,* scullion, varlet, orig. man's short tunic, from obs. F *jupeau,*)]

gyp[2]**,** *v.t.* (*coll.*) to cheat, swindle. *n.* a swindle. [perh. from *gipsy*]

gyp[3]**,** *n.* (*coll.*) pain. **to give someone gyp,** to cause (someone) pain.

gypsum, *n.* a mineral consisting of hydrous sulphate of lime, which when deprived of its water by heat and calcined forms plaster of Paris. *v.t.* to manure with gypsum. **gypseous, gypsous,** *a.* **gypsiferous,** *a.* [L, from Gr. *gupsos,* chalk]

gypsy, GIPSY.

gyrate, *a.* circular, convoluted; of a plant, circinate; moving round in a circle. *v.i.*, to rotate, revolve, whirl, in either a circle or a spiral. **gyration,** *n.* **gyrational,** *a.* **gyratory,** *a.* **gyre,** *n.* a gyration, a revolution. *v.t.* to turn round; to whirl. *v.i.* to turn or move in a circle. **gyral,** *a.* **gyrally,** *adv.* [L *gȳrātus,* p.p. of *gȳāre,* from GYRUS]

gyre-carline, *n.* (*Sc.*) a witch, a hag. [Icel. *gȳgr,* witch, *karlinna,* CARLINE[1]]

gyrfalcon, GERFALCON.

gyro-, *comb. form* round, curved; relating to revolutions. **gyro-compass,,** *n.* a navigating compass consisting of an electrically driven gyroscope the axle of which orientates the sensitive element. [Gr. *guros,* circle, ring]

gyrograph, *n.* an instrument for recording revolutions.

gyroidal, *a.* arranged or moving spirally.

gyromancy, *n.* divination performed by walking round in a circle or ring until one falls from dizziness.

gyron, *n.* (*Her.*) a triangular charge formed by two lines meeting at the fesse-point. **gyronny,** *a.* [F]

gyroplane, *n.* an aeroplane deriving its lift from the reaction of the air on freely rotating rotors in a horizontal plane, a rota-plane, a helicopter.

gyroscope, *n.* a heavy fly-wheel rotated (usu. electrically) at very high speed and supported on an axis at right angles to the plane of the wheel. Any alteration of direction of the axis of rotation is resisted by the turning movement. It is used as a controlling or stabilizing device or as a compass in ships, aeroplanes etc. **gyroscopic,** *a.*

gyrose, *a.* (*Bot.*) marked with wavy lines; circinate.

gyrostabilizer, -iser, *n.* a gyroscopic device for steadying the roll of a vessel.

gyrostat, *n.* Lord Kelvin's modification of the gyroscope, for illustrating the dynamics of rotating bodies. **gyrostatic,** *a.*

gyrus, (*pl.* **gyri**) (*Anat.*) a rounded serpentine ridge bounded by grooves or fissures, esp. a convolution of the brain. [L, from Gr. *guros,* a ring, a circle]

Gysi, *n.* **Gregor** (1948–), East German politician, elected leader of the Communist Party in Dec. 1989 following the resignation of Egon Krenz. A lawyer, Gysi had acted as defence counsel for dissidents during the 1960s.

gyte[1]**,** *a.* (*Sc.*) mad, crazy. [etym. unknown]

gyte[2]**,** *n.* (*Sc.*) a child; a first-year boy at Edinburgh High School. [corr. of GET]

gytrash, *n.* (*Sc.*) a ghost, a spectre. [etym. doubtful]

gyve, *n.* (*usu. in pl.*) a fetter, a shackle. †*v.t.* to fetter, to enchain; to entangle. [ME *guive,* etym. doubtful]

H

H, h, the eighth letter of the English alphabet (*pl.* **aitches, Hs, H's**), is mostly in English a simple breathing at the beginning of a word or syllable, as in *help*, *hard*, *hope* etc. **H** is commonly joined to other consonants to form digraphs, as *ch* in *child*, *chill*; *sh* in *shin*, *ship*; *th* in *this*, *that*, *think*; joined with *p*, and sometimes with *g*, it gives the sound of *f*, as in *philosophy*, *enough*; sometimes the latter digraph is silent, as in *bough*, *plough*. *Ch* is common in words derived from the Greek, and in such cases in usu. sounded as *k*, as in *chemistry*, *chyle* etc.; the Scottish and German *ch* (represented as *kh* in the scheme of pronunciation adopted here) is a guttural spirant corresponding to the Greek χ, as in *clachan*, *Reichstag*. **H-bomb,** *n.* a hydrogen bomb. **to drop one's hs,** to fail to give the breathing in words beginning with the letter *h*; to speak incorrectly.

ha[1], *int.* an exclamation denoting surprise, joy, suspicion or other sudden emotion; †expressing interrogation; an inarticulate sound expressive of hesitation; when repeated, **ha ha!** it denotes laughter. *n.* the exclamation so defined, or the sound of it. *v.i.* to express surprise, wonder etc.; to hesitate. [onomat., common to Teut., Gr., L etc.]

ha[2], (*abbr.*) hectare.

ha', (*Sc.*) HALL.

haaf, *n.* deep-sea fishing ground (off Orkney and Shetland). [Icel. *haf,* the high sea]

Haakon I, *n.* **(the Good)** (*c.* AD 915–961), king of Norway from about AD 935. The son of Harald Hárfagri ('Finehair') (*c.* AD 850–930), king of Norway, he was raised in England. He seized the Norwegian throne and tried unsuccessfully to introduce Christianity to Norway. His capital was at Trondheim.

Haakon IV (1204–63), *n.* king of Norway from 1217, the son of Haakon III. Under his rule, Norway flourished both militarily and culturally; he took control of the Faroe Islands, Greenland, 1261, and Iceland, 1262–64. His court was famed throughout N Europe.

Haakon VII *n.* (1872–1957), king of Norway from 1905. Born Prince Charles, the second son of Frederick VIII of Denmark, he was elected king of Norway on separation from Sweden, and in 1906 he took the name Haakon. In World War II he refused to surrender to Germany and, when armed resistance in Norway was no longer possible, carried on the struggle from Britain until his return in 1945.

haar, *n.* (*dial. esp. Sc.*) a wet mist, esp. a sea-fog. [perh. from Icel. *hārr*]

Haarlem, *n.* industrial town in the W Netherlands, 20 km/12 miles west of Amsterdam; population (1988) 214,000. At Velsea to the north a road-rail tunnel runs under the North Sea Canal, linking N and S Holland. Industries include chemicals and pharmaceuticals.

hab., (*abbr.*) Habakkuk.

habanera, *n.* a Cuban dance in slow duple time. [Sp. Havanan (dance)]

habble, (*Sc.*) HOBBLE.

habeas corpus, *n.* a writ to produce a prisoner before a court, with particulars of the day and cause of his arrest and detention, in order that the justice of this may be determined. **Habeas Corpus Act,** Act 31 Charles II, c. 2 (1679), authorizing this. [L, thou mayest have the body]

Haber, *n.* **Fritz** (1868–1934), German chemist whose conversion of atmospheric nitrogen to ammonia opened the way for the synthetic fertilizer industry. His study of the combustion of hydrocarbons led to the commercial 'cracking' or fractionating of natural oil into its components, for example diesel, petrol, and paraffin.

Habsburg, Hapsburg, *n.* European royal family, former imperial house of Austria-Hungary. The name comes from the family castle in Switzerland. The Habsburgs held the title Holy Roman emperor (1273–91, 1298–1308, 1438–1740, and 1745–1806). They ruled Austria from 1278, under the title emperor 1806–1918.

hack[1], *v.t.* to cut irregularly or into small pieces; to chop, to notch; to cut unskilfully; to kick (a player's shins) at football; to mangle in uttering. (*sl.*) tolerate; cope with; *v.i.* to cut or chop away at anything; to emit a short dry cough. (*Comput.*) to use computers as a hobby, esp. in order to manipulate another computer system illegally. *n.* an irregular cut, a gash, a notch, a dent; the result of a kick (on the shins etc.); a mattock or large pick, a miner's pick with a chisel edge at one end; †a stammering. **hack-saw,** *n.* a hand-saw used for cutting metal. **hacker,** *n.* one who writes computer programs as a hobby; one who uses a computer to gain access to another computer system, often for illegal purposes; **hacking,** *a.* slashing, chopping, mangling; short, dry and intermittent (of a cough). **hacking jacket, coat,** *n.* a short jacket with a vent or vents at the back, worn for riding. [ME *hakken,* OE *-haccian* (cp. Dut. *hakken,* Dan. *hakke,* G *hacken*)]

hack[2], *n.* a hackney, a horse for hire; a horse for general purposes, esp. as dist. from a hunter or racer; (*N Am.*) a hackney-carriage; one who earns money from routine literary or journalistic work. *v.t.* to let out for hire; to make a hack of; to make common, to hackney. *v.i.* to be let out for hire; to ride a hack or (*N Am.*) in a hack; to ride at the pace of an ordinary hack; to be common or vulgar; to live as a prostitute. **hack-work,** *n.* work done by a literary or journalistic hack.

hack[3], *n.* a rack or grated frame, a hatch; a drying-frame for fish; a frame for drying bricks; a feeding-rack or manger; (*Hawking*) a feeding-board for hawks, also the state of partial liberty in which young hawks are kept. *v.t.* to keep young hawks at hack. **at hack,** (*Hawking*) to be at liberty but obedient to the falconer. [var. of HATCH[1]]

hackamore, *n.* a rope with a loop used instead of a bit on a horse unused to a bridle. [Sp. *jáquima*]

hackberry, *n.* a N American tree of the genus *Celtis,* related to the elms; called also the nettle-tree, sugarberry, hog berry. [var. of HAGBERRY]

hackbut, *n.* a harquebus. **hackbuteer, hackbutier**, *n.* [MF *haquebute*, OF *haquebusche*, see HARQUEBUS]

hackery, *n.* a rude E Indian two-wheeled car.

hackle[1], *n.* an instrument with sharp steel spikes for dressing or combing (flax etc.); fibrous substance unspun, as raw silk; a long shining feather on a cock's neck; a fly for angling, dressed with this; the hairs on a cat's or dog's neck. *v.t.* to dress or comb (flax or hemp) with a hackle; to tie a hackle on (an artificial fly). **to raise the hackles,** anger. **with his hackles up,** (of a dog, cock etc.) ready to fight. [ME *hachele,* cogn. with MHG *Hachele* (G *Hechel,* cp. Dut. *hekel*)]

hackle[2], *v.t.* to hack, to mangle. **hackler,** *n.* **hackly,** *a.* broken or jagged as if hacked; (*Cryst.*) breaking with a peculiarly uneven surface.

hacklet, *n.* the kittiwake. [etym. unknown]

Hackman, *n.* **Gene** (1931–), US character actor. He became a star as 'Popeye' Doyle in *The French Connection* (1971) and continued to play major roles in films such as *Bonnie and Clyde* (1967), *The Conversa-*

tion (1974), and *Mississippi Burning* (1988).

hackmatack, *n.* the American larch; the tamarack. [Am. Ind.]

hackney, *n.* a horse kept for riding or driving; a horse kept for hire; a hackney-carriage. *v.t.* †to carry in a hackney-carriage; †to use much; (*usu. in p.p.*) to make stale, trite or commonplace. **hackney-carriage, -coach,** *n.* a passenger road-vehicle licensed for hire. **hackney-coachman,** *n.* †**hackney-man,** *n.* one who lets out hackneys. **hackneyed,** dull or stale from over-use, trite. [ME *Hakeney,* Hackney, in E London]

had, *past, p.p.* HAVE. **you've had it,** (*coll.*) there's no chance of your getting it now; you've had your chance and lost it; something unpleasant is going to happen to you. [HAVE]

haddie, (*Sc.*) HADDOCK.

haddin', hadding, (*Sc.*) HOLDING.

haddock, *n.* a sea-fish, *Gadus aeglefinus,* allied to the cod and fished for food. [ME]

hade, *n.* the inclination of a fault or vein from the vertical, complementary to the dip. **hading,** *n.* [etym. doubtful]

Hades, *n.* in Greek mythology, the underworld where spirits went after death, usually depicted as a cavern or pit underneath the earth. It was presided over by the god Hades or PLUTO (Roman DIS).

Hadith, *n.* a collection of the teachings of Mohammed and stories about his life, regarded by Muslims as a guide to living second only to the Koran.

hadji, *n.* a Muslim who has performed the pilgrimage to Mecca; a title conferred on such a man. **hadj,** *n.* a pilgrimage to Mecca. [Arab. *hājī*]

Hadlee, *n.* **Richard John** (1951–), New Zealand cricketer. In 1987 he surpassed Ian Botham's world record of 373 wickets in test cricket. He retired from international cricket in 1990.

Hadrian, *n.* (AD 76–138), Roman emperor from AD 117. Born in Spain, he was adopted by his relative, the emperor Trajan, whom he succeeded. He abandoned Trajan's conquests in Mesopotamia and adopted a defensive policy, which included the building of Hadrian's Wall in Britain. **Hadrian's Wall,** *n.* Roman fortification built AD 122–126 to mark England's northern boundary and abandoned about 383; its ruins run 185 km/115 miles from Wallsend on the river Tyne to Maryport, W Cumbria. At least in part, the wall was covered with a glistening, white coat of mortar.

hadron, *n.* an elementary particle taking part in strong nuclear interactions. [Gr. *hadros,* heavy]

hadrosaur, *n.* (*Palaeont.*) a genus of gigantic fossil saurians from the Cretaceous strata of N America. [mod. L *hadrosaurus* (Gr. *hadros,* thick, *sauros,* lizard)]

hae, (*Sc.*) HAVE.

haecceity, *n.* (*Phil.*) the quality of being a particular thing, individuality. [med. L *hæcceitas,* thisness (Duns Scotus), from *haec,* fem. of *hīc,* this]

Haeckel, *n.* **Ernst Heinrich** (1834–1919), German scientist and philosopher. His theory of 'RECAPITULATION' has been superseded, but stimulated research in embryology.

haem, *n.* red organic compound containing iron, found in haemoglobin.

haema-, haemat-, haemato-, (*esp. N Am.*) **hema-** etc. *comb. form.* consisting of or containing blood; pertaining to or resembling blood. [Gr. *haima haimatos,* blood]

haemal, *a.* of or pertaining to the blood; on or pertaining to the side of the body containing the heart and great blood-vessels. [as prec.]

haematemesis, (*esp. N Am.*) **hematemesis,** *n.* a vomiting of blood.

haematic, *a.* of or pertaining to the blood; acting on the blood; containing blood; blood-coloured. *n.* a medicine acting on the blood. **haematics,** *n.* the branch of physiology which treats of the blood.

haematin, *n.* an amorphous substance associated with haemoglobin in the blood; haemotoxylin.

haematite, *n.* native sesquioxide of iron, occurring in two forms, red and brown, a valuable iron-ore. **haematitic,** *a.*

haemato- HAEMA-.

haematoblast, *n.* one of the minute colourless disks, smaller than the ordinary corpuscles, found in the blood. **haematoblastic,** *a.*

haematocele, *n.* cavity containing blood.

haematocrit, *n.* an instrument for separating blood cells from plasma to measure their relative proportions. [Gr. *kritēs,* judge]

haematocyte, *n.* a blood corpuscle. **haematocytometer,** *n.* an instrument for determining the number of corpuscles in a given quantity of blood.

haematoid, *a.* having the appearance of blood.

haematology, (*esp. N Am.*) **hematology,** *n.* the branch of physiology dealing with blood.

haematosin, *n.* haematin.

haematosis, *n.* the formation of blood or of blood corpuscles; the conversion of venous into arterial blood.

haematoxylin, *n.* a dye obtained from logwood. **haematoxylic,** *a.* [Gr. *xulon,* wood]

haematozoa, *n.pl.* parasites found in the blood.

haematuria, *n.* the presence of blood in the urine.

haemo-, (*esp. N Am.*) **hemo-,** short form of HAEMATO-.

haemochrome, *n.* the colouring matter of the blood.

haemocyanin, *n.* an oxygen-bearing substance containing copper, found in arthropods and molluscs. [HAEMO-, Gr. *kuanos,* blue]

haemocyte, *n.* a blood cell, esp. of an invertebrate animal.

haemodynamics, *n.* the dynamics of the circulation of the blood.

haemoglobin, (*esp. N Am.*) **hemo-,** *n.* (*Chem.*) the colouring matter of the red corpuscles of the blood.

haemolysis, *n.* the release of haemoglobin from red blood cells.

haemony, *n.* an unidentified plant having supernatural properties, mentioned by Milton (*Comus,* I. 638). [prob. from Gr. *haimōnios,* blood-red]

haemophilia, (*esp. N Am.*) **hemophilia,** *n.* a constitutional tendency to haemorrhage. **haemophiliac,** *n.* a person suffering from this. also *a.*

haemoptysis, *n.* (*Path.*) a spitting or coughing up of blood from the lungs.

haemorrhage, (*esp. N Am.*) **hemorrhage,** *n.* abnormal discharge of blood from the heart, arteries, veins or capillaries. **haemorrhagic** , *a.* [MF *hemorrhagie,* late L *haemorrhagia,* Gr. *haimorrhagia* (HAEMO-, *-rhagia,* from stem of *rhēgnunai,* to break)]

haemorrhoids, (*esp. N Am.*) **hemorrhoids,** *n.pl.* (*Path.*) piles. **haemorrhoidal,** *a.* [formerly *emorods, emoroydes,* OF *emoroyde,* L *haemorrhoidae,* (Gr. *haimorrhoïdēs* pl.) adj., discharging blood (HAEMO-, *-rhoos,* flowing, from *rheein,* to flow)]

haemostatic, *a.* serving to stop haemorrhage. *n.* a medicine for doing this; (*pl.*) the branch of physiology relating to the hydrostatics of blood. **haemostasia,** *n.* congestion of blood; stoppage of the flow of blood by means of constriction or compression of an artery.

haeremai, (*New Zealand*) *int.* welcome! [Maori]

haffet, *n.* (*Sc.*) the side of the head, the temple. [earlier *halfhed,* OE *healf-hēafod* (half-head)]

hafflin, HALFLING.

hafiz, *n.* one knowing the Koran by heart (a Muslim title). [Pers.]

Hâfiz, *n.* **Shams al-Din Mohammed** (*c.* 1326–1390), Persian lyric poet, who was born in Shiraz and taught in a Dervish college there. His *Diwan,* a collection of short odes, extols the pleasures of life.

hafnium, *n.* metallic element occurring in zirconium ores. [L *Hafniae,* Copenhagen]

haft, *n.* a handle, esp. of a dagger, knife or tool; (*Sc.*) a dwelling, a lodging. *v.t.* to set in or fit with a handle; †to drive in to the hilt; (*Sc.*) to establish as in a residence, to settle, to accustom to. [OE *hæft,* from root of *hebban,* to HEAVE]

hag[1], *n.* a witch; a fury; an ugly old woman; an eel-like fish, *Myxine glutinosa,* of low organization, parasitic within the bodies of other fishes; †a kind of phosphoric light appearing on horses' manes, hair etc. *v.t.* †to frighten, to torment; to sweat (work-people). †**hag-born,** *a.* born of a hag. **hag-ridden,** *a.* suffering from nightmare. **hag-weed,** *n.* the broom, *Cytisus scoparius*. **haggish,** *a.* **haggishly,** *adv.* [perh. shortened from OE *haegtesse*]

hag[2], *n.* a break or soft place in a bog; one of the turfy hillocks of firmer ground in a bog. *v.t., v.i.* to hack, to chop. [Sc. and North., perh. from Icel. *hogg,* a cut or gap, from *hoggva,* cogn. with OE *heawan,* to HEW]

Hag., (*abbr.*) Haggai.

Haganah, *n.* Zionist military organization in Palestine. It originated under Turkish rule before World War I to protect Jewish settlements, and many of its members served in the British forces in both world wars. After World War II it opposed the British authorities only passively. It formed the basis of the Israeli army after Israel was established in 1948.

hagberry, *n.* the bird-cherry, *Prunus padus;* (*N Am.*) the hackberry. [from Scand. (cp. Dan. *haeggebaer*)]

hagbut, HACKBUT.

Haggadah, *n.* in Judaism, the legendary part of the Talmud not concerned with religious law, but devoted to folklore and stories of heroes. **Haggadic, -ical,** *a.* **Haggadist,** *n.* **Haggadistic,** *a.*

haggard[1], *a.* wild-looking; anxious, careworn or gaunt from fatigue, trouble etc.; wild (of a hawk). *n.* a wild or untrained hawk. **haggardly,** *adv.* **haggardness,** *n.* [F *hagard* (perh. conn. with OHG *Haga,* HEDGE, whence *faucon hagard,* hedge-falcon)]

haggard[2], *n.* (*Ireland, Isle of Man*) a stack-yard. [cp. Icel. *heygarthr* (*hey,* hay, *garthr,* GARTH)]

Haggard, *n.* **H(enry) Rider** (1856–1925), English novelist. Born in Norfolk, he held colonial service posts in Natal and the Transvaal (1875–79), then returned to England to train as a barrister. He used his South African experience in his romantic adventure tales, including *King Solomon's Mines* (1885) and *She* (1887).

haggis, *n.* a Scottish dish, made of liver, lights, heart etc., minced with onions, suet, oatmeal etc., boiled in a sheep's stomach. [Sc., etym. doubtful]

haggle, *v.t.* to hack, to mangle. *v.i.* to, wrangle, esp. over a bargain; (*Sc.*) to struggle onwards. *n.* a wrangle about terms. **haggler,** *n.* [prob. freq. of HAG[2]]

hagiarchy, *n.* government by priests; the order of priests or holy men. [foll., Gr. *archē,* rule, from *archein,* to reign]

hagio-, *comb. form.* pertaining to saints or to holy things. [Gr. *hagios,* holy]

hagiocracy, *n.* government by priests or holy persons.

Hagiographa, *n.pl.* the third and last of the Jewish divisions of the Old Testament, comprising the books not included in 'the Law' and 'the Prophets,' i.e. consisting of the Psalms, Proverbs, Job, Song of Songs, Ruth, Lamentations, Ecclesiastes, Esther, Daniel, Ezra, Nehemiah and Chronicles. **hagiographical,** *a.* [late L, from Gr. (HAGIO-, *graphé,* writing)]

hagiography, *n.* biography of saints; a series of lives of saints; any biography that treats its subject as excessively good, noble etc.; †the Hagiographa. **hagiographer, hagiographist,** *n.* **hagiographic, -ical,** *a.*

hagiolatry, *n.* the worship of saints. **hagiolater,** *n.*

hagiology, *n.* literature relating to the lives and legends of saints; a work on the lives of saints. **hagiologic, ical,** *a.* **hagiologist** *n.*

hagioscope, *n.* an oblique opening in the wall of a church to enable persons in the transept or aisles to see the high altar, a squint.

haglet, HACKLET.

Hague, The, *n.* (Dutch **Gravenhage** or **Den Haag**) seat of the Netherlands government, linked by canal with Rotterdam and Amsterdam; population (1988) 680,000. It is also the seat of the United Nations International Court of Justice.

hah, ha ha HA[1].

ha-ha, *n.* a hedge, fence or wall sunk between slopes. [F *haha,* a sudden obstacle that laughs at one]

Hahn, *n.* **Otto** (1879–1968), West German physical chemist, who discovered nuclear fission. Nobel prize for chemistry 1944.

haiduck, haiduk, HEYDUCK.

Haifa, *n.* port in NE Israel; population (1987) 223,000. Industries include oil refining and chemicals.

Haig[1], *n.* **Alexander (Meigs)** (1924–), US general and Republican politician. He became President Nixon's White House chief of staff at the height of the Watergate scandal, was NATO commander (1974–79), and was secretary of state to President Reagan (1981–82).

Haig[2], *n.* **Douglas, 1st Earl Haig** (1861–1928), British army officer, commander-in-chief in World War I. His Somme (France) offensive in the summer of 1916 made considerable advances only at enormous cost, and his Passchendaele (Belgium) offensive (Jul.–Nov. 1917) achieved little at huge loss. He was created field marshal in 1917.

haik[1], *n.* a strip of woollen or cotton cloth worn as an upper garment by Arabs over the head and body. [Arab. *hayk,* from *hak,* to weave]

haik[2], HAKE[2].

haiku, *n.* a Japanese verse of 17 syllables. [Jap.]

hail[1], *n.* frozen rain or particles of frozen vapour falling in showers; (*fig.*) a great number of violent or abusive words etc. *v.i.* (*impers.*) to pour down hail; to come down with swiftness or violence. *v.t.* to pour down or out, as hail. **hailstone,** *n.* a single pellet of hail. **hailstorm,** *n.* **haily,** *a.* [OE *hagol*]

hail[2], *v.t.* to call to (a person at a distance); to greet, designate (as); to welcome, to salute. *v.i.* to come (as a ship). *int.* an address of welcome or salutation. *n.* a salutation; a shout to attract attention. **hail fellow well met,** on easy, familiar terms. **hail Mary** AVE MARIA. **to hail a ship,** to call to those on board. **to hail from,** to come from (a place designated). **within hail,** within the reach of the voice. [Icel. *heill,* HALE[1], used ellipt. as a greeting (cp. OE *wes hāl,* be whole, good health)]

Haile Selassie, *n.* **Ras Tafari ('the Lion of Judah')** (1892–1975), emperor of Ethiopia (1930–74). He pleaded unsuccessfully to the League of Nations against Italian conquest of his country 1935–36, and lived in the UK until his restoration in 1941. He was deposed by a military coup and died in captivity. Followers of Rastafarianism believe that he was the Messiah, the incarnation of God (Jah).

Hailsham, *n.* **Quintin Hogg, Baron Hailsham of St Marylebone** (1907–), British lawyer and Conservative politician. The 2nd Viscount Hailsham, he renounced the title in 1963 to re-enter the House of Commons, and was thereby enabled to contest the Conservative Party leadership elections, but took a life peerage in 1970 on his appointment as Lord Chancellor (1970–74). He was Lord Chancellor again (1979–87).

hain, *v.t.* (*Sc.*) to protect; to save, to preserve. **haining,** *n.* (*Sc.*) an enclosure. [Icel. *hegna,* from Teut. *hag-,* fence (cp. HEDGE)]

Hainan, *n.* island in the South China Sea; area 34,000 sq km/13,124 sq miles; population (1986) 6,000,000. The capital is Haikou. In 1987 Hainan was designated a Special Economic Zone.

Haiphong, *n.* industrial port in N Vietnam; population (1980) 1,305,000. It has shipyards, and industries include cement, plastics, phosphates, and textiles.

hair, *n.* a filament composed of a tube of horny, fibrous substance, with a central medulla enclosing pigment cells, growing from the skin of an animal; (*collect.*) the mass of such filaments forming a covering for the head or the whole body; (*Bot.*) hair-like cellular processes on the surface of plants; (*fig.*) something very small or fine, a hair's breadth; †haircloth; †course, tendency, grain. **against the hair,** against the grain. **by a hair,** by a very small margin. **keep your hair on,** (*coll.*) don't lose your temper. **to get in one's hair,** to become a nuisance, cause irritation. **hair of the dog,** (*coll.*) small amount of what has proven harmful, esp. of alcohol during a hangover. **to make one's hair curl,** (*coll.*) to shock extremely. **to let one's hair down,** (*coll.*) to talk without restraint; to forget ceremony. **not to turn a hair,** not to show any sign of fatigue or alarm. **to a hair,** to an extreme nicety, exactly. **to split hairs,** to quibble about trifles; to be over-nice. **hair-breadth, hair's breadth,** *n.* the breadth of a hair; a very minute distance. **hairbrush,** *n.* a brush for the hair. **hair-brush,** *n.* a brush made of hair. **haircloth,** *n.* cloth made wholly or in part of hair. **hair-compasses,** *n.pl.* compasses that can be finely adjusted. **hair-cut,** *n.* the act or style of cutting a man's hair. **hair-do,** *n.* (*coll.*) a woman's hairdressing. **hair-dresser,** *n.* one who dresses and cuts hair. **hairdressing,** *n.* **hair-dryer, -drier,** *n.* an electric device for drying the hair, either a hand-held one that blows warm air, or a hood that covers the head. **hair-grass,** *n.* tall, tufted grass of the genus *Aira.* †**hair-lace,** *n.* a fillet for tying up the hair. **hair-lead,** *n.* (*Print.*) a very fine lead for spacing out type. **hair-letter,** *n.* (*Print.*) a very thin-faced type. **hair-line,** *n.* the up-stroke of a letter; a fishing-line of horse-hair; the edge of the hair on a person's head, esp. the forehead. **hair-net,** *n.* net, sometimes invisible, to keep the hair in place. **hair-oil,** *n.* oil for dressing the hair. **hair-pencil,** *n.* a fine brush made of hair for painting. **hair-piece,** *n.* a piece of false hair worn to change the style of the natural hair. **hairpin,** *n.* a pin for fastening the hair. **hairpin bend,** a V-shaped turn in a road. **hair-pointed,** *a.* (*Bot.*) terminating in a very fine weak point. **hair-powder,** *n.* a white powder formerly worn on the hair by fashionable men and women. **hair-raising,** *a.* inspiring fear. **hair-raisingly,** *adv.* **hair-shirt,** *n.* a shirt made of horse-hair, worn as a penance. **hair-space,** *n.* the thinnest space used by printers. **hair-splitting,** *n.* the practice of making minute distinctions. *a.* quibbling. **hair-spray,** *n.* lacquer for the hair sprayed from an aerosol can. **hair-spring,** *n.* the fine steel spring regulating the balance-wheel in a watch. **hair-stroke,** *n.* a hair-line in penmanship or on type, a serif. **hairstyle,** *n.* a particular way of arranging the hair. **hair-trigger,** *n.* a secondary trigger for releasing a main trigger by very slight pressure. **hair-wave,** *n.* a wave-like appearance given to the hair. **hair-worm,** *n.* a member of a genus of simple thread-like nematoid worms found in stagnant and slow-running water. **haired,** *a.* having hair (*usu. in comb.*, as *greyhaired*). **hairless,** *a.* **hair-like,** *n.* **hairy,** *a.* covered with hair; consisting of or resembling hair; (*coll.*) difficult, exciting or dangerous. **hairiness,** *n.* [OE *hǣr, hēr* (cp. Dut. and G *Haar,* Icel. *hār*)]

hairst, HARVEST.

haith, *int.* by my faith! [Sc., corr. of FAITH]

Haiti, *n.* Republic of (*République d'Haïti*) country in the Caribbean, occupying the W part of the island of Hispaniola, to the E is the Dominican Republic. **area** 27,750 sq km/10,712 sq miles. **capital** Port-au-Prince. **physical** mainly mountainous. **population** (1985) 5,272,000; annual growth rate 2.5%. **exports** coffee, sugar, sisal, cotton, cocoa, rice. **language** French (official, spoken by the bourgeoisie), creole (spoken by 90% black majority). **religion** Roman Catholic (official, but opposed to the regime).

Haitink, *n.* **Bernard** (1929–), Dutch conductor of the Concertgebouw Orchestra, Amsterdam, from 1964, and music director of the Royal Opera House, Covent Garden, London, from 1986.

haka, *n.* a ceremonial Maori dance. [Maori]

hake¹, *n.* a fish, *Merlucius vulgaris,* allied to the cod. *v.i.* to fish for hake. [etym. doubtful (cp. obs. *haked,* OE *hacod,* the pike)]

hake², haik², *n.* a wooden frame for drying; a cheese-rack; a manger; a mill-hatch. [HACK³]

hakeem, *n.* (in Muslim countries) a physician. [Arab. *hakīm,* wise, from *hakama,* to exercise authority]

hakim, *n.* (in Muslim countries) a governor; a judge. [Arab. *hākim,* as prec.]

Hakluyt, *n.* **Richard** (1553–1616), English geographer whose chief work is *The Principal Navigations, Voyages and Discoveries of the English Nation* (1598–1600). He was assisted by Sir Walter Raleigh.

Halab, *n.* Arabic name of Aleppo, a city in Syria.

Halabja, *n.* Kurdish town near the Iran border in Sulaymaniyah province, NE Iraq. In Aug. 1988 Iraqi planes dropped poison gas, killing 5000 of its inhabitants.

Halachah, Halakah, *n.* a body of traditional laws, supposed to be of Mosaic origin, included in the Mishna. **Halachic,** *a.* **Halachist,** *n.* [Heb. *halākāh,* the rule one walks by, from *hālak,* to walk]

halal, *n.* meat which is prepared in accordance with Muslim law. *v.t.* to prepare (meat) in this way. *a.* of meat, prepared in this way. [Arab. *halāl,* lawful]

halation, *n.* (*Phot.*) a blurring in a negative caused by the reflection of a strong light from the back of the plate during exposure. [HALO, -ATION]

halberd, *n.* a weapon consisting of a combination of spear and battle-axe, mounted on a pole 5 to 7 ft. in length. **halberdier,** *n.* one armed with a halberd. [OF *halebarde,* MHG *helmbarde* (*helm,* helmet, or perh. *helm,* handle, *barde,* a broad axe)]

halcyon, *n.* the kingfisher, supposed by the ancients to make a floating nest at the winter solstice, and to have the power of calming the sea while it was breeding; calm, peace; (*Zool.*) the genus of birds containing the Australasian king-fishers. *a.* peaceful, happy, pleasant. **halcyon days,** *n.pl.* the period of time (about a fortnight) during which the halcyon was traditionally supposed to breed; hence, a time of prosperity, peace and happiness. [L, from Gr. *alkuōn,* kingfisher]

hald, (*Sc.*) HOLD.

Haldane¹, *n.* **J(ohn) B(urdon) S(anderson)** (1892–1964), English scientist and writer. A geneticist, Haldane was best known as a popular science writer of such books as *The Causes of Evolution* (1933) and *New Paths in Genetics* (1941).

Haldane², *n.* **Richard Burdon, Viscount Haldane** (1856–1928), British Liberal politician. As secretary for war (1905-12), he sponsored the army reforms that established an expeditionary force, backed by a territorial army and under the unified control of an imperial general staff. He was Lord Chancellor (1912–15) and in the Labour government of 1924. His writings on German philosophy led to popular accusations of his being pro-German.

hale¹, *a.* sound and vigorous, robust (esp. of elderly people). **haleness,** *n.* [North., from OE *hāl,* WHOLE]

hale², *v.t.* to drag, to draw violently. [OF *haler,* from OHG *halōn* (G *holen,* cp. Dut. *halen,* OE *ge-holian*)]

Hale¹, *n.* **George Ellery** (1868–1938), US astronomer, who made pioneer studies of the Sun and founded three major observatories. In 1889, he invented the spectroheliograph, a device for photographing the Sun at particular wavelengths.

Hale², *n.* **Nathan** (1755–76), US nationalist, hanged by the British as a spy in the War of American Independence. Reputedly his final words were 'I regret that I have but one life to give for my country.'

Halévy, *n.* **Ludovic** (1834–1908), French novelist and librettist. He collaborated with Hector Crémieux in the libretto for Offenbach's *Orpheus in the Underworld*; and with Henri Meilhac on librettos for Offenbach's *La Belle Hélène* and *La Vie parisienne*, and for Bizet's *Carmen*.

Haley, *n.* **Bill** (1927–1981), US pioneer of rock and roll, originally a western-swing musician. His songs 'Rock Around the Clock' (1954) (recorded with his group the Comets and featured in the 1955 film *Blackboard Jungle*) and 'Shake, Rattle and Roll' (1955) came to symbolize the beginnings of the rock-and-roll era.

half, *n.* (*pl.* **halves**) one of two equal parts into which a thing is or may be divided; a moiety; a half-year, a term; (*coll.*) a half-pint; †a side, a part. *a.* consisting of or forming a half. *adv.* to the extent or degree of a half; to a certain extent or degree; partially, imperfectly (*often in comb.*). †*v.t.* to halve. **better half,** one's wife. **by halves,** badly, imperfectly. **half past,** half an hour past as in *half past three,* 3.30. **half three,** (*Naut.*) three and a half fathoms; (*coll.*) half past three. **not half,** (*sl.*) not at all; (*iron.*) rather. **one's other half,** one's spouse or partner. **to cry halves,** to claim an equal share. **to go halves,** to share equally (with or in). **too clever, cocky etc. by half,** far too clever, cocky etc. **half-and-half,** *n.* a mixture of two malt liquors, esp. of porter and ale; an insincere person. *a.* languid, spiritless. **half-back,** *n.* (*Football, hockey etc.*) a position behind the forwards; one who plays in this position. **half-baked,** *a.* not quite baked; inexperienced; not thorough; (*sl.*) half-witted, silly. **half-binding,** *n.* binding in which the backs and corners are of leather and the sides of paper or cloth. **half-blast,** *n.* (*Golf*) a shot played with half the force of a blast. **half-blood,** *n.* relationship between two persons having but one parent in common; one so related; a half-breed. *a.* born of the same father or mother; half-blooded. **half-blooded,** *a.* born of different races; †partly of noble and partly of mean birth. **half-blown,** *a.* having its blossom partially expanded. **half-blue,** *n.* a person who has represented Oxford or Cambridge University at a minor sport or as a substitute. **half board,** *n.* in hotels etc. the provision of bed, breakfast and one main meal per day. **half-boot,** *n.* a boot reaching high up the ankle. **half-bound,** *a.* applied to a book bound in half-binding. **half-brassy shot,** *n.* (*Golf*) a brassy shot played with a half swing. **half-bred,** *a.* imperfectly bred; wanting in refinement; of mixed breed, mongrel. **half-breed,** *n.* an offspring of parents of different races, *esp.* of different colours. *a.* half-blooded. **half-brother,** *n.* a brother by one parent only. **half-butt,** *n.* a billiard cue intermediate in length between an ordinary cue and a long butt. **half-calf,** *a.* half-bound in calf. *n.* this kind of binding. **half-caste,** *n.* a half-breed, esp. one born of a Hindu and a European. †**half-checked,** prob orig. *half-cheeked, a.* (*Shak.*) with only one cheek or end-piece left (of bridles). †**half-cheek,** *n.* a face in profile. **half-cloth,** *a.* bound with cloth sides. *n.* this style of binding. **half-cock,** *n.* the position of the cock of a fire-arm when retained by the first notch, so that it cannot be moved by the trigger. **go off at half-cock, go off half-cocked,** to fail as a result of being too impetuous. **half-crown,** *n.* a British silver coin, value *c.* 12p. **half-dead,** almost dead; (*coll.*) nearly exhausted. **half-dime,** *n.* (*N Am.*) five cents. **half-dozen,** *n., a.* six. **half-face,** *n.* the face as seen in profile; †a miserable look. *a.* half-faced. †**half-faced,** *a.* showing the face in profile; half-hidden; miserable, thin-faced. **half-guinea,** *n.* an English gold coin, value *c.* 50p, not now in circulation. **half-hardy,** *a.* (of a plant) able to survive outside except in the severest frosts. **half-hearted,** *a.* luke-warm, indifferent; poor-spirited, timorous; †ungenerous. **half-heartedly,** *adv.* **half-heartedness,** *n.* **half-holiday,** *n.* the latter half of a working day taken as a holiday; a day on which this is allowed. **half-hour,** *n.* thirty minutes. **half-inch,** *v.t.* (*sl.*) to steal, to purloin. **half-iron shot,** *n.* (*Golf*) an iron shot played with a half swing. †**half-kirtle,** *n.* a woman's jacket or short-skirted gown. **half-landing,** *n.* a landing half-way up a flight of stairs. **half-length,** *n.* a portrait showing only the upper half of the body. *a.* consisting of only half the full length. **half-life,** *n.* the time taken for the radiation from a radioactive substance to decay to half its initial value. **half-light,** *n.* dim light as at dawn or dusk. **half mast,** the middle of or half-way up the mast, the position of a flag denoting respect for a dead person, thus. **half-mast high. half-moon,** *n.* the moon at the quarters when but half is illuminated; a crescent-shaped thing; (*Fort.*) a lunette. *a.* crescent-shaped. **half-mourning,** *n.* a mourning costume of black relieved by grey. **half-nelson,** *n.* (*Wrestling*) a grip in which one arm is driven through the corresponding arm of an opponent and the hand pressed on the back of his neck. **half-note,** *n.* (*Mus.*) a minim; a semitone. †**half-part,** *n.* a moiety; an equal share, half. **half-pay,** *n.* a reduced allowance to an officer retired or not in active service. *a.* entitled to half-pay, on half-pay. †**half-pike,** *n.* a spear-headed weapon about half the length of the pike. **half-price,** *n.* a reduced charge to children for admission to an entertainment or for railway travelling etc. or for persons admitted to an entertainment when half over. **half-round,** *a.* semicircular. *n.* (*Arch.*) a semicircular moulding; †**half-rounding,** *a.* forming into a semi-circle. **half-saved,** *a.* (*sl.*) half-witted. **half-seas-over,** *a.* slightly drunk. **half-servo,** *n.* (*Motor.*) a vacuum or mechanically aided foot-brake which still requires a certain amount of foot pressure. **half-shaft,** *n.* (*Motor.*) a small axle that connects the rear wheel to the differential (or universal joint if there is one). **half-shift,** *n.* (*Mus.*) a move of the hand upward on a violin to reach a high note. †**half-sighted,** *a.* having short or imperfect sight. **half-sister,** *n.* a sister by one parent only. **half-speed, -shaft,** *n.* the cam shaft of a four-stroke cycle combustion engine, rotating at half the rate of the crank shaft. **half-starved,** *a.* poorly fed, not having sufficient food. **half-step,** *n.* (*Mus.*) a semi-tone. †**half-strained,** *a.* half-bred; imperfect. **half-sword,** *n.* half-sword, *n.* half the length of a sword. **at half-sword,** at close quarters. **half term,** *n.* short holiday half-way through a school term. **half-tide,** *n.* half the time of a tide, about six hours; the tide midway between flow and ebb. **half-timbered,** *a.* (*Build.*) having the foundations and principal supports of timber, and the interstices of the walls filled with plaster or brickwork. **half-time,** *n.* the time at which the first half of a game is completed; half the ordinary time allotted. **half-timer,** *n.* (*formerly*) a child attending school for half-time and engaged in some occupation the rest of the day. **half-title,** *n.* (*Print.*) a short title of a book, printed on the recto preceding the title page; a title printed on the recto preceding a separate section of a book. **half-track,** *n.* (*Motor.*) a vehicle running on one pair of wheels and one pair of caterpillar tracks. **half-tone,** *a.* of or pertaining to a process by which printing blocks are made with the shaded portions in small dots, by photographing on to a prepared plate through a finely-ruled screen or grating. **half-tone block,** *n.* **half-truth,** *n.* a statement suppressing part of the truth. **half-volley,** *n.* a stroke in tennis in which a ball is hit immediately after it bounces. **half-way,** *adv.* in the middle; at half the distance. **half-way house,** *n.* an inn half-way between two towns etc; a compromise; short-term accommodation provided for people leaving institutions such as prisons or mental hospitals as rehabilitation for going back into the community. *a.* equi-distant from two extremes. †**halfwit,** *n.* a silly fellow. **half-witted,** *a.* weak in the intellect, imbecile. †**half-world,** *n.* a hemisphere. **half-yearly,** *a.* happening every six months. *adv.* twice in every year. †**halfen,** *a.* half. †**halfendale,** *adv.* by half, nearly all. [OE *healf, half* (cp. Dut. *half,* Icel. *hālfr,* G *half*)]

halfling, *n.* (*Sc. and North.*) a stripling; a witling; †half of an old silver penny. *a.* half grown.

halfpenny, *n.* an English copper coin, half the value of a penny; †a small fragment. *a.* of the value or price of a halfpenny; trumpery, almost worthless. **halfpenny-worth, ha'p'worth,** *n.* as much as can be bought for a halfpenny; a very small amount.

halibut, *n.* a large flat-fish, *Hippoglossus vulgaris,* sometimes weighing from 300 to 400 lb. (135–180 kg), much esteemed for food. **halibut oil,** *n.* (*Med.*) extract from the liver of this fish, rich in vitamins A and D. [ME *hali,* holy, and *butte,* a flounder, perh. cogn. with BUTT[1]]

Halicarnassus, *n.* ancient city in Asia Minor (now Bodrum in Turkey), where the tomb of Mausolus, built about 350 BC by widowed Queen Artemisia, was one of the Seven Wonders of the World.

halicore, *n.* (*Zool.*) a genus of sirenians, comprising the dugong. [Gr. *hals halos,* sea, *korē,* maiden]

halide, *n.* a binary salt of halogen.

halidom, *n.* a holy relic or sacred thing; a holy place, a sanctuary; lands belonging to a religious foundation. †**by my halidom,** an oath. [OE *hāligdōm* (HOLY, DOM)]

halieutic, *a.* pertaining to fishing. *n.pl.* the art of fishing; a treatise on this. [L *halieuticus,* Gr. *halieutikos,* from *halieutēs,* a fisherman, from *halieuein,* to fish]

Halifax[1], *n.* woollen textile town in W Yorkshire, England; population (1981) 87,500.

Halifax[2], *n.* capital of Nova Scotia, E Canada's main port; population (1986) 296,000. Its industries include lumber, steel, and sugar refining.

halitosis HALITUS.

halitus, *n.* a vapour, an exhalation. **halitous,** *a.* like breath; vaporous; produced by breathing. **halitosis,** *n.* offensive breath. [L, breath, from *halāre,* to breathe]

hall, *n.* a large room, esp. one in which public meetings are held, the large public room in a palace, castle etc.; a large building in which public business is transacted; the building occupied by a guild etc.; (*Univ. etc.*) a large room in which scholars dine in common, hence the dinner itself; a manor-house or mansion; a room or passage at the entrance of a house; (*N Am.*) a connecting passage between rooms, a landing; a room forming the entry area of a house; the room in a mansion in which the servants dine etc.; (*Univ.*) a building for undergraduates or other students; a college or department of a university. **hallmark,** *n.* an official stamp stamped by the Goldsmiths' Company and Government assay offices on gold and silver articles to guarantee the standard; any mark of genuineness. *v.t.* to stamp with this. **hallway,** *n.* (*esp. N Am.*) an entrance hall. **hallmote,** *n.* the court of a lord of a manor. [OE *heall* (cp. Dut. and Dan. *hal,* Icel. *hall*), cogn. with *helan,* to cover]

Hall[1], *n.* **Charles** (1863–1914), US chemist who developed a process for the commercial production of aluminium in 1886.

Hall[2], *n.* **Peter (Reginald Frederick)** (1930–), English theatre, opera, and film director. He was director of the Royal Shakespeare Theatre in Stratford-on-Avon (1960–68) and developed the Royal Shakespeare Company as director (1968–73) until appointed director of the National Theatre 1973–88, succeeding Laurence Olivier.

hallan, *n.* (*Sc. and North.*) a wall or partition between the door and the fire-place. **hallan-shaker,** *n.* a sturdy beggar. [perh. dim. of HALL]

Hall effect, *n.* production of a voltage across a conductor or semiconductor carrying a current at right-angles to a surrounding magnetic field. It was discovered 1897 by the US physicist Edwin Hall (1855–1938).

Hallel, *n.* a hymn of praise sung at the four great Jewish feasts, consisting of Ps. cxiii–cxviii. [see HALLELUJAH]

Hallelujah, *n., int.* an ascription of praise to God, sung at the commencement of many psalms and in hymns of praise. **Hallelujah-lass,** *n.* a female member of the Salvation Army who takes part in the public services. [Heb. *halelū jāh,* praise Jehovah]

Haller, *n.* **Albrecht von** (1708–77), Swiss physician and scientist, founder of modern neurology. He studied the muscles and nerves, and concluded that nerves provide the stimulus which triggers muscle contraction. He also showed that it is the nerves, not muscle or skin, that permit sensation.

Halley, *n.* **Edmund** (1656–1742), English scientist. In 1682 he observed the comet named after him, predicting that it would return 1759. **Halley's comet,** *n.* a comet which orbits the Sun about every 76 years. It is the brightest, most famous, and most conspicuous of the periodical comets. Recorded sightings go back over 2000 years. It travels around the Sun in the opposite direction to the planets. Its orbit is inclined at almost 20° to the main plane of the Solar System and ranges between the orbits of Venus and Neptune. It will next reappear 2061.

halliard, HALYARD.

hallo, *int.* an exclamation of surprise; an informal greeting; a preliminary summons and answer when telephoning; a call for attention; a call to cheer on dogs. *n.* this cry. *v.i.* (*past, p.p.* **halloed**) to cry 'hallo'; to cheer dogs on with cries; to call out loudly. *v.t.* to shout loudly to; to cheer, or urge on; to chase with shouts. [imit., cp. OF *halloer*]

hallow, *v.t.* to make sacred or worthy of reverence; to revere; to consecrate, to sanctify. †*n.* a saint. **Hallowe'en,** *n.* the evening of 31 Oct., immediately preceding the Christian feast of Hallowmas or All Saints' Day. Customs associated with Hallowe'en in the US and the UK include children wearing masks or costumes, and 'trick or treating', going from house to house collecting sweets, fruit, or money. **Hallowmas,** *n.* the feast of All-Hallows or **Hallow-Day**. [OE *hālgian,* from *hālig,* HOLY]

Hallstatt, *n.* archaeological site in Upper Austria, SW of Salzburg. The salt workings date from prehistoric times, and in 1846 over 3000 graves were discovered, belonging to a 9th–5th cent. BC Celtic civilization transitional between the Bronze and Iron ages. **Hallstattian,** *a.* denoting the first period of the Iron Age, typified by weapons found in the necropolis of Hallstatt.

hallucinate, †*v.i.* to wander in mind; to blunder, to stumble. *v.t.* to affect with hallucination. **hallucination,** *n.* an apparent sense perception or appearance of an external object arising from disorder of the brain, an illusion. **hallucinatory,** *a.* **hallucinogen,** *n.* a drug etc. that induces hallucinations. **hallucinogenic,** *a.* inducing hallucinations. [L *hallūcinātus,* p.p. of *hallūcinārī, alūcinārī*]

hallux, *n.* (*pl.* **-uces**) the great toe; the digit corresponding to this (as in some birds). [L *allex*]

halm, HAULM.

halma, *n.* a game for two or four played on a board with 256 squares. [Gr., leap, from *allesthai,* to leap]

hal(o), *n.* (*pl.* **-loes**) a luminous circle round the sun or moon caused by the refraction of light through mist; a nimbus or bright disk surrounding the heads of saints etc.; (*fig.*) an ideal glory investing an object. †*v.t.* to surround with or as with a halo. *v.i.* to be formed into a halo. **haloscope,** *n.* an instrument for showing phenomena connected with haloes, parhelia etc. [F, from L *halō,* acc. of *halōs,* orig. a round threshing-floor]

hal(o)- *comb. form.* pertaining to salt or the sea; pertaining to a halogen. [Gr. *hals,* salt]

halogen, *n.* an element or other radical which by combination with a metal forms a salt; fluorine chlorine, bromine and iodine. **halogenous,** *a.*

haloid, *a.* resembling common salt. *n.* a salt formed by the union of a halogen with a metal.

halomancy, *n.* divination by salt.

haloscope HALO.

halothane, *n.* a volatile liquid used as a general anaesthetic. [HALO-, ETHANE]

halotrichite, *n.* iron alum, occurring in fibrous masses. **halotrichine,** *n.* a variety of this.

†**hals,** *n.* the neck; the throat; a neck or strait. [OE *hals, heals* (cp. Icel. and OHG *hals,* also L *collum*)]

†**halse,** *v.t.* to beseech, to adjure; to salute, to greet; to embrace. [OE *hālsian*]

Hals, *n.* **Frans** (*c.* 1581–1666), Flemish-born painter of portraits, such as the *Laughing Cavalier* (1624, Wallace Collection, London), and large groups of military companies, governors of charities, and others (many examples in the Frans Hals Museum, Haarlem, Holland). In the 1620s he experimented with genre scenes.

halser, HAWSER.

halt[1], *a.* limping, lame, cripplied. *v.i.* to limp, to be lame; to doubt, to hesitate; to be defective, to fall or come short; to be faulty in measure or rhyme. *n.* the act of limping; lameness; (*collect.*) lame persons generally; a disease in sheep. **halting,** *a.* **haltingly,** *adv.* [OE *healt, halt* (cp. Icel. *haltr,* Dan. *halt*)]

halt[2], *n.* a stop or interruption in activity or motion; (*Rail.*) a minor stopping-place, without a siding. *v.i.* to come to a stand, esp. of soldiers; (*Mil. command*) cease marching, come to a stand. *v.t.* to cause to stop. **to call a halt (to something),** to cause something to end. **halting-place,** *n.* [G *Halt,* a stoppage, cogn. with HOLD]

halter[1], *n.* a headstall and strap or rope by which an animal is fastened; a rope to hang malefactors; hence, death by hanging. *v.t.* to put a halter upon; to tie up with a halter. **halter-break,** *v.t.* to train (a horse) to submit to the halter. [OE *hælfter* (cp. G *Halfter*), cogn. with HELVE]

haltere, halter[2], *n.* (*pl.* **halteres**) either of two modified hind wings on dipterous insects, used for maintaining balance in flight. [Gr., a balancing weight held by jumpers, from *hallesthai,* to leap]

halve, *v.t.* to divide into two equal parts; to share equally; to lessen by half, to reduce to half; to join (timbers) together by chopping away half the thickness of each; (*Golf*) to win the same number of holes, or to reach a hole in the same number of strokes, as the other side. [ME *halven,* from HALF]

halyard, *n.* a rope or tackle for hoisting or lowering yards, sails or flags. [ME *halier* (HALE[1]) assim. to YARD[1]]

ham[1], *n.* the hind part of the thigh; (*usu. in pl.*) the thigh and buttock; the thigh of an animal, esp. of a hog, salted and dried in smoke, or otherwise cured; an amateur radio operator; a ham actor; the acting of a ham actor. *v.t., v.i.* to act in a clumsy or exaggerated way. **ham actor,** *n.* a bad, inexperienced actor; amateur actor; tyro. **ham-fisted** (*adj.*) (*coll.*) clumsy; inept. **hammy,** *a.* [OE *hamm* (cp. Dut. *ham,* Icel. *höm,* G *Hamme*)]

ham[2], *n.* (*Hist.*) a village, a town (now only in place-names, as *Cheltenham*). [OE *hām,* HOME]

hamadryad, *n.* (*pl.* **-ads, -des**) (*Gr. Myth.*) a dryad or wood-nymph, who lived and died with the tree in which she lived; an Indian venomous snake, *Hamadryas elaps;* an Arabian and Abyssinian baboon, *Cynocephalus hamadryas*. [L *hamadryas,* pl. *-ades,* Gr. *hamadruades* (*hama,* with, *drus,* tree)]

Hamaguchi, *n.* **Hamaguchi Osachi** (also known as Hamaguchi Yuko) (1870–1931), Japanese politician and prime minister 1929–30. His policies created social unrest and alienated military interests. His acceptance of the terms of the London Naval Agreement 1930 was also unpopular. Shot by an assassin Nov. 1930, he died of his wounds nine months later.

hamartiology, *n.* (*Theol.*) the doctrine of sin; a treatise on sin. [Gr. *hamartia,* sin]

hamate, *a.* hooked; furnished with a hook; hook-shaped. **hamiform**, *a.* [L *hāmātus,* from *hāmus,* a hook]

Hamburg[1], *n.* largest port of Europe, in West Germany, on the Elbe; population (1988) 1,571,000. Industries include oil, chemicals, electronics, and cosmetics.

Hamburg[2], *n.* a variety of black hothouse grape; a small black or speckled variety of domestic fowl. **Hamburg lake,** *n.* a deep purplish red. **hamburger,** *n.* a flat cake of minced beef, fried and often served in a bun. [German city]

hame, *n.* one of the pair of curved bars of wood or metal fixed on the collar of a draught-horse, to which the traces are connected. [cogn. with Dut. *haam*]

hamesucken, *n.* (*Sc. Law*) the crime or felony of assaulting a man in his own house. [OE *hāmsōcn* (*hām,* HOME[1], *sōcn,* seeking, assault)]

ham-fisted HAM.

Hamilcar Barca *n.* (*c.* 270–228 BC), Carthaginian general, father of Hannibal. From 247 BC to 241 BC he harassed the Romans in Italy and then led an expedition to Spain, where he died in battle.

Hamilton[1], *n.* capital (since 1815) of Bermuda, on Bermuda Island; population (1980) 1617. It was founded in 1612.

Hamilton[2], *n.* town in Strathclyde, Scotland; population (1981) 52,000. Industries include textiles, electronics, and engineering.

Hamilton[3], *n.* port in Ontario, Canada; population (1986) 557,000. Linked with Lake Ontario by the Burlington Canal, it has a hydro-electric plant, and steel, heavy machinery, electrical, chemical, and textile industries.

Hamilton[4], *n.* **Alexander** (1757–1804), US politician, who influenced the adoption of a constitution with a strong central government, and was the first secretary of the treasury (1789–95). He led the Federalist Party, and incurred the bitter hatred of Aaron Burr when he voted against Burr and in favour of Jefferson for the presidency in 1801.

Hamilton[5], *n.* **Emma** (born **Amy Lyon**) (1765–1815), English courtesan. In 1782 she became the mistress of Charles Greville, and in 1786 of his uncle Sir William Hamilton, the British envoy at Naples, who married her 1791. After Admiral Nelson's return from the Nile (1798) she became his mistress and their daughter, Horatia, was born in 1801.

Hamilton[6], *n.* **James, 1st Duke of Hamilton** (1606–49), Scottish adviser to Charles I, he led an army against the Covenanters (1639), and subsequently took part in the negotiations between Charles and the Scots. In the second Civil War he led the Scottish invasion of England, but was captured at Preston and executed.

Hamilton[7], *n.* **Richard** (1922–), English artist, a pioneer of pop art. His collage *Just what is it that makes today's homes so different, so appealing?* (1956) (Kunsthalle, Tübingen) is often cited as the first pop art work.

Hamilton[8], *n.* **William Rowan** (1805–65), Irish mathematician, whose formulation of Isaac Newton's mechanics proved adaptable to quantum theory, and whose 'quarternion' theory was a forerunner of the branch of mathematics known as vector analysis.

Hamite, *n.* member of an African people, descended, according to tradition, from Ham, son of Noah in the Bible: they include the ancient Egyptians, and the Berbers and Tuareg of N Africa. Hamitic languages are related to the Semitic. **Hamitic**, *a.* of or belonging to Ham, his supposed descendants, or the languages spoken by them. **Hamito-Semitic languages,** a family of languages spoken throughout the world but commonly associated with North Africa and Western Asia. It has two main branches, the *Hamitic* languages of North Africa and the *Semitic* languages originating in Syria, Mesopotamia, Palestine, and Arabia, but now found from Morocco in the west to the Arabian or Persian Gulf in the east. The scripts of Arabic and Hebrew run from right to left.

Hamlet, *n.* tragedy by William Shakespeare, first performed in 1602. Hamlet, after much hesitation, avenges the murder of his father, the king of Denmark, by the king's brother Claudius, who has married his mother. The play ends with the death of all three.

hamlet, *n.* a small village; a little cluster of houses in the country. [OF *hamelet,* dim. of *hamel* (F *hameau*), from Teut. (cp. OFris. and OE *hām,* HOME[1])]

hammal, *n.* an Oriental porter; a palanquin-bearer. [Arab. *hammāl,* from *hamala,* to carry]

hammam, *n.* an Oriental bath-house; a Turkish bath. [Arab. *hāmmam*]

Hammarskjöld, *n.* **Dag** (1905–61), Swedish secretary-general of the United Nations (1953–61). Over the SUEZ CRISIS 1956 he opposed Britain. His attempts to solve the problem of Congo (now Zaïre), where he was killed in a plane crash, were criticized by the USSR. Nobel Peace Prize 1961.

hammer, *n.* a tool for driving nails, beating metals etc., consisting of a head, usu. of steel, fixed at right angles on a handle; a machine, part of a machine or other appliance, performing similar functions, as a steam-hammer; the part of a gun-lock for exploding the charge; the striker of a bell etc.; an auctioneer's mallet; a metal ball, approx. 16 lb (7.3 kg) in weight, attached to a handle by a long wire and thrown in an athletics contest; the contest in which it is thrown; (*Elec.*) the trembler of a magnetic make-and-break mechanism. *v.t.* to strike, beat or drive with or as with a hammer; to forge or form with a hammer; (*fig.*) to work (out) laboriously in the mind; (*coll.*) to defeat easily; (*Stock Exch.*) to declare a defaulter. *v.i.* to work or beat with or as with a hammer; to make a noise like a hammer; to work hard (at). **hammer and sickle,** the emblem symbolic of worker and peasant adopted on the flag etc. of USSR. **hammer and tongs,** with great noise and vigour; violently. **to bring to the hammer,** to put up for auction. **to come under the hammer,** to be sold by auction. **to hammer home,** to stress greatly. **up to the hammer,** first-rate. **hammer-beam,** *n.*

(*Arch.*) a short beam projecting horizontally from a wall, in place of a tie-beam, to support the timbers of a roof. **hammer break,** *n.* (*Elec.*) an interrupter in which the motion of an automatically vibrating hammer interrupts contact. **hammer-cloth,** *n.* the cloth covering the driver's seat in a horse-drawn coach. **hammer-harden,** *v.t.* (*Metal.*) to harden a metal by hammering it in the cold state. **hammer-head,** *n.* the head of a hammer; a S African bird; a shark with a head like a hammer, also called **hammer-fish. hammer-headed,** *a.* **hammer-lock,** *n.* (*Wrestling*) a grip in which one man's arm is held twisted and bent behind his back by his opponent. **hammerman, -smith,** *n.* one who works with a hammer. **hammer-toe,** *n.* (*Med.*) a malformation of the foot consisting of permanent angular fixing of one or more toes. **hammerwort,** *n.* the common pellitory (*Parietaria*). **hammerer,** *n.* **hammering,** *n.* (*coll.*) a clear defeat. **hammerless,** *a.* [OE *hamor* (cp. Dut. *hamer,* Icel. *hamarr,* G *Hammer*)]

Hammerstein, *n.* **Oscar II** (1895–1960), US lyricist and librettist, who collaborated with Jerome Kern on *Show Boat* (1927), and with Richard Rodgers.

Hammett, *n.* **Dashiell** (1894–1961), US crime novelist, whose books include *The Maltese Falcon* (1930), *The Glass Key* (1931), and the *The Thin Man* (1932).

hammochrysos, *n.* a mineral known to the ancients, perhaps yellow micaceous schist. [Gr. *hammochrūsos* (*hammos,* sand, *chrusos,* gold)]

hammock, *n.* a swinging or suspended bed made of canvas or network, and hung by hooks or other contrivance from a roof, ceiling, tree etc. **hammock-batten,** *n.* one of the strips of wood from which hammocks are slung. **hammock-chair,** *n.* a frame-work supporting canvas on which one may sit or recline. **hammock-netting,** *n.pl.* (*Naut.*) orig. a row of stanchions supporting a netting, now long racks, in which the hammocks are stowed during the day. **hammock-rack.** HAMMOCK-BATTEN. [Sp. *hamaca,* prob. from Carib.]

Hammond organ, *n.* an electric organ invented in the US by Laurens Hammond (1934) and widely used in gospel music. A precursor of the synthesizer.

Hammurabi, *n.* king of Babylon from *c.* 1792 BC. He united his country and took it to the height of its power, although his consolidation of the legal code was bloodthirsty in its punishments.

hamose, -mous *a.* (*Bot.*) curved like a hook; having hooks. [L *hāmus,* a hook]

Hampden, *n.* **John** (1594–1643), English politician. His refusal in 1636 to pay SHIP MONEY made him a national figure. In the Short and Long parliaments he proved himself a skilful debater and parliamentary strategist. Charles's attempt to arrest him and four other leading MPs made the Civil War inevitable. He raised his own regiment on the outbreak of hostilities, and on 18 June 1643 was mortally wounded at the skirmish of Chalgrove Field in Oxfordshire.

Hampden Park, *n.* Scottish football ground, opened 1903, home of Queen's Park AFC and the national Scottish team. It plays host to the Scottish FA Cup and League Cup final each year as well as semi-final and other matches.

hamper¹, *n.* a large, coarsely made wickerwork basket, with a cover; a package of groceries etc. put together for a special occasion. *v.t.* †to put into or enclose in a hamper; (*facet.*) to load with hampers. [formerly *hanaper, hanper,* OF *hanapier,* HANAPER]

hamper², *v.t.* to impede the movement or free action of; to obstruct or impede (movement etc.); to hinder, to shackle, to fetter; †to put out of order. *n.* anything which hampers or impedes free action; (*Naut.*) rigging, equipment or other gear of a cumbrous kind. [etym. doubtful (cp. LG *hampern,* Dut. *haperen,* to stop, to fail)]

Hampshire, *n.* county of S England. **area** 3770 sq km/1455 sq miles. **towns** administrative headquarters Winchester; Southampton, Portsmouth, Gosport. **population** (1987) 1,537,000. **products** agricultural; oil from refineries at Fawley; chemicals, pharmaceuticals, electronics.

Hampton Court Palace, *n.* former royal residence near Richmond, London, built 1515 by Cardinal Wolsey, and presented by him to Henry VIII in 1525. Henry subsequently enlarged and improved it. In the 17th cent. William and Mary made it their main residence outside London, and the palace was further enlarged by Christopher Wren, although only part of his intended scheme was completed.

hamshackle, *v.t.* to fasten the head (of an ox, horse etc.) to one of its forelegs. [etym. doubtful, perh. conn. with prec.]

hamster, *n.* a rat-like rodent of the genus *Cricetus,* esp. *C. frumentarius,* with large cheek-pouches in which it carries grain for food during hibernation. [G]

hamstring, *n.* one of the tendons of the thigh muscle behind the knee; (*Quadrupeds*) the large tendon at the back of the hock in the hind leg. *v.t.* to lame or disable by cutting or severing the hamstring. [HAM¹, STRING]

hamulus, *n.* (*pl.* **-li,** -lī), a little hook; (*Bot.*) a hooked bristle; (*Anat.*) a hook-like process; (*Surg.*) an instrument for extracting the foetus. **hamular, hamulose,** *a.* [L, dim. of *hāmus,* hook]

hanap, *n.* a drinking-vessel, a goblet. [OF, from Teut. (cp. OHG *Hnapf,* Dut. *nap.* OE *hnæp*)]

hanaper, *n.* a hamper; a basket or wicker case for documents and valuables; the office of the old Court of Chancery dealing with the sealing etc. of charters and other documents (abolished in 1842). [OF *hanapier,* from *hanap,* see prec.]

hanaster, hanster HANSE.

Hanbury-Tenison, *n.* **(Airling) Robin** (1936–), Irish adventurer, explorer, and writer, who made the first land crossing of South America at its widest point, 1958. He explored the southern Sahara intermittently during 1962–66, and in South America sailed in a small boat from the Orinoco River to Buenos Aires, 1964–65. After expeditions to Ecuador, Brazil, and Venezuela, he rode across France in 1984 and along the Great Wall of China in 1986. In 1969 he became chairman of Survival International, an organization campaigning for the rights of threatened tribal peoples.

hance, *n.* (*Naut.*) the curved rise or fall as in bulwarks, fife-rails etc.; (*Arch.*) the haunch of an arch. **hanced,** *a.* (*Arch.*). [perh. through an A-F *haunce,* from OF *hauce,* from *haucer* (F *hausser*), late L *altiāre,* from *altus,* high]

Hancock, *n.* **John** (1737–1793), US revolutionary politician. He advocated resistance to the British as president of the Continental Congress, 1775–77, and was the first to sign the Declaration of Independence in 1776. Because he signed it in a large, bold hand (in popular belief, so that it would be big enough for George III to see), his name became a colloquial term for a signature in the US. He was governor of Massachusetts (1780–85 and 1787–93).

hand¹, *n.* the part used for grasping and holding, consisting of the palm and fingers, at the extremity of the human arm; a similar member terminating the limbs of monkeys; the end of a limb, esp. a fore-limb, in other animals, when serving as a prehensile organ; power of execution, skill, performance, handiwork; a pledge of marriage; possession, control, authority, power (*often in pl.*); source, person; (*pl.*) operatives, labourers, crew of a ship, players, persons engaged in a game etc.; a part, a share, a turn, an innings; an act of helping; a game at cards; the cards held by a player; a part in a game of cards; one of the players in a game of cards; a player's turn to serve the ball at tennis, rackets etc.; style of workmanship, handwriting etc.; signature; a lineal measure of 4 ins. (10 cm), a palm (measuring horses); a handful; a handle or helve; the pointer or index finger of a watch, clock or counter; five of any article of sale; a bundle of tobacco leaves; a shoulder (of pork); side direction (right or left); a round of applause. **a good hand,** skilful, expert (at). **all hands,** (*Naut.*) the entire crew. **at, on all hands,** by all parties; from all quarters. †**at any hand,** at any rate. **at first, second hand,** as the original purchaser, owner, hearer etc., or as one deriving or learning through another party. **at hand,** near, close by; available. **at the hand** or **hands of,** from, through; by the means or instrumentality of. **by hand,** with the hands (as dist. from instruments or machines); by messenger or agent; by artificial rearing (of children or the young of the lower animals). **clean hands,** innocence, freedom from guilt. **for one's own hand,** (to play or act) for one's personal advantage. **from hand to hand,** from one person to another, bandied about. **from hand to mouth,** without provision for the future. **hand in glove,** on most intimate terms (with). **hand in hand,** with hands mutually clasped; (*fig.*) in union, unitedly. **hand over hand,** by passing the hands alternately one above or before the other, as in climbing; (*fig.*) with rapid, unchecked progress. **hand to hand,** at close quarters; in close fight. **hands off!** stand off! don't touch! **hands up!** show hands, those who assent etc.; show hands to preclude resistance. **heavy on hand,** hard to manage. **in hand,** in a state of preparation or execution; in possession; under control. **light on hand,** easy to manage. **on hand,** in present possession; in stock. **on one's hands,** (left) to one's responsibility; (left) unsold. **on the one hand, on the other,** from this point of view, from that. **out of hand,** done, ended, completed; at once, directly, extempore; out of control. **(the) upper hand,** dominance; mastery. **to ask** or **give the hand of,** to ask or give in marriage. **to bear in hand,** to help. **to be on the mending hand,** (*N Am.*) to be in a fair way of recovery. **to bite the hand that feeds one,** to be ungrateful to a benefactor. **to change hands,** to become someone else's property. **to come cap in hand,** to come humbly, to come seeking a favour. **to come to hand,** to be received; to arrive. **to force one's hand,** to make one take action against his or her will. **to hand,** near; available. **to have a hand for,** to be skilful at. **to have a hand in,** to have a share in; to be mixed up with. **to have one's hands full,** to be fully occupied. **to join hand in hand,** to act in concert. **to know like the back, palm of one's hand,** to be very familiar with something. **to lay hands on,** to touch; to assault; to seize; to lay the hands on the head of (in ordination, confirmation etc.). **to lend a hand,** to help, to give assistance. **to one's hand,** ready, in readiness. †**to put, stretch forth one's hand against,** to use violence against; to attack. **to set the hand to,** to undertake; to engage in. **to shake hands,** to clasp each other's right hand in token of friendship etc. **to show etc. one's hand,** to reveal one's plans, resources etc. †**to strike hands,** to make a bargain; to become surety. **to take a hand,** to take part in a game, esp. of cards. **to take by the hand,** to take under one's protection, care or guidance. **to take in hand,** to undertake, to attempt. **to take one in hand,** to deal with, to manage; to discipline. **to tie one's hands,** to prevent one from taking action. **to wash one's hands of,** to declare oneself no longer responsible for; to renounce for ever. **to win hands down,** without an effort, easily (of a jockey). **under one's hand,** with one's proper signature. **with a heavy hand,** oppressively; unstintedly, without sparing. **with a high hand,** arbitrarily, arrogantly. **handbag,** *n.* a small bag for carrying things with the hand. **hand-ball,** *n.* a ball played with the hand; a game played with this between goals. **handbarrow,** *n.* a kind of stretcher, having a pair of handles at each end, adapted to be carried by two men. **handbell,** *n.* a small bell rung with the hand, esp. one of a series played musically. **handbill,** *n.* a small printed sheet for circulating information. **handbook,** *n.* a small book or treatise on any subject, a compendium, a manual. **hand-brace,** *n.* a tool for boring. **handbrake,** *n.* (*Motor.*) a brake worked by a hand lever. **hand('s)-breadth,** *n.* a linear measurement equal to the breadth of the hand. **hand-canter,** *n.* a gentle canter. **hand-car,** *n.* (*Rail.*) a small hand-propelled truck running on the rails, used by workers on the line. **hand-cart,** *n.* a two-wheeled vehicle for carrying parcels or goods, pushed or drawn by hand. **handcuff,** *n.* (*usu. pl.*) a manacle for the wrists, consisting of a chain and locking-rings. *v.t.* to secure with handcuffs. **handfast,** *v.t.* to bind by a contract or engagement; to betroth, to pledge; to marry. *n.* a hold or grasp with the hand; custody, constraint, confinement; a contract, a pledge; a marriage engagement. †*a.* made fast by contract; betrothed. **hand-gallop,** *n.* a slow and easy gallop. **hand-gear,** *n.* (*Mech.*) gear worked by hand, with a view to starting or checking some other machinery operated by power. **hand-glass,** *n.* a small mirror with a handle; a magnifying glass for holding in the hand; (*Hort.*) a bell-glass or glazed frame, for the protection of plants; (*Naut.*) a half-minute glass, used to measure time in running out the log-line. **hand-grenade,** *n.* a grenade for throwing, by hand. **hand-grip,** *n.* grasp or seizure with the hands; (*esp. N Am.*) a suitcase, a large bag for holding luggage, equipment etc. **hand-gun,** *n.* a gun that can be held and fired in one hand. **handhold,** *n.* something for the hand to hold on by (in climbing etc.). **hand-lead,** *n.* (*Naut.*) a small lead for sounding. **hand-line,** *n.* a line worked by the hand, esp. a fishing-line without a rod. **hand-loom,** *n.* a loom worked by hand. **hand-made,** *a.* produced by hand, not by machinery. †**handmaid, -maiden,** *n.* a female servant or attendant. **hand-me-downs,** *n.pl.* (*coll.*) second-hand clothes. **hand-mill,** *n.* a small mill worked by hand; a quern. **hand-organ,** *n.* a barrel-organ worked by a handle. **handout,** *n.* information handed out to the press; financial help given esp. to the poor. **handover,** *n.* an act of handing over; transfer. **hand-pick,** *v.t.* to choose carefully. **hand-press,** *n.* a press, esp. for printing, worked by the hand, as dist. from one worked by steam, water etc. **handpromise,** *n.* a solemn form of betrothal among the Irish peasantry. **handrail,** a rail protecting stairs, landings etc. **hand-sale,** *n.* a sale confirmed by the shaking of hands. **handsaw,** *n.* a saw riveted at one end to a handle, and adapted to be used by one hand. **hand-screw,** *n.* a jack-screw for raising heavy weights; (*Motor.*) a screw, generally for brake adjustment, which can be turned by hand. **handset,** *n.* the receiver of a telephone. **hand-shake,** *n.* a shake of another's hand as a greeting. **hand-spike,** *n.* a bar, usu. of wood shod with steel, used as a lever for lifting, heaving etc. **hands-on,** *a.* having, through practical experience. **handstand,** *n.* the act of balancing upright on one's hands. **handstaves,** *n.pl.* (*Bibl.*) probably javelins. **handwriting,** *n.* writing done by hand; the style of writing peculiar to a person. **handed,** *a.* having a hand of a certain kind (*in comb.,* as *free-handed*); †having the hands joined. **-hander** *comb. form.* blow, stroke etc. using the stated hand. **handful,** *n.* as much as can be held in the hand; a small number or quantity; (*coll.*) a troublesome person or task. **handless,** *a.* [OE *hand, hond* (cp. Dut. and G *Hand,* Icel. *hönd, hand*)]

hand[2], *v.t.* to give, deliver or transmit with the hand; to assist or conduct with the hand (into, out of etc.); (*Naut.*) to furl; †to seize, to lay hands on; †to handle. †*v.i.* to co-operate; to agree. **to hand down,** to transmit, to give in succession; to pass on. **to hand in,** to deliver to an office etc. **to hand it to,** to give someone credit, to acknowledge someone's superiority, victory etc. **to hand over,** to deliver to a person. [from prec.]

Handel, *n.* **Georg Friedrich** (1685–1759), German composer, who became a British subject 1726. His first opera, *Almira,* was performed in Hamburg 1705. In 1710 he was appointed Kapellmeister to the elector of Hanover (the future George I of England). In 1712 he settled in England, where he established his popularity with works such as the *Water Music* 1717 (written for George I). His great choral works include the *Messiah* (1742) and the oratorios *Samson* (1743), *Belshazzar* (1745), *Judas Maccabaeus* (1747), and *Jephtha* (1752).

handicap, *n.* †an old game at cards; a race or contest in which an allowance of time, distance or weight is made to the inferior competitors; the heavier conditions imposed on a superior competitor; any physical or mental disability; a disadvantage. *v.t.* to impose heavier weight or other disadvantageous conditions on a competitor; to put at a disadvantage. **handicapped,** *a.* having a physical or mental disability. **handicapper,** *n.* [from the drawing of lots out of a hat or cap]

handicraft, *n.* skill in working with the hands; manual occupation or trade; †a handicraftsman. *a.* pertaining to manual labour. **handicraftsman,** *n.* one employed in a handicraft. [OE *handcræft*]

handily HANDY.

handiwork, *n.* work done by the hands; the product of one's hands, labour or effort. [OE *handgeweorc* (HAND[1], *weorc,* collect. WORK)]

Handke, *n.* **Peter** (1942–), Austrian novelist and playwright, whose first play *Insulting the Audience* (1966) was an example of 'anti-theatre writing'. His novels include *Die Hornissen/The Hornets* (1966) and *The Goalie's Anxiety at the Penalty Kick* (1970). He directed and scripted the film *The Left-handed Woman* (1979).

handkerchief, *n.* (*pl.* **-chiefs, -chieves**) a piece of cloth, silk, linen or cotton, carried about the person for wiping the nose, face etc.; a neckcloth, a neckerchief. **to throw the handkerchief to,** to call upon a player to take a turn, esp. to pursue one (in certain games); to single out patronizingly. [HAND[1], KERCHIEF]

handle, *v.t.* to touch, to feel with, to wield or use with the hands; to treat (well, ill etc.); to deal with, to manage, to treat of; to deal in. *v.i.* to work with the hands; to be handled (of a vehicle) to respond in a specified way to control by a driver. *n.* that part of a vessel, tool or instrument, by which it is grasped and held in the hand; an instrument or means by which anything is done; (*sl.*) name, title. **a handle to one's name,** (*sl.*) a title. **to fly off the handle,** to become angry, to go into a rage. **to give a handle,** to furnish an occasion or advantage that may be utilized. **handle-bar,** *n.* a horizontal bar with grips at each end for steering a bicycle, motorcycle etc. **handlebar moustache,** *n.* a thick, wide moustache that curls upwards at each end. **handler,** *n.* one who handles; (*Tanning*) a tan-pit containing a weak ooze. **handling,** *n.* the action of touching, feeling etc. with the hand; (*Art.*) the art of managing the pencil; characteristic style of painting, composing, manipulating etc.; the responsiveness of a vehicle to a driver's control. [OE *handlian,* from HAND[1] (cp. Dut. *handelen,* G *handeln*)]

handrail HAND[1].

handsel, *n.* a gift for luck, esp. on the first Monday in the New Year; earnest money; the first sale, present, use etc.; (*fig.*) a foretaste. *v.t.* to give a handsel to; to use for the first time; to be the first to use. **handsel Monday,** *n.* (*Sc.*) the first Monday of the New Year, when presents were commonly given to servants, children etc. [perh. from Scand. (cp. Icel. *handsal,* Dan. *handsel,* an earnest, OE *handselen,* delivery into the hand)]

handshake etc. HAND[1].

handsome, *a.* †handy, convenient, suitable; well formed, finely featured, good-looking; noble; liberal, generous; ample, large; (*N Am.*) showing skill and cleverness, adroit. **handsomely,** *adv.* **handsomeness,** *n.*

handwriting HAND[1].

handy, *a.* ready or convenient to the hand; close at hand; dexterous, skilful with the hands; near, convenient. **handy-dandy,** *n.* a children's game, in which one child has to guess in which hand of the other some small article is held. **handy-man,** *n.* a man who does odd jobs; a man who is good at DIY. **handily,** *adv.* **handiness,** *n.*

handywork HANDIWORK.

hang[1], *v.t.* (*past, p.p.* **hung;** for put to death and as imprecation **hanged**) to suspend; to attach loosely to a point of support above the centre of gravity; to fasten so as to leave movable (as a bell, gate, the body of a coach etc.); to suspend by the neck on a gallows as capital punishment; to cause to droop; to cover or decorate with anything suspended; to attach, to fasten. *v.i.* to be suspended; to depend, to dangle, to swing; to cling; to be executed by hanging; to droop, to bend forwards; to project (over), to impend; to be fixed or suspended with attention; to depend (as on a basis etc.); to be in suspense; †to be delayed. **hang! hang it! I'll be hanged!** forms of imprecation or exclamation. **to go hang,** (*coll.*) to be neglected. **to hang about, around,** to loiter, to loaf. **to hang back,** to act reluctantly, to hesitate. **to hang down,** to decline, to droop. **to hang fire,** said of a fire-arm when the charge does not ignite immediately; (*fig.*) to hesitate; to be wanting in life or spirit. **to hang heavy,** to go slowly (as time). **to hang in,** (*esp. N Am. coll.*) to persist. **to hang in doubt,** to be in suspense. **to hang on,** to grasp or hold; to persist; to depend on; (*coll.*) to wait. **to hang on to,** keep holding; retain, to spend time. **to hang on, upon,** to adhere closely to; to be a weight or drag on; to rest, to dwell upon. **to hang out,** to suspend from a window etc.; to protrude loosely (of a tongue); (*sl.*) to live. **to hang over,** to be overhanging or impending; to spend time. **to hang together,** to be closely united; to be consistent. **to hang up,** to suspend; to put aside, to leave undecided; to defer indefinitely; to replace a telephone receiver and so end the call. (*Austral.*) to tie a horse to a post. **hangman,** *n.* a public executioner. **hang-bird,** *n.* a bird building a hanging nest, esp. the Baltimore oriole. **hang-dog,** *n.* a low, base fellow; *a.* base, sullen. **hang-glider,** *n.* a type of large kite controlled by the person suspended beneath it in a harness; the person who flies it. **hang-gliding,** *n.* **hang-nail** AG-NAIL. **hang-nest** *n.* a bird constructing a pendulous nest; the nest of such a bird; the hangbird. **hang-net,** *n.* a net with a large mesh hanging vertically on stakes. **hangout,** *n.* (*coll.*) haunt. **hangover,** *n.* (*coll.*) the after-effects of a drinking-bout. **hang-up,** *n.* (*coll.*) a source of neurosis or anxiety. **hung over,** *a.* suffering from a hangover. **hung up,** *a.* nervous, tense, obsessed. **hanger** *n.* one who hangs or causes to be hanged; that on which a thing is hung or suspended; a pot-hook; a double curve (ʃ) in writing; a short, curved sword or cutlass, orig. hung from the belt; a sloping wood or grove (largely in place-names). **hanger-on,** *n.* one who hangs on or sticks to a person, place etc.; a dependant, a parasite. **hanging,** *n.* the act of suspending; an execution by the gallows; an exhibition; (*pl.*) fabrics hung up to cover or drape a room. *a.* suspended, dangling; steep, inclined; †foreboding death by the halter; deserving death by the halter; punishable with hanging. **hanging-bird** HANG-BIRD. **hanging buttress,** a buttress supported on a corbel. **hanging committee,** a committee appointed to arrange pictures in an exhibition. **hanging garden,** a garden rising in terraces one above the other. **hanging guard,** a position of defence with the broadsword. **hanging valve,** a hinged valve falling by the action of gravity. [from two OE verbs. *hangian,* intr., and the causal *hōn,* and in North. Eng. from Icel. *hengja,* whence the p.p. *hung*]

hang[2], *n.* a slope, a declivity; mode of hanging; general tendency, drift or bent. **to get the hang of,** to understand the drift or connexion of; to get the knack of. [from prec.]

hangar, *n.* a large shed, esp. for aircraft. [F, etym. doubtful]

Hangchow, *n.* former name for HANGZHOU.

Hangzhou, *n.* (formerly **Hangchow**) port and capital of Zhejiang province, China; population (1986) 1,250,000. It has jute, steel, chemical, tea, and silk industries.

hank, *n.* a coil or skein; two or more skeins of yarn, silk, wool or cotton, tied together (840 yd. (750 m) of cotton yarn, 560 yd. (500 m) of worsted); a coil or bundle (as of fish); a withe for fastening a gate; (*Naut.*) one of the hoops or rings to which a fore-and-aft sail is bent. †*v.t.* to form into hanks; to fasten. [cp. Icel. *hōnk,* Dan. and LG *Hank*]

hanker, *v.i.* to have strong desire or longing (after). **hankering,** *n.* **hankeringly,** *adv.* [etym. doubtful, prob. cogn. with Dut. *hunkeren*]

hanky-panky, *n.* jugglery, trickery, fraud; (*coll.*) improper activity esp. of a sexual kind. [coined on anal. of HOCUS-POCUS]

Hanley, *n.* **Ellery** (1961–), English rugby league player, a regular member of the Great Britain team since 1984 and the inspiration behind his club Wigan's rise to the top in the 1980s.

Hannibal *n.* (247–182 BC), Carthaginian general from 221 BC, son of Hamilcar Barca. His siege of Saguntum (now Sagunto, near Valencia) precipitated the 2nd Punic War. Following a campaign in Italy (after crossing the Alps in 218 BC with 57 elephants), Hannibal was the victor at Trasimene in 217 BC and Cannae in 216 BC, but he failed to take Rome. In 203 BC he returned to Carthage to meet a Roman invasion but was defeated at Zama in 202 BC and exiled in 196 BC at Rome's insistence.

Hanoi, *n.* capital of Vietnam, on the Red River; population (1979) 2,571,000. Industries include textiles, paper, and engineering.

Hanover[1]**,** *n.* industrial city, capital of Lower Saxony, West Germany; population (1988) 506,000. Industries include machinery, vehicles, electrical goods, rubber, textiles, and oil refining. **Hanoverian**[1]**,** *a.* of or pertaining to Hanover. *n.* a native or inhabitant of Hanover.

Hanover[2]**,** *n.* German royal dynasty that ruled Great Britain and Ireland (1714–1901). Under the Act of Settlement (1701), the succession passed to the ruling family of Hanover, Germany, on the death of Queen Anne. On the death of Queen Victoria the crown passed to Edward VII of the house of Saxe-Coburg. **Hanoverian**[2]**,** *a.* of or pertaining to Hanover. *n.* an adherent of the House of Hanover, the dynasty that came to the throne of Great Britain and Ireland in 1714.

Hansard, *n.* the official report of the proceedings of the British Parliament, named after Luke Hansard (1752–1828), printer of the House of Commons *Journal* from 1774. The first official reports were published from 1803 by the political journalist Cobbett, who during his imprisonment 1810–12 sold the business to his printer, Thomas Curson Hansard, son of Luke Hansard. The publication of the debates remained in the hands of the family until 1889, and is now the responsibility of the Stationery Office. The name *Hansard* was officially adopted 1943. **Hansardize, -ise,** *v.t.* to produce the official record of an MP's former utterances in order to confute him.

Hanse, Hansa, *n.* a corporation or guild of merchants; the Hanseatic League; the entrance-fee of a mediaeval guild. **Hanse Towns,** *n.pl.* the towns which confederated to form the Hanseatic League. **Hanseatic,** *a.* **Hanseatic League,** *n.* a confederation of N European trading cities from the 12th cent. to 1669. At its height in the later 14th cent. the Hanseatic League included over 160 towns, among them Lübeck, Hamburg, Cologne, Breslau, and Cracow. The basis of its power was its monopoly of the Baltic trade and its relations with Flanders and England. The decline of the Hanseatic League from the 15th cent. was caused by the movement of trade routes and the development of national states. †**hanaster, hanster,** *n.* (*Oxford*) the ancient name for persons who paid the entrance-fee of the guild-merchant and were admitted as freemen of the city. [OF, from OHG *Hansa,* a company]

Hansel and Gretel, a fairy tale, collected by the Grimm brothers. Hansel and Gretel are children abandoned in the forest by their poor parents. They find a cottage made of gingerbread and are captured by the child-eating witch who lives there, but escape by wit and ingenuity. The happy ending reunites them with their parents. The story was made into a children's opera by Humperdinck in 1893.

Hansom, *n.* **Joseph Aloysius** (1803–82), British architect. His works include the Birmingham town hall 1831, but he is remembered as the introducer of the **hansom cab** in 1834, a two-wheel carriage with a seat for the driver on the outside.

han't, (*sl.*) HAVE NOT.

hant, *n.* (*N Am. dial.*) a ghost. [HAUNT]

hantle, (*Sc. and North.*) *n.* a good many; a good deal. [etym. unknown]

Hants, (*abbr.*) Hampshire.

Hanukkah, *n.* eight-day festival in Judaism which takes place at the beginning of Dec. It celebrates the recapture of the Temple in Jerusalem by Judas Maccabeus in 164 BC.

Hanuman, *n.* in the Sanskrit epic *Rāmāyana*, the Hindu monkey god and king of Hindustan (N India). He assisted Rama (an incarnation of the god Vishnu) to recover his wife Sita, abducted by Ravana of Lanka (modern Sri Lanka). **hanuman,** *n.* entellus monkey.

hap[1]**,** *n.* chance, luck; that which happens or chances; a casual event. *v.i.* (*past, p.p.* **happed**) to befall, to happen by chance. **hapless,** *a.* unhappy, unfortunate, luckless. **haplessly,** *adv.* **haply,** *adv.* by hap; perhaps. [prob. from Icel. *happ* (cp. OE *gehæp,* fit)]

hap[2]**,** *v.t.* (*Sc.*) to cover over; to wrap up. *n.* a covering. [etym. unknown]

hapalote, *n.* (*Austral.*) a genus of non-marsupial rodents, also known as jumping mice.

haphazard, *n.* mere chance, accident. *a.* happening by chance; random. **at haphazard,** by chance, casually. **haphazardly,** *adv.* **haphazardness,** *n.*

haplo-, *comb. form.* single, simple.

haplodont, *a.* having the crowns of the molar teeth simple, not ridged. *n.* one of the Haplodontidae, an American family of marmot-like rodents regarded as a connecting-link between the beavers and the squirrels.

haplography, *n.* inadvertent writing of a word or letter once which should be written twice, as *superogatory* for *supererogatory*.

haploid, *a.* having half the usual number. **haplology,** *n.* the omission in speech of one or more similar sounds or syllables; having a single set of unpaired chromosomes.

haply HAP[1].

ha'p'orth HALFPENNY.

happen, *v.i.* to fall out; to hap; to chance (to); to light (upon). **happening,** *n.* (*usu. in pl.*) something that happens, a chance occurrence; (*coll.*) a spontaneous event, performance etc. *a.* (*esp. N Am. sl.*) trendy, modern.

happy, *a.* lucky, fortunate; prosperous, successful; enjoying pleasure from the fruition or expectation of good; contented, satisfied; apt, felicitous; favourable; dexterous, ready, skilful; (*coll.*) slightly drunk; (*in comb.*) in a dazed state. †*v.t.* to make happy. **happy-go-lucky,** *a.* careless, thoughtless, improvident. **happy dispatch** HARA-KIRI. **happily,** *adv.* **happiness,** *n.* [HAP[1], -Y]

happy hour, *n.* a period when a bar etc. sells drinks at reduced prices to attract customers. **happy hunting-ground,** (*coll.*) an area of activity offering easy rewards.

Hapsburg, *n.* English form of HABSBURG.

haptic, *a.* relating to the sense of touch. [Gr. *haptein,* to touch]

hapuka, *n.* a New Zealand fish, the grouper. [Maori]

Haq, *n.* **Fazlul** (1873–1962), leader of the Bengali Muslim peasantry. He was a member of the Viceroy's Defence Council, established 1941, and was Bengal's first Indian prime minister (1937–43).

haquebut, HACKBUT.

†**haqueton,** ACTON.

hara-kiri, *n.* a Jap. method of suicide by disembowelling; happy dispatch. [Jap. *hara,* belly, *kiri,* cutting]

haram HAREM.

harangue, *n.* a declamatory address to a large assembly; a noisy and vehement speech, a tirade. *v.i.* to make an harangue. *v.t.* to address in an angry, vehement way. **haranguer,** *n.* [MF, from med. L *harenga* or It. *aringa,* prob. from OHG *Hring,* a ring (of people)]

Harare, *n.* capital of Zimbabwe, on the Mashonaland plateau about 1525 m/5000 ft. above sea level; population (1982) 656,000. It is the centre of a rich farming area (tobacco and maize), with metallurgical and food processing industries.

harass, *v.t.* to torment by or as by importunity; to worry, to molest; to tire out with care or worry; (*Mil.*) to worry by repeated attacks. †*n.* harassment. **harassed,** *a.* **harasser,** *n.* **harassment,** *n.* the act of harassing; the state of being harassed. [MF *harasser,* perh. from OF *harer,* to hound a dog on]

Harbin *n.* (formerly **Haerhpin** and **Pinkiang**), port on the Songhua river, NE China; capital of Heilongjiang province; population (1986) 2,630,000. Industries include metallurgy, machinery, paper, food processing, and sugar refining, and it is a major rail junction. Harbin was developed by Russian settlers after Russia was granted trading rights there in 1896, and more Russians arrived as refugees after the October Revolution in 1917.

harbinger, *n.* one who went before to provide lodgings for an approaching guest; a precursor; one who or that which goes before and foretells what is coming. *v.t.* to precede as harbinger; to announce the approach of. [ME *herbergeour,* OF *herbergere,* from *herberge* (F *auberge*), OHG *Heriberga* (*hari,* army, *bergan,* to shelter)]

harbour, (*N Am.*) **harbor**, *n.* a refuge, esp. a refuge or shelter for ships; a port or haven; an asylum, shelter, security; †a lodging, an inn. *v.t.* to shelter, to entertain, to cherish, to foster; †to trace (a hart or hind) to its covert. *v.i.* †to come to anchor in a harbour; to take shelter, to lodge. **habour-dues,** *n.pl.* charges for mooring or accommodating a ship in a harbour. **harbour-master,** *n.* an official having charge of the berthing and mooring of ships in a harbour. **harbour-watch,** *n.* (*Naut.*) ANCHOR-WATCH, ANCHOR. **harbourage,**, *n.* shelter, harbour, refuge. **harbourer,** *n.* one who harbours another; one who traces a hart or hind to its covert. **harbourless,** *a.* [ME *hereberge,* perh. from OE (*here,* army, *beorg,* shelter), cp. *prec.*]

Harcourt, *n.* **William Vernon** (1827–1904), British Liberal politician. Under Gladstone he was home secretary (1880–85) and chancellor of the Exchequer (1886 and 1892–95). He is remembered for his remark in 1892: 'We are all Socialists now.'

hard, *a.* firm, solid, compact; not yielding to pressure; difficult of accomplishment, comprehension or explanation; laborious, fatiguing, toilsome; intricate, perplexing; harsh, severe, galling, inflexible, cruel, unfeeling; sordid, miserly, stingy; difficult to bear, oppressive, unjust; (of a drug) highly addictive and harmful; coarse, unpalatable; rough and harsh to the palate, the touch etc.; containing mineral salts unfitting it for washing (of water); (*Phon.*) sounded gutturally (as *c* and *g* when not pronounced like *s* and *j*), aspirated (as *k, t, p,* compared with *g, d, b*); (*Art.*) adhering too rigidly to the mere mechanism of art. *adv.* forcibly, violently; strenuously, severely; with effort or difficulty; close, near; (*Naut.*) as hard as possible, to the utmost limit. *n.* something that is hard; a firm landing-place, jetty or roadway; (*coll.*) hard cash; (*sl.*) hard labour. **hard and fast,** strict; that must be strictly adhered to. **hard-a-lee, -a-port, -a-starboard, -a-weather, down,** (*Naut.*) as far as it will go in the direction indicated (of the tiller). **hard by,** close by; close at hand. **hard put to it,** in straits, in difficulties. **hard upon,** close behind. **hard of hearing,** rather deaf. **to die hard,** to die only after a struggle, or impenitent. **to go hard with,** to fare ill with. **hard-bake,** *n.* a kind of toffee in which blanched almonds are mixed. **hardback,** *n.* a book with a stiff binding. **hardbacked,** *a.* **hard-baked,** *n.* cooked until hard. **hard-beam** HORNBEAM under HORN. **hard-bitten,** *a.* used to hard biting; tough, resolute. **hardboard,** *n.* a form of compressed fibreboard. **hard-boiled,** *a.* boiled until hard; (*sl., coll.*) hard, sophisticated, unemotional, callous; shrewd, hard-headed. **hard case,** *n.* a tough or violent person; (*Austral.*) an amusing fellow. **hard coal,** *n.* anthracite, non-bituminous coal. **hard cash,** *n.* money in the form of coins and notes. **hard cheese,** (*coll.*) hard luck. **hard copy,** (*Comput.*) copy that can be ready without the use of a word processor etc. **hardcore,** *n.* refuse stone, brickbats etc., crushed to form the substratum of a road; members of a group devoted to their beliefs and resistant to change. *a.* loyal to beliefs and resistant to change; of pornography, sexually explicit. **hard currency,** *n.* (*Fin.*) coin, metallic money; currency unlikely to depreciate suddenly or fluctuate in value. **hard doer,** *n.* (*Austral.*) a smart Alec, a tough nut. **hard drinker,** *n.* a drunkard. **hard-earned,** *a.* earned with difficulty. †**hard-faced,** *a.* having a harsh or stern face. **hard-favoured, -featured,** *a.* of harsh features; ill-looking, ugly. **hard fern,** a fern of the genus *Lomaria,* esp. *L. spicant* or *L. blechnum.* **hard-fisted,** *a.* having hard, strong hands; close, miserly. **hard-fought,** *a.* closely contested. **hard-got, -gotten,** *a.* hard-earned. **hard-grained,** *a.* having a close, firm grain; (*fig.*) unattractive. **hardhack,** *n.* (*N Am.*) New England shrub, *Spiraea tomentosa.* **hard-handed,** *a.* having hard, rough hands; (*fig.*) harsh, severe. **hard hat,** *n.* a protective helmet, such as worn on construction sites. **hard-head,** *n.* a hard-headed person; the menhaden and other fishes. †**hard-heads,** *n.* a manner of fighting in which the combatants dashed their heads together. **hard-headed,** *a.* matter-of-fact, practical, not sentimental. **hard-hearted,** *a.* cruel, unfeeling, pitiless. **hardheartedly,** *adv.* **hardheartedness,** *n.* **hard hit,** seriously damaged, especially by monetary losses; smitten with love. **hard-hitting,** *a.* forceful; effective. **hard labour,** *n.* enforced labour, esp. when added to imprisonment. **hard-line,** *a.* (of a policy) uncompromising; extreme. **hard-liner,** *n.* a person following a hard-line policy. **hard lines,** *n.pl.* hard luck. **hard luck,** *n.* misfortune, lack of success. **hard metal,** *n.* sintered tungsten carbide, for high-speed cutting tools. **hard-mouthed,** *a.* insensible to the action of the bit (of a horse); (*fig.*) harsh, severe in language. **hard-nosed,** *a.* (*coll.*) unsentimental; tough. **hard-on,** *n.* (*sl.*) an erect penis. **hard pad,** *n.* a form of distemper in dogs. **hard pan,** *n.* (*N Am.*) a firm subsoil of sand or gravel; a firm foundation. **hard porn,** *n.* (*coll.*) sexually explicit pornography. **hard pressed,** *a.* closely pressed; in straits. **hard sell,** *n.* (*coll.*) aggressive selling, advertising etc. **hard-set,** *a.* rigid, stony, inflexible; firmly set (as an egg). **hard-shell,** *a.* having a hard shell (as a crab); (*fig.*) rigid, unyielding, uncompromising; (*Amer.*) a term applied to a strict sect of Baptists. **hard shoulder,** *n.* an extra lane beside the nearside lane of a motorway etc. used for stopping in emergencies. **hard standing,** *n.* a hard surface, e.g. tarmac, on which a vehicle etc. may stand. **hard-tack,** *n.* coarse ship-biscuit. **hard-up,** *a.* in great want, esp. of money; very poor; as far as possible to windward (of the tiller). **hard-valve,** *n.* a thermionic valve which is very highly exhausted of gas. **hardware,** *n.* articles of metal, ironmongery etc.; items of machinery, weaponry etc. (*Comput.*) the physical apparatus of a computer system, contrasted with the programs for it (cp. SOFTWARE). **hardwareman,** *n.* one who deals in hardware; **hard-wearing,** *a.* durable. **hard wheat,** *n.* a type of wheat with hard kernels that are high in gluten, used for making bread and pasta. **hard-won,** *a.* won with difficulty. **hardwood,** *n.* close-grained wood from deciduous trees, as dist. from pines etc. **hardwooded,** *a.* **hard-working,** *a.* working hard and diligently. **hard water,** *n.* water which from holding mineral salts in solution is unfit for washing purposes. **hardish,** *a.* **hardly,** *adv.* with difficulty; harshly, rigorously; unfavourably; scarcely, not quite. **hardness,** *n.* **hardly earned,** *a.* earned with difficulty. [OE *heard* (cp. Dut. *hard,* Icel. *harthr,* G *hart,* also Gr. *kratus,* strong)]

hardanger, *n.* decorative needlework in square and diamond patterns, originally done at Hardanger. *a.* on this pattern (of needlework designs). [city in Norway]

harden, *v.t.* to make hard or harder; to temper (tools); to confirm (in effrontery, wickedness, obstinacy etc.); to make firm; to make insensible, unfeeling or callous. *v.i.* to become hard or harder; to become unfeeling or inured; to become confirmed (in vice); (of prices) become stable. **hardener,** *n.* one who or that which hardens, esp. one who tempers tools; (*Phot.*) chemical placed in gelatine negatives to prevent the film melting in hot weather.

Hardenberg, *n.* **Karl August von** (1750–1822), Prussian politician, foreign minister to King Frederick William III of Prussia during the Napoleonic Wars. He later became chancellor. His military and civic reforms were restrained by the reactionary tendencies of the king.

Hardicanute *n.* (*c.* 1019–1042), king of England from 1040. Son of Canute, he was king of Denmark from 1028. In England he was known as a harsh ruler.

Hardie, *n.* **(James) Keir** (1856–1915), Scottish socialist, member of Parliament for West Ham, London, (1892–95) and for Merthyr Tydfil, Wales, from 1900. Born in Lanarkshire, he worked in the mines as a boy, and in 1886 became secretary of the Scottish Miners' Federation. In 1888 he was the first Labour candidate to stand for Parliament; he entered Parliament independently as a Labour member in 1892 and was a chief founder of the Independent Labour Party in 1893.

Harding, *n.* **Warren G(amaliel)** (1865–1923), 29th president of the US (1921–23), a Republican. He was born in Ohio, and entered the US Senate in 1914. As president he concluded the peace treaties of 1921 with Germany, Austria and Hungary, and in the same year called the Washington Conference. He opposed US membership of the League of Nations. There were charges of corruption among members of his cabinet (the TEAPOT DOME SCANDAL).

hardock, *n.* (*Shak.*) a coarse kind of plant, prob. the burdock. [prob. from OE *hār,* hoar, DOCK[1]]

Hardouin-Mansart (1646–1708), *n.* French architect, royal architect to Louis XIV from 1675. He designed the lavish baroque extensions to the palace of Versailles (from 1678) and the Invalides Chapel in Paris (1680–91).

hards, *n.pl.* the coarse or refuse part of flax or wool. [OE *heordan* (cp. MDut. *heerde, herde*), not cogn. with HARD]

hardship, *n.* that which is hard to bear, as privation, suffering, toil, fatigue, oppression, injury, injustice.

hardy, *a.* bold, over-confident, audacious; inured to fatigue, robust; (of plants) capable of bearing exposure to winter weather. *n.* an ironsmith's chisel fixed upright, usu. in a **hardy-hole** or socket in an anvil, for cutting metal etc. **hardy annual,** an annual plant that may be sown in the open; a question that crops up annually or periodically. **hardihood,** †**hardiesse**, *n.* boldness, daring; audacity, effrontery. **hardily,** *adv.* in a daring or audacious manner. †**hardiment, hardiness,** *n.* [F *hardi,* orig. p.p. of *hardir,* from Teut. (OHG *hartjan,* to make strong, cp. OE *heard,* HARD)]

Hardy[1], *n.* **Oliver** (1892–1957), US film comedian, member of the duo Laurel and Hardy.

Hardy[2], *n.* **Thomas** (1840–1928), English novelist and poet. His novels, set in rural 'Wessex' (his native West Country), portray intense human relationships played out in a harshly indifferent natural world. They include *Far From the Madding Crowd* (1874), *The Return of the Native* (1878), *The Mayor of Casterbridge* (1886), *The Woodlanders* (1887), *Tess of the D'Urbervilles* (1891), and *Jude the Obscure* (1895). His poetry includes the *Wessex Poems* (1898), the blank-verse epic *The Dynasts* (1904–08), and several volumes of lyrics.

hare, *n.* a long-eared short-tailed rodent of the genus *Lepus,* with cleft upper lip, esp. *L. timidus,* similar to but larger than the rabbit. **hare and hounds,** a paper-chase. **to run with the hare and hunt with the hounds,** to keep in with both sides. **jugged hare** JUG[1]. **hare-bell,** *n.* the blue-bell of Scotland, *Campanula rotundifolia,* the round-leaved bell-flower. †**hare-brain,** *a.* hare-brained. *n.* a hare-brained person. **hare-brained,** *a.* (*coll.*) rash, giddy, flighty. †**hare-hearted,** *a.* timid, fearful, timorous. **hare-lip,** *n.* a congenital fissure of the upper lip. **hare-lipped,** *a.* **hare's-foot,** *n.* a species of clover, *Trifolium arvense;* a tropical American cork-tree, *Ochroma lagopus.* [OE *hara* (cp. Dut. *haas,* Dan. and Swed. *hare,* G *Hase*)]

Hare, *n.* **David** (1947–), British dramatist and director, whose plays include *Slag* (1970), *Teeth 'n' Smiles* (1975), *Pravda* (1985) (with Howard Brenton), and *Wrecked Eggs* (1986).

Hare Krishna, *n.* popular name for a member of the International Society for Krishna Consciousness, derived from their chant.

harem, *n.* the apartments reserved for the women in a Muslim household; the occupants of these; a Muslim sanctuary (usu. **haram,** hərahm'). [Arab. *haram,* from *harama,* be prohibited]

Hare's apparatus, *n.* in physics, a specific kind of hydrometer used to compare the relative densities of two liquids, or to find the density of one if the other is known. It was invented by US chemist Robert Hare (1781–1858).

Hargobind *n.* (1595–1644), Indian religious leader, sixth guru (teacher) of Sikhism (1606–44). He encouraged Sikhs to develop military skills in response to growing persecution. At the festival of DIWALI, Sikhs celebrate his release from prison.

Hargraves, *n.* **Edward Hammond** (1816–91), Australian prospector, born in England. In 1851 he found gold in the Blue Mountains of New South Wales, thus beginning the first Australian gold rush.

Hargreaves, *n.* **James** (died 1778), English inventor, who co-invented a carding machine in 1760. About 1764 he invented his 'spinning-jenny', which enabled a number of threads to be spun simultaneously by one person.

haricot, *n.* a stew or ragout of meat, usu. mutton, with beans and other vegetables; the kidney or French bean, *Phaseolus vulgaris.* **haricot-bean,** *n.* [F, etym. doubtful]

haridan, HARRIDAN.

Harijan, *n.* member of the Indian caste of untouchables. The name was coined by Mahatma Gandhi.

hari-kari, HARA-KIRI.

hark, *v.i.* to listen. *v.t.* to listen to (usu. in imper., listen). **hark forward! hark away!** cries to urge hounds. **hark back!** calling hounds back when they have passed the scent, hence **to hark back,** to return to some point or matter from which a temporary digression has been made. [ME *herkien* (cogn. with OFris. *herkia,* MDut. *horken,* G *horchen*)]

harken, HEARKEN.

Har Krishen *n.* (1656–64), Indian religious leader, eighth guru (teacher) of Sikhism (1661–64), who died at the age of eight.

harl[1], *n.* filaments of flax; fibrous substance; a barb of a feather, esp. one from a peacock's tail used in making artificial flies. [cp. MLG *Herle, Harl,* LG *Harl*]

harl[2], *v.t.* (*Sc. and North.*) to drag along the ground; to rough-cast (a wall) with lime. *v.i.* to drag oneself; (*Angling*) to troll. *n.* the act of harling; a small amount or quantity. [etym. unknown]

Harleian, *a.* of or pertaining to Robert and his son Edward Harley and the library collected by them, now in the British Museum. [Robert *Harley,* Earl of Oxford, 1661–1724]

Harlem Globetrotters, *n. pl.* US touring basketball team who play exhibition matches worldwide. Comedy routines as well as their great skills are a feature of the games. They were founded by Abraham Saperstein (1903–1966) in 1927.

Harlem Renaissance, *n.* a movement in US literature in the 1920s that used black life and traditional black culture as its subject matter; it was an early manifestation of black pride in the US. The centre of the movement was the Harlem area of New York City.

harlequin, *n.* the leading character in a pantomime or harlequinade, adopted from Italian comedy; supposed to be invisible to the clown, he is dressed in a mask, parti-coloured and spangled clothes, and bears a magic wand; a buffoon; the harlequin duck. *v.i.* to act as a harlequin. †*v.t.* to conjure away as with a harlequin's wand. **harlequin duck,** *n.* a sea-duck with variegated plumage, *Histronicus minutus,* of the northern hemisphere. **harlequina**, **harlequiness**, *n. fem.* **harle-**

quinade, *n.* that part of a pantomime in which the harlequin and clown play the principal parts; an extravaganza; a piece of fantastic conduct. **harlequinesque**, *a.*

harlot, *n.* a woman who prostitutes herself for hire. †*v.i.* to play the harlot. **harlotry,** *n.* the practices or trade of a harlot; lewdness, incontinence; †ribaldry. [OF, orig. masc., vagabond, rogue, cp. It. *arlotto* (etym. doubtful)]

Harlow, *n.* **Jean** (1911–37), stage name of Harlean Carpenter, US film actress, the first 'platinum blonde'. Her films include *Hell's Angels* (1930), *Dinner At Eight* (1934), and *Saratoga* (1937).

harm, *n.* hurt, injury, damage, evil. *v.t.* to injure, hurt or damage. **out of harm's way,** safe. **harmful,** *a.* hurtful, injurious, detrimental. **harmfully,** *adv.* **harmfulness,** *n.* **harmless,** *a.* not hurtful or injurious; uninjured, unharmed. **harmlessly,** *adv.* **harmlessness,** *n.* [OE *hearm* (cp. Icel. *harmr,* G *Harm*)]

harmala, harmel, *n.* wild rue. **harmaline**, *n.* a white crystalline alkaloid obtained from the seeds of this. [late L and Gr. *harmala,* from Sansk. (cp. Arab. *harmil*)]

harman, *n.* (*sl.*) a policeman. †**harman-beck,** *n.* a parish constable or beadle. †**harmans,** *n.pl.* the stocks.

harmattan, *n.* a dry hot wind blowing from the interior of Africa to the upper Guinea coast in December, January and February. [Fanti *haramata*]

harmonic, *a.* pertaining to harmony or music; concordant, harmonious. *n.* a harmonic tone; †(*pl.*) the science of musical sounds. *n.pl.* (*Radio.*) frequencies which are multiples of a main frequency; the waves that are incidental to the main waves of a transmitter. **harmonic progression,** *n.* a series of numbers whose reciprocals are in arithmetical progression, as 1/5, 1/7, 1/9 etc. **harmonic quantities,** *n.pl.* numbers or quantities having this relation. **harmonic proportion,** *n.* the relation of three consecutive terms of a harmonic progression. **harmonic tones,** *n.pl.* tones produced by the vibration of aliquot parts of a string, column of air etc. **harmonical,** *a.* **harmonically,** *adv.* **harmonica, -on**, *n.* a musical instrument of various kinds, as musical glasses, mouth-organ, a series of glass or metal plates of graduated lengths played on with a small mallet etc. **harmonious** HARMONY. **harmonist**[1] HARMONY. [L *harmonicus,* Gr. *harmonikos,* from *harmonia,* HARMONY]

harmoniphon, *n.* a small musical instrument with reeds or reeds and pipes, played by means of a keyboard. [Gr. *harmonia,* HARMONY, *-phōnos,* sounding, from *phōnē,* a sound]

Harmonist, -nite, *n.* one of a communistic sect founded by the brothers Rapp, who emigrated from Württemberg to the US in 1803, and settled in Harmony. [*Harmony,* Pennsylvania]

harmonium, *n.* a keyed musical wind-instrument whose tones are produced by the forcing of air through free reeds. [F]

harmonograph, *n.* an instrument for determining the resultant of two simple harmonic motions in different planes.

harmonometer, *n.* an instrument for measuring the harmonic relation of sounds.

harmony, *n.* the just adaptation of parts to each other, so as to form a complete, symmetrical or pleasing whole; the agreeable combination of simultaneous sounds, music; an arrangement of musical parts for combination with an air or melody; the science dealing with musical combination of sounds; concord or agreement in views, sentiments etc.; a literary work showing the agreement between parallel or corresponding passages of different authors, esp. of the Gospels. **harmony of the spheres,** the theory derived from Pythagoras that the revolving spheres in which the heavenly bodies were supposed to be carried round the earth emitted musical sounds varying according to their magnitude, velocity and relative distance. **pre-established harmony,** (*Phil.*) according to Leibnitz, a harmony established between mind and matter by God at the Creation. **harmonious**, *a.* concordant, having harmony; having parts adapted and proportioned to each other, symmetrical; without discord or dissension; musical, tuneful. **harmoniously,** *adv.* **harmoniousness,** *n.* **harmonist**, *n.* one skilled in harmony; a musical composer; one who treats of and shows the agreement between corresponding passages of different authors. **harmonistic**, *a.* **harmonize, -ise,** *v.t.* to make harmonious; to arrange in musical concord, to add the proper accompaniment to; to adjust in proper proportions; to cause to agree (with). *v.i.* to agree in sound or effect; to live in peace and concord; to correspond, to be congruous (with). **harmonization, -isation,** *n.* **harmonizer, -iser,** *n.* [F *harmonie,* L and Gr. *harmonia* (*harmos,* a fitting or joining, from the root *ar-,* to fit)]

harmost, *n.* (*Gr. Hist.*) a Spartan governor of a subject city, island etc. **harmosty,** *n.* [Gr. *harmostēs,* from *harmozein,* to fit, to put in order]

harmotome, *n.* (*Min.*) a vitreous hydrous silicate of aluminium and barium characterized by cross-shaped crystals, sometimes called cross-stone. [F, from Gr. *harmos,* joint, *-tomos,* cutting, from *temnein,* to cut]

harness, *n.* the working gear of a horse or other draught-animal; the accoutrement of a knight or man-at-arms, arms and armour; working apparatus or equipment in various mechanical operations; an arrangement of straps etc. to hold a person or thing safely, e.g. in a pram, car seat etc; a device in a loom for raising and lowering the warp-threads; business equipment. *v.t.* to equip with armour; to put harness on (a horse etc.); to utilize natural forces, e.g. water, for motive power. **in harness,** at work. **to die in harness,** to continue to the last in one's business or profession. **harness-cask, -tub,** *n.* (*Naut.*) a large cask or tub with a rimmed cover, containing the supply of salt meat for immediate use. **harness racing,** *n.* a type of trotting with horses harnessed to a two-wheeled trap. **harnesser,** *n.* **harnessry,** *n.* [MG and OF *harneis,* etym. doubtful]

harns, *n.pl.* (*Sc.*) brains. [from MG *hœrnes,* prob. from Scand. (cp. Icel. *hjarne,* OHG *hirni,* G *Hirn*)]

haro, *int.* a call for help or to raise a hue-and-cry; (*Channel Islands*) a cry constituting a form of legal appeal against encroachment on property. [OF, etym. doubtful]

Harold I *n.* (died 1040), king of England from 1035. The illegitimate son of Canute, known as Harefoot, he claimed the throne in 1035 when the legitimate heir Hardicanute was in Denmark. In 1037 he was elected king.

Harold II *n.* (*c.* 1020–66), king of England from Jan. 1066. He succeeded his father Earl Godwin 1053 as earl of Wessex. In 1063 William of Normandy (William I) tricked him into swearing to support his claim to the English throne, and when the Witan elected Harold to succeed Edward the Confessor, William prepared to invade. Meanwhile, Harold's treacherous brother Tostig (died 1066) joined the king of Norway, Harald III Hardrada (1015–66), in invading Northumbria. Harold routed and killed them at Stamford Bridge 25 Sept. Three days later William landed at Pevensey, Sussex; Harold was killed at the Battle of Hastings 14 Oct. 1066.

harp, *n.* a musical instrument of triangular shape, with strings which are plucked by the fingers. *v.i.* to play upon a harp. **to harp on,** to dwell incessantly upon anything. **harp-seal,** *n.* an Arctic seal with dark bands on its back resembling the former saddle shape of a harp. **harp-shell,** *n.* a tropical genus of molluscs. **harper, harpist,** *n.* a player on the harp. **harpress**, *n.fem.* a female harp-player. [OE *hearpe* (cp. Dut. *harp.* Icel. *harpa,* G *Harfe*)]

harpings, *n.pl.* the fore parts of the wales encompassing the bow or extensions of the rib-bands of a vessel. [prob. from prec.]

harpoon, *n.* a barbed, spearlike missile weapon with a line attached, used for striking and killing whales etc. *v.t.* to strike, catch or kill with a harpoon. **harpoon-**

gun, *n.* a gun for firing a harpoon. **harpoon-rocket,** *n.* a combination of bomb and lance for killing whales. **harpooneer**, †**harpooner,** *n.* [F *harpon,* from *harpe,* a claw, late L and Gr. *harpē,* a sickle]

harpsichord, *n.* a stringed instrument with a keyboard actuating quills that pluck instead of hammers that strike, similar in form to the pianoforte, by which it was superseded. [OF *harpechorde* (*harpe,* HARP, *chorde,* CHORD1)]

Harpy, *n.* (*pl.* **-pies**) in early Gr. mythology, a wind spirit; in later legend a fabulous monster represented with the face of a woman, the body of a vulture and fingers armed with sharp claws; **(harpy)** an extortioner, a rapacious person or animal; a harpy-eagle. **harpy-eagle,** *n.* a crested eagle, *Thrasaëtus harpyia,* from S America. **harpy-footed,** *a.* with claws like a harpy. [OF *harpie,* L *harpyiae,* Gr. *harpuiai* (pl.), from the root *harp-,* to seize]

harquebus, *n.* an old kind of musket fired from a forked hand-rest or tripod. **harquebusade,** *n.* the discharge from a harquebus; †a vulnerary water for the cure of gunshot wounds. **harquebusier,** *n.* [F *harquebuse,* It. *arcobugio* (*arco,* bow, *bugio,* a hole), a pop. corr. of MHG *Haekbüsse,* see HACKBUT]

harr, HAAR.

Har Rai (1630–61), *n.* Indian religious leader, seventh guru (teacher) of Sikhism (1644–61).

harridan, *n.* a worn-out haggard old woman; an old vixen; an ill-tempered woman. [prob. from MF *haridelle,* a worn-out horse]

Harrier, *n.* the only truly successful vertical take-off and landing fixed-wing aircraft, often called the jump jet. Built in Britain, it made its first flight in 1966. It has a single jet engine and a set of swivelling nozzles. These deflect the jet exhaust vertically downwards for take-off and landing, and to the rear for normal flight. Designed to fly from confined spaces with minimal ground support, it refuels in midair.

harrier1, *n.* a variety of dog, smaller than the foxhound, used for hare-hunting by mounted huntsmen; (*pl.*) a pack of such hounds, or a club of cross-country or hare-and-hounds runners. [HARE, -ER]

harrier2, *n.* one who harries or plunders; a falconoid bird of the genus *Circus*. [HARRY1, -ER]

Harriman, *n.* **(William) Averell** (1891–1986), US diplomat, administrator of lend-lease in World War II, Democratic secretary of commerce in Truman's administration, 1946–1948, negotiator of the Nuclear Test Ban Treaty with the USSR in 1963, and governor of New York (1955–58).

Harris1, *n.* **Arthur Travers** (1892–1984), British marshal of the Royal Air Force in World War II. Known as 'Bomber Harris', he was commander-in-chief of Bomber Command (1942–45).

Harris2, *n.* **Joel Chandler** (1848–1908), US author of the tales of 'Uncle Remus', based on black folklore, about Br'er Rabbit and the Tar Baby.

Harris3, *n.* **Richard** (1932–), Irish film actor known for playing rebel characters in such films as *This Sporting Life* (1963); *Il Deserto rosso/The Red Desert* (1964); *Camelot* (1967); *Cromwell* (1970); *Robin and Marion* (1976); *Tarzan the Ape Man* (1981).

Harrison1, *n.* **Benjamin** (1833–1901), 23rd president of the US (1889–93), a Republican. He called the first Pan-American Conference, which led to the establishment of the Pan American Union, to improve inter-American cooperation, and develop commercial ties. In 1948 this became the Organization of American States.

Harrison2, *n.* **(Reginald Carey) 'Rex'** (1908–90), British actor. His successes include *French Without Tears* (1936) and the musical *My Fair Lady* (stage 1956, film 1964). Films include *Blithe Spirit* (1944) and *Cleopatra* (1962).

Harrison3, *n.* **William Henry** (1773–1841), 9th president of the US (1841). Elected 1840 as a Whig, he died a month after taking office. Benjamin Harrison was his grandson.

Harris Tweed®, *n.* a type of tweed woven in the Outer Hebrides.

Harrovian, *a.* of or pertaining to Harrow School. *n.* a person educated there. [*Harrow*-on-the-Hill, Middlesex]

harrow1, *n.* a large rake or frame with teeth, drawn over ground to level it, stir the soil, destroy weeds or cover seed. *v.t.* to draw a harrow over; to torment, to cause anguish or suffering to. **under the harrow,** in distress or tribulation. **harrowing,** *a.* causing anguish or torment. [MG *harwe,* etym. doubtful]

harrow2, *v.t.* to plunder, to spoil, to harry, to pillage. [HARRY1]

harrumph, *v.i.* to make a sound as if clearing one's throat, often to indicate disapproval. [imit.]

harry1, *v.t.* to plunder, to pillage, to lay waste; to harass. *v.i.* to make plundering excursions. [OE *hergian,* cogn. with *here,* army]

harry2, (*Sc.*) HARROW1.

Harry-long-legs DADDY-LONG-LEGS.

harsh, *a.* rough to the touch or other senses; discordant, irritating; austere, morose, severe; rigorous, inclement; unfeeling. †**harsh-resounding,** *a.* grating on the ear. †**harshen,** *v.t.* to make harsh. **harshly,** *adv.* **harshness,** *n.* [ME *harsk,* from Scand. (cp. Dan. *harsk,* Swed. *härsk,* G *harsch*)]

harslet HASLET.

hart, *n.* a stag, esp. a male red deer, from its fifth year onwards. **hart of ten,** a hart with ten tines on its antlers. **hart's-tongue,** *n.* a fern, *Scolopendrium vulgare,* with tongue-shaped leaves. [OE *heort, heorot,* from OTeut. *herut,* horned (cp. L *cervus,* stag, *keras -atos,* horn)]

Hart, *n.* **Gary** (1936–), US Democrat politician, senator for Colorado from 1974. In 1980 he contested the Democratic nomination for the presidency, and stepped down from his Senate seat in 1986 to stand, again unsuccessfully, in the 1988 presidential campaign.

hartal, *n.* a boycott in India, carried out by closing shops. [Hind. *hāt,* shop, *tālā,* bolt]

hartebeest, *n.* the S African *Alcephalus caama,* the commonest of the larger antelopes. [S Afr. Dut. (*hert,* hart, *beest,* beast)]

Hartley, *n.* **L(eslie) P(oles)** (1895–1972), English novelist, noted for his exploration of the sinister. His books include the trilogy *The Shrimp and the Anemone* (1944), *The Sixth Heaven* (1946), and *Eustace and Hilda* (1947), on the intertwined lives of a brother and sister. Later books include *The Boat* (1949), *The Go-Between* (1953), and *The Hireling* (1957).

hartshorn, *n.* a preparation from shavings or chippings of the horns of the hart; spirit of hartshorn. **salt of hartshorn,** impure carbonate of ammonia. **spirit of hartshorn,** a solution of ammonia in water, smelling-salts.

harum-scarum, *a.* giddy, hare-brained. *n.* a giddy, hare-brained person. [prob. compounded from HARE and SCARE]

Harun al-Rashid *n.* (AD 763–AD 809), caliph of Baghdad from AD 786 of the Abbasid dynasty, a lavish patron of music, poetry, and letters, known from the *Arabian Nights* stories.

haruspex, *n.* (*pl.*-**pices**) an ancient Etruscan or Roman soothsayer who divined the will of the gods by inspecting the entrails of victims. **haruspicy,** *n.* [L, lit. inspector of entrails (root from Sansk. *hird,* entrails, L *spic-,* to behold)]

harvest, *n.* the season of reaping and gathering crops, esp. of corn; ripe corn or other agricultural products gathered and stored; the yield of any natural product for the season; the product or result of any labour or conduct. *v.t.* to reap and gather in, as corn, grain etc.; to garner, to lay up; to receive as payment, penalty etc. **harvest-bug, -louse, -mite, -tick,** *n.* a minute tick, mite or acaridan which burrows in or attaches itself to the skin during late summer and autumn, setting up an irritating itch. **harvest feast,** *n.* a merry-making at the completion of the harvest. **harvest festival,** *n.* a religious service of thanksgiving for the harvest. **harvest**

home, *n.* the close of harvesting; a merry-making in celebration of this. **harvest lord,** *n.* the leading reaper whose motions regulate the others. **harvestman,** *n.* a labourer in the harvest; an arachnid with long slender legs. **harvest month,** *n.* the month of harvest, usually September. **harvest moon,** the moon at its full about the time of the autumnal equinox. **harvest mouse,** a very small fieldmouse, *Mus messorius,* which makes a nest usually among wheat-stalks. **harvest queen,** *n.* a person or image representing Ceres, the goddess of fruits, flowers etc. on the last day of harvest. **harvester,** *n.* a reaper; a reaping and binding machine; a harvest-bug. †**harvestless,** *a.* barren. [OE *hærfest* (cp. Dut. *herfst,* Icel. *haust,* G *Herbst*), from Teut. root *harb-* (cp. L *carpere,* to pluck)]

harvey, harveyize, -ise, *v.t.* to harden (steel plates for armoured ships) by a patent process of cementation; to fit a ship with plates hardened by this process. [H.A. *Harvey* 1824–93, of New Jersey, inventor]

Harvey[1], *n.* **Laurence (Lauruska Mischa Skikne)** (1928–73), British film actor of Lithuanian descent who worked both in England (*Room at the Top*, 1958) and in Hollywood (*The Alamo*, 1960; *The Manchurian Candidate*, 1962).

Harvey[2], *n.* **William** (1578–1657), English physician who discovered the circulation of blood. In 1628 he published his great book *De Motu Cordis/On the Motion of the Heart*.

Harwell, *n.* the main research establishment of the United Kingdom Atomic Energy Authority, situated near the village of Harwell in Oxfordshire.

Haryana, *n.* state of NW India. **area** 44,200 sq km/ 17,061 sq miles. **capital** Chandigarh. **population** (1981) 12,851,000. **products** sugar, cotton, oilseed, textiles, cement, iron ore. **language** Hindi.

has, HAVE. **has-been,** (*coll.*) one whose days of success, fame etc. are past; a not-so-young person.

hasard, HAZARD.

Hasdrubal Barca *n.* (died 207 BC), Carthaginian general, son of HAMILCAR BARCA and brother of HANNIBAL. He remained in command in Spain when Hannibal invaded Italy, and, after fighting there against the SCIPIOS until 208, marched to Hannibal's relief. He was defeated and killed in the Metaurus valley, NE Italy.

Hašek, *n.* **Jaroslav** (1883–1923), Czech writer. His masterpiece is the anti-authoritarian comic satire on military life under Austro-Hungarian rule, *The Good Soldier Schweik* (1923). During World War I he deserted to the Russians, and eventually joined the Bolsheviks.

hasel, HAZEL.

hash[1], *n.* meat, specially such as has already been cooked, cut into small pieces, mixed with vegetables and stewed etc.; (*N Am.*) shepherd's pie; a second preparation of old matter; (*coll.*) a mess, a muddle. *v.t.* to cut or chop up in small pieces; to mince. **to settle one's hash,** (*coll.*) to defeat a person completely. **hashmagandy,** *n.* (*Austral.*) bush stew. [OF *hachis*]

hash[2], *n.* (*coll.*) hashish.

hashish, *n.* the tender tops and sprouts of Indian hemp, *Cannabis indica* (see BHANG), used as a narcotic for smoking, chewing etc. [Arab. *hashīsh*]

Hasid, *n.* (*pl.* **-im**) a member of any of several mystical Jewish sects. **Hasidic,** *a.* [Heb. *hāsid,* pious]

hask, *n.* a case or basket made of rushes or flags etc. [prob. conn. with HASSOCK]

haslet, harslet, *n.* a part of the entrails, liver, heart etc. of an animal, usu. a hog, for roasting. [ME and OF *hastelet,* from *haste,* a spit, L *hasta,* a spear]

hasp, *n.* a fastening, esp. a clamp or bar hinged at one end, the other end passing over a staple, where it is secured by a pin, key or padlock; a skein of yarn. *v.t.* to fasten, shut or secure with a hasp. [OE *hæpse* (cp. Dut. *haspel,* Icel. *hespa,* G *Haspe*)]

Hassam, *n.* **Childe** (1859–1935), US impressionist painter and printmaker. He was profoundly influenced by a visit to Paris in 1866. He became one of the members of 'the Ten', a group of American impressionists who exhibited together until World War I.

Hassan II *n.* (1930–), king of Morocco from 1961; from 1976 he undertook the occupation of Western Sahara.

Hassidim, Chasidim,*n.* a mystic sect of ultra-conservative Orthodox Jews (see JUDAISM), founded in 18th-cent. Poland, which stressed intense emotion as a part of worship. Many of their ideas are based on the KABBALA.

hassle, *n.* (*coll.*) an argument; something causing difficulty or problems. *v.i.* to argue; to behave in a difficult or destructive way. *v.t.* to cause difficulty or problems for; to harass. [etym. doubtful]

hassock, *n.* a small stuffed footstool or cushion for kneeling on in church; a matted tuft of rank grass, a tussock; (*local*) soft calcareous sandstone separating the beds of Kentish rag. [OE *hassuc,* etym. doubtful, not from W *hesg,* sedges]

hast, HAVE.

hastate, *a.* triangular, like the head of a spear. [L *hastātus*, from *hasta,* spear]

haste, *n.* hurry, speed of movement of action, urgency, precipitance. *v.i.* to make haste. **to make haste,** to be quick; to be in a hurry. **hasten,** *v.t.* to cause to hurry; to urge or press on; to expedite. *v.i.* to move with haste or speed. **hastener,** *n.* **hasting,** *a.* hurrying; moving or acting hastily; coming early to maturity. *n.* (*prov.*) a fruit coming early to maturity, esp. a kind of early pea. **hasty,** *a.* hurried, quick; eager, precipitate; rash, inconsiderate; irritable; ripening early. †**hasty-footed,** *a.* nimble, swift. **hasty pudding,** flour stirred into boiling milk and the mixture boiled quickly. **hastily,** *adv.* **hastiness,** *n.* [OF *haste* (F *hâte*), whence *haster,* from WG *Haisti-,* violence (cp. OE *hæst*)]

hastelet HASLET.

Hastings[1], *n.* **Warren** (1732–1818), British colonial administrator. A protégé of Lord Clive, who established British rule in India, Hastings carried out major reforms, and became governor of Bengal in 1772 and governor general of India in 1774. Impeached for corruption on his return to England in 1785, he was acquitted in 1795.

Hastings[2], **Battle of,** battle on 14 Oct. 1066 at which William the Conqueror defeated Harold, king of England. The site is 10 km/6 miles inland of Hastings, at Senlac, Sussex; it is marked by Battle Abbey.

hasty etc. HASTE.

hat, *n.* a covering for the head, usu. having a crown or top and a continuous brim; the dignity of a cardinal, from the broad-brimmed scarlet hat worn by cardinals; a specified function. *v.t.* to provide, fit or cover with a hat. **at the drop of a hat** DROP. **old hat,** outdated, old-fashioned; familiar and dull. **to hang up one's hat,** to make oneself at home (in another's house). **to pass, send round the hat,** to ask for subscriptions, charity etc. **to raise the hat to,** to salute. **to talk through one's hat,** to talk about something one does not understand. **to throw one's hat into the ring,** to enter a contest, election etc. **hatband,** *n.* a band round a hat (esp. a black one as a sign of mourning). **hat block,** *n.* a block or mould for shaping or ironing hats. **hat-peg, -rack, -rail, -stand,** *n.* a contrivance or piece of furniture for hanging hats on. **hat trick,** *n.* the feat of taking three wickets with consecutive balls (from its being held to entitle the bowler to the reward of a new hat); the feat of one player scoring three goals etc. in one match; three successes in any area of activity. **hatful,** *n.* **hatless,** *a.* **hatter, hat-maker,** *n.* a maker of hats; (*Austral.*) a miner who works by himself; a bush recluse. [OE *hæt,* cogn. with HOOD]

hatch[1], *n.* a half-door, a wicket; an opening in a roof for access to the outside; an opening in a wall between two rooms; a flood-gate or a grated opening in a weir used for a fish-trap; (*Naut.*) a hatch-way, or a trap-door or shutter to cover this. †*v.t.* to fasten (a door etc.). **to be under hatches,** (*Naut.*) to be confined below; to be in a state of bondage or repression. **hatchback,** *n.* a car with a door at the back that opens upwards. **hatch-boat,** *n.* a kind of half-decked fishing-boat with a well for fish. **hatchway,** *n.* a large opening in the deck of a ship for lowering cargo etc. [OE *hæce* (cp. Dut. *hek,* Swed. *häck*), prob. conn. with OE *haca,* the bolt of a door]

hatch[2], *v.t.* to produce from eggs by incubation or artificial heat; to produce young from (eggs); to evolve, to contrive, to devise. *v.i.* to produce young (of eggs); to come out of the egg; to be developed from ova, cells of a brood-comb etc. *n.* act of hatching; a brood hatched. **to count one's chickens before they are hatched** CHICKEN. **hatches, matches and dispatches,** (*coll.*) newspaper announcements of births, marriages and deaths. **hatchery,** *n.* a place where fish ova are hatched artificially. [ME *hacchen* (cp. Swed. *häcka,* Dan. *hække*)]

hatch[3], *v.t.* to mark with fine lines, parallel or crossing each other; †to engrave, to chase; to inlay with thin strips of another material. *n.* a fine line in drawing or engraving. **hatched moulding,** *n.* (*Arch.*) ornamentation with a series of cuts or grooves crossing each other, common in Norman work. **hatching,** *n.* shading produced by lines crossing each other at more or less acute angles. [F *hacher,* see HASH]

hatchel, *v.t.* to dress flax; to heckle, to worry. [HACKLE[1]]

hatchet, *n.* a small axe with a short handle for use with one hand. **to bury, take up the hatchet,** to make peace or war. **to throw the hatchet,** to tell lies or fabulous stories. **hatchet-face,** *n.* a narrow face with sharp, prominent features. **hatchet-faced,** *a.* **hatchet job,** *n.* (*coll.*) a damaging attack on someone's reputation, argument etc. **hatchet-man,** *n.* (*coll.*) a person hired to carry out violent or illegal tasks; a person appointed to sack people in an organization. [F *hachette,* dim. of *hache* a sickle]

hatchment, *n.* a funeral escutcheon or panel bearing the coat of arms of a deceased person placed on the front of his house, in a church etc. [corr. of ACHIEVEMENT]

hate, *n.* extreme dislike or aversion; detestation. (*coll.*) a hated thing or person. *v.t.* to dislike exceedingly; to abhor, to detest. **hatable,** *a.* **hateful,** *a.* causing hate; odious, detestable; feeling hatred. **hatefully,** *adv.* **hatefulness,** *n.* †**hateless,** *a.* **hater,** *n.* †**hatesome,** *a.* hateful. **hatred,** *n.* exceeding dislike or aversion; active malevolence, animosity, enmity. [OE *hete,* from Teut. root *hat-,* whence *hatian,* to hate]

hath, HAVE.

Hathaway, *n.* **Anne** (1556–1623), wife of the English dramatist Shakespeare from 1582.

hatha yoga, *n.* a form of yoga involving physical exercises and breathing control. [Sansk. *hatha,* force, YOGA]

Hathor, *n.* in ancient Egyptian mythology, the sky-goddess, identified with ISIS.

hatred HATE.

Hatshepsut *n.* (*c.* 1540–*c.* 1481 BC), queen of Egypt during the 18th dynasty. She was the daughter of Thothmes I, with whom she ruled until the accession to the throne of her husband and half-brother Thotmes II. Throughout his reign real power lay with Hatshepsut, and she continued to rule after his death, as regent for her nephew Thotmes III.

Hattersley, *n.* **Roy** (1932–), British Labour politician. On the right wing of the Labour Party, he was prices secretary (1976–79), and in 1983 became deputy leader of the party.

Hatton, *n.* **Derek** (1948–), British left-wing politician, former deputy leader of Liverpool Council. A notorious member of the Militant Tendency, Hatton was removed from office and expelled from the Labour Party in 1987.

hauberk, *n.* a coat of mail, sometimes without sleeves, formed of interwoven steel rings. [OF *hauberc,* OHG *Halsberg* (*Hals,* neck, cp. HALS, *bergan,* cogn. with OE *beorgan,* to protect, see BURY)]

haugh, *n.* (*Sc. and North.*) a piece of low-lying land, esp. by a river. [prob. from OE *healh,* nook, corner]

Haughey, *n.* **Charles** (1925–), Irish Fianna Fáil politician of Ulster descent. Dismissed in 1970 from Jack Lynch's cabinet for alleged complicity in IRA gun-running, he was afterwards acquitted. Prime minister (1979–81, Mar.–Nov. 1982, and 1986–).

haughty, *a.* proud, arrogant, disdainful, supercilious; proceeding from or expressing disdainful pride; †lofty, high; †bold. **haughtily,** *adv.* **haughtiness,** *n.* [earlier *haught,* F *haut,* L *altus,* high]

haul, *v.t.* to pull or drag with force; to transport or move by dragging. *v.i.* to pull or drag (at or upon) with force; to alter the course of a ship. *n.* a hauling, a pull; the drawing of a net; the amount that is taken or stolen at once; take, acquisition. **a long haul,** (*coll.*) a long and wearisome task, journey etc. **to haul over the coals,** to take to task, to reprimand. **to haul up,** to bring for trial in a court of law. **to haul the wind,** to turn the head of the ship nearer to that point from which the wind blows. **haulabout,** *n.* a large steel coal-barge or lighter equipped with transporters. **haulage,** *n.* **hauler, haulier,** *n.* one who hauls, esp. a workman who hauls trucks to the bottom of the shaft in a coal-mine; a person or business that transports goods by lorry. [var. of HALE[2]]

haulm, *n.* a stem, a stalk; (*collect.*) the stems or stalks of peas, beans, potatoes etc. [OE *healm* (cp. Dut. and G *Halm,* Icel. *hālmr,* also L *culmus,* Gr. *kalamos,* reed)]

haunch, *n.* that part of the body between the ribs and the thigh; the buttock, the basal joint; the leg and loin of an animal as meat; (*Arch.*) the shoulder of an arch; †the rear, the hind part. **haunch-bone,** *n.* **haunched,** *a.* having haunches. [OF *hanche,* from Teut. (cp. OHG *Anchā*]

haunt, *v.t.* to frequent, to resort to often; to frequent the company of; to visit frequently, to recur to the mind of frequently in an irritating way; to frequent as a ghost or spirit; †to practise, to pursue. *v.i.* to stay or be frequently (about, in etc.). *n.* a place to which one often or customarily resorts; a resort, a den, a feeding-place for animals etc.; †practice, use; habit of frequenting a place; (*N Am.*) a ghost. **haunter,** *n.* **haunting,** *a.* **hauntingly,** *adv.* [OF *hanter,* etym. doubtful]

Hausa, *n.* (*pl.* **Hausa**) a member of a Muslim people occupying a large area of West Africa, esp. N Nigeria; their language, an Afro-Asiatic language which is a *lingua franca* of W Africa.

hausen, *n.* the huso. [G, from OHG *Hûso,* HUSO]

Hausfrau, *n.* a housewife. [G]

Haussa, HAUSA.

Haussmann, *n.* **Georges Eugène, Baron Haussmann** (1809–91), French administrator, who re-planned mediaeval Paris (1853–70), with wide boulevards and parks. The cost of his scheme and his authoritarianism caused opposition, and he was made to resign. **haussmannize,** *v.t.* to reconstruct or improve (a town, suburbs, streets etc.) by opening out and re-building.

haustellum, *n.* (*pl.* **-lla**) (*Zool.*) the sucking organ of certain insects and crustaceans. **haustellate,** *a.* [dim. from L *haustrum,* from *haurīre,* to draw (water)]

haustorium, *n.* (*Bot.*) a rootlet or sucker of a parasitic plant. [from L *haustor,* a drawer, as prec.]

hautboy, *n.* an oboe; an organ stop with a thin, soft tone; a tall species of strawberry, *Fragaria elatior.* [F *hautbois* (*haut,* L *altus,* high, *bois,* late L *boscus,* wood)]

haute couture , *n.* the designing and making of exclusive trend-setting fashions; the designers and houses creating such fashions. [F *haute,* high, *couture,* sewing]

haute cuisine, *n.* cooking of a very high standard. [F *haute,* high, *cuisine,* cooking]

haute ecole, *n.* difficult feats of horsemanship; a method of teaching these. [F]

Haute-Normandie, Upper Normandy, *n.* coastal region of NW France lying between Basse-Normandie and Picardy and bisected by the Seine; area 12,300 sq km/4,757 sq miles; population (1986) 1,693,000. It consists of the *départements* of Eure and Seine-Maritime; its capital is Rouen. Major ports include Dieppe and Fécamp. The area is noted for its beech forests.

hauteur, *n.* haughtiness, lofty manners or demeanour. [F, from *haut,* high]

haut monde, *n.* high society. [Fr. *haut,* high, *monde,* world]

haut-ton, *n.* high fashion; people of the most approved fashion. [F *haut,* high, *ton,* TONE, fashion]

haüyne, *n.* (*Min.*) a vitreous silicate of aluminium and sodium with calcium sulphate, found in igneous rocks. [F, from R.J. *Haüy* 1743–1822, French mineralogist]

Havana[1], *n.* capital and port of Cuba; population (1986) 2,015,000. Products include cigars and tobacco.

Havana[2], **Havana cigar,** *n.* a cigar made at Havana or elsewhere in Cuba.

have, *v.t.* (*2nd sing.* **hast,** *3rd sing.* **has,** †**hath;** *past* **had,** *2nd sing.* **hadst,** *p.p.* **had**) to possess, to hold as owner; to enjoy, to suffer, to experience; to receive, to get, to obtain; to require, to claim; to hold mentally, to retain; to entertain; to maintain; to hold as part, appurtenance, quality etc., to contain, to comprise; to know, to understand, to be engaged in; to vanquish, to hold at one's mercy; to circumvent, to cheat, to bring forth, to bear; (*sl.*) to engage in sexual intercourse with. *v.i.* (*usu. in imper.*) to go, to betake oneself, to get (at, after, with etc.). *aux.* used with past participles to denote the completed action of verbs. *n.* (*sl.*) a take-in, a do, a sell. **had I known,** if I had known. †**have after,** follow, let us follow. †**have at,** (*imper.*) assail, encounter. **have done,** stop, cease. †**have with you,** I will go with you; come on, agreed. **I had a lief,** I would as willingly. **I had better,** it would be wiser or better (to do, go etc.). **I had rather,** I would prefer to. **let him have it,** (*coll.*) punish, censure or abuse him; give it him. **you've had it** HAD. **the haves and the have-nots,** the propertied classes and the unpropertied. **to be had,** to be taken in. **to have a care,** to be cautious. **to have it in one,** to be capable, have the ability. **to have it in for,** to want to harm somebody. **to have it off, away,** (*sl.*) to have sexual intercourse. **to have it out,** to settle a quarrel or dispute by fighting, debate etc. **to have it that,** to maintain or argue that. **to have nothing for it,** to have no alternative. **to have on,** to wear; to have planned; to deceive, trick. **to have pain,** to suffer. **to have pleasure,** to enjoy. **to have to do,** to be obliged to do. **to have someone up,** (*coll.*) to cause someone to be prosecuted in court. **haveless,** *a.* †having little or nothing; (*Sc.*) shiftless, careless. **having,** *n.* possession, goods, property; (*pl.*) endowments, qualities; (*Sc. usu. in pl.*) behaviour; good manners. †*a.* grasping, covetous. [OE *habban* (cp. Dut. *hebban,* Icel. *hafa,* G *haben,* and perh. L *habēre*)]

Havel, *n.* **Vaclav** (1936–), Czech playwright and politician, president from Dec. 1989. His plays include *The Garden Party* (1963) and *Largo Desolato* (1985), about a dissident intellectual, Havel became widely known as a human-rights activist. He was imprisoned (1979–83 and again 1989) for support of Charter 77 (see CZECHOSLOVAKIA).

havelock, *n.* a light covering for the cap hanging over the neck, worn as a protection against sunstroke. [General Sir H. *Havelock* 1795–1857]

haven, *n.* a port, a harbour; a station or refuge for ships; a refuge, an asylum. *v.t.* to shelter. †**havenage,** *n.* harbour dues. **havener,** *n.* the overseer of a haven. [OE *hæfene* (cp. Dut. *haven,* Icel. *höfn,* G *Hafen*)]

haver[1], *n.* (*Sc. Law*) one who holds a deed or document.

haver[2], *n.* (*Sc. and North.*) (*usu. pl.*) nonsense, foolish talk. *v.i.* to talk nonsense. **haverel, haverer,** *n.* [etym. unknown]

Havers, *n.* **Robert Michael Oldfield, Baron Havers** (1923–), British lawyer, Lord Chancellor (1987–88). After a successful legal career he became Conservative MP for Wimbledon in 1970 and was solicitor-general under Edward Heath and attorney-general under Margaret Thatcher. He was made a life peer in 1987 and served briefly, and unhappily, as Lord Chancellor before retiring in 1988.

haversack, *n.* a strong canvas bag to hold rations etc. on march. [F *havresac,* G *Habersack* (*Haber,* oats, *Sack,* SACK[1])]

Haversian, *a.* (*Anat.*) applied to certain passages etc. in the substance of the bones. **Haversian canals,** *n.pl.* a network of canals in bone conveying and protecting the blood-vessels. [Clopton *Havers* (d. 1702), English physician]

havildar, *n.* a sergeant of a regiment of infantry in India. [Pers. *hawāl-dār,* from Arab. *hawālah,* charge, Pers. *dār,* holding]

having HAVE.

†**haviour,** *n.* possession, property; behaviour, manners. [A-F *aveir* (F *avoir*), to have]

havoc, *n.* widespread destruction; devastation, waste; chaos. †*v.t.* to lay waste; to devastate. **to cry havoc,** to give the signal for violence or devastation. **to play havoc with,** to damage; to upset. [A-F *havok,* OF *havot,* plunder, prob. from Teut. and cogn. with HEAVE]

haw[1], *n.* the berry or fruit of the hawthorn; a hedge, an enclosed field or yard. [OE *haga* (cp. Icel. *hagi,* Dut. *haag,* G *Hag*)]

haw[2], *int., n.* a sound expressive of hesitation in speaking. *v.i.* to utter this sound, to speak with hesitation. [imit.]

haw[3], *n.* (*Farriery*) the nictitating membrane or third eyelid (of a horse etc.); (*often in pl*) a disease of this characterized by inflammation, enlargement etc. [etym. unknown]

Hawaii, *n.* Pacific state of the US; nickname Aloha State. **area** 16,800 sq km/6485 sq miles. **capital** Honolulu on Oahu. **towns** Hilo. **physical features** Hawaii consists of a chain of some 20 volcanic islands, of which the chief are: Hawaii itself, noted for *Mauna Kea* 4201 m/13,788 ft., the world's highest island mountain (site of a UK infrared telescope) and Mauna Loa, 4170 m/13,686 ft., the world's largest active volcanic crater; Maui second largest island; Oahu third largest, with the greatest concentration of population and tourist attractions, for example, Waikiki beach, and site of Pearl Harbor; Kauai; and Molokai. **population** (1987) 1,083,000 of whom about 34% are European, 25% Japanese, 14% Filipino, 12% Hawaiian, and 6% Chinese. **products** sugar, coffee, pineapples, bananas, flowers, offshore cobalt, nickel, and manganese deposits. **language** English. **religion** Christianity; minority Buddhism. **history** a kingdom until 1893, Hawaii became a republic 1894, ceded itself to the US 1898, and became a state 1959. **Hawaiian,** *a.* of or pertaining to Hawaii. *n.* a native or inhabitant of Hawaii.

hawbuck, *n.* a clown, a rustic.

hawfinch, *n.* the common grosbeak, *Coccothraustes coccothraustes.*

haw-haw[1], **Lord Haw Haw,** name given derisively to William Joyce (hanged 1946), who broadcast anti-British propaganda from Germany during the war of 1939–45.

haw-haw[2], HA-HA.

hawk[1], *n.* a name for many species of raptorial birds allied to the falcons; a bird of prey with short, rounded wings used in falconry; a rapacious person, a sharper. *v.i.* to hunt birds etc. by means of trained hawks or falcons; to attack on the wing, to soar (at). *v.t.* to pursue or attack on the wing. **to know a hawk from a handsaw,** to be intelligent and discriminating. **hawk-bell,** *n.* a small bell on the foot of a hawk. **hawk-eyed,** *a.* having sharp sight. **hawk-moth,** *n.* a moth of the family Sphingidae, the flight of which is not unlike that of a hawk in quest of prey. †**hawk-nose,** *n.* one who has a hooked nose. **hawk-nosed,** *a.* **hawk's-beard,** *n.* the composite genus *Crepis,* related to the hawkweeds. **hawking,** *n.* falconry. [OE *hafoc, heafoc* (cp. Dut. *havic,* Icel. *haukr,* G *Habicht*), prob. from Teut. root *haf-,* to seize, cp. L *capere*]

hawk[2], *v.i.* to clear or try to clear the throat in a noisy manner. *v.t.* to force (up) phlegm from the throat. *n.* an effort to force up phlegm from the throat. [prob. imit.]

hawk[3], *v.t.* to carry about for sale, to cry for sale; to carry or spread about. [HAWKER[2]]

hawk[4], *n.* a plasterer's board with handle underneath, for carrying plaster, mortar etc. [etym. doubtful]

Hawke, *n.* **Bob (Robert)** (1929–), Australian Labor politician, on the right wing of the party. He was president of the Australian Council of Trade Unions (1970–80), and became prime minister 1983.

hawked[1], (*Sc., North*) *a.* streaked, spotted. **hawkey, -kie**, *n.* a cow with a white or white-striped face; a pet name for a cow. [etym. unknown]

hawked[2], *a.* curved like a hawk's bill.

hawker[1], *n.* one who practises the sport of hawking; a falconer.

hawker[2], *n.* one who travels with any beast of burden or mechanically propelled vehicle licensed to carry goods for sale in the street or from house to house. [prob. from G (cp. LG *Höker,* Dut. *heuker,* G *Höker*)]

Hawking, *n.* **Stephen** (1942–), English physicist, who has researched black holes and gravitational field theory. His books include *A Brief History of Time* (1988).

Hawkins[1], *n.* **Anthony Hope,** real name of British novelist ANTHONY HOPE.

Hawkins[2], *n.* **Coleman (Randolph)** (1904–69), US virtuoso tenor saxophonist. He was until 1934 a soloist in the swing band led by Fletcher Henderson (1898–1952), and was an influential figure in bringing the jazz saxophone to prominence as a solo instrument.

Hawkins[3], *n.* **Jack** (1910–73), British film actor, usually cast in authoritarian roles. His films include *The Cruel Sea* (1953), *The League of Gentlemen* (1959), *Zulu* (1963), *Waterloo* (1970). After 1966 his voice had to be dubbed following an operation for throat cancer that removed his vocal chords.

Hawkins[4], *n.* **John** (1532–95), English navigator, born in Plymouth. Treasurer to the navy (1573–89), he was knighted for his services as a commander against the Spanish Armada in 1588.

Hawkins[5], *n.* **Richard** (*c.* 1562–1622), English navigator, son of John Hawkins. He held a command against the Spanish Armada 1588, was captured in an expedition against Spanish possessions (1593–94) and not released until 1602. He was knighted 1603.

Hawks, *n.* **Howard** (1896–1977), US director and producer of a wide range of films, including *Bringing Up Baby* (1936), *Ball of Fire* (1942), *The Big Sleep* (1946), and *Gentlemen Prefer Blondes* (1953).

Hawksmoor, *n.* **Nicholas** (1661–1736), English architect, assistant to Wren in London churches and St Paul's Cathedral; joint architect with VANBRUGH of Castle Howard and Blenheim Palace.

hawkweed, *n.* any plant of the composite genus *Hieracium.*

Haworth, *n.* **Norman** (1883–1950), English organic chemist who was the first to synthesize a vitamin (vitamin C), in 1933. He shared a Nobel prize in 1937.

hawse, *n.* (*Naut.*) that part of the bow in which the hawseholes are situated; the distance between a ship's head and the anchors by which she rides; the situation of the cables when a ship is moored from the bows with two anchors. **hawsehole,** *n.* a hole in each bow through which a cable or hawser can be passed. **to come in at the hawseholes,** to enter the naval service at the lowest grade. [prob. from Icel. *hals,* neck, cp. HALS]

hawser, *n.* a cable, used in warping and mooring. [OF *haucier* (F *hausser*), late L *altiāre,* to raise, from L *altus,* high]

hawthorn, *n.* a thorny, rosaceous shrub or tree belonging to the genus *Crataegus,* bearing white or pink flowers which develop into haws. Other names are whitethorn and may. [OE *hægthorn* (HAW[1], THORN)]

Hawthorne, *n.* **Nathaniel** (1804–64), US writer of *The Scarlet Letter* (1850), a powerful novel of Puritan Boston. He wrote three other novels, including *The House of the Seven Gables* (1851), and many short stories, including *Tanglewood Tales* (1853), classic legends retold for children.

hay[1], *n.* grass cut and dried for fodder; †growing grass. *v.t.* to make (grass etc.) into hay; to supply or feed with hay. *v.i.* to make hay. **to make hay,** to turn, toss and expose mown grass to the sun for drying. **to make hay of,** to throw into confusion. **to make hay while the sun shines,** to take advantage of every favourable opportunity. **hay-asthma** HAY-FEVER. **haybox,** *n.* an air-tight box, with a thick layer of hay, used for keeping food hot, and for continuing the process of slow cooking after the food has been removed from the fire. **haycock,** *n.* a conical heap of hay. **hay-fever,** *n.* a severe catarrh with asthmatic symptoms, frequent in summer and probably caused by the inhalation of pollen. **hayfield,** *n.* a field where hay is being made. **hayfork,** *n.* a fork for turning over or pitching hay. **hayknife,** *n.* a large, broad knife with a handle set crosswise, used for cutting hay out of a stack. **hayloft,** *n.* a loft for storing hay. **haymaker,** *n.* one employed in making hay; a machine for tossing hay; a kind of country dance; (*coll.*) a swinging punch. **haymaking,** *n.* **haymow,** *n.* a hayrick; a mass of hay laid up in a barn. **hayrick, haystack,** *n.* a pile of hay in the open air, built with a conical or ridged top, and thatched to keep it dry. **hayseed,** *n.* (*N Am., sl.*) a yokel, rustic. **haysel,** *n.* hay harvest. **haywire,** *a.* (*coll.*) crazy, mad; chaotic, disordered. [ME *hey,* OE *hīeg,* cogn. with HEW]

hay[2], *n.* a country dance with a winding movement. **†hay-de-guy, -guise** , *n.* a frolicsome dance of the 16th and early 17th cents. [etym. doubtful]

†hay[3], *n.* a hedge, a fence. **†hayward,** *n.* a parish or town officer in charge of fences, enclosures, commons etc., and responsible for the impounding of stray cattle etc. [OE *hege,* cogn. with *haga,* HAW[1]]

hay[4], *n.* a home-thrust in fencing. [It. *hai,* thou hast it (cp. L. *habet*)]

Hay, *n.* **Will** (1888–1949), British comedy actor. Originally a music hall comedian, from the 1930s he made many films in which he usually played incompetents in positions of authority, incl. *Good Morning Boys* (1937); *Oh Mr Porter* (1938); *Ask a Policeman* (1939); *The Ghost of St Michaels* (1941); *My Learned Friend* (1944).

Hayden[1], *n.* **Sterling,** (1916–86), stage name of John Hamilton, US film actor who played leading roles in Hollywood in the 1940s and early 1950s. Although later seen in some impressive character roles, his career as a whole failed to do justice to his talent. His work includes *The Asphalt Jungle* (1950), *Johnny Guitar* (1954), *Dr Strangelove* (1964), and *The Godfather* (1972).

Hayden[2], *n.* **William (Bill)** (1933–), Australian Labor politician. He was leader of the Australian Labor Party and of the opposition (1977–83), and minister of foreign affairs 1983. He became Governor-General 1989.

Haydn, *n.* **Franz Joseph** (1732–1809), Austrian composer. A teacher of both Mozart and Beethoven, he was a major exponent of the classical sonata form in his numerous chamber and orchestral works (he wrote over 100 symphonies). He also composed choral music, including the oratorios *The Creation* (1798) and *The Seasons* (1801). He was the first great master of the string quartet.

Hayes, *n.* **Rutherford B(irchard)** (1822–93), 19th president of the US (1877–81), a Republican. Born in Ohio, he was a major-general on the Union side in the Civil War. During his presidency federal troops (see RECONSTRUCTION) were withdrawn from the Southern states and the Civil Service reformed.

haymaker, hayrick, haysel HAY[1].

Hays Office, *n.* film-regulation body in the US. Officially known as the Motion Picture Producers and Distributors of America, it was created 1922 by the major film companies to improve the industry's image and provide internal regulation. It terminated in 1945.

hayward HAY[3].

haywire HAY[1].

Hayworth, *n.* **Rita** (1918–87), stage name of Magarita

Carmen Cansino, US film actress who gave vivacious performances in 1940s musicals and romantic dramas such as *Gilda* (1946) and *The Lady from Shanghai* (1948).

hazard, *n.* a game at dice; danger, risk; chance, casualty; the stake in gaming; one of the winning openings in a tennis-court; difficulties, obstacles, bunkers etc. on a golf-course; (*Billiards*) a stroke putting a ball into a pocket; **a winning hazard** is when the player pockets the object ball, a **losing hazard** when his own ball runs into a pocket off the object ball. *v.t.* to risk; to expose to chance or danger; to run the risk of; to venture (an act, statement etc.). *v.i.* to run a risk, to venture. **at all hazards,** in spite of any risk. **chicken-hazard** CHICKEN. **to run the hazard,** to run the risk. **hazardable,** *a.* †**hazardize, -ise,** *n.* a hazardous situation. **hazardous,** *a.* full of hazard, danger, or risk. **hazardously.** *adv.* **hazardousness,** *n.* **hazardry,** *n.* gambling, dicing; rashness, temerity. [OF *hasard,* perh. from Arab. *al zahr,* the die]

haze[1], *n.* want of transparency in the air, a very thin mist or vapour, usu. due to heat; obscurity or indistinctness of perception. *v.t.* to make hazy. **hazy,** *a.* misty; thick with haze; dim, vague, indistinct, obscure; (*sl.*) rather drunk; muddled. **hazily,** *adv.* **haziness,** *n.* [etym. unknown]

haze[2], *v.t.* (*Naut.*) to harass or punish with overwork; to play practical jokes on. *v.i.* (*N Am.*) to bully, to tease; to riot, to frolic (about). **hazer,** *n.* **hazing,** *n.* [etym. doubtful, cp. OF *haser,* to irritate, to annoy]

hazel, *n.* a shrub or small tree of the genus *Corylus,* esp. the European *C. avellana,* bearing the hazel nut; a reddish-brown colour. *a.* reddish-brown. **hazel-eyed,** *a.* having light-brown eyes. **hazelnut,** *n.* the fruit of the hazel, the cob-nut. **hazeline,** *n.* a distilled product of wych-hazel used in medicine. [OE *hæsel* (cp. Icel. *hasl,* Dut *hazel,* G *Hasel*)]

hazing HAZE[2].

Hazlitt, *n.* **William** (1778–1830), British essayist and critic, noted for his invective, scathing irony and gift for epigram. His critical essays include *Characters of Shakespeare's Plays* (1817–18), *Lectures on the English Poets* (1818–19), *English Comic Writers* (1819), and *Dramatic Literature of the Age of Elizabeth* (1820). Other notable works are *Table Talk* (1821–22); *The Spirit of the Age* (1825), and *Liber Amoris* (1823).

hazy HAZE[1].

HB, (*abbr.*) (of pencils) hard and black.

h & c, (*abbr.*) hot and cold (water).

HC, (*abbr.*) House of Commons.

hdqrs, (*abbr.*) headquarters.

He, (*chem. symbol*) helium.

he, *pron.* (*obj.* **him** *poss.* **his,** *pl.* **they,** *obj.* **them,** *poss.* **their**), the male person or animal referred to. *n.* a male person; a children's game of chasing to touch another player. **he-cat, -goat** etc., *n.* a male cat, goat, etc. **he-man,** *n.* (*coll.*) a virile man. **he-oak,** *n.* an Australian tree, *Casuarina stricta.* [OE *hē* cogn. with OFris. and OS *hi, he*]

head[1], *n.* the foremost part of the body of an animal, the uppermost in man, consisting of the skull, with the brain and the special sense-organs; any part, organ or thing of an analogous kind; a measure of length equal to a head, esp. in a horse race; the upper part of anything, the top; the upper end of a valley, lake, gulf etc.; the front part of a ship, plough, procession, column of troops etc.; a ship's toilet; a promontory; the capital of a pillar etc.; the part of a bed where the head rests; the more honourable end of a table etc.; the obverse of a coin or medal; the knobbed end of a nail etc.; the striking part of a tool; the part of a machine tool etc. that holds a drill or cutter; the device on a tape recorder that can record sound, or play back or erase recorded sound; the globular cluster of flowers or leaves at the top of a stem; the first or most honourable place, the forefront, the place of command; a chief, a ruler, a principal or leader; a head teacher of a school; a person, an individual; a single one (as of cattle); a main division, a topic, a category; a culmination, a crisis, a pitch; the ripened part of an ulcer or boil; froth on liquor; pressure of water available for driving mills; available steam-pressure; liberty, licence, freedom from restraint; an aptitude for something specified; the mind, the understanding, the intellect, esp. as distinguished from the feelings; one's life; a bundle of flax about 2 ft. (60 cm) long; (*sl.*) addict, devotee, fan. **from head to foot,** over the whole person. **head and ears,** the whole person; completely. **head and shoulders,** by the height of the head and shoulders; by a great margin; †by force, by hook or by crook. **head over heels,** turning upside down; completely (in love). **off one's head,** out of one's mind; wildly excited, demented. **out of one's own head,** by one's own invention; of one's own accord. **over head and ears,** deeply (immersed). **over someone's head,** beyond someone's understanding; appealing to a higher authority than someone. **to come to a head,** to suppurate (of an ulcer or boil); hence, to ripen; to reach a crisis or culminating point. **to give someone, let someone have his head,** to give liberty or licence to; to let (a horse) go as he pleases. **to go to one's head,** (of a success etc.) make one vain, arrogant etc. **to have one's head screwed on the right way,** to be sensible, well-balanced. **to hold one's head high,** to retain one's dignity. **to keep one's head,** to remain calm. **to lose one's head,** to be carried away by excitement; to lose one's presence of mind; to be decapitated. **to make head,** to push forward; to struggle (against) effectually. **to raise, rear its (ugly) head,** to become apparent, esp. in an ominous way. **to turn someone's head,** to cause someone to be vain or infatuated. **headache,** *n.* neuralgic or other persistent pain in the head; (*coll.*) a source of worry. **headachy,** *a.* suffering from or tending to cause headache. **headband,** *n.* a fillet or band for the hair; a band at the top and bottom inside the back of a book; the band connecting a pair of receivers or ear-phones. **headbanger,** *n.* (*sl.*) a person who makes violent head movements in time to pop music; a stupid, crazy or violent person. **headboard,** *n.* a panel at the head of a bed. **headborough,** *n.* the chief man of a tithing; a petty constable. **head case,** *n.* (*coll.*) a mad or foolish person. **headcheese,** *n.* (*N Am.*) portions of the head and feet of swine cut up fine, boiled and pressed into a mass, brawn. **head cold,** *n.* a cold affecting the head, not the chest. **head count,** *n.* a count of all the people etc. present. **head-dress,** *n.* covering and ornaments for the head, esp. of a woman. **headfast,** *n.* a rope to make fast the head of a vessel to some fixed object. **head-first, -foremost,** *adv.* with the head in front (of a plunge); precipitately. **head-frame,** *n.* (*Mining*) a frame over a pit-shaft to which the hoisting pulleys are attached. **head-gear,** *n.* the covering, dress or ornaments of the head; a bridle; (*Mining*) machinery at the top of a shaft or boring. **head-house,** *n.* (*Mining*) a house which houses the head-frame. **headhunt,** *v.t., v.i.* to seek and recruit business executives. **head-hunters,** *n.pl.* several races or tribes, notably the Dyaks of Borneo and Celebes, so called from their practice of making hostile raids in order to secure human persons and heads as trophies; an agency that specializes in seeking and recruiting business executives. **head-hunting,** *n.* **head-knee,** *n.* (*Shipbuilding*) a timber which is laid edgeways to the cutwater and stem. **headland,** *n.* a point of land projecting into the sea, a cape, a promontory; a ridge or strip of unploughed land at either end of a field, where the plough is turned. **headlight, -lamp,** *n.* the lamp carried at the front of a locomotive, motor-car etc. **headline,** *n.* the line at the head of a page or paragraph giving the title etc.; news set out in large, heavy type. **to hit the headlines,** to gain notoriety, to get notice in the press. **headlong,** *adv.* head-foremost; violently, hastily, rashly. *a.* steep, precipitous; violent, precipitate; rash, thoughtless. **head-lugged,** *a.* lugged, dragged or drawn along by the head. **headman,** *n.* a chief, a leader, a head worker. †**head-mark,** *n.* a feature of the face or head which marks individuality.

headmaster, headmistress, *n.* the principal master or mistress at a school. **headmastership,** *n.* **head-money,** *n.* a capitation tax or payment. **headmost,** *a.* most forward, most advanced. **head-mould, -moulding** HOOD-MOULD under HOOD. **head-on,** *a.* head to head; (of a collision) with the front of one vehicle hitting that of another. **headphone,** *n.* a telephone receiver to fit to the head. **headpiece,** *n.* armour for the head, a helmet; (*coll.*) the head, the intellect; an ornamental engraving at the head of a chapter etc. **headrace,** *n.* a race that leads water to a water-wheel. **head-resistance,** *n.* (*Aviat.*) resistance offered by the air to the wings and body of an aeroplane when flying level. **headrest,** *n.* a padded support for the head, esp. at the top of a seat in a vehicle. **head-room,** *n.* room or space for the head in a low tunnel etc. **head-sail,** (*Naut.*) *n.* any of the foresails. **head sea,** *n.* a heavy sea running directly against a ship's course. **headset,** *n.* a set of earphones joined by a band over the head. **head-shake,** *n.* a significant shake of the head. **heads-man,** *n.* one who cuts off heads, an executioner; (*Mining*) a labourer who conveys coal from the working to the horse-way; (*Whaling*) the man who takes charge of a boat after the whale has been struck. **head-spring,** *n.* the source of a stream; source, origin. **headstall,** *n.* the bridle without the bit and reins. **head start,** *n.* an advantage given or taken at the begining of a race etc.; an advantageous beginning to any enterprise. **headstock,** *n.* the part supporting the end or head, esp. the end of a revolving spindle; the portion of a lathe that contains the mandrel; the part which supports the cutters in a planing-machine. **headstone,** *n.* a stone at the head of a grave; the principal stone in a building; a cornerstone. **headstrong,** *a.* ungovernable, obstinate, intractable, self-willed. **head teacher,** *n.* a headmaster or headmistress. **head-tire,** *n.* attire for the head. **head-up,** *n.* (of an instrument display) visible without a driver, pilot etc. having to look down at instruments. **head-voice,** *n.* (*Singing, etc.*) sounds produced above the chest register. **head-water,** *n.* (*usu. pl.*) the upper part of a stream near its source. **headway,** *n.* motion ahead, rate of progress; head-room. **headwind,** *n.* a contrary wind. **headword,** *n.* one constituting a heading, esp. in a dictionary. **head-work,** *n.* brain-work; (*Arch.*) head-like ornament on the keystone of an arch. **headworker,** *n.* **head-workman,** *n.* a chief workman. **headage,** *n.* a payment per capita for animals. **headed,** *a.* having a head; having intellect or mental faculties (*esp. in comb.*, as *hard-headed*). **headless,** *a.* without a head; having no leader; †foolish, rash, obstinate, groundless. **headship,** *n.* the office of a head teacher. **heady,** *a.* headstrong, precipitate; violent, impetuous, intoxicating, inflaming, exhilarating. **headily,** *adv.* **headiness,** *n.* [OE *hēafod* (cp. Dut. *hoofd,* Icel. *haufoth,* G *Haupt*)]

head², *v.t.* to lead, to be the leader to, to direct; to move, travel in a specified direction; to be or form a head to; to provide with a head; to put or to be a heading to a chapter, etc.; to get ahead of; to lop (as trees); to oppose, to check; to strike (a ball) with the head; †to behead. *v.i.* to go or tend in a direction; to form a head. **to head back, off,** to intercept, to get ahead of and turn back or aside. **to head up,** to be in charge of (a team of people etc.). **heading,** *n.* the action of the verb TO HEAD; an inscription at the head of an article, chapter etc.; a running title; the pieces which compose a cask-head; (*Mining*) the end or the beginning of a drift or gallery; a gallery, drift or adit; (*Football*) the act of hitting the ball with the head; the compass bearing of an aircraft etc. [from prec.]

Head, *n.* **Bessie** (1937–), South African writer living in exile in Botswana. Her novels include *When Rain Clouds Gather* (1969), *Maru* (1971), and *A Question of Power* (1973).

-head, -hood, *suf.* denoting state or quality, as in *godhead, maidenhead, childhood, manhood.* [OE *-hād* (ME *-hod*), cogn. with Goth. *haidux,* manner, way]

header, *n.* one who puts or fixes a head on anything; a plunge or dive head-foremost; a brick or stone laid with its end in the face of the wall; (*Mech.*) a reaper that clips off the corn heads only; a machine for heading nails, rivets etc.; a tube or water-chamber in a steam boiler into which either end of a stack of water tubes is secured in such a manner that the steam and water can go from one tube or coil to another; (*coll.*) an act of heading a ball.

Headingley, *n.* Leeds sports centre, home of the Yorkshire County Cricket club and Leeds Rugby League club. The two venues are separated by the large stand.

headquarters, *n.pl.* the residence of the commander-in-chief of an army; the place whence orders are issued; the centre of authority. **headquarters staff,** the staff attached to the commander-in-chief of an army.

heal¹, *v.t.* to make whole, to restore to health; to cure (of disease etc.); to cause to cicatrize; to reconcile; to free from guilt, to purify. *v.i.* to grow or become sound or whole. **heal-all,** *n.* a universal remedy. **healable,** *a.* **healer,** *n.* **healing,** *a.* tending to heal; soothing, mollifying. **the healing art,** the art of medicine. **healingly,** *adv.* **healsome,** *a.* wholesome. [OE *hǣlan,* cogn. with HALE, WHOLE]

heal², HELE.

Heal, *n.* **Ambrose** (1872–1959), English cabinet-maker who took over the Heal's shop from his father and developed it into the renowned London store. He initially designed furniture in the Arts and Crafts style, often in oak, and in the 1930s he started using materials such as tubular steel.

heald, *n.* a heddle. [etym. doubtful]

Healey, *n.* **Denis (Winston)** (1917–), British Labour politician. While minister of defence (1964–70) he was in charge of the reduction of British forces east of Suez. He was chancellor of the Exchequer (1974–79). In 1976 he contested the party leadership, losing to James Callaghan, and again in 1980, losing to Michael Foot, to whom he was deputy leader (1980–83). In 1987 he resigned from the shadow cabinet.

health, *n.* a state of bodily or organic soundness, freedom from bodily or mental disease or decay; physical condition (good, bad etc.); a toast wishing that one may be well, prosperous etc. **health farm,** *n.* an establishment, often in the country, where clients can diet, exercise, relax etc. **health food,** *n.* types of food, e.g. organically grown or with no synthetic ingredients, regarded as promoting health. **health-resort,** *n.* a place where sick, delicate or convalescent people stay for the benefit of their health. **health visitor,** *n.* a nurse specializing in preventive medicine, who visits people in their own homes. **healthful,** *a.* promoting health, either physical or spiritual; salubrious; healthy. **healthfully,** *adv.* **healthfulness,***n.* **†healthless,** *a.* unhealthy, unwholesome. **†healthsome,** *a.* healthy, wholesome. **healthy,** *a.* enjoying good health; hale, sound; promoting health, salubrious, salutary. **healthily,** *adv.* **healthiness,** *n.* [OE *hǣlth,* from *hāl,* WHOLE]

Heaney, *n.* **Seamus (Justin)** (1939–), Irish poet, born in County Derry, who has written powerful verse about the political situation in Northern Ireland. Collections include *North* (1975), *Field Work* (1979), and *Station Island* (1984). In 1989, he was elected professor of poetry at Oxford University.

heap, *n.* a pile or accumulation of many things placed or thrown one on another; (*coll.*) a large number, a lot, a crowd, a good many times, a good deal. *v.t.* to throw (together) or pile (up) in a heap; to load or overload (with); to pile (upon). **struck all of a heap,** (*coll.*) staggered, flabbergasted. **†heapy,** *a.* lying in heaps; heaped. [OE *hēap* (cp. Dut. *hoop,* Swed. *hop,* G *Haufe*)]

hear, *v.t.* (*past & p.p.* **heard**) to perceive by the ear, to perceive the sound of; to listen to, to attend to; to listen to as a judge etc.; to understand by listening; to be a hearer of; to pay regard to, to heed, to obey; to be informed of by report; to receive a communication (from). *v.i.* to have the sense of hearing; to be told, to be informed (of, about etc.). **hard of hearing,** *a.* having defective hearing. **hear! hear!** listen! a form of applause or ironical approval. **hearable,** *a.* **hearer,** *n.* one who hears; one of an audience. **hearing,** *n.* the act of perceiving sound; the sense by which sound is perceived; audience, attention; a judicial trial or investigation; earshot. **hearing-aid,** *n.* a mechanical or electrical device for assisting the deaf to hear. **hearing-impaired,** *a.* (*euphem.*) having defective hearing. [OE *hīeran* (cp. Dut. *hooren,* Icel. *heyra,* G *horen*)]

hearken, †*v.t.* to hear, to regard. *v.i.* to listen attentively (to). **hearkener,** *n.* [OE *heorcnian,* as HARK]

hearsay, *n.* common talk, report or gossip. *a.* told or given at second-hand.

hearse, *n.* a vehicle in which the dead are taken to the place of burial; †a framework or canopy (orig. like an ancient harrow) for candles etc. formerly placed over the bier or coffin at the funeral of a great person; †a coffin, a bier. *v.t.* to carry in or on a hearse to the grave; †to entomb; to put in or under a hearse. **hearse-cloth,** *n.* a pall. **hearselike,** *a.* funereal. [OF *herce,* It. *erpice,* L *hirpicem,* nom. *hirpex,* a harrow]

Hearst, *n.* **William Randolph** (1863–1951), US newspaper proprietor, celebrated for his introduction of banner headlines, lavish illustration, and the sensationalist approach known as 'yellow journalism'.

heart, *n.* the central organ of circulation, which it keeps going by its rhythmical contraction and dilatation; the mind, the soul; the emotions or affections, esp. the passion of love; sensibility, tenderness, courage, spirit; zeal, ardour; the breast as seat of the affections; the central part; strength, efficacy, fertility; a term of endearment; anything heart-shaped; (*pl.*) a suit of cards marked with figures like hearts. †*v.t.* to hearten. *v.i.* to grow into a compact head or mass, as a plant. **after one's own heart,** exactly as one desires. **a heart of gold,** a quality of kindness, helpfulness etc. **at heart,** in reality, truly, at bottom; in the inmost feelings. **by heart,** by rote, by or from memory. **from (the bottom of) one's heart,** with absolute sincerity; fervently. **heart and hand,** with enthusiastic energy. **heart and soul,** devotedly. **heart of oak,** a man of courage. **in (good) heart,** in good spirits; in good condition, fertile. **in one's heart,** inwardly, secretly. **near one's heart,** very dear to one. **out of heart,** in low spirits, depressed; exhausted of fertility (of land). **to break the heart of,** to cause the greatest grief to. **to cross one's heart,** to promise or aver something solemnly. **to eat one's heart out,** to brood over or pine away through trouble; be envious. **to find in one's heart,** to be willing. **to get, learn by heart,** to commit to memory. **to give, lose one's heart to,** to fall deeply in love with. **to have at heart,** to be earnestly set upon, to cherish (a design etc.). **(not) to have one's heart in,** (not) to be fully committed or devoted to. **to have one's heart in one's mouth,** to be violently frightened or startled. **(not) to have the heart to,** (not) to be able or have the courage to (do something unkind or unpleasant). **to lose heart,** to become discouraged. **to make one's heart bleed,** (*iron.*) to distress. **to one's heart's content,** as much as one likes. **to set the heart at rest,** to tranquillize, to console. **to set the heart on,** to want very much. **to speak to one's heart,** to comfort, to encourage, to cheer. **to take heart,** to pluck up courage. **to take to heart,** to be greatly affected by. **to wear one's heart upon one's sleeve,** to be excessively frank and unreserved; to reveal one's inmost feelings and thoughts. **with all one's heart,** very willingly; completely, utterly. **heartache,** *n.* anguish of mind. **heart attack,** *n.* an acute loss of normal function in the heart. **heartbeat,** *n.* a pulsation of the heart; an emotion. **heart-block,** *n.* a condition in which the atria and the ventricles of the heart do not beat in coordination. **heart-blood** HEART'S BLOOD. **heartbreak,** *n.* overpowering sorrow. **heartbreaker,** *n.* one who or that which breaks the heart; a kind of curl; a love-lock. **heart-breaking,** *a.* **heart-broken,** *a.* **heartburn,** *n.* a burning pain in the stomach arising from indigestion. †**heart-burned,** *a.* having the heart inflamed; suffering from heart-burn. **heart-burning,** *a.* inflaming or distressing the heart. *n.* heartburn; secret enmity; envy. **heart-cam** HEART-WHEEL. †**heart-dear,** *a.* sincerely beloved. **heart disease,** *n.* a generic term for various affections of the heart. †**heart-easing,** *a.* comforting, consoling, pacifying. **heart-failure,** *n.* a condition in which the heart fails to function normally, often leading to death. **heartfelt,** *a.* deeply felt, sincere. †**heart-grief,** *n.* affliction of the heart. **heartland,** *n.* (*often pl.*) the central or most important part of a country. **heart–lung machine,** *n.* a machine that adopts the function of a patient's heart and lungs during heart surgery. **heart-rending,** *a.* heart-breaking, intensely afflictive. †**heart-robbing,** *a.* ecstatic. **heart's blood,** *n.* the life-blood; life; †soul, essence. **heart-searching,** *n.* an anguished examination of one's feelings etc. **heart-seed,** *n.* climbing plants of the genus *Cardiospermum.* **heart-sick,** *a.* pained in mind; deeply afflicted. **heart-sickness,** *n.* **heart-sore,** *n.* a cause of deep sorrow. *a.* grieved at heart. **heart-stricken** HEART-STRUCK. **heart-strings,** *n.pl.* the sensibilities; pity, compassion; one's deepest affections. †**heart-struck,** *a.* overwhelmed with anguish, grief or terror; struck to the heart. †**heart-swelling,** *a.* rankling in the heart. **heart-throb,** *n.* a person, e.g. a film-star, adulated by many. **heart-to-heart,** *n., a.* (a conversation) of a searching and intimate nature. **heart-warming,** *a.* inspiring emotional approval. **heart-wheel,** *n.* a form of cam-wheel for converting uniform rotary motion into uniform reciprocating rectilinear motion. **heart-whole,** *a.* having the affections free, not in love; undaunted; sincere. **heartwood,** *n.* duramen. **hearted,** *a.* **-hearted,** *comb.form.* having emotions of the specified kind. †**heartedness,** *n.* sincerity, zeal. [OE *heorte* (cp. Dut. *hart,* Icel. *hjarta,* G *Herz;* also L *cordis,* Gr. *kardia*)]

heartburn HEART.

hearten, *v.t.* to encourage, to inspirit, to stir up. *v.i.* to cheer (up). **heartener,** *n.* **heartening,** *a.* **hearteningly,** *adv.* [OE *hiertan,* as prec.]

hearth, *n.* the floor of a fireplace; that part of a reverberatory furnace in which the ore is laid, or in a blast furnace the lowest part through which the metal flows; the fireside, the domestic circle, the home. **hearth-broom, -brush,** *n.* a small brush for sweeping up ashes. †**hearth-money, -tax,** *n.* a tax on domestic hearths imposed 1662–89. **hearth-rug,** *n.* a rug placed in front of a fireplace. **hearthstone,** *n.* the stone forming the hearth; a soft kind of stone for whitening hearths etc. [OE *hearth* (cp. Dut. *haard,* Swed. *hard,* G *Herd*)]

heartless, *a.* destitute of feeling or affection; insensible, pitiless, cruel; faint-hearted, spiritless. **heartlessly,** *adv.* **heartlessness,** *n.*

heartlet, *n.* a little heart, a nucleus.

Heart of Darkness, a story by Joseph Conrad, published 1902. Marlow, the narrator, tells of his journey by boat into the African interior to meet a company agent, Kurtz, who exercises great power over the indigenous people by barbaric means.

heartsease, *n.* peace of mind; the wild pansy, *Viola tricolor.*

†**heartsome,** *a.* encouraging, unspiriting; merry, cheerful. [HEART, -SOME]

hearty, *a.* proceeding from the heart, sincere; cordial, good-natured, kindly; healthy; of keen appetite; full, abundant, satisfying; boisterous; irritatingly cheerful. *n.* (*Naut.*) a brave, hearty fellow; an extrovert person, esp. a sporty one. **my hearties,** (*Naut.*) a friendly mode of address. †**hearty-hale,** *a.* good for the heart. **heartily,** *adv.* **heartiness,** *n.*

heast, HEST.

heat, *n.* a form of energy, probably consisting in the vibration of the ultimate molecules of bodies or of the ether, capable of melting and decomposing matter, and transmissible by means of radiation, conduction or convection; hotness, the sensation produced by a hot body; hot weather; an inflamed condition of the skin, flesh etc.; redness, flush, high colour; hotness or pungency of flavour; violence, vehemence, fury; anger; intense excitement; warmth of temperament; animation, fire; sexual excitement in animals, esp. in females; a single course in a race or other contest; (*sl.*) coercive pressure; (*sl.*) searches etc. by police after a crime. *v.t.* to make hot; to inflame, to cause to ferment; to excite. *v.i.* to become hot; to become inflamed or excited. **more heat than light,** more anger or vehemence than enlightenment. **on heat,** (*Biol.*) of a female animal when sexually excited. **to take the heat out of,** to make less emotional or vehement. **heat-engine,** *n.* an engine driven by hot air, steam or other agent for converting heat into mechanical energy. **heat exchanger,** *n.* a device that transfers heat from one fluid to another. **heat pump,** *n.* a machine for transferring heat from a low temperature to a higher temperature, for the purpose of space or water heating. **heat-shield,** *n.* a shield that protects from high temperatures, e.g. those produced by a spacecraft re-entering the earth's atmosphere. **heatspot,** *n.* a freckle; an urticarious pimple attributed to heat. **heat-stroke,** *n.* prostration from excessive heat. **heat-treat,** *v.t.* to heat and cool (metals) in order to change their properties. **heat treatment,** *n.* **heat-unit,** *n.* the quantity of heat required to raise the temperature of one unit of water (usu. 1 lb, 0.45 kg) through one degree. **heat-wave,** *n.* a wave of radiant heat; an unbroken spell of hot weather. **heated,** *a.* passionate, angry. **heatedly,** *adv.* **heater,** *n.* one who or that which heats; a heating-apparatus; a block of iron made red-hot and then placed in an urn or a smoothing-iron; (*N Am., sl.*) a pistol. **heating,** *a.* promoting warmth or heat; exciting; stimulating. [OE *hætu,* from *hāt,* HOT]

heath, *n.* an open space of country, esp. if covered with shrubs and coarse herbage; any plant belonging to the genus *Erica,* or the allied genus *Calluna,* consisting of narrow-leaved evergreen shrubs with wiry stems and red or reddish flowers. **one's native heath,** one's home country or area. **heath-bell,** *n.* a flower growing on a heath, esp. on heather. **heath-berry,** *n.* a berry growing on low shrubs common on heaths, as the bilberry, cranberry etc. **heath-fowl, -game,** *n.* the black grouse. **heath-hen,** *n.* the female of the black grouse; (*N Am.*) various species of grouse. **heath-pea,** *n.* a perennial herb, *Lathyrus macrorhizus,* of the bean family, with pea-like edible tubers. **heath-plant,** *n.* heather. **heath-pout,** *n.* a heath-bird, esp. the female and the young. **heathy,** *a.* [OE *hǣth*]

Heath, *n.* **Edward (Richard George)** (1916–), British Conservative politician, party leader (1965–75). As prime minister (1970–74) he took the UK into the European Community, but was brought down by economic and industrial-relations crises at home.

heathen, *n.* a Gentile; one who is not Christian, Jewish or Muslim; a pagan, an idolater; an unenlightened or barbarous person. *a.* gentile; pagan; unenlightened; barbarous. **the heathen,** (*collect.*) heathen peoples. **heathendom,** †**heathenesse,** *n.* the portion of the world in which heathenism is dominant; heathens collectively; heathenism. **heathenish,** *a.* of or belonging to heathens; barbarous, rapacious, cruel. **heathenishly,** *adv.* **heathenishness,** *n.* **heathenism, heathenry,** *n.* the moral or religious state or practices of heathens; debased moral condition. **heathenize, -ise,** *v.t.* to render heathen. [OE *hǣthen* (cp. Dut. *heiden,* Icel. *heithimr,* G *Heide*), cogn. with prec.]

heather, *n.* heath, esp. *Calluna vulgaris,* called in the north ling. **to set the heather on fire,** to create a disturbance. **to take to the heather,** to become an outlaw. **heather-ale,** *n.* a liquor formerly brewed from heather-flowers. **heather-bell,** *n.* the cross-leaved heather, *Erica tetralix;* sometimes applied to *E. cinera.* **heather-mixture, -stockings, -tweed, -wool,** *n.* a fabric or garment of a speckled colour supposed to resemble heather. **heathery,** *a.* abounding in heather. [etym. doubtful]

Heath Robinson, *a.* (of an apparatus) ingenious and extremely complex. [*Heath Robinson,* 1872–1944, English cartoonist who drew such devices]

†**heaume,** *n.* a large helmet coming down to the shoulders. [F, from OF *helme,* HELM[1]]

heave, *v.t.* (*past, p.p.* **heaved,** †**hove**) to lift, to raise, with effort; to utter or force from the breast; (*coll., orig Naut.*) to throw, to cast (something heavy); (*Naut.*) to hoist (as the anchor), to haul; (*Geol.*) to fracture and displace (strata); to elevate, to exalt. *v.i.* to rise; to rise and fall with alternate or successive motions; to pant; to retch, to vomit. *n.* an upward motion or swelling; the act of heaving; a sigh; an effort to vomit; amount of displacement of a vein or stratum, esp. measured in a horizontal direction. **give, get the heave-ho,** (*coll.*) dismiss/be dismissed from employment. **heave ho!** sailor's cry in hauling up the anchor. **to heave down,** to careen. **to heave in, into sight,** to come into sight. **to heave out,** to throw out. **to heave to,** (*Naut.*) to bring the head (of a ship) to the wind and so stop her motion; to bring a ship to a standstill. **heave-offering,** *n.* a Judaic offering which was consecrated by lifting up before the Lord. **heaver,** *n.* one who or that which heaves (*esp. in comb.,* as *coal-heaver*). [OE *hebban* (cp. Dut. *heffen,* Icel. *hefja,* G *heben,* also L *capere,* to take, Gr. *kōpē,* handle)]

heaven, *n.* the sky, the firmament (*often in pl.*); the atmosphere enveloping the earth regarded as the region in which the clouds float, the winds blow etc.; the abode of God and the blessed; the place of supreme felicity; any place or state of extreme joy or pleasure; God, providence; †the pagan divinities or their abode; (*Anc. Cosmog.*) one of several revolving spheres in which the heavenly bodies were carried round the earth. *int.* expressing surprise. **Good heavens!** an exclamation. **heaven of heavens, seventh heaven,** the highest of the seven heavens believed by the later Hebrews and the Muslims to be the dwelling-place of God; a state of supreme felicity. **to move heaven and earth,** to overcome very great difficulties. **heaven-born,** *a.* derived from heaven; inspired. **heaven-bred,** *a.* of divine origin. **heaven-directed,** *a.* pointing towards the sky; directed by heaven. **heaven-fallen,** *a.* fallen or driven from heaven. †**heaven-hued,** *a.* blue, azure **heaven-sent,** *a.* (of an opportunity etc.) coming at an opportune moment. **heavenly,** *a.* pertaining to the heavens, celestial; inhabiting heaven; situated in the heavens (as the planets, stars etc.); divine; superhuman; supremely blest or excellent; (*coll.*) highly pleasing, delicious. †*adv.* in the manner of heaven; divinely, celestially. **heavenly body,** *n.* a sun, star, planet or other mass of matter, distinct from the earth. **heavenly host,** *n.* the angels. **heavenly minded,** *a.* having the affections fixed upon heaven and heavenly things; pure, holy, pious. **heavenly mindedness,** *n.* **heavenliness,** *n.* **heavenward,** *a.* and *adv.* **heavenwards,** *adv.* [OE *heofon, hefon* (etym. doubtful)]

heaves, *n.pl.* an asthmatic disease in horses, broken wind. **heavy[1],** *a.* affected with the heaves. [HEAVE]

Heaviside layer, *n.* a layer in the upper atmosphere that reflects radio waves, thus enabling reception round the curved surface of the earth. [British physicist O. *Heaviside,* 1850–1925]

heavy[1] HEAVES.

heavy[2], *a.* having great weight, weighty, ponderous; of a large and ponderous kind (as metal, artillery etc.); of great density or specific gravity, dense; not properly raised (as bread); (of the ground) soft and wet; of full body (as wines etc.); great, powerful, forcible, violent; concerned with large amounts or dealings; unwieldy, clumsy; plentiful, abundant; large in amount; weighed down, loaded (with); not easily borne; oppressive, grievous, severe; burdensome, obstructive, clogging; difficult; drowsy, dull, sluggish, stupid; tedious; doleful, depressing, depressed; excessively serious, sombre; threatening, louring; †deep, loud; †pregnant. *n.* (*coll.*) a thug, villain; (*Sc.*) a type of strong beer. †*adv.* heavily, with great weight. **the Heavies,** *n.pl.* the Dragoon Guards. **time hangs heavy,** time passes tediously. **to make heavy weather,** to make a labour of a task. **heavy-armed,** *a.* bearing heavy armour or arms. **heavy breather,** *n.* a person who makes obscene telephone calls, panting audibly while doing so. **heavy-duty,** *a.* designed to sustain more than usual wear. **heavy-handed,** *a.* clumsy, awkward; oppressive. †**heavy-headed,** *a.* dull, stupid, drowsy. **heavy-hearted,** *a.* dejected. **heavy laden,** *a.* burdened with depression. **heavy metal,** *n.* a metal with a high specific gravity; a type of loud rock music with a strong beat. **heavy spar,** *n.* barytes. **heavy swell,** *n.* (*sl.*) a person dressed in the height of fashion. **heavy water,** *n.* (*Phys.*) deuterium oxide, a liquid similar to ordinary water, with density about 10% greater. **heavyweight,** *n.* a person or animal of more than average weight, esp. a jockey above the average or a boxer weighing over 12 st. 10 lb (80·74 kg); (*coll.*) a person of great power, influence or intellect. **heavy wet,** *n.* (*sl.*) a drink of strong malt liquor, esp. stout. **heavily,** *adv.* **heaviness,** *n.* **heavyish,** *a.* [OE *hefig,* cogn. with HEAVE]

hebdomad, *n.* a week, a period of seven days (alluding to Daniel's prophecy, Dan. ix.27); a group of seven things; (*Gnostic Phil.*) a group of seven spirits dwelling in the seven planets, also the demiurge. **hebdomadal,** *a.* consisting of seven days; meeting or occurring weekly. **Hebdomadal Council,** a board meeting weekly which manages the principal affairs of the Univ. of Oxford. **hebdomadally,** *adv.* **hebdomadary,** *a.* hebdomadal. *n.* a member of a chapter or convent whose week it is to officiate in the choir. [L and Gr. *hebdomasados* (*hegdomos,* seventh, from *hepta,* seven)]

Hebe, *n.* (*Gr. Myth.*) the goddess of youth, daughter of Zeus and Hera and cupbearer to the gods of Olympus; (*facet.*) a waitress, a barmaid; (*Astron.*) the sixth asteroid. **hebetic,** *a.* pertaining to youth or pubescence. [Gr., youthful prime]

Hebei, *n.* (formerly) **Hopei** or **Hupei,** province of N China. **area** 202,700 sq km/78,242 sq miles. **capital** Shijiazhuang. **population** (1986) 56,170,000. **products** cereals, textiles, iron, steel.

†**hebenon,** *n.* perh. henbane. [Shak., a nonce-word, occurring only in *Hamlet,* 1, 5]

hebetate, *v.t.* to make blunt or dull; to stupefy. *v.i.* to become blunt or dull. **hebetant,** *a.* †**hebetation,** *n.* †**hebetude,** *n.* obtuseness, stupidity. [L *hebetātus,* p.p. of *hebetāre,* from *hebes -etis,* blunt]

hebetic HEBE.

Hebraic, *a.* pertaining to the Hebrews, their mode of thought, or language. **Hebraically,** *adv.* **Hebraism,** *n.* the thought or religion of the Hebrews; a Hebrew characteristic; a Hebrew idiom or expression. **Hebraist,** *n.* one learned in the Hebrew language and literature; one who conforms or adheres to Jewish ideas or religious observances. **Hebraistic, -ical,** *a.* **Hebraistically,** *adv.* **hebraize, -ise,** *v.t.* to convert into a Hebrew idiom; to give a Hebrew character to. *v.i.* to become Hebrew; to act according to Hebrew manners or fashions. [late L *Hebraicus,* Gr. *Hebraikos*]

Hebrew, Israelite, *n.* one of a Semitic people living in Palestine at the time of the Old Testament, and who traced their ancestry to Abraham. The term was formerly used to describe Jews; the Hebrew language. **Hebrew Bible,** *n.* the sacred writings of Judaism, known to Christians as the Old Testament. It includes the Torah (the first five books, ascribed to Moses), historical and prophetic books, and psalms, all in the Hebrew language. **Hebrew language,** *n.* a member of the Hamito-Semitic language family spoken in W Asia by the ancient Hebrews, sustained for many centuries as the liturgical language of Judaism, and revived and developed in the 20th cent. as modern Israeli Hebrew, the national language of the state of Israel. It is the original language of the Old Testament of the Bible.

Hebridean, *a.* of or pertaining to the Hebrides, islands off the West coast of Scotland. [*Hebrides,* erron. for L *Hebudes* (Pliny), *Hebudae,* Gr. *Heboudai*]

Hebrides, *n. pl.* group of over 500 islands (fewer than 100 inhabited) off W Scotland; total area 2900 sq km/1120 sq miles. The Hebrides were settled by Scandinavians in the 6th–9th cents., and passed under Norwegian rule from about 890–1266. The **Inner Hebrides** are divided between Highland and Strathclyde regions, and include Skye, Mull, Jura, Islay, Iona, Rum, Raasay, Coll, Tiree, Colonsay, Muck, and uninhabited Staffa. The **Outer Hebrides** form the islands area of the Western Isles administrative area, separated from the Inner Hebrides by the Little Minch. They include Lewis with Harris, North Uist, South Uist, Barra, and St Kilda.

Hecate, *n.* (*Gr. Myth.*) a mysterious goddess, sometimes identified with Artemis and the moon, holding sway in earth, heaven and the underworld, and represented as triform; a hag, a witch. **Hecataean,** *a.* [Gr. *Hekatē*]

hecatomb, *n.* (*Gr. Ant.*) the sacrifice of 100 oxen or other beasts; any great sacrifice. [L *hecatombē,* Gr. *hekatombē* (*hekaton,* a hundred, *bous,* ox)]

†**hecatontome,** *n.* (*Milton*) a large quantity (lit. 100) of books. [Gr. *hekaton,* a hundred, *tomos,* TOME]

hech, *int.* (*Sc.*) an exclamation, chiefly of surprise. [HEIGH]

†**hecht,** (*Sc.*) HEIGHT.

Hecht, *n.* **Ben** (1893–1964), US film screenwriter and occasional director, who was formerly a journalist. His play *The Front Page* was adapted several times for the cinema by other writers. His screenplays for such films as *Gunga Din* (1939), *Spellbound* (1945), and *Actors and Sin* (1952) earned him a reputation as one of Hollywood's best writers.

heck[1], *n.* a rack for fodder; a hatch; a grated contrivance in a stream, used as a fish-trap or to obstruct the passage of fish. [OE *hæce,* HATCH[1]]

heck[2], *int.* (*coll. euphem.*) an exclamation of irritation, used instead of *hell.*

heckle, *v.t.* to hackle; to worry (a public speaker) by inconvenient questions. **heckler,** *n.* **heckling,** *n.*

hectare, *n.* a measure of area equal to 100,000 sq. metres or 2·471 acres. [F]

hectic, *a.* (*Path.*) habitual, continual (of fever); consumptive; pertaining to consumption; (*coll.*) full of excitement, exciting, wild. *n.* a hectic fever; a hectic patient; the morbid flush in hectic fever and consumption. **hectic fever,** a fever attendant on phthisis, dysentery etc. †**hectical, hectoid,** *a.* **hectically,** *adv.* [F *hectique,* late L *hecticus,* Gr. *hektikos,* from *hexis,* habit of body, from *hexein,* fut. of *echein,* to have, to hold]

hecto-, *comb. form.* a hundred. [Gr. *hekaton,* a hundred]

hectogram, *n.* a weight of 100 grams or 3·52 oz av.

hectograph, *n.* a machine for multiplying copies of writings or drawings. **hectographic,** *a.*

hectolitre, *n.* a liquid measure containing 100 litres or 3·531 cu. ft.

hectometre, *n.* a measure of length equal to 100 metres or 109·3633 yds.

Hector, *n.* in Greek mythology, a Trojan prince, son of King Priam, who, in the siege of Troy, was the foremost warrior on the Trojan side until he was killed by Achilles.

hector, *n.* a bully, a blusterer. *v.t.* to bully, to treat with insolence. *v.i.* to play the bully, to bluster. **hectorer,** *n.* †**hectorism,** *n.* bluster, bullying. [Gr. *Hectōr,* the son of Priam and Hecuba, the bravest of the Trojan warriors in Homer's *Iliad*]

hectostere, *n.* a solid measure of 100 cu. m or 3531·66 cu. ft.

Hecuba, *n.* in Greek mythology, the wife of King Priam, and mother of Hector and Paris.

Hedda Gabler, *n.* a play by Henrik Ibsen, first produced in 1891. Trapped in small-town society, Hedda Gabler takes out her spiritual and sexual frustrations on everyone from her feeble-minded academic husband to the reformed alcoholic writer Lörborgo. When her mean-spirited revenge schemes backfire, she commits suicide.

heddle, *n.* (*Weaving*) one of the sets of parallel cords or wires forming loops for the warp-threads of a loom. [perh. from an OE *hefedl,* earlier form of *hefeld*]

hedera, *n.* a genus of climbing plants containing two species, the common and the Australian ivy. **hederaceous**, †**hederal,** *a.* **hederiferous**, *a.* [L]

hedge, *n.* a fence of bushes or small trees; a barrier of any kind; a means of securing oneself against loss; a shifty or non-committal statement. *v.t.* to fence (in) with or separate (off) by a hedge; to surround or enclose with or as with a hedge; to secure oneself against loss (on a speculation etc.) by transactions that would compensate one. *v.i.* to plant or repair hedges; to skulk in a hedge; to act in a shifty way, to avoid making a decisive statement. **hedge-bill,** *n.* a billhook for trimming hedges. **hedge-born,** *a.* of low or mean birth. **hedge-creeper,** *n.* one who skulks under hedges for evil purposes. **hedge-hop,** *v.i.* to fly very low over fields etc. **hedge-hopper,** *n.* †**hedge hyssop,** *n.* a scrophulareous plant, *Gratiola officinalis,* having medicinal properties. †**hedge-marriage,** *n.* an irregular marriage performed by a hedge-priest; a clandestine marriage. †**hedge note,** *n.* poor, inferior writing. **hedge-priest,** *n.* a poor, illiterate priest, or sham priest, formerly common in Ireland. **hedgerow,** *n.* a row of shrubs planted as a hedge. **hedge-school,** *n.* a low-class school such as was formerly conducted in the open air in the country parts of Ireland. **hedge-schoolmaster,** *n.* **hedge-sparrow,** *n.* a common European bird, *Accentor modularis,* one of the warblers. **hedging-bill,** *n.* a hedge-bill. **hedgeless,** *a.* **hedger,** *n.* one who makes or trims hedges. [OE *hecg* (cp. Dut. *hegge,* Icel. *heggr,* G *Hecke*), cogn. with *hāga,* HAW[1]]

hedgehog, *n.* a small insectivorous mammal, *Erinaceus europaeus,* covered above with spines, and able to roll itself up into a ball; a spiny fish, *Diodon hystrix;* a plant with spiny seed-vessels, *Medicago intertexta;* an irritable, quarrelsome person; (*Mil.*) a line formed by a number of fortified points. **hedgehog thistle,** *n.* a spiny globular plant of the cactus family.

Hedin, *n.* **Sven Anders** (1865–1952), Swedish archaeologist, geographer, and explorer in central Asia and China. Between 1891 and 1908 he explored routes across the Himalayas and produced the first maps of Tibet. During 1928–33 he travelled with a Sino-Swedish expedition which crossed the Gobi Desert. His publications include *My Life as Explorer* (1925) and *Across the Gobi Desert* (1928).

hedonic, *a.* of or pertaining to pleasure. *n.pl.* the science of pleasure; the branch of ethics dealing with the relations of duty and pleasure. **hedonism**, *n.* (*Phil.*) the doctrine that pleasure is the chief good. **hedonist**, *n.* **hedonistic**, *a.* **hedonistically,** *adv.* [Gr. *hēdonikos,* from *hēdonē,* pleasure]

-hedral, *comb. form.* having the specified number of sides.

-hedron, *comb. form.* a solid figure having the stated number of sides.

hedyphane, *n.* a massive, colourless variety of mimetite, containing calcium; a variety of green lead-ore. [Gr. *hēdus,* sweet, *-phanēs,* appearing (*phainein,* to show)]

heebie-jeebies, *n. pl.* (*coll.*) a feeling of anxiety or apprehension. [coined by W. De Beck, 1890–1942, an American cartoonist]

heed, *v.t.* to regard, to take notice of. †*v.i.* to take notice, to pay attention. *n.* care, attention; careful consideration. **to take, give,** or **pay heed to,** to take notice of, pay regard to. **heedful,** *a.* circumspect, wary; attentive, regardful (of). **heedfully,** *adv.* **heedfulness,** *n.* †**heediness,** *n.* heedfulness. **heedless,** *a.* careless; thoughless; negligent (of). **heedlessly,** *adv.* **heedlessness,** *n.* [OE *hēdan* (cp. Dut. *hoeden,* G *hūten,* from *hut,* protection), prob. cogn. with HOOD]

heehaw, *v.i.* to bray like an ass. *n.* an ass's bray; a loud and foolish laugh. [imit.]

heel[1], *n.* the rounded hinder part of the foot in man; the corresponding part of the hind limb in quadrupeds, often above the foot; (*pop.*) the hinder part of a quadruped's foot; (*pl.*) the feet, esp. the hind feet of animals; the hinder part of a shoe, stocking etc. covering the heel; a block built up of pieces of leather to raise the hinder part of a boot or shoe from the ground; a heel-like protuberance, knob or part, such as the lower end of a mast, the hindermost part of a ship's keel, the cusp of a molar tooth, the crook in the head of a golf-club; (*coll.*) the crusty end of a loaf of bread, the latter part, the tail-end of anything; (*sl.*) a contemptible person. *v.t.* to add a heel to; to arm (a game-cock) with a spur; to follow close on the heels; (*Football*) to pass the ball out from a scrimmage with the heels; (*Golf*) to hit the ball with the heel of a club. *v.i.* to dance. **at someone's heels,** close behind someone. **come to heel, to heel,** come close behind, so as to be under control (direction to a dog). **head over heels** HEAD. **on the heels of,** following closely after. **to be down, out at heel,** to be trodden or worn down at the back (of shoes etc.); to be slipshod or slovenly; to be in unfortunate circumstances. **to cool one's heels,** to be made to wait. **to dig one's heels in,** to be obstinate. **to lay, clap by the heels,** to arrest, to imprison. **to show a clean pair of heels, to take to one's heels,** to run away. **to turn on one's heel,** to turn round sharply. **heel-ball,** *n.* a composition of hard wax and lamp-black, used to give a smooth surface to heels, and for taking rubbings of inscriptions etc. **heel-piece,** *n.* a piece of leather on the heel of a shoe; †the end, the conclusion. **heel-tap,** *n.* a thickness of leather in a shoe-heel; a small quantity of liquor left in the bottom of a glass. **heeler,** *n.* one who puts heels on boots; †a game-cock that strikes well with his heels or spurs; (*N Am., sl.*) a political hanger-on. **-heeled,** *comb. form.* having heels of the specified type, e.g. *high-heeled.* [OE *hēla* (cp. Dut. *hiel,* Icel. *hœll*), allied to *hōh,* HOUGH]

heel[2], *v.i.* (*Naut.*) to incline or cant over to one side. *v.t.* to make (a vessel) do this. *n.* an inclination to one side (of a ship, etc.). [ME *helden,* OE *hyldan,* cogn. with *heald,* sloping]

heeze, (*Sc.*) *v.t.* to raise, to heave up. *n.* a lift. [HOISE]

Hefei (formerly **Hofei**), *n.* capital of Anhui province, China; population (1984) 853,000. Products include textiles, chemicals, and steel.

heft[1], *n.* the act of heaving; a lift, a push; an effort, an exertion; weight, heaviness. *v.t.* to try the weight of by lifting. [from HEAVE]

heft[2], HAFT.

hefty, *a.* (*coll.*) strong, muscular, powerful; big. [HEFT[1]]

Hegel, *n.* **Georg Wilhelm Friedrich** (1770–1831), German philosopher, who conceived of consciousness and the external object as forming a unity, in which neither factor can exist independently, mind and nature being two abstractions of one indivisible whole. Hegel believed development took place through dialectic: contradiction and the resolution of contradiction. For Hegel, the task of philosophy was to comprehend the rationality of what already exists, but leftist followers, including Marx, used Hegel's dialectic to attempt to show the inevitability of radical change, and attacked both religion and the social order. **Hegelian,** *a.* pertaining to Hegel or his philosophy. *n.* one who accepts the teaching of Hegel. **Hegelianism,** *n.* the philosophical system of Hegel.

hegemony, *n.* leadership, predominance, esp. applied to the relation of one state to another or to a confederation. **hegemonic**, *a.* [Gr. *hēgemonia, from hēgemōn,* leader, from *hēg-*, stem of *agein,* to lead]

Hegira, *n.* the flight of Mohammed from Mecca to Medina, 19 July 622, from which the Muslim era is computed; a hurried escape from a dangerous situation. [med. L, from Arab. *hijrah,* from *hajara,* to separate]

hegumen, *n.* the head of a monastery in the Greek Church. [med. L *hēgūmenus,* Gr. *hēgoumenos,* orig. pres.p. of *hegeisthai,* to lead]

Heidegger, *n.* **Martin** (1889–1976), German philosopher. In *Being and Time* (1927), he used the methods of Husserl's phenomenology to explore the structures of human existence. His later writings meditated on the fate of a world dominated by science and technology.

Heidi, *n.* novel for children by the Swiss writer, Johanna Spyri (1827–1901) published in 1881. Heidi, a orphan, shares a simple life with her grandfather high on a mountain bringing happiness to those around her. Three years spent in Frankfurt as companion to a crippled girl, Clara, convince Heidi that city life is not for her and she returns to her mountain home.

heifer, *n.* a young cow that has not yet calved. [OE *hēahfore,* etym. doubtful]

heigh, *int.* an exclamation calling attention or expressing inquiry or encouragement. **heigh-ho,** *int.* an expression of disappointment, weariness or regret. [imit.]

heighday, HEYDAY.

height, *n.* the quality or state of being high; the distance of the top of an object above its foot, basis or foundation; altitude above the ground, sea-level or other recognized level; an elevated position; an eminence, a summit; stature; elevation in rank, office, society etc.; the fullest extent or degree. **at its height,** at its highest degree; at the culminating point. **the height,** the fullest extent. **heighten,** *v.t.* to make high or higher, to raise, to elevate; to increase, to enhance, to intensify, to accentuate, to emphasize; to exaggerate. *v.i.* to rise; to increase, to augment; to intensify. [OE *hīehtho,* from *hēah,* HIGH]

Heike monagatori, *n.* Japanese chronicle, written down in the 14th century but based on oral legend describing events that took place 200 years earlier, that recounts the struggle for control of the country between the rival Genji (Minamoto) and Heike (Taira) dynasties. The conflict resulted in the end of the Heian period, and the introduction of the first *shogunate* (military dictatorship). Many subsequent Japanese dramas are based on material from the chronicle.

Heilongjiang (formerly **Heilungkiang**), *n.* province of NE China, in Manchuria. **area** 463,600 sq km/178,950 sq miles. **capital** Harbin. **population** (1986) 33,320,000. **products** cereals, gold, coal, copper, zinc, lead, cobalt.

Heine, *n.* **Heinrich** (1797–1856), German romantic poet and journalist, who wrote *Reisebilder* (1826) and *Buch der Lieder/Book of Songs* (1827). From 1831 he lived mainly in Paris, as a correspondent for German newspapers. Schubert and Schumann set many of his songs to music.

Heinkel, *n.* **Ernst** (1888–1958), German aircraft designer who pioneered jet aircraft. He founded his firm 1922, and built the first jet aircraft 1939 (developed independently of the Whittle jet of 1941). During World War II his company was Germany's biggest producer of warplanes.

heinous, *a.* abominable, flagrant, atrocious; wicked in the highest degree. **heinously,** *adv.* **heinousness,** *n.* [OF *haïnos,* from *haïne,* hate, from *haïr,* to hate]

heir, *n.* one who by law succeeds or is entitled to succeed another in the possession of property or rank; one who succeeds to any gift, quality etc.; †child, product. *v.t.* to be heir to, to inherit. **heir apparent,** *n.* the heir who will succeed on the death of the present possessor. **heir-at-law,** *n.* one who inherits property by right of descent. **heir presumptive,** *n.* one whose actual succession may be prevented by the birth of someone else nearer akin to the present possessor of the title, estate etc. **heirdom,** *n.* **heiress,** *n.* a female heir. **heirless,** *a.* **heirship,** *n.* [OF, from late L *hērem,* L *hērēdem,* acc. of *hērēs*]

heirloom, *n.* a chattel which descends with an estate to an heir; any possession that has remained in a family for several generations. [LOOM[1]]

Heisenberg, *n.* **Werner Carl** (1901–76), German physicist. He was an originator of quantum mechanics and the formulator of the uncertainty principle. Nobel prize 1932.

heist, *n.* (*esp. N Am.*) a robbery. *v.t.* to steal. [var. of HOIST]

Hejira, HEGIRA.

Hekmatyar, *n.* **Gulbuddin** (1949–), Afghani Islamic fundamentalist guerrilla leader, leading the fundamentalist faction of the Hizb-i Islami (Islamic Party), dedicated to the overthrow of the Soviet-backed communist regime in Kabul. He refused to countenance participation in any interim 'national unity' government which includes Afghani communists.

Hel, Hela *n.* in Norse mythology, the goddess of the underworld.

helco-, *comb. form.* *(Path.)* of or relating to an ulcer or ulcers. **helcoid,** *a.* like an ulcer. [Gr. *helkos,* ulcer]

helcology, *n.* the branch of pathology relating to ulcers; a treatise on this subject.

helcoplasty, *n.* the grafting of a strip of healthy skin on an ulcer. [Gr. *plastos,* formed from *plassein,* to mould]

helcosis, *n.* an ulceration. **helcotic,** *a.*

held, *past & p.p.* HOLD[1].

heldentenor, *n.* (a man with) a strong tenor voice, suitable for Wagnerian roles. [G, hero tenor]

Helen, *n.* in Greek mythology, the daughter of Zeus and Leda, and the most beautiful of women. She married Menelaus, king of Sparta, but during his absence was the mistress of Paris, prince of Troy. This precipitated the Trojan War. Afterwards she returned to Sparta with her husband.

Helena, St, *n.* (*c.* 248–328), Roman empress, mother of Constantine the Great, and a convert to Christianity. According to legend, she discovered the true cross of Jesus in Jerusalem. Her feast day is 18 Aug.

heli- HELICOPTER.

heliacal, †**heliac,** *a.* closely connected with the sun; rising just before the sun. **heliacal rising, setting,** the apparent rising or setting of a star when it first becomes perceptible or invisible in rays of the sun. **heliacally,** *adv.* [Gr. *hēliakos,* from *hēlios,* sun]

helianthus, *n.* (*Bot.*) a genus of plants containing the sunflower. [Gr. *anthos,* flower]

helical, *a.* like a helix; spiral. **helical gears,** (*Mach.*) gear-wheels in which the teeth are set at angle to the axis. **helically,** *adv.* **helicograph,** *n.* an instrument for describing spirals. **helicoid,** *a.* **-coidal,** *a.* [L *helix -icis,* see HELIX]

Heliconian, *a.* of or pertaining to Helicon or the Muses. [L *Helicōnius,* Gr. *Helikōnios,* from *Helikōni,* a mountain in Boeotia, the fabled seat of Apollo and the Muses]

helicopter, *n.* an aircraft with one or more powerdriven airscrews mounted on vertical axes with the aid of which it can take-off or land vertically. **helicopter gunship,** *n.* a heavily-armed helicopter for attacking ground forces. **helicopter pad, helipad,** *n.* an area, e.g. on the roof of a building, where helicopters can take off and land. **heli-,** *comb. form.* pertaining to helicopters. **helipad** HELICOPTER PAD. **heliport,** an airport for the landing and departure of helicopters. [HELIX, Gr. *pteron,* a wing]

heli(o)-, *comb. form.* pertaining to the sun; produced by the sun. [Gr. *hēlios,* the sun]

heliocentric, *a.* having reference to the sun as centre; regarded from the point of view of the sun. **heliocentrically,** *adv.*

heliochrome, *n.* a photograph representing an object in the natural colours. **heliochromic,** *a.* pertaining to heliochromy. **heliochromotype,** *n.* a heliochrome. **heliochromy,** *n.* a photographic process by which the natural colours of objects are reproduced. [Gr. *chrōma,* colour]

heliogram HELIOGRAPH.

heliograph, *n.* an engraving obtained by a process in which a prepared plate is exposed to the light; an instrument for obtaining photographs of the sun; an apparatus for signalling by reflecting flashes of sunlight. *v.i.* to signal with this, to photograph by a heliographic process. **heliogram,** *n.* a message transmitted by heliograph. **heliographic, -ical,** *a.* **heliography,** *n.* the operation of signalling with the heliograph; the process of engraving by exposure by light; a description of the sun.

heliogravure, *n.* photoengraving; an engraved plate or print obtained by this.

heliolatry, *n.* sun-worship. **heliolater,** *n.* **heliolatrous,** *a.* [HELIO-, -LATRY]

heliology, *n.* the science of the sun.

heliometer, *n.* an instrument for measuring small angles in the heavens, such as the angular distance between stars, the diameter of stars etc.; orig. for measuring the diameter of the sun. **heliometric, -ical,** *a.*

heliophilous, *a.* attracted by or turning towards the sunlight. **heliophobous, -bic,** *a.* disliking or turning away from the sunlight.

Heliopolis, *n.* ancient Egyptian centre (biblical On) of the worship of the sun god Ra, NE of Cairo and near the modern village of Matariah.

Helios, *n.* in Greek mythology, the sun-god and father of PHAETHON, thought to make his daily journey across the sky in a chariot.

helioscope, *n.* a form of reflecting telescope for viewing the sun. **helioscopic,** *a.*

heliosis, *n.* spots caused on leaves etc. by the concentration of the sun's rays shining through glass, water-drops etc.; sunstroke.

heliostat, *n.* an instrument, comprising a mirror turned by clockwork, by which the rays of the sun are continuously reflected in a fixed direction. [Gr. *statos,* standing]

heliotherapy, *n.* (*Med.*) curative treatment by exposing the body to the rays of the sun.

heliothermometer, *n.* a thermometer with a blackened bulb for registering the effect of atmospheric absorption on solar radiation.

heliotrope, *n.* a genus of tropical or subtropical plants belonging to the borage family, whose flowers turn with the sun, those cultivated being varieties of *Heliotropium peruvianum;* formerly applied to the sunflower, marigold etc.; a purple tint characteristic of heliotrope flowers; a red-spotted variety of quartz, also called blood-stone; †an apparatus for reflecting the sun's rays, a kind of heliograph; †an ancient form of sundial. **heliotropic, -ical,** *a.* pertaining to or manifesting heliotropism. **heliotropism, heliotropy,** *n.* movement of leaves or flowers towards the sun. [L *heliotropium,* Gr. *heliotropion* (*trop-,* stem of *trepein,* to turn)]

heliotype, *n.* a picture obtained by printing from a gelatine surface in the same way as from a lithographic stone; this process. **heliotypic,** *a.* **heliotypography, heliotypy,** *n.*

heliozoan, *a.* (*Zool.*) pertaining to the Heliozoa, a group of Protozoa with threadlike radiating processes, also called sun-animalcules. *n.* one of this class. **heliozoic,** *a.* [Gr. *zōā,* pl. of *zōon,* animal]

helipad, *n.* a helicopter pad.

heliport, *n.* airport for the landing and departure of helicopters.

†**helispheric, -ical** *a.* winding round a globe spirally. [HELIX, SPHERICAL]

helium, *n.* a gaseous inert element, at. no. 2; chem. symbol He, discovered by Lockyer in the atmosphere of the sun by means of the solar spectrum, and afterwards found in the atmosphere and occluded to certain minerals. [Gr. *hēlios,* sun]

helix, *n.* (*pl.* **-lices**) a spiral line, as of wire or rope in coil; (*Anat.*) the rim or fold of the external ear; (*Arch.*) the small volute under the abacus of a Corinthian column, and other spiral ornaments; (*Zool.*) a genus of molluscs, containing the common snails. [L, from Gr.]

hell[1]**,** *n.* the place of punishment for the wicked after death; the place or state of the dead; a place of extreme misery, pain or suffering; torment, torture; a gambling-house; in prisoner's base and other games, the place for those who have been caught. *int.* an exclamation expressing anger, annoyance etc. **a hell of a, helluva something,** (*coll.*) a very good, bad, remarkable etc. thing of its kind. **as hell,** (*coll.*) extremely. **come hell or high water,** (*coll.*) whatever may happen. **for the hell of it,** for amusement. **hell for leather,** (*coll.*) very fast. **hell to pay,** unpleasant consequences. **like hell,** (*coll.*) very hard, much etc; used to deny a statement made by another. **to play hell with,** (*coll.*) to harm or damage; to scold. **what the hell,** what does it matter? **what, where, why etc. the hell?** (*coll.*) used as an intensifier. **hell-bent,** *adj.* recklessly intent (on). †**hell-black,** *a.* as black as hell. **hell-born, -bred,** *a.* of villainous origin. **hell-brewed,** *a.* prepared in hell. †**hell-broth,** *n.* a magical composition for evil purposes. **heli-cat,** *n.* a witch, a hag. **hell-fire,** *n.* the torments of hell. **hell-fired,** *a.* damned. **hell-gate,** *n.* the entrance to hell. †**hell-hag,** *n.* a mischievous, wicked old woman. **hell-hated,** *a.* abhorred like hell. †**hell-hound,** *n.* a fiend of hell; an agent of hell. †**hell-kite,** *n.* a person of extreme cruelty. **hell's angel,** *n.* a member of an often violent gang wearing leather and riding motorcycles. **hell's bells, teeth,** *int.* an exclamation expressing anger, annoyance etc. **hell-weed,** *n.* the dodder and other plants. **hellish,** †**helly,** *a.* pertaining to hell; infernal; detestable; atrociously wicked. **hellish(ly),** *adv.* **hellishness,** *n.* **hell-ward,** *a., adv.* [OE *hel* (cp. Dut. and Icel. *hel,* OHG *Hella,* G *Hölle*), from *hel-,* to hide, whence OE *hēlan,* see HELE]

hell[2]**,** HELE.

hellebore, *n.* any plant of the ranunculaceous genus *Helleborus,* containing *H. niger,* the Christmas rose, and the hellebore of the ancients, *H. officinalis,* which with other plants of the same genus or of *Veratrum* was supposed by the ancients to be a cure for insanity. †**helleborize, -ise,** *v.t.* to treat or dose with hellebore, as for madness. †**helleborism,** *n.* [L *helleborus,* Gr. *helleboros*]

Hellene, *n.* (*pl.* **-llenes**) an ancient Greek, one of Greek descent whether inhabiting Europe or Asia Minor; a citizen of modern Greece. **Hellenic,** *a.* **Hellenic period** *n.* the classical period of ancient Greek civilization, from the first Olympic Games 776 BC until the death of Alexander the Great 323 BC. **Hellenism,** *n.* a Greek idiom, phrase, peculiarity or custom; cultivation of Greek ideas, language, style etc.; Greek civilization or culture; Greek nationalism. **Hellenist,** *n.* one who adopted the Greek language, dress, customs etc., esp. a Greek Jew in the early days of Christianity; one who is learned in the Greek language and literature. **Hellenistic,** *a.* **Hellenistic period,** *n.* the period in Greek civilization from the death of Alexander 323 BC until the accession of the Roman emperor Augustus 27 BC. Alexandria in Egypt was the centre of culture and commerce during this period, and Greek culture spread throughout the Mediterranean region. **Hellenistically,** *adv.* **hellenize, -ise,** *v.i.* to adopt or follow Greek habits; to use or study the Greek language. *v.t.* to permeate with Greek ideas, culture etc.; to make Greek. **hellenization, -isation,** *n.* [Gr. *Hellēn*]

Heller, *n.* **Joseph** (1923–), US novelist. He drew on his experiences in World War II to write *Catch-22* (1961), satirizing war and bureaucratic methods.

Hellespont, *n.* former name of the Dardanelles, the strait which separates Europe from Asia.

hellicat, *a.* (*Sc.*) giddy-headed, flighty. *n.* a hell-cat. [var. of Sc. *halok, halokit,* etym. unknown]

Hellman, *n.* **Lillian** (1907–84), US playwright, whose work is largely concerned with contemporary political and social issues. *The Children's Hour* (1934), *The Little Foxes* (1939), and *Toys in the Attic* (1960) are all examples of the 'well-made play'.

hello, HALLO.

helm[1]**,** *n.* a helmet; †the upper part of a retort or alembic; (*Cumb. and Westmor.*) a cloud gathering over the northern Pennines before or during a storm. **helm-cloud,** *n.* **helm-wind,** *n.* a violent easterly wind blowing down from the Pennines. **helmed,** *a.* helmeted. **helmless,** *a.* [OE, Dut., G, cogn. with *helan,* see HELE]

helm[2]**,** *n.* the instrument or apparatus by which a vessel is steered; the rudder and its operative parts, such as the tiller or wheel; the tiller; a position of management or direction; †a helmsman. *v.t.* to guide, to steer; to manage. **to put up (down) the helm,** (*Naut.*) to bring the rudder to leeward (windward). †**helmage,** *n.* guidance; direction; management. **helmless,** *a.* **helms-**

man, *n.* the man who steers. [OE *helma* (cp. Icel. *hjalm*)]

Helmand, *n.* the longest river in Afghanistan. Rising in the Hindu Kush, W of Kabul, it flows SW for 1125 km/703 miles before entering the marshland surrounding Lake Saberi on the Iranian frontier.

helmet, *n.* a piece of defensive armour for the head; a hat of similar form made of felt, cork, pith or metal, worn as a protection against the sun or by policemen etc.; the hooded upper lip of some flowers; a helmet-shell. **helmet-shell,** *n.* a tropical mollusc belonging to the genus *Cassis*. **helmeted,** *a.* wearing a helmet. [obs. F *healmet,* dim. of *helm,* HELM[1]]

Helmholtz, *n.* **Hermann Ludwig Ferdinand von** (1821–94), German physiologist, physicist, and inventor of the ophthalmoscope. He was the first to explain how the cochlea of the inner ear works, and the first to measure the speed of nerve impulses. In physics, he formulated the law of conservation of energy, and did important work in thermodynamics.

helminth, *n.* a worm, esp. a parasitic intestinal worm. **helminthagogue,** *n.* (*Med.*) a medicine to expel worms; an anthelmintic. **helminthic,** *a.* relating to intestinal worms. **helminthite,** *n.* (*Geol.*) a sinuous mark on sandstone supposed to be a fossil worm-track. **helminthoid,** *a.* **helminthology,** *n.* the study of intestinal worms. **helminthological,** *a.* **helminthologist,** *n.* **helminthous,** *a.* [Gr. *helmins -minthos,* cogn. with HELIX]

Helmont, *n.* **Jean Baptiste van** (1577–1644), Belgian doctor. He was the first to realize that gases exist apart from the atmosphere, and claimed to have coined the word 'gas' (from the Greek 'chaos').

Héloïse, *n.* (1101–64), abbess of Paraclete in Champagne, correspondent and lover of Abelard. She became deeply interested in intellectual study in her youth. After her affair with Abelard, and the birth of a son, Astrolabe, she became a nun in 1229, and with Abelard's assistance, founded a nunnery at Paraclete. Her letters show her strong and pious character.

helot, *n.* a serf or bond slave in ancient Sparta; a slave or serf. **helotism,** *n.* the system of serfdom in Sparta or elsewhere. **helotry,** *n.* helots collectively; bond slaves or serfs. **helotize, -ise,** *v.t.* [L *Hēlōtēs,* Gr. *Heilōtes,* pl. of *Hielōs,* prob. orig. an inhabitant of *Helos,* a Laconian town whose inhabitants were enslaved by the Spartans]

help, *v.t.* (†*past* **holp,** †*p.p.* **holpen**) to assist, to aid; to further; to supply succour or relief to in time of distress; to remedy, to prevent. *v.i.* to lend aid or assistance; to be of use; to avail. *n.* aid or assistance; succour, relief; escape, remedy; a helper; a domestic servant; a helping (of food etc.). **a helping hand,** an act of assisting. **it cannot be helped,** there is no remedy; it cannot be prevented or avoided. **so help me God,** a strong oath or asseveration. **to help off,** to help (a person) to remove or take off (a garment etc.); to help to get rid of. **to help on,** to forward, to advance; to help (a person) put on (a garment etc.). **to help oneself,** to take or do without assistance; to take without permission, authority etc. **to help out,** to help to complete or to get out of a difficulty. **to help over,** to enable to surmount. **to help to,** to supply with, to furnish with. **to help up,** to raise, to support. **helpline,** *n.* a telephone service offering advice or counselling to callers. **helper,** *n.* **helpful,** *a.* giving help, useful, serviceable, beneficial. **helpfully,** *adv.* **helpfulness,** *n.* **helping,** *n.* a portion of food given at table. **helpless,** *a.* wanting power to help oneself; affording no help; irremediable, †unavailing; †destitute. **helplessly,** *adv.* **helplessness,** *n.* [OE *helpan*]

Helpmann, *n.* **Robert** (1909–86), Australian dancer, choreographer, and actor. The leading male dancer with the Sadler's Wells Ballet, London 1933–50, he partnered Margot Fonteyn in the 1940s.

helpmate, *n.* a helper; a partner or helpful companion, esp. a spouse. **helpmeet,** *n.* a helpmate (formed by a misunderstanding of Gen. ii.18, 'help meet for him').

Helsinki, *n.* (Swedish **Helsingfors**) capital and port of Finland; population (1988) 490,000, metropolitan area 978,000. Industries include shipbuilding, engineering, and textiles. The homes of the architect Eliel Saarinen and the composer Jean Sibelius outside the town are museums. **Helsinki Conference,** *n.* international conference (1975) at which 35 countries, including the USSR and the US, attempted to reach agreement on cooperation in security, economics, science, technology, and human rights.

helter-skelter, *adv.* in great hurry and confusion. *a.* hurried and confused. *n.* hurry; a fun-fair amusement consisting of a tower with a spiral slide. [imit.]

helve, *n.* the handle of a weapon or tool. *v.t.* to fit a helve to. **helve-hammer,** *n.* a trip hammer. **helver,** *n.* (*Mining*) a helve. [OE *hielf* (cp. MDut. *helve*), cogn. with HALTER]

Helvetian, *a.* Swiss. *n.* a Swiss; one of the ancient Helvetii. **Helvetic,** *a.* Helvetian. *n.* a Swiss Protestant, a Zwinglian. [L *Helvētius*]

Helvetius, *n.* **Claude Adrien** (1715–71), French philosopher. In *De l'Esprit* (1758) he argued that self-interest, however disguised, is the mainspring of all human action, that since conceptions of good and evil vary according to period and locality there is no absolute good or evil. He also believed that intellectual differences are only a matter of education.

hem[1], *n.* the edge or border of a garment or piece of cloth, esp. when doubled and sewn in to strengthen it. *v.t.* (*past, p.p.* **hemmed**) to double over and sew in the border of; to enclose or shut (in, about or round). **hemmer,** *n.* one who or that which hems; an attachment to a sewing-machine for hemming. **hem-line,** *n.* the hemmed bottom edge of a skirt or dress. **hem-stitch,** *n.* an ornamental stitch made by drawing out parallel threads and fastening the cross threads. *v.t.* to hem with this. [OE *hemm, hem* (cp. G *hemmen,* to stop, to check)]

hem[2], *int., n.* a voluntary short cough, uttered by way of warning, encouragement etc. *v.i.* to cry 'hem'; to hesitate. †*v.t.* to clear the throat by hemming. [imit.]

hema-, hemat-, hemato- etc. HAEMA-.

he-man HE.

hematite, HAEMATITE.

heme HAEM.

hemeralopia, *n.* a pathological condition in which the eyes see badly by daylight and better by night or artificial light; also applied to night-blindness or nyctalopia. [from Gr. *hēmeralops* (*hēmera,* day, *alaos,* blind, *ops,* eye)]

hemi-, *pref.* half, halved; pertaining to or affecting one half. [Gr. *hēmi-*]

hemianopsia, *n.* paralysis of the optic nerve causing obscuration of half of the field of vision. **hemianoptic, hemiopic,** *a.*

hemicrania, *n.* headache affecting only one side of the head. **hemicranial,** *a.* [L *hēmicrānia,* Gr. *hēmikrania* (*kranion,* skull)]

hemicycle, *n.* a semicircle; a semicircular arena, room or division of a room. **hemicyclic,** *a.* (*Bot.*) having the parts of the inflorescence arranged in spirals or in spirals and whorls. [F *hémicycle,* L *hēmicyclium,* Gr. *hemikuklion*]

hemidemisemiquaver, *n.* a note equal in time to half a demisemiquaver.

hemihedral, *a.* (*Cryst.*) having only half the normal number of planes or facets. **hemihedrism,** *n.* **hemihedron,** *n.* [Gr. *hedra,* seat, base]

hemimetabola, *n.* a section of insects that undergo incomplete metamorphosis. **hemimetabolic, hemimetabolous,** *a.* [Gr. *metabolos,* changeable]

Hemingway, *n.* **Ernest** (1898–1961), US writer. War, bullfighting, and fishing became prominent themes in his short stories and novels, which included *A Farewell to Arms* (1929), *For Whom the Bell Tolls* (1940), and *The Old Man and the Sea* (1952). His short, deceptively simple sentences attracted many imitators. Nobel prize 1954.

hemione, hemionus, *n.* the dziggetai, a species of wild ass. [L *hemionus,* Gr. *hemionos* (HEMI-, *onos,* ass)]

hemiopia, hemiopsia, HEMIANOPSIA.

hemiplegia, †hemiplegy, *n.* paralysis of one side of the body. **hemiplegic**, *a.* [Gr. *hēmiplēgia* (*plēgē*, stroke, from *plēssein,* to strike)]

Hemiptera, *n.pl.* (*sing.* **hemipteron**), an order of insects with suctorial mouth-organ, and usually having four wings, the upper pair partly horny and partly membranous, comprising bugs, lice etc. **hemipter,** *n.* one of this order of insects. **hemipteral, -terous,** *a.* **hemipteran,** *n.* **hemiperist,** *n.* [HEMI-, Gr. *pteron,* wing]

hemisphere, *n.* the half of a sphere or globe, divided by a plane passing through its centre; half of the terrestrial or the celestial sphere; a map or projection of either of these; cerebral hemisphere. **hemispheric, -al**, *a.* **hemispheroid**, *n.* **hemispheroidal**, *a.* [F *hémisphère,* Gr. *hemisphaira*]

hemistich, *n.* half a verse, usu. as divided by the caesura; an imperfect verse. **hemistichal,** *a.* [L *hēmistichium,* Gr. *hēmistichion* (*stichos,* a row)]

hemitrope, *a.* used of a crystal looking as if the one half were turned round upon the other. *n.* a crystal of this form. **hemitropic**, *a.* hemitrope. **hemitropal, hemitropous**, *a.* hemitropic; (*Bot.*) used of a half-inverted ovule. [F *hémitrope* (Gr. *-tropos,* turning, from *trepein,* to turn)]

hemlock, *n.* the poisonous umbelliferous genus *Conium,* esp. *C. maculatum,* the common hemlock; a poison obtained from it; (*N Am.*) the hemlock fir or spruce. **hemlock fir, spruce,** or **tree,** *n.* a N American conifer, *Abies canadensis.* [OE *hemlic, hymlic,* etym. unknown]

hemmer HEM[2].

hemo- HAEMA-.

hemorrhage etc., HAEMORRHAGE.

hemorrhoids etc., HAEMORRHOIDS.

hemp, *n.* an Indian herbaceous plant, *Cannabis sativa;* the fibre of this, used for making ropes, coarse fabrics etc.; applied also to other vegetable fibres used for cloth or cordage; bhang, hashish; **hemp-agrimony,** *n.* a composite plant, *Eupatorium cannabinum.* **hemp-nettle,** *n.* a coarse plant of the labiate genus *Galeopsis.* **hemp-palm,** *n.* an Indian and Chinese palm, *Chamaerops excelsa,* which yields fibre for cordage. **hemp-seed,** *n.* the seed of hemp, much used as food for cage-birds; a person destined for the gallows. **hempen,** *a.* made of or resembling hemp. **†hempen candle,** *n.* (*Shak.*) the hangman's rope. **†hempy,** *a.* like or of the nature of hemp; (*Sc.*) deserving to be hanged, roguish, mischievous. *n.* (*Sc.*) a rogue, a mischievous young person. [OE *henep* (cp. Dut. *hennep,* Icel. *hampr,* G *Hanf,* also Gr. *kannabis*)]

hen, *n.* the female of any bird, esp. the domestic fowl; a female bird (*in comb.,* as *guinea-hen, pea-hen*); in parts of Scotland a term of endearment or friendliness to a woman. **hen and chickens,** *n.pl.* one of the houseleeks, esp. *Sempervivum globiferum;* a cultivated variety of daisy with a large flower-head encircled by smaller ones; the ground-ivy. **hen-bane,** *n.* a plant of the genus *Hyoscyamus,* esp. *H. niger;* a poisonous drug obtained from *H. niger.* **henbit,** *n.* a species of dead-nettle, *Lamium amplexicaule;* the ivy-leaved speedwell, *Veronica hederifolia.* **hen-coop,** *n.* a coop or cage for fowls. **†hen-driver, -harrier,** *n.* the blue hawk, *Circus cyaneus.* **hen-house,** *n.* a fowl-house. **hen-mould,** *n.* black spongy soil. **hen-party,** *n.* (*sometimes derog.*) a party for women only. **henpeck,** *v.t.* to govern or rule (of a wife who has the upper hand of her husband). *n.* a wife who domineers over or nags at her husband. **hen-roost,** *n.* a place for fowls to roost in. **hen-toed,** *a.* having the toes turned in. **hen-wife, -woman,** *n.* a woman who has the charge of fowls. **hennery,** *n.* an enclosed place or run for fowls. **henny,** *a.* hen-like. *n.* a hen-like male fowl. [OE *henn,* from *hana,* cock (cp. Dut. *hen,* Icel. *haena,* G *Henne*), cogn. with L *canere,* to sing]

Henan (formerly **Honan**), *n.* province of E central China. **area** 167,000 sq km/64,462 sq miles. **capital** Zhengzhou. **population** (1986) 78,080,000. **products** cereals, cotton.

hence, *adv.* from this place, time, source or origin; in consequence of this, consequently, therefore. *int.* away, away with, begone, depart. **henceforth, henceforward,** *adv.* from this time on. [ME *hennes, henne,* OE *heonan, heonane,* from *hi-,* root of HE, HIS etc.]

henchman, *n.* a squire, a page; a male servant or attendant; a faithful follower; a political worker, esp. in the US. [ME *henxtman, henxman* (OE *hengest,* horse, MAN)]

†hend, *v.t.* to seize, to take, to lay hold on. [from OE *gehendan,* from HAND, or Icel. *henda*]

hendeca-, *comb. form.* eleven. [Gk. *hendeka,* eleven]

hendecagon, *n.* a plane rectilinear figure of 11 sides or angles. [Gr. *hendeka,* eleven, gōnia, angle]

hendecasyllable, *n.* a verse or line of 11 syllables. **hendecasyllabic**, *a.* containing 11 syllables; *n.* a hendecasyllabic verse. [L *hendecasyllabus,* Gr. *hendekasullabos hendeka,* eleven]

Henderson, *n.* **Arthur** (1863–1935), British Labour politician, born in Glasgow. He worked 20 years as an iron-moulder in Newcastle, entered Parliament (1903), and contributed to Labour's political organization. He was home secretary in the first Labour government, and was foreign secretary 1929–31, when he accorded the Soviet government full recognition. Nobel Peace Prize 1934.

hendiadys, *n.* a rhetorical figure representing one idea by two words connected by a conjunction, e.g. 'by hook or crook'. [late L, from Gr. *hen dia duoin,* one by two]

Hendrix, *n.* **Jimi (James Marshall)** (1942–70), US rock guitarist, songwriter, and singer, legendary for his virtuoso experimental technique and flamboyance.

Hendry, *n.* **Stephen** (1970–), Scottish snooker player of exceptional talent. He succeeded Steve Davis at the top of the top-ranking list during the 1989–90 season.

henequen, *n.* sisal hemp. [Sp. *jehiquen*]

Heng, *n.* **Samrin** (1934–), Cambodian politician. A former Khmer Rouge commander (1976–78), who had become disillusioned by its brutal tactics, he led an unsuccessful coup against Pol Pot (1978) and established the Kampuchean People's Revolutionary Party (KPRP) in Vietnam, before returning, in 1979, to head the new Vietnamese-backed government.

henge, *n.* a circle of stones or staves of prehistoric date. [backformation from *Stonehenge*]

Hengist, *n.* legendary leader, with his brother Horsa, of the Jutes, who originated in Jutland, and settled in Kent about AD 450, the first Anglo-Saxon settlers in Britain.

hen-harrier HEN.

Henlein, *n.* **Konrad** (1898–1945), Sudeten-German leader of the Sudeten Nazi Party inside Czechoslovakia, and closely allied with Hitler's German Nazis. He was partly responsible for the destabilization of the Czech state 1938 which led to the Munich Agreement and secession of the Sudetenland to Germany.

Henley Royal Regatta, a rowing festival in the UK on the river Thames inaugurated 1839. It is as much a social as a sporting occasion. The principal events are the solo *Diamond Challenge Sculls*, and the *Grand Challenge Cup*, the leading event for eights. The regatta is held in July.

henna, *n.* the Egyptian privet, *Lawsonia ermis;* a dye obtained from this plant used largely for dyeing hair, also in the East for dyeing parts of the body. [Arab. *hinnā*]

hennery, henny HEN.

henotheism, *n.* worship of or ascription of supreme power to one out of several gods, a phase intermediate between polytheism and monotheism. **henotheist**, *n.* **henotheistic**, *a.* [Gr. *heis henos,* one, THEISM]

henpeck HEN.

Henri, *n.* **Robert** (1865–1929), US painter, a leading figure in the transition between 19th-cent. conventions and modern art in America. He was a principal member of the ASHCAN SCHOOL.

Henrietta Maria, *n.* (1609–69), queen of England

1625–49. The daughter of Henry IV of France, she married Charles I of England 1625. As she used her influence to encourage him to aid Roman Catholics and make himself an absolute ruler, she became highly unpopular and had to go into exile 1644–60. She returned to England at the Restoration, but retired to France 1665.

henry, *n.* (*pl.* **-ries**) unit of inductance; inductance of a circuit in which a change of current of 1 ampere per second induces e.m.f. of 1 volt. [US physicist J *Henry*, 1797–1878]

Henry, *n.* eight kings of England:

Henry I, *n.* (1068–1135), king of England from 1100. Youngest son of William I, he succeeded his brother William II. He won the support of the Saxons by granting them a charter and marrying a Saxon princess. An able administrator, he established a professional bureaucracy and a system of travelling judges. He was succeeded by Stephen.

Henry II, *n.* (1133–89), king of England from 1154, when he succeeded Stephen. He was the son of Matilda and Geoffrey of Anjou (1113–51). He curbed the power of the barons, but his attempt to bring the church courts under control had to be abandoned after the murder of Becket. During his reign the English conquest of Ireland began. He was succeeded by his son Richard I.

Henry III, *n.* (1207–72), king of England from 1216, when he succeeded John, but he did not assume royal power until 1227. His subservience to the papacy and his foreign favourites led to de Montfort's revolt (1264). Henry was defeated at Lewes, Sussex, and imprisoned. He was restored to the throne after a royalist victory at Evesham 1265. He was succeeded by his son Edward I.

Henry IV, *n.* **(Bolingbroke)** (1367–1413), king of England from 1399, the son of John of Gaunt. In 1398 he was banished by Richard II for political activity, but returned 1399 to head a revolt and be accepted as king by Parliament. He was succeeded by his son Henry V.

Henry V, *n.* (1387–1422), king of England from 1413, son of Henry IV. Invading Normandy (1415), he captured Harfleur, and defeated the French at AGINCOURT. He invaded again (1417–19), capturing Rouen. He married Catherine of Valois 1420, to gain recognition as heir to the French throne. He was succeeded by his son Henry VI.

Henry VI, *n.* (1421–71), king of England from 1422, son of Henry V. He assumed royal power 1442, and identified himself with the party opposed to the continuation of the French war. After his marriage 1445, he was dominated by his wife, Margaret of Anjou. The unpopularity of the government, especially after the loss of the English conquests in France, encouraged Richard, Duke of York to claim the throne, and though York was killed 1460, his son Edward IV proclaimed himself king 1461. Henry was captured 1465, temporarily restored 1470, but again imprisoned 1471 and then murdered.

Henry VII, *n.* (1457–1509), king of England from 1485, son of Edmund Tudor, Earl of Richmond (*c.* 1430–56), and a descendant of John of Gaunt. He spent his early life in Brittany until 1485, when he landed in Britain to lead the rebellion against Richard III which ended with Richard's defeat and death at Bosworth. Yorkist revolts continued until 1497, but Henry restored order after the Wars of the Roses by the Star Chamber, and achieved independence from Parliament by amassing a private fortune through confiscations. He was succeeded by his son Henry VIII.

Henry VIII, *n.* (1491–1547), king of England from 1509, when he succeeded his father Henry VII and married Catherine of Aragon, the widow of his brother. His Lord Chancellor, Cardinal Wolsey, was replaced by Thomas More 1529, for failing to persuade the pope to grant Henry a divorce. After 1532 Henry broke with the Catholic church, proclaimed himself head of the church, and dissolved the monasteries. After divorcing Catherine, his wives were Anne Boleyn, Jane Seymour, Anne of Cleves, Catherine Howard, and Catherine Parr. He was succeeded by his son Edward VI.

Henry, *n.* four kings of France:

Henry I, *n.* (1005–60), king of France from 1031, who spent much of his reign in conflict with William I the Conqueror, then duke of Normandy.

Henry II, *n.* (1519–59), king of France from 1547. He captured the fortresses of Metz and Verdun from the Holy Roman emperor Charles V, and Calais from the English. He was killed in a tournament.

Henry III, *n.* (1551–89), king of France from 1574. He fought both the Huguenots (headed by his successor, Henry of Navarre) and the Catholic League (headed by the Duke of Guise). Guise expelled Henry from Paris 1588 but was assassinated. Henry allied with the Huguenots under Henry of Navarre to besiege the city, but was assassinated by a monk.

Henry IV, *n.* (1553–1610), king of France from 1589. Son of Antoine de Bourbon and Jeanne, queen of Navarre, he was brought up as a Protestant, and from 1576 led the Huguenots. On his accession he settled the religious question by adopting Catholicism while tolerating Protestantism. He restored peace and strong government to France, and brought back prosperity by measures for the promotion of industry and agriculture, and the improvement of communications. He was assassinated by a Catholic fanatic.

Henry, *n.* seven Holy Roman emperors:

Henry I, *n.* **(the Fowler)** (*c.* AD 876–AD 936), king of Germany from AD 919, and duke of Saxony from AD 912. He secured the frontiers of Saxony, ruled in harmony with its nobles, and extended German influence over the Hungarians, the Danes, and Slavonic tribes in the east. He was about to claim the imperial crown when he died.

Henry II, *n.* **(the Saint)** (AD 973–1024), king of Germany from 1002, Holy Roman emperor from 1014, when he recognized Benedict VIII as pope. He was canonized 1146.

Henry III, *n.* **(the Black)** (1017–56), king of Germany from 1028, Holy Roman emperor from 1039, who raised the empire to the height of its power, and extended its authority over Poland, Bohemia, and Hungary.

Henry IV, *n.* (1050–1106), Holy Roman emperor from 1056, who was involved from 1075 in a struggle with the papacy (see GREGORY VII).

Henry V, *n.* (1081–1125), Holy Roman emperor from 1106. He continued the struggle with the church until the settlement of the investiture contest in 1122.

Henry VI, *n.* (1165–97), Holy Roman emperor from 1190. As part of his plan for making the empire universal, he captured and imprisoned Richard I of England, and compelled him to do homage.

Henry VII, *n.* (1269–1313), Holy Roman emperor from 1308. He attempted unsuccessfully to revive the imperial supremacy in Italy.

Henry[1], *n.* **(Charles Albert David)** known as **Harry** (1984–), prince of the United Kingdom; second child of the Prince and Princess of Wales.

Henry[2], *n.* **Joseph** (1797–1878), US physicist, inventor of the electromagnetic motor (1829), and a telegraphic apparatus. He also discovered the principle of electromagnetic induction, roughly at the same time as Faraday, and the phenomenon of self-induction. A unit of inductance (HENRY) is named after him.

Henry[3], *n.* **O.** (1862–1910), pen name of William Sydney Porter, US short story writer, whose collections include *Cabbages and Kings* (1904) and *The Four Million* (1906). His stories are in a colloquial style and noted for their skilled construction with twist endings.

Henry[4], *n.* **Patrick** (1736–99), US politician, who in 1775 supported the arming of the Virginia militia against the British by a speech ending: 'Give me liberty or give me death!' He was governor of the state (1776–79 and 1784–86).

Henry[5], *n.* **William** (1774–1836), British chemist. In 1803 he formulated **Henry's law**: when a gas is dissolved in a liquid at a given temperature, the mass which dissolves is in direct proportion to the gas pressure.

Henry the Navigator, *n.* (1394–1460), Portuguese prince. He set up a school for navigators 1419 and under his patronage, Portuguese seamen explored and colonized Madeira, the Cape Verde Islands, and the Azores; they sailed down the African coast almost to Sierra Leone.

hent, *v.t.* to take hold of; to seize, to get possession of. *n.* seizing, seizure, grasp. [OE *hentan,* cp. HEND]

Henze, *n.* **Hans Werner** (1926–), German composer whose large and varied output includes orchestral, vocal, and chamber music. He uses traditional symphony and concerto forms, and incorporates a wide range of styles including jazz.

hep, *a.* (*esp. N Am.* (*dated*) *sl.*) aware of, informed of, wise to. **hep-cat,** *n.* a jazz dancer or player; a jazz fiend.

†**hepar,** *n.* (*Chem.*) liver of sulphur, and other metallic sulphides, so called from their reddish-brown colour; (*Homoeopathy*) calcium sulphide. **heparin,** *n.* (*Med.*) substance extracted from this which prevents blood-clotting. [med. L, from Gr., the liver]

hepatic, *a.* of or belonging to the liver; resembling the liver in colour or form; (*Bot.*) pertaining to the liverworts. †**hepatic air, gas,** *n.* sulphuretted hydrogen. [as prec.]

hepatica, *n.* (*pl.* **-cae** -sē) a sub-genus of the genus *Anemone* containing the liverleaf, *Anemone* or *Hepatica triloba;* the common liverwort *Marchantia polymorpha;* (*pl.*) a sub-class of cryptogams comprising the liverworts, moss-like plants having no lid or operculum such as that characteristic of mosses.

hepatite, *n.* (*Min.*) a variety of barytes giving out a fetid odour when heated; liverstone. [as prec.]

hepatitis, *n.* (*Med.*) inflammation or congestion of the liver.

hepatize, -ise, *v.t.* to convert the lungs into a substance like liver; to impregnate with sulphuretted hydrogen. **hepatization, -isation,** *n.*

hepat(o)-, *comb. form.* liver. [late L *hēpaticus,* Gr. *hēpatikos,* from *hēpar hēpatos,* the liver]

hepatocele, *n.* (*Path.*) hernia of the liver. [-CELE]

hepatocystic, *a.* relating to the liver and the gall-bladder. [CYSTIC]

hepatogastric, *a.* relating to the liver and the stomach. [GASTRIC]

hepatology, *n.* the branch of medical science relating to the liver. **hepatologist,** *n.* [-LOGY]

hepatorrhoea, *n.* (*Path.*) a morbid flow of bile, bilious diarrhoea. [Gr. *rhoia,* a flowing, from *rheein,* to flow]

hepatoscopy, *n.* divination by inspection of an animal's liver. [-SCOPY]

Hepburn[1]**,** *n.* **Audrey (Audrey Hepburn-Rushton)** (1929–), British actress of Anglo-Dutch descent who tended to play innocent, child-like characters. Slender and doe-eyed, she set a different style from the pneumatic stars of the 1950s. After playing minor parts in British films in the early 1950s, she became a Hollywood star in such films as *Funny Face* (1957), *My Fair Lady* (1964), *Wait Until Dark* (1968), and *Robin and Marian* (1976).

Hepburn[2]**,** *n.* **Katharine** (1909–), US actress, who appeared in such films as *The African Queen* (1951), *Guess Who's Coming to Dinner* (1967), and *On Golden Pond* (1981). She won four Academy Awards.

Hephaestus, *n.* in Greek mythology, the god of fire and metalcraft (Roman Vulcan), son of Zeus and Hera; he was lame, and married Aphrodite.

Hepplewhite, *n.* **George** (d. 1786), English furniture maker. He developed a simple, elegant style, working mainly in mahogany or satinwood, adding delicately inlaid or painted decorations of feathers, shells, or wheat-ears. His book of designs, *The Cabinetmaker and Upholsterer's Guide* (1788), was published posthumously.

hepta-, *comb. form.* consisting of seven. [Gr. *hepta,* seven]

heptachord [hep'təkawd), *n.* (*Mus.*) a series of seven notes; the interval of a seventh; an instrument with seven strings. [Gr. *heptachordos* (*chordē,* CHORD)]

heptad, *n.* a sum or group of seven; a week; (*Chem.*) an atom with a valency of seven. (*Mus.*) a scheme of seven tones comprising all from which consonant triads with the tonic may be formed. [Gr. *heptas -tados,* as prec.]

heptaglot, *n.* a book in seven languages. *a.* in seven languages. [Gr. *glōtta,* tongue]

heptagon, *n.* a plane rectilinear figure having seven sides and seven angles. **heptagonal,** *a.* [Gr. *gōnia,* angle)]

heptagynia, *n.pl.* (*Bot.*) a Linnaean order containing plants which have seven pistils. **heptagyn,** *n.* a plant of this order. **heptagynian, heptagynous,** *a.* [Gr. *gunē,* woman, female]

heptahedron, *n.* (*Geom.*) a solid figure having seven sides. **heptahedral,** *a.* [Gr. *hedra,* seat, base]

heptamerous, *a.* having seven parts or members. †**heptamerede,** *n.* that which divides into seven parts. [Gr. *meros,* part]

heptameter, *n.* a verse of seven metrical feet.

heptandria, *n.pl.* (*Bot.*) a Linnaean class of plants containing those with seven stamens. **heptandrous, -drian,** *a.* [Gr. *anér andros,* man, male]

heptane, *n.* a hydrocarbon of the methane series.

heptarchy, *n.* a government by seven rulers; a country under seven rulers; the seven kingdoms established in Britain by the Angles and Saxons, i.e. Kent, Sussex, Wessex, Essex, Mercia, Northumbria and East Anglia, which flourished for various periods from the 5th to the 8th cents. †**heptarch,** †**heptarchist,** *n.* a governor of one division of a heptarchy. **heptarchic, -al,** *a.* [Gr. *-archia,* government, from *archein,* to rule]

heptastich, *n.* (*Pros.*) a poem of seven verses. [Gr. *stichos,* a row]

heptasyllabic, *a.* seven-syllabled. *n.* a verse of seven syllables. [Gr. *heptasullabos*]

Heptateuch, *n.* the first seven books of the Old Testament. [Gr. *heptateuchos* (HEPTA-, *teuchos,* book)]

Hepworth, *n.* **Barbara** (1903–75), British sculptor. She developed a distinctive abstract style, creating hollowed forms of stone or wood with spaces bridged by wires or strings; many later works are in bronze.

her, *pron.* the possessive, dative or accusative case of the personal pronoun SHE; used in the possessive as an adj., and absolutely in the form **hers**, when the noun is not expressed. [OE *hire,* gen. and dat. of *hēo,* she.]

Hera, *n.* in Greek mythology, a goddess, sister-consort of Zeus, mother of Hephaestus, Hebe, and Ares; protector of women and marriage, and identified with Roman Juno.

Heraclean, *a.* pertaining to Heracles. **Heracleid,** *n.* one of the descendants of Heracles; one of the Dorian aristocracy who claimed this origin. **Heracleidan,** *a.* [L *Hēraclēus,* Gr. *Hērakleios,* from *Hēraklēs*]

Heracles, *n.* in Greek mythology, a hero (Roman Hercules), son of Zeus and Alcmene, famed for strength. While serving Eurystheus, king of Argos, he performed 12 labours, including the cleansing of the Augean stables.

Heraclius, *n.* (*c.* AD 575–AD 641), Byzantine emperor from AD 610. His reign marked a turning point in the empire's fortunes. Of Armenian descent, he recaptured Armenia AD 622, and other provinces AD 622–628 from the Persians, but lost them to the Arabs AD 629–41.

Heraklion, *n.* alternative name for IRÁKLION.

herald, *n.* an officer whose duty was to proclaim peace or war, to challenge to battle and to carry messages between sovereigns and princes; an officer whose duty it is to superintend state ceremonies, such as coronations, installations etc., to grant, record and blazon arms, trace genealogies etc.; a messenger; a harbinger, a precursor. *v.t.* to act as herald to; to proclaim; to announce; to introduce, to usher in. **herald-moth,** *n.* a noctuid moth, *Gonoptera libatrix,* which appears in the autumn and is supposed to be a forerunner of winter.

Heralds' College, *n.* another name for the College of Arms, a royal corporation, founded in 1483, consisting of the Earl Marshal, the Kings-of-Arms, the heralds and pursuivants, whose duty now is to record pedigrees and grant armorial bearings. [OF *heralt, heraut,* prob. from Teut.]

heraldry, *n.* the art and study of armorial bearings etc.; pomp, ceremony etc.; the office of a herald; heraldic bearings, emblazonment; †a coat of arms, **heraldic,** *a.* pertaining to heraldry or heralds. **heraldically,** *adv.* [as prec.]

Herat, *n.* capital of Herat province, and the largest city in W Afghanistan, on the N banks of the Hari Rud; population (1980) 160,000. A principal road junction, it was a great city in ancient and mediaeval times.

herb, *n.* a plant producing shoots of only annual duration; herbage, grass and other green food for cattle; a plant having medicinal, culinary or aromatic properties, a simple. **herb beer,** *n.* a teetotal beverage made from herbs. **herb bennet,** *n.* the wood avens, *Geum urbanum.* †**herb grace,** †**herb of grace,** *n.* rue, *Ruta graveolens;* applied to other herbs. **herb Paris,** *n.* a herb, *Paris quadrifolia,* growing in woods, with four leaves in the form of a cross and a terminal green flower. **herb Robert,** *n.* common wild flower *Geranium robertianum* found throughout Europe and central Asia, and naturalized in North America. About 30 cm/1 ft high, it bears hairy leaves and small pinkish to purplish flowers, and has a reddish hairy stem. When rubbed, the leaves have a strong smell. **herbaceous,** *a.* pertaining to herbs; of the nature of herbs; †herbivorous. **herbage,** *n.* herbs collectively; grass, pasture; (*Law.*) the right of pasture in the forest or on the grounds of another. †**herbaged,** *a.* grassy, verdant. **herbal,** *a.* pertaining to herbs. *n.* a book containing the names of plants, with a description of their properties, medicinal and other virtues etc. **herbalist,** *n.* one skilled in the knowledge of herbs and their qualities; a collector of plants; an early botanist; a dealer in medicinal herbs. †**herbar,** †**-er,** *n.* a garden; a herb; an arbour. **herbarium,** *n.* (*pl.* **-ia**) a systematic collection of dried plants; a case or room for the preservation of dried plants. †**herbary,** *n.* a garden of herbs; a herbarium; a herbal. **herbescent,** *a.* growing into a herb, becoming herbaceous. **herbicide,** *n.* a chemical that destroys vegetation, used to control weeds. **herbicidal,** *a.* **herbiferous,** *a.* producing vegetation. **herbous, herby,** *a.* of the nature of or like herbs; abounding in herbs. [ME and OF *erbe,* L *herba,* grass]

Herbert¹, *n.* **George** (1593–1633), English poet. His volume of religious poems, *The Temple,* appeared in 1633, shortly before his death. His poems depict his intense religious feelings in clear, simple language.

Herbert², *n.* **Wally (Walter)** (1934–), British surveyor and explorer. His first surface crossing by dog sledge of the Arctic Ocean 1968–69, from Alaska to Spitsbergen via the North Pole, was the longest sustained sledging journey (6000 km/3800 miles) in polar exploration.

herbivora, *n.pl.* (*Zool.*) animals, esp. mammals, feeding on grass or plants. **herbivore,**, *n.* one of the herbivora. **herbivorous,** *a.* [L *herbivorus,* herb-eating]

herborize, -ise, *v.t.* to search for or collect plants, to botanize. **herborist,** *n.* **herborization, -isation,** *n.* the act or practice of botanizing; (*erron.*) arborization.

Herculanean, *a.* of or pertaining to Herculaneum.

Herculaneum, *n.* ancient city of Italy between Naples and Pompeii. Along with Pompeii, it was buried when Vesuvius erupted in AD 79. It was excavated from the 18th cent. onwards.

Hercules, *n.* Roman form of HERACLES; a man of enormous strength; in astronomy, the fifth-largest constellation, lying in the northern hemisphere. Despite its size it contains no prominent stars. Its most important feature is a globular cluster of stars 22,500 light years away, one of the best examples in the sky. **Hercules beetle,** *n. Dynastes* or *Megasoma hercules,* a Brazilian arboreal beetle 5–6 in. (12–15 cm) long, with hornlike projections on the head and thorax. **Hercules club,** *n.* the American prickly ash, or other shrubs or trees; a big cudgel. **Herculean,** *a.* pertaining to Hercules; exceedingly strong or powerful; exceedingly great, difficult or dangerous (as the labours of Hercules). [L, from Gr. *Hēraklēs*]

Hercynian, *a.* a term applied to an extensive forest in Germany, the remains of which still exist in Swabia, the Harz Mountains etc. [L *Hercynia* (*silva*), Gr. *Herkunios* (*drumos*)]

herd¹, *n.* a number of beasts or cattle feeding or driven together; a crowd of people, a rabble. *v.i.* to go in herds or companies; to associate; to act as a herd or shepherd. *v.t.* to tend or watch (cattle etc.); to form or bring into a herd; to drive in a herd. **the herd,** *n.* the masses. **herd-book,** *n.* a book containing the pedigrees of high-bred cattle. †**herd-groom,** *n.* a herd, a shepherd; a shepherd-lad. **herd instinct,** *n.* (*Psych.*) the instinct that urges men and animals to react to contagious impulses and follow their leader. **herdsman,** †**herdman,** *n.* one who tends domestic animals, esp. cattle. [OE *heord* (cp. Icel. *hjörd,* G *Herde*)]

herd², *n.* a keeper of a herd (*usu. in comb.,* as *shepherd, swineherd*). [OE *hierde* (cp. Icel. *hirthir,* G *Hirte*)]

Herder, *n.* **Johann Gottfried von** (1744–1803), German poet, critic, and philosopher. Herder's critical writings indicated his intuitive rather than reasoning trend of thought. He collected folk songs of all nations 1778 and in the *Ideen zur Philosophie der Geschichte der Menschheit/Outlines of a Philosophy of the History of Man* (1784–91) he outlined the stages of human cultural development.

herdic, *n.* (*N Am.*) a two- or four-wheeled horse-drawn carriage, with a low-hung body, back entrance and side seats, largely used as a public conveyance. [Peter *Herdic* of Pennsylvania, the inventor]

Herdwick, *n.* a hardy breed of sheep raised in the mountainous parts of Cumberland and Westmorland; †the district under the charge of a herd; †a pasture-ground. [HERD², WICK²]

here, *adv.* in this place; to this place, hither, in this direction; in the present life or state; at this point; on this occasion; from this, hence. *n.* this place, point or time. **here and now,** right now, the present. **here and there,** in this place and that; hither and thither. **here goes,** *int.* said by a speaker who is about to do something. **here we go again,** *int.* meaning the same unpleasant, predictable etc. thing is about to happen again. **neither here nor there,** without reference to the point; irrelevant. **hereabouts, -about,** *adv.* somewhere about or near this place. **hereafter,** *adv.* for the future; in a future state. *n.* a future state; the future life. †**hereat,** *adv.* at this. †**hereaway,** *adv.* hereabouts. **hereby,** *adv.* by this, by means or by virtue of this; †close by. **herein,** *adv.* in this; here. **hereinafter,** later or below in this (writing, book, document etc.). **hereinbefore,** *adv.* †**hereof,** *adv.* of this; concerning this. †**hereon,** *adv.* on or concerning this. †**hereout,** *adv.* out of this place. **hereto,** *adv.* up to this place, point or time; (attached) to this; †hitherto. **heretofore,** *adv.* below in this (document etc.). **hereunto,** *adv.* up to this; hereto. **hereupon,** *adv.* upon this, after this, at this, in consequence of this. **herewith,** *adv.* with this. [OE *hēr* (Dut. and G *hier,* Icel. *hēr*)]

hereditable, *a.* that may be inherited. **hereditably,** *adv.* **hereditability,** *n.* [F *héréditable,* from L *hērēditāre,* from *hērēs hērēdis,* an HEIR]

hereditament, *n.* any property that may be inherited; real property. [med. L *hērēditāmentum,* as prec.]

hereditary, *a.* descending or passing by inheritance; transmitted by descent from generation to generation; holding or deriving by inheritance. **Hereditary Grand Almoner** ALMONER. **hereditarily,** *adv.* **hereditariness,** *n.* [L *hērēditārius,* as foll.]

heredity, *n.* the tendency to transmit individual characteristics to one's offspring; the tendency in an organism to resemble the parent. **hereditarian,** *n.* one who believes in this tendency. [F *hérédité,* L *hērēditātem* nom. *-tas,* from *hērēs hērēdis,* HEIR]

Hereford and Worcester, county in W central England. **area** 3930 sq km/1517 sq miles. **towns** administrative headquarters Worcester; Hereford, Kidderminster, Evesham, Ross-on-Wye, Ledbury. **products** mainly agricultural, apples, pears, and cider; hops and vegetables; Hereford cattle; carpets, porcelain, some chemicals and engineering. **population** (1987) 665,000.

hereof, hereon, hereout HERE.

heresiarch, *n.* a leader of a sect of heretics; a prominent or leading heretic. **heresiographer,** *n.* a writer on heresies. **heresiography,** *n.* **heresiologist,** *n.* **heresiology,** *n.* the study of the history of heresy; a treatise on this. [as foll.]

heresi(o)-, *comb. form.* pertaining to heresy.

heresy, *n.* departure from what is held to be true doctrine, esp. when such opinions lead to division in the Christian Church. **heresy-hunter,** *n.* one who pries for and searches out heretical opinions in others. [OF *heresie,* L *haeresis,* Gr. *hairesis,* from *haireisthai,* to choose]

heretic, *n.* one who holds unorthodox opinions, esp. in religious matters. **heretical,** *a.* **heretically,** *adv.* [F *hérétique,* L *haereticus,* Gr. *hairetikos,* as prec.]

hereto, heretofore, hereunder, hereunto, hereupon, herewith HERE.

Hereward, *n.* **the Wake** (11th cent.) English leader of a revolt against the Normans 1070; whose stronghold in the Isle of Ely was captured by William the Conqueror 1071. Hereward escaped, but his fate is unknown.

heriot, *n.* (*Law*) a fine, such as the best beast, payable to the lord of the manor on the decease of the tenant. **heriotable,** *a.* subject to heriot. [corr. of OE *heregeatwe,* military apparel (*here,* army, *geatwe,* equipments)]

†**herisson,** *n.* (*Fort.*) a beam armed with iron spikes used to block up a passage. [F *hērisson,* var. of URCHIN]

heritable, *a.* capable of being inherited; (*Law*) passing by inheritance, esp. of lands and appurtenances as dist. from movable property; capable of inheriting by descent. **heritably,** *adv.* by inheritance. [F *héritable,* from *hériter,* L *hērēditāre,* see HEREDITABLE]

heritage, *n.* land or other property that passes by descent or course of law to an heir; (*Sc. Law*) heritable estate, realty; share, portion, lot; anything passed from one generation to another; (*Bibl.*) the people of God, the Israelites, the Church. **heritor,** *n.* one who inherits; (*Sc. Law*) a landholder in a parish. **heritrix,** *n.* an heiress. [OF, as prec.]

herl, HARL[1].

herling, *n.* (*Sc.*) the young of the sea-trout.

herm(a), *n.* (*pl.* **-mae**) (*Gr. and Rom. Ant.*) a statue of a head, usu. of Hermes, placed on a square pillar and set as a boundary etc. **Hermaean, Hermaic,** *a.* [L, var. of HERMES]

hermandad, *n.* (*Sp. Hist.*) a popular league or association formed to resist oppression, esp. by the cities of Castile against the nobles. [Sp., a fraternity, from *hermano,* brother]

hermaphrodite, *n.* a human being or an animal combining in itself both male and female organs; one in which the organs of both sexes are normally combined in the same individual; a plant having the stamens and pistils in the same floral envelope; a person or thing in which opposite qualities are embodied; a vessel having the special rig of two kinds of craft, esp. a hermaphrodite brig. *a.* possessing to a greater or less extent the characteristics of both sexes, or other opposite attributes, in a single individual. **hermaphrodite brig,** *n.* a vessel square-rigged on the foremast and schooner-rigged on the mainmast. **hermaphroditic, -ical,** *a.* **hermaphroditism,** *n.* [L *Hermaphroditus,* Gr. *-ditos* (*Hermēs, Aphroditē*)]

Hermaphroditus, *n.* in Greek mythology, the son of Hermes and Aphrodite. He was loved by a nymph who prayed for eternal union with him, so that they became one body with dual sexual characteristics, hence the term HERMAPHRODITE.

hermeneutic, *a.* interpreting, explaining, explanatory. *n.pl.* the art or science of interpretation, esp. of Scripture. **hermeneutical,** *a.* **hermeneutically,** *adv.* †**hermeneutist,** *n.* [Gr. *hermēneutikos,* from *hermēneutēs, hermēneus,* interpreter]

Hermes, *n.* (*pl.* **-mae, -mai**) (*Gr. Myth*) son of Zeus and Maia, messenger of the gods of Olympus, god of science, commerce etc., identified by the Romans with Mercury, the Egyptian god Thoth, identified with Hermes, called by the Neo-Platonists Hermes Trismegistus or Thrice-great, and supposed to be the originator of art, magic, religion etc. [cp. HERM(A)]

hermetic, *a.* of or belonging to alchemy; fitting by or as by fusion so as to be air-tight. *n.pl.* alchemy, chemistry. **hermetic art,** *n.* alchemy; chemistry. **hermetism,** *n.* **hermetist,** *n.* **hermetically,** *adv.* [low L *hermĕticus,* from HERMES *Trismegistus*]

hermit, *n.* a person who retires from society to live in solitary contemplation or devotion, esp. an early Christian anchorite; †a beadsman. **hermit-crab, -lobster,** *n.* the genus *Pagurus,* esp. *P. bernhardus,* named thus because they live in abandoned univalve shells. **hermitage**[1], *n.* the cell or habitation of a hermit. **hermitess,** *n. fem.* **hermitical,** *a.* [F *hermite,* L. *her-, erēmīta,* Gr. *erēmitēs,* from *erēmos,* deserted]

Hermitage[2], *n.* a type of French wine, of two kinds, red and white. [name of a hill near Valence capped by the ruins of a supposed hermit's cell]

hermitical HERMIT.

hern[1] HERON.

hern[2], (*dial.*) HERS.

hernia, *n.* (*pl.* **-nias, -niae**) rupture; the protrusion of any organ, or part of an organ, from its natural place. **hernial, herniary,** *a.* **herniology,** *n.* the branch of science dealing with hernia; a treatise on ruptures. **herniotomy,** *n.* operation for strangulated hernia. [L]

†**hernshaw,** †**heronsew,** *n.* a young heron; a heron. [OF *heronceau,* dim. of *hairon,* HERON]

hero, *n.* (*pl.* **heroes**) a person of extraordinary valour, fortitude or enterprise; the principal male character in a novel, play, poem etc.; orig., in Greek mythology, a man of superhuman powers, often deified or regarded as a demigod after death (cp. HEROINE). **hero-worship,** *n.* the deification of a hero; excessive devotion shown to a person who is regarded as a hero. **hero-worshipper,** *n.* **heroify,** *v.t.* to make into a hero. **heroine,** *n.* a heroic woman; the principal female character in a literary work or an episode of actual life. **heroism,** *n.* the quality, character or conduct of a hero; extreme bravery. **heroize, -ise,** *v.t.* to regard or treat as a hero, to make heroic. *v.i.* to show oneself off as a hero. [MF *heroē* (F *héros*), L *hērōem* nom. *hērōs,* Gr. *hērōs*]

Hero and Leander, in Greek mythology, a pair of lovers. Hero was a priestess of Aphrodite at Sestos on the Hellespont, in love with Leander on the opposite shore at Abydos. When he was drowned while swimming across during a storm, she threw herself into the sea out of grief.

Herod, *n.* **the Great** (74–4 BC), king of the Roman province of Judaea, S Palestine, from 40 BC. With the aid of the triumvir Mark Antony he established his government in Jerusalem 37 BC. He rebuilt the Temple in Jerusalem, but his Hellenizing tendencies made him suspect to orthodox Jewry. His last years were a reign of terror, and St Matthew in the New Testament alleges that he ordered the slaughter of all the infants in Bethlehem to ensure the death of Jesus, whom he foresaw as a rival. He was the father of Herod Antipas.

Herod Agrippa I, *n.* (10 BC–AD 44), Jewish ruler of Palestine from AD 14. His real name was Marcus Julius Agrippa, erroneously called 'Herod' in the Bible. Grandson of Herod the Great, he was made tetrarch (governor) of Palestine by the Roman emperor Caligula and king by Claudius in AD 41. He put St James to death and imprisoned St Peter, both apostles. His son was Herod Agrippa II.

Herod Agrippa II, *n.* (*c.* AD 40–93), king of Chalcis (now S Lebanon), son of Herod Agrippa I, he was appointed by Claudius about AD 50. In AD 60 he tried the apostle St Paul. He helped the Roman emperor Titus take Jerusalem in AD 70, then went to Rome where he died.

Herod Antipas, *n.* (21 BC–AD 39), tetrarch (governor) of the Roman province of Galilee, N Palestine, 4 BC–AD 9, son of Herod the Great. He divorced his wife to marry his niece Herodias, who got her daughter Salome to ask for John the Baptist's head when he reproved Herod's action. In AD 38 Herod Antipas went to Rome to try to get the emperor Caligula to give him the title of king, but was banished.

Herodian, *a.* of or pertaining to Herod, his family or the party supporting him; like Herod, blustering, swaggering (cp. OUT-HEROD). *n.* a member of the party supporting Herod (Matt. xxii.15–16; Mark iii.6, xii.13).

Herodotus, *n.* (*c.* 484–424 BC), Greek historian. His history deals with the Greek-Persian struggle which culminated in the defeat of the Persian invasion attempts 490 BC and 480 BC. Herodotus was the first historian to apply critical evaluation to his material.

heroic, *a.* pertaining to or becoming a hero; having the qualities or attributes of a hero; producing heroes; relating to or describing the deeds of heroes; bold, vigorous, attempting extreme deeds or methods. *n.pl.* heroic verses; high-flown or bombastic language or sentiments. **heroic age,** *n.* the age in which heroes or demigods were supposed to have lived, esp. the age of Greece closing with the deeds celebrated in the *Iliad* and *Odyssey*. **heroic size,** *n.* of sculpture, between life-size and colossal. **heroic verse,** the metre of heroic or epic poetry; in English, German and Italian poetry, the five-foot iambic; in French, the Alexandrine, and in Latin and Greek the hexameter. **heroical,** *a.* **heroically,** *adv.* †**heroicalness,** *n.* **heroicomic, -ical,** *a.* combining the heroic and the comic; mockheroic, burlesque. [L *hērōicus,* Gr. *hērōikos*]

heroin, *n.* a derivative of morphine, a white crystalline powder, used as an anodyne, a sedative and as an addictive drug. [prob. as prec., from its effect on the personality]

heron, †**hern,** *n.* a long-legged, long-necked wading bird of the genus *Ardea,* esp. *A. cinerea,* the common European heron. **heronry,** *n.* a place where herons breed. [OF *hairon,* through pop. L or It. from OHG *Hegir* (cp. Icel. *hegri,* also OE *higora,* a magpie)]

heronsew, †**heronshaw,** HERNSHAW.

herpes, *n.* a skin complaint consisting of vesicles grouped on an inflamed surface such as the lip. **herpes simplex,** *n.* an acute viral disease, often transmitted sexually, resembling herpes. **herpes zoster,** *n.* SHINGLES. **herpetic,** *a.* **herpetiform,** *a.* **herpetography,** *n.* [L, from Gr. *herpēs -ētos,* from *herpein,* to creep]

herpestes, *n.* a genus of small carnivorous mammals of the subfamily Herpestinae, containing the ichneumons and the mongooses. [Gr., as prec.]

herpet(o)-, *comb. form.* pertaining to reptiles; pertaining to herpes. [Gr. *herpeton,* a reptile, from *herpein,* to creep]

herpetology, *n.* the natural history of reptiles. **herpetoid,** *a.* having the shape of a snake. **herpetologic, -ical,** *a.* **herpetologist,** *n.*

Herr, *n.* (*pl.* **Herren**) German title corresponding to the English Mr. [G]

Herrenvolk, *n.* the master race, esp. the Aryan race as conceived by Nazi ideology. [G]

herring, *n.* a clupeoid marine fish, *Clupea harengus,* of the N Atlantic, moving in large shoals and spawning near the coast. **herring-bone,** *a.* like the spine and bones of a herring; denoting a kind of masonry in which the stones etc. are set obliquely in alternate rows. **herring-bone stitch,** *n.* a kind of cross-stitch used in mending sails and for ornamental purposes. *v.t.* to sew or stitch with herring-bone stitch. **herring-gull,** *n.* a large sea-gull, *Larus argentatus,* feeding on herrings. **herring-pond,** *n.* (*facet.*) the ocean, the North Atlantic, the North Sea and English Channel. [OE *hæring* (cp. Dut. *haring,* G *Häring*), etym. doubtful]

Herriot, *n.* **Edouard** (1872–1957), French Radical politician. He was briefly prime minister (1924–25, 1926, and 1932). As president of the chamber of deputies in 1940 he opposed the policies of the right-wing Vichy government, was arrested and later taken to Germany until released 1945 by the Soviets.

Herrnhuter, *n.* a Moravian, a member of the sect calling themselves the United Brethren. [*Herrnhut,* Saxony, their first settlement]

herry, (*Sc.*) HARRY[1].

hers HER.

†**hersall,** (*Spens.*) short for REHEARSAL.

Herschel[1], *n.* **John Fredrick William** (1792–1871), English scientist and astronomer, who discovered thousands of close double stars, clusters, and nebulae, reported 1847. His inventions include astronomical instruments, sensitized photographic paper, and the use of sodium thiosulphite for fixing it. **Herschelian[1],** *a.*

Herschel[2], *n.* **William** (1738–1822), German-born British astronomer. He was a skilled telescope-maker, and pioneered the study of binary stars and nebulae. In 1781, he discovered Uranus. **Herschelian[2],** *a.*

Herschelite, *n.* an orthorhombic, colourless or white translucent silicate of aluminium, calcium and sodium. [Sir John *Herschel,* 1792–1871]

herse, *n.* cheval de frise; †a portcullis with iron bars like a harrow placed above gates and lowered as a barrier. [F *herse,* see HEARSE]

herself, *pron.* the reflexive form of SHE, used to give emphasis in either the nominative or the objective case; her usual self. **by herself,** alone, unaided. [OE *hire self*]

Hertfordshire, *n.* county in SE England. **area** 1634 sq km/631 sq miles. **towns** administrative headquarters Hertford; St Albans, Watford, Hatfield, Hemel Hempstead, Bishop's Stortford, Letchworth. **population** (1986) 986,000. **products** engineering, aircraft, electrical goods, paper and printing; general agriculture.

Herts, (*abbr.*) Hertfordshire.

hertz, *n.* (*pl.* **hertz**) a standard unit of frequency equal to one cycle per second. [Heinrich *Hertz,* 1857–94, German physicist]

Hertzian, *a.* (*Elec.*) pertaining to Hertz or the phenomena of electromagnetic vibrations discovered by him. **Hertzian telegraphy,** *n.* wireless telegraphy. **Hertzian waves,** *n.pl.* radio waves, wireless waves first studied by Hertz. [from prec.]

Hertzog, *n.* **James Barry Munnik** (1866–1942), South African politician, prime minister 1924–39, founder of the Nationalist Party 1913 (the United South African National Party from 1933). He opposed South Africa's entry into both World Wars.

Hertzsprung-Russell diagram, *n.* in astronomy, a graph on which the surface temperatures of stars are plotted against their luminosities. Most stars, including the Sun, fall into a narrow band called the main sequence. When a star grows old it moves from the main sequence to the upper right part of the graph, into the area of the giants and supergiants. At the end of its life, as the star shrinks to become a white dwarf, it moves again, to the bottom left area. It is named after the Dane Ejnar Hertzsprung and the American Henry Norris Russell, who independently devised it in the years 1911–13.

Herzl, *n.* **Theodor** (1860–1904), Austrian founder of the Zionist movement. The Dreyfus case convinced him that the only solution to the problem of anti-Semitism was the resettlement of the Jews in a state of their own. His book *Jewish State* (1896) launched political Zionism, and he was the first president of the World Zionist Organization (1897).

Heseltine, *n.* **Michael** (1933–), English Conservative politician. Secretary of State for the Environment 1979–83, he succeeded John Nott as Minister for Defence Jan. 1983 but resigned Jan. 1986 over the Westland affair.

Heshvan, *n.* the second month of the Jewish civil year

and the eighth month of the Jewish ecclesiastical year. [Heb.]

Hesiod, *n.* (7th cent. BC) one of the earliest of the poets of ancient Greece. He is supposed to have lived a little later than Homer, and according to his own account he was born in Boeotia. He is the author of *Works and Days*, a poem that tells of the country life, and the *Theogony*, an account of the origin of the world and of the gods.

hesitate, *v.i.* to stop or pause in action; to be doubtful or undecided; to be reluctant (to); to stammer. **hesitant,** *a.* hesitating, dubious, vacillating, undecided. **hesitance, -tancy,** *n.* **hesitantly,** *adv.* **hesitatingly,** *adv.* **hesitation,** *n.* **hesitative,** *a.* **hesitator,** *n.* [L *haesitātus,* p.p. of *haesitāre,* freq. of *haerēre,* to stick, cling]

Hesper, Hesperus, *n.* the evening star. **Hesperian,** *a.* (*poet.*) situated at or in the west, western. *n.* an inhabitant of a western country. [L *Hesperus,* Gr. *hesperos,* evening, the evening star]

Hesperides, *n.pl.* (*Gr. Myth.*) the daughters of Hesperus, possessors of the garden of golden fruit watched over by a dragon at the western extremity of the earth; †the garden so watched over. [L, from Gr., pl. of *hesperis,* western]

hesperidium, *n.* (*pl.* **-dia**) a citrus fruit, e.g. the orange, with a leathery rind and a pulp divided into sections. [from prec.]

Hesperis, *n.* a genus of cruciferous plants comprising the rockets and dame's violet. [see prec.]

hesperornis, *n.* a fossil genus of toothed birds from the chalk of N America. [Gr. *hesperos,* see HESPER, *ornis,* bird]

Hess¹, *n.* **Victor** (1883–1964), Austrian physicist, who emigrated to the US shortly after sharing a Nobel prize in 1936 for the discovery of cosmic radiation.

Hess², *n.* (**Walter Richard**) **Rudolf** (1894–1987), German Nazi leader. In 1932 he was appointed deputy Führer to Hitler. On 10 May 1941 he landed by air in the UK with compromise peace proposals and was held prisoner of war until 1945, when he was tried at Nuremberg as a war criminal and was sentenced to life imprisonment. He died in Spandau prison, Berlin.

Hesse, *n.* **Hermann** (1877–1962), German-born writer who became a Swiss citizen 1923. He was a conscientious objector in World War I and a pacifist opponent of Hitler. His works include *Siddhartha* (1922) and *Steppenwolf* (1927). Nobel prize 1946.

Hessian, *a.* of or belonging to Hesse. *n.* a native or inhabitant of Hesse; (*not caps.*) a coarse cloth made of hemp and jute; (*pl.*) Hessian boots; (*N Am.*) a mercenary politician, a hireling. **Hessian boot,** *n.* a high boot with tassels, fashionable early in the 19th cent. **Hessian fly,** *n.* a small fly or midge, *Cecidomyia destructor,* the larva of which attacks wheat in the US. [*Hesse* in Germany, -IAN]

hest, *n.* a command, an injunction. [OE *hǣs,* from *hātan,* see HIGHT²]

hesternal, *a.* of yesterday. [L *hesternus*]

Hestia, *n.* in Greek mythology, the goddess (Roman Vesta) of the hearth, daughter of Kronos (Roman Saturn) and Rhea.

Heston, *n.* **Charlton** (1924–), stage name of Charles Carter, US film actor who often starred in biblical and historical epics (as Moses, for example, in *The Ten Commandments*, 1956, and the title role in *Ben-Hur*, 1959).

Hesvan, HESHVAN.

hetaera, *n.* (*pl.* **-rae**) one of a class of highly educated courtesans in ancient Athens. **hetaerism,** *n.* recognized concubinage; community of women within the limits of the tribe. **hetaerist,** *n.* **hetaeristic,** *a.* **hetaerocracy,** *n.* [Gr. *hetaira,* fem. of *hetairos,* companion]

heterauxesis, *n.* (*Bot.*) irregular or unsymmetrical growth. [Gr. *auxesis,* growth]

heter(o)-, *comb. form.* different, dissimilar; irregular, abnormal; erroneous. [Gr. *heteros,* other]

heteroblastic, *a.* (*Biol.*) derived from unlike cells, dist. from homoblastic. **heteroblasty,** [Gr. *blastos,* germ]

heterocarpous, *a.* producing fruit of more than one kind. [Gr. *karpos,* fruit]

heterocercal, *a.* of fish, having the upper lobe of the tail longer than the lower. **heterocerc,** *n.* a heterocercal fish. **heterocercality,** *n.* [Gr. *kerkos,* tail]

heterochromous, *a.* of different colours. [Gr. *chrōma,* colour]

heterochronic, *a.* occurring at irregular intervals or at abnormal times, irregular, intermittent. **heterochronia, heterochronism, heterochrony,** *n.* **heterochronistic, heterochronous,** *a.*

heteroclite, *a.* deviating from the ordinary rules or forms; anomalous, irregular. *n.* a word that deviates from the ordinary forms of inflexion; a person or thing deviating from the ordinary forms. **heteroclitic,** *a.* [Gr. *klinein,* to learn]

heterocyclic, *a.* of organic chemical compounds with a ring structure of atoms of different kinds in the molecules.

heterodactyl, *a.* having the toes different in number or form on the fore and hind legs. **heterodactylous,** *a.*

heterodont, *a.* having teeth of different forms, dist. from homodont. *n.* a heterodont animal.

heterodox, *a.* contrary to received or established doctrines, principles or standards; heretical; not orthodox. **heterodoxy,** *n.* [Gr. *heterodoxos* (from *dokein,* to think)]

heterodyne, *n.* a beat frequency caused in a radio receiver by the interplay of two alternating currents of similar frequencies. [Gr. *dynamis,* power]

heteroecious, *a.* of parasitic fungi, developing at different times on different hosts. **heteroecism,** *n.* **heteroecismal,** *a.* [Gr. *oikia,* dwelling]

heterogamous, *a.* having flowers or florets sexually different, as in certain Compositae, where the disk-florets are male and the ray-florets neuter or female. **heterogamy,** *n.* [Gr. *gamos,* marriage]

heterogeneous, †heterogene, †heterogeneal. *a.* diverse in character, structure or composition; (*Math.*) of different kinds, dimensions or degrees; incommensurable. **heterogeneously,** *adv.* **heterogeneousness, heterogeneity,** *n.* [Gr. *genos,* kind]

heterogenesis, *n.* the production of offspring differing from the parent; abiogenesis, spontaneous generation; alternation of generations. **heterogenetic,** *a.* **heterogenist,** *n.* a believer in heterogenesis.

heterogonous, *a.* of certain flowers, stamens and pistils dimorphous or trimorphous so as to ensure cross-fertilization. **heterogonism, heterogony,** *n.* [Gr. *gonos,* off-spring]

heterograft, *n.* a tissue graft from a member of one species onto a member of another.

heterography, *n.* heterogeneous or incorrect spelling; the employment of the same letters to represent different sounds as *g* in *go* and *gin*.

heterolith, *n.* a stony concretion composed of organic or other non-mineral matter. [-LITH]

heterologous, *a.* consisting of different elements, or of the same elements combined in different proportions; (*Path.*) differing in structure from normal tissue. **heterology,** *n.*

Heteromera, *n.pl.* a section of Coleoptera, having five joints in the first four tarsi, and four in the other two. **heteromeran,** *n.* [mod. L, as foll.]

heteromerous, *a.* differing in number, form or character of parts. **heteromeran,** *a.* [Gr. *meros,* part]

heteromorphic, -ous, *a.* differing from the normal form; having dissimilar forms; of insects, having different forms at different stages of development. **heteromorphism, heteromorphy,** *n.* the quality of being heteromorphic; existence in different forms. **heteromorphosis,** *n.* abnormal shape, structure etc.; deformity; assumption by an organ of the functions properly belonging to another. [Gr. *morphē,* form]

heteronomous, *a.* subject to the law or rule of another, not autonomous; (*Biol.*) having different laws of growth, diverging from the type. **heteronomy,** *n.* [Gr. *nomos,* law]

heteronym, *n.* a word spelt the same way as another

but differing in sound and meaning, as *gill* (gil), a breathing-organ, and *gill* (jil), a measure. **heteronymous**, *a.* **heteronymy,**, *n.* [Gr. *heterōnumos* (*onoma,* name)]

heteroousian, *a.* having a different nature or essence. *n.pl.* a sect holding that the Son was of a different essence from the Father, an Arian. [Gr. *heteroousios* (*ousia,* essence)]

heteropathic, *a.* allopathic. **heteropathy**, *n.*

heterophemy, *n.* the action or habit of saying or writing differently from what one intends. **heterophemism**, *n.* **heterophemist**, *n.* **heterophemistic**, *a.* **heterophemize, -ise**, *v.i.* [Gr. *-phēmia,* from *phēmē,* voice]

heterophyllous, *a.* having leaves of different form on the same plant. **heterophylly**, *n.* [Gr. *phullon,* leaf]

heteroplasm, heteroplasia, *n.* a morbid formation of tissue foreign to the part where it occurs. **heteroplastic**, *a.*

heteropod, *a.* belonging to the Heteropoda. *n.* one of the Heteropoda. **Heteropoda**, *n.pl.* a group of Gasteropoda having the foot modified into a swimming-organ. **heteropodous**, *a.*

Heteroptera, *n.pl.* a sub-order of Hemiptera in which the wings are of dissimilar parts, comprising the bugs. **heteropterous,** *a.* [Gr. *pteron,* wing]

heterorhizal, *a.* having the root springing from any part of the spore. [Gr. *rhiza,* root]

heteroscian, *a.* used of a part of the earth's surface where the shadows fall in an opposite direction relatively to another part. *n.* a person living in such part of the globe. [med. L *heteroscius,* Gr. *heteroskios* (*skia,* shadow)]

heterosexual, *a.* having or concerning sexual attraction to the opposite sex. *n.* a heterosexual person. **heterosexuality**, *n.* **heterosexism,** *n.* prejudice against those who are not heterosexual (cp. HOMOSEXUAL).

heterosis, *n.* abnormal vigour or stength typical of a hybrid plant or animal. [HETERO-, -OSIS]

heterosporous, *a.* having two kinds of spores. [Gr. *sporos,* seed]

heterostrophic, *a.* of spiral shells, in a different direction. **heterostrophous**, *a.* **heterostrophy**, *n.* [Gr. *strophos,* turning]

heterostyled, *a.* heterogonous, the styles or pistils on different plants of the species differing in length so as to promote cross-fertilization. **heterostylism**, *n.*

heterotaxy, *n.* deviation of organs or parts from ordinary arrangement. **heterotaxic**, *a.* [Gr. *taxis,* arrangement]

heterotomic, heterotomous, *a.* (*Min.*) having an abnormal cleavage; (*Bot.*) having the perianth unequally or unsymmetrically divided. [Gr. *-tomos,* cut, from *temnein,* to cut]

heterotopy, heterotopism, *n.* (*Path.*) misplacement of an organ etc.; occurrence of a growth in an abnormal position; (*Biol.*) variation from the normal sequence of development resulting in displacement of the order or place of phenomena. **heterotopic**, **heterotopous**, *a.* [Gr. *-topia,* from *topos,* place]

heterotropal, -tropous, *a.* lying parallel with the hilum (as some embryos). [Gr. *-tropos,* turning, from *trepein,* to turn]

heterotrophy, *n.* (*Bot.*) abnormal mode of obtaining nourishment.

heterousian, HETEROOUSIAN.

hetman, *n.* a commander or leader of the Cossacks. [Pol.]

het up, (*coll.*) excited, agitated, annoyed.

heuchera, *n.* a genus of herbaceous plants of the saxifrage family, with roundish leaves and scapes of red, white or green flowers rising directly from the root-stock. [J *Heucher,* 1677–1747, German botanist]

heugh[1], *n.* (*Sc.*) a crag; a craggy glen or gorge, a cleuch; a coal-pit, a pit. [from ME *hōgh,* OE *hōh*]

heugh[2], *int.* hallo! (an exclamation of surprise). [imit.]

heulandite, *n.* a monoclinic, transparent brittle mineral, consisting chiefly of silica, alumina and lime, occurring chiefly in amygdaloid rock. [H *Heuland,* English mineralogist]

heuristic, *a.* serving or tending to find out; not correct or provable, but aiding the discovery of truth. *n.* the branch of logic dealing with discovery and invention, also called **heuretic**. [from Gr. *heuriskein,* to find]

hew, *v.t.* (*p.p.* **hewed, hewn**) to cut (down, away, off etc.) with an axe or similar tool; to hack, to chop; to make or fashion with toil and exertion. *n.* the act of hewing; a cut or gash; destruction by hewing. **hewer,** *n.* one who hews; a miner who cuts coal from the seam. [OE *hēawan* (cp. Dut. *houwen,* Icel. *hōggva,* G *hauen*)]

Hewish, *n.* **Antony** (1924–), British radio-astronomer, who was awarded, with Martin Ryle, the Nobel prize for physics 1974 for his work on pulsars.

hex, *v.i.* (*N Am.*) to practise witchcraft. *v.t.* to cast a spell on; jinx. *n.* a person who practices witchcraft; a spell. [Pennsylvania Dutch, orig. from G *Hexe,* witch]

hex(a)-, *comb. form.* six. [Gr. *hex,* six]

hexachord, *n.* (*Mus.*) an interval of four tones and a semitone; a scale or diatonic series of six notes with a semitone between the third and the fourth.

hexad, *n.* a group of six; an atom with a valency of six. [Gr. *hexas -ados,* from *hex,* six]

hexadactylic hexadactylous , *a.* having six fingers or toes.

hexaemeron, *n.* a period of six days, esp. the six days of the Creation; a history of this period. **hexaemeric,** *a.* [late L, from Gr. (*hēmera,* day)]

hexagon, *n.* a plane figure having six sides and six angles. **hexagonal**, *a.* [Gr. *gōnia,* angle]

hexagram, *n.* a figure formed by two equilateral triangles whose points coincide with those of a regular hexagon; (*Geom.*) one of various six-sided figures; (*Chinese Lit.*) one of 64 figures each formed by six parallel lines on which the *I Ching* or *Book of Changes* is based.

Hexagynia, *n.pl.* a Linnaean order of plants having six styles. **hexagyn,** *n.* a plant belonging to this order **hexagynian, hexagynous**, *a.* having six styles. [Gr. *gunē,* woman, female]

hexahedron, *n.* a solid body of six sides, esp. a regular cube. **hexahedral,** *a.* [Gr. *hedra,* seat, base]

hexahemeron, HEXAEMERON.

hexameter, *n.* the heroic verse of the Greeks and Romans consisting of six feet, of which the first four were dactyls or spondees, the fifth normally a dactyl (though sometimes a spondee, and then the fourth was a dactyl), and the sixth a spondee or trochee. *a.* hexametric. **hexametric, -ical**, *a.* **hexametrist,** *n.* [L, from Gr. *hexametros* (*metron,* see METER)]

Hexandria, *n.pl.* a Linnaean class containing plants with six stamens. **hexander,** *n.* any plant of this order. **hexandrian, -drous,** *a.* having six stamens. [Gr. *anēr andros,* man, male]

hexane, *n.* a hydrocarbon of the methane series.

hexangular, *a.* having six angles.

hexapetalous, *a.* having six petals. **hexapetaloid,** *a.*

hexaphyllous, *a.* having six leaves or sepals. [Gr. *phullon,* leaf]

hexapla, *n.* an edition of a book, esp. of the Scriptures, having six versions in parallel columns (orig. the title of Origen's text of the Old Testament). **hexaplar, hexaplarian, -plaric,** *a.* [Gr. neut. pl. of *hexaplous,* six-fold (*hex,* six, *-ploos,* fold)]

hexapod, *n.* an animal having six feet; one of the Hexapoda or insects. *a.* having six legs; belonging to the Hexapoda. **hexapodal, -podous**, *a.* **hexapody,** *n.* a verse of six feet. [Gr. *pous podos,* foot]

hexastich, *n.* a poem or poetical passage of six lines or verses. **hexastichic**, *a.* [Gr *-stichos* (*stichos,* a row)]

hexastyle, *n.*, *a.* (a portico or temple) having six columns. [Gr. *stūlos* pillar]

Hexateuch, *n.* the first six books of the Old Testament. [Gr. *teuchos,* book]

hey, *int.* an exclamation of joy, surprise, interrogation, encouragement etc.; (*esp. N Am.*) an exclamation used to attract someone's attention, often used meaninglessly. [ME *hei*]

hey-day[1], *int.* an exclamation of cheerfulness, wonder etc.

hey-day[2], *n.* the prime, the time of unexhausted spirits, vigour, prosperity etc. [perh. HIGH-DAY]

Heydrich, *n.* **Reinhard** (1904–42), German Nazi. As head of party's security service and Heinrich Himmler's deputy, he was instrumental in organizing the final solution. While deputy 'protector' of Bohemia and Moravia from 1941, he was ambushed and killed by three members of the Czech forces in Britain, who had landed by parachute. Reprisals followed, including several hundred executions and the massacre of Lidice.

heyduck, *n.* one of a class of mercenaries in Hungary who were granted lands and the rank of nobles in 1605. [Boh., Pol. *hajduk,* from Magyar *hajdú,* pl. *-duk,* orig. robber, brigand]

Heyerdahl, *n.* **Thor** (1914–), Norwegian ethnologist, who sailed on the raft *Kon Tiki* (1947) from Peru to the Tuamotu Islands along the Humboldt Current, and in 1969–70 used ancient-Egyptian-style papyrus-reed boats to cross the Atlantic. He attempted to prove that ancient civilizations could have travelled the oceans.

hey-ho, HEIGH-HO.

hey presto, *int.* PRESTO[2].

Heywood, *n.* **Thomas** (*c.* 1570– *c.* 1650), English actor and dramatist. He wrote or adapted over 220 plays, including the domestic tragedy *A Woman kilde with kindnesse* (1607).

Hezekiah, *n.* in the Old Testament or Jewish Bible, king of Judah from 719 BC. Against the advice of the prophet Isaiah he rebelled against Assyrian suzerainty in alliance with Egypt, but was defeated by Sennacherib. He carried out religious reforms.

Hf, (*chem. symbol*) hafnium.

Hg, (*chem. symbol*) mercury.

HGV, (*abbr.*) heavy goods vehicle.

HH, (*abbr.*) Her/His Highness; His Holiness (the Pope); of pencils, extra hard.

hi, *int.* an exclamation, usu. calling attention, also expressing surprise, derision etc. [cp. HEY]

hiatus, *n.* a gap, a break, a lacuna in a manuscript, connected series etc.; the coming together of two vowels in successive syllables or words. **hiatus hernia,** *n.* a hernia caused when part of the stomach protrudes through the oesophagal opening in the diaphragm. [L, from *hiāre,* to yawn]

Hiawatha, *n.* legendary 16th-cent. N American Indian teacher and Onondaga chieftain, who is said to have welded the Six Nations of the Iroquois into the league of the Long House, as the confederacy was known in what is now upper New York State. He is the hero of Longfellow's epic poem *The Song of Hiawatha*.

†**hibernacle,** *n.* winter quarters; winter shelter, covering etc. **hibernaculum,** *n.* the winter quarters of a hibernating animal; a bud or bulb sheltering the future plant; winter quarters, shelter, covering etc. [L *hībernāculum,* from *hīberna,* see foll.]

hibernate, *v.i.* to pass the season of winter in sleep or torpor, as some animals; (*fig.*) to live in seclusion or remain inactive at a time of stress. **hibernal,** *a.* pertaining to winter. **hibernant,** *a.* hibernating. **hibernation,** *n.* [L *hībernātus,* p.p. of *hībernāre,* from *hīberna,* winter quarters, orig. neut. pl. of *hībernus,* wintry]

Hibernian, *a.* pertaining to Ireland. *n.* a native or inhabitant of Ireland. **Hibernianism, Hibernicism,** *n.* a phrase, mode of speech, or other peculiarity of the Irish. **Hibernicize, -ise,** *v.t.* to render Irish. **Hibernization, -isation,** *n.* [L *Hibernia, Iverna,* Gr. *Iernē,* from OCelt.]

Hiberno-, *comb. form.* pertaining to or connected with Ireland. **Hiberno-Celtic,** *a.* pertaining to the Irish Celts. *n.* the native Irish language.

hibiscus, *n.* a genus of mostly tropical mallows, with large showy flowers. [L, from Gr. *hibiskos*]

hic, *int.* a sound like a hiccup, denoting interruption, as in the speech of a drunken person. [imit.]

hiccatee, *n.* a freshwater tortoise of the Antilles. [native name]

hiccup, *n.* a short, audible catching of the breath due to spasmodic contraction of the diaphragm and the glottis; a series of sudden, rapid and brief inspirations, followed by expiration accompanied by noise. *v.i.* to have or utter a hiccup. *v.t.* to utter with a hiccup. **hiccupy,** *a.* [imit., cp. HIC (spelling *hiccough* due to confusion with COUGH)]

hic jacet, *n.* an epitaph, tombstone or place of sepulture, from the first two words of a memorial inscription. [L, here lies]

hick, *n.* (*esp. N Am.*) a farmer, countryman, yokel. *a.* rustic, rural. [etym. doubtful]

Hick, *n.* **Graeme** (1966–), Rhodesian-born cricketer who became Zimbabwe's youngest professional cricketer at the age of 17. A prolific batsman, he joined Worcestershire, England, in 1984. He achieved the highest score in England in the 20th cent. in 1988 against Somerset, 405 not out.

hickey, *n.* (*N Am., coll.*) device, gadget; lovebite. [etym. unknown]

Hickok, *n.* **'Wild Bill' (James Butler)** (1837–76), US pioneer and law enforcer, a legendary figure in the Wild West. In the Civil War he was a sharpshooter and scout for the Union army, and then served as marshal in Kansas, killing many outlaws. He was shot from behind while playing poker in Deadwood, South Dakota.

hickory, *n.* a name for several N American trees of the genus *Carya,* allied to the walnuts, esp. *C. alba,* the timber of which is tough and elastic. **hickory shirt,** a shirt of striped or check cotton. [N Am. Ind. *pohickery*]

hickwall, hickway, *n.* the green woodpecker, *Picus viridis.* [etym. doubtful]

hid, *past, p.p.* HIDE[1].

hidalgo, *n.* a Spanish nobleman of the lowest class, a gentleman by birth. **hidalgoish,** *a.* **hidalgoism,** *n.* [Sp., earlier *hijodalgo,* L *fīlius dē aliquō,* son of something]

Hidalgo y Costilla, *n.* **Miguel** (1753–1811), Catholic priest, known as 'the Father of Mexican Independence'. A symbol of the opposition to Spain, he rang the church bell in Sept. 1810 to announce to his parishioners in Dolores that the revolution against the Spanish had begun. He was captured and shot the following year.

hidden, *p.p.* HIDE[1].

hide[1], *v.t.* (*past* **hid,** *p.p.* **hidden, hid**) to conceal; to put out of or withhold from sight; to secrete, to cover up; to keep secret, to withhold from the knowledge (of); to suppress. *v.i.* to lie concealed, to conceal oneself. *n.* a place of concealment for observing wild life. **neither hide nor hair of someone,** nothing at all of someone. **hide-and-seek,** *n.* a children's game in which one hides and the others try to find; evasion. **hideaway,** *n.* a concealed or secluded place. **hideout,** *n.* a place where someone can hide or take refuge. **hiddenly,** *adv.* **hiddenmost,** *a.* **hiddenness,** *n.* **hider,** *n.* one who hides. **hiding,** *n.* concealing, lying in concealment. **hiding-place, hidey-hole,** *n.* a secret chamber, priest's hiding-place. [OE *hydan,* cogn. with Gr. *keuthein*]

hide[2], *n.* the skin of any animal, raw or dressed; (*coll.*) the human skin. *v.t.* (*coll.*) to flog. **hide-bound,** *a.* said of an animal the skin of which adheres so closely to the ribs and back as to be raised with difficulty; having the bark so close and tight as to impede growth (of trees); narrow-minded, bigoted, obstinate; †penurious. **hiding,** *n.* (*coll.*) a thrashing, a flogging. [OE *hȳd* (cp. Dut. *huid,* Icel. *hūth,* G *Haut,* also L *cutis,* Gr *kutos*)]

hide[3], *n.* a certain portion of land variously estimated at from 60 to 120 acres (24 to 48 ha), orig. enough to support a family and its dependants. [OE *hīd higid,* from *hīw-,* family]

hideous, *a.* horrible, frightful or shocking to eye or ear; ghastly, grim. **hideously,** *adv.* **hideousness,** *n.* [ME *hidous,* OF *hidos* (F *hideux*), *hisdos* (acc. to OED from *hisde, hide,* horror, fear; acc. to Brachet etc. from L *hispidus,* rough)]

hidlings, *adv.* (*Sc., North.*) secretly, clandestinely. *a.* hidden, clandestine, furtive. *n.* furtiveness. **in hidlings,** on the quiet, secretly. [HIDE[1]]

hidrosis, *n.* (esp. excessive) sweating. **hidrotic,** *a.* causing perspiration. *n.* a sudorific. [late L *hidrōticus,* Gr. *hidrōtikos,* from *hidrōs -drōtos,* sweat]

hie[1], *v.i.* (*pres.p.* **hying**) to hasten, to hurry. †*v.t.* to urge (on). †*n.* haste, speed. [OE *hīgian* (cp. Dut. *hijgen,* to haul)]

hie[2], *int.* (*Sc., North.*) the call to a horse to turn to the left, opposed to hup. [cp. HI]

hielaman, *n.* the narrow wooden or bark shield of the Australian Aborigines. [Austral. Abor.]

hieland, -er HIGHLAND, HIGHLANDER, see HIGH[1].

hiemal, *a.* wintry. [L *hiems,* winter]

Hieracium, *n.* the hawk-weed genus of Compositae. *n.* any plant of this genus. [L, from Gr. *hierākion, hierāx,* hawk]

hiera-picra, *n.* a purgative made from aloes and canella bark. [Gr. *hierā,* sacred, *pikrā,* bitter]

hierarch, *n.* the chief of a sacred order, one who has authority in sacred things, a chief priest, prelate or archbishop. **hierarchic, -ical,** *a.* of or pertaining to a hierarch or hierarchy. **hierarchism,** *n.* hierarchical principles, power or character. [med. L *hierarcha,* Gr. *hierarchēs* (*hieros,* sacred, *-archēs,* ruling, from *archein,* to govern)]

hierarchy, *n.* a rank or order of sacred persons; any one of three orders of angels; government in sacred matters; priestly or ecclesiastical government; organization in grades or orders, esp. of a priesthood; the bishops collectively of a province. **hierarchal, hierarchical,** *a.* [F *hierarchie,* from L, from Gr. *hierarchia,* as prec.]

hieratic, *a.* pertaining to the priesthood, priestly; applied to the written characters employed in Egyptian records and to early styles in Egyptian and Greek art. **hieratically,** *adv.* [L *hierātikos,* Gr. *hierātikos,* from *hierasthai,* to be priest, from *hieros,* holy]

hier(o)-, *comb.form.* sacred; pertaining to sacred things. [Gr. *hieros,* holy]

hierocracy, *n.* government by priests, hierarchy.

hieroglyph, *n.* the figure of an animate or inanimate object used to represent a word, sound etc., a kind of writing practised by the ancient Egyptians, the Aztecs and others; a character or symbol employed to convey a secret meaning; (*usu. in pl., facet.*) illegible writing. *v.t.* to represent by or in hieroglyphs. **hieroglyphic,** *a.* written in or covered with hieroglyphs; written in characters difficult to decipher; mysterious, emblematic, esoteric. *n.* (*usu. in pl.*) hieroglyphs; hieroglyphic writing. **hieroglyphical,** *a.* **hieroglyphically,** *adv.* **hieroglyphist,** *n.* a writer of hieroglyphs; one skilled in deciphering hieroglyphs. [late L *hieroglyphikos,* Gr. *hierogluphikos* (HIER(O)-, *gluphē,* carving)]

hierogram, *n.* a sacred writing, character or symbol. **hierogrammatic, -ical,** *a.* **hierogrammatist,** *n.* **hierograph,** *n.* a hierogram. **hierographer,** *n.* **hierographic, -ical,** *a.* **hierography,** *n.*

hierolatry, *n.* the worship of sacred persons or things, esp. the worship of saints. [HIER(O)-, -LATRY]

hierology, *n.* a discourse on sacred matters; the science of hieroglyphics, esp. of the ancient writings of the Egyptians; the science or study of religious or of sacred literature. **hierologic, -ical,** *a.* **hierologist,** *n.* [late Gr. *hierologia*]

hieromancy, *n.* divination by observing things offered in sacrifice. [HIER(O)-, -MANCY]

Hieronomian, *a.* of or pertaining to St Jerome. *n.* a Hieronymite. **Hieronymic,** *a.* **Hieronymite,** *n.* one of a monastic order named after St Jerome. *a.* belonging to such an order. [L *Hieronymus,* Jerome]

hierophant, *n.* one who teaches or explains the mysteries of religion; a priest who acted as initiator to the Eleusinian mysteries. **hierophantic,** *a.* [late L and Gr. *hierophantēs* (*phainein,* to show)]

†**hieroscopy,** *n.* hieromancy.

Hierosolymitan, *a.* belonging to Jerusalem. *n.* a native or inhabitant of Jerusalem. **Hierosolymite,** *n., a.* [late L *Hīerosolymītānus,* from *Hierosolyma,* Gr. *Hierosoluma,* Jerusalem]

hierurgy, *n.* a holy work, sacred performance; worship. **hierurgical,** *a.* [Gr. *hierourgia,* religious worship]

hi-fi, *n.* any equipment for high-quality sound reproduction. *a.* HIGH FIDELITY.

Higgins, *n.* **Jack,** pseudonym of British novelist HARRY PATTERSON.

higgle, *v.i.* to make a fuss about trifles as in striking a bargain. **higgler,** *n.* one who higgles; a huckster, a pedlar. [prob. a form of HAGGLE]

higgledy-piggledy, *adv.* (*coll.*) in confusion, topsy-turvy. *a.* confused, jumbled about anyhow. *n.* a jumble. [etym. doubtful]

high[1], *a.* lofty, elevated; situated at a great elevation; rising or extending upwards for or to a specified extent; upper, inland; exalted in rank, position, or office; chief; of noble character or purpose; proud, lofty in tone or temper, arrogant; great, extreme, intense; full, complete, consummate; far advanced (of time); expensive, costly (in price); lively, animated; boisterous, violent; (*Mus.*) sharp, acute in pitch; esp. of meat, tainted, approaching putrefaction, strong-smelling; chief, principal; (*coll.*) under the influence of alcohol or drugs; in a nervous, hysterical state. *adv.* to a great altitude, aloft; in or to a high degree; eminently, greatly, powerfully; at a high price; at or to a high pitch. **from on high,** from aloft, from heaven. **high and dry,** (*Naut.*) out of the water; aground; left behind, stranded, of no account in affairs. **high and low,** of people, all sorts and conditions; †(*sl.*) false dice loaded for throwing high or low; everywhere. **high and mighty,** arrogant. **on high,** aloft; to or in heaven. **on one's high horse,** arrogant, affecting superiority, giving oneself airs. **the Most High,** the Supreme Being, God. **to be riding high,** to be in a state of good fortune or prosperity. **to hightail it,** (*sl.*) to run away. **to play high,** to play or gamble for heavy amounts; to play a high card. **to run high,** to have a strong current; to be at high tide; to be in a state of excitement. **with a high hand,** in an arrogant or arbitrary manner. **high-aimed,** *a.* having lofty aims. **high altar,** *n.* the principal altar. **high-bailiff,** *n.* the chief officer of certain corporations. **high-ball,** *n.* iced whisky and soda in a tall glass. **high-blower,** *n.* a horse that flaps his nostrils with a blowing noise. **high-blown,** *a.* swelled out with wind or with pride. **high-born,** *a.* of noble birth. **high-boy,** *n.* (*N Am.*) a tall-boy. **high-bred,** *a.* of pure blood or extraction. **high-brow,** *n.* (*coll.*) an intellectually superior person; a person who takes an intellectual or academic line in conversation. *a.* intellectual, superior. **high camp,** *n., a.* (of or displaying) sophisticated camp style, behaviour, etc. **high-caste,** *a.* belonging to a high caste. **high-chair,** *n.* a baby's chair with a tray, raised on long legs to table height. **High Church,** *n.* one of the three great schools in the Anglican Church, distinguished by its maintenance of sacerdotal claims and assertion of the efficacy of the sacraments. *a.* belonging to the High Church party, hence, **High Churchism, High Churchman. high-class,** *a.* of high quality, refinement, sophistication etc. **high-coloured,** *a.* having a strong deep colour; flushed; represented in strong or forcible language. **high command,** *n.* the supreme headquarters of the armed forces. **high commissioner,** *n.* the chief representative of one Commonwealth country in another. †**high constable** CONSTABLE. **High Court (of Justice),** *n.* the Supreme Court. **high cross,** *n.* the cross formerly erected in market-places. **high day,** *n.* a feast, a festival; broad daylight, noon. **high-energy,** *a.* concerning elementary particles accelerated in a particle accelerator. **high-energy, hi-NRG music,** up-tempo dance music, usu. recorded. **higher education,** *n.* education after secondary schools, e.g. at a college or university. **higher-up,** *n.* a person in a position of greater authority or higher rank. **high-explosive,** *n.* an explosive of extreme rapidity and great destructive energy. *a.* exploding with great violence and rapidity. **highfalutin,** *a.* bombastic, affected.

n. bombast. **high fidelity,** *a.* reproducing sound with very little distortion. **high-five (sign),** *n.* (*esp. N Am.*) a gesture of victory, greeting etc. in which two people slap the palms of their hands together above their heads. **high-flier,** *n.* one with high qualifications, or who is likely to achieve high position. **high-flown,** *a.* proud, turgid, bombastic. †**high-flushed,** *a.* elated, excited. **high frequency,** *n.* any frequency of alternating current above the audible range, from about 12,000 cycles per second upward. **High German,** *n.* the form of German spoken in central and southern Germany, regarded as standard speech. **high-handed,** *a.* overbearing, domineering, arbitrary. **high-hat,** *n.* (*coll.*) one with an air of affected superiority. **highjack** HIJACK. **high jinks,** *n.pl.* high festivities or revelry; great sport. **high-level,** *a.* placed, done etc. at a high level; having a high rank. **high-level language,** *n.* (*Comput.*) a language in which each word is equal to several machine instructions, making it closer to human language. **high life,** *n.* the style of living or the manners of the fashionable world; the fashionable classes. **highlight,** *n.* the most brilliantly lit spot in a photograph or picture; (*pl.*) streaks of artificial light colour in dark hair; a moment or event of particular importance or interest. *v.t.* to put emphasis on; to put highlights in (hair). **high living,** *n.* living in extravagance and luxury. **high-lows,** *n.pl.* laced boots reaching to the ankle. **High Mass,** *n.* a Mass in which the celebrant is attended by deacon and sub-deacon, usu., but not necessarily, sung at the high altar. **high-mettled,** *a.* full of fire, spirited. **high-minded,** *a.* magnanimous; †proud, arrogant. **high-mindedly,** *adv.* **high-mindedness,** *n.* **high noon,** *n.* the time when the sun is in the meridian. **high-octane,** *a.* (of petrol) of high efficiency. **high-pitched,** *a.* aspiring, haughty; steeply sloping (of roofs); (*Mus.*) acute, tuned high. **high-power(ed),** *a.* (*coll.*) having or showing great energy or vigour. **high pressure,** *n.* a pressure of more than about 50 lb per sq. in. (22.68 kg per 6.45 sq. cm). **high-pressure,** *a.* working at such pressure; working with abnormal energy. **high priest,** *n.* a chief priest, esp. the head of the Jewish hierarchy. **high priesthood,** *n.* **high-principled,** *a.* having high or noble principles. **high-proof,** *a.* highly rectified; containing much alcohol. **high-reaching,** *a.* reaching to a great height; aspiring, ambitious. **high relief** ALTO-RILIEVO. †**high-resolved,** *a.* very resolute. **high-rise,** *a.* (in a building) having many storeys **high road,** *n.* a main road, a highway. **high school,** *n.* a secondary school. **high seas,** *n.* the open sea or ocean; (*Law*) the waters beyond low-water mark. **high-seasoned,** *a.* strongly seasoned, piquant; lewd, obscene. **high-seated,** *a.* seated aloft, lofty. **high sheriff** SHERIFF. **high-sounding,** *a.* pompous, ostentatious. **high-speed,** *a.* moving or operating at a high speed; (of photographic film) requiring brief exposure. **high-spirited,** *a.* having a lofty or courageous spirit; bold, daring. **high spot,** *n.* the outstanding characteristic of a thing. **high steel,** *n.* steel containing a relatively high proportion of carbon. **high-stepper,** *n.* a horse that lifts its feet well off the ground in trotting; a person of a dashing or showy walk or bearing. **high street,** *n.* the principal street (often used as the proper name of a street). **high-strung,** *a.* highly strung. **high table,** *n.* the table for the fellows of a college etc. †**high tasted,** *a.* having a strong taste; piquant. **high tea,** *n.* tea at which meat is served. **high tech**, *n.* advanced technology. **high-tech,** *a.* **high tension,** *n.* steady and high voltage. **high-tension battery,** *n.* a battery of dry cells or accumulators used to provide high-tension supply. **high tide,** *n.* high water; the tide at its full; †a holiday. **high time,** *n.* fully time. **high-toned,** *a.* high in pitch; strong in sound; morally or culturally elevated. **high treason** TREASON. **high-up,** *n.* a person of high rank or authority. **high-velocity,** *a.* applied to projectiles with a low trajectory and long range; applied to guns firing such projectiles. **high water,** *n.* the utmost flow of the tide; the time when the tide is at its full. **high-water mark,** *n.* the level reached by the tide at its utmost height. **high wire,** *n.* a tightrope high above the ground. **high-wrought,** *a.* wrought with great skill; inflamed to a high degree (of feelings). **highly,** *adv.* in a high degree, extremely, intensely; honourably, favourably. **highly-strung,** *a.* of a nervous and tense disposition. †**highmost,** *a.* highest, topmost. **highness,** *n.* the quality or state of being high; a title of honour given to princes and others of high rank (used with a possessive pronoun); height. †**hight**[1], HEIGHT. [OE *hēah* (cp. Dut. *hoog,* Icel. *hār,* G *hoch*)]

high[2], HIE[2].

Highland, *a.* pertaining to the Highlands of Scotland. **Highland Clearances**, *n. pl.* the forced removal of tenants from large estates in Scotland during the early 19th cent., as landowners 'improved' their estates by switching from arable to sheep farming. It led ultimately to widespread emigration to N America. **Highland fling,** *n.* a hornpipe, peculiar to the Sc. Highlanders. **Highland Games**, *n. pl.* traditional Scottish outdoor gathering which includes tossing the caber, putting the shot, running, dancing, and bagpipe playing. The most famous is the Braemar Gathering. **Highland Region**, *n.* administrative region of Scotland. **area** 26,100 sq km/10,077 sq miles. **towns** administrative headquarters Inverness; Thurso, Wick. **population** (1987) 201,000. **products** oil services, winter sports, timber, livestock, grouse and deer hunting, salmon fishing.

Highlander, *n.* an inhabitant of the Highlands of Scotland.

Highlands, *n.* general name for the plateau of broken rock which covers almost all of Scotland, and extends S of the Highland region itself.

Highsmith, *n.* **Patricia** (1921–), US crime novelist. Her first book *Strangers on a Train* (1950) was filmed by Hitchcock, and she excels in tension and psychological exploration of character, notably in her series dealing with the amoral Tom Ripley, including *The Talented Mr Ripley* (1956), *Ripley Under Ground* (1971), and *Ripley's Game* (1974).

†**hight**[2], *v.i.* (*3rd sing. past*) to be named or called; to promise. *v.t.* to call, to name; to promise; to mean, to purport. [the only instance in English of a passive verb; from OE *hātte,* I am or was called, from *hātan,* to call, to be called]

highty-tighty, HOITY-TOITY.

highway, *n.* a public road open to all passengers; a main route either by land or by water. **highway code,** *n.* the official guide and instructions for proper behaviour on the road to avoid accidents etc. **highwayman,** *n.* one who robs on the highway.

HIH, (*abbr.*) His/Her Imperial Highness.

hijack, *v.t.* to steal goods in transit; to take over a vehicle, aircraft etc. by force, esp. to divert it from its route. *n.* an act of hijacking. **hijacker,** *n.* [etym. unknown]

Hijra, Hijrah, HEGIRA.

hike, *n.* a ramble, a walking-tour; (*N Am., coll.*) an increase, e.g. in prices. *v.i.* to go for a hike. *v.t.* to hoist, lift, throw up; (*N Am., coll.*) to increase. **hiker,** *n.*

hilar, *a.* pertaining to the hilum. [HIL-UM, -AR]

hilarious, *a.* cheerful, mirthful, merry; enjoying or provoking laughter. **hilariously,** *adv.* **hilariousness, hilarity,** *n.* [L *hilaris -us,* Gr. *hilaros*]

Hilary Term, *n.* one of the four terms of the High Court of Justice etc. in England (11 Jan.–31 Mar.); the spring term at Oxford and Dublin universities. [(L *Hilarius*) St. *Hilary* of Poitiers, d. 367, whose festival occurs on 13 Jan.]

Hilbert, *n.* **David** (1862–1943), German mathematician, who founded the formalist school with the publication of *Grundlagen der Geometrie/Foundations of Geometry* (1899), which was based on Hilbert's idea of postulates. He attempted to put mathematics on a logical foundation through defining it in terms of a number of basic principles, which Gödel later showed to be impossible; none the less, his attempt greatly influenced 20th-cent. mathematicians.

hilch, *v.i.* (*Sc.*) to limp, to hobble. *n.* a hobble.

hilding, *n.* a base, cowardly fellow; a mean wretch, a

worthless person; a jade. *a.* mean, base. [perh. from ME *helden,* OE *hieldan,* to bend, to yield]

hill, *n.* a natural elevation on the surface of the earth, a small mountain; a heap, a mound; (*N Am.*) a cluster of plants, roots etc., with earth heaped round them. *v.t.* to form into hills, heaps or mounds; to heap (up). **(as) old as the hills,** (*coll.*) very old. **over the hill,** of an age when one has lost one's vigour, energy etc. **hill billy,** *n.* (*N Am.*) a rustic from the mountain country. **hill-folk, -people,** *n.* (*collect.*) a name sometimes given to the Cameronians, who held their conventicles secretly among the hills; the fairies or elves, or a class of beings intermediate between elves and human beings. **hill-side,** *n.* the slope or declivity of a hill. **hill-top,** *n.* **hillock,** *n.* a little hill or mound. **hillocky,** *a.* **hilly,** *a.* **hilliness,** *n.* [OE *hyll* (cp. MDut. *hil, hille,* L *collis*)]

Hill[1], *n.* **David Octavius** (1802–70), Scottish photographer who, in collaboration with Adamson, made extensive use of the calotype process in their large collection of portraits taken in Edinburgh 1843–48.

Hill[2], *n.* **Rowland** (1795–1879), British Post Office official who invented adhesive stamps and prompted the introduction of the penny prepaid post in 1840 (previously the addressee paid on receipt).

Hillary, *n.* **Edmund** (1919–), New Zealand mountaineer. In 1953, with Nepalese Sherpa mountaineer Tenzing Norgay, he reached the summit of Mount Everest, the world's highest peak. As a member of the Commonwealth Transantarctic Expedition 1957–58, he was the first person since Scott to reach the South Pole overland, on 3 Jan. 1958.

Hilliard, *n.* **Nicholas** (*c.* 1547–1619), English miniature portraitist and goldsmith, court artist to Elizabeth I from about 1579. His sitters included Francis Drake and Walter Raleigh.

hillo, -loa, HALLO.

Hillsborough Agreement, *n.* another name for the ANGLO-IRISH AGREEMENT.

hilt, *n.* the handle of a sword or dagger. **up to the hilt,** to the fullest extent. **hilted,** *a.* [OE, perh. related to HELVE]

hilum, *n.* the spot upon a seed where it was attached to the placenta; a small aperture or a small depression in a body organ. [L, a trifle, a whit]

him, *pron.* the objective or accusative case of HE. **himself,** *pron.* an emphatic or reflexive form of the personal pronoun of the 3rd pers. sing. masc.; his usual self. **by himself,** alone, unaccompanied; unaided. [HE]

Himachal Pradesh, *n.* state of NW India. **area** 55,700 sq km/21,500 sq miles. **capital** Simla. **population** (1981) 4,238,000, mainly Hindu. **products** timber, grain, rice, fruit. **language** Pahari.

Himalayan, *a.* pertaining to the Himalayas; vast, gigantic. **Himalayan pine,** *n.* the Nepal nutpine, *Pinus gerardiana.* **Himalayan primrose, cowslip,** *n.* a large yellow primula, *P. sikkimensis.* [Sansk. *Himālaya* (*hima,* snow, *ālaya,* abode)]

Himalayas, *n. pl.* vast mountain system of central Asia, extending from the Indian states of Kashmir in the W to Assam in the E, covering the S part of Tibet, Nepal, Sikkim, and Bhutan. It is the highest mountain range in the world. The two highest peaks are Mount Everest and Kangchenjunga. Other major peaks include Makalu, Annapurna, and Nanga Parbat, all over 8000 m/ 26,000 ft.

himation, *n.* (*pl.* **-tia**) the ordinary outer garment in ancient Greece, an oblong piece of cloth thrown over the left shoulder. [Gr.]

Himmler, *n.* **Heinrich** (1900–45), German Nazi leader, head of the SS elite corps from 1929, the police and the Gestapo secret police from 1936. During World War II he replaced Göring as Hitler's second-in-command. He was captured May 1945, and committed suicide.

himself HIM.

Himyarite, *n.* one of an ancient Semitic race in southern Arabia. *a.* pertaining to this race. **Himyaritic, Himyaric,** *a.* [*Himyar,* traditionary king of Yemen]

hin, *n.* a Jewish measure for liquids, containing rather more than a gallon (4.5 l). [Heb. *hīn*]

hinau, *n.* a New Zealand tree the bark of which yields a black dye. [Maori]

Hīnayāna, *n.* Mahāyāna Buddhist name for Theravāda Buddhism.

hind[1], *n.* the female of the deer, esp. the red deer. †**hindberry,** *n.* the raspberry. [OE (cp. Dut. and G *Hinde,* Icel., Dan. and Swed. *hind*)]

hind[2], *n.* an agricultural labourer, a farm-servant, esp. (*Sc., North.*) one in charge of two horses and allotted a house on the farm; a peasant, a rustic, a boor; †a menial. [ME *hine,* OE *hīna,* gen. pl. of *hīwa,* a domestic]

hind[3], **hinder,**[1] *a.* pertaining to or situated at the back or rear. **hind-afore, hind-foremost, hind-first,** *a., adv.* back to front. **hinder end,** *n.* the posteriors. **hindquarters,** *n.pl.* the posterior of an animal. **hindsight,** *n.* wisdom after the event, the reverse of foresight. **hinderings,** *n.pl.* (*Sc.*) the posteriors. **hindermost, hindmost,** *a.* the last; that is or comes last of all. [OE *hindan*]

Hindemith, *n.* **Paul** (1895–1963), German composer. His neo-classical, contrapuntal works include chamber ensemble and orchestral pieces, such as the *Symphonic Metamorphosis on Themes of Carl Maria von Weber* (1944), and the operas *Cardillac* (1926, revised 1952), and *Mathis der Maler/Mathis the Painter* (1938).

Hindenburg, *n.* **Paul Ludwig Hans von Beneckendorf und Hindenburg** (1847–1934), German field marshal and right-wing politician. During World War I he was supreme commander and, together with Ludendorff, practically directed Germany's policy until the end of the war. He was president of Germany 1925–33.

Hindenburg Line, *n.* German western line of World War I fortifications built 1916–17.

hinder[1] HIND[3].

hinder[2], *v.t.* to obstruct, to impede; to prevent from proceeding or moving. *v.i.* to cause a hindrance; to interpose obstacles or impediments. **hinderer,** *n.* **hindrance,** *n.* the act of hindering; that which hinders; an impediment, an obstacle. [OE *hindrian*]

Hindi, *n.* a member of the Indo-Iranian branch of the Indo-European language family, the official language of the Republic of India, although resisted as such by the Dravidian-speaking states of the south. Hindi proper is used by some 30% of Indians, in such N states as Uttar Pradesh and Madhya Pradesh. [Hind., from Pers. *hind,* India]

hindrance HINDER[2].

hindsight HIND[3].

Hindu, Hindoo, *n.* a native of India, not of Parsee, Muslim or Christian descent; an Aryan still adhering to Hinduism. *a.* pertaining to the Hindus. **Hinduism,** *n.* the Hindu polytheistic system of Brahminism modified by Buddhism and other accretions. **Hinduize, -ise,** *v.t.* **Hindustan,** *n.* ('land of the Hindus') a term loosely applied to the whole of India, but more specifically to the plain of the Ganges and Jumna rivers, or that part of India N of the Deccan. **Hindustani,** *a.* of or belonging to Hindustan, Indian. *n.* a native of Hindustan proper; a member of the Indo-Iranian branch of the Indo-European language family, closely related to Hindi and Urdu and originating in the bazaars of Delhi. It serves as a *lingua franca* in many parts of the Republic of India. [HINDI]

Hindu Kush, *n.* mountain range in central Asia; length 800 km/500 miles; greatest height Tirich Mir 7690 m/ 25,239 ft., Pakistan. The Khyber Pass, a narrow defile (53 km/33 miles long), separates Pakistan from Afghanistan, and was used by Zahir and other invaders of India. The present road was built by the British in the Afghan Wars.

Hine, *n.* **Lewis** (1874–1940), US sociologist. He recorded in photographs child labour conditions in US factories at the beginning of this century, leading to a change in the law.

hinge, *n.* the joint or mechanical device on which a door or lid turns; a natural articulation fulfilling similar functions; a piece of gummed paper for sticking a stamp in an album etc.; the point on which anything depends or turns. *v.t.* to furnish with or as with a hinge; †to cause to bend. *v.i.* to turn on or as on a hinge; to depend (upon). **to be off the hinges,** to be in a state of mental or physical disorder; to be out of working order. **hinged,** *a.* **hingeless,** *a.* [ME *heng,* cogn. with HANG]

Hinkler, *n.* **Herbert John Louis** (1892–1933), Australian pilot who in 1928 made the first solo flight from England to Australia. He was killed while making another attempt to fly to Australia.

hinny¹, *n.* the offspring of a stallion and a she-ass. [L *hinnus* (Gr. *hinnos, ginnos*)]

hinny², *v.i.* to neigh, to whinny. [F *hennir,* L *hinnīre*]

hinny³, (*Sc.*) HONEY.

Hinshelwood, *n.* **Cyril** (1897–1967), British chemist. Hinshelwood shared the 1956 Nobel Chemistry Prize with Nikolay Semenov for his work on chemical chain reactions. He also studied the chemistry of bacterial growth.

hint, *n.* a slight or distant allusion; an indirect (usu. pointed) mention or suggestion. *v.t.* to mention indirectly, to suggest, to allude to. *v.i.* to make remote allusion. **to hint at,** to make slight but pointed allusion to. **hinter,** *n.* **hintingly,** *adv.* [prob. from HENT¹]

hinterland, *n.* the region situated behind that on the coast or that along a navigable river. [G (*Hinter-,* HINDER¹, LAND)]

hip¹, *n.* the projecting fleshy part covering the hip-joint; the haunch; the external angle formed by the meeting sides of a roof; a rafter along the edge of this; a truncated gable; a hip-lock. *v.t.* to throw by a hip-lock; (*Arch.*) to furnish with a hip. **to catch, have on, upon the hip,** to have at a disadvantage. **to smite hip and thigh,** to overthrow completely, to slaughter without mercy. **hip-bath,** *n.* a bath in which the body can be immersed to the hips. **hip-disease,** *n.* a scrofulous disease of the hip-joint attacking the bones. **hip-flask,** *n.* a flask, usu. containing spirits, carried in a pocket at the hip. **hip-hop,** *n.* a form of music and dancing originating among black and Hispanic youngsters in New York. **hip-huggers,** *n.pl.* (*N Am., coll.*) hipsters. **hip-joint,** *n.* the articulation of the femur and the thigh-bone. **hip-lock,** *n.* in wrestling, a grip in which one tries to throw one's opponent by putting a leg or hip in front of him. **hip-roof,** *n.* a roof rising directly from the walls on every side and consequently having no gable. **hipped¹,** *a.* having the hip dislocated or sprained; (*Arch.*) furnished with a hip; (*in comb.*) having hips of the specified kind (as *wide-hipped*). **hipped roof** HIP-ROOF. **hipsters,** *n.pl.* trousers that start at the hips, not the waist. [OE *hype* (cp. Dut. *heup,* Dan. *hofte,* G *Hüfte*)]

hip², *n.* the fruit of the dog-rose. [OE *hēope*]

†**hip³,** *n.* melancholia, the blues. *v.t.* (*usu. in p.p.* **hipped²**) to affect with melancholia; to irritate, to provoke. **hippish,** *a.* [short for HYPOCHONDRIA]

hip⁴, *int.* an exclamation, usu. twice or three times repeated, introducing a hurrah.

hip⁵, *adv.* (*esp. N Am.* (*dated*), *sl.*) aware, in the know. **hippie, hippy,** *n.* a member of the youth culture of the 1960s, which stressed universal love and brotherhood, rejection of middle-class values, the wearing of long hair and colourful clothes, and the use of drugs. **hipster,** *n.* one who knows what's what, one in the know. [HEP]

hipe, *v.t.* in wrestling, to throw (one's opponent) by lifting and putting the knee between his thighs. *n.* a throw of this kind; (*old Mil. sl.*) a rifle. [HIP¹]

hipp- HIPPO-.

Hipparchos, (*acronym*) *H*igh *P*recision *Par*allax *Co*llecting *S*atellite, launched by the European Space Agency in Aug. 1989. Named after the Greek astronomer HIPPARCHUS, it is the world's first astronometry satellite designed to provide the first measurements of the positions and apparent motions of stars from space. The accuracy of these measurements will be far greater than from ground-based telescopes. However, because of engine failure, Hipparchos is making more limited orbits than had been planned, which may restrict the data it is able to provide.

Hipparchus¹, *n.* (*c.* 190–*c.* 120 BC), Greek astronomer, who invented trigonometry, calculated the lengths of the solar year and the lunar month, discovered the precession of the equinoxes, made a catalogue of 800 fixed stars, and advanced Eratosthenes' method of determining the situation of places on the Earth's surface by lines of latitude and longitude.

Hipparchus², *n.* (*c.* 555–514 BC), Greek tyrant. Son of Pisistratus, he was associated with his elder brother Hippias as ruler of Athens 527–514 BC. His affection being spurned by Harmodius, he insulted her sister, and was assassinated by Harmodius and Aristogiton.

Hipparion, *n.* an extinct quadruped of the Miocene and Pliocene ages probably representing a stage in the evolution of the horse. [Gr., pony]

hippic, *a.* pertaining to horses or to horse-racing. [Gr. *hippikos,* see HIPP(O)-]

hippie HIP⁵.

hippo, *n.* (*coll.*) short for HIPPOPOTAMUS.

hipp(o)-, *comb. form.* pertaining to or resembling a horse. [Gr. *hippos,* a horse]

hippocampus, *n.* (*pl.* **-pi**) a genus of small teleostean fishes, with a head and neck somewhat like that of a horse, and a prehensile tail, the sea-horse; one of two eminences on the floor of the lateral ventricle of the brain. **hippocampus major,** *n.* a large white eminence extending the whole length of the cornu in the cerebrum. **hippocampus minor,** *n.* a curved and pointed longitudinal eminence on the inner side of the posterior cornu, projecting backwards into the posterior lobe of the cerebrum. †**hippocamp,** *n.* a sea-monster. [late L, from Gr. *hippokampos* (HIPPO-, *kampos,* sea-monster)]

hippocentaur, *n.* a centaur. [L *hippocentaurus,* Gr. *hippokentauros*]

hippocras, *n.* a cordial made of wine and spices. [earlier *ypocras,* OF *ipocras,* from *Hippocrătes,* Gr. physician born about 460 BC, perh. from being strained through Hippocrates' sleeve, a woollen bag]

Hippocrates, *n.* (*c.* 460–*c.* 370 BC), Greek physician, often called the founder of medicine. Important Hippocratic ideas include cleanliness (for patients and physicians), moderation in eating and drinking, letting nature take its course, and living where the air is good. **Hippocratic, -ical, -cratian,** *a.* of or pertaining to Hippocrates. **Hippocratic oath,** *n.* an oath taken by a physician binding him to observe the code of medical ethics, secrecy etc., first drawn up in the 4th or 5th cent. BC, possibly by Hippocrates.

hippocrene, *n.* a spring on Mount Helicon in Greece, a supposed source of poetic inspiration. [L from Gr. *hippos,* horse, *krēnē,* a fountain]

hippocrepian, *a.* like a horseshoe in shape. [Gr. *krēpis,* shoe]

†**hippodame,** *n.* (*Spens.*) a hippocampus. **hippodamist,** *n.* a horse-tamer. **hippodamous,** *a.* [Gr. *hippodamos* (HIPPO-, *damaein,* to tame, to subdue)]

hippodrome, *n.* (*Gr. and Rom. Ant.*) a circus for equestrian games and chariot races; a circus. **hippodromic,** *a.* **hippodromist,** *n.* a circus rider or horse-trainer. [F, from L, from Gr. *hippodromos* (*dromos,* a course)]

hippogriff, *n.* a fabulous creature, half horse and half griffin; a winged horse. [F *hippogriffe*]

hippology, *n.* the study of the horse. **hippological,** *a.* **hippologist,** *n.*

Hippolytus, *n.* in Greek mythology, the son of Theseus, who cursed him for his supposed dishonourable advances to his stepmother Phaedra. Killed by Poseidon as he rode near the sea in his chariot, he was restored to life when his innocence was proven.

hippomanes, *n.* a substance supposed to possess aphrodisiac qualities, obtained from a mare or the forehead of a recently dropped foal, formerly used in preparing love-potions. [Gr. HIPPO-, *mainesthai,* to go mad]

hippopathology, *n.* the pathology of the horse; veterinary medicine.

hippophagy, -agism, *n.* the act or practice of feeding on horseflesh. **hippophagist**, *n.* **hippophagistical**, **hippophagous**, *a.* [Gr. *phagein,* to eat]

hippophile, *n.* a lover of horses.

hippophobia, *n.* dislike, fear of horses.

hippopotamus, *n.* (*pl.* **-es, -mi,**) a gigantic African pachydermatous quadruped of amphibious habits, with a massive, heavy body, short, blunt muzzle and short limbs and tail. **hippopotamic**, **hippopotamoid**, *a.* [L, from Gr. *hippopotamos* (*potamos,* river)]

hippuric, *a.* of hippuric acid, contained in the urine of horses. [Gr. *ouron,* urine]

Hippuris, *n.* a genus of plants containing the mare's-tail, common in pools and marshes. [L, from Gr. (*oura,* tail)]

hippurite, *n.* a fossil mollusc of the genus *Hippurites,* from cretaceous strata. [Gr. *hippouros,* as prec.]

hippy HIP[5].

hipster HIP[1], HIP[5].

hircine, *a.* goatish; strong smelling. **hircinous**, *a.* **hircocervus**, *n.* a fabulous creature, half goat, half stag. **hircosity**, *n.* [L *hircīnus,* from *hircus,* he-goat]

hire, *n.* the price paid for labour or services or the use of things; the engagement of a person or thing for such a price; a reward; a bribe. *v.t.* to procure at a certain price or consideration for temporary use; to employ (a person) for a stipulated payment; to grant the use or service of for a stipulated price; to bribe; to engage (a servant etc.). **on hire,** for hiring. **hire car,** *n.* a car hired usu. for a short period. **hire purchase,** *n.* a method by which payments for hire are accepted as instalments of the price and the article eventually becomes the property of the hirer. **hireable,** *a.* **hireless,** *a.* gratuitous, unpaid. **hireling**, *n.* one who serves for hire; a mercenary; a prostitute. *a.* mercenary. **hirer,** *n.* one who hires or lets on hire. [OE *hӯr* (cp. Dut. *huur,* Dan. *hyre,* G *Heuer*)]

Hirohito, *n.* (1901–89), emperor of Japan from 1926. He succeeded his father Yoshihito. After the defeat of Japan 1945 he was made to reject belief in the divinity of the emperor and Japanese racial superiority, and accept the 1946 constitution greatly curtailing his powers. He was succeeded by his son Akihito.

Hiroshige, *n.* **Andō** (1797–1858), Japanese artist whose landscape prints, often using snow or rain to create atmosphere, were highly popular in his time, notably *Tōkaidō gojūsan-tsugi/53 Stations on the Tokaido Highway* (1833).

Hiroshima, *n.* industrial city (cars) and port on the S coast of Honshu, Japan, destroyed by the first wartime use of an atomic bomb, 6 Aug. 1945. The city has largely been rebuilt since the war; population (1987) 1,034,000.

hirple, *v.i.* (*Sc., North.*) to walk with a limping or halting gait. *n.* such a gait. [etym. unknown]

hirrient, *a.* (*Phon.*) trilled. *n.* a trilled sound. [L *hirriens -entem,* pres.p. of *hirrīre,* to snarl]

hirsle, *v.i.* (*Sc., North.*) to slide or graze (along, down etc.). *v.t.* to move (something or someone) in a rough, rubbing manner. [cp. Icel. *hrista,* to shake]

hirsute, *a.* rough, hairy, unshorn; (*Bot.*) covered with bristles. **hirsuteness,** *n.* [L *hirsūtus*]

hirudin, *n.* a substance secreted by the salivary gland of the leech, preventing blood-clotting. [L *hirūdō -dinis,* a leech]

hirundine, *a.* like a swallow. [L *hirundo,* a swallow]

his, *pron., a.* of or belonging to him; used absolutely as in *this is his,* this belongs to him. †**hisn,** †**his'n,** *pron.* (*prov.*) his (used absolutely). [OE, gen. of *hē,* HE]

Hispanic, *a.* pertaining to Spain or the Spanish people. **Hispanicism**, *n.* a Spanish idiom. **Hispanicize, -ise,** *v.t.* **Hispanophile**, *n., a.* (one) fond of Spain. [L *Hispānicus,* from *Hispānia,* Spain]

Hispano-Suiza, *n.* car designed by a Swiss engineer Marc Birkigt (1878–1947), who emigrated to Barcelona, where he founded a factory which produced cars (*c.* 1900–38), legendary for their handling, elegance, and speed.

hispid, *a.* rough, bristly. [L *hispidus*]

hiss, *v.i.* to make a sound like that of the letter *s,* by forcing out the breath between the tongue and the upper teeth; to make a sibilant sound, vocally as do geese, or by rapid motion through the air, as an arrow etc.; to express disapprobation by making such a sound. *v.t.* to utter with a hissing sound; to condemn by hissing; to drive (away etc.) thus. *n.* a hissing sound; an expression of derision or disapprobation. **hissingly,** *adv.* [imit.]

Hiss, *n.* **Alger** (1904–), US diplomat and liberal Democrat, a former State Department official, controversially imprisoned 1950 for allegedly having spied for the USSR.

hist, *int.* silence! hush! listen! *v.t.* to urge or incite with this sound. [imit.]

histic, *a.* of or pertaining to tissue. **histioid**, *a.* **histiology**, etc. HISTOLOGY. [as foll.]

histo-, *comb. form.* pertaining to organic tissues. [Gr. *histos,* web]

histochemistry, *n.* the application of chemistry to organic tissue.

histocompatibility, *n.* the compatibility of tissues that allows one to be grafted successfully onto another.

histogen, *n.* an area of tissue on a plant from which a specific part develops.

histogenesis, *n.* the science of the origin of tissues. **histogenetic**, *a.* **histogeny**, *n.* histogenesis; the formation and development of the organic tissues.

histogram, *n.* a pictorial method of showing the distribution of various quantities, e.g. rainfall month by month.

histography, *n.* a description of or treatise on organic tissues.

histology, *n.* the science of organic tissues. **histologic, histological**, *a.* **histologically,** *adv.* **histologist,** *n.*

histolysis, *n.* the decay and dissolution of organic tissue. **histolytic**, *a.*

histone, *n.* any of various water-soluble proteins found in cell nuclei.

histopathology, *n.* (the study of) changes in tissue accompanying disease. **histopathological**, *a.* **histopathologist,** *n.*

historian, *n.* a writer of history; one versed in history. **historiated**, *a.* ornamented with figures (as illuminated capitals etc.). [F *historien,* from L *historia,* HISTORY]

historic, *a.* celebrated in history, associated with historical events, important, momentous. **historic infinitive,** *n.* (*Gr. Gram.*) the infinitive verb used for the indicative. **historic present,** *n.* (*Gr. Gram.*) the present tense used in a past sense. **historic tenses,** *n.pl.* (*Gram.*) the tenses normally employed to express past events. **historical,** *a.* pertaining to or of the nature of history, distinguished from legendary, fictitious etc. **historical novel,** *n.* a novel set in the past, using actual historical events and characters as background. **historical picture,** *n.* a picture representing a historical event. **historically,** *adv.* **historicism,** *n.* a theory that all political and social events are historically determined. **historicist,** *n.* **historicity**, *n.* historical existence. [L *historicus,* Gr. *historikos,* see HISTORY]

historiette, *n.* a short history; a tale. [F]

historiographer, *n.* a writer of history, esp. an official historian; an expert on historical method. **historiographic, -ical**, *a.* **historiography,** *n.* [late L *historiographus*]

history, *n.* a systematic record of past events, esp. those of importance in the development of men or peoples; a study of or a book dealing with the past of any country, people, science, art etc.; past events, esp. regarded as material for such a study; an eventful past, an interesting career; an historical play; a story; a record, e.g. of someone's past medical treatment. †*v.t.* to relate or record, to chronicle. **to make history,** to do something momentous. [L and Gr. *historia,* from *histōr,* knowing, cogn. with *id-, eidenai,* to know]

histrion, †**-trio**, *n.* (*usu. derog.*) a stage-player. **histrionic**, *a.* pertaining to actors or acting; theatrical; stagey, affected, unreal. *n.pl.* the art of theatrical representation; theatricals; an ostentatious display of usu. false emotion. **histrionically,** *adv.* **histrionicism, histrionism,** *n.* stage representation; feigned representation; histrionics. [F *histrion* or L *histrio -ōnem*]

hit, *v.t.* (*past, p.p.* **hit**) to strike; to strike or touch with a blow or missile after taking aim; to attain to; to guess; to affect, to wound; (*esp. N Am., sl.*) to kill; to encounter, meet. *v.i.* to strike (at, against etc.); to come into collision (against); to agree, to suit, to fall in with. *n.* a blow, a stroke; a touch with the sword or stick in fencing; a lucky chance; a felicitous expression or turn of thought; a successful effort; a best-selling book, record etc. **hit and miss,** succeeding and failing in a haphazard way. **hit-and-run,** *a.* of a driver, causing an accident and not stopping to help the injured; of an accident, involving a hit-and-run driver. **to hit below the belt** BELT. **to hit it off with, together,** to agree. **to hit off,** to represent or describe rapidly or cleverly. **to hit on, upon,** to light or chance on; to discover by luck. **to hit out,** to strike out straight from the shoulder. **to hit the bottle** BOTTLE. **to hit the nail on the head** NAIL. **to hit the road** ROAD. **to make a hit,** to be a sudden success, to become popular. **hit list,** *n.* (*coll.*) a list of people to be killed, sacked etc. **hit man,** *n.* (*coll.*) a hired professional killer; a person who undertakes unpleasant tasks. **hit parade,** *n.* a list of the currently most popular recordings of pop music. [prob. from Scand. (cp. Dan. *hitte*)]

hitch, *v.t.* to fasten loosely; to make fast by a hook, loop etc.; to pull up with a jerk; to drag (in); (*coll.*) to obtain (a lift) by hitch-hiking. *v.i.* to move with jerks; to become entangled or caught; (*coll.*) to work pleasantly together; to interfere (as horses); (*coll.*) to hitch-hike. *n.* a catch, a stoppage; an impediment, a temporary difficulty; the act of catching, as on a hook; a pull or jerk up; (*Naut.*) various species of knot by which a rope is bent to a spar or to another rope. **to get hitched,** (*sl.*) to get married. **hitch-hike,** *v.i.* to travel by obtaining lifts from passing motorists. **hitch-hiker, hitch-hiking,** *n.* **hitchy,** *a.* **hitchily,** *adv.* [etym. doubtful]

Hitchcock, *n.* **Alfred** (1899–1980), English director of suspense films, noted for his camera work, and for making 'walk-ons' in his own films. His films include *The Thirty-Nine Steps* (1935), *The Lady Vanishes* (1939), *Rebecca* (1940), *Strangers on a Train* (1951), *Psycho* (1960), and *The Birds* (1963).

†**hithe,** *n.* a small port or haven (common in place-names, as *Rotherhithe*). [OE *hȳth*]

hither, *adv.* to this place, end or point; in this direction. *a.* situated on this side; the nearer (of two objects) to the speaker. **hither and thither,** to this place and that; here and there. †**hithermost,** *a.* nearest in this direction. **hither side,** *n.* the nearer side. **hitherto,** *adv.* up to this place, limit or time. †**hitherward,** *adv.* in this direction. [OE *hider*]

Hitler, *n.* **Adolf** (1889–1945), German Nazi dictator, born in Austria. Führer (leader) of the Nazi party from 1921, author of *Mein Kampf/My Struggle* (1925–27). Chancellor of Germany from 1933 and head of state from 1934, he created a dictatorship by playing party and state institutions against each other, and continually creating new offices and appointments. His position was not seriously challenged until the 'Bomb Plot', 20 July 1944. In foreign affairs, he reoccupied the Rhineland and formed an alliance with the Italian fascist Mussolini, 1936, annexed Austria, 1938, and occupied Sudetenland under the Munich Agreement. The rest of Czechoslovakia was annexed Mar. 1939. The Hitler–Stalin pact was followed in Sept. by the invasion of Poland and the declaration of war by Britain and France (see WORLD WAR II). He committed suicide as Berlin fell. **Hitlerite,** *n.* supporter of Adolf Hitler (1889–1945) and of German National Socialism. **Hitlerism,** *n.* the ideology of National Socialism as propounded by Adolf Hitler.

Hitler–Stalin pact, *n.* nonaggression treaty between Germany and the USSR signed 25 Aug. 1939. It secretly allowed for the partition of Poland between the two countries and formed a sufficient security in the east for Hitler's declaration of war on Poland, 1 Sept. 1939. This alliance of two apparently inimical ideologies was ended only by the German invasion of the USSR on 22 June 1941.

Hittite, *n.* member of a group of peoples who inhabited Anatolia and N Syria from the 3rd to the 1st millennium BC. The city of Hattusas (now Boğazköy in central Turkey) became the capital of a strong kingdom, which overthrew the Babylonian empire. After a period of eclipse the Hittite New Empire became a great power (about 1400–1200 BC) which successfully waged war with Egypt. The Hittite language is an Indo-European language. *a.* of or pertaining to the Hittites.

HIV, (*abbr.*) human immunodeficiency virus, the virus which causes AIDS.

hive, *n.* an artificial structure for housing bees; a swarm of bees inhabiting a hive; a place swarming with busy occupants; †a kind of bonnet or other object resembling a hive. *v.t.* to put into or secure in a hive; to house as in a hive; to store up for future use. *v.i.* to enter or live in a hive; to take shelter or swarm together, as bees. **to hive off,** to assign part of a firm's work to a subsidiary company; to divert (assets) from one concern to another. **hiveless,** *a.* **hiver,** *n.* one who collects bees into hives. **hiveward,** *adv.* [OE *hȳf* (cp. Dut. *huif,* Icel. *hūfr,* also L *cupa,* a tub)]

hives, *n.* an eruptive disease characterized by scattered vesicles filled with a fluid; applied also to inflammation of the bowels or of the larynx. [etym. doubtful]

hl, (*abbr.*) hectolitre.

HM, (*abbr.*) His (or Her) Majesty.

HMC, (*abbr.*) His (or Her) Majesty's Customs.

HMI, (*abbr.*) His (or Her) Majesty's Inspector, Inspectorate (of schools).

HMS, (*abbr.*) His (or Her) Majesty's Ship or Service.

HMSO, (*abbr.*) His (or Her) Majesty's Stationery Office.

HNC, (*abbr.*) Higher National Certificate.

HND, (*abbr.*) Higher National Diploma.

Ho, (*chem. symbol*) holmium.

ho, *int.* an exclamation to call attention, or to denote exultation, surprise etc.; a cry used by teamsters to stop their teams. **ho! ho!** *int.* expressing amusement, derision etc. **eastward, westward ho!** *int.* (*Naut.*) eastward or westward away. [cp. Icel. *hō, hōa*]

hoactzin, hoatzin, *n.* a S American bird, *Opisthocomus hoazin* or *O. cristatus,* with a harsh hissing cry. [prob. native, onomat.]

hoar, *a.* white, grey or greyish-white; grey with age; ancient; white with foam. †*v.i.* to become mouldy or musty. †*v.t.* to make hoary or white; to make mouldy. *n.* hoariness; antiquity; hoar-frost, rime. **hoar-frost,** *n.* frozen dew, white frost. **hoar-headed** HOARY. **hoarstone,** *n.* a landmark; a stone marking out the boundary of an estate. [OE *hār* (cp. Icel. *hārr,* also G *Hehr,* august)]

hoard, *n.* a stock, a store, a quantity of things, esp. money, laid by; an accumulated stock of anything. *v.t.* to collect and lay by; to store up. *v.i.* to amass and store up anything of value. **hoarder,** *n.* [OE *hord,* whence *hordian,* to hoard (cp. Icel. *hodd,* G *Hort*)]

hoarding, †**hord,** *n.* a temporary screen of boards round or in front of a building where erections or repairs are in progress; a large screen for posting bills on. [from OF *hourd, hurt,* scaffold, or Dut. *horde,* hurdle]

hoarhound, HOREHOUND.

hoarse, *a.* of the voice, harsh, rough; grating, discordant; having such a voice, as from a cold. **hoarse-sounding,** *a.* **hoarsely,** *adv.* **hoarsen,** *v.t., v.i.* **hoarseness,** *n.* [ME *hors, hos,* OE *hās* (cp. Dan. *hæs,* G *heiser*)]

hoarstone HOAR.

hoary, *a.* white or whitish-grey as with age; white- or grey-headed; of great antiquity; venerable; (*Nat. Hist.*) covered with very short dense hairs, which give an appearance of whiteness to the surface; †mouldy, musty. **hoary-headed,** *a.* grey-headed. **hoariness,** *n.*

[HOAR]

hoast, *v.i.* (*Sc.*) to cough. [prob. from Icel. *hōsta* (cp. OE *hwōstan*)]

†**hoastman,** *n.* a member of a merchant-guild in Newcastle-upon-Tyne, orig. charged with the duty of receiving strangers, and afterwards with the control of the trade in coal. [HOST, guest, MAN]

hoax, *n.* a deception meant as a practical joke. *v.t.* to play a practical joke upon, to take in for sport. **hoaxer,** *n.* [perh. corr. of HOCUS]

hob[1], *n.* the projecting side of a grate, or the top of this, on which things are placed to be kept warm; a peg or iron pin used as a mark in quoits and other games; a hardened, threaded spindle by which a comb or chasing-tool may be cut; the runner of a sledge. [identified by Skeat with HUB[1]]

hob[2], *n.* an elf, a sprite; a rustic; a male ferret. **hobbish,** *a.* **hob-job,** *n.* (*dial.*) an odd job. **hob-jobbing,** *n.* **hob-jobber,** *n.* [var. of *Rob,* short for ROBIN, *Robert*]

Hoban, *n.* **James C.** (1762–1831), Irish-born architect who emigrated to the US. His best-known building is the White House, Washington DC, and he also worked on the Capitol and other public buildings.

hob-a-nob, HOB-NOB.

Hobart, *n.* capital and port of Tasmania, Australia; population (1986) 180,000. Products include zinc, textiles, and paper. Founded 1804 as a pearl colony, it was named after Lord Hobart, then Secretary of State for the Colonies.

Hobbema, *n.* **Meindert** (1638–1709), Dutch landscape painter. He was a pupil of Ruisdael and his early work is derivative, but later works are characteristically realistic and unsentimental.

Hobbes, *n.* **Thomas** (1588–1679), English political philosopher, and the first thinker since Aristotle to attempt to develop a comprehensive theory of nature, including human behaviour. In *The Leviathan* (1651) he advocates absolutist government as the only means of ensuring order and security; he saw this as deriving from the social contract. He was tutor to the exiled Prince Charles. **Hobbesian,** *a.* concerning the philosopher Hobbes or his political philosophy. **Hobbism,** *n.* the system of philosophy contained in or deduced from the writings of Hobbes, esp. his teachings with regard to absolute monarchy.

hobbinoll, *n.* a rustic. [name of a rustic in Spenser's *Shepherd's Calendar*]

Hobbit, The (or *There and Back Again*), *n.* a fantasy for children by J.R.R. Tolkien, published in the UK, 1937. It describes the adventures of Bilbo Baggins, a 'hobbit' (small humanoid) in an ancient world, Middle-Earth, populated by dragons, dwarves, elves, and other mythical creatures, including the wizard Gandalf. *The Hobbit,* together with Tolkien's later trilogy *The Lord of the Rings* (1954–55), achieved cult status in the 1960s.

hobble, *v.i.* to walk lamely or awkwardly; to walk with unequal and jerky steps; to move in a halting or irregular way; to run lamely (as verses). *v.t.* to cause to hobble; to shackle the legs of (horses etc.) to prevent straying; to perplex. *n.* an awkward, uneven or limping gait; a difficulty, a perplexity; a rope, shackle, clog etc. for hobbling an animal. **hobble-skirt,** *n.* a skirt fitting closely round the legs and ankles, usu. confined to a wide band causing the wearer to hobble. **hobbler,** *n.* one who hobbles; an unlicensed pilot, a hoveller; a casual dock-labourer. **hobblingly,** *adv.* **hobbly,** *a.* causing to hobble; full of holes, rough. [cp. Dut. *hobbelen,* to toss or rock about, to stammer]

hobbledehoy, *n.* a raw, awkward young fellow. **hobbledehoyhood**, **-ism,** *n.* **hobbledehoyish,** *a.* [etym. doubtful]

hobby[1], *n.* †a strong, active, middle-sized horse; an easy ambling horse; a hobby-horse; any recreation or pursuit, plan or object; †an early form of velocipede. **hobby-horse,** *n.* orig. a figure rudely imitating a horse used in morris-dances, pantomime etc.; a child's rocking-horse, or a horse's head on a stick for a child to bestride in play; a horse on a merry-go-round; a hobby; a topic to which one constantly reverts; †a buffoon. **hobbyism,** *n.* **hobbyist,** *n.* **hobbyless,** *a.* [OF *hobin,* perh. var. of ROBIN]

hobby[2], *n.* a small species of falcon, *Falco subbuteo.* [OF *hobet,* prob. from *hober,* to move about (cp. Dut. *hobbelen,* see HOBBLE)]

hobgoblin, *n.* a kind of goblin, elf or fairy, esp. one of a frightful appearance.

hobhoy HAUTBOY.

hobnail, *n.* a short thick nail with a large head, used for heavy boots; a clown, a clod-hopper. *v.t.* to set or stud (boots) with hobnails; to trample. **hobnailed,** *a.* set with hobnails; of the liver, rough and uneven, as if studded with hobnails.

hob-nob, *v.i.* to drink familiarly, or to associate familiarly (with). †*adv.* (*Shak.*) give it or take it. [earlier *hab nab* (OE *habban,* to HAVE, *nabban,* not to have)]

hobo, *n.* (*pl.* **-boes**) (*esp. N Am.*) a vagrant, a tramp. [etym. unknown]

Hobson-Jobson, *n.* the practice of assimilating foreign words and modifying them to approximate to familiar sounds in the native language. [Anglo-Indian approximation to Arab. *Yā Hasan Yā Hosain,* a lament for the grandsons of Mohammed]

Hobson's choice CHOICE.

Hochhuth, *n.* **Rolf** (1931–), Swiss dramatist, whose controversial play *Soldaten/Soldiers* (1968) implied that the British politician Churchill was involved in a plot to assassinate the Polish general Sikorski.

Ho Chi Minh, *n.* (1890–1969), adopted name of Nguyen That Tan, North Vietnamese Communist politician, president from 1954. He was trained in Moscow, and headed the communist Vietminh from 1941. Having campaigned against the French (1946–54), he became president and prime minister of the republic at the armistice. Aided by the communist bloc, he did much to develop industrial potential. He relinquished the premiership 1955, but continued as president.

Ho Chi Minh City (formerly **Saigon**), chief port and industrial city of S Vietnam; population (1985) 3,500,000. Industries include shipbuilding, textiles, rubber, and food products. Saigon was the capital of the Republic of Vietnam (South Vietnam), 1954–76, when it was renamed.

Ho Chi Minh Trails, North Vietnamese troop and supply routes to South Vietnam via Laos during the Vietnam War.

hock[1], *n.* the joint between the knee and the fetlock in the hind leg of quadrupeds; (*Sc.*) the posterior part of the knee-joint in man. *v.t.* to hamstring. [OE, *hoh,* cogn. with HEEL[1]]

hock[2], *n.* a kind of light wine, still or sparkling, made at Hochheim in Nassau; any white wine of the Rhine region. [formerly *hockamore,* G *Hochheimer*]

hock[3], *v.t.* (*coll.*) to pawn. *n.* the state of being pawned or pledged; prison.

†**hock-day,** *n.* a festival held on the second Tuesday after Easter, when money was levied, with a good deal of horse-play, on passers-by for pious uses; it was traditionally believed to have been on that day that the English overcame the Danes. [etym. doubtful]

hockey[1], *n.* a game of ball played with a club having a curved end. [perh. conn. with F *hoquet,* a crook, or with HOOK]

hockey[2], *n.* (*dial.*) harvest-home, or the feast celebrating this. [etym. unknown]

hockle, *v.t.* to hamstring; to hough. [etym. doubtful; perh. from HOCK[1]]

Hockney, *n.* **David** (1937–), British painter, printmaker, and designer, resident in California. In the early 1960s he contributed to the pop art movement. His portraits and views of swimming pools and modern houses reflect a preoccupation with surface pattern and effects of light. He has produced etchings, photo collages, and sets for opera.

hocus, *v.t.* to take in, to impose upon; to stupefy with liquor treated with drugs; to put a drug into (liquor). *n.* a cheat, an impostor; drugged liquor. **hocus pocus,**

n. an expression used by jugglers in playing tricks; a juggler; a juggler's trick, a fraud, a hoax. *v.i.* to juggle. *v.t.* to cheat, to trick. [from the mock L *hocus pocus*]

hod, *n.* a wooden holder shaped like a trough and fixed on a long handle, for carrying mortar or bricks on the shoulder; a coal-scuttle. **hod-carrier, hodman,** *n.* a labourer who carries a hod for bricklayers etc.; a drudge, a hack; (*Univ. sl.*) a scholar from Westminster School admitted to Christ Church, Oxford. [prob. from obs. *hot,* OF *hotte,* from Teut. (cp. MDut. *hodde,* G *Hotte*)]

hodden, *n.* (*Sc.*) a coarse woollen cloth such as would be produced by a handloom. *a.* attired in this; plain, homely. **hodden grey,** *n.* grey hodden manufactured from undyed wool. [etym. doubtful]

Hodeida, *n.* (or **Al Hudaydah**) Red Sea port of North Yemen; population(1986) 155,000. It trades in coffee and spices.

hodge, *n.* a typical countryman; the agricultural labouring class. [corr. of ROGER]

hodge-podge, *n.* a hotchpotch; a mixture or medley. †**hodge-pudding,** *n.* a pudding consisting of a medley of ingredients.

Hodgkin, *n.* **Alan Lloyd** (1914–), British physiologist engaged in research with Andrew Huxley on the mechanism of conduction in peripheral nerves, 1946–60. In 1963 they shared the Nobel Prize for Physiology and Medicine with John Eccles.

Hodgkin's disease, *n.* rare form of cancer (also known as lymphadenoma), mainly affecting the lymph nodes and spleen. It undermines the immune system, leaving the sufferer more susceptible to infection. However, it responds well to radiotherapy and cytotoxic drugs, and long-term survival is usual.

hodiernal, *a.* pertaining to the present day. [L *hodiernus,* from *hodiē,* today]

hodman HOD.

†**hodmandod,** *n.* a snail. [var. of obs. *dodman,* a snail]

hodograph, *n.* the curve traced by the end of lines, drawn from a fixed point, representing in magnitude and direction the velocity of a moving point. **hodographic,** *a.* **hodographically,** *adv.* [Gr. *hodos,* way, -GRAPH]

hodometer, ODOMETER.

hodoscope, *n.* any device for tracing the path of a charged particle. [Gr. *hodos,* way]

Hodza, *n.* **Milan** (1878–1944), Slovak politician and prime minister of Czechoslovakia from Feb. 1936. He and President Beneš were forced to agree to the secession of the Sudeten areas of Czechoslovakia to the Germans before resigning 22 Sept. 1938 (see MUNICH AGREEMENT).

hoe[1], *n.* a tool used to scrape or stir up earth around plants, cut weeds up from the ground etc. *v.t.* (*pres.p.* **hoeing**) to scrape or loosen (ground), cut (weeds), or dig (up) with a hoe. *v.i.* to use a hoe. **hoe-cake,** *n.* (*N Am.*) a cake of Indian meal, orig. cooked on a hoe. **hoedown,** *n.* (*esp. N Am.*) a social gathering for square-dancing. [F *houe,* OHG *houwa,* to HEW]

hoe[2], *n.* a promontory, a protecting ridge. [OE *hoh,* a heel]

Hofei, *n.* former name of HEFEI.

Hoffman, *n.* **Dustin** (1937–), US actor, who won Academy Awards for his performances in *Kramer vs Kramer* (1979) and *Rain Man* (1988). His other films include *The Graduate* (1967) and *Midnight Cowboy* (1969).

Hoffmann[1], *n.* **E(rnst) T(heodor) A(madeus)** (1776–1822), German composer and writer. He composed the opera *Undine* (1816) and many fairy stories, including *Nüssknacker/Nutcracker* (1816). His stories inspired Offenbach's *Tales of Hoffmann.*

Hoffmann[2], *n.* **Josef** (1870–1956), Austrian architect, one of the founders of the Wiener Werkstätte, and a pupil of Otto Wagner.

Hofmann, *n.* **Hans** (1880–1966), German-born abstract expressionist painter, active in Paris and Munich from 1915 until 1932, when he moved to the US. He was influential among New York artists in the 1930s.

Hofstadter, *n.* **Robert** (1915–), US high energy physicist who revealed the structure of the atomic nucleus. He demonstrated that the nucleus is composed of a high energy core and a surrounding area of decreasing density. Nobel physics prize 1961.

hog, *n.* a swine, esp. a castrated boar meant for killing; (*N Am.*) any kind of pig; a young sheep or bullock, usu. of a year old; a dirty, filthy, gluttonous or low fellow; a scrub-broom for cleaning a ship's bottom under water; in curling, a stone that fails to pass the hog-score. *v.t.* (*past, p.p.* **hogged**) to cut short like the bristles of a hog; to cause (a ship, keel etc.) to rise in the middle and droop at the ends; to clean (a ship's bottom) under water by scraping; to keep greedily to oneself. *v.i.* to droop at both ends; to carry the head down and back up (of animals). **hog in armour,** (*facet.*) an awkward, ungainly person; the nine-banded armadillo, *Tatusia novemcincta.* **to go the whole hog,** to do a job completely; to make no compromise or reservations. **hogback, hog's back,** *n.* a long ridged hill; (*Geol.*) a monocline; an eskar. **hog-backed,** *a.* **hog cholera,** *n.* swine fever. **hog-fish,** *n.* a fish with dorsal spine or bristles on the head. **hog-frame,** *n.* a fore-and-aft frame forming a truss in the main frame of a vessel of light draught to prevent vertical flexure. **hogmane,** *n.* a horse's mane cut so as to stand erect. **hog-pen,** *n.* a pigsty. **hog-plum,** *n.* a name for several species of W Indian trees and their fruit, which is used for feeding hogs. **hog-reeve,** *n.* a district official who adjudicated on the damage done by stray hogs. **hog-ringer,** *n.* one who puts rings on hogs' snouts. **hog's back** HOGBACK. †**hog's-bean,** *n.* henbane. **hog-score,** *n.* in curling, a line drawn across the rink which a stone must pass in order to count. †**hog-shearing,** *n.* much ado about nothing. **hog-skin,** *n.* tanned pig's skin. **hog's-lard,** *n.* the rendered fat of the hog. **hog's pudding,** *n.* a pudding of various ingredients stuffed like a sausage into a hog's entrail. **hogtie,** *v.t.* to tie the feet of (an animal or person); to make helpless. **hog-wash,** *n.* the refuse of a kitchen or brewery, used for feeding hogs; (*sl., coll.*) bad liquor; (*coll.*) anything worthless. **hogweed,** *n.* a name applied to many coarse plants, esp. the cow-parsnip. **hoggish,** *a.* having the qualities or manners of a hog; brutish, gluttonous, filthy, selfish. **hoggishly,** *adv.* **hoggishness,** *n.* **hoglike,** *a.* [etym. doubtful]

Hogarth, *n.* **William** (1697–1764), British painter and engraver, who produced portraits and moralizing genre scenes, such as the series *A Rake's Progress* (1735).

Hogg[1], *n.* **James** (1770–1835), Scottish novelist and poet, known as the 'Ettrick Shepherd'. Born in Ettrick Forest, Selkirkshire, he worked as a shepherd at Yarrow (1790–99), and until the age of 30, he was illiterate. His novel *Confessions of a Justified Sinner* (1824) is a masterly portrayal of personified evil.

Hogg[2], **Quintin** HAILSHAM, LORD.

hogger, *n.* (*Sc.*) a stocking without a foot, worn by coal-miners as an anklet; a pipe connexion of india-rubber etc. **hogger-pipe,** *n.* the upper terminal pipe of a mining pump. **hogger-pump,** *n.* the top pump in the sinking pit of a mine. [etym. doubtful]

hoggerel, *n.* a sheep in its second year. **hogget,** *n.* a yearling sheep; a year-old colt.

hoggin, hoggins, *n.* screened gravel for footpaths. [etym. doubtful]

hogmanay, *n.* in Scotland, the last day of the year; an entertainment or a present given on that day. [acc. to OED from OF *aguillaneuf,* the last day of the year, from the shout with which new year's gifts were given and asked (cp. Norman *hoguinané*)]

hogshead, *n.* a measure of capacity containing 52½ imperial gal. (238.7 l); a large cask; a butt. [HOG, HEAD (etym. doubtful)]

Hohenlinden, Battle of, in the French Revolutionary Wars, a defeat of the Austrians by the French, 3 Dec. 1800, which, on top of the defeat at Marengo, led the Austrians to make peace at the Treaty of Lunéville 1801.

Hohenstaufen, *n.* German family of princes, several

members of which were Holy Roman emperors (1138–1208 and 1214–54). They were the first German emperors to make use of associations with Roman law and tradition to aggrandize their office. Among the most notable were Conrad III, Frederick I (Barbarossa), the first to use the title Holy Roman emperor, Henry VI and Frederick II. The last of the line, Conradin, was executed 1268 while attempting to gain his Sicilian inheritance.

Hohenzollern, *n.* German family, originating in Württemberg, the main branch of which held the titles of elector of Brandenburg from 1415, king of Prussia from 1701, and German emperor from 1871. The last emperor, Wilhelm II, was dethroned 1918. Another branch of the family were kings of Romania (1881–1947).

Hohhot, *n.* (formerly **Huhehot**) city and capital of Inner Mongolia (*Nei Mongol*) autonomous region, China; population (1984) 778,000. Industries include textiles, electronics, and dairy products. There are Lamaist monasteries and temples here.

ho hum, *int.* used to express a feeling of tedium, lack of interest, resignation etc.

hoick, *v.t.* (*coll.*) to pull up or out of; to force an aeroplane upwards; to pull.

hoiden, HOYDEN.

hoiho, *n.* a New Zealand species of penguin. [Maori]

hoi polloi, *n.* (*often derog.*) the common herd; the masses. [Gr., the many]

hoist, †**hoise**, *v.t.* to raise up; to lift by means of tackle; to run up (a sail or flag); to lift on to the back of another person for the purpose of flogging. *n.* the act of lifting or hoisting up; an apparatus for hoisting or raising; a lift or elevator; (*Naut.*) the vertical height of a yard, sail or flag. **hoist with his own petard** PETARD. [formerly *hysse*, perh. from MDut. *hyssen* (cp. Icel. *hisa*, Swed. and Norw. *hissa*, G *hissen*)]

hoity-toity, *int.* an exclamation of astonishment mixed with disapproval and contempt. *a.* flighty; petulant. *n.* a romp, a frolic; a rumpus. [prob. from obs. *hoit*, to romp]

hokey, *a.* (*N Am.*) sentimental, corny; false, phoney. [from HOKUM, -Y]

hokey-pokey, *n.* a cheap confection like stiff ice-cream sold by street vendors. [corr. of HOCUS POCUS]

Hokkaido, *n.* most northerly of the four main islands of Japan, separated from Honshu to the S by Tsugaru Strait and from Sakhalin to the N by Soya Strait; area 83,500 sq km/32,231 sq miles, population (1986) 5,678,000 including 16,000 Ainus. The capital is Sapporo. Natural resources include coal, mercury, manganese, oil and natural gas, timber, and fisheries. Coal mining and agriculture are the main industries.

hokum, *n.* (*esp. N Am., coll.*) bunkum; a foolish stage or book plot; counterfeit culture. [*ho*cus-pocus, bun*kum*]

Hokusai, *n.* **Katsushika** (1760–1849), Japanese artist, the leading printmaker of his time. He is known for *Fugaku Sanjū-rokkei/36 Views of Mount Fuji* (about 1823–29), but he produced outstanding pictures of almost every kind of subject – birds, flowers, courtesans, scenes from legend and everyday life, and so on.

hol- HOL(O)-.

holarctic, *a.* of or pertaining to the entire northern region of the globe. [HOL-, ARCTIC]

Holbein[1]**,** *n.* **Hans, the Elder** (*c.* 1464–1524), German painter, active in Augsburg. His works include altarpieces, such as that of *St Sebastian*, 1516 (Alte Pinakothek, Munich). He also painted portraits and designed stained glass.

Holbein[2]**,** *n.* **Hans, the Younger** (1497/98–1543), German painter and woodcut artist; the son and pupil of Hans Holbein the Elder. He travelled widely in Europe, and was active in England 1527–28 and 1532–43; he was court painter to Henry VIII from 1536. He painted outstanding portraits of Erasmus, Thomas More, and Thomas Cromwell; a notable woodcut series is *Dance of Death* (*c.* 1525).

hold[1]**,** *v.t.* (*past, p.p.* **held** held, †*p.p.* **holden**) to grasp and retain; to keep in, to confine; to enclose, to contain; to be able to contain, to keep from running or flowing out; to keep back, to restrain; to keep in a certain manner or position; to retain possession or control of; to occupy, to possess; to regard, to believe; to maintain (that); to judge, to assert (that); to carry on; to celebrate; to use, to employ (as language); (*coll.*) to lay, to wager, to accept as a bet or wager; (*Comput.*) retain (data) in a storage device after copying it into another storage device. *v.i.* to maintain a grasp or attachment; to continue firm, not to break; to adhere (to); to maintain a course; to be valid or true, to stand; to be fit or consistent; (*usu. in imper.*) to stop, to stay, to refrain. **hold hard!** (*coll.*) stop. **hold it!** stop! **to hold a wager,** to bet. **to hold back,** to restrain; to retain in one's possession; to keep oneself in check. **to hold by,** to hold to, to adhere to. **to hold forth,** to stretch or put forward; to propose, to offer; to speak in public; to harangue, to dilate. **to hold good, true,** to remain valid; to apply; to be relevant. **to hold in,** to restrain, to restrain oneself; to keep quiet, to keep silent. **to hold in esteem** etc., to regard with esteem etc. **to hold of, from,** or **under,** to derive title from. **to hold off,** to keep at a distance; to remain at a distance; to delay. **to hold on,** to continue or proceed without interruption; (*coll.*) to stop; to wait. **to hold on one's way,** to keep going steadily. **to hold one's head (high),** to conduct oneself proudly or arrogantly. **to hold one's own,** to maintain one's position. **to hold one's tongue,** to be silent. **to hold out,** to hold forward, to offer; to bear, to endure; to persist, not to yield. **to hold out on,** (*coll.*) not to tell someone about something. **to hold over,** to keep back or reserve, to defer; (*Law*) to keep possession of after the expiration of one's term. **to hold to,** to bind by (bail, one's statement etc.); to adhere to. **to hold together,** to keep in union, cause to cohere; to continue united; to cohere. **to hold up,** to raise or lift up; to support, to encourage; to sustain; to show forth, to exhibit (to ridicule etc.); to stop on the highway and rob; to keep from falling; of the weather, to keep fine; to continue the same speed. **to hold water** WATER. **to hold with,** to approve of, to side with. **hold-all,** *n.* a hand-bag or case for carrying clothes etc. **hold-back,** *n.* a restraint, a check, a hindrance. **holdfast,** *n.* a means by which something is clamped to another; a support. **hold-up,** *n.* a delay; a robbery, esp. armed. **holder,** *n.* one who or that which holds; a tenant, occupier or owner; a contrivance by or in which anything is kept or held; the payee of a bill of exchange or promissory note. [OE *healdan*]

hold[2]**,** *n.* the act of seizing or grasping in the hands; a grasp, a clutch; mental grasp; a support, anything to hold by or support oneself by; moral influence; custody, possession; a refuge, a fortified place. **no holds barred,** observing no rules. **on hold,** of a telephone call(er), waiting to be connected; deferred until later. **to get hold of,** to grasp; to get in contact with. [from prec.]

hold[3]**,** *n.* the interior cavity of a ship, in which the cargo is stowed. [HOLE[1]]

Holden, *n.* **William** (1918–81), stage name of William Franklin Beedle, US film actor, a star in the late 1940s and 1950s. One of his best roles was as the leader of *The Wild Bunch* (1969), and he also played leading roles in *Sunset Boulevard* (1950), *Stalag 17* (1953), and *Network* (1976).

holding, *n.* a hold, a grasp; tenure or occupation; that which is held, esp. land, property, stocks or shares; †the burden of a song. **holding company,** *n.* a company formed to acquire the majority of shares in one or more subsidiary companies. **holding pattern,** *n.* the course an aircraft takes while waiting to land.

hole[1]**,** *n.* a hollow place or cavity; (*Austral.*) a pool; an aperture, an orifice, a perforation; a wild animal's burrow; a mean habitation; a small pit or hollow into which the ball has to be driven in various games; in golf, one of the points made by the player who drives his ball from one hole to another with the fewest strokes, the distance between two consecutive holes; a dingy, disreputable place; a difficulty, a fix. *v.t.* to form a hole or holes in; to tunnel; to put or drive into a hole; to undercut a coal-seam. *v.i.* to go into a hole; to hibernate; in golf, to drive one's ball into a hole. **to hole out,** in golf, to play the ball into the hole. **to hole up,** to go into hiding. **to make a hole in,** to take or consume a large part of. **to pick holes in,** to find fault with. **hole-and-corner,** *a.* secret, clandestine. **hole-in-the-wall,** *a.* hard to find, out of the way. **holing-axe,** *n.* a tool for cutting holes in posts. **holing-pick,** *n.* a pick for undercutting coal. **holey,** *a.* [OE *hol* (cp. Dut. and Icel. *hol*)]

†**hole**[2]**,** WHOLE.

holibut, HALIBUT.

holiday, *n.* a day of exemption from work; a day of amusement or pleasure; any period devoted to this; a vacation. *a.* pertaining to or befitting a holiday. **holiday camp,** *n.* an enclosed area with accommodation, entertainment facilities etc. for holidaymakers. **holidaymaker,** *n.* a person taking a holiday away from home. [OE *hæligdæg,* holy day]

Holiday, *n.* **Billie** (1915–59), stage name of Eleanor Gough McKay, US jazz singer, also known as 'Lady Day'. She made her debut in Harlem clubs and became known for her emotionally charged delivery and idiosyncratic phrasing; she brought a blues feel to performances with swing bands. Songs she made her own include 'Strange Fruit' and 'I Cover the Waterfront'.

holier-than-thou HOLY.

holily etc. HOLY.

holiness HOLY.

Holinshed, *n.* **Ralph** (*c.* 1520– *c.* 1580), English historian. He was probably born in Cheshire, went to London as assistant to a printer, and in 1578 published two volumes of the *Chronicles of England, Scotland and Ireland*, which were largely used by Shakespeare for his history plays.

holism, *n.* (*Phil.*) the tendency in nature to evolve wholes that are more than the sum of the parts; a form of medical treatment concerned with the whole person rather than with one part of the body. [HOLO-, -ISM]

holk, HOWK.

Holkeri, *n.* **Harri** (1937–), Finnish politician, prime minister from 1987. Joining the centrist National Coalition Party (KOK) at an early age, he eventually became its national secretary.

holla, HALLO.

holland, *n.* coarse unbleached linen with a glazed surface, first made in Holland. **Hollander,** *n.* a native of Holland; a Dutch ship. **Hollandish,** *a.* **hollands,** *n.* a kind of gin made in Holland.

Holland[1]**,** *n.* **Henry Richard Vassall Fox, 3rd Baron** (1773–1840), British Whig politician. He was Lord Privy Seal (1806–07). His home at Holland House, London, was for many years the centre of Whig political and literary society.

Holland[2]**,** *n.* **John Philip** (1840–1914), Irish engineer who developed some of the first submarines. He began work in Ireland in the late 1860s and emigrated to the US 1873. His first successful boat was launched 1881 and, after several failures, he built the *Holland* (1893), which was bought by the US Navy two years later. He continued to build submarines for various navies but died in poverty after his company failed because of financial difficulties.

Holland[3]**,** *n.* **Sidney George** (1893–1961), New Zealand politician, leader of the National Party (1940–57) and prime minister (1949–57).

hollandaise, *a.* of sauce, made with butter, egg-yolk and lemon-juice or vinegar. [F]

holler, (*N Am.*) HALLO.

Hollerith, *n.* **Herman** (1860–1929), US inventor of a mechanical tabulating machine, the first device for data processing. Hollerith's tabulator was widely publicized after being successfully used in the 1890 census. The firm he established, the Tabulating Machine Company, was later one of the founding companies of International Business Machines (IBM).

hollo, holloa, hollow[1] HALLO.

hollow[2]**,** *a.* containing a cavity or empty space; not solid; excavated, sunken, concave; empty, vacant; deep, low (of sounds); insincere, not genuine. *n.* a depression or unoccupied space; a cavity, a hole, a basin; a valley. *v.t.* to make hollow, to excavate. **to beat etc. someone hollow,** (*coll.*) to beat etc. someone completely. **hollow-eyed,** *a.* having sunken eyes. **hollow-hearted,** *a.* insincere, false. **hollow square,** *n.* a body of troops drawn up in the form of a square with a vacant space in the middle. **hollow-ware,** *n.* castiron culinary vessels, such as pots, kettles etc. **hollowly,** *adv.* **hollowness,** *n.* [ME *holwe,* OE *holge,* dat. of *holh,* prob. a form of *hol,* HOLE[1]]

holly, *n.* a shrub or tree of the genus *Ilex,* esp. *I. aquifolium,* a tree with glossy, prickly leaves and scarlet or, more rarely, yellow berries. **holly oak** HOLM[2]. [OE *holen*]

Holly, *n.* **Buddy** (1936–1959), stage name of Charles Hardin Holley, US rock-and-roll singer, guitarist, and songwriter, born in Lubbock, Texas. He had a distinctive, hiccuping vocal style and was an early experimenter with recording techniques. Many of his hits with his band, the Crickets, such as 'That'll Be the Day' (1957), 'Peggy Sue' (1957), and 'Maybe Baby' (1958), have become classics. He was killed in a plane crash.

hollyhock, *n.* a tall garden plant, *Althaea rosea,*with red, pink and yellow flowers. [ME *holihoc* (*holi,* HOLY, *hoc,* mallow)]

Hollywood, *n.* suburb of Los Angeles, California, US, the centre of the US film industry from 1911.

holm[1]**,** *n.* flat ground, liable to flooding, along the side of a river; an island in a river or estuary. [Icel. *hōlmr,* perh. cogn. with OE *holm,* sea, and L *culmen,* mountain-top]

holm[2]**,** *n.* the ilex or evergreen oak, *Quercus ilex,* often called **holm-oak**. [corr. of OE *holen,* HOLLY]

Holmes, Sherlock, *n.* fictitious private detective, created by the English writer Arthur Conan Doyle in *A Study in Scarlet* (1887) and recurring in novels and stories until 1914. His ability to make inferences from slight clues always astonishes the narrator, Dr Watson.

holmium, *n.* a metallic element of the rare-earth group, at. no. 67; chem. symbol Ho. [L *Holmia,* Stockholm]

hol(o)- *comb. form.* entire, complete; completely. [Gr. *holos,* whole]

holoblastic, *a.* having the whole mass directly formative (of an ovum), undergoing segmentation throughout. [Gr. *blastos,* germ]

holobranchiate, *a.* (*Zool.*) having complete gills.

holocaust, *n.* a sacrifice entirely consumed by fire; a wholesale sacrifice of life, or general destruction, esp. by fire; the wholesale slaughter of Jews in Europe by the Nazis in the 1940s. [F *holocauste,* L *holocaustum,* Gr. *holokauston* (HOL(O)-, *kaiëin* fut. *kausō,* to burn)]

Holocene, *n.* the most recent period of geological time, that began 10,000 years ago, the second epoch of the Quaternary period when glaciers retreated, and the climate became warmer and humans developed significantly. *a.* of or concerning this period. [HOLO-, Gr. *kainos,* new]

holocryptic, *a.* wholly secret, unintelligible, or undecipherable. [CRYPTIC]

hologram, *n.* (a photographic reproduction of) a pattern produced by the interference between a beam of coherent light (e.g. from a laser) and a direct beam of such light reflected off an object; a three-dimensional image produced by illuminating this reproduction.

holograph, *a.* wholly in the handwriting of the author or signatory. *n.* a document, letter etc. so written. **holographic,** *a.* **holography,** *n.* the technique of making or using a hologram. [late L *holographus,* Gr. *-phos* (*graphein,* to write)]

holohedral, *a.* of crystals, having the full possible number of planes symmetrically arranged. **holohedrism,** *n.* **holohedron,** *n.* [Gr. *hedra,* seat, base]

holometabola, *n.pl.* a division containing those insects which undergo complete metamorphosis. **holometabolic, holometabolous,** *a.* **holometabolism,** *n.* [Gr. *metabolos,* undergoing change]

holometer, *n.* an instrument for taking all kinds of measurements.

holomorphic, *a.* (*Math.*) having the properties of an entire function, being finite, continuous and one-valued for all finite values of the variable; of crystals, holohedral or holosymmetrical. [Gr. *morphē,* shape]

Holophane®, *n.* a globe or shade for a lamp made of clear glass with prismatic corrugations for refracting, reflecting, illuminating or diffusing the light. [Gr. *phainein,* to shine]

holophotal, *a.* utilizing the whole of the available light, applied to the illuminating apparatus in lighthouses. **holophotally,** *adv.* **holophote,** *n.* an apparatus of this kind. **holophotometer,** *n.* [Gr. *phōs phōtos,* light]

holophrasis, *n.* the expression of a whole sentence in a single word. **holophrase, holophrasm,** *n.* **holophrastic,** *a.* [Gr. *phrasis,* see PHRASE]

holophyte, *n.* a plant that obtains food like a green plant, esp. by photosynthesis. **holophytic,** *a.*

holorhinal, *a.* having the nasal bones almost or entirely uncleft. [Gr. *rhis rhinos,* the nose]

holosymmetrical, *a.* of crystals, wholly symmetrical, holohedral.

holothurian, *a.* belonging to the Holothuroidea, a class of echinoderms comprising the sea-slugs. *n.* an animal of this class. [mod. L *holothūria,* Gr. *holothouria,* pl. of *-rion,* zoophytes]

holotype, *n.* the original specimen from which a new species is derived.

†holp, †holpen HELP.

hols, *n.pl.* (*coll.*) school holidays.

Holst, *n.* **Gustav(us Theodore von)** (1874–1934), English composer. He wrote operas, including *Savitri* (1916) and *At the Boar's Head* (1925), ballets, choral works, including *Hymns from the Rig Veda* (1911) and *The Hymn of Jesus* (1920), orchestral suites, including *The Planets* (1918), and songs. He was a lifelong friend of Ralph Vaughan Williams, with whom he shared an enthusiasm for English folk music. His musical style, although tonal and drawing on folk song, tends to be severe.

Holstein, *n.* **Friedrich von** (1839–1909), German diplomat and foreign-affairs expert. He refused the post of foreign minister, but played a key role in German diplomacy from the 1880s until his death.

holster, *n.* a leather case, usu. attached to the saddle-bow, to hold a pistol. **holstered,** *a.* [Dut. (cp. Icel. *hulstr,* case, OE *heolstor,* a hiding-place, a covering)]

holt¹, *n.* a wood, a grove, a copse; a plantation. [OE (cp. Dut. *hout,* timbers, Icel. *holt,* a copse, G *Holz*)]

holt², *n.* a burrow, a hole; a covert, a shelter; †a hold, grasp. [prov. corr. of HOLD¹]

Holt, *n.* **Harold Edward** (1908–67), Australian Liberal politician, prime minister 1966–67.

Holtby, *n.* **Winifred** (1898–1935), English novelist, poet, and journalist. She was an ardent advocate of women's freedom and racial equality, and wrote the novel *South Riding* (1936), set in her native Yorkshire. Her other works include an analysis of women's position in contemporary society *Women and a Changing Civilization* (1934).

holus-bolus, *adv.* all at once, at one gulp. [mock L, from WHOLE (cp. HOCUS POCUS)]

holy, *a.* sacred; set apart for the service of God or other sacred use; morally pure; free from sin or sinful affections; of high spiritual excellence. **Holy Cross Day,** *n.* the festival of the Exaltation of the Cross, 14 Sept. **Holy of holies,** the innermost and most sacred apartment of the Jewish Tabernacle and the Temple, where the ark was kept; the inmost shrine. **Holy Roman Empire,** name applied to the empire of Charlemagne and his successors, and to the German empire (962–1806), both being regarded as a revival of the Roman Empire. At its height it comprised much of western and central Europe. **Holy Alliance,** *n.* a 'Christian Union of Charity, Peace, and Love' initiated by Alexander I of Russia 1815 and signed by every crowned head in Europe. The alliance became associated with Russian attempts to preserve autocratic monarchies at any price, and an excuse to meddle in the internal affairs of other states. **Holy City,** *n.* Jerusalem. **holy cross,** *n.* the cross on which Christ was put to death. **†holy-cruel,** *a.* cruel through being too rigidly virtuous. **holy day,** *n.* a day commemorating some religious event; †a holiday. **Holy Family,** *n.* the infant Jesus with Joseph and Mary. **Holy Ghost, Holy Spirit,** *n.* the third Person of the Trinity. **Holy Grail** GRAIL. **holy Joe,** *n.* (*coll., derog.*) a priest; a pious or sanctimonious person. **Holy Land,** *n.* Palestine. **holy office,** *n.* the Inquisition. **holy orders** ORDERS. **Holy Roller,** (*coll., derog.*) *n.* a member of an excessively zealous religious sect. **holy rood,** *n.* a cross or crucifix, esp. one on the rood-beam in churches. **Holy Saturday,** *n.* the Saturday before Easter. **Holy See,** *n.* the bishopric of Rome, the Pope's see. **Holy Shroud,** TURIN SHROUD. **Holy Thursday,** *n.* in the English Church, Ascension Day; in the Roman Catholic Church, Maundy Thursday, the Thursday in Holy Week. **holy war,** *n.* a war waged on behalf of a religion. **holy water,** *n.* water blessed by a priest, used in the Roman and Greek ritual. **Holy Week,** *n.* in the Christian church, the last week of Lent, when Christians commemorate the events that led up to the crucifixion of Jesus, the week from Palm Sunday to Holy Saturday inclusive. **holy well,** *n.* a well reputed to be invested with miraculous qualities. **Holy Willie,** *n.* a hypocritically pious person. **holy writ,** *n.* sacred scriptures, esp. the Bible. **holier,** *comp. a.* more holy. **holier-than-thou,** *a.* convinced of one's moral superiority, sanctimonious. **holily,** *adv.* **holiness,** *n.* the state of being holy, sanctity; moral purity or integrity; the state of being consecrated to God or His worship; that which is so consecrated. **his Holiness,** a title of the Pope, †given formerly to the Greek emperors and other sacred and ecclesiastical dignitaries. [OE *hālig* (cp. Dut. and G *heilig,* Icel. *heilagr*)]

Holy Loch, *n.* a US nuclear-submarine base on the river Clyde in Scotland.

Holyoake, *n.* **Keith Jacka** (1904–83), New Zealand National Party politician, prime minister 1957 (for two months) and 1960–72.

Holyrood House, *n.* royal residence in Edinburgh, Scotland. The palace was built 1498–1503 on the site of a 12th-century abbey by James IV. It has associations with Mary Queen of Scots and Charles Edward, the Young Pretender.

holystone, *n.* a soft sandstone used for scrubbing the decks of vessels. *v.t.* to scrub with this.

hom- HOM(O)-.

homage, *n.* the service paid and fealty professed to a sovereign or superior lord; respect paid by external action; deference, obeisance, reverence, worship. *v.t.* to pay homage or respect to. **homager,** *n.* one who does homage; one who holds a fee by homage. [OF, from late L *homāticum, homināticum,* from *homo hominis,* man]

hombre, *n.* (*N Am., coll.*) man.

Homburg, *n.* a trilby hat. [German city]

home¹, *n.* one's own house or abode; the abode of the family to which one belongs; one's own country; the place of constant residence, of commonest occurrence, or where anything is indigenous; a place or state of rest or comfort; a charitable institution of rest or refuge for orphans, the destitute or the afflicted; in various games, the goal or den. *a.* connected with, carried on or produced at home or in one's native country; domestic, opposed to foreign; personal, touching the heart or conscience; a football match won by a home team. *adv.* to one's home or country; to the point, pointedly, closely, intimately. **at home,** in one's own house; accessible to visitors; in one's own area, country etc.; at one's ease, comfortable; conversant with. **at-home,** *n.* a gathering or party held in one's own home.

home and dry, safe after having successfully come through an experience. **last** or **long home,** the grave. **nothing, not much etc. to write home about,** (*coll.*) not very impressive, great etc. **to bring home to one,** to convince. **to come home to one,** to reach one's heart or conscience. **home base, plate,** *n.* the rubber plate on which the batter stands in baseball. **home-born,** *a.* native, domestic, natural. **home-bound,** *a.* weather bound; kept at home. **home-bred,** *a.* bred at home, not foreign; natural, native; not polished by travel. **home-brew,** *n.* a beverage brewed at home. **home-brewed,** *a.* brewed at home or for consumption at home. *n.* home-brewed ale. **home circuit,** *n.* (*Law*) the circuit comprising the Home Counties. **home-comer,** *n.* **home-coming,** *n., a.* a return to, or arrival at home. **Home Counties,** *n.pl.* the counties in close proximity to London, England: Hertfordshire, Essex, Kent, Surrey, and formerly Middlesex. **home economics,** *n.* the study of how to run a home, including cookery, child-care etc. **home farm,** *n.* a farm attached to and run by the owner of a large country estate. **home-felt,** *a.* felt in one's heart, inward, private. **home ground,** *n.* a familiar topic or subject. **home-grown,** *a.* grown in one's own garden, area, country etc. **Home Guard,** *n.* unpaid force formed in Britain in May 1940, to repel the expected German invasion, and known until July 1940 as the Local Defence Volunteers. It consisted of men aged 17–65 who had not been called up, formed part of the armed forces of the crown, and was subject to military law. Over 2 million strong in 1944, it was disbanded 31 Dec. 1945, but revived 1951, then placed on a reserve basis 1955, and ceased activities 1957. **home-keeping,** *a.* staying at home, untravelled. **homeland,** *n.* one's native land; in S Africa, a semi-autonomous state reserved for Black Africans. **home-lot,** *n.* (*N Am.*) a piece of land allotted for a residence as distinguished from the rest of a farm. **home-made,** *a.* made at home; not manufactured abroad. **homemaker,** *n.* (*esp. N Am.*) a housewife. **Home Office,** *n.* the department of the Secretary of State for Home Affairs, dealing with police administration, prisons, factories, licensing etc.; the building occupied by this. **Home Rule,** *n.* the slogan of the Irish nationalist movement (1870–1914); it stood for the repeal of the Act of Union of 1801 and the establishment of an Irish parliament within the framework of the British Empire. The slogan was popularized after 1870 by Isaac Butt (1813–79) and Parnell, his successor in the nationalist leadership. Gladstone's Home Rule bills (1886 and 1893) were both defeated; Asquith's Home Rule bill became law in 1914, but was suspended during World War I. After 1918 the demand for an independent Irish republic replaced that for home rule. **home run,** *n.* a hit in baseball that allows the batter to make a complete circuit and score a run. **home-sick,** *a.* **home-sickness,** *n.* a vehement desire to return home, causing depression of spirits and affecting physical health. **home signal,** *n.* (*Railway*) a signal that must on no account be passed if it is against a train, distinguished from distance signal. **home-sitter** HOUSE-SITTER. **home-speaking,** *n.* plain direct speech that goes to the heart or conscience. **home-spun,** *a.* spun or wrought at home; home-made; plain, unaffected, rude. *n.* cloth spun at home. **homestall,** *n.* a homestead; a farmyard. **homestead**, *n.* a house, esp. a farmhouse, with the buildings attached; (*N Am.*) a lot granted for the residence and maintenance of a family, under the Homestead Act, 1862; (*Austral.*) the owner's house on a sheep station. *v.t.* to occupy as a homestead. **homesteader,** *n.* **homesteading,** *n.* **home straight, stretch,** *n.* the last section of a race-course before the winning-post is reached; the last phase of any enterprise. **home truth,** *n.* an unwelcome truth expressed in a pointed way. **home unit,** *n.* (*Austral.*) one of a number of separate apartments in the same building each under individual ownership. **homework,** *n.* study exercises to be done at home. **to do one's homework,** to prepare well. **homeless,** *a.* **homely,** *a.* plain, without affectation, unpretending; unadorned, unvarnished; (*N Am.*) plain in looks. †*adv.* plainly, simply. **homeliness,** *n.* **homeward,** *adv.* towards home. *a.* being or going in the direction of home. **homeward-bound,** *a.* returning home from abroad. **homewards,** *adv.* **homish, homy,** *a.* [OE *hām* (cp. Dut. *heem,* Icel. *heimr,* G *Heim*)]

home², *v.i.* of pigeons, to fly home; to go home; to dwell; to long for home. *v.t.* to send (pigeons) home; to provide with a home; to direct onto a target, e.g. with a navigational device. **homer¹**, *n.* a homing pigeon. **homing device,** *n.* (*Mil.*) the mechanism for the automatic guiding of missiles. [from prec.]

Home, *n.* **Alec Douglas-Home, Baron Home of the Hirsel** (1903–), British Conservative politician. He was foreign secretary (1960–63), and succeeded Macmillan as prime minister 1963. He renounced his peerage (as 14th Earl of Home) to fight (and lose) the general election 1964, and resigned as party leader 1965. He was again foreign secretary 1970–74, when he received a life peerage. His brother is the playwright William Douglas-Home.

homelyn, *n.* the spotted ray, *Raia maculata,* a European sea-fish used for food. [etym. unknown]

homeo-, *comb. form.* similar. [Gr. *homoios,* of the same kind, similar]

homeomorphous, *a.* similar in form and structure (esp. of crystals differing in chemical composition). **homeomorphism,** *n.* [Gr. *morphē,* shape]

homeopathy, *n.* the system which aims at curing diseases by administering in small doses medicines which would produce in healthy persons symptoms similar to those they are designed to remove. **homeopath**, *n.* a homeopathist. **homeopathic**, *a.* belonging to homeopathy; (*fig.*) infinitesimally small, like a dose given in homeopathy. **homeopathically,** *adv.* **homeopathist,** *n.* one who practises or believes in homeopathy. [Gr. *homoiopatheia*]

homeoplastic, *a.* of tumours etc., similar in structure to the surrounding tissue.

homeostasis, *n.* the keeping of an even level. **homeostatic**, *a.* [Gr. *stasis,* standing still]

homeozoic, *a.* containing similar forms of life (of regions of the earth). [Gr. *zōē,* life]

homer¹ HOME².

homer², *n.* a Hebrew liquid measure of 75⅝ gal (343.8 l); a dry measure of 11²/₉ bush. (4 hl). [Heb. *khōmer*]

Homer¹, *n.* legendary Greek epic poet of the 8th cent. BC; according to tradition a blind minstrel and the author of the *Iliad* and the *Odyssey*. **Homeric**, *a.* pertaining to Homer or his poems; resembling Homer's poems in style. **Homeridae**, *n.pl.* the literary successors or reputed descendants of Homer; the rhapsodists who recited his poems, supposed by some critics to have been joint-authors of the Homeric poems. **Homerist**, *n.* **Homerology**, *n.* **Homerologist,** *n.* [L *Homēricus,* Gr. *Homērikos,* from *Homeros,* Homer]

Homer², *n.* **Winslow** (1836–1910), US painter and lithographer, known for his seascapes, both oils and watercolours, which date from the 1880s and 1890s.

homestall, homestead HOME¹.

Homestead Act, the, in US history, an act of Congress 1862 to encourage the settlement of land in the west by offering 65-hectare/160-acre plots cheaply or even free to those willing to cultivate and improve the land. By 1900 about 32,400,000 hectares/80,000,000 acres had been disposed of.

homicide, *n.* the act of killing a human being; one who kills another, a man-slayer. **homicidal**, *a.* [F, from L *homicīdium,* manslaughter, *homīcida,* man-slayer (HOMO, man)]

homiletic, *a.* pertaining to homilies. *n.pl.* the art of preaching; sacred eloquence; the art or method of presenting spiritual truths to an audience in the most effective form **homilist**, *n.* [Gr. *homīlētikos,* from *homīleein,* to hold converse with, from *homīlos,* assembly (*homos,* like, *eilein,* to crowd together)]

homily, *n.* a religious discourse; a sermon, esp. on some practical subject; a tedious moral exhortation. **Books of Homilies,** two books published in England by authority in 1547 and 1562, to be read in churches when no sermon was prepared. [OF *omelie* (F *homélie*), L *homīlia,* as prec.]

hominid, *n.* a creature of the genus *Homo;* a man-like fossil. [HOMO]

hominy, *n.* maize hulled and coarsely ground, boiled with water or milk for food. [N Am. Ind.]

homish HOME[1].

hommack, HUMMOCK.

Homo, *n.* (*pl.* **homines**) man, the genus of which man is the only living species. **Homo sapiens,** *n.* man as a species. [L]

homo, *n.* (*coll. derog.*; *often offensive*) short for HOMOSEXUAL.

hom(o)-, *comb. form.* noting likeness or sameness. [Gr. *homos,* same]

homobaric, *a.* of uniform weight. [BARIC[1]]

homoblastic, *a.* derived from the same kind of cells. **homoblasty,** *n.* [Gr. *blastos,* a germ]

homocentric, *a.* concentric.

homocercal, *a.* equally lobed, as the tail of the whiting; having an equally-lobed tail. [Gr. *kerkos,* a tail]

homochromy, *n.* the resemblance of an animal's colour to the colour of its surroundings.

homocyclic, *a.* of an organic compound, having a closed chain of atoms of the same kind.

homodermic, *a.* derived from the same primary blastoderm or germ-layer. **homodermatous, homodermous,** *a.* (*Zool.*) having the skin or integument structurally uniform.

homodont, *a.* having the teeth all alike or nearly alike, opp. to heterodont.

homodromous, homodromal, *a.* turning in the same direction, as leaf spirals; having the power and the weight moving in the same direction on the same side of the fulcrum. **homodromy,** *n.* [Gr. *dromos,* running]

homoeo- HOMEO-.

homoerotic, *a.* of or concerning sexual attraction to the same sex. **homoeroticism,** *n.*

homogamous, *a.* having all the florets of a capitulum hermaphrodite; having the stamens and pistils ripe at the same time. [Gr. *gamos,* marriage]

homogeneous, homogeneal, *a.* composed of the same or similar parts or elements; of the same kind or nature throughout; (*Math.*) having all its terms of the same degree; commensurable. **homogeneously,** *adv.* **homogeneousness, homogeneity,** *n.* [Gr. *homogenēs* (*genos,* kind)]

homogenesis, *n.* reproduction characterized by the likeness of the offspring to the parent and correspondence in the course of its development.

homogenetic, *a.* pertaining to or characterized by homogenesis; corresponding in structure so as to show community of descent; (*Geol.*) similar in structural relations prob. owing to community of origin. **homogenetical, homogenous,** *a.* **homogenist,** *n.* one who believes in community of origin. **homogenize, -ise,** *v.t.* **homogeny,** *n.*

homograft, *n.* a tissue graft from one organism to a member of the same species.

homograph, *n.* a word which has the same form as another, but a different origin and meaning; a method of telegraphic signalling.

homoio- HOMEO-.

homoiousian, *a.* having a similar nature or substance. *n.* one who asserted that the Son of God is of a substance similar to but not the same as that of the Father. [Gr. *homoiousios* (HOMEO-, *ousia,* essence); cp. HOMOOUSIAN]

homologate, *v.t.* to admit, to concede; to approve, to confirm. **homologation,** *n.* [late L *homologātus,* p.p. of *homologāre,* Gr. *homologein*]

homologous, *a.* having the same relative position, proportion, value, structure etc **homological,** *a.* characterized by homology; homologous. **homologically,** *adv.* **homologize, -ise,** *v.i.* to be homologous. *v.t.* to make homologous. **homologue,** *n.* something that is homologous; the same organ in different animals under every variety of form and function. **homology,** *n.* correspondence; identity of relation between parts developed from the same embryonic structures, as the arm of a man, the foreleg of a quadruped, and the wing of a bird [Gr. *homologos* (HOM(O)-, *logos,* ratio)]

homologumena, *n.pl.* those books of the New Testament the canonicity of which was accepted at once [Gr. *homologoumena,* neut. pl. p.p. of *homologein,* see HOMOLOGATE]

homomorphic, homomorphous, *a.* analogous, identical or closely similar in form. **homomorphism,** *n.* [Gr. *morphē,* shape]

homonomous, *a.* subject to the same law of growth. **homonomy,** *n.* [Gr. *homonomos* (*nomos,* law)]

homonym, *n.* a word having the same sound and perhaps the same spelling as another, but differing in meaning. **homonymic, homonymous,** *a.* **homonymously,** *adv.* **homonymy,** *n.* the state of being homonymous; a sameness of name with difference of meaning; ambiguity. [late L *homōnymum,* Gr. *homōnumon* (HOMO-, *onuma,* name)]

homoousian, *a.* consubstantial, of the same substance or essence, opposed to homoiousian. *n.* one who held the second Person of the Trinity to be of the same substance as the Father. [Gr. *homoousios* (*ousia,* essence)]

homophone, *n.* a letter or word agreeing in sound with another, but having a different meaning, as *heir* and *air.* **homophonic,** *a.* (*Mus.*) having the same pitch; in unison, opp. to polyphonic. **homophonous,** *a.* having the same sound; homophonic. **homophony,** *n.* identity of sound; (*Mus.*) unison. [Gr. *homophōnos*)]

homoplastic, *a.* similar in structure though not homogenetic. **homoplasmy, homoplasy,** *n.*

Homoptera, *n.pl.* a suborder of Hemiptera having the wings uniform throughout. **homopterous,** *a.* [Gr. *pteron,* wing]

homosexual, *n., a.* (a person) sexually attracted by those of the same sex. **homosexuality,** *n.*

homotaxis, *n.* (*Geol.*) arrangement of strata in different localities in the same relative position in the geological series. **homotaxial, -eous, -ic,** *a.* **homotaxially,** *adv.* [Gr. *taxis*]

homotonous, *a.* of the same tenor or tone; equable. **homotonously,** *adv.* **homotony,** *n.*

homotopy, *n.* repetition of the ontogenetic changes in an organism in a sequence corresponding to that in which they occurred in the parent. **homotopic,** *a.* [Gr. *topos,* place]

homotropal, -ropous, *a.* turning in the same direction; of seeds, having the radicle turned towards the hilum. [Gr. *-tropos,* turning]

homotype, *n.* a part or organ having the same structure or relative position to that of another. **homotypal, homotypic, -ical,** *a.* **homotypy,** *n.*

Homs, Hums, *n.* city, capital of Homs district, W Syria, near the Orontes River; population (1981) 355,000. Silk, cereals and fruit are produced in the area, and industries include silk textiles, oil refining, and jewellery. Zenobia, Queen of Palmyra, was defeated at Homs by the Roman emperor Aurelian, 272.

homunculus, homuncle, *n.* a little man; a dwarf; a manikin. **homuncular,** *a.* [L *homunculus,* dim. of HOMO]

homy HOME[1].

Hon., (*abbr.*) Honourable.

hon., (*abbr.*) honourable; honorary.

Honan, *n.* former name of HENAN.

honcho, *n.* (*pl.* **-chos**) a boss, chief; a controller. [Jap.]

Honda, *n.* Japanese motorcycle and car manufacturer. They also make racing cars. Their racing motorcycles were first seen in Europe at the 1959 Isle of Man TT races. Mike Hailwood and Tom Phillis were their first world champions 1961. They pulled out of motorbike racing 1967 but returned 1979 to become one of the top teams.

Honduras, *n.* Republic of (*República de Honduras*),

area 112,100 sq km/43,282 sq miles. **capital** Tegucigalpa. **towns** San Pedro Sula; ports Henecan (on Pacific), La Ceiba. **physical** mountainous; 45% forest. **population** (1985) 4,370,000 (90% mestizo, 10% Indians and Europeans); annual growth rate 3.4%. **exports** coffee, bananas, timber (including mahogany, rosewood). **language** Spanish. **religion** Roman Catholic.

hone[1], *n.* a stone for giving an edge to a cutting tool. *v.t.* to sharpen on a hone. [OE *hān* (cp. Icel. *hein*)]

†**hone**[2], *v.i.* to moan, to whine; to pine. [perh. from OF *hogner,* from *hon,* a cry, a complaint]

Honecker, *n.* **Erich** (1912–), East German communist politician, in power 1973–89, elected chair of the council of state (head of state) 1976. He governed in an outwardly austere and efficient manner and, while favouring East-West detente, was a loyal ally of the USSR. In Oct. 1989, following a wave of pro-democracy demonstrations, he was replaced as SED leader and head of state by Egon Krenz, and in Dec. expelled from the Communist Party.

Honegger, *n.* **Arthur** (1892–1955), Swiss composer, one of Les Six. His work was varied in form, for example, the opera *Antigone* (1927), the ballet *Skating Rink* (1922), the oratorio *Le Roi David/King David* (1921), programme music *Pacific 231* (1923), and the *Symphonie liturgique/Liturgical Symphony* (1946).

Hōnen, *n.* (1133–1212), Japanese Buddhist monk who founded the Pure Land school of Buddhism.

honest, *a.* upright, fair, truthful, trustworthy in dealings, business or conduct; just, equitable; open, frank, candid, sincere, honourable; chaste, of women, virtuous; unimpeached, unstained; worthy. *int.* used to affirm the honesty of a statement. **honest-to-God, honest-to-goodness,** *a.* genuine, outright. **honest to goodness,** absolutely genuine. **to make an honest woman of,** to marry (a woman). **to make, turn an honest penny,** (*coll.*) to seize an opportunity to make profit. **honestly,** *adv.* **honesty,** *n.* the quality or state of being honest; integrity, sincerity, uprightness; chastity; a cruciferous garden plant, *Lunaria biennis,* bearing flat, round, semi-transparent seed-pods. [OF *honeste,* L *honestus,* from *honos,* HONOUR]

honey, *n.* a sweet viscid product collected from plants by bees, and largely used as an article of food; sweetness; a term of endearment. †*v.t.* to speak fondly to; to coax. *v.i.* to use endearing language; to talk or behave fondly. **honey-bag,** *n.* the receptacle for honey in a bee. **honey-bear,** *n.* a S American quadruped, also called the kinkajou, which destroys the nests of bees. **honey-bee,** *n.* a bee that produces honey. **honey-buzzard,** *n.* a British raptorial bird, *Pernis apivora,* which feeds on the larvae of bees and wasps. **honeycomb,** *n.* a waxy substance formed in hexagonal cells by the hive-bee, for the reception of honey and for the eggs and larvae; anything similarly perforated, esp. flaws in a metal casting. *v.t.* to fill with holes or cavities. **honey-dew,** *n.* a saccharine substance found on the leaves of some plants; something extremely sweet, nectar; a kind of tobacco moistened with molasses and pressed into cakes. **honeydew melon,** *n.* a type of melon with sweet flesh and a greenish rind. **honey-guide,** *n.* the genus *Indicator,* S African cuckoos, whose cry is supposed to indicate the nests of bees. **honey-harvest,** *n.* honey collecting, the time for collecting honey. †**honey-heavy,** *a.* heavy and somewhat oppressive. **honey-locust,** *n.* a large American tree, *Gleditschia triacanthus,* of the family Leguminosae. **honey-mouthed,** *a.* sweet and smooth in speech. **honey-sac** HONEY-BAG. **honey-stalk,** *n.* the flower of clover. **honeysuckle,** *n.* the genus *Lonicera,* esp. *L. periclymenum,* the woodbine, a wild climbing plant with sweet-scented flowers; (*Austral.*) any one of the Banksia shrubs. **honey-sweet,** *a.* very dear; sweet as honey. **honey-tongued,** *a.* smooth in speech; honey-mouthed. **honey-wort,** *n.* two cultivated plants of the borage family, *Cerinthe major* and *C. minor,* both attractive to bees. **honeyed,** *a.* sweetened with honey; of words, ingratiating. †**honeyedness,** *n.* sweetness. **honeyless,** *a.* [OE *hunig* (cp. Dut. and G *Honig,* Icel. *hunang*)]

honeymoon, *n.* the first month after marriage; the period immediately following marriage spent by the married couple by themselves away from home. *v.i.* to spend the honeymoon (in, at etc.). **honeymooner,** *n.* **honeymoon period,** *n.* a period of goodwill and harmony at the start of a new business appointment, relationship etc.

hong, *n.* the Chinese name for a foreign factory, warehouse or other mercantile establishment. [Chin. *hang,* row, series]

Hong Kong, *n.* British crown colony in SE Asia, comprising Hong Kong island, the Kowloon peninsula, and the mainland New Territories. **area** 1070 sq km/413 sq miles. **capital** Victoria (popularly Hong Kong City). **towns** Kowloon, Tsuen Wan (in the New Territories). **population** (1986) 5,431,000; 57% Hong Kong Chinese, most of the remainder refugees from the mainland. **exports** textiles, clothing, electronic goods, clocks, watches, cameras, plastic products; a large proportion of the exports and imports of S China are transshipped here, and the Chinese special economic zone of Shenzen is only 40 km/25 miles away; tourism is important. **languages** English and Chinese. **religion** Confucianist, Buddhist, Taoist, with Muslim and Christian minorities.

Honiara, *n.* port and capital of the Solomon Islands, on the NW coast of Guadalcanal island; population (1985) 26,000.

honied, HONEYED, see HONEY.

honi soit qui mal y pense, shame be to him who thinks evil of it (motto of the Order of the Garter). [F]

Honiton (lace), *n.* a kind of lace with floral sprigs.

honk, *n.* the cry of the wild goose; any similar cry or noise, esp. that of a vehicle's horn. *v.t., v.i.* to (cause to) make this noise. *v.i.* (*sl.*) to vomit. **honker,** *n.* [imit.]

honky, honkie, *n.* (*N Am., derog., sl.*) a white person.

honky-tonk, *n.* (*esp. N Am.*) a disreputable nightclub, bar etc; a type of ragtime piano-playing, esp. on a cheap upright piano. *a.* of a piano, of such a kind; of music, of this type of ragtime.

Honolulu, *n.* (Hawaiian 'sheltered bay') capital city and port of Hawaii, US, on the S coast of Oahu; population (1980) 365,000. It is a holiday resort, noted for its beauty and tropical vegetation, with some industry. 11 km/7 miles SW is Pearl Harbor with naval and military installations.

honor, (*N Am.*) HONOUR.

honorable, (*N Am.*) HONOURABLE.

honorarium, *n.* (*pl.* **honorariums, -ria**) a fee or payment for the services of a professional person. [late L, as foll.]

honorary, *a.* done, made, or conferred as a mark of honour; holding a title or an office without payment or without undertaking the duties; depending on honour, not enforceable by law (of duties or obligations). †**honorificabilitudinity** HONOUR. [L *honorārius,* from *honos,* HONOUR]

honoris causa, gratia, for the sake of honour, honorary. [L]

honour, *n.* respect, esteem, reverence; reputation, glory, distinction, a mark or token of distinction; high rank; nobleness of mind, probity, uprightness; conformity to the accepted code of social conduct; chastity, reputation of chastity (in women); (*pl.*) courteous attentions paid to guests etc.; (*Univ., pl.*) a distinction awarded for higher proficiency than that required for a pass; one who or that which confers honour, position etc.; an ornament; a title of address given to certain officers, as a county court judge etc.; in golf, the right of driving off first; (*pl.*) the four highest trump cards; †a seigniory of several manors, held under one baron or lord-paramount. *v.t.* to treat with reverence or respect; to bestow honour upon; to dignify, to glorify, to exalt; to acknowledge; to accept and pay when due (as a bill). **honour bright,** (*coll.*) on one's honour. **honours of war,** a distinction or privilege granted to an enemy who has surrendered on terms. **in honour of,** to celebrate. **on, upon one's honour,** a declaration pledging one's honour or reputation to the accuracy or good faith of a statement. **to do the honours,** to perform the courtesies required of a master or mistress at a dinner, reception etc. **funeral** or **last honours,** marks of respect paid to the deceased at a funeral. **honour-point,** *n.* (*Her.*) the point immediately above the centre or fesse-point of a shield. **honours easy,** *n.pl.* in a card game, honours equally divided. **honours list,** *n.* the list of people who have received honours, e.g. knighthoods etc., from the Queen. **honorific,** *a.* conferring or doing honour. *n.* an honorific title etc. **honorifically,** *adv.* †**honorificabilitudinity,** *n.* honourableness (often cited as the longest word in the English language). **honourer,** *n.* [OF *onor, honur,* L *honōrem,* nom. *honos*]

honourable, *a.* worthy of honour; illustrious, of distinguished rank, noble; conferring honour; actuated by principles of honour, upright; consistent with honour or reputation; accompanied or performed with or as with marks of honour; proceeding from a laudable cause; not base; a title of respect or distinction borne by the children of peers below the rank of marquess, maids of honour, Justices of the High Court etc. **Honourable Company of Edinburgh Golfers,** *n.* the oldest golf club in the world. They were formed in 1744 as the Gentleman Golfers of Edinburgh and played over the Leith links. They drew up the first set of golf rules, which were later accepted by the ruling body of the Royal and Ancient Club of St. Andrews. †**honourableness,** *n.* **honourably,** *adv.*

Honshu, *n.* principal island of Japan. It lies between Hokkaido to the NE and Kyushu to the SW; area 231,100 sq km/89,205 sq miles, including 382 smaller islands; population (1986) 97,283,000. A chain of volcanic mountains runs along the island, which is subject to frequent earthquakes. The main cities are Tokyo, Yokohama, Osaka, Kobe, Nagoya, and Hiroshima.

Honthorst, *n.* **Gerrit van** (1590–1656), Dutch painter who used extremes of light and shade, influenced by Caravaggio; with Terbrugghen he formed the Utrecht school.

hooch, hootch, *n.* (*N Am.*) crude alcoholic liquor. [*hooch*inoo, spirits made by the Hootchinoo tribe of Alaska]

Hooch, *n.* **Pieter de** (1629–84), Dutch painter, active in Delft and, later, Amsterdam. The harmonious domestic interiors and courtyards of his Delft period were influenced by Vermeer.

hood, *n.* a loose covering for the head and back of the neck, separate, or an appendage to a cloak or overcoat; an appendage to an academic gown marking a degree; anything more or less resembling a hood, as the blinding-cap on a hawk, a carriage-top, a paper cornet etc.; (*N Am.*) the bonnet of a motor-car; a hoodlum. *v.t.* to dress in a hood; to put a hood on; to blind, to cover. **hoodman,** *n.* one blindfolded in blind-man's buff. †**hoodman-blind,** *n.* blind-man's buff. **hood-mould, -moulding,** *n.* a band or moulding over the head of a door, window or other opening, a drip-stone. **hood-wink,** *v.t.* to blindfold; to deceive, to take in. **hooded,** *a.* covered with a hood; blinded; (*Bot.*) hood-shaped, cucullate. **hooded snake,** *n.* a snake of the Elapidae family, having the power of dilating the loose skin of the neck into a kind of cowl or hood. **hoodie, hoody-crow,** *n.* the hooded crow, *Corvus cornix.* **hoodless,** *a.* [OE *hōd* (cp. Dut. *hoed,* G *Hut*)]

-hood, -HEAD.

hoodlum, *n.* (*N Am., coll.*) a street rowdy, a hooligan, esp. one of a gang of street ruffians who flourished in San Francisco during the 1870s and 1880s. **hoodlumism,** *n.* [etym. unknown]

hoodoo, *n.* bad luck; the cause of bad luck, a Jonah. *v.t.* to bring bad luck; to cast a spell on something. [variant of VOODOO]

hoodwink HOOD.

hooey, *n.* bosh, nonsense. [onomat.]

hoof, *n.* (*pl.* **hoofs, hooves**) the horny sheath covering the feet of horses, oxen etc.; an animal with hoofs; (*facet.*) a human foot; (*Geom.*) an ungula. *v.t.* to strike or attack with the hoof; (*sl.*) to kick. *v.i.* to walk, to go afoot; (*sl.*) to kick (out). **on the hoof,** of livestock, alive; (*coll.*) while standing up or moving around. **to hoof it,** (*coll.*) to walk, to tramp it. **hoof-bound,** *a.* having a painful dryness and contraction of the hoof, causing lameness. **hoof-pad,** *n.* a pad fastened on a horse-shoe to prevent injury by interference. **hoof-pick,** *n.* a pointed or hooked instrument for removing stones etc. from a horse's hoof. **hoofed,** *a.* **hoofer,** *n.* (*N Am., coll.*) a dancer. [OE *hōf* (Dut. *hoef,* Icel. *hōfr,* G *Huf*)]

hoo(h)-ha, *n.* (*coll.*) fuss, noisy excitement. [onomat.]

hook, *n.* a curved piece of metal or other material by which an object is caught or suspended; a bent and pointed wire, usu. barbed, for catching fish; a trap, a snare; a curved instrument for cutting grass or corn, a sickle; a sharp bend; a cape, a headland; (*sl.*) a catch, an imposture; an advantage; (*sl.*) a repetitive catchy musical phrase. *v.t.* to catch, grasp or hold with or as with a hook; to fasten with a hook or hooks; (*esp. passive; coll.*) to attract or cause to become addicted; (*sl.*) to snatch, to steal, to pilfer; in golf, to drive (the ball) widely to the left; in football, to pull (the ball) in with the foot in a certain manner. *v.i.* to fit or fasten (on) with or as with hooks. **believe** etc. **something hook, line and sinker,** believe etc. something completely. **by hook or by crook,** by fair means or foul. **hook and eye,** a metal hook and corresponding loop for fastening a dress. **Hook of Holland,** the corner of Holland projecting into the North Sea. **off the hook,** ready-made; of a telephone receiver, not on its rest. **on one's own hook,** (*sl.*) on one's own account. **to hook it, to sling one's hook,** (*sl.*) to decamp; to run away. **hook-nosed,** *a.* having an aquiline nose. **hook-pin,** *n.* an iron pin with a hooked head used in building and carpentry. **hook-up,** *n.* a radio network, a series of connected stations. **hook-worm,** *n.* a parasite infesting men and animals. **hooked,** *a.* bent; furnished with hooks. **hookedness,** *n.* the state of being hooked. †**hooky,** *a.* [OE *hōc* (cp. Dut. *hoek,* Icel. *haki,* G *Haken*)]

hooka(h), *n.* a tobacco-pipe in which the smoke passes through water. [Arab. *huqqah,* a casket, a bowl]

Hooke, *n.* **Robert** (1635–1703), English scientist and inventor, originator of Hooke's law. His inventions included a telegraph system, the spirit-level, marine barometer, and sea gauge. He coined the term 'cell' in biology. **Hooke's law,** *n.* in physics, law stating that the tension in a lightly stretched spring is proportional to its extension from its natural length.

hooker¹, *n.* (*N Am., sl.*) a prostitute.

hooker², *n.* a two-masted Dutch coasting or fishing vessel; a one-masted fishing smack. [Dut. *hoeker,* from *hoek,* HOOK]

Hooker, *n.* **Joseph Dalton** (1817–1911), English botanist who travelled to the Antarctic and made many botanical discoveries, documented in *Flora Antarctica* (1844–47). His works include *Genera Plantarum* (1862–63) and *Flora of British India* (1875–97). In 1865 he succeeded his father, William Jackson Hooker (1785–1865), as director of the Royal Botanic Gardens, Kew, England.

hookey, hooky, *n.* (*N Am.*) truant, esp. in the phrase **to play hookey.**

hookum, *n.* a command, an order. [Hind.]

Hoolee, *n.* the great Hindu festival in honour of Krishna. [Hind. *hōlī*]

hooligan, *n.* one of a gang of street roughs given to violent attacks on persons. **hooliganism,** *n.* [prob. from the name of a rowdy family (cp. Ir. *Houlihan*) in a comic song pop. in music-halls, *c.* 1885]

hoop¹, *n.* a strip of wood or metal bent into a band or ring to hold the staves of casks etc. together; a circular strip of whalebone etc. used to expand the skirts of women's dresses; a large iron or wooden ring for a child to trundle; a small iron arch used in croquet; a hank; a band on a wooden anchor-stock; a strap round an eccentric. *v.t.* to bind or fasten with hoops; to encircle. **to go, be put etc. through the hoop,** to go, be put etc. through an ordeal. **hoop-iron,** *n.* flat, thin bar-iron such as is used for hooping barrels. **hoop-la,** *n.* game of winning small objects by throwing rings over them. **hoop-petticoat, -skirt,** *n.* a woman's dress expanded by means of a hoop. **hooper,** *n.* one who hoops casks; a cooper. [OE *hōp* (cp. Dut. *hoep*)]

hoop[2], **hooping-cough** WHOOP.

Hooper, *n.* **John** (*c.* 1495–1555), English Protestant reformer and martyr, born in Somerset. He adopted the views of Zwingli and was appointed bishop of Gloucester 1550. He was burned to death for heresy.

hoopoe, *n.* a bird, *Upupa epops,* a rare British visitant with large crest and fine plumage. [earlier *hoope,* F *huppe,* L *upupa,* onomat.]

hoorah, hooray, *int.* HURRAH. **Hooray Henry,** , *n.* an extrovert, sporty person, esp. a student.

hoosegow, *n.* (*N Am. sl.*) a prison. [Sp. *juzgado,* courtroom]

Hoosier, *n.* (*N Am.*) a native of the state of Indiana. [etym. unknown]

hoot[1], *v.i.* to shout or make loud cries in derision or contempt; to cry as an owl; to make a sound like this. *v.t.* to shout (down, out, away etc.) in contempt or derision; express by hooting. *n.* a cry like that of an owl; an inarticulate shout in contempt or derision. *a.* (*coll.*) something or someone very amusing. **not to care two hoots,** (*coll.*) not to care at all. **hooter,** *n.* one who or that which hoots; a steam-whistle or siren, esp. one used to give notice to workpeople of the beginning or end of work-time. [ME *houten,* perh. from Scand., or imit.]

hoot[2], **hoots,** *int.* (*Sc., North.*) an exclamation of disgust, impatience.

hoove, *n.* a disease in cattle in which the stomach is distended with gas. [OE *hōf-*, stem of HEAVE]

Hoover[1], *n.* **Herbert (Clark)** (1874–1964), 31st president of the US (1929–33), a Republican. Secretary of commerce 1921–28. He lost public confidence after the stock-market crash of 1929, when he opposed direct government aid for the unemployed in the depression that followed.

Hoover[2], *n.* **J(ohn) Edgar** (1895–1972), US director of the Federal Bureau of Investigation (FBI) from 1924. He built up a powerful network for the detection of organized crime. His drive against alleged communist activities after World War II, and his opposition to the Kennedy administration and others brought much criticism over abuse of power.

Hoover[3], *n.* **William Henry** (1849–1932), US manufacturer, known for his association with the vacuum cleaner. Hoover soon became a generic name for vacuum cleaner.

Hoover®, *n.* a vacuum-cleaner. *v.t., v.i.* to clean with a vacuum-cleaner.

Hoover Dam, *n.* the highest concrete dam in the US, 221 m/726 ft., on the Colorado River at the Arizona-Nevada border, built 1931–36. Known as Boulder Dam 1933–47, its name was restored by President Truman as the reputation of the former president, Herbert Hoover, was revived. It impounds Lake Meade, and has a hydro-electric power capacity of 1300 megawatts.

Hooverville, *n.* colloquial term for any shantytown built by the unemployed and destitute in the US during the Depression 1929–33, named after the US president Herbert Hoover, whose policies were blamed for the plight of millions.

hop[1], *v.i.* (*past, p.p.* **hopped**) to spring, leap or skip on one foot; to skip with both feet (as birds) or with all four feet (as quadrupeds); to limp; †to dance. *v.t.* to jump lightly or skip over; (*esp. N Am.*) to ride on (a bus etc.). *n.* a jump, spring, or light leap on one foot; (*coll.*) a dance; a short trip by aircraft, a short run, a quick passage; a distance easily covered in a few paces. **hop, skip** (or **step**), **and a jump,** orig. a game or athletic feat in which as much ground as possible was covered by these three movements. **to hop the twig,** (*sl.*) to die; to give one's creditors the slip. **to catch on the hop,** to catch by surprise, esp. in the midst of a prank. **hop-o'-my-thumb,** *n.* a person of restricted growth, a dwarf. **hopper,** *n.* one who hops; a hopping insect, a flea, the larva of a cheese-fly etc. **hopping mad,** *a.* (*coll.*) very angry. [OE *hoppian* (cp. Dut. *hoppen,* Icel. and Swed. *hoppa,* G *hopfen*)]

hop[2], *n.* a perennial climbing plant, *Humulus lupulus,* the mature cones of which are used in brewing. *v.t.* to impregnate with hops. *v.i.* to pick hops. **hop-back,** *n.* (*Brewing*) a vessel to receive the infusion of malt and hops. **hop-bind, -bine,** *n.* the stem of the hop. **hop-fly, -louse,** *n.* an aphis, *Phorodon humuli,* destructive of hops. **hop-picker,** *n.* one who gathers hops; a machine for this purpose. **hop-pillow,** *n.* a pillow stuffed with hops for inducing sleep. **hop-pocket,** *n.* a coarse sack for hops; a half-sack, or 168 lb (76 kg), a measure of capacity for hops. **hop-pole,** *n.* a training pole for hops. **hop-tree,** *n.* an American shrub, *Ptelea trifoliata,* the bitter fruit of which is used as a substitute for hops. **hop-yard, -garden,** *n.* a field where hops are grown. **hoppy,** *a.* tasting of hops. **hop-vine** HOP-BIND. [MDut. *hoppe* (cp. G *Hopfen*)]

hope[1], *n.* an expectant desire; confidence in a future event; a ground for expectation, trust or confidence; that in which one confides; a person or thing that is the object of someone's hopes. *v.i.* to have confidence; to trust with confidence; to look (for) with desire or expectation, to trust (in). *v.t.* to expect with desire; to look forward to with trust; (*coll.*) to think, to suppose; †to expect. **hope chest,** *n.* (*N Am.*) bottom drawer. **to hope against hope,** to cling to a slight chance. **hopeful,** *a.* full of hope; giving rise to hope. **hopefully,** *adv.* in a hopeful way; one hopes. **hopefulness,** *n.* **hopeless,** *a.* destitute of hope, despairing; affording no hope, desperate; (*coll.*) incompetent or showing incompetence. **hopelessly,** *adv.* **hopelessness,** *n.* [OE *hopa* (cp. Dut. *hoop,* Swed. *hopp,* G *Hoffe*), whence *hopian,* to hope]

hope[2] FORLORN HOPE.

hope[3], *n.* a small enclosed valley, the upper part of a dale (often used in place-names). [OE *-hop,* in *fennhop* etc.]

Hope[1], *n.* **Anthony** (1863–1933), pen name of Anthony Hope Hawkins, English novelist, whose romance *The Prisoner of Zenda* (1894), and its sequel *Rupert of Hentzau* (1898), introduced the imaginary Balkan state of Ruritania.

Hope[2], *n.* **Bob** (1904–), stage name of Leslie Townes Hope, US comedian. His film appearances include a series of 'road' films with Bing Crosby.

Hopei, *n.* former name of HEBEI.

Hope's apparatus, *n.* in physics, an apparatus used to demonstrate the temperature at which water has its maximum density. It is named after Thomas Charles Hope (1766–1844).

Hopewell, *n.* N American Indian culture about AD 200, noted for burial mounds up to 12 m/40 ft. high, and also for Serpent Mound, Ohio.

Hopi, *n.* indigenous American people, numbering approximately 6000, who live mainly in mountain villages in the SW US. Their language belongs to the Uto-Aztecan family. The Hopi live in the middle of the Navajo (or Dineh) reservation.

Hopkins[1], *n.* **Anthony** (1937–), Welsh actor. Among his stage appearances are *Equus*, *Macbeth*, *Pravda*, and the title role in *King Lear*. His films include *The Lion in Winter* (1968), *A Bridge Too Far* (1977), and *The Elephant Man*.

Hopkins[2], *n.* **Gerard Manley** (1844–89), English poet. His work, marked by its religious themes and use of natural imagery, includes 'The Wreck of the Deutschland' (1876) and 'The Windhover' (1877). His employment of 'sprung rhythm' greatly influenced later 20th-century poetry.

Hopkins[3], *n.* **Harry L(loyd)** (1890–1946), US government official. Originally a social worker, in 1935 he became head of WPA (Works Progress Administration), which was concerned with Depression relief work. After a period as secretary of commerce 1938–40, he was appointed supervisor of the lend-lease programme 1941, and undertook missions to Britain and the USSR during World War II.

hoplite, *n.* a heavy-armed soldier in ancient Greece. [Gr. *hoplitēs,* from *hoplon,* weapon]

hopper[1] HOP[1].

hopper[2], *n.* a hop-picker; a funnel-shaped vessel for feeding material to a machine; a funnel or trough for passing grain etc. through a mill into vehicles; a barge for receiving and dumping mud, sand etc. from a dredging-machine; a tilting bottom in a barge, car etc. for discharging refuse. **hopper-boy,** *n.* a revolving rake in a grinding-mill, drawing the meal over a discharge-opening in the floor.

Hopper[1], *n.* **Dennis** (1936–), US film actor and director who caused a sensation with *Easy Rider* (1969), the archetypal 'road' film, but whose later *The Last Movie* (1971) was poorly received by the critics. He made a comeback in the 1980s. His work as actor includes *Rebel Without a Cause* (1955), *The American Friend/Der amerikanische Freund* (1977), and *Blue Velvet* (1986).

Hopper[2], *n.* **Edward** (1882–1967), US painter and etcher, whose views of New York in the 1930s and 1940s captured the loneliness and superficial glamour of city life, as in *Nighthawks* 1942 (Art Institute, Chicago).

hopple, *v.t.* to fetter (a horse, cattle etc.) by tying the feet together. *n.* a shackle or fetter used for this purpose. [etym. doubtful, cp. the later HOBBLE]

Hoppus foot, *n.* a unit of volume for timber equal to 1.27 cu. ft. (0.034 cu. m). [Edward *Hoppus,* 18th cent. English surveyor]

hopscotch, *n.* a children's game in which a stone is driven by the foot of a player hopping from one compartment to another of a figure scotched or traced on the ground. [HOP[1]]

Horace, *n.* (65–8 BC), Roman lyric poet and satirist. He became a leading poet under the patronage of the emperor Augustus. His works include *Satires* (35–30 BC), the four books of *Odes* (*c.* 24–25 BC), *Epistles*, a series of verse letters, and a critical work *Ars Poetica.* **Horatian**, *a.* pertaining to or resembling the Latin poet Horace or his poetry.

horal, horary, *a.* relating to an hour; pertaining to the time by the clock; occurring every hour; †lasting for an hour. [late L *hōrālis, hōrārius,* from *hōra,* HOUR]

†hord HOARDING.

horde, *n.* a nomadic tribe or clan; a gang, a multitude (usu. in contempt). *v.i.* to live in hordes; to gather together in gangs. [F, from Turk. *ordū,* camp (cp. URDU)]

Hordern, *n.* **Michael** (1911–), English actor who appeared in stage roles such as Shakespeare's Lear and Prospero. His films include *The Man Who Never Was* (1956), *The Spy Who Came in From the Cold* (1965), *The Bed Sitting Room* (1969) and *Joseph Andrews* (1977).

Hordeum, *n.* a genus of grasses typified by wild barley. **hordeaceous**, *a.* **hordeiform**, *a.* **hordein**, *n.* a protein found in barley grains. [L, barley]

Hore-Belisha, *n.* **Leslie, Baron Hore-Belisha** (1895–1957), British politician. A National Liberal, he was minister of transport 1934–37, introducing Belisha beacons to mark pedestrian crossings. As war minister from 1937, until removed by Chamberlain 1940 on grounds of temperament, he introduced peacetime conscription 1939.

horehound, *n.* a labiate herb, *Marrubium vulgare,* with woolly stem and leaves and aromatic juice, used as a tonic and a remedy for colds etc.; applied to various allied herbs. [OE *hārehūne* (*hār,* HOAR, *hūne,* etym. unknown)]

horizon, *n.* the circular line where the sky and the earth seem to meet; the great circle parallel to it, the centre of which is the centre of the earth; the boundary of one's mental vision, experience etc. **horizonless,** *a.* [F, from late L *horīzontem,* nom. *-zōn,* Gr. *horizōn,* from *horizein,* to bound, from *horos,* a limit]

horizontal, *a.* pertaining or relating to the horizon; situated at or near the horizon; parallel to the horizon, level, flat, plane; measured or contained in a plane of the horizon. *n.* a horizontal line, plane, bar etc.; a Tasmanian shrub with horizontal branches. **horizontality**, *n.* **horizontally,** *adv.* [from prec.]

hormone, *n.* a secretion from an internal gland having the property of stimulating vital and functional activity. **hormonal**, *a.* **hormonally,** *adv.* **hormone replacement therapy (HRT)**, the use of oral oestrogen to help limit the thinning of bone that occurs in women after menopause. The treatment was first used in the 1970s. [from Gr. *hormaein,* to arouse, to stimulate]

horn, *n.* a projecting bony growth, usu. pointed and in pairs on the heads of certain animals; the substance of which such growths are composed; anything made of or like a horn in shape, as a powder-flask or a drinking-vessel; an organ or growth resembling horns, as the feeler of a snail etc.; an extremity of a curved object, as of the moon when on the wane or waxing; a wing of an army; the imaginary projection on the forehead of a cuckold; a branch of a lake, inlet of the sea or stream; a metal wind instrument, orig. of horn; one of the alternatives of a dilemma. *a.* made of horn. *v.t.* to furnish with horns; to cuckold; to gore; to square (a vessel's frame with the line of the keel). **to horn in,** (*coll.*) to push in, to intrude. **horn of plenty** CORNUCOPIA. **to draw, pull in one's horns,** to repress one's ardour; to curtail one's expenses; to draw back, to check oneself. **horn-bar,** *n.* a cross-bar in a carriage. **horn-beak,** *n.* the garfish. **hornbeam,** *n.* a small tree, *Carpinus betulus,* yielding tough timber; other trees of the same family. **hornbill,** *n.* one of the family Bucerotidae, birds with bone-crested bills from India and the Indian Archipelago. **horn-blower,** *n.* one who plays a horn. **hornbook,** *n.* an alphabet with the Lord's Prayer etc., formerly printed on a slip of paper, fastened to a board and covered with horn to prevent its being torn; hence, a primer. **horn-core,** *n.* a process of the frontal bone supporting permanent horns as distinct from antlers. **horn-distemper,** *n.* a disease of cattle affecting the horn-core. **hornfels**, *n.* a compact rock formed by heat metamorphosing clay rocks. **horn-fish,** *n.* the garfish; the sand-pike, and other fishes. **horn-foot, -ed,** *a.* having a hoof; hoofed. **horn-mad,** *a.* furiously mad (like horned beasts, used by Shakespeare with allusion to cuckoldom). **horn-maker,** *n.* a maker of horns, esp. for drinking; a cuckolder. **†hornmercury,** *n.* calomel. **horn-owl** HORNED OWL. **hornpipe,** *n.* an old wind instrument; a lively dance, usu. for one person, popular among sailors; the music for such a dance. **horn-plate,** *n.* an axle-guard, on a railway carriage, locomotive etc. **horn-rimmed,** *a.* esp. of spectacles, having rims made of (a material resembling) horn. **horn-rims,** *n.pl.* horn-rimmed spectacles. **horn-shavings,** *n.pl.* scrapings from horns used for manure. **†hornsilver,** *n.* chloride of silver, from its horn-like appearance when fused. **hornslate,** *n.* grey siliceous stone. **hornstone,** *n.* chert. **hornwork,** *n.* an outwork consisting of two half-bastions and a curtain. **hornwrack,** *n.* a sea-mat. **horned,** *a.* furnished with horns; having projections or extremities like horns. **horned horse,** *n.* the gnu. **horned owl,** *n.* one of several species of owl having large ear-tufts and called long-eared owls. **horned screamer,** *n.* a S American grallatorial bird, *Palamedea cornuta,* with a horn on its forehead, and a piercing voice. **horned snake, viper,** *n.* an Indian or African viper of the genus *Cerastes* with horns over the eyes. **horned toad,** *n.* a small American toadlike lizard covered with spines. **hornedness**, *n.* **horner,** *n.* one who works or deals in horns; one who blows a horn; †a cuckold-maker. **hornful,** *n.* as much as a drinking-horn will hold. **hornish,** *a.* **hornless,** *a.* **horny,** *a.* made of or like horn; callous; having or abounding in horns; (*esp. N Am., sl.*) sexually excited; causing sexual excitement; lustful. **hornily,** *adv.* **horniness,** *n.* [OE (cp. Icel., Dan., Swed., and G *Horn;* cogn. with L *cornu,* Gr. *keras*)]

Horn, *n.* **Philip de Montmorency, Count of Horn** (1518–68), Flemish politician. He held high offices under the Holy Roman emperor Charles V and his son Philip II. From 1563 he was one of the leaders of the opposition to the rule of Cardinal Granvella (1517–86) and to the introduction of the Inquisition. In 1567 he was arrested together with the Resistance leader Egmont, and both were beheaded in Brussels.

hornblende, *n.* a dark-coloured mineral consisting of silica, magnesia, lime and iron. **horneblende schist,** a metamorphic schistose rock composed principally of hornblende. [G *Horn* (HORN, BLENDE)]

hornet, *n.* a large social wasp, *Vespa crabro,* or the American *V. maculata,* with a formidable sting; a person who makes himself very disagreeable. **to stir up a hornet's nest,** to excite (often unintentionally) the animosity of a large number of people. [OE *hyrnet* (cp. G *Hornisse*)]

Hornie, *n.* (*Sc.*) the devil, usu. **Auld Hornie.**

Horniman, *n.* **Annie Elizabeth Frederika** (1860–1937), English pioneer of repertory theatre, who subsidized the Abbey Theatre, Dublin, and founded the Manchester company.

horning, *n.* the appearance of the moon when in the form of a crescent; in Scottish law, a summons to a debtor to pay within a certain time, under pain of imprisonment.

hornito, *n.* a small smoking mound or fumerole produced by volcanic action. [Sp., dim. of *horno,* ult. from L *furnus,* oven, see FURNACE]

hornswoggle, *v.t.* (*esp. N Am., coll.*) to cheat, deceive. [etym. unknown]

Hornung, *n.* **E(rnest) W(illiam)** (1866–1921), English novelist, who at the prompting of Conan Doyle created 'A.J. Raffles', the gentleman-burglar, and his assistant Bunny Manders in *The Amateur Cracksman* (1899).

horo-, *comb. form.* pertaining to times or seasons, or to the measurement of time. [Gr. *hōra,* a season, an hour]

horography, *n.* the art of constructing clocks, watches etc. [-GRAPHY]

horologe, *n.* an instrument for showing the hour, a time-piece. **horologer, †horologiographer, horologist,** *n.* one skilled in horology; a maker of horologes. **horological,** *a.* **†horologiography,** *n.* the art of constructing instruments to show the hour; an account of such instruments. **horologiographic,** *a.* **horology,** *n.* the art of measuring time, or of constructing instruments to indicate time. [OF, from L *hōrologium,* Gr. *hōrologion* (HORO-, *legein,* to tell)]

horometry, *n.* the art or practice of measuring time. **horometrical,** *a.*

horopito, *n.* the New Zealand pepper tree. [Maori]

horoscope, *n.* an observation of the sky and the configuration of the planets at a particular time, esp. at the moment of one's birth, in order to foretell one's future; a scheme of the 12 houses or signs of the zodiac, in which is marked the disposition of the heavens at a particular moment. **horoscopic, -ical,** *a.* **horoscopy,** *n.* the pretended art of predicting the future by the disposition of the stars; a horoscope. [F, from L *hōroscopus,* Gr. *hōroskopos* (*skopos,* observer)]

Horowitz, *n.* **Vladimir** (1904–89), US pianist, born in Kiev, Ukraine. He made his debut in the US 1928 with the New York Philharmonic Orchestra. Renowned for his commanding virtuoso style, he was a leading interpreter of Liszt, Schumann, and Rachmaninov.

horrendous, *a.* (*coll.*) awful; horrifying. [L *horrendus,* ger. of *horrēre,* to bristle]

horrent, *a.* (*poet.*) bristling; erect, as bristles. [L *horrens -ntem,* pres.p. of *horrēre,* to bristle, to shudder]

horrible, *a.* causing or tending to cause horror; dreadful, shocking, harrowing; (*coll.*) extremely unpleasant, awful. **horribleness,** *n.* **horribly,** *adv.* [OF, from L *horribilis,* as prec.]

horrid, *a.* causing horror; shocking; †rough, bristly; (*coll.*) nasty, unpleasant, frightful. **horridly,** *adv.* **horridness,** *n.* [L *horridus,* as prec.]

horrify, *v.t.* to strike with horror; (*coll.*) to scandalize. **horrifyingly,** *adv.* **horrific,** *a.* **horrifically,** *adv.* **horrification,** *n.* [L *horrificāre* (*horrēre,* to bristle, *-ficāre, facere,* to make)]

horripilation, *n.* a sensation of a creeping or motion of the hair of the body, caused by disease, terror etc. **horripilant,** *a.* **horripilate,** *v.t., v.i.* [late L *horripilātio,* from *horripilāre* (as prec., *pilus,* hair)]

horrisonant, *a.* having a dreadful sound. [L *horrēre,* to bristle, *sonans -ntem,* pres.p. of *sonāre,* to sound]

horror, *n.* a shaking, shuddering or shivering; dread or terror, mingled with detestation or abhorrence; that which excites terror or repulsion. *a.* esp. of a cinema film, depicting gruesome, frightening, often paranormal events. **the horrors,** *n.pl.* the blues; delirium tremens. **horror-stricken, -struck,** *a.* overwhelmed with horror. [OF *horrour,* L *horrōrem,* nom. *-or,* as prec.]

hors, *prep.* outside, out of. *adv.* out of, beyond. **hors concours,** *a.* not for competition. **hors de combat,** *a.* out of the battle, disabled. **hors d'oeuvre,** *n.* (*pl.* **hors d'oeuvres**) a dish not forming part of the regular course, served as relish before or during a meal. [F, earlier *fors,* L *foris*]

horse, *n.* a solid-hoofed quadruped, *Equus caballus,* with mane and tail of long coarse hair, domesticated and employed as beast of draught and burden; the adult male of the species; (*collect.*) cavalry; a frame or other device used as a support; a vaulting-block; a wooden frame on which soldiers were made to sit astride as a punishment; a currier's trestle; a slanting board on which pressmen place sheets to be printed; other appliances of analogous use in various trades etc.; (*Mining*) a mass of rock, clay etc., forming an obstruction; (*Naut.*) an iron bar on which slides the sheet-block of a fore-and-aft sail; a foot-rope beneath a yard or bowsprit; a breast-rope in the chains; (*sl.*) work charged for before being executed; also called 'dead-horse'; (*sl.*) heroin. *v.t.* to provide with a horse or horses; to cover (said of a stallion); to carry on the back; to put astride of anyone for flogging. *v.i.* to mount or ride on horsebac. **a dark horse,** (*coll.*) a person who is secretive or reserved. **a Trojan horse,** something apparently innocuous that introduces potential danger, harm etc., as the huge wooden horse in which the Greeks entered Troy. **horse and foot,** cavalry and infantry. **on horseback,** mounted on a horse. **to change horses in midstream,** to alter plans, views, loyalties etc. in the middle of a project. **to eat like a horse,** (*coll.*) to eat very much. **to hold one's horses,** (*coll.*) to stop; hesitate; refrain from acting. **to flog a dead horse** FLOG. **to look a gift horse in the mouth,** to criticize something freely offered. **to mount, ride the high horse,** to be arrogant; to put on consequential airs. **to take horse,** to mount for the purpose of riding; to travel on horseback. **horse artillery,** *n.* field artillery with the gunners mounted. **horseback,** *n.* the back of a horse. **horse bean,** *n.* a coarse variety of bean, *Faba vulgaris,* used for feeding horses. **horse block,** *n.* a block or stage to assist a person in mounting on horseback. **horse boat,** *n.* a ferry-boat drawn by horses; a boat for transporting horses across water. **horse box,** *n.* a closed van or car for taking horses by rail; a compartment for horses on ship-board, or a box-like structure for slinging horses on board; (*facet.*) a large pew. **horse-boy,** *n.* a stable-boy. **horse brass,** *n.* a brass decoration originally hung on a horse's harness. **horse-breaker,** *n.* one whose occupation it is to break in or to train horses. **horse-car,** *n.* a tram-car drawn by a horse or horses. **horse chestnut,** *n.* a large variety of chestnut, *Aesculus hippocastanum,* with coarse, bitter fruit; its fruit. **horse-cloth,** *n.* a rug to cover a horse. **horse-coper,** *n.* a horse-dealer. **horse-coping,** *n.* **horse-dealer,** *n.* one who deals in horses. **horse-doctor,** *n.* a veterinary surgeon. **horse-drench,** *n.* a dose of liquid physic for a horse; the apparatus by which it is administered. **horse-faced,** *a.* having a long, coarse face. **horse-flesh,** *n.* the flesh of the horse, used as food; (*collect.*) horses. **horsefly,** *n.* any large fly that irritates horses. **Horse Guards,** *n.pl.* the brigade of cavalry of the English household troops, esp. the 3rd Regiment, the Royal Horse Guards; their barracks or headquarters; formerly, the office of the Commander-in-Chief in Whitehall; the military authorities of the War Department. **horsehair,** *n.* the long hair of the mane and tail of horses. *a.* made of this. **horsehoe,** *n.* a hoe drawn by horses. **horse-knacker** KNACKER. **horse-latitudes,** *n.pl.* the region of calms on the northern edge of the north-east trade winds, said to be so called because the old navigators frequently threw overboard there the horses they were carrying to America and the W Indies. **horselaugh,** *n.* a loud, coarse laugh. **horse-leech,** *n.* a farrier; a large kind of leech which is often drawn in by horses and cattle when drinking; (*fig.*) a rapacious person, a blood-sucker (in alln. to Prov. xxx.15). **horse-litter,** *n.* a litter borne by horses. **horse-load,** *n.* a load for a horse. **horse mackerel,** *n.* the cavally, *Caranx trachurus,* and other fishes. **horseman,** *n.* one skilled in riding or the management of horses; †a horse-soldier; a variety of the domestic pigeon. **horsemanship,** *n.* **horse marine,** *n.* one of a mythical body of troops; one out of his element. **horse-mill,** *n.* a mill turned by horse-power. **horse-milliner,** *n.* one who deals in fancy trappings and decorations for horses. **horse opera,** *n.* a wild west film. **horseplay,** *n.* rough, boisterous play. **horse-pond,** *n.* a pond for watering and washing horses. **horse-power,** *n.* the power a horse can exert, used as a unit of measurement of the rate of doing mechanical work, equivalent to 33,000 foot-pounds (44.7 kJ) per minute; mechanical power expressed in such units; a mechanical contrivance by which a horse is made to drive machinery. **horse-race,** *n.* a race between horses with riders. **horse-racing,** *n.* **horse-radish,** *n.* a plant, *Cochlearia armoracia,* with a pungent, acrid root, used as a condiment. **horse-rake,** *n.* a rake drawn by horses. **horse-rider,** *n.* a person riding a horse. **horse-riding,** *n.* **horse-road, -way,** *n.* a road or way by which horses may travel. **horse-sense,** *n.* (*coll.*) rough, practical common sense. **horseshit,** *n.* (*esp. N Am., taboo, sl.*) nonsense; rubbish. **horseshoe,** *n.* a shoe for horses; anything resembling this in shape. *a.* shaped like this. **horseshoe bat,** *n.* any of several Old World insectivorous bats with a horseshoe-shaped growth round the nostrils. **horseshoe crab,** *n.* any of several types of crab of N America and Asia with a heavily armoured crescent-shaped body. **horse-shoeing,** *n.* the act or occupation of shoeing horses. **horse-stinger,** *n.* (*dial.*) a dragon-fly. **horsetail,** *n.* the tail of a horse; this used as a Turkish standard or token of rank; a plant of the cryptogamous genus *Equisetum,* with whorls of branches like the hairs in a horse's tail. **horse trading,** *n.* hard bargaining. **horse-whip,** *n.* a whip for driving horses. *v.t.* to flog with a horsewhip; to thrash. **horsewoman,** *n.fem.* a woman skilled in riding and managing horses. **horseless,** *a.* **horseless carriage,** *n.* a vehicle driven by mechanical means, not pulled by a horse. **horsy,** *a.* of the nature of a horse; pertaining to or fond of horses or horse-racing; resembling a horse; coarse in behaviour. **horsily,** *adv.* **horsiness,** *n.* [OE *hors* (cp. Icel. *hross,* OHG *hros,* Dut. *ros,* G *Ross*)]

horst, *n.* a raised block of land separated by faults from the surrounding land. [G]

Horst-Wessel-Lied, *n.* song introduced by the Nazis as a second German national anthem. The text was written by Horst Wessel (1907–30), a Nazi 'martyr', to a traditional tune.

hortative, hortatory, *a.* giving or containing advice or encouragement. **hortation,** *n.* [L *hortātīvus,* from *hortārī,* to EXHORT]

Horthy de Nagybánya, *n.* **Nicholas** (1868–1957), Hungarian politician and admiral. Leader of the counter-revolutionary White government, he became regent 1920 on the overthrow of the communist Bela Kun regime by Romanian intervention. He represented the conservative and military class, and retained power until World War II, trying (although allied to Hitler) to retain independence of action. In 1944 Hungary was taken over by the Nazis and he was deported to Germany.

horticulture, *n.* the art of cultivating or managing gardens. **horticultural,** *a.* **horticulturist,** *n.* [L *hortus,* garden, CULTURE]

hortus siccus, *n.* a collection of dried plants arranged systematically. [L, dry garden, see prec.]

Horus, *n.* in ancient Egyptian mythology, the hawkheaded sun god, son of Isis and Osiris, of whom the pharaohs were thought to be the incarnation.

hosanna, *n.* an acclamatory prayer for blessing; a shout of praise and adoration. [late L and Gr., from Heb. *hōshī 'āh-nnā,* save, we pray]

hose, *n.* (*collect.*) orig., close-fitting breeches or trousers reaching to the knees; stockings; (*sing. with pl.* **hoses**) flexible tubing for water or other fluid, as for fire-engine service; the part of a spade, golf-club etc., in which the handle is inserted. *v.t.* to water or drench with a hose; to provide with hose. **hose-man,** *n.* a fireman who works the hose. **hose-pipe,** *n.* **hose-cart, -truck,** *n.* vehicles for carrying hose. **hose-reel,** *n.* a drum (usu. on a cart or truck) for carrying hose; the vehicle itself. **hoseless,** *a.* **hosier,** *n.* one who deals in hosiery. **hosiery,** *n.* (*collect.*) stockings and other underclothing; a factory for such goods; the shop or business of a hosier. [OE *hosa* (cp. Dut. *hoos,* Icel. *hosa,* G *Hose*)]

Hoskins, *n.* **Bob** (1942–), British character actor who progressed to fame from a series of supporting roles. Films include *The Long Good Friday* (1980), *The Cotton Club* (1984), *Mona Lisa* (1985), *A Prayer for the Dying* (1987), *Who framed Roger Rabbit?* (1988).

hospice, *n.* a convent or other place for the reception and entertainment of travellers on some difficult or dangerous road or pass, as among the Alps; a home for the needy or afflicted; a nursing home or hospital for the terminally ill. [F, from L *hospitium,* from *hospes -pitis,* guest]

hospitable, *a.* entertaining or disposed to entertain strangers or guests with kindness. **hospitableness,** *n.* **hospitably,** *adv.* †**hospitage,** *n.* hospitality; a place of hospitality. **hospitality,** *n.* liberal entertainment of strangers or guests. [F, from late L *hospitāre,* to receive as a guest, as prec.]

hospital, *n.* †a place of shelter or entertainment, a hospice; an institution for the reception and treatment of the sick or injured; applied to some almshouses, orphanages and other charitable foundations. **hospital fever,** *n.* a kind of typhus fever caused by the effluvia from diseased bodies in hospitals. **Hospital Saturday, Sunday,** *n.* a day set apart for the collection of money in support of hospitals. **hospitalize, -ise,** *v.t.* to send to hospital; to admit for hospital treatment. **hospitalization, -isation,** *n.* [OF, from late L *hospitāle,* from L pl. *hospitālia,* as HOSPICE]

hospitality HOSPITABLE.

hospitaller, *n.* one residing in a hospital for the reception of the poor or strangers; (*Hist.*) one of a religious brotherhood whose office was to relieve the poor, strangers and the sick. **Knights Hospitallers,** *n.pl.* a military and charitable religious brotherhood established in the Middle Ages, esp. the Knights Hospitallers of St John of Jerusalem founded *c.* 1048.

hospitium, HOSPICE.

hospodar, *n.* Lord, a title borne by the princes or governors of Wallachia and Moldavia. [Slav.]

host[1], *n.* one who entertains another; the landlord of an inn; the compere of a TV or radio show; an animal or plant on which another is parasitic; an organism into which an organ or tissue is grafted or transplanted. †*v.i.* to take up one's abode, to lodge. †*v.t.* to lodge, to entertain; to be the compere of. **to reckon without one's host,** to overlook important considerations. **hostess,** *n.* a female host; the landlady of an inn or hotel; a woman employed to attend to the comfort of travellers on passenger planes, ships etc.; a woman paid to entertain customers in a bar, nightclub etc [OF *hoste* (F *hôte*), L *hospitem* nom. *-pes,* a host, a guest]

host[2], *n.* an army; a great number, a multitude. **the heavenly host, host of heaven,** *n.* the angels and archangels; the stars, planets etc. †**hosting,** *n.* a mustering of armed men; a military expedition, a foray. [OF, from L *hostem* enemy]

host[3], *n.* the consecrated bread or wafer used in the Eucharist. †**hostie**, *n.* the host. [ME *oste,* OF *oiste,* L *hostia,* sacrificial victim]

hostage, *n.* a person given or seized in pledge for the performance of certain conditions or for the safety of others. **hostages to fortune,** *n.pl.* those dearest to one, one's wife and children. **to give a hostage to fortune,** put oneself at a disadvantage by risking the loss of someone or something valued highly. **hostageship,** *n.* **hostage-taker,** *n.* **hostage-taking,** *n.* [OF (F *ôtage*), ult. from L *obsidātus,* hostageship, from *obses obsidis,* a hostage]

hostel, *n.* an inn; a house or extra-collegiate hall for the residence of students etc.; a place of residence not run commercially, esp. for the homeless; youth hostel. †**hosteler,** *n.* an inn-keeper, an ostler; a student in a hostel. **hostelling,** *n.* the practice of staying at youth hostels when travelling. **hostelry,** *n.* an inn. [OF, as HOSPITAL]

hostess HOST[1].

†**hostie** HOST[3].

hostile, *a.* pertaining to an enemy; showing enmity; unfriendly; inimical. **hostile witness,** *n.* a witness whose evidence is unfavourable to the party which has called him. **hostilely,** *adv.* **hostility,** *n.* enmity; antagonism; state of war; (*pl.*) acts of war. [L *hostilis,* from *hostis,* HOST[2]]

†**hosting** HOST[2].

hostler, OSTLER.

hot, *a.* having a high temperature; having much sensible heat; producing a sensation of heat; burning, acrid, pungent; ardent, impetuous; passionate, fierce; eager, enthusiastic; (*coll.*) exciting, excited, trying, arduous; sexually excited; (*Hunting*) of scent, strong; (*Dancing*) highly elaborated, florid; of animals, rutty; of news, fresh, recent; (*sl.*) of stolen goods, easily identifiable; wanted by the police; (*coll.*) very good; (*coll.*) radioactive. *adv.* hotly; ardently, eagerly; fiercely, angrily. *v.t.* (*past, p.p.* **hotted**) to make hot. **hot under the collar,** indignant, angry. **the hots,** (*esp. N Am., sl.*) strong (sexual) desire. **in hot water,** WATER. **to give it one hot,** to punish, censure or abuse severely. **to hot up,** to become more intense, exciting etc. **to make a place too hot to hold one,** to make it too uncomfortable for one to stay. **hot air,** *n.* (*coll.*) boastful, empty talk. **hot-air,** *a.* using hot air. **hotbed,** *n.* a bed of earth heated by means of fermenting manure, used for raising early and tender plants; (*fig.*) of disease, vice etc., any place which favours rapid growth. **hot blast,** *n.* a heated blast of air introduced into a smelting furnace. **hot-blooded,** *a.* excitable, irritable, passionate. **hot-brained,** *a.* violent, hotheaded. **hot-cockles,** *n.pl.* a child's game in which one covers his eyes and guesses who strikes him. **hot-cross bun,** *n.* a spicy yeast bun with a cross marked on the top, eaten esp. on Good Friday. **hot dog,** *n.* a hot sausage sandwiched in a roll. **hot-dogging,** *n.* performance of acrobatic manoeuvres whilst skiing, skating or skateboarding. **hot favourite,** *n.* the horse, runner etc. most likely to win in a race etc. **hot-flue,** *n.* a heated chamber for drying printed calicoes etc. **hot flush,** a sudden feeling of warmth accompanied by blushing, associated in women with the menopause. **hot-foot,** *adv.* very hastily, swiftly. **to hotfoot it,** (*sl.*) to run; go quickly. **hot gospeller,** *n.* (*coll.*) a tub-thumping preacher; a revivalist. **hot-head,** *n.* **hot-headed,** *a.* fiery, impetuous, passionate. **hothouse,** *n.* a plant-house where a relatively high artificial temperature is maintained to facilitate growth. *a.* (*coll.*) too sensitive, delicate. **hot line,** *n.* a telephone line for swift communication in emergencies, esp. the one between Washington and Moscow. **hot-mouthed,** *a.* headstrong, ungovernable. **hot music,** *n.* swing or jazz music in which the performers break free from the score and interpolate variations without losing the rhythm or melody; music that excites the dancers. **hot plate,** *n.* a round plate, electrically heated, on top of a cooker; a portable heatable plate for keeping food warm. **hotpot,** *n.* meat cooked with potatoes in a closed pot in an oven. **hot potato** POTATO. **hot-press,** *n.* a machine for giving a gloss to paper or linen by pressure between heated metal plates and glazed boards. *v.t.* to subject to this process. **hot rod,** *n.* (*coll.*) a car with an engine considerably modified to increase its performance greatly. **hot-rodder,** *n.* **hot-short,** *a.* of iron, brittle when hot. **hotshot** *n.* (*esp. N Am., coll.*) an important, often ostentatious, person. **hot-spirited,** *a.* having a fiery spirit. **hotspot,** *n.* a point in an engine etc. with an (excessively) high temperature; a lively nightclub or similar; a place of potential trouble; (*coll.*) a warm, sunny place, esp. a holiday resort. **hotspur,** *n.* a man of hot and hasty valour; a hot-headed person. **hot stuff,** *n.* (*sl.*) an impressive or excellent thing; very attractive woman. **hot-tempered,** *a.* quick to anger; irascible. **hot tub,** *n.* a Jacuzzi. **hot-wall,** *n.* a wall with included flues to assist in ripening the fruit of trees trained against it. **hot-water bottle,** *n.* a usu. rubber vessel containing hot water, used for warming a bed. **hot well,** *n.* the reservoir for warm water from the condenser in a condensing engine; a natural warm spring. **hotly,** *adv.* **hotness,** *n.* [OE *hāt* (cp. Dut. *heet,* Icel. *heitr,* G *heiss*)]

hotchpot, *n.* (*Law*) a general commixture of property in order to secure equal division (among heirs of an intestate person etc.). [F *hochepot* (*hocher,* to shake, toss together, from Teut., cp. Flem. *hutsen,* POT)]

hotchpotch, *n.* a confused mixture, a jumble; a dish composed of various ingredients, esp. thick broth made with mutton or other meat and vegetables. [corr. of prec.]

hotel, *n.* a commercial establishment providing accommodation, meals etc. for travellers; in France, a town residence or mansion. **hôtel-de-ville,** *n.* a town-hall. **hôtel-dieu,** *n.* (*pl.* **hôtels-dieu**) a hospital. **hotelier,** *n.* a hotel-keeper. [F, from OF *hostel,* see HOSTEL]

Hotol, *n.* a space craft designed to take off and land like a conventional aircraft, carrying payloads into low-earth orbit. [*ho*rizontal *t*ake-*o*ff and *l*anding]

Hottentot, *n.* a member of a South African people inhabiting the SW corner of the continent when Europeans first settled there. The language resembles Bushman, and has mainly monosyllabic roots with explosive consonants which produce clicking sounds. **Hottentot cherry,** *n.* a glabrous Cape shrub, *Cassine maurocenia,* with a cherry-like fruit. [Dut., prob. a stammerer (cp. *hateren,* to stammer)]

houdah, HOWDAH.

Houdini, *n.* **Harry** (1874–1926), stage name of Erich Weiss, US escape artist and conjurer. He attained fame by his escapes from ropes and handcuffs, from trunks under water, from straitjackets and prison cells.

Houdon, *n.* **Jean-Antoine** (1741–1828), French sculptor, a portraitist who made characterful studies of Voltaire and a neo-classical statue of George Washington, commissioned 1785.

houff, HOWFF.

hough, HOCK[1].

houhere, hohere, *n.* the ribbon-wood tree of New Zealand. [Maori]

hound, *n.* a dog used in hunting (*usu. in comb.,* as *bloodhound, deerhound, foxhound* etc.); one of those who chase the hares in hare and hounds; a mean, contemptible fellow. *v.t.* to hunt or chase with or as with hounds; to set on the chase; to incite to pursuit; to urge or cheer (on). **hound's tongue,** *n.* a coarse, hairy plant, of the borage family, with dull-red flowers; the genus *Cynoglossum,* comprising this. **hound-fish,** *n.* a dog-fish. **houndish,** *a.* [OE *hund* (cp. Dut. *hond,* Icel. *hundr,* G *Hund*), prob. allied to L *canis,* Gr. *kuōn*]

Houphouët-Boigny, *n.* **Felix** (1905–), Ivory Coast right-wing politician. He held posts in French ministries, and became president of the Republic of the Ivory Coast on independence 1960. He was re-elected for a sixth term 1985 representing the sole legal party.

hour, *n.* the 24th part of a natural day, the space of 60 minutes; the point of time indicated by a clock etc.; a particular time; 15° of longitude; (*pl.*) times appointed for work, attendance at office etc.; in the Roman Catholic Church, certain prayers to be said at fixed times of the day; the distance travelled in an hour; (*Myth.*) goddesses of the seasons and hours. **at all hours,** at all times. **at the eleventh hour,** at the last moment (with alln. to the parable of the vineyard, Matt. xx). **on the hour,** at exactly one, two etc. o'clock. **the hour,** the present time. **the small hours,** the early hours of the morning. **to keep good** or **regular hours,** to be home at night early or punctually. **hour-angle,** *n.* the angular distance of a heavenly body east or west of the meridian. **hour-circle,** *n.* a great circle passing through the celestial poles, a meridian (24 of which are usu. marked on the globe); a circle on an equatorial telescope indicating the hour-angle of an object. **hour-glass,** *n.* a glass having two bulbs and a connecting opening through which the sand in one bulb runs into the other, used for measuring small periods of time. *a.* of a woman's figure, having a narrow waist and large bust and hips. **hour-hand,** *n.* that hand which shows the hour on a clock or watch, dist. from minute-hand. **hourplate,** *n.* the dial of a clock or watch. **hourly,** *a.* happening or done every hour; continual. *adv.* hour by hour; frequently. [OF *hure, ure,* L, Gr. *hōra,* hour]

houri, *n.* a nymph of the Muslim paradise; a beautiful woman. [F, from Pers. *hūrī,* from Arab. *haurā,* having gazelle-like eyes]

house[1], *n.* a building for shelter or residence; a dwelling, a place of abode; a building used for a specified purpose (as *bake-house, carriage-house, coffee-house, farm-house, hen-house, public-house, warehouse*); the abode of a religious fraternity, a monastery; the fraternity itself; a household; a family or stock, esp. a noble family; an assembly, esp. one of the legislative assemblies of a country; a quorum of a legislative body; a theatre; the audience at a place of entertainment; manner of living, table; a commercial establishment; a square on a chess-board; the game of lotto; the station of a planet in the heavens; a twelfth part of the heavens; (*usu.* **House**) a type of disco or pop music characterized by electronically synthesized effects. **a halfway house,** a compromise. **house and home,** an emphatic expression for home. **house of call,** a house where journeymen of a particular trade meet when out of employment, and where they may be engaged. **house of cards,** a structure built of playing cards; any scheme or enterprise of an insecure or precarious kind. **house of correction,** a prison; a penitentiary. **house of God,** a church, a place of worship. **house of ill fame,** a brothel. †**house of office,** a privy. **house of the ascendant** ASCENDANT. **house-to-house,** performed at every house (of an enquiry etc.). **like a house on fire,** very quickly and successfully. **on the house,** esp. of alcoholic drinks, given for no payment. **(as) safe as houses,** completely safe. **the House,** Christ Church, a college of Oxford Univ.; (*coll.*) the Stock Exchange; (*euphem.*) the workhouse. **to bring down the house** BRING. **to keep house,** to maintain or manage a household. **to keep open house,** to provide hospitality for all comers. **to keep the house,** to be confined through illness. **to put, set etc. one's house in order,** to settle one's affairs. **house-agent,** *n.* one who sells and lets houses, collects rents etc. **house arrest,** *n.* detention in one's own home under guard. **house-boat,** *n.* a boat or barge with a cabin or house for living in. **house-bote,** *n.* the amount of wood for repairs and fuel which a tenant is allowed to take from the land. **housebound,** *a.* unable to leave one's house, e.g. because of a disability. **housebreaker,** *n.* one who breaks into and robs houses in daytime; a workman employed to pull down houses. **housebreaking,** *n.* **house-broken,** *a.* HOUSE-TRAINED. **house-coat,** *n.* a woman's long over-garment, worn in the house. **house-dog,** *n.* a dog kept to guard the house. **house-father,** *n.* a man in charge of children in an institution. **house-flag,** *n.* (*Naut.*) the particular flag of an owner or firm. **house-fly,** *n.* the common fly, *Musca domestica*. **house guest,** *n.* a guest in a private house. **house-husband,** *n.* a married man who stays at home to run a household instead of having a paid job. **houseleek,** *n.* a plant with thick, fleshy leaves, *Sempervivum tectorum,* growing on the tops of walls and houses in Britain. **houseman,** *n.* HOUSE-SURGEON. **house martin,** *n.* a black and white bird, *Delichon urbica,* with a forked tail, resembling a swallow. **housemaster** *n.* a master in charge of a house of residence at a boarding-school. **housemistress,** *n.* **house-minder,** *n.* HOUSE-SITTER. **housemind,** *v.i.* **house-mother,** *n.* a woman in charge of children in an institution. **houseparent,** *n.* a house-father or house-mother. **house-party,** *n.* a party of guests at a country house. **house-physician** HOUSE-SURGEON. **house plant,** *n.* a plant for growing indoors. **house-proud,** *a.* taking a pride in the care and embellishment of a home. **house-room,** *n.* accommodation in a house. **house-sitter,** *n.* a person who stays in a house to look after it while the occupier is away. **house-sit,** *v.i.* **house-sparrow,** *n.* the common sparrow, *Passer domesticus*. **house-steward,** *n.* one who manages the internal affairs of a large establishment. **house-surgeon, -physician,** *n.* the resident surgeon or physician in a hospital. **house-tax,** *n.* a tax on inhabited houses. **house-top,** *n.* the top or roof of a house. **house-trained,** *a.* of an animal, trained not to foul places indoors; of a person, well-mannered. **house-warming,** *n.* a feast or merry-making on going into a new house. **house-work,** *n.* work connected with housekeeping. **house-wright,** *n.* one who builds houses. †**housage**, *n.* rent or charge for housing goods. **houseful,** *n.* as many or as much as a house will hold. **houseless,** *a.* destitute of house or shelter. [OE *hūs* (cp. Dut. *huis*, Icel. *hūs*, G *Haus*)]

house[2], *v.t.* to place or store in a house; to lodge, contain; to shelter; (*Naut.*) to put (a gun) in a secure state or position. *v.i.* to have a lodging, to dwell; to take shelter. [OE *hūsian,* as prec.]

household, *n.* those who live together under the same roof and compose a family; a domestic establishment; (*pl.*) flour of the second quality, seconds. *a.* pertaining to the house and family, domestic. **household bread,** *n.* bread made in the house; bread of the second quality. **household gods,** *n.pl.* (*Rom. Ant.*) the lares and penates; (*fig.*) the most valued possessions of a home. **household troops,** *n.pl.* troops specially employed to guard the person of the sovereign. **household name, word,** *n.* a familiar name or word. **householder,** *n.* the head of a household, the occupier of a house.

housekeeper, *n.* a female servant who manages the affairs of a household; a person in charge of a house, place of business etc.; †a householder; †one who keeps at home. **housekeeping,** *n.* the care of a household; domestic economy.

†**housel,** *n.* the Eucharist. *v.t.* to administer the sacrament to; to prepare for a journey. **houseling, housling,** *n., a.* [OE *hūsel* (cp. Icel. *hūsl,* Goth. *hunsl,* a sacrifice)]

housemaid, *n.* a female servant employed to keep a house clean etc., esp. one in charge of reception-rooms and bedrooms. **housemaid's knee,** inflammation of the knee-cap, due to much kneeling.

housewife, *n.* a married woman who stays at home to run a household instead of having a paid job; a domestic manager; a case for holding pins, needles and the like. **housewifely,** *a.* pertaining to a housewife or good domestic management, thrifty. *adv.* like a housewife, thriftily. **housewifery**, *n.* the business of a housewife; female management of domestic affairs.

housey-housey, BINGO[2].

housing[1], *n.* lodging, shelter, accommodation.

housing[2], *n.* a cloth covering for a horse; (*pl.*) trappings for horses. [OF *houce*]

housing association, *n.* a non profit-making body which builds or renovates dwellings and lets them at a reasonable rent. **housing estate,** *n.* a planned residential area; such an estate built by a local authority.

Housman, *n.* **A(lfred) E(dward)** (1859–1936), English poet and classical scholar. His *A Shropshire Lad* (1896), a series of deceptively simple nostalgic ballad-like poems, was popular during World War I. It was followed by *Last Poems* (1922), and *More Poems* (1936).

Houston[1], *n.* port in Texas, US; population (1981) 2,891,000; linked by canal to the Gulf of Mexico. It is an agricultural centre, and industries include petrochemicals, chemicals, plastics, synthetic rubber, and electronics.

Houston[2], *n.* **Sam** (1793–1863), US general who won Texas' independence from Mexico 1836 and was president of the Republic of Texas (1836–45). Houston, Texas, is named after him.

houyhnhnm, *n.* one of the race of horses with the finer human characteristics, in Swift's *Gulliver's Travels.* [imit., coined by Jonathan *Swift,* Anglo-Irish satirist, 1667–1745]

Hova, *n.* one of the dominant class in Madagascar. [Malagasy]

hove[1], *past* HEAVE.

hove[2], *v.t.* to heave, to swell, to inflate. (*Sc.*) [prob. from HEAVE]

†**hove**[3], *v.i.* to hover; to linger, to remain about (as lying in wait). [etym. unknown]

hovel, *n.* a shed or outhouse open at the sides; a miserable dwelling-house; a conical building enclosing the ovens in a porcelain-factory. *v.t.* to shelter in or as in a hovel; to carry up the exposed sides of (a chimney) so as to prevent smoking. [etym. doubtful]

Hovell, *n.* **William Hilton** (1786–1875), explorer of Australia with Hamilton Hume.

hoveller, *n.* an unlicensed boatman or pilot, esp. one who plunders wrecks; a small coaster. [etym. doubtful]

hover, *v.i.* to hang or remain (over or about) fluttering in the air or on the wing; to loiter (about); to be irresolute, to waver. **Hovercraft®,** *n.* an aircraft supported above land or water on a cushion of air which it generates itself. **hoverfly,** *n.* any brightly-coloured fly of the family Syrphidae, which hover and dart. **hoverport,** *n.* a place where passengers enter and leave hovercraft. [prob. from HOVE[3]]

how[1], *adv.* in what way or manner; by what means; to what extent, degree etc.; in what proportion; in what condition; by what name; at what price. *n.* the way, manner, means (of becoming, happening, doing etc.). **and how!** *int.* (*sl.*) and how much more! **how about?** used to suggest a possible choice. **how come?** (*coll.*) how does it, did that etc. happen? **how-do-you-do?** how are you? a conventional form of greeting. **how-d'ye-do,** *n.* (*coll.*) an awkward situation. **how's that?** used in cricket to ask for the batsman to be given out. **howbeit,** †**howbe,** *adv.* nevertheless, however it may be. **however,** *adv.* in whatever manner or degree; †at all events; nevertheless, notwithstanding. **howsoever,** *adv.* in whatsoever manner; however; to what extent or degree soever; †at all events. **how-to,** *a.* (*coll.*) of a book etc. containing instructions on how things are done. [OE *hū* (cp. Dut. *hoe*), cogn. with WHO]

how[2], *n.* (*North.*) a hill, esp. a low one; a hillock; a barrow or tumulus. [Icel. *haugr,* prob. cogn. with HIGH]

how[3], HOWE.

Howard[1], *n.* **Catherine** (*c.* 1520–1542), queen consort of Henry VIII of England from 1540. In 1541 the archbishop of Canterbury, Thomas Cranmer, accused her of being unchaste before marriage to Henry, and she was beheaded (1542) after Cranmer made further charges of adultery.

Howard[2], *n.* **Charles, 2nd Baron Howard of Effingham and 1st Earl of Nottingham** (1536–1624), English admiral, a cousin of Queen Elizabeth I. He commanded the fleet against the Spanish Armada while Lord High Admiral (1585–1618).

Howard[3], *n.* **Ebenezer** (1850–1928), English town planner and founder of the ideal of the garden city, through his book *Tomorrow* (1898) (republished as *Garden Cities of Tomorrow*, 1902).

Howard[4], *n.* **John** (1726–90), English philanthropist whose work to improve prison conditions is continued today by the Howard League for Penal Reform.

Howard[5], *n.* **Trevor (Wallace)** (1916–89), English actor, whose films include *Brief Encounter* (1945), *Sons and Lovers* (1960), *Mutiny on the Bounty* (1962), *Ryan's Daughter* (1970), and *Conduct Unbecoming* (1975).

howdah, *n.* a seat, usu. canopied, carried on an elephant's back. [Pers. *haudah,* Arab. *haudaj*]

howdy[1], *n.* (*esp. N Am.*) a greeting. [short for HOW-D'YE-DO, see HOW[1]]

howdy[2], **-die,** (*Sc.*) *n.* a midwife. [etym. doubtful]

howe, *n.* (*Sc.*) a hollow, a valley, a dell. [prob. from OE *hol,* HOLE[1]]

Howe[1], *n.* **Elias** (1819–67), US inventor, in 1846, of a sewing machine using double thread.

Howe[2], *n.* **Geoffrey** (1926–), British Conservative politician. Under Heath he was solicitor-general 1970–72 and minister for trade 1972–74; as chancellor of the Exchequer 1979–83 under Thatcher, he put into practice the monetarist policy which reduced inflation at the cost of a rise in unemployment. In 1983 he became foreign secretary, and in 1989 he unexpectedly became deputy prime minister and leader of the House of Commons.

Howe[3], *n.* **James Wong** (1899–1976), adopted name of Wong Tung Jim, Chinese-born director of film photography, who lived in the US from childhood. One of Hollywood's best camera operators, he is credited with introducing the use of hand-held cameras and deep focus. His work ranges from *The Alaskan* (1924) to *Funny Lady* (1975).

Howe[4], *n.* **William, 5th Viscount Howe** (1729–1814), British general. During the War of American Independence he won the Battle of Bunker Hill 1775, and as commander-in-chief in America 1776–78 captured New York and defeated Washington at Brandywine and Germantown. He resigned in protest at lack of home government support.

Howells, *n.* **William Dean** (1837–1920), US novelist and editor. The 'dean' of US letters in the post-Civil War era, and editor of the *Atlantic Monthly*, he championed the realist movement in fiction and encouraged many younger authors. He wrote 35 novels, 35 plays, and many books of poetry, essays, and commentary.

however HOW[1].

howff, *n.* (*Sc.*) a resort, a haunt; a meeting place; a public house. *v.i.* to frequent a place. [etym. doubtful]

howitzer, *n.* a short, light or heavy piece of ordnance with a high trajectory and low muzzle velocity. [formerly *howitz, G Haublitze,* Boh. *haufnice,* sling]

howk, *v.t.* (*Sc.*) to dig (up or out). *v.i.* to burrow. [cogn. with HOLE]

howker, HOOKER.

howl, *v.i.* to utter a protracted hollow cry; to cry as a dog or wolf; to wail; to make a wailing sound like the wind. *v.t.* to utter in wailing or mournful tones. *n.* the cry of a wolf or dog; a protracted, hollow cry, esp. one of anguish, distress or derision. **howler,** *n.* one who howls; a S American monkey, *Mycetes ursinus;* (*coll.*) a ludicrous blunder. **howling,** *a.* that howls; wild and dreary (of a desert etc.); (*sl.*) extreme, glaring. [ME *houlen,* imit. (cp. Dut. *huilen,* Icel. *ȳla,* G *heulen,* also L *ululāre,* Gr. *hulaein*)]

howlet, *n.* an owlet. [perh. from F *hulotte,* or from OWL]

howsoever HOW[1].

†**hox,** *v.t.* to hock, to hamstring. [earlier *hoxen,* OE *hōhseono* (*hōh,* HOUGH, *seono,* SINEW)]

Hoxha, *n.* **Enver** (1908–85), Albanian Communist politician, the country's leader from 1954. He founded the Albanian Communist Party 1941, and headed the liberation movement 1939–44. He was prime minister 1944–54, combining with foreign affairs 1946–53, and from 1954 was first secretary of the Albanian Party of Labour. In policy he was a Stalinist, and independent of both Chinese and Soviet communism.

hoy[1], *n.* a one-masted coasting-vessel; a barge or lighter (usu. distinguished as *anchor-hoy*, *gun-hoy* etc.). [MDut. *hoei*, etym. doubtful]

hoy[2], *int.* an exclamation to draw attention etc.; (*Naut.*) a hail. [cp. Dut. and Dan. *hui*]

hoya, *n.* a genus of tropical climbing shrubs with pink, white or yellow flowers, called by gardeners wax-flowers. [Thomas *Hoy*, *d.* 1821, gardener]

hoyden, *n.* a boisterous girl; a romp; †a clown, a lout. *a.* boisterous, bold. *v.i.* to romp roughly or indecently. **hoydenhood**, **hoydenism,** *n.* **hoydenish,** *a.* **hoydenishness,** *n.* [etym. doubtful]

Hoyle, *n.* **Fred(erick)** (1915–), English astronomer and writer. In 1948 he joined with Hermann Bondi and Thomas Gold in developing the steady-state theory. In 1957, with Geoffrey and Margaret Burbidge and William Fowler, he showed that chemical elements heavier than hydrogen and helium are built up by nuclear reactions inside stars. He has created controversy by suggesting that life originates in the gas clouds of space, and is delivered to the Earth by passing comets.

HP, hp, (*abbr.*) high pressure; horsepower; hire purchase; Houses of Parliament.

HQ, (*abbr.*) headquarters.

HR, (*abbr.*) Home Rule; House of Representatives.

HRH, (*abbr.*) His/Her Royal Highness.

HRT, (*abbr.*) hormone replacement therapy.

hrw, (*abbr.*) heated rear window (of a car).

Hsuan Tung, *n.* name adopted by Henry P'U-I on becoming emperor of China 1908.

ht, (*abbr.*) high tension.

Hua Guofeng, *n.* (formerly **Hua Kuofeng**) (1920–), Chinese politician, leader of the Chinese Communist Party (CCP) 1976–81, premier 1976–80. He dominated Chinese politics 1976–77, seeking economic modernization without major structural reform. From 1978 he was gradually eclipsed by Deng Xiaoping. Hua was ousted from the Politburo Sept. 1982, but remained a member of the CCP Central Committee.

Huallaga River, *n.* a tributary of the Marayon in NE Peru. The upper reaches of the river valley are renowned for the growing of coca, a major source of the drug cocaine.

Huang He *n.* (formerly **Hwang-ho**), river in China; length 5,464 km/3,395 miles. It gains its name (meaning 'yellow river') from its muddy waters. Formerly known as 'China's sorrow' because of disastrous floods, it is now largely controlled through hydro-electric works and flood barriers.

Huáscar, *n.* (*c.* 1495–1532), king of the Incas. He shared the throne with his half-brother Atahualpa from 1525, but the latter overthrew and murdered him during the Spanish conquest.

hub[1], *n.* the central part of a wheel from which the spokes radiate, the nave; a place of central importance; a mark at which quoits are thrown. **hub-cap,** *n.* a (decorative) plate or disk covering the hub of a wheel. [etym. unknown]

hub[2], **hubby**, *n.* (*coll.*) husband.

Hubbard, *n.* **L(afayette) Ron(ald)** (1911–86), US science-fiction writer of the 1930s–1940s, founder in 1954 of Scientology.

Hubble, *n.* **Edwin Powell** (1889–1953), US astronomer, who discovered the existence of other galaxies outside our own, and classified them according to their shape. He proposed that the universe was expanding, a theory since confirmed. **Hubble's constant,** *n.* in astronomy, a measure of the rate at which the universe is expanding, named after Edwin Hubble. Modern observations suggest that galaxies are moving apart at a rate of 50–100 km/30–60 miles per second for every million parsecs of distance. This would mean that the universe, which began at one place according to the Big Bang theory, is between 10 billion and 20 billion years old.

hubble bubble, *n.* a tobacco-pipe in which the smoke is drawn through water, making a bubbling noise, a kind of hookah; a bubbling noise; a hubbub, an uproar; a jabbering or chattering. [onomat.]

hubbub, *n.* a confused noise; a noisy disturbance; a tumult, an uproar. **hubbuboo,** *n.* a howling; a hubbub. [onomat., perh. suggested by an Irish word]

hubby, *n.* HUB[2].

Hubei, *n.* (formerly **Hupei**) province of central China, through which flow the Chang Jiang and its tributary the Han Shui. **area** 187,500 sq km/72,375 sq miles. **capital** Wuhan. **population** (1986) 49,890,000. **products** beans, cereals, cotton, rice, vegetables, copper, gypsum, iron ore, phosphorus, salt.

hubris, *n.* insolent pride or security, arrogance. **hubristic,** *a.* [Gr.]

huckaback, *n.* a coarse linen or cotton cloth, with a rough surface, used for table-cloths and towels. [etym. doubtful]

huckle, *n.* the hip, the haunch. **huckle-backed, -shouldered,** *a.* (*dial.*) round-shouldered. **huckle-bone,** *n.* the hip-bone; the knuckle-bone or astragalus in a quadruped. [prob. dim. of obs. *huck*, which Skeat identifies with HOCK[1], see HOUGH]

huckleberry, *n.* the edible fruit of species of *Gaylussacia*, low shrubs of the family Vacciniaceae, bearing dark-blue berries; the fruit of the blueberry and other species of the allied Vaccinium. [prob. corr. of HURTLEBERRY]

huckster, *n.* a retailer of small goods, a pedlar, a hawker; a mean, trickish, mercenary fellow; (*N Am.*) a person who produces advertising material for radio or TV. *v.i.* to deal in petty goods; to bargain, to haggle. †**hucksterage,** *n.* petty dealing; higgling, bargaining. **hucksterer,** *n.* **hucksteress,** *n. fem.* **huckstery,** *n.* [etym. doubtful (conn. by Skeat with MDut. *hucken*, to stoop or bow, cp. Icel. *hokra* and HAWKER[2])]

huddle, *v.t.* to throw or crowd (together, up etc.) promiscuously; to do or make hastily and carelessly; to coil (oneself up) anyhow; to put (on) hurriedly or anyhow. *v.i.* to gather or crowd (up or together) promicuously; to hurry. *n.* a confused crowd; disorder, confusion; (*coll.*) a secretive discussion between a group of people. [cp. LG *hudern*, to shelter, to cover up (*hûden*, to HIDE)]

Hudibrastic, *a.* resembling *Hudibras* in style or metre. [Butler's *Hudibras* (1663–78), a satire against the Puritans]

Hudson[1], *n.* **Henry** (*c.* 1565– *c.* 1611), English explorer. Under the auspices of the Muscovy Company 1607–08, he made two unsuccessful attempts to find the Northeast passage to China. In Sept. 1609, commissioned by the Dutch East India Company, he reached New York Bay and sailed 240 km/150 miles up the river that now bears his name, establishing Dutch claims to the area. In 1610, he sailed from London in the *Discovery* and entered what is now the Hudson Strait. After an icebound winter, he was turned adrift by a mutinous crew in what is now Hudson Bay.

Hudson[2], *n.* **Rock** (1925–85), stage name of Roy Scherer Jr., US film actor, a big star from the mid-1950s to the mid-1960s, seen at his best in several melodramas directed by Douglas Sirk and three comedies co-starring Doris Day (including *Pillow Talk*, 1959).

Hudson[3], *n.* **W(illiam) H(enry)** (1841–1922), Anglo-US author, born of US parents at Florencio near Buenos Aires, Argentina. He was inspired by recollections of early days in Argentina to write the romances *The Purple Land* (1885) and *Green Mansions* (1904), and his autobiographical *Far Away and Long Ago* (1918). He wrote several books on birds, and on the English countryside, for example, *Nature in Down-Land* (1900) and *A Shepherd's Life* (1910).

Hudson Bay, *n.* inland sea of NE Canada, linked with the Atlantic by Hudson Strait, and with the Arctic by Foxe Channel; area 1,233,000 sq km/476,000 sq miles. It is named after Henry Hudson.

Hudson's Bay Company, *n.* a chartered company founded by Prince Rupert 1670 to trade in furs with

North American Indians. In 1783 the rival North West Company was formed, but in 1851 this became amalgamated with the Hudson's Bay Company. It is still Canada's biggest fur company, but today also sells general merchandise in towns through department stores and has oil and natural gas interests.

hue¹, *n.* colour, tint; a compound colour, esp. one in which a primary predominates. **hued,** *a.* having a particular hue (*esp. in comb.*, as *light-hued*). **hueless,** *a.* [OE *hīw* (cp. Swed. *hy,* Goth. *hiwi,* form, appearance)]

†**hue²,** *n.* a loud shout or cry, a clamour. **hue and cry,** *n.* (*Law*) a cry or general summons to pursue a felon or offender; a clamour or outcry (against); a great stir or alarm. **huer,** *n.* (*now chiefly Cornish*) a person stationed on a high point to give notice of the movements of a shoal of fish. [OF *hu* (*huer,* to shout), imit.]

huff, *v.t.* †to blow or puff (*usu. with* up); to bully, to hector; in draughts, to remove (one's opponent's piece) from the board when he omits to capture with it; (*usu. in p.p.*) to offend. *v.i.* to take offence; †to be puffed up, to bluster. *n.* a sudden fit of anger or petulance; (*Draughts*) the act of huffing; †a boaster, a braggart. **huffer,** *n.* a blusterer. **huffish, huffy,** *a.* **huffily, huffishly,** *adv.* **huffiness, huffishness,** *n.* [imit.]

hug, *v.t.* (*past, p.p.* **hugged**) to embrace closely; to clasp or squeeze tightly; to hold fast or cling to, to cherish; to congratulate (oneself); of a ship, to keep close to (the shore). †*v.i.* to cuddle, to huddle, to lie close. *n.* a close embrace, a particular grip in wrestling. **huggable,** *a.* **to hug oneself,** to congratulate oneself complacently. **hug-me-tight,** *n.* a woollen wrap or shawl. [etym. doubtful]

huge, *a.* very large; enormous, immense. **hugely,** *adv.* in a huge manner; (*coll.*) exceedingly, extremely. **hugeness,** *n.* [OF *ahuge,* etym. unknown]

hugger-mugger, *n.* secrecy, privacy, disorder, confusion. *a.* clandestine; confused, slovenly. *adv.* secretly, clandestinely; confusedly. *v.i.* to act clandestinely; to muddle. *v.t.* to hush up. [prob. rhyming redupl. of HUG]

Hughes¹, *n.* **Howard** (1905–76), US tycoon. Inheriting wealth from his father, who had patented a successful oil-drilling bit, he created a legendary financial empire. A skilled pilot, he manufactured and designed aircraft, and made the classic film *Hell's Angels* (1930) about aviators of World War I; later successes include *Scarface* (1932) and *The Outlaw* (1943). From his middle years he was a recluse.

Hughes², *n.* **Richard (Arthur Warren)** (1900–76), English writer. His study of childhood, *A High Wind in Jamaica*, was published 1929, and the trilogy *The Human Predicament* 1961–73.

Hughes³, *n.* **Ted** (1930–), English poet, Poet Laureate from 1984. His work includes *The Hawk in the Rain* (1957), *Lupercal* (1960), *Wodwo* (1967), and *River* (1983), and is characterized by its harsh portrayal of the crueller aspects of nature. He was born in Mytholmroyd, West Yorkshire. In 1956 he married the poet Sylvia Plath.

Hughes⁴, *n.* **Thomas** (1822–96), English writer of the children's book *Tom Brown's School Days* (1857), a story of Rugby school under Thomas Arnold. It had a sequel, *Tom Brown at Oxford* (1861).

Hughes⁵, *n.* **William Morris** (1864–1952), Australian politician, prime minister 1915–23; originally Labor, he headed a national cabinet. After resigning as prime minister 1923, he held many other cabinet posts 1934–41.

Hugo, *n.* **Victor (Marie)** (1802–85), French poet, novelist, and dramatist. The *Odes et poésies diverses* appeared 1822, and his verse play *Hernani* (1830) established him as the leader of French romanticism. More volumes of verse followed between his series of dramatic novels which included *The Hunchback of Notre Dame* (1831) and *Les Misérables* (1862). Originally a monarchist, he became in later years an ardent republican, and was a senator under the Third Republic. He died a national hero.

Huguenot, *n.* French Protestant in the 16th cent.; the term referred mainly to Calvinists. Severely persecuted under Francis I and Henry II, the Huguenots survived both an attempt to exterminate them (the Massacre of St Bartholomew, 24 Aug. 1572) and the religious wars of the next 30 years. In 1598 Henry IV (himself formerly a Huguenot) granted them toleration under the Edict of Nantes. Louis XIV revoked the edict, 1685, attempting their forcible conversion, and 400,000 emigrated. **Huguenotism,** *n.*

huh, *int.* used to express surprise, contempt disbelief etc.

Huhehot, *n.* former name of HOHHOT.

huia-bird, *n.* a New Zealand bird of the starling family. [Maori]

hula, *n.* a Hawaiian dance performed by women. **Hula Hoop®,** *n.* a light hoop kept in motion by swinging round the waist. **hula skirt,** *n.* a grass skirt worn by hula dancers. [HAWAIIAN].

hulk, *n.* the hull or body of a ship, especially an unseaworthy one; an old ship used as a store, formerly as a prison, or for other purposes; a bulky and unwieldy ship; any unwieldy object or person. **the hulks,** *n.pl.* old dismasted ships formerly used as convict prisons. **hulking,** *a.* bulky, unwieldy, awkward. [OE *hulc* (cp. late L *hulka,* OF *hulke,* Dut. *hulk*), perh. from Gr. *holkos,* a ship that is towed, from *helkein,* to draw]

hull¹, *n.* the outer covering of anything, especially of a nut or seed; the pod, shell or husk. *v.t.* to strip the hull or husk off. **hully,** *a.* having hulls or husks. [OE *hulu,* cogn. with *helan,* to HELE]

hull², *n.* the body of a ship. *v.t.* to pierce the hull of with a cannon-ball. *v.i.* to float or drive to and fro helplessly, like a dismasted ship. **hull down,** *adv.* of a ship, so far off that only the masts and sail are visible. [prob. the same as prec., but confused with HOLE¹, HOLD³]

Hull¹, *n.* (officially **Kingston upon Hull**), city and port, through which the river Humber flows, administrative headquarters of Humberside, England; population (1986) 258,000. It is linked with the south bank of the estuary by the Humber Bridge. Industries include fish processing, vegetable oils, flour milling, electricals, textiles, paint, pharmaceuticals, chemicals, caravans, and aircraft.

Hull², *n.* **Cordell** (1871–1955), US Democrat politician, born in Tennessee. He was a member of Congress 1907–33, and, as Roosevelt's secretary of state 1933–44, was identified with the Good Neighbour Policy of non-intervention in Latin America, and opposed German and Japanese aggression. In his last months of office he paved the way for a system of collective security, for which he was called 'father' of the United Nations. Nobel peace prize 1945.

hullabaloo, *n.* an uproar. [redupl. of HULLO]

hullo, -loa HALLO.

Hulme, *n.* **Keri** (1947–), New Zealand novelist. She won the Booker Prize with her first novel *The Bone People* (1985).

hum¹, *v.i.* (*past, p.p.* **hummed**) to make a prolonged murmuring sound like a bee; to sing with the lips closed; to make an inarticulate sound in speaking, from embarrassment or hesitation; (*sl.*) to smell unpleasant. *v.t.* to utter in a low murmuring voice, to applaud, disapprove etc. by emitting such a sound. *n.* a low droning or murmuring sound; the act of humming; an inarticulate expression of hesitation, disapproval etc.; †strong ale mixed with spirits, **to hum and ha,** to hesitate in speaking; to refrain from giving a decided answer. **to make things hum,** to stir (people etc.) into activity (prob. from the humming of a top spinning rapidly). **hummer,** *n.* one who or that which hums; a humming insect; a humming-bird. [imit.]

hum², *int.* expressing hesitation, disapproval, etc. [var. of HEM²]

†**hum³,** *v.t.* (*sl.*) to impose upon; to humbug. *n.* a hoax, a humbug. [identified with prec. by Skeat]

human, *a.* pertaining to man or mankind; having the

nature; qualities or characteristics of man; of or pertaining to mankind as dist. from divine, animal or material. *n.* (*coll.*) a human being. **human being,** *n.* a member of the human race; a person. **human nature,** *n.* all those characteristics considered typical of human beings, esp. the weaknesses. **human rights,** *n.pl.* the rights of an individual to freedom of speech, freedom of movement, justice etc. **Universal Declaration of Human Rights,** charter of civil and political rights drawn up by the United Nations 1948. They include the right to life, liberty, education, and equality before the law; to freedom of movement, religion, association, and information; and to a nationality. Under the European Convention of Human Rights 1950, the Council of Europe established the **European Commission of Human Rights** (headquarters in Strasbourg, France), which investigates complaints by states or individuals, and its findings are examined by the **European Court of Human Rights** (established 1959), whose compulsory jurisdiction has been recognized by a number of states, including the UK. **humankind,** *n.* mankind, the human race. **humanly,** *adv.* after the manner of men; according to the knowledge or capacity of men; from the human point of view. **humanness,** *n.* **humanoid,** *a.* like a human in form or attributes. **humanoid,** *n.* [MF *humain,* L *hūmānus,* cogn. with HOMO]

humane, *a.* having the feelings proper to man; tender, compassionate, kind, gentle; elevating, refining; polite, elegant; relieving distress, aiding those in danger etc. **humane killer,** *n.* an instrument for slaughtering animals painlessly. **Humane Society,** *n.* a society that campaigns for humane behaviour, esp. in the treatment of animals. **humanely,** *adv.* **humaneness,** *n.* [as prec., differentiated in meaning late]

humanism, *n.* a moral or intellectual system that regards the interests of mankind as of supreme importance, in contradistinction to individualism or theism; humanitarianism; devotion to humanity or human interests; culture derived from literature, esp. the Greek and Latin classics. **humanist,** *n.* one versed in human history or the knowledge of human nature; one versed in the humanities, esp. one of the classical scholars of Renaissance times. **humanist, -istic,** *a.* **humanistically,** *adv.*

humanitarian, *a.* humane; pertaining to the humanitarians. *n.* one who professes the 'Religion of Humanity'; one who believes that Christ was a mere man; one who believes in the perfectibility of humanity; a philanthropist. **humanitarianism,** *n.* [foll., -ARIAN]

humanity, *n.* human nature; (*collect.*) mankind, the human race; kindness, benevolence, humaneness; humanism; (*Sc.*) Latin and Latin literature, in contradistinction to divinity; †good breeding, politeness. **the humanities,** *n.pl.* the study of literature, music, history etc. distinguished from social or natural sciences. **humanize, ise,** *v.t.* to render human; to give human character or expression to; to render humane. *v.i.* to become human or humane. **humanization, -isation,** *n.* [F *humanité,* L *hūmānitātem,* nom. *-tas,* from *hūmānus,* HUMAN]

humanoid HUMAN.

Humber Bridge, *n.* a suspension bridge with twin towers 163 m/535 ft. high, which spans the estuary of the river Humber in NE England. When completed 1980, it was the world's longest bridge with a span of 1410 m/4628 ft.

Humberside, *n.* county of NE England. **area** 3510 sq km/1355 sq miles. **towns** administrative headquarters Kingston upon Hull; Grimsby, Scunthorpe, Goole, Cleethorpes. **population** (1987) 847,000. **products** petrochemicals, refined oil, processed fish, cereals, root crops, cattle.

humble[1], *a.* having or showing a sense of lowliness or inferiority, modest; of lowly condition, kind, dimensions etc.; submissive, deferential. *v.t.* to lower; to bring to a state of subjection or inferiority; to abase. **humble-mouthed,** *a.* humble in speech. **humble pie,** *n.* a pie made of the umbles or entrails of the deer. **to eat humble pie,** to submit oneself to humiliation or insult; to apologize humbly (the phrase is said to have arisen from the fact that at hunting-feasts humble pie was given to the menials). **humble plant,** *n.* the sensitive plant, *Mimosa pudica.* **humbleness, †humblesse,** *n.* **humbler,** *n.* **humbly,** *adv.* [OF, from L *humilis, -lem,* from HUMUS]

humble[2], HUMMEL.

humble-bee, *n.* a bumble-bee. [obs. *humble,* freq. of HUM[1], BEE]

Humboldt, *n.* **Friedrich Heinrich Alexander, Baron von Humboldt** (1769–1859), German botanist and geologist who explored the regions of the Orinoco and the Amazon in S America 1800–04, and gathered 60,000 plant specimens. On his return, Humboldt devoted 21 years to writing an account of his travels.

humbug, *n.* a hoax; an imposition under fair pretences; a spirit of deception or trickery, sham; an impostor; a sweet highly flavoured with peppermint. *int.* nonsense. *v.t.* (*past, p.p.* **humbugged**) to impose upon, to hoax; to take in; to cajole (into, out of etc.). *v.i.* to behave in a fraudulent or misleading manner. **humbuggable,** *a.* **humbugger,** *n.* **humbuggery,** *n.* [etym. doubtful]

humbuzz, *n.* (*dial.*) the cockchafer; a piece of notched wood whirled swiftly round to make a humming sound, also called a bull-roarer.

humdinger, *n.* (*coll.*) an excellent person or thing.

humdrum, *a.* dull, commonplace, tedious. *n.* a dull, stupid fellow; dull, tedious talk; dullness. *v.i.* to proceed or while away the time in a humdrum manner. **humdrumness,** *n.*

humdudgeon, *n.* (*Sc.*) a causeless outcry; an imaginary illness.

Hume[1], *n.* **Basil** (1923–), British Roman Catholic cardinal from 1976. A Benedictine monk, he was abbot of Ampleforth in Yorkshire 1963–76, and in 1976 became archbishop of Westminster, the first monk to hold the office.

Hume[2], *n.* **David** (1711–76), Scottish philosopher. *A Treatise of Human Nature* (1740) is a central text of British empiricism. Hume denies the possibility of going beyond the subjective experiences of 'ideas' and 'impressions'. The effect of this position is to invalidate metaphysics. **Humean,** *a.* of or pertaining to his philosophical doctrines. **Humism,** *n.* **Humist,** *n.*

Hume[3], *n.* **Joseph** (1777–1855), British Radical politician. Born at Montrose, Scotland, he went out to India as an army surgeon in 1797, made a fortune, and on his return bought a seat in Parliament. In 1818 he secured election as a Philosophic Radical and supported many progressive measures.

humectant, *a.* moistening. *n.* a diluent; a substance that increases the fluidity of the blood. **humectate,** *v.t.* **humectation,** *n.* a making wet or moist. **humective,** *a.* [L *hūmectans -antem,* pres.p. of *hūmectāre,* from *hūmēre,* to be moist (cp. HUMID)]

humerus, *n.* the long bone of the upper arm, articulating above with the scapula and below with the radius and the ulna; the corresponding bone in the foreleg of quadrupeds. **humeral,** *a.* pertaining to the shoulder. *n.* a humeral veil. **humeral veil,** *n.* in the Roman Catholic Church, an oblong scarf worn by priests and deacons at various ceremonies. [L, shoulder (cp. Gr. *ōmos*)]

humhum, *n.* a plain, coarse cotton Indian cloth.

Humian, HUMEAN under HUME[2].

humic, *a.* pertaining to mould or earth. **humic acid,** *n.* an acid formed from mould by the action of an alkali. **humify,** *v.i.* to turn into mould. **humification,** *n.* [from HUMUS]

humid, *a.* moist, damp; rather wet. **humidify,** *v.t.* **humidification,** *n.* **humidistat,** HYGROMETER. **humidity, †humidness,** *n.* the state of being humid; a measure of the amount of moisture in the atmosphere. **humidor,** *n.* a container constructed to keep its contents in a moist state; a box for keeping cigars moist; a contrivance for keeping the air moist. [L *hūmidus,* from *hūmēre,* to be moist]

humify etc. HUMIC.

humiliate, *v.t.* to lower in self-esteem, to mortify; to humble, to lower in condition, to abase. **humiliating,** *a.* **humiliation,** *n.* [L *humiliātus,* p.p. of *humiliāre* (*humilis,* HUMBLE[1])]

humility, *n.* the state of being humble; modesty, a sense of unworthiness; self-abasement. [F *humilité,* L *humilitātem* nom. *-tas,* as prec.]

Humism, etc. HUMEAN under HUME[2].

hummel, *a.* hornless (of cattle). *v.t.* to separate or free (barley) from the awns. **hummeller,** *n.* [cp. LG *Hummel,* hornless beast]

humming, *a.* that hums; of ale, strong; (*sl.*) vigorous, hard (of blows). **humming-bird,** *n.* one of the family Trochilidae, diminutive birds, mostly tropical, of brilliant plumage and very rapid flight. **humming-top,** *n.* a hollow top with a hole in the side, which emits a humming noise in spinning.

hummock, *n.* a mound or hillock, a protuberance formed by pressure in an icefield; (*N Am.*) an elevation in a swamp or bog, esp. if wooded. *v.t., v.i.* to form hummocks (of an ice-field). **hummocky,** *a.* [etym. doubtful; prob. of naut. orig. earlier than HUMP]

hummum, HAMMAM.

hummus, *n.* a kind of Middle Eastern hors d'oeuvre consisting of pureed chick-peas, sesame oil, garlic and lemon. [Turk.]

humor, HUMOUR.

humoral, *a.* pertaining to or proceeding from the bodily humours. **humoralism,** *n.* the doctrine that all diseases proceed from affections of the humours, humoral pathology. **humoralist,** *n.* **humoralistic,** *a.* **humorism,** *n.* humoralism; humorousness. [F, from L *humor,* HUMOUR]

humoresque, *n.* a musical composition of a humorous or capricious character. *a.* (*Lit.*) humorous in style. [G *Humoreske*]

humorist, *n.* one who displays humour in his conversation, writings etc.; a facetious person, a wag, a droll; a whimsical person; (*Med.*) †a humoralist. **humoristic,** *a.* [F *humoriste,* med. L *hūmorista,* as prec.]

humorous, *a.* full of humour; tending to excite laughter; jocular; whimsical, capricious, crotchety; †humoral; †humid, moist. **humorously,** *adv.* **humorousness,** *n.*

humour, (*esp. N. Am.*) **humor**, *n.* mental disposition, frame of mind, mood; bias, caprice, whim; drollery, comicality; the capacity of perceiving the ludicrous elements in life or art; playful yet sympathetic imagination or mode of regarding things, delighting in the absurdity of incongruities; moisture, animal fluids; †(*pl.*) the four bodily fluids supposed to produce diversity of temperament. *v.t.* to fall in with the humour of; to indulge, to give way to, to make concessions to. **out of humour,** in an ill-temper, displeased. **humoured,** *a.* having a certain humour (*usu. in comb.*, as *good-humoured*). **humouredly,** *adv.* **humourless,** *a.* **humoursome**, *a.* led by caprice or fancy, whimsical; humorous. **humoursomely,** *adv.* **humoursomeness,** *n.* [AF, from OF *humor* (F *humeur*), L *hūmōrem,* moisture (cp. HUMID)]

humous, HUMUS.

hump, *n.* a swelling or protuberance, esp. on the back; a rounded hillock; (*coll.*) a fit of annoyance, ill-temper or the blues. *v.t.* to make (the back) hump-shaped; (*coll.*) to carry on the back; (*sl.*) to have sexual intercourse with. *v.i.* (*sl.*) to have sexual intercourse. **over the hump,** (*coll.*) past the difficult or critical stage of something. **humpback,** *n.* a crooked back; a person having a humpback; an American whale, *Megaptera nodosa*, also called the humpbacked whale. **humpback bridge,** *n.* a small, narrow bridge with steep inclines on either side leading to its centre. **humpbacked,** *a.* **humped,** *a.* having a hump. **humpless,** *a.* **humpy,** *a.* having many humps; (*coll.*) irritable; depressed. [cp. Dut. *homp,* Norw. *hump*]

Humperdinck, *n.* **Engelbert** (1854–1921), German composer. He wrote the operas *Hänsel and Gretel* (1893), and *Königskinder/King's Children* (1910).

humph, *int.* expressing doubt, disapproval etc. [var. of HUM[2]]

humpty-dumpty, *n.* a short, squat person; anyone or anything that having fallen down cannot be put back or mended (from the nursery rhyme in which the name stands for an egg); a low stool formed by a big cushion. *a.* short and squat; mechanical in rhythm, like nursery doggerel. [prob. HUMPY, DUMPY]

humpy, *n.* an Aborigine hut; a shack, a lean-to. [Austral. Abor.]

humus, *n.* soil or mould, esp. that largely composed of decayed vegetation. **humous,** *a.* [L, earth]

Hun, *n.* (*coll., derog.*) a German; barbarian, destroyer, savage; a member of any of a number of nomad Mongol peoples who first appeared in history in the 2nd cent. BC raiding across the Great Wall into China. They entered Europe about AD 372, settled in Hungary, and imposed their supremacy on the Ostrogoths and other Germanic peoples. Under the leadership of Attila they attacked the Byzantine Empire, invaded Gaul, and threatened Rome, but after his death in 453 their power was broken by a revolt of their subject peoples. The White Huns or Ephthalites, a kindred people, raided Persia and N India in the 5th-6th cents. **Hunnish,** *a.* [OE *Hūne,* med. L *Hunni,* prob. from native name *Chunni, Chuni*]

Hunan *n.* province of S central China. **area** 210,500 sq km/81,253 sq miles. **capital** Changsha. **population** (1985) 55,610,000. **products** rice, tea, tobacco, cotton; non-ferrous minerals.

hunch, *n.* a hump; a lump, a thick piece; a push with the elbow; an intuition. *v.t.* to crook, to arch (esp. the back); to bend or thrust out into a hump; to push with the elbow, to shove. **hunchback,** *n.* a person with a humped back. **hunchbacked,** *a.* **hunchy,** *a.* [etym. doubtful, perh. var. of HUMP]

hundred, *n.* the cardinal number representing 10 times 10; the product of 10 multiplied by 10; (*coll.*) a hundred pounds (money); an administrative division of a county in England, supposed to have originally contained 100 families or freemen. **Chiltern Hundreds** CHILTERN. **Hundred Days,** the period 20 Mar.–22 June 1815, from Napoleon's escape from Elba to his abdication. **Hundred Years' War**, the series of conflicts between England and France (1337–1453). **hundreds and thousands,** tiny strips or balls of sugar coated with different colours, used esp. for cake decoration. **hundredweight,** *n.* a weight of 112 lb av. (50·8 kg). **hundredfold,** *n.* **hundredth,** *a.* the ordinal of a hundred. *n.* one of a hundred equal parts; the one after the ninety-ninth in a series. [OE *hundred* (*hund,* hundred, *-red,* a reckoning or account, cp. G *Rede*)]

hung, *past* HANG. *a.* of an election, not resulting in a clear majority for any party; of a Parliament, produced by such an election, of a jury, unable to reach a verdict.

Hungarian, *a.* pertaining to Hungary. *n.* a native or inhabitant of Hungary; the Hungarian language, a member of the Finno-Ugric language group, spoken principally in Hungary but also in parts of Czechoslovakia, Romania, and Yugoslavia. Known as *Magyar* among its speakers, Hungarian is written in a form of the Roman alphabet in which *s* corresponds to English *sh*, and *sz* to *s*. [late L *Hungaria,* Hungary (from *Hungari, Ugri,* Magyars), -AN]

Hungary, *n.* Hungarian Republic (*Magyar Köztársaság*), country in central Europe, bordered to the N by Czechoslovakia, NE by the USSR, E by Romania, S by Yugoslavia, and W by Austria. **area** 93,032 sq km/35,910 sq miles. **capital** Budapest. **towns** Miskolc, Debrecen, Szeged, Pécs. **physical** Great Hungarian Plain covers E half of country; Bakony Forest; rivers Danube, Tisza; Lake Balaton. **population** (1988) 10,604,000 (Magyar 92%, Romany 3%, German 2.5%. A Hungarian minority in Romania has caused some friction between the two countries); annual growth rate 0%. **exports** machinery, vehicles, chemicals, textiles. **language** Hungarian (or Magyar), one of the few languages of Europe with non-Indo-European origins. It is grouped with Finnish and Estonian in the Finno-Ugrian family. **religion** Roman Catholic 50%, other Christian denominations 25%.

hunger, *n.* a craving for food; a painful sensation caused by the want of food; †a famine; any strong desire. *v.i.* to feel the pain or sensation of hunger; to crave for food; to desire or long eagerly. *v.t.* to make hungry, to starve; to compel, drive etc. (into, out of etc.) by hunger. **hunger-bitten,** *a.* pinched with hunger. **hunger march,** *n.* a march of the unemployed to protest against their lot. **hunger strike,** *n., v.i.* a refusal to take food, usu. as a protest. **hunger-striker,** *n.* †**hungered,** †**a-hungered,** *a.* hungry. †**hungerly,** *a.* hungry, weak, thin. *adv.* hungrily. [OE *hungor* (cp. Icel. *hungr,* Dut. *honger,* G *Hunger*), whence *hyngran,* to hunger]

hungry, *a.* feeling a sensation of hunger; having a keen appetite; showing hunger, emaciated, thin; causing hunger; longing or craving eagerly; barren, poor (of soil). **hungry rice,** a grain like millet raised in W Africa. **hungrily,** *adv.* **hungriness,** *n.* [OE *hungrig*]

hunk, *n.* (*coll.*) a large piece; a big, strong, sexually attractive man. [Flem. *hunke*]

hunker, *v.i.* (*Sc.*) to squat on the calves or heels. *n.pl.* the haunches. **on one's hunkers,** squatting down. [etym. doubtful; cp. Dut. *huiken,* G *hocken*]

hunks, *n.* a stingy person. [etym. doubtful]

hunky-dory, *a.* (*esp. N Am., coll.*) satisfactory, fine. [etym. doubtful]

hunt, *v.t.* to chase (as wild animals) for the purpose of catching and killing; to employ (horses, dogs etc.) in hunting; to pursue or chase in or over (a district etc.); to search for, to seek after. *v.i.* to follow the chase; to pursue game or wild animals; to search (after or for); of a machine etc., to vary in speed of operation. *n.* hunting, the chase; a pack of hounds; a group of people who regularly go hunting together; a district hunted by a pack of hounds; †the game captured or killed in the chase. **to hunt down,** to bring to bay; to destroy by persecution or violence. **to hunt out,** to track out, to find by searching. **to hunt up,** to search for. **to hunt the fox, hare, slipper, squirrel,** various games in which a player or an object is hunted out. **hunt ball,** *n.* a ball given by the members of a hunt. **hunt-counter,** *n.* a dog that runs back on the scent; a blunderer. †**hunt's-up,** *n.* a tune used to rouse huntsmen in the morning; a reveille. **hunter,** *n.* one who follows the chase; a huntsman; a horse trained for hunting; one who searches or seeks for anything (*usu. in comb.,* as *fortune-hunter*); a hunting-watch. **hunter-killer,** *n.* a naval craft designed to pursue and destroy enemy craft. **hunter's moon,** *n.* the full moon after harvest moon. **hunting,** *a.* chasing game or wild animals; pertaining or given to hunting; (*N Am.*) shooting (birds etc.). **hunting box, -lodge, -seat,** *n.* a temporary residence for the hunting-season. **hunting-cat,** *n.* a cheetah. **hunting-crop,** *n.* a riding-rod with a loop at the end for attaching a thong. **hunting-ground,** *n.* ground or region where one hunts; (*fig.*) a likely place for finding anything. **hunting-horn,** *n.* a bugle or horn used in the chase; the second pommel of a side-saddle. **hunting knife,** *n.* a knife used for killing game at bay, or skinning it. **hunting-watch,** *n.* a watch with a metal cover over the face. **huntress,** *n.* **huntsman,** *n.* one who hunts; the servant who manages the hounds, esp. the foxhounds. **huntsmanship,** *n.* [OE *huntian,* cogn. with *hentan,* to HENT[1]]

Hunt[1], *n.* **(James Henry) Leigh** (1784–1859), English poet and essayist. Convicted for libel against the Prince Regent in his Liberal newspaper *The Examiner*, he was imprisoned 1813. The friend and, later, enemy of Byron, he also knew Keats and Shelley.

Hunt[2], *n.* **William Holman** (1827–1910), British painter, one of the founders of the Pre-Raphaelite Brotherhood 1848. Obsessed with realistic detail, he travelled to Syria and Palestine to paint biblical subjects from 1854 onwards. His works include *The Awakening Conscience*, 1853 (Tate Gallery, London) and *The Light of the World*, 1854 (Keble College, Oxford).

Hunter, *n.* **John** (1728–93), Scottish surgeon, pathologist, and comparative anatomist. His main contribution to medicine was his insistence on rigorous scientific method. He was also the first to understand the nature of digestion.

Hunterian, *a.* of or pertaining to John Hunter (1728–93), Scottish surgeon, or his museum of anatomical and pathological specimens in London; or to his brother William Hunter (1718–83) or his museum of natural history at Glasgow. [pers. name *Hunter*]

Huntingdonshire, *n.* former English county, merged 1974 in a much enlarged Cambridgeshire.

Huntington's chorea, *n.* a rare hereditary disease which begins in middle age. It is characterized by uncontrolled involuntary movements and rapid mental degeneration progressing to dementia. There is no known cure.

huntress, huntsman HUNT.

Hunts., (*abbr.*) Huntingdonshire.

Hunyadi, *n.* **János Corvinus** (1387–1456), Hungarian politician and general. Born in Transylvania, reputedly the son of the emperor Sigismund, he won battles against the Turks from the 1440s. In 1456 he defeated them at Belgrade, but died shortly afterwards of the plague.

Hunza, *n.* small state on the NW frontier of Kashmir, under the rule of Pakistan.

Huon pine, *n.* a large Tasmanian yew, *Dacrydium franklinii,* valued for its finely-marked wood, used in cabinet-making, boat-building etc. [river *Huon,* Tasmania]

hup, *int.* (*Sc.*) a call to a horse to turn to the right. *v.i.* to call thus to a horse.

Hupei, *n.* former name of HEBEI.

hurcheon, *n.* (*Sc., North.*) a hedgehog; an urchin. [ONorth.F *herichon,* OF *heriçun* (F *hérisson*), URCHIN]

Hurd, *n.* **Douglas (Richard)** (1930–), English Conservative politician, foreign secretary from 1989 and home secretary 1986–89. He entered the House of Commons 1974, representing Witney from 1983.

hurdies, *n.pl.* (*Sc.*) the buttocks, the haunches. [etym. unknown]

hurdle, *n.* a movable framework of withes or split timber serving for gates, enclosures etc.; a barrier like this for jumping over in racing; (*Hist.*) a frame or sledge on which criminals were drawn to execution; a barrier or obstacle. *v.t.* to enclose, hedge or barricade with hurdles; leap over; surmount. **hurdle-race,** *n.* a race over hurdles or fences. **hurdler,** *n.* one who runs in such races; a hurdle-maker. [OE *hyrdel,* dim. (cp. Dut. *horde,* Icel. *hürth,* G *Hürde,* also L *crātis*)]

hurds, HARDS.

hurdy-gurdy, *n.* orig. a stringed musical instrument like a rude violin, sounded by a rosined wheel turned by the left hand, the right playing on keys; a barrel-organ, or other similar instrument which is played with a handle. [prob. imit.]

hurl, *v.t.* to throw with violence; to drive or fling with great force; to utter or emit with vehemence. *v.i.* †to move rapidly, to whirl; to play the game of hurling. *n.* the act of throwing with great force; †a tumult. **hurler,** *n.* one who hurls or plays at hurling. **hurley,** *n.* (*Ir.*) hockey, hurling; a hockey-stick. **hurling,** *n.* throwing, flinging with violence; an Irish game resembling hockey in which two teams of 15 players each equipped with sticks try to score goals. [prob. imit., cp. HURTLE]

hurly-burly, *n.* a tumult, commotion, uproar. †**hurly,** *n.* [perh. from prec., or from OF *hurlee,* a howling, from *hurler,* to howl, L *ululāre,* imit.]

Huron, *n.* second largest of the Great Lakes of North America, on the US-Canadian border; area 60,000 sq km/23,160 sq miles. It includes Georgian Bay, Saginaw Bay, and Manitoulin Island. **Huronian,** *a.* (*Geol.*) of or pertaining to Lake Huron; formerly applied to the archaean strata of Canada. **Huronite,** *n.* an impure feldspar from Lake Huron.

hurrah, hurray, *int.* an exclamation of joy, welcome, applause etc. *v.i.* to utter hurrahs. *v.t.* to salute with hurrahs. *n.* a shout of hurrahs. [earlier HUZZA (cp. Swed., Dan., and G *hurra*)]

hurricane, †**hurricano**, *n.* a storm with violent wind with a mean velocity of over 75 mph (120 kph); an extremely violent gale, orig. a W Indian cyclone; anything that sweeps along violently. **hurricane-deck,** *n.* the upper deck above the cabins of a river steamer; a raised deck on an ocean steamer. **hurricane-lamp,** *n.* a lamp designed to keep alight in a wind. [Sp. *huracan,* from Carib.]

hurry, *v.t.* to impel to greater speed, to accelerate; to push forward; to drive or cause to act or do carelessly or precipitately; to draw (a wagon) in a mine. *v.i.* to hasten; to move or act with excessive haste. *n.* the act of hurrying; urgency, bustle, precipitation; eagerness (to do etc.); (*coll.*) need for haste; a river-staging for loading vessels, or a shute for loading coal into a hold; (*Mus.*) a tremolo passage by the orchestra accompanying a dramatic situation. **not in a hurry,** (*coll.*) not soon, not easily. **hurry-scurry,** *adv.* in a hurry or bustle; confusedly. *n.* a confused bustle. *v.i.* to make haste, to act with disorderly haste. **hurryingly,** *adv.* **hurried,** *a.* impelled to speed; done in a hurry; hasty. **hurriedly,** *adv.* **hurriedness,** *n.* **hurrier,** *n.* [imit.]

hurst, *n.* a wood, a thicket; a wooded eminence (a frequent element in place-names); a hillock, a knoll; (*dial.*) a sandbank in a river. [OE *hyrst* (cp. MHG *Hurst,* LG and MDut. *horst*)]

hurt, *v.t.* (*past, p.p.* **hurt**) to cause pain, injury, loss or detriment to; to damage; to grieve or distress (as the feelings). *v.i.* (*usu. impers.*) to be painful, to cause pain. *n.* a wound; an injury, damage, harm; anything that causes pain, injury, or detriment. **hurter**[1], *n.* one who hurts. **hurtful,** *a.* causing hurt; mischievous, noxious. **hurtfully,** *adv.* **hurtfulness,** *n.* **hurtless,** *n.* **hurtlessly,** *adv.* **hurtlessness,** *n.* [prob. from OF *hurter* (F *heurter*), to knock or push, etym. doubtful]

hurter[2], *n.* a timber placed at the foot of a slope or platform to prevent the wheels of gun-carriages from injuring the parapet; the shoulder or the reinforcing piece on an axle. [F *hurteoir,* as prec.]

hurtle, *v.t.* to strike or dash against with violence; to move or whirl with great force. *v.i.* to rush with great force and noise; to make a crashing noise. *n.* a loud, crashing noise; a collision, a shock. [prob. a freq. of HURT]

hurtleberry, var. of WHORTLEBERRY.

Husák, *n.* **Gustáv** (1913–), leader of the Communist Party of Czechoslovakia (CCP) 1969–87 and president 1975–89. After the 1968 Prague Spring of liberalization, his task was to restore control, purge the CCP, and oversee the implementation of a new, federalist constitution. He was deposed in the popular uprising of Nov.–Dec. 1989.

husband, *n.* a man joined to a woman in marriage; †a good and frugal manager; (*Naut.*) a ship's husband (see SHIP). *v.t.* to manage with frugality, to economize. †to till; †to cultivate; (*facet.*) to provide with a husband; to be a husband to, to marry. **husbandage,** *n.* commission to the ship's husband. **husbandhood, -ship,** *n.* **husbandless,** *a.* having no husband. **husband-like,** *a.* **husbandly,** *a.* frugal, economical; husbandlike. [OE *hūsbonda,* (*hūs,* HOUSE, *bonda,* from Icel. *bōndi,* from *būa,* to dwell)]

husbandry, *n.* the business of a farmer, agriculture; the products of farming; economy, esp. domestic; frugality, careful management. **husbandman,** *n.* a farmer, a tiller of the soil; a good economist. [as prec.]

Huscarls, *n. pl.* Anglo-Danish warriors, in 10th-cent. Denmark and early 11th-cent. England. They formed the bulk of English royal armies until the Norman Conquest.

hush[1], *v.t.* to make silent; to repress the noise of. *v.i.* to be still or silent. *n.* silence, stillness. *int.* silence! be still! †*a.* silent, quiet. **to hush up,** *v.t.* to keep concealed, to suppress. **hushaby,** *int.* used in lulling to sleep. *n.* a lullaby. **hush-hush,** *a.* (*coll.*) very secret. **hush-money,** *n.* a bribe paid to secure silence (about a scandal etc.). **hushed,** *a.* [from obs. adj. *husht,* imit., cp. HIST]

hush[2], *n.* a smooth, swift rush of water; (*Mining*) a rush of water let out from a dam. *v.t.* (*Mining*) to let out (water) from a dam, esp. to clear away soil, stones etc. [onomat.]

husk, *n.* the dry external integument of certain fruits or seeds; a mere frame, shell or worthless part; a disease in cattle. *v.t.* to strip the husk from. **husked,** *a.* having or covered with a husk; stripped of a husk. **husker,** *n.* **husking,** *n.* the act of stripping off husks; (*N Am.*) a husking-bee. **husking-bee,** *n.* (*N Am.*) a gathering of friends at a farmer's house to husk maize. **husky,** *a.* abounding in husks; consisting of or resembling husks; rough; dry, hoarse, rough and harsh in sound; (*esp. N Am., coll.*) strong, stalwart. **huskily,** *adv.* **huskiness,** *n.* [perh. from OE *hūs,* HOUSE (cp. EFris. *hüske,* G *Häuschen,* little house)]

Huskisson, *n.* **William** (1770–1830), British conservative politician, financier, and advocate of free trade. He served as secretary to the Treasury 1807–09 and colonial agent for Ceylon (now Sri Lanka). He was active in the Corn Law debates and supported their relaxation in 1821.

husky, *n.* (*Canada*) an Indian sledge-dog; an Eskimo; the Eskimo language. [perh. corr. of ESKIMO]

huso, *n.* the beluga or great sturgeon, *Acipenser huso.* [med. L, from OHG]

huss, *n.* any of various kinds of dogfish. [ME *husk*]

Huss, *n.* **John** (*c.* 1373–1415), Bohemian church reformer, rector of Prague University from 1402, who was excommunicated for attacks on ecclesiastical abuses. He was summoned before the Council of Constance 1414, defended the English reformer Wycliffe, rejected the pope's authority, and was burned at the stake. His followers were called Hussites.

hussar, *n.* originally a light horseman, and applied to the national cavalry of Hungary; now, a soldier of a light cavalry regiment in European armies. [Hung. *huszar,* OServ. *husar,* Ital. *corsaro,* or late Gr. *choursarios,* med. L *cursārius,* CORSAIR]

Hussein[1], *n.* **(ibn Ali)** (*c.* 1854–1931), leader of the Arab revolt 1916–18 against the Turks. He proclaimed himself king of the Hejaz 1916, accepted the caliphate 1924, but was unable to retain it due to internal fighting. He was deposed 1924 by Ibn Saud.

Hussein[2], *n.* **(ibn Talal)** (1935–), king of Jordan from 1952. Great-grandson of Hussein ibn Ali, he became king after the mental incapacity of his father Talal. By 1967 he had lost all his kingdom west of the Jordan river in the Arab-Israeli Wars, and in 1970 suppressed the Palestine Liberation Organization acting as a guerrilla force against his rule on the remaining East Bank territories. In recent years, he has become a moderating force in Middle Eastern politics.

Hussein[3], *n.* **Saddam** (1937–), Iraqi left-wing politician, in power from 1968, president from 1979. Ruthless in the pursuit of his objectives, he fought a bitter war against Iran 1980–88 and has dealt harshly with Kurdish rebels seeking a degree of independence.

Husserl, *n.* **Edmund (Gustav Albrecht)** (1859–1938), German philosopher, regarded as the founder of phenomenology, a philosophy concentrating on what is consciously experienced.

hussif, HOUSEWIFE.

Hussite, *n.* a follower of John Huss. Opposed to both German and papal influence in Bohemia, the Hussites waged successful war against the Holy Roman Empire from 1419, but Roman Catholicism was finally re-established 1620.

hussy, *n.* a pert, forward girl; a worthless woman; †a housewife. [corr. of HOUSEWIFE]

husting, *n.* (*Hist.*) a meeting for deliberative purposes, a council; (*pl.*) a platform from which, before the Ballot Act of 1872, candidates addressed the electors during parliamentary elections; proceedings at an election; a court held in the City of London, formerly the principal and highest court in the City. [OE *hūsting,* Icel. *hūsthing* (*hūs,* HOUSE, *thing,* an assembly)]

hustle, *v.t.* to shake together in confusion; to jostle, to push violently; to hurry or cause to move quickly; (*sl.*) to acquire (something) by aggressive or dishonest means. *v.i.* to press roughly; to move (along) with difficulty; to act with energy; to give the appearance of being busy; to push one's way in an unceremonious or unscrupulous way; (*sl.*) to make a living by aggressive or dishonest means; (*esp. N Am., sl.*) to engage in prostitution. *n.* hustling. **hustler,** *n.* [Dut. *hutselen,* freq. of *hutsen*]

Huston, *n.* **John** (1906–87), US film director, screenwriter, and actor. An impulsive and individualistic film-maker, he often dealt with the themes of greed, treachery, human relationships, and the loner. His works as a director include *The Maltese Falcon* (1941) (his debut), *The Treasure of the Sierra Madre* (1947, for which he won an Academy Award), *The African Queen* (1951), and *Prizzi's Honor* (1984).

†**huswife,** etc. HOUSEWIFE.

hut, *n.* a small, rude house, a mean dwelling; a cabin, a hovel; (*Mil.*) a small temporary camp-shelter or house. *v.t.* to place (troops) in huts. *v.i.* to lodge in huts. **hut circle,** *n.* a circle of stones or earth indicating the site of a prehistoric hut. **hutment,** *n.* a camp of huts. [F *hutte,* from MHG *Hütte*]

hutch, *n.* a coop or box-like pen for small animals; a chest, box, bin or other receptacle; a hut, a hovel, a small mean house; a kneading-trough; a bolting hutch; in mining, a truck, a trough for washing ore. *v.t.* to store, as in a hutch; to wash (ore) in a hutch. [OF *huche,* low L *hūtica,* etym. doubtful]

Hutton[1], *n.* **James** (1726–97), Scottish geologist, known as the 'founder of geology', who formulated the concept of uniformitarianism. In 1785 he developed a theory of the igneous origin of many rocks. **Huttonian,** *a.* of or pertaining to Hutton and his theory of the plutonic or volcanic origin of unstratified rocks. *n.* an adherent of this theory. **Huttonianism,** *n.*

Hutton[2], *n.* **Leonard** (1916–), English cricketer, born in Pudsey, West Yorkshire. He captained England in 23 test matches 1952–56 and was England's first professional captain. In 1938 at the Oval he scored 364 against Australia, a world record test score until beaten by Gary Sobers 1958.

Huxley[1], *n.* **Aldous (Leonard)** (1894–1963), English writer. The satirical disillusion of his witty first novel, *Crome Yellow* (1921), continued throughout *Antic Hay* (1923), *Those Barren Leaves* (1925), and *Point Counter Point* (1928). *Brave New World* (1932) concerns the reproduction of the human race by mass production in the laboratory.

Huxley[2], *n.* **Andrew** (1917–), English physiologist, awarded the Nobel prize for medicine 1963, with Hodgkin and Eccles, for work on nerve impulses.

Huxley[3], *n.* **Julian** (1887–1975), English biologist, first director-general of UNESCO, and a founder of the World Wildlife Fund (now the World Wide Fund for Nature).

Huxley[4], *n.* **Thomas Henry** (1825–95), English scientist and humanist. Following the publication of Charles Darwin's *On the Origin of Species* (1859), he became known as 'Darwin's bulldog', and for many years was the most prominent and popular champion of evolution. In 1869, he coined the word 'agnostic' to express his own religious attitude.

Hu Yaobang, *n.* (1915–89), Chinese politician, Communist Party (CCP) chairman 1981–87. A protégé of the communist leader Deng Xiaoping, Hu presided over a radical overhaul of the party structure and personnel 1982–86.

Huygens, *n.* **Christiaan** (1629–95), Dutch mathematical physicist and astronomer, who propounded the wave theory of light. He developed the pendulum clock, discovered polarization, and observed Saturn's rings.

Huysmans, *n.* **J(oris) K(arl)** (1848–1907), French novelist of Dutch ancestry. *Marthe* (1876), the story of a courtesan, was followed by other realistic novels, including *À rebours/Against Nature* (1884), a novel of self-absorbed aestheticism which symbolized the 'decadent' movement.

huzza, *int.* a cry of joy, applause etc. *v.i.* to shout 'huzza'. *v.t.* to applaud or greet with this cry. *n.* a shout of 'huzza'. [imit.]

huzzy, HUSSY.

hw, (*abbr.*) hit wicket.

Hwang-Ho, *n.* former name of the HUANG HE.

HWM, (*abbr.*) *n.* high water mark.

hwyl, *n.* passion or fervour, esp. in rhetoric. [Welsh]

hyacinth, *n.* a plant of the genus *Hyacinthus,* esp. *H. orientalis,* a beautiful bulbous-rooted flowering plant of the order Lilaceae; a flower mentioned by the ancients, said to have sprung from the blood of the youth Hyacinth, beloved of Apollo, and to bear the letters AI (alas!) on its petals; a precious stone known to the ancients; a brownish, orange or reddish variety of zircon; a colour ranging from purplish-blue to violet. †**hyacine,** *n.* (*Spens.*) hyacinth. **hyacinthian, hyacinthine** , *a.* resembling the hyacinth (the flower or the gem) in colour; (of hair) curling richly (after an epithet of Homer's of doubtful meaning). [F *hyacinthe,* L *hyacinthus,* Gr. *huakinthos,* a flower, prob. iris or larkspur]

Hyades, Hyads, *n.pl.* a cluster of stars, including Aldebaran, in the head of Taurus, supposed by the ancients to bring rain when they rose with the sun. It is 130 light years away and contains over 200 stars, although only about a dozen are visible to the naked eye. [Gr. *Huades,* cogn. with *hus,* a sow (pop. derived from *huein,* to rain)]

hyaena, HYENA.

hyal- HYAL(O)-.

hyalescence, *n.* the process of becoming transparent. **hyalescent,** *a.* [HYALINE]

hyalin, *n.* an opalescent nitrogenous compound similar to chitin, the chief constituent of hydatid cysts. **hyalose,** *n.* a sugar allied to glucose obtained from this. [Gr. *hualos,* glass]

hyaline, *a.* glassy, transparent, crystalline; vitreous. *n.* the glassy surface of the sea; the clear sky or atmosphere; the pellucid substance determining the fission of cells. **hyaline cartilage,** *n.* a translucent cartilage found in joints and respiratory passages, containing little fibrous tissue. **hyalite,** *n.* a glassy variety of opal. [L *hyalīnus,* Gr. *hualinos,* from *hualos,* glass or crystal]

hyalitis, *n.* inflammation of the vitreous matter of the eye.

hyal(o)-, *comb. form.* colourless, transparent, crystalline; vitreous. [Gr. *hualos,* glass]

hyalograph, *n.* an instrument for etching on glass. **hyalography,** *n.*

hyaloid, *a.* glassy, vitriform. *n.* the hyaloid membrane. **hyaloid coat, membrane,** *n.* the transparent membrane enclosing the vitreous humour of the eye. **hyaloid humour, body,** *n.* the vitreous humour.

hyaloplasm, *n.* the clear, fluid constituent of cytoplasm.

hyalose HYALIN.

hyberbola, *n.* (*pl.* **-las, -lae**) a plane curve formed by cutting a cone when the intersecting plane makes a greater angle with the base than the side of the cone makes. **hyperbolic,** *a.* pertaining to or of the nature of an hyperbola. **hyperboliform,** *a.* having the form of a hyperbola. **hyperboloid,** *n.* a solid formed by the revolution of a hyperbola about its axis. [Gr. *huperbolē,* see foll.]

hybernate, HIBERNATE.

Hyblaean, Hyblan, *a.* of or pertaining to Hybla, a town in ancient Sicily, famous for its honey. [L *Hyblaeus,* from *Hybla,* Gr. *Hublē*]

hybrid, *a.* produced by the union of two distinct species, varieties etc.; produced by cross-fertilization or interbreeding; mongrel, cross-bred; derived from incongruous sources. *n.* a mongrel; an animal or plant produced by the union of two distinct species, varieties etc.; one of mixed nationality; a word compounded from different languages; anything composed of heterogeneous parts or elements. **hybridity,** *n.* the state or quality of being hybrid. **hybridism,** *n.* hybridity; the act or process of interbreeding, hybridization. **hybridist,** *n.* **hybridize, -ise,** *v.t.* to produce by the union of different species or varieties; to produce by cross-fertilization or interbreeding. *v.i.* to produce hybrids, to be capable of cross-fertilization or interbreeding. **hybridizable, -isable,** *a.* **hybridization, -isation,** *n.* **hybridizer, -iser,** *n.* †**hybridous,** *a.* [L *hybrida,* mongrel]

hydatid, *n.* a watery cyst occurring in animal tissue, esp. one resulting from the development of the embryo of a tapeworm. **hydatic,** *a.* **hydatidiform, hydatiform,** *a.* resembling a hydatid. [Gr. *hudatis -tidos,* a watery vesicle, cogn. with *hudōr,* water]

hydatism, *n.* (*Med.*) a sound produced by the effusion of fluid in a cavity of the body. **hydato-,** *comb. form.* [Gr. *hudatismos,* from *hudōr hudatos,* water]

hydatoid, *a.* resembling water. *n.* the membrane surrounding the aqueous humour of the eye, or the humour itself.

Hyderabad¹, *n.* capital city of the S central Indian state of Andhra Pradesh, on the Musi; population (1981) 2,528,000. Products include carpets, silks, and metal inlay work. It was formerly the capital of the state of Hyderabad. Buildings include the Jama Masjid mosque and Golconda fort.

Hyderabad², *n.* city in Sind province, SE Pakistan; population (1981) 795,000. It produces, gold, pottery, glass, and furniture. The third largest city of Pakistan, it was founded 1768.

Hyder Ali, *n.* (*c.* 1722–82), Indian general, sultan of Mysore from 1759. In command of the army in Mysore from 1749, he became the ruler of the state 1759, and rivalled British power in the area until his triple defeat by Sir Eyre Coote 1781 during the Anglo-French wars. He was the father of Tippu Sultan.

hydr- HYDR(O)-.

hydra, *n.* in Greek mythology, a water-serpent with many heads, each of which, when cut off, was succeeded by two, destroyed by Hercules; a water-serpent; an evil or calamity difficult to extinguish; (*Astron.*) one of the 15 ancient southern constellations; a genus of freshwater polyps which multiply when divided. **hydra-headed,** *a.* having many heads; hence, difficult to get rid of; spreading. **hydra-tainted,** *a.* poisonous, deadly. **hydroid,** *a.* hydra-like; allied to the genus *Hydra*. *n.* a hydrozoan; a member of the genus *Hydra*. [L, from Gr. *hudra,* cogn. with *hudōr,* water]

hydracid, *n.* (*Chem.*) an acid containing hydrogen but no oxygen. *a.* of or pertaining to a hydracid.

hydragogue, *n.* an active purgative, causing a large secretion of fluid. [F, from L *hydragōgus,* Gr. *hudragōgos* (HYDR-, *agein,* to lead)]

hydrangea, *n.* a genus of flowering shrubs of the saxifrage family, from Asia and America. [HYDR-, Gr. *angeion, angos,* a vessel]

hydrant, *n.* a spout or discharge-pipe, usu. with a nozzle for attaching hose, connected with a water-main for drawing water.

hydranth, *n.* a polyp in a hydroid colony specialized for feeding. [HYDRA-, Gr. *anthos,* flower]

hydrargyrum, *n.* mercury, quicksilver. **hydrargyrate, -gyric,** *a.* [L *hydrargyrus,* Gr. *hudrarguros* (HYDR-, *arguros,* silver)]

hydrastine, *n.* a bitter alkaloid prepared from the root of a N American plant, *Hydrastis canadensis,* used as a tonic and febrifuge. [mod. L *Hydrastis*]

hydrate, *n.* a compound of water with an element or another compound. *v.t.* to combine with water to form a hydrate. **hydration,** *n.*

hydraulic, *a.* pertaining to fluids in motion, or to the power exerted by water conveyed through pipes or channels; operating or operated by such power. *n.pl.* the science of water or other liquids both at rest and in motion, esp. the conveyance of water through pipes etc., and the practical application of water-power. **hydraulic cement, mortar,** *n.* a cement or mortar which hardens under water. **hydraulic lift,** *n.* a lift worked by means of water-power. **hydraulic press,** *n.* a heavy pressing machine worked by water-power. **hydraulic ram,** *n.* a machine by which the fall of a column of water supplies power to elevate a portion of the water to a greater height than that at the source. **hydraulically,** *adv.* **hydraulician,** *n.* [L *hydraulicus,* Gr. *hudraulikos* (HYDR-, *aulos,* pipe)]

hydraulico-, *comb. form.*

hydrazine, *n.* a colourless corrosive liquid that is a strong reducing agent, used esp. in rocket fuel. [HYDR-, AZO-, -INE]

hydria, *n.* (*pl.* **-iae**), in ancient Greece, a water-jar or pitcher. †**hydriad,** *n.* a water-nymph. [L, from Gr. *hudria,* from *hudōr,* water]

hydric, *a.* of, pertaining to or containing hydrogen in chemical combination. **hydride,** *n.* a compound of hydrogen with another element or radical. **hydriodic,** *a.* of, pertaining to, or containing hydrogen and iodine in chemical combination. **hydriodate, hydriodide,** *n.*

hydro, *n.* (*coll.*) a hydropathic establishment. [short for HYDROPATHIC]

hydr(o)-, *comb. form.* pertaining to or connected with water; containing hydrogen in chemical combination; of a mineral, containing water as a constituent; dropsical; belonging to the genus *Hydra* or the class Hydrozoa. **hydro-aeroplane,** *n.* an aeroplane adapted for rising from or descending upon the surface of water. [AEROPLANE] **hydro-barometer,** *n.* an instrument for determining the depth of the sea by its pressure. [BAROMETER] [Gr. *hudōr hudatos,* water]

hydrobromic, *a.* composed of hydrogen and bromine. **hydrobromate, hydrobromide,** *n.*

hydrocarbon, *n.* a compound of carbon and hydrogen. **hydrocarbide,** *n.* **hydrocarbonaceous,** *a.* **hydrocarbonate,** *n.* **hydrocarbonic,** *a.*

hydrocele, *n.* an accumulation of fluid, often swollen and painful, in a saclike cavity, esp. in the scrotum.

hydrocephalus, -cephaly, *n.* dropsy of or water on the brain. **hydrocephalic, hydrocephaloid, hydrocephalous,** *a.* pertaining to or akin to hydrocephalus. [Gr. *hudrokephalon*]

hydrochloric, *n.* a compound of chlorine and hydrogen. **hydrochloric acid,** *n.* a solution of hydrogen chloride in water, a strong corrosive acid.

hydrochloride, *n.* a compound of hydrochloric acid, esp. with an organic base.

hydrocortisone, *n.* the steroid hormone naturally secreted by the adrenal cortex, synthesized to treat e.g. rheumatoid arthritis.

hydrocyanic, *a.* formed by the combination of hydrogen and cyanogen. **hydrocyanic acid, hydrocyanate,** *n.*

hydrodynamics, *n.* the science which deals with water and other liquids in motion. **hydrodynamic, -ical,** *a.* pertaining to hydrodynamics; derived from the force of water.

hydroelectric, *a.* pertaining to electricity generated from water-power. **hydroelectrically,** *adv.* **hydroelectricity,** *n.*

hydro-extractor, *n.* an apparatus for removing moisture from yarns and fabrics during the process of manufacture.

hydrofluoric, *a.* consisting of fluorine and hydrogen.

hydrofoil, *n.* a fast vessel with one or more pairs of vanes attached to its hull which lift it out of the water at speed; such a vane.

hydrogel, *n.* protoplasm comprising gelatine or albumen in a jelly-like state with water filling the interstices. [HYDR(O)-, *gel-,* from L *gelāre,* to freeze]

hydrogen, *n.* (*Chem.*) an invisible, inflammable, gaseous element, the lightest of all known bodies, which in combination with oxygen produces water. **hydrogen bomb,** *n.* an exceedingly powerful bomb in which an immense release of energy is obtained by the conversion by fusion of hydrogen nuclei into helium nuclei. **hydrogen chloride,** *n.* a colourless pungent corrosive gas obtained from the interaction of sulphuric acid and sodium chloride. **hydrogen cyanide,** *n.* a colourless poisonous liquid faintly redolent of bitter almonds. **hydrogen peroxide** PEROXIDE. **hydrogen sulphide,** *n.* a colourless poisonous gas smelling of rotten eggs. **hydrogenate, -nize, -nise** , *v.t.* to cause to combine with hydrogen; to charge with hydrogen.

hydrogenation, -genization, -isation, *n.* **hydrogenous,** *a.* [F *hydrogène*]
hydrography, *n.* the science and art of studying, surveying and mapping seas, lakes, rivers and other waters, and their physical features, tides, currents etc. **hydrograph,** *n.* a chart or diagram setting forth hydrographic phenomena. **hydrographer,** *n.* **hydrographic, -ical,** *a.* **hydrographically,** *adv.*
hydroid HYDRA.
hydrokinetic, *a.* relating to the motion of liquids. **hydrokinetics,** *n.* the kinetics of liquids.
hydrology, *n.* the science of water, its properties, phenomena, laws and distribution. **hydrological,** *a.* **hydrologically,** *adv.* **hydrologist,** *n.*
hydrolysis, *n.* the formation of an acid and a base from a salt by the action of water. **hydrolyse, -lyze,** *v.t.* to subject to hydrolysis. **hydrolytic,** *a.* **hydrolytically,** *adv.* [Gr. *lusis,* loosening, from *luein,* to loose]
†**hydromancy,** *n.* divination by means of water. **hydromantic,** *a.*
hydromania, *n.* morbid craving for water. **hydromaniac,** *n.* **hydromaniacal,** *a.*
hydromechanics, *n.* the mechanics of liquids. **hydromechanical,** *a.*
hydromel, *n.* a drink consisting of honey diluted with water. [L, from Gr. *hudromeli* (HYDR(O)-, *meli,* honey)]
hydrometallurgy, *n.* extraction of metal from ore by treatment with fluid.
hydrometamorphism, *n.* metamorphism of igneous rocks by the agency of water. **hydrometamorphic,** *a.*
hydrometeor, *n.* a meteorological phenomenon produced by water-vapour, as rain, snow etc. **hydrometeoric,** *a.* **hydrometeorology,** *n.* **hydrometeorological,** *a.*
hydrometer, *n.* an instrument for determining the specific gravity of liquids or solids by means of flotation. **hydrometric, -ical,** *a.* **hydrometry,** *n.* the art or process of measuring the specific gravity of fluids etc.
hydromotor, *n.* a motor for propelling vessels by means of a jet of water emitted at the stern.
hydromyd, *n.* one of the Australian genus *Hydromys* comprising the water-rats and beaver-rats. [Gr. *mus,* MOUSE]
hydronaut, *n.* a person trained to operate vessels for exploring the ocean's depths.
hydropathy, *n.* the treatment of disease by the internal and external application of water. **hydropath, hydropathist,** *n.* one who practises or believes in hydropathy. **hydropathic,** *a.* pertaining to hydropathy. *n.* an establishment for the hydropathic treatment of disease. **hydropathically,** *adv.*
hydrophane, *n.* an opal which becomes translucent when immersed in water. **hydrophanous,** *a.* becoming more translucent or brighter when immersed in water. [Gr. *phanēs,* clear, from *phainein,* to show]
hydrophid, *n.* one of the Hydrophidae, a family of small sea-snakes from Indian and Australian seas. [Gr. *ophis,* serpent]
hydrophilic, *a.* having a great affinity for water.
hydrophilous, *a.* of a plant, growing in or pollinated by water. [HYDR(O)-, -PHILOUS]
hydrophobia, *n.* an unnatural dread of water, a symptom of rabies resulting from the bite of a rabid animal; rabies; dread of water. **hydrophobic,** *a.* of or concerning hydrophobia; repelling water. [L, from Gr. *hudrophobia*]
hydrophone, *n.* an instrument for detecting sound by water, used in naval warfare to locate submarines etc.; an instrument for detecting the sound of running water, used to discover leaks etc. [Gr. *phōnē,* voice, sound]
hydrophore, *n.* an instrument for obtaining specimens of water from any given depth. [Gr. *hudrophoros*]
hydrophthalmia, *n.* enlargement of the eyeball by the increase of its fluid contents. **hydrophthalmic,** *a.*
hydrophyte, *n.* an aquatic plant. **hydrophytic,** *a.* **hydrophytography, hydrophytology,** *n.* the study of these plants. [Gr. *phyton,* plant]
hydropic, *a.* dropsical; resembling dropsy. †**hydropical,** †**hydroptic,** *a.* hydropic. †**hydropsy,** *n.* dropsy. [ME and OF *ydropique,* L *hydrōpicus,* Gr. *hudrōpikos,* from *hudrops* (*hudōr,* water)]
hydroplane, *n.* a light motor-boat capable of rising partially above the surface of water; a flat fin for governing the vertical direction of a submarine; a plane for lifting a boat partially from the water, so as to diminish the resistance and increase the speed. *v.i.* of a boat, to move across the water like a hydroplane. [cp. HYDRO-AEROPLANE, see HYDRO-]
hydropneumatic, *a.* pertaining to or produced by the combined action of water and air.
hydroponics, *n.pl.* the cultivation of plants without soil in water containing chemicals. **hydroponic,** *a.* **hydroponically,** *adv.* [Gr. *ponos,* work]
hydropower, *n.* hydroelectric power.
hydropsy HYDROPIC.
hydroquinone, *n.* a compound derived from quinone, employed in the development of photographs.
hydroscope, *n.* a water-clock or clepsydra; a hygroscope; an instrument for viewing underwater. [Gr. *hudroskopos*]
hydrosol, *n.* a solution of a colloid in water.
hydrosome, *n.* the colonial organism of a hydrozoan. **hydrosomal, hydrosomatous,** *a.* [HYDRA, Gr. *soma,* body]
hydrosphere, *n.* the watery envelope of the earth.
hydrostat, *n.* an electrical contrivance for detecting the presence of water; an apparatus to prevent the explosion of steam-boilers. [Gr. *statos,* standing]
hydrostatic, -ical, *a.* pertaining or relating to hydrostatics; pertaining to the pressure and equilibrium of liquids at rest. **hydrostatic balance,** *n.* a balance for weighing substances in water to ascertain their specific gravities. **hydrostatic paradox,** *n.* the principle that any quantity of liquid, however small, may be made to balance any weight. **hydrostatic press,** *n.* a hydraulic press. **hydrostatically,** *adv.* **hydrostatics,** *n.* the science concerned with the pressure and equilibrium of liquids at rest.
hydrosulphuric, *a.* containing hydrogen and sulphur.
hydrotelluric, *a.* composed of hydrogen and tellurium.
hydrotherapeutic, *a.* pertaining to the therapeutic application of water; hydropathic. **hydrotherapist,** *n.* **hydrotherapeutics, hydrotherapy,** *n.*
hydrothermal, *a.* relating to the action of heated water, esp. on the materials of the earth's crust. **hydrothermally,** *adv.*
hydrothorax, *n.* an abnormal accumulation of fluid in the chest.
hydrotropism, *n.* the tendency in the growing parts of plants to turn towards or away from moisture. **hydrotropic,** *a.* **hydrotropically,** *adv.* [Gr. *-tropos,* a turning, from *trepein,* to turn]
hydrous, *a.* containing water.
hydrovane, HYDROFOIL.
hydroxide, *n.* a compound formed by the union of a basic oxide with the molecules of water; †a hydrate.
hydroxy-, *comb. form.* containing the radical hydroxyl. **hydroxyl,** *n.* the monad radical formed by the combination of one atom of hydrogen and one of water occurring in many chemical compounds.
Hydrozoa, *n.pl.* a class of coelenterates, principally marine, comprising the hydra, medusa, jelly-fish etc. **hydrozoan,** *n., a.* **hydrozoic,** *a.* [Gr. *zōon* (pl. *zōa*), an animal]
†**hydruret,** HYDRIDE.
†**hyemal,** etc. HIEMAL.
hyena, *n.* a genus of carnivorous quadrupeds allied to the dog, with three modern species, the striped *Hyena striata,* the spotted *H. crocuta,* and the brown hyena, *H. brunnea* (the first is also called the laughing hyena); a ferocious or treacherous person; applied also to the thyacine. **hyena-dog,** *n.* a S African quadruped, also called the hunting-dog. **hyenaish,** *a.* **hyenaism,** *n.* **hyena-like,** *a.* [L *hyaena,* Gr. *huaina,* sow-like, from *hus,* a sow]
hyetal, *a.* of or belonging to rain; relating to the rainfall

of different countries. [as foll.]

hyet(o)-, *comb. form.* pertaining to rain or rainfall. [Gr. *huetos,* rain]

hyetograph, *n.* a self-recording instrument that registers rainfall. **hyetographic, -ical**, *a.* **hyetography**, *n.* the branch of meteorology concerned with the distribution and mapping of the rainfall.

hyetology, *n.* the science of rainfall.

hyetometer, *n.* a rain-gauge.

Hygeia, *n.* the goddess of health. **hygeian**, *a.* relating to Hygeia, the goddess of health; pertaining to hygiene. †**hygeist**, *n.* [Gr. *Hugeia, Hugieia,* from *hugiēs*, healthy]

hygiene, *n.* the science of the prevention of disease; the art of preserving health, esp. of the community at large; practices that promote health; sanitary science. **hygienic**, *a.* **hygienics,** *n.* hygiene. **hygienically,** *adv.* **hygienist**, *n.* **hygiology**, *n.* a treatise on hygiene; hygiene. [F *hygiène,* Gr. *hugienē technē,* the art of health, as prec.]

hygristor, *n.* an electronic component whose resistance varies with humidity. [HYGR-, *resistor*]

hygr(o)-, *comb. form.* moist, pertaining to or denoting the presence of moisture. [Gr. *hugros,* wet]

hygrodeik, *n.* a hygrometer indicating the degree of atmospheric humidity by an index set according to the heights of a wet or dry bulb thermometer. [Gr. *deiknunai,* to show]

hygrograph, *n.* a self-recording hygrometer.

hygrology, *n.* the branch of physics relating to humidity, esp. of the atmosphere.

hygrometer, *n.* an instrument for measuring the moisture of the air etc. **hygrometric, -ical**, *a.* **hygrometrically,** *adv.* **hygrometry,** *n.* the branch of physics concerned with the measurement of moisture, esp. of the air.

hygrophanous, *a.* of plants, minerals etc., appearing transparent when wet and opaque when dry. **hygrophaneity,** *n.* [Gr. *phanein,* to appear]

hygrophilous, *a.* living or growing in moist places.

hygroscope, *n.* an instrument for indicating the degree of moisture in the atmosphere. **hygroscopic, -ical**, *a.* pertaining to or indicated by the hygroscope; imbibing moisture from the atmosphere (of bodies); perceptible or liable to detection through moisture. **hygroscopically,** *adv.* **hygroscopicity**, *n.*

hygrostat, *n.* a hygrometer; a device for maintaining constant humidity. **hygrostatics**, *n.* hygrometry.

hying HIE.

hyl- HYLO-.

hyleg, *n.* the planet ruling, or in the sign of the zodiac above the eastern horizon, at the hour of a person's nativity. [Pers. *hailāj*]

hylic, *a.* of or relating to matter; material. **hylicism**, **hylism**, *n.* **hylicist**, *n.* a philosopher who assigns a material basis to being, as water or air. [Gr. *hulikos,* as foll.]

hylo-, *comb. form.* of matter; pertaining to wood. [Gr. *hule,* matter]

hylogenesis, *n.* the origin of matter. **hylogeny**, *a.*

hyloism, *n.* hylotheism.

hylomorphism, *n.* the philosophy that finds the first cause of the universe in matter. **hylomorphic, -ical,** *a.* **hylomorphist,** *n.*

hylophagous, *a.* feeding on wood. [-PHAGOUS]

hylotheism, *n.* the system which regards God and matter as identical; pantheism. **hylotheist,** *n.*

hylotomous, *a.* of certain insects, wood-cutting. [Gr. *temnein*, to cut]

hylozoism, *n.* the doctrine that matter is necessarily endowed with life. **hylozoic,** *a.* **hylozoist, hylozoistic**, *a.* [Gr. *zoe,* life]

Hymen[1], *n.* in Greek mythology, either the son of Apollo and one of the Muses, or of Dionysus and Aphrodite. He was the god of marriage, and in art is represented as a youth carrying a bridal torch. **hymeneal**, **†-an,** *a.* pertaining to marriage. *n.* a marriage song. **hymeneally,** *adv.* [L, from Gr. *humēn*]

hymen[2], *n.* a membrane stretched across the vaginal entrance; the fine pellicle enclosing a flower in the bud. [Gr. *humēn,* a membrane]

hymenium, *n.* (*pl.* **-nia, -niums**) (*Bot.*) the spore-bearing stratum or surface in fungi. **hymeniferous**, *a.* [Gr. *humenīon,* dim. of *humēn,* HYMEN[1]]

hymeno-, *comb. form.* membranous. [Gr. *humēn humenos,* a membrane]

hymenogeny, *n.* the production of membranes by the simple contacts of two liquids.

hymenography, *n.* a description of membranes.

hymenoid, *a.* of the nature or having the structure of a membrane.

hymenology, *n.* the branch of anatomical science that treats of membranes. **hymenological**, *a.*

hymenomycete, *n.* one of the Hymenomycetae, an order of fungi characterized by an exposed hymenium. **hymenomycetal, -toid, -tous**, *a.* [Gr. *muketes,* mushroom]

hymenophyllaceous, *a.* belonging to or having the characteristics of the Hymenophyllaceae or filmy ferns. [Gr. *phullon,* a leaf]

Hymenoptera, *n.pl.* an order of insects having four membranous wings, as the bee, wasp, ant etc. **hymenopteral, -ous,** *a.* **hymenopteran,** *n., a.* [Gr. *pteron,* a wing]

hymn, *n.* a song or ode in praise or adoration of God or some deity; a sacred or solemn song or ode, esp. a religious song not taken from the Bible. *v.t.* to praise or worship in hymns; to sing hymns to; to express in hymns. *v.i.* to sing hymns. **hymn-book,** *n.* a book of hymns. **hymnal**, *n.* a collection of hymns, esp. for public worship. **hymnary**, *n.* a hymnal. **hymnic,** *a.* **hymnist,** *n.* a composer of hymns. **hymno-,** *comb. form.* pertaining to a hymn or hymns. **hymnody,** *n.* the singing of hymns; the composition of hymns; hymns collectively; hymnology. **†hymnodist,** *n.* **†hymnography**, *n.* the art or act of writing hymns. **hymnographer,** *n.* **hymnology**, *n.* the composition or the study of hymns; hymns collectively. **hymnologic,** *a.* **hymnologist,** *n.* [OF *hymne,* L *hymnus,* Gr. *humnos*]

hyoid, *a.* (*Anat.*) resembling the Greek letter upsilon (υ) in shape; pertaining to the hyoid bone. **hyoid bone,** *n.* the bone supporting the tongue. [F *hyoïde,* L *hyoīdes,* Gr. *huoeidēs* (letter υ -OID)]

hyoscyamine, *n.* a white crystalline alkaloid obtained from the seeds of henbane, *Hyoscyamus niger,* highly poisonous, used as a sedative. **hyoscine**, *n.* a strong narcotic drug, scopolamine. [Gr. *huoscuamos* (*huos,* gen. of *hus,* sow, *kuamos,* bean)]

hyp, HIP[3].

hyp- HYPO-.

hypabyssal, *a.* of igneous rock, formed at a moderate distance below the surface of the earth.

hypaethral, HYPETHRAL.

hypalgia, *n.* reduction of or freedom from pain. **hypalgic,** *a.* [Gr. *-algia algos,* pain]

hypallage, *n.* the interchange of natural or grammatical relations between terms in a sentence. [L *hypallagē,* Gr. *hupallagē* (HYPO-, *allagē,* change, from *allassein,* to change)]

hype[1], *n.* (*coll.*) exaggerated or false publicity used to sell or promote; a deception, a swindle. *v.t.* (*sometimes with up, coll.*) to sell or promote something or somebody by using exaggerated or false publicity.

hype[2], *n.* (*coll.*) short for HYPODERMIC NEEDLE, see HYPODERM. **hyped up,** *a.* (*sl.*) full of nervous excitement.

hyper-, *comb. form.* above, beyond; excessive, beyond measure. [L, from Gr. *huper*]

hyperacidity, *n.* excessive acidity in the digestive tract, esp. in the stomach.

hyperactive, *a.* abnormally active. **hyperactivity**, *n.*

hyperacute, *a.* morbidly or excessively acute. **hyperacuity**, *n.*

hyperaemia, *n.* morbid or excessive accumulation of blood. **hyperaemic,** *a.*

hyperaesthesia, *n.* morbid or excessive sensibility, esp. of the nerves. **hyperaesthetic**, *a.*

hyperalgesia, *n.* a condition of exaggerated sensibility to pain.

hyperbaric, *a.* esp. of oxygen, of higher than normal pressure. **hyperbarically,** *adv.*

hyperbaton, *n.* a figure by which words are transposed or inverted from their natural and grammatical order. **hyperbatic**, *a.* **hyperbatically,** *adv.* [L, from Gr. *huperbaton* (*bainein,* to go)]

hyperbole, *n.* a figure of speech expressing much more than the truth; rhetorical exaggeration. **hyperbolic, -ical**, *a.* of the nature of hyperbole. **hyperbolically,** *adv.* **hyperbolism,** *n.* the use of hyperbole; a hyperbolic expression. **hyperbolist,** *n.* †**hyperbolize, -ise,** *v.i.* to use hyperbolical language. *v.t.* to express in hyperbolical language. [L, from Gr. *huperbolē,* (HYPER-, *ballein,* to throw)]

hyperborean, *a.* belonging to or inhabiting the extreme north; in Greek myths, of or pertaining to the Hyperboreans. *n.* one living in the extreme north; in Greek myths, one of a people supposed to live in a land beyond the north wind, distinguished for piety and happiness. **hyperboreanism,** *n.* [late L *hyperboreānus,* L *hyperboreus,* Gr. *huperboreos* (HYPER-, *Boreas,* the north wind)]

hypercatalectic, *a.* of a line of verse, having a final redundant syllable. [late L *hypercatalēcticus*]

hypercharge, *n.* an interaction between elementary particles that is a weak force tending to oppose gravitational attraction between objects.

hypercritic, *n.* one unreasonably critical; a captious censor. †*a.* hypercritical. **hypercritical,** *a.* unreasonably critical; captiously censorious, over-nice. **hypercritically,** *adv.* **hypercriticism,** *n.* **hypercriticize, -ise,** *v.t.* to criticize captiously. *v.i.* to be hypercritical.

hyperdulia, *n.* in the Roman Catholic Church, the particular veneration made to the Virgin Mary, dist. from that paid to the saints and from the worship paid to God.

hyperemia, HYPERAEMIA.

hyperesthesia, HYPERAESTHESIA.

hyperfocal distance, *n.* the distance beyond which objects appear sharply defined through a lens focused at infinity.

hyperglycaemia, *n.* an excessive level of sugar in the blood. [HYPER-, GLYCO-, -AEMIA]

hypericum, *n.* a genus of herbaceous plants or shrubs typified by the St John's wort. [L, from Gr. *hupereikon* (*ereikē,* heath)]

hyperinflation, *n.* a very high level of inflation in an economy.

hyperinosis, *n.* a morbid state of the blood characterized by excess of fibrin. **hyperinosed**, **hyperinotic**, *a.* [Gr. *is inos,* fibre, -OSIS]

hypermarket, *n.* a very large self-service store selling a wide range of household and other goods, usually on the outskirts of a town or city.

hypermetrical, *a.* of a line of verse, having a redundant syllable or syllables; of such a syllable, redundant. †**hypermeter**, *n.* [Gr. *hupermetros*]

hypermetropia, *n.* an abnormal state of the eye characterized by long-sightedness, opposed to myopia. **hypermetropic**, *a.* **hyperopia**, *n.* **hyperopic**, *a.* [Gr. *hupermetros,* as prec., *ōps ōpos,* eye]

hyperon, *n.* an elementary particle of the baryon group with a greater mass than a proton or a neutron.

hyperoodon, *n.* a genus of cetaceans comprising the bottle-nosed whales. [Gr. *huperōos,* upper, superior, *odous odontos,* tooth]

hyperphasia, *n.* (*Path.*) lack of control over the organs of speech. **hyperphasic**, *a.* [Gr. *phasis,* speaking]

hyperphysical, *a.* supernatural.

hyperplasia, *n.* (*Path.*) excessive growth due to abnormal multiplication of cells. **hyperplasm**, *n.* **hyperplasic, hyperplastic**, *a.* [Gr. *plasis,* formation, from *plassein,* to mould]

hypersarcoma, **hypersarcosis**, *n.* a fleshy excrescence; proud flesh.

hypersensitive, *a.* excessively or morbidly sensitive. **hypersensitiveness, hypersensitivity**, *n.*

hypersonic, *a.* of speeds, higher than Mach 5. **hypersonically,** *adv.*

hyperspace, *n.* space that has more than three dimensions.

hypersthene, *n.* (*Min.*) an orthorhombic, foliated, brittle mineral allied to hornblende, with a beautiful pearly lustre. **hypersthenic**[1], *a.* **hypersthenite,** *n.* (*Min.*) a variety of pyroxenite mainly composed of hypersthene. [F *hypersthène* (Gr. *sthenos,* strength)]

hypertension, *n.* abnormally high blood pressure. **hypertensive,** *a.* suffering from hypertension.

hyperthermia, *n.* abnormally high body temperature. [Gr. *thermē,* heat]

hyperthesis, *n.* transposition of a letter from one syllable to another. **hyperthetic**, *a.* [Gr. *hyperthesis* (*thesis,* placing, from *tithenai,* to put)]

hyperthyroidism, *n.* excessive activity of the thyroid gland, causing an accelerated metabolic rate, nervousness etc.

hypertonic, *a.* of muscles, being excessively tense; of a solution, more concentrated than a surrounding medium or than another liquid.

hypertrophy, *n.* excessive development or enlargement. *v.t.* to affect with hypertrophy. *v.i.* to be affected by hypertrophy. **hypertrophic, -ical**, **hypertrophous,** *a.* [Gr. *-trophia,* from *trephein,* to nourish]

hyperventilation, *n.* excessive breathing, causing excessive loss of carbon dioxide in the blood.

hypethral, *a.* open to the sky, roofless (esp. of a temple or sanctuary not intended to be roofed). **hypaethron,** *n.* a temple with a central space open to the sky. [L *hypaethrus,* Gr. *hupaithros* (HYPO-, *aithēr,* ETHER)]

hyphen, *n.* a short stroke (-) joining two words or parts of words. *v.t.* to join by a hyphen. **hyphenic,** *a.* **hyphenate, hyphenize, -ise,** *v.t.* **hyphenation, hyphenization, -isation,** *n.* [L, from Gr. *huphen*]

hypnagogic, hypnogogic, *a.* of or concerning the state of drowsiness before sleep. [Gr. *agōgos,* leading, from *agein,* to lead]

hypn(o)-, *comb. form.* sleep. [Gr. *hupnos*]

hypnogenesis, *n.* inducement of hypnotic sleep. **hypnogeny**, *n.* **hypnogenetic,** *a.*

hypnology, *n.* the study of the phenomena of sleep; a treatise on sleep. **hypnologist,** *n.*

hypnopompic, *a.* of or concerning the state of drowsiness between sleep and waking. [Gr. *pompé,* sending, procession]

hypnosis, *n.* inducement of sleep; a morbid state of sleep; a state resembling sleep in which the subconscious mind responds to external suggestions and forgotten memories are recovered.

hypnotherapy, *n.* treatment by hypnotism.

hypnotic, *a.* causing sleep; soporific; of, pertaining to or inducing hypnotism. *n.* a medicine that produces sleep; an opiate.

hypnotism, *n.* an artificial method of inducing sleep or hypnosis; sleep artificially produced. **hypnotist,** *n.* **hypnotize, -ise,** *v.t.* to affect with hypnotism. **hypnotizable,** *a.* **hypnotizability, -isability**, *n.* **hypnotization, -isation,** *n.* **hypnotizer, -iser,** *n.*

hypnum, *n.* (*pl.* **-nums, -na**) a genus of pleurocarpous mosses known as feather-moss. [Gr. *hupnon*]

hypo[1], *n.* common term for sodium thiosulphate, the normal fixing solution in photography. [abbr. sodium hyposulphite]

hypo[2], *n.* (*coll.*) short for HYPODERMIC NEEDLE.

hyp(o)-, *comb. form.* under, below; less than; (*Chem.*) denoting compounds having a lower degree of oxidation in a series. [Gr. *hupo,* under]

hypoblast, *n.* the innermost membrane of the blastoderm. **hypoblastic**, *a.* [Gr. *blastos,* sprout]

hypobole, *n.* a mode of reasoning in which several things seemingly opposed to the argument are mentioned and then refuted. [Gr. *hupobolē* (ballein, to throw)]

hypobranchial, *a.* (*Anat.*) situated below the gills or branchiae. *n.pl.* in fish, the lower and inner part of the branchial arch.

hypocaust, *n.* in ancient Roman buildings, a space or

series of channels under the floor by which heat was conducted from a furnace to heat a building, room, bath etc.; a stove. [late L *hypocaustum,* Gr. *hupokauston* (*kaiein,* fut. *kaus-,* to burn)]

hypochlorite, *n.* a salt or ester of hypochlorous acid. **hypochlorous acid,** *n.* an unstable acid formed when chlorine dissolves in water, used as a bleach, disinfectant etc.

hypochondria, *n.* a morbid condition characterized by excessive anxiety with regard to the health, and depression of spirits, see also HYPOCHONDRIUM. **hypochondriac,** *a.* produced or characterized by hypochondria; having a disordered mind; causing melancholy; pertaining to, connected with or situated in the hypochondria. *n.* a person affected with hypochondria. †**hypochondriacal,** *a.* **hypochondriacally,** *adv.* **hypochondriasis,** †**hypochondriacism,** *n.* †**hypochondriast,** *n.* **hypochondrium,** *n.* (*pl.* **-dria**), either of the two regions of the abdomen situated to the right and left under the costal cartilages and short ribs. [late L, pl., from Gr. *hupochondria,* pl., the soft parts below the cartilage (*chondros,* cartilage, esp. that of the breast-bone)]

hypocist, *n.* an astringent inspissated juice obtained from the fruit of *Cytinus hypocistis,* a plant from southern France. [F *hypociste,* L *hypocistis,* Gr. *hupokistis*]

hypocorism, *n.* a pet name. **hypocoristic,** *a.* [Gr. *hupokorizesthai,* from *korizesthai,* to caress, from *koros,* boy, *koré,* girl]

hypocrisy, *n.* dissimulation; a feigning to be what one is not; a pretence to virtue or goodness. **hypocrite,** *n.* one who practises hypocrisy; a dissembler. **hypocritical,** *a.* **hypocritically,** *adv.* [OF *hypocrisie,* L *hypocrisis,* Gr. *hupokrisis,* acting of a part, from *hupokrinesthai* (*krinein,* to judge, decide)]

hypocycloid, *n.* a curve generated by a point on the circumference of a circle rolling round the inside of the circumference of another circle. **hypocycloidal,** *a.*

hypoderm, hypoderma, *n.* (*pl.* **-mata**) (*Zool.*) a layer beneath the outer integument, as the inner membrane lining the elytra of beetles; (*Bot.*) the cellular layer beneath the epidermis of leaves etc. **hypodermal,** *a.* hypodermic. **hypodermic,** *a.* pertaining to parts underlying the skin. *n.* (a drug introduced into the system by) an injection under the skin; (*coll.*) a hypodermic syringe. **hypodermic injection,** *n.* an injection (of narcotics, antitoxins etc.) beneath the skin. **hypodermic needle,** *n.* (the hollow needle of) a hypodermic syringe. **hypodermic syringe,** *n.* a small syringe with a hollow needle for giving hypodermic injections. **hypodermically,** *adv.* [Gr. *derma,* skin]

hypogastrium, *n.* (*Anat.*) the middle part of the lowest zone into which the abdomen is divided. **hypogastric,** *a.* **hypogastrocele,** *n.* (*Path.*) hernia in the region of the hypogastrium. [Gr. *hupogastrion* (*gastēr,* belly)]

hypogean, -geal, -geous, *a.* existing or growing underground; subterranean. **hypogene, hypogenic,** *a.* applied to rocks that were formed under the surface; plutonic. [L *hypogēus,* Gr. *hupogeios* (*gē,* earth)]

hypogeum, *n.* (*pl.* **-gea**) (part of) a building below the level of the ground.

hypoglossal, *a.* under the tongue. **hypoglossal nerve,** the motor nerve of the tongue. **hypoglossus,** *n.* (*Anat.*) the hypoglossal nerve. [Gr. *glossa,* tongue]

hypoglycaemia, *n.* an abnormally low level of sugar in the blood.

hypognathous, *a.* having a lower mandible longer than the upper. **hypognathism,** *n.* [Gr. *gnathos,* jaw]

hypogynous, *a.* of stamens, growing from below the base of the ovary; of plants, having the stamens so situated.

hypolimnion, *n.* the lower, colder layer of water below the thermocline of a lake. [Gr. *limné,* lake]

hypomania, *n.* the mental state of over-excitability. **hypomanic,** *a.*

hyponasty, *n.* more active growth of a plant-organ on the under side causing a tendency to upward curvature. [Gr. *nastos,* solid, from *nassein,* to press]

hypophosphate, *n.* a salt of hypophosphoric acid. **hypophosphite,** *n.* a salt of hypophosphorous acid. **hypophosphoric, hypophosphorous,** *a.* **hypophosphoric acid,** *n.* an acid formed by action of water and oxygen on phosphorus. **hypophosphorous acid,** *n.* a weak acid composed of hydrogen, phosphorus and oxygen.

hypophysis, *n.* (*pl.* **-physes**) the pituitary gland; a cell in the embryo, in flowering plants, from which the root and root-cap are developed; in mosses, an enlarged part of the pedicel beneath the capsule. **hypophyseal, -physial,** *a.* [Gr. *hupophusis* (*phusis,* from *phuein,* to grow)]

hypoplasia, *n.* underdevelopment of an organ or part. [Gr. *plasis,* formation]

hyposensitize, -ise, *v.t.* to reduce the sensitivity of, to desensitize.

hypostasis, *n.* (*pl.* **-stases**) that which forms the basis of anything; in metaphysics, that by which a thing subsists, substance as distinguished from attributes; the essence or essential principle; the personal subsistence, as opposed to substance, of the Godhead; one of the persons of the Trinity; congestion of the blood (in an organ) by weight. **hypostatic, -ical,** *a.* pertaining to hypostasis; constitutive or elemental; constituting a distinct personality or substance. **hypostatic union,** *n.* union of the divine and human natures in Christ. **hypostatically,** *adv.* **hypostasize, -ise,** *v.t.* to attribute proper personal existence to; to treat as or make into a substance. **hypostasization, -isation,** *n.* [late L, from Gr. *hupostasis,* (*statis,* standing, basis)]

hypostome, *n.* a part or organ situated below the mouth, as the proboscis of Hydrozoa, the under lip of a trilobite etc. **hypostoma,** *n.* (*pl.* **-stomata**). [Gr. *stoma,* mouth]

hypostyle, *a.* having the roof supported by pillars. *n.* a building with a roof or ceiling supported by pillars; a covered colonnade; a pillared hall. [Gr. *stulos,* pillar]

hyposulphite, *n.* a thiosulphate, a salt of hyposulphurous acid. **hyposulphuric acid,** *n.* acid containing two more atoms of oxygen per molecule than sulphuric acid. **hyposulphurous acid,** *n.* an unstable acid containing one more sulphur atom per molecule than sulphuric acid.

hypotaxis, *n.* subordinate construction in syntax, opp. to parataxis. **hypotactic,** *a.*

hypotension, *n.* abnormally low blood pressure.

hypotenuse, *n.* the side of a right-angled triangle opposite to the right angle. [F *hypoténuse,* late L *hypotenusa,* Gr. *hupoteinousa,* fem. p.p. of *hupoteinein* (*teinein,* to stretch)]

hypothalamus, *n.* a region at the base of the brain controlling autonomic functions, e.g. hunger, thirst.

hypothec, *n.* (*esp. Sc., Law*) a security in favour of a creditor over the property of his debtor, while the property continues in the debtor's possession. **hypothecary,** *a.*of or pertaining to a pledge or hypothecation. **hypothecate,** *v.t.* to pledge or mortgage in security for some debt or liability. **hypothecation,** *n.* **hypothecator,** *n.* [F *hypothèque,* late L *hypothēca,* Gr. *hupothēkē* (HYPO-, *thēkē,* from *tithenai,* to place)]

hypothermia, *n.* subnormal body temperature, esp. when induced for surgical purposes. [Gr. *therme,* heat]

hypothesis, *n.* (*pl.* **-theses**) a proposition assumed for the purpose of argument; a theory assumed to account for something not understood; a mere supposition or assumption. **hypothesize, -ise,** *v.i.* to form hypotheses. *v.t.* to assume. **hypothetic, -ical,** *a.* founded on or of the nature of a hypothesis; conjectural, conditional. **hypothetically,** *adv.* [L, from Gr. *hupothesis* (HYPO-, THESIS)]

hypothyroidism, *n.* underactivity of the thyroid gland.

hypotonic, *a.* of muscles, deficient in tension; of a solution, less concentrated than a surrounding medium or than another liquid.

hypotrachelium, *n.* a groove round the junction of the capital and shaft in a Doric column. [Gr. *hupotrachelion* (HYPO-, *trachelos,* neck)]

hypotyposis, *n.* (*pl.* **-oses**) a vivid or forcible description of a scene, so as to present it attractively to the mind. [Gr. *hupotupōsis*]

hypoxia, *n.* a deficiency of oxygen reaching the body tissues.

hypozoic, *a.* (*Geol.*) situated beneath the strata that contain organic remains. **Hypozoa**, *n.pl.* Protozoa. **hypozoan,** *n.*, *a.*

hyps(o)-, *comb. form.* height. [Gr. *hupsos,* height]

hypsography, *n.* the branch of geography concerned with the altitudes above sea-level. **hypsographical**, *a.*

hypsometer, *n.* an instrument for measuring heights above sea-level by observing the boiling-point of water with a delicate thermometer and so determining the relative atmospheric pressure. **hypsometric, -ical**, *a.* **hypsometry,** *n.* the art of measuring heights by observing differences in barometric pressures at different altitudes.

hypural, *a.* (*Ichthyol.*) situated below the tail, as the bones supporting the fin-rays. [HYPO-, Gr. *oura,* tail]

hyrax, *n.* a genus of small hare-like quadrupeds, comprising the Syrian rock-rabbit or cony of Scripture and the S African rock-badger. **hyracid**, *a.* **hyracoid**, *n.*, *a.* [Gr. *hurax,* shrew-mouse]

hyson, *n.* a kind of green tea. **hyson-skin,** *n.* the inferior grade of this. [Chin. *hei-ch'un,* bright spring]

hy-spy, *n.* hide-and-seek. [I SPY]

hyssop, *n.* a labiate plant, *Hyssopus officinalis,* with blue flowers; in Biblical times, an unidentified plant the twigs of which were used for sprinkling in Jewish rites of purification. [L *hyssōpus,* Gr. *hussōpos,* perh. from Heb.]

hyster- HYSTERO.

hysterectomy, *n.* the removal of the womb by surgery. [HYSTER-, Gr. *ektomē* (*ek,* out, *temnein,* to cut)]

hysteresis, *n.* the tendency of a magnetic substance to remain in a certain magnetic condition, 'the lag of magnetic effects behind their causes'. **hysteresial,** *a.* [Gr. *husterēsis,* from *husteros,* late]

hysteria, *n.* a nervous disorder, occurring in paroxysms, and often simulating other diseases. **hysteric**, *n.* one subject to hysteria. *a.* hysterical. *n.pl.* a fit or fits of hysteria, hysteria. **hysterical,** *a.* pertaining to or affected with hysteria; morbidly emotional or excitable. **hysterical fit,** *n.* an emotional paroxysm of crying, laughing etc., occurring in hysteria. **hysterically,** *adv.* **hysterics,** *n.pl.* a hysterical fit; (*coll.*) a fit of uncontrollable laughter. **hysterogenic**, *a.* producing hysteria. **hysterogenous**, *a.* **hysterogeny**, *n.* **hysteroid**, *a.* resembling hysteria. [mod. L, from Gr. *hustera,* the womb (from its having been attributed formerly to disturbance of the womb)]

hysteritis, *n.* inflammation of the uterus. [as foll., -ITIS]

hystero-, hyster-, *comb. form.* womb; hysteria. [Gr. *hustera,* womb]

hysterogenetic, *a.* (*Bot.*) later in origin or development. **hysterogenic**, *a.* [Gr. *husteros,* later, GENETIC]

hysteroid HYSTERIA.

hysterology, *n.* the branch of medical science concerned with the uterus; a treatise on this. [HYSTERO-, -LOGY]

hysteron proteron, *n.* a figure of speech in which what should follow comes first; an inversion of the natural or logical order. [Gr. *husteron,* latter, *proteron,* former]

hysterotomy, *n.* delivery of a child through the walls of the abdomen; hysterectomy. [HYSTERO-, -TOMY]

hythe, HITHE.

I

I[1], **i**, the ninth letter and the third vowel in the English alphabet (*pl.* **Is, I's**), has two principal sounds: long, as in *bīnd, fīnd;* short, as in *fin, bin, win* etc.; and three minor sounds: (1) as in *dirk*, (2) as in *intrigue* , and (3) the consonantal sound of *y*, as in *behaviour*, *onion*; the Roman numeral symbol for one; (*Math.*) the symbol for the square root of minus one.

I[2], *nom. sing. 1st pers. pron.* (*obj.* **me**, *poss.* **my**, *pl. nom.* **we**, *obj.* **us**, *poss.* **our**) in speaking or writing denotes oneself. *n.* (*Metaph.*) the self-conscious subject, the ego. [OE *ic* (cp. Dut. *ik*, Icel. *ek*, G *ich*, L *ego*, Gr. *egō*)]

I[3], (*abbr.*) Institute; Island; Italy.

I[4], (*chem. symbol*) iodine.

-i, *suf.* indicating plural of L nouns in *-us* or *-er*, as *fungi, hippopotami;* also of It. nouns and adjectives in *-o* or *-e, banditti, literati.* [L]

Ia., (*abbr.*) Iowa.

-ia, *suf.* forming abstract nouns, as *mania, militia;* names of countries etc., as *Australia, Bulgaria, Helvetia;* names of diseases, as *hysteria, malaria, neuralgia;* names of botanical genera etc., as *Begonia, Gaillardia, Saponaria;* names of alkaloids, as *morphia, strychnia;* (*pl.* of L *-ium,* Gr. *-ion*) *bacteria, mammalia, regalia, reptilia.* [L and Gr.]

IAEA, (*abbr.*) International Atomic Energy Agency.

-ial, *suf.* forming adjectives, as *celestial, terrestrial.* [L *-iālis, -iāle*]

iambus, iamb, *n.* (*pl.* **-buses**) a poetic foot of one short and one long, or one unaccented and one accented syllable. **iambic,** *a.* of or pertaining to the iambus; composed of iambics. *n.* an iambic foot; an iambic verse. †**iambically,** *adv.* **iambist,** *n.* **iambize, -ise,** *v.t.* **iambographer**, *n.* a writer of iambics. [L, from Gr. *iambos,* an iambic verse, a lampoon, from *iaptein,* to assail]

-ian, *suf.* forming nouns or adjectives, as *Athenian, Baconian, Bristolian, Cantabrigian.* [L *-ānus,* -AN, with a euphonic or connective *-i-*]

Iaşi, *n.* (German **Jassy**) city in NE Romania, capital of Moldavia; population (1985) 314,000. It has chemical, machinery, electronic, and textile industries.

-iasis, *comb. form.* indicating a disease, as *elephantiasis, phthiriasis.* [L, from Gr. *-iasis,* from *iāsthai,* to heal]

IATA, (*abbr.*) International Air Transport Association.

iatric, -ical, *a.* pertaining to physicians or medicine. †**iatraliptic**, *a.* curing by the application of ointments and friction. †**iatrarchy**, *n.* the medical hierarchy. **iatrochemical,** *a.* pertaining to the application of chemistry to medicine. **iatrochemist,** *n.* **iatrochemistry,** *n.* **iatrogenic**, *a.* resulting unintentionally from medical treatment. **iatrogenically,** *adv.* **iatrogenicity**, *n.* **-iatrology**, *n.* the science of or a treatise on medicine. **-iatrics,** *comb. form.* indicating medical care, as *paediatrics.* **-iatry,** *comb. form.* indicating healing treatment, as *psychiatry.* [*iātrikos,* as prec., *aleptes,* anointer]

IBA, (*abbr.*) Independent Broadcasting Authority.

Ibadan, *n.* city in SW Nigeria and capital of Oyo state; population (1981) 2,100,000. Industries include chemicals, electronics, plastics, and vehicles.

Iban, *n.* (formerly known as **Dayak**) a people of central Borneo. Approximately 250,000 Iban live in the interior uplands of Sarawak, while another 10,000 live in the border area of W Kalimantan. The Iban speak languages belonging to the Austronesian family.

Ibáñez, *n.* **Vincente Blasco** (1867–1928), Spanish novelist and politician, born in Valencia. He was actively involved in revolutionary politics. His novels include *La barraca/The Cabin* (1898), the best of his regional works; *Sangre y arena/Blood and Sand* (1908), the story of a famous bullfighter; and *Los cuatro jinetes del Apocalipsis/The Four Horsemen of the Apocalypse* (1916), a product of the effects of World War I.

Ibarruri, *n.* **Dolores** (1895–1989), known as La Pasionaria ('the passion flower') Spanish Basque politician, journalist, and orator. In 1936 she helped to establish the Popular Front government, and was a Loyalist leader in the Civil War. When Franco came to power in 1939 she left Spain for the USSR, where she was active in the Communist Party. She returned to Spain in 1977 after Franco's death, and was re-elected to the Cortes (at the age of 81) in the first parliamentary elections for 40 years.

Iberian, *a.* of or pertaining to ancient Iberia in Europe, comprising modern Spain and Portugal, or ancient Iberia in Asia, now Transcaucasian Georgia. *n.* one of the inhabitants of ancient Iberia in Europe, or in Asia; one of an ancient race, chiefly dolichocephalic, who inhabited western Europe and probably entered the British Isles early in the Neolithic period, variously identified with the Silures, the modern Basques etc., but not recognized as a definite ethnological group by most recent authorities; the language of ancient Iberia. **Iberian Peninsula,** *n.* Spain and Portugal. [L *Ibēria,* from Gr. *Ibēres,* -AN]

Iberis, *n.* (*Bot.*) a genus of crucifers comprising the candytufts. [as prec.]

ibex, *n.* the name given to several species of wild goats inhabiting the mountain regions of Europe and Asia, of which the best known is the common ibex or steenbok, *Capra ibex.* [L]

ibid., (*abbr.*) ibidem.

ibidem, *adv.* in the same place (as in a book, page etc.). [L *ibi,* there, *-dem,* suf. as in *īdem,* the same]

ibis, *n.* any of a genus (*Ibis*) of heron-like wading birds belonging to the family Ibididae, esp. *I. religiosa,* the sacred ibis, which was venerated by the ancient Egyptians. [L and Gr., prob. of Egyptian orig.]

Ibiza, *n.* one of the Balearic Islands, a popular tourist resort; area 596 sq km/230 sq miles; population (1986) 45,000. The capital and port, also called Ibiza, has a cathedral.

-ible, *suf.* as in *edible, risible.* **-ibility**, *suf.* **-ibly**, *suf.* [L *-ibilis,* -ABLE]

Iblees, *pl.* EBLIS.

Iblis EBLIS.

IBM, (abbr.) International Business Machines.

Ibn Battuta, *n.* (1304–68), Arab traveller born in Tangiers. In 1325, he went on an extraordinary 120,675 km/75,000 miles journey via Mecca to Egypt, E Africa, India, and China, returning some 30 years later. During this journey he also visited Spain and crossed the Sahara to Timbuktu. The narrative of his travels, *The Adventures of Ibn Battuta,* was written with an assistant, Ibn Juzayy.

Ibn Saud, *n.* (1880–1953), first king of Saudi Arabia from 1932. His father was the son of the sultan of Nejd, at whose capital, Riyadh, Ibn Saud was born. In 1891 a rival group seized Riyadh, and Ibn Saud went into exile with his father, who resigned his claim to the throne in his favour. In 1902 Ibn Saud recaptured Riyadh and recovered the kingdom, and by 1921 he had brought all central Arabia under his rule. In 1924 he invaded the Hejaz, of which he was proclaimed king in 1926.

Ibn Sina, *n.* Arabic name of Avicenna, scholar and translator.

Ibo, Ebo, *n.* a black African people living in SE Nigeria; person of Ibo culture from Nigeria's East-Central State (*pl.* **Ibo, Ibos**). Primarily cultivators, they inhabit the richly forested tableland, bound by the River Niger to the W and the Cross River to the E. They are divided into five main divisions, and their languages belong to the Kwa branch of the Niger-Congo family. *a.* of the Ibo.

Ibrahim, *n.* **Abdullah** (1934–), South African pianist and composer, formerly known as 'Dollar' Brand. He first performed in the US in 1965, and has had a great influence on the fusion of African rhythms with American jazz. His compositions range from songs to large works for orchestra.

Ibsen, *n.* **Henrik (Johan)** (1828–1906), Norwegian playwright and poet, whose realistic and often controversial plays revolutionized European theatre. Driven into exile 1864–91 by opposition to the satirical *Love's Comedy* (1862), he wrote the verse dramas *Brand* (1866) and *Peer Gynt* (1867), followed by realistic plays dealing with social issues, including *Pillars of Society* (1877), *The Doll's House* (1879), *Ghosts* (1881), *An Enemy of the People* (1882), and *Hedda Gabler* (1891). By the time of his return to Norway, he was recognized as the country's greatest living writer.

-ic, *suf.* of, pertaining to, like, as in *alcoholic, algebraic, domestic, Miltonic, plutonic;* (*Chem.*) in acids etc., denoting a higher state of oxidation than the suffix *-ous;* forming names of sciences, arts etc., as *arithmetic, epic, logic, music;* (*later in pl.*) as acoustics, *aesthetics, economics, metaphysics, politics;* (*recent var.*) *aesthetic, metaphysic* etc. [L *icus* (sometimes through F *-ique*), usu. from Gr. *-ikos*]

i/c, (*abbr.*) in charge.

ICA, (*abbr.*) Institute of Chartered Accountants; Institute of Contemporary Arts.

-ical, *suf.* forming adjectives, as *algebraical, comical, historical, political.* **-ically,** *suf.* forming adverbs, as *historically, politically.* [-IC, -AL]

ICAO, (*abbr.*) International Civil Aviation Organization.

Icarus¹, *n.* in Greek mythology, the son of Daedalus, who died when he flew too near the sun using wings made from feathers fastened with wax. **Icarian,** *a.* soaring too high; rash or adventurous in flight.

Icarus², *n.* in astronomy, an Apollo asteroid 1.5 km/1 mile in diameter, discovered 1949. It orbits the Sun every 409 days ata distance of between 2.0 and 0.19 astronomical units (about 150 million km). It is the only asteroid known to approach the Sun closer than the planet Mercury.

ICBM, (*abbr.*) intercontinental ballistic missile.

ice, *n.* water congealed by cold; a frozen confection of cream, syrup etc., ice-cream; a confection of sugar etc. used for coating cakes etc. *v.t.* to cover or cool with ice; to convert into ice; to coat with concreted sugar; to frost; to freeze. *v.i.* to freeze; to become covered with ice. **dry ice,** frozen carbon dioxide. **on ice,** in abeyance. **on thin ice,** in a vulnerable or dangerous situation. **to break the ice** BREAK. **to cut no ice,** (*coll.*) to fail to make an impression, to be unimportant. **young ice,** ice which has formed recently. **ice age,** *n.* a glacial period. **Ice Age, Little,** *n.* period of particularly severe winters that gripped N Europe between the 13th and 17th (or 16th and 19th) cent. **ice-axe,** *n.* an axe shaped like a pickaxe, used by mountain-climbers for cutting steps on glaciers etc. **ice-bird,** *n.* an Arctic seabird, the little auk or sea-dove. **ice-blink,** *n.* a luminous reflection over the horizon from snow- or ice-fields. **ice-boat,** *n.* a boat for travelling on ice; a heavily-built boat for breaking a passage through ice. **ice-bound,** *a.* completely surrounded with ice; fringed or edged with ice; unable to get out because of ice. **icebox,** *n.* the freezing compartment of a refrigerator; a portable insulated box containing ice; (*chiefly N Am.*) a refrigerator. **ice-breaker,** *n.* a ship with a reinforced hull for forcing a channel through ice; (*coll.*) something that encourages a relaxed atmosphere among a group of people. **ice-brook,** *n.* a frozen stream or brook. **ice bucket, pail,** *n.* a bucket containing ice, for keeping wine etc. cool. **ice-cap,** *n.* a mass of ice and snow permanently covering an area. **ice-cave,** *n.* a cave in which ice remains unmelted throughout the year. **ice-claw,** *n.* an apparatus for lifting blocks of ice. **ice-cream,** *n.* cream or custard flavoured and artificially frozen. **ice-drift,** *n.* masses of floating ice. **ice-fall,** *n.* a shattered part of a glacier where it descends a steep slope. **ice-field,** *n.* a large expanse of ice, esp. such as exist in the Polar regions. **ice-floe, -pack,** *n.* a sheet of floating ice. **ice-foot,** *n.* a hill or wall of ice along the shore in Polar regions. **ice hockey,** *n.* a type of hockey played on ice by teams of skaters. **ice-house,** *n.* a repository for the storage of ice. **ice lolly,** *n.* (*coll.*) a flavoured piece of ice or ice-cream on a stick. **iceman,** *n.* one who deals in ice or ices; one skilled in traversing or navigating through ice. **ice-pack,** *n.* ICE-FLOE; a bag etc. containing ice applied to a part of the body to reduce swelling or ease pain. **ice pail** ICE BUCKET. **ice pick,** *n.* a pointed tool for splitting ice. **ice-plant,** *n.* a creeping plant, *Mesembryanthemum crystallinum,* whose leaves have a glistening lustre somewhat like ice. **ice rink,** *n.* a rink for ice-skating. **ice-river,** *n.* a glacier. **ice-saw,** *n.* a saw for cutting through ice in order to free ships. **ice-show,** *n.* (*Theat.*) a performance on ice by actors wearing skates. **ice skate,** *n.* a boot with a blade attached for skating on ice. **ice-skate,** *v.i.* **ice-skater,** *n.* **ice-spar,** *n.* a vitreous orthoclase. **ice-stream,** *n.* a stream of drifting ice-floes. **ice-wall,** *n.* a rampart of ice-blocks piled up on the shore. **ice-water, iced water,** *n.* water from melted ice; water cooled by ice. **icing,** *n.* a coating of concreted sugar. **icing sugar,** *n.* powdered sugar used for icing cakes etc. **icy,** *a.* pertaining to or consisting of ice; like ice, frozen; (*fig.*) frigid, chilling. **icily,** *adv.* **iciness,** *n.* [OE *īs* (cp. Dut *ijs,* Icel. *īss,* G *Eis*)]

-ice, *suf.* forming nouns, as *justice, malice, novice, service.* [OF *-ice,* L *itia, -itius, -itium*]

iceberg, *n.* a large mass of ice, usu. floating on the sea at high latitudes, usu. formed by detachment from a glacier; a cold and unresponsive person. **tip of the iceberg,** the part of an iceberg visible above the water; the most obvious part of a huge problem etc. [prob. from Dut. *ijsberg* (*ijs,* ICE, *berg,* hill)]

Iceland, *n.* Republic of, island in the N Atlantic, situated S of the Arctic Circle, between Greenland and Norway. **area** 103,000 sq km/39,758 sq miles. **capital** Reykjavik. **physical** warmed by the Gulf Stream; glaciers and lava fields cover 75% of the country. **exports** cod and other fish products. **population** (1987) 247,400; annual growth rate 1.2%. **language** Icelandic, the most archaic Scandinavian language, in which some of the finest sagas were written. **religion** Evangelical Lutheran. **Iceland lichen, moss,** *n.* an edible moss or lichen, *Cetraria islandica,* growing in the northern and mountainous parts of Europe, used as a medicine. **Iceland poppy,** *n.* the yellow Arctic poppy. **Iceland spar,** *n.* a transparent variety of calcite. **Icelander,** *n.* a native or inhabitant of Iceland. **Icelandic,** *n.* a member of the N Germanic branch of the Indo-European language family, spoken only in Iceland and the most conservative in form of the Scandinavian languages. *a.* pertaining to Iceland. [Icel. *Island* (*iss,* ICE, LAND)]

Iceni, *n.pl.* an ancient people of E England, who revolted against occupying Romans under Boudicca.

I Ching, *n.* an ancient Chinese method of divination employing a set of symbols, 8 trigrams and 64 hexagrams, together with the text known as the *I Ching* which serves to interpret them. [Chin., book of changes]

ichneumon, *n.* a small carnivorous animal, *Herpestes ichneumon,* related to the mongoose, found in Egypt, where it was formerly held sacred on account of its devouring crocodiles' eggs; the ichneumon-fly, which lays its eggs in or upon the larvae of other insects, upon which its larvae will feed. **ichneumonidan,** *a.* pertaining to the Ichneumonidae. *n.* an insect of this family. **ichneumonid**, *n.* **ichneumonology**, *n.* the branch of entomology dealing with the Ichneumonidae. **ichneumon-fly,** *n.* a hymenopterous insect belonging to the family Ichneumonidae. [L, from Gr. *ichneumōn,* from *ichneuein,* to track, from *ichnos,* a track]

ichnite, ICHNOLITE.

ichnography, *n.* the art of drawing ground-plans etc. **ichnograph**, *n.* a ground-plan. **ichnographic, -ical,** *a.* **ichnographically,** *adv.* [Gr. *ichnos,* a track]

ichnolite, ichnite, *n.* a stone with the impression of a footprint. [as prec.]

ichnology, ichnolithology, *n.* the department of palaeontology that treats of and classifies fossil footprints. **ichnological, ichnolithological**, *a.* [as prec.]

ichor, *n.* (*Gr. Myth.*) the ethereal fluid which took the place of blood in the veins of the gods; a thin watery humour like serum; a watery acrid discharge from a wound etc. **ichorology**, *n.* (*Path.*). **ichorous,** *a.* [Gr. *ichōr*]

ichthy-, ichthyo-, *comb. form.* pertaining to fish; fish-like. [Gr. *ichthus,* a fish]

ichthyic, *a.* pertaining to fishes; having the characteristics of a fish.

ichthyodorulite, -dorylite, *n.* a fossil spine of a fish or fish-like vertebrate. [Gr. *doru,* spear]

ichthyography, *n.* a description of or a treatise on fishes. **ichthyographer,** *n.*

ichthyoid, *a.* resembling fish. *n.* a vertebrate of fishlike form.

ichthyol, *n.* a brownish-black substance, obtained by distilling a bituminous shale containing fish-remains, from the Tyrol, used as an application in skin diseases. [L *oleum,* OIL]

ichthyolatry, *n.* the worship of fishes, or of a fish god such as Dagon. **ichthyolater,** *a.* **ichthyolatrous,** *a.*

ichthyolite, *n.* a fossil fish; an impression of a fossil fish. **ichthyolitic**, *a.*

ichthyology, *n.* the branch of zoology concerned with fishes; the natural history of fishes. **ichthyologic, -ical**, *a.* **ichthyologist,** *n.* one versed in ichthyology.

ichthyomancy, *n.* divination by means of the entrails or the heads of fish. **ichthyomantic**, *a.*

ichthyomorphic, *a.* having the form of a fish; (*Zool.*) having the characteristics of fishes.

ichthyophagy, *n.* the practice of eating fish; fish diet. **ichthyophagist**, *n.* **ichthyophagous**, *a.* [through F *ichtyophagie* or directly from Gr. *ichthuophagia* (ICHTHYO-, *-phagia,* from *phagein,* to eat)]

ichthyopsida, *n.pl.* (*Zool.*) according to Huxley's terminology, the lowest of the three main divisions of vertebrates, comprising fishes, amphibians, and fish-like vertebrates, the other two divisions being Mammalia and Sauropida. [Gr. *opsis,* appearance]

ichthyornis, *n.* an extinct bird having biconcave vertebrae and socketed teeth. [Gr. *ornis,* a bird]

ichthyosaurus, *n.* a genus of gigantic fossil marine reptiles, chiefly from the Lias. **ichthyosaur**, *n.* any species of the order Ichthyosauria of which the type genus is *Ichthyosaurus*. [Gr. *sauros,* lizard]

ichthyosis, *n.* a hereditary skin disease, marked by thick, hard, imbricated grey scales. **ichthyotic**, *a.*

ichthyotomy, *n.* the dissection of fishes. **ichthyotomist,** *n.*

ichthys, *n.* a symbol in the form of a fish, connected with Christ because the Greek letters ιχθυϑ gave the initials of the Greek words meaning 'Jesus Christ, Son of God, Saviour'. [Gr. *ichthus,* a fish]

ICI, (*abbr.*) Imperial Chemical Industries.

-ician, *suf.* indicating a specialist in a subject, as in *beautician*.

icicle, *n.* a hanging conical point of ice, formed by dripping water freezing. [OE *īses giecel* (*īses,* gen. of *īs,* ICE, *giecel,* cogn. with Icel. *jökull,* icicle, glacier, orig. dim. of *jaki,* a piece of ice)]

icily, icing etc. ICE.

icky, *a.* (*coll.*) cloying; over-sentimental. [perh. alt. of *sticky*]

-icle, *suf.* diminutive, as in *particle, versicle.* [L *-iculus, -iculum, -icula*]

icon, ikon, *n.* in the Eastern Church, a sacred image, picture, mosaic, or monumental figure of a holy personage, usu. regarded as endowed with miraculous attributes (see also EIKON); a symbol; a hero-figure; a pictorial representation of a facility available to the user of a computer system. **iconic**, *a.* pertaining to or consisting of figures or pictures; (*Art*) following a conventional pattern or type, as busts, memorial effigies etc. **iconic memory,** *n.* the continuation of a sense impression after the stimulus has disappeared. [late L *īcōn,* Gr. *eikon,* image, likeness]

icono-, *comb. form.* of or pertaining to images or idols. [as prec.]

iconoclasm, *n.* the breaking of idols; attack on or disregard of established opinions etc. **iconoclast**, *n.* a breaker of images, esp. one of the religious zealots in the Eastern Empire who attacked the worship of images during the 8th and 9th cents.; an assailant or despiser of established practices etc. **iconoclastic**, *a.* **iconoclastically,** *adv.* [Gr. *klasma,* from *klaein,* to break]

iconography, *n.* a treatise on or the study of pictures, statues, engravings on gems, symbolism etc.; the illustration of a subject by means of figures etc.; a book or other collection of figures, drawings etc.; pictorial matter relating to a subject. **iconographer,** *n.* **iconographic, -ical,** *a.* [Gr. *ikonographia*]

iconolatry, *n.* adoration of images. **iconolater,** *n.*

iconology, *n.* the science or study of images, pictures etc.; symbolism. **iconological**, *a.* **iconologist,** *n.*

iconomachy, *n.* war against images or idols. [late Gr. *eikonomachia* (*-machia,* from *machesthai,* to fight)]

iconomatic, *a.* denoting a kind of writing in which pictures or figures of objects represent phonetic elements, a stage of writing intermediate between picture-writing and phonetic writing. [Gr. *onoma,* name]

iconometer, *n.* an instrument for measuring the size or distance of an object; a directvision viewfinder. **iconometry,** *n.*

iconophile, *n.* a connoisseur of pictures, prints etc. **iconophilism, -phily,** *n.* **iconophilist,** *n.*

iconoscope, *n.* a type of electron camera.

iconostasis, *n.* (*pl.* **-ses**) in the Eastern Church, a screen on which icons are placed separating the sanctuary from the rest of the church. [late Gr. *eikonostasis* (Gr. *stasis,* standing, position)]

icosahedron, *n.* (*pl.* **-dra, -drons**) (*Geom.*) a solid figure having 20 plane sides; a regular solid contained by 20 equilateral triangles. **icosahedral,** *a.* [Gr. *eikosaedron* (*eikosi,* twenty, *hedra,* seat, base)]

Icosandria, *n.pl.* (*Bot.*) a Linnaean class containing plants with 20 or more stamens inserted on the calyx. **icosander**, *n.* a plant of the class Icosandria. **icosandrous, -drian,** *a.* [Gr. *eikosi,* twenty, *anēr andros,* man, male]

-ics, *suf.* (*usu. sing. in constr.*) indicating a science or art, as *linguistics;* indicating specified activities, as *acrobatics;* indicating matters etc. relating to, as *mechanics*. [-IC]

icterus, *n.* jaundice; a disease of plants characterized by yellowness of the leaves; a genus of American birds belonging to the Icteridae, and including the orioles. **icteric,** *a.* affected with jaundice; good against jaundice; belonging to the Icteridae. *n.* a remedy for jaundice. **icterical,** *a.* icteric. **icterine,** *a.* †**icteritious,** *a.* yellow; resembling the skin in jaundice. **icteroid,** *a.* [L, from Gr. *ikteros,* jaundice]

ictus, *n.* (*pl.* **ictuses, ictus**) the stress, beat, or rhythmical accent in metre; the beat of the pulse. †**ictic,** *a.* [L, a stroke, from *icere,* to strike]

icy ICE.

ID, (*abbr.*) identification.

Id., (*abbr.*) Idaho.

I'd, *contr. form. I had* or *I would.*

id[1], *n.* (*Biol.*) a unit of germplasm (according to Weismann's theory of heredity); (*Psych.*) the instinctive impulses of the individual. [from IDIOPLASM]

id.[2], (*abbr.*) idem, the same.
-id, *suf.* forming adjectives denoting the quality orig. expressed by a Latin verb, as *acid, frigid, morbid, tepid;* (*Bot.*) denoting a member of an order, as *amaryllid* (Amaryllidaceae), orchid (Orchidaceae); (*Zool.*) member of a family, as *arachnid* (Arachnida). [F *-ide,* L *idus,* ult. from Gr. *-id-,* nom. *-is,* pl. *-idēs*]
IDA, (*abbr.*) International Development Association.
-idae, *suf.* indicating membership of a specified zoological family.
Idaho, *n.* state of NW US; nickname Gem State. **area** 216,500 sq km/ 83,569 sq miles. **capital** Boise. **towns** Pocatello, Idaho Falls. **products** potatoes, wheat, livestock, timber, silver, lead, zinc, antimony. **population** (1984) 1,001,000. **religion** Christian, predominantly Mormon. **history** first permanently settled 1860 after the discovery of gold, Idaho became a state 1890.
Idalian, *a.* pertaining to Idalia or to Aphrodite or Venus. [*Idalia,* a mountain in Cyprus, sacred to Aphrodite]
ide, *n.* a northern European fish, *Leuciscus idus,* of the carp family. [Swed. *id*]
-ide, *suf.* indicating chemical compounds of an element with another element or a radical, as *chloride, fluoride, oxide.* [-ID]
idea, *n.* a mental image, form, or representation of anything; a notion, a conception, a supposition; a more or less vague opinion, belief, or fancy; a plan, an intention or design; a view, a way of thinking or conceiving (something); (*Platonic*) the archetype or perfect and eternal pattern of which actual things are imperfect copies; (*Cartesian etc.*) the immediate object of cognition, present in consciousness as representing an actual thing; (*Kantian etc.*) a conception or ideal of the pure reason transcending mere experience. **not my** etc. **idea of,** not what I etc. expect something or someone to be like. **the very idea!,** that is ridiculous. **to get ideas,** (*coll.*) to become over-ambitious; to develop the wrong expectations or impressions. **to have no idea,** to be unaware of what is going on; (*coll.*) to be innocent or stupid. **what's the big idea?** (*coll.*) what is the purpose of this? **idea'd, ideaed,** *a.* **ideate,** *n.* (*Phil.*) the actual existence correlating with an idea. *v.t.*, to form in ideas, to imagine; to apprehend and retain mentally. *v.i.* to form ideas. **ideation,** *n.* **ideational,** *a.* **idealess,** *a.* destitute of ideas. [late L, from Gr. (*idein,* to see)]
ideal, *a.* consisting of, existing in, or pertaining to ideas, mental; visionary, fanciful; reaching one's standard of perfection; (*Phil.*) of or pertaining to idealism or the Platonic ideas. *n.* an imaginary standard of perfection; an actual thing realizing this. **idealism,** *n.* the practice of forming ideals; the quest of an ideal; (*Art*) the representation of things in conformity with an ideal standard of perfection; (*Phil.*) the doctrine that in external perceptions the objects immediately known are ideas. **idealist,** *n.* **idealistic,** *a.* **idealistically,** *adv.* **ideality,** *n.* the quality of being ideal; (*Art*) capacity to form ideals. **idealize, -ise,** *v.t.* to make ideal; (*Art.*) to portray in conformity with an ideal. *v.i.* to form ideals. **idealization, -isation,** *n.* the representing of an object in accordance with one's desires or ideals. **idealizer, -iser,** *n.* **ideally,** *adv.* in an ideal manner; intellectually, mentally. †**idealness,** *n.*
idée fixe, *n.* a fixed idea, monomania. [F]
idem, *n.* the same (word, author, book etc.). [L]
identical, *a.* absolutely the same, not different (though viewed or found under different conditions); similar in essentials; uniform in quality, appearance etc.; (*Math.*) expressing identity. **identical twins,** *n.pl.* uniovular or similar twins, having developed from a single oocyte. **identic,** *a.* (*Diplom.*) identical. **identic note,** *n.* a note or expression or opinion in precisely similar terms (addressed simultaneously by the representatives of several powers to another). **identically,** *adv.* **identicalness,** *n.* [formerly *identic,* F *identique,* late L *identicus,* formed from *identitas,* IDENTITY]
identify, *v.t.* to consider or represent as precisely the same (with); to determine or prove the identity of; to prove to be the same (with); to unite or associate (oneself) closely (with a party, interests etc.). *v.i.* to associate oneself (with); to consider oneself to be at one (with). **identifiable,** *a.* **identifiably,** *adv.* **identification,** *n.* the act of identifying; the state of being identified; a proof of identity; the assumption of the characteristics of another, esp. of an admired person. **identification parade,** *n.* a number of persons assembled by the police and among whom a witness is invited to identify a suspect. **identifier,** *n.* [F *identifier,* late L *identificāre*]
identikit, *n.* a set of facial features on transparent slips, used to compose a likeness, esp. of a criminal suspect; a portrait built up in this way. *adj.* pertaining to such portraits; (*coll.*) conforming to an unimaginative pattern. [from *Identi-Kit,* trademark]
identity, *n.* the state of being identical; absolute sameness; one's individuality; (*Alg.*) absolute equality between two expressions; an equation expressing such equality. **old identity,** an old inhabitant. **identity crisis,** *n.* a state of psychological confusion resulting from a failure to reconcile discordant elements in one's personality. **identity element,** *n.* a mathematical element belonging to a set and which leaves any other member of that set unchanged when combining with it. [F *identité,* late L *identitātem* nom. *-tas,* from L IDEM]
ideo-, *comb. form.* pertaining to or expressing ideas. [IDEA]
ideograph, ideogram, *n.* a symbol, figure etc., suggesting or conveying the idea of an object, without expressing its name. **ideographic, -ical,** *a.* **ideographically,** *adv.* **ideography,** *n.* a system of or a treatise on ideographic writing.
ideology, *n.* the science of ideas, esp. that enunciated by Condillac; abstract or fanciful theorizing; the political or social philosophy of a nation, movement, group etc. **ideological,** *a.* **ideologically,** *adv.* **ideologist, ideologue,** *n.* a supporter of an ideology; one who treats of ideas; a theorist, a visionary. **ideologize, -ise,** *v.t.*
ideo-metabolic, *a.* denoting the influence of psychological, esp. emotional, states on the metabolic processes.
ideo-motor, ideo-muscular, *a.* (*Psych.*) denoting unconscious muscular movements due to the concentration of attention on an idea.
ideopraxist, *n.* one who puts ideas into practice. [Gr. *praxis,* doing]
Ides, *n.pl.* in the ancient Roman calendar, the 15th of March, May, July, October, and 13th of the other months. [F, from L *īdūs*]
id est, that is, that is to say (usu. written i.e.). [L]
idio-, *comb. form.* individual, peculiar. [Gr. *idios,* peculiar to oneself]
†**idiocrasy,** *n.* idiosyncrasy. †**idiocratic, -ical,** *a.* peculiar in constitution. [Gr. *idiokrāsia* (*krāsis,* CRASIS)]
idiocy IDIOT.
idioelectric, *a.* applied to substances electric by virtue of their own peculiar properties, and which are readily electrified by friction. *n.* an idoelectric substance.
idiograph, *n.* a private mark or signature, esp. a trademark. **idiographic,** *a.* [Gr. *ideographon*]
idiolect, *n.* a form of speech or language peculiar to an individual. **idiolectal, -tic,** *a.*
idiom, *n.* a mode of expression, esp. an irregular use of words, peculiar to a language; a peculiarity of expression or phraseology; a dialect, a peculiar speech or language; a mode of artistic expression characteristic of a particular person or school. **idiomatic, -ical,** *a.* peculiar to or characteristic of a language; dialectal, vernacular; expressed in idioms. **idiomatically,** *adv.*
idiomorphic, *a.* (*Min.*) having a distinctive form of its own, esp. distinctive faces of crystallization.
idiopathy, *n.* a primary disease, one not occasioned by another; †a characteristic affection or disposition peculiar to an individual. †**idiopathetic, idiopathic, -ical,** *a.* **idiopathically,** *adv.*
idioplasm, *n.* the portion of protoplasm derived from

the parent organism, and supposed to determine the character of the individual, distinguished from that which is due to the development of the individual. **idioplasmatic**, *a.*

idiosyncrasy, *n.* individual quality, habit, or attitude of mind; a characteristic peculiar to an individual; (*Med.*) individual temperament or constitution; esp. an abnormal sensitivity to a particular food, drug etc. **idiosyncratic, -ical**, *a.* **idiosyncratically,** *adv.* [Gr. *idiosunkrāsia*]

idiot, *n.* a person of weak or defective understanding; one belonging to the lowest grade of mental defectives; one destitute of reason or intellectual powers; a stupid, silly person. *a.* idiotic. **idiot board,** *n.* (*coll.*) an autocue. **idiot box,** *n.* (*sl.*) a television set. **idiot tape,** *n.* a computer tape printing out information in an unbroken stream, lacking any line breaks. **idiocy,** †**idiotcy,** *n.* **idiotic, -ical**, *a.* resembling or characteristic of an idiot; foolish, silly, absurd. **idiotically,** *adv.* †**idiotism,** *n.* an idiom; an idiosyncrasy; idiocy. **idiotize, -ise,** *v.i.* to become idiotic. *v.t.* to make an idiot of; to make a fool of. [F, from L *idiōta,* Gr. *idiōtēs,* a private person, hence one who is ignorant or not an expert, from *idios,* see IDEO-]

idle, *a.* doing nothing; disengaged, inactive, not occupied, free; not in use; averse to work, lazy; useless, vain, ineffectual; unfruitful, barren; trifling, without foundation. *v.i.* to spend time in idleness; †to move about aimlessly or lazily; of machinery, to run slowly without the transmission being engaged. *v.t.* to spend (time) in idleness; to cause to idle. *n.* the act of idling, indolence. **to idle away,** to spend in idleness. †**idle-headed,** †**-pated,** *a.* foolish, unreasonable; delirious, infatuated. **idle-pulley,** *n.* a pulley able to rotate freely as a means of guiding or controlling the tension of a belt. **idle-tongs** LAZY-TONGS. **idle-wheel,** *n.* a cogged wheel between two others for transmitting motion. †**idle-worms,** *n.pl.* worms supposed to breed in the fingers of lazy persons. **idleness,** †**idlesse**, *n.* **idler,** *n.* one who spends his or her time in idleness; (*Naut.*) a person not required to keep night watch. **idly,** *adv.* [OE *idel,* empty, vain (cp. Dut. *ijdel,* G *eitel,* also Gr. *itharos,* pure)]

Ido, *n.* an artificial international language based on Esperanto.

idocrase, *n.* (*Min.*) Vesuvianite. [F (Gr. *eidos,* form, *krāsis,* CRASIS)]

idol, *n.* an image, esp. one worshipped as a god; a false god; a person or thing loved or honoured excessively; (*Phil.*) a false conception, a misleading tendency, a fallacy. **idolater**, *n.* one who worships idols; a pagan; an adorer, an extravagant admirer. **idolatress,** *n. fem.* †**idolatrize, -ise,** *v.i.* to practise idolatry. *v.t.* to adore; to worship as an idol. **idolatrous,** *a.* **idolatrously,** *adv.* **idolatry,** *n.* †**idolish,** *a.* idolatrous, pagan, heathenish. **idolism,** *n.* idolatry; idolization; a vain opinion or fancy. †**idolist,** *n.* an idolater. **idolize, -ise,** *v.t.* to worship as an idol; to make an idol of; to love or venerate to excess. **idolization, -isation,** *n.* **idolizer, -iser,** *n.* [OF *idole,* L *īdōlum -lon,* Gr. *eidōlon,* from *eidos,* form]

idolon, idolum, *n.* (*pl.* **-la**) an image, an appearance; a phantom, an apparition; (*Phil.*) a fallacious appearance or misconception, classified by Bacon as *idola tribūs, specūs, fori, theatri,* idols of the tribe, the cave, the marketplace, and the theatre, that is, limitations of the human mind, personal prejudices, fallacies due to the influence of words and phrases, and philosophic and logical misconceptions.

†**idoneous,** *a.* proper, suitable. [L *idoneus*]

idrialite, *n.* (*Min.*) a greyish crystalline hydrocarbon found in the mines of Idria, also called inflammable cinnabar. **idrialin,** *n.* a crystalline compound which is an essential constituent of idrialite. [*Idria,* in Austria, -LITE]

idyll, *n.* a short pastoral poem; a brief, artistic, and picturesque narrative or description of rustic life, either in verse or prose; a work of art, esp. a musical piece, of a similar character; a scene, episode, or situation suitable for the tone of such a composition. **idyllic,** *a.* pertaining to or suitable for an idyll; perfect in harmony, peace, beauty etc. **idyllically,** *adv.* **idyllist,** *n.* **idyllize, -ise,** *v.t.* [L *īdyllium,* Gr. *eidullion,* dim. of *eidos,* form]

i.e., (*abbr.*) id est.

-ie, *suf.* -Y.

IEEE, (*abbr.*) Institute of Electrical and Electronic Engineers.

-ier, *suf.* denoting occupation, profession etc., as in *bombardier, brigadier, chevalier, financier*. [F *-ier* or -EER]

if, *conj.* on the supposition that, providing that, in case that; even on the supposition, allowing that; whenever, at the time when; whether; also used in an exclamatory sense, as *if only you were here!*. *n.* (*coll.*) an uncertain or doubtful factor; a condition. **as if,** as it would be if. **ifs and ans,** things that might have been. **ifs and buts,** objections. [OE *gif* (cp. Dut. *of,* Icel. *ef, if,* G *ob*)]

-iferous, *suf.* -FEROUS.

iffy, *a.* (*coll.*) doubtful, uncertain; risky.

-iform, *suf.* -FORM.

Ifugao, *n.* people of N Luzon in the Philippines, numbering approximately 70,000. Their language belongs to the Austronesian family.

igloo, *n.* an Eskimo hut, often built of snow. [Eskimo]

†**ignaro,** *n.* (*pl.* **-ros**) an ignorant person. [It., from L *ignārus,* IGNORANT]

Ignatian, *a.* pertaining to St Ignatius, Bishop of Antioch or to St Ignatius of Loyola, founder of the Society of Jesus. *n.* a follower of the latter, a Jesuit. **Ignatian Epistles,** *n.pl.* epistles advocating episcopacy attributed to St. Ignatius of Antioch. [*Ignatius,* -AN]

Ignatius Loyola, St *n.* (1491–1556), Spanish soldier converted 1521 to the Roman Catholic religious life after being wounded in battle, and founder of the Jesuit order in 1540. Feast day 31 July.

Ignatius of Antioch, St *n.* (1st–2nd cent. AD), Christian martyr. Traditionally a disciple of St John, he was bishop of Antioch, and was thrown to the wild beasts in Rome. He wrote seven epistles, important documents of the early Christian church. Feast day 1 Feb.

igneous, *a.* containing or of the nature of fire; emitting fire; (*Geol.*) produced by volcanic action. [L *igneus,* from *ignis,* fire]

†**ignescent,** *a.* emitting sparks when struck, as with steel; scintillating. *n.* a mineral emitting sparks when struck.

†**igniferous,** *a.* producing fire.

†**ignigenous,** *a.* produced by fire.

†**ignipotent,** *a.* ruling over fire.

ignis fatuus, *n.* (*pl.* **ignes fatui**), an apparent flame probably due to the spontaneous combustion of inflammable gas, floating above the ground in marshes etc.; a delusive object or aim. [L, foolish fire (see FATUOUS)]

ignite, *v.t.* to set on fire; to render luminous or red with heat. *v.i.* to take fire; to become red with heat. **ignitable, ignitible,** *a.* **ignitability, ignitibility**, *n.* **ignition,** *n.* the act of igniting; the state of being ignited; the mechanism for igniting the explosive mixture in the internal-combustion engine. **ignition-box, -chamber,** *n.* the chamber in an engine, gun etc., in which combustion takes place. **ignition key,** *n.* the key that operates the ignition system in a motor vehicle. **igniter,** *n.* person who or that which sets on fire, esp. a contrivance for igniting powder in an explosive, firing the gases in an internal-combustion engine etc. [L *ignītus,* p.p. of *ignīre,* from *ignis,* fire]

ignoble, *a.* of humble or mean birth; mean, base, despicable, unworthy, dishonourable. †*v.t.* to make ignoble; to dishonour. **ignobility**, **ignobleness,** *n.* **ignobly,** *adv.* [F, from *ignōbilis* (IN-[1], *gnōbilis, nōbilis,* NOBLE)]

ignominy, †**ignomy**, *n.* public disgrace or shame; dishonour, infamy; an act deserving disgrace; (*coll.*) contemptuous treatment. **ignominious**, *a.* **ignominiously,** *adv.* **ignominiousness,** *n.* [F *ignominie,* L *ignōminia* (IN-², *gnōmen, nōmen,* name, from *gnōscere,* to know)]

ignoramus, *n.* (*pl.* **-muses**) an ignorant fellow; a stupid person, a fool; †(*Law*) 'we know nothing of it', the endorsement on a bill by the grand jury when there was not sufficient evidence to support the charge. †*a.* ignorant. [L, we do not know]

ignorance, *n.* the state of being ignorant; want of knowledge (of). **ignorant,** *a.* destitute of knowledge, unconscious (of); illiterate, uninstructed, uneducated; †done inadvertently. †*n.* an ignorant person. **ignorantism,** *n.* obscurantism. **ignorantly,** *adv.* [F, from L *ignōrantia,* from *ignōrans -ntem,* ignorant]

Ignorantine, *n.* a member of a Roman Catholic order originally founded (1495) to minister to the sick poor, later devoted to the teaching of poor children and called Brethren of the Christian Schools. *a.* pertaining to this order. [F *ignorantin,* from *ignorant,* IGNORANT]

ignoratio elenchi, the fallacy of arguing to the wrong point. [L]

ignore, *v.t.* to pass over without notice, to disregard; deliberately to pay no attention; (*Law*) to throw out (a bill) as unsupported by sufficient evidence. **ignorable,** *adj.* **ignoration,** *n.* [F *ignorer,* L *ignōrāre* (IN-², *gnō-,* stem of *gnoscere,* to know)]

Iguaçu Falls, Iguassú Falls *n.* waterfall in South America, on the border between Brazil and Argentina. The falls lie 19 km above the junction of the Iguaç with the Paraná. They are divided by forested rocky islands and form a spectacular tourist attraction. The water plunges in 275 falls, many of which have separate names. They have a height of 82m/269 ft, and a width about 4 km/2.5 miles.

iguana, *n.* any of a genus (*Iguana*) of large American lizards, esp. *I. tuberculata,* of South and Central America and the West Indies. [Sp., from Carib. *iwana*]

iguanodon, *n.* a genus of extinct gigantic lizards. [IGUANA, Gr. *odous odontos,* tooth]

IJsselmeer, *n.* lake in the Netherlands, formed 1932 after the Zuider Zee was cut off by a dyke from the North Sea; freshwater since 1944. Area 1217 sq km/470 sq miles.

IKBS, (*abbr.*) intelligent knowledge-based system, alternative name for the more usual KBS (knowledge-based system).

ikebana, *n.* the Japanese art of arranging flowers. [Jap.]

Ikhnaton, Akhenaton, *n.* (14th cent. BC) king of Egypt of the 18th dynasty (*c.* 1379–62 BC), who may have ruled jointly for a time with his father Amenhotep III. He developed the cult of the sun, Aton rather than the rival cult of Ammon. Some historians believe that his neglect of imperial defence for religious reforms led to the loss of most of Egypt's possessions in Asia. His favourite wife was Nefertiti, and two of their six daughters were married to his successors Smenkhare and Tutankaton (later known as Tutankhamen).

ikon ICON.

il-¹, *pref.,* as in *illation, illuminate.* [IN-¹]

il-², *pref.,* as in *illiberal, illicit.* [IN-²]

-il, -ile, *suf.* that may be, capable of being, pertaining to etc., as in *civil, fossil, docile, fragile, Gentile, puerile, senile.* [OF *-il,* F *-ile,* L *-īlis* (*-ilis* in OF became *-le,* as in *humble,* L *humilis,* HUMBLE¹, *frail, fragilis,* FRAIL¹)]

ILEA, *n.* (*abbr.*) Inner London Education Authority (abolished 1990 and replaced by smaller borough-based education authorities).

ileac, etc. ILIAC.

Ile-de-France, *n.* region of N France; area 12,000 sq km/4632 sq miles; population (1986) 10,251,000. It includes the French capital, Paris, and the towns of Versailles, Sèvres, and St-Cloud, and is comprised of the *départements* of Essonne, Val-de-Marne, Val d'Oise, Ville de Paris, Seine-et-Marne, Hauts-de-Seine, Seine-Saint-Denis, and Yvelines. From here the early French kings extended their authority over the whole country.

ileo-, *comb. form.* (*Anat., Path.*) ileum.

ileocaecal, *a.* pertaining to the ileum and the caecum. **ileocaecal valve,** *n.* a membrane covering the opening of the ileum into the caecum.

ileum, *n.* (*pl.* **ilea**) the portion of the small intestine communicating with the larger intestine. [late L, from L *īlia,* pl., the flanks, the groin (modified in form by confusion with *īleus,* Gr. *eileos,* see ILIAC)]

†ileus, ILIAC.

ilex, *n.* (*pl.* **-lexes**) the holm-oak; a genus of trees or shrubs with coriaceous leaves, typified by the holly. [L]

iliac, *a.* of or belonging to the ileum or smaller intestines; pertaining to the ilium or hip-bone. **†iliac passion,** *n.* pains due to obstruction of the bowels. **iliac region,** *n.* the part of the abdomen between the ribs and the hips. [F *iliaque,* late L *īliacus,* from L *īlia,* see ILIUM (meaning as if from L *īleos,* Gr. *eileos,* pain in the intestines)]

Iliad, *n.* an epic poem, usually ascribed to Homer, consisting of 24 books, describing the incidents of the 10th and last year of the siege of Troy; a long narrative or series of events, esp. of a mournful kind. [L *Ilias -adis,* Gr. *Ilias,* adj., of Ilium or Troy]

ilio-, *comb. form.* pertaining to or situated near the *ilium.*

ilium, *n.* (*pl.* **-ia**) the upper part of the hip-bone. [L, a part of the abdomen (cp. ILEUM)]

ilk, *a.* the same. **of that ilk,** of the same name (used when the surname of a person is the same as the name of his estate). **that ilk,** (*coll., erron.*) that family or kind. [OE *ilca* (pron. stem *i-, -lic,* LIKE¹)]

ilka, *a.* (*Sc.*) each, every. [*aelc,* EACH, A]

I'll, *contr. form.* of *I will* or *I shall.*

Ill., (*abbr.*) Illinois.

ill, (*comp.* **worse,** *superl.* **worst**) *a.* unwell, sick, diseased; bad morally, evil; malevolent, hostile, adverse; tending towards evil, noxious, mischievous, harmful; unfortunate, unfavourable, unlucky; not right, faulty, inferior, incorrect, improper; unskilful; awkward, cross (in temper); †unwholesome. *adv.* (*comp.* **worse,** *superl.* **worst**) not well, badly; not rightly; not easily; imperfectly, scarcely; unfavourably, in bad part or humour. *n.* evil; injury, harm; wickedness; (*pl.*) misfortunes. **ill at ease,** uncomfortable, anxious. **to be taken ill,** to fall sick. **to speak ill,** to speak (of, about) unfavourably. **to take ill, to take in ill part,** to take offence at. **ill-advised,** *a.* imprudent; injudicious. **ill-advisedly,** *adv.* **ill-affected,** *a.* not friendly disposed; disaffected, †affected with bad impressions. **ill-assorted,** *a.* poorly matched; not compatible. **ill blood, ill feeling,** *n.* resentment, displeasure, enmity. **†ill-boding,** *a.* inauspicious. **ill-bred,** *a.* brought up badly; rude, unmannered, offensive. **ill breeding,** *n.* want of good breeding; rudeness. **ill-conditioned,** *a.* having a bad temper or disposition; in a bad physical condition. **ill-considered,** *a.* done without careful thought; misconceived. **ill-defined,** *a.* poorly defined; lacking a clear outline. **ill-disposed,** *a.* wickedly or maliciously inclined; unfavourably inclined (towards). **ill fame,** *n.* disrepute. **ill-fated,** *a.* unfortunate, unlucky. **ill-favoured,** (*Sc.*) **ill-faurd,** *a.* ugly, deformed; forbidding, repulsive; unattractive, objectionable. **†ill-favouredly,** *adv.* **ill-favouredness,** *n.* **ill-feeling** ILL BLOOD. **ill-founded,** *a.* lacking any foundation in fact, not substantiated. **ill-got, ill-gotten,** *a.* obtained in an improper way. **ill humour,** *n.* bad temper. **ill-humoured,** *a.* **ill-humouredly,** *adv.* **ill-judged,** *a.* not well-judged; injudicious, unwise. **ill luck,** *n.* bad luck, misfortune. **ill-manned,** *a.* (*Naut.*) having an insufficient crew. **ill-mannered,** *a.* rude, boorish. **ill-matched,** *a.* not well-matched or suited. **ill-mated,** *a.* badly joined or mated. **ill nature,** *n.* evil disposition; lack of kindness or good feeling. **ill-natured,** *a.* of a churlish disposition, bad-tempered; expressive of or indicating ill nature; †not yielding to culture, intractable. **ill-naturedly,** *adv.* **ill-naturedness,** *n.* **ill-omened,** *a.* unlucky, inauspicious, of evil augury. **ill-starred,** *a.* born under the influence of an unlucky planet, hence unlucky. **ill temper,** *n.* **ill-tempered,** *a.* having a bad temper, sour, peevish. **ill-timed,** *a.* done, said, or attempted, at an unsuitable time. **ill-treat** ILL USE. **ill treatment** ILL USAGE. **ill turn,** *n.* an ill-natured act or treatment; †an attack of illness. **ill usage,** *n.* unkind treatment. **ill use,** *v.t.* to treat badly. **ill-versed,** *a.* uninstructed, lacking skill (in). **ill will,** *n.* malevolence, enmity. [ME, from Icel. *illr*]

†illapse, *n.* a gliding of one thing into another; influx, inspiration. *v.i.* to fall, to glide (into). [L *illapsus,* p.p. of *illābī* (IL-¹, LAPSE)]

†illaqueate, *v.t.* to ensnare, to entrap. **†illaqueation,** *n.* [L *illaqueātus,* p.p. of *illaqueāre* (IL-¹, *laqueāre,* from *laqueus,* noose, snare)]

illation, *n.* deduction; a deduction, an inference. **illative,** *a.* denoting, expressing, or of the nature of an inference; of some Finno-Ugrian languages, denoting a noun case expressing motion or direction. *n.* that which denotes inference, as an illative particle; the illative case. **illatively,** *adv.* [F, from late L *illatiōnem,* nom. *-tio* (IL-¹, *lāt-,* p.p. stem of *ferre,* to bear)]

Illawarra Shorthorn, *n.* a noted breed of Australian dairy cattle. [Illawarra, New South Wales]

illegal, *a.* not according to law; contrary to law, unlawful. **illegality,** *n.* **illegalize, -ise,** *v.t.* to render illegal. **illegally,** *adv.* [med. L *illegālis*]

illegible, *a.* that cannot be read or deciphered. **illegibility, -ibleness,** *n.* **illegibly,** *adv.*

illegitimate, *a.* not lawfully begotten; born out of wedlock; contrary to law or recognized usage; irregular, improper; illogical, contrary to logical rules, unsound. *n.* an illegitimate child, a bastard; one of illegitimate status, *v.t.*, to render or declare illegitimate. **illegitimacy,** *n.* the state of being illegitimate. **illegitimately,** *adv.* **illegitimation,** *n.* **illegitimatize, -ise,** *v.t.* to illegitimate.

illiberal, *a.* not generous, petty, sordid; narrow-minded, niggardly, stingy; not catholic; rude, vulgar, not characterized by wide views or by culture. **illiberality,** *n.* **illiberalize, -ise,** *v.t.* to render illiberal. **illiberally,** *adv.* [F *illibéral*]

Illich, *n.* **Ivan** (1926–), US radical philosopher and activist, born in Austria. His works, which include *Deschooling Society* (1971), *Towards a History of Need* (1978), and *Gender* (1983), are a critique against modern economic development, especially in the Third World.

illicit, *a.* not allowed or permitted; unlawful. **illicitly,** *adv.* **illicitness,** *n.* [F *illicite,* L *illicitus*]

illimitable, *a.* boundless, limitless. **illimitability, illimitableness,** *n.* **illimitably,** *adv.* **†illimitation,** *n.* absence of or freedom from limitation. **†illimited,** *a.* unlimited, infinite. **illimitedly,** *adv.* **illimitedness,** *n.*

illinium, *n.* promethium.

Illinois, *n.* midwest state of the US; nickname Inland Empire/Prairie State. **area** 146,100 sq km/56,395 sq miles. **capital** Springfield. **towns** Chicago, Rockford, Peoria, Decatur. **population** (1987) 11,582,000. **products** soybeans, cereals, meat and dairy products, machinery, electric and electronic equipment.

illiquid, *a.* of assets, not easily convertible into cash; of a company etc., lacking liquid assets; (*Law*) not clearly proved or manifest. **illiquidity,** *n.*

†illision, *n.* a striking or dashing against. [L *illīsio -ōnem,* from *illīdere* (IL-¹, *laedere,* to strike)]

illiterate, *a.* unlearned, ignorant of letters; unable to read or write; ignorant in a specific subject; rude, uncultivated. *n.* an ignorant or uneducated person, esp. one unable to read. **illiterately,** *adv.* **illiteracy, illiterateness,** *n.* [L *illīterātus*]

illness, *n.* the state of being ill, sickness, physical indisposition; †unfavourableness, depravity; †badness (of the weather).

illogical, *a.* ignorant or careless of the rules of logic; contrary to reason. **illogically,** *adv.* **†illogicalness, illogicality,** *n.*

illude, *v.t.* to deceive, to cheat; to mock. [L *illūdere* (*lūdere,* to play)]

illume, *v.t.* to illuminate, to lighten or brighten up; (*fig.*) to enlighten. [shortened form of ILLUMINE]

illuminate, *v.t.* to throw light upon; to light up; to adorn (buildings, streets etc.) with festal lamps; to adorn (a manuscript etc.) with coloured pictures, letters etc.; to enlighten mentally or spiritually; to make illustrious. *v.i.* to adorn manuscripts etc. with coloured pictures, letters etc. *a.* lit up; claiming enlightenment; initiated into something esoteric. *n.* an initiate. **illuminable,** *a.* **illuminant,** *a.* illuminating. *n.* that which illuminates. **illuminating,** *a.* lighting up; enlightening. **illumination,** *n.* lighting up; enlightenment; a source of light; (*often pl.*) a display of ornamental lights; the adornment of manuscripts etc. with ornamental coloured letters and pictures; clarification; illuminance. **illuminative,** *a.* **illuminator,** *n.* [L *illūminātus,* p.p. *illūmināre* (*lūmināre,* from *lūmen -inis,* light)]

Illuminati, *n.pl.* a name given to several sects and secret societies professing to have superior enlightenment, esp. a German society of deists and republicans founded by Adam Weishaupt in 1776; hence any persons who affect to possess extraordinary knowledge or gifts. **illuminee,** *n.* one of the Illuminati. **illuminism,** *n.* the principles or doctrines of the Illuminati. **illuminist,** *n.* **†illuminize, -ise,** *v.t.* to initiate into or instruct in the doctrines of the Illuminati. *v.i.* to become an illuminist. [L, pl. of *illūminātus,* or It., pl. of *illuminato,* as prec.]

illumine, *v.t.* to illuminate; to enlighten; to brighten. [F *illuminer*]

illus., (*abbr.*) illustrated; illustration.

illusion, *n.* the act of deceiving; that which deceives; a false show, a delusion; a conjuring trick; an unreal image presented to the vision; esp. a deceptive sensuous impression; (*Psych.*) a wrong interpretation of what is perceived through the senses. **illusionism,** *n.* a theory that regards the external world as a mere illusion of the senses; the artistic practice of aiming to give an illusion of reality. **illusionist,** *n.* one given to illusions, a visionary; one who produces illusions, as a conjurer; a believer in illusionism. **illusive, illusory,** *a.* delusive, deceptive. **illusively, illusorily,** *adv.* **illusiveness, illusoriness,** *n.* [F, from L *illūsiōnem,* nom. *-sio,* from *illūdere,* to ILLUDE]

illustrate, *v.t.* to make clear, to explain or elucidate by means of examples, figures etc.; to embellish or elucidate by pictures etc.; †to illuminate; †to make celebrated, to glorify. †*a.*, illustrious, glorified. **illustration,** *n.* the act of illustrating; the state of being illustrated; that which illustrates, an example, a typical instance; an engraving or drawing illustrating a book or article in a periodical; an embellishment. **illustrational, illustrative, †illustratory,** *a.* **illustratively,** *adv.* **illustrator,** *n.* [L *illustrātus,* p.p. of *illustrāre* (*lustrāre*)]

illustrious, *a.* distinguished, famous; conferring lustre, renown, or glory; brilliant. **illustriously,** *adv.* **illustriousness,** *n.* [L *illustris* (*-lustris,* from stem of *lux,* light, *lūcidus,* bright)]

Illyria, *n.* ancient name for the eastern coastal region on the Adriatic, N of the Gulf of Corinth, conquered by Philip of Macedon. It became a Roman province AD 9. The Albanians are the survivors of its ancient peoples.

ILP, (*abbr.*) International Labour Party.

ILS, (*abbr.*) instrument landing system.

I'm, contr. form of *I am.*

im-¹, *pref.* (before *b, m, p*), as in *imbibe, imbrue.* [IN-¹]

im-², *pref.* (before *b, m, p*), as in *immaculate, impossible.* [IN-²]

image, *n.* the visible representation or similitude of a person or thing; a likeness, an effigy, a statue, esp. one intended for worship, an idol; a copy, a counterpart; the living embodiment of a particular quality; an idea, a conception; a mental picture; a persistent mental conception; the impression given to others of a person's character etc.; an expanded metaphor or simile; a lively description; the figure of an object formed (through the medium of a mirror, lens etc.) by rays of light; a mental representation of a sense impression. *v.t.* to make an image of; to mirror; to portray; to represent mentally; to conceive in the mind; to typify, to symbolize; to represent a part of the body pictorially for medical purposes. **image-maker,** *n.* a public relations expert employed to improve the impression that someone, e.g. a politician, makes on the general public. **image orthicon,** *n.* type of television camera tube. **image-worship,** *n.* idolatry. **imageable,** *a.* **imageless,** *a.* **imagery,** *n.* an image; (*collect.*) images, statues; appearance, imitation; figures evoked by the fancy; rhetorical figures, figurative description. **imagism,** *n.* **imagist,** *n.* a follower of a poetical school that seeks to express itself through clear and precise images of nature etc. **imagistic,** *a.* [F, from L *imāginem,* nom. *imāgo,* prob. from *im-,* root of IMITATE]

imaginable etc. IMAGINE.

imaginal IMAGO.

imagine, *v.t.* to form an image of in the mind, to conceive, to form an idea of; (*coll.*) to suppose, to think; to believe without any justification; to conjecture, to guess; to plot, to devise. *v.i.* to form images or ideas in the mind. **imaginable,** *a.* that can be imagined. **imaginably,** *adv.* **imaginary,** *a.* existing only in imagination or fancy; not real, esp. a mathematical quantity or value assumed as real for the purposes of an equation etc. **imaginary number,** *n.* a number involving the square root of a negative number. **imaginarily,** *adv.* **imaginariness,** *n.* **imagination,** *n.* the act or process of imagining; the power of imagining; the mental faculty that forms ideal images or combinations of images from the impressions left by sensuous experience; fancy, fantasy; the constructive or creative faculty of the mind; a mental image; a fanciful opinion, a fancy; †a contrivance, a plot. **imaginative,** *a.* endowed with imagination; creative, constructive; produced or characterized by imagination; †imaginary; †*n.* imagination. **imaginatively,** *adv.* **imaginativeness,** *n.* **imaginer,** *n.* **imagining,** *n.* imagination; a conception, an idea. †**imaginist,** *n.* **imaginal,** *a.* [F *imaginer,* L *imāginārī*]

imagism, *n.* a movement in Anglo-American poetry which flourished in London 1912–14 and affected much British and US poetry and critical thinking thereafter. A central figure was Ezra Pound, who asserted principles encouraging free verse, hard imagery, and poetic impersonality.

imago, *n.* (*pl.* **-goes, -gines**) the adult, fully-developed insect after its metamorphoses; an idealized type of a parent or other person exercising a persistent influence in the subconscious. **imaginal,** *a.* pertaining to the imago or perfect form of an insect. [L, IMAGE]

imam, *n.* a person who leads congregational prayer in a mosque; the title of various Muslim rulers and founders. **imamate, imamship,** *n.* [Arab. *imām,* from *amma,* to precede]

imbalance, *n.* a lack of balance.

imbalm, imbank, imbar, imbargo, imbark, imbathe, EMBALM etc.

imbecile, *a.* mentally weak, half-witted; stupid, fatuous; physically weak. *n.* one mentally weak; one who, though mentally deficient, shows signs of rudimentary intelligence; a stupid or foolish person. **imbecilely,** *adv.* †**imbecilitate,** *v.t.* to render feeble or weak. **imbecility,** *n.* [F *imbécille* (now *imbécile*), L *imbecillum,* nom. *-lus,* etym. doubtful]

imbed, imbellish, EMBED etc.

imbibe, *v.t.* to drink in; to draw in, to absorb; to receive into the mind. *v.i.* (*facet.*) to drink; to indulge in a drinking session. **imbiber,** *n.* **imbibition,** *n.* absorption; drinking in; (*facet.*) drinking. **water of imbibition,** the quantity of water absorbed by rocks and remaining present above the level of saturation. [through F *imbiber* or directly from L *imbibere* (*bibere,* to drink, to BIB)]

imbitter, imblaze, imbody, imbolden, EMBITTER etc.

†**imbosk,** *v.t.* to hide (oneself) as in an ambush. *v.i.* to lie concealed. [It. *imboscare* (*bosco,* wood, BUSH[1])]

imbosom, imbound, imbow, imbrangle, EMBOSOM etc.

imbricate[1], *v.t.* to lap (leaves, scales on fish etc.) the one over the other like tiles. *v.i.* to be arranged in this position. **imbrication,** *n.* **imbricative,** *a.* [L *imbricātus,* p.p. of *imbricāre,* from *imbrex -bricis,* a tile, from *imber -bris,* shower]

imbricate[2], *a.* arranged in an imbricated fashion.

imbroglio, *n.* (*pl.* **-lios**) a complicated plot, as of a play or novel; a perplexing or confused state of affairs; a disorderly heap; a misunderstanding. [It. (IM-[1], *broglio,* BROIL[1])]

imbrown, EMBROWN.

imbrue, *v.t.* to steep, to soak or moisten (in or with blood, carnage etc.); to stain, to dye (in or with); †to pour out. †**imbruement,** *n.* [OF *embruer, -breuver, -beuvrer,* causal of *bevre* (F *boire*), L *bibere,* to drink]

imbrute, *v.t.* to brutalize. *v.i.* to become brutalized.

imbue, *v.t.* to saturate (with); to dye (with); to tinge strongly (with); to inspire, to impregnate (with). †**imbuement,** *n.* [L *imbuere* (*buere,* rel. to *bibere,* to drink)]

imburse, *v.t.* to furnish with money; to stow away. †**imbursement,** *n.* [late L *imbursāre* (IM-[1], *bursa,* PURSE)]

IMF, (*abbr.*) International Monetary Fund.

Imhotep, *n.* (*c.* 2800 BC), Egyptian physician and architect, adviser to King Zoser (3rd dynasty). He is thought to have designed the step pyramid at Sakkara, and his tomb (believed to be in the N Sakkara cemetery) became a centre of healing. He was deified as the son of Ptah and was identified with Aesculapius, the Greek god of medicine.

imide, *n.* a compound derived from ammonia by the replacement of two atoms of hydrogen by a metal or organic radical. [altered from AMIDE, see AMIC]

imido-, *comb. form.* imide.

imidogen, *n.* the hypothetical radical representing ammonia deprived of two atoms of hydrogen as explained above.

imit., (*abbr.*) imitation; imitative.

imitate, *v.t.* to produce a likeness of in form, colour, or appearance; to follow the example of; to mimic, to ape. **imitable,** *a.* **imitability,** *n.* **imitation,** *n.* the act of imitating; a copy or likeness; (*Mus.*) the repetition of a phrase or subject by another part or key. **imitative,** *a.* given to or aiming at imitation; done in imitation (of); counterfeit. **imitatively,** *adv.* **imitativeness,** *n.* **imitator,** *n.* **imitatress,** *n. fem.* [L *imitātus,* p.p. of *imitārī*]

immaculate, *a.* spotlessly clean or tidy; pure; free from blemish; absolutely faultless; (*Biol.*) not spotted. **Immaculate Conception,** *n.* in the Roman Catholic Church, the doctrine (made an article of faith in 1854) that the Virgin Mary was conceived and born free from original sin. **immaculacy, -lateness,** *n.* **immaculately,** *adv.* [L *immaculātus* (*macula,* spot)]

†**immalleable,** *a.* not malleable.

†**immanation,** *n.* a flowing in. [L *mānāre,* to flow (on anal. of EMANATION)]

†**immane,** *a.* monstrous, prodigious, immense; savage, cruel. †**immanely,** *adv.* †**immanity,** *n.* [L *immānis* (*mānus,* hand)]

immanent, *a.* remaining within, inherent, not transient; in-dwelling; (*Theol.*) present throughout the universe as an essential sustaining spirit. **immanence, -ency,** *n.* **immanently,** *adv.* [late L *immanens -ntem,* pres.p. of *immanēre* (*manēre,* to remain)]

immantle, *v.t.* to wrap in or as in a mantle.

immarginate, *a.* (*Bot.*) not having a rim or edge.

immaterial, *a.* not consisting of matter; incorporeal; spiritual; irrelevant, unimportant. **immaterialism,** *n.* the doctrine that there is no material substance, and that all being may be reduced to mind and ideas in mind; the doctrine that affirms the existence of spirit independently of matter, spiritism. **immaterialist,** *n.* **immateriality,** *n.* the quality of being immaterial. **immaterialize, -ise,** *v.t.* to make immaterial. **immaterially,** *adv.* [MF *immatériel,* from med. L *immateriālis* (MATERIAL)]

immature, *a.* not mature, not ripe, imperfect; not fully developed; lacking the appropriate maturity of character etc.; †premature. **immaturely,** *adv.* **immaturity, immatureness,** *n.* [L *immātūrus* (MATURE)]

immeasurable, *a.* that cannot be measured; immense. **immeasurability, -ableness,** *n.* **immeasurably,** *adv.*

†**immeasured,** *a.* unmeasured; immeasurable.

immediate, *a.* situated in the closest relation; not separated by any space etc.; acting or acted upon by direct agency, direct; proximate, next, present; done or occurring at once, without delay, instant. **immediacy,** *n.* **immediately,** *adv.* without delay, at once, closely or directly; just close by. *conj.* as soon as. **immediateness,** *n.* **immediatism,** *n.* (*US Hist.*) the doctrine of the abolitionists who advocated immediate emancipation of slaves. **immediatist,** *n.* [MF *immédiat,* med. L *immediātus* (MEDIATE)]

†**immedicable,** *a.* that cannot be healed; incurable. [F, from L *immedicābilis*]

†**immemorable,** *a.* not memorable, not worthy of remembrance. [L *immemorābilis*]

immemorial, *a.* beyond memory or record; extending or existing beyond the reach of record or tradition. **immemorially,** *adv.* [MF *immémorial,* med. L *immemorālis*]

immense, *a.* huge, vast, immeasurable; (*coll.*) very great, very large; (*sl.*) very good, excellent. **immensely,** *adv.* **immenseness, immensity,** *n.* [F, from L *immensus* (*mensus,* p.p. of *metīrī,* to measure, to METE)]

†**immensurable,** *a.* immeasurable. [late L *immensūrābilis*]

immerge, *v.t.* to immerse. *v.i.* (*Astron.*) to disappear in the shadow of or behind another heavenly body, opp. to *emerge.* [L *immergere* (*mergere,* to plunge, to sink)]

immerse, *v.t.* to plunge, to dip (into or under water or other fluid); to baptize in this manner; to involve or absorb deeply (in difficulty, debt, study, etc.). **immersible,** *a.* **immersion,** *n.* the act of immersing; the state of being immersed; baptism by plunging completely under water; the state of being deeply involved (in thought etc.); the disappearance of a celestial body behind or into the shadow of another; a language-teaching method involving the exclusive use of the language concerned in the learning situation. **immersion heater,** *n.* an electrical appliance that is immersed in a tank etc. to heat the water contained therein. **immersion lens,** *n.* the object-glass of a high-powered microscope that carries a drop of cedarwood oil between it and the cover-glass. **immersionist,** *n.* one who believes in baptism by immersion. [L *immersus,* p.p. of *immergere,* to IMMERGE]

†**immesh,** ENMESH.

†**immethodical,** *a.* not methodical; confused. †**immethodically,** *adv.*

†**immew,** *v.t.* to mew up or confine.

immigrate, *v.i.* to come into a foreign country for settlement there. *v.t.* to bring into a foreign country for settlement. **immigrant,** *n.* one who immigrates. **immigration,** *n.* [L *immigrātus,* p.p. of *immigrāre* (*migrāre,* to MIGRATE)]

imminent, *a.* impending; close at hand; overhanging; †intent (upon). **imminence, -ency,** *n.* **imminently,** *adv.* [L *imminens -ntem,* pres.p. of *imminēre* (*minere,* cp. EMINENT)]

†**immingle,** *v.t.* to intermingle, to mix together.

immiscible, *a.* not capable of being mixed. **immiscibility,** *n.* **immiscibly,** *adv.*

†**immit,** *v.t.* to send or put in; to inject. †**immission,** *n.* [L *immittere* (*mittere,* to send)]

immitigable, *a.* incapable of mitigation or softening down. **immitigably,** *adv.* [L *immītigābilis*]

immix, *v.t.* to mix or mingle together; to blend (with); to involve (with). †**immixable,** *a.* **immixture,** *n.* [obs. p.p. *immixt,* L *immixtus,* from *immiscēre* (*miscēre,* to mix)]

immobile, *a.* not mobile, immovable; impassible; (*coll.*) not moving. **immobility,** *n.* **immobilize, -ise,** *v.t.* to render immovable; to withdraw (specie) from circulation; to render (troops) incapable of being moved. **immobilization, -isation,** *n.* [F, from L *immōbilis*]

immoderate, *a.* excessive; unreasonable. **immoderacy, immoderateness, immoderation,** *n.* **immoderately,** *adv.* [L *immoderātus*]

immodest, *a.* not modest, forward, pretentious; unchaste, indelicate, indecent. **immodestly,** *adv.* **immodesty,** *n.* [F *immodeste,* L *immodestus*]

immolate, *v.t.* to kill in sacrifice, to offer up; to sacrifice (to). **immolation,** *n.* **immolator,** *n.* [L *immolātus,* p.p. of *immolāre* (*molāre,* to sprinkle with meal, to sacrifice, from *mola,* meal)]

immoral, *a.* not moral; inconsistent with or contrary to (esp. sexual) morality; licentious, vicious. **immoralism,** *n.* the rejection of morality. **immoralist,** *n.* **immorality,** *n.* **immorally,** *adv.*

immortal, *a.* not mortal, not subject to death; imperishable; relating to immortality; eternally famous; (*coll.*) not changing, constants, †excessive, grievous. *n.* one who is immortal, esp. one of the ancient gods; (*pl.*) the royal bodyguard in ancient Persia; the 40 members of the French Academy. **immortality,** *n.* the state of being immortal; exemption from annihilation or oblivion. **immortalize, -ise,** *v.t.* to make immortal; to perpetuate the memory of. †*v.i.* to become immortal. **immortalization, -isation,** *n.* **immortally,** *adv.* with endless existence; (*coll.*) extremely, excessively. [L *immortālis*]

immortelle, *n.* a plant with flowers that keep their shape and colour for a long period after being gathered, an 'everlasting', esp. *Helichrysum orientale.* [F, fem. of *immortel,* IMMORTAL]

immovable, *a.* that cannot be moved; firmly fixed; steadfast; unchanging, unalterable; unfeeling; (*Law*) not liable to be removed. **immovability, -ableness,** *n.* **immovably,** *adv.* in an immovable manner.

immune, *a.* free or exempt (from); highly resistant to (a disease etc.); pertaining to immunity. *n.* one who is not liable to infection. **immunist,** *n.* **immunity,** *n.* freedom or exemption from any obligation, duty, or office; exemption from a penalty, taxation etc.; freedom from liability to infection. **immunize, -ise,** *v.t.* **immunization, -isation,** *n.* the conferring of immunity to a disease by artificial means. [L *immūnis* (IM-[2], *mūnis,* serving, rel. to *mūnus,* service, duty)]

immuno-, *comb. form.* immunity; immune.

immunoglobulin, *n.* one of five classes of proteins showing antibody activity.

immunology, *n.* the scientific study of immunity. **immunological,** *a.* **immunologically,** *adv.* **immunologist,** *n.*

immunosuppressive, *a.* pertaining to a drug that minimizes the body's natural reactions to a foreign substance, esp. the rejection of a transplanted organ. **immunosuppression,** *n.*

immunotherapy, *n.* the treatment of disease through the stimulation of the patient's own natural immunity.

immure, *v.t.* to shut in or up; to surround, as with a wall; to confine. †*n.* a wall. **immurement,** *n.* [F *emmurer,* med. L *immūrāre* (*mūrāre,* from *mūrus,* wall)]

immutable, *a.* unchangeable, not susceptible to change or variation, invariable. **immutability, -ableness,** *n.* **immutably,** *adv.* [F, from *immūtābilis*]

imp, *n.* a young or little devil; a little malignant spirit; a mischievous child; †a graft; †an offspring; †a child. *v.t.* to supply (esp. the wing of a falcon) with new feathers; †to strengthen, to eke out; †to graft. **impish,** *a.* having the characteristics of an imp; mischievous. **impishly,** *adv.* **impishness,** *n.* [OE *impa,* shoot, graft, *impian,* to graft, prob. from Gr. *emphuein,* to implant]

imp., (*abbr.*) imperative; imperfect; imperial; impersonal.

†**impacable,** *a.* that cannot be appeased. [L *pācāre,* to pacify, from *pax pācem,* PEACE]

impact, *n.* a forcible striking (upon or against), a collision; effect, influence. *v.t.,* to press or drive firmly together, to pack firmly in. **impacted,** *a.* of a tooth, wedged in such a way as to be unable to come through the gum; of a fracture, having jagged ends that are wedged into each other. **impaction,** *n.* [L *impactus,* p.p. of *impingere,* to IMPINGE]

impair[1], *v.t.* to diminish in excellence, value, strength etc.; to damage, to injure. †*v.i.* to become worse, to be lessened. **impairment,** *n.* [OF *empeirer,* late L *impēiōrāre* (IM-[1], *pejor,* worse)]

†**impair**[2], *a.* unsuitable; odd, unequal. *n.* an odd number, thing, person etc. [F (*pair,* L *par*)]

impala, *n.* a large antelope of southern and eastern Africa. [Zulu]

impale, *v.t.* to transfix, esp. to put to death by transfixing with a sharp stake; (*Her.*) to arrange two coats of arms on one shield, divided by a vertical line; to render helpless, as though by impaling; †to fence, to enclose. **impalement,** *n.* [F *empaler* (IM-[1], *pal,* L *pālus,* a stake)]

impalpable, *a.* not perceptible to the touch; not coarse; not to be readily apprehended by the mind, intangible. **impalpability,** *n.* **impalpably,** *adv.* [F, from L *impalpābilis*]

impaludism, *n.* the morbid condition disposing to intermittent fever and enlarged spleen to which those living in marshy regions are liable. [L *palus palūdis,* marsh]

impanate, *a.* (*Eccles.*) embodied in bread. *v.t.* to embody in bread. **impanation,** *n.* the doctrine of the local union of the body of Christ with the consecrated elements in the Eucharist. [med L *impānātus,* p.p. of *impānāre* (*pānis,* bread)]

impanel, EMPANEL.

imparadise, *v.t.* to put in a place or state of perfect happiness; to make perfectly happy.

†**imparasite,** *n.* an insect that is not a parasite (applied to those whose larvae feed upon dead insects).

imparipinnate, *a.* (*Bot.*) pinnate with an odd terminal leaflet. [L *impar,* see foll., PINNATE]

imparisyllabic, *a.* not having the same number of syllables. *n.* a noun not having the same number of syllables in all its cases. [L *impar* (IM-[2], PAR, SYLLABIC)]

†**imparity,** *n.* disparity, inequality, disproportion; difference in degree, rank, power etc.; oddness, indivisibility into equal parts. [late L *imparitas*]

impark, *v.t.* to form (land) into a park; to enclose (animals) in a park. **imparkation,** *n.* [A-F *emparker,* OF *emparquer*]

†**imparl,** *v.i.* to talk together, to consult (with); (*Law*) to have delay for the adjustment or compromise of a suit. †**imparlance,** *n.* conversation, parley; (*Law*) time granted for the compromise of a suit, the continuance of a cause till another day. [MF *emparler* (*parler,* to speak)]

impart, *v.t.* to grant or bestow a share of; to communicate the knowledge of; to give, to bestow; †to share with. *v.i.* to give a portion. **impartance, impartation, impartment,** *n.* the act of imparting. **imparter,** *n.* †**impartible**[1], *a.* **impartibility,** *n.* [OF *impartir,* L *impartīre* (*partīre,* to PART)]

impartial, *a.* not partial; not favouring one party or one side more than another; equitable, disinterested. **impartiality, impartialness,** *n.* **impartially,** *adv.*

impartible[2], *a.* not subject to or capable of partition. **impartibility,** *n.* [late L *impartībilis*]

impassable, *a.* that cannot be passed; †unable to pass, as a coin. **impassability, -ableness,** *n.* **impassably,** *adv.*

impasse, *n.* a blind alley; an insurmountable obstacle; deadlock. [F *passer,* to PASS)]

impassible, *a.* insensible to pain or suffering; incapable of being injured; not subject to feeling or passion. **impassibility, -ibleness,** *n.* **impassibly,** *adv.* [F, from L *impassibilis*]

impassion, *v.t.* to rouse the deepest feelings of, to stir to ardour or passion. **impassionable,** *a.* †**impassionate,** *a.* strongly or deeply affected or moved. *v.t.*, to impassion. **impassioned,** *a.* charged with passion. [It. *impassionare* (*passione,* PASSION)]

impassive, *a.* not affected by pain, feeling, or passion; apathetic; unmoved, serene. **impassively,** *adv.* **impassiveness, impassivity,** *n.*

impaste, *v.t.* to make into paste; (*Paint.*) to lay on colours thickly and boldly. **impastation,** *n.* (*Ceram.*) the act or process of making into a paste; a combination of materials of different colours or consistencies baked and united by a cement. **impasto,** *n.* the application of a thick layer or body of pigment, to give relief etc.; paint so applied. [It. *impastare* (IM-[1], *pasta,* PASTE)]

impatient, *a.* not able to wait or to endure; fretful; not patient or tolerant (of); eager (for or to); †intolerable. †*n.* one who is impatient. **impatience,** †**-ency,** *n.* **impatiently,** *adv.* [F, from L *impatientem,* nom. *-iens*]

impave, *v.t.* (*poet.*) to set in a pavement.

impavid, *a.* fearless, bold. **impavidly,** *adv.* [L *impavidus* (*pavidus,* fearful)]

impawn, *v.t.* to deposit as security; to pledge.

impeach, *v.t.* to charge with a crime or misdemeanour; to bring a charge of maladministration or treason against; to accuse, to charge, to find fault; to call in question; to bring discredit upon. **impeachable,** *a.* **impeacher,** *n.* **impeachment,** *n.* the act of impeaching; the arraignment before a proper tribunal for maladministration or treason; an accusation; a calling in question; †hindrance, obstruction. [OF *empescher* (F *empêcher*), late L. *impedicāre* (*pedica,* fetter, from *pēs pedis,* foot) (Brachet, however, connects the word with a late L *impactāre,* from *impactus,* p.p. of *impingere,* to impinge)]

impearl, *v.t.* to form into pearls or pearl-like drops; to adorn with pearls.

impeccable, *a.* not liable to fall into sin; blameless; faultless. **impeccability,** *n.* **impeccably,** *adv.* **impeccant,** *a.* sinless, impeccable. †**impeccance, -ancy,** *n.* [L *impeccābilis*]

impecunious, *a.* destitute of money; short of money. **impecuniosity, impecuniousness,** *n.* **impecuniously,** *adv.*

impede, *v.t.* to hinder, to obstruct. **impedance,** *n.* resistance to alternating current, esp. due to inductance or capacitance together with ohmic resistance. **impediment,** *n.* that which impedes; hindrance, obstruction; a speech defect; an obstacle to lawful marriage. **impedimenta,** *n.pl.* baggage, supplies for an army on the march; things that impede progress. **impedimental,** *a.* [L *impedīre* (*pēs pedis,* foot), to entangle the feet]

impel, *v.t.* (*past, p.p.* **impelled**) to drive or push forward; to drive or urge (to an action or to do). **impellent,** *a.* that impels. *n.* one who or that which impels. **impeller,** *n.* a person or thing that impels; a rotor. [L *impellere* (*pellere,* to drive)]

impend, *v.i.* to threaten, to be imminent; to hang (over), to be suspended (over). **impendence, -ency,** *n.* **impendent, impending,** *a.* [L *impendēre* (*pendēre,* to hang)]

impenetrable, *a.* that cannot be penetrated or pierced; inscrutable, incomprehensible; not penetrable to ideas etc., dull, obtuse, stupid; (*Phys.*) preventing any other substance from occupying the same place at the same time. **impenetrability, -ableness,** *n.* **impenetrably,** *adv.* [F *impénétrable,* L *impenetrābilis*]

impenetrate, *v.t.* to penetrate deeply into.

impenitent, *a.* not penitent, not contrite. *n.* a hardened sinner. **impenitence, -ency,** *n.* **impenitently,** *adv.* [L *impaenitentem,* nom. *-tens*]

impennate, *a.* (*Ornith.*) wingless; belonging to the Impennes, a family of swimming birds having short wings covered with scale-like feathers, containing the auks, penguins etc. *n.* one of these birds. †**impennuous,** *a.* wingless.

imper., (*abbr.*) imperative.

imperative, *a.* (*Gram.*) expressive of command; authoritative, peremptory; obligatory; urgent. *n.* that mood of a verb which expresses command, entreaty, or exhortation; something absolutely essential or very urgent. **categorical imperative** CATEGORICAL. **imperatival,** *a.* (*Gram.*) **imperatively,** *adv.* **imperativeness,** *n.* [late L *imperātivus,* from *imperāre,* to command (*parāre,* to make ready)]

imperator, *n.* (*Rom. Hist.*) a title originally bestowed upon a victorious leader on the field of battle by his soldiers; afterwards the equivalent of the modern 'emperor'. **imperatorial,** *a.* **imperatorially,** *adv.* **imperatrix,** *n.* an empress. [L, as prec.]

imperceivable, *a.* imperceptible.

imperceptible, *a.* not perceptible; not easily apprehended, indistinguishable; insignificant, extremely slight, small, or gradual. **imperceptibility, -ibleness,** *n.* **imperceptibly,** *adv.* **imperceptive,** *a.*

impercipient, *a.* not perceiving; not having power to perceive. *n.* an unperceiving person.

imperf., (*abbr.*) imperfect.

imperfect, *a.* not perfect, defective; incomplete, not fully made, done etc.; unfinished; lacking some part or member; (*Gram.*) expressing action as continuous and not completed; (*Mus.*) diminished; less than a semitone; of a cadence, passing to a dominant chord from another, esp. a tonic, chord. *n.* the imperfect tense; a verb in this tense. **imperfectible,** *a.* incapable of being perfected. **imperfectibility,** *n.* **imperfect tense,** *n.* a tense expressing or denoting an uncompleted action or state, usu. relating to past time. **imperfection,** *n.* a moral or physical fault; a defect; a deficiency. **imperfective,** *a.* denoting that aspect of a verb which shows that the action is in progress. *n.* the imperfective aspect of a verb, or a verb in this aspect. **imperfectively,** *adv.* **imperfectly,** *adv.* **imperfectness,** *n.* [OF *imparfait,* L *imperfectus,* assim. to L]

imperforate, *a.* not perforated; not separated by rows of perforations, as stamps; (*Anat.*) having no opening or normal orifice etc. **imperforable,** *a.* that cannot be perforated. **imperforation,** *n.* imperforate condition.

imperial, *a.* of or pertaining to an empire, an emperor, or other supreme ruler; pertaining to the British Empire, as dist. from any particular kingdom, dominion, colony etc.; suitable to or like an emperor; sovereign, supreme; lordly, majestic; of weights and measures, conforming to official British nonmetric standards. *n.* a baggage-case on a travelling carriage; an outside seat on a diligence or coach; a size of paper about 22 × 30 in. (57 × 76 cm); a tuft of hair on a man's chin (named from Napoleon III); (*G Hist.*) an adherent of the emperor's party, one of the Imperialist troops. **Imperial City,** *n.* Rome; a city that was an independent member of the Holy Roman Empire. **imperial federation,** *n.* a scheme for the consolidation of the British Empire, on the basis of joint control and a share in the cost of imperial defence by the Colonies. **imperialism,** *n.* government by an emperor; imperial spirit, state, or authority; the policy of imperial federation; the policy of extending the British Empire; the policy of extending the authority of a nation by means of colonies or dependencies. **imperialist,** *n.* a supporter of imperialism; (*Hist.*) an adherent of the emperor, esp. during the Thirty Years' War; an advocate of imperial rule. **imperialistic,** *a.* **imperialistically,** *adv.* **imperiality,** *n.* imperial power or authority. **imperialize, -ise,** *v.t.* to render imperial. **imperialization, -isation,** *n.* **imperially,** *adv.* [OF, from L *imperiālis,* from IMPERIUM]

Imperial War Museum, *n.* British military museum, founded 1917. It includes records of all operations fought by British forces since 1914. Its present building (formerly the Royal Bethlehem, or Bedlam, Hospital) in Lambeth Road, London, was opened 1936. It was rebuilt and enlarged 1989.

imperil, *v.t.* (*past, p.p.* **imperilled**) to endanger.

imperious, *a.* arbitrary, dictatorial, overbearing; haughty, arrogant; urgent, pressing; †imperial. **imperiously,** *adv.* **imperiousness,** *n.* [L *imperiōsus,* from IMPERIUM]

imperishable, *a.* enduring permanently; not subject to decay. **imperishability, -ableness,** *n.* **imperishably,** *adv.*

imperium, *n.* absolute command, authority, or rule. **imperium in imperio,** an independent authority within the dominion of another authority. [L, command, supreme authority]

impermanent, *a.* not permanent. **impermanence,** *n.* **impermanently,** *adv.*

impermeable, *a.* not allowing passage, esp. of a fluid, impervious. **impermeability, †-ableness,** *n.* **impermeably,** *adv.* **impermeator,** *n.* a contrivance for lubricating the cylinder of a steam engine by the forcing in of oil. [F *imperméable,* late L *impermeābilis*]

impermissible, *a.* not permissible. **impermissibility,** *n.*

impers., (*abbr.*) impersonal.

imperscriptible, *a.* not derived from written authority. [L *perscrībere* (PER-, *scribēre,* to write, p.p. *scriptus*)]

impersonal, *a.* without personality; not relating to any particular person or thing; lacking in human warmth; (*Gram.*) applied to verbs used only in the third person singular in English with the neuter pronoun *it* as the nominative. *n.* an impersonal verb. **impersonality,** *n.* **impersonalize, ise,** *v.t.* to make impersonal. **impersonally,** *adv.* [late L *impersōnālis*]

impersonate, *v.t.* to invest with personality; to personify; to represent in character, to personate; to imitate the mannerisms of, esp. for entertainment. **impersonation,** *n.* **impersonator,** *n.* **impersonify,** *v.t.* to personify.

impertinent, *a.* not pertinent, not pertaining to the matter in hand; trifling, frivolous; offensive, impudent, insolent. *n.* an officious or unmannerly person; a meddler, an intruder. **impertinence, †-ency,** *n.* **impertinently,** *adv.* [F, from L *impertinentem,* nom. *-ens*]

imperturbable, *a.* that cannot be easily disturbed or excited; unmoved, calm, cool. **imperturbability, -ableness, †imperturbation,** *n.* **imperturbably,** *adv.* [late L *īmperturbābilis*]

impervious, *a.* not penetrable; not receptive or open (to). **imperviously,** *adv.* **imperviousness,** *n.* [L *impervius*]

impeticos, *v.t.* (*Shak.*) to put in one's pocket. [comic perversion of IMPOCKET, with alln. to PETTICOAT]

impetigo, *n.* (*pl.* **-tigines**), a clustered yellow-scaled pustular eruption on the skin. **impetiginous,** *a.* [L, from *impetere,* to assail (*petēre,* to seek)]

impetrate, *v.t.* to obtain by petition or entreaty. **impetration,** *n.* the act of obtaining by petition or entreaty; †(*Law*) the obtaining, by petition from the court of Rome, of benefices and Church offices in England, the disposition of which by law belonged to lay patrons. **impetrative, -atory,** *a.* [L *impetrātus,* p.p. of *impetrāre* (*patrāre,* to bring to pass)]

impetuous, *a.* moving with violence or great speed; acting violently or suddenly, hasty, impulsive, precipitate. **impetuously,** *adv.* **impetuosity, impetuousness,** *n.* [F *impetueux -euse,* L *impetuōsus,* from foll.]

impetus, *n.* the force with which a body moves or is impelled; impulse, driving force; stimulus. [L (*petere,* to seek)]

impeyan, *n.* an East Indian pheasant, *Lophophorus impeyanus,* with brilliant plumage and crested head. [Lady *Impey,* wife of Sir Elijah Impey, 1732–1809, who tried to introduce it to England]

imphee, *n.* the African or Chinese sugar-cane. [Natal native *imfe*]

impi, *n.* a body of southern African native fighters. [Zulu]

†impicture, *v.t.* to stamp or impress with a picture or resemblance of. [PICTURE]

impiety, *n.* the quality of being impious; an impious act; want of filial affection or of reverence towards God. [F *impieté,* L *impietātem,* nom. *-tas,* from *impius,* IMPIOUS]

impignorate, *v.t.* (*Sc.*) to pawn or pledge; to mortgage. **impignoration,** *n.* [med. L *impignorātus,* p.p. of *impignorāre* (*pignus -noris,* a pledge)]

impinge, *v.i.* to come into collision, to strike (on, against etc.); to encroach (on); to have an effect (on). **impingement,** *n.* **†impingent,** *a.* [L *impingere* (*pangere,* to drive, fasten)]

impious, *a.* wanting in piety or reverence, esp. towards God; irreverent, profane. **†impiously,** *adv.* **impiousness,** *n.* impiety. [L *impius*]

impish IMP.

impiteous, *a.* (*poet.*) pitiless, ruthless.

implacable, *a.* not to be appeased; inexorable, unrelenting. **implacability**, **-ableness,** *n.* **implacably,** *adv.* [F, from L *implācābilis*]

implacental, *a.* without a placenta (used of marsupials and monotremes).

implant, *v.t.* to plant for the purpose of growth; to set or fix (in); to engraft; to inculcate, to instil. *n.* something engrafted, esp. surgically. †**implantation,** *n.* [F *implanter,* late L *implantāre*]

implausible, *a.* not having an appearance of truth and credibility. **implausibility**, †**-ibleness,** *n.* **implausibly,** *adv.*

†**implead,** *v.t.* to bring an action against; to accuse, to impeach. *v.i.* to bring an action. †**impleader,** *n.* [ME *enpleden,* A-F *enpleder,* OF *empleidier*]

impledge, *v.t.* to pledge, to pawn.

implement, *n.* a tool, a utensil; an instrument used in labour; (*fig.*) an instrument, an agent; (*pl.*) things that serve for equipment, furniture, use etc.; (*Sc. Law*) fulfilment, complete performance. *v.t.* to fulfil; to carry into effect; to complete, to supplement. **implemental**, *a.* **implementation,** *n.* **implementiferous**, *a.* of strata, containing stone implements. [L *implēmentum,* a filling up or accomplishing, from *implēre* (*plēre,* to fill)]

implete, *v.t.* (*N Am.*) to fill up. **impletion,** *n.* the act of filling; fullness. [L *implētus,* p.p. of *implēre* (*plēre,* to fill)]

†**implex,** *a.* involved, complicated. †**implexion,** *n.* **implexous**, *a.* (*Bot.*) folded or plaited. [L *implexus,* p.p. of *implectere* (*plectere,* to plait)]

implicate, *v.t.* to enfold, to entangle, to entwine; to involve, to bring into connection with; to show to be involved. *n.*, that which is involved or implied. **implication,** *n.* the act of implicating; the state of being implicated; entanglement; an inference. **implicative,** *a.* [L *implicātus,* p.p. of *implicāre* (*plicāre,* to fold)]

implicit, *a.* implied; understood or inferable; tacitly contained but not expressed; depending upon complete belief or trust in another; hence, unquestioning, unreserved. **implicitly,** *adv.* **implicitness,** *n.* [L *implicitus,* var. of *implicātus,* see prec.]

implied etc. IMPLY.

implode, *v.t.*, *v.i.* to burst inwards; to sound by implosion. **implosion**, *n.* imploding; the inward release of obstructed breath involved in the articulation of certain stop consonants. **implosive,** *n.*, *a.* [L *plodere,* to clap]

implore, *v.t.* to call upon in earnest supplication; to ask for earnestly. *v.i.* to entreat, to beg, to supplicate. **imploration,** *n.* †**implorator**, *n.* one who implores. †**imploratory**, *a.* earnestly imploring. **implorer,** *n.* one who implores; a suppliant. **imploringly,** *adv.* **imploringness,** *n.* [F *implorer,* L *implorāre* (*plorāre,* to weep)]

implosion IMPLODE.

impluvium, *n.* a cistern or basin for receiving the rainwater in the open central part of the court or atrium of an ancient Roman house. [L, from *impluere* (*pluere,* to rain)]

imply, *v.t.* to involve or contain by implication; to signify; to import; to mean indirectly, to hint; †to enfold, to entangle. **implied,** *a.* contained in substance or essence, though not actually expressed. **impliedly,** *adv.* [OF *emplier,* L *implicāre,* see IMPLICATE]

impolarizable, -isable, *a.* (*Elec.*) in-capable of polarization (as some voltaic batteries).

impolder, empolder, *v.t.* to form into a polder; to reclaim (land) from the sea.

impolicy, *n.* the quality of being impolitic or inexpedient.

impolite, *a.* not polite, ill-mannered. **impolitely,** *adv.* **impoliteness,** *n.* [L *impolītus*]

impolitic, *a.* not politic; injudicious, inexpedient. **impoliticly,** *adv.*

imponderable, *a.* not having sensible weight; very light; (*fig.*) incalculable. *n.* a body or agent without sensible weight (as light, heat, electricity); an element or factor whose importance cannot be assessed or evaluated. **imponderabilia**, *n.pl.* imponderables. **imponderability**, **-ableness,** *n.* †**imponderous,** *a.* †**imponderousness,** *n.*

†**impone,** *v.t.* to impose; to stake, to wager. **imponent,** *a.* that imposes. *n.* one who imposes. [L *impōnere* (*pōnere,* to place)]

imporous, *a.* lacking pores; close and compact in texture. **imporosity,** *n.*

import[1], *v.t.* to bring (goods) from a foreign country (into); to introduce; to imply, to signify, to mean; to concern, to be of interest to. *v.i.* to be important, to matter. **importable,** *a.* **importability**, *n.* **importation,** *n.* the act or practice of importing; that which is imported. **importer,** *n.* one who imports goods. [F *importer,* L *importāre* (*portāre,* to bring)]

import[2], *n.* that which is imported from abroad (*usu. pl.*); importation; that whch is signified or implied; importance, moment, consequence. **importance**, *n.* the quality of being important; weight, authority, consequence; personal consideration, self-esteem, pretentiousness; †pressing solicitation. †**importancy,** *n.* importance; an important matter.

important, *a.* of great moment or consequence, weighty; of great personal consequence, pretentious; notable, eminent; †urgent. **importantly,** *adv.* †**importless,** *a.* without import; insignificant.

importunate, *a.* unreasonably and pertinaciously solicitous or urgent; unendurable, troublesome. †*v.t.*, to importune. **importunately,** *adv.* **importunacy,** †**importunateness, importunity**, *n.* [L *importūnus,* unfit, unsuitable, rel. to *portus,* PORT[1]]

importune, *a.* untimely; importunate; violent, grievous; pertinacious, irksome. *v.t.* to solicit pertinaciously or urgently; to press with solicitation; †to mean, to signify. †*v.i.* to be importunate. †**importunely,** *adv.* inopportunely; importunately. **importuner,** *n.* [as prec.]

importunity IMPORTUNATE.

impose, *v.t.* †to lay or place upon; to set, to attach; to lay (as a burden, tax, toll etc.) upon; to force (views etc.) upon; to palm off (upon); to arrange (pages of type) in a forme for printing. *v.i.* to impress oneself (upon); to practise trickery or deception (upon). **to impose on, upon,** to cheat, to deceive; to take advantage of. **imposer,** *n.* **imposing,** *a.* commanding; impressive, majestic. **imposing-stone,** *n.* a slab of stone or metal on which type is made up into formes. **imposingly,** *adv.* **imposingness,** *n.* [F *imposer,* L *impōnere* (cp. COMPOSE)]

imposition, *n.* the act of imposing or placing upon; that which is laid or placed upon; an unfair and excessive burden; an exercise enjoined as a punishment in schools etc.; a duty, a tax, an impost; a deceit, an imposture, a fraud; the process of assembling pages in type on the stone and then locking them into a chase, the whole then becoming a forme. **imposition of hands,** (*Eccles.*) the laying on of hands in the ordination ceremony etc.

impossible, *a.* not possible; (*loosely*) impracticable, not feasible; that cannot be done, thought, endured etc.; outrageous, monstrous; (*Math.*) imaginary. †*n.* an impossibility. **impossibility**, *n.* **impossibly,** *adv.* [F, from L *impossibilis*]

impost[1], *n.* that which is imposed or levied as a tax, a tribute, a duty (esp. on imported goods); (*Racing*) a weight carried by a horse in a handicap. [OF (F *impôt*), late L *impostum,* L *impositum,* nom. *-tus,* p.p. of *impōnere,* to IMPOSE]

impost[2], *n.* the upper member of a pillar or entablature on which an arch rests. [F *imposte,* It. *imposta,* as prec.]

impostor, *n.* one who falsely assumes a character; a deceiver by false pretences. **impostorship,** *n.* **impostrous,** *a.* **imposture**, *n.* deception by the assumption of a false character, imposition; a fraud, a swindle. [F *imposteur,* late L *impostor,* from *impōnere,* to IMPOSE; assim. to L]

†**impostume,** †**-thume**, *n.* a collection of purulent matter in any part of the body; an abscess. *v.i.* to

impostumate. **impostumate,** *v.i.* to form an abscess, to gather. *v.t.* to affect with an abscess. **impostumation,** *n.* [OF *empostume, apostume,* L and Gr. *apostēma* (APO-, *sta-,* base of *istanai,* to stand)]

impotent, *a.* wanting in physical, intellectual, or moral power; of the male, lacking the power of sexual intercourse. *n.* one who is sexually impotent. **impotence, -ency,** *n.* **impotently,** *adv.* [F, from L *impotentem,* nom. *-tens*]

impound, *v.t.* to shut up (cattle) in a pound; to confine; to collect and confine or retain (water) in a reservoir, mill-pond etc.; to take possession of or confiscate (a document etc.). **impoundable,** *a.* **impoundage,** *n.* the act of impounding. **impounder,** *n.* **impoundment,** *n.*

impoverish, *v.t.* to make poor; to exhaust the strength, fertility, or resources of. **impoverisher,** *n.* **impoverishment,** *n.* [OF *empoveriss-,* part. stem of *empoverir* (*povre, pauvre,* POOR)]

impracticable, *a.* not possible to be effected by the means at command; not feasible; unsuitable for a particular purpose; impassable; intractable, stubborn. **impracticability, -ableness,** *n.* **impracticably,** *adv.*

impractical, *a.* unpractical. **impracticality, impracticalness,** *n.*

imprecate, *v.t.* to invoke (as an evil on); to invoke a curse on. *v.i.* to curse. **imprecation,** *n.* the act of imprecating; a prayer for evil to fall on anyone; a curse. **imprecatory,** *a.* involving a curse. [L *imprecātus,* p.p. of *imprecārī* (*precārī,* to PRAY)]

impregnable[1], *a.* that cannot be stormed or taken by assault; able to resist all attacks, invincible. **impregnability,** *n.* **impregnably,** *adv.* [OF *imprenable* (*prendre,* L *prehendere,* to seize), *-g-* as in REIGN, SOVEREIGN, etc.]

impregnate, *v.t.* to make pregnant; to fertilize, to fecundate; to render fruitful or fertile; to infuse the particles or qualities of any other substance into; to saturate (with); to imbue, to inspire (with). †*a.*, impregnated, pregnant; imbued, inspired (with). **impregnable**[2], *a.* able to be impregnated. **impregnation,** *n.* [late L *impraegnātus,* p.p. of *impraegnāre* (*praegnāre,* to be PREGNANT[1])]

impresario, *n.* (*pl.* **-rios**) one who organizes or manages a concert, an opera company etc. [It *impresa,* IMPRESE]

imprescriptible, *a.* that cannot be lost or impaired by usage or claims founded on prescription. **imprescriptibility,** *n.* [F (PRESCRIPTIBLE)]

†**imprese, impress**[1], *n.* an heraldic device; a motto. [It. *impresa,* undertaking, device, fem. of *impreso,* undertaken, cp. EMPRISE]

†**impress**[2], *v.t.* to press or stamp (a mark etc., in or upon); to produce (a mark or figure) by pressure; to fix deeply (in or on the mind); to affect strongly. **to impress on,** to emphasize to (someone); to urge, insist. **impressible,** *a.* capable of being impressed; yielding to pressure; susceptible. †**impressibly,** *adv.* **impression,** *n.* the act of impressing; the mark made by impressing; a copy taken from type, an engraved plate etc.; the visible or tangible effect of an action etc.; (*collect.*) copies constituting a single issue of a book, engraving etc., esp. a reprint from standing type, as dist. from an edition; effect produced upon the senses, feelings etc.; an indistinct notion, a slight recollection, belief etc.; a mental effect of a previous experience; an imitation or impersonation. **impressionable,** *a.* easily impressed, impressible. **impressionability,** *n.* **impressionism,** *n.* an artistic movement that began in France acting on the principle that the hand should paint what the eye sees, thus ruling out all conventions of lighting and composition. **impressionist,** *n.*, *a.* pertaining to impressionism. **impressionary, impressionistic,** *a.* **impressionistically,** *adv.* **impressive,** *a.* adapted to make an impression on the mind; commanding; inspiring; leaving a deep impression; †impressible. **impressively,** *adv.* **impressiveness,** *n.* [L *impressāre,* freq. of *imprimere* (*premere,* to PRESS)]

impress[3], *n.* the act of marking by pressure; a mark or stamp made by pressure; a stamp, an impression; a characteristic mark.

impress[4], *v.t.* to compel (seamen) to enter the public service; to seize or set apart (goods, property etc.) for the public service. **impressment,** *n.*

imprest, *n.* a loan, an advance, esp. for carrying on any of the public services. **bill of imprest,** an order entitling the bearer to have money paid in advance. **imprest bill,** *n.* a bill of imprest. **imprest office,** *n.* a former department of the Admiralty which advanced money to paymasters and other officers. [PREST, prob. after obs. *iprest,* in ready money]

imprimatur, *n.* a licence to print a book, granted by the authorities, esp. of the Roman Catholic Church, where there is a censor of the press; (a mark of) sanction or approval. [L, let it be printed, from *imprimere,* to IMPRESS[2]]

imprimis, *adv.* first in order. [L (*primis*), among the first things]

imprint, *v.t.* to impress, to stamp; to print; to impress (on or in the mind). *n.*, a mark, stamp, or impression; the name of the printer or publisher of a book, periodical etc., with the place and usu. the date of publication (on the title-page or at the end of a book). **imprinting,** *n.* the process by which young animals develop the tendency to recognize and be attracted to members of their own species. [OF *empreinter, empreindre,* L *imprimere,* to IMPRESS[2]]

imprison, *v.t.* to put into prison; to confine, to hold in custody or captivity. **imprisonment,** *n.* [OF *emprisoner*]

improbable, *a.* not likely to be true; not likely to happen. **improbability,** *n.* **improbably,** *adv.* [L *improbābilis*]

improbation, *n.* (*Sc. Law*) the proving of falsehood or forgery; an action to set aside a deed on account of falsity or forgery. **improbative, -atory,** *a.* tending to disprove. [L *improbātio,* from *improbāre,* to disapprove, from *improbus,* wicked (*probus,* good, see PROBITY)]

improbity, *n.* want of probity; dishonesty. [L *improbitās,* from *improbus,* see prec.]

impromptu, *adv.* off-hand, without previous study. *a.* done or said off-hand, extempore. *n.* (*pl.* **-tus**) an extemporaneous composition, performance, act etc. **impromptuary,** *a.* **impromptuist,** *n.* an improvisator. [L *in promptū,* in readiness (*promptū,* abl. of *-tus,* from *prōmere,* to PROMPT)]

improper, *a.* not proper; unsuitable, unfit; unbecoming, indecent; not accurate, erroneous. **improper fraction,** *n.* a fraction the numerator of which is equal to or greater than the denominator. **improperly,** *adv.* [F *impropre*]

impropriate, *v.t.* to convert (esp. ecclesiastical property) to one's own or to private use; to place the revenues, profits etc., of in the hands of a layman. *a.*, vested in a layman. **impropriation,** *n.* **impropriator,** *n.* one, esp. a layman, to whom church lands or an ecclesiastical benefice are impropriated. [L *propriāre,* to appropriate, from *proprius,* one's own]

impropriety, *n.* the quality of being improper; an unbecoming act, expression etc.; indecency. [L *improprietās*]

improve, *v.t.* to make better; to increase the value, goodness, or power of; to turn to profitable account; to take advantage of, to utilize. *v.i.* to grow or become better; to recover from illness, to regain health or strength; to increase in value, to rise, to be enhanced. **to improve on, upon,** to make something better than; to make use of for edification; to draw a moral from. **improvable,** *a.* admitting of improvement or amelioration; capable of being used to advantage. **improvability,** †**-ableness,** *n.* **improvement,** *n.* the act of improving; advancement in value, goodness, knowledge etc.; profitable use or employment; progress, growth, increase; that which is added or done to anything in order to improve it; a beneficial or valuable addition or substitute; the practical application of a discourse.

improver, *n.* one who or that which improves; a worker who accepts low wages in order to learn a trade, esp. an apprentice in millinery or dressmaking. **improving,** *a.* tending to improve. **improving lease,** *n.* (*Sc. Law*) a lease granted for a longer period to encourage a tenant to make improvements. **improvingly,** *adv.* [ME *emprowen,* A-F *emprouwer,* from OF *prou,* profit, perh. from L *prōd-* (*prōdesse,* to be useful or profitable to)]

improvident, *a.* not provident; neglecting to make provision for future exigencies; thriftless; careless, heedless. †**improvided**, *a.* unforeseen, unexpected. **improvidence,** *n.* want of foresight or thrift. **improvidently,** *adv.*

improvise, *v.t.* to compose and recite or sing off-hand; to extemporize; to do, produce, or prepare on the spur of the moment. **improvisate**, *v.t.* to improvise. †*a.*, improvised, impromptu. **improvisation**, *n.* **improvisator**, *n.* **improvisatore**, *n.* (*pl.* **-ori**) one who improvises; a versifier who can compose verses extemporaneously on any given subject. **improvisatorial**, **improvisatory**, *a.* pertaining to improvisation. **improvisatrice**, *n.* (*pl.* **-ci**) a female improvisatore. †**improviso,** *a.* impromptu, extemporaneous. [F *improviser,* It. *improvvisare,* from *improvviso,* L *imprōvīsus* (*prōvīsus,* p.p. of *prōvidēre,* to see ahead, to PROVIDE)]

imprudent, *a.* wanting in foresight or discretion; rash, incautious, indiscreet. **imprudence,** *n.* **imprudently,** *adv.* [L *imprūdens -ntem*]

impudent, *a.* wanting in shame or modesty; impertinent, insolent. **impudence,** †**-ency,** *n.* **impudently,** *adv.* **impudicity**, *n.* immodesty, shamelessness. [F, from L *impudentem,* nom. *-dens* (*pudens,* pres.p. of *pudēre,* to feel shame)]

impugn, *v.t.* to call in question, to contradict, to gainsay; †to oppose. **impugnable,** *a.* **impugner,** *n.* **impugnment,** *n.* [F *impugner,* L *impugnāre* (*pugnāre,* to fight)]

impuissant, *a.* powerless, impotent. **impuissance,** *n.* [F]

impulse, *n.* the application or effect of an impelling force; influence acting suddenly on the mind tending to produce action; a sudden tendency to action; stimulus, inspiration; a large force acting for an extremely short time, the momentum due to such a force; a disturbance passing along a nerve or muscle; †attack, onset. **impulsion**, *n.* the act of impelling; the state of being impelled; impetus; an impelling force; a compulsion; instigation, incitement. **impulsive**, *a.* communicating impulse, urging forward; resulting from or liable to be actuated by impulse rather than reflection; acting momentarily, not continuous. **impulsively,** *adv.* **impulsiveness,** *n.* [L *impulsus,* from *impellere,* to IMPEL]

impunity, *n.* exemption from punishment, penalty, injury, damage, or loss. [F *impunité,* L *impūnītātem,* nom. *-tās* (*poena,* Gr. *poinē,* penalty)]

impure, *a.* not pure; mixed with foreign matter, adulterated; defiled, unclean, unchaste; not grammatically correct; mixed with other colours. **impurely,** *adv.* †**impureness,** *n.* **impurity,** *n.* [L *impūrus*]

†**impurple,** EMPURPLE.

impute, *v.t.* to ascribe, to attribute; to set to the account or charge of; (*Theol.*) to ascribe (righteousness, guilt etc.) on account of another; †to charge. **imputable,** *a.* **imputability**, *n.* **imputation,** *n.* the act of imputing; that which is imputed as a charge or fault; reproach, censure; (*Theol.*) the attributing of righteousness or personal guilt and its consequences to a person or persons, on account of another. **imputative,** *a.* coming by imputation. **imputatively,** *adv.* **imputer,** *n.* [F *imputer,* L *imputāre* (*putāre,* to reckon)]

in, *prep.* within, inside of, contained or existing within; denoting presence or situation within the limits of time, place, circumstance, reason, tendency, ratio, relation etc.; pregnant with. *adv.* within or inside some place; indoors, at home; in office; in favour; in fashion; in season; into the bargain, over and above; (*Cricket*) at the wicket. *a.* directed inwards; internal, living inside (as a hospital); fashionable; understood by a select group. *n.pl.* the political party in office. †*v.t.* to take in, to harvest. **in absentia**, not being present. **in any case,** whatever happens. **in as much as, inasmuch as,** seeing that, since; in so far as. **in cash,** (*coll.*) supplied with money. **in itself,** by itself, apart from other things or considerations, absolutely. **in on,** (*coll.*) sharing in. **in so** (or **as**) **far as, insofar as,** in such measure as. **not in it,** (*sl.*) not in the running, standing no chance of success. **in that,** seeing that; since. **in the air,** floating, current (as a rumour etc.). **in the name of,** under the authority of. **to be in for,** to be committed to or involved in; to be entered for (a race etc.). **to be in for it,** to be certainly heading for trouble. **to be in with,** to be on intimate terms with. **to keep the fire in,** to keep the fire burning. **in-and-in,** *a.*, *adv.* from closely related parents. †*n.* a game played by three persons with four dice. **in-and-out,** *a.*, *adv.* alternately in and out (as in running); now in, now out. **in-depth,** *a.* detailed, thorough, comprehensive. **in-fighting,** *n.* behind-the-scenes squabbling or jockeying for power within a group etc. **in-flight,** *a.* available during an aeroplane flight. **in-house,** *a.* pertaining to, or employed, within a particular organization, company etc. **in-off,** *n.* billiards or snooker shot that falls into a pocket after striking another ball. **inpass,** *n.* (*Rugby football*) a pass from back to the centre. **in-patient,** *n.* a person residing inside a hospital and receiving regular treatment. **in-phase,** *a.* of two electric currents, alternating simultaneously. **in-player,** *n.* (*Rackets*) the server. **in-service,** *a.* performed whilst remaining in one's ordinary employment. **in-shoot,** *n.* (*Baseball*) the act of moving the ball swiftly inwards; a ball so moved. **in-tray,** *n.* a tray holding letters and documents still to be dealt with. [OE, Dut., G, Goth., cogn. with L *in,* Gr. *en*]

in., (*abbr.*) inch, inches.

in-[1], *pref.* in; into; within; on; against, towards; as in *indicate, induce.* [OE *in-,* or OF *in-, en-,* or directly from L *in-*]

in-[2], *pref.* un-, not, without, as in *incomprehensible.* [L, not]

-in[1], *suf.* (*Chem.*) denoting neutral compounds, and usu. dist. from alkaloids and basic compounds in -INE, as *albumin, casein.* [INE]

-in[2], *comb. form.* indicating a gathering for common activity.

-ina[1], *suf.* denoting the feminine, as *tsarina,* and proper names, as *Thomasina.* [L *-īna,* fem. of *-īnus*]

-ina[2], *suf.* (*Zool.*) forming names of groups of animals, usu. from the name of a genus, as *globigerina.* [L *-īna,* neut. pl. of *-īnus*]

inability, *n.* the state of being unable (to do, understand etc.); lack of power or means.

†**inabstinence,** *n.* lack of abstinence.

inaccessible, *a.* not accessible; that cannot be reached, attained, or approached; not affable, not encouraging advances. **inaccessibility**, **-ibleness,** *n.* **inaccessibly,** *adv.* [F, from late L *inaccessibilis*]

inaccurate, *a.* not accurate. **inaccuracy,** *n.* want of accuracy; an inaccurate statement, an error. **inaccurately,** *adv.*

inaction, *n.* inactivity, idleness, sloth; sluggishness, supineness. **inactive,** *a.* not active; sluggish, inert; idle, indolent; chemically or biologically lacking in reactivity; not in active service. **inactively,** *adv.* **inactivity**, *n.*

inadaptable, *a.* not adaptable. **inadaptability**, *n.* **inadaptation,** *n.*

inadequate, *a.* not adequate; insufficient, unequal; unable to cope. **inadequately,** *adv.* **inadequacy, inadequateness,** *n.*

inadherent, *a.* (*Bot.*) not adherent, free.

inadhesive, *a.* not adhesive.

inadmissible, *a.* that cannot be admitted, allowed, or received. **inadmissibility**, *n.*

inadvertent, *a.* not paying attention; heedless, careless, negligent; of actions, unintentional, accidental. **inadvertence, -ency,** *n.* **inadvertently,** *adv.*

inadvisable, UNADVISABLE.

†**inaidable,** *a.* that cannot be aided, helpless.

inalienable, *a.* that cannot be alienated or transferred. **inalienability**, *n.* **inalienably,** *adv.*
inalterable, *a.* incapable of alteration. **inalterability**, *n.* **inalterably,** *adv.*
inamorato, *n.* (*pl.* **-tos**) a lover. **inamorata**, *n. fem.* [It. *innamorato,* p.p. of *innamorare* (*amore,* L *amor -em,* love)]
inane, *a.* empty, void; purposeless, senseless; silly, fatuous. *n.* infinite void space. **inanely,** *adv.* **inanition**, *n.* emptiness, voidness; exhaustion from want of food or nourishment. **inanitiate**, *v.t.* **inanity**, *n.* [L *inānis,* empty]
inanga, *n.* the New Zealand whitebait. [Maori]
inanimate, *a.* not animate, not living; not endowed with animal life; void of animation, dull, lifeless. †**inanimated,** *a.* lifeless. **inanimately,** *adv.* **inanimateness, inanimation,** *n.* [L *inanimātus*]
inanition, inanity INANE.
inappeasable, *a.* not to be appeased.
inappellable, *a.* beyond appeal; absolute, final. **inappellability**, *n.*
inappetence, *n.* lack of appetence or appetite. **inappetent,** *a.*
inapplicable, *a.* not applicable; irrelevant. **inapplicability**, †**-ableness,** *n.* **inapplicably,** *adv.* †**inapplication**, *n.* want of application, energy, or assiduity.
inapposite, *a.* not apposite; not pertinent. **inappositely,** *adv.* **inappositeness,** *n.*
inappreciable, *a.* not appreciable, not perceptible; too insignificant to be considered. **inappreciably,** *adv.* **inappreciation,** *n.* want of appreciation; inability to appreciate properly. **inappreciative,** *a.*
inapprehensible, *a.* unintelligible, not to be apprehended or understood. **inapprehension**, *n.* want of apprehension. **inapprehensive,** *a.* not apprehensive; regardless (of danger etc.). **inapprehensiveness,** *n.*
inapproachable, *a.* inaccessible; unrivalled. **inapproachably,** *adv.*
inappropriate, *a.* not appropriate, unsuitable. **inappropriately,** *adv.* **inappropriateness,** *n.*
inapt, *a.* not apt; unsuitable. **inaptitude, inaptness,** *n.* **inaptly,** *adv.*
inarable, *a.* not fit for tillage.
inarch, *v.t.* to graft by inserting a scion, without separating it from the parent tree, into a stock growing near.
inarm, *v.t.* to encircle with the arms, to embrace.
inarticulate, *a.* not articulated, not jointed; belonging to the Inarticulata, a division of brachiopoda having non-articulated valves; not uttered with distinct articulation, indistinct, dumb, speechless; unable to express oneself clearly. **inarticulacy**, **inarticulateness,** *n.* **inarticulately,** *adv.* †**inarticulation,** *n.* indistinctness of sounds in speaking. [L *inarticulātus*]
inartificial, *a.* devoid of art, unaffected, artless, simple, natural. **inartificially,** *adv.* [L *inartificiālis*]
inartistic, *a.* not designed, done etc., according to the principles of art; not having artistic taste or ability. **inartistically,** *adv.*
inasmuch, IN AS MUCH AS under IN.
inattention, *n.* want of attention; heedlessness, negligence; disregard of courtesy. **inattentive,** *a.* **inattentively,** *adv.* **inattentiveness,** *n.*
inaudible, *a.* not audible, so low as not to be heard. **inaudibility**, *n.* **inaudibly,** *adv.* [L *inaudībilis*]
inaugurate, *v.t.* to install or induct into an office solemnly or with appropriate ceremonies; to commence, introduce, or celebrate the opening of with some degree of formality, solemnity, pomp, or dignity. **inaugural,** *a.* pertaining to or performed at an inauguration. *n.* an inaugural address. **inauguration,** *n.* the act of inaugurating; a formal or solemn commencement. **inaugurator,** *n.* **inauguratory,** *a.* [L *inaugurātus,* p.p. of *inaugurāre* (*augurāre,* to take omens, from AUGUR)]
†**inaurate,** *a.* covered with gold, gilt. [L *inaurātus,* p.p. of *inaurāre* (*aurāre,* from *aurum,* gold)]
inauspicious, *a.* unlucky, unfortunate; ill-omened, unfavourable. **inauspiciously,** *adv.* **inauspiciousness,** *n.*
inauthentic, *a.* not authentic or genuine.
in banco regis, in the King's Bench. [L]
inbeing, *n.* inherence; inherent existence; essence, essential nature. [BEING]
inbent, *a.* bent inwards.
inboard, *adv.* within the sides or towards the middle of a ship, aircraft, or vehicle. *a.* situated thus. *prep.* inside, within (a ship etc.).
inbond, *a.* a term applied to a stone or brick laid lengthwise across a wall, also called a header, opp. to *outbond.*
inborn, *a.* innate, naturally inherent.
inbreak, *n.* the act of breaking in; an inroad, an incursion. †**inbreaking,** *n., a.*
†**inbreathe,** *v.t.* to breathe into, to draw in (breath); (*fig.*) to inspire.
inbred, *a.* innate, inborn, natural.
inbreed, *v.t.* to breed or produce within; to breed from animals nearly related. **inbreeding,** *n.*
in-by, -bye, *adv.* (*Sc.*) towards the inside, towards the middle of a house, mine etc.
inc., (*abbr.*) incorporated.
Inca, *n.* the title given to the sovereigns of Peru up to the conquest under Pizarro, AD 1531; one of the royal race formerly dominant in Peru. **Inca art,** *n.* art of the Inca people of the Peruvian Andes, South America, of the 11th–16th centuries. The main sites are Cuzco, the old capital, and Machu Picchu, a fortified mountain settlement. Inca artisans produced technically brilliant, highly finished masonry, with large blocks of stone fitted together with great precision. Animal and human figures are frequent sculptural subjects. [Quechua]
†**incage,** ENCAGE.
incalculable, *a.* not calculable, not to be reckoned or estimated in advance; too vast or numerous to be calculated; not to be reckoned upon, uncertain. **incalculability**, **-ableness,** *n.* **incalculably,** *adv.*
†**incalescent,** *a.* becoming warm; increasing in heat. †**incalescence,** *n.* [L *incalescens -ntem* pres.p. of *incalescere* (*calescere,* freq. of *calere,* to be hot)]
in camera CAMERA.
incandesce, *v.i.* to glow with heat. *v.t.* to cause to glow with heat. **incandescence,** *n.* **incandescent,** *a.* glowing with heat; intensely luminous with heat; strikingly radiant or bright. **incandescent lamp,** *n.* an electric or other lamp in which a filament or mantle is made intensely luminous by heat. [L *incandescere* (*candescere,* incept. of *candēre,* to be white)]
incantation, *n.* a formula, said or sung, supposed to add force to magical ceremonies, a charm. †**incantator**, *n.* †**incantatory**, *a.* [F, from L *incantātiōnem,* nom. *-tio,* from *incantāre,* see ENCHANT]
incapable, *a.* not physically, intellectually, or morally capable (of); wanting in power, ability, or fitness (of doing, committing etc.); not susceptible (of); legally incapacitated; unable to take care of oneself; incapacitated by drink. *n.* one who is incapable. †**incapability**, †**-ableness,** *n.* **incapably,** *adv.* [F, from med. L *incapabilis*]
†**incapacious,** *a.* not capacious; not roomy. †**incapaciousness,** *n.* [L *incapax*]
incapacitate, *v.t.* to render incapable, to disable; to render unfit, to disqualify (for, from etc.). **incapacitated,** *a.* **incapacitation,** *n.* [from foll.]
incapacity, *n.* want of capacity; inability, incompetency; legal disqualification. [F *incapacité*]
incarcerate, *v.t.* to imprison; (*fig.*) to shut up or confine. †*a.*, imprisoned, shut up; confined. **incarceration,** *n.* **incarcerator,** *n.* [med. L *incarcerātus,* p.p. of *incarcerāre* (*carcer,* prison)]
incardinate, *v.t.* in the Roman Catholic Church, to institute as principal priest, deacon etc., of a particular church, diocese etc.; to raise to the rank of cardinal. [med. L *incardinātus,* p.p. of *incardināre* (*cardo -dinis,* hinge, see CARDINAL)]
†**incarnadine,** *a.* of a flesh or carnation colour. †*v.t.* to dye this colour; to tinge with red. [F *incarnadin,* It. *incarnadino, -tino,* from *incarnato,* INCARNATE]
incarnate, *a.* invested or clothed with flesh, embodied

in flesh, esp. in human form; typified, personified; (*esp. Bot.*) flesh-coloured, pink. *v.t.*, to clothe with flesh; to embody in flesh; to embody (an idea) in a living form; to be the embodiment of. **incarnant,** *a.* promoting the formation of flesh (over a wound etc.). *n.* an agent promoting this. **incarnation,** *n.* the act of assuming flesh; embodiment, esp. in human form; Christ's assumption of human nature; a vivid exemplification or personification; carnation, flesh-colour; the process of healing wounds, and filling or covering the damaged part with new flesh. [L *incarnātus,* p.p. of *incarnāre* (*caro carnis,* flesh)]

incase, ENCASE.

†**incatenation,** *n.* a linking together. [med. L *incatēnātio,* from *incatēnāre* (*catēna,* a CHAIN)]

incautious, *a.* wanting in caution; rash, unwary. †**incaution,** *n.* lack of caution. **incautiously,** *adv.* **incautiousness,** *n.*

incavate, *v.t.* to hollow, to make hollow. *a.*, hollowed, bent inwards. **incavation,** *n.* [L *incavātus,* p.p. of *incavāre* (*cavāre,* to hollow, from *cavus,* CAVE[1])]

incave ENCAVE.

incavo, *n.* (*pl.* **-cavi**) the incised portion of an intaglio. [It.]

†**incede,** *v.i.* to move in a majestic way. **incedingly,** *adv.* [L *incēdere* (*cēdere,* to go)]

incendiary, *a.* pertaining to the malicious burning of property; exciting or tending to excite factions, seditions or quarrels; inflammatory; igniting readily. *n.* one who maliciously sets fire to property etc.; an incendiary bomb; one who excites factions, seditions etc. **incendiary bomb,** *n.* a bomb containing violently incendiary materials that are scattered in flames on detonation. **incendiarism,** *n.* †**incendious,** *a.* †**incendiously,** *adv.* [L *incendiārius,* from *incendium,* a conflagration, from *incendere,* see foll.]

incense[1], *n.* a mixture of fragrant gums, spices etc. used for producing perfumes when burnt, esp. in religious rites; the smoke of this; flattery; an agreeable perfume; any offering to a superior being; the resin or gum of olibanum. *v.t.* to perfume with or as with incense; to offer incense to. **incense-boat,** *n.* a small boat-shaped vessel for holding incense. **incense-breathing,** *a.* exhaling sweet odours. **incense-tree,** *n.* one of various trees producing incense. **incense wood,** *n.* the wood of *Icica keptaphylla,* a S American tree. **incensation,** *n.* the offering of incense as an act of divine worship, or as a ceremonial adjunct. **incenser, -sory,** *n.* a censer. [ME and OF *encens,* L *incensum,* that which is burnt, neut. p.p. of *incendere,* to burn (*-candere,* to burn, rel. to *candēre,* to glow)]

incense[2], *v.t.* to inflame, to exasperate, to provoke, to enrage. †**incensement,** *n.* **incension,** *n.* the act of setting on fire; the state of being on fire. [from OF *incenser,* or directly L *incensus,* p.p. of *incendere,* see prec.]

incentive, *a.* inciting, urging. *n.* that which acts as a motive, incitement or spur. [L *incentīvus,* setting a tune, from *incinere* (*canere,* to sing)]

incept, *v.i.* at Cambridge University, to be finally admitted to the degree of Master or Doctor. *v.t.* (*Biol.*) to receive, to take in. [L *inceptus,* p.p. of *incipere,* to begin (*capere,* to take)]

inception, *n.* a commencement; at Cambridge University, the act or ceremony of incepting. **inceptive,** *a.* beginning, commencing; (*Gram.*) denoting the beginning of an action. *n.* a verb that denotes the beginning of an action.

inceptor, *n.* one at the point of taking his or her degree in Arts at Cambridge University.

†**incertain,** UNCERTAIN.

incertitude, *n.* uncertainty. [F (late L *certitūdo,* from *certus,* CERTAIN)]

incessant, *a.* unceasing, unintermittent, perpetual. **incessantly,** *adv.* †**incessably,** *adv.* unceasingly, continually. **incessancy,** †**incessantness,** *n.* [late L *incessans -antem* (*cessans -antem,* pres.p. of *cessāre,* to CEASE)]

incest, *n.* sexual intercourse between persons related within the prohibited degrees of matrimony. **incestuous,** *a.* guilty of or involving incest; of a group etc., inward-looking, closed to external influences etc. **incestuously,** *adv.* †**incestuousness,** *n.* [F *inceste,* L *incestus,* from *incestus -tum,* adj. (*castus,* CHASTE)]

inch[1], *n.* the 12th part of a linear foot; the least quantity or degree; the unit of measurement of the rainfall, the quantity that would cover the surface of the ground to the depth of one inch (2·54 cm); the pressure, atmospheric or other, equivalent to the weight of a column of mercury one inch (2.54 cm) high in a barometer; (*pl.*) stature. *v.t.* to drive by inches or small degrees. *v.i.* to move thus. **by inches, inch by inch,** bit by bit; gradually, by very small degrees. **every inch,** entirely, from head to foot. **(by) inchmeal,** by inches, bit by bit. **inch-measure, -rule, -tape,** *n.* a measure divided into inches. **inch-stuff,** *n.* (*Carp.*) deal in planks 1 in (2·54 cm) thick. **incher,** *n.* (*usu. in comb.,* as *six-incher*). [OE *ynce,* L *uncia*]

inch[2], *n.* an island. [Gael. *innis* (cp. Ir. *inis,* W *ynys,* also L *insula*)]

†**inchase,** ENCHASE.

inchmeal INCH[1].

inchoate, *a.* only begun, commenced; existing only in elements, incomplete, undeveloped. *v.t.* to begin, to originate. **inchoately,** *adv.* **inchoateness,** *n.* **inchoation,** *n.* an inception, a beginning. **inchoative,** *a.* incipient; indicating the beginning of an action. *n.* an inchoative verb. [L *inchoātus, incohātus,* p.p. of *incohāre,* to begin]

Inchon, *n.* (formerly **Chemulpo**) chief port of Seoul, South Korea; population (1985) 1,387,000. It produces steel and textiles.

†**inch-pin,** *n.* the sweetbread of a deer. [etym. doubtful]

incident, *a.* falling or striking (on or upon); likely to happen; naturally; appertaining or belonging (to); consequent (on); occasional, fortuitous. *n.* that which falls out or happens; a fortuitous event; a concomitant or subsidiary event; an occurrence, esp. one of a picturesque or striking nature; a minor event causing a public disturbance; (*Law*) a privilege, burden etc. legally attaching to property etc.; all circumstances attendant upon the fall of a bomb in an air-raid. **incidence,** *n.* the act or state of falling on or upon; (*Phys.*) the direction in which a body, or a ray of light, heat etc. falls upon any surface; scope, bearing, range; frequency of occurrence; †an incident. **angle of incidence,** an angle formed by the line of incidence of a ray of light, heat etc. moving to strike a plane and the perpendicular to that plane. **line of incidence,** the line in which a ray of light, heat etc. moves to strike a plane. †**incidency,** *n.* an incident; incidence. **incidental,** *a.* casual, accidental, contingent; undesigned, fortuitous, not essential; concomitant, naturally connected with or related (to); occasional. *n.* something that is incidental; (*pl.*) casual expenses. **incidentally,** *adv.* †**incidentalness,** *n.* [F, from L *incidentem,* nom. *dens,* pres.p. of *incidere* (*cadere,* to fall)]

incinerate, *v.t.* to reduce to ashes. **incineration,** *n.* **incinerator,** *n.* a receptacle in which refuse etc. is burned. [med. L *incinerātus,* p.p. of *incinerāre* (L *cinis cineris,* ashes)]

incipient, *a.* beginning, in the first stages. **incipiently,** *adv.* **incipience, -ency,** *n.* [L *incipiens -entem,* pres.p. of *incipere,* to INCEPT]

incipit, here begins (a book, manuscript etc.). [L, as prec.]

incircle, ENCIRCLE.

incise, *v.t.* to cut into, to engrave, to carve (with an inscription, pattern etc.); to engrave. **incision,** *n.* the art of incising; a cut, a gash made by surgery in the body; separation of the parts of any substance by a sharp instrument; †sharpness, trenchancy, decision. **incisive,** *a.* having the quality of cutting into; having a sharp cutting edge; (*fig.*) sharp, penetrating; trenchant, acute. **incisively,** *adv.* **incisiveness,** *n.* [F *inciser,* from L *incīsus,* p.p. of *incīdere* (*caedere,* to cut)]

incisor, *n.* a tooth adapted for cutting or dividing the food, one of those between the canines. †**incisory,** *a.*

incisive. †**incisure**, *n.* an incision, a notch.

incite, *v.t.* to stir up, to urge; to stimulate, to prompt, to encourage (to action, to do etc.). **incitant**, *a.* exciting, stimulating. *n.* a stimulant. **incitation**, *n.* the act of inciting; that which incites; an incitement. **incitement,** *n.* a stimulus, an incentive, a motive. **inciter,** *n.* **incitingly,** *adv.* [F *inciter,* L *incitāre* (CITE)]

†**incivil,** *a.* rude, unpolished. **incivility**, *n.* want of civilization; rudeness, impoliteness; an act of rudeness. **incivilization, -isation**, *n.* lack of civilization; barbarism. [F, from L *incivīlis*]

incivism, *n.* want of good citizenship or of patriotism, esp. as interpreted on the principles of the French Revolution.

incl., (*abbr.*) including.

inclasp, ENCLASP.

inclave, ENCLAVE.

in-clearing, *n.* the amount received in cheques etc. payable by a particular bank. **in-clearer,** *n.*

inclement, *a.* without clemency, merciless; rough, severe; boisterous, stormy. **inclemently,** *adv.* **inclemency**, *n.* [F, from L *inclemens -ntem*]

incline[1], *v.i.* to deviate from any direction that is regarded as the normal one; to lean, to bend down or forwards; to be disposed (to); to have a propensity, proneness or inclination. *v.t.* to cause to deviate from a line or direction; to give an inclination or leaning to; to direct; to cause to bend (the head or body) down, to bow or stoop; to dispose, to turn. **inclinable**, *a.* having a tendency; inclined, disposed, willing (to). **inclinableness,** *n.* **inclination**, *n.* the act of inclining or bending; a deviation from any direction regarded as the normal one; leaning or bent of the mind or will; disposition, proclivity, propensity (to, for etc.); liking, affection (for); (*Geom.*) the mutual approach or tendency of two bodies, lines or planes towards each other, esp. as measured by the angle between them. **inclinational,** *a.* **inclinatorium**, *n.* a dipping-compass. †**inclinatory,** *a.* having the quality of leaning or inclining. **inclined,** *a.* **inclined plane,** *n.* one of the mechanical powers, consisting of a plane set at an acute angle to the horizon. **incliner,** *n.* **inclinograph**, *n.* an instrument for recording the declinations of a compass. **inclinometer**, *n.* an instrument for detecting the vertical intensity of the magnetic force, a dipping-compass; a clinometer; an instrument that indicates the angle an aircraft is making with the horizon. [F *incliner,* L *inclināre* (*clināre,* to bend)]

incline[2], *n.* an inclination; an inclined plane, a slope, a gradient.

inclose, ENCLOSE.

include, *v.t.* to contain, to hold, to comprise, to comprehend as a component part, member etc.; to put in or classify as part of a set etc.; to enclose, to confine within; †to conclude, to terminate. **includable, -dible,** *n.* **included,** *a.* enclosed; contained, comprehended; of the style and stamens of a plant, not projecting beyond the mouth of the corolla. **inclusion**, *n.* the act of including; the state of being included; something included. **inclusive**, *a.* including, containing, comprehending (usu. with *of*); comprehending in the total sum or number; including everything; including the limits specified. **inclusive terms,** *n.* terms including all subsidiary charges (at a hotel etc.). **inclusively,** *adv.* **inclusiveness,** *n.* [L *inclūdere* (*claudere,* to shut), p.p. *inclūsus*]

incog., (*abbr.*) incognito.

incogitable, *a.* not cogitable, not thinkable. †**incogitability**, *n.* †**incogitant,** *a.* thoughtless; not thinking. †**incogitative,** *a.* [late L *incōgitābilis*]

incognito, *a., adv.* living or going under an assumed name or character. *n.* (*pl.* **-tos**) a person who is unknown or under an assumed name or character; the state of being unknown or in disguise; an assumed identity. *adv.* with one's real name etc., unknown or disguised. **incognita**, *n., a., adv., fem.* [It., from L *incognitus* (IN-[2], *cognitus,* p.p. of *cognōscere,* see COGNITION)]

incognizable, -isable, *a.* not cognizable, not capable of being perceived or apprehended. **incognizance, -isance,** *n.* **incognizant, -isant,** *a.* **incognoscible**, *a.* not cognoscible, beyond cognition. **incognoscibility,** *n.*

incoherent, *a.* lacking cohesion; loose, disconnected, inconsistent; inarticulate, rambling. **incoherence, -ency, incohesion**, *n.* **incoherently,** *adv.* **incohesive,** *a.*

incombustible, *a.* incapable of being burnt or consumed by fire. *n.* an incombustible thing, substance etc. **incombustibility**, *n.* **incombustibly,** *adv.* [F, from med. L *incombustibilis*]

income, *n.* the amount of money (usu. annual) accruing as payment, profit, interest etc. from labour, business, profession, or property; †advent, arrival; (*Sc.*) a tumour or similar bodily affection, an ailment that comes on with no apparent cause. **income support,** *n.* in Britain a social security payment made to the unemployed or people on low incomes, such as part-time workers. **income-tax,** *n.* a tax levied for State purposes on incomes above a certain amount. [IN-[1], COME]

incomer, *n.* one who comes in, an immigrant; an intruder; one who succeeds another as a tenant, esp. a stranger by birth etc. **incoming,** *a.* coming in or entering into possession; accruing; succeeding. *n.* an entrance or arrival; (*usu. pl.*) income, gain, revenue.

incommensurable, *a.* having no common measure (with another integral or fractional number or quantity); not fit or worthy to be measured (with). *n.* one or two (or more) quantities that have no common measure. **incommensurability**, *n.* **incommensurably,** *adv.* **incommensurate,** *a.* not commensurate; incommensurable. inadequate (to or with). **incommensurately**, *adv.* **incommensurateness,** *n.* [F, from late L *incommensūrābilis*]

†**incommiscible,** *a.* that cannot be mixed together. [L *incommiscibilis*]

incommode, *v.t.* to cause trouble or inconvenience to; to disquiet, to embarrass, to disturb, to hinder. †**incommodation,** *n.* **incommodious,** *a.* not commodious; inconvenient; cramped, too small. **incommodiously,** *adv.* **incommodiousness,** *n.* **incommodity**, *n.* inconvenience, incommodiousness; anything that causes this. [F *incommoder,* L *incommodāre* (*commodāre,* from *commodus,* COMMODIOUS)]

incommunicable, *a.* that cannot be communicated to, or shared with another. **incommunicability**, **-ableness,** *n.* **incommunicably,** *adv.* **incommunicative,** *a.* not communicative; not disposed to intercourse, communion or fellowship with others, reserved. †**incommunicatively,** *adv.* **incommunicativeness,** *n.*

incommunicado, *a.* with no means of communication with the outside world; in solitary confinement. [Sp.]

incommutable, *a.* not commutable; that cannot be exchanged with another; that cannot be changed. **incommutability**, *n.* **incommutably,** *adv.* [F, from L *incommūtābilis*]

incompact, *a.* not compact; loosely organized, combined etc.; incoherent. **incompactly,** *adv.* **incompactness,** *n.*

incomparable, *a.* not to be compared (to or with); unequalled, peerless. **incomparableness,** *n.* **incomparably,** *adv.* †**incompared,** *a.* unmatched, matchless. [F, from L *incomparābilis*]

incompatible, *a.* inconsistent with something else; incapable of subsisting with something else; unable to cooperate or work together; mutually intolerant; not suited for use together because of harmful effects; incongruous, discordant. *n.* an incompatible person or thing. **incompatible terms,** *n.pl.* (*Log.*) terms which cannot both be affirmed of the same subject. **incompatibility**, †**-ibleness,** *n.* **incompatibly,** *adv.* [F, from L *incompatibilis*]

incompetent, *a.* lacking adequate power, means, capacity, or qualifications (to do); grossly lacking in ability or fitness for a task; wanting legal fitness or qualification. *n.* an incompetent person. **incompetence, -ency,** *n.* **incompetently,** *adv.* lacking competence; (*coll.*) inefficiently. [F *incompétent,* L *incompetentem,* nom. *-ens*]

incomplete, *a.* not complete, not perfect. **incomplete flower,** *n.* one destitute of calyx, corolla, or of both. **incompletely,** *adv.* **incompleteness, incompletion,** *n.* [L *incomplētus*]

†**incompliant,** *a.* indisposed to yield to solicitation or request. †**incompliance,** *n.* †**incompliantly,** *adv.*

incomposite, *a.* not composite; not properly composed. [L *incompositus*]

incomprehensible, *a.* that cannot be comprehended, conceived or understood, inconceivable; †(*Athanasian Creed*) unlimited, boundless. **incomprehensibility, -ibleness,** *n.* **incomprehensibly,** *adv.* **incomprehension,** *n.* want of comprehension; failure to understand. †**incomprehensive,** *a.* not comprehensive or inclusive; not understanding. †**incomprehensively,** *adv.* †**incomprehensiveness,** *n.* [F, from L *incomprehensibilis*]

incompressible, *a.* not compressible; strongly resisting compression. **incompressibility,** *n.*

incomputable, *a.* not computable; incalculable.

inconceivable, *a.* not conceivable, incomprehensible; hence, incredible, most extraordinary. **inconceivability, -ableness,** *n.* **inconceivably,** *adv.*

inconclusive, *a.* not conclusive; of evidence etc., not cogent or decisive. **inconclusively,** *adv.* **inconclusiveness,** *n.*

incondensable, *a.* not condensable, not reducible from the liquid to a solid condition.

incondite, *a.* irregular, ill-composed, unfinished, crude. [L *inconditus* (*conditus,* p.p. of *condere,* to put together)]

inconformity, *n.* lack of conformity, correspondence or similarity (to or with); non-conformity.

incongruous, *a.* not congruous, not agreeing or harmonizing; unsuitable, inconsistent; not fitting, improper, out of place. †**incongruent,** *a.* **incongruity, incongruousness,** †**incongruence,** *n.* **incongruously,** *adv.* [L *incongruus*]

inconscient, *a.* unconscious. †**inconscious** etc. UNCONSCIOUS.

inconsecutive, *a.* not consecutive, not in regular order. **inconsecutively,** *adv.* **inconsecutiveness,** *n.*

inconsequent, *a.* not following regularly from the premises, irrelevant; illogical; disconnected. **inconsequence,** *n.* **inconsequential,** *a.* not consequential, inconsequent; of no consequence, trivial. **inconsequentiality,** *n.* **inconsequentially,** *adv.* **inconsequently,** *adv.* [L *inconsequens -entem*]

inconsiderable, *a.* not deserving consideration or notice; insignificant, unimportant, trivial; small. **inconsiderableness,** *n.* **inconsiderably,** *adv.* [F *inconsidérable* (CONSIDERABLE)]

inconsiderate, *a.* not considerate; hasty, incautious; having no consideration for the feelings of others. **inconsiderately,** *adv.* **inconsiderateness, -ation,** *n.* [L *inconsiderātus*]

inconsistent, *a.* discordant, incongruous; not suitable, incompatible (with); self-contradictory, not agreeing with itself or oneself; not uniform, changeable, unsteady. **inconsistency,** †**-ence,** *n.* **inconsistently,** *adv.*

inconsolable, *a.* of a person, grief etc., not to be consoled. **inconsolability, -ableness,** *n.* **inconsolably,** *adv.* [F, from L *inconsōlābilis*]

inconsonant, *a.* not consonant, discordant (with). **inconsonance,** *n.* †**inconsonantly,** *adv.* [F]

inconspicuous, *a.* not conspicuous; not easy to see; (*Bot.*) small in size, obscure in colour etc. **inconspicuously,** *adv.* **inconspicuousness,** *n.* [L *inconspicuus*]

inconstant, *a.* not constant, changeable, fickle; variable, unsteady, irregular. **inconstancy,** *n.* **inconstantly,** *adv.* [F, from L *inconstāntem,* nom. *-tāns*]

inconsumable, *a.* not consumable; indestructible; (*Polit. Econ.*) not intended for consumption. **inconsumably,** *adv.*

incontestable, *a.* indisputable, undeniable, unquestionable. **incontestability,** *n.* **incontestably,** *adv.* †**incontested,** *a.* uncontested, undisputed.

incontinent, *a.* not restraining (esp. sexual) the passions or appetites; licentious, unchaste; (*Med.*) not able to restrain natural evacuations. †*adv.* incontinently. †*n.* an unchaste person. **incontinence,** †**-ency,** *n.* **incontinently,** *adv.* unchastely; at once, straightway, immediately. [F, from L *incontinentem,* nom. *-ens*]

incontrollable, *a.* not controllable. **incontrollably,** *adv.*

incontrovertible, *a.* that cannot be controverted; incontestable, indisputable. **incontrovertibility, -ibleness,** *n.* **incontrovertibly,** *adv.*

inconvenience, *n.* the quality or state of being inconvenient; that which inconveniences, a cause of difficulty. *v.t.* to put to inconvenience; to incommode, to embarrass. **inconvenient,** *a.* not convenient, incommodious; causing or tending to cause trouble, uneasiness or difficulty; inopportune, awkward. **inconveniently,** *adv.*

inconvertible, *a.* incapable of being converted into or exchanged for something else, esp. money. **inconvertibility,** †**-ibleness,** *n.* **inconvertibly,** *adv.*

incoordinate, *a.* not coordinate. **incoordination,** *n.*

incoronate, *a.* crowned. **incoronation,** *n.* [med. L *incorōnātus*]

†**incorporal** INCORPOREAL.

incorporate[1], *a.* combined into one body or corporation, closely united; of a society, company etc., made into a corporation; †closely combined or associated (with); †embodied. [late L *incorporātus,* p.p. of *incorporāre* (*corpus -poris,* body)]

incorporate[2], *v.t.* to unite, combine or mingle into one mass or body (with); to combine into one body (with); to form into a legal corporation; to receive into a corporation; to embody. *v.i.* to become united or incorporated (with another substance, society etc.) so as to form one body; (*N Am.*) to form a limited company. **incorporated, incorporation,** *n.* the act of incorporating; the state of being incorporated; embodiment; formation of or reception into a corporate body; a corporate body, a corporation. *a.* (*N Am.*) of a joint stock company, limited. **incorporative,** *a.* incorporating or tending to incorporate; applied to languages such as the Basque and those of the N American Indians, which run a whole phrase into one long word. **incorporator,** *n.*

†**incorporate**[3], *a.* incorporeal, not embodied in matter. [CORPORATE]

incorporeal, *a.* not corporeal; immaterial; (*Law*) lacking material existence of itself but based on something material. †**incorporal,** *a.* †**incorporeality, -reity,** *n.* immateriality. **incorporeally,** *adv.* [L *incorporeus* (*corpus -poris,* body, see CORPOREAL)]

incorrect, *a.* not in accordance with truth, propriety etc.; faulty, wrong, inaccurate, inexact; improper, unbecoming; not corrected. **incorrectly,** *adv.* **incorrectness,** *n.* [L *incorrectus*]

incorrigible, *a.* incapable of being amended or improved; bad beyond hope of amendment. *n.* one who is incorrigible. **incorrigibility,** †**-ibleness,** *n.* **incorrigibly,** *adv.* [F, from L *incorrigibilis*]

incorrodible, *a.* that cannot be corroded. **incorrosive,** *a.*

incorrupt, *a.* not corrupt; not decayed, marred or impaired; pure, untainted; not depraved; above the influence of bribery. †**incorrupted,** *a.* **incorruptible,** *a.* incapable of corruption, decay or dissolution; eternal; not to be bribed; high-principled. **incorruptibility,** *n.* **incorruptibly,** *adv.* **incorruption,** *n.* freedom from corruption. †**incorruptive,** *a.* **incorruptly,** *adv.* **incorruptness,** *n.* [L *incorruptus*]

incrassate, *a.* (*Nat. Hist.*) thick, thickened (in form). †*v.t.* to make thick or thicker; to thicken (as fluids) by mixture or evaporation. †*v.i.* to become thick or thicker. **incrassation,** *n.* **incrassative,** *a.* [L *incrassātus,* p.p. of *incrassāre* (*crassāre,* to make thick, from *crassus,* CRASS)]

increase[1], *v.i.* to grow; to become greater in bulk,

quantity, number, value, degree etc.; to multiply by the production of young. *v.t.* to make greater in number, bulk, quantity etc.; to add to, to extend, to enlarge, to intensify. **increasable,** *a.* †**increaseful,** *a.* prolific, fruitful. **increasingly,** *adv.* [A-F *encress-*, OF *encreis-*, stem of *encreistre* (cp. F *croître*), L *increscere* (IN-[1], *crescere,* to grow)]

increase[2]**,** *n.* the act, state or process of increasing; growth, multiplication; that which is added; increment; produce, crops; progeny; profit.

incredible, *a.* not credible; passing belief; (*coll.*) extraordinarily great, astounding. **incredibility,** †**-ibleness,** *n.* **incredibly,** *adv.* [F, from L *incrēdibilis*]

incredulous, *a.* indisposed to believe, sceptical (of); unbelieving; †incredible. **incredulity, incredulousness,** *n.* **incredulously,** *adv.* [L *incrēdulus*]

increment, *n.* the act or process of increasing; an addition, an increase; the amount of increase; (*Math.*) the finite increase of a variable. **unearned increment,** (*Polit. Econ.*) an increase of value or wealth accruing without labour or effort, as by the increase in the value of land near a populous place. **incremental,** *a.* [L *incrēmentum,* from *increscere,* to INCREASE]

increscent, *a.* increasing, growing; (*Her.*) of the moon, waxing, represented with the horns towards the dexter side. *n.* (*Her.*) the moon represented thus. [L *increscens -entem,* pres.p. of *increscere,* to INCREASE]

incriminate, *v.i.* to charge with a crime, to criminate; to involve (a person) in a charge. **incrimination,** *n.* **incriminatory,** *a.* [med. L *incrimінātus,* p.p. of *incrimināre* (CRIMINATE)]

incroach, ENCROACH.

incrustation, *n.* the act or process of encrusting; a crust or hard coating on a surface etc.; a facing or lining of foreign material, as marble, stone etc., on masonry etc. **incrust,** ENCRUST. [late L *incrustātio,* from *incrustāre,* to ENCRUST]

incubate, *v.t.* to sit on (eggs) in order to hatch; to hatch by sitting on or by artificial means; to cause (bacteria etc.) to develop; to evolve (a plan etc.) by meditation. *v.i.* to sit on eggs for hatching, to brood; to undergo incubation. **incubation,** *n.* the act or process of incubating or hatching; brooding, as of a hen upon eggs; the brooding of the Holy Spirit over chaos at the Creation; meditation on a scheme etc.; (*Path.*) the period between infection and the development of symptoms of a disease; (*Gr. Ant.*) the act of sleeping for oracular dreams. **incubative, -atory,** *a.* **incubator,** *n.* an apparatus for hatching eggs by artificial heat, for developing bacteria etc., or rearing a child prematurely born; one that incubates, esp. a brooding hen. [L *incubātus,* p.p. of *incubāre* (*cubāre,* to lie)]

incubous, *a.* having the tip of one leaf lying over the base of the leaf above it.

incubus, *n.* (*pl.* **-bi, -buses**) a demon supposed (esp. in the Middle Ages) to have sexual intercourse with men or women at night, credited with the power of producing supernatural births; a nightmare; any person, thing or influence that oppresses, harasses or restrains, such as a nightmare. [late L, nightmare, as INCUBATE]

inculcate, *v.t.* to impress (upon the mind) by emphasis or frequent repetition; to enforce, to instil. **inculcation,** *n.* **inculcator,** *n.* [L *inculcātus,* p.p. of *inculcāre* (*calcāre,* to tread, from *calx calcis,* heel)]

inculpate, *v.t.* to charge with participation in a crime, to incriminate. †**inculpable,** *a.* †**inculpably,** *adv.* **inculpation,** *n.* **inculpatory,** *a.* [late L *inculpātus,* p.p. of *inculpāre* (*culpa,* fault)]

incumbent, *a.* lying or resting (on); pressing or weighing (upon); imposed (upon) as a duty or obligation; currently holding a post or office; (*Bot.*) used of anthers when they lie against the inner side of the filament; of the wings of insects when they fold along the body. *n.* a person in possession of an office etc., esp. a clergyman holding a benefice. **incumbency,** *n.* the act, state, sphere or period of holding a benefice as incumbent; an ecclesiastical benefice. [L *incumbens -entem,* pres.p. of *incumbere* (*cumbere,* to lie)]

†**incumber,** ENCUMBER.

incunabula, *n.pl.* (*sing.* **-lum**) the beginning (of a race, art, development etc.); examples of books etc., printed during the early period of the art, esp. before AD 1500. **incunabular,** *a.* [L, swaddling clothes (*cūnābula,* dim. of *cūnae,* cradle)]

incur, *v.t.* (*past, p.p.* **incurred**) to render oneself liable to (risk, injury, punishment etc.); to bring upon oneself, to run into. **incurrable,** *a.* [L *incurrere* (IN-[1], *currere,* to run)]

incurable, *a.* that cannot be cured or healed; irremediable, hopeless, irreparable. *n.* one suffering from an incurable disease. **incurability, -ableness,** *n.* **incurably,** *adv.* [OF, from L *incūrābilis*]

incurious, *a.* not curious or inquisitive; indifferent, heedless. **incuriosity, incuriousness,** *n.* **incuriously,** *adv.* [L *incūriōsus*]

incursion, *n.* a sudden inroad, a raid; an irruption; a brief and temporary exploration (into a subject etc.). **incursive,** *a.* [F, from L *incursiōnem,* nom. *-sio,* from *incurrere,* see INCUR]

incurve, *v.t.* to cause to curve inwards; to make crooked. **incurvate,** *v.t.* to cause to turn or bend from a straight course or line, esp. to bend inwards. *a.,* curved inward. **incurvation,** *n.* †**incurvity,** *n.* [L *incurvāre*]

incus, *n.* (*pl.* **-cudes**) one of the small bones of the middle ear or tympanum which receives vibrations, as an anvil, from the malleus. [L, anvil]

incuse, *v.t.* to impress (a device etc.) by stamping; to stamp with a device etc. *a.* stamped or impressed (on a coin etc.). *n.* an impression made by stamping (on a coin etc.). [L *incūsus,* p.p. of *incūdere,* to forge, from prec.]

Ind.[1]**,** (*abbr.*) Independent; India; Indiana.

ind.[2]**,** (*abbr.*) independent.

indaba, *n.* (*S Afr.*) a council; a conference. [Zulu, topic]

†**indagate,** *v.t.* to seek or search out, to investigate. **indagation,** *n.* **indagator,** *n.* [L *indāgātus,* p.p. of *indāgāre,* to trace out]

indebted, *a.* being under a debt or obligation (to or for); owing money (to). **indebtedness,** *n.* [ME *endetted,* OF *endetté,* p.p. of *endetter* (EN-, *dette,* DEBT)]

indecent, *a.* unbecoming, unseemly; offensive to modesty or propriety; immodest, grossly indelicate, obscene. **indecent exposure,** *n.* the offence of exposing a part of the body, esp. the genitals, publicly in breach of accepted standards of decency. **indecency,** *n.* **indecently,** *adv.* [F *indécent,* L *indecentem,* nom. *-cens* (DECENT)]

indecipherable, *a.* not decipherable, illegible.

indecision, *n.* want of decision; wavering of the mind, irresolution. **indecisive,** *a.* not decisive, final, or conclusive; irresolute, vacillating, hesitating. **indecisively,** *adv.* **indecisiveness,** *n.* [F *indécision*]

indeclinable, *a.* (*Gram.*) not varied by terminations, having no inflections. *n.* an indeclinable word. **indeclinably,** *adv.* [F *indéclinable,* L *indēclīnābilis*]

indecorous, *a.* violating propriety, decorum or good manners. **indecorously,** *adv.* **indecorousness,** *n.* **indecorum,** *n.* violation of decorum or propriety; an indecorous act. [*indecōrus*]

indeed, *adv.* in reality, in truth, of a truth, in point of fact, actually (expressing emphasis, interrogation, concession etc.). *int.* expressing surprise, irony, interrogation etc.

indef., (*abbr.*) indefinite.

indefatigable, *a.* not yielding to fatigue or exertion; unwearied, unremitting. **indefatigability, -ableness,** *n.* **indefatigably,** *adv.* [obs. F *indéfatigable,* L *indēfatigābilis* (*defatigāre,* to wear out, from *fatigāre,* to FATIGUE)]

indefeasible, *a.* not defeasible, incapable of being annulled or forfeited. **indefeasibility,** *n.* **indefeasibly,** *adv.*

indefectible, *a.* not liable to defect, decay or failure; faultless, flawless. **indefectibility,** *n.* †**indefective,** *a.* free from defect. [F *indéfectible*]

indefensible, *a.* incapable of being defended, excused

or justified. **indefensibly,** *adv.* **indefensibility,** *n.* †**indefensive,** *a.* defenceless.

indefinable, *a.* that cannot be defined. **indefinably,** *adv.*

indefinite, *a.* not limited or defined, not determinate; vague, uncertain, large beyond the comprehension of humans; infinite, without limit; of certain adjectives, adverbs and pronouns, not defining or determining the persons, things etc. to which they apply; also applied to tenses like the Greek aorist and English past by which an action is expressed but not when it is continuous or complete; (*Bot.*) not constant in number (used of floral organs, esp. stamens, usu. more than 20 in number); (*Math.*) without definite or conceivable limits. **indefinitely,** *adv.* **indefiniteness, -finitude,** *n.* [L *indēfīnītus*]

indehiscent, *a.* of seed-capsules etc., not splitting open to set free the seeds.

indelible, *a.* that cannot be blotted out or effaced. **indelible pencil,** *n.* a pencil that makes ineffaceable marks. **indelibility, †-ibleness,** *n.* **indelibly,** *adv.* [earlier *indeleble,* L *indēlēbilis* (*dēlēbilis,* from *dēlēre,* to DELETE)]

indelicate, *a.* wanting in delicacy; coarse, unrefined; offensive to modesty or propriety. **indelicacy,** *n.* **indelicately,** *adv.*

indemnify, *v.t.* to secure from or compensate for damage, loss, penalty or responsibility. **indemnification,** *n.* [L *indemnis* (*damnum,* loss)]

indemnity, *n.* security against damage, loss or penalty; indemnification or compensation for damage, loss or penalties incurred; a sum paid as such compensation, esp. by a defeated state to the conqueror as a condition of peace; legal exemption from liabilities or penalties incurred.

indemonstrable, *a.* that cannot be demonstrated; assumed as self-evident, axiomatic. **indemonstrability,** *n.*

indent[1], *v.t.* to notch or cut into as with teeth; (*Print.*) to set in farther from the margin than the rest of the paragraph; to indenture; to order by an indent; to execute or draw up (a contract etc.) in exact duplicate. *v.i.* to make an indent or order (upon); †to wind in and out, to run zigzag; to requisition. **indentation,** *n.* the act of indenting; a notch, dent or incision, esp. in a margin; a deep recess, esp. in a coast-line; a zigzag moulding. **indented,** *a.* notched, serrated, zigzag, winding; bound by an indenture. **indenter,** *n.* **indention,** *n.* (*Print.*) the setting in of a line of print farther from the margin; indentation. [acc. to Skeat from low L *indentāre,* to notch or cut into like teeth (*dens dentis,* tooth)]

indent[2], *n.* a notch in the margin of anything; an indentation or recess; an official order for stores; an order for goods, esp. one from abroad; (*N Am.*) †an indented certificate for the principal or interest of the public debt.

indent[3], *v.t.* to dent; to make a dent in; to mark with a dent. *n.* a dent.

indenture, *n.* (*Law*) an agreement or contract under seal, esp. one binding an apprentice to a master (so called because the two documents had their edges cut or indented exactly alike so as to correspond with each other); an official voucher, certificate, register etc.; an indentation. *v.t.* to bind (esp. an apprentice) by an indenture. †*v.i.* to run in and out in a zigzag course.

independence, *n.* the quality or state of being independent; income sufficient to make one independent of others, a competency. **Independence Day,** *n.* a day set apart for publicly celebrating the attainment of national independence; esp. 4 July, the day on which the American colonies declared their independence in 1776. **independency,** *n.* independence; the principles of the Independents or Congregationalists; †an independent State. **independent,** *a.* not dependent upon or subject to the control, power or authority of another, not subordinate; free to manage one's own affairs without the interference of others; not affiliated with or part of a larger organization; not depending on anything for its value, cogency etc.; having or affording the means of independence; self-asserting, self-reliant; free from bias or prejudice; pertaining to the Independents or Congregationalists. *n.* one who exercises his or her judgment and choice of action without dependence on any person, party etc.; a Congregationalist. **independently,** *adv.*

Independent Labour Party, (ILP) British socialist party, founded in Bradford 1893 by the Scottish Member of Parliament Keir Hardie. In 1900 it joined with trades unions and Fabians in founding the Labour Representation Committee, the nucleus of the Labour Party. Many members left the ILP to join the Communist Party 1921, and in 1932 all connections with the Labour Party were severed. After World War II the ILP dwindled, eventually becoming extinct. James Maxton (1885–1946) was its chair 1926–46.

Independent Television, *n.* (formerly the Independent Broadcasting Authority) in the UK, the orporate body established by legislation to provide commercially funded television (ITV from 1955) and local radio (ILR from 1973) services. During the 1980s this role was expanded to include the setting up of Channel 4 (launched 1982) and the provision of services broadcast directly by satellite into homes (DBS). Government proposals in 1988 recommended replacing the IBA and the Cable Authority (body established 1984 to develop cable TV services) with an Independent Television Commission (ITC) to oversee all commercial TV services. Commercial radio, to include three new national services, would be overseen by a separate new radio authority.

in-depth IN.

indescribable, *a.* not describable, too fine or too bad for description, passing description; (*sl., pl.*) trousers. **indescribability,** *n.* **indescribably,** *adv.* †**indescriptive,** *a.* not furnishing proper description (of).

indesignate, *a.* indefinite in quantity; not qualified.

indestructible, *a.* incapable of being destroyed. **indestructibility,** *n.* **indestructibly,** *adv.*

indeterminable, *a.* that cannot be determined or defined; that cannot be terminated as a dispute. **indeterminably,** *adv.* [L *indēterminābilis*]

indeterminate, *a.* not determinate; indefinite, undefined, not precise; (*Math.*) having no fixed value. **indeterminate vowel,** *n.* a vowel with an obscure or slurred sound, as the *a* in *advice.* **indeterminately,** *adv.* **indeterminacy, indeterminateness,** *n.* [L *indēterminātus*]

indetermination, *n.* lack of determination, vacillation. **indetermined,** *a.* not determined; indefinite.

indeterminism, *n.* (*Ethics*) the theory that conduct is not solely determined by motives, esp. that the will is able to choose between motives. **indeterminist,** *n.* **indeterministic,** *a.*

index, *n.* (*pl.* **indexes,** *Math.* **indices**) that which serves to point out or indicate; the forefinger; a hand (as of a watch etc.), an arm or a pointer, that directs to anything; a table of the contents of a book in alphabetical order with page-references; anything that indicates or denotes (an inner meaning, character etc.); (*Alg.*) the exponent of a power; the decimal number expressing the ratio between the length and breadth of a skull; a numerical scale indicating the relative changes in the cost of living etc., by reference to a given base level; (*dated sl.*) the face. *v.t.* to provide with an index; to enter in an index; to relate to an index, index-link. **index expurgatorius,** in the Roman Catholic Church, a list of passages from current literature condemned to be expunged as heretical. **index librorum expurgandorum** , in the Roman Catholic Church, a list of books to be read only in expurgated editions. **index librorum prohibitorum,** a list of books forbidden to be read by Roman Catholics on pain of excommunication (abolished in 1966). **index of a globe,** a little style on the north, serving to point to certain divisions of the hour-circle when the globe is turned. **index of a logarithm,** the integral part of the logarithm. **index of refraction,** (*Opt.*) the ratio of the sines of the angles of incidence and refraction. **the Index** INDEX EXPURGATORIUS, LIBRORUM etc. **index-finger,** *n.* the forefinger, from its being used in pointing. †**index-learning,** *n.* superficial knowledge. **index-linked,** *a.* increasing or decreasing in direct relation to changes in an index, esp. the cost of living index. **index number,** *n.* an indicator of the relative change in the price or value of something by reference to an earlier period, usu. taken to be 100. **index point,** *n.* a sub-division of a track on a compact disc. **indexation,** *n.* the act of linking wages, rates of interest etc. to the cost of living index. **indexer,** *n.* one who makes an index. **indexical,** *a.* pertaining to or of the form of an index. **indexless,** *a.* [L *index -dicis,* a forefinger, an informer (*indicāre,* to INDICATE)]

India, *n.* country in S Asia, having borders to the N with Afghanistan, China, Nepal, and Bhutan, to the E with Burma, and to the NW with Pakistan. **area** 3,166,829 sq km/1,222,396 sq miles. **capital** New Delhi. **towns** Bangalore, Hyderabad, Ahmedabad; ports Calcutta, Bombay, Madras, Kanpur, Pune, Nagpur. **physical** Himalaya mountains on the N border; plains around rivers Ganges, Indus, Brahmaputra; Deccan peninsula S of the Narmada River, plateau between the W and E Ghats mountain ranges. **territories** Andaman and Nicobar Islands, Lakshadweep. **exports** tea, coffee, fish, iron ore, leather, textiles, polished diamonds. **population** (1985) 750,900,000; annual growth rate 1.9%. **language** Hindi (official), English, and 14 other recognized languages: Assamese, Bengali, Gujarati, Kannada, Kashmiri, Malayalam, Marathi, Oriya, Punjabi, Sanskrit, Sindhi, Tamil, Telugu, Urdu. **religion** Hindu 80%, Sunni Muslim 10%, Christian 2.5%, Sikh 2%. **East India Company,** a chartered company (1600–1858) established for trading with India and later armed with territorial powers. **Further India,** the region between India and China. **India ink** INDIAN INK. **India-man,** *n.* (*pl.* **-men**) a large ship employed in the Indian trade. **india-matting,** *n.* matting made from *Papyrus corymbosus.* **India Office,** *n.* the department of the British Government formerly dealing with affairs of India. **India of the Princes**, the 562 Indian states ruled by princes during the period of British control. They occupied an area of 715,964 sq miles (45% of the total area of pre-partition India) and had a population of over 93 million. At the partition of British India in 1947 the princes were given independence by the British government, but were advised to adhere to either India or Pakistan. Between 1947 and 1950 all except Kashmir were incorporated in either country. **India paper,** *n.* a fine paper, imported from China, used by engravers for taking proofs. **Oxford India paper,** a very thin, tough, and opaque paper made by the Oxford University Press. **India proof,** *n.* a proof on India paper. **india-rubber,** *n.* a soft, elastic substance obtained from the coagulated juice of certain tropical plants, usu. called rubber. **india-rubbery,** *a.* **Indian,** *a.* belonging to the East or West Indies, to the natives of India, or to the aboriginal inhabitants of America. *n.* a native of India; one of the aboriginal inhabitants of America or the West Indies. **Indian art**, *n.* the painting, sculpture, and architecture of India. Indian art dates back to the ancient Indus Valley civilization of about 3000 BC. Sophisticated artistic styles emerged from the 1st cent. AD. Buddhist art includes sculpture and murals. Hindu artists created sculptural schemes in caves and huge temple complexes; the Hindu style is lively, with voluptuous nude figures. The Islamic Mogul Empire of the 16th–17th cent. created an exquisite style of miniature painting, inspired by Persian examples. **Indian National Congress,** Indian political organization founded in 1885 and reformed in 1916, to work for the political progress and final independence of India. **Red Indian,** one of the aboriginal inhabitants of N America, a N American Indian. **Indian berry,** *n.* cocculus indicus, or the climbing shrub *Anamirta cocculus* which bears this. **Indian club,** *n.* a bottle-shaped club used in gymnastic exercises. **Indian corn,** *n.* maize. **Indian cress,** *n.* a Peruvian climbing plant of the genus *Tropaeolum,* the best known being *T. major,* the nasturtium. **Indian date,** *n.* the tamarind. **Indian file,** *n.* single file. **Indian fire,** *n.* a brilliant white signal light composed of sulphur, realgar and nitre. **Indian ink,** *n.* a black pigment, composed of lamp-black and animal glue, manufactured in China and Japan, there used for writing etc., and employed in Europe in water-colour painting. **Indian languages**, *n.pl.* traditionally, the languages of the subcontinent of India; since 1947, the languages of the Republic of India. These number some 200, depending on whether a variety is classified as a language or a dialect. They divide into five main groups, the two most widespread of which are the Indo-European languages (mainly in the north) and the Dravidian languages (mainly in the south). **Indian meal,** *n.* meal made from maize. **Indian Mutiny**, *n.* the revolt 1857–58 of the Bengal army against the British in India. The movement was confined to the north, from Bengal to the Punjab, and central India. The majority of support came from the army and recently dethroned princes, but in some areas it developed into a peasant rising or general revolt. It included the seizure of Delhi by the rebels, and its siege and recapture by the British, and the defence of Lucknow by a British garrison. The mutiny led to the end of rule by the East India Company and its replacement by direct crown administration. **Indian Ocean**, *n.* ocean between Africa and Australia, with India to the N, and the S boundary being an arbitrary line from Cape Agulhas to S Tasmania; area 73,500,000 sq km/ 28,371,000 sq miles; average depth 3872 m/12,708 ft. The greatest depth is the Java Trench 7725 m/25,353 ft. **Indian rope-trick,** *n.* the supposed Indian feat of climbing an unsupported rope. **Indian-rubber** INDIA-RUBBER. **Indian summer,** *n.* summer-like weather, occurring late in autumn.

Indiana, *n.* state of the midwest US; nickname Hoosier State. **area** 93,700 sq km/36,168 sq miles. **capital** Indianapolis. **towns** Fort Wayne, Gary, Evansville, South Bend. **population** (1988) 5,575,000. **products** cereals, building stone, machinery, electrical goods, coal, steel, iron, chemicals.

Indianapolis Raceway, *n.* US motor sport circuit, built 1910 following the success of Brooklands in the UK. The Indianapolis 500 is staged here at the end of May each year as part of the Memorial Day celebrations.

Indic, *a.* originating or existing in India; pertaining to the Indian branch of the Indo-European languages. *n.* this group of languages. [L and Gr., from *Indos,* the Indus, Pers. *hind,* Sansk. *sindhu,* river]

indic., (*abbr.*) indicative.

indican, *n.* the natural glucoside contained in the indigo-plant and other plants, by the decomposition of which indigo is yielded; a normal constituent of urine. **indicanein,** *n.* [L *indicum,* INDIGO, -AN]

indicant, *a.* indicating or pointing out, esp. suggesting a specific disease or remedy. *n.* that which indicates a disease or its remedy.

indicate, *v.t.* to show, to point out; to be a sign or token of; (*Med.*) to point out or suggest (as a remedy); to state briefly, to suggest. **indication,** *n.* the act of indicating; that which indicates; intimation; a symptom suggesting certain treatment. **indicative**, *a.* applied to that mood of a verb which affirms, denies or asks questions; (*sometimes pron.* in'dikātiv) indicating; denoting something not visible or obvious. *n.* the indicative mood. **indicatively,** *adv.* **indicator,** *n.* one who or that which indicates; a reagent used to indicate, by change of colour, the presence of an acid, alkali etc.; an instrument attached to apparatus, machinery, a vehicle etc., to indicate or record pressure, speed, number etc.; a device for indicating the times of departure etc. of trains; a device, esp. a flashing light, on a vehicle to show an intention to change direction; a statistic such as the level of industrial production that indicates the condition of a national economy. **indicatory,** *a.* [L *indicātus,* p.p. of *indicāre* (*dicāre,* to point out)]

indices INDEX.
indicium, *n.* (*pl.* **-cia**) an indicating sign or mark; a symptom. [L, from *indic-*, INDEX]
indict, *v.t.* to charge with a crime or misdemeanour, esp. by means of an indictment. **indictable,** *a.* of a person, liable to be indicted; of an offence, forming a ground of indictment. **indictably,** *adv.* †**indictee,** *n.* a person indicted. **indicter,** *n.* **indictment,** *n.* the act of indicting; a formal accusation of a crime or misdemeanour, presented upon oath by the grand jury to a court; the document embodying this; (*Sc. Law*) a process by which a criminal is brought to trial at the instance of the Lord Advocate. [OF *enditer,* INDITE]
indiction, *n.* a period of 15 years arbitrarily fixed by Constantine the Great as a fiscal arrangement, beginning 1 Sept. 312, adopted by the Popes as part of their chronological system; a land-tax imposed by the Roman emperors at the beginning of each of these periods; a year in one of these cycles reckoned from the beginning; †a proclamation. **indictive,** *a.* proclaimed, declared publicly. [through F or directly from L *indictio -ōnem,* from *indīcere,* to appoint (*dīcere,* to say)]
Indies, *n.pl.* India and the neighbouring regions, also called the East Indies; the West Indies. [pl. of *Indie,* INDIA]
indifferent, *a.* impartial, unbiased, neutral; having no inclination or disinclination (to); unconcerned, apathetic; neither good nor bad; of no importance, of little moment (to); of a barely passable quality, not good; (*Chem., Elec. etc.*) neutral, not active. *n.* a neutral person. **indifference,** *n.* the quality or state of being indifferent; impartiality, neutrality, absence of inclination or disinclination; lack of interest or attention (to or towards); unconcern, inattention; mediocrity; unimportance, insignificance. **indifferential,** *a.* **indifferentiated,** *a.* **indifferentism,** *n.* systematic indifference, esp. with regard to religious belief. **indifferentist,** *n.* **indifferently,** *adv.* [F, from L *indifferentem,* nom. *-ens*]
indigenous, *a.* native, not exotic; natural, innate (to). **indigene,** *n.* **indigenously,** *adv.* [L *indigenus* (*indi-, indu,* IN-[1], *gen-,* root of *gignere,* to produce)]
indigent, *a.* in want, poor, needy, necessitous; in need (of); destitute (of). **indigence,** †**-ency,** *n.* **indigently,** *adv.* [F, from L *indigentem,* nom. *-gens* (*indi-,* as prec., *egēre,* to be in want, in need)]
indigest, *a.* undigested. †*n.* a shapeless, undigested mass. *v.t.* to fail to digest. **indigested,** *a.* not digested; not reduced to order, not methodized; crude; shapeless; not digested (in the stomach). **indigestible,** *a.* not easily digested; hard to understand or to follow; not acceptable. *n.* an indigestible substance or thing. **indigestibility,** *n.* **indigestibly,** *adv.* **indigestion,** *n.* difficulty of digestion, dyspepsia; want of proper digestive power; the state of being undigested, unorganized or immature. **indigestive,** *a.* [L *indīgestus* (*dīgestus,* p.p. of *dīgerere,* to DIGEST)]
indignant, *a.* feeling or showing indignation, esp. at meanness, injustice etc., or with a person acting meanly etc. †**indignance,** *n.* **indignantly,** *adv.* **indignation,** *n.* a mingled feeling of anger and disdain; the feeling excited by that which is unworthy, mean, base or unjust. **indignation-meeting,** *n.* a public meeting to protest against some abuse. [L *indignans -antem,* pres.p. of *indignārī*]
indignity, *n.* undeserved contemptuous treatment; an act of incivility, a slight, an insult.
indigo, *n.* (*pl.* **-gos, -goes**) a beautiful and very durable blue dye obtained from the indigo-plant, largely used in calico printing etc.; a deep-blue colour. *a.* of a deep-blue colour. **native indigo,** (*Austral.*) the poisonous Darling pea. **indigo-bird,** *n.* a N American finch, *Cyanospiza cyanea.* **indigo-blue,** *n.* the colour or the colouring-matter of indigo. **indigo-plant,** *n.* a plant of the genus *Indigofera,* esp. *I. tinctoria.* **indigo-white,** *n.* a colourless crystalline powder obtained by the reduction or deoxidation of indigo. **indigotic,** *a.* [formerly *indico,* Sp., from L *indicum,* Gr. *indikon,* Indian]
indirect, *a.* not direct, deviating from a direct line; not straight or rectilinear; not resulting directly or immediately from a cause; of taxes, not paid directly to the Government, but in the form of increased prices etc.; (*Gram.*) in oblique oration or reported speech; not fair, not honest, not open or straightforward. **indirect evidence, testimony,** *n.* evidence deduced from collateral circumstances. **indirect object,** *n.* (*Gram.*) the person or thing indirectly affected by an action though not the direct object of the verb. **indirect speech,** *n.* the reporting of spoken or written discourse by indicating what was meant rather than by repetition of the exact words. †**indirection,** *n.* dishonest or indirect means. **indirectly,** *adv.* **indirectness,** *n.* [F, from L *indīrectus*]
indiretin, *n.* a resinous compound obtained by the decomposition of indican. [*indi-, Indus,* root of INDIGO, L *rhetinē,* RESIN]
indirubin, *n.* a brownish-red amorphous compound obtained by the decomposition of indican. [*indi-,* as prec. L *ruber,* red]
indiscernible, *a.* not discernible, not distinguishable, not visible. *n.* an indiscernible thing. **indiscernibleness,** *n.* **indiscernibly,** *adv.*
indiscerptible, *a.* not to be destroyed by dissolution of parts. **indiscerptibility,** *n.*
indiscipline, *n.* want of discipline. **indisciplinable,** *a.* incapable of being disciplined or improved by discipline.
indiscoverable, *a.* not discoverable.
indiscreet, *a.* wanting in discretion; injudicious, incautious; foolish, rash. **indiscreetly,** *adv.* **indiscreetness,** *n.* indiscretion. **indiscretion,** *n.* want of discretion; imprudence, rashness; an indiscreet act, indiscreet conduct. [L *indiscrētus*]
indiscrete, *a.* not discrete or separated.
indiscriminate, *a.* wanting in discrimination; making no distinction; confused, promiscuous. **indiscriminately,** *adv.* **indiscriminateness, -ation,** *n.* **indiscriminating, -ative,** *a.*
indispensable, *a.* that cannot be dispensed with; absolutely necessary or requisite; †not admitting dispensation; *n.pl.* (*sl.*) trousers. **indispensability, -ableness,** *n.* **indispensably,** *adv.* [med. L *indispensābilis*]
indispose, *v.t.* to make disinclined or unfavourable; to render unfit or unable (for or to); to make slightly ill. **indisposed,** *a.* disinclined, unwilling, unfavourable; slightly ill. †**indisposedness, indisposition,** *n.* disinclination, aversion, unsuitableness; a slight illness.
indisputable, *a.* not disputable; too clear to admit of question or dispute. **indisputability, -ableness,** *n.* **indisputably,** *adv.* †**indisputed,** *a.*
indissociable, *a.* not to be separated or disassociated.
indissoluble, *a.* not dissoluble; not to be dissolved or disintegrated; stable, binding, subsisting and binding for ever. **indissolubility, indissolubleness,** *n.* **indissolubly,** *adv.* [F, from L *indissolūbilis*]
indistinct, *a.* not distinct, obscure; not readily distinguishable; confused, faint. †**indistinction,** *n.* want of distinction or distinctness; inability to distinguish. **indistinctive,** *a.* not distinctive. **indistinctively,** *adv.* **indistinctly,** *adv.* **indistinctness,** *n.* [F, from L *indistinctus*]
indistinguishable, *a.* not distinguishable. **indistinguishably,** *adv.* †**indistinguished,** *a.* indistinct, confused.
indistributable, *a.* that cannot be distributed.
indite, *v.t.* to put in words, to compose; to set down, to write; †to indict; †to dictate; †to invite. †**inditement,** *n.* the act of inditing; an indictment. **inditer,** *n.* [OF *enditer,* late L *indictāre* (*dictāre,* to DICTATE)]
indium, *n.* a soft, silver-white metallic element, at. no. 49; chem. symbol In, occurring in minute quantities in zinc ores. [L *ind-icum,* see INDIGO]
individual, *a.* subsisting as a single indivisible entity; single, particular as opp. to general; separate or distinct; characteristic of a particular person or thing, distinctive; †indivisible. *n.* a single person, animal or thing, esp. a single human being; a single member of a

species, class etc.; a person; the result of the development of a single ovum; an organism that has attained separate existence. **individual psychology,** *n.* a system founded by the Viennese psychologist Adler which considers the main factor of neurosis to be fear, and the desire for power to be the driving force behind every motive. **individualism,** *n.* individuality; conduct or feeling centred in self, egoism, self-interest, selfishness; idiosyncrasy, personal peculiarity; an attitude, tendency or system in which each individual works for his or her own ends; independent action as opposed to cooperation, or as opp. to collectivism or Socialism. **individualist,** *n.* **individualistic,** *a.* **individualistically,** *adv.* **individuality,** *n.* separate or distinct existence; distinctive character, strongly-marked personality. **individualize, -ise,** *v.t.* to mark out or distinguish from other individuals; to connect with one particular individual; to package separately; to make so as to suit the needs of a particular person. **individualization, -isation,** *n.* **individually,** *adv.* separately, in an individual capacity. **individuate,** *v.t.* to give the character of individuality to; to make an individual or a distinct entity. **individuation,** *n.* **principle of individuation,** (*Scholastic Phil.*) the principle individuating an *ens* from all other *entia.* [med. L *indīviduālis,* from *indīviduus,* indivisible (*dīvidere,* to DIVIDE)]

indivisible, *a.* not divisible; that cannot be exactly divided. *n.* that which is indivisible, an infinitely small quantity or particle. **indivisibility,** *n.* **indivisibly,** *adv.* †**indivision,** *n.* the state of being undivided. [F, from L *indīvīsibilis*]

Indo-, *comb.form* Indian; derived from, belonging to, or connected with India. [INDIA]

Indo-Aryan, *a.* pertaining to the Indian division of the Aryan family of races.

Indochina, French *n.* former collective name for Cambodia, Laos, and Vietnam, which became independent after World War II. **Indochina War,** *n.* war 1946–1954 between France, the occupying colonial power, and nationalist forces of what was to become Vietnam. **Indochinese,** *a.* pertaining to the southeastern peninsula of Asia or Further India, its people or their languages.

indocile, *a.* not docile; not capable of being instructed. †**indocible,** *a.* **indocility,** *n.* [F, from L *indocilis*]

indoctrinate, *v.t.* to instruct in any body of doctrine; to imbue with the distinctive principles of any system; to brainwash. **indoctrination,** *n.*

Indo-Eur., (*abbr.*) Indo-European.

Indo-European, *a.* of or pertaining to the family of languages spoken over most of Europe and over Asia as far as northern India. *n.pl.* a family of languages that includes some of the world's leading classical languages (Sanskrit and Pali in India, Zend Avestan in Iran, Greek and Latin in Europe), as well as several of the most widely spoken languages (English worldwide; Spanish in Iberia, Latin America, and elsewhere; and the Hindi group of languages in N India).

Indo-Germanic languages, *n.pl.* former name for the Indo-European languages.

indole, *n.* a white or yellowish crystalline heterocyclic compound derived from coal tar. [INDIGO]

indolent, *a.* habitually idle or lazy; (*Path.*) causing no pain. **indolent tumour,** *n.* a tumour causing no pain. **indolence,** †**-ency,** *n.* **indolently,** *adv.* [late L *indolens -entem*]

in Domino, in the Lord. [L]

indomitable, *a.* untamable, unconquerable; indefatigable. **indomitably,** *adv.* [late L *indomitābilis* (*domitāre,* to tame)]

Indonesia, *n.* Republic of, country in SE Asia, made up of over 3000 islands situated on the equator, between the Indian and Pacific Oceans. **area** 1,919,443 sq km/740,905 sq miles. **capital** Jakarta. **towns** ports Surabaya, Semarang. **physical** comprises 13,677 tropical islands, including the greater part of the Sunda Islands to the W of the Moluccas, both the Greater Sundas (including Java and Madura, part of Kalimantan/Borneo, Sumatra, Sulawesi and Belitung) and the Lesser Sundas/Nusa Tenggara (including Bali, Lombok, Sumba, Timor), as well as Malaku/Moluccas and part of New Guinea (Irian Jaya). **population** (1987) 172,250,000 (including 300 ethnic groups); annual growth rate 2%. **exports** coffee, rubber, palm oil, coconuts, tin, tea, tobacco, oil, liquid natural gas. **language** Indonesian, closely allied to Malay. **religion** Muslim 90%, Buddhist, Hindu, and Pancasila (a secular official ideology). **Indonesian,** *a.* pertaining to the East Indian islands forming the Republic of Indonesia. *n.* an inhabitant of Indonesia; the language. [Gr. *nesos,* an island]

indoor, *a.* being or done within doors. **indoor relief,** *n.* (*formerly*) relief granted to paupers domiciled in a workhouse. **indoors,** *adv.* within a house or building.

indorsation, *n.* the act or process of endorsing. **indorse,** ENDORSE.

Indra, *n.* Hindu god of the sky, shown as a four-armed man on a white elephant, carrying a thunderbolt. The intoxicating drink soma is associated with him.

indraught, *n.* an inward flow, draught or current.

indrawn, *a.* drawn in.

indri, indris, *n.* the babacoote, a Madagascan lemur. [Malagasy *indry,* lo! look! (mistaken for the name)]

indubitable, *a.* not doubtful, unquestionable; too evident to admit of doubt. **indubitability, -ableness,** *n.* **indubitably,** *adv.* †**indubitate,** *a.* [F, from L *indubitābilis*]

induce, *v.t.* to lead by persuasion or reasoning, to prevail on; to bring about, to cause; to bring on or speed up (labour) by artificial means, as by the use of drugs; (*Elec.*) to produce by induction; (*Log.*) to derive as a deduction, opp. to *deduce.* **inducement,** *n.* the act of inducing; that which induces; a motive, a reason, an incitement; (*Law*) a preamble or statement of facts introducing other material facts. **inducer,** *n.* **inducible,** *a.* [L *indūcere* (*dūcere,* to lead), p.p. *inductus*]

induct, *v.t.* to introduce (as into a benefice or office); to put in actual possession of an ecclesiastical benefice or of any office, with the customary forms and ceremonies. *v.i.* (*N Am.*) to enlist for military training. **inductance,** *n.* the tendency of an electric circuit to oppose any change in the current passing through it. **induction,** *n.* the process of adducing facts to prove a general statement; (*Log.*) the process of inferring a law or general principle from particular instances, as dist. from *deduction;* a general statement or conclusion attained by this kind of reasoning; the proving of the universal truth of a theorem by showing it to be true of any case in a series or of a particular case; the production of an electric or magnetic state by the proximity or movement of an electric or magnetized body; instalment in an office or benefice; an introduction, a prologue, prelude; (*N Am.*) enlistment for military training; †a beginning, a preliminary measure. **induction coil,** *n.* an apparatus for producing currents by electromagnetic induction. **induction motor,** *n.* an electric motor in which an electromagnetic flux is set up by currents in a primary winding, and this induces currents in a secondary winding, such that interaction of currents with flux produces rotation. **inductional,** *a.* **inductive,** *a.* (*Log.*) proceeding or characterized by induction; (*Elec.*) pertaining to, producing or susceptible of induction; leading or drawing on; †introductory, beginning. **inductive method,** *n.* (*Log.*) the process of reasoning from particular instances to general principles. **inductive sciences,** *n.pl.* sciences based on induction from positive fact. **inductively,** *adv.* **inductivity,** *n.* **inductor,** *n.* one who inducts a clergyman into office; any part of an electrical apparatus acting inductively. **inductorium,** *n.* (*pl.* **-ria**) an induction coil. **inductory,** *a.* **inductric,** *a.* (*Elec.*). [L *inductus,* see prec.]

inductile, *a.* not ductile. **inductility,** *n.*

indue, ENDUE.

indulge, *v.t.* to yield, esp. unduly, to the desires, humours or wishes of, to humour (in or with); to favour; to gratify (one's desires, weakness etc.); to harbour, to entertain, to foster. *v.i.* to yield to one's desires (in); †to yield or grant compliance (to); to take alcoholic drink, esp. in excess. **indulgence**, *n.* the act or practice of indulging, yielding or complying to desires etc.; an indulgent act, a favour or privilege granted; a pleasurable thing or habit indulged in; liberality, tolerance, leniency; in the Roman Catholic Church, a remission of the punishment still due to sin after sacramental absolution. **Declaration of Indulgence,** (*Eng. Hist.*) a proclamation granting religious liberty, esp. that of Charles II in 1672 suspending the penal laws against Nonconformists and recusants, and that of James II in 1687 in favour of Roman Catholics. **indulgenced,** *a.* of certain prayers, religious objects etc., bestowing an indulgence. †**indulgency,** *n.* **indulgent,** *a.* indulging or disposed to indulge the wishes, humours or caprices of others; not exercising restraint or control. †**indulgential**, *a.* relating to indulgences. **indulgently,** *adv.* **indulger,** *n.* one who indulges (in). [L *indulgēre*]

induline, *a.* one of a series of blue, blue-black and grey dye-stuffs related to aniline. [*ind-icum,* see INDIGO, *-ul-*, dim. suf., -INE]

indult, *n.* an indulgence or privilege granted by the Pope, exempting from some canonical duty or authorizing something not normally permitted. [F, from L *indultum,* p.p. of *indulgēre,* to INDULGE]

indumentum, *n.* (*pl.* **-ta**) a covering, as of hair, feathers etc. †**indument**, *n.* [L, from *induere,* to ENDUE]

induna, *n.* a leader or general of an impi. [Zulu]

induplicate, *a.* of leaves and flowers in aestivation, having the edges folded in.

indurate, *v.t.* to make hard, to harden; to render obdurate or unfeeling. *v.i.* to become hard; to become fixed or inveterate, as a custom. †*a.*, hardened; obstinate, callous. **induration,** *n.* insensibility. **indurative,** *a.* [L *indūrātus,* p.p. of *indūrāre* (*dūrāre,* to make hard)]

Indus, *n.* river in Asia, rising in Tibet and flowing 3180 km/1975 miles to the Arabian Sea. In 1960 the use of its waters, including those of its five tributaries, was divided between India (rivers Ravi, Beas, Sutlej) and Pakistan (rivers Indus, Jhelum, Chenab). **Indus Valley Civilization,** *n.* a prehistoric culture existing in the NW Indian subcontinent about 2500–1600 BC. Remains include soapstone seals with engravings of elephants and snakes.

indusium, *n.* (*pl.* **-sia**) (*Bot.*) a hairy cup enclosing a stigma; a shield or scale covering the fruit-cluster in some ferns; the larval case of an insect. **indusial,** *a.* of limestone in Auvergne, consisting in large measure of the fossil larva-cases of the caddisworm. **indusiate**, *a.* (*Bot.*) having an indusium. **indusiform**, **indusioid**, *a.* (*Bot.*). [L, from *induere,* to ENDUE]

industry, *n.* diligence, assiduity, steady application to any business or pursuit; useful work, esp. mechanical and manufacturing pursuits as dist. from agriculture and commerce; any branch of these; (*Polit. Econ.*) the employment of labour in production; any field of activity as organized for economic gain. **industrial**, *a.* pertaining to industry, to productive occupations or to produce; characterized by advanced and sophisticated industries. *n.* a person engaged in an industrial occupation; (*pl.*) shares or securities relating to industrial enterprises. **industrial action,** *n.* action taken by employees to try to coerce their employer into complying with demands or as a protest, esp. a strike or go-slow. **industrial archaeology,** *n.* the study of the remains of past industrial activity. **industrial estate,** *n.* an industrial area specially planned to provide employment in factories of different kinds. **industrial exhibition,** *n.* an exhibition of industrial products, machinery, appliances etc. **industrial relations,** *n.* a general term covering the relationships between employer and employees. **Industrial Revolution**, *n.* the sudden acceleration of technical and economic development that took place in Britain from the second half of the 18th cent. The great initial invention was the steam engine, originally developed for draining mines (see NEWCOMEN) but rapidly put to use in factories and on the railways (see WATT, ARKWRIGHT, CROMPTON, TREVITHICK). This transferred the balance of political power from the landowner to the industrial capitalist and created an urban working class. From 1830 to the early 20th cent., the Industrial Revolution spread to Europe, its colonies, the US, and Japan. **industrial school,** *n.* a school for teaching trades to neglected or convicted children. **Industrial Workers of the World**, (IWW) a US labour movement founded 1905, popularly known as the Wobblies. The IWW was dedicated to the overthrow of capitalism but divided on tactics and gradually declined in popularity after 1917. At its peak (1912–15) the organization claimed to have 100,000 members, mainly in western mining and lumber areas, and in the textile mills of New England. Demonstrations were violently suppressed by the authorities. **industrialism,** *n.* a state of society in which the object of statesmanship is the success of industrial pursuits, the opposite to militarism; the modern industrial system. **industrialist,** *n.* a person engaged in management or ownership in industry. **industrialize, -ise,** *v.t.* **industrialization, -isation,** *n.* **industrially,** *adv.* **industrious**, *a.* characterized by industry; diligent and assiduous in business or study. **industriously,** *adv.* **industriousness,** *n.* [F *industrie,* L *industria* (prob. *indu, in,* in, *struere,* see CONSTRUCT)]

induviae, *n.pl.* the withered remains of leaves which remain and decay on the stem of some plants. **induviate,** *a.* [L, clothing, from *induere,* to ENDUE]

indwell, *v.t.* (*past, p.p.* **indwelt,**) to abide in; (*usu. fig.*) to inhabit. *v.i.* to dwell (in the soul etc.). **indweller,** *n.*

Indy, *n.* **(Paul Marie Théodore) Vincent d'** (1851–1931), French composer. He studied under César Franck, and was one of the founders of the *Schola Cantorum*. His works include operas (*Fervaal*, 1897), symphonies, tone poems (*Istar*, 1896), and chamber music.

-ine, *suf.* pertaining to, of the nature of; forming adjectives, as *crystalline, divine, equine, hyacinthine, marine;* forming feminine nouns, as *heroine, landgravine,* abstract nouns, as *discipline, medicine;* (*Chem.*) names of alkaloids and basic substances, as *cocaine, morphine*. [L *-īnus, īnus;* or from F *-ine,* L *īna*]

inebriate, *v.t.* to make drunk; to intoxicate or exhilarate. *a.*, (*lit.* or *fig.*) intoxicated, drunk. *n.* a habitual drunkard. **inebriant,** *a.* intoxicating. *n.* anything which intoxicates. **inebriation,** *n.* **inebriety**, *n.* intoxication; habitual drinking.

ineconomy, *n.* lack of economy. **ineconomical**, *a.*

inedible, *a.* not edible. **inedibility**, *n.*

inedited, *a.* not edited or revised, not published.

ineffable, *a.* unspeakable, unutterable, beyond expression. **ineffableness,** *n.* **ineffably,** *adv.* [F, from L *ineffābilis* (*effārī,* EF-, *fārī,* to speak)]

ineffaceable, *a.* that cannot be rubbed out. **ineffaceably,** *adv.*

ineffective, *a.* not producing any or the desired effect; inefficient; not having artistic effect. **ineffectively,** *adv.* **ineffectiveness,** *n.*

ineffectual, *a.* not producing any effect; powerless, vain. †**ineffectuality**, **ineffectualness,** *n.* **ineffectually,** *adv.*

inefficacious, *a.* not efficacious; producing no result or effect. **inefficacy**, *n.*

inefficient, *a.* not efficient; wanting in ability or capacity. **inefficiently,** *adv.* **inefficiency,** *n.*

inelastic, *a.* wanting in elasticity. **inelasticity**, *n.*

inelegant, *a.* not elegant; wanting in grace, polish, refinement etc. **inelegance,** †**-ancy,** *n.* **inelegantly,** *adv.* [F *inélégant,* L *inelēgantem,* nom. *-gans*]

ineligible, *a.* not eligible; not capable of being selected or preferred. **ineligibility**, *n.* **ineligibly,** *adv.*

ineluctable, *a.* not to be escaped; not to be overcome by struggling. [L *inēluctābilis* (*ēluctārī,* E-, *luctārī,* to struggle)]

inept, *a.* not apt, fit or suitable; clumsy, incompetent; silly, absurd. **ineptitude**, **ineptness,** *n.* **ineptly,** *adv.*

[L *ineptus* (*aptus*, APT)]

inequable, *n.* unfair; not uniform.

inequality, *n.* want of equality; difference, diversity, irregularity, variability, unevenness (of dimensions, position, intensity etc.); disparity; inadequacy, incompetency; unfairness, partiality; (*Astron.*) deviation from uniformity of motion in a heavenly body. [OF *inéqualité* (F. *inégalité*), L. *inaequālitas*]

inequilateral, *a.* not equilateral; having unequal sides.

inequitable, *a.* not equitable, not fair or just. **inequitably,** *adv.* **inequity,** *n.* a want of equity; injustice, unfairness.

ineradicable, *a.* that cannot be eradicated. **ineradicably,** *adv.*

inerrable, *a.* exempt from error; infallible. **inerrability, inerrancy,** *n.* **inerrably,** *adv.* **inerrant,** *a.* **inerrantist,** *n.* (*N Am.*) a person who believes in the inerrancy of the Bible. **inerratic,** *a.* not wandering; fixed, as a star. [L *inerrābilis* (*errāre*, to ERR)]

inert, *a.* lacking inherent power of motion or active resistance to motive power applied; motionless, slow, sluggish; indisposed to move or act; (*Chem.*) destitute of active chemical powers, neutral. **inert gas,** *n.* any of a group of gaseous elements that react very little with other elements and include helium, neon, argon, krypton, xenon and radon. **inertia,** *n.* inertness; that property of a body by which it persists in an existing state of rest or of uniform motion in a straight line, unless an external force changes that state. **vis inertiae,** the resistance of matter to a force operating to move it. **inertia-reel seat belt,** *n.* a type of vehicle seat-belt in which the belt unwinds freely except when the violent deceleration of the vehicle causes it to lock. **inertia selling,** *n.* the practice of sending unsolicited goods to householders and requesting payment if the goods are not returned. **inertial,** *a.* **inertial navigation,** *n.* a system of gyroscopic guidance for aircraft, missiles etc., that dispenses with magnetic compass or ground-based radio direction. **inertly,** *adv.* **inertness,** *n.* [L *iners -ertem* (*ars*, ART[2])]

inescapable, *a.* inevitable, not to be escaped.

inescutcheon, *n.* a small escutcheon borne within a shield.

inessential, *a.* unessential; not indispensable.

inestimable, *a.* that cannot be estimated; too valuable or excellent to be valued or rated. **inestimably,** *adv.* [F, from L *inaestimābilis*]

ineunt, *a.* entering. *n.* (*Math.*) a point of a curve. [L *ineuntem*, nom. *iniens*, pres.p. of *inīre* (*īre*, to go)]

inevitable, *a.* that cannot be avoided or prevented; (*coll.*) customary, wonted. **inevitability, -ableness,** *n.* **inevitably,** *adv.* [L *inēvītābilis* (*ēvītāre*, to avoid)]

inexact, *a.* not exact, not precisely accurate. **inexactitude, inexactness,** *n.* **inexactly,** *adv.*

inexcusable, *a.* not to be excused or justified. **inexcusability, -ableness,** *n.* **inexcusably,** *adv.* [F, from L *inexcūsābilis*]

inexecutable, *a.* incapable of being performed. **inexecution,** *n.* failure to perform.

inexertion, *n.* want of exertion or effort.

inexhausted, *a.* not exhausted. **inexhaustible,** *a.* that cannot be exhausted; unfailing, unceasing. **inexhaustibility, -ibleness,** *n.* **inexhaustibly,** *adv.* **inexhaustive,** *a.* inexhaustible; not exhausting (the subject etc.). **inexhaustively,** *adv.*

inexistent[1], *a.* not existing, non-existent. **inexistence** *n.*

inexistent[2], *a.* existent in or within. **inexistence,** *n.*

inexorable, *a.* incapable of being persuaded or moved by entreaty or prayer; unbending, inflexible, relentless. **inexorability,** *n.* **inexorably,** *adv.* [F, from L *inexōrābilis* (*ōrāre*, to pray)]

inexpansible, *a.* not capable of being expanded. **inexpansive,** *a.*

inexpedient, *a.* not expedient; unadvisable, disadvantageous, unprofitable. **inexpedience, -ency,** *n.* **inexpediently,** *adv.*

inexpensive, *a.* not expensive; cheap. **inexpensively,** *adv.* **inexpensiveness,** *n.*

inexperience, *n.* want of knowledge gained by experience. **inexperienced,** *a.* [F *inexpérience*, L *inexperientia*]

inexpert, *a.* not expert, unskilful. **inexpertly,** *adv.* [OF, from L *inexpertus*]

inexpiable, *a.* that cannot be expiated or atoned for; implacable. **inexpiably,** *adv.* [L *inexpiābilis*]

inexplicable, *a.* not capable of being made plain or intelligible; not to be explained. *n.pl.* (*sl.*) trousers. **inexplicability, †-ableness,** *n.* **inexplicably,** *adv.* [F, from L *inexplicābilis*]

inexplicit, *a.* not definitely or clearly stated. **inexplicitly,** *adv.* **inexplicitness,** *n.*

†inexplorable, *a.* not capable of being explored, inscrutable.

inexplosive, *a.* not explosive.

inexpressible, *a.* not expressible; incapable of being expressed or described; unutterable, unspeakable. *n.pl.* (*sl.*) trousers. **inexpressibly,** *adv.* **inexpressive,** *a.* **inexpressively,** *adv.* **inexpressiveness,** *n.*

inexpugnable, *a.* not expugnable, impregnable. **inexpugnably,** *adv.* [F, from L *inexpugnābilis*]

inextinguishable, *a.* incapable of being extinguished. **inextinguishably,** *adv.*

in extremis, at the point of death. [L]

inextricable, *a.* that cannot be disentangled or solved; inescapable. **inextricably,** *adv.* [F, from L *inextricābilis*]

inf., (*abbr.*) infinitive.

INF, (*abbr.*) intermediate nuclear forces.

infall, *n.* a hostile descent, an inroad; the place where the water enters a reservoir etc., an inlet.

infallible, *a.* exempt from liability to error or to failure; certain not to fail. **infallibilism,** *n.* **infallibilist,** *n., a.* **infallibility, †-ibleness,** *n.* **papal infallibility,** the dogma that the Roman Pontiff, when he defines a doctrine regarding faith or morals to be held by the universal Church, is infallible. **infallibly,** *adv.* [F, from med. L *infallibilis*]

infamous, *a.* having a reputation of an ill kind; notoriously vile; detestable, scandalous; (*Law*) branded with infamy by conviction for a crime. **†infame, infamize, -ise,** †(*Shak.*) **†infamonize, -ise,** *v.t.* to make infamous; to defame. **infamously,** *adv.* **infamy,** *n.* total loss of reputation or character; public reproach; extreme baseness; an infamous act; (*Law*) loss of character or position attaching to a convict. [OF *infameux*, med. L *infamōsus*, L *infāmis*]

infant, *n.* a child during the earliest years of its life (*usu.* a babe, *also*, a child less than seven years old); (*Law*) a minor; †the child of a king or prince. *a.* young, tender; pertaining to or designed for infants. †*v.t.* to bear or bring forth (as a child); to produce. **infancy,** *n.* **infantile,** *a.* pertaining to infants or infancy; characteristic of infancy, childish. **infantile paralysis,** *n.* poliomyelitis. **infantilism,** *n.* **infantine,** *a.* [OF *enfant*, L *infantem*, nom. *-fans* (*fans*, pres.p. of *fārī*, to speak)]

infanta, *n.* (in Spain and Portugal) any royal princess (usu. the eldest) except an heiress-apparent. **infante,** *n.* any son of the king except the heir-apparent. [Sp. and Port., as prec.]

infanticide, *n.* murder of a new-born infant; the practice of killing new-born children; the murderer of an infant. **infanticidal,** *a.* [late L *infanticīdium*]

infantry, *n.* (*collect.*) foot-soldiers, usu. armed with small arms or rifle and bayonet; (*facet.*) children. **light infantry,** infantry formerly equipped and trained for rapid evolutions. **mounted infantry,** infantry mounted for rapid transportation, but fighting on foot. **infantryman,** *n.* a soldier in an infantry regiment. [F *infanterie*, Ital. *infanteria*, from *infante*, a youth, a foot-soldier, as INFANT]

infarct, *n.* an area of tissue that is dying from lack of a blood supply. **infarction,** *n.* [med. L, *infarctus* (*farctus*, stuffed)]

infatuate, *v.t.* to deprive of judgment, to affect with folly or extravagance; to inspire with an extravagant passion. †*a.*, affected with folly or infatuation. **infatuatedly,** *adv.* **infatuation** *n.* [L *infatuātus*, p.p. of *infatuāre* (*fatuus,* FATUOUS)]

infect, *v.t.* to act upon by contagion or infection; to taint with the germs of disease; to corrupt, to affect (with depravity etc.); to imbue (with noxious opinions etc.); to taint with crime or illegality. †*a.* infected. **infectedly,** *adv.* **infection,** *n.* the act or process of infecting, esp. the communication of disease by means of water, the atmosphere etc., as distinct from *contagion;* that which infects, infectious matter; an infectious disease; moral contamination; the act of diffusing or instilling (esp. evil qualities) by means of example etc. **infectious,** *a.* infecting or capable of infecting; likely to communicate disease; liable to be communicated by the atmosphere, water etc.; of feelings etc., apt to spread, catching. **infectiously,** *adv.* **infectiousness,** *n.* **infective,** *a.* infectious. **infectiveness, infectivity,** *n.* [L *infectus,* p.p. of *inficere,* to taint (*facere,* to make)]

†**infecund,** *a.* not fecund; barren. †**infecundity,** *n.* [L *infēcundus* (FECUND)]

infeft, *v.t.* (*Sc.*) to enfeoff. **infeftment,** *n.* (*Sc. Law*) the act of giving symbolic possession of heritable property. [var. of ENFEOFF]

infelicitous, *a.* not felicitous; unfortunate; inappropriate, inept. **infelicitously,** *adv.* **infelicity,** *n.* unhappiness, misery; misfortune; inappropriateness, ineptness. [FELICITOUS]

infer, *v.t.* (*past, p.p.* **inferred**) to deduce as a fact, consequence or result; to conclude; to prove, to imply; †to bring in, to adduce. *v.i.* to draw inferences. **inferable, inferrable,** *a.* **inference,** *n.* the act of inferring; that which is inferred from premises, a conclusion or deduction. **inferential,** *a.* **inferentially,** *adv.* [L *inferre* (*ferre,* to bear, to bring)]

inferior, *a.* lower in place, rank, value, quality, degree etc.; subordinate; of mediocre or poor quality; (*Astron.*) within the earth's orbit; below the horizon; (*Bot.*) growing below another organ, as the calyx or the ovary; (*Print.*) set below ordinary letters or below the line, as the figures in H_2SO_4. *n.* a person who is inferior to another in station etc.; a subordinate. **inferiority,** *n.* **inferiority complex,** *n.* a suppressed sense of inferiority which produces as compensation some abnormal reaction such as megalomania, assertiveness, or the like. **inferiorly,** *adv.* [L, comp. of *inferus,* low, nether]

infernal, *a.* pertaining to hell or the lower regions; worthy of hell, hellish; detestable, diabolical; (*coll.*) abominable, confounded. **infernal machine,** *n.* an explosive machine employed for the purposes of assassination or wilful damage. **infernally,** *adv.* **inferno,** *n.* (*pl.* **-nos**) hell, esp. as conceived by Dante; any place supposed to resemble hell; a blaze or conflagration. [F, from L *infernālis,* from *infernus, inferus,* lower]

inferrable INFERABLE under INFER.

infertile, *a.* not fertile; unfruitful. **infertility,** *n.* [F, from late L *infertilis*]

infest, *v.t.* to overrun, to swarm over or about, to haunt, so as to harass, annoy or injure; †to attack, to harass, to plague; †to infect. **infestation,** *n.* **infester,** *n.* [F *infester,* L *infestāre,* from *infestus,* hostile]

infeudation, *n.* the granting of or putting one in possession of an estate in fee; the granting of tithes to laymen. [med. L *infeudātio,* from *infeudāre* (*feudum,* FEUD[2])]

infibulate, *v.t.* to fasten with or as with a clasp. †**infibulation,** *n.* the act of confining or fastening the sexual organs with a clasp or buckle to prevent copulation. [L *infībulātus,* p.p. of *infībulāre* (*fībula,* a clasp)]

infidel, *a.* disbelieving in a given form of faith (that of the person using the epithet), esp. rejecting the Christian religion; rejecting revelation, agnostic, sceptical; also non-Jewish or non-Muslim. *n.* one who disbelieves in a given form of faith; (*Hist.*) a Turk, a pagan, a Jew; one who rejects revelation, an agnostic, a sceptic; a non-Muslim or a non-Jew. **infidelity,** *n.* disbelief in a religion (as Christianity); breach of trust, disloyalty, deceit, esp. unfaithfulness to the marriage vow. **infidelize, -ise,** *v.t.* [OF *infidele,* from L *infidēlis* (*fidēlis*)]

infield[1], *n.* land near home or the base, as distinct from *outfield;* (*Sc.*) land under tillage; (*Cricket*) the part of the field close to the wicket; (*Baseball*) the ground within the base lines. **infielder,** *n.* (*Baseball*) one of the players in the infield.

infield[2], *v.t.* to enclose, to make into a field.

infighting, *n.* fighting or boxing at close quarters, so that blows from the shoulder are impossible; IN.

infill, *v.t.* to fill in; to fill up. *n.* also **infilling,** closing up gaps, esp. between houses; material for filling up holes etc.

infiltrate, infilter, *v.t.* to cause to enter by penetrating the pores or interstices of; to enter or permeate in this way; to pass or cause to pass secretly through (enemy lines etc.); to gain access or cause to gain access secretly to. *v.i.* to pass or percolate (into) thus. **infiltration,** *n.*

infin., (*abbr.*) infinitive.

infinitate, *v.t.* (*Log.*) to render infinite, to make (a proposition) infinite in extent by prefixing a negative. **infinitant,** *a.* **infinitation,** *n.* [med. L *infīnītātus,* p.p. of *infīnītāre,* from *infīnītus,* see foll.]

infinite, *a.* having no bounds or limits, endless; indefinitely great or numerous; (*Gram.*) not limited by person, mood etc.; (*Mus.*) a term applied to certain forms of the canon in which the ending leads back to the beginning; (*Math.*) greater than any assignable quantity. *n.* infinite space, infinity; a vast or infinite amount; (*Math.*) an infinite quantity. **the Infinite,** the infinite Being, God. **the infinite,** infinite space. **infinitely,** *adv.* **infiniteness,** *n.* **infinitesimal,** *a.* infinitely small; (*coll.*) insignificant; negligible; (*Math.*) less than any assignable quantity. *n.* a quantity less than any assignable quantity. **infinitesimally,** *adv.* **infinity, infinitude,** *n.* boundlessness; an infinite quantity or distance; a boundless expanse, vastness, immensity. [L *infīnītus*]

infinitive, *a.* (*Gram.*) unlimited; applied to that mood of a verb which expresses the action without regard to any person etc. *n.* the infinitive mood; a verb in this mood. **infinitival,** *a.* **infinitively, infinitivally,** *adv.* [L *infīnītīvus,* as prec.]

infinitude, infinity INFINITE.

infirm, *a.* lacking bodily strength or health, esp. through age or disease; weak-minded, irresolute; uncertain, unstable. †*v.t.* to weaken, to enfeeble. **infirmary,** *n.* a hospital or establishment in which the sick or injured are lodged and nursed. **infirmarian,** *n.* one in charge of an infirmary or of the sick, esp. in connection with a religious order in the Middle Ages. **infirmity,** *n.* **infirmly,** *adv.* [L *infirmus*]

infix, *v.t.* to fasten or fix in; to implant firmly; to insert (an infix) in a word. *n.,* (*Gram.*) a modifying element in the body of a word, in certain languages.

in flagrante (delicto), whilst actually committing the misdeed. [L]

inflame, *v.t.* to cause to blaze, to kindle; to cause inflammation in, to render morbidly hot by exciting excessive action in the blood-vessels and tissues; to excite, to stir up to passion etc.; to intensify, to aggravate. *v.i.* to burst into a blaze; to become inflamed; to become excited. [OF *enflamber,* L *inflammāre* (*flammāre,* from *flamma,* FLAME)]

inflammable, *a.* that may be easily set on fire; readily enkindled, excited or morbidly inflamed. *n.* something that catches fire easily. †**inflammable air,** *n.* hydrogen. **inflammability, -ableness,** *n.* †**inflammably,** *adv.*

inflammation, *n.* an abnormal condition characterized by heat, redness, swelling, pain and loss of function in the part affected; the act of inflaming or the state of being inflamed. **inflammatory,** *a.* tending to inflame; exciting or arousing passions. [INFLAME]

inflate, *v.t.* to distend with air or wind; to puff out; (*fig.*) to puff up, to elate; to raise (prices, reputation etc.) artificially or excessively. **inflatable,** *a.* that can be inflated. *n.* an inflatable toy, esp. an imitation castle etc. for children to jump or climb on; anything inflatable. **inflatant,** *n.* that which inflates (a balloon etc.). **inflated,** *a.* distended with air; tumid, bombastic, turgid; expanded or raised artificially; (*Bot.*) hollow and distended. **inflation,** *n.* the act of inflating, the state of being inflated; an increase in price above the real value; an expansion of credit. **inflationary,** *a.* **inflationism,** *n.* **inflationist,** *n.* one who favours an increased issue of paper money. **inflator,** *n.* [L *inflātus,* p.p. of *inflāre* (*flāre,* to blow)]

inflatus, *n.* a breathing into; (*fig.*) inspiration.

inflect, *v.t.* to bend, to curve; to turn from a straight or direct course; to modulate (as the voice); (*Gram.*) to change the terminations of (words) for purposes of declension or conjugation. **inflectedness,** *n.* **inflection, inflexion,** *n.* the act of inflecting; the state of being inflected; modulation of the voice; the variation of the termination of nouns etc. in declension, and of verbs in conjugation; (*Opt.*) diffraction; change from concave to convex in a curve. **inflectional, inflexional,** *a.* pertaining to or having grammatical inflections. **inflectionless, inflexionless,** *a.* **inflective,** *a.* capable of bending; (*Gram.*) inflectional. **inflector,** *n.* **inflexed,** *a.* bent, curved; (*Bot.*) bent inwards. †**inflexure,** *n.* a bend, a curve, a bow. [L *inflectere* (*flectere,* to bend), p.p. *inflexus*]

inflexible, *a.* incapable of being bent or curved; that will not yield to prayers or entreaties; firm of will or purpose. **inflexibility,** *n.* **inflexibly,** *adv.*

inflexion INFLECT.

inflict, *v.t.* to impose upon as a penalty or punishment; to cause to feel or experience (something of an unpleasant nature); †to afflict. **inflictable,** *a.* **inflicter,** *n.* **infliction,** *n.* the act of inflicting; a punishment inflicted; (*coll.*) a trouble, an annoyance. **inflictive,** *a.* [L *inflictus,* p.p. of *inflīgere* (*flīgere,* to dash)]

in-flight IN.

inflorescence, *n.* the act or process of flowering; the arrangement of flowers upon a branch or stem; the collective flower or flowers of a plant. [F, from L *inflōrescens,* pres.p. of *inflōrēscere*]

inflow, *n.* flowing in; influx; (*Aviat.*) the increase in air velocity in front of an air-screw produced by its rotation. *v.i.*, to flow in.

influence, *n.* agency or power (upon) serving or tending to affect, modify or control; power to move, direct or control, ascendency (over); the effect of such power; an ethereal fluid supposed to flow from the stars and to affect character and control human destinies; energy affecting other bodies, as electric and magnetic induction; a person, thing, feeling etc., exercising moral power (over). *v.t.* to exercise influence upon; to modify (motives etc.) to any end or purpose; to bias, to sway. **influencer,** *n.* **influential,** *a.* **influentially,** *adv.* [OF, from late L *influentia* (*fluere,* to flow)]

influent, *a.* flowing in; influential. *n.* a tributary, an affluent. [as prec.]

influenza, *n.* a catarrhal inflammation of the mucous membranes of the air-passages, attended by fever and nervous prostration, contagious and infective; (*fig.*) an epidemic. [It., as INFLUENCE]

influx, *n.* a flowing of or as of water (into); the point of inflow (of a stream); an introduction in abundance, an infusion; †influence. **influxion,** *n.* **influxive,** *a.* [late L *influxus,* p.p. of *influere,* see INFLUENCE]

info, *n.* (*coll.*) short for INFORMATION.

infold, ENFOLD.

in-folio, *n.* a folio volume. [F (L *in folio,* see FOLIO)]

infopreneur, *n.* (*coll.*) a person engaged in business activity in the field of information technology. **infopreneurial,** *adj.*

inforce, ENFORCE.

inform[1], *v.t.* to animate, to imbue (with feeling, vitality etc.); to communicate knowledge to, to tell; to give form or shape to. *v.i.* to take form or shape; to disclose facts, to bring a charge (against). **to inform against,** to lay an information against. **informant,** *n.* **informatics,** *n.* information science or technology. **information,** *n.* the act of informing or communicating knowledge etc.; intelligence communicated; notice, knowledge acquired; facts, data; a complaint or accusation presented to a court or magistrate as a preliminary to criminal proceedings. **information retrieval,** *n.* the storage, classification and access to computerized information. **information science,** *n.* the computerized processing and communication of data; the study of this. **information technology,** *n.* the gathering, processing and communication of information through computing and telecommunications combined. **information theory,** *n.* mathematical theory on the subject of transmission, storage, retrieval and decoding of information. **informational,** *a.* **informative,** *a.* conveying information or instruction; †having power to animate or give vitality. **informatory,** *a.* affording knowledge or information. **informed,** *a.* having information; apprized of the facts; educated, enlightened; †formed, shaped. **informer,** *n.* one who informs, esp. one who lays an information against a person offending against the law or any penal statute. **common informer,** one who makes a business of detecting offenders and laying information against them, usu. for the sake of reward. [OF *enformer,* L *informāre* (*formāre,* from *forma,* FORM)]

†**inform**[2], *a.* without regular form; shapeless. [L *informis* (*forma,* FORM)]

informal, *a.* not in accordance with official, proper or customary forms; without formality. **informality,** *n.* **informally,** *adv.*

infra, *adv.* of a passage in a book etc., below, further on. [L]

infra-, *pref.* below, beneath. [L, as prec.]

infra-costal, *a.* situated below the ribs.

infraction, *n.* the act of breaking or violating; violation, infringement. **infract,** *v.t.* (*N Am.*) to infringe. †**infractor,** *n.* **infractous,** *a.* (*Bot.*). [F, from L *infractiōnem,* nom. *-tio,* from *infringere,* to INFRINGE]

infra dig, beneath one's dignity, undignified. [short for L *infrā dignitātem,* beneath the dignity (of)]

infrahuman, *a.* having qualities or characteristics inferior to human.

infralapsarian, *n.* one of a branch of Calvinists who held that God, having permitted the Fall, then decreed the salvation of the elect (see also SUBLAPSARIAN, SUPRALAPSARIAN). *a.* belonging to the infralapsarians or their doctrine. **infralapsarianism,** *n.* [L *lapsus,* fall, see LAPSE]

inframaxillary, *a.* situated under the jaw; pertaining to the lower jawbone. *n.* the lower jawbone.

†**inframundane,** *a.* lying beneath the world.

infranchise, ENFRANCHISE.

infrangible, *a.* that cannot be broken, that cannot be infringed or violated. **infrangibility,** *n.* **infrangibly,** *adv.*

infra-orbital, *a.* situated below the orbit of the eye.

infra-red rays, *n.pl.* invisible radiations beyond the visible spectrum at the red end.

infrarenal, *a.* situated below the kidneys.

infra-scapular, *a.* situated below the shoulder-blade.

infrasonic, *a.* having a frequency below the usual audible limit.

infrasternal, *a.* situated below the breastbone.

infrastructure, *n.* underlying structure or basic framework; the network of communications etc. systems essential for industry, military operations etc.

infrequent, *a.* rare, uncommon, unusual. **infrequency,** †**-ence,** *n.* †**infrequently,** *adv.* [L *infrequens -entem*]

infringe, *v.t.* to break (a law, compact, contract etc.); to violate, to neglect to obey, to transgress; †to destroy; †to hinder, to obstruct. *v.i.* to encroach, to intrude (upon). **infringement,** *n.* **infringer,** *n.* [L *infringere* (*frangere,* to break)]

infructuous, †**-tuose,** *a.* not fruitful; fruitless, unprofitable. **infructuosity,** *n.* **infructuously,** *adv.* [L *infructuōsus*]

infula, *n.* (*Rom. Ant.*) a fillet worn by priests and victims; one of the ribbons hanging from a bishop's mitre. [L]

infundibulum, *n.* (*pl.* **-bula**) (*Anat.*) any funnel-shaped part; the siphon or funnel of a cephalopod, the gastric cavity in the ctenophora. **infundibular, -ulate, -uliform,** *a.* funnel-shaped. [L, a funnel, from *infundere* (*fundere*, to pour)]

infuriate, *v.t.* to provoke to madness or fury. *a.*, infuriated, enraged, mad. **infuriatingly,** *adv.* [late L *infuriātus,* p.p. of *infuriāre* (*furia*, FURY)]

†**infuscate,** *v.t.* to make black or dusky; to darken, to obscure. *a.*, darkened, clouded. †**infuscation,** *n.* [L *infuscātus,* p.p. of *infuscāre* (*fuscus*, dark-brown)]

infuse, *v.t.* to pour (into); to inculcate, to implant; to steep in liquid so as to obtain an extract or infusion. **infuser,** *n.* **infusion,** *n.* the act of infusing; instillation, inculcation; the act or process of steeping; the liquid extract obtained by steeping any substance; that which is instilled or implanted, an admixture, a tincture; †immersion. **infusionism,** *n.* (*Theol.*) the doctrine that the human soul is an emanation from or an influx of the divine substance. **infusionist,** *n.* **infusive,** *a.* having the power of infusing. †*n.* an infusion. [F *infuser,* L *infūsus,* p.p. of *infundere* (*fundere*, to pour)]

infusible, *a.* that cannot be fused or melted. **infusibility,** *n.*

infusoria, *n.pl.* (*Zool.*) the name first given by Otto Frederick Müller to the protozoa developed in infusions of decaying organic matter. **infusorial,** *a.* (*Zool.*) pertaining to the infusoria; (*Geol.*) containing or composed of infusoria. **infusorian,** *n., a.* **infusory,** *a.* [mod. L, pl. of *infūsōrium,* from *infūsus,* see INFUSE]

-ing, *suf.* forming verbal nouns, as *cleansing, hunting;* denoting occupations, as *bricklaying, lumbering, soldiering;* denoting the results, material used etc., as *painting, roofing, scaffolding, washing.* [OE *-ende*]; used as a gerund, as *in coming, my having written, to begin writing* etc.; as participial adjectives, as *charming, fleeting, horrifying;* forming diminutives, as *farthing, lording, shilling;* patronymics etc., as *atheling, gelding, whiting.* [OE [1] *-ung, -ing,* ending of verbal nouns; [2] *-ende,* part. ending, later *-inde,* confused with *-ing,* -ING [1]; [3] *-ing, -ung,* forming nouns with sense of belonging to, of the kind of, the son of etc.]

ingate, *n.* entrance, way in; the aperture in a mould at which the metal enters.

ingathering, *n.* the act of gathering or collecting, esp. of getting in the harvest.

ingeminate, *v.t.* to redouble, to repeat, to reiterate. **ingemination,** *n.* [L *ingeminātus,* p.p. of *ingemināre*]

ingender, ENGENDER.

†**ingenerate,** *v.t.* to generate or produce within; to engender. *a.*, inborn, innate. †**ingenerable,** *a.* that can be ingenerated. [L *ingenerātus,* p.p. of *ingenerāre* (*generāre*, GENERATE)]

Ingenhousz, *n.* **Jan** (1730–99), Dutch physician and plant physiologist who established that in the light plants absorb carbon dioxide and give off oxygen.

ingenious, *a.* possessed of natural capacity or talent; skilful, clever, esp. in inventing or contriving; cleverly designed; †ingenuous. **ingeniously,** *adv.* **ingeniousness, ingenuity,** *n.* [L *ingeniōsus,* from *ingenium,* genius]

ingénue, *n.* an ingenuous or naive girl, esp. such a character on the stage. [F, as INGENUOUS]

ingenuous, *a.* open, candid, frank, sincere; of honourable or noble extraction. **ingenuously,** *adv.* **ingenuousness,** *n.* [L *ingenuus,* free-born, frank (*gen-*, base of *gignere,* to produce, to beget)]

ingest, *v.t.* to take (food) into the stomach. **ingesta,** *n.pl.* (*Physiol.*) food; that which is taken into the body. **ingestible,** *a.* **ingestion,** *n.* **ingestive,** *a.* [L *ingestus,* p.p. of *ingerere* (*gerere*, to carry)]

ingle[1], *n.* a fire on the hearth; (*erron.*) a fireplace. **ingle-cheek,** *n.* the jamb of a fireplace. **ingle-nook,** *n.* a chimney-corner. **ingle-side,** *n.* [Sc., etym. doubtful, perh. from Gael. *aingeal,* fire]

†**ingle**[2], *n.* a male favourite or paramour. *v.t.* to coax, to wheedle. [etym. doubtful, perh. rel. to MDut. *ingel, engel,* ANGEL (Skeat)]

inglobate, *a.* formed into a globe (as by gravitation).

inglorious, *a.* not glorious; shameful, ignominious. **ingloriously,** *adv.* **ingloriousness,** *n.* [L *inglōriōsus*]

ingluvies, *n.* the crop of birds; the stomach of ruminants. **ingluvial,** *a.* [L, maw, craw, prob. rel. to *glutīre,* to swallow]

ingoing, *a.* going in, entering. *n.* entrance.

ingot, *n.* a mass of cast metal, esp. steel, gold or silver; a bar of gold or silver for assaying; †a mould. [prob. from OE IN, *goten,* p.p. of *gēotan,* to pour, to fuse (Skeat)]

ingraft, etc. ENGRAFT.

ingrail, ENGRAIL.

ingrain[1] *a.* dyed in the grain or yarn before manufacture; thoroughly imbued, inherent, inveterate. *n.* a yarn or fabric dyed with fast colours before manufacture. **ingrain carpet,** *n.* a carpet manufactured from wool dyed in the grain, the pattern showing through the fabric. **ingrained** , *a.* deeply imprinted; complete, total; of dirt etc., worked into the fibres, pores etc. [orig. *in grain,* F *en graine,* see GRAIN [1]]

ingrain[2], ENGRAIN.

ingrate, *a.* unpleasant to the senses; ungrateful; unpleasant. *n.* an ungrateful person. †**ingrateful,** *a.* [L *ingrātus* (*grātus*, pleasing)]

ingratiate, *v.t.* to insinuate (oneself) into goodwill or favour (with) another. **ingratiating,** *a.* **ingratiatingly,** *adv.* [It. *ingratiāre* (L *in grātiam,* into favour, see GRACE)]

ingratitude, *n.* want of gratitude. [F, from late L *ingrātitūdo,* from *ingrātus,* INGRATE]

ingravescent, *a.* of an illness, increasing in severity. **ingravescence,** *n.* [L *ingravescens -entem,* pres.p. of *ingravescere* (*gravis*, heavy)]

ingredient, *n.* that which enters into a compound as an element, a component part. †*a.* forming a component part. [F, from L *ingredientem,* nom. *-ens,* pres.p. of *ingredī* (*gradī*, to walk), p.p. *ingressus*]

Ingres, *n.* **Jean Auguste Dominique** (1780–1867), French painter, a student of David and leading exponent of the neo-classical style. He studied and worked in Rome about 1807–20, where he began the *Odalisque* series of sensuous female nudes, then went to Florence, and returned to France 1824. His portraits painted in the 1840s–50s are meticulously detailed and highly polished.

ingress, *n.* the act of entering, entrance; power or liberty of entrance. **ingression,** *n.* **ingressive,** *a.* [L *ingressus,* see prec.]

ingroove, ENGROOVE.

†**ingross,** ENGROSS.

ingrowing, *a.* growing inwards of a toe-nail etc., growing abnormally into the flesh. **ingrown,** *a.* **ingrowth,** *n.*

inguinal, *a.* of, pertaining to or situated near the groin. **inguino-,** *comb. form.* [L *inguinālis,* from *inguen -guinis,* the groin]

ingulf, ENGULF.

ingurgitate, *v.t.* to swallow down greedily; (*fig.*) to engulf. *v.i.* to eat greedily, to gorge. **ingurgitation,** *n.* [L *ingurgitātus,* p.p. of *ingurgitāre* (*gurges gurgitis,* a whirlpool)]

inhabit, *v.t.* to live or dwell in; to occupy as a place of settled residence. †*v.i.* to live, to dwell, to reside. **inhabitable**[1], *a.* fit for habitation. **inhabitancy,** †**-ance,** *n.* domiciliation or residence for a considerable period, esp. such as confers the rights of an inhabitant; †a habitation. **inhabitant,** *n.* **inhabitation,** *n.* the act of inhabiting; the state of being inhabited; a dwelling; †population. **inhabitativeness, inhabitiveness,** *n.* **inhabiter,** *n.* **inhabitress,** *n. fem.* [ME *enhabiten,* OF *enhabiter,* L *inhabitāre* (*habitāre*, to dwell, see HABIT)]

†**inhabitable**[2], *a.* not habitable, uninhabitable. [F, from L *inhabitābilis*]

inhale, *v.t.* to breathe in, to draw into the lungs; to inspire, as distinct from *exhale.* **inhalant,** *n., a.* **inhalation,** *n.* **inhaler,** *n.* one who inhales; a respirator; an instrument for enabling the inhalation of medicated vapours etc. [L *inhālāre* (*hālāre*, to breathe)]

Inhambane, *n.* seaport on the SE coast of Mozambique, 370 km/231 miles NE of Maputo. Population

(1980) 56,000.

inharmonious, *a.* not harmonious; unmusical. **inharmonic, -ical,** *a.* **inharmoniously,** *adv.* †**inharmony,** *n.*

inhaust, *v.t.* to draw or drink in. [L *haustus,* p.p. of *haurire,* to draw (cp. EXHAUST)]

inhere, *v.i.* to belong or exist (in) as an attribute or quality; to be an essential or necessary part (in); to be vested (in). **inherence, -ency,** *n.* **inherent,** *a.* permanently belonging (in or to); not to be removed, inseparable; naturally conjoined or attached (to); innate, inborn. **inherently,** *adv.* [L *inhaerēre* (*haerēre,* to stick)]

inherit, *v.t.* to receive by legal succession as the representative of a former possessor; to derive from one's ancestors by genetic transmission; to take over (a position etc.) from a predecessor; †to put in possession. *v.i.* to take or come into possession as an heir. **inheritable,** *a.* capable of inheriting or of being inherited. **inheritability,** *n.* **inheritably,** *adv.* **inheritance,** *n.* the act of inheriting; that which is inherited; a hereditary succession to an estate etc.; the right of an heir to succeed; the hereditary derivation of characteristics of one generation from another; †acquisition, ownership. **inheritor,** *n.* **inheritress, -trix,** *n. fem.* [OF *enheriter* (late L *hērēditāre,* from *hēres -ēdis,* HEIR)]

inhesion, *n.* inherence. [late L *inhaesio,* from *inhaerēre,* to INHERE]

inhibit, *v.t.* to restrain, to hinder, to put a stop to (an action, nervous process etc.); to prohibit, to forbid, to interdict; (*Eccles.*) to prohibit (a priest) from exercising his office. **inhibiter, -tor,** *n.* **inhibition,** *n.* the act of inhibiting; the state of being inhibited; †a writ to inhibit a judge from proceeding further in a cause, now called prohibition; an order forbidding a priest to exercise his functions; (*Sc. Law*) a writ to prevent a person from burdening his or her heritable property to the prejudice of a creditor; (*Psych.*) habitual shrinking from some action which is instinctively thought of as a thing forbidden; the partial or complete stoppage of a physical process by a nervous influence. **inhibitory, inhibitive,** *a.* [L *inhibitus,* p.p. of *inhibēre* (*habēre,* to have, to hold)]

inhospitable, *a.* not inclined to show hospitality to strangers; affording no shelter, desolate. **inhospitableness,** *n.* **inhospitably,** *adv.*

in-house IN.

inhuman, *a.* destitute of a feeling of kindness towards one's fellow-creatures; brutal, savage, unfeeling; not human. **inhumanity,** *n.* **inhumanly,** *adv.* [F *inhumain,* L *inhūmānus*]

inhumane, *a.* lacking in humanity.

inhume, *v.t.* to bury, to inter. †**inhumate,** *v.t.* **inhumation,** *n.* [F *inhumer,* L *inhumāre* (*humus,* the ground)]

inimical, *a.* having the temper or disposition of an enemy; adverse, unfavourable (to). **inimicality, inimicalness,** *n.* **inimically,** *adv.* [late L *inimīcālis,* from *inimīcus* (*amīcus,* friend)]

inimitable, *a.* that cannot be imitated; superb. **inimitability, -ableness,** *n.* **inimitably,** *adv.* [F, from L *inimitābilis*]

inion, *n.* (*Anat.*) the ridge of the occiput. [Gr.]

iniquity, *n.* want of equity, gross injustice; unrighteousness, wickedness, crime. **iniquitous,** *a.* **iniquitously,** *adv.* **iniquitousness,** *n.* [OF *iniquité,* L *inīquitātem,* nom. *-tas,* from *inīquus* (*aequus,* just)]

initial, *a.* beginning; incipient; placed at or pertaining to the beginning. *n.* the first letter of a word; (*pl.*) the first letters of a Christian name and surname. *v.t.* (*past, p.p.* **initialled**) to mark with one's initials, as a guarantee of correctness, a sign of ownership etc. **initially,** *adv.* at the beginning. [L *initiālis,* from *initium,* beginning (*īre,* to go)]

initiate, *v.t.* to begin or originate; to set afoot, to start; to instruct in the rudiments or principles; to admit (into a society or association or mysteries or secret science), usu. with ceremonial rites. *v.i.* to do the first act; to perform the first rite. *a.* initiated; †unpractised, new. *n.*, one who is newly initiated, a novice. **initiation,** *n.* a beginning; the making one acquainted with new principles, rites etc.; admission into a new society or association; the ceremony by which one is so admitted. **initiative,** *a.* serving to begin or initiate; initiatory. *n.* the first step or action in any business; power or right to take the lead or originate (esp. legislation); the energy and resourcefulness typical of those able to initiate new projects etc. **on one's own initiative,** without being prompted by others. **initiator,** *n.* one who initiates. **initiatrix,** *n.fem.* **initiatory,** *n., a.*

inject, *v.t.* to throw or force (into); to introduce (as a liquid) by mechanical means; to charge (with a liquid) by injection; to interject; to add, insert. **injection,** *n.* the act of injecting; that which is injected; the introduction of colouring substance or a therapeutic agent into the body; the spraying of oil fuel into the cylinder of a compression ignition engine; the forcing of cold water into the condenser of a steam-engine. **injection-cock, -pipe,** *n.* the cock or pipe through which water is injected into a condenser. **injection engine,** a steam-engine with a condenser in which steam is condensed by this means. **injection moulding,** *n.* the manufacture of rubber or plastic items by the injection of heated material into a mould. **injector,** *n.* one who or that which injects; a mechanical apparatus for supplying the boiler of a steam-engine with water to make steam; an injection nozzle. [L *injectus,* p.p. of *injicere* (*jacere,* to throw)]

injelly, *v.i.* to imbed in jelly.

injoin, ENJOIN.

†**injoint,** *v.i.* to join (with).

injudicious, *a.* not judicious; void of judgment, rash, hasty; done without judgment, unwise. **injudicial,** *a.* not judicial. **injudiciously,** *adv.* **injudiciousness,** *n.*

Injun, *n.* (*facet.; sometimes offensive.*) a N American Indian.

injunction, *n.* the act of enjoining; that which is enjoined; (*Law*) a writ or process whereby a party is required to do or (more usually) to refrain from doing certain acts; an admonition, direction or order. **injunct,** *v.t.* (*coll.*) to restrain by a legal injunction. **injunctive,** *a.* **injunctively,** *adv.* [late L *injunctio,* from *injungere,* to ENJOIN]

injure, *v.t.* to do wrong or harm to; to hurt, to damage; to slander, to depreciate; to impair or diminish. **injurer,** *n.* **injurious,** *a.* that injures or tends to injure; wrongful, hurtful, pernicious, detrimental; insulting, abusive. **injuriously,** *adv.* **injuriousness,** *n.* [from INJURY]

injury, *n.* a wrong; that which occasions loss, detriment or mischief; damage, hurt, harm; †an insult, an affront. **injury time,** *n.* time added on to normal playing time in soccer, rugby etc. to compensate for interruptions to play on account of injuries. [A-F *injurie,* L *injūria* (*jūs jūris,* justice, right)]

injustice, *n.* the quality of being unjust, lack of right or equity, unfairness; violation of justice, a wrong. [F, from L *injustitia*]

ink, *n.* a coloured, usu. black, liquid or viscous material used in writing or printing; the dark fluid exuded by a cuttle-fish to cover its escape. *v.t.* to blacken, daub or cover with ink (as type etc.); to mark (in or over) with ink. **printer's ink** PRINTER. **ink-bag,** *n.* the ink-bladder of a cuttle-fish and other cephalopods. **ink-blot,** *n.* **ink-blot test** RORSCHACH TEST. **ink-cap,** *n.* a mushroom of the genus *Coprinus.* **ink-eraser,** *n.* india-rubber treated with fine sand, used for rubbing out ink-marks. †**ink-fish,** *n.* the cuttle-fish. †**inkhorn,** *n.* a small vessel, formerly made of horn, to hold ink; a portable writing-case. †**inkhorn mate, varlet,** *n.* a pedantic fellow, a scribbler. **inkhorn terms,** *n.pl.* pedantic, high-sounding terms. **inking-roller,** *n.* (*Print.*) a roller receiving the ink from the inking-table and transferring it to the type. **inking-table,** *n.* a slab on which printing-ink is spread to be taken up by the inking-roller. **ink-pencil,** *n.* a copying-pencil. **ink-slinger,** *n.* a writer, esp. a newspaper editor or reporter. **inkstand,** *n.* a stand for one or more inkpots, usu. with a place for pens. **inkwell,** *n.* a container for ink often let into a school desk. **inker,** *n.* an inking-roller; a device for recording telegraphic messages in ink. **inkless,** *a.* **inky,** *a.* of the nature of or resembling ink; discoloured with ink; black as ink; †black, gloomy, miserable. **inkies**, *n.pl.* (*Cinema, dated*) studio slang for incandescent lights. **inkiness,** *n.* [OF *enque* (F *encre*), late L *encaustum,* purple ink used by the Roman emperors, from Gr. *enkaustos,* burnt in, see ENCAUSTIC]

Inkatha, *n.* South African political organization formed 1975 by Chief Gatsha Buthelezi, leader of six million Zulus, the country's biggest ethnic group. Inkatha aims to create a nonracial democratic political situation. Because Inkatha has tried to work with the white regime, Buthelezi has been regarded as a collaborator by blacks and the United Democratic Front. The term Inkatha is from the grass coil worn by Zulu women for carrying head loads; its many strands give it strength.

Inkerman, Battle of, a battle of the Crimean War, fought on 5 Nov. 1854, during which an attack by the Russians on Inkerman Ridge, occupied by the British army besieging Sebastopol, was repulsed.

†**inkle,** *n.* a broad linen tape; (*Shak.*) prob. a kind of crewel or worsted. [etym. doubtful]

inkling, *n.* a hint, a whisper, an intimation; a mere suspicion (of); (*dial.*) a desire, an inclination. [ME *inclen,* to hint at]

INLA, (*abbr.*) Irish National Liberation Army.

inlace, ENLACE.

inlaid INLAY.

inland, *a.* remote from the sea; situated in the interior of a country; carried on within a country, domestic, not foreign; †refined, civilized. *adv.* in or towards the interior of a country. *n.* the interior of a country; (*Sc.*) the mainland as dist. from outer islands; †demesne land. **inland revenue,** *n.* taxes and duties levied on home trade etc., not foreign. **Inland Revenue,** *n.* in Britain, the government department responsible for collecting these. **inlander,** *n.* **inlandish,** *a.*

in-law, *n.* (*pl.* **in-laws**) (*coll.*) a relation by marriage.

inlay, *v.t.* (*past, p.p.* **inlaid**) to lay or insert in; to decorate by inserting different materials into a groundwork, leaving the surfaces even; to fasten a print, picture etc. evenly (into a page or sheet). *n.*, material inlaid or prepared for inlaying. **inlayer**, *n.* **inlaying**, *n.* the business of an inlayer; inlaid work.

inlet, *n.* a means of entrance, admission, entrance; a passage allowing fuel etc. into a machine; a small arm of the sea; a creek. *a.* let in.

inlier, *n.* (*Geol.*) an isolated portion of an underlying bed, which has become surrounded by a later formation.

inly, *adv.* inwardly, internally; closely, deeply. *a.* †inward, internal, secret. [OE *inlīce* (IN, -LY)]

inlying, *a.* lying inside.

inmate, *n.* one who dwells in the same house as another; a resident or occupant, esp. of a prison etc. †*a.* dwelling or resident under the same roof (with).

in memoriam, in memory of; as a memorial. [L]

inmost, innermost, *a.* remotest from the surface; most inward; deepest, most heartfelt, most secret. [OE *innemest*]

inn, *n.* a public house providing lodging and entertainment for travellers; †lodging, abode; †a place of residence or hostel for students. †*v.i.* to stay at an inn. †*v.t.* to lodge and entertain. **Inns of Chancery,** colleges in which young students formerly began their law studies, now occupied as chambers by lawyers etc.; the societies formerly occupying these buildings. **Inns of Court,** four corporate societies in London (*Inner Temple, Middle Temple, Lincoln's Inn, Gray's Inn*), which have the exclusive right of admitting persons to practise at the bar; the buildings belonging to such societies. **innkeeper,** †**innholder,** *n.* [OE, cogn. with IN]

innards, *n.pl.* (*coll.*) entrails; the components of a machine etc.

innate, *a.* inborn, natural; native, not acquired. **innate ideas,** *n.pl.* (*Phil.*) general notions which (according to the Stoics and other philosophers) are inborn or developed by intuition in all humans, opp. to acquired ideas. **innately,** *adv.* **innateness,** *n.* [L *innātus (nātus,* p.p. of *nascī,* to be born)]

inner, *a.* interior; farther inward or nearer the centre; internal; spiritual; dark, hidden, esoteric. *n.* that part of a target immediately outside the bull's eye; a shot striking that part. **inner man,** *n.* the inner or spiritual part of a person; (*coll.*) the stomach, the appetite for food. **inner tube,** *n.* an inflatable tube inside a tyre. **innerly,** *a.* (*Sc.*) intimate, familiar; kindly. †*adv.* inwardly. **innerliness,** *n.* **innermost** INMOST. [OE *innera,* comp. of IN]

innervate, *v.t.* to give a nerve impulse to; to supply with nerves or nerve filaments. **innervation,** *n.* **innerve,** *v.t.* to give nerve to, to invigorate, to strengthen.

Inness, *n.* **George** (1825–94), US landscape painter influenced by the Hudson River school. His early works such as *The Delaware Valley*, 1865 (Metropolitan Museum of Art, New York) are on a grand scale and show a concern for natural effects of light. Later he moved towards impressionism.

inning, *n.* †the gathering in of crops, harvest; (*pl.*) (*Cricket*) the time or turn for batting of a player or a side; the time during which a party or person is in possession, in power etc.; †lands recovered from the sea.

innkeeper INN.

innocent, *a.* free from moral guilt; guiltless (of); blameless, sinless; pure, unspotted, guileless; naive or credulous; devoid (of); of a tumour, not malignant; (*dial.*) weak in intellect. †*n.* an innocent person, esp. a child; (*dial.*) an imbecile, idiot. **Massacre of the Innocents,** Innocents' Day. **Innocents' Day,** *n.* the festival (28 Dec.) commemorating the massacre of the children of Bethlehem by Herod (Matt. ii.16). **innocence,** †-**ency,** *n.* **innocently,** *adv.* [F, from L *innocentem,* nom. *-cens* (*nocens,* pres.p. of *nocēre,* to hurt)]

Innocent, *n.* thirteen popes including Innocent III.

Innocent III, *n.* (1161–1216), pope from 1198 who asserted papal power over secular princes, especially over the succession of Holy Roman Emperors. He also made King John of England his vassal, compelling him to accept Langton as archbishop of Canterbury. He promoted the fourth Crusade and crusades against the non-Christian Livonians and Letts, and Albigensian heretics.

innocuous, *a.* having no injurious qualities, harmless; (*Zool.*) belonging to the Innocua or harmless serpents. **innocuously,** *adv.* **innocuousness,** *n.* [L *innocuus*]

innominate, *a.* not named; nameless. **innominate artery,** *n.* a large but short artery which is given off from the arch of the aorta. **innominate bone,** *n.* the hipbone. [late L *innōminātus nōminātus,* p.p. of *nōmināre,* to NOMINATE)]

innovate, *v.i.* to introduce alterations (in anything); to put forward novelties. *v.t.* to alter or change, by the introduction of something new. **innovation,** *n.* **innovative, -atory,** *a.* **innovator,** *n.* [L *innovātus,* p.p. of *innovāre* (*novāre,* to make new, from *novus,* new)]

innoxious, *a.* harmless, innocuous. **innoxiously,** *adv.* **innoxiousness,** *n.* [L *innoxius*]

Innsbruck, *n.* capital of Tirol State, W Austria, population (1981) 117,000. It is a tourist and winter sports centre, and a route junction for the Brenner Pass. The 1964 and 1976 Winter Olympics were held here.

innuendo, *n.* (*pl.* **-dos, -does**) an indirect or oblique hint or intimation; an insinuation. *v.t.* to insinuate. *v.i.* to make innuendoes. [L *innuendō,* by way of intimation, abl. gerund of *innuere* (*nuere,* to nod)]

Innuit, Inuit, *n.* (*pl.* **Innuit, Innuits**) (one of) a N American or Greenland Eskimo people. [Eskimo]

innumerable, *a.* countless, numberless; indefinitely numerous. †**innumerableness,** *n.* **innumerably,** *adv.* †**innumerous,** *a.* [F, from L *innumerābilis*]

innumerate, *a.* ignorant of or unskilled in mathematics or science.

inobservant, *a.* not observant; heedless. **inobservance,** *n.* want of observance (of a law etc.). †**inobservation,** *n.* [L *inobservans -antem*]

inobtrusive, UNOBTRUSIVE.

inocular, *a.* inserted in the inner margin of the eye, as the antennae of some insects.

inoculate, *v.t.* to communicate a disease to (humans or the lower animals) by the introduction of infectious matter, in order to induce a mild form of the disease and render the subject immune against further attack; (*fig.*) to impregnate, to infect, to imbue (with); (*Hort.*) to graft on by the insertion of buds. *v.i.* to graft trees by budding; to practise inoculation. **inoculable,** *a.* **inoculation,** *n.* **inoculative,** *a.* **inoculator,** *n.* [L *inoculātus,* p.p. of *inoculāre,* to engraft (*oculus,* eye)]

inodorous, *a.* without smell, odourless. [L *inodōrus*]

in-off, IN.

inoffensive, *a.* giving no offence; unobjectionable, harmless. **inoffensively,** *adv.* **inoffensiveness,** *n.*

†**inofficial,** UNOFFICIAL.

inofficious, *a.* without office, inoperative; (*Law*) regardless of natural obligation and duty. [L *inofficiōsus*]

inoperable, *a.* that cannot be operated on. **inoperability, -ableness,** *n.* **inoperably,** *adv.*

inoperative, *a.* not in operation; producing no result.

inoperculate, *a.* (*Conch., Bot.*) without an operculum or lid. **inopercular,** *a.*

inopportune, *a.* not opportune; unseasonable. **inopportunely,** *adv.* **inopportuneness, -tunity,** *n.* [F, from late L *inopportūnus*]

inorb, *v.t.* to place in or as in an orb, to ensphere.

inordinate, *a.* irregular, disorderly; excessive, immoderate, passing all bounds. **inordinately,** *adv.* **inordinateness,** †**-nation,** *n.* [L *inordinātus, ordinātus,* p.p. of *ordināre,* from *ordo -inis,* ORDER)]

inorganic, *a.* not organic, not having the organs or instruments of life; not having organic structure, e.g. rocks, metals etc.; not resulting from natural growth. **inorganic chemistry** CHEMISTRY. **inorganically,** *adv.* without organization. **inorganizable, -isable,** *a.* **inorganization, -isation,** *n.* †**inorganized, -ised,** *a.*

inornate, *a.* not ornate. [L *inornātus*]

inosculate, *v.i.* to become united (with, as two vessels) by the mouth of one fitting into the mouth of the other, or by a duct; to anastomose. *v.t.* to cause to unite (as two vessels) in an animal body; to blend. **inosculation,** *n.* [L *osculātus,* furnished with a mouth, from *osculum,* dim. of *os,* mouth]

inositol, *n.* a member of the vitamin B complex, found in most plant and animal tissues. [Gr. *īs, īnos,* a muscle]

inotropic, *a.* of or directing contraction of the heart muscle. [Gr. *īs īnos,* a muscle]

inoxidize, -ise, *v.t.* to render incapable of or not liable to oxidizing. **inoxidable, inoxidizable, -isable,** *a.* **inoxidized, -ised,** *a.*

inpass, in-patient, in-phase, in-player IN.

inpouring, *n.* a pouring in. *a.* that pours in.

input, *n.* the amount put into (a machine, the body etc.); a place where energy, information etc. goes into a system; data fed into a computer; the process of entering such data; (*Sc.*) a contribution. *a.* pertaining to computer input. *v.t.* to put into (esp. a computer).

inquest, *n.* a judicial inquiry or investigation into a matter, usu. an inquiry before a jury, esp. a coroner's inquest; the jury itself; an inquiry, an investigation. **coroner's inquest,** a judicial inquiry before a coroner and a jury into death occurring suddenly, from violence, an unknown cause or in a prison; also into cases of treasure trove. **grand inquest,** a grand jury; the House of Commons. **great inquest,** the Last Judgment. [OF *enqueste,* med. L *inquesta,* orig. fem. of *inquistus,* L *inquīsītus,* p.p. of *inquīrere,* to INQUIRE]

inquiet, *a.* unquiet. †*v.t.* to disquiet, to disturb. **inquietude,** *n.* restlessness, uneasiness (bodily or mental). [L *inquiētus*]

inquiline, *n.* an animal living in the abode of another, as certain beetles in ants' nests, or certain insects in the galls of other insects. **inquilinous,** *a.* [L *inquilīnus,* a sojourner, for *incolīnus,* from *incolere* (*colere,* to dwell)]

inquire, *v.i.* to ask questions (of); to seek information by asking questions (about or after); to investigate (into); †to seek or search (out). *v.t.* to ask information about; to search out, to find out; to ask (what, whether, how etc.); †to ask, to interrogate; †to call. †**inquirable,** *a.* that may be inquired into. †**inquiration,** *n.* (*dial.*). **inquirer,** *n.* **inquiring,** *a.* given to inquiry; inquisitive. **inquiringly,** *adv.* **inquiry,** *n.* the act of inquiring; a question, an interrogation; a searching for truth, information or knowledge; examination of facts or principles; a judicial investigation. **court of inquiry,** a court appointed to make a legal investigation into charges against soldiers, usu. before proceedings are instituted before a court-martial. [ME *enquere,* OF *enquerre,* L *inquīrere* (*quaerere,* to seek)]

inquirendo, *n.* (*Law*) an authority given in general to some person or persons to inquire into something for the benefit of the Crown. **de lunatico inquirendo,** a writ to inquire into the sanity of a person said to be incapable of managing his or her estate. [L, by inquiring, abl. gerund of *inquīrere*]

in re, in the matter (of). [L]

INRI, (*abbr.*) Jesus of Nazareth King of the Jews. [L *Iesus Nazarenus Rex Iudaeorum*]

inroad, *n.* a hostile incursion; a sudden or desultory invasion; (*fig.*) an encroachment.

inroll, ENROL.

inrush, *n.* an irruption; an inpouring.

insalivate, *v.t.* to mix (food) with saliva during eating. **insalivation,** *n.*

insalubrious, *a.* not salubrious, unhealthy. **insalubriously,** *adv.* **insalubrity,** *n.* [L *insalūbris*]

insane, *a.* deranged in mind. mad; exceedingly rash or foolish; †causing insanity. †**insane root,** *n.* (*Shak.*) hemlock. **insanely,** *adv.* **insanity, insaneness,** †**insanie,** *n.* madness, mental derangement. [L *insanus*]

insanitary, *a.* not sanitary. **insanitation,** *n.*

insatiable, *a.* that cannot be satisfied or appeased; immoderately greedy (of). **insatiability, -ableness,** *n.* **insatiably,** *adv.* **insatiate,** *a.* never satisfied; insatiable. †**insatiately,** *adv.* †**insatiety,** *n.* [F, from L *insatiābilis*]

insconce, ENSCONCE.

inscribe, *v.t.* to write, carve or engrave (in or upon a stone, paper or other surface); to mark (a stone etc. with writing or letters); to address, to dedicate (as a book to a friend); to enter in or on a book, list etc., esp. to register the names of shareholders; to issue (loans) with the names of holders so registered; (*Geom.*) to delineate (a figure) within another so that it touches the boundary surfaces of the latter. **inscribable,** *a.* **inscriber,** *n.* [L *inscrībere* (*scrībere,* to write), p.p. *inscriptus*]

inscription, *n.* the art or act of inscribing; that which is inscribed, as a dedicatory address, the words on the reverse of some coins and medals, or the titular line or lines of an illustration. **inscriptional, inscriptive,** *a.*

†**inscroll,** *v.t.* to inscribe on a scroll.

inscrutable, *a.* incapable of being penetrated or understood; unfathomable, mysterious. **inscrutability, -ableness,** *n.* **inscrutably,** *adv.* [F, from late L *inscrūtābilis* (*scrūtābilis,* from *scrūtārī,* to search)]

†**insculp,** *v.t.* to insculpture; to carve. †**insculpture,** *n.* an engraving, an inscription. *v.t.* to engrave, to inscribe, to carve (upon). [L *insculpere* (*sculpere,* to carve)]

insect, *n.* one of the Insecta, a class of articulate, usu. winged animals, with three pairs of legs, and divided into three distinct segments, the head, thorax and abdomen; used incorrectly of other articulated animals resembling these, as a spider or centipede; a small or contemptible person or creature. **insect-powder,** *n.* a powder for destroying insects such as fleas, bugs etc. **insectarium,** *n.* (*pl.* **-riums, -ria**) an insectary. **insectary,** *n.* a place for keeping or breeding insects. †**insected,** *a.* segmented like an insect. **insecticide,** *n.*

a preparation for killing insects. **insecticidal,** *a.* **insectifuge,** *n.* a substance for keeping insects away. **insectile,** *a.* of the nature of insects. *n.* an insect. **insectology,** *n.* entomology, esp. in its economic relations. **insectologist,** *n.* [F *insecte,* L *insectum,* neut. p.p. of *insecāre* (*secāre,* to cut)]

insection, *n.* a cutting in; an incision. [see prec.]

Insectivora, *n.pl.* (*Zool.*) an order of mammals containing the moles, shrews, hedgehogs etc. that feeds on insects. **insectivore,** *n.* a member of the Insectivora. **insectivorous,** *a.* feeding on insects; belonging to the Insectivora. [from L *insectivorus,* insect-eating, see -VOROUS]

insecure, *a.* not secure, not safe; apprehensive of danger; not effectually guarded; not strongly fixed or supported; lacking in self-confidence. **insecurely,** *adv.* **insecurity,** *n.* [L *insēcūrus*]

inselberg, *n.* an isolated steep rocky hill in a flat plain. [G *Insel,* island, *Berg,* mountain]

inseminate, *v.t.* to impregnate, esp. by artificial means; to sow (in the soil); to implant (in the mind etc.). **insemination,** *n.* [L *insēminātus,* p.p. of *insēmināre* (*sēmināre,* to sow, from *sēmen -minis,* seed)]

insensate, *a.* lacking sensation, inanimate or unconscious; wanting in sensibility, unfeeling; besotted, foolish, mad. **insensately,** *adv.* [late L *insensātus*]

insensible, *a.* that cannot be perceived or felt; imperceptible, inappreciable; destitute of the power of feeling or perceiving, unconscious; unaware; indifferent, heedless (of, how etc.); not susceptible of feeling, emotion or passion, callous, apathetic. **insensibility,** *n.* lack of feeling, emotion or passion; unconsciousness; insusceptibility or indifference (to). **insensibilize, -ise,** *v.t.* **insensibilization, -isation,** *n.* **insensibly,** *adv.* imperceptibly, gradually. [F, from L *insensibilis*]

insensitive, *a.* not sensitive (to). **insensitiveness,** *n.*

insentient, *a.* not sentient, inanimate.

inseparable, *a.* incapable of being separated; (*Gram.*) incapable of being employed separately (as the prefixes DIS-, RE-). *n.* (*usu. pl.*) things which cannot be separated; persons who are constantly together. **inseparable accident,** *n.* (*Log.*) an attribute inseparable from its subject. **inseparability,** **†-ableness,** *n.* **inseparably,** *adv.* [F, from L *insēparābilis*]

insert, *v.t.* to set or place (in, amongst etc.); to introduce (in or into). *n.* something inserted; a printed sheet etc. placed inside the leaves of a newspaper, periodical etc. **inserted,** *a.* placed or set in or upon; (*Bot.*) growing from or upon a part. **inserter,** *n.* **insertion,** *n.* the act of inserting; that which is inserted, an intercalation, a passage etc. introduced (in or into); a band of lace or embroidery inserted in a dress, handkerchief, fancy work etc.; (*Anat., Bot. etc.*) the manner in which one part is inserted into or adheres to another. [L *insertus,* p.p. of *inserere* (*serere,* to join)]

in-service IN.

Insessores, *n.pl.* an order of birds with feet adapted for perching and walking, more generally called Passeres. **insessorial,** *a.* [mod. L, pl. of *insessor,* from *insidēre* (*sedēre,* to sit)]

inset[1], *v.t.* (*past, p.p.* **inset**) to set or fix (in), to insert (in).

inset[2], *n.* that which is set or fixed in; an insertion, as a piece let into a dress etc., a small map or diagram set within a larger one, a page or number of pages inserted in a book, newspaper etc.

in-shoot IN.

inshore, *a., adv.* on, near or towards the shore.

inside[1], *a.* situated within; interior, internal, inner; indoor; (*coll.*) of a crime, organized with the help of someone trusted or employed by the victim. *n.* the inner or interior part; the inner side, surface, part etc. (of); (*Print.*) the side of a sheet containing the second page; the middle part (of); (*pl.*) the contents; (*pl.*) the bowels; a passenger travelling inside. **inside information,** *n.* confidential knowledge not generally accessible. **inside out,** having the inner side turned out and vice versa. **to know inside out,** (*coll.*) to have thorough knowledge of. **insider,** *n.* one inside; one who belongs to a society, clique etc.; one who has inside information. **insider dealing, trading,** *n.* the criminal practice of conducting share deals on the basis of inside information.

inside[2], *adv.* in or into the interior, within; indoors; (*coll.*) in or into prison. *prep.* within, on the inner side of, into. **inside of a mile, an hour etc.,** (*coll.*) within or in less than a mile, an hour etc.

insidious, *a.* lying in wait; treacherous, sly; working secretly or deceptively; intended to deceive or betray; harmful but attractive; working gradually but dangerously. **insidiously,** *adv.* **insidiousness,** *n.* [L *insidiōsus,* from *insidiae,* an ambush, a snare, from *insidēre* (*sedēre,* to sit)]

insight, *n.* power of observation or discernment of the real character of things; penetration; awareness, esp. self-awareness. **insightful,** *a.*

insignia, *n.pl.* (*in N Am. often sing. in constr.*) badges of office or honour; distinguishing marks or signs (of). [L, pl. of *insigne,* remarkable (*signum,* SIGN)]

insignificant, *a.* unimportant, trivial; contemptible; tiny; without meaning. **insignificantly,** *adv.* **insignificance, -ancy,** *n.* **†insignificantive,** *a.* not expressing by external signs.

insincere, *a.* not sincere; false, dissembling; hypocritical, deceitful. **insincerely,** *adv.* **insincerity,** *n.* [L *insincērus*]

†insinew, *v.t.* to strengthen, to invigorate. **insinewed,** *a.* (*Shak.*) joined together, allied (?).

insinuate, *v.t.* to introduce (into favour, office etc.) by gradual and artful means; to indicate indirectly or obliquely; to hint or suggest by remote allusion. *v.i.* to make way (into) by indirect means; to work into one's affections by artful means. **insinuatingly,** *adv.* **insinuation,** *n.* the art or power of insinuating; a hint, an indirect suggestion. **insinuative,** *a.* **insinuator,** *n.* [L *insinuātus,* p.p. of *insinuāre* (*sinuāre,* to wind, from *sinus,* a curve)]

insipid, *a.* tasteless, savourless; wanting in life or animation, dull, vapid. **insipidity, insipidness,** *n.* **insipidly,** *adv.* [F *insipide,* late L *insipidus* (*sapidus,* well-tasting)]

insist, *v.i.* to dwell, to dilate (on); to be emphatic, positive, urgent or persistent (on or upon). *v.t.* to maintain emphatically; to urge strongly or without accepting any refusal. **to insist on,** to demand emphatically; to assert positively. **insistence, -ency,** *n.* **insistent,** *a.* **insistently,** *adv.* [F *insister,* L *insistere* (*sistere,* to set, causal of *stāre,* to stand)]

in situ, in the proper, appropriate or destined position. [L]

insnare, ENSNARE.

insobriety, *n.* want of sobriety; intemperance (usu. in drinking).

insofar IN.

†insolate, *v.t.* to expose to the sun's rays (for bleaching etc., or as a form of medical treatment). **insolation,** *n.* exposure to the sun; sunstroke; solar radiation falling on a given surface. [L *insolātus,* p.p. of *insōlāre* (*sol,* sun)]

insole, *n.* the inner sole of a boot or shoe; a strip of waterproof or other material placed inside a shoe.

insolent, *a.* showing overbearing contempt; impudent, offensive, insulting. **insolently,** *adv.* **insolence,** *n.* [F, from L *insolentum,* nom. *-lens* (*solens,* pres.p. of *solēre,* to be wont)]

†insolidity, *n.* want of solidity; flimsiness, weakness.

insoluble, *a.* that cannot be dissolved; that cannot be solved; inexplicable. **insolubility, insolubleness,** *n.* **insolubly,** *adv.* [F, from L *insolūbilis*]

insolvable, *a.* that cannot be solved or explained, insoluble; that cannot be dissolved; that cannot be paid, discharged or cashed. **insolvability,** *n.* **insolvably,** *adv.*

insolvent, *a.* not able to discharge all debts or liabilities; pertaining to insolvents. *n.* a debtor unable to pay his or her debts. **insolvency,** *n.*

insomnia, *n.* sleeplessness; chronic inability to sleep or sleep well. **insomniac,** *n.* †**insomnious,** *a.* †**insomnolence, -ency,** *n.* [L, from *insomnis,* sleepless (*somnus,* sleep)]

insomuch, *adv.* so, to such a degree, in such wise (that).

insouciant, *a.* careless, unconcerned. **insouciance,** *n.* [F (*souciant,* caring, from *soucier,* L *sollicitāre,* to make anxious)]

Insp., (*abbr.*) Inspector.

inspan, *v.t.* (*past, p.p.* **inspanned**) (*S Afr.*) to yoke (horses, oxen etc.) to a wagon etc.; to harness draught animals to (a wagon). *v.i.* to harness or yoke up draught animals. [Dut. *inspannen* (IN, SPAN[1])]

inspect, *v.t.* to look closely into; to scrutinize carefully; to view and examine officially. †*v.i.* to inquire (into or among). **inspectable,** *a.* **inspection,** *n.* the act of inspecting; a careful, narrow or critical examination or survey; an official examination. †**inspective,** *a.* **inspector,** *n.* one who inspects; an overseer, a superintendent; a police officer usu. ranking next below a superintendent. **inspectoral, -orial,** *a.* **inspectorate, inspectorship,** *n.* **inspectress,** *n. fem.* [L *inspectāre,* freq. of *inspicere* (*specere,* to look)]

inspire, *v.t.* to breathe or take (as air) into the lungs, to breathe into; to instil or infuse (ideas, feelings etc.) into, esp. by or as by supernatural agency; to imbue or animate (with); to infuse or instil (as emotion in or into); to convey privately suggestions or material for (an article on Government affairs etc.). *v.i.* to take air into the lungs. **inspirable,** *a.* **inspiration,** *n.* the act of drawing air into the lungs; an act of inspiring, breathing in or infusing feelings, ideas etc.; a person that inspires others; supernatural influence, esp. that exerted by the Holy Spirit on certain teachers and writers so as to impart a certain divine element to their utterances; the feeling, ideas or other influences imparted by or as by divine agency; an inspiring idea. **inspirational,** *a.* **inspirationally,** *adv.* **inspirationist,** *n.* one who holds that every word of the Bible is inspired. **inspirationism,** *n.* **inspirator,** *n.* a device or apparatus for drawing in air, steam etc., a variety of injector for steam-boilers; a kind of respirator. **inspiratory,** *a.* pertaining to inspiration; aiding in the process of inspiration. **inspired,** *a.* inhaled, infused; imparted, actuated or produced by or as by supernatural agency. **inspirer,** *n.* **inspiringly,** *adv.* [OF *enspirer,* L *inspirāre* (*spirāre,* to breathe)]

inspirit, *v.t.* to infuse spirit, life or animation into; to inspire, to encourage (to action or to do). **inspiriting,** *a.*

inspissate, *v.t.* to thicken, to render more dense, to bring to a greater consistence by boiling or evaporation. *a.*, thickened, rendered more dense. **inspissation,** *n.* [late L *inspissātus,* p.p. of *inspissāre* (*spissus,* thick)]

inst., (*abbr.*) instant (this month).

instability, *n.* want of stability or firmness; lack of mental or emotional consistency; the tendency of an aeroplane to depart involuntarily from the set line of flight. [F *instabilité, L instābilitātem,* nom. *-tas*]

†**instable,** UNSTABLE.

install, *v.t.* (*past, p.p.* **installed**) to induct or invest by placing (in an office, charge or dignity) with customary ceremonies; to set or establish in an office etc.; to put (apparatus etc.) in position for use. **installation,** *n.* the act of installing; a piece or complex of machinery; a military base etc. †**instalment[1],** installation. [F *installer,* low L *installāre* (*stallum,* STALL[1])]

instalment[2], *n.* a part of a debt or sum due paid at successive periods; a part (of anything) supplied at different times; part of a serial story etc. **instalment plan,** *n.* (*N Am.*) the hire-purchase system. [perh. from an obs. verb *install,* to arrange or fix, as a payment]

instance, *n.* an example, illustrative case or precedent; situation; solicitation or asking; suggestion, prompting; (*Law*) a process or suit; †a cause, a motive; †a proof; †presence, present time. *v.t.* to bring forward as an instance or example. **at the instance of,** at the suggestion or desire of. **for instance,** for example. **in the first instance,** at the first stage, in the first place. **instancy,** *n.* urgency. [F, from L *instantia,* as foll.]

instant, *a.* pressing, urgent, importunate, immediate; esp. of food, processed so as to be quickly and easily prepared; present, current, still going on, of the current month. *n.* a particular point of time; a moment, a very brief space of time; †instance; †a pressing application. **instantaneous,** *a.* happening or done in an instant or immediately; (*Dynam.*) relating to a particular instant. **instantaneously,** *adv.* **instantaneity, instantaneousness,** *n.* **instantly,** *adv.* immediately; without delay. [F, from L *instantem,* nom. *-stans* (*stāre,* to stand)]

instanter, *adv.* at once, immediately. [L]

instar, *n.* (*Zool.*) a stage in development; the form of an insect or other arthropod after each successive stage. [L, resemblance, form]

instate, *v.t.* to put in a certain place, office, condition etc., to install; †to invest.

†**instauration,** *n.* renewal, restoration. **instaurator,** *n.* [L *instaurātio,* from *instaurāre* (*-staurāre,* see RESTORE)]

instead, *adv.* in the place, stead or room of; as an alternative or substitute.

instep, *n.* the arched upper side of the human foot, near the ankle; the part of a shoe, stocking etc., corresponding to this; the front part of the hind leg of a horse reaching from the ham to the pastern-joint; anything shaped like a human instep. [IN, STEP, or perh. STOOP, bend]

instigate, *v.t.* to incite, to urge on (to an action or to do); to provoke or bring about (an action, esp. of an evil kind). **instigation,** *n.* **instigator,** *n.* [L *instīgātus,* p.p. of *instīgāre* (*stig-,* cp. Gr. *stig-,* root of *stizein,* to prick)]

instil, *v.t.* (*past, p.p.* **instilled**) to pour by drops (into); to infuse slowly and gradually (into the mind of a person). **instillation, instilment,** *n.* **instillator,** *n.* [F *instiller,* L *instillāre* (*stillāre,* to drop)]

instinct, *n.* a natural impulse, esp. in the lower animals, leading them without reasoning or conscious design to perform certain actions tending to the welfare of the individual or the perpetuation of the species; an innate or intuitive impulse, tendency or aptitude; intuition, unreasoning perception of rightness, beauty etc. *a.*, animated or impelled from within; moved or imbued (with). **instinctive,** *a.* prompted by instinct; spontaneous, impulsive. **instinctively,** *adv.* **instinctual,** *a.* pertaining to instinct. [through F *instinct* or directly from L *instinctus,* from *instinguere,* as INSTIGATE]

instipulate, *a.* (*Bot.*) destitute of stipules.

institor, *n.* (*Law, esp. Sc.*) an agent, a factor. **institorial,** *a.* [L, from *insistere,* to INSIST]

institute, *v.t.* to set up, to establish, to originate, to set in operation, to start, to begin; to nominate, to appoint (to or into), esp. to invest with the spiritual part of a benefice. *n.* a society established for the promotion or furtherance of some particular object (usu. literary or scientific); the building in which such a society meets; an established law, precept or principle; (*pl.*) a book of elements or principles, esp. of jurisprudence or medicine. **Institute for Advanced Study,** a department of Princeton University, US, established 1933, to encourage gifted scientists to further their research uninterrupted by teaching duties or an imposed research scheme. Its first professor was Alfred Einstein. **institution,** *n.* the act of instituting; that which is instituted; an established order, law, regulation or custom; a society or association for the promotion of some particular object; the building in which such a society meets; a building for the recipients of indoor public relief, a workhouse, orphanage etc.; the act or ceremony of investing a clergyman with the spiritual part of a benefice; (*coll.*) a familiar custom, person etc. **institutional,** *a.* pertaining to an institution; of organized churches etc., finding expression in this; routine or unimaginative. **institutional religion,** *n.* the form of religion that expresses itself through ritual and church services. **institutionalism,** *n.* **institutionalist,** *n.* **institutionalize, -ise,** *v.t.* to make an institution of; to confine to an institution. **institutionalization, -isation,** *n.* **institutionally,** *adv.* [L *institūtus,* p.p. of *instituere* (*statuere,* to place, from *status,* see STATUS)]

instruct, *v.t.* to teach, to educate (in a subject); to inform; to furnish with orders or directions; to supply (a solicitor, counsel etc.) with information relating to a case. †**instructible,** *a.* **instruction,** *n.* the act of instructing; teaching, education; a code directing a computer to perform a certain operation; (*pl.*) directions, orders, injunctions; directions to a solicitor, counsel etc. **instructional,** *a.* **instructive,** *a.* conveying instruction. **instructively,** *adv.* **instructiveness,** *n.* **instructor,** *n.* one who instructs; (*N Am.*) a college teacher having a rank inferior to professor. **instructress,** *n. fem.* [L *instructus,* p.p. of *instruere* (*struere,* to pile up)]

instrument, *n.* that by means of which work is done or any object or purpose effected; a tool, a mechanical implement, esp. one for scientific and other delicate operations; a contrivance for producing musical sound; (*Law*) a document giving formal expression to an act; an agent, a person used as a means by another. *v.t.* (*Mus.*) to arrange (music) for instruments; to equip with instruments. **stringed instrument,** a musical instrument in which sounds are generated by the vibration of strings. **wind instrument,** one in which the agency is a column of air vibrating in a tube. **Instrument Landing System,** *n.* a landing aid for aircraft that uses radio beacons on the ground and instruments on the flight deck. One beacon (localizer) sends out a vertical radio beam along the centre line of the runway. Another beacon (glide slope) transmits a beam in the plane at right-angles to the localizer beam at the ideal approach-path angle. The pilot can tell from the instruments how to manoeuvre to attain the correct approach path. **instrumental,** *a.* serving as instrument or means (to some end or in some act); of errors, etc., pertaining or due to the instrument used; pertaining to or produced by musical instruments; (*Gram.*) denoting the means or instrument, as certain cases in Sanskrit etc. *n.* (*Gram.*) the instrumental case; a piece of music for instruments as opposed to voices. **instrumentalist,** *n.* one who plays an instrument. **instrumentality,** *n.* **instrumentally,** *adv.* **instrumentation,** *n.* the arrangement of music for several instruments in combination; the art or manner of using an instrument or instruments; instrumentality. [F, from L *instrūmentum,* from *instruere,* see prec.]

insubordinate, *a.* not submissive to authority; disobedient, disorderly. **insubordinately,** *adv.* **insubordination,** *n.*

insubstantial, *a.* unsubstantial, unreal; flimsy or slight. **insubstantiality,** *n.* **insubstantiate,** *v.t.* **insubstantiation,** *n.* [late L *insubstantiālis*]

insufferable, *a.* not to be borne or endured; detestable, intolerable. **insufferably,** *adv.*

insufficient, *a.* not sufficient; deficient, inadequate. **insufficiency, -ence,** *n.* **insufficiently,** *adv.* [OF, from L *insufficientem,* nom. *-ens*]

insufflate, *v.t.* (*Med.*) to blow or breathe (air, vapour, powder etc.) into an opening, cavity etc.; to treat (a person, organ etc.) by insufflation. **insufflator,** *n.* an instrument used for this purpose. **insufflation,** *n.* the act of blowing or breathing upon or into; (*Med.*) blowing or breathing (therapeutic vapour etc.) into the lungs etc.; (*Eccles.*) a symbolic breathing upon a person. [L *insufflātus,* p.p. of *insufflāre* (*flāre,* to blow)]

insular, *a.* pertaining to or of the nature of an island; pertaining to or like the inhabitants of an island; narrow, contracted (in outlook). **insularism, -larity,** *n.* **insularly,** *adv.* [L *insulāris,* from *insula,* island]

insulate, *v.t.* to make into an island; to place in a detached situation or position; to isolate; (*Phys.*) to separate from other bodies by a nonconductor, so as to prevent the passage of electricity or heat. **insulation,** *n.* **insulator,** *n.* [L *insulātus,* made like an island, as prec.]

insulin, *n.* a hormone produced in the pancreas which regulates the metabolism of sugar and fat and is employed in the treatment of diabetes. [L *insula,* an island]

insult[1], *v.t.* to treat with gross indignity, insolence or contempt; to affront; †to assail. *v.i.* to use insults; to glory, to triumph (over); †to make an attack (upon). **insultable,** *a.* †**insultant,** *a.* **insulter,** *n.* **insultingly,** *adv.* †**insultment,** *n.* [F *insulter,* L *insultāre,* freq. of *insilīre* (*salīre,* to leap)]

insult[2], *n.* an affront, an indignity; an insulting act or speech; †an attack, an assault.

insuperable, *a.* insurmountable, invincible; †unsurpassable. **insuperability,** *n.* **insuperably,** *adv.* [F, from L *superābilis*]

insupportable, *a.* insufferable, intolerable; incapable of being sustained or defended; †irresistible. †**insupportableness,** *n.* **insupportably,** *adv.*

insuppressible, *a.* that cannot be suppressed. †**insuppressive,** *a.*

insure[1], *v.t.* to secure compensation, whole or partial, for loss or injury of (property, life etc.) by paying a periodical premium; to secure the payment of (a specified sum) in the event of loss, injury etc. (said of the owner or the insurance company); to furnish (a person) with an insurance policy. *v.i.* to take out an insurance policy. **the insured,** the person to whom compensation for fire etc. will be paid; the person whose life is insured. **insurability,** *n.* **insurable,** *a.* **insurance,** *n.* the act of insuring against damage or loss; a contract by which a company, in consideration of a sum of money, becomes bound to indemnify the insured against loss by fire, shipwreck etc.; the sum so insured; the premium so paid. **insurance company,** *n.* a company which insures persons against loss or damage. **insurance policy** POLICY[2]. **insurer,** *n.* [var. of ENSURE]

insure[2], ENSURE.

insurgent, *a.* rising up against the constituted government, rebellious; of waves, surging or rushing in. *n.* one who rises up against established government or authority; a rebel. **insurgence, -ency,** *n.* [L *insurgens -entem,* pres.p. of *insurgere* (*surgere,* to rise)]

insurmountable, *a.* that cannot be surmounted, passed over or overcome. **insurmountability,** *n.* **insurmountably,** *adv.*

insurrection, *n.* the act of rising in open opposition to established authority; uprising, rebellion in the initial stage. **insurrectional, -tionary,** *a.* **insurrectionist,** *n.* [F, from L *insurrectiōnem,* nom. *-tio,* from *insurgere,* see INSURGENT]

insusceptible, *a.* not susceptible (of); incapable of being moved by any feeling or impression. **insusceptibility,** *n.* †**insusceptive,** *a.*

int., (*abbr.*) interjection.

intact, *a.* untouched; unimpaired, uninjured; entire. **intactness,** *n.* [L *intactus* (*tactus,* p.p. of *tangere,* to touch)]

intaglio, *n.* (*pl.* **-lios**) a figure cut or engraved in a hard substance; the act or process of producing this; a gem with a figure cut or engraved into it; (*N Am.*) a rotogravure. *v.t.* to cut or engrave in this manner. **intagliated,** *a.* carved or engraved on a hard surface. [It., from *intagliare,* to cut, to engrave, late L *intaleāre,* to cut, from *talea,* a twig]

intail, ENTAIL.

intake, *n.* that which is taken in; the point where a tube or woven article narrows; a place where water is taken in, an inlet; an air-shaft in a mine; the point at which fuel enters an engine; a quantity of new members (of a school etc.); land enclosed, esp. a tract taken in from a moorland and cultivated.

intangible, *a.* not tangible; imperceptible to the touch, impalpable; not to be grasped mentally; unfounded. **intangibility,** *n.* **intangibly,** *adv.* [med. L *intangibilis*]

integer, *n.* the whole of anything; a whole number as distinguished from a fraction. [L (*tag-,* root of *tangere,* to touch)]

integrable, *a.* capable of being integrated.

integral, *a.* whole, entire, complete; necessary to completeness, an essential part of a whole; (*Math.*) pertaining to or constituting an integer; pertaining to or produced by integration. *n.* (*Math.*) the limit of the sum of a series of values of a differential $f(x)\ dx$ when x varies by indefinitely small increments from one given value to another (cp. DIFFERENTIAL); a whole, a total, an integer; †an integral part. **integral calculus,** *n.* a method of summing up differential quantities. **integrality**, *n.* [INTEGER]

integrand, *n.* (*Math.*) an expression to be integrated.

integrant, *a.* making part of a whole; necessary to constitute an entire entity. **integrant parts,** *n.pl.* parts into which a body may be reduced, each remaining of the same nature as the whole.

integrate, *v.t.* to make into a whole, to complete by addition of the parts; to combine into a whole; to indicate the whole or mean value of; to end the racial segregation of; (*Math.*) to find the integral of. *a.*, made up of integrant parts; whole, entire, complete. **integrated circuit,** *n.* a minute electronic circuit in or on a slice of semiconductor material. **integration,** *n.* the making into a whole; the unification of all elements in a society, esp. of white and coloured; (*Math.*) the act or process of integrating. **integrative,** *a.* **integrator,** *n.* one who or that which integrates; a device or instrument for determining the value of an integral, as an area, rate of speed etc. [INTEGER]

integrity, *n.* entireness, completeness; soundness; genuine, unadulterated state; probity, rectitude, high principle. [F *integrité,* from L *integritātem,* wholeness, nom. *-tas,* from prec.]

integument, *n.* a covering, esp. a natural one; the skin; the outer covering of a seed, the husk, rind etc. **integumentary**, *a.* [L *integumentum,* from *integere* (*tegere,* to cover)]

intellect, *n.* the faculty of the human mind by which it understands and reasons, as dist. from the faculty of feeling and willing; the understanding; the philosophic mind; intellectual people collectively; †(*pl.*) wits, senses; †meaning, purport. **intellection,** *n.* the act or process of understanding or comprehending, esp. as distinct from sensation or imagination. **intellective,** *a.* pertaining to or produced by the intellect; having power to understand. †**intellectively,** *adv.* **intellectual**, *a.* possessing intellect in a high degree; pertaining to or performed by the intellect; appealing to or perceived by the intellect. *n.* an intellectual person; (*pl.*) the most enlightened people (in a country etc.). **intellectualism,** *n.* the cultivation of the intellect; the doctrine that knowledge is exclusively or principally derived from pure reason. **intellectualist,** *n.* **intellectuality**, *n.* **intellectualize, -ise,** *v.t.* to make intellectual; to treat intellectually; to give an intellectual character or significance to. *v.i.* to become intellectual; to employ the intellect. **intellectualization, -isation,** *n.* **intellectually,** *adv.* [L *intellectus,* as INTELLIGENT]

intelligence, *n.* the exercise of the understanding; intellectual power; capacity for the higher functions of the intellect; acquired knowledge; quickness or sharpness of intellect; news, information, notice, notification; a department concerned with gathering secret or little-known information of importance for military activity; such information; an intelligent being, esp. an incorporeal or spiritual being regarded as pure intellect. **intelligence office,** *n.* an office where information may be obtained, esp. (*N Am.*) with reference to servants. **intelligence quotient (IQ),** *n.* a number denoting a person's intelligence by dividing the mental age by the age in years. **intelligence test,** *n.* a psychological test to determine a person's relative mental capacity. **intelligencer,** *n.* one who conveys intelligence; a messenger, a spy. **intelligential**, *a.* [F, from L *intelligentia,* as foll.]

intelligent, *a.* endowed with understanding; sagacious, sensible, clever, quick. **intelligential** INTELLIGENCE. **intelligently,** *adv.* **intelligentsia, -gentzia**, *n.* people who claim or possess enlightenment or culture. [L *intelligens -entem,* pres.p. of *intelligere,* to understand (INTER-, *legere,* to gather, to choose)]

intelligible, *a.* capable of being understood, comprehensible; plain, clear; apprehensible only by the intellect, as distinct from *sensible*. **intelligibility**, †**-ibleness,** *n.* **intelligibly,** *adv.* [F, from L *intelligibilis,* as prec.]

intemperate, *a.* not exercising due moderation or self-restraint; indulging any appetite or passion in excess; addicted to excessive indulgence in alcoholic liquors; immoderate, excessive, exceeding proper bounds; violent, inclement. **intemperance,** *n.* want of moderation or self-restraint, esp. excessive indulgence in alcoholic liquors. **intemperately,** *adv.* †**intemperateness,** *n.* [L *intemperātus*]

†**intempestive,** *a.* unseasonable. [L *intempestīvus* (*tempestīvus,* from *tempus,* time, season)]

intend, *v.t.* to propose, to plan; to signify, to mean; to design (for); to destine (for); to mean, to have a certain intention; †to extend; †to bend, to direct (one's course etc.); †to intensify; to look after, to superintend. *v.i.* †to direct one's course, to proceed (towards, for etc.); †to start (for etc.); †to attend. **intendancy,** *n.* superintendence; a body of intendants; the position or office of intendant. **intendant,** *n.* a superintendent or manager. **intended,** *n.* (*coll.*) a person whom one is expecting to marry. **intendedly,** *adv.* †**intender,** *n.* †**intendiment,** *n.* attention, consideration; intendment, knowledge, skill. **intendment,** *n.* (*Law*) true intent or meaning as determined by the law; †intention, purpose. [F *entendre, intendere,* to stretch to, to direct (*tendere,* to stretch, see TEND[1])]

†**intenerate,** *v.t.* to make tender, to soften. [L *tener,* tender]

†**intenible,** *a.* (*Shak.*) incapable of holding or containing.

intense, *a.* raised to a high pitch; strained, forced; violent, vehement; extreme in degree; severe, immoderate, excessive; ardent, eager, fervent; strongly or deeply emotional. †**intensate,** *v.t.* to intensify. **intensative** INTENSIVE. **intensely,** *adv.* **intenseness,** *n.* **intensify**, *v.t.* to render more intense; (*Phot.*) to increase the density of (a negative) so as to produce stronger contrasts. *v.i.* to become more intense. **intensification**, *n.* **intensifier,** *n.* **intensity,** *n.* the condition or quality of being intense; an extreme degree of force or strength; magnitude of force per unit. [F, from L *intensus,* p.p. of *intendere,* to INTEND]

intension, *n.* the act of straining or stretching; the state of being strained or stretched; tension; intense exertion or concentration (of will etc.); intensity, high degree (of a quality), as distinct from *extension*; (*Log.*) the content of a notion. **intensive**, *a.* admitting of intension; concentrated, thorough, as opp. to extensive; unremitting; characterized by intensity; (*chiefly in comb.*) utilizing one specified element in production proportionately more than others; (*Econ.*) conducive to high productiveness within a narrow area; pertaining to methods (of inoculation etc.) in which injections, doses etc. are successively increased; (*Gram.*) serving to intensify, or to add force or emphasis. *n.* an intensive particle, word or phrase. **intensive cultivation,** *n.* the system whereby land is kept under cultivation by a rotation of crops and manuring. **intensive therapy unit**, a high-technology facility for treating the critically ill or injured. **intensively,** *adv.*

intent[1], *a.* having the mind bent or strained on an object; sedulously applied (on); fixed, resolved, earnest. **intently,** *adv.* **intentness,** *n.* [L *intentus,* p.p. of *intendere,* to INTEND]

intent[2], *n.* design, purpose, intention; meaning, drift. **to all intents and purposes,** practically, really, in reality. **to the intent that,** in order that. [OF *entent, entente,* intention, meaning, L *intentus,* a stretching out, late L, intention, from *intendere,* to INTEND]

intention, *n.* determination to act in some particular manner; purpose, design, intent; (*pl.*) (*coll.*) designs with regard to marriage; (*Log.*) a general concept; in the Roman Catholic Church, special purpose to perform any act of devotion with a particular object in view; ultimate aim or object; (*Med.*) a process of healing wounds. **first intentions,** (*Log.*) primary conceptions formed by the application of the mind to the objects themselves. **second intentions,** secondary conceptions formed by the action of the mind upon first intentions and their inter-relations. **to heal by first intention,** (*Med.*) to cicatrize without suppuration. **to heal by second intention,** to unite by granulation after suppuration. **intentional,** *a.* done with design or purpose. **intentionality,** *n.* **intentionally,** *adv.* **intentioned,** *a.* (*chiefly in comb.*, as *well-intentioned*). †**intentive,** *a.* attentive; intent. †**intentively,** *adv.* †**intentiveness,** *n.*

inter, *v.t.* (*past, p.p.* **interred**) to bury; to place in a grave or tomb; to put out of sight. **interment,** *n.* [OF *interrer,* late L *interrāre* (*terra,* earth)]

inter-, *pref.* between, among; with, into or upon each other; as *intercede, intercostal, international, interstellar, intertexture, interwoven.* [L]

interact[1], *v.i.* to act reciprocally; to act on each other. **interaction,** *n.* **interactionism,** *n.* the theory that mind and body interact, opp. to *automatism* and *phenomenal parallelism.* **interactionist,** *n.* **interactive,** *a.* capable of mutual action; permitting continuous mutual communication between computer and user.

interact[2], *n.* the interval between two acts of a play; an interlude.

inter alia, among other things. [L]

interbed, *v.t.* (*past, p.p.* **interbedded**) (*Geol.*) to interstratify.

interblend, *v.t.* to mingle with one another. *v.i.* to blend together.

interbreed, *v.t.* to breed by crossing different subvarieties or species of animals or plants. *v.i.* to breed together.

intercalary, intercalar, *a.* inserted between or amongst others, as a day inserted in the calendar to make this correspond with the solar year; of a year, containing such an addition; inserted, interpolated. **intercalate,** *v.t.* to insert between or amongst others (esp. a day etc. into a calendar); to interpolate, to insert anything in an unusual or irregular way. **intercalation,** *n.* **intercalative,** *a.* [L *intercalārius,* from *intercalāre* (*calāre,* to proclaim), p.p. *intercalātus*]

intercede, *v.i.* to plead (with someone) in favour of another; to mediate; †to intervene. †**intercedent,** *a.* **interceder,** *n.* [F *intercéder,* L *intercēdere* (*cēdere,* to go), p.p. *intercessus*]

intercellular, *a.* (*Biol. etc.*) situated between or among cells.

intercensal, *a.* pertaining to the interval between two censuses.

intercept, *v.t.* to stop, take or seize by the way or in passage; to obstruct, to stop, to shut off; (*Math.*) to mark off or include between two points etc. *n.* (*Math.*) the part of a line that is intercepted. **interception,** *n.* **interceptive,** *a.* **interceptor,** *n.* one who or that which intercepts; a swift aeroplane for purposes of pursuit. [L *interceptus,* p.p. of *intercipere* (*capere,* to take)]

intercerebral, *a.* connecting two parts of the brain.

intercession, *n.* the act of interceding; a prayer offered for others. **intercessional,** *a.* [L *intercessio,* see INTERCEDE]

intercessor, *n.* one who intercedes; a mediator; one who administered a bishopric during the vacancy of a see. †**intercessorial, intercessory,** *a.*

interchange, *v.t.* to exchange with each other, to give and take; to put each (of two things) in the place of the other, to cause to alternate. *v.i.* to alternate. *n.*, reciprocal exchange; alternate succession, alternation; a junction of two or more roads designed to prevent traffic streams crossing one another. **interchangeable,** *a.* **interchangeability, -ableness,** *n.* **interchangeably,** *adv.* †**interchangement,** *n.* **interchanger,** *n.* [OF *entre-changier* (*changier,* to CHANGE)]

intercilium, *n.* the part between the eyebrows. [L *cilium,* eyelid]

intercipient, *a.* intercepting. †*n.* one who or that which intercepts. [L *intercipiens -entem,* pres.p. of *intercipere,* to INTERCEPT]

intercitizenship, *n.* (*N Am.*) the right to citizenship in any state.

intercity, *a.* existing or carried on between different cities.

interclavicle, *n.* a median bony plate attached to the clavicles, in many reptiles. **interclavicular,** *a.*

intercollegiate, *a.* existing or carried on between colleges.

intercolline, *a.* lying between hills formed of volcanic matter. [L *collīnus,* from *collis,* hill]

intercolonial, *a.* existing or carried on between colonies.

intercolumnar, *a.* placed between columns; situated between the columns of the external abdominal ring. **intercolumniation,** *n.* the spacing of columns in a building; the interval between two columns.

intercom, *n.* a system of intercommunication in aircraft etc. [*inter*nal *com*munication]

†**intercommune,** *v.i.* to have mutual intercourse or communion (with); †(*Sc. Hist.*) to have intercourse with rebels. **letters of intercommuning,** writs issued by the Scottish Privy Council forbidding anyone to harbour or communicate with persons therein denounced. **intercommunion,** *n.* the partaking of communion in common between members of different Churches or sects.

intercommunicate, *v.i.* to hold or enjoy mutual communication; to have free passage to and from each other. *v.t.* to give or communicate mutually. **intercommunicable,** *a.* **intercommunication,** *n.* **intercommunion** INTERCOMMUNE.

intercommunity, *n.* the quality of being common to various persons or of holding things in common.

intercomparison, *n.* mutual comparison.

interconnect, *v.i.* to connect (with) by links or parts acting reciprocally. **interconnectedness,** *n.* **interconnection,** *n.*

intercontinental, *a.* existing between or connecting different continents or persons belonging thereto.

interconvertible, *a.* convertible into each other.

intercostal, *a.* situated between the ribs; between the framework of the keel of a ship. *n.pl.* the intercostal muscles; (*Shipbuilding*) the parts between the frames.

intercourse, *n.* reciprocal dealings, association, communication etc., between persons, nations etc.; spiritual communion; copulation, sexual intercourse. [OF *entrecours,* late L *intercursus,* commerce, L, intervention (COURSE)]

intercrop, *n.* a crop raised between the rows of another crop; a quickly-maturing crop between crops grown in a regular series. *v.t.* (*past, p.p.* **intercropped**) to raise (a crop) in this way. *v.i.* to plant intercrops.

intercross, *v.t.* to cross each other; to cause to interbreed. *v.i.* to interbreed. *n.* an instance of cross-breeding.

intercurrent, *a.* occurring between or among; intervening; occurring during the progress of another disease, occurring at different seasons. **intercurrence,** *n.* [L *intercurrens -entem,* pres.p. of *intercurrere* (*currere,* to run)]

intercut, *v.t.* (*pres.p.* **intercutting,** *past, p.p.* **intercut**) to alternate (contrasting camera shots) by cutting.

interdeal, *v.i.* (*past, p.p.* **interdealt**) to have reciprocal dealings (with). †*n.* mutual dealing, traffic. [DEAL[1]]

interdenominational, *a.* existing or carried on between different denominations.

interdental, *a.* situated between teeth (of an animal or a machine); (*Phon.*) sounded between the teeth.

interdepartmental, *a.* involving or carried on between different departments.

interdepend, *v.i.* to depend upon each other. **interdependent,** *a.* **interdependently,** *adv.* **interdependence,** *n.*

interdict, *n.* a prohibitory decree; (*Rom. Law*) a decree of the praetor pronounced between two litigants, sometimes enjoining, but more frequently forbidding something to be done; (*Sc. Law*) an order of the Court of Session equivalent to an injunction; in the Roman Catholic Church, a sentence by which places or persons are debarred from ecclesiastical functions and privileges. *v.t.*, to forbid, to prohibit; to restrain (from); to lay under an interdict. **interdiction,** *n.* **interdictory**, *a.* [L *interdictum,* a decree, from *interdictus,* p.p. of *interdīcere,* to impose, to forbid by a decree (*dīcere,* to say)]

interdigital, *a.* situated between the fingers. **interdigitate,** *v.t.* to insert between the fingers; to interlock. *v.i.* to interlock, as when the fingers of one hand are inserted between those of the other. [L *interdigitālis* (*digitus,* finger, see DIGIT)]

interdisciplinary, *a.* involving two or more disciplines or fields of study.

interest¹, *n.* lively, sympathetic or curious attention; the power of eliciting such attention; personal concern, sympathy; something in which one has a personal concern; participation in advantages, benefits or profits; (*often pl.*) benefit, advantage, behoof; proprietary right or concern, a share, a portion or stake (in); (*collect.*) those having a concern in a particular business etc.; influence with or over others; payment for the use of borrowed money or on a debt. **compound interest** COMPOUND. **simple interest** SIMPLE. **to take an interest in,** to pay sympathetic or curious attention to. **interest group,** *n.* a group of people concerned to defend a common interest. [earlier *interess,* altered after OF *interest* (F *intérêt*), L *interesse,* to concern (INTER-, *esse,* to be)]

interest², *v.t.* to arouse or hold the attention or curiosity of; to concern; to cause to participate (in). **interested,** *a.* having the interest excited; concerned (in); having an interest, concern or share in; liable to be biased through personal interest, not disinterested. **interestedly,** *adv.* **interesting,** *a.* arousing interest, attention or curiosity. **to be in an interesting condition,** to be pregnant. **interestingly,** *adv.* [earlier *interess* (influ. by prec. or formed from the p.p. *interess'd*), as prec.]

interface, *n.* (*Geom., Cryst.*) a surface lying between two spaces; the point at which independent systems meet and act on each other; an electrical circuit linking computers or other devices. **interfacial,** *a.* included between two faces of a crystal etc.; pertaining to an interface. **interfacing,** *n.* stiffening material inserted between layers of fabric.

interfemoral, *a.* situated or extending between the thighs.

interfere, *v.i.* to come into collision, to clash (with); to intermeddle (with); (*coll.*) to assault sexually; to interpose, to intervene (in); (*Phys.*) to act reciprocally, to modify each other; of a horse, to strike the hoof against the opposite fetlock. **interference,** *n.* the act of interfering; meddling; hindrance; (*Radio.*) the spoiling of reception by atmospherics or by other signals; (*N Am.*) an appeal against a patent by the holder of a prior patent. **interferer,** *n.* **interfering,** *a.* inclined to interfere; officious. *n.* interference. **interferingly,** *adv.* **interferometer,** *n.* an optical instrument for accurate measuring, esp. of the wavelength of light. [OF *entreferir* (*ferir,* L *ferīre,* to strike), to exchange blows]

interferon, *n.* an antiviral substance produced in living cells in humans and other creatures in response to infection from various viruses.

interfluent, *a.* flowing between; flowing together or into each other. †**interfluous,** *a.* [L *interfluens -entem,* pres.p. of *interfluere* (*fluere,* to flow)]

interfoliaceous, *a.* situated between opposite leaves.

interfrontal, *a.* situated between the two frontal bones.

interfuse, *v.t.* to cause to flow into each other; to commix or intersperse; to blend together. *v.i.* to blend into each other. **interfusion,** *n.* [L *interfūsus,* p.p. of *interfundere* (*fundere,* to pour)]

intergalactic, *a.* between galaxies.

interglacial, *a.* occurring or formed between two of the glacial periods.

interglandular, *a.* situated between glands.

intergrade, *n.* an intermediate grade. *v.i.* to pass into or mingle gradually with another form. **intergradation,** *n.*

interim, *n.* the meantime; the intervening time or period. *a.* temporary, provisional. [L, in the meantime (*-im,* adv. suf.)]

interior, *a.* internal, inner; inland; remote from the coast, frontier or exterior; domestic, as dist. from foreign; pertaining to the inner consciousness, the soul or spiritual matters. *n.* the internal part of anything, the inside; the central or inland part of a country; the inside of a building or room, esp. as portrayed in a picture, photograph etc.; the domestic affairs of a country; the government department dealing with these; the inward nature, the soul. **interior angle,** *n.* the angle between two sides of a polygon. **interior-sprung,** *a.* of a mattress etc., having springs. **interiority,** *n.* **interiorly,** *adv.* [L, compar. of *inter,* see INTER-]

interjacent, *a.* lying between or among; intervening. †**interjacency,** *n.* [L *interjacens -entem,* pres.p. of *interjacēre* (*jacēre,* to lie)]

interject, *v.t.* to throw in (an abrupt remark etc.); to insert, to interpose. **interjection,** *n.* the act of interjecting; an exclamation, a word thrown in to express feeling, and which is differentiated as a separate part of speech. **interjectional, -jectory, -jectural,** *a.* **interjectionally,** *adv.* [L *interjectus,* p.p. of *interjicere* (*jacere,* to throw)]

†**interjoin,** *v.t.* to join with one another. **interjointal,** *a.* occurring between the joint planes in rocks.

interlace, *v.t.* to lace or weave together; to interweave; to entangle together; (*fig.*) to intermix. *v.i.* to be interwoven (with each other); to intersect in a complicated fashion. *v.t.* to intersect. **interlaced arches,** *n.* arches, usu. semicircular which intersect each other. **interlacement,** *n.* [ME *entrelace,* F *entrelacer* (*lacer,* to LACE)]

interlard, *v.t.* †to mix with alternate layers of fat; to diversify (a conversation, passage in a book etc., with unusual phrases etc.); to intersperse. [F *entrelarder* (*larder,* to LARD)]

interleaf, *n.* a leaf, usu. blank, inserted among others for purposes of illustration etc. **interleave,** *v.t.* to insert (a blank leaf or leaves) between the leaves of.

interline, *v.t.* to write or print between the lines of; to insert between lines; to write or print in alternate lines; to insert a lining between the outer cloth and the lining of (a garment). **interlineal, -linear,** †**-lineary,** *a.* **interlineation,** *n.* **interlining,** *n.* [prob. from late L *interlineāre* (after MF *entreligner*)]

Interlingua, *n.* an artificial language based on Latin roots. [L *lingua,* tongue]

interlink, *v.t.* to connect (together or with) by links. *n.* an intermediate link.

interlobate, *a.* (*Geol.*) formed or lying between loops or lobes, usu. the terminal lobes of a moraine.

interlobular, *a.* situated or occurring between the lobes of a gland or other organ.

interlocation, *n.* the act of placing between, intercalating or interposing.

interlock, *v.t.* to connect firmly together by reciprocal engagement of parts; to link or lock together. *v.i.* to engage with each other by reciprocal connections. *n.*, the state of being interlocked; a device in a logic circuit preventing the initiation of an activity in the absence of certain preceding events. **interlocking system,** (*Railway*) a method of connecting points and signals by interlocking mechanism so as to keep the signal at danger until each movement has been completed and to prevent the movement of two points at once.

interlocution, *n.* conversation, dialogue, discussion; †(*Law*) an intermediate decree. **interlocutor,** *n.* one who takes part in a conversation; the compere of a minstrel show; (*Sc. Law*) an interlocutory or interim decree in a case. **interlocutory,** *a.* consisting of dialogue; (*Law*) intermediate, not final. **interlocutress, -trice, -trix,** *n. fem.* [L *interlocūtio* (*loquī,* to speak)]

interloper, *n.* one who interlopes or thrusts him- or herself into a place, office, affairs etc., without a right; an intruder; one who trades without a licence or infringes upon another's business. **interlope,** *v.i.* to run between parties and intercept the advantage that one would gain from the other; to traffic without a proper licence; to forestall others; to intrude. [prob. from *inter-* and *-loper* (cp. Dut. *loopen,* OE *hlēapen,* to LEAP)]

interlude, *n.* a pause or a short entertainment between the acts of a play, or between a play and the after-piece; an interval; a piece of instrumental music played between the acts of a drama, between the verses of a hymn, portions of a church service etc.; an incident, esp. an amusing one, coming between graver events; a dramatic representation, usu. farcical, intervening between the acts of the mystery-plays and moralities. [med. L *interlūdium* (*lūdus,* play)]

interlunar, †-nary, *a.* pertaining to the time when the moon, about to change from old to new, is invisible.

intermarriage, *n.* marriage between persons of different families, tribes, castes or nations; marriage between persons closely akin. **intermarry,** *v.i.* of different families, tribes etc., to become connected by marriage; to marry within the family etc.; (*Law*) to marry.

intermaxillary, *a.* situated between the maxillae or jaw-bones. *n.* the intermaxillary bone.

intermeddle, *v.i.* to interfere improperly or officiously (with). †*v.t.* to intermix, to intermingle. **intermeddler,** *n.* [A-F *entremedler,* OF *entremesler*]

intermediary, *a.* being, coming or acting between; intermediate; mediatory. *n.* an intermediate agent, a go-between; intermediation. **intermediate, †-medial,** *a.* coming or being between; intervening, interposing. *n.* an intermediate thing. *v.i.*, to act as intermediary; to mediate (between). **Intermediate Nuclear Forces Treaty**, an agreement signed 8 Dec. 1987 between the US and the USSR to eliminate all ground-based nuclear missiles in Europe that were capable of hitting only European targets (including European Russia). It reduced the countries' nuclear arsenals by some 2000 (4% of the total). The treaty included provisions for each country to inspect the other's bases. A total of 1269 weapons (945 Soviet, 234 US) was destroyed in the first year of the treaty. **intermediate technology,** *n.* technology as adapted for the conditions and requirements of developing nations. **intermediately,** *adv.* **-mediateness, -mediation,** *n.* **†intermediacy**, [F *intermédiaire,* from L *intermedius* (*medius,* middle)]

intermedium, *n.* (*pl.* **-media**) an intermediate agent or agency; an intermediate bone of the wrist or ankle.

intermembral, *a.* (*Biol.*) subsisting between members.

interment INTER.

intermezzo, *n.* (*pl.* **-mezzi, -mezzos**) a short dramatic or other entertainment between the acts of a play; a short movement connecting the main divisions of a large musical composition. [It., pop. var. of *intermedio,* L *intermedius,* INTERMEDIARY]

intermigration, *n.* reciprocal migration.

interminable, *a.* endless; tediously protracted. **interminableness,** *n.* **interminably,** *adv.* **†interminate**, *a.* having no limits; (*Alg.*) interminable, as a recurring decimal. [late L *interminābilis* (*termināre,* to TERMINATE)]

intermingle, *v.t.* to mingle together, to intermix. *v.i.* to be mingled (with).

intermit, *v.t.* (*past, p.p.* **intermitted**) to cause to cease for a time; to suspend. *v.i.* to cease or relax at intervals (as a fever, pain etc.). **intermittence, intermission**, *n.* the act or state of intermitting; temporary cessation of a paroxysm; a pause; an interlude; an interval between acts of a play etc.; (*N Am.*) school break; †disuse; †interference. **†intermittent, †intermissive,** *a.* ceasing or relaxing at intervals. *n.* an intermittent fever. **intermittently,** *adv.* [L *intermittere* (*mittere,* to send), p.p. *-missus*]

intermix, *v.t.* to mix together, to intermingle. *v.i.* to be intermingled. **intermixture**, *n.*

intermobility, *n.* capacity (of atoms etc.) to move about among themselves.

intermolecular, *a.* between molecules.

intermundane, *a.* being or existing between worlds.

intermural, *a.* situated between walls. [L *intermūrālis*]

intermuscular, *a.* lying between the muscles.

intermutation, *n.* interchange of elements.

intern, *v.t.* to send to or confine in the interior of a country; to keep under restraint; to confine aliens (in time of war), political opponents, prisoners of war etc. *n.*, (also **interne,** (*N Am.*)) an assistant surgeon or physician resident in a hospital. **internee**, *n.* one who is interned. **internment,** *n.* **internment camp,** *n.* a camp for the internment of aliens in time of war, or of prisoners of war. **internship**, *n.* (*N Am.*). [F *interner,* from L *internus,* INTERNAL]

internal, *a.* situated in the inside; of or pertaining to the inside, inherent, intrinsic; domestic as opp. to foreign; pertaining to the inner being, inward. *n.pl.* the internal organs, the entrails; intrinsic or essential qualities. **internal-combustion engine,** *n.* an engine in which mechanical energy is produced by the combustion or explosion of a mixture of air and gas, oil-vapour etc. in its cylinder. **internal evidence,** *n.* evidence derived from what the thing itself contains. **internality**, *n.* **internalize, -ise,** *v.t.* to assimilate (an idea etc.) into one's outlook, to contain (an emotion) within oneself instead of expressing it. **internally,** *adv.* [med. L *internālis,* from *internus,* inward]

internat., (*abbr.*) international.

international, *a.* pertaining to, subsisting or carried on between, or mutually affecting different nations; known or famous in more than one country; pertaining to the INTERNATIONAL; a person belonging to different nations, as a native or a citizen; a match between two national teams; one who has taken part in such a match. **the International,** *n.* a society (called in full the International Working Men's Association) for promoting the joint political action of the working classes throughout the world. The First International (1862–73) was Marxist in principle; the Second (1889–) was French socialist; the Third (1918–43), also known as the Comintern, was Russian communist. **International Bank for Reconstruction and Development,** official name of the World Bank. **International Brigade**, *n.* international volunteer force on the Republican side in the Spanish Civil War 1936–39. **International Civil Aviation Organization**, agency of the United Nations, established 1947 to regulate safety and efficiency and air law; headquarters Montreal. **International Court of Justice,** the principal judicial organ of the United Nations, inaugurated in 1946. **International Date Line,** a line roughly along the 180th meridian, east and west of which the date is one day different. **International Development Association**, (IDA) an agency of the United Nations, established in 1960, and affiliated to the World Bank. **International Finance Corporation**, United Nations agency affiliated to the World Bank. It was set up in 1956 to facilitate loans for private investment to developing countries. **International Fund for Agricultural Development**, agency of the United Nations, established 1977, to provide funds for benefiting the poor in developing countries. **International Labour Organization,** an independent body established at Geneva at the same time as the League of Nations, with the object of raising the level of the standard of labour conditions throughout the world. **International Maritime Organization**, a United Nations agency concerned with world shipping. Established in 1958, it has its headquarters in London, England. **International Monetary Fund**, (IMF) a specialized agency of the United Nations, headquarters Washington DC, established under the 1944 Bretton Woods agreement and operational since 1947. It seeks to promote international monetary cooperation and the growth of world trade, and to smooth multilateral payment arrangements among member states. IMF stand-by loans are available to members in balance of payments difficulties (the amount being governed by the member's quota), usually on the basis of acceptance of instruction on stipulated corrective measures. **International Phonetic Alphabet,** a series of symbols intended to give an accurate representation of human speech sounds. **international law,** *n.* an accepted system of laws or jurisprudence regulating intercourse between nations. **Internationale**, *n.* the French socialist hymn adopted by the International. **internationalism,** *n.* the promotion of community of interests between nations; the principles or objects advocated by the Internationalists. **internationalist,** *n.* an advocate of internationalism; a member of the International; one versed in international law. **internationality**, *n.* **internationalize, -ise,** *v.t.* to make international; to bring under the joint protection or control of different nations. **internationalization, -lisation,** *n.* **internationally,** *adv.*

interne, *n.* an intern.

internecine, *a.* deadly, destructive; mutually destructive. †**internecive**, *a.* [L *internecīnus* (*necāre,* to kill)]

internee INTERN.

interneural, *a.* situated between two nerves or neural processes; applied to the spines supporting the rays of the dorsal fin of fishes.

internment INTERN.

internode, *n.* (*Anat.*) a part between two nodes or joints; a part of a stem between two nodes or leaf-knots. **internodal**, *a.*

internuncio, *n.* (*pl.* **-cios**) a messenger between two parties; an ambassador of the Pope sent to a court when there is no nuncio present or to minor states; an envoy or minister representing a government. **internuncial,** *a.* pertaining to an internuncio or his functions; (*Physiol.*) communicating between different parts (as nerves). [It. *internunzio,* L *internuntius* (*nuntius,* see NUNCIO)]

interoceanic, *a.* situated between or connecting two oceans.

interoceptive, *a.* of or being stimuli developing inside the viscera.

interocular, *a.* situated between the eyes.

interorbital, *a.* situated between the orbits of the eyes.

interosseal, -sseous, *a.* situated between bones.

interpage, *v.t.* to insert pages between other pages (in a book); to insert on intermediate pages.

interparietal, *a.* situated between the parietal bones of the skull. *n.* an interparietal bone, esp. in fishes.

interpellate, *v.t.* to interrogate, esp. to interrupt discussion etc. in order to demand a statement or explanation from (a minister). **interpellant,** *n., a.* **interpellation,** *n.* **interpellator,** *n.* [L *interpellātus* (*pellāre,* var. of *pellere,* to drive)]

interpenetrate, *v.t.* to penetrate thoroughly, to permeate; to penetrate (each other). *v.i.* to penetrate each other. **interpenetration,** *n.* **interpenetrative,** *a.*

interpetiolar, *a.* situated between petioles.

interpilaster, *n.* the space between two pilasters.

interplanetary, *a.* pertaining to the regions between the planets.

interplay, *n.* reciprocal action between parts or things.

interplead, *v.i.* to take legal proceedings in order to discuss and determine an incidental issue. **interpleader**, *n.* a suit by which the claims of two parties to money or property are determined, in order that a third party, on whom the claim is made, may know to which party payment is due. [A-F *enterpleder*]

†**interpledge,** *v.t.* to pledge mutually.

interpleural, *a.* situated between the pleurae of the right and left lungs.

Interpol, *n.* the *Inter*national Criminal *Pol*ice Commission, that ensures cooperation between police forces in the suppression and detection of crime.

interpolar, *a.* situated between the poles (of a galvanic battery etc.).

interpolate, *v.t.* to insert (esp. a spurious word or passage) in (a book or document); to insert or intercalate; to alter or corrupt; (*Math.*) to introduce (intermediate terms) in a series. *v.i.* to make interpolations. **interpolation,** *n.* the act of interpolating; that which is interpolated; (*Math.*) the operation of finding terms (conformable to the law of the series) between any two consecutive terms of a series. **interpolator,** *n.* [L *interpolātus,* p.p. of *interpolāre* (*polāre,* rel. to *polīre,* to POLISH)]

interpose, *v.t.* to place between or among; to put forward (as an objection, veto, obstruction etc.) by way of intervention or interference. *v.i.* to intervene, to intercede, to mediate between; to remark by way of interruption, to interrupt. **interposal,** *n.* **interposer,** *n.* **interposition**, *n.* the act of interposing; intervention, mediation; that which is interposed. [F *interposer*]

interpret, *v.t.* to explain the meaning of; to translate from one language into another; to expound, to make intelligible; to find out the meaning of, to construe or understand (in a particular way); to represent the meaning of, or one's idea of, artistically. *v.i.* to act as an interpreter. **interpretable,** *a.* **interpretation,** *n.* **interpretative**, *a.* **interpretatively,** *adv.* **interpreter,** *n.* one who interprets, esp. one employed to translate orally to persons speaking a foreign language. **interpretership,** *n.* **interpretress**, *n. fem.* [F *interpréter,* L *interpretārī,* from *interpres -pretis* (*-pret-,* cogn. with Sansk. *prath-,* to spread abroad)]

interprovincial, *a.* existing, carried on etc., between different provinces.

interpubic, *a.* situated between the right and left pubic bones.

interpunctuate, *v.t.* to insert the punctuation marks in or between. **interpunctuation,** †**interpunction,** *n.*

interracial, *a.* between different races.

interradial, *a.* (*Zool.*) situated between the radii or rays. *n.* an interradial part (in a crinoid). **interradially,** *adv.* **interradius**, *n.* (*pl.* **-dii**) an interradial part (as in an echinoderm).

interradiate, *v.i.* to radiate into each other. **interradiation,** *n.*

interramal, *a.* (*Ornith.*) situated between two rami or branches, as of the lower jaw.

interregnum, *n.* (*pl.* **-nums, -na**) the period between two reigns, ministries or governments; a suspension or interruption of normal authority, succession etc.; an interval, a pause. †**interregnal,** *a.* †**interreign**, *n.* [L (*regnum,* REIGN)]

interrelation, *n.* mutual relation. **interrelationship,** *n.*

interrex, *n.* (*pl.* **interreges**) one who governs during an interregnum; a regent. [L *rex,* king]

interrog., (*abbr.*) interrogative.

interrogate, *v.t.* to put questions to; to examine in a formal manner. *v.i.* to ask questions. **interrogable,** *a.* †**interrogant,** *n.* an interrogator. **interrogation,** *n.* the act of interrogating; a question put; (*Gram.*) the sign (?) marking a question. **interrogational,** *a.* **interrogative,** *a.* denoting a question; expressed in the form or having the character of a question. *n.* (*Gram.*) a word used in asking questions. **interrogatively,** *adv.* **interrogator,** *n.* **interrogatory**, *a.* interrogative. *n.* a question; an inquiry; (*Law*) a question or set of questions put formally to a defendant etc. [L *interrogātus,* p.p. of *interrogāre* (*rogāre,* to ask)]

interrupt, *v.t.* to stop or obstruct by breaking in upon; to break the continuity of; to cause a break or gap in; to obstruct (a view etc.); (*coll.*) to disturb. *v.i.* to make interruption. †*a.* interrupted. †*n.* a gap, a chasm. **interruptedly,** *adv.* **interrupter,** *n.* **interruptible,** *a.* **interruption,** *n.* **interruptive, -tory,** *a.* **interruptively,** *adv.* [L *interruptus,* p.p. of *interrumpere* (*rumpere,* to break)]

interscapular, *a.* situated between the shoulder blades. *n.* an interscapular feather.

intersecant, *a.* intersecting. *n.pl.* intersecting lines.

intersect, *v.t.* to pass or cut across; to divide by cutting or passing across. *v.i.* to cut or cross each other. **intersection**, *n.* the act or state of intersecting;, a crossroads; (*Geom.*) the point or line in which two lines or planes cut each other. **intersectional,** *a.* [L *intersectus,* p.p. of *intersecāre* (*secāre,* to cut)]

intersegmental, *a.* situated between two segments.

interseptal, *a.* situated between or pertaining to septa or partitions. [L *intersaeptum,* a partition, the diaphragm, -AL]

intersex, *n.* an individual developing certain characters of the opposite sex. **intersexual,** *a.* intermediate in sexual characters between male and female. **intersexuality**, *n.* **intersexually,** *adv.*

intersidereal, *a.* interstellar.

interspace¹, *n.* intervening space; an interval between two things or occurrences. **interspatial,** *a.* **interspatially,** *adv.*

interspace², *v.t.* to put a space or spaces between; to fill the intervals between.

interspecific, *a.* subsisting between different species.

intersperse, *v.t.* to scatter here and there (among etc.); †to diversify or variegate (with scattered objects, colours etc.). **interspersion,** *n.* [L *interspersus,* p.p. of *interspergere* (*spargere,* to scatter)]

interspinal, -spinous, *a.* situated between spines or spinal processes.

interstate, *a.* (*N Am.*) subsisting, maintained or carried on between states. **The Interstate Commerce Act,** in US history, an act of Congress in 1887 responding to public concern regarding alleged profiteering and malpractice by railroad companies. It required all charges to be reasonable and fair, and established the Interstate Commerce Commission to investigate railroad management. The act proved difficult to enforce. **Interstate Commerce Commission,** *n.* US authority which regulates all traffic between states. ICC regulations cover routes, services, bills of lading, mergers, and rates charged to users.

interstellar, -ary, *a.* situated between or passing through the regions between the stars.

interstice, *n.* a space, opening, crevice etc., between things near together or between the component parts of a body. **interstitial,** *a.* of, pertaining to, occupying or forming interstices. [MF, from L *interstitium,* from *intersistere* (*sistere,* to place, causal from *stāre,* to stand)]

interstratify, *v.t.* (*usu. in p.p.*) (*Geol.*) to stratify between or among other strata. **interstratification,** *n.*

intertarsal, *a.* situated between the bones of the ankle.

intertergal, *a.* situated between the terga or tergites of an arthropod.

intertidal, *a.* situated between the low-water and high-water marks.

intertie, *n.* a horizontal timber framed between two posts to tie them together; a binding joist.

intertransverse, *a.* situated between the transverse processes of the vertebrae.

intertribal, *a.* occurring or carried on between different tribes.

intertrigo, *n.* (*pl.* **-gos**) inflammation of the skin through the rubbing of two parts together. [L *interterīgo* (*terere,* to rub)]

intertropical, *a.* situated within or between the tropics. **intertropics,** *n.pl.*

intertwine, *v.t.* to entwine or twist together. *v.i.* to be twisted together. *n.* an intertwinement. **intertwinement,** *n.* an intertwining. **intertwiningly,** *adv.*

intertwist, *v.t.* to twist together. **intertwistingly,** *adv.*

interunion, *n.* reciprocal union.

interurban, *a.* between cities.

interval, *n.* intermediate space, distance or time; a break, a gap; a pause or interlude; the extent of difference between two things, persons etc.; the difference of pitch between two sounds; the break between scenes or acts of a play etc.; (*N Am.*) an intervale. *v.t.* to separate or interrupt at intervals. **at intervals,** from time to time; with spaces in between. **intervallic,** *a.* †**intervallum,** *n.* (*pl.* **-lla**) an interval. [OF *intervalle, entreval,* L *intervallum,* the space between palisades or ramparts (*vallum,* rampart)]

intervale, *a.* (*N Am.*) a tract of low or plain ground between hills or along the banks of rivers. [var. of prec., assim. to VALE]

interveined, *a.* intersected as with veins.

intervene, *v.i.* to come in as an extraneous feature or thing; to come or be situated (between); to occur between points of time or events; to happen or break in so as to interrupt or disturb, to interfere, to interpose; to practise intervention. **intervener,** *n.* one who intervenes, esp. in a law-suit. **intervenient,** *a.* **intervention,** *n.* the act of intervening; violating a sovereign state's independence by interfering in its domestic or external affairs; the practice of the EEC of buying and storing surplus products when the market price is low; the action of a central bank in buying large quantities of a currency in order to prevent its international value from falling. **interventionism,** *n.* **interventionist,** *n.* [L *intervenīre* (*venīre,* to come), p.p. *interventus*]

interventricular, *a.* situated between the ventricles (of the heart or the brain).

intervertebral, *a.* situated between vertebrae.

interview, *n.* a meeting between two persons face to face; a conference; a formal meeting between some person and a press representative employed to obtain information or opinions for publication; the article describing this or recording the result; a meeting in which an employer questions a candidate for a job in order to test the candidate's suitability. *v.t.* to have an interview with, esp. in order to obtain matter for publication or to test a candidate's suitability for a post. **interviewee,** *n.* **interviewer,** *n.* [OF *entrevue,* from *entrevoir* (*voir,* L *vidēre,* to see)]

intervisible, *a.* said of two surveying stations, each of which is visible from the other.

intervocal, *a.* occurring between vowels. **intervocalic,** *a.*

intervolve, *v.t.* to involve or wind one (thing) within another. [L *volvere,* to roll]

interwar, *a.* occurring in the period between World Wars I and II.

interweave, *v.t.* (*p.p.* **-woven**) to weave together; to blend or mingle closely together.

interwind, *v.t.* to wind together.

interwork, *v.t.* (*past, p.p.* **-wrought, -worked**) to work things together or into each other. *v.i.* to work reciprocally, to interact.

interzonal, *a.* between zones in occupied territory.

intestacy, *n.* lack of a will or testament.

intestate, *a.* dying without having made a will; not disposed of by will. *n.* an intestate person. †**intestable,** *a.* legally incompetent to make a will or benefit by one. [L *intestātus* (*testātus,* p.p. of *testārī,* to witness, to make a will)]

intestine, *a.* internal, domestic, not foreign; civil, †innate. *n.* (*usu. pl.*) the long membranous tube from the stomach to the anus; the bowels, the guts. **intestinal,** *a.* pertaining to the intestines. **intestinally,** *adv.* [L *intestīnus,* from *intus,* within]

inthral, etc. ENTHRAL.

Intifada, *n.* Palestinian uprising; also the title of the involved Liberation Army of Palestine, a loosely organized group of adult and teenage Palestinians active since 1987 in attacks on Israeli troops in the occupied territories of Palestine. Their campaign for self-determination includes stone-throwing and petrol bombing. Measures taken by the Israeli government to prevent violence include fining parents of stone-throwing children up to $2000. [Arab.]

intil, *prep.* (*Sc.*) into.

intimate¹, *v.t.* to make known, to announce; to signify, to indicate, to hint. **intimation,** *n.* [late L *intimātus,* p.p. of *intimāre,* from *intimus,* within]

intimate², *a.* close in friendship or fellowship; familiar, confidential; private, personal; having an atmosphere conducive to close personal relationships; pertaining to one's inner being; adhering closely; internal, inward; having sexual relations. †*n.* a familiar friend or associate. **intimacy,** *n.* **intimately,** *adv.* [as prec.]

intimidate, *v.t.* to frighten, to make fearful, to dishearten, to cow; to deter (from an action or doing). **intimidation,** *n.* **intimidator,** *n.* **intimidatory,** *a.* [med. L *intimidātus,* p.p. of *intimidāre* (*timidus,* TIMID)]

intimity, *n.* the quality of being intimate; inwardness; privacy. [F *intimité,* from *intime,* L *intimus,* inmost]

intinction, *n.* the method of administering the Eucharist by dipping the bread in the wine. [late L *intinctio,* from *intingere* (*tinguere,* to moisten)]

intituled, *a.* chiefly of Acts of Parliament, having a specified name or title, entitled. [F *intitulé,* L *intitulāre,* to ENTITLE]

into, *prep.* expressing motion or direction towards the interior, or change from one state to another; entrance; penetration; insertion; inclusion or comprehension; (*sl.*) very keen on; indicating the dividend in division. [OE *in to* (IN, adv., TO)]

intoed, *a.* having the toes turned inwards.

intolerable, *a.* not tolerable, unendurable; †enormous, monstrous, extreme. **intolerableness,** *n.* **intolerably,** *adv.* [F, from L *intolerābilis*]

intolerant, *a.* not tolerant (of); not enduring or allowing difference of opinion, teaching or worship; bigoted. *n.* one who is intolerant, a bigot. **intolerance, intoleration,** *n.* **intolerantly,** *adv.* [F, from L *intolerantem,* nom. *-ans*]

†intomb, ENTOMB.

intone, *v.i.* to recite or chant prayers etc. in a monotone; to give a musical tone to one's delivery. *v.t.* to recite or chant in a monotone. **intonate,** *v.i.* to sound the notes of the musical scale; to intone. *v.t.* to intone. **intonation,** *n.* modulation of the voice, accent; intoning; the opening phrase of a plain-song melody, usu. sung by a priest or chorister; the mode of producing sound from a voice or an instrument, esp. as regards correctness of pitch. [med. L *intonāre* (*in tonum,* in tone (*tonus,* TONE))]

intort, *v.t.* to twist, to twine, to involve. **intorsion, -tion,** *n.* a winding, bending or twisting; the twisting of any part of a plant upon itself. [L *intortus,* p.p. of *intorquere* (*torquere,* to twist)]

in toto, *adv.* completely.

intoxicate, *v.t.* to make drunk; to excite to enthusiasm; to make delirious, as with joy; (*Med.*) to poison. †*a.* intoxicated, delirious. **intoxicant,** *n., a.* **†intoxicatedly,** *adv.* **intoxicating,** *a.* tending to intoxicate. **intoxicatingly,** *adv.* **intoxication,** *n.* the act of intoxicating; the state of being intoxicated; excitement, elation. [med. L *intoxicātus,* p.p. of *intoxicāre,* to smear with poison *toxicāre,* from *toxicum,* Gr. *toxikon,* from *toxa,* arrows)]

intra-, *pref.* within, on the inside. **intra-abdominal,** *a.* situated inside the abdomen. **intra-arterial,** *a.* occurring within an artery. **intra-capsular,** *a.* situated or occurring inside a capsule. **intra-cardiac, -cardial,** *a.* situated or occurring inside the heart. **intracellular,** *a.* situated or occurring in a cell. [L *intrā,* within]

intracommunity, *a.* situated or occurring inside the European Economic Community (EEC).

intractable, *a.* unmanageable, indocile, refractory. **intractability, -ableness,** *n.* **intractably,** *adv.* [F, from L *intractābilis*]

intrados, *n.* (*pl.* **intrados, intradoses**) the under surface or curve of an arch (cp. EXTRADOS). [F (*dos,* the back)]

intramundane, *a.* existing within this world or the material world.

intramural, *a.* situated or happening within the walls or boundaries, as of a city, town, institution etc.; situated or occurring within the walls of an organ etc.

intransigent, *a.* irreconcilable; uncompromising, obdurate, inflexible. *n.* an irreconcilable; an uncompromising adherent of any creed (political, artistic etc.). **intransigency, intransigentism,** *n.* **intransigentist,** *n.* **intransigently,** *adv.* [F *intransigeant,* Sp. *intransigente* (L *transigens -entem,* pres.p. of *transigere,* to come to an understanding, to TRANSACT)]

intransitive, *a.* not passing on or over; (*Gram.*) denoting action confined to the agent. *n.* an intransitive verb. **intransitively,** *adv.* **intransitiveness, intransitivity,** *n.* [L *intransitīvus* (TRANSITIVE)]

intransmissible, *a.* not transmissible.

†intransmutable, *a.* not transmutable. **intransmutability,** *n.*

intrant, *n.* one who enters on a duty, property etc., esp. one who enters a college, society etc. [L *intrans -entem,* pres.p. of *intrāre,* to ENTER]

intranuclear, *a.* situated within the nucleus of a cell.

intra-ocular lens, *n.* an artificial lens implanted into the eye after the removal of the natural lens, as in cataract surgery etc.

intraparietal, *a.* situated or occurring within walls, private; situated within the walls of an organ, esp. within the parietal lobe of the brain.

intrapreneur, *n.* one who initiates or manages a new business or division within an existing firm. **intrapreneurial,** *a.* **intrapreneurship,** *n.*

intraspecific, *a.* relating to the internal development of a species.

intratelluric, *a.* occurring, existing or formed in the interior of the earth.

intratropical, *a.* situated or happening within the tropics.

intra-urban, *a.* existing or carried on within a city.

intrauterine, *a.* situated inside the uterus. **intrauterine device,** *n.* a metal or plastic coil, loop or ring, placed in the uterus to prevent conception.

intravascular, *a.* situated or occurring within a vessel, esp. a blood-vessel.

intravenous, *a.* into a vein or veins. **intravenously,** *adv.*

intrepid, *a.* fearless, brave, bold. **intrepidity,** *n.* **intrepidly,** *adv.* [L *intrepidus* (TREPID)]

intricate, *a.* entangled, involved, complicated; obscure. **intricacy,** *n.* **intricately,** *adv.* [L *intricātus,* p.p. of *intricāre* (*tricae,* hindrances, wiles)]

intrigant, *n.* an intriguer. **intrigante,** *n. fem.* [F *intriguant, -nte,* pres.p. of *intriguer,* see foll.]

intrigue, *v.i.* to carry on a plot or scheme to effect some object by underhand means; to carry on a secret love affair. *v.t.* to perplex; to fascinate; †to render intricate. *n.,* the act of intriguing; a plot to effect some object by underhand means; secret love; a liaison. **intriguer,** *n.* **†intriguery,** *n.* **intriguingly,** *adv.* [F *intriguer,* It. *intrigare,* L *intricāre,* see INTRICATE]

†intrince, †intrinse, *a.* (*Shak.*) intricate. [prob. from INTRINSICATE]

intrinsic, †-ical, *a.* inward, inherent; belonging to the nature of a thing; essential; genuine, real; †intimate, familiar. **intrinsically,** *adv.* [F *intrinsèque,* L *intrinsecus* (INTRA-, *secus,* following, rel. to *secundus,* SECOND[1] *sequī,* to follow)]

†intrinsicate, †-secate, *a.* (*Shak.*) entangled, perplexed. [perh. from It. *intrinsecato,* familiar, confused with *intricato,* INTRICATE]

intro, *n.* (*pl.* **intros**) (*coll.*) introduction.

intro-, *pref.* in, into; inward. [L *intrō,* to the inside, rel. to *intrā,* in]

intro-active, *a.* acting internally; acting upon itself.

introcession, *n.* (*Path.*) a going inwards or shrinking of parts. [CESSION (after L *intrōcēdere,* to go in, from *cēdere,* to go)]

introduce, *v.t.* to bring or lead in; to usher in; to insert; to bring into use or notice; to cause (a person) to discover; to make known, esp. (a person) in a formal way (to another); to bring before the public; to bring out into society; to bring before Parliament; to preface; to present (a programme etc.); †to occasion; to induce. **introducer,** *n.* **introduction,** *n.* the act of introducing; formal presentation of a person to another; a preface or preliminary discourse; an elementary treatise. **letter of introduction,** a letter introducing a friend to a third person. **introductive, -tory,** *a.* **introductively, -torily,** *adv.* [L *intrōdūcere* (*dūcere,* to lead), p.p. *introductus*]

introflexed, *a.* (*Bot.*) bent inwards.

†introgression, *n.* entrance. [L *intrōgressus,* p.p. of *intrōgredī* (*gradī,* to walk)]

introit, *n.* a psalm or antiphon sung or recited as the priest approaches the altar to begin the Mass. [F *introït,* L *introitus,* from *introīre,* to enter (*īre,* to go)]

introject, *v.t.* to assimilate unconsciously into one's personality. **introjection,** *n.*

intromit, *v.t.* (*past, p.p.* **intromitted**) to send in; to admit, to allow to enter; to insert. *v.i.* (*Sc. Law*) to intermeddle (with another's property). **intromission,** *n.* **intromittent,** *a.* [L *intrōmittere* (*mittere,* to send), p.p. *intrōmissus*]

intron, *n.* a section of a nucleic acid not coding information for protein synthesis.

introrse, *a.* (*Bot.*) turned towards the axis. [L *introrsus,* adv., from *introversus* (*versus,* towards)]

introspect, *v.t.* to look into or within; to examine one's own mind and its working. **introspection,** *n.* **introspectionist,** *n.* one who introspects; one who employs introspection as a psychological instrument. **introspective,** *a.* **introspectively,** *adv.* **introspectiveness,** *n.* [L *intrōspectus,* p.p. of *intrōspicere* (*specere,* to look)]

introsusception, *n.* the act of taking or receiving in or within, †intussusception. [L *susceptio,* from *suscipere* (SUS-, *capere,* to take)]

introvert¹, *v.t.* to turn inwards; to turn (the mind or thoughts) inwards; to turn (an organ or a part) in upon itself; to turn inside out; (*Pros. etc.*) to invert (verses etc.). **introversible,** *a.* **introversion,** *n.* [L *intrōvertere* (*vertere,* to turn)]

introvert², *n.* a part or organ that is introverted or introversible; a person who is interested chiefly in his or her own mental processes and standing with other people, this making the person shy and unsociable (cp EXTROVERT). **introversive, -vertive,** *a.*

intrude, *v.t.* to thrust or force (into); to force in (volcanic rock etc.) into sedimentary strata; †to invade. *v.i.* to thrust oneself or force one's way (into); to force oneself (upon others); to enter without invitation; †to encroach. **intruder,** *n.* [L *intrūdere* (*trūdere,* to thrust)]

intrusion, *n.* the act of intruding; an encroachment; (*Geol.*) the penetration of volcanic rocks into sedimentary strata; (*Law*) unlawful entry by a stranger upon lands or tenements, invasion, usurpation; the settlement of a minister in the Scottish Church in opposition to the wishes of the congregation. **†intrusionist,** *n.* in the Scottish Church, one who favoured settlement of a minister in a church or congregation without the consent of the congregation.

intrusive, *a.* tending to intrude; entering without invitation or welcome. **intrusive rocks,** *n.pl.* igneous rocks which have forced their way into sedimentary strata. **intrusively,** *adv.* **intrusiveness,** *n.*

intrust, ENTRUST.

intubate, *v.t.* to insert a tube into (the larynx), as in a case of diphtheria. **intubation,** *n.* **intubator,** *n.* an instrument for inserting a tube thus. [L *tuba,* TUBE, -ATE]

intuition, *n.* immediate perception by the mind without reasoning; the power of the mind for such perception; instinctive knowledge; a truth so perceived; †the action of looking upon, a sight. **intuit,** *v.t.* to know by intuition. *v.i.* to acquire knowledge by means of intuition. **intuitional,** *a.* **intuitionalism,** *n.* the doctrine that the perception of truth, or of certain truths, is by intuition. **intuitionalist,** *n.* **intuitionism,** *n.* intuitionalism; an extreme form of this held by Reid and other Scottish philosophers, that the objects of sense-perception are known intuitively as real. **intuitionist,** *n.* **intuitive,** *a.* perceived by intuition; perceiving by intuition; seeing immediately and clearly. **intuitively,** *adv.* **intuitiveness,** *n.* **intuitivism,** *n.* the doctrine that ideas of right and wrong are intuitive. [F, from med. L *intuitiōnem,* nom. *-tio,* from *intuērī* (*tuērī,* to look)]

intumesce, *v.i.* to swell up, to become tumid; to enlarge or expand by heat. **intumescence,** *n.* **intumescent,** *a.* [L *intumescere* (*tumescere,* incept. of *tumēre,* to become tumid)]

inturn, *n.* an inward turn, bend, step etc. **inturned,** *a.*

intussuscept, *v.t.* (*Path.*) to receive within itself or another part; to invaginate. **intussusception,** *n.* reception within; the taking in of anything (as of ideas into the mind); the reception of foreign matter (as food) by an organism and its conversion into living tissue; the accidental insertion or protrusion of an upper segment of the bowels into a lower. **intussusceptive,** *a.* [L *intus,* within, *susceptus,* p.p. of *suscipere* (SUS-, *capere,* to take)]

intwine, ENTWINE.

intwist, ENTWIST.

inuendo, INNUENDO.

Inuit INNUIT.

Inula, *n.* a genus of Compositae comprising the elecampane. **inulinaceous,** *a.* [L, elecampane]

inulin, *n.* a soluble, white starchy powder, obtained from the roots of elecampane and other Compositae.

inunction, *n.* anointing or smearing with ointment, oil etc. [L *inunctio,* from *inunguere* (*unguere,* to ANOINT)]

inundate, *v.t.* to overflow, to flood; to submerge, to deluge; to overwhelm. **†inundant,** *a.* overflowing. **inundation,** *n.* a flood, a deluge. [L *inundātus,* p.p. of *inundāre* (*unda,* a wave)]

inurbane, *a.* discourteous, rude, unpolished. **inurbanely,** *adv.* **†inurbanity,** *n.* [L *inurbānus*]

inure, *v.t.* to use or practise habitually; to accustom, to habituate, to harden (to); †to exercise; to practise. *v.i.* (*Law*) to come into operation; to take or have effect. **inurement,** *n.* practice, use, habit. [ME *enuren,* to habituate (*en-,* in, *ure,* to use, from OF *euvre,* habit, work, L *opera,* works)]

inurn, *v.t.* to place in a cinerary urn; to bury.

†inusitate, *a.* unusual; out of use. † **inusitation,** *n.* disuse. [L *inūsitātus* (*ūsitātus,* p.p. of *ūsitāri,* freq. of *ūtī,* to USE)]

in utero, in the uterus. [L]

inutile, *a.* useless. **inutility,** *n.* [L *inūtilis* (*ūtilis,* useful)]

inutterable, UNUTTERABLE.

in vacuo, in a vacuum. [L]

invade, *v.t.* to enter (a country) as an enemy; to enter by force; to assail; to encroach on, to violate. *v.i.* to make an invasion. **invader,** *n.* [F *invader,* L *invādere* (*vādere,* to go)]

invaginate, *v.t.* to put into or as into a sheath; to introvert or turn (a tubular sheath) upon itself. **invaginable,** *a.* **invagination,** *n.* [L *vagīna,* a sheath, -ATE]

invalid¹, *a.* of no force, weight or cogency; null. **invalidate,** *v.t.* to weaken or destroy the validity of, to render not valid; to overthrow. **invalidation,** *n.* **invalidator,** *n.* **invalidity, invalidness,** *n.* **invalidly,** *adv.* [L *invalidus*]

invalid², *a.* infirm or disabled through ill-health or injury. *n.* an infirm or disabled person. *v.t.* to disable by illness or injury; to register or discharge as unfit for military or naval duty on account of illness etc. *v.i.* to become an invalid; to be enrolled as such. **invalidism,** *n.* chronic ill health, esp. neurotic. **invalidity,** *n.* **invalidity pension, benefit,** *n.* money paid by the government to someone who is chronically ill or disabled. [as prec.]

Invalides, Hôtel des, a building in Paris, S of the Seine, founded in 1670 as a home for disabled soldiers. The church Dôme des Invalides contains the tomb of Napoleon I. The military government of Paris has its headquarters at Les Invalides.

invaluable, *a.* precious above estimation; priceless. **invaluably,** *adv.*

Invar®, *n.* a nickel-steel alloy with small coefficient of expansion.

invariable, *a.* not variable, uniform; not liable to change; (*Math.*) fixed, constant. *n.* (*Math.*) a constant quantity. **invariability, -ableness,** *n.* **invariably,** *adv.* **invariant,** *a.* not varying or subject to variation. *n.* (*Math.*) that which remains fixed and unchanged though its constituents may vary. **†invaried,** *a.* unvaried; invariable. [F]

invasion, *n.* the act of invading; a hostile attack upon or entrance into the territory of others; infringement, violation; the approach or assault of anything dangerous or pernicious. **invasive,** *a.* [F, from L *invāsiōnem,* nom. *-sio,* from *invādere,* to INVADE]

invecked, invected, *a.* (*Her.*) bordered by a line of convex arcs or scallops; of a border-line, curved in this way, opp. to *engrailed.* [L *invectus,* as foll.]

invective, *n.* a violent expression of censure or abuse; vituperation. *a.* abusive. **invectively,** *adv.* [F, from late L *invectīva,* fem. adj. from *invectus,* p.p. of *invehere,* see foll.]

inveigh, *v.t.* to utter or make use of invectives; to declaim censoriously and abusively (against). **inveigher,** *n.* [L *invehī,* to attack, to abuse, refl. of *vehere* (*vehere,* to carry)]

inveigle, *v.t.* to seduce, to wheedle, to entrap (into an action, fault etc.). **inveiglement,** *n.* **inveigler,** *n.* [prob. from F *aveugler* (altered to *enveoglir*), to blind, from *aveugle,* low L *aboculum,* nom. *-lus* (AB-[1], *oculus,* eye)]

invent, *v.t.* to devise or contrive (a new means, instrument etc.); to concoct, to fabricate; †to meet with; †to discover. †**inventful,** *a.* †**inventible,** *a.* **invention,** *n.* the act of inventing; the production of something new; the faculty or power of inventing, inventiveness; that which is invented, a contrivance; a fabrication, a fiction, a scheme; a discovery, a finding; a short piece of music, usu. in double counterpoint. **Invention of the Cross,** the finding of the true Cross by Helena, the mother of Constantine the Great, AD 326; the festival (3 May) commemorating this. **inventive,** *a.* quick at contrivance; able to invent; ready at expedients, ingenious; imaginative; characterized by creative skill. **inventively,** *adv.* **inventiveness,** *n.* **inventor,** *n.* **inventress,** *n. fem.* [F *inventer,* L *inventus,* p.p. of *invenīre,* to find, to invent (*venīre,* to come)]

inventory, *n.* a detailed list or catalogue of goods and chattels; the articles enumerated in such a list; (*chiefly N Am.*) the quantity or value of a firm's current assets in terms of raw materials and stock; these assets individually; the material in a nuclear reactor. *v.t.* to enter in an inventory; to make a list, catalogue or schedule of. **inventorial,** *a.* **inventorially,** *adv.* [med. L *inventōrium,* from *inventus,* as prec.]

inveracity, *n.* untruthfulness.

Invergordon Mutiny, *n.* incident in the British Atlantic Fleet, Cromarty Firth, Scotland, 15 Sept. 1931. Ratings refused to prepare the ships for sea following the government's cuts in their pay; the cuts were consequently modified.

Inverness, *n.* town in Highland region, Scotland, lying in a sheltered site at the mouth of the Ness; population (1985) 58,000. A tourist centre with tweed, tanning, engineering, and distilling industries. **Inverness cape,** *n.* a kind of sleeveless cloak with a cape hanging loosely over the shoulders.

Inverness-shire, *n.* largest of the former Scottish counties, it was merged in Highland region 1975.

inverse, *a.* opposite in order or relation; contrary, inverted. *n.* that which is inverted; the direct opposite of; (*Math.*) the result of inversion. **inverse proportion, ratio,** *n.* (*Math.*) the ratio of the reciprocals of two quantities. **inversely,** *adv.* [F *inverse,* L *inversus,* as INVERT]

inversion, *n.* the act of inverting; reversal of order, place or relation; (*Gram.*) reversal of the natural order of words in a sentence; (*Mus.*) the process or result of altering or reversing the relative position of the elements of a chord etc.; the rearrangement of molecular structure taking place when starch, dextrin or sugar is boiled with a dilute acid; the overturning of strata by igneous agency; (*Math.*) the operation of changing the order of the terms, so that the antecedent takes the place of the consequent and the reverse in both ratios; the assumption of the characteristics of the other sex; a military movement by which the order of companies in line is inverted. **inversive,** *a.*

invert[1], *v.t.* to turn upside down; to place in a contrary position or order; to reverse; to transpose (a chord, interval, part for a voice etc.); †to divert. **inverted commas** QUOTATION MARKS. **invertedly,** *adv.* **inverter, -tor,** *n.* a device that converts direct current into alternating current. **invertible,** *a.* [L *invertere* (*vertere,* to turn)]

invert[2], *n.* an inverted arch, esp. such as forms the bottom of a sewer etc.; one with inverted sexual instincts, a homosexual. **invert sugar,** *n.* a mixture of laevulose and dextrose. **invertase,** *n.* an enzyme able to convert sucrose into invert sugar. **invertend,** *n.* (*Log.*) a proposition from which another is derived by inversion.

invertebrate, *a.* destitute of a backbone or vertebral column; lacking strength or firmness. *n.* an invertebrate animal; an irresolute person. †**invertebral,** †**invertebrated,** *a.* **Invertebrata,** *n.pl.* a former subdivision of the animal kingdom, containing animals without a vertebral column.

invest, *v.t.* to clothe (with or in); to cover (with or as with a garment); to clothe or endue (with office, authority, dignity etc.); to surround, beleaguer, besiege; to employ (money in remunerative property, business, stocks etc.); to devote (effort etc.) to a project etc. for future rewards; †to give, to bestow. *v.i.* to make an investment; (*coll.*) to spend money (as in a small purchase). **investable,** *a.* **investive,** *a.* **investment,** *n.* the act of laying out money; money invested; that in which money is invested; the act of surrounding or besieging; investiture; †clothing, covering. **investment trust,** *n.* a financial enterprise which invests its subscribers' capital in securities and distributes the net return among them. **investor,** *n.* [F *investir,* L *investīre* (*vestīre,* to clothe)]

investigate, *v.t.* to search or trace out; to examine or inquire into closely. *v.i.* to research or make investigation. †**investigable,** *a.* **investigation,** *n.* **investigative, -gatory,** *a.* **investigator,** *n.* [L *investigātus,* p.p. of *investīgāre* (*vestigāre,* to track, see VESTIGE)]

investiture, *n.* the act of investing, esp. the ceremonial of investing (with office, rank etc.); the state of being invested; that with which one is invested or endued; (*Feudal Law*) the open delivery of possession. [F, from med. L *investītūra,* from *investīre,* to INVEST]

investment INVEST.

inveterate, *a.* long-established; firmly established by long continuance, deeply-rooted, obstinate, confirmed by long use; habitual; determinedly settled in a habit; †malignant, virulent. †*v.t.,* to establish firmly by long continuance. **inveteracy, inveterateness,** *n.* **inveterately,** *adv.* †**inveteration,** *n.* [L *inveterātus,* p.p. of *inveterāre* (*vetus veteris,* old)]

invexed, *a.* (*Her.*) arched or concave. [late L *invexus,* L *invectus,* p.p. of *invehere* (*vehere,* to carry)]

invidious, *a.* tending to incur or provoke envy or ill-will; likely to give offence; offending through real or apparent unfairness or injustice; †envious; †enviable. **invidiously,** *adv.* **invidiousness,** *n.* [L *invidiōsus,* from *invidia,* ENVY]

invigilate, *v.i.* to keep a watch over students during an examination. *v.t.* to supervise. **invigilation,** *n.* **invigilator,** *n.* [L *invigilātus,* p.p. of *invigilāre* (*vigilāre,* to watch, see VIGIL)]

invigorate, *v.t.* to give vigour or strength to; to animate, to encourage. **invigorant,** *a.* **invigoratingly,** *adv.* **invigoration,** *n.* **invigorative,** *a.* **invigorator,** *n.* [L *vigor*]

invincible, *a.* not to be conquered. **invincibility, -ibleness,** *n.* **invincibly,** *adv.* [F, from L *invincibilis*]

inviolable, *a.* not to be violated, profaned or dishonoured; not to be broken or disturbed. **inviolability,** †**-ableness,** *n.* **inviolably,** *adv.* **inviolate,** †**-lated,** *a.* not violated or profaned; unbroken. **inviolacy, inviolateness,** *n.* **inviolately,** *adv.* [F, from L *inviolābilis*]

invisible, *a.* not visible; imperceptible to the eye; too small, distant, misty etc. to be seen; (*coll.*) not in sight, away, not at home; not recorded in published accounts; not showing in statistics; pertaining to services as opposed to goods, as *invisible earnings.* **the invisible,** the invisible world; the supreme Being. **invisible ink,** *n.* ink that does not show until heated or otherwise treated. †**invised,** *a.* unseen; invisible. **invisibility, -ibleness,** *n.* **invisibly,** *adv.* [F, from L *invīsibilis*]

invitatory, *a.* containing or using invitation. *n.* an invitatory psalm, antiphon etc., esp. the psalm *Venite exultemus Domino.*

invite[1], *v.t.* to solicit the company of (to or in); to request courteously (to do something); to solicit; to allure, to attract; to tempt; to draw upon one, esp. unintentionally. *v.i.* to give invitation; to allure, to tempt. **invitation,** *n.* the act of inviting; words, written or oral, with which one is invited; allurement; attraction. **invitee,** *n.* one invited. **inviter,** *n.* **inviting,** *a.* that invites; seductive; physically attractive. **invitingly,**

adv. **invitingness,** *n.* [F *inviter,* L *invītāre,* to bid, rel. to *-vītus,* willing (in *invītus,* unwilling)]
invite², *n.* (*coll.*) an invitation.
in vitro, in an artificial environment outside the body. **in vitro fertilization (IVF)**, literally, fertilization 'in glass', i.e. allowing eggs and sperm to fuse in a laboratory to form embryos. The embryos produced may then either be reimplanted into the womb of the otherwise infertile mother, or used for research. The first baby to be produced in the UK by this method, Louise Brown, was born in 1978.
in vivo, in the body. [L]
invocation, *n.* the act of invoking; a supplication or call, esp. to God; a petition addressed to a muse, saint etc., for help or inspiration; the calling up of a spirit by incantation; †a judicial call, demand or order. † **invocable**, *a.* †**invocate**, *v.t.* to invoke, to call upon; to address in prayer. **invocatory**, *a.* [F, from L *invocātiōnem,* nom. *-tio,* from *invocāre,* to INVOKE]
invoice, *n.* a list of goods dispatched, with particulars of quantity and price, sent to a consignee. *v.t.* to enter (goods) in an invoice; to send an invoice to. [prob. from earlier *invoyes,* pl. from F *envoi,* see ENVOY¹]
invoke, *v.t.* to address in prayer; to solicit earnestly for assistance and protection; to call upon solemnly; to call on as a witness, to appeal to as an authority; to summon by magical means; †to call for judicially. [F *invoquer,* L *invocāre* (*vocāre,* to call)]
involucre, *n.* a whorl of bracts surrounding the flowers of certain Compositae and other plants; the indusium of ferns; a membranous envelope or cover of certain parts and organs. **involucel**, **-cellum**, *n.* a secondary involucre. **involucellate**, **involucral**, **involucrate**, *a.* **involucret,** *n.* [F, from L *involūcrum,* from *involvere* (*volvere,* to roll)]
involuntary, *a.* done unintentionally, not from choice, not spontaneous; independent of will or volition; †unwilling. **involuntarily,** *adv.* **involuntariness,** *n.* [L *involuntārius*]
involute, *a.* rolled up, folded; rolled inward at the margin, as certain leaves, petals etc.; complicated, involved. *n.* (*Math.*) a curve traced by the end of a string unwinding itself from another curve, which is called the *evolute.* **involuted, -lutive,** *a.* [L *involūtus,* p.p. of *involvere,* to INVOLVE]
involution, *n.* the act of involving; the state of being involved; complication, entanglement, intricacy; a rolling up or curling of parts; anything folding up or enveloping; a complicated grammatical construction; the shrinking of a bodily organ, e.g. of the uterus after pregnancy; (*Math.*) the act or process of raising a quantity to any power.
involve, *v.t.* to enwrap, to enfold or envelop (in); to entangle (in); to implicate (in); to include (in); to commit (as oneself) emotionally; to comprise as a logical or necessary consequence; to imply, to entail; to complicate, to make intricate; (*Math.*) to raise to any power. **involvedness,** *n.* **involvement,** *n.* the act of involving; the state of being involved, esp. financially. [F *involver,* from L. *involvere* (*volvere,* to roll)]
invulnerable, *a.* incapable of being wounded or injured. **invulnerably,** *adv.* **invulnerability**, **-ableness,** *n.* [F, from L *invulnerābilis*]
†**invultuation,** *n.* the practice of pricking or stabbing the wax or clay image of an enemy, in the belief that his or her death would thereby be magically brought about. [low L *invultuātiōnem,* nom. *-tio,* from *invultuāre* (*vultus,* face)]
inward, *a.* internal; situated or being within; towards the interior, connected with the mind or soul; †intimate; †domestic; †confidential. *adv.* inwards. **inwardly,** *adv.* internally, within; towards the centre; in one's thoughts and feelings, mentally, secretly; †intimately. **inwardness,** *n.* the inner quality or essence (of); the quality of being inward; the mental and spiritual nature; †familiarity, intimacy. **inwards,** *adv.* towards the interior, internal parts or centre; in the mind or soul. *n.* the viscera; †intellectual parts. [OE *innanweard*]
inweave, *v.t.* to weave in or together; to interlace (with).
inwick, *n.* (*Curling*) a stroke in which the stone strikes the inside of another and glances off it to the tee. *v.i.* to make an inwick; of the stone, to glance off another stone and reach the tee.
inworn, *a.* worn or pressed in; inveterate.
inwrap, ENWRAP.
inwreathe, ENWREATHE.
inwrought, *a.* of a pattern etc., wrought or worked in among other things; of a fabric, adorned with work or figures.
inyala, *n.* the S African antelope.
Io, *n.* in astronomy, the third largest moon of the planet Jupiter, 3600 km/2240 miles in diameter, orbiting in 1.77 days at a distance of 413,000 km/257,000 miles. It is the most volcanically active body in the Solar System, covered by hundreds of vents that erupt not lava but sulphur, giving Io an orange-coloured surface.
iodal, *n.* an oily liquid obtained by treating iodine with alcohol and nitric acid, analogous to chloral.
iodate, *n.* a salt of iodic acid.
iodic, *a.* belonging to, or containing, iodine.
iodide, *n.* a compound of iodine with an element or radical.
iodine, *n.* a non-metallic bluish-black element, yielding violet fumes when heated, and resembling bromine and chlorine in chemical properties, used in photography. It is largely used in medicine for its antiseptic and disinfectant qualities. [F *iode,* Gr. *iōdēs, ioeidēs* (*ion,* a violet, *eidos,* appearance), -INE]
iodism, *n.* the morbid effects of overdoses of iodine or iodic preparations.
iodize, -ise, *v.t.* to treat with iodine; to prepare with iodine. **iodization, -isation,** *n.*
iod(o)-, *comb.form* pertaining to iodine.
iodoform, *n.* an iodine compound resembling chloroform in its antiseptic effects. **iodoformin,** *n.*
iodol, *n.* an antiseptic compound of iodine.
iodopsin, *n.* a light-sensitive pigment in the retinal cones.
iolite, *n.* a blue orthorhombic transparent or translucent silicate of aluminium, iron and magnesium. [Gr. *ion,* as foll., -LITE]
-ion, *suf.* [F *-ion,* L *iōnem,* nom. *-io* (cp. -ATION, -ITION, -TION)]
ion, *n.* an electrically charged atom or group of atoms formed, for example, by the solution of a salt in water. **ion exchange,** *n.* a process by which ions are exchanged between a solution and a solid or another liquid, as used in the softening of water etc. **ionic,** *a.* **ionic bond,** *n.* bond within a chemical compound produced by the transfer of electrons, such that the resulting ions are held together by electrostatic attraction. **ionizable, -isable,** *a.* **ionize, -ise,** *v.t.* to convert into an ion or ions. **ionization, -isation,** *n.* [Gr. *ion,* neut. pres.p. of *ienai,* to go]
Iona, *n.* an island in the Inner Hebrides; area 850 hectares. It is the site of a monastery founded 563 by St Columba, and a centre of early Christianity. It later became a burial ground for Irish, Scottish, and Norwegian kings. It has a 13th-cent. abbey.
Ionesco, *n.* **Eugène** (1912–), Romanian-born French dramatist, a leading exponent of the theatre of the absurd. Most of his plays are in one act and concern the futility of language as a means of communication. These include *La Cantatrice chauve/The Bald Prima Donna* (1950) and *La Leçon/The Lesson* (1951).
Ionian, *a.* pertaining to Ionia, a district of Asia Minor, or to the Ionians. *n.* a member of the division of the Hellenic race which settled in Attica and the northern coast of the Peloponnesus and founded colonies on the shores of the Mediterranean and Euxine and esp. in Asia Minor. **Ionian mode,** *n.* (*Mus.*) one of the ancient Greek modes, characterized as soft and effeminate; the last of the ecclesiastical modes, commencing on C, corresponding in tonality with the major diatonic scale in modern music. **Ionic,** *a.* Ionian. **Ionic dialect,** the Greek dialect spoken in Ionia. **Ionic foot,** *n.* a me-

trical foot of four syllables (either *ionic a majore,* two long and two short, or *ionic a minore,* two short and two long). **Ionic metre,** *n.* metre consisting of Ionic feet. **Ionic order,** *n.* one of the five orders of architecture, the distinguishing characteristic of which is the volute on both sides of the capital. **Ionic sect, school,** *n.* the first school of Greek philosophy, founded by Thales of Miletus, the distinctive characteristic of which was its inquiry into the material and formative constitution of the universe. **ionicism,** *n.* **ionicist,** *n.* **ionicize, -ise,** *v.t.* **ionicization, -isation,** *n.* [L *Iōnius,* Gr. *Iōnios* (*Ionia*).

Ionic, ionicize etc. IONIAN.

ionic, ionize, ionization ION.

ionosphere, *n.* the region surrounding the earth at a height of from 6 miles (about 9·5 km) to about 250 miles (400 km) in which ionized layers of gas occur. **ionospheric,** *a.*

-ior, *suf.* as in *junior, superior, warrior.* [[1] L *-ior,* compar. suf. of adjectives; [2] var. of -IOUR]

iota, *n.* the Greek letter ι, which, being frequently indicated by a dot under other letters (as ω), known as **iota subscript,** has come to mean a jot, very small quantity. **iotacism,** *n.* [Gr.]

IOU, *n.* a formal acknowledgment of debt, bearing these letters, the sum involved and the debtor's signature. [*I owe you*]

-iour, *suf.* as in *behaviour, saviour.* [OF *-ur, -or* (F. *-eur*), L *-ātōrem,* nom. *-ātor*]

-ious, *suf.* characterized by, full of; forming adjectives, as *ambitious, cautious, suspicious.* [L *-iōsus* (cp. F *-ieux*), *-i-,* -OUS]

IOW, (*abbr.*) Isle of Wight.

Iowa, *n.* state of the midwest US; nickname Hawkeye State. **area** 145,800 sq km/56,279 sq miles. **capital** Des Moines. **towns** Cedar Rapids, Davenport, Sioux City. **population** (1984) 2,837,000. **products** cereals, soya beans, meat, wool, chemicals, machinery, electrical goods.

IPA, (*abbr.*) International Phonetic Alphabet.

ipecacuanha, ipecac, *n.* the dried root of *Cephaelis ipecacuanha,* a cinchonaceous plant from Brazil, used in medicine as an emetic and purgative. **ipecacuanhic,** *a.* [Port., from Tupí *ipekaaguené*]

†**ipocras,** HIPPOCRAS.

Ipomoea, *n.* a genus of Convolvulaceae, with many species. [Gr. *ip-,* stem of *ips,* worm, *omoios,* like]

ipse dixit, *n.* a mere assertion; a dogmatic statement. [L, he himself has said it]

ipsissima verba, *n.pl.* the precise words. [L]

ipso facto, by that very fact. [L]

IQ, (*abbr.*) Intelligence Quotient.

Iqbāl, *n.* **Muhammad** (1875–1938), Islamic poet and thinker. His literary works, in Urdu and Persian, were mostly verse in the classical style, suitable for public recitation. He sought through his writings to arouse Muslims to take their place in the modern world.

IR, (*abbr.*) Inland Revenue.

Ir, (*chem. symbol*) iridium.

Ir., (*abbr.*) Ireland; Irish.

ir-[1], *pref.* (*before r*) as in *irradiate.* [see IN-[1]]

ir-[2], *pref.* (*before r*) as in *irrelevant, irreligion.* [see IN-[2]]

IRA, (*abbr.*) Irish Republican Army.

†**iracund,** *a.* angry, passionate. [L *īracundus,* from *īra,* IRE]

irade, *n.* a written decree of a Muslim ruler. [Turk., from Arab. *irādah,* desire]

Iráklion, Heraklion, *n.* largest city and capital (since 1971) of Crete, Greece; population (1981) 102,000.

Iran, *n.* Islamic Republic of (until 1935 **Persia**). **area** 1,648,000 sq km/636,128 sq miles. **capital** Tehran. **towns** Isfahan, Mashhad, Tabriz, Shiraz, Ahwaz; chief port Abadan. **physical** plateau surrounded by mountains, including Elburz and Zagros; Lake Rezayeh; Dasht-Ekavir Desert. **population** (1988) 53,920,000 (including minorities in Azerbaijan, Baluchistan, Khuzestan/Arabistan, and Kurdistan); annual growth rate 2.9%. **exports** carpets, cotton textiles, metalwork, leather goods, oil, petrochemicals. **languages** Farsi, Kurdish, Turkish, Arabic, English, French. **religion** Shi'ite Muslim (official). **Irangate, or Contragate,** *n.* a US political scandal involving senior members of the Reagan administration. The Congressional Joint Investigative Committee reported, in November 1987, that the President bore 'ultimate responsibility' for allowing a 'cabal of zealots' to seize control of the administration's policy, but found no firm evidence that President Reagan had actually been aware of the Contra diversion. Colonel Oliver North was tried and convicted in May 1989 on charges of obstructing Congress and unlawfully destroying government documents. Admiral John Poindexter faced trial in 1990. **Iranian,** *a.* of or belonging to Iran; pertaining to the inhabitants or language of Iran. *n.* a member of the Iranian race; a native of Iran; a branch of the Indo-European family of languages including Persian; the modern Persian language. [Pers.]

Iran-Iraq War, Gulf War, *n.* war between Iran and Iraq (1980–88), claimed by the former to have begun with the Iraq offensive 21 Sept. 1980, and by the latter with the Iranian shelling of border posts 4 Sept. 1980. Occasioned by a boundary dispute over the Shatt-al-Arab waterway, it fundamentally arose because of Iran's encouragement of the Shi'ite majority in Iraq to rise against the Sunni government of Saddam Hussein. An estimated 1 million people died in the war.

Iraq, *n.* Republic of. **area** 434,924 sq km/167,881 sq miles. **capital** Baghdad. **towns** Mosul and port of Basra. **physical** mountains in N, desert in W; wide valley of rivers Tigris and Euphrates NW–SE. **exports** dates (80% of world supply), wool, oil. **population** (1987) 17,093,000; annual growth rate 3.6%. **language** Arabic (official). **religion** Shi'ite Muslim 60%, Sunni Muslim 30%, Christian 3%. **Iraqi,** *a.* (pertaining to) a native or inhabitant of Iraq; (pertaining to) the form of Arabic spoken in Iraq.

irascible, *a.* easily excited to anger; passionate, irritable. **irascibility, -ibleness,** *n.* **irascibly,** *adv.* **irate,** *a.* angry, enraged. [F, from L *īrascibilis,* from *īrasci,* to be angry, from *īra,* IRE]

IRBM, (*abbr.*) Intermediate Range Ballistic Missile.

ire, *n.* anger, passion. **ireful,** *a.* **irefully,** *adv.* †**irefulness,** *n.* [OF, from L *īra*]

†**irenic** , †**-ical,** *a.* pacific; promoting peace. **irenicon,** EIRENICON. [Gr. *eirēnikos,* from *eirēnē,* peace]

Ireland[1], *n.* one of the British Isles, lying to the west of Great Britain, from which it is separated by the Irish Sea. It comprises the provinces of Ulster, Leinster, Munster, and Connacht, and is divided between the Republic of Ireland, which occupies the south, central, and northwest of the island, and Northern Ireland, which occupies the northeast corner and forms part of the United Kingdom. **Ireland, Northern,** *n.* constituent part of the UK. **area** 13,460 sq km/5,196 sq miles. **capital** Belfast. **towns** Londonderry, Enniskillen, Omagh, Newry, Armagh, Coleraine. **exports** engineering, especially shipbuilding including textile machinery, aircraft components; linen and synthetic textiles; processed foods, especially dairy and poultry products – all affected by the 1980s depression and political unrest. **population** (1986) 1,567,000. **language** English. **religion** Protestant 54%, Roman Catholic 31%. The creation of Northern Ireland dates from 1921 when the mainly Protestant counties of Ulster withdrew from the newly established Irish Free State. Spasmodic outbreaks of violence by the IRA continued, but only in 1968–69 were there serious disturbances arising from Protestant political dominance and discrimination against the Roman Catholic minority in employment and housing. British troops were sent to restore peace and protect Catholics, but disturbances continued and in 1972 the parliament at Stormont was prorogued, and superseded by direct rule from Westminster. **Ireland, Republic of** (Irish **Éire**) *n.* **area** 68,900 sq km/26,595 sq miles. **capital** Dublin. **towns** ports Cork, Dún Laoghaire, Limerick, Waterford. **physical** central plateau with hills; rivers Shannon, Liffey, Boyne. **exports** livestock, dairy products, Irish whiskey, microelectronic components and assemblies, mining and engineering products, chemicals, tobacco, clothing; tourism is important. **population** (1988) 3,540,000; annual growth rate 1.2%. **language** Irish and English (both official). **religion** Roman Catholic.

Ireland[2], *n.* **John (Nicholson)** (1879–1962), English composer. His works include the mystic orchestral prelude *The Forgotten Rite* (1917) and the piano solo *Sarnia* (1941). Benjamin Britten was his pupil.

Irene[1], *n.* in Greek mythology, goddess of peace (Roman Pax).

Irene[2], **St**, *n.* (*c.* 752–*c.* 803), Byzantine emperor 797–802. The wife of Leo IV (750–780), she became regent for their son Constantine (771–805) on Leo's death. In 797 she deposed her son, had his eyes put out, and assumed full title of *basileus* (emperor), ruling in her own right until deposed and exiled to Lesvos by a revolt of 802. She was made a saint by the Greek Orthodox church for her attacks on iconoclasts.

Ireton, *n.* **Henry** (1611–51), English Civil War general. He joined the Parliamentary forces and fought at Edgehill 1642, Gainsborough 1643, and Naseby 1645. After the Battle of Naseby, Ireton, who was opposed to the extreme republicans and Levellers, strove for a compromise with Charles I, but then played a leading role in his trial and execution.

Irgun, *n.* short for Irgun Zvai Leumi (National Military Society), a Jewish guerrilla group active against the British administration in Palestine (1946–48). Their bombing of the King David Hotel in Jerusalem, 22 July 1946, cost 91 lives.

Irian Jaya, *n.* the western portion of the island of New Guinea, part of Indonesia. **area** 420,000 sq km/162,000 sq miles. **capital** Jayapura. **population** (1980) 1,174,000.

Iricism, IRISHISM under IRISH.

iridescent, *a.* exhibiting changing colours like those of the rainbow. **iridescence**, *n.* **iridescently**, *adv.* [Gr. *īris īridos*, IRIS]

iridium, *n.* a shining white metallic element belonging to the platinum group, at. no.77; chem. symbol Ir. **iridize, -ise**, *v.t.* to tip (a pen) with iridium. [as prec.]

irid(o)-, *comb.form* of or pertaining to the iris of the eye; of or pertaining to iridium. [Gr. *īris īridos*, IRIS]

iridology, *n.* a diagnostic technique in alternative medicine involving studying the iris of the eye. **iridologist**, *n.*

iridosmine, *n.* a native alloy of iridium and osmium, used for the points of gold pens.

iridotomy, *n.* incision of the iris to relieve occlusion of the pupil etc. **iridotome**, *n.* a knife used for this.

iris, *n.* (*pl.* **irises, irides,**) (*Gr. Myth.*) the rainbow personified as a goddess, the messenger of the gods; the rainbow; an appearance resembling the rainbow, an iridescence; the circular coloured membrane or curtain surrounding the pupil of the eye; a genus of plants of the family Iridaceae, with tuberous roots, sword-shaped leaves, and large variously-coloured flowers, the commonest British species being *Iris pseudacorus,* yellow flag; a flower of this genus, a fleur-de-lis or flower-de-luce; a rock-crystal with iridescent properties. **iris diaphragm**, *n.* an adjustable diaphragm regulating the entry of light into an optical instrument. **irisated**, *a.* exhibiting prismatic colours. **irisation**, *n.* **iriscope**, *n.* an instrument for exhibiting the prismatic colours. **irised**, *a.* containing colours like the rainbow. [Gr. *īris īridos*]

Irish, *a.* of or pertaining to Ireland or its inhabitants; like an Irishman. *n.* a native of Ireland; the Irish language; (*N Am. sl.*) temper, contentiousness. (*collect.*) the people of Ireland. **Irish coffee**, *n.* a drink made of sweetened coffee mixed with Irish whiskey and topped with cream. **Irish Gaelic**, *n.* first official language of the Irish Republic, but much less widely used than the second official language, English. **Irish language**, *n.* a common name for Irish Gaelic. At one time, especially in the form 'Erse', also a name for the Gaelic of Scotland. **Irishman, -woman**, *n.* a native of Ireland; one of Irish race. **Irish moss** CARRAGEEN. **Irish National Liberation Army**, (INLA) a guerrilla organization committed to the end of British rule in Northern Ireland and the incorporation of Ulster into the Irish Republic. The INLA was a 1974 offshoot of the Irish Republican Army. Among the INLA's activities was the killing of British politician Airey Neave in 1979. **Irish Republican Army**, (IRA) militant Irish nationalist organization, whose aim is to create a united Irish socialist republic including Ulster. The paramilitary wing of Sinn Féin, it was founded 1919 by Michael Collins, and fought a successful war against Britain 1919–21. It came to the fore again 1939 with a bombing campaign in Britain, and was declared illegal in Eire. Its activities intensified from 1968 onwards, as the civil-rights disorders in Northern Ireland developed. In 1970 a group in the north broke away to become the Provisional IRA; their commitment is to the expulsion of the British from Northern Ireland. In 1974 a further breakaway occurred, of the left-wing Irish Republican Socialist Party with its paramilitary wing, the Irish National Liberation Army. **Irish stew**, *n.* a stew of vegetables and meat boiled together. **Irishism**, *n.* a mode of expression or idiom peculiar to the Irish, esp. a 'bull'. **Irishize, -ise**, *v.t.* †**Irishry**, *n.* the people of Ireland as opposed to English settlers. [OE *Iras*, pl.]

iritis, *n.* inflammation of the iris of the eye. [IRIS, -ITIS]

irk, *v.t.* to tire, to bore; to annoy, to disgust. *v.i.* to become tired or worried. **irksome**, *a.* wearisome, tedious, tiring; †tired. **irksomely**, *adv.* **irksomeness**, *n.* [MG *irken*, etym. doubtful]

Irkutsk, *n.* city in S USSR; population (1987) 609,000. It produces coal, iron, steel, and machine tools. Founded 1652, it began to grow after the Trans-Siberian railway reached it 1898.

IRO, (*abbr.*) Inland Revenue Office.

iron, *n.* a malleable tenacious metallic element used for tools etc. the commonest and most useful of all the metals; an article, tool, utensil etc., made of iron; an implement for smoothing clothes; a metal-headed golf club used for lofting; (*pl.*) fetters. *a.* made or composed of iron; like iron, robust, strong, inflexible, or unyielding, merciless. *v.t.* to furnish or cover with iron; to fetter with irons; to smooth with a smoothing-iron. **flat-iron, smoothing-iron,** an iron implement that is heated for smoothing cloth. **in irons,** in fetters. **to have (too) many irons in the fire,** to be attempting or dealing with (too) many projects at the same time; to have several expedients. **to iron out,** *v.t.* to correct (defects etc.); to find a solution to (problems etc.). **to pump iron** PUMP. **iron age,** *n.* the late prehistoric age when weapons and many implements began to be made of iron; (*Gr. Myth.*) the last of the four ages of the world, described by Hesiod, Ovid etc., in which oppression and vice prevailed. **iron-bark,** *n.* an Australian eucalyptus with a hard, firm bark. **iron-bound,** *a.* bound with iron; of a coast, surrounded with rocks; unyielding, hard and fast. **ironclad,** *n.* a war-vessel having the parts above water plated with iron. *a.* covered or protected with iron. **Iron Cross,** *n.* a Prussian war-medal first struck in 1813 and revived in 1870. **Iron Curtain,** *n.* in Europe after World War II, the division between capitalist West and communist East. The term was first used by the UK prime minister Winston Churchill in a speech at Fulton, Missouri, US, 1946; (**iron curtain**) any similar barrier to communication. **Iron Duke,** *n.* the first Duke of Wellington. **iron-filings,** *n.pl.* fine particles of iron made by filing. **iron-fisted,** *a.* close-fisted, covetous. †**iron-flint,** *n.* ferruginous quartz. **iron-founder,** *n.* one who makes iron castings. **iron-foundry,** *n.* **iron-gang,** *n.* (*Austral. hist.*) a gang of convicts in chains. **iron-grey,** *n.* a grey colour like that of iron freshly broken; a horse of this colour. *a.* of an iron-grey colour. **Iron Guard,** *n.* profascist group controlling Romania in the 1930s. To counter its influence, King Carol II established a dictatorship 1938 but the Iron Guard forced him to abdicate 1940. **iron hand,** *n.* strict control, often tyranny. **the iron hand in the velvet glove,** strict control which is at first concealed. **ironheart,** *n.* a hard-wood New Zealand tree. **iron-hearted,** *a.* hard-hearted, cruel. **iron-heater,** *n.* the piece of metal heated in the fire for a laundress's box-iron. **iron horse,** *n.* (*dated, coll.*) a railway locomotive. **iron-liquor,** *n.* acetate of iron, used by dyers as a mordant. **iron lung,** *n.* a mechanical device employed for maintaining or assisting respiration. **iron man,** *n.* a self-acting spinning mule; (*N Am. sl.*) a dollar. **iron-master,** *n.* a manufacturer of iron. **ironmonger,** *n.* one who deals in ironware or hardware. **ironmongery,** *n.* **iron-mould,** *n.* a spot on cloth etc. caused by ink or rust. *v.t.* to stain (as cloth) with ink or rust. *v.i.* to be stained in this way. **iron rations,** *n.pl.* complete emergency rations packed in a sealed case. **iron-sand,** *n.* sand full of particles of iron, usu. magnetite. †**iron-sick,** *a.* applied to a ship with bolts and nails so corroded with rust as to cause her to leak. **iron-smith,** *n.* a worker in iron. **iron-stone,** *n.* an iron-ore containing oxygen and silica. **ironware,** *n.* goods made of iron, hardware. †**iron-witted,** *a.* unfeeling, insensible. **iron-wood,** *n.* the popular name given to several very hard and heavy woods. **ironwork,** *n.* anything made of iron; (*pl., often sing. in constr.*) an establishment where iron is manufactured, wrought or cast. **ironer,** *n.* one who irons or smooths (linen etc.) with a flat-iron; a machine for ironing. **ironing,** *n.* **ironing-board,** *n.* **irony**[1], *a.* consisting of, containing, or resembling iron. [OE *īren, īsen, īsern* (cp. Dut. *ījzer,* Icel. *jārn, īsarn,* G *eīsen*]

iron., (*abbr.*) ironically.

ironic, ironical IRONY.

Ironside, Ironsides, *n.* one of Cromwell's troopers; a hardy veteran.

irony[1] IRON.

irony[2], *n.* an expression intended to convey the opposite to the literal meaning; the use of such expressions; language having a meaning or implication for those who understand different from the ostensible one, or different from that of which the speaker is conscious; subtle sarcasm in which apparent praise really conveys disapprobation. **irony of fate, circumstances,** the apparent malice or perversity of events not under human control. **Socratic irony** SOCRATIC. **ironic, -ical,** *a.* **ironically,** *adv.* **ironist,** *n.* **ironize, -ise,** *v.i.* [F *ironie,* L *īronīa,* Gr. *eirōneia,* from *eirōn,* a dissembler]

Iroquois, *n.* confederation of North American Indians, the Six Nations (Cayuga, Mohawk, Oneida, Onondaga, and Seneca, with the Tuscarora from 1715), traditionally formed by Hiawatha (actually a priestly title) 1570.

irradiate, *v.t.* to shed light upon; to make bright or brilliant; (*fig.*) to light up (a subject etc.); to brighten up (a face, expression etc.); to subject to sunlight or ultraviolet rays; to expose food to low levels of gamma radiation in order to sterilize and preserve it. †*v.i.* to shine. †*a.* made brilliant or bright. **irradiant,** *a.* **irradiance,** †**-ancy, irradiation,** *n.* **irradiative,** *a.* [L *irradiātus,* p.p. of *irradiāre* (*radius,* RAY[1])]

irradicate, *v.t.* to fix firmly, to enroot. [L *rādīcātus,* p.p. of *rādīcāre,* to take root, from *rādix rādīcem,* root]

irrational, *a.* not rational; without reason or understanding; illogical, contrary to reason, absurd; not expressible by a whole number or common fraction, not commensurable with a finite number. *n.* an irrational number; absurd. **irrationalism,** *n.* **irrationalist,** *n.* **irrationality,** *n.* **irrationalize, -ise,** *v.t.* **irrationally,** *adv.* [L *irrātiōnālis*]

Irrawaddy, *n.* (Burmese **Ayeryarwady**) chief river of Burma, flowing roughly N to S for 2090 km/1300 miles across the centre of the country into the Bay of Bengal. Its sources are the Mali and N'mai rivers; its chief tributaries are the Chindwin and Shweli.

irreceptive, UNRECEPTIVE.

irreciprocal, *a.* not reciprocal.

irreclaimable, *a.* incapable of being reclaimed; obstinate, inveterate. **irreclaimability,** *n.* **irreclaimably,** *adv.*

irrecognizable, -isable, *a.* unrecognizable. **irrecognizability, -isability,** *n.* **irrecognizably, -isably,** *adv.* **irrecognizant, -isant,** *a.* **irrecognition,** *n.*

irreconcilable, *a.* incapable of being reconciled; implacably hostile; incompatible, inconsistent, incongruous; (*Math.*) independent, never coinciding within given limits. *n.* one who cannot be reconciled, appeased or satisfied, an intransigent. **irreconcilability, -ableness,** *n.* **irreconcilably,** *adv.* †**irreconciled,** *a.* **irreconcilement,** *n.*

irrecoverable, *a.* that cannot be recovered; irreparable. **irrecoverableness,** *n.* **irrecoverably,** *adv.*

irrecusable, *a.* not to be refused or rejected. [F, from late L *irrecūsābilis* (*recūsāre,* to refuse)]

irredeemable, *a.* not redeemable; not terminable by payment of the principal (as an annuity); not convertible into cash (as a banknote); irreclaimable; beyond redemption, offering no scope for salvage or rectification. **irredeemability, -ableness,** *n.* **irredeemably,** *adv.*

irredentist, *n.* one of a party formed about 1878 to bring about the inclusion of all Italian-speaking districts in the kingdom of Italy. **irredentism,** *n.* [It. *irredentista,* from *Italia irredenta,* unredeemed Italy]

irreducible, *a.* not reducible; not to be lessened; not to be brought to a required condition etc.; (*Surg.*) not giving way to treatment; (*Math.*) not to be simplified. **irreducibility, -ibleness,** *n.* **irreducibly,** *adv.* †**irreduction,** *n.*

irreformable, *a.* unalterable; incapable of being reformed.

irrefragable, *a.* incapable of being refuted; undeniable, unanswerable. **irrefragability,** †**-ableness,** *n.* **irrefragably,** *adv.* [late L *irrefrāgābilis*]

irrefrangible, *a.* not to be broken, inviolable; not susceptible of refraction.

irrefutable, *a.* incapable of being refuted. **irrefutability,** *n.* **irrefutably,** *adv.* [F, from L *irrefutābilis*]

irreg., (*abbr.*) irregular, irregularly.

irregular, *a.* not regular, not according to rule or established principles or custom; departing from rules, not in conformity with law, duty etc., lawless, disorderly; not according to type, abnormal, asymmetrical; not straight, not direct, not uniform; (*Gram.*) deviating from the common form in inflection; not belonging to the regular army. *n.* one who does not conform to established rule, discipline, authority etc.; (*pl.*) irregular troops. **irregularity,** *n.* **irregularly,** *adv.* †**irregulous,** *a.* lawless, licentious. [OF *irreguler,* late L *irrēgulāris*]

irrelative, *a.* no relative, unconnected; (*Metaph.*) having no relations, absolute. *n.* that which is without relations. **irrelated,** *a.* **irrelation,** *n.* **irrelatively,** *adv.*

irrelevant, *a.* not applicable or pertinent, not to the point; having no application (to the matter in hand). **irrelevance, -ancy,** *n.* **irrelevantly,** *adv.*

irreligion, *n.* indifference or hostility to religion. **irreligionist,** *n.* **irreligious,** *a.* **irreligiously,** *adv.* **irreligiousness,** *n.* [F *irréligion,* L *irreligiōnem,* nom. *-gio*]

irremediable, *a.* incurable, irreparable; incapable of being remedied or corrected. **irremediableness,** *n.* **irremediably,** *adv.* [MF *irrémédiable,* L *irremediābilis*]

irremissible, *a.* that cannot be remitted or pardoned. **irremissibility,** *n.* **irremissibly,** *adv.* †**irremissive,** *a.* unremitting. [F *irrémissible,* L *irremissibilis*]

irremovable, *a.* that cannot be removed or displaced, permanent, immovable; †inflexible, determined. **irremovability,** *n.* **irremovably,** *adv.*

irreparable, *a.* incapable of being repaired, remedied or restored. **irreparableness,** †**-ability,** *n.* **irreparably,** *adv.* [F, from L *irreparābilis*]

irrepealable, *a.* incapable of being repealed, irrevocable. **irrepealability,** *n.* **irrepealably,** *adv.*

irreplaceable, *a.* not to be made good in case of loss. **irreplaceably,** *adv.*

irreprehensible, *a.* free from blame. **irreprehensibly,** *adv.* [late L *irreprehensibilis*]

irrepressible, *a.* not to be repressed. **irrepressibility,** *n.* **irrepressibly,** *adv.*

irreproachable, *a.* blameless, faultless. **irreproachability, -ableness,** *n.* **irreproachably,** *adv.* [F *irre-*

prochable]

irresistible, *a.* that cannot be resisted; not to be withstood; extremely attractive or alluring. †**irresistance,** *n.* **irresistibility**, **-ibleness,** *n.* **irresistibly,** *adv.* [late L *irresistibilis*]

†**irresoluble,** *a.* incapable of being resolved into its elements; indissoluble; insoluble in water.

irresolute, *a.* not resolute; undecided, hesitating. **irresolutely,** *adv.* **irresoluteness, -lution,** *n.* [L *irresolūtus*]

irresolvable, *a.* incapable of being resolved, insoluble; not to be analysed or separated into elements. **irresolvability**, *n.*

irrespective, *a.* not respective, regardless of, without reference to; irrespectively; †disrespectful. **irrespectively,** *adv.* without regard to circumstances or conditions.

irrespirable, *a.* not fit to be breathed.

irresponsible, *a.* not responsible; not trustworthy; performed or acting without a proper sense of responsibility; lacking the capacity to bear responsibility. **irresponsibility**, *n.* **irresponsibly,** *adv.*

irresponsive, *a.* not responsive (to). **irresponsiveness,** *n.*

irretentive, *a.* not retentive. **irretention, irretentiveness,** *n.*

irretrievable, *a.* not to be retrieved; irreparable. **irretrievability**, *n.* **irretrievably,** *adv.*

irreverent, *a.* lacking in reverence; disrespectful; proceeding from irreverence. **irreverence,** *n.* **irreverential**, *a.* **irreverently,** *adv.* [F *irrévérent*, L *irreverentem*, nom. *-ens*]

irreversible, *a.* not reversible; irrevocable. **irreversibility**, †**-ibleness,** *n.* **irreversibly,** *adv.*

irrevocable, *a.* incapable of being revoked or altered, unalterable. **irrevocability**, **-ableness,** *n.* **irrevocably,** *adv.* [F, from L *irrevocābilis*]

irrigate, *v.t.* to water (land) by causing a stream to flow over it; of streams, to supply (land) with water; to moisten (a wound etc.) with a continuous jet or stream of antiseptic fluid; to refresh or fertilize the mind as with a stream. **irrigable,** *a.* **irrigant,** *a.* irrigating. *n.* a ditch for irrigation. **irrigative,** *a.* **irrigation,** *n.* **irrigator,** *n.* †**irriguous**, *a.* [L *irrigātus*, p.p. of *irrigāre* (*rigāre,* to moisten)]

†**irrision,** *n.* mockery, derision. [L *irrīsio- ōnem*, from *irrīdēre* (*rīdēre,* to laugh)]

irritate[1], *v.t.* to excite to impatience or ill-temper; to fret, to annoy, to exasperate; to stir up, to excite; to cause an uneasy sensation in (the skin, an organ etc.); to stimulate (an organ) artificially. **irritable,** *a.* easily provoked, fretful; easily inflamed or made painful, highly sensitive; of nerves, muscles etc., responsive to artificial stimulation. **irritability**, †**-ableness,** *n.* **irritably,** *adv.* **irritancy,** *n.* **irritant,** *n., a.* **irritation,** *n.* **irritative,** †**-atory,** *a.* [L *irrītātus*, p.p. of *irrītāre,* prob. freq. of *irrīre, hirrīre,* to snarl]

irritate[2], *v.t.* (*Sc. Law*) to render null and void. **irritancy,** *n.* nullification, invalidity. [L *irritātus,* p.p. of *irritāre,* from *irritus,* invalid (*ratus,* established)]

irruption, *n.* a bursting in; a sudden invasion or incursion. **irrupt, irruptive,** *a.* [F, from L *irruptiōnem,* nom. *-tio,* from *irrumpere* (*rumpere,* to break), p.p. *irruptus*]

Irving[1], *n.* **Henry** (stage name of John Brodribb) (1838–1905), English actor. He established his reputation from 1871, chiefly at the Lyceum Theatre in London, where he became manager 1878. He staged a series of successful Shakespearean productions, including *Romeo and Juliet* (1882), with himself and Ellen Terry playing the leading roles. In 1895 he was the first actor to be knighted.

Irving[2], *n.* **Washington** (1783–1859), US essayist and short-story writer. He published a mock-heroic *History of New York* in 1809, supposedly written by the Dutchman 'Diedrich Knickerbocker'. In 1815 he went to England where his publications include the *Sketch Book of Geoffrey Crayon, Gent.* (1820), which contained such stories as 'Rip van Winkle' and 'The Legend of Sleepy Hollow'.

Irvingite, *n.* a member of a religious body known as the Catholic Apostolic Church, of which Irving was an early leader. **Irvingism,** *n.* [Edward *Irving,* 1792–1834, minister of the Church of Scotland]

Is., (*abbr.*) Isaiah; Island(s).

is, *3rd. pers. sing. pres. ind.* [see AM, BE]

is- IS(O)-.

Isaac, *n.* in the Old Testament, Hebrew patriarch, son of Abraham and Sarah, and father of Esau and Jacob.

Isaacs, *n.* **Alick** (1921–67), Scottish virologist who with Jean Lindemann, discovered interferon in 1957; a naturally-occurring substance found in cells infected with viruses. The full implications of this discovery are still being investigated.

Isabel, Isabella, *n., a.* greyish-yellow, light buff or straw colour. **Isabelline**, *a.* [female name]

Isabella I, *n.* **the Catholic** (1451–1504), queen of Castile from 1474, after the death of her brother Henry IV. By her marriage with Ferdinand of Aragon 1469, the crowns of two of the Christian states in the Spanish peninsula were united. In her reign the Moors were finally driven out of Spain; she introduced the Inquisition into Castile, and the persecution of the Jews, and gave financial encouragement to Columbus. Her youngest daughter was Catherine of Aragon, first wife of Henry VIII of England.

Isabella II, *n.* (1830–1904), queen of Spain from 1833, when she succeeded her father Ferdinand VII (1784–1833). The Salic Law banning a female sovereign had been repealed by the Cortes (Spanish parliament), but her succession was disputed by her uncle Don Carlos de Bourbon (1788–1855). After seven years of civil war the Carlists were defeated. She abdicated in favour of her son Alfonso XII in 1868.

isagogic, *a.* introductory. *n.pl.* preliminary investigation regarding the Scriptures, the department of biblical study concerned with literary history, authorship etc. [L *īsagōgicus,* Gr. *eisagōgikos,* from *eisagōgē,* introduction (*eis,* into, *agōgē,* from *agein,* to lead)]

Isaiah, *n.* (8th century BC), in the Old Testament, the first major Hebrew prophet. The son of Amos, he was probably of high rank, and lived largely in Jerusalem.

isandrous, *a.* having the stamens all similar and equal in number to the petals. [Gr *isos,* equal, *anēr andros,* a male]

isantherous, *a.* having equal anthers.

isanthous, *a.* having regular flowers. [Gr. *anthos,* flower]

isatin, *n.* a compound obtained by oxidizing indigo, crystallizing in yellowish-red prisms. **Isatis**, *n.* a genus of cruciferous herbs, comprising *I. tinctoria,* the woad, cultivated for dyeing. [L and Gr. *isatis,* -IN]

Isaurian, *n.* an 8th-cent. Byzantine imperial dynasty, originating in Asia Minor.

ISBN, (*abbr.*) International Standard Book Number.

ischaemia, (*esp. N Am.*) **ischemia**, *n.* a shortage of blood in part of the body. **ischaemic,** *a.* [Gr. *ischein,* to restrain, *haima,* blood]

ischialgia, *n.* pain in the hip-joint, sciatica. [Gr. *-algia, algos,* pain]

ischiatic, *n.* pertaining to the ischium, the hips, or to sciatica. [med. L *ischiaticus, ischiadicus,* Gr. *ischiadikos,* from *ischias -ados,* pain in the hip, from *ischion,* hip]

ischium, *n.* (*pl.* **ischia**) one of the posterior bones of the pelvic girdle. **ischial,** *a.* [Gr. *ischion,* hip]

ischuria, *n.* retention or suppression of the urine. **ischuretic**, *a.* relieving ischuria. *n.* an ischuretic medicine. [L *ischūria,* Gr. *ischouiar* (*ischein,* to hold, *ouria,* URINE)]

-ise[1], *suf.* forming abstract nouns, as *franchise, merchandise.* [OF *-ise,* L *-ītia, -itia, -icia, -itium, -icium* (cp. -ICE)]

-ise[2] -IZE.

isenergic, *a.* (*Phys.*) of or indicating equal energy. [Gr. *isos,* equal, ENERGIC]

isentropic, *a.* having equal entropy. [Gr. *isos,* equal, *entropē,* a turning about]

Isfahan, Eşfahan, *n.* industrial (steel, textiles, carpets) city in central Iran; population (1986) 1,001,000. It was the ancient capital (1598–1722) of Abbas the Great, and its features include the Great Square, Grand Mosque, and Hall of Forty Pillars.

-ish[1], *suf.* of the nature of, pertaining to; rather, somewhat; as in *childish, English, outlandish, reddish, yellowish.* [OE *isc* (cp. Dut. and G *-isch,* Icel. *-iskr,* also Gr. *iskos*)]

-ish[2], *suf.* forming verb, as *cherish, finish, punish.* [F *-iss-*, in pres.p. etc. of verbs in *-ir,* L incept. suf. *-isc-*]

Isherwood, *n.* **Christopher (William Bradshaw)** (1904–86), English novelist. Educated at Cambridge, he lived in Germany (1929–33) just before Hitler's rise to power, a period which inspired *Mr Norris Changes Trains* (1935) and *Goodbye to Berlin* (1939), creating the character of Sally Bowles (the basis of the musical *Cabaret*, 1968). Returning to England, he collaborated with Auden in three verse plays.

Ishiguro, *n.* **Kazuo** (1954–), Japanese-born British novelist. His novel *An Artist of the Floating World* won the 1986 Whitbread Prize, and *The Remains of the Day* won the Booker Prize of 1989.

Ishmael, *n.* in the Old Testament, son of Abraham and his wife Sarah's Egyptian maid Hagar; traditional ancestor of Mohammed and the Arab people. He and his mother were driven out by Sarah's jealousy. Muslims believe that it was Ishmael, not Isaac, whom God commanded Abraham to sacrifice, and that Ishmael helped Abraham build the Kaaba in Mecca. **Ishmaelite**, *n.* a descendant of Ishmael; one at war against society. **Ishmaelitish,** *a.*

Ishtar, *n.* goddess of love and war worshipped by the Babylonians and Assyrians, and personified as the legendary queen Semiramis.

Isiac, *a.* of or pertaining to Isis. *n.* a priest or worshipper of Isis, the principal Egyptian goddess. [L *īsiacus,* Gr. *isiakos,* from ISIS]

isidium, *n.* (*pl.* **-dia**) a coral-like growth on the thallus of lichens acting as soredia. [mod.L, from *Isis -idis*]

Isidore of Seville, *n.* (*c.* 560–636), writer and missionary. His *Ethymologiae* was the model for later mediaeval encyclopedias and helped to preserve classical thought into the Middle Ages, and his *Chronica Maiora* remains an important source for the history of Visigothic Spain. **Isidorian**, *a.* of or pertaining to St Isidore or to his collection of canons and decretals (applied to the interpolated collection later recognized as the pseudo-Isidorian or false decretals).

isinglass, *n.* a gelatinous substance prepared from the swimming-bladders of the sturgeon, cod, and other fish, used for making jellies, glue etc. [said to be a corr. of MDut. *huyzenglas* (cp. G *Hausenblase*), sturgeon's bladder]

Isis, *n.* the principal goddess of ancient Egypt. She was the daughter of Geb and Nut (earth and sky), and as the sister-wife of Osiris searched for his body after his death at the hands of his brother Set. Her son Horus then defeated and captured Set, but cut off his mother's head because she would not allow Set to be killed.

Iskandariya, *n.* Arabic name for Alexandria, Egypt.

Islam, *n.* religion founded in the Arabian peninsula in the early 7th cent. It emphasizes the oneness of God, his omnipotence, benificence, and inscrutability. The sacred book is the Koran of the prophet Mohammed, the Prophet or Messenger of Allah. There are two main Muslim sects: Sunni and Shi'ite. Other schools include Sufism, a mystical movement originating in the 8th century; the Muslim World. **Islamic,** *a.* **Islamic art,** *n.* art, architecture, and design of Muslim nations and territories. Because the Koran forbids representation in art, Islamic artistry was channelled into calligraphy and ornament. Despite this, there was naturalistic Persian painting, which inspired painters in the Mogul and Ottoman empires. Ceramic tiles decorated mosques and palaces from Spain (Alhambra, Granada) to S Russia and Mogul India (Taj Mahal, Agra). Wood, stone, and stucco sculpture ornamented buildings. Islamic artists produced excellent metalwork and, in Persia in the 16th–17th cent., woven textiles and carpets. **Islamicize, -ise,** *v.t.* Islamize. **Islamism,** *n.* **Islamist, Islamite**, *n.* **Islamitic**, *a.* **Islamize, -ise,** *v.t.* to convert to Islam. [Arab. *islām,* submission, from *salama,* he was resigned, whence SALAAM]

Islamabad, *n.* capital of Pakistan from 1967, in the Potwar district, at the foot of the Margala Hills and immediately NW of Rawalpindi; population (1981) 201,000. The city was designed by Constantinos Doxiadis in the 1960s. The Federal Capital Territory of Islamabad has an area of 907 sq km/350 sq miles, and a population (1985) of 379,000.

island, *n.* a piece of land surrounded by water; anything isolated or resembling an island; an area in the middle of a highway which divides the traffic and affords a refuge for the pedestrian; (*N Am.*) wood surrounded by prairie; a cluster of cells, mass of tissue etc., different in formation from those surrounding it. †*v.t.* to form into an island; to isolate; to dot as with islands. **Islands of the Blest,** (*Gr. Myth.*) imaginary islands situated in the western ocean, supposed to be the abode of good men after death. **islander,** *n.* [ME *iland,* OE *īgland* (*īg, īeg,* LAND), cp. Icel. *eyland,* Dut. *eiland* (*s* introd. by conf. with foll.)]

isle, *n.* an island, esp. a small island. †*v.t.* to form into an island; to isolate. **islesman,** *n.* an islander, esp. belonging to the Hebrides, Orkneys or Shetlands. **islet**, *n.* a little island. **islets of Langerhans,** groups of endocrine cells in the pancreas that secrete insulin, discovered by Paul *Langerhans* (1847–88), German anatomist. [ME *ile,* OF *ile, isle,* L *insula*]

Isle of Man, MAN, ISLE OF.

Isle of Wight, *n.* WIGHT, ISLE OF.

ism, *n.* (*usu. derog.*) a doctrine or system of a distinctive kind. **ismatic, -ical,** *a.* **ismaticalness,** *n.* [as foll.]

-ism, *suf.* forming abstract nouns denoting doctrine, theory, principle, system etc., as *altruism, Conservatism, Socialism, spiritualism, Gallicism, scoundrelism.* [F *-isme,* L *-ismus,* Gr. *-ismos* or *-isma,* from verbal ending *-izein*]

Ismail, *n.* (1830–95), khedive (governor) of Egypt 1866–79. A grandson of Mehemet Ali, he became viceroy of Egypt in 1863 and in 1866 received the title of khedive from the Ottoman sultan. In 1875 Britain, at Prime Minister Disraeli's suggestion, bought the khedive's Suez Canal shares for £3,976,582, and Anglo-French control of Egypt's finances was established. In 1879 the UK and France persuaded the sultan to appoint Tewfik, his son, khedive in his place.

Ismail I, *n.* (1486–1524), shah of Persia from 1501, founder of the Safavi dynasty, who established the first national government since the Arab conquest, and Shiite Islam as the national religion.

Ismaili, *n.* one of a sect of Shiite Muslims whose spiritual leader is the Aga Khan. **Ismailism**, *n.* **Ismailitic**, *a.*

isn't, is not.

ISO, *n.* in photography, a numbering system for rating the speed of films, devised by the International Standards Organization.

is(o)-, *comb.form* equal; having the same number of parts; indicating an isomeric substance. [Gr. *isos*]

isobar, *n.* a line on a map connecting places having the same mean barometric pressure, or the same pressure at a given time. **isobaric**, **isobarometric**, *a.* of equal barometric pressure; pertaining to isobars. [Gr. *baros,* weight]

isobathytherm, *n.* a line connecting points having the same temperature in a vertical section of a part of the sea. **isobathythermal**, *a.*

isobront, *n.* a line connecting points at which a peal of thunder is heard simultaneously.

isochasm, *n.* a line connecting points having an equal frequency of auroras. **isochasmic,** *a.*

isocheim, *n.* a line connecting places having the same mean winter temperature. **isocheimal**, **isocheimenal**, *a.* marking equal winters. *n.* an isocheimenal line. [Gr. *cheima,* winter (cp. L *heims*)]

isochor, *n.* a line (on a diagram representing relations between pressure and temperature) connecting the points denoting equal volumes. **isochoric**, *a.* [Gr. *chōra,* space]

isochromatic, *a.* of the same colour.

isochronal, -chronous, -chronic, *a.* denoting or occupying equal spaces of time; having regular periodicity. **isochronism**, *n.* the occupying of an equal space of time; regular periodicity (as the swinging of a pendulum). **isochronously,** *adv.*

isochroous, *a.* having a uniform colour throughout. [Gr. *chroa,* colour]

isoclinal, -clinic, *a.* having the same inclination or dip; having the same magnetic inclination; (*Geol.*) having the same angle or dip.

Isocrates, *n.* (436–338 BC), Athenian orator, a pupil of Socrates. He was a professional speechwriter and teacher of rhetoric.

isocrymal, *a.* connecting points having the same temperature at the coldest season. *n.* an isocrymal line. **isocryme**, *n.* [Gr. *krumos,* cold]

isodiametric, *a.* (*Bot., Cryst.*) equal in diameter.

isodimorphism, *n.* (*Cryst.*) isomorphism between substances that are dimorphous. **isodimorphic**, *a.* characterized by isodimorphism.

isodomon, -omum, *n.* a method of building practised by the ancient Greeks, with blocks of equal length, the vertical joints being above the middle of the blocks immediately below. **isodomous,** *a.* [Gr. *isodomon* (L *-domum*), from *domos,* a layer or course]

isodont, *a.* having the teeth all alike. **isodontous**, *a.* [Gr. *odous odontos,* tooth]

isodynamic, *a.* having equal force, esp. of terrestrial magnetism.

isoelectric, *a.* having identical electric potential.

isogamy, *n.* the conjugation of two cells or protoplasmic masses not differentiated into male or female. **isogamous,** *a.* [Gr. *gamia,* marriage]

isogeny, *n.* general similarity of origin; general correspondence or homology. **isogeneic, -genous,** *a.*

isogeotherm, *n.* a line connecting places having the same mean temperature below the surface. **isogeothermal, -thermic,** *a.*

isogloss, *n.* a line on a map separating off one region from another region differing from it in a specific dialectal feature. **isoglossal**, **-glottic**, *a.* [Gr. *glossa,* tongue]

isognathous, *a.* having the jaws projecting equally. [Gr. *gnathos,* jaw]

isogon, *n.* a geometrical figure having the angles all equal. **isogonal**, *a.* equiangular; isogonic. **isogonic**, *a.* connecting points (on the earth's surface) having the same magnetic declination or variation from true north. *n.* an isogonic line.

isogonism, *n.* the production of like sexual individuals from different stocks, as in certain hydrozoa. **isogonic**, *a.* [Gr. *gonos, gonē,* offspring]

isohel, *n.* a line connecting places having equal amounts of sunshine. [Gr. *hēlios,* sun]

isohyet, *n.* a line connecting places having equal amounts of rainfall. **isohyetal,** *a.* [Gr. *hyetos,* rain]

isolate, *v.t.* to place in a detached situation; (*Elec.*) to insulate; (*Chem.*) to obtain in an uncombined form; to subject to quarantine. **isolability**, *n.* **isolable,** *a.* **isolation,** *n.* **isolationism,** *n.* **isolationist,** *n.* one who believes in the policy of holding aloof from all political entanglements with other countries. **isolator,** *n.* [F *isoler,* It. *isolare,* L *insulāre,* to INSULATE]

isoleucine, *n.* an essential amino acid.

isomeric, -ical, *a.* (*Chem.*) having identical elements, molecular weight and proportions, with difference in physical characteristics or chemical properties owing to different grouping; of atomic nuclei, having the same numbers of protons and neutrons but different energy states. **isomer**, *n.* a compound, chemical group, atom etc. isomeric with one or more other compounds etc. **isomerism**, *n.* **isomerous**, *a.* (*Chem.*) isomeric; (*Bot., Zool. etc.*) having the parts or segments equal in number. [Gr. *isomerēs* (ISO-, *meros,* share)]

isometric, -ical, *a.* of equal measure. **isometric line,** *n.* a line on a graph representing variations of pressure and temperature at a constant volume. **isometric projection,** *n.* (*Eng.*) a drawing in approximate perspective from which lengths can be scaled. **isometrics,** *n. sing.* a system of exercises in which the muscles are strengthened as one muscle is opposed to another or to a resistant object.

isomorphism, *n.* (*Cryst.*) the property of crystallizing in identical or nearly identical forms; (*Math.*) identity of form and construction between two or more groups. **isomorphic, -phous,** *a.* [Gr. *morphē,* form]

-ison, *suf.* as in *comparison, orison*. [F *-aison, -eison, -ison,* L *-ātiōnem, -etiōnem, -itiōnem*]

isonomy, *n.* equality of political or legal rights. [Gr. *isonomia* (*nomos,* law)]

isopathy, *n.* the theory that disease may be cured by a product of the same disease. **isopathic**, *a.*

isoperimetrical, *a.* having equal perimeters. **isoperimetry**, *n.* the science of perimetrical figures.

isopleth, *n.* a line on a map connecting points at which a variable such as humidity has a constant value. **isoplethic**, *a.* [Gr. *plēthos,* quantity]

isopod, *n.* one of the Isopoda or sessile-eyed crustaceans characterized by seven pairs of thoracic legs almost of the same length. *a.* isopodous. **isopodan**, *n., a.* **isopodous**, *a.* [Gr. *pous podos,* a foot]

isopolity, *n.* equality or reciprocity of civil rights between different states.

isoprene, *n.* a hydrocarbon of the terpene group used esp. in synthetic rubber.

isoprinosine, (*esp. N Am.*) **-nocine,** *n.* an antiviral drug used in treatment of the early symptoms of AIDS.

isopterous, *a.* (*Ent.*) having the wings equal. [Gr. *pteron,* wing]

isorhythmic, *a.* (*Pros.*) having the same number of time units in the thesis and arsis as a dactyl and an anapaest; composed in the same rhythm, structure etc.

isosceles, *a.* of a triangle, having two sides equal. [late L *īsoscelēs,* Gr. *isoskelēs,* lit. equal-legged (*skelos,* leg)]

isoseismal, *a.* connecting points at which an earthquake has been of the same intensity. *n.* an isoseismal line. **isoseismic,** *a.*

isosmotic, *a.* equal in osmotic pressure.

isostatic, *a.* (*Geol.*) in equilibrium owing to equality of pressure on every side, as that normally prevailing in the crust of the earth. **isostasy**, *n.*

isotheral, *a.* connecting points having the same mean summer temperature. *n.* an isotheral line. [Gr. *theros,* summer]

isotherm, *n.* a line on a globe or map passing over places having the same mean temperature. **isothermal**, *n., a.*

isotonic, *a.* having equal tones; of muscles, having equal tension or tonicity; of the corpuscles of the blood, isosmotic. **isotonicity**, *n.* [Gr. *isotonos*]

isotope, *n.* one of a set of species of atoms of a chemical element having the same atomic number but differing in atomic weight etc. **isotopic, -ical**, *a.* **isotopy**, *n.* [Gr. *topos,* place]

isotropic, *a.* manifesting the same physical properties in every direction. **isotropism, -tropy**, *n.* **isotropous**, *a.* [Gr. *isotropos* (*tropos,* way, from *trepein,* to turn)]

I-spy, HY-SPY.

Israel[1], *n.* (*collect.*) the Israelites, the Jewish people; an autonomous country founded in Palestine in 1948. **Israeli**, *n., a.* (an inhabitant) of the State of Israel. **Israelite**, *n.* a descendant of Israel, a Jew. **Israelitic**, **Israelitish**, *a.* [L and Gr. *Isrāēl,* Heb. *yisrāēl,* striver with God]

Israel[2], *n.* State of (*Medinat Israel*). **area** 20,800 sq km/ 8029 sq miles (as at 1949 armistice). **capital** Jerusalem (not recognized by the United Nations). **towns** ports Tel Aviv/Jaffa, Haifa, Eilat; Bat-Yam, Holon, Ramat Gan, Petach Tikva, Beersheba. **physical** coastal plain of Sharon between Haifa and Tel Aviv noted since ancient times for fertility; high arid region in south and centre; river Jordan Rift Valley along the east is below sea level. **population** (1988) 4,442,000 (including 750,000 Arab Israeli citizens and over 1 million Arabs in the occupied territories); under the Law of Return 1950, 'every Jew shall be entitled to come to Israel as an immigrant', those from the East and E Europe are *Ashkenazim*, and from Spain, Portugal, and Arab N Africa are *Sephardim* (over 50% of the population is now of Sephardic descent). An Israeli-born Jew is a *Sabra*; about 500,000 Israeli Jews are resident in the US. Annual growth rate 1.8%. **exports** citrus and other fruit, avocados, chinese leaves, fertilizers, plastics, petrochemicals, textiles, electronics (military, medical, scientific, industrial), electro-optics, precision instruments, aircraft and missiles. **language** Hebrew and Arabic (official); Yiddish, European and W Asian languages. **religion** Israel is a secular state, but the predominant faith is Judaism; also Sunni Muslim, Christian, and Druse.

Israels, *n.* **Jozef** (1824–94), Dutch painter. In 1870 he settled in The Hague and became a leader of the Hague school of landscape painters, who shared some of their ideals with the Barbizon school in France. Israels's sombre and sentimental scenes of peasant life recall Millet.

Issei, *n.* Japanese immigrant in the US. [Jap., first generation]

Issigonis, *n.* **Alec** (1906–88), British engineer who designed the Morris Minor 1948 and the Mini-Minor 1959 cars, thus creating modern economy motoring and adding the word 'mini' to the English language.

issue, *n.* the act of passing or flowing out; egress, outgoing, outflow; that which passes or flows out; a discharge, as of blood; way or means of exit or escape; outlet; the mouth of a river; progeny, offspring; the produce of the earth; profits from land or other property; result, consequence; the point in debate; (*Law*) the point between contending parties; the act of sending, giving out or putting into circulation; publication; that which is published at a particular time; the whole quantity or number sent out at one time. *v.i.* to pass or flow out; to be published; to emerge (from); to be descended; to proceed, to be derived (from); to end or result (in). *v.t.* to send out; to publish; to put into circulation. **at issue,** in dispute; at variance. **side issue,** a less important issue arising from the main business or topic. **to join, take issue,** to take opposite sides upon a point in dispute; (*Law*) to submit an issue jointly for decision. **issuable,** *a.* **issuance,** *n.* the act of issuing. **issuant,** *a.* (*Her.*) emerging or issuing (from a chief). **issueless,** *a.* **issuer,** *n.* [OF, from pop. L *exūtus,* L *exitus,* from *exīre* (EX-, *īre,* to go)]

-ist, *suf.* denoting an agent, adherent, follower etc., as *Baptist, botanist, Calvinist, fatalist, monogamist, Socialist.* [F *-iste,* L *-ista,* Gr. *-istēs*]

Istanbul, *n.* city and chief seaport of Turkey; population (1985) 5,495,000. It produces textiles, tobacco, cement, glass, and leather. Founded as Byzantium about 660 BC, it was renamed Constantinople AD 330, and was the capital of the Byzantine Empire until captured by the Turks, 1453. As Istamboul it was capital of the Ottoman Empire until 1922.

-ister, *suf.* denoting an agent etc., as *chorister, sophister.* [OF *-istre,* var. of prec.]

isthmus, *n.* (*pl.* **-muses**) a neck of land connecting two larger portions of land; (*Anat. etc.*) a narrow passage or part between two larger cavities or parts. **Isthmian,** *a.* pertaining to an isthmus, esp. to the Isthmus of Corinth in Greece. **Isthmian games,** *n.pl.* games celebrated in ancient times at Corinth in the first and third years of each Olympiad, forming one of the four great Panhellenic festivals. **isthmitis,** *n.* inflammation of the fauces. [L, from Gr. *isthmos*]

istle, *n.* a species of Mexican agave, or the tough wiry fibre of its leaves, used for cordage etc. [Mex. Sp. *ixtli*]

It., (*abbr.*) Italy; Italian.

it[1], *3rd pers. neut. pron.* (*poss.* **its,** *pl.* **they,** *poss.* **their,** *obj.* **them**) the thing spoken about (ref. to noun mentioned or understood); the person understood (esp. questions and replies, also as subject of a verb the actual subject of which follows, usu. in apposition or introduced by 'that'); the grammatical subject of an impersonal verb; the indefinite object of an intransitive or transitive verb (as *to rough it, to fight it out*); the player in a children's game chosen to oppose the others; that which corresponds precisely to what one has been seeking; personal magnetism, charisma, sex appeal. [OE *hit,* neut. of *hē,* HE]

it[2], *n.* (*coll.*) Italian vermouth.

itacism, *n.* pronunciation of the Greek η as ē (cp. ETACISM under ETA). [Gr. *ēta,* η (cp. IOTACISM under IOTA)]

itacolumite, *n.* a granular quartzose slate which in thin slabs is sometimes flexible. [*Itacolumi,* mountain in Brazil]

Itagaki, *n.* **Taisuke** (1837–1919), Japanese military and political leader, the founder of Japan's first political party, the Jiyuto (Liberal Party) in 1875. Involved in the overthrow of the Tokugawa shogunate and the Meiji restoration, Itagaki became a champion of democratic principles although continuing to serve in the government for short periods.

Itaipu, *n.* the world's largest dam, situated on the Paraná River, SW Brazil.

ital., (*abbr.*) italics.

Italian, *a.* pertaining to Italy. *n.* a native of Italy; the Italian language. **Italian architecture,** *n.* architecture of the Italian peninsula after the fall of the Roman Empire. In the earliest styles – byzantine, romanesque, and gothic – the surviving buildings are mostly churches. From the renaissance and baroque periods there are also palaces, town halls, and so on. **Italian art,** *n.* painting and sculpture of Italy from the early Middle Ages to the present. Schools of painting arose in many of the city states, particularly Florence and Siena and, by the 15th cent., Venice. Florence was a major centre of the renaissance, along with Venice, and Rome was the focus of the high renaissance and baroque styles. **Italian handwriting,** *n.* the cursive writing adopted from Italy, opp. to Gothic. **Italian iron,** *n.* a cylindrical iron for fluting frills etc. **Italian language,** *n.* a member of the Romance branch of the Indo-European language family. With a strong infusion of Latin for religious, academic and educational purposes, the written standard has tended to be highly formal and divorced from the many regional dialects (often mutually unintelligible) that are still largely the everyday usage of the general population. **Italian Somaliland,** *n.* former Italian Trust Territory on the Somali coast of Africa extending to 502,300 sq km/ 194,999 sq miles. Established in 1892, it was extended in 1925 with the acquisition of Jubaland from Kenya; administered from Mogadishu; under British rule 1941-50. Thereafter it reverted to Italian authority before uniting with British Somaliland in 1960 to form the independent state of Somalia. **Italian warehouse,** *n.* a shop for the sale of oils, macaroni, dried fruits etc. †**Italianate,** *v.t.* to render Italian. *a.,* Italianized. **Italianism,** *n.* **Italianize, -ise,** *v.i., v.t.* [L *Italiānus*]

italic, *a.* applied to a sloping type (*thus*), introduced by the Venetian printer Aldus Manutius, *c.* 1500; pertaining to ancient Italy or the Italian races or their languages, esp. as distinguished from Roman. *n.pl.* italic letters or type. **italicize, -ise,** *v.t.* to print in italics; to emphasize. **italicism, italicization, -isation,** *n.* [L *Italicus,* Gr. *Italikos,* as prec.]

Italiot, *a.* pertaining to the Greek colonies in Italy. *n.* a native or inhabitant of these. [Gr. *Italiōtēs,* from *Italia,* Italy]

Italo-, *comb. form* Italian.

Italy, *n.* Republic of. **area** 301,300 sq km/116,332 sq miles. **capital** Rome. **towns** Milan, Turin; ports Naples, Genoa, Palermo, Bari, Catania. **physical** mountainous (Maritime Alps, Dolomites, Apennines); rivers Po, Adige, Arno, Tiber, Rubicon; islands of Sicily, Sardinia, Elba, Capri, Ischia. **population** (1988) 57,397,000; annual growth rate 0.1%. **exports** wine, fruit, vegetables, textiles (Europe's largest silk producer), leather goods, motor vehicles, electrical goods, chemicals, marble (Carrara), sulphur, mercury, iron, steel. **language** Italian, derived from Latin. **religion**

Roman Catholic 90%.

ITC, (*abbr.*) Independent Television Commission.

itch, *v.i.* to have a sensation of uneasiness in the skin exciting a desire to scratch the part; to feel a constant teasing desire (for etc.). *n.* a sensation of uneasiness in the skin causing a desire to scratch; an uneasy desire or craving (for etc.); a contagious skin-disease produced by the itch-mite *Sarcoptes scabiei.* **itchiness,** *n.* **itchy,** *a.* [OE *giccan* (cp. Dut. *jeuken,* G *jucken*)]

-ite, *suf.* belonging to, a follower of, as *Browningite, Pre-Raphaelite, Spinozite;* denoting fossils, minerals, chemical substances, explosives etc., as *belemnite, ichnite, dolomite, quartzite.* [F *-ite,* L *-ita,* Gr. *-itēs*]

item, *n.* a separate article or particular in an enumeration; an individual entry in an account, schedule etc.; a paragraph or detail of news in a newspaper; (*sl.*) an acknowledged couple; a well-established grouping. **item,** *adv.* likewise, also. *v.t.* to make a note or memorandum of. **itemize, -ise,** *v.t.* to set forth in detail. [L, in like manner, cp. *ita,* so, from *is,* he, with adv. suf. *-tem*]

iterate, *v.t.* to repeat, to say, make or do over and over again. **iterant,** *a.* repeating, iterating. **iteration,** *n.* **iterative,** *a.* [L *iterātus,* p.p. of *iterāre,* from *iterum,* again]

Ithuriel's spear, *n.* test of genuineness. [angel in *Paradise Lost*]

ithyphallic, *a.* of or pertaining to the erect phallus carried in Bacchic processions; in the metre of Bacchic verse; grossly indecent. *n.* a poem in this metre or style. [L *ithyphallicus,* Gr. *ithuphallikos* (*ithus,* straight, *phallikos,* from PHALLUS)]

itinerant, *a.* passing or moving from place to place; travelling on a circuit. *n.* one who journeys from place to place; a travelling preacher, a strolling player etc. **itineracy, itinerancy,** *n.* †**itinerantly,** *adv.* [L *itinerans -antem,* pres.p. of *itinerāri,* from *iter itineris,* a journey]

itinerary, *n.* an account of places and their distances on a road, a guide-book; a route taken or to be taken; an account of travels; †in the Roman Catholic Church, a form of prayer for clerics when travelling. *a.* pertaining to roads or to travel. **itinerate,** *v.i.* to journey from place to place; to preach on circuit. **itineration,** *n.*

-ition, *suf.* [F *-ition,* L *-itiōnem,* -ION]

-itious, *suf.* as in *adventitious, factitious, ambitious, nutritious.* [[1] L *-icius* or *-īcius;* [2] L *-ōsus,* -OUS, added to stems in *-it-*]

-itis, *suf.* denoting inflammation, as *gastritis, peritonitis.* [mod. L *-ītis,* Gr. *-itis,* orig. fem. of adjectives in *-itēs* (qualifying *nosos,* disease)]

ITN, (*abbr.*) Independent Television News.

Ito, *n.* **Hirobumi** (1841–1909), Japanese politician, prime minister and a key figure in the modernization of Japan, he was also involved in the Meiji restoration under Mutsuhito 1866–68 and in government missions to the US and Europe in the 1870s. As minister for home affairs, he drafted the Meiji constitution in 1889 and oversaw its implementation as prime minister the following year. While resident-general in Korea, he was assassinated by a Korean nationalist.

-itous, *suf.* [F *-iteux,* L *-itōsus* (*-it-,* OUS)]

its, *poss.* IT.

it's, contr. form of *it is.*

itself, *pron.* (*usu. in apposition*) used emphatically; used reflexively. **by itself,** alone, separately. **in itself,** independently of other things; in its essential qualities.

itsy-bitsy, *a.* (*coll.*) tiny.

ittria, etc. YTTRIA.

ITU, (*abbr.*) intensive therapy unit.

-ity, *suf.* [F *-ité,* L *-itātem,* nom. *-itas,* see -TY]

IUD, (*abbr.*) intrauterine device.

-ium, *suf.* used chiefly to form names of metals, as *aluminium, lithium, sodium.* [L]

Ivan III, *n.* **the Great** (1440–1505), grand duke of Muscovy from 1462, who revolted against Tatar overlordship by refusing tribute to Grand Khan Ahmed 1480. He claimed the title of tsar, and used the double-headed eagle as the Russian state emblem.

Ivan IV, *n.* **the Terrible** (1530–84), grand duke of Muscovy from 1533, he assumed power 1544, and was crowned as first tsar of Russia 1547. He conquered Kazan 1552, Astrakhan 1556, and Siberia 1581. His last years alternated between debauchery and religious austerities.

I've, contr. form of *I have.*

-ive, *suf.* disposed, serving or tending to; of the nature or quality of; as *active, massive, pensive, restive, talkative;* forming nouns, as *captive, detective.* [F *-if,* fem. *-ive,* L *-ivus*]

Ives[1], *n.* **Charles (Edward)** (1874–1954), US composer who experimented with atonality, quarter tones, clashing time signatures, and quotations from popular music of the time. He wrote five symphonies, including *Holidays Symphony* (1904–13), chamber music, including the *Concord Sonata,* and the orchestral *Three Places in New England* (1903–14) and *The Unanswered Question* (1908).

Ives[2], *n.* **Frederic Eugene** (1856–1937), US inventor who developed the halftone process of printing photographs in 1878. The process uses a screen to break up light and dark areas into different-sized dots. By 1886 he had evolved the halftone process now generally in use. Among his many other inventions was a three-colour printing process.

IVF, *n.* (*abbr.*) in vitro fertilization.

ivied IVY.

ivory, *n.* the hard white substance composing the tusks of the elephant, the narwhal etc.; the colour of ivory; (*pl.*) (*sl.*) teeth, billiard-balls, dice, keys of a piano etc. *a.* consisting, made of or resembling ivory. **black ivory,** black African slaves. **vegetable ivory,** the hard albumen of ivory-nuts. **ivory-black,** *n.* a kind of bone-black made of calcined ivory. **ivory-nut,** *n.* the seed of a tropical American palm, *Phytelephas macrocarpa.* **ivory tower,** *n.* a shelter from realities. **ivory turner,** *n.* a worker in ivory. [A-F *ivorie,* OF *yvoire* (F *ivoire*), L *eboreus,* made of ivory, from *ebur eboris,* ivory]

Ivory Coast, *n.* Republic of. **area** 322,463 sq km/ 124,471 sq miles. **capital** Abidjan; capital designate Yamoussoukro. **towns** Bouaké. **physical** tropical rainforest (diminishing as it is exploited) in the S; savanna and low mountains in the N. **population** (1988) 11,630,000; annual growth rate 3.7%. **exports** coffee, cocoa, timber, petroleum. **language** French (official). **religion** animist 65%, Muslim 24%, Christian 11%.

IVP, (*abbr.*) intravenous pyelogram (an X-ray of the kidneys).

ivy, *n.* (*pl.* **ivies**) an evergreen climbing plant, *Hedera helix,* usu. having five-angled leaves, and adhering by aerial rootlets. **ivy-bush,** *n.* a large bunch of ivy formerly hung in front of a tavern; a painted sign representing this. **ivy-geranium,** *n.* the ivy-leaved pelargonium. **Ivy League,** *n.* a collective term for eight long-established East Coast private universities in the US (Harvard, Yale, Princeton, Pennsylvania, Columbia, Brown, Dartmouth and Cornell). **ivy-mantled,** *a.* overgrown with ivy. **ivied,** *a.* [OE *ifig*]

iwis, *adv.* certainly (often spelt erron. *I wis*). [OE *gewis,* certain (cp. Dut. *gewis,* G *gewiss*)]

Iwo Jima, *n.* largest of the Japanese Volcano Islands in the W Pacific Ocean, 1222 km/764 miles S of Tokyo; area 21 sq km/8 sq miles. Annexed by Japan 1891, it was captured by the US 1945 after heavy fighting. It was returned to Japan 1968.

IWW, (*abbr.*) Industrial Workers of the World.

Ixia, *n.* a genus of S African bulbous flowering plants of the iris family. [Gr.]

Ixion, *n.* in Greek mythology, a king whom Zeus punished for his crimes by binding him to a fiery wheel rolling endlessly through the underworld.

ixolite, *n.* (*Min.*) an amorphous mineral resin found in bituminous coal, of greasy lustre and hyacinth-red colour. [G *ixolyt* (Gr. *ixos,* mistletoe, birdlime, -LITE)]

Iyar, *n.* the eighth month of the Jewish civil, and the second of the ecclesiastical year.

izard, *n.* a kind of antelope related to the chamois, inhabiting the Pyrenees. [F *isard,* etym. doubtful]

-ize, -ise, *suf.* forming verbs denoting to speak or act as; to follow or practise; to come to resemble to come into such a state; (*transitively*) to cause to follow, resemble or come into such a state; as *Anglicize, Christianize, evangelize, Hellenize.* [F *-iser,* late L *-izāre,* Gr. *-izein*]

Izmir, *n.* (formerly **Smyrna**) port and naval base in Turkey; population (1985) 1,490,000. Products include steel, electronics, and plastics. The largest annual trade fair in the Middle East is held here. Headquarters of North Atlantic Treaty Organization SE Command.

Iznik, *n.* town in Turkey; modern name of ancient Nicaea.

Izod Test, *n.* a test to determine particular characteristics of structural materials.

Izvestia, *n.* the official organ of the legislature of the USSR. [Rus., news]

†**izzard,** *n.* the letter *z.* [formerly *ezod,* F *ézed,* Gr. *zēta*]

J

J[1], **j**, the 10th letter in the English alphabet (*pl.* **jay's, Js, J's**), has the sound of a voiced explosive consonant, that of *g* in *gem*
J[2], symbol for current density; joule.
J., (*abbr.*) Journal; Judge; Justice.
JA, (*abbr.*) Judge Advocate.
jaal-goat, *n.* a type of ibex or goat found in Ethiopia and southern Egypt.
jab , *v.t.* to poke violently; to stab; to thrust (something) roughly (into). *n.* a sharp poke, a stab, a thrust; (*coll.*) a vaccination or injection. [prob. imit. (cp JOB[2])]
jabber, *v.i.* to talk volubly and incoherently; to chatter; to utter nonsensical or unintelligible sounds. *v.t.* to utter rapidly and indistinctly, *n.* rapid, indistinct, or nonsensical talk; gabble. **jabberer**, *n.* †**jabberment**, *n.* [prob. onomat., cp. GABBLE]
jabbernowl, JOBBERNOWL.
jabberwock, *n.* a fabulous monster created by Lewis Caroll in the poem *Jabberwocky*. **jabberwocky** *n.* nonsense, gibberish.
jabble, *v.i.* (*Sc.*) to splash, to dash in wavelets. *n.* a splashing; an agitation. [prob. onomat. (cp. DABBLE)]
jabiru, *n.* a bird of the genus *Mycteria,* S American stork-like wading-birds. [Tupi-Guarani]
jaborandi, *n.* the dried leaflets of certain species of *Pilocarpus,* tropical American shrubs, used as sudorific and diuretic drugs. [Tupi-Guarani]
jabot, *n.* a lace frill worn at the neck of a woman's bodice; a ruffle on a shirt front. [F, etym. unknown]
jacamar, *n.* any bird of the tropical American genus *Galbula,* resembling the kingfisher. [F, from Tupi-Guarani]
jacana, *n.* any bird of the grallatorial genus *Parra,* from the warmer parts of N and S America. [Port. *jaçaná,* Tupi-Guarani *jasaná*]
jacaranda, *n.* a genus of tropical American trees of the order Bignoniaceae yielding fragrant and ornamental wood. [Tupi-Guarani]
Jacchus, *n.* a small squirrel-like S American monkey. [Gr. *Iakkos,* Bacchus]
†**jacent**, *a.* recumbent, lying at length. [L *jācens -ntem,* pres.p. of *jacēre,* to lie]
jacinth, *n.* a variety of zircon; †a hyacinth. [OF *jacinthe,* HYACINTH]
jack[1], *n.* familiar or diminutive for John; hence, a fellow, one of the common people; a labourer, an odd-job man; a sailor; a pike, esp. a young or small one; the knave of cards; a contrivance for turning a spit; a contrivance for lifting heavy weights; a device for lifting a carriage-wheel etc.; a lever or other part in various machines; a wooden frame on which wood or timber is sawn; (*Mining*) a gad, a wooden wedge; a small flag [cp. UNION JACK]; a small white ball at which bowlers aim; (*N Am. sl.*) money. *v.t.* to lift, hoist, or move with a jack; (*sl.*) to resign, to give (up). **before one can say Jack Robinson,** quite suddenly and unexpectedly. **every man jack,** every individual. **cheap-jack** CHEAP. **steeple-jack** STEEPLE. **yellow jack,** yellow fever. **jack-a-dandy,** *n.* a little foppish fellow. †**Jack-a-Lent,** *n.* a puppet thrown at in Lenten games; (*fig.*) a simple fellow. **jack-bean,** *n.* a climbing plant of the *Camavali* genus. **jack-block,** *n.* a block for raising and lowering the top gallant mast. **jack-boot,** *n.* a large overall boot reaching to the thigh, worn by fishermen; a large boot with a front piece coming above the knee; (*fig.*) unintelligent and inhuman behaviour in dictatorial rule (from the high boots worn by German soldiers). **jack-by-the-hedge,** *n.* hedge garlic, *Sisymbrium alliaria.* **jack-chain,** *n.* (*Forestry*) an endless spiked chain which carries logs from one point to another. **jack-flag,** *n.* a flag hoisted at the spiritsail top-mast head. **Jack Frost,** *n.* frost personified. **jack-hammer,** *n.* a hand-held compressed-air hammer used for drilling rock. **jack-high,** *a., adv.* (*Bowls*) the distance up the green to the jack. **Jack-in-office,** *n.* one who assumes authority on account of holding a petty office. **jack-in-the-box,** *n.* a grotesque figure that springs out of a box when the lid is raised; a kind of firework; a large wooden male screw turning in a nut. **Jack-in-the-green,** *n.* a chimney-sweep enclosed in a framework covered with leaves, in old-fashioned May-day festivities. **Jack Ketch,** *n.* the public hangman. **jack-knife,** *n.* a large clasp-knife, esp. orig. one with a horn handle, carried by seamen. *v.i.* to double up like a jack-knife; of an articulated vehicle, to turn or rise and form an angle of 90° or less when out of control. **Jack of all trades,** *n.* one who can turn his hand to any business. **jack o' lantern,** *n.* an ignis fatuus. **jack-plane,** *n.* the first and coarsest of the joiner's bench-planes. **jackpot,** *n.* the money pool in card games and competitions; a fund of prize-money. **jack-pudding,** *n.* a merry-andrew. **Jack Russell,** *n.* a breed of small terrier introduced by John Russell in the 19th cent. **jack-screw,** *n.* a lifting implement worked by a screw. †**jack-smith,** *n.* one who makes roasting jacks. **jack-snipe,** *n.* a small European species of snipe. **jack-staff,** *n.* a flagstaff on the bowsprit cap for flying the jack, **jack-stay,** *n.* (*Naut.*) a rib or plate with holes, or a rod running through eye-bolts, passing along the upper side of a yard, to which the sail is bent. **jack-straw,** *n.* †a scare-crow; a person of no weight or substance, also a straw or twig used in jack-straws or spillikins, a children's game. **jack-tar** TAR[2]. **jack the lad,** *n.* an adventurous stylish young man. **jack-towel,** *n.* a long round towel on a roller. **Jacky,** *n.* (*Austral. coll.*) an Aboriginal man. [prob. dim. of *John* (E.W.B. Nicholson traced it (1892) to *Jackin, Jankin, John*), but perh. conn. with F *Jacques,* James, L *Jacōbus,* Gr. *Jakōbos,* Jacob]
jack[2], *n.* an E Indian fruit, like a coarser bread-fruit. **jack-tree,** *n.* [Port. *jaca,* Malayalam *chukka*]
jackal, *n.* a gregarious animal, *Canis aureus,* closely allied to the dog; one who does dirty work or drudgery for another (from the belief that the jackal hunts up prey for the lion). [Turk. *chakāl,* Pers. *shaghāl*]
jackanapes, *n.* a pert fellow; a coxcomb; †an ape. [*Jack Napes,* nickname of William de la Pole, Duke of Suffolk *d.* 1450, whose badge was a clog and chain such as was commonly used for a tame ape]
Jack and the Beanstalk, English fairy tale. Jack is the lazy son of a poor widow. When he exchanges their cow for some magic beans, the beans grow into a beanstalk that Jack climbs to a realm above the clouds. There he tricks a giant out of various magical treasures before finally killing him by cutting down the beanstalk.
jackaroo , *n.* (*Austral. sl*) a new-comer, a novice. **jillaroo,** *n.fem.* [*Jack; kangaroo*]
jackass, *n.* a male ass; a stupid ignorant fellow. **laughing jackass,** the Australian giant kingfisher, so called from its discordant cry. **jackass fish,** *n.* the edible 'morwong' of Australia and New Zealand. **jackass rabbit,** *n.* a male rabbit.
jackdaw, *n.* the smallest of the British crows, *Corvus monedula.*
jacket, *n.* a short coat or sleeved outer garment for men

or women; the coat of an animal; a wrapper, a cover; an outer covering of paper put on a book bound in cloth or leather; (*coll.*) the skin of a potato; an exterior covering or casing esp. a covering round a boiler, steam-pipe, cylinder of an internal-combustion engine etc., to prevent radiation of heat. *v.t.* to envelop in a jacket; (*coll.*) to thrash. **to dust one's jacket** DUST. **jacketed,** *a.* wearing a jacket. **jacketing,** *n.* (*coll.*) a thrashing. [OF *jaquette,* dim of *jaque,* JACK[2]]

jack-flag etc. JACK[1].

jacko, JOCKO.

jack o' lantern etc. JACK[1].

Jackson[1], *n.* **Alexander Young** (1882–1974). Canadian landscape painter, a leading member of the Group of Seven who aimed to create a specifically Canadian school of landscape art.

Jackson[2], *n.* **Andrew** (1767–1845), 7th president of the US 1829–37, a Democrat. He was born in South Carolina. He defeated a British force at New Orleans in 1815 (after the official end of the war in 1814) and was involved in the war which led to the purchase of Florida in 1819. After an unsuccessful attempt in 1824, he was elected president in 1828. Governing through a 'kitchen cabinet', he also made use of the presidential veto to oppose the renewal of the US bank charter. Re-elected in 1832, he continued his struggle against the power of finance. **Jacksonian Democracy,** *n.* in US history, a term describing the populist, egalitarian spirit pervading the presidencies of Andrew Jackson and Martin Van Buren, 1833–1841, which encouraged greater participation in the democratic process. Recent studies have questioned the professed commitment to popular control, emphasizing Jackson's alleged cult of personality.

Jackson[3], *n.* **Glenda** (1936–), British actress. She has made many stage appearances, including *Marat/Sade* (1966), and her films include the Oscar-winning *Women in Love* 1971.

Jackson[4], *n.* **Jesse** (1941–), US Democrat politician, campaigner for minority rights. He contested his party's 1984 and 1988 presidential nominations in an effort to increase voter registration and to put black issues on the national agenda. He is a notable public speaker.

Jackson[5], *n.* **John Hughlings** (1835–1911), English neurologist and neurophysiologist. As a result of his studies of epilepsy, Jackson demonstrated that particular areas of the cerebral cortex (outer mantle of the brain) control the functioning of particular organs and limbs.

Jackson[6], *n.* **Michael** (1958–), US rock singer and songwriter, known for his meticulously choreographed performances. He had his first solo hit in 1971; his worldwide popularity reached a peak with the albums *Thriller* (1982) and *Bad* (1987).

Jackson[7], *n.* **Thomas Jonathan** (1824–1863), known as 'Stonewall' Jackson, US Confederate general. In the American Civil War he acquired his nickname and his reputation at the Battle of Bull Run, from the firmness with which his brigade resisted the Northern attack. In 1862 he organized the Shenandoah valley campaign, and assisted Lee's invasion of Maryland. He helped to defeat Gen Joseph E Hooker's Union army at the battle of Chancellorsville, Virginia, but was fatally wounded by one of his own men in the confusion of battle.

Jacksonville, *n.* port, resort, and commercial centre in Florida, US; population (1980) 541,000. The port has naval installations and ship repair yards. To the N the Cross-Florida Barge Canal links the Atlantic with the Gulf of Mexico.

Jack the Ripper, popular name for the unidentified mutilator and murderer of five women prostitutes in the Whitechapel area of London in 1888.

Jacob[1], *n.* in the Old Testament, Hebrew patriarch, son of Isaac and Rebecca, who obtained the rights of seniority from his twin brother Esau by trickery. He married his cousins Leah and Rachel, serving their father Laban seven years for each, and at the time of famine in Canaan joined his son Joseph in Egypt. His 12 sons were the traditional ancestors of the 12 tribes of Israel.

Jacob[2], *n.* **François** (1920–), French biochemist who, with Jacques Monod, did pioneering research in molecular genetics and showed how the production of proteins from DNA is controlled.

Jacobean, *n.* a style in the arts, particularly in architecture and furniture, during the reign of James I (1603–25) in England. Following the general lines of Elizabethan design, but using classical features more widely, it adopted many motifs from Italian renaissance design. *a.* belonging to the reign of James I.

Jacobin, *n.* a dominican friar; a member of a revolutionary republican club, that met in the hall of the Jacobin friars, in the Rue St Jacques, Paris, 1789–94; an extreme revolutionist, a violent republican; a variety of hooded pigeon. **Jacobinic, †-ical,** *a.* **Jacobinism** *n.* **Jacobinize, -ise,** *v.t.* [F, from low L *Jacōbinus,* as prec.]

Jacobite, *n.* a partisan of James II after his abdication, or of the Stuart pretenders to the throne. *a.* pertaining to or holding the opinions of the Jacobites. **Jacobitic, -ical,** *a.* **Jacobitism,** *n.* [L *Jacōbus,* James, -ITE]

Jacob's ladder, *n.* a garden plant, *Polemonium caeruleum,* with closely pinnate leaves; a rope ladder with wooden rounds. [with alln. to the patriarch Jacob's dream (Gen. xxviii.12)]

Jacob's staff, *n.* †a pilgrim's staff; †a staff containing a concealed dagger; a cross-staff, an instrument for measuring distances and heights. [with alln. to St James the Less, whose emblem was a pilgrim's staff and a scallop]

Jacobus, *n.* a gold coin struck in the reign of James I. [L, see JACOBITE]

jaconet, *n.* a fine, close, white cotton cloth, rather heavier than cambric. [corr. from Hind. *Jagganāthī,* whence JUGGERNAUT]

Jacquard, *n.* **Joseph Marie** (1752–1834), French textile manufacturer, who invented a punched-card system for programming designs on a carpet-making loom. In 1804 he constructed looms that used a series of punched cards which controlled the pattern of longitudinal warp threads depressed before each sideways passage of the shuttle. On later machines the punched cards were joined to form an endless loop which represented the 'program' for the repeating pattern of a carpet.

Jacquard loom, *n.* a loom for weaving figured fabrics. **jacquard** *n.* fabric woven in such a manner. [French inventor J.M. *Jacquard*]

jacquerie, *n.* a revolt of the peasants against the nobles in France, in 1357–8; any peasant revolt. [F, from *Jacques,* a peasant]

jactation, *n.* the act of throwing; agitation of the body in exercise, as in riding; jactitation; †boasting, bragging. **jactitation,** *n.* restlessness, a tossing or twitching of the body or limbs; (*Law*) a false pretension to marriage. [L *jactātio,* from *jactāre,* to throw, freq. of *jacere,* see foll.]

†jaculate, *v.t.* to throw, dart, or hurl. † **jaculation,** *n.* **jaculator,** *n.* one who throws or darts; the archer-fish. **†jaculatory,** *a.* throwing or darting out suddenly; ejaculatory. [L *jaculātus,* p.p. of *jaculārī,* from *jaculum,* javelin, from *jacere,* to throw]

Jacuzzi®, *n.* a type of bath or small pool with a mechanism which makes the water swirl round; this mechanism itself; a bathe in such a bath.

Jacuzzi, *n.* **Candido** (1903–1986), Italian-born US inventor and engineer, who invented the Jacuzzi, which he developed for his 15-month-old son, a sufferer from rheumatoid athritis.

jade[1], *n.* a broken-down, worthless horse; (*playfully or in contempt*) an old woman, a wench, a young woman. *v.t.* to overdrive; (*usu. in p.p.*) to tire out. *v.i.* to become weary. **jadedly,** *adv.* **jadedness,** *n.* **†jadery,** *n.* **jadish,** *a.* [etym. doubtful]

jade[2], *n.* a green, massive, sometimes cryptocrystalline, silicate of lime and magnesia, used for ornamental purposes; applied to other minerals of a similar appearance. [F, from Sp. *piedra di ijada* (stone of the side), L ILIUM (because supposed to cure colic)]

Jade Emperor, *n.* in Chinese religion, the supreme god, Yu Huang, of pantheistic Taoism, who watches over human actions and is the ruler of life and death.

jaeger, *n.* a huntsman; a sharpshooter; an attendant waiting on a person of quality. [G from *jagen,* hunt]

Jaeger®, *n.* a woollen material used in clothes-making, orig. one containing no vegetable fibre. [from Dr Gustav *Jaeger*, the manufacturer]

Jaffa 1, Jaffa orange, *n.* a type of orange from *Jaffa* in Israel.

Jaffa 2, (Biblical name **Joppa**) *n.* port in W Israel, part of Tel Aviv-Jaffa from 1950.

Jaffna, *n.* capital of Jaffna district, Northern Province, Sri Lanka. The focal point of Hindu Tamil nationalism and the scene of recurring riots during the 1980s.

jag, *n.* a notch; a ragged piece, tooth, or point; a stab, a prick; (*esp. Sc.*) a vaccination or injection; (*sl.*) a bout of drinking or drug-taking. *v.t.* to cut or tear raggedly; to cut into notches, to form denticulations in. **jagged,** *a.* having notches; ragged, sharply uneven; (*Bot.*) cut coarsely. **jaggedly,** *adv.* **jaggedness,** *n.* **jagger,** *n.* one who or that which jags; a toothed chisel. **jaggy,** *a.* [prob. imit.]

†**jaggery,** *n.* a coarse dark-brown kind of sugar made in India from the juice of certain palms. [Port. *jágara,* Canarese *sharkare,* Hind. *shakkar,* Sansk. *çarkarā,* SUGAR]

Jagan 1, *n.* **Cheddi** (1918–), Guyanese left-wing politician. Educated in British Guyana and the US, he led the People's Progressive Party from 1950, and in 1961 he became the first prime minister of British Guyana.

Jagan 2, *n.* **Janet** (1920–), Guyanese left-wing politician, wife of Cheddi Jagan. She was general secretary of the People's Progressive Party 1950–70.

jaguar, *n.* a S American feline animal, *Felis onca,* resembling the leopard. [Tupi-Guarani *yagouara*]

Jaguar, *n.* British car manufacturer, which has enjoyed a long association with motor racing. They were one of the most successful companies in the 1950s and won the Le Mans 24 Hour race five times 1951–58.

jaguarundi, *n.* a S American wild cat.

Jah, *n.* Jehovah. **Jahveh,** *n.* (*form adopted by Bibl. critics*). **Jahvism, Jahvist,** *n.* [Heb. *Yah,* shortened form of *Yahiveh,* JEHOVAH]

Jahad, JIHAD.

Jahangir, *n.* **'Conqueror of the World'** (1569–1627), name adopted by Salim. Third Mughal emperor of India from 1605, when he succeeded his father Akbar the Great. He designed the Shalimar Gardens in Kashmir and buildings and gardens in Lahore.

Jahweh, JEHOVAH.

jai-alai, *n.* a game played by two or four players on a court, who wear woven baskets tied to their wrists and using these hurl a ball at the walls. [Sp., from Basque *jai,* festival, *alai,* merry]

jail, gaol, *n.* a prison, a public place of confinement for persons charged with or convicted of crime. **jail-bird,** *n.* one who has been to prison; an inveterate criminal. **jail-break,** *n.* an escape from jail. **jail-delivery,** *n.* a commission empowering judges to try the prisoners in a place, and so clear the jail. **jail-fever,** *n.* an old name for typhus formerly endemic in jails. **jailer, gaoler,** *n.* the keeper of a prison. **jaileress, gaoleress,** *n. fem.* [A-F *gaole,* OF *jaiole* (F *geôle*), late L *gabiola,* dim. of *gabia,* L *cavea,* CAGE]

Jain, Jaina, *n.* a professor of Jainism. *a.* of or belonging to the Jains or Jainism. **Jainism,** *n.* Indian religion, sometimes regarded as an offshoot from Hinduism. Jains believe that non-injury to living beings is the highest religion, and their code of ethics is based on sympathy and compassion. They also believe in karma. In Jainism there is no deity, and like Buddhism it is a monastic religion. Jains number about 3.3 million. **Jainist,** *n.* [Hindi, from Sansk. *jaina,* pertaining to a Buddha or Saint, *jina*]

Jaipur, *n.* capital of Rajasthan, India; population (1981) 1,005,000. Formerly the capital of the state of Jaipur, it was merged with Rajasthan in 1949. Products include textiles and metal products.

Jakarta, Djakarta *n.* capital of Indonesia on the NW coast of Java; population (1980) 6,504,000. Industries include textiles, chemicals, and plastics; a canal links it with its port of Tanjung Priok where rubber, oil, tin, coffee, tea, and palm oil are among its exports; also a tourist centre.

jake, *a.* (*coll.*) honest; correct; very good.

†**jakes,** *n.* a privy; excrement. [etym. doubtful perh. from F *Jacques* James]

Jakeš, *n.* **Miloš** (1922–), Czech communist politician, a member of the Politburo from 1981 and party leader 1987–89. A conservative, he supported the Soviet invasion of Czechoslovakia in 1968. He was forced to resign in Nov 1989 following a series of pro-democracy mass rallies.

Jalalabad, *n.* capital of Nangarhar province, E Afghanistan, on the road from Kabul to Peshawar in Pakistan. The city was beseiged by mujaheddin rebels in 1989 after the withdrawal of Soviet troops from Afghanistan.

jalap, *n.* the dried tubercles of *Exogonium purga,* used as a purgative. **jalapin,** *n.* an amorphous glucoside existing in jalap root. [F, from Sp. *jalapa, Xalapa,* Aztec *Xalapan,* place in Mexico]

jalopy, *n.* (*coll.*) a much-worn automobile. [etym. unknown]

jalouse, *v.t.* (*Sc.*) to suspect; to surmise. [F *jalouser,* from *jaloux,* JEALOUS]

jalousie, *n.* a louvre blind, a Venetian shutter. **jaloused,** *a.* [F, JEALOUSY]

jam 1, *v.t.* (*past, p.p.* **jammed**) to wedge or squeeze (in or into); to squeeze, to compress between two surfaces; to squeeze together; to block up by crowding into; to make (a machine etc.) immovable or unworkable by forcible handling; to prevent clear radio reception of a signal by transmitting an interfering signal on the same wavelength. *v.i.* of a machine etc. to become immovable or unworkable by rough handling; of a jazz musician to improvise freely; to take part in a jam session; *n.* a crush, a squeeze; a stoppage in a machine due to jamming; a crowd, a press; congestion as in traffic jam. **to be in a jam,** to be in a predicament. **jam-packed,** *a.* very crowded; filled to capacity. **jam session,** *n.* (*coll.*) an improvised performance by jazz musicians. [prob. imit.]

jam 2, *n.* a conserve of fruit made by boiling with sugar. **jam-jar,** *n.* **jam-pot,** *n.* **jammy,** (*coll.*) sticky (with jam); lucky; desirable. [prob. JAM 1]

Jamaica, *n.* island in the Caribbean, to the S of Cuba, and to the W of Haiti. **area** 11,425 sq km/4,410 sq miles **capital** Kingston. **towns** Montego Bay, Spanish Town, St Andrew. **physical** mountainous. **population** (1987) 2,300,000 (a mixture of several ethnic groups); annual growth rate 1.5%. **exports** sugar, bananas, bauxite, rum, coffee, coconuts, liqueurs, cigars. **language** English, Jamaican creole. **religion** Protestant 70%, Rastafarian. **Jamaica pepper,** *n.* Allspice; pimento.

jamb, *n.* one of the upright sides of a doorway, window, or fireplace; †a piece of armour for the leg; (*Her.*) a leg. [F *jambe,* leg, late L *gamba,* a hoof, prob. from Celt. (cp. W *cam,* crooked)]

jambalaya, *n.* a Southern US dish consisting of meat, sea-food, rice, onions etc. [F, Provençal *jambalaia*]

†**jambeaux, giambeaux,** *n.pl.* leg or shin-pieces of armour; leggings. [A-F from prec.]

†**jambee,** *n.* a walking-stick or cane from the Jambi district. [*Jambi,* in Sumatra]

jambok, SJAMBOK.

jamboree, *n.* a Scouts rally; a frolic.

James 1, St, *n.* **the Great** (d. AD 44), a New Testament apostle, originally a Galilean fisherman, he was the son of Zebedee and brother of the apostle John. He was put to death by Herod Agrippa. Patron saint of Spain. Feast day 25 July.

James 2, St, *n.* **the Just** (1st cent. AD), the New Testament brother of Jesus, to whom Jesus appeared after the Resurrection. Leader of the Christian church in Jerusalem, he was the author of the biblical Epistle of James.

James[1], *n.* **Henry** (1843–1916), US novelist, who lived in Europe from 1875 and became a naturalized British subject 1915. His novels deal with the impact of European culture on the US soul. They include *The Portrait of a Lady* (1881), *Washington Square* (1881), *The Bostonians* (1886), *The Ambassadors* (1903), and *The Golden Bowl* (1904). He also wrote more than a hundred shorter works of fiction, notably the supernatural tale *The Turn of the Screw* (1898).

James[2], *n.* **Jesse** (1847–1882), US bank and train robber, born in Missouri and a leader (with his brother Frank) of the Quantrill gang. Jesse was killed by an accomplice; Frank remained unconvicted and became a farmer.

James[3], *n.* **M(ontague) R(hodes)** (1862–1936), British writer, theologian, linguist, and medievalist. He wrote *Ghost Stories of an Antiquary* (1904) and other supernatural tales.

James[4], *n.* **William** (1842–1910), US psychologist and philosopher, brother of the novelist Henry James. He turned from medicine to psychology and taught at Harvard 1872–1907. His books include *Principles of Psychology* (1890), *The Will to Believe* (1897), and *Varieties of Religious Experience* (1902), one of the most important works on the psychology of religion.

James Edward Stuart *n.* (1688–1766), British prince, known as the Old Pretender (for Jacobites James III). Son of James II, he was born at St James's Palace and after the revolution of 1688 was taken to France. He landed in Scotland in 1715 to head a Jacobite rebellion, but withdrew for lack of support. In his later years he settled in Rome.

James I[1], *n.* **the Conqueror** (1208–1276), king of Aragon from 1213, when he succeeded his father. He conquered the Balearic Islands and took Valencia from the Moors, dividing it with Alfonso X of Castile by a treaty of 1244. Both these exploits are recorded in his autobiography *Llibre deis feyts*. He largely established Aragon as the dominant power in the Mediterranean.

James I[2], *n.* (1394–1437), king of Scotland 1406–37, who assumed power 1424. He was a cultured and strong monarch, whose improvements in the administration of justice brought him popularity among the common people. He was assassinated by a group of conspirators led by the Earl of Atholl.

James I[3], *n.* (1566–1625), king of England from 1603 and Scotland (James VI) from 1567. The son of Mary, Queen of Scots, and Lord Darnley, he succeeded on his mother's abdication from the Scottish throne, assumed power 1583, established a strong centralized authority, and in 1589 married Anne of Denmark (1574–1619). As successor to Elizabeth in England, he alienated the Puritans by his High Church views and Parliament by his assertion of divine right, and was generally unpopular because of his favourites, such as Buckingham, and because of his schemes for an alliance with Spain. He was succeeded by his son Charles I.

James II[1], *n.* (1430–1460), king of Scotland from 1437, who assumed power 1449. The only surviving son of James I, he was supported by most of the nobles and parliament. He sympathized with the Lancastrians during the War of the Roses, and attacked English possessions in S Scotland. He was killed while besieging Roxburgh Castle.

James II[2], *n.* (1633–1701), king of England and Scotland (**James VII**) from 1685, second son of Charles I. He succeeded Charles II. James married Anne Hyde 1659 (1637–71, mother of Mary II and Anne) and Mary of Modena 1673 (mother of James Edward Stuart). He became a Catholic 1671, which led first to attempts to exclude him from the succession, then to the rebellions of Monmouth and Argyll, and finally to the Whig and Tory leaders' invitation to William of Orange to take the throne in 1688. James fled to France, led a rising in Ireland 1689, but after defeat at the Battle of the Boyne 1690 remained in exile in France.

James III, *n.* (1451–1488), king of Scotland from 1460, who assumed power 1469. His reign was marked by rebellions by the nobles, including his brother Alexander, duke of Albany. He was murdered during a rebellion.

James IV, *n.* (1473–1513), king of Scotland from 1488, who married Margaret (1489–1541, daughter of Henry VII) in 1503. He invaded England 1513, but was defeated and killed at Flodden.

Jameson, *n.* **Leander Starr** (1853–1917), British colonial administrator. In South Africa, early in 1896, he led the Jameson Raid from Mafeking into Transvaal, in support of the non-Boer colonists there, in an attempt to overthrow the government, for which he served some months in prison. Returning to South Africa, he succeeded Cecil Rhodes as leader of the Progressive Party of Cape Colony, where he was prime minister 1904–08.

James V, *n.* (1512–1542), king of Scotland from 1513, who assumed power 1528. Following an attack on Scottish territory by Henry VIII's forces, he was defeated near the border at Solway Moss 1542.

James VI, JAMES I OF ENGLAND.

James VII, JAMES II OF ENGLAND.

Jammu and Kashmir, *n.* state of N India. **area** 101,300 sq km/39,102 sq miles; another 78,900 sq km/ 30,455 is occupied by Pakistan, and 42,700 sq km/ 16,482 by China. **capital** Srinagar (winter); Jammu (summer). **towns** Leh. **population** (1981) 5,982,000 (Indian-occupied territory). **products** timber, grain, rice, fruit, silk, carpets.

jampan, *n.* a sedan-chair borne on two bamboo poles by four men. **jampanee**, *n.* one of the bearers of a jampan. [Bengali *jhāmpān,* Hind. *jhappān*]

Jan., (*abbr.*) January.

Janáček, *n.* **Leoš** (1854–1928), Czech composer. He became director of the Conservatoire at Brno in 1919 and professor at the Prague Conservatoire in 1920. His music, highly original and influenced by Moravian folk music, includes arrangements of folk songs, operas (*Jenufa* 1904, *The Cunning Little Vixen* 1924), and the choral *Glagolitic Mass* (1927).

Janam Sakhis, *n.* a collection of stories about the life of Nanak, the first guru (teacher) of Sikhism.

Janata, *n.* alliance of political parties in India formed 1971 to oppose Indira Gandhi's Congress Party. Victory in the election brought Morarji Desai to power as prime minister but he was unable to control the various groups within the alliance and resigned 1979. His successors fared little better and the elections of 1980 overwhelmingly returned Indira Gandhi to office.

jane, *n.* (*Am., Austral. sl.*) a woman. [name]

Jane Eyre, *n.* a novel by Charlotte Brontë, published 1847. Jane, an orphan, is engaged as governess to Mr Rochester's ward Adèle. Rochester and Jane fall in love, but their wedding is prevented by the revelation that Rochester already has a wife. Jane flees, but later returns to find the house destroyed by fire and Rochester blinded in a vain attempt to save his wife. Jane and Rochester marry.

jangle, *v.i.* to sound harshly or discordantly; to wrangle, to bicker; †to chatter. *v.t.* to cause to sound discordantly; to utter harshly. *n.* wrangling, bickering; discordant sound, as of bells out of tune; noisy chatter. **jangler,** *n.* a wrangler. [OF *jangler,* prob. onomat.]

janissary JANIZARY.

janitor, *n.* a doorkeeper; caretaker, porter; (*Sc.*) the caretaker of a school. **janitorial**, *a.* **janitorship,** *n.* **janitress**, **-trix**, *n. fem.* [L from *jānua,* door]

janizary, janissary, *n.* a soldier of the old Turkish infantry forming the Sultan's bodyguard (originally young prisoners trained to arms), disbanded in 1826. †**janizarian**, *a.* [Turk. *yeni-tsheri* (*yeni,* new, *tscheri,* soldiery)]

Jannequin, *n.* **Clament** (*c.* 1472– *c.* 1560), French composer. He studied with Josquin Desprez and is remembered for choral works that incorporate images from real life, such as birdsong and the cries of street vendors.

Jannings, *n.* **Emil** (1882–1950), stage name of Theodor Emil Jarenz. German actor whose greatest success was in silent films of the 1920s, as in *The Last Command* (1928). In *Der blaue Engel/The Blue Angel* (1930) he played a schoolteacher who loses his head over Marlene Dietrich. He remained in Germany during the Nazi era.

jannock[1], *n.* (*North., chiefly Lancs.*) oaten bread, an oaten loaf.

jannock[2], *a.*, *adv.* fair, straightforward.

Jansen, *n.* **Cornelius** (1585–1638). Dutch Roman Catholic theologian, founder of Jansenism with his book *Augustinus* 1640. He became professor at Louvain, Belgium, in 1630, and bishop of Ypres, Belgium, in 1636. **Jansenism**, *n.* Christian teaching of Cornelius Jansen, which divided the Roman Catholic Church in France in the mid-17th cent. Emphasizing the more predestinatory approach of Augustine's teaching, as opposed to that of the Jesuits, Jansenism was supported by the philosopher Pascal and Antoine Arnauld (a theologian linked with the abbey of Port Royal). Jansenists were excommunicated in 1719. **Jansenist**, *n.*

Jansky, *n.* **Karl Guthe** (1905–1950), US radio engineer, who discovered that the Milky Way galaxy emanates radio waves.

janty, jantily etc. JAUNTY.

January, *n.* the name given to the first month of the year. [L *jānuārius,* from foll.]

janus, *n.* an ancient Roman deity presiding over doors and gates, and usually represented with two heads looking in opposite directions. **Janus-cloth,** *n.* a fabric with different colours on opposite sides. [L]

jap, *a.*, *n.* (*derog. or offensive*) short form of JAPANESE. **Jap silk,** *n.* a pure silk fabric plainly woven from net silk yarns.

japan, *n.* an intensely hard varnish, or varnishing liquid, made from linseed oil, resin, shellac etc.; orig. a hard, black varnish obtained from *Stagmaria verniciflua;* work varnished and figured in the Japanese style. *v.t.* (*past, p.p.* **japanned**) to cover with or as with japan. **Japan earth,** Catechu. **Japanize, -ise,** *v.t.* **Japanization, -isation,** *n.* **japanner,** *n.* one whose business is to japan goods; †a shoeblack. [island empire lying east of China]

Japan, *n.* country in E Asia, occupying a group of islands situated in the N Pacific, to the E of North and South Korea. **area** 377,815 sq km/145,837 sq miles. **capital** Tokyo. **towns** Fukuoka, Kitakyushu, Kyoto, Sapporo; ports Osaka, Nagoya, Yokohama, Kobe, Kawasaki. **physical** mountainous, volcanic; comprises over 1,000 islands, of which the chief are Hokkaido, Honshu, Shikoku, Kyushu, Ryukyu. **population** (1987) 122,264,000; annual growth rate 0.7%. **exports** televisions, cassette and video recorders, radios, cameras, computers, robots, other electronic and electrical equipment, cars and other vehicles, ships, iron, steel, chemicals, textiles. **language** Japanese. **religion** Shinto and Buddhist (often combined), Christian (minority). 30% of the population claim to have a personal religious faith. **Japan Current,** (Kuroshio) *n.* warm ocean current flowing from Japan to North America. **Japanese,** *a.* pertaining to Japan or its people *n.* a native or inhabitant of Japan; the language of Japan. **Japanese art,** *n.* the painting, sculpture, and design of Japan. Japanese art was early influenced by China. Painting developed a distinct Japanese character, bolder and more angular, with the spread of Zen Buddhism in the 12th cent. Ink painting and calligraphy flourished, followed by book illustration and decorative screens. Japanese prints developed in the 17th cent, with multicolour prints invented around 1765. Buddhist sculpture proliferated from 580, and Japanese sculptors excelled at portraits. Japanese pottery stresses simplicity. **Japanese cedar,** *n.* a tall Japanese conifer. **Japanese language,** *n.* a traditionally isolated language of E Asia, spoken almost exclusively in the islands of Japan. Possibly related to Korean, Japanese is culturally and linguistically influenced by Mandarin Chinese and written in Chinese-derived ideograms as well as syllabic alphabets.

jape, *v.i.* to jest, to play tricks. †*v.i.* to mock, to deride, to cheat. *n.* a jest, a trick, a joke. **japer,** *n.* [OF japer, to yelp]

Japhetic, *a.* of, pertaining to, or descended from Japheth, the third son of Noah.

Japji, *n.* Sikh morning hymn which consists of verses from the beginning of the holy book *Guru Granth Sahib.*

Japonic, *a.* Japanese. **japonica**, *n.* the Japanese quince, *Phyrus Japonica,* a common garden shrub. **japonically,** *adv.* **japonicize, -ise,** *v.i.* [F *Japon*]

jar[1], *v.i.* (*past, p.p.* **jarred**) to emit a harsh or discordant sound; to vibrate harshly; to be discordant, disagreeable, or offensive; to disagree, to clash, to be inconsistent (with). *v.i.* to cause to shake or tremble; to give a shock to; †to offend, to displease. *n.* a harsh vibration as from a shock; a harsh discordant sound; a shock; a disagreement, a conflict of opinions or interests. **jarringly,** *adv.* [prob. onomat.]

jar[2], *n.* a vessel of glass or earthenware of various shapes and sizes, used for various domestic purposes; (*coll.*) (a glass of) alcoholic drink. **jarful,** *n.* [F *jarre,* prob. through Sp. *jarra,* from Arab. *jarrah*]

jar[3], *n.* a word found only in the phrase 'on the jar', partly closed, ajar [cp. AJAR[1]]. [CHAR[2]]

jardiniere, *n.* an ornamental pot or stand for growing flowers in a room etc. [F, fem. of *jardinier,* gardener]

jargon[1], *n.* unintelligible talk; gibberish, gabble; debased or illiterate speech or language; any professional, technical or specialized language. *v.i.* to talk unintelligibly; (of birds) to twitter. **jargoner,** *n.* **jargonesque**, **jargonic**, *a.* **jargonist,** *n.* **jargonize, -ise,** *v.i.* **jargonization, -isation,** *n.* [OF *jargon, gargon,* etym. doubtful]

jargon[2], *n.* a transparent, colourless or smoky variety of zircon found in Sri Lanka. [F, from It. *giargone*]

jargonelle, *n.* a kind of early pear. [F]

jarl, *n.* a Norse or Dutch nobleman or chieftain, an earl or count. [Icel., EARL]

jarrah, *n.* the W Australian mahogany gum-tree, *Eucalyptus marginata.* [Austral. abor. *jerryh*]

Jarrett, *n.* **Keith** (1945–), US jazz pianist and composer, an eccentric innovator who performs both alone and with small groups. *The Köln Concert* (1975) is a characteristic solo live recording.

jarringly JAR[1].

Jarry, *n.* **Alfred** (1873–1907), French satiric dramatist, whose *Ubu Roi* 1896 foreshadowed the Theatre of the Absurd and the French Surrealist movement.

Jaruzelski, *n.* **Wojciech** (1923–), Polish general, communist leader from 1981, president from 1985. He imposed martial law for the first year of his rule, suppressed the opposition, and banned trade union activity, but later released many political prisoners. In 1989, elections in favour of *Solidarity* forced Jaruzelski to speed up democratic reforms, overseeing a transition to a new form of 'socialist pluralist' democracy.

jarvey, *n.* (the driver of) a hackney-coach or Irish jaunting-car. [pers. name *Jarvis*]

Jarvik 7, *n.* the first successful artificial heart intended for permanent implantation in a human being. Made from polyurethane plastic and aluminium, it is powered by compressed air. Dr Barney Clark became the first person to receive a Jarvik 7 in Salt Lake City in Dec 1982; it kept him alive for 112 days.

Jas, (*abbr.*) James.

jasey, *n.* a familiar name for a worsted wig. [said to be a corr. of *Jersey,* as being made of Jersey yarn]

jasmine, *n.* any plant of the genus *Jasminum,* many of which are climbers with sweetscented white or yellow flowers, esp. the common white *J. officinale.* [F *jasmin, jassemin, jessemin,* Arab. *yāsmīn*]

Jason, *n.* in Greek mythology, leader of the Argonauts who sailed in the Argo to Colchis of the Golden Fleece.

jaspé, *a.* (*Ceram.*) having an appearance like jasper; of mottled appearance. [F *jasper,* to marble]

jasper, *n.* an impure variety of quartz, of many colours and shades, opaque even in thin splinters; a greenish marble, with small red spots; (*Am. sl.*) a fellow, a man. †**jasperated**, *a.* mixed with jasper. **jasperite**, *n.* a red variety of jasper found near Lake Superior. **jasperize, -ise**, *v.t.* †**jaspery,** †**jaspidean, -eous**, *a.* like jasper; of the nature of or containing jasper. **jaspoid**, *a.* resembling jasper. **jasperous,** *a.* †**jasponyx**, *n.* jasper marked like the human nail. [OF *jaspre, jaspe,* L and Gr. *iaspis* Oriental in origin (cp. Arab. *yasb,* Pers. *yashp,* Heb. *yāshpeh)*]

Jataka, *n.* collections of Buddhist legends compiled at various dates in several countries; the oldest and most complete has 547 stories. They were collected before AD 400.

jato, *n.* (acronym) *j*et *a*ssisted *t*ake-*o*ff.

†**jaunce,** *v.i.* to make a horse prance. [prob. from an OF *jancer*]

jaunder, *v.i.* to gossip, to chat. *n.* idle talk. [Sc., etym. unknown]

jaundice, *n.* a condition due to obstruction of the bile or absorption of the colouring matter into the blood, characterized by yellowness of the skin, diarrhoea and general debility; a mental attitude or condition, such as that caused by jealousy, prejudice etc., which warps the vision. *v.t.* to affect with or as with jaundice; to poison the mind with jealousy, prejudice etc. **jaundiced,** *a.* [ME *jaunys,* F *jaunisse,* from *jaune,* L *galbinus,* from *galbus,* yellow]

jaunt, *v.i.* to ramble or rove about; to take a short excursion. *n.* a ramble, an excursion, a short journey, a trip. **jaunting-car,** *n.* an Irish horse-drawn vehicle having two seats, back to back, over the wheels, and a seat for the driver in front. [perh. conn. with JAUNCE]

jaunty, *n.* the head of a ship's police. *a.* sprightly, airy, self-satisfied, perky. **jauntily,** *adv.* **jauntiness,** *n.* [earlier *janty,* F *gentil,* see GENTEEL]

Jaurès, *n.* **Jean Léon** (1859–1914), French socialist politician and advocate of international peace. He was a lecturer in philosophy at Toulouse until his election in 1885 as a deputy (member of parliament). In 1893 he joined the Socialist Party, established a united party, and in 1904 founded the newspaper *L'Humanité,* becoming its editor until his assassination.

Java, Jawa, *n.* the most important island of Indonesia, situated between Sumatra and Bali. **area** (with the island of Madura) 132,000 sq km/51,000 sq miles. **capital** Jakarta (also capital of Indonesia). **towns** ports include Surabaja and Semarang. **physical** about half the island is under cultivation, the rest being thickly forested. Mountains and sea breezes keep temperatures down, but humidity is high, with heavy rainfall from Dec to Mar. **population** (with Madura) (1980) 91,270,000; including people of Javanese, Sundanese, and Madurese origin, with differing languages. **exports** rice, coffee, cocoa, tea, sugar, rubber, quinine, teak, and petroleum. **religion** predominantly Muslim. **Javanese**, *a.* of or pertaining to Java. *n.* a native of Java; the language of Java.

†**javel,** *n.* a low fellow, a tramp. [etym. unknown]

javelin, *n.* a light spear thrown by the hand, used as a weapon or in field events; (**the javelin**) the competitive sport of javelin-throwing. *v.t.* to wound or pierce with or as with a javelin. **javelin-men,** *n.pl.* a sheriff's retinue, now the escort of a judge at assizes. [F *javeine,* It. *giavelina,* prob. from Celt. (cp. Ir. *gabhla,* spear, Gael. *gobhal,* a fork)]

Javelle water, *n.* a solution of sodium hypochlorite used in disinfecting and bleaching. [*Javel,* a former French village]

jaw¹, *n.* one of two bones or bony structures in which the teeth are fixed, forming the framework of the mouth; (*pl.*) the mouth; (*fig., pl.*) the narrow opening of a gorge, narrow valley etc.; one of two opposing members of a vice or similar implement or machine; (*Naut., pl.*) the concave or forked end of a boom or gaff; (*pl.*) a narrow opening or entrance. (*sl.*) abuse, wrangling, long-winded talk; a lecture. *v.i.* (*coll.*) to talk lengthily; †to rail. *v.t.* to abuse; to lecture. **hold your jaw,** (*sl.*) shut up. **jaw-bone,** *n.* one of the pair of bones forming the lower jaw. **jaw-breaker,** *n.* (*coll.*) an unpronounceable word. **jaw-lever,** *n.* an instrument for opening the mouths of cattle for the administration of medicine. **jaw-tooth,** *n.* a molar. **jawed,** *a.* having jaws (*usu. in comb.*, as *heavy-jawed*). [etym. doubtful, perh. rel. to CHEW]

jaw², *n.* (*Sc.*) a wave, a billow; a quantity of water poured out. *v.i.* to dash, to plunge, to surge. *v.t.* to cause to surge; to pour out. **jaw-box, -hole, -tub,** *n.* a sink. [etym. unknown]

jay, *n.* a chattering bird, *Garrulus glandarius,* of brilliant plumage; a bird of several allied genera; (*fig.*) an impudent chatterer; a loud, coarse woman. **jay-walker,** *n.* (*coll.*) a pedestrian who crosses the street heedless of the traffic. **jay-walk,** *v.i.* [OF *jay* (F *geai*), etym. doubtful]

Jayawardene, *n.* **Junius Richard** (1906–), Sri Lankan politician. Leader of the United Nationalist Party from 1973, he became prime minister 1977, and the country's first president 1978–88.

jazerant, *n.* a light coat of armour composed of small plates of metal, usu. fastened to a flexible lining. [OF *jaserant,* prob. from Sp. *jazarino,* Algerian, from Arab. *al-jazīrah,* Algiers]

jazz, *n.* syncopated music of black American origin; the form of dancing that goes to this music; vividness; garishness; liveliness; (*sl.*) rigmarole; (*sl.*) insincere talk. **to jazz up,** quicken the tempo of (a piece of music); to make more attractive, livelier, colourful etc. **jazz-man,** *n.* a jazz musician. **jazz rock,** *n.* music which is a mixture of jazz and rock. **jazzy,** *a.* *v.i.* to dance jazz. [Creole *jazz,* to speed up, prob. of Af. origin]

JC (*abbr.*) Jesus Christ; Julius Caesar; Justice Clerk.

JCB® *n.* a type of construction machine with a hydraulically operated shovel at the front and an excavator at the back. [*J*oseph *C*yril *B*amford b. 1916. British manufacturer]

J-curve, *n.* in economics, a graphic illustration of the likely effect of a currency devaluation on the balance of payments. Initially, there will be a deterioration as import prices increase and export prices decline, followed by a decline in import volume and upsurge of export volume.

jealous, *a.* suspicious or apprehensive of being supplanted in the love or favour (of a wife, husband, lover or friend); suspicious or apprehensive (of a rival); solicitous or anxiously watchful (of one's honour, rights etc.); envious (of another or another's advantages etc.); (*Bibl.*) requiring exclusive devotion (of God). **jealously,** *adv.* †**jealousness, jealousy,** *n.* [ME and OF *gelos,* late L *zēlōsus,* from *zēlus,* ZEAL)

Jeames, *n.* a footman, a flunkey. [after Thackeray's *Jeames* (James) de la Pluche]

jean, *n.* a twilled undressed cloth with cotton warp; (*pl.*) a garment or garments made of this; close-fitting casual trousers usu. made of this. [ME *Gene,* It. *Genova,* Genoa]

Jeans, *n.* **James Hopwood** (1877–1946), British mathematician and scientist. In physics, he contributed work on the kinetic theory of gases, and forms of energy radiation; and in astronomy, on giant and dwarf stars, the nature of spiral nebulae, and the origin of the cosmos. He also did much to popularize astronomy.

Jedda, JIDDAH.

jeep, *n.* (*US mil.*) a fast, light car; a utility motor-van. [*G.P.*, initials of General Purposes]

jeer¹, *v.i.* to scoff, to mock (at). *v.t.* to scoff at, to make a mock of, to deride. *n.* a scoff, a gibe, a taunt, mockery. **jeerer,** *n.* **jeeringly,** *adv.* [etym. doubtful]

jeer², *n.* tackle for joisting, swaying, and lowering lower yards [etym. doubtful]

Jefferson, *n.* **Thomas** (1743–1826), 3rd president of the US 1801–09, founder of the Democratic Party. Born in Virginia into a wealthy family. He published *A Summary View of the Rights of America* (1774) and as a member of the Continental Congresses of 1775–76 was largely responsible for the drafting of the Declaration of Independence. He was governor of Virginia 1779–81, ambassador to Paris 1785–89, secretary of state 1789–93, and vice president 1797–1801.

jeffersonite, *n.* a greenish-black variety of pyroxene. [Thomas JEFFERSON]

Jeffreys[1], *n.* **George, 1st Baron** (1648–1689), British judge. Born in Denbighshire, Wales, he became Chief Justice of the King's Bench in 1683, and presided over numerous political trials, notably those of Sidney, Oates, and Baxter, becoming notorious for his brutality.

Jeffreys[2], *n.* **Alec John** (1950–), British geneticist, who discovered the DNA probes necessary for accurate genetic fingerprinting so that a murderer or rapist could be identified by traces of blood, tissue, or semen.

Jehosophat, *n.* 4th king of Judah (*c.* 873–849 BC); he allied himself with Ahab, king of Israel, in the war against Syria.

Jehovah, Jahweh, *n.* the most sacred name given in the Old Testament to God, esp. regarded as the God of the Jewish people, **Jehovist,** *n.* the presumed author, or one of the authors, of the Jehovistic portions of the Pentateuch. **Jehovistic**, *a.* a term used regarding portions of the Pentateuch in which the name of Jehova is habitually employed (cp. ELOHIST). **Jehovah's Witnesses,** *n.* a millenarian sect, the International Bible Students' Association, founded by the American Pastor C. T. Russell (1852–1916). [Heb. *Yahōvāh)*

Jehu, *n.* king of Israel (*c.* 842–815 BC), he led a successful rebellion against the family of Ahab and was responsible for the death of Jezebel. He was noted for his furious chariot-driving; a coachman, a driver, esp. one who drives fast or furiously.

jejune, *a.* bare, meagre, scanty; wanting in substance; devoid of interest or life. **jejunely,** *adv.* **jejuneness,** *n.* [L *jējūnus,* fasting, etym. doubtful]

jejunum, *n.* the second portion of the small intestine between the duodenum and the ileum. **jejuno-,** *comb. form* pertaining to the jejunum.

Jekyll, *n.* **Gertrude** (1843–1932), English landscape gardener and writer. She created over 200 gardens, many in collaboration with the architect Edwin Lutyens.

Jekyll and Hyde, a person with a split personality, one side evil the other good. [from R.L. Stevenson's *The Strange Case of Dr Jekyll and Mr Hyde*]

jelly, *n.* any gelatinous substance, esp. that obtained by decoction from animal matter; a conserve made of the inspissated juice of fruit boiled with sugar. *v.i.* to turn into jelly. *v.t.* to convert into jelly. **jelly-baby,** *n.* a sweet made of jelly and shaped like a baby. **jelly-bag, -cloth,** *n.* a bag or cloth used for straining jelly. **jelly bean,** *n.* a sugar-coated, bean-shaped sweet filled with jelly. **jelly-fish,** *n.* the popular name of the medusas and other coelenterates. **jellygraph**, *n.* an apparatus, whose essential parts are a sheet of jelly and a special kind of ink, used for multiplying copies of writing. **jell, gell**, *v.i.* (*coll.*) to jelly. **jellify,** *v.t.*, *v.i.* [F *gelée,* frost, L *gelāta,* fem. p.p. of *gelāre,* to freeze]

jemadar, *n.* an officer in the Indian army. [Hind.]

jemimas, *n.pl.* (*coll.*) elastic-sided boots; long galoshes for boots.

jeminy, GEMINI.

jemmy[1], *n.* a short, stout crowbar, used by burglars; a baked sheep's head; a great-coat. [dim. of *James*]

jemmy[2], (*dial.***)** *a.* spruce, neat. **jemminess,** *n.* [cp. JIMP]

Jenkins, *n.* **Roy (Harris)** (1920–), British politician. He became a Labour minister 1964, was home secretary 1965–67 and 1974–76, and chancellor of the Exchequer 1967–70. He was president of the European Commission 1977–81. In 1981 he became one of the founders of the Social Democratic Party and was elected 1982, but lost his seat 1987.

Jenner, *n.* **Edward** (1749–1823), English physician who pioneered vaccination. In Jenner's day, smallpox was a major killer. His discovery that inoculation with cowpox gives immunity to smallpox was a great medical breakthrough. He coined the word vaccination from the Latin word for cowpox *vaccina*.

jennet, *n.* a small Spanish horse. [F *genet,* Sp. *ginete,* orig. light-armed horseman, perh. from Arab. *Zenāta,* Barbary tribe famous for horsemanship]

jenneting, *n.* an early kind of apple. [prob. from F *jeanneton,* from *Jeannet, Jean* (cp. *pomme de St Jean,* St John's apple)]

jenny, *n.* a popular name for a female ass, animal, bird etc.; a spinning-jenny; a travelling crane; (*Billiards*) a stroke pocketing the ball from an awkward position. **jenny-ass,** *n.* a female ass. **jenny-long-legs,** *n.* (*Sc.*) a cranefly. **jenny-wren,** *n.* a wren. [familiar form of *Jane, Jennifer* or *Janet*]

†**jeofail,** *n.* an error or oversight in pleading or other proceeding. [A-F *jeo fail,* OF *je faille,* I fail]

jeopardy, *n.* exposure to danger, loss, or injury; risk, hazard, danger, peril. †**jeopard, jeopardize, -ise,** *v.t.* to put in jeopardy; to risk. **jeopardous,** *a.* **jeopardously,** *adv.* [OF *jeu parti,* divided or even game (*jeu,* L *jocus,* game, *parti,* L *partītus,* p.p. of *partīrī,* to PART)]

jequirity, *n.* a tropical twining shrub, *Abrus precatorius* or Indian liquorice, with parti-coloured seeds or beans which are used for ornaments and for medicinal purposes. **jequirity-beans,** *n.pl.* [Tupi-Guarani, *jekiriti*]

Jerablus, *n.* ancient Syrian city, adjacent to Carchemish on the Euphrates.

jerboa, *n.* a small mouse-like rodent, *Dipus Aegyptius,* with long and hind legs adapted for leaping. [Arab. *yarbū',* the flesh of the loins, from the powerful muscles of its hind leg]

jereed, -id, *n.* a javelin, used in Iran and Turkey, esp. in games; a game with this. [Arab. *jarīd*, orig. a stripped palm-branch]

jeremiad, *n.* a lamentation, esp. over modern degeneracy, in the style of the prophet Jeremiah. [F *jérémiade*]

Jeremiah, *n.* (7th cent. BC), Old Testament Hebrew prophet, whose ministry continued 626–586 BC. He was imprisoned during Nebuchadnezzar's siege of Jerusalem on suspicion of intending to desert to the enemy. On the city's fall, he retired to Egypt; a prophet of doom; a pessimistic person.

jerfalcon, GERFALCON.

Jericho, *n.* Israeli-administered town in Jordan, N of the Dead Sea. It was settled by 8000 BC, and by 6000 BC had become a walled city with 2000 inhabitants. In the Old Testament it was the first Canaanite stronghold captured by the Israelites, its walls, according to the Book of Joshua, falling to the blast of Joshua's trumpets. Successive archaeological excavations since 1907 show that the walls of the city were destroyed many times.

jerk[1], *v.t.* to pull, push, or thrust sharply; to throw with a sharp, suddenly arrested action. *v.i.* to move with jerks. *n.* a sharp, sudden push or tug; a twitch, a spasmodic movement due to involuntary contraction of a muscle; (*sl.*) a stupid, ignorant or contemptible person. (*pl.*) violent twitches or spasmodic movements of the face or members, often due to religious excitement. **jerk off,** (*sl.*) to masturbate. **jerker,** *n.* **jerky,** *a.* **jerkily,** *adv.* **jerkiness,** *n.* [prob. onomat.]

jerk[2], *v.t.* to cut (beef) into long pieces and dry in the sun. **jerked beef,** *n.* Charqui. [corr. from Am. Sp. *cha quear,* from CHARQUI]

jerk[3], JERQUE.

jerkin[1], *n.* a short coat or jacket, formerly often made of leather; a close waistcoat. †**jerkinet,** *n.* a woman's jacket or blouse. [etym. unknown]

jerkin[2], GERFALCON.

jerkin-head, *n.* (*Arch.*) a combination of truncated gable and hipped roof. [etym. doubtful]

jeroboam, *n.* a drinking-bowl or beaker or great size; a wine-bottle holding 10–12 quarts (about 12 l). [in alln. to I Kings ix.28]

Jeroboam, *n.* first king of Israel c. 922–901 BC after the split with Judah.

Jerome, St *n.* (c. 340–420), one of the early Christian leaders and scholars known as the Fathers of the

Church. His Latin versions of the Old and New Testaments form the basis of the Roman Catholic Vulgate. He is usually depicted with a lion. Feast day 30 Sept.

Jerome, *n.* **Jerome K(lapka)** (1859–1927), English journalist and writer. His works include the humorous essays *Idle Thoughts of an Idle Fellow* (1889), the novel *Three Men in a Boat* (1889), and the play *The Passing of the Third Floor Back* (1907).

jerque, *v.t.* to search (a vessel or her papers) for unentered goods. **jerquer,** *n.* a custom-house searcher. [etym. doubtful]

Jerry[1], *n.* (*esp. war sl., often derog.*) a German soldier. [perh. from GERMAN]

jerry[2], *a.* cheaply and badly built, flimsy. *n.* (*sl.*) a chamber-pot. **jerry-builder,** *n.* a speculative builder of cheap and inferior houses. **jerry-building,** *n.* **jerry-built,** *a.* **jerry-shop,** *n.* a beerhouse. [prob. fam. form of *Jeremiah*]

jerrymander, GERRYMANDER.

jersey, *n.* a close-fitting woollen knitted tunic worn in athletic exercises; knitted garment worn on the upper part of the body; fine wool yarn and combed wool, as that produced in Jersey. **Jersey cow,** *n.* one of a breed of dairy cattle originating from Jersey. [the island of *Jersey*]

Jersey, *n.* largest of the Channel Islands; capital St Helier; area 117 sq km/45 sq miles; population (1986) 80,000. It is governed by a lieutenant-governor representing the English Crown and an assembly. Like Guernsey, it is famous for its cattle.

jerupigia GEROPIGIA.

Jerusalem, *n.* ancient city of Palestine, divided 1948 between Jordan and the new republic of Israel; area (pre-1967) 37.5 sq km/14.5 sq miles, (post-1967) 108 sq km/42 sq miles, including areas of the West Bank; population (1989) 500,000, about 350,000 Israelis and 150,000 Palestinians. In 1950 the western New City was proclaimed as the Israeli capital, and, having captured from Jordan the eastern Old City 1967, Israel affirmed 1980 that the united city was the country's capital; the United Nations does not recognize the claim. **Jerusalem artichoke,** *n.* a species of sunflower, *Helianthus tuberosus,* the tuberous roots of which are edible; the tuber of it eaten as a vegetable. [perh. corr. of It. *girasole articiocco*]

Jervis, *n.* **John, Earl of St Vincent** (1735–1823), English admiral. A rigid disciplinarian, he secured the blockage of Toulon in 1795, and the defeat of the Spanish fleet off Cape St Vincent 1797, in which Nelson played a key part.

jess, *n.* (*falconry*) a short leather or silk ribbon which was tied round each leg of a hawk, and to which the leash was usually attached. **jessed,** *a.* having jesses on (said of a hawk); (*Her.*) with jesses of a specified tincture. [OF *ges.* obj. *gel,* L *jactus -tum,* a cast, from *jacere,* to throw]

jessamine, JASMINE.

jessamy, *n.* jasmine; a fop, a dandy. [corr. of prec]

jessant, *a.* (*Her.*) issuing or springing (from). [OF *iessant,* pres.p. of *issir,* to ISSUE]

Jesse, *n.* a genealogical tree representing the genealogy of Christ, esp. in the form of a large brass candlestick with many branches. **Jesse-window,** *n.* a window of which the tracery and glazing represent a genealogical tree of Jesse. [the father of David (Is. xi.I)]

jesserant, JAZERANT.

Jessop, *n.* **William** (1745–1814), British canal engineer, who built the first canal in England entirely dependent on reservoirs for its water supply (the Grantham Canal 1793–97), and who designed (with Thomas Telford) the 302 m/1,000 ft long Pontcysyllte aqueduct over the river Dee.

jest, *n.* a joke, something ludicrous said or done to provoke mirth; a jeer, a taunt; a laughing-stock; a prank, a frolic; †a masque, a masquerade. *v.i.* to joke; to utter jests; to provoke mirth by ludicrous actions or words; to make game, to jeer (at). **in jest,** as a jest or joke; not seriously or in earnest. **jest-book,** *n.* a collection of jokes or jocular tales or sayings. **jester,** *n.* one who jests or jokes, a buffoon, esp. one formerly retained by persons of high rank to make sport. **jestingly,** *adv.* [OF *jeste,* orig. an exploit, L *gesta,* neut. pl. p.p. of *gere,* to do]

Jesuit, *n.* a member of the Society of Jesus, a Roman Catholic order founded in 1534 by Ignatius Loyola; (*fig.*) a crafty, insidious person, a subtle casuist or prevaricator. **Jesuits' bark,** *n.* Cinchona bark. †**Jesuitess,** *n. fem.* a member of an order of nuns, abolished by Pope Urban VIII in 1630. **Jesuitic, -ical,** *a.* craft, cunning, designing. **Jesuitically,** *adv.* **Jesuitism, Jesuitry,** *n.* **Jesuitize, -ise,** *v.t., v.i.*

Jesus, *n.* (*c.* 4 BC–AD 29 or 30), Jewish preacher on whose teachings Christianity was founded. According to the accounts of his life in the four Gospels, he was born in Bethlehem, Palestine, son of God and the Virgin Mary, and brought up as a carpenter in Nazareth. After adult baptism, he gathered 12 disciples, but his preaching antagonized the authorities and he was executed. Three days after the Crucifixion there came reports of his resurrection and, later, of his ascension to heaven.

JET, *n.* Joint European Torus.

jet[1], *n.* a black compact variety of lignite susceptible of a brilliant polish, formerly much used for articles of personal ornament. *a.* the colour of jet. **jet-black,** *a.* **jetty**[2], *a.* [OF *jaiet,* L *gagātem,* nom. *-tēs,* Gr. *gagatēs,* from *Gagai,* in Lycia]

jet[2], *v.i.* (*past, p.p.* **jetted**) to spurt or shoot out, to come out in a jet or jets; †to shoot forward, to jut out; (*Shak.*) to encroach (upon); †to strut, to swagger; to travel by jet-plane. *v.t.* to send out in a jet or jets. *n.* a sudden spurt or shooting out of water or flame, esp. from a small orifice; a spout or nozzle for the discharge of water etc.; a channel for passing molten metal into a mould; also the piece of metal remaining in the aperture after the metal is cold, the spruce; (*coll.*) a jet-propelled plane. **jet-foil,** *n.* a hydrofoil powered by a jet of water. **jet-lag,** *n.* the exhaustion caused by the body's inability to adjust to the time-zone changes involved in long-distance air-travel. **jet-plane,** *n.* a jet-propelled plane. **jet-propelled,** *a.* descriptive of an aircraft vehicle propelled by heating and expanding air which is directed in a jet from the rear of the plane. **jet propulsion,** *n.* **jet-set,** *n.* fashionable people who can afford constant travel by jet-plane. **jet-ski,** *n.* a small powered water vehicle with a flat heel shaped like a water-ski. **jet-skiing,** *n.* [OF *jetter* (F *jeter*), L *jactāre,* freq. of *jacere,* to throw]

jeté, *n.* a leap from one foot to another in ballet. [Fr. thrown]

jetsam, *n.* goods, cargo etc., thrown overboard in order to lighten a ship in distress and subsequently washed ashore. **flotsam and jetsam** FLOTSAM. [var. of foll.]

jettison, *n.* the casting of goods overboard to lighten a vessel in distress. *v.t.* to throw (goods) overboard in order to lighten a vessel; to drop (anything unwanted) from an aircraft or spacecraft in flight; to cast aside to rid oneself of. [A-F *getteson,* OF *getaison,* L *jactātiōnem,* nom. *-tio,* from *jactāre,* freq. of *jacere,* to throw]

jetty[1], *n.* a structure of stone or timber projecting into water and serving as a mole, pier, or wharf; a landing pier; (*Arch.*) a part of a building which juts beyond the ground-plan. [OF *getee* (F *jetée*), p.p. of *jeter,* to throw, see JET[2]]

jetty[2] JET[1].

jeu, *n.* (*pl.* **jeux**) a game, a play, a jest. **jeu de mots,** *n.* a pun. **jeu d'esprit,** *n.* a witticism, a witty sally. [F, from L *jocus*]

jeunesse dorée, *n.* gilded youth. [F.]

Jew, *n.* originally a member of the kingdom of Judah, but later used for all adherents of the Mosaic Law, frequently also called 'Israelite' or 'Hebrew'; now applied to professing members of the synagogue and, loosely, to descendants of the Hebrew tribe; (*offensive*) a usurer, a person who drives a hard bargain. **(jew)** *v.t.* (*offensive*) to drive a hard bargain, to cheat. **jewfish,** *n.* the name given to several large edible fish caught in Australian waters; the kingfish of S Australia and

Victoria. **jew's-ear,** *n.* a tough edible fungus, *Hirneola auricula Judoe,* growing on elder and elm-trees. **jew's harp,** *n.* a musical instrument held between the teeth, the sound produced by the vibrations of a metal tongue set in motion by the forefinger. **jew's-mallow,** *n.* a plant, *Corchorus capsularis,* used in the East as a potherb. **Jewess,** *n.fem.* **jewing,** *n.* the wattles at the base of the beak in some domestic pigeons (supposed to have some resemblance to a hooked nose). **Jewish,** *a.* [A-F *Jeu, Geu,* OF *giu* (F *juif*), L *Iudaeus -um,* Gr. *Ioudaios,* Heb. *y'hudah,* Judah, son of Jacob]

jewel, *n.* a precious stone, a gem; a personal ornament containing a precious stone or stones; (*fig.*) a person or thing of very great value or excellence. *v.t.* to adorn with or as with jewels; to fit (a watch) with jewels in the pivot-holes. **jewel in the crown,** (*Hist.*) any of the countries of the British Empire, esp. India; (*fig.*) the most highly-prized, beautiful etc. one of a collection or group. **jewel-block,** *n.* a block at the yard-arm of a ship, for the halyard of a studding-sail yard to pass through. **jewel-case,** *n.* **Jewel-house, -office,** *n.* the place (in the Tower of London) where the Crown Jewels are deposited. **jewel-like,** *a.* **jeweller,** *n.* a maker of or dealer in jewels. **jewellery, jewelry,** *n.* (*collect.*) jewels in general; the art or trade of a jeweller. [A-F *juel,* OF *joïel, joel,* etym. doubtful; perh. from late L *jocāle,* from L *jocāre,* to play (whence *juer, jouer*), or dim. of *joie,* L *gaudium,* joy]

Jewish Agency, *n.* body created by the British mandate power in Palestine 1929 to oversee the administration of the Jewish population and immigration. In 1948 it took over as the government of an independent Israel.

Jewry, *n.* (*collect.*) the Jews or the land where they dwell or dwelt; (*Hist.*) Judaea; the Jews' quarter in a town or country. [OF *juierie*]

jewstone, *n.* a local name for a black basalt found in the Clee Hills, Shropshire; the fossil spine of a sea-urchin or echinus, formerly used as a medicine. [W *ddu,* black]

Jezebel, *n.* a wicked, bold, or vicious woman, esp. a woman who paints her face. [wife of Ahab, king of Israel, I Kings, xvi.31]

Jiang, *n.* **Zemin** (1926–), Chinese political leader. The son-in-law of Li Xiannian, he joined the Chinese Communist Party's politburo in 1967 after serving in the Moscow embassy and as mayor of Shanghai. He succeeded Zhao Ziyang as party leader after the Tian'anmen Square massacre of 1989. A cautious proponent of economic reform coupled with unswerving adherence to the party's 'political line', he subsequently also replaced Deng Xiaoping as head of the influential central military commission.

Jiang Jie Shi, *n.* alternative transcription of Chinese leader Chiang Kai-shek.

Jiang Qing, *n.* (formerly **Chiang Ching**) (1913–), Chinese communist politician, wife of the party leader Mao Zedong. In 1960 she became minister for culture, and played a key role in the 1966–69 Cultural Revolution as the leading member of the Shanghai-based Gang of Four, who attempted to seize power 1976. Jiang was imprisoned.

Jiangsu, *n.* (formerly **Kiangsu**), province on the coast of E China. **area** 102,200 sq km/39,449 sq miles. **capital** Nanjing. **population** (1986) 62,130,000. **products** cereals, rice, tea, cotton, soya, fish, silk, ceramics, textiles, coal, iron, copper, cement.

Jiangxi, *n.* (formerly **Kiangsi**), province of SE China. **area** 164,800 sq km/63,613 sq miles. **capital** Nanchang. **population** (1986) 35,090,000. **products** rice, tea, cotton, tobacco, porcelain, coal, tungsten, uranium.

jib¹, *n.* a large triangular sail set on a stay between the fore-topmast-head and bowsprit or jib-boom in large vessels and between the masthead and the bowsprit in smaller ones; the extended arm of a crane or derrick. **the cut of one's jib,** (*orig. Naut. sl.*) one's physical appearance. **jib-boom,** *n.* a movable spar running out beyond the bowsprit. **jib-door,** *n.* a door flush with the wall on both sides, and usu. papered or painted over so as to be concealed. [etym. doubtful; perh. abbr. of GIBBET, or from JIB²]

jib², *v.t.* (*past, p.p.* **jibbed**) to shift (a boom, yard or sail) from one side of a vessel to the other. *v.i.* to swing round (of a sail etc.). Cp. GYBE [cp. Dan. *gibbe,* Dut. *gijpen*]

jib³, *v.i.* to move restively sideways or backwards, as a horse; (*fig.*) to make difficulties (at some task, course, person etc.); of a horse etc., to stop short and refuse to move forwards; (*with* **at**) of a person, to refuse to do (something). **jibber,** *n.* a horse that jibs. [etym. doubtful]

jibbah, *n.* long, loose coat worn by Mohammedans; a loose overall or pinafore. [Ar.]

jibber², GIBBER.

jibe, GIBE.

jiblet, GIBLET.

Jiddah, Jedda, *n.* port in Hejaz, Saudi Arabia, on the E shore of the Red Sea; population (1986) 1,000,000. Industries include cement, steel, and oil refining. Pilgrims pass through here on their way to Mecca.

jiff, jiffy, *n.* (*coll.*) a moment, an instant, an extremely short time. [etym. unknown]

Jiffy-bag®, *n.* a kind of strong padded envelope.

jig, *n.* a lively dance for one or more performers; the music for such a dance; a fish-hook with a weighted shank, used for snatching at fish; a device for holding an object and guiding a cutting-tool in a machine for the manufacture of standard parts. *v.i.* (*past, p.p.* **jigged**) to dance a jig; to skip about. *v.t.* to sing or play in jig time; to jerk up and down rapidly; to separate finer and coarser qualities of (ore etc.) by treatment in a jigger; (*fig.*) to cheat, to hoax. **jig-saw,** *n.* a vertically-reciprocating saw moved by a vibrating lever or crank-rod, used for cutting scrolls, fretwork etc. **jigsaw puzzle,** *n.* a puzzle to put together a picture cut into irregularly shaped pieces. **jigging,** *n.* **jigging-machine,** *n.* an apparatus for sifting ore in water, a jigger. †**jiggish,** *a.* resembling or fitted for a jig; playful, frisky. [etym. doubtful]

jigger¹, *n.* one who or that which jigs; a sieve shaken vertically in water to separate the contained ore; the man using such sieve; (*Naut.*) small tackle used for holding on to the cable as it is heaved in, and similar work; a small sail, usu. set on a jigger-mast; a small smack carrying this; a potter's wheel on which earthen vessels are shaped; a throwing-wheel; (*sl.*) a rest for a billiard-cue; (*coll.*) any kind of mechanical contrivance, implement etc.; (*Golf*) an iron club coming between a mid-iron and a mashie; a machine for dyeing cloth; a small measure of spirits. **jigger-mast,** *n.* a small mast at the stem of a yawl, a small mizen-mast.

jigger², CHIGOE.

jiggered, *a.* very surprised, confounded. **I'm jiggered,** a mild oath expressing surprise etc. [etym. doubtful]

jiggery-pokery, *n.* underhand goings-on. [onomat.]

jiggle, *v.t.* to jerk or rock lightly to and fro. [freq. of JIG]

jig-jog, *n.* a jogging, jolting motion.

jigot, GIGOT.

jihad, jehad, *n.* a holy war proclaimed by Muslims against unbelievers or the enemies of Islam; (*fig.*) a war or crusade on behalf of a principle etc. [Arab. *jihād*]

Jilin, *n.* (formerly **Kirin**). province of NE China in central Manchuria. **area** 187,000 sq km/72,182 sq miles. **capital** Changchun. **population** (1986) 23,150,000.

Jill, GILL³.

jillaroo JACKAROO.

jilliflower, GILLY-FLOWER.

jilt, *n.* a woman who capriciously or wantonly gives her lover encouragement and then throws him over. *v.t.* to throw over or discard (one's lover). *v.i.* to play the jilt. [prob. from a dim. (*-et*) of JILL]

jimcrack, GIMCRACK.

Jim Crow, *n.* originally a derogatory US term for a black person. Jim Crow laws are laws designed to deny civil rights to blacks or to enforce the policy of segregation, which existed in parts of the US until Supreme

Court decisions and civil-rights legislation of the 1950s and 1960s (Civil Rights Act 1964, Voting Rights Act 1965) denied their legality; (*Mach.*) an implement for bending or straightening rails; a planing-machine with a cutting-tool adapted for turning about and cutting both ways; (*Mining*) a crowbar with an iron claw like a burglar's jemmy.

jim-jams, *n.pl.* (*coll.*) fluster, jumpiness; delirium tremens.

jimmy, JEMMY[1]. **Jimmy Woodser,** *n.* (*Austral. coll.*) a drink one pays for oneself; a drink taken alone.

jimp, *a.* (*Sc., North.*) neat, spruce, comely; slender, scant; short in measure or weight. *adv.* scarcely. *n.* a witty jest; a quirk. **jimply,** *adv.* [etym. unknown]

Jinan, *n.* (formerly **Tsinan**). city and capital of Shandong province, China; population (1986) 1,430,000. It has food processing and textile industries.

jingal GINGAL. **jingko** GINGKO.

jingle, *v.i.* to make a clinking or tinkling sound like that of small bells, bits of metal etc.; to correspond in sound, rhyme etc.; also, to rhyme, alliterate etc. (both in a depreciative sense). *v.t.* to cause to make such a clinking or tinkling sound. *n.* a tinkling metallic sound; a correspondence or repetition of sounds in words, esp. of a catchy inartistic kind; doggerel; a simply rhythmical verse, esp. one used in advertising; a covered two-wheeled Irish or Australian horse-drawn vehicle. **jingle-jangle,** *n.* **jingling-match,** *n.* an obsolete game in which a player carrying a bell is chased by others blind-folded. [imit.]

Jingo, *n.* (*pl.* **-goes**) a word used as a mild oath; one of a party advocating a spirited foreign policy, esp. those who championed the cause of the Turks during and after the Russian-Turkish war of 1877–8 (in this sense derived directly from the refrain of a song then popular); a person given to (excessive) belligerent patriotism. *a.* pertaining to the Jingoes. **jingoish,** *a.* **Jingoism,** *n.* the (excessive) belligerent patriotism of Jingoes; a foreign policy based on this. **jingoist,** *n.* **jingoistic,** *a.* [prob. conjurer's nonsense]

jink, *v.i.* (*Sc.*) to move nimbly; to dance, to fling; to dodge. *v.t.* to dodge; to cheat, to take in; (*Football*) to trick an opponent. *n.* a slip, an evasion, a dodging turn, a dodge. **high jinks,** pranks, frolics. [prob. onomat.]

jinker, *n.* (*Austral.*) a sort of two-wheeled bogey for transporting heavy logs and timber.

Jinnah, *n.* **Muhammad Ali** (1876–1948), Indian politician, Pakistan's first governor general from 1947. He became president of the Muslim League in 1916 and from 1934 he was elected annually as president. He advised the UK government on the need for a separate state of Pakistan 1942, and at the 1946 conferences in London he insisted on the partition of British India into Hindu and Muslim states.

jinnee, *n.* (*pl.* **jinn,** often taken for sing.) one of a race of spirits or demons in Muslim mythology supposed to have the power of assuming human or animal forms [cp. GENIE]. [Arab. *jinnī*]

jinrickshaw, jinrickisha, RICKSHAW.

Jinsha Jiang, *n.* river of China, which rises in SW China, and forms the Chang Jiang (Yangtze) at Yibin.

jinx, *n.* (*sl.*) a person or thing that brings ill luck.

Jiricna, *n.* **Eva** (19??–), Czechoslovak architect, who has worked in the UK since 1968. Her striking fashion shops, bars, and cafés for Joseph Ettedgui (1900–) are built in a highly refined modernist style.

jit, *n.* a type of beat music that originated in Zimbabwe.

jitney, *n.* (*N Am. sl.*) a motor-car.

jitters, *n.pl.* (*sl.*) nervous apprehension. **jitter-bug,** *n.* a person who spreads alarm; a dancer who greatly exaggerates swing dancing. **jittery,** *a.*

jiu-jitsu, JU-JITSU.

Jivaro, *n.* American Indian peoples of E Ecuador and N Peru. They live by farming, hunting, fishing, and weaving; the Jivaro language belongs to the Andean-Equatorial family. They were formerly famous for preserving the hair and shrunken skin of the heads of their enemies as battle trophies.

jive, *n.* a style of lively, jazz-style music; dancing to such music; (*sl.*) misleading talk; jargon. *v.i.* to dance to jive music; (*sl.*) to mislead. **jiver,** *n.* **jiving,** *n.* [etym. doubtful]

jizz, *n.* the characteristic features, appearance, behaviour etc. which distinguish a bird from other species. [etym. doubtful]

jo, *n.* (*Sc.*) one's sweetheart; one's delight. [JOY]

joanna, *n.* (*sl.*) a piano.

Joan of Arc, St, (1412–1431), French military leader. In 1429 at Chinon, NW France, she persuaded Charles VII that she had a divine mission to expel the English from France (see Hundred Years' War) and secure his coronation. She raised the siege of Orléans, defeated the English at Patay, north of Orléans, and Charles was crowned in Reims. However, she failed to take Paris, and was captured in May 1430 by the Burgundians, who sold her to the English. She was found guilty of witchcraft and heresy by a tribunal of French ecclesiastics who supported the English. She was burned at the stake in Rouen on 30 May 1431. In 1920 she was canonized.

Job, *n.* (*c.* 5th cent. BC), in the Old Testament, Jewish leader who in the Book of Job questioned God's infliction of suffering on the righteous and endured great sufferings himself; (*fig.*) an uncomplaining sufferer or victim. **Job's comforter,** *n.* a false friend who lacerates one's feelings whilst pretending to sympathize. **Job's news,** *n.* ill tidings. **Job's post,** *n.* a bearer of ill tidings. **jobe,** *v.t.* to reprove, to reprimand. **jobation,** *n.* a long-winded reproof, a lecture.

job[1], *n.* a piece of work, esp. one done for a started price; an occupation; a responsibility or duty; (*coll.*) a difficult task; a piece of work or business yielding unfair profit or advantage, esp. one in which public interests are sacrificed to personal gain; (*coll.*) a situation; (*sl.*) a crime, esp. a robbery; *a.* applied to collections of things sold together; let on hire. *v.t.* (*past, p.p.* **jobbed**) to let out (as work) by the job; to let out thus for hire; to hire thus; to buy up in miscellaneous lots and retail; to deal in (stocks); to deal with in an underhand way for one's private benefit. *v.i.* to buy and sell as a broker; to do job-work; to let or hire by the job; to make profit corruptly out of a position of trust, esp. at public expense. **a bad** or **good job,** (*coll.*) a sad, an unfortunate, or a satisfactory turn of affairs. **to do the job for one,** to ruin or kill one. **to job out,** to sublet a piece of work. **job centre,** *n.* government-run centres where information about available jobs is displayed. **job lot,** *n.* a miscellaneous lot of goods bought cheap in the expectation of random profit. **jobmaster,** *n.* one who lets out carriages or horses. **job-printer,** *n.* [see JOBBING HOUSE]. **job-sharing,** *n.* the division of one job by two or more people who work hours complementary to each other. **job-work,** *n.* work done or paid for by the job **jobber,** *n.* one who does small jobs; a jobmaster; one who deals in stocks and shares on the Stock Exchange; one who uses a position of trust, esp. a public office, commission etc., to private advantage; one who does dishonourable work. **jobber's turn,** *n.* a term denoting the middle price between which a jobber is prepared to buy or sell. **jobbery,** *n.* **jobbing,** *n.* **jobbing house,** a printing-office where miscellaneous work (as distinct from newspapers or books) is done. [etym. unknown]

job[2], *v.t.* to stab, poke or prod with a sharp instrument; to drive (a sharp instrument) in. *v.i.* to stab or thrust (at). *n.* a sudden stab, poke or prod. [prob. onomat. (cp. JAB)]

jobber JOB[1].

jobbernowl, *n.* a blockhead. [F *jobard,* a fool, from *jobe,* silly, NOLL]

Jock, *n.* (*coll.*) a soldier of a Scottish regiment. [pers. name]

jockey, *n.* a professional rider in horse-races; (*contemp.*) a groom, a lad, an under-strapper; †a horse-dealer; one given to sharp practice, prob. from the bad reputation of horse-dealers, a cheat. *v.t.* to deceive in a bargain; to employ sharp practices against; to outwit, out-manoeuvre etc.; to cheat; (*Horse-racing*) to jostle by riding against. *v.i.* to be tricky; to play a tricky game. **disk-jockey** DISK. **to jockey for position,** to try by skill to get an advantageous position; to gain an unfair advantage. **jockey-pulley,** *n.* (*Motor.*) a pulley that rotates on a spring-loaded mounting. used to keep a belt taut on two fixed pulleys. **jockeydom, jockeyism, jockeyship,** *n.*

jocko, *n.* a chimpanzee. [F, from Bantu *engeco* or *nchenko*]

jockstrap, *n.* support for the genitals worn by men engaged in athletic or sporting activity. [sl. *jock*, penis + *strap*]

jockteleg, *n.* (*Sc.*) a large clasp-knife. [said by Lord Hailes to be a corr. of *Jacques de Liège,* name of cutler]

jocose, *a.* humorous, facetious; given to jokes or jestings; containing jokes, amusing. **jocosely,** *adv.* **jocoseness, jocosity,** *n.* †**jocoserious,** *a.* partaking of mirth and sadness. [L *jocōsus,* from *jocus,* JOKE]

jocular, *a.* addicted to jesting; merry, facetious, amusing; embodying a joke. **jocularity** , *n.* **jocularly,** *adv.* †**joculator,** *n.* a professional jester. †**joculatory,** *a.*

jocund, *a.* sportive, gay; inspiring mirth. **jocundity,** *n.* **jocundly,** *adv.* [OF *jocond,* L *jūcundus,* from *juvāre,* to help, to delight]

jodel, YODEL.

jodhpurs, *n.pl.* long riding-breeches fitting closely from knee to the ankle. [place in India]

Jodl, *n.* **Alfred** (1892–1946), German general, born in Aachen. In World War II he drew up the Nazi government's plan for the attack on Yugoslavia, Greece, and the USSR, and in Jan. 1945 became chief of staff. He headed the delegation that signed Germany's surrender in Reims on 7 May 1945. He was tried for war crimes in Nuremberg 1945–46, and hanged.

Jodrell Bank, *n.* site in Cheshire, England, of the Nuffield Radio Astronomy Laboratories of the University of Manchester. Its largest instrument is the 76 m/250 ft radio dish, completed 1957 and modified 1970. A 38 m '3 25 m/125 ft '3 82 ft elliptical radio dish was introduced 1964, capable of working at shorter wavelengths.

joe[1], joey[1], *n.* (*old sl.*) a fourpenny or threepenny bit. [*Joseph* Hume, MP 1836]

Joe[2], *n.* a male christian name. **Joe Bloggs,** *n.* a typical or ordinary person. **Joe Miller,** *n.* an old joke, a chestnut. **Joe-Millerism,** *n.* **Joe Public,** *n.* the general public. **Joe Soap,** *n.* one who does menial tasks; one who is taken advantage of. [*Joseph Miller,* 1684–1738, comedian, whose name was attached to a jest-book (1739)]

joey[2], *n.* a young kangaroo. [Austral. Abor. *joè*]

Joffre, *n.* **Joseph Jacques Césaire** (1852–1931), marshal of France during World War I. He was chief of general staff 1911. The German invasion of Belgium 1914 took him by surprise, but his stand on the Marne resulted in his appointment as supreme commander of all the French armies 1915. His failure to make adequate preparations at Verdun 1916 and the military disasters on the Somme led to his replacement by Nivelle Dec. 1916.

jog, *v.t.* (*past, p.p.* **jogged**) to push or jerk lightly, usually with the hand or elbow; to nudge, esp. to excite attention; to stimulate (one's memory or attention). *v.i.* to move with an up-and-down leisurely pace; to walk or trudge idly, heavily, or slowly (on, along etc.); to go, to depart, to be off; to run at a steady, slow pace for exercise. *n.* a light push or nudge to arouse attention; a leisurely trotting or jogging motion. **to be jogging,** to take one's departure. **to jog on,** to get along (somehow or in some specified manner). **jog-trot,** *n.* a slow, easy, monotonous trot; humdrum progress; slow routine. *a.* (*fig.*) monotonous. **jogger,** one who jogs (for exercise). **jogger's knee, nipple** etc., *n.* an injured or damaged knee, nipple etc. caused by jogging. **jogging,** *n.* the act of jogging, esp. as a form of exercise. *a.* **jogging-suit,** *n.* a garment like a track-suit worn when jogging. [prob. onomat. (cp. F. *choquer*)]

joggle, *v.t.* to shake, push, nudge or jerk slightly; (*Build.*, perh. from JAG) to unite by means of joggles, to prevent sliding. *v.i.* to shake slightly, to totter. *n.* a joint in stone or other material to prevent sliding of one piece over another; a notch, projection, dowel etc., used to form such joints. [prob. freq. of prec.]

†**Johannes,** *n.* an old Portuguese coin (of Joannes V). [L *Joannes,* JOHN]

Johannesburg, *n.* largest city of South Africa, situated on the Witwatersrand in Transvaal; population (1985) 1,609,000. It is the centre of a large gold mining industry; other industries include engineering works, meat-chilling plants, and clothing factories.

Johannine, *a.* of or pertaining to the Apostle John, or (rarely) to John the Baptist. **Johannean,** *a.* [as prec., -INE]

Johannisberger, *n.* a fine white Rhenish wine. [G, from *Johannisberg,* a vineyard near Wiesbaden]

John, *n.* a male Christian name. **John-a-Dreams,** (*Shak.*) a dreamy fellow. **John-a-Nokes,** and **John-a-Stiles,** John at the oak and John at the stile, two fictitious parties to an imaginary action at law. **John Barleycorn** BARLEY[1]. **John Bull** BULL[1]. **John Chinaman,** *n.* (*offensive*) a Chinaman. **John Collins,** an alcoholic drink based on gin. **John Company,** *n.* [after Dut. *Jan Kompanie*], a familiar name for the East India Company. **John Doe,** *n.* the fictitious plaintiff in an (obsolete) action for ejectment, the defendant being called Richard Roe. **John Dory** DORY[1]. **Johnian,** *a.* of or pertaining to St John's College, Cambridge. *n.* a member or student of this. **Johnny,** *n.* (*sl.*) a fellow, a chap; a toff, a swell, a young man about town; (*sl.*) a condom. **Johnny cake,** *n.* (*N Am.*) a maize cake baked on the hearth; (*Austral.*) a similar wheat-meal cake. **johnny-come-lately,** *n.* a newcomer. **Johnny Crapaud,** *n.* (*offensive*) a Frenchman. **Johnny Raw,** *n.* a raw beginner, a novice. [OF *Jehan* (F *jean*), late L *Johannes,* L *Joannes,* Gr. *Jōannēs,* Heb. *Yōchānāni,* Jah is gracious]

John, St, *n.* (1st cent. AD), New Testament apostle. Traditionally, he wrote the fourth Gospel and the Johannine Epistles when bishop of Ephesus, and the Book of Revelation while exiled to the Greek island of Patmos. His emblem is an eagle, his feast day 27 Dec.

John[1], *n.* **Augustus (Edwin)** (1878–1961), British painter of landscapes and portraits, including *The Smiling Woman* 1910 (Tate Gallery, London) of his second wife, Dorelia. He was the brother of Gwen John.

John[2], *n.* **Elton** (1947–), stage name of Reginald Dwight. English pop singer, pianist, and composer, noted for his melodies and elaborate costumes and glasses. His lyrics are written by Bernie Taupin.

John[3], *n.* **Gwen** (1876–1939), British painter who lived in France for most of her life. Many of her paintings depict Dominican nuns (she converted to Catholicism 1913); she also painted calm, muted interiors.

John[4], *n.* **(John Lackland)** (1167–1216), king of England from 1199. He lost Normandy and almost all of the other English possessions in France to the French, and succeeded in provoking Pope Innocent III to excommunicate England 1208–13. After the revolt of the barons he was forced to seal the Magna Carta 1215 at Runnymede on the Thames.

John Bull, *n.* an imaginary figure used as a personification of England. The name was popularized by Dr Arbuthnot's *History of John Bull* (1712). He is represented as a prosperous farmer of the 18th cent.

John I, *n.* (1357–1433), king of Portugal from 1385. An illegitimate son of Pedro I, he was elected by the Cortes. His claim was supported by an English army against the rival king of Castile, thus establishing the Anglo-Portuguese Alliance of 1386. He married Philippa of Lancaster, daughter of John of Gaunt.

John II, *n.* (1319–1364), king of France from 1350. He was defeated and captured by the Black Prince at Poitiers 1356. Released 1360, he failed to raise the money for his ransom and returned to England 1364, where he died.

John III, *n.* **Sobieski** (1624–1696), king of Poland from 1674. He became commander-in-chief of the army 1668 after victories over the Cossacks and Tatars. A victory over the Turks 1673 helped to get him elected to the Polish throne, and he saved Vienna from the besieging Turks 1683.

John IV, *n.* (1603–1656), king of Portugal from 1640. Originally Duke of Braganza, he was elected king when the Portuguese rebelled against Spanish rule. His reign was marked by a long war against Spain, which did not end until 1668.

John VI, *n.* (1769–1826), king of Portugal, and regent for his insane mother Maria I from 1799 until her death 1816. He fled to Brazil when the French invaded Portugal 1807, and did not return until 1822. On his return Brazil declared its independence, with John's elder son Pedro as emperor.

John XXII, *n.* (1249–1334), pope 1316–34. He spent his papacy in Avignon, France, engaged in a long conflict with the Holy Roman emperor, Louis of Bavaria, and the Spiritual Franciscans, a monastic order who preached the absolute poverty of the clergy.

John XXIII, *n.* **Angelo Giuseppe Roncalli** (1881–1963), pope from 1958. He improved relations with the USSR in line with his encyclical *Pacem in Terris/Peace on Earth* (1963), established Roman Catholic hierarchies in newly emergent states, and summoned the Second Vatican Council, which reformed church liturgy and backed the ecumenical movement.

John of Damascus, St (*c.* 676–*c.* 754), Eastern Orthodox theologian and hymn writer, a defender of image worship against the iconoclasts. He was born in Damascus, Syria. Feast day 4 Dec. Contained in his *The Fountain of Knowledge* is *An Accurate Exposition of the Orthodox Faith*, an important chronicle of theology from the 4th–7th cents.

John of Gaunt, (1340–1399), English politician, born in Ghent, fourth son of Edward III, duke of Lancaster from 1362. During Edward's last years, and the years before Richard II attained the age of majority, he acted as head of government, and Parliament protested against his corrupt rule. He supported the religious reformer Wycliffe against ecclesiastical influence at court.

John of Salisbury, (*c.* 1115–1180), English philosopher and historian. His *Policraticus* portrayed the church as the guarantee of liberty against the unjust claims of secular authority.

John of the Cross, St, (1542–1591), Spanish Roman Catholic Carmelite friar from 1564, who was imprisoned several times for attempting to impose the reforms laid down by St Teresa. His verse describes spiritual ecstasy. Feast day 24 Nov.

John Paul I, *n.* **Albino Luciani** (1912–1978), pope 26 Aug.–28 Sept. 1978. His name was chosen as the combination of his two immediate predecessors.

John Paul II, *n.* **Karol Wojtyla** (1920–), pope 1978– , the first non-Italian to be elected pope since 1522. He was born near Kraków, Poland. He has been criticized for his upholding of the tradition of papal infallibility and condemnation of artificial contraception, women priests, married priests, and modern dress for monks and nuns. He has warned against involvement of priests in political activity.

John the Baptist, St, (*c.* 12 BC–*c.* AD 27), in the New Testament, an itinerant preacher. After preparation in the wilderness, he proclaimed the coming of Jesus Christ, baptized him in the river Jordan, and was executed by Herod Antipas at the request of Salome. His emblem is a lamb. Feast day 24 June.

Johns¹, *n.* **'Captain' W(illiam) E(arl)** (1893–1968), British author, from 1932, of popular novels of World War I flying ace Captain James Bigglesworth ('Biggles'), now sometimes criticized for chauvinism, racism, and sexism. Johns retired from the RAF 1930.

Johns², *n.* **Jasper** (1930–), US artist. He rejected the abstract in favour of such simple subjects as flags, maps and numbers so that the viewer's concentration would be entirely directed to the craftsmanship of the artist. He uses encaustic pigments to create a rich surface, with unexpected delicacies of colour.

Johnson¹, *n.* **Amy** (1904–1941), British aviator. She made a solo flight from Croydon, S London, to Australia 1930, in 19.5 days, and in 1932 made the fastest ever solo flight to Cape Town, South Africa. Her plane disappeared over the English Channel in World War II while she was serving with the Air Transport Auxiliary.

Johnson², *n.* **Andrew** (1808–1875), 17th president of the US 1865–69, a Democrat. He was born in Raleigh, North Carolina, and was a congressman from Tennessee 1843–53, governor of Tennessee 1853–57, senator 1857–62, and became vice-president 1864. He succeeded to the presidency on Lincoln's assassination. His conciliatory policy to the defeated South after the Civil War involved him in a feud with the radical Republicans, culminating in his impeachment before the Senate 1868, which failed to convict him by one vote.

Johnson³, *n.* **Ben** (1961–), Jamaican-Canadian sprinter. In 1987, he broke the world record for the 100 metres, running it in 9.83 seconds. At the Olympic Games 1988, he again broke the record, but was disqualified and suspended for using anabolic steroids to enhance his performance.

Johnson⁴, *n.* **Eastman** (1824–1906), US painter born in Germany, trained in Düsseldorf, The Hague, and Paris. Painting in the open air, he developed a fresh and luminous landscape style.

Johnson⁵, *n.* **Jack** (1878–1968), US heavyweight boxer. He overcame severe racial prejudice to become the first black heavyweight champion of the world 1908 when he travelled to Australia to challenge Tommy Burns. The US authorities wanted Johnson 'dethroned' because of his color but could not find suitable challengers until 1915, when he lost the title in a dubious fight decision to the giant Jess Willard.

Johnson⁶, *n.* **Lyndon (Baines)** (1908–1973), 36th president of the US 1963–69, a Democrat. He was born in Stonewall, Texas, elected to Congress 1937–49 and to the Senate 1949–60. He stood as vice president 1960, bringing crucial Southern votes to J F Kennedy, after whose assassination he succeeded as president. After the Tonkin Gulf Incident, the escalation of US involvement in the Vietnam War eventually dissipated the support won by his Great Society legislation (civil rights, education, alleviation of poverty), and he declined to stand for re-election 1968.

Johnson⁷, *n.* **Philip Cortelyou** (1906–), US architect, who invented the term 'international style'. Originally designing in the style of Mies van der Rohe, he later became an exponent of Post-Modernism. His best known building is the giant AT&T building in New York 1978, a pink skyscraper with a Chippendale-style cabinet top.

Johnson⁸, *n.* **Samuel** (1709–1784), known as **'Dr Johnson'**, English lexicographer, author, and critic, also a brilliant conversationalist and the dominant figure in 18th-cent. London literary society. His *Dictionary*, published 1755, remained authoritative for over a century, and is still remarkable for the vigour of its definitions. In 1764 he founded the 'Literary Club', whose members included Reynolds, Burke, Goldsmith, Garrick, and Boswell, Johnson's biographer. **Johnsonian,** *a.* pertaining to Dr Samuel Johnson or his style; pompous, inflated, abounding in words of classical origin. **Johnsonism,** *n.* **Johnsonese,** *n.*

Johnson⁹, *n.* **Uwe** (1934–), German novelist, who left East Germany for West Berlin 1959, and wrote of the division of Germany in, for example, *Anniversaries* (1977).

join, *v.t.* to connect, to fasten together, to unite; to couple, to associate; to unite (two persons, or a person or persons with or to) in marriage etc.; to begin, to engage in (battle etc.); to become a member (of a club etc.). *v.i.* to be contiguous or in contact; to become associated or combined (with etc.) in views, partnership, action etc.; to become a member of (a society etc.); †to begin battle. *n.* a joint; a point, line, or mark of junction. †**join-, joining-hand,** *n.* writing in which the letters are joined, cursive writing. **to join hands,** to clasp hands (with); (*fig.*) to come to an understanding or combine (with). **to join issue** [ISSUE]. **to join up,** (*coll.*) to enlist. **joinant,** *a.* (*Her.*) conjoined. **joinder,** *n.* †the act of joining; conjunction; the coupling of two things in one suit or action, or two or more parties as defendants in a suit; the acceptance by a party in an action of the challenge in his adversary's demurrer or last pleading. **joiner,** *n.* one who joins; a carpenter who makes articles of furniture, finishes woodwork etc.; (*N Am.*) a carpenter; a person who likes joining clubs etc.. **joinery,** *n.* [OF *joign-*, stem of *joindre,* L *jungere* (p.p. *junctus*)]

joint, *n.* a junction or mode of joining parts together; the place where two things are joined together; the union of two bones in an animal body; an analogous point or mechanical device connecting parts of any structure, whether fixed or movable; one of the pieces into which a butcher cuts up a carcass; this piece as served at table; a node; an internode; a natural fissure or line of parting traversing rocks in a straight and well-determined line; (*N Am. sl.*) an eating-house; a low and usu. illicit opium or gambling den; (*sl.; often derog.*) a place, building etc; (*sl.*) a bar or nightclub; (*sl.*) a marijuana cigarette. *a.* of, belonging to, performed or produced by different persons in conjunction; sharing or participating (with others). *v.t.* to form with joints or articulations; to connect by joints; to plane and prepare (boards etc.) for joining; to point (masonry); to divide or cut (meat) into joints, to disjoint. **out of joint,** dislocated, out of order. **to put someone's nose out of joint,** to upset, disconcert, or supplant a person. **universal joint,** a joint in which one part is able to swivel in all directions as in a ball and socket joint. **joint-action,** *n.* the joining of several actions in one. **Joint European Torus,** *n.* an experimental nuclear fusion machine, known as JET. **joint-heir,** *n.* an heir having a joint interest with another. **joint-stock,** *n.* stock or capital divided into shares and held jointly by several persons, hence **joint-stock company, firm** etc. **joint-stool,** *n.* a stool made with parts jointed (orig. *joined*) together. **joint-tenancy,** *n.* (*Law.*) tenure of an estate by unity of interest, title, time, and possession. **joint-tenant,** *n.* **jointweed,** *n.* the mare's-tail or *Equisetum;* (*N Am.*) a herb, *Polygonella articulatum,* of the buckwheat family. **jointed,** *a.* having joints, esp. of a specified kind. **jointedly,** *adv.* **jointer,** *n.* one who or that which joints; (*Carp.*) a long plane used to true the edges of boards to be joined; a pointing tool used by masons and bricklayers. **jointing,** *n., a.* **jointing-plane,** *n.* **jointing-rule,** *n.* a straight rule used in marking the joints of brickwork. **jointless,** *a.* **jointly,** *adv.* together or in conjunction with others. **jointress,** †**jointuress,** *n. fem.* a woman who has a jointure. **jointure,** *n.* an estate in lands or tenements, settled upon a woman in consideration or marriage, which she is to enjoy after her husband's decease. *v.t.* to settle a jointure upon. [OF, p.p. of *joindre,* see prec.]

Joinville, *n.* **Jean, Sire de Joinville** (1224–1317), French historian, born in Champagne. He accompanied Louis IX on the crusade of 1248–54, which he described in his *History of St Louis.*

joist, *n.* one of a series of parallel horizontal timbers to which floor-boards or the laths of a ceiling are nailed. *v.t.* to furnish with joists. [ME and OF *giste* (F *gîte*), a bed, a place to lie in, from *gesir,* L *jacēre,* to lie]

jojoba, *n.* a desert shrub native to Arizona, Mexico and California, whose edible seeds provide waxy oil similar to spermaceti, used in cosmetics, toiletries etc.. [Mex. Sp.]

joke, *n.* something said or done to excite laughter or merriment; a jest; a ridiculous incident, circumstance etc. *v.i.* to make jokes, to jest. *v.t.* to crack jokes upon; to rally, to banter. **practical joke,** a trick played on a person to raise a laugh at his expense. **jokee,** *n.* one on whom a joke is played. **jokeless,** *a.* **jokelet,** *n.* **joker,** one who jokes, a jester; (*sl.*) a fellow; (*Cards*) an extra card (often printed with a comic device) used with various values in some games. **jokesman, jokesmith, jokester, jokist,** *n.* **jokesome,** *a.* **jokingly,** *adv.* **joky,** *a.* [L *jocus*]

jokul, *n.* a glacier or snow mountain in Iceland. [Icel. *jökull,* icicle, glacier, dim. of *jaki,* piece of ice (cp. ICICLE)]

†**jole, joll,** JOWL.

Joliot-Curie, *n.* **Irène** (1897–1956) and **Frédéric Joliot-Curie** (1900–1958), French physicists who made the discovery of artificial radioactivity for which they were jointly awarded the 1935 Nobel chemistry prize. Irene was the daughter of Marie Curie and began work at her mother's Radium Institute in 1921. In 1926 she married Frédéric, a pupil of her mother and they began a long and fruitful collaboration. Notably, in 1934 they found that certain elements exposed to radiation themselves become radioactive.

jolly, *a.* merry, mirthful, gay, jovial, festive; inspiring or expressing mirth; (*coll.*) pleasant, agreeable, charming; remarkable, extraordinary; (*iron.*) nice, precious; (*sl.*) slightly drunk; †gallant; †wanton, amorous; †fine in appearance; †plump, buxom. *adv.* (*coll.*) very, exceedingly. *v.i.* to be jolly, to make merry. *v.t.* (*sl.*) to banter, to joke, to rally; to treat agreeably so as to keep in good humour or secure a favour (usu. with *along*). **jolly Roger,** *n.* a pirate's flag with skull and cross-bones. **jollify,** *v.i.* to make merry; to tipple. *v.t.* to make (a person) merry, esp. with drink. **jollification,** *n.* merry-making, a jolly party. **jollily,** *adv.* †**jolliment, jolliness, jollity,** *n.* [OF *jolif, joli,* gay, fine, etym. doubtful]

jolly-boat, *n.* a small boat for the general work of a ship. [cp. Dan. *jolle,* Dut. *jol,* YAWL]

Jolson, *n.* **Al** (1886–1950), stage name of Asa Yoelson. Russian-born singer and entertainer, who lived in the US from childhood. Formerly a Broadway star, he gained instant cinema immortality as the star of the first talking picture, *The Jazz Singer* (1927).

jolt, *v.t.* to shake with sharp, sudden jerks, as in a carriage along a rough road; to disturb, to shock. *v.i.* to move thus. *n.* a sudden shock or jerk. **jolter-,** †**jolthead,** *n.* a blockhead, a dolt. **jolter,** *n.* **joltingly,** *adv.* [etym. doubtful, perh. conn. with JOWL]

Jonah, *n.* (7th cent. BC), Hebrew prophet whose name is given to a book in the Old Testament. According to this, he fled by ship in order to evade his mission to prophesy the destruction of Nineveh. The crew threw him overboard in a storm, as a bringer of ill fortune, and he spent three days and nights in the belly of a whale before coming to land; a bringer of bad luck.

Jonathan[1], *n.* the American people; a typical American; a kind of late-ripening red apple. [prob. from *Jonathan* Trumbull 1710–85, Governor of Connecticut, to whom Washington frequently referred for advice]

Jonathan[2], *n.* **Chief (Joseph) Leabua** (1914–1987), Lesotho politician. As prime minister of Lesotho 1965–86, he played a pragmatic role, allying himself in turn with South Africa, then with the Organization of African Unity. His rule was brought to an end by a coup in 1986.

Jones[1], *n.* **Charles Martin ('Chuck')** (1912–), US film animator and cartoon director who worked at Warner Brothers with characters such as Bugs Bunny, Daffy Duck, Wile E. Coyote and Elmer Fudd.

Jones[2], *n.* **Inigo** (1573–*c.* 1652), English architect. Born in London, he studied in Italy, and was influenced by the works of Palladio. He was employed by James I to design scenery for Ben Jonson's masques. In 1619 he designed his English Renaissance masterpiece, the banqueting-room at Whitehall, London.

Jones[3], *n.* **John Paul** (1747–1792), Scottish-born American naval officer in the War of Independence 1775. Heading a small French-sponsored squadron in the *Bonhomme Richard*, he captured the British warship *Serapis* 23 Sept. 1779 in a bloody battle off Scarborough.

Jones[4], *n.* **Robert Tyre ('Bobby')** (1902–1971), US golfer. He was the game's greatest amateur player, who never turned professional but won 13 major amateur and professional tournaments, including the Grand Slam of the amateur and professional opens of both the US and Britain 1930.

Jonestown, *n.* commune of the People's Temple Sect, NW of Georgetown, Guyana, established 1974 by the American Jim Jones (1933–78), who originally founded the sect among San Francisco's black community. After a visiting US congressman was shot dead, Jones enforced mass suicide on his followers by instructing them to drink cyanide; 914 died, including over 240 children.

Jongkind, *n.* **Johan Bartold** (1819–1891), Dutch painter active mainly in France. His studies of the Normandy coast show a keen observation of the natural effects of light. He influenced the Impressionist painter Monet.

jongleur, *n.* an itinerant minstrel or reciter of the Middle Ages, esp. in N France. [F, from OF *jogleor,* JUGGLER]

jonquil, *n.* the rush-leaved narcissus, *Narcissus jonquilla,* with two to six flowers on a stem. [F *jonquille,* Sp. *junquillo,* dim. of *junco,* L *jucus,* rush]

Jonson, *n.* **Ben(jamin)** (1572–1637), English dramatist, poet, and critic. *Every Man in his Humour* (1598) established the English 'comedy of humours', in which each character embodies a 'humour', or vice, such as greed, lust, or avarice. This was followed by *Every Man out of his Humour* (1599), *Cynthia's Revels* (1600) and *Poetaster* (1601). His first extant tragedy is *Sejanus* (1603), with Burbage and Shakespeare as members of the original cast. The plays of his middle years include *Volpone, or The Fox* (1606), *The Alchemist* (1610), and *Bartholomew Fair* (1614).

Joplin[1], *n.* **Janis** (1943–1970), US blues and rock singer, born in Texas. She was lead singer with the San Francisco group Big Brother and the Holding Company 1966–68. Her biggest hit, Kris Kristofferson's 'Me and Bobby McGee', was released on the posthumous *Pearl* LP 1971.

Joplin[2], *n.* **Scott** (1868–1917), US ragtime pianist and composer in Chicago. His 'Maple Leaf Rag' (1899) was the first instrumental sheet music to sell a million copies, and 'The Entertainer', as the theme tune of the film *The Sting* 1973, revived his popularity. He was an influence on Jelly Roll Morton and other early jazz musicians.

Jordaens, *n.* **Jacob** (1593–1678), Flemish painter, born in Antwerp. His style follows Rubens, whom he assisted in various commissions. Much of his work is exuberant and on a large scale, including scenes of peasant life, portraits, and mythological subjects.

jordan, *n.* a chamber-pot. [doubtfully conjectured to mean orig. a Jordan-vessel, i.e., one in which pilgrims brought water from the River Jordan for baptismal purposes]

Jordan, Hashemite Kingdom of, a country in SW Asia. **area** 89,206 sq km/34,434 sq miles (West Bank, incorporated into Jordan 1950 but occupied by Israel since 1967, area 5879 sq km/2269 sq miles). **capital** Amman. **towns** Zarqa, Irbid, Aqaba (the only port). **physical** mostly desert. **population** (1988) 2,970,000 (including Palestinian refugees); West Bank (1988) 866,000; annual growth rate 3.7%. **exports** potash, phosphates, citrus. **language** Arabic. **religion** Sunni Muslim.

Jörgensen, *n.* **Jörgen** (1779–1845), Danish sailor who in 1809 seized control of Iceland, announcing it was under the protection of England. His brief reign of corruption ended later the same year when he was captured by an English naval ship and taken to London, where he was imprisoned.

jorum, *n.* a large bowl or drinking-vessel; its contents. [prob. from *Joram* in the Bible, II Sam. viii.10]

Joseph[1], *n.* a man of invincible chastity (alln. to Gen. xxxix.12); an 18th-cent. caped riding-dress for ladies, having buttons down to the skirts. [the patriarch JOSEPH[3] (alln. to Gen. xxxvii.3)]

Joseph[2], *n.* in the New Testament, the husband of the Virgin Mary, a descendant of King David, and a carpenter by trade. Although Jesus was not the son of Joseph, Joseph was his legal father. According to Roman Catholic tradition, he had a family by a previous wife, and was an elderly man when he married Mary.

Joseph[3], *n.* in the Old Testament, the 11th and favourite son of Jacob, sold into Egypt by his jealous half-brothers. After he had risen to power there, they and his father joined him to escape from famine.

Joseph[4], *n.* **Keith (Sinjohn)** (1918–), British Conservative politician. A barrister, he entered parliament 1956. He held ministerial posts 1962–64, 1970–74, 1979–81, and was secretary of state for education and science 1981–86. He was made a life peer 1987.

Joseph I, *n.* (1678–1711), holy Roman emperor from 1705, and king of Austria, of the house of Habsburg. He spent most of his reign involved in fighting the War of Spanish Succession.

Joseph II, *n.* (1741–1790), holy Roman emperor from 1765, son of Francis I (1708–1765). The reforms he carried out after the death of his mother, Maria Theresa, in 1780, provoked revolts from those who lost privileges.

Josephine, *n.* **Marie Josèphe Rose Tascher de la Pagerie** (1763–1814), empress of France 1804–1809. Born on Martinique, she married in 1779 Alexandre de Beauharnais, and in 1796 Napoleon, who divorced her in 1809 because she had not produced children.

Joseph of Arimathaea, St, (1st cent. AD), in the New Testament, a wealthy Jew, member of the Sanhedrin (supreme court), and secret supporter of Jesus. On the evening of the Crucifixion he asked the Roman procurator Pilate for Jesus's body and buried it in his own tomb. Feast day 17 Mar.

Josephson, *n.* **Brian** (1940–), British physicist, a leading authority on superconductivity. In 1973 he shared a Nobel prize for his theoretical predictions of the properties of a supercurrent through a tunnel barrier. **Josephson junction,** *n.* a device used in 'superchips' (large and complex integrated circuits) to speed the passage of signals by a phenomenon called 'electron tunnelling'. Although these superchips respond a thousand times faster than the silicon chip, they have the disadvantage that the components of the Josephson junctions operate only at temperatures close to absolute zero.

Josephus, *n.* **Flavius** (37–*c.* 100 AD), Jewish historian and general, born in Jerusalem. He became a Pharisee, and commanded the Jewish forces in Galilee in the revolt against Rome from 66 (which ended in mass suicide at Masada). When captured, he gained the favour of Vespasian and settled in Rome as a citizen. He wrote *Antiquities of the Jews*, an early history to AD 66; *The Jewish War*, and an autobiography.

josh, *v.t.* (*N Am. sl.*), to make fun of, to ridicule. *n.* a friendly joke. [etym. uncertain]

Joshua, *n.* (13th cent. BC), in the Old Testament, successor of Moses, who led the Jews in their conquest of the land of Canaan. The city of Jericho was the first to fall: according to the Book of Joshua, the walls crumbled to the blast of his trumpets.

Josiah, *n.* (*c.* 647–609 BC), king of Judah. Grandson of Manasseh and son of Amon, he succeeded to the throne when eight. The discovery of a Book of Instruction (probably Deuteronomy, a book of the Old Testament) during repairs of the Temple in 621 BC stimulated thorough reform, which included the removal of all sanctuaries except that of Jerusalem. He was killed in a clash at Megiddo with Pharaoh-nechoh, king of Egypt.

joskin, *n.* (*sl.*) a bumpkin, a yokel.

Josquin Desprez, des Prés *n.* (1440–1521), Franco-Flemish composer. His music combines a technical mastery with the feeling for words that became a hallmark of renaissance vocal music. His works, which include 18 masses, over 100 motets, and secular vocal works, are characterized by their vitality and depth of feeling.

joss, *n.* a Chinese idol. **joss-house,** a Chinese temple. **joss-stick,** *n.* a stick of perfumed material burnt as incense, orig. in China. [corr. of Port. *deos*. L *deus,* God]

jostle, *v.t.* to push against, to hustle; to elbow. *v.i.* to push (against, along etc.); to hustle, to crowd. *n.* a hustling; a collision, a conflict. [formerly *justle,* freq. of *just,* JOUST]

jot, *n.* a tittle, an iota. *v.t.* to write (down a brief note or memorandum of). **jotter,** *n.* a pad or exercise-book for taking notes etc. **jotting,** *n.* a note or memorandum. [L and Gr. *iōta,* the letter *i*]

Joubert, *n.* **Petrus Jacobus** (1831–1900), Boer general in South Africa. He opposed British annexation of the Transvaal 1877, proclaimed its independence 1880, led the Boer Commandos in the First South African War against the British 1880–81, defeated Jameson 1896, and fought in the Second South African War.

jougs, *n.pl.* an iron collar attached by a chain to a post, corresponding to the English pillory. [Sc., prob. from F *joug,* L *jugum,* YOKE]

†**jouisance,** *n.* jollity, mirth. [F *jouissance,* from *jouir,* to enjoy]

jouk, *v.i.* (*Sc.*) to dodge, to duck; to skulk, to hide. *v.t.* to dodge, to evade. *n.* a dodge, a quick movement; the slip. **joukery, joukery-cookery, joukery-pawkery,** *n.* [etym. doubtful]

joul, JOWL.

Joule, *n.* **James Prescott** (1818–1889), British physicist whose work on the relations between electrical, mechanical, and chemical effects led to the discovery of the first law of thermodynamics.

joule, *n.* orig. the unit of electrical energy, the work done in 1 second by a current of 1 ampere against a resistance of 1 ohm; the SI unit of work and energy, equal to the work done when a force of 1 newton advances its point of application 1 metre. **joulemeter,** *n.* [Dr J.P. *Joule*]

Joule-Thomson effect, *n.* in physics, the fall in temperature of a gas as it expands adiabatically (without loss or gain of heat to the system) through a narrow jet. It can be felt when, for example, compressed air escapes through the valve of an inflated bicycle tyre. Only hydrogen does not exhibit the effect. It is the basic principle of most refrigerators.

jounce, *v.t., v.i.* to jolt or shake. *n.* a jolt, a shake. [etym. doubtful]

Jounieh, *n.* a port on the Mediterranean coast of Lebanon, 15 km/9 miles N of Beirut. The centre of an anti-Syrian Christian enclave.

journal, *n.* an account of daily transactions; (*Bookkeeping*) the book from which daily entries are posted up in the ledger; a daily record of events, a diary; a record of events or news, properly one published daily, but now extended to any newspaper or other periodical published at regular intervals; the transactions of a learned society etc.; a log-book or daily register of the ship's course and distance etc.; the part of a shaft that rests on the bearings. **journal-box,** *n.* the metal case in which the journal moves. **journalese,** (*derog.*) a superficial style of writing full of cliches etc., regarded as being typical of writing in newspapers etc.. **journalist,** *n.* an editor of or contributor to a newspaper or other journal; one who keeps a diary. **journalism,** *n.* **journalistic,** *a.* **journalize, -ise,** *v.t.* (*book-keeping*) to enter in a journal; to enter in a diary. *v.i.* to follow the profession of a journalist; to keep a journal or diary. [OF, from L *diurnālis,* DIURNAL]

journey, *n.* passage or travel from one place to another, esp. by land as dist. from a voyage; the distance travelled in a given time; †a day's work or travel; a round of work, a turn, a spell. *v.i.* to travel; to make a journey. †**journeybated,** *a.* worn out with a journey. **journeyman,** *n.* a mechanic or artisan who has served his apprenticeship and works for an employer; a mere drudge, hack or hireling. **journey-work,** *n.* work performed for hire (*lit. and fig.*). †**journeyer,** *n.* [OF *jornée,* late L *jornāta, diurnāta,* a day's work as prec.]

joust, just[2], *v.i.* to tilt, to encounter on horseback with lances. *n.* a tilting-match; a combat between knights or men-at-arms on horseback. [OF *jouster* (F *jouter*), from low L *juxtāre,* to approach, from *juxtā,* near]

Jove, *n.* Jupiter, the chief of the Roman divinities. **Jovian,** *a.* pertaining to or like Jupiter; pertaining to the planet Jupiter. **jovial,** *a.* mirthful, merry, joyous; †(*Astrol.*) under the influence of the planet Jupiter; †propitious. **joviality, jovialness,** *n.* good humour. **jovially,** *adv.* [L *Jovem,* acc of OL *Jovis,* JUPITER]

Jovian, *n.* (331–364), Roman emperor from 363. Captain of the imperial bodyguard, he was chosen as emperor by the troops after Julian's death in battle with the Persians. He concluded an unpopular peace and restored Christianity as the state religion.

jow, *v.t.* (*Sc.*) to knock, to strike. *v.t.* to rock, to swing. *n.* a stroke, esp. of a bell. [perh. of var. of foll.]

Jowett, *n.* **Benjamin** (1817–1893), English scholar. He promoted university reform, including the abolition of the theological test for degrees, and translated Plato, Aristotle, and Thucydides.

jowl, *n.* the (lower) jaw; (*often pl.*) the cheek; the throat or neck, esp. of a double-chinned person; the dewlap; the crop or wattle of a fowl; the head and shoulder of fish. †*v.t.* to bump, to dash (together, against etc.). **cheek by jowl,** with the cheeks close together; close together. **jowler,** *n.* a dog with heavy jowls. [ME *chowl, chavel,* OE *cēafl,* jaw, blended obscurely with ME *cholle,* OE *ceolur,* throat]

joy, *n.* the emotion produced by gratified desire, success, happy fortune, exultation etc.; gladness, happiness, delight; a cause of joy or happiness; †mirth, gaiety. *v.i.* to rejoice. *v.t.* to gladden; to congratulate; to enjoy. **to have no joy,** (*coll.*) to be unsuccessful in a task etc. **joy-bells,** *n.pl.* peals rung on festive occasions. **joy-ride,** *n.* (*coll.*) a ride in a car for pleasure, especially when unauthorized. **joy-stick,** *n.* the control-lever of an aeroplane; a lever for controlling the movement of a cursor on a computer screen. †**joyance,** *n.* **joyful,** *a.* **joyfully,** *adv.* **joyfulness,** *n.* **joyless,** *a.* **joylessly,** *adv.* **joylessness,** *n.* **joyous,** *a.* joyful; causing joy. **joyously,** *adv.* **joyousness,** *n.* [OF *joie,* L *gaudia,* orig. pl. of *gaudium*]

Joyce, *n.* **James (Augustine Aloysius)** (1882–1941), Irish writer, born in Dublin, who revolutionized the form of the English novel with his 'stream of consciousness' technique. His works include *Dubliners* 1914 (short stories), *Portrait of the Artist as a Young Man* 1916, *Ulysses* 1922 and *Finnegans Wake* 1938.

JP, (*abbr.*) Justice of the Peace.

JP, *n.* abbreviation for **justice of the peace**.

Jr., jr., (*abbr.*) junior.

Juan Carlos, *n.* (1938–), king of Spain. The son of Don Juan, pretender to the Spanish throne, he married in 1962 Princess Sofia, eldest daughter of King Paul of Greece. In 1969 he was nominated by Franco to succeed on the restoration of the monarchy intended to follow Franco's own death; his father was excluded because of his known liberal views. He became king in 1975 and has sought to steer his country from dictatorship to democracy.

Juárez, *n.* **Benito** (1806–1872), Mexican politician, president 1861–64 and 1867–72. In 1861 he suspended repayments of Mexico's foreign debts, which prompted a joint French, British, and Spanish expedition to exert pressure. French forces invaded and created an empire for Maximilian, brother of the Austrian emperor. After their withdrawal in 1867, Maximilian was executed, and Juárez returned to the presidency.

juba[1], *n.* a mane, as of a horse; a loose beard or tuft of awns (as on certain grasses, maize etc.). **jubate,** *a.* maned; fringed with or as with mane. [L]

juba[2], *n.* a characteristic Negro dance.

jube, *n.* a rood-loft or gallery dividing the choir from the nave. [F *jubé,* L *jubē,* imper. of *jubēre,* to command, from the formula, *jubē, domine, benedīcere*]

jubilate[1], *v.i.* to exult; to express intense joy. **jubilance, jubilation,** *n.* **jubilant,** *a.* **jubilantly,** *adv.* [L *jūbilātus,* p.p. of *jūbilāre,* from *jūbilum,* a shout of joy]

jubilate[2], *n.* the 100th Psalm used as canticle in the evening service of the Church of England, from its Latin commencing words *Jubilate Deo;* (*fig.*) a shout of joy or exultation. [L, shout ye for joy, as prec.]

jubilee, *n.* the most important festival among the Jews, proclaimed by the sound of a trumpet, and celebrated every 50th year to commemorate their deliverance from Egyptian slavery; the 50th anniversary of an event of public interest; a season of great public rejoicing or festivity; an outburst of joy; in the Roman Catholic Church, a year of special indulgence or remission of the guilt of sin, formerly periodical now occasional. **diamond jubilee,** a 60th anniversary. **golden jubilee,** a jubilee, a 50th anniversary. **silver jubilee,** a 25th anniversary, esp. of a marriage. [OF *jubilé,* late L *jūbilaeus* (assim. to *jūbil, see* JUBILATE[1]), Gr. *iōbēlaios,* pertaining to the jubilee, from *ibōbēlos,* Heb. *yōbēl,* orig., ram, ram's horn-trumpet]

Judaea, JUDAH.

Judaeo-, *comb.form* of or relating to the Jews or Judaism. [Gr. *Iudaios*; see JUDAIC]

Judaeophobe, *n.* one who fears or dislikes the Jews. **Judaeophobia,** *n.*

Judah, Judaea, *n.* district of S Palestine. After the death of King Solomon 937 BC, Judah adhered to his son Rehoboam and the Davidic line, whereas the rest of Israel elected Jeroboam as ruler of the northern kingdom. In New Testament times, Judah was the Roman province of Judaea, and in current Israeli usage it refers to the southern area of the West Bank.

Judah Ha-Nasi, *n.* **'the Prince'** (*c.* AD 135–*c.* 220), Jewish scholar who with a number of colleagues edited the collection of writings known as the Mishna, which formed the basis of the Talmud, in the 2nd century AD.

Judaic, -ical, *a.* pertaining to the Jews, Jewish. **Judaically,** *adv.* **Judaism,** *n.* the religious doctrines and rites of the Jews, according to the law of Moses; conformity to such doctrines and rites. **Judaist,** *n.* **Judaize, -ise,** *v.t.* and *i.* **Judaization, -isation,** *n.* **Judaizer, -iser,** *n.* [L *Judāicus,* Gr. *Ioudaïkos,* from *Ioudais,* JEW]

Judas, *n.* the name of several persons mentioned in the New Testament, esp. the disciple who betrayed Christ; a traitor. **Judas-coloured,** *a.* red, reddish (from a tradition that Judas had red hair). †**Judas-hole,** *a.* a small hole cut in a door etc. to enable a person to pry into a room. **Judas-tree,** the leguminous tree, *Cercis siliquastrum,* which flowers before the leaves appear (traditionally the tree on which Judas hanged himself). [L *Jūdas,* Gr. *Ioudas,* Heb. y'hūdāh, Judah]

judder, *v.i.* to wobble; to vibrate; in singing to make rapid changes in intensity during the emission of a note. *n.* a wobble; the vibration of an aircraft. [prob. *jar* + *shudder*]

Jude, St, *n.* (lived 1st cent.), supposed brother of Jesus Christ and writer of Epistle in the New Testament; patron saint of lost causes. Feast day 28 Oct.

judge, *n.* a civil officer invested with power to hear and determine causes in a court of justice; one authorized to decide a dispute or contest; (*N Am.*) any person who sits in judgment, from a Supreme Court judge to a local magistrate; one skilled in deciding on relative merits, a connoisseur; (*Jewish Hist.*) a chief civil and military magistrate among the Jews, from the death of Joshua to the Kings. *v.t.* to decide (a question); to hear or try (a cause); to pass sentence upon; to examine and form an opinion upon (an exhibition etc.); to criticize; (*coll.*) to consider, to estimate, to decide; (*Jewish Hist.*) to act as chief magistrate over, to rule. *v.i.* to hear and determine a case; to give sentence; to form or give an opinion; to come to a conclusion; to criticize, to be censorious; sit in judgment. **judge advocate,** *n.* an officer in charge of proceedings at a court martial. **judges' rules,** *n. pl.* in English law, a set of rules governing the behaviour of the police towards suspects. **judger,** *n.* **judgeship,** *n.* **judgingly,** *adv.* **judgmatic, -ical,** *a.*, **-ally,** *adv.* **judgment, judgement,** *n.* the act of judging; a judicial decision, a sentence of a court of justice; discernment, discrimination; the capacity for arriving at reasonable conclusions leading to well-adapted behaviour, especially as indicated by conduct in the practical affairs of life; criticism; the critical faculty; opinion, estimate; a misfortune regarded as sent by God. **judgment of Solomon,** any judgment designed to reveal the false claimant, after Solomon in I Kings iii.16–28. **Last Judgment,** the judgment of mankind by God at the end of the world. **Judgment Day,** *n.* the day of this. **judgment debt,** *n.* a debt secured by a judge's order, under which an execution can be levied at any time. **judgment seat,** *n.* the seat or bench on which judges sit; (*fig.*) a court, a tribunal. [ME and OF *juge,* L *iūdex -icem,* (*jūs,* law, *dic-,* root of *dicāre,* to point out. cp. INDICATE)]

Judica, *n.* passion Sunday. [words of the introit, *Judica me,* judge me]

judicature, *n.* the administration of justice by trial and judgment; the authority of a judge; a court of justice; the jurisdiction of a court. **Supreme Court of Judicature in England,** the court established by Acts in 1873 and 1875, combining the functions of the former Courts of Chancery, King's Bench, Common Pleas, Exchequer, Admiralty etc. †**judicable,** *a.* †**judicative,** *a.* †**judicatory,** *a.* pertaining to the administration of justice. *n.* a court of justice; the administration of justice. [F, from med. L *jūdicātura,* from *judicāre,* to JUDGE]

judicial, *a.* pertaining or proper to courts of law or the administration of justice; proceeding from a court of justice; showing judgment; critical, discriminating; impartial. **judicial factor,** *n.* (*Sc. Law*) an administrator appointed by the Court of Session to manage estates. **judicial murder,** *n.* capital punishment inflicted as the result of a legal but unjust sentence. **judicial separation,** *n.* separation of married persons by order of the Divorce Court. **judicially,** *adv.* **judiciary,** *n.* judicial; passing judgment. *n.* the judicature. **judicious,** *a.* sagacious, clear-headed, discerning; wise, prudent; done with reason or judgment. †**judicial, judiciously,** *adv.* **judiciousness,** *n.* [L *jūdiciālis,* from *jūdicium,* a trial, a judgment, from *jūdex,* JUDGE]

judicium Dei, the judgment of God. [L.]

Judith, *n.* in Christian legend, a woman who saved her community from a Babylonian siege by killing the enemy general, Holofernes. The Book of Judith is part of the Apocrypha, a section of the Old Testament.

judo, *n.* a modern sport derived from a form of ju-jitsu. [Jap.]

Judy, *n.* the name of Punch's wife in the Punch and Judy show; (*derog.*) a woman, a wench, a sweetheart. [short for *Judith*]

jug[1], *n.* a vessel, usually with a swelling body, narrow neck, and handle, for holding liquors; (*sl.*) a prison, a lock-up. *v.t.* (*usu. in p.p.*) to stew (a hare) in a jug or jar; (*sl.*) to imprison. **jugful,** *n.* [etym. doubtful]

jug[2], *v.i.* of the nightingale etc. to make a sound like 'jug'. **jug-jug,** *n.* [imit.]

jugal, *a.* pertaining to the cheek-bone. [L *jugālis,* from *jugum,* yoke]

jugate, *a.* (*Bot.*) having leaflets in pairs. [L *jugātus,* p.p. of *jugāre,* to couple as prec.]

juggernaut, *n.* Vishnu in his eighth avatar; his idol at Krishna or Puri in Orissa, which is annually dragged in a procession on a huge car, under the wheels of which fanatics are said to have thrown themselves; (*fig.*) a belief, institution etc., to which one is ruthlessly sacrificed or by which one is ruthlessly destroyed; a very large articulated lorry (causing damage to the environment). [Hindi, *Jagganāth,* Sansk. *Jagganātha,* lord of the world (*jugat,* world, *nātha,* lord)]

juggins, *n.* (*coll.*) a blockhead, a dolt.

juggle, *v.i.* to play tricks by sleight of hand, to conjure; to throw in the air and catch several objects, such as balls, continuously so that some are in the air all the time; to practise artifice or imposture (with). *v.i.* to deceive by trickery; to obtain, convey etc. (away, out of etc.) by trickery; to manipulate (facts, figures etc.) in order to deceive; to try to keep several things (such as jobs etc.) going at the same time. *n.* a trick by sleight of hand; an imposture. **juggler,** *n.* **jugglery,** *n.* [from OF *jogleor,* juggler, late L *ioculator -torem* from *joculāre,* L *joculārī,* to jest, from *joculus,* dim. of *jocus,* JOKE]

juglans, *n.* a genus of trees containing the walnuts. **juglandaceous,** *a.* [L, the walnut (*Jovis glans,* Jove's acorn)]

Jugoslav, YUGOSLAV.

Jugoslavia YUGOSLAVIA.

jugular, *a.* belonging to the neck or throat; (*Ichthyol.*) having the ventral fins anterior to the pectoral. *n.* a jugular vein. **to go for the jugular,** to attack someone where he/she is most vulnerable or most likely to be harmed. **jugular veins,** *n.pl.* the veins of the neck which return the blood from the head. **jugulate,** *v.t.* to kill; (*Med.*) to put an end to (a disease etc.) by drastic measures. [L *jugūlum,* the collarbone, -AR]

Jugurtha, *n.* (d. 104 BC), king of Numidia, N Africa, who, after a long resistance, was betrayed to the Romans in 107 BC and put to death.

juice, *n.* the watery part of vegetable or the fluid part of animal bodies; (*sl.*) electricity, electric current, petrol; the essence or characteristic element of anything. **to juice up,** (*sl.*) to make more lively. **to step on the juice,** (*sl.*) to accelerate a motor-car. **juiceless,** *a.* **juicy,** *a.* abounding in juice, succulent; interesting esp. in a titillating or scandalous way; (*coll.*) profitable. **juiciness,** *n.* [OF *jus,* L *jūs,* soup, sauce]

ju-jitsu, *n.* the Japanese art of wrestling, based on the principle of making one's opponent exert his strength to his own disadvantage. [Jap.]

ju-ju, *n.* a fetish, an idol credited with supernatural power; the ban or taboo worked by this. [Hausa, perh. from F *joujou,* a toy]

jujube, *n.* the berry-like fruit of *Zizyphus vulgaris* or Z. *jujuba,* spiny shrubs of the buckthorn family, dried as a sweetmeat; a lozenge of sweetened gum-arabic or gelatine flavoured with or imitating this. [F, from late L *jujuba,* L *zizyphum,* Gr. *zizuphon*]

juke-box, *n.* a kind of large automatic record player, usu. in a public place, in which coins are inserted and buttons pressed to select the relevant tunes. [Gullah *juke,* disorderly, of W Afr. origin]

Jul., (*abbr.*) July.

julep, *n.* a sweet drink, esp. a preparation with some liquid used as a vehicle for medicine, a stimulant composed of spirit, usu. flavoured with mint. [F, from Sp. *julepe,* Arab. *julāb,* Pers. *julāb* (*gul,* rose, *āb,* water)]

Julian, *a.* pertaining to or originated by Julius Caesar. **Julian calendar,** *n.* the calendar instituted by him in 46 BC. **Julian year,** *n.* the year of this, containing 365¼ days.

Julian, *n.* (*c.* 331–363), Roman emperor, called the 'Apostate'. Born in Constantinople, the nephew of Constantine the Great, he was brought up as a Christian but early in life became a convert to paganism. Sent by Constantius to govern Gaul in 355, he was proclaimed emperor by his troops in 360, and in 361 was marching on Constantinople when Constantius' death allowed a peaceful succession. He revived pagan worship and refused to persecute heretics. He was killed in battle against the Persians.

Juliana, *n.* (1909–), queen of the Netherlands. The daughter of Queen Wilhelmina (1880–1962), she married Prince Bernhard of Lippe-Biesterfeld in 1937 and ruled 1948–80, when she abdicated and was succeeded by her daughter Beatrix.

julienne, *n.* a clear soup from meat with chopped or shredded vegetables; a variety of pear. [F, from *Jules* or *Julien*]

Julius II, *n.* (1443–1513), pope 1503–13, a politician who wanted to make the Papal States the leading power in Italy, and formed international alliances first against Venice and then against France. He began the building of St Peter's Church, Rome, in 1506, and was the patron of the artists Michelangelo and Raphael.

July, *n.* the seventh month of the year. [AF *Julie,* L *Jūlius,* after *Jūlius* Caesar]

July Revolution, *n.* the French revolution 27–29 July 1830 in Paris which overthrew the restored Bourbon monarchy of Charles X and substituted the constitutional monarchy of Louis Philippe, whose rule (1830–48) is sometimes referred to as the July Monarchy.

jumble, *v.t.* to mix confusedly; to throw or put together without order. †*v.i.* to be mixed in a confused way; to move (about, along etc.) confusedly. *n.* a confused mixture; a muddle, disorder, confusion; articles donated to, or suitable for, a jumble-sale. **jumble-sale,** *n.* a sale of miscellaneous articles at a bazaar etc. **jumbleshop,** *n.* †**jumblement,** *n.* **jumbly,** *a.* [prob. onomat.]

jumbo, *n.* a huge, unwieldly person, animal or thing, used as the proper name of a famous elephant (sold from the Zoological Gardens, London, to Barnum and killed by accident in 1885); an over-sized object. **jumbo jet,** *n.* a very large jet-propelled aircraft, **jumbo-size(d),** *a.* of much larger than usual size. **jumboesque,** *a.* **jumboism,** *n.* [etym. doubtful]

jumbuck, *n.* a sheep. [Austral. Abor. pidgin English]

jumelle, *a.* twin, paired. *n.* a gimmal; a pair of opera-glasses; (*pl.*) the side-pieces of a loom carrying the cylinders. [F, from L *gemellus,* GIMMAL]

jump[1], *v.i.* to throw oneself from the ground by a sudden movement of the muscles of the legs and feet; to spring, to leap, to bound; to move suddenly (along, up, out) with such springs or bounds; to start or rise (up) abruptly; (*fig.*) to agree, to tally (with or together). *v.t.* to pass over or cross by leaping; to cause to leap over; to skip (a chapter, pages etc.). †*adv.* exactly. *n.* the act of jumping; a leap, a spring, a bound; a start, an involuntary nervous movement, esp. (*pl.*) convulsive twitching as in delirium tremens; a sudden rise (in price, value etc.); a break, a gap; (*Geol.*) a fault; †risk, hazard. **to jump a claim,** to seize upon a mining claim by force or fraud. **to jump at,** to accept eagerly; to reach hastily (as a conclusion). **to jump down one's throat,** to answer or interrupt violently. **to jump on** or **upon,** to reprimand, abuse, or assail violently; to pounce upon. **to jump one's bail, country, town,** etc. to abscond. **to jump ship,** of a sailor etc., to leave a ship without permission, to desert. **to jump the gun,** to get off one's mark in a race too soon; to take action prematurely. **to jump the queue,** to get ahead of one's turn. **to jump to it,** (*coll.*) to act swiftly. **jump-seat,** *n.* a movable seat; an open buggy with a shifting seat or seats. **jump-start,** *v.t.* to start (a car) by pushing it and then engaging gear. **jump-suit,** *n.* a one-piece garment consisting of combined trousers and top. **jumpable,** *a.* **jumped-up,** *a.* up-start. **jumper**[1], *n.* one who or that which jumps or leaps; (*pl.*) certain Welsh Methodists in the 18th cent. and other religious sects who danced or jumped during worship; a hopper, a jumping insect; a tool or implement worked with a jumping motion; a quarryman's boring-tool. **jumping,** *n., a.* **jumping bean** or **seed,** *n.* the seed of various plants belonging to the Euphorbiaceae, which jump about through the movements of larvae inside them. **jumping-deer,** *n.* the black-tailed deer found west of the Mississippi. **jumping-jack,** *n.* a toy figure whose limbs move when a string is pulled. **jumping-rope,** *n.* (*N Am.*) a skipping-rope. **jumpy,** *a.* moving or proceeding with jumps and jerks; (*coll.*) nervous, easily startled. **jumpiness,** *a.* [prob. onomat. (cp. G dial. *gumpen,* Dan. *gumpe,* Swed. dial. *gumpa*)]

jumper[2], *n.* a loose, coarse outer jacket worn by sailors, labourers etc.; a woman's knitted or crocheted woollen upper garment; (*N Am.*) a pinafore dress. **jumper-suit,** *n.* a woman's jacket and skirt made of a stockingette material.

juncaceous, *a.* of or resembling rushes; belonging to the family Juncaceae. **juncal,** *a.* [L *juncus,* rush, -ACEOUS]

junco, *n.* the snow-bird, a genus of N American finches. [Sp., from L *juncus,* rush]

junction, *n.* the act of joining or the state of being

joined, a combination; a joint, a point or place of union, esp. the point where lines of railway meet. **junction box,** *n.* an earthed box in which wires and cables can be safely connected. [L *junctio,* from *jungere,* to JOIN]

juncture, *n.* a junction, a union; the place, line, or point at which two things are joined, a joint, an articulation; a point of time marked by the occurrence of critical events or circumstances. [L *junctūra,* as prec.]

June, *n.* the sixth month of the year. **June-bug,** *n.* an insect or beetle that appears about June, chiefly in the US. [L *Jūnius*]

Jung, *n.* **Carl Gustav** (1875–1961), Swiss psychiatrist, who collaborated with Freud until their disagreement in 1912 about the importance of sexuality in causing psychological problems. He studied religion and dream symbolism, and saw the unconscious as a source of spiritual insight. He also distinguished between introversion and extroversion. Works include *Modern Man in Search of a Soul* 1933. **Jungian,** *a.* pertaining to Jung's psychoanalytical style.

jungle, *n.* land covered with forest trees or dense, matted vegetation; a place of ruthless competition; anything difficult to negotiate, understand etc; a confusing mass. **jungle-bear,** *n.* the Indian sloth-bear, *Prochylus labiatus*. **jungle-cat,** *n.* the marsh lynx, *Felis chaus*. **jungle-fever,** *n.* a remittent tropical fever. **jungle-fowl,** *n.* an E Indian bird, *Gallus sonnerati,* and others of the same genus; the Australian mound-bird, *Megapodius tumulus*. **jungle juice,** *n.* (*sl.*) alcoholic liquor, esp. of poor quality or home-made. **jungle-cock, -hen,** *n.* **jungled,** *a.* **jungli,** *a.* uncouth, unrefined. **jungly,** *a.* [Hind. *jangal,* from Sansk. *jangala,* desert]

Jungle Book, The, a collection of short stories for children by Rudyard Kipling, published in two volumes in 1894 and 1895. Set in India, the stories feature a boy, Mowgli, reared by wolves and the animals he encounters in the jungle. The stories inspired the formation by Baden Powell of the Wolf Cub division of the Boy Scout movement.

junior, *a.* the younger (esp. as distinguishing a son from his father of the same name or two of the same surname); lower in standing. *n.* one younger or of lower standing than another; (*N Am.*) a son. **junior common room,** *n.* (in some colleges and universities) a common room for the use of students. **junior school,** *n.* (in England and Wales), a school for pupils aged about 7 to 11. **junior service,** *n.* the Army. **juniorate,** *n.* (*Society of Jesus*) a two years' course of higher studies for juniors before they enter the priesthood. **juniorship,** *n.* [L *jūnior,* comp. of *juvenis,* young]

juniper, *n.* a genus of prickly evergreen shrubs, comprising *Juniperus communis,* the berries of which are used to flavour gin. [L *jūniperus,* etym. doubtful]

junk[1], *n.* a flat-bottomed vessel with lug-sails, used in the Chinese seas. [Port. and Sp. *junco,* Jav. *jong*]

junk[2], *n.* a lump or chunk of anything. **junk-bottle,** *n.* (*N Am.*) a stout bottle of green or black glass. [prob. corr. of CHUNK]

junk[3], *n.* pieces of old cable and rope cut into lengths for making mats, swabs, gaskets, fenders, oakum etc.; rubbish, valueless odds and ends; salt beef supplied to ships bound on long voyages, from its being as tough as old rope; (*sl.*) a narcotic drug; (*sl.*) drugs. *v.t.* to cut into junks; (*sl.*) to discard, abandon. **junk bond,** *n.* a bond giving a high yield but low security. **junk-dealer,** *n.* a marine-store dealer. **junk food,** *n.* food of little nutritional value, quick to prepare. **junk mail,** *n.* unsolicited mail usu. advertising material. **junk-ring,** *n.* a steam-tight packing round a piston. **junk-shop,** *n.* a shop where second-hand goods of all kinds are sold. **junk-wad,** *n.* an oakum wad for a nuzzle-loading gun, placed between the charge and the ball. **junkie, junky,** (*sl.*) *n.* a drug addict. [etym. doubtful]

junker, *n.* a young German noble; a member of the German reactionary aristocratic party. **junkerdom, junkerism,** *n.* [G (*jung,* YOUNG, HERR)]

Junkers, *n.* **Hugo** (1859–1935), German aeroplane designer. In 1919 he founded in Dessau the aircraft works named after him. Junkers planes, including dive bombers, night fighters, and troop carriers, were used by the Germans in World War II.

junket, *n.* a dish of curds sweetened and flavoured, and served with cream; a sweetmeat, delicacy, a confection; a feast, a banquet, an entertainment; a supposed business trip (at public expense) which is really for pleasure. *v.i.* to feast, to picnic, to make good cheer. *v.t.* to regale at a feast. **junketer,** *n.* †**junketing,** *n.* [MF *juncade* (cp. Norm. patois *jonquette*), Prov. *joncada,* It. *giuncata,* p.p. of *giuncare,* from *giunco,* L *juncus,* rush]

Juno, *n.* the wife of Jupiter, identified with the Greek Hera; a beautiful queenly woman; the third asteroid. [L]

junta, *n.* a legislative or administrative council, esp. in Spain, Italy, and S America; a group, esp of military officers who take control of a country e.g. after a coup. [Sp., from L *juncta,* fem. p.p. of *jungere,* to JOIN]

junto, *n.* a secret political or other council; a cabal, clique, a faction. [erron. from prec.]

jupati-palm, *n.* the S American palm yielding raffia fibre. [S Am. native *jupati,* PALM]

jupe, *n.* a woman's skirt; †a loose jacket or tunic; †(*Sc.*) a woman's long jacket. [F, from OF *juppe,* Arab. *jubbah*]

Jupiter[1], **Jove,** *n.* in mythology, chief god of the Romans, identified with the Greek Zeus. He was god of the sky, associated with lightning and thunderbolt, protector in battle and bestower of victory. He was the son of Saturn, married his sister Juno, and reigned on Mount Olympus as lord of heaven.

Jupiter[2], *n.* the fifth planet from the Sun, and the largest in the solar system (equatorial diameter 142,800 km/88,700 miles), with a mass more than twice that of all the other planets combined, 318 times that of the Earth's. It takes 11.86 years to orbit the Sun, at an average distance of 778 million km/484 million miles, and has at least 16 moons. It is largely composed of hydrogen and helium, liquefied by pressure in its interior, and probably with a rocky core larger than the Earth. Its main feature is the Great Red Spot, a turbulent storm of rising gas 14,000 km/8500 miles wide and some 30,000 km/20,000 miles long.

jupon, *n.* a skirt or petticoat; †a sleeveless surcoat worn outside armour; earlier a tunic worn underneath the armour. [F, from JUPE]

jural, *a.* of or relating to law or jurisprudence, esp. with regard to rights and obligations. [L *jūs jūris,* law, -AL]

Jura mountains, *n. pl.* series of parallel mountain ranges running SW–NE along the French-Swiss frontier between the Rhône and the Rhine, a distance of 250 km/156 miles. The highest peak is Crête de la Neige, 1723 m/5650 ft.

jurassic, *n.* period of geological time 213–144 million years ago; the middle period of the mesozoic era. Climates worldwide were equable creating forests of conifers and ferns, dinosaurs were abundant, birds evolved, and limestones and iron ores were deposited.

jurat, *n.* a person under oath; a member of a corporation corresponding to an alderman, esp. of the Cinque Ports; a magistrate in the Channel Islands. **jurant,** *a.* taking an oath. *n.* one who takes an oath. **juratory,** *a.* containing an oath. [F, from med. L *jurātus,* one who is sworn, orig. p.p. of L *jurāre,* to swear]

juridical, *a.* pertaining to the administration of justice, to courts of justice, or to jurisprudence. **juridically,** *adv.* [L *jūridicus* (*jūs jūris,* law, *dic-,* stem of *dicāre,* to proclaim)]

jurisconsult, *n.* one learned in law, esp. civil or international law; a jurist. [L *jūrisconsultus* (*jūris,* as prec., *consultus,* see CONSULT)]

jurisdiction, *n.* the legal power or right of administering justice, making and enforcing laws, or exercising other authority; the district or extent within which such power may be exercised. **jurisdictional,** *a.* **jurisdictive,** *a.* having jurisdiction. [F, from L *jūrisdictiōnem,* nom. -*tio* (*jūris,* see JURIDICIAL, *dictio,* DICTION)]

jurisprudence, *n.* the science or philosophy of law; the science of the laws, constitutions, and right of men; the legal system of a particular country. **jurisprudent,** *n., a.* **jurisprudential**, *a.* [L *jūrisprudentia*]

jurist, *n.* one learned in the law; a writer on legal subjects; a student of law. **juristic, -ical,** *a.* **juristically,** *adv.* [F *juriste,* med. L *jūrista,* from *jūs jūris,* law]

juror, *n.* one who serves on a jury; one who takes an oath. [A-F *jurour,* OF *jureor,* L *jūrātōrem,* nom. -*tor,* from *jūrāre,* to swear]

Jurrassic, *a.* belonging to the oolitic limestone formation well developed in the Jura Mts; belonging to the second period of the Mesozoic era. *n.* the Jurassic system or period, coming between the Triassic and the Cretaceous. [F *Jurassique,* from *Jura* (cp. LIASSIC under LIAS)]

jury, *n.* a body of persons selected according to law and sworn to try, and give a true verdict upon, questions put before them; a body of persons selected to award prizes at public shows, exhibitions etc. **common, petty, transverse,** or **trial jury,** a jury usu. of 12 persons who (by a unanimous or majority verdict) determine the question of fact in a trial. **grand jury,** a jury (usu. of 12 to 23) who decide by a majority whether there is prima facie ground for an indictment before it goes to trial. **jury of matrons,** married women who have borne children, formerly empanelled in cases where pregnancy is pleaded in stay of execution. **special jury,** a jury composed of persons of a certain class or station. **jury-box,** *n.* the enclosure in a court where the jury sits. **juryman,** *n.* **jurywoman,** *n.fem.* [A-F *juree,* OF *jurée,* an oath, an inquest, a body of sworn men, p.p. of *jurer,* L *jūrāre,* to swear]

jury-mast, *n.* a temporary mast erected in place of one carried away. **jury-rudder,** *n.* [etym. doubtful (Skeat proposes *ajúry-mast,* from OF *ajuirie,* aid, succour, from L *adjūtare,* to AID)]

jussive, *a.* (*Gram.*) expressing command. *n.* a form or construction expressing command. [L *juss-us,* p.p. of *jubēre,* to command]

just[1], *a.* acting according to what is right and fair; fair, equitable, impartial, upright, honest; exact, accurate, precise; fit, proper, suitable; merited, deserved; righteous. *adv.* exactly, precisely; barely, only, with nothing to spare; precisely at the moment; only a moment ago, a very little time ago; (*coll.*) perfectly, quite. **just about,** *a.* nearly; more or less. **just now,** a very little time since, but a moment ago; at this instant. **just so,** *adv.* exactly; that is right; with great precision. **justly,** *adv.* **justness,** *n.* [F *juste,* L *justus,* from *jūs,* right]

just[2] JOUST.

justice, *n.* the quality of being just; fairness in dealing with others; uprightness, rectitude, honesty; just requital of deserts; the authoritative administration or maintenance of law and right: a person legally commissioned to hold courts, hear causes, and administer justice between individuals; a magistrate; a judge, esp. of the Supreme Court of Judicature in England. **Justice of the Peace,** a local magistrate commissioned under the Great seal to keep the peace and try cases of felony and other misdemeanours. **Lord Chief Justice,** a judge combining the former functions of President of the King's Bench and of the Court of Common Pleas. **to do justice to,** to treat fairly; to treat appreciatively. **to do oneself justice,** to acquit oneself worthily of one's ability. **Justice-Clerk,** *n.* (*Sc. Law*) the President of the Outer House or Second Division of the Court of Session, and Vice-President of the High Court of Justiciary. **Justice-General,** *n.* the highest judge in Scotland, Lord President of the Court of Session. †**justicer** *n.* a justiciary. **justiceship,** *n.* **justiciable**, *a.* liable to be tried in a court of justice. *n.* one subject to (another's) jurisdiction. **justiciar**, *n.* a chief officer or deputy of the Crown (under the Norman and Plantagenet kings) who exercised both judicial and administrative powers. **justiciary**, *n.* an administrator of justice, a justiciar. *a.* pertaining to the administration of justice. **High Court of Justiciary,** the supreme court of Scotland in criminal causes. [OF, from L *justitia,* from *justus,* just]

justify, *v.t.* to prove or show to be just or right; to vindicate, to make good, to show grounds for; to exonerate; (*Theol.*) to declare free from the penalty of sin; to adjust and make (lines or type) even in length. *v.i.* to coincide or range uniformly (of lines of type). **justifiable,** *a.* **justifiability**, **justifiableness,** *n.* **justifiably,** *adv.* **justification**, *n.* **justificative, justificatory,**, *a.* †**justificator, justifier,** *n.* [F *justifier,* L *justificāre* (*jūs,* JUSTICE, *facere,* to make)]

Justin, St, *n.* (*c.* 100–*c.* 163), one of the early Christian leaders and writers known as the Fathers of the Church. Born in Palestine of a Greek family, he was converted to Christianity and wrote two *Apologies* in its defence. He spent the rest of his life as an itinerant missionary, and was martyred in Rome. Feast day 1 June.

Justinian I, *n.* (483–562), Byzantine emperor from 527. He recovered N Africa from the Vandals, SE Spain from the Visigoths, and Italy from the Ostrogoths, largely owing to his great general Belisarius. He ordered the codification of Roman law, which has influenced European jurisprudence.

justle, JOSTLE.

justly, justness JUST[1].

Just So Stories, a collection of stories for small children by Rudyard Kipling, published in 1902. Many of the stories offer amusing explanations of how certain animals acquired their characteristic appearance, such as 'How the Leopard got his Spots', and 'How the Camel got his Hump'. They originated in stories which the author told to his children.

jut, *v.i.* to project, to protrude; to stick (out). *n.* a projection; a protruding point or part. **jut-window,** *n.* a projecting window. [var. of JET[2]]

Jute, *n.* member of a Germanic people who originated in Jutland but later settled in Frankish territory. They occupied Kent, SE England, about 450, according to tradition, and conquered the Isle of Wight and the opposite coast of Hampshire in the early 6th cent.

jute, *n.* the fibre from the inner bark of two plants, *Corchorus capsularis* and *C. olitorius,* from which fabrics, paper and cordage are prepared. [Bengali *jhōto* (pop. *jhūto*), Sansk. *jūta, jatā,* a braid of hair]

Jutland, *n.* (Danish **Jylland**), a peninsula of N Europe; area 29,500 sq km/11,400 sq miles. It is separated from Norway by the Skagerrak, from Sweden by the Kattegat, with the North Sea to the west. The larger northern part belongs to Denmark, and the southern part to West Germany.

Jutland, Battle of, naval battle of World War I, fought between England and Germany on 31 May 1916, off the W coast of Jutland. Its outcome was indecisive, but the German fleet remained in port for the rest of the war.

Juvenal, *n.* (*c.* 60–AD 140), Roman satirist and poet, born probably at Aquinum. His genius for satire brought him to the unfavourable notice of the emperor Domitian. Juvenal's 16 extant satires give an explicit and sometimes brutal picture of the decadent Roman society of his time.

juvenescent, *a.* growing or being young. **juvenescence,** *n.* [L *juvenescere,* as prec.]

juvenile, *a.* young, youthful; befitting or characteristic of youth. *n.* a young person; a book for children; an actor who usually performs the part of a young person. **juvenile court,** *n.* a court for young people under 17 years of age. **juvenile offender,** *n.* a criminal under 17 years of age. **juvenileness,** *n.* **juvenilely,** *adv.* **juvenilia,** *n.pl.* writings etc., produced in youth. **juvenility,** *n.* [L *juvenīlis,* from *juvenis,* JUVENAL]

juxtapose, *v.t.* to place (a thing) next to or (things) side by side. **juxtaposition,** *n.* [F *juxtaposer* (L *juxtā,* next, F *poser,* to put)]

K

K¹, k¹, the 11th letter and eighth consonant of the English alphabet, is a voiceless guttural mute (*pl.* **Ks, K's, Kays**)
K², (*abbr.*) the solar constant; Kaon; Kelvin scale; Kilo-; King; 1024 words, bytes or bits; Knight; Köchel (catalogue of Mozart's work).
K³, (*chem. symbol*) potassium.
K2, *n.* second highest mountain in the world, about 8900 m/29,210 ft, in the Karakoram range, Kashmir, N India; it is also known as Dapsang (Hidden Peak) and formerly as Mount Godwin-Austen (after the son of a British geologist). It was first climbed 1954 by an Italian expedition.
ka, *n.* the double of the personality in ancient Egyptian mythology, born with but surviving the individual. [Egypt?]
Kaaba, CAABA.
kaama, *n.* the hartebeest. [Bantu]
kaava, KAVA.
kabbala, kabala, CABBALA.
Kabinda, CABINDA.
kabuki, *n.* a highly-stylized, traditional and popular form of Japanese drama, based on legend and acted only by men, in elaborate costumes. [Jap. *kabu,* music, *n. ki,* art]
Kabul, *n.* capital of Afghanistan, 2100 m/6900 ft above sea level, on the river Kabul; population (1984) 1,179,300. Products include textiles, plastics, leather, and glass. It commands the strategic routes to Pakistan via the Khyber Pass.
Kabyle, *n.* one of the agricultural branch of the Berber people inhabiting the highlands of Algeria; the Berber dialect spoken by the Kabyles. [F, from Arab. *Qabāil,* pl. of *qabīla,* tribe]
Kádár, *n.* **János** (1912–1989), Hungarian Communist leader, in power 1956–88, after suppressing the national rising. As Hungarian Socialist Workers' Party (HSWP) leader and prime minister 1956–58 and 1961–65, Kádár introduced a series of market-socialist economic reforms, while retaining cordial political relations with the USSR.
kaddish, *n.* a form of thanksgiving and prayer used by the Jews, esp. in mourning. [Aram. *qaddīsh,* holy]
kadi, CADI.
kadjibut, *n.* a small tree or shrub yielding an oil useful in treating skin diseases. [Malay, *kaju puleh,* white tree]
kae, *n.* (*Sc.*) a jackdaw. [cp. Dut. *ka,* Dan. *kaa,* Norw. *kaae*]
Kafir¹, Kaffir, *n.* (*now offensive*) one of a S African Bantu people; their language; (*pl.*) S African mining shares. *a.* of or pertaining to the Kafirs. **kaffir beer**, *n.* a S African beer made from kaffir corn or millet. **kaffirboom**, *n.* a S African tree. **kaffir bread**, *n.* the pith of S African cycads. **kaffir corn**, *n.* a variety of sorghum cultivated in S Africa. [Arab. *kāfir,* infidel]
kafir², *n.* a native of Kafiristan in E Afghanistan; (*offensive*) an infidel. [Arab. *kāfir,* infidel]
Kafka, *n.* **Franz** (1883–1924), Czech novelist, born in Prague, who wrote in German. His three unfinished allegorical novels *Der Prozess/The Trial* (1925), *Das Schloss/The Castle* (1926), and *Amerika/America* (1927), were posthumously published despite his instructions that they should be destroyed. His short stories include 'Die Verwandlung'/'The Metamorphosis' (1915), in which a man turns into a beetle. **kafkaesque**, *a.* of or like the ideas and work of Franz Kafka, esp. his ideas concerning the alienation of man.
kaftan, CAFTAN.
kago, *n.* (*pl.* **-gos**), a Japanese basket-work palanquin slung on a pole and carried by men. [Jap. *kango*]
kagool, kagoule, CAGOULE.
kahawai, *n.* the New Zealand salmon. [Maori]
kahikatea, *n.* the white pine of New Zealand. [Maori]
Kahn, *n.* **Louis** (1901–1974), US architect, born in Estonia. He developed a classically romantic style, in which functional 'servant' areas, such as stairwells and air ducts, featured prominently, often as tower-like structures surrounding the main living and working, or 'served', areas. His works are characterized by an imaginative use of concrete and brick and include the Salk Institute for Biological Studies, La Jolla, California, and the British Art Centre at Yale University.
kai, *n.* a general word for 'food' in New Zealand and the South Sea Islands. [Maori]
kaiak, KAYAK, CAÏQUE.
Kaifu, *n.* **Toshiki** (1932–), Japanese conservative politician, prime minister from 1989. A protégé of former premier Takeo Miki, he was selected as a compromise choice as Liberal Democratic Party president and prime minister in Aug. 1989, following the resignation of Sosuke Uno. Kaifu is Japan's first premier without World War II military experience.
kaikomoko, *n.* the New Zealand ribbonwood tree. [Maori]
kail, KALE.
kaim KAME.
kaiman, CAYMAN.
kain CAIN².
kainga, *n.* a Maori settlement, village. [Maori]
kainite, *n.* hydrous chlorosulphate of magnesium and potassium, used as a fertilizer. [G *kainit* (Gr. *kainos,* new)]
Kairouan, *n.* Muslim holy city in Tunisia, N Africa, S of Tunis; population (1984) 72,200. It is a noted centre of carpet production. The city, said to have been founded 617 AD, ranks after Mecca and Medina as a place of pilgrimage.
Kaiser¹, *n.* an emperor; the emperor of Germany or Austria; the head of the Holy Roman Empire. **the Kaiser's war**, the 1914–18 war. **Kaiserdom**, *n.* **Kaiserin**, *n.* the wife of the Kaiser. **Kaiserism**, *n.* **Kaisership**, *n.* [G, from L, *Caesar*]
Kaiser², *n.* **Georg** (1878–1945), German playwright, the principal writer of German Expressionism. His large output includes *Die Bürger von Calais/The Burghers of Calais* (1914), and *Gas* (1918–20).
kaitaka, *n.* a mat used as a cloak. [Maori]
kajawah, *n.* a pannier carried in pairs on a camel, horse or mule, used by women and children. [Hind. and Pers.]
kajeput, CAJUPUT.
kaka, *n.* a New Zealand parrot belonging to the genus *Nestor*. **kaka beak**, *n.* a shrub with beak-shaped flowers, found in New Zealand. **kakapo**, *n.* (*pl.* **pos**) the ground- or owl-parrot of New Zealand. **kakariki**, *n.* a small green parrot; a green lizard. [Maori]
Kakadu, *n.* a national park E of Darwin in the Alligator Rivers Region of Arnhem Land, Northern Territory, Australia. Established in 1979, it overlies one of the richest uranium deposits in the world. As a result of this, it has become the focal point of controversy between conservationists and mining interests.
kakemono, *n.* a Japanese wall-picture mounted on rollers for putting away. [Jap.]
kaki, *n.* the Chinese date-plum or Japanese persimmon.

[Jap.]

kakistocracy, *n.* government by the worst citizens. **kakistocrat**, *n.* [Gr. *kakistos,* superl. of *kakos,* bad, -CRACY]

kakodyl, CACODYL.

kal., (*abbr.*) kalends.

kala-azar, *n.* a chronic tropical disease with a high mortality. [Hind.]

Kalahari Desert, *n.* semi-desert area forming most of Botswana, and extending into Namibia, Zimbabwe, and South Africa; area about 900,000 sq km/347,400 sq miles. The only permanent river, the Okavango, flows into a delta in the NW forming marshes rich in wildlife. Its inhabitants are the nomadic Bushmen.

kalanchoe, *n.* a succulent plant grown indoors or in a greenhouse, with pink, red or yellow flowers. [Chin.]

kale, kail, *n.* (*Sc., North.*) cabbage; a cabbage with crinkled leaves, borecole; (*Sc.*) cabbage soup. **Scotch kale,** kale with purplish leaves. **kale-yard,** *n.* a kitchen-garden. **kale-yard school,** *n.* a group of novelists and writers depicting the homely life of Scottish lowlanders, with liberal use of broad dialect. [var. of COLE]

kaleidophone, *n.* an instrument for exhibiting the character of sound-waves by means of a vibrating bar or plate armed with a reflector. [Gr. *kalos,* beautiful, *eidos,* appearance, -PHONE]

kaleidoscope, *n.* an instrument showing by means of bits of coloured glass and a series of reflecting surfaces, an endless variety of symmetrical forms; any complex, changing pattern. **kaleidoscopic**, **-ical,** *a.* **kaleidoscopically,** *adv.*

kalendar, etc. CALENDAR.

kalends CALENDS.

kalevala, *n.* the land of the legendary finnish hero Kaleva; the epic which recounts his exploits. [finnish *Kaleva,* a hero, *la,* place]

Kalf, *n.* **Willem** (1619–1693), Dutch painter, active in Amsterdam from 1653. He specialized in still lifes set off against a dark ground.

Kalgan, *n.* city in NE China, now known as Zhangjiakou.

Kali, *n.* in Hindu mythology, the goddess of destruction and death. She is the wife of Siva.

kali, *n.* the salt-wort, *Salsola kali,* from which soda-ash was obtained. **kaligenous**, *a.* **kalinite**, *n.* (*Min.*) native potash alum. [Arab. *qalī,* see ALKALI]

kalian, *n.* an Iranian form of hookah. [Arab. *qalyan*]

Kālidāsa, *n.* Indian epic poet and dramatist. His works, in Sanskrit, include the classic drama *Sakuntala,* the love story of King Dushyanta for the nymph Sakuntala.

kalif, CALIPH.

Kalimantan, *n.pl.* provinces of the republic of Indonesia occupying part of the island of Borneo. **area** 543,900 sq km/210,000 sq miles. **towns** Banjermasin and Balikpapan. **physical features** mostly low-lying, with mountains in the N. **population** (1980) 6,723,086. **products** petroleum, rubber, coffee, copra, pepper, timber.

Kalinin, *n.* **Mikhail Ivanovich** (1875–1946), Soviet politician, founder of the newspaper *Pravda.* He was prominent in the October Revolution, and in 1919 became head of state (president of the Central Executive Committee of the Soviet government until 1937, then president of the Presidium of the Supreme Soviet until 1946).

Kali-Yuga, *n.* in Hinduism, the last of the four *yugas* (ages) that make up one cycle of creation. The Kali-Yuga, in which Hindus believe we are now living, is characterized by wickedness and disaster, and leads up to the destruction of this world in preparation for a new creation and a new cycle of *yugas*.

Kalki, *n.* in Hinduism, the last avatar (manifestation) of Vishnu, who will appear at the end of the Kali-Yuga, or final age of the world, to destroy it in readiness for a new creation.

kalmia, *n.* a genus of smooth, evergreen N American flowering shrubs. [Peter *Kalm,* 1715–79, Swed. naturalist, professor at Abo]

Kalmuck, *n.* one of a Mongol people living in a region extending from W China to the Volga; a coarse shaggy cloth like bearskin; a coarse, coloured cotton made in Iran. [Rus. *Kalmuikū*]

kalology, *n.* the science or theory of beauty. [Gr. *kalos,* beautiful]

kalong, *n.* the Malay fox-bat, *Pteropus edulis*. [Malay]

kalpa, *n.* a day of Brahma, or a period of 4,320,000 years, constituting the age or cycle of a world. [Sansk.]

Kaltenbrunner, *n.* **Ernst** (1901–1946), Austrian Nazi leader. After the annexation of Austria 1938 he joined police chief Himmler's staff, and as head of the Security Police (SD) from 1943 was responsible for the murder of millions of Jews and Allied soldiers in World War II. After the war, he was tried at Nuremberg, and hanged.

†**kam,** *a.* crooked. *adv.* awry, askew. **clean kam,** quite away from the purpose. [cp. W, Gael. and Manx *cam*]

Kama, *n.* the god of love in the puranas; impure or sensual desire. **Kamasutra**, *n.* an ancient Hindu book on erotic love. [Sansk.]

kamala, *n.* an orange dye obtained from the down on the fruit capsules of the E Indian tree, *Rottlera tinctoria,* belonging to the Euphorbiaceae or spurge family. [Sansk.]

kamaraband, CUMMERBUND.

Kamchatka, *n.* mountainous peninsula separating the Bering Sea and Sea of Okhotsk, forming (together with the Chukchi and Koryak national districts) a region of the USSR. Its capital Petropavlovsk is the only town; agriculture is possible only in the South . Most of the inhabitants are fishers and hunters.

kame, kaim, *n.* a long mound of glacial detritus, an eskar. [Sc. and North., var. of COMB[1]]

kameez, *n.* a type of loose tunic with tight sleeves worn by women in S Asia. [Urdu *kamis*]

Kamenev, *n.* **Lev Borisovich** (1883–1936), Russian leader of the Bolshevik movement after 1917 who, with Stalin and Zinoviev, formed a ruling triumvirate in the USSR after Lenin's death 1924. His alignment with the Trotskyists led to his dismissal from office and from the Communist Party by Stalin 1926. Tried for plotting to murder Stalin, he was condemned and shot 1936.

kamerad, *int.* comrade; a German form of surrender or appeal for quarter. *v.i.* to surrender. [G]

kami, *n.* a Japanese title, equivalent to lord, given to nobles, ministers, governors etc.; in Shinto, a divinity, a god. [Jap.]

kamichi, *n.* a S American bird, the horned screamer. [F, from Brazil]

kamikaze, *n.* a Japanese airman or plane performing a suicidal mission in World War II. *a.* pertaining to a kamikaze; (*coll.*) suicidal, self-destructive. [Jap. *kami,* divine, *kaze,* wind]

Kampala, *n.* capital of Uganda; population (1983) 455,000. It is linked by rail with Mombasa. Products include tea, coffee, textiles, fruit, and vegetables.

kampong, *n.* a Malay village. [Malay]

kamptulicon, *n.* a floor-covering of india-rubber, gutta-percha, and cork, pressed into sheets. [Gr. *kampt-os,* flexible, *oul-os,* thick, *-ikon,* neut. adj. suf.]

Kampuchean, *n.* a native or inhabitant of Kampuchea, SE Asia. *a.* of or from Kampuchea.

Kamseen, kamsin KHAMSIN.

Kanaka , *n.* a Sandwich islander; a South Sea islander; one of these employed as an indentured labourer on the Queensland sugar-plantations. [Hawaiian, a man]

Kananga, *n.* chief city of Kasai Occidental region, W central Zäire; situated on the Lulua river; population (1984) 291,000. It was known as Luluabourg until 1966.

Kanarese, Canarese, *n.* (*pl.* **-rese**) a member of Kannada-speaking people living largely in Kanara in southern India; the Kannada language. *a.* of or from the Kanara area.

Kanchenjunga, KANGCHENJUNGA.

Kandinsky, *n.* **Wassily** (1866–1944), Russian painter, a pioneer of abstract art. Born in Moscow, he travelled widely, settling in Munich 1896. He was joint originator of the **Blaue Reiter** movement 1911–12. For some years he taught at the Bauhaus, then, in 1933, settled in Paris.

Kandy, *n.* city in central Sri Lanka, former capital of the kingdom of Kandy 1480–1815; population (1985) 140,000. Products include tea. One of the most sacred Buddhist shrines is situated at Kandy, and the chief campus of the University of Sri Lanka (1942) is at Peradenia, 5 km/3 miles away.

kang, *n.* a brick structure in Chinese houses for sleeping on, warmed by a fire inside in cold weather; a large Chinese water-jar. [Chin.]

kanga, khanga, *n.* a piece of brightly coloured cotton worn as a woman's dress in E Africa. [Swahili]

kangaroo, *n.* a name for several marsupial quadrupeds peculiar to Australia, Tasmania, New Guinea and adjacent islands, distinguished by their large hind limbs, used for leaping, and short limbs, almost useless for walking; (*pl.*) Australian mining shares; dealers in these. **kangaroo-apple,** *n.* an Australian shrub with fruit like an apple. **kangaroo-bicycle,** *n.* an obsolete form of bicycle with sloping backbone, a forerunner of the modern safety. **kangaroo closure,** *n.* the parliamentary procedure whereby the chairman or speaker decides what shall be discussed (e.g. which clauses of a Bill) and what passed over. **kangaroo court,** *n.* an irregular court, set up by e.g. the mob, prisoners, or strikers; a court where a fair trial is impossible. **kangaroo-dog,** *n.* a kind of greyhound used in Australia for hunting. **kangaroo-grass,** *n.* an Australian fodder-grass. **kangaroo paw,** *n.* any of several Australian plants with green and red flowers. **kangaroo-rat,** *n.* a small Australian marsupial, an American pouched burrowing-mouse. [prob. from Abor. name]

Kangchenjunga, Kanchenjunga, *n.* Himalayan mountain on the Nepál–Sikkim border, 8598 m/20,208 ft high, 120 km/75 miles SE of Everest. The name means 'five treasure houses of the great snows'. Kangchenjunga was first climbed by a British expedition 1955.

Ka Ngwane, *n.* black homeland in Natal province, South Africa; achieved self-governing status 1971; population (1985) 392,800.

kanji, *n.* (*pl.* **-ji, -jis**) a script for representing Japanese syllables derived from Chinese orthography. [Chin. *han,* Chinese, *tsû,* word]

Kannada, *n.* an important Dravidian language spoken in the Mysore area of southern India. [Kanarese *Kannada*]

Kano, *n.* capital of Kano state in N Nigeria, trade centre of an irrigated area; population (1983) 487,100. Products include bicycles, glass, furniture, textiles, and chemicals. Founded about 1000 BC, Kano is a walled city, with New Kano extending beyond the walls. Goods still arrive by camel train to a market place holding 20,000 people.

kanoon, *n.* a kind of dulcimer or zither with 50 or 60 strings. [Pers. and Arab. *qānūn*]

Kanpur (formerly **Cawnpore**), *n.* capital of Kanpur district, Uttar Pradesh, India, SW of Lucknow, on the river Ganges; a commercial and industrial centre (cotton, wool, jute, chemicals, plastics, iron, steel); population (1981) 1,688,000.

Kansas, *n.* state of central US; nickname Sunflower State. **area** 213,200 sq km/82,295 sq miles. **capital** Topeka. **towns** Kansas City, Wichita, Overland Park. **physical features** undulating prairie; rivers Missouri, Kansas, and Arkansas. **population** (1985) 2,450,000. **products** wheat, cattle, coal, petroleum, natural gas, aircraft.

Kansas City, *n.* twin city in the US at the confluence of the Missouri and Kansas rivers, partly in Kansas and partly in Missouri; a market and agricultural distribution centre and, next to Chicago, the chief livestock centre of the US. Kansas City, Missouri, has car assembly plants and Kansas City, Kansas, has the majority of offices; population (1980) of Kansas City (Kansas) 161,087, Kansas City (Missouri) 448,159, metropolitan area 1,327,000. The city was founded as a trading post by French fur trappers about 1826.

Kansu, *n.* alternative spelling for Chinese province Gansu.

Kant, *n.* **Immanuel** (1724–1804), German philosopher, who believed that knowledge is not merely an aggregate of sense impressions, but is dependent on the conceptual apparatus of the human understanding, which is itself not derived from experience. In ethics, Kant argued that right action cannot be based on feelings or inclinations, but conforms to a law given by reason, the *categorical imperative*. **Kantian,** *a.* pertaining to the philosophy of Kant. *n.* a Kantist. **Kantianism, †Kantism,** *n.* **Kantist,** *n.*

kantikoy, *n.* a N American Indian ceremonial dance; a meeting for dancing, a dancing match. [Algonkin]

Kanto, *n.* flat, densely populated region of E Honshu island, Japan; population (1986) 37,156,000; area 32,377 km2/12,505 sq miles. Chief city is Tokyo.

KANU, *n.* short for Kenya African National Union, political party founded 1944 and led by Jomo Kenyatta from 1947, when it was the Kenya African Union; it became KANU on independence. The party formed Kenyatta's political power base in 1963 when he became prime minister; in 1964 he became the first president of Kenya.

kaolin, *n.* a porcelain clay (also used medicinally as a poultice or internally) derived principally from the decomposition of feldspar, China clay. **kaolinic,** *a.* **kaolinize, -ise,** *v.t.* **kaolinization, -isation,** *n.* [F, from Chin. *kaoling,* name of a mountain whence orig. obtained (*kao,* high, *ling,* ridge or hill)]

kaon, *n.* an unstable type of meson, also called K-meson. [K + on]

kapellmeister, *n.* the musical director of a choir, band or orchestra. [G (*kapelle,* med. L *capella,* CHAPEL, *meister,* MASTER)]

kapnography, *n.* drawing or writing on a smoked surface with a pointed instrument, shading with further films of carbon from a flame, and varnishing. **kapnographic,** *a.* [Gr. *kapnos,* smoke]

kapok, *n.* a fine woolly or silky fibre enveloping the seeds of a tropical silk-cotton tree, used for stuffing cushions etc. [Malay *kāpoq*]

kappa, *n.* the tenth letter of the Greek alphabet.

kaput, *adv.* finished, done for, smashed up. [G slang]

karabiner, *n.* a metal clip with a spring inside it, for attaching to a piton, used in mountaineering. [G *Karabinerhaken,* carbine hook]

Karachi, *n.* largest city and chief seaport of Pakistan, and capital of Sind province, NW of the Indus delta; industry (engineering, chemicals, plastics, textiles); population (1981) 5,208,000. It was the capital of Pakistan 1947–59.

Karaite, *n.* a member of a Jewish sect who hold by the literal inspiration of the Scriptures, rejecting rabbinical tradition. **Karaism,** *n.* [Heb. *q'rāīm,* readers, -ITE]

Karajan, *n.* **Herbert von** (1908–1989), Austrian conductor. He was conductor of the Berlin Philharmonic Orchestra 1955–89. He directed the Salzburg Festival from 1964 and became director of the Vienna State Opera in 1976. He is associated with the classical and romantic repertoire – Beethoven, Brahms, Mahler, and Richard Strauss.

Karakoram, *n.* mountain range in central Asia, divided among China, Pakistan, and India. Peaks include K2, Masharbrum, Gasharbrum, and Mustagh Tower. Ladakh subsidiary range is in NE Kashmir on the Tibetan border.

karakul, caracul, *n.* a breed of sheep from the Bukhara district of Central Asia; the fleece prepared as fur from the lambs of these sheep. [*Karakul,* a village in Bukhara, USSR]

Karamanlis, *n.* **Constantinos** (1907–), Greek politician of the New Democracy Party. A lawyer and an anti-communist, he was prime minister Oct. 1955–Mar. 1958, May 1958–Sept. 1961, and Nov. 1961–June 1963 (when he went into self-imposed exile). He was recalled as prime minister on the fall of the regime of the 'colonels' in July 1974, and was president 1980–85.

karat, CARAT.

karate, *n.* a traditional Japanese martial art, based on blows and kicks. **karate chop,** *n.* a downward blow with the side of the hand. [Jap., empty hand]

Karelia, *n.* Autonomous Republic of the Russian Soviet Republic (RSFSR), in NW USSR. **area** 172,400 sq km/66,550 sq miles. **capital** Petrozavodsk. **towns** Vyborg. **physical features** mainly forested; Lake Ladoga. **population** (1986) 787,000. **products** fishing, timber, chemicals, coal.

Karelian bear dog, medium-sized dog, about 60 cm/2 ft high, used to protect Russian settlements from bears. Rather like a husky, the dog is a 'national treasure'. It was not exported until 1989 when some were sent to Yellowstone Park, US, to keep bears away from tourists.

Karen, *n.* a people of the Far East, numbering 1.9 million alone, also living in Thailand, and the Irrawaddy delta. Their language belongs to the Sino-Thai family. In 1984 the Burmese government began a large-scale military campaign against the Karen National Liberation Army (KNLA), the armed wing of the Karen National Union (KNU).

Karg-Elert, *n.* **Sigfrid** (1877–1933), German composer. After studying at Leipzig he devoted himself to the European harmonium. His numerous concert pieces and graded studies exploit a range of impressionistic effects such as the 'endless chord'.

Karl-Marx-Stadt (formerly **Chemnitz**), *n.* town in East Germany, capital of Karl-Marx-Stadt county, on the river Chemnitz, 65 km/40 miles SSE of Leipzig. It is an industrial centre (engineering, textiles, chemicals); population (1986) 314,000. It came within the Soviet zone of occupation after World War II, and was renamed 1954. Karl-Marx-Stadt county has an area of 6010 sq km/2320 sq miles, and a population of 1,870,000.

Karloff, *n.* **Boris (William Henry Pratt)** (1887–1969), British actor who mostly worked in the US. He is chiefly known for his role as the monster in *Frankenstein* (1931); most of his subsequent roles were in horror films, although he also played some conventional parts. He appeared in *Scarface* (1932), *The Lost Patrol* (1934), and *The Body Snatcher* (1945).

karma, *n.* in Buddhism, the results of action, ethical causation as determining future existence, esp. the cumulative consequence of a person's acts in one stage of existence as controlling his or her destiny in the next. [Sansk.]

Karmal, *n.* **Babrak** (1929–), Afghan communist politician. In 1965 he formed what became the banned People's Democratic Party of Afghanistan (PDPA) 1977. As president 1979–86, with Soviet backing, he sought to broaden the appeal of the PDPA but encountered wide resistance from the mujaheddin Muslim guerrillas.

Karmathian, *n.* one of a Muslim rationalistic sect, with pantheistic and socialistic tenets, founded in the 9th cent. [*Karmat,* the founder]

Karnataka (formerly (until (1973)) **Mysore**), *n.* state in SW India. **area** 191,800 sq km/74,035 sq miles. **capital** Bangalore. **products** mainly agricultural, but its minerals include manganese, chromite, and India's only sources of gold and silver. **population** (1981) 37,043,000. **language** Kannada.

karoo, karroo, *n.* one of the waterless S African tablelands, esp. the Great Karoo in the middle of Cape Colony. [Hottentot in orig.]

kaross, *n.* a S African native mantle or jacket made of skins with the hair left on. [Afrikaans *karos*]

karri, *n.* a W Australian timber tree. [Austral. Abor.]

kars(e)y, CARSEY.

karst, *n.* the characteristic scenery of a limestone region with underground streams, caverns and potholes forming a drainage system. [*Karst,* limestone plateau east of the Adriatic]

kart, *n.* a go-kart. **karting,** *n.* go-kart racing.

kartel, *n.* a kind of wooden hammock swung in a S African ox-wagon. [S Afr. Dut., said to be from Port. *catel,* Tamil *kaṭṭil,* bedstead]

karyo- CARYO-, *comb. form* relating to the changes which occur in the structure of a cell.

karyokinesis, *n.* the series of changes that take place in indirect or mitotic cell-division. **karyokinetic,** *a.* [Gr. *kinēsis,* motion, from *kinein,* to move]

karyoplasm, *n.* the protoplasm in the nucleus of a cell.

karyotype, *n.* the chromosomes of a cell. **karyotypic,** *a.*

kasbah, casbah, *n.* the castle or fortress in a N African city, or the area around it. [Arab.]

Kashmir, *n.* CASHMERE.

kashmiri, *n.* a native or inhabitant of Kashmir; the language of Kashmir. [*Kashmir,* India]

kashruth, kashrut, *n.* the state of being kosher; the Jewish dietary rules. [Heb?]

katabasis, a moving down. katabatic, *a.* [Gk. **katabainein,** to descend]

katabolism, *n.* the process of change by which complex organic compounds break down into simpler compounds, destructive metabolism. [Gr. *katabolē,* from *kataballein* (CATA-, *ballein,* to throw)]

katakana, *n.* a Japanese syllabary. [Jap.]

katalysis, katalytic etc. CATALYSIS.

katathermometer, CATA-, *n.* an instrument for indicating the evaporating and cooling power of the air.

kathak, *n.* a type of Indian classical dance involving mime. [Sans.]

kation, CATION.

katipo, *n.* a venomous spider found in New Zealand and Australia. [Maori]

katydid, *n.* a large green orthopterous insect, *Curtophyllum concavum,* common in N America. [imit. of its stridulating cry]

katzenjammer, *n.* a hangover; emotional distress. [G, cat's misery]

kauri, *n.* a New Zealand coniferous forest-tree, *Dammaris australis*. **kauri-gum,** *n.* a resinous gum from the kauri. **kauri-pine,** *n.* [Maori]

kava, kaava, *n.* a beverage prepared from the chewed or pounded roots of a Polynesian shrub. **kava-ring,** *n.* a gathering for the ceremonial drinking of kava. [Polynesian]

kavass, *n.* a Turkish armed constable, courier or attendant. [Turk. *gawwās,* bow-maker, from Arab. *qaws,* a bow]

kayak, *n.* the Eskimo and Alaskan canoe, made of sealskins stretched upon a light wooden framework. [Eskimo]

kayo, *n.* the spoken form of K.O., knockout. *v.t.* to knock someone out.

Kazakhstan, *n.* constituent republic of the USSR in Soviet Central Asia. **area** 2,717,300 sq km/1,049,150 sq miles. **capital** Alma-Ata. **towns** Karaganda, Semipalatinsk, Petropavlovsk. **physical** second largest republic in the USSR; Caspian and Aral seas, Lake Balkhash; Steppe region. **population** (1987) 16,244,000; Russian 41%, Kazakh 36% Ukrainian 6%. **products** second only to Ukraine as a grain producer; copper, lead, zinc, manganese, coal, oil. **language** Russian; Kazakh, related to Turkish.

Kazan[1], *n.* capital of the Tatar Autonomous Republic in Russian SFSR, USSR, on the river Volga; population (1987) 1,068,000. It a transport, commercial, and industrial centre (engineering, oil refining, petrochemical, textiles, large fur trade). Formerly capital of a Tatar khanate, Kazan was captured by Ivan IV 'the Terrible' 1552.

Kazan[2], *n.* **Elia** (1909–), US stage and film director, a founder of the Actors Studio 1947. Plays he directed include *The Skin of Our Teeth* (1942), *A Streetcar Named Desire* (1947), and *Cat on a Hot Tin Roof* (1955); films include *Gentlemen's Agreement* (1948), *East of Eden* (1954), and *The Visitors* (1972).

Kazantzakis, *n.* **Nikos** (1885–1957), Greek writer of poems, for example, *I Odysseia/The Odyssey* (1938), which continues Homer's *Odyssey*, and novels, for example, *Zorba the Greek* (1946).

kazi, CARSEY.

kazoo, *n.* (*pl.* **-zoos**) a tube of metal or plastic with a membrane covering a hole in the side, through which one sings or hums to produce sound. [perh. imit. of sound]

KB, (*abbr.*) King's Bench; Knight Bachelor; Knight of the Bath.

KBE, (*abbr.*) Knight Commander of the Order of the British Empire.

KC, (*abbr.*) King's Counsel.

kc, (*abbr.*) kilocycle.

kcal, (*abbr.*) kilocalorie.

KCB, (*abbr.*) Knight Commander of the Order of the Bath.

kea, *n.* a green and blue mountain parrot, *Nestor notabilis,* of New Zealand, feeding on carrion and attacking living sheep for their kidney-fat. [Maori, imit. of cry]

Kean, *n.* **Edmund** (1787–1833), British tragic actor, noted for his portrayal of villainy in the Shakespearean roles of Shylock, Richard III, and Iago.

Keane, *n.* **Mary Nesta 'Molly'** (1905–), Irish novelist, whose comic novels of Anglo-Irish life, include *Good Behaviour* (1981), *Time After Time* (1983), and *Loving and Giving* (1988). She also writes under the name M. J. Farrell.

Keaton, *n.* **Buster** (1896–1966), stage name of Joseph Frank Keaton. US comedian and actor. After being a star in vaudeville, he took up a career in 'Fatty' Arbuckle comedies, and became one of the great comedians of the silent film era, with an inimitable deadpan expression masking a sophisticated acting ability. His films include *One Week* (1920), *The Navigator* (1924), *The General* (1927), and *The Cameraman* (1928).

Keats, *n.* **John** (1795–1821), English poet, a leading figure of the Romantic movement. He published his first volume of poetry 1817; this was followed by *Endymion*, *Isabella*, and *Hyperion* (1818), 'The Eve of St Agnes', his odes 'To Autumn', 'On a Grecian Urn', and 'To a Nightingale', and 'Lamia' (1819). His final volume of poems appeared in 1820.

keb, *v.i.* (*Sc., North.*) to cast a lamb prematurely or dead. *n.* a ewe that has kebbed. [etym. doubtful]

kebab, *n.* (also **shish kebab**) small pieces of meat, with vegetables, cooked on skewers. [Arab. *kabāb,* roast meat]

kebbie, *n.* (*Sc., North.*) a cudgel.

kebbuck, *n.* (*Sc.*) a cheese. [etym. doubtful]

keck¹, *v.i.* to retch, to heave; to make a retching sound. [imit.]

keck², †**kecksy,** †**kecky** KEX, KEXY.

keckle, *v.i.* (*Sc.*) to cackle; to giggle, to chuckle. *v.t.* to utter with a keckle. *n.* a short, chuckling laugh. [var. of CACKLE]

ked, kade, *n.* a sheep-tick. [etym. doubtful]

kedge, *n.* a small portable anchor, used in warping. *v.t.* to move (a ship) by a light cable attached to kedge. *v.i.* of a ship, to move in this way. **kedger,** *n.* a kedge. [cp. CADGE]

kedgeree, *n.* a stew of rice, pulse, onions etc., a common dish in India; a dish of fish, rice etc. [Hind. *khichrī*, Sansk. *k'rsara*]

†**keech,** *n.* the fat of an ox or cow, rolled in a lump; a term of contempt. [etym. doubtful]

keek, *v.i.* (*Sc., North.*) to peep, to pry. *n.* a peep. **keek-hole,** *n.* **keeking-glass,** *n.* a looking-glass. **keeker,** *n.* (*Coal-min.*) an inspector or overlooker. [ME *kyken* (cp. Dut. *kijken,* LG *kîken*)]

keel¹, *n.* the principal timber of a ship, extending from bow to stern and supporting the whole structure; the structure corresponding to this in an iron vessel; a ship; the two lower petals of a papilionaceous corolla; a projecting ridge or longitudinal process. *v.i.* of a ship, to roll on her keel; to turn (over), to careen. *v.t.* to turn up the keel of, to turn over or keel upwards. **false keel,** a supplementary keel fastened below the true keel to protect this and promote stability. **on an even keel,** calm, steady, well-balanced. **to keel over,** to capsize; to turn over; (*coll.*) to fall over. **keelboat,** *n.* (*N Am.*) a large covered river-boat without sails. **keelhaul,** *v.t.* to punish by dragging under water on one side of the ship and up again on the other. †**keelage,** *n.* a toll paid by vessels entering a harbour. **keeled,** *a.* having a keel; (*Bot. etc.*) carinate. **keelless,** *a.* [prob. from Icel. *kjölr*]

keel², *n.* a lighter or flat-bottomed barge, esp. one of those used for loading colliers in the Tyne. **keeler, keelman,** *n.* [prob. from MDut. *kiel* (cp. OE *cēol,* ship)]

†**keel³,** *v.t.* to cool; to keep from boiling over by scumming; to mitigate, to lessen. [OE *cēlan,* cogn. with *cōl,* COOL]

keel⁴, *n.* (*Sc.*) ruddle. *v.t.* to mark with this. [etym. unknown]

Keeler, *n.* **Christine** (1942–), British model and call girl of the 1960s. She became notorious in 1963 after revelations of an affair with a Soviet attaché and the war minister John Profumo, who resigned after admitting lying to the House of Commons about their relationship. Her patron, the osteopath Stephen Ward, convicted of living on immoral earnings, committed suicide and Keeler was subsequently imprisoned for related offences.

keelhaul KEEL¹.

keelie, *n.* (*Sc.*) a kestrel; a city-bred hooligan, particularly one from Glasgow or surrounding area.

keeling, *n.* (*Sc.*) a cod, esp. a kind of small cod. [etym. doubtful]

keelivine, *n.* (*Sc., North.*) a lead-pencil. [etym. unknown]

keelson KELSON.

keen¹, *a.* having a sharp edge or point; of an edge, sharp; sensitive, acute, penetrating; of cold etc., biting, piercing, intense; bitter, acrimonious; enthusiastic; eager, ardent (on); †fierce, bold. **keen on,** interested in; **keen prices,** *n.pl.* low, competitive prices. **keen-set,** *a.* eager; hungry. **keen-witted,** *a.* **keenly,** *adv.* **keenness,** *n.* [OE *cēne* (cp. Dut. *koen,* Icel. *koenn, koenn,* G *kühn,* bold, daring)]

keen², *n.* lamentation over the body of a deceased person. *v.i.* to raise the keen. *v.t.* to mourn with the keen; to utter with keening. **keener,** *n.* a professional mourner. [Ir. *caoine,* from *caoinim,* to weep]

keep¹, *v.t.* (*past, p.p.* **kept**), to hold, to retain; to have in charge; to guard, preserve, protect; to maintain; to observe, to pay proper regard to; to fulfil, to celebrate; to supply with the necessaries of life; to protect; to tend, to look after; to remain in; to have in pay; to make business entries in; to have regularly on sale; to restrain (from); to detain (in custody etc.); to reserve (for); to refrain from divulging; to preserve; to write (a diary); to associate with; to stock. *v.i.* to continue or retain one's place (in, on etc.); to remain; to continue to be (in a specified condition etc.); to remain unspoiled, untainted etc.; to adhere (to); to restrict oneself (to); to lodge, to reside; keep your hair on HAIR. **to keep at,** to persist. **to keep a term,** to reside in college etc. during a term. **to keep away,** to prevent from approaching. **to keep back,** to restrain, to hold back; to reserve; to keep secret. **to keep body and soul together,** to survive, to maintain life. **to keep cave,** (*School sl.*) to keep a lookout. **to keep company with** COMPANY. **to keep down,** to repress, to subdue; to keep (expenses etc.) low. **to keep from,** to abstain or refrain from; not to tell (someone about something). **to keep house,** to manage a household. **to keep in,** to repress, to restrain; to confine, esp. after school-hours; to maintain (a fire); to remain indoors. **to keep in with,** to remain on friendly terms with. **to keep in touch with,** to maintain connection with. **to keep off,** to hinder from approach; to avert; to remain at a distance. **to keep on,** to continue to employ etc.; to continue (doing etc.), to persist. **to keep oneself to oneself,** to avoid other people. **to keep one's feet** FOOT. **to keep one's hand in,** to keep oneself in practice. **to keep on foot,** to maintain, to support (as a standing army). **to keep out,** to hinder from entering or taking possession (of). **to keep school, shop etc.,** to conduct a school, shop etc., on one's own account. **to keep someone going in (something),** to keep supplied. **to keep tabs on,** (*coll.*) to keep a check on. **to keep time,** to go accurately; to go rhythmically. **to keep to,** to adhere strictly to. **to keep together,** to remain or cause to remain together. **to keep the pot boiling,** (*coll.*) to go on (doing); to keep the game alive. **to keep under,** to hold down. **to keep up,** to maintain; to keep in repair or good condition; to prevent from falling or diminishing; to carry on; to cause to stay up at night; to bear up; to go on at the same pace (with). **to keep up with the Joneses,** (*coll.*) to keep on the same social level as one's friends and neighbours. **keep fit,** *n.* physical exercises to keep one fit and healthy. **keepnet,** *n.* a net kept in the water by anglers, where they put the fish they have caught to keep them alive. **keepsake,** *n.* anything kept or given to be kept for the sake of the giver; an illustrated or decorated gift-book, usu. containing extracts in verse and prose of a sentimental character, in fashion early in the 19th cent. **keeper,** *n.* one who or that which keeps; one who retains others (esp. lunatics) in custody or charge; one who has the charge, care or superintendence of anything, esp. of a park; a gamekeeper; a ring worn to protect another, esp. a wedding-ring; the bar of soft iron used to prevent permanent magnets from losing magnetism; a position in some games. **Keeper of the Great Seal,** the officer of State who holds the Great Seal; the Lord Chancellor. **keepership,** *n.* **keeping,** *n.* the action of holding, guarding, preserving etc.; charge, custody, guardianship; harmony, accord; consistency, congruity. *a.* that can be kept, as fruit. **in, out of keeping,** in or not in harmony (with), esp. in painting. **kept,** *a.* **kept woman,** *n.* a woman supported financially by the man whose mistress she is. [OE *cēpan,* etym. doubtful]

keep[2]**,** *n.* subsistence, maintenance; food required for subsistence; a donjon, the main tower or stronghold of a mediaeval castle; †care, heed. **keeps,** *n.pl.* **for keeps,** permanently. [from prec.]

keeshond, *n.* a small breed of dog, with a heavy coat, pointed muzzle, and erect ears. [Dutch *kees,* cornelius, *hond,* dog]

keeve, *n.* a large tub or vat, esp. a mash-tub. *v.t.* to put in a keeve; (*dial.*) to tilt up (as a cart). [OE *cyf*]

kef, keif KIEF.

keffiyeh, *n.* a Bedouin Arab's kerchief headdress. [Arab. *kaffiyah*]

kefir, *n.* a species of koumiss produced by fermenting milk, used medicinally, esp. as a food for invalids. [Causasian]

keg, *n.* a small cask or barrel. **keg beer,** *n.* any beer kept in pressurized kegs. [formerly *cag* (cp. Icel. *kaggi,* Swed. *kagge*)]

Keillor, *n.* **Garrison** (1942–), US writer and humorist. His hometown is Anoka, Minnesota, in the American Midwest. It inspired his Lake Wobegon stories, including *Lake Wobegon Days* 1985 and *Leaving Home* 1987, often started as radio monologues about 'the town that time forgot, that the decades cannot improve'.

keir, *n.* a vat for bleaching-liquor, in cloth-, paper-making etc. [cp. Icel. *ker,* Swed. and Dan. *kar*]

†**kell,** *n.* a woman's hair-net or cap; a film, a web, a cocoon; a caul. [North. var. of ME *calle,* CAUL]

Keitel, *n.* **Wilhelm** (1882–1946), German field marshal in World War II, chief of the supreme command from 1938. He signed Germany's unconditional surrender in Berlin 8 May 1945. Tried at Nuremberg for war crimes, he was hanged.

Kekulé, *n.* **Friedrich August** (1829–1896), German chemist whose theory 1858 of molecular structure revolutionized organic chemistry. He proposed two resonant forms of the benzene ring.

Kellogg–Briand pact, *n.* an agreement 1927 between the US and France to renounce war and seek settlement of disputes by peaceful means. It took its name from the US secretary of state Frank B. Kellogg (1856–1937) and the French foreign minister Aristide Briand (1862–1932). Other powers signed in Aug. 1928, making a total of 67 signatories. The pact made no provision for measures against aggressors and became ineffective in the 1930s.

Kells, Book of, an 8th-cent. illuminated manuscript of the Gospels produced at the monastery of Kells in County Meath, Ireland. It is now in Trinity College library, Dublin.

Kelly[1]**,** *n.* **(Edward) Ned** (1854–1880), Australian bushranger. The son of an Irish convict, he wounded a police officer in 1878 while resisting the arrest of his brother Daniel for horse-stealing. The two brothers escaped and carried out bank robberies. Kelly wore a distinctive home-made armour. In 1880 he was captured and hanged.

Kelly[2]**,** *n.* **'Gene' (Eugene Curran)** (1912–), US film actor, dancer, choreographer, and director. A major star of the 1940s and 1950s in a series of MGM musicals, including *Singin' in the Rain* (1952), his subsequent attempts at straight direction were less well received.

Kelly[3]**,** *n.* **Grace (Patricia)** (1928–1982), US film actress, Princess of Monaco from 1956. She starred in *High Noon* (1952), *The Country Girl* (1954), for which she received an Academy Award, and *High Society* (1955). When she married Prince Rainier of Monaco she retired from acting.

keloid, *n.* a hard, pinkish growth of scar tissue, usu. occurring in dark-skinned people. [Gr. *khēlē,* claw]

kelp, *n.* the calcined ashes of seaweed, from which carbonate of soda was obtained for glass- and soap-making, now chiefly used for obtaining iodine; the large, coarse seaweed from which kelp is produced. [ME *culp,* etym. unknown]

kelpie, *n.* a water-spirit usu. in the form of a horse, supposed to haunt fords, and to rejoice in the drowning of wayfarers; (*Austral.*) a smooth-haired variety of sheep-dog. [etym. doubtful]

kelson, keelson, *n.* a longitudinal piece placed along the floor-timbers of a ship binding them to the keel. [KEEL[1], *-son,* etym. doubtful (cp. Swed. *kölsvin,* Dut. *kolzwijn,* G *kielschwein*)]

kelt[1]**,** *n.* (*Sc.*) a spent salmon or sea-trout. [etym. unknown]

kelt[2]**,** *n.* (*Sc.*) cloth of native black wool. [etym. doubtful (cp. Ir. and Gael. *cealt*)]

Kelt[3] **Keltic** etc. CELT[1].

Kelvin, *a.* referring to a thermometer scale in which zero is absolute zero. **Kelvin,** *n.* the basic SI unit of temperature. [Lord *Kelvin*]

Kelvin, *n.* **William Thomson, 1st Baron Kelvin** (1824–1907), Irish physicist, who pioneered the absolute scale of temperature. His work on the conservation of energy 1851 led to the second law of thermodynamics.

Kemal Atatürk, ATATÜRK.

Kemalist, *n.* an adherent of Kemal Atatürk (1882–1938), first president of the Turkish republic.

†**kemb,** COMB[1].

Kemble[1]**,** *n.* **Charles** (1775–1854), English actor and theatre manager, younger brother of Philip Kemble. His greatest successes were in romantic roles with his daughter Fanny Kemble.

Kemble[2]**,** *n.* **'Fanny' (Frances Anne)** (1809–1893), English actress, daughter of Charles Kemble. She first appeared as Shakespeare's Juliet in 1829.

Kemble[3]**,** *n.* **(John) Philip** (1757–1823), English actor and theatre manager. He excelled in tragic roles, especially Shakespearean, including Hamlet and Coriolanus. As manager of Drury Lane 1788–1803 and Covent Garden 1803–17 in London, he introduced many innovations in theatrical management, costume, and scenery.

kemp, *n.* the coarse rough hairs of wool; (*pl.*) knotty hairs that will not felt. **kempy,** *a.* [prob. from Icel. *kampr,* beard, whisker]

Kempe, *n.* **Margery** (*c.* 1373–*c.* 1439), English Christian mystic. She converted to religious life after a period of mental derangement, and travelled widely as a pilgrim. Her *Boke of Margery Kempe* about 1420 describes her life and experiences, both religious and worldly. It has been called the first autobiography in English.

Kempis, THOMAS À KEMPIS.

ken[1], *v.t.* (*past, p.p.* **kenned**) (*chiefly Sc.*) to be acquainted with; to understand; to know; to see at or from a distance; to descry; †to teach. †*v.i.* to look round. *n.* view, sight; range of sight or knowledge, apprehension. **beyond one's ken,** beyond the limits of one's knowledge or experience. **in one's ken,** within the limits of one's knowledge. **kenning,** *n.* a metaphorical name or phrase for something, in Old English and Old Norse poetry. [immediate source doubtful (cp. OE *cennan,* to make known, to declare, Goth. *kannjan,* Dut. and G *kennen,* Icel. *kenna,* to know)]

ken[2], *n.* (*sl.*) a low tavern or lodging-house.

kenaf, *n.* the fibre from the E Indian hibiscus, used in ropes. [Pers.]

Kendal green, *n.* green cloth, orig. made at Kendal for foresters. [*Kendal,* Westmorland]

Kendall, *n.* **Edward** (1886–1972), US biochemist. Kendall isolated in 1914 the hormone thyroxin, the active compound of the thyroid gland. He went on to work on secretions from the adrenal gland, among which he discovered a compound E, which was in fact the steroid cortisone. For this Kendall shared the 1950 Nobel prize for medicine with Philip Hench (1896–1965) and Tadeus Reichstein.

Kendo, *n.* the Japanese martial art of fencing, usu. with pliable bamboo staves, occasionally with swords. [Jap.]

Kendrew, *n.* **John** (1917–), British biochemist. Kendrew began, in 1946, the ambitious task of determining the 3-dimensional structure of the major muscle protein, myoglobin. This was completed in 1959 and won for Kendrew a share of the 1962 Nobel chemistry prize with Max Perutz.

Keneally, *n.* **Thomas Michael** (1935–), Australian novelist, who won the Booker Prize with *Schindler's Ark* (1982), a novel based on the true account of Polish Jews saved from the gas chambers in World War II by a German industrialist.

Kennedy[1], *n.* **Edward (Moore)** (1932–), US Democrat politician. He aided his brothers John and Robert Kennedy in the presidential campaign of 1960, and entered politics as a senator from Massachusetts 1962. He failed to gain the presidential nomination 1980, largely because of feeling about his delay in reporting a car crash at Chappaquiddick Island, near Cape Cod, Massachusetts, in 1969, in which his passenger, Mary Jo Kopechne, was drowned.

Kennedy[2], *n.* **John F(itzgerald)** (1917–1963), 35th president of the US 1961–63, a Democrat. Kennedy was the first Roman Catholic and the youngest person to be elected president. In foreign policy he carried through the unsuccessful Bay of Pigs invasion of Cuba, and in 1963 secured the withdrawal of Soviet missiles from the island. His programme for reforms at home, called the New Frontier, was posthumously executed by Lyndon Johnson. Kennedy was assassinated while on a state visit to Dallas, Texas, on 22 Nov. 1963 by Lee Harvey Oswald (1939–1963), who was in turn shot dead by Jack Ruby.

Kennedy[3], *n.* **Joseph (Patrick)** (1888–1969), US industrialist and diplomat; ambassador to the UK 1937–40. A self-made millionaire, he groomed his four sons from an early age for careers in politics. His eldest son, Joseph Patrick Kennedy Jr (1915–44), was killed in action with the naval air force in World War II. Among his other children were John, Robert, and Edward.

Kennedy[4], *n.* **Robert F(rancis)** (1925–1968), US Democrat politician and lawyer. He was campaign manager for his brother John F Kennedy 1961, and as attorney general 1961–64 pursued a racket-busting policy and promoted the Civil Rights Act of 1964. When Johnson preferred Hubert H Humphrey for the 1964 vice-president nomination, Kennedy resigned and was elected senator for New York. In 1968 he campaigned for the Democratic party's presidential nomination, but was assassinated by Sirhan Bissara Sirhan (1944–), a Jordanian Arab.

Kennedy Space Center, the NASA launch site on Merritt Island, near Cape Canaveral, Florida, used for Apollo and space-shuttle launches.

kennel[1], *n.* a house or shelter for a dog or hounds; a place where dogs are bred or boarded; a hovel, a wretched haunt or den; a pack of hounds; †the hole of a fox or other animal. *v.i.* to lie or lodge in or as in a kennel. *v.t.* to confine in or as in a kennel. **kennel-maid, -man,** *n.* one who works in a kennel looking after the dogs. [O.North.F *kenil,* OF *chenil,* low L *canīle,* from L *canis,* dog]

kennel[2], *n.* a gutter, the watercourse at the side of a street; a puddle. †**kennel-raker,** *n.* a scavenger. [ME and OF *canel,* CHANNEL[1]]

kennel-coal, CANNEL.

Kennelly–Heaviside layer, *n.* former term for the E-layer, the lower regions of the ionosphere, which refract radio waves allowing their reception around the surface of the Earth. The Kennelly–Heaviside layer approaches the Earth by day and recedes from it at night.

Kenneth I, *n.* Kenneth MacAlpin, king of Scotland. Traditionally, he is regarded as the founder of the Scottish kingdom by virtue of his final defeat of the Picts about 844. He invaded Northumbria six times, and drove the Angles and the Britons over the river Tweed.

kenosis, *n.* Christ's relinquishment of the divine nature at the incarnation. **kenotic,** *a.* **kenoticist, kenotist,** *n.* [Gr. *kenōsis,* from *kenoein,* to empty]

kenotron, *n.* a thermionic valve which is exhausted to a high vacuum and has an incandescent filament as cathode and a molybdenum or tungsten anode acting as a rectifier. [as prec.]

kenspeckle, *a.* (*Sc.*) conspicuous; easily recognized. [ON *kennispeki,* power of recognition]

Kent, *n.* county in SE England, nicknamed the 'garden of England'. **area** 3730 sq km/1440 sq miles. **towns** administrative headquarters Maidstone; Canterbury, Chatham, Rochester, Tunbridge Wells; resorts Folkestone, Margate, Ramsgate. **products** hops, apples, soft fruit (on the weald), coal, cement, paper. **population** (1987) 1,511,000. **Kentish,** *a.* pertaining to the county of Kent. **Man of Kent,** a native of Kent born east of the Medway. **Kentish man,** *n.* a native of Kent born west of the Medway. **Kentish rag,** *n.* a calcareous rock belonging to the lower Greensand. [OE *Centisc* (*Cent,* Kent, -ISH)]

kent[1], *n.* a staff, a pole, esp. a long leaping-staff or a punting-pole. *v.t., v.i.* to punt. [etym. doubtful]

kent[2], *a.* (*Sc.*) known, recognized. [KEN[1]]

kentledge, *n.* pigs of iron used for permanent ballast, laid over the kelson-plates. [etym. unknown]

Kentucky, *n.* state of S Central US. **area** 104,700 sq km/40,414 sq miles. **capital** Frankfort. **towns** Louisville, Lexington-Fayette, Owensboro, Covington, Bowling Green. **products** tobacco, cereals, steel goods, textiles, transport vehicles. **population** (1987) 3,727,000.

Kenya, *n.* Republic of **area** 582,600 sq km/224,884 sq miles. **capital** Nairobi. **towns** Kisumu, port Mombasa. **physical** mountains and highlands in the W and centre; coastal plain in S; the N is arid. **population** (1988 est) 22,800,000 (the dominant ethnic group is the Kikuyu); annual growth rate 4.1%. **exports** coffee, tea, sisal, pineapples. **language** Kiswahili (official), 21% Kikuyu, 14% Luhya, English is spoken in commercial centres. **religion** indigenous religions with Christian and Muslim minorities.

Kenyatta, *n.* **Jomo** (*c.* 1889–1978), assumed name of Kamau Ngengi. Kenyan nationalist politician, prime minister from 1963 as well as first president of Kenya from 1964 until his death. He led the Kenya African Union from 1947 (KANU from 1963) and was active in liberating Kenya from British rule.

kep, *v.t.* (*Sc.*) to catch; to intercept, to stop. *n.* a catch.

[var. of KEEP[1]]

kephalic, CEPHALIC

képi, *n.* a French flat-topped military hat with a horizontal peak. [F, from G Swiss *käppi,* dim. of *kappe,* CAP[1]]

Kepler, *n.* **Johann** (1571–1630), German mathematician and astronomer. **Kepler's laws,** *n.pl.* concerning the revolution of planets round the sun: (1) the orbit of each planet is an ellipse with the sun at one of the foci; (2) the radius vector of each planet sweeps out equal areas in equal times; (3) the squares of the periods of the planets are proportional to the cubes of their mean distances from the sun.

kept, *past, p.p.* KEEP[1].

Kerala, *n.* state of SW India, formed 1956 from the former princely states of Travancore and Cochin. **area** 38,900 sq km/15,015 sq miles. **capital** Trivandrum. **population** (1981) 25,403,000. **products** tea, coffee, rice, oilseed, rubber, textiles, chemicals, electrical goods. **language** Kannada, Malayalam, Tamil.

keramic CERAMIC.

keratin, *n.* a nitrogenous substance, the chief constituent of hair, feathers, claws and horns. **keratinous,** *a.* **keratinization, -isation,** *n.* the formation of keratin; the state of becoming horny. **keratinize, -ise,** *v.i.* **keratitis,** *n.* inflammation of the cornea of the eye. **keratose,** *n.* the substance of the skeleton of horny sponges. *a.* horny. **keratosis,** *n.* a horny growth on the skin, e.g. a wart; the skin condition causing this symptom. [Gr. *keras keratos,* horn, -IN]

kerb, *n.* a row of stones set as edging to a pavement etc. **kerb-crawling,** *n.* the act of driving along slowly with the intention of enticing someone into the car for sexual purposes. **kerb-crawler,** *n.* **kerb-drill,** *n.* a pedestrian's procedure, as looking to the left and right, for crossing a road in safety, esp. as taught to and used by children. **kerb-merchant, -trader, -vendor,** *n.* someone who sells goods on the pavement. **kerbside,** *n., a.* **kerb-stone,** *n.* **kerb-stone broker,** a stockbroker who is not a member of the Stock Exchange. [var. of CURB[1]]

kerchief, *n.* (*pl.* **-chiefs**) a cloth to cover the head; a handkerchief, a napkin. **kerchiefed,** *a.* [ME *curchef, coverchef,* OF *couvrechief* (*couvrir,* to COVER, *chief,* L *caput,* head)]

Kerekou, *n.* **Mathieu (Ahmed)** (1933–), Benin socialist politician and soldier, president from 1980. In 1972, when deputy head of the Dahomey army, he led a coup to oust the ruling president and establish his own military government. He embarked on a programme of 'scientific socialism', changing his country's name to Benin to mark this change of direction. Re-elected president 1984, in 1987 he resigned from the army and confirmed a civilian administration.

kerel, *n.* (*S Afr.*) a young man. [Afrikaans]

Kerensky, *n.* **Alexander Feodorovich** (1881–1970), Russian politician, premier of the second provisional government before its collapse Nov. 1917, during the Russian Revolution. He lived in the US from 1918.

kerf, *n.* the slit, notch or channel made by a saw or axe in cutting; the spot where something has been cut or lopped off; a cutting or lopping; a quantity of hay, straw etc., cut for thatching etc.; a heap of clay, ashes etc., exposed to the weather until suitable for use in brick-making. [OE *cyrf,* cogn. with CARVE]

kerfuffle, *n.* commotion, fuss. [Sc. *curfuffle, carfuffle*]

kerion, *n.* an inflammation of the hair-follicles of the scalp, causing baldness. [Gr., honeycomb]

kerite, *n.* artificial caoutchouc used as an insulating material in telegraphy. [Gr. *kēros,* wax, -ITE]

Kerkira, *n.* Greek form of Corfu, an island in the Ionian Sea.

kermes, *n.* the dried bodies of the females of an insect, *Coccus ilicis,* yielding a red or scarlet dye. **kermes oak,** *n.* a shrubby, dwarf mediterranean oak. [F *kermès,* Arab. and Pers. *qirmiz,* CRIMSON]

kermis, kermess, kirmess, *n.* in the Netherlands, a fair or outdoor festival or merrymaking, orig. a church festival. [Dut. *kirk,* CHURCH, *mis,* MASS[1]]

Kern, *n.* **Jerome (David)** (1885–1945), US composer. He wrote the operetta *Show Boat* (1927), which includes the song 'Ol' Man River'.

kern[1], kerne, *n.* a light-armed Irish foot-soldier; a country lout; †a vagabond. **kernish,** *a.* [Ir. *ceatharn*]

kern[2], *n.* the projecting part of a piece of printing type. **kerned,** *a.* [F *carne,* L *cardinem,* nom. *cardo,* hinge]

kernel, *n.* the substance, usu. edible, contained in the shell of a nut or the stone of a fruit; that which is enclosed in a shell, husk, integument etc.; the nucleus, core, gist or essence. *v.i.* to ripen or harden into kernels. **kernelled,** *a.* having a kernel. **kernel-less,** *a.* **kernelly,** *a.* [OE *cyrnel,* dim. of CORN[1]]

kerosene, kerosine, *n.* an oil distilled from petroleum, coal or bituminous shale, chiefly used for burning in lamps. [Gr. *kēros,* wax]

Kerouac, *n.* **Jack** (1923–1969), US novelist, who epitomized the beat generation of the 1950s. His books include *On the Road* (1957), and *Big Sur* (1963).

Kerr, *n.* **Deborah** (1921–), British actress, who often played genteel, ladylike roles. Her performance in British films such as *Major Barbara* (1940), *Black Narcissus* (1946) led to starring parts in Hollywood films such as *From Here to Eternity* (1953), *Quo Vadis* (1951), and *The King and I* (1956).

Kerry, *n.* county of Munster province, Republic of Ireland, E of Cork. **area** 4,700 sq km/1,814 sq miles. **county town** Tralee. **physical** W coastline deeply indented, N part low-lying, but in the S are the highest mountains in Ireland including Carrantuohill 1041 m/3417 ft, the highest peak in Ireland; many rivers and lakes. **population** (1986) 124,000. **products** engineering, woollens, shoes, cutlery; tourism. **Kerry blue** *n.* a large, grey-blue, longhaired breed of terrier.

kerry, *n.* any of a breed of small black dairy cattle, from Ireland. [County Kerry]

kersey, *n.* a coarse woollen cloth, usu. ribbed. *a.* made of kersey; homely, plain. [place in Suffolk]

kerseymere, CASSIMERE.

Kertesz, *n.* **André** (1894–1986), US photographer. A master of the 35-mm format camera, he recorded his immediate environment (Paris, New York) with wit and style.

kerygma, *n.* in the early Christian church, the teaching of the Gospel. **kerygmatic,** *a.* [Gk. **kerygma,** proclamation]

Kesp®, *n.* a textured vegetable protein used as a meat substitute.

Kesselring, *n.* **Albert** (1885–1960), German field marshal in World War II, commander of the Luftwaffe (air force) 1939–40, during the invasions of Poland and the Low Countries and the early stages of the Battle of Britain. He later served under Field Marshal Rommel in N Africa, took command in Italy 1943, and was commander in chief on the western front Mar. 1945. His death sentence for war crimes at the Nuremberg trials 1947 was commuted to imprisonment, and he was released 1952.

kestrel, *n.* a small species of hawk, *Falco tinnunculus.* [prob. from OF *cresserelle,* etym. doubtful]

†**ket,** *n.* carrion; filth, trash. [Sc. and North. (cp. mod. Icel. *ket,* flesh)]

keta, *n.* the dog-salmon. [Rus.]

ketch, *n.* a fore-and-aft rigged two-masted vessel. [formerly CATCH]

ketchup, *n.* a sauce, usu. prepared from mushrooms, tomatoes etc.; tomato sauce. [Malay *kēchap,* perh. from Chin. *kôe-chiap,* fish-brine]

ketone, *n.* one of a class of organic compounds, usu. formed by oxidation of a secondary alcohol. **ketone body,** *n.* a compound produced in the liver from fatty acids, found in the blood and urine in abnormal amounts in people unable to use glucose, such as diabetics. **ketonic,** *a.* **ketosis,** *n.* the excessive formation of ketone bodies, as in diabetes. [G *keton,* ACETONE]

ketter KILTER.

†**kelty,** *n.* (*Sc.*) a bumper imposed as a fine; the draining off of a glass or bumper. [prob. from *Keltie,* pers. name]

kettle, *n.* a metallic vessel for heating water or other liquid. **a pretty kettle of fish,** a pretty mess, a muddle, a troublesome state of affairs. **kettledrum,** *n.* a drum made of a thin hemispherical shell of copper or brass, with a parchment head; †an afternoon tea party. **kettle-drummer,** *n.* **kettleholder,** *n.* a thick piece of cloth for protecting the hand in holding a hot kettle. [OE *cetel* or Icel. *ketill* (cp. Dut. *ketel,* G *kessel*)]

keuper, *n.* the upper portion of the Triassic, consisting chiefly of marls and sandstones. [G, mining term]

kevel, *n.* (*Naut.*) a belaying-cleat, usu. fixed in pairs. [O.North.F *keville* (F *cheville*), L *clāvicula,* dim. of *clāvis,* key]

Kew Gardens, *n.* popular name for the Royal Botanic Gardens, Kew, Surrey. They were founded 1759 by the mother of George III as a small garden and passed to the nation by Queen Victoria 1840. By then they were almost at their present size of 149 hectares and since 1841 have been open daily to the public. They contain a collection of over 25,000 living plant species and many fine buildings. Much of the collection of trees was destroyed by a gale 1987. The gardens are also a centre for botanical research.

Kewpie doll®, *n.* a plump baby-doll with hair in a top-knot. [Cupid]

kex, *n.* the dry hollow stem of umbelliferous plants, as the hemlock, the cow-parsnip, or the angelica. **kexy,** *a.* [etym. unknown]

key¹, *n.* a portable instrument, usu. of metal, for working the bolt of a lock to and fro; a tool or instrument by which something is screwed up or turned; that which gives access to or opportunity for something; a place whose military occupation gives control over a region of land or sea; that which explains anything difficult; a solution, an explanation; a translation; a series of solutions of problems etc.; a piece of wood or metal let transversely into the back of a board to prevent warping; a keystone; the first coat of plaster on a wall or ceiling which goes between the laths and binds the whole together; a small lever actuated by the fingers in operating certain instruments, machines etc.; one of several systems of musical notes having definite tonic relations among themselves and to one fundamental note called the key-note; the general tone or style (of a picture, literary composition, speech etc.). *v.t.* to fasten (on, in etc.) with a key, bolt, wedge etc.; (*Mus.*) to tune, to regulate; (*fig.*) to stir (up) to an action etc. **House of Keys,** the representative branch of the legislature in the Isle of Man. **power of the keys,** the supreme ecclesiastical authority claimed by the Pope (Matt. xvi.19). **St Peter's keys,** the cross-keys on the Papal arms symbolizing this. **to have the key of the street,** to be homeless. **to key in,** to enter data into a computer using a keyboard. **to key up,** to brace up, to incite, to encourage. **keyboard,** *n.* the range of keys on a piano, organ, typewriter etc. *v.t.* to set (text) in type using a keyboard. **keyboarder,** *n.* **key-bugle,** *n.* a keyed bugle. **key-cold,** *a.* cold as a key; lifeless. **key colour,** *n.* the leading colour of a picture. **key fruit,** *n.* a winged fruit, like that of the sycamore, which hangs like bunches of keys. **key-grip,** *n.* the person in a television studio or on a film set responsible for setting up scenery and camera tracks. **keyhole,** *n.* the hole in a lock, door, cover etc., by which a key is inserted. **key industry,** *n.* an industry upon which the other interests and the economic welfare of a country depend. **key-money,** *n.* a premium demanded, in addition to rent, for the granting or renewal of a tenancy. **key-note,** *n.* (*Mus.*) the fundamental note of a key; the general tone or spirit (of a picture, poem etc.). **keypad,** *n.* a small device with a push-button keyboard for operating, for example, a television or teletext system. **key-person,** *n.* an indispensable worker. **key punch,** *n.* a keyboard operated manually and used to put data onto punched cards. *v.t.* to transfer data in this way. **key-ring,** *n.* a ring for carrying keys upon. **key-seat,** *n.* (*Mach.*) a groove to receive a key for preventing a wheel or other part from sliding. **key signature,** *n.* the sharps and flats on the musical stave, showing the key of a piece of music. **keystone,** *n.* the central stone of an arch locking the others together; the fundamental element, principle etc. **key-stroke,** *n.* the operation of a key on a keyboard-operated machine. **keyed,** *a.* **keyless,** *a.* not having a key; wound without a key (as a clock or watch). [OE *cæg,* etym. doubtful]

key², *n.* a low island, esp. of coral, on the coast of Florida. [var. of CAY]

Keynes, *n.* **John Maynard, 1st Baron Keynes** (1883–1946), English economist, whose *The General Theory of Employment, Interest, and Money* (1936) proposed the prevention of financial crises and unemployment by adjusting demand through government control of credit and currency. He is responsible for that part of economics now known as macroeconomics. **Keynesian economics,** *n.* the economic theory of J. M. Keynes which argues that a fall in national income, lack of demand for goods, and rising unemployment should be countered by increased government expenditure to stimulate the economy. It is opposed by monetarists.

keystone KEY¹.

KG, (*abbr.*) Knight of the Order of the Garter.

kg, (*abbr.*), keg; kilogram.

KGB, (*abbr.*) Soviet secret police. [Rus. *komitet gosudarstvennoi bezpasnosti* State Security Committee]

KGC, (*abbr.*) Knight Grand Cross.

Khabarovsk, *n.* territory of the Russian Soviet Federal Socialist Republic bordering the Sea of Okhotsk and drained by the Amur; area 824,600 sq km/318,501 sq miles; population(1985) 1,728,000. Capital is Khabarovsk. Mineral resources include gold, coal and iron ore.

Khachaturian, *n.* **Aram Il'yich** (1903–1978), Armenian composer. His use of folk themes is shown in the ballets *Gayaneh* 1942, which includes the 'Sabre Dance', and *Spartacus* 1956.

khaddar, khadi, *n.* hand-woven cloth. [Hind.]

Khaddhafi, Gaddafi, Qaddafi, *n.* **Moamer al** (1942–), Libyan revolutionary leader. Overthrowing King Idris 1969, he became virtual president of a republic, although he nominally gave up all except an ideological role 1974. He favours territorial expansion in N Africa reaching as far as Zaïre, has supported rebels in Chad, and proposed mergers with a number of countries. His theories, based on those of the Chinese communist leader Mao Zedong, are contained in a *Green Book.*

khaki, *a.* dust-coloured, dull-yellow. *n.* cloth or cotton material of this colour, used for army uniforms. [Hind., dusty, from *khāk,* dust]

khalif, CALIPH.

Khalifa, *n.* **Abdullah el Taaisha** (1846–1899), Sudanese dervish leader, successor to the Mahdi as Sudanese ruler from 1885, he was defeated by the British general Kitchener at Omdurman 1898, and later killed in Kordofan.

Khalistan, *n.* projected independent Sikh state.

Khalka, *n.* the official language of the Mongolian People's Republic.

Khalsa, *n.* the brotherhood of the Sikhs, created by Guru Gobind Singh at the festival of Baisakhi in 1699. The Khalsa was originally founded as a militant group to defend the Sikh community from persecution.

Khama, *n.* **Seretse** (1921–1980), Botswanan politician, prime minister of Bechuanaland 1965 and first president of Botswana from 1966 until his death.

khamsin, kamseen, kamsin, *n.* a hot southerly wind blowing in Egypt for some 50 days in March to May. [Arab., fifty]

Khan¹, *n.* **Imran** (1952–), Pakistani cricketer. He played county cricket for Worcestershire and Sussex in the UK, and made his test debut for Pakistan 1971, subsequently playing for his country 75 times. In first-class cricket he has scored over 16,000 runs and taken over 1,200 wickets.

Khan², *n.* **Jahangir** (1963–), Pakistani squash player, who won the world open championship a record six times 1981–85 and 1988.

Khan³, *n.* **Liaquat Ali** (1895–1951), Indian politician, deputy leader of the Muslim League Party 1941–47, first prime minister of Pakistan from 1947. He was assassinated by a Muslim fanatic.

khan[1], *n.* orig. a prince, a lord, a chief; now a title (in India, Central Asia etc.) equivalent to 'esquire'; †a king or emperor, esp. the chief rulers of Tartar, Turkish, and Mongol tribes. **khanate**, *n.* [Turk. *khān*, perh. orig. *khāqan*]

khan[2], *n.* a caravanserai. [Arab. *khān*]

Khardungla Pass, *n.* road linking the Indian town of Leh with the high-altitude military outpost on the Siachen Glacier at an altitude of 5662 m/1744 ft in the Karakoram range, Kashmir. It is possibly the highest road in the world.

Kharg Island, *n.* a small island in the Persian Gulf used by Iran as a deepwater oil terminal. Between 1982 and 1988 Kharg Island came under frequent attack during the Gulf War.

Kharkov, *n.* capital of the Kharkov region, Ukraine, USSR, 400 km/250 miles E of Kiev; population (1987) 1,587,000. It is an important railway junction and industrial city (engineering, tractors), close to the Donets Basin coalfield and Krivoy Rog iron mines. Kharkov was founded 1654 as a fortress town. Its university dates from 1805.

Khartoum, *n.* capital and trading centre of Sudan, at the junction of the Blue and White Nile; population (1983) 476,000, and of Khartoum North, across the Blue Nile, 341,000. It was founded 1830 by Mehemet Ali.

kheda, *n.* an enclosure used in Bengal and other parts of India for catching elephants. [Hind.]

Khedive, *n.* the official title of the Governor of Egypt, conferred upon Ismail Pasha in 1867 by the Porte. **Khediva, Khediviah,** *n.* the wife of the Khedive. **khedival, khedivial,** *a.* **khedivate,** *n.* [F *khédive,* Turk. (Pers.) *khedīv*]

Khe Sanh, *n.* in the Vietnam War, US Marine outpost near the Laotian border and just south of the demilitarized zone between North and South Vietnam. Garrisoned by 4000 Marines, it was attacked unsuccessfully by 20,000 North Vietnamese troops 21 Jan–7 Apr. 1968.

Khirbet Qumran QUMRAN.

Khmer, *n.* a member of a people inhabiting Kampuchea, formerly Cambodia; the official language of Kampuchea. *a.* pertaining to this people or their language. **Khmer Rouge**, *n.* communist movement in Cambodia (Kampuchea), which formed the largest opposition group against the US-backed regime led by Lon Nol 1970–75. By 1974 the Khmer Rouge controlled the countryside and in 1975 the capital Phnom Penh was captured and Sihanouk installed as head of state. Internal disagreements led to the creation of the Pol Pot government 1976 and mass deportations and executions of an estimated 1 million people 1975–79. From 1978, when Vietnam invaded the country, the Khmer Rouge conducted a guerrilla campaign against the Vietnamese forces. Pol Pot retired as military leader 1985 and was succeeded by the more moderate Khieu Samphan. **khmerian,** *a.*

Khoisan, *n.* a family of African languages which includes Hottentot and Bushman languages.

Khomeini, *n.* **Ayatollah Ruhollah** (1900–1989), Iranian Shi'ite Muslim leader, born in Khomein, central Iran. Exiled for opposition to the Shah from 1964, he returned when the Shah left the country 1979, and established a fundamentalist Islamic republic. His rule was marked by a protracted war with Iraq, and suppression of opposition within Iran.

Khorana, *n.* **Har Gobind** (1922–), Indian biochemist, who in 1976 led the team that first synthesized a biologically active gene.

Khrushchev, *n.* **Nikita Sergeyevich** (1894–1971), Soviet politician, secretary general of the Communist Party 1953–64, premier 1958–64. In 1956 he was the first official to denounce Stalin. A personal feud with Mao Zedong led to a breach in Soviet relations with China 1960. Khrushchev's foreign policy was one of peaceful coexistence with the West, marred by the crisis when he attempted to supply missiles to Cuba and US pressure compelled their withdrawal 1962.

khud, *n.* a deep ravine or chasm; a steep descent. [Hind.]

Khufu, *n.* (*c.* 3000 BC), Egyptian king of Memphis, who built the largest of the pyramids, known to the Greeks as the pyramid of Cheops (the Greek form of Khufu).

Khulna, *n.* capital of Khulna region, SW Bangladesh, situated close to the Ganges delta; population (1981) 646,000. Industry includes shipbuilding and textiles; it trades in jute, rice, salt, sugar, and oilseed.

khutbah, khotbah, khotbeh, *n.* Muslim prayer and sermon in the mosque on Friday. [Arab.]

Khwarizmi, al-, *n.* **Muhammad ibn-Musa** (780–c. 850), Arab mathematician who lived and worked in Baghdad. He introduced the algorithm (a word based on his name), the word algebra (*al-jabr*, in an adaptation of an earlier Indian text), the Hindu decimal system, and the concept of zero into Arab mathematics. He compiled astronomical tables, and put forward Arabic numerals.

Khyber Pass, *n.* pass 53 km/33 miles long through the mountain range that separates Pakistan from Afghanistan. The Khyber Pass was used by invaders of India. The present road was constructed by the British during the Afghan Wars.

kHz, (*abbr.*) kilohertz.

kiak, KAYAK.

kiang, *n.* an Asian wild ass. [Tibetan]

Kiangsi, *n.* former spelling of Jiangxi, province of China.

Kiangsu, *n.* former spelling of Jiangsu, province of China.

kia ora, *int.* (*New Zealand*) your health! [Maori]

kiaugh, *n.* (*Sc.*) care, trouble. [etym. doubtful]

kibble[1], *n.* a strong iron (formerly wooden) bucket for raising ore from a mine. **kibble-chain,** *n.* a chain for drawing this up. [cp. G *Kübel*]

kibble[2], *v.t.* to grind (grain, beans etc.) coarsely. [etym. unknown]

kibbutz, *n.* (*pl.* **kibbutzim**) a communal agricultural settlement in Israel. **kibbutznik,** *n.* someone who lives and works on a kibbutz. [Heb.]

kibe, *n.* a chap occasioned by cold; an ulcerated chilblain. **to tread on** or **gall one's kibes,** to irritate one's feelings. **kibed, kiby,** *a.* affected with kibes. [perh. from W. *cibi* (*cib*, a cup, a husk)]

kibitka, *n.* a tartar circular tent, usu. made of latticework and felt; a Russian wheeled vehicle with a tent-like covering, used as a sledge in snowy weather. [Rus.]

kibitzer, *n.* (*N Am.* (*coll.*)) an interfering looker-on, a meddler; a spectator. **kibitz,** *v.i.* [Yiddish, fr. G, a looker-on]

kiblah, *n.* the direction of the Caaba at Mecca, to which Muslims turn during prayer. [Arab. *qiblah*]

kibosh, kybosh, *n.* (*sl.*) bosh, humbug. **to put the kibosh on,** to checkmate, to do for; to put an end to. [etym. unknown]

kick[1], *v.t.* to strike with the foot; to push, move, or drive, by kicking; to strike in recoil; (*coll.*) to free oneself of a bad habit, addiction etc. *v.i.* to strike out with the foot or feet; to recoil, as a gun; to show opposition, dislike etc. (against, at etc.); to be alive and well; to make a sudden violent movement. *n.* the act of kicking; a blow with the foot; a recoil (of a gun); the erratic course of an arrow owing to wrong handling of the bow; a transient high-voltage discharge in an inductive electric current; a stimulating reaction to alcohol or pungent seasoning; a sudden thrill of excitement; an enthusiastic, short-lived interest. **a kick in the teeth,** a rebuff. **to get a kick out of,** to get enjoyment from. **to kick ass,** (*sl.*) to make one's presence felt in a forceful manner, to show that one is in control. **to kick off,** to throw off by kicking; (*Football*) to give the ball the first kick. **to kick one's heels,** to stand idly waiting. **to kick out,** to eject or dismiss contumeliously or with violence. **to kick over the traces,** to throw off any means of restraint or control. **to kick up a dust, fuss, rumpus** etc. DUST. **to kick up one's heels,** to enjoy oneself with no inhibitions. **to kick upstairs,** (*coll.*) to promote, often to a less active or less powerful post. **kickback,** *n.* a strong reaction to something; a sum paid to another person, confidentially, for favours past or future. **kickdown,** *n.* a way of changing gear in an automatic car, by pressing the accelerator pedal right down. **kick-off,** *n.* (*Football*) the first kick in the game. **kick-pleat,** *n.* a pleat at the back of a tight skirt. **kick-start,** *n.* the starting of an engine by kicking down a pedal. *v.t.* to start (an engine) thus. **kick-starter,** *n.* a pedal for kickstarting, e.g. a motorcycle. **kickable,** *a.* **kicker,** *n.* one who or that which kicks; a horse given to kicking. [ME *kiken*]

kick², *n.* the pushed-in base of a glass bottle. [perh. from prec.]

kickshaw, *n.* something fantastical, a trifle; a light, unsubstantial dish. [corr. of F *quelque chose,* something]

kid¹, *n.* the young of the goat; leather from the skin of this; (*pl.*) gloves of this leather; (*coll.*) a child. *v.i.* (*past, p.p.* **kidded**) to bring forth a kid or kids. †**kid-fox,** *n.* a young fox. **kid glove,** *n.* a glove made of kid. *a.* too fastidious for common tasks etc. **with kid gloves,** very carefully or tactfully. **kidskin,** *n.* a smooth, soft leather from a young goat. **kids' stuff,** *n.* (*coll.*) something suitable for children; something childish or very easy. **kiddy,** *n.* a little child. **kiddy-wink, kiddiewink,** *n.* a child, kiddy. **kidling,** *n.* [ME *kid, kide* (cp. Norw., Swed. and Dan. *kid,* Icel. *kith,* G *Kitze*)]

kid², *n.* a small wooden tub, esp. one used at mess by sailors. [prob. var. of KIT¹]

kid³, *n.* a faggot, a bundle. [etym. doubtful]

kid⁴, *v.t.* (*past, p.p.* **kidded**) (*coll.*) to humbug, to hoax; to pretend; to deceive for fun. *v.i.* to joke. *n.* a deception, a fraud. **kidder¹,** *n.* **kiddingly,** *adv.* **kidology,** *n.* (*coll.*) the art or practice of kidding, bluffing. [perh. from KID¹]

Kidd, *n.* **'Captain' (William)** (*c.* 1645–1701), Scottish pirate, born in Greenock, who settled in New York. In 1696 he was commissioned by the governor of New York to suppress pirates, but he became a pirate himself. Arrested 1699, he was taken to England and hanged.

†**kidder²,** *n.* a dealer in corn, esp. an engrosser of corn to enhance its price. [etym. unknown]

Kidderminster, *a.* of or pertaining to Kidderminster. *n.* two-ply ingrain carpet orig. made there. [town in Hereford and Worcs.]

kiddle, *n.* a weir or dam in a river with traps or nets for catching fish; a set of stake-nets for the same purpose on a beach. [OE *kidel,* OF *quidel,* later *quideau,* etym. doubtful]

kidnap, *v.t.* to steal (a child); to carry off by force or illegally, to abduct. **kidnapper,** *n.* [KID¹, *nap,* NAB]

kidney, *n.* an oblong flattened glandular organ embedded in fatty tissue in the lumbar region on each side of the spine, and serving to secrete urine and remove nitrogenous matter from the blood; anything resembling a kidney; temperament, kind, fashion; †(*sl.*) a waiter. **kidney bean,** *n.* the name of two species of *Phaseolus,* the dwarf French bean and the scarlet runner. **kidney-form, -shaped,** *a.* **kidney machine,** *n.* a machine used to carry out blood dialysis in cases of kidney failure. **kidney-potato,** *n.* an oval-shaped potato. **kidney stone,** *n.* a hard mass in the kidney. **kidney-vetch,** *n.* a leguminous plant, *Anthyllis vulneraria* or lady's fingers. **kidney-wort,** *n.* the navelwort, *Cotyledon umbilicus;* the star saxifrage, *Saxifraga stellaris.*

kief, kif, kef, *n.* the drowsy, dreamy, trance-like condition produced by the use of bhang etc.; dreamy repose, happy idleness; Indian hemp, smoked in Morocco and Algeria to produce this condition. [Arab. *kaif*]

Kiefer, *n.* **Anselm** (1945–), German painter. He studied under Joseph Beuys, and his works include monumental landscapes on varied surfaces, often with the paint built up into relief with other substances. Much of his highly expressionist work deals with recent German history.

kiekie, *n.* a New Zealand climber, *Freycinetia banksii,* the berries of which are eaten and the leaves used for baskets etc. [Maori]

Kierkegaard, *n.* **Søren Aabye** (1813–1855), Danish philosopher, considered to be the founder of existentialism. He disagreed with Hegel, arguing that no system of thought could explain the unique experience of the individual. He defended Christianity, suggesting that God cannot be known through reason, but only through a 'leap of faith'. He believed that God and exceptional individuals were above moral laws.

kieselguhr, *n.* diatomite. [G *Kiesel,* flint, *Gur,* loose earth]

Kiev, *n.* capital of Ukraine, industrial centre (chemicals, clothing, leatherwork) and third largest city of the USSR, on the confluence of the Desna and Dnieper rivers; population (1987) 2,554,000. Founded in the 5th cent., Kiev replaced Novgorod as the capital of Slav-dominated Russia in 882, and was the original centre of the Orthodox Christian faith in 988.

Kigali, *n.* capital of Rwanda, central Africa; population (1981) 157,000. Products include coffee and minerals.

kike, *n., a.* (*offensive*) Jew. [possibly from *-ki* ending of many Jewish immigrants names in the US at the end of the 19th cent.]

Kikuyu, *n.* a Bantu-speaking people of Kenya, E Africa; a member of this people; its language. [Bantu]

Kildare, *n.* county of Leinster province, Republic of Ireland, S of Meath. **area** 1,690 sq km/652 sq miles. **county town** Naas. **physical** wet and boggy in the north. **population** (1986) 116,000. **products** oats, barley, potatoes, cattle.

kilderkin, *n.* a small barrel, usu. of 18 gals. (81·8 l); a liquid measure of this capacity. [corr. of MDut. *kindeken,* dim. of *kintal,* OF QUINTAL]

kilerg, *n.* a unit of measurement of work, 1000 ergs. [*kil-,* KILO-, ERG]

kiley, KYLIE.

Kilimanjaro, *n.* volcano in Tanzania, the highest mountain in Africa, 5,900 m/19,364 ft.

Kilkenny, *n.* county of Leinster province, Republic of Ireland, E of Tipperary. **area** 2,060 sq km/795 sq miles. **county town** Kilkenny. **population** (1986) 73,000. **products** agricultural, coal.

kill, *v.t.* to deprive of life; to put to death; to slay; to put an end to, to destroy, to quell; to deaden, to still (pain etc.); to neutralize (effects of colour etc.); to pass or consume (time) idly; to discard, to cancel; to cause pain or discomfort; to mark a paragraph or article not to be used; to order type to be distributed; (*coll.*) to overwhelm with admiration, astonishment, personal charms etc.; in lawn tennis, to strike (the ball) so forcibly that it cannot be returned. *v.i.* to put to death; to slaughter, esp. in sport; (*sl.*) to fascinate, to do execution. *n.* the act of killing; an animal or number of animals killed, esp. in sport; an animal used as a bait in hunting wild beasts; (*Lawn Tennis, Rackets*) the hitting of a ball in such a manner that it cannot be returned. **to be in at the kill,** to be present at the end or conclusion of something. **to kill off,** to get rid of by killing. **to kill oneself,** (*coll.*) to over-exert oneself. **to kill the sea,** to make the sea become calmer. **to kill the skin,** in leather manufacturing, to remove the natural grease from the skin. **to kill the wind,** (*Naut.*) to check wind-velocity. **to kill time,** to pass time idly. **to kill two birds with one stone,** to achieve two things with a single action. †**to kill up,** to exterminate. **kill-devil,** *n.* an artificial spinning bait used in angling. **kill-joy,** *n.* a person who sheds a general depression on company, a wet blanket. **killer,** *n.* **killer bee,** *n.* an African honey-bee which is very aggressive when disturbed. **killer whale,** *n.* a black-and-white toothed whale, *Orcinus orca,* found in most seas. **killing,** *ger.* the number of animals killed by sportsmen; the precaution against the evolution of gas in steel during the process of manufacture; (*Bridge*) a heavy defeat of a contract. *a.* that kills; fascinating, irresistibly charming; (*coll.*) excruciatingly funny. **to make a killing,** to make a large profit. **killingly,** *adv.* [etym. doubtful, prob. not rel. to QUELL]

killas, *n.* clay-slate. [Cornish]

killdee, killdeer, *n.* a N American ring-plover, *Aegialites vocifera.* [imit. of the cry]

killick, *n.* a stone or small anchor used for mooring a fishing-boat. [etym. unknown]

killifish, *n.* a minnow-like fish of the genus *Fundulus* used as bait and to control mosquitoes. [Dut. *kille,* river]

killogie, *n.* (*Sc.*) the sheltered space in front of the fireplace in a kiln. [KILN, *logie,* the space by the fire]

kiln, *n.* a furnace, oven or stove for calcining, drying, hardening etc., esp. a lime-kiln. *v.t.* to dry or bake in a kiln. **brick-kiln,** a kiln for baking bricks. **lime-kiln,** a kiln for calcining lime. **kiln-dry,** *v.t.* to dry in a kiln. **kiln-dried,** *a.* **kiln-hole,** *n.* the mouth of a kiln. [OE *cyln, cyline,* L *culīna,* kitchen]

kilo-, *comb. form* **kilobit,** *n.* a unit fo computer information equal to 1024 bits. **kilobyte,** *n.* a unit of computer storage equal to 1024 bytes. **kilocalorie,** *n.* 1000 units of heat CALORIE. **kilocycle,** *n.* (*Elec.*) 1000 cycles per second, a unit for measuring the frequency of alternating current. **kilodyne,** *n.* a unit of force equivalent to 1000 dynes. **kilo-electron-volt,** *n.* the energy of an electron accelerated through 1000 volts. **kilogram,** *n.* a measure of weight, 1000 grams or 2·2046 lb. av., the SI base unit of mass. **kilogram-metre,** *n.* a unit of measurement of work, the energy expended in raising one kilogram to the height of one metre. **kilohertz,** *n.* 1000 hertz, a unit used to measure the frequency of radio waves. **kilojoule,** *n.* a unit equal to 1000 joules. **kilolitre,** *n.* a liquid measure, 1000 litres. **kilometre,** *n.* a measure of distance, 1000 metres or 0·621 mile. **kilometrical,** *a.* **kiloton,** *n.* a measure of explosive power, equivalent to 1000 tons of TNT. **kilovolt,** *n.* a unit of electromotive force equivalent to 1000 volts. **kilowatt,** *n.* a unit of measurement of electrical energy, 1000 watts. **kilowatt hour,** *n.* a unit of energy or work equivalent to that performed by 1 kilowatt acting for 1 hour. [F, from Gr. *chilioi,* a thousand]

kilt, *v.t.* to tuck up (the skirts of a dress); to gather together (the material of a dress) into vertical pleats. *n.* a kind of short skirt usu. of tartan cloth gathered in vertical pleats, worn as part of male dress by the Highlanders of Scotland. **kiltie,** *n.* (*coll.*) a soldier of a kilted regiment. **kilted,** *a.* [cp. Dan. *kilte,* Icel. *kilting,* a skirt)]

kilter, kelter, *n.* (*coll.*) good condition, fitness, form. [etym. unknown]

Kilvert, *n.* **Francis** (1840–1879), British clergyman, noted for a diary recording social life on the Welsh border 1870–79 published in 1938–39.

kimberlite, *n.* a diamond-bearing clay-like substance, called miners 'blue earth' or 'blue ground', found in S Africa. [*Kimberley,* S Afr.]

kimbo, AKIMBO.

Kim Dae Jung, *n.* (1924–), South Korean social-democratic politician. As a committed opponent of the regime of Gen Park Chung Hee, he suffered imprisonment and exile. He was a presidential candidate in 1971 and 1987.

Kim Il Sung, *n.* (1912–), North Korean communist politician and marshal. He became prime minister 1948 and president 1972, retaining the presidency of the Communist Workers' Party. He likes to be known as the 'Great Leader' an has campaigned constantly for the reunification of Korea. His son Kim Jong Il (1942–), known as the 'Dear Leader', has been named as his successor.

Kimmeridge clay, *n.* (*Geol.*) a thick bed of Upper Oolitic clay or bituminous shale, occurring near Kimmeridge, on the Dorset coast. **Kimmeridgian,** *a.*

kimono, *n.* (*pl.* **-nos**) a loose robe fastened with a sash, the principal outer garment of Japanese costume. [Jap.]

Kim Young Sam, *n.* (1927–), South Korean democratic politician. A member of the National Assembly from 1954 and president of the New Democratic Party (NDP) from 1974, he lost his seat and was later placed under house arrest because of his opposition to President Park Chung Hee. In 1983 he led a pro-democracy hunger strike but in 1987 failed to defeat Roh Tae-Woo in the presidential election. In 1990 he merged the ruling party to form the new Democratic Liberal Party (DLP).

kin, *n.* stock, family; relations or connections collectively, kindred; a relation, a connection. *a.* of the same family, nature, or kind; akin. **kith and kin** KITH. **near of kin,** closely related. **next of kin** the nearest blood relation. **kinsfolk,** *n.* (*collect.*) family relations, kindred. **kinsman, -woman,** *n.* **kinless,** *a.* [OE *cynn* (cp. Dut. *kunne,* Icel. *kyn*), cogn. with L *genus,* Gr. *genos*]

-kin, *dim. suf.* as in *bumpkin, buskin, cannikin, catkin.* [cog. with MDut. *-kijn,* OHG *-chîn,* G *-chen*]

kinaesthesis, (esp. N Am.) **kinesthesis , kinaesthesia,** *n.* the muscular sense, the perception of muscular movement. **kinaesthetic,** *a.* [Gr. *kinein,* to move, Gr. *aesthesis,* perception]

kinase, *n.* a chemical in the body which converts a zymogen into an enzyme; an enzyme that facilitates the transfer of phosphates from ATP. [*Kinetic, -ase*]

Kincardineshire, *n.* former county of E Scotland, merged in 1975 in Grampian region. The county town was Stonehaven.

kinchin, *n.* a little child. **kinchin-cove,** *n.* a little man; a raw thief. **kinchin-lay,** *n.* stealing money from children. **kinchin-mort,** *n.* a baby girl. [perh. from G *Kindchen* or MLG *kindekin,* little child]

kincob, *n.* a rich E Indian stuff interwoven with gold or silver thread. [Hind. *kimkhāb*]

kind, *n.* race, genus, species, natural group; sort, class, variety; manner, fashion, way; †nature; †natural way, natural propensity or inclination; †parentage, descent. *a.* disposed to do good to others; sympathetic, benevolent, tender; proceeding from or characterized by goodness of heart; †affectionate. †*v.t.* to beget. **after its kind,** according to its nature. **a kind of,** a sort of; roughly or approximately of the description or class expressed. **in kind,** of payment, wages etc.; in produce or commodities; in the same way or manner. **to differ in kind,** to differ in nature, not merely in degree. **kind-hearted,** *a.* sympathetic. **kindheartedness,** *n.* †**kind-less,** *a.* unnatural; unparalleled. **kindly,** *a.* kind, good-natured, benovelent, genial, beneficial; favourable, auspicious; †native, akin, natural. *adv.* in a considerate or tolerant way. **to take kindly,** to react favourably. **to take kindly to,** to take a favourable view of something. **kindly,** *adv.* **kindliness,** *n.* **kindness,** *n.* [OE *cynd, gecynd,* cogn. with KIN]

kindergarten, *n.* a school for infants and young children, in which knowledge is imparted chiefly by simple object-lessons, by toys, games, singing and work. **kindergartenism,** *n.* **kindergartener,** *n.* [G, children's garden]

kindle[1], *v.t.* to set fire to; to light; to inflame, to inspire (the passions etc.); to excite, to stir up (to action or feeling); to light up or illumine. *v.i.* to take fire, to begin to burn or flame; to become inflamed or excited; to become illumined. **kindler,** *n.* **kindling,** *n.* the act of setting on fire; wood, shavings etc., for lighting fires, firewood. [prob. from Icel. *kynda,* -LE]

†**kindle[2],** *n.* a brood, a litter. *v.t.* to bring forth, to bear. *v.i.* to bring forth young. [from KIND]

kindly KIND.

kindred, *n.* relationship by blood or marriage; affinity or likeness of character; (*collect.*) relatives, kin; †family, race, descent. *a.* related by blood; congenial, sympathetic; of like nature or qualities. [KIN, *-red,* OE *-raeden,* condition]

kine, *n.pl.* cow[1].

kinematics, *n.sing.* the science of pure motion, admitting conceptions of time and velocity but excluding that of force. **kinematic,** *a.* pertaining to movement or to kinematics. **kinematical,** *a.* **kinematically,** *adv.* [Gr.

kinēma -matos, movement, from *kinein,* to move]

kinesi-, *comb. form* movement. [Gr. *kinēsis,* motion, from *kinein,* to move]

kinesiology, *n.* the study of human movement and anatomy. **kinesiologist,** *n.*

kinesipathy, *n.* the treatment of disease by muscular movements; cure by gymnastic exercises. **kinesipath, kinesipathist,** *n.*

kinesis, *n.* movement under stimulus. **kinesics,** *n.sing.* the study of body movements as non-verbal communication.

kinesitherapy, *n.* kinesipathy.

kinetic, *a.* of or producing motion; due to or depending upon motion. **kinetic art,** *n.* art, e.g. sculpture, which has moving parts. **kinetic energy,** *n.* the energy possessed by a body by virtue of its motion. **kinetic pressure,** *n.* the increase in pressure when a stream of fluid meets an obstruction. **kinetic theory,** *n.* a theory which accounts for the behaviour of gases, vapours, liquids etc. in terms of the motions of molecules or atoms comprising them. **kinetically,** *adv.* **kinetics,** *n.sing.* that branch of dynamics which treats of forces imparting motion to or influencing motion already imparted to bodies. [Gr. *kinētikos,* as prec.]

kineto-, *comb. form* pertaining to motion; pertaining to kinetics.

kinetogenesis, *n.* the theory that animal structures originated and were developed through movements.

kinetograph, *n.* a camera for obtaining photographs of objects in motion. **kinetographer,** *n.* **kinetographic,** *a.* **kinetography,** *n.*

kinetoscope, *n.* a device for exhibiting pictures taken by the kinetograph, an early form of cinematograph; an instrument for combining arcs of different radii into continuous curves.

king, *n.* the male sovereign of a nation, esp. a hereditary sovereign of an independent State; one who or that which is pre-eminent in any sphere; a card bearing a representation of a king, usu. ranking next to the ace and before the queen; (*Chess*) a piece which has to be protected from checkmate; (*Draughts*) a piece which has been crowned and is entitled to move in any direction. *v.i.* to act as king, to govern; to play the king. *v.t.* to make a king of; to raise to a throne. **King Charles's spaniel** SPANIEL. **King James Version,** the authorized version of the Bible. **King-of-Arms,** *n.* a senior herald. **king of beasts,** the lion. **king of birds,** the eagle. **King of Kings,** God, the title of various Oriental monarchs. **king of metals,** gold. **King of Terrors,** death. **King of the Castle,** *n.* a children's game; the most important person in a group. **king of the forest,** the oak. **king-bird,** *n.* an American tyrant flycatcher, *Tyrannus carolinensis;* a king bird of Paradise, *Paradisea regia.* **king-bolt,** *n.* a main or central pin, bolt or pivot. **king-cobra,** *n.* a large, venomous cobra. **King Country,** *n.* the name given to a central part of North Island, New Zealand. **king-crab,** *n.* a large crustacean with a carapace shaped like a horseshoe, of the genus *Limulus.* **king-craft,** *n.* the art of governing; kingly statesmanship. **king-cup,** *n.* the bulbous buttercup, *Ranunculus bulbosus,* the marsh marigold, *Caltha palustris,* and some allied species. **kingfish,** *n.* a food and game fish. **kingfisher,** *n.* any bird of the genus *Alcedo,* esp. *A. ispida,* a small British bird with brilliant blue and green plumage, subsisting on fish. **kingklip,** *n.* an eel-like fish. **king-maker,** *n.* one who sets up kings, esp. Richard Neville, Earl of Warwick, who supported the Houses of York and Lancaster alternately in the Wars of the Roses. **king penguin,** the largest of the penguins, *Aptenodytes longirostris* or *A. patagonica,* also called the emperor penguin. **king-pin,** *n.* the centre pin in ninepins; (*coll.*) a most important person. **kingpost,** *n.* the middle post of a roof, reaching from the ridge to the tie-beam; a strut to which an aeroplane's bracing wires are fixed. **king prawn,** *n.* a large prawn. **King's Bench** BENCH. **King/Queen's Champion,** *n.* in English history, ceremonial office held by virtue of possessing the lordship of Scrivelsby, Lincolnshire. Sir John Dymoke established his right to champion the monarch on coronation day 1377 and it is still held by his descendant. **King's Counsel** COUNSEL. **King's evidence** EVIDENCE. **King's evil,** *n.* scrofula, formerly believed to be cured by the royal touch. **King's highway,** *n.* a public road, a right-of-way. **king-size, king-sized,** *a.* of beds etc., larger than is usual. **king's spear,** *n.* the white asphodel, *Asphodelus albus.* **king's yellow,** orpiment or yellow arsenic used as a pigment. **kingdom,** *n.* the territory under rule of a king; the position or attributes of a king; sovereign power or authority; a domain, a territory; the highest and most comprehensive of the divisions into which natural objects are arranged. **kingdom come,** the world to come. **United Kingdom,** Great Britain and Northern Ireland. **kingdomed,** *a.* in the condition of a kingdom; †furnished with a kingdom. **kinghood,** *n.* **kingless,** *a.* **kinglet,** *n.* a petty king; the golden-crested wren, *Regulus cristatus.* **king-like,** *a.* †**kingling,** *n.* **kingly,** *a., adv.* **kingliness, kinglihood,** *n.* **kingship,** *n.* **kingwood,** *n.* a fine, hard wood from Brazil, used for turning and cabinet work. [OE *cyning* (*cyn,* KIN, -ING), cp. Dut. *koning,* Icel. *konungr,* G *könig*]

King[1], *n.* **Billie Jean** (born Moffitt) (1943–), US lawn tennis player. She won a record 20 Wimbledon titles 1961–79 and 39 Grand Slam titles.

King[2], *n.* **Martin Luther, Jr** (1929–1968), US civil-rights campaigner, black leader, and Baptist minister. He first came to national attention as leader of the Montgomery, Alabama, bus boycott 1955, and was one of the organizers of the massive (200,000 people) march on Washington DC 1963 to demand racial equality. An advocate of nonviolence, he was awarded the Nobel Peace Prize 1964. He was assassinated. The third Monday in Jan. is celebrated as Martin Luther King Day, a public holiday in the US.

King[3], *n.* **William Lyon Mackenzie** (1874–1950), Canadian Liberal prime minister 1921–26, 1926–30, and 1935–48. He maintained the unity of the English- and French-speaking populations, and was instrumental in establishing equal status for Canada with Britain.

King Lear, *n.* tragedy by William Shakespeare, first performed 1605–06. Lear, king of Britain, favours his grasping daughters Goneril and Regan with shares of his kingdom but refuses his third, honest daughter, Cordelia, a share. Rejected by Goneril and Regan, the old and unbalanced Lear is reunited with Cordelia but dies of grief when she is murdered.

Kingsley[1], *n.* **Ben (Krishna Banji)** (1944–), British film actor of Indian descent, who usually plays character parts. He played the title role of *Gandhi* 1982 and also appeared *Betrayal* 1982, *Testimony* 1987, and *Pascali's Island* 1988.

Kingsley[2], *n.* **Charles** (1819–1875), English author. Rector of Eversley, Hampshire 1842–75, he was known as the 'Chartist clergyman' because of such social novels as *Alton Locke* 1850. His historical novels include *Westward Ho!* 1855 and, for children, *The Water-Babies* 1863.

Kingston, *n.* capital and principal port of Jamaica, West Indies; the cultural and commercial centre of the island; population (1983) 101,000, metropolitan area 525,000. Founded 1693, Kingston became the capital of Jamaica 1872.

Kingston-upon-Hull, *n.* official name of Hull, city in Humberside in NE England.

Kingstown, *n.* capital and principal port of St Vincent and the Grenadines, West Indies, in the SW of the island of St Vincent; population (1987) 29,000.

kinin, *n.* a hormone which causes dilation of the blood vessels; a plant hormone which promotes cell division and slows down the aging process in plants. [Gr. *kinema,* movement, -IN]

kink, *n.* a twist or abrupt bend in a rope, thread, wire etc.; a prejudice, a crotchet, a whim. *v.i.* to twist or run into kinks. *v.t.* to cause to kink. **kinkle,** *n.* a slight twist; an arrangement of bricks in an oven or for drying, courses being laid at opposite angles in alternate courses. **kinky,** *a.* twisted; curly; given to abnormal sexual practices; provocative. **kinkily,** *adv.* **kinkiness,** *n.* [prob. from Dut. *kink* (cp. Dan., Swed., Norse and G *Kink*)]

kinkajou, *n.* an arboreal carnivorous quadruped, *Cercoleptes caudivolvulus,* of S and Central America, allied to the racoon, with long body and prehensile tail. [F *quincajou,* from Algonquian]

Kinki, *n.* region of S Honshu island, Japan; population(1986) 21,932,000; area 33,070 sq km/12,773 sq miles. Chief city is Osaka.

kinless KIN.

kinnikinic, *n.* the leaves of the sumach or the bark of willow or cornel, dried and prepared for smoking; one of various plants used for this purpose. [Algonquin]

Kinnock, *n.* **Neil** (1942–), British Labour politician, party leader from 1983. Born and educated in Wales, he was elected to represent a Welsh constituency in Parliament 1970 (Islwyn from 1983). A noted orator, he was further left than prime ministers Wilson and Callaghan, but as party leader (in succession to Michael Foot) adopted a more moderate position, initiating a major policy review 1988–89.

kino, *n.* an astringent gum used for tanning or dyeing and in medicine, obtained from certain Indian, African and Australian trees. [prob. W Afr.]

Kinross-shire, *n.* former county of E central Scotland, merged in 1975 in Tayside region. Kinross was the county town.

Kinsey, *n.* **Alfred** (1894–1956), US researcher, whose studies of male and female sexual behaviour 1948–53, based on questionnaires, were the first serious published research on this topic.

kinsfolk KIN.

Kinshasa, (formerly) **Léopoldville,** *n.* capital of Zaïre on the river Zaïre, 400 km/250 miles inland from Matadi; population (1984) 2,654,000. Industries include chemicals, textiles, engineering, food processing, and furniture. It was founded by the explorer Henry Stanley 1887.

Kinski, *n.* **Klaus** (1926–), German actor who has appeared in several Werner Herzog films such as; *For a Few Dollars More* (1965), *Dr Zhivago* (1965), *Aguirre Wrath of God* (1972), *Nosferatu* (1978), and *Venom* (1982).

kiosk, *n.* an open pavilion or summerhouse; a light ornamental structure for the sale of newspapers etc.; a public telephone booth; band-stand. [F *kiosque,* Turk. *kiushk,* Pers. *kūshk,* palace, villa]

kip¹, *n.* the hide of a calf or of small cattle, used for leather; leather made from such skins. **kip-leather, kip-skin,** *n.* [etym. doubtful]

kip², *n.* (*sl.*) a common lodging-house; a bed; a brothel; a (period of) sleep. *v.i.* (*past, p.p.* **kipped**) to lie down to sleep; to sleep. **to kip down,** to go to sleep. [cp. Dan. *kippe*]

kip³, *n.* a wooden bat for tossing coins in the game of two-up. [Austral.]

kipe, *n.* an osier basket for catching fish. [OE *cype*]

Kipling, *n.* **(Joseph) Rudyard** (1865–1936), British writer, born in India. His stories for children include the *Jungle Books* (1894–1895), *Stalky and Co* (1899), and the *Just So Stories* (1902). Other works include the novel *Kim* (1901), poetry, and the unfinished autobiography *Something of Myself* (1937). In his heyday he enjoyed enormous popularity, but was subsequently denigrated for alleged 'jingoist imperialism'. Nobel prize 1907.

kippage, *n.* (*Sc.*) a state of excitement or rage, a tantrum. [corr. of EQUIPAGE]

kipper, *n.* a male salmon during the spawning season; a salmon or herring split open, salted, and smoke-dried *v.t.* to cure and preserve (salmon, herrings etc.) by rubbing with salt, pepper etc., and drying or smoking. **kipperer,** *n.* [etym. doubtful; identity with OE *cypera,* a kind of salmon, uncertain]

kir, *n.* a drink, made from white wine and cassis. [F. *Kir,* 1876–1968, mayor of Dijon, France, who invented it]

Kirbigrip®, kirby grip, *n.* a type of hair-grip.

Kirchner, *n.* **Ernst Ludwig** (1880–1938), German expressionist artist, a leading member of the group Die Brücke in Dresden and later in Berlin. He suffered a breakdown during World War I and settled in Switzerland, where he committed suicide.

Kirghiz, *n.* a pastoral people who inhabit the Central Asian region bounded by the Hindu Kush, Himalayas, and the Tian Shan mountains. The Kirghiz are Sunni Muslims and their Turkic language belongs to the Altaic family.

Kirghizia, *n.* constituent republic of the USSR from 1936, part of Soviet Central Asia. **area** 198,500 sq km/ 76,641 sq miles. **capital** Frunze. **physical** mountainous, an extension of the Tian Shan range. **population** (1987) 4,143,000; Kirghiz 48% (related to the Kazakhs, they are of Mongol-Tatar origin), Russian 26%, Uzbek 12%, Ukrainian 3%, Tatar 2%. **products** cereals, sugar, cotton, coal, oil, sheep, yaks, horses. **language** Kirghiz. **religion** Sunni Muslim.

Kiribati, Republic of, an independent country in the central Pacific. **area** 717 sq km/277 sq miles. **capital** and port Bairiki (on Tarawa Atoll). **physical** comprises 33 Pacific islands: the Gilbert, Phoenix, and Line Islands, and Banaba (Ocean Island). **population** (1987) 66,250; annual growth rate 1.7%. **exports** copra. **language** English and Gilbertese (official). **religion** Christian, both Roman Catholic and Protestant.

Kirin, *n.* former name for Jilin, Chinese province.

Kirk, *n.* **Norman** (1923–1974), New Zealand Labour politician. He led the Labour party from 1965, and was prime minister 1972–74.

kirk, *n.* (*Sc., North.*) a church, the Established Church of Scotland, esp. in contradistinction to the Church of England or the Scottish Episcopal Church. **at kirk and market,** (*Sc. coll.*) on all occasions. **Auld Kirk,** the Established Church of Scotland. **Free Kirk,** the Free Church of Scotland. **kirkman,** *n.* **kirk-session,** *n.* the lowest court in the Kirk of Scotland and other Presbyterian Churches consisting of the minister and elders. [var. of CHURCH]

Kirkcudbright, *n.* former county of S Scotland, merged 1975 in Dumfries and Galloway region. The county town was Kirkcudbright.

kirn¹, *n.* (*Sc.*) a harvest home; the last sheaf of the harvest. **to win, get the kirn,** to cut the last armful of corn; to finish the harvest. **kirn-baby,** *n.* an image dressed up with corn, carried before reapers to the harvest home. **kirn-dolly,** *n.* a doll made from the last corn cut. [etym. doubtful]

kirn², CHURN.

Kirov, *n.* **Sergei Mironovich** (1886–1934), Russian Bolshevik leader, who joined the Communist party in 1904 and took a prominent part in the 1917–20 civil war. His assassination 1934, which was possibly engineered by Stalin, led to the political trials held during the next four years.

kirsch, kirschwasser, *n.* an alcoholic liqueur distilled from the fermented juice of the black cherry. [G (*Kirsche,* cherry, *Wasser,* water)]

kirtle, *n.* an upper garment of various kinds; a woman's gown or petticoat; a man's short jacket. *v.t.* to dress in a kirtle. [OE *cyrtel*]

Kishi, *n.* **Nobusuke** (1896–1987), Japanese politician and prime minister 1957–60. A government minister during World War II and imprisoned 1945, he was never put on trial and returned to politics 1953. During his premiership, Japan began a substantial rearmament programme and signed a new treaty with the US, which gave greater equality in the relationship between the two states.

Kishinev, *n.* capital of the Moldavian Republic, USSR; population (1987) 663,000. Industries include cement, food processing, tobacco, and textiles.

kismet, *n.* fate, destiny. [Turk. *qismet,* Pers. *qismat,* Arab. *qisma(t),* from *qasama,* to divide]

kiss, *n.* a caress or salute with the lips; a mere touch of the moving balls; a confection of sugar, white of eggs etc. *v.t.* to salute or caress by pressing or touching with the lips; to touch or graze in passing (of a ball or balls). *v.i.* to join lips in affection or respect; of moving balls, to come in contact. **kiss and sell,** (*coll.*) the practice of revealing details of one's sexual relationships for money, as to a newspaper. **kiss-and-tell,** (*coll.*) the practice of publishing memoirs, etc. that describe, one's sexual relationships or other confidential matters. **kiss in the ring,** a game for a number of young people in which the player chases and kisses one of the opposite sex. **kiss of death,** something which will inevitably lead to failure. **kiss of life,** mouth-to-mouth resuscitation. **kiss of peace,** a ceremonial entrance in the Christian church. **to kiss away,** to wipe away by kissing. **to kiss hands,** to kiss one's sovereign's hands when one accepts office. **to kiss the book,** to touch the Bible with the lips in taking an oath. **to kiss the dust,** to be conquered, to yield; to die, to be slain. **to kiss the ground, earth,** to bow down, to prostrate oneself; to be conquered. **to kiss the rod,** to submit tamely to punishment. **kissagram,** *n.* a greetings service where the person employed to deliver the greeting kisses the person who is celebrating. **kiss-curl,** *n.* a curl hanging over the forehead, in front of the ear, or at the nape of the neck. **kiss-me-quick,** *n.* the wild pansy or heartsease, *Viola tricolor;* a small old-fashioned bonnet. **kisser,** *n.* one who kisses; (*sl.*) the mouth. **kissing,** *n., a.* †**kissing-comfits,** *n.pl.* perfumed sugar-plums. **kissing-cousin,** *n.* a relation familiar enough to be kissed on meeting. **kissing-crust,** *n.* the soft portion of the crust of a loaf where it touched another loaf in baking. **kissing-gate,** *n.* a gate hung in a U- or V-shaped enclosure. **kissable,** *a.* [OE *coss,* whence the v. *cyssan*]

Kissinger, *n.* **Henry** (1923–), German-born US diplomat. In 1969 he was appointed assistant for National Security Affairs by President Nixon, and was secretary of state 1973–77. His missions to the USSR and China improved US relations with both countries, and he took part in negotiating US withdrawal from Vietnam 1973 and in Arab-Israeli peace negotiations 1973–75. Nobel Peace Prize 1973.

kist, CIST.

kistvaen, *n.* a cist, a tomb formed of stone slabs. [W *cist faen* (*cist,* chest, *faen, maen,* stone)]

Kiswahili, *n.* another name for Swahili language.

kit¹, *n.* a wooden tub, a milk-pail, a tub for pickled fish, butter etc.; a chest, a box; that which contains the necessaries, tools etc., for a particular purpose; hence, an outfit, esp. the equipment of a soldier; the bag or valise containing these; (*coll.*) the whole lot; pieces of equipment, sold as a set, and ready for assembly. **to kit out, up,** to fit out with the necessary clothes or equipment. **kit-bag,** *n.* a strong bag for holding a person's gear, esp. a serviceman's. **kit-boat, -car,** *n.* a boat or car assembled from a set of pieces by an amateur. [MDut. *kitte,* a wooden bowl or tub]

kit², *n.* a small violin used by dancing-masters. [etym. doubtful]

kit³, *n.* a kitten. **kit-cat¹,** *n.* the game of tip-cat. [short for KITTEN]

Kitaj, *n.* **Ron B.** (1932–), US painter and printmaker, active in Britain. His work is mainly figurative, and his distinctive decorative pale palette was in part inspired by studies of the Impressionist Degas.

Kitakyushu, *n.* industrial (coal, steel, chemicals, cotton thread, plate glass, alcohol) city and port in Japan, on the Hibiki Sea, N Kyushu, formed 1963 by the amalgamation of Moji, Kokura, Tobata, Yawata, and Wakamatsu; population (1987) 1,042,000. A tunnel 1942 links it with Honshu.

Kitasato, *n.* **Shibasaburo** (1852–1931), Japanese bacteriologist who discovered the plague bacillus. Kitasato was the first to grow the tetanus bacillus in pure culture. He and the German bacteriologist Behring discovered that increasing non-lethal doses of tetanus toxin gives immunity to the disease.

kit-cat², *n.* a portrait of a particular size, rather less than half-length; a size of canvas 28 by 36 in. (about 70 by 90 cm), used for portraits, that size being adopted by Kneller for the portraits he painted of the Kit-cat Club; a member of this club. **Kit-cat Club,** a club founded in 1688 by Whig politicians, meeting at a pie-house near Temple Bar kept by Christopher Cat or catling. [*Kit* (or Christopher) *Cat* or *Catling*]

kitchen, *n.* the room in a house etc. where food is cooked. †*v.t.* to regale or feed in a kitchen. **kitchen-dresser** DRESSER². **Kitchen Dutch,** *n.* a mixture of Dutch or Kaffir with English. **kitchen-garden,** *n.* a garden in which fruit and vegetables are cultivated for the table. **kitchen-knave,** *n.* a scullion. **kitchen-maid,** *n.* a female servant whose business it is to assist the cook. **kitchen-midden** [Dan. *kjökken-mödding*], *n.* a prehistoric refuse-heap, or shell-mound, first noticed on the coast of Denmark, and since found in the British Isles etc. **kitchen range,** *n.* a kitchen grate with oven, boiler etc., for cooking. **kitchen sideboard,** *n.* (*N Am.*) a dresser. **kitchen sink,** *a.* of a type of British drama which depicts the reality and often sordid quality of family life. **kitchen-stuff,** *n.* fat collected from dripping-pans; materials for cooking, esp. vegetables. **kitchen tea,** *n.* (*Austral., New Zealand*) a party held before a wedding to which the guests bring gifts of kitchenware. **kitchen unit,** *n.* a complete set of modern kitchen furniture. **kitchenware,** *n.* the pots, pans, china and cutlery used in the kitchen. **kitchen-wench,** *n.* **kitchener,** *n.* a close cooking-range; one employed in a kitchen, esp. that of a monastery. **kitchenette,** *n.* a small kitchen and scullery. [OE *cycene,* late L, *cucīna,* L *coquīna,* from *coquere,* to cook]

Kitchener, *n.* **Horatio Herbert, Earl Kitchener of Khartoum** (1850–1916), British soldier and administrator. He defeated the Sudanese dervishes at Omdurman 1898 and re-occupied Khartoum. In South Africa, he was chief of staff 1900–02 during the Boer War, and commanded the forces in India 1902–09. He was appointed war minister on the outbreak of World War I, and drowned when his ship was sunk on the way to Russia.

kite, *n.* a medium-sized bird of the raptorial genus *Milvus,* esp. *M. ictinus,* the common or European kite or glede; a greedy or rapacious person, a sharper; a device consisting of a light frame of wood and paper constructed to fly in the air by means of a string; (*sl.*) an aircraft; (*Comm. sl.*) an accommodation note or bill; (*pl.*) light sails, set only in very light winds, above the other sails. *v.i.* to fly like a kite; (*sl.*) to fly a kite. *v.t.* (*sl.*) to issue or convert into an accommodation bill. **to fly a kite,** to try how the wind blows; (*Comm. sl.*) to raise money on an accommodation bill; to find out about a situation, public opinion etc. **kite-balloon,** *n.* an observation-balloon moored to the ground. **kite-flyer,** *n.* **kite-flying,** *n.* flying and controlling a kite; the circulation of rumours to test public opinion. **kite-mark,** *n.* a kite-shaped mark indicating that goods conform in all particulars with the specifications of the British Standards Institution. [OE *cȳta*]

kith, *n.* kindred. **kith and kin,** close friends and relations; relatives only. [OE *cythth,* knowledge, native country, from *cūth,* known (*cunnan,* to know)]

kithe, KYTHE.

kitling, *n.* (*dial.*) a kitten. **kittle¹,** *v.i.* (*Sc.*) to kitten. [prob. from Icel. *ketlingr,* dim. of *köttr,* cat]

kitmutgar, *n.* a male servant. [Hind.]

kitsch, *n.* art or literature that is inferior or in bad taste, and designed to appeal to popular taste. **kitschy,** *a.* [G]

kitten, *n.* the young of the cat; a playful girl. *v.i.* to bring forth young, as a cat. **to have kittens,** (*coll.*) to be over-excited, very annoyed etc. **kittenish,** *a.* **kitty,** *n.* a pet-name for a kitten. [ME *kitoun,* OF *chitoun* (F *chaton*), from *chat,* cat]

kittiwake, *n.* a seagull of the genus *Rissa,* esp. *R. tridactyla,* common on the British coasts. [imit. of its cry]

kittle¹ KITLING.

kittle², *v.t.* (*now chiefly Sc.*) to tickle; to excite a pleasant sensation in, to rouse. *a.* ticklish, awkward to deal with, intractable. **kittly,** *a.* [etym. doubtful, perh. from a non-extant OE *citelian,* or from Scand. (cp. Icel. *kitla,* Swed. *kittla*)]

kitty¹ KITTEN.

kitty[2], *n.* the pool into which each player puts a stake in poker, and other games; a common fund of money.

kiwi, *n.* the New Zealand apteryx or wingless bird; (*coll.*) a New Zealander. [Maori]

kiwi fruit, *n.* the edible green fruit of the Chinese gooseberry, an Asiatic climbing plant.

KKK, (*abbr.*) Ku Klux Klan.

kl., (*abbr.*) kilolitre.

Klammer, *n.* **Franz** (1953–), Austrian skier, who won a record 35 World Cup downhill races between 1974 and 1985. Olympic gold medallist 1976.

Klan KU KLUX KLAN.

Klaproth, *n.* **Martin Heinrich** (1743–1817), German chemist who first identified the elements uranium, zirconium, cerium, and titanium.

klaxon®, *n.* a loud horn formerly used on cars.

Klee, *n.* **Paul** (1879–1940), Swiss painter. He settled in Munich 1906, joined the Blaue Reiter group 1912, and worked at the Bauhaus school of art and design 1920–31, returning to Switzerland 1933. His style in the 1920s and 1930s was dominated by humorous linear fantasies.

Kleenex®, *n.* (*pl.* **Kleenex, Kleenexes**) soft paper tissue used as a handkerchief etc.

Klein[1], *n.* **Melanie** (1882–1960), Austrian child psychoanalyst. She pioneered child psychoanalysis and play studies, and was influenced by Sigmund Freud's theories. She published *The Psychoanalysis of Children* in 1960.

Klein[2], *n.* **Yves** (1928–1962), French painter of bold abstracts and provocative experimental works, including imprints of nude bodies.

Klein bottle, *n.* in mathematics, a one-sided surface surrounding a three-dimensional space, formed by putting the narrow end of tapered tube through the surface of the tube, then stretching it to fit into the other end. [Felix *Klein*, 1849–1925, G mathematician]

kleisto- CLEISTO-.

Klepht, *n.* one of the Greeks who refused to submit to the Turks after the conquest (15th cent.), and carried on a predatory existence in the mountains. [mod. Gr. *klephtēs*, Gr. *kleptēs*, thief]

klepsydra, CLEPSYDRA.

kleptomania, *n.* a form of insanity or mental aberration displaying itself in an irresistible propensity to steal. **kleptomaniac**, *n.* [Gr. *kleptēs*, as KLEPHT, -MANIA]

Klieglight, *n.* a powerful arc lamp used as floodlighting in a film studio. [John *Kliegl*, 1869–1959, and Anton *Kliegl*, 1872–1927, inventors]

Klimt, *n.* **Gustav** (1862–1918), Austrian painter, influenced by jugendstil ('Youth Style', a form of art nouveau); a founder member of the Vienna sezession group 1897. His works include mosaics, and his paintings have a similar jewelled effect, for example *The Kiss* 1909 (Musée des Beaux-Arts, Strasbourg). He painted many portraits.

Klinefetter's syndrome, *n.* an abnormality in a man, with infertility and small testicles as symptoms, characterized by two X and a single Y chromosomes. [Harry *Klinefetter*, b. 1912, US physician]

klipdas, *n.* the Cape hyrax, *Hyrax capensis*. [Afrikaans]

klipspringer, *n.* a small South African antelope, *Oreotragus saltator*. [Afrikaans *klip*, rock, SPRINGER]

Klondike, Klondyke *n.* former gold-mining area in Yukon, Canada, and named after the river valley where gold was found 1896. About 30,000 people moved there during the following 15 years. Silver is still mined there; a source of wealth. *v.t.*, *v.i.* to export (usu. fish) directly from Scotland to the Continent.

kloof, *n.* (*S Afr.*) a ravine, gully or mountain gorge. [Dut., cleft]

Klopstock, *n.* **Friedrich Gottlieb** (1724–1803), German poet, whose religious epic *Der Messias/The Messiah* (1748–73) and *Oden/Odes* (1771) anticipated Romanticism.

Klosters, *n.* alpine skiing resort NE of Davos in E Switzerland.

klystron, *n.* an electron tube used to amplify or generate microwaves. [Gr. *klyster*, syringe]

km, (*abbr.*) kilometre.

knack, *n.* a trick or adroit way of doing a thing; dexterity, adroitness; a habit, a mannerism; †a toy, a knick-knack. †**knacker**[1], *n.* a maker of knick-knacks; (*pl.*) two pieces of wood used as castanets. **knackish, knacky**, *a.* **knackiness**, *n.* [prob. onomat.]

knacker[2], *n.* a dealer in worn-out horses; a horse-slaughterer; a dealer in second-hand goods, houses, ships etc. **knackery**, *n.* [perh. from prec., a dealer in KNACKS]

knackwurst, *n.* a spicy sausage. [G *knacken*, to crackle, *wurst*, sausage]

knag, *n.* a knot in wood; a knob, a peg; the shoot of a deer's horn; the rough or rugged top of a hill or rock. **knagged, knaggy**, *a.* [cp. G *knagge*, Norw. and Swed. *knagg*]

knap[1], *n.* a protuberance, a knob; a hill-crest, rising ground. [OE *cnæpp*, prob. cogn. with Icel. *knappr*, Dan. *knap*, a KNOB]

knap[2], *v.t.* (*past, p.p.* **knapped**) to break into pieces, esp. with a sharp snapping noise; to break, flake, or chip flint; to strike smartly. *v.i.* to make a sharp, cracking noise. **knapper, flint-knapper**, *n.* one who breaks flints; one who shapes gun-flints, flint implements etc. †**knap-bottle**, *n.* the bladder-campion, *Silene inflata*. †**knapple**, *v.i.* to break off with a sharp, cracking noise. [imit., cp. Dut. *knappen*]

knapsack, *n.* a case or bag for clothes etc., carried on the back during a march by soldiers or tourists etc. **knapsackwise**, *adv.* [cp. Dut. *knapzak* (*knappen*, to snap, to bite, to eat, *zak*, SACK[1])]

knapweed, *n.* a composite plant with purple globular flowers, of the genus *Centaurea*, esp. *C. nigra*, the black knapweed and *C. scabiosa*, the great knapweed. [formerly *knopweed* (KNOP, WEED)]

†**knar, gnar**, *n.* a knot in wood; a protuberance on the trunk or branch of a tree; a tough, thickset, rough fellow. [ME *knarre* (cp. LG *knarre*, Dut. *knar*)]

†**knarled**, GNARL.

knave, *n.* a deceitful, cunning fellow, a rogue; a court-card with a representation of a soldier or servant, the jack; †a boy; †a servant. **knave-bairn, -child**, *n.* a male child. **knave-ship**, *n.* the quality of being a knave; (*Sc.*) a portion of corn or meal paid to a miller's servant as his due. **knavery**, *n.* dishonesty. **knavish**, *a.* fraudulent. **knavishly**, *adv.* **knavishness**, *n.* [OE *cnafa*, a boy (cp. Dut. *knaap*, Icel. *knapi*, G, *knabe*)]

knead, *v.t.* to work up (flour, clay etc.) with the hands into a plastic mass; to work or incorporate into dough: to shape, fashion, mingle or blend by this method; to work thus on (the muscles etc.) in massage. **kneadable**, *a.* **kneader**, *n.* **kneading-trough**, *n.* a trough in which dough is worked up. [OE *cnedan* (cp. Dut. *kneden*, G *kneten*)]

knee, *n.* the joint of the thigh or femur with the leg; a joint roughly corresponding to this in animals; the part of a garment covering the knee; a piece of timber or metal cut or cast with an angle like that of the knee to connect beams etc.; anything resembling a knee in shape or function; †a genuflection; †a courtesy. *v.t.* to touch or strike with the knee; to fasten or strengthen (beams etc.) with knees; (*coll.*) to cause (trousers) to bag at the knees. **on the knees of the gods**, as yet undetermined. **to bring to one's knees**, to reduce to submission. **to give a knee to**, to support on one's knee during a pause in a fight or contest; to act as second to. **knee-breeches**, *n.pl.* breeches reaching just below the knee. **knee-cap**, *n.* a padded cover for the knee; the heart-shaped sesamoid bone in front of the knee-joint; *v.t.* to shoot or injure someone in the knees. **knee-capping**, *n.* †**knee-crooking**, *a.* prone to bend the knee; cringing. **knee-deep**, *a.* sunk in as far as the knees. **knee-high**, *a.* coming up to the knee. **knee-hole**, *n.* the hole between the pedestals of a writing-table or desk. **knee-hole table**, *n.* **knee-holly, -holm**, *n.* butcher's broom, *Ruscus aculeatus*. **knee-jerk**, *n.* a reflex kick of the lower part of the leg; (*coll.*) a reflex, an automatic reaction. **knee-joint**, *n.* the articulation of the femur with the tibia; a joint between two pieces hinged together. **knee-jointed,** *a.* (*Bot.*) forming an obtuse angle like the knee. **knee-length,** *a.* reaching down to, or up to, the knee. **knee-pan,** *n.* the knee-cap or socket of the knee. **knees-up,** *n.* a party. **knee-swell,** *n.* (*N Am., Organ etc.*) a lever for working the swell operated by the knee. **knee-tribute,** *n.* reverence shown by kneeling. **kneed,** *a.* (*usu. in comb.*, as *loose-kneed*). [OE *cnēo, cnēow* (cp. Dut. and G *knie,* Icel. *knē*, also L *genu,* Gr. *gonu*)]

kneel, *v.i.* (*past, p.p.* **knelt**), to bend or incline the knees; to fall on the knees; to support the body on the knees. **kneeler,** *n.* one who kneels; a stool or cushion for kneeling on; a name given to certain catechumens and penitents allowed to be present at certain parts of the liturgy, and to receive the benediction. [OE *cnēowlian,* from *cnēow,* KNEE]

knell, *v.i.* to ring, to toll, as a funeral bell; to sound in a mournful or ominous manner. *v.t.* to proclaim or summon by or as a knell. *n.* the sound of a bell when struck, esp. at a death or funeral; an evil omen, a death-blow. [OE *cnyllan,* from Teut. *knel-* (cp. Dut. and G *knallen,* Swed. *knalla*), imit. in orig.]

Kneller, *n.* **Godfrey** (1646–1723), German-born painter, who lived in London from 1674. He was court portraitist to Charles II, James II, William III, and George I.

knelt, *past, p.p.* KNEEL.

Knesset, *n.* the single-chamber parliament of the state of Israel. [Heb., assembly]

knew, *past* KNOW.

Knickerbocker, *n.* a New Yorker of original Dutch descent; (*pl.*) loose breeches gathered in below the knee. **knickerbocker glory,** *n.* a large ice-cream sundae, with fruit and jelly. [imag. author of Washington Irving's *History of New York*]

knickers, *n.pl.* women's underpants. **to get one's knickers in a twist,** (*coll.*) to be over-anxious, upset etc.

knick-knack, *n.* any little ornamental article; a showy trifle. **knickery-knackery,** *n.* [redupl. of KNACK]

knife, *n.* (*pl.* **knives**) a blade with one edge sharpened, usu. set in a handle; a cutting-blade forming part of a machine; †a sword or dagger. *v.t.* to cut out (shoemaker's work etc.); to prune, to cut back; (*sl.*) to stab or cut with a knife. **the knife,** surgical operations. **to have one's knife in someone,** to be vindictive towards someone. **under the knife,** (*coll.*) undergoing a surgical operation. **war to the knife,** mortal combat. **knife-bayonet,** *n.* a bayonet with a broad blade that enables it to be used as a dagger. **knife-board,** *n.* a board covered with leather or composition to clean knives on; (*coll.*) a long seat for passengers on the roof of an omnibus etc. **knife-boy,** *n.* a boy employed to clean table-knives. **knife-edge,** *n.* the edge of a knife; a hard steel edge used as fulcrum for a balance, pendulum etc.; a difficult situation where things could go either right or wrong. **knife-grass,** *n.* (*Bot.*) a tropical American sedge with knife-like edges. **knife-grinder,** *n.* one who grinds or sharpens knives, esp. an itinerant knife-sharpener. **knife-machine,** *n.* a machine for cleaning knives. **knife money,** *n.* knife-shaped bronze money current in China about 300 BC. **knife-pleat,** *n.* a single, narrow pleat. **knife-rest,** *n.* a support for a carving knife or fork at table. **knife switch,** *n.* a switch consisting of knife-like pieces hinged at one end, and having contact at the other with springs. **knife tool,** *n.* a small wheel used in seal engraving. [OE *cnīf* (cp. Dut. *knijf,* Icel. *knīfr, hnīfr,* G *kneif*)]

knight, *n.* a man of gentle birth, usu. one who had served as page and esquire, admitted to an honourable degree of military rank, with ceremonies or religious rites; one who holds a corresponding non-hereditary dignity conferred by the sovereign or his representative, and entitling the possessor to the title of 'Sir' prefixed to his name; one of the class of Equites in ancient Rome; an Athenian citizen of the middle class, as constituted by Solon; (*Chess*) a piece shaped like a horse's head entitled to move two squares straight and one at right-angles; a chivalrous or quixotic person; one acting as chevalier to a lady. *v.t.* to create or dub (a person) a knight. †**knight of the post,** a rogue, one well acquainted with the whipping-post; one who gave false evidence for hire. **knight of the road,** a footpad, a highwayman; a tramp. **knight of the shire,** (*Hist.*) a representative of an English county in Parliament. **knight-bachelor** BACHELOR. **knight-banneret,** *n.* a knight holding the rank of banneret. **knight-errant,** *n.* a mediaeval knight who wandered about in quest of adventures to show his prowess and generosity. **knight-errantry,** *n.* **knight-head,** *n.* (*Naut.*) one of a pair of vertical posts supporting the bow-sprit (the tops were formerly ornamented with figures resembling human heads). †**knight-marshal,** *n.* an official in the household of the British sovereign having cognizance of offences committed within the royal verge. **knight service,** *n.* (*Feud. Law*) tenure of land on condition of military service. **knight's fee,** *n.* (*Feud. Law*) the amount of land for which the services of a knight were accorded. **knight's progress,** *n.* in chess, a combination of moves which allow a knight to visit every square on the board. **knightage**, *n.* knights collectively. **knighthood**, *n.* **knightlike,** *a.* **knightly,** *a., adv.* **knightliness,** *n.* [OE *cniht,* a boy, a servant (cp. Dut. and G *knecht,* Swed. *knekt,* soldier)]

kniphofia, *n.* the red-hot poker. [J.H. *Kniphof,* 1704–63, G professor of medicine]

knit, *v.t.* (*past, p.p.* **knit, knitted**) to form into a fabric or form (a fabric, garment etc.) by looping or knotting a continuous yarn or thread; to join closely together, to unite; to make close or compact; to contract into folds or wrinkles; †to compound, to mix. *v.i.* to make a textile fabric by interweaving yarn or thread; to grow together; to become closely united. *n.* style of knitting; texture; a knitted garment. †*a.* allied, connected. **to knit up,** to repair by knitting; to conclude, to wind up (a speech, argument etc.). **knitwear,** *n.* knitted clothes, usu. sweaters. **knitter,** *n.* one who knits; a knitting machine. **knitting,** *n.* **knitting-machine,** *n.* an apparatus for mechanically knitting jerseys etc. **knitting-needle, -pin,** *n.* a long eyeless needle of metal, bone, wood etc., used in knitting. [OE *cnyttan* (cp. MDut. *knutten,* Icel. *knytja,* G *kntten*), rel. to KNOT[1]]

knitch, *n.* (*dial.*) a bundle, a faggot. [etym. doubtful]

knittle, *n.* a small line such as is used for slinging a hammock.

knives, *pl.* KNIFE.

knob, *n.* a rounded protuberance, usu. at the end of something; a rounded handle of a door, lock, drawer etc.; (*N Am.*) a rounded hill, a knoll; an ornamental terminal boss; a small lump (of coal, sugar etc.). *v.t.* (*past, p.p.* **knobbed**) to furnish with a knob or knobs. *v.i.* to become knobby; to bulge or bunch (out). **with knobs on,** even more so. **knobstick,** *n.* a knobbed stick used as a weapon; (*sl.*) a worker who refuses to join a strike. **knobbed, knobby,** *a.* **knobbiness,** *n.* **knobble,** *n.* a small knob. **knobbly,** *a.* **knoblike,** *a.* [cogn. with KNOP (cp. G *knobbe,* Dut. *knobbel*)]

knobkerrie, *n.* the round-headed club used as a weapon by S African tribesmen. [Afrikaans *knopkirie*]

knock, *v.t.* to strike, to hit, to give a hard blow to; to drive or force by striking; to cause to strike together. *v.i.* to strike hard or smartly (at, against, together etc.); to collide. *n.* a blow; a rap, esp. on a door for admission. **knock-for-knock,** *a.* of an agreement between vehicle insurance companies by which each company pays for the damage sustained to a vehicle insured by them irrespective of legal liability. **to knock about, around,** to strike with repeated blows; to handle violently; (*coll.*) to wander about; to lead an irregular life. **to knock back,** to drink quickly; to cost; to reject; to shock. **to knock cold,** to shock. **to knock down,** to fell with a blow; to prostrate (with astonishment etc.); to sell (with a blow of the hammer) to a bidder at an auction; (*coll.*) to call upon (for a song); to lower in price, quality etc. **to knock off,** to strike off; to dispatch, to do or finish quickly; to cease work; to leave off (work); to deduct. **to knock one's head**

against, to come into collision with (awkward facts etc.). **to knock on the head,** to stun or kill with a blow on the head; to frustrate, to spoil, to defeat. **to knock out,** to force or dash out with a blow; to disable by a particular blow. **to knock out of time,** to disable (an opponent) so that he is unable to respond when 'time' is called. **to knock sideways,** to knock off course. **to knock someone into the middle of next week,** (*coll.*) to butt someone very hard. **to knock the bottom out of,** to refute (an argument). **to knock together,** to put hastily or roughly into shape. **to knock under,** to acknowledge oneself beaten. **to knock up,** to strike or force upwards; to arouse by knocking; to fatigue, to wear out, to exhaust; to put together or make up hastily; to make (a score of runs) at cricket; (*sl.*) to make (someone) pregnant. **knock-about,** *a.* noisy, rough, violent; suitable for rough usage, as clothes; irregular, bohemian. *n.* a noisy, boisterous performance or performer (at a music-hall etc.); a light, partly-decked yacht or sailing-boat. **knockback,** *n.* a rejection. **knock-down,** *a.* of a blow, overwhelming; of a price at auction, reserve or minimum. *n.* a knock-down blow; a free fight. **knock-knees,** *n.pl.* knees bent inwards in walking. **knock-kneed,** *a.* **knock-on,** *n.* in Rugby, playing the ball with the hand or arm. **knock-on effect,** *n.* an indirect result of an action. **knock-out,** *a.* of a blow, disabling. *n.* a knock-out blow; (*sl.*) a marvel, wonder; (*sl.*) one of a gang who combine to keep bidding low at auctions and afterwards sell the purchases among themselves, dividing the profits; the sale at which the goods so obtained are resold; an auction at which this practice is carried on. **knock-out drops,** *n.pl.* (*sl.*) a drug put into someone's drink secretly. **knocker,** *n.* one who knocks; a hammer-like attachment to an outer door to give notice that someone desires admittance; a gnome or goblin who indicates the presence of hidden ore by knocking. (*pl.*) (*sl.*) a woman's breasts. **on the knocker,** promptly, at once. **knocking,** *n.* explosions in the cylinder of an internal combustion engine due to over-compression of the mixture of air and petrol vapour before sparking. **knocking copy,** *n.* publicity aimed at undermining a competing product. **knocking-shop,** *n.* (*sl.*) a brothel. [OE *cnocian, cnucian* (cp. Icel. *knoka*), prob. imit.]

knoll[1], *n.* a rounded hill; a mound, a hillock. **knolly,** *a.* [OE *cnoll* (cp. Dut. *knol,* a turnip, Swed. *knöl*, G *knollen*)]

knoll[2], *v.t.* to ring; to toll or sound out (hours); to proclaim or summon by ringing; to ring a bell or knell for. *v.i.* to sound (as a bell). **knoller,** *n.* [var. of KNELL]

knop, *n.* a knob, a button; a bunch of leaves, flowers, or similar ornaments; †a bud. **knopped,** *a.* adorned with knops. [perh. rel. to KNAP[1] (cp. Dut. and Dan. *knop,* G *knopf*)]

†**knosp,** *n.* a knob, a boss; an ornamental flower-bud or boss. [prob. from G *knospe*]

Knossos, *n.* the chief city of Minoan Crete, near present-day Iráklion, 6 km/4 miles SE of Candia. The archaeological site excavated by Arthur Evans 1899–1935, dates from about 2000 BC, and includes the palace throne room and a labyrinth, legendary home of the Minotaur.

knot[1], *n.* the interlacement or intertwining of a rope or ropes, cords etc., so as to fasten one part to another part of the rope etc. or to another object; an ornamental bow or interlacement of a ribbon etc. on a dress; (usu. **porters' knot, shoulder-knot**) a kind of double shoulder-pad, with a loop passing round the forehead, used by London market-porters for carrying burdens; a difficulty, a perplexity, a problem; something not easily solved; the gist or kernel of a matter; anything resembling a knot; an irregular or twisted portion in a tree caused by branches, buds etc. a tangle; a node or joint in a stem; a protuberance or excrescence; a flower-bud; a hard cross-grained part in a piece of wood, caused by interlacing fibres; a hard lump in the body of an animal; a group, a cluster; a division of the log-line marked off by knots, used as a unit for measuring speed; (*loosely*) a nautical mile per hour. *v.t.* (*past, p.p.* **knotted**) to tie in a knot or knots; to fasten with a knot; to intertwine; to make (fringe) by means of knots; to knit (the brows); to join together closely or intricately; to entangle, to perplex. *v.i.* of plants, to form knots; to make knots for fringe. **at a rate of knots,** very fast. **to tie someone up in knots,** to confuse someone completely. **knot-garden,** *n.* a formal garden. **knot-grass,** *n.* a prostrate plant, *Polygonum aviculare,* with internodes and white, pink, crimson or green inconspicuous flowers. **knot-hole,** *n.* a hole in wood where a knot used to be. **knot-work,** *n.* ornamental fringe made by knotting cords together; representation of this in painting or carving; a kind of ornamental needlework. **knotless,** *a.* **knotted,** *a.* **get knotted!,** an expression of anger, exasperation etc. **knotter,** *n.* **knotting,** *n.* fancy knotted work; the removal of knots from textile fabrics. **knotty,** *a.* full of knots; rugged, rough; intricate; perplexing, difficult of solution. **knottiness,** *n.* †**knottypated,** *a.* blockheaded. [OE *cnotta* (cp. Dut. *knot,* G *knoten*)]

knot[2], *n.* a small wading-bird, *Tringa canutus,* of the snipe family, visiting Britain in the late summer and autumn. [etym. unknown]

knout, *n.* a whip or scourge formerly used as an instrument of punishment in Russia. *v.t.* to punish with the knout. [F, from Rus. *knutu*]

know, *v.t.* (*past* **knew,** *p.p.* **known**) to have a clear and certain perception of; to recognize from memory or description, to identify; to be convinced of the truth or reality of; to be acquainted with; to have personal experience of; to be familiar with; to be on intimate terms with; to be aware of; to understand from learning or study; †to have sexual intercourse with; to be informed of. *v.i.* to have knowledge; to be assured (of); †to be acquainted. *n.* knowledge, knowing. **in the know,** in the secret; acquainted with what is going on. **to know better,** to be well informed (to believe etc.). **to know how many beans make five,** to have one's wits about one. **to know of,** to be informed of; †to ask, to inquire. **to know the ropes,** (*coll.*) to be acquainted with the particular conditions of any affair or proceeding. **to know what's what,** to be wideawake; to know the ways of the world; to appreciate a good thing. **to know which side one's bread is buttered,** to appreciate what is in one's best interests. **to not know someone from Adam,** to have no idea at all who somebody is. **what do you know?,** an expression of incredulity. **you never know,** things are never certain. **know-all,** *n.* (*derog.*) someone who thinks they know everything. **know-how,** *n.* (*coll.*) specialized skill, expertise. **know-it-all,** *n.* (*derog.*) a know-all. **know-nothing,** *n.* an ignorant person; an agnostic. **knowable,** *a.* **knowability, knowableness,** *n.* **knower,** *n.* **knowing,** *a.* intelligent; conscious; skilful, experienced; sharp, cunning, wideawake; (*coll.*) smart, stylish. **there is no knowing,** one can never tell. **knowingly,** *adv.* **knowingness,** *n.* [OE *cnāwan* (cp. Icel. *knā,* OHG *chnāan,* cogn. with L *gnōscere,* Gr. *gignōskein,* Sansk. *jnā-*)]

knowledge, *n.* the result of knowing; that which is known; certain or clear apprehension of truth or fact; cognition, the process of knowing; familiarity gained by actual experience; learning; erudition, science, the sum of what is known; information, notice; range or scope of information; †sexual intercourse. **to the best of my** etc. **knowledge,** as far as I etc. know. **knowledgeable,** *a.* (*coll.*) sharp, intelligent. **knowledgeably,** *adv.* [ME *knowledge* (KNOW, *-lege,* etym. doubtful)]

known, *p.p.* KNOW.

Knox[1], *n.* **John** (*c.* 1505–1572), Scottish Protestant reformer, founder of the Church of Scotland. He spent several years in exile for his beliefs, including a period in Geneva where he met John Calvin. He returned to Scotland 1559 to promote Presbyterianism.

Knox[2], *n.* **Ronald Arbuthnott** (1888–1957), British Roman Catholic scholar, whose translation of the Bible (1945–49) was officially approved by the Roman

Catholic Church.
knt., (*abbr.*) knight.
knub, *n.* a lump, a knob; (*usu. pl.*) the waste silk produced in winding off from the cocoon, the innermost wrapping of the chrysalis. [var. of KNOB]
knubble, nubble, *v.t.* to beat.
knuckle, *n.* one of the joints of a finger, esp. at the base; the middle or tarsal joint of a quadruped; a joint of meat comprising this and adjoining parts; a knuckle-shaped joint or part in a structure, machinery etc.; †a joint in a plant stem. *v.t.* to hit with the knuckles. *v.i.* to submit, to yield (with *down* or *under*); to keep the knuckles on the ground in a game of marbles. **near the knuckle,** verging on the indecent. **to knuckle down,** to get down to some hard work. **to knuckle under,** to bow to the pressure of authority. **knuckle-bone,** *n.* a bone forming the knuckle of a sheep or other animal; (*pl.*) a game played with such bones. **knuckle-duster,** *n.* an iron instrument to protect the knuckles, and to add force to a blow. **knucklehead,** *n.* (*coll.*) an idiot. **knuckleheaded,** *a.* **knuckle-joint,** *n.* a joint in which a projection on one part lies between two projections in the other, and is held in place by a screw or pin. **knuckle sandwich,** *n.* (*sl.*) a punch. **knuckly,** *adv.* [ME *knokil* (cp. MDut. *knökkel,* LG *knukkel,* G *knochel,* rel. to G *knochen,* bone)]
knur, knurr, knar, nur, nurr, *n.* a hard swelling on the trunk of a tree; a knot; a hard concretion; the hard ball used in knur and spell. **knur and spell,** a northern ball-game, in some respects resembling trap-ball and in others somewhat like golf. [ME *knor* (cp. Dut. *knor,* Dan. *knort,* G *knorren*)]
knurl, *n.* a knot, a lump, an excrescence; a bead or ridge produced on a metal surface as a kind of ornamentation; a hunch-backed dwarf; a surly, obstinate fellow. *v.t.* to make knurls, beadings, or ridges. **knurled,** *a.* milled. **knurled work,** *n.* woodwork shaped on the lathe into a series of knots or knurls. **knurly,** *a.* [prob. from prec.]
k.o., (*abbr.*) knock-out.
koa, *n.* an acacia used for cabinet-work and building, from the Sandwich Isles. [Hawaiian]
koala, koala bear, *n.* an Australian marsupial, not unlike a small bear, with dense fur, which feeds on eucalyptus leaves. [Abor. kūlā]
koan, *n.* a problem with no logical answer, used for meditation by Zen Buddhists. [Jap.]
kob, *n.* an African water-antelope of the genus *Kobus.* [African name]
Kobe, *n.* deep water port in S Honshu, Japan; population (1987) 1,413,000. Port Island, created 1960–68 from the rock of nearby mountains, area 5 sq km/2 sq miles, is one of the world's largest construction projects.
København, *n.* Danish name for Copenhagen, capital of Denmark.
kobold, *n.* a German house-spirit, corresponding to the English Robin Goodfellow, and the Scottish brownie; a gnome or goblin haunting mines and hidden lodes. [G, etym. unknown]
Koch, *n.* **Robert** (1843–1910), German bacteriologist. Koch and his assistants devised the means to culture bacteria outside the body, and formulated the rules for showing whether or not a bacterium is the cause of a disease. Nobel Prize for Medicine 1905.
Köchel number, *n.* a number given to the works of Mozart in the Köchel catalogue of his compositions. [Ludwig von *Köchel,* d. 1877, Austrian cataloguer of Mozart's work]
kochia, *n.* an annual, ornamental plant with purple-red foliage in the late summer. [N. D. J. *Koch,* 19th cent. G, botanist]
Kodály, *n.* **Zoltán** (1882–1967), Hungarian composer. With Bartók, he recorded and transcribed Magyar folk music, the scales and rhythm of of which he incorporated in a deliberately nationalist style. His works include the cantata *Psalmus Hungaricus* (1923), a comic opera *Háry János* (1925–27), and orchestral dances and variations.
kodiak, kodiak bear, *n.* a brown bear found in Alaska and the neighbouring Aleutian Islands, esp. Kodiak Island.
koeksister, *n.* (*S Afr.*) a cake made with sweetened dough. [Afrikaans, *koek* cake, *sissen,* to sizzle]
koel, *n.* an E Indian or Australasian cuckoo of the genus *Eudynamis.* [Hind. *kôīl,* from Sansk. *kokila*]
Koestler, *n.* **Arthur** (1905–1983), Hungarian author. Imprisoned by the Nazis in France 1940, he escaped to England. His novel *Darkness at Noon* (1941) is a fictional account of the Stalinist purges, and draws on his experiences as a prisoner under sentence of death during the Spanish Civil War. He also wrote extensively about creativity, parapsychology, politics, and culture. He committed suicide with his wife.
koff, *n.* a two-masted Dutch fishing-vessel, with a spritsail on each mast. [Dut.]
koh-i-noor, *n.* a famous Indian diamond which became one of the British Crown jewels on the annexation of the Punjab in 1849; anything splendid or unexampled in its own kind. [Pers. *kōh-i-nūr,* mountain of light]
kohl, *n.* fine powder of antimony used to darken the eyelids. [Arab. *kuh'l, koh'l*]
Kohl, *n.* **Helmut** (1930–), West German conservative politician, leader of the Christian Democratic Union (CDU) from 1976, and chancellor from 1982.
kohlrabi, *n.* the turnip-stemmed cabbage, *Brassica oleracea caulorapa.* [G, from It. *cavoli rapa,* cole-rape]
Koine, *n.* a Greek dialect used as a common language in the E Mediterranean during the Hellenistic and Roman periods; a lingua franca. [Gr. *koine dialektos,* common dialect]
kokanee, *n.* a salmon from one of the land-locked lakes in NW America. [*Kokanee,* creek, in British Columbia]
Kokoschka, *n.* **Oskar** (1886–1980), Austrian expressionist painter and writer, who lived in the UK from 1938. Initially influenced by the Vienna sezession painters, he developed a disturbingly expressive portrait style. His writings include several plays.
kokra, *n.* the wood of an E Indian tree, *Aporosa dioica,* used for flutes etc. [Hind.]
kola COLA.
Kolchak, *n.* **Alexander Vasilievich** (1875–1920), Russian admiral, was commander of the White forces in Siberia during the Russian Civil War. He proclaimed himself Supreme Ruler of Russia 1918, but was later handed over to the Bolsheviks by his own men and shot.
kolinsky, *n.* (*pl.* **-kies**) a type of Asian mink; the fur from this mink. [Rus. **kolinski,** from the Kola peninsula]
kolkhoz, *n.* (*pl.* **-hozy**, **-hozies**) a cooperative or collective farm in the USSR. [Rus. abbr. for *kollektivnoe khozyaistvo,* collective farm]
Koller, *n.* **Carl** (1857–1944), Austrian ophthalmologist who introduced local anaesthesia 1884.
Kollontai, *n.* **Alexandra** (1872–1952), Russian revolutionary, politician, and writer. In 1905 she published *On the Question of the Class Struggle*, and was the only female member of the first Bolshevik government as Commissar for Public Welfare. She campaigned for domestic reforms such as acceptance of free love, simplification of divorce laws, and collective childcare.
Kollwitz, *n.* **Käthe** (1867–1945), German sculptor and printmaker Her early series of etchings of workers and their environment are realistic and harshly expressive. Later themes include war, death, and maternal love.
Kol Nidre, *n.* the service marking the beginning of Yom Kippur; the opening prayer of this service. [Aram. *kol nidre,* all the vows]
komodo dragon, *n.* the largest known lizard *Veranus komodoensis,* from Indonesia. [*Komodo* Island, Indonesia]
Komsomol, *n.* Russian name for the USSR's All-Union Leninist Communist Youth League. Founded in 1918, it acts as the youth section of the Communist party; a member of this.

Kong Zi, *n.* Pinyin form of Confucius, Chinese philosopher.

Koniev, *n.* **Ivan Stepanovich** (1898–1973), soviet marshal, who in World War II liberated Ukraine from the invading German forces 1943, and advanced from the south on Berlin to link up with the British-US forces.

koniscope, *n.* an instrument for indicating the amount of dust in the atmosphere. [Gr. *konis,* dust]

Konoe, *n.* **Fumimaro** (1891–1946), Japanese politician and prime minister. Entering politics in the 1920s, Konoe was active in trying to curb the power of the army in government, and preventing an escalation of the war with China. He was prime minister for periods in the late 1930s, but finally resigned 1941 over differences with the army. He helped to engineer the fall of the Tojo government 1944, but committed suicide after being suspected of war crimes.

Kon-Tiki, *n.* legendary sun king who ruled the country later occupied by the Incas, and was supposed to have migrated out into the Pacific. The name was used by explorer Thor Heyerdahl for his raft which sailed from Peru to the Pacific Islands 1947.

koodoo, *n.* a S African antelope, *Strepsiceros kudu,* with white stripes. [Afrikaans *koedoe,* from Xhosa]

kook, *n.* (*coll.*) an eccentric, mad, or foolish person. **kookie, kooky,** *a.* [prob. from *cuckoo*]

kookaburra, *n.* the laughing jackass; Australian kingfisher. [Austral. Abor.]

koolah, *n.* a small tailless Australian marsupial, *Phascolarctos cinereus.* [Abor. name]

koomis KUMISS.

kopeck, kopek, *n.* Russian coin, the hundredth part of a rouble. [Russ. *kopeika*]

kopje, koppie, *n.* a small hill. [Dut., dim. of *kop,* head (cp. COP[1])]

Koran, *n.* the Muslim sacred scriptures consisting of the revelations delivered orally by Mohammed and collected after his death. **Koranic,** *a.* [Arab. *qurān,* from *qara'a,* to read]

Korbut, *n.* **Olga** (1955–), Soviet gymnast, who attracted world attention at the 1972 Olympic Games with her 'cheeky' floor routine, and won three gold medals.

Korda, *n.* **Alexander** (1893–1956), Hungarian-born British film producer and director, a dominant figure during the 1930s and 1940s. His films include *The Private Life of Henry VIII* (1933), *The Third Man* (1950), and *Richard III* (1956).

Korea, North, *n.* **Democratic People's Republic of. area** 120,538 sq km/46,528 sq miles. **capital** Pyongyang. **physical** mountainous. **population** (1988) 21,890,000; annual growth rate 2.5%. **exports** coal, iron, copper, textiles, chemicals. **language** Korean. **religion** traditionally Buddhist and Confucian.

Korea, South, *n.* **Republic of. area** 99,022 sq km/38,222 sq miles. **capital** Seoul. **towns** Taegu, ports Pusan, Inchon. **physical** mountainous. **population** (1987) 42,082,000; annual growth rate 1.6%. **exports** steel, ships, chemicals, electronics, textiles, plastics. **language** Korean. **religion** traditionally Buddhist and Confucian.

Korean, *a.* pertaining to Korea, its people, or its language. *n.* a person living in Korea. **Korean language,** *n.* the language of Korea, written from the 5th cent. AD in Chinese characters until the invention of an alphabet by King Sejong 1443. The linguistic affiliations of Korean are unclear, but it appears to be distantly related to Japanese. **Korean War,** *n.* war 1950–53 between North Korea (supported by China) and South Korea, aided by the United Nations (including the UK, though the troops were mainly US). North Korean forces invaded the South 25 Jun 1950, and the Security Council of the United Nations, owing to a walk-out by the USSR, voted to oppose them. After a 'concertina' campaign up and down the peninsula (initially led by the US general Douglas MacArthur), which ended in the restoration of the original boundary on the 38th parallel, an armistice was signed with the North, although South Korea did not participate in this.

korfball, *n.* a game not unlike basket-ball, with teams of six men and six women. [Dut. *korfball,* basket-ball]

korma, *n.* an Indian dish composed of braised meat or vegetables cooked in spices and a yoghurt or cream sauce.

Kornberg, *n.* **Arthur** (1918–), US biochemist. In 1956, while working on enzymes at Washington University, Kornberg discovered the enzyme DNA-polymerase which enabled molecules of DNA to be synthesized for the first time. For this work Kornberg shared the 1959 Nobel Physiology or Medicine Prize with Severo Ochoa.

Korngold, *n.* **Erich Wolfgang** (1897–1957), Austrian-born composer. He began composing operas while still in his teens and in 1934 moved to Hollywood to become a composer for Warner Brothers. His film scores combine a richly orchestrated and romantic style, reflecting the rapid changes of mood characteristic of screen action.

Korolev, *n.* **Sergei Pavlovich** (1906–1966), Soviet designer of the first Soviet intercontinental missile, used 1957 to launch the first Sputnik satellite, and 1961 to launch the Vostok spacecraft (also designed by Korolev).

Kosciusko, *n.* highest mountain in Australia (2229 m/7316 ft), in New South Wales.

Kosciuszko, *n.* **Tadeusz** (1746–1817), Polish revolutionary leader, defeated by combined Russian and Prussian forces 1794, and imprisoned until 1796. He fought for the US in the War of Independence.

kosher, *a.* permitted, right; (*coll.*) genuine, above-board; of food or a shop where it is sold, fulfilling the requirements of the Jewish law. *n.* a kosher shop or food. *v.t.* to make kosher. [Heb. *kāshēr,* right]

kosmos, COSMOS.

Kosovo, *n.* autonomous region (since 1974) in S Serbia, Yugoslavia; capital Priština; area 10,900 sq km/4207 sq miles; population (1986) 1,800,000. Products include wine, nickel, lead, and zinc. Largely inhabited by Albanians and bordering on Albania, there are demands for unification with that country, while in the late 1980s Serbians were agitating for Kosovo to be merged with the rest of Serbia.

Kossuth, *n.* **Lajos** (1802–1894), Hungarian nationalist. He proclaimed Hungarian independence of Habsburg rule 1849, and when the Hungarians were later defeated, fled first to Turkey, and then to Britain.

Kosygin, *n.* **Alexei Nikolaievich** (1904–1980), Soviet politician, prime minister 1964–80. He was elected to the Supreme Soviet 1938, became a member of the Politburo 1946, deputy prime minister 1960, and succeeded Khrushchev as premier.

koto, *n.* (*pl.* **-tos**) a Japanese stringed instrument with a wooden body and 13 silk strings. [Jap.]

kotow, kowtow, , *n.* the ancient Chinese method of obeisance by kneeling or prostrating oneself, and touching the ground with the forehead. *v.i.* to perform the kotow; to act obsequiously. [Chin. *k'o-t'ou* (*k'o,* knock, *t'ou,* the head)]

kotuku, *n.* a white heron found in New Zealand. [Maori]

koumiss KUMISS.

kourbash, *n.* a hide whip used as an instrument of punishment in Turkey and Egypt. [Arab.]

Kourou, *n.* river and second-largest town of French Guiana, NW of Cayenne, site of the Guiana Space Centre of the European Space Agency. Situated near the equator, it is an ideal site for launches of satellites into geostationary orbit.

kowhai, *n.* (*pl.* **-hais**) a small shrub with clusters of golden flowers found in Australasia and Chile. [Maori]

Kowloon, *n.* peninsula on the Chinese coast forming part of the British crown colony of Hong Kong; the town of Kowloon is a residential area.

kowtow KOTOW.

kr[1], (*chem. symbol*) krypton.

kr[2], (*abbr.*) krona; krone; kreutzer.

kraal, *n.* a S African village or group of huts enclosed by a palisade; a hut; an enclosure for cattle or sheep. [Afrikaans, from Port. CORRAL]

kraft, *n.* strong, brown, wrapping paper. [G, *Kraft,* strength]

kragdadige, *n.* (*S Afr.*) someone who advocates hard-line policies.

kragdadigheid, *n.* a hard-line attitude, esp. of a government towards demands for liberalization. [Afrikaans, *kragdadig,* firm]

krait, *n.* a poisonous rock snake. [Hind.]

kraken, *a.* a fabulous sea-monster, said to have been seen at different times off the coast of Norway. [Norw.]

Kraków, Cracow, *n.* city in Poland, on the Vistula; population (1985) 716,000. It is an industrial centre producing railway wagons, paper, chemicals, and tobacco. It was capital of Poland c. 1300–1595.

krantz, krans, kranz, *n.* a precipitous acclivity, esp. of crags walling in a valley. [Afrikaans, from Dut. *krans,* coronet, chaplet (cp. G *Kranz*)]

krasis, CRASIS.

Krasnodar, *n.* territory of the Russian Soviet Federal Socialist Republic in the N Caucasus, adjacent to the Black Sea; area 83,600 sq km/32,290 sq miles; population(1985) 4,992,000. Capital is Krasnodar. In addition to stock rearing and the production of grain, rice, fruit and tobacco, oil is refined.

Krasnoyarsk, *n.* territory of the Russian Soviet Federal Socialist Republic in central Siberia stretching N to the Arctic Ocean; area 2,401,600 sq km/927,617 sq miles; population (1985) 3,430,000. Capital is Krasnoyarsk. It is drained by the Yenisei river. Mineral resources include gold, graphite, coal, iron ore and uranium.

kraut, *n.* (*offensive*) a German. [from *sauerkraut*]

Krebs, *n.* **Hans** (1900–1981), German-born British biochemist. In 1953 he shared a Nobel prize in medicine for discovering the citric acid cycle, also known as Krebs' cycle, by which food is converted into energy in living tissues. **Krebs' cycle,** or **citric acid cycle** *n.* part of the chain of biochemical reactions through which organisms break down food using oxygen (aerobically) to release energy. It breaks down food molecules in a series of small steps, producing energy-rich molecules of ATP.

Kreisler, *n.* **Fritz** (1875–1962), Austrian violinist and composer, renowned as an interpreter of Brahms and Beethoven. From 1911 he was one of the earliest recording artists of classical music, some of which he composed himself.

Kremlin, *n.* the citadel of a Russian town, esp. that of Moscow enclosing the old imperial palace, now government buildings etc.; the Russian Government. **Kremlinologist,** *n.* **Kremlinology,** *n.* the study of the Soviet government and Soviet politics. [F, from Rus. *kreml,* citadel]

Krenek, *n.* **Ernst** (1900–), Austrian-born composer. His jazz opera *Jonny spielt auf/Johnny plays up* (1927) received international acclaim.

kreng, *n.* the carcass of a whale after the blubber has been removed. [Dut.]

Krenz, *n.* **Egon** (1937–), East German communist politician. A member of the Socialist Unity Party (SED) from 1955, he joined its politburo in 1983 and became known as a hardline protégé of Erich Honecker, succeeding him as party leader and head of state in 1989 after widespread pro-democracy demonstrations. Pledging a 'new course', Krenz opened the country's western border and promised more open elections, but his conversion to genuine pluralism proved weak in the face of popular protest and he resigned after a few weeks in Dec 1989, as party general secretary and head of state. He was replaced by Manfred Gerlach (1928–) and Gregor Gysi (1948–) respectively.

kreuzer, *n.* a copper coin (earlier silver), formerly current in Germany and Austria. [G, from *Kreuz,* cross]

krill, *n. collect.* tiny shrimplike crustaceans, the main food of whales. [Norw. *krill,* young fish]

krimmer, *n.* the tightly curled black or grey fleece from a type of lamb found in the Crimean. [G, *krim,* Crimea]

kris, CREESE.

Krishna, *n.* incarnation of the Hindu god Vishnu. The devotion of the bhakti movement is usually directed towards Krishna; an example of this is the International Society for Krishna Consciousness. Many stories are told of Krishna's mischievous youth, and he is the charioteer of Arjuna in the *Bhagavad-Gītā.* **Krishna Consciousness Movement,** popular name for the International Society for Krishna Consciousness. **Krishnaism,** *n.* the worship of Krishna. **krishnaist, Krishnaite,** *n.*

Kristallnacht, *n.* the 'night of [broken] glass' 9–10 Nov 1938 when the Nazi Sturmabteilung (SA) militia in Germany and Austria mounted a concerted attack on Jews, their synagogues, and their property. It followed the murder of a German embassy official in Paris by a Polish-Jewish youth. Subsequent measures included legislation against Jews owning businesses.

Kristiansen, *n.* **Ingrid** (1956–), Norwegian athlete, an outstanding long-distance runner at 5,000 m, 10,000 m, marathon, and cross-country running. She has won all the world's leading marathons. In 1986 she knocked 45.68 seconds off the world 10,000 m record.

kromesky, *n.* chicken minced and rolled in bacon, then fried. [Rus.]

krone, krona, *n.* a silver coin of Denmark, Norway and Sweden; a German gold coin; an Austrian silver coin. [G, crown]

Kronos, Cronus, *n.* in Greek mythology, ruler of the world and one of the Titans. He was the father of Zeus, who overthrew him.

Kronstadt uprising, *n.* revolt in Mar. 1921 by sailors of the Russian Baltic Fleet at their headquarters in Kronstadt, outside Petrograd (now Leningrad). On the orders of the leading Bolshevik Trotsky, Red Army troops, dressed in white camouflage, crossed the ice to the naval base and captured it on 18 Mar. The leaders were subsequently shot.

Kroo, *n.* one of a Negro people on the coast of Liberia, famous for their skill as seamen. *a.* of or pertaining to the Kroos. [W Afr. native]

Kropotkin, *n.* **Peter Alexeivich, Prince Kropotkin** (1842–1921), Russian anarchist. Imprisoned for revolutionary activities 1874, he escaped to the UK in 1876, and later moved to Switzerland. Expelled from Switzerland, he went to France, where he was imprisoned 1883–86. He lived in Britain until 1917, when he returned to Moscow. Among his works are *Mutual Aid* (1902) and *Modern Science and Anarchism* (1903).

Kruger, *n.* **Stephanus Johannes Paulus** (1825–1904), president of the Transvaal 1883–1900. He refused to remedy the grievances of the Uitlanders (English and other non-Boer white residents), and so precipitated the Second South African War. **Krugerrand,** *n.* a coin minted in S Africa containing 1 oz. of gold. **Kruger telegram,** *n.* message sent by Kaiser Wilhelm II of Germany to President Kruger of the Transvaal 3 Jan. 1896 congratulating him on defeating the Jameson raid of 1895. The text of the telegram provoked indignation, in Britain and elsewhere, and represented a worsening of Anglo-German relations, in spite of a German government retraction.

krummhorn, *n.* †a wind instrument with a curved tube, and a tone like that of a clarinet; an organ stop consisting of reed pipes, with a similar tone. [G (*krumm,* crooked)]

Krupp, *n.* German steelmaking armaments firm, founded in the early 19th cent., and developed by Alfred Krupp (1812–87) by pioneering the Bessemer steelmaking process. It developed the long-distance artillery used in World War I, and supported Hitler's regime in preparation for World War II, after which the head of the firm was imprisoned.

kryo-, *comb. form* cryo-.

kryometer, *n.* a thermometer for measuring low temperatures, esp. below freezing-point.

krypton, *n.* an inert gaseous element, at no. 38; chem. symbol Kr, discovered by Ramsay in 1898 as a constituent of the atmosphere. [Gr. *krypton,* neut. of *kruptos,* concealed (cp. CRYPT)]

Kshatriya, *n.* the warrior caste in the Hindu caste system. [Sansk. *kshatra,* rule]

kt, (*abbr.*) karat; knot; knight.

Kuala Lumpur, *n.* capital of the Federation of Malaysia; population (1985) 1,103,000. The city developed after 1873 with the expansion of tin and rubber trading; these are now its major industries. Formerly within the state of Selangor, of which it was also the capital, it was created a federal territory 1974; area 240 sq km/93 sq miles.

Kuanyin, *n.* transliteration of Guanyin, goddess of mercy in Chinese Buddhism.

Kublai Khan, *n.* (1216–1294), Mongol emperor of China from 1259. He completed his grandfather Genghis Khan's conquest of N China from 1240, and on his brother Mungo's death 1259, established himself as emperor of China. He moved the capital to Peking and founded the Yuan dynasty, successfully expanding his empire into Indochina, but was defeated in an attempt to conquer Japan 1281.

Kubrick, *n.* **Stanley** (1928–), US director, producer, and screenwriter. His films include *Paths of Glory* (1957), *Dr Strangelove* (1964), *2001: A Space Odyssey* (1968), *A Clockwork Orange* (1971), and *The Shining* (1979).

kudos, *n.* glory, fame, credit. [Gr.]

kudu, KOODOO.

kudzu, *n.* an ornamental plant, with edible tubers, found in China and Japan. [Jap.]

Kuhn[1], *n.* **Richard** (1900–1967), Austrian chemist. Working at Heidelberg University in the 1930s Kuhn succeeded in determining the structures of vitamins A, B_2, and B_6. For his success he was awarded the 1938 Nobel Chemistry Prize, but could not collect it until after World War II.

Kuhn[2], *n.* **Thomas S.** (1922–), US historian and philosopher of science, who showed that social and cultural conditions affect the directions of science. *The Structure of Scientific Revolutions* 1962 argued that even scientific knowledge is relative, dependent on the paradigm (theoretical framework) that dominates a scientific field at the time.

Kuibyshev, Kuybyshev, *n.* capital of Kuibyshev region, USSR, and port at the junction of the rivers Samara and Volga, situated in the centre of the fertile middle Volga plain; population (1987) 1,280,000. Its industries include aircraft, locomotives, cables, synthetic rubber, textiles, fertilizers, petroleum refining, and quarrying. It was provisional capital of the USSR 1941–43.

Ku-Klux-Klan, *n.* a secret society formed in the Southern States after the American Civil War of 1861–65 to keep down the black population. Suppressed by the US government in 1871 but revived since then with the aim of preserving white supremacy. **klanism,** *n.* **klansman,** *n.* **Ku Klux Klanner,** *n.* [Gr. *kuklos,* circle, CLAN]

kukri, *n.* a curved knife broadening at the end, used by the Gurkhas. [Hind.]

kulak, *n.* a prosperous Russian peasant. [Rus.]

kultur, *n.* a concept of German culture held by militant Nazis. **kulturkampf,** *n.* a conflict between secular and religious authorities, over, for example, education; a conflict between the German government and the Catholic Church at the end of the 19th cent. [G]

kumara, kumera, *n.* (*New Zealand*) the sweet potato. [Maori]

Kumasi, *n.* town in Ghana, W Africa, capital of Ashanti region, with trade in cocoa, rubber, and cattle; population (1984) 350,000.

kumiss, koumiss, *n.* a spirituous liquor made by Tartars from fermented mare's milk. [Tartar *kumiz*]

kummel, *n.* a liqueur flavoured with caraway-seeds made in Germany and Russia. [G]

kummerbund, CUMMERBUND.

kumquat, CUMQUAT.

Kun, *n.* **Béla** (1885–1938), Hungarian politician who created a Soviet republic in Hungary Mar. 1919, which was overthrown Aug. 1919 by a Western blockade and Romanian military actions. The succeeding regime under Admiral Horthy effectively liquidated both socialism and liberalism in Hungary.

Kundera, *n.* **Milan** (1929–), Czech writer, born in Brno. His first novel *The Joke* (1967) brought him into official disfavour in Prague, and, unable to publish further works, he moved to France. His novels include *The Book of Laughter and Forgetting* (1979) and *The Unbearable Lightness of Being* (1984).

Kung, *n.* an aboriginal people of southern Africa, formerly known as Bushman. They still live nomadically, especially in the Kalahari Desert. Although formerly numerous, only some 26,000 now remain. They are traditionally hunters and gatherers, and speak a Khoisan language. Their early art survives in cave paintings.

Küng, *n.* **Hans** (1928–), Swiss Roman Catholic theologian, who was barred from teaching by the Vatican 1979 'in the name of the Church' because he had cast doubt on papal infallibility, and on whether Christ was the son of God.

kung fu, *n.* a Chinese martial art. [Chin. *ch'üan fa,* boxing principles]

Kunming, (formerly **Yunnan**) *n.* capital of Yunnan province, China, on Lake Dian Chi, about 2000 m/ 6300 ft above sea level; population (1986) 1,490,000. Industries include chemicals, textiles, and copper smelted with nearby hydroelectric power.

Kuomintang, *n.* the Chinese Nationalist party founded by Sun Yat Sen in 1891 and replaced by the Communist Party in 1948.

kuo-yü, *n.* a form of Mandarin taught all over China. [Chin. *Kuo-yü,* lit. national language]

kurbash, KOURBASH.

kurchatovium, *n.* the chemical element at no. 104, whose discovery was claimed by the Soviets in 1966, also called rutherfordium. [I. V. Kurchatov, 1903–1960, Soviet physicist]

Kurd, *n.* a native or inhabitant of Kurdistan. **Kurdish,** *a.* pertaining to the Kurds or Kurdistan; *n.* their language. [Arab.]

Kurdistan, Kordestan, *n.* hilly region in SW Asia in the neighbourhood of Mt Ararat, where the borders of Iran, Iraq, Syria, Turkey, and the USSR meet; area 192,000 sq km/74,600 sq miles; total population around 18 million.

kuri, *n.* (*New Zealand*) a mongrel dog. [Maori]

Kuril Islands, *n.pl.* chain of about 50 small islands stretching from the NE of Hokkaido, Japan, to the S of Kamchatka, USSR; area 14,765 sq km/5700 sq miles; population (1970) 15,000. Some of them are of volcanic origin. Two of the Kurils are claimed by both Japan and the USSR.

Kuropatkin, *n.* **Alexei Nikolaievich** (1848–1921), Russian general. He made his reputation during the Russo-Turkish War 1877–78, was commander in chief in Manchuria 1903, and resigned after his defeat at Mukden in the Russo-Japanese War. During World War I he commanded the armies on the N front until 1916.

Kurosawa, *n.* **Akira** (1929–), Japanese director whose film *Rashomon* introduced Western audiences to Japanese cinema. Epics such as *Seven Samurai* (1954) combine spectacle with intimate human drama. His other films include *Drunken Angel* (1948), *Yojimbo* (1961), *Kagemusha* (1981), and *Ran* (1985).

kurrajong, currajong, *n.* (*Austral.*) any of several trees and shrubs with fibrous bark. [Abor.]

kursaal, *n.* a public room for the use of visitors, esp. at German health resorts. [G (*Kur,* CURE, *Saal,* room)]

kurta, *n.* a loose tunic worn in India. [Hindi]

kurtosis, *n.* the distribution and density of points around the mean. [Gr. *kurtos,* arched]

kuru, *n.* a disease, usu. fatally, of the nervous system occurring in the inhabitants of eastern New Guinea. [New Guinea native, trembling]

Kutuzov, *n.* **Mikhail Larionovich, Prince of Smolensk** (1745–1813), commander of the Russian forces in the Napoleonic Wars. He commanded an army corps at Austerlitz, and the retreating army in 1812. After the burning of Moscow he harried the French throughout their retreat, and later took command of the united Prussian armies.

Kuwait, State of, country in SW Asia. **area** 17,819 sq km/6878 sq miles. **capital** Kuwait (also chief port). **physical** hot desert. **population** (1988) 1,960,000 (40% Kuwaitis, 30% Palestinians); annual growth rate 5.5%. **exports** oil. **language** 78% Arabic, 10% Kurdish, 4% Farsi. **religion** Sunni Muslim, with Shi'ite minority. **Kuwait City**, (formerly **Qurein**) *n.* capital of the State of Kuwait, on the S shore of Kuwait Bay; population (1985) 44,300, plus the suburbs of Hawalli, population (1985) 145,100, Jahra, population (1985) 111,200, and as-Salimiya, population (1985) 153,400. Kuwait is a banking and investment centre.

Kuznetsk Basin, *n.* industrial area in Kemorovo region, S USSR. Abbreviated to Kuzbas.

Kuznetsov, *n.* **Anatoli** (1930–1979), Russian writer. His novels *Babi Yar* (1966), describing the wartime execution of Jews at Babi Yar, near Kiev, and *The Fire* (1969), about workers in a large metallurgical factory, were seen as anti-Soviet. He lived in Britain from 1969.

kv, (*abbr.*) kilovolt.

kvass, *n.* beer made from rye. [Rus.]

kvetch, *v.i.* (*coll.*) to whine, to complain, **kvetcher,** *n.* a complainer. [Yiddish[

kW, (*abbr.*) kilowatt.

kwacha, *n.* the unit of currency in Zambia and Malawi. [native name, dawn]

Kwa Ndebele, *n.* black homeland in Transvaal province, South Africa; achieved self-governing status 1981; population (1985) 235,800.

Kwangchow, *n.* former name of Guangzhou, city in China.

Kwangchu, Kwangju, *n.* capital of South Cholla province, SW South Korea; population (1985) 906,000. It is at the centre of a rice-growing region. A museum in the city houses a huge collection of Chinese porcelain dredged up 1976 after lying for over 600 years on the ocean floor.

Kwangsi-Chuang, *n.* former name of Guanxi Zhuang, region of China.

Kwangtung, *n.* former name of Guangdong, province of China.

Kwannon, Kannon, *n.* in Japanese Buddhism, a female form (known to the West as 'goddess of mercy') of the bodhisattva Avalokiteśvara. Sometimes depicted with many arms extending compassion.

kwashiorkor, *n.* a nutritional disease caused by lack of protein. [Ghanaian]

Kwa Zulu, *n.* black homeland in Natal province, South Africa; achieved self-governing status 1971; population (1985) 3,747,000.

Kweilin, *n.* former name of Guilin in China.

kwela, *n.* Zulu, jazz-type, folk music. [Bantu]

kWh, (*abbr.*) kilowatt hour.

KWIC, (*acronym*) *k*ey*w*ord *i*n *c*ontext.

Kwik Cricket, *n.* a form of cricket devised for children. It is played with a soft ball and a major feature is that all players get a chance to bat and bowl.

KWOC, (*acronym*) *k*ey*w*ord *o*ut of *c*ontext.

kyanite, CYANITE.

kyanize, -ise, *v.t.* to impregnate (wood) with a solution of mercuric chloride (corrosive sublimate) to prevent dry-rot. **kyanization, -isation,** *n.* [J. H. *Kyan,* 1774–1830, British inventor]

kyat, *n.* the unit of currency in Burma.

†**kye, kyen,** KINE, COW[1].

Kyd, *n.* **Thomas** (*c.* (1557–1595), English dramatist, author in about 1588 of a bloody revenge tragedy *The Spanish Tragedy*, which anticipated elements present in Shakespeare's *Hamlet*.

kyle, *n.* a narrow channel. [Gael. *caol,* narrow]

kylie, *n.* a boomerang. [W Austral. Abor.]

kyloe, *n.* one of a small Highland breed of cattle. [Sc., etym. doubtful]

kymograph, *n.* an instrument for recording wave-like oscillations, as of the pulsation of the blood in a living body. **kymographic,** *a.* [Gr. *kuma,* a wave]

Kymric, CYMRIC.

Kyoto, *n.* former capital of Japan 794–1868 on Honshu island, linked by canal with Biwa Lake; population (1987) 1,469,000. Industries include silk weaving and manufacture, porcelain, bronze, and lacquer ware.

kyphosis, *n.* a condition of the spine resulting in a hunched back. **kyphotic,** *a.* [Gr, *kyphos,* hump].

Kyprianou, *n.* **Spyros** (1932–), Cypriot politician. Foreign minister 1961–72, he founded the Democratic Front (DIKO) in 1976. He was president 1977–88.

Kyrie, Kyrie eleison (ilā'ison, -zon), *n.* this phrase used as a short petition in the liturgies of the Eastern and Western Churches, at the beginning of the Mass; a musical setting of this. [Gr. *Kurie eleēson,* Lord have mercy]

kyte, *n.* (*Sc., North.*) the belly, the paunch, the stomach. [etym. doubtful]

kythe, *v.t.* (*Sc., North.*) to make known. *v.i.* to show oneself, to appear. [OE *cȳthan,* to make known; see CAN[2]]

kyu, *n.* in Judo, a grade for a beginner. [Jap.]

Kyushu, *n.* most southerly of the main islands of Japan, separated from Shikoku and Honshu by Bungo Channel and Suo Bay, but connected to Honshu by bridge and rail tunnel. **area** 42,150 sq km/16,270 sq miles including about 370 small islands. **capital** Nagasaki. **towns** Fukuoka, Kumamoto, Kagoshima. **physical** mountainous, volcanic, with sub-tropical climate. **population** (1986) 13,295,000. **products** coal, gold, silver, iron, tin, rice, tea, timber.

L

L¹, l¹, the 12th letter of the English alphabet (*pl.* **Els, Ls, L's**), commonly described as a semi-vowel or liquid, but more accurately as a voiced or sonorous consonant, having the value of an unstressed vowel in such words as *cattle, trouble;* an L-shaped thing, part or building; a rectangular joint; the Roman numeral for 50.

L², (*abbr.*) Lady; Lake; Latin; Law; Learner (driver); Liberal; Libra (pound); Licentiate; Lira; London; Longitude.

l², (*abbr.*) latitude; league; left; length; line; link; litre(s).

†**la¹**, *int.* Lo! see! behold! (*derisively etc.*) really! [OE *lā*]

la², lah, *n.* the name for the sixth note of the scale in solmization. [It., orig. first syl. of L *labii,* one of the words of the gamut]

LA, (*abbr.*) Los Angeles.

La, (*chem. symbol*) lanthanum.

laager, *n.* a defensive encampment, esp. one formed with wagons, armoured vehicles etc. *v.t.* to form into a laager; to encamp (a body of people) in a laager. *v.i.* to encamp. [Afrikaans *lager* (cp. G *Lager,* Dut. *leger,* LEAGUER)]

Lab¹, (*abbr.*) Labour; Labrador.

lab², short for LABORATORY.

labarum, *n.* the imperial standard of Constantine the Great (bearing the cross and a monogram of the Greek name of Christ), adopted by him after his conversion to Christianity; a banner resembling this used in religious processions. [L, from Gr. *labaron,* etym. unknown]

labdacism, LAMBDACISM under LAMDA.

labdanum, LADANUM.

labefaction, *n.* a weakening; decay; downfall, ruin. [more correctly *labefactation,* L *labefactātio,* from *labefactāre* (*labāre,* to totter, *facere,* to make)]

label, *n.* a narrow strip of cloth, paper, parchment or other material, attached to an object to indicate contents, destination, ownership or other particulars; a descriptive phrase associated with a person, group etc.; a slip of paper, parchment etc., attached to a document to carry the appended seal; an addition to a document, as a codicil; an adhesive stamp; a moulding over a doorway or window, a dripstone; (*Her.*) a fillet, with pendants or points, used as marks of cadency; a brass rule with sights, formerly used to take altitudes; a firm's tradename (esp. of a record company); a character or set of characters which indicates the start of an instruction in a computer program. *v.t.* (*past, p.p.* **labelled**) to affix a label to; to describe, to categorize. **labeller,** *n.* [OF, a ribbon, a fillet (etym. doubtful)]

labellum, *n.* (*pl.* **-lla,** -lə) the lower part of the corrolla in an orchidaceous flower. [L, dim. of LABRUM]

labial, *a.* of or pertaining to the lips; of or pertaining to the labium, serving as or resembling a lip; having lips or lip-like edges (as an organ flue-pipe); formed or modified in sound by the lips. *n.* a sound or letter representing a sound formed with the lips, as *b, f, v, p, m* or *w*. **labialism,** *n.* **labialization, -isation,** *n.* **labialize, -ise,** *v.t.* **labially,** *adv.* by means of the lips. **labiate,** *a.* (*Bot.*) having lips or parts like lips, esp. having a corolla with an upper and lower part like a pair of lips; belonging to the natural order Labiatae, the mint family. [late L *labiālis,* from L LABIUM]

labile, *a.* unstable, liable to chemical or other change. [L *lābilis,* from *lābī,* to fall]

labio-, *comb. form* labial. [LABIUM]

labiodental, *a.* produced by the agency of lips and teeth. *n.* a letter or sound so produced, as *f* or *v*.

labium, *n.* (*pl.* **-bia,** -biə) (*Anat.*) a lip or lip-like part, as of the female genitals; the lower surface of the mouth in insects, crustaceans etc.; the inner lip of a univalve shell; the lower lip of a labiate corolla. [L, lip]

Labor, Knights of, *n.* in US history, a national labour organization founded by a Philadelphia tailor Uriah Stephens in 1869 and committed to cooperative enterprise, equal pay for both sexes, and the establishment of an eight-hour day. The Knights grew rapidly in the mid-1880s under Terence V. Powderly (1849–1924) but gave way to the American Federation of Labor after 1886.

laboratory, *n.* a room or building in which chemical or other scientific experiments are conducted; a manufactory of chemical articles, explosives, fireworks etc. [med. L *labōrātōrium,* from *labōrāre,* to LABOUR]

laborious LABOUR.

Labor Party, *n.* in Australia, political party based on socialist principles. It was founded in 1891 and first held office in 1904. It formed governments during 1929–31 and 1939–49, but in the intervening periods internal discord provoked splits, and reduced its effectiveness as a political force. It returned to power under Gough Whitlam 1972–75, and again under Bob Hawke from 1983.

labour, (esp. *N. Am.*) **labor,** *n.* physical or mental exertion, esp. in obtaining the means of subsistence; the performance of work, toil; work to be done, a task, esp. a task requiring great effort; travail, the pains of childbirth; the element contributed by toil to production, esp. in opp. to capital; of the Labour Party, its members, causes or ideals; (*collect.*) workers. *a.* pertaining to labour or to the Labour Party. *v.i.* to work hard; to exert oneself; to move or proceed with difficulty; to be burdened or oppressed with difficulties; of ships, to move heavily and slowly or to pitch or roll heavily; to be in travail or the pains of childbirth. *v.t.* to fabricate, to work out laboriously; to elaborate, to deal with in much detail or at great length; †to till; †to belabour. **labour of love,** work done without expectation of payment. **labour camp,** *n.* a penal establishment where prisoners are forced to labour. **Labour Day,** *n.* a public holiday honouring working people, esp. May; (*N Am.*) the first Monday in September. **Labour Exchange,** *n.* the former name for an office established by the State for the registration of unemployed people and assistance in procuring them employment. **labour market,** *n.* the supply of unemployed labour in relation to the demand. **Labour Party,** *n.* a British political party representing 'workers by hand or brain', composed of the chief socialist organizations and supported by the trade unions. Formed in 1900, it received its name in 1906 and first came into power in 1924. **labour-saving,** *a.* **laborious,** *a.* working hard or perseveringly; industrious, assiduous; betraying marks of labour, laboured; difficult, hard, arduous, fatiguing. **laboriously,** *adv.* **laboriousness,** *n.* **laboured,** *a.* showing signs of strain or effort, not spontaneous. **labourer,** *n.* one who labours; esp. one who performs work requiring manual labour but little skill. **labourite,** *n.* a follower or member of the Labour Party. †**labourless,** *a.* †**laboursome,** *a.* [OF, from L *labōrem,* acc. of *labor,* whence *labōrāre,* F *labourer,* to labour]

Labrador, *n.* area of NE Canada, part of the province of Newfoundland, lying between Ungava Bay on the

NW, the Atlantic on the E, and the Strait of Belle Isle on the SE; area 266,060 sq km/102,699 sq miles; population (1976) 33,052. It consists primarily of a gently sloping plateau with an irregular coastline of numerous bays, fjords, and inlets, and cliffs 60 m/200 ft to 120 m/400 ft high. Industries include fisheries, timber and pulp, and many minerals. Hydroelectric resources include Churchill Falls on Churchill River, where one of the world's largest underground power houses is situated. The Canadian Air Force base in Goose Bay is on land claimed by the Innu (or Montagnais-Naskapi) Indian people, who call themselves a sovereign nation (in 1989 numbering 9500). **Labrador retriever,** *n.* a type of retriever dog of either a golden or black colour. **labradorite**, *n.* a feldspar from Labrador and other places, exhibiting a brilliant display of colour.

labrum, *n.* (*pl.* **-bra**) a lip or lip-like part, as in insects, crustaceans etc. **labret**, *n.* a plug of stone, shell etc., inserted into the lip as an ornament, as among the peoples of Alaska. **labrose**, *a.* having thick lips. [L cogn. with LABIUM]

La Bruyère, *n.* **Jean de** (1645–1696), French essayist. He was born in Paris, studied law, took a post in the revenue office, and in 1684 entered the service of the house of Condé. His *Caractères* (1688), satirical portraits of contemporaries, made him many enemies.

laburnum, *n.* a poisonous tree or shrub, *Cytisus laburnum,* has racemes of yellow flowers. [L]

labyrinth, *n.* a structure similar to that constructed by Daedalus, in Crete, composed of intricate winding passages, rendering it difficult to penetrate to the interior and equally difficult to return, a maze; a complication, an intricate combination, arrangement etc.; the internal portion of the ear. *v.t.* to enclose in or as in a labyrinth. **labyrinthal,** †**labyrinthian**, †**labyrinthic, -ical**, **labyrinthine**, *a.* **labyrinthitis**, *n.* an inflammation of the inner ear. **labyrinthodont**, *n.* a fossil amphibian, so called from the labyrinthine structure seen in a cross-section of a tooth. [F *labyrinthe,* L *labyrinthus,* Gr. *laburinthos,* etym. doubtful]

lac¹, *n.* a resinous incrustation caused, chiefly on the banyan-tree, by the parasitic insect *Coccus lacca;* a similar exudation or resin otherwise produced; ware coated with lac or lacquer. **lac-dye, lac-lake,** *n.* colouring matters obtained from lac and used in dyeing scarlet or purple. **laccic**, *a.* **laccin**, *n.* the colouring principle in lac. [Hind. *lākh,* from Sansk. *lākshā*]

lac² LAKH.

Laccadive, Minicoy, and Amindivi Islands, former name of Indian island group Lakshadweep.

laccolite, -lith, *n.* an intrusive mass of lava penetrating between strata and raising the surface into domes. [Gr. *lakkos,* reservoir, -LITE]

lace, *n.* a cord or string used to bind or fasten, esp. by interweaving, as a shoe-lace etc.; a kind of ornamental network of threads of linen, cotton, gold or silver wire or other suitable material, forming a fabric of open texture; an ornamental braid or edging for uniforms etc.; †a snare, a noose, a gin. *v.t.* to fasten by means of a lace or string through eyelet-holes etc.; to compress or tighten by lacing; to intertwist or interweave (with thread etc.); to trim or adorn with lace; to embellish with or as with stripes; to flavour or fortify by adding spirits to; to beat, to thrash; to trap, to ensnare; to embroil in. *v.i.* to compress the waist by tightening laces; of boots etc., to fasten with laces; to lash (into). **lacebark,** *n.* the inner bark of a W Indian shrub, *Lagetta lintearia,* which resembles coarse lace; (*Austral.*) the ribbon-wood tree. **lace-boot,** *n.* a boot fastened by a lace. **lace-frame,** *n.* a machine used in lacemaking. **lace-glass, lace-glass,** *n.* Venetian glass decorated with lace-like patterns. **lace-maker,** *n.* **laceman,** *n.* one dealing in lace. **lace-pillow,** *n.* a cushion on which various kinds of lace are made. **lace-ups,** *n.pl.* shoes or boots fastened by laces. **lace-wing, lace-wing fly,** *n.* any of various flying insects with veiny wings, esp. any of the families Chrysopidae and Hemerobiidae. **lace-winged,** *a.* **laced,** *a.* having laces. **lacing,** *n.* a fastening by a cord passing through holes etc.; a lace or cord for fastening; various interlacing structures of timber, iron etc., in mining, shipbuilding etc.; a dose of spirit added to a liquor to strengthen or flavour it; a thrashing. **lacy,** *a.* like lace. [OF *las* (L *laqueus,* nom. *-us,* a noose), whence OF *lacier* (F *lacer*), to ensnare]

lacerate, *v.t.* to tear, to mangle; to rend, to harrow, to wound. **lacerable,** *a.* **lacerant,** *a.* agonizing, traumatic. **lacerate, -ated**, *a.* torn, mangled; (*Bot.*) having the edge in irregular segments, as if torn. **laceration,** *n.* **lacerative,** *a.* [L *lacerātus,* p.p. of *lacerāre,* from lacer, torn (cp. Gr. *lakeros*)]

Lacerta, *n.* the typical genus of the Lacertilia, an order of reptiles containing the lizards, iguanas etc.; the Lizard, a constellation in the N hemisphere. **lacertian**, *n., a.* **lacertillian**, **-tine**, **-toid**, *a.* [L, lizard]

lacet, *n.* work with braid or tape made into designs with crochet or lace-stitches. *a.* of or pertaining to this.

laches, *n.* negligence, neglect to do; in law, culpable negligence or remissness. [OF *laschesse,* from *lasche,* L *laxus,* LAX (with transposition of *cs* (*x*) to *sc*)]

lachesis, *n.* one of the three Fates in Greek mythology; a genus of venomous rattlesnakes, with the rudiments of a rattle, from Surinam and Brazil. [Gr.]

Lachish, *n.* ancient city SW of Jerusalem, destroyed 589 BC, where inscribed potsherds have been found that throw light on Hebrew manuscripts and the early development of the alphabet.

Lachryma Christi, *n.* a sweet white wine from S Italy. [L, Christ's tears]

lachrymal, lacrimal, lacrymal, *a.* pertaining to tears; of glands, ducts etc., secreting or conveying tears. *n.* a bone near the tear-producing glands; a lachrymatory; (*pl.*) outbursts of weeping; (*pl.*) lachrymal organs. †**lachrymary,** *a.* **lachrymation,** *n.* **lachrymatory,** *a.* of, pertaining to or causing tears. *n.* a small glass vessel found in ancient tombs, said to be intended for holding tears, but prob. for perfumes or ointments. **lachrymose**, *a.* shedding or ready to shed tears; sad, mournful. **lachrymosely,** *adv.* [med. L *lacrymālis,* from L *lacryma,* tear (cp. Gr. *dakru*)]

lacing LACE.

lacinia, *n.* (*pl.* **-niae**) an incision or slash in a leaf or petal; a slender lobe like the result of slashing or cutting; (*Ent.*) the blade of a maxilla. **laciniate**, **-ated**, *a.* **laciniation,** *n.* [L, lappet]

lack, *n.* deficiency, want, need (of); that which is needed; †blame, reproach. *v.t.* to be in need of, to be deficient in; to be without; to feel the want of. *v.i.* to be deficient (in); to be wanting; †to be absent. **lackall,** *n.* one perfectly destitute. †**lack-beard,** *n.* †**lackbrain,** *n.* †**lackland,** *a.* having no property or estate. †**lack-linen,** *a.* destitute of a shirt. **lacklustre,** *a.* wanting brightness or lustre. **lacking,** *a.* [cp. Dut. and LG *lak*]

lackadaisical, *a.* affectedly pensive, languishing or sentimental; listless, absent-minded. **lackadaisically,** *adv.* **lackadaisicalness,** *n.* **lackaday**, *int.* [obs. *lackadaisy*]

†**lacker,** LACQUER.

lackey, *n.* a footman, a menial attendant; a servile follower. *v.t.* to follow or attend as a servant; to attend servilely. *v.i.* to act as a lackey; to act servilely. [F *laquais,* etym. doubtful]

Laclos, *n.* **Pierre Choderlos de** (1741–1803), French author. An army officer, he wrote a single novel in letter form, *Les Liaisons dangereuses/Dangerous Liaisons* (1782), an analysis of moral corruption.

lacmus, LITMUS.

laconic, -ical, *a.* pertaining to Laconia or Sparta or its inhabitants; hence brief, sententious, pithy, concise. **laconically,** *adv.* **laconicism**, **laconism**, *n.* a concise, pithy or sententious style; a laconic saying. [L *lacōnicus,* Gr. *Lakōnikos,* from *Lakōn,* Spartan]

lacquer, *n.* a varnish composed of shellac dissolved in alcohol and coloured with gold, gamboge, saffron etc., used to coat articles of metal or wood; (also **hair lacquer**) a similar substance used to keep a hairstyle in place; a hard glossy varnish made from black resin; woodwork coated with such a varnish, usu. decorated

with inlaid figures. *v.t.* to cover with lacquer. **lacquerer,** *n.* [MF *lacre,* Port. *lacre,* var. of *lacca,* from LAC[1]]
lacrimal, LACHRYMAL.
lacrosse, *n.* a Canadian ball-game resembling hockey, but played with a crosse or stringed bat. **lacrosse stick,** *n.* [F, the CROSSE]
lacrymal, LACHRYMAL.
lact- LACT(O)-.
lactate, *v.i.*, to secrete or produce milk. *n.* a salt of lactic acid. **lactation,** *n.* the act or process of giving suck to an infant; the secretion and excretion of milk.
lacteal, *a.* pertaining to milk; milky; conveying chyle. *n.pl.* the vessels which convey chyle from the alimentary canal. **lacteous,** *a.* milky; lacteal.
lactescent, *a.* turning to milk; having a milky appearance or consistence; yielding milky juice. **lactescence,** *n.*
lactic, *a.* pertaining to milk; contained in or derived from sour milk. **lactic acid,** *n.* a colourless liquid acid produced in tissue by the anaerobic breakdown of carbohydrates and also formed during the souring of milk.
lactific, lactiferous, *a.* carrying or producing milk or milky juice.
lact(o)-, *comb. form* pertaining to milk.
lactoflavin, *n.* an earlier name for riboflavin.
lactogenic, *a.* inducing lactation.
lactometer, *n.* a kind of hydrometer for showing the specific gravity and consequent value of different samples of milk.
lactoscope, *n.* an instrument for determining the quality of milk by ascertaining its relative opacity.
lactose, *n.* milk-sugar, the form in which sugar occurs in milk.
Lactuca, *n.* a genus of plants containing the lettuce. **lactucic**, *a.* [L]
lacuna, *n.* (*pl.* **-nae, -nas**) a gap, an hiatus; a vacancy; a cavity, a small pit or depression. **lacunal, -nary, -nate, -nose,** *a.* pertaining to or containing lacunae. **lacunar,** *a.* lacunal. *n.* a ceiling having sunk or hollowed compartments; (*pl.*) the panels or compartments of this. [L, from *lacus,* LAKE[1]]
lacustrine, *a.* of or pertaining to or living on or in a lake. **lacustrine age,** *n.* that of the lake dwellings. **lacustral,** *a.* **lacustrian,** *n., a.* [from L *lacus,* LAKE, onomat. of *palustrine,* from *palus*]
lacy LACE.
lad, *n.* a boy, a youth, a stripling; (*coll.*) a fellow, a companion, a mate. **laddie,** *n.* familiar or affectionate term. **lad's love,** *n.* (*dial.*) the southern wood. [ME *ladde,* perh. rel. to *lad, led,* p.p. of *leden,* to LEAD]
ladanum, labdanum, *n.* an odorous, resinous substance, which exudes from the leaves and twigs of various kinds of cistus; †laudanum. [L *lādanum,* Gr. *ladanon, lēdanon,* from *lēdon,* mastic]
Ladd, *n.* **Alan** (1913–1964), US actor whose first leading role, the professional killer in *This Gun for Hire* (1942), made him a star. His career declined after the mid-1950s although his last role, in *The Carpetbaggers* (1964), was one of his best. His other films include *The Blue Dahlia* (1946) and *Shane* (1953).
ladder, *n.* a device of wood, iron, rope etc., usu. portable and consisting of two long uprights, connected by rungs or cross-pieces, which form steps by which one may ascend; a vertical rent in a stocking or tights; anything serving as a means of ascent. *v.t.* to ascend by ladder; to equip with a ladder. *v.i.* of stockings, tights, knitted fabrics etc.; to form a rent through the snapping of a longitudinal thread. *n.* **ladder-proof,** *a.* descriptive of fabrics that are unlikely to ladder. **ladder-stitch,** *n.* a cross-bar stitch used in embroidery and fancy-work. **laddered, laddery,** *a.* [OE *hlǣder* (cp. Dut. *ladder,* G *Leiter*), cogn. with Gr. *klimax,* CLIMAX]
laddie LAD.
lade, *v.t.* (*p.p.* **laden**) to put a load or burden on; to put a cargo or freight on board; to ship (goods) as cargo; (*esp. in p.p.*) to load, to weigh down; to lift or throw out or in (as water) with a ladle, bowl etc. **laden,** *a.* weighed down, loaded; encumbered. **lading,** *n.* cargo. **bill of lading** BILL3. [OE *hladan* (cp. Dut. and G *laden,* Icel. *hlather*]
la-di-da, lah-di-dah, *a.* (*sl.*) affectedly genteel, swaggering, pretentious, foppish. *n.* such a person. [imit. of affected speech]
ladify LADY.
Ladin, *n.* the Rhaeto-Romanic language spoken in the Engadine and part of Tyrol; one who speaks this. [L *Latīnus,* Latin]
lading LADE.
Ladino, *n.* the old Castilian language; a Spanish–Portuguese dialect spoken by Turkish Jews; a Sp. American of mixed (white and Indian) descent. [Sp. and It., from L *Latinus,* LATIN]
Ladins, *n.* ethnic community (about 16,000) in the Dolomites whose language (Ladin) derives directly from Latin; they descend from the Etruscans and other early Italian tribes, and have links with the speakers of Romansch.
ladle, *n.* a large spoon with which liquids are lifted out or served from a vessel; a pan or bowl with a long handle to hold molten metal; the float-board of a mill-wheel. *v.t.* to serve out or transfer with a ladle. **to ladle out,** to give or hand out freely; to distribute liberally. **ladleful,** *n.* [OE *hlœdel,* from *hladan,* to LADE]
Ladoga, (Russian **Ladozhskoye**) *n.* largest lake on the continent of Europe, in the USSR, just NE of Leningrad; area 18,400 sq km/7100 sq miles. It receives the waters of the Svir, which drains Lake Onega, and other rivers, and runs to the Gulf of Finland by the river Neva.
ladrone, *n.* a thief, a highwayman, a brigand;, a rascal, a rogue, a vagabond. [Sp., from L *latrōnem,* nom. *latro,* robber]
lady, *n.* (*pl.* **ladies**) a gentle-woman; a woman of refinement or social standing; a wife; an object of romantic love, a mistress, girlfriend, sweetheart; the mistress of a house or family; a title prefixed to the surname or territorial title of the wife of a knight or any superior to him in rank, or the Christian name of the daughter of an earl, marquess or duke, or to the Christian name of the husband if a son of marquess or duke; also in such titles as lady mayoress; (*pl.*) the ladies' room, a public lavatory for women. **lady-in-waiting,** a lady attending on a queen or princess. **Lady of the Lamp,** name given to Florence Nightingale in the Crimean War by wounded soldiers whom she used to visit in the wards at night, carrying a lantern. **my lady, your ladyship,** forms of address for those holding the title. **Our Lady,** the Virgin Mary. **painted lady** PAINT. **Ladies' Gallery,** *n.* a gallery in the House of Commons, formerly screened off by a grille and the only place where women were admitted. **ladies' man,** *n.* one attentive to women; one who enjoys the company of women. **lady-altar,** *n.* the altar of a chapel (usu. in a cathedral or large church) dedicated to the Virgin Mary. **lady-bird, -bug,** *n.* a small red coleopterous insect, of the genus *Coccinella,* with black spots. **lady-chair,** *n.* a seat made by interlacing two people's arms for carrying an injured person. **Lady chapel,** *n.* a chapel dedicated to the Virgin Mary (usu. in a cathedral or large church). **lady-cow** LADYBIRD. **Lady Day,** *n.* the Feast of the Annunciation of the Virgin Mary, 25 Mar. **lady-fern,** *n.* a tall slender fern, *Asplenium filix-foemina.* **ladyfly** LADYBIRD. **lady-killer,** *n.* (*facet.*) one who devotes himself to conquests of women; one who is irresistibly fascinating to women. **lady-love,** *n.* a female sweetheart. **lady's bedstraw,** the herb bedstraw. **lady's cushion,** the thrift or sea-pink; mossy saxifrage. **lady's finger,** the kidney vetch; okra. **lady's maid,** a female attendant on a lady, esp. at the toilet. **lady's mantle,** the rosaceous herb, *Alchemilla vulgaris.* **lady's slipper,** *n.* an orchid of the genus *Cypripedium.* **lady's-smock, lady-smock,** *n.* the cuckoo flower, *Cardamine pratensis.* **lady's-tresses,** *n.pl.* orchidaceous plants of the genus *Spiranthes;* grasses of the genus *Briza.* **ladified,** *a.* affecting the manners and air of a fine lady. **ladify,** *v.t.* to make a lady of; to treat

as a lady. **ladyhood**, *n.* **ladyish,** *a.* having the manners and air of a fine lady. **ladyism,** *n.* **ladylike,** *a.* **ladyship,** *n.* the title of a lady. [OE *hlǣfdīge* (*hlāf,* LOAF, *-dīge,* prob. kneader, cp. DOUGH)]

Laënnec, *n.* **René Théophile Hyacinthe** (1781–1826), French physician, inventor of the stethoscope 1814. He introduced the new diagnostic technique of auscultation (evaluating internal organs by listening with a stethoscope) in his book *Traité de l'auscultation médiaté* 1819, which quickly became a medical classic.

laesa majestas LESE-MAJESTY.

Laetare, *n.* the fourth Sunday in Lent, so called from the first word of the introit of the Mass on that day. [L, to rejoice]

laevo-, lev(o)-, *comb. form.* left, as opposed to right; noting the turning of a ray of polarized light to the left, as opp. to DEXTRO-. **laevo-glucose**, *n.* laevulose. **laevo-gyrate**, **-gyrous,** *a.* **laevorotatory**, *a.* turning the plane of polarization to the left. **laevorotation,** *n.* [L *laevus,* left]

laevulose, *n.* a sugar or glucose distinguished from dextrose by its turning the plane of polarization to the left.

Lafayette[1], *n.* **Marie Joseph Gilbert de Motier, Marquis de Lafayette** (1757–1834), French soldier and politician. He fought against Britain in the American War of Independence. During the French Revolution he sat in the National Assembly as a constitutional royalist, and in 1789 was given command of the National Guard. In 1792 he fled the country after attempting to restore the monarchy, and was imprisoned by the Austrians until 1797. He supported Napoleon during the Hundred Days, sat in the chamber of deputies as a Liberal from 1818, and played a leading part in the revolution of 1830.

Lafayette[2], *n.* **Marie-Madeleine, Comtesse de Lafayette** (1634–1693), French author. Her *Mémoires* of the French court are keenly observed, and her *La Princesse de Clèves* (1678) is the first French psychological novel and *roman à clef* (novel with a 'key') in that real-life characters (including La Rochefoucauld, who was for many years her lover) are presented under fictitious names.

La Fontaine, *n.* **Jean de** (1621–1695), French poet. He was born at Château-Thierry, and from 1656 lived largely in Paris, the friend of Molière, Racine, and Boileau. His works include *Fables* (1668–94), and *Contes* (1665–74), a series of witty and bawdy tales in verse.

Lafontaine, *n.* **Oskar** (1943–), West German socialist politician, federal deputy chair of the Social Democrat Party (SPD) from 1987. Leader of the Saar regional branch of the SPD from 1977 and former mayor of Saarbrucken, he was dubbed 'Red Oskar' because of his radical views on defence and environmental issues. His attitude mellowed after becoming minister-president of Saarland in 1985. He is a likely future candidate for chancellor.

Laforgue, *n.* **Jules** (1860–1887), French poet, who pioneered free verse and who greatly influenced later French and English writers.

lag[1], *a.* last; long-delayed; †slow, sluggish, tardy. *v.i.* (*past, p.p.* **lagged**) to loiter, to move slowly; to fall behind. *n.* retardation of current or movement; delay in response; an interval; one who or that which lags behind or comes last, the last comer; †the lag-end; the grey lag. **lag of the tide,** the interval by which the tide lags behind the mean time during the first and third quarters of the moon. †**lag-end,** *n.* the hinder part; the fag-end; the dregs. **laggard**, *a.* slow, sluggish, backward; wanting in energy. *n.* a slow, sluggish fellow; a loiterer. **lagger,** *n.* **lagging,** *n., a.* **laggingly,** *adv.* [etym. doubtful, perh. from LAST[1] or LACK]

lag[2], *v.t.* (*sl.*) to arrest; to send to penal servitude; to steal. *n.* a convict; a long-term prisoner, a gaol-bird; †a sentence of transportation. [etym. doubtful]

lag[3], *n.* a stave, lath or strip of wood, felt etc.; one of the pieces of the non-conducting jacket of a boiler or cylinder. *v.t.* to cover or encase with lags or lagging, esp. to preserve against freezing. **lagger,** *n.* one who insulates with lagging. **lagging,** *n.* insulating material. [Icel. *lögg,* the end of a cask]

lagan, *n.* wreckage or goods lying at the bottom of the sea, usu. marked by a float or buoy. [A-F (cp. Icel. *lögn,* pl. *lagnir,* nets laid in the sea, cogn. with LIE[2])]

Lagash, *n.* Sumerian city north of Shatra, Iraq, of great importance under independent and semi-independent rulers from about 3000–2700 BC. Besides objects of high artistic value, it has provided about 30,000 clay tablets giving detailed information on temple administration. It was discovered 1877 and excavated by Ernest de Sarzec, then French consul in Basra.

lagena, *n.* (*pl.* **-nae**) a Roman amphora; the termination of the cochlea in birds and reptiles. **lageniform**, *a.* [L, an amphora]

lager, lager beer, *n.* a light beer, the ordinary beer of Germany. **lager lout,** *n.* (*sl.*) a youth who behaves like a hooligan, esp. when having drunk too much alcohol, esp. lager or beer. [G *Lager-bier* (*Lager,* a store)]

Lagerkvist, *n.* **Pär** (1891–1974), Swedish author of lyric poetry, dramas, including *The Hangman* (1935), and novels, such as *Barabbas* (1950). Nobel prize (1951).

Lagerlöf, *n.* **Selma** (1858–1940), Swedish novelist. She was originally a schoolteacher, and in 1891 published a collection of stories of peasant life, *Gösta Berling's Saga*. She was the first woman to receive a Nobel prize, in 1909.

laggard etc. LAG[1].

laggen, laggin, *n.* (*Sc.*) the angle between the side and bottom of a wooden dish; †the projecting rim of staves at the end of a cask etc. [var. of LAGGING]

lagging LAG[1,3].

lagomorph, *n.* any gnawing mammal with two pairs of upper incisors (e.g. hares, rabbits). **lagomorphic, -phous**, *a.* [Gr. *lagōs,* hare, *morphē,* form]

lagoon, *n.* a shallow lake near a river or the sea, due to the infiltration or overflow of water from the larger body; the water enclosed by an atoll or coral island. [F *lagune,* It. and Sp. *laguna,* L LACUNA]

Lagos, *n.* chief port and former capital of Nigeria, located at the western end of an island in a lagoon and linked by bridges with the mainland via Iddo Island; population (1983) 1,097,000. Industries include chemicals, metal products, and fish.

Lagrange, *n.* **Joseph Louis** (1736–1813), French mathematician, who predicted the existence of Lagrangian points 1772. His *Mécanique analytique* (1788) applied mathematical analysis, using principles established by Newton, to such problems as the movements of planets when affected by each other's gravitational force. He presided over the commission that introduced the metric system 1793. **Lagrangian points**, *n.pl.* five points in space where a small body can remain in a stable orbit with two much more massive bodies. Three of the points, L1–L3, lie on a line joining the two bodies. The other two points, L4 and L5, which are the most stable, lie either side of the line. Their existence was predicted 1772 by Lagrange.

lagrimoso, *a., adv.* (*Mus.*) solemnly, plaintively. [It., as LACHRYMOSE]

La Guardia, *n.* **Fiorello (Henrico)** (1882–1947), US Republican politician, mayor of New York 1933–1945. Elected against the opposition of the powerful Tammany Hall Democratic Party organization, he cleaned up the administration, suppressed racketeering, and organized unemployment relief, slum-clearance schemes, and social services. Although nominally a Republican, he strongly supported Roosevelt's New Deal. La Guardia Airport, New York, is named after him.

lah-di-dah LA-DI-DA.

Lahore, *n.* capital of the province of Punjab and second city of Pakistan; population (1981) 2,920,000. Industries include engineering, textiles, carpets, and chemicals. It is associated with Mogul rulers Akbar, Jahangir, and Aurangzeb, whose capital it was in the 16th–17th centuries.

laic, laical etc. LAY[2].

laid, *past, p.p.* LAY[1]. *a.* lying down; placed or pressed down, set out. **laid back,** *a.* (*coll.*) relaxed, casual.

laid paper, *n.* paper made with a ribbed surface, marked by the wires on which the pulp is laid, opp. to *wove paper*.

Lailat ul-Barah, *n.* Muslim festival, the Night of Forgiveness, which takes place two weeks before the beginning of the fast of Ramadan (the ninth month of the Islamic year) and is a time for asking and granting forgiveness.

Lailat ul-Isra Wal Mi'raj, *n.* Muslim festival that celebrates the prophet Mohammed's Night Journey.

Lailat ul-Qadr, *n.* Muslim festival, the Night of Power, which celebrates the giving of the Koran to Mohammed. It usually falls at the end of Ramadan.

lain, *past, p.p.* LIE[2].

Laing, *n.* **R(onald) D(avid)** (1927–1989), Scottish psychoanalyst, originator of the 'social theory' of mental illness, for example that schizophrenia is promoted by family pressure for its members to conform to standards alien to themselves. His books include *The Divided Self* 1960 and *The Politics of the Family* 1971.

lair[1], *n.* the den or retreat of a wild beast; a pen or shed for cattle on the way to slaughter or the market; †a resting-place; †a tomb; †a litter. *v.i.* to go to or lie in a lair; to make one's lair (in). *v.t.* to place in a lair. **lairage,** *n.* [OE *leger,* a bed (cp. Dut. *leger,* G *Lager,* LAAGER), cogn. with LIE[2]]

†**lair[2],** *n.* mire, mud; soil, earth; (*Sc.*) a quagmire. *v.i.* to sink or stick in a quagmire. [Icel. *leir*]

lair[3], *n.* (*Austral. coll.*) an over-dressed man. **all laired up,** dressed in a flashy manner. **lairy,** *a.* flashy.

laird, *n.* (*Sc.*) the owner of a landed estate; a landlord. **lairdship,** *n.* [var. of LORD]

laissez-aller, *n.* unrestraint; absence of conventionality. [F, let (them or things) go (*laissez,* imper. of *laisser,* to let, *aller,* to go)]

laissez-faire, *n.* the principle of non-interference, esp. by the Government in industrial and commercial affairs. *a.* [F *faire,* to do]

laity LAY[2].

lake[1], *n.* a large sheet of water entirely surrounded by land; a large amount of wine, milk etc., a commodity surplus. **Lake District, lakeland,** *n.* the mountainous district occupied by the English lakes formerly in Cumberland, Westmorland and Lancashire, now in Cumbria. **lake-dwellers,** *n.pl.* the prehistoric inhabitants of dwellings built on piles on the shallow edges of lakes. **lake-dwellings,** *n.pl.* **Lake Poets,** *n.pl.* **Lake School,** *n.* Coleridge, Southey and Wordsworth, grouped as a school by the *Edinburgh Review* because they happened to live in the Lake District. **lake-settlement,** *n.* **lake-trout,** *n.* a fish of the salmon family living in lakes, esp. *Salmo ferox*. **laker,** *n.* one of the Lake Poets; a lake fish; a boat for lakes; one who boats on lakes. **lakeless,** *a.* **lake-like,** *a.* **lakelet,** *n.* **laky,** *a.* [OF *lac,* L *lacum,* nom. *lacus*]

lake[2], *n.* a crimson pigment, orig. derived from lac or cochineal; an insoluble coloured pigment formed by a soluble dye mixed with a mordant; the colour of these, carmine. [var. of LAC[1]]

Lake, *n.* **Veronica** (1919–1973), stage name of Constance Frances Marie Ockelman, US film actress, who co-starred with Alan Ladd in several films during the 1940s, including *The Blue Dahlia* (1946). Her other work includes *Sullivan's Travels* (1942) and *I Married a Witch* (1942).

Lake District, *n.* region in Cumbria, England; area 1800 sq km/700 sq miles. It embraces the the principal English lakes separated by wild uplands rising to many peaks, including Scafell Pike 978 m/3210 ft.

lakh, lac, *n.* the number 100,000 (usu. of rupees, taka). [Hind., from Sansk. *lākshā*]

Lakshadweep, *n. pl.* group of 36 coral islands, 10 inhabited, in the Indian Ocean, 320 km/200 miles off the Malabar coast; area 32 sq km/12 sq miles; population (1981) 40,000. The administrative headquarters is on Kavaratti Island. Products include coir, copra, and fish. The religion is Muslim. The first Western visitor was Vasco da Gama 1499. It was British from 1877 until Indian independence, and created a Union Territory of the Republic of India 1956. Formerly known as the Laccadive, Minicoy, and Amindivi Islands, they were renamed Lakshadweep 1973.

Lakshmi, *n.* Hindu goddess of wealth and beauty, consort of Vishnu; her festival is Diwali.

laky LAKE[1].

Lalande, *n.* **Michel de** (1657–1726), French organist and compose, of church music for the court at Versailles.

Lalique, *n.* **René** (1860–1945), French designer of art nouveau glass, jewellery, and house interiors.

Lallan, Lallans, *n.* the Lowlands of Scotland; the broad Scots dialect, esp. its modern literary use. [Sc.]

lallation, *n.* pronunciation of *r* as *l*. **lalling,** *n.* the continuous repetition of a single sound, as in infants. [F, from L *lallāre,* to sing (a lullaby)]

Lalo, *n.* **(Victor Antoine) Edouard** (1823–1892), French composer. His Spanish ancestry and violin training are evident in the *Symphonie Espagnole* 1873 for violin and orchestra, and *Concerto for cello and orchestra* 1877. He also wrote an opera, *Le Roi d'Ys* 1887.

lalopathy, *n.* any speech disorder.

Lam, *n.* **Wilfredo** (1902–1982), Cuban abstract painter. Influenced by surrealism in the 1930s (he lived in Paris 1937–41), he created a semi-abstract style using mysterious and sometimes menacing images and symbols mainly taken from Caribbean tradition. His *Jungle* series, for example, contains voodoo elements.

lam[1], *v.t.* (*past, p.p.* **lammed**) (*coll.*) to thrash, to wallop. **to lam it into,** to thrash. **lamming,** *n.* a beating. [cp. Icel. *lemja,* OE *lemian,* to LAME]

lam[2], *n.* (*N Am. sl.*) a quick escape, hasty flight, esp. from the law. *v.i.* (*past, p.p.* **lammed**) to depart quickly, to escape. [perh. from LAW[1]]

lama[1], *n.* a Tibetan or Mongolian Buddhist priest or monk. **Dalai Lama,** the chief lama of Tibet. **Teshu Lama,** that of Mongolia. **Lamaism,** *n.* the religion of Tibet and Mongolia, a form of Mahāyāna Buddhism. Buddhism was introduced into Tibet AD 640, but the real founder of Lamaism was the Indian missionary Padma Sambhava who began his activity about 750. The head of the church is the Dalai Lama, who is considered an incarnation of the Bodhisattva Avalokiteśvara. **lamaist,** *n., a.* **lamaistic,** *a.* **lamaserai, -sery,** *n.* a lamaist monastery. [Tibetan *blama* (*b* silent)]

lama[2], LLAMA.

lamantin, *n.* the manatee. [F]

Lamarck, *n.* **Jean Baptiste de** (1744–1829), French naturalist, whose theory of evolution, known as Lamarckism, was based on the idea that acquired characters are inherited. His works include *Philosophie Zoologique/Zoological Philosophy* (1809) and *Histoire naturelle des animaux sans vertèbres/Natural History of Invertebrate Animals* (1815–22). **Lamarckian,** *a.* of or pertaining to Lamarck. *n.* an adherent of Lamarck's theories. **Lamarckianism, Lamarckism,** *n.* a theory of evolution, now discredited, advocated during the early 19th cent. by Lamarck. It differed from the Darwinian theory of evolution in that it was based on the idea that acquired characters were inherited: he argued that particular use of an organ or limb strengthens it, and that this development may be 'preserved by reproduction'. For example, he suggested that giraffes have long necks because they are continually stretching them to reach high leaves; according to the theory, giraffes that have lengthened their necks by stretching will pass this characteristic on to their offspring.

Lamartine, *n.* **Alphonse de** (1790–1869), French poet. He wrote romantic poems, *Méditations* (1820), followed by *Nouvelles Méditations/New Meditations* (1823), *Harmonies* (1830), and others. His *Histoire des Girondins/History of the Girondins* (1847) influenced the revolution of 1848.

lamasery LAMA[1].

Lamb[1], *n.* **Charles** (1775–1834), English essayist and critic. He collaborated with his sister Mary (1764–1847) on *Tales from Shakespeare* (1807), and his

Specimens of English Dramatic Poets (1808) helped to revive interest in Elizabethan plays. As 'Elia' he contributed essays to the *London Magazine* from 1820 (collected 1823 and 1833).

Lamb[2], *n.* **Willis** (1913–), US physicist who revised the quantum theory of Dirac. The hydrogen atom was thought to exist in either of two distinct states carrying equal energies. More sophisticated measurements by Lamb in 1947 demonstrated that the two energy levels were not equal. This discrepancy, since known as the Lamb shift, won for him the 1955 Nobel physics prize.

lamb, *n.* the young of a sheep; the flesh of this used for food; one as innocent and gentle as a lamb; a member of a church flock; a term of endearment; †(*iron.*) a cruel, merciless person; †a dupe. *v.i.* to bring forth lambs. *v.t.* to tend ewes at lambing. **like a lamb to the slaughter,** defenceless, innocent, unresisting. **the Lamb, Lamb of God,** Christ. **lamb-ale,** *n.* a rural festivity at sheep-shearing. **lambskin,** *n.* the skin of a lamb dressed as a leather with the fleece on. **lamb's tails,** *n.pl.* catkins of hazel and filbert. **lamb's-wool,** *n.* wool from lambs used for hosiery; ale mixed with sugar, nutmeg and the pulp of roasted apples. *a.* made of lamb's wool. **lambhood, lambkin,** *n.* **lamb-like,** *a.* [OE (cp. Dut. *lam,* Icel. *lamb,* G *Lamm*)]

lambast, lambaste, *v.t.* to beat; to give a verbal thrashing to.

lambative LAMBITIVE under LAMBENT.

lambda, *n.* the 11th letter of the Greek alphabet (λ) transliterated as Roman *l;* a symbol denoting wavelength. **lambda particle,** *n.* an elementary particle, a hyperon, that has no charge. **lambdacism, labdacism,** *n.* the too frequent repetition or improper pronunciation of the letter *l*; lallation. **lambdoid, -oidal,** *a.* resembling the Greek letter lambda (λ) in form, as the suture between the parietal and the occipital bones of the skull. [Gr., rel. to Heb. *lāmedh*]

lambent, *a.* playing or moving about, touching slightly without burning, as flame or light; softly radiant; light, sparkling, as wit. **lambency,** *n.* **lambently,** *a.* †**lambitive, lambative,** *a.* to be taken by licking. *n.* a medicine to be taken thus. [L *lambens -entis,* pres.p. of *lambere,* to lick]

lambert, *n.* a former measure of the luminous intensity or brightness of a surface, one lumen for every square centimetre. [after the G scientist J.H. *Lambert,* 1728–77]

Lambeth, *n.* a London borough south of the Thames. **Lambeth Conference,** *n.* meeting of bishops of the Anglican Communion every ten years, presided over by the archbishop of Canterbury; its decisions are not binding. **Lambeth degree,** *n.* an honorary degree conferred by the Archbishop of Canterbury. **Lambeth palace,** *n.* the palace of the Archbishop of Canterbury; the chief hierarchy of the Church of England.

lambrequin, *n.* a strip of cloth or other material worn as covering over a helmet for protection from heat; (*Her.*) the floating wreath of a helmet; an ornamental strip of drapery over a door, window, mantelshelf etc. [F, etym. doubtful]

lame, *a.* disabled in one or more of the limbs, esp. the foot or leg; limping, halting; not running smoothly or evenly; unsatisfactory; imperfect. *v.t.* to make lame; to cripple, to disable. **lame duck,** *n.* a defaulter on the Stock Exchange; a weak, ineffective or disabled person. **lamely,** *adv.* **lameness,** *n.* **lamish,** *a.* [OE *lama* (cp. Dut. *lam,* Icel. *lami,* G *lahm*)]

lamé, *n.* a fabric containing metallic threads. [F, from L *lāmina,* a thin plate]

lamella, *n.* (*pl.* **-llae**) a thin plate, layer or scale. **lamellar, lamellate, -ated, lamellose,** *a.* **lamellarly,** *adv.* [L, dim. of LAMINA]

lamelli-, *comb. form* pertaining to thin layers, scales etc.

lamellibranch, *n.* one of the Lamellibranchiata, a class of molluscs breathing by two pairs of plate-like gills. **lamellibranchiate,** *a.* pertaining to the Lamellibranchiata. *n.* any individual of the Lamellibranchiata. [Gr. *branchia,* gills]

lamellicorn, *a.* pertaining to the Lamellicornia, a group of beetles having short antennae terminated by a short lamellated club. *n.* a lamellicorn beetle. **lamellicornate, -cornous,** *a.* **lamelliferous, lamelliform,** *a.* [L *cornu,* a horn]

lamellirostral, *a.* pertaining to the Lamellirostres, a group of birds (acc. to Cuvier) having lamellose bills, containing the ducks, geese etc.

lament, *v.i.* to mourn, to wail; to feel or express sorrow. *v.t.* to bewail, to mourn over; to deplore, to grieve for. *n.* sorrow expressed in cries or complaints; an elegy, a dirge; a mournful song or melody. **lamentable,** *a.* to be lamented; mournful, sad; very unfortunate, deplorable. **lamentably,** *adv.* **lamentation,** *n.* the act of lamenting; an audible expression of grief; a wail. **Lamentations,** *n. sing.* the book of the Old Testament containing the lamentations of Jeremiah. **lamented,** *a.* mourned for; deceased, late. †**lamentedly,** *adv.* **lamenter,** *n.* **lamenting,** *n., a.* **lamentingly,** *adv.* [F *lamenter,* L *lāmentārī,* from *lāmentum,* a wail]

lameter, lamiter, *n.* (*chiefly Sc.*) a lame person, a cripple. [LAME (*-eter,* etym. doubtful)]

lametta, *n.* gold, silver or brass foil or wire. [It., dim. of *lama,* L LAMINA]

lamia, *n.* in classical mythology, a lascivious evil spirit in the form of a serpent with a woman's head; a sorceress, a witch. [L, from Gr.]

lamina, *n.* (*pl.* **-nae, -nas**) a thin plate, layer, coat, leaf, flake, stratum etc. **laminable,** *a.* **laminal, laminar, -nary,** *a.* **laminar flow,** *n.* a smooth liquid flow following the shape of a stream-lined surface. **laminarian,** *a.* pertaining to the genus *Laminaria,* a genus of algae with a flat ribless expansion in place of leaves, or to the sea-depths where these occur. **laminarize, -ise,** *v.t.* to form (a surface) for a laminar flow. **laminate,** *v.t.* to beat, press or roll into thin plates; to cut or split into thin layers or sheets; to produce by joining successive layers or sheets. *v.i.* to split into thin plates. *a.*, consisting of, or having laminae, laminated. *n.* an article or material produced by laminating. **laminated,** *a.* laminate. **lamination,** *n.* **laminator,** *n.* one who produces laminates. **laminitis,** *n.* an inflammation of the sensitive tissue lining a horse's hoof. **laminiferous, laminose,** *a.* [L]

Lammas, Lammas Day, *n.* 1 Aug., the day on which first-fruits were offered in Anglo-Saxon times; the Roman Catholic feast of St Peter celebrated on the same day. **Lammas -tide,** *n.* the season around Lammas, harvest time. [OE *hlāfmœsse* (LOAF[1], MASS[1])]

lammergeyer, -geier, *n.* the great bearded vulture, *Gypaëtus barbatus,* an inhabitant of lofty mountains of S Europe, Asia and N Africa. [G *Lämmergeier* (*Lämmer,* lambs, *Geier,* vulture)]

Lamming, *n.* **George** (1927–), Barbadian novelist, author of the autobiographical *In the Castle of my Skin* (1953), describing his upbringing in the small village where he was born. He later moved to London.

lamp[1], *n.* a vessel for the production of artificial light, esp. by the combustion of oil with a wick; any vessel enclosing a gas-jet, incandescent wire or other source of artificial light; any of various usu. movable holders with fittings for one or more electric light bulb, as a *table lamp, standard lamp;* an electric device which emits, esp. infrared or ultraviolet light waves, as a *sun lamp;* any source of light, as the sun, moon etc.; a source of intellectual or spiritual light; (*pl.*) *sl.* the eyes. *v.i.* to shine; to give light. *v.t.* to supply with lamps; to light, to illuminate. **to smell of the lamp,** to show signs of laborious preparation (as a sermon, speech etc.). **lamp-black,** *n.* amorphous carbon, obtained by the imperfect combustion of oil or resin used as a pigment or filler. **lamp-chimney, -glass,** *n.* the upright chimney surrounding the wick and flame of an oil lamp. **lamp-light,** *n.* the light from a lamp or lamps. **lamp-lighter,** *n.* one employed to light the public lamps. **lamp-post, -standard,** *n.* a pillar supporting a street lamp. **lampshade,** *n.* a cover for a lamp which softens or directs the light emitted by the electric bulb.

†**lamping,** *a.* shining, sparkling. [OF *lampe,* L and Gr. *lampas,* from *lampein,* to shine]
lamp[2], *v.i.* to go rapidly or jauntily; to go with long strides. [Sc., etym. doubtful]
lampad, *n.* a lamp, a torch. **lampadary,** *n.* in the Greek Church, an officer who attended to the lighting of the church and carried a lighted taper before the patriarch. [Gr. *lampas -pados,* LAMP[1]]
lampadedromy, *n.* an ancient Greek torch-race; a race in which a lighted torch was passed from hand to hand. [Gr. *lampadēdromia* (*-dromia,* from *dramein,* to run)]
lampadomancy, *n.* divination by the flame of a torch or lamp.
lampas[1], **-passe,** *n.* a swelling of the roof of the mouth in horses. [F, etym. doubtful]
lampas[2], *n.* a flowered silk or woollen cloth used in upholstery. [F, etym. doubtful]
Lampedusa, *n.* **Giuseppe Tomasi di** (1896–1957), Italian aristocrat, author of *The Leopard* 1958, a novel set in his native Sicily in the period after it was annexed by Garibaldi 1860, which chronicles the reactions of an aristocratic family to social and political upheavals.
lampern, *n.* the river lamprey, *Petromyzon fluviatilis.* [OF *lamproyon,* dim. of *lampreie*]
lampion, *n.* a small coloured globe or cup with wick etc., used in illuminations. [F, from It. *lampione,* from *lampa,* LAMP[1]]
lampoon, *n.* a scurrilous personal satire. *v.t.* to write lampoons upon; to abuse with personal satire. **lampooner, -nist,** *n.* †**lampoon(e)ry,** *n.* [F *lampon,* from *lampons,* let us drink (*lamper,* to booze, perh. a var. of *lapper,* to lap up)]
lamprey, *n.* an eel-like fish with a suctorial mouth, belonging to the genus *Petromyzon.* [OF *lampreie* (F *lamproie*), It. *lampreda,* late L *lampetra* (*lambere,* to lick, *petra,* rock)]
lana, *n.* the close-grained, tough wood of a S American tree, *Genipa americana.* **lana dye,** *n.* a pigment obtained from the fruit of this. [native name]
Lanarkshire, *n.* former inland county of Scotland, merged 1975 in the region of Strathclyde. The county town was Lanark.
lanate, lanose, *a.* woolly, covered with curly hairs. †**lanary,** *n.* a wool-store. [L *lānātus,* from *lāna,* wool]
Lancashire, *n.* county in NW England. **area** 3040 sq km/1173 sq miles. **towns** administrative headquarters Preston, which forms part of Central Lancashire New Town (together with Fulwood, Bamber Bridge, Leyland, and Chorley), Lancaster, Accrington, Blackburn, Burnley; ports Fleetwood and Heysham; seaside resorts Blackpool, Morecambe, and Southport. **population** (1987) 1,381,000. **products** formerly a world centre of cotton manufacture, this has been replaced with newer varied industries.
Lancaster, Duchy and County Palatine of, created in 1351, and attached to the crown since 1399. The office of Chancellor of the Duchy is actually a 'sinecure', usually held by a member of the Cabinet with a special role outside that of the regular ministries, for example, Harold Lever as financial adviser to the Wilson-Callaghan governments from 1974.
Lancasterian, *a.* of or pertaining to Joseph Lancaster or his monitorial system of education. [Joseph *Lancaster,* 1778–1838]
Lancastrian, *a.* pertaining to the family descended from John of Gaunt, Duke of Lancaster. *n.* an adherent of this, one of the Red Rose party in the Wars of the Roses; a native of Lancashire.
lance, *n.* a thrusting weapon consisting of a long shaft with a sharp point, formerly the weapon of knights, later used by some regiments of cavalry; a similar weapon used for killing a harpooned whale, for spearing fish etc.; a lancet; a lancer. *v.t.* to pierce with or as with a lance; (*Surg.*) to open with a lancet; †to hurl or fling (a lance). **lance-corporal,** *n.* a private who performs the duties and holds the rank of a corporal. **lance-sergeant,** *n.* an acting sergeant. **lance-snake,** *n.* a venomous American snake, the fer-de-lance, of the genus *Bothrops,* allied to the rattlesnake. **lance-wood,** *n.* the tough, elastic wood of *Duguetia quitarensis* and other S American and W Indian trees. **lancer,** *n.* a cavalry soldier armed with a lance; (*pl.*) a particular set of quadrilles; the music for this. **lanciform,** *a.* having a lance shape. [F, from L *lancea*]
†**lancegay,** *n.* a kind of spear. [OF *lancegaye,* corr. of *lancezagaye* (LANCE, *zagaye,* ASSAGAI)]
lancelet, *n.* a small transparent iridescent fish, *Amphioxus lanceolatus,* of very low organization.
Lancelot of the Lake, in British legend the most celebrated of King Arthur's knights, the lover of Queen Guinevere. Originally a folk-hero, he was introduced into the Arthurian cycle of tales in the 12th cent.
lanceolate, -ated, *a.* tapering to a point at each end. [L *lanceolātus,* from *lanceola,* dim. of *lancea,* LANCE]
lancet, *n.* a sharp surgical instrument, used in bleeding, cutting of abscesses, tumours etc.; a lancet-window or arch. *a.* lancet shaped. **lancet arch,** *n.* an arch with a sharply pointed top. **lancet window,** *n.* a high narrow window with a sharply pointed arch. **lanceted,** *a.* [OF *lancette,* dim. of LANCE]
lancinate, *v.t.* to tear, to lacerate. **lancinating,** *a.* of a pain, piercing, cutting, keen. **lancination,** *n.* [L *lancinātus,* p.p. of *lancināre,* to rend]
Lancs., (*abbr.*) Lancashire.
Land[1], *n.* (*pl.* **Länder**) federal unit of West Germany.
Land[2], *n.* **Edwin** (1909–), US inventor of the Polaroid camera 1947, which develops the film inside the camera and produces an instant photograph.
land, *n.* the solid portion of the earth, esp. of the earth's surface, as distinct from the oceans and seas; the ground, the soil, a tract of country, esp. a rural or agricultural area; a country, a district, a region; a nation, a people; landed property, real estate; (*pl.*) estates. *v.t.* to set or place on shore; to bring to shore; to set down from a vehicle; to bring to or place in a certain position; to deal (a blow); to bring (fish) to land; to win, attain, capture or secure (e.g. a prize, a business deal). *v.i.* to come or go ashore; to disembark; to find oneself in a certain position; to alight. *a.* belonging to the land; terrestrial. **land of milk and honey,** the fertile land promised by God to the Israelites; any extremely fertile land; a place, country offering wealth and ease. **land of nod,** the land to which Cain was exiled after killing Abel; the state of being asleep. **land of the living,** the present life. **land of the midnight sun,** Norway. **to land up,** to end up. **to land with,** to burden with. **to make land, to make the land,** to come in sight of land as one's ship approaches it from the sea. **to see how the land lies,** to assess how matters stand or the state of play of a situation (before acting). **land-agent,** *n.* one employed to manage land for the proprietor, a steward; an agent for the sale of land. **Land Army,** *n.* a national organization of war-time volunteer farm-workers. **land bank,** *n.* a bank lending money on the security of land. **land-breeze,** *n.* a wind blowing seawards off the land. **land-crab,** *n.* a crab of the family Gecarcinidae, which lives mainly on land, visiting the sea chiefly for breeding. **landfall,** *n.* approach to land after a voyage; the first land descried after a voyage; a sudden transference of property in land by the death of a rich man; a landslip. **landfill,** *n.* the practice of burying rubbish under layers of earth; a rubbish dump where refuse is buried; the rubbish so buried. **landfilling,** *n.* **land-fish,** *n.* one who is as much out of his or her element as a fish out of water. **land-flood,** *n.* an overflow of water on land. **land-force,** *n.* a military force employed on land. †**land-gavel,** *n.* (*Hist.*) a tax, tribute or rent on land. **land-girl,** *n.* a girl or woman employed in farm-work during the two World Wars. **land-grabber** GRAB. **land-grabbing,** *n., a.* **landholder,** *n.* one who owns or (usu.) rents land. **landholding,** *n., a.* **land-hunger,** *n.* the desire to acquire land. **land-hungry,** *a.* eager to acquire land. **land-jobber,** *n.* one who speculates in land. **landlady,** *n.* a woman who keeps an inn or lodging-house; a woman who lets houses, lodgings etc. **Land League,** *n.* an association formed in Ireland in 1879 to agitate for a settlement of the land question, by

reducing rents, introducing peasant proprietorship etc., suppressed in 1881. **land-line,** *n.* an overland telecommunications cable or wire. **landlocked,** *a.* enclosed by land; isolated from the sea. **landlord,** *n.* a man who lets houses, lodgings etc.; the master of an inn or of a lodging-house. **landlordism,** *n.* the proceedings or authority of land-owners as a body or class; the system under which land is owned by individuals to whom tenants pay a fixed rent. **land-lubber,** *n.* (*derog.*) a landsman, one unused to the sea or ships. †**landman,** *n.* one who lives on the land, a countryman, a peasant. **landmark,** *n.* anything set up to mark the boundaries of land; a prominent object on land serving as a guide; a conspicuous object in a place or district; an important event in history etc. **landmass,** *n.* a large area of land uninterrupted by the sea. **land-measuring,** *n.* **land-mine,** *n.* a mine set in the ground to explode under advancing troops etc. *v.t.* to place land-mines. **landowner,** *n.* **landownership,** *n.* **land-owning,** *a.* **land-rail,** *n.* the corn-crake. †**land-raker,** *n.* a vagabond. **land-rat,** *n.* a rat living on land; hence, a thief, a robber. †**land-reeve,** *n.* an assistant to a land-steward. **land reform,** *n.* a redistribution of land or adjustment of land-rent. **Land Registry,,** *n.* an official body set up 1925 to register legal rights to land in England and Wales. There has been a gradual introduction, since 1925, of compulsory registration of land in different areas of the country. This requires the purchaser of land to register details of his title and all other rights (such as mortgages and easements) relating to the land. Once registered, the title to the land is guaranteed by the Land Registry. This makes buying and selling of land easier and cheaper. **land-roll, -roller,** *n.* a roller for crushing clods. **land-scrip,** *n.* (*N Am.*) a certificate entitling the holder to become the owner of a specified amount of public land. **land-shark,** *n.* a person who preys on seamen ashore; a land-grabber. **landslide,** *n.* a landslip; a political debacle. **landslip,** *n.* the sliding down of a considerable portion of ground from a higher to a lower level; the ground thus slipping. **landsman,** *n.* one who lives on land; one unused to the sea and its ways. **land-spring,** *n.* a spring of water appearing only after a heavy rain. **land-steward,** *n.* one who manages a landed estate. **land-surveying,** *n.* measuring and mapping of land. **land-surveyor,** *n.* one who measures and draws plans of land. **land-tax,** *n.* a tax assessed upon land and property. **land-waiter,** *n.* a custom-house officer who watches the landing of dutiable goods. **landwind,** *n.* a wind blowing off the land. **landed,** *a.* having an estate in land; consisting of real estate. **lander,** *n.* one who lands or disembarks; (*coll.*) a strong blow. **landing,** *n.* the act of going or setting on land, esp. from a vessel or aircraft; a pier, wharf, jetty or other place for disembarking or alighting; (*N Am.*) the platform of a railway-station; a level space at the top of a flight of stairs or between flights. **landing beam,** *n.* a radio beam that guides an aircraft to ground. **landing-craft,** *n.* a small naval vessel for making shore landings (with troops, equipment etc.). **landing-field,** *n.* an area for the landing or take-off of aircraft. **landing-gear,** *n.* apparatus of an aircraft employed in its landing. **landing-net,** *n.* a small bag-net used to take fish from the water when hooked. **landing-place,** *n.* a place for landing. **landing-stage,** *n.* a platform, fixed or floating, on which passengers and goods are disembarked. **landing-strip,** *n.* a strip of ground for aircraft landings and take-offs; an airstrip. **landless,** *a.* **landward,** *a.*, *adv.* **landwards,** *adv.* [OE (cp. Dut., Icel., G etc., *Land*)]

landamman(n), *n.* the chief magistrate in some of the Swiss cantons. [Swiss G]

landau, *n.* a four-wheeled horse-drawn carriage with a folding top that may be opened and thrown back. **landaulet,** *n.* a small landau. **landaulette,** *n.* a motor-car with a covering or hood, fixed in front, movable behind. [*Landau,* Germany, where the landau was orig. made]

landdros(t), *n.* a district magistrate, civil commissioner, fiscal agent etc., in S Africa. [Afrikaans]

lande, *n.* a heathy and sandy plain; a moor. [F, see LAWN[1]]

landfall, landfill etc. LAND.

landgrave, *n.* a German title, dating from the 12th cent., orig. used to distinguish a governor of a province from inferior counts. **landgraviate, landgraveship,** *n.* **landgravine,** *n.* the wife of a landgrave. [MHG *lantgrave* (G *Landgraf*), cp. Dut. *landgraaf*]

landing, landlady, landmark etc. LAND.

Landsat, *n.* a series of satellites used for monitoring earth resources. The first was launched in 1972.

Landsborough grass, *n.* (*Austral.*) the rich fodder grass of Queensland.

landscape, †**skip,** *n.* a picture representing country scenery; a view, esp. a picturesque view of country scenery. *v.t.* to develop the natural beauty of (an area) by landscape-gardening. **landscape architecture, landscape-gardening,** *n.* the art of laying out grounds so as to develop their natural beauties. **landscape-gardener,** *n.* **landscape-marble,** *n.* a variety of marble with dendriform markings. **landscape-painter, landscapist,** *n.* a painter of landscapes. [Dut. *land-schap* (LAND, SHIP)]

Landseer, *n.* **Edwin Henry**(1802–1873), English painter and sculptor, who achieved popularity with sentimental studies of animals. His sculptures include the lions in Trafalgar Square, London, 1859.

Landsteiner, *n.* **Karl** (1868–1943), Austrian immunologist, who discovered the ABO blood group system 1900–02, and aided in the discovery of the Rhesus blood factors 1940. He discovered the polio virus.

lane[1], *n.* a narrow road, way or passage, esp. between hedges; a narrow street; a passage between persons or objects; a prescribed route, as for ocean liners; a division of a road for a single stream of traffic. [OE (cp. OFris. *lana*, Dut. *laan*)]

lane[2], LONE.

Lanfranc, *n.* (*c.* 1010–1089), Italian archbishop of Canterbury from 1070; he rebuilt the cathedral, replaced English clergy by Normans, enforced clerical celibacy, and separated the ecclesiastical from the secular courts.

Lang[1], *n.* **Andrew** (1844–1912), Scottish historian and folklore scholar. His writings include historical works, anthropological essays, (such as *Myth, Ritual and Religion* (1887) and *The Making of Religion* (1898), novels, and a series of children's books, beginning with the *Blue Fairy Tale Book* 1889.

Lang[2], *n.* **Fritz** (1890–1976), Austrian film director. His German films include *Metropolis* (1927), and the series of *Dr Mabus* films, after which he fled from the Nazis to Hollywood 1936. His US films include *Fury* (1936), *You Only Live Once* (1937), and *The Big Heat* (1953).

lang (*Sc.*) LONG[1]. **langsyne,** *adv.* (*Sc.*) long since, long ago. *n.* time long ago.

lang., (*abbr.*) language.

Lange, *n.* **David (Russell)** (1942–), New Zealand socialist politician, Labour Party leader from 1983. Lange, a barrister, was elected to the House of Representatives 1977. Labour had a decisive win in the 1984 general election on a non-nuclear defence policy, which Lange immediately put into effect, despite criticism from other Western countries, particularly the US. He introduced a free-market economic policy and was re-elected 1987.

Langland, *n.* **William** (*c.* 1332–*c.* 1400), English poet. His alliterative *Vision concerning Piers Plowman* appeared in three versions between about 1362 and 1398, but some critics believe he was only responsible for the first. It condemns the social and moral evils of 14th-cent. England.

langlauf, *n.* cross country skiing. **langlaufer,** *n.* [G *lang,* long, *Lauf,* run, race]

langouste, *n.* the spiny lobster. **langoustine,** *n.* the smaller Norway lobster. [F]

†**langrage, -ridge,** *n.* canister or case-shot loaded with bolts, nails and pieces of iron, formerly used against rigging. [etym. unknown]

†**langspiel,** *n.* a kind of harp formerly used in the Shetland Isles. [Norw. *langspil*]

Langton, *n.* **Stephen** (*c.* 1150–1228), English priest. When in 1207 Innocent III secured his election as archbishop of Canterbury, King John refused to recognize him, and Langton was not allowed to enter England until 1213. He supported the barons in their struggle against John, and was mainly responsible for the Magna Carta.

Langtry, *n.* **Lillie** (1853–1929), English actress, and mistress of the future Edward VII. She was known as the 'Jersey lily' from her birthplace, and was considered to be one of the most beautiful women of her time.

language, *n.* human speech; the communication of ideas by articulate sounds or words; the vocabulary peculiar to a nation, tribe or people; the vocabulary appropriate to a particular science, profession etc.; the phrases and manner of expression peculiar to an individual; literary style; the phraseology or wording (of a book, passage, speech etc.); any formal or informal method of communicating ideas by symbols, gestures etc.; †a nation. **bad language,** swearing. **to speak the same language,** (*fig.*) to have a similar background; to have the same habits of mind, tastes etc. **language laboratory,** *a.* a place where languages are taught with the aid of tape recorders, headphones etc. **language-teacher,** *n.* **languaged,** *a.* (*usu. in comb.* as *well-languaged*). **languageless**, *a.* [F *langage,* from *langue,* L *lingua,* tongue]

langue, *n.* in linguistics, language regarded as an abstract system tacitly shared by a speech community. **langue d'oc**, *n.*; (*collect.*) mediaeval Southern French dialects, esp. the Provençal language, so called from the use of the word *oc,* yes, instead of *oïl* or *oui.* **langue docian**, *a.* **langue d'oïl**, **d'oui**, *n.* Northern French, that spoken north of the Loire in the Middle Ages, the original of modern French. [F, see prec.]

languet, -ette, *n.* a tongue-shaped part; a small metal tongue on a sword-hilt fitting over the scabbard; the tongue of an organ flue-pipe or the reed of a harmonium; the tongue of a balance; one of a row of tongue-like appendages along the dorsal edge of the bronchial sac of ascidians. [F *languette,* dim. of *langue,* as prec.]

languid, *a.* faint, relaxed, lacking energy; indisposed to exertion; spiritless, lacking animation, listless, dull; sluggish, slow. **languidly,** *adv.* **languidness,** *n.* [L *languidus,* as foll.]

languish, *v.i.* to become weak, feeble or sluggish; to lose vitality, energy or animation; to fall off, to fade, to grow slack; to droop, to pine (for); to put on a languid expression, to affect a tender, wistful or sentimental air. *n.* languishment; the act of languishing; a soft, tender look. **languisher,** *n.* **languishingly,** *adv.* **languishment,** *n.* [F *languiss-*, stem. of *languir,* L *languēre,* rel. to *laxus,* LAX]

languor, *n.* languidness, lassitude, faintness, laxity, inertness; debility; softness, tenderness of mood or expression; oppressive stillness (of the air etc.). **languorous,** *a.* **languorousness,** *n.* [OF, from L *languor -ōrem,* as prec.]

langur, *n.* any of several Asiatic monkeys having long tails and a circle of long hair around the face. [Hind. *lāgūr*]

laniard LANYARD.

laniary, *a.* adapted for tearing. *n.* a canine tooth in the Carnivora; †a slaughter-house, a shambles. †**laniate,** *v.t.* [L *laniārius,* pertaining to a butcher, *lanius,* from *laniāre,* to tear]

laniferous, lanigerous, *a.* bearing wool. [L *lāna,* wool]

lank, *a.* lean, long and thin, shrunken-looking; of hair, long and straight; †languid, drooping, limp. *v.i.* to be or become lank; to shrink or fall away. **lankly,** *adv.* **lankness, lankiness,** *n.* **lanky,** *a.* [OE *hlanc*]

lanner, *n.* the female of a falcon, *Falco lanarius.* **lanneret,** *n.* the male *Falco lanarius,* which is smaller than the female. [OF *lanier,* prob. ident. with *lanier,* cowardly]

lanolin, -line, *n.* an unctuous substance forming the basis of ointments etc., extracted from wool. [L *lāna,* wool, *oleum,* oil]

Lansbury, *n.* **George** (1859–1940), British Labour politician, leader in the Commons 1931–35. In 1921, while Poplar borough mayor, he went to prison with most of the council rather than modify their policy of more generous unemployment relief. He was MP 1910–12, and 1922–40; he was leader of the parliamentary Labour party 1931–35, but resigned (as a pacifist) in opposition to the party's militant response to the Italian invasion of Abyssinia (present-day Ethiopia).

lansquenet, *n.* a mercenary foot-soldier of Germany and France (15th–17th cent.); a cardgame of German origin, consisting largely of betting. [F, from G *Landsknecht* (LAND, *knetcht,* servant, cp. KNIGHT)]

Lantana, *n.* a genus of shrubs of the Verbena family, able to bloom continuously.

lantern, *n.* a case with transparent sides or panes for holding and protecting a light; the upper chamber of a lighthouse containing the light; a glazed structure on the top of a dome or roof, for the admission of light and air; a magic lantern. *v.t.* to furnish or provide with a lantern. **Chinese lantern** CHINA. **dark lantern** DARK. **magic lantern,** an apparatus with a lens through which a magnified image from a glass slide is cast on a screen by a powerful light. **lantern-fly,** *n.* an insect of the tropical genus *Fulgora,* formerly believed to produce light. **lantern-jawed,** *a.* having a long, thin face. **lantern-jaws,** *n.pl.* **lantern slide,** *n.* the glass slide holding the image projected by a magic lantern. **lantern-wheel,** *n.* a form of cog-wheel acting as a pinion to a spur-wheel. [F *lanterne,* L *lanterna,* prob. from Gr. *lamptēr,* from *lampein,* to shine (see LAMP[1])]

lanthanum, *n.* a metallic divalent element, at. no. 57; chem. symbol La, usu. occurring with didymium and cerium in cerite. **lanthanides**, **-noids**, **-nons**, *n.pl.* a group of rare metallic elements, at. nos. 58 to 71, rare earths. [from Gr. *lanthanein,* to lurk, to escape detection (from the lateness of its discovery in 1839)]

†**lanthorn,** LANTERN.

lanugo, *n.* pre-natal hair; a fine down. **lanuginose**, †**-ginous,** *a.* downy, covered with soft downy hair. [L lānūginōsus, from *lānūgo -ginis,* down, from *lāna,* wool]

lanx, *n.* (*Rom. Ant.*) a large dish or platter for serving meat. [L]

lanyard, laniard, *n.* (*Naut.*) a short cord, line or gasket for seizing or lashing; cord for firing a gun; cord to which a whistle or knife is attached. [earlier *lannier,* F *lanière* (assim. to YARD[1])]

Lanzhov, (formerly **Lanchow**) *n.* capital of Gansu province, China, on the Yellow river, 190 km/120 miles south of the Great Wall; population (1986) 1,350,000. Industries include oil refining, chemicals, fertilizers, and synthetic rubber.

Lao, *n. a.* the people or language of Laos in S E Asia. **Laotian**, *n.* a native of Laos, a Lao. *a.* pertaining to Laos or its people.

Laodicean, *a.* lukewarm in religion, politics etc. *n.* a person of this character. [ref. to the Christians of the ancient city of Laodicea (Rev. iii.15–16)]

Laois, Laoighis, *n.* county in Leinster province, Republic of Ireland. **area** 1720 sq km/664 sq miles. **county town** Portlaoise. **physical** flat except for the Slieve Bloom mountains in the NW. **population** (1986) 53,000. **products** sugarbeet, dairy products, woollens, agricultural machinery.

Laos, *n.* People's Democratic Republic of, landlocked country in SE Asia, bordered to N by China, E by Vietnam, S by Kampuchea, and W by Thailand. **area** 236,790 sq km/91,400 sq miles. **capital** Vientiane. **towns** Luang Prabang, the former royal capital. **physical** high mountains in the E; Mekong River in the W; jungle. **population** (1989) 3,923,000; annual growth rate 2.6%. **exports** tin, teak. **language** Lao. **religion** traditionally Theravada Buddhist.

lap[1], *n.* a loose hanging part of a garment or other object; the part of the person from the waist to the knees in sitting, esp. as a place for holding an object, a reposing child etc.; a place where anything rests or lies securely; that part of anything that extends over something else, the overlap; the amount of overlap; a continuous band of cotton-fibre; the length of rope, cord, thread etc., making one turn round a wheel, roller etc.; one round of a race-course, running track etc.; a wheel, disc or piece of leather made to rotate, for polishing gems, metal articles etc. *v.t.* (*past, p.p.* **lapped**) to wrap, to twist, to roll (around, about etc.); to lay (one thing) partly over another; to fold, to bend over; to enfold, to enwrap, to surround, to involve; to cause to overlap; to tie, to bind; to get ahead of by a lap or laps; to polish with a lap. *v.i.* to be turned over; to lie partly over something else, to overlap. **in the lap of the gods,** outside human control, up to chance. **lap of honour,** a victory circuit made by a winning contestant (e.g. around a racing track). **lap of luxury,** a state of wealth and ease. **the last lap,** the beginning of the end, closing stages. **to drop in someone's lap,** to give someone responsibility for something, a situation etc. **lap-dog,** *n.* a small pet dog. **lap-joint,** *n.* a joint in which one part laps over the other. **lap-jointed,** *a.* **lap-robe,** *n.* (*N Am.*) a travelling rug. **lapstone,** *n.* a stone held in the lap by a shoemaker for hammering leather on. **lap-streak,** *a.* clinker-built. *n.* a clinker-built boat. **lap-top,** *a.* of a portable computer etc., (theoretically) small enough to be held and operated on a person's lap. **lap-work,** *n.* work constructed with lap-joints; work polished by lapping. **lapful,** *n.* **lapper,** *n., a.* [OE *lœppa* (cp. Dut. and Dan. *lap,* G *Lappen*)]

lap², *v.i.* (*past, p.p.* **lapped**) to take up liquid with the tongue; to drink by lifting with the tongue; to beat gently (as waves on the shore) with a sound as of lapping. *v.t.* to lick or take up with the tongue; to drink or consume by lapping. *n.* the act of lapping; a lick; the amount taken up by this; food or drink that can be lapped up, esp. liquid food for animals; a weak kind of drink [cp. CAT-LAP]; the sound of water beating softly on a beach. [OE *lapian* (cp. Icel. *lepja,* OHG *laffan,* L *lambere,* Gr. *laptein*)]

lap³, lapje, lappie, *n.* (*S Afr.*) a small rag or cloth, a patch. [Afrikaans, from Dut. *lap,* rag, patch]

laparectomy, *n.* excision of a part of the intestine at the side.

laparo-, *comb. form* pertaining to the intestines or abdomen. [Gr. *lapara,* the flank, from *laparos,* soft]

laparoscope, *n.* an optical instrument for the internal examination of the body's organs. **laparoscopy**, *n.* an internal examination using a laparoscope.

laparotomy, *n.* incision into the cavity of the abdomen to form an artificial anus. **laparotomist,** *n.* **laparotomize, -mise,** *v.t.*

La Paz, *n.* city in Bolivia, 3800 m/12,400 ft above sea level; population (1985) 992,600. Products include textiles and copper. Founded by the Spanish 1548, it has been the seat of government since about 1900.

lapel, *n.* that part of a garment made to lap or fold over, esp. the fold on the front of a coat or jacket below the collar. **lapelled,** *a.* [LAP¹, -EL]

lapidary, *n.* one who cuts, polishes or engraves gems; a dealer in or connoisseur of gems. *a.* pertaining to the art of cutting, engraving or polishing gems; inscribed on or suitable for inscription on stones; hence, formal or monumental in style. **lapidary-bee,** *n. Bombus lapidarius,* which nests in or among stones. **lapidarian**, *a.* **lapidate,** *v.t.* to stone, esp. to kill by stoning. **lapidation,** *n.* **lapideous**, *a.* stony. †**lapidescent**, *a.* turning into stone, having the quality of converting into stone. *n.* a liquid converting substances into stone. **lapidescence,** *n.* **lapidicolous**, *a.* dwelling under or among stones. **lapidify**, *v.t.* to form or convert into stone. *v.i.* to become petrified. **lapidific, -ical**, *a.* **lapidification**, *n.* †**lapidist,** *n.* a lapidary. **lapidose**, *a.* stony; growing in stony soil.

lapilli, *n.pl.* volcanic ashes, consisting of small, angular, stony or slaggy fragments. **lapilliform**, *a.* [L, pl. of *lapillus,* dim. of *lapis,* stone]

lapis lazuli, *n.* a rich blue silicate of alumina, lime and soda; a pigment made from this; its colour. [med. L, stone of azure (*lapis,* stone, *lazulum,* azure)]

lapje, lappie LAP³.

Laplace, *n.* **Pierre Simon, Marquis de Laplace** (1749–1827), French astronomer and mathematician. In 1796, he theorized that the Solar System originated from a cloud of gas (the nebular hypothesis). He studied the motion of the Moon and planets, and published a five-volume survey of celestial mechanics, *Traité de méchanique céleste* (1799–1825). Among his mathematical achievements was the development of probability theory.

Lapland, *n.* region of Europe within the Arctic Circle in Norway, Sweden, Finland, and USSR, without political definition. Its chief resources are chromium, copper, iron, timber, hydroelectric power, and tourism. There are about 20,000 Lapps, who live by hunting, fishing, reindeer herding, and handicrafts. **Laplander**, **Lapp,** *n.* a native or inhabitant of Lapland; one belonging to the race inhabiting Lapland. **Laplandish, Lapp, Lappish,** *a.* [Swed. *Lappland*]

La Plata, *n.* capital of Buenos Aires province, Argentina; population (1980) 560,300. Industries include meat packing and petroleum refining. It was founded 1882.

La Plata, Río de, (or **River Plate**) estuary in South America into which the rivers Paraná and Uruguay flow; length 320 km/200 miles and width up to 240 km/150 miles. The basin drains much of Argentina, Bolivia, Brazil, Uruguay, and Paraguay, who all cooperate in its development.

lappel, LAPEL.

lapper LAP¹.

lappet, *n.* a little lap, fold or loose part of a garment or head-dress; a flap; a loose, fleshy process, a lobe, a wattle; a cloth, usually of the muslin type, on which is woven a small pattern. **lappeted,** *a.*

lapse, *v.i.* to slide, to glide, to pass insensibly or by degrees; to pass away, to fall back or away; to fall into disuse, decay or ruin; to make a slip or fault, to fail in duty; to pass from one proprietor to another by omission, negligence or failure of a patron, legatee etc.; to become void. †*v.t.* to allow to slide or slip away; to catch, to seize. *n.* the act of lapsing, gliding, slipping or gradually falling (away, from etc.); easy, smooth and almost imperceptible movement, gentle flow etc.; the imperceptible passage of time; a mistake, a slip, an error, a fault, deviation from what is right; a falling into disuse, neglect, decay or ruin; termination of a right or privilege through desuetude. **lapse rate,** *n.* the rate of change of atmospheric factors (e.g. temperature, humidity) with changing altitude. **lapsable, -sible,** *a.* **lapser,** *n.* **lapsus,** *n.* (*pl.* **lapsus**) a lapse, a slip. **lapsus calami**, a slip of the pen. **lapsus linguae**, a slip of the tongue. **lapsus memoriae** , a slip of the memory. [L *lapsāre,* freq. of *lābī* (p.p. *lapsus*), to glide]

Laputan, -tian, *a.* pertaining to Laputa the flying island in Swift's *Gulliver's Travels*; visionary, chimerical. *n.* an inhabitant of Laputa; a visionary.

lapwing, *n.* a bird of the genus *Vanellus,* of the plover family, esp. *V. cristatus,* a British bird, the peewit. [OE *hlēapewince* (*hlēapan,* to LEAP), WING]

lar, *n.* (*pl.* **lares**) a tutelary Roman divinity, usu. a deified ancestor or hero; (*pl.* **lars**) the white-handed gibbon. **lares and penates,** the home or the valued household possessions contained in it; household gods or their representations. [L]

larboard, *n.* former name for the port or left side of a vessel to a person standing on deck and facing the bow. *a.* pertaining to the left side of a vessel. [ME *ladeborde* (etym. doubtful), assim. to STARBOARD]

larceny, *n.* the unlawful taking away of another's personal goods with intent to convert them for one's own use, theft. **grand larceny,** theft of anything over a value fixed by statute (in England before 1827, one shilling). **petty larceny,** theft of anything under a value of (formerly) one shilling. **larcener, -nist,** *n.* **larcenous,** *a.* **larcenously,** *adv.* [A-F *larcin,* OF *larrecin,* L *latrōcinium,* from *latro,* robber]

larch, *n.* a tree of the coniferous genus *Larix,* having deciduous bright-green foliage and tough, durable timber and yielding Venetian turpentine. [G *lärche,* L *laricem,* nom. *larix*]

lard, *n.* the rendered fat of pigs; †the flesh of swine, pork, bacon. *v.t.* to fatten; to cover or smear with lard; to insert strips of bacon in (a fowl etc.) before roasting; to intermix or garnish (writing, talk etc.) with foreign phrases, flowery speech etc.; †to make rich or fertile. †*v.i.* to grow fat. **lardaceous,** *a.* of the nature or consisting of lard. **lardon, -doon,** *n.* a strip of bacon for larding fowls etc. **lardy,** *a.* **lardy cake,** *n.* a rich cake made from yeast, lard, flour, dried fruits etc. [OF, from L *lardum,* rel. to Gr. *laros,* pleasant to the taste, *larinos,* fat]

larder, *n.* a room where meat and other provisions are kept, a pantry. †**larderer,** *n.* [A-F, from OF *lardier,* med. L *lardārium,* as prec.]

lares, *n.pl.* LAR.

Largactil®, *n.* chlorpromazine, a tranquillizer.

large, *a.* great in size, number, quantity, extent or capacity; big, bulky; wide, extensive; abundant, ample, copious; liberal, generous, lavish, prodigal; wide in range or comprehension, comprehensive, far-seeing; †free, unrestrained, licentious. **as large as life,** unmistakably present or real. **at large,** at liberty, free; freely, without restraint; diffusely, with ample detail. **by and large** BY. **larger than life,** remarkably vivid or eye-catching. **large calorie,** *n.* 1,000 calories, a kilocalorie. **large-handed,** *a.* profuse; †rapacious, greedy. **large-hearted,** *a.* having a liberal heart or disposition. **large-heartedness,** *n.* **large intestine,** *n.* in the digestive system, that part of the intestine comprising the caecum, colon and rectum. **large-minded,** *a.* **large-mindedness,** *n.* **large-paper,** *a.* applied to books, prints etc., having wider margins than the ordinary. **large-scale,** *a.* extensive; detailed. **largely,** *adv.* to a large extent. **largen,** *v.t., v.i.* (*poet.*). **largeness,** *n.* **largish,** *a.* [F, from L *larga,* fem. of largus]

Large Electron–Positron collider, (LEP) the world's largest particle accelerator, in operation from 1989 at the CERN laboratories near Geneva. It occupies a tunnel 3.8 m/12.5 ft wide and 27 km/16.7 miles long, which is buried 180 m/590 ft underground and forms a ring consisting of eight curved and eight straight sections. In 1989 the LEP was used to measure the mass and lifetime of the Z particle, carrier of the weak nuclear force.

largess, -gesse, *n.* a present, a reward, a generous bounty (usu. from a superior to inferiors); liberality, esp. in giving. †**largition,** *n.* the bestowing of largess. [F *largesse,* as prec.]

largo, *adv.* (*Mus.*) slowly, broadly, in an ample, dignified style. *n.* (*pl.* **-gos**) a piece of music played in this manner. **larghetto,** *adv.* somewhat slow. **larghissimo,** *adv.* very slowly. [It., from L *largus,* LARGE]

Largo Caballero, *n.* **Francisco** (1869–1946), Spanish socialist and leader of the Spanish Socialist Party (PSOE). He became prime minister of the popular-front government elected Feb 1936 and remained in office for the first ten months of the Civil War before being replaced by Juan Negrin (1887–1956) May 1937.

lariat, *n.* a rope for picketing horses in camp; a lasso. *v.t.* to secure or catch with a lariat. [Sp. *la reata,* the rope or tie (see REATA)]

La Rioja, *n.* region of N Spain; area 5000 sq km/1930 sq miles; population (1986) 263,000.

Larionov, *n.* **Mikhail Fedorovich** (1881–1964), Russian painter, active in Paris from 1919. He pioneered a semi-abstract style known as **Rayonnism** with his wife Natalia Goncharova, in which subjects appear to be deconstructed by rays of light from various sources.

lark¹, *n.* any bird of the genus *Alauda,* with five British species, esp. the skylark, *A. arvensis.* **to get up with the lark,** to rise very early in the morning. **lark('s)-heel,** *n.* the larkspur; the nasturtium or Indian cress, *Tropaeolum majus.* **lark-heeled,** *a.* having long back claws. **larkspur,** *n.* a plant with spur-shaped calyx belonging to the genus *Delphinium,* esp. *D. ajacis.* [OE *laferce, lāwerce* (cp. Dut. *leeuwerik,* G *Lerche,* Icel. *laeverki,* Swed. *lärka*)]

lark², *n.* a prank, a frolic, a spree. *v.i.* to sport, to frolic. **larker,** *n.* **larkish, larky,** *a.* (*coll.*) [etym. doubtful]

Larkin, *n.* **Philip** (1922–1985), English poet. His perfectionist, pessimistic verse includes *The North Ship* 1945, *The Whitsun Weddings* 1964, and *High Windows* 1974. He edited *The Oxford Book of 20th-Century English Verse* 1973.

larn, *v.i.* (*dial., facet.*) to learn. *v.t.* to teach.

La Rochefoucauld, *n.* **François, duc de La Rochefoucauld** (1613–1680), French writer. *Réflexions, ou sentences et maximes morales/Reflections, or Moral Maxims* (1665) is a collection of brief, epigrammatic, and cynical observations on life and society, with the epigraph 'Our virtues are mostly our vices in disguise'. He was a lover of Mme de Lafayette.

larrigan, *n.* a high leather boot worn by woodsmen etc. [etym. unknown]

larrikin, *n.* (*chiefly Austral.*) a rowdy youngster, a young hooligan. **larrikinism,** *n.* [perh. dim. of pers. name *Larry*]

larrup, *v.t.* (*coll.*) to thrash, to flog, to lash. **larruper,** *n.* **larruping,** *n.* [dial., etym. unknown]

Larsson, *n.* **Carl** (1853–1919), Swedish painter, engraver, and illustrator. He is remembered for his watercolours of domestic life, delicately coloured and full of detail, illustrating his book *Ett Hem/A Home* (1899).

Lartigue, *n.* **Jacques-Henri** (1894–1986), French photographer. He began taking extraordinary and humorous photographs of his family at the age of seven, and went on to make autochrome colour prints of women.

Larus, *n.* a genus of swimming-birds, containing the seagulls. **larine, laroid,** *a.* [late L, from Gr. *laros*]

larva, *n.* (*pl.* **-vae**) the first condition of an insect on its issuing from the egg, when it is usually in the form of a grub, caterpillar or maggot; sometimes used of the half-developed state of other invertebrates that undergo metamorphosis. **larval,** *a.* **larvate,** †**-ated,** *a.* wearing a mask. †**larve,** *n.* a larva; †a mask. **larvicidal,** *a.* killing larvae. **larvicide,** *n.* a preparation for this purpose. **larviform,** *a.* **larvigerous, larviparous,** *a.* producing larvae. [L, a ghost, a mask]

laryngectomy, *n.* the surgical removal of the larynx.

laryng(o)-, *comb. form* pertaining to the larynx. [Gr. *larunx -ngos*]

laryngology, *n.* the branch of medical science dealing with the windpipe and its diseases. **laryngological,** *a.* **laryngologist,** *n.*

laryngophony, *n.* the sound of the voice as heard through the stethoscope over the larynx. [Gr. *phonia,* sounding, from *phonein,* to speak]

laryngoscope, *n.* an instrument with a reflecting mirror for obtaining a view of the larynx. **laryngoscopic,** *a.* **laryngoscopist,** *n.* **laryngoscopy,,** *n.*

laryngotomy, *n.* the operation of making an incision into the larynx in order to provide an artificial channel for breathing.

larynx, *n.* (*pl.* **larynges, larynxes**) the vocal organ, consisting of the upper part of the windpipe, containing the vocal cords. **laryngeal, -gal,** *a.* pertaining to the larynx; glottal. [Gr. *larunx -ngos*]

lasagna, *n.* a baked dish consisting of wide flat strips of pasta layered with bolognese and béchamel sauces. **lasagne,** *n.* lasagna; the strips of pasta used in this dish. [It.]

la Salle, *n.* **René Robert Cavelier, Sieur de la Salle** (1643–1687), French explorer. He made an epic voyage through North America, exploring the Mississippi River down to its mouth, and in 1682 founded Louisiana.

lascar, *n.* an E Indian sailor. [prob. from Pers. *lashkarī,* a soldier, from *lashkar,* army]

Las Casas, *n.* **Bartolomé de** (1474–1566), Spanish missionary, historian, and colonial reformer, known as the Apostle of the Indies. He was the first European to call for the abolition of Indian slavery in Latin America. He took part in the conquest of Cuba 1513, but subsequently worked for American Indian freedom in the Spanish colonies. *Apologetica historia de las Indias* (first published 1875–76) is his account of Indian traditions and his witnessing of Spanish oppression of the Indians.

Lascaux, *n.* cave system near Montignac in the Dordogne, SW France, discovered 1940. It has rich paintings of buffalo, horses, and red deer of the Upper Palaeolithic period, about 18,000 BC.

lascivious, *a.* lewd, wanton, lustful; exciting or provoking lust. **lasciviously,** *adv.* **lasciviousness,** *n.* [late L *lascīviōsus,* from L *lascīvia,* from *lascīvus,* sportive, lustful]

laser, *n.* an instrument which amplifies light waves by stimulation to produce a powerful, coherent beam of monochromatic light, an optical maser; a similar instrument for producing other forms of electromagnetic radiation. *v.i.* to be capable of functioning as a laser. **laser printer,** *n.* a computer printer using a laser beam. [acronym for *l*ight *a*mplification by *s*timulated *e*mission of *r*adiation]

lash, *n.* the thong or flexible part of a whip; a whip, a scourge; a stroke with a whip; flogging; an eyelash; a stroke of satire; sarcasm, satire, vituperation; †a leash, a snare. *v.t.* to strike or flog with anything pliant and tough; to whip; to drive with or as with a whip; to beat or dash against; to throw or dash out suddenly or with a jerk; to fasten or bind with a rope or cord; to assail fiercely with satire. *v.i.* to use a whip; to strike, fling or kick violently (at, out etc.); to fling out satire or sarcasm. **to lash out,** to kick, strike out physically or verbally; to be unruly; to be extravagant with money. **lasher,** *n.* one who lashes or flogs; a rope, binding material for securing or fastening; the water rushing over a weir; the water below a weir. **lashing,** *n.* a rope or gasket by which anything is secured; a whipping, a flogging; (*pl.*) (*coll.*) abundance, a plentiful supply. **lashless,** *a.* [etym. obscure, perh. from OF *lache,* whence *lachier,* var. of *lacier,* to LACE, or imit.]

lasket, *n.* a loop of line at the foot of a sail by which an additional piece of sail is attached. [perh. from F *lacet,* LATCHET]

Las Palmas, (or **Las Palmas de Gran Canaria**) *n.* tourist resort on the NE coast of Gran Canaria, Canary Islands; population (1986) 372,000. Products include sugar and bananas.

laspring, *n.* young salmon of the first year. [OE *leax,* a salmon]

lasque, *n.* a thin, flat diamond; an ill-formed or veiny diamond.

lass, *n.* a young woman, a girl; a sweetheart; a servant-maid. **lassie,** *n.* (*Sc.*). [ME *lasce,* cogn. with Icel. *löskr,* weak]

Lassa fever, *n.* an often fatal tropical viral disease characterized by fever and muscle pain and transmitted by rats etc. [*Lassa,* a village in N Nigeria]

Lassalle, *n.* **Ferdinand** (1825–1864), German socialist. He was imprisoned for his part in the Revolution of 1848, during which he met Marx, and in 1863 founded the General Association of German Workers (later the Social-Democratic Party). His publications include *The Working Man's Programme* (1862), and *The Open Letter* (1863). He was killed in a duel arising from a love affair.

lassitude, *n.* weariness, lack of energy or animation; languor. [F, from L *lassitūdo,* from *lassus,* weary]

lasso, *n.* (*pl.* **lasso(e)s**) a rope of untanned hide with a running noose, used for catching cattle, horses etc. *v.t.* to catch with a lasso. [OSp. *laso* (Sp. *lazo*)]

Lassus, (or **Lasso**) *n.* **Roland de** (*c.* 1532–1594), Franco-Flemish composer. His works include polyphonic sacred music, songs, and madrigals, including settings of poems by his friend Ronsard.

last[1], *a.* coming after all others or at the end; closing, final; pertaining to the end, esp. of life or of the world; conclusive, definitive; utmost, extreme; lowest, meanest; only remaining; furthest from the thoughts; least likely etc.; next before the present, most recent. *n.* the end, the conclusion; the last moment, hour, day etc.; death; (*ellipt.*) the last thing done, mentioned etc., or the last doing, mention etc. *adv.* on the last time or occasion; for the last time; after all others; †lately. **at last,** in the end, ultimately. **at long last,** in the end, after long delay. **on one's last legs,** in an extreme stage of exhaustion; on the verge of ruin. **to breathe one's last,** to die. **to the last,** to the end; till death. **Last Day,** *n.* the Day of Judgment. **last ditch,** *a.* of an attempt, effort etc., done or made at the final moment or as a last resort. **last minute,** *a.* made or done at the latest possible time. **last post,** *n.* (*Mil.*) the bugle-call signalling the time of turning-in; a bugle-salute at military funerals. **last rites,** *n.pl.* religious rites for the dying. **last straw,** *n.* the limit of endurance or patience. **Last Supper,** *n.* the supper shared by Christ and his disciples the evening before his crucifixion. **last word,** *n.* a concluding statement; a final decision; the latest improvement, most up-to-date model. **lastly,** *adv.* at last; finally. [OE *latost, lœtest,* superl. of *lœt,* LATE]

last[2], *n.* a shaped wooden block on which boots and shoes are fashioned or repaired. [OE *lāst,* foot-track, *lœste,* fem., shoemaker's last (cp. Dut. *leest,* Icel. *leistr,* G *Leisten*)]

last[3], *n.* a certain weight or quantity, varying in different commodities; †a unit in measuring the cargo or burden of a ship; †a load, a burden. **lastage,** *n.* a cargo, a load; ballast; tonnage; †a payment for the right of loading (a vessel) with goods. [OE *hlœst,* rel. to *hladan,* to LADE (cp. Dut., G, Swed., and Dan. *last*)]

last[4], *v.i.* to continue in existence, to go on; to hold out, to continue unexhausted or unimpaired, to endure; †to reach, to extend. †*n.* continuance; endurance. **to last out,** to endure to the end, to persevere, to survive. **laster,** *n.* a person or thing which lasts (out). **lasting,** *a.* continuing in existence; enduring, permanent, durable. *n.* †endurance, continuance, permanence; a durable woollen fabric used in making women's shoes. **lastingly,** *adv.* **lastingness,** *n.* [OE *lǣstan,* from *lāst,* see LAST[2]]

Las Vegas, *n.* city in Nevada, US, known for its nightclubs and gambling casinos; population (1986) 202,000.

Lat.[1], (*abbr.*) Latin.

lat.[2], (*abbr.*) latitude.

Latakia, *n.* a superior kind of Syrian tobacco. [a port in Syria]

latch, *n.* a fastening for a door, gate etc., consisting of a bolt and catch; a spring-lock fastening with the shutting of a door and opened with a key. *v.t.* to fasten with a latch; †to catch, to seize. **on the latch,** fastened by the latch only, not locked. **to latch onto,** to understand the meaning of; to attach oneself to. **latchkey,** *n.* key of latch on front door. **latchkey child,** *n.* one who lets him- or herself into the house after school, one with working parents. [ME *lacche,* from *lacchen,* OE *lœccan,* to catch (prob. blended with OF *lache,* LACE)]

latchet, *n.* a string for a shoe or sandal. [OF *lachet, lacet*]

late, *a.* coming after the proper or usual time; slow, tardy, backward, long delayed; far on towards the close or end; far on in any period; far advanced, far on in development; existing at a previous time but now gone or ceased; deceased, departed; lately or recently alive, in office etc.; recent in date. *adv.* after the proper or usual time; at or till a late hour, season, stage etc.; (*poet.*) a short time ago, lately, recently; †formerly, of old. **at the latest,** no later than. **of late,** a short time ago, lately, recently; latterly, formerly. **the late,** the recently deceased, resigned etc.; the recent. **the latest,** *n.* (*coll.*) the most recent news. **lately,** *adv.* **laten,** *v.t., v.i.* **lateness,** *n.* **latish,** *a., adv.* [OE *lœt* (cp. Dut. *laat,* Icel. *latr,* G *lass,* cogn. with L *lassus,* weary)]

lateen, *a.* a term applied to a triangular sail, inclined at an angle of about 45°, used principally in the Mediterranean. *n.* a vessel so rigged. [F *latine,* fem. of *atin,* LATIN]

La Tène, *a.* of the later European Iron Age from the 5th cent. to 1st cent. BC. [*La Tène,* near Neuchâtel, Switzerland]

La Tène, *n.* prehistoric settlement at the east end of Lake Neuchâtel, Switzerland, which has given its name to a culture of the Iron Age. The culture lasted from the 5th cent. BC to the Roman conquest; sites include Glastonbury Lake village, England.

latent, *a.* hidden or concealed; not seen, not apparent; dormant, not active, potential. **latent heat** HEAT. **latent period,** *n.* the length of time between stimulation and reaction. **latency, †-ence,** *n.* **latently,** *adv.* **latescent,** *a.* becoming latent or obscure. **latescence,** *n.* [L *latens -ntem,* pres.p. of *latēre,* to lie hid]

-later, *comb. form* as *idolater* etc. [see -LATRY]

lateral, *a.* of, pertaining to, at, from or towards the side. *n.* a part, member, process, shoot etc., situated or developing at the side; a lateral consonant. **lateral axis,** *n.* the cross-wise axis of an aircraft. **lateral line,** *n.* a sensory organ on the side of fish for detecting changes in water pressure or movement through vibrations. **lateral thinking,** *n.* a way of thinking which seeks to solve problems by finding new perspectives rather than following conventional or strictly logical lines of thought. **laterality,** *n.* physical one-sidedness. **laterally,** *adv.* **lateri-, latero-,** *comb. form.* [L *laterālis,* from *latus lateris,* side]

Lateran, *n.* a cathedral church at Rome, dedicated to St John the Baptist. *a.* pertaining to this. **Lateran Council,** *n.* name given to five general oecumenical councils held in the church of St John Lateran. **Lateran Treaty,** *n.* a treaty concluded between the Italian State and the Papacy (1929) establishing the sovereign state of the Vatican City. [after the Roman *familia* of the Plautii *Laterani,* on the site of whose palace the church is built]

laterite, *n.* a red porous rock, composed of silicate of alumina and oxide of iron, found in extensive beds in India and SW Asia. **lateritic,** *a.* [L *later,* brick, -ITE]

latescent LATENT.

latex, *n.* (*pl.* **-texes, -tices**) the juice of milky plants, esp. rubber trees; a similar emulsion of a polymer in a watery liquid. **laticiferous,** *a.* conveying or producing latex. [L, liquid, fluid]

lath, *n.* (*pl.* **laths**) a thin strip of wood, esp. such as one nailed to rafters to support tiles or to the studs of partitions to support plastering; anything of similar dimensions or used for the same purposes. *v.t.* to cover or line with laths. **lath-work,** *n.* a lining of laths to receive plaster. **lathen,** *a.* **lathing,** *n.* **lathy,** *a.* thin as a lath; made of lath or laths. [cp. OE *lœth,* Dut. *lat,* G *Latte*]

lathe[1], *n.* a machine for turning and polishing wood, ivory, metal etc.; a potter's wheel; the swing-frame or batten of a loom. *v.t.* to work an object on a lathe. [cp. Dan. *lad* in *dreie-lad,* turning wheel (perh. however from OE *hlœd-whēogl,* lade-wheel, a wheel for drawing water)]

lathe[2], *n.* a former division of Kent. [OE *lœth,* cp. Icel. *lāth*]

lather, *n.* froth or foam made by soap moistened with water or caused by profuse sweating; (*coll.*) a flustered or excited state. *v.i.* to form a lather, as with soap and water; of soap, to form lather; of a horse, to become covered with lather. *v.t.* to cover with lather; (*coll.*) to thrash, to flog. **lathering,** *n.* a beating. **lathery,** *a.* [OE *lēathor* (cp. Icel. *lauthr, löthr,* also Gr. *loutron,* bath, L *lavare,* to wash)]

lathi, lathee, *n.* a long, heavy stick. [Hind.]

laticiferous LATEX.

laticlave, *n.* a broad purple stripe worn on the front of the tunic, as a mark of senatorial rank in ancient Rome. [late L *lāticlāvium, lāticlāvus,* (*lātus,* broad, *clāvus,* stripe)]

Latimer, *n.* **Hugh** (1490–1555), English Christian church reformer and bishop. After his conversion to Protestantism 1524 he was imprisoned several times but was protected by Cardinal Wolsey and Henry VIII. He was burned for heresy.

Latin, *a.* of or pertaining to ancient Latium or ancient Rome, the inhabitants or their language; of, pertaining to or expressed in the language of the ancient Romans; pertaining to one or any of the (Romance) languages derived from this or the peoples who speak them; of the Roman Catholic Church. *n.* the Latin language, the language or inhabitants of ancient Latium and Rome; one belonging to a people whose language derives from Latin; (*N Am.*) a Latin American; a Roman Catholic. **Classical Latin,** that of the golden age of Latin literature (*c.* 75 BC to AD 175). **dog Latin,** Latin of a barbarous or illiterate kind. **Late Latin,** that of the period *c.* AD 175–600. **Low Latin,** Mediaeval Latin, esp. of a debased or semi-popular kind. **Mediaeval Middle Latin,** that of the Middle Ages (*c.* AD 600–1500). **Modern New Latin,** that of periods after AD 1500. **thieves' Latin,** cant or jargon employed as a secret language by thieves. **Vulgar Latin,** colloquial Latin. **Latin America,** *n.* the parts of America where the official language is derived from Latin (e.g. Spanish, Portuguese). **Latin-American,** *n., a.* a citizen of or pertaining to the states of Latin America. **Latin Church,** *n.* the Church of the West, the Roman Catholic Church. **Latin cross** CROSS. **Latin peoples,** *n.pl.* those whose language is of Latin origin, the French, Spanish, Portuguese and Italians. **Latin Quarter,** *n.* a left-bank district of Paris surrounding the Sorbonne, famous for students, artists etc., and bohemianism. **Latin Union,** *n.* a monetary alliance established in 1865 between France, Belgium, Italy and Switzerland with a view to maintaining a similar standard of currency. **latian,** *a.* belonging to Latium, Italy. **Latinate,** *a.* imitating or derived from Latin. **Latinism,** *n.* **Latinist,** *n.* **latinity,** *n.* quality of Latin style or idiom, or of Latin scholarship. **latinize, -ise,** *v.t.* to give a Latin form to (a word, phrase etc.); to translate into Latin; to bring into conformity with the ideas, customs, forms etc., of the Romans, the Latin peoples or the Roman Catholic Church. *v.i.* to use Latin words, idioms or phrases. **latinization, -isation,** *n.* **latinizer, -iser,** *n.* [F, from L *Latīnus,* from *Latium,* a region in Italy]

latipennate, *a.* broad-winged. **latirostral, -trate, -trous,** *a.* having a wide or broad beak. [L *lātus,* broad, -PENNATE]

latish LATE.

latitude, *n.* breadth, width; extent, scope, comprehensiveness; looseness of application or meaning; absence of strictness, laxity, freedom from rule, restraint or limits; extent of deviation from a standard or rule; the angular distance of a celestial body from the ecliptic; angular distance on a meridian, angular distance of a place north or south of the equator; (*pl.*) regions, climates, esp. with reference to distance from the equator or the tropics. **latitudinal,** *a.* **latitudinally,** *adv.* **latitudinarian,** *n.* one who does not attach great importance to dogmas; one of a party in the Church of England (mid-17th cent.) who aimed at a comprehensive system which should embrace those points on which Christians are agreed. *a.* wide in range or scope; not confined within narrow limits; free from prejudice, attaching little importance to speculative opinions; lax; libertine. **latitudinarianism,** *n.* **latitudinous,** *a.* [F, from L *lātitūdo,* from *lātus,* broad]

La Tour, *n.* **Georges de** (1593–1652), French painter active in Lorraine. He was patronized by the duke of Lorraine and perhaps also by Louis XIII. Many of his pictures are illuminated by a single source of light, with deep contrasts of light and shade. They range from religious paintings to genre scenes.

latria, *n.* in the Roman Catholic Church, that supreme worship which can lawfully be offered to God alone [cp. DULIA, HYPERDULIA]. [late L, see -LATRY]

latrine, *n.* a lavatory, a toilet, esp. in an army or prison camp. [F, from L *lātrīna* (*lavātrīna*), from *lavāre,* to wash]

La Trobe, *n.* **Charles Joseph** (1801–1875), Australian administrator. He was superintendent of Port Phillip district 1839–51 and first lieutenant-governor of Victoria 1851–54. The Latrobe River is named after him, and flows generally SE through Victoria to Lake Wellington.

-latry, *comb. form* pertaining to worship, as in *bibliola-*

try, idolatry, zoolatry. [Gr. *-latreia* (*-later*, Gr. *-latrēs*, worshipper)]

latten, *n.* a finer kind of brass, of which the incised plates for sepulchral monuments, crosses etc., were made; metal in thin sheets. *a.* made of latten. [OF *laton* (F *laiton*), prob. cogn. with *latte*, LATH, from Teut.]

latter, *a.* coming or happening after something else; last-mentioned; late, modern, present; lately done or past; later, second, second-mentioned; pertaining to the end of a period, life, the world etc. †**latter-born,** *a.* last-born, youngest. **latter-day,** *a.* modern, recent. **Latter-day Saints,** see below. **latter-end,** *n.* death; the end. **latterly,** *adv.* †**lattermath**, *n.* aftermath. [OE *lœtra*, compar. of *lœt*, LATE]

Latter-day Saint, *n.* member of a US-based Christian sect, the Mormons.

lattice, *n.* a structure of laths or strips of metal or wood crossing and forming open work; in a crystal, the geometric pattern of molecules, atoms or ions, or of the points around which they vibrate; in a nuclear reactor, the structural arrangement of fissile and non-fissile material in a geometric pattern. *a.* consisting of or furnished with lattice-work. *v.t.* to furnish with a lattice or lattice-work; to intertwine. **lattice bridge,** *n.* one built of lattice girders. **lattice bar, beam, frame, girder,** *n.* a beam or girder consisting of bars connected together by iron lattice-work. **lattice-window,** *n.* a window consisting of small (usu. diamond-shaped) panes set in strips of lead. **lattice-work,** *n.* the arrangement of laths etc., forming a lattice. **latticed,** *a.* **latticing,** *n.* [ME *latis*, OF *lattis*, from *latte*, see LATTEN]

Latvia, *n.* constituent republic of W USSR from 1940. **area** 63,700 sq km/24,595 sq miles. **capital** Riga. **towns** Daugavpils, Liepaja, Jelgava, Ventspils. **physical** lakes, marshes, wooded lowland. **population** (1987) 2,647,000; Lett 54%, Russian 33%. **products** meat and dairy products, communications equipment, consumer durables, motorcycles, locomotives. **language** Latvian. **religion** mostly Lutheran Protestant with a Roman Catholic minority. **Latvian**, *n.* a native or inhabitant of Latvia (Lettland); the language of Latvians. *a.* of or pertaining to Latvia, its people or its language. **Latvian language**, *n.* the language of Latvia; with Lithuanian it is one of the two surviving members of the Baltic branch of the Indo-European language family.

Latynina, *n.* **Larissa Semyonovna** (1935–), Soviet gymnast, winner of more Olympic medals than any person in any sport. She won 18 between 1956–64, including nine gold medals. She won a total of 12 individual Olympic and world championship gold medals.

Laud, *n.* **William** (1573–1645), English priest. As archbishop of Canterbury from 1633, his High Church policy, support for Charles I's unparliamentary rule, censorship of the press, and persecution of the Puritans, all aroused bitter opposition, while his strict enforcement of the statutes against enclosures and of laws regulating wages and prices alienated the propertied classes. His attempt to impose the use of the Prayer Book on the Scots precipitated the English Civil War. Impeached by Parliament, 1640, he was imprisoned in the Tower, condemned to death by a bill of attainder, and beheaded.

laud, *v.t.* to praise, to celebrate, to extol. *n.* praise; thankful adoration; worship consisting of praise; a song of praise, a hymn; (*pl.*) the psalms immediately following matins. **laudable,** *a.* praiseworthy, commendable. **laudableness, laudability**, *n.* **laudably,** *adv.* **laudation,** *n.* the act of praising; praise. **laudative, laudatory,** *a.*, †*n.* **lauder,** *n.* [L *laudāre*, from *laus laudis*, praise]

laudanum, *n.* opium prepared in alcohol, tincture of opium; †ladanum. [prob. var. of LADANUM or LABDANUM]

Lauderdale, *n.* **John Maitland, Duke of Lauderdale** (1616–1682), Scottish politician. Formerly a zealous Covenanter, he joined the Royalists 1647, and as high commissioner for Scotland 1667–1679 persecuted the Covenanters. He was created duke of Lauderdale 1672, and was a member of the Cabal ministry 1667–73.

laugh, *v.i.* to express amusement, scorn or exultation by inarticulate sounds and the convulsive movements of the face and body which are the involuntary effects of such emotions; to deride, jeer or scoff (at); to be or appear happy, sparkling or sportive, as a brook or stream. *v.t.* to express by laughing; to utter with laughter; to move or influence by ridicule or laughter. *n.* the action of laughing; an act or explosion of laughter; manner of laughing; entertainment. **to have the last laugh,** to be ultimately triumphant after a former setback. **to laugh at,** to mock, to deride, to ridicule. **to laugh away,** to dismiss with a laugh; to pass (time) away in jesting. **to laugh down,** to suppress or silence with derisive laughter. **to laugh in, up, one's sleeve,** to be inwardly amused while one's expression remains serious or demure. **to laugh in someone's face,** to show someone open contempt or ridicule. **to laugh off,** to treat as of trifling importance. **to laugh on the other side of one's face, on the wrong side of one's mouth,** to be made to feel vexation or disappointment after mirth or satisfaction; to cry. **to laugh out of court,** to treat as not worth considering or listening to. **to laugh over,** to talk about or recall to mind with amusement. **to laugh to scorn,** to treat with the utmost contempt. **laughable,** *a.* exciting laughter; comical, ridiculous. **laughableness,** *n.* **laughably,** *adv.* **laugher,** *n.* **laughing,** *n.*, *a.* **no laughing matter,** something serious, not a proper subject for levity. **laughing-gas,** *n.* nitrous oxide, used as an anaesthetic (so-called because when inhaled it produces violent exhilaration). **laughing hyena** HYENA. **laughing jack-ass** JACKASS under JACK[1]. **laughing-stock,** *n.* an object of ridicule; a butt. **laughingly,** *adv.* **laughter,** *n.* †**laughterless**, *a.* **laughy,** *a.* (*coll.*) prone to laughing. [OE *hlehhan* (cp. Dut. and G *lachen*, Icel. *hlœja*), prob. from an Aryan imit. base *klak-* (cp. Gr. *klōssein*, to cluck)]

Laughton, *n.* **Charles** (1899–1962), English actor, who became a US citizen 1950. Initially a classical stage actor, his dramatic film roles included the king in *The Private Life of Henry VIII* (1933), Captain Bligh in *Mutiny on the Bounty* (1935), Quasimodo in *The Hunchback of Notre Dame* (1939), and Gracchus in *Spartacus* (1960).

launce[1], *n.* a sand-eel. [perh. var. of LANCE (cp. LANCELET)]

†**launce**[2], *n.* a balance. [L, LANX]

launch[1], *v.t.* to throw, to hurl, to propel; to cause to glide into the water (e.g. a vessel), or take off from land (e.g. a space rocket); to start or set (a person etc.) going; to fulminate; †to lance; to introduce a new product or publication onto the market, usu. with a publicity campaign. *v.i.* of a ship, rocket etc., to be launched; to put to sea; to put forth, to enter on a new sphere of activity; to expatiate, to burst (out); †to dart or dash forwards. *n.* the act or occasion of launching a ship, rocket, product etc. **to launch into,** to propel oneself into a new activity, career etc. with vigour and enthusiasm; to embark on a long speech, story or explanation. **launch(ing)-pad, -site,** *n.* a platform or place from which a rocket is launched; the initiating event or starting place or point which propels a new activity or from which it gets underway. **launcher,** *n.* the apparatus for launching a rocket, vessel etc. [ONorth.F *lanchier*, var. of *lancier* (F *lancer*), to LANCE[1]]

launch[2], *n.* the largest boat belonging to a man-of-war; a large open pleasure-boat propelled by steam, electricity or internal-combustion engine. [Sp. and Port. *lancha*, perh. from Malay *lanchār*, swift]

†**laund,** *n.* an open space in a wood or forest, a glade. [LAWN[1]]

launder, *v.t.* to wash and iron (clothing, linen etc.); (*coll.*) to legitimize illegally-acquired money by transferring it through banks, foreign institutions etc. *v.i.* to wash and iron clothing, linen etc.; to become clean and ready for use by washing and ironing. *n.* a trough or gutter for carrying water. **launderer, laun-**

dress, *n.* one who washes and irons (clothes, linen etc.). **launderette**, *n.* (*orig. trademark*) an establishment containing coin-operated washing-machines etc., for public use. **Laundromat**®, *n.* a launderette. **laundry**, *n.* a room or establishment where clothes are washed and ironed; the batch of clothes sent to or received from a laundry, a washing. †a laundress. **laundry-maid,** *n.* **laundry-man, -woman,** *n.* one who is employed in a laundry or who delivers washing. [ME *lavender,* a launder, OF *lavandier,* fem. *-diere,* late L *lavandārius,* from *lavanda,* things to be washed, from *lavāre,* to wash]

laura, *n.* an aggregation of separate cells tenanted by monks, esp. in the desert. [Gr., passage, alley]

Laurasia, *n.* former land mass or supercontinent, consisting of what are now North America, Greenland, Europe, and Asia. It made up the northern half of Pangaea, the 'world continent' that is thought to have existed between 250 and 200 million years ago. The southern half was Gondwanaland.

laureate, *a.* crowned or decked with laurel; worthy of laurels, eminent, distinguished, esp. as a poet; consisting or made of laurels. *n.* one crowned with laurel; a Poet Laureate. †*v.t.*, to crown with laurel; to confer a degree on, together with a wreath of laurel. **Poet Laureate** POET. **laureateship,** *n.* † **laureation,** *n.* [L *laureātus,* from *laurea,* a laurel-wreath, fem. of *laureus,* adj., from *laurus*]

laurel, *n.* a glossy-leaved evergreen shrub, *Laurus nobilis,* also called bay-tree; (*sing. or pl.*) the foliage of this, esp. in the form of a wreath, conferred as a distinction on victorious competitors in the ancient classical games, on heroes, poets etc.; (*sing. or pl.*) the honours conferred by this; any other species of the genus *Laurus;* the common laurel or cherry laurel, *C laurocerasus;* any of various trees and shrubs resembling the laurel. **to look to one's laurels,** to guard against rivalry, to take care not to lose one's pre-eminence. **to rest on one's laurels,** to retire from active life or to cease from one's efforts. **laurel water,** *n.* water distilled from the leaves of the *Cerasus laurocerasus,* used as a sedative or narcotic. **laurelled,** *a.* crowned with laurel. **lauric acid,** *n.* an insoluble crystalline substance used in the manufacture of cosmetics and detergents. [ME *laurer,* F *laurier,* prob. through a L *laurārius,* from *laurus*]

Laurel and Hardy, Stan Laurel (1890–1965) and **Oliver Hardy** (1892–1957), US film comedians (Laurel was English-born). Their films include many short silent films, as well as *Way Out West* (1937), and *A Chump at Oxford* (1940).

Laurence, *n.* **Margaret** (1926–1987), Canadian writer, whose novels include *A Jest of God* (1966) and *The Diviners* (1974). She also wrote short stories set in Africa, where she lived for a time.

Laurentian, *a.* a term designating a vast series of rocks north of the St Lawrence River, older than the Cambrian; relating to the St Lawrence River; relating to Lorenzo de'Medici or the library he established.

laurestine, laurustinus, *n.* an ornamental evergreen shrub, *Viburnum tinus,* with pinkish-white winter flowers and dark-blue berries. [L *laurus,* laurel, *tīnus,* a plant, prob. laurus-tinus]

Laurier, *n.* **Wilfrid** (1841–1919), Canadian politician, leader of the Liberal Party 1887–1919 and prime minister 1896–1911. The first French-Canadian to hold the office, he encouraged immigration into Canada from Europe and the US, established a separate Canadian navy, and sent troops to help Britain in the Boer War.

Laurus, *n.* a genus of plants containing the laurels, bay-tree etc. **lauraceous,** *a.* [L]

Lausanne, *n.* resort and capital of Vaud canton, W Switzerland, above the N shore of Lake Geneva; population (1987) 262,000. Industries include chocolate, scientific instruments, and publishing.

lauwine, *n.* an avalanche. [G]

lav, *n.* (*coll.*) short for LAVATORY.

lava, *n.* (*pl.* **-vas**) molten matter flowing in streams from volcanic vents or solidified by cooling. **lava-cone,** *n.* a volcanic cone formed by successive outflows of lava. **lava-flow, -stream,** *n.* **lavaform,** *a.* having the form of lava. **lava-like,** *a.* [It., from *lavare,* to wash, see LAVE]

lavabo, lavatory LAVE[1].

Laval, *n.* **Pierre** (1883–1945), French right-wing politician. He was prime minister and foreign secretary 1931–32, and again 1935–36. In World War II he joined Pétain's Vichy government as vice-premier June 1940; dismissed Dec 1940, he was reinstated by Hitler's orders as head of the government and foreign minister 1942. After the war he was executed.

La Vallière, *n.* **Louise de la Baume le Blance, Duchesse de la Vallière** (1644–1710), mistress of the French king Louis XIV; she gave birth to four children 1661–74. She retired to a convent on her supersession by Mme de Montespan.

lave[1], *v.i.* to wash oneself; to bathe. *v.t.* to wash or flow against, as the sea, streams etc.; to ladle, scoop or bale (out, up etc.). **lavabo,** *n.* (*pl.* **-bos**) the washing of the celebrant's hands, in the Roman Catholic and other churches, after the offertory and before the Eucharist; the towel used in this ceremony, also the basin; a washing-trough or basin, often with running water, in monasteries. **lavation,** *n.* the act of washing. **lavatory,** *n.* a room or place for washing; a room with a toilet and usu. a washhand basin; a toilet; a piscina, a ritual vessel for washing. **lavatory paper,** *n.* toilet paper. **lavatorial,** *a.* **lavement,** *n.* **laver[1],** *n.* †a vessel in which to wash, a piscina; a brazen vessel, containing water for the Jewish priests to wash when they offered sacrifices; a font. [prob. from OE *lafian* (cp. Dut. *laven,* G *laben*), coalescing with foll., or from F *laver,* L *lavāre* (cp. Gr. *louein*)]

lave[2], *n.* (*Sc.*) what is left over, the residue, the rest (of things or of persons). [OE *lāf,* remains, remainder]

lavender, *n.* a sweet-scented flowering shrub, *Lavandula vera,* cultivated for its oil which is used in perfumery; the flower and stalks or the oil used for perfuming linen etc.; the colour of the flowers, a pale lilac. *a.* of the colour of lavender blossoms, pale lilac. *v.t.* to perfume or sprinkle with lavender. **lavender-cotton** *n.* santo-lin or ground-cypress. **lavender-water,** *n.* a liquid perfume, consisting of essential oil of lavender, ambergris, and spirits of wine. [A-F *lavendre* (F *lavande*), med. L *lavendula,* perh. from L *lividus,* LIVID (cp. var. *livendula*)]

laver[1] LAVE[1].

laver[2], *n.* a name given to various marine algae, esp. *Porphyra laciniata, P. vulgaris* and other edible species. [L]

laverock, var. of LARK[1].

lavish, *a.* spending or giving with profusion; prodigal, spendthrift, unrestrained; existing or produced in profusion; excessive, super-abundant. *v.t.* to expend or bestow profusely; to be excessively free or liberal with, to squander. **lavisher,** *n.* **lavishly,** *adv.* †**lavishment, lavishness,** *n.* [orig. a noun, lavishness, from OF *lavache, lavasse,* a deluge of words, from *laver,* L *lavāre,* see LAVE[1]]

Lavoisier, *n.* **Antoine Laurent** (1743–1794), French chemist. He proved that combustion needed only a part of 'air' which he called oxygen, thereby destroying the theory of phlogiston (an imaginary 'fire element' released during combustion). With Laplace, he showed that water was a compound of oxygen and hy rogen. In this way he established the modern basic rules of chemical combination.

†**lavolta,** †**lavolt,** *n.* an old Italian dance for two persons, with much high leaping, popular in the 16th cent. [It. *la,* the, *volta,* turn]

Lavrentiev, *n.* **Mikhail** (1900–), Soviet scientist, who developed the Akademgorodok ('Science City') in Novosibirsk, Russia from 1957.

Law, *n.* **Andrew Bonar** (1858–1923), British Conservative politician, born in New Brunswick, Canada. He made a fortune in Scotland as a banker and iron-merchant, and entered Parliament 1900. Elected leader of the opposition 1911, he became colonial secretary in Asquith's coalition government 1915–16. Chancellor of the Exchequer 1916–19, and Lord Privy Seal 1919–21 in Lloyd George's coalition. He formed a Conservative Cabinet 1922, but resigned on health grounds.

law[1], *n.* a rule of conduct imposed by authority or accepted by the community as binding; a system of such rules regulating the intercourse of mankind, of individuals within a State, or of States with one another; the controlling influence of this; the condition of order and stability it secures; the practical application of these rules, esp. by trial in courts of justice, litigation, judicial process; the interpretation or the science of legal principles and enactments, jurisprudence; legal knowledge; the legal profession; rules governing the conduct of a profession, art, association, sport, game or other activity or department of life; the orderly recurrence of natural phenomena as the uniform results of corresponding conditions; a generalized statement of such conditions and their consequences; the will of God as set forth in the Pentateuch, esp. in the Commandments; (*Ethics*) a principle of conduct emanating from the conscience; a start or an allowance of time given in a hunt or race. *v.t., v.i.* (*coll.*) to go to law, to take legal proceedings. **canon, civil, common, international, martial law** CANON, CIVIL, COMMON, INTERNATIONAL, MARTIAL. **law of averages,** the principle that extremes cancel one another out thereby reaching a balance. **law of supply and demand,** the principle that the price of a commodity or service is governed by the relationship between the amount of demand for it and the quantity which can be supplied. **law of the jungle,** rules necessary for survival or success in adverse conditions or circumstances. **laws of motion** MOTION. **the law,** the police; a policeman. **to go to law,** to take legal proceedings. **to have the law of, on,** to take legal proceedings against; to summon the police. **to lay down the law,** to talk or direct in a dictatorial manner. **to take the law into one's own hands,** to try to secure satisfaction or retaliation by one's own methods or actions. **law-abiding,** *a.* obedient to the law. **law-abidingness,** *n.* **law-book,** *n.* a treatise on law. **law-binding,** *a.* a binding in plain sheep or calf used largely for law-books. **law-breaker,** *n.* one who violates the law. **law-calf** LAW-BINDING. **Law Commissions**, *n.pl.* in Britain, statutory bodies established 1965 (one for England and Wales and one for Scotland) which consider proposals for law reform and publish their findings. They also keep British law under constant review, looking for ways in which it can be simplified or finding obsolete laws which should be repealed. †**law-day,** *n.* a day on which a court sat, esp. a leet or sheriff's court; a day of open court. **law-French,** *n.* Anglo-Norman terms and phrases used in law. **lawgiver,** *n.* one who makes or enacts laws, a legislator. †**lawgiving,** *a.* **law-hand,** *n.* handwriting used in legal documents. **law-Latin,** *n.* the debased Latin used in legal documents. **Law-Lord,** *n.* a member of the House of Lords qualified to deal with the judicial business of the House. **law-maker,** *n.* a legislator. **law-making,** *n.* **lawman,** *n.* (*N Am.*) a law enforcement officer. **law merchant,** *n.* mercantile law. **law-monger,** *n.* a pettifogging lawyer. **law officer,** *n.* a public legal functionary, esp. the Attorney-General and Solicitor-General. **law stationer,** *n.* one who deals in stationery used in legal work. **lawsuit,** *n.* an action in a court of law. **law-term,** *n.* a word or phrase used in law; one of the periods appointed for the sitting of the Law Courts. **law-writer,** *n.* one who writes on law; one who copies or engrosses legal documents. **lawful,** *a.* conformable to law; allowed by law; legitimate; valid, rightful; †law-abiding; loyal, faithful. **lawfully,** *adv.* **lawfulness,** *n.* †**lawing,** *n.* litigation; (*Sc.*) a tavern reckoning. **lawless**, *a.* regardless of or unrestrained by the law, unbridled, licentious; not subject to or governed by law; illegal; anomalous, irregular; †outlawed. **lawlessly,** *adv.* **lawlessness,** *n.* **lawyer**, *n.* one who practises law, esp. an attorney or solicitor; one versed in the law; (*NT*) a professional expounder of the Mosaic law; (*N Am.*) the black-necked stilt, *Himantopus nigricollis*. **lawyer-like, lawyerly,** *a.* [OE *lagu,* from old Icel., cogn. with LAID, LAY[1]]

†**law**[2], *n.* (*Sc., North.*) a hill, esp. a rounded or conical hill of moderate size. [OE *hlæw*]

lawine, LAUWINE.

lawks, *int.* (*dial.*) an old exclamation of surprise or wonder. [corr. of ALACK or LORD]

lawn[1], *n.* †an open space between woods, a glade in a forest; a grassy space kept smooth and closely mown in a garden or pleasure-ground. **lawn-mower,** *n.* a machine for mowing a lawn. **lawn-sprinkler,** *n.* a device with a perforated revolving collar for watering lawns. **lawn-tennis,** *n.* a game somewhat resembling real tennis, orig. played on a lawn but now frequently on a hard court. **lawny**, *a.* [ME *laund,* OF *launde,* from Celt. (cp. Bret. *lann,* W *llan*)]

lawn[2], *n.* a cotton or linen fabric, finer than cambric (e.g. used for the sleeves of an Anglican bishop's rochet). **lawny**, *a.* [OF *Lan,* now *Laon,* a town N-W of Rheims]

Lawrence[1], *n.* **D(avid) H(erbert)** (1885–1930), English writer, who in his work expressed his belief in emotion and the sexual impulse as creative and true to human nature. His novels include *Sons and Lovers* (1913), *The Rainbow* (1915), *Women in Love* (1921), and *Lady Chatterley's Lover* (1928). Lawrence also wrote short stories, for example 'The Woman Who Rode Away', and poetry.

Lawrence[2], *n.* **Ernest O(rlando)** (1901–1958), US physicist. His invention of the cyclotron pioneered the production of artificial radioisotopes.

Lawrence[3], *n.* **Thomas** (1769–1830), British painter, the leading portraitist of his day. He became painter to George III in 1792 and president of the Royal Academy 1820.

Lawrence[4], *n.* **T(homas) E(dward)** (1888–1935), British soldier, known as 'Lawrence of Arabia'. Appointed to the military intelligence department in Cairo during World War 1, he took part in negotiations for an Arab revolt against the Turks, and in 1916 attached himself to the emir Faisal. He showed himself a guerrilla leader of genius, combining raids on Turkish communications with the stirring up of revolt among the Arabs. In 1935 he was killed in a motorcycle accident.

lawrencium, *n.* a radioactive element, at. no. 103; chem. symbol Lr, with a short half-life, orig. produced in America. [after Ernest O. *Lawrence*]

Lawson, *n.* **Nigel** (1932–), British Conservative politician. A former financial journalist, he was financial secretary to the Treasury 1979–81, secretary of state for energy 1981–83, and chancellor of the Exchequer 1983. He resigned in 1989 after criticism of his policy of British membership of the European Monetary System by government advisor Alan Walters.

lawyer LAW[1].

lax, *a.* slack, loose, not tight, firm or compact; porous; not exact, not strict; negligent, careless; equivocal, ambiguous, vague; relaxed in the bowels. †**laxation,** *n.* **laxative,** *a.* opening or loosening the bowels. *n.* a laxative medicine. †**laxist,** *n.* one of a school of Roman Catholic theologians, who held that merely probable opinions might be followed in cases of doubt, esp. in ethical matters. **laxity, laxness,** *n.* **laxly,** *adv.* [L *laxus,* cogn. with *languēre,* to LANGUISH]

Laxness, *n.* **Halldor** (1902–), Icelandic novelist, who wrote about Icelandic life in the style of the early sagas. Nobel prize 1955.

lay[1], *v.t.* (*past, p.p.* **laid**) to cause to lie; to place in a prostrate or recumbent position; to bury; to drop (as eggs); to put down, to place, to deposit; to stake, to wager; to set, to apply; to dispose regularly, to put in proper position; to spread on a surface; to beat down, to prostrate; to overthrow; to cause to settle (as dust); to cause to be still, to allay, to calm; to exorcize; to put or bring into a certain state or position; to put forward, to present; †to charge, to impute; to impose, to enjoin, to inflict; to bring down (a weapon, blows etc., on); to think out, to devise, to plan, to prepare; (*Mil.*) to point (a gun); (*Hort.*) to propagate by layers; (*Lit.*) to locate (a scene, story etc.); (*sl.*) to have sexual intercourse with. *v.i.* to drop or deposit eggs; (*nonstandard or Naut.*) to lie; to make a bet. *n.* the way, direction or position in which a region or object is situated; the direction the strands of a rope are twisted; (*sl.*) particular business, occupation, job etc. (*sl.*) an act of sexual intercourse; (*sl.*) a sexual partner. **in lay,** of hens, laying eggs. **to lay about one,** to hit out on all sides; to fight vigorously. **to lay a cable,** to bury or sink an electric cable; to twist the strands of a cable. †**to lay apart,** to put away. **to lay aside, away,** to reject, to abandon, to put away. **to lay bare,** to reveal; to strip. **to lay before,** to exhibit to; to bring to the notice of. **to lay by,** to save; to reserve for a future occasion. **to lay by the heels** HEEL[1]. **to lay down,** to put down; to resign, to surrender; to draft, to delineate (as the lines of a ship); to declare, to affirm, to assert; to formulate, to deposit; to pay; to wager; to sacrifice; to put down the main structural parts of; to store (wine etc.); to stipulate. **to lay down the law** LAW[1]. **to lay fast,** to seize and keep fast, to prevent from escaping. **to lay for,** (*coll.*) to lie in wait for. **to lay hands on** HAND[1]. **to lay heads together,** to deliberate, to confer. **to lay hold of, on,** to seize, to catch; to grasp; to utilize, to make a pretext of. **to lay in,** to store, to stock oneself with. **to lay into,** to assault physically or verbally. **to lay it on,** to speak or flatter extravagantly; to charge exorbitantly. **to lay low,** to fell or destroy; to cause to become weak or ill. **to lay off,** to suspend from employment; to desist; to avoid. **to lay on,** to impose, to inflict; to deal (blows etc.); to supply (as water or gas); to prepare or arrange for printing. **to lay oneself open to,** to expose oneself to (criticism, attack etc.). **to lay oneself out,** to busy or exert onself to do something. **to lay open,** to cut so as to expose the interior of; to expose, to reveal; to explain. **to lay out,** to arrange according to plan; to spread out; to expound, to explain; to expend; to dress in grave-clothes and dispose for burial; to knock to the ground or render unconscious. **to lay over,** to spread over, to overlay; (*N Am.*) to stop over during a journey; to postpone. **to lay siege to,** to besiege; to importune. **to lay the table,** to set a table with cutlery, crockery etc. for a forthcoming meal. **to lay to,** to apply vigorously; to check the motion of a ship. **to lay together,** to place side by side; to add together. **to lay to sleep, rest,** to bury. **to lay under,** to subject to. **to lay up,** to store, to treasure, to save; of illness, to confine to one's bed or room; to dismantle and place in dock. **to lay waste,** to ravage, to devastate. **layabout,** *n.* an idle person, a lounger. **lay-by,** *n.* a widening of a road to enable vehicles to stop without holding up traffic. **lay-days,** *n.pl.* a certain number of days allowed for loading or unloading a ship. **lay-out,** *n.* the make-up of a printed page; a planned arrangement of buildings etc.; that which is set out or displayed. **laystall,** *n.* a place where dung or refuse is kept. **layer,** *n.* one who or that which lays; a thickness or anything spread out (usu. one of several), a stratum, a bed; a shoot laid with part of its length on or beneath the surface of the ground in order that it may take root; an artificial oyster-bed; a tanning-pit; the areas between contours on a map marked by distinctive colouring. *v.t.* to propagate by layers; to place, cut or form in layers. *v.i.* of growing corn etc., to be laid flat by weather, weak growth etc. **layering,** *n.* a method of propagation in which shoots and stems are pegged to the ground and left until they root, when they can be separated; any method employing layers. **laying,** *n.* the act or period of setting, placing or depositing; the act or period of depositing eggs; the eggs laid; the twisting of yarns into a strand or of strands into a rope. **laying on of hands,** sacramental imposition of hands for healing or other purposes. [OE *lecgan* (cp. Dut. *leggen,* Icel. *leggja,* G *legen*), casual of LIE[2]]

lay[2], *a.* pertaining to the people as distinct from the clergy; non-professional, lacking specialized knowledge; (*Cards*) other than trumps. **lay brother, sister,** *n.* a brother or sister in a monastery, under vows and wearing the habit of the order, engaged chiefly in manual labour and exempt from other duties. **lay communion,** *n.* communicating of the laity at the Eucharist; membership of the church as a layman. **lay elder,** *n.* a ruling elder in the Presbyterian Church. **layman, laywoman,** *n.* one of the people, as distinguished from the clergy; a non-professional, one not an expert. **lay reader,** *n.* a member of the Church of England laity authorized to conduct certain religious services; a layman in the Roman Catholic Church who reads the epistle at Mass. **lay sister** LAY BROTHER. **laic, -ical,** *a.* lay, not clerical, secular. *n.* a layman. **laically,** *adv.* **laicization, -isation,** *n.* **laicize, -ise,** *v.t.* to render lay or secular; to throw open or hand over to the laity. **laity,** *n.* (*collect.*) the people, as distinct from the clergy; laymen and laywomen, those not belonging to a particular profession. [F *lai,* L *lāicus,* Gr. *laikos,* from *laos,* the people]

lay[3], *n.* a lyric song or ballad; a short narrative poem for singing or recitation; song, singing (of birds etc.). [OF *lai,* prob. from OHG *leth, leich* (not rel. to G *Lied*)]

lay[4], *past* LIE[2].

lay[5], LEY.

Layamon, *n.* (lived about 1200), English poet, author of the *Brut,* a chronicle of about 30,000 alliterative lines on the history of Britain from the legendary Brutus onwards, which gives the earliest version of the Arthurian story in English.

layer LAY[1].

layette *n.* the outfit for a new-born infant. [F, dim. of OF *laye* (cp. OHG *lada*)]

lay figure, *n.* a jointed figure of the human body used by artists for hanging drapery on etc.; a puppet, a nonentity; an unreal character in a story etc. [*lay,* from obs. *layman,* Dut. *leeman,* joint-man (*lid,* joint, *lith,* limb, MAN) FIGURE]

laying LAY[1].

layman LAY[2].

laystall LAY[1].

lazar, *n.* a person infected with a loathsome disease, esp. a leper. **lazar-house,** *n.* a lazaretto. **Lazarists,** *n.pl.* the popular name for the Congregation of Priests of the Mission, founded by St Vincent de Paul in 1624. **lazarus-house,** *n.* [F *lazare,* from name *Lazarus* (Luke xvi.20)]

lazaretto, lazaret, *n.* (*pl.* **-ttos**) a hospital (chiefly abroad) for persons suffering from some contagious disease; a ship or other place of quarantine; a storeroom for provisions in large merchant-vessels. [F *lazaret,* It. *lazzaretto,* as prec.]

lazarone, LAZZARONE.

Lazarus, *n.* in the New Testament (John 11), a friend of Jesus, raised by him from the dead. Lazarus is also the name of a beggar in a parable told by Jesus (Luke 16).

Lazarus, *n.* **Emma** (1849–1887), US poet, author of the poem on the base of the Statue of Liberty which includes the words: 'Give me your tired, your poor/Your huddled masses yearning to breathe free.'

laze LAZY.

Lazio, (Roman **Latium**) *n.* region of W central Italy; area 17,200 sq km/6639 sq miles; capital Rome; population (1988) 5,137,000. Products include olives, wine, chemicals, pharmaceuticals, and textiles. Home of the Latins from the 10th cent. BC, it was dominated by the Romans from the 4th cent. BC.

lazuli LAPIS LAZULI.

lazulite, *n.* an azure-blue to pale greenish-blue mineral, composed of phosphate of aluminium and magnesium. [med. L *lazulum,* LAPIS LAZULI, -ITE]

lazy, *a.* idle, indolent, slothful, disinclined for labour or exertion; disposing to idleness or sloth. **laze,** *v.i.* to be lazy; to live in idleness. *v.t.* to waste or spend in idleness. *n.* a time or spell of idleness. **lazy-bed,** *n.* a bed in which seed potatoes are placed on the surface of the ground and covered with soil from trenches dug on each side. **lazy-bones,** *n.* a lazy fellow, an idler. **lazy daisy,** *n.* a type of embroidery stitch. **lazy Susan,** *n.* a revolving tray for a dining table with compartments for various condiments. **lazy-tongs,** *n.pl.* tongs consisting of levers, in pairs, crossing one another and turning on a pin like scissors, for picking up distant objects. **lazily,** *adv.* **laziness,** *n.* [etym. doubtful]

lazzarone, *n.* (*pl.* **-ni**) one of the poorer class of Neapolitans who depend upon begging for their living. [It., from *lazzaro,* LAZAR]

lb, (*abbr.*) in cricket, leg-bye; pound(s).

lbw, (*abbr.*) in cricket, leg before wicket.

LC, (*abbr.*) Legislative Council; Lord Chamberlain; Lord Chancellor.

lc, (*abbr.*) left centre; letter of credit; *loco citato,* in the place cited; lower case (*type*).

LCC, (*abbr.*) London County Council.

lcd, LCD, (*abbr.*) Liquid Crystal Display; lowest common denominator.

LCJ, (*abbr.*) Lord Chief Justice.

lcm, LCM, (*abbr.*) least, lowest common multiple.

L Cpl, (*abbr.*) Lance-Corporal.

L-dopa, *n.* chemical, normally produced by the body, which is converted in the brain to dopamine, and is essential for local movement.

LDR, *n.* a light-dependent resistor, or a resistor which conducts electricity better when light falls on it. They are made from semiconductors, such as cadmium sulphide, and are used in electric eye burglar alarms and light meters.

LDS, (*abbr.*) Latter-day Saints; *laus Deo semper,* praise be to God for ever.

lea[1]**,** *n.* a meadow; grassland; open country. [OE *lēah* (cp. OHG *lôh,* also L *lūcus,* grove, glade)]

lea[2]**,** *n.* land left untilled, fallow land, grass-land. *a.* fallow, unploughed. [OE *lǣge* in *lǣghrycg,* lea-rig (*lǣg-, liegan,* to LIE[2])]

LEA, (*abbr.*) Local Education Authority.

Leach, *n.* **Bernard** (1887–1979), British potter. His simple designs, which were inspired by a period of study in Japan, pioneered a modern revival of the art. He established the Leach Pottery at St Ives, Cornwall, in 1920.

leach[1]**,** *v.t.* to wash or wet by letting liquid percolate through; to wash out or separate (a soluble constituent) by percolation; to strain or drain (liquid) from some material (*usu.* out or away). *v.i.* of liquid in any material, to drain out. *n.* a tub, vat or other vessel used for leaching; the solution obtained by leaching, a leachate or the substance which is leached. **leach-tub,** *n.* a tub for leaching ashes in. **leachate,** *n.* the substance obtained by leaching; the percolating liquid used in leaching. **leachy,** *a.* [prob. from OE *leccan,* to water]

leach[2]**,** LEECH[1].

Leacock, *n.* **Stephen Butler** (1869–1944), Canadian humorist, whose writings include *Literary Lapses* 1910, *Sunshine Sketches of a Little Town* 1912, and *Frenzied Fiction* 1918.

lead[1]**,** *n.* a soft malleable and ductile, bluish-grey, heavy metal; in printing, a thin plate of type-metal used to separate lines; blacklead, plumbago or graphite, used in lead-pencils; (*pl.*) strips of lead used for covering a roof; a roof, esp. a flat roof, or part of a roof, covered with lead; a plummet, usu. consisting of a mass of lead, used for sounding; the metal strips or cames holding the glass in diamond-paned windows; lead bullets or (fishing) weights. *a.* pertaining to or containing lead; consisting more or less of lead. *v.t.* to cover, fasten, weight, frame or fit with lead; to space out (as lines of type) by inserting leads. **blacklead** BLACK. **red lead, white lead,** RED, WHITE. **to swing the lead,** to malinger. **lead-arming,** *n.* a piece of tallow etc., pressed into the lower part of the sounding-lead, to ascertain the nature of the sea-bottom. **lead-glance,** *n.* galena or lead-ore. **leadglass,** *n.* glass containing lead oxide. **lead-line,** *n.* a sounding-line. **lead-oxide,** *n.* litharge, a yellow crystalline material substance used in the manufacture of glass and paint. **lead paint,** *n.* paint with a lead base. **lead-pencil,** *n.* a pencil containing a slip of graphite or blacklead. **lead-poisoning,** *n.* poisoning caused by the prolonged absorption of lead into the system. **leadsman,** *n.* the sailor who heaves the lead in sounding. **leaded,** *a.* set in or fitted with lead; separated by leads, as lines of printing. **leaden,** *a.* made of lead; of the colour of lead, dark; heavy as lead; heavy, slow, burden-some; inert, indisposed to action or exertion. *v.t., v.i.* to make or become leaden. †**leaden-hearted,** *a.* destitute of feeling. †**leaden-heeled,** †**-paced,** †**-stepping,** *a.* moving slowly; slow, tardy. **leadenly,** *adv.* **leadenness,** *n.* **leading,** *n.* strips of lead inserted between lines of print, leads; the space introduced between lines of type by inserting leads; the lead strips framing panes of glass or covering a roof. **leadless,** *a.* **leady,** *a.* [OE *lēad* (cp. Dut. *lood,* Dan. *lod,* G *Lot*)]

lead[2]**,** *v.t.* (*past, p.p.* **led**) to conduct, to guide by the hand or by showing the way; to direct the movements of; to be in command of; to direct or induce by persuasion, instruction or advice; to keep in front of, to take the first place among; to be at the head of, to direct by example; to point out, to indicate, esp. by going in advance; to pass or spend (time etc.); to cause to spend or pass; to draw or drag after one; to begin a round at cards with; to transport (as hay etc.) in a cart. *v.i.* to act as conductor or guide; to go in advance; to be the commander, head or foremost person in any undertaking etc.; to be the first player in a game of cards, to play in a specified way; to go towards, to extend, to reach (to); to tend (to) as a result. *n.* guidance, direction, esp. by going in front; the first place, precedence, command, leadership; the leading role; an example; a clue; a way, passage, channel, esp. through ice; an artificial water-course, esp. a mill-race; a cord for leading a dog; a principal conductor for distribution of current in an electrical installation; in cards, the first play or the right to this; the direction in which a rope runs; the main story in a newspaper. *a.* principal, chief, main, leading. **to lead astray,** to lead into error. **to lead by the nose,** to cause to follow unthinkingly. **to lead captive,** to take captive. **to lead off,** to make a start. **to lead on,** to entice, to draw further towards some end; to fool or trick. **to lead the way,** to go first so as to point the way; to take the precedence. **to lead up to,** to conduct conversation towards (some particular subject); to conduct towards; to pave the way for; in cards, to play so as to induce an opponent to play (a certain card). **lead-in,** *n.* an introduction to a topic; the electric conductor connecting a radio transmitter or receiver with an outside aerial or transmission cable. **lead-off,** *n.* a start, a beginning; a leading motion. **lead time,** *n.* the interval between the design and manufacture of a product. **leadable,** *a.* **leader,** *n.* one who or that which leads; a guide, a conductor; a chief, a commander; the leading counsel in a case; the senior counsel of a circuit; a chief editorial article in a newspaper; the principal first violin of an orchestra; (*N Am.*) a conductor of an orchestra; a blank strip of film or tape preceeding or following the recorded material; the foremost horse, or one of the foremost horses abreast, in a team; in printing, a row of dots to lead the eye across a page or column; a trace on a fishing-line; a small vein of ore, usu. leading to a lode; the terminal bud or shoot at the apex of a stem or branch. **leaderless,** *a.* **leadership,** *n.* **leading,** *a.* guiding, conducting; alluring, enticing; chief, principal. *n.* the action of the verb TO LEAD; guidance, influence. **leading aircraftman, aircraftwoman,** *n.* a rank in the British Air Force below senior aircraftman. **leading article,** *n.* a leader in a newspaper. **leading business,** *n.* the chief role in a play etc. **leading case,** *n.* in law, a case that forms a precedent for the decision of others. **leading edge,** *n.* (*Aviat.*) the foremost edge of an aerofoil (e.g. of a wing, propeller blade). **leading lady, man** etc., *n.* persons taking the chief role in a play. **leading light,** *n.* an expert in a particular field; an influential or prominent member of a movement, group etc. **leading motive** LEIT-MOTIV. **leading note,** *n.* the seventh note of the major and minor scales. **leading question,** *n.* a question (esp. in cross-examination) that suggests a certain answer. **leading-**

rein, *n.* a rein for leading a horse by. **leading-reins, -strings,** *n.pl.* strings by which children were formerly supported when learning to walk or by which they are restrained when walking. **to be in leading-strings,** to be in a state of dependence on others. †**leadingly,** *adv.* **led,** *a.* under another's influence or leading. [OE *lǣdant,* causal of *līthan,* to go (cp. Dut. *leiden,* G *leitan,* to lead, OHG *līdan,* to go)]

leaden LEAD[1].

leading LEAD[2].

leaf, *n.* (*pl.* **leaves**) one of the expanded (usu. lateral) organs of plants which aid in the functions of assimilation of food-materials, transpiration and absorption of carbon dioxide from the atmosphere; anything resembling this; a petal, scale or sepal; (*collect.*) foliage; a sheet of paper in a book or manuscript, usu. comprising two pages; a thin sheet of metal or other material; a valved, hinged, sliding or detachable member of a bridge, table, door, shutter, screen etc. *v.i.* to shoot out or produce leaves or foliage. **to leaf through,** to turn the pages of a book, magazine etc., in a casual way, to browse through. **to take a leaf out of someone's book,** to follow the example of, to imitate. **to turn over a new leaf,** to change one's mode of life or conduct for the better; to make a new start. **leaf-bridge,** *n.* a bridge with a rising leaf or leaves swinging vertically on hinges. **leaf-bud,** *n.* a bud developing into a leaf. **leaf curl,** *n.* a disease of plants which causes curling of the leaves. **leaf-cutter,** *n.* any of various insects (as a bee or ant) which cut out sections of leaves. **leaf-hopper,** *n.* any of various jumping insects belonging to the order Orthoptera that suck plant juices. **leaf-insect,** *n.* an insect having camouflaged wing covers resembling leaves. **leaf-metal,** *n.* metal, esp. (imitation) silver or gold, beaten into thin sheets and used for decoration etc. **leaf miner,** *n.* any of various insects that as larvae bore into and eat leaf tissue. **leaf-mould,** *n.* decayed leaves reduced to mould and used as compost. **leaf-roll,** *n.* a form of potato virus. **leaf-spring,** *n.* a spring consisting of several broad, flat pieces of metal. **leaf-stalk,** *n.* a petiole supporting a leaf. **leaf-work,** *n.* decorative work embodying designs from leaves. **leafage,** *n.* **leafed, leaved,** *a.* (*usu. in comb.,* as *thick-leafed*). **leafless,** *a.* **leaflessness,** *n.* **leaflet,** *n.* a small leaf; a one-page handbill, circular etc.; a pamphlet; one of the primary divisions of a compound leaf. *v.i.* to distribute leaflets. **leaflike,** *a.* **leafy,** *a.* **leafiness,** *n.* [OE *lēaf* (cp. Dut. *loof* Icel. *lauf,* G *Laub*)]

league[1], *n.* a combination or union for mutual help or protection or the pursuit of common interests; a treaty or compact of alliance or confederation; a category, class or group; an association of clubs that play matches against one another, as *football league, rugby league. v.i.* to join in a league, to confederate. *v.t.* to combine together (with). **in league with,** having formed an alliance with, usu. for a dubious purpose. **League of Nations,** an international organization formed in 1920 pledged to cooperate in securing peace and the rigorous observance of treaties by its member states. It came to an end in 1946 when the United Nations was founded. **not in the same league,** not in the same class, not on the same level of excellence etc. **league match,** *n.* a match between clubs in the same league. **league table,** *n.* a table of competitors in a league listed in order of performance; a list showing the order of achievement, merit, performance etc. **leaguer**[1], *n.* a party to a league; a league member. [F *ligue,* It. *liga,* L *ligāre* to tie, to bind]

league[2], *n.* an old measure of distance, varying in different countries (in England usu. about three land or nautical miles, about 4·8 km). [perh. through Prov. *legua,* from late L *leuga,* prob. from Gaulish]

†**leaguer**[2], *n.* a siege; the camp of a besieging army. *v.t.* to beleaguer. [Dut. *leger,* cp. LAIR[1], LAAGER]

leak, *v.i.* to let liquid, gas etc., pass in or out through a hole, crevice or fissure; to ooze, as water, through a hole or fissure; (*sl.*) †to urinate. *v.t.* to cause or allow to enter or pass out; to divulge (confidential information). *n.* a crevice or hole which admits water or other fluid; the oozing of water or other fluid through such crevice; (*sl.*) urination; the divulgence of confidential information; a loss of electric current from a conductor. **to leak out,** to become gradually known or public, esp. in an underhand manner. **to spring a leak,** to open or crack so as to admit or let out water. **leakage,** *n.* a leak; the quantity that escapes by a leak; an allowance at a certain rate per cent for loss by leaking etc. **leaker,** *n.* **leakiness,** *n.* **leaky,** *a.* [cp. Icel. *leka,* Dut. *lekken,* G *lecken,* also OE *leccan,* to wet]

Leakey[1], *n.* **Louis (Seymour Bazett)** (1903–1972), British archaeologist, born in Kabete, Kenya. In 1958, with his wife Mary Leakey, he discovered gigantic animal fossils in Olduvai Gorge, as well as many early remains of a human type.

Leakey[2], *n.* **Mary** (1913–), British archaeologist. In 1948 she discovered, on Rusinga Island, Lake Victoria, E Africa, the prehistoric ape skull known as Proconsul, about 20 million years old; and human remains at Laetolil, to the south, about 3,750,000 years old.

Leakey[3], *n.* **Richard** (1944–), British archaeologist, son of Louis and Mary Leakey. In 1972 he discovered at Lake Turkana, Kenya, an ape-form skull, estimated to be about 2.9 million years old; it had some human characteristics and a brain capacity of 800 cu cm. In 1984 his team found an almost complete skeleton of *Homo erectus* some 1.6 million years old.

leal, *a.* (*Sc.*) loyal, true. **leally,** *adv.* **lealty,** *n.* [A-F, from OF *leel,* as LOYAL]

†**leam, leme,** *n.* a gleam, a light, a glow; brightness. *v.i.* to shine. [OE *lēoma* (cp. Icel. *liome,* also L *lūmen*), cogn. with *lēoht,* LIGHT[1]]

lean[1], *v.i.* (*past, p.p.* **leaned, leant**) to incline one's body from an erect attitude; to incline one's body so as to rest (against or upon); to deviate from a straight or perpendicular line or direction; to depend (upon) as for support; to have a tendency or propensity (to or towards). *v.t.* to cause to incline; to support, to rest (upon or against). *n.* a leaning, inclination, slope or deviation. **to lean on,** (*coll.*) to coerce, threaten (someone). **lean-to,** *n.* a building with a roof supported by another building or wall. **leaning,** *n.* inclination, partiality, propensity (towards or to). [OE *hlinian, hleonian,* whence *hlǣnan,* to cause to lean (cogn. with L *inclīnāre,* Gr. *klinein*)]

lean[2], *a.* thin, lank; of meat, not fat, consisting of muscular tissue; wanting in plumpness; meagre, poor; unproductive, sterile; unprofitable, unremunerative. *n.* the part of meat that consists of muscular tissue without fat; in printing, work or copy unremunerative to the compositor. †**lean-witted,** *a.* silly, stupid, foolish. **leanly,** *adv.* **leanness,** *n.* †**leany,** *a.* [OE *hlǣne,* etym. doubtful]

Lean, *n.* **David** (1908–), English film director. His films, noted for their atmospheric quality, include *Brief Encounter* (1946), *The Bridge on the River Kwai* (1957) (Academy Award), *Lawrence of Arabia* (1962) (Academy Award), and *A Passage to India* (1985).

leap , *v.i.* (*past, p.p.* **leapt, leaped**) to jump, to spring upwards or forwards; to rush, to fly, to dart; to pass over an interval, esp. in music; to make a sudden transition. *v.t.* to jump or spring over or across; to cause to jump or spring; in music, to pass from one note to another by an interval which is greater than a degree of the scale; of male animals, †to copulate with. *n.* the act of leaping; a jump, a spring, a bound; the space passed over by leaping; a space or interval; a collection of leopards; †copulation (of the lower mammals); a sudden transition; an increase; a place of leaping. **a leap in the dark,** a hazardous step or action, one whose consequences cannot be foreseen. **by leaps and bounds** BOUND[1]. **leap-day,** *n.* 29 February. **leap-frog,** *n.* (*Mil.*) the deploying of units in advance of each other in turns; a game in which one stoops down and another vaults over. *v.t., v.i.* to vault in this way. **leap year,** *n.* an intercalary year of 366 days, which adds one day to February every four years (leap year is every year the number of which is a multiple of four, except those divisible by 100 and not by 400). **leaper,** *n.* **leaping,** *n.* **leaping-fish,** *n.* a small E Indian fish, *Salarias tridactylus,* which goes on land and moves along by leaps. **leapingly,** *adv.* [OE *hlēapan* (cp. Dut. *loopen,* Icel. *hlaupa,* G *laufen,* to run)]

Lear, *n.* **Edward** (1812–1888), English artist and humorist. His *Book of Nonsense* 1846 popularized the limerick. He first attracted attention by his paintings of birds, and later turned to landscapes. He travelled in Italy, Greece, Egypt, and India, publishing books on his travels with his own illustrations, and spent most of his later life in Italy.

learn, *v.t.* (*past, p.p.* **learnt, learned**) to acquire knowledge of or skill in by study, experience or instruction; to fix in the memory; to find out, to be informed of, to ascertain; †to teach, to tell. *v.i.* to acquire knowledge or skill; to receive instruction. **learnable,** *a.* **learned,** *a.* having acquired learning by study; skilled, skilful (in); erudite; characterized by great learning or scholarship; of words etc., introduced or chiefly used by learned people. **learnedly,** *adv.* **learnedness,** *n.* **learner,** *n.* †**learner-like,** *a.* **learning,** *n.* the act of learning; knowledge acquired by study; erudition; scholarship. [OE *leornian* (cp. G *lernen*), cogn. with LORE, cp. OE *lǣran,* to teach]

lease¹, *n.* a letting or renting of land, houses, offices etc. for a specified period; the written contract for, the term of or the rights of tenure under such letting. *v.t.* to grant or to take or hold under lease. **a new lease of life,** an anticipated spell of life or enjoyment (e.g. after recovery from illness or release from trouble). **leaseback,** *n.* an arrangement whereby the seller of a property leases it back from the buyer. **leasehold,** *n.* tenure by lease; property held by lease. *a.* held thus. **leaseholder,** *n.* **leasable,** *a.* [A-F *lesser* (F *laisser*), L *laxāre,* to loose, from *laxus,* LAX]

†**lease²,** *v.i.* to glean. [OE *lesan,* to gather]

leash, *n.* a thong by which a hound or a hawk is held; a set of three animals; a lead for a dog or other animal; that which controls or restrains as if by a leash. *v.t.* to bind, hold or fasten (as) by a leash. **straining at the leash,** anxious or impatient to begin. [OF *lesse* (F *laisse*), late L *laxa,* orig. fem. of *laxus,* LAX]

†**leasing,** *n.* (*dial.*) a lie; falsehood. [OE *lēasung,* from *lēasian,* to lie, from *lēas,* false, destitute of, -LESS]

leasow, -sowe, *n.* (*dial.*) pasture, meadowland. *v.t., v.i.* to pasture. [OE *lǣswe,* oblique case of *lǣs*]

least, *a.* smallest; less than all others in size, amount, degree, quantity, value, importance etc. *adv.* in the smallest or slightest degree. *n.* the smallest amount, degree etc. **at (the) least,** at or in the lowest degree; at any rate. **in the least,** in the slightest degree, at all. **least(a)ways** (*dial.*) †**leastwise,** *adv.* at least; or rather. [OE *lǣst, lœ̄sast,* superl. of *lǣs,* LESS]

leat, *n.* (*dial.*) a water-course conveying water to a mill etc. [OE *gelǣt,* cross-roads, *wæter-gelǣt,* water-conduit, from *lǣtan,* see LET¹]

leather, *n.* the tanned or dressed skin or hide of an animal; dressed hides collectively; an article or part made of leather (*often in comb.*, as *stirrup-leather*); (*pl.*) a pair of leather breeches or leggings; (*sl.*) a cricket- or football; (*facet.*) one's skin. *a.* made of leather. *v.t.* to cover or furnish with leather; to thrash, as with a leather strap. **fair, white leather,** leather with its natural colour. **patent leather,** PATENT. **leather-back,** *n.* a leathery, soft-shelled turtle. **leather-carp,** *n.* a variety of the common carp in which almost all trace of scales is lost. **leather-cloth,** *n.* a fabric covered with a waterproof composition to resemble leather. **leather-coat,** *n.* an apple with a tough skin, esp. the golden russet. **leather-head,** *n.* a blockhead; an Australian bird without head feathers. **leather-jacket,** *n.* an Australian tree, *Eucalyptus resinifera;* the larva of a crane-fly; one of various fishes. **leather-neck,** *n.* (*Austral.*) a handyman; (*sl.*) a US marine. **leather-wood,** *n.* a N American shrub, *Dirca palustris,* the tough bark of which was used by the Indians for thongs. **Leatherette**®, *n.* a kind of imitation leather. **leatheriness,** *n.* **leathering,** *n.* a beating. **leathern,** *a.* **leathery,** *a.* [OE *lether* (cp. Dut. and G *Leder,* Icel. *lethr*)]

leave¹, *n.* liberty or permission; permission to be absent from duty; the period of this; the act of departing, a formal parting, a farewell, an adieu; a holiday. **by, with your leave,** with your permission. **French leave** FRENCH. **on leave,** absent from duty by permission; on holiday. **to take leave of one's senses,** to think or act contrary to reason. **to take (one's) leave,** to say good-bye; to depart. **leave-taking,** *n.* a parting; a farewell. [OE *lēaf,* cogn. with *lēof,* pleasing, LIEF]

leave², *v.t.* (*past, p.p.* **left²**) to allow to remain, to go without taking; to bequeath, to part from at death; to refrain from removing, consuming or interfering with; to depart from, to quit; to withdraw from, to forsake, to abandon; to cease to live or work at or belong to; to desist from, to cease, to discontinue; to commit, to entrust, to refer for consideration, approval etc. *v.i.* to depart, to go away; to cease, to discontinue. **to leave alone,** not to interfere with; to have no dealings with. **to leave be,** to avoid disturbing or interfering. **to leave behind,** to go away without; to outstrip; to leave as a record, mark, consequence etc. **to leave go,** to let go. **to leave off,** to desist from, to discontinue; to cease to wear. **to leave out,** to omit. **to leave over,** to leave for future consideration etc. **to leave unsaid,** to refrain from stating. **to leave well alone,** to leave be. **leaver,** *n.* **leaving,** *n.* the act of departing; (*pl.*) residue, remnant, refuse, offal. [OE *lǣfan* (cp. Icel. *leifa,* Goth. *-laibjan*), cogn. with *lāf,* LAVE²]

leaven, *n.* fermenting dough or any other substance (e.g. yeast) mixed with other dough, a batter etc. in order to cause fermentation and make it lighter; any influence tending to cause a general change. *v.t.* to raise and make light (as) with leaven; to imbue, to pervade with an influence causing change. **leavening,** *n.* leaven. †**leavenous,** *a.* [F *levain,* L *levāmen,* from *levāre,* to live]

leaves, LEAF.

Leavis, *n.* **F(rank) R(aymond)** (1895–1978), English literary critic, and co-founder (with his wife Q. D. Leavis) and editor of the controversial review *Scrutiny* 1932–53. He championed the work of D. H. Lawrence and James Joyce, and in 1962 attacked C. P. Snow's theory of 'Two Cultures'. His other works include *New Bearings in English Poetry* (1932) and *The Great Tradition* (1948). He was a lecturer at Cambridge university.

Lebanon, Republic of, country in W Asia bordering the E Mediterranean. **area** 10,452 sq km/4034 sq miles. **capital** and port Beirut. **towns** ports Tripoli, Tyre, Sidon. **physical** valley N–S between mountain ranges. **population** (1985 est) 3,500,000 (including 350,000 Palestinian refugees, many driven out, killed in fighting or massacred 1982–85); annual growth rate -0.1%. **exports** citrus and other fruit; industrial products to Arab neighbours. **language** Arabic (official); French and English. **religion** Muslim 57% (Shi'ite 33%, Sunni 24%), Christian (Maronite and Orthodox) 40%, Druse 3%. **Lebanese,** *a.* pertaining or belonging to Lebanon. *n.* the people of the Lebanon.

Lebedev, *n.* **Peter Nikolaievich** (1866–1912), Russian physicist. He proved by experiment, and then measured, the minute pressure which light exerts upon a physical body.

Lebensraum, *n.* theory developed by Hitler for the expansion of Germany into E Europe, and used by the Nazis to justify their annexation of neighbouring states on the grounds that Germany was overpopulated. [G, living-space]

Lebowa, *n.* black homeland in Transvaal province, South Africa; achieved self-governing status 1972; population (1985) 1,836,000.

Le Brun, *n.* **Charles** (1619–1690), French artist, painter to Louis XIV from 1662. In 1663 he became director of the French Academy and of the Gobelin factory, which produced art, tapestries, and furnishings for the new palace of Versailles.

Le Carré, *n.* **John** (pseudonym of **David John Cornwell**) (1931–), English thriller writer. His low-key realistic accounts of complex espionage include

The Spy Who Came in from the Cold (1963), *Tinker Tailor Soldier Spy* (1974), *Smiley's People* (1980), and *The Little Drummer Girl* (1983). He was a member of the Foreign Service 1960–64.

Le Chatelier's principle, (or **Le Chatelier-Braun principle**), in science, the principle that if a change in conditions is imposed on a system in equilibrium, the system will react to counteract that change and restore the equilibrium.

lecher, *n.* a man addicted to lewdness, a fornicator. †*v.i.* to practise lewdness. **lech, letch,** *v.i.* (*sl.*) to lust (after); to act lecherously. *n.* a lecher; a lascivious act. **lecherous,** *a.* **lecherously,** *adv.* †**lecherousness, lechery,** *n.* [OF *lecheor,* from *lechier,* to lick, to live in gluttony, OHG *leccôn,* to LICK]

lecithin, *n.* a nitrogenous fatty substance containing phosphorus found in the cellular tissue of animal and vegetable bodies. [Gr. *lekithos,* yolk of an egg]

Leclanché, *n.* **Georges** (1839–1882), French engineer. In 1866 he invented a primary electrical cell, which is still the basis of most dry batteries. **Leclanché Cell,** *n.* a primary cell consisting of a carbon cathode covered with manganese dioxide, all in a porous pot, and a zinc anode dipping into ammonium chloride solution.

Leconte de Lisle, Charles Marie René (1818–1894), French poet. He was born on Réunion, settled in Paris 1846 and headed Les Parnassiens 1866–76. His work drew inspiration from the ancient world, as in *Poèmes antiques/Antique Poems* (1852), *Poèmes barbares/Barbaric Poems* (1862), and *Poèmes tragiques/Tragic Poems* (1884).

Le Corbusier, *n.* (1887–1965), (assumed name of **Charles-Édouard Jeanneret**), Swiss architect. His functionalist approach to town planning in industrial society, was based on the interrelation between modern machine forms and the techniques of modern architecture. His concept, *La Ville Radieuse*, developed in Marseille (1945–50) and Chandigarh, India, placed buildings and open spaces with related functions in a circular formation, with buildings based on standard sized units mathematically calculated according to the proportions of the human figure.

lectern, *n.* a reading-desk from which parts of a church service, esp. the lessons, are said or sung; (*Sc.*) the precentor's desk; any similar reading desk. [OF *letrun,* late L *lectrum,* from *lect-,* p.p. stem of *legere,* to read]

lection, *n.* a reading or variation in a text; a portion of Scripture to be read in a church service, a lesson. **lectionary,** *n.* a collection of passages of Scripture for daily services. **lector,** *n.* a cleric in minor orders whose duty it was to read the lessons; a reader, esp. in a German university. **lectorate, lectorship,** *n.* [OF, from L *lectiōnem,* nom. as prec.]

lectual, *a.* (*Path.*) that confines to bed. [late L *lectuālis,* from *lectus,* bed]

lecture, *n.* a formal expository or instructive discourse on any subject, before an audience or a class; a reproof, a reprimand. *v.i.* to deliver a lecture or lectures; to give instruction by means of lectures. *v.t.* to instruct by lectures; to reprimand. **to read one a lecture,** to reprimand one. **lecturer,** *n.* **lectureship,** *n.* the academic office of a lecturer. [F, from late Latin *lectūra,* from *lectus,* p.p. of *legere,* to read]

lecythus, lekythos, *n.* (*pl.* **-thi**) (*Gr. Ant.*) a narrow-necked vase or flask for oil, unguents etc. [late L *lēcythus,* Gr. *lēkuthos*]

LED, (*abbr.*) light-emitting diode.

led, LEAD[2].

Leda, *n.* in Greek mythology, wife of Tyndareus, by whom she was the mother of Clytemnestra. By Zeus, who came to her as a swan, she was the mother of Helen of Troy, and Castor and Pollux.

Lederberg, *n.* **Joshua** (1925–), US geneticist who showed that bacteria can reproduce sexually, combining genetic material so that offspring possess characteristics of both parent organisms.

lederhosen, *n.* leather shorts with braces, the trad. male dress of Austria and Bavaria. [G, leather trousers]

ledge, *n.* a shelf or shelf-like projection ; a shelf-like ridge or outcrop of rock; a metal-bearing stratum of rock. **ledged,** *a.* **ledgeless,** *a.* **ledgy,** *a.* [prob. from ME *leggen,* to LAY[1]]

ledger, *n.* the principal book in a set of account-books, in which is entered a record of all trade transactions; a large flat stone as for an altar-table or grave; a horizontal pole parallel to the walls in scaffolding, to support the putlogs; (*Angling*) a ledger-line or tackle; †a resident ambassador. †*a.* resident, as an ambassador. *v.i.* to fish with a ledger-tackle. **ledger-bait,** *n.* fishing bait fixed or made to remain on the bottom; hence **ledger-hook, -line, -tackle. ledger-, legerline,** *n.* in musical notation, an additional short line above or below the stave to express ascending or descending notes. [prob. from ME *leggen,* as prec., after MDut. *ligger* (Dut. *legger*), that which lies in a place]

Ledru-Rollin, *n.* **Alexandre Auguste** (1807–1874), French politician and contributor to the radical and socialist journal *La Réforme*. He became minister for home affairs in the provisional government formed 1848 after the overthrow of Louis Philippe and the creation of the Second Republic, but he opposed the elected president Louis Napoleon.

Le Duc Tho, *n.* (1911–), North Vietnamese diplomat, who was joint winner (with US secretary of state Kissinger) of the Nobel Peace Prize 1973 for his part in the negotiations to end the Vietnam War. He indefinitely postponed receiving the award.

Ledum, *n.* a genus of low shrubs of the heath family. [mod. L, from Gr. *lēdon,* mastic]

Lee[1], *n.* **Bruce** (stage name of **Lee Yuen Kam**) (1941–1973), US 'Chinese Western' film actor, an expert in kung fu who popularized the oriental martial arts in the West.

Lee[2], *n.* **Christopher** (1922–), British film actor, whose tall, gaunt figure was memorable in the title role of *Dracula* 1958 and its sequels. He has not lost his sinister image in subsequent Hollywood productions. His other films include *Hamlet* 1948, *The Mummy* 1959, *Julius Caesar* 1970, and *The Man with the Golden Gun* 1974.

Lee[3], *n.* **Laurie** (1914–), English writer, born near Stroud, Gloucestershire. His works include the autobiographical novel *Cider with Rosie* 1959, a classic evocation of childhood; nature poetry such as *The Bloom of Candles* 1947, and travel writing including *A Rose for Winter* 1955.

Lee[4], *n.* **Robert E(dward)** (1807–1870), US Confederate general in the American Civil War, a military strategist. As military adviser to Jefferson Davis, president of the Confederacy, and as commander of the army of N Virginia, he made several raids into Northern territory, but was defeated at Gettysburg and surrendered 1865 at Appomattox.

lee[1], *n.* the side or quarter opposite to that against which the wind blows, opp. to windward or weather side; the sheltered side; shelter, protection. *a.* pertaining to the side or quarter away from the wind; sheltered. **under the lee of,** on the sheltered side of; protected from the wind by. **lee-board,** *n.* a board let down on the lee-side of a flat-bottomed vessel to prevent a leeward drift. **lee-gage, -gauge,** *n.* position to leeward of another ship. **lee shore,** *n.* the shore on the lee side of a vessel; the shore towards which the wind blows. **lee side,** *n.* the lee of a vessel. **lee tide,** *n.* a tide running in the same direction as the wind blows. **leeward,** *a.* relating to, in or facing the lee side. *adv.* towards the lee side. *n.* the lee side or direction. **leeway,** *n.* the leeward drift of a vessel; allowable scope or toleration inside defined limits. **to make up leeway,** to recover lost ground or time. [OE *hlēo, hlēow,* a covering, shelter (cp. Icel. *hlē,* lee, *hly,* warmth, shelter)]

lee[2], LEES.

Lee and Yang, Tsung Dao (1926–) and **Chen Ning** (1922–), Chinese physicists who studied how parity operates at the nuclear level. They found no proof for the claim, made by Wigner, that nuclear processes were indistinguishable from their mirror images, and that elementary particles made no distinction between left and right. In 1956 they predicted that parity was not conserved in weak interactions. Nobel prize 1957.

leech[1], *n.* †a physician, a healer; an aquatic annelid of the suctorial order Hirudinea, employed for the local extraction of blood; one who abstracts or absorbs the gains of others; one who clings tenaciously to another. *v.t.* to apply leeches to, as in phlebotomy; to cling to or prey on. **leechcraft,** *n.* the art of healing; medicine. [OE *lǣce,* rel. to *lācnian,* to heal (cp. Icel. *laeknir,* Dan. *laege,* a physician)]

leech[2], *n.* the perpendicular ledge of a square sail; the after edge of a fore-and-aft sail. [cp. Icel. *līk,* Dut. *ijk,* G *Liek*]

Leeds, *n.* city in W Yorkshire, England, on the river Aire; population (1984) 712,200. Industries include engineering, printing, chemicals, glass, and woollens.

leek, *n.* a culinary vegetable, *Allium porrum,* allied to the onion, with a cylindrical bulb, the national emblem of Wales. [OE *lēac* (cp. Dut. *look,* Icel. *laukr,* G *Lauch*)]

Lee Kuan Yew, *n.* (1923–), Singapore politician, prime minister from 1959. Lee founded the anti-communist Socialist People's Action Party 1954 and entered the Singapore legislative assembly 1955. He was elected the country's first prime minister 1959, and took Singapore out of the Malaysian federation 1965.

leer, *n.* an oblique, sly or arch look; a look expressive of a feeling of malice, lasciviousness or triumph; †the face, the countenance, hue, complexion. *v.i.* to look with a leer. †to allure with sly or arch looks. **leeriness,** *n.* **leering,** *n., a.* **leeringly,** *adv.* **leery,** *a.* knowing, sly. **to be leery of,** to be wary of. [OE *hlēor,* the cheek, the face, the look]

lees, *n.pl.* dregs, the sediment of liquor which settles to the bottom. [formerly *lee,* OF *lie,* Gaulish L *lia,* perh. from Celt.]

†**leese,** *v.t.* (*past* **lore** *p.p.* **loren, lorn**) to lose. [OE *lēosan* (in belēosan, *forlēosan*), cp. LEASING]

†**leet[1],** *n.* a court leet; a court of record; the jurisdiction of a court leet; a day on which a court leet is held. [prob. from A-F *lete,* OE *lǣth,* LATHE[2]]

†**leet[2],** *n.* (*Sc.*) a list of candidates for any office. **short leet,** the final select list of such candidates. [perh. from ÉLITE]

Lee Teng-hui, *n.* (1923–), Taiwanese right-wing politician, vice president 1984–88, president and Kuomintang party leader from 1988. Lee, the country's first island-born leader, is viewed as a reforming technocrat.

Leeuwenhoek, *n.* **Anton van** (1632–1723), Dutch pioneer of microscopic research. He ground his own lenses, some of which magnified up to 200 times. With these he was able to see individual red blood cells, sperm, and bacteria, achievements not repeated for more than a century.

leeward, leeway LEE[1].

Leeward Islands, *n. pl.* group of islands, part of the Society Islands, in French Polynesia, S Pacific; general term for the northern half of the Lesser Antilles in the West Indies; former British colony in the West Indies (1871–1956) comprising Antigua, Montserrat, St Christopher/St Kitts-Nevis, Anguilla, and the Virgin Islands.

leeze, LIEF.

Lefebvre, *n.* **Mgr Marcel** (1905–), French Catholic priest. Ordained in 1929, he was a missionary and an archbishop in West Africa until 1962. He opposed the liberalising reforms of the Second Vatican Council 1962–65 and formed the 'Priestly Cofraternity of Pius X'. In 1976, he was suspended by Pope Paul VI for continuing the unauthorised ordination of priests at his Swiss headquarters. His defiance continued and in June 1988 he was excommunicated by Pope John Paul II, in the first formal schism within the Roman Catholic Church since 1870.

left[1], *a.* of, pertaining to or situated on the side that is to the east when one faces south, opp. to right; correspondingly situated in relation to the front or the direction of anything; radical, politically innovative; of or pertaining to socialism or communism. *adv.* on or towards the left. *n.* the side opposite to the right; the left hand; a left-handed blow; the left wing of an army; the party which sits on the left of the president in a legislative assembly; the progressive, democratic or socialist party, wing or faction. **Left Bank,** *n., a.* a district in Paris on the south bank of the Seine, famous for artists. **left hand,** *a.* situated on or pertaining to the left side; executed by the left hand. *n.* the left side, direction or region. **left-handed,** *a.* using the left hand more readily than the right; moving from right to left; for the left hand; of a blow, delivered with the left hand; awkward, clumsy, stupid; insincere, malicious, sinister; ambiguous, equivocal; of marriages, morganatic, fictitious. **a left-handed compliment,** one which couches a jibe or reproach. **left-handedly,** *adv.* **left-handedness,** *n.* **left-hander,** *n.* a left-handed person or a left-handed blow. **leftward,** *adv., a.* **leftwards,** *adv.* **left-wing,** *n.* the left side of an army or sports pitch; the part of a building which projects to the left. *a.* pertaining to, active in or sympathetic to the political left (of a party); playing on the left-wing. **left-winger,** *n.* a person belonging to the left-wing (of a political party) or sympathetic to left-wing policies. **leftism,** *n.* the policies and principles of the political left. **leftist,** *n., a.* **lefty,** *n.* (*derog.*) a left-winger, a leftist. *a.* left-wing. [OE *left, lyft,* weak, worthless]

left[2], left-luggage, *n.* luggage deposited temporarily at a railway station etc. **left-luggage office,** *n.* **left-off,** *a.* discarded as no longer serviceable, laid aside. **left-over,** *n.* (*usu. pl.*) a remainder, esp. of uneaten food. [*past, p.p.* LEAVE[2]]

leg, *n.* one of the limbs by which humans and other mammals walk, esp. the part from the knee to the ankle; the analogous member in other species; an animal's hind leg (esp. the upper portion) which is eaten as meat; the part of a garment that covers the leg; anything resembling a leg in form or function; one of a set of posts or rods supporting a table, bed, chair etc.; a limb of a pair of compasses etc.; the course and distance run by a vessel on one tack; a stage in a long-distance flight, journey, race etc.; in cricket, that part of the field to the rear and left of a batsman; a fielder in such part; in a contest, any of a series of events, games etc. **a leg up,** assistance; a boost. **leg-and-leg,** *adv.* equal (in a race, card-game etc.). **leg before wicket** (lbw) in cricket, stoppage by the batsman's leg of a ball when it would have hit the wicket. **leg-of-mutton,** *a.* of a sleeve etc., shaped like a leg of mutton. **not to have a leg to stand on,** to have no support or basis for one's position (e.g. in a controversy). **to be on one's last legs** LAST[1]. **to find one's legs,** to attain ease or mastery. **to get on one's legs,** to stand up, esp. to make a speech. **to pull someone's leg,** to hoax, to make a fool of; to tease. **to shake a leg,** (*often int.*) to hurry up. **to show a leg,** to get out of bed; to make an appearance. **to stretch a leg,** to take exercise, esp. after inactivity. **leg-break,** *n.* in cricket, a ball which breaks from the leg side. **leg-bye,** *n.* (lb) in cricket, a run scored for a ball that touches the batsman. **leg-guard,** *n.* in cricket, baseball etc., a pad to protect the leg from knee to ankle. **leg-iron,** *n.* a fetter for the leg. **leg-rest,** *n.* a support for an injured leg. **legroom,** *n.* space for the legs (e.g. in a car). **leg show,** *n.* entertainment involving the exhibition of women's legs. **legwarmers,** *n.pl.* long footless stockings usu. worn over outer garments. **legwork,** *n.* work involving much travel on foot; groundwork. **legged,** *a.* (*usu. in comb.*, as *four-legged*). **legging,** *n.* (*usu. pl.*) gaiters; a covering of leather, stretch cotton etc. for the legs. **leggy,** (*coll.*) having long legs; of plants, spindly. **legginess,** *n.* **legless,** *a.* without legs; (*coll.*) very drunk. [Icel. *leggr*]

leg., (*abbr.*) legal; legate; legato; legislation.

legacy, *n.* a bequest; property bequeathed by will; anything left or handed on by a predecessor; †a legateship. **legacy-duty,** *n.* (*formerly*) a tax on legacies, usu. at graduated rates, increasing in proportion as relationship diminishes. **legacy-hunter,** *n.* one who pays court to another in the hope of receiving a legacy. **legatee,** *n.* one to whom a legacy is bequeathed. **legator,** *n.* [OF *legacie,* legateship, med. L *lēgātia,* L *lēgātus,* LEGATE]

legal, *a.* of, pertaining to, or according to law; lawful, legitimate; recognized or sanctioned by the law; appointed or laid down by the law; concerned with the law, characteristic of lawyers; belonging or conformable to the Mosaic law, or the principle of salvation by works, not by grace. **legal aid,** *n.* financial assistance for legal proceedings granted to those with low incomes. **legal tender,** money which a creditor is bound to accept in discharge of a debt. **legalese,** *n.* the language of legal documents. **legalism,** *n.* strict adherence to law and formulas; (*Theol.*) the doctrine of justification by works; respect for the letter rather than the spirit of religious or ethical laws. **legalist,** *n.* **legalistic,** *a.* **legalistically,** *adv.* **legality,** *n.* **legalization, -isation, legalize, -ise,** *v.t. n.* **legally,** *adv.* [F *légal,* L *lēgālis,* from *lex lēgis*]

legate, *n.* a papal emissary; an ambassador, an envoy; a lieutenant or deputy attached to a Roman general or governor; the governor of a papal province. **legateship,** *n.* **legatine,** *a.* **legation,** *n.* the act of sending one as legate or deputy, a diplomatic mission; a diplomatic representative and his or her delegates the official residence of a diplomatic representative; a legateship. [OF *legat,* L *lēgātus,* orig. p.p. of *lēgāre,* to appoint, to commission]

legatee etc. LEGACY.

legato, *adv., a.* (*Mus.*) in an even gliding manner without a break. *n.* this style of playing. **legatissimo,** *adv., a.* as smoothly as possible. [It., bound, p.p. of *legare,* L *ligāre,* see LIGATE]

legend, *n.* †a chronicle, biography or series of selections from the lives of saints or sacred history, formerly read in the refectories of religious houses, and as lessons at matins; a traditional story, esp. one popularly accepted as true; a myth, a fable; traditional or non-historical story-telling or literature; an inscription on a coat of arms, round the field of a medal or coin, beneath an illustration; one who is renowned for outstanding deeds or qualities, whether real or fictitious etc. **legendary,** *a.* **legendist,** *n.* **legendry,** *n.* [OF *legende,* med. L *legenda,* that which is to be read, from L *legere,* to read]

leger, LEDGER.

Léger, *n.* **Fernand** (1881–1955), French painter, associated with cubism. From around 1909 he evolved a characteristic style, composing abstract and semi-abstract works with cylindrical forms, reducing the human figure to robot components.

legerdemain, *n.* sleight of hand, a trick in which the eye is deceived by the quickness of the hand, conjuring; jugglery, sophistry. [OF *legier de main* (F *léger*), light of hand]

legging, leggy LEG.

leghorn, *n.* a plait of the straw of bearded Italian wheat cut green and bleached, used for bonnets and hats; a hat made of this plait; a breed of domestic fowl. [*Leghorn* (*Livorno*), Italy]

legible, *a.* that may be read; easily decipherable; clear, plain, evident. **legibleness, legibility,** *n.* **legibly,** *adv.* [OF, from late L *legibilis,* from *legere,* to choose, to read]

legion, *n.* a division of the ancient Roman army, varying, at different periods, from 3000 to 6000 men; a military force, esp. in France and other foreign countries; a host, a vast army or multitude. **American Legion,** an association of US war veterans. **British Legion,** an association of ex-Service men and women formed after World War I. **Foreign Legion,** corps of foreign volunteers in the French army. **Legion of Honour,** a French order of merit founded by Napoleon I as a reward for services or merit, civil or military. **legionary,** *a.* pertaining to a legion or legions; consisting of one or more legions. *n.* a soldier of a legion; a member of the Legion of Honour. **legioned,** *a.* formed or drawn up in legions. **legionnaire,** *n.* a legionary. **Legionnaire's disease,** *n.* a serious, sometimes fatal disease resembling pneumonia, caused by *Legionella* bacteria (so named because of its occurrence at an American Legion convention in 1976). [OF, from L *legiōnem,* nom. *legio,* from *legere,* to choose]

legislate, *v.i.* to make or enact a law or laws; to issue instructions; to make allowance for. **legislation,** *n.* the act or process of making laws; laws or prospective laws. **legislative,** *a.* enacting laws; having power to legislate; enacted by or pertaining to legislation. *n.* the legislative power or function; the legislature. **legislatively,** *adv.* **legislator,** a lawgiver, a member of a legislative assembly. **legislatorial,** *a.* †**legislatorship,** *n.* **legislatress,** †**-trix** , *n.fem.* **legislature,** *n.* a body of people in which is vested the power or right to enact, alter, repeal or suspend laws. [L *lex lēgis,* law, *latum* serving as a verbal noun of *ferre,* to bear]

legist, *n.* one learned in the law. [OF *legiste,* med. L *lēgista,* from *lex lēgis,* law]

legit, *a.* (*coll.*) short for LEGITIMATE. *n.* the legitimate theatre.

legitim, -time, *n.* (*Sc. Law*) the portion of a person's property that must be inherited by the children.

legitimate¹, *a.* lawful; legal, properly authorized; lawfully begotten, born in wedlock, legally descended; of a title to sovereignty, derived from strict hereditary right; proper, regular, natural; conformable to accepted usage; following by logical sequence; pertaining to formal or serious theatre rather than television, cinema, variety etc. *n.* one who is legitimate; (*sl.*) the legitimate drama. **legitimate drama,** *n.* the body of plays of recognized merit; plays belonging to the recognized canons of dramatic art. **legitimacy, legitimately,** *adv.* **legitimateness,** *n.* **legitimation, legitimization, -isation,** *n.* **legitimism,** *n.* the doctrine of hereditary monarchical government and divine right. **legitimist,** *n., a.* **legitimize,** *v.t.* to render legitimate. [med. L *lēgitimātus,* p.p. of *lēgitimāre,* from L *lēgitimus,* as prec.]

legitimate², *v.t.* to make lawful; to render legitimate; to invest with the rights of one legitimately born; to justify, to serve as justification for.

Legnano, Battle of, defeat of Holy Roman emperor Frederick I (Barbarossa) by members of the Lombard League 1176 at Legnano, NW of Milan. It was a major setback to the emperor's plans for imperial domination in Italy.

Lego®, *n.* a building toy mainly consisting of connecting plastic bricks.

Le Guin, *n.* **Ursula K(roeber)** (1929–), US writer of science fiction and fantasy. Her novels include *The Left Hand of Darkness* 1969, which questions sex roles; the *Earthsea* trilogy 1968–72; and *The Dispossessed* 1974, which contrasts an anarchist and a capitalist society.

legume, *n.* the fruit or pod of a leguminous plant; a two-valved fruit, usu. dehiscent along its face and back, and bearing its seeds on either margin of the ventral suture (as the pod of the pea); any of various vegetables used as food, esp. pulses. **legumin,** *n.* a protein resembling casein, contained in leguminous and other seeds. **leguminous,** *a.* producing legumes; pertaining to the Leguminosae, an order of herbs, shrubs and trees bearing legumes. [F *légume,* L *legūmen,* pulse, from *legere,* to gather]

Leh, *n.* capital of Ladakh region, E Kashmir, India, situated E of the Indus, 240 km/150 miles E of Srinagar. Leh is the nearest supply base to the Indian army outpost on the Siachen Glacier.

Lehár, *n.* **Franz** (1870–1948), Hungarian composer. He wrote many operettas, among them *The Merry Widow* (1905), *The Count of Luxembourg* (1909), *Gypsy Love* (1910), and *The Land of Smiles* (1929). He also composed songs, marches, and a violin concerto.

Le Havre, *n.* industrial port (engineering, chemicals, oil refining) in Normandy, NW France, on the Seine; population (1982) 255,000.

lei, *n.* a garland or necklace of flowers. [Hawaiian]

Leibniz, *n.* **Gottfried Wilhelm** (1646–1716), German mathematician and philosopher. Independently of, but concurrently with, Newton he developed calculus. In his metaphysical works, such as *The Monadology* (1714), he argued that everything consisted of innumerable units, *monads*, whose individual properties determined their past, present, and future. **Leibnitzian, -nizian,** *a.* pertaining to the German philosopher Leibniz or his philosophy. *n.* a follower of Leibnitz or his philosophy. **Leibnitzianism,** *n.*

Leicester[1], *n.* a type of cheese resembling cheddar; a breed of sheep with a long fleece. [after the English county of *Leicester*]

Leicester[2], *n.* industrial city (food processing, hosiery, footwear, engineering, electronics, printing, plastics) and administrative headquarters of Leicestershire, England, on the river Soar; population (1983) 282,300.

Leicester[3], *n.* **Robert Dudley, Earl of Leicester** (*c.* (1532–1588), English courtier. Son of the duke of Northumberland, he was created Earl of Leicester 1564. Queen Elizabeth I gave him command of the army sent to the Netherlands 1585–87, and of the forces prepared to resist the threat of Spanish invasion 1588.

Leicestershire, *n.* county in central England. **area** 2,550 sq km/984 sq miles. **towns** administrative headquarters Leicester; Loughborough, Melton Mowbray, Market Harborough. **population** (1987) 879,000. **products** horses, cattle, sheep, dairy products, coal.

Leichhardt, *n.* **Friedrich** (1813–1848), Prussian-born Australian explorer. In 1843, he walked 965 km/600 miles from Sydney to Moreton Bay, Queensland, and in 1844 went from Brisbane to Arnhem Land, but disappeared during a further expedition from Queensland in 1848.

Leics (*abbr.*) Leicestershire.

Leigh, *n.* **Vivien** (1913–1967), British actress, born Vivien Mary Hartley. Noted for her fragile beauty and vivacity, she is remembered for her Oscar-winning roles as Scarlett O'Hara in *Gone With the Wind* (1939) and as Blanche du Bois in *A Streetcar Named Desire* (1951).

Leinster, *n.* SE province of the Republic of Ireland, comprising the counties of Carlow, Dublin, Kildare, Kilkenny, Laois, Longford, Louth, Meath, Offaly, Westmeath, Wexford, Wicklow; area 19,635 sq km/ 7581 sq miles; capital Dublin; population (1981) 1,790,521.

leiotrichi, *n.* a primary division of mankind comprising the races characterized by having smooth hair. **leiotrichous,** *a.* [Gr. *leios,* smooth, *trich-,* stem of *thrix,* hair]

leipoa, *n.* a genus of mound-birds, containing the native pheasant of Australia, *Leipoa ocellata.* [Gr. *leipein,* to forsake, to leave, *ōon,* an egg]

Leipzig, *n.* capital of Leipzig county, East Germany, 145 km/90 miles SW of Berlin; population (1984) 1,384,050. Products include furs, leather goods, cloth, glass, cars, and musical instruments.

leister, *n.* (*Sc.*) a pronged fishing-spear. *v.t.* to spear with a leister. [Icel. *liôstr,* from *liôsta,* to strike]

leisure, *n.* freedom from business, occupation or hurry; time at one's own disposal, unoccupied time; opportunity, convenience. *a.* unoccupied, free, idle. **at leisure,** at one's ease or convenience; without hurry; deliberately. **leisure centre,** *n.* a complex containing facilities for sports, entertainments, meetings etc. **leisure wear,** *n.* casual clothing. **leisurable,** *a.* **leisurably,** *adv.* **leisured,** *a.* **leisureless,** *a.* **leisureliness,** *n.* **leisurely,** *a., adv.* [OF *leisir,* orig. inf. verb, L *licēre,* to be allowed]

leitmotiv, -motif, *n.* the leading, representative or recurring theme in a composition, orig. a musical theme invariably associated with a certain person, situation or idea throughout an opera etc. [G (*leit,* leading, MOTIVE)]

Leitrim, *n.* county in Connacht province, Republic of Ireland, bounded on the NW by Donegal Bay. **area** 1526 sq km/589 sq miles. **county town** Carrick-on-Shannon. **population** (1986) 27,000. **products** potatoes, cattle, linen, woollens, pottery, coal, iron, lead.

lek[1], *n.* a unit of Albanian currency.

lek[2], *n.* an area where certain species of birds (esp. black grouse) assemble for sexual display and courtship.

lekythos, LECYTHUS.

Lely, *n.* **Peter** (1618–1680), adopted name of Pieter van der Faes. Dutch painter, active in England from 1641, who painted fashionable portraits in Baroque style. His subjects included Charles I, Cromwell, and Charles II.

LEM, (*abbr.*) lunar excursion module.

Lemaître, *n.* **Georges Édouard** (1894–1966), Belgian cosmologist who proposed the Big Bang theory of the origin of the universe 1927.

†**leman,** *n.* a sweetheart of either sex; a gallant, a mistress; a concubine, a paramour. [ME *lemman, leofman* (OE *lēof,* dear)]

Léman, Lac, *n.* French name for Lake Geneva.

Le Mans, *n.* industrial town in Sarthe *département,* France; population (1982) 150,000, conurbation 191,000. It has a motor racing circuit where the annual endurance 24-hour race (established 1923) for sports cars and their prototypes is held.

lemma, *n.* (*pl.* **-mmass, -mmata**) an auxiliary proposition taken to be valid in order to demonstrate some other proposition; a theme, a subject, esp. when prefixed as a heading. [L and Gr. *lēmma,* from *lambanein,* to take]

lemming, *n.* a small rodent of northern Europe, *Myodes lemmus,* allied to the mouse and rat, remarkable for migrating at certain periods in immense multitudes; someone who dashes headlong into situations without forethought. [Norw.]

Lemmon, *n.* **'Jack' (John Uhler III)** (1925–), US character actor, often cast as the lead in comedy films such as *Some Like it Hot* (1959) but equally skilled at straight drama, as in *The China Syndrome* (1979).

Lemnian, *a.* of or pertaining to Lemnos, an island in the Aegean Sea. *n.* an inhabitant of Lemnos. **Lemnian earth,** *n.* a medicinal earth obtained from Lemnos. **Lemnian ruddle,** *n.* a reddish ochre found with this and used as a pigment.

lemniscate, *n.* a curve of the general form of a figure 8 (∞). **lemniscate function,** *n.* an elliptic function used in mathematical formulae expressing the properties of such curves. [L *lēmniscātus,* from *lēmniscus,* Gr. *lēmniskos,* ribbon]

lemniscus, *n.* (*pl.* **-ci**) (*Rom. Ant.*) a fillet or ribbon; the character ÷ employed by ancient textual critics; (*Anat., Zool.*) a bundle of fibres or ribbon-like appendages. [see prec.]

lemon, *n.* the oval acid fruit of *Citrus limonum;* the tree bearing this; the pale yellow colour of a lemon; (*sl.*) someone who or that which is disappointing, unpleasant, useless. *a.* pertaining to the lemon; of the colour of a lemon; lemon flavoured. **salt of lemon** SALT. **lemon cheese, curd,** *n.* a spread made from lemon, butter, eggs and sugar. **lemon-dab,** LEMON-SOLE. **lemon-drop,** *n.* a lemon-flavoured hard sweet. **lemon-grass,** *n.* the lemon-scented hardy grass from the tropics which yields an essential oil. **lemon-peel,** *n.* the peel or rind of the lemon (either fresh or dried, preserved and candied) used as a flavouring material. **lemon-plant, -verbena,** *n.* a South American shrub cultivated for its lemon-scented foliage. **lemon-squash,** *n.* a sweet concentrated lemon drink. **lemon-squeezer,** *n.* **lemon-wood,** *n.* a small New Zealand tree, the Maori tarata. **lemonade,** *n.* lemon-juice or flavouring mixed with still or aerated water and sweetened. **lemony,** *a.* [F *limon,* med. L *limōnem,* nom. *limo,* Oriental in orig. (cp. Arab. *laimūn,* Pers. *līmū*)]

Le Mond, *n.* **Greg** (1961–), US racing cyclist, the first American to win the Tour de France 1986.

lemon-sole, lemon-dab *n.* a flat-fish with brown markings valued as a food. [prob. from F *limande,* a mud-fish]

lemur, *n.* any member of a genus of arboreal nocturnal animals allied to the monkeys commonly found in Madagascar. **lemurid,** *n.* **lemuroid,** *n., a.* **lemures,** *n.pl.* a term applied by the Romans to spectres or spirits of the dead. [L *lemures,* ghosts]

Lena, *n.* longest river in Asiatic Russia, 4400 km/2730 sq miles, with numerous tributaries. Its source is near Lake Baikal and it empties into the Arctic Ocean through a delta 400 km/240 miles wide. It is ice-covered for half the year.

Lenard, *n.* **Phillip** (1862–1947), German physicist who investigated the photoelectric effect and cathode rays. Nobel physics prize 1905.

Lenclos, *n.* **Ninon de** (1615–1705), French courtesan. As the recognized leader of Parisian society, she was the mistress in turn of many highly placed men, including General Condé and the writer La Rochefoucauld.

lend, *v.t.* (*past, p.p.* **lent**) to grant for temporary use; to grant the use of on condition of repayment or compensation; to let out (money) at interest; to furnish, to contribute, esp. for temporary service; to accommodate (oneself); †to devote. *v.i.* to make loans. **to lend a hand** HAND[1]. **to lend an ear,** to listen. **to lend oneself, itself, to,** to have the right qualities for; to be appropriate for using. **Lend-Lease,** *n.* the provision of military and other equipment by the US to the allied countries of Europe during World War II. *v.t.* to provide an ally with military equipment during wartime. **lendable,** *a.* **lender,** *n.* one who lends, esp. money upon interest. **lending,** *n.* **lending library,** *n.* a library from which books can be borrowed freely or for a subscription. [ME *lenen,* OE *lǣnan* (cp. Dut. *leenen,* Icel. *lāna,* G *lehnen*)]

Lendl, *n.* **Ivan** (1960–), Czechoslovakian lawn tennis player who is the top money winner of all time in the men's game. He has won seven Grand Slam singles titles including the US and French titles three times each. He has won more than $14 million.

Leng, *n.* **Virginia** (1955–), British showjumping rider, born in Malta. She has won world, European, and most major domestic championships.

Lenglen, *n.* **Suzanne** (1899–1938), French tennis player, Wimbledon singles and doubles champion 1919–23 and 1925, and Olympic champion 1921. She became professional 1926. She also introduced modern sports clothes, designed by Jean Patou.

length, *n.* measure or extent from end to end, as distinguished from breadth or thickness; the longest line that can be drawn from one extremity of anything to the other; a definite portion of the linear extent of anything; the state of being long; extent of time, duration, long continuance; the distance anything extends; extent or degree of action etc.; the quantity of a vowel or syllable; the distance traversed by a cricket ball before striking the ground; in racing, the linear measure of the body of a horse, boat etc.; **arm's length** ARM[1]. **at length,** to the full extent, in full detail; at last. **to go to any length,** to stop at no obstacle; to be restrained by no scruples. **lengthen,** *v.t.* to make long or longer; to draw out, to extend; to protract. *v.i.* to grow longer. **lengthener,** *n.* †**lengthful,** *a.* **lengthways, lengthwise,** *adv., a.* **lengthy,** *a.* long and tedious; prolix. **lengthily,** *adv.* **lengthiness,** *n.* [OE *lengthu,* from *lang,* LONG[1] (cp. Dut. *lengte,* Icel. *lengd*)]

lenient, *a.* mild, gentle; merciful, clement; †soothing, emollient, mitigating. †*n.* an emollient preparation or application. **lenience, -ency,** *n.* **leniently,** *adv.* **lenitive,** *a.* having the power or quality of softening or mitigating; mitigating, palliative. *n.* a lenitive medicine or application. **lenity,** *n.* [L *lēniens -ientem,* pres.p. of *lēnīre,* to soothe, from *lēnis,* soft, gentle]

Lenin, *n.* **Vladimir Ilyich** (1870–1924), adopted name of Vladimir Ilyich Ulyanov. Soviet communist politician and theoretician. Active in the 1905 Revolution, Lenin had to leave Russia when it failed, settling in Switzerland 1914. He returned to Russia after the February revolution and in Nov. 1917 he became leader of a Soviet government, concluded peace with Germany, and organized a successful resistance to White Russian (pro-Tsarist) uprisings and foreign intervention. His modification of traditional Marxist doctrine to fit conditions prevailing in Russia became known as Marxism-Leninism, the basis of communist ideology.

Leningrad, *n.* capital of the Leningrad region, at the head of the Gulf of Finland; population (1987) 4,948,000. Industries include shipbuilding, machinery, chemicals, and textiles. Originally called St Petersburg, it was renamed Petrograd 1914, and Leningrad 1924.

Lennon, *n.* **John** (1940–1980), Rock singer and songwriter, former member of the Beatles.

leno, *n.* (*pl.* **-nos**) an open cotton fabric resembling fine muslin. [perh. corr. of F *linon*]

lenocinium, *n.* (*Sc. Law*) a husband's connivance at his wife's adultery. [L, the trade of a pimp]

Le Nôtre, *n.* **André** (1613–1700), French landscape gardener, creator of the gardens at Versailles and Les Tuileries.

lens, *n.* (*pl.* **lenses**) a piece of transparent substance, usu. glass or a combination of such (**compound lens**), with the surface or both surfaces curved so as to change the direction of rays of light, and diminish or increase the apparent size of objects viewed through it; the crystalline body (**crystalline lens**) in the eye through which rays of light are focused on the retina. A device (**electrostatic** or **electromagnetic lens**) for converging beams of electrons and other charged particles; a device for directing sound waves. **lensed,** *a.* **lensless,** *a.* [L *lens lentis,* seed of lentil]

Lent[1], *n.* a fast of 40 days (excluding Sundays) from Ash Wednesday to Easter Eve; a season of penitence and fasting in commemoration of Christ's fasting in the wilderness. **Lent-lily,** *n.* the daffodil. **Lent term,** *n.* the school and university term in which Lent falls. **lenten,** *a.* of, pertaining to or used in Lent; sparing, meagre. **Lenten fare,** *n.* a meatless diet. [ME *lenten,* OE *lencten,* spring (cp. Dut. *lente,* G *Lenz,* prob. cogn. with LONG[1], because the days lengthen in spring)]

lent[2], *past, p.p.* LEND.

-lent, *suf.* full, as in *corpulent, opulent, violent.* [L *-lentus*]

lentamente LENTO.

lenten LENT[1].

lent(i)-, *comb. form* pertaining to a lens.

lenticel, *n.* a lens-shaped mass of cells in the bark of a plant, through which respiration takes place. **lenticellate,** *a.* [F *lenticelle,* dim. from L *lentēm,* nom. *lens*]

lenticula, *n.* a lenticel; a small lens; a freckle. **lenticular,** *a.* resembling in shape a lentil or lens doubly convex; of or pertaining to the lens of the eye. **lenticularly,** *adv.*

lentiform, shaped like a lens.

lentigo, *n.* (*pl.* **lentigines**) a freckle, freckly eruption. **lentiginous, -nose,** *a.* [L, from *lens lentis,* LENS]

lentil, *n.* a small branching leguminous plant, *Ervum lens;* (*pl.*) the seeds of this plant, largely used for food. [OF *lentille,* L *lenticula*]

lentisk, *n.* the mastic tree, *Pistacia lentiscus.* [F *lentisque,* L *lentiscum,* nom. *-cus*]

lentivirus, *n.* any of a family of viruses that include the AIDS virus and others which affect cattle, goats and sheep. [L *lentus,* slow, VIRUS]

lento, *adv., a.* (*Mus.*) slow(ly). *n.* (*pl.* **-tos, -ti**) a piece of music played in this way. **lentamente,** *adv.* (*Mus.*) slowly; in slow time. **lentando,** *adv.* (*Mus.*) with increasing slowness. **lentissimo,** *adv., a.* very slow(ly). [It., from L *lentus,* slow]

lentoid, pertaining to a lens.

lentor, *n.* slowness, sluggishness (of temperament, vital functions etc.); viscidity. †**lentous,** *a.* [L *lentus,* slow]

l'envoy, †**lenvoy,** ENVOY[1].

Lenz's law, *n.* in physics, law stating that the direction of an electromagnetically induced current (generated by moving a magnet near a wire or a wire in a magnetic field) will oppose the motion producing it.

Leo, *n.* one of the 12 zodiacal constellations, the Lion; the fifth sign of the zodiac. **leonid,** *n.* one of the meteors that appear in numbers radiating from the constellation Leo. **leonine**, *a.* pertaining to or like a lion; majestic, undaunted; (**Leonine**) of or pertaining to, one of the Popes Leo, esp. Leo I; describing pentameter or hexameter Latin verse the last word of which rhymes with that preceding the caesura. **Leonine City,** *n.* the portion of Rome comprising the Vatican which was walled by Leo IV. [L *leo leōnis*]

Leo I, *n.* **St, (the Great)** (*c.* 390–461), pope from 440 who helped to establish the Christian liturgy. Leo summoned the Chalcedon Council where his Dogmatical Letter was accepted as the voice of St Peter. Acting as ambassador to the emperor Valentinian III (425–455), Leo saved Rome from devastation by the Huns by buying off their king, Attila, with large sums of money.

Leo III, *n.* **the Isaurian** (*c.* 680–740), Byzantine emperor and soldier. He seized the throne 717, successfully defended Constantinople against the Saracens 717–18, and attempted to suppress the use of images in church worship.

Leo III, *n.* (*c.* 750–816), pope from 795. After the withdrawal of the Byzantine emperors, the popes had become the real rulers in Rome. Leo III was forced to flee because of a conspiracy in Rome, and took refuge at the court of Charlemagne. He returned to Rome 799, and crowned Charlemagne emperor on Christmas Day 800, establishing the secular sovereignty of the pope over Rome under the suzerainty of the emperor.

Leo X, *n.* **Giovanni de' Medici** (1475–1521), pope from 1513. The son of Lorenzo the Magnificent of Florence, he was created a cardinal at 13. He bestowed on Henry VIII of England the title of Defender of the Faith, but later excommunicated him. A patron of the arts, he sponsored the rebuilding of St Peter's Church, Rome. He raised funds for this by selling indulgences, a sale that led the religious reformer Martin Luther to rebel against papal authority. He condemned Luther in the bull *Exsurge domine* (1520) and excommunicated him 1521.

León, *n.* city in W Nicaragua, population (1985) 101,000. Industries include textiles and food processing. Founded 1524, it was capital of Nicaragua until 1855.

Leonard, *n.* **Elmore** (1925–), US author of westerns and thrillers, marked by vivid dialogue, for example *Stick* (1983) and *Freaky Deaky* (1988).

Leonard, *n.* **Sugar Ray** (1956–), US boxer. In 1988 he became the first man to win world titles at five officially recognized weights. In 1976 he was Olympic light-welterweight champion and won his first professional title in 1979 when he beat Wilfred Benitez for the WBC welterweight title. He has since won titles at junior-middleweight (WBA version) 1981, middleweight (WBC) 1987, light-heavyweight (WBC) 1988, and super-middleweight (WBC) 1988. In 1989 he drew with Thomas Hearns.

Leonardo da Vinci, (1452–1519), Italian painter, sculptor, architect, engineer, and scientist, one of the greatest figures of the Italian renaissance, active in Florence, Milan, and from 1516 in France. As state engineer and court painter to the duke of Milan, he produced the *Last Supper* mural about 1495 (Sta Maria delle Grazie, Milan), and on his return to Florence painted the *Mona Lisa* about 1503–06 (Louvre, Paris). His notebooks and drawings show an immensely inventive and enquiring mind, studying aspects of the natural world from anatomy to aerodynamics.

Leoncavallo, *n.* **Ruggiero** (1857–1919), Italian operatic composer, born in Naples. He played in restaurants, composing in his spare time, until in 1892 *Pagliacci* was performed. His other operas include *La Bohème* (1897) (contemporary with Puccini's version) and *Zaza* (1900).

León de los Aldamas, *n.* industrial city (leather goods, footwear) in central Mexico; population (1986) 947,000.

Leone, *n.* **Sergio** (1928–1989), Italian film director, responsible for popularizing 'spaghetti' westerns (westerns made in Italy and Spain, usually with a US leading actor and a European supporting cast and film crew) and making a world star of Clint Eastwood. His films include *Per un Pugno di Dollari/A Fistful of Dollars* (1964), *Cera una Volta il West/Once upon a Time in the West* (1968), and *Cera una Volta il America/Once upon a Time in America* (1984).

Leonidas, *n.* (died 480 BC), king of Sparta. He was killed while defending the pass of Thermopylae with 300 Spartans, 700 Thespians, and 400 Thebans against a huge Persian army.

Leonov, *n.* **Aleksei Arkhipovich** (1934–), Soviet cosmonaut. In 1965 he was the first person to walk in space, from *Voskhod 2*.

leopard, *n.* a large mammal, *Felis pardus,* of the cat family from Africa and S Asia, having a pale fawn to tan coat with dark spots, the panther; a leopard-like animal, as the **American leopard** or jaguar, the **hunting leopard** or cheetah, and the **snow leopard** or ounce; in heraldry, a lion passant guardant, as in the English royal arms. **leopard's bane,** *n.* a plant of the composite genus *Doronicum;* other composite plants, also herb Paris. **leopardess,** *n.fem.* [OF, from late L *leopardus,* late Gr. *leopardos* (LION, PARD[1])]

Leopardi, *n.* **Giacomo, Count Leopardi** (1798–1837), Italian romantic poet. The first collection of his uniquely pessimistic poems, *Versi/Verses*, appeared (1824), and was followed by his philosophical *Operette Morali/Minor Moral Works* (1827), in prose, and *Canti/Lyrics* (1831).

Leopold I[1], *n.* (1640–1705), holy Roman emperor from 1658, in succession to his father Ferdinand III. He warred against Louis XIV of France and the Ottoman Empire.

Leopold I[2], *n.* (1790–1865), king of Belgium from 1831, having been elected to the throne on the creation of an independent Belgium. Through his marriage, when prince of Saxe-Coburg, to Princess Charlotte Augusta, he was the uncle of Queen Victoria, and exercised considerable influence over her.

Leopold II[1], *n.* (1747–1792), holy Roman emperor in succession to his brother Joseph II, he was the son of Empress Maria Theresa. His hostility to the French Revolution led to the outbreak of war a few weeks after his death.

Leopold II[2], *n.* (1835–1909), king of Belgium from 1865, son of Leopold I. He financed the journalist Stanley's explorations in Africa, which resulted in the foundation of the Congo Free State (now Zaïre), from which he extracted a huge fortune by ruthless exploitation.

Leopold III, *n.* (1901–1983), king of Belgium from 1934, he surrendered to the Germans 1940. Postwar charges against his conduct led to a regency by his brother Charles, and his eventual abdication 1951 in favour of his son Baudouin.

Léopoldville, *n.* former name (until 1966) of Kinshasa, city in Zaïre.

leotard, *n.* a close-fitting garment resembling a swimsuit, worn during exercise, dance practice etc. [Jules *Léotard,* F trapeze artist]

Lepanto, Battle of, sea battle 7 Oct 1571, fought in the Mediterranean Gulf of Corinth off Lepanto (Italian name of the Greek port of *Naupaktos*), then in Turkish possession, between the Ottoman Empire and forces from Spain, Venice, Genoa, and the Papal States, jointly commanded by Don John of Austria. The combined western fleets delivered a crushing blow to Muslim sea power. The Spanish writer Cervantes was wounded in the battle.

Le Pen, *n.* **Jean-Marie** (1928–), French extreme right-wing politician. In 1972 he formed the French National Front, supporting immigrant repatriation and capital punishment; the party gained 10% of the national vote in the 1986 election. Le Pen was elected to the European Parliament 1984.

Lepenski Vir, *n.* the site of Europe's oldest urban settlement (6th millennium BC), now submerged by an artificial lake on the Danube.

leper, *n.* one affected with leprosy; one who is deliberately avoided by others. †*a.* leprous. **leprosarium, le-**

proserie, -sery, *n.* a leper hospital. **leprose,** *a.* scaly. **leprosity,** *n.* scaliness. **leprosy,** *n.* a chronic disease, usu. characterized by shining tubercles of various sizes, thickening of the skin, loss of feeling, and ulceration and necrosis of parts. **leprous,** *a.* †**leprously,** *adv.* †**leprousness,** *n.* [OF *lepre,* leprosy, L and Gr. *lepra,* fem. of *lepros,* from *lepos,* scale]

†**lepid,** *a.* pleasant, merry; jocose, facetious. [L *lepidus*]

lepid(o)-, *comb. form* having scales; resembling scales. [Gr. *lepis lepidos,* a scale]

Lepidodendron, *n.* a genus of fossil plants so named from the scars on the stems where the leaves were attached. **lepidodendroid,** *n., a.* [Gr. *dendron,* tree]

lepidolite, *n.* a pinky-violet mica containing lithium.

Lepidoptera, *n.pl.* an order of insects, characterized by having four wings clothed with minute powder-like scales, containing the butterflies and moths. **lepidopteral, -an,** *n., a.* **lepidopterist,** *n.* **lepidopterology,** *n.* **lepidopterous,** *a.* [Gr. *pteron,* wing]

lepidosaurian, *a.* pertaining to the Lepidosauria, a subclass of reptiles having a scaly integument. *n.* a member of this subclass.

lepidosiren, *n.* a genus of dipnoan fishes with one species, *Lepidosiren paradoxa,* the S American mudfish, from the river Amazon. [SIREN]

lepidote, *a.* scaly.

leporide, *n.* an animal supposed to be a hybrid between a hare and a rabbit. [F *léporide,* as foll.]

leporine, *a.* of or pertaining to hares, having the nature or form of a hare. *n.* a leporide. [L *leporīnus,* from *lepus leporis,* hare]

leprechaun, *n.* in Irish folklore, a brownie or dwarfish sprite who performs domestic tasks, mends shoes etc. [Ir.]

leprosy LEPER.

-lepsy, *suf.* a seizure, as in *epilepsy, catalepsy.* [Gr. *lēpsis, lambanein,* to seize]

Leptis Magna, *n.* ruined city in Libya, 120 km/75 miles E of Tripoli. It was founded by the Phoenicians, then came under Carthage, and in 47 BC under Rome.

lepto-, *comb. form* fine, small, thin, delicate; narrow, slender. [Gr. *leptos*]

leptocardian, *a.* belonging to the Leptocardii, the lowest division of vertebrates, typified by the lancelet. *n.* an individual of this class. [Gr. *kardia,* heart]

leptocephalic, *a.* having a long and narrow scull. **leptocephalid,** *n.* one of a family of eel-like fishes, the Leptocephalidae. **leptocephaloid,** *n., a.* **leptocephalous,** *a.*

leptocercal, *a.* slender tailed. [Gr. *kerkos,* tail]

leptodactyl, *a.* having long, slender toes. *n.* a bird having such toes. **leptodactylous,** *a.* [Gr. *daktulos,* digit]

lepton, *n.* (*pl.* **lepta**) a small ancient-Greek coin, the mite of the New Testament parable, now worth one-hundredth of a drachma; (*pl.* **leptons**) any of a various elementary particles (e.g. electron, muon) insensitive to the strong interaction. [Gr., neut. of *leptos,* LEPTO-]

leptorrhine, *a.* having a long, narrow nose. [Gr. *rhis rhinos,* nose]

leptosome, *n.* someone of slender build, narrow chested etc. [Gr. *soma,* body]

leptosperm, *n.* a plant of the Australian genus *Leptospermum,* of myrtaceous shrubs and trees.

leptospirosis, *n.* any of various infectious diseases transmitted by animals and caused by bacteria. [Gr. *speira,* a coil]

†**lere,** *v.t.* to teach; to learn. [OE *lǣran* (cp. LEARN and LORE)]

Lermontov, *n.* **Mikhail Yurevich** (1814–1841), Russian Romantic poet and novelist. In 1837 he was put into active military service in the Caucasus for a revolutionary poem on the death of Pushkin, which criticized Court values, and for participating in a duel. In 1838 he published the psychological novel *A Hero of Our Time* (1840) and a volume of poems *October* (1840).

lerp, *n.* (*Austral.*) an edible saccharine substance secreted by a desert insect. [Austral. Abor., sweet]

Le Sage, *n.* **Alan René** (1668–1747), French novelist and dramatist. Born in Brittany, he abandoned law for literature. His novels include *Le Diable boîteux/The Devil upon Two Sticks* (1707) and his picaresque masterpiece *Gil Blas* (1715–1735), much indebted to Spanish originals.

lesbian, *n.* a female homosexual. *a.* **lesbianism,** *n.* [Gr. island of *Lesbos,* home of Sappho]

Lesbos, *n.* ancient name of Lesvos, an island in the Aegean Sea.

lese-majesty, *n.* an offence against the sovereign power or its representative, high treason. [F *lèse-majesté,* L *laesa mājestās* (*laesa,* hurt, violated, fem. p.p. of *laedere,* see foll.)]

lesion, *n.* a hurt, an injury; physical change in a tissue or organ due to injury. [F *lésion,* L *laesiōnem,* nom. *-sio,* from *laedere,* to injure]

Les Miserables, *n.* a novel by Victor Hugo, published 1862. On release from prison, Jean Valjean attempts to hide his past by assuming a series of false identities. He cares for a young girl, Cossette, who believes Valjean to be her father. When she marries he reveals the truth but dies a broken man.

Lesotho, Kingdom of, landlocked country in southern Africa, an enclave within South Africa. **area** 30,355 sq km/11,717 sq miles. **capital** Maseru. **physical** mountainous. **population** (1987) 1,627,000; annual growth rate 2.5%. **exports** wool, mohair, diamonds. **language** Sesotho and English (official). **religion** Christian 70% (Roman Catholic 40%).

less, *a.* smaller; of smaller size, extent, amount, degree, importance, rank etc. *prep.* minus, with deduction of. *adv.* in a smaller or lower degree; not so much. *n.* a smaller part, quantity or number; the smaller, the inferior, the junior etc., of things compared; (*coll.*) enough. *conj.* unless. **less and less,** gradually diminishing. **nothing less,** anything else (than), anything rather; (*coll.*) nothing of a smaller or milder kind. **lessen,** *v.t.* to make less or diminish in size, extent, number, quantity or degree; to reduce, to depreciate, to degrade. *v.i.* to become less in size, extent, number, degree or quantity; to decrease, to shrink. **lesser,** *a.* less, smaller; inferior. [double comp.] [OE (*læssa,* a. *lǣs* adv.]

-less, *suf.* devoid of, free from, as in *fearless, godless, sinless, tireless.* [OE *lēas,* loose, free from, cogn. with LOOSE]

lessee, *n.* one to whom a lease is granted. **lesseeship,** *n.* [A-F, from OF *lessé,* p.p. of *lesser,* to LEASE[1]]

lessen, lesser LESS.

Lesseps, *n.* **Ferdinand, Vicomte de Lesseps** (1805–1894), French engineer, constructor of the Suez Canal 1859–69; he began the Panama Canal 1879, but failed when he tried to construct it without locks.

Lessing, *n.* **Doris (May) (**born **Taylor)** (1919–), British novelist, born in Iran. Concerned with social and political themes, particularly the place of women in society, her work includes *The Grass is Singing* (1950), *The Golden Notebook* (1962), *The Good Terrorist* (1985), and the five-novel series *Children of Violence* (1952–69). She has also written an 'inner space fiction' series *Canopus in Argus Archives* (1979–83), and under the pen name 'Jane Somers', *The Diary of a Good Neighbour* (1981).

Lessing, *n.* **Gotthold Ephraim** (1729–1781), German dramatist and critic. His plays include *Miss Sara Sampson* (1755), *Minna von Barnhelm* (1767), *Emilia Galotti* (1772); and the verse play *Nathan der Weise* (1779). His works of criticism *Laokoon* (1766) and *Hamburgische Dramaturgie* (1767–68) influenced German literature. He also produced many theological and philosophical writings.

lesson, *n.* any exercise done, or portion of a book learnt, read or recited by a pupil to a teacher; the amount or duration of instruction given to a pupil at one time; (*pl.*) a course of instruction (in any subject); a portion of Scripture read in divine service; a reprimand, admonition or lecture; an occurrence or example taken as a warning or caution. *v.t.* to teach, to instruct; to discipline; to admonish, to lecture. [OF *le-*

con, L *lectiōnem,* nom. *-tio,* from *legere,* to read, p.p. *lectus*]

lessor, *n.* one who grants a lease. [A-F, from *lesser,* to LEASE[1]]

lest, *conj.* for fear that; in case; so that not; (after words expressing alarm, anxiety etc.) that. [ME *leste lesthe,* OE *thȳ lǣs the,* the (instrumental) less that]

Lesvos, *n.* Greek island in the Aegean Sea, near the coast of Turkey. **area** 2154 sq km/831 sq miles. **capital** Mytilene. **population** (1981) 104,620. **products** olives, wine, grain.

let[1], *v.t.* (*pres.p.* **letting,** *past, p.p.* **let**) to permit, to allow, to suffer (to be or do); to give leave to; to cause to; to grant the use, occupation or possession of for a stipulated sum, to lease; to give out on contract. *aux.v.* used in the imperative mood, with the force of prayer, exhortation, assumption, permission or command. *v.i.* to be let or leased, for rent. *n.* a letting. **let alone,** not to mention; much less. **to let alone,** to leave without interference; not to do or deal with; not to mention. **to let be,** not to interfere with. **to let blood,** to bleed. **to let down,** to allow to sink or fall; to humiliate; to fail (someone). **to let drive** DRIVE. **to let drop, fall,** to drop; to mention by or as if by accident. **to let fly** FLY[2]. **to let go,** to release; to relinquish hold of; to cease to retain; to dismiss from the mind; to drop anchor. **to let in,** to allow to enter; to insert; to cheat, to defraud. **to let in for,** to involve (someone) in something unpleasant, difficult etc. **to let in on,** to allow to be involved in. **to let into,** to admit to; to admit to knowledge of. **to let loose,** to free from restraint, to release. **to let off,** to suffer to go free; to refrain from punishing or to punish lightly; to pardon, to excuse; to discharge, to fire off (an arrow, gun etc.). **to let on,** to divulge, to let out; to pretend. **to let oneself go,** to give way to any impulse; to lose interest in maintaining one's appearance. **to let out,** to open the door for; to suffer to escape; to divulge; to enlarge (as a dress); to lease or let on hire. **to let rip,** (*coll.*) to explode into action or speech without restraint. **to let slip,** to allow to escape; to lose, to miss; to reveal inadvertently. **to let up (on),** to become less (severe), to abate. **let-down,** *n.* a disappointment. **let up,** *n.* a cessation, an alleviation. [OE *lǣtan* (cp. Dut. *laten,* Icel. *lāta,* G *lassen*)]

let[2], *n.* †a hindrance, an obstacle; in tennis etc., a stoppage, hindrance etc., requiring the ball to be served again; a rally or service affected by this. †*v.t.* (*pres.p.* **letting,** *past, p.p.* **letted, let**) to hinder, to impede, to obstruct, to prevent. †*v.i.* to cause obstruction. [OE *lettan* (cp. Dut. *letten,* Icel. *letja*), rel. to LATE]

-let, *suf.* diminutive, as in *bracelet, cutlet, tartlet.* [OF *-let, -lete, -et* (L *-ellus, -ella, -ellum,* -ET)]

letch, LECH, under LECHER.

lethal, *a.* deadly, fatal, mortal. **lethality,** *n.* **lethally,** *a.* †**lethe,** *n.* death. **lethiferous,** *a.* [F, from L *lēthālis, lētālis,* from *lētum,* death]

lethargy, *n.* morbid drowsiness; unnatural sleepiness; a state of torpor, apathy, dullness or inactivity. †*v.t.* to affect with lethargy. **lethargic, -ical,** *a.* **lethargically,** *adv.* **lethargied,** *a.* **lethargize, -ise,** *v.t.* **lethargus,** *n.* sleeping-sickness. [L and Gr. *lēthargia,* from *lēthargos,* forgetting, from foll.]

Lethe, *n.* in Greek mythology, a river of Hades whose waters produced forgetfulness in those who drank them; forgetfulness, oblivion. **Lethean,** *a.* [L, from Gr. *lēthē,* forgetfulness, *lēth-, lath-,* root of *lanthanesthai* to forget]

lethiferous LETHAL.

Lett, *n.* a member of a people largely inhabiting Latvia (Lettland), a Latvian. **Lettic,** *a.* of the group of languages to which Latvian (Lettish) belongs (also containing Lithuanian and Old Prussian. **Lettish,** *n., a.* Latvian. [G *Lette,* native *Latvi*]

letter, *n.* a mark or character employed to represent a sound in speech; one of the characters in the alphabet; a written message or communication; the literal or precise meaning of a term or terms, distinguished from the spirit; a character used in printing, type, fount of type; (*pl.*) literature, literary culture; learning, erudition; †an inscription, lettering; a degree, membership, title etc. abbreviated after a surname. *v.t.* to impress, mark or stamp with letters. **letter of attorney** ATTORNEY[2]. **letter of credit** CREDIT. **letter of marque (and) reprisal,** a privateer's commission to seize and plunder the merchant ships of a hostile state. **letter of the law,** literal or precise definition of the law. **letters of administration,** a document issued by a court authorizing a person to administer an intestate estate. **letters of credence,** a document held by a diplomat presenting his or her credentials to a foreign government. **man of letters,** an author; a scholar. **letter-board,** *n.* a board on which pieces of type for distribution are placed. **letter bomb,** *n.* an explosive device contained in an envelope, which detonates when opened. **letter-book,** *n.* a book in which copies of letters are kept. **letter-box,** *n.* a box for the reception of letters. **letter-card,** *n.* a folded card with gummed edges for sending by post as a letter. †**letter-carrier,** *n.* a postman. **letterhead,** *n.* notepaper with a printed heading; the heading on such notepaper. **letter-perfect,** *a.* of actors etc., having learnt one's part thoroughly; word perfect. **letterpress,** *n.* matter printed by ink on raised type; printed matter other than illustrations. **letters patent** PATENT. **lettered,** *a.* marked or impressed with letters; learned, erudite; pertaining to or suited for literature or learning. **lettering,** *n.* the act or technique of impressing or marking with letters; an inscription, a title. **letterless,** *a.* having received no letters; illiterate, ignorant. [OF *lettre,* L *littera*]

lettre de cachet CACHET.

lettuce, *n.* a crisp-leaved garden plant of the genus *Lactuca,* esp. *L. sativa,* much used for salad. [ME *letuce,* ult. from L *lactūca,* cogn. with *lac lactis,* milk]

leu, *n.* (*pl.* **lei**) the monetary unit of Romania equal to 100 bani [Rom., lion]

leucaemia, -chaemia, leukaemia, (*esp. N Am.*) **-emia,** *n.* a cancerous disease in which leucocytes multiply causing loss of red corpuscles, hypertrophy of the spleen etc.

leucin, -cine, *n.* a white crystalline substance obtained from the decomposition of animal fibre. **leucic, leucinic,** *a.*

leucite, *n.* a dull, glassy silicate of aluminium and potassium, occurring at Mt Vesuvius and Monte Somma. **leucitic,** *a.*

leuc(o)-, leuk(o)-, *comb. form* white, pale. [Gr. *leukos*]

leucocyte, *n.* a white corpuscle or blood cell. **leucocytic,** *a.*

leucocythaemia, *n.* leucaemia. [Gr. *-haima,* blood]

leucocytogenesis, *n.* the production of leucocytes.

leucocytolysis, *n.* the destruction of leucocytes.

leucocytosis, *n.* a condition characterized by an increase in the number of white corpuscles in the blood.

leucoma, *n.* a white opaque spot in the cornea, due to a wound, inflammation etc. [Gr. *leukōma,* from *leukos,* see prec.]

leucorrhoea, *n.* a mucous discharge from the vagina, commonly called whites. **leucorrhoeal, -rrhoeic,** *a.* [Gr. *rhoia,* a flow]

leucosis, *n.* pallor, whiteness; the morbid condition resulting in albinism. **leucism,** *n.* **leucous,** *a.* [Gr. *leukōsis,* from *leukoun,* to make white, from *leukos,* white]

leucotomy, LOBOTOMY.

leukaemia LEUCAEMIA.

lev, *n.* (*pl.* **leva**) the monetary unit of Bulgaria equal to 100 stotinki. [Bulg., lion]

Lev., (*abbr.*) Leviticus.

Levant[1], *n.* the eastern part of the Mediterranean with the adjoining countries; a levanter or easterly wind in the Mediterranean; levant morocco MOROCCO. **levanter,** *n.* a native or inhabitant of the Levant; an easterly wind in the Mediterranean. **levantine,** *a.* pertaining to the Levant. [F, from It. *levante,* L *levantem,* nom. *-vans,* pres.p. of *levāre,* to raise]

levant[2], *v.t.* to abscond, to run away, esp. with gambling liabilities undischarged. **levanter,** *n.* [Sp. *levantar,* to break up (camp, house etc.), from *levar,* to raise, as prec.]

levator, *n.* a muscle that raises some part of the body. [late L, from *levāre* to raise]

Le Vau, *n.* **Louis** (1612–1670), French architect, who drafted the plan of Versailles, and built the Louvre and Les Tuileries in Paris.

levee[1], *n.* †the action of rising; a morning or early afternoon reception held by a sovereign or person of high rank; a general reception or assembly of visitors. [F *levé* or *lever,* rising]

levee[2], *n.* the natural bank of a river formed by the deposition of silt; an artificial bank to prevent overflow and flooding; a quay, a landing place on a river. [F *levée,* p.p. of *lever,* to raise]

level, *n.* a horizontal line or plane or plane surface; a line or plane at all points at right angles to the vertical; an instrument for determining whether a surface or a series of objects are horizontal; the altitude of any point or surface; level country; a stage or degree of progress or rank; a position on a scale of values; a horizontal gallery or passage in a mine. *a.* horizontal, even, not higher or lower at any part, flat; of an evenness with something else (e.g. the top of a cup, spoon); equal in rank or degree; equable, uniform, well-balanced. *v.t.* (*past, p.p.* **levelled**) to make horizontal; to reduce to a horizontal plane; to bring (up or down) to the same level; to make smooth or even; to point (a gun) in taking aim; to aim, to direct (an attack, satire etc.); to raze, to overthrow, to make level (with the ground etc.), to knock down; to bring to an equality of state, rank, condition, or degree. †*v.i.* to aim or point a gun; to conjecture, to guess. **on the level,** honest, genuine. **to do one's level best,** to do the best one can. **to find one's level,** to settle in a position, office, rank etc. suitable for one's abilities, qualities, powers. **to level off,** to make flat; to reach and stay in a state of equilibrium. **to level with,** (*sl.*) to be honest with, to come clean. **level crossing,** *n.* a level place where a road crosses a railway line. **level-headed,** *a.* sensible, shrewd, untemperamental. **levelheadedly,** *adv.* **level-headedness,** *n.* **level pegging,** *a.* equal; of contestants etc., at the same level or at the same place in a race etc. **leveller,** *n.* one who or that which levels; one who wishes to destroy all social distinctions (esp. during the English Civil War); that which does so. **levelling-rod, -staff,** *n.* a pole used in surveying. **levelly,** *adv.* **levelness,** *n.* [OF *livel* (F *niveau*), L *lībella,* dim. of *lībra,* balance, a level]

Levellers, *n.pl.* the democratic party in the English Revolution. They found wide support among Cromwell's New Model Army and the yeoman farmers, artisans, and small traders, and proved a powerful political force 1647–49. Their programme included the establishment of a republic, government by a parliament of one house elected by male suffrage, religious toleration, and sweeping social reforms.

lever, *n.* a bar of wood, metal, or other rigid substance, having a fixed point of support (or fulcrum), used to overcome a certain resistance (or weight); a part of a machine, instrument etc., acting on the same principle; anything that brings power or influence to bear. *v.t.* to move or lift with or as with a lever. *v.i.* to use a lever. **lever escapement,** *n.* an escapement in which two levers connect the pallet and balance. **lever watch,** *n.* a watch with a lever escapement. **leverage,** *n.* the action of a lever; the mechanical power or advantage gained by the use of a lever; an arrangement of levers; means of accomplishing, influencing etc. [OF *leveor,* from *lever,* to raise]

leveret, *n.* a hare in its first year. [A-F, from OF *levrete,* dim. of *levre* (F *lièvre*), L *leporem,* nom. *lepus,* hare]

Leverrier, *n.* **Urbain Jean Joseph** (1811–1877), French astronomer, who predicted the existence and position of Neptune.

Lévesque, *n.* **René** (1922–1987), French-Canadian politician. In 1968 he founded the Parti Québecois, with the aim of an independent Quebec, but a referendum rejected the proposal 1980. He was premier of Quebec 1976–85.

Levi, *n.* **Primo** (1919–1987), Italian novelist. He joined the anti-Fascist resistance during World War II, was captured and sent to Auschwitz concentration camp. He wrote of these experiences in *Se questo e un uomo/If This is a Man* (1947).

leviable LEVY.

leviathan, *n.* a huge aquatic monster (perh. the Nilotic crocodile) described in The Book of Job; anything huge or monstrous, esp. a huge ship, a whale, the state. [late L, from Heb. *livyāthān,* etym. doubtful]

levigate, *v.t.* to make smooth; to grind or rub down to an impalpable powder, esp. in liquid or a moist state. *a.*, smooth. **levigable,** *a.* **levigation,** *n.* [L *lēvigātus, p.p. of lēvigāre,* from *lēvis,* smooth]

†**levin,** *n.* lightning; a flash of lightning. †**levin-brand,** *n.* a thunderbolt. [ME *levene,* etym. doubtful]

Levi-Montalcini, *n.* **Rita** (1909–), Italian neurologist who discovered nerve growth factor, a substance that controls how many cells make up the adult nervous system. Nobel prize 1986.

levirate, *n.* an ancient law of the Hebrews and others binding a man to marry the widow of his dead brother if the orig. marriage was childless. *a.* leviratical. **leviratic, -ical,** *a.* **leviration,** *n.* [L, *levir,* brother-in-law (cp. Sansk. *dēvar,* Gr. *daēr*)]

Levis®, *n.pl.* a type of (blue) denim jeans.

Lévi-Strauss, *n.* **Claude** (1908–), French anthropologist, who sought to find a universal structure governing all societies, reflected in the way myths are created. His works include *Tristes Tropiques* (1955), and *Mythologiques/Mythologies* (1964–71).

levitate, *v.t., v.i.* to (cause to) rise or float in the air, as a body through supernatural causes. **levitation,** *n.* **levitational,** *a.* **levitator,** *n.* [L *levis,* light, after GRAVITATE]

Levite, *n.* in the Old Testament or Hebrew Bible, one of the tribe or family of Levi, esp. one of those who acted as assistants to the priests in the Jewish temple; a priest, a parson, a clergyman. **Levitic, -ical,** *a.* pertaining to the Levites; pertaining to the book of Leviticus or the laws contained in it; †priestly. **Levitical degrees,** *n.pl.* degrees of relationship which according to the Levitical law precluded marriage. **Levitically,** *adv.* **Leviticus,** *n.* the third book of the Pentateuch, containing the Levitical law and ritual. **levitism,** *n.* [L *Levīta,* Gr. *Leuitēs,* from *Leui,* Heb. *Lēvī,* son of Jacob]

levity, *n.* (*rare*) lightness of weight; lightness of disposition, conduct or manner; want of seriousness or earnestness, thoughtlessness, frivolity. [OF *levité,* L *levitātem,* nom. *-tas,* from *levis,* light]

levo- LAEVO-.

levulose, LAEVULOSE.

levy, *n.* the act of raising or collecting (e.g. a tax, a fine, a fee); that which is so raised or collected; a body of troops called out for military service. *v.t.* to raise, to collect together, to enlist (as an army); to begin to wage (war); to impose and collect (as a tax or forced contribution); to seize (property) by a judicial writ etc. **to levy war,** to wage war. **leviable,** *a.* [F *levée,* fem. p.p. of *lever,* L *levāre,* to raise]

lewd, *a.* lascivious, unchaste, indecent; depraved, wicked, worthless. **lewdly,** *adv.* **lewdness,** *n.* †**lewdster,** *n.* a lecher. [OE *lǣwede,* lay, belonging to the laity]

Lewes, Battle of, battle 1264 caused by the baronial opposition to Henry III, led by Simon de Montfort, earl of Leicester (1208–65). The king was defeated and captured at the battle.

Lewes, *n.* **George Henry** (1817–1878), English philosopher and critic. From acting he turned to literature and philosophy; his works include a *Biographical History of Philosophy* (1845–46), and *Life and Works of Goethe* (1855). He married in 1840, but left his wife in 1854 to form a life-long union with the writer Mary Ann Evans (George Eliot), whom he had met in 1851.

Lewis[1], *n.* **Cecil Day** DAY LEWIS.

Lewis[2], *n.* **Carl (Frederick Carleton)** (1961–), US athlete. At the 1984 Olympic Games he equalled Jesse Owens' performance, winning gold medals in the 100 and 200 metres, sprint relay, and long jump. In the

1988 Olympics, he repeated his golds in the 100 metres and long jump, and won a silver in the 200 metres.

Lewis[3], *n.* **C(live) S(taples)** (1898–1963), British academic and writer, born in Belfast. His books include the medieval study *The Allegory of Love* (1936), and the space fiction *Out of the Silent Planet* (1938). He was a committed Christian and wrote essays in popular theology such as *The Screwtape Letters* (1942) and *Mere Christianity* (1952); the autobiographical *Surprised by Joy* (1955); and a series of books of Christian allegory for children, set in the magic land of Narnia, including *The Lion, the Witch, and the Wardrobe* (1950).

Lewis[4], *n.* **(Harry) Sinclair** (1885–1951), US novelist. He made a reputation with *Main Street* (1920), depicting American small-town life; *Babbitt* (1922), the story of a real-estate dealer of the Midwest caught in the conventions of his milieu; and *Arrowsmith* (1925), a study of a scientist. Nobel prize 1930.

Lewis[5], *n.* **Jerry Lee** (1935–), US rock-and-roll and country singer and pianist. His trademark was the 'pumping piano' style in hits such as 'Whole Lotta Shakin' Going On' and 'Great Balls of Fire' (1957); later recordings include 'What Made Milwaukee Famous' 1968.

Lewis[6], *n.* **Jerry** (1926–), stage name of Joseph Levitch. US comic actor, formerly in partnership with Dean Martin (1946–1956). He enjoyed great commercial success as a solo performer and was revered by French critics, but his later films, such as *The Nutty Professor* (1963), were less well received in the US.

Lewis[7], *n.* **Meriwether** (1774–1809), US explorer. He was commissioned by president Thomas Jefferson to find a land route to the Pacific with William Clark (1770–1838). They followed the Missouri River to its source, crossed the Rocky Mountains (aided by Indian girl Sacajawea) and followed the Columbia River to the Pacific, then returned overland to St Louis 1804–06.

Lewis[8], *n.* **(Percy) Wyndham** (1886–1957), English writer and artist, who pioneered Vorticism. He was noted for the hard and aggressive style of both his writing and his painting. His literary works include the novels *Tarr* (1918) and *The Childermass* (1928), the essay *Time and Western Man* (1927), and autobiographies.

lewis, *n.* a hoisting device for heavy stone blocks employing metal, usu. curved pieces which fit into and grasp the stone; the son of a Freemason. [perh. from the inventor]

Lewis gun, *n.* a portable gas-operated machine-gun invented by Col. Isaac Newton Lewis (1858–1931).

lewisite, *n.* a poisonous liquid used in chemical warfare obtained from arsenic and acetylene.

Lewton, *n.* **Val** (1904–1951), stage name of Vladimir Ivan Leventon. Russian-born US film producer, responsible for a series of atmospheric 'B' horror films made for RKO in the 1940s, including *Cat People* (1942) and *The Body Snatcher* (1946). He co-wrote several of his films under the adopted name of Carlos Keith.

lexicon, *n.* a dictionary (usu. applied to Greek, Hebrew, Arabic or Syriac). **lexical**, *a.* pertaining to the words of a language, as opp. to grammar; pertaining to a lexicon or lexicography. **lexically,** *adv.* **lexicography**, *n.* the art or process of compiling lexicons or dictionaries. **lexicographer,** *n.* **lexicographic, -ical**, *a.* **lexicographist**, *n.* **lexicology**, *n.* that branch of learning concerned with the derivation, signification and application of words. **lexicologist**, *n.* **lexigram**, *n.* a sign representing a word. **lexigraphy**, *n.* a system of writing in which each word is represented by a distinct character. **lexigraphic, -ical**, *a.* **lexis,** *n.* the complete vocabulary of a language, individual or subject. [Gr. *lexikon,* orig. neut. of *lexikos,* pertaining to words, from *lexis,* a saying, a word, from *legein,* to speak]

ley, *n.* pasture land; fallow land; a ley-line. **ley-line,** *n.* a straight line across the landscape joining two landmarks, supposed to be of prehistoric origin. *a.* cultivated for pasture; fallow. [LEA[2]]

Leyden, *n.* **Lucas van** LUCAS VAN LEYDEN.

Leyden jar, *n.* a glass bottle or jar coated inside and out with tinfoil used as an electrical condenser. [invented in *Leyden,* Holland, in 1745]

leze-majesty, LESE-MAJESTY.

LF, (*abbr.*) low frequency.

lf, (*abbr.*) light face (type).

LG, (*abbr.*) Low German.

LH, Lh, (*abbr.*) left hand, luteinizing hormone.

Lhasa, *n.* (the 'Forbidden City') capital of the autonomous region of Tibet, China, at 5,000 m/16,400 ft; population (1982) 105,000. Products include handicrafts and light industry.

lherzolite, *n.* a greenish-grey igneous rock composed of pyroxene, chrysolite, diallage and picotite. [Lake *Lherz,* in the Pyrenees]

Li, (*chem. symbol*) lithium.

li, *n.* a Chinese measure of weight, the thousandth part of a liang; a Chinese measure of distance, rather more than one-third of a mile (0.5 km). [Chin.]

liable, *a.* bound or obliged in law or equity; responsible (for); subject or amenable (to); exposed or open (to); tending, apt or likely (to). **liability**, *n.* the state of being liable; that for which one is liable; (*pl.*) debts, pecuniary obligations. **limited liability,** responsibility for debts of a company only to a specified amount, in proportion to the amount of stock held; hence, **limited (liability) company**. [perh. from non-extant A-F *liable,* or med. L *ligābilis* (F *lier,* L *ligāre,* to bind)]

liaison, *n.* an illicit initimacy between a man and woman; a bond, a connection; (*Cookery*) a thickening, usu. made of yolk of egg; the carrying on of the sound of a final consonant to a succeeding word begining with a vowel or *h* mute; communication between military units; communication and contact between units, groups etc. **liaison officer,** *n.* an officer acting as go-between for forces or bodies of men under different commands; a person in charge of communication between units, groups etc. **liaise,** *v.i.* to form a liaison; to maintain communication and contact. [F, from L *ligātiōnem,* nom. *-tio,* from *ligāre,* to bind]

liana, liane, *n.* a general name for the climbing and twining plants common in the forests of tropical America. **lianoid,** *a.* [F *liane,* prob. from *lier,* L *ligāre,* to bind]

liang, *n.* a Chinese weight, equal to about $1\frac{1}{3}$ oz. av. (38g); this weight of silver as money of account. [Chin.]

Liaoning, *n.* province of NE China. **area** 151,000 sq km/58,300 sq miles. **capital** Shenyang. **towns** Anshan, Fushun, Liaoyang. **population** (1986) 37,260,000. **products** cereals, coal, iron, salt, oil.

Liaquat Ali Khan, *n.* (1895–1951), Indian Muslim nationalist politician, prime minister of Pakistan from independence 1947. The chief lieutenant of Muhammad Jinnah, he was a leader of the Muslim League. He was assassinated.

liar, *n.* one who knowingly utters falsehoods, esp. one addicted to lying. [OE *lēogere,* from *lēogan,* to LIE[1]]

†**liard,** *n.* a former French coin worth a quarter of a sou. [F, perh. from *liard,* grey, LYART]

Lias, *n.* the lowest series of rock strata of the Jurassic system. **Liassic**, *a.* [F *liais,* etym. doubtful]

lib[1], (*abbr.*) Liberal.

†**lib**[2], *v.t.* to castrate, to geld. [cp. EFris. *lübben,* MDut. *lubben*]

Lib[3], **lib**, (*coll.*) short for LIBERATION.

libation, *n.* a sacrificial offering to a deity involving the pouring of oil or wine; the liquid poured; (*usu. facet.*) an (alcoholic) beverage; the act of drinking this. **libate,** *v.t., v.i.* **libatory**, *a.* [L *lībātio,* from *lībāre,* to sip, to pour out (cp. Gr. *leibein*)]

†**libbard,** LEOPARD.

libber, *n.* (*coll.*) short for LIBERATIONIST.

Libby, *n.* **Willard Frank** (1908–1980), US chemist, whose development of radiocarbon dating 1947 won him a Nobel prize 1960.

libeccio, *n.* the south-west wind. [It., from L *libs,* Gr. *lips*]

libel, *n.* a defamatory writing, print, picture or publication of any kind, containing any malicious statements or representations tending to bring any person into ridicule, contempt or disrepute; the act or crime of publishing a libel; the written statement containing a plaintiff's allegations; an unfair representation or defamatory statement. *v.t.* (*past, p.p.* **libelled**) to publish a libel; to defame, to misrepresent; to bring a suit against by means of a written complaint. *v.i.* to spread libels or defamatory statements. †**libellant,** *n.* one who brings a libel suit. **libellee,** *n.* **libeller, libel(l)ist,** *n.* one who libels; **libellous,** *a.* **libellously,** *adv.* [OF, from L *libellum,* nom. *-lus,* dim. of *liber,* book]

liber, *n.* the bast or inner bark of exogens. [L, bark]

liberal, *a.* generous, open-handed, bountiful, munificent; ample, abundant, profuse; free, open, candid; favourable to liberty and progress; not strict, narrow or literal; broad-minded, unprejudiced; favourable to freedom and democratic government, opposed to aristocratic privileges; esp. of education, befitting a gentleman, not technical, tending to free mental development; of or pertaining to a Liberal Party. *n.* **Liberal Party,** *n.* in the UK, a political party, the successor to the Whig Party, with an ideology of liberalism. In the 19th cent. it was the party of the left, representing the interests of commerce and industry. Its outstanding leaders were Palmerston, Gladstone, and Lloyd George. From 1914 it declined, and the rise of the Labour Party pushed the Liberals into the middle ground. The Liberals joined forces with the Social Democratic Party (SDP) for the 1983 and 1987 elections. In the 1987 election the Alliance, as they were jointly known, achieved 22 seats and 22.6% of votes. In 1988, a majority of the SDP voted to merge with the Liberals to form the Social and Liberal Democrats (called Liberal Democrats for short). **Liberal Party, Australian,** *n.* political party established 1944 by Robert Menzies, after a Labor landslide, and derived from the former United Australia Party. After the voters rejected Labor's extensive nationalization plans, the Liberals were in power 1949–72 and 1975–83, and were led in succession by H. E. Holt, J. G. Gorton, Sir William McMahon (1908–), Sir Billy Snedden (1926–), and Malcolm Fraser. **Liberal Unionist,** *n.* a member of the Liberal Party who seceded in 1886 and supported the conservatives in opposing the adoption of the Home Rule Bill. **liberalism,** *n.* **liberalist,** *n.* **liberalistic,** *a.* **liberality,** *n.* the quality of being liberal; bounty, munificence, generosity; largeness or breadth of views, catholicity; freedom from prejudice. **liberalization, -isation,** *n.* **liberalize, -ise,** *v.t.* **liberally,** *adv.* **liberalness,** *n.* [OF, from L *līberālis,* from *līber,* free]

liberate, *v.t.* to set at liberty; to release from domination, injustice, restraint or confinement; (*euphem. or facet.*) to steal; to set free from chemical combination. **liberated,** *a.* freed, having liberty; pertaining to peoples freed from foreign domination, of women freed from trad. sexual roles etc. **liberation,** *n.* **animal liberation** ANIMAL. **gay liberation** GAY. **women's liberation** WOMAN. **liberation theology,** *n.* the theory (orig. amongst the Roman Catholic clergy of Latin America) that political involvement to effect social equality and justice is a necessary part of Christianity. *n.* **liberationism,** *n.* **liberationist,** *n.* one who seeks or supports the causes of equality, freedom or liberty (e.g. *women's liberationist, gay liberationist*). **liberator,** *n.* **liberatory,** *a.* [L *līberātus,* from *līberāre,* as prec.]

Liberia, *n.* Republic of, country in W Africa, bounded to the N and NE by Guinea, E by the Ivory Coast, S and SW by the Atlantic, and NW by Sierra Leone. **area** 111,370 sq km/42,989 sq miles. **capital** Monrovia. **physical** forested highlands; swampy coast where six rivers end. **population** (1988) 2,436,000 (95% belonging to the indigenous peoples); annual growth rate 3.2%. **exports** iron ore, rubber, diamonds, coffee, cocoa, palm oil. **language** English (official). **religion** Muslim 20%, Christian 15%, traditional 65%.

libertarian LIBERTY.

libertine, *n.* †a freedman; (*formerly*) a free-thinker in religious matters; one free in moral practice; a debauchee, a profligate; one free from restraint. *a.* loose, licentious, dissolute; free from restraint. **libertinage, libertinism,** *n.* licentiousness. [L *lībertīnus,* a freedman, from *lībertus* (*līber,* free)]

liberty, *n.* the quality or state of being free from captivity, bondage, subjection or despotic control; freedom of choice, opinion or action; permission granted to do any act; free time; (*pl.*) rights, privileges or exemptions, enjoyed by grant or prescription; a place or district within which certain privileges or immunities are enjoyed; a breach of decorum; †a district beyond a debtors' prison where prisoners were sometimes allowed to reside. **at liberty,** free; having the right (to do etc.); disengaged, not occupied. **cap of liberty** CAP. **civil liberty,** the freedom of the individual as embodied in the law. **liberty of the press,** freedom of the press to publish without government censorship or interference. **to set at liberty** to free from confinement or restraint. **to take liberties (with),** to be unduly familiar or presumptious (with); to transgress rules or usages; to falsify. **to take the liberty,** to venture; to do something without permission. **liberty bodice,** *n.* a sleeveless bodice worn as an undergarment, esp. by children. **liberty hall,** *n.* a place where one may do as one pleases. **liberty horse,** *n.* a riderless circus horse. **liberty man,** *n.* a sailor having permission to go ashore. **liberty ship,** *n.* a prefabricated, mass-produced cargo ship produced during World War II. **libertarian,** *a.* pertaining to liberty, inculcating the doctrine of free will. *n.* an advocate of the doctrine of free will; an advocate of liberty. **libertarianism,** *n.* **liberticide,** *n.* destruction of liberty; one who destroys liberty. *a.* destroying liberty. [F *liberté,* L *lībertātem,* nom. *-tas,* from *līber,* free]

libidinous, *a.* characterized by lewdness or lust, lustful; lascivious. **libidinously,** *adv.* **libidinousness,** *n.* [L *libīdinōsus,* from *libīdo -dinis,* lust]

libido, *n.* (*pl.* **-dos**) the will to live, life force; in psychoanalysis, the life force deriving from biological impulses; the sexual drive. **libidinal,** *a.* [L, desire]

LIBOR, *n.* acronym for London Interbank Offered Rates, loan rates for a specified period which are offered to first-class banks in the London interbank market. Banks link their lending to LIBOR as an alternative to the base lending rate when setting the rate for a fixed term, after which the rate may be adjusted.

Libra, *n.* (*gen.* **-rae**) faint constellation of the zodiac, in the southern hemisphere near Scorpius. It represents the scales of justice. The Sun passes through Libra during Nov. In astrology, the dates for Libra are between about 23 Sept. and 23 Oct.

libra, *n.* (*pl.* **-rae**) an ancient Roman pound; hence, a pound weight (*lb*), a pound sterling (£). [L]

library, *n.* a collection of books, esp. classified, or otherwise organized, and catalogued, to facilitate use either by the public or by private persons; a building, room, or series of rooms containing such a collection; an institution established for the formation or maintenance of such a collection; a series of books similar in subject, literary form etc., issued (usu. in similar format) by a publisher; a collection of computer software, films, records, tapes etc. **circulating library** CIRCULATE. **free library** PUBLIC LIBRARY. **lending library** LENDING. **public library,** a library open to members of the public. **reference library** REFERENCE. **library science,** *n.* (*N Am.*) librarianship, its practices and principles. **librarian,** *n.* one who has charge of a library. **librarianship,** *n.* [F *librarie,* L *librārius,* pertaining to books, from *liber,* book, orig. bark]

librate, *v.i.* to be poised; to move as a balance, to oscillate, to swing or sway. **libration,** *n.* **libration of the moon,** a real or apparent oscillation by which parts near the edges of the moon's disc are alternately visible and invisible. **librational, libratory** *a.* [L *lībrātus,* p.p. of *lībrāre,* to poise, from *lībra,* balance]

libretto, *n.* (*pl.* **-tti, -ttos**) the words of an opera, oratorio etc.; a book containing such words. **librettist,** *n.* one who writes a libretto. [It., dim. of *libro,* L *liber,* book]

Libreville, *n.* capital of Gabon, on the estuary of the river Gabon; population (1985) 350,000. Products include timber, oil, and minerals. It was founded 1849 as a refuge for slaves freed by the French.

Librium®, *n.* a tranquillizing drug containing chlordiazepoxide.

Libya, Socialist People's Libyan Arab State of the Masses, country in N Africa. **area** 1,759,540 sq km/ 679,182 sq miles. **capital** Tripoli. **towns** ports Benghazi, Misurata. **physical** desert; mountains in N and S. **population** (1986) 3,955,000 (including 500,000 foreign workers); annual growth rate 3.9%. **exports** oil, natural gas. **language** Arabic. **religion** Sunni Muslim. **Libyan,** *a.* of or pertaining to Libya, its language or its people. *n.* a native or inhabitant of Libya; a Hamitic language of ancient Libya, now extinct.

lice, (*pl.*) LOUSE.

licence, *n.* authority, leave, permission; consent or permission granted by a constituted authority (to marry, drive a motor vehicle, possess a firearm, own a dog, carry on a business etc.); a document containing such permission; unrestrained liberty of action, disregard of law or propriety; abuse of freedom, licentiousness; in literature or art, deviation from the ordinary rules or mode of treatment; pemitted freedom of thought or action. **special licence,** *n.* a licence authorizing a marriage without banns. [F, from L *licentia,* from *licēre,* to be allowed or lawful]

license, *v.t.* to authorize by a legal permit; to allow, to permit, esp. to allow entire freedom of action, comment etc. **license plate,** *n.* (*chiefly N Am.*) the number plate on a vehicle. **licensed,** *a.* **licensable,** *a.* **licensed victualler,** *n.* one who holds a licence to sell spirits, wines, beer etc. **licensee,** *n.* one holding a licence (esp. a publican). **licenser,** *n.* one who grants a licence or has the authority to do so. †**licensure,** *n.* the act of licensing, esp. to preach. **licentiate,** *n.* one holding a certificate of competence in some profession from a university or other collegiate body; in the Presbyterian Church, one who has a licence to preach; a higher degree conferred by some European universities; the holder of such a degree. *v.t.*, to give a licence to. †**licentiation,** *n.* **licentious,** *a.* lascivious, dissolute, profligate, loose; unrestrained by rule or accepted laws of style etc. **licentiously,** *adv.* **licentiousness,** *n.*

lich, *n.* a dead body, a corpse. **lich-gate, lych-gate,** *n.* a churchyard gate with a roof, under which a coffin used to be placed while the introductory portion of the burial service was read. **lich-owl,** *n.* the screech-owl, supposed to foretell death. **lich-stone,** *n.* a stone at the lich-gate, on which the coffin is placed. †**lich-wake** LYKE-WAKE. [OE *līc,* body, orig. form (cp. Dut. *lijk,* Icel. *līk,* G *Leiche*)]

lichee LITCHI.

lichen, *n.* a cryptogamic thallophytic plant of the order Lichenaceae, parasitic fungi on algal cells covering rocks, tree-trunks etc., with variously coloured crusts; a papular inflammatory eruption of the skin. **lichened,** *a.* **lichenin,** *n.* a kind of starch occurring in Iceland moss and other lichens. **lichenism,** *n.* **lichenist,** *n.* **lichenoid, -nose, -nous,** *a.* **lichenology,** *n.* that branch of botany which deals with lichens. **lichenologist,** *n.* [L *līchēn,* Gr. *leichēn,* prob. rel. to *leichein,* to lick]

Lichfield, *n.* **Patrick Anson, 5th Earl of Lichfield** (1939–), British photographer, known for portraits of the rich and famous.

Lichtenstein, *n.* **Roy** (1923–), US Pop artist. His reputation was made with an exhibition in New York 1962. He used advertising and comic-strip imagery, often focusing on popular ideals of romance and heroism, as in *Whaam!,* 1963 (Tate Gallery, London).

licit, *a.* lawful, allowed. **licitly,** *adv.* [L *licitus,* p.p. of *licēre,* to be allowed]

lick, *v.t.* to draw or pass the tongue over; to take in or lap (up) with the tongue; of flame etc., to stroke or pass lightly over; (*sl.*) to chastise, to beat, to overcome, to surpass. *v.i.* of flames etc., to make a licking motion; (*sl.*) to beat, to win; to lap. *n.* the act of licking; a slight smear or coat (as of paint); a salt-lick; (*coll.*) a smart blow or slap; (*coll.*) great exertion, effort or pace. **a lick and a promise,** (*coll.*) a quick or superficial wash. **salt lick** SALT. **to lick into shape,** to give form or method to (from the notion that young bears are born shapeless, and are licked into shape by their dam). **to lick one's lips,** to anticipate or remember something with pleasure. **to lick one's wounds,** to withdraw after a defeat to recuperate physically or mentally. **to lick someone's boots, shoes,** to be servile towards. **to lick the dust,** to be beaten, to be killed; †to act in a servile manner. **to lick up,** to consume, to devour. **lickspittle,** *n.* an abject parasite or toady. **licker,** *n.* **licking,** *n.* a beating, a defeat. **to take a licking,** to take a beating. [OE *liccian* (cp. Dut. *likken,* G *lecken,* also Gr. *leichein,* L *lingere*)]

lickerish, liquorish, *a.* greedy; pleasing to the taste, dainty; lecherous. **lickerishly,** *adv.* **lickerishness,** *n.* †**lickerous,** *a.* [North. var. of OF *lecheros,* LECHEROUS]

lickety-split, *adv.* (*chiefly N Am. coll.*) speedily; very quickly. [LICK, SPLIT]

†**licorice** LIQUORICE.

lictor, *n.* a civil officer who attended the chief Roman magistrates, and bore the fasces as a sign of authority. [L, rel. to *ligāre,* to bind]

lid, *n.* a hinged or detachable cover or cap, usu. for shutting a vessel, container or aperture; an eyelid; (*Bot.*) an operculum; a curb, a restraint. **to blow, lift, take the lid off,** (*coll.*) to reveal, uncover (esp. something clandestine or corrupt). **to flip one's lid,** (*sl.*) to go berserk, mad. **to put the (tin) lid on it,** (*coll.*) to curb, to put an end to; to be a final blow, misfortune etc. **lidded,** *a.* **lidless,** *a.* uncovered, bare. [OE *hlid* (cp. Dut. *lid,* Icel. *hlith,* G *-lid,* in *Augenlid*)]

Liddell Hart, *n.* **Basil** (1895–1970), British military scientist. He was an exponent of mechanized warfare, and his ideas were adopted in Germany 1935 in creating the 1st Panzer Division, combining motorized infantry and tanks. From 1937 he advised the UK War Office on army reorganization.

Lidice, *n.* Czechoslovakian mining village, replacing one destroyed by the Nazis 10 Jun 1942 as a reprisal for the assassination of Heydrich. The men were shot, the women sent to concentration camps, and the children taken to Germany. The officer responsible was hanged 1946.

lido, *n.* (*pl.* **-dos**) a bathing-beach, an out-door swimming pool. [Resort near Venice]

Lie, *n.* **Trygve (Halvdan)** (1896–1968), Norwegian Labour politician and diplomat. He became the first secretary-general of the United Nations 1946–53, when he resigned over Soviet opposition to his handling of the Korean War.

lie[1], *v.i.* (*pres.p.* **lying,** *past, p.p.* **lied**) to say or write anything with the deliberate intention of deceiving; to convey a false impression, to deceive. *v.t.* to take (away) or get (oneself into or our of) by lying. *n.* an intentional violation of the truth; a false statement deliberately made for the purpose of deception; a deception, an imposture. **to give someone the lie,** to accuse of deliberate falsehood. **to give the lie to,** to show to be false; to disprove; to accuse of lying. **white lie,** a pardonable fiction or misstatement. **lie-detector,** *n.* a device for monitoring physiological changes taken as evidence of mental stress accompanying the telling of lies, a polygraph. [OE *lēogan* (cp. Dut. *liegen,* G *lügen*), whence *lyge,* a lie, *lēogere,* LIAR]

lie[2], *v.i.* (*pres.p.* **lying,** *past* **lay,** *p.p.* **lain,** †**lien**[2]) to rest or place oneself in a reclining or horizontal posture; to be situated or fixed in a specified condition or direction; to sleep, to lodge, to encamp (usu. at a specified place); to rest, to remain, to abide; to exist, to be, to reside, in a specified state, position, relation etc.; of an action, objection etc., to be sustainable. *n.* position, arrangement, direction, manner of lying; the retiring-place or lair (of an animal). **lie of the land,** the posture of affairs. **to lie at one's heart,** to be a source of anxiety, care, or desire. **to lie at someone's door,** to be the direct responsibility of someone. **to lie by,** to be or stay near; to be put aside; to rest; to be quiet; to remain unused. **to lie down,** to go to rest; †to sink into the grave; (*in pres.p.*) to submit tamely. **to lie hard, heavy on,** to oppress, to be a weight upon. **to lie in,** to be in childbed; to remain in bed later than normal. **to lie in one,** to be in one's power or capacity. **to lie in the way,** to be an obstacle or impediment. **to lie in wait,** to wait in ambush or concealment. **to lie low,** to remain in hiding; to conceal one's knowledge or intentions in order to outwit, forestall etc. **to lie off,** of a vessel to stay at a distance from the shore or another ship. **to lie on, upon,** to be incumbent upon; to depend or be dependent upon. **to lie on one's hands,** to remain unsold or undisposed of; of time, to hang heavy. **to lie on the head of,** to be imputable or chargeable to. **to lie over,** to remain unpaid; to be deferred. **to lie to,** to be checked or stopped in her course, as a ship by backing the yards or taking in sail. **to lie under,** to be subject to or oppressed by. **to lie up,** to rest, to stay in bed or in one's room to recuperate; of a ship, to go into dock. **to lie with,** to lodge or sleep with; to have sexual intercourse with; to belong to, to depend on. **lie-a-bed,** *n.* a late riser. **lie-in,** *n.* a longer than normal stay in bed. **lying-in,** *n.* (*pl.* **lyings-in**) confinement in childbirth. [OE *licgan* (cp. Dut. *liggen,* Icel. *liggja,* G *liegen,* cogn. with Gr. *lechos,* L *lectus,* bed)]

Liebig, *n.* **Justus, Baron von Liebig** (1803–1873), German chemist, a major contributor to agricultural chemistry. He introduced the theory of radicals, and discovered chloroform and chloral.

Liebknecht[1], *n.* **Karl** (1871–1919), German socialist, son of Wilhelm Liebknecht. A founder of the German Communist Party, originally known as the Spartacus League (see SPARTACIST), he led an unsuccessful revolt in Berlin 1919, and was murdered by army officers.

Liebknecht[2], *n.* **Wilhelm** (1826–1900), German socialist. A friend of the communist theoretician Marx, with whom he took part in the revolution of 1848; he was imprisoned for opposition to the Franco-Prussian War. He was the father of Karl Liebknecht.

Liechtenstein, Principality of, landlocked country in W central Europe. **area** 160 sq km/62 sq miles. **capital** Vaduz. **physical** Alpine; includes part of Rhine Valley. **population** (1987) 27,700 (33% foreign); annual growth rate 1.4%. **exports** microchips, precision engineering, processed foods, postage stamps; easy tax laws make it an international haven for foreign companies and banks. **language** German. **religion** Roman Catholic.

Lied, *n.* (*pl.* **Lieder,**) a German song or ballad. [G]

lief, *adv.* willingly, gladly, freely. †*a.* dear, beloved; willing, ready, blessed. †*n.* a sweetheart, a dear friend. [OE *lēof* (cp. Dut. *lief,* G *lieb*), cogn. with LOVE]

liege, *n.* bound by some feudal tenure, either as a vassal or as a lord; pertaining to such tenure. *n.* a vassal bound to do service to his lord; a lord, a superior, a sovereign; a law-abiding citizen, a subject. **liegedom,** *n.* **liegeless,** *a.* **liegeman,,** *n.* a liege vassal. [OF *lige,* prob. from OHG *ledig,* free]

Liège, *n.* industrial city (weapons, textiles, paper, chemicals), capital of Liège province in Belgium, SE of Brussels, on the Meuse; population (1988) 200,000. The province of Liège has an area of 3,900 sq km/1,505 sq mi, and a population (1987) of 992,000.

lien[1], *n.* (*Law*) a right to detain the goods of another until some claim has been satisfied; (*coll.*) an option. [F, from L *ligāmen,* a band, from *ligāre,* to bind]

lientery, *n.* diarrhoea in which the food passes rapidly through the bowels undigested. **lienteric,** *a.* [F *lienterie,* Gr. *leienteria* (*leios,* smooth, *entera,* bowels)]

†**lier,** *n.* one who lies (usu. in adv. phrases, as *lier in wait*). [LIE[2], -ER]

lierne, *n.* a cross-rib connecting the main ribs in Gothic vaulting, introduced about the middle of the 14th cent. [F, etym. doubtful]

lieu, *n.* place, stead, room. **in lieu of,** instead of. [F, from L *locum,* nom. *locus,* place]

lieutenant, *n.* an officer acting as deputy or substitute to a superior; an army officer ranking next below a captain; a naval officer ranking next below a lieutenant-commander. **Deputy-Lieutenant,** an officer appointed by the Lord-Lieutenant of a county to act, in certain cases, as his deputy. **Lord-Lieutenant** LORD. **second-lieutenant,** the lowest commissioned rank in the British army. **lieutenant-colonel,** *n.* an officer next in rank below a colonel, in actual command of a battalion. **lieutenant-commander,** *n.* a naval officer ranking between a lieutenant and a commander. **lieutenant-general,** *n.* an army officer next in rank below a general and above a major-general. **lieutenant-governor,** *n.* a deputy governor; the acting governor in subordination to a governor-general; (*N Am.*) the deputy to a state governor. **lieutenancy,** †**-antry,** †**lieutenantship,** *n.* [F (LIEU, TENANT), cp. LOCUM TENENS]

†**liever.** [comp. of LIEF]

Lifar, *n.* **Serge** (1905–1986), Russian dancer and choreographer. Born in Kiev, he studied under Nijinsky, joined the Diaghilev company 1923, and was *maître de ballet* at the Paris Opéra 1930–44 and 1947–59.

life, *n.* (*pl.* **lives**) the state or condition of being alive; the state of an organism in which it is capable of performing its animal or vegetable functions; animate existence; the period of such existence, any specified portion of a person's existence; the average period which a person of a given age may expect to live; a person considered as object of a policy of assurance; the period of time for which an object functions or operates; the living form; (*collect.*) animated existence, living things; mode, manner or course of living; the vehicle or source of life; the animating principle, the essential or inspiring idea (of a movement etc.); animation, vivacity, spirit; one who or that which imparts spirit or animation; the active side of existence; human affairs; a narrative of one's existence, a biography; (*coll.*) a life sentence; one of the points or chances to which each player is entitled in a game that are lost in certain contingencies. *a.* for the duration of one's life; in drawing, sculpture etc., taken from life. **a matter of life and death,** one of utmost urgency. **for one's life, for dear life,** with extreme vigour, in order to escape death. **for the life of me, upon my life,** as if my life depended upon it. **high life,** the habits of fashionable society. **not on your life,** under no circumstances. **the life and soul of,** one who is the chief source of amusement or interest, esp. at a party. **the life of Riley,** (*coll.*) an easy, carefree existence. **the time of one's life,** an experience of unequalled pleasure. **to bring to life,** to restore (an unconscious or apparently lifeless person). **to come to life,** to revive from such a state. **to the life,** of a portrait etc., as if the original stood f. before one. **life-annuity,** *n.* a sum of money paid yearly during the portion of a person's life from a specified age to death. **life-assurance, insurance,** *n.* insurance providing for the payment of a specified sum to a beneficiary on the policy holder's death, or to the policy holder on reaching a certain age. **life-belt,** *n.* a belt of buoyant or inflated material for supporting a person in the water. **life-blood,** *n.* the blood necessary to life; that which is essential to existence, success or strength. **lifeboat,** *n.* a boat specially constructed for saving life in storms and heavy seas. **lifebuoy** BUOY. **life cycle,** *n.* the series of changes in the form and function of an organism etc. during its lifetime. **life-estate,** *n.* a property that is held only until one's death, and then reverts to a specified heir. **life-force,** *n.* a vital urge supposed to be inherent in living organisms. **life-giving,** *a.* inspiriting, invigorating, animating. **lifeguard,** *n.* a bodyguard; an attendant at a bathing beach or pool who renders aid to swimmers in difficulties. **Life Guards,** *n.pl.* a regiment of cavalry forming part of the bodyguard of the British sovereign, hence **Life Guardsman,** *n.* **life-insurance** LIFE-ASSURANCE. **life-interest,** *n.* an interest or estate terminating with the life of a person. **life-jacket,** *n.* a sleeveless jacket used as a life-belt. **life-line,** *n.* a rope used for saving life; a rope used as an additional safeguard; a vital line of communication. **lifelong, livelong,** *a.* lasting throughout life. **life-peer,** *n.* **life-peerage,** *n.* a peerage lapsing with the death of the holder. **life-preserver,** *n.* (*N Am.*) a life-belt, life-jacket etc.; a loaded stick or cane for defending one's life. **life raft,** *n.* a raft kept on board ships etc. for use in emergencies. **liferent,** *n.* (*Sc. Law*) a rent to which one is entitled for one's life. **liferenter,** *n.* **life-saver,** *n.* one who saves a persons life; a person trained to rescue swimmers or bathers from drowning; (*coll.*) one who or that which provides help in distress. **life-saving,** *a.* **life science,** *n.* a science that deals with the structure and function of living organisms, such as biology, medicine, anthropology or zoology. **life-size(d),** *a.* representing the actual size of an object. **life span,** *n.* the length of time during which an organism, machine etc. lives or functions. **life style,** *n.* the attitudes, behaviour, surroundings etc. characteristic of an individual or group. **life support,** *a.* pertaining to a device or system which maintains a person's life, e.g. during a serious illness. **life-table,** *n.* a table of statistics showing the average expectation of life at different ages. **lifetime,** *n.* the duration of one's life; the length of time something functions. **life-weary,** *a.* **life-work,** *n.* the work to which one devotes the best part of one's life. †**lifeful,** *a.* **lifeless,** *a.* destitute or deprived of life; dead, inanimate; inorganic, inert; deprived of physical energy; dull, heavy, spiritless, vapid. **lifelessly,** *adv.* **lifelessness,** *n.* **lifelike,** *a.* like a living being; of a portrait, like the original. **lifelikeness,** *n.* **lifer,** *n.* one sentenced to imprisonment for life. [OE *līf* (cp. Icel. *līf,* OFris. *līf,* Dut. *lijf,* G *Leib,* cogn. with LIVE, LEAVE[2], from Aryan root *leip-*), cp. Gr. *aleiphein,* to anoint, *liparēs,* persistent]

LIFFE, *n.* acronym for London International Financial Futures Exchange, one of the exchanges in London where futures contracts are traded. It opened Sept. 1982.

Liffey, *n.* river in E Ireland, flowing from the Wicklow mountains to Dublin Bay; length 80 km/50 miles.

lift[1], *v.t.* to raise to a higher position, to elevate; to hold or support on high; to raise or take up from the ground, to pick up; (*coll.*) to carry off, to steal, to appropriate, to plagiarize; to raise, rescind or remove; to exalt, to elate; †to bear, to support. *v.i.* to perform or attempt to perform the act of raising something; to rise, as a ship on the waves or a sail in the wind; to rise and disperse, as a mist. *n.* the act of lifting; the degree of elevation; a rise in the height of the ground; a hoisting-machine, an elevator for persons, goods or material; assistance in lifting; a helping hand; a layer of material inserted in the heel of a shoe, esp. to increase the height of the wearer; a rise in spirits, morale; a rise in condition; a ride in a vehicle as a passenger for part or all of a journey; the component of the aerodynamic force on an aircraft or aerofoil acting upwards at right angles to the airflow and opposing the pull of gravity. **to lift the hand,** to strike a blow (at). **lift-lock,** *n.* a canal lock. **lift-off,** *n.* the take-off of an aircraft, rocket or missile; the instant at which this occurs. **lift off,** *v.i.* **lift-pump,** *n.* a pump that lifts to its own level, distinguished from a *force-pump*. [Icel. *lypta,* rel. to *lopt,* the air, and foll.]

†**lift[2],** *n.* the sky, the upper regions of the air. [OE *lyft,* cogn. with prec. and with LOFT]

Ligachev, *n.* **Egor (Kuzmich)** (1920–), Soviet politician. He joined the Communist Party 1944, and has been a member of the Politburo since 1985. He is regarded as the chief conservative ideologist, and the leader of conservative opposition to President Gorbachev.

ligament, *n.* anything which binds; a bond, a tie; a short band of fibrous tissue by which bones are bound together; any tough bands or tissues holding parts together. **ligamental, -tary, -tous,** *a.* [F, from L *ligāmentum,* from *ligāre,* see LIGATE]

ligand, *n.* a single atom, molecule, radical or ion attached to a control atom to form a co-ordination complex. [L *ligandus,* from *ligāre,* see foll.]

ligate, *v.t.* to tie with a ligature. **ligation,** *n.* **ligature,** *n.* that which binds, esp. a thread or cord to tie arteries or veins or a wire used in removing tumours; anything that unites, a bond; (*Print.*) two or more letters cast on one shank, as *ff, ffi;* (*Mus.*) a tie connecting notes, a slur. *v.t.* to bind with a ligature. [L *ligātus,* p.p. of *ligāre,* to tie]

liger, *n.* a cross between a lion and a tigress.

Ligeti, *n.* **György (Sándor)** (1923–), Hungarian-born Austrian composer who developed a dense, highly chromatic, polyphonic style in which melody and rhythm are sometimes lost in shifting blocks of sound. He achieved international prominence with *Atmosphères* (1961) and *Requiem* (1965), which were used for Kubrick's film epic *2001: A Space Odyssey*. Other works include an opera *Le Grand Macabre* (1978), and *Poème symphonique* (1962), for 100 metronomes.

light[1], *n.* electromagnetic radiation which, by acting on the retina, stimulates the sense of sight; the sensation produced by the stimulation of the visual organs; the state or condition in which things are visible, opp. to darkness; the amount of illumination in a place or required by a person; a source of light, a lamp, a candle, the sun etc.; daylight; that by which light is admitted into a place, a window, a division of a window, esp. a perpendicular division in a mullioned window, a pane or glazed compartment in a greenhouse; exposure, publicity, general knowledge; point of view, aspect; mental illumination, elucidation, enlightenment; one who enlightens, a model, an example; (*pl.*) one's intellectual powers or capacity; (*pl. sl.*) eyes, optics; the manner in which the light falls on a picture; the illuminated part of a picture; brightness on the face or in the eyes; something that kindles or ignites. *a.* having light, bright, clear, not dark; pale-coloured, fair. *v.t.* (*past, p.p.* **lit, lighted**) to kindle, to set fire to; to give light to; to fill (up); with light; to conduct with a light; to brighten. *v.i.* to take fire, to begin to burn; to be illuminated; to brighten (up). (*coll.*) to decamp, to make tracks, to hurry away. **according to one's lights,** according to one's information or knowledge of a situation. **between the lights,** in the twilight. **in the light of,** considering, allowing for. **light-emitting diode,** a semiconductor junction which emits light when an electric current passes through it, used in indicators and the displays of calculators, watches etc. **lighting-up time,** the time of day when vehicles are required by law to show their lights. **lights out,** a signal indicating when lights are to be put out; the time when residents in an institution (e.g. a boarding school) are expected to retire for the night. **to bring to light,** to discover, to detect, to disclose. **to come to light,** to become known. **to light up,** (*coll.*) to light a cigarette, pipe etc.; to illuminate; to switch on (car) lights; to become cheerful or animated suddenly. **to see (the) light,** to come into existence, to be born; to come into view; to be published; to be enlightened. **to shed, throw light (up)on,** to elucidate, to explain. **to stand in one's own light,** to frustrate one's own purposes or wishes. **light-bulb,** *n.* a glass bulb filled with a low density gas and containing a metal filament which glows when an electric current is passed through it. **lighthouse,** *n.* a tower or other structure which supports a powerful light for the warning and guidance of ships at sea. **light pen,** *n.* a pen-shaped photoelectric device which when pointed at a visual display unit senses whether a spot is illuminated, used for creating or entering information on a computer esp. in graphics and design. **lightship,** *n.* a moored vessel carrying a light to give warning or guidance to mariners. **light show,** *n.* a display of multi-coloured lights or visual effects using laser beams etc., esp. at a pop concert. **light-year,** *n.* the distance (about 6,000,000,000,000 miles or 9460×10^9 km) travelled by light in one year;

(*pl. coll.*) a long way away from. **lit-up,** *a.* (*coll.*) slightly drunk. **lighting,** *n.* **lightish,** *a.* **lightless,** *a.* [OE *lēoht* (cp. Dut. and G *Licht,* Icel. *ljos, logi,* L *lux,* Gr. *leukos,* white)]

light², *a.* of small weight, not heavy; easy to be lifted, carried, moved, handled etc.; not burdensome, easily borne; easy to be performed; not cumbersome, adapted for small loads; of troops, lightly armed and equipped; nimble, active, quick; of low specific gravity; short in weight, below the standard weight; not heavily laden; adapted for rapid movement; employed in or adapted for easy work; not massive, not heavy in construction or appearance; graceful, elegant; of fabrics, thin, delicate; loose or sandy, as soil; of bread, not dense; of wine, beer etc., not strong; easily digested; not forcible or violent, gentle, slight; not intense or emphatic; of little consequence, unimportant, trivial; thoughtless, flighty, frivolous; volatile, fickle; wanton, unchaste; cheerful, merry, airy; dizzy, giddy, deranged, delirious. **to make light of,** to disregard, to slight; to treat as pardonable or excusable. **light-armed,** *a.* †**light-brain,** *n.* an empty-headed person. **light engine,** *n.* an engine running light, that is, with no train attached. **light-fingered,** *a.* dextrous in stealing; given to thieving. **light-foot,** *a.* nimble, active. †*n.* a name for the hare, also for the deer. **light-footed,** *a.* **light-handed,** *a.* light of touch, light in handling; short of the proper complement of workers. **light-handedly,** *adv.* **light-handedness,** *n.* **light-headed,** *a.* delirious; †unsteady, loose, thoughtless. **light-headedness,** *n.* light-hearted, *a.* free from care or anxiety; merry, cheerful. **light-heartedly,** *adv.* **light-heartedness,** *n.* **light-heeled,** *a.* nimble, quick-moving, light-footed. **light-legged,** *a.* swift of foot, active. **light literature,** *n.* books intended for entertainment; sometimes applied to belles-lettres as a class. **light-minded,** *a.* fickle, unsteady, volatile. **light-mindedly,** *adv.* **light-mindedness,** *n.* **light railway,** *n.* a railway, usu. less than the standard gauge, adapted for light traffic. **light-spirited,** *a.* cheerful, merry. **light-weight,** *n.* an animal or person below average weight; a professional boxer weighing not more than 135 lb (61.2 kg) or 132 lb (60 kg) if amateur; (*coll.*) a person of small importance or ability. *a.* light in weight; trivial. **light-winged,** *a.* having swift wings; volatile. **lightish,** *a.* **lightly,** *adv.* in a light manner. **lightness,** *n.* [OE *lēoht* (cp. Icel. *lēttr,* G *leicht,* Sansk. *laghu,* Gr. *elachus*)]

light³, *v.i.* of a bird, to descend as from flight, to settle; to alight, to dismount; to come down; to chance (upon). *v.t.* (*Naut.*) to lift or help to move (along etc.). **to light into,** (*sl.*) to attack physically or verbally. **to light out,** (*sl.*) to leave in a hurry. **to light up,** (*Naut.*) to slacken. [*lihtan,* orig. to lighten or relieve of a burden, as prec.]

lighten¹, *v.i.* to become light, to brighten; to emit lightning, to flash; to shine out. *v.t.* to illuminate, to enlighten. [OE *lēohtan*]

lighten², *v.t.* to reduce in weight; to reduce the weight or load of; to relieve, to mitigate, to alleviate; to cheer. *v.i.* to be lightened, to grow lighter; to become less burdensome. [LIGHT², -EN]

lighter¹, *n.* a pocket appliance for lighting cigarettes, pipe etc.; one who or that which ignites.

lighter², *n.* a large, open, usu. flat-bottom boat, used in loading and unloading ships; a heavy barge for carrying railway trains etc. *v.t.* to carry or remove in a lighter. **lighterage,** *n.* **lighterman,** *n.* [perh. from Dut. *lichter* or LIGHT², -ER]

lightning, *n.* the dazzling flash caused by the discharge of electricity between clouds or from a cloud to the earth; (*poet.*) lightening, brightening. *a.* very fast or sudden. **lightning-arrester,** *n.* a contrivance for deflecting the electrical discharge in thunder-storms and protecting electrical instruments. **lightning-bug,** *n.* a fire-fly. **lightning-conductor, -rod,** *n.* a wire or rod for carrying the electric discharge to earth and protecting a building, mast etc., against damage. **lightning strike,** *n.* workers' strike without notice being given.

lights, *n.pl.* the lungs of animals, esp. as food for cats etc. [LIGHT²]

lightsome¹, *a.* light-hearted, playful; airy, graceful, nimble. **lightsomely,** *adv.* **lightsomeness,** *n.* [LIGHT²]

†**lightsome²,** *a.* luminous, light-giving; bright, lighted up.

lign- LIGN(O)-.

lign-aloes, *n.* the bitter drug aloe; a fragrant Mexican wood. [late L *lignum aloēs,* trans. of Gr. *xulaloē,* wood of the aloe]

ligneous, *a.* made or consisting of wood; resembling wood; woody. **lignescent,** *a.* **ligniferous,** *a.* **ligniform,** *a.* **lignify,** *v.t., v.i.* **lignification,** *n.*

lignin, *n.* a complex organic material which forms the woody cell walls of certain plants.

ligniperdous, *a.* destructive of wood, as certain insects. [L *perdere,* to destroy]

lignite, *n.* a partially carbonized coal showing fibrous woody structure, usu. of Cretaceous or Tertiary age. **lignitic,** *a.*

lignivorous, *a.* feeding on wood.

lign(o)-, *comb. form* pertaining to wood. [L *lignum,* wood]

lignocaine, *n.* a local anaesthetic.

lignum, *n.* wood. **lignum vitae** , *n.* the very hard and heavy wood of various tropical American trees, e.g. *Guaiacum officinale.*

ligule, *n.* a membranous process at the top of the sheath beneath the blade of a grass; one of the rays of a composite plant. **ligula,** *n.* (*pl.* **-lae**) a tongue-like organ or part. **ligular, liguliform,** *a.* **ligulate, -ated,** *a.* (*Bot.*) strap-shaped; having a ligule or ligula. [L, dim. of *lingua,* tongue]

Liguria, *n.* coastal region of NW Italy, which includes the resorts of the Italian Riviera, lying between the western Alps and the Mediterranean Gulf of Genoa. The region comprises the provinces of Genova, La Spezia, Imperia, and Savona, with a population (1988) of 1,750,000 and an area of 5,418 sq km/2,093 sq miles. Genoa is the chief town and port.

ligurite, *n.* an apple-green variety of titanite, ranking as a gem, found in the Apennines. [*Liguria,* in northern Italy]

like¹, *a.* resembling, similar; such as; almost the same as; equal or nearly equal in quantity, quality, or degree; characteristic of; disposed towards, inclined to; †probable, likely. *adv.* †in the same manner as; (*used ellipt. as prep. or conj., coll.*) as, in the manner of, to the same extent or degree as; as it were, so to speak; †likely, probably. *n.* a counterpart; a similar or equal thing, person or event; a stroke that brings the number of strokes on that side up to an equality with the other. **had like,** came near to; was or were nearly; had a narrow escape of. **something like,** (*with emphasis on* like) in some way or nearly resembling; first-rate, highly satisfactory. **the likes of,** (*coll., usu. derog.*) people like you or me. **to feel like,** to feel as if one resembled; to feel as if one were the same as; to feel disposed or inclined to. **to look like,** to resemble in appearance; to have the appearance of; to seem likely. **like-minded,** *a.* having similar disposition, opinions, purpose etc. **likely,** *a.* probable, credible, plausible; liable, to be expected (to); promising, suitable, well-adapted. *adv.* probably. **likelihood, likeliness,** *n.* **liken,** *v.t.* to compare, to represent as similar (to); †to make like. **likeness,** *n.* similarity, resemblance; a picture or other representation of a person or thing; form, appearance, guise. **likewise,** *adv., conj.* in like manner; also, moreover, too. [OE *līc* in *gelīc* (cp. Dut. *gelijk,* Icel. *līkr, glīkr,* G *gleich,* also LICH)]

like², *v.t.* to be pleased with; to be inclined towards or attracted by; to enjoy; to be fond of; (*usu. impers.*) †to be pleasing to, to suit. *v.i.* to be pleased; to choose; †to thrive. *n.* liking; a longing desire; (*usu. pl.*) predilection. **likeable,** *a.* **likeableness,** *n.* **liking** *n.* the state of being pleased; inclination, fondness, regard, fancy; †state of the body. **to one's liking,** to one's taste. [OE *līcian* (cp. Dut. *lijken,* Icel. *līka*) as prec.]

-like, *suf.* forming adjectives, as in *childlike, saintlike,* *warlike;* forming adverbs, as in *childlike she replied.* [LIKE[1]]

Likud, *n.* alliance of right-wing Israeli political parties that defeated the Labor Party coalition in the May 1977 election, and brought Menachem Begin to power. In 1987, Likud were part of an uneasy national coalition with Labor, formed to solve Israel's economic crisis. In 1989, another coalition was formed under Shamir.

lilac, *n.* a shrub of the genus *Syringa,* esp. *S. vulgaris,* with very fragrant pale violet or purple flowers, white in cultivated varieties. *a.* of the colour of lilac. [F and Sp., from Arab. and Pers. *līlăk,* var. of *nīlak,* dim. of *nīl,* blue, indigo]

Lilburne, *n.* **John** (1614–1657), English republican agitator. He was imprisoned 1638–40 for circulating Puritan pamphlets, fought in the Parliamentary army in the Civil War, and by his advocacy of a democratic republic won the leadership of the Levellers. He was twice tried for sedition and acquitted; nonetheless after his acquittal he was imprisoned 1653–55.

Lilienthal, *n.* **Otto** (1848–1896), German aviation pioneer, who inspired the Wright brothers. He made and successfully flew many gliders before he was killed in a glider crash.

Lille, *n.* (Flemish **Ryssel**), industrial city (textiles, chemicals, engineering, distilling), capital of Nord-Pas-de-Calais, France; population (1982) 174,000, metropolitan area 936,000. The world's first entirely automatic underground system was opened here 1982.

Lilliputian, *a.* of or pertaining to Lilliput, an imaginary country in Swift's *Gulliver's Travels,* the inhabitants of which were pygmies; pygmy, diminutive. *n.* a native of Lilliput; a pygmy; a very small person.

lills, *n.pl.* very small pins. [etym. unknown]

Lilo ®, *n.* a type of inflatable mattress used in camping, on the beach etc.

Lilongwe, *n.* capital of Malawi since 1975; population (1985) 187,000. Products include tobacco and textiles.

lilt, *v.i.* to sing in cheerful, lively style; to jerk, to spring. *v.t.* to sing in a lively style. *n.* a lively tune; the melody, rhythm or cadence of a song. [ME *lulte,* etym. doubtful]

lily, *n.* a flower or plant of the bulbous genus *Lilium,* producing white or coloured flowers of great beauty, esp. the Madonna lily, *L. candidum;* applied to various plants having resemblances, as the Lent-lily or daffodil, the water-lily etc.; (*Her.*) the fleur-de-lis; hence (*pl.*) the royal arms of France; a person or thing of unsullied whiteness or purity; a fair complexion. *a.* pure white; pure, unsullied. **lily of the valley,** a fragrant spring-flowering plant of the genus *Danvallaria,* with a scape of white hanging cuplike flowers. **to gild, paint the lily,** to try to improve what is already perfect. **lily-handed,** *a.* having delicate hands. **lily-iron,** *n.* the detachable barbed head of a harpoon. **lily-livered,** *a.* cowardly. **lily-pad,** *n.* the broad floating leaf of the water-lily. **lily-white,** *a.* pure white; (*coll.*) irreproachable. **liliaceous,** *a.* pertaining to lilies, or the Liliaceae, an order of endogens. **lilied,** *a.* lilylike in complexion; †full of or covered with lilies. [OE *lilie,* L *līlium,* Gr. *leirion*]

Lima, *n.* capital of Peru, and industrial city (textiles, chemicals, glass, cement), with its port at Callao; population (1988) 418,000, metropolitan area 4,605,000. Founded by the conquistador Pizarro 1535, it was rebuilt after destruction by an earthquake 1746. **Lima bean,** *n.* an edible climbing bean, *Phaseolus lunatus.*

limaceous, *a.* pertaining to the genus *Limax* or the family Limacidae which contains the slugs. **limaciform,** *a.* **limacoid,** *n., a.* **limaçon,** *n.* (*Math.*) a particular curve based on the union of two ovals. [L *līmax -ācis,* slug or snail, -ACEOUS]

limb[1], *n.* one of the articulated extremities of an animal, an arm, leg or wing; a main branch of a tree; a member, branch or arm of a larger group or institution; (*coll.*) an impish child or urchin. *v.t.* to tear the limbs from, to dismember. **out on a limb,** in a predicament, isolated. †**limb-meal,** *adv.* limb from limb. **limbed,** *a.* (*usu. in comb.*) having limbs, as *large-limbed.* **limbless,** *a.* [OE *lim* (cp. Icel. *limr*)]

limb[2], *n.* an edge or border; the outermost edge of the sun, moon etc.; the graduated arc of a sextant etc.; the expanded portion of a gamosepalous corolla, petal etc. **limbate,** *a.* bordered, having a differently-coloured border. **limbation,** *n.* **limbic, limbiferous, limbous,** *a.* [L *limbus,* border, edging]

limber[1], *n.* the detachable part of a gun-carriage consisting of two wheels and ammunition-box. *v.t.* to attach the limber to the gun (usu. with *up*). *v.i.* to fasten (up) the limber and gun. [formerly *limmer, lymor,* perh. from F *limonière,* from *limon,* shaft]

limber[2], *n.* (*Naut.*) a gutter on each side of the kelson for draining; (*pl.*) the gutters and holes in the floor-timbers. **limber-passage,** *n.* [perh. a corr. of F *lumière,* light, hole]

limber[3], *a.* flexible, lithe. **to limber up,** *v.i.* to stretch and flex the muscles in preparation for physical exercise. [etym. doubtful]

limbo[1], *n.* the edge or uttermost limit of hell, the abode of those who died unbaptized through no fault of their own, such as the just before Christ and infants; prison, confinement; a place of neglect or oblivion; an uncertain or transitional state. [L, abl. of *limbus,* see LIMB[2]]

limbo[2], *n.* a West Indian dance in which the participants bend backwards and pass under a bar. [etym. doubtful]

Limbourg brothers, *n. pl.* Franco-Flemish painters, **Pol, Herman,** and **Jan** (Hennequin, Janneken), active in the late 14th and early 15th cent., first in Paris, then at the ducal court of Burgundy. They produced richly detailed manuscript illuminations, including two Books of Hours.

Limburg, *n.* southernmost province of the Netherlands in the plain of the Maas (Meuse); area 2170 sq km/838 sq miles; population (1988) 1,095,000. Its capital is Maastricht, the oldest city in the Netherlands. Manufacture of chemicals has now replaced coal mining but the coal industry is still remembered at Kerkrade, alleged site of the first European coal mine. The marl soils of S Limburg are used in the manufacture of cement and fertilizer. Mixed arable farming and horticulture are also important.

Limburger, *n.* a white cheese with a strong taste and smell. [*Limburg,* Belgium]

lime[1], *n.* a caustic earth, mainly calcium oxide (**quicklime**), obtained by burning calcium carbonate (usu. in limestone form), used in building and agriculture; bird-lime; calcium hydroxide (**slaked lime**), a white powder obtained by the action of water on quicklime. *v.t.* to smear with bird-lime; to ensnare; to manure with lime; to spread lime over (land); to dress (hides) in lime and water. **lime-burner,** *n.* one who burns limestone to make lime. **lime-cast,** *n.* a covering of lime in the form of mortar. *a.* of a building, covered with this. **lime-kiln,** *n.* a kiln in which limestone is calcined and reduced to lime. **limelight,** *n.* a light produced by projecting a jet of ignited hydrogen and oxygen upon a ball of lime, making it incandescent; the glare of publicity. **lime-pit,** *n.* a pit for liming hides. **limestone,** *n.* any rock the basis of which is carbonate of lime, esp. mountain limestone, the principal rock of the Carboniferous series. **lime-twig,** *n.* a twig smeared with bird-lime to catch birds. **limewash,** *n.* whitewash. *v.t.* to whitewash. **lime-water,** *n.* a solution of lime in water used medicinally and for refining sugar. **lime-wort,** *n.* the brook-lime. **limy,** *a.* viscous, tenacious; of the nature of, resembling or containing lime. **liminess,** *n.* [OE *līm* (cp. Dut. *lijm,* Icel. *līm,* G *Leim,* also L *līmus,* mud, LOAM)]

lime[2], *n.* the linden-tree. **lime-tree,** *n.* [perh. var. of OE *lind,* LINDEN]

lime[3], *n.* a small tropical citrus tree; the greenish-yellow fruit of this tree with acid flesh. **lime-juice,** *n.* the juice of the lime used as a beverage. **limey,** *n.* (*N Am. sl.*) a British sailor (from the former use of lime juice on British ships to prevent scurvy); any British person. [F, from Sp. *lima,* Arab. *līmah* (cp. LEMON)]

lime-hound, LYAM-HOUND.

limelight LIME[1].

limen, *n.* (*Psych.*) the stage of consciousness at which a given stimulus begins to produce sensation and below which it is imperceptible. **liminal, liminary,** *a.* [L, threshold]

Limerick[1]**,** *n.* a nonsense verse, usu. of five lines, the first, second and fifth, and the third and fourth of which rhyme together respectively. [said to be from the chorus 'Will you come up to *Limerick*?' sung at the end of impromptu verses at convivial parties in Ireland]

Limerick[2]**,** *n.* county town of Limerick, Republic of Ireland, the main port of W Ireland, on the Shannon estuary; population (1986) 77,000. It was founded in the 12th century.

Limerick[3]**,** *n.* county in SW Republic of Ireland, in Munster province. **area** 2690 sq km/1038 sq miles. **county town** Limerick. **physical** fertile, with hills in the south. **population** (1986) 164,000. **products** dairy products.

limit, *n.* a boundary, a line, point or edge marking termination or utmost extent; a restraint, a check; that which has bounds, a district, a period etc.; (*sl.*) a person, demand, opinion or the like, of an exaggerated kind. *v.t.* to set a limit or bound to; to confine within certain bounds; to restrict (to); to serve as boundary or restriction to. †**limitable,** *a.* **limitarian,** *a.* (*Theol.*) tending to limit. *n.* one who believes in limited redemption. **limitary,** *a.* stationed at the limits (of a guard); limited, circumscribed; limiting, confining. **limitation,** *n.* the act of limiting; the state of being limited; that which limits; a restriction; (*Law*) the period within which an action must be brought and beyond which it may not lie. **statute of limitation,** a statute fixing such periods. **limitative,** *a.* **limited,** *a.* having or being limited, narrow; restricted; confined; (*coll.*) not very clever or well-read. *n.* a limited company. **limited edition,** *n.* an edition of a book, print etc. of which only a small number is issued. *a.* **limited liability** LIABLE. **limited monarchy,** *n.* a monarchy in which the power of the sovereign is limited by a constitution. **limited redemption,** (*Theol.*) the doctrine that only a portion of the human race can be saved. **limitedly,** *adv.* **limitedness,** *n.* **limiter,** †**limitour,** *n.* one who or that which limits; †a friar licensed to beg or exercise his functions within certain limits. **limitless,** *a.* [F *limite,* L *līmitem,* nom. *līmes,* rel. to LIMEN]

limitrophe, *a.* on the border, adjacent (to). [F, from late L *līmi trophus,* L *līmes līmitis,* LIMIT, Gr. *-trophos,* feeding, from *trephein,* to feed]

limma, *n.* (*pl.* **-mmata**) (*Mus.*) the semitone in the Pythagorean scale; (*Gr. Pros.*) a time or pause unexpressed by a syllable, indicated by the mark ʌ. [late L, from Gr. *leimma,* remnant, from *leipein,* to leave]

limmer, *n.* (*Sc.*) a jade, a huzzy; a strumpet; a rogue, a scoundrel. [etym. doubtful]

limn, *v.t.* to paint or draw, to depict, to portray; †to paint in water-colour, †to illuminate (a book, manuscript etc.). **limner,** *n.* [ME *limnen,* contr. from *luminen,* OF *luminer*]

limnology, *n.* the study of the physical, biological, geographical etc. features of lakes, ponds and other freshwater bodies. **limnological,** *a.* **limnologist,** *n.* [*limnē,* lake, -LOGY]

limonite, *n.* a hydrated sesquioxide of iron, orig. bog iron-ore. [Gr. *leimōn,* meadow]

Limousin, *n.* former province and modern region of central France; area 16,900 sq km/6544 sq miles; population (1986) 736,000. It consists of the *départements* of Corréze, Creuse, and Haute-Vienne. Chief town is Limoges. A thinly populated and largely unfertile region, it is crossed by the mountains of the Massif Central. Fruit and vegetables are produced in the more fertile lowlands. Kaolin is mined.

limousine, *n.* a large opulent car (orig. having a closed body with a separate driver's seat), esp. one with a glass partition dividing the driver from the passengers. [F, orig. a coarse cape or cloak of wool or goat's hair]

limp[1]**,** *v.i.* to walk lamely; to halt; of verse, logic etc., to be irregular; to proceed with difficulty. *n.* the act of limping; a limping step or walk. **limpingly,** *adv.* [etym. doubtful, cogn. with MHG *limphin*]

limp[2]**,** *a.* wanting in stiffness, flaccid, flexible, pliable; lacking in firmness; of book covers, not stiffened by boards. **limply,** *adv.* **limpness,** *n.* [etym. doubtful]

limpet, *n.* any individual of the genus of gastropods *Patella,* having an open conical shell, found adhering firmly to rocks; a tenacious person or thing. **limpet mine,** *n.* an explosive device which clings to a ship's hull, tank etc. by magnetic or adhesive means. [ME *lempet,* OE *lempedu,* late L *lampēdra,* limpet, LAMPREY]

limpid, *a.* clear, pellucid, transparent; lucid, perspicuous. **limpidly,** *adv.* **limpidness, limpidity,** *n.* [F *limpide,* L *limpidus,* rel. to *lympha,* LYMPH]

Limpopo, *n.* river in SE Africa, rising in the Transvaal and reaching the Indian Ocean in Mozambique; length 1600 km/1000 miles.

limp-wort, LIME-WORT, under LIME[1].

limy LIME[1].

lin, LINN.

linage, *n.* amount of printed matter reckoned by lines; payment by the line.

Lin Biao, *n.* (1907–1971), Chinese politician and general. He joined the Communists 1927, became a commander of Mao Zedong's Red Army, and led the Northeast People's Liberation Army in the civil war after 1945. He became defence minister 1959, and as vice chairman of the party 1969, he was expected to be Mao's successor, but he lost favour, perhaps because of his control over the army. After an attempted coup failed, he was reported to have been killed in an aeroplane crash in Mongolia 17 Sept. 1971.

linch, *n.* a ledge; a linchet; a steep bank or ridge; an unploughed strip between fields. **linchet,** *n.* an unploughed strip serving as a boundary; a cultivation terrace on the side of a steep hill. [OE *hlinc,* cp. LINKS]

linchpin, *n.* a pin serving to hold a wheel on the axle; someone or something essential to an organization etc. [OE *lynis,* an axle-tree (cp. Dut. *luns,* G *Lünse*) PIN]

Lincoln, *n.* **Abraham** (1809–1865), 16th president of the US 1861–65. In the US Civil War, his chief concern was the preservation of the Union from which the Confederate (Southern) slave states had seceded on his election. In 1863 he announced the freedom of the slaves with the Emancipation Proclamation. He was re-elected 1864 with victory for the North in sight, but assassinated at the end of the war.

Lincoln green, *n.* bright green cloth formerly made at Lincoln; its colour.

Lincolnshire, *n.* county in E England. **area** 5890 sq km/2274 sq miles. **towns** administrative headquarters Lincoln; resort Skegness. **physical** Lincoln Wolds, marshy coastline, the Fens in the SE, rivers Witham and Welland. **population** (1987) 575,000. **products** cattle, sheep, horses, cereals, flower bulbs, oil.

lincrusta, *n.* a canvas-backed material with designs in bold relief, used for decorating walls and ceilings. [L *linum,* thread, *crusta,* skin, crust]

Lincs, (*abbr.***)** Lincolnshire.

linctus, *n.* (*pl.* **-tuses**) a syrupy cough medicine. [L, a licking, from *lingere,* to lick]

Lindbergh, *n.* **Charles (Augustus)** (1902–1974), US aviator, who made the first non-stop solo flight across the Atlantic (New York-Paris) 1927 in the *Spirit of St Louis.*

linden, *n.* a tree of the genus *Tilia,* esp. *T. europaea,* with soft timber, heart-shaped leaves, and small clusters of delicately-scented flowers, the lime-tree. [OE *lind* (cp. Dut. and G *Linde,* Gr. *elatē,* fir)]

line[1]**,** *n.* a thread or string; a rope, a piece of rope used for sounding or other purposes; a cord, string, wire etc. used for specific purposes, as with hooks for fishing, with a plumb for testing verticality; a clothes-line; a cord for measuring etc.; a wire or cable for telegraph or telephone; the route traversed by this; a rule or direction; (*pl.*) one's lot in life; a thread-like mark; such a mark drawn by a pencil, pen, graver or other instrument; a streak, narrow band, seam, furrow, wrinkle etc. resembling this; (*Math.*) that which has length without breadth or thickness; the boundary of a surface; the track of a moving point; the curve connecting a series of points; the equator; shape of contour, outline, lineament; (*pl.*) the plan or outlines shown in the sections of a ship; a scheme, a plan, design; a limit, a boundary; a row or continuous series of letters, words, people or other objects; a short letter, a note; a single verse of poetry; (*pl.*) a piece of poetry, a specified quantity of verse or prose for a school student to copy out as an imposition; (*pl.*) a certificate of marriage; (*pl.*) a series of trenches, ramparts etc.; a double row of men ranged as in order of battle; the aggregate of troops in an army apart from support units etc.; a row of ships drawn up in order; a series of persons related in direct descent or succession, family, lineage; a series of ships or public conveyances plying between certain places or under one management; a railway track; a railway system under one management; a certain branch of business, a certain class of goods, a stock of these, an order for these; field of activity, province; particular interest; the twelfth part of an inch; (*coll.*) pertinent facts; (*sl.*) smooth talk; one of the horizontal lines on a television screen, traced by a scanning electron beam, which creates the picture. *v.t.* to draw lines upon, to cover with lines; to mark (in, off etc.) with lines; to spread out, extend or post (troops etc.) in line. *v.i.* to come or extend into line; of troops, to form a line beside or along. **hard lines** HARD. **line of distance** DISTANCE. **one's line of country,** one's special field of interest. **to line one's pocket** POCKET. **to line up,** to arrange, to array; to align; to queue; to take the side of or against. **to read between the lines,** to detect the hidden or unexpressed meaning of a letter, speech etc. **line block,** *n.* a printing block on which the black and white parts only of a subject are reproduced. **line-drawing,** *n.* a drawing with pen or pencil. **line-engraving,** *n.* an engraving with incised lines. **line frequency,** *n.* (*TV*) the frequency with which the lines in a scanned image are repeated. **lineman,** *n.* one employed in the maintenance and repair of a line of railway, telegraph etc.; (*Surveying*) one who carries the line or chain. **line-out,** *n.* a method of restarting a match in Rugby Union when the ball has gone out of play, by throwing it in between the forwards of each team lined up facing the touchline. **line printer,** *n.* a high-speed output device, used esp. in conjunction with a computer, which prints copy a whole line at a time. **linesman,** *n.* a lineman; in lawn tennis, football etc., an official who has to note when and where a ball crosses a line. **line-up,** *n.* a row or group of persons assembled for a particular purpose; (*esp. N Am.*) a queue; an identification parade. [ult. from L *līnea,* fem. of *līneus,* flaxen, from *līnum,* flax, through OE *line,* and in later senses F *ligne*]

line², *n.* the fine long fibre of flax separated from the tow. *v.t.* to put a covering of different material on the inside of (a garment, box etc.); to serve as such a covering for; to fill the inside of. **liner**, *n.* one who makes or fits linings; a lining of a cylinder; one cylinder lining another; a strip of metal put between parts to adjust them; the friction substance of a brake. **lining,** *n.* the covering of the inside of anything; that which is within, contents. [OE *līn,* flax (cp. Dut. *lijn,* OHG *lin,* Icel. *līn*) perh. from or cogn. with L *līnum,* see prec.]

line³, *v.t.* to cover, to impregnate (a bitch). [F *ligner,* cp. LINE¹]

lineage, *n.* descendants in a direct line from a common progenitor, ancestry, pedigree. [OF *lignage* (LINE¹, -AGE)]

lineal, *a.* ascending or descending in the direct line of ancestry, opp. to collateral; linear. **lineality,** *n.* **lineally,** *adv.* [F *linéament,* late L *līneālis,* from *līnea,* LINE¹]

lineament, *n.* (*usu. pl.*) characteristic lines or features; outline, contour. [F *linéal,* L *līneāmentum,* from *lineāre,* from *līnea,* LINE¹]

linear, *a.* composed of or having the form of lines; having a straight or lengthwise direction; of one dimension; of mathematical functions, expressions etc., containing only first degree terms, and able to be represented on a graph as a straight line; narrow, slender with parallel sides. **linear accelerator,** *n.* an apparatus for accelerating charged particles along a straight line by applying high-frequency potential between electrodes placed at intervals along their path. **Linear B,** *n.* an ancient script from the 2nd millennium BC found in Crete and the Greek mainland, apparently a form of Mycenaean Greek modified from the earlier **Linear A. linear motor,** *n.* an electric motor in which the stator and rotor are linear, producing direct thrust without the use of gears. **linear perspective,** *n.* perspective dealing with the apparent positions, magnitudes and forms of objects, opp. to *aerial perspective*. **linear programming,** *n.* a method of solving practical problems in economics etc., using mathematical models involving complex interactions of linear equations. **linearly,** *adv.* **lineate,** *a.* of leaves, marked with lines, esp. long straight lines. **lineation,** *n.* **lineolate,** *a.* marked with minute lines. [L *līneāris,* as prec.]

lineman LINE¹.

linen, *n.* a cloth made of flax; (*collect.*) articles chiefly made of linen, esp. underclothing, sheets, table cloths etc. *a.* made of flax; white, blanched. **linen-draper,** *n.* [OE *līnen,* adj. (*līn,* LINE², -EN)]

liner¹ LINE².

liner², *n.* one of a regular line of passenger ships or aircraft; colouring material for pencilling the eyebrows; a slab of metal on which pieces of marble etc., are fastened for polishing.

linesman LINE¹.

ling¹, *n.* a long slender food-fish, *Molva vulgaris,* found in the northern seas. [cp. E Fris. and Dut. *leng,* G *Länge,* Icel. *langa,* cogn. with LONG]

ling², *n.* heather or heath, *Calluna vulgaris*. [Icel. *lyng*]

-ling¹, *suf.* forming nouns (now only with a diminutive force), as *darling, gosling, lordling, youngling*. [OE and OHG *-ling*]

-ling², *suf.* forming adverbs, as *darkling*. [OE *-linga, -lunga,* adverbial suffix]

lingam, linga, *n.* the phallus representative of the god Siva, in Hindu mythology. [Sansk., a mark, a penis]

lingel, *n.* (*Sc.*) a cobbler's waxed thread. [OF *ligneul,* ult. from L *linea,* LINE¹]

linger, *v.i.* to delay going, to tarry, to loiter; to be long in going or coming, to hesitate; to be protracted. *v.t.* to spend or pass (time) wearily or in delays. **lingerer,** *n.* **lingeringly,** *adv.* [ME *lengen,* OE *lengan,* to protract (cp. Icel. *lengja,* G *längen*), from *lang,* LONG]

lingerie, *n.* women's underwear and nightclothes. [F, from *linge,* linen]

lingo, *n.* (*pl.* **-goes**) a foreign language, peculiar dialect or technical phraseology. [prob. corr. of *lingua,* see LINGUA FRANCA]

†**lingot,** *n.* an ingot. [F, from INGOT]

lingua, *n.* the tongue.

lingua franca, *n.* a mixture of Italian with French, Greek, Arabic etc., used in Mediterranean ports; a language serving as a medium of communication between different peoples; any hybrid language with this function. [It., Frankish tongue]

lingual, *a.* pertaining to the tongue; (*phon.*) formed by the tongue. *n.* a letter or sound produced by the tongue, as *t, d, n, l, r*. **lingually,** *adv.* **linguiform**, *a.* having the form of a tongue. [med. L *linguālis,* from *lingua,* tongue]

linguist, *n.* one skilled in languages. **linguistic**, *a.* of or pertaining to linguistics. **linguistically,** *adv.* **linguistics,** *n.pl.* the science of languages; comparative grammar.

lingula, *n.* (*pl.* **-lae**) a tongue-shaped part; (**lingula**) a genus of brachiopods, largely fossil. **lingula flags,** *n.pl.* (*Geol.*) a series of flagstones and slates in N Wales containing immense numbers of fossil lingulae. **lingular,** *a.* **lingulate**, *a.* tongue-shaped. [L, dim. of *lingua,* see prec.]

linhay, *n.* a shed, usu. a lean-to, open at the sides for cattle or carts. [etym. doubtful]

liniment, *n.* a liquid preparation, usu. with oil, for rubbing on bruised or inflamed parts, embrocation. [F, from L *linīmentum,* from *linīre,* to anoint]

lining LINE3.

link1, *n.* a ring or loop of a chain; a connecting part in machinery etc. or in a series, sequence, argument etc.; one-hundredth of a surveyor's chain equal to 7·92 in. (about 20 cm); a unit in a communications system. *v.t.* to connect or attach (to, together, up etc.) by or as by a link or links. *v.i.* to be connected. **missing link,** the creature formerly conjectured (and subsequently discovered) to have existed linking man and the anthropoid ape; any piece of information required to complete a chain of connection or argument. **linkman,** *n.* a television or radio presenter who provides continuity between separate items (e.g. of news, sport) in a broadcast. **link-up,** *n.* a connection, joint. **linkage,** *n.* the act or manner of linking or being linked; a system of links; the product of magnetic flux and the total number of turns in a coil; the occurrence of two genes on the same chromosome so that they tend to be inherited together. **linker,** *n.* (*Comput.*) a programme which joins separately assembled or compiled modules into a single executable programme. [Icel. *hlekkr* (OIcel. *hlenkr*), cp. Swed. *länk,* OE *hlence* (cogn. with G *Gelenk,* joint)]

link2, *n.* a torch made of tow and pitch, used formerly for lighting persons in the streets. **link-boy, -man,** *n.* a boy or man carrying a link. [etym. doubtful, perh. a use of prec.]

links, (*Sc.*) *n.pl.* flattish or undulating sandy ground near the seashore, covered with coarse grass etc.; hence a golf-course. [from OE *hlinc,* LINCH]

Linlithgowshire, *n.* former name of West Lothian, now included in Lothian region, Scotland.

linn, *n.* a waterfall, a torrent; a pool, esp. one below a fall; a precipice or precipitous ravine. [OE *hlynn,* torrent, confused with Gael. *linne,* Ir. *linn,* W *llyn,* a pool]

Linnaeus, *n.* **Carolus (Carl von Linné)** (1707–1778), Swedish naturalist and physician. His botanical work *Systema Naturae* (1758) contained his system for classifying plants and animals into groups depending on the number of stamens in their flowers, providing a much-needed framework for identification. He also devised the concise and precise system for naming plants and animals, using one Latin (or Latinized) word to represent the genus and a second to distinguish the species. **Linnaean, Linnean,** *a.* of or pertaining to Linnaeus or his system of classification and naming of plants and animals. *n.* a follower of Linnaeus.

linnet, *n.* a common finch, *Linota cannabina,* with brownish plumage. [OF *linette* (F *linotte*), from *lin,* flax (see LINEN), on which it feeds]

lino, *n.* short for LINOLEUM. **linocut,** *n.* an engraving on linoleum in the manner of a woodcut.

linoleum, *n.* a preparation of oxidized linseed-oil mixed with ground cork and laid upon fabric, used as a floor covering. [L *līnum,* flax, *oleum,* OIL]

Linotype®, *n.* a typesetting machine once used for producing castings or slugs of whole lines of words; type produced by such a method. [LINE1, OF, TYPE]

Lin Piao, *n.* alternative form of Lin Biao.

linsang, *n.* a kind of civet cat common in Borneo and Java; a related African species. [Javanese]

linseed, *n.* the seed of the flax-plant. **linseed-cake,** *n.* the solid mass left after the oil has been pressed out of flax-seed. **linseed-oil,** *n.* the oil expressed from linseed. [ME *lin-seed* (OE *līn,* LINE2, SEED]

linsey-woolsey, *n.* a coarse fabric of linen or cotton warp with wool filling; a motley composition, a jargon. [prob. formed from LINE2 and WOOL, with a jingling suf., or perh. from a place-name as *Lindsey*]

†**linstock,** *n.* a forked staff to hold a lighted match for firing a gun. [formerly *lintstock,* Dut. *lontstok* (*lont,* match, *stok,* stick)]

lint, *n.* the down of linen cloth scraped on one side, or cotton substitute, used for dressing wounds etc. [rel. to LINE2, perh. through F *linette* or *lin,* linen]

lintel, *n.* the horizontal beam or stone over a door or window. **lintelled,** *a.* [OF, from med. L *lintellus,* prob. for *līmitellus,* dim. of *līmes,* LIMIT]

lintie, lintwhite, *n.* (*Sc.*) a linnet. [OE *līnetwige*]

Linz, *n.* industrial port (iron, steel, metalworking) on the river Danube in N Austria; population (1981) 199,900.

lion, *n.* a large and powerful carnivorous quadruped, *Felis leo,* usu. brown or tawny, with tufted tail and (in the adult male) a long mane, inhabiting southern Asia and Africa; the sign of the zodiac and constellation Leo; the British national emblem; (*pl.*) sights to be seen by visitors (from the lions formerly kept at the Tower of London); a courageous person; an eminent celebrity, an object of general attention. **the lion's mouth,** a dangerous place. **the lion's share,** the largest part or the whole. **lion-heart,** *n.* **lion-hearted,** *a.* having great courage. †**lion-sick,** *a.* sick of a proud heart. **lion's-provider,** *n.* the jackal (see JACKAL); a tool, a sycophant. **lioncel,** *n.* (*Her.*) a small lion, esp. one of several borne on the same coat of arms. **lionesque, lion-like,** *a.* **lioness,** *n.fem.* **lionet,** *n.* a young lion. **lionhood, -ship,** *n.* **lionize, -ise,** *v.t.* to treat as an object of interest or curiosity; to visit or show off (a place or sights) to visitors. *v.i.* to visit the objects of interest or curiosity in a place. [A-F *liun* (OF *leon*), L *leōnem,* nom. *leo,* Gr. *leōn leontos*]

lip, *n.* one of the two fleshy parts enclosing the opening of the mouth; the edge or margin of an orifice, chasm etc.; (*pl.*) the projecting lobes of a bilabiate corolla; (*pl.*) the mouth, as organ of speech; (*sl.*) impudence, cheek. *v.t.* (*past, p.p.* **lipped**) to touch with the lips; to kiss; of water, to lap against; to breathe, whisper, murmur. *v.i.* of water, to lap. **to bite one's lips,** to express vexation, to repress anger, laughter or other emotion. **to hang on one's lips,** to listen eagerly for every word spoken. **to keep a stiff upper lip,** to be self-reliant, inflexible, unflinching. †**to make a lip,** to pout the lips in sullenness or contempt. **to smack one's lips,** to anticipate or recall with relish. **lip-deep,** *a.* in up to the lips; only from the lips, superficial, insincere. **lip-gloss,** *n.* a cosmetic which makes the lips glossy. **lip-reading,** *n.* the practice of following what is said by observing the movements of the speaker's lips. **lipsalve,** *n.* ointment for the lips; compliments, flattery. **lip service,** *n.* flattery, servile agreement a sentiment etc. expressed but not put into practice. **lipstick,** *n.* a stick of cosmetic for colouring the lips. **lip-sync, -synch,** *v.t.* to synchronize the movement of the lips with a prerecorded soundtrack (of words, music etc.) on film or television. **lipless,** *a.* **lipped** *a.* (*usu. in comb.,* as *thick-lipped*). [OE *lippa* (cp. Dut. *lip,* Dan. *laebe,* G *Lippe,* also L *labium, labrum*)]

lip- LIP(O).

lipase, *n.* an enzyme which decomposes fats.

Li Peng, *n.* (1928–), Chinese communist politician, a member of the Politburo from 1985, and head of government from 1987. He is the adopted son of the communist leader Zhou Enlai. During the pro-democracy demonstrations 1989 he supported the massacre of students by Chinese troops, and the subsequent executions of others.

lipid, *n.* any of various organic compounds which are esters of fatty acids, and are important structural components of living cells. **lipidic,** *a.*

lip(o)-, *comb. form* fat, fatty. [Gr. *lipos,* fat]

Li Po, *n.* (705–762), Chinese poet. He wrote in traditional forms, but his exuberance, the boldness of his imagination, and the intensity of his feeling have won him recognition as perhaps the greatest of all Chinese poets. Although he was mostly concerned with higher themes, he also celebrated the joys of drinking.

lipogenesis, *n.* the formation of fat. **lipogenic,** *a.*

lipogram, *n.* a writing in which a particular letter is omitted. **lipogrammatic,** *a.* **lipogrammatism,** *n.* **lipogrammatist,** *n.* [Gr. *lipogrammatos,* wanting a letter (*leipein,* to leave, *gramma -atos,* letter)]

lipography, *n.* the accidental omission of a letter or letters in writing.
lipohaemia, *n.* prevalence of fatty matter in the blood.
lipoid, *a.* fat-like. *n.* a fat-like substance, a lipid.
lipoma, *n.* (*pl.* **-mata**) a fatty tumour. **lipomatosis,** *n.* excessive growth of fatty tissue. **lipomatous,** *a.*
lipoprotein, *n.* a protein which includes a lipid.
lippen, *v.i.* (*Sc.*) to confide, to rely, to depend (on, to etc.). *v.t.* to entrust. [etym. doubtful]
Lippi[1], *n.* **Filippino** (1457–1504), Italian painter of the Florentine school, trained by Botticelli. He produced altarpieces and several fresco cycles, full of detail and drama, elegant and finely drawn. He was the son of Filippo Lippi.
Lippi[2], *n.* **Filippo** (1406–1469), Italian Florentine painter, called Fra (Brother) Filippo, born in Florence and patronized by the Medici. He was a monk, but was tried in the 1450s for abducting a nun (the mother of his son Filippino). He is best known for his altarpieces, notably Madonnas and groups of saints.
†**lippitude,** *n.* blearedness; soreness of the eyes; chronic ophthalmia. [L *lippitūdo,* from *lippus,* blear-eyed]
Lippizaner, *n.* a breed of horses (usu. white or grey in colour) used, esp. by the Spanish Riding School in Vienna for dressage displays. [G, after *Lippiza,* Yugoslavia where orig. bred]
Lippman, *n.* **Gabriel** (1845–1921), French doctor, who invented the direct colour process in photography. Nobel prize 1908.
lippy, (*Sc.*) *n.* †a basket; an old dry-measure equal to a quarter of a peck. [dim. of obs. *leap,* OE *lēap* (cp. Icel. *laupr*)]
liq., (*abbr.*) liquid; liquor.
liquate, *v.t.* to melt; to liquefy (metals) in order to purify. †*v.i.* to melt, to liquefy. †**liquable,** *a.* **liquation,** *n.* [L *liquātus,* p.p. of *liquāre,* to melt, cogn. with LIQUOR]
liquefy, liquify, *v.t.* to melt, to dissolve; to convert from a solid (or gaseous) to a liquid form. *v.i.* to become liquid. **liquefacient,** *n.* that which liquefies. *a.* serving to liquefy. **liquefaction,** *n.* **liquefactive,** *a.* **liquefiable,** *a.* **liquefier,** *n.* **liquescence,** †**-ency,** *n.* **liquescent,** *a.* [F *liquéfier,* L *liquefacere* (*liquāre,* to become fluid, *facere,* to make)]
liqueur, *n.* an alcoholic cordial sweetened or flavoured with aromatic substance and drunk in small quantities; *v.t.* to treat or flavour with this. **liqueur brandy,** *n.* brandy of special quality drunk as a liqueur. **liqueur-glass,** *n.* a small glass for drinking liqueurs. [F, LIQUOR]
liquid, *a.* fluid; flowing or capable of flowing, watery; transparent, limpid, clear; of vowels, not guttural, fluent, smooth, easily pronounced; of assets, readily convertible into cash; of principles etc., unstable, changeable. *n.* a substance whose molecules are incompressible and inelastic and move freely among themselves, but cannot escape as in a gaseous state; a letter pronounced with a slight contact of the organs of articulation, as *l, r,* and sometimes *m, n.* **liquid crystal,** *n.* a liquid with physical, esp. optical, properties analogous to crystals. **liquid crystal display,** a display, esp. in electronic calculators, using liquid crystal cells which change their reflectivity in an electric field. **liquid paraffin,** *n.* an oily liquid obtained from petroleum distillation and used as a laxative. **liquidate,** *v.t.* to pay off (a debt etc.); to wind up (a bankrupt estate etc.); to suppress; to assassinate. *v.i.* of a company, to have its debts, liabilities and assets liquidated. **liquidation,** *n.* **liquidator,** *n.* the person officially appointed to effect a liquidation. **liquidity, liquidness,** *n.* **liquidize, -ise,** *v.t.* to reduce to liquid; to liquefy; to pulverize (food) into a liquid. **liquidizer, -iser,** *n.* a kitchen appliance with blades and various attachments for chopping or puréeing vegetables, blending soup etc. **liquidly,** *adv.* [OF *liquide,* L *liquidus,* from *liquēre,* cp. LIQUEFY, LIQUATE]
liquidambar, *n.* any of a genus, *Liquidambar,* of tropical trees, several species of which yield a fragrant resin or balsam called storax; the resin so produced. [LIQUID, med. L *ambar,* AMBER]
liquor, *n.* a liquid or fluid substance, esp. the liquid part of anything as of a solution, a secretion, food etc.; a solution or dilution; an alcoholic drink, usu. not including wine or beer; an aqueous solution of a drug. *v.t.* to moisten, to wet, to steep; to grease, to dress (leather etc.). **liquor-up,** *v.i.* to take a lot of drink. **liquorish**[1], *a.* fond of liquor. **liquorishly,** *adv.* **liquorishness,** *n.* [A-F *licur* (F LIQUEUR), L *liquor,* from *liquēre,* see LIQUID]
liquorice, licorice, *n.* the root of a bean-like plant of the genus *Glycyrrhiza;* its dried root; an extract from the root used in medicine and confectionery; liquorice flavoured sweets. [A-F *lycorys* (F *liquerice*), late L *liquiritia,* Gr. *glukurrhiza* (*glukus,* sweet, *rhiza,* root)]
liquorish[1] LIQUOR.
liquorish[2] LICKERISH.
lira, *n.* (*pl.* **lire, liras**) the standard unit of currency in Italy; the standard monetary unit of Turkey. [It., from L *libra,* a pound]
liriodendron, *n.* a genus of N American trees and containing the tulip tree. [Gr. *leirion,* LILY, *dendron,* tree]
lis FLEUR-DE-LIS.
Lisbon (Portuguese **Lisboa**), *n.* city and capital of Portugal, in the SW on the tidal lake and estuary formed by the Tagus; population (1981) 817,627. Industries include steel, textiles, chemicals, pottery, shipbuilding, and fishing. It has been capital since 1260, and reached its peak of prosperity in the 16th cent.
lisle, *n.* a fine, hard cotton thread. [*Lisle,* an old name for *Lille* in France]
Lisp, *n.* a computer-programming language for list processing used primarily in artificial-intelligence (AI) research. Developed in the 1960s, and until recently common only in university laboratories, Lisp is more popular in the US than in Europe, where the language Prolog is often preferred for AI work.
lisp, *v.i.* to pronounce *s* and *z* with the sound of *th* or *dh;* to speak affectedly or imperfectly as a child. *v.t.* to pronounce with a lisp. *n.* the act or habit of lisping; the speech-defect which causes one to lisp. **lisper,** *n.* **lispingly,** *adv.* [OE *wlispian*]
lissom, lissome, *a.* Lithe, supple, nimble. **lissomness,** *n.* [var. of LITHESOME]
list[1], *n.* a number (of people, places, objects) written down in order. *v.t.* to enter in a list; to arrange in a list. **list price,** *n.* a price as listed in a catalogue etc. **listed,** *a.* entered in a list; of buildings architecturally important and officially protected from demolition or significant alteration. **listing,** *n.* the act or fact of entering in a list; (*pl.*) a published list of current plays, films, exhibitions, radio and TV programmes etc.
list[2], *n.* the border, edge or selvedge of cloth; a strip of this used as material; a boundary, a limit; (*pl.*) the palisades enclosing a piece of ground for a tournament, the ground so enclosed; a scene of contest, an area. *v.t.* to cover or line with list (as the edge of a door); to sew together so as to form a border; (*N Am.*) to prepare (land) for corn or cotton by making alternate beds and furrows. **to enter the lists,** to enter into a contest. **lister,** *n.* (*N Am.*) a plough specially designed for throwing up ridges. [OE *līste* (cp. Dut. *lijst,* G *Leiste,* OHG *lista,* whence It. *lista,* F *liste,* whence the sense of roll or catalogue)]
list[3], *v.t.* (3rd *sing.* **list, listeth,** *past* **list, listed**) to please, to be pleasing to. *v.i.* to please, to choose, to be disposed. *n.* desire, pleasure, inclination. **listless,** *a.* careless, heedless; indifferent to what is going on; inattentive, languid. **listlessly,** *adv.* **listlessness,** *n.* [OE *lystan* (cp. Dut. *lusten,* Icel. *lysta,* G *lüsten*), from *lust,* see LUST]
list[4], *n.* a leaning over (of a ship, building etc.). *v.i.* to lean over, to careen. *v.t.* to careen or heel (a ship) over. [perh. from prec. n.]
†**list**[5], *v.i.* to listen. *v.t.* to listen to. [OE *hlystan,* from *hlyst,* hearing (cp. Icel. *hlust,* ear), cogn. with L *cluere,* Gr. *kluein*]
listen, *v.i.* to give ear or attention (to), to hearken; to heed, to obey, to follow. *n.* an act of listening. **to listen in,** to listen to radio; to tap a telephone

message. †*v.t.* to hearken to. **listener,** *n.* one who listens, esp. to broadcasting. **listening,** *a.* **listening post,** *n.* a position where men are posted to overhear what the enemy is saying or planning. [ONorthum. *lysna* (cp. OE *hlosnian*), cogn with LIST[4]]

Lister, *n.* **Joseph, 1st Baron Lister** (1827–1912), British surgeon, and founder of antiseptic surgery. He introduced dressings soaked in carbolic acid and strict rules of hygiene to combat the increase in wound sepsis (the number of surgical operations had increased considerably, following the introduction of anaesthetics). He was much influenced by Louis Pasteur's work on bacteria.

Listeria, *n.* a genus of bacteria found in the environment and in contaminated food; (**listeria**) a member of this genus. **listeriosis**, *n.* a serious disease caused by the presence of Listeria monocytogenes in certain contaminated foods.

Liszt, *n.* **Franz** (1811–1886), Hungarian pianist and composer. An outstanding virtuoso of the piano, he was an established concert artist by the age of 12. His expressive, romantic, and frequently chromatic works includes piano music (*Transcendental Studies* 1851), symphonies, piano concertos and organ music.

lit, *past, p.p.* LIGHT[1], LIGHT[3].

lit., (*abbr.*) literal(ly); literature; litre.

litany, *n.* a solemn form of supplicatory prayer, used in public worship, esp. a series of short invocations with fixed responses in the Prayer Book; a long, usu. boring, list or catalogue. **lesser litany,** the Kyrie Eleison, or the response 'Lord have mercy upon us'. **litany-desk, -stool,** *n.* the desk or stool at which the clergyman reciting the litany kneels. [ME and OF *letanie* (F *litanie*), med. L *litanīa,* Gr. *litaneia,* from *litaneuein,* to pray, from *litanos,* a suppliant, from *litē,* prayer]

litchi, lichee, lychee, *n.* the Chinese tree, *Nephelium litchi,* bearing an edible fruit; the fruit of this tree which has a hard, scaly skin and a soft white pulp. [Chin. *li-chi*]

-lite, *suf.* forming names of minerals, as *aerolite, coprolite, radiolite.* [F, from Gr. *lithos,* stone]

liter LITRE.

literacy LITERATE.

literal, *a.* according to the primitive or verbal meaning; not figurative or metaphorical; following the exact words (as a translation); consisting of or expressed by letters; unimaginative, prosaic, matter-of-fact. *n.* a misprint or misspelling of a word. **literalism,** *n.* the interpretation or understanding of words and statements in a literal sense; realistic or unimaginative portrayal in art or literature. **literalist,** *n.* **literality**, **literalness,** *n.* **literalize, -ise,** *v.t.* **literally,** *adv.* [OF, from L *litterālis,* from *littera,* LETTER]

literary, *a.* of or pertaining to literature or writing; derived from, versed or engaged in literature; well-read; consisting of written or printed compositions; of language, formal not colloquial in style. **literary agent,** *n.* one who manages the business affairs of an author. [L *litterārius,* as prec.]

literate, *a.* instructed in letters or literature, esp. able to read and write; †literary. *n.* one able to read and write; a person of liberal education; a candidate for Holy orders who is not a graduate. **literacy,** *n.* **literati**, *n.pl.* the learned; men and women of letters. **literation,** *n.* representation (of a language etc.) by means of letters. **literator,** *n.* a literary man, a *littérateur;* an elementary teacher; a sciolist, a pretender to learning. **literature,** *n.* (*collect.*) the written or printed productions of a country or period or pertaining to a particular subject; printed matter; the class of writings distinguished for beauty of form or expression, as poetry, novels, essays etc.; the production of literary works; the literary profession; literary culture. **literose**, *a.* affecting literary tastes. **literosity**, *n.* [L *litterātus,* as LITERARY]

literatim, *adv.* letter for letter, literally. [L]

-lith, *suf.* as in *monolith.*

lith[1], (*abbr.*) lithograph; lithography.

lith[2], *n.* (*Sc.*) a joint, a limb; a division. [OE]

lithaemia, *esp. N Am.* **-emia** *n.* excess of lithic or uric acid in the blood. **lithaemic,** *a.* [LITH-, Gr. *haima,* blood]

lithagogue, *n.* (*Surg.*) expelling or tending to expel stone from the kidneys or bladder. [LITH-, Gr. *agōgos,* drawing forth, from *agein,* to draw]

litharge, *n.* lead monoxide. [OF *litarge,* L *lithargyrus,* Gr. *litharguros* (LITH-, *arguros,* silver)]

lithe , *a.* flexible, limber, supple. **lithely,** *adv.* **litheness,** *n.* **lithesome,** *a.* **lithesomeness,** *n.* [OE *līthe,* cogn. with L *lentus*]

†**lither,** *a.* depraved, dissolute; lazy; yielding, pliant; supple, nimble. †**litherly,** *a., adv.* [OE *lythre* (cp. G *liederlich*)]

lithia, *n.* oxide of lithium. [formerly *lithion,* Gr. *litheion,* neut. adj. stony, from *lithos,* stone]

lithiasis, *n.* the formation of calculi in the bladder and urinary passages. [Gr., from *lithiân,* from *lithos,* stone]

lithic[1], *a.* pertaining to or composed of stone or calculi.

lithium, *n.* the lightest metallic element, at. no. 3; chem. symbol Li; a member of the alkali series, used, esp. in alloys and batteries. **lithic[2],** *a.* [*lithia,* -IUM]

litho, *n., a., adv.* (*pl.* **lithos**) short for LITHOGRAPH, -GRAPHIC, -GRAPHY.

lith(o)-, *comb. form* pertaining to stone; calculus. [Gr. *lithos,* a stone]

lithocarp, *n.* a fossil fruit. [Gr. *karpos,* fruit]

lithochromatics, *n.pl.* the art of painting in oil upon stone and taking impressions therefrom. **lithochromatic,** *a.*

lithoclast, *n.* an instrument for breaking up stone in the bladder.

lithodome, *n.* any member of the genus *Lithodomus,* small molluscs which excavate and live in rocks, shells etc. [Gr.]

lithogenous, *a.* stone-producing; forming coral.

lithoglyph, *n.* a carving on stone, esp. a gem. **lithoglyphic,** *a.* [Gr. *gluphein,* to carve]

lithoglyphite, *n.* a fossil substance resembling carving.

lithograph, *v.t.* to engrave or draw on stone or metal and transfer to paper etc., by printing; to print by lithography. *n.* an impression from a drawing on stone or metal. **lithographer**, *n.* **lithographic, -ical**, *a.* **lithographic stone,** a slaty limestone from the upper bed of the Jurassic formation, used in lithography. **lithographically,** *adv.* **lithography**, *n.* the art or process of making a lithograph.

lithoid, lithoidal, *a.* resembling a stone in nature or structure.

litholabe, *n.* an instrument for grasping a stone in lithotomy. [Gr.]

lithology, *n.* the science of the composition, structure and classification of rocks, petrology; the branch of medical science dealing with calculus. **lithologic, -ical**, *a.* **lithologist,** *n.*

lithomancy, *n.* divination by means of stones.

lithomarge, *n.* a hydrated silicate of alumina related to or identical with kaolin.

lithophagous, *a.* eating or perforating stones (as some molluscs). [LITHO-, -PHAGOUS]

lithophane, *n.* ornamental porcelain suitable for lamps, windows and other transparencies.

lithophotography, PHOTOLITHOGRAPHY.

lithophyl, *n.* a fossil leaf or impression of a leaf. [LITHO, Gr. *phullon,* leaf]

lithophyte, *n.* a calcareous polyp, as some corals; a plant that grows on stone.

lithosis, *n.* a disease of the lungs caused by tiny particles of stone; grinders' and stone-masons' disease. [Gr. *lithosis,* turning into stone]

lithosphere, *n.* the outer, rocky shell of the earth, the crust of the earth.

lithotint, *n.* a process of drawing and printing coloured pictures on lithographic stone; such a drawing.

lithotome, *n.* a natural stone so formed as to appear to have been cut artificially; an instrument used for cutting the bladder in lithotomy. **lithotomy**, *n.* the surgical removal of stone in the bladder. **lithotomic**, *a.* **lithotomist**, *n.* [Gr. *lithotomos,* stone-cutting (LITHO-, *tomos,* cutting, from *temnein,* to cut)]

lithotripsy LITHOTRITY.

lithotrity, lithotripsy, *n.* the operation of crushing stones in the bladder, kidney or gall-bladder to small fragments by means of instruments. **lithotripter, -triptor,** *n.* a device which uses ultrasound to crush kidney etc. stones without the need for surgery. **lithotritic, lithotriptic, lithontriptic**, *n., a.* a medicine that crushes stones in the bladder etc. [Gr. *tribein,* to rub]

lithotype, *n.* a stereotype made with shellac, sand, tar and linseed-oil, pressed hot on a plaster mould taken from type; an etched stone surface for printing; a machine for preparing a lithographic transfer-sheet. *v.t.* to prepare for printing by lithotypes. **lithotypy**, *n.* [LITHO-, TYPE]

Lithuania (Russian **Litovskaya**), *n.* constituent republic of the W USSR from 1940. **area** 65,200 sq km/ 25,300 sq miles. **capital** Vilnius. **towns** Kaunas, Klaipeda. **physical** river Niemen; 25% forested; lakes, marshes, and complex sandy coastline. **population** (1984) 3,500,000 million, 80% Lithuanian. **products** bacon, dairy products, cereals, potatoes, heavy engineering, electrical goods, cement. **religion** only Soviet republic that is predominantly Roman Catholic.

Lithuanian, *a.* pertaining to Lithuania. *n.* a native or inhabitant of Lithuania; the language of Lithuania. **Lithuanian language**, *n.* an Indo-European language spoken by the people of Lithuania that through its geographical isolation has retained many ancient features of the Indo-European language family. It acquired a written form in the 16th cent., using the Latin alphabet, and is currently spoken by some 3–4 million people.

litigate, *v.t.* to contest in a court of law. *v.i.* to go to law; to carry on a lawsuit. **litigable,** *a.* **litigant,** *n., a.* **litigation,** *n.* **litigious**, *a.* fond of litigation; quarrelsome, contentious; subject or open to legal dispute; pertaining to litigation. **litigiously,** *adv.* **litigiosity**, **litigiousness,** *n.* [L *lītigātus,* p.p. of *lītigāre,* from *līs, lītis,* lawsuit]

litmus, *n.* a substance obtained from *Roccella tinctoria* or other lichens, turned red by acids or blue by alkalis. **litmus-paper,** *n.* unsized paper stained with litmus, used to test the acidity or the alkaline nature of a solution. [of Scand. orig. rel. to ON *litmosi,* herbs used in dyeing, *litr,* colour, *musi,* moss]

litotes, *a.* (*Rhet.*) an understatement by which an affirmative is expressed by negation of its contrary, or a weaker expression used to suggest a stronger one, as, 'Something has happened to him', meaning 'He is dead.'. [Gr., from *lītos,* smooth, meagre]

litre,, (*esp. N Am.*) **liter** *n.* the unit of capacity in the metric system, equal to a cubic decimetre, or about $1\frac{3}{4}$ pints. [F, late L *lītra,* from Gr. *litra,* a pound]

LittD, LitD, (*abbr.*) Doctor of Letters, Doctor of Literature.

litter, *n.* a couch in which a person may be carried by animals or on men's shoulders. A stretcher used for transporting the sick or wounded; straw, hay or other soft material used as a bed for horses, cattle etc. or as a covering for plants; refuse, rubbish, odds and ends scattered about; hence, a state of disorder or untidiness; the young brought forth by a sow, bitch, cat etc. at one birth. *v.t.* to supply (beasts) with litter; to spread bedding for; to scatter (things) about carelessly; to make (a place) untidy with articles scattered about; to bring forth (said esp. of the sow, dog, cat etc., applied in contempt to human beings); †to carry in a litter. *v.i.* to bring forth a litter of young. **litter-bug, -lout,** *n.* (*coll.*) one who drops rubbish in public places. **littery,** *a.* [A-F *littere,* OF *litiere,* med. L *lectāria,* from *lectus,* bed]

littérateur, *n.* an author, professional writer. [F, from L *litterator -orem,* from *littera,* LETTER]

little, *a.* (*comp.* **less**), †**lesser,** (*coll.*) **littler,** *superl.* **least,** (*coll.*) **littlest**) small, not great or big in size, extent, amount or quantity; short in duration; short in distance; of small dignity, weight or importance; slight, inconsiderable, insignificant, petty; narrow, mean, contemptible, paltry; smaller than normal, diminutive, short in stature; young like a child, weak; (*coll.*) entitled to indulgence or forbearance, calling for amusement. *adv.* in a small degree; not much, slightly; not at all. *n.* a small amount, quantity, space, distance, time etc.; only a trifle. **by little and little, little by little,** by small degrees. **in little,** in miniature. **little or nothing,** scarcely anything. **make little of,** to treat as insignificant; to disparage. **not a little,** a great deal; extremely. **Little Bear** (*N Am.* **Little Dipper**), *n.* Ursa Minor. **Little Bighorn**, *n.* site in Montana, US, of Gen. George Custer's defeat by the Sioux Indians 25 June 1876 under chiefs Crazy Horse and Sitting Bull, known as Custer's last stand. **little-ease,** *n.* bodily discomfort; a form of punishment, as the pillory, the stocks or a cell too small for the inmate. **little-endian,** *n.* one of the political faction in Swift's *Gulliver's Travels* who maintained that eggs should be broken at the small end; one who disputes about trifles. **little Englander,** *n.* an opponent of British expansion overseas in the 19th cent. **Little Entente**, *n.* the name given to a series of alliances between Czechoslavakia, Romania and Yugoslavia (1920–21) for mutual security and the maintenance of existing frontiers. Reinforced by the Treaty of Belgrade 1929, the entente collapsed with Yugoslav co-operation with Germany 1935–38 and the Anglo-French abandonment of Czechslovakia 1938. **Little-go** GO[2]. **little people,** *n.pl.* the fairies. **little woman,** *n.* (*facet.*) one's wife. **littleness,** *n.* [OE *lȳtel, lytel,* cogn. the *lūtan,* to LOUT]

Littlewood, *n.* **Joan** (1914–), English theatre director. She was responsible for many vigorous productions at the Theatre Royal, Stratford (London) (1953–75), such as *A Taste of Honey* (1959), *The Hostage* (1959–60), and *Oh, What a Lovely War* (1963).

littoral, *a.* pertaining to the shore, esp. the zone between high- and low-water marks. *n.* a coastal region. [L *littorālis, lītorālis,* from *lītus -toris,* shore]

liturgy, *n.* a form of public worship, the entire ritual for public worship or the set of formularies in which this is set forth; the Mass, the formulary of the Eucharist; in ancient Greece, a public duty discharged at his own cost by a wealthy Athenian citizen in rotation, such as the building of a warship, production of a play etc. **liturgic,** *a.* liturgical, pertaining to a liturgy or liturgies. *n.pl.* the study or doctrine of liturgies. **liturgical,** *a.* **liturgically,** *adv.* **liturgiology**, *n.* the study of liturgy. **liturgiologist,** *n.* **liturgist,** *n.* [through F *liturgie* or directly from med. L *lītūrgia,* Gr. *leitourgia,* a public service, from *leitourgos* (*leitos,* public, *ergon,* work)]

Liu Shaoqi, *n.* (formerly **Liu Shao-chi**) (1898–1969), Chinese communist politician, in effective control of government 1960–65. A labour organizer, he was a firm proponent of the Soviet line of development based around disciplined one-party control, the use of incentive gradings, and priority for industry over agriculture. This was opposed by Mao Zedong, but began to be implemented when Liu was in power as state president 1960–65. In 1967, during the Cultural Revolution, Liu was brought down.

live[1], *a.* alive, living; burning, ignited; ready for use; charged with electricity (as a wire); unexploded (as a shell); full of energy, of present interest etc.; of a radio, television broadcast, transmitted at the actual time of an event, not a recording; relating to a living performance of a play, concert etc. as opposed to a film, or radio or television broadcast. **live axle,** *n.* driving shafts in back axle. **live-bait,** *n.* live fish, worms etc., used as bait in fishing. *v.t.* to fish with this. **live-box,** *n.* a case in which living microscopic objects are confined for observation. **live-cartridge,** *n.* one containing a bullet. **live feathers, hair etc.** *n.* feathers, hair etc., plucked from a living fowl or animal. **live-oak,** *n.* a N American evergreen tree, esp. *Quercus virens,* valuable for shipbuilding. **live rail,** *n.* a rail charged with an electric current. **livestock,** *n.* animals kept for farming or domestic purposes. **live wire,** *n.* a wire through which an electric current is flowing; (*coll.*) an energetic person. **liven,** *v.t.* to make lively, to enliven. *v.i.* to cheer (up). [ALIVE]

live², *v.i.* to have life; to be alive; to exist in such a way as to be capable of performing the animal or vegetable functions; to continue in life or as in life; to remain in operation or as an active principle; to reside, to dwell (at, in etc.); to be nourished, to subsist (upon); to depend for subsistence (upon); to receive or gain a livelihood (by); to pass or conduct one's life in a particular condition, manner etc.; to live strenuously, to enjoy life intensely; to continue alive, to survive. *v.t.* to pass, to spend (a specified kind of life); to remain alive through; to survive; to manifest, express, or effect, by living. **live and let live,** to wink at the deficiencies of others in return for indulgence of one's own. **to live down,** to falsify or efface the recollection of (scandal etc.) by one's conduct. **to live in, out,** to reside or not at one's place of work. **to live it up,** (*coll.*) to live extravagantly, to excess. **to live together,** to cohabit. **to live up to,** to be worthy of, to conform to a prescribed standard. **to live with,** to cohabit; to accept or tolerate. **liveable,** *a.* worth living (of life); fit to live in; fit to live with. **liveablenss,** *n.* **lived,** *a. in comb.* as *long-lived.* **liver,** *n.* one who lives; a resident, a dweller; one who spends his life in a specified way (as a *good liver*). [OE *lifian, libban* (cp. Dut. *leven,* Icel. *lifa,* G *leben*), cogn, with LIFE]

livelihood, *n.* means of subsistence. [OE *līflād,* (LIFE, *lād,* course, cogn. with LOAD and LODE)]

livelong, *a.* long-lasting; the whole, entire, the whole length of. [orig. *lief-long* (LIEF, LONG¹)]

lively, *a.* life-like, actual, vivid; full of life, brisk, active, vigorous; animated, vivacious, bright; striking, forcible, exciting. **livelily,** *adv.* **liveliness,** *n.* [OE *liflīc*]

liven LIVE¹.

liver¹ LIVE².

liver², *n.* a glandular organ in the abdominal cavity of vertebrates which secretes the bile and purifies the blood; the flesh of this from a sheep, calf etc., used as food; (*coll.*) a distorted liver; applied to certain liver-coloured sulphides or other compounds of specified elements. *a.* liver-coloured. **liver-colour,** *n.* the colour of the liver; a reddish-brown. **liver-coloured,** *a.* **liver-complaint,** *n.* a disordered state of the liver. **liver-fluke,** *n.* a parasitic worm causing disease in the human liver. **liver-grown,** *a.* having an enlarged liver. **liver-leaf,** *n.* (*N Am.*) one of the Hepaticae or anemones. **liver salts,** *n.pl.* a preparation of mineral salts used to relieve indigestion. **liver sausage, liverwurst,** *n.* sausage made from liver. **liver spot,** *n.* a liver-coloured spot which appears on the skin in old age. **liver-vein,** *n.* (*Shak.*) the way of a man in love. **liver-wing,** *n.* the right wing of a cooked fowl; (*facet.*) the right arm. **liverwort,** *n.* (*Bot.*) any plant of the Hepaticae family, cryptogamic plants. **livered,** *a. in comb.*, as *white-livered,* cowardly. **liverish,** *a.* having a disordered liver; irritable. [OE *lifer* (cp. Dut. *lever,* Icel. *lifr,* G *Leber*)]

liver³, *n.* a fabulous bird, supposed to have given its name to Liverpool, and still commemorated in the arms of that town. [from *Liverpool*]

Livermore Valley, *n.* valley in California, US, site of the Lawrence Livermore Laboratory. Part of the University of California, it shares with Los Alamos Laboratory, New Mexico, all US military research into nuclear warheads and atomic explosives. It also conducts research into nuclear fusion, using high-integrity lasers.

Liverpool¹, *n.* **Robert Banks Jenkinson, 2nd Earl Liverpool** (1770–1825), British Tory politician. He entered Parliament 1790, and was foreign secretary 1801–03, home secretary 1804–06 and 1807–09, war minister 1809–12, and prime minister 1812–27. His government conducted the Napoleonic Wars to a successful conclusion, but its ruthless suppression of freedom of speech and of the press aroused such opposition that during 1815–20 revolution frequently seemed imminent.

Liverpool², *n.* city, seaport, and administrative headquarters of Merseyside, NW England; population (1984) 497,300. In the 19th and early 20th cent., it exported the textiles of Lancashire and Yorkshire, and is the UK's chief Atlantic port with miles of specialized, mechanized quays on the river Mersey.

Liverpudlian, *n.* a native or inhabitant of Liverpool. [*Liverpool* (with PUDDLE, for POOL), -IAN]

livery, *n.* a distinctive dress worn by the servants of a particular person or the members of a city company, orig. a ration or allowance of clothing, food etc. to retainers of a baron or knight; any distinctive dress, guise or outward appearance; the privileges of a city company or guild; (*Law*) delivery of property; a writ granting possession; †allowance for keeping and feeding a horse. †*v.t.* to dress or clothe in or as in livery. **at livery,** kept at a stable for the owner at a fixed charge. **livery company,** *n.* one of the guilds or companies of the City of London that formerly had a distinctive costume. **liveryman,** *n.* one who wears a livery (as a footman etc.); a freeman of the City of London, who is entitled to wear the livery of the company to which he belongs and to vote in the election of Lord Mayor, sheriffs, chamberlain etc. **livery-servant,** *n.* a servant wearing a livery. **livery-stable,** *n.* a stable where horses are kept for owners at livery or let out on hire. **liveried,** *a.* [A-F *liveré,* OF *livrée,* fem. p.p. of *livrer,* late L *līberāre,* to give, to DELIVER]

Livia Drusilla, *n.* (58 BC–AD 29), Roman empress, wife of Augustus from 39 BC, she was the mother by her first husband of Tiberius and engaged in intrigue to secure his succession to the imperial crown. She remained politically active to the end of her life.

livid, *a.* of a leaden colour; black and blue, discoloured (as by a bruise); (*coll.*) furious, very angry. **lividity,** †**lividness,** *n.* **lividly,** *adv.* [L *līvidus*]

living, *a.* alive, having life; flowing, running; in a state of combustion; vivifying, quickening; operative, active, efficient; alive now, existing, contemporary; true to life, exact (of a portrait). *n.* the state of being alive, existence; livelihood, the power of continuing life; the benefice of a clergyman; manner of life. **living death,** *n.* a life of unmitigated suffering. **living rock,** *n.* rock in its native state or location (prob. from the obs. idea that rock grows). **living-room,** *n.* a family sitting-room. **living wage,** *n.* the lowest wage on which it is possible to maintain oneself and family. †**livingly,** *adv.* [LIVE², -ING]

Livingston, *n.* industrial new town (electronics, engineering) in W Lothian, Scotland, established 1962; population (1985) 40,000.

Livingstone¹, *n.* **David** (1813–1873), Scottish missionary explorer. In 1841, he went to Africa, reached Lake Ngami 1849, followed the Zambezi to its mouth, saw the Victoria Falls 1855, and went to East and Central Africa 1858–64, reaching Lakes Shirwa and Malawi. From 1866, he tried to find the source of the river Nile, and reached Ujiji Oct 1871.

Livingstone², *n.* **Ken(neth)** (1945–), British left-wing Labour politician. He was leader of the Greater London Council (GLC) 1981–86 and a member of Parliament from 1987.

Livonia, *n.* former region in Europe on the E coast of the Baltic Sea comprising most of present-day Latvia and Estonia. Conquered and converted to Christianity in the early 13th cent. by the Livonian Knights, a crusading order, Livonia was independent until 1583, when it was divided between Poland and Sweden. In 1710 it was occupied by Russia, and in 1721 was ceded to Peter the Great.

livre, *n.* an old French coin, replaced by the franc in 1795. [F, from L LIBRA]

Livy, *n.* **Titus Livius** (59 BC–AD 17), Roman historian, author of a *History of Rome* from the city's foundation to 9 BC, based partly on legend. It was composed of 142 books, of which 35 survive, covering the periods from the arrival of Aeneas in Italy to 293 BC and from 218–167 BC.

Li Xiannian, *n.* (1905–), Chinese politician, member of the Chinese Communist Party (CCP) Politburo from 1956. He fell from favour during the 1966–69 Cultural

Revolution, but was rehabilitated as finance minister 1973, supporting cautious economic reform. Li was state president 1983–88.

lixiviate, *v.t.* to leach, to dissolve out by lixiviation; to impregnate with salts by lixiviation. †**lixivial, -ious,** *a.* †**lixiviate,** *n., a.* **lixiviation,** *n.* the process of separating a soluble from an insoluble material by a washing or filtering action; leaching. **lixivium,** *n.* water impregnated with alkaline salts from wood-ash. [from mod. L *lixīviāre,* from *lixīvium,* neut. adj., from *lix,* ashes, lye]

lizard, *n.* any member of the reptilian order Lacertilia, esp. of the typical genus *Lacerta,* having a long, scaly body and tail, and four limbs, each with five toes of unequal length. **lizard-stone,** *n.* a variety of serpentine found in the Lizard peninsula in Cornwall. [OF *lesard,* L *lacerta -tus*]

Lizard Point, *n.* most southerly point of England in Cornwall. The coast is broken into small bays overlooked by two cliff lighthouses.

LJ, (*abbr.*) Lord Justice.

Ljubljana, *n.* (German **Laibach**) capital and industrial city (textiles, chemicals, paper, leather goods) of Slovenia, Yugoslavia; population (1981) 305,200. It has a nuclear research centre and is linked with S Austria by the Karawanken road tunnel under the Alps (1979–83).

LL, (*abbr.*) Late Latin; Low Latin; Lord-Lieutenant.

ll., (*abbr.*) of print, lines.

llama, *n.* a domesticated Peruvian wool-bearing animal, *Lama glama,* resembling a camel, but humpless and smaller, used as a beast of burden; its wool, material made from this. [Sp., from Peruv.]

llano, *n.* a level, treeless steppe or plain in the northern part of S America. **llanero,** *n.* one who lives on the llanos of S America. [Sp., from L *plānum,* PLAIN¹]

LLB, (*abbr.*) Bachelor of Laws. [L *Legum Baccalaureus*]

LLD, (*abbr.*) Doctor of Laws. [L *Legum Doctor*]

Llewellyn, *n.* **Richard** (1907–1983), pen name of Richard Vivian Llewellyn Lloyd. Welsh writer. *How Green Was My Valley* 1939, a novel about a S Wales mining family, was made into a play and a film.

Llewelyn I, *n.* (1173–1240), King of Wales from 1194, who extended his rule to all Wales not in Norman hands, driving the English from N Wales 1212, and taking Shrewsbury 1215. During the early part of Henry III's reign, he was several times attacked by English armies. He was married to Joanna, illegitimate daughter of King John.

Llewelyn II, *n.* (*c.* 1225–1282), King of Wales from 1246, grandson of Llewelyn I. In 1277 Edward I of England compelled Llewelyn to acknowledge him as overlord and to surrender S Wales. His death while leading a national uprising ended Welsh independence.

LLM, (*abbr.*) Master of Laws. [L *Legum Magister*]

Lloyd, Selwyn SELWYN LLOYD.

Lloyd George, *n.* **David** (1863–1945), Welsh Liberal politician, prime minister 1916–22. A pioneer of social reform, as chancellor of the Exchequer 1908–15 he introduced old-age pensions 1908 and health and unemployment insurance 1911. High unemployment, intervention in the Russian Civil War, and use of the Black and Tans in Ireland eroded his support as prime minister, and creation of the Irish Free State 1921, and his pro-Greek policy against the Turks caused the collapse of his coalition government.

Lloyd's, *n.* a corporation, having offices at the Royal Exchange, dealing with marine insurance, the classification and registration of vessels etc. **Lloyd's List,** *n.* a newspaper, orig. started by Edward Lloyd in 1696 as **Lloyd's News,** devoted to maritime intelligence. **Lloyd's Register,** *n.* an annual alphabetical list of shipping belonging to all nations, classified according to seaworthiness. [Edward *Lloyd,* who kept a coffee-house frequented by shippers in the 17th cent.]

Lloyd Webber, *n.* **Andrew** (1948–), English composer. His early musicals, with lyrics by Tim Rice, include *Joseph and the Amazing Technicolor Dreamcoat* (1968); *Jesus Christ Superstar* (1970); and *Evita* (1978), based on the life of the Argentinian leader Eva Perón. He also wrote *Cats* (1981), *The Phantom of the Opera* (1986), and *Aspects of Love* (1989).

Llull, *n.* **Ramon** (1232–1316), Catalan scholar and mystic. In 1262, he became a monk and later a missionary in N Africa and Asia. He produced treatises on theology, mysticism, and chivalry in Catalan, Latin, and Arabic. His *Ars Magna* is one of the greatest medieval encyclopedias.

lm, (*symbol*) lumen.

lo, *int.* See! Behold! Observe! [OE *lā,* perh. blended with ME *lo,* short for loke, OE *lōca,* LOOK]

loach, *n.* any of the Cobitidae, a group of the carp family, esp. *Nemachilus barbatulus,* a small British river-fish. [F *loche,* etym. unknown]

load, *n.* a burden; that which is laid on or put in anything for conveyance; as much as can be carried at a time; hence, a measure of weight varying according to the material carried; that which is borne with difficulty; that which presses upon, obstructs or resists; the downward pressure of a superstructure; the resistance to an engine or motor apart from friction; the power output of a machine, circuit etc.; a device which receives power; any mental burden; (*coll., pl.*) heaps, lots, any amount. *v.t.* to put a load upon or in; to put (a load or cargo) on or in a ship, vehicle etc.; to add weight to, to make heavy or heavier, to weight; to weigh down, to encumber, to oppress; to charge (a gun etc.); to put a film, cartridge etc. in a camera; to fill to overflowing; to cover, to heap or overwhelm (with abuse, honours etc.); to adulterate, esp. with something to increase strength or weight; to add charges to an insurance premium; (*Comput.*) to transfer a programme into the memory, usu. from tape or disk. *v.i.* to take in a load or cargo (usu. with *up*); to charge a firearm. **to get a load of,** (*sl.*) to listen to, pay attention to. **to have a load on,** (*sl.*) to be drunk. **to load the dice against someone,** (*fig.*) to prejudice someone's chances of success. **load-displacement, -draught, -line,** *n.* a ship's displacement when fully loaded, or the line to which she sinks. **loaded,** *a.* biased, weighted in a certain direction; likely to cause argument; (*coll.*) wealthy; (*sl.*) drunk or drugged. **loaded dice,** *n.pl.* dice so weighted that they fall with a required face up. **loaded question,** *n.* a question with hidden implications designed to trap the answerer. **loader,** *n.* one who or that which loads; a person employed to load a sportsman's gun; a loading-machine; *in comb.,* as *breech-* or *muzzle-loader.* **loading,** *n.* a load, a burden; also *in comb.,* as *breech-loading.* **loading-coil,** *n.* an extra coil inserted in an electrical circuit to increase the inductance. **loading-gauge,** *n.* a gauge indicating the height to which railway-trucks can be loaded so that they can pass bridges and tunnels safely. [OE *lād,* way, course, cogn. with LEAD² and LODE]

loadsa, *n.* (*sl.*) short for *a load of;* also *comb. form,* e.g. *loadsamoney.*

loadstar, LODESTAR under LODE.

loadstone, LODESTONE.

loaf¹, *n.* (*pl.* **loaves**) a shaped mass of bread, esp. of a standard size or weight; a moulded mass of any material, esp. a conical mass of refined sugar; the head of a cabbage or lettuce; (*sl.*) the head or brains. **loaf-sugar,** *n.* **sugar-loaf,** *n.* **loaves and fishes,** personal gains, material benefits, as an inducement in religious profession or public service. [OE *hlāf* (cp. Icel. *hleifr,* G *Leib*)]

loaf², *v.i.* to lounge or idle about. *v.t.* to spend or pass (time away) idly. *n.* a saunter, an idle time, a loafing. **loafer,** *n.* one who loafs, an idler; a low leather shoe similar to a moccasin. [etym. doubtful]

loam, *n.* soil consisting of sand and clay loosely coherent, with admixture of organic matter or humus; in brickmaking etc., a mixture of sand and clay with chopped straw, used for making moulds. *v.t.* to cover with loam. **loamy,** *a.* **loaminess,** *n.* [OE *lām* (cp. Dut. *leem,* G *Lehm*) cogn. with *līm,* LIME]

loan, *n.* the act of lending; the state of being lent; that which is lent, esp. a sum of money lent at interest;

permission to make use of; a word, myth, custom etc., adopted from another people. *v.t.* to grant the loan of. **loan-collection,** *n.* a set of pictures etc. lent by the owners for public exhibition. **loan-office,** *n.* an office where loans are negotiated; an office for receiving subscriptions to a public loan; a pawn-shop. **loan shark,** *n.* (*coll.*) one who lends money at excessive or illegal interest rates. **loan-society,** *n.* a society lending money to members who repay by instalments. **loan translation,** *n.* a compound word or phrase which is a literal translation of the corresponding elements of a foreign expression (e.g. *Superman* from G *Übermensch*), also called a CALQUE. **loan-word,** *n.* a word borrowed from another language. **loanable,** *a.* **loanee,** *n.* **loaner,** *n.* [OE *lān,* (cp. Dut. *leen,* Icel. *lān,* G *Lehn*), cogn. with *leōn,* to lend, also with Gr. *leipein,* L *linquere,* to leave]

loath, loth, *a.* unwilling, averse, reluctant. **nothing loath,** quite willing; willingly. **loathness,** *n.* unwillingness, reluctance. [OE *lāth* (cp. Dut. *leed,* Icel. *leithr*), cogn. with G *Leid,* sorrow]

loathe, *v.t.* to feel disgust at; to abhor, to detest. *v.i.* to feel disgust (at). **loather,** *n.* †**loathful,** *a.* full of loathing, disgusting; (*Sc.*) reluctant, bashful. †**loathfully,** *adv.* **loathfulness,** *n.* **loathing,** *a.* abhorring. *n.* disgust, aversion, abhorrence. **loathingly,** *adv.* †**loathly,** *a.* creating loathing, loathsome. †*adv.* unwillingly. †**loathliness,** *n.* **loathsome,** *a.* causing loathing or disgust; odious, detestable. **loathsomely,** *adv.* **loathsomeness,** *n.* [OE *lathian,* from prec.]

loave, *v.i.* to expand into a head (of cabbages etc.). [LOAF[1]]

loaves, LOAF[1].

lob, *n.* a heavy, dull, stupid fellow; anything thick and heavy; (*Cricket*) a slow underhand ball; (*Lawn-tennis*) a ball pitched high into the air. *v.t.* (*past, p.p.* **lobbed**) †to hang or allow to droop heavily; (*Cricket or Lawn-tennis*) to bowl a lob. *v.i.* to make a lob. [etym. doubtful, perh. onomat.]

lobar, lobate LOBE.

lobby, *n.* (*pl.* **-bbies**) a passage, corridor or vestibule, usu. opening into several apartments; a small hall or ante-room; that part of a hall of a legislative assembly to which the public are admitted; also one of two corridors to which members go to vote (also **division lobby**); a group of people who try to influence legislators on behalf of special interests. *v.i.* to solicit the votes of members. *v.t.* to influence or solicit (members); to secure the passage of (a Bill) by lobbying. **lobby correspondent,** *n.* a reporter who covers parliamentary affairs. **lobby-member,** *n.* a person who frequents the lobbies of a legislative assembly to solicit the votes of members. **lobby system,** *n.* the system which allows correspondents access to political information on condition that the source remains anonymous. **lobbyist,** *n.* [low L *lobia,* LODGE]

lobe, *n.* any rounded and projecting or hanging part; a division of a bodily organ; the soft lower part of the ear; a rounded division of a leaf. **lobar, lobate,** *a.* **lobed,** *a.* **lobelet.** [F, from late L *lobus,* Gr. *lobos,* lobe or pod. cogn. with L *legūmen,* LEGUME, cp. *legula,* lobe of ear]

lobectomy, *n.* (*pl.* **-mies**) the surgical removal of a lobe from an organ or gland.

lobelia, *n.* a genus of herbaceous and brilliant flowering plants. [Matthias de *Lobel,* 1538–1616, botanist]

loblolly, *n.* thick gruel; a name for various US pine trees. **loblolly man, boy,** *n.* a man or boy who attends on the ship's surgeon. [etym. doubtful]

lob(o)- *comb. form* pertaining to a lobe. [see LOBE]

lobotomy, *n.* a surgical incision into the lobe of an organ or gland; an operation in which the fibres connecting the frontal lobes of the brain to the rest of the brain are cut; formerly used in the treatment of severe depression. **lobotomize, -ise,** *v.t.* to perform a lobotomy on; (*coll.*) to render dull or harmless.

lobscouse, *n.* (*Naut.*) a hash of meat with vegetables of various kinds and ship's biscuit. [G *labskaus*]

lobster, *n.* a large marine long-tailed and stalk-eyed decapod crustacean of the genus *Homarus,* esteemed for food; (*sl.*) a British soldier, orig. one of a regiment of Cromwell's cuirassiers. **lobster-pot,** *n.* a wickerwork trap for lobsters. [OE *loppestre,* corr. of L *locusta,* LOCUST]

lobule, *n.* (a subdivision of) a small lobe. **lobular, lobulated,** *a.*

lobworm, *n.* a large earthworm, used as bait by anglers; a lugworm.

local, *a.* of or pertaining to a place; pertaining to, existing in or peculiar to a particular place or places; pertaining to a part, not the whole (as a disease etc.); (*Math.*) of or pertaining to a *locus. n.* an inhabitant of a particular place; a professional person practising there; a train serving a suburban district; an examination held in a provincial centre; a postage-stamp valid in certain districts; an item of local news; a public-house; locale. **local anaesthesia,** *n.* anaesthesia affecting only a particular area of the body and not involving general unconsciousness. **local anaesthetic,** *n.* **local authorities,** *n.pl.* the elected bodies which administer local government, district councils. **local colour,** *n.* features characteristic of a place or district emphasized in a literary work in order to promote actuality; (*Painting*) the colour of individual objects considered apart from the general colour-scheme. **local government,** *n.* administration of towns, districts etc. by elective councils; decentralization, opp. to centralization. **Local Group,** *n.* in astronomy, a cluster of about three dozen galaxies that includes our own. Like other groups of galaxies, the Local Group is held together by the gravitational attraction among its members, and does not expand with the expanding Universe. **local time,** *n.* time calculated on the noon of the meridian of a place, as against standard time. **locale, local,** the scene or locality of an event etc. **localism,** *n.* the state of being local; affection for a place; limitations due to confinement to a place, provincialism; a local idiom, custom etc. **locality,** *n.* particular place or region, site, geographical position; existence in a certain portion of space; limitation to a place. **localize, -ise,** *v.t.* to make local; to ascertain or indicate the exact place or locality of; to identify with a place; to restrict to a particular place; to decentralize; to concentrate (attention) upon. **localizable, -isable,** *a.* **localization, -isation,** *n.* **locally,** *adv.* [F, from L *locālis,* from *locus,* place]

Locarno, Pact of, a series of diplomatic documents initialled in Locarno 16 Oct 1925 and formally signed in London 1 Dec 1925. The pact settled the question of French security, and the signatories – Britain, France, Belgium, Italy, and Germany – guaranteed the existing frontiers between Germany and France, and Germany and Belgium. The prime mover in the pact was British foreign secretary Austen Chamberlain. Following the signing of the pact, Germany was admitted to the League of Nations.

locate, *v.t.* to set or place in a particular locality; (*in p.p.*) to situate; to discover or determine the site of; to settle, to take up residence. **location,** *n.* situation or position; a tract of land marked out, a place of settlement or residence; (*Cinema*) a site outside the studio grounds where a scene is shot; (*Comput.*) a specific area in memory capable of holding a unit of information, e.g. a word. **on location,** outside the studio (of filming etc.). **locative,** *a.* (*Gram.*) denoting place. *n.* a case denoting place. [from L *locus,* place]

loc. cit., (*abbr.*) loco citato. [L, in the place cited]

loch, *n.* a lake, a narrow or land-locked arm of the sea in Scotland. **lochan,** *n.* a small lake, a tarn; a pond. [Gael.]

lochia, *n.pl.* the uterine evacuations which follow childbirth. **lochial,** *a.* [Gr., from *lochos,* a childbed]

Lochner, *n.* **Stephan** (d. 1451), German painter, active in Cologne, a master of the International Gothic style. Most of his work is still in Cologne, for example the *Virgin in the Rose Garden* (Wallraf-Richartz Museum).

Loch Ness, *n.* lake in Highland region, Scotland, forming part of the Caledonian Canal; 36 km/22.5 miles long, 229m/754 ft deep. There have been unconfirmed reports of a Loch Ness monster since the 15th cent.

loci, *pl.* of LOCUS.

lock[1], *n.* a device for fastening doors etc., usu. having a bolt moved by a key of a particular shape; a mechanical device for checking or preventing movement, as of a carriage-wheel; the firing-apparatus of a gun; an enclosure in a canal, between gates, for raising and lowering vessels by the introduction or liberation of water; an air-tight antechamber to a caisson or tunnel; the oblique position of a fore-axle to a rear-axle in turning; (*fig.*) a fastening together or interlocking; a block, a jam; a hug or grapple in wrestling; in Rugby, a player in the second row of a scrum (**lock forward**). *v.t.* to fasten with a lock; to shut (up a house, box, contents of these etc.) thus; to prevent passage (in, out etc.) by fastening doors etc. with locks; to shut (in), enclose or hem (in); to bind or fix together, to fasten by means of mechanism or parts that engage together; (*in p.p.*) to embrace, to tangle together; to furnish with locks (as a canal); to seize the sword-arm of and disarm (an antagonist) in fencing. *v.i.* to become fastened by or as by a lock; to intertwine. **lock, stock and barrel,** the whole lot. **to lock on (to),** to track automatically (an object) by means of a radar beam or sensor. **to lock up, in, away,** to close, fasten or secure with lock and key; to invest (money) so that it cannot be readily realized; (*fig.*) to make unavailable. **lock-chain,** *n.* one for locking the wheels of a vehicle. **lock-fast,** *n.* secured by a lock. **lock-gate,** *n.* the gate of a canal-lock. **lock hospital,** *n.* a hospital for the treatment of venereal diseases, (orig. a hospital in Southwark, London). **lockjaw,** *n.* a symptom of tetanus in which the muscles of the jaw are violently contracted and its motion suspended; tetanus. **lock-keeper,** *n.* one who attends to a canal-lock. **lockman,** *n.* (*Isle of Man*) an officer corresponding to sheriff. **lock-nut,** *n.* a check-nut screwed over another. **lock-out,** *n.* the temporary discharge of workers by employers to bring them to terms. *v.t.* to try to coerce workers by closing a works or factory. **lock-paddle,** *n.* a sluice for filling and emptying a lock-chamber. **lock-sill,** *n.* a piece of timber at the bottom of a canal-lock, against which the gates shut. **locksman,** *n.* a lock-keeper. **locksmith,** *n.* a maker and repairer of locks. **lock-spring,** *n.* a spring for closing a watch-case. **lock-stitch,** *n.* a sewing-machine stitch which locks two threads together. **lock-up,** *n.* a place where prisoners are temporarily confined; time for locking up; a small garage; the investing of capital in such a way that it cannot be realized; the amount so invested. *a.* that may be locked. **lock-up shop,** *n.* shop having access only from the street, with no connection with the rest of the building. **lockage,** *n.* the works of a canal-lock; the rise and fall in a canal through the working of locks; a toll for passing through locks. [OE *loc* (cp. Icel. *loka,* lock, *lok,* lid, G *Loch*)]

lock[2], *n.* a tuft of hair, wool or similar substance; a tress, ringlet; a love-lock; (*pl.*) hair. [OE *locc* (cp. Dut. *lok,* Icel. *lokkr,* G *Locke*), cogn. with Gr. *lugos,* a withy, and *lugizein,* to bend]

lockage LOCK[1].

Locke, *n.* **John** (1632–1704), English philosopher. His *Essay concerning Human Understanding* (1690) maintained that experience was the only source of knowledge (empiricism), and that 'we can have knowlege no farther than we have ideas' prompted by such experience. *Two Treatises on Government* (1690) was influential in forming modern ideas of liberal democracy. **Lockian,** *a.* characteristic of the teaching of Locke or his followers. **Lockist,** *n.*

locker, *n.* one who or that which locks; a cupboard, chest or other closed receptacle, with lock and key; a chest or compartment on a ship for locking up stores etc. **not a shot in one's locker,** (having) no money in one's pocket. **locker room,** *n.* a room with lockers for storing clothes and other belongings.

locket, *n.* a small gold or silver case, worn as an ornament and adapted to contain hair, a miniature etc.; a plate or band on a scabbard to which the hook is fastened. [F *loquet,* dim. of OF *loc,* latch, from Teut. (cp. Icel. *loka,* LOCK[1])]

lockjaw LOCK[1].

†**lockram,** *n.* a coarse linen cloth. [F *locrenan,* from *Locronan,* Brittany, where orig. made]

loco[1], *n.* short for LOCOMOTIVE.

loco[2], *a.* (*esp N Am. sl.*) insane, mad; affected with loco disease. *n.* (also **loco-plant, -weed**) any of several leguminous plants of NW America which cause loco disease in livestock when ingested. **loco disease,** *n.* a disease of cattle, sheep and horses, affecting the brain and characterized by paralysis of the limbs and impaired vision and caused by the ingestion of locoweed. [Sp., insane]

locomobile, *a.* able to change place. *n.* a locomotive vehicle. **locomobility,** *n.*

locomotion, *n.* the act or power of moving from place to place; moving about, travel, travelling. **locomote,** *v.i.* to move from one place to another. **locomotive,** *a.* of or pertaining to locomotion; moving from place to place, not stationary; having the power of locomotion, or causing locomotion; pertaining to travel. *n.* a self-propelling machine, esp. a railway engine; an animal capable of locomotion. **locomotively,** *adv.* **locomotivity**, **locomotiveness,** *n.* **locomotor,** *a.* of or pertaining to locomotion. *n.* one who or that which is capable of locomotion. **locomotor ataxy** *n.* a nervous disorder characterized by inability to coordinate the movements of the limbs; constitutional unsteadiness in the use of the limbs. **locomotory,** *a.* [L *locō,* abl. of *locus,* place, MOTION]

loculus, *n.* (*pl.* **-li**) a small cavity, a cell; a separate chamber or cell in a large tomb; (*Biol. etc.*) one of numerous cavities in various organisms. **loculament,** *n.* one of the cells of a seed-vessel. **locular, loculate,** *a.* [L, dim. of LOCUS]

locum, locum tenens, *n.* (*pl.* **-tenentes**), a deputy or substitute, esp. one acting in the place of a doctor or clergyman. **locum-tenency**, *n.* [L, holding place (see foll.)]

locus, *n.* (*pl.* **-ci**) the exact place, the locality (of); (*Math.*) the line generated by a point, or the surface generated by a line, moving according to specified conditions; the location of a particular gene on a chromosome. **locus citatus**, the passage quoted. **locus classicus**, the best or most authoritative passage quoted as an instance or illustration. **locus in quo**, the scene of some event. **locus poenitentiae**, (*Law*) an opportunity for withdrawing at an early stage. **locus standi**, recognized place or position authorizing intervention, application to a court etc. [L]

locust, *n.* a winged insect of various species allied to the grasshopper, which migrates in vast swarms and is very destructive to vegetation; applied to certain US and Australian grasshoppers; a locust-tree. **locust-bean,** *n.* the sweet pod of the carob. **locust-bird, -eater,** *n.* one of various species of birds that feed on locusts. **locust-tree,** the carob; the N American acacia, *Robinia pseudacacia;* applied to various W Indian trees. [L *locusta,* lobster, locust]

locution, *n.* style of speech, mode of delivery; a phrase or expression considered with regard to style or idiom. **locutor**, *n.* a spokesman. [L *locūtio,* from *loquī,* to speak]

locutory, *n.* a conversation-room or parlour in a monastery; a grille at which inmates and visitors might converse. [med. L *locūtōrium,* from L *locūtor,* see prec.]

lode, *n.* an open ditch or watercourse for draining; a reach of water in a canal; a vein bearing metal. **lodestar,** *n.* a guiding star or one that is steered by, usu. the pole-star; one's aim, ambition or guiding principle. **lodestone,** *n.* magnetic oxide of iron, a natural magnet; something that attracts. [OE *lād,* see LOAD]

loden, *n.* a thick soft waterproof woollen cloth used for making coats; a greyish-green colour typical of this cloth. [G, from OHG *liodo,* thick cloth]

Lodge[1], *n.* **David (John)** (1935–   ), British novelist, short story writer, and critic. Much of his fiction concerns the role of Catholicism in mid-20th-cent. England, exploring the situation both through broad comedy and parody, as in *The British Museum is Falling Down* (1967), and realistically, as in *How Far Can You Go?* (1980).

Lodge[2], *n.* **Henry Cabot** (1850–1924), US historian, Republican senator from 1893, and chairman of the Senate Foreign Relations Committee after World War I, who influenced the US to stay out of the League of Nations 1920.

lodge, *n.* a temporary residence; a cottage, a hut, a cabin, a small house in a park; a gate-keeper's or gardener's cottage; a small house attached or pertaining to a larger; a room or apartment for a porter in a college, chambers etc.; (*Freemasonry etc.*) a local branch or place of meeting of certain societies; a beaver's or otter's lair; a N Am. Indian wigwam, the family that lives in it. *v.t.* to supply with temporary quarters, esp. for sleeping; to receive as an inmate, usu. for a fixed charge; to entertain as a guest; to establish in temporary or permanent quarters; to accommodate with rooms etc.; to deposit, to leave for security (in, with etc.); to deposit in court or with a prosecuting officer (as a complaint); to implant, to fix; to beat down (crops, of wind). *v.i.* to reside temporarily, esp. to have sleeping quarters; to reside as an inmate at a fixed charge; to stay or become fixed (in); of crops, to be laid flat. **lodger,** *n.* one who rents and occupies furnished rooms. **lodging,** *n.* a temporary residence; a room or rooms hired in another's house (*usu. in pl.*). **lodging-house,** *n.* **lodgement,** *n.* the act of lodging; the state of being lodged; an accumulation of matter that remains at rest, a deposit; an entrenchment hastily constructed to defend captured enemy territory; (*fig.*) a position, advantage or foothold secured. [OF *loge,* low L *lobia,* LOBBY, from Teut. (cp. OHG *louba,* G *Laube,* cogn. with *laub,* LEAF)]

Łódź, *n.* industrial town (textiles, machinery, dyes) in central Poland, 120 km/75 miles SW of Warsaw; population (1984) 849,000.

loess, *n.* a deposit of clay, loam, sand etc., in the Rhine, Mississippi and other river-valleys. [G *Löss*]

Loewe, *n.* **Frederick** (1901–1988), US composer of musicals, born in Berlin. Son of an operatic tenor, he studied under Busoni, and in 1924 went with his father to the US. In 1942 he joined forces with the lyricist Alan Jay Lerner (1918–86), and their joint successes include *Brigadoon* (1947), *Paint Your Wagon* (1951), *My Fair Lady* (1956), *Gigi* (1958), and *Camelot* (1960).

Loewi, *n.* **Otto** (1873–1961), German physiologist, whose work on the nervous system established that a chemical substance is responsible for the stimulation of one neurone by another.

loft, *n.* the room or air space under a roof; an elevated gallery in a church or hall; a room over a barn or stable; a pigeon-house, hence, a flock of pigeons; (*Golf*) a backward inclination of the face of a club, a lofting stroke. *v.t.* to strike (the ball) so that it rises high in the air; to provide (pigeons) with a loft. **lofter,** *n.* (*Golf*) a club for lofting. **lofty,** *a.* very high, towering, of imposing height; elevated in character, sentiment, style etc., sublime; high-flown, grandiose; haughty, arrogant. **loftily,** *adv.* **loftiness,** *n.* [Icel. *lopt* (pronun. loft), orig. the sky (cp. LIFT[1])]

Lofting, *n.* **Hugh** (1886–1947), English writer and illustrator of children's books, especially the 'Dr Dolittle' series, in which the hero can talk to animals. Lofting was born in Maidenhead, Berkshire, was originally a civil engineer, and went to the US 1912.

log[1], *n.* a bulky piece of unhewn timber; a block; a device (orig. a piece of wood with a line attached) used for ascertaining the rate of a ship's motion; a detailed record of the voyage of a ship or flight of an aircraft; a log-book; any record of performance; a dolt, a blockhead. *v.t.* (*past, p.p.* **logged**) to cut into logs; to enter in the log-book; to make (a specified distance) by the log (of a ship etc.). **to log on,** to identify oneself to a computer system in order to gain access to files; (*coll.*) to begin work etc., **to log off,** to close computer files at the end of a session of work; (*coll.*) to finish work etc. **to sleep like a log,** to be in a deep sleep. **log-book,** *n.* a book, in which an official diary of events occurring in a ship's voyage or aircraft's flight is kept; the registration documents of a motor vehicle. **log-cabin, -house, -hut,** *n.* one built of logs. **log-canoe,** *n.* a dug-out. **logjam,** *n.* (*N Am.*) a blockage in a river caused by floating logs; a deadlock, a standstill. **log-line,** *n.* a knotted line, fastened to the log for finding the speed of the vessel. **log-man,** *n.* one employed to carry logs. **log-reel,** *n.* the reel on which the log-line is wound. **log-roll,** *v.i.* **log-roller,** *n.* **log-rolling,** *n.* mutual assistance in collecting logs for burning; (*N Am.*) mutual political assistance in carrying legislative measures; a sport in which two opponents attempt to spin each other off a floating log on which both are standing. **logwood,** *n.* the wood of a tropical US tree, *Haematoxylon campeachianum,* used as a dark-red dye-stuff. **logger,** *n.* a lumberman. **logging,** *n.* [ME *logge*]

log[2], *n.* short for LOGARITHIM.

loganberry, *n.* a permanent hybrid obtained by crossing the raspberry and a species of blackberry; the fruit of this. [J.H. *Logan,* 1841–1928, US horticulturalist]

logan-stone, *n.* a rocking-stone. [obs. *logging,* pres.p. of *log* (prob. onomat.), rock, STONE]

logaoedic, *a.* in ancient prosody, applied to lines consisting of a mixture of dactyls and trochees. *n.* a line of this character. [late L *logaoedicus,* Gr. *logaoidikos* (*logos,* speech, *aoidē,* song)]

logarithm, *n.* the exponent of the power to which a fixed number, called the base, must be raised to produce a given number (tabulated and used as a means of simplifying arithmetical processes by enabling addition and subtraction to be substituted for multiplication and division). **logarithmic,** *a.* **logarithmic scale,** *n.* a scale of measurement in which an increase of one unit represents a tenfold increase in the quantity measured. **logarithmically,** *adv.* [Gr. *log-os,* word, ratio, *arithmos,* number]

loge, *n.* a box in the theatre. [F; see LODGE]

loggerhead, *n.* a large marine turtle; a tool consisting of a long handle with a bulbous iron head for heating liquids, melting tar etc.; an idiot. **at loggerheads,** in conflict, locked in dispute. [dial. *logger,* from LOG[1], HEAD]

loggia, *n.* (*pl.* **-gias, -gie**) an open corridor, gallery or arcade along the front of a large building; an open balcony in a theatre or concert hall. [It., LODGE]

logia, *pl.* of LOGION.

logic, *n.* the science of reasoning, correct thinking, proving and deducing; a treatise on this; a particular mode or system of reasoning; reasoning, argument etc. considered with regard to correctness or incorrectness; force of argument; force of circumstances, situation etc. (*Comput.*) the elementary principles for performing arithmetical and logical operations in a computer. **logic circuit,** *n.* an electronic circuit used in computers which performs logical operations on its two or more inputs. **logical,** *a.* pertaining to, used in or according to the rules of logic, consistent or accurate in reasoning; reasonable; versed or skilled in accurate reasoning; (*Comput.*) of, performed by or used in logic circuits. **logical positivism,** *n.* a philosophical school based on linguistic analysis which demands that meaningful statements must be empirically verifiable, so rejecting metaphysics etc. as nonsense. **logicality, logicalness,** *n.* **logically,** *adv.* **logician,** *n.* one skilled in logic. [OF *logique,* L *logica,* Gr. *logikē* (*technē*), the art of reasoning (*logikos,* pertaining to reasoning, from LOGOS)]

logion, *n.* (*pl.* **-gia**) a traditional saying, revelation or truth, esp. one of those ascribed to Christ but not recorded in the Gospels. [Gr., oracle, dim. of LOGOS]

-logist, *suf.* as in *anthropologist.* [-LOGY, -IST]

logistics, *n.pl.* the art of arithmetical calculation; a system of arithmetic in which the logarithms of sexagesimal numbers are employed; the branch of strategy concerned with the moving and supply of troops; the planning and organization of any complex enterprise. **logistic,** *a.* pertaining to proportion; applied to logarithms of sexagesimal numbers or fractions; pertaining to logistics. [LOGIC]

loglog, *n.* the logarithm of a logarithm.

Logo, *n.* a computer-programming language designed to teach mathematical concepts. Developed about 1970 at the Massachusetts Institute of Technology, it became popular in schools and with home computer users because of its 'turtle graphics' feature. This allows the user to write programs that create line drawings on a computer screen, or drive a small mobile robot (a 'turtle' or a 'buggy') around the floor.

logo, *n.* (*pl.* **-gos**) short for LOGOTYPE.

logo-, *comb. form* pertaining to words; wordy. [LOGOS]

logogram, *n.* a sign representing a word, esp. in shorthand; a puzzle in verse containing words synonymous with others formed from the transposition of the letters of an original word to be found out. **logograph,** *n.* a logogram; a logotype. **logographer,** *n.* a prose-writer, esp. one of the historians preceding Herodotus, also a professional speech-writer. **logographic, -ical,** *a.* **logography,** *n.* a method of printing in which a type represents a word instead of a letter.

logogryph, *n.* a word-puzzle, a logogram. [F *logogriphe,* Gr. *griphos,* basket, riddle]

logomachy, *n.* contention about words, controversy hingeing on verbal matters. **logomachist,** *n.* **logomachize, -ise,** *v.i.* [Gr. *logomachia* (*-machia,* battle, from *machesthai,* to fight)]

logomania, *n.* a form of insanity or organic disease of the nervous system characterized by uncontrollable loquacity. [-MANIA]

logorrhoea, *n.* excessive or uncontrollable talkativeness; rapid and incoherent speech.

logos, *n.* in Greek philosophy, the divine reason implicit in and governing the cosmos; (*Theol.*) the Divine Word, the Son of God, the Second Person of the Trinity. [Gr., word, speech, reason, cogn with *legein,* to speak]

logotype, *n.* (*Print.*) a type having two or more letters cast in one piece, but not as a ligature, as *are, was* etc.; a symbol or simple design identifying a company, organization etc.

-logue, *suf.* as in *epilogue, prologue.* [Gr. *-logos -on,* see LOGOS]

logwood LOG[1].

-logy, *suf.* forming names of sciences and departments of knowledge, and nouns denoting modes of speaking, as *astrology, eulogy, tautology.* [Gr. *-logia, -logos,* see LOGOS (older examples through F *-logie,* med. L *-logia*)]

†**loimic,** *a.* pertaining to the plague or to contagious diseases. [Gr. *loimikos,* from *loimos,* plague]

Lohengrin, *n.* son of Parsifal, hero of a late 13th-cent. legend, on which Wagner based his German opera *Lohengrin* (1847). He married Princess Elsa, who broke his condition that she never ask his origin, and he returned to the temple of the Holy Grail.

loin, *n.* the part of the body of a human being or quadruped lying between the lower ribs and the hip-joint; (*pl.*) this part as representing strength and generative power; a joint of meat from this part. **to gird up the loins,** to prepare oneself for a great effort. **loincloth,** *n.* a cloth worn round the loins as an elementary kind of garment. [OF *loigne,* ult. from L *lumbus,* cogn. with OE *lendenu,* and Dut. *lende*]

Loire, *n.* the longest river in France, rising in the Cévennes at 1350 m/4430 ft and flowing for 1050 km/650 miles first north then west until it reaches the Bay of Biscay at St Nazaire, passing Nevers, Orléans, Tours, and Nantes. It gives its name to the *départements* of Loire, Haute-Loire, Loire-Atlantique, Indre-et-Loire, Maine-et-Loire, and Saône-et-Loire. There are many chateaux and vineyards along its banks.

loiter, *v.i.* to linger, to dawdle; to move or travel with frequent halts; to spend time idly; to be dilatory. *v.t.* to waste or consume (time) in trifles; to idle (time) away. **loiterer,** *n.* **loiteringly,** *adv.* [perh. from MDut. *loteren* (Dut. *lenteren*), cp. WFlem. *lutteren,* Norw. *lutra*]

Loki, *n.* in Norse mythology, one of the Aesir, but the cause of dissension among the gods, and the slayer of Balder. His children are the Midgard serpent Jörmungander which girdles the earth, the wolf Fenris, and Hela, goddess of death.

Lok Sabha, *n.* the lower chamber of the Indian parliament. [Hind. *lok,* people, *sabha,* house]

loligo, *n.* a genus of cephalopods containing the calamaries or squids. [L]

loll, *v.i.* of the tongue, to hang from the mouth; to stand, sit or lie in a lazy attitude, to lounge. *v.t.* to allow (the tongue) to hang from the mouth; to let (one's head or limbs) hang or recline lazily (on or against). **loller,** *n.* **lollingly,** *adv.* [prob. imit. (cp. MDut. *lollen,* Icel. *lolla,* also LULL)]

Lollard, *n.* one of a sect of English religious reformers in the 14th and 15th cents., followers of John Wyclif (?1330–84). **Lollardism, Lollardy,** *n.* [MDut. *lollaerd,* from *lollen,* to hum (conf. with LOLLER under LOLL)]

lollipop, *n.* a flat or round boiled sweet stuck on the end of a stick; an ice lollipop; a piece of popular classical music. **lollipop man, woman, lady,** *n.* (*coll.*) one who conducts children safely across roads by controlling traffic using a pole with a disc on the top. [etym. doubtful]

lollop, *v.i.* to loll about; to roll or flop about heavily; to go or do in a lounging or idle way. [from LOLL]

lolly, *n.* a lollipop, a sweet on a stick; an ice lolly; (*sl.*) money.

Lombard[1], *n.* one of the Teutonic Longobardi who conquered Italy in the 6th cent.; a native of Lombardy; †a money-lender or banker (a profession exercised in London during the Tudor period by Italians from Lombardy); †a bank, a money-lender's office or a pawnshop. *a.* of or pertaining to the Lombards or to Lombardy. **Lombard league,** *n.* an association of N Italian communes established 1164 to maintain their independence against the holy Roman emperors' claims of sovereignty. **Lombard Street,** the banking centre of the City of London fomerly occupied by Lombard merchants and money-lenders. **Lombardic,** *a.* Lombard, applied esp. to a style of architecture flourishing in Italy, 7th–13th cents., a school of Italian painters of the 15th and 16th cents., and a style of handwriting used in mediaeval manuscripts. **Lombardy poplar,** *n.* a variety of poplar tree with erect branches. [F, from It. *Lombardo,* late L *Longo-, Langobardus* (Teut. *lang-,* LONG[1], *Bardi,* L, name of the people)]

Lombard[2], *n.* **Carole** (1908–1942), stage name of Jane Alice Peters. US comedy film actress. Her successful career, which included starring roles in some of the best comedies of the 1930s, was tragically cut short by her death in a plane crash; her films include *Twentieth Century* (1934), *My Man Godfrey* (1936), and *To Be or Not To Be* (1942).

†**lombard,** *n.* a mediaeval species of artillery. [Sp. *lombarda*]

Lombardy, (Italian **Lombardia**), *n.* region of N Italy, including Lake Como; capital Milan; area 23,900 sq km/9225 sq miles; population (1988) 8,886,000. It is the country's chief industrial area (chemical, pharmaceuticals, engineering, textiles).

Lomé, *n.* capital and port of Togo; population (1983) 366,000. It is a centre for gold, silver, and marble crafts; major industries include steel production and oil refining. **Lomé Convention,** *n.* convention 1975 that established economic cooperation between the EEC and African, Caribbean, and Pacific countries. It was renewed 1979 and 1985.

loment, *n.* an indehiscent legume, separating by a transverse articulation between each seed. **lomentaceous,** *a.* **lomentum,** *n.* (*pl.* **-ta**). [L *lōmentum,* bean-meal, used as a cosmetic, from *lavāre* (p.p. *lōtum*), to wash]

Lomond, Loch, *n.* largest freshwater Scottish lake, 37 km/21 miles long, area 70 sq km/27 sq miles, divided between Strathclyde and Central regions. It is overlooked by the mountain Ben Lomond 296.5 m/973 ft and linked to the Clyde estuary.

London[1], *n.* the capital of England and the United Kingdom, on the river Thames; area 1580 sq km/610 sq miles; population (1987) 6,770,000, larger metropolitan area about 9 million. The City of London, known as the 'square mile', area 677 acres, is the financial and commercial centre of the UK. Greater London from 1965 comprises the City of London and 32 boroughs. Popular tourist attractions include the Tower of London, St Paul's Cathedral, Buckingham Palace, and Westminster Abbey. Roman Londinium was established soon after the Roman invasion AD 43; in the 2nd century London became a walled city; by the 11th century, it was the main city of England and gradually extended beyond the walls to link with the originally separate Westminster. **London-clay,** *n.* a formation of a lower Eocene age in SE England. **London particular,** *n.* (*old coll.*) dense yellow fog. **London pride,** *n.* an Irish saxifrage, *Saxifraga umbrosa,* cultivated in gardens. **Londoner,** *n.* a native, inhabitant or citizen of London. [L *Londinium,* perh. of Celt. orig.]

London[2], *n.* **Jack (John Griffith)** (1876–1916), US novelist, born in San Francisco. He is best known for adventure stories, for example, *The Call of the Wild* (1903), *The Sea Wolf* (1904), and *White Fang* (1906).

Londonderry, former name (until 1984) of the county and city of Derry in Northern Ireland.

London Working Men's Association, *n.* campaigning organization for political reform, founded June 1836 by William Lovett and others, who in 1837 drew up the first version of the People's Charter (see Chartism). It was founded in the belief that popular education, achieved through discussion and access to a cheap and honest press, was a means of obtaining political reform. By 1837 the LWMA had 100 members.

lone, *a.* (*chiefly poet. or rhet.*) solitary, retired, uninhabited, lonely, deserted; without company or a comrade; unmarried, widowed. **lone hand,** (*Cards*) one played without help from one's partner's cards. †**loneness,** *n.* **lonesome,** *a.* lonely, unfrequented; adapted for solitude. †**lonesomely,** *adv.* **lonesomeness,** *n.*

lonely, *a.* solitary, unfrequented, sequestered; companionless, lone; addicted to solitude or seclusion. **lonely hearts,** *a.* of, or for people seeking friendship or marriage. **loneliness,** *n.*

Long, *n.* **Huey** (1893–1935), US Democratic politician, nicknamed 'the Kingfish', governor of Louisiana 1928–31, US senator for Louisiana 1930–35. A legendary public speaker, he was popular with poor white voters for his programme of social and economic reform, which he called the 'Share Our Wealth' programme, and which represented a significant challenge to Roosevelt's New Deal, but his own extravagance, including the state capitol building at Baton Rouge built of bronze and marble, was widely criticized, and he was also accused of corruption. He was assassinated.

long[1], *a.* of considerable or relatively great linear extent; of great extent in time; of a specified linear extent or duration in time; protracted in sound, not short; stressed (of vowels or syllables); delayed in coming, dilatory; far-reaching; lengthy, verbose, tedious. *adv.* to a great extent in distance or time; for a long time; by a long time; throughout a specified period; having a large holding of securities or a commodity in anticipation of a price rise. *n.* anything that is long, esp. a period, interval etc.; (*Pros.*) a long syllable; (*Mus.*) a note equal in common time to two breves; the long summer vacation at a university. **before long,** soon, shortly. **in the long run,** in the end, eventually. **long-drawn-out,** prolonged, extended to great length. **no longer,** formerly but not now. **so long!,** (*coll.*) goodbye. **to make a long nose,** to cock a snook. **the long and the short of it,** the whole matter in a few words. **long ago,** *n.* the distant past. *a.* of the distant past. **longboat,** *n.* the largest boat on a sailing vessel. **longbow,** *n.* a long powerful bow drawn by hand used as a weapon in mediaeval England. **longcase clock,** *n.* a grandfather clock. **longcloth,** *n.* a type of fine, soft cotton cloth made in strips. **long-dated,** *a.* of securities, not due for redemption in less than 15 years. **long-distance,** *a.* from, or at long range. **long-distance call,** (*N Am.*) a telephone call over a large distance. **long dozen,** *n.* thirteen. **long face,** *n.* a gloomy or dejected expression. **long firm** FIRM[2]. **longhand,** *n.* ordinary writing opp. to shorthand. **long haul,** *n.* a journey (esp. the transport of goods) over a great distance; a difficult or extended period of time. **long-headed,** *a.* shrewd, sensible, far-sighted; dolichocephalous. **long hop,** *n.* a short-pitched cricket ball making a long bounce. **longhorn,** *n.* any of several breeds of cattle with long horns; a beetle with long antennae. **long hundred,** *n.* one hundred and twenty. **Long Island,** *n.* island off the coast of Connecticut and New York, US, separated from the mainland by Long Island Sound; area 3627 sq km/1400 sq miles. It includes two boroughs of New York City (Queens and Brooklyn), John F. Kennedy airport, suburbs, and resorts. **long johns,** *n.pl.* underpants with long legs. **longjump,** *n.* an athletic event involving a horizontal jump for distance from a running start. **long-lived,** *a.* enjoying long life. **Long March,** *n.* in Chinese history, the 10,000 km/6000 miles trek undertaken 1934–35 by Mao Zedong and his communist forces from SE to NW China, under harassment from the Guomindang nationalist army. **long metre,** *n.* hymn stanza consisting of four 8-syllable lines. **long odds,** *n.* unequal or unfavourable odds (in betting.) **long off** or **on,** *n.* in cricket, the fielder to the left or right rear of the bowler. **Long Parliament,** *n.* the English Parliament 1640–53 and 1659–60, which continued through the Civil War. After the Royalists withdrew in 1642, and the Presbyterian right was excluded in 1648, the remaining Rump ruled England until expelled by Cromwell in 1653. Reassembled 1659–60, the Long Parliament initiated the negotiations for the restoration of the monarchy. **long-playing,** *a.* of or relating to a fine-grooved gramophone record. **long-range,** *a.* involving or fit for an extended distance or period of time. **longship,** *n.* a long open sturdy vessel with oars and a square sail used esp. by the Vikings for carrying warriors. **long shot,** *n.* a camera shot from a long distance; a random guess, a remote possibility. **long-sighted,** *a.* able to see to a great distance; shrewd, far-sighted. **long-standing,** *a.* of long duration. **long staple,** *n.* a type of long-fibred cotton. **long stop,** *n.* in cricket, a fielder positioned to stop balls which pass the wicket-keeper. **long-suffering,** *a.* patient, enduring. **long suit,** *n.* the most numerous suit in a hand of cards: a person's special interest or skill. **long-term,** *a.* of a policy looking to the future rather than the immediate present. **long vacation,** *n.* the long summer holidays of universities, schools etc. **long wave,** *n.* a radio wave with a wavelength of 1000 m or more. **long weekend,** *n.* a holiday which extends over several days including a weekend. **long-winded,** *a.* wordy, tiresome. **longish,** *a.* †**longly,** *adv.* for a long time; at great length, wearisomely. **longways, -wise,** *adv.* [OE *lang* (cp. Dut., G and Dan. *lang,* Icel. *langr,* also L *longus*)]

long[2], *v.i.* to have an earnest desire (for); to yearn (to or for). **longing,** *a.* **longingly,** *adv.* [OE *longian,* perh. rel. to prec.]

†**long**[3], *a.* †**long of,** on account or because of. [shortened form of ME *ilong,* OE *gelang,* ALONG]

long., (*abbr.*) longitude.

longanimity, *n.* long-suffering, forbearance. **longanimous,** *a.* [late L *longa- nimitās,* from *long animus* (*longus,* LONG[1], ANIMUS)]

Longchamp, *n.* French horseracing course situated at the Bois de Boulogne, near Paris. Most of the major races in France are run at Longchamp including the most prestigous open-age group race in Europe, the *Prix de L'Arc de Triomphe*, which attracts a top-quality field every Oct.

longe LUNGE[2].

longeron, *n.* longitudinal spar of an aeroplane's fuselage. [F, girder]

longevity, *n.* great length of life. **longeval,** *a.* long-lived. †**longevous,** *a.* [L *longaevus* (*longus,* LONG[1], *aevum,* age)]

Longfellow, *n.* **Henry Wadsworth** (1807–1882), US poet, born in Portland, Maine. He is remembered for ballads ('Excelsior' and 'The Wreck of the Hesperus'), the narrative *Evangeline* (1847), and his metrically haunting *The Song of Hiawatha* (1855).

Longford, *n.* county of Leinster province, Republic of Ireland. **area** 1040 sq km/401 sq miles. **county town** Longford. **population** (1986) 31,000.

longi-, *comb. form.* [L *longus,* LONG[1]]

longicaudal, longicaudate, *a.* long-tailed.

longicorn, *a.* pertaining to the Longicornes, a division of beetles with large filiform antennae. *n.* a beetle of this division.

longimanous, *a.* having long hands.

Longinus, *n.* **Dionysius** (lived 1st cent. AD), Greek critic, author of a treatise *On the Sublime,* which influenced Dryden and Pope.

longipennate, *a.* having long wings.

longiroster, *n.* any individual of the Longirostres, a family of wading-birds having a long, slender bill. **longirostral,** *a.*

longitude, *n.* †length; angular distance of a place E or W of a given meridian, usu. that of Greenwich; (*Astron.*) distance in degrees on the ecliptic from the vernal equinox to the foot of a perpendicular from, or circle of latitude of, a heavenly body. **longitudinal,** *a.* pertaining to longitude or length; running lengthwise. **longitudinal wave,** *n.* a wave in which the particles of the medium vibrate in the same direction as the advance of the wave. **longitudinally,** *adv.* [F, from L *longitūdinem,* nom. *-tūdo,* from *longus,* LONG[1]]

Longobard, LOMBARD[1].

longshore, *a.* of or belonging to, existing or working on the shore. **longshoreman,** *n.* a landsman working on the shore; a man who works in or about boats along the shore; a stevedore; one employed in fishing from the shore; (*N Am.*) a docker, labourer. [shortened from ALONG SHORE]

Lonsdale, *n.* **Hugh Cecil Lowther, 5th Earl of Lonsdale,** (1857–1944), British sporting enthusiast. The Lonsdale Belts in boxing, first presented 1909, are named after him.

loo[1]**,** *n.* (*coll.*) a lavatory. [etym. doubtful]

loo[2]**,** *n.* a round game at cards; the pool in this game into which penalties are paid; the penalty. *v.t.* to cause to pay this penalty, to beat at loo. **loo-table,** *n.* a table for loo; a round table. [short from obs. *lanterloo,* F *lanturelu,* orig. nonsense, the refrain of a 17th-cent. song]

looby, *n.* an awkward, clumsy fellow; a lubber. †**loobily,** *a.* [rel. to LUBBER]

loof[1]**,** *n.* (*Sc.*) the palm of the hand. [from Icel. *lōfe* (cp. OHG *laffa,* oar-blade, OSlav. *lapa,* paw)]

loof[2]**,** LUFF.

loofah, *n.* the fibre of the sponge-gourd, *Luffa cylindrica,* used as a flesh-brush. [Arab. *lūfa,* plant]

look, *v.i.* to direct the eye (towards, at etc.) in order to see an object; to exercise the sight; to gaze, to stare; to stare in astonishment, wonder etc.; to direct the mind or understanding, to give consideration; to face, to front, to be turned or have a particular direction (towards, to, into etc.); to suggest, to have a particular tendency; to seem, to appear; to watch; to take care; †to expect, to anticipate. *v.t.* to express or show by the looks; to view, to inspect, to examine; †to search for. *n.* the act of looking or seeing, a glance; (*usu. in pl.*) appearance, esp. of the face, aspect, mien; expression of the eye and countenance; general appearance. **look before you leap,** be cautious before acting. **on the look out,** on the watch. **to look after,** to search, to seek, to attend to; to take care of. **to look down upon,** to despise; to assume superiority over. **to look for,** to seek; to hope for; to expect, anticipate, be on the watch for. **to look forward to,** to anticipate or hope for with pleasure. **to look in,** to call, to pay a brief visit; to watch television. **to look in the face** FACE. **to look into,** to inspect carefully, to investigate; to examine the inside of. **to look on,** to be a mere spectator; to regard, to consider (as, with etc.). **to look out,** to be on the watch, to be prepared (for); to put one's head out of window etc.; to choose by selection. **to look over,** to examine; to overlook or excuse. **to look through,** to see or direct the eyes through; to penetrate with one's sight or insight; to examine the contents of. **to look to, unto,** to take heed, to attend; to keep a watch over; to rely upon (for). **to look up,** to search for; to pay a visit to; to improve, to become more prosperous; (*with* **to**) to admire or respect. **to look upon,** to regard (as or with). **look-alike,** *n.* somebody or something who or that closely resembles another; a double. **look alive** ALIVE. **look here,** *v.i.* (*imper.*) give heed! pay attention! **look in,** *n.* a call, a short visit; a chance, as of winning in a game. **look lively,** *v.i.* (*coll.*) make haste. **look sharp,** *v.i.* (*imper.*) bestir yourself, be quick! **look-out,** *n.* a watch; a person engaged in watching or looking out; a place from which watch or observation is kept; a view, a prospect; (*fig.*) future prospect; one's personal affair or concern. *v.i.* (*imper.*) be careful. **look-see,** *n.* (*coll.*) an inspection. **looker,** *n.* an observer; (*coll.*) an attractive person, esp. a woman. **looker-on,** *n.* a mere spectator. †**looking-for,** *n.* expectation. **looking-glass,** *n.* a mirror. [OE *lōcian* (cp. G dial. *lugen*)]

loom[1]**,** *n.* a machine in which yarn or thread is woven into a fabric; the handle or inboard part of an oar. [OE *gelōma,* orig. a tool or implement (cp. *andlōma*)]

loom[2]**,** *v.i.* to appear indistinctly or faintly in the distance; to appear larger than the real size, as in a mist; †to appear to the mind faintly or obscurely; †to shine. *n.* the first indistinct appearance, as of land at sea. [cp. EFris. *lōmen,* Swed. dial. *loma,* to move slowly, OHG *luomen,* to be weary]

loom[3]**,** *n.* a guillemot. [Icel. *lōmr*]

loon[1]**,** *n.* (*Sc., North.*) a rogue, a scamp, a worthless person; (*coll.*) a daft or eccentric person. [etym. doubtful]

loon[2]**,** *n.* the great northern diver, *Colymbus glacialis;* the grebe; the guillemot. [corr. of LOOM[3]]

loony, *n., a.* (*sl.*) a lunatic a foolish person. **loony-bin,** *n.* (*sl.*) a mental hospital. [short for LUNATIC

loop[1]**,** *n.* a folding or doubling of a string, rope etc. across itself to form a curve or eye; a noose, a bight; anything resembling this; a ring, eye or curved piece by which anything is hung up, fastened, held etc.; a stitch in crochet or knitting; a hinge of a door; a loop-line; a length of film or tape joined end to end to form a continuous strip; (*Skating*) a curve performed on one edge and crossing itself; a flight manoeuvre comprising a complete revolution in flight in a vertical plane, the upper surface of the aircraft being on the inside of the circle; a loop-shaped intrauterine contraceptive device; (*Comput.*) a set of instructions repeated in a programme until a specific condition is met; *v.t.* to form into a loop or loops; to fasten or secure with loops. *v.t.* to make a loop; **to loop the loop,** to travel round in a vertical loop in an aeroplane etc. **loop-line,** *n.* a railway, telegraph-line etc. diverging from the main line and joining it again. **loop-work,** *n.* fancy-work with loose stitches. **looped,** *a.* **looper,** *n.* one who or that which loops; the larva of the geometer moth, which moves by drawing up the hinder part of its body to the head, forming a loop; a part in a sewing-machine for making loops; an instrument for looping pieces together in making rag-carpets. **loopy,** *a.* (*coll.*) slightly mad. [prob. from Celt. (cp. Gael. and Ir. *lub*)]

†**loop**[2]**, loop-hole,** *n.* an aperture in a wall for shooting or looking through or for admission of light; an outlet, a means of evasion or escape. *v.t.* to make loop-holes in. [prob. rel. to MDut. *lūpen* (Dut. *luipen*), to watch, to peer (cp. Dut. *gluip,* a narrow opening)]

†**loord,** *n.* a stupid good-for-nothing fellow. [F *lourd,* heavy]

Loos[1]**,** *n.* **Adolf** (1870–1933), Viennese architect. He rejected the ornamentation and curved lines of the

Viennese *Jugendstil* (see ART NOUVEAU). His most important buildings are private houses on Lake Geneva 1904 and the Steiner House in Vienna 1910, but his main importance is as a polemicist; for example the article *Ornament and Crime* 1908.

Loos[2], *n.* **Anita** (1888–1981), US writer, author of the humorous fictitious diary *Gentlemen Prefer Blondes* (1925).

loose, *a.* not tied, fastened or confined; unfastened, freed, detachable, hanging partly free; not fixed or tight; not crowded together, not compact or dense; relaxed, slack; careless, slovenly; straggling, rambling; not strict; vague, indefinite; incorrect; ungrammatical; dissolute, wanton; lax in the bowels, opp. to costive. *v.t.* to undo, to untie, to unfasten; to release, to set at liberty, to unbind; to dissolve; to relax; to free from obligation or burden; to discharge; †to forgive, to absolve. †*v.i.* to set sail. *n.* release, discharge, vent; †the issue or conclusion. **at a loose end,** with nothing to do. **on the loose,** on the spree. **to break loose,** to escape from captivity. **to give a loose to,** to give free vent to (one's tongue, feelings etc.). **to let loose** LET[1]. **to loosen up,** to relax, to become less shy or restrained. **to set loose,** to set at liberty. **loose box** BOX[2]. **loose change,** *n.pl.* coins kept for small items of expenditure. **loose cover,** *n.* an easily removable cloth cover for a chair, sofa etc. **loose-leaf,** *a.* bound so that pages may be inserted or removed. **loose-limbed,** *a.* having flexible or supple limbs. **loosely,** *adv.* **loosen,** *v.t., v.i.* **loosener,** *n.* **looseness,** *n.* **loosish,** *a.* [Icel. *lauss* (cogn. with OE *lēas,* G *los*), cp. Gr. *leuin*]

loosestrife, *n.* any of a genus of plants of the primrose family, esp. *Lysimachia vulgaris* with yellow flowers; a water-side plant, *Lythrum salicaria,* with red or purple flowers. [(LOOSE, STRIFE), erron. translation of late L *lysimachia,* Gr. *lusimachion,* from *Lusimachos,* a pers. name (*lusi-,* from *luein,* to loose, *machē,* strife)]

loot, *n.* booty, plunder, esp. from a conquered city; stolen money, jewellery etc.; (*coll.*) money. *v.t.* to plunder, to pillage, esp. a city; to carry off as plunder. *v.i.* to plunder. **looter,** *n.* one who loots, a pillager. [Hind. *lut*]

lop[1], *v.t.* (*past, p.p.* **lopped**) to cut off the top or extremities of; to trim (trees, shrubs etc.) by cutting; to cut off (as a person's head); to omit a part of. *v.i.* to cut (at) as if to lop. *n.* (*usu. in pl.*) that which is lopped. **lop and top,** trimmings of trees. **lopper,** *n.* [etym. doubtful, perh. *n.* from *v.*]

lop[2], *v.i.* to hang down limply; to flop, to droop; to hang or idle (about). *v.t.* to allow to hang down; to let fall. *n.* a lop-eared rabbit. **lop-ear,** *n.* a lop. **lop-eared,** *a.* having hanging ears. **lop-sided,** *a.* heavier on one side than the other; not symmetrical; ill-balanced. **lop-sidedly,** *adv.* **lop-sidedness,** *n.* [etym. doubtful, prob. onomat.]

lope, *v.i.* to gallop, swing or move (along) with long strides or leaps. *n.* motion of this kind. **loper,** *n.* [ON *hlaupa,* var. of LEAP, LOUP[1]]

Lope de Vega (Carpio), *n.* **Felix** (1562–1635), Spanish poet and dramatist, founder of modern Spanish drama. He was born in Madrid, served with the Armada 1588, and in 1613 took holy orders. He wrote epics, pastorals, odes, sonnets, and novels, and reputedly over 1,500 plays (of which 426 are still in existence), mostly tragi-comedies. He set out his views on drama in *Arte nuevo de hacer comedias/The New Art of Writing Plays* (1609), while re-affirming the classical form. *Fuenteovejuna* (1614) has been acclaimed as the first proletarian drama.

López[1], *n.* **Carlos Antonio** (1790–1862), Paraguayan dictator (in succession to his uncle José Francia) from 1840. He achieved some economic improvement; he was succeeded by his son Francisco López.

López[2], *n.* **Francisco Solano** (1827–1870), Paraguayan dictator in succession to his father Carlos López. He involved the country in a war with Brazil, Uruguay, and Argentina, during which approximately 80% of the population died.

Lopez[3], *n.* **Nancy** (1957–), US golfer, who turned professional 1977 and became in 1979 the first woman to win $200,000 in a season. She has twice won the US LPGA title and has won over 35 tour events.

lopho-, *comb. form* having a crest; crested. [Gr. *lophos,* crest]

lophobranchiate, *a.* belonging to or like the Lophobranchiata, a division of teleosteous fishes having the gills arranged in tufts. *n.* a fish in this division.

lophodont, *a.* having ridges on the crowns of the crowns of the molar teeth. *n.* an animal with such teeth. [Gr. *odous odontos,* tooth]

loquacious, *a.* talkative, garrulous, chattering; apt to disclose secrets. **loquaciously,** *adv.* **loquaciousness, loquacity,** *n.* [L *loquax -ācis,* from *loquī,* to talk, -ACIOUS]

loquat, *n.* a Chinese and Japanese tree, *Eriobotrya japonica;* its yellow edible fruit. [Chin. *luh kwat,* lit. rush orange]

loral, lorate LORE[2].

Lorca, *n.* **Federico García** (1898–1936), Spanish poet and playwright, born in Granada. *Romancero gitano/Gipsy Ballad-book* (1928) shows the influence of the Andalusian songs of the area. In 1929–30 Lorca visited New York, and his experiences are reflected in *Poeta en Nuevo York.* He returned to Spain, founded a touring theatrical company, and wrote plays such as *Bodas de sangre/Blood Wedding* (1933) and *La casa de Bernarda Alba/The House of Bernarda Alba* (1936). His poems include a 'Lament' for the bullfighter Mejías. He was shot by the Falangists during the Spanish Civil War.

lorcha, *n.* a light Chinese coaster of European build rigged like a junk. [Port., etym. doubtful]

Lord, *n.* in the UK, prefix used informally as alternative to the full title of a marquess, earl, or viscount; normally also in speaking of a baron, and as a courtesy title before the forename and surname of younger sons of dukes and marquesses.

lord, *n.* a ruler, a master; one possessing supreme power, a sovereign; God; Jesus Christ; a feudal superior, the holder of a manor; (*facet.*) one's husband; a nobleman, a peer of the realm; a courtesy-title given to the son of a duke or marquis, or the son of an earl holding a barony; a title of honour conferred on certain official personages, as Lord Chief Justice, Lord Commissioner, Lord Mayor, Lord Rector etc.; (*pl.*) the peers, the members of the House of Lords. *v.i.* to play the lord (over). *v.t.* to raise to the peerage. *int.* an exclamation of surprise or dismay ((*coll.*) **lor, lordy**). **drunk as a lord,** very drunk. **House of Lords,** the upper legislative chamber in the UK comprising the lords spiritual and temporal. †**lord of misrule,** one who superintended the games and revels at Christmas. **lords and ladies,** the wild arum lily, *Arum maculatum.* **my lord,** a formula for addressing a nobleman (not a duke), bishop, lord mayor or judge of the Supreme Court. **to live like a lord,** to live affluently. **Lord Advocate,** *n.* chief law officer of the Crown in Scotland. **Lord Chancellor,** CHANCELLOR. **Lord-Lieutenant,** *n.* an official representing the sovereign, and the chief executive authority and head of the magistracy in a county. **Lord Mayor,** *n.* the chief magistrate of London, York and certain other large towns. **Lord Rector,** *n.* the elected head officer of certain Scottish universities. **Lord's Cricket Ground,** the headquarters of Marylebone Cricket Club and of cricket generally. **Lord's day,** *n.* Sunday. **Lord's Prayer,** *n.* the prayer taught by Jesus Christ to his disciples (Math. vi.9–13, Luke xi.2–4). **lords spiritual,** *n.pl.* the archbishops and bishops having seats in the House of Lords. **Lord's Supper,** *n.* the Eucharist. **Lord's table,** *n.* the altar in a Christian church; the Eucharist. **lords temporal,** *n.pl.* lay peers having seats in the House of Lords. †**lording,** *n.* a lord used as a respectful mode of address. **lordless,** *a.* **lordlet, lordling,** *n.* **lord-like,** *a., adv.* **lordly,** *a.* becoming or befitting a lord; noble, grand, magnificent; superb, lofty, proud, haughty, insolent. *adv.* proudly; imperiously; arrogantly. **lordli-**

ness, *n.* **lordolatry,** *n.* **lordship,** *n.* **your, his lordship,** a formula used in speaking deferentially to or of a lord. [OE *hlāford* (*hlāf*, LOAF[1], WARD)]

lordosis, *n.* curvature of a bone, esp. of the spine forward. **lordotic,** *a.* [Gr., from *lordos,* bent backwards]

lore[1], *n.* learning; the collective traditions and knowledge relating to a given subject; †erudition, scholarship; †admonition, instruction. [OE *lār* (cogn. with LEARN)]

lore[2], *n.* a strap-like part, the surface between the eye and the beak in birds, the corresponding part in snakes. **loral,** *a.* pertaining to the lore. **lorate,** *a.* strap-shaped. [F, from L *lōrum,* a strap]

Lorelei, *n.* in Germanic folklore, a river nymph of the Rhine who lures sailors on to the rock where she sits combing her hair; a siren. She features in several poems, including 'Die Lorelei' by the Romantic writer Heine. The Lurlei rock S of Koblenz is 130 m/430 ft high.

Loren, *n.* **Sophia,** (1934–), stage name of Sofia Scicolone. Italian film actress who achieved fame under the guidance of her husband, producer Carlo Ponti. Her work includes *Aida* (1953), *The Key* (1958), *La Ciocara/Two Women* (1961), *Judith* (1965), and *Firepower* (1979).

Lorentz, *n.* **Hendrik Antoon** (1853–1928), Dutch physicist, winner (with his pupil Pieter Zeeman) of the Nobel physics prize 1902 for his work on the Zeeman effect.

Lorenz[1], *n.* **Konrad** (1903–1989), Austrian ethologist. Director of the Max Planck Institute for the Physiology of Behaviour in Bavaria 1955–73, he wrote the studies of ethology (animal behaviour) *King Solomon's Ring* (1952) and *On Aggression* (1966). In 1973 he shared a Nobel prize with N Tinbergen and Karl von Frisch.

Lorenz[2], *n.* **Ludwig Valentine** (1829–1891), Danish mathematician and physicist. He developed mathematical formulae to describe phenomena such as the relation between refraction of light and the density of a pure transparent substance, and the relation between a metal's electrical and thermal conductivity and temperature.

Lorenzetti[1], *n.* **Ambrogio** (*c.* 1319–1347), Italian painter active in Siena and Florence. His allegorical frescoes *Good and Bad Government* 1337–39 (Palazzo Pubblico, Siena) include a detailed panoramic landscape, and a view of the city of Siena that shows an unusual mastery of spatial effects.

Lorenzetti[2], *n.* **Pietro** (*c.* 1306–1345), Italian painter of the Sienese school, active in Assisi. His frescoes in the Franciscan basilica, Assisi reflect Giotto's concern with mass and weight. He was the brother of Ambrogio Lorenzetti.

lorette, *n.* a courtesan. [Church of Notre Dame de *Lorette* (*Loretto*), Paris, near which they lived]

lorgnette, *n.* a pair of eye-glasses with a long handle; an opera-glass. [F, from *lorgner,* squint]

lorica, *n.* a cuirass; the carapace of a crustacean, the sheath of certain infusorians and rotifers. **loricate,** *a.* covered with defensive plates, scales or other natural armour. *v.t.*, to plate or coat over; to encrust. **lorication,** *n.* [L *lōrīca,* from *lōrium,* strap]

lorikeet, *n.* a genus of brightly-coloured parrots belonging to the Malay Archipelago. [dim. of LORY (*-keet,* as PARRAKEET)]

†**lorimer,** †**loriner,** *n.* a maker of bits and spurs, a spurrier; applied also to makers of small ironwork. [OF *loremier, lorenier* (F *lorimer*), from *lorain,* med. L *loranum,* a bridle, from L *lōrum,* thong]

loriot, *n.* the golden oriole. [F, from OF *l'oriot,* the ORIOLE]

loris, *n.* a lemur of Sri Lanka, usu. called the slender loris; also the slow lemur or E Indian loris. [F, prob. from MDut. *loeris,* a clown]

†**lorn,** *a.* lost, abandoned, forlorn. [p.p. of obs. *leese* (OE *loren,* p.p. of *lēosan,* to LOSE[1])]

Lorrain, Claude CLAUDE LORRAIN.

Lorraine, *n.* former province and modern region of NE France in the upper reaches of the Meuse and Moselle rivers; bounded to the N by Belgium, Luxembourg, and West Germany and to the E by Alsace; area 23,600 sq km/9095 sq miles; population (1986) 2,313,000. It consists of the *départements* of Meurthe-et-Moselle, Meuse, Moselle, and Vosges, and its capital is Nancy. There are deposits of coal, iron-ore and salt; grain, fruit and livestock are important. In 1871 the region was ceded to Germany as part of Alsace-Lorraine.

Lorraine, Cross of, heraldic cross with double cross-bars, emblem of the medieval French nationalist Joan of Arc. It was adopted by the Free French forces in World War II.

Lorre, *n.* **Peter** (1904–1964), stage name of Lazlo Löwenstein. Hungarian character actor, whose bulging eyes and sinister voice made him one of cinema's most memorable performers. He made several films in Germany before moving to Hollywood in 1935. He appeared in *M* (1931), *Mad Love* (1935), *The Maltese Falcon* (1941), *Casablanca* (1942), *Beat the Devil* (1953), and *The Raven* (1963).

lorry, *n.* (*pl.* **-rries**) a large motor vehicle for carrying heavy loads. [etym. doubtful]

lory, *n.* a brilliantly coloured parrot-like bird of various genera of Loriinae, found in SE Asia and Australia. [Malay *lūri*]

Los Alamos, *n.* town in New Mexico, US, which has had a centre for atomic and space research since 1942. In World War II, the atom (nuclear fission) bomb was designed there (under Oppenheimer), working on data from other research stations; the hydrogen bomb was also developed there.

Los Angeles, *n.* city and port in SW California, US; population of urban area (1980) 2,967,000, the metropolitan area of Los Angeles-Long Beach 9,478,000. Industries include aerospace, electronics, chemical, clothing, printing, and food-processing. Features include the suburb of Hollywood, centre of the film industry since 1911; the Hollywood Bowl concert arena; observatories at Mt Wilson and Mt Palomar; Disneyland; the Huntingdon Art Gallery and Library; and the Getty Museum,

lose[1], *v.t.* (*past, p.p.* **lost**) to be deprived of; to part with accidentally or as a forfeit, penalty etc.; to be freed from; to miss, to stray from, to be unable to find; to fail to gain, win, hear, obtain or enjoy; to fail to keep possession of, to fail to hold or grasp; to spend uselessly, to waste; (*in p.p.*) to cause to disappear, to die or to perish; to cause one the loss of; to make (oneself or itself) disappear; †to dislodge. *v.i.* to fail to be successful, to be beaten; to suffer loss; to be worse off (by); of a clock etc., to run slow. **to lose ground** GROUND[1]. **to lose oneself,** to lose one's way; to be bewildered. **to lose out,** (*coll.*) to make a loss; to fail to take advantage of. **losable,** *a.* **loser,** *n.* one who loses; a person, horse, boat etc. failing to win a race; (*coll.*) a failure; (*Billiards*) a losing hazard; (*pl.*) the beaten party in a game, battle etc. **losing,** *pres.p.* **losing game,** *n.* a hopeless game or contest. **losingly,** *adv.* **lost,** *a.* unable to find the way; no longer possessed or known; missing; confused, helpless; ruined, destroyed; insensible; engrossed. **to be lost in,** to be engrossed in; to merge or be obscured in. **lost cause,** *n.* a futile endeavour. **lost soul,** *n.* one who is damned or beyond redemption. [OE *losian,* to escape (from), becoming transitive by gradually superseding the obs. *leese,* OE *lēosan*]

†**lose[2],** *n.* praise, fame, renown. [OF *los,* L *laudēs,* pl. of *laus,* praise]

†**losel,** *n.* a worthless fellow; a scamp, a ne'er-do-well; a lazy vagabond. *a.* worthless, lazy. [rel. to OE *-lēosan,* see LOSE[1]]

Losey, *n.* **Joseph** (1909–1984), US film director. Black-listed as a former Communist in the McCarthy era, he settled in England, where his films included *The Servant* (1963) and *The Go-Between* (1971).

losh, *int.* (*Sc.*) indicating surprise. [distortion of LORD]

loss, *n.* the act or state of losing or being lost; failure to win or gain; that which is lost or the amount of this; detriment, disadvantage; wasted expenditure, effort etc. **loss adjuster,** *n.* one who assesses losses through fire, theft etc. for an insurance company. **loss leader,** *n.* an article sold at a loss to attract customers. **to bear a loss,** to sustain a loss without giving way; to make good a loss. **to be at a loss,** to be embarrassed or puzzled, to be at fault. [OE *los,* dissolution, rout, dispersion, from *-lēosan,* see LOSE[1] (cp. Icel. *los*)]

löss, LOESS.

lost, *past, p.p.* LOSE[1].

Lost Generation, the, the disillusioned US literary generation of the 1920s, especially those who went to live in Paris. The phrase is attributed to the writer Gertrude Stein in Ernest Hemingway's novel of 1920s Paris, *The Sun Also Rises* 1926.

Lot, *n.* in the Old Testament or Hebrew Bible, Abraham's nephew, who escaped the destruction of Sodom. Lot's wife was turned into a pillar of salt when she turned around to look at Sodom.

lot, *n.* anything, such as a die, paper or other object, used in determining chances; choice or decision by chance drawing of these; the chance, share or fortune falling to anyone; one's fortune, destiny or condition in life; a distinct portion, collection or parcel of things offered for sale, esp. at auction; a parcel of land; a number or quantity of things or persons; a considerable quantity or amount, a great deal (*often in pl.*); one's proportion of a tax, a due; †a lottery prize; a plot of land in the vicinity of a film studio on which special exterior sets are built. *v.t.* to divide into lots; to apportion. **a bad lot, a nice lot,** a person of bad or doubtful character. **the lot,** the whole quantity. **to cast lots,** to determine by the throw of a die or other contrivance. **to draw lots,** to determine by drawing one name etc. from a number. **lotsa,** *n.* (*sl.*) short for *lots of;* also *comb. form,* e.g. *lotsalolly*. **lotta,** *n.* (*sl.*) short for *a lot of*. [OE *hlot* (cp. Dut. *lot,* Icel. *hluti,* G *loos*)]

†lote, LOTUS.

loth LOATH.

Lothair, *n.* (825–869), king of Lotharingia (called after him, and later corrupted to Lorraine, now part of Alsace-Lorraine) from 855, when he inherited from his father, the holy Roman emperor Lothair I, a district W of the Rhine, between the Jura mountains and the North Sea.

Lothair I, *n.* (795–855), holy Roman emperor from 817 in association with his father Louis I. On Louis' death, the empire was divided between Lothair and his brothers; Lothair took N Italy and the valleys of the rivers Rhône and Rhine.

Lothair II, *n.* (*c.* 1070–1137), holy Roman emperor from 1133 and German king from 1125. His election as emperor, opposed by the Hohenstaufens, was the start of the feud between Guelph and Ghibelline.

Lothario, *n.* a libertine, a seducer. [character in Nicholas Rowe's tragedy *Fair Penitent*]

Lothian, *n.* region of Scotland. **area** 1,800 sq km/695 sq miles. **towns** administrative headquarters Edinburgh; Livingston. **population** (1987) 744,000 **area** 135,900 sq km/52,457 sq miles. **products** bacon, vegetables, coal, whisky, engineering, electronics.

lotion, *n.* a medicinal or cosmetic liquid application for external use. †the act of washing. [L *lōtio,* from *lavāre* (p.p. *lōtus*), to wash]

lottery, *n.* a method of allotting valuable prizes by chance or lot among purchasers of tickets; the drawing of lots; a mere hazard. **lottery-wheel,** *n.* a drum-like wheel used for shuffling lottery-tickets. **lotto,** *n.* a game of chance, played with disks placed on cards divided into numbered squares. [It., from Teut. (cpHG *Hlōz,* LOT)]

Lotto, *n.* **Lorenzo** (*c.* 1480–1556), Italian painter, born in Venice, active in Bergamo, Treviso, Venice, Ancona, and Rome. His early works were influenced by Giovanni Bellini; his mature style belongs to the high renaissance. He painted dignified portraits, altarpieces, and frescoes.

lotus, *n.* (*pl.* **lotuses**) in Greek legend, a name for several plants the fruit of which was said to induce a dreamy languor in those who ate it; the Egyptian or Indian water-lily; an architectural representation of this; a genus of leguminous plants containing the bird's-foot trefoil. **lotus-eater,** *n.* one of the Lotophagi, mentioned in Homer's *Odyssey,* who lived on the fruit of the lotus; (*fig.*) one who gives himself up to dreamy ease. **lotus-eating,** *n., a.* **lotus-land,** *n.* **lotus position,** *n.* a position used in yoga in which one sits cross-legged with each foot nestled against or on top of the opposite thigh. **Lotus Sutra,** *n.* an important scripture of Mahāyāna Buddhism, particularly in China and Japan. It is Buddha Śākyamuni's final teaching, emphasizing that everyone can attain Buddhahood with the help of bodhisattvas. The original is in Sanskrit (*Saddharmapundarīka Sūtra*) and thought to date to some time after 100 BC. [L, from Gr. *lōtos*]

louche, *a.* morally suspect; seedy; sinister. [F, lit., cross-eyed, from L *luscus,* one-eyed]

loud, *a.* powerful in sound, sonorous; noisy, clamorous; conspicuous, ostentatious, flashy (of attire, manners etc.). **loud-hailer,** *n.* a megaphone with a built-in amplifier and microphone. **loudmouth,** *n.* (*coll.*) somone who brags or talks offensively in a loud voice. **loudspeaker,** *n.* an electromechanical device which converts electrical signals into audible sound. **louden,** *v.t., v.i.,* to make or become louder. **loudish,** *a.* **loudly,** *adv.* **loudness,** *n.* [OE *hlūd* (cp. Dut. *luid,* G *laut*), cogn. with Gr. *kluein,* hear, L *cluēre*]

lough, *n.* a lake, an arm of the sea in Ireland. [Ir. *loch* or Northum. *luh*]

Louis, *n.* **Joe** (1914–1981), US boxer, born Joseph Louis Barrow. Nicknamed the 'Brown Bomber'. He was world heavyweight champion between 1937–49 and made a record 25 successful defences (a record for any weight).

louis, louis d'or, *n.* (*unchanged in pl.*) an old French gold coin issued from Louis XIII to Louis XVI, worth at different times 20 or 23 francs, superseded by the 20-franc piece. **Louis Treize, Quatorze, Quinze,** or **Seize,** Louise XIII, XIV, XV or XVI (used to denote styles of furniture fashionable in those reigns). [F *Louis,* name of many French kings, *d'or,* of gold]

Louis I, *n.* **the Pious** (788–840), holy Roman emperor from 814, when he succeeded his father Charlemagne.

Louis II, *n.* **the Stammerer** (846–879), king of France from 877, son of Charles the Bald, he was dominated by the clergy and nobility.

Louis III, *n.* (863–882), son of Louis II, from 879 he ruled N France while his brother Charloman (866–84) ruled S France. His resistance to the Normans made him a hero of epic poems.

Louis IV, *n.* (921–954), king of France from 936. His reign was marked by rebellion of nobles. As a result of his liberality they were able to build up powerful feudal lordships.

Louis VII, *n.* (*c.* 1120–1180), king of France from 1137, who led the Second Crusade.

Louis X, *n.* **the Stubborn** (1289–1316), king of France who succeeded his father Philip IV 1314. His reign saw widespread noble discontent.

Louis XI, *n.* (1423–1483), king of France from 1461. He broke the power of the nobility (headed by Charles the Bold) by intrigue and military power.

Louis XII, *n.* (1462–1515), king of France from 1499, he was duke of Orléans until he succeeded his cousin Charles VIII to the throne. His reign was devoted to Italian wars.

Louis XIII, *n.* (1601–1643), king of France from 1610 (in succession to his father Henry IV), assuming royal power in 1617; he was under the political control of Richelieu from 1624–42.

Louis XIV, *n.* (**the Sun King**) (1638–1715), king of France from 1643, when he succeeded his father Louis XIII. Until 1661 France was ruled by the chief minister, Mazarin, but later Louis took absolute power. Throughout his reign he was engaged in unsuccessful expansionist wars – 1667–68, 1672–78, 1688–97, and 1701–13 (the War of the Spanish Succession) – against various European alliances, always containing Britain and the Netherlands. He was a patron of the arts.

Louis XV, *n.* (1710–1774), king of France from 1715, with the Duke of Orléans as regent until 1723. Great-grandson of Louis XIV. Indolent and frivolous, Louis left government in the hands of his ministers, the Duke of Bourbon and Cardinal Fleury (1643–1743). On the latter's death he attempted to rule alone, but became entirely dominated by his mistresses, Mme de Pompadour and Mme Du Barry. His foreign policy led to Canada and India being lost to France.

Louis XVI, *n.* (1754–1793), king of France from 1774; grandson of Louis XV. He was dominated by his queen, Marie Antoinette, and the finances fell into such confusion that in 1789 the States General had to be summoned, and the French Revolution began. Louis was sentenced to death for treason in Jan. 1793, and guillotined.

Louis XVII, *n.* (1785–1795), nominal king of France, the son of Louis XVI. During the French Revolution he was imprisoned with his parents in 1792, and probably died in prison.

Louis XVIII, *n.* (1755–1824), king of France 1814–24. Younger brother of Louis XVI; he assumed the title of king of France in 1795, having fled into exile in 1791 during the French Revolution, but became king only on the fall of Napoleon I in Apr. 1814.

Louisiana, *n.* southern state of the US. **area** 125,675 sq km/48,523 sq miles. **capital** Baton Rouge. **towns** New Orleans, Shreveport. **population** (1987), 4,461,000. **products** rice, cotton, sugar, maize, oil, natural gas, sulphur, salt, processed foods, petroleum products, timber, paper. **Louisiana Purchase**, *n.* the sale by France in 1803 to the US of an area covering about 2,144,000 sq km/828,000 sq miles, including the present-day states of Louisiana, Missouri, Arkansas, Iowa, Nebraska, North Dakota, South Dakota, and Oklahoma.

lounder, *n.* (*Sc.*) a heavy blow. *v.t.* to beat, to thrash. [etym. doubtful, prob. onomat.]

lounge, *v.i.* to idle about, to saunter; to move lazily; to loll or recline. *v.t.* to idle (time) away. *n.* the act of lounging; a saunter; a place for lounging; the sitting-room in a house; (also **lounge-bar**) a more comfortable and expensive section of a public house or hotel; a sofa with a back and one raised end. **lounge-lizard,** *n.* a gigolo; a hanger-on. **lounge suit,** *n.* a man's suit for daily wear. **lounger,** *n.* one who lounges; a comfortable sofa or extending chair for relaxing on; a loose fitting garment. **loungingly,** *adv.* [etym. unknown]

loup[1], **(***Sc.***)** *v.t., v.i.* to leap. **loup-the-dike,** *a.* runaway, skittish, giddy. [from Icel. *hlaupa,* to LEAP]

†**loup**[2], LOOP[1].

loupe, *n.* a small magnifying glass used by jewellers, watchmakers etc. [F]

lour, lower[3], *v.i.* to appear dark or gloomy; to frown, to scowl; to look threatening (of clouds, weather etc.). *n.* a scowl; sullenness; gloominess (of weather etc.). **louring, loury,** *a.* **louringly,** *adv.* [ME *louren* (cp. LG *lūren,* M.Dut. *loeren,* G *lauern,* to lie in wait)]

Lourdes, *n.* town in SW France with a Christian shrine to St Bernadette which has a reputation for miraculous cures; population (1982) 18,000.

Lourenço Marques, *n.* former name of Maputo, capital of Mozambique.

louse, *n.* (*pl.* **lice**) an insect of the genus *Pediculus,* three species of which are parasitic on man; applied to various parasites infesting animals, birds, fish and plants; (*sl.*) a mean, contemptible person. *v.t.*, to clean from lice; (*with up* ((*sl.*))) to spoil, make a mess of. **lousy,** *a.* infested with lice; (*sl.*) low, mean, or obscene; (*sl.*) bad, inferior. (*sl.*) swarming or excessively supplied (with). **lousily,** *adv.* **lousiness,** *n.* [OE *lūs* (cp. Dut. *luis,* Icel. *lūs,* G *Laus*)]

lout, *v.i.* to bend, to bow, to stoop. †*v.t.* to treat as a lout; to make a fool of. *n.* an awkward, crude person; an oaf; a clown, a bumpkin. **loutish,** *a.* **loutishly,** *adv.* **loutishness,** *n.* [OE *lūtan* (cp. Icel. *lūta*)]

Louth, *n.* smallest county of the Republic of Ireland, in Leinster province; county town Dundalk; area 820 sq km/317 sq miles; population (1986) 92,000.

louver, *n.* a turret on the roof of a mediaeval hall, with openings for the escape of smoke; an opening in a chimney pot etc. to let out smoke; (*pl.*) louvre-boards. **louvre-boards,** *n.pl.* sloping overlapping boards across a window to exclude rain but allow the passage of air. **louvre-door, -window,** *n.* a door, window covered by louvre-boards. **louvred,** *a.* [ME and OF *lover,* med. L *lōdium,* etym. doubtful]

Louvre, *n.* French art gallery, former palace of the French kings, in Paris. It was converted by Napoleon to an art gallery 1793, and houses the sculpture *Venus de Milo* and Leonardo da Vinci's *Mona Lisa*.

lovage, *n.* a name applied to various umbelliferous herbs, used in salads and for flavouring food, esp. *Levisticum officinale;* the genus *Levisticum.* [ME *loveache,* OF *levesche,* ult. from L *ligusticum,* Ligurian]

love, *n.* a feeling of deep regard, fondness and devotion (for, towards etc.); deep affection, usu. accompanied by yearning or desire for; affection between persons of the opposite sex, more or less founded on or combined with desire or passion; a personification of this or of Cupid, usu. in the form of a naked winged boy; a beloved one, a sweetheart (as a term of endearment); (*coll.*) a delightful person, a charming thing; in games, no points scored, nil; †traveller's joy, *Clematis vitalba. v.t.* to have strong affection for, to be fond of, to be in love with; to like greatly, to delight in, to have a strong partiality or predilection for. *v.i.* to be in love. **for love or money,** by some means or other. **for the love of,** for the sake of (esp. in adjuration). **labour of love,** work done for its own sake, for love of some other person or from devotion to a cause. **love-in-a-mist,** *n.* the fennel-flower, *Nigella damascena.* **love-in-idleness,** *n.* the pansy or heartsease, *Viola tricolor.* **there's no love lost between them,** they have anything but love for each other. **to give, send one's love,** to give, send an affectionate message. **to fall in love,** to become enamoured. **to make love to,** to woo, to pay court or attentions to; to have sexual intercourse with. **to play for love,** to play without stakes. **love-affair,** *n.* a romantic or sexual attachment between two people, often temporary in nature. **love all,** *n.* in games, nothing scored on either side. †**love-apple,** the tomato. **love-begotten,** *a.* illegitimate. **love-bird,** *n.* a short-tailed parrot of the African genus *Agapornis* or the American *Psittacus,* from the attachment they show to their mates. **love-bite,** *n.* a temporary red or purple mark on the skin caused by a partner biting or sucking it during love-making. †**love-broker,** *n.* a go-between for lovers; a procurer. **love-child** *n.* an illegitimate child. †**love-drink,** *n.* a philtre. **love-feast,** *n.* a religious meeting such as the agape held by Methodists etc. **love game,** *n.* a game in which the loser has not scored. **love-god,** *n.* cupid. †**love-juice,** *n.* a lotion supposed to produce love. **love-knot,** *n.* an intricate bow or knot (a token of love). **love-letter,** *n.* a letter between lovers or professing love. **love-lies-bleeding,** *n.* a species of amaranth, esp. *Amaranthus caudatus.* †**love-line,** *n.* a love-letter. **love-lock,** *n.* a curl or tress hanging at the ear or on the forehead. **love-lorn,** *a.* forsaken by one's love; pining-away for love. **love-making,** *n.* courtship, amorous attentions; sexual play or intercourse between partners. **love-match,** *n.* a marriage for love, not other considerations. **love-monger,** *n.* a love-broker. **love-nest,** *n.* a secret place where lovers meet, esp. for illicit sexual relations. †**love-prate,** *n.* idle talk about love. **love seat,** *n.* a small sofa or double-chair for two people. **love-shaft,** *n.* a shaft of love, esp. Cupid's arrow. **lovesick,** *a.* languishing with love; expressive of languishing love. **love-sickness,** *n.* **love-song,** *n.* a song expressing love. **love-spring,** *n.* the beginnings of love. **love-story,** *n.* a story dealing mainly with romantic love. †**love-suit,** *n.* courtship. **love-token,** *n.* a present in token of love. **lovable, loveable,** *a.* worthy of love; amiable. **lovableness,** *n.* **lovably,** *adv.* **loveless,** *a.* destitute of love; not loving; not loved. **lovelessly,** *adv.* **lovelessness,** *n.* **lovely,** *a.* beautiful and attractive, inspiring admiration and affection, winsome, tempting, delightful; †affectionate, loving. *adv.* so as to excite love or admiration. *n.* a beautiful woman. **lovelily,** *adv.* **loveliness,** *n.* **lover,** *n.* one who loves, one in love (used only of the man); a suitor or woman's sweetheart; a paramour, a gallant; one fond of anything; (*pl.*) a pair of sweethearts. †**lovered,** *a.* having a lover. **loverless,** *a.* **loverlike,** *a., adv.* **loverly,** *a., adv.* †**lovesome,** *a.* lovely. **lovey,** *n.* (*coll.*) a person who is loved, a term of endearment. **lovey-dovey,** *a.* (*coll.*) loving, affectionate. **loving-cup,** *n.* a large two- or three-handled drinking-vessel passed round with wine at a banquet. **lovingly,** *adv.* **lovingness,** *n.* [OE *lufu,* whence *lufigan, lufian,* to love (cp. Dut. *lieven,* G *lieben*), rel. to LIEF]

Lovecraft, *n.* **H(oward) P(hillips)** (1890–1937), US writer of horror fiction, whose stories of hostile, supernatural forces, known collectively as the *Cthulhu Mythos*, have lent names and material to many other writers in the genre. Much of his work on this theme was collected in *The Outsider and Others* (1939).

Lovelace[1], *n.* a fascinating or accomplished libertine. [character in Samuel Richardson's *Clarissa*]

Lovelace[2], *n.* **Richard** (1618–1658), English poet. Imprisoned 1642 for petitioning for the restoration of royal rule, he wrote 'To Althea from Prison', and in a second term in jail 1648 revised his collection *Lucasta* (1649).

low[1], *a.* (*comp.* **lower**[1], *superl.* **lowest**) not reaching or situated far up; not high or tall, below the usual or normal height; below or little above a given surface or level; not elevated; of the sun, moon etc., near the horizon; near the equator; below the common standard in rank, condition, quality, character etc.; humble, mean, degraded; base, dishonourable; not sublime, not exalted; coarse, vulgar; not advanced in civilization; not high in organization; lacking in vigour, weak, feeble; badly nourished; affording poor nourishment; of sounds, not raised in pitch, deep, produced by slow vibrations, not loud or intense, soft; not large in amount, scanty, nearly exhausted; moderate, cheap; in the Church of England, inclined to evangelical doctrine, not favouring sacerdotal pretensions not characterized by elaborate ritual. *adv.* not on high; in or to a low position; deeply; at a low price; in a humble rank or position; of humble birth; with a subdued voice, in low tones; softly, quietly; on a poor diet; of or in times approaching our own. *n.* a low position or level; an area of low atmospheric pressure. **at lowest,** to mention or judge by the least possible amount etc. **to bring low,** to reduce in wealth, position, health etc. **to lay low,** to overthrow; to kill. **to lie low,** to crouch; to be prostrate or abased; to be dead; (*coll.*) to keep quiet, to do nothing for the moment, to await one's opportunity. **low birth,** *n.* humble parentage. **low born,** *a.* **low-bred,** *a.* vulgar in manners, ill-bred. **low-brow,** *n.* a person making no claims to intellectuality. *a.* unintellectual; assuming no airs of intellectual superiority. **low-browed,** *a.* having a low brow or forehead; beetling; having a low entrance etc. **Low Church,** the evangelical party in the Church of England. **Low Churchman,** *n.* **low comedy,** *n.* comedy bordering on farce, hence **low comedian. Low Countries,** *n.pl.* a collective name for Belgium, Luxemburg and the Netherlands. **low-cut,** *a.* of a dress etc., cut low at the neck, exposing part of the shoulders and breast. **low-down,** *a.* degraded, mean, abject. *adv.* meanly, ungenerously, contemptibly. *n.* (*coll.*) the inner history, real facts. **Low Dutch** DUTCH. **low frequency,** *n.* term denoting a radio frequency lying between 300 and 30 kHz. **Low German** GERMAN. **low-key, -keyed,** *a.* of low intensity; undramatic; restrained. **lowland,** *n.* low-lying or level country. *a.* pertaining to a lowland or the Lowlands. **Lowlands,** *n.pl.* the eastern and southern or less mountainous parts of Scotland. **Lowlander,** *n.* **Low Latin** LATIN. **low latitudes,** *n.pl.* latitudes near the Equator. **low-level language,** *n.* computer programming language that corresponds more to machine code than to human language. **low life,** *n.* (*pl.* **lifes**) a mean or low state of life; persons of a low position in life. **low-loader,** *n.* a road or rail vehicle with a low platform for heavy loads. **low Mass,** *n.* mass said without music and without elaborate ritual. **low-minded,** *a.* having a crude mind and character. **low-neck, -necked,** *a.* of a woman's dress, cut low at the neck. **low-pitched,** *a.* having a low tone or key; low angular elevation in a roof. **low profile,** *n.* a reserved or inconspicuous attitude or manner to avoid attention or publicity. **low-profile,** *a.* **low relief,** *n.* bas-relief. **low-rise,** *a.* of buildings, having only one or two storeys. **low-spirited,** *a.* dejected in spirit. **Low Sunday, Week,** *n.* the Sunday or week next after Easter. **low-tension,** *a.* having, generating or operating at a low voltage. **low tide,** *n.* the lowest point of the ebb tide; the level of the sea at ebb tide. **low-velocity,** *a.* applied to projectiles propelled at a comparatively low velocity and having a high trajectory. **low-voiced,** *a.* having a soft, gentle voice. **low water,** *n.* low tide; hence, **low-water mark,** *n.* **low wine,** *n.* a liquor produced by the first distillation of alcohol. **lower**[1], *comp. a.* **lower case,** *n.* (*Print.*) the type case which contains the small letters; the small letters. **Lower Chamber, House,** *n.* the second of two legislative chambers, as the House of Commons. **lower deck,** *n.* the deck just above the hold of a ship; petty officers and men of the Royal Navy. **lower world,** *n.* the earth. **lower**[2], *v.t.* to bring down in height, force, intensity, amount, price, estimation etc.; to haul or let down; to reduce the condition of. *v.i.* to become lower or less; to sink, to fall. **lowermost,** *a.* **lowish,** *a.* **lowly,** *a.* humble, modest, unpretentious; low in size, rank or condition; low, mean, inferior. *adv.* humbly, modestly; †in a low or inferior way. †**lowlihead, -hood, lowliness,** *n.* **lowlily,** *adv.* **lowness,** *n.* [late OE *lāh,* Icel. *lāgr* (cp. Dut. *laag*), cogn. with LIE[1]]

low[2], *v.i.* to utter the moo of cow. *v.t.* to utter with such a sound. *n.* the moo of a cow. **lowing,** *n.* [OE *hlōwan* (cp. Dut. *lōeien,* OHG *hlōjan*), cogn, with L *clāmāre,* Gr. *kalein,* to call]

low[3], *n.* (*Sc.*) flame; a blaze. *v.i.* to flame, to blaze (up). [from Icel. *loge* (cp. OFris. *loga,* G *Lohe*), cogn. with L *lux,* LIGHT[1]]

low[4], *n.* a rounded hill. †a barrow or tumulus. [OE *hlāw, hlǣw,* LAW[2]]

Lowell[1], *n.* **Amy (Lawrence)** (1874–1925), US poet, who succeeded Ezra Pound as leader of the Imagists. Her works, in free verse, include *Sword-Blades and Poppy Seed* (1916).

Lowell[2], *n.* **Robert (Traill Spence)** (1917–1977), US poet whose work includes *Lord Weary's Castle* 1946 and *For the Union Dead* 1964. A Roman Catholic convert from 1940, he was imprisoned in 1943 as a conscientious objector.

lower[1,2] LOW[1].

lower[3] LOUR.

Lower Saxony, (German **Niedersachsen**), *n. Land* of N West Germany. **area** 47,400 sq km/18,296 sq miles. **capital** Hanover. **towns** Brunswick, Osnabrück, Oldenburg, Göttingen, Wolfsburg, Salzgitter, Hildesheim. **population** (1988) 7,190,000. **products** cereals, cars, machinery, electrical engineering. **religion** 75% Protestant, 20% Roman Catholic.

lown, *a.* (*Sc.*) quiet, tranquil, serene; gentle, calm. *n.* quietness, tranquillity; shelter. *v.i.* to become calm. [etym. doubtful, prob. from Icel.]

Lowry, *n.* **L(aurence) S(tephen)** (1887–1976), British painter. Born in Manchester, he lived mainly in nearby Salford. He painted northern industrial townscapes and town life. His characteristic style of matchstick figures and almost monochrome palette emerged in the 1920s.

lox[1], *n.* a kind of smoked salmon. [Yiddish *laks,* from MG *lans,* salmon]

lox[2], *n.* liquid oxygen, used in rocket fuels. [*l*iquid *ox*ygen]

loxodrome, *n.* RHUMBLINE; also **loxodromic curve, line, spiral.** [Gr. *loxos,* oblique, *dromos,* course, from *dramein,* to run]

Loy, *n.* **Myrna** (1905–), stage name of Myrna Williams. US film actress who played Nora Charles in the *Thin Man* series (1943–47) co-starring William Powell. Her other films include *The Mask of Fu Manchu* (1932) and *The Rains Came* (1939).

loyal, *a.* faithful, true, constant, in a trust or obligation (to); faithful to one's sovereign, government or country. †*n.* a loyal subject, esp. in a time of disaffection. **loyalism,** *n.* **loyalist,** *n.* a patriotic supporter of sovereign or government; (with *caps*) in Northern Ireland, a Protestant who supports Ulster's union with Britain; in the American War of Independence, a colonial supporter of Britain; a republican supporter in the Spanish Civil War. **loyalize, -ise,** *v.t.* **loyally,** *adv.* **loyalty,** *n.* [F, from L *lēgālis,* LEGAL]

Loyola IGNATIUS LOYOLA.

lozenge, *n.* a rhombus or oblique-angled parallelogram; (*Her.*) a diamond-shaped bearing, appropriated to the arms of spinsters and widows; a rhomb-shaped facet in a cut gem; a small rhomb-shaped pane of glass; a confection or medicated sweet etc. in a tablet of this shape. **lozenge moulding,** *n.* (*Arch.*) an ornament enclosing diamond-shaped panels. **lozenge-shaped,** *a.* **lozenged,** *a.* shaped like a rhomb or diamond; arranged in series of lozenges in alternate colours; having diamond panes. **lozengewise,** *adv.* **lozengy,** *a.* (*Her.*) divided lozengewise. [OF *losenge,* Prov. *lauza,* tombstone, prob. from L *lapis -idem,* stone]

LP, *n.* a *l*ong-*p*laying record, usu. 12 in. (30 cm) in diameter and designed to rotate at 33.3 revolutions per minute.

LPG, (*abbr.*) liquid petroleum gas.

Lr, (*chem. symbol*) lawrencium.

LSD, *n.* **lys**ergic acid **d**iethylamide, a psychedelic drug and a hallucinogen. Colourless, odourless, and easily synthesized, it is non-addictive, but its effects are unpredictable. Its use is illegal in most countries.

L.S.D., £.s.d., l.s.d., (*abbr.*) librae, solidi, denarii. [L, pounds, shillings and pence]

LSE, (*abbr.*) London School of Economics.

LSI, *n.* large-scale integration, the technology by which whole electrical circuits can be etched into a piece of semiconducting material just a few millimetres square.

LSO, (*abbr.*) London Symphony Orchestra.

Lt, (*abbr.*) Lieutenant.

Ltd, (*abbr.*) limited liability.

Lu, (*chem. symbol*) lutetium.

Luanda, (formerly **Loanda**) *n.* capital and industrial port (cotton, sugar, tobacco, timber, paper, oil) of Angola; population (1988) 1,200,000. It was founded 1575 and became a Portuguese colonial administrative centre as well as an outlet for slaves transported to Brazil.

lubber, *n.* a lazy, clumsy fellow; an awkward lout; a bad seaman. **lubber's hole,** *n.* a hole in the top through which sailors can reach the masthead without climbing the futtock-shrouds. **lubber's line,** *n.* the mark inside a compass-case which shows the direction of the ship's head. **lubberlike,** *a.* **lubberly,** *a.* like a lubber. *adv.* clumsily. **lubberliness,** *n.* [etym. doubtful, prob. rel. to LOB]

Lubbers, *n.* **Rudolph (Frans Marie)** (1939–), Netherlands politician. He became minister for economic affairs 1973 and prime minister 1983.

Lubitsch, *n.* **Ernst** (1892–1947), German film director, who worked in the US from 1921. Starting as an actor in silent films in Berlin, he turned to writing and directing, including *Die Augen der Mummie Ma/The Eyes of the Mummy* (1918) and *Die Austernprinzessin/The Oyster Princess* (1919). In the US he directed *The Marriage Circle* (1924), *The Student Prince* (1927). His sound films include *Design for Living* (1933), *Ninotchka* (1939), and *To Be or Not to Be* (1942).

lubricate, *v.t.* to make smooth or slippery by means of grease, oil or similar substance, in order to reduce friction; to bribe; (*sl.*) to drink. †*a.*, slippery, smooth; oily. †**lubric,** †**-ical,** *a.* smooth and slippery; changeable, deceitful; lascivious. **lubricant,** *n., a.* **lubrication,** *n.* **lubricator,** *n.* one who or that which lubricates. **lubricity,** *n.* smoothness; slipperiness; shiftiness, instability; lewdness, lasciviousness. **lubricious,** *a.* [L *lūbricātus,* p.p. of *lūbricāre,* from *lūbricus,* slippery, cogn. with SLIP]

Lucan, *a.* pertaining to the evangelist St Luke. [L *Lūcas,* Luke, -AN]

Lucan, *n.* **Marcus Annaeus Lucanus** (AD 39–65), Latin poet, born in Cordova, a nephew of Seneca and favourite of Nero until the emperor became jealous of his verse. He then joined a republican conspiracy and committed suicide on its failure. His epic *Pharsalia* deals with the civil wars of Caesar and Pompey.

lucarne, *n.* a dormer or garret window, a light in a spire. [F, etym. doubtful]

Lucas, *n.* **George** (1944–), US director and producer. His films, often on science fiction themes and using special effects, include *THX 1138* (1971), *American Graffiti* (1973), and the *Star Wars* trilogy (1977–83).

Lucas van Leyden, (1494–1533), Dutch painter and printmaker, active in Leiden and Antwerp. He was a pioneer of Netherlandish genre scenes, for example *The Chess Players* (Staatliche Museen, West Berlin). His woodcuts and engravings were inspired by Dürer, whom he met in Antwerp 1521. Lucas was an influence on Rembrandt.

luce, *n.* a pike, esp. when full-grown; a figure of a pike used as an armorial bearing. [OF *lus,* L *lūcius*]

Luce, *n.* **Henry Robinson** (1898–1967), US publisher, founder of the magazine *Time* (1923), and of the pictorial weekly *Life* (1936).

lucent, *a.* shining, bright, luminous, resplendent. **lucency,** *n.* [L *lūcens -ntis,* pres.p. of *lūcēre,* to shine (*lux lūcis,* light, cogn. with Gr. *leukos,* white)]

lucerne, *n.* purple medick, *Medicago sativa,* a fodder-plant. [F *luzerne,* etym. unknown]

Lucerne, (German **Luzern**), *n.* capital and tourist centre of Lucerne canton, Switzerland, on the Reuss where it flows out of Lake Lucerne; population (1987) 161,000. It developed around the Benedictine monastery, established about 750, and owes its prosperity to its position on the St Gotthard road and railway.

Lucian, *n.* (*c.* 125–*c.* AD 190), Greek writer of satirical dialogues, in which he pours scorn on all religions. He was born at Samosata in Syria, and for a time was an advocate at Antioch, settling in Athens about 165. He later occupied a post in Egypt, where he died.

lucid, *a.* bright, shining, radiant; clear, transparent, perspicuous, easily understood; sane. **lucidity, lucidly,** *adv.* †**lucidness,** *n.* [L *lūcidus,* from *lūcēre,* see LUCENT]

Lucifer, *n.* the morning star; Satan, the chief of the rebel angels; a match tipped with combustible substance and ignited by friction. **lucifer-match,** *n.* **Luciferian,** *a.* †**luciferous,** *a.* bearing or giving light; making plain or clear; Satanic, devilish. [-FEROUS]. †**lucific,** *a.* †**luciform,** *a.* [L, light-bringing (*lūci-*, see LUCENT, *-fer,* from *ferre,* to bring)]

lucifugous, *a.* of certain animals, shunning the light

lucigen, *n.* a lamp in which oil is mixed with air.

luck, *n.* chance, accident, as bringer of fortune, whether good or bad; what happens to one, fortune, hap; the supposed good or evil tendency of fortuitous events as regards a person; good fortune, success. **down on one's luck,** not having much luck. **to luckout,** (*sl.*) to be successful or fortunate, esp. by chance. **to luck into,** (*sl.*) to acquire or achieve by good fortune or chance. **to push one's luck** PUSH. **to try one's luck,** to attempt something. **tough luck,** an expression of sympathy for another person. **luck-money, -penny,** *n.* a small sum returned to the buyer 'for luck' by the person who receives money on a sale or contract. **luckily,** *adv.* fortunately (for). **luckiness,** *n.* **luckless,** *a.* unfortunate. **lucklessly,** *adv.* **lucky,** *a.* characterized or usually attended by good-luck; favoured by fortune; successful, esp. by a fluke or more than is deserved; bringing luck, auspicious; (*Sc.*) full to the brim, abundant. **lucky-bag,** *n.* a bag containing miscellaneous articles in which one may dip on paying a small sum; a receptacle for lost property on a warship. **lucky dip,** *n.* receptacle containing an assortment of articles, for one of which one dips blindly. [Dut. *luk, geluk* (cp. G *Glück*), etym. doubtful]

Lucknow, *n.* capital and industrial city (engineering, chemicals, textiles, many handicrafts) of the state of Uttar Pradesh, India; population (1981) 1,007,000. During the Indian Mutiny against British rule, it was besieged 2 Jul–16 Nov 1857.

lucrative, *a.* producing gain, profitable, bringing in money; †greedy of gain. **lucratively,** *adv.*

lucre, *n.* pecuniary gain or advantage, usu. as an object of greed. [F, from L *lucrum* (cp. Gr. *leia,* booty, *apolauein,* to enjoy, G *Lohn,* reward)]

Lucretia, *n.* Roman woman, the wife of Collatinus, said to have committed suicide after being raped by Sextus, son of Tarquinius Superbus. According to tradition, this incident led to the dethronement of Tarquinius and the establishment of the Roman Republic 509 BC.

Lucretius, *n.* **(Titus Lucretius Carus)** (*c.* 99–55 BC), Roman poet and Epicurean philosopher, whose *De Rerum Natura/On the Nature of Things* envisaged the whole universe as a combination of atoms, and had some concept of evolutionary theory.

lucubrate, *v.i.* to study by lamplight; to produce lucubrations. *v.t.* to compose or elaborate, as by night study. **lucubration,** *n.* night work, night study; that which is composed at night; composition of a learned or too elaborate and pedantic character. [L *lūcubrātus,* p.p. of *lūcubrāre,* from *lux lūcis,* light]

luculent, *a.* clear, lucid, plain, manifest. **luculently,** *adv.* [L *lūculentus,* from *lux lūcis,* light]

Lucullus, *n.* **Lucius Licinius** (110–56 BC), Roman general and consul. As commander against Mithridates of Pontus 74–66 he proved to be one of Rome's ablest generals and administrators, until superseded by Pompey. He then retired from politics. His wealth enabled him to live a life of luxury, and Lucullan feasts became legendary.

lucumo, *n.* one of the Etruscan nobles who were at once priests and princes. [L]

Lüda, (formerly **Hüta**), *n.* industrial port (engineering, chemicals, textiles, oil refining, shipbuilding, food processing) in Liaoning, China, on Liaodong Peninsula, facing the Yellow Sea; population (1986) 4,500,000. It comprises the naval base of Lüshun (known under 19th-cent. Russian occupation as Port Arthur) and the commercial port of Dalien (formerly Talien/Dairen).

Luddite, *n.* a member of a band of workmen who organized riots (1811–16) for the destruction of machinery as a protest against unemployment; any opponent of technological change. **Luddism,** *n.* [supposedly after Ned *Ludd,* fl. 1779, a Leicestershire workman who destroyed machinery]

Ludendorff, *n.* **Erich von** (1865–1937), German general, chief of staff to Hindenburg in World War I, and responsible for the eastern-front victory at Tannenberg 1914. After Hindenburg's appointment as chief of general staff and Ludendorff's as quartermaster-general 1916, he was also politically influential. He took part in the Nazi rising in Munich 1923, and sat in the Reichstag (parliament) as a right-wing Nationalist.

ludicrous, *a.* adapted to excite laughter or derision; comical, ridiculous. **ludicrously,** *adv.* **ludicrousness,** *n.* **ludicro-,** *comb. form.* [L *lūdicrus,* from *lūdi-,* stem of *lūdus,* play]

ludo, *n.* a game played with counters on a specially chequered board. [L *ludo,* I play]

Ludwig I, *n.* (1786–1868), king of Bavaria 1825–48, succeeding his father Maximilian Joseph I. He made Munich an international cultural centre, but his association with the dancer Lola Montez, who dictated his policies for a year, led to his abdication 1848.

Ludwig II, *n.* (1845–1886), king of Bavaria from 1864, when he succeeded his father Maximilian II. He supported Austria during the Austro-Prussian War 1866, but brought Bavaria into the Franco-Prussian War as Prussia's ally, and in 1871 offered the German crown to the king of Prussia. He was the composer Wagner's patron, and built the Bayreuth theatre for him. Declared insane 1886, he drowned himself soon after.

Ludwig III, *n.* (1845–1921), king of Bavaria 1913–1918, when he abdicated upon the formation of a republic.

Luening, *n.* **Otto** (1900–), US composer. He studied in Zurich, and privately with Busoni. In 1949 he joined the staff at Columbia University, and in 1951 began a series of pioneering compositions for instruments and tape, some in partnership with Vladimir Ussachevsky (*Incantation* 1952, *Poem in Cycles*, and *Bells* 1954). In 1959 he became co-director, with Babbitt and Ussachevsky, of the Columbia-Princeton Electronic Music Center.

lues, *n.* plague, contagious disease, infection, contagion, now used only for syphilis. **luetic,** *a.* [L]

luff, *n.* that part of a ship's bows where the timbers begin to curve in towards the stem; the weather-edge of a fore-and-aft sail; the part of a ship facing into, towards the wind; the act of sailing close to the wind. *v.i.* to bring a ship's head or to steer nearer the wind. *v.t.* to bring (a ship's head) or the head of (ship) nearer the wind; to turn (the helm) so as to do this. **luff-tackle,** *n.* a large tackle composed of a double and single block. **luffing-match,** *n.* a struggle to secure the windward position. [ME *luff, lof(f)* from OF *lof;* perh. derived from MDut. *loef,* peg of a tiller]

luffa, LOOFAH.

†**luffer,** LOUVER.

Luftwaffe, *n.* the German Air Force before and during World War II. [G *Luft,* air, *Waffe,* weapon]

lug[1], *n.* a large marine worm, *Arenicola marina,* burrowing in the sand, used for bait. **lugworm,** *n.* [cp. LOG[1]]

lug[2], LUG-SAIL.

lug[3], *v.t.* (*past, p.p.* **lugged**) to drag, to pull, esp. roughly or with exertion; to tug, to haul; (*fig.*) to drag in, to insert unnecessarily. *v.i.* to drag; to move heavily or slowly. *n.* a drag or tug. [prob. from Scand. (cp. Swed. and Norw. *lugga,* to pull by the hair, *lugg,* the forelock)]

lug[4], *n.* a projecting part; a projecting part of a machine made to hold or grip another part; the lobe of the ear; (*coll.* or *Sc.*) the ear; a pliable rod or twig; a measure of land; unlooped handle of a pot. **lug-mark,** *n.* a mark cut in the ear of a sow, sheep etc., for identification. [etym. doubtful]

luge, *n.* a small one-man toboggan. *v.t.* to toboggan in one of these. [F]

Luger ®, *n.* a type of German automatic pistol.

luggage, *n.* anything heavy and cumbersome to be carried; the baggage of any army; a traveller's trunks, suitcases etc. **luggage-van,** *n.* a railway carriage for luggage, bicycles, etc.

lugger, *n.* a small vessel with two or three masts, a running bowsprit and lug-sails.

Lugosi, *n.* **Bela** (1882–1956), stage name of Bela Ferenc Blasko. Hungarian film actor who appeared in Hungarian and German films before going to Hollywood in 1921. His most famous role was *Dracula* (1930), followed by horror roles in *Son of Frankenstein* (1939), *The Body Snatcher* (1945), and *Bride of the Monster* (1956).

lug-sail, *n.* a four-cornered sail bent to a yard lashed obliquely to the mast. [etym. doubtful, perh. from LUG[3]]

lugubrious, *a.* mournful, dismal, funereal. **lugubriously,** *adv.* **lugubriousness,** *n.* [L *lūgubris,* from *lūgēre,* to mourn]

Lu Hsün, *n.* former transcription of Chinese writer Lu Xun.

Lukács, *n.* **Georg** (1885–1971), Hungarian philosopher, one of the founders of 'Western' or 'Hegelian' Marxism, a philosophical current opposed to the Marxism of the official communist movement.

Luke, St, *n.* (1st cent. AD), traditionally the compiler of the third Gospel and of the Acts of the Apostles in the New Testament. He is the patron saint of painters; his emblem is a winged ox, and his feast day 18 Oct.

lukewarm, *a.* moderately warm; tepid; indifferent, cool. *n.* a person who is indifferent or unenthusiastic. **lukewarmly,** *adv.* **lukewarmness,** *n.* [ME *luke,* tepid, prob. cogn. with OE *hleow,* LEE[1], WARM]

lull, *v.t.* to sooth to sleep, to calm, to quiet. *v.i.* to subside, to become quiet. *n.* a temporary calm; an intermission or abatement. **lullaby,** *n.* a refrain or song for lulling a child to sleep. *v.t.* to sing to sleep. **lullingly,** *adv.* [imit. (cp. Swed. *lulla,* MDut. *lullen,* G *lallen,* Gr. *lalein*)]

Lully, *n.* **Jean-Baptiste** (1632–1687), adopted name of Giovanni Battista Lulli. French composer of Italian origin who was court composer to Louis XIV. He composed music for the ballet, for Molière's plays, and established French opera with such works as *Alceste* (1674) and *Armide et Renaud* (1686). He was also a ballet dancer.

lulu, *n.* (*coll.*) an extremely good or bad person or thing.

lum, *n.* (*Sc.*) a chimney. **lum-hat,** *n.* a top-hat.

lumbago, *n.* rheumatism in the lumbar region. [L *lumbus,* loin]

lumbar, *a.* pertaining to portion of the body between the lower ribs and the upper part of the hipbone. *n.* a lumbar nerve, vertebra, artery etc. **lumbar puncture,** *n.* the insertion of a needle between two lumbar vertebrae to withdraw cerebrospinal fluid.

lumber[1], *v.i.* to move heavily, cumbrously or clumsily; to make a heavy rumbling noise. **lumbering,** *a.* **lumberingly,** *adv.* **lumbersome,** *a.* [etym. doubtful, perh. imit. (cp. Swed. dial. *lomra,* to roar, Icel. *hljōmr,* a sound) or freq. of LAME]

lumber[2], *n.* discarded articles of furniture and other rubbish taking up room; useless and cumbersome things; rubbish, refuse; superfluous bulk or fat, esp. in horses; (*N Am.*) timber sawn into marketable shape. *v.t.* to fill with lumber; to encumber, to obstruct; to heap up in a disorderly way; to cut and prepare timber for the market. **lumber camp,** *n.* a lumberman's camp. **lumber-dealer,** *n.* a timber merchant. **lumberjack, lumberman,** *n.* one who is employed in lumbering. **lumber-jacket,** *n.* a man's loose-fitting jacket in a heavy, usu. chequered material that fastens up to the neck; a woman's cardigan similarly fastened. **lumbermill,** *n.* a saw-mill. **lumber-room,** *n.* a room for the storage of lumber, trunks etc. **lumber-yard,** *n.* a timber yard. [etym. doubtful, perh. var. of LOMBARD[1], the room where the Lombard bankers stored their unredeemed pledges, or from prec.]

Lumbini, *n.* birthplace of Buddha in the foothills of the Himalayas near the Nepalese-Indian frontier. A sacred garden and shrine were established 1970 by the Nepalese government.

lumbrical, *a.* pertaining to, or resembling, a worm; applied to certain muscles. *n.pl.* four vermiform muscles, two of the foot and two of the hand, which help to flex the digits. **lumbriciform,** *a.* resembling a worm, vermiform. [L *lumbrīcus,* worm, -AL]

lumen, *n.* (*pl.* **-mens, -mina**) the SI unit of luminous flux, being the quantity of light emitted per second in a solid angle of one steradian by a uniform point-source having an intensity of one candela; (*Anat.*) the cavity of a tubular organ; a cavity within a plant cell wall. **luminel, luminal,** *a.* **luminance,** *n.* a measure, in candela/cm^2, of the luminous intensity of any surface in a given direction per unit of projected area. **luminant,** *n., a.* [L, light]

Lumet, *n.* **Sidney** (1924–), US film director. His films, sometimes marked by a heavy-handed seriousness, have met with varying critical and commercial success. They include *Twelve Angry Men* (1957), *Fail Safe* (1964), *The Deadly Affair* (1967), and *Network* (1976).

Lumière, *n.* **Auguste Marie** (1862–1954) and **Louis Jean** (1864–1948), French brothers who pioneered cinematography. In 1895 they patented their cinematograph, a combined camera and projector that operated at 16 frames per second, and opened the world's first cinema in Paris to show their films. The Lumière's first films were short static shots of everyday events such as *La Sortie des Usines Lumière* (1895) about workers leaving a factory and *L'Arroseur Arrosé* (1895), the world's first fiction film. Production was abandoned in 1900.

luminary, *n.* any body yielding light, esp. a heavenly body; one who enlightens mankind or is a brilliant exponent of a subject. **luminesce,** *v.i.* to exhibit luminescence. **luminescence,** *n.* the emission of light at low temperatures by processes other than incandescence, e.g. by chemical action. **luminescent,** *a.* **luminiferous,** *a.* giving, yielding or transmitting light. **luminist,** *n.* an artist who makes special use of light-effects. **luminosity,** *n.* being luminous; the measure of the amount of light emitted by a star irrespective of its distance from the earth. **luminous,** *a.* emitting light; shining brightly, brilliant; lucid, perspicuous, shedding light (on a subject etc.). **luminous flux,** *n.* a measure of the rate of flow of luminous energy. **luminous intensity,** *n.* a measure of the amount of light radiated in a given direction from a point source. **luminous paint,** *n.* a paint containing phosphorescent compounds which cause it to glow in the dark after exposure to light. **luminously,** *adv.* **luminousness,** *n.* [OF *luminarie,* med. L *lūminārium,* L *lūmināre,* from *lūmen -inis,* light]

lumme, lummy, *int.* an exclamation of surprise. [contr. of *Lord love me*]

lummox, *n.* (*coll.*) a clumsy person. [etym. unknown]

lump[1], *n.* a small mass of matter of no definite shape; a mass, a quantity, a heap, a lot; a swelling, a protuberance; a heavy, stupid person. *v.t.* to put together in a lump, to form into a mass; hence, to take collectively, to treat as all alike. *v.i.* to form or collect into lumps; to move (about) heavily or clumsily. **in the lump,** the whole taken together; altogether, in gross. **the lump,** the collective group of self-employed workers in the building trade. **lump-sugar,** *n.* loaf sugar broken into small lumps. **lump sum,** *n.* the whole amount of money taken together, as opp. to instalments. **lumpectomy,** *n.* the removal by surgery of a cancerous lump in the breast. **lumper,** *n.* one who lumps things together; a labourer who loads or unloads ships; (*sl.*) a militiaman; a small contractor or sweater who takes work in the lump and puts it out. **lumping,** *a.* large, heavy; big, bulky, plentiful. **lumpish,** *a.* like a lump; gross; lazy, inert; stupid. **lumpishly,** *adv.* **lumpishness,** *n.* **lumpy,** *a.* full of lumps; (*Naut.*) running in short waves that do not break. **lumpily,** *adv.* **lumpiness,** *n.* [etym. doubtful, prob. from Scand. (cp. Swed. dial. and Norw. *lump,* block, stump, Dan. *lumpe*)]

lump[2], *v.t.* (*coll.*) to dislike, to put up with. **like it or lump it,** put up with it as there is no alternative. [etym. doubtful, prob. imit.]

lump[3], lumpfish, *n.* a suctorial fish, *Cyclopterus lumpus,* of northern seas. [cp. MDut. *lompe,* G *lump,* F *lompe*]

lumpen, *a.* (*coll.*) stupid, oafish; denoting a degraded section of a particular social and economic grouping. **lumpenproletariat,** *n.* the very poorest section of the urban population, composing criminals, vagabonds etc. [G *Lumpen,* rags]

Lumumba, *n.* **Patrice** (1926–1961), Congolese politician, prime minister of Zaïre 1960. Imprisoned by the Belgians, but released in time to attend the conference giving the Congo independence 1960, he led the National Congolese Movement to victory in the subsequent general election. He was deposed in a coup d'état, and murdered some months later.

lunacy, *n.* unsoundness of mind, insanity, formerly supposed to be caused by the moon; gross folly, senseless conduct. **master in lunacy,** a person appointed to inspect lunatic asylums or investigate cases of alleged insanity. [see LUNATIC]

luna moth, *n.* a large N American moth with crescent-shaped markings on its forewings.

lunar, *a.* of, pertaining to, caused or influenced by the moon; resembling the moon. *n.* a lunar distance or observation. **lunar caustic,** *n.* nitrate of silver fused at a low heat. **lunar cycle** CYCLE. **lunar distance,** *n.* the angular distance of the moon from the sun, a planet or a star, used at sea in finding longitude. **lunar month,** *n.* the period of a complete revolution of the moon, 29½ days, (*pop.*) four weeks. **lunar observation,** *n.* observation of the moon's distance from the sun or a star to find the longitude. **lunar year,** *n.* a period of twelve lunar months. **lunarian,** *n.* an inhabitant of the moon; one using the lunar method of finding longitude; a lunarist. **lunarist,** *n.* an investigator of the moon; one who believes that the weather is largely affected by the moon. **lunary,** *a.* lunar. *n.* the moonwort. **lunate,** †**-nated, luniform,** *a.* crescent-shaped. **lunation,** *n.* the period between two returns of the moon, a lunar month. [L *Lūnārus,* from *lūna,* the moon]

lunatic, *a.* insane; mad, frantic, crazy, extremely foolish. *n.* an insane person. **lunatic asylum,** *n.* (*offensive*) formerly the name for a hospital for the care and treatment of the mentally ill. **lunatic fringe,** *n.* members of society or of a group regarded as holding extreme or fanatical views. [F *lunatique,* late L *lūnāticus,* as prec.]

lunation LUNAR.

lunch, *n.* a light repast between breakfast and dinner; a midday meal; (*N Am.*) a snack. *v.i.* to take lunch. *v.t.* to provide lunch for. **luncheon,** *n.* lunch (in more formal usage). **luncheon meat,** *n.* a type of pre-cooked meat, usu. pork minced with cereal, served cold. **luncheon voucher,** *n.* a voucher given to employees which can be used to pay for take-away food or a meal in a restaurant. [etym. doubtful, prob. a var. of LUMP[1], a lump or slice, as of bread]

lune, *n.* (*Geom.*) a figure enclosed by two intersecting arcs; anything in the shape of a half-moon; †(*pl.*) fits of lunacy, crotchets, freaks. [F, from L *lūna,* moon]

lunette, *n.* a semicircular aperture in a concave ceiling; a crescent-shaped or semicircular space or panel for a picture or decorative painting; a horseshoe lacking the branches; (*Fort.*) an advanced work of two faces and two flanks; a flattened watch-glass; a blinder for a draught horse; the hole for the neck in a guillotine. [F]

lung, *n.* one of the two organs of respiration in vertebrates, situated on each side of the chest; an analogous organ in invertebrates; (*fig.*) an open space in or near a city. **lung-fish,** *n.* a dipnoan, having lungs as well as gills. **lung-grown,** *a.* having the lungs adhering to the pleura. **lung-power,** *n.* strength of voice. **lungwort,** *n.* a lichen, *Sticta pulmonacea,* growing on the trunks of trees; the genus *Pulmonaria,* of the borage family, formerly held to be good for pulmonary diseases. **lunged,** *a.* **lungless,** *a.* [OE *lungen* (cp. Dut. *long,* Icel. *lunga,* G *Lunge*), cogn. with LIGHT[2], cp. LIGHTS]

lunge[1], *n.* a sudden thrust with a sword etc.; a sudden forward movement, a plunge. *v.i.* to make a lunge; to plunge or rush forward suddenly. [earlier *allonge,* see ALLONGE]

lunge[2], longe, *n.* a long rope or rein used in training horses. *v.t.* to drive a horse round in a circle at the end of a lunge. [F *longe,* var. of *loigne,* LUNE[2]]

lungi, *n.* a long cloth used as a loincloth or sash, sometimes as a turban. [Hind.]

luniform LUNAR.

lunisolar, *a.* pertaining to, or compounded of the revolutions of, the sun and the moon. **lunisolar period, year,** *n.* a period of 532 years found by multiplying the cycle of the sun by that of the moon. [L *lūna,* moon, *sōl,* sun]

lunt, *n.* a matchcord for firing cannon; flame, smoke. *v.i.* to flame, to emit smoke. [Dut. *lont* (see LINSTOCK)]

lunula, *n.* a crescent-shaped mark, spot or part, esp. at the base of a fingernail. **lunular, lunulate, -nulated,** *a.* **lunule,** *n.* **lunulet,** *n.* a small semicircular spot, of different colour from the other parts, on some insects. [L, dim. of *lūna,* moon]

Lupercalia, *n.* Roman festival celebrated 15 Feb. It took place at the Lupercal, the cave where Romulus and Remus were supposedly suckled by the wolf (*lupus*). Lupercalia included feasting, dancing, and sacrificing goats. Priests ran round the city carrying whips made from the hides of the sacrificed goats, a blow from which was believed to cure sterility in women.

lupin, lupine, *n.* a leguminous plant of the genus *Lupinus,* with spikes of white or coloured flowers, grown in flower-gardens and for fodder. **lupinin,** *n.* (*Chem.*) a bitter glucoside obtained from *L. albus* and *L. luteus.* [L *lupīnus*]

lupine, *a.* pertaining to wolves; like a wolf. [L *lupīnus,* from *lupus,* wolf]

lupoid, lupous LUPUS.

lupulin, *n.* the bitter essence of hops; a yellow granular aromatic powder containing that essence. **lupulite,** *n.* lupulin. [mod. L *lupulus,* hop, -IN]

lupus, *n.* a spreading tuberculous or ulcerous inflammation of the skin, usually of the face. **lupoid, lupous,** *a.* [L, wolf]

lurch[1], *n.* a losing position in the game of cribbage and some other games; †a swindle. **to leave in the lurch,** to leave in difficulties. [F *lourche,* a 16th-cent. game like backgammon, etym. doubtful]

lurch[2], *v.i.* of a ship, to roll suddenly to one side; to stagger. *n.* a sudden roll sideways, as of a ship; a stagger. [etym. doubtful]

†**lurch[3],** *v.i.* to lie in wait; to steal, to rob; to play tricks. *v.t.* to overreach, to cheat, to rob; to take or gain privily; to filch, to steal. **lurcher,** *n.* one who lurks about to steal or entrap; a dog supposed to be a cross between a collie and a greyhound; †a glutton. [var. of LURK]

†**lurdan, lurdane, lurden,** *a.* stupid, lazy, useless. *n.* a blockhead. [OF *lourdin,* from *lourd,* heavy]

lure[1], *n.* an object resembling a fowl, used to recall a hawk; hence, an enticement, an allurement. *v.t.* to attract or bring back by a lure; to entice. *v.t.* to call or tempt an animal, esp. a hawk. [OF *leurre,* prob. from Teut. (cp. G *Luder,* bait)]

lure[2], *n.* a trumpet with long, curved tube, used in Scandinavia for calling cattle home. [Icel. *lūthr*]

Lurex ®, *n.* (a fabric made from) a thin plastic-coated metallic thread.

lurid, *a.* of a pale yellow colour, wan, gloomy; ghastly, unearthly; shocking in detail; of a story etc., sensational; (*Bot.*) of a dirty brown colour. **luridly,** *adv.* **luridness,** *n.* [L *lūridus,* perh. cogn. with Gr. *chlōros,* green]

lurk, *v.i.* to lie hid; to lie in wait; to be latent, to exist unperceived; †to move about furtively. **lurker,** *n.* **lurking,** *a.* **lurking-hole, -place,** *n.* [etym. doubtful, perh. cogn. with LOUR (cp. Norw. and Swed. dial. *lurka,* G *lauern*)]

Lusaka, *n.* capital of Zambia from 1964 (of N Rhodesia 1935–64), 370 km/230 miles NE of Livingstone; commercial and agricultural centre (flour mills, tobacco factories, vehicle assembly, plastics, printing); population (1987) 819,000.

luscious, *a.* very sweet, delicious; sweet to excess; cloying, fulsome, over-rich in imagery, sensuousness etc. (of music, poetry etc.); †lascivious, voluptuous. **lusciously,** *adv.* **lusciousness,** *n.* [etym. doubtful]

lush[1], *a.* luxuriant in growth; succulent, juicy. **lushness,** *n.* [var. of obs. *lash,* OF *lasche* (F *lâche*), L *laxus,* LAX]

lush[2], *n.* (*sl.*) a heavy drinker, an alcoholic. *v.i.* to drink. *v.t.* to ply with liquor. **lushy,** *a.* drunk. [etym. doubtful]

Lusitania, *n.* ocean liner sunk by a German submarine 7 May 1915 with the loss of 1200 lives, including some Americans; its destruction helped bring the US into World War I.

lusk, luskish *a.* sluggish, indolent. **luskishness,** *n.* [etym. doubtful]

lust, *n.* a powerful desire for sexual pleasure, concupiscence, lasciviousness; sensual appetite; passionate desire for; †vigour. *v.i.* to have powerful or inordinate desire (for or after). †**luster,** *n.* **lustful,** *a.* **lustfully,** *adv.* **lustfulness,** *n.* †**lustick,** *a.* **lustiness,** *n.* **lustily,** *adv.* **lustless,** *a.* listless; joyless; free from lust. **lusty,** *a.* full of health and vigour. [OE (cp. Dut., Swed. and G *Lust*), cogn. with LIST[2]]

lustre[1], *n.* brightness, splendour, luminousness, gloss, sheen, bright light; the reflection of a light; a chandelier ornamented with pendants of cut glass; a cotton, woollen or other fabric with a glossy surface; a glossy enamel on pottery etc.; illustriousness, radiant beauty. **lustreless**, *a.* **lustrous**, *a.* **lustrously**, *adv.* [F, from L *lūstrāre,* to lighten, illumine (cogn. with *lux lūcis,* light)]

lustre[2], **lustrum**, *n.* a purification; an expiatory offering made by the Roman censors every five years; a period of five years. **lustral**, *a.* pertaining to or used in purification; pertaining to a lustrum. **lustrate**, *v.t.* to purify. †*v.i.* to go about inspecting for cleansing purposes. **lustration**, *n.* cleansing, esp. ceremonial cleansing. [L *lustrum,* prob. from *luere,* to wash (cogn. with *lavāre,* to wash, see LAVE[1])]

lustrine, lustring, *n.* a glossy silk fabric. [F *lustrine,* from LUSTRE[1]]

lustrum LUSTRE.

lusty LUST.

lute[1], *n.* a stringed instrument with a pear-shaped body and a long fretted fingerboard. *v.t.* to play on or as on the lute. *v.i.* to sound sweetly, like a lute. **lute-string**, *n.* a string of a lute; a noctuid moth with string-like markings on its wings. †**lutanist, lutenist**, †**luter, lutist**, *n.* a lute-player. [F *lut* (now *luth*), Prov. *laut,* Sp. *laud,* Arab. *al-'ūd,* the lute, orig. wood]

lute[2], *n.* a composition of clay or cement used to secure the joints of vessels and tubes, or as a covering to protect retorts etc. from fire; a rubber washer. *v.t.* to seal up or coat with lute. †**lutation**, *n.* the act or process of luting. †**lutose**, *a.* muddy, covered with clay or mud; (*Ent.*) covered with a powder resembling this. [OF *lut,* from L *lutum,* mud]

luteal, *a.* of or pertaining to the corpus luteum. **luteinize, -ise**, *v.t., v.i.* to produce or form corpora lutea. **luteinization, -isation**, *n.* **luteinizing hormone**, *n.* a hormone secreted from the front lobe of the pituitary gland which stimulates, in females, ovulation and the development of corpora lutea and, in males, maturation of the interstitial cells of the testes and androgen production. [L *lūteus,* yellow, *lūteum,* egg yolk]

lute-string LUTE[1].

lutestring, *n.* [corr. of LUSTRING].

Lutetian, *a.* Parisian. [L *Lutetia Parisiorum,* Paris]

lutetium, lutecium, *n.* an extremely rare metallic element, at. no.71; chem. symbol Lu; of the lanthanides, discovered in 1907 by Georges Urbain (1872–1938), a French chemist. [L *Lutetia,* Paris]

Luther, *n.* **Martin** (1483–1546), German Christian church reformer, a founder of Protestantism. When a priest at the university of Wittenberg 1517, he attacked the sale of indulgences in 95 theses and defied papal condemnation; the Holy Roman emperor Charles V summoned him to the Diet of Worms 1521, where he refused to retract his objections. After the drawing up of the Augsburg Confession 1530, he gradually retired from the Protestant leadership. **Lutheran**, *a.* of or belonging to Luther or his doctrines. *n.* a follower of Luther; a member of the Church based on Luther's religious doctrines. **Lutheranism, -therism**, *n.* a form of Protestant Christianity derived from the life and teaching of Martin Luther; it is sometimes called Evangelical to distinguish it from the other main branch of European Protestantism, the Reformed. The most generally accepted statement of Lutheranism is that of the Augsburg Confession 1530 but Luther's Shorter Catechism also carries great weight. It is the largest Protestant body, including some 80 million persons, of whom 40 million are in Germany, 19 million in Scandinavia, 8.5 million in the US and Canada, with most of the remainder in central Europe.

Luthuli, Lutuli, *n.* **Albert** (1899–1967), South African politician, president of the African National Congress from 1952. Luthuli, a Zulu tribal chief, preached non-violence and multiracialism. Arrested 1956, he was never actually tried for treason, although he suffered certain restrictions from 1959. He was under suspended sentence for burning his pass (an identity document required of non-white South Africans) when awarded the Nobel Peace Prize 1960.

Lutine bell, *n.* a bell recovered from the ship *Lutine* and rung at Lloyd's in London before important announcements, such as the loss of a vessel.

lutist LUTE[1].

Lutosławski, *n.* **Witold** (1913–), Polish composer and conductor, born in Warsaw. His early music, dissonant and powerful (*First Symphony* 1947), was criticized by the communist government, so he adopted a more popular style. With the lifting of artistic repression, he quickly adopted avant-garde techniques, including improvisatory and aleatoric forms. He has written chamber, vocal, and orchestral music, including three symphonies, *Livre pour orchestre* (1968) and *Mi-parti* (1976).

Lutyens, *n.* **Edwin Landseer** (1869–1944), English architect. His designs ranged from picturesque to Renaissance style country houses and ultimately evolved into a classical style as in the Cenotaph, London, and the Viceroy's House, New Delhi.

lutz, *n.* in figure-skating, a jump from one skate with one, two or three rotations and a return to the other skate. [etym. doubtful, perh. from Gustave *Lussi,* b.1898, Swiss skater who invented it]

lux, *n.* (*pl.* **lux, luxes**) the SI unit of illumination equal to one lumen per square metre. [L *lūx,* light]

luxate, *v.t.* to put out of joint, to dislocate. †*a.* out of joint. **luxation**, *n.* [L *luxātus,* p.p. of *luxāre,* to put out of joint, from *luxus,* Gr. *loxos, oblique*]

luxe, *n.* luxury, sumptuousness, superfine elegance. [F, from L *luxux*]

Luxembourg, *n.* capital of Luxembourg; population (1985) 76,000. The 16th-cent. Grand Ducal Palace, European Court of Justice, and European Parliament secretariat are situated here, but plenary sessions of the parliament are now held only in Strasbourg. Products include steel, chemicals, textiles, and processed food. **Luxembourg Accord**, *n.* French-initiated agreement in 1966 that a decision of the Council of Ministers of the European Community may be vetoed by a member whose national interests are at stake.

Luxembourg, Grand Duchy of, landlocked country in W Europe. **area** 2,586 sq km/998 sq miles. **capital** Luxembourg. **physical** on the river Moselle; part of the Ardennes (Oesling) forest in the north. **population** (1989) 380,000; annual growth rate 0%. **exports** pharmaceuticals, synthetic textiles; international banking is very important; Luxembourg is economically linked with Belgium. **language** French (official); local Letzeburgesch; German. **religion** Roman Catholic.

Luxembourg, Palais du, palace in Paris, France, in which the Senate sits. Built 1615 for Marie de' Medici by Salomon de Brosse, it was later enlarged.

Luxemburg, *n.* **Rosa** (1870–1919), Polish-born German communist, collaborator with Karl Liebknecht in founding the Spartacus League in 1918 (see SPARTACIST), and murdered with him during the Jan. 1919 Berlin workers' revolt.

Luxor, (Arabic **al-Uqsur**) *n.* village in Egypt on the E bank of the Nile near the ruins of Thebes.

Lu Xun, *n.* pen name of Chon Shu-jêu (1881–1936), Chinese short story writer. His three volumes of satirically realistic stories, *Call to Arms*, *Wandering*, and *Old Tales Retold*, reveal the influence of Gogol. He is one of the most popular of modern Chinese writers.

luxury, *n.* habitual indulgence in dainty and expensive pleasures; luxurious living; that which is delightful, esp. to the appetite; luxuriousness; †luxuriance, exuberance. **luxuriant**, *a.* abundant in growth; plentiful, copious, profuse, exuberant; fertile, prolific, rank; ornate, florid, extravagant, sumptuous. **luxuriance, -iancy**, *n.* **luxuriantly**, *adv.* **luxuriate**, *v.i.* to feed or live luxuriously; to revel, to indulge oneself to excess. †**luxuriation**, *n.* **luxurious**, *a.* **luxuriously**, *adv.* **luxuriousness**, *n.* †**luxurist**, *n.* [L *luxurians -iantem,* pres.p. of *luxuriāre,* from *luxuria, luxus,* extravagance, sumptuousness]

luzerne, LUCERNE.

Luzon, *n.* largest island of the Philippines; area 108,130 sq km/41,750 sq miles; capital Quezon City; population (1970) 18,001,270. The chief city is Manila, capital of the Philippines. Products include rice, timber, and minerals. It has US military bases.

LV, (*abbr.*) *l*uncheon *v*oucher.

LW, (*abbr.*) long wave; low water.

lx, (*phys. symbol*) lux.

-ly, *suf.* forming adjectives, as *ghastly, godly, manly,* or adverbs, as *badly, heavily, mightily.* [OE †*-līc,* a., LIKE[1]; *līce,* adv.]

lyam, *n.* a leash for holding hounds. **lyam-hound,** *n.* a blood-hound. [OF *liem* (F *lien*), see LIEN[1]]

†lyard,, †lyart, *a.* roan, dappled; grey; grey-headed. *n.* a dapple-grey horse. [OF *liart,* etym. doubtful]

lycanthropy, *n.* insanity in which the patient believes himself a wolf or some other animal, whose instincts and habits he assumes; belief in a form of witchcraft by which men or women transform themselves into wolves. **lycanthrope,** *n.* a werewolf, one suffering from lycanthropy. **lycanthropic,** *a.* **lycanthropist,** *n.* [Gr. *lukanthrōpos* (*lukos,* wolf, *anthrōpos,* man)]

lycée, *n.* a French State secondary school. [F]

lyceum, *n.* the garden at Athens in which Aristotle taught; hence, the Aristotelean philosophy or philosophic school; a place devoted to instruction; an institution for literary instruction or mutual improvement by means of lectures, libraries etc.; a lycée. [L *lycēum,* Gr. *Lukeion,* nom. *-os,* pertaining to Apollo, whose temple was adjoining]

†lych, lych-gate etc. LICH.

Lyceum, *n.* an ancient Athenian gymnasium and garden, with covered walks, where Aristotle taught. It was SE of the city and named after the nearby temple of Apollo Lyceus.

lychee LITCHI.

lychnis, *n.* a genus of plants belonging to the family Silenaceae, comprising the campions. [L, from Gr. *luchnis,* from *luchnos,* lamp]

lycopod, *n.* a club-moss, a member of the genus *Lycopodium,* or the order Lycopodiaceae. **lycopodiaceous,** *a.* **lycopodium,** *n.* a genus of perennial plants comprising the club-mosses; an inflammable yellow powder in the spore-cases of some species, used for making fireworks and as an absorbent in surgery. [mod. L *lycopodium* (Gr. *lukos,* wolf, *pous podos,* foot, from the claw-like shape of root)]

Lycra®, *n.* a synthetic elastic fibre and material used in swimwear and other tight-fitting garments.

Lycurgus, *n.* Spartan lawgiver. He is said to have been a member of the royal house, who, while acting as regent, gave the Spartans their constitution and system of education. Many scholars believe him to be purely mythical.

lyddite, *n.* a powerful explosive composed mainly of picric acid, used in shells. [*Lydd,* in Kent]

Lydgate, *n.* **John** (*c.* 1370– *c.* 1450), English poet. He was a Benedictine monk, and later prior. His numerous works were often translations or adaptations, such as *Troy Book,* and *Falls of Princes.*

Lydia, *n.* ancient kingdom in Anatolia (7th–6th cent. BC), with its capital at Sardis. The Lydians were the first Western people to use standard coinage. Their last king, Croesus, was conquered by the Persians 546 BC. **Lydian,** *a.* pertaining to Lydia, in Asia Minor, whose inhabitants were noted for effeminacy and voluptuousness; hence, effeminate, soft, voluptuous; (*Mus.*) applied to one of the modes in Greek music, and the third ecclesiastical mode. *n.* a native or inhabitant or the language of Lydia. **Lydian-stone,** *n.* (*Min.*) basanite.

lye, *n.* an alkaline solution leached from wood ashes or other alkaline substance; a lixivium, a detergent. [OE *lēag* (cp. Dut. *loog,* G *Lauge*), prob. cogn. with LAVE[1] and LATHER]

Lyell, *n.* **Charles** (1797–1875), Scottish geologist. In his book *The Principles of Geology* (1830–33), he opposed Cuvier's theory that the features of the Earth were formed by a series of catastrophes, and expounded Hutton's view, known as uniformitarianism, that past events were brought about by the same processes that occur today – a view that influenced Charles Darwin's theory of evolution.

lying[1], *n.* the act or habit of telling lies; a lie. *a.* telling lies; false, deceitful. **lyingly,** *adv.*

lying[2], *n.* the act or state of being recumbent; a place to lie in. **lying-in,** *n.* child-bed; lying in childbirth; hence **lying-in hospital. low-lying,** *a.* situated at a low level.

†lyke, LICH.

lyke-wake, *n.* a night watch over a dead body. [LICH, WAKE[2]]

Lyly, *n.* **John** (*c.* (1553–1606), English playwright and author of the romance *Euphues, or the Anatomy of Wit* (1578). Its elaborate stylistic devices gave rise to the word 'euphuism' for an affected rhetorical style.

lyme-grass, *n.* a coarse grass of the genus *Elymus,* planted in sand in order to bind it. [etym. doubtful, perh. from LIME[1]]

Lymeswold®, *n.* a mild, blue, soft cheese.

lymph, *n.* water or any clear transparent fluid; the comparatively transparent, colourless, alkaline fluid in the tissues and organs of the body, bearing a strong resemblance to blood without the red corpuscles; matter containing the virus of a disease, obtained from a diseased body or by culture, and used in vaccination. **lymph gland, node,** *n.* any of the small localized masses of tissue distributed along the lymphatic vessels that produce lymphocytes. **lymphatic,** *a.* pertaining to, containing, secreting or conveying lymph; phlegmatic, sluggish, flabby-tissued (of temperament etc., formerly supposed to be so affected by excess of lymph). *n.* †a madman, an enthusiast; a vessel that conveys lymph. **lymphatic system,** *n.* the network of capillary vessels that conveys lymph to the venous system. **lymphocyte,** *n.* a type of white blood cell formed in the lymph nodes, which forms part of the body's immunological defence against infection. **lymphoid,** *a.* containing or resembling lymph. **lymphoma,** *n.* (*pl.* **-phomas, -phomata,** -tə) a tumour of lymphoid tissue. **lymphomatous,** *a.* **lymphomatoid,** *a.* [L *lympha,* prob. cogn. with *limipidus,* LIMPID]

†lymphad, *n.* (*Sc.*) a one-masted galley; (*Her.*) this as a charge. [corr. of Gael. *longfhada*]

Lynch, *n.* **'Jack' (John)** (1917–), Irish politician, born in Cork. A noted Gaelic footballer and a barrister, in 1948 he entered the parliament of the republic as a Fianna Fáil member, and was prime minister 1966–73 and 1977–79.

lynch, *v.t.* to judge and punish, esp. to execute, by lynch law. **lynch law,** *n.* summary punishment without trial or upon trial by a self-appointed court. [Charles *Lynch,* 1742–1820, a Virginian farmer who inflicted summary punishment on lawless persons during the American War of Independence]

lynx, *n.* one of several species of animals of the cat tribe, characterized by tufted ear-tips, short tail and extremely sharp sight. **lynx-eyed,** *n.* having sharp sight. **lyncean,** *a.* pertaining to the lynx; lynx-eyed, sharp-sighted. [L, from Gr. *lunx,* rel. to *lussein,* to see (cp. with G *Luchs,* OE *lox*)]

Lyon[1], *n.* the chief of the Scottish heralds, also called **Lyon King of Arms.** [LION]

Lyon[2], (English **Lyons**) *n.*industrial city (textiles, chemicals, machinery, printing) and capital of Rhône *département,* Rhône-Alpes region, and third largest city of France, at the confluence of the Rhône and Saône, 275 km/170 miles NNW of Marseille; population (1982) 418,476, conurbation 1,221,000. Formerly a chief fortress of France, it was the ancient Lugdunum, taken by the Romans 43 BC.

Lyons, *n.* **Joseph** (1848–1917), British entrepreneur, founder of the catering firm of J Lyons 1894. He popularized 'tea-shops', and the 'Corner Houses' incorporating several restaurants of varying types were long a feature of London life.

lyophil, lyophilic, *a.* of a colloid, easily dispersed in a solvent. **lyophilize, -ise,** *v.t.* to freeze-dry. **lyophiliza-**

tion, -isation, *n.* **lyophobe, lyophobic**, *a.* of a colloid, not easily dispersed in a solvent [Gr. *lȳē*, separation, *phileein,* to love, *phobeein,* to fear]

Lyra, *n.* small but prominent constellation of the northern hemisphere, representing the lyre of Orpheus. Its brightest star is Vega.

lyre, *n.* a stringed musical instrument of the harp kind, anciently used as an accompaniment to the voice. **lyre-bird,** *n.* an insectivorous Australian bird, *Menura superba,* having the 16 tail-feathers of the male disposed in the form of a lyre. **lyrate**, **-rated**, *a.* shaped like a lyre. **lyric**, *a.* relating to or suited for the lyre; intended to be sung or fitted for expression in song; of a poem expressing the individual emotions of the poet; writing poetry of this kind. *n.* a lyric poem; a song; (*pl.*) verses used in lyric poetry; the words of a popular song. **lyrical,** *a.* lyric; effusive. **lyrically,** *adv.* **lyricism**, *n.* **lyrico-**, *comb. form.* **lyrist,** *n.* [F, from L *lyra,* Gr. *lura*]

Lysander, *n.* (died 395 BC), Spartan general. He brought the Peloponnesian War to a successful conclusion by capturing the Athenian fleet at Aegospotami 405 BC, and by starving Athens into surrender in the following year. He then aspired to make Sparta supreme in Greece and himself supreme in Sparta; he set up puppet governments in Athens and her former allies, and tried to secure for himself the Spartan kingship, but he was killed in battle with the Thebans.

Lysenko, *n.* **Trofim Denisovich** (1898–1976), Soviet biologist, who believed in the inheritance of acquired characters and used his position under Stalin to officially exclude Mendel's theory of inheritance. He was removed from office president of the Academy of Agricultural Sciences, after the fall of Khrushchev 1964.

Lysippus, *n.* (4th century BC), Greek sculptor. He made a series of portraits of Alexander the Great (Roman copies survive) and is also known for the *Apoxyomenos*, an athlete (copy in the Vatican), and a colossal *Hercules* (lost).

lysis, *n.* the gradual decline in the symptoms of a disease, opp. to crisis; the destruction of cells by the action of a lysin. **lyse**, *v.t.* to cause to undergo lysis. **-lysis**, *comb. form.* denoting a breaking down, loosening or disintegration. **-lyse, -lyze**, *comb. form.* to cause or undergo loosening or decomposition through lysis. **lysergic acid diethylamide** LSD. **lysimeter**, *n.* an instrument for measuring the rate of percolation of rain through soil. **lysin**, *n.* a substance, esp. an antibody, which causes the disintegration of cells. **lysine**, *n.* an amino acid obtained from dietary sources which is essential to nutrition in humans. **lysol**, *n.* a mildly astringent solution of cresol and soap, used as a disinfectant.

-lyst, -lyte, *comb. form* denoting a substance capable of being broken down.

lythe, *n.* (*Sc., Ir.*) the pollack. [Sc.]

-lytic, -lytical, *comb. form* of or producing decomposition.

M

M[1], **m**, the thirteenth letter of the alphabet, M, m (*pl.* **Ems, M's, Ms**), has but one sound, that of a labial nasal, as in *man, time;* (*Print.*) an em; (*Roman numeral*) 1000. **M roof,** *n.* a roof formed by the junction of two parallel ridges with a cross section like a broad M. **M & B,** a proprietary drug of the sulphanilamide group (initials of makers May & Baker).

M[2], (*abbr.*) Majesty; (G) mark; Master; (F) Monsieur; (UK) motorway; the Roman numerall 1000.

m, (*abbr.*) male; married; masculine; (*Mech.*) mass; maiden over; metre(s); mile(s); milli-; minute(s); month(s); moon; meridian.

ma, *n.* childish shortening of MAMMA[1].

MA, (*abbr.*) Master of Arts.

ma'am, *n.* (*coll.*) Madam (used by servants etc., and at Courts in addressing the queen or a royal princess). [MADAM]

maar, *n.* a volcanic crater without a cone of lava, caused by a single explosion. [G]

Mabinogion, the, a collection of mediaeval Welsh myths and folk tales put together in the mid-19th cent. and drawn from two manuscripts: *The White Book of Rhydderch* (1300–25) and *The Red Book of Hergest* (1375–1425).

Mabuse, *n.* **Jan** (adopted name of Jan Gossaert) (*c.* 1478– *c.* 1533), Flemish painter, active chiefly in Antwerp. His common name derives from his birthplace, Maubeuge. His visit to Italy in 1508 with Philip of Burgundy started a new vogue in Flanders for Italianate ornament and classical influence in painting, including sculptural nude figures.

MAC, *n.* a European standard for satellite broadcasting. [acronym for *m*ultiplex *a*nalogue *c*omponents]

macabre, *a.* gruesome. **macabrely,** *adv.* **macaberesque,** *a.* [F]

macaco[1], *n.* orig. a South African monkey, now any monkey of the genus *Macacus*. [Port., monkey]

macaco[2], *n.* applied to various kinds of lemur. [F]

McAdam, *n.* **John Loudon** (1756–1836), Scottish engineer. The word 'macadamizing' was coined for his system of constructing roads of broken granite.

macadam, *n.* broken stone for macadamizing; a road made by macadamizing. *v.t.* to macadamize. **tar macadam** TAR[1]. **macadamize, -ise,** *v.t.* to make, cover or pave (a road) with layers of broken stone so as to form a smooth hard surface. **macadamization, -isation,** *n.* **macadamizer, -iser,** *n.* [J.L. *McAdam,* 1756–1836, road-engineer]

Macao, *n.* a Portuguese possession on the south coast of China, about 65 km/40 miles west of Hong Kong, from which it is separated by the estuary of the Canton River; it consists of a peninsula and the islands of Taipa and Colôane. **area** 17 sq km/7 sq miles. **capital** Macao, on the peninsula. **population** (1986) 426,000. **language** Cantonese; Portuguese (official). **religion** Buddhist, with 6% Catholic minority.

macaque MACACO[1].

macarize, -ise, *v.t.* to bless, to make or to pronounce happy. **macarism,** *n.* [Gr. *makarizein,* from *makar,* blessed]

macaroni, *n.* an Italian pasta made of fine wheaten flour formed into long slender tubes; (*pl.* **-nies**) a medley; a crested variety of penguin; a fop, a dandy. †*a.* foppish, fashionable, affected. **macaronic,** *a.* †of, pertaining to or like macaroni; †of, pertaining to or like a macaroni; consisting of a jumble of incongruous words, as of different languages, or of modern words Latinized or Latin words modernized, in burlesque poetry. *n.* a confused medley or jumble; (*pl.*) macaronic verse. **macaroni cheese,** *n.* a dish of macaroni in a cheese sauce. [It. *maccaroni* (now *maccheroni, pl.,* see foll.) perh. from earlier *maccare,* L *mācerāre,* to MACERATE]

macaroon, *n.* a small sweet cake or biscuit made of flour, almonds, sugar etc. [F *macaron,* It. *maccarone,* sing. of *maccaroni,* as prec.]

MacArthur, *n.* **Douglas** (1880–1964), US general in World War II, commander of US forces in the Far East and, from Mar. 1942, of the Allied forces in the SW Pacific. After the surrender of Japan he commanded the Allied occupation forces there. During 1950 he commanded the UN forces in Korea, but in Apr. 1951, after expressing views contrary to US and UN policy, he was relieved of all his commands by President Truman.

macartney, *n.* the fireback pheasant, *Euplocamus ignitus*. [George, 1st Earl *Macartney,* 1737–1806, introducer]

macassar, *n.* an oil for the hair, orig. brought from *Macassar,* in the island of Celebes also called **macassar oil**.

Macaulay, *n.* **Thomas Babington, Baron Macaulay** (1800–59), English historian, essayist, poet and politician, secretary of war (1839–41). His *History of England* in five volumes (1849–51) celebrates the Glorious Revolution of 1668 as the crowning achievement of the Whig party.

macaw, *n.* a S American parrot, of various species distinguished by their large size and beautiful plumage. [Port. *macao,* prob. from Tupí-Guaraní]

macaw-tree, *n.* a palm of the genus *Acrocomia,* esp. *A. fusiformis* or *A. lasiospatha*. [prob. Carib., TREE]

Macbeth, *n.* king of Scotland from 1040. The son of Findlaech, hereditary ruler of Moray, he was commander of the forces of Duncan I, King of Scotia, whom he killed in battle (1040). His reign was prosperous until Duncan's son Malcolm III led an invasion and killed him at Lumphanan. Shakespeare's tragedy *Macbeth* was based on the 16th-cent. historian Holinshed's *Chronicles*.

Maccabees, *n.* Jewish family, sometimes known as the **Hasmonaeans**. It was founded by the priest Mattathias (d. 166 BC) who, with his sons, led the struggle for Jewish independence against the Syrians in the 2nd cent. BC. This story is told in the book of Maccabees in the Apocrypha. Judas (d. 161 BC) reconquered Jerusalem 165 BC, and Simon (d. 135 BC) established Jewish independence in 142 BC. **Maccabean,** *a.*

McCarthy[1], *n.* **Joseph R(aymond) 'Joe'** (1909–57), US right-wing Republican politician, whose unsubstantiated claim (1950) that the State Department had been infiltrated by Communists started a wave of anticommunist hysteria, wild accusations and blacklists, which continued until he was discredited in 1954.

McCarthy[2], *n.* **Mary (Therese)** (1912–89), US novelist and critic. Much of her work looks probingly at US society, for example the novels *The Groves of Academe* (1952), which describes the anticommunist witch-hunts of the time (see McCARTHYISM), and *The Group* (1963), which follows the post-college careers of eight women.

McCarthyism, *n.* intolerance of liberalism; the hunting down of suspected Communists and their dismissal from public employment. [J. *McCarthy,* see above]

McCartney, *n.* **Paul** (1942–), Rock singer, songwriter, and bass guitarist, former member of the Beatles, and leader of the pop group Wings (1971–81). His subsequent solo hits have included collaborations with Michael Jackson and Elvis Costello.

McClellan, *n.* **George Brinton** (1826–85), US Civil War general, commander in chief of the Union forces (1861–62). He was dismissed by President Lincoln when he delayed five weeks in following up his victory over the Confederate general Lee at Antietam. He was the unsuccessful Democrat presidential candidate against Lincoln in 1864.

McClure, *n.* **Robert John le Mesurier** (1807–73), Irish-born British admiral and explorer. While on an expedition (1850–54) searching for John Franklin, he was the first to pass through the Northwest Passage.

maccoboy, *n.* a rose-scented snuff, orig. grown at Macouba, in Martinique.

McCowen, *n.* **Alec** (1925–), British actor. His Shakespearean roles include Richard II and the Fool in *King Lear*; he is also noted for his dramatic one-man shows.

McCoy REAL.

MacCready, *n.* **Paul** (1925–), US designer of the *Gossamer Condor* aircraft which made the first controlled flight by human power alone in 1977. His *Solar Challenger* flew from Paris to London under solar power; and in 1985 he constructed a powered replica of a pterodactyl.

McCullers, *n.* **Carson (Smith)** (1917–67), US novelist. Most of her writing (including her best-known novels *The Heart is a Lonely Hunter* (1940) and *Reflections in a Golden Eye* (1941)) is set in the Southern states, where she was born, and deals with spiritual isolation, containing elements of sometimes macabre violence.

McDiarmid, *n.* **Hugh** (pen name of Christopher Murray Grieve (1892–1978), Scottish nationalist and Marxist poet. His works include *A Drunk Man looks at the Thistle* (1926) and two *Hymns to Lenin* (1930, 1935).

Macdonald[1], *n.* **Flora** (1722–90), Scottish heroine who rescued Prince Charles Edward Stuart, the Young Pretender, after his defeat at Culloden in 1746. Disguising him as her maid, she escorted him from her home in the Hebrides to France. She was arrested, but released in 1747.

MacDonald[2], *n.* **(James) Ramsay** (1866–1937), British Labour politician. He joined the Independent Labour Party in 1894, and became first secretary of the new Labour Party in 1900. In Parliament he led the party (1906–14) and (1922–31), and was prime minister of the first two Labour governments, Jan.–Oct. 1924 and 1929–31, and of a coalition (1931–35), for which he left the party.

Macdonald[3], *n.* **John Alexander** (1815–91), Canadian Conservative politician. He was born in Glasgow but taken to Ontario as a child. In 1857 he became prime minister of Upper Canada. He took the leading part in the movement for federation, and in 1867 became the first prime minister of Canada. He was defeated in 1873, but returned to office in 1878, and retained it until his death.

McDowell, *n.* **Malcolm** (1943–), British actor who played the rebellious hero in the film *If* (1969) and confirmed his acting abilities in Stanley Kubrick's *A Clockwork Orange* (1971).

Mace®, *n.* a liquid causing the eyes to run and a feeling of nausea, used in self-defence, riot control etc.

mace[1], *n.* a mediaeval weapon shaped like a club with a heavy metal head, usu. spiked; an ornamented staff of office of analogous shape; a mace-bearer; a flat-headed stick formerly used in billiards; a similar stick used in bagatelle. **mace-bearer,** *n.* a person who carries the mace before a judge etc. †**mace-proof,** *n.* secure against arrest. **macer,** *n.* a mace-bearer; (*Sc.*) an officer who keeps order in courts of law. [OF (F *masse*), from L. *matea*, known from its dim. *mateola*, a mallet]

mace[2], *n.* a spice made from the dried covering of the nutmeg. †**mace-ale,** *n.* ale spiced with mace. [F *macis*]

macedoine, *n.* a dish of mixed vegetables; a medley. [F, Macedonian, from the mixture of nationalities in Macedonia]

Macedonia[1], *n.* (Serbo-Croat **Makedonija**) a federal republic of Yugoslavia. **area** 25,700 sq km/9,920 sq miles. **capital** Skopje. **physical** mountainous; chief rivers Struma and Vardar. **population** (1981) 2,040,000, including 1,280,000 Macedonians, 380,000 Albanians and 90,000 Turks. **language** Macedonian, closely allied to Bulgarian and written in Cyrillic. **religion** Macedonian Orthodox Christian.

Macedonia[2], *n.* (Greek **Makedhonia**) mountainous region of N Greece, bounded to the W and N by Albania and Yugoslavia; population (1981) 2,122,000; area 34,177 sq km/13,200 sq miles. Chief city is Thessaloniki. Fertile valleys produce grain, olives, grapes, tobacco and livestock. Mt Olympus rises to 2918 m/9570 ft on the border with Thessaly.

Macedonia[3], *n.* an ancient region of Greece, forming parts of modern Greece, Bulgaria and Yugoslavia. Macedonia gained control of Greece after Philip II's victory at Chaeronea in 338 BC. His son, Alexander the Great, conquered a vast empire. Macedonia became a Roman province in 146 BC.

macerate, *v.t.* to soften by steeping; to separate the parts of by a digestive process; to make lean, to cause to waste away; †to harass. *v.i.* to undergo maceration. **maceration,** *n.* [L *mācerātus*, p.p. of *mācerāre*]

Mach MACH NUMBER.

machair, *n.* a strip of land just above the high-water mark along a sandy shore, used for pasturage. [Gael.]

Machairodus, *n.* the sabre-toothed lion or tiger, an extinct genus. [Gr. *machaira*, sabre, *odous*, tooth]

machan, *n.* an elevated platform for tiger-shooting. [Hind.]

Machel, *n.* **Samora** (1933–86), Mozambique nationalist leader, president (1975–86). Machel was active in the liberation front Frelimo from its conception in 1962, fighting for independence from Portugal. He became Frelimo leader (1966), and Mozambique's first president, from independence until his death in a plane crash near the South African border.

machete, *n.* a broad knife or cutlass used in tropical America as a weapon, to cut down sugar canes etc. [Sp.]

Machiavel, *n.* an unscrupulous intriguer; an intriguing and unscrupulous statesman or politician. **Machiavellian,** *n., a.* **Machiavellianism, Machiavellism,** *n.* [Niccolò MACHIAVELLI]

Machiavelli, *n.* **Niccolò** (1469–1527), Italian politician and author, whose name is now synonymous with cunning and cynical statecraft. In his most important political works, *Il principe/The Prince* (1513) and *Discorsi/Discourses* (1531), he discusses ways in which rulers can advance the interests of their states (and themselves) through an often amoral and opportunist manipulation of other people.

machinate, *v.i.* to contrive, to plot, to intrigue. **machination,** *n.* (*often pl.*). **machinator,** *n.* [L *māchinātus*, p.p. of *māchinārī*, to contrive, see foll.]

machine, *n.* a mechanical apparatus by which motive power is applied; any mechanism, simple (as a lever or tool) or compound, for applying or directing force; a person who acts mechanically and without intelligence; any organization of a complex character designed to apply power of any kind; a bicycle or tricycle; (*Sc.*) a light vehicle; in classical Greek theatre, a contrivance for effecting change of scenery or introducing a supernatural being; hence, supernatural agency in a poem etc. *v.t.* to effect by means of machinery; to print by machinery; to sew with a sewing-machine. *v.i.* to be employed in or upon machinery. **machine code, language,** *n.* a set of instructions for coding information in a form usable by a computer. **machine-gun,** *n.* a light piece of ordnance loaded and fired automatically. **machine-gunner,** *n.* **machine head,** *n.* (*Mus.*) a simple worm and tooth-wheel mechanism fitted to the head of a bass viol or other instrument for stretching the strings to the required pitch. **machine-made,** *a.* made by machinery, as distinct from *hand-made*. **machine-readable,** *a.* of data, in a form usable by a computer. **machine-ruler,** *n.* a machine for ruling paper. **machine-shop,** *n.* a large workshop where machines are made or repaired. **machine-tool,** *n.* a machine for doing work with a tool, such as a chisel, plane, drill etc. **machine-work,** *n.* **machineable,** *a.* **machinery,** *n.* (*collect.*) machines; the parts or mechanism of a machine; mechanical combination; any combination to keep anything in action or to effect a purpose; the means and combinations, esp. supernatural, employed to develop a plot in a poem etc. **machinist,** *n.* one who constructs machines; one versed in the principles of machinery; one who works or tends a machine, esp. a sewing-machine. **machinize, -ise,** *v.t.* to convert to machinery. [F, from L *māchina,* Gr. *mēchanē,* from *mēchos,* means, contrivance, cogn. with MAY [1]]

machiocolate, *v.t.* to furnish with machicolations. **machicolation,** *n.* an aperture between the corbels supporting a projecting parapet, through which missiles were hurled upon assailants; a parapet or gallery with a series of such apertures. **machicoulis,** *n.* a machicolation. [low L *machicolātus*]

machismo, *n.* aggressivearrogant assertiveness, often associated with masculinity. [Mex. Sp., from Sp. *macho,* male]

Mach number, *n.* a number representing the ratio of the velocity of a body in a certain medium to the velocity of sound in the same medium. [Ernst *Mach,* Austrian physicist, 1838–1916]

macho, *a.* showing machismo. [MACHISMO]

Machtpolitik, *n.* (G) power politics.

Machu Picchu, *n.* a ruined Inca city in Peru, built *c.* 1500 AD, NW of Cuzco, discovered in 1911 by Hiram Bingham. It stands at the top of 300 m/1000 ft high cliffs, and contains the well-preserved remains of houses and temples.

MacInnes, *n.* **Colin** (1914–76), English novelist, son of the novelist Angela Thirkell. He made a reputation with sharp depictions of London youth and subcultures of the 1950s, such as *City of Spades* (1957) and *Absolute Beginners* (1959).

Macintosh, *n.* **Charles** (1766–1843), Scottish manufacturing chemist who invented a waterproof fabric lined with a rubber that was used for raincoats – hence 'mackintosh'. Other waterproofing processes have now largely superseded this method.

mack, mac, *n.* (*coll.*) short for MACKINTOSH.

Mackay of Clashfern, *n.* **Baron James Peter Hymers** (1927—), Scottish lawyer and Conservative politician. The son of a railway signalman, he won first class honours in mathematics and statistics and after a period of teaching and research switched to law, being called to the Bar in 1955. Ten years later he became a QC and in 1979 was unexpectedly made Lord Advocate for Scotland, and a life peer. He became Lord Chancellor in 1987, and in 1989 announced a reform package to end legal restrictive practices, including prohibiting the barristers' monopoly of advocacy in the higher courts, promoting the combination of the work of barristers and solicitors in 'mixed' practices, and allowing building societies and banks to do property conveyancing, formerly limited to solicitors. The plans met with fierce opposition.

Macke, *n.* **August** (1887–1914), German painter, a founder member of the Blaue Reiter group in Munich. With Franz Marc he developed a semi-abstract style comprising cubist and Fauvist characteristics.

McKellen, *n.* **Ian** (1939–), British actor, whose stage roles include Richard II and Edward II, and Mozart in the stage version of *Amadeus*. His films include *Priest of Love* (1982) and *Plenty* (1985).

Mackendrick, *n.* **Alexander** (1912–), American-born, Scottish director responsible for some of Ealing Studio's finest comedies, including *Whisky Galore* (1949) and *The Man in the White Suit* (1951). He later made several films in America like *Mandy* (1952) and *Sweet Smell of Success* (1957) before becoming a film lecturer.

Mackensen, *n.* **August von** (1849–1945), German field marshal. During World War I he achieved the breakthrough at Gorlice and the conquest of Serbia (1915), and in 1916 played a major role in the overthrow of Romania. After the war Mackensen retained his popularity to become a folk hero of the German army.

Mackenzie¹, *n.* **Compton** (1883–1972), Scottish author. His parents were actors. He was educated at Magdalen College, Oxford University, and published his first novel *The Passionate Elopement* in 1911. Later works were *Carnival* (1912), *Sinister Street* (1913–14) (an autobiographical novel); and the comic *Whisky Galore* (1947). He published his autobiography in ten 'octaves' (volumes) (1963–71).

Mackenzie², *n.* **William Lyon** (1795–1861), Canadian politician, born in Scotland. He emigrated to Canada in 1820, and led the rebellion of 1837–38, an unsuccessful attempt to limit British rule and establish more democratic institutions in Canada. After its failure he lived in the US until 1849, and in 1851–58 sat on the Canadian legislature as a Radical. He was grandfather of W.L. Mackenzie King, the Liberal prime minister.

Mackenzie River, *n.* a river in the Northwest Territories, Canada, flowing from Great Slave Lake NW to the Arctic Ocean; about 1800 km/1120 miles long. It is the main channel of the Finlay-Peace-Mackenzie system, 4241 km/2635 miles long.

mackerel, *n.* a well-known sea-fish, *Scomber scomber,* moving in shoals in the N Atlantic and coming inshore in summer to spawn, valuable as a food-fish. **mackerel-breeze, -gale,** *n.* a strong fresh breeze good for mackerel-fishing. **mackerel-shark,** *n.* the porbeagle. **mackerel-sky,** *n.* a sky with small roundish masses of cirrocumulus, frequent in summer. [OF *makerel* (F *maquereau*)]

mackinaw, *n.* (*N Am.*) a heavy woollen blanket. [Michilli-*mackinac,* island in Lake Michigan where they were first distributed to Indians]

McKinley, Mount, *n.* a peak in Alaska, US, the highest in North America, 6194 m/20,320 ft; named after US president William McKinley.

McKinley, *n.* **William** (1843–1901), 25th president of the US, 1897–1901, a Republican. He was born in Ohio, and elected to Congress in 1876. His period as president was marked by the US's adoption of an imperialist policy, as exemplified by the Spanish-American War of 1898 and the annexation of the Philippines. He was assassinated in Buffalo, New York.

mackintosh, macintosh, *n.* a water-proof material made of rubber and cloth; a coat or cloak made of this, a raincoat. [Charles *Mackintosh,* 1766–1843, inventor]

Mackintosh, *n.* **Charles Rennie** (1868–1928), Scottish Art Nouveau architect, designer and painter, who exercised considerable influence on European design. His chief work includes the Glasgow School of Art (1896).

mackle, *n.* in printing, a blurred impression, causing printed matter to appear double. *v.t.* to spot, stain, blur. [see MACULE under MACULA]

Mackmurdo, *n.* **Arthur H.** (1851–1942), English designer and architect. He founded the Century Guild in 1882, a group of architects, artists and designers inspired by William Morris and John Ruskin. His book and textile designs are forerunners of Art Nouveau.

Maclaine, *n.* **Shirley** (stage name of Shirley MacLean Beaty) (1934–), US actress, sister of Warren Beatty. She has played both comedy and dramatic roles. Her many offscreen interests have limited her film appearances, which include *The Trouble with Harry* (1955), *The Apartment* (1960), and *Terms of Endearment* (1983).

McLaren, *n.* racing car company, makers of the most successful Formula One Grand Prix car of the 1980s. The team was founded in 1966 by the New Zealand driver Bruce McLaren, and by 1988 had won more than 80 Grand Prix races. McLaren was killed in an accident in 1970, and Ron Dennis became the team manager. McLaren world champions have been: Emerson Fittipaldi (1974), James Hunt (1976), Nikki

Lauda (1984), Alain Prost (1985, 1986, and 1989) and Ayrton Senna (1988).

macle, *n.* a twin crystal; (*Her.*) a mascle. **macled,** *a.* (*Cryst.*) hemitropic; (*Her.*) mascled. [F, from MACULA]

Maclean[1], *n.* **Alistair** (1922–87), Scottish adventure novelist. His first novel, *HMS Ulysses* (1955) was based on wartime experience. It was followed by *The Guns of Navarone* (1957), and other adventure novels. Many of his books were made into films.

Maclean[2], *n.* **Donald** (1913–83), British spy, who worked for the USSR while in the UK civil service. He defected to the USSR in 1951 together with Guy Burgess.

MacLennan, *n.* **Robert (Adam Ross)** (1936–), Scottish centrist politician. Member of parliament for Caithness and Sutherland from 1966. He left the Labour Party for the Social Democrats (SDP) in 1981, and was SDP leader in 1988 during merger negotiations with the Liberals. He then became a member of the new Social and Liberal Democrats.

McLuhan, *n.* **(Herbert) Marshall** (1911–80), Canadian theorist of communication, noted for his views on the effects of technology on modern society. He coined the phrase 'the medium is the message', meaning that the form rather than the content of information is crucial. His works include *The Gutenberg Galaxy* (1962) (in which he coined the phrase 'the global village' for the modern electronic society), *Understanding Media* (1964), and *The Medium is the Massage* (sic) (1967).

MacMahon, *n.* **Marie Edmé Patrice Maurice, Comte de MacMahon** (1808–93), marshal of France. Captured at Sedan in 1870 during the Franco-Prussian War, he suppressed the Paris Commune after his release, and as president of the republic (1873–79) worked for a royalist restoration until forced to resign.

MacMillan[1], *n.* **Kirkpatrick,** Scottish blacksmith, who invented the bicycle in 1839. His invention consisted of a 'hobby-horse' that was fitted with treadles and propelled by pedalling.

Macmillan[2], *n.* **(Maurice) Harold, 1st Earl of Stockton** (1894–1986), British Conservative politician. As minister of housing (1951–54) he achieved the construction of 300,000 new houses per year. He was chancellor of the Exchequer (1955–57), and became prime minister (1957) on Eden's resignation after the Suez crisis. At home, he furthered domestic expansion. Internationally, he attempted unsuccessfully to negotiate British entry to the European Community, and encouraged the transition to independence of British colonies in Africa.

MacMillan[3], *n.* **Kenneth** (1929–), Scottish choreographer. After studying at the Sadler's Wells Ballet School he was director of the Royal Ballet (1970–77) and then principal choreographer.

McNaghten rules, *n.pl.* (*Law*) rules governing the degree of responsibility of a mentally abnormal criminal defendant. [defendant in a lawsuit of 1843]

MacNeice, *n.* **Louis** (1907–63), British poet, born in Belfast. He made his debut with *Blind Fireworks* (1929) and developed a polished ease of expression, reflecting his classical training, as in *Autumn Journal* (1939). Unlike many of his contemporaries, he was politically uncommitted. Later works include the play *The Dark Tower* (1947), written for radio, for which he also wrote features (1941–49); a verse translation of Goethe's *Faust*, and the radio play *The Administrator* (1961). He also translated the Greek classics.

McPhee, *n.* **Colin** (1900–64), US composer. His studies of Balinese music (1934-36) produced two works, *Tabuh-tabuhan* for two pianos and orchestra (1936) and *Balinese CeremonialMusic* for two pianos (1940), which influenced Cage and later generations of US composers.

Macpherson, *n.* **James** (1736–96), Scottish writer and forger, author of *Fragments of Ancient Poetry collected in the Highlands of Scotland* (1760), followed by the epics *Fingal* (1761) and *Temora* (1763), which he claimed as the work of the 3rd-cent. bard Ossian. After his death they were shown to be forgeries.

Macquarie, *n.* **Lachlan** (1761–1834), Scottish administrator in Australia. He succeeded Bligh as governor of New South Wales in 1808, raised the demoralized settlement to prosperity, and did much to rehabilitate ex-convicts. In 1821 he returned to Britain in poor health, exhausted by struggles with his opponents. Lachlan River and Macquarie River and Island are named after him.

McQueen, *n.* **Steve (Terrence Steven)** (1930–80), US actor. He was one of the most popular film stars of the 1960s and 1970s, admired for his portrayals of the strong, silent loner, and noted for performing his own stunt work. After television success in the 1950s he became a film star with *The Magnificent Seven* (1960). His films include *The Great Escape* (1963), *Bullitt* (1968), *Papillon* (1973) and *The Hunter* (1980).

macr- MACR(O)-.

macramé, *n.* a fringe or trimming of knotted thread or cord; knotted work. [Turk. *marqrama*]

Macready, *n.* **William Charles** (1793–1873), British actor. He made his debut at Covent Garden, London, in 1816. Noted for his roles as Shakespeare's tragic heroes (Macbeth, Lear and Hamlet), he was partly responsible for persuading the theatre to return to the original texts of Shakespeare and abandon the earlier, bowdlerized versions.

macro, *n.* (*pl.* **macros**) a computer instruction that represents a sequence of instructions.

macr(o)- *comb. form* great, large (as distinct from small). [Gr. *makros,* long]

macrobiote, *n.* one who lives long. **macrobiotic,** *a.* of a diet, consisting chiefly of whole grains or of vegetables grown without chemical additives; concerning such a diet. **macrobiotics,** *n.sing.*

macrocephalic, -lous, *a.* largeheaded. **macrocephalism,** *n.*

macrocosm, *n.* the great world, the universe, as distinct from *microcosm;* the great whole of any body etc., esp. as imagined on a small scale by a part. **macrocosmic,** *a.*

macrocrystalline, *a.* having crystals visible to the naked eye.

macrocyte, *n.* a large, red blood-corpuscle.

macrodactylic, -lous, *a.* having long fingers or toes.

macrodiagonal, *n.* the longer diagonal of a rhombic prism.

macroeconomics, *n. sing.* the study of economics on a large scale, e.g. of national economies.

macro instruction, MACRO.

macrometer, *n.* an instrument with two telescopes used by surveyors for measuring distant objects.

macromolecule, *n.* a large complex molecule formed from a number of simple molecules.

macron, *n.* a short horizontal line put over a vowel (as ē) to show that it is pronounced with a long sound. [Gr. neut. a. of *makros,* long]

macrophage, *n.* a large phagocytic cell found in connective tissue. [Gr. *phagein,* to eat]

macropod, *a.* long-footed. *n.* a long-footed animal, esp. a spider-crab. **macropodal, -dous,** *a.* large-footed, as an embryo with the radicle large relatively to the cotyledon, or a leaf with a long foot-stalk. [Gr. *pous podos,* foot]

macropterous, *a.* long-winged. [Gr. *pteron* a wing]

macroscopic, *a.* visible with the naked eye, as distinct from *microscopic*. **macroscopical,** *a.* **macroscopically,** *adv.*

macrosporange, -angium, *n.* a sporangium or capsule containing macrospores.

macrospore, *n.* a relatively large spore, as in the club-mosses etc.; (*Zool.*) one of the spore-like parts resulting from the division of a monad.

macrostructure, *n.* the structure, e.g. of a body part or the soil, revealed by visual examination, with little or no magnification. **macrostructural,** *a.*

macrurus, *a.* long-tailed; of or belonging to the *Macrura,* a division of decapod crustaceans comprising the lobsters and shrimps. [Gr. *oura,* tail]

macula, *n.* (*pl.* **-lae**) a spot, as on the skin, the surface of the sun etc. **macula lutea**, *n.* a small yellowish spot near the centre of the retina of the eye, where vision is especially acute. **macular,** *a.* **maculate**, *v.t.* to spot, to stain. *a.*, spotted, stained, impure. **maculation,** *n.* **macule**, *n.* a spot, a stain; a mackle. [L]

MAD, (*abbr.*) mutual assured destruction, a theory of nuclear deterrence based on the ability of each side to inflict an unacceptable level of damage on the other.

mad, *a.* (*comp.* **madder**[1], *superl.* **maddest**) disordered in mind, lunatic, insane, crazy; furious, frantic, wildly excited; of animals, rabid; extravagant, infatuated, inflamed, wild, frolicsome; exceedingly foolish, very unwise; (*coll.*) enraged, annoyed, vexed. *v.i.* to be or go mad; to act madly. *v.t.* to make mad. **like mad,** (*coll.*) violently, wildly, excitedly. **madbrain, madbrained,** *a.* hot-headed, eccentric. **madcap,** *a.* mad, eccentric. *n.* a person of wild and eccentric habits. **mad-doctor,** (*coll.*) a doctor attending lunatics. **mad-headed,** *a.* **madhouse,** *n.* a lunatic asylum; a scene of confusion or uproar. **madman,** *n.* **madwoman,** *n. fem.* **madden,** *v.t., v.i.* **maddening,** *a.* **maddeningly,** *adv.* †**madding,** *a.* furious, raging, acting madly. **madly,** *adv.* in an insane manner; (*coll.*) extremely. **madness,** *n.* [OE *gemǣdd, gemæded,* p.p. of *gemædan* (cp. Icel. *meiddr,* OHG *gameit,* cogn. with L *mūtāre,* to change)]

Madagascar, *n.* Democratic Republic of (*Repoblika Demokratika n'i Madagaskar*), an island in the Indian Ocean, off the coast of E Africa, about 400 km/280 miles from Mozambique. **area** 587,041 sq km/226,598 sq miles. **capital** Antananarivo. **towns** chief port Toamasina. **physical** central highlands; humid valleys and coastal plains. **exports** coffee, sugar, spice, textiles. **population** (1988) 10,919,000; annual growth rate 2.8%. **language** Malagasy (of the Malayo-Polynesian family, official); French and English. **religion** animist 50%, Christian 40%, Muslim 10%.

madam, *n.* a polite form of address to a woman; the formal opening of a letter to a woman; (*coll.*) a brothel keeper; (*coll.*) an impertinent girl. [OF *ma dame,* my lady (see DAME)]

Madame, *n.* the French title for married women and mode of address to a woman; †the title of a French princess, esp. the eldest daughter of the king or the dauphin. [F, as prec.]

Madame Bovary, *n.* a novel by Flaubert, published in France (1857). It aroused controversy by its portrayal of a country doctor's wife driven to suicide by a series of unhappy love affairs.

madarosis, *n.* loss of the hair, esp. of the eyebrows. [Gr. (*madaros,* bald, -OSIS)]

madder[1] MAD.

madder[2], *n.* a shrubby climbing-plant of the genus *Rubia,* esp. *R. tinctoria,* the root of which is used in dyeing; the dye obtained from this plant. **madder-bleach**, *n.* a style of bleaching cotton. **madder-print,** *n.* cloth or cotton treated by madder-printing. [OE *maedere* (cp. Icel. *mathra,* Swed. *madra*)]

made, *a.* p.p. of MAKE[2]. **made to measure,** clothes, footwear etc., made according to the customer's measurements. **made dish,** *n.* one made up of various ingredients. **made ground, earth,** *n.* ground that has been formed artificially. **made man, woman,** *n.* a person whose success is assured. **made-up,** *a.* of complexion etc., artificial; of a story etc., invented, coined.

Madeira[1], *n.* a white wine made in Madeira. **madeira cake,** *n.* a light, spongy cake without fruit. [Port., wood, timber (the island being well wooded), L *matēria,* MATTER]

Madeira[2], *n.* a group of islands forming an autonomous region of Portugal off the NW coast of Africa, about 420 km/260 miles N of the Canary Islands. Madeira, the largest, and Porto Santo, are the only inhabited islands. The Desertas and Selvagens are uninhabited islets. Their mild climate makes them an all-year-round resort. **area** 796 sq km/308 sq miles. **capital** Funchal, on Madeira. **physical** Pico Ruivo, on Madeira, is the highest mountain at 1861 m/6056 ft. **products** madeira (a fortified wine), sugar cane, fruit, fish, handicrafts. **population** (1986) 269,500.

Madeira River, *n.* a river of W Brazil; length 3250 km/2020 miles. It is formed by the rivers Beni and Mamoré, and flows NE to join the Amazon.

madeleine, *n.* a small sponge cake, often coated with jam and coconut. [F]

Mademoiselle, *n.* (*pl.* **mesdemoiselles**, a title given to an unmarried Frenchwoman; a French teacher or governess. [F (*ma,* MY, *demoiselle,* see DAMSEL) (cp. MADAME)]

maderize, -ise, *v.i.* of white wine, to go reddish and flat-tasting through oxidation. [*Madeira,* which has a reddish colour]

Maderna, *n.* **Bruno** (1920–73), Italian composer and conductor. He studied with Malapiero and Scherchen, and collaborated with Berio in setting up an electronic studio in Milan. His compositions combine advanced techniques with an elegance of sound, and include a pioneering work for live and pre-recorded flute, *Musica su due dimensioni* (1952), numerous concertos, and the aleatoric *Aura* for orchestra (1974).

madge, *n.* the barn-owl; the magpie. [fam. form of *Margaret*]

madhouse MAD.

Madhya Pradesh, *n.* a state of central India. **area** 442,800 sq km/170,921 sq miles. **capital** Bhopal. **towns** Indore, Jabalpur, Gwalior, Durg-Bhilainagar, Raipur, Ujjain. **products** cotton, oilseed, sugar, textiles, engineering, paper, aluminium. **population** (1981) 52,132,000. **language** Hindi.

madia, *n.* a plant, *Madia sativa,* allied to the sunflowers, cultivated for the oil it yields. [Chilean Sp. *madi*]

†**madid,** *a.* wet, moist. [L *madidus,* from *madēre,* to be wet]

Madison, *n.* **James** (1751–1836), 4th president of the US (1809–17). In 1787 he became a member of the Philadelphia Constitutional Convention and took a leading part in drawing up the US constitution and the Bill of Rights. As secretary of state in Jefferson's government (1801–09), his main achievement was the Louisiana Purchase. He was elected president in 1808 and re-elected in 1812. During his period of office the War of 1812 with Britain took place.

Madison Square Garden, venue in New York, built as a boxing arena and also used for concerts. The current 'Garden' is the fourth to bear the name and staged its first boxing match in 1968. It is situated over Pensylvania Station on 7th Avenue, New York City.

madman MAD.

Madoc, Prince, *n.* legendary prince of Gwynedd, Wales, supposed to have discovered the Americas and been an ancestor of a group of light-skinned, Welsh-speaking Indians in the American West.

Madonna, *n.* the Virgin Mary; a picture or statue of the Virgin Mary. **Madonna lily,** *n.* the white lily, *Lilium candidum.* [It. (*ma, mia,* MY, *donna,* L *domina,* lady)]

Madras[1], *n.* a large bright-coloured handkerchief worn on the head by Afro-Caribbeans; a fine cotton or silk fabric. [from foll.]

Madras[2], *n.* an industrial port (cotton, cement, chemicals, iron and steel) and capital of Tamil Nadu, India, on the Bay of Bengal; population (1981) 4,277,000. Fort St George (1639) remains from the East India Company when Madras was the chief port on the E coast. Madras was occupied by the French (1746–48), and shelled by the German ship *Emden* in 1914, the only place in India attacked in World War I.

madrepore, *n.* a perforated coral or the animal producing such. **madreporic, madreporiform**, *a.* **madreporid,** *n., a.* **madreporigenous**, *a.* **madreporite,** *n.* a fossil madrepore; a calcareous rock of columnar structure; the madreporic tubercle in echinoderms. [F *madrépore,* It. *madrepora* (*madre,* matter, *poro,* L *porus,* PORE[1], or late L *pōrus,* Gr. *pōros,* calcareous stone)]

Madrid, *n.* industrial city (leather, chemicals, furniture, tobacco, paper) and capital of Spain and Madrid province; population (1986) 3,124,000. Built on an elevated plateau in the centre of the country, at 655 m/

2183 ft it is the highest capital city in Europe and has excesses of heat and cold. Madrid province has an area of 8000 sq km/3088 sq miles, and a population of 4,855,000. Madrid began as a Moorish citadel captured by Castile in 1083, became important in the times of Charles V and Philip II and was designated capital 1561.

madrigal, *n.* a short amorous poem; an unaccompanied vocal composition in five or six parts; (*loosely*) a part-song, a glee. [It. *madrigale,* perh. from *mandria,* herd, flock, fold, L and Gr. *mandra,* fold etc.]

madroño, *n.* a large evergreen tree, *Arbutus menziesii,* of N California, with hard wood, and edible berries. [Sp.]

Madurai, *n.* a city in Tamil Nadu, India; site of the 16th–17th cent. Hindu temple of Sundareswara, and of Madurai University (1966); cotton industry; population (1981) 904,000.

maduro, *n.* a type of dark, strong cigar. [Sp. *maduro,* ripe; cf. MATURE]

madwort, *n.* alyssum; also the catchweed, *Asperugo procumbens.* [MAD, WORT, perh. translating Gr. *alusson* (A-, priv., *lussa,* rabies)]

Maecenas, *n.* a munificent patron of literature or art. [a Roman knight, *c.* 70–8 BC, patron of Horace and Virgil]

maelstrom, *n.* a dangerous whirlpool off the coast of Norway; a turmoil, an overwhelming situation. [Dut. (now *maalstroom* (*malen,* to grind, to whirl, *stroom,* stream)]

maenad, *n.* (*pl.* **-nads**) a woman who took part in the orgies of Bacchus, a bacchante; a frenzied woman. [L *Maenas -adis,* Gr. *Mainas -ados,* from *mainesthai,* to rave]

maestoso, *adv.* (*Mus.*) with dignity, grandeur and strength. [It., MAJESTIC]

maestro, *n.* (*pl.* **-tros, -tri,**) a master in any art, esp. in music; a great composer or conductor. [It.]

mae west, *n.* an airman's life-jacket [named thus because, when inflated, it resembles the bosom of the US actress Mae West, 1892–1980]

maffick, *v.i.* (*coll.*) to celebrate an event uproariously. **mafficker,** *n.* **mafficking,** *n.* [from *Mafeking,* in South Africa, besieged by the Boers and relieved 16 May 1900, which event was celebrated with wild rejoicings]

maffled, *a.* confused, muddled. **maffling,** *n.* a simpleton. [p.p. of obs. *maffle,* to stammer (cp. Dut. *maffelen*)]

Mafia, *n.* active hostility to the law and its agents, widespread especially among the population of Sicily, where it frequently leads to violent crimes; a secret criminal society based on this, engaged in international organized crime, esp. in the US. **Mafioso** , *n.* (*pl.* **Mafiosi,**) a member of the Mafia. [Sicilian It.]

mag¹, *n.* (*sl.*) a half-penny. **magflying,** *n.* pitch-and-toss. [etym. doubtful]

mag², *n.* the magpie; (*Shooting*) a magpie; the long-tailed titmouse; †a chatterbox. *v.i.* to chatter. [short for *Margaret*]

mag³, *n.* (*coll.*) short for MAGAZINE.

Magadha, *n.* a kingdom of ancient India, roughly corresponding to the middle and southern parts of modern Bihar. It was the scene of many incidents in the life of Buddha, and was the seat of the Maurya dynasty, founded by Chandragupta in the 3rd cent. BC.

magazine, *n.* a place for storage, a depot, a warehouse; a building or apartment for military stores, esp. ammunition; a storeroom for explosives etc. aboard ship; the chamber holding cartridges in a magazine-gun; a light-tight receptacle or enclosure for holding exposed or unexposed films or plates; a periodical publication or broadcast containing miscellaneous articles by different people. **magazine-gun,** *n.* a rifle or other gun fed with cartridges from a magazine. [F *magasin,* It. *magazzino,* Arab. *makhāzīn, pl.* of *makhzan,* storehouse, from *khazn,* a laying up]

magdalen, *n.* a reformed prostitute; an asylum for such women. **Magdalen** (Oxford), **Magdalene** (Cambridge) **College,** *both pron*[Mary *Magdalene,* or of *Magdala* (Luke viii.2), identified with the woman mentioned in Luke vii. 37–50]

Magdalenian, *a.* of or pertaining to the period of Upper Palaeolithic culture, succeeding the Solutrian period, typified by the implements and weapons of bone, horn, ivory and stone, and carvings and engravings found at this station. [rock-shelter of *La Madeleine,* Dordogne, France]

Magdeburg, *n.* an industrial city (vehicles, paper, chemicals, iron, steel, textiles, machinery) and port on the river Elbe, in East Germany, capital of Magdeburg county; population (1986) 289,000. Magdeburg was a member of the Hanseatic League, and has a 13th-cent. Gothic cathedral. Magdeburg county has an area of 11,530 sq km/4451 sq miles, and a population of 1,250,000.

mage, *n.* a magician. [L MAGUS]

Magellan, *n.* **Ferdinand** (1480–1521), Portuguese navigator. In 1519 he set sail in the *Victoria* from Seville with the intention of reaching the East Indies by a westerly route. He sailed through the **Magellan Strait** at the tip of South America, crossed an ocean he named the Pacific, and in 1521 reached the Philippines, where he was killed in a battle with the islanders. His companions returned to Seville in 1522, completing the voyage under del Cano.

Magellanic Clouds, *n.pl.* in astronomy, the two nearest galaxies. They are irregularly shaped, and appear as detached parts of the Milky Way, in the southern constellations Dorado and Tucana.

magenta, *n.* an aniline dye of a brilliant crimson colour. [after a city in Italy near which the Austrians were defeated in a bloody battle by the French and Sardinians in 1859]

maggot, *n.* a grub, a worm, esp. the larva of the cheese- or flesh-fly; a whim, a crotchet; †a whimsical person. **†maggot-pie,** *n.* the magpie. **maggoty,** *a.* **maggotiness,** *n.* [perh. corr. of ME *maddock, mathek* (cp. Icel. *mathkr,* OE *mathu*)]

Maghreb, *n.* a name for NW Africa (Arabic 'far west', 'sunset'). The Maghreb powers – Algeria, Libya, Morocco, Tunisia and Western Sahara – agreed on economic coordination (1964–65), with Mauritania cooperating from 1970. Chad and Mali are sometimes included.

magi, magian etc. MAGUS.

magic, *n.* the pretended art of employing supernatural power to influence or control events; sorcery, witchcraft; any agency, power or action that has astonishing results. *a.* pertaining to or used in magic; using magic; exercising supernatural powers; produced by magic; (*coll.*) used as a form of approval. *v.t.* to affect or move by magic. **black magic** BLACK. **white magic** WHITE. **magic circle,** *n.* one possessing properties analogous to those of the magic square. **magic lantern,** *n.* an apparatus with a lens through which a magnified image from a glass slide is on a screen by a powerful light. **magic mushroom,** *n.* a type of fungus containing a hallucinogenic substance. **magic square,** *n.* a series of numbers so disposed in a square that the totals, taken perpendicularly, horizontally or diagonally, are equal. **magical,** *a.* **magically,** *adv.* **magician,** *n.* [F *magique,* L *magicus,* Gr. *magikos,* from *magos,* MAGUS]

Magic Mountain, The, a novel by Thomas Mann, published in Germany (1924). It is an ironic portrayal of the lives of inmates in a Swiss sanatorium, showing the futility of their sheltered existence.

Maginot Line, *n.* French fortification system along the German frontier from Switzerland to Luxembourg built (1929–36) under the direction of the war minister, André Maginot. It consisted of semi-underground forts joined by underground passages, and protected by antitank defences; lighter fortifications continued the line to the sea. In 1940 the Germans pierced the Belgian frontier line and outflanked the Maginot Line.

magisterial, *a.* pertaining to or befitting a master or magistrate; authoritative, commanding; dictatorial, domineering; oracular. **magisterially,** *adv.* **ma-**

gisterium, *n.* the teaching authority in the Roman Catholic Church; †**magistery,** *n.* mastership, authority; in alchemy, a master-principle of nature, esp. the principle of transmuting substances or a substance, such as the philosopher's stone, possessing this. [med. L *magisteriālis,* L *magisterius,* from *magister,* MASTER]

magistral, *a.* of or like a master, magisterial; of a medicine, specially prescribed or devised, not in the ordinary pharmacopoeia; †acting as a sovereign remedy. †*n.* a magistral preparation; a sovereign remedy. [L *magistrālis,* as prec.]

magistrand, *n.* an Arts student in the fourth year at Aberdeen or St Andrews Universities. [from med. L *magistrandus,* ger.p. of *magistrārī,* to become an MA (see MASTER)]

magistrate, *n.* a public officer, commissioned to administer the law, a Justice of the Peace. **magistrates' court,** *n.* a court of summary jurisdiction for minor offences and preliminary hearings. **magistracy, magistrateship, magistrature,** *n.* †**magistratic, -ical,**, *a.* [F *magistrat,* L *magistrātus,* as MASTER]

Maglemosian, *a.* of a transitional culture between the Palaeolithic and Neolithic, represented by finds at Maglemose in Denmark.

magma, *n.* (*pl.* **-mas, -mata**) a crude mixture of mineral or organic matter in a thin paste; (*Pharmacy*) a confection, a thick residuum etc.; the molten semi-fluid matter below the earth's crust. [L, from Gr., from *massein,* to knead]

Magna Carta, *n.* the Great Charter of English liberties sealed by King John on 15 June 1215; any fundamental constitution guaranteeing rights and privileges. [med. L, great CHARTER]

magna cum laude, with great distinction. [L]

magnalium, *n.* an alloy of magnesium and aluminium.

magnanerie, *n.* silkworm culture; a silkworm house. [F, from *magnan,* silkworm]

magnanimous, *a.* great-minded, elevated in soul or sentiment; brave, generous. **magnanimity,** *n.* **magnanimously,** *adv.* [L *magnanimus* (*magnus,* great, *animus,* soul)]

magnate, *n.* a person of rank, distinction or great wealth. [late L *magnas -nātem,* from *magnus,* great]

magnes, *n.* a magnet. [L, MAGNET]

magnesia, *n.* oxide of magnesium, a white alkaline antacid earth; hydrated carbonate of magnesia, used as an antacid and laxative. **magnesian,** *a.* **magnesite,**, *n.* native magnesium carbonate. [med. L, from Gr., fem. of *Magnēsios,* of or pertaining to Magnesia in Thessaly (applied to two minerals, the lodestone and a silver-like stone, perh. talc)]

magnesium, *n.* a divalent metallic element, at. no.12; chem. symbol Mg, the base of magnesia. **magnesium ribbon, wire,** *n.* magnesium prepared for burning as an illuminant.

magnet, *n.* the lodestone; a body, usu. of iron or steel, to which the properties of the lodestone, of attracting iron and pointing to the poles, have been imparted; a thing or person exercising a powerful attractive influence. **magnetic,** *a.* pertaining to a magnet or magnetism; having the properties of a magnet; attractive; mesmeric. *n.* any metal capable of receiving the properties of the lodestone; (*pl.,* sing. in constr.) the science or principles of magnetism. **magnetic battery,** *n.* a combination of magnets with their poles similarly arranged. **magnetic dip,** *n.* the angle between the earth's magnetic field and the horizontal. **magnetic disk** DISK. **magnetic equator,** *n.* a line round the globe where the magnetic needle has no dip. †**magnetic fluid,** *n.* a fluid formerly supposed to account for magnetism. **magnetic flux,** *n.* a measure of the strength of a magnetic field over a given area. **magnetic friction,** *n.* the reaction of a strong magnetic field on an electric discharge. **magnetic iron,** *n.* magnetite. **magnetic mine,** *n.* a submarine mine detonated by the passing over it of a metal ship. **magnetic needle,** *n.* a slender poised bar of magnetized steel, as in the mariner's compass, pointing north and south. **magnetic north, south,** or **pole,** *n.* two nearly opposite points of the earth's surface where the magnetic needle dips vertically. **magnetic resonance,** *n.* the vibration of electrons, atoms, molecules or nuclei in a magnetic field in response to various radiation frequencies. **magnetic screen,** *n.* a screen of soft iron cutting off a magnetic needle from the influence of a magnet. **magnetic storm,** *n.* a disturbance of the earth's magnetism setting up an oscillation of the magnetic needle. **magnetic tape,** *n.* a tape covered with a magnetic powder used for the recording and reproduction of sound and television pictures. **magnetical,** *a.* **magnetically,** *adv.* **magnetism,** *n.* the property whereby certain bodies, esp. iron and its compounds, attract or repel each other according to certain laws; the science treating of this property, its conditions or laws; the attractive power itself; personal attractiveness, charm. **magnetist,** *n.* one skilled in the science of magnetism or in animal magnetism. **magnetite,** *n.* magnetic oxide of iron. **magnetize, -ise,** *v.t.* to communicate magnetic properties to; to attract as with a magnet; to mesmerize. *v.i.* to become magnetic. **magnetization, -isation,** *n.* **magnetizer, -iser,** *n.* [OF *magnete,* L *magnēs -nētis,* Gr. *magnēs -nētos,* (stone) of magnetite, see prec.]

magneto, *n.* (*pl.* **-tos**) a magneto-electric machine (esp. the igniting apparatus of an internal-combustion engine). **magneto-electricity,** electricity generated by the inductive action of magnets; the science treating of such electricity. **magneto-electric-telegraph,** *n.* a system of telegraphy in which magneto-electric machines, not voltaic batteries, produce the current. **magneto-ignition,** *n.* ignition by a magneto-generated spark in a petrol engine. **magneto-pointer,** *n.* the index of a magneto-electric dial telegraph. **magneto-printer,** *n.* a printing-telegraph worked by a magneto-electric machine. [MAGNET]

magnetograph, *n.* an instrument for measuring magnetic forces, esp. terrestrial magnetism.

magnetometer, *n.* a device for measuring the intensity or direction of a magnetic field, esp. of the earth. **magnetometry,** *n.*

magneton, *n.* the unit of magnetic moment.

magnetophone, *n.* an instrument on the principle of the telephone for producing loud musical tones. **magneto-phonograph,** *n.* a phonograph which records speech magnetically.

magnetoscope, *n.* an instrument which shows the presence of magnetic force-lines.

magnetron, *n.* a thermionic tube for generating very high frequency oscillations.

†**magnific, -ical,** *a.* magnificent, grand, sublime. †**magnifically,** *adv.* [F *magnifique,* L *magnificus* (*magnus,* -FIC)]

Magnificat, *n.* the song of the Virgin Mary on her visit to her cousin Elizabeth shortly after the Annunciation (Luke i.46–55), so called from the first word in the Latin version; a setting of the same to music. [L, 3rd sing. pres. of *magnificāre,* to MAGNIFY]

magnification MAGNIFY.

magnificent, *a.* grand in appearance, majestic, splendid; characterized by sumptuousness, luxury, splendour or generous profusion; (*coll.*) first-rate, excellent. **magnificence,** *n.* **magnificently,** *adv.* [OF, from L *magnificent-,* stem of *magnificentior,* compar. of *magnificus,* MAGNIFIC]

magnifico, *n.* a grandee, orig. of Venice. [It.]

magnify, *v.t.* to increase the apparent size of (an object) as with an optical instrument; to make greater, to increase; to extol, to glorify; to exaggerate. *v.i.* to increase the apparent size of objects. **magnifying glass,** *n.* an optical lens for magnifying objects. **magnification,** *n.* **magnifier,** *n.* [F *magnifier,* L *magnificāre* (*magnus,* great, *-ficāre, facere,* to make)]

magniloquent, *a.* using high-flown, pompous or bombastic language. **magniloquence,** *n.* **magniloquently,** *adv.* [L *magniloquus* (*magnus,* great, *-loquus,* assim. to *loquens -entem,* pres.p. of *loquī,* to speak)]

magnitude, *n.* size, bulk, extent, quantity, amount; anything that can be measured; importance; the order of brilliance of a star. **of the first magnitude,** among the best, worst, most important etc. of its kind. [L *magnitūdo,* from *magnus,* great, -TUDE]

Magnolia, *n.* a genus of beautiful flowering trees or shrubs, chiefly N American. [P. *Magnol,* 1638–1715, French botanist]

Magnox, *n.* an early type of nuclear reactor used in the UK, for example in Calder Hall, the world's first commercial nuclear power station. This type of reactor uses uranium fuel encased in tubes of magnesium alloy called Magnox. Carbon dioxide gas is used as a coolant to extract heat from the reactor core.

magnum, *n.* a bottle containing two quarts; two quarts; a wine bottle containing the equivalent of two normal bottles (about 1½ litres); a large-calibre pistol. [L, orig. neut. sing. of *magnus,* great]

magnum bonum, *n.* the name applied to large kinds of plums and and potatoes. [neut. sing. of *magnus,* great, and *bonus,* good]

magnum opus, *n.* the greatest work of a writer, painter etc. [L, great work]

Magog GOG AND MAGOG.

magot, *n.* the tailless Barbary ape. *Macacus inuus,* of Gibraltar and N Africa. [F]

magpie, *n.* a well-known chattering bird, *Pica caudata,* with black and white plumage; a chatterer; a person who collects and hoards trifles; a variety of domestic pigeon resembling a magpie; (*Austral.*) the black and white crow-shrike; in rifle-shooting, a shot that hits the outermost division but one of the target. **magpie lark,** *n.* the Austral. peewee. [MAG[2], PIE[1]]

magra, *n.* an Australian Aboriginal woman's sling for carrying a child. [Abor.]

Magritte, *n.* **René** (1898–1967). Belgian Surrealist painter. His paintings focus on visual paradoxes and everyday objects taken out of context. Recurring motifs include bowler hats, apples and windows.

maguey, *n.* a type of agave whose leaves yield fibre used to make an alcoholic drink. [Sp., from Taino]

magus, *n.* (*pl.* **-gi**) a member of the priestly caste among the Medes and Persians; a magician. **the Magi,** the three holy men of the East who brought presents to the infant Saviour. **magian,** *n., a.* **magianism,** *n.* [L, from Gr. *magos,* OPers. *magus*]

Magyar, *n.* one of the Mongoloid race (entering Europe in 884), dominant in Hungary; a Magyar blouse or bodice. *a.* pertaining to a type of blouse in which the sleeves and the rest of the garment are all one piece. **Magyarism,** *n.* **Magyarize, -ise,** *v.t.* [native name]

Mahabad, *n.* a Kurdish town in Azerbaijan, W Iran, population (1983) 63,000. Occupied by Russian troops in 1941 it formed the centre of a short-lived Kurdish republic (1945-46) before being reoccupied by the Iranians. In the 1980s Mahabad was the focal point of resistance by Iranian Kurds against the Isalmic republic.

Mahābhārata, *n.* a Sanskrit Hindu epic consisting of 18 books, probably composed in its present form about 300 BC. It forms with the *Ramayana* the two great epics of the Hindus. It deals with the fortunes of the rival families of the Kauravas and the Pandavas, and contains the *Bhagavad-Gītā*, or *Song of the Blessed*, an episode in the sixth book.

Mahādeva, *n.* a title given to the Hindu god Siva. [Sansk., great god].

Mahādevī, *n.* a title given to Sakti, the consort of the Hindu god Siva. She is worshipped in many forms, including her more active manifestations as Kali or Durga and her peaceful form as Parvati. [Sansk., great goddess].

Mahan, *n.* **Alfred Thayer** (1840–1914), US naval officer and military historian, author of *The Influence of Sea Power upon History* (1890), in which he propounded a global strategy based on the importance of sea power.

Maharajah, *n.* a title assumed by some Indian princes. **Maharani,** *n.* a princess; the wife of a Maharajah. [Sansk. *mahā-rājā* (*mahā,* great, RAJAH)]

Maharashtra, *n.* a state in W central India. **area** 307,800 sq km/118,811 sq miles. **capital** Bombay. **towns** Pune, Nagpur, Ulhasnagar, Sholapur, Nasik, Thana, Kolhapur, Aurangabad, Sangli, Amravati. **products** cotton, rice, groundnuts, sugar, minerals. **population** (1981) 62,694,000. **language** Marathi 50%. **religion** Hindu 80%, Parsee, Jain and Sikh minorities.

maharishi, *n.* a Hindu religious teacher. [Sansk. *mahā,* great, *rishi,* sage]

Mahatma, *n.* in esoteric Buddhism, an adept of the highest order. [Sansk. *mahātman* (*mahā,* great, *ātman,* soul)]

Mahāyāna, *n.* one of the two major forms of Buddhism, common in N Asia (China, Korea, Japan and Tibet). Veneration of bodhisattvas is important in Mahāyāna, as is the idea that everyone has within them the seeds of Buddhahood.

Mahdi, *n.* in Islam, the title of a coming messiah who will establish the reign of justice on Earth. It has been assumed by many Muslim leaders, notably the Sudanese sheik Muhammad Ahmed (1848–85), who headed a revolt in 1881 against Egypt and in 1885 captured Khartoum. **Mahdism,** *n.* **Mahdist,** *n.* [Arab. *mahdīy,* he who is divinely guided]

Mahfouz, *n.* **Naguib** (1911–), Egyptian novelist and playwright. His novels, which deal with the urban working class, include a semi-autobiographical trilogy (1957), *Children of Gebelawi* (1959) (banned in Egypt because of its treatment of religious themes), and *Respected Sir* (1988). Nobel prize 1988.

mahjong, mahjongg, *n.* a Chinese table game played with 144 pieces called tiles. [Chin., sparrow]

Mahler, *n.* **Gustav** (1860–1911), Austrian composer and conductor. His ten symphonies, the moving *Das Lied von der Erde/Song of the Earth* (1909), and his song cycles display a synthesis of Romanticism and new uses of chromatic harmonies and musical forms.

mahlstick MAULSTICK.

Mahmud, *n.* two sultans of the Ottoman Empire:

Mahmud I, *n.* (1696–1754), Ottoman sultan from 1730. After restoring order to the empire in Istanbul (1730), he suppressed the Janissary rebellion (1731) and waged war against Persia (1731–46). He led successful wars against Austria and Russia, concluded by the Treaty of Belgrade (1739). He was a patron of the arts and also carried out reform of the army.

Mahmud II, *n.* (1785–1839), Ottoman sultan from 1808 who attempted to westernize the declining empire, carrying out a series of far-reaching reforms of civil service and army. In 1826 he destroyed the Janissaries. Wars against Russia (1807–12) led to losses of territory. The pressure for Greek independence after 1821 led to conflict with Britain, France and Russia, leading to the destruction of the Ottoman fleet at the Battle of Navarino in 1829 and defeat in the Russo-Turkish war (1828–29), and he was forced to recognize Greek independence in 1830.

mahoe, *n.* the New Zealand white-wood tree. [Maori]

mahogany, *n.* the hard, fine-grained wood of *Swietenia mahagoni,* a tree of tropical America, largely used in making furniture; the tree itself; applied also to other trees yielding similar wood; a dining-table; the colour of mahogany, reddish-brown. [prob. native Am.]

Mahomedan, -etan, etc. MOHAMMEDAN.

mahout, *n.* an elephant-driver or keeper. [Hind. *mahāwat*]

Mahratta MARATHA.

mahseer, *n.* a large and powerful East Indian river-fish, *Barbus tor,* somewhat like the barbel. [Hindi *mahāsir,* perh. from Sansk. *mahāçiràs*), big-head]

maid, *n.* a girl, a young unmarried woman, a virgin; a female servant; †a man who has not known woman. **maid of all work,** a general servant. **maid of honour,** an unmarried lady attending upon a royal personage; (*esp. N Am.*) an unmarried attendant of a bride; a variety of cheese-cake. **old maid,** an elderly spinster. **†maid-child,** *n.* **maid-servant,** *n.* **maid's sickness** CHLOROSIS. **maidhood** MAIDENHEAD. [shortened from MAIDEN]

maidan, *n.* a parade ground. [Pers.]

maiden, *n.* a girl; a spinster; an apparatus for washing linen; †a machine used in Scotland for beheading, not so efficient as the guillotine. *a.* of or pertaining to a maid; unmarried; of female animals, unmated; first, new, unused, untried; of a city or fortress, never captured; of a horse, never having won a prize; of a race, open to such horses; **maiden assize,** *n.* an assize at which there are no cases. **maiden name,** *n.* the surname of a woman before marriage. **maiden over,** *n.* (*Cricket*) an over in which no runs are scored. **maiden speech,** *n.* the first speech made by a nember of Parliament in the House. †**maiden-tongued,** *a.* speaking in a gentle and insinuating manner. **maiden voyage,** *n.* a first voyage (of a ship). **maidenhead, maidenhood,** the state of being a maid or virgin, virginity; the virginal membrane; †newness, freshness. **maidenish,** *a.* **maidenlike,** *a.* **maidenly,** *a., adv.* **maidenliness,** *n.* [OE *mægden,*dim. of *mægth* (cp. Dut. *maagd,* G *Magd*) cogn. with MAY[1]]

maidenhair, *n.* a fern with delicate fronds, esp. *Asplenium trichomanes* or *Adiantum capillus-Veneris.* **maidenhair tree,** *n.* a gingko.

maieutic, *a.* helping to bring forth or evolve (applied to the system pursued by Socrates, in which he endeavoured to bring out latent ideas by persistent questioning). **maieutics,** *n.sing.* [Gr. *maieutikos,* from *maieuesthai,* to act as a midwife, from *maia,* midwife]

maigre, *a.* of food, esp. soup, suitable for fast days, not made from meat nor containing gravy; applied to fast days. *n.* a large Mediterranean fish, *Sciaena aquila.* [F *maigre,* lean]

mail[1], *n.* defensive armour for the body, formed of rings, chains or scales; any defensive covering. *v.t.* to invest in or as in mail. **mailed,** *a.* clad in mail. **mailed fist,** *n.* the application of physical force. [OF *maille,* L *macula,* spot, mesh]

mail[2], *n.* a bag for the conveyance of letters etc.; the letters etc. conveyed by the post; the system of conveying letters etc., the post, esp. for abroad; a mail-train or ship. *v.t.* to send by mail, to post. **mail-cart,** *n.* a cart for carrying the mail; a light vehicle for carrying children. **mail-coach,** *n.* **mailman,** *n.* (*N Am.*) a postman. **mail-merge,** *n.* the automatic merging of names and addresses from a computer file with the text of a letter etc. **mail order,** *n.* the ordering of goods to be sent by post. **mail-train,** *n.* **mailable,** *a.* **mailing list,** *n.* a list of names and addresses of people to whom letters, advertising material are to be posted. [OF *male* (F *malle*), from Teut. (cp. Dut. *maal,* OHG *malha*)]

†**mail**[3], *n.* rent, tribute, tax. [late OE and Icel. *māl* (cp. OE *mæl,* speech)]

Mailer, *n.* **Norman** (1923–), US writer and journalist. He gained wide attention with his novel of World War II *The Naked and the Dead* (1948). A social commentator in the US literary and political scene, he has run for mayor of New York and has expressed radical sexual views.

maillot, *n.* tights for a ballet-dancer; a tight-fitting swimsuit. [F, swaddling-clothes, a swimsuit]

maim, *v.t.* to deprive of the use of a limb; to cripple, to mutilate. *n.* a serious, esp. a disabling mutilation or injury; an essential defect. **maimedness,** *n.* [ME *mahaym,* from OF *mahaignier,* etym. doubtful]

Maimonides, *n.* **Moses** (Moses Ben Maimon) (1135–1204), Jewish rabbi and philosopher, born in Córdoba, Spain. Known as one of the greatest Hebrew scholars, he attempted to reconcile faith and reason; his philosophical classic is *More nevukhim/The Guide to the Perplexed* (1176–91), which helped to introduce the theories of Aristotle into mediaeval philosophy.

main[1], *a.* of force, concentrated or fully exerted; principal, chief, most important; †mighty, powerful. **mainboom,** *n.* the lower spar of a small vessel on which the mainsail is extended. **mainbrace,** *n.* a brace attached to the mainyard of a sailing ship. **to splice the mainbrace,** to serve an extra rum ration (on a ship). **main chance** CHANCE. †**main-course,** *n.* the mainsail of a square-rigged ship. **main-deck,** *n.* the deck below the spar-deck in a man-of-war; the portion of the upper deck between poop and forecastle on a merchant man. **mainframe,** *n.* a large, powerful computer; the central processing and storage unit of a computer. **mainland,** *n.* the principal body of land as opposed to islands etc. **mainlander,** *n.* the Tasmanian term for a resident on the Australian continent. **main line,** *n.* a primary railway route. **mainline,** *v.t., v.i.* (*sl.*) to inject (a narcotic drug etc.) into a vein. **mainliner,** *n.* **mainmast,** *n.* the principal mast of a ship. **mainsail,** *n.* a sail bent to the main-yard of a square-rigged ship; the sail set on the after part of the mainmast of a fore-and-aft rigged vessel. **mainsheet,** *n.* the rope that extends and fastens the mainsail. **mainspring,** *n.* the chief spring of a watch etc. **mainstay,** *n.* the stay from the main-top to the foot of the foremast; the chief support. **main store,** *n.* the central storage facility of a computer. **main-top,** *n.* a platform above the head of the lower mainmast. **main-yard,** *n.* the yard on which the mainsail is extended. **mainly,** *adv.* principally, chiefly; in the main; greatly, strongly. [from Icel. *megn,* strong, or foll., or from both]

main[2], *n.* strength, force, violent effort; the main or high sea, the ocean; a chief sewer, conduit, conductor, electric cable etc. **in the main,** for the most part. **Spanish Main** SPANISH. **with might and main,** with all one's strength. [OE *mægen,* cogn. with MAY[1]]

†**main**[3], *n.* a throw at dice, or a number (5–9) called by the caster before throwing; a match at cock-fighting; a match in various sports. [etym. doubtful]

Maine, *n.* northeasternmost state of the US, largest of the New England states; nickname Pine Tree State. **area** 86,200 sq km/33,273 sq miles. **capital** Augusta. **towns** Portland, Lewiston, Bangor. **physical** Appalachian Mountains; Acadia National Park; 80% of the state is forested. **products** dairy and market garden produce, paper, pulp, timber, textiles; tourism and fishing are also important. **population** (1986) 1,174,000.

mainland, mainly etc. MAIN[1].

†**mainour,** *n.* (*Law*) stolen property found in the hands of the thief. [A-F *meinoure,* OF *maneuvre,* MANOEUVRE]

†**mainprize,** *n.* (*Law*) releasing a prisoner by becoming surety for his appearance; a writ commanding bail to be accepted. [A-F and OF *mainprise,* from *mainprendre* (*main,* a hand, *prendre,* to take)]

mains, *n.pl.* (*Sc.*) a home-farm. [DOMAIN]

mainsail, mainstay etc. MAIN[1].

mainstream, *n.* the most important aspects of a culture, society etc. *a.* concerning the mainstream; of jazz music, of the type prevalent between early and modern jazz.

maintain, *v.t.* to hold, preserve or carry on in any state; to sustain, to keep up; to support, to provide with the means of living; to keep in order, proper condition or repair; to assert, to affirm, to support by reasoning, argument etc.; †to represent. **maintainable,** *a.* **maintainer,** *n.* **maintenance,,** *n.* the act of maintaining; means of support; (*Law*) an officious intermeddling in a suit in which the person has no interest. **cap of maintenance** CAP[1]. **maintenance man,** *n.* a workman employed to keep machines etc., in working order. **maintained school,** *n.* one receiving financial support from the state or from a local authority. [F *maintenir,* L *manūtenēre* (*manū,* with the hand, abl. of *manus, tenēre,* to hold)]

Maintenon, *n.* **Françoise d'Aubigné, Marquise de Maintenon** (1653–1719), second wife of Louis XIV of France from 1684, and widow of the writer Paul Scarron (1610–60). She was governess to the children of Mme de Montespan by Louis, and his mistress from 1667. She secretly married the king after the death of Queen Marie Thérèse in 1683. Her political influence was considerable, and, as a Catholic convert from Protestantism, her religious opinions were zealous.

maiolica, majolica[1], *n.* Staffordshire name for ceramic ware decorated with coloured lead glazes. [MAJOLICA[2]]

maire, *n.* a close-grained New Zealand tree the wood of which is used for many purposes. [Maori]

maisonette, maisonnette, *n.* part of a house let separately; a small house. [F *maison,* house]

†**maister, maistery** etc. MASTER.

maître d'hôtel, *n.* (*pl.* **maitres d'hôtel**) a head waiter; a major-domo. [F, master of house]

Maitreya, *n.* the Buddha to come, 'the kindly one', an important figure in all forms of Buddhism; he is known as *Mi-lo-fo* in China and *Miroku* in Japan. Buddhists believe that a Buddha appears from time to time to maintain knowledge of the true path; Maitreya is the next future Buddha.

maize, *n.* Indian corn, *Zea mays.* **maizena,** *n.* maize-starch prepared for food. [Sp. *maiz,* Cuban Sp. *mahiz*]

Maj., (*abbr.*) Major.

majesty, *n.* the quality of inspiring awe or reverence; impressive dignity, grandeur, stateliness; sovereign power and dignity, esp. (*with poss. pron.*); a title of kings, queens and emperors; in religious art, a representation of the Father or the Son in glory. **majestic** †**-al,** *a.* **majestically,** *adv.* †**majesticalness,** *n.* [F *majesté,* L *majestas, majestātem,* cogn. with MAJOR]

Maj.-Gen., (*abbr.*) Major-General.

Majlis, *n.* the Iranian legislative assembly. [Pers. assembly]

majolica[1] MAIOLICA.

majolica[2], *n.* a fine enamelled Italian pottery, said to have come orig. from Majorca, or an imitation of this. [It. *maiolica,* prob. *Majorca*]

major, *a.* greater in number, quantity, extent or importance; of considerable importance; serious; main, principal; (*Mus.*) standard, normal, applied to a third consisting of four semitones; of full legal age (18 years). *n.* the first premise of a regular syllogism containing the major term; a person of full legal age; an officer next above captain and below lieutenant-colonel; (*N Am.*) a subject of specialization at a college or university; a person specializing in such a subject. **major axis,** *n.* the axis passing through the foci (in a conic section). **major-domo,,** *n.* (*chiefly It. and Sp.*) the chief officer of a royal or princely household; one who takes charge of a household, a steward. **major-general,** *n.* an officer commanding a division, ranking next below lieutenant-general. **major interval,** *n.* (*Mus.*) an interval greater by a semitone than the minor interval of the same denomination. **major league,** *n.* a league of the highest classification in US sport, esp. baseball. **major mode,** *n.* (*Mus.*) the mode in which the third and sixth tones of the scale form major intervals with the key-note. **major premise,** *n.* in logic, the premise containing the major term. **major suit,** *n.* in contract bridge, spades or hearts, which have a higher value than clubs and diamonds. **major term,** *n.* in logic, that term which forms the predicate of the conclusion. **majorat,** *n.* in continental law, the right of primogeniture. **majorate,** *n.* the rank or office of a major. **majorette,,** *n.* one of a group of girls in scanty uniforms, who march in parades twirling batons, playing instruments etc. **majority,** *n.* the greater number; the greater part, more than half; the amount of the difference between the greater and the less number, esp. of votes in an election; full age; majorate; †superiority; †ancestry. **the majority,** the dead. **to join the majority,** to die. **majority verdict,** *n.* one reached by a majority of a jury. [L, comp. of *magnus,* great]

Major, *n.* **John** (1943–), British Conservative politician, briefly foreign secretary (1989) and then chancellor of the Exchequer from 1989.

Majorca, *n.* (Spanish **Mallorca**) largest of the Balearic Islands, belonging to Spain, in the W Mediterranean. **area** 3,640 sq km/1,405 sq miles. **capital** Palma. **products** olives, figs, oranges, wine, brandy, timber, sheep; tourism is the mainstay of the economy **population** (1981) 561,215.

majuscule, *n.* (*Palaeont.*) a capital or large letter, as in Latin MSS. before the introduction of minuscules. [F, from L *mājuscula,* fem. of *-ulus,* dim. of *mājor,* see prec.]

Makarios III, *n.* (1913–77), Cypriot politician, Greek Orthodox archbishop (1950–77). A leader of the Resistance organization EOKA, he was exiled by the British to the Seychelles (1956–57) for supporting armed action to achieve union with Greece (*enosis*). He was president of the republic of Cyprus (1960–77) (briefly deposed by a Greek military coup Jul.–Dec. 1974).

Makarova, *n.* **Natalia** (1940–), Russian ballerina. She danced with the Kirov Ballet (1959–70), then sought political asylum in the West. Her roles include the title role in *Giselle,* and Aurora in *The Sleeping Beauty.*

†**make**[1], *n.* one's equal, like or match; a mate, a husband or wife. †**makeless,** *a.* matchless, unequalled. [OE *gemaca* (*gamaec,* equal, well-matched, cp. Dut. *gemac,* G *Gemach,* OHG *gimah*)]

make[2], *v.t.* (*past, p.p.,* **made,** †*2nd, 3rd sing.* **makest, maketh**) to frame, construct, produce; to bring into existence, to create; to give rise to, to effect, to bring about; to execute, to perform, to accomplish (with nouns expressing action); to result in, to cause to be or become; to compose (as a book, verses etc.); to prepare for use; to establish, to enact; to raise to a rank or dignity; to constitute, to form, to become, to turn out to be; to gain, to acquire; to move or proceed (towards etc.); (*Cards*) to win (a trick) or cause (a card) to win, to shuffle; to score; to cause, to compel (to do); to cause to appear, to represent to be; to reckon, to calculate or decide to be; to conclude, to think; to reach the end of; to amount to, to serve for; to travel over (a distance etc.); to fetch, as a price; (*Naut.*) to come near; to arrive at; to infuse (tea); (*sl.*) to succeed in seducing. *v.i.* to go, move, tend or lie (in a specified direction); to contribute, to have effect (for or to); to rise, to flow (of the tide); (*usu. with a.*) to do, to act in a specified way, as *make bold. n.* form, shape; arrangement of parts; making; style; disposition, mental or moral constitution; making of electrical contact, completion of a circuit. **on the make,** (*coll.*) intent on personal profit, after the main chance. **to make account of,** to esteem; to consider. **to make against,** to be unfavourable to, to tend to injure. **to make as if,** to pretend, to feint. **to make at,** to attack. **to make away,** to hurry away. **to make away with,** to get rid of, to kill; to waste, to squander. **to make believe** BELIEVE. **to make bold** BOLD. **to make do (with),** to be satisfied with (something) not completely adequate. **to make for,** to conduce to; to corroborate; to move toward; to attack. **to make free,** to venture (to). **to make free with,** to treat without ceremony. **to make good** GOOD. **to make hay of** HAY[1]. **to make headway,** to advance. **to make it,** (*coll.*) to reach an objective; to succeed. **to make light of** LIGHT[2]. **to make like,** (*esp. N Am.*) to pretend; to imitate. **to make love** LOVE. **to make merry,** to feast, to be jovial; to make much of, to treat with fondness or favour; to treat as of great importance. **to make no doubt,** to be sure. **to make of,** to understand, interpret; to attach a specified degree of importance to. **to make off,** to run away; to abscond. **to make out,** to understand, to decipher; to prove, to establish; to claim or allege; to draw up; (*coll.*) to be successful; (*N Am., coll.*) to engage in necking or petting; (*sl.*) to have sexual intercourse. **to make over,** to transfer. **to make place, room,** to move so as to leave space (for). **to make sail,** to set more sails; to set sail. **to make sure of,** to consider as certain. **to make tea,** to infuse tea. **to make the grade** GRADE. **to make the most of,** to use to the best advantage. **to make up,** to compose; to compound; to collect together; to complete; to supply (what is wanting); to compensate; to settle, to adjust; to repair; of an actor, to dress up, to prepare the face to represent a character; to apply cosmetics to the face; to fabricate, to concoct; to arrange (as type) in columns or pages. **to make up one's mind,** to decide, to resolve. **to make up to,** to make advances to. **to make water,** to urinate; (*Naut.*) to leak. **to make way,** to make room, to open a passage; to progress. **to make with,** (*N Am., coll.*) to show, produce. **to make words,** to multiply words; to raise a quarrel. †**makebate,** *n.* a breeder of quarrels. **make-believe,** *n.* a pretending, a pretence, a sham. *a.* unreal; counterfeit. *v.t., v.i.* to pretend. **makeshift,** *n.* a temporary expedient; †a thief, a rogue. *a.* used as a makeshift. **make-up,** *n.* the arrangement of type into columns or pages; the manner in which an actor's face is made to represent a character; the material used for this; a made-up story, a fiction; cosmetics for use on the face; a person's character or temperament. **make-weight,** *n.* that which is thrown into a scale to make weight; a stop-gap; anything that counterbalances, a counterpoise. **maker,** *n.* one who makes; **(Maker)** the Creator, God. **to meet one's Maker,** to die. **making,** *n.* the act of constructing, producing, causing etc.; possibility or opportunity of success or full development; (*pl.*) composition, essential qualities; (*pl.*) profits, earnings. **in the making,** gradually developing or being made. **making-up,** *n.* balancing of accounts. [OE *macian* (cp. Dut. *maken,* G *machen*), cogn. with MATCH[1]]

mako, *n.* a small New Zealand tree; a kind of shark. [Maori]

mal- MAL(E)-.

Malabo, *n.* port and capital of Equatorial Guinea, on the island of Bioko; population (1983) 15,253. It was founded in the 1820s by the British as Port Clarence. Under Spanish rule it was known as Santa Isabel (until 1973).

malacca, *n.* a palm-stem used as a walking-stick. [town and district in Malay peninsula]

malachite, *n.* a bright green monoclinic carbonate of copper. [OF *melochite* (Gr. *malachē,* mallow)]

malaco-, *comb.form* soft. [Gr. *malakos*]

malacoderm, *n.* a soft-skinned animal, esp. one of the Malacodermata or sea-anemones.

malacolite, *n.* a greenish calcium-magnesium variety of pyroxene.

malacology, *n.* the natural history of the Mollusca. **malacological,** *a.* **malacologist,** *n.*

malacopterygian, *a.* belonging to the Malacopyterygii, a group of soft-finned fishes. *n.* any individual of this group. **malacopyterygious,** *a.* [Gr. *pteryx,* a wing]

malacostomous, *a.* having soft jaws without teeth (as some fish). [Gr. *stoma,* an orifice]

malacostracan, *a.* of or belonging to the Malacostraca, a division of crustaceans containing crabs, lobsters etc. *n.* a member of this division. **malacostracous,** *a.* **malacostracology,** *n.* crustaceology. **malacostracological,** *a.* **malacostracologist,** *n.* [Gr. *ostrakon,* a shell]

malacozoic, *a.* of or belonging to the Malacozoa, or soft-bodied animals, i.e. the Mollusca.

maladaptation, *n.* defective adaptation.

maladjusted, *a.* unable to adjust oneself to the physical or social environment. **maladjustment,** *n.*

maladministration, *n.* defective of vicious management, esp. of public affairs. **maladminister,** *v.t.*

maladroit, *a.* awkward, clumsy. **maladroitly,** *adv.*

malady, *n.* a disease, an ailment, esp. a lingering or deep-seated disorder; a moral defect or disorder. [F *maladie,* from *malade,* sick, late L *male habitus* (MAL(E)-, *habitus,* p.p. of *habēre,* to have, hold, keep)]

mala fide, *a., adv.* (done) in bad faith. [L]

Malaga[1], *n.* white wine imported from Malaga. [see foll.]

Málaga[2], *n.* an industrial seaport (sugar refining, distilling, brewing, olive-oil pressing, shipbuilding) and holiday resort in Andalusia, Spain; capital of Málaga province on the Mediterranean; population (1986) 595,000. Founded by the Phoenicians and taken by the Moors in 711, Málaga was capital of the Moorish kingdom of Malaga from the 13th cent. until captured 1487 by Ferdinand and Isabella.

Malagasy, *a.* of or pertaining to Madagascar or its inhabitants or language, *n.* (*pl.* **Malagasy**) a native or the Malayo-Polynesian language of Madagascar.

malaise, *n.* a feeling of uneasiness, esp. as premonition of a serious malady; (a feeling) of sickness. [F (OF *mal,* as MAL(E)-, *aise,* EASE)]

Malamud, *n.* **Bernard** (1914–86), US novelist. He first attracted attention with *The Natural* (1952), taking a professional baseball player as his hero. Later works, often dealing with Jewish immigrant tradition, include *The Assistant* (1957), *The Fixer* (1966), *Dubin's Lives* (1979), and *God's Grace* (1982).

malander, *n.* (*now always pl.*) a scaly eruption at the back of the knee in horses. [F *malandre*]

†**malapert,** *a.* pert, impudent, saucy, forward. *n.* a pert, saucy person. †**malapertly,** *adv.* †**malapertness,** *n.* [OF *mal appert* (MAL(E)-, *espert,* EXPERT)]

malaprop, malapropism, *n.* grotesque misapplication of words; a word so misapplied. **malapropian,** *a.* [Mrs *Malaprop* in Sheridan's *The Rivals,* see foll.]

malapropos, *adv.* unseasonably, unsuitably, out of place. *a.* unseasonable etc. *n.* an unseasonable or inopportune thing, remark, event etc. [F *mal à propos* (MAL(E)-, APROPOS)]

malar, *a.* pertaining to the cheek or cheek-bone. *n.* the bone which forms the prominence of the cheek. [L *māla* (prob. rel. to MAXILLA), cheek, -AR]

malaria, *n.* the unpleasant, harmful air arising from marshy districts, formerly believed to produce fevers etc.; applied to various kinds of fever of an intermittent and remittent nature, now known to be due to a parasite introduced by the bite of mosquitoes. **malarial, -rian, -rious,** *a.* [It. *mal'aria* (MAL-, AIR)]

malark(e)y, *n.* (*esp. N Am., coll.*) foolish or insincere talk; nonsense.

malassimilation, *n.* imperfect assimilation, esp. of nutriment.

malate MALIC.

Malathion®, *n.* an insecticide used for house-flies and garden pests.

Malatya, *n.* capital of a province of the same name in E central Turkey, lying W of the river Euphrates; population (1985) 251,000.

Malawi[1], *n.* Republic of (*Malaŵi*), a country in SE Africa, bordered N and E by Tanzania, S and W by Mozambique, and W by Zambia. **area** 118,000 sq km/ 45,560 sq miles. **capital** Lilongwe. **towns** Blantyre-Limbe. **physical** occupies the mountainous west side of Lake Malawi. **exports** tea, tobacco, cotton, groundnuts, sugar. **population** (1985) 7,059,000; annual growth rate 3.1%. **language** English (official); Chichewa. **religion** Christian 50%; Muslim 30%.

Malawi[2] (or **Nyasa**), **Lake,** *n.* African lake, bordered by Malawi, Tanzania and Mozambique, formed in a section of the Great Rift Valley. It is about 500 m/1650 ft above sea level and 560 km/350 miles long, with an area of 37,000 sq km/14,280 sq miles. It is intermittently drained to the south by the river Shiré into the Zambezi.

Malay, *a.* of or pertaining to the predominant race in Malaysia and Indonesia. *n.* a member of this race; their language. **Malay language,** *n.* a member of the Western or Indonesian branch of the Malayo-Polynesian language family, used in the Malay peninsula and many of the islands of Malaysia and Indonesia. It can be written with either Arabic or Roman scripts. **Malayan,** *n., a.* [native *Malayu*]

Malayala(a)m, *n.* the language of Malabar, a Dravidian dialect akin to Tamil. **Malayalim,** *n.pl.* the Dravidians of Malabar speaking this. [native name]

Malayo-Polynesian (or **Austronesian),** *n.* a family of languages spoken in Malaysia, the Indonesian archipelago, parts of Indo-China, Taiwan, Madagascar, Melanesia and Polynesia (excluding Australia and most of New Guinea). The group contains some 500 distinct languages, including Malay in Malaysia, Bahasa in Indonesia, Fijian, Hawaiian and Maori.

Malaysia, *n.* a country in SE Asia, comprising the Malay Peninsula, bordered to the N by Thailand and surrounded E, S and W by the South China Sea; and the states of Sabah and Sarawak, which occupy the N part of the island of Borneo, the S being part of Indonesia. **area** 329,759 sq km/127,287 sq miles. **capital** Kuala Lumpur. **towns** Kuching in Sarawak and Kota Kinabalu in Sabah. **physical** comprises W Malaysia (the nine Malay states – Perlis, Kedah, Johore, Selangor, Perak, Negri Sembilan, Kelantan, Trengganu, Pahang – plus Penang and Malacca); and E Malaysia (Sarawak and Sabah); 75% of the area tropical jungle; a central mountain range; swamps in the E. **exports** pineapples, palm oil, rubber, timber, petroleum (Sarawak), bauxite. **population** (1988) 16,968,000 (Malaysian 47%, Chinese 32%, Indian 8%, and indigenous peoples – Dayaks, Ibans – of E Malaysia 10%); annual growth rate 2.5%. **language** Malay (official, usually written in Arabic characters); in Sarawak English is also official. **religion** Muslim (official).

Malcolm, *n.* four kings of Scotland, including:

Malcolm III, *n.* (called **Canmore**) (*c.* 1031–93), king of Scotland from 1054, the son of Duncan I (d. 1040); he was killed at Alnwick while invading Northumberland.

Malcolm X, *n.* (assumed name of Malcolm Little) (1926–65), US black nationalist leader. While serving a prison sentence for burglary (1946–53) he joined the Black Muslims sect. On his release he campaigned for black separatism, condoning violence in self-defence, but in 1964 modified his views to found the Islamic-socialist Organization of Afro-American Unity, preaching racial solidarity. A year later he was assassinated by Black Muslim opponents while addressing a rally in Harlem, New York. His *Autobiography of Malcolm X* was published in 1964.

malconformation, *n.* imperfect conformation, disproportion of parts.

malcontent, *a.* discontented, esp. with the government or its administration. *n.* one who is discontented, esp. with the government. **malcontented,** *a.* **malcontentedly,** *adv.* **malcontentedness,** *n.* [OF (MAL-, CONTENT[1])]

mal de mer, seasickness. [F]

Maldives, *n.pl.* Republic of (*Divehi Jumhuriya*), a group of 1196 islands in the N Indian Ocean, about 640 km/400 miles SW of Sri Lanka, only 203 of which are inhabited. **area** 298 sq km/115 sq miles. **capital** Malé. **physical** comprises 1200 coral islands, grouped into 12 clusters of atolls, largely flat, none bigger than 13 sq km/5 sq miles. **exports** coconuts, copra, bonito (fish related to tuna); tourism. **population** (1988) 200,000; annual growth rate 3.2%. **language** Divehi (related to Sinhalese). **religion** Islam.

male, *a.* pertaining to the sex that begets young or has organs for impregnating ova; of organs, adapted for fertilization; of flowers, having stamens but no pistil; consisting of or pertaining to individuals of this sex; (*Mech.*) designed for entering a correlative female part; masculine, virile. *n.* one of the male sex; a plant, or part of a plant, that bears the fecundating organs. **male chauvinist (pig),** a man with an arrogant belief in the superiority of the male sex. **male fern,** *n.* a fern, *Nephrodium filix-mas,* with the fronds clustered in a crown. **male menopause,** *n.* a (supposed) period in a man's middle life when he experiences an emotional crisis focused on diminishing sexual prowess. **male screw,** *n.* one whose threads enter the grooves of a corresponding screw. [OF, from L *masculum,* nom. *-lus,* from *mās,* male]

mal(e)-, *comb. form* bad(ly); evil; faulty; abnormal. [L *male,* ill, badly]

Malé, *n.* capital of the Maldives in the Indian Ocean; population (1985) 38,000. It trades in copra, breadfruit and palm products.

malediction, *n.* a curse, an imprecation. **maledictory,** *a.* [F, from L *maledictio -ōnem,* from *maledīcere* (*dīcere,* to speak)]

malefactor, *n.* an evil-doer, a criminal. † **malefaction,** *n.* **maleficent,** *a.* hurtful, mischievous, causing evil (to). **maleficence,** *n.* [L *factor,* from *facere,* to do)]

malefic, *a.* mischief-making, harmful, hateful. [L *maleficus*]

maleic, *a.* applied to an acid obtained by the dry distillation of malic acid. [F *maléique,* from *malique,* MALIC]

malevolent, *a.* wishing evil or injury to others; ill-disposed, envious, malicious, spiteful. **malevolence,** *n.* **malevolently,** *adv.* [L *malevolens -entem* (*volens,* pres.p. of *velle,* to wish)]

malfeasance, *n.* evil-doing, esp. illegal conduct by a public official. [from OF *malfaisant* (*faisant,* pres.p. of *faire,* to do)]

malformation, *n.* faulty formation; a faulty structure or irregularity of form. **malformed,** *a.*

malfunction, *n.* defective function or operation. *v.i.* to operate defectively.

malgré, MAUGRE. **malgré lui,** *adv.* in spite of oneself. [F]

Malherbe, *n.* **François de** (1555–1628), French poet and grammarian, born in Caen. He became court poet about 1605 under Henry IV and Louis XIII. He advocated reform of language and versification, and established the 12-syllable Alexandrine as the standard form of French verse.

Mali[1], *n.* Republic of (*République du Mali*), a landlocked country in NW Africa, bordered to the NE by Algeria, E by Niger, SE by Burkina Faso, S by the Ivory Coast, SW by Senegal and Guinea, and W and N by Mauritania. **area** 1,240,142 sq km/478,695 sq miles. **capital** Bamako. **physical** river Niger in S; savanna; part of the Sahara in N. **exports** cotton, groundnuts, livestock. **population** (1988) 7,784,000; annual growth rate 2.8%. **language** French (official), Bambara. **religion** Sunni Muslim 65%, animist 35%.

Mali[2], ancient, *n.* a Muslim empire in NW Africa during the 7th–15th cent. Thriving on its trade in gold, it reached its peak in the 14th cent. under Mansa Musa (reigned 1312–37), when it occupied an area covering present-day Senegal, Gambia, Mali and S Mauritania. Mali's territory was similar to (though larger than) that of the Ghana Empire, and gave way in turn to the Songhai Empire.

malic, *a.* of malic acid, derived from fruit. **malate,** *n.* a salt or ester of malic acid. [F *malique,* from L *mālum,* apple]

malice, *n.* a disposition to injure others, active malevolence; (*Law*) a premeditated design to do evil or injure another. †*v.t.* to bear malice towards. **malice aforethought,** *n.* (*Law*) a premeditated wish to commit an illegal act, esp. murder. **malicious,** *a.* **maliciously,** *adv.* †**maliciousness,** *n.* [F, from L *malitia,* from *malus,* bad]

malign, *a.* unfavourable, pernicious, malignant, hurtful; †malevolent. *v.t.* to speak evil of, to slander, †*v.i.* to be malicious. **maligner,** *n.* **malignly,** *adv.* [OF *maligne,* L *malignus* (*mali-,* MALE-, *genus,* cp. BENIGN)]

malignant, *a.* actuated by extreme enmity or malice; exercising a pernicious influence, virulent; of a disease, tumour etc., resisting treatment and threatening life. *n.* a malevolent person, esp. applied by the Puritans to a Royalist in the time of the Civil War. **malignancy,** *n.* **malignantly,** *adv.* **malignity,** *n.*

malinger, *v.i.* to pretend illness in order to shirk work. **malingerer,** *n.* [F *malingre,* sickly, etym. doubtful]

Malinowski, *n.* **Bronislaw** (1884–1942), Polish anthropologist, one of the founders of the theory of functionalism in the social sciences. His study of the peoples of the Trobriand Islands led him to see customs and practices in terms of their function in creating and maintaining social order.

malism, *n.* the doctrine that on the whole this is a bad world. [L *malus,* bad]

†**malison,** *n.* a curse, a malediction. [OF *maleison,* MALEDICTION]

†**malkin,** *n.* a kitchen-wench; a slattern; a mop; a scarecrow, esp. one representing a woman. [dim. of *Matilda* or *Maud*]

mall, *n.* a public walk, orig. a place where pall-mall was played; (*esp. N Am.*) a street or area of shops reserved for pedestrians; †the game of pall-mall; †the mallet used in this. [MAUL]

mallander, MALANDER.

mallard, *n.* a wild drake; a wild duck; the flesh of this. [OF *malart,* perh. from OHG proper name *Madehart*]

Mallarmé, *n.* **Stéphane** (1842–98), French poet who founded the Symbolist school with Verlaine. His belief that poetry should be evocative and suggestive was reflected in *L'Après-midi d'un faune/Afternoon of a Faun* (1876), which inspired Debussy. Later publications are *Poésies complètes/Complete Poems* (1887), *Vers et prose/Verse and Prose* (1893), and the prose *Divagations/Digressions* (1897).

Malle, *n.* **Louis** (1932–), French film director. After a period as assistant to Robert Bresson, he directed *Les Amants/The Lovers* (1958), audacious in its time for its explicitness. His subsequent films, made in France and the US, include *Zazie dans le métro* (1961), *Viva Maria* (1965), *Pretty Baby* (1978), *Atlantic City* (1980), and *Au Revoir les enfants* (1988).

malleable, *a.* capable of being rolled out or shaped by hammering without being broken; easily influenced by outside forces, pliant. **malleability**, **†malleableness,** *n.* **†malleate,** *v.t.* **†malleation**, *n.* [OF, prob. from L *malleābilis,* from *malleāre,* from *malleus,* hammer]

mallecho MICHING MALICHO.

mallee, *n.* one of various dwarf species of eucalyptus growing in the deserts of Victoria and S Australia. **mallee-bird, -fowl, -hen,** *n.* a mound-bird. **mallee-scrub,** *n.* [Abor.]

malleiform MALLEUS.

mallemuck, *n.* the fulmar. [Dut. *mallemok* (*mal,* foolish, *mok,* gull)]

mallender MALANDER.

malleolus, *n.* one of two bony processes extending either side of the ankle. **malleolar,** *a.* [L, dim. of MALLEUS]

mallet, *n.* a light hammer, usu. of wood; a long-handled wooden one for striking the ball in croquet or polo. [F *maillet,* dim. of *mail,* MAUL]

malleus, *n.* one of the small bones of the tympanum. **malleiform,** *a.* [L, hammer]

Mallorca, *n.* Spanish form of Majorca, an island in the Mediterranean.

mallow, -lows, *n.* a plant of various species belonging to the genus *Malva,* usu. with pink or mauve flowers and hairy stems and foliage, and having emollient properties whence perhaps its name. [OE *mealwe,* L *malva* (cp. Gr. *malachē,* perh. rel. to *malakos,* soft)]

malm, *n.* a soft, friable chalky rock or loam, used with clay and sand for brick-making. *v.t.* to mix (clay, chalk etc.) to make malm for bricks; to cover brick-earth with this. [OE *mealm* (cp. Icel. *mālmr,* Goth. *malma,* from Teut. *mal-,* to grind)]

Malmaison, *n.* a variety of blush-rose; a variety of carnation like this in colour. [house near Paris of the Empress Josephine]

Malmö, *n.* an industrial port (shipbuilding, engineering, textiles) in SW Sweden; population (1988) 231,000.

malmsey, *n.* a strong sweet white wine now chiefly made in the Canaries and Spain. [ult. from med. L *malmasia,* corr. of Gr. *Monembasia,* Napoli di Monemvasia, town in Morea, Greece (cp. *malvoisie*)]

malnutrition, *n.* insufficient or defective nutrition.

malodorous, *a.* having an unpleasant smell. **malodour,** *n.* an offensive odour.

Malory, *n.* **Thomas** (15th cent.), English author of the prose romance *Le Morte d'Arthur* (about 1470). It is a translation from the French, modified by material from other sources, and deals with the exploits of King Arthur's knights of the Round Table and the quest for the Grail.

Malpighi, *n.* **Marcello** (1628–94), Italian physiologist, who made many discoveries (still known by his name) in his microscope studies of animal and plant tissues. **Malpighian**, *a.* applied to certain corpuscles, layers and other structures, in the spleen and kidneys.

malpractice, *n.* illegal or immoral conduct, esp. improper treatment of a case by a physician, lawyer etc.

malpresentation, *n.* an abnormal position of the foetus at birth.

Malraux, *n.* **André** (1901–76), French novelist. He became involved in the nationalist and communist revolution in China in the 1920s, reflected in *La Condition humaine/Man's Estate* (1933); *L'Espoir/Days of Hope* (1937) is set in Civil War Spain. He was minister of cultural affairs (1960–69).

malt, *n.* grain, usually barley, steeped in water and fermented, dried in a kiln and used for brewing and distilling; malt-liquor. *a.* pertaining to, containing or made of malt. *v.t.* to convert into malt; to treat with malt. *v.i.* to be converted into malt; (*facet.*) to drink malt-liquor. **malt extract,** *n.* a thick, sticky liquid made from malt, taken as a health food. **malt-floor,** *n.* the floor in a malt-house on which the grain is spread to germinate. **malt-horse,** *n.* a horse employed in grinding malt; a dull, stupid fellow. **malt-house, maltings,** *n.* building where malt is prepared and stored. **malt-liquor,** *n.* liquor made from malt by fermentation, beer, stout etc. **malt whisky,** *n.* whisky distilled from malted barley. **†malt-worm,** *n.* a tippler. **maltings** MALT-HOUSE. **maltster,** *n.* a man whose occupation is to make malt. **malty,** *a.* [OE *mealt* (cp. Dut. *mout,* Icel. *malt,* G *Malz*), cogn. with OHG *malz,* soft, and MELT]

Malta, *n.* Republic of (*Repubblika Ta'Malta*), an island in the Mediterranean, S of Sicily, E of Tunisia, and N of Libya. **area** 320 sq km/124 sq miles. **capital** Valletta. **physical** includes the island of Gozo 67 sq km/26 sq miles and Comino 2.5 sq km/1 sq miles. **exports** vegetables, knitwear, handmade lace, plastics, electronic equipment. **population** (1987) 346,000; annual growth rate 0.7%. **language** Maltese (related to Arabic, with Phoenician survivals and influenced by Italian). **religion** Roman Catholic. **Malta fever,** *n.* a fever common in Malta and other places in the Mediterranean, said to be conveyed by goat's milk. **Maltese,** *a.* pertaining to Malta or its inhabitants. *n.* a native of Malta; the Maltese language or the people; a Maltese dog. **Maltese cross** CROSS[1]. **Maltese dog,** *n.* a small variety of spaniel with long silky hair.

Malta, Knights of, *n.* another name for members of the military-religious order of the Hospital of St John of Jerusalem.

maltha, *n.* a bituminous cement used by the ancients; applied to various kinds of mineral pitch. [L, from Gr.]

Malthus, *n.* **Thomas Robert** (1766–1834), English economist and cleric, whose *Essay on the Principle of Population* (1798, revised 1803) argued for population control, since populations increase in geometric ratio, and food only in arithmetic ratio. He saw war, famine and disease as necessary checks on population growth. **Malthusian**, *a.* pertaining to or supporting the teachings of Malthus. *n.* a follower of Malthus; one who holds that some check is necessary to prevent over-population. **Malthusianism,** *n.*

maltose, *n.* a sugar obtained by the action of malt or diastase on starch paste. [F (MALT, -OSE)]

maltreat, *v.t.* to ill-treat; to abuse. **maltreatment,** *n.* [F *maltraiter,* L *male tractāre* (MAL(E)-, TREAT)]

maltster, malty MALT.

Maluku, Moluccas, *n.pl.* group of Indonesian islands. **area** 74,500 sq km/28,764 sq miles. **capital** Ambon, on Amboina. **population** (1980) 1,411,000.

malvaceous, *a.* belonging to or resembling the genus *Malva* or the family Malvaceae, comprising the mallows. [late L *malvaceus,* from *malva,* MALLOW]

malversation, *n.* fraudulent conduct or corruption in a position of trust, esp. corrupt administration of public funds. [F *malverser* (L *male,* badly, *versārī,* to behave, freq. of *vertere,* to turn), -ATION]

Malvinas, *n.pl.* Argentinian name for the Falkland Islands.

mam, *n.* (*dial.*) mother.

mama MAMMA[1].

mamba, *n.* any of various African poisonous snakes of the genus *Dendroaspis*. [Zulu *im mamba,* large snake]

mambo, *n.* a W Indian syncopated dance or dance tune, like the rumba. *v.i.* to dance the mambo.

mamelon, *n.* a small rounded hill or mound, from its resemblance to a woman's breast. [F, a teat, from *mamelle,* L MAMILLA]

Mameluke, *n.* one of the mounted soldiers of Egypt (orig. Circassian slaves) who formed the ruling class in that country, destroyed by Mehmet Ali in 1811. [Arab.

mamlūk, slave, from *malaka,* to possess]

Mamet, *n.* **David** (1947–), US playwright. His plays, with their vivid, freewheeling language and sense of ordinary US life, include *American Buffalo* (1977), *Sexual Perversity in Chicago* (1978), and *Glengary, Glen Ross* (1984).

mamilla, *n.* a nipple or teat; a nipple-shaped organ or part. **mamillary, mamillate, mamillated, mamilliform,** *a.* [L, dim. of MAMMA[2]]

mamma[1], *n.* mother (used chiefly by young children). **mammy,** *n.* (*dial.*) mother; (*N Am.*) a black woman working as a children's nurse in a white family. [reduplication of instinctive sound made by infants]

mamma[2], *n.* (*pl.* **-mae,** -ē) the milk-secreting organ in mammals. **mammary,** *a.* of or concerning the mammae. **mammary gland,** *n.* a mamma. **mammifer,** *n.* **mammiferous,** *a.* (*Zool.*) Mammalian; (*Anat.*) bearing the breasts. **mammiform,** *a.* in shape like a breast. [L]

mammal, *n.* (*Zool.*) any individual of the Mammalia. **Mammalia,** *n.pl.* the class of animals having milk-secreting organs for suckling their young, the highest division of vertebrates. **mammalian,** *a.* **mammaliferous,** *a.* of rocks, containing mammalian remains. **mammalogy,** *n.* **mammalogist,** *n.* **mammography,** *n.* examination of the breasts by X-ray. **mammogram,** *n.* [sing. from mod. L *mammālia,* neut. pl. of late L *mammālis,* from L MAMMA[2]]

mammee, *n.* a tropical American tree, *Mammea americana,* bearing edible pulpy fruit. [through F *mammée* or Sp. *mamey,* from Haitian]

†**mammer,** *v.i.* to hesitate, to stand muttering. [imit. with freq. suf. -ER]

mammifer MAMMA[2].

mammillary MAMILLA.

†**mammock,** *n.* a shapeless piece. *v.t.* to tear in or into pieces. [etym. unknown]

mammon, *n.* riches personified as an idol or an evil influence (orig. a Syrian god of riches). **mammonish,** *a.* **mammonism,** *n.* **mammonist, -nite,** *n.* **mammonize, -ise,** *v.t.* [L *mammōna,* Gr. *mamōnas,* Aram. *māmōnā,* riches]

mammoth, *n.* a large extinct species of elephant, *Elephas primigenius, a.* gigantic, huge. [Russ. *mammat* (now *mamont*)]

mammy (*dial.*) MAMMA[1].

Mamoulian, *n.* **Rouben** (1898–1987), Armenian film director who lived in the US from 1923. After several years on Broadway he turned to films, making the first sound version of *Dr Jekyll and Mr Hyde* (1932) and *Queen Christina* (1933). His later work includes *The Mark of Zorro* (1940) and *Silk Stockings* (1957).

man, *n.* (*pl.* **men,**) a human being, a person; (*collect.*) mankind, the human race; an adult male of the human race; an individual, one; one with manly qualities; manhood; (*dial., coll.*) a husband; a man-servant, a valet, a workman; a person under one's control; †a vassal, a tenant; (*pl.*) soldiers, esp. privates; (*pl.*) pieces used in playing chess or draughts; (*in comb.*) a ship, as *man-of-war, merchantman* etc. *v.t.* (*past, p.p.* **manned**) to furnish with a man or men, esp. for defence or other military service; to fortify the courage of (esp. oneself); †to tame. **as one man,** all together, in unison. **inner man** INNER. **man about town,** a fashionable idler. **man alive!** an expression of remonstration, often sarcastic. **man and boy,** from boyhood upwards. **man in the street,** *n.* an ordinary person. **man of letters,** a writer, literary critic etc. **man of straw,** a man of no substance; a false argument or adversary put forward for the sake of being refuted. **man of the world,** an experienced person, sophisticated and urbane. **man to man,** as between individual men, one with or against the other; with complete frankness. **man-to-man,** *adj.* **to a man,** without exception. **to be one's own man,** to be of independent mind. **man-at-arms,** *n.* a heavily-armed mounted soldier, esp. in the Middle Ages. **man-child,** *n.* a male child. **man-day,** *n.* the amount of work done by one person in one day. **man-eater,** *n.* a cannibal; a tiger, shark etc., that devours human beings; a horse that bites. **man-eating,** *a.* **Man Friday,** *n.* a personal servant, factotum. **man-handle,** *v.t.* to move by man-power alone; (*coll.*) to handle roughly, to maltreat. **man-hater,** *n.* one (usu. a woman) who hates men. **manhole,** *n.* a hole in a floor, drain or parts of machinery etc., to allow entrance for cleansing and repairs. **man-hour,** *n.* the amount of work done by one person in one hour. **manhunt,** *n.* a large-scale search for a person, e.g. an escaped prisoner. **man-jack,** *n.* a person. **man-made,** *a.* made by man, not natural, artificial. **man-midwife,** *n.* **man-milliner,** *n.* a man who makes or sells millinery; one who busies himself with trifles. **man-of-war, man-o'-war,** *n.* a warship belonging to a navy. **manpower,** *n.* amount of men available for any purpose. **man-rope,** *n.* a rope at the side of a gangway etc. **manservant,** *n.* **man-sized,** *a.* of a suitable size for a man; (*coll.*) large. **manslaughter,** *n.* the killing of a human being or beings; (*Law*) the unlawful killing of a person but without malice. **man-slayer,** *n.* one who kills a human being or commits manslaughter. **man-tiger,** *n.* a lycanthrope or were-wolf assuming the form of a tiger. **man-trap,** *n.* a trap set for poachers etc. **manful,** *a.* brave, courageous; resolute, manly. **manfully,** *adv.* **manfulness,** *n.* **manhood,** *n.* the state of being a man; the state of being a male person of full age; manliness, courage, resolution. **manhood suffrage,** *n.* the right of voting granted to every citizen of full age not disqualified by crime etc. **mankind,** *n.* the human species;, men collectively as distinct from humanity. **manlike,** *a.* **manly,** *a.* having the finer qualities characteristic of a man, courageous, resolute, magnanimous; befitting a man; mannish. **manliness,** *n.* **manned,** *a.* furnished with a crew, workers etc., of a spacecraft, having a human pilot or crew. **mannish,** *a.* esp. of a woman, masculine, characteristic of a man. **mannishly,** *adv.* **mannishness,** *n.* **manward,** *a., adv.* [OE *mann* (cp. Dut. and Swed. *man,* G *Mann*)]

Man, Isle of, an island in the Irish Sea, a dependency of the British crown, but not part of the UK. **area** 570 sq km/220 sq miles. **capital** Douglas. **towns** Ramsey, Peel, Castletown. **exports** light engineering products. **population** (1986) 64,000. **language** English (Manx, nearer to Scottish than Irish Gaelic, has been almost extinct since the 1970s).

mana, *n.* spiritual power exerted through man or inanimate objects; power, authority. [Polynesian]

manacle, *n.* (*usu. pl.*) a handcuff, a fetter. *v.t.* to put manacles on; to fetter. [OF *manicle,* L *manicula,* dim. of *manus,* hand]

manage, *v.t.* to conduct, to direct, to carry on, to control; to conduct the affairs of; to handle, to wield; to bring or keep under control; to lead or guide by flattery etc.; to break in, to train (as a horse); to deal with, to make use of; †to husband, to use cautiously. *v.i.* to direct affairs; to contrive (to do etc.); to get on (with or without); to succeed (with). *n.* management; manège. **manageable,** *a.* **manageability, manageableness,** *n.* **manageably,** *adv.* **management,** *n.* the act of managing; conduct, administration; those who manage, a board of directors etc.; skilful employment of means; †skill, ingenuity. **management consultant,** *n.* a person who advises on the efficient management of a business company or institution. **manager,** *n.* one who manages, esp. a business, institution etc.; (*Law*) one appointed to administer a business in chancery etc.; (*usu. with* good, bad etc.) one skilled in economical management; (*pl.*) a committee appointed by either House of Parliament to perform a duty concerning both Houses. **manageress,** *n.* a female manager, esp. of a retail shop, canteen, restaurant etc. **managerial,** *a.* **managership,** *n.* **managing,** *a.* having the management or control of a business, department etc.; careful, economical. [It. *maneggiare,* from L *manus,* hand]

Managua, *n.* the capital and chief industrial city of Nicaragua, on the lake of the same name; population (1985) 682,000. It has twice been destroyed by earthquake and rebuilt, in 1931 and 1972; it was also badly damaged by civil war in the late 1970s.

Manama, *n.* (Arabic **Al Manamah**) capital and free trade port of Bahrain, on Bahrain Island; handles oil and entrepôt trade; population (1988) 152,000.

mañana, *n.* tomorrow, presently, later on; procrastination. [Sp., from L *māne*]

manatee, *n.* the sea-cow, a large herbivorous sirenian. [Sp. *manati,* Carib. *manatoui*]

Manaus, *n.* the capital of Amazonas, Brazil, on the Rio Negro, near its confluence with the Amazon; population (1980) 612,000. It can be reached by sea-going vessels, although 1600 km/1000 miles from the Atlantic. Formerly a centre of the rubber trade, it developed as a tourist centre in the 1970s.

manche, *n.* a sleeve, with long hanging ends; in heraldry, a bearing representing such a sleeve; the neck of a violin etc. [F, from L *manica,* from *manus,* hand]

Manchester[1]**,** *n.* port in NW England, on the river Irwell, 50 km/31 miles E of Liverpool. It is a manufacturing (textile machinery, chemicals, rubber, processed foods) and financial centre; population (1985) 451,000. It is linked by the Manchester Ship Canal, built 1894, to the river Mersey and the sea. **Manchester goods,** *n.pl.* cotton textiles. **Manchesterism,** *n.* the doctrines of the school of thought of Cobden and Bright advocating Free Trade and the principle of laissez-faire.

Manchester[2]**, Greater,** *n.* a former (1974–86) metropolitan county of NW England, replaced by a residuary body in 1986 which covers some of its former functions. **area** 1,290 sq km/498 sq miles. **towns** administrative headquarters Manchester; Bolton, Oldham, Rochdale, Salford, Stockport and Wigan. **products** industrial. **population** (1987) 2,580,000.

manchet, *n.* a small loaf of fine wheaten bread. *a.* of bread, fine and white. [etym. doubtful]

manchette, *n.* an ornamental cuff or trimming for a sleeve. [F, dim. of MANCHE]

manchineel, *n.* a W Indian tree, *Hippomane mancinella,* with a poisonous sap and apple-like fruit; its timber used for cabinet work. [F *mancenille,* Sp. *manzanilla,* dim. of *manzana,* L *matiāna,* a certain kind of apple, from *Matius,* name of a Roman gens]

Manchu, *n.* ruling dynasty in China (1644–1912), originally a nomadic people from Manchuria, they established power through a series of successful invasions from the north.

Manchukuo, *n.* former Japanese puppet state in Manchuria 1932–45.

Manchuria, *n.* European name for the NE region of China (provinces of Heilongjiang, Jilin and Liaoning). It was united with China by the Manchu dynasty (1644), but as the Chinese Empire declined Japan and Russia were rivals for its control. The Russians were expelled after the Russo-Japanese War, and in 1932 Japan consolidated its position by creating a puppet state, Manchukuo, which disintegrated on the defeat of Japan in World War II.

mancipate, *v.t.* under Roman law, to hand over, to deliver possession, by the formal method of mancipation. **mancipable,** *a.* **mancipant,** *n.* **mancipation,** *n.* the formal method of transferring property required by Roman law. **mancipative, -tory,** *a.* [L *manipātus,* p.p. of *mancipāre,* as foll.]

manciple, *n.* a steward, a purveyor of stores, esp. for a college, inn of court etc. [OF *manciple,* L *mancipium,* from *manceps,* a buyer, a manager (*manus,* hand, *capere,* to take)]

Mancunian, *n.* a native or citizen of Manchester. *a.* of Manchester. [mod. L *Mancunium,* Manchester]

-mancy, *suf.* divination by, as in *necromancy, pyromancy.* [Gr. *manteia,* divination, from *manteuesthai,* to prophesy, from *mantis,* prophet]

mandala, *n.* any of various symbols used to represent the universe in Buddhism or Hinduism, used as an aid to meditation. [Sansk., circle]

Mandalay, *n.* chief town of Upper Burma, on the river Irrawaddy, about 495 km/370 miles N of Rangoon; population (1983) 533,000.

mandamus, *n.* a writ issued from a higher court directed to a person, corporation or inferior court, requiring them to do some particular thing therein specified which appertains to their office or duty. [L, we command (cp. MANDATE)]

mandarin, *n.* a Chinese official; a grotesque ornament or statuette in Chinese costume; (**Mandarin**) the chief dialect of the Chinese language; a mandarin orange; a dye the colour of this; a mandarin duck; a liqueur flavoured with juice of the mandarin orange; a high-ranking public servant; an influential, often reactionary (literary) figure. **mandarin collar,** *n.* a stiff, narrow stand-up collar. **mandarin duck,** *n.* a brightly-coloured Asiatic duck, *Aix galericulata.* **mandarin orange,** *n.* a small flattish sweet Chinese orange, *Citris nobilis,* of a dark-yellow colour. **mandarinate,** *n.* the office of a mandarin; mandarins collectively. [Port. *mandarim,* from Malay and Hindi *mantrī,* Sansk., *mantrin,* counsellor, from *man,* to think, cogn. with MIND]

mandate, *n.* an authoritative charge, order or command; (*Law*) a judicial command to an officer or a subordinate court; a contract of bailment by which the mandatary undertakes to perform gratuitously a duty regarding property committed to him; a rescript of the Pope; a direction from electors to a representative or a representative body to undertake certain legislation etc.; the authority given (esp. formerly by the League of Nations) to a larger power to govern another country in trust for its native inhabitants; a country ruled in this way. **mandatary,** *n.* **mandator,** *n.* **mandatory,** *a.* containing, or of the nature of a mandate; bestowing a mandate; obligatory, compulsory. [L *mandātum,* neut. p.p. of *mandāre,* to command (*manus,* hand, *dare,* to give)]

Mandela[1]**,** *n.* **Nelson (Rolihlahla)** (1918–), South African politician and lawyer. As organizer of the banned African National Congress (ANC), he was acquitted of treason in 1961, but was jailed for life in 1964 on charges of sabotage and plotting to overthrow the government. In prison he became a symbol of unity for the anti-apartheid movement. He was released in 1990.

Mandela[2]**,** *n.* **Winnie (Nomzamo)** (1934–), civil rights activist in South Africa and wife of Nelson Mandela. A leading spokesperson for the African National Congress during her husband's imprisonment in 1964, she was jailed for a year and put under house arrest several times.

Mandelshtam, *n.* **Osip Emilevich** (1891–1938), Russian poet. Son of a Jewish merchant, he was sent to a concentration camp by the Communist authorities in the 1930s, where he died. His posthumously published work with its classic brevity established his reputation as one of the greatest modern Russian poets. His wife Nadezhda's memoirs of her life with her husband, *Hope Against Hope,* were published in 1970, but in the USSR only in 1988.

mandible, *n.* the jaw, the under jaw in vertebrates, the upper or lower in birds, and the pair in insects. **mandibular, -late, -lated,** *a.* [L *mandibula,* from *mandere,* to chew]

mandolin, *n.* a musical instrument with a deep almond-shaped body and two or three pairs of metal strings. [F *mandoline,* It. *mandolino,* dim. of *mandola, mandora,* var. of PANDORA (cp. BANDORE)]

mandragora, *n.* †the mandrake; (**Mandragora**) a genus of thick, fleshy-rooted plants yielding a narcotic poison; a narcotic. [OE and late L, from Gr. *mandragoras*]

mandrake, *n.* the plant *Mandragora officinarum,* the root of which was anciently believed to be like the human form and to shriek when pulled up. [ME *mandrage,* from prec. (cp. Dut. *mandrage*)]

mandrel, *n.* an arbor or axis on which work is fixed for turning; the revolving spindle of a circular saw; a cylindrical rod or core round which metal or other material is forged or shaped; a miner's pick. [perh. corr. of F *mandrin*]

mandrill, *n.* a ferocious W African baboon, *Cynocepha-*

lus maimon. [MAN, DRILL⁴]

manducate, *v.t.* to chew, to eat. **manducable,** *a.* **manducation,** *n.* **manducatory,** *a.* [L *mandūcātus,* p.p. of *mandūcāre,* to chew]

mane, *n.* the long hair on the neck of some animals, as the horse; long, thick hair on a person's head. **mane-sheet,** *n.* a covering for the upper part of a horse's head. **maned,** *a.* (*usu. in comb.*) having a mane, as *thick-maned.* **maneless,** *a.* [OE *manu* (cp. Dut. *mane,* Icel. *mōn,* pl. *manar,* G *Mähne*), cogn. with Sansk. *manyā,* nape of the neck, L *monīle,* necklace]

manège, *n.* a school for training horses or teaching horsemanship; the training of horses; horsemanship. *v.t.* to manage; to break in and train (a horse). [F]

manes, *n.pl.* the spirits of the dead, esp. of ancestors worshipped as tutelary divinities; the shade of a deceased person regarded as an object of reverence. [L]

Manet, *n.* **Edouard** (1832–83), French painter, active in Paris. Rebelling against the academic tradition, he developed a clear and unaffected Realist style. He went on to become a leading spirit in the impressionist movement. His subjects were chiefly modern, such as *Un bar aux Folies-Bergère/Bar at the Folies-Bergère* (1882).

maneuver, (*N Am.*) MANOEUVRE.

manful, etc. MAN.

manga, *n.* a flowing robe like a poncho; (*Eccles.*) a case or covering for a processional cross. [Sp., from L *manica,* sleeve]

mangabey, *n.* an African monkey of the genus *Cercocebus.* [part of Madagascar]

manganese, *n.* a metallic element, at. no.25; chem. symbol Mn, of a greyish-white colour; the oxide of this occurring as a black mineral, used in glass-making. **manganate,** *n.* a salt of manganic acid. **manganesian, -nesic, manganic,** *a.* **manganiferous,** *a.* **Manganin**®, *n.* an alloy of manganese, copper and nickel with a high electrical resistance. **manganite,** *n.* grey manganese ore. [F *manganèse,* corr. of MAGNESIA]

mangaroo, *n.* (*Austral.*) a small flying phalanger. [Abor.]

mange, *n.* a skin disease occurring in cattle, dogs etc. **mangy,** *a.* infected with the mange; mean, squalid. **manginess,** *n.* [ME *manjewe,* OF *manjue,* from *manjuer* (F *manger,* to eat), L *mandūcāre,* to MANDUCATE]

mangel-wurzel, *n.* a large-rooted variety of the common beet, *Beta vulgaris,* cultivated as fodder for cattle. [G *Mangoldwurzel* (*Mangold,* beet, *Wurzel,* root)]

manger, *n.* a trough for horses or cattle to eat out of. **dog in a manger** DOG. [OF *mangeure,* from *manger,* to eat, see MANGE]

mangetout, *n.* a type of pea which is eaten complete with the pod. [F, eat all]

mangle¹, *v.t.* to lacerate, to mutilate; to disfigure by hacking; to mar, to ruin, to destroy the symmetry or completeness of, by blundering etc. [A-F *mangler, mahangler,* freq. of OF *mahaignier,* to MAIM]

mangle², *n.* a rolling-machine for pressing and smoothing damp linen. *v.t.* to press and smooth with a mangle; to calender. **mangler,** *n.* [Dut. *mangel* whence *mangelen,* to mangle), late L *manganum,* Gr. *manganon,* see MANGONEL]

mango, *n.* (*pl.* **-goes**) an E Indian tree, *Mangifera indica,* or its fruit; (*N Am.*) a green musk-melon pickled. **mango-fish,** *n.* an E Indian food-fish, *Polynemus paradiseus,* of a beautiful yellow colour. **mango-trick,** *n.* an Indian juggler's trick of making a mango-tree appear to spring up and bear fruit. [Port. *manga,* Malay *mañggā,* Tamil *mānkāy* (*mān,* mango-tree, *kay,* fruit)]

mangonel, *n.* a mediaeval engine for throwing missiles. [OF, from late L *mangona, mango -ōnem,* Gr. *manganon*]

mangosteen, *n.* an E Indian tree, *Garcinia mangostana,* or its orange-like fruit, with a sweet, juicy pulp. [Malay *manggustan*]

mangrove, *n.* a tropical tree of the genus *Rhizophora,* esp. *R. mangle,* growing in muddy places by the coast, the bark of which is used for medicine and in tanning. [etym. doubtful]

mangy etc. MANGE.

manhandle, manhole, manhood, manhunt MAN.

Manhattan¹, *n.* a cocktail containing whisky, vermouth and sometimes a dash of bitters. [*Manhattan,* borough of New York City]

Manhattan², *n.* an island 20 km/12.5 miles long and 4 km/2.5 miles wide, lying between the Hudson and East rivers and forming a borough of the city of New York, US; population (1980) 1,428,000. It includes the Wall Street business centre and Broadway theatres.

Manhattan Project, *n.* code name for the development of the atom bomb in the US in World War II, to which the scientists Fermi and Oppenheimer contributed.

mania, *n.* a form of mental disorder characterized by hallucination, emotional excitement and violence; (*coll.*) an infatuation, a craze. **maniac,** *a.* affected with mania, insane, raving. *n.* a madman, a raving lunatic. **maniacal,** *a.* **maniacally,** *adv.* **manic,** *a.* of or affected by mania; (*coll.*) over-excited, wildly energetic. **manic-depressive,** *n., a.* (a person) suffering from alternating bouts of mania and depression. [L and Gr., cogn. with *mainesthai,* to be mad]

-mania, *comb. form* denoting special kinds of derangement, hallucination, infatuation or excessive enthusiasm, as in *erotomania, kleptomania, megalomania, monomania.* **-maniac,** *suf.* forming nouns and adjectives. [as prec.]

Manichaean, *a.* pertaining to Manichaeism. *n.* a believer in Manichaeism, **Manichaeism,** *n.* a religious doctrine, widely prevailing in the 3rd–5th cent., that the universe is controlled by two antagonistic powers, light or goodness, identified with God, and darkness, chaos or evil. **Manichee,** *n.* [L *Manichaeus,* late Gr. *Manichaios,* from name of founder]

manicure, *n.* one who undertakes the treatment of the hands and finger-nails as a business; the care of the hands, nails etc. *v.t.* to treat the hands and finger-nails. **manicurist,** *n.* [F (L *manus,* hand, *cura,* care)]

manifest, *a.* not concealed; plainly apparent, clear, obvious; †detected. *v.t.* to make manifest, to show clearly; to display, to exhibit, to evince; to be evidence of; to reveal or exhibit (itself); to record in a ship's manifest. *v.i.* to make a public demonstration of opinion; of a spirit, to reveal its presence. *n.* a list of a ship's cargo for the use of the custom-house officers; a list of passengers on an aircraft; †a manifesto. **manifestable,** *a.* **manifestation,** *n.* manifesting or being manifested; a public demonstration. **manifestative,** *a.* **manifester,** *n.* **manifestly,** *adv.* **manifestness,** *n.* [through F *manifeste* or directly from L *manifestus* (prob. *mani-, manu, manus,* hand, *festus,* struck, cogn. with DEFEND)]

manifesto, *n.* (*pl.* **-to(e)s**) a public declaration, esp. by a political party, government, sovereign or other authoritative body, of opinions, motives or intentions. †*v.i.* to issue a manifesto. [It.]

manifold, *a.* of various forms or kinds; many and various, abundant; shown, applied or acting in various ways. *n.* that which is manifold; (*Phil.*) a sum or aggregate of sense-impressions etc.; (*Math.*) manifoldness; a copy made by a manifold writer; a tube or system of tubes for conveying steam, gas etc., in an engine, motor etc. *v.t.* to multiply, esp. by a manifold writer. **manifold writer,** *n.* an apparatus for making several copies of a document at once. **manifolder,** *n.* **manifoldly,** *adv.* **manifoldness,** *n.* the state of being manifold; (*Math.*) a conception of space or magnitude comprehending several particular concepts. [OE *manigfeald*]

Manihot, *n.* a genus of tropical American spurges, including manioc. [MANIOC]

manikin, *n.* a little man, a dwarf; an anatomical model exhibiting the parts, organs and structure of the human body; a lay figure; a small tropical American passerine bird. [Dut. *manneken,* dim. of *man* (cp. F *mannequin*)]

Manila¹, *n.* an industrial port (textiles, tobacco, distilling, chemicals, shipbuilding) and capital of the Philippines, on the island of Luzon; population (1980) 5,926,000.

Manila[2], **Manilla**[1], *n.* a kind of cheroot made at *Manila* (capital of Philippine Islands); Manila hemp; a rope of this. **Manila hemp,** *n.* hemp made from the fibre of *Musa textilis,* used for making rope. **Manila man,** *n.* (*Austral., coll.*) a native of the East Indies. **Manila paper,** *n.* a strong brown paper, orig. made from Manila hemp.

manilla[2], *n.* a metal ring worn by Africans on the legs or arms; a piece of metal shaped like a ring horseshoe formerly used as a medium of exchange among the natives of the W African coast. [Sp., from It. *maniglia* (perh. dim. of L *manus,* hand or from *monīlia,* pl. of *monīle,* necklace)]

†**manille,** *n.* in ombre or quadrille, the highest but one trump or honour. [corr. of Sp. *malilla,* dim. of *mala,* L *malus,* bad]

manioc, *n.* the cassava, *Manihot utilissima;* meal made from the root of this. [Port., from Tupí-Guaraní]

maniple, *n.* a strip worn as a eucharistic vestment on a priest's left arm; a subdivision of the Roman legion consisting of 60 to 120 men with their officers; †a handful. **manipular**, *a.* [OF, from L *manipulus,* handful (*mani-, manus-,* hand, *-pulus,* form of root *plē-,* to fill, as in *plēnus,* full)]

maniplies MANYPLIES.

manipulate, *v.t.* to operate on with or as with the hands, to handle, to treat, esp. skilfully or dexterously; to manage, influence or tamper with by artful or sly means. *v.i.* to use the hands skilfully, as in scientific experiments etc. **manipular**, *a.* **manipulation,** *n.* **manipulative, -tory** *a.* **manipulator,** *n.* [prob. from MANIPULATION, from F *manipuler,* from L *manipulus,* see MANIPLE]

Manipur, *n.* NE state of India. **area** 22,400 sq km/8,646 sq miles. **capital** Imphal. **products** grain, fruit, vegetables, sugar, textiles, cement. **population** (1981) 1,434,000. **language** Hindi. **religion** Hindu 70%.

manis, *n.* a genus of edentate mammals, containing the scaly ant-eaters. [mod. L, prob. from MANES]

Manitoba, *n.* prairie province of Canada. **area** 650,000 sq km/250,900 sq miles. **capital** Winnipeg. **exports** grain, manufactured foods, beverages, machinery, furs, fish, nickel, zinc, copper, and the world's largest caesium deposits. **population** (1986) 1,071,000.

manitou, *n.* among certain American Indians a spirit or being endowed with supernatural power; an amulet, a fetish. [Algonkin *manitu*]

mankind, manlike, etc. MAN.

Manley, *n.* **Michael** (1924–), Jamaican politician, prime minister (1972–80) and from 1989, adopting more moderate socialist policies. His father, **Norman Manley** (1893–1969), was founder of the People's National Party and prime minister (1959–62).

Mann[1], *n.* **Anthony** (adopted name of Emil Anton Bundmann) (1906–67), US film director who made a series of violent but intelligent 1950s Westerns starring James Stewart, such as *Winchester '73* (1950). He also directed one of the best film epics, *El Cid* (1961). His other films include *The Glenn Miller Story* (1954) and *A Dandy in Aspic* (1968).

Mann[2], *n.* **Thomas** (1875–1955), German novelist and critic, concerned with the theme of the artist's relation to society. His first novel was *Buddenbrooks* (1901) which, followed by *Der Zauberberg/The Magic Mountain* (1924), led to a Nobel prize 1929. Later works include *Dr Faustus* (1947) and *Die Bekenntnisse des Hochstaplers Felix Krull/Confessions of Felix Krull* (1954). Notable among his short stories is *Der Tod in Venedig/Death in Venice* (1913).

manna, *n.* the food miraculously supplied to the Israelites in the wilderness; divine food, spiritual nourishment, as the Eucharist; a sweetish exudation, of a slightly laxative nature, from certain species of ash, chiefly *Fraxinus ornus.* **Hebrew, Jews'** or **Persian manna,** or **manna of Mount Sinai,** an exudation from an Arabian variety of tamarisk, *Tamarix gallica.* **manna from heaven,** anything very advantageous and unexpected. **manna-croup,** *n.* coarse-ground granular wheat-meal, separated by bolting. **manna gum,** *n.* dried sap of the eucalyptus, lerp. **manniferous**, *a.* bearing or yielding manna. [late L and Gr., from Heb. *mān* (said to be from Heb. *mān hu,* what is this?; but more prob. the same as Arab. *mann,* applied to Hebrew or Persian manna)]

mannequin, *n.* a woman employed to wear and display clothes. [F, a lay figure]

manner, *n.* the mode in which anything is done or happens; method, style, mannerism; practice, habit, use, custom; demeanour, bearing, address; sort, kind; (*pl.*) conduct in social intercourse, behaviour, deportment; politeness, habits showing good breeding; general modes of life, social conditions. **all manner of,** all kinds of. **by no manner of means,** under no circumstances. **in a manner,** in a certain way, somewhat, so to speak. **to the manner born,** (*Shak.*) born to follow a certain practice or custom; (as if) accumstomed to something from birth. **what manner of,** what kind of. **mannered,** *a.* (*usu. in comb.*) having manners, as *ill-mannered;* having or betraying mannerism, affected. **mannerism,** *n.* excessive adherence to the same manner or peculiarity; peculiarity of style; a 16th-cent. art style (see below). **mannerist,** *n.* **manneristic, -ical,** *a.* **mannerless,** *a.* devoid of manners or breeding. **mannerly,** *a.*, †*adv.* **mannerliness,** *n.* [OF *maniere,* from L *manuārius,* pertaining to the hand, from *manus,* hand]

Mannerheim, *n.* **Carl Gustav Emil von** (1867–1951), Finnish general and politician, leader of the conservative forces in the civil war (1917–18) and regent (1918–19). He commanded the Finnish army (1939–40) and (1941–44) and was president of Finland (1944–46).

mannerism, *n.* in painting and architecture, a style characterized by a subtle but conscious breaking of the 'rules' of classical composition, for example, displaying the human body in a distorted pose, off-centre, and using harsh, non-blending colours. The term was coined by Vasari and used to describe the 16th-cent. reaction to the peak of Renaissance classicism as achieved by Raphael, Leonardo and early Michelangelo.

Mannheim, *n.* **Karl** (1893–1947), Hungarian sociologist, who settled in the UK in 1933. In *Ideology and Utopia* (1929) he argued that all knowledge, except in mathematics and physics, is ideological, a reflection of class interests and values; that there is no such thing as objective knowledge or absolute truth.

mannikin MANIKIN.

Manning, *n.* **Henry Edward** (1808–92), English priest, one of the leaders of the Oxford Movement. In 1851 he was converted to Roman Catholicism, and in 1865 became archbishop of Westminster. He was created a cardinal in 1875.

mannish etc. MAN.

mannite, *n.* a sweetish substance obtained from manna. **mannitose,** *n.*

manoao, *n.* the yellow pine of New Zealand. [Maori]

Manoel, *n.* two kings of Portugal:

Manoel I, *n.* (1469–1521), king of Portugal from 1495, when he succeeded his uncle John II (1455–95). He was known as 'the Fortunate', because his reign was distinguished by the discoveries made by Portuguese navigators and the expansion of the Portuguese empire.

Manoel II, *n.* (1889–1932), king of Portugal (1908–10). He ascended the throne on the assassination of his father, Carlos I, but was driven out by a revolution in 1910, and lived in England.

manoeuvre, *n.* a tactical movement or change of position by troops or warships; (*pl.*) tactical exercises in imitation of war; skilful or artful management; a trick, a stratagem. *v.i.* to perform manoeuvres; to manage with skill; to employ stratagem. *v.t.* to cause (troops) to perform manoeuvres; to move, drive or effect by means of strategy or skilful management; to manipulate. **manoeuvrable,** *n.* **manoeuvrability**, *n.* **manoeuvrer,** *n.* [F, from late L *manopera,* from *manoper-*

āre, L *manū operārī* (*manū,* abl. of *manus,* hand, *operārī,* to work)]

manometer, *n.* an instrument for measuring the pressure of a gas. **manometric,** *a.* **manometry,** *n.* [F *manomètre* (Gr. *manos,* thin, rare, -METER)]

manor, *n.* a landed estate consisting of a demesne and certain rights over lands held by freehold tenants etc., orig. a barony held by a lord and subject to the jurisdiction of his court-baron; (*N Am.*) a tract of land occupied in perpetuity or for long terms by tenants who pay a fee-farm rent to the proprietor; (*sl.*) a police district. **lord of the manor,** a person or corporation holding the rights of a manor. **manor-house,** *n.* **manorial,** *a.* pertaining to a manor. **manpower** MAN. [OF *manoir,* mansion, from L *manēre,* to remain, dwell]

manqué, *a.* having the potential to be, but not actually being, something specified, as in *actor manqué.* [F, having failed]

mansard roof, *n.* a roof with two sets of rafters on each side, the lower nearly vertical, the upper much inclined, giving space for attics. [F *mansarde* after F. *Mansard,* 1598–1666, French architect]

Mansart, *n.* **Jules Hardouin** (1646–1708), French architect of the palace of Versailles and Grand Trianon, and designer of the Place de Vendôme and the Place des Victoires, Paris.

manse, *n.* the residence of a clergyman, esp. a Presbyterian minister. [med. L *mansa,* a house, a farm, from *manēre,* to dwell, p.p. *mansus*]

Mansell, *n.* **Nigel** (1954–), English motor-racing driver. Runner-up in the world championship on two occasions.

Mansfield¹, *n.* **Jayne** (stage name of Vera Jayne Palmer) (1933–67), US actress who had a short career as a kind of living parody of Marilyn Monroe in films including *The Girl Can't Help It* (1956) and *Will Success Spoil Rock Hunter?* (1957).

Mansfield², *n.* **Katherine** (pen name of Kathleen Beauchamp) (1888–1923), New Zealand writer, who lived most of her life in England. Her delicate artistry emerges not only in her volumes of short stories, such as *In a German Pension* (1911), *Bliss* (1920) and *The Garden Party* (1923), but in her *Letters* and *Journal.*

mansion, *n.* a residence of considerable size and pretensions; a manor-house; (*pl.*) a large building or set of buildings divided into residential flats; (*poet.*) a place of abode. **mansion-house,** *n.* a manor-house; an official residence, esp. of the Lord Mayors in London and Dublin. †**mansionry,** *n.* [OF, from L *mansio, -ōnem,* as prec.]

man-sized, manslaughter MAN.

†**mansuete,** *a.* tame, gentle. †**mansuetude,** *n.* [L *mansuētus,* p.p. of *mansuescere,* to tame (*manus,* hand, *suescere,* to accustom)]

Manson, *n.* **Patrick** (1844–1922), Scottish physician, who showed that insects are responsible for the spread of diseases like elephantiasis and malaria.

manta (ray), *n.* any of various very large rays of the family *Mobulidae.* [Sp., cloak, see MANTLE¹]

Mantegna, *n.* **Andrea** (*c.* 1431–1506), Italian Renaissance painter and engraver, active chiefly in Padua and Mantua, where some of his frescoes remain. Paintings such as *The Agony in the Garden* (about 1455, National Gallery, London) reveal a dramatic linear style, mastery of perspective and strongly Classical architectural detail.

mantel, *n.* the ornamental facing round a fireplace with the shelf above it. **mantel-board,** *n.* a mantelshelf or a shelf resting on it, formerly draped. **mantelpiece,** *n.* a mantel; a mantel-tree. **mantelshelf,** *n.* the shelf above a fireplace. †**mantel-tree,** *n.* the beam forming the lintel of a fireplace. [var. of MANTLE¹]

mantelet, *n.* a short mantle; a bullet-proof shield, enclosure or shelter. [OF, dim. of prec.]

mantic, *a.* pertaining to prophecy or divination. [Gr. *mantikos,* from *mantis,* prophet]

manticore, *n.* a fabulous monster with a human head, a lion's body and the tail of a scorpion. [L *manticora,* Gr. *matichōras, mantichoras,* prob. from O Pers.]

mantilla, *n.* a woman's light cloak or cape; a veil for the head and shoulders, worn in Spain and Italy. [Sp., dim. of *manta,* MANTLE¹]

mantis, *n.* (*pl.* **mantis**) a genus of carnivorous orthopterous insects, which hold their forelegs as if in prayer lying in wait for other insects as prey. [Gr., prophet]

mantissa, *n.* the decimal or fractional part of a logarithm. [L, make-weight]

mantle¹, *n.* a sleeveless cloak or loose outer garment; a covering; a conical or tubular network coated with refractory earth placed round a gas-jet to give an incandescent light; a covering or concealing skin, part or organ, as the fold enclosing the viscera in the Mollusca; a symbol of leadership, power or authority; the layer of the earth between the crust and the core. **mantle rock,** *n.* unconsolidated rock at the earth's surface. [OF *mantel* (F *manteau*), L *mantellum,* whence also OE *mentel*]

mantle², *v.t.* to clothe in or as in a mantle; to cover, to envelop, to conceal; to suffuse. *v.i.* to be overspread or suffused (as with a blush); to suffuse the cheeks; of a blush, of liquids, to become covered or coated; to stretch the wings (as a hawk on its perch). **mantlet** MANTELET. **mantling,** *a.* foaming, creamy, suffusing. *n.* material for mantles; in heraldry, drapery or scroll-work round an achievement. [as prec.]

Manton, *n.* a fowling-piece made by Manton. [Joseph *Manton, c.* 1766–1835, gunsmith]

Mantoux test, *n.* a test for past or present tuberculosis conducted by injecting tuberculin beneath the skin. [C. *Mantoux,* 1877–1956, French physician]

mantra, *n.* a Hindu formula or charm; a Vedic hymn of praise; a word or phrase chanted inwardly in meditation. [Sansk., from *man,* to think]

mantrap MAN.

†**mantua,** *n.* a woman's loose gown worn in the 17th and 18th cents. **mantua-maker,** *n.* a dressmaker. [corr. of F *manteau,* MANTLE, confused with *Mantua* in Italy]

Manu, *n.* in Hindu mythology, the founder of the human race, who was saved by Brahma from a deluge.

manual¹, *a.* pertaining to or performed with the hands; involving physical exertion; not mechanical or automatic. **sign manual** SIGN. **manual alphabet** FINGER ALPHABET. **manual exercise,** *n.* the drill by which soldiers are taught to handle their rifles etc. properly. **manually,** *adv.* [F *manuel,* L *manuālis,* from *manus,* hand]

manual², *n.* a small book or handy compendium, a handbook; a fire-engine worked by hands; a service book, esp. that used by priests in the mediaeval church; an organ keyboard played by the hands. **manual engine,** *n.* a fire-engine worked by hand.

manubrium, *n.* (*pl.* **-bria, -briums**) (*Anat., Zool.*) a handle-like part or process, as the presternum in mammals, the peduncle hanging from the umbrella in medusae; the handle of an organ-stop. **manubrial,** *a.* [L, a haft, a handle from *manus,* hand]

manucode, *n.* the Australian rifle-bird or bird of paradise.

manufacture, *n.* the making of articles by means of labour or machinery, esp. on a large scale; industrial production; any particular branch of this; (*pl.*) the products of industry or any particular industry. *v.t.* to make or work up into suitable forms for use; to produce or fashion by labour or machinery, esp. on a large scale; to produce (pictures, literature etc.) in a mechanical way; to fabricate, to invent (a story, evidence etc.). *v.i.* to be occupied in manufacture. **manufactory,** *n.* a factory, †**manufactural,** *a.* **manufacturer,** *n.* **manufacturing,** *n.* [F, from L *manū,* by hand, abl. of *manus,* hand, *factūra,* from *facere,* to make]

manuka, *n.* the New Zealand tea-tree. [Maori]

manumit, *v.t.* (*past, p.p.* **manumitted**) to release from slavery. **manumission,** *n.* [L *manūmittere* (*manū,* abl. of *manus,* hand, *mittere,* to send)]

manumotor, *n.* a wheeled carriage worked by the

hands of the rider. **manumotive,** *a.* [L *manū,* as prec.]

manure, *v.t.* to enrich (a soil) with fertilizing substances. *n.* any substance, as dung, compost or chemical preparations, used to fertilize land. †**manurance,** *n.* manuring; cultivation or tillage; (*Law*) tenure or occupation. **manurer,** *n.* **manurial,** *a.* [corr. of MANOEUVRE]

manus, *n.* the hand or a corresponding part in an animal. [L]

manuscript, *a.* written by hand. *n.* a book or document written by hand, not printed; copy for a printer. [med. L *manuscriptus* (*manū,* abl. of *manus,* hand, *scriptus,* p.p. of *scrībere,* to write)]

Manutius, *n.* **Aldus** (1450–1515), Italian printer, established in Venice (which he made the publishing centre of Europe) from 1490; he introduced italic type and was the first to print books in Greek.

manward MAN.

Manx, *a.* pertaining to the Isle of Man, or its inhabitants or its language. *n.* the Celtic language spoken by natives of Man; the people of the Isle of Man. **Manx cat,** *n.* a tailless variety of domestic cat. **Manxman,** *n.* **Manx shearwater,** *n.* a long-winged black and white shearwater of the N Atlantic. **Manxwoman,** *n. fem.* [earlier *Maniske,* Icel. *manskr*]

many, *a.* numerous; comprising a great number. *n.* a multitude; a great number. **the many,** the majority; the multitude, the common crowd. **too many,** superfluous, not wanted, in the way; (*coll.*) too clever, too able or skilful (for). **many-headed,** *a.* of a mob etc., fickle. **many-headedness,** *n.* **many-sided,** *a.* having many sides, aspects etc.; widely sympathetic, versatile, liberal. **many-sidedness,** *n.* [OE *manig* (cp. Dut. *menig,* Dan. *mange,* G *manch*)]

manyplies, *n.* the third stomach of a ruminant, the omasum. [MANY, *plies,* pl. of PLY¹]

manzanilla, *n.* a very dry sherry. [Sp., camomile]

Manzoni, *n.* **Alessandro, Count Manzoni** (1785–1873), Italian poet and novelist, best known for his historical romance, *I promessi sposi/The Betrothed* (1825–27), set in Spanish-occupied Milan during the 17th cent. Verdi's *Requiem* commemorates him.

Maoism, *n.* a form of communism based on the ideas and teachings of the Chinese communist leader Mao Zedong. It involves an adaptation of Marxism to suit conditions in China and apportions a much greater role for agriculture and the peasantry in the building of socialism, thus effectively bypassing the capitalist (industrial) stage envisaged by Marx. **Maoist,** *n., a.* (an adherent) of Maoism.

Maori, *n., a.* (a member) of a Polynesian people of New Zealand, who form about 10% of the population; (1986) 294,200. In recent years there has been increased Maori consciousness, and a demand for official status for the Maori language and review of the Waitangi Treaty of 1840 (under which the Maoris surrendered their lands to British sovereignty). The **Maori Unity Movement/Kotahitanga** was founded (1983) by Eva Rickard. The Maoris claim 70% of the country's land, and have secured a ruling that the fishing grounds of the far north belong solely to local tribes. **Maori chief,** *n.* a New Zealand flat fish. **Maori hen,** *n.* the flightless wood hen of New Zealand. **Maoriland,** *n.* New Zealand. **Maorilander,** *n.* a white person native of New Zealand. **Maori language,** *n.* a member of the Polynesian branch of the Malayo-Polynesian language family. **Maoritanga,** *n.* Maori culture.

Mao Zedong, *n.* (formerly **Mao Tse-tung**) (1893–1976), Chinese political leader and Marxist theoretician. A founder of the Chinese Communist Party (CCP) (1921), Mao soon emerged as its leader. He organized the Long March (1934–36) and the war of liberation (1937–49), and headed the CCP and government until his death. His influence diminished with the failure of his 1958–60 Great Leap Forward, but he emerged dominant again during the 1966–69 Cultural Revolution. Mao adapted communism to Chinese conditions, as set out in the *Little Red Book.*

map, *n.* a representation of a portion of the earth's surface or the heavens, upon a plane; any delineation; a mathematical function. *v.t.* (*past, p.p.* **mapped**) to represent or set down in a map; to plan (out) in exact detail; (*Math.*) to assign (each of the elements of a set) to each of the elements in a different set. **off the map,** *adv.* (*coll.*) of no account, not worth consideration, remote; out-of-the-way. **to put on the map,** to cause to become important or well-known. †**mapless,** *a.* **maplike,** *a.* **mapper, mappist,** *n.* †**mappery,** *n.* [L *mappa,* orig. napkin]

Mapai, *n.* (Miphlegeth Poolei Israel) the Israeli Workers' Party or Labour Party, founded in 1930. Its leading figure until 1965 was David Ben Gurion. In 1968, the party allied with two other democratic socialist parties to form the Israeli Labour Party, led initially by Levi Estikol and later Golda Meir.

maple, *n.* a tree or shrub of the genus *Acer;* the wood of this. **maple leaf,** *n.* the emblem of Canada. **maple-sugar,** *n.* a coarse sugar obtained from *Acer saccharinum* and other maples. [OE in *mapulder* and *mapeltrēow*]

Mappa Mundi, *n.* a 13th-cent. map of the world, one of the best-known mediaeval world maps. It is circular, and shows Asia at the top, with Europe and Africa below, and Jerusalem at the centre. It was drawn by David de Bello, a canon at Hereford Cathedral, who left the map to the cathedral. In 1988 there were plans to sell the map to raise money for repairs.

Maputo, *n.* (formerly until (1975) **Lourenço Marques**) capital of Mozambique, and Africa's second largest port, on Delagoa Bay; population (1986) 883,000. Linked by rail with Zimbabwe and South Africa, it is a major outlet for minerals, steel, textiles, processed foods and furniture.

maquette, *n.* a sculptor's preliminary model in clay, wax etc.; a preliminary sketch. [F, from It. *machietta,* little spot]

maqui, *n.* a Chilean evergreen shrub, the berries of which produce a wine used in adulteration. [Chilean Sp.]

maquillage, *n.* (the technique of applying) make-up, cosmetics. [F]

maquis, *n.* scrub or bush in Corsica; the name taken by those surreptitiously resisting the German invaders of France etc., in 1940–45. [F]

Maquis, *n.* the French Resistance movement that fought against German occupation during World War II.

Mar., (*abbr.*) March.

mar, *v.t.* to spoil, to ruin; to disfigure. *n.* a blemish, a drawback. **marplot,** *n.* one who spoils a plot or undertaking by interference. [OE *merran* (cp. MDut. *merren,* to hinder, Dut. *marren,* to tarry)]

Mara, *n.* in Buddhism, a supernatural being who attempted to distract the Buddha from the meditations that led to his enlightenment. In Hinduism, a goddess of death.

marabou, *n.* a W African stork, *Leptoptilus marabou,* the downy feathers from under the wings and tail of which are used for trimming hats etc.; the adjutant-bird. [from foll., because of Islamic belief that the stork is a holy bird]

marabout, *n.* a Muslim hermit or saint, esp. one of a priestly caste in N Africa; the tomb or dwelling of such a saint. [F, from Port. *marabuto,* Arab. *murābit*]

maraca, *n.* a hollow gourd or shell containing beads, shot etc., shaken as a percussive accompaniment to music, esp. in Latin America. [Port. *maracá,* from Tupí]

Maracaibo, *n.* an oil-exporting port in Venezuela, on the channel connecting Lake Maracaibo with the Gulf of Venezuela; population (1981) 889,000.

Maracaibo, Lake, *n.* a lake in a rich oil-producing region in NW Venezuela; area 14,000 sq km/5,400 sq miles.

Maradona, *n.* **Diego** (1960–), Argentinian footballer who helped his country to win the World Cup in 1986.

maranatha ANATHEMA.

maraschino, *n.* a cordial or liqueur distilled from bitter cherries grown in Dalmatia. [It., a. from *marasca, amarasca,* a sharp black cherry, from *amaro,* L *amārus,* bitter]

marasmus, *n.* wasting away of the body. **marasmic,** *a.* [Gr. *marasmos,* from *marainein,* to wither away]

Marat, *n.* **Jean Paul** (1743–93), French Revolutionary leader and journalist. He was elected in 1792 to the National Convention, where he carried on a long struggle with the Girondins, ending in their overthrow in May 1793. In July he was murdered by Charlotte Corday.

Maratha, *n.* a member of a people of SW India, esp. the state of Maharashtra. **Marathi,** *n.* their Sanskritic language.

marathon, *n.* any task or contest; requiring great endurance. [*Marathon* in Greece]

Marathon, Battle of, (490 BC), fought between the Greeks, who were ultimately victorious, and invading Persians on the plain of Marathon, NE of Athens. Before the battle, news of the Persian destruction of the Greek city of Eretria was taken from Athens to Sparta by a courier, Pheidippides, who fell dead on arrival. His feat is commemorated by the **marathon race**.

maraud, *v.i.* to rove in quest of plunder; to make a raid (on). *v.t.* to plunder. †*n.* a raid, a foray. **marauder,** *n.* [F *marauder,* from *maraud,* rogue, etym. doubtful]

†**maravedi,** *n.* a former Spanish copper coin worth less than a farthing; a former Spanish gold coin. [Sp. from Arab. *Murābitīn,* pl. of *murābit,* MARABOUT, the name of a Moorish dynasty at Cordova, 1087–1147]

marble, *n.* a fine-grained or crystalline limestone capable of taking a fine polish; (*usu. pl.*) a piece of sculpture in this material; a type of smoothness, hardness or inflexibility; a small ball of marble, glass or other hard substance used as a toy; (*pl., coll.*) one's sanity, one's wits. *v.t.* to stain or vein (end-papers of books etc.) to look like marble. *a.* composed of marble; veined like marble; hard, unfeeling; †pure, pellucid. **marble-edged,** *a.* marbled. **marble-hearted,** *a.* hard-hearted. **marbleize, -ise,** *v.t.* (*N Am.*) **marbler,** *n.* **marbling,** *n.* the veined or speckled appearance of marble. **marbly,** *a.* [OF *marbre,* L *marmor,* cogn. with Gr. *marmaros,* sparkling, *marmairein,* to sparkle, to glisten]

Marble Arch, *n.* a triumphal arch in London designed by John Nash to commemorate Nelson's victories. Intended as a ceremonial entry to Buckingham Palace, in 1851 it was moved to Hyde Park at the end of Oxford Street.

Marburg disease, *n.* a viral disease of central Africa, first occurring in Europe in 1967 among research workers in Germany working with African green monkeys, hence its common name *green monkey disease.* It is characterized by haemorrhage of the mucous membranes, fever, vomiting and diarrhoea; mortality is high.

marc, *n.* the compressed residue of grapes left after pressing, in the making of wine or oil; liqueur-brandy made from this. [F *marcher,* to tread]

Marc, *n.* **Franz** (1880–1916), German expressionist painter, associated with Kandinsky in founding the *Blaue Reiter* movement. Animals played an essential part in his view of the world and bold semi-abstracts of red and blue horses are characteristic of his work.

Marcaña Stadium, *n.* the world's largest football stadium, in Rio de Janeiro, Brazil, built in 1950. It has a capacity of 175,000 but held a world record 199,854 spectators for the 1950 World Cup final between Brazil and Uruguay.

†**marcantant,** *n.* (*Shak.*) a merchant. [corr. of It. *mercatante,* MERCHANT]

marcasite, *n.* pyrites, esp. a white orthorhombic form of iron pyrites, used for making ornaments. [med. L *marcasīta,* etym. doubtful]

marcato, *a.* of musical notes, heavily accented. *adv.* (played) with a heavy accent. [It. *marcare,* to mark]

Marceau, *n.* **Marcel** (1923–), French mime artist. He is the creator of the clown-harlequin Bip and mime sequences such as 'Youth, Maturity, Old Age and Death'.

marcel, *n.* a style of permanent wave hairdresssing. **marcel wave,** *n.* a permanent wave. [*Marcel,* a French hairdresser]

marcescent, *a.* of blooms, leaves etc., withering without falling. **marcescence,** *n.* †**marcescible,** *a.* [L *marcescēns -entem,* pres.p. of *marcescere,* freq. of *marcēre,* to wither]

March[1], *n.* the third month of the year. **March chick,** *n.* a precocious young person. [A-F *marche* (F *mars*), from L *Martius,* pertaining to Mars]

march[2], *n.* (*pl.* **-ches**) the frontier or boundary of a territory; (*often pl.*) a borderland or debatable land between two countries, as the border country of England and Wales. *v.i.* to border (upon) or have a common frontier (with). **Lord Marcher,** (*pl.* **Lords Marchers**) Lords holding jurisdiction and privileges on the Welsh border. **marchman,** *n.* **marcher,** *n.* an officer or warden having jurisdiction over marches; an inhabitant of a march. [F *marche,* MARK[1]]

march[3], *v.i.* to move with regular steps as soldiers; to walk in a grave, deliberate or determined manner. *v.t.* to cause to move (on, off etc.) in military order. *n.* the act of marching; a stately, deliberate or measured movement, esp. of soldiers; the distance marched in a day; progress, advance; (*Mus.*) a composition for accompanying a march. **on the march,** advancing steadily; making progress. **to steal a march on,** to gain an advantage over. **march past,** *n.* a marching of troops in a review past a superior officer etc. [F *marcher,* etym. doubtful]

Marchais, *n.* **Georges** (1920–), leader of the French Communist Party (PCF) from 1972. Under his leadership, the party committed itself to a 'transition to socialism' by democratic means and entered into a union of the left with the Socialist Party (PS). This was severed in 1977, and the PCF returned to a more orthodox pro-Moscow line, since when its share of the vote has decreased.

Marchantia, *n.pl.* a genus of Hepaticae or liverworts. [Nicholas *Marchant* (fl. 17th cent.), French botanist]

Marche, *n.* region of E central Italy consisting of the provinces of Ancona, Ascoli Piceno, Macerata and Pesaro e Urbino; capital Ancona; area 9700 sq km/3744 sq miles; population (1988) 1,429,000.

marchioness, *n.* the wife or widow of a marquis, or a woman holding this rank in her own right. [low L *marchiōnissa,* from *marchio -ōnem,* MARQUESS; see MARQUIS]

marchpane MARZIPAN.

Marciano, *n.* **'Rocky'** (Rocco Francis Marchegiano) (1923–69), US boxer, world heavyweight champion 1952–56. He retired after 49 professional fights, the only heavyweight champion to retire undefeated.

†**marcid,** *a.* wasted, withered; causing wasting (as fever). † **marcidity,** *n.* [L *marcidus*]

Marconi, *n.* **Guglielmo** (1874–1937). Italian pioneer in the invention and development of wireless telegraphy. In 1895 he achieved wireless communication over more than a mile, and in England in 1896 he conducted successful experiments that led to the formation of the company that became Marconi's Wireless Telegraph Company Ltd. He shared the Nobel Prize for Physics in 1909.

marconigram, *n.* a message sent by the Marconi system of wireless telegraphy. [Guglielmo *Marconi,* see prec.]

Marconi Scandal, *n.* a scandal in 1912 in which UK chancellor Lloyd George and two other government ministers were found by a French newspaper to have dealt in shares of the US Marconi company shortly before it was announced that the Post Office had accepted the British Marconi company's bid to construct an imperial wireless chain. A parliamentary select committee, biased towards the Liberal government's interests, found that the other four wireless systems were technically inadequate and therefore the decision to adopt Marconi's tender was not the result of ministerial corruption. The scandal did irreparable harm to Lloyd George's reputation.

Marcos, *n.* **Ferdinand** (1917–89), Filipino right-wing politician, president (1965–86), when he was forced into exile in Hawaii. He was backed by the US when in power, but in 1988 US authorities indicted him and his wife for racketeering and embezzlement, and at her trial in 1990 she was accused of stealing $105 million.

Marcus Aurelius Antoninus, *n.* (AD 121–80), Roman emperor from 161 and Stoic philosopher. Although considered one of the best of the Roman emperors, he persecuted the Christians for political reasons. He wrote philosophical *Meditations*.

Mardi Gras, *n.* Shrove Tuesday; the carnival celebrated at this time. [F, fat Tuesday]

mare, *n.* the female of the horse or other equine animal. **mare's-nest,** *n.* a discovery that turns out a hoax or a delusion. **mare's-tail,** *n.* an aquatic plant, *Hippuris vulgaris;* long fibrous cirrus-clouds, supposed to prognosticate rain. [OE *mere* (cp. Dut. *merrie,* Icel. *merr,* G *Mähre*)]

maremma, *n.* (*pl.* **-me**) a marshy and usu. malarious region by the seashore. [It.]

†**mareschal** MARSHAL.

Marengo, Battle of, defeat of the Austrians by the French emperor Napoleon on 14 Jun. 1800, as part of his Italian campaign, near the village of Marengo in Piedmont, Italy.

Margaret[1]**, St,** *n.* (1045–93), queen of Scotland, the granddaughter of King Edmund Ironside of England. She went to Scotland after the Norman Conquest, and soon after married Malcolm III. The marriage of her daughter Matilda to Henry I united the Norman and English royal houses.

Margaret[2]**,** *n.* **(Rose)** (1930–), princess of the UK, younger daughter of George VI. In 1960 she married Anthony Armstrong-Jones, later created Lord Snowdon, but in 1976 they agreed to live apart, and were divorced in 1978. Their children are **David, Viscount Linley** (1961–) and **Lady Sarah Armstrong-Jones** (1964–).

Margaret[3]**,** *n.* (1282–90), queen of Scotland from 1285, known as *the Maid of Norway*. Margaret was the daughter of Eric II, king of Norway, and Princess Margaret of Scotland. When only two years of age she became queen of Scotland on the death of her grandfather, Alexander III, but died in the Orkneys on a voyage to her kingdom.

Margaret of Anjou, *n.* (1430–82), queen of England from 1445, wife of Henry VI of England. After the outbreak of the Wars of the Roses in 1455, she acted as the leader of the Lancastrians, but was defeated and captured at the battle of Tewkesbury (1471) by Edward IV.

margaric, *a.* pertaining to pearl, pearly. **margarate,** *n.* a salt of margaric acid. **margarin,** *n.* margarate of glyceryl. [Gr. *margar,* in *margaritēs,* pearl]

margarine , *n.* an emulsion of edible oils and fat with water or skimmed milk or other substances with or without the addition of colouring matter, capable of being used for the same purposes as butter. [F *margarin*]

margarita, *n.* a cocktail made from tequila and lemon (or other fruit) juice. [from the woman's name]

margarite, *n.* †a pearl; pearl mica, a hydrous silicate. **margaritiferous,** *a.* [OF, from L *margarīta,* as MARGARIC]

margay, *n.* a S American tiger-cat, *Felis tigrina*. [F, from Tupi *mbaracaïa*]

marge[1] MARGIN.

marge[2]**,** *n.* (*coll.*) short for MARGARINE.

margin, *n.* an edge, a border, a brink; the blank space round the printed matter on a page; the space of time or the range of conditions within which a thing is just possible; an allowance of time, money, space etc. for contingencies, growth etc.; the difference between cost and selling price; a sum deposited with a broker to protect him against loss; the lowest amount of profit allowing an industry etc. to continue. *v.t.* to furnish with a margin; to enter on the margin. *v.i.* to deposit margin on stock. **marginal,** *a.* of, pertaining to or at the margin; written or printed on the margin; near the limit; (*coll.*) small, slight; of land, difficult to cultivate. *n.* a marginal constituency. **marginal constituency,** *n.* a parliamentary constituency where there is only a small difference between the totals of votes cast for the two leading candidates. **marginalia,** *n.pl.* marginal notes. **marginalize, -ise,** *v.t.* to reduce in influence, power, importance etc. **marginally,** *adv.* **marginate, -ated,** *a.* having a margin; edged. *v.t.*, to furnish with a margin. **margination,** *n.* [L *margo -ginis*]

margrave, *n.* orig. a lord or governor of a march or border province, now a German title of nobility. **margravate, margraviate,** *n.* **margravine,** *n. fem.* [Dut. *markgrave* (now *markgraaf*) (MARK[1], GRAVE[4])]

Margrethe II, *n.* (1940–), queen of Denmark from 1972, when she succeeded her father Frederick IX. In 1967, she married the French diplomat Count Henri de Laborde de Monpezat, who took the title Prince Hendrik. Her heir is Crown Prince Frederick (1968–).

marguerite, *n.* the ox-eye daisy and other wild or cultivated varieties of chrysanthemum. [F, from L *margarīta,* L, Gr. *margaritēs,* from *margaron,* pearl]

Marguerite of Navarre, *n.* (also known as **Margaret d'Angoulême**) (1492–1549), queen of Navarre from 1527, French poet, and author of the *Heptaméron* (1558), a collection of stories in imitation of Boccaccio's *Decameron*. The sister of Francis I of France, she was born in Angoulême. Her second husband (1527) was Henri d'Albret, king of Navarre.

Marian, *a.* pertaining to the Virgin Mary, to Mary I of England or Mary Queen of Scots. *n.* an adherent or defender of either of the two last. **Marian year,** *n.* the year as reckoned from beginning on 25 Mar., the Feast of the Annunciation. [L *Marīa,* -AN]

Mariana Islands, *n.pl.* (or **Marianas**) archipelago in the NW Pacific, divided politically into **Guam** and the **Northern Marianas**, a commonwealth in union with the US of 16 mountainous islands, extending 560 km/350 miles north from Guam. **area** 480 sq km/185 sq miles. **capital** Garapan on Saipan. **products** sugar, coconuts, coffee. **population** (1988) 21,000, mainly Micronesian. **language** 55% Chamorro, English. **religion** mainly Roman Catholic.

Mariana Trench, *n.* the lowest region on the Earth's surface; the deepest part of the sea floor. The trench is 2400 km/1500 miles long and is situated 300 km/200 miles E of the Mariana Islands, in the NW Pacific Ocean. Its deepest part is the gorge known as the Challenger Deep, which extends 11,034 m/36,201 ft below sea level.

Marianne, *n.* symbolic figure of the French republic, dating from the Revolution. Statues of her adorn public buildings in France. Her name combines those of the Virgin Mary and St Anne.

Maria Theresa, *n.* (1717–80), empress of Austria from 1740, when she succeeded her father, the Holy Roman Emperor Charles VI; her claim to the throne was challenged and she became embroiled, first in the War of the Austrian Succession (1740–48), then in the Seven Years' War (1756–63); she remained in possession of Austria but lost Silesia. The rest of her reign was peaceful and, with her son Joseph II, she introduced social reforms.

mariculture, *n.* the cultivation of marine organisms in their own natural environment. [L *mare,* the sea, CULTURE]

Marie Antoinette, *n.* (1755–93), queen of France from 1774. She was the daughter of Empress Maria Theresa of Austria, and married Louis XVI of France in 1770. With a reputation for frivolity and extravagance, she meddled in politics in the Austrian interest, and helped provoke the French Revolution of 1789. She was tried for treason in Oct 1793 and guillotined.

Marie de France, *n.* (*c.* 1150–1215), French poet, thought to have been the half-sister of Henry II of England, and abbess of Shaftesbury (1181–1215). She wrote *Lais* (verse tales which dealt with Celtic and

Arthurian themes) and *Ysopet*, a collection of fables.

Marie de' Medici, *n.* (1573–1642), queen of France, wife of Henry IV from 1600, and regent (after his murder) for their son Louis XIII. She left the government to her favourites, the Concinis, until in 1617 Louis XIII seized power and executed them. She was banished, but after she led a revolt in 1619, Richelieu effected her reconciliation with her son, but when she attempted to oust him in 1630, she was exiled.

Marie Louise, *n.* (1791–1847), queen consort of Napoleon I from 1810 (after his divorce from Josephine), mother of Napoleon II. She was the daughter of Francis I of Austria and on Napoleon's fall returned to Austria. In 1815 she was granted the duchy of Parma.

Mariette, *n.* **Auguste Ferdinand François** (1821–81), French egyptologist, whose discoveries from 1850 included the 'temple' between the paws of the Sphinx. He founded the Egyptian Museum in Cairo.

marigold, *n.* a plant bearing a bright yellow flower, *Calendula officinalis;* applied to other composite yellow-flowered plants. **marsh marigold** MARSH. [*Mary,* the Virgin Mary, GOLD]

marihuana, marijuana, *n.* dried leaves of Indian hemp, used to make cigarettes smoked as a narcotic. [Sp.]

marimba, *n.* a musical instrument of the nature of a xylophone.

Marin, *n.* **John** (1870–1953), US painter, known for seascapes in watercolour and oil, influenced by impressionism. He visited Europe (1905–11), and began his paintings of the Maine coast in 1914.

marina, *n.* a docking area for yachts and pleasure boats. [It. and Sp. from L; see MARINE]

marinade, marinate, *n.* a pickle of vinegar, oil etc. flavoured with wine and spices; fish or meat pickled in this. *v.t.*, to pickle in marinade. [F, from Sp. *marinada,* from *marinar,* to pickle in brine, from *marino,* as foll.]

marine, *a.* pertaining to, found in or produced by the sea; used at sea or in navigation, nautical, naval; serving on shipboard. *n.* the shipping, fleet or navy of a country; (*pl.*) troops for service on board warships; a member of the Royal Marines; a specialist in commando and amphibious operations; a seascape. **horse-marine** HORSE. **mercantile marine** MERCANTILE. **tell it to the marines,** an expression of incredulity and derision (from the sailor's contempt for landsmen). **marine glue,** *n.* a glue made of rubber, shellac and oil which resists the action of water. **marine store,** *n.* a place where old ship's stores are bought and sold; (*pl.*) old ship's materials as articles of merchandise. **mariner,** *n.* a seaman, a sailor. **master mariner,** the captain of a merchant ship. [F *marin,* fem. *-ine,* L *marīnus,* from *mare,* the sea]

Mariner spacecraft, *n.* series of US space probes that explored the planets Mercury, Venus and Mars (1962–75).

Marinetti, *n.* **Filippo Tommaso** (1876–1944), Italian author, who in 1909 published the first manifesto of futurism, which called for a break with tradition in art, poetry and the novel, and glorified the machine age.

Marini, *n.* **Marino** (1901–80), Italian sculptor. Influenced by ancient art, he developed a distinctive horse-and-rider theme and a dancers series, reducing the forms to an elemental simplicity. He also produced fine portraits in bronze.

Marinism, *n.* excessive literary ornateness and affectation. **Marinist,** *n.* [Giambattista *Marini,* 1569–1625, Italian poet, -ISM]

Mariolatry, *n.* idolatrous worship of the Virgin Mary. **Mariolater,** *n.* [Gr. *Maria,* Mary, -LATRY]

marionette, *n.* a puppet moved by strings. [F *marionnette,* dim. of *Marion*]

Mariotte, *n.* **Edme** (1620–84), French physicist and priest known for his statement in 1676 of Boyle's law about the volume of gas, formulated in 1672. He had earlier, in 1660, discovered the eye's blind spot.

mariput, *n.* the African zoril, *Zorilla capensis*. [native name]

†**marish,** *n.* a marsh. *a.* marshy. [OF *mareis, maresche,* med. L *mariscus,* MARSH]

Marist, *n.* a member of the Roman Catholic congregation of Mary for teaching and foreign missions. *a.* pertaining or devoted to this or to the Virgin Mary.

marital, *a.* pertaining to marriage or to a husband. **maritally,** *adv.* [F, from L *marītālis,* from *marītus,* husband]

maritime, *a.* pertaining to, connected with or bordering on the sea; of countries, cities etc., having a navy or commerce by sea. [F, from L *maritimus* (*mare,* the sea, *-timus,* cp. *ultimus*)]

Marivaux, *n.* **Pierre Carlet de Chamblain de** (1688–1763), French novelist and dramatist. His sophisticated comedies include *Le Jeu de l'amour et du hasard/The Game of Love and Chance* (1730) and *Les Fausses confidences/False Confidences* (1737); his novel, *La Vie de Marianne/The Life of Marianne* (1731–41) has autobiographical elements. Marivaux gave the word *marivaudage* (over-subtle lovers' conversation) to the French language.

marjoram, *n.* a herb of the genus *Origanum* of the mint family, esp. *O. vulgare,* the wild marjoram, and *O. majorana,* sweet marjoram, a fragrant plant used as a herb in cooking. [OF *marjorane,* med. L *majorāna,* etym. doubtful]

mark¹, *n.* a visible sign or impression, as a stroke, cut, dot etc.; an indication, symbol, character, brand, device or token; a target, an object to aim at; (*coll.*) a victim, esp. of fraud; the point to be reached; a limit, a standard; a starting-line in a race; a distinguishing sign, a seal etc.; a character made by one who cannot write; a number or sign indicating merit in an examination; a distinguishing feature, a characteristic, a symptom; (*Boxing*) the pit of the stomach; (*Rugby*) an indentation made in the ground by the heel of a player who has secured a fair catch; †a tract of land held in common by the ancient Teutonic community; a boundary, frontier or limit. *v.t.* to make a mark on; to distinguish or designate or indicate, by a mark or marks; to select, to single out; to pay heed to; to indicate or serve as a mark to; to characterize, to be a feature of; to express or produce by marks; to record (points in games); to award (merit in examination); in football, hockey etc., to keep close to an opponent so as to be ready to tackle him. *v.i.* to observe something critically, to take note. **below, not up to, the mark,** not equal to a desired standard. **beside, wide, of the mark,** not hitting the object; not to the point, irrelevant. **man of mark,** a distinguished or famous man. **on your marks,** an order from the starter in a race to the runners to take their position on the starting-line. **save the mark,** an exclamation of irony, deprecation or contempt, perh. orig. used in archery. **to make one's mark,** to do something that brings fame, recognition etc. **to mark down, up,** *v.t.* to lower or raise the price. **to mark out,** to set out boundaries and levels for a proposed building; to set out lines and marks on material as a guide for cutting, drilling or other operations. **to mark time,** to move the feet alternately as in marching, without changing position; to pause until further progress can be made. **to toe the mark,** to touch a chalk line with the toes so as to be in rank abreast with others; to do one's duty, to perform one's obligations. **mark-down,** *n.* the amount by which a price is reduced. **mark-up,** *n.* the amount by which a price is increased. **marked,** *a.* noticeable, definite; of a person, destined to suffer misfortune, attack, suspicion etc. **markedly**, *adv.* **markedness**, *n.* **marker,** *n.* one who marks; a counter used in card-playing; one who notes the score at billiards; a book-mark. [OE *mearc* (cp. Dut. *mark,* neut. *merk,* Icel. *mark,* G *Mark,* neut. *Marke,* OTeut. *markā*), whence *mearcian,* to mark]

mark², *n.* the name of several coins of various values, esp. that of the Federal Republic of Germany and of the German Democratic Republic; (*Hist.*) English money of account valued at 13s. 4d. (67p); a unit of weight (about ½ or 2/3 lb.) (227 or 300g) formerly used for gold and silver. [OE *marc* (Icel. *mörk,* Dan., Swed., Dut. *mark,* G *Mark*)]

Mark, St, *n.* (lived 1st cent. AD), in the New Testament,

Christian apostle and evangelist, whose name is given to the second Gospel. It was probably written 65–70 AD, and used by the authors of the first and third Gospels. He is the patron saint of Venice, and his emblem is a winged lion; feast day 25 Apr.

Mark Antony, *n.* **Marcus Antonius** (83–30 BC), Roman politician and soldier. He was tribune and later consul under Julius Caesar, serving under him in Gaul. In 44 BC he tried to secure for Caesar the title of king. After Caesar's assassination, he formed the Second Triumvirate with Octavian (Augustus) and Lepidus. In 42 he defeated Brutus and Cassius at Philippi. He took Egypt as his share of the empire and formed a liaison with Cleopatra. In 40 he returned to Rome to marry Octavia, the sister of Augustus. In 32 the Senate declared war on Cleopatra. Antony was defeated by Augustus at the battle of Actium 31 BC. He returned to Egypt and committed suicide.

market, *n.* a meeting for buying and selling; the place for this; an open space or large building in which cattle, provisions or other commodities are offered for sale; a county or locality regarded as a place for buying and selling commodities in general or a particular form of merchandise; demand for a commodity, value as determined by this. *v.i.* to buy or sell in a market. *v.t.* to sell in a market. **to come into** or **put on the market,** to be offered or to offer for sale. †**market-bell,** *n.* a bell rung at the beginning of a market. **market-cross,** *n.* a cross set up in a market place. **market-day,** *n.* **market-garden,** *n.* a garden in which vegetables and fruit are raised for market. **market-gardener,** *n.* **market overt,** *n.* open market. **marketplace,** *n.* a market square etc.; the sphere of commercial trading. **market-price, -rate,** *n.* **market research,** *n.* research into public demand, need etc. for particular commercial goods. **market town,** *n.* a town having the privilege of holding a public market. **marketable,** *a.* **marketability, marketableness,** *n.* **marketably,** *adv.* **marketer,** *n.* **marketing,** *n.* the processes involved in selling goods, e.g. promotion, distribution etc. [late OE and ONorth.F (F *marché*), from L *mercātus,* p.p. of *mercārī,* to trade (cp. MERCANTILE)]

Markevich, *n.* **Igor** (1912–83), Russian-born composer and conductor. He composed the ballet *L'Envol d'Icare* (1932), and the cantata *Le Paradis Perdu* (1933–35) to words by Milton. After World War II he concentrated on conducting.

markhor, *n.* a wild mountain goat, *Capra falconeri,* inhabiting the border-land of India, Iran and Tibet. [Pers. *mārkhōr,* serpent-eater]

Markievicz, *n.* **Constance Georgina, Countess Markievicz** (born Gore Booth) (1868–1927), Irish nationalist, who married the Polish count Markievicz in 1900. Her death sentence for taking part in the Easter Rising of 1916 was commuted, and after her release from prison in 1917 she was elected to the Westminster Parliament as a Sinn Féin candidate in 1918 (technically the first British woman member of Parliament), but did not take her seat.

marking, *a.* producing a mark. *n.* (*often in pl.*) marks or colouring, esp. on natural objects. **marking-ink,** *n.* an indelible ink for marking linen etc. **marking-nut,** *n.* the nut of *Semecarpus anacardium,* the juice of which produces an indelible ink. [MARK[1]]

markka, *n.* the Finnish unit of currency. [MARK[2]]

Markova, *n.* **Alicia** (adopted name of Lilian Alicia Marks (1910–), British ballet dancer. Trained by Pavlova, she was ballerina with Diaghilev's company (1925–29), was the first resident ballerina of the Vic-Wells Ballet (1933–35), partnered Anton Dolin in their own Markova-Dolin Company (1935–37), and danced with the Ballet Russe de Monte Carlo (1938–41) and Ballet Theatre, US (1941–46). She is associated with the great classical ballets, especially *Giselle*.

Markov chain, *n.* a sequence of events in which the probability of each event is dependent on the event immediately preceding it. [Andrei *Markov,* 1856–1922, Russian mathematician]

Marks, *n.* **Simon, 1st Baron of Broughton** (1888–1964), English chain-store magnate. His father, Polish immigrant Michael Marks, had started a number of 'penny bazaars' with Yorkshireman Tom Spencer in 1887; Simon Marks entered the business in 1907 and built up a national chain of Marks and Spencer stores.

marksman, †**markman,** *n.* one skilled in aiming at a mark; one who shoots well. **marksmanship,** *n.* **markswoman,** *n. fem.*

marl, *n.* clay containing much calcareous matter, much used as a fertilizer; (*poet.*) earth. *v.t.* to manure with marl. **marlpit,** *n.* **marlstone,** *n.* sandy, calcareous and ferruginous strata dividing the upper from the lower Lias clays. **marlaceous,** *a.* **marlite,** *n.* a variety of marl that remains solid after exposure to the air. **marlitic,** *a.* **marly,** *a.* [OF *marle,* late L *margila,* dim. of *marga,* perh. from Gaulish]

Marlborough, *n.* **John Churchill, 1st Duke of Marlborough** (1650–1722), English soldier, created a duke 1702 by Queen Anne. He was granted the Blenheim mansion in Oxfordshire in recognition of his services, which included defeating the French army outside Vienna in the Battle of Blenheim (1704), during the War of the Spanish Succession.

Marley, *n.* **Bob (Robert Nesta)** (1945–80), Jamaican reggae singer, a Rastafarian whose songs, many of which were topical and political, popularized reggae in the UK and the US in the 1970s. One of his best-known songs is 'No Woman No Cry'; his albums include *Natty Dread* (1975) and *Exodus* (1977).

marlin, *n.* any of various large oceanic fishes with a long upper jaw. [MARLINE-SPIKE]

marline, *n.* (*Naut.*) a small two-stranded line, used for lashing etc. **marline-spike,** *n.* a pointed iron pin for opening the strands of rope in splicing. [Dut. *marlijn* (*marren,* to tie, LINE[1])]

Marlowe, *n.* **Christopher** (1564–93), English poet and dramatist. His work includes the blank-verse plays *Tamburlaine the Great* (about 1587), *The Jew of Malta* (about 1589), *Edward II* and *Dr Faustus* (both about 1592), the poem *Hero and Leander* (1598), and a translation of Ovid's *Amores*.

marmalade, *n.* a jam or preserve prepared from fruit, esp. oranges or lemons, boiled with the sliced rind. *a.* of cats, having streaks of orange and brown. [F *marmelade,* Port. *marmelada* (*marmelo,* quince, L *melimēlum,* Gr. *melimēlon,* from *meli,* honey, and *mēlon,* apple)]

Marmara, *n.* a small inland sea separating Turkey in Europe from Turkey in Asia, connected through the Bosporus with the Black Sea, and through the Dardanelles with the Aegean; length 275 km/170 miles, breadth up to 80 km/50 miles.

marmarize, -ise etc. MARMOREAL.

Marmite®, *n.* a savoury yeast extract used as a spread or for flavouring.

marmolite, *n.* a laminated variety of serpentine of a pearly green colour. [from Gr. *marmairein,* to shine, -LITE]

Marmontel, *n.* **Jean François** (1723–99), French novelist and dramatist. He wrote tragedies and libretti, and contributed to the *Encyclopédie*; in 1758 he obtained control of the journal *Le Mercure/The Mercury*, in which his *Contes moraux/Moral Studies* (1761) appeared. Other works include *Bélisaire/Belisarius* (1767), and *Les Incas/The Incas* (1777).

marmoreal, -ean, *a.* like marble, esp. cold, smooth or polished, pure white; made of marble. **marmoraceous,** *a.* †**marmorate, †-rated,** *a.* **marmarize, -ise,** *v.t.* to convert (limestone) into marble by metamorphism. **marmarosis,** *n.* this process. [L *marmoreus,* from *marmor,* MARBLE]

marmose, *n.* one of various S American pouchless opossums, as *Didelphys dorsigera* or *D. murina.* [F, ult. from foll.]

marmoset, *n.* a small tropical American monkey of various species belonging to the *Hapalidae,* called squirrel-monkeys from their bushy tails. [OF, a grotesque image (etym. doubtful, prob. conn. with *marmot,* a little child)]

marmot, *n.* a squirrel-like rodent about the size of a rabbit, esp. *Arctomys marmotta,* the Alpine marmot. [F *marmotte,* Romansch *murmont* (L *mūrem,* nom. *mūs,* MOUSE, *montis,* gen. of *mons,* MOUNTAIN)]

Marne, Battles of the, in World War I, two unsuccessful German offensives: **First Battle** 6–9 Sept. 1914, von Moltke's advance was halted by the British Expeditionary Force and the French under Foch; **Second Battle** 15 Jul.–4 Aug. 1918, Ludendorff's advance was defeated by British, French and US troops under the French general Pétain, and German morale crumbled.

marocain, *n.* a cloth similar in structure to crêpe de Chine, but made from coarser yarns. [F *maroquin,* from *Maroc,* Morocco]

Maronite, *n.* a member of a Christian sect deriving from refugee Monothelites (Christian heretics) of the 7th cent. They were subsequently united with the Roman Catholic Church, and number about 400,000 in Lebanon and Syria, with an equal number scattered overseas in S Europe and the Americas. [late L *Marōnīta,* from *Marōn,* a 5th-cent. Syrian monk, the founder, or the 7th-cent. patriarch of the same name]

maroon¹, *a.* of a brownish-crimson colour. *n.* this colour; a detonating firework. [F *marron,* It. *marrone,* chestnut, etym. unknown]

maroon², *n.* one of a group of descendants of fugitive slaves in the W Indies and Guyana; one who has been marooned. *v.t.* to put ashore and abandon on a desolate island. **marooner,** *n.* [F *marron,* fugitive, corr. of Sp. *cimarron,* savage, etym. doubtful (perh. from *cima,* mountain-top, L *cyma,* Gr. *kūma,* wave)]

maroquin, *n.* Morocco leather. [F, a., from *Maroc,* Morocco]

marplot MAR.

marque, *n.* a brand, model or type. **letter of marque** LETTER. [OF, from Prov. *marca,* from *marcar,* to seize, perh. rel. to MARK¹]

marquee, *n.* a large field-tent. [from MARQUISE under MARQUIS, regarded as pl.]

Marquesas Islands, *n.pl.* (French **Iles Marquises**) island group in French Polynesia, lying north of the Tuamotu Archipelago; area 1270 sq km/490 sq miles; population (1983) 6500. The administrative headquarters is Atuona on Hiva Oa. It was annexed by France in 1842.

marquetry, *n.* work inlaid with different pieces of fine wood, ivory, plates of metal, steel etc. [F *marqueterie,* from *marqueter,* to inlay, to spot, from *marquer,* to MARK¹]

Márquez, *n.* **Gabriel García** see GARCÍA MÁRQUEZ.

marquis, marquess, *n.* a title or rank of nobility in England, ranking next below a duke and above an earl. **marquessate, marquisate,** *n.* **marquise,** *n.* (F) a marchioness; a marquise-ring; †a large tent, a marquee. **marquise-ring,** *n.* a finger-ring set with gems in a pointed oval cluster. [OF *marchis* (F *marquis*), low L *marchensis,* warden or prefect of the marches, from *marcha,* MARCH¹, MARK¹]

marquisette, *n.* a finely-woven mesh fabric used for clothing, curtains and mosquito-nets.

Marquoi's scale, *n.* an instrument for drawing equidistant parallel lines. [prob. from F *marquoir,* a marker]

Marrakesh, *n.* a historic town in Morocco in the foothills of the Atlas mountains, about 210 km/130 miles south of Casablanca; population (1982) 549,000. It is a tourist centre, and has textile, leather and food processing industries. Founded 1062, it has a mediaeval palace and mosques, and was formerly the capital of Morocco.

marram, *n.* bent-grass. [ON *marr,* sea; *halmr,* haulm]

Marrano, *n.* one of the Spanish and Portuguese Jews converted by force to Christianity in the 14th and 15th cent., many of whom secretly preserved their adherence to Judaism and carried out Jewish rites. Under the Spanish Inquisition thousands were burned at the stake.

marriage, *n.* the legal union of a man and woman, wedlock; the act or ceremony of marrying, a wedding, a nuptial celebration; sexual union; close conjunction or union; in bezique etc., the declaration of a king and queen of the same suit. **civil marriage** CIVIL. **marriage of convenience,** a marriage contracted for advantage rather than for love; any union that is made to secure an advantage. **marriage articles, contract,** *n.(pl.)* a contract embodying the marriage settlement made before marriage. **marriage favour** WEDDING- FAVOUR. **marriage guidance,** *n.* counselling and advice given to couples with marital problems. **marriage licence,** *n.* a licence for the solemnization of a marriage without the proclamation of banns. **marriage lines,** *n.pl.* (*coll.*) a marriage certificate. **marriage partner,** *n.* a spouse. **marriage settlement,** *n.* an arrangement made before marriage securing a provision for the wife and sometimes for future children. **marriageable,** *a.* fit or of age for marriage; (*Bot. etc.*) suitable for close union. [F *mariage,* low L *marītāticum,* from *marītus,* husband, see MARITAL]

married MARRY¹.

marrons glacés, *n.pl.* chestnuts coated with sugar. [F]

marrow¹, *n.* a fatty substance contained in the cavities of bones; the essence, the pith; the pulpy interior of a fruit etc.; a vegetable marrow. **marrow-bone,** *n.* a bone containing marrow; (*pl.*) the knees. **marrowfat,** *n.* a large variety of pea. **marrowless,** *a.* **marrowy,** *a.* [OE *mearg* (cp. Dut. *merg,* Icel. *mergr,* G *Mark*)]

†**marrow²,** *n.* (*esp. Sc.*) a match, a mate, a partner; a husband or wife; one's equal or peer; one of a pair. [etym. doubtful]

marry¹, *v.t.* to unite as man and wife; to give in marriage; to take for one's husband or wife; to join closely together, to unite intimately. *v.i.* to enter into the state of wedlock. **to marry into,** to gain (esp. money) by marrying; to join (a family) by marrying. **married,** *a.* united in marriage; pertaining to married persons, conjugal. *n.* a married person. [F *marrier,* L *marītāre,* from L *marītus,* husband, see MARITAL]

†**marry²,** *int.* indeed, forsooth. [corr. of *Mary,* the Virgin]

Mars¹, *n.* in Roman mythology, the god of war, after whom the month of March is named. He is equivalent to the Greek Ares.

Mars², *n.* the fourth planet from the Sun, average distance 227,800,000 km/141,500,000 miles. It revolves around the Sun in 687 Earth days, and has a rotation period of 24 hr 37 min. It is much smaller than Venus or Earth, with diameter 6780 km/4210 miles, and mass 0.11 that of Earth. Mars is slightly pear-shaped, with a low, level northern hemisphere, comparatively uncratered and geologically 'young', and a heavily cratered 'ancient' southern hemisphere.

Marsala, *n.* a white fortified wine somewhat like sherry, made at *Marsala* in Sicily.

Marseillaise, *n.* the national anthem of the French Republic, composed by Rouget de l'Isle and introduced into Paris by the Marseillaise contingent in 1792. [F]

marseille, marseilles, *n.* a stiff and heavy cotton fabric quilted in the loom. [see foll.]

Marseille, *n.* the chief seaport of France, industrial centre (chemicals, oil refining, metallurgy, shipbuilding, food processing), and capital of the *département* of Bouches-du-Rhône, on the Golfe du Lion, Mediterranean Sea; population (1982) 1,111,000.

marsh, *n.* a tract of low land covered wholly or partially with water. **marsh-fire, -light,** *n.* a will-o'-the-wisp. **marsh-gas,** *n.* carburetted hydrogen evolved from stagnant water. **marsh-harrier,** *n.* a hawk, *Circus aeruginosus.* **marshland,** *n.* **marsh-mallow,** *n.* a shrubby herb, *Althaea officinalis,* growing near salt marshes; a confection made from its root. **marsh-marigold,** *n.* a ranunculaceous plant, *Caltha palustris,* with bright yellow flowers, growing in marshy places. **marshy,** *a.* **marshiness,** *n.* [OE *mersc, merisc,* from Teut. *mari-* MERE¹ (cp. MARISH)]

Marsh, *n.* **Ngaio** (1899–1982), New Zealand writer of detective fiction. Her first detective novel *A Man Lay Dead* (1934) introduced her protagonist Chief Inspector Roderick Alleyn.

marshal, *n.* an officer regulating ceremonies and directing processions; an officer of state with functions varying by country and period; an earl-marshal; a provost-marshal; a military officer of the highest rank; a field-marshal; (*N Am.*) a civil officer corresponding to an English sheriff. *v.t.* (*past, p.p.* **marshalled**) to arrange or rank in order; to conduct in a ceremonious manner; (*Her.*) to dispose in order, as the coats in a shield. *v.i.* to assemble, to take up a position (of armies, processions etc.). †**knight marshal** KNIGHT. **Marshal of the Air,** the highest rank in the RAF, corresponding in rank to Field-Marshal in the Army. **marshaller,** *n.* **marshalling yard,** *n.* a place where goods trucks are sorted according to their destination, and goods trains made up. **marshalship,** *n.* [OF *mareschal,* OHG *marahschalh, marah,* horse, cogn. with MARE, *scalh,* cogn. with OE *sceale,* servant]

†**marshalsea,** *n.* a former court and a prison in Southwark controlled by the knight marshal. [as prec.]

Marshall¹, *n.* **George Catlett** (1880–1959), US general and diplomat. He was army chief of staff in World War II, secretary of state (1947–49), and secretary of defence, Sept. 1950–Sept. 1951. He initiated the **Marshall Plan** 1947 and received the Nobel Peace prize 1953.

Marshall², *n.* **John** (1755–1835), US jurist. As chief justice of the Supreme Court (1801–35), he established the power and independence of the Supreme Court. He laid down interpretations of the US constitution in a series of important decisions which have since become universally accepted.

Marshall³, *n.* **John Ross** (1912–88), New Zealand National Party politician, noted for his negotiations of a free-trade agreement with Australia. He was deputy to K.J. Holyoake as prime minister and succeeded him Feb.–Nov. 1972.

Marshall aid, *n.* economic aid for warstricken countries in Europe given by the US according to a plan initiated by G. C. *Marshall* (1881–1959), US statesman, in 1947.

Marshall Islands, *n.pl.* the Radak (13 islands) and Ralik (11 islands) chains in the W Pacific. **area** 180 sq km/69 sq miles. **capital** Majuro. **products** copra, phosphates, fish, tourism. **population** (1988) 41,000.

Marshall Plan, *n.* a programme of US financial aid to Europe, set up at the end of World War II, totalling $12,000 million (1948–52). Officially known as the European Recovery Programme, it was initiated by George Marshall in a speech at Harvard in June 1947, but was in fact the work of a State Department group led by Dean Acheson.

marsipobranch, *n.* one of the Marsipobranchii, vertebrates with sacciform gills, as the lampreys and shags. **marsipobranchiate,** *n., a.* [Gr. *marsipos,* see foll., *branchia,* gills]

Marston Moor, Battle of, battle fought in the English Civil War on 2 July 1644 on Marston Moor, 11 km/7 miles W of York. The Royalists were completely defeated by the Parliamentarians and Scots.

marsupial, *a.* of or resembling a pouch; belonging to the order Marsupialia, carrying the young in a pouch, as the kangaroos and opossums. *n.* any individual of the Marsupialia. **marsupium,** *n.* (*pl.* **marsupia**) a pouch for carrying the imperfectly developed young of marsupial animals; a pouch-like part or organ in other animals. [L *marsūpium,* Gr. *marsupion,* dim. of *marsipos,* purse, bag, -AL]

mart, *n.* a market, a marketplace; an auction-room; traffic, purchase and sale. [prob. from Dut. *markt,* MARKET]

martagon, *n.* the Turk's-cap lily, *Lilium martagon.* [F, from Turk. *martagān,* a kind of turban]

†**martel,** *n.* a hammer. *v.t.* to strike, to hammer. [OF (F *marteau*), from pop. L (cp. L *martulus*)]

martello, *n.* a martello tower. **martello tower,** *n.* a circular, isolated tower of masonry, erected on the coast to oppose the landing of invaders. [corr. of *Mortella,* from a tower at Cape Mortella in Corsica captured by the British in 1793–94]

marten, *n.* a small carnivorous mammal, *Mustela martes,* allied to the weasel, with a valuable fur. [ME *martren,* OF *matrine,* marten's fur, fem. of *matrin,* a., from *martre,* from OTeut. *marthuz* (cp. Dut. *marter,* G *Marder,* OE *mearth*)]

Martens, *n.* **Wilfried** (1936–), prime minister of Belgium from 1979, member of Social Christian Party. He was president of the Dutch-speaking CVP (1972–79) and, as prime minister, headed six coalition governments in the periods 1979–81, 1981–85, and from 1985.

martensite, *n.* a constituent of steel that has been rapidly cooled, a solid solution of carbon in iron. [Adolf *Martens,* d.1914, German metallurgist]

martext, *n.* a blundering or ignorant preacher. [MAR, TEXT]

martial, *a.* pertaining to or suited for war; military; warlike, courageous, bellicose; under the influence of the planet Mars. **martial art,** *n.* any of the various forms of single combat pursued as a sport, e.g. judo, karate. **martial law,** *n.* military law abrogating ordinary law for the time being, proclaimed in time of war, insurrection or like emergency. **martialism,** *n.* **martialist,** *n.* **martialize, -ise,** *v.t.* **martially,** *adv.* [F, from L *Martiālis,* from MARS]

Martial, *n.* **(Marcus Valerius Martialis)** (41–104), Latin epigrammatist. His poetry, often bawdy, reflects contemporary Roman life.

Martian, *n.* an inhabitant of the planet Mars. *a.* of the planet or god Mars. [L *Martius*]

martin, *n.* a bird allied to the swallow, *Chelidon urbica.* [F, St *Martin,* Bishop of Tours, 4th cent.]

Martin, St, *n.* (316–400), bishop of Tours, France, from about 371, and founder of the first monastery in Gaul. He is usually represented as tearing his cloak to share it with a beggar. His feast day is Martinmas, 11 Nov.

Martin V, *n.* (1368–1431), pope from 1417. A member of the Roman family of Colonna, he was elected during the Council of Constance, and ended the Great Schism between the rival popes of Rome and Avignon.

martinet, *n.* a strict disciplinarian. [Gen. *Martinet,* a very strict officer under Louis XIV]

Martinet, *n.* **Jean** (d. 1672), French inspector-general of infantry under Louis XIV, whose constant drilling brought the army to a high degree of efficiency.

martingale, *n.* a strap fastened to a horse's girth to keep the head down; (*Naut.*) a lower stay for the jib-boom or flying jib-boom; the system of doubling stakes after every loss in gambling. [F, etym. doubtful]

Martini®¹, *n.* Italian vermouth; a cocktail based on this. [name of It. firm]

Martini², *n.* **Simone** (*c.* 1284–1344), Italian painter, one of the great masters of the Sienese school. A pupil of Duccio, he continued the graceful linear pattern of Sienese art, but introduced a fresh element of naturalism. His patrons included the city of Siena, the king of Naples and the pope. Two of his frescoes are in the Palazzo Pubblico in Siena: the *Maestà* about 1315 and the horseback warrior *Guidoriccio da Fogliano* (the attribution of the latter is disputed). He died at the papal court in Avignon.

Martinique, *n.* a French island in the West Indies (Lesser Antilles). **area** 1,079 sq km/417 sq miles. **capital** Fort-de-France. **products** sugar, cocoa, rum, bananas, pineapples. **population** (1984) 327,000.

Martinmas, *n.* the feast of St Martin, 11 Nov. †**Martlemass,** *n.*

Martins, *n.* **Peter** (1946–), Danish-born US dancer, choreographer and director, principal dancer with the New York City Ballet from 1965 and its joint director from 1983.

Martinu, *n.* **Bohuslav (Jan)** (1890–1959), Czech composer, who studied in Paris. He left Czechoslovakia after the Nazi occupation of 1939. The quality of his music varies but at its best it is richly expressive and has great vitality. His works include the operas *Julietta* (1937) and *The Greek Passion* (1959), symphonies and chamber music.

martlet, *n.* a swift, *Cypselus apus;* (*Her.*) a swallow-like bird without feet. [F *martelet*, prob. corr. of *martinet*, dim. of MARTIN]

martyr, *n.* one who suffers death or persecution in defence of his faith or principles, esp. one of the early Christians who suffered death for their religion. *v.t.* to put to death for adherence to one's religion or principles; to persecute, to torture. **a martyr to,** a continual sufferer from. **martyrdom,** *n.* **martyrium, martyry,** *n.* a chapel or shrine built in honour of a martyr. **martyrize, -ise,** *v.t.* **martyrolatry,** *n.* worship of martyrs. **martyrology,** *n.* a list or history of martyrs. **martyrological,** *a.* **martyrologist,** *n.* [OE and L, from Gr. *martur, martus,* a witness]

marvel, *n.* a wonderful or astonishing thing; a prodigy; †wonder, astonishment. *v.i.* (*past, p.p.* **marvelled**) to be astonished (at or that); to be curious to know (why etc.). **marvellous,** *a.*, †*adv.* **marvellously,** *adv.* **marvellousness,** *n.* [OF *merveille,* L *mīrābilia,* pl. of *mīrābilis,* wonderful, from *mīrārī,* to wonder, from *mīrus,* wonderful]

Marvell, *n.* **Andrew** (1621–78), English metaphysical poet and satirist. His poems include 'To His Coy Mistress' and 'Horatian Ode upon Cromwell's Return from Ireland'. He was committed to the Parliamentary cause, and was Member of Parliament for Hull from 1659. He devoted his last years mainly to verse satire and controversial prose works.

Marvin, *n.* **Lee** (1924–87), US film actor who began his career playing violent, often psychotic villains and progressed to playing violent, occasionally psychotic heroes. His work includes *The Big Heat* (1953), *The Killers* (1964), and *Cat Ballou* (1965).

Marx, *n.* **Karl (Heinrich)** (1818–83), German philosopher, economist, and social theorist, whose account of change through conflict is known as historical, or dialectical, materialism. His *Das Kapital/Capital* (1867–95) is the fundamental text of Marxist economics, and his systematic theses on class struggle, history and the importance of economic factors in politics have exercised an enormous influence on later thinkers and political activists.

Marx Brothers, *n.pl.* US film comedians: **Leonard 'Chico'** (from the 'chicks' (girls) he chased) (1891–1961); **Arthur 'Harpo'** (from the harp he played) (1893–1964); **Julius 'Groucho'** (1890–1977); **Milton 'Gummo'** (from his gumshoes or galoshes) (1894–1977), who left the team early on, and **Herbert 'Zeppo'** (born at the time of the first zeppelins) (1901–79), part of the team until 1934. Their films include *Animal Crackers* (1932), *Duck Soup* (1933), *A Night at the Opera* (1935), and *Go West* (1937).

Marxism, *n.* a philosophical system, developed by the 19th-cent. German social theorists Marx and Engels, also known as **dialectical materialism**, under which matter gives rise to mind (materialism) and all is subject to change. As applied to history, it supposes that the succession of feudalism, capitalism, socialism, and finally the classless society is inevitable. The stubborn resistance of any existing system to change necessitates its complete overthrow in the **class struggle** – in the case of capitalism, by the proletariat – rather than gradual modification. **Marxian,** *a.* **Marxist,** *n., a.* **Marxism–Leninism,** *n.* the political ideology developed by Lenin from the theories of Marx.

Mary¹, *n.* **Queen of Scots** (1542–87), queen of Scotland (1542–67). Also known as **Mary Stuart**, she was the daughter of James V. Mary's connection with the English royal line from Henry VII made her a threat to Elizabeth I's hold on the English throne, particularly as she represented a champion of the Catholic cause. She was married three times. After her forced abdication she was imprisoned but escaped 1568 to England. Elizabeth I held her prisoner, while the Roman Catholics, who regarded Mary as rightful queen of England, formed many conspiracies to place her on the throne, and for complicity in one of these she was executed.

Mary², *n.* in the New Testament, the mother of Jesus through divine intervention, wife of Joseph. The Roman Catholic Church maintains belief in her Immaculate Conception and bodily assumption into heaven, and venerates her as a mediator. Feast day 15 Aug.

Mary³, *n.* **Duchess of Burgundy** (1457–82), daughter of Charles the Bold. She married Maximilian of Austria (1477), thus bringing the Low Countries into the possession of the Habsburgs and, ultimately, of Spain.

Mary⁴, *n.* **Queen** (1867–1953), consort of George V of the UK. The daughter of the Duke and Duchess of Teck, the latter a grand-daughter of George II, in 1891 she became engaged to the Duke of Clarence, eldest son of the Prince of Wales (later Edward VII). After his death 1892, she married 1893 his brother George, Duke of York, who succeeded to the throne in 1910.

Mary⁵, *n.* two queens of England:

Mary I, *n.* (1516–58), queen of England from 1553. She was born at Greenwich, the daughter of Henry VIII by Catherine of Aragon. When Edward VI died, she secured the crown without difficulty in spite of the conspiracy to substitute Lady Jane Grey. In 1554 she married Philip II of Spain, and as a devout Catholic obtained the restoration of papal supremacy. She was succeeded by her half-sister Elizabeth I.

Mary II, *n.* (1662–94), queen of England, Scotland and Ireland from 1688. She was the elder daughter of James II, and in 1677 was married to her cousin, William III of Orange. After the 1688 revolution she accepted the crown jointly with William.

Maryland, *n.* state of the eastern US; nickname Old Line State or Free State. **area** 31,600 sq km/12,198 sq miles. **capital** Annapolis. **towns** Baltimore, Silver Spring, Dundalk, Bethesda. **products** fruit, cereals, tobacco, fish, oysters. **population** (1986) 4,463,000.

Mary Magdalene, St, *n.* the woman who according to the New Testament was present at the Crucifixion and was the first to meet the risen Jesus. She is often identified with the woman of St Luke's gospel who anointed Jesus' feet, and her symbol is a jar of ointment; feast day 22 July.

Mary of Modena, *n.* (1658–1718), queen consort of England and Scotland. She was the daughter of the Duke of Modena, Italy, and married James, Duke of York, later James II, in 1673. The birth of their son James Francis Edward Stuart was the signal for the revolution of 1688 which overthrew James II. Mary of Modena fled to France.

marzipan, *n.* a confection of almonds, sugar and white of egg. [F *marcepain* (now *massepain*), etym. doubtful, cp. It. *marciapane,* G *Marzipan*]

Masaccio, *n.* (Tomaso di Giovanni di Simone Guidi) (1401–28), Florentine painter, a leader of the early Italian Renaissance. His frescoes in Sta Maria del Carmine, Florence, 1425–28, which he painted with Masolino da Panicale (*c.* 1384–1447), show a decisive break with Gothic conventions. He was the first painter to apply the scientific laws of perspective, newly discovered by the architect Brunelleschi.

Masai, *n.pl.* a dark Hamito-Negroid people inhabiting Kenya and Tanzania. [native name]

Masaryk¹, *n.* **Tomáš (Garrigue)** (1850–1937), Czech nationalist politician. He directed the Czech revolutionary movement against the Austrian Empire, founding with Beneš and Stefanik the Czechoslovak National Council, and in 1918 was elected first president of the newly formed Czechoslovak Republic. Three times re-elected, he resigned in 1935 in favour of Beneš.

Masaryk², *n.* **Jan (Garrigue)** (1886–1948), Czech politician, son of Tomáš Masaryk. He was foreign minister from 1940, when the Czech government was exiled in London in World War II. He returned in 1945, retaining the post, but as a result of communist political pressure committed suicide.

masc., (*abbr.*) masculine.

Mascagni, *n.* **Pietro** (1863–1945), Italian composer of the one-act opera *Cavalleria rusticana/Rustic Chivalry*, first produced in Rome in 1890.

mascara, *n.* a dark cosmetic for eyelashes etc. [Sp., mask]

mascle, *n.* a lozenge-shaped plate or scale used in 13th cent. armour; (*Her.*) a lozenge perforated. **mascled,**

masculy, *a.* [F, etym. doubtful, perh. corr. of MACLE]

mascon, *n.* one of the concentrations of dense material just beneath the moon's surface. [*mass con*centration]

mascot, *n.* an object or person that acts as a talisman and brings luck. [F dial. *mascotte,* perh. rel. to Prov. *masco,* witch]

masculine, *a.* belonging to or having the characteristic qualities of the male sex; strong, robust, vigorous; manly, spirited; mannish, forward, coarse; (*Gram.*) denoting the male gender. *n.* the masculine gender; a masculine word. **masculine rhyme,** *n.* a rhyme on a word ending with a stressed syllable. **masculinely,** *adv.* **masculineness, masculinity**, *n.* [F *masculin,* L *masculīnus,* see MALE]

Masefield, *n.* **John** (1878–1967), English poet and novelist. His works include novels (*Sard Harker*, 1924), critical works (*Badon Parchments*, 1947), children's books (*The Box of Delights*, 1935), and plays. He was Poet Laureate from 1930.

maser, *n.* a device similar to a laser used for amplifying microwave radiation. [acronym for *m*icrowave *a*mplification by *s*timulated *e*mission of *r*adiation]

Maserati, *n.* Italian racing-car company, founded (1926) by the six Maserati brothers. The most outstanding Maserati was the 250F Grand Prix car, which the Argentinian Juan Manuel Fangio drove during his world-championship-winning year, 1957. The company withdrew from Grand Prix racing at the end of 1957.

Maseru, *n.* capital of Lesotho, South Africa, on the Caledon river; population (1986) 289,000. It is a centre for trade and diamond processing.

mash¹, *n.* a mass of ingredients crushed and mixed into a pulp; a mixture of bran and hot water for horses; crushed or ground grain or malt steeped in hot water to form wort; †a confused mixture, a mess. *v.t.* to crush into a pulpy mass; to make an infusion of (malt) in hot water; to infuse (tea). *v.i.* to be in process of infusion (of tea). **mash-tub, -vat,** *n.* a brewer's tub or vat in which malt is mashed. †**mashy,** *a.* [OE *masc-, max-,* in *maxwyrt,* mash-wort (cp. Dan. and Swed. dial. *mask,* G *Maische*), prob. cogn. with MIX]

mash², *v.t.* (*sl.*) to ogle, to flirt with. *n.* the object of such attention. **to be mashed on,** (*dated*) to be in love with. **masher,** *n.* a vulgar fop or lady-killer. [etym. doubtful]

mashie, mashy, *n.* in golf, an iron club with a deep short blade, lofted. [perh. corr. of F *massue,* a club]

Mashraq, *n.* the Arab countries of the E Mediterranean: Egypt, Sudan, Jordan, Syria and Lebanon. The term is contrasted with Maghreb, Arab countries of NW Africa. [Arab., east]

Masire, *n.* **Quett Ketumile Joni** (1925–), president of Botswana from 1980. He was a journalist before entering politics, sitting in the Bangwaketse Tribal Council and then the Legislative Council. In 1962, with Seretse Khama, he founded the Botswana Democratic Party (BDP) and in 1965 was made deputy prime minister. After independence, in 1966, he became vice-president and, on Khama's death in 1980, president. Masire maintained his predecessor's policy of nonalignment and helped Botswana become one of the most stable states in Africa.

masjid, *n.* a mosque. [Arab.]

mask¹, *n.* a covering for the face, for protection or to conceal one's identity; a face-guard; an impression of a face in plastic material; a reproduction of a face used as a gargoyle or part of a moulding; a disguise, a pretence, a subterfuge; a masque; in photography, an opaque screen for framing the image in lantern slides, a silhouette used in printing to cover part of the plate; the head of a fox. *v.t.* to cover with a mask; (*in p.p.*) to disguise with a mask; to hide, screen or disguise; to watch (a hostile force) so as to hinder its effective action. *v.i.* to go in disguise. **masked ball,** *n.* a ball attended by guests wearing masks. **masker,** *n.* a masquer. [F *masque,* from Sp. *máscara* (see MASQUERADE) or med. L *mascus, masca,* etym. doubtful]

mask², *v.t.* (*Sc., North.*) to infuse (tea). [var. of MASH¹]

Maskelyne, *n.* **Nevil** (1732–1811), English astronomer, who accurately measured the distance from the Earth to the Sun by observing a transit of Venus across the Sun's face, 1769. In 1774, he measured the mass of the Earth by noting the deflection of a plumbline near Mount Schiehallion in Scotland.

maskinonge, *n.* a large pike inhabiting the Great Lakes of N America. [Algonkin]

maslin, *n.* (*dial.*) a mixture of grain, esp. wheat and rye. *a.* made of this; mingled, mixed. [acc. to OED, from OF *mesteillon,* late L *mistiliō -ōnem,* from L *mistus,* p.p. of *miscēre,* to MIX]

masochism, *n.* a variety of sexual perversion in which a person takes delight in being dominated or cruelly maltreated by another. **masochist,** *n.* **masochistic,** *a.* **masochistically,** *adv.* [L. von Sacher-*Masoch,* 1836–95, Austrian novelist, who described it]

mason, *n.* a craftsman who works in stone; a Freemason. *v.t.* to build with masonry. **masonic,** *a.* pertaining to Freemasonry. **masonry,** *n.* the art or occupation of a mason; mason's work, stonework; Freemasonry. [OF *maçon,* med. L *maciō -ōnem*]

Mason, *n.* **James** (1909–84), British actor who portrayed romantic villains in British films of the 1940s. After *Odd Man Out* (1947) he worked in the US, notably in *A Star is Born* (1954). Other films include *The Wicked Lady* (1946), *Lolita* (1962), and *Cross of Iron* (1977).

Mason–Dixon line, *n.* the boundary drawn between Pennsylvania and Maryland in 1763–67 by Charles Mason and Jeremiah Dixon, regarded as the dividing line between the Northern states and the Southern slave states prior to the American civil war.

Masorah, Massorah, *n.* a mass of traditional criticism and illustrative matter on the text of the Hebrew Bible, compiled before the 10th cent. **Masorete**, *n.* one of the scholars who contributed to this. **Masoretic**, *a.* [Heb. *māsōreth*]

masque, *n.* a play or dramatic entertainment, usu. presented by amateurs at court or in noblemen's houses, the performers wearing masks, orig. in dumb show, later with dialogue, poetical and musical accompaniments. **masquer,** *n.* [F, see MASK¹]

masquerade, *n.* a ball or assembly at which people wear masks; disguise, pretence. *v.i.* to wear a mask or disguise, to pass oneself off in a false guise. **masquerader,** *n.* [Sp. *mascarada,* from *máscara,* perh. from Arab. *maskhara,* a buffoon]

Mass¹, *n.* the celebration of the Eucharist in the Roman Catholic Church (also applied by some to the Anglican communion service); the office for this; a setting of certain portions of this to music. **black mass** BLACK. **High Mass** HIGH¹. **Low Mass** LOW¹. **mass-bell,** *n.* the sanctus bell. **mass-book,** *n.* a missal. [OE *mæsse,* eccles. L *missa,* fem. p.p. of *mittere,* to send]

mass², *n.* a body of matter collected, concreted or formed into a coherent whole of indefinite shape; a compact aggregation of things; a great quantity or amount; the greater proportion, the principal part or the majority (of); volume, bulk, magnitude; (*Phys.*) the quantity of matter which a body contains. *v.t.* to form or gather into a mass; to concentrate (as troops). *v.i.* to gather into a mass. **in the mass,** in the aggregate. **the great mass,** the great majority; the bulk. **the masses,** the ordinary people; the populace. **mass defect,** *n.* the difference in mass between a nucleus and its constituent particles. **mass media,** *n.pl.* the means of communication with large numbers of people, i.e. radio, TV, newspapers etc. **mass meeting,** *n.* a large meeting for some specific purpose. **mass observation,** *n.* method of obtaining public opinion by observing and interviewing people of various modes of life. **mass-produce,** *v.t.* **mass-producer,** *n.* **mass production,** *n.* the production of standardized articles in large quantities in which the processes are reduced to simple, usually mechanical, operations performed often along a conveyor belt. **mass radiography,** *n.* the X-ray screening of large numbers of people by mobile units. **mass spectrograph,** *n.* an instrument for separating charged particles into a ray spectrum according to their mass and for detecting them photographically. **mass spectrometer,** *n.* an instrument like a mass spectrograph which detects particles photographically or electrically. **massive,** *a.* heavy, weighty, ponderous; bulky; substantial, solid; (*coll.*) very large; (*Psych.*) applied to sensations of large magnitude; (*Min.*) without definite crystalline form. **massively,** *adv.* **massiveness,** *n.* **massless,** *a.* **massy,** *a.* **massiness,** *n.* [F *masse,* L *massa,* prob. from Gr. *maza,* a barley-cake, rel. to *massein,* to knead]

Mass., (*abbr.*) Massachusetts.

Massachusetts, *n.* New England state of the US; nickname Bay State or Old Colony. **area** 21,500 sq km/8299 sq miles. **capital** Boston. **towns** Worcester, Springfield, New Bedford, Brockton, Cambridge. **products** electronic and communications equipment, shoes, textiles, machine tools, building stone, cod. **population** (1985) 5,819,000.

massacre, *n.* indiscriminate slaughter; carnage, wholesale murder. *v.t.* to kill or slaughter indiscriminately. [F, from OF *maçacre,* etym. doubtful]

massage, *n.* treatment by rubbing or kneading the muscles and body, usu. with the hands. *v.t.* to subject to this treatment; to manipulate or misrepresent (esp. statistics). **massage parlour,** *n.* a place where massages are administered; (*euphem. coll.*) a kind of brothel. **massagist, masseur,** *n.* one skilled in massage. **masseuse,,** *n.fem.* [F, from *masser,* to apply massage, perh. from Port. *amassar,* to knead, from *massa,* dough, MASS[2]]

massé, *n.* in billiards, a stroke with the cue held vertically. [F, p.p. of *masser,* to make such a stroke, from *masse,* MACE[1]]

Massenet, *n.* **Jules Emile Frédéric** (1842–1912), French composer of opera, ballets, oratorios and orchestral suites.

masseter, *n.* the muscle which raises the lower jaw. [Gr. *masētēr,* from *masāsthai,* to chew]

masseur etc. MASSAGE.

Massey, *n.* **Vincent** (1887–1967), Canadian Liberal Party politician. He was the first Canadian to become governor general of Canada (1952–59).

massicot, *n.* yellow protoxide of lead, used as a pigment. [F, etym. doubtful]

massif, *n.* the main or central mass of a mountain or range. [F]

Massif Central, *n.* a mountainous plateau region of S central France; area 93,000 sq km/36,000 sq miles, highest peak Puy de Sancy 1886 m/6188 ft. It is a source of hydroelectricity.

Massine, *n.* **Léonide** (1895–1979), Russian choreographer and dancer with the Ballets Russes. He was a creator of comedy in ballet and also symphonic ballet using concert music.

massive etc. MASS[2].

Masson, *n.* **André** (1896–1987), French artist and writer, a leader of surrealism until 1929. His interest in the unconscious led him to experiment with 'automatic' drawing – simple pen and ink work, and later multitextured accretions of pigment, glue and sand.

Massorah, etc. MASORAH.

mast[1], *n.* a long pole of timber, or iron or steel tube, placed upright in a ship to support the yards, sails etc.; a tall, slender structure carrying a TV or radio aerial. **masthead,** *n.* the top of a mast, usu. of the lower-mast as a place for a look-out etc., or of the topmast; the name of a newspaper or periodical as printed at the top of the front page. *v.t.* to send to the masthead as a punishment. **masted,** *a.* furnished with a mast or masts. **mastless,** *a.* [OE *mæst* (cp. Dut., Swed., Dan. *mast,* G *Mast*)]

mast[2], *n.* the fruit of the oak and beech or other forest trees. [OE *mæst* (cp. G *Mast*), prob. cogn. with Sansk. *mēda,* fat]

mastaba, *n.* an ancient Egyptian tomb or chapel covering a sepulchral pit, used for the deposit of offerings. [Arab.]

mastectomy, *n.* surgical removal of the breast. **radical mastectomy,** surgical removal of the breast including some of the pectoral muscles and the lymph nodes of the armpit. [Gr. *mastos,* breast; *ektomē,* a cutting-out]

master, *n.* one who has control or authority over others; an employer; the head of a household; the owner of a slave, dog, horse etc.; one who has secured the control or upper hand; one thoroughly acquainted with or skilled in an art, craft etc., a great artist; a schoolmaster, a teacher, a tutor, an expert, a proficient; the highest degree in arts and surgery; a title given to the head of certain colleges, corporations etc.; a title of certain judicial officers; a title prefixed to the names of young gentlemen; (*Sc.*) the courtesy title of a viscount's or baron's eldest son; the captain of a merchant vessel; an officer who navigates a ship of war under the direction of the captain; †a respectful form of address. *a.* having control or authority; employing workmen; in charge of work or of workmen. *v.t.* to become the master of; to overpower, to defeat; to subdue, to bring under control; to become thoroughly conversant with or skilled in using; to be the master of, to rule as a master. **Little Masters** LITTLE. **Master of Arts** ART[2]. **master of ceremonies** CEREMONY. **master of foxhounds, harriers** etc., one elected to control a hunt. **master of the horse,** an officer of the royal household, formerly in charge of the horses; in ancient Rome, an officer appointed by a dictator to command the cavalry. **master of the revels,** a court official who had charge of entertainments etc. **Old Masters,** the great painters of the 13th–17th cents.; their pictures. **to be one's own master,** to be free to do as one likes. **master-at-arms,** *n.* a first-class petty officer acting as head of the ship's police. **master-builder,** *n.* a builder who employs workmen; the chief builder, the architect. **master-carpenter,** *n.* one who works on his own account; one employing other carpenters; a skilled carpenter. **master-class,** *n.* the class that exerts control in a society; a lesson, esp. in music, given by a leading expert to gifted students. **master-hand,** *n.* an expert; the hand or skill of an expert. **master-key,** *n.* a key which opens all the locks of a set, opened each by a separate key. **master-mason,** *n.* a Freemason who has attained the third degree. **mastermind,** *n.* the ruling mind or intellect. *v.t.* to direct, plan. **masterpiece,** *n.* a performance superior to anything of the same kind; an achievement showing surpassing skill. **master race,** *n.* the Aryan race, regarded by Nazi ideology as superior to all others; any race regarded as superior. **master sergeant,** *n.* a senior non-commissioned officer in the US army. **master-spring,** *n.* the spring which sets in motion or regulates the whole. **master-stroke,** *n.* an instance of great skill, mastery etc. **masterwork,** *n.* a masterpiece. **masterdom, masterhood,** *n.* **masterful,** *a.* expressing mastery; domineering, self-willed. **masterfully,** *adv.* **masterfulness,** *n.* **masterless,** *a.* **masterly,** *a.*, †*adv.* with the skill of a master. **masterliness,** *n.* †**masterous,** *a.* **mastership,** *n.* **mastery,** *n.* [ME *meister,* through OE *mægester* or OF *maistre, meistre* (or both), from L *magister* (cogn. with *magis,* more, Gr. *megas,* great)]

Master of the King's/Queen's Musick, appointment to the British royal household, the holder composing appropriate music for state occasions. The first was Nicholas Lanier, appointed by Charles I in 1626; the composer Malcolm Williamson was appointed in 1975.

Master of the Rolls, title of an English judge ranking immediately below the Lord Chief Justice. He presides over the Court of Appeal, besides being responsible for Chancery records and for the admission of solicitors.

Masters, *n.* **Edgar Lee** (1869–1950), US poet. In his *Spoon River Anthology* (1915), the people of a small town tell of their frustrated lives.

masterwort, *n.* a herb of the parsley family, esp. *Peucedanum ostruthium,* formerly cultivated as a pot-herb, now used as a stimulant.

mastic, *n.* a resin exuding from a Mediterranean evergreen tree, *Pistacia lentiscus,* chiefly used for varnish; a putty-like preparation used for bedding windowframes etc. in buildings; a liquor flavoured with gum mastic used in Greece and the Levant. **masticic**, *a.* **masticin**, *n.* that portion of mastic insoluble in alcohol. [F, from late L *mastichum,* earlier *masticha,* Gr. *mastichē,* etym. doubtful]

masticate, *v.t.* to grind and crush with the jaw, to chew. **masticable,** *a.* **masticability**, *n.* **mastication,** *n.* **masticator,** *n.* **masticatory,** *a.* [late L *masticātus,* p.p. of *masticāre,* perh. as prec. or rel. to Gr. *mastax -akos,* the jaw]

mastiff, *n.* a large dog of great strength and courage, characterized by drooping ears, used as a watch-dog. [A-F and OF *mastin* (F *mâtin*), through a late L *mansuētīnus,* from *mansuētus,* MANSUETE]

mastitis, *n.* inflammation of the breast or udder. [Gr. *mastos,* breast, rel. to *madaein* and L *madēre,* to be moist, -ITIS]

mastodon, *n.* an extinct mammal closely allied to the elephant, with nipple-shaped crests on the molar teeth. **mastodontic**, *a.* [Gr. *odous odontos,* tooth]

mastodynia, *n.* neuralgia in the breast. [Gr. *odunē,* pain]

mastoid (process), *n.* a process of bone behind the ear.

Mastroianni, *n.* **Marcello** (1924–), Italian film actor, famous for his carefully understated roles as an unhappy romantic lover in such films as *La Dolce Vita* (1959) and *La Notte/The Night* (1961).

masturbate, *v.i.* to excite one's genitals, usu. with the hand, to obtain sexual pleasure. *v.t.* to do this for (oneself or another). **masturbation,** *n.* **masturbator,** *n.* [L *masturbātus,* p.p. of *masturbārī,* etym. doubtful]

mat¹, *n.* a coarse fabric of fibre, rushes, hemp, wire etc. or of perforated rubber etc., used as a carpet, to wipe shoes on, for packing etc.; (*Naut.*) a mass of old rope etc. to prevent chafing; a flat piece of cork, wood etc. placed under a dish or similar object; a tangled mass of anything. *v.t.* (*past, p.p.* **matted**) to cover or lay with mats; to twist or twine together. *v.i.* of hair etc., to become twisted into a mat. **matting,** *n.* matwork; mats; material for mats; the making of mats; a coarse fabric of rushes, bast, hemp etc. esp. for packing and covering. [OE *meatte, matte,* late L *matta,* perh. from Semitic (cp. Heb. *mattāh* a bed, a thing spread out)]

mat², *a.* dull, lustreless, not glossy. *n.* a dull, lustreless surface, groundwork, border etc., esp. in metal roughened or frosted. *v.t.* to dull; to give a wet surface or appearance to. [F, prob. from OF *mat,* mated at chess, see CHECKMATE]

matador, *n.* in Spanish bullfights the man who has to kill the bull; one of the three principal cards at ombre and quadrille; a game played with dominoes. [Sp.]

Mata Hari, *n.* ('Eye of the Day'), stage name of Gertrud Margarete Zelle (1876–1917), Dutch courtesan, dancer and probable spy. In World War I she appears to have been a double agent, in the pay of both France and Germany. She was shot by the French on espionage charges.

match¹, *n.* a person or thing, equal, like, or corresponding to another; a counterpart, a facsimile; one able to cope with another; a contest of skill, strength etc.; a pairing or alliance by marriage; one eligible for marrying; †a bargain, an agreement. *v.t.* to be a match for; to compare as equal; to oppose as equal; to oppose (against or with) as a rival, opponent etc.; to be the equal of, to correspond, to join. *v.i.* to agree, to be equal, to tally (of different things or persons); †to be married. **to meet one's match,** to encounter someone who is equal to or better than one in combat, skill, argument etc. **matchboard,** *n.* a board having a tongue along one edge and a corresponding groove on the other for fitting into similar boards. **matchmaker,** *n.* one fond of planning and bringing about marriages. **matchmaking,** *n.*, *a.* **match point,** *n.* the point that needs to be won in order for a match to be won in tennis, squash etc. **matchable,** *a.* **matcher,** *n.* **matchless,** *a.* without equal, incomparable. **matchlessly,** *adv.* **matchlessness,** *n.* [OE *mæcca* (cp. Icel. *maki,* a mate, *makr,* suitable), cogn. with MAKE²]

match², *n.* a small strip of wood or taper tipped with combustible material for producing or communicating fire; a fuse burning at a uniform rate for firing charges. **matchbox,** *n.* a box for holding matches. **matchlock,** *n.* the lock of an obsolete musket fired by means of a lighted match; a musket so fired. **matchstick,** *n.* the wooden part of a match. **matchwood,** *n.* wood suitable for making matches; wood reduced to small splinters. [OF *mesche* (F *mèche*), wick, etym. doubtful]

matchet MACHETE.

mate¹, *v.t.* to checkmate; to confound, to paralyse. *a.* confounded, paralysed. *n.* a checkmate. **fool's mate** FOOL. **smothered mate** SMOTHER. [from CHECKMATE]

mate², *n.* a companion, a comrade, a fellow-worker, an equal, a match; a spouse; a suitable partner, esp. in marriage; one of a pair of the lower animals, esp. birds, associated for breeding; an officer in a merchant ship ranking below the captain; an assistant to the surgeon, cook etc.; an assistant to a plumber etc. *v.t.* to match, to couple; to join together in marriage; to pair (birds); to vie with. *v.i.* to pair. **mateless,** *a.* **mat(e)y,** *a.* (*coll.*) friendly. [prob. MLG (cp. LG *maat,* MDut. *maet*), cogn. with MEAT]

mate³, maté, *n.* paraguay-tea, an infusion of the leaves of *Ilex paraguayensis,* a Brazilian holly; this shrub; the vessel in which the tea is made. [Sp. *mate,* from Quechua *mati*]

matelassé, *a.* having a raised pattern as in quilting. *n.* a variety of silk and wool fabric with such a pattern. [F, from *matelas,* MATTRESS]

matelot, *n.* (*coll. facet.*) a sailor. [F, etym. unknown]

matelote, *n.* a dish of fish with wine, seasoning etc. [F, from prec.]

mater, *n.* (*pl.* **-tres**) (*usu. facet.*) a mother (cp. DURA MATER, PIA MATER). **materfamilias,** *n.* the mother of a family. [L]

material, *a.* pertaining to or consisting of matter; corporeal, substantial; pertaining to or concerning the physical nature or the appetites of man; sensual, unspiritual, pertaining to the matter or essence of a thing, not to the form; important, momentous, essential. *n.* the substance or matter from which anything is made; stuff, fabric; elements or component parts (of); notes, ideas etc. for a written or oral composition; a person or persons suitable to fulfil a specified function after training etc. **raw material** RAW. **materialism,** *n.* the theory that there is nothing in the universe but matter, that mind is a phenomenon of matter, and that there is no ground for assuming a spiritual First Cause; regard for secular to the neglect of spiritual interests; (excessive) devotion to the pursuit of material wealth and physical well-being. **dialectical materialism** DIALECTICAL. **materialist,** *n.* **materialistic,** *a.* **materialistically,** *adv.* **materiality,** *n.* **materialize, -ise,** *v.t.* to make material, to invest with matter or corporeity; to cause (a spirit) to become material or to appear; to make materialistic. *v.i.* of a spirit, to appear; to become actual fact. **materialization, -isation,** *n.* **materially,** *adv.* in a material way; to a significant extent. [OF *materiel,* late L *māteriālis,* from *māteria,* MATTER]

materia medica, *n.* a general term for the different substances employed in medicine; the scientific study of such substances. [L]

materiel, *n.* the material, supplies, machinery or instruments, as distinguished from the personnel or persons, employed in an art, business, military or naval activity etc. [F, see MATERIAL]

maternal, *a.* motherly; pertaining to a mother or to maternity; connected or related on the mother's side. **maternally,** *adv.* **maternity,** *n.* motherhood; motherliness. **maternity leave,** *n.* paid leave granted to a woman having a baby. [F *maternel,* late L *māternālis,* L *māternus,* from MATER]

mat(e)y MATE².

†math¹, *n.* a mowing. [OE *mæth*]

math², *n.* (*N Am., coll.*) short for MATHEMATICS.

mathematical, *a.* pertaining to mathematics; rigidly precise or accurate. **mathematically,** *adv.* **mathematician**, *n.* [OF *mathematique,* L *mathēmaticus,* Gr. *mathēmatikos,* from *mathē-,* stem of *manthanein,* see foll.]

mathematics, *n.* the science of quantity, magnitude as expressed by numbers; the mathematical calculations involved in a particular problem, area of study etc. **applied mathematics,** the application of pure mathematics to branches of physical research, as mechanics, astronomy etc. **pure mathematics,** the abstract science of magnitudes etc.

Mather, *n.* **Cotton** (1663–1728), US theologian and writer. He was a Puritan minister in Boston, and wrote over 400 works of history, science, annals and theology, including *Magnalia Christi Americana/The Great Works of Christ in America* (1702), a vast compendium of early New England history and experience. Mather appears to have supported the Salem witch-hunts.

mathesis, *n.* learning, esp. knowledge of mathematics. **mathetic,** *a.* [Gr., cogn. with *manthanein,* to learn]

maths, *n.* (*coll.*) short for MATHEMATICS.

matico, *n.* a Peruvian shrub, *Piper angustifolium,* the leaves of which are a powerful styptic. [Sp. *yerba Matico* (*yerba,* herb, *Matico,* dim. of *Mateo,* Matthew)]

Matilda[1], *n.* (*Austral., coll.*) a swag, a bag of belongings. **waltzing Matilda,** carrying the swag (q.v.).

Matilda[2], *n.* (1102–67), claimant to the throne of England. On the death of her father, Henry I, in 1135, the barons elected her cousin Stephen to be king. Matilda invaded England in 1139, and was crowned by her supporters, 1141. Civil war ensued until in 1153 Stephen was finally recognized as king, with Henry II (Matilda's son) as his successor.

matinal, *a.* of, pertaining to or occurring in the afternoon. [see MATINS]

matinée, *n.* an afternoon performance. **matinée jacket,** *n.* an infant's top garment of wool or material. [F, morning]

matins, *n.pl.* one of the canonical hours of the Roman Catholic breviary, properly recited at midnight but also at daybreak; the daily office of morning prayer in the Anglican Church; a morning song as of birds; †morning, dawn. [F *matines,* fem. pl., eccles. L *mātūtinas,* acc. fem. pl. of *mātūtinus,* of the morning]

Matisse, *n.* **Henri** (1869–1954), French painter, sculptor, illustrator and designer. He settled in the south of France in 1914. His work concentrates on designs that emphasize curvaceous surface patterns, linear arabesques and brilliant colour. Subjects include odalisques (women of the harem), bathers and dancers; later works include pure abstracts, as in his collages of coloured paper shapes and the designs (1949–51) for the decoration of a chapel for the Dominican convent in Vence, near Nice.

Mato Grosso, *n.* an area of SW Brazil, now forming two states, with their capitals at Cuiaba and Campo Grande. The forests, now depleted, supplied rubber and rare timbers; diamonds and silver are mined. [Port., dense forest]

†**matrass,** *n.* a round or oval glass vessel with a long neck, used for distilling. [F *matras,* etym. doubtful]

matr(i)-, matro-, *comb.form* mother. [L *māter*]

matriarch, *n.* a woman regarded as at once ruler and mother; a venerable or patriarchal lady. **matriarchal,** *a.* **matriarchalism,** *n.* **matriarchalist,** *n.* **matriarchate,** *n.* **matriarchy,** *n.* a social system in which the mother is head of the family, or in which descent is reckoned through the female line. [MATR(I)-, *-arch,* as in PATRIARCH]

matric, *n.* (*coll.*) short for MATRICULATION.

matricide, *n.* one who murders his mother; the murder of a mother. **matricidal,** *a.* [F, from L *mātricīda* (MATR(I)-, -CIDE)]

matriculate, *v.t.* to enter in a register, to admit to membership of a body or society, esp. a college or university. *v.i.* to be admitted as a member or student; to pass the examination formerly required to ensure such admission. *a.* matriculated. *n.* one who has matriculated. **matricular,** *n., a.* **matriculation,** *n.* the examination that must be passed to matriculate; the act of matriculating. [med. L *mātrīculātus,* p.p. of *mātrīculāre,* from *mātrīcula,* register, dim. of MATRIX]

matrilineal, *a.* by succession through the mother. **matrilineally,** *adv.* [LINEAL]

matrimony, *n.* the act of marrying; the state of being married, marriage, wedlock; a card-game; the combination of king and queen of one suit in this and other games; slices of cake and bread-and-butter eaten together; †a partner in marriage. **matrimonial, †-nious,** *a.* **matrimonially,** *adv.* [OF *matrimonie,* L *mātrimōnium,* from *māter mātris,* mother]

matrix, *n.* the womb; a place where anything is generated or developed; (*Biol.*) the formative part from which a structure is produced, intercellular substance; a mould in which anything, esp. type or a die, is cast or shaped; the concave bed into which a stamp or die fits; a mass of rock in which a mineral or fossil is embedded, also the impression left by a fossil, crystal etc. after its removal from the rock; an array of numbers or symbols with special mathematical properties. [L; see MATR(I)-]

matro- MATR(I)-.

matron, *n.* a married woman, esp. an elderly one; (*formerly*) the head of the nursing staff in a hospital; the female superintendent of an institution. **matron of honour,** a bride's principal married attendant at a wedding. **matronage,** *n.* **matronal,** *a.* **matronhood, matronship,** *n.* **matronize, -ise,** *v.t.* to render matronlike; to chaperon; (*facet.*) to patronize. **matronlike,** *a.* **matronly,** *a., adv.* **matronymic,** *n.* a name derived from the mother or ancestress. [F *matrone,* L *mātrōna*]

Matsudaira, *n.* **Tsuneo** (1877–1949), Japanese diplomat and politician who became the first chair of the Japanese Diet (parliament) after World War II.

Matsukata, *n.* **Masayoshi** (1835–1924), prince of Japan. As a politician, he paved the way for the modernization of the Japanese economy in the 1880s.

Matsuoka, *n.* **Yosuke** (1880–1946), Japanese politician. As foreign minister (1927–29), he was largely responsible for the increasingly belligerent attitude towards China. His attempts to deal with Japan's worsening economic situation led to inflation and civil unrest.

Matsys, *n.* (also **Massys** or **Metsys**) Quentin (1464/65–1530), Flemish painter, born in Louvain, active in Antwerp. He is known for religious subjects such as the *Lamentation* (1511, Musées Royaux, Antwerp) and portraits set against landscapes or realistic interiors.

matt MAT[2].

mattamore, *n.* an underground storage-place for grain. [F *matamore,* Arab. *matmūrah,* from *tamara,* to store up]

matte, *n.* an impure metallic product containing sulphur, from the smelting of ore, esp. copper. [F, from G, MAT[1]]

matter, *n.* that which constitutes the substance of physical things; that which has weight or mass, occupies space and is perceptible by the senses; physical substance as distinguished from thought, mind, spirit etc.; meaning, sense or substance (of a book, discourse etc.); (*Log.*) content as opposed to form; a subject for thought or feeling; an object of or for attention; an affair, a business; the cause or occasion of or for difficulty, regret etc.; importance, moment; an indefinite amount, quantity or portion; (*Print.*) type set up; (*Law*) a statement or fact forming the ground of an action etc.; purulent substance in an abscess, pus. *v.i.* to be of moment, to signify; †to form pus. **a matter of course,** what may be expected in the natural course of events. **a matter of fact,** a reality, a fact. **for that matter,** so far as that is concerned. **in the matter of,** as regards. **no matter,** it does not matter; regardless of. **matter-of-fact,** *a.* treating of or adhering to facts or realities; not fanciful or imaginary; commonplace, prosaic, plain, ordinary. †**matterful,** *a.* †**matterless,** *a.* unimportant. **mattery,** *a.* full of matter or pus, purulent. [ME and OF *matere,* F *matière,* L *māteria,* stuff, esp. for building]

Matterhorn, *n.* (French **le Cervin** Italian **il Cervino**) mountain peak in the Alps on the Swiss-Italian border;

4478 m/14,690 ft.

Matthau, *n.* **Walter** (stage name of Walter Matuschanskavasky) (1922–), US character actor, impressive in both comedy and dramatic roles. He gained film stardom in the 1960s after his stage success in *The Odd Couple* (1965), and went on to act in, among others, *Kotch* (1971) and *Charley Varrick* (1973).

Matthew, St, *n.* Christian apostle and evangelist, the traditional author of the first Gospel. He is usually identified with Levi, who was a tax collector in the service of Herod Antipas, and was called by Jesus to be a disciple as he sat by the Lake of Galilee receiving customs dues. His emblem is a man with wings; feast day 21 Sept.

Matthews, *n.* **Stanley** (1915–), English footballer who played for Stoke City, Blackpool and England. He played nearly 700 Football League games, and won 54 international caps. He was the first European Footballer of the Year in 1956.

Matthias Corvinus, *n.* (1440–90), king of Hungary from 1458. His aim of uniting Hungary, Austria and Bohemia involved him in long wars with the Holy Roman Emperor and the kings of Bohemia and Poland, during which he captured Vienna (1485) and made it his capital. His father was János Hunyadi.

matting MAT[1].

mattock, *n.* a kind of pick with one broad adze-edged end, for loosening ground, severing roots etc. [OE *mattuc,* etym. doubtful]

mattoid, *a.* semi-insane. *n.* a stupid or foolish person regarded by Lombroso, the Italian criminologist and alienist, as semi-insane. [It. (*matto,* foolish)]

mattress, *n.* a case of coarse material stuffed with hair, wool etc., used for the bottom of a bed; a similar appliance called a spring, box or interior-sprung mattress. [OF *materas* (F *matelas*), It. *materasso,* Arab. *matrah,* a place where anything is thrown, from *taraha,* to throw]

maturate, *v.t.* to mature; to promote suppuration in. *v.i.* to ripen, to suppurate perfectly. **maturation,** *n.* **maturative,** *n., a.* [L *mātūrātus,* p.p. of *mātūrāre,* to MATURE]

mature, *a.* ripe, ripened; completely developed; fully grown; fully elaborated, considered etc.; become payable (as a bill); in a state of perfect suppuration. *v.t.* to bring to a state of ripeness or complete development; to bring to a state of suppuration. *v.i.* to become ripened or fully developed; of a bill, to become payable. **maturation,** *n.* the attainment of maturity, the completion of growth. **maturely,** *adv.* **matureness, maturity,** *n.* **maturescence,** *n.* †**maturescent,** *a.* [L *mātūrus,* ripe, whence *mātūrāre,* to ripen]

Mature, *n.* **Victor** (1915–), US actor, film star of the 1940s and early 1950s. He gave memorable performances in, among others, *My Darling Clementine* (1946), *Kiss of Death* (1947), and *Samson and Delilah* (1949).

matutinal, matutine, *a.* pertaining to the morning; early. [L *mātūtīnālis,* from *mātūtīnus,* pertaining to *Mātūta,* goddess of dawn (rel. to *mātūrus,* early)]

maty MATE[2].

matzo, *n.* (*pl.* **matzoth, -os**) (a thin wafer of) unleavened bread, eaten esp. at the Passover. [Heb. *matsāh*]

Mauchly, *n.* **John William** (1907–80), US physicist and engineer. He constructed in 1946 the first general-purpose computer, the ENIAC, in collaboration with John Eckert (1919–). Their company was bought by Remington Rand (1950), and they built the Univac 1 computer in 1951 for the US census.

maud, *n.* (*Sc.*) a grey-striped plaid worn by shepherds etc., or used as a travelling rug. [etym. unknown]

maudlin, *a.* muddled with drink; characterized by sickly sentimentality, mawkish; †weeping, tearful. *n.* mawkish sentimentality. [OF *mawdeleine,* L *Magdalēnē,* MAGDALEN]

Maugham, *n.* **(William) Somerset** (1874–1965), English writer. His work includes the novels *Of Human Bondage* (1915), *The Moon and Sixpence* (1919), and *Cakes and Ale* (1930); short stories *The Trembling of a Leaf* (1921), *Ashenden* (1928); and plays *Lady Frederick* (1907), *Our Betters* (1923).

†**maugre,** *prep.* in spite of. [OF *maugré, malgré* (*mal,* L *malus -um,* bad, *gré,* L *gratus -um,* pleasing)]

maul, *n.* a heavy wooden hammer, a beetle; a loose scrum in Rugby; a tussle, struggle. *v.t.* to beat, to bruise (as with a maul); to handle roughly; to damage. [ME *malle,* OF *mail,* L *malleus -um,* hammer]

maulstick, *n.* a light stick with a round pad at the end used as a rest for the right hand by painters. [Dut. *maalstok* (*malen,* to paint, STICK[1])]

Mau Mau, *n.* a name given by white settlers to a Kenyan secret guerrilla society with nationalist aims (1952–60), an offshoot of the Kikuyu Central Association banned in World War II. Attacks on other Kikuyu (about 1000 killed) were far more common than on whites (about 100 killed).

maun, *aux. v.* (*esp. Sc.*) must. [ON *man,* must, will]

Mauna Kea, *n.* an astronomical observatory in Hawaii, US, built on a dormant volcano at 4200 m/13,784 ft above sea level. Because of its elevation high above clouds, atmospheric moisture and artificial lighting, Mauna Kea is ideal for infrared astronomy. The first telescope on the site was installed in 1970.

Mauna Loa, *n.* an active volcano rising to a height of 4169 m/13,678 ft on the Pacific island of Hawaii; it has numerous craters, including the second largest active crater in the world.

maund, *n.* an Asian measure of weight varying from place to place—in India 83 lb (37 kg). [Hind. *man*]

maunder, *v.i.* to grumble, to mutter; to talk incoherently, to ramble; to act or move about aimlessly. *v.t.* to utter in a grumbling or incoherent manner. **maunderer,** *n.* [perh. imit.]

maundy, *n.* the ceremony of washing the feet of poor people on Holy Thursday, in commemoration of Christ's performing this office for His disciples; a distribution of alms following this. **maundy money, penny,** *n.* silver money specially struck and distributed on Maundy Thursday. **Maundy Thursday,** *n.* the day before Good Friday, when the royal alms or maundy money is distributed by the royal almoner. [OF *mandé,* L *mandātum,* MANDATE]

Maupassant, *n.* **Guy de** (1850–93), French author who established a reputation with the short story 'Boule de Suif/Ball of Fat' (1880) and wrote some 300 short stories in all. His novels include *Une Vie/A Woman's Life* (1883) and *Bel-Ami* (1885).

mauresque MORESQUE.

Mauriac, *n.* **François** (1885–1970), French novelist. His novel *Le Baiser au lépreux/A Kiss for the Leper* (1922) describes the conflict of an unhappy marriage. The irreconcilability of Christian practice and human nature are examined in *Fleuve de feu/River of Fire* (1923), *Le Désert de l'amour/The Desert of Love* (1925) and *Thérèse Desqueyroux* (1927). Nobel Prize for Literature 1952.

Mauritania, *n.* Islamic Republic of (*République Islamique de Mauritanie*), a country in NW Africa, bordered to the NE by Algeria, E and S by Mali, SW by Senegal, W by the Atlantic Ocean and NW by Western Sahara. **area** 1,030,700 sq km/397,850 sq miles. **capital** Nouakchott. **physical** valley of river Senegal in south; the rest is arid. **exports** iron ore, fish. **population** (1988) 1,894,000 (30% Arab Berber, 30% black Africans, 30% Haratine – descendants of black slaves, who remained slaves until 1980); annual growth rate 2.9%. **language** Arabic (official), French. **religion** Sunni Muslim.

Mauritius, *n.* State of, an island in the Indian Ocean, E of Madagascar. **area** 2,040 sq km/787 sq miles; the island of Rodrigues is part of Mauritius and there are several small island dependencies. **capital** Port Louis. **physical** a mountainous, volcanic island surrounded by coral reefs. **exports** sugar, knitted goods; tourism is increasingly important. **population** (1987) 1,041,000; annual growth rate 1.9%. **language** English (official); creole French. **religion** Hindu 45%, Christian 30%,

Muslim 15%.

Maurois, *n.* **André** (pen name of Emile Herzog) (1885–1967), French novelist and writer, whose works include the semi-autobiographical *Bernard Quesnay* (1926), and fictionalized biographies, such as *Ariel* (1923), a life of Shelley.

Mauroy, *n.* **Pierre** (1928–), French socialist politician, prime minister (1981–84). He oversaw the introduction of a radical reflationary programme.

Maurya dynasty, *n.* an Indian dynasty (*c.* 321–*c.* 185 BC), founded by Chandragupta Maurya (321–*c.* 279 BC) on the basis of a highly organized aristocracy, which ruled much of the Indian continent until the murder of the emperor Brhadratha in 185 BC and the creation of the Suringa dynasty. After the death of Emperor Asoka, the empire was riven by dynastic disputes.

Mauser ®, *n.* a variety of military magazine rifle. **Mauser pistol,** *n.* [Paul *Mauser,* 1838–1914, G inventor]

mausoleum, *n.* (*pl.* **-lea, -leums**) the stately tomb of Mausolus, king of Caria, erected by his widow Artemisia, and reckoned one of the seven wonders of the world; a sepulchral monument of considerable size or architectural pretensions. †**mausolean,** *a.* [L, from Gr. *Mausōleion,* from *Mausōlos*]

mauvais quart d'heure, a brief unpleasant experience. [F, bad quarter of an hour]

mauve, *n.* a purple- or lilac-coloured aniline dye; the colour of this. *a.* of this colour. [F, from L *malva,* MALLOW]

maverick, *n.* (*N Am.*) an unbranded beast; anything got hold of dishonestly; an irresponsible or independent person. *v.t.* to brand (a stray beast); hence, to seize or appropriate illegally. [Samuel *Maverick,* Texan cattle-raiser, who refrained from branding his stock, *c.* 1840]

mavis, *n.* the song-thrush. [F *mauvis* (cp. Sp. *malvis*), etym. doubtful]

mavourneen, *n.* (*Ir.*) my dear one. [Ir. *mo mhurnin*]

maw, *n.* the stomach of lower animals, esp. the fourth stomach of ruminants; the crop of birds; (*facet.*) the human stomach; the mouth. **mawworm,** *n.* an intestinal worm. [OE *maga* (cp. Dut. *maag,* Icel. *mage,* G *Magen*)]

†**mawk,** *n.* a maggot. [Icel. *mathkr* (cp. OE *mathu, matha*)]

mawkin MALKIN.

mawkish, *a.* apt to cause satiety or loathing; sickly, insipid; falsely or feebly sentimental. **mawkishly,** *adv.* **mawkishness,** *n.*

Mawson, *n.* **Douglas** (1882–1958), Australian explorer, born in Britain, who reached the magnetic South Pole on Shackleton's expedition of 1907–09.

maxi, *n., a.* short for MAXIMUM, esp. (*n.*) a coat, skirt etc. reaching the ankles.

maxi-, *comb.form* very large or long.

maxilla, *n.* (*pl.* **-lae**) one of the jaw-bones, esp. the upper in mammals. **maxillary,** *n.* the part of the skull that forms the upper jaw. *a.* pertaining to a jaw or maxilla. **maxilliferous,** *a.* **maxilliform,** *a.* **maxilliped,** *n.* a foot-jaw or limb modified into a maxillary organ, in Crustacea. **maxillo-,** *comb.form.* [L]

Maxim, *n.* an automatic single-barrelled quick-firing machine-gun. [Sir Hiram S *Maxim,* 1840–1916, inventor]

maxim, *n.* a general principle of a practical kind; a rule derived from experience; (*Law*) an established or accepted principle. **maximist, maxim-monger,** *n.* **maximistic,** *a.* [F *maxime,* L *maxima,* fem. superl. of *magnus,* great]

maximal, *a.* of the greatest, largest etc. size, rate etc.; of an upper limit. **maximally,** *adv.*

Maximalist, *n.* an adherent of the extremist section of the former Social Revolutionary Party in Russia. [MAXIMUM]

Maximilian, *n.* (1832–67), emperor of Mexico 1864–67. He accepted that title when the French emperor Napoleon III's troops occupied the country, but encountered resistance from the deposed president Juárez. In 1866, after the French troops withdrew on the insistence the US, Maximilian was captured by Mexican republicans and shot.

Maximilian I, *n.* (1459–1519), Holy Roman Emperor from 1493, the son of Emperor Frederick III. He had acquired the Low Countries through his marriage to Mary of Burgundy, 1477; he married his son Philip I (the Handsome) to the heiress to the Spanish throne, and undertook long wars with Italy and Hungary in attempts to extend Habsburg power. He was the patron of the artist Dürer.

maximin, *n.* the maximum of a set of minima, esp. of minimum gains in game theory. [*maxi*mum, *min*imum]

maximum, *n.* (*pl.* **-ma**) the greatest quantity or degree attainable in any given case. *a.* greatest; at the greatest or highest degree. **maxima and minima,** the greatest and least values of a variable quantity. **maximum thermometer,** *n.* one automatically recording the highest temperature reached during a given period. **maximize, -ise,** *v.t.* to raise to a maximum; to increase to the utmost extent; to hold rigorous opinions in matters of faith. *v.i.* to interpret doctrines in the most rigorous way. [L, neut. superl. of *magnus,* great]

maxwell, *n.* a unit of magnetic flux. [J.C. *Maxwell,* 1831–79]

Maxwell[1], *n.* **(Ian) Robert** (1923–), Czech-born British publishing and newspaper proprietor, chief executive of Maxwell Communications Corporation, and owner of several UK national newspapers, including the *Daily Mirror.* He was Labour Member of Parliament for Buckingham (1964–70).

Maxwell[2], *n.* **James Clerk** (1831–79), Scottish physicist. He contributed to every branch of physical science, particularly gases, optics, colour sensation, electricity and magnetism. His theoretical work in magnetism prepared the way for wireless telegraphy and telephony.

Maxwell-Boltzmann distribution, *n.* basic equation concerning the distribution of velocities of the molecules of a gas.

May[1], *n.* the fifth month of the year; the springtime of life, youth; hawthorn blossom, from its appearing in May; Mayday festivities; (*pl.*) at Cambridge University, the Easter term examinations, the boat-races held in May Week. †*v.i.* to engage in the festivities of Mayday. **Queen of the May** MAY-QUEEN. **May-apple,** *n.* a N American herb (*Podophyllum peltatum*) with a single white flower and an edible egg-shaped fruit. **may-blossom,** *n.* hawthorn bloom. **May-bug,** *n.* the cockchafer. **Mayday,** *n.* the first of May as a spring festival or, in some countries, as a public holiday in honour of workers. **mayduke,** *n.* a variety of cherry said to have been introduced from Médoc. **mayflower,** *n.* a flower blooming in May, as the cowslip, lady's smock or hawthorn; (*N Am.*) the trailing arbutus, *Epigaea repens.* **mayfly,** *n.* an ephemeral insect, esp. *Ephemera vulgata* or *E. dania;* an angler's fly made in imitation of this; the caddis-fly. **May-games,** *n.pl.* games held on Mayday. †**May-lady** MAY-QUEEN. **may-lily,** *n.* the lily of the valley. †**May-morn,** *n.* freshness, vigour. **maypole,** *n.* a pole decorated with garlands etc., round which people dance on Mayday. **May-queen,** *n.* a young girl chosen to act as queen of the games on Mayday. **May Week,** *n.* at Cambridge University, the boat-race week held in June. **mayer,** *n.* [F *mai,* L *Māius,* perh. pertaining to *Māia*]

may[2], *aux.v.* (*2nd sing.* **mayest,** mā'əst, †**mayst,** *past* **might,** mīt) expressing possibility, ability, permission, desire, obligation, contingency or uncertainty. **maybe,** *adv.* perhaps, possibly. †**mayhap,** *conj.* peradventure. [OE *mæg,* 1st sing. of *magan,* to be able, past *mihte, meahte* (cp. Dut. *mag, mocht, mogen,* Icel. *mā, megom, mātte,* G *mag, mochte, mögen*)]

†**may**[3], *n.* a maiden, a girl. [OE *mæg,* kinswoman (see MAIDEN)]

Maya, *n.* member of an American Indian civilization originating in the Yucatan Peninsula about 2600 BC, with later sites in Mexico, Guatemala and Belize, and enjoying a classical period (325–925 AD), after which it declined. The Maya constructed stone buildings and stepped pyramids without metal tools; used hieroglyphic writing in manuscripts, of which only three survive; were skilled potters, weavers and farmers; and regulated their rituals and warfare by observations of the planet Venus.

maya, *n.* in Hinduism, the world as perceived by the senses, regarded as illusory. [Sansk.]

Mayan art, *n.* art of the Central American civilization of the Maya, between about AD 300 and 900. Mayan figures have distinctive squat proportions and squared-off composition. Large, steeply inclined pyramids were built, for example at Chichén Itzá, decorated with sculpture and inscription.

maybe MAY[2].

Mayday, *n.* the international radiotelephone distress signal. [F *m'aider,* help me]

May Day, *n.* first day of May. In many countries it is a public holiday in honour of labour.

Mayer[1], *n.* **Julius Robert von** (1814–78), German physicist who in 1842 anticipated Joule in deriving the mechanical equivalent of heat, and Helmholtz in the principle of conservation of energy.

Mayer[2], *n.* **Louis Burt** (adopted name of Eliezer Mayer) (1885–1957), US film producer and distributor. He founded a production company in 1917 and in 1924 became vice-president of the newly formed MGM. Something of a tyrant, he built up his studio into one of Hollywood's finest through the use of top talent and good judgment of audience tastes.

mayflower MAY[1].

mayhem, *n.* (*formerly*) the offence of maiming a person; wilful damage; a state of disorder or confusion.

Mayo, *n.* a county in Connacht province, Republic of Ireland. **area** 5,400 sq km/2,084 sq miles. **towns** administrative town Castlebar. **products** sheep and cattle farming; fishing. **population** (1986) 115,000.

mayonnaise, *n.* a thick sauce or salad-dressing made of egg-yolk, vinegar etc.; a dish with this as a dressing, as *egg mayonnaise*. [F, etym. doubtful]

mayor, *n.* the chief officer of a city or borough. **Lord Mayor** LORD. **mayoral,** *a.* **mayoralty,** *n.* **mayoress,** *n.* a female mayor; the wife of a mayor, or a woman who assists the mayor in official duties. [F *maire*]

maypole MAY[1].

mayst MAY[2].

mayweed, *n.* the stinking camomile, *Anthemis cotula;* other composite plants, esp. the feverfew. [obs. *maythe,* OE *magothe,* WEED]

mazard, *n.* †the head, the skull; †the face; a small kind of black cherry. [etym. doubtful, perh. var. of MAZER]

Mazarin, *n.* **Jules** (1602–61), French politician, who succeeded Richelieu as chief minister of France in 1642. His attack on the power of the nobility led to the Fronde and his temporary exile, but his diplomacy achieved a successful conclusion to the Thirty Years' War, and, in alliance with Cromwell during the British protectorate, he gained victory over Spain.

mazarine, *n., a.* a deep rich blue. [etym. doubtful]

maze, *n.* a labyrinth, a confusing network of winding and turning passages; a state of bewilderment, uncertainty, perplexity. *v.t.* to bewilder, to confuse. †*v.i.* to be bewildered; to wind about perplexedly. **mazeful,** *a.* **mazy,** *a.* involved, winding, perplexing, intricate; giddy, dizzy. **the mazy,** (*facet.*) the dance, dancing. **mazily,** *adv.* **maziness,** *n.* [etym. doubtful]

†**mazer,** *n.* a large cup or drinking-vessel, orig. made of maple-wood. [OF *masere,* prob. from OHG *masar,* a knot in wood, maple-wood (cp. G *Maser,* Icel. *mösurr*)]

Mazowiecki, *n.* **Tadeusz** (1927–), Polish politician, founder member of Solidarity, and Poland's first postwar noncommunist prime minister from 1989.

mazurka, *n.* a lively Polish dance like the polka; the music for this. [Pol., a woman of the province Mazovia (cp. POLONAISE)]

mazy MAZE.

Mazzini, *n.* **Giuseppe** (1805–72), Italian nationalist. He was a member of the revolutionary society, the Carbonari, and founded in exile the nationalist movement *Giovane Italia/Young Italy* (1832). Returning to Italy on the outbreak of the 1848 revolution, he headed a republican government established in Rome, but was forced into exile again on its overthrow in 1849. He acted as a focus for the movement for Italian unity.

MB, (*abbr.*) Bachelor of Medicine (L *Medicinae Baccalaureus*); megabyte.

Mbabane, *n.* capital (since 1902) of Swaziland, 160 km/100 miles west of Maputo, in the Dalgeni Hills; population (1986) 38,000.

MBE, (*abbr.*) Member of (the Order of) the British Empire.

Mboya, *n.* **Tom** (1930–69), Kenyan politician, a founder of the Kenya African National Union (KANU), and minister of economic planning (opposed to nationalization) from 1964 until his assassination.

mbx, *n.* a message transferred from one computer terminal to another. *v.t.* to send messages, information, tc. between computer terminals. [*mailbox*]

MC, (*abbr.*) Master of Ceremonies; Member of Congress; Military Cross.

MCC, (*abbr.*) Marylebone Cricket Club.

MCP, (*abbr.*) male chauvinist pig.

MD, (*abbr.*) Doctor of Medicine (L *Medicinae Doctor*); Managing Director.

Md., (*abbr.*) Maryland (US).

MDMA, *n.* a psychedelic drug, also known as ecstasy.

ME, (*abbr.*) Mechanical Engineer; Military Engineer; Middle English; myalgic encophalomyelitis.

Me., (*abbr.*) Maine (US).

me[1], *pers. pron.* the dative and objective of the first personal pronoun. [OE *mē, mec,* acc. (cp. Dut. *mij,* Swed. and Dan. *mig,* G *mich,* dat. *mir,* L *mē,* dat. *mihi,* Gr. *me, eme, moi, emoi*)]

me[2] MI.

mea culpa, by my fault. [L]

mead[1], *n.* a fermented liquor made from honey, water and spices. [OE *medu*]

mead[2], *n.* a meadow. [see foll.]

meadow, *n.* a tract of land under grass, esp. if grown for hay; low, rich, moist ground, esp. near a river. **meadow-lark,** *n.* an American songbird, *Sturnella magna*. **meadow pipit,** *n.* a brown and white European songbird. **meadow-saffron,** *n.* a plant of the genus *Colchicum,* esp. *C. autumnale*. **meadow-sweet,** *n.* a rosaceous plant, *Spiraea ulmaria,* with white, plumy, fragrant flowers. **meadowy,** *a.* [OE *mǣdwe,* dat. of *mǣd,* cogn. with MOW[3]]

meagre, *a.* lean, thin, wanting flesh; destitute of richness, fertility or productiveness; poor, scanty. †*v.t.* to make meagre. **meagrely,** *adv.* **meagreness,** *n.* [ME and OF *megre, maigre,* L *macer macrum,* cogn. with Gr. *makros,* long]

meal[1], *n.* food taken at one of the customary times of eating, a repast; the occasion or usual time of this; (*dial.*) the yield of milk from a cow at one milking. *v.i.* to have a meal. **to make a meal of,** to exaggerate the importance, difficulty etc. of. **meals-on-wheels,** *n.* a scheme by which pre-cooked meals are delivered by vehicles to the house-bound, needy etc. **meal ticket,** *n.* a ticket given in exchange for a meal, often at a subsidized price; (*coll., often derog.*) a person upon whom one can depend for financial support. **meal-time,** †**-tide,** *n.* [OE *mǣl*]

meal[2], *n.* the edible portion of grain or pulse ground into flour. **meal-ark** *n.* (*Sc.*) a receptacle for meal. **meal-man, meal-monger,** *n.* one who deals in meal. **meal-worm,** *n.* the larva of a beetle that infests meal. **mealy,** *a.* of, containing or resembling meal; powdery, friable, floury; farinaceous; besprinkled with or as with meal, spotty; pale (of the complexion); mealy-mouthed. **mealy bug,** *n.* an insect infesting vines and hothouse plants. **mealy-mouthed,** *a.* soft-spoken, hypocritical. **mealiness,** *n.* [OE *melu* (cp. Dut. and Dan. *meel,* G *Mehl*), cogn. with L *molere,* to grind]

mealie, *n.* (*usu. pl.*) maize. [Afrikaans *milje,* Port. *milho,* MILLET]

mean[1], *v.t.* (*past, p.p.* **meant**) to have in the mind; to purpose, to intend; to design, to destine (for); to denote, to signify; to intend to convey or to indicate. *v.i.* to have a specified intention or disposition. **to mean business** BUSINESS. **to mean well,** to have good intentions. **meaning,** *n.* that which is meant, significance, import. *a.* significant, expressive. **meaningful,** *a.* **meaningfully,** *adv.* **meaningfulness,** *n.* **meaningless,** *a.* **meaninglessly,** *adv.* **meaninglessness,** *n.* **meaningly,** *adv.* [OE *mǣnan* (cp. Dut. *meenen,* Dan. *mene,* G *meinen*)]

mean², *a.* occupying a middle position; equidistant from two extremes; not extreme, moderate, not excessive; intervening; (*Math.*) intermediate in value between two extremes, average. *n.* the middle point, state, course, quality or degree between two extremes; (*Math.*) a quantity intermediate between two extremes, an average. **means,** *n.pl.* that by which anything is done or a result attained; available resources, income, wealth. **(a man etc.) of means,** a wealthy man etc. **by all means,** certainly, undoubtedly. **by any means,** in any way possible, somehow; at all. **by fair means or foul,** by any means whatsoever. **by means of,** by the agency or instrumentality of. **by no means,** certainly not, on no account whatever. **means-test,** *n.* the official investigation into the means of a person applying for pension, dole etc. **meantime, -while,** *adv.* in the intervening time. *n.* the interval between two given times. [OF *meien, moien* (F *moyen*), late L *mediānus,* L *medius,* middle]

mean³, *a.* low in quality, capacity, value, rank etc.; inferior, poor, inefficient, shabby; low-minded, petty, stingy; shabby, contemptible, miserly; ignoble, of no account, disreputable; despicable; (*coll.*) having or showing great skill, excellent. **mean-born,** *a.* of humble birth. **mean-spirited,** *a.* **mean-spiritedly,** *adv.* **meanie**, *n.* (*coll.*) a petty-minded or miserly person. **meanly,** *adv.* **meanness,** *n.* [OE *mǣne, gemǣne* (cp. Dut. *gemeen,* Icel. *meinn,* G *gemein*), cogn. with L *commūnis,* COMMON]

meander, *n.* (*usu. pl.*) a tortuous or intricate course or bend; (*usu. pl.*) a winding, a circuitous path or movement, a deviation; a decorative pattern, fretwork etc. composed of intricately interlacing lines; †a maze, a labyrinth. *v.i.* to wander, wind or flow in a tortuous course. **meandering, †meandrian, meandriform,** *a.* **meandrine**, *a.* meandering; belonging to the *Meandrina,* a genus of tropical corals, in appearance somewhat resembling the convolutions of the brain. [L *Meander,* Gr. *Maiandros,* a winding river in Phrygia]

meanie MEAN³.

means MEAN².

meant, *past, p.p.* MEAN¹.

measles, *n.pl.* a contagious viral disease, indicated by a red papular rash, usu. attacking children; applied to the effects of a cystic worm in swine and oxen. **German measles** GERMAN. **measled,** *a.* **measly,** *a.* infected with measles; (*coll.*) worthless, paltry, meagre. [ME *maseles* (cp. Dut. *mazelen*), from OTeut. *masmæs,* whence MAZER]

measure, *n.* the extent or dimensions of a thing as determined by measuring; the measurements necessary to make an article of dress; a standard of measurement; a definite unit of capacity or extent; an instrument for measuring, as a rod, tape etc., or a vessel of standard capacity; a system of measuring; the act of measuring, measurement; a quantity measured out taken as a rule or standard; prescribed or allotted extent, length or quantity; limit, moderation, just degree or amount; metre, poetical rhythm; an action to achieve a purpose; a law, a statute, an Act of Parliament; (*Geol.*) (*pl.*) a series of beds, strata; (*Mus.*) time, pace, the contents of a bar; †a slow and stately dance. *v.t.* to determine the extent or quantity of by comparison with a definite unit or standard; to take the dimensions of; to weigh, to judge, to value or estimate by comparison with a rule or standard; to serve as the measure of; to allot or apportion by measure; to travel over, to cover; to survey, look up and down; to bring into competition (with); †to regulate, to keep within bounds; †to set to metre. *v.i.* to take measurements; to be in extent, to show by measurement. **beyond measure,** exceedingly, excessively. **for good measure,** as an additional amount. **in a measure,** to some extent, in a certain degree. **short measure,** less than the due amount. **to measure one's length,** to fall prostrate. **to measure swords,** of duellists, to see whether the swords are of the same length; to try one's strength with or against. **to measure up to,** to be adequate for. **to take measures,** to adopt means, to take steps (to). **to take someone's measure,** to measure someone for clothes; to find out what kind of a person someone is. **within measure,** in moderation. **without measure,** immoderately. **measurable,** *a.* **measurably,** *adv.* **measured,** *a.* of definite measure; deliberate and uniform; rhythmical; well-considered, carefully weighed. **measureless,** *a.* **measurement,** *n.* **measurer,** *n.* **measuring,** *n., a.* **measuring jug,** *n.* a graduated jug used for measuring ingredients in cooking. [OF *mesure,* L *mensūra,* from *mens-,* p.p. stem of *mētīrī,* to measure]

meat, *n.* the flesh of animals, usu. excluding fish and fowl, used as food; solid food of any kind; the partaking of food, a meal; the edible part of a nut, egg, shellfish etc.; the substance of sth, the pith. **after, before, meat,** immediately after, before, a meal. **strong meat** STRONG. **to sit at meat,** to sit at table. **meat-ball,** *n.* a ball of minced meat, eaten e.g. with a sauce and spaghetti; (*esp. N Am. sl.*) a stupid or foolish person. **meat-biscuit,** *n.* dried meat mixed with meal and baked. **meat-eater,** *n.* a person who eats meat; a carnivore. **meat loaf,** *n.* a loaf-shaped mass of minced or chopped meat, cooked and often eaten cold. **meat-safe,** *n.* a cupboard, usu. of wire gauze or perforated zinc, for storing meat. **meat-salesman,** *n.* one who receives carcases and sells them to butchers. **meaty,** *a.* containing much meat; of or like meat; substantial, pithy. **meatiness,** *n.* [OE *mete*]

Meath, *n.* a county in the province of Leinster, Republic of Ireland. **area** 2,340 sq km/903 sq miles. **county town** Trim. **products** sheep, cattle. **population** (1986) 104,000.

meatus, *n.* (*pl.* **-tus**) (*Anat.*) a passage, channel or tubular canal. **auditory meatus,** the passage of the ear. [L, from *meāre,* to flow]

Mecca¹, *n.* (*fig.*) a holy place; the object of one's aspirations; a place frequently visited. [see foll.]

Mecca², *n.* (Arabic **Makkah**) city in Saudi Arabia and, as birthplace of Mohammed, the holiest city of the Islamic world; population (1974) 367,000. In the centre of Mecca is the Great Mosque, in whose courtyard is the Kaaba.

Meccano®, *n.* a set of toy engineering parts that can be built up into various mechanical models.

mechanic, *n.* an artisan; a skilled workman; one who is employed or skilled in repairing or maintaining machines; (*pl.*) the branch of physics treating of the motion and equilibrium of material bodies; also the science of machinery; (*pl.*) the practical details of an operation, project etc. *a.* mechanical; industrial; pertaining to or of the nature of machinery, machine-like; †vulgar, low. **mechanical,** *a.* pertaining to mechanics; in accordance with physical laws; acting or affected by physical power without chemical change; pertaining to or acting as machinery or mechanism; produced by machinery; of or pertaining to handicraft; working with tools or machinery; machine-like, automatic, done from force of habit; slavish, unoriginal; †vulgar, rude, base. †*n.* a mechanic. **mechanical arts,** *n.pl.* those in which the hands and body are chiefly concerned. **mechanical engineering,** *n.* the branch of engineering concerned with the design and production of machinery. **mechanical powers,** *n.pl.* the simple machines, the wedge, the inclined plane, the screw, the lever, the wheel and axle and the pulley. **mechanical transport,** *n.* road transportation by motor vehicles. **mechanicalism,** *n.* **mechanicalist, mechanist,** *n.* a mechanician; a supporter of the mechanical philosophy. **mechanically,** *adv.* **mechanicalness,** *n.* **mechanician**, *n.* **mechanico-,** *comb.form.* [L *mēch-*

anicus, Gr. *mēchanikos,* from *mēchanē,* MACHINE]

mechanism, *n.* the structure or correlation of parts of a machine; machinery; a system of correlated parts working reciprocally together, as a machine; in art, mechanical execution as distinguished from style etc., technique; the philosophical doctrine that phenomena can be explained purely in terms of mechanical or biological interactions. **mechanistic,** *a.* **mechanistically,** *adv.*

mechanize, -ise, *v.t.* to make mechanical; to equip (troops) with mechanical transport. **mechanization, -isation,** *n.*

mechan(o)-, *comb.form* pertaining to mechanics or machinery.

mechanography, *n.* reproduction of a work of art, a writing etc. by mechanical means. **mechanograph,** *n.*

mechanotherapy, *n.* the treatment of disease through the agency of mechanical appliances.

mechanotropism, *n.* the bending of tendrils or other plant organs through reaction to contact or other mechanical stimulus.

Mechlin, *n.* a light lace made at Mechlin. [*Mechlin* (Malines), near Brussels]

Mechnikov, *n.* **Elie** (1845–1916), Russian scientist who discovered the function of white blood cells and phagocytes. After leaving Russia and joining Pasteur in Paris, he described how these 'scavenger cells' can attack the body itself (autoimmune disease).

Mecklenburg, *n.* the historic name of an area of the Baltic coast of Germany. It was formerly the two grand duchies of Mecklenburg-Schwerin and Mecklenburg-Strelitz, which became free states of the Weimar Republic (1918–34), and were joined 1946 (with part of Pomerania) to form a region of East Germany. In 1952 it was split into the counties of Rostock, Schwerin and Neubrandenburg.

meconic, *a.* contained in or derived from the poppy. **meconin,** *n.* a neutral substance existing in opium. **meconium,** *n.* inspissated poppy juice; the first faeces of infants consisting of excretions from the liver etc. **Meconopsis,** *n.* a genus of flowering plants related to and resembling the poppy. [Gr. *mēkōn,* poppy]

MEd, (*abbr.*) Master of Education.

med., (*abbr.*) medical, medicine; mediaeval; medium.

medal, *n.* a piece of metal, often in the form of a coin, stamped with a figure and inscription to commemorate some illustrious person or event. †**medalet,** *n.* a small medal. **medalled,** *a.* **medallic,** *a.* **medallion,** *n.* a large medal; (*Arch.*) a tablet or panel, usually round or oval, containing painted or sculptured figures, decorations etc. **medallist,** *n.* one who designs or engraves medals; a collector of or dealer in medals; one who has gained a medal. †**medallurgy,** *n.* the art of engraving or stamping medals. [F *médaille,* It. *medaglia,* pop. L *metallea,* L *metallum,* METAL]

Medan, *n.* seaport and economic centre of the island of Sumatra, Indonesia; population (1980) 1,379,000. It trades in rubber, tobacco and palm oil.

Medawar, *n.* **Peter (Brian)** (1915–87), Brazilian-born British immunologist, who, with Burnet, discovered that the body's resistance to grafted tissue is undeveloped in the newborn child, and studied the way it is acquired.

meddle, *v.i.* to interfere (in) officiously; to concern or busy oneself (with) unnecessarily; †to mix. **meddler,** *n.* **meddlesome,** *a.* **meddlesomeness,** *n.* [A-F *medler,* OF *mesler* (F *mêler*), med. L *misculāre,* L *miscēre,* to mix]

Mede, *n.* a member of a people of NW Iran who first appeared in the 9th cent. BC as tributaries to Assyria, with their capital at Ecbatana (now Hamadán). Allying themselves with Babylon, they destroyed the Assyrian capital of Nineveh, 612 BC, and extended their conquests into central Anatolia. In 550 BC they were overthrown by the Persians, with whom they rapidly merged.

Medea[1], *n.* in Greek mythology, the sorceress daughter of the king of Colchis. When Jason reached the court, she fell in love with him, helped him acquire the golden fleece, and they fled together. When Jason married Creusa, Medea killed his bride with the gift of a poisoned garment, and also killed her own two children by Jason.

Medea[2], *n.* a tragedy by Euripedes, produced in 431 BC. It deals with the later part of the legend of Medea – her murder of Jason's bride and of her own children.

Medellín, *n.* industrial town (textiles, chemicals, engineering, coffee) in the Central Cordillera, Colombia, 1538 m/5048 ft above sea level; population (1985) 2,069,000. It is a centre of the Colombian drug trade, and there has been considerable violence in the late 1980s.

media[1], *pl.* MEDIUM.

media[2] MASS[2].

media[3], *n.* (*pl.* **-iae**) (*Anat.*) the middle coat or tunic of a vessel; (*Phon.*) a voiced mute, *g, d* or *h,* regarded as intermediate between smooth and rough or aspirate. [L, fem. of *medius,* middle]

mediacy MEDIATE.

mediaeval, medieval, *a.* of, or pertaining to, or characteristic of the Middle Ages. *n.* one who lived in the Middle Ages. **medi(a)eval history,** *n.* history from the fall of Rome (AD 476) until the Renaissance (15th cent.). **medi(a)evalism,** *n.* **medi(a)evalist,** *n.* **medi(a)evalize, -ise,** *v.t.* **medi(a)evally,** *adv.* [L *medius,* middle; *aevum,* age]

medial, *a.* pertaining to or situated in the middle, intermediate; mean or average. *n.* a medial letter; (*Phon.*) a media. [late L *mediālis,* see MEDIA[1]]

median, *a.* (*Anat.*) situated in the middle, esp. in the median plane, dividing the body longitudinally into two equal halves; (*Geol.*) intermediate, as a line or zone between the extreme limits of winds, calm belts etc. *n.* a straight line joining the vertex of a triangle to the mid-point of the opposite side. **medianly,** *adv.*

mediant, *n.* (*Mus.*) the third tone of any scale. [It. *mediante,* late L *medians -antem,* pres.p. of *mediāre,* to MEDIATE]

mediastinum, *n.* (*pl.* **-na**) a membranous septum or cavity between the two main parts of an organ etc., esp. the folds of the pleura between the right and left lung. **mediastinal,** *a.* [L, neut. of *mediastīnus,* orig. a common servant, a drudge]

mediate, *a.* situated in the middle or between two extremes; intervening, indirect, secondary; serving or acting as an intervening or indirect means or agency; effected or connected by such means. *v.t.,* to interpose between (parties) in order to reconcile them; to effect by means of intervention. *v.i.* to interpose (between) in order to reconcile parties etc.; to serve as connecting link or medium (between). **mediacy,** *n.* **mediately,** *adv.* **mediateness,** *n.* **mediation,** *n.* **mediator,** *n.* **mediatorial,** *a.* **mediatorially,** *adv.* **mediatorship, mediatory,** *a., n.* **mediatrix,** †**mediatress,** *n. fem.* [late L *mediātus,* p.p. of *mediāre,* from *medius,* middle]

mediatize, -ise, *v.t.* to render dependent; to disestablish politically and subject to a larger State, leaving the ruler a nominal sovereignty. **mediatization, -isation,** *n.* [F *médiatiser,* from *médiat,* MEDIATE]

medic, *n.* (*coll.*) a medical student; a physician; a doctor.

medical, *a.* pertaining to, connected with or employed in medicine; curative, healing, medicinal; pertaining to medicine as opposed to surgery etc. *n.* (*coll.*) a medical student; an examination to ascertain a person's state of physical fitness. **medical certificate,** *n.* a document issued by a doctor stating that a person is unfit for work etc. **medical examiner,** *n.* (*N Am.*) a public official, usu. a physician, appointed to inquire into cases of sudden or suspicious death. **medical jurisprudence** FORENSIC MEDICINE. **medicable,** *a.* able to be treated or cured. **medically,** *adv.* **medicament,** *n.* a healing substance or application. **medicamental,** *a.* **medicamentally,** *adv.* **medicaster,** *n.* a quack. **medicate,** *v.t.* to impregnate with anything medicinal; to treat medically. **medication,** *n.* a medicine or drug; treatment with medicine or drugs. **medicative,** *a.* [F *médical,* late L *medicālis,* from *medicus,* a physician, cognate with *medēre,* to heal]

Medicare, *n.* (*N Am.*) government-sponsored health insurance. [*medical care*]

Medicean, *a.* of or pertaining to the Medici, a wealthy family who were rulers of Florence in the 15th and 16th cents.

Medici[1], *n.* a noble family of Florence, the city's rulers from 1434 until they died out in 1737. Family members included Catherine de' Medici, Pope Leo X, Pope Clement VII, Marie de' Medici.

Medici[2], *n.* **Lorenzo de',** the Magnificent (1449–92), Italian politician, ruler of Florence from 1469. He was also a poet and a generous patron of the arts.

Medici[3], *n.* **Cosimo de'** (1389–1464), Italian politician and banker. Regarded as the model for Machiavelli's *The Prince,* he dominated the government of Florence from 1434 and was a patron of the arts. He was succeeded by his inept son **Piero de' Medici** (1416–69).

medicine, *n.* a substance, usu. taken internally, used for the alleviation or removal of disease; the art or science of preserving health and curing or alleviating disease, esp. as distinguished from surgery and obstetrics; a term applied by the N American Indians to anything supposed to possess supernatural powers or influence, a charm, a fetish. *v.t.* to treat or cure with or as with medicine. **a taste of one's own medicine,** unpleasant treatment given to one in retaliation. **medicine ball,** *n.* a heavy ball thrown from one person to another as physical exercise. **medicine chest,** *n.* a box, cupboard etc. containing medicine, bandages etc. **medicine-man,** *n.* a witch-doctor; a magician. **medicinable,** *a.* **medicinal,** *a.* **medicinally,** *adv.* **medico,** *n.* (*facet.*) a physician; a doctor; a medical student. [OF *medecine,* L *medicīna,* from *medicus,* see MEDICAL]

medick, *n.* a plant of the genus *Medicago,* allied to the clover, esp. *M. sativa,* lucerne. [L *mēdica,* Gr. *Mēdikē,* fem. of *-kos,* (grass) of Media]

medico MEDICINE.

medico-, *comb.form* medical.

medieval MEDIAEVAL.

Medina, *n.* (Arabic **Madinah**) Saudi Arabian city, about 355 km/220 miles N of Mecca; population (1974) 198,000. It is the second holiest city in the Islamic world, containing the tomb of Mohammed. It produces grain and fruit.

medio-, *comb.form* situated in or pertaining to the middle. [L *medius,* middle]

mediocre, *a.* of middling quality; indifferently good or bad, average, commonplace. **mediocrity,** *n.* the state of being mediocre; a mediocre person. [F *médiocre,* L *mediocris -crem,* from *medius,* as prec.]

meditate, *v.i.* to ponder, to engage in thought (upon); to muse, to cogitate; to engage in contemplation, esp. on religious or spiritual matters. *v.t.* to dwell upon mentally; to plan, to design, to intend. **meditation,** *n.* **meditative,** *a.* **meditatively,** *adv.* **meditativeness,** *n.* **meditator,** *n.* [L *meditātus,* p.p. of *meditārī,* cogn. with Gr. *medesthai,* to think about]

Mediterranean[1], *a.* inland; surrounded by or lying between lands; pertaining to the Mediterranean Sea or the countries surrounding it. [L *mediterrāneus* (*medi-,* MEDIO-, *terra,* land)]

Mediterranean[2], *n.* an inland sea separating Europe from N Africa, with Asia to the E; extreme length 3700 km/2300 miles; area 2,966,000 sq km/1,145,000 sq miles. It is linked to the Atlantic (at the Strait of Gibraltar), Red Sea and Indian Ocean (by the Suez Canal), Black Sea (at the Dardanelles and Sea of Marmara). The main subdivisions are the Adriatic, Aegean, Ionian and Tyrrhenian seas.

medium, *n.* (*pl.* **-dia, -diums**) anything serving as an intermediary, agent or instrument; instrumentality, agency; an intervening substance or element, such as the air or ether, through which forces act, impressions are conveyed etc.; a substance in which germs are developed; a means of communication; an instrument of exchange, as money; a middle or intermediate object, quality, degree etc.; a size of paper, $23\frac{1}{2}\times18\frac{1}{2}$ in. (59·5×47 cm), between demy and royal; (*Painting*) a liquid vehicle for dry pigments; the middle term of a syllogism; (*pl.* **-diums**) a person claiming to receive communications from the spirit world. *a.* intermediate in quantity, quality or degree; average, moderate; middling, mediocre. **medium-range,** *a.* of a missile, having a range between 300 and 3100 miles (about 500 to 5000 km). **medium waves,** *n. pl.* radio waves of between 300 kHz and 3 mHz. **mediumism, mediumship,** *n.* **mediumistic,** *a.* of the nature of, or pertaining to, a spiritualistic medium. **mediumize, -ise,** *v.t.* to act as a spiritualistic medium. [L, neut. of *medius,* middle]

Medjidie, *n.* a Turkish order of knighthood established by Sultan Abdul-Medjid in 1851; a Turkish coin first minted by Sultan Abdul-Medjid. [Turk. *mejīdie*]

medlar, *n.* a rosaceous tree, *Pyrus germanica,* the fruit of which is eaten when beginning to decay. [A-F *medler,* OF *meslier,* L *mespila,* Gr. *mespilē*]

medley, *n.* a mixed or confused mass, esp. of incongruous objects, persons, materials etc.; a musical or literary miscellany. *a.* mixed, multifarious, motley. *v.t.* to make a medley of. [A-F *medlee,* OF *meslee* (F *mêlée*), as MEDDLE]

Médoc, *n.* a red wine from *Médoc,* a district in Gironde, SW France.

medulla, *n.* (*pl.* **-llas, -llae,**) the marrow of bones, esp. that of the spine; the spinal cord; the inner part of certain organs, as the kidneys; the pith of hair; the internal tissue or pith of plants. **medulla oblongata,** *n.* the elongated medulla or continuation of the spinal cord forming the hindmost segment of the brain. **medullary, medullar,** *a.* **medullated, medullose,** *a.* **medullin,** *n.* cellulose or lignin from the pith of certain plants. [L, prob. rel. to *medius,* middle]

medusa, *n.* (*pl.* **-sae**) a jellyfish. **medusal, medusiform,** *a.* **medusan, -oid,** *n., a.* [L, from Gr. *Medousa,* one of the three Gorgons whose head (which turned beholders to stone) was cut off by Perseus and placed by Athene on her aegis]

Medvedev, *n.* **Vadim** (1929–), Soviet politician. He was deputy chief of propaganda (1970–78), was in charge of party relations with communist countries (1986–88), and in 1988 was appointed by the Soviet leader Gorbachev to succeed the conservative Ligachev as head of ideology. He adheres to a firm Leninist line.

meed, *n.* reward, recompense, esp. for merit; †merit, worth. **meedless,** *a.* [OE *mēd* (cp. G *Miete,* also Gr. *misthos,* Sansk. *mīdha,* reward)]

meek, *a.* mild, submissive, humble, tame, gentle, forbearing. †**meeken,** *v.t.* **meekly,** *adv.* **meekness,** *n.* [MG *meoc,* Icel. *mjūkr* (cp. Swed. *mjūk,* Dan. *myg*)]

meerkat, *n.* a small, carnivorous lemur-like mammal of southern Africa. [Dut., sea-cat]

meerschaum, *n.* a white compact hydrous silicate of magnesia, used for tobacco-pipes; a pipe made of this. [G, sea-foam (*Meer,* sea, *Schaum,* foam)]

meet[1], *a.* fit, proper, suitable. **meetly,** *adv.* **meetness,** *n.* [MG *mēte,* OE *gemǣte,* fitting well, cogn. with METE]

meet[2], *v.t.* (*past, p.p.* **met**) to come face to face with; to go to a place so as to join or receive; to reach and touch or unite with (of a road, railway, etc.); to encounter, to confront, to oppose; to experience; to refute; to answer, to satisfy; to pay, to discharge. *v.i.* to come together; to assemble; to come into contact; to be united. *n.* a meeting of persons and hounds for hunting, or of cyclists, athletes etc.; the persons assembled or the place appointed for a meet; (*Austral.*) an appointment. **to meet halfway,** to compromise with. **to meet one's maker** MAKE. **to meet the eye** or **ear,** to be seen or heard. **to meet with,** to come across; to experience; to encounter, to engage. †**well met,** welcome (a greeting). **meeting,** *n.* a coming together, an assembly; the persons assembled; a duel; a race-meeting; a conflux, intersection. **meeting-house,**

n. a dissenting place of worship, esp. of Quakers. [OE *mētan* (cp. Dut. *mœten,* Icel. *mœta,* Swed. *möta*), cogn. with *mōt, gemōt,* MOOT]

meg(a)-, megal(o)-, *comb. form* great, large; one million; (*coll.*) great in number, significance, impressiveness etc. [Gr. *megas,* fem. *megalē,* great]

mega, *a.* (*coll.*) very large in number; very important. [as prec.]

megabit, *n.* (*Comput.*) one million bits; 2^{20} bits.

megabyte, *n.* (*Comput.*) one million bytes; 2^{20} bytes.

megacephalic, megacephalous, *a.* large-headed.

megacycle, *n.* a frequency of a million cycles per second, a megahertz.

megadeath, *n.* one million deaths, esp. in nuclear war.

megadyne, *n.* one million dynes.

megafog, *n.* a fog-signal equipped with several megaphones.

megahertz, *n.* a unit of frequency equal to one million hertz.

Megalichthys, *n.* a genus of fossil ganoid fishes, from the coal-measures.

megalith, *n.* a great stone; a megalithic monument, as a cromlech, stone circle etc. **megalithic,** *a.*

megalomania, *n.* a form of mental disorder characterized by self-exaltation; a craze for over-statement etc. **megalomaniac,** *n., a.*

megalopolis, *n.* a large, densely-populated urban area.

Megalosaurus, *n.* an extinct genus of gigantic carnivorous lizards from the Oolite.

megaparsec, *n.* one million parsecs.

megaphone, *n.* an apparatus for enabling persons to converse at a long distance; a large speaking-trumpet.

megapod, *n.* an Australian or Malaysian mound-bird.

megascope, *n.* a form of solar microscope for throwing enlarged images on a screen; an enlarging camera. **megascopic,** *a.*

megass, *n.* fibrous residue after sugar has been extracted from the cane. [etym. unknown]

megastar, *n.* a very popular, internationally-known star of the cinema, theatre etc. **megastardom,** *n.*

Megatherium, *n.* a genus of extinct gigantic sloth-like edentates from S America. **megatherial,** *a.*

megaton, *n.* one million tons; a unit of explosive power in nuclear weapons, equal to a million tons of TNT.

megavolt, *n.* one million volts.

megawatt, *n.* one million watts.

megerg, *n.* one million ergs.

Megger®, *n.* an instrument for measuring high resistances.

Meghalaya, *n.* state of NE India. **area** 22,500 sq km/ 8,685 sq miles. **capital** Shillong. **products** potatoes, cotton, jute, fruit. **minerals** coal, limestone, white clay, corundum, sillimanite. **population** (1981) 1,328,000, mainly Khasi, Jaintia, and Garo. **religion** Hindu 70%.

Megiddo, *n.* site of a fortress town in N Israel, where Thothmes III defeated the Canaanites about 1469 BC; the Old Testament figure Josiah was killed in battle about 609 BC; and in World War I the British field marshal Allenby broke the Turkish front in 1918. It is identified with Armageddon.

megilp, *n.* a vehicle for colours, consisting of a compound of linseed-oil and mastic varnish. [etym. doubtful]

megohm, *n.* one million ohms.

megrim, *n.* a migraine; a sudden attack due to congestion of the brain causing a horse at work to reel or fall, staggers; (*pl.*) low spirits, depression; a whim, a fad. [corr. of *migrane,* F *migraine,* L *hēmicrania,* Gr. *hēmikrania* (HEMI-, *kranion,* skull)]

†**meinie,** *n.* a household; a body of household attendants; a retinue. [OF *meyné, mesnie,* ult. from L *mansio -ōnem,* MANSION]

Mehemet Ali, *n.* (1769–1849), pasha (governor) of Egypt from 1805, and founder of the dynasty that ruled until 1953. An Albanian in the Ottoman service, he had originally been sent to Egypt to fight the French. As pasha, he established a European-style army and navy, fought his Turkish overlord, 1831 and 1839, and conquered Sudan.

Meier, *n.* **Richard** (1934–), US architect, whose white designs spring from the poetic modernism of the Le Corbusier villas of the 1920s. His abstract style is at its most mature in the *Museum für Kunsthandwerk* (Museum of Arts and Crafts), Frankfurt, West Germany, which was completed in 1984.

Meiji era, *n.* in Japanese history, the reign of Emperor Mutsuhito, 1867–1912.

Meikle, *n.* **Andrew** (1719–1811), Scottish millwright who in 1785 designed and built the first practical threshing machine for separating cereal grains from the husks.

Meinhof, *n.* **Ulrike** (1934–1976), West German urban guerrilla, member of the Baader-Meinhof gang in the 1970s.

Mein Kampf, *n.* book written by Adolf Hitler (1924) during his jail sentence for his part in the abortive 1923 Munich beer-hall putsch. Part autobiography, part political philosophy, the book outlines Hitler's ideas of German expansion, anti-communism and anti-Semitism. [G, my struggle]

meiosis, *n.* litotes, depreciative hyperbole; the stage of a malady when the symptoms tend to abate; the diminution of the number of chromosomes in the cell nucleus. [Gr., from *meioun,* to lessen, from *meiōn,* less]

Meir, *n.* **Golda** (1898–1978), Israeli Labour (*Mapai*) politician, born in Russia. She was foreign minister, 1956–66 and prime minister, 1969–74, resigning after criticism of the Israelis' lack of preparation for the 1973 Arab-Israeli War.

Meissen, *n.* a type of fine porcelain first produced at *Meissen* near Dresden in the 18th century.

Meistersinger, *n.* one of a group of German lyric poets, singers, and musicians of the 14th–16th centuries, who formed guilds for the revival of minstrelsy. Hans Sachs was a Meistersinger, and Richard Wagner's opera, *Die Meistersinger von Nüremberg* (1868) depicts the tradition.

Mekele, *n.* capital of Tigray region, N Ethiopia. Population (1984) 62,000.

Mekong, *n.* river rising as the Za Qu in Tibet and flowing to the South China Sea, through a vast delta (about 200,000 sq km/77,000 sq miles); length 4425 km/2750 miles. It is being developed for irrigation and hydroelectricity by Cambodia, Laos, Thailand and Vietnam.

melamine, *n.* a white crystalline compound used for making synthetic resins; a resin made from this, used in moulded products, adhesives, coatings etc. [G *Melamin*]

melampod, *n.* black hellebore. [L *melampodium,* Gr. *melampodion* (*melas -anos,* black, *pous podos,* foot)]

melampyre, *n.* the cow-wheat, *Melampyrum boreale,* a herbaceous scrophulareous woodland plant. [Gr. *melampūron* (*melas -anos,* black, *pūros,* wheat)]

melan- MELAN(O)-.

melanaemia, (*esp. N Am.*) **melanemia,** *n.* a morbid condition in which the blood contains an excessive proportion of black colouring-matter. **melanaemic,** *a.* [MELAN-, Gr. *haima,* blood]

melancholia, *n.* a mental disorder, often preceding mania, characterized by lowness of spirits, frequently with suicidal tendencies (formerly supposed to be due to excess of black bile). [as foll.]

melancholy, *n.* a gloomy, dejected state of mind; sadness, gloom, depression, despondency; (*poet.*) pensive contemplation; melancholia. *a.* sad, gloomy, depressed in spirits; mournful, saddening; pensive; afflicted with melancholia. **melancholic,** *a.* **melancholically,** *adv.* [OF *melancolie,* L and Gr. *melancholia* (MELAN-, *cholos,* bile)]

Melanchthon, *n.* **Philip** (assumed name of Philip Schwarzerd) (1497–1560), German theologian who helped Luther prepare a German translation of the New Testament. In 1521 he issued the first systematic formulation of Protestant theology, and composed the Confession of Augsburg (1530).

Melanesian, *a.* of or pertaining to Melanesia, the group of islands in the Pacific ocean lying to the east of New

Guinea. *n.* a native or inhabitant of Melanesia. [Gr. *melas -anos,* black, *nēsos,* an island]

mélange, *n.* a mixture, medley or miscellany; a mixed worsted yarn. [F, from *mêler,* to mix, see MEDDLE]

melanic, *a.* black, dark-complexioned; applied to the black pigment characteristic of melanosis. **melanin,** *n.* a black or dark brown pigment occurring in the hair and skin of dark-skinned races. **melanism,** *n.* excess of colouring-matter in the skin, hair and tissues; a disease producing blackness in plants. **melanistic,** *a.* **melanoid,** *a.* **melanoma,** *n.* a malignant tumour with dark pigmentation, esp. on the skin. **melanosis,** *n.* an organic affection, characterized by a deposit of black pigment in the tissues; black cancer. **melanotic,** *a.* **melanous,** *a.* dark or sallow-complexioned. **melanuria,** *n.* a disorder characterized by blackness of the urine. **melanuric,** *a.* [MELAN-, -IC]

melanism MELANIC.

melanite, *n.* a black variety of garnet.

melan(o)-, *comb.form* dark, black.

melanochroi, *n.pl.* a subdivision of the leiotrichi, comprising the races with dark hair and pale complexion. **melanochroic, melanochrous,** *a.* [pl. of Gr. *melanochroos* (*chroa,* skin, or *ōchros,* pale)]

melasma, *n.* a skin disease characterized by excess of black pigment. [Gr., from *melas,* black]

melatonin, *n.* a hormone produced by the pineal gland. [Gr. *melas,* black]

Melba toast, *n.* very thin crisp toast. [named after Dame Nellie *Melba,* 1861–1931, Austral. operatic soprano]

Melbourne, *n.* capital of Victoria, Australia, near the mouth of the river Yarra; population (1986) 2,943,000. Industries include engineering, shipbuilding, electronics, chemicals, food processing, clothing and textiles.

Melchite, Melkite, *n.* member of a Christian church in Syria, Egypt, Lebanon and Israel. The Melchite Church was founded in Syria in the 6th–7th cents. after accepting Byzantine rule at the council of Chalcedon 451 (unlike the Maronites). In 1754 some Melchites broke away to form a Uniate Church with Rome; the remainder belong to the Orthodox Church.

meld¹, *v.t., v.i.* (*Cards*) to declare for a score. [G *melden,* to announce]

meld², *v.t., v.i.* to mix, blend, combine. [*melt,* weld²]

mêlée, *n.* a confused hand-to-hand fight, an affray. [F]

Meliboean, *a.* alternately responding. [*Meliboeus,* shepherd in Virgil's first Eclogue]

melic, *a.* for singing, applied to certain Greek lyric poetry. [Gr. *melikos,* from *melos,* song]

Méliès, *n.* **Georges** (1861–1938), French film pioneer, born in Paris. From 1896–1908 he made over 1000 films, mostly fantasies, such as *Le Voyage dans la Lune/A Trip to the Moon* (1902). He developed trick effects such as slow motion, double exposure and dissolves, and in 1897 built Europe's first film studio at Montreuil.

melilot, *n.* a plant of the leguminous genus *Melilotus.* [OF, from late L and Gr. *melilōtos* (*meli,* honey, LOTUS)]

melinite, *n.* a French explosive containing picric acid; a soft unctuous clay like yellow ochre. [F *mélinite* (Gr. *mēlinos,* from *mēlon,* apple)]

meliorate, *v.t.* to make better. *v.i.* to grow better. **melioration,** *n.* **meliorism,** *n.* the doctrine that society etc. may be improved by persistent practical effort. **meliorist,** *n.* [late L *meliōrātus,* p.p. of *meliōrāre,* from L *melior,* better]

meliphagous, *a.* belonging to the family of birds Meliphagidae or honey-eaters. [Gr. *meli,* honey, *-phagos,* eating, from *phagein,* to eat]

melisma, *n.* (*pl.* **-mata**) a melodic embellishment; a group of notes sung to a single syllable. **melismatic,** *a.* [Gr., a song tune]

†**mell,** *v.t.* to mix, to mingle. *v.i.* to meddle, to concern oneself (with); to mingle, esp. in combat; to mix or associate (with). [OF *meller,* var. of *mesler,* to MEDDLE]

melliferous, *a.* producing or yielding honey. †**mellific,** *a.* **mellification,,** *n.* †**melligenous** , *a.* **mellivorous,** *a.* [L *mellifer* (*mel mellis,* honey, -FEROUS)]

mellifluous, *a.* flowing smoothly and sweetly. **mellifluent,** *a.* **mellifluence,** *n.* [L *mellifluus* (*mel mellis,* honey, *fluere,* to flow)]

mellite, *n.* native mellitate of aluminium, honeystone. **mellitate, mellate,** *n.* a salt of mellitic acid. **mellitic,** *a.* applied to an acid found in mellite in combination with aluminium. [L *mel mellis,* honey, -ITE]

Mellon, *n.* **Andrew William** (1855–1937), US financier who donated his art collection to found the National Gallery of Art, Washington DC, 1941. His son, **Paul Mellon** (1907–) was its president (1963–79). He funded Yale University's Centre for British Art, New Haven, Connecticut, and donated important works of art to both collections.

mellophone, *n.* a brass musical instrument similar in tone to a French horn. [*mellow*, -PHONE]

mellow, *a.* fully ripe, pulpy, sweet; of earth, rich, friable; of tones and colours, soft and rich; ripened or softened by age and experience; genial, kindly; (*coll.*) jolly, half tipsy. *v.t.* to ripen, mature, soften. *v.i.* to become ripe, mature or softened, by age etc. **mellowly,** *adv.* **mellowness,** *n.* **mellowy,** *a.* [perh. from OE *melo,* MEAL², perh. conf. with *mearu,* tender]

melodeon, -dion, *n.* a wind-instrument with a row of reeds and a keyboard. [earlier *melodium,* Latinized from MELODY]

melodic, melodious etc. MELODY.

melodrama, *n.* a sensational play, film, novel etc. with a plot characterized by startling situations; orig. a dramatic composition with songs intermixed; sensational and extravagant events, behaviour or speech. **melodramatic,** *a.* **melodramatically,** *adv.* **melodramatist,** *n.* **melodramatize, -ise,** *v.t.* [earlier *melodrame,* F *mélodrame* (Gr. *melos,* song, DRAMA)]

melody, *n.* an agreeable succession of sounds, esp. of simple tones in the same key, an air or tune; a simple setting of words to music; the chief part in harmonic music, the air; music. **melodic, melodious,** *a.* of, characterized by or producing melody; musical, sounding sweetly. **melodiously,** *adv.* **melodiousness,** *n.* **melodist,** *n.* **melodize, -ise,** *v.t. v.i.* [OF *melodie,* late L and Gr. *melōdia,* from *melōdos,* singing, musical (*melos,* song, *ōdē,* see ODE)]

melon, *n.* a kind of gourd, esp. *Cucumis melo,* the musk-melon, and *Citrullus vulgaris,* the water-melon. **melon-cactus, -thistle,** *n.* a tropical American cactaceous plant. [OF, from late L *mēlo -ōnem,* for *mēlopepo,* Gr. *mēlopepōn* (*mēlon,* apple, fruit, *pepōn,* a kind of gourd)]

Melpomene, *n.* (*Gr. Myth.*) the Muse of tragedy. [Gr. *Melpomenē*]

melt, *v.i.* (*p.p.* **melted, molten**), to pass from a solid to a liquid state by heat; to dissolve; to be dissipated, to disappear, to vanish (away); to be softened to kindly influences, to give way; to dissolve in tears; to dissolve or blend (into); *v.t.* to make liquid by heat; to dissolve; to soften to tenderness; to dissipate. *n.* a period of melting, a thaw. **meltdown,** *n.* the melting of fuel rods in a nuclear reactor, often causing the escape of radiation into the environment; an economic collapse. **melting-point,** *n.* the temperature at which a solid begins to melt. **melting-pot,** *n.* a crucible; a situation or place where there is a mixture of races, cultures, ideas etc. **in the melting-pot,** with an undecided future. **meltwater,** *n.* water produced by melting snow or ice, esp. from a glacier. **melter,** *n.* **meltingly,** *adv.* **meltingness,** *n.* [OE *meltan,* intr., and *mieltan,* tr. (cp. Icel. *melta*), cogn. with Gr. *meldein,* to melt, and L *mollis,* soft]

melton, *n.* a jacket worn in hunting; a stout make of cloth without nap, used largely for overcoats. [*Melton* Mowbray, in Leicestershire]

Melville, *n.* **Herman** (1819–91), US writer, whose *Moby-Dick* (1851) was inspired by his whaling experiences in the South Seas, the setting for other fiction, such as *Typee* (1846) and *Omoo* (1847). He published several volumes of verse, and short stories (*The Piazza Tales*, 1856). *Billy Budd* was completed just before his death and published 1924.

member, *n.* a limb, a part or organ of the body; the penis; a component part or element of an organism or complex whole; one belonging to a society or body; a branch or division of a society or organization; a set of figures or symbols forming part of a mathematical expression. **Member of Parliament,** one representing a constituency in the House of Commons. **memberless,** *a.* **membership,** *n.* the state of being a member; (a number of) members. **membral,** *a.* (*Anat., Zool.*). [F *membre,* L *membrum*]

membrane, *n.* a thin sheet of tissue lining or covering parts of an organism; a morbid tissue produced in certain diseases; a skin of parchment or vellum. **membranaceous, membraneous, membraniform, membranous,** *a.* of or like a membrane; very thin, translucent. [L *membrāna,* as prec.]

memento, *n.* (*pl.* **-os, -oes**), a memorial, a souvenir, a reminder. **memento mori,** *n.* an emblem of mortality, esp. a skull (L., remember you must die). [L, imper. of *meminisse,* to remember]

Memlinc, *n.* (**Memling**) **Hans** (*c.* 1430–94), Flemish painter, born near Frankfurt-am-Main, Germany, but active in Bruges. He painted religious subjects and portraits. Some of his works are in the Hospital of St John, Bruges, including the *Adoration of the Magi* (1479).

memo, *n.* (*pl.* **memos**) short for MEMORANDUM.

memoir, *n.* (*usu. pl.*) an account of events or transactions in which the narrator took part; an autobiography or a biography; a communication to some learned society on a special subject. **memoirist,** *n.* [F *mémoire,* L *memoria,* MEMORY]

memorabilia, *n.pl.* things worthy to be remembered. [L, memorable things, as foll.]

memorable, *a.* worthy to be remembered; notable, remarkable. †**memorableness, memorability,** *n.* **memorably,** *adv.* [L *memorābilis,* from *memorāre,* to call to remembrance, from *memor,* see MEMORY]

memorandum, *n.* (*pl.* **-dums, -da**) a note to help the memory; a brief record or note; a short informal letter, usu. unsigned, with the sender's name etc. printed at the head; (*Law*) a summary, outline or draft of an agreement etc. [L, neut. ger. of *memorāre,* see prec.]

memorial, *a.* preservative of memory; commemorative; preserved in memory. *n.* that which preserves the memory of something; a monument, festival etc. commemorating a person, event etc.; a written statement of facts, esp. of the nature of a petition, remonstrance etc.; an informal diplomatic paper; (*usu. pl.*) a chronicle or record. **Memorial Day** DECORATION DAY. **memorialist,** *n.* **memorialize, -ise,** *v.t.* [OF, L *memoriālis*]

memorize, -ise, *v.t.* to commit to memory; to learn by heart.

memory, *n.* the mental faculty that retains and recalls previous ideas and impressions; the exercise of this faculty, remembrance, recollection; something that is remembered; the state of being remembered; posthumous reputation; the period during which anything is remembered; (*Comput.*) a device for storing data in a computer; the capacity of a material to return to its former condition after distortion; †a memorial, a memento. †**memorative,** *a.* [A-F *memorie,* OF *memoire,* L *memoria,* from *memor,* mindful, redupl. of *mer-,* to remember (cp. Gr. *merimna,* care, thought)]

Memphis[1]**,** *n.* a ruined city beside the Nile, 19 km/12 miles south of Cairo, Egypt. Once the centre of the worship of Ptah, it was the earliest capital of a united Egypt under King Menes about 3200 BC, but was superseded by Thebes under the new empire, 1570 BC. It was later used as a stone quarry, but the 'cemetery city' of Sakkara survives, with the step pyramid built for King Zoser by Imhotep, probably the world's oldest stone building.

Memphis[2]**,** *n.* industrial city (pharmaceuticals, food processing, cotton, timber, tobacco) on the Mississippi River, in Tennessee, US; population (1986) 960,000.

mem sahib, *n.* a term formerly applied to European married women living in India. [ma'am, SAHIB]

men, *pl.* MAN.

menace, *n.* a threat; (*coll.*) a nuisance. *v.t.* to threaten. **menacer,** *n.* **menacing,** *a.* **menacingly,** *adv.* [OF, from L *mināćia,* from *minax -ācis* threatening, from *minae,* threats]

ménage, *n.* a household; housekeeping, household management. **ménage à trois,** an arrangement whereby a couple live together with the lover of one or both of them (F, household of three). [OF, earlier *mesnage, maisnage,* pop. L *mansiōnāticum* from *mansio,* MANSION]

menagerie, *n.* a collection of wild animals; a place or enclosure where wild animals are kept. [F *ménagerie,* as prec.]

menagogue, *n.* a medicine that promotes the flow of the menses. [F *ménagogue* (Gr. *mēn,* month, *agōgos* leading)]

Menander, *n.* (*c.* 342–291 BC), Greek comic dramatist, born in Athens. Of his 105 plays only fragments (many used as papier-mâché for Egyptian mummy cases) and Latin adaptations were known prior to the discovery (1957) of the *Dyscholos/The Bad-Tempered Man.*

menarche, *n.* the first onset of menstruation in a woman's life. **menarcheal,** *a.* [L, from Gr. *mēn,* month, *archē,* beginning]

Mencken, *n.* **H(enry) L(ouis)** (1880–1956), US essayist and critic, known as 'the sage of Baltimore'. His unconventionally phrased, satiric contributions to *Smart Set* and *US Mercury* (both of which periodicals he edited) aroused great controversy. His book *The American Language* (1918) is often revised.

mend, *v.t.* to repair, to restore, to make good; to improve, to make better; to correct, to amend. *v.i.* to grow better, to improve; to amend, to recover health. *n.* the act or process of mending; improvement; a repaired part (in a garment etc.). **on the mend,** improving, recuperating. **to mend one's fences** FENCE. **mendable,** *a.* **mender,** *n.* [from AMEND]

mendacious, *a.* given to lying, untruthful. **mendaciously,** *adv.* **mendacity,** *n.* [L *mendax -ācis,* lying, cogn. with *mentīrī,* to lie, -OUS]

Mendel, *n.* **Gregor Johann** (1822–84), Austrian biologist, founder of genetics. His experiments with successive generations of peas gave the basis for his theory of particulate inheritance rather than blending, involving dominant and recessive characters. His results, published 1865–69, remained unrecognized until early this century.

mendelevium, *n.* an artificially-produced transuranic element, at. no. 101; chem. symbol Md. [Russian chemist D.I. *Mendeleyev,* see foll.]

Mendeleyev, *n.* **Dmitri Ivanovich** (1834–1907). Russian chemist who framed the periodic law in chemistry which states that the chemical properties of the elements depend on their relative atomic masses. This law is the basis of the periodic table of elements.

Mendelism, *n.* a theory of heredity based on researches and generalizations by G. J. *Mendel* (see above), showing that the characters of the parents of cross-bred offspring reappear by certain proportions in successive generations according to definite laws. **Mendelian,** *a.* **Mendelize, -ise,** *v.t.*

Mendelssohn (-Bartholdy), *n.* **(Jakob Ludwig) Felix** (1809–47), German composer, also a pianist and conductor. Among his many works are *A Midsummer Night's Dream* (1827); the *Fingal's Cave* overture (1832); and five symphonies, which include the Reformation (1830), the Italian (1833), and the Scottish (1842).

Mendes, *n.* **Filho Francisco 'Chico' ,** Brazilian environmentalist and labour leader. Opposed to the destruction of Brazil's rainforests, he organized itinerant rubber tappers into the Workers' Party (PT) and was assassinated.

Mendès-France, *n.* **Pierre** (1907–82), French prime minister and foreign minister (1954–55). He extricated France from the war in Indochina, and prepared the way for Tunisian independence.

mendicant, *a.* begging; reduced to beggary. *n.* a beggar; a member of a mendicant order. **mendicant orders,** *n.pl.* monastic orders subsisting on alms. **mendicancy,** *n.* **mendicity**, *n.* [L *mendīcans -antem,* pres.p. of *mendīcāre,* from *mendīcus,* beggar]

Mendoza, *n.* **Antonio de** (*c.* (1490–1552), first Spanish viceroy of New Spain (Mexico), 1535–51. He attempted to develop agriculture and mining and supported the church in its attempts to convert the Indians. The system he established lasted until the 19th cent. He was subsequently viceroy of Peru, 1551–52.

Menem, *n.* **Carlos Saul** (1935–), Argentinian politician, president from 1989; leader of the Peronist (Justice Party) movement. As president, he improved relations with the United Kingdom.

Menes, *n.* (*c.* 3200 BC), traditionally, the first king of the first dynasty of ancient Egypt. He is said to have founded Memphis and organized worship of the gods.

menfolk, *n.pl.* the men, esp. of a particular family or community.

Mengistu, *n.* **Haile Mariam** (1937–), Ethiopian soldier and socialist politician, head of state from 1977 (president from 1987). As an officer in the Ethiopian army, he took part in the overthrow in 1974 of Emperor Haile Selassie and in 1977 led another coup, becoming head of state. He was confronted with severe problems of drought and secessionist uprisings, but survived with help from the USSR and the West. In 1987 civilian rule was formally reintroduced, but with the Marxist-Leninist Workers' Party of Ethiopia the only legally permitted party.

Mengs, *n.* **Anton Raffael** (1728–79), German neoclassical painter, born in Bohemia. He was court painter in Dresden (1745) and in Madrid (1761); he then worked alternately in Rome and Spain. The ceiling painting *Parnassus* (1761, Villa Albani, Rome) is an example of his work.

menhaden, *n.* a N American sea-fish allied to the herring. [Am. Ind. *munnawhattsang*]

menhir, *n.* a prehistoric monument consisting of a tall upright stone. [Bret. *men,* stone, *hir,* long]

menial, *a.* pertaining to or suitable for servants; servile, low, mean. *n.* a domestic servant; one doing servile work. **menially,** *adv.* [A-F, as MEINIE]

meningitis MENINX.

meninx, *n.* (*pl.* **meninges**) one of the three membranes enclosing the brain and spinal cord, comprising the dura mater, arachnoid and pia mater. **meningeal**, *a.* **meningitis**, *n.* inflammation of the meninges. **meningocele**, *n.* protrusion of the meninges through the skull. [Gr.]

meniscus, *n.* (*pl.* **-sci**) a lens convex on one side and concave on the other; the top of a liquid column made convex or concave by capillarity (as mercury in a barometer). **meniscal,** *a.* [Gr. *mēniskos,* a crescent, dim. of *mēnē,* moon]

menisperm, *n.* a plant of the Menispermaceae, containing the cocculus indicus. [Gr. *mēnē,* as prec., SPERM]

Mennonite, *n.* a member of a Protestant Christian sect, originating in Zürich in 1523. Members refuse to hold civil office or do military service, and reject infant baptism. They were later named Mennonites after Menno Simons (1496–1559), leader of a group in Holland. [*Menno* Simons, 1496–1561, its first leader]

menology, *n.* a calendar of months, esp. the martyrology of the Greek Church. [late Gr. *mēnologion* (*mēn mēnos,* month, -LOGY)]

menopause, *n.* final cessation of the menses, change of life. [Gr. *mēn mēnos,* month]

menorah, *n.* a candelabrum with several branches, used in Jewish worship. [Heb., candlestick]

menorrhagia, *n.* excessive flow of the menses. [Gr. *-ragia,* from *rhēgnunai* to break forth]

menorrhoea, *n.* ordinary flow of the menses. [Gr. *rhoia,* flow]

Mensa International, *n.* an organization founded in the UK in 1945 with membership limited to those passing an 'intelligence' test. Criticized by many who believe that intelligence is not satisfactorily measured by IQ tests alone.

mensal[1]**,** *a.* of, pertaining to or used at the table. [L *mensa,* table]

mensal[2]**,** *a.* monthly. [as foll.]

menses, *n.pl.* the periodic flow of blood from the uterus of women, usu. occurring once every lunar month. **menstrual, menstruous,** *a.* monthly; pertaining to the menses. **menstruant,** *a.* **menstruate,** *v.i.* to undergo menstruation. **menstruation,** *n.* the menses. [L, pl. of *mensis,* month]

Menshevik, *n.* member of the minority of the Russian Social Democratic Party, who split from the Bolsheviks in 1903. The Mensheviks believed in a large, loosely organized party, and that before socialist revolution could occur in Russia, capitalist society must develop further. During the Russian Revolution they had limited power and set up a government in Georgia, but were suppressed in 1922. [Rus., member of a minority, from *men'she,* fewer]

mens sana in corpore sano , a sound mind in a sound body, used to suggest that mental well-being is dependent on physical fitness. [L]

menstruate etc. MENSES.

menstruum, *n.* (*pl.* **-trua**) any fluid that dissolves a solid, a solvent. [L, neut. of *menstruus,* monthly, from *mensis,* month (from the alchemistic analogy with the menstrual flow)]

mensurable, *a.* measurable; (*Mus.*) having rhythm and measure. **mensurability**, *n.* **mensural,** *a.* [late L *mensūrābilis,* from *mensūrāre* to measure, from *mensūra,* MEASURE]

mensuration, *n.* the act or practice of measuring; the branch of mathematics concerned with the determination of lengths, areas and volumes. [late L *mensūrātio,* as prec.]

-ment, *suf.* forming nouns denoting result, state, action etc., as in *agreement, bereavement, enticement, impediment ornament*. [OF, from L *-mentum*]

mental[1]**,** *a.* pertaining to the mind, intellectual; due to or done by the mind; of or concerning psychiatric illness; slightly deranged in mind. **mental age,** *n.* the intellectual maturity of an individual expressed in terms of the average intellectual maturity of a child of a specified age. **mental arithmetic,** *n.* arithmetic done in the head, without writing it down or using a calculator. **mental science,** *n.* psychology, mental philosophy. **mentalism,** *n.* the theory that nothing exists outside the mind. **mentalist,** *n.* **mentality**, *n.* mental attitude or disposition. **mentalize, -ise,** *v.t.* **mentalization, -isation,** *n.* **mentally,** *adv.* **mentation,** *n.* mental action; cerebration. [F, from late L *mentālis,* from *mens mentis* mind]

mental[2]**,** *a.* of or pertaining to the chin. [F, from L *mentum,* chin]

menthol, *n.* a waxy crystalline substance obtained from oil of peppermint, used as a local anaesthetic for neuralgia etc. **mentholated,** *a.* esp. of cigarettes, treated with menthol. [G (L *mentha,* MINT[2], -OL)]

mention, *n.* a concise notice, allusion to (or of); a naming. *v.t.* to refer to, to allude to; to indicate by naming without describing. **honourable mention,** a distinction sometimes awarded to a competitor who has just failed to win a prize. **mention in dispatches,** (*Mil.*) reference by name (in official dispatches) to an officer who has done well in battle. **mentionable,** *a.* [F, from L *mentio -ōnem,* rel. to *mens mentis* see MENTAL[1]]

mentor, *n.* a faithful monitor, a wise counsellor. †**mentorial**, *a.* **mentorship,** *n.* [F, from Gr. *Mentōr,* counsellor to Telemachus]

menu, *n.* a bill of fare; (*Comput.*) a list of alternative operations, topics etc. which the operator can choose from. [F, orig. small, L *minūtus,* MINUTE[1]]

Menuhin, *n.* **Yehudi** (1916–), US violinist. A child prodigy, he achieved great depth of interpretation, and was often accompanied on the piano by his sister Hephzibah (1921–81). He conducted his own chamber orchestra and founded a school in Surrey, England in 1963 for training young musicians.

Menzies[1]**,** *n.* **Robert Gordon** (1894–1978), Australian politician, leader of the United Australia (now Liberal) Party and prime minister (1939–41) and (1949–66).

Menzies[2], *n.* **William Cameron** (1896–1957), US art director of films, later a film director, who was one of Hollywood's most imaginative and talented designers. He was responsible for the sets of such films as *Gone With the Wind* (1939) and *Foreign Correspondent* (1940). His films as director include *Things to Come* (1936) and *Invaders from Mars* (1953).

meow MIAOW.

MEP, (*abbr.*) Member of the European Parliament.

Mephistopheles, *n.* a tempter; a diabolical person. **Mephistophelian, -lean,** *a.* sardonical, cynically sceptical, scoffing. [the spirit in ancient legend to whom Faust sells his soul, etym. doubtful]

mephitis, *n.* a foul, offensive or pestilential exhalation; (**Mephitis**) a genus of American carnivores containing the skunks. **mephitic, -ical,** *a.* **mephitism,** *n.* [L]

-mer, *comb.form.* (*Chem.*) a substance of a specified type.

Mercalli scale, *n.* one used to measure the *intensity* of an earthquake. It differs from the Richter scale, which measures *magnitude*. It is named after the Italian seismologist Giuseppe Mercalli (1850–1914).

mercantile, *a.* commercial, pertaining to buying and selling; mercenary. **mercantile marine** MERCHANT SERVICE. **mercantilism,** *n.* **mercantilist,** *n.* [F, from It. *mercantile,* from *mercante,* MERCHANT]

†**mercatante** MARCANTANT (*Shak.*).

Mercator, *n.* **Gerardus** (1512–94), latinized form of the name of the Flemish map-maker Gerhard Kremer. He devised the first modern atlas, showing **Mercator's projection** in which the parallels and meridians on maps are drawn uniformly at 90°. It is often used for navigational charts, because compass courses can be drawn as straight lines, but the true area of countries is increasingly distorted the further N or S they are from the equator.

Mercedes-Benz, *n.* a German car-manufacturing company created by a merger of the Daimler and Benz factories in 1926. The first cars to carry the Mercedes name were those built by Gottlieb Daimler, 1901. In the 1930s Mercedes-Benz dominated Grand Prix races. The W196, which made its debut 1954, was one of the finest racing cars of the postwar era. Following a disaster at Le Mans 1955, when 80 spectators lost their lives after an accident involving a Mercedes, the company withdrew from motor sport until 1989.

mercenary, *a.* hired or serving for money; done from or actuated by motives of gain; venal. *n.* one who is hired, esp. a soldier hired in foreign service. **mercenarily,** *adv.* **mercenariness,** *n.* [L *mercēnārius,* from *merces -cēdis* reward, from *merx -cis,* see foll.]

mercer, *n.* one who deals in silk, cotton, woollen and linen goods. **mercery,** *n.* [F *mercier,* through pop. L *merciarius,* from L *merx mercis,* MERCHANDISE]

mercerize, -ise, *v.t.* to treat cotton fabrics with an alkaline solution in preparation for dyeing. **mercerization, -isation,** *n.* [J. *Mercer,* 1791–1866, patentee of process]

merchandise, *n.* articles of commerce; commodities for purchase; †trade, commerce. *v.t. v.i.* to trade, to barter. **merchandiser,** *n.* **merchandising,** *n.* promotion and advertising of goods for sale. [F *marchandise,* as foll.]

merchant, *n.* one who carries on trade on a large scale, esp. with foreign countries; (*N Am., Sc.*) a shopkeeper, a tradesman; †a merchant vessel; †a fellow; (*coll.*) one given to, as *speed merchant*. *a.* mercantile, commercial. **merchant bank,** *n.* a private bank whose business chiefly involves dealing in bills of exchange and underwriting new security issues. **merchant banker,** *n.* **merchantman,** *n.* a merchant ship. **merchant navy,** *n.* collective name for sea-going vessels other than those of the Royal Navy. **merchant prince,** *n.* a wealthy merchant. **merchant service,** *n.* personnel etc. of shipping employed in commerce. **merchant ship,** *n.* ship for conveying merchandise. **merchantable,** *a.* **merchantlike,** *a.* [OF *marchand, marchant,* from L *mercans -antem,* pres.p. of *mercāri,* to trade, from *merx mercis,* MERCHANDISE]

Merchant, *n.* **Ismael** (1936–), Indian film producer, known for his stylish collaborations with James Ivory on films including *Shakespeare Wallah* (1965), *The Europeans* (1979), *Heat and Dust* (1983), *A Room with a View* (1986), and *Maurice* (1987).

Merchants Adventurers, *n.* trading company founded in 1407 and consisting of guilds and traders in many N European ports. In direct opposition to the Hanseatic League, it came to control 75% of English overseas trade by 1550.

Mercia, *n.* an Anglo-Saxon kingdom that emerged in the 6th cent. By the late 8th cent. it dominated all England south of the Humber, but from about 825 came under the power of Wessex. Mercia eventually came to denote an area bounded by the Welsh border, the river Humber, East Anglia and the river Thames.

merciful etc. MERCY.

Merckx, *n.* **Eddie** (1945–), Belgian cyclist known as 'the Cannibal'. He won the Tour de France a joint record five times (1969–74).

mercury, *n.* a liquid, silvery, toxic, metallic element, at. no. 80; chem. symbol Hg; (**Mercury**) the Roman god of commerce, identified with the Greek Hermes, the messenger of the gods; a planet (see separate article below); a messenger; a common title for a newspaper. **mercurial,** *a.* pertaining to the god Mercury; flighty, volatile, fickle; pertaining to, consisting of or caused by mercury. *n.* a preparation containing mercury, used as a drug. **mercurialism,** *n.* a morbid condition due to excessive use of mercurial drugs. †**mercurialist,** *n.* **mercuriality,** *n.* **mercurialize, -ise,** *v.t.* **mercurially,** *adv.* **mercuric,** *a.* containing mercury in the divalent state. †**mercurify,** *v.t.* to obtain mercury from (metallic minerals); to mercurialize. †**mercurification,** *n.* **mercurous,** *a.* containing mercury in the monovalent state. [A-F *Mercurie,* OF *Mercure,* L *Mercurius*]

Mercury, *n.* in astronomy, the closest planet to the Sun, at an average distance of 58,000,000 km/36,000,000 miles. Its diameter is 4880 km/3030 miles, its mass 0.056 that of Earth. Mercury orbits the Sun every 88 days, and spins on its axis every 59 days. On its sunward side the surface temperature reaches over 400°C, but on the 'night' side it falls to –170°C. Mercury has an atmosphere with minute traces of argon and helium. The US space probe Mariner 10 (1974) discovered that its surface is cratered by meteorite impacts. Mercury has no moons.

Mercury project, *n.* the US project to put a human in space in the one-seat Mercury spacecraft (1961–63).

mercy, *n.* a disposition to temper justice with mildness; forbearance, clemency, compassion; an act of clemency, pity or compassion; pardon, forgiveness; control, discretion, liberty to punish or spare; (*coll.*) something to be thankful for. **at the mercy of,** wholly in the power of. **for mercy's sake,** an exclamation or appeal for mercy, or of expostulation. **sister of mercy** SISTER. **mercy dash, flight,** etc., *n.* a trip, flight etc. to bring help to a sick or injured person. **mercy killing,** *n.* euthanasia. **mercy-seat,** *n.* (*Bibl.*) the covering of the ark of the Covenant; the throne of God as dispenser of mercy. **merciful,** †**merciable,** *a.* **mercifully,** *adv.* **mercifulness,** *n.* †**mercify,** *v.t.* **merciless,** *a.* **mercilessly,** *adv.* **mercilessness,** *n.* [F *merci,* L *merces -cēdem,* reward, late L, pity, from *merx -cis,* MERCHANDISE]

merdivorous, *a.* feeding upon dung. [L *merda,* dung; *vorare,* to devour]

mere[1], *n.* a lake, a pool. [OE (cp. Dut. *meer,* G *Meer,* Icel. *marr,* L *mare,* sea)]

mere[2], *a.* such and no more; absolute, unqualified. **merely,** *adv.* purely, only, solely. [L *merus,* pure, unadulterated]

mere[3], *n.* a boundary; a boundary-stone; a landmark. †*v.t.* to limit, to mark off. †**mere-stone,** *n.* [OE *mǣre, gemǣre* (cp. MDut. *mere, meer,* Icel. *landa-mæri,* also

L *mūrus,* wall)]

mere[4] MERI.

-mere, *comb.form* part, segment. [Gr. *meros,* part]

meretricious, *a.* pertaining to or befitting a harlot; alluring by false or empty show; unreal, tawdry. **meretriciously,** *adv.* **meretriciousness,** *n.* [L *meretrīcius,* from *meretrix -trīcis,* harlot, from *merērī,* to earn, see MERIT]

merganser, *n.* the goosander and other diving or fish-eating ducks belonging to the genus *Mergus.* [L *mergus,* a diving-bird, *anser,* goose]

merge, *v.t.* to cause to be swallowed up or absorbed, to sink (in a larger estate, title etc.). *v.i.* to be absorbed or swallowed up; to lose individuality or identity (in). **mergence,** *n.* **merger,** *n.* the merging of an estate, limited company etc. into another; extinction, absorption. [L *mergere,* to dip (partly through low F *merger*)]

Mergenthaler, *n.* **Ottmar** (1854–99), German-American who invented a typesetting method. He went to the US in 1872 and developed the first linotype machine (for casting metal type in complete lines), 1876–86.

meri, mere, *n.* a war-club; a greenstone trinket shaped like this. [Maori]

mericarp, *n.* one of the two carpels forming the fruit of umbelliferous plants. [F *méricarpe* (Gr. *meros,* part, *karpos,* fruit)]

Mérida, *n.* capital of Yucatán state, Mexico, a centre of the sisal industry; population (1986) 580,000.

meridian, *a.* pertaining to midday or to a geographical or astronomical meridian, or to the point or period of highest splendour or vigour. *n.* a great circle drawn through the poles and the zenith of any given place on the earth's surface; the line in which the plane of this circle intersects the earth's surface; the time when the sun or other heavenly body crosses this; midday, noon; culmination, zenith, point of highest splendour or vigour. **first, prime, meridian,** a meridian from which longitude is reckoned, usu. that of Greenwich. **meridional,** *a.* pertaining to a meridian; highest, culminating; pertaining to the south, esp. of Europe; running north and south, as a mountain range. *n.* an inhabitant of the south, usu. of the south of France. **meridionality,** *n.* **meridionally,** *adv.* [OF *meridien,* L *merīdiānus,* from *merīdiēs,* midday (*medius,* middle, *diēs,* day)]

Mérimée, *n.* **Prosper** (1803–70), French author. Among his works are the stories *Colomba* (1841), *Carmen* (1846), and the *Lettres à une inconnue/Letters to an Unknown Girl* (1873).

meringue, *n.* a confection of white of eggs, sugar etc., used as icing; a cake made of this. [F, etym. doubtful]

merino, *n.* a breed of sheep introduced from Spain, valuable for their fine wool; a fine woollen dress-fabric, orig. of this wool; a fine woollen yarn used for hosiery. *a.* pertaining to this breed of sheep; made of merino. **pure merino,** (*Austral., coll.*) descendant of an early settler with no convict connection. [Sp., prob. from L *mājōrīnus* (perh. overseer or major-domo), from *mājor,* greater]

meristem, *n.* vegetable tissue or cells in process of growth. **meristematic,** *a.* [from Gr. *meristos,* from *merizein,* to divide (ending assim. to PHLOEM, XYLEM)]

merit, *n.* the quality of deserving, desert; excellence deserving honour or reward; worth, worthiness; a reward or recompense, a mark or award of merit; (*pl.*) the essential rights and wrongs of a case. *v.t.* to deserve, to earn; to be entitled to receive as a reward; to have a just title to. *v.i.* to acquire merit. **Order of Merit** ORDER. **merited,** *a.* **meritocracy,** *n.* (a society ruled by) those who have gained their positions through talent, intellect or industriousness, not through their family background, inherited wealth etc.; the rule of such people. **meritocrat,** *n.* **meritocratic,** *a.* **meritorious,** *a.* deserving reward; praiseworthy. **meritoriously,** *adv.* **meritoriousness,** *n.* [OF *merite,* L *meritum,* neut. p.p. of *merērī,* to earn, perh. cogn. with Gr. *meros,* a share, whence *meiresthai,* to receive a portion]

†**merk,** *n.* an old Scottish silver coin. [MARK[2]]

merle, *n.* (*poet.*) the blackbird. [OF, from L *merula*]

merlin, *n.* the smallest of the European falcons, *Falco aesalon,* and other falcons of the subdivision *Aesalon.* [A-F *merilun,* OF *esmerillon,* prob. from Teut.]

Merlin, *n.* a legendary magician and counsellor to King Arthur. Welsh bardic literature has a cycle of poems attributed to him, and he may have been a real person. He is said to have been buried in a cave in the park of Dynevor Castle, Dyfed.

†**merling,** *n.* the whiting. [OF *merlanke* (F *merlan*), from MERLE]

merlon, *n.* the part of an embattled parapet between two embrasures. [F, from It. *merlone,* from *merlo, merla,* battlement, prob. from *mergola,* dim. of L *mergae,* pl., a pitchfork]

mermaid, *n.* a fabulous marine creature, having the upper half like a woman and the lower like a fish. **mermaid's purse** SEA-PURSE. **mermaiden,** *n.* **merman,** *n. masc.* [MERE[1], MAID (cp. OE *mere-wīf,* mere-woman)]

mero-, *comb.form* partly. [Gr. *meros,* part, portion]

meroblast, *n.* an ovum only a part or portion of which is directly germinal. **meroblastic,** *a.* undergoing or involving cleavage in part of the ovum only.

Meroe, *n.* ancient city in Sudan, on the Nile near Khartoum, capital of Nubia from about 600 BC to 350 AD. Tombs and inscriptions have been excavated, and iron-smelting slag heaps have been found.

merogony, *n.* the growth of an organism from a portion of the ovum not containing a nucleus. **merogonic,** *a.*

merohedral, *a.* of crystals, having less than the number of faces belonging to the type.

meroistic, *a.* of the ovaries of certain insects, secreting vitilligenous cells as well as ova.

meropidan, *a.* of or pertaining to the Meropidae, a family of birds containing the bee-eater. *n.* a bird of this family. [mod. L *Meropidae,* from Gr. *merops,* bee-eater, -AN]

merosome, *n.* a segment of the body of a segmented animal, as the ring of a worm. **merosomal,** *a.* [Gr. *sōma,* body]

Merovingian dynasty, *n.* a Frankish dynasty, named after its founder, Merovech (5th century AD). His descendants ruled France from the time of Clovis (481–511) to 751. [F *Merovingien,* med. L *Merovingī,* from Teut.]

merriment etc. MERRY[2].

merry[1], *n.* the wild black cherry. [F *merise,* taken as pl.]

merry[2], *a.* joyous, gay, jovial, mirthful; causing merriment; (*coll.*) slightly tipsy; †sarcastic. **the more the merrier,** the pleasure will be greater, the more people are involved. **to make merry** MAKE[2]. **to make merry over,** to make a laughing matter of. **merry-andrew,** *n.* a buffoon, a jester, esp. one assisting a mountebank or quack. **merry-dancers,** *n.pl.* the aurora borealis. **merry England,** *n.* an idealized image of England as it used to be, esp. in Elizabethan times. **merry-go-round,** *n.* a revolving frame with seats or wooden horses on which persons ride at fairs etc.; (*coll.*) a traffic roundabout. **merry-make,** *v.i.* to make merry. *n.* a merry-making. **merry-maker,** *n.* **merry-making,** *a.* making merry, jovial. *n.* merriment; a festivity. †**merryman,** *n.* a merry-andrew. **merrythought,** *n.* the furcula or forked bone in the breast of a bird. **merrily,** *adv.* **merriment, merriness,** *n.* [OE *myrige,* whence MIRTH, prob. from OTeut. *murgjo-,* lasting a short time, cogn. with Gr. *brachus,* short]

Mersey, *n.* river in NW England; length 112 km/70 miles. Formed by the confluence of the Goyt and Etherow rivers, it flows W to join the Irish Sea at Liverpool Bay. It is linked to the Manchester Ship Canal.

Mersey beat, *n.* a type of pop music of the mid-1960s that originated in the NW of England (also called the **Liverpool sound** or, elsewhere, beat music), drawing on US styles. It was almost exclusively performed by all-male groups, of whom the most famous was the Beatles.

Merseyside, *n.* former (1974–86) metropolitan county of NW England, replaced by a residuary body in 1986 which covers some of its former functions. **area** 650 sq km/251 sq miles. **towns** administrative headquarters Liverpool; Bootle, Birkenhead, St Helens, Wallasey, Southport. **products** chemicals, electrical goods, vehicles. **population** (1987) 1,457,000.

merulidan, *a.* of or pertaining to the Turdidae or Merulidae, a family of birds comprising the thrush and blackbird. *n.* a bird of this family. [mod. L *Merulidae,* from L *merula,* MERLE]

Merv, *n.* an oasis in Soviet Turkmenistan, a centre of civilization from at least 1200 BC, and site of a town founded by Alexander the Great. Old Merv was destroyed by the emir of Bokhara in 1787, and the modern town of Mary, founded by the Russians in 1885, lies 29 km/18 miles west.

merycism, *n.* a disorder in which food is brought back from the stomach and chewed again. [Gr. *mērukismos,* from *mērukizein,* to ruminate]

mes- MESO-.

mesa, *n.* a tableland; a plateau with steep sides. [Sp., table]

mesail, *n.* the visor of a helmet, esp. if made in two parts. [F *mésail,* prob. from OF *muçaille,* from *mucier,* to hide]

mésalliance, *n.* marriage with one of inferior social position. [F (*més-,* MIS-[1], ALLIANCE)]

mesaraic, *a.* mesenteric. [med. L *mesaraïcus,* Gr. *mesaraïkos,* from *mesaraion* (*meson,* middle, *araia,* the belly)]

mescal, *n.* a small globular cactus of the southern US and Mexico, the tubercles of which are chewed for their hallucinogenic effects; an alcoholic liquor distilled from Agave. **mescal button,** *n.* the tubercle of the mescal cactus. **mescaline,** *n.* a hallucinogenic substance derived from mescal buttons. [Mex. Sp., from Nahuatl *mexcalli*]

Mesdames MADAME.

Mesdemoiselles, *pl.* MADEMOISELLE.

†**meseems,** *v. impers.* it seems to me. [ME, dat., SEEM]

Mesembrianthemum, *n.* a genus of very succulent plants, with thick, fleshy leaves and brilliant flowers, containing the ice-plant or fig-marigold. [Gr. *mesēmbria,* noon, *anthemon,* flower]

mesencephalon, *n.* the mid-brain. **mesencephalic,** *a.* [Gr. *mesos,* middle, ENCEPHALON]

mesentery, *n.* a fold of the peritoneum investing the small intestines and connecting them with the wall of the abdomen. **mesenteric,** *a.* **mesenteritis,** *n.* inflammation of the mesentery. [med. L *mesenterium,* Gr. *mesenterion* (*mesos,* middle, *enteron,* entrail)]

mesh, *n.* the space or interstice between the threads of a net; (*pl.*) network; a trap, a snare; the engagement of gear-teeth etc.; interlacing structure. *v.t.* to catch in a net, to ensnare; to engage (of gear-teeth etc.). *v.i.* to coordinate (with); of gear-teeth etc., to engage. **in mesh,** of cogs, engaged. **mesh-work,** *n.* **meshy,** *a.* [perh. from OE *max* (cp. Dut. *maas,* G *Masche*), or from MDut. *maesche*]

mesial, *a.* pertaining to, situated or directed towards the middle, esp. the middle line of the body; median. **mesially,** *adv.* [Gr. *mesos,* middle, -IAL]

Mesmer, *n.* **Friedrich Anton** (1733–1815), Austrian physician who was an early experimenter in hypnosis, formerly (and popularly) called *mesmerism* after him.

mesmerism, *n.* the art or power of inducing an abnormal state of the nervous system, in which the will of the patient is controlled by that of the agent; the hypnotic state so induced. **mesmeric,** *a.* **mesmerist,** *n.* **mesmerize, -ise,** *v.t.* to hypnotize; to occupy (someone's attention) totally. **mesmerization, -isation,** *n.* **mesmerizee, -isee,** *n.* **mesmerizer, -iser,** *n.* [F. A. *Mesmer,* see above]

mesne, *a.* middle, intermediate. **mesne lord,** *n.* in feudal law, one holding of a superior lord. **mesne profits,** *n.pl.* the profits of an estate received by a person wrongfully in possession. [F, legal var. of A-F *meen,* MEAN[1]]

mes(o)-, *comb.form* intermediate, in the middle; pertaining to the middle. [Gr. *mesos,* middle]

mesoblast, *n.* the intermediate layer of the blastoderm of the embryo. **mesoblastic,** *a.* [-BLAST]

mesocarp, *n.* the middle layer of a pericarp. [Gr. *karpos,* fruit]

mesocephalic, *a.* intermediate between dolichocephalic and brachycephalic (of skulls). **mesocephalism, mesocephaly,** *n.* **mesocephalous,** *a.*

mesode, *n.* in Greek verse, a passage between the strophe and antistrophe in a choral ode. **mesodic,** *a.* [Gr. *mesōdos* (MES(O)-, ODE)]

mesoderm, *n.* the mesoblast; (*Bot.*) the middle layer of the bark, of the wall of a sporecase etc. **mesodermal, -dermic,** *a.*

mesogaster, *n.* a membrane attaching the stomach to the dorsal wall of the abdomen. **mesogastric,** *a.* [Gr. *gastēr,* stomach]

Mesolithic, *a.* intervening between the Neolithic and Palaeolithic divisions of the stone age. [Gr. *lithos,* stone]

mesomorphic, *a.* having a muscular physique. **mesomorph,** *n.* **mesomorphy,** *n.* [-MORPHIC under -MORPH]

meson, *n.* a particle intermediate in mass between a proton and an electron.

mesophloeum, *n.* the middle or green layer of bark in exogens. [Gr. *phloios,* bark]

mesophyll, *n.* the inner parenchymatous tissue of a leaf. [Gr. *phullon,* leaf]

mesophyte, *n.* a plant that grows in conditions where there is a moderate supply of water. [-PHYTE]

mesoplast, *n.* the nucleus of a cell.

Mesopotamia, *n.* the land between the rivers Tigris and Euphrates, part of modern Iraq. Here the civilizations of Sumer and Babylon flourished, and some consider it the site of the earliest civilization.

mesosphere, *n.* the region of the earth's atmosphere above the stratosphere.

mesothelioma, *n.* a tumour of the lining of the lungs, heart or stomach, often caused by blue asbestos dust.

mesothorax, *n.* in insects, the middle segment of the thorax bearing the anterior legs and the middle wings.

Mesozoic, *a.* belonging to the second great geological epoch, secondary.

mesquit, *n.* either of two leguminous shrubs or trees growing in the SW United States and as far south as Peru, the larger yielding the sweetish screw-pod used for fodder. **mesquit-bean,** *n.* **mesquit-grass,** *n.* [Mex. Sp. *mezquite*]

mess, *n.* a dish or a portion of food sent to table at one time; liquid or semi-liquid food, esp. for animals; a quantity of such food; a number of persons who sit down to table together (used esp. of soldiers and sailors); a meal taken thus; officers' living quarters; a state of dirt and disorder; a muddle, a difficulty; †a set or party of four, orig. one of the parties into which a company was divided at a banquet etc. *v.i.* to take a meal or meals in company, esp. of soldiers etc.; to muddle or potter (about). *v.t.* to mix together, to muddle, to jumble; to dirty, to soil. **to mess about,** (*coll.*) to tumble about; to treat roughly; to treat improperly or inconsiderately; to potter about. **to mess up,** (*coll.*) to ruin, spoil. **to mess with,** (*coll.*) to interfere with. **messmate,** *n.* a member of the same mess; an associate; a parasite which does not actually feed on the body of its host, a commensal. **messy,** *a.* dirty, muddled; complicated and difficult to handle. **messiness,** *n.* a state of dirt or disorder. [OF *mes,* late L *missum,* neut. p.p. of *mittere,* to send]

message, *n.* a communication, oral or written, from one person to another; the truths, ideas or opinions of a writer or inspired person; the chief theme of a play, novel etc.; †a messenger; (*Naut.*) a rope from the capstan to the cable for lifting the anchor. [F, from pop. L *missāticum,* as prec.]

Messalina, *n.* **Valeria** (*c.* AD 22–48), third wife of the Roman emperor Claudius, whom she dominated. She was notorious for her immorality, forcing a noble to marry her in AD 48, although still married to Claudius, who then had her executed.

messan, *n.* (*Sc.*) a lap-dog. **messan-cur, -dog, -tyke,**

n. [prob. from Gael. *measan*]

messenger, *n.* one who carries a message or goes on an errand. **queen's, king's, messenger,** official bearer of Foreign Office dispatches to foreign countries. **messenger RNA,** *n.* a type of RNA that carries genetic information from DNA to the ribosomes for the synthesis of protein. [F *messager,* see MESSAGE]

Messerschmidt, *n.* **Willy** (1898–1978), German plane designer, whose ME-109 was a standard Luftwaffe fighter in World War II, and whose ME-262 (1942) was the first mass-produced jet fighter.

Messiaen, *n.* **Olivier** (1908–), French composer and organist. His theories of melody, harmony, and rhythm, drawing on medieval and oriental music, have inspired contemporary composers such as Boulez and Stockhausen. Among his better-known works are the *Quatuor pour la fin du temps* (1941), the large-scale *Turangalîla Symphony* (1949), and several organ pieces.

Messiah, Messias, *n.* the Anointed One, Christ, as the promised deliverer of the Jews; an expected saviour or deliverer. **messiahship,** *n.* **messianic,** *a.* of, or inspired by the hope of, a Messiah; marked by great zeal in support of a cause. [F *Messie,* L and Gr. *Messīas,* Heb. *māshīah,* from *māshah,* to anoint]

Messier, *n.* **Charles** (1730–1817), French astronomer, who discovered 15 comets and in 1781 published a list of 103 star clusters and nebulae. Objects on this list are given M (for Messier) numbers which astronomers still use today, such as M1, the Crab Nebula, and M31, the Andromeda Galaxy.

Messieurs, *n.pl.* sirs; gentlemen (pl. of Mr, usu. abbr. to **Messrs**). [see MONSIEUR]

Messina, Strait of, a channel in the central Mediterranean separating Sicily from mainland Italy; in Greek legend a monster (Charybdis), who devoured ships, lived in the whirlpool on the Sicilian side, and another (Scylla), who devoured sailors, in the rock on the Italian side. The classical hero Odysseus passed safely between them.

messmate MESS.

Messrs, MESSIEURS.

messuage, *n.* (*Law*) a dwelling-house with the adjacent buildings and curtilage for the use of the household. [A-F *mesuage,* perh. scriptorial corr. of *mesnage,* but acc. to Skeat from OF *masuage,* med. L *mansuāgium,* from *mansa,* see MANSE]

mestee, *n.* the offspring of a white and a quadroon, an octoroon. [Sp. *mestizo,* see foll.]

mestizo, *n.* one of mixed Spanish or Portuguese and Indian blood; applied also to one of mixed Chinese and Philippine blood. **mestiza,** *n. fem.* [Sp., mongrel, from pop. L *mixtīcius, mixtus,* p.p. of *miscēre,* to mix]

Met, *n.* (*coll.*) the (London) Metropolitan Police; the Metropolitan Opera, New York.

met, *past, p.p.* MEET[2].

met(a)-, meth-, *comb.form* on; with, among or between; after (implying change or transposition). [Gr.]

metabasis, *n.* (*Rhet.*) transition from one subject to another; (*Med.*) change of remedies. [Gr.]

Metabola, *n.* a division of insects containing those undergoing complete metamorphosis. **metabolian,** *n.* one of the Metabola. [as foll.]

metabolism, *n.* the continuous chemical change going on in living matter, either constructive, by which nutritive material is built up into complex and unstable living matter, or destructive, by which protoplasm is broken down into simpler and more stable substances. **metabolic,** *a.* **metabolite,** *n.* a substance involved in or produced by metabolism. **metabolize, -ise,** *v.t.* [Gr. *metabolē,* change, rel. to *metaballein,* to change (MET(A)-, *ballein,* to throw), -ISM]

metacarpus, *n.* the part of the hand between the wrist and the fingers. **metacarpal,** *a.*

metacentre, *n.* the point in a floating body slightly out of equilibrium where the vertical drawn through the centre of gravity when it is in equilibrium intersects the vertical passing through the centre of buoyancy.

metachrosis, *n.* change of colour, as in certain lizards.

metagalaxy, *n.* the universe beyond our galaxy. **metagalactic,** *a.*

metage, *n.* official measurement, esp. of coal; toll charged for measuring.

metagenesis, *n.* alternation of like and unlike generations. **metagenetic, metagenic,** *a.*

metal, *n.* one of a class of elementary substances which usu. present in various degrees certain physical characters, as lustre, malleability and ductility, possessed by the six metals known to the ancients, viz. gold, silver, copper, iron, lead and tin; a compound of the elementary metals, an alloy; broken stone for road-making etc.; molten glass ready for blowing or casting; the effective power of the guns of a warship; (*pl.*) rails of a railway etc.; mettle, essential quality. *v.t.* (*past, p.p.* **metalled**) to furnish or fit with metal; to cover or repair (a road) with metal. **metallic,** *a.* **metallic currency,** *n.* money composed of gold, silver etc., as opp. to paper. **metalliferous,** *a.* bearing or yielding metal. **metalline,** *a.* **metalling,** *n.* broken stones etc. used in making or mending roads. †**metallist,** *n.* **metallize, -ise,** *v.t.* to form into a metal; to give metallic properties to; to vulcanize. **metallization, -isation,** *n.* [OF, from L *metallum,* Gr. *metallon,* mine, mineral, perh. rel. to *metallan,* to search after]

metalanguage, *n.* a language or system of symbols used to speak about another language.

metalepsis, *n.* the substitution of one word for another that is itself figurative, or the union of two or more tropes of a different kind in one word. **metaleptic, -ical,** *a.* **metaleptically,** *adv.* [L and Gr. *metalēpsis,* from *metalambanein,* to substitute (MET(A)-, *lambanein,* to take)]

metallo-, *comb.form* metal. **metallography,** *n.* the science of metals, esp. the microscopic study of their internal structure. **metalloid,** *n., a.* **metalloidal,** *a.* **metallophone,** *n.* a piano with metal bars instead of wires; a musical instrument like the xylophone with metal bars.

metallurgy, *n.* the science of metals; the art of separating metals from ores; the art of working in metal. **metallurgic, -ical,** *a.* **metallurgist,** *n.* [Gr. *metallourgos* (*metallon,* mineral, *-ergos,* working)]

metamere, *n.* one of a series of similar parts of a body. **metameric,** *a.* of, pertaining to, or of the nature of a metamere; having the same composition and molecular weight, isomeric but different in chemical properties. **metamerism,** *n.* [Gr. *meros,* part]

metamorphose, *v.t.* to change into a different form; to transmute. *v.i.* to undergo change into a different form. **metamorphic,** *a.* causing or showing the results of metamorphosis; transforming or transformed. **metamorphism,** *n.* change in the structure of rocks, caused usu. by heat. **metamorphology,** *n.* the science of the metamorphoses of organisms. **metamorphosis,** *n.* a change of form; the result of such a change; transformation, as of a chrysalis into a winged insect; a complete change of character, purpose etc. [F *métamorphoser,* from L and Gr. *metamorphōsis,* transformation, from *metamorphoun* (MET(A)-, *morphē,* form)]

metaphor, *n.* a figure of speech by which a word is transferred from one object to another, so as to imply comparison. **metaphoric, -ical,** *a.* **metaphorically,** *adv.* †**metaphorist,** *n.* [F *métaphore,* L and Gr. *metaphora* (MET(A)-, *pherein,* to bear)]

metaphrase, *v.t.* to translate literally. *n.* (also **metaphrasis**) a literal translation. **metaphrastic,** *a.* **metaphrist,** *n.* [Gr. *metaphrasis* (MET(A)-, *phrazein,* to speak)]

metaphysics, *n. sing.* the philosophy of being and knowing; the theoretical principles forming the basis of any particular science; the philosophy of mind; anything vague, abstract and abstruse. **metaphysical,** *a.* of or pertaining to metaphysics; transcendental, dealing with abstractions; abstruse, over-subtle; imaginary, fantastic; of the group of 17th cent. poets noted for their intellectual tone and ingenious imagery. **me-**

taphysically, *adv.* **metaphysician,** *n.* **metaphysicize, -ise,** *v.t., v.i.* [formerly *metaphysic,* med. L *metaphysica,* Gr. *metaphusika* (*meta ta phusika,* after physics, or coming next after the study of natural science)]

metaphyte, *n.* a multicellular plant, as distinct from *protophyte.*

metaplasia, *n.* change of one form of tissue into another. [Gr.]

metaplasm, *n.* the formative material of protoplasm; change in a word by alteration of a letter or syllable. **metaplastic,** *a.*

metapolitics, *n. sing.* abstract political theories of an impractical nature.

metapophysis, *n.* a tubercular prominence on the vertebrae. [Gr.]

metapsychology, *n.* the body of theory on psychological matters. **metapsychological,** *a.*

metastable, *a.* seeming stable because passing slowly from one state to another. **metastability,** *n.*

Metastasio, *n.* pen name of Pietro Trapassi (1698–1782), Italian poet and the leading librettist of his day, creating 18th-cent. Italian *opera seria* (serious opera).

metastasis, *n.* metabolism; a change in the seat of a disease, esp. cancer, from one organ to another. **metastasize, -ise,** *v.i.* **metastatic,** *a.*

metatarsus, *n.* that part of the foot between the tarsus and the toes, in man consisting of five long bones. **metatarsal,** *a.*

metatheory, *n.* a theory used to discuss the nature of another theory or theories.

metathesis, *n.* the transposition of sounds or letters in a word; the surgical removal of a morbific agent etc. from one place to another; interchange of radicals or groups of atoms in a compound with others. **metathetic,** *a.*

metathorax, *n.* the posterior segment of the thorax in an insect.

metatome, *n.* (*Arch.*) the space between two dentils.

metayer, *n.* a cultivator paying a certain proportion of the produce to the landlord, who provides seed, stock etc. **metayage,** *n.* [F, from med. L *medietārius,* from *medietas,* MOIETY]

Metazoa, *n.pl.* a primary division of the animal kingdom including all animals which have many-celled bodies and differentiated tissues, as distinct from *Protozoa.* **metazoan,** *a.* pertaining to the Metazoa. *n.* any individual of the Metazoa. **metazoic,** *a.* [Gr. *zōa,* pl. of *zōon,* animal]

mete¹, *v.t.* to measure; to allot, to apportion (out); to appraise; to be the measure of. †*v.i.* to measure; to aim. †**metewand,** †**meteyard,** *n.* a measuring-rod. [OE *metan* (cp. Dut. *meten,* G *messen*)]

mete², *n.* a limit, a boundary. [OF, from L *meta,* a goal]

metempirics, *n. sing.* the science of things lying beyond the bounds of experience; one who believes in this. **metempiric, -ical,** *a.* **metempiricism,** *n.* **metempiricist,** *n.*

metempsychosis, *n.* the passage of the soul after death from one animal body to another. [late L, from Gr. *metempsuchōsis*]

metensomatosis, *n.* the transference of the elements of one body into another body as by decomposition and assimilation. [Gr.]

meteor, *n.* a luminous body appearing for a few moments in the sky and then disappearing, a shooting-star; any atmospheric phenomenon, as rain, hail etc.; anything which transiently dazzles or strikes with wonder. **meteoric,** *a.* pertaining to or consisting of meteors; resembling a meteor; brilliant but fading quickly, dazzling; of or pertaining to the atmosphere or its phenomena. **meteorically,** *adv.* **meteorite,** *n.* a fallen meteor; stone, metal or a compound of earth and metal, that has fallen upon the earth from space. **meteorolite,** *n.* **meteorograph,** *n.* an instrument for recording meteorological phenomena. **meteorography,** *n.* **meteoroid,** *n.* **meteoroidal,** *a.* [Gr. *meteōron,* n. from a. *meteōros,* raised (META-, *eōra,* var. of *aiōra,* from *aeirein,* to raise)]

meteorology, *n.* the science of the atmosphere and its phenomena, esp. for the purpose of forecasting the weather; the general character of the weather in a particular place. **meteorologic, -ical,** *a.* **Meteorological Office,** *n.* a government department responsible for issuing weather forecasts, storm warnings etc. **meteorologically,** *adv.* **meteorologist,** *n.*

meter¹, *n.* one who or that which measures, esp. an instrument for registering the quantity of gas, water, electric energy etc. supplied. *v.t.* to measure by means of a meter. **meterage,** *n.*

meter² METRE¹.

meter³ METRE².

-meter¹, *suf.* a measuring instrument, as *barometer, thermometer.* [Gr. *metron,* measure]

-meter², *comb.form* a verse metre with a specified number of feet.

metewand, meteyard METE¹.

meth- MET(A)- before aspirates.

methadone, *n.* a synthetic drug similar to morphine, but less addictive, often used in the treatment of addiction.

methane, *n.* (*Chem.*) a light, colourless gas, methyl hydride or carburetted hydrogen, produced by the decomposition or dry distillation of vegetable matter, one of the chief constituents of coal-gas, and also of fire-damp and marsh-gas. **methanometer,** *n.* [METHYL, -ANE]

methanol, *n.* a colourless, volatile liquid used as a solvent or as fuel.

†**metheglin,** *n.* a variety of mead, orig. Welsh. [W *meddyglyn* (*meddyg,* L *medicus,* healing, *llyn,* liquor)]

methinks, *v.impers.* (*past* **-thought**) it seems to me; I think.

method, *n.* mode of procedure, way or order of doing; an orderly, systematic or logical arrangement; orderliness, system; a system or the basis of a system of classification. **method acting,** *n.* an actor's identification of himself with the part rather than giving just a technical performance. **methodical,** *a.* done according to a method; habitually proceeding in a systematic way. **methodically,** *adv.* **Methodism,** *n.* the doctrines, practices or Church system of the Methodists. **Methodist,** *n.* a strict observer of method in philosophical inquiry or medical practice; a member of any of the religious bodies that have grown out of the evangelical movement begun in the middle of the 18th cent. by John Wesley (1703–91), his brother Charles, and George Whitefield (1714–70). **methodistic, -ical,** *a.* **methodistically,** *adv.* **methodize, -ise,** *v.t.* to reduce to order; to arrange systematically. **methodizer, -iser,** *n.* **methodology,** *n.* the branch of logic dealing with the methods of accurate thinking; the methods used in a particular project, discipline etc. [F *méthode,* L *methodus,* Gr. *methodos* (METH-, *hodos,* way)]

Methodius, St, *n.* (*c.* 825–84), Greek Christian bishop, who with his brother Cyril translated much of the Bible into Slavonic. Feast day 14 Feb.

methomania, *n.* craving for intoxicating drink. [Gr. *methē,* drink, drunkenness, -MANIA]

methought METHINKS.

meths, *n.pl.* (*coll.*) short for METHYLATED SPIRIT(S).

Methuselah, *n.* in the Old Testament, a Hebrew patriarch who lived before the Flood; his supposed age of 969 years made him a byword for longevity.

methyl, *n.* the hypothetical radical of wood spirit, formic acid and many other organic compounds. **methylic,** *a.* [F *méthyle,* from *methylène* (Gr. *methu,* wine, *hulē,* wood)]

methylate, *v.t.* to mix or saturate with methyl alcohol. **methylated spirit,** *n.* spirit of wine, mixed with 10% of methyl alcohol so as to be rendered unfit to drink and accordingly duty-free.

methylene, *n.* a hypothetical organic radical in which two atoms of hydrogen are in chemical combination with one atom of carbon, occurring in numerous compounds.

metic, *n.* an immigrant, a resident alien. [Gr. *metoikos,* resident alien]

meticulous, *a.* cautious or over-scrupulous about trivial details, finical; very careful; †timid. **meticulously,** *adv.* **meticulousness,** *n.* [L *meticulōsus,* from *metus,* fear]

métier, *n.* trade, profession, one's particular 'line'. [F, earlier *mestier,* pop. L *misterium,* L *ministerium,* MINISTRY]

métif, *n.* an octoroon. [MESTIZO]

métis, *n.* one of mixed blood, esp. (in Canada) the offspring of a European and an American Indian. [F, MESTIZO]

metonic, *a.* pertaining to *Meton,* Athenian astronomer, applied to the cycle of 19 Julian years at the end of which the new and full moons recur on the same dates.

metonymy, *n.* a figure in which one word is used for another, as the effect for the cause, the material for the thing made etc., e.g. 'bench' for 'magistrates'. **metonymic, -ical,** *a.* **metonymically,** *adv.* [late L *metōnymia,* Gr. *metōnumia* (MET(A)-, *onoma,* Aeolic *onuma,* name)]

metope¹, *n.* the space between the triglyphs in a Doric frieze. [Gr. *metopē* (MET(A)-, *opē,* hole for a beam)]

metope², *n.* the face or front (of a crab). **metopic,** *a.* frontal. **metopism,** *n.* persistence of the frontal suture. **metoposcopy,** *n.* the study of physiognomy. **metoposcopic,** *a.* **metoposcopist,** *n.* [Gr. *metōpon,* forehead]

metre¹, (*esp. N Am.*) **meter,** *n.* the rhythmical arrangement of syllables in verse; verse; any particular form of poetic rhythm. **metric,** *a.* metrical. *n.* (*usu. pl.*) the science or art of metre, prosody. **metrical,** *a.* of, pertaining to or composed in metre; of or pertaining to measurement. **metrically,** *adv.* **metrician, metrist,** *n.* one skilled in metres; a versifier. **metrify,** *v.t.* [OF, from L *metrum,* Gr. *metron,* measure]

metre², (*esp. N Am.*) **meter,** *n.* the standard measure of length in the metric system, orig. the ten-millionth part of the quadrant of a meridian, 39·37 in., now defined as the distance travelled by light in a vacuum in 1/299, 792, 458 of a second. **metre-ampere,** *n.* a measure of the power which a transmitter radiates. **metre-bridge,** *n.* (*Elec.*) wheatstone bridge of slide-wire pattern with 1-m length wire. **metric,** *a.* **metric system,** *n.* a system of weights and measures in which ascending units carry Greek prefixes and descending units Latin prefixes. Units are multiples of ten times the basic unit. **metric ton** TONNE. **metricate,** *v.t.* to convert to the metric system. **metrication,** *n.* [F *mètre,* as prec.]

metro, *n.* (*pl.* **metros**) an underground railway network in a city. [F *métro,* abbr. of *chemin de fer métropolitain,* metropolitan railway]

metro-, *comb.form* measuring. [Gr. *metron,* measure]

Metro-Goldwyn-Mayer, *n.* (MGM) a US film-production company (1924–1970s), when it was taken over by United Artists. MGM was formed by the amalgamation of the Metro Picture Corporation, the Goldwyn Picture Corporation, and Louis B Mayer Pictures. One of the most powerful Hollywood studios of the 1930s to the 1950s, it produced such prestige films as *David Copperfield* (1935) and *The Wizard of Oz* (1939). Among its stars were Greta Garbo, James Stewart and Elizabeth Taylor.

metrograph, *n.* a contrivance on a locomotive recording the speed achieved with the number and duration of the stoppages.

metromania, *n.* a passion for writing verses.

metronome, *n.* an instrument for indicating and marking time in music by means of a pendulum. **metronomic,** *a.* **metronomically,** *adv.* **metronomy,** *n.* [F *métronome* (Gr. *nomos,* law, rule)]

metronymic, *a.* of names, derived from the name of a mother or maternal ancestor. *n.* a name so derived. **metronymy,** *n.* [Gr. *mētrōnumikos* (*mētēr -tros,* mother, *onoma, onuma,* name)]

metropolis, *n.* the chief town or capital of a country; the seat or see of a metropolitan bishop; a centre or focus of activity etc.; a large town. [L and Gr. *mētropolis,* mother-state (*mētēr -tros,* mother, *polis,* city)]

metropolitan, *a.* pertaining to a capital city or to an archbishopric; forming part of a sovereign state as distinct from its colonies. *n.* a bishop having authority over other bishops in a province, in the Western Church an archbishop, in the ancient and the modern Greek Church ranking above an archbishop and next to a patriarch. **metropolitanate,** *n.* †**metropolite,** *n.* **metropolitic,** †**-ical,** *a.*

Metropolitan Opera Company, the foremost opera company in the US, founded 1883 in New York. The Metropolitan Opera House (opened 1883) was demolished in 1966, and the company transferred to the Lincoln Center.

-metry, *suf.* science of measuring, as *geometry, trigonometry.* [Gr. *metria,* measurement, from *metrēs,* measurer, see -METER¹]

Metternich, *n.* **Klemens (Wenzel Lothar), Prince von Metternich** (1773–1859), Austrian foreign minister from 1809 until the 1848 revolution forced him to flee to the UK. At the Congress of Vienna (1815) he advocated cooperation by the great powers to suppress democratic movements.

mettle, *n.* quality of temperament or disposition; constitutional ardour; spirit, courage; †stuff, material one is made of. **to put on one's mettle,** to test one's courage, determination etc. **mettled, mettlesome,** *a.* high-spirited, fiery, ardent. **mettlesomeness,** *n.* [var. of METAL]

†**meuse,** *n.* a gap in a fence etc. through which a hare runs; a way of escape, a loophole. [OF *muce,* from *musser, muchier,* to hide (cp. MICHE, MOUCH)]

mew¹, *n.* a kind of sea-gull, esp. *Larus canus.* [OE *mǣw* (cp. Dut. *meeuw,* Icel. *mar,* G *Möwe*)]

mew², *v.i.* to cry 'mew' as a cat. *n.* this cry of the cat. [imit.]

mew³, *n.* a cage for hawks, esp. whilst moulting; a place of confinement; a den; (*pl.*) royal stables in London (built on the spot where the royal hawks were formerly mewed); (*pl.*) stables for carriage-horses etc.; a row of dwellings, garages etc. converted from these; (*pl., N Am.*) a back alley. *v.t.* †to moult, to shed (the feathers); to put (a hawk) in a mew or cage; to shut (up), to confine. †*v.i.* to shed the feathers. [OF *mue,* from *muer,* L *mūtāre,* to change]

mewl, *v.i.* to cry, whine or whimper, as a child; to mew, as a cat. **mewler,** *n.*

Mexican, *a.* of or pertaining to Mexico. *n.* a native or inhabitant of Mexico.

Mexican Empire, *n.* a short-lived empire (1822–23) following the liberation of Mexico from Spain. The empire lasted only eight months, under the revolutionary leader Iturbide.

Mexican War, *n.* a war between the US and Mexico (1846–48), begun when Gen. Zachary Taylor invaded New Mexico. Mexico City was taken, 1847, and under the Treaty of Guadaloupe-Hidalgo, Mexico lost Texas, New Mexico and California (half its territory) to the US for $15 million compensation.

Mexico, *n.* United States of (*Estados Unidos Mexicanos*), a country in Central America, bordered N by the US, E by the Gulf of Mexico, SE by Belize and Guatemala, and SW and W by the Pacific Ocean. **area** 1,958,201 sq km/755,866 sq miles. **capital** Mexico City. **towns** Guadalajara, Monterrey; port Veracruz. **physical** partly arid central highlands flanked by Sierra Madre mountain ranges E and W; tropical coastal plains. **exports** silver, gold, lead, uranium, oil, natural gas, traditional handicrafts, fish, shellfish. **population** (1989) 88,087,000 (a minority are *criollos* of Spanish descent, 12% are American Indian, and the majority are of mixed descent; 50% of the total are under 20 years of age); annual growth rate 2.6%. **language** Spanish (official); Indian languages include Nahuatl, Maya, and Mixtec. **religion** Roman Catholic.

Mexico City, *n.* (Spanish **Ciudad de México**) capital, and industrial (iron, steel, chemicals, textiles) and cultural centre of Mexico, 2255 m/7400 ft above sea level on the southern edge of the central plateau; population (1986) 18,748,000. It is thought to be the most polluted city in the world.

Meyerbeer, *n.* **Giacomo** (adopted name of Jakob Liebmann Beer) (1791–1864), German composer. He is renowned for his spectacular operas, including *Robert le Diable* (1831) and *Les Huguenots* (1836). From 1826 he lived mainly in Paris, returning to Berlin after 1842 as musical director of the Royal Opera.

MEZ, (*abbr.*) Central European Time (G *M*itteleuropäische Zeit).

mezereon, *n.* a small ornamental shrub, *Daphne mezereum.* [med. L, from Arab. *māzaryūn*]

mezuza(h), *n.* a small case containing extracts from Scripture fixed to the doorpost by Jews as a sign of their piety. [Heb., doorpost]

mezzanine, *n.* a storey intermediate in level between two main storeys, usu. between the ground and first floors; a window in such a storey; a floor beneath the stage of a theatre from which the traps etc. are worked. **mezzanine-floor, -window,** *n.* [F, from It. *mezzanino,* dim. of *mezzano,* L *mediānus,* MEDIAN]

mezza voce, *a., adv.* (singing or sung) softly; quiet(ly). [It., half voice]

mezzo, *a.* half or medium. [It., from L *medius,* middle]

mezzo forte, *a., adv.* in music, moderately loud(ly).

mezzo-rilievo, *n.* (*pl.* **-os**) half-relief, sculpture in which the figures stand out from the background to a half of their proportions.

mezzo-soprano, *n.* a voice lower than a soprano and higher than a contralto; a singer with such a voice.

mezzotint, †**mezzotinto** , *n.* a process of engraving in which a copper plate is uniformly roughened so as to print a deep black, lights and half-lights being then produced by scraping away the burr; a print from this. *v.t.* to engrave in mezzotint. [It. *mezzotinto*]

mf, (*abbr.*) mezzo forte.

Mfecane, *n.* in African history, a series of disturbances in the early 19th cent. among communities in what is today the eastern part of South Africa. They arose when chief Shaka conquered the Nguni peoples between the Tugela and Pongola rivers, then created by conquest a centralized, militaristic Zulu kingdom from several communities, resulting in large-scale displacement of people.

Mg, (*chem. symbol*) magnesium.

mg, (*abbr.*) milligram.

Mgr, (*abbr.*) Monsignor.

MHD, (*abbr.*) magnetohydrodynamics.

mho, *n.* (*formerly*) unit of conductivity, now **siemens**. [*ohm* reversed]

MHz, (*abbr.*) megahertz.

mi, *n.* the third note of the diatonic scale. [It., orig. first syl. of L *mīra,* see GAMUT]

MI5, (*abbr.*) the British government agency for counter-espionage.

MI6, (*abbr.*) the British government agency for espionage.

Miami, *n.* a city and port in Florida, US; population (1984) 383,000. It is the hub of finance, trade and air transport for Latin America and the Caribbean.

Miandad, *n.* **Javed** (1957–), Pakistani test cricketer, his country's leading run-maker. He scored a century on his test debut in 1976 and has since gone on to be one of a handful of players to make 100 test appearances. He has captained his country. His highest score of 311 was made when he was aged 17.

miaow, *n.* the cry of a cat. *v.i.* of a cat, to cry 'miaow'.

miasma, *n.* (*pl.* **-mata**) poisonous or infectious exhalation, malaria. †**miasm**, *n.* **miasmal, miasmatic, -ical, miasmatous, miasmic, miasmous,** *a.* **miasmology**, *n.* [Gr., from *miainein,* to pollute]

miaul, *v.i.* of a cat, to cry 'miaow'. *v.t.* to sing or utter with the voice of a cat. **miauler,** *n.* a cat.

mica, *n.* a name for a group of silicates having a perfect basal cleavage into thin, tough and shining plates, formerly used instead of glass. **mica-schist, -slate,** *n.* **micaceous,** *a.* [L, a crumb]

mice, *pl.* MOUSE.

mich MICHE.

Mich., (*abbr.*) Michigan (US).

Michael[1], *n.* in the Bible, an archangel, referred to as the guardian angel of Israel. In the New Testament Book of Revelation he leads the hosts of heaven to battle against Satan. In paintings he is depicted with a flaming sword and sometimes a pair of scales. Feast day 29 Sept. (Michaelmas).

Michael[2], *n.* **Mikhail Fyodorovich Romanov** (1596–1645), tsar of Russia from 1613. He was elected tsar by a national assembly, at a time of chaos and foreign invasion, and was the first of the house of Romanov, which ruled until 1917.

Michael[3], *n.* (1921–), king of Romania (1927–30) and (1940–47). The son of Carol II, he succeeded his grandfather as king in 1927, but was displaced when his father returned from exile, 1930. In 1940 he was proclaimed king again on his father's abdication, and in 1944 overthrew the fascist dictatorship of Ion Antonescu (1882–1946) and enabled Romania to share in the victory of the Allies at the end of World War II. He abdicated and left Romania in 1947.

Michaelmas, *n.* the feast of St Michael the Archangel, 29 Sept.; autumn. **Michaelmas daisy,** *n.* the wild aster, *Aster tripolium* also various perennial cultivated asters. [L *Michael,* Heb. *Mīkhāel,* who is like God, MASS[1]]

miche, *v.i.* to hide, to skulk, to play truant. **micher,** *n.* [prob. from ONorth. F *muchier,* OF *mucier* (F *musser*), from Teut. (cp. OHG *mūhōn,* to hide, G dial. *maucheln,* to hide, to cheat)]

Michelangelo (Buonarroti), *n.* (1475–1564), Italian sculptor, painter, architect and poet, active in his native Florence and in Rome. His giant talent dominated the High Renaissance. The marble *David* (1501–04) (Accademia, Florence) set a new standard in nude sculpture. His massive figure style was translated into fresco in the Sistine Chapel (1508–12 and 1536–41, Vatican). Other works in Rome include the dome of St Peter's basilica.

Michelson, *n.* **Albert Abraham** (1852–1931), German-born US physicist. In conjunction with Edward Morley, he performed in 1887 the *Michelson–Morley experiment* to detect the motion of the Earth through the postulated ether (a medium believed to be necessary for the propagation of light). The failure of the experiment indicated the nonexistence of the ether, and led Einstein to his theory of relativity. Nobel prize 1907.

Michigan, *n.* a state of the US, bordered by the Great Lakes, Ohio, Indiana, Wisconsin and Canada; nickname Great Lake State or Wolverine State. **area** 151,600 sq km/58,518 sq miles. **capital** Lansing. **towns** Detroit, Grand Rapids, Flint. **products** cars, iron, cement, oil. **population** (1986) 9,145,000.

Michigan, Lake, *n.* lake in north central US, one of the Great Lakes; area 58,000 sq km/22,390 sq miles. Chicago and Milwaukee are its main ports.

miching malicho, sneaking or stealthy mischief. [Shak. (MICHE, -ING, *malicho,* of uncertain meaning)]

Mick, *n.* (*sl. often offensive*) an Irishman.

Mickey Finn, *n.* (*esp. N Am.*) a doped drink.

Mickiewicz, *n.* **Adam** (1798–1855), Polish revolutionary poet, whose *Pan Tadeusz* (1832–34) is Poland's national epic. He died at Constantinople while raising a Polish corps to fight against Russia in the Crimean War.

mickle, *a.* (*chiefly Sc.*) much, great. *n.* a large amount. [OE *micel, mycel*]

micky, *n.* (*Austral. sl.*) a young wild bull; (*N Am. sl.*) an Irish lad. **to take the micky out of,** (*coll.*) to debunk; to tease. **micky-taking,** *n.* [fam. form of *Michael,* see MICHAELMAS]

micracoustic, *a.* serving to increase small or indistinct sounds. *n.* an instrument for augmenting sounds for the partially deaf. [F *micracoustique*]

micro, *n.* (*coll.*) short for MICROCOMPUTER.

micr(o)-, *comb.form* noting smallness; pertaining to small things (as opposed to large ones). [Gr. *mikros,* small]

microbe, *n.* any minute organism, esp. a bacterium or

microzyme causing disease or fermentation. **microbial, -ian, -bic,** *a.* **microbiology,** *n.* **microbiologist,** *n.* [F (MICR(O)-, Gr. *bios,* life)]

microcephalic, *a.* having an unusually small skull. **microcephalous,** *a.* **microcephaly,** *n.*

microchip, *n.* a chip of silicon etc. bearing many integrated circuits.

microchronometer, *n.* one for measuring minute intervals of time.

microcircuit, *n.* a very small integrated circuit on a semiconductor.

microclimate, *n.* the climate of a very small area.

micrococcus, *n.* (*pl.* **-cocci**) one of a genus of minute spherical bacteria, usu. regarded as fission-fungi.

microcomputer, *n.* a small computer with one or more microprocessors.

microcosm, *n.* the universe on a small scale; man as an epitome of the macrocosm or universe; a little community; a representation (of) in little. **microcosmic,** *a.* **microcosmography,** *n.* **microcosmology,** *n.* [F *microcosme,* med. L *microcosmus,* Gr. *mikrokosmos* (MICR(O)-, COSMOS)]

microcrith, *n.* (*Chem.*) the weight of an atom of hydrogen. [Gr. *krithē,* barley-corn]

microcyte, *n.* (*Path.*) a small red blood-corpuscle, such as appear in cases of anaemia. **microcythaemia, microcytosis,** *n.*

microdont, *a.* having abnormally small teeth. [Gr. *odous odontos,* tooth]

microdot, *n.* a photographic image reduced to the size of a dot, e.g. for espionage purposes.

microelectronics, *n. sing.* electronics as applied to microcircuits.

microfarad, *n.* a unit of electrical capacitance, one millionth of a farad.

microfiche, *n.* a sheet of film bearing miniature photographs of documents etc. [F *fiche,* sheet of paper]

microfilm, *n.* a strip of cinematograph film on which successive pages of a document or book are photographed for purposes of record.

microgeology, *n.* the department of geology dealing with microscopic structures.

micrograph, *n.* a kind of pantograph for extremely minute engraving; a very small picture, photograph etc. **micrography,** *n.* a description of microscopic objects. **micrographer,** *n.* **micrographic,** *a.*

microgroove, *n.* the groove of a long-playing gramophone record.

microhm, *n.* a unit of electrical measurement, one millionth of an ohm.

microinstruction, *n.* a computer instruction that activates a particular circuit to execute part of an operation specified by a machine instruction.

microlight, *n.* a very small light aircraft for one or two people.

microlite, *n.* a native salt of calcium found in small crystals; microlith.

microlith, *n.* one of the microscopic bodies found in vitreous feldspar, hornblende etc. **microlithic,** *a.* applied to a particular style of funeral monuments, in which extremely small stones are used.

micrology, *n.* the branch of science dealing with microscopic objects; excessive concern with petty matters, over-minuteness, hair-splitting. **micrological,** *a.* **micrologically,** *adv.* **micrologist,** *n.*

micrometer, *n.* an instrument to measure small distances or objects. **micrometric, -ical,** *a.*

micron, *n.* one millionth of a metre, the unit of length in microscopic research.

Micronesia, *n.pl.* islands in the Pacific Ocean lying N of Melanesia, including the Federated States of Micronesia, Belau, Kiribati, the Mariana and Marshall Islands, Nauru and Tuvalu.

Micronesia, Federated States of, a self-governing island group (Kosrae, Ponape, Truk and Yap) in the W Pacific; capital Kolonia, on Ponape; area 700 sq km/ 270 sq miles; population (1988) 86,000. It is part of the US Trust Territory. Purchased by Germany from Spain, 1898, they were occupied in 1914 by Japan. They were captured by the US in World War II, and became part of the US Trust Territory of the Pacific, 1947. Micronesia became internally self-governing from 1979, and in free association with the US from 1986 (there is US control of military activities in return for economic aid). The people are Micronesian and Polynesian, and the main languages are Kosrean, Ponapean, Trukese and Yapese, although the official language is English.

microorganism, *n.* an organism of microscopic size.

microphone, *n.* an instrument for converting sound into electrical waves; the mouthpiece for broadcasting. **microphonic,** *a.* pertaining to the microphone; behaving in a manner similar to a microphone. *n.pl.* the branch of acoustics dealing with the magnifying of weak sounds.

microphotography, *n.* the photography of objects on a minute scale; the photography of microscopic objects. **microphotograph,** *n.*

microphylline, *a.* (*Bot.*) composed of or having minute leaflets or scales. **microphyllous,** *a.* having small leaves. [Gr. *phullon,* leaf]

microphyte, *n.* a microscopic vegetable organism, esp. a bacterium.

micropodal, *a.* having abnormally small feet. [Gr. *pous podos,* foot, -AL]

microprocessor, *n.* an integrated circuit operating as the central processing unit of a microcomputer.

micropsia, *n.* (*Path.*) a state of vision in which objects appear unnaturally small. [Gr. *-opsia,* vision]

micropterous, *a.* having small wings or fins. [Gr. *pteron,* wing]

micropyle, *n.* a minute opening in the external membrane of the ovum by which spermatozoa may enter; (*Bot.*) the foramen in an ovule by which the pollen reaches the apex of the nucleus; the aperture representing this in the ripe seed. [Gr. *pulē,* gate]

microscope, *n.* an optical instrument by which objects are so magnified that details invisible to the naked eye are clearly seen. **microscopic,** *a.* pertaining to the microscope; too small to be visible except by the aid of a microscope. **microscopically,** *adv.* **microscopy,** *n.* **microscopist,** *n.*

microsecond, *n.* one millionth of a second.

microseism, *n.* a slight tremor or vibration of the earth's crust. **microseismic,** *a.* **microseismograph,** *n.* an instrument for recording microseisms. **microseismology,** *n.* **microseismometry,** *n.* [Gr. *seismos,* earthquake]

microsoma, *n.* (*pl.* **-somata,** -tə) one of the minute granules in the endoplasm of protoplasmic cells. **microsomatous,** *a.* **microsome,** *n.*

microspectroscope, *n.* a combination of microscope and spectroscope for examining minute traces of substances.

microsporangium, *n.* a sporangium containing microspores.

microspore, *n.* a small spore, sexual in function, as in the *Selaginellae;* a parasitic fungus with small spores; a spore-like body in certain protozoans. **microsporous,** *a.*

microsurgery, *n.* surgery performed using a microscope and special small instruments.

microtome, *n.* an instrument for cutting thin sections for microscopic examination. **microtomic, -ical,** *a.* **microtomist,** *n.* **microtomy,** *n.*

microwave, *n.* an electromagnetic wave with a wavelength between 30 cm and 1 mm; (*coll.*) a microwave oven. **microwave oven,** *n.* one that cooks food with microwaves.

microzoa, *n.pl.* microscopic animals. **microzoal, microzoic,** *a.* **microzoan,** *n.* **microzoid,** *n., a.*

microzyme, *n.* any of the minute organisms floating in the air, probably the germs of certain infectious diseases.

micturition, *n.* a frequent desire to urinate; (*loosely*) the act of urinating. **micturate,** *v.i.* to urinate. [L *micturīre,* desiderative of *mingere,* to make water, -ITION]

mid, *a.* (*superl.* **midmost**) (*usu. in comb.*) middle. †*n.* the middle. *prep.* (*poet.*) amid. †**mid-age,** *n.* middle age. **midday,** *n.* noon. *a.* pertaining to noon. **mid-heaven,** *n.* **mid-iron,** *n.* an iron golf club with a moderate amount of loft. **mid-off,** *n.* (*Cricket*) the fieldsman to the left of the bowler. **mid-on,** *n.* the fieldsman to the right of the bowler. (These definitions apply only when the batsman is right-handed.) [OE *mid, midd*]

Midas, *n.* a fabulously rich man. **the Midas touch,** the facility for making money or achieving success. [legendary king of Phrygia granted the power of turning all he touched into gold]

MIDAS, *n.* (*acronym*) *M*issile *D*efence *A*larm *S*ystem.

Mid-Atlantic Ridge, the ocean ridge, formed by the movement of plates described by plate tectonics, that runs along the centre of the Atlantic Ocean, parallel to its edges, for some 14,000 km/8800 miles – almost from the Arctic to the Antarctic.

midden, *n.* a dunghill. **kitchen-midden** KITCHEN. [ME *midding*]

middle, *a.* (*superl.* **middlemost**) placed equally distant from the extremes; intervening; intermediate; of verbs, between active and passive, reflexive. *n.* the point equally distant from the extremes; the waist; the midst, the centre. *v.t.* to place in the middle; (*Naut.*) to fold or double in the middle; in football, to pass or return the ball to midfield from one of the wings. **in the middle of,** during, while. **middle age,** *n.* the period of life between youth and old age, or about the middle of the ordinary human life (35–55). **middle-aged,** *a.* **Middle Ages,** *n.pl.* the period of European history between the fall of the Roman Empire in the 5th century and the Renaissance in the 15th. **Middle America,** *n.* the midwestern region of the US; the middle class of the US. **middle C,** *n.* the white note at the centre of the piano keyboard, indicating the division between left and right-hand regions and corresponding to the treble and bass staves of printed music. **middle class,** *n.* the class between the leisured class and artisans, the bourgeoisie. **middle-class,** *a.* **middle-distance** DISTANCE. **Middle English** ENGLISH. **middle finger,** *n.* the second finger (third from the little finger inclusive). **Middle Kingdom,** *n.* see separate article below. **middleman,** *n.* an agent, an intermediary; one through whose hands a commodity passes between the producer and the consumer. **middle name,** *n.* any name between a person's first given name and his or her family name; (*coll.*) one's most typical quality. **middle-of-the-road,** *a.* moderate; having a wide appeal. **middle term,** *n.* the term of a syllogism that appears in both major and minor premises. **Middle Way,** *n.* the path to enlightenment, taught by Buddha, which avoids the extremes of indulgence and asceticism. **middling,** *a.* of middle size, quality or condition; mediocre; moderately good, second-rate. *adv.* moderately, tolerably. **fair to middling** FAIR[1]. **middlingly,** *adv.* **middlings,** *n.pl.* the coarser part of flour; the middling grade of other commodities. [OE *middel* (cp. Dut. *middle,* G *Mittel*)]

Middle East, *n.* indeterminate area now usually taken to include the Balkan States, Egypt and SW Asia. Until the 1940s, this area was generally called the Near East, and the term Middle East referred to the area from Iran to Burma.

Middle Kingdom, *n.* **Egyptian** a period of Egyptian history extending from the late 11th to the 13th dynasty (roughly 2040–1670 BC); **Chinese** Chinese term for China and its empire up to 1912, describing its central position in the Far East.

Middlesex, *n.* a former English county, absorbed by Greater London in 1965. Contained within the Thames basin, it provided good agricultural land before it was built over. It was settled in the 6th cent. by Saxons, and its name comes from its position between the kingdoms of the East and West Saxons.

Middleton, *n.* **Thomas** (*c.* 1570–1627), English dramatist. He produced numerous romantic plays, tragedies, and realistic comedies, both alone and in collaboration. The best-known are *A Fair Quarrel* and *The Changeling* (1622) with Rowley; *The Roaring Girl* with Dekker; and *Women Beware Women* (1621).

Middx, (*abbr.*) Middlesex.

middy[1], MIDSHIPMAN.

middy[2], *n.* (*Austral., coll.*) a glass of beer; a 10 oz. (approx. 300 ml.) pot or container.

midfield, *n.* the central area of a sports pitch, esp. a football pitch; the players with positions between the attackers and defenders, esp. in football.

midge, *n.* a gnat or other minute fly; a tiny person. **midget,** *n.* a very small person. *a.* very small. [OE *mycg*]

Mid Glamorgan, *n.* a county in S Wales. **area** 1020 sq km/394 sq miles. **towns** administrative headquarters Cardiff; resort Porthcawl; Aberdare, Merthyr Tydfil, Bridgend, Pontypridd. **products** the north was formerly an important coal (Rhondda) and iron and steel area; Royal Mint at Llantrisant; agriculture in the south; Caerphilly noted for mild cheese. **population** (1987) 535,000. **language** 8% Welsh, English.

MIDI, *n.* (*Comput.*) an interface which allows computer control of electronic key-boards and other musical instruments. [acronym for *M*usical *I*nstrument *D*igital *I*nterface]

Midi, *n.* the South of France. [F]

midi-, *comb.form* of middle size; of a skirt etc., reaching to the mid-calf. **midi,** *n.* a midi-skirt, midi-dress etc. **midi-bus,** *n.* a bus larger than a minibus, but smaller than a standard bus. **midi system,** *n.* a compact hi-fi stacking unit.

Midi-Pyrénées, *n.* a region of SW France; area 45,300 sq km/17,486 sq miles; population (1986) 2,355,000. Its capital is Toulouse, and it consists of the *départements* of Ariège, Aveyron, Haute-Garonne, Gers, Lot, Haute-Pyrénées, Tarn and Tarn-et-Garonne. Towns include Montauban, Cahors, Rodez and Lourdes. The region includes a number of spa towns, winter resorts and prehistoric caves.

midland, *a.* situated in the middle or interior of a country; surrounded by land. *n.* the interior of a country; (*pl.*) the midland counties of England.

Midlands, *n.pl.* area of England corresponding roughly to the Anglo-Saxon kingdom of Mercia. **E Midlands** Derbyshire, Leicestershire, Northamptonshire, Nottinghamshire. **W Midlands** the former metropolitan county of West Midlands created from parts of Staffordshire, Warwickshire and Worcestershire; and (often included) **S Midlands** Bedfordshire, Buckinghamshire and Oxfordshire.

midnight, *n.* the middle of the night, twelve o'clock; intense darkness. *a.* pertaining to or occurring in the middle of the night; very dark. **midnight sun,** *n.* the sun visible around midnight in summer in the polar regions.

mid-off, -on MID.

Midrash, *n.* the ancient Jewish commentaries on the Bible, in the form of sermons in which allegory and legendary illustration are used. They were compiled mainly in Palestine between AD 400 and 1200.

midrib, *n.* the continuation of the petiole to the apex of a leaf.

midriff, *n.* the diaphragm. [OE *midrif, -hrif* (*mid, hrif,* belly)]

midship, *n.* the middle part of a ship or boat. *a.* situated in or belonging to this. **midshipman,** *n.* formerly an officer ranking between a cadet and a sublieutenant, a young officer under instruction on shipboard. **midshipmite,** *n.* (*facet.*) a very young or small midshipman. **midships** AMIDSHIPS.

midst, *n.* the middle. *prep.* in the middle of, amidst. †*adv.* in the middle. **in the midst of,** among, surrounded by or involved in. [earlier *middest* (OE *middes,* gen. of MID used adverbially, prob. confused or blended with superl. of MID)]

midstream, *n.* the middle of a stream. *adv.* in the middle of a stream. **to change horses in midstream** HORSE.

midsummer, *n.* the middle of summer, esp. the period

of the summer solstice, about 21 June. **midsummer day,** *n.* 24 June.

midway, *a.* situated in the middle or the middle of the way. *adv.*, in the middle; half-way.

Midway Islands, *n.pl.* two islands in the Pacific, 1800 km/1120 miles NW of Honolulu; area 5 sq km/2 sq miles; population (1980) 500. They were annexed by the US 1867, and are now administered by the US Navy. The naval **Battle of Midway**, 3–6 June 1942, between the US and Japan, was the turning point in the Pacific in World War II.

midweek, *n.* the middle of the week, i.e. Tuesday, Wednesday, Thursday.

Midwest, Middle West, *n.* a large area of N central US. It is loosely defined, but is generally taken to comprise the states of Ohio, Indiana, Illinois, Michigan, Iowa, Wisconsin, Minnesota and sometimes Nebraska. It tends to be conservative socially and politically, and isolationist. Traditionally its economy is divided between agriculture and heavy industry.

midwife, *n.* (*pl.* **-wives**) a woman who assists at childbirth; any person who helps to bring something forth. *v.i.* to perform the office of a midwife. *v.t.* to assist in childbirth. **midwifery,** *n.* [OE *mid,* with (cp. G *mit,* also Gr. *meta*), WIFE]

midwinter, *n.* the middle of winter, esp. the winter solstice, 21 Dec.

mien, *n.* air or manner; appearance, deportment, demeanour, bearing, carriage. [F *mine* or shortened from DEMEAN]

Mies van der Rohe, *n.* **Ludwig** (1886–1969), German architect who practised in the US from 1937. He was director of the Bauhaus, 1929–33. He became professor at the Illinois Technical Institute, 1938–58, for which he designed new buildings on characteristically functional lines from 1941. He also designed the bronze-and-glass Seagram building in New York (1956–59).

miff, *n.* a petty quarrel; a huff. *v.i.* to be vexed (with or at). *v.t.* to vex, to annoy slightly, to offend. [prob. imit. of instinctive expression of annoyance]

Mifune, *n.* **Toshiro** (1920–), Japanese actor who appeared in several films directed by Kurosawa, including *Rashomon* (1950) and *Throne of Blood* (1957). He has also appeared in European and American films.

might[1], *n.* strength, force; power, esp. to enforce will or arbitrary authority. **with might and main,** with all one's strength. †**mightful,** *a.* **mighty,** *a.* strong, powerful; very great, huge, immense; (*coll.*) great, considerable. *adv.* (*coll.*) exceedingly, very. **mightily,** *adv.* **mightiness,** *n.* [OE *miht,* cogn. with *megan,* MAY[1] (cp. G *Macht,* Dan. *magt*)]

might[2], *past* MAY[1].

mignon, *a.* delicate and small, dainty. [F]

mignonette, *n.* an annual plant, *Reseda odorata,* with fragrant greenish flowers. [F, dim. of prec.]

migraine, *n.* a recurrent severe headache, esp. on one side of the head only, often accompanied by nausea and visual disturbances. [F *migraine,* see MEGRIM]

migrate, *v.i.* to remove from one country, place or habitation to another; of birds, fishes etc., to pass from one region to another according to the season; to pass from one part of the body to another. **migrant,** *n., a.* **migration,** *n.* **migrator,** *n.* **migratory,** *a.* [L *migrātus,* p.p. of *migrāre,* to wander]

Mihailovič, *n.* **Draza** (1893–1946), Yugoslav soldier, leader of the guerrilla Chetniks of World War II against the German occupation. His feud with Tito's communists led to the withdrawal of Allied support and that of his own exiled government from 1943. He turned for help to the Italians and Germans, and was eventually shot for treason.

mihanere, *n.* a convert to Christianity. [Maori]

mikado, *n.* the Emperor of Japan. [Jap. (*mi,* august, *kado,* gate, door)]

mike, *n.* (*coll.*) short for MICROPHONE.

mil., (*abbr.*) military.

mil, *n.* a unit of length, a thousandth part of an inch (0·0254 mm), in measuring wire; a proposed basis of British decimal coinage, £0·001; in pharmacy, a millilitre. [L *mille,* a thousand]

miladi, milady, *n.* (formerly used in France) my lady (used as address or appellation).

milage, MILEAGE under MILE.

Milan, *n.* (Italian **Milano**) an industrial city (aircraft, cars, locomotives, textiles), financial and cultural centre, capital of Lombardy, Italy; population (1988) 1,479,000.

milch, *a.* giving milk. **milch-cow,** *n.* a cow kept for milk; a person from whom money is easily obtained. [OE *meolc, melc,* cogn. with MILK]

mild, *a.* gentle in manners or disposition; tender, pacific, clement, placid, bland, pleasant; of fruit, liquor etc., soft, not harsh, sharp or strong; of beer, not bitter, not strongly flavoured with hops; moderate, not extreme, tame; moderate in degree; demulcent, lenitive; of medicines, operating gently. **draw it mild,** (*coll.*) do not exaggerate. **milden,** *v.t., v.i.* **mildly,** *adv.* **to put it mildly,** without exaggerating. **mildness,** *n.* [OE *milde* (cp. Dut., G, Dan. and Swed. *mild,* Icel. *mildr*), cogn. with Gr. *malthakos*]

mildew, *n.* a deleterious fungoid growth on plants, cloth, paper, food etc. after exposure to damp. *v.t.* to taint with mildew. *v.i.* to be tainted with mildew. **mildewy,** *a.* [OE *meledēaw,* honeydew, cp. OHG *militou* (*milith,* cp. Gr. *meli,* honey, DEW)]

mile, *n.* a measure of length or distance, 1760 yds. (1·609 km); orig. a Roman measure of 1000 paces, about 1620 yds. (1·481 km). **geographical, nautical, mile,** one sixtieth of a degree, acc. to the British Admiralty 6080 ft., or 2026⅔ yds. (1·853 km). **mil(e)ometer,** *n.* a device for recording the number of miles travelled by a vehicle. **milepost, milestone,** *n.* a post or stone marking the miles on a road. **mileage,** *n.* the number of miles concerned; an allowance paid for the number of miles travelled; the distance travelled by a vehicle on one gallon or litre of petrol; the benefit to be derived from something. **miler,** *n.* a person, animal or thing qualified to run or travel a mile, or (*in comb.*) a specified number of miles (as *ten-miler*). **miles,** *adv.* (*coll.*) considerably, very much. [OE *mīl,* L *mīlia,* pl. of *mille,* a thousand (paces)]

Miles, *n.* **Bernard (Baron Miles)** (1907–), English actor and producer. He appeared on stage as Briggs in *Thunder Rock* (1940) and Iago in *Othello* (1942), and his films include *Great Expectations* (1947). He founded a trust that in 1959 built the City of London's first new theatre for 300 years, the Mermaid.

Milesian, *a.* Irish. *n.* an Irishman. [*Milesius,* legendary king of Spain, whose sons are said to have conquered Ireland about 1300 BC, -AN]

milfoil, *n.* the yarrow, *Achillea millefolium,* named because the leaves are thrice pinnatifid; the genus *Achillea;* applied to some other plants. [OF, from L *millefolium* (*mille,* thousand, *folium,* leaf)]

miliary, *a.* like millet seed; of a medical condition, attended with an eruption like millet seeds. [L *miliārius,* from *milium,* MILLET]

milieu, *n.* environment, surroundings, setting. [F, middle, from *mi,* middle, *lieu,* place]

militant, *a.* fighting; combative, warlike, military. *n.* a militant person. **Church militant,** the body of Christians on earth. **militant suffragette,** *n.* one of the female advocates of woman suffrage (1905–18) who undertook violent means to gain a hearing. **militancy,** *n.* **militantly,** *adv.* [L *mīlitans, -antem,* pres.p. of *mīlitāre,* to MILITATE]

Militant Tendency, *n.* a faction formed within the British Labour Party, aligned with the publication *Militant.* It became active in the 1970s, with radical socialist policies based on Trotskyism, and gained some success in local government, for example in the inner-city area of Liverpool. In the mid-1980s the Labour Party considered it to be an organization within the party and banned it.

military, *a.* pertaining to soldiers, arms or warfare; soldierly, warlike, martial; engaged in war. *n.* (*collect.*)

soldiers generally; the army; troops. **Military Cross (Medal),** *n.* a British army decoration awarded for conspicuous courage under fire. **military fever,** *n.* enteric or typhus. **military honours,** *n.pl.* courtesies paid to a soldier or person of high rank at funerals, weddings, toasts etc. **military police,** *n.* a police force for enforcing discipline in the army. **military service,** *n.* service (usu. compulsory) in the armed forces; the service due in time of war from a vassal to his superior. **military tenure,** *n.* tenure by this. **militaria**, *n.pl.* military uniforms, medals etc. of the past that are of interest to collectors. **militarism,** *n.* military spirit; military or warlike policy; domination by the military or the spirit of aggression. **militarist,** *n.* **militarize, -ise,** *v.t.* **militarization, -isation,** *n.* [F *militaire,* L *mīlitāris,* from *mīles mīlitis,* soldier]

militate, *v.i.* to be or stand opposed; to have weight or influence, to tell (against). [L *mīlitātus,* p.p. of *mīlitāre,* from *mīles mīlitis,* soldier]

militia, *n.* a military force consisting of the body of citizens not enrolled in the regular army; the former constitutional force of England, consisting usu. of volunteers enrolled and disciplined, but called out only in case of emergency, superseded by the Territorial Army in 1907. **militiaman,** *n.* [L, as prec.]

milk, *n.* the whitish fluid secreted by female mammals for the nourishment of their young, esp. that of the cow; the white juice of certain plants or fruits; an emulsion made from herbs, drugs etc., esp. for cosmetic purposes. *v.t.* to draw milk from; to plunder (creditors); to exploit or get money out of (a person) in an underhand or disreputable way; (*sl.*) to tap (a telegraph wire or message); †to give milk to; †to suck. *v.i.* to yield milk. **milk-and-water,** *n.* milk diluted with water; namby-pamby or mawkish talk, sentiment etc. *a.* namby-pamby, weak, twaddling. **milk chocolate,** *n.* chocolate made with milk. **milk-fever,** *n.* a fever attacking women when milk is first secreted after childbirth. **milk float,** *n.* a usu. electrically-propelled vehicle for delivering milk to houses. **†milk-livered,** *a.* cowardly. **milkmaid,** *n.* a woman employed in dairywork. **milkman,** *n.* a man who sells milk; a dairy worker. **milk-punch,** *n.* spirits mixed with milk and sweetened. **milk-run,** *n.* a regular journey to deliver milk; a routine trip, flight etc. **milk-shake,** *n.* a drink of milk, flavouring and ice-cream, shaken up in a machine. **milk-sickness,** *n.* a fatal spasmodic cattle disease, sometimes communicated to man, peculiar to the Western States of the US. **milksop,** *n.* an effeminate person. **milk-sugar,** *n.* (*Chem.*) lactose. **milk-thistle,** *n.* a thistle-like herb of the aster family, *Silbyum marianum.* **milk-tooth,** *n.* one of the temporary teeth in young mammals; the foretooth of a foal. **milk-vetch,** *n.* a plant of the leguminous genus *Astragalus,* supposed to increase milk-bearing in goats. **milkweed,** *n.* a plant, of various species, with milky juice. **milkwort,** *n.* a plant of the genus *Polygala,* formerly believed to promote the secretion of milk, esp. *P. vulgaris,* a small plant with blue, white or pink flowers. **milker,** *n.* **milky,** *a.* consisting of, mixed with or resembling milk; mild, effeminate; white, opaque, clouded (of liquids); of cattle, yielding milk; timid. **Milky Way,** *n.* see below. **milkily,** *adv.* **milkiness,** *n.* [OE *meolc* (cp. Dut. and Dan. *melk,* G *Milch,* Icel. *mjōlk,* cogn. with Gr. *amelgein,* L *mulgēre,* to milk)]

Milky Way, *n.* the faint band of light crossing the night sky, consisting of stars in the plane of our galaxy. The name Milky Way is often used for the galaxy itself. It is a spiral galaxy, about 100,000 light years in diameter, containing at least 100 billion stars. The Sun is in one of its spiral arms, about 25,000 light years from the centre.

mill[1], *n.* a machine for grinding corn to a fine powder; a building with machinery for this purpose; a machine for reducing solid substances of any kind to a finer consistency; a building fitted up with machinery for any industrial purpose, a factory; (*sl.*) a fight with fists. *v.t.* to grind (as corn); to produce (flour) by grinding; to serrate the edge of (a coin); to full (cloth); (*sl.*) to thrash, to pummel. *v.i.* to move slowly (around). **to go, be put through the mill,** to undergo a harrowing, exhausting etc. experience. **millboard,** *n.* thick pasteboard used by bookbinders for book-covers. **mill-cog,** *n.* a cog of a mill-wheel. **mill-dam,** *n.* a wall or dam built across a stream to divert it to a mill; a millpond. **mill-hand,** *n.* a factory worker. **millpond,** *n.* **mill-race,** *n.* the canal or the current of water for driving a mill-wheel. **mill-rind,** *n.* an iron fitting for fixing an upper millstone to the spindle. **millstone,** *n.* one of a pair of circular stones for grinding corn; a very burdensome person or thing. **to see far into a millstone,** to be remarkably acute. **millstone grit,** *n.* a coarse quartzose sandstone used for making millstones. **mill-tail,** *n.* the stream flowing from a mill-wheel. **mill-tooth,** *n.* a molar tooth. **mill-wheel,** *n.* a large wheel moved by water, flowing over or under it, for driving the machinery in a mill. **millwright,** *n.* one who constructs or repairs the machinery of mills. **milled,** *a.* passed through a mill; of coins, having the edges serrated; of cloth, fulled. **miller,** *n.* one who keeps or works in a flour mill; one who works any mill; applied to various moths and other insects with white or powdery wings etc. **miller's thumb,** *n.* the bullhead, *Cottus gobio.* [OE *myln,* from late L *mulīna, molīna,* L *mola,* a mill (*molere,* to grind)]

mill[2], *n.* a money of account in the US, the thousandth part of a dollar or tenth of a cent. [short for L *millēsimum,* thousandth, from *mille,* a thousand]

Mill[1], *n.* **James** (1773–1836), Scottish philosopher and political thinker who developed the theory of utilitarianism. He is remembered for his political articles, and for the rigorous education he gave his son John Stuart Mill.

Mill[2], *n.* **John Stuart** (1806–73), English philosopher and economist, who wrote *On Liberty* (1859), the classic philosophical defence of liberalism, and *Utilitarianism* (1863), a version of the 'greatest happiness for the greatest number' principle in ethics. His progressive views inspired *On the Subjection of Women* (1869). In his social philosophy, he gradually abandoned the Utilitarians' extreme individualism for an outlook akin to liberal socialism, while still laying great emphasis on the liberty of the individual; this change can be traced in the later editions of *Principles of Political Economy* (1848).

Millais, *n.* **John Everett** (1829–96), British painter, a founder member of the Pre-Raphaelite Brotherhood (PRB) in 1848. By the late 1850s he had dropped out of the PRB and his style became more fluent and less detailed.

millennium, *n.* (*pl.* **-nniums, -nnia**) a period of 1000 years, esp. that when Satan shall be bound and Christ reign on earth (in allusion to Rev. xx.1–5). **millenarian,** *a.* consisting of 1000 years; pertaining to the millennium. *n.* one who believes in this. **millenarianism,** *n.* **millenary,** *n., a.* **millennial,** *a.* pertaining to the millennium. *n.* a thousandth anniversary. **millennialist,** *n.* [L *mille,* thousand, *annus,* year]

millepede, MILLIPEDE.

†millepore, *n.* any coral of the genus *Millepora,* the surface of which is full of minute pores. **milleporite,** *n.* a fossil millepore. [L *mille,* thousand, *porus,* PORE[1]]

miller MILL[1].

Miller[1], *n.* **Arthur** (1915–), US playwright. His plays deal with family relationships and contemporary American values, and include *Death of a Salesman* (1949) and *The Crucible* (1953), based on the Salem witch trials and reflecting the communist witch-hunts of Senator McCarthy. He was married (1956–61) to the film star Marilyn Monroe, for whom he wrote the film *The Misfits* (1960).

Miller[2], *n.* **Glenn** (1904–44), US trombonist and, as bandleader, exponent of the big-band swing sound from 1938. He composed his signature tune 'Moonlight Serenade' (a hit 1939). He disappeared without trace on a flight between England and France during World War II.

Miller[3], *n.* **Stanley** (1930–), US chemist. In the early

1950s, under laboratory conditions, he tried to imitate the original conditions of the Earth's atmosphere (a mixture of methane, ammonia and hydrogen), added an electrical discharge, and waited. After a few days he found that amino acids, the ingredients of protein, had been formed.

millesimal, *a.* consisting of one-thousandth parts. *n.* a thousandth. **millesimally,** *adv.* [L *millēsimus,* thousandth, from *mille,* thousand]

millet, *n. Panicum miliaceum* of E Indian origin, or its nutritive seeds; applied to some other species of grasses bearing edible seeds. **millet-grass,** *n.* a tall N American grass, *Milium effusum.* [F, dim. of *mil,* L *milium* (cp. Gr. *melinē*)]

Millet, *n.* **Jean François** (1814–75), French painter, a leading member of the Barbizon school, painting scenes of peasant life and landscapes. *The Angelus* (1859, Musée d'Orsay, Paris) brought him great success and was widely reproduced in his day.

Millett, *n.* **Kate** (1934–), US radical feminist lecturer, writer and sculptor, whose book *Sexual Politics* (1970) was a landmark in feminist thinking. She was a founding member of the National Organization of Women (NOW). Later books include *Flying* (1974), *The Prostitution Papers* (1976), and *Sita* (1977).

milli-, *comb. form* one-thousandth. [L *mille,* a thousand]

milliard, *n.* one thousand millions. [F, from L *mille,* a thousand]

†**milliary,** *a.* pertaining to or denoting a mile, esp. a Roman mile; pertaining to a millennium. *n.* a milestone. [L *milliārius,* from *mille,* a thousand (paces)]

millibar, *n.* one-thousandth of a bar, equivalent to the pressure exerted by a column of mercury about 0·03 in. (0·762 mm) high. [L *mille,* a thousand; BAR[3]]

millicurie, *n.* one-thousandth of a curie.

milligram, *n.* one-thousandth of a gram, 0·0154 of an English grain.

Millikan, *n.* **Robert Andrews** (1868–1953), US physicist, awarded a Nobel prize, 1923, for his determination of the electric charge on an electron by his oil-drop experiment (which took him five years up to 1913 to perfect).

millilitre, *n.* one-thousandth of a litre, 0·06103 cu. in.

millimetre, *n.* one-thousandth of a metre, or 0·03937 in.

milliner, *n.* one who makes and sells hats, bonnets etc. for women; †a haberdasher. **millinery,** *n.* [prob. *Milaner,* a dealer in Milan wares, such as silk and ribbons.]

milling, *n.* the act or process of working a mill or mills; the serrated edging of a coin.

million, *n.* one thousand thousand, esp. of pounds, francs or dollars; an indefinitely great number. **the million,** the multitude, the masses. **millionaire,** *n.* a man who has a million pounds, francs or dollars; one immensely rich. **millionairess,** *n. fem.* **millionary,** *a.* pertaining to or consisting of millions. *n.* a millionaire. **millionfold,** *a., adv.* **millionocracy,** *n.* government by millionaires. **millionth,** *n., a.* [F, from It. *millione,* from L *mille,* thousand]

millipede, *n.* a segmented myriapod, esp. of the genus *Iulus;* any articulate animal with numerous feet. [L *millipeda,* wood-louse (*mille,* thousand, *pes pedis,* foot)]

millisecond, *n.* one-thousandth of a second.

millocrat, *n.* a wealthy mill-owner; one of the mill-owning class. **millocracy, millocratism,** *n.*

Mills-bomb, *n.* a type of hand grenade. [from name of inventor, Sir W. *Mills,* 1856–1932]

millwright MILL[1].

Milne, *n.* **A(lan) A(lexander)** (1882–1956), English writer. His books for children were based on the teddy bear and other toys of his son Christopher Robin (*Winnie-the-Pooh*, 1926, and *The House at Pooh Corner*, 1928). He also wrote children's verse (*When We Were Very Young*, 1924, and *Now We Are Six*, 1927) and plays, including an adaptation of Kenneth Grahame's *The Wind in the Willows* as *Toad of Toad Hall* (1929).

milometer MILE.

milord, *n.* my lord (applied to rich Englishmen).

Miłosz, *n.* **Czesław** (1911–), Polish writer, born in Lithuania. He became a diplomat before defecting and taking US nationality. His poetry in English translation includes *Selected Poems* (1973) and *Bells in Winter* (1978). Among his novels are *The Seizure of Power* (1955) and *The Issa Valley* (1981). Nobel prize 1980.

milreis, *n.* a former Portuguese coin. [Port. (*mil,* thousand, REIS[1])]

Milstein, *n.* **César** (1927–), Argentinian molecular biologist who developed monoclonal antibodies, giving immunity against specific diseases. He shared a Nobel prize 1984.

milt, *n.* the spleen; the spermatic organ of a male fish; the soft roe of fishes. *v.t.* to impregnate with milt (as fish ova). **milter,** *n.* [OE *milte* (cp. Dut. and Dan. *milt,* G *Milz*), prob. cogn. with MELT]

Milton, *n.* **John** (1608–74), English poet. His early poems include the pastoral *L'allegro* and *Il penseroso* (1632), the masque *Comus* (1633), and the elegy *Lycidas* (1637). His later works include *Paradise Lost* (1667), *Paradise Regained* (1677), and the classic drama, *Samson Agonistes* (1677). **Miltonic, Miltonian,** *a.* of or resembling the style of the poet John *Milton*; elevated, stately and sonorous, sublime. **Miltonism,** *n.*

milvine, *a.* of or belonging to the *Milvinae* or kites. *n.* a bird of this family. [L *milvus,* kite, -INE]

Milwaukee, *n.* industrial (meatpacking, brewing, engineering, textiles) port in Wisconsin, US, on Lake Michigan; population (1980) 1,207,000.

mim, *a.* (*Sc.*) prim, demure, quiet, precise. [prob. imit.]

mime, *n.* a simple kind of farce characterized by mimicry and gesture, popular among the ancient Greeks and Romans; any communication through facial expression, gesture etc. and without words; an actor in mime; a mimic, a clown or buffoon. *v.i.* to act in mime; to play the mime. *v.t.* to mimic. [L *mīmus,* Gr. *mīmos*]

MIMechE, (*abbr.*) Member of the Institute of Mechanical Engineers.

mimeograph, *n.* a duplicating apparatus in which a paraffin-coated sheet is used as a stencil for reproducing written or typewritten matter. *v.t.* to reproduce by means of this. [Gr. *mīmeesthai,* to imitate, -GRAPH]

mimesis, *n.* mimicry; imitation of or close natural resemblance to the appearance of another animal or of a natural object; the imitation of nature in art. **mimetic,** *a.* **mimetically,** *adv.* [Gr., from *mīmos,* MIME]

mimetite, *n.* a native arsenate of lead. [G *Mimetit,* Gr. *mīmētēs,* imitator, as prec., -ITE]

mimic, *a.* given to imitation; imitative; imitating, counterfeit. *n.* one who mimics; †an actor, mime. *v.t.* (*past, p.p.* **mimicked**) to imitate, esp. in order to ridicule; to ape, to copy; to resemble closely (of animals, plants etc.). **mimicry,** *n.* [L *mīmicus,* Gr. *mīmikos,* from *mīmos,* MIME]

miminy-piminy, *a.* too fastidious, finical; affectedly nice or delicate. *n.* writing or diction of this character. [imit., cp. MIM]

Mimosa, *n.* a genus of leguminous shrubs, including the sensitive plant, *Mimosa pudica.* [L *mīmus,* MIME, *-ōsa,* -OSE]

Mimulus, *n.* a genus of plants with a mask-like corolla, comprising the monkey-flower. [dim. of L *mīmus,* MIME]

mina[1], *n.* a Greek weight of 100 drachmae, or about 1 lb. avoirdupois (0·454 kg); a coin worth 100 drachmae. [L, from Gr. *minā*]

mina[2], *n.* one of various Eastern and Australian passerine birds. **minabird,** *n.* Also **myna, mynah.** [Hind. *maina*]

minacious, *a.* threatening. **minaciously,** *adv.* **minacity,** *n.* [L *minax -ācis*]

minaret, *n.* a lofty slender turret on a mosque, from which the muezzin summons the people to prayers. [F *minaret* or Sp. *minarete,* from Arab. *manārat,* rel. to *nār,* fire]

minatory, *a.* threatening, menacing. [late L *minātōrius,* from *minārī,* to threaten]

minauderie, *n.* affectation, coquettish airs. [F, from

minauder, to put on airs, from *mine,* MIEN]

mince, *v.t.* to cut or chop into very small pieces; to utter or pronounce with affected delicacy; to minimize, to palliate, to gloss over; to restrain (one's words) for politeness' sake. *v.i.* to talk with affected elegance; to walk in a prim and affected manner. *n.* minced meat; mincemeat. **not to mince matters,** to speak plainly. **mincemeat,** *n.* meat chopped into very small pieces; a filling for pies etc. composed of suet, raisins, currants, candied-peel etc. chopped fine; very fine or small pieces or fragments. **to make mincemeat of,** to crush or destroy completely. **mince-pie,** *n.* a small pie filled with mincemeat. **mincing,** *a.* affectedly elegant. **mincingly,** *adv.* [OF *mincier,* pop. L *minūtiāre,* from MINUTIA]

mind, *n.* a person's intellectual powers; the understanding, the intellect; the soul; intellectual capacity; recollection, memory; one's candid opinion; sanity; disposition, liking, way of feeling or thinking; intention, purpose; desire, inclination. *v.t.* to heed, to regard; to pay attention to, to apply oneself to; (*coll.*) to object to; (*coll.*) to look after; †to remember, to bear in mind. *v.i.* to take care, to be on the watch. **absence, presence, of mind** ABSENT[2], PRESENCE. **in one's mind's eye,** in one's imagination. **in two minds,** unable to choose between two alternatives. **to bring, call, to mind** CALL[1]. **to cast one's mind back** CAST[1]. **to cross one's mind** CROSS[2]. **to have (half) a mind,** to be inclined (to). **to make up one's mind** MAKE[2]. **to one's mind,** in one's opinion. **to put in mind,** to remind (of). **to put out of one's mind,** to stop thinking about. **to speak one's mind,** to express one's candid opinion (of or about). **mind-blowing,** *a.* of or inducing a state like that produced by psychedelic drugs. **mind-boggling,** *a.* amazing, astonishing. **mind-reader,** *n.* a person who claims to know what others are thinking. **mind-reading,** *n.* **minded,** *a.* (*usu. in comb.,* as *evil-minded*). **minder,** *n.* one who watches over someone or something; (*sl.*) a bodyguard; an aide to a politician etc. **mindful,** *a.* attentive, heedful. **mindfully,** *adv.* **mindfulness,** *n.* **mindless,** *a.* done for no reason; done without need for thought; heedless, regardless. **mindlessly,** *adv.* **mindlessness,** *n.* [OE *gemynd,* cogn. with *munan,* to think, to remember (cp. OHG *gimunt,* Goth. *gamunds,* memory, from root *men-, mun-,* cp. L *mens,* mind]

Mindanao, *n.* the second-largest island of the Philippines. **area** 94,627 sq km/36,526 sq miles. **towns** Davao, Zamboanga. **physical** mountainous rainforest. **products** pineapples, coffee, rice, coconut, rubber, hemp, timber, nickel, gold, steel, chemicals, fertilizer. **population** (1980) 10,905,250.

mine[1], *poss. pron.* belonging to me. †*a.* my (used before vowels and sometimes *h*). [OE *mīn*]

mine[2], *v.t.* to dig into or burrow in; to obtain by excavating in the earth; to make by digging; to undermine, to sap; to set with mines. *v.i.* to dig a mine, to engage in digging for ore etc.; to burrow; to practise secret methods of inquiry. *n.* an excavation in the earth for the purpose of obtaining minerals; a rich deposit of minerals suitable for mining; crude ironstone; an excavation under an enemy's works for blowing them up, formerly to form a means of entering or to cause a collapse of the wall etc.; a receptacle filled with explosive, floating in the sea or buried in the ground, which is exploded by contact; a rich source of wealth, or of information etc. **mine-captain,** *n.* the overseer of a mine. **mine-crater,** *n.* one formed by the explosion of a mine. **mine-layer,** *n.* a ship employed to lay mines. **mine-sweeper,** *n.* a trawler or other vessel employed to clear mines laid by the enemy. **miner,** *n.* one who digs for minerals; one who works in mines; a soldier employed to lay mines; (*Austral.*) a variety of honey-eater bird. **mining,** *n.* [F *miner* (cp. It. *minare,* Sp. *minar*), etym. doubtful]

mineral, *n.* an inorganic body, homogeneous in structure, with a definite chemical composition, found in the earth; any inorganic substance found in the ground; (*pl.*) mineral waters; †a mine. *a.* pertaining to or consisting of minerals; impregnated with mineral matter. **mineral caoutchouc,** *n.* elaterite. **mineral green,** *n.* arsenite of copper. **mineral jelly,** *n.* a soft, soap-like substance obtained from the residue of petroleum. **mineral kingdom,** *n.* the inorganic kingdom of Nature. **mineral oil,** *n.* any oil derived from minerals; (*N Am.*) liquid paraffin. **mineral salt,** *n.* the salt of a mineral acid; native salt. **mineral water,** *n.* water naturally impregnated with mineral matter; an artificial imitation of this. †**mineralist,** *n.* **mineralize, -ise,** *v.t.* to convert into a mineral; to give mineral qualities to; to impregnate with mineral matter. *v.i.* to become mineralized; to study mineralogy. **mineralization, -isation,** *n.* **mineralizer, -iser,** *n.* **mineralogy,** *n.* the science of minerals, their nature and properties. **mineralogical,** *a.* **mineralogically,** *adv.* **mineralogist,** *n.* [F *minéral,* med. L *minerāle,* neut. of *minerālis,* from *minera,* from prec.]

Minerva, *n.* in ancient Roman mythology, the goddess of intelligence, and of the handicrafts and arts, counterpart of the Greek Athena. From the earliest days of ancient Rome, there was a temple to her on the Capitol.

minestrone, *n.* a thick soup of vegetables, pasta, etc. [It.]

minge, *n.* (*taboo sl.*) the female genitals.

mingle, *v.t.* to mix up together; to blend (with); †to associate; †to debase by mixture. *v.i.* to be mixed, blended or united (with). †*n.* a mixture; a medley. **mingler,** *n.* **minglingly,** *adv.* [freq. of ME *mengen,* OE *mengan*]

Mingus, *n.* **Charles** (1922–79), US bass player and composer. He was influential for his experimentation with atonality and dissonant effects, opening the way for the new style of free collective jazz improvisation of the 1960s.

mingy, *a.* (*coll.*) mean, stingy. **minginess,** *n.* [onomat.]

mini, *n.* (*coll.*) a mini-skirt; a small car.

mini-, *comb. form* smaller than the usual size.

miniate, *v.t.* to paint with vermilion; to illuminate. [L *miniātus,* p.p. of *miniāre,* from *minium,* cinnabar, native red lead]

miniature, *n.* a small-sized painting, esp. a portrait on ivory, vellum etc., orig. a small picture in an illuminated manuscript; the art of painting on a small scale; an image on a greatly reduced scale; a reproduction on a small scale. *a.* represented on a very small scale. *v.t.* to portray in miniature. **miniature camera,** *n.* a camera using film negative material usu. of 35 mm. **miniaturist,** *n.* **miniaturize, -ise,** *v.t.* to make or construct on a smaller scale; to reduce the size of. **miniaturization, -isation,** *n.* [med. L *miniātūra,* as prec.]

minibus, *n.* a small bus.

minicab, *n.* a taxi that can be ordered by telephone, but may not cruise in search of passengers.

minicomputer, *n.* a small digital computer.

minify, *v.t.* to make little or less; to represent (a thing) as of less size or importance than it is. [L *minor,* less]

minikin, *n.* a little darling; a pet; a diminutive thing; a small sort of pin. *a.* tiny, delicate; affected, mincing. [Dut. *minnekyn,* a cupid, dim. of *minne,* love, see KIN]

minim, *n.* a musical note of the value of two crotchets or half a semi-breve; an apothecaries' fluid-measure, one drop, or one sixtieth of a drachm (0·059 g); a down-stroke in writing; an insignificant person, a dwarf, a pigmy; a member of an order of hermits founded by St Francis of Paula (1416–1507). [OF *minime,* L *minimus,* very small]

minimal, *a.* pertaining to or being a minimum; least possible; smallest, very small. **minimal art, minimalism,** *n.* a movement beginning in the late 1960s in abstract art and music towards a severely simplified composition. In painting, it emphasized geometrical and elemental shapes. In sculpture, Carl André focused on industrial materials. In music, Philip Glass and Steve Reich attempted to depart from complexity with repetitive rhythms and harmonies. **minimalist,** *n.* a person ready to accept the minimum; one who practises minimal art.

minimize, -ise, *v.t.* to reduce to the smallest possible amount or degree; to belittle. **minimization, -isation,** *n.*

minimum, *n.* (*pl.* **-mums, -ma**) the smallest amount or degree possible or usual. *a.* least possible. **minimum lending rate,** the minimum rate at which the Bank of England will discount bills. **minimum thermometer,** *n.* one automatically recording the lowest temperature reached in a given period. **minimum wage,** *n.* the rate of wages established by law or collective bargaining below which workers cannot be employed.

minimus, *n.* a being of the smallest size. *a.* applied to the youngest of several boys of the same name in a school.

minion, *n.* a darling, a favourite; a servile dependant; a size of printing type between nonpareil and brevier. **minions of the moon,** highwaymen, footpads. [F *mignon,* etym. doubtful]

minipill, *n.* a low-dose oral contraceptive pill without oestrogen.

miniscule MINUSCULE.

mini-series, *n.* a television programme in several parts, usu. shown on consecutive nights.

†**minish,** *v.t.* to diminish; to reduce in power etc. *v.i.* to diminish. [OF *menuisier*]

mini-skirt, *n.* a skirt with the hem far above the knees.

minister, *n.* one charged with the performance of a duty, or the execution of a will etc.; a person entrusted with the direction of a state department; a person representing his government with another state, an ambassador; the pastor of a church, esp. a Nonconformist; one who acts under the authority of another, a subordinate, an instrument; a servant. *v.i.* to render aid, service or attendance; to contribute, to be conducive (to); to serve as minister. †*v.t.* to furnish, to supply. **ministerial,** *a.* pertaining to a minister of state or of religion; pertaining to the ministry, esp. in contradistinction to the opposition; subsidiary, instrumental; pertaining to the execution of a legal mandate etc. **ministerialist,** *n.* **ministerially,** *adv.* **ministrant,** *n., a.* **ministration,** *n.* **ministrative,** *a.* **ministress,** *n. fem.* **ministry,** *n.* the act of ministering; administration; the ministers of state or of religion collectively. [F *minister,* L *minister,* from *minus,* less (cp. *magister,* from *magis*)]

miniver, *n.* a kind of fur used for ceremonial robes; applied to the Siberian squirrel and its fur. [A-F *meniver,* F *menu vair* (*menu,* little, small, *vair,* a kind of fur, from L *varius,* VARIOUS)]

mink, *n.* a name for several species of *Putorius,* amphibious stoat-like animals esteemed for their fur. *n., a.* (of) this fur. [cp. LG *mink,* Swed. *menk*]

Minn., (*abbr.*) Minnesota (US).

Minneapolis, *n.* city in Minnesota, US, forming with St Paul the Twin Cities area; population (1980) 371,000, metropolitan area 2,114,000.

Minnelli¹, *n.* **Liza** (1946–), US actress and singer, daughter of Judy Garland and the director Vincente Minnelli. She gave a star-making performance in the musical *Cabaret* (1972). Her subsequent films include *New York* (1977) and *Arthur* (1981).

Minnelli², *n.* **Vincente** (1910–86), US film director, who specialized in musicals and occasional melodramas. His best films, such as *Meet Me in St Louis* (1944) and *The Band Wagon* (1953), display a powerful visual flair.

Minnesinger, *n.* any of a group of German lyric poets of the 12th and 13th cents. who, in their songs, dealt mainly with the theme of courtly love without revealing the identity of the object of their affections. Minnesingers included Dietmar von Aist, Friedrich von Hausen, Heinrich von Morungen, Reinmar and Walther von der Vogelweide. [G (*Minne,* love, SINGER)]

Minnesota, *n.* a state of the northern midwest US; nickname North Star or Gopher State. **area** 218,700 sq km/84,418 sq miles. **capital** St Paul. **towns** Minneapolis, Duluth, Bloomington, Rochester. **products** cereals, potatoes, livestock, pulpwood, iron ore (60% of US output), farm and other machinery. **population** (1987) 4,246,000.

minnow, *n.* a small fish common all over Europe, *Leuciscus phoxinus;* (*loosely*) any tiny fish; an insignificant person or thing. [cp. OHG *minewa* and OE *myne*]

Minoan, *a.* pertaining to ancient Crete or its people. *n.* an inhabitant of ancient Crete; their language. **Minoan period,** *n.* the Bronze Age of Crete, loosely 2500–1200 BC.

Minoan civilization, *n.* a Bronze Age civilization on the Aegean island of Crete. The name is derived from Minos, the legendary king of Crete, reputed to be the son of the god Zeus. The civilization is divided into three main periods: early Minoan, about 3000–2200 BC, middle Minoan, about 2200–1580 BC; and late Minoan, about 1580–1100 BC. The Minoan language was deciphered by Michael Ventris.

minor, *a.* less, smaller (not used with *than*); petty, comparatively unimportant; (*Mus.*) less by a semitone; †under age. *n.* a person under age; a minor term or premise in logic; a minor key or a composition or strain in this; a Minorite. **minor canon,** *n.* a clergyman, not a member of the chapter, assisting in the daily service at a cathedral. **minor key,** *n.* (*Mus.*) a key in which the scale has a minor third. **minor premise,** *n.* the premise containing the minor term of a syllogism. **minor suit,** *n.* in bridge, clubs or diamonds. **minor term,** *n.* the subject of the conclusion of a categorical syllogism. **Minorite,** *n.* a Franciscan friar. **minority,** *n.* the smaller number, esp. the smaller of a group or party voting together in an election, on a Bill etc.; the state of being under age; the period of this. [L]

Minorca, *n.* (Spanish **Menorca**) second largest of the Balearic Islands in the Mediterranean. **area** 689 sq km/266 sq miles. **towns** Mahon, Ciudadela. **products** copper, lead, iron, tourism. **population** (1985) 55,500. **Minorca (fowl),** *n.* a black variety of domestic fowl from Spain. [one of the Balearic Isles]

Minotaur, *n.* in Greek mythology, a monster, half man and half bull, offspring of Pasiphaë, wife of King Minos of Crete, and a bull. It lived in the labyrinth at Knossos and its victims were seven girls and seven youths, sent in annual tribute by Athens, until Theseus killed it, with the aid of Ariadne, the daughter of Minos. [Gr. *Minōtauros* (*Minōs,* the king of Crete, husband of Pasiphaë, *tauros,* bull)]

Minsk, *n.* an industrial city (machinery, textiles, leather; centre of the Soviet computer industry) and capital of the Byelorussian Republic, USSR; population (1987) 1,543,000.

minster, *n.* the church of a monastery; a cathedral or other large and important church. [OE *mynster,* L *monastērium,* MONASTERY]

minstrel, *n.* one of a class of men in the Middle Ages who lived by singing and reciting; a travelling gleeman, musician, performer or entertainer; a poet; a musician; one of a troupe of entertainers with blackened faces. **minstrelsy,** *n.* the art or occupation of minstrels; a body of minstrels; minstrels collectively; a collection of ballad poetry; †musical instruments. [OF *menestral,* late L *ministeriālis -lem,* MINISTERIAL under MINISTER]

mint¹, *n.* a place where money is coined, usu. under state authority; a source of invention or fabrication; a great quantity, supply or amount. *v.t.* to coin, to stamp (money); to invent, to coin (a phrase etc.). *a.* of a book, coin etc., in its unused state; as new. **in mint condition,** as perfect as when first produced. **mintman,** *n.* a man versed in coins or coining. **mint-mark,** *n.* a mark distinguishing the coins struck at a particular mint; a distinctive mark of origin. †**mint-master,** *n.* **mintage,** *n.* coining; coinage; a fee paid for minting a coin. **minter,** *n.* [OE *mynet,* L *monēta,* MONEY]

mint², *n.* any plant of the aromatic genus *Mentha,* esp. *M. viridis,* the garden mint, from which an essential oil is distilled. **mint-julep,** *n.* spirits, sugar and pounded ice flavoured with mint. **mint-sauce,** *n.* mint chopped up with vinegar and sugar, used as a sauce with roast lamb. [OE *minte* (L *menta, mentha,* Gr. *mintha*)]

Minto, *n.* **Gilbert, 4th Earl of** (1845–1914), British colonial administrator who succeeded Curzon as viceroy of

India, 1905–10. With John Morley, secretary of state for India, he co-sponsored the Morley Minto reforms of 1909. The reforms increased Indian representation in government at provincial level, but also created separate Muslim and Hindu electorates which, it was believed, helped the British Raj in the policy of divide and rule.

Mintoff, *n.* **Dom (Dominic)** (1916–), Labour prime minister of Malta (1971–84). He negotiated the removal of British and other foreign military bases (1971–79), and made treaties with Libya.

Minton, *n.* **Thomas** (1765–1836), English potter. He first worked at the Caughley porcelain works, but in 1789 established himself at Stoke-on-Trent as an engraver of designs (he originated the 'willow pattern') and in the 1790s founded a pottery there, producing high-quality bone china, including tableware.

minuend, *n.* the quantity from which another is to be subtracted. [L *minuendus,* ger. of *minuere,* to DIMINISH]

minuet, *n.* a slow stately dance in triple measure; music for this or in the same measure. [F *menuet,* dim. of *menu,* MINUTE[1]]

minus, *prep., a.* less by, with the deduction of; (*coll.*) short of, lacking; negative. *n.* the sign of subtraction (−). [L, neut. of MINOR]

minuscule, *a.* small; miniature (esp. applied to mediaeval script). *n.* a minute kind of letter in cursive script of the 7th–9th cent.; a small or lower-case letter; anything very small. [F, from L *minuscula,* fem. dim. of MINOR]

minute[1], *a.* very small; petty, trifling; particular, exact, precise. **minutely,** *adv.* **minuteness,** *n.* [L *minūtus,* p.p. of *minuere,* to DIMINISH]

minute[2], *n.* the 60th part of an hour; a very small portion of time, an instant; an exact point of time; the 60th part of a degree; a memorandum; an official memorandum of a court or other authority; (*pl.*) official records of proceedings of a committee etc. *v.t.* to write minutes of; to take a note of; to time to the exact minute. **up to the minute,** very modern. **minute-book,** *n.* a book in which the minutes of meetings are recorded. **minute-glass,** *n.* a sandglass running 60 seconds. **minute-gun,** *n.* a gun fired at intervals of one minute as a signal of distress or mourning. **minute-hand,** *n.* the hand pointing to minutes in a clock or watch. **minute-man,** *n.* in the US, an enrolled militiaman of the Revolutionary period who held himself ready for service at a minute's notice. **minute steak,** *n.* a thin steak that can be cooked quickly. **minute-watch,** *n.* a watch on which the minutes are marked. †**minute-while,** *n.* a minute's time. **minutely,** *a., adv.* every minute. [F, from late L *minūta,* as prec.]

minutia, *n.* (*usu. pl.* **-tiae**) small and precise or trivial particulars. [L, smallness, as MINUTE[1]]

minx, *n.* a pert girl, a jade, a hussy. [per. corr. of LG *minsk,* a man, a pert female (cp. G *Mensch*)]

Miocene, *n.* fourth epoch of the Tertiary period of geological time, 25–5 million years ago. The name means 'middle recent'. At this time grasslands spread over the interior of continents, and hoofed mammals rapidly evolved. [Gr. *meiōn,* less, *kainos,* new]

miosis MEIOSIS.

MIPS, (*acronym*) (*Comput.*) *m*illion *i*nstructions *p*er *s*econd.

Mira, *n.* (or **Omicron Ceti**) the brightest long-period pulsating variable star, located in the constellation Cetus. Mira was the first star discovered to vary in brightness over a regular period.

Mirabeau, *n.* **Honoré Gabriel Riqueti, Comte de** (1749–91), French politician, leader of the National Assembly in the French Revolution. He wanted to establish a parliamentary monarchy on the English model. From May 1790 he secretly acted as political adviser to the king.

miracle, *n.* a wonder, a marvel, a prodigy; a marvellous event or act due to supernatural agency; an extraordinary occurrence; of cleverness etc., an extraordinary example; a miracle play. †*v.i.* (*Shak.*) to render or seem miraculous. †**miracle-monger,** *n.* **miracle play,** *n.* a mediaeval dramatic representation, usu. dealing with historical or traditional events in the life of Christ or of the Saints. **miraculous,** *a.* **miraculously,** *adv.* **miraculousness,** *n.* [OF, from L *mīrăculum,* as foll.]

mirador, *n.* a belvedere turret or gallery, commanding an extensive view. [Sp., from *mirar,* to look, L *mīrārī,* as foll.]

mirage, *n.* an optical illusion by which images of distant objects are seen as if inverted, esp. in a desert where the inverted sky appears as a sheet of water. [F, from *se mirer,* to see oneself in a mirror, L *mīrārī,* to wonder at, to gaze]

Miranda, *n.* **Carmen** (stage name of Maria de Carmo Miranda da Cunha) (1909–55), Portuguese dancer and singer who lived in Brazil from her childhood. Successful in Brazilian films, she went to Hollywood 1939 via Broadway and appeared in over a dozen musicals, including *Down Argentine Way* 1940 and *The Gang's All Here* 1943.

MIRAS, (*acronym*) *m*ortgage *i*nterest *r*elief *a*t *s*ource.

mire, *n.* wet, clayey soil, swampy ground, bog; mud, dirt. *v.t.* to plunge in mire; to soil with mire; to involve in difficulties. *v.i.* to sink in mire. **mire-crow,** *n.* the laughing gull, *Larus ridibundus.* **miry,** *a.* **miriness,** *n.* [ME, from Icel. *mȳrr* (cp. Swed. *myra* and OE *mēos,* MOSS)]

mirepoix, *n.* (*pl.* **mirepoix**) a sauce of sautéed root vegetables. [prob. named after Duc de *Mirepoix,* 18th cent. French general]

mirific, *a.* wonderful, marvellous; wonder-working. [L *mirificus,* wonder-working]

mirk etc. MURK.

miro, *n.* the New Zealand robin. [Maori]

Miró, *n.* **Joan** (1893–1983), Spanish surrealist painter, born in Barcelona. In the mid-1920s he developed a distinctive abstract style with amoeba shapes, some linear, some highly coloured, generally floating on a plain ground.

mirror, *n.* an appliance with a polished surface for reflecting images; a looking-glass; anything that reflects objects; an exemplar, a pattern, a model. *v.t.* to reflect in or as in a mirror. **mirror writing,** *n.* handwriting from right to left, as if reflected in a mirror. [OF *mirour* (F *miroir*), prob. through a non-extant pop. L *mīrātōrium,* from *mīrārī,* see MIRAGE]

mirth, *n.* merriment, jollity, gaiety, hilarity. **mirthful,** *a.* **mirthfully,** *adv.* **mirthfulness,** *n.* **mirthless,** *a.* **mirthlessness,** *n.* [OE *myrgth,* cogn. with MERRY[2]]

MIRV, *n.* a missile with two or more warheads designed to strike separate targets. [acronym for *m*ultiple *i*ndependently-targetable *r*e-entry *v*ehicle]

miry MIRE.

mirza, *n.* a Persian title of honour, prince; doctor. [Pers.]

mis-[1], *pref.* wrongly, badly, amiss, unfavourably. [two prefixes have coalesced; OE *mis-,* wrongly, amiss (cp. Dut., Dan. and Icel. *mis-,* G *miss-*); OF *mes-,* L *minus,* less]

mis-[2] MIS(O)-.

misadventure, *n.* bad luck; ill fortune; an unlucky chance or accident. †**misadventured, -turous,** *a.* [OF *mesaventure*]

misadvise, *v.t.* to advise wrongly; to give bad advice to. **misadvice,** *n.* **misadvised,** *a.* ill-advised, ill-directed. †**misadvisedly,** *adv.* **misadvisedness,** *n.*

†**misaim,** *v.i.* to aim amiss.

misalign, *v.t.* to align wrongly.

misalliance, *n.* an improper alliance, esp. by marriage. **misallied,** *a.*

†**misallotment,** *n.* a wrong allotment.

misandry, *n.* a hatred of men. [MIS-[2] Gr. *anēr andros,* a man]

misanthrope, *n.* a hater of mankind; one who has a morbid dislike of his fellow-men. **misanthropic, -ical,** *a.* **misanthropist,** *n.* **misanthropize, -ise,** *v.i.* **misanthropy,** *n.* [Gr. *misanthrōpos* (*miseein,* to hate, *anthrōpos,* man)]

misapply, *v.t.* to apply wrongly. **misapplication,** *n.*

misappreciate, *v.t.* to fail to appreciate rightly or fully.

misappreciation, *n.* **misappreciative,** *a.*
misapprehend, *v.t.* to misunderstand. **misapprehension,** *n.* **misapprehensive,** *a.* **misapprehensively,** *adv.*
misappropriate, *v.t.* to apply to a wrong use or purpose (esp. funds to one's own use). **misappropriation,** *n.*
misarrange, *v.t.* to arrange wrongly. **misarrangement,** *n.* **misarray,** *v.t.*
misbecome, *v.t.* to be improper or unseemly to, to ill become. **misbecomingly,** *adv.* †**misbecomingness,** *n.*
misbegotten, †**misbegot,** *a.* begotten unlawfully, illegitimate, bastard; hideous, despicable.
misbehave, *v.i.* to behave (oneself) ill or improperly. **misbehaved,** *a.* guilty of misbehaviour, ill-mannered. **misbehaviour,** *n.*
misbelief, *n.* false or erroneous belief. **misbelieve,** *v.t.* **misbeliever,** *n.*
misbeseem, *v.t.* to misbecome.
misborn, *a.* base-born; born to evil or misfortune. **misbirth,** *n.*
misc., (*abbr.*) miscellaneous; miscellany.
miscalculate, *v.t.* to calculate wrongly. **miscalculation,** *n.*
miscall, *v.t.* to misname; to abuse, to call (someone) names.
miscarry, *v.i.* to be carried to the wrong place; to fail, to be unsuccessful; to be delivered of a child prematurely. **miscarriage,** *n.* an act or instance of miscarrying; failure; the (accidental) premature expulsion of a foetus before it can survive outside the womb. **miscarriage of justice,** a mistake or wrong committed by a court of justice.
miscast, *v.t.* to cast or add up wrongly; to cast (a play or an actor) inappropriately.
miscegenation, *n.* intermarriage or interbreeding between people of different races. [L *miscēre,* to mix, *genus,* race, -ATION]
miscellaneous, *a.* consisting of several kinds; mixed, multifarious, diversified; various, many-sided. **miscellanea,** *n.pl.* a collection of miscellaneous literary compositions. **miscellaneously,** *adv.* **miscellaneousness,** *n.* **miscellany,** *n.* a mixture of various kinds, a medley, a number of compositions on various subjects in one volume. **miscellanist,** *n.* [L *miscellāneus,* from *miscellus,* mixed, from *miscēre,* to mix]
mischance, *n.* misfortune, ill-luck. †*v.i.* to happen unfortunately. **mischancy,** *a.* (*Sc.*) [OF *meschance*]
†**mischarge,** *v.t.* to charge wrongly. *n.* a wrong charge.
mischief, *n.* harm, injury, damage; vexatious action or conduct, esp. a vexatious prank; (*euphem.*) the devil. †*v.t.* (also †**mischieve**) to hurt, to harm. **mischief-maker,** *n.* one who stirs up ill-will. **mischief-making,** *n., a.* **mischievous,** *a.* making mischief; naughty; of a child, full of pranks, continually in mischief; arch, roguish; vexatious. **mischievously,** *adv.* **mischievousness,** *n.* [OF *meschief* (MIS-[1], CHIEF, aim, result)]
misch metal, *n.* an alloy of cerium with other rare earth metals, used for cigarette-lighter flints. [G *mischen,* to mix]
miscible, *a.* that may be mixed (with). **miscibility,** *n.* [F, from L *miscēre,* to mix, -BLE]
miscolour, *v.t.* to misrepresent. **miscoloration,** *n.* discoloration.
miscomprehend, *v.t.* to comprehend wrongly, to misunderstand. **miscomprehension,** *n.*
miscompute, *v.t.* to compute wrongly. †*n.* a miscalculation. **miscomputation,** *n.*
misconceive, *v.t.* to have a wrong idea of, to misapprehend. **misconception,** *n.*
misconduct[1], *n.* improper conduct, esp. adultery; mismanagement.
misconduct[2], *v.t.* to mismanage. *v.i.* to misbehave.
misconstrue, *v.t.* to mistake the meaning of; to put a wrong interpretation or construction upon. **misconstruction,** *n.*
miscopy, *v.t.* to copy incorrectly.
miscounsel, *v.t.* to advise wrongly.
miscount[1], *v.t.* to count wrongly; to estimate or regard wrongly. *v.i.* to make a false account.
miscount[2], *n.* a mistake in counting, esp. of votes.
miscreant, *n.* †an unbeliever, infidel or heretic; a vile wretch, a scoundrel. *a.* †infidel; abandoned, vile. †**miscreance,** †**miscreancy,** *n.* [OF *mescreant* (*creant,* L *crēdens -entem,* pres.p. of *crēdere,* to believe)]
miscreate, *v.t.* to create wrongly or badly. †**miscreated,** †**miscreate,** *a.* deformed, shapeless. **miscreation,** *n.* **miscreative,** *a.*
miscreed, *n.* a false or mistaken creed.
miscue, *n.* in billiards, snooker etc., failure to strike a ball properly with the cue. *v.i.* to make a miscue.
misdate, *v.t.* to date wrongly. *n.* a wrong date.
misdeal, *v.t.* to deal wrongly (as cards). *v.i.* to make a misdeal. *n.* a wrong or false deal.
misdecision, *n.* a wrong decision.
misdeed, *n.* an evil deed, a crime. [OE *misdǣd*]
misdeem, *v.t.* to judge wrongly; to have wrong views about; to mistake (for someone or something else). *v.i.* to have a wrong idea or judgment (of).
misdemean, *v.t.* to misconduct (oneself). **misdemeanant,** *n.* **misdemeanour,** *n.* misbehaviour, misconduct; (*Law*) an indictable offence of less gravity than a felony.
misdescribe, *v.t.* to describe wrongly.
†**misdesert,** *n.* ill-desert.
†**misdevotion,** *n.* misdirected devotion.
misdirect, *v.t.* to direct wrongly. **misdirection,** *n.*
†**misdistinguish,** *v.i.* to make erroneous distinctions (concerning).
misdivision, *n.* wrong or erroneous division.
misdo, *v.t.* to do wrongly. *v.i.* to commit a crime. **misdoer,** *n.* **misdoing,** *n.*
†**misdoubt,** *v.t.* to have doubts or misgiving as to the truth or fact of; to suspect, surmise or apprehend. *v.i.* to have suspicions or misgivings. *n.* doubt, hesitation; suspicion.
†**mise,** *n.* a treaty, esp. a settlement by arbitration or compromise; (*Law*) the issue in a writ of right; (*usu. pl.*) cost, expense. [OF, from p.p. of *mettre,* to put, L *mittere,* to send]
miseducate, *v.t.* to educate wrongly. **miseducation,** *n.*
mise en scène, the scenery and general setting of a play; the visible surroundings of an event. [F]
misemploy, *v.t.* to misapply, to misuse. **misemployment,** *n.*
misentry, *n.* an erroneous entry.
miser[1], *n.* one who denies himself the comforts of life for the sake of hoarding; an avaricious person; a wretched person. **miserly,** *a.* **miserliness,** *n.* [L, wretched]
miser[2], *n.* a large auger for well-boring. [etym. unknown]
miserable, *a.* very wretched or unhappy, distressed; causing misery, distressing; sorry, despicable, worthless; very poor or mean. *n.* a miserable person, a wretch. †**miserableness,** *n.* **miserably,** *adv.* [F *misérable,* L *miserābilis,* from *miserērī,* to pity, from *miser,* wretched]
misère, *n.* a declaration in solo whist etc. by which a player undertakes not to take a single trick. [F]
miserere, *n.* the 51st Psalm, beginning with this word in the Vulgate; a musical setting of this psalm; a prayer or cry for mercy; a misericord. [L, have mercy, imper. of *miserērī,* see MISERABLE]
misericord, *n.* an apartment in a monastery for monks to whom special indulgences were granted; a bracketed projection on the underside of the seat of a choir-stall, to afford rest to a person standing; a small, straight dagger for giving the coup de grâce; †mercy. [OF, from L *misericordia,* from *misericors -cordis* (*miseri-,* stem of *miserērī,* see MISERABLE, *cor cordis,* heart)]
miserly MISER[1].
misery, *n.* great unhappiness or wretchedness of mind or body; affliction, poverty; misère; (*coll.*) an ill-tempered, gloomy person; †miserliness, avarice. [OF,

from L *miseria,* from *miser,* wretched]
†**misesteem,** *v.t.* to esteem wrongly. *n.* want of esteem, disrespect; disregard.
misestimate, *v.t.* to estimate wrongly. *n.*, a wrong estimate.
misexpress, *v.t.* to express (oneself) wrongly. **misexpression,** *n.*
†**misfall,** *v.t.* to befall unluckily.
†**misfare,** *v.i.* to fare ill. *n.* misfortune, mishap. [OE *misfaran*]
misfeasance, *n.* (*Law*) a trespass, a wrong, esp. negligent or improper performance of a lawful act. [OF *mesfaisance,* from *mesfaire* (*faire,* L *facere,* to do)]
misfire1, *n.* failure to go off or explode (of a gun, charge etc.); in a motor-vehicle engine, failure to fire in the correct ignition sequence.
misfire2, *v.i.* to fail to go off; to fail to achieve the intended effect; of a motor-vehicle engine, to fail to fire correctly.
misfit1, *n.* a bad fit; a garment that does not fit properly; an awkward person.
misfit2, *v.t.*, *v.i.* to fail to fit.
misform, *v.t.* to form badly or amiss. **misformation,** *n.*
misfortune, *n.* ill luck, calamity; a mishap, a disaster. †**misfortuned,** *a.*
misgive, *v.t.* (*impers.*) to fill (one's mind) with doubt or suspicion. **misgiving,** *n.*
misgo, *v.i.* to go wrong.
misgovern, *v.t.* to govern ill; to administer unfaithfully. †**misgovernance, misgovernment,** *n.* **misgoverned,** *a.* badly governed, rude.
misguide, *v.t.* to guide wrongly; to lead astray. **misguidance,** *n.* **misguided,** *a.* foolish. **misguidedly,** *adv.*
mishandle, *v.t.* to handle roughly; to ill-treat.
mishanter, *n.* (*Sc.*) misadventure, mischance. [earlier *misaunter,* MISADVENTURE]
mishap, *n.* a mischance; ill luck. †**mishappen,** *v.i.*
Mishima, *n.* **Yukio** (1925–70), Japanese novelist, whose work often deals with sexual desire and perversion, as in *Confessions of a Mask* (1949) and *The Temple of the Golden Pavilion* (1956). He committed hara-kiri (ritual suicide) as a demonstration against the corruption of the nation and the loss of the samurai warrior tradition.
mishit, *v.t.* to hit wrongly. *n.*, an instance of hitting wrongly.
mishmash, *n.* a hotchpotch, a jumble. [redupl. of MASH1]
Mishmee, Mishmi, *n.* the dried root of *Coptes teeta,* a bitter tonic. **mishmee-bitter,** *n.* [mountains east of Assam]
Mishna, *n.* a collection of commentaries on written Hebrew law, consisting of discussions between rabbis handed down orally from their inception in 70 AD until about 200, when, with the Gemara, the discussions in schools of Palestine and Babylon on law, it was committed to writing to form the Talmud. **Mishnic,** *a.* [Heb. *mishnah,* a repetition, instruction, from *shānāh,* to repeat]
misinform, *v.t.* to give erroneous information to. **misinformant, misinformer,** *n.* **misinformation,** *n.*
misintelligence, *n.* false information; lack of intelligence. [F *mésintelligence*]
misinterpret, *v.t.* to interpret wrongly; to draw a wrong conclusion from. **misinterpretation,** *n.* **misinterpreter,** *n.*
misjoin, *v.t.* to join or connect badly or improperly. **misjoinder,** *n.* (*Law*) the improper uniting of parties or things in a suit or action.
misjudge, *v.t.* to judge erroneously; to form an erroneous opinion of. **misjudgment,** *n.*
misken, *v.t.* (*Sc.*) to fail to recognize; to pretend not to know. [KEN1]
misknow, *v.t.* to misunderstand; to know imperfectly. **misknowledge,** *n.*
mislay, *v.t.* (*past, p.p.* **-laid**) to lay in a wrong place or in a place that cannot be remembered; to lose.
misle, MIZZLE1.
mislead, *v.t.* (*past, p.p.* **misled**) to lead astray; to cause to go wrong, esp. in conduct; to deceive, to delude. **misleader,** *n.* **misleading,** *a.* **misleadingly,** *adv.*
mislike, *v.t.* to dislike. *v.i.* to feel dislike or aversion. *n.* dislike, aversion. [OE *mislīcian*]
mislippen, *v.t.* (*Sc.*) to deceive; to neglect, not to attend to; to suspect. [LIPPEN]
mismanage, *v.t.*, *v.i.* to manage badly. **mismanagement,** *n.* **mismanager,** *n.*
mismarriage, *n.* an unsuitable, incongruous or unfortunate marriage.
mismatch1, *v.t.* to match unsuitably.
mismatch2, *n.* an unsuitable match. †**mismatchment,** *n.*
mismate, *v.t.* (*in p.p.*) to mate or match unsuitably.
mismeasure, *v.t.* to measure wrongly; to form an erroneous measurement of. **mismeasurement,** *n.*
misname, *v.t.* to call by a wrong name.
misnomer, *n.* a mistaken or misapplied name or designation; an incorrect term. [OF *mesnommer* (*nommer,* L *nōmināre,* to name)]
miso, *n.* a food paste made from soya beans fermented in brine, used for flavouring. [Jap.]
mis(o)-, *comb. form* dislike; hatred. [Gr. *mīseein,* to hate]
misogamy, *n.* hatred of marriage. **misogamist,** *n.* [Gr. *gamos,* marriage]
misogyny, *n.* hatred of women. **misogynic,** *a.* **misogynist,** *n.* [Gr. *mīsogunēs* (*gunē,* woman)]
misology, *n.* hatred of reason or knowledge. [Gr. *mīsologia* (-LOGY)]
misoneism, *n.* hatred of what is new. **misoneist,** *n.* [It. *misoneismo* (Gr. *neos,* new, -ISM]
misotheism, *n.* hatred of God. **misotheist,** *n.* [Gr. *mīsotheos, theos,* god (see THEISM2)]
misplace, *v.t.* to mislay; to set on or devote to an undeserving object. *v.i.* to misapply terms. **misplacement,** *n.*
misplay, *n.* wrong or foul play.
†**misplead,** *v.t.*, *v.i.* to plead wrongly. **mispleading,** *n.* an error in pleading.
†**mispoint,** *v.t.* to punctuate improperly.
misprint1, *v.t.* to print incorrectly.
misprint2, *n.* a mistake in printing.
misprision1, *n.* (*Law*) an offence under the degree of capital but bordering thereon, esp. one of neglect or concealment; †mistake, misconception. **misprision of treason** or **felony,** concealment of treason or felony without actual participation. [OF *mesprision* (MIS-1, L *prensio -ōnem,* see PRISON)]
†**misprision**2, *n.* scorn, contempt; undervaluing, failure to appreciate. [from MISPRIZE1]
misprize1, *v.t.* to undervalue, to slight, to despise. †*n.* neglect; contempt. [OF *mespriser*]
†**misprize**2, *n.* a mistake. [OF *mesprise* (F *méprise*), from *mesprendre* (L *prendere,* to take)]
mispronounce, *v.t.* to pronounce wrongly. **mispronunciation,** *n.*
misproportion, *v.t.* to proportion wrongly.
†**misproud,** *a.* viciously proud.
mispunctuate, *v.t.*, *v.i.* to punctuate wrongly.
misquote, *v.t.* to quote erroneously. **misquotation,** *n.*
misread, *v.t.* (*past, p.p.* **-read**) to read incorrectly; to misinterpret. **misreading,** *n.*
†**misreckon,** *v.t.* to miscalculate. †**misreckoning,** *n.*
misrelate, *v.t.* to relate inaccurately. **misrelation,** *n.*
misremember, *v.t.* to remember imperfectly; (*dial.*) to forget. **misremembrance,** *n.*
misreport, *v.t.* to report wrongly; †to slander. *n.* a false report.
misrepresent, *v.t.* to represent falsely or incorrectly. **misrepresentation,** *n.* **misrepresentative,** *n.*, *a.* **misrepresenter,** *n.*
misrule, *n.* bad government; disorder, confusion, tumult, riot. *v.t.* to rule incompetently, misgovern. **lord of misrule** LORD.
Miss, *n.* (*pl.* **misses**) a title of address for an unmarried woman or girl; (*coll.*) a girl; used before the name of a place, activity etc. to refer to a young woman who re-

presents that place, activity etc., often in beauty contests; †a kept mistress. **missish,** *a.* like a self-conscious young girl; prim, affected. **missishness,** *n.* **missy,** *n.* (*coll.*) a form of address to a young woman or little girl. †*a.* missish. [contr. of MISTRESS]

miss, *v.t.* to fail to reach, hit, meet, perceive, find, or obtain; to fall short of, to let slip, to overlook; to fail to understand; to omit; to escape, to dispense with; to feel or perceive the want of. *v.i.* to fail to hit the mark; to be unsuccessful; †to go astray, to err. *n.* a failure to hit, reach, obtain etc.; †loss, want, feeling of loss; †error, mistake. **a miss is as good as a mile,** escape or failure, no matter how narrow the margin, is the point of importance. **to give a miss,** in billiards, to avoid hitting the object ball in order to leave one's own in a safe position; not to take an opportunity to see, visit, enjoy etc. **to go missing,** to disappear or be lost. **to miss fire,** to fail to go off (of a gun, explosive etc.). **to miss out,** to omit; to fail to receive or enjoy. **to miss stays,** of a sailing-vessel, to fail in trying to go on another tack. **to miss the boat, bus,** to miss an opportunity. **missing,** *a.* that misses; lost, wanting; absent, not in its place. **missing link,** *n.* something required to complete a series; a hypothetical form connecting types that are probably related, as man and the anthropoid apes. †**missingly,** *adv.* [OE *missan* (cp. Dut. and G *missen,* Icel. *missa*), cogn. with OE *mis-,* see MIS-[1]]

Miss., (*abbr.*) Mississippi (US).

missal, *n.* the book containing the service of the Mass for the whole year; a mediaeval illuminated manuscript. [late L *missāle,* orig. neut. a. from *missa,* MASS[1]]

missel-thrush MISTLE.

misshape, *v.t.* (*p.p.* **misshapen**) to shape ill; to deform. *n.* deformity. **misshapen,** *a.*

missile, *a.* that may be thrown or discharged. *n.* a weapon or other object projected or propelled through the air, esp. a rocket-propelled weapon, often with a nuclear warhead. **missil(e)ry,** *n.* (the design, use or study of) missiles. [L *missilis,* from *miss-,* p.p. stem of *mittere,* to send]

mission, *n.* a sending or being sent; the commission, charge or office of a messenger, agent etc.; a person's appointed or chosen end, a vocation; a body of persons sent on a diplomatic errand, an embassy or legation; a body of missionaries established in a district at home or sent to a foreign country to spread religious teaching; their field of work; a missionary station; a religious organization in the Roman Catholic Church ranking below that of a regular parish; a series of special services for rousing spiritual interest. **missionary**, *a.* pertaining to missions, esp. those of a religious nature; pertaining to the propagation of religion or other moral, social or political influence. *n.* one sent to carry on such work. **missionary box,** *n.* a box for contributions to missionary work. **missionary position,** *n.* (*coll.*) the conventional position for sexual intercourse, lying down with the woman on her back and the man on top of her. **missioner,** *n.* a missionary; one in charge of a parochial mission. [L *missio -ōnem,* as prec.]

missis, missus, *n.* (*coll.*) the mistress of a household; a wife. [corr. of MISTRESS]

missish MISS[1].

Mississippi[1], *n.* river in the US, the main arm of the great river system draining the US between the Appalachian and the Rocky mountains. The length of the Mississippi is 3780 km/2350 miles; of the Mississippi-Missouri 6020 km/3740 miles.

Mississippi[2], *n.* a state of the southern US; nickname Magnolia State. **area** 123,600 sq km/47,710 sq miles. **capital** Jackson. **towns** Biloxi, Meridian, Hattiesburg. **products** cotton, sweet potatoes, sugar, rice, canned sea food at Biloxi, timber, pulp, oil, natural gas, chemicals. **population** (1985) 2,657,000.

Mississippian, *n.* a US term for the lower Carboniferous period of geological time, named after the state of Mississippi.

missive, *n.* a message, a letter; †a messenger. *a.* sent or for sending. **letter, letters, missive,** a letter or letters sent by an authority, esp. from the sovereign to a dean and chapter nominating someone for the office of bishop; (*Sc. Law*) a document given by the parties to a contract etc. [F, from med. L *missīvus,* as MISSILE]

Missouri, *n.* a state of the central US; nickname Show Me State. **area** 180,600 sq km/69,712 sq miles. **capital** Jefferson City. **towns** St Louis, Kansas City, Springfield, Independence. **products** meat and other processed food, aerospace and transport equipment, lead, clay, coal. **population** (1986) 5,066,000.

Missouri Compromise, *n.* (*US Hist.*) the solution by Congress (1820–21) of a sectional crisis caused by the 1819 request from Missouri for admission to the union as a slave state, despite its proximity to existing non-slave states. The compromise was the simultaneous admission of Maine as a non-slave state.

Missouri River, *n.* a river in central US, a tributary of the Mississippi, which it joins at St Louis; length 3725 km/2328 miles.

misspeak, *v.i.* to speak wrongly; to speak evil. *v.t.* to speak or pronounce incorrectly.

misspell, *v.t.* to spell incorrectly. **misspelling,** *n.*

misspend, *v.t.* (*past, p.p.* **-spent**) to spend ill; to waste.

misstate, *v.t.* to state wrongly. **misstatement,** *n.*

†**misstep,** *n.* a false step.

missuit, *v.t.* to suit ill.

mist, *n.* visible watery vapour in the atmosphere at or near the surface of the earth; a watery condensation dimming a surface; a suspension of a liquid in a gas; a watery film before the eyes; anything which dims, obscures or darkens. *v.t.* to cover as with mist. *v.i.* to be misty. **mistful,** *a.* **mistlike,** *a., adv.* **misty,** *a.* characterized by or overspread with mist; vague, dim, indistinct, obscure. **mistily,** *adv.* **mistiness,** *n.* [OE, cp. Icel. *mistr,* Swed. and Dut. *mist,* cogn. with Gr. *omichlē*]

mistake, *v.t.* (*past* **-took,** *p.p.* **-taken**) to take or understand wrongly; to take in a wrong sense; to take one person or thing for another. *v.i.* to be in error; to err in judgment or opinion; †to transgress. *n.* an error of judgment or opinion; a misunderstanding, a blunder. **mistakable,** *a.* **mistakably,** *adv.* **mistaken,** *a.* wrong in judgment, opinion etc. **mistakenly,** *adv.* **mistakenness,** *n.* **mistaker,** *n.* [Icel. *mistaka*]

Mister, *n.* the common form of address prefixed to men's names or certain official titles (abbr. in writing to MR). *v.t.* to speak of or address (someone) as 'Mister'. [var. of MASTER]

†**mister,** *n.* a trade, craft; manner, kind; (*Sc.*) need, necessity. †*v.t.* to occasion loss to. †*v.i.* to be needed; to require. [OF *mestier* (F *métier*), L *ministerium,* MINISTRY under MINISTER]

misterm, *v.t.* to misname; to apply a wrong term to.

misthink, *v.i.* to think wrongly. *v.t.* to misjudge, to think ill of. †**misthought,** *n.*

mistic, mistico, *n.* a small coasting-vessel used in the Mediterranean. [Sp. *mistico,* prob. from Arab. *misteh,* from *sataha,* to flatten]

mistime, *v.t.* to say or do inappropriately or not suitably to the time or occasion.

mistitle, *v.t.* to call by a wrong title.

mistle, mistle-thrush, *n.* the largest of the European thrushes, *Turdus viscivorus,* feeding largely on mistletoe-berries. [OE *mistel,* basil, mistletoe (cp. G *Mistel-drossel*)]

mistletoe, *n.* a plant, *Viscum album,* parasitic on the apple and other trees, bearing white glutinous berries used in making bird-lime. [OE *misteltān* (prec., *tān,* twig)]

mistral, *n.* a cold dry NW wind of S France. [F and Prov., from L *magistrālis,* MAGISTRAL]

Mistral, *n.* **Gabriela** (pen name of Lucila Godoy de Alcayaga) (1889–1957), Chilean poet, who wrote *Sonnets of Death* (1915). Nobel Prize for Literature 1945. She was consul of Chile in Spain, and represented her country at the League of Nations and the United Nations.

mistranslate, *v.t.* to translate wrongly. **mistranslation,** *n.*

mistreat, *v.t.* to ill-treat. **mistreatment,** *n.*

mistress, *n.* a woman who has authority or control; the female head of a family, school etc.; a woman having the control or disposal (of); a woman who has mastery (of a subject etc.); a female teacher; a woman beloved and courted, a sweetheart; a woman with whom a man has a long-term extramarital relationship; a title of address to a married woman (abbr. in writing to MRS, mis'iz); †a patroness. **Mistress of the Robes,** a lady of the royal household nominally in charge of the Queen's wardrobe. **mistress-ship,** *n.* [ME and OF *maistresse* (MASTER, -ESS)]

mistrial, *n.* an abortive or inconclusive trial.

mistrust, *v.t.* to regard with doubt or suspicion. *n.* distrust, suspicion. **mistrusted,** *a.* **mistrustful,** *a.* **mistrustfully,** *adv.* **mistrustfulness,** *n.* **mistrustingly,** *adv.* **mistrustless,** *a.*

mistryst, *v.t.* to fail to keep an engagement with; to trouble, embarrass or perplex.

mistune, *v.t.* to tune wrongly; to make discordant.

misunderstand, *v.t.* (*past, p.p.* **-stood**) to misconceive, to misapprehend, to mistake the meaning or sense of. **misunderstanding,** *n.* **misunderstood,** *a.*

misuse, *v.t.* to use or treat improperly; to apply to a wrong purpose; to ill-treat. *n.*, improper use; abuse. **misusage,** *n.*

misventure, *n.* a misadventure. **misventurous,** *a.*

miswend, *v.i.* (*p.p.* **miswent**) to go astray; to go wrong, to go to ruin.

misword, *v.t.* to word incorrectly.

miswrite, *v.t.* to write incorrectly.

†**miswrought,** *a.* badly wrought.

MIT, (*abbr.*) Massachusetts Institute of Technology.

Mitchell¹, *n.* **Arthur** (1934–), US dancer, director of the Dance Theater of Harlem, which he founded with Karel Shook in 1968. Mitchell was a principal dancer with the New York City Ballet (1956–68), creating many roles in Balanchine's ballets.

Mitchell², *n.* **Margaret** (1900–49), US novelist, born in Atlanta, Georgia, which is the setting for her one book *Gone With the Wind* (1936), a story of the US Civil War.

Mitchell³, *n.* **R(eginald) J(oseph)** (1895–1937), British aircraft designer, whose Spitfire fighter was a major factor in winning the Battle of Britain.

Mitchum, *n.* **Robert** (1917–), US film actor, a star for over 30 years. His films include *Out of the Past* (1947), *The Night of the Hunter* (1955), and *Farewell My Lovely* (1975).

mite¹, *n.* a very small coin, orig. Flemish; a half or smaller portion of a farthing; a small contribution; a minute amount, a tiny thing, esp. a child. [OE (cp. LG *mite,* Dut. *mijt,* OHG *mīza,* gnat)]

mite², *n.* a name common to the minute arachnids of the Acarida, esp. those infesting cheese. **mity,** *a.* [OF *mite,* prob. cogn. with prec.]

miter MITRE.

Mitford sisters, *n.pl.* the six daughters of Lord Redesdale, including: **Nancy** (1904–73), author of the semi-autobiographical *The Pursuit of Love* (1945) and *Love in a Cold Climate* (1949), and editor and part author of *Noblesse Oblige* (1956) elucidating 'U' (upper-class) and 'non-U' behaviour; **Diana** (1910–) who married Oswald Mosley; **Unity** (1914–48), who became an admirer of Hitler; and **Jessica** (1917–), author of the autobiographical *Hons and Rebels* (1960) and *The American Way of Death* (1963).

Mithraism, *n.* the ancient Persian worship of Mithras. His cult was introduced into the Roman Empire in 68 BC, spread rapidly particularly among soldiers, and by about 250 AD rivalled Christianity in strength. **Mithraist,** *n.* [L and Gr. *Mithrās,* OPers. *Mithra*]

Mithras, *n.* in Persian mythology, the god of light. Mithras represented the power of goodness, and promised his followers compensation for present evil after death. Mithras was said to have captured and killed the sacred bull, from whose blood all life sprang. **mithraic,** *a.*

mithridate, *n.* an antidote against poison. **mithridatic,** *a.* **mithridatism,** *n.* **mithridatize, -ise,** *v.t.* to render immune against poison by taking larger and larger doses of it. [*Mithridates* VI, see foll.]

Mithridates VI Eupator, *n.* known as **the Great** (132–63 BC), king of Pontus (NE Asia Minor, on the Black Sea) from 120 BC. He massacred 80,000 Romans in overrunning the rest of Asia Minor and went on to invade Greece. He was defeated by Sulla in the First Mithridatic War (88–84); by Lucullus in the Second (83–81); and by Pompey in the Third (74–64). He was killed by a soldier at his own order rather than surrender.

mitigate, *v.t.* to make less rigorous or harsh; to relax (severity); to alleviate (pain, violence etc.); to soften, to diminish, to moderate. *v.i.* to become assuaged, relaxed or moderated. †**mitigable,** *a.* †**mitigant,** *n.*, *a.* **mitigation,** *n.* **mitigative, mitigatory,** *a.* **mitigator,** *n.* [L *mītigātus,* p.p. of *mītigāre,* from *mītis,* gentle]

mitochondrion, *n.* a spherical or rodlike organism, found in cytoplasm, whose function is energy production.

mitokinetic, *a.* productive of mitosis. [MITOSIS, KINETIC]

mitosis, *n.* (*pl.* **-oses**) indirect cell-division; the appearance of the nucleus during karyokinesis. **mitotic,** *a.* [Gr. *mitos,* a thread, -OSIS]

mitrailleuse, *n.* a breech-loading machine-gun consisting of several barrels united, for firing simultaneously or in succession. **mitraille,** *n.* small shot from this. **mitrailleur,** *n.* [F, from *mitrailler,* to fire small missiles, from *mitraille,* from MITE²]

mitral, *a.* of or resembling a mitre. **mitral valve,** *n.* the valve between the left auricle and ventricle of the heart, which prevents the blood flowing back into the auricle.

mitre, (*esp. N Am.*) **miter,** *n.* a tall ornamental cap shaped like a cleft cone rising into two peaks, worn as symbol of office by bishops; the dignity of a bishop; a joint at an angle (usu. of 90°), as the corner of a picture-frame, each jointing surface being cut at an angle to the piece on which it is formed; hence, an angle of 45°. *v.t.* to confer a mitre upon; to join with a mitre; to shape off at an angle of 45°. **mitre-block, -box,** *n.* a block or box used to guide the saw in cutting mitres. **mitre-joint,** *n.* **mitre-wheel,** *n.* a bevelled cog-wheel engaged with another at an angle of 45°. **mitrewort** BISHOP'S-CAP. **mitred,** *a.* wearing a mitre, of episcopal rank; joined or cut at an angle of 45°. **mitriform,** *a.* (*Bot.*) mitre-shaped. [OF *mitre*]

Mitre, *n.* **Bartólomé** (1821–1906), Argentinian president (1862–68). In 1852 he helped overthrow the dictatorial regime of Juan Manuel de Rosas and in 1861 unify Argentina. Mitre encouraged immigration and favoured growing commercial links with Europe. He is seen as a symbol of national unity.

mitt, *n.* a kind of glove or covering, usu. of lace or knitting, for the wrist and palm; a thick mitten worn by the catcher in baseball; (*sl.*) a hand. **frozen mitt,** (*sl.*) a snub. [see foll.]

mitten, *n.* a glove with a thumb but no fingers; (*sl.*) a boxing-glove. **to give, get, the mitten,** (*sl.*) to reject (a lover) or dismiss (from office etc.) or to be rejected or dismissed. [OF *mitaine,* etym. doubtful]

Mitterrand, *n.* **François** (1916–), French socialist politician, president from 1981. He held ministerial posts in 11 governments (1947–58). He founded the French Socialist Party (PS) 1971. In 1985 he introduced proportional representation, allegedly to weaken the growing opposition from left and right.

mittimus, *n.* (*Law*) a warrant of commitment to prison; †a writ to remove records from one court to another; (*coll.*) dismissal. [L, we send, from *mittere,* see MISSION]

mity MITE².

mix, *v.t.* to put together or blend into one mass or compound; to mingle or incorporate (several substances, quantities or groups) so that the particles of each are indiscriminately associated; to compound by mingling various ingredients; to cross (breeds); to join; (*Mus.*) to combine individual instruments, voices etc. electronically. *v.i.* to become united; to be mingled (with or together); to be associated or have intercourse (with); to copulate; †to join (in battle etc.). *n.* an act or process of mixing; a mixture, a combination; mixed ingredients, e.g. for a cake, sold pre-packed; (*Mus.*) the sound produced by mixing electronically. **to mix up,** to mix thoroughly; to confuse, to bewilder; to involve (in an (esp. dubious) undertaking or with an (esp. undesirable) person). **mixed-up,** *a.* confused, chaotic, muddled; in emotional turmoil. **mixable,** *a.* **mixed,** *a.* consisting of various kinds or constituents; promiscuous, of company, not select; not wholly good or bad, not of consistent quality; (*coll.*) confused, bewildered, muddled. **mixed bathing,** *n.* bathing of both sexes together. **mixed blessing,** *n.* something that has advantages and disadvantages. **mixed doubles,** *n.pl.* (*Tennis*) matches with a man and woman player as partners on each side. **mixed farm,** *n.* a farm combining arable and livestock production. **mixed marriage,** *n.* one in which the contracting parties are of different creeds or races. **mixed mathematics** MATHEMATICS. **mixed metaphor,** *n.* one that brings together incongruous concepts. **mixed school,** *n.* one at which boys and girls are educated together. **mixed train,** *n.* a train composed of both passenger and goods wagons. **mixedly,** *adv.* **mixer,** *n.* a person or thing that causes mixing, that mixes; a person with social tact; one who gets on well with all sorts of people; (*coll.*) a person who stirs up trouble; a non-alcoholic drink suitable for mixing with alcoholic drinks; a kitchen appliance for mixing food ingredients. [back-formation from obs. *mixt,* F *mixte,* L *mixtus,* p.p. of *miscēre,* to mix]

Mix, *n.* **'Tom' (Thomas)** (1880–1940), US actor, a cowboy star of silent films. At their best his films, such as *The Range Riders* (1910) and *King Cowboy* (1928), were fast-moving and full of impressive stunts.

mixen, *n.* a dunghill. [OE]

mixture, *n.* that which is mixed; a mixing, compound; gas or vaporized oil mixed with air to form the explosive charge in an internal-combustion engine.

Mizoguchi, *n.* **Kenji** (1898–1956), Japanese film director whose *Ugetsu Monogatari* (1953) confirmed his international reputation. He also directed *Blood and Soul* (1923), *The Poppies* (1935), and *Street of Shame* (1956).

Mizoram, *n.* a state of NE India. **area** 21,100 sq km/ 8,145 sq miles. **capital** Aizawl. **products** rice, hand loom weaving. **population** (1981) 488,000. **religion** 84% Christian.

mizzen, mizen, *n.* a fore-and-aft sail set on the mizzen-mast, also called the **mizzen-sail**. **mizzen-mast,** *n.* the aftermost mast of a three-masted ship. **mizzen-rigging, -top, -yard,** *n.* [F *misaine,* It. *mezzana,* fem. of *mezzano*]

mizzle¹, *v.i.* to rain in very fine drops, to drizzle. *n.* very fine rain. **mizzly,** *a.* [cp. Dut. dial. *miezelen*]

mizzle², *v.i.* (*sl.*) to decamp. [etym. doubtful]

Mk, (*abbr.*) mark; markka.

MKS units, *n.pl.* the metric system of units based on the *m*etre, *k*ilogram and *s*econd as units of length, mass and time.

MLA, (*abbr.*) Member of the Legislative Assembly; Modern Languages Association.

Mladenov, *n.* **Petar** (1936–), Bulgarian Communist politician, secretary general of the Bulgarian Communist Party from Nov. 1989 after the resignation of Zhivkov.

MLF, (*abbr.*) multilateral (nuclear) force.

MLitt, (*abbr.*) Master of Letters (L *Magister Litterarum*).

Mlle(s), (*abbr.*) Mademoiselle; Mesdemoiselles.

MLR, (*abbr.*) minimum lending rate.

MM, (*abbr.*) Messieurs.

mm, (*abbr.*) millimetre.

Mme(s), (*abbr.*) Madame; Mesdames.

mmHg, (*abbr.*) millimetre of mercury.

Mn, (*chem. symbol*) manganese.

mnemonic, *a.* pertaining to or aiding the memory. *n.* an aid to memory; (*pl.*) the art of or a system for aiding or strengthening memory. **mnemonist,** *n.* **mnemotechny,** *n.* the art of developing the memory. **mnemotechnic,** *n.pl., a.* [Gr. *mnēmonikos,* from *mnēmōn,* mindful (*mnāsthai,* to remember)]

MO, (*abbr.*) Medical Officer; modus operandi; money order.

Mo, (*chem. symbol*) molybdenum.

Mo., (*abbr.*) Missouri (US).

mo¹, *n.* (*coll.*) moment, as in *just a mo.*

†mo², *n., a., adv.* more. [OE *mā,* MORE¹]

mo., (*abbr.*) month(s).

moa, *n.* an extinct, flightless bird of the genus *Dinornis.* [Maori]

Moab, *n.* an ancient country in Jordan E of the S part of the river Jordan and the Dead Sea. The inhabitants were closely akin to the Hebrews in culture, language and religion, but were often at war with them, as recorded in the Old Testament. Moab eventually fell to Arab invaders. The **Moabite Stone**, discovered in 1868 at Dhiban, dates from the 9th cent. BC and records the rising of Mesha, king of Moab, against Israel.

moan, *n.* a low prolonged sound expressing pain or sorrow; a complaint; †grief, woe. *v.i.* to utter a moan or moans; to complain, grumble. *v.t.* to lament, to deplore; to mourn; to utter moaningly. **moaner,** *n.* **moanful,** *a.* **moanfully, moaningly,** *adv.* [cogn. with OE *mǣnan,* to moan]

moat, *n.* a ditch round a castle, fort etc., usu. filled with water. *v.t.* to surround with or as with a moat. [OF *mote,* a dike, a mound]

mob¹, *n.* a disorderly or riotous crowd, a rabble; the masses, the lower orders; a gang of criminals engaged in organized crime; (*coll., derog.*) a group or class (of people of a specified kind). *v.t.* (*past, p.p.* **mobbed**) to attack in a mob; to crowd roughly round and annoy. *v.i.* to gather together in a mob. **the heavy mob,** (*coll., facet.*) (a group of) people with the power to frighten or coerce. **the mob, Mob,** (*chiefly N Am.*) the Mafia; organized crime. **mob law,** *n.* the rule of the mob; lynch law. **mobbish,** *a.* **mobbism,** *n.* **mobocracy,** *n.* rule by mob or by the lower orders. **mobsman,** *n.* **mobster,** *n.* a member of a criminal mob. [contr. from L *mōbile* (*vulgus*), the fickle (crowd)]

†mob², *n.* a mob-cap. †*v.t.* to muffle up (the head). **mob-cap,** *n.* a plain indoor cap or head-dress for women, usu. tied under the chin. **†moble,** *v.t.* to wrap in a hood. [cp. Dut. *mopmuts,* woman's night-cap]

mobbee, mobie, *n.* spirituous liquor distilled from the batata; (*N Am.*) the juice of apples or peaches distilled to make apple or peach brandy. [Carib *mabi,* batata]

mobile, *a.* movable, free to move; easily moved; easily changing (as expression); that may be moved from place to place (as troops); †fickle, excitable. *n.* that which moves or causes motion; an artistic concoction of dangling wires etc. **mobility,** *n.* **mobilize, -ise,** *v.t.* to make mobile; to put into circulation; to put (troops, a fleet etc.) in a state of readiness for active service; to put into action. **mobilizable, -isable,** *a.* **mobilization, -isation,** *n.* [L *mōbilis,* from *movēre,* to MOVE]

Möbius, *n.* **Augustus Ferdinand** (1790–1868), German mathematician, inventor of the Möbius strip and considered one of the founders of topology.

Möbius strip, *n.* a long, rectangular strip of paper twisted through 180° and joined at the ends, to form a one-sided surface bounded by one continuous curve. [A.F. *Möbius,* see prec.]

moble MOB².

mobocracy MOB¹.

Mobutu, *n.* **Sese-Seko-Kuku-Ngbeandu-Wa-Za-Banga** (1930–), Zaïrean president from 1965. He assumed the presidency by coup, and created a unitary state under his centralized government. He abolished secret voting in elections in 1976 in favour of a system of acclamation at mass rallies. His personal wealth is estimated at $3–4 billion, and more money is spent on the presidency than on the entire social-services budget. The harshness of some of his policies has attracted widespread international criticism.

moccasin, *n.* a foot-covering, usu. of deer-skin or soft leather in one piece, worn by N American Indians; a bedroom slipper of soft leather made of one piece. [Powhatan *mockasin*]

Mocha, *n.* a choice quality of coffee, orig. from Mocha. [fortified seaport in SW Arabia]

mocha, *n.* a dendritic variety of chalcedony. [prob. as prec.]

mock, *v.t.* to deride, to laugh at; to mimic, esp. in derision; to defy contemptuously; to delude, to take in. *v.i.* to express ridicule, derision or contempt. *a.* sham, false, counterfeit; imitating reality. *n.* a derision, a sneer; that which is derided; an imitation; an examination taken as practice prior to an official one. **mock-turtle soup,** a soup prepared from calf's head, veal etc. to imitate turtle soup. **mock-heroic,** *a.* burlesquing the heroic style. *n.* a burlesque of the heroic style. **mock-orange,** *n.* the common syringa, *Philadelphus coronarius,* the flowers of which smell like orange-blossoms. **mock sun,** *n.* a parhelion. **mock-up,** *n.* a full-size dummy model; an unprinted model of a book. **mock-velvet,** *n.* an imitation of velvet. **mockable,** *a.* **mocker,** *n.* **to put the mockers on,** (*sl.*) to cause to fail; to make impossible. **mockery,** *n.* the act of mocking; ridicule, derision; a subject of ridicule; a delusive imitation; a futile effort. **mocking,** *n., a.* **mocking-bird,** *n.* an American song-bird, *Mimus polyglottus,* with great powers of mimicry; the lyre-bird of Australia; a small New Zealand bird that imitates voices etc. **mockingly,** *adv.* [OF *mocquer* (F *moquer*), perh. from pop. L *muccāre,* to wipe the nose, L *muccus,* see MUCUS]

mod[1], *n.* a Highland gathering analogous to a Welsh eisteddfod. [Gael. *mòd,* cogn. with MOOT]

mod[2], *n.* a member of a youth group of the 1960s, who wore smart casual clothes, rode motor-scooters and were often involved in fights with gangs of rockers, a rival youth group. [*mod*ern]

MOD, (*abbr.*) Ministry of Defence.

modal, *a.* pertaining to mode, form or manner, as opp. to substance; of a verb, pertaining to mood or denoting manner. *n.* a modal proposition or verb. **modal proposition,** *n.* a proposition that affirms or denies with some qualification. **modalism,** *n.* the doctrine that the three Persons of the Trinity are merely different modes of being. **modalist,** *n.* **modality,** *n.* **modally,** *adv.* [med. L *modālis,* from L *modus,* MODE]

mod. con., *n.* (*coll.*) a modern device or appliance that gives comfort, convenience etc. [*mod*ern *con*venience]

mode, *n.* manner, method, way of doing, existing etc.; style; common fashion, prevailing custom; an operational state; one of the systems of dividing the octave, the form of the scale; the character of the connection in or the modality of a proposition; an open-work filling in lace; †(*Gram.*) mood; a kind of silk, alamode. [F, from L *modus, -um,* rel. to Gr. *mēdos* plan, and Eng. METE[2]]

model, *n.* a representation or pattern in miniature, in three dimensions, of something to be made on a larger scale; a figure in clay, plaster etc. for execution in durable material; a thing or person to be represented by a sculptor or painter; one employed to pose as subject to an artist; one employed to wear clothes to display their effect; a standard, an example regarded as a canon of artistic execution; a particular style or type, e.g. of a car or a garment; a description or representation of something that cannot be observed directly; a set of postulates, mathematical equations etc. used e.g. to predict developments in the economy; (*euphem.*) a prostitute. *a.* serving as a model or example; worthy of imitation, perfect. *v.t.* (*past, p.p.* **modelled**) to shape, mould or fashion in clay etc.; to form after or upon a model; to give a plan or shape to (a document, book etc.); to display (clothes) by wearing them. *v.i.* to make a model or models; to act as a mannequin. **modeller,** *n.* [OF *modelle,* It. *modello,* dim. of *modo,* as prec.]

Model Parliament, *n.* English parliament set up in 1295 by Edward I; it was the first to include representatives from outside the clergy and aristocracy, and was established because Edward needed the support of the whole country against his opponents: Wales, France and Scotland. His sole aim was to raise money for military purposes, and the parliament did not pass any legislation.

modem, *n.* a device used to transmit and receive data, esp. between two computers over a telephone line. [*mo*dulator *dem*odulator]

modena, *n.* a deep crimson or purple. [Italian city of *Modena*]

moderate, *a.* keeping within bounds; temperate, reasonable, mild; not extreme or excessive; of medium quantity or quality. *n.* one of moderate views in politics, religion etc. *v.t.,* to reduce to a calmer, less violent, energetic or intense condition; to restrain from excess; to temper, to mitigate. *v.i.,* to become less violent; to quiet or settle down; to preside as a moderator. **moderant,** *n.* a moderate; something that moderates. **moderately,** *adv.* with moderation; not excessively, fairly. **moderateness,** *n.* **moderation,** *n.* the act of moderating; the quality or state of being moderate; temperance; self-restraint; (*pl.*) the first public examination for a degree at Oxford. **moderatism,** *n.* **moderato,** *adv.* (*Mus.*) in moderate time. **moderator,** *n.* one who or that which moderates; one who presides at a meeting, esp. the presiding officer at a court of the Presbyterian Church; one whose task is to ensure fairness and consistency in the way examination papers are set and marked; one who superintends certain examinations for degrees and honours at Oxford and Cambridge Univs.; †an umpire, an arbitrator. **moderatorship,** *n.* **moderatrix,** *n. fem.* [L *moderātus,* p.p. of *moderārī,* from *moder-,* stem of *modestus,* MODEST, cogn. with *modus,* MODE]

modern, *a.* pertaining to the present or recent time; late, recent; not ancient, old-fashioned or obsolete; being or concerning the present or most recent form of a language; †commonplace, trite. *n.* a person of modern times; an exponent of modernism (as artist, writer etc.). **modern history,** *n.* history from AD 1517 to the present day. **modern languages,** *n.pl.* those that are still in current use, esp. as a subject of study. **modern pentathlon,** *n.* a sports contest involving swimming, cross-country running, fencing, equestrian steeplechasing and shooting. **modernism,** *n.* a modern mode of expression or thought; a modern term or idiom; in art and literature, the conscious rejection of traditional forms and use of new forms of expression; a tendency towards freedom of thought and the acceptance of the results of modern criticism and research in religious matters. **modernist,** *n.* **modernity, modernness,** *n.* **modernize, -ise,** *v.t., v.i.* **modernization, -isation,** *n.* **modernizer, -iser,** *n.* **modernly,** *adv.* [F *moderne,* late L *modernus,* from *modo,* just now]

modest, *a.* humble, unassuming or diffident in regard to one's merits or importance; not presumptuous, forward or arrogant; bashful, retiring; restrained by a sense of propriety; decorous, chaste; moderate, not extreme or excessive. **modestly,** *adv.* **modesty,** *n.* the quality of being modest; a sense of propriety; delicacy; chastity. **modesty vest,** *n.* a narrow piece of lace worn over the bosom with an open dress. [F *modeste,* L *modestus,* as MODERATE]

modicum, *n.* a little; a small amount, a scanty allowance. [L, neut. of *modicus,* moderate, as prec.]

modify, *v.t.* to alter, to make different; to change to a moderate extent the form, character or other qualities of; to reduce in degree or extent; to moderate, to tone down; (*Gram.*) to qualify the sense of, to alter (a vowel) by umlaut. **modifiable,** *a.* **modifiability,** *n.* **modification,** *n.* †**modificative,** *n., a.* †**modificator,** *n.* **modificatory,** *a.* **modifier,** *n.* a word or phrase that modifies another. [F *modifier,* L *modificāre* (*modus,* MODE, -FY)]

Modigliani, *n.* **Amedeo** (1884–1920), Italian artist, active in Paris from 1906. He painted and sculpted graceful nudes and portrait studies. His paintings have a distinctive soft, elongated, linear style.

modillion, *n.* an ornamental bracket beneath the cornice of a Corinthian or other order. [It. *modiglione,* etym. doubtful]

modiolus, *n.* the central column round which the cochlea of the ear winds. **modiolar,** *a.* [L, bucket on waterwheel, dim. of *modius,* a corn-measure]

modish, *a.* fashionable; stylish. **modishly,** *adv.* **modishness,** *n.* **modist,** *n.* a follower of the fashion. [MODE, -ISH[1]]

modiste, *n.* a milliner or dressmaker. [F]

Mods, *n.pl.* short for MODERATIONS.

modulate, *v.t.* to adjust, to regulate; to vary or inflect the sound or tone of; (*Mus.*) to change the key of. *v.i.* (*Mus.*) to pass from one key to another. **modulation,** *n.* the act of modulating or being modulated; alterations in the amplitude or frequency of an electrical wave at a different frequency, usually at a lower. **modulative,** *a.* **modulator,** *n.* one who or that which modulates; (*Mus.*) a chart of the modulations in the tonic sol-fa system; (*Radio.*) a transmitter valve which superinduces microphone signals on the high-frequency carrier. [L *modulātus,* p.p. of *modulārī,* to measure, from MODULUS]

module, *n.* a measure or unit of proportion, esp. (*Arch.*) the semidiameter or other unit taken as a standard for regulating the proportions of a column; any element or unit that forms part of a larger system, e.g. a space-craft, an educational course; †(*fig.*) an image or counterfeit. **modular,** *a.* [F, as foll.]

modulus, *n.* (*pl.* **-li**) (*Math. etc.*) a constant number or coefficient expressing a force, effect, function, etc.; a constant multiplier in a function of a variable; the numerical value of quantity. **modular,** *a.* [L, dim. of foll.]

modus, *n.* (*pl.* **-di**), mode, manner, way; money compensation in lieu of tithe. [L, MODE]

modus operandi, the way one does something; the way a thing works. [L, method of operating]

modus vivendi, way of living; a compromise or temporary arrangement pending a final settlement of matters in dispute. [L, way of living]

mofette, *n.* an exhalation of noxious gas from the earth; a fissure giving vent to such gas. [F, from It. *mofetta*]

moff, *n.* a Circassian silk stuff. [etym. doubtful]

mog, moggy, *n.* (*coll.*) a cat.

Mogadishu, Mugdisho, *n.* capital and chief port of Somalia; population (1988) 1,000,000. It is a centre for oil refining, food processing, and uranium mining.

Mogadon®, *n.* a proprietary drug used to treat insomnia.

Mogul, *n.* a Mongolian; a follower of Baber, descendant of Tamerlane, or of Genghis Khan; a powerful and influential entrepreneur. **Great Mogul,** the emperors of Delhi (1526–1857), formerly sovereigns of the greater part of Hindustan. [Pers. *mugul,* Mongol]

MOH, (*abbr.*) Medical Officer of Health.

Mohács, Battle of, Austro-Hungarian defeat of the Turks (1687) which effectively marked the end of Turkish expansion into Europe. It is also the site of a Turkish victory in 1526. Mohács is now a river port on the Danube in Hungary.

mohair, *n.* the hair of the angora goat; a fabric made from it; an imitation of this fabric in cotton and wool. [Arab. *mukhayyar* (assim. to HAIR)]

Mohamad, *n.* **Mahathir bin** (1925–), prime minister of Malaysia from 1981 and leader of the United Malays' National Organization (UMNO). His 'look east' economic policy emulates Japanese industrialization.

Mohammed, Muhammad, *n.* (*c.* 570–632), founder of Islam, born in Mecca on the Arabian peninsula. In about 616 he claimed to be a prophet and that the *Koran* was revealed to him by God (it was later written down by his followers). He fled from persecution to the town now known as Medina in 622: the flight, **Hegira,** marks the beginning of the Islamic era.

Mohammedan, *a.* pertaining to Mohammed or Mohammedanism. *n.* a follower of Mohammed, a Muslim; an adherent of Mohammedanism, Islam. **Mohammedanism, †-medism,** *n.* the Muslim religion founded by Mohammed (*c.* 570–632). **Mohammedanize, †-medize, -ise,** *v.t.* [Arab. *Muhammad,* praiseworthy, from *hamada,* to praise]

Moharram, *n.* the first month (30 days) of the Muslim year; the first 10 days of this observed as a fast in memory of the martyrdom of Husain, the son of Ali. [Arab. *muharram,* sacred]

Mohawk, *n.* the name of a tribe of N American Indians; their language; (*Skating*) a stroke from either edge to the same edge on the other foot, but in the opposite direction. [from the native name]

Mohenjo Daro, *n.* the site of a city (about 2500–1600 BC) on the lower Indus, Pakistan, where excavations from the 1920s have revealed the Indus Valley civilization. The most striking artistic remains are soapstone seals of elephants and snakes.

Mohican, *n.* a N American Indian of a tribe living in the Hudson river valley; the language of this tribe. *a.* of this tribe or its language. [from a native name]

mohican, *n.* a punk hairstyle in which the head is bald apart from a narrow central strip of erect hair from front to rear, often brightly coloured.

Mohock, *n.* a name given to a set of aristocratic ruffians who infested the streets of London at night early in the 18th cent. [corr. of MOHAWK]

Moholy-Nagy, *n.* **Laszlo** (1895–1946), US photographer, born in Hungary. He lived in Germany (1923–29), where he was a member of the Bauhaus school, and fled from the Nazis in 1935. Through the publication of his illuminating theories and practical experiments, he had great influence on 20th-cent. photography and design.

Mohorovičić discontinuity, *n.* (also **Moho** or **M-discontinuity**) boundary that separates the Earth's crust and mantle, marked by a rapid increase in the speed of earthquake waves. It follows the variations in the thickness of the crust and is found approximately 32 km/20 miles below the continents and about 10 km/6 miles below the oceans. It is named after the Yugoslav geophysicist Andrija Mohorovičić (1857–1936) who suspected its presence after analysing seismic waves from the Kulpa Valley earthquake (1909).

mohr, *n.* a W African gazelle, *Gazella mohr.* [Arab.]

Mohs, *n.* **Friedrich** (1773–1839), German mineralogist, who in 1812 devised **Mohs' scale** of hardness for minerals (in ascending order): 1 talc; 2 gypsum; 3 calcite; 4 fluorite; 5 apatite; 6 orthoclase; 7 quartz; 8 topaz; 9 corundum; 10 diamond.

Moi, *n.* **Daniel arap** (1924–), Kenyan politician, president from 1978. Originally a teacher, he became minister of home affairs in 1964, vice-president in 1967, and succeeded Kenyatta as president.

moider, *v.t.* (*dial.*) to confuse, to muddle; to weary; to labour (one's life etc.) away. *v.i.* to ramble, to talk incoherently. [perh. conn. with MUDDLE]

moidore, *n.* (*Hist.*) a Portuguese gold coin. [Port. *moeda d'ouro* (*moeda,* L *monēta,* MONEY, *de,* of, *ouro,* L *aurum,* gold)]

moiety, *n.* a half; a part or share. [OF *moitié,* L *medietas -tātem,* middle point, half, from *medius,* see MEDIUM]

moil, *v.i.* to toil, to drudge, to work hard. *v.t.* to weary, to fatigue; †to moisten, to bedaub, to defile. [OF *moiller* (F *mouiller*), to wet, to paddle through mud, from L *mollis,* soft]

moineau, *n.* a small flat bastion. [F, sparrow]

moire, *n.* watered silk; a watered appearance on textile fabrics or metals. **moire antique,** *n.* a heavy, watered silk. **moiré,** *v.t.* to give a watered appearance to. *a.* watered (of silk, surfaces of metal etc.). *n.* a surface or finish like watered silk. [F, prob. a form of MOHAIR]

Moissan, *n.* **Henri** (1852–1907), French chemist. For his preparation of pure fluorine in 1886, Moissan was awarded the 1906 Nobel Chemistry Prize. He also attempted to create artificial diamonds by rapidly cooling mixtures of carbon heated to high temperatures. His claims of success were treated with suspicion.

moist, *a.* moderately wet, damp, humid; rainy; discharging pus etc.; †fresh, new. **moisten,** *v.t., v.i.* **moistener,** *n.* †**moistful,** *a.* **moistify,** *v.t.* **moistness, moisture,** *n.* **moistureless,** *a.* **moisturize, -ise,** *v.t.* to add moisture to. **moisturizer, -iser,** *n.* anything which moisturizes, esp. a cosmetic cream or lotion. **moisty,** *a.* [OF *moiste* (F *moite*), perh. from late L *muccidus,* L *mūcidus,* MUCID]

Mojave Desert, *n.* an arid region in S California, US, part of the Great Basin; area 38,500 sq km/15,000 sq miles.

moke, *n.* (*sl.*) a donkey; (*Austral.*) an inferior horse. [etym. unknown]

moki, *n.* a variety of New Zealand fish. [Maori]

moko, *n.* tattooing; the Maori method of doing this. [Maori]

mol, (*chem. symbol*) MOLE4.

mol., (*abbr.*) molecular; molecule.

molar1, *a.* having power to grind; grinding. *n.* one of the back or grinding teeth. **molary,** *a.* [L *molāris,* from *mola,* mill]

molar2, *a.* of or pertaining to mass; acted on or exerted by a large mass or masses. [MOLE2, -AR]

molasses, *n.pl.* (*usu. sing. in constr.*) the viscid, dark-brown uncrystallizable syrup drained from sugar during the refining process; treacle. [Port. *melaço,* late L *mellāceum,* must, from *mel,* honey]

mold MOULD.

Moldavia1, *n.* a constituent republic of the Soviet Union from 1940. **area** 33,700 sq km/13,012 sq miles. **capital** Kishinev. **products** wine, tobacco, canned goods. **population** (1987) 4,185,000; 64% Moldavians (a branch of the Romanian people) Ukrainian 14%, Russian 13%, Gagauzi 4%, Jewish 2%. **language** Moldavian, allied to Romanian. **religion** Russian Orthodox.

Moldavia2, *n.* a former principality in Eastern Europe, on the river Danube, occupying an area divided today between the Soviet republic of Moldavia and modern Romania. It was independent between the 14th and 16th cents., when it became part of the Ottoman Empire. In 1940 the E part, Bessarabia, became part of the Soviet Union, whereas the W part remained in Romania.

mole1, *n.* a spot on the human skin, usu. dark-coloured and sometimes covered with hair. [OE *māl*]

mole2, *n.* a pile of masonry, such as a breakwater, pier or jetty before a port; a port, a harbour. [F *môle,* L *mōles,* mass, etym. doubtful]

mole3, *n.* a small soft-furred burrowing mammal of the genus *Talpa,* esp. *T. europaea;* a spy or subversive person working within an organization on behalf of a rival organization, enemy etc. *v.t.* to burrow or ferret (something out). **mole-cricket,** *n.* a burrowing cricket of the genus *Gryllotalpa,* esp. *G. vulgaris.* **mole-eyed,** *a.* having very small eyes or imperfect vision. **molehill,** *n.* a hillock thrown up by a mole burrowing underground; an unimportant or very small matter, problem etc. **mole-rat,** *n.* a mouse-like burrowing rodent, *Spalax typhlus.* **moleskin,** *n.* the skin of the mole used as fur; a kind of fustian, dyed after the surface has been shaved; (*pl.*) clothes, esp. trousers, of this material. [cp. MDut. and LG *mol*]

mole4, *n.* the basic SI unit of substance, being the amount of substance of a system which contains as many specified elementary entities as there are atoms in 0·012 kg of carbon-12.

molecule, *n.* one of the structural units of which matter is built up; the smallest quantity of substance capable of separate existence without losing its chemical identity with that substance; a particle. **molecular,** *a.* **molecular attraction,** *n.* the force by which molecules of bodies act upon each other; cohesion. **molecular biology,** *n.* the study of the structure and chemical organization of living matter, esp. of nucleic acids and protein synthesis. **molecular weight,** *n.* the weight of a molecule of any substance in terms of one-twelfth of the mass of an atom of the isotope carbon-12. **molecularity,** *n.* [F *molécule,* dim. from L *mōles,* see MOLE2]

molendinaceous, *a.* (*Bot.*) resembling the sails of a windmill (applied to the wings of certain seeds). †**molendinar,** *a.* of or pertaining to a mill. *n.* a molar. †**molendinary,** *a.* [med. L *molendīnum,* a mill, from *molere,* to grind]

moleskin MOLE3.

molest, *v.t.* to trouble, to disturb, to harm; to assault or attack, esp. for sexual purposes. **molestation,** *n.* **molester,** *n.* †**molestful,** *a.* [OF *molester,* L *molestāre,* from *molestus,* troublesome]

Molière, *n.* (pen name of Jean Baptiste Poquelin) (1622–73), French satirical playwright from whose work modern French comedy developed. One of the founders of the Illustre Théâtre (1643), he was later its leading actor. In 1655 he wrote his first play, *L'Etourdi,* followed by *Les Précieuses ridicules* (1659). His satires include *L'Ecole des femmes* (1662), *Le Misanthrope* (1666), *Le Bourgeois gentilhomme* (1670), and *Le Malade imaginaire* (1673).

molimen, *n.* (*pl.* **-mina**) (*Physiol.*) an effort, esp. a periodical effort of the system as in the catamenial discharge. [L, effort, from *mōīrī,* to make an effort]

moline, *a.* of the arms of a heraldic cross, shaped like a mill-rind. *n.* a moline cross. [cp. F *moulin,* late L *molīna,* MILL1]

Molinism1, *n.* the doctrine taught by the Spanish Jesuit Luis *Molina* (1535–1600) that the efficacy of divine grace depends on free acceptance by the will. **Molinist,** *n.*

Molinism2, *n.* quietism. **Molinist,** *n.* [Miguel de *Molinos,* 1640–97, the quietist]

Molise, *n.* a mainly agricultural region of S central Italy, comprising the provinces of Campobasso and Isernia; area 4400 sq km/1698 sq miles; population (1988) 335,000. Its capital is Campobasso.

moll, *n.* (*sl.*) a wench, a prostitute; a gangster's girl-friend. [fam. form of *Mary*]

Mollah MULLAH.

mollify, *v.t.* to soften, to assuage; to pacify, to appease. †**mollient,** *a.* **mollifiable,** *a.* **mollification,** *n.* **mollifier,** *n.* [F *mollifier,* L *mollificāre* (*mollis,* soft, *-ficāre,* from *facere,* to make)]

mollusc, *n.* any animal of the Mollusca. **Mollusca,** *n.pl.* a division of invertebrates comprising those with soft bodies, as snails, mussels, cuttlefishes etc. **molluscan, molluscoid,** *n., a.* **Molluscoidea,** *n.pl.* a former group of invertebrates, containing the Brachiopoda and Polyzoa. **molluscous,** *a.* [L *molluscus,* softish, from *mollis,* soft]

molly1, *n.* an effeminate fellow, one who likes to be coddled, a milksop; (*dated sl.*) a wench, a prostitute. **molly-coddle,** *n.* a milksop. *v.t.* to coddle. [form of *Mary*]

molly2, *n.* the fulmar; a convivial meeting on board one of a company of whalers. [corr. of MALLEMUCK]

Molly Maguires, the, (*US Hist.*) a secret Irish coalminers' organization in the 1870s which staged strikes and used violence against coal-company officials and property in the anthracite fields of Pennsylvania, prefiguring a long period of turbulence in industrial relations. The movement was infiltrated by Pinkerton agents (detectives) and in 1876 trials led to convictions and executions.

Moloch, Molech, *n.* an idol of the Phoenicians, worshipped in Jerusalem in the 7th cent. BC, to which human sacrifices were offered; a devouring influence such as overbearing wealth, tyranny etc.; an Australian spiny lizard, *Moloch horridus.* [Heb. *molek*]

molossus, *n.* (*pl.* **molossi,** -ī) (*Pros.*) a foot composed of three long syllables, or a spondee and a half. [Gr.]

Molotov, *n.* **Vyacheslav Mikhailovich** (assumed name of V. M. Skryabin) (1890–1986), Soviet communist politician. He was chair of the Council of People's Commissars (prime minister), 1930–41, and foreign minister, 1939–49, during which period he negotiated a non-aggression treaty with Germany (the Hitler–Stalin pact), and again, 1953–56. In 1957 he was expelled from the government for Stalinist activities.

Molotov cocktail, *n.* a home-made weapon consisting of a bottle filled with petrol, plugged with a rag as a wick, ignited, and thrown as a grenade. Resistance groups during World War II named them after the Soviet foreign minister Molotov.

molten, *a.* made of melted metal; melted by heat. **molten sea,** *n.* the brazen laver of the Mosaic ritual (see I Kings vii.25). **moltenly,** *adv.* [p.p. of MELT]

Moltke[1], *n.* **Helmuth Carl Bernhard, Count von Moltke** (1800–91), Prussian general. He entered the Prussian army in 1821, became chief of the general staff 1857, and was responsible for the Prussian strategy in the wars with Denmark (1863–64), Austria (1866), and France (1870–71). He was created a count in 1870 and a field marshal in 1871.

Moltke[2], *n.* **Helmuth Johannes Ludwig von Moltke** (1848–1916), German general (nephew of Count von Moltke, the Prussian general), chief of the German general staff (1906–14). His use of Schlieffen's plan for a rapid victory on two fronts failed and he was superseded.

molto, *adv.* (*Mus.*) much, very. [It.]

Moluccas, *n.* another name for MALUKU, Indonesia.

moly, *n.* a fabulous herb with white flower and black root, given to Ulysses to counteract the spells of Circe; wild garlic. [L, from Gr. *mōlu*]

molybdenum, †**molybdena,** *n.* (*Chem.*) a rare metallic element, at. no.42; chem. symbol Mo, found in combination as molybdenite. **molybdate,** *n.* **molybdenite,** *n.* a sulphide or native disulphide of molybdenum. **molybdenous,** *a.* **molybdic, -dous,** *a.* **molybdo-,** *comb. form.* [L *molybdaena,* Gr. *molubdaina,* from *molubdos,* lead]

mom, *n.* (*N Am., coll.*) mother.

Mombasa, *n.* an industrial port (oil-refining, cement) in Kenya (serving also Uganda and Tanzania), built on Mombasa Island and adjacent mainland; population (1984) 481,000.

†**mome**, *n.* a blockhead. [etym. doubtful]

moment, *n.* a minute portion of time, an instant; importance, consequence; the measure of a force by its power to cause rotation; †momentum. **at the moment,** at the present, just now. **moment of a force,** the product of a force and the perpendicular from the point of application to the point of action. **moment of truth,** a moment when something important must be decided, a difficult task undertaken etc. **the moment,** the right time for anything, the opportunity. **this moment,** at once. **momentaeous, momentary,** *a.* lasting only for a moment; done or past in a moment; transient, ephemeral. **momentarily,** *adv.* for a moment; (*N Am.*) immediately. **momentariness,** *n.* **momently,** *adv.* from moment to moment; at any moment, for a moment. **momentous,** *a.* weighty, important. **momentously,** *adv.* **momentousness,** *n.* [F, from L MOMENTUM]

momentum, *n.* (*pl.* **-ta**) impetus, power of overcoming resistance to motion; the quantity of motion in a body, the product of the mass and the velocity. [L, for *movimentum* (*movēre,* to MOVE, -MENT)]

momma, *n.* (*N Am., coll.*) mother.

Momus, *n.* a Greek divinity, the son of Night, the god of blame and ridicule; a fault-finding or querulous person. [Gr. *Mōmos*]

Mon., (*abbr.*) Monday.

mon- MON(O)-.

monachal, *a.* monastic. **monachism,** *n.* monasticism; monkery, monkishness. **monachist,** *n.* **monachize, -ise,** *v.t., v.i.* [med. L *monachālis,* from *monachus,* MONK]

monacid, *a.* capable of saturating one molecule of a monobasic acid.

Monaco, *n.* Principality of, a small sovereign state, forming an enclave in southern France, with the Mediterranean to the S. **area** 1.95 sq km/0.75 sq mile. **capital** Monaco-Ville. **town** Monte Carlo, noted for its film festival, motor races and casino. **physical** steep slope. **exports** some light industry, but economy depends on tourism and gambling. **population** (1989) 29,000; annual growth rate -0.5%. **language** French. **religion** Roman Catholic.

monactinal, *n.* of a sponge-spicule, single-rayed, rod-shaped. **monactine,** *a.* **monactinellid,** *a.* of or pertaining to the **Monactinellida,** a Palaeozoic order of sponges. *n.* a sponge of this order. [Gr. *aktis aktinos,* ray]

monad, *n.* a simple, indivisible unit; one of the primary elements of being, esp. according to the philosophy of Leibnitz; a univalent atom, radical or element; an elementary, single-celled organism. **monadic, -ical,** *a.* **monadism,** *n.* **monadology,** *n.* the theory or doctrine of monads. [late L and Gr. *monad-,* nom. *monas,* from *monos,* sole]

monadelphous, *a.* having the stamens united by their filaments; of stamens, having the filaments united. [MON-, Gr. *adelphos,* brother]

Monaghan, *n.* (Irish **Mhuineachain**) a county of the NE Republic of Ireland, province of Ulster; area 1290 sq km/498 sq miles; population (1986) 52,000. The county town is Monaghan. The county is low and rolling, and includes the rivers Finn and Blackwater. Products include cereals, linen, potatoes and cattle.

monandry, *n.* that form of marriage in which one woman has only one husband at a time; the quality of being monandrous. **monandrous,** *a.* (*Bot.*) having only one stamen. [Gr. *anēr andros,* male]

monanthous, *a.* bearing only one flower (on each stalk).

monarch, *n.* a sole ruler; a hereditary sovereign, as emperor, empress, king or queen; the chief of its class; a large red and black butterfly, *Danais archippus.* **monarchic, -ical,, monarchal,** *a.* **monarchically,** †**monarchally,** *adv.* **monarchism,** *n.* **monarchist,** *n.* **monarchize, -ise,** *v.t.* †**Monarcho,** *n.* a crack-brained Italian who thought himself emperor of the world; (*Shak.*) a pretendèr. **monarchy,** *n.* government in which the supreme power is vested in a monarch; a state under this system, a kingdom; supreme control. [F *monarque,* L *monarche,* Gr. *monarchēs* (MON-, *archein,* to rule)]

monastery, *n.* a residence for a community, esp. of monks, living under religious vows of seclusion. †**monasterial,** *a.* **monastic,** *a.* monasterial; in bookbinding, applied to an antique style of tooling without gold. **monastical,** *a.* **monastically,** *adv.* **monasticism,** *n.* the theory and system of the monastic life. **monasticize, -ise,** *v.t.* **monasticon,** *n.* a book treating of monasteries. [med. L *monastērium,* Gr. *monastērion,* from *monazein,* to live alone, from *monos,* see MONAD]

Monastir, *n.* a resort town on the Mediterranean coast of Tunisia, 18 km/11 miles S of Sousse. Summer residence of the president of Tunisia.

monatomic, *a.* having one atom in the molecule; univalent.

monaural, *a.* having or using one ear; of reproduced sound, not stereophonic.

Monck, or **Monk,** *n.* **George, 1st Duke of Albemarle** (1608–69), English soldier. During the Civil War he fought for King Charles I, but after being captured changed sides and took command of the Parliamentary forces in Ireland. Under the Commonwealth he became commander in chief in Scotland, and in 1660 he led his army into England and brought about the restoration of Charles II.

Mond, *n.* **Ludwig** (1839–1909), German chemist who perfected a process for recovering sulphur during the manufacture of alkali.

Monday, *n.* the second day of the week, following Sunday. **Mondayish,** *a.* miserable, reluctant to start the week's work. [OE *Mōnandæg* (*Mōnan,* gen. of *Mōna,* moon, DAY)]

monde, *n.* society; one's circle or set. [F, from L *mundus -um,* the world]

Mondrian, *n.* **Piet** (Pieter Mondriaan) (1872–1944), Dutch painter, a pioneer of abstract art. He lived in Paris (1919–38), then in London, and from 1940 in New York. He was a founder member of the de Stijl movement and chief exponent of neo-plasticism, a rigorous abstract style based on the use of simple geometric forms and pure colours.

Monegasque, *a.* pertaining to the principality of Monaco. *n.* a native or inhabitant of Monaco. [F]

Monera, *n.pl.* a class of amoebiform Protozoa of the most elementary organization. **moneral, -eric, -eran,** *a.* [Gr. *monērēs,* single, from *monos,* sole]

monergism, *n.* the Lutheran doctrine that regeneration is entirely the work of the Holy Spirit, as distinct from *synergism.* [Gr. *ergon,* work, -ISM]

Monet, *n.* **Claude** (1840–1926), French painter, a pioneer of impressionism and a lifelong exponent of its ideals; his painting *Impression, Sunrise* (1872) gave the movement its name. In the 1870s he began painting the same subjects at different times of day to explore the effects of light on colour and form; the *Haystacks* and *Rouen Cathedral* series followed in the 1890s, and from 1899 a series of *Water Lilies* painted in the garden of his house at Giverny in Normandy.

monetary, *a.* of or pertaining to money or the coinage. **monetarism,** *n.* the economic theory that advocates strict control of the money supply as the best method of regulating the economy. **monetarist,** *n., a.* **monetize, -ise,** *v.t.* to give a standard value to (a metal) as currency; to form into coin. **monetization, -isation,** *n.* [L *monētārius,* from *monēta,* see foll.]

money, *n.* (*pl.* **moneys,** erroneously **monies**) coin or other material used as medium of exchange; banknotes, bills, notes of hand and other documents representing coin; wealth, property, regarded as convertible into coin; (*with pl.*) coins of a particular country or denomination; (*pl.*) sums of money, receipts or payments. **for my etc. money,** in my etc. opinion. **money of account,** a denomination (as of the guinea), not actually coined, but used for convenience in keeping accounts. **money-bag,** *n.* a bag for money; (*pl.*) wealth; (*pl., sing. in constr.*) a rich or miserly person. **money-box,** *n.* a box with a slit through which savings or contributions are put in. **money-changer,** *n.* one who changes foreign money at a fixed rate. **money-grubber,** *n.* a person who saves or amasses money in sordid ways. **money-lender,** *n.* a person whose business is to lend money at interest. **money-making,** *n., a.* highly profitable (business). **money-market,** *n.* the field of operation of dealers in stocks etc., the financial world. **money-matter,** *n.* an affair involving money. **money-order,** *n.* an order for money, granted at one post-office and payable at another. **money-spider, -spinner,** *n.* a small spider, *Aranea scenica,* supposed to bring good luck; one who makes great profits. **money's-worth, †moneyworth,** *n.* full value, an equivalent for money paid. **moneywort,** *n.* a trailing plant, *Lysimachia nummularia,* with round glossy leaves. **moneyed,** *a.* rich; consisting of money. **moneyer,** *n.* a banker; an authorized coiner of money. **moneyless,** *a.* [ME and OF *moneie* (F *monnaie*), L *monēta,* mint, money, orig. name of Juno in whose temple money was coined]

monger, *n.* a trader, a dealer (now only in comb., as *ironmonger, scandalmonger*). [OE *mangere;* from *mangian,* to traffic, from L *mango,* a dealer]

mongol, *n.* a person suffering from mongolism. *a.* of or being a sufferer from Down's syndrome. **mongolism,** *n.* DOWN'S SYNDROME. **mongoloid,** *n., a.*

Mongol, *n.* person of Mongol culture from Central Asia. Mongols, who comprise a number of distinct ethnic groups, live in the Mongolian People's Republic, the USSR, and China. The Mongol language belongs to the Altaic family. **Mongolian,** *a.* pertaining to the straight-haired yellow-skinned peoples of Asia. *n.* a Mongol; the language of the Mongols or of the Mongolian stock.

Mongol Empire, *n.* an empire established by Genghis Khan, who extended his domains from Russia to N China and became khan of the Mongol tribes in 1206. His grandson Kublai Khan conquered China and used foreigners such as Marco Polo as well as subjects to administer his empire. In 1367 the Mongols lost China and suffered defeats in the West in 1380; the empire broke up soon afterwards.

Mongolia[1], *n.* Mongolian People's Republic (*Bügd Nayramdakh Mongol Ard Uls*), a country in E central Asia, bounded N by the USSR and S by China. **area** 1,567,000 sq km/605,000 sq miles. **capital** Ulaanbaatar (formerly Ulan Bator). **towns** Darkhan, Choybalsan. **physical** a high plateau with steppe (grasslands). **exports** meat and butter; varied minerals; furs. **population** (1989) 2,093,000; annual growth rate 2.8%. **language** Khalkha Mongolian (official), Chinese, Russian. **religion** formerly Tibetan Buddhist Lamaist, suppressed in the 1930s.

Mongolia[2], Inner, *n.* (Chinese **Nei Mongol**) autonomous region of NE China from 1947. **area** 450,000 sq km/173,700 sq miles. **capital** Hohhot. **physical** grassland and desert. **products** cereals under irrigation; coal; reserves of rare earth oxides europium, and yttrium at Bayan Obo. **population** (1986) 20,290,000.

Mongoloid, *n.* a former racial classification, based on physical features, used to describe people of E Asian and North American origin.

mongoose, *n.* an ichneumon, *Herpestes griseus,* found in Africa, S Europe and SE Asia, which feeds on venomous snakes. [Marathi *mangūs*]

mongrel, *a.* of mixed breed, arising from the crossing of two varieties; of mixed nature or character. *n.* anything, esp. a dog, of mixed breed. **mongrelism,** *n.* **mongrelize, -ise,** *v.t.* **mongrelly,** *adv.* [prob. cogn. with OE *mang,* a mixture]

monial, *n.* a mullion. [OF, etym. unknown]

moni(c)ker, *n.* (*sl.*) name. [etym. unknown]

moniliform, *a.* shaped like a necklace or string of beads. [L *monīle,* necklace]

†moniment MONUMENT.

moniplies MANYPLIES.

monism, *n.* the doctrine that all existing things and activities are forms of manifestations of one ultimate principle or substance; any philosophic theory such as idealism, pantheism or materialism, opposed to dualism. **monist,** *n.* **monistic,** *a.* [Gr. *monos,* one]

monition, *n.* a warning; an intimation or notice; (*Civil Law*) a summons or citation; a formal letter from a bishop or court warning a clergyman to abstain from certain practices. **monitive,** *a.* [F, from L *monitio -ōnem,* from *monēre,* to warn]

monitor, *n.* one who warns or admonishes; a senior pupil appointed to keep order in a school or to look after junior classes; one whose duty it is to listen to foreign or other broadcasts; a detector for radioactivity; an ironclad of low draught having revolving turrets; (**Monitor**) a genus of large tropical lizards found in Asia, Africa and Australia; a television screen used e.g. in a studio or with a computer for displaying and checking pictures or information. *v.t., v.i.* to listen to (radio broadcasts) in order to glean information. **monitorial,** *a.* **monitorially,** *adv.* **monitorship,** *n.* **monitory,** *a.* giving warning or admonition. *n.* a warning or admonition from a bishop, pope etc. **monitress,** *n. fem.*

monk, *n.* a member of a religious community of men, living apart under vows of poverty, chastity and obedience; a patch of print with too much ink. **monkfish,** *n.* any of various anglerfish of the *Lophius* genus. **monk's-hood,** *n.* a plant of the genus *Aconitum,* esp. *A. napellus* (from its hooded sepals). **monkdom,** *n.* **monkery,** *n.* (*derog.*) monasticism; monkish practices; monks collectively. **monkhood, monkship,** *n.* **monkish,** *a.* **monkishness,** *n.* [OE *munec, munuc,* L and Gr. *monachos,* from *monos,* alone]

Monk, *n.* **Thelonious** (1917–82), US jazz pianist and composer. Working in Harlem, New York, during the Depression, he took part in developing the jazz style known as *bebop* or *bop*. He became popular in the 1950s, and is remembered for numbers such as 'Round Midnight', 'Blue Monk', and 'Hackensack'.

monkey, *n.* a quadrumanous mammal of various species and families ranging from the anthropoid apes to the lemurs; (*coll.*) a rogue, an imp; an ape, a mimic; a pile-driving machine; a monkey-jar; a mixture of hydrochloric acid and zinc used in soldering; (*sl.*) a sum of £500 or $500. *v.t.* to mimic, to ape; to meddle with, to interfere with. *v.i.* to play foolish or mischievous tricks. **to get, put, one's monkey up,** (*coll.*) to be angry or to enrage. **to make a monkey of,** to cause to seem foolish. **monkey-block,** *n.* a single block strapped to a swivel. **monkey-bread,** *n.* the fruit of the baobab tree, *Adansonia digitata.* **monkey-business,** *n.* devious or underhand behaviour; mischievous behaviour. **monkey-engine,** *n.* a pile-driving machine. **monkey-flower,** *n.* a plant of the genus *Mimulus.* **monkey-jacket,** *n.* a pea-jacket worn by sailors etc. **monkey-jar,** *n.* a globular earthenware vessel used in tropical countries for cooling water. **monkey-puzzle,** *n.* the Chilean pine, *Araucaria imbricata,* having spiny leaves and branches. **monkey-rail,** *n.* a light rail running above the quarter-rail of a ship. **monkey-wrench,** *n.* a spanner with a movable jaw. **monkey-ish,** *a.* **monkeyishness,** *n.* **monkeyism,** *n.* [prob. from LG]

monkish etc. MONK.

Monmouth, *n.* **James Scott, Duke of Monmouth** (1649–85), claimant to the English crown, the natural son of Charles II and Lucy Walter. After James II's accession in 1685, he landed at Lyme Regis, Dorset, claimed the crown, and raised a rebellion, which was crushed at Sedgemoor in Somerset. Monmouth was executed with 320 of his accomplices.

Monmouthshire, *n.* a former county of Wales, which in 1974 became, minus a small strip on the border with Mid Glamorgan, the new county of Gwent.

mono, *n., a.* monophonic (sound).

mon(o)-, *comb. form* alone, single; as in *monograph, monosyllable.* [Gr. *monos*]

monobasic, *a.* with one base or replaceable atom.

monoblastic, *a.* (*Biol.*) having a single germ-layer. [Gr. *blastos,* sprout]

monoblepsis, *n.* a defective state of vision in which objects can be seen clearly only when one eye is used. [Gr. *blepsis,* vision]

monobloc, *n.* denoting a type of internal-combustion engine having all its cylinders cast in one piece.

monocardian, *a.* having a single heart.

monocarp, *n.* a monocarpic plant. **monocarpic, -pous,** *a.* bearing fruit but once, and dying after fructification.

monocentric, *a.* (*Biol.*) having a single centre; (*Anat.*) unipolar.

monocephalous, *a.* having one head; (*Bot.*) having a single head of flowers.

monoceros, *n.* a one-horned creature, the unicorn; †a sea-unicorn, a sword-fish or narwhal; the constellation Unicorn. **monocerous,** *a.* [Gr. *keras,* a horn]

monochlamydeous, *a.* having a single floral envelope, as a calyx, but no corolla. [see CHLAMYS]

monochord, *n.* a musical instrument with one string; an apparatus for determining the ratios of musical intervals.

monochromatic, *a.* of light, presenting rays of one colour only; painted etc. in monochrome. **monochromator,** *n.* a spectroscope capable of segregating for use a narrow portion of spectrum. **monochrome,** *n.* a painting in tints of one colour only; any representation in one colour. *a.* monochromic. **monochromic,** *a.* executed in one colour. **monochromy,** *n.*

monocle, *n.* an eye-glass for one eye.

monocleid, monocleide, *n.* a cabinet in which all the drawers are shut simultaneously by one key. [Gr. *kleis -eidos,* a key]

monoclinal, *a.* (*Geol.*) of strata, dipping continuously in one direction. **monocline,** *n.* a monoclinal fold, a hogback. **monoclinic, -clinate,** *a.* (*Cryst.*) having two oblique axes and a third at right angles to these. [Gr. *klinein,* to bend]

monoclinous, *a.* (*Bot.*) hermaphrodite; (*Geol.*) monoclinal. [Gr. *klinē,* couch]

monoclonal antibody, *n.* an antibody composed of cells derived from a single cell.

monocoque, *n.* (*Aviat.*) a form of stream-lined fuselage shaped like an elongated egg; an aeroplane with such a fuselage; a car or vehicle with a body and chassis manufactured as an integrated structure; a boat with a hull all made of one piece.

monocotyledon, *n.* a plant having a single cotyledon. **monocotyledonous,** *a.*

monocracy, *n.* government by a single person. **monocrat,** *n.*

monocular, *a.* one-eyed; for use with one eye only. **monocularity,** *n.* **monocule,** MONOCULUS. **monoculist,** *n.* **monoculous,** *a.* **monoculus,** *n.* a one-eyed creature, a cyclops; a bandage for one eye; (**Monoculus**) a Linnaean genus containing the water-fleas. [late L *monoculus,* see MONOCLE]

monoculture, *n.* the cultivation of a single type of crop; the area where it is grown.

monocycle, *n.* a unicycle.

monocyte, *n.* the largest white blood-cell in vertebrate blood.

monodactylous, *a.* having but one finger, toe or claw. [Gr. *monodaktulos* (*daktulos,* finger)]

monodelph, *n.* a mammal belonging to the Monodelphia, a division of Mammalia in which the uterus and vagina are single. **monodelphian,** *n., a.* **monodelphic, -phous,** *a.* [F *monodelphe,* mod. L *Monodelphia* (Gr. *delphus,* womb)]

Monodon, *n.* a genus of cetaceans containing only the narwhal. [Gr. *odous odontos,* tooth]

monodrama, *n.* a dramatic piece for one performer only. **monodramatic,** *a.*

monody, *n.* an ode, usu. of a mournful character, for a single actor; a song for one voice, or a musical composition in which one voice predominates; a mournful or plaintive song or poetical composition, a threnody. **monodic,** *a.* **monodist,** *n.*

Monoecia, *n.pl.* a Linnaean class, comprising plants in which the stamens and pistils are in distinct flowers. **monoecious,** *a.* belonging to the Monoecia; having separate male and female flowers on the same plant; (*Zool.*) hermaphrodite. [mod. L (Gr. *oikos,* house)]

monofil, *n.* a single strand of synthetic fibre.

monogamy, *n.* marriage to one wife or husband only; (*rare*) the practice of marrying only once; (*Zool.*) the habit of pairing with a single mate. **monogamic,** *a.* **monogamist,** *n.* **monogamous,** *a.* [F *monogamie,* L and Gr. *monogamia* (Gr. *gamos,* marriage)]

monogenesis, *n.* generation from one parent, asexual reproduction; development of an organism from a parent resembling itself. **monogenetic, monogenic, monogenous,** *n.* **monogenism, -geny,** *n.* the doctrine that all human beings are descended from a single pair. **monogenist,** *n.*

monoglot, *a.* speaking only one language. *n.* a monoglot person. [Gr. *monoglōttos* (*glōtta,* tongue)]

monogony, *n.* asexual propagation. **monogonic,** *a.* [Gr. *-gonia,* begetting, from *gon-, gen-,* to beget]

monogram, *n.* a character composed of two or more letters interwoven; a single character representing a word etc. **monogrammatic,** *a.* [late L *monogramma,* Gr. *monogrammon*]

monograph, *n.* a treatise on a single thing or class of things. *v.t.* to treat of in a monograph. **monographer, -phist,** *n.* **monographic, -ical,** *a.* **monographically,** *adv.*

Monogynia, *n.pl.* a Linnaean order containing plants having flowers with one pistil. **monogyn,** *n.* a plant of this kind. **monogynian, -gynous,** *a.* **monogyny,** *n.* the practice of mating with only one female. [mod. L, from *monogynus* (Gr. *gunē,* woman)]

monohull, *n.* a vessel with a single hull, contrasted with a catamaran, trimaran etc.

monoïdeism, *n.* fixation of the mind upon one idea, esp. in monomania or hypnotic condition.

monokini, *n.* a one-piece bathing garment for a woman, usu. similar to the bottom half of a bikini. [MON(O)-, bi*kini*]

monolatry, *n.* worship of one god, esp. among many. **monolater, -trist,** *n.* **monolatrous,** *a.*

monolayer, *n.* a single layer of atoms or molecules adsorbed on a surface.

monolingual, *a.* using or expressed in only one language. **monolingualism,** *n.*

monolith, *n.* a monument or other structure formed of a single stone. **monolithic,** *a.* of or like a monolith; consisting of a large and undifferentiated whole, often entailing inflexibility. [F *monolithe* or L *monolithus,* Gr. *monolithos,* made of a single stone]

monologue, *n.* a dramatic scene in which a person speaks by himself; a dramatic piece for one actor; a soliloquy; a long speech in conversation. **monological**, *a.* **monologist, -guist**, *n.* **monologize, -gise** , *v.i.* †**monology**, *n.* [F, one who likes to hear himself talk, Gr. *monologos*]

†**monomachy,** *n.* a single combat, a duel. **monomachist,** *n.* [F *monomachie,* L and Gr. *monomachia,* from *monomachos,* one fighting alone (*machesthai,* to fight)]

monomania, *n.* mental derangement on one subject only. **monomaniac**, *n., a.* **monomaniacal**, *a.*

Monomark®, *n.* one of a system of registered combinations of numbers, serving to identify property or manufactured goods.

monomer, *n.* a chemical compound that can undergo polymerization. **monomerous**, *a.* of flowers, having one member in each whorl; (*Ent.*) of tarsi, single-jointed; having the tarsi single-jointed. [Gr. *monomerēs* (*meros,* part)]

monometallism, *n.* a one-metal standard of value for coinage. **monometallic**, *a.* **monometallist,** *n.*

monometer, *n.* a verse consisting of one foot; metre of this kind. **monometric**, *a.* in this metre; (*Cryst.*) having the axes equal or similar, isometric. [L, from Gr. *monometros*]

monomial, *n.* a mathematical expression consisting of a single term. *a.* consisting of a single term.

monomorphic, -phous, *a.* having the same structure or morphological character, esp. throughout successive stages of development. **monomorphism,** *n.*

monomyary, *a.* belonging to the Monomyaria, a section of bivalves in which there is only one abductor muscle, as in the oyster. *n.* a bivalve of this section. **monomyarian**, *n., a.* [Gr. *mus,* muscle]

mononuclear, *a.* having only one nucleus.

mononym, *n.* a name consisting of a single word. **mononymic**, *a.* **mononymize, -ise**, *v.t.* **mononymization, -isation**, *n.* **mononymy**, *n.* [Gr. *onoma,* Aeolic *onuma,* name]

monoousious, *a.* of God the Father and God the Son, having the same substance. [late Gr. *monoousios* (MON(O)-, *ousia,* essence)]

monopathy, *n.* disease affecting only one organ or function; †solitary suffering or sensibility. **monopathic**, *a.*

monopetalous, *a.* having the petals coherent in a single corolla.

monophagous, *a.* feeding on only one type of food.

monophobia, *n.* morbid dread of being alone.

monophone, *n.* a monophonous sound; a homophone. **monophonic**, *a.* of sound, reproduced through only one electronic channel; homophonic. **monophonous**, *a.* homophonous; (*Mus.*) producing only one tone at a time.

monophthong, *n.* a simple or single vowel sound; two written vowels pronounced as one. **monophthongal**, *a.* [Gr. *monophthongos* (*phthongos,* sound)]

monophyletic, *a.* pertaining to a single family or race or descended from one parental form. [Gr. *phuletikos,* from *phulē,* tribe]

monophyllous, *a.* having or formed of one leaf. [Gr. *phullon,* leaf]

monophyodont, *a.* having only one set of teeth, as the Cetacea. *n.* a monophyodont animal. [Gr. *phuein,* to generate, *odous odontos,* tooth]

Monophysite, *n.* a member of a group of Christian heretics of the 5th–7th cents. who taught that Jesus had one nature, in opposition to the orthodox doctrine laid down at the Council of Chalcedon in 451, that he had two natures, the human and the divine. Monophysitism developed as a reaction to Nestorianism and led to the formal secession of the Coptic and Armenian churches from the rest of the Christian church. Monophysites survive today in Armenia, Syria and Egypt. **monophysitic, -ical**, *a.* **monophysitism,** *n.* [eccles. L *Monophysīta,* eccles. Gr. *Monophysītēs* (*phusis,* nature, from *phuein,* see prec., -ITE)]

monoplane, *n.* an aircraft with one supporting plane.

monoplast, *n.* a structure or organism consisting of a single cell. **monoplastic**, *a.*

monoplegia, *n.* paralysis of a single part or limb. [Gr. *plēgē,* stroke]

monopode, *n.* an animal having one foot; one of a fabulous race of men having one foot with which they shaded themselves against the heat of the sun. **monopodous**, *a.* [Gr. *pous podos,* foot]

monopole, *n.* a radio aerial consisting of one, usu. straight, element.

Monopolies and Mergers Commission, *n.* a British government body re-established in 1973 under the Fair Trading Act and, since 1980, embracing the Competition Act. Its role is to investigate and report when there is a risk of creating a monopoly following a company merger or takeover, or when a newspaper or newspaper assets are transferred. It also investigates companies, nationalized industries or local authorities which are suspected of operating in a non-competitive way. The US equivalent is the Federal Trade Commission.

monopoly, *n.* an exclusive trading right in a certain commodity or class of commerce or business, usu. conferred by government; a company or combination enjoying this; the subject of such a right; exclusive possession, control or enjoyment (of); (**Monopoly®**) a board game for two or more people, who throw dice to move their pieces round a board marked with the names of streets etc., the object being to accumulate capital through buying the property on which the pieces land. **monopolism**, *n.* **monopolist**, *n.* **monopolistic**, *a.* **monopolize, -ise**, *v.t.* to obtain or possess a monopoly of; to engross the whole of (attention, conversation etc.). **monopolization, -isation**, *n.* [late L *monopōlium,* Gr. *monopōlion* (*pōleein,* to sell)]

monopolylogue, *n.* a dramatic entertainment in which one performer takes many parts. **monopolylogist**, *n.*

monopteros, *n.* a circular temple composed of columns supporting a roof. **monopteral**, *n., a.* **monopterous**, *a.* of seeds, one-winged. [late L *monopteros* (Gr. *pteron,* wing)]

monoptote, *n.* a word having a single case-form. **monoptotic**, *a.* [late L *monoptōtus,* Gr. *monoptōtos* (*ptōtos,* falling, rel. to *piptein,* to fall)]

monorail, *n.* a railway with a track consisting of a single rail. *a.* consisting of one rail. **monorailway**, *n.*

monorchid, *n.* a person or animal having only one testicle. **monorchidism, monorchism,** *n.* [Gr. *monorchis* (*orchis,* testicle)]

monorganic, *a.* of a disease, affecting one organ or set of organs.

monorhine, *a.* having a single nasal passage. *n.* one of the Monorhina, a section of monorhine vertebrates comprising the lampreys and hags. [Gr. *rhis rhīnos,* nose]

monorhyme, *n.* a composition in which all the lines end in the same rhyme. *a.* having but one rhyme. [F *monorime*]

monosaccharide, *n.* a sugar that cannot be hydrolysed to form simpler sugars.

monosepalous, *a.* having one sepal.

monoski, *n.* a single ski on which both the skier's feet are placed. *v.i.* to use a monoski. **monoskier,** *n.*

monosodium glutamate, *n.* a salt of glutamic acid used as a flavour-enhancing food additive.

monospermous, *a.* having but one seed. **monospermal, -matous, -mic,** *a.* [Gr. *sperma,* seed]

monospherical, *a.* consisting of a single sphere.

monosporous, *a.* having only one spore.

monostich, *n.* a single metrical line forming a complete composition, as an epigram. *a.* consisting of a single metrical line. **monostichous**, *a.* (*Bot., Zool. etc.*) having, arranged in or consisting of a single row or layer. [late L *monostichum,* Gr. *monostichon* (*stichos,* row)]

monostrophic, *a.* having only one form of strophe. [Gr. *monostrophikos*]

monostyle¹, *a.* (*Arch.*) of a single shaft. [Gr. *stulos,* pillar]

monostyle², *a.* built in the same style throughout. **monostylar,** *a.* [STYLE¹]

monosyllable, *n.* a word of one syllable. **monosyllabic,** *a.* of one syllable; speaking in words of a single syllable. **monosyllabically,** *adv.* **monosyllabism,** *n.* **monosyllabize, -ise,** *v.t.*

monosymmetric, *a.* (*Cryst.*) monoclinic. **monosymmetrical,** *a.* (*Bot.*) divisible into symmetrical halves in only one plane. **monosymmetry,** *n.*

monotelephone, *n.* a telephone which carries sounds of one pitch only.

monotessaron, *a.* a continuous narrative embodying the stories in the four Gospels. [med. L, Gr. *tessares,* four, after DIATESSARON]

monothalamous, *a.* possessing a single chamber, as some shells. **monothalamic,** *a.* monothalamous; of certain fruits, developed from a single pistil.

monotheism, *n.* the doctrine that there is only one God. **monotheist,** *n.* **monotheistic,** *a.* **monotheistically,** *adv.*

monothelete, -lite, *n.* one of a sect arising in the 7th cent. who maintained that Christ has but one will, as distinct from *dyothelete*. **monotheletic, -litic,** *a.* **monothelism, -theletism,** *n.* [med. L *monothelīta,* late Gr. *monothelētēs* (*thelein,* to will)]

monotint, *n.* a picture or other representation in one colour.

monotone, *n.* continuance of or repetition in the same tone; a succession of sounds of the same pitch; intoning of words on a single note; monotony; monotint. *a.* monotonous. *v.t., v.i.* to chant, recite or speak in the same tone or note. **monotonic,** *a.* **monotonize, -ise,** *v.t.* **monotonous,** *a.* wearisome through sameness, tedious; unvarying in pitch. **monotonously,** *adv.* **monotonousness, monotony,** *n.* [late Gr. *monotonos,* monotonous]

Monotremata, *n.pl.* a sub-class of mammals having only one aperture or vent for the genital organs and the excretions. **monotrematous,** *a.* **monotreme,** *n., a.* [Gr. *trēma -atos,* perforation, hole]

Monotype®, *n.* a type-setting machine that casts and sets single printing-types.

monovalent UNIVALENT.

monoxide, *n.* an oxide containing one atom of oxygen in combination with a radical. **monox(y)-,** *comb. form.*

monozygotic, *a.* from a single zygote.

Monroe¹, *n.* **James** (1758–1831), 5th president of the US (1817–25), born in Virginia. He served in the War of Independence, was minister to France (1794–96), and in 1803 negotiated the Louisiana Purchase. He was secretary of state (1811–17). His name is associated with the Monroe Doctrine.

Monroe², *n.* **Marilyn** (stage name of Norma Jean Mortenson or Baker) (1926–62), US film actress, who made comedies such as *The Seven Year Itch* (1955), *Bus Stop* (1956), and *Some Like It Hot* (1959). Her second husband was baseball star Joe di Maggio, and her third Arthur Miller.

Monroe Doctrine, *n.* the principle that non-American powers should not intervene in affairs in either of the American continents, formulated by Monroe in 1823. [James *Monroe*, see above]

Monrovia, *n.* capital and port of Liberia; population (1985) 500,000. Industries include rubber, cement and petrol processing.

Monseigneur, *n.* (*pl.* **Messeigneurs**) a French title of honour given to high dignitaries, esp. in the Church. [F *mon,* my, SEIGNEUR]

Monsieur, *n.* (*pl.* **Messieurs**) the French title of address, Mr or Sir; a Frenchman; †the title of a French king's second son or next younger brother. [F *mon,* my, *sieur,* as prec.]

Monsignor, *n.* (*pl.* **Monsignori**) a title given to Roman Catholic prelates, officers of the Pope's court and others. [It.]

monsoon, *n.* a wind in SW Asia and the Indian Ocean, blowing from the south-west from April to October accompanied by heavy rainfall, and from the north-east the rest of the year; applied to other periodical winds. [MDut. *monssoen,* Port. *monção,* Arab. *mausim,* time, season]

monster, *n.* something misshapen, abnormal, out of the ordinary course of nature; an abortion, a deformed creature; an imaginary animal, usually compounded of incongruous parts, such as a centaur, griffin, mermaid, gorgon etc.; an abominably cruel or depraved person; a person, animal or thing of extraordinary size; †a prodigy, a marvel, a portent. *a.* of extraordinary size, huge. †*v.t.* to make monstrous. †**monsterful,** *a.* [OF *monstre,* L *monstrum,* a portent or omen, from *monēre,* to warn]

monstrance, *n.* an open or transparent vessel in which the Host is carried in procession or exposed for adoration, esp. in a Roman Catholic church. [OF, from med. L *monstrantia,* from *monstrāre,* to show]

monstrous, *a.* unnatural in form; out of the ordinary course of nature; enormous, huge; shocking, atrocious, outrageous; absurd, incredible; †full of monsters. †*adv.* extraordinarily, very, exceedingly. †**monstriferous,** *a.* **monstrosity,** *n.* the quality of being monstrous; a monster, an abortion; a deformity, a distortion. **monstrously,** *adv.* **monstrousness,** *n.* [OF *monstreux,* late L *monstrōsus,* from *monstrum,* MONSTER]

mons veneris, *n.* (*pl.* **montes veneris**) the pad of fatty tissue over the pubic bone of the human female. [L, mount of Venus]

Mont., (*abbr.*) Montana (US).

montage, *n.* cutting and assembling of shots taken when making a cinema picture; an artistic, literary or musical work consisting of heterogeneous elements in juxtaposition.

montagnard, *n.* a mountaineer, an inhabitant of mountain country; (*F. Hist.*) a member of the 'Mountain' or extreme democratic wing in the Revolutionary Legislative Assembly (1791–2). [F, from *montagne,* MOUNTAIN]

Montaigne, *n.* **Michel Eyquem de** (1533–92), French writer, regarded as the creator of the essay form. In 1580 he published the first two volumes of his *Essais*, the third volume appeared in 1588. Montaigne deals with all aspects of life from an urbanely sceptical viewpoint. Through the translation by John Florio in 1603, he influenced Shakespeare and other English writers.

Montana¹, *n.* a state of the western US on the Canadian border; nickname Treasure State. **area** 381,200 sq km/147,143 sq miles. **capital** Helena. **towns** Billings, Great Falls, Butte. **physical** mountainous forests in the west, rolling grasslands in the east. **products** wheat under irrigation, cattle, wool, copper, oil, natural gas. **population** (1986) 819,000.

Montana², *n.* **Joe** (1956–), US American footballer. He appeared in three winning Super Bowls with the San Francisco 49ers (1982, 1985 and 1989), winning the Most Valuable Player award in the first two, and setting a record for passing yardage in 1989.

Montand, *n.* **Yves** (1921–), French actor and singer who achieved fame in the thriller *La Salaire de la Peur/The Wages of Fear* (1953) and continued to be popular in French and American films, including *Let's Make Love* (1960) (with Marilyn Monroe), *Grand Prix* (1966), *Le Sauvage/The Savage* (1976), *Jean de Florette* (1986), *Manon des Sources* (1986).

montane, *a.* of or pertaining to mountainous regions. [L *montānus,* from *mons montis,* MOUNT]

Montanism, *n.* the doctrine of a religious sect founded in the 2nd cent. by *Montanus* of Phrygia, who claimed the gift of prophecy and taught asceticism. **Montanist,** *n.*

†**montant,** *n.* an upright cut or thrust in fencing; (*Carp.*) an upright part in framing. *a.* rising; (*Her.*) ascending. [F, pres.p. of *monter,* to MOUNT]

Mont Blanc, *n.* (Italian **Monte Bianco**) the highest

mountain in the Alps, between France and Italy; height 4807 m/15,772 ft.

montbretia, *n.* a bulbous-rooted plant with orange flowers of the genus *Montbretia*; a similar plant of the genus *Crocosmia*. [A.F.E. Coquebert de *Montbret*, 1780–1801, French botanist]

Montcalm, *n.* **Louis-Joseph de Montcalm-Gozon, Marquis de** (1712–59), French general, appointed military commander in Canada 1756. He won a succession of victories over the British during the French and Indian War, but was defeated in 1759 by Wolfe at Québec, where both he and Wolfe were killed; this battle marked the end of French rule in Canada.

monte, *n.* a Spanish game of chance with 45 cards, resembling faro; in Latin America, a tract of wooded country. **three-card monte,** a Mexican game of sleight-of-hand with three cards. [Sp., mountain, as MOUNT]

Monte Carlo, *n.* a town and resort in Monaco, known for its gambling; population (1982) 12,000.

montem, *n.* a custom formerly observed at Eton College of collecting money, called 'salt money', at a mound called Salt Hill, to defray the expenses of the senior scholar at King's College, Cambridge. [L *ad montem*, to the hill]

Montenegro, *n.* (Serbo-Croat **Crna Gora**) a constituent republic of Yugoslavia. **area** 13,800 sq km/5,327 sq miles. **capital** Titograd. **town** Cetinje. **physical** mountainous. **population** (1986) 620,000, including 400,000 Montenegrins, 80,000 Muslims, and 40,000 Albanians. **language** Serbian variant of Serbo-Croat. **religion** Serbian Orthodox.

montero, *n.* a Spanish huntsman's cap with flaps and a round crown. [Sp., a huntsman, a mountaineer, from *monte*, MOUNT]

Monterrey, *n.* industrial city (iron, steel, textiles, chemicals, food processing) in NE Mexico; population (1986) 2,335,000.

Montessori, *n.* **Maria** (1870–1952), Italian educationalist. From her experience with mentally handicapped children, she developed the *Montessori method*, an educational system for all children based on a more informal approach, incorporating instructive play and allowing children to develop at their own pace.

Monteverdi, *n.* **Claudio (Giovanni Antonio)** (1567–1643), Italian composer. He contributed to the development of the opera with *Orfeo* (1607) and *The Coronation of Poppea* (1642). He also wrote madrigals, motets and sacred music, notably the *Vespers* (1610).

Montevideo, *n.* capital and chief port (grain, meat products, hides) of Uruguay, on Río de la Plata; population (1985) 1,250,000. It was founded in 1726.

Montezuma II, *n.* (1466–1520), Aztec emperor (1502–20). When the Spanish conquistador Cortés invaded Mexico, Montezuma was imprisoned and killed during the Aztec attack on Cortés' force as it tried to leave Tenochtitlán, the Aztec capital city.

Montfort, *n.* **Simon de Montfort, Earl of Leicester** (*c.* 1208–65), English politician and soldier. From 1258 he led the baronial opposition to Henry III's misrule during the second Barons' War and in 1264 defeated and captured the king at Lewes, Sussex. In 1265, as head of government, he summoned the first parliament in which the towns were represented; he was killed at the Battle of Evesham during the last of the Barons' Wars.

Montgolfier[1], *n.* a balloon inflated and raised by heated air, called fully **Montgolfier balloon**. [J.M. and J.E. *Montgolfier*, see foll.]

Montgolfier[2], *n.* **Joseph Michel** (1740–1810) and **Étienne Jacques** (1745–99), French brothers whose hot-air balloon was used for the first successful human flight 21 Nov. 1783.

Montgomery[1], *n.* **Bernard Law, 1st Viscount Montgomery of Alamein** (1887–1976), British field marshal. In World War II he commanded the 8th Army in N Africa in the Second Battle of El Alamein (1942). As commander of British troops in N Europe from 1944, he received the German surrender on 1945.

Montgomery[2], *n.* **Henry ('Robert')** (1904–81), US film actor of the 1930s and 1940s. He directed some of his later films, such as *Lady in the Lake* (1947), before leaving the cinema for television and politics. His other films include *Night Must Fall* (1937) and *Mr and Mrs Smith* (1941).

Montgomeryshire, *n.* a former county of N Wales, included in Powys in 1974.

month, *n.* one of the twelve parts into which the year is divided, orig. the period of one revolution of the moon round the earth; four weeks. **month of Sundays,** an indefinitely long period. †**month's mind,** *n.* mass said for a deceased person a month after death; a desire, a liking, an inclination. †**monthling,** *n.* that which lasts for a month, esp. a child a month old. **monthly,** *a.* done in or continuing for a month; happening or payable once a month. *adv.* once a month. *n.* a periodical published every month; (*pl.*) the menses. **monthly nurse,** *n.* a nurse attending women during the month after confinement. **monthly rose,** *n.* the Indian or China rose, erroneously supposed to flower monthly. [OE *mōnath* (cp. Dut. *maand*, G *Monat*, Icel. *mānuthr*, also L *mensis*), cogn. with MOON]

monticle, -cule, *n.* a little hill, a mound, a hillock, esp. a small volcanic cone. †**monticulate,** †**-lous,** *a.* having little knobs or projections. [F *monticule*, late L *monticulus*, dim. of *mons -tem*, MOUNT]

montmorillonite, *n.* a soft clayey mineral, a hydrated silicate of aluminium, the chief constituent of bentonite and fuller's earth. [*Montmorillon* in France]

†**montoir,** *n.* a horse-block; a stone or step used in mounting a horse. [F, from *monter*, to MOUNT]

monton, *n.* a heap of ore, a batch under process of amalgamation. [Sp., from *monte*, MOUNT]

montre, *n.* in an organ, a flue-stop the pipes of which are visible in the external case. [F, from *montrer*, L *monstrāre*, to show]

Montreal, *n.* an inland port, industrial city (aircraft, chemicals, oil and petrochemicals, flour, sugar, brewing, meat packing) of Québec, Canada, on Montreal Island at the junction of the Ottawa and St Lawrence rivers; population (1986) 2,921,000.

Montrose, *n.* **James Graham, 1st Marquess of Montrose** (1612–50), Scottish soldier. Son of the 4th earl of Montrose. He supported the Covenanters against Charles I, but after 1640 changed sides. Defeated in 1645 at Philiphaugh, he escaped to Norway. Returning in 1650 to raise a revolt, he survived shipwreck only to have his weakened forces defeated, and (having been betrayed to the Covenanters) was hanged in Edinburgh.

Montserrat, *n.* a volcanic island in the West Indies, one of the Leeward group, a British crown colony; capital Plymouth; area 110 sq km/42 sq miles; population (1985) 12,000. Practically all buildings were destroyed by Hurricane Hugo, Sept. 1989.

monture, *n.* a setting or frame; the way (a gem etc.) is set. [F, from *monter*, to MOUNT]

monument, *n.* anything by which the memory of persons or things is preserved, esp. a building or permanent structure; anything that serves as a memorial of a person, event or of past times; a document, a record; a distinctive mark; (*N Am.*) a natural or artificial landmark; †a tomb; †a statue, an effigy; †a portent. **the Monument,** a column in London commemorating the Great Fire of 1666. **monumental,** *a.* serving as a monument; stupendous (as of ignorance). **monumental mason,** *n.* a stone-mason who engraves and erects tombstones etc. **monumentalize, -ise,** *v.t.* to commemorate with a monument. **monumentally,** *adv.* [L *monumentum*, from *monēre*, to remind]

-mony, *suf.* forming nouns, as *ceremony*, *matrimony*, *parsimony*. [L *-monium*, *-monia*]

monyplies MANYPLIES.

moo, *v.i.* to make a noise like a cow. *n.* the sound 'moo'. [imit.]

mooch, *v.i.* (*coll.*) to wander aimlessly, amble; to cadge. *v.t.* (*coll.*) to cadge; to steal. **moocher,** *n.* [prob. from F *muchier*, to lurk, hide]

mood¹, *n.* a verb-form expressing the manner in which the act, event or fact is conceived, whether as actual, contingent, possible, desirable etc.; the nature of the connection between antecedent and consequent in a proposition, modality; the form of a syllogism with regard to the quantity and quality of the propositions; (*Mus.*) mode. [var. of MODE, assim. to foll.]

mood², *n.* temper of mind, disposition, humour; a morbid state of mind; a favourable state of mind; the expression of mood in art, literature etc. *a.* expressing a mood. **in the mood,** inclined (to or for). **moody,** *a.* indulging in moods or humours; peevish, sullen, out of temper. †**moody-mad,** *a.* mad with passion. **moodily,** *adv.* **moodiness,** *n.* [OE *mōd* (cp. Dut. *moed*, Icel. *mōthr*, Dan. and Swed. *mod*, G *Mut*)]

Moog®, *n.* a type of music synthesizer. [Robert *Moog*, born 1934, US engineer]

mool, Sc. var. of MOULD¹.

moolah, *n.* (*sl.*) money. [etym. unknown]

moon¹, *n.* the earth's satellite (see separate article, below); the satellite of any planet; a lunar month; anything shaped like a moon or crescent. *v.i.* to wander (about) or stare in a listless manner; (*sl.*) to expose one's buttocks to others. *v.t.* to pass (time) in this way. **blue moon** BLUE. **cycle of the moon** CYCLE. **full moon,** the moon with its face fully illuminated. **new moon,** the moon at the beginning of its course with its face invisible or partially illuminated. **over the moon,** (*coll.*) very pleased or happy. **moonbeam,** *n.* **moon-blind,** *a.* suffering from moon-eye; blind from sleeping under the moon's rays. **moon-blindness,** *a.* **moon-calf,** *n.* a blockhead; a born fool; †a creature deformed in the womb; a monstrosity; a false conception. **moon-daisy, -flower,** *n.* the ox-eye daisy. **moon-eye,** *n.* an affection of the eyes in horses; an eye affected with this; applied to two N American freshwater fish. **moon-eyed,** *a.* purblind, dim-eyed; round-eyed. **moon-fish,** *n.* any fish that is silvery and disk-shaped, e.g. the opah or the platy. **moon-glade,** *n.* the track of moonlight on water. **moonlight,** *n., a.* **moonlight flit,** *n.* a removal of household furniture after dark to escape paying rent. *v.t.* see below. **moonlighter,** *n.* a member of gangs of ruffians who committed violent nocturnal outrages on tenants in Ireland who had transgressed the mandates of the Land League; a person in full-time work who has a second, part-time job (in the evening). **moonlighting,** *n.* **moonlight,** *v.i.* **moonlit,** *a.* **moonraker,** *n.* a foolish person (from the Wiltshire legend that some stupid rustics mistook the reflection of the moon in the water for a cheese). **moonrise,** *n.* the rising of the moon; the time of this. **moonseed,** *n.* a plant of the genus *Menispermum.* **moonshine,** *n.* moonlight; unreality, visionary ideas, nonsense; smuggled or illicitly-distilled spirits; †a month. **moonshiner,** *n.* an illicit distiller; a smuggler, esp. of spirits. **moonshiny,** *a.* **moonshot,** *n.* the launching of a space-craft to the moon. **moonstone,** *n.* a variety of feldspar with whitish or opalescent reflections. **moonstruck, -stricken,** *a.* affected by the moon; deranged, lunatic; fanciful, sentimental. **moon-trefoil,** *n.* medick, *Medicago arborea.* **moonwort,** *n.* a fern, *Botrychium lunaria*; honesty, *Lunaria biennis;* applied to other plants. **mooned,** *a.* shaped like the moon, crescent-shaped; moonlit. †**moonish,** *a.* fickle, changeable, capricious. **moonless,** *a.* **moony,** *a.* like the moon; crescent-shaped; like moonlight; moonstruck, listless, dreamy, silly; (*sl.*) tipsy. **moonily,** *adv.* **mooniness,** *n.* [OE *mōna* (cp. Dut. *maan*, Icel. *māni*, Goth. *mēna*, G *Mond*), cogn. with Gr. *mēnē*, L *mensis*, MONTH]

moon², *n.* the natural satellite of Earth, 3476 km/2160 miles in diameter, with a mass an eighth that of Earth. Its average distance from Earth is 384,400 km/238,900 miles, and it orbits every 27.32 days (the **sidereal month**). It spins on its axis so that it keeps one side permanently turned towards Earth. The Moon is thought to have no air or water.

Moon¹, *n.* **Sun Myung** (1920–), Korean industrialist and founder of the Unification Church (**Moonies**) 1954. From 1973 he launched a major mission in the US and elsewhere. The church has been criticized for its manipulative methods of recruiting and keeping members. He was convicted of tax fraud in the US 1982.

Moon², *n.* **William** (1818–94), English inventor of the Moon alphabet for the blind. Devised in 1847, it uses only nine symbols in different orientations. From 1983 it has been possible to write it with a miniature typewriter.

Moonie, *n.* (*coll.*) a member of the Unification Church, whose followers give all their possessions to it and live in communes. [Sun Myung *Moon*, see above]

Moon probe, *n.* a spacecraft used to investigate the Moon. Early probes flew past the Moon or crash-landed on it, but later ones achieved soft landings or went into orbit. Soviet probes included the long Lunik/Luna series. US probes (Ranger, Surveyor, Lunar Orbiter) prepared the way for the Apollo crewed flights.

moonshee MUNSHI.

moor¹, *v.t.* to secure (a ship, boat etc.) with chains, ropes or cable and anchor. *v.i.* to secure a ship in this way, to anchor; to lie at anchor or secured by cables etc. **moorage,** *n.* **mooring,** *n.* (*usu. pl.*) the place where a ship is moored; anchors, chains etc. by which a ship is moored. [prob. from a non-extant OE *mārian* (cp. *mǣrels*, mooring-rope, and MDut. *maren*, to tie)]

moor², *n.* a tract of wild open land, esp. if overgrown with heather. **moor-cock, -fowl,** *n.* the male of the red grouse, *Lagopus scoticus.* **moor game,** *n.* red grouse. **moor-hen,** *n.* the red female of this; the water-hen. **moorland,** *n., a.* **moorman, moorsman,** *n.* **moorswoman,** *n. fem.* [OE *mōr* (cp. Dut. *moer*, G *Moor*)]

Moor, *n.* any of the Muslims who conquered Spain and occupied its southern part from 711 to 1492. They were of mixed Arab and Berber origin. The name was originally applied to an inhabitant of the Roman province of Mauritania, in NW Africa. **Moorish,** *a.* [L *Maurus*]

Moorcock, *n.* **Michael** (1939–), English writer, associated with the 1960s new wave in science fiction, editor of the magazine *New Worlds* (1964–69). He wrote the Jerry Cornelius novels, collected as *The Cornelius Chronicles* (1977), and *Gloriana* (1978).

Moore¹, *n.* **Dudley** (1935–), British actor and comedian, formerly teamed with comedian Peter Cook, who became a Hollywood star after appearing in *10* (1979). His subsequent films, mostly comedies, include *Bedazzled* (1968), *Arthur* (1981), and *Santa Claus* (1985).

Moore², *n.* **Henry** (1898–1986), British sculptor. His subjects include the reclining nude, mother and child groups, the warrior, and intelocking abstract forms. As an official war artist during World War II, he did a series of drawings of London's air-raid shelters. Many of his postwar works are in bronze or marble, including monumental semi-abstracts such as *Reclining Figure* (1957–58) (outside UNESCO, Paris), and often designed to be placed in landscape settings.

Moore³, *n.* **John** (1761–1809), British general, born in Glasgow. In 1808 he commanded the British army sent to Portugal in the Peninsular War. After advancing into Spain he had to retreat to Corunna in the NW, and was killed in the battle fought to cover the embarkation.

Moore⁴, *n.* **(John) Jeremy** (1928–), British major general of the Commando Forces, Royal Marines, 1979–82. He commanded the land forces in the UK's conflict with Argentina over the Falklands 1982.

Moore⁵, *n.* **Marianne** (1887–1972), US poet. She edited the literary magazine *Dial* (1925–29), and published volumes of witty and intellectual verse including *Observations* (1924), *What are Years* (1941), and *A Marianne Moore Reader* (1961).

Moore⁶, *n.* **Roger** (1928–), British actor who starred in the television series *The Saint* (1962–70), and assumed the film role of James Bond in 1973 in *Live and Let Die*. His films include *Diane* (1955), *Gold* (1974), *The Wild Geese* (1978) and *Octopussy* (1983).

Moorhouse, *n.* **Adrian** (1964–), English swimmer

who won the 100 metres breaststroke at the 1988 Seoul Olympics.

moorstone, *n.* a kind of granite, chiefly from Cornwall.

moose, *n.* (*pl.* **moose**) a large animal, *Alces americana*, allied to the elk, inhabiting the colder parts of N America. [Algonkin *musu*]

moot, *v.t.* to raise for discussion; to suggest; †to debate. *v.i.* to argue or plead on a supposed case. *n.* formerly, an assembly of freemen in a township, tithing etc.; a law students' debate on a supposed case. *a.* open to discussion or argument. **moot case, point,** *n.* a debatable case or point; an open question. **moot court,** *n.* a meeting in an inn of court for discussing points of law. †**moot hall,** *n.* a hall of meeting; a town-hall; a judgment-hall. †**mootable,** *a.* **mooter,** *n.* [OE *mōtian*, rel. to *gemōt*, an assembly (cp. Dut. *gemoet*)]

mop¹, *n.* a bundle of rags, coarse yarn etc. fastened to a long handle, and used for cleaning floors etc.; applied to various similar implements; a thick mass, as of hair; a mop-fair. *v.t.* (*past, p.p.* **mopped**) to wipe, clean or dry with or as with a mop. **to mop up,** to wipe up with or as with a mop; to clear (a place) of enemy troops etc.; (*sl.*) to seize, to appropriate, to get hold of; to worst, to dispatch. **mop-board,** *n.* (*N Am.*) a narrow skirting round a room. **mop-fair,** *n.* an annual fair at which servants are hired. **mop-head,** *n.* a thick head of hair; a person with such a head. **mopstick,** *n.* the handle of a mop; in a pianoforte, a rod working the damper in an old-fashioned movement. [15th cent. *mappe*, L *mappa*, see NAPKIN]

†**mop²,** *v.i.* to make wry faces or grimaces. *n.* a grimace, a wry face. **mops and mows,** grimaces. [prob. imit. of pouting]

mope, *v.i.* to be dull or dispirited. *v.t.* to make dull or dispirited (*usu. refl., p.p.*). *n.* one who mopes; (*pl.*) ennui, the blues. **mope-eyed,** *a.* purblind, short-sighted. **moper,** *n.* **mopish,** *a.* **mopishly,** *adv.* **mopishness,** *n.* [etym. doubtful]

moped, *n.* a motorized pedal cycle, less than 50cc.

mopoke, morepork, *n.* (*Austral.*) a night-jar, *Podargus cuvieri*; applied to other birds; (*New Zealand*) a small owl. [imit. of cry]

moppet, *n.* a pet, a darling (applied to children, young girls etc.); a variety of lap-dog; †a rag doll; †an effeminate man. **mops,** *n.* a pug-dog. **mopsy,** *n.* a pet, a dear; a slatternly woman. [perh. dim. of MOP²]

mopus, *n.* (*pl.* **-uses**) (*sl.*) a small coin; (*pl.*) money. [etym. doubtful]

moquette, *n.* a woven fabric of wool and hemp or linen with a velvety pile, used for carpets. [F, etym. doubtful]

MOR, (*abbr.*) middle-of-the-road (music), used esp. in broadcasting parlance.

mora¹, *n.* (*Sc. Law*) delay, esp. if due to negligence; (*Pros., pl.* **morae**) a unit of time equal to a short syllable. [L]

mora², *n.* an Italian game in which one has to guess the number of fingers held up by another player, popular also in China and other countries. [It.]

mora³, *n.* a tall S American tree, *Mora excelsa*, the timber of which is used for shipbuilding. [Tupí-Guaraní *moiratinga*, white-tree]

moraine, *n.* the debris of rocks brought down by glaciers. **morainal, morainic,** *a.* [F]

moral, *a.* pertaining to character and conduct as regards the distinction between right and wrong; conforming to or regulated by right, good, virtuous, esp. in sexual relations; subject to the rules of morality, distinguishing between right and wrong; based on morality; concerned with or treating of conduct or morality; conveying a moral; probable, virtual; (esp. of support) psychological rather than practical; †moralizing. *n.* the moral lesson taught by a story, incident etc.; (*pl.*) moral habits, conduct, behaviour, esp. in sexual relations; (*pl.*) ethics, moral science; (*sl.*) counterpart, likeness, double (prob. corr. of MODEL). †*v.i.* to moralize. **moral certainty,** *n.* probability that leaves little doubt. **moral courage,** *n.* fortitude in matters of life and conduct, esp. in resisting unjust or iniquitous opposition, odium and abuse, as opp. to physical courage. **moral defeat** MORAL VICTORY. **moral faculty,** *n.* the capacity to distinguish between right and wrong. **moral judgment,** *n.* judgment as to the rightness or wrongness of an act. **moral majority,** *n.* (*esp. N Am.*) the majority of the country's population, regarded as acting on and favouring adherence to strict moral principles. **moral philosophy, science,** *n.* ethics. **Moral Rearmament** BUCHMANISM. **moral victory,** *n.* an indecisive result or a partial success the moral effects of which are equivalent to victory. **moralism,** *n.* morality distinguished from religion or divested of religious teaching; †a moral maxim. **moralist,** *n.* a person who teaches morality or behaves in accordance with moral rules. **moralistic,** *a.* **moralistically,** *adv.* **morality,** *n.* the doctrine, principles or practice of moral duties; moral science, ethics; morals, moral conduct, esp. in sexual relations; moralizing; a kind of drama (popular in the 16th cent.) in which the characters represent virtues, vices etc. **moralize, -ise,** *v.t.* to interpret or apply in a moral sense; to provide with moral lessons; to render moral. *v.i.* to make moral reflections (on). **moralization, -isation,** *n.* **moralizer, -iser,** *n.* **morally,** *adv.* according to morality; practically, virtually. [F, from L *mōrālis*, from *mōs mōris*, custom]

morale, *n.* mental or moral condition; courage and endurance in supporting fatigue and danger, esp. of troops in war.

morality, moralize MORAL.

Moral ReArmament, *n.* international anticommunist movement calling for 'moral and spiritual renewal'. It was founded by the Christian evangelist F. N. D. Buchman in 1938.

Morandi, *n.* **Giorgio** (1890–1964), Italian still-life painter and etcher, whose subtle studies of bottles and jars convey a sense of calm and repose.

morass, *n.* a swamp, a bog; anything that is confused or complicated, esp. when it impedes progress. **morass ore,** *n.* bog iron-ore. †**morassy,** *a.* [Dut. *moeras*, earlier *moerasch*, OF *maresche*, MARISH]

†**morat,** *n.* a kind of mead flavoured with mulberries. [med. L *mōrātum*, from *mōrus*, mulberry]

moratorium, *n.* a legal act authorizing a debtor or bank to defer or suspend paymentfor a time; any deferment, delay or temporary suspension. [L, from *morārī*, to delay, from MORA¹]

Moravia¹, *n.* (Czech **Morava**) district of central Europe, from 1960 two regions of Czechoslovakia: **South Moravia** (Czech **Jihomoravský**) **area** 15,030 sq km/5802 sq miles. **capital** Brno. **population** (1986) 2,075,000. **North Moravia** (Czech **Severomoravský**) **area** 11,070 sq km/4273 sq miles. **capital** Ostrava. **population** (1986) 1,957,000. **products** maize, grapes, wine in the south; wheat, barley, rye, flax, sugarbeet in the north; coal and iron.

Moravia², *n.* **Alberto** (pen name of Alberto Pincherle) (1907–), Italian novelist. His first successful novel was *Gli indifferenti/The Time of Indifference* (1929). However, its criticism of Mussolini's regime led to the government censoring his work until after World War II. Later books include *La romana/Woman of Rome* (1947), *La ciociara/Two Women* (1957), and *La noia/The Empty Canvas* (1961), a study of an artist's obsession with his model.

Moravian, *a.* pertaining to Moravia, the Moravians or their dialect of Czech. *n.* a native of Moravia; (*pl.*) a Protestant sect founded in Saxony in the 18th cent. by emigrants from Moravia adhering to the doctrines taught by John Hus (1369–1415). [*Moravia*, in modern Czechoslovakia]

moray, *n.* a brightly-patterned coastal eel of the family Muraenidae. [Port. *moreia*, L *mūraena*, Gr. *muraina*]

Moray, *n.* **Earl of Moray** another spelling of MURRAY, regent of Scotland (1567–70).

Morazán, *n.* **Francisco** (1792–1842), Central American politician, born in Honduras. He was elected president of the United Provinces of Central America in 1830. In the face of secessions he attempted to hold the union together by force but was driven out by the Guatemalan dictator Carrera. Morazán was eventually captured and executed in 1842.

morbid, *a.* sickly, unhealthy, diseased; pathological; unhealthily preoccupied with unpleasant matters, esp. with death. **morbidity,** *n.* unhealthiness, prevalence of morbid conditions; morbidness. **morbidly,** *adv.* **morbidness,** *n.* **morbiferal, -ferous,** *a.* causing disease. **morbific,** *a.* producing disease. **morbilliform, morbillous,** *a.* like morbilli or measles. **morbose,** *a.* **morbosity,** *n.* [L *morbidus*, from *morbus*, disease]

morbidezza, *n.* the delicate quality in the rendering of flesh-tints in painting that gives the effect of life. [It.]

morceau, *n.* (*pl.* **-eaux**) a small piece, a short literary or musical composition. [F]

morcellement, *n.* division of property, esp. land, into small portions. [F]

mordant, *a.* biting, caustic, pungent; causing pain or smarting; serving to fix colours etc. *n.* a substance for fixing colouring-matter in dyeing; an adhesive substance used in applying gold-leaf; acid or other corrosive used by etchers. **mordacious,** *a.* biting, acrid; sarcastic. **mordaciously,** *adv.* **mordacity, mordancy,** *n.* **mordantly,** *adv.* †**mordicant,** *a.* biting, sharp, acrid. *n.* a mordant. †**mordicancy,** *n.* †**mordication,** *n.* [F, pres.p. of *mordre*, L *mordēre*, to bite]

mordent, *n.* (*Mus.*) a rapid alternation of a note with the one immediately below it, a kind of trill the character indicating this. [G, from It. *mordente*, as prec.]

more[1], *a.* (*superl.* **most**) greater in quantity, extent degree, number, importance etc.; additional, extra. *adv.* in or to a greater degree, extent, or quantity (used to form compar. of most adjectives and adverbs of more than one syllable); further, besides, again. *n.* a greater quantity, amount, number or degree; an additional quantity. **more and more,** with continual increase. **more by token,** as further proof. **more or less,** to a greater or less extent; about; thereabouts. **more's the pity** PITY. **more than,** very. **no more,** nothing in addition; no longer existing, dead. **mor(e)ish,** *a.* (*coll.*) of food, causing one to want more; delicious. [OE *māra* (cp. MDut. *mêre,* Icel. *meire,* Goth. *maiza*), from an adverbial form *maiz,* whence MO[2]]

†**more**[2], *n.* a root, a tree-stock; a plant. [OE *more, moru* (cp. G *Möhre,* carrot)]

More[1], *n.* **Kenneth** (1914–82), British actor, a film star of the 1950s, cast as leading man in adventure films and light comedies such as *Genevieve* (1953), *Doctor in the House* (1954), and *Northwest Frontier*. His film career declined in the 1960s, although he played occasional character parts.

More[2], *n.* **(St) Thomas** (1478–1535), English politician and author. From 1509 he was favoured by Henry VIII and employed on foreign embassies. He was a member of the privy council from 1518 and Lord Chancellor from 1529 but resigned over Henry's break with the pope. For refusing to accept the king as head of the church, he was executed. The title of his political book *Utopia* (1516) has come to mean any supposedly perfect society.

Moreau[1], *n.* **Gustave** (1826–98), French Symbolist painter. His works are biblical, mythological and literary scenes, richly coloured and detailed, and atmospheric.

Moreau[2], *n.* **Jeanne** (1928–), French actress who has appeared in international films, often in passionate roles. Her work includes *Les Amants/The Lovers* (1958), *Jules et Jim/Jules and Jim* (1961), *Chimes at Midnight* (1966), and *Querelle* (1982).

moreen, *n.* a stout woollen or wool and cotton stuff for hangings etc. [etym. doubtful]

morel[1], *n.* an edible fungus, *Morchella esculenta,* and other species of *Morchella*. [F *morille,* prob. from Teut., cogn. with MORE[2]]

morel[2], *n.* the black nightshade, *Solanum nigrum,* and other species of nightshade. [OF *morele,* It. *morello,* perh. from L *mōrum,* mulberry]

morello, *n.* a bitter dark-red cherry. [prob. from It. *amarella,* dim. of L *amarus,* bitter, and It. *morello,* blackish]

moreover, *adv.* besides, in addition, further.

morepork MOPOKE.

mores, *n.pl.* the customs and conduct which embody the fundamental values of a social group. [L, pl. of *mōs,* custom]

moresque, *a.* Moorish in style and decoration. *n.* Moorish decoration, as the profusely ornamented work in the Alhambra. [F, from It. *Moresco*]

Morgagni, *n.* **Giovanni Battista** (1682–1771), Italian anatomist. As professor of anatomy at Padua, Morgagni carried out large numbers of autopsies, and developed the view that disease was not an imbalance of the body's humours but a result of alterations in the organs. His work formed the basis of morbid anatomy and pathology.

Morgan[1], *n.* **Henry** (*c.* 1635–88), Welsh buccaneer in the Caribbean. He made war against Spain, capturing and sacking Panama (1671). In 1674 he was knighted and appointed lieutenant-governor of Jamaica.

Morgan[2], *n.* **John Pierpont** (1837–1913), US financier and investment banker whose company (sometimes criticized as 'the money trust') wielded great influence over US corporate economy after the Civil War, being instrumental in the formation of many trusts to stifle competition. He set up the US Steel Corporation in 1901.

Morgan[3], *n.* **Thomas Hunt** (1866–1945), US geneticist, awarded a Nobel prize in 1933 for his pioneering studies in classical genetics. He was the first to work on the fruit fly, *Drosophila*, which has since become a major subject of genetic studies. He helped establish that the genes were located on the chromosomes, discovered sex chromosomes, and invented the techniques of genetic mapping.

Morgana FATA MORGANA.

morganatic, *a.* applied to a marriage between a man of high rank and a woman of inferior station, by virtue of which she does not acquire the husband's rank and neither she nor the children of the marriage are entitled to inherit his title or possessions. **morganatically,** *adv.* [low L *morganātica,* MHG *morgengâbe,* morning-gift]

Morgan le Fay, *n.* in the romance and legend of Arthur, an enchantress and healer, ruler of Avalon and sister of the king, whom she tended after his final battle. In some versions of the legend she is responsible for the suspicions held by the king of his wife Guinevere.

morgen, *n.* a unit of land measurement based on area that can be ploughed by one team in one morning. In SE Africa, Holland and parts of the US it is slightly over two acres (8094 sq.m). [G, morning]

morgue, *n.* a mortuary; a building or room where the bodies of unknown persons found dead are exposed for identification; a stock of files, clippings etc. kept by a newspaper for reference. [F, etym. unknown]

MORI®, (*abbr.*) Market and Opinion Research Institute.

†**Morian,** *a.* Moorish. *n.* a Moor. [OF *Morien,* from late L *Maurītānus* or *-tānius,* country of the *Maurī* or Moors]

moribund, *a.* in a dying state; lacking vitality and energy. †*n.* a dying person. [L *moribundus,* from *morī,* to die]

†**morion,** *n.* a helmet having no beaver or visor. [F, from Sp. *morrion,* perh. from *morra,* crown of the head]

Moriori, *n.pl.* the original inhabitants of New Zealand before the arrival of the Maoris. [Maori]

†**Morisco,** †**Morisk,** *a.* Moorish. *n.* a Moor, esp. one of the Moors remaining in Spain after the conquest of Granada; the language of the Moors; a morris dance; †a morris dancer; Moresque ornament or architecture. [Sp. *morisco,* from *Moro,* MOOR[1]]

morish MORE[1].

†**morkin,** *n.* an animal that has died from disease or accident. †**morling,** †**mortling,** *n.* a sheep that has died of disease; wool from such sheep. [ME *mortkyn,* A-F *mortekine,* OF *mortecine,* L *morticīna,* carrion, from *mors mortis,* death]

Morisot, *n.* **Berthe** (1841–95), French Impressionist painter, who specialized in pictures of women and children.

Morley[1], *n.* **Edward** (1838–1923), US physicist who collaborated with Michelson on the Michelson–Morley experiment 1887. In 1895 he established precise and accurate measurements of the densities of oxygen and hydrogen.

Morley[2], *n.* **Malcolm** (1931–), British painter, active in New York from 1964. He coined the term Super-realism for his work in the 1960s.

Morley[3], *n.* **Robert** (1908–), British actor and playwright, active in both Britain and the US. His film work has been mainly character roles, including films such as *Marie Antoinette* (1938), *The African Queen* (1952), and *Oscar Wilde* (1960).

Morley[4], *n.* **Thomas** (1557–1602), English composer. A student of Byrd, he became organist at St Paul's Cathedral, London, and obtained a monopoly on music printing. A composer of the English madrigal school, he also wrote sacred music, songs for Shakespeare's plays and a musical textbook.

morlop, *n.* a jasper pebble found in New South Wales. [etym. doubtful]

mormaor, *n.* (*Sc. Hist.*) a high steward, usu. hereditary, of a province, before the introduction of feudalism. [Gael. *mormaer* (*mor,* great, *maor,* steward)]

†**mormo,** *n.* a bugbear. [Gr.]

Mormon, *n.* a member of an American religious body, founded by Joseph Smith in 1830, now calling themselves the Latter-day Saints, who claim continuous divine revelation through their priesthood, and formerly practised polygamy; a polygamist. **Mormonism,** *n.* [from a mythic personage, author of the *Book of Mormon,* containing the alleged divine revelations on which their creed was based]

morn, *n.* (*poet.*) morning. **the morn,** (*Sc.*) tomorrow. [OE *morgen* (cp. Dut., Dan. *morgen,* G *Morgen,* Icel. *morginn,* perh. from root *mergh-,* to blink or twinkle)]

mornay, *a.* served with a cheese sauce. [perh. Philippe de *Mornay,* French Huguenot leader]

†**morne[1],** *n.* the blunted head of a tilting lance. **morné,** *a.* (*Her.*) applied to a lion rampant without teeth or claws. **morned,** *a.* blunted (of a spear). [F, from *morner,* to blunt]

morne[2], *a.* dreary, doleful. [F, prob. cogn. with MOURN]

morning, *n.* the first part of the day, beginning at twelve o'clock at night and extending to twelve noon, or from dawn to midday; the early part of a period or epoch; (*poet.*) dawn. *a.* pertaining to or meant to be taken or worn in the morning. **good morning,** a salutation. **in the morning,** tomorrow morning. **morning call,** *n.* a social visit usu. paid in the afternoon. **morning coat,** *n.* a tail-coat with cutaway front. **morning dress,** *n.* men's clothes worn on formal occasions during the day, esp. for weddings etc. **morning-glory,** *n.* various climbing or twining plants, species of *Ipomoea* and *Pharbitis.* **morning prayer,** *n.* in the Anglican Church, matins. **morning room,** *n.* a sitting-room used in the morning. **morning sickness,** *n.* nausea and vomiting frequently accompanying early pregnancy. **morning star,** *n.* the planet Venus when visible in the east at dawn; †a weapon consisting of a ball with spikes, united by a chain to a staff. **morning watch,** *n.* (*Naut.*) the watch from 4 to 8 am. [ME *morwening,* dawning (*morwen,* MORN, -ING)]

Moro[1], *n.* a member of a Muslim people of the S Philippines; the language of this people. *a.* of this people or its language. [Sp., Moor, L *maurus*]

Moro[2], *n.* **Aldo** (1916–78), Italian Christian Democrat politician. Prime minister (1963–68) and (1974–76), he was expected to become Italy's president, but he was kidnapped and shot by Red Brigade urban guerrillas.

Moroccan Crises, *n.pl.* two periods of international tension (1905 and 1911) following German objections to French expansion in Morocco. Their wider purpose was to break up the Anglo-French Entente of 1904, but both crises served to reinforce the entente and isolate Germany.

morocco, *n.* a fine leather from goat- or sheep-skin, tanned with sumach and dyed (formerly made in Morocco). **French morocco,** an inferior small-grained kind of Levant morocco. **Levant morocco,** a high grade of morocco with large grain, properly made with the skin of the Angora goat. **Persian morocco,** an inferior kind finished on one side of the skin only. [It. *Marocco,* ult. from native *Marrākesh*]

Morocco, *n.* Kingdom of (*al-Mamlaka al-Maghrebia*), a country in N Africa, bordered N and NW by the Mediterranean, E and SE by Algeria, and S by Western Sahara. **area** 458,730 sq km/177,070 sq miles. **capital** Rabat. **towns** Marrakesh, Fez, Kenes; ports Casablanca, Tangier. **physical** mountain ranges NE–SW; plains in W. **economy** dates, figs, cork, wood pulp, canned fish, phosphates, tourism. **population** (1989 est.) 25,380,000; annual growth rate 2.5%. **language** Arabic (official) 75%, Berber 25%, French, Spanish. **religion** Sunni Muslim.

moron, *n.* a feeble-minded person; an adult with the mentality of the average child aged between eight and twelve; (*coll.*) a very stupid or foolish person. **moronic,** *a.* **moronism,** *n.* [Gr. *mōros,* stupid]

morone MAROON[1].

Moroni, *n.* capital of the Comoros Republic, on Njazídja (Grand Comore); population (1980) 20,000.

morose, *a.* peevish, sullen; gloomy, churlish; given to morbid brooding. **morosely,** *adv.* **moroseness,** *n.* [L *mōrōsus,* from *mōs mōris,* manner, self-will]

morph, *n.* the phonological representation of a morpheme. [Gr. *morphē,* form]

-morph, *comb. form* denoting shape or structure. **-morphic, -morphous,** *a.* **-morphism, -morphy,** *n.*

morph- MORPH(O)-.

morpheme, *n.* a linguistic element that can carry meaning and cannot be divided into smaller such elements. **morphemic,** *a.* **morphemics,** *n.pl.*

Morpheus, *n.* (*Ovid*) the god of dreams. **in the arms of Morpheus,** asleep. [L, prob. from Gr. *morphē,* form]

morphic, *a.* morphological. [Gr. *morphē,* form]

morphine, morphia, *n.* the alkaloid constituting the narcotic principle of opium, used in medicine as a sedative. **morphinism,** *n.* addiction to the abuse of morphine. **morphinist,** *n.* **morphinize, -ise,** *v.t.* [G *Morphin,* as prec.]

morphino- *comb. form.* pertaining to morphine or morphia.

morphinomania,, morphiomania, *n.* a craving for morphia and its sedative effect. **morphino-, morphiomaniac,** *n.*

morph(o)-, *comb. form* form, pertaining to form.

morphogenesis, *n.* the development of the form of an organism during its growth to maturity. **morphogenetic,** *a.*

morphography, *n.* descriptive morphology. **morphographer,** *n.*

morphology, *n.* the branch of biology dealing with the form of organisms; the science of the forms of words; the science of the forms of rocks etc. **morphologic, -ical,** *a.* **morphologically,** *adv.* **morphologist,** *n.*

morphosis, *n.* the mode or order of development of an organ or organism. **morphotic,** *a.*

Morrigan, *n.* in Celtic mythology, a goddess of war and death who could take the shape of a crow.

morris, *n.* a grotesque dance; a rustic dance in which the performers formerly represented characters from folk legends, usu. performed by six men, one of them in girl's clothing; any similar dancing performance. *v.i.* (*sl.*) to decamp. **morris dance,** *n.* †**morris-pike,** *n.* a pike supposed to be of Moorish origin. [var. of MORISCO, Moorish]

Morris[1], *n.* **Henry** (1889–1961), British educationalist. He inspired and oversaw the introduction of the 'village college' and community school education, which he saw as regenerating rural life.

Morris[2], *n.* **William** (1834–96), English designer, socialist and poet, who shared the Pre-Raphaelite painters' fascination with mediaeval settings. His first book of verse was *The Defence of Guenevere* (1858). In 1862 he founded a firm for the manufacture of furniture, wallpapers and the like, and in 1890 he set up the Kelmscott Press to print beautifully decorated books. The prose romances *A Dream of John Ball* (1888) and *News from Nowhere* (1891) reflect his socialist ideology. He also lectured on socialism.

Morris chair, *n.* an armchair with an adjustable back. [William *Morris*, see above]

Morrison[1], *n.* **Herbert Stanley, Baron Morrison of Lambeth** (1888–1965), British Labour politician. He was secretary of the London Labour Party (1915–45), and a member of the London County Council (1922–45). He entered Parliament in 1923, and in 1955 was defeated by Gaitskell in the contest for leadership of the party.

Morrison[2], *n.* **Toni** (1931–), US novelist, whose fiction records black life in the South. Her works include *The Song of Solomon* (1978), *Tar Baby* (1981), and *Beloved* (1987), based on a true story about infanticide in Kentucky, which won the Pulitzer prize in 1988.

Morrison shelter, *n.* an indoor air-raid shelter in the form of a steel table. [Herbert *Morrison*, British minister responsible for its introduction in 1941]

Morris tube, *n.* a small-bore barrel for fixing on a large-bore rifle or gun for practice at close range at a miniature target. [Richard *Morris*, inventor (1881)]

morro, *n.* (*pl.* **-rros**) a small promontory or hill. [Sp.]

morrow, *n.* the day next after the present, the following day; the succeeding period; †morning, morn. [ME *morwe, morwen,* MORNING]

Morse[1], *n.* the Morse telegraph; (*coll.*) a message sent by the Morse code. **Morse finger, Morse key, paralysis,** forms of a nervous disease, also called telegraphist's cramp, due to the reaction of prolonged muscular strain upon the controlling mechanism in the brain. **Morse alphabet, code,** *n.* a system of expressing messages by the recording telegraph invented by Morse in combinations of dots and dashes. [S.F.B. *Morse*, see below]

Morse[2], *n.* **Samuel (Finley Breese)** (1791–1872), US inventor. In 1835 he produced the first adequate electric telegraph, and in 1843 was granted $30,000 by Congress for an experimental line between Washington and Baltimore. With his assistant Alexander Bain he invented the Morse code. He was also a respected portrait painter.

morse[1], *n.* the walrus. [Lapp. *morsa* or Finn. *mursu*]

morse[2], *n.* the clasp of a cope. [OF *mors,* from L *morsus,* bite, from *mordēre,* to bite]

morsel, *n.* a mouthful, a bite; a small piece of food; a small quantity, a piece. †**morsure,** *n.* biting. [OF, dim. of *mors,* MORSE[3]]

†**morsing,** *n.* (*Sc.*) the act of priming a gun. **morsing-hole,** *n.* the touch-hole of a gun. **morsing-horn, -powder,** *n.* the powder-horn and powder used for this. [obs. *mors,* F *amorcer,* to prime]

mort[1], *n.* a note sounded on the horn at the death of the deer. [F, from L *mors mortis,* death]

mort[2], *n.* a salmon in the third year. [etym. unknown]

mort[3], *n.* a woman or girl; a harlot. [etym. unknown]

mortal, *a.* subject to death, causing death, deadly, fatal; inveterate, implacable; involving physical or spiritual death (as a sin or crime); pertaining to death; liable to death, hence human; (*coll.*) extreme, excessive; long and tedious; (*coll.*) very drunk. *n.* a being subject to death; a human being; (*facet.*) a person. *adv.* (*coll.*) exceedingly, extremely. **mortality,** *n.* the quality of being mortal; human nature; (*collect.*) human beings; loss of life, esp. on a large scale; the number of deaths in a given period, the death-rate. †**mortalize, -ise,** *v.t.* **mortally,** *adv.* in a fatal way; (*coll.*) exceedingly, greatly. [OF, from L *mortālis,* from *mors mortis,* death]

mortar, *n.* a vessel in which substances are pounded with a pestle; a short piece of ordnance used for throwing shells at a high angle; a device for firing pyrotechnic shells; a cement, made of lime, sand and water, for joining bricks etc. in building. *v.t.* to join, plaster or close up with mortar. **mortar-board,** *n.* a square board for holding mortar; a square-topped academic cap. **mortarless,** *a.* **mortary,** *a.* [OE *mortere,* or F *mortier,* L *mortārium,* etym. doubtful]

mortgage, *n.* the grant of an estate or other immovable property in fee as security for the payment of money, to be voided on the discharge of the debt or loan; the loan thus made. *v.t.* to grant or make over property on mortgage; to pledge, to plight (oneself etc. to or for). **mortgage rate,** *n.* the rate of interest charged by building societies, banks etc. for mortgage loans. **mortgageable,** *a.* **mortgagee,** *n.* the one who accepts a mortgage. **mortgagor, mortgager,** *n.* the one who mortgages his property. [OF (*mort,* L *mortuus,* dead, from *mors mortis,* death, GAGE[1])]

mortice MORTISE.

mortician, *n.* (*N Am.*) an undertaker. [L *mors mortis,* death]

mortier, *n.* a cap of state formerly worn by legal and other functionaries in France. [F, as MORTAR]

mortify, *v.t.* to subdue (the passions etc.) by abstinence or self-discipline; to humiliate, to chagrin, to wound. *v.i.* to lose vitality, to decay, to gangrene. †**mortiferous,** *a.* bringing or producing death; fatal, mortal, deadly. **mortification,** *n.* †**mortifiedness,** *n.* **mortifier,** *n.* **mortifyingly,** *adv.* [F *mortifier,* L *mortificāre* (*mors mortis,* death, *-ficāre, facere,* to make)]

Mortimer[1], *n.* **Roger de, 8th Baron of Wigmore and 1st Earl of March** (*c.* 1287–1330), English politician and adventurer. He opposed Edward II and with Edward's queen, Isabella, led a rebellion against him (1326), bringing about his abdication. From 1327 Mortimer ruled England as the queen's lover, until Edward III had him executed.

Mortimer[2], *n.* **John** (1923–), English barrister and writer. His works include the plays *The Dock Brief* (1958) and *A Voyage Round My Father* (1970), the novel *Paradise Postponed* (1985), and the television series *Rumpole of the Bailey*, from 1978, centred on a fictional barrister.

mortise, *n.* a hole cut in timber or other material to receive a tenon. *v.t.* to cut a mortise in; to join by means of mortise and tenon. **mortise-chisel,** *n.* one with a stout blade for cutting mortises. **mortise lock,** *n.* one set into a mortise in the edge of a door, so that the lock mechanism is enclosed by the door. [F *mortaise,* etym. unknown]

†**mortling** MORLING under MORKIN.

mortmain, *n.* possession or tenure of lands or tenements by an ecclesiastical or other corporation who cannot alienate. **in mortmain,** in unalienable possession. [A-F *morte mayn,* OF *mortemain,* med. L *mortua manus,* dead hand]

Morton, *n.* **Jelly Roll** (stage name of Ferdinand Joseph La Menthe) (1885–1941), US jazz pianist, singer, and composer. Influenced by Scott Joplin, he played a major part in the development of jazz from ragtime to swing by improvising and imposing his own personality on the music. His band from 1926 was called the Red Hot Peppers.

mortuary, *n.* a building for the temporary reception of the dead; †a fee paid to a parson of a parish on the death of a parishioner; †a burial-ground. *a.* pertaining to death or the burial of the dead. [A-F *mortuarie,* L *mortuārius,* from *mortuus,* dead]

morula, *n.* (*pl.* **-las, -lae**) the stage of development in which an ovum has become completely segmented; an ovum at this stage; any of various kinds of tuberculous affections of the skin. [mod. L, dim. of *mōrum,* mulberry]

Morus, *n.* a genus of trees, containing the mulberry. [L *mōrus,* mulberry tree]

morwong, *n.* an edible fish found off the coasts of Australia and New Zealand. [Austral. Abor.]

Mosaic[1], *a.* pertaining to Moses or to the law given through him. **Mosaism, Mosaist,** *n.* [*Moses,* -IC]

mosaic[2], *a.* a term applied to any work in which a pattern or representation is produced by the junction of small pieces of differently-coloured marble, glass or stone; tesselated, inlaid. *n.* a pattern, picture etc. produced in this style; a viral disease of plants in which the leaves display a mottled yellowing; an organism, or part of one, consisting of tissues with different genetic constitutions. *v.t.* to decorate with mosaic; to combine into or as into a mosaic. **mosaically,** *adv.* **mosaicist, mosaist,** *n.* [F *mosaique,* med. L *mōsāicus, mūsāicus,* as from a late Gr. *mousaikos, mouseios,* pertaining to the Muses]

mosasaurus, *n.* a large fossil marine reptile of the Cretaceous period, first found near Maastricht on the Meuse. [L *Mosa,* Meuse or Maas, Gr. *sauros,* lizard]

moschate, *a.* having a musky smell. **moschatous, moschiferous,** *a.* [med. L *moschus,* musk]

moschatel, *n.* a small perennial herb, *Adoxa moschatellina,* with yellowish-green flowers and a musky scent. [F *moscatelle,* It. *moscatella,* dim. of *moscato,* MUSK]

Moscow[1], *n.* (*Austral., coll.*) a pawnshop. **gone to Moscow,** pawned.

Moscow[2], *n.* (Russian **Moskva**) capital of the USSR and of the Moskva region, on the Moskva river 640 km/400 miles SE of Leningrad; population (1987) 8,815,000. Its industries include machinery, electrical equipment, textiles, chemicals and many food products.

Moseley, *n.* **Henry Gwyn-Jeffreys** (1887–1915), English physicist who, 1913–14, devised the series of atomic numbers, leading to the modern periodic table of the elements. He did valuable work on atomic structure.

moselle, *n.* a white wine made in the Moselle district. [F, name of river]

Moses[1], *n.* (*c.* 13th cent. BC), Hebrew lawgiver and judge who led the Israelites out of Egypt to the promised land of Canaan. On Mount Sinai he claimed to have received from Jehovah the **Ten Commandments** engraved on tablets of stone. The first five books of the Old Testament – in Judaism, the *Torah* – are ascribed to him.

Moses[2], *n.* **Ed(win Corley)** (1955–), American track athlete and 400 metres hurdler. Between 1977 and 1987 he ran 122 races without defeat.

Moses[3], *n.* **'Grandma'** (born Anna Mary Robertson) (1860–1961), US painter. She was self-taught, and began full-time painting in about 1927, after many years as a farmer's wife. She painted naive and colourful scenes from rural American life.

mosey, *v.i.* (*esp. N Am., coll.*) to walk, amble. [etym. unknown]

Moslem MUSLIM.

Mosley, *n.* **Oswald (Ernald)** (1896–1980), British politician, founder of the British Union of Fascists (BUF). He was a Member of Parliament (1918–31), then led the BUF until his internment (1940–43), when he was released on health grounds. In 1946 Mosley was denounced when it became known that Italy had funded his prewar efforts to establish fascism in Britain, but in 1948 he resumed fascist propaganda with his Union Movement, the revived BUF.

moslings, *n.pl.* thin shreds of leather shaved off by the currier in dressing skins. [prob. corr. from MORSEL]

mosque, *n.* a Muslim place of worship. [F *mosquée* (later *mosque*), It. *moschea,* Arab. *masgid,* MASJID]

mosquito, *n.* (*pl.* **-toes**) an insect of the genus *Culex* or allied genera, with a proboscis for piercing the skin of animals and sucking their blood. **mosquito-net,** *n.* a fine-mesh netting round a bed, over windows etc. to ward off mosquitoes. [Sp., dim. of *mosca,* L *musca,* fly]

Mosquito Coast, *n.* the Caribbean coast of Honduras and Nicaragua, characterized by swamp, lagoons and tropical rain forest. A largely undeveloped territory occupied by Mosquito Indians, Garifunas and Zambos, many of whom speak English. Between 1823 and 1860 Britain maintained a protectorate over the Mosquito Coast which was ruled by a succession of 'Mosquito Kings'.

moss, *n.* a bog, a peat-bog, wet, spongy land; a low, tufted, herbaceous plant of the cryptogamous class Musci, usually growing on damp soil or the surface of stones, trees etc. *v.t.* to cover with moss. **mossback,** *n.* (*N Am., coll.*) an old-fashioned or conservative person. **mossbacked,** *a.* **mossbunker,** *n.* the menhaden. **mossclad,** *a.* **moss-grown,** *a.* **moss-hag,** *n.* a pit or cutting in a moss from which peat has been taken; a mass of firm heathery ground in a peat-moss. **moss-rose,** *n.* a variety of *Rosa centifolia,* with moss-like calyx. **moss stitch,** *n.* a stitch in knitting consisting of alternating plain and purl stitches. **moss-trooper,** *n.* a common name for the marauders who formerly infested the borders of England and Scotland. **mossy,** *a.* **mossiness,** *n.* [OE *mos,* bog (cp. Dut. *mos,* Icel. *mosi,* G *Moos,* also OE *mēos,* moss, G *Mies,* lichen)]

Mössbauer, *n.* **Rudolf** (1929–), German physicist who discovered in 1958 that in certain conditions a nucleus can be stimulated to emit very sharply defined beams of gamma rays. This became known as the **Mössbauer effect**. Such a beam was used in 1960 to provide the first laboratory test of Einstein's General Theory of Relativity. For his work on gamma rays Mössbauer shared the 1961 Nobel physics prize with Hofstadter.

most[1], *a.* greatest in amount, number, extent, quality, degree etc. *adv.* in the greatest or highest degree (forming the superl. of most adjectives and adverbs of more than one syllable); (*coll.*) very. *n.* the greatest number, quantity, amount etc.; the best, the worst etc.; the majority. **at most,** at the utmost extent; not more than. **for the most part,** in the main; usually. **to make the most of,** to use to the best advantage. **mostly,** *adv.* chiefly, mainly; on most occasions; usually. [OE *mǣst* (cp. Dut. *meest,* Icel. *mestr,* G *meist*), cogn. with MORE[1]]

most[2], *adv.* (*N Am., coll.*) short for ALMOST.

-most, *suf.* forming superlatives of adjectives and adverbs denoting position, order etc., as in *hindmost, inmost, utmost.* [OE *-mest,* double superl. suf. (*-ma,* OTeut. *-mo-,* -EST, OTeut. *-isto*), conn. with MOST[1]]

Mostel, *n.* **'Zero' (Samuel Joel)** (1915–77), US comedian and actor, active mainly in the theatre. His film work includes *Panic in the Streets* (1950), *A Funny Thing Happened on the Way to the Forum* (1966), *The Producers* (1967), and *The Front* (1976).

MOT, (*abbr.*) Ministry of Transport; (*coll.*) short for MOT test. **MOT test,** *n.* a test of the roadworthiness of a motor vehicle more than three years old, administered under the authority of the Department of the Environment.

mot[1], *n.* a witty or pithy saying; †a motto. [F, a word, It. *motto,* L *muttum,* from *muttīre,* to murmur]

†**mot**[2], *n.* a note on a bugle. [as prec.]

motatorious, *a.* of the legs of insects, in continual motion, vibratile. **motatory,** *a.* [L *mōtātor,* from *mōtāre,* freq. of *movēre,* to MOVE, -OUS]

mote[1], *n.* a particle of dust, a speck, a spot; anything proverbially small. **moted, motty,** *a.* (*Sc.*) [OE *mot* (cp. Dut. *mot,* sawdust, dirt, LG *mut,* dust)]

†**mote**[2], *n.* a mound, an embankment; a tumulus. [ME and OF *mote* (F *motte*), clod, mound, castle, prob. identical with MOAT]

mote[3], MAY[1], MUST[3].

motel, *n.* a roadside hotel or furnished cabins where motorists may put up for the night.

motet, *n.* a vocal composition in harmony, of a sacred character. [F, dim. of MOT[1]]

moth, *n.* one of a group of nocturnal or crepuscular Lepidoptera, distinguished from butterflies by not having knotted antennae, comprising a small insect breeding in cloth, furs etc., on which the larvae feed; that which gradually eats, consumes or wears away anything. **moth-ball,** *n.* a ball of naphthalene or similar substance that keeps away clothes-moths. *v.t.* to lay up in moth-balls; to lay up for later use; to spray with a plastic for laying-up and preserving. **to put into moth-balls,** to defer execution of (a plan, project etc.). **moth-eaten,** *a.* eaten into holes by moths; ragged. **mothy,** *a.* full of moths; moth-eaten. [F, dim. of MOT[1]]

mother[1], *n.* a female parent; the source or origin of anything; a motherly woman; a woman performing the function of a mother; the head of a religious community; a contrivance for rearing chickens artificially; short for MOTHERFUCKER; †hysteria. *v.t.* to act as mother towards; to adopt as a son or daughter; (*lit. or fig.*) to profess oneself to be mother of; to give birth to. *a.* holding the place of a mother; giving birth or origin; native, natural, inborn, vernacular. **every mother's son,** all without exception. **Mother Carey's chicken** CHICKEN. **to be mother,** to pour, esp. tea. **mother-cell,** *n.* (*Biol.*) one that produces other cells by division. **Mother Church,** *n.* the Church regarded as having the status and authority of a parent; one from which others have sprung. **mother complex,** *n.* (*Psych.*) the Oedipus complex. **mother country,** *n.* one's native country; a country in relation to its colonies. **mothercraft,** *n.* application of scientific methods in rearing children. **mother earth,** *n.* the earth regarded as parent of all that lives on her surface; (*facet.*) the ground. **motherfucker,** *n.* (*N Am., taboo sl.*) an offensive or unpleasant person or thing. **Mother Hubbard,** *n.* the old woman in a nursery rhyme; a woman's flowing gown or cloak. **Mothering Sunday,** *n.* the mid-Lent Sunday, when mothers traditionally receive presents from their children. **mother-in-law,** *n.* (*pl.* **mothers-in-law**) the mother of one's wife or husband. **motherland,** *n.* one's native country. **mother language** MOTHER TONGUE. **mother-liquor, -water,** *n.* the portion of a mixed solution which remains after the less soluble salts or other bodies have crystallized out. **mother lode,** *n.* in mining, the main lode of a system. **mother-of-chapel** CHAPEL. **mother-of-pearl,** *n.* the iridescent nacreous or pearly substance forming the internal layer of many shells. *a.* (*usu. in comb.*) made of this. **mother-of-thousands,** *n.* a perennial herb of the genus *Linaria,* having ivy-shaped leaves, and usu. with yellow or bluish flowers. **Mother's Day,** *n.* (*US and Canada*) the second Sunday in May, set apart for the remembrance of one's mother; Mothering Sunday. **mother's help,** *n.* a person whose job is to help look after children. **mother ship,** *n.* one which supplies a number of other ships with stores, ammunition etc. **mother superior,** *n.* a woman having charge of a community of women in religious orders. **mother-to-be,** *n.* a pregnant woman. **mother tongue,** *n.* one's native language; a language from which others have sprung. **mother wit,** *n.* natural sagacity, common sense. **motherwort,** *n.* a plant, *Leonurus cardiaca,* supposed to be of efficacy for diseases of the womb; the mugwort, *Artemisia vulgaris.* **motherhood,** *n.* **motherless,** *a.* **motherlike,** *a., adv.* **motherly,** *a., adv.* **motherliness,** *n.* [OE *mōder, mōdor* (cp. Dut. *moeder,* Icel. *mōthur,* G *Mutter*), cogn. with L *māter,* Gr. *mētēr*]

mother[2], *n.* a thick slimy substance forming in various liquids during fermentation. *v.i.* to become mothery (as vinegar). **mothery,** *a.* [prob. same as prec. (cp. MDut. *moeder,* Dut. *maer,* G *Mutter*)]

mothy MOTH.

motif, *n.* the dominant feature or idea in a literary, musical or other artistic composition; a theme in music; an ornamental piece of lace etc. sewn on a dress. [F, MOTIVE]

motile, *a.* capable of motion. **motility,** *n.* [L *mōt-,* stem, *movēre,* to move, -ILE]

motion, *n.* the act, process or state of moving; passage of a body from place to place; change of posture; a gesture; an evacuation of the bowels; a combination of moving parts in a machine etc.; a proposal, esp. in a deliberative assembly; (*Law*) an application to a court for a rule or order; impulse, instigation. *v.t.* to direct by a gesture; †to propose. *v.i.* to make significant gestures; †to make proposals. **angular motion,** motion of a body as measured by the increase of the angle made with some standard direction by a line drawn from the body to a fixed point. **in motion,** moving; not at rest. **laws of motion,** three axioms laid down by Sir Isaac Newton: (1) every body remains in a state of rest or of uniform motion in the same direction, unless it is compelled to change that state; (2) change of motion is proportional to the force applied, and takes place in the direction of the straight line in which the force acts; (3) to every action there is always an equal and contrary reaction. **to go through the motions,** to do something without enthusiasm or conviction. **to put in motion,** to set going or in operation. **motion picture,** *n.* a cinematograph film. **motion sickness,** *n.* nausea induced by travelling in a car, ship, aircraft etc. **motion study,** *n.* the study of repetitive movement in industrial work with a view to the elimination of unnecessary movement. **motional,** *a.* †**motioner, -nist,** *n.* **motionless,** *a.* [F, from L *motio -ōnem,* as prec.]

motive, *a.* causing or initiating motion; tending to cause motion; pertaining to movement; †pertaining to a motive or motives. *n.* that which incites to action, or determines the will; cause, ground, incentive; in art, the predominant idea, feeling etc., motif. *v.t.* (*usu. pp.*) to furnish with an adequate motive (as a story, play etc.). **motive power,** *n.* the power by which mechanical motion is imparted; any impelling force; the act of motivating; a method of employing posters, loud-speakers etc. in factories to induce workers to speed up output. **motivate,** *v.t.* to motive; to instigate; to provide an incentive. **motivation,** *n.* **motiveless,** *a.* **motivelessness,** *n.* **motivity,** *n.* [OF *motif,* med. L *mōtīvus -vum,* from *mot-,* stem of *movēre,* to MOVE]

mot juste, *n.* the appropriate or felicitous word or phrase. [F]

motley, *a.* variegated in colour; dressed in particoloured clothes; heterogeneous. *n.* the particoloured dress of fools or jesters; a fool, a jester; a heterogeneous mixture. **man of motley,** a jester. **to wear motley,** to play the fool. **motley-minded,** *a.* having the fickle and inconstant mind of a fool or jester. [etym. doubtful, perh. rel. to MOTE[1,2]]

motmot, *n.* a S American and Mexican bird allied to the kingfishers, a sawbill. [imit.]

motocross, *n.* the sport of racing on motor-cycles over rough ground. [*motor, cross*-country]

motograph, *n.* a device invented by Thomas Edison (1847–1931), US inventor, in which friction is reduced periodically between two conductors, used as a receiver for an electric telegraph or telephone. **motographic,** *a.* [L *mōt-, mōtus,* p.p. of *movēre,* to MOVE]

motophone, *n.* a sound-engine actuated by aerial waves, invented by Thomas Edison. [see prec.]

motor, *n.* that which imparts motive power, esp. a machine imparting motion to a vehicle or vessel (usu. excluding steam-engines); a device that converts electrical energy into mechanical energy; (*coll.*) a motor-car; a muscle for moving some part of the body; a nerve exciting muscular action. *a.* causing or imparting motion. *v.i.* to drive or ride in a motor-car. *v.t.* to convey in a motor-car. **motor torpedo boat,** a light, fast naval vessel equipped chiefly with torpedoes. **motorboat,** *n.* a boat propelled by a motor carried by itself. **motor-bus, -cab, -car, -coach, -cycle, -truck,** etc., *n.* various kinds of vehicle propelled by their own motor. **motorcade,** *n.* a procession of motor-cars. **motor caravan,** *n.* a motor-vehicle fitted with sleeping accommodation, cooking facilities etc. **motordrome,** *n.* an enclosure or track where motor-vehicles compete or are tested. **motor launch,** *n.* a motor-driven small boat, for plying between vessels and the shore. **motorman,** *n.* a man in charge of a motor, esp. of an electric tram or train. **motormouth,** *n.* (*sl.*) a very talkative person; a loud mouth. **motor nerve,** *n.* an efferent nerve that excites muscular activity. **motor-scooter,** *n.* a small motor-cycle, usu. with fairing reaching from below the handlebars in a curve to under the rider's feet. **motorway,** *n.* a road for fast motor traffic, usu. with a relatively high speed limit. **motorial,** *a.* **motorist,** *n.* a driver of a motor-car. **motorize, -ise,** *v.t.* to equip (troops) with petrol-driven vehicles. **motory,** *a.*

[L, from *movēre,* to MOVE]

Motown, *n.* a form of music containing elements of rhythm and blues and pop, often combined with the rhythm of gospel music. [*mo*tor *town,* the nickname of Detroit, Michigan, where this originated]

Mott, *n.* **Nevill Francis** (1905–), British physicist noted for his research on the electronic properties of metals, semiconductors and noncrystalline materials. He shared the Nobel Prize for Physics 1977.

mottle, *v.t.* to blotch, to variegate with spots of different colours or shades of colour. *n.* a blotch or patch of colour; a spotted, blotched or variegated appearance on a surface. [prob. from MOTLEY]

motto, *n.* (*pl.* **-toes**) a short pithy sentence or phrase expressing a sentiment or maxim; a principle or maxim adopted as a rule of conduct; a joke, verse or maxim contained in a paper cracker; (*Her.*) a word or sentence used with a crest or coat of arms. †**mottoed,** *a.* [It., as MOT[1]]

motty MOTE[1].

mouch MOOCH.

mouchoir, *n.* a handkerchief. [F, from *moucher,* to wipe the nose]

moue, *n.* a small pouting grimace. [F, cp. MOW[2]]

mouflon, moufflon, *n.* a wild sheep, *Ovis musimon,* of Sardinia and Corsica. [F, from late L *mufron*]

moujik MUZHIK.

moulage, *n.* in the US, a section of a police force that specializes in taking plaster casts of footprints etc.; a plaster cast thus made. [F, cast from a mould]

mould[1], *n.* fine soft earth, easily pulverized, suitable for tillage; the earth, the ground; the grave. **mould-board,** *n.* the curved plate in a plough which turns the furrow-slice over. **mould-warp,** *n.* the mole. [OE *molde* (cp. Dut. *moude,* Icel. *mold,* Dan. *muld*), cogn. with L *molere,* to grind, Eng. MEAL[1]]

mould[2], *n.* a hollow shape into which molten metal or other substance is poured in a fluid state to cool into a permanent shape; a templet used by plasterers for shaping cornices etc.; various analogous appliances used in trades and manufactures; a tin, wooden or earthenware vessel for shaping puddings etc.; (*Arch.*) a moulding or group of mouldings; physical form, shape, build; character, nature. *v.t.* to form into a particular shape; to fashion, to make, to produce; to give a particular character to; to shape (bread) into loaves. **mould candle,** *n.* a candle made in a mould. **mould-loft,** *n.* a large room in a dockyard, in which the several parts of a ship are laid off on full-size drawings. **mouldable,** *a.* that may be moulded. **moulder[1],** *n.* **moulding,** *n.* the act or process of shaping anything in or as in a mould; anything formed in or as in a mould; an ornamental part of a cornice, capital, arch, woodwork etc., usu. in the form of continuous grooves and projections, showing in profile a complex series of curves. [ONorth.F *molde,* OF *modle,* L MODULUS]

mould[3], *n.* a minute fungoid growth forming a woolly or furry coating on matter left in the damp. **mouldy,** *a.* covered with mould; (*coll.*) bad, poor, nasty; (*coll.*) mean, shabby. **mouldiness,** *n.* [prob. from *mould, mouled,* p.p. of ME *moulen,* to become mouldy (cp. Swed. *mögla,* Dan. *muggeh,* also Eng. MUGGY)]

moulder[1] MOULD[2].

moulder[2], *v.i.* to turn to dust by natural decay; to crumble; to waste away gradually. [prob. from MOULD[1]]

moulding MOULD[2].

mouldy MOULD[3].

moulin, *n.* a vertical pit in a glacier engulfing water from the surface. [F, a mill]

moulinet, *n.* a machine for turning the drum of a hoisting-machine; a kind of turnstile; †a machine for bending a crossbow. [dim. of prec.]

moult, *v.i.* to cast the feathers, hair, skin, horns etc. (of certain birds and animals). *v.t.* to shed or cast. *n.* the act of moulting. [ME *mouten,* OE *bemūtian,* L *mūtāre,* to change]

mound[1], *n.* an artificial elevation of earth, stones etc.; a hillock, a knoll; a barrow, a tumulus. *v.t.* to heap up in a mound or mounds; to furnish, enclose or protect with a mound. **mound-bird,** *n.* a bird of Australia and the Pacific islands laying large eggs in mounds to hatch by themselves. [etym. doubtful, acc. to Skeat from A-F *mund,* var. of *munt,* OF *mont,* MOUNT]

mound[2], *n.* a ball or globe representing the earth, usu. of gold and surmounted by a cross, used as part of regalia, an orb. [F *monde,* L *mundus,* the world]

mount, *n.* a high hill; a mountain (in poetry, or as first part of a proper name); in palmistry, one of the fleshy protuberances on the palm of the hand; a figure of a green hill occupying the base of a shield; that upon which anything is mounted; a gummed hinge for affixing stamps, photographs etc. to a page; the margin round a picture; a cardboard etc. upon which a drawing is placed; a slide upon which something is placed for microscopic examination; the parts by which various objects are prepared for use, strengthened or ornamented; a horse with the appurtenances necessary for riding; a horse-block or other means of mounting on horseback. *v.i.* to rise, to ascend; to soar; to get on horseback; to rise in amount. *v.t.* to ascend, to climb; to ascend upon, to get on; to form a path up; to copulate with; to raise; to prepare for use; to put into working order; to put (a picture) on a mount; to affix (a stamp, photograph etc.) with mounts; to stage (a play); to put (someone) on a horse; to furnish with a horse or horses. **mount!** get on horseback! **to mount guard,** to go on duty as sentry. **mountable,** *a.* **mounted,** *a.* on horseback; placed on a mount. **mounter,** *n.* **Mountie, Mounty,** *n.* (*coll.*) a member of the Royal Canadian Mounted Police. **mounting,** *n.* [OE *munt,* L *mons montis*]

mountain, *n.* a natural elevation of the earth's surface rising high above the surrounding land; a large heap or pile; something of very great bulk; an excessive supply, esp. of an agricultural product. **the Mountain,** the extreme democratic party in the first French Revolution, from their occupying the highest seats in the National Convention. **mountain ash,** *n.* the rowan (*Austral.*) various kinds of Eucalyptus. **mountain bicycle, bike,** *n.* an ATB (q.v.) for use on rugged terrain. **mountain biking,** *n.* **mountain-chain,** *n.* a range or series of mountains. **mountain cork, leather, paper, wood,** *ns.* varieties of asbestos, sufficiently light to float in water. **mountain dew,** *n.* Scotch whisky, in former times often secretly distilled in the mountains. **mountain flour,** *n.* bergmehl. **mountain-high,** *a., adv.* esp. of waves, high as mountains. **mountain limestone,** *n.* carboniferous limestone. **mountains high** MOUNTAIN-HIGH. **mountain sickness,** *n.* a feeling of indisposition, varying in different people, brought on by ascending into rarefied mountain air. **mountain-side,** *n.* **mountain soap,** *n.* a soft, earthy, brownish-black mineral, used in crayon painting. **mountaineer,** *n.* one who dwells among mountains; one who climbs mountains for amusement or scientific purposes. **mountaineering,** *n.* †**mountainet,** *n.* **mountainous,** *a.* full of mountains; exceedingly large; †inhabiting mountains. **mountainously,** *adv.* **mountainousness,** *n.* [OF *montaigne* (F *montagne*), pop. L *montānea,* L *montāna,* pertaining to a mountain, from *mons montis,* mountain]

†**mountant[1],** *a.* mounting; lifted up. [F]

mountant[2], *n.* an adhesive substance for mounting photographs etc.

Mountbatten, *n.* **Louis, 1st Earl Mountbatten of Burma** (1900–79), British admiral. In World War II he became chief of combined operations (1942) and commander in chief in SE Asia (1943). As last viceroy of India (1947) he oversaw the transition to independence, becoming first governor-general of India (until 1948). He was chief of UK Defence Staff, 1959–65. Mountbatten was killed by an Irish Republican Army bomb aboard his yacht at Mullaghmore, County Sligo.

mountebank, *n.* a quack doctor, orig. one who proclaimed his nostrums from a platform; a boastful pretender, a charlatan. *v.t.* to cheat by false boasts or pretences. **mountebankery, -kism,** *n.* [It. *montambanco* (*monta in banco,* to mount on a bench)]

Mountie MOUNT.

Mount St Helens, a volcanic mountain in Washington state, US. When it erupted in 1980 after being quiescent since 1857, it devastated an area of 600 sq km /230 sq miles and its height was reduced from 2950 m/9682 ft to 2560 m/8402 ft.

moup, *v.t.* (*Sc.*) to nibble; to mumble. *v.i.* to associate (with). [etym. unknown]

mourn, *v.i.* to express or feel sorrow or grief; to wear mourning. *v.t.* to grieve or sorrow for; to deplore; to utter mournfully. **mourner,** *n.* **mournful,** *a.* **mournfully,** *adv.* **mournfulness,** *n.* **mourning,** *a.* grieving, sorrowing; expressive of grief or sorrow. *n.* grief, sorrow, lamentation; the customary dress, usu. black, worn by mourners. **in mourning,** wearing mourning garments. **mourning-band,** *n.* a band of black material worn esp. round the sleeve to show that one is in mourning. **mourning-brooch,** *n.* a jet brooch. **mourning-coach,** *n.* a black coach, drawn by black horses, used at funerals. **mourning-dove,** *n.* the Carolina turtle dove, *Columba carolinensis,* so called from its plaintive note. **mourning-paper,** *n.* note-paper edged with black, used during a period of mourning. **mourning-ring,** *n.* a black ring worn as memorial of a deceased person. **mourningly,** *adv.* [OE *murnan*]

mousaka MOUSSAKA.

mouse, *n.* (*pl.* **mice**) a small rodent quadruped of various species belonging to the genus *Mus,* esp. *M. musculus,* the common house mouse; applied to similar animals, as the shrews, voles etc.; (*sl.*) a black eye; (*coll.*) a shy or inconspicuous person; (*Comput.*) a device that allows manual control of the cursor and selection of computer functions without use of the keyboard. *v.i.* (mowz) to hunt for or catch mice; to hunt, to watch craftily, to prowl (about). *v.t.* to hunt for persistently; to rend or pull about as a cat does a mouse. **mouse-colour,** *n.* darkish grey with a tinge of brown. **mouse-ear,** *n.* a popular name for several plants, from the shape and velvety surface of their leaves (usu. attrib. as *mouse-ear chickweed, mouse-ear hawkweed*). †**mousefall,** *n.* a mouse-trap. **mousetail,** *n.* a plant of the ranunculaceous genus, *Myosurus.* **mouse-trap,** *n.* **mouser,** *n.* a cat good at catching mice. **mousy,** *a.* of a drab grey or brown colour; (*coll.*) shy, timid or inconspicuous. **mousiness,** *n.* [OE *mūs* (cp. Dut. *muis,* Icel. *mūs,* pl. *mȳss,* G *Maus,* L and Gr. *mūs*)]

mousquetaire, MUSKETEER.

moussaka, mousaka, *n.* a Greek dish of layered meat, aubergines, tomatoes and a white sauce. [Gr.]

mousse, *n.* a dish of flavoured cream whipped and frozen; any of various light, stiff liquid preparations, e.g. used for hair-styling or cosmetic purposes. [F, froth]

mousseline, *n.* fine French muslin. **mousseline-de-laine,** *n.* an untwilled woollen dress-fabric resembling muslin. **mousseline-de-soie,** *n.* a thin silk fabric resembling muslin in texture, usu. figured. [F]

moustache, *n.* the hair on the upper lip of men; applied to growths of hair on various animals, esp. round the mouth. **moustache-cup,** *n.* a drinking-cup with a guard to keep liquid from wetting the moustache. **moustached,** *a.* [F, from It. *mostaccio*]

Moustier, Le, *n.* a cave in the Dordogne, SW France, with prehistoric remains, giving the name **Mousterian** to the flint-tool culture of Neanderthal peoples; the earliest ritual burials are linked with Mousterian settlements.

mouth, *n.* the opening at which food is taken into the body with the cavity behind containing the organs of mastication, insalivation and speech; anything analogous to a mouth; a person regarded as needing to be fed; the opening of a vessel, pit, cave or the like; the outfall of a river; †a cry, a voice. *v.t.*, to utter pompously or in an elaborate or constrained manner, to declaim; to take up or seize with the mouth; to chew or roll with the mouth; to train (a horse) to the use of the bit; †to insult. *v.i.* to talk pompously or affectedly; to make grimaces; †to bill and coo. **down in the mouth** DOWN3. **to give mouth,** of a dog, to bark or bay. **to keep one's mouth shut,** not to speak, esp. not to reveal secrets. **to laugh on the wrong side of the mouth** LAUGH. **to make mouths, to make a wry mouth,** to make grimaces. **to shoot one's mouth off,** to speak boastfully or ill-advisedly. **to stop the mouth of,** to put to silence. **mouth-breather,** *n.* one who usually breathes through the mouth. **mouth-filling,** *a.* filling the mouth; inflated; sonorous. **mouth-organ,** *n.* a small musical instrument, played by blowing on metallic reeds. **mouthpiece,** *n.* a tube by which a cigar or cigarette is held in the mouth; that part of a musical instrument put between the lips; a spokesman for others. **mouth-to-mouth,** *a.* of resuscitation, carried out by breathing air into someone's mouth directly, with mouths in contact. **mouthwash,** *n.* an antiseptic liquid used to cleanse the mouth. **mouth-watering,** *a.* (appearing to be) delicious. **mouth-wateringly,** *adv.* **mouthable,** *a.* **mouthed,** *a.* (*usu. in comb.*) having a mouth, as *big-mouthed.* †**mouther,** *n.* **mouthful,** *n.* an amount that fills the mouth; (*coll.*) a word or phrase that is pompous or difficult to say; (*coll.*) an abusive tirade. **mouthless,** *a.* **mouthy,** *a.* talkative; ranting, bombastic. [OE *mūth* cogn. with L *mentum,* chin]

move, *v.t.* to cause to change position or posture; to carry, lift, draw or push from one place to another; to put in motion, to stir; to cause (the bowels) to act; to incite, to incline, to prompt, to rouse (to action); to excite, to provoke (laughter etc.); to prevail upon; to affect with feelings, usu. of tenderness, to touch; to propose, to submit for discussion; †to apply to. *v.i.* to change place or posture; to go from one place to another; to advance, to progress; to change one's place of residence; to change the position of a piece at chess etc.; to make an application, appeal etc.; to begin to act; to take action, to proceed; to be moved, to have an evacuation (of the bowels); to live, to exercise one's activities (in or among); to bow. *n.* the act of moving; the right to move (in chess etc.); proceeding, action, line of conduct; a step, a device to obtain an object; a change of abode. **move on,** a policeman's order to a person not to stand in one place. **on the move,** stirring; moving from place to place, travelling about. **to get a move on,** (*coll.*) to hurry. **to make a move,** to go, to leave the table etc.; to start; to begin to go; to move a piece at chess etc. **to move heaven and earth,** to make every effort, to leave no stone unturned (to secure an object). **to move the goalposts** GOAL. **movable,** *a.* capable of being moved; occurring at varying times (as a festival); †changeable, inconstant. *n.* anything that can be moved or removed, esp. a movable or portable piece of furniture etc. that is not a fixture; (*pl.*) goods, furniture, chattels etc., as distinct from houses and lands, personal as distinct from real property; (*Sc. Law*) not heritable, as distinguished from heritable property. **movable feast,** *n.* a festival the date of which varies; (*facet.*) a meal taken at irregular times. **movability, movableness,** *n.* †**movably,** *adv.* **movement,** *n.* the act or process of changing position, place or posture; a military evolution; change in temper, disposition, feeling etc.; manner or style of moving; action, incident or process of development in a story etc.; the working mechanism of a watch, clock, machine etc., or a connected group of parts of this; a connected series of impulses, efforts and actions, directed to a special end; a tendency in art, politics, literature etc., either actively promoted or occurring spontaneously; the people involved in this; activity in a market, esp. change of value; the mode or rate of a piece of music, also a section of a large work having the same general measure or time. **mover,** *n.* one who or that which moves; a cause or source of motive power; a proposer (of a resolution etc.); one who originates or instigates. **moving,** *a.* causing motion; in motion; impelling, persuading; pathetic, affecting. **moving-coil microphone,** a type of microphone in which currents at audio-frequencies are generated by the moving of a coil of wire hanging in a magnetic field. **moving staircase,** *n.* an escalator. **movingly,** *adv.* [OF *movoir* (F *mouvoir*), L *movēre*]

movie, *n.* (*esp. N Am.*) a cinema film. [*mov*ing picture, -IE]

Movietone®, *n.* a system of producing sound films.

moving MOVE.

mow¹, *n.* a heap or pile of hay, corn or other field produce; a stack. †*v.t.* to put in a mow or mows. [OE *mūga* (cp. Icel. *mūge,* a swathe, Swed. and Norw. *muga*)]

†**mow²,** *n.* a wry face, a grimace. *v.i.* to make grimaces. **mops and mows** MOP². [OF *moue, moe,* mouth, pout, perh. from MDut. *mouwe,* etym. doubtful]

mow³, *v.t.* to cut down (grass, corn etc.) with a scythe, mowing-machine etc.; to cut the grass off (a lawn etc.); to destroy indiscriminately; to cut (down) in great numbers. *v.i.* to cut grass by mowing. **mower,** *n.* **mowing,** *n.* the act of cutting with a scythe or mowing-machine; land from which grass is cut. *a.* of land, crops etc., intended to be mown. [OE *māwan* (cp. Dut. *maaien,* G *mahen,* also Gr. *amaein* and L *mētere,* to reap)]

Mow Cop, *n.* the site in England of an open-air religious gathering on 31 May 1807 that is considered to be the start of Primitive Methodism. Mow Cop is a hill at the S end of the Pennines on the Cheshire-Staffordshire border and dominates the surrounding countryside. It remained a popular location for revivalist meetings.

moxa, *n.* a downy material obtained from the dried leaves of *Artemisia,* esp. *A. moxa* and *A. chinensis,* burnt on the skin as a cautery or counter-irritant for gout etc. **moxibustion,** *n.* cauterization by means of moxa. [Jap. *mokusa* (*moe kusa,* burning herb)]

moya, *n.* mud ejected from volcanoes. [prob. S Am.Sp.]

Mozambique, *n.* People's Republic of (*República Popular de Moçambique*), a country in SE Africa, bordered to the N by Zambia, Malawi and Tanzania, E by the Indian Ocean, S by South Africa and E by Swaziland and Zimbabwe. **area** 799,380 sq km/308,561 sq miles. **capital** and chief port Maputo. **towns** ports Beira, Nacala. **physical** mostly flat; mountains in W. **exports** sugar, cashews, tea, cotton, copra, sisal. **population** (1989) 15,259,000 (mainly indigenous Bantu peoples; Portuguese 50,000); annual growth rate 2.8%. **language** Portuguese (official). **religion** animist 69%, Roman Catholic 21%, Muslim 10%.

Mozarab, *n.* one of those Christians in Spain after the Moorish conquest who were allowed the exercise of their religion in return for allegiance to the Moors. **Mozarabic,** *n.* [Sp. *Mozárabe,* Arab. *musta 'rib,* desiderative from *arab,* ARAB]

Mozart, *n.* **Wolfgang Amadeus** (1756–91), Austrian composer and performer who showed astonishing precocity as a child and was an adult virtuoso. He was trained by his father, Leopold Mozart (1719–87). From an early age he composed prolifically, his works including 27 piano concertos, 23 string quartets, 35 violin sonatas and more than 50 symphonies, including the E flat K543, G minor K550, and C major K551 ('Jupiter') symphonies, all composed in 1788. His operas include *Idomeneo* (1781), *Le Nozze di Figaro/The Marriage of Figaro* (1786), *Don Giovanni* (1787), *Così fan tutte/Thus Do All Women* (1790), and *Die Zauberflöte/The Magic Flute* (1791). Strongly influenced by Haydn, Mozart's music marks the height of the Classical age in its purity of melody and form.

mozetta, *n.* a short cape with a small hood worn by cardinals, bishops, abbots etc. in the Roman Catholic Church. [It. *mozzetta,* dim. of *mozza,* see AMICE¹]

mozzarella, *n.* a soft white unsalted curd cheese. [It.]

MP, (*abbr.*) Member of Parliament; Military Police.

mp, (*abbr.*) melting-point; (*Mus.*) mezzo piano.

mpg, (*abbr.*) miles per gallon.

mph, (*abbr.*) miles per hour.

MPhil, (*abbr.*) Master of Philosophy.

MPLA, *n.* (Portuguese *Movimento Popular de Libertacão de Angola,* Popular Movement for the Liberation of Angola) socialist organization founded in the early 1950s that sought to free Angola from Portuguese rule 1961–75 before being involved in the civil war against its former allies UNITA and FNLA 1975–76. The MPLA took control of the country but UNITA guerrilla activity continues, supported by South Africa.

mpret, *n.* an Albanian ruler. [Albanian corrupt. of L *imperator*]

Mr MISTER¹.

MRC, (*abbr.*) Medical Research Council.

MRCP, (*abbr.*) Member of the Royal College of Physicians.

MRCS, (*abbr.*) Member of the Royal College of Surgeons.

MRCVS, (*abbr.*) Member of the Royal College of Veterinary Surgeons.

Mrs MISTRESS.

MS¹, (*abbr.*) (*pl.* **MSS**) manuscript.

MS², (*abbr.*) multiple sclerosis.

Ms, (*abbr.*) a title used before the name of a woman in order not to distinguish her marital status.

MSc, (*abbr.*) Master of Science.

MS-Dos, (*abbr.*) Microsoft Disc Operating System, an operating system widely used on microcomputers.

Mt, (*abbr.*) Mount.

MTB, (*abbr.*) motor torpedo boat.

mu, *n.* the Greek letter M, μ.

Mubarak, *n.* **Hosni** (1928–), Egyptian politician, president from 1981. He commanded the air force (1972–75) (and was responsible for the initial victories in the Egyptian campaign of 1973 against Israel), when he became an active vice-president to Sadat, and succeeded him on his assassination. He has continued to pursue Sadat's moderate policies, and has significantly increased the freedom of the press and of political association.

mucedinous, *a.* mouldy, mildewy; of or like mould or mildew. [L *mūcēdo -dinis,* from *mūcēre,* to be mouldy, from MUCUS]

much, *a.* great in quantity or amount; long in duration; †numerous, many. *adv.* in or to a great degree or extent; almost, nearly, about. *n.* a great quantity, a great deal; something uncommon. **a bit much,** (*coll.*) rather excessive, unreasonable etc. **as much,** an equal quantity. **not much,** (*sl.*) certainly not, not likely. **not up to much,** (*coll.*) not very good, of poor quality. **to make much of** MAKE². **too much,** more than enough. **muchness,** *n.* **much of a muchness,** practically the same, very nearly alike. [ME *moche, miche, michel,* OE *micel,* MICKLE]

mucic, *a.* applied to an acid formed by the oxidation of milk, sugar and various gums. [F *mucique,* from L MUCUS]

mucid, *a.* mouldy, musty. †**mucidness,** *n.* **mucidous, muciferous, mucific,** *a.* [L *mūcidus,* from *mūcēre,* to be mouldy, as prec.]

mucilage, *n.* a gummy or viscous substance from the seeds, bark or roots of various plants; gum prepared for use; a viscous lubricating secretion in animal bodies. **mucilaginous,** *a.* [F, from L *mūcilāgo -ginis,* as prec.]

muciparous etc. MUCUS.

mucivorous, *a.* of some insects, feeding on the juices of plants.

muck, *n.* dung or manure; refuse, filth; anything filthy, disgusting or nasty; (*coll.*) untidiness; (*coll.*) money. *v.t.* to make dirty; (*sl.*) to bungle, to make a mess of. **in a muck sweat,** (*sl.*) sweating, esp. with fear. **to muck about** MESS ABOUT. **to muck in,** (*coll.*) to help others to do something. **to muck out,** to clean (esp. a stable). **muck-heap, -hill,** *n.* **muckrake,** *v.i.* to stir up scandal. **muckraker,** *n.* **muckraking,** *n.* **muckworm,** *n.* a worm found in dung-heaps; a miser. **mucker,** *n.* (*sl.*) a bad fall, esp. in the mud; (*coll.*) a friend. **to come a mucker,** to have a bad fall; to come to grief. **to go a mucker,** to plunge; to be extravagant. **mucky,** *a.* **muckiness,** *n.* [prob. from Scand. (cp. Icel. *myki,* dung, Norw. *myk,* Dan. *mög*)]

muckle, (*Sc.*) MICKLE.

Mucor, *n.* a genus of fungi comprising the moulds, growing on substances in a state of decay; animal mucus.

mucosaccharine, SACCHARINE.

mucous, *a.* pertaining to, like or covered with mucus; secreting mucus; slimy, viscid. **mucous membrane,** *n.* the membranous lining of the cavities and canals of the body.

mucro, *n.* (*pl.* **mucrones**) a sharp point, process, or organ. **mucronate, -cronated,** *a.* terminating abruptly in a point. **mucronately,** *adv.* [L]

mucus, *n.* the viscid secretion of the mucous membrane; applied to other slimy secretions in animals and fishes; gummy matter found in all plants, soluble in water but not in alcohol. **muciparous,** *a.* secreting mucus. **mucoid,** *a.* **mucosity,** *n.* **muculent,** *a.* [L *mūcus, muccus,* cogn. with Gr. *mussesthai,* L *ēmungere,* to blow the nose]

mud, *n.* moist, soft earth, or earthy matter; mire; anything that is worthless or defiling. †*v.t.* to bury in or bedaub with mud; to make turbid or foul. **mud in your eye!** used facetiously as a toast. **to throw mud,** to make disgraceful imputations. **mud-bath,** *n.* a bath of mineral water and mud in which patients are immersed for medicinal purposes. **mudcart,** *n.* **mudfish,** *n.* a New Zealand fish that burrows in the mud at a distance from water. **mudflap,** *n.* a flap hanging behind the road-wheel of a vehicle to prevent mud etc. being thrown behind. **mud-flat,** *n.* a flat expanse of mud revealed by the ebb-tide. **mudguard,** *n.* a board or strip of metal fastened over a wheel of a carriage or cycle to protect persons riding from mud. **mud-hole,** *n.* a place full of mud; an opening in a boiler for discharging sediment. **mudlark,** *n.* one who cleans out sewers, or fishes up pieces of coal, metal etc. from the mud of tidal rivers; a street arab; (*Austral.*) the pee-wee. **mudpack,** *n.* a cosmetic containing fuller's earth, applied in paste form to the face. **mud pie,** *n.* a heap of mud shaped by a child to resemble a pie. **mudslinger,** *n.* one who throws mud, a slanderer. **mudslinging,** *n.* **mud-valve** MUD-HOLE. **muddy,** *a.* covered or foul with mud; of the colour of mud; resembling mud; turbid, cloudy; confused, muddled, obscure. *v.t.* to make muddy or foul; to confuse; †to muddle, to confuse. †**muddy-brained,** †**-headed,** *a.* †**muddy-mettled,** *a.* dull-spirited. **muddily,** *adv.* **muddiness,** *n.* [cp. LG *mudde, mōde*]

muddle, *v.t.* to confuse, to bewilder, to stupefy; to make half drunk; to mix (up), to jumble (together) confusedly; to make a mess of, to bungle, to waste, to squander; †to make muddy or turbid. *v.i.* to act or proceed in a confused or bungling way; †to become muddy; to become confused. *n.* a mess; a state of confusion or bewilderment. **to muddle on, along,** to get along somehow. **to muddle through,** to attain a desired result without any efficiency or organization. **muddle-headed,** *a.* **muddle-headedly,** *adv.* **muddle-headedness,** *n.* **muddler,** *n.* [freq. from prec.]

mudir, *n.* a governor of a village or canton in Turkey; a governor of a province in Egypt. **mudirate, mudirieh,** *n.* [Turk. and Arab., from *adāra,* to administer]

muesli, *n.* a breakfast cereal of rolled oats, nuts, dried fruit etc. [Swiss G.]

muezzin, *n.* a Muslim crier of the hour of prayer. [Arab. *mu'azzin, mu'aththin,* from *azana, athana,* to call, to proclaim]

muff¹, *n.* a covering, usu. cylindrical, of fur or other material, carried by women, in which the hands are placed to keep them warm. **muffatee,** *n.* a small muff or woollen cuff worn on the wrist; †a muffler for the neck. [prob. from Dut. *mof,* F *moufle,* to MUFFLE]

muff², *n.* an awkward or stupid fellow; a bungling action, esp. failure to catch the ball at cricket. *v.t.* to miss (a catch) or to fail to catch (the ball) at cricket; to bungle or fail in. *v.i.* to fail, to bungle badly. [etym. doubtful]

muffin, *n.* a plain, light, spongy, round cake, usu. toasted and eaten hot with butter. **muffin-bell,** *n.* a bell rung by a street muffin-man. **muffin-man,** *n.* one who sells muffins. **muffineer,** *n.* a castor for sprinkling salt or sugar on muffins etc. [perh. rel. to OF *moufflet,* soft bread]

muffle¹, *v.t.* to wrap or cover (up) closely and warmly; to wrap up the head of so as to silence; to wrap up (oars, bells etc.) so as to deaden the sound; to dull, to deaden. *n.* a muffler, a boxing-glove; a large mitten; anything employed to deaden sound; an oven or receptacle placed in a furnace used in operations in which the pottery etc. is not in direct contact with the products of combustion. **muffler,** *n.* a wrapper or scarf for the throat; a boxing-glove; a mitten, a thick stuffed glove; a pad or other contrivance for deadening sound, as in a piano; (*N Am.*) the silencer on a motor-vehicle; a bandage for blindfolding. [perh. from OF *mofle, moufle,* med. L *muffula,* a winter glove, a mitten, etym. unknown]

muffle², *n.* the thick, naked upper lip and nose of ruminants and rodents. [F *mufle,* etym. doubtful]

mufti, *n.* an official interpreter or expounder of the Koran and Muslim law; civilian dress worn by servicemen off duty, ordinary dress as distinguished from that worn on state or ceremonial occasions. [Arab. *muftī*]

mug¹, *n.* a drinking-cup, usu. cylindrical without a lip; the contents of this; a cooling drink; (*sl.*) the face or mouth; (*coll.*) a dupe, a gullible person. *v.i.* to make faces, to grimace. [cp. LG *mokke, mukke,* Norw. *mugga, mugge,* Swed. *mugg*]

mug², *v.i.* (*coll.*) to study hard, to grind. *v.t.* to work or get up (a subject). *n.* one who works hard for examinations, esp. one who neglects outdoor sports.

mug³, *v.t.* to rob (someone) violently or by threatening violence, esp. in the street. **mugger,** *n.*

Mugabe, *n.* **Robert (Gabriel)** (1925–), Zimbabwean politician, prime minister from 1980 and president from 1987. He was in detention in Rhodesia for nationalist activities (1964–74), then carried on guerrilla warfare from Mozambique. As leader of ZANU he was in alliance with Joshua Nkomo of ZAPU from 1976, and the two parties merged in 1987.

mugger¹ MUG³.

mugger², *n.* an E Indian crocodile, *Crocodilus palustris,* with a broad snout. [Hind. *magar*]

muggins, *n.* a children's card-game; a game of dominoes; (*sl.*) a fool, a simpleton. [etym. doubtful, perh. from the surname *Muggins*]

Muggletonian, *n.* one of a sect founded in 1657 who believed the statements of Lodowicke *Muggleton* (1609–98) and his coadjutor Reeve that they were the two witnesses mentioned in Rev. xi.3–6.

muggy, *a.* damp and close, sultry; moist, damp, mouldy (of hay etc.). **mugginess,** *n.* [cp. Icel. *mugga,* Norw. *mugg,* drizzle]

Mughal emperors, *n.pl.* N Indian dynasty (1526–1857), established by Zahir ('Baber'). They were descendants of Tamerlane, the 14th-cent. Mongol leader, and ruled until the last Mughal emperor was dethroned and exiled by the British 1857; they included Akbar, Aurangzeb and Shah Jehan. They were Muslims.

mugwort, *n.* a herb of the genus *Artemisia,* esp. *A. vulgaris,* the motherwort. [*mucg-wyrt* (cp. LG *mugge,* Dut. *mug,* MIDGE, WORT)]

mugwump, *n.* in the US, an independent member of the Republican party; one who abstains from voting or otherwise declines to be led by party politics; a consequential person; †a person of importance, a leader. *v.i.* to act like a mugwump; to assert one's independence. [Algonkin *mugquomp,* a chief]

Muhammad MOHAMMED.

mujaheddin, mujahedeen, *n.pl.* Islamic fundamentalist guerillas. [lit. "holy warriors"]

Mujibur Rahman, *n.* **Sheik** (1921–75), Bangladeshi nationalist politician, president 1975. He was arrested several times for campaigning for the autonomy of East Pakistan. He won the elections in 1970 as leader of the Awami League, but was again arrested when negotiations with the Pakistan government broke down. After the civil war, 1971, he became prime minister of the newly independent Bangladesh. He was presidential dictator, Jan.–Aug. 1975, when he was assassinated.

Mukalla, *n.* seaport capital of the Hadhramaut coastal region of South Yemen; on the Gulf of Aden 480 km E of Aden; population (1984) 158,000.

Mukden, Battle of, the taking of Mukden (now Shenyang), NE China, the capital of the Manchu emperors, from Russian occupation by the Japanese, 20 Feb.–10 Mar. 1905, during the Russo-Japanese War. Mukden was later the scene of a surprise attack on 18 Sept. 1931 by the Japanese on the Chinese garrison, which marked the beginning of their invasion of China.

mulatto, *n.* the offspring of a white and a black. *a.* of this colour, tawny, esp. when intermediate in colour between the parents. [Sp. *mulato,* from *mulo,* MULE[1]]

mulberry, *n.* any tree of the genus *Morus,* bearing a collective fruit like a large blackberry; its fruit; the colour of this; the code name for the pre-fabricated port towed across to France for the invasion of 1944. [prob. from OHG *mūlberi, mūrberi* (*mūr,* L MORUS, *beri,* BERRY), cp. G *Maulbeere,* and OE *mōrbēam*]

Mulberry Harbour, *n.* a prefabricated floating harbour, used on D-day in World War II, to assist in the assault on the German-held French coast of Normandy.

mulch, *n.* a surface layer of dead vegetable matter, manure etc. to keep the ground or the roots of plants moist. *v.t.* to cover with mulch. [prob. from the obs. a. *mulch,* soft]

mulct, *n.* a fine, esp. for an offence or misdemeanour. *v.t.* to punish with a fine or forfeiture; to deprive (a person of); to swindle. †**mulctuary,** *a.* [L *mulcta,* a fine, whence *mulctāre,* to fine]

Muldoon, *n.* **Robert David** (1921–), New Zealand National Party politician, prime minister (1975–84).

mule[1], *n.* the offspring of a male ass and a mare; also a hinny; a stupidly stubborn or obstinate person; a hybrid between different animals or plants; an instrument for cotton-spinning. **mule-bird, -canary,** *n.* a cross between a canary and a goldfinch. **mule-deer,** *n.* the N American blacktail, *Cariacus macrotis.* **mule-spinner,** *n.* **mule-twist,** *n.* yarn spun on a mule. **mulewort,** *n.* a fern of the genus *Hemionitis.* **muleteer,** *n.* a mule-driver. **mulish,** *a.* like a mule; obstinate, sullen. **mulishly,** *adv.* **mulishness,** *n.* [OE *mūl,* or OF *mul, mule,* L *mūlus*]

mule[2], *n.* a backless shoe or slipper. [OF, from L *mulleus,* a magistrate's shoe]

muley, *n.* a hornless cow; any cow. *a.* hornless. [var. of Sc. and Ang.-Ir. *moiley,* from *moil,* Ir. *maol* (cp. W *moll,* bald)]

mulga, *n.* an Australian acacia, used as fodder. **mulga grass,** *n.* a fodder grass. [Abor.]

†**muliebrity,** *n.* womanhood; effeminacy. †**mulierosity,** *n.* excessive fondness for women. [L *muliebritas,* from *muliebris,* pertaining to women, from *mulier,* woman]

mulish etc. MULE[1].

mull[1], *v.t.* to warm (wine, beer etc.), sweeten and flavour with spices. **muller[1],** *n.* [etym. doubtful]

mull[2], *v.t.* to miss, to fail in (a catch etc. in a game). *n.* a failure, a miss; a mess, a muddle. [etym. doubtful]

mull[3], *n.* a thin soft muslin. [earlier *mulmull,* Hindi *malmal*]

mull[4], *n.* (*Sc.*) a snuff-box made of horn; a snuff-box. [var. of MILL[1]]

mull[5], *v.t.* (*usu. followed by over*) to ponder, consider. [etym. doubtful]

mull[6], (*Sc.*) a promontory. [prob. from Gael. *maol* or ON *mūli,* a snout]

Mullah, *n.* an honorary title in Muslim countries for persons learned in theology and sacred law, and for ecclesiastical and civil dignitaries. [Arab. *maulā,* a judge (in Pers., Turk. and Hind. *mullā*)]

mullein, *n.* a herbaceous plant with woolly leaves and tall spikes of yellow flowers, sometimes called Aaron's rod; other plants of the genus *Verbascum.* [A-F *moleyne* (F *molène*), perh. from *mol,* L *mollis,* soft]

muller[1] MULL[1].

muller[2], *n.* a stone with a flat surface, used to grind and mix pigment etc. on a slab. [perh. from *moloir,* grinding, from OF *moldre* (F *moudre*), L *molere,* to grind]

Müller, *n.* **Johannes Peter** (1801–58), German comparative anatomist whose studies of nerves and sense organs opened a new chapter in physiology by demonstrating the physical nature of sensory perception. His name is associated with a number of discoveries, including the Müllerian ducts in the mammalian foetus and the lymph heart in frogs.

mullet[1], *n.* a fish living near coasts and ascending rivers, belonging either to the genus *Mullus* and family Mullidae or the genus *Mugil* and the family Mugilidae, the former distinguished as red and the latter as grey mullet. [ME and OF *mulet,* dim. of L *mullus* (cp. Gr. *mullos*)]

mullet[2], *n.* (*Her.*) the figure of a five-pointed star, supposed to resemble the rowel of a spur; the mark of cadency indicating a third son. [OF *molette,* rowel, etym. doubtful]

mulligatawny, *n.* an E Indian highly-flavoured curry-soup. [Tamil *milagutannīr,* pepper-water]

mulligrubs, *n.pl.* depression, the blues; a pain in the stomach, colic. [facet. coinage]

Mulliken, *n.* **Robert Sanderson** (1896–1986), US chemist and physicist, who received the 1966 Nobel Prize for Chemistry for his development of the molecular orbital theory.

mullion, *n.* a vertical bar separating the compartments of a window. *v.t.* to divide or separate by mullions. [formerly *muniall,* prob. var. of MONIAL]

mullock, *n.* (*Austral.*) rock containing no gold; mining refuse from which the gold has been extracted; (*dial.*) rubbish; a muddle. [from obs. or dial. *mull,* dust, powder, from the root *mul,* to grind, cogn. with MEAL[2]]

†**mulse,** *n.* wine heated and sweetened with honey. [L *mulsum,* neut. p.p. of *mulcere,* to sweeten]

Mulready, *n.* **William** (1786–1863), Irish painter of rural scenes, active in England. In 1840 he designed the first penny-postage envelope, known as the **Mulready envelope**.

Mulroney, *n.* **Brian** (1939–), Canadian politician. A former businessman, he replaced Joe Clark as Progressive Conservative party leader in 1983, and achieved a landslide in the 1984 election to become prime minister. He won the 1988 election on a platform of free trade with the US, but with a reduced majority.

mult- MULT(I)-.

multangular, *a.* having many angles. **multangularly,** *adv.*

multanimous, *a.* many-sided mentally. [L *animus,* mind]

multarticulate, *a.* many-jointed.

multeity, *n.* the quality or state of being manifold; a manifold thing. [as foll.]

mult(i)-, *comb. form* many, several. [L *multus,* many, much]

multiaxial, *a.* having many axes or lines of growth.

multicamerate, *a.* having many chambers or cells.

multicapitate, *a.* many-headed.

multicapsular, *a.* (*Bot.*) having many capsules.

multicarinate, *a.* of a conch, having many ridges.

multicauline, *a.* (*Bot.*) having many stems.

†**multicavous,** *a.* full of holes or cavities. [L *multicavus* (*cavus,* CAVE[1])]

multicellular, *a.* many-celled.

multicentral, *a.* having many centres (of development etc.).

multicharge, *a.* having or firing several charges in rapid succession (of a gun).

multicipital, *a.* (*Bot.*) having many heads. [as BICIPITAL, see BICEPS]

multicolour, -ed, *a.* of or in many colours; many-coloured.

multicostate, *a.* having many ribs. [see COSTA]

multicuspid, -date, *a.* of teeth, having more than two cusps. [see CUSP]

multicycle, *n.* a velocipede having four or more wheels, usu. for carrying a number of men for military purposes.
multicylinder, *a.* of steam-engines, having a number of cylinders.
multidentate, *a.* having many teeth or tooth-like processes.
multidenticulate, *a.* having many denticulations or a finely indented margin.
multidigitate, *a.* having many fingers or finger-like processes.
multidimensional, *a.* having more than three dimensions.
multifaced, *a.* of some crystals, having many faces.
multifaceted, *a.* of a gem, having many facets; having many aspects or factors.
multifarious, *a.* having great multiplicity, variety or diversity. **multifariously,** *adv.* **multifariousness,** *n.* [L *multifārius* (MULT(I)-, *-fārius,* perh. rel. to *fārī,* to speak), cp. *multifāriam,* adv.]
multifid, multifidous, *a.* (*Bot., Zool. etc.*) having many divisions; cleft into parts, lobes, segments etc. [*fid-,* stem of *findere,* to cleave]
multifil, *n.* a multiple strand of synthetic fibre.
multiflagellate, *a.* having many flagella.
multiflorous, *a.* having many flowers. [late L *multiflōrus* (L *flōs flōris,* flower)]
multiflue, *a.* having many flues.
multifoil, *a.* having more than five foils. *n.* an ornament having more than five foils.
multifold, *a.* many times doubled.
multiform, *a.* having many forms. **multiformity,** *n.*
multiganglionate, *a.* having many ganglia.
multigenerate, *a.* generated in many different ways.
multigenerous, *a.* having many kinds. [L *multigenerus*]
multigranulate, *a.* containing or consisting of many grains.
multigym, *n.* a versatile exercise apparatus used for toning various muscle groups.
multigyrate, *a.* having many gyri or convolutions.
multihull, *n.* a vessel with more than one hull.
multijugous, *a.* (*Bot.*) having many pairs of leaflets. [L *jugum,* yoke, pair]
multilateral, *a.* many-sided; of an agreement or treaty in which more than two states participate.
multilineal, multilinear, *a.* having many lines.
multilingual, *a.* in many languages; able to speak, or speaking, several languages.
multilobate, -lobular, *a.* manylobed.
multilocular, -late, *a.* divided into many chambers.
multiloquent, -quous, *a.* talkative, loquacious. **multiloquence,** *n.*
multimedia, *a.* combining different media such as television, video, computer graphics.
multi-millionaire, *n.* one who possesses several millions.
multimodal, *a.* having more than one maximum (of statistical curves exhibiting the relative frequency of certain characters in organisms). **multimodalism,** *n.*
multinational, *n., a.* (a company) operating in several countries.
multinodal, -date, *a.* having many knots or nodes.
multinomial, *a.* having many terms. *n.* a quantity of more than two terms, connected by the signs plus or minus.
multinominal, †-nous, *a.* having many names.
multinucleate, -ated, *a.* of cells, having several nuclei. **multinucleolate,** *a.*
multiovulate, *a.* having many ovules. **multiovulation,** *n.*
multiparous, *a.* bringing forth many at a birth; bearing or having borne more than one child. **multipara,** *n.* a woman who has borne more than one child. **multiparity,** *n.* [L *multiparus*]
multipartite, *a.* divided into many parts; having several parts or divisions.
multiped, *a.* having many feet. *n.* an animal having many feet. [L *pēs pedis,* foot]
multiplane, *n.* an aeroplane having more than one plane.
multiple, *a.* manifold; numerous and multifarious; having many parts, components or relations. *n.* a quantity that contains another a number of times without a remainder. **multiple-choice,** *a.* of a test etc., giving a number of different answers, from which the candidate must choose the correct one. **multiple mark,** *n.* the sign × indicating multiplication. **multiple personality,** *n.* a condition occasioned by the splitting of the normal organization of mental life into a number of distinct parts, each of which is comparable with an individual personality. **multiple-poinding,** *n.* (*Sc. Law*) an action in which several claimants to a fund or property are compelled to come into court and settle their claims together. **multiple sclerosis,** *n.* a progressive disease causing paralysis, speech and visual defects etc., caused by the loss of myelin sheath from nerve tissue in the brain and spinal cord. **multiple star,** *n.* three or more stars in close proximity to each other due to their gravitational force. **multiple store,** *n.* a number of retail stores under the same ownership. **multiplicity,** *n.* the quality of being many or manifold; many of the same kind. [F, from late L *multiplus* (MULT(I)-, *-plus,* see DUPLE)]
multiplex[1]**,** *a.* manifold; multiple; of a channel, cable etc., allowing more than one signal to be transmitted simultaneously.
multiplex[2]**,** *n.* a cinema complex with a number of screens showing different films.
multiply, *v.t.* to add (a quantity called the multiplicand) to itself a certain number of times (called the multiplier) so as to produce a quantity called the product; to make more numerous, to increase in number or quantity. *v.i.* to increase in number or extent; to increase by propagation. **multiplicable, †multipliable,** *a.* **multiplicand,** *n.* the quantity to be multiplied. **†multiplicate,** *a.* **multiplication,** *n.* **multiplication table,** *n.* a table exhibiting the products of quantities taken in pairs, usually to 12 times 12. **multiplicative,** *a.* **multiplier, †multiplicator,** *n.* one who or that which multiplies or increases; the number by which the multiplicand is multiplied; an instrument for intensifying an electric current. **multiplying,** *n., a.* **multiplying glass, lens,** *n.* a lens with a number of facets giving many reflections of an object. [OF *multiplier,* L *multiplicāre* (MULT(I)-, *plicāre,* to fold)]
multipolar, *a.* (*Physiol., Elec.*) having more than two poles.
multiprogramming, *n.* the handling of several computer programs simultaneously by interleaving them in a single system.
multipurpose, *a.* serving several purposes.
multiracial, *a.* incorporating several racial groups.
multiradial, *a.* having many radii.
multiradiate, *a.* having many rays.
multiradicate, *a.* having many roots. **multiradicular,** *a.*
multiramified, *a.* having many ramifications or branches. **multiramose,** *a.*
multirole, *a.* having several different roles or uses.
multisaccate, *a.* having many sacs.
multisect, *a.* divided into many parts or segments. **multisection,** *n.* [L *sectus,* p.p. of *secāre,* to cut]
multiseptate, *a.* (*Bot. etc.*) having many septa or divisions.
multiserial, †-riate, *a.* having many series or rows.
multisiliquose, -quous, *a.* having many pods or seed-vessels.
multisonous, *a.* having many sounds; sounding much. **multisonant,** *a.* [L *multisonus* (*sonus,* see SOUND)]
multispiral, *a.* of an operculum, having many spirals or convolutions.
multistage, *a.* having many stages; of a rocket, having several sections which fall off in series at set points during flight.
multistaminate, *a.* having many stamens.
multistorey, *a.* having several storeys, esp. of a carpark. *n.* a multistorey car-park.
multistriate, *a.* marked with numerous striae or

streaks.
multisulcate, *a.* many-furrowed.
multisyllable, *n.* a polysyllable. **multisyllabic,** *a.*
multitasking, *n.* of a computer, the carrying out of several tasks simultaneously.
multitentaculate, *a.* having many tentacles.
multititular, *a.* having many titles.
multitrack, *a.* of a sound recording, using several different tracks blended to produce the final sound.
multituberculate, *a.* having many tubercles (as teeth).
multitubular, *a.* having many tubes.
multitude, *n.* the state of being numerous; a great number; a very large crowd or throng of people; the common people. **multitudinism,** *n.* the doctrine that the welfare of the many is of higher importance than that of the individual. **multitudinist,** *n.* **multitudinous,** *a.* very numerous; †pertaining to or composing a multitude. **multitudinously,** *adv.* **multitudinousness,** *n.* [F, from L *multitūdo -dinem* (MULT(I)-, -TUDE)]
multiuser, *a.* of a computer system, designed for use by several people simultaneously.
†**multivagant,** *a.* much-wandering. †**multivagous,** *a.* [L *multivagus* (MULT(I)-, *vagus,* wandering, from *vagārī,* to wander)]
multivalent, *a.* having several degrees of valency; (*Chem.*) having a valency greater than unity. **multivalence, -valency,** *n.*
multivalve, *a.* having many valves. *n.* an animal having a shell of many valves or pieces; a multivalve shell. **multivalvular,** *a.*
†**multiversant,** *a.* assuming many shapes, protean. [L *versans -antem,* pres.p. of *vertere,* to turn]
multivious, *a.* having many ways; pointing in several directions. [L *via,* way]
multivocal, *a.* susceptible of several interpretations; ambiguous. *n.* an ambiguous word. [cp. EQUIVOCAL]
†**multocular,** *a.* having many eyes.
multum in parvo, *adv.* much in little. [L]
multungulate, *a.* having more than two functional hoofs. *n.* a multungulate mammal, as an elephant or tapir.
multure, *n.* (*Sc.*) the toll or percentage paid for grinding grain at a mill; the percentage of ore paid to the owner of a pulverizing-mill for grinding. **multurer,** *n.* (*Sc.*) one who has corn ground at a certain mill to which he pays multure, usu. on the terms of his lease. [OF *moulture* (F *mouture*), med. L *molitūra,* from *molere,* to grind]
mum[1], *a.* silent. *int.* silence, hush! *v.i.* to act in dumb-show; to play as a mummer. **mum's the word,** a phrase used to ask for silence or discretion. †**mumbudget,** *n.* an expression impressing silence and secrecy. †**mumchance,** *n.* a game of hazard with cards or dice; a silent, tongue-tied person. *a.* silent. [onomat. (cp. G *mumm,* Dut. *mommen,* to mum)]
mum[2], *n.* a strong, sweet beer, orig. made in Brunswick. [G *Mumme*]
mum[3], *n.* an informal term for MOTHER. **mummy,** *n.* a child's word for MOTHER.
mumble, *v.i.* to speak indistinctly; to mutter; to speak with the lips closed. *v.t.* to mutter indistinctly or inarticulately; to chew or mouth gently. *n.* indistinct utterance; a mutter. †**mumble-news,** *n.* a tale-bearer. **mumblement,** *n.* **mumbler,** *n.* **mumbling,** *n., a.* **mumblingly,** *adv.* [ME *momelen,* from MUM[1]]
mumbo-jumbo, *n.* a W African idol, deity or malignant spirit; an absurd object of popular veneration; (*coll.*) incomprehensible or nonsensical language. [etym. doubtful]
mummer, *n.* an actor in dumb-show, esp. one of a number of people who formerly went from house to house at Christmas in fantastic disguises performing a kind of play; (*derog.* or *facet.*) an actor. **mummery,** *n.* the act or performance of mumming; tomfoolery, hypocritical parade of ritual etc. [OF *momeur,* from *momer,* to mum, perh. from Teut. (cp. MUM[1])]
mummy[1], *n.* a body of a person or animal preserved from decay by embalming, esp. after the manner of the ancient Egyptians; (*Hort.*) a kind of wax used in grafting; a bituminous pigment giving a rich brown tint; dried flesh, like that of a mummy; a dried-up person or body. *v.t.* to mummify. **mummy-case,** *n.* a wooden or papier-mâché case, usu. semi-human in shape, and decorated with hieroglyphics, in which Egyptian mummies were preserved. **mummiform,** *a.* **mummify,** *v.t.* **mummification,** *n.* [F *momie,* med. L *mumia,* Arab. *mūmiyā,* from *mūm,* wax used in embalming]
mummy[2] MUM[3].
mump[1], *v.i.* to beg in a whining tone. *v.t.* to obtain by begging; to overreach. **mumper,** *n.* a beggar. [perh. from Dut. *mompen,* to cheat]
mump[2], *v.i.* to sulk, to mope; (*dial.*) to mumble, to munch; †to grimace. *v.t.* (*dial.*) to munch. *n.pl.* (*sing. in constr.*) the sulks; a contagious disease characterized by a swelling and inflammation in the parotid and salivary glands. **mumpish,** *a.* †**mumpishly,** *adv.* [etym. doubtful, perh. imit. (identified with prec. by Skeat)]
munch, *v.t.* to chew audibly; to eat with much movement of the jaws. *v.i.* to chew audibly or with much movement of the jaws; to work the jaws up and down (as an aged person in talking). **muncher,** *n.* [prob. onomat.]
Munch, *n.* **Edvard** (1863–1944), Norwegian painter. He studied in Paris and Berlin, and his best works date from 1892–1908, when he lived mainly in Germany. His paintings often focus on neurotic emotional states. The *Frieze of Life* (1890s), a sequence of highly charged, symbolic paintings, includes some of his favourite images, for example *Skriket/The Scream* (1893). He reused these in etchings, lithographs and woodcuts.
Münchhausen, *n.* **Karl Friedrich, Freiherr (Baron) von** (1720–97), German soldier, born in Hanover. He served with the Russian army against the Turks, and after his retirement in 1760 told exaggerated stories of his campaigning adventures. This idiosyncrasy was utilized by the German writer Rudolph Erich Raspe (1737–94) in his extravagantly fictitious *Adventures of Baron Munchausen* (1785), which he wrote in English while living in London.
Münchhausen's syndrome, *n.* a syndrome in which the patient repeatedly simulates illness in order to obtain hospital treatment. [Baron *Münchhausen,* see prec.]
mundane, *a.* belonging to this world, earthly, worldly; matter-of-fact; prosaic, everyday, banal; (*Astrol.*) pertaining to the horizon. **mundanely,** *adv.* **mundaneness, mundanity,** *n.* [F *mondain,* L *mundānus,* from *mundus,* the world]
†**mundify,** *v.t.* to cleanse, to purify. †**mundificant,** †**mundificative,** *n., a.* †**mundification,** *n.* †**mundatory,** *a.* cleansing. *n.* that which cleanses or purifies. [F *mondifier,* L *mundificāre* (*mundus,* clean, *-ficāre,* from *facere,* to make)]
†**mundungus,** *n.* ill-smelling tobacco. [Sp. *mondongo,* tripe, black-pudding]
mung bean, *n.* (the seed of) an E Asian bean plant, *Phaseolus aureus,* used as a forage plant and as the main source of beansprouts.
mungo, *n.* woollen cloth made of second-hand material (of rather higher grade than shoddy). [etym. doubtful]
mungoose MONGOOSE.
Munich[1], *n.* an act of appeasement, so called from the attempt to buy peace from Hitler at *Munich* in 1938.
Munich[2], *n.* (German **München**) an industrial city (brewing, printing, precision instruments, machinery, electrical goods, textiles), capital of Bavaria, West Germany, on the river Isar; population (1986) 1,269,400.
Munich Agreement, *n.* a pact signed on 29 Sept. 1938 by the leaders of the UK (N. Chamberlain), France (Daladier), Germany (Hitler) and Italy (Mussolini), under which Czechoslovakia was compelled to surrender its Sudeten-German districts (the **Sudetenland**) to Germany. Chamberlain claimed it would guarantee 'peace in our time', but it did not prevent Hitler from seizing the rest of Czechoslovakia in Mar.

1939.

municipal, *a.* pertaining to the government of a town or city or to local self-government in general; †pertaining to the internal government of a state, kingdom or nation. **municipalism,** *n.* **municipalist,** *n.* **municipality,** *n.* a town, city or district having a charter of incorporation or enjoying local self-government. **municipalize, -ise,** *v.t.* **municipally,** *adv.* [F, from L *mūnicipālis,* from *mūniceps -cipis,* a citizen of a town having the rights of Roman citizenship (*mūnia,* civic offices, pl. of *mūnus,* duty, *capere,* to take)]

munificent, *a.* liberal, generous, bountiful; characterized by splendid liberality. **munificence,** *n.* **munificently,** *adv.* [L *mūnificus* (*mūnus,* duty, -FIC), after MAGNIFICENT]

muniment, *n.* a title-deed, charter or record kept as evidence or defence of a title; †a fortification, a stronghold; help, support, defence. **muniment-room, -house,** *n.* a strongroom or building in which muniments are preserved. [OF, from L *mūnīmentum,* from *mūnīre,* to fortify]

munition, *n.* (*usu. pl.*) military stores of all kinds; anything required for an undertaking; †a stronghold. *v.t.* to furnish with munitions. [F, from L *mūnitio -ōnem,* as prec.]

munnion MULLION.

Munro, *n.* **H(ugh) H(ector)** British author who wrote under the pen name Saki.

munshi, *n.* a native secretary, teacher of languages or interpreter, in India. [Hind.]

Munster, *n.* southern province of Republic of Ireland, comprising the counties of Clare, Cork, Kerry, Limerick, North and South Tipperary and Waterford; area 24,140 sq km/9318 sq miles; population (1986) 1,019,000.

muntin, *n.* a vertical strip dividing panels in a door or panes in a sash window. [MONTANT]

muntjak, *n.* a small Asiatic deer, *Cervulus muntjac.* [Sunda *minchek*]

muon, *n.* a subatomic particle, an unstable lepton with a mass approx. 207 times that of the electron. [contr. of *mu-meson,* cp. MU]

Muraena, *n.* a genus of marine eels. [L, from Gr. *muraina,* fem. of *(s)mūros,* sea-eel]

murage, *n.* a toll formerly paid for the repair or maintenance of the walls of a town. [OF, from *mur,* L *mūrus -um,* wall]

mural, *a.* pertaining to, on or like a wall. *n.* a large painting, mosaic etc. on a wall. **mural arc, circle, quadrant,** *n.* a graduated arc, circle or quadrant, formerly fixed to a wall in the plane of the meridian, for determining altitudes and zenith distances. **mural crown,** *n.* a crown, indented and embattled, given to the Roman soldier who first mounted a breach in storming a town. [F, from L *mūrālis,* as prec.]

Murasaki, *n.* **Shikibu** (*c.* 978–*c.* 1015), Japanese writer, a lady at the court. Her masterpiece of fiction, *The Tale of Genji,* is one of the classic works of Japanese literature, and may be the world's first novel.

Murat, *n.* **Joachim** (1767–1815), king of Naples from 1808. An officer in the French army, he was made king by Napoleon, but deserted him in 1813 in the vain hope that the Allies would recognize him. In 1815 he attempted unsuccessfully to make himself king of all Italy, but when he landed in Calabria in an attempt to gain the throne he was captured and shot.

Muratorian, *a.* of or pertaining to the Italian scholar L. A. *Muratori* (1672–1750). **Muratorian fragment, canon,** *n.* the oldest Western canon of the New Testament writings (compiled *c.* AD 170, and edited by Muratori).

Murcia, *n.* an autonomous region of SE Spain; area 11,300 sq km/4362 sq miles; population (1986) 1,014,000. It includes the cities Murcia and Cartagena, and produces esparto grass, lead, zinc, iron and fruit.

murder, *n.* homicide with malice aforethought. *v.t.* to kill (a human being) with malice aforethought; to slay barbarously; to spoil, to mar, by blundering or clumsiness; to mangle, to ruin. **capital murder** CAPITAL. **murder will out,** a hidden matter will certainly come to light. **to get away with murder,** (*coll.*) to do something criminal, outrageous etc. without being punished. **murderer,** *n.* **murderess,** *n. fem.* **murderous,** *a.* **murderously,** *adv.* [OE *morthor* (cp. Goth. *maurthr,* Dut. *moord,* Icel. *morth,* L *mors mortis,* death), whence *myrthrian,* to murder (cp. Goth. *maurthrjan*)]

Murdoch[1], *n.* **Iris** (1919–), British novelist, born in Dublin. Her novels combine philosophical speculation with often outrageous situations and tangled human relationships. They include *The Sandcastle* (1957), *The Sea, The Sea* (1978), and *The Book and the Brotherhood* (1987).

Murdoch[2], *n.* **Rupert** (1931–), Australian entrepreneur and newspaper owner, with interests in Australia, the UK and the US. Among his UK newspapers are the *Sun,* the *News of the World,* and *The Times*; in the US, he has a 50% stake in 20th Century Fox, and he also owns publishing companies. He is chief executive of Sky Television, the UK's first satellite television service.

mure, *v.t.* to immure, to shut up; to wall in. †*n.* a wall. [F *murer,* L *mūrāre,* from *mūrus,* wall]

Murex, *n.* (*pl.* **Murices**), a genus of molluscs, one species of which yields a purple dye. [L, prob. cogn. with Gr. *muax*]

murgeon, *n.* (*Sc.*) (*pl.*) grimaces, smirks, antics. *v.t.* to make grimaces at. [etym. doubtful]

muriate, *n.* chloride (now used only commercially). **muriate of soda,** common salt. **muriated,** *a.* impregnated with chloride (of mineral waters). **muriatic,** *a.* derived from sea-water or brine; hydrochloric. **muriatiferous,** *a.* [F, from *muriatique,* L *muriāticus,* pickled in brine, from *muria,* brine]

muricate, *a.* (*Bot.*) armed with sharp points or prickles. [L *mūricātus,* shaped like the *mūrex,* see MUREX]

muriform, *a.* (*Bot.*) arranged like bricks in a wall. [L *mūrus,* wall]

Murillo, *n.* **Bartolomé Estebán** (1617–82), Spanish painter, active mainly in Seville. He painted sweetly sentimental pictures of the Immaculate Conception; he also specialized in studies of street urchins.

murk, *n.* darkness. †*a.* murky; thick, obscure. **murky,** *a.* dark, gloomy; unclear, hazy. **murkily,** *adv.* **murkiness,** *n.* [OE *mirce* (cp. Icel. *myrkr,* Dan. and Swed. *mörk*)]

Murmansk, *n.* a seaport in NW USSR, on the Barents Sea; population (1987) 432,000. It is the largest city in the Arctic, the USSR's most important fishing port, and base of the icebreakers that keep the Northeast Passage open.

murmur, *n.* a low, confused, continuous or repeated sound, as of running water; a half-suppressed protest or complaint, a grumble; a subdued speech; an abnormal sound heard on auscultation of the heart, lungs or arteries. *v.i.* to make a low continued noise, like that of running water; to mutter in discontent; to find fault. *v.t.* to utter in a low voice. **murmurer,** *n.* a grumbler, a complainer. **murmuringly,** *adv.* **murmurous,** *a.* [F *murmure,* L *murmur,* whence *murmurāre* (cp. Gr. *mormurein,* to boil up (as waves))]

Murnau, *n.* **F. W.** (assumed name of Friedrich Wilhelm Plumpe) (1889–1931), German silent-film director, whose 'subjective' use of a moving camera to tell the story, through expressive images and without subtitles, in *Der letzte Mumm/The Last Laugh* (1924) made him famous. Other films include *Nosferatu* (1922), a version of the Dracula story.

Murphy, *n.* **Audie** (1924–71), US actor and war hero, who starred mainly in low-budget Western films. His work includes *The Red Badge of Courage* (1951), *The Quiet American* (1958), and *The Unforgiven* (1960).

murrain, *n.* an infectious disease among cattle. *a.* affected with murrain. [OF *morine,* perh. rel. to L *morī,* to die]

Murray[1], *n.* the principal river of Australia, 2575 km/1600 miles long. It rises in the Australian Alps near Mount Kosciusko and flows west, forming the boundary between New South Wales and Victoria, and reaches the sea at Encounter Bay, South Australia. With its main tributary, the Darling, it is 3750 km/2330 miles long.

Murray², *n.* **James Augustus Henry** (1837–1915), Scottish philologist. He was the first editor of the *Oxford English Dictionary* (originally the *New English Dictionary*) from 1878 until his death; the first volume was published in 1884.

Murray³, *n.* **James Stuart, Earl of Murray,** or **Moray** (1531–70), regent of Scotland from 1567, an illegitimate son of James V. Murray was one of the leaders of the Scottish Reformation, and after the deposition of his half-sister Mary Queen of Scots, he became regent. He was assassinated by one of her supporters.

Murray cod, *n.* a freshwater fish found in the *Murray* River, Australia.

Murrayfield, *n.* a Scottish rugby ground and home of the national team. It staged its first international in 1925 when Scotland beat England 14–11. The capacity is approximately 70,000.

murrey, *a.* of a dark-red colour. [OF *moré, morée,* L *mōrātus, -ta,* from *mōrum,* mulberry]

murrhine, *a.* a term applied to a delicate kind of Eastern ware made of fluorspar. [L *murrhinus,* from *murra,* late Gr. *morria,* a material of which costly vases were made]

murrnong, *n.* a sweet, edible tuberous root found in S Australia. [Austral. Abor.]

Murrumbidgee oyster, *n.* a raw egg taken with vinegar. **Murrumbidgee whaler,** *n.* a tramp, a hobo. [Austral. river]

†**murther** MURDER.

Musca, *n.* (*pl.* **-cae**) a genus of dipterous insects containing the house-flies. **muscae volitantes,** *n.pl.* black specks or motes apparently moving before the eyes. [L]

muscadel, *n.* a kind of rich wine made from muscadine grapes; the grapes from which such wine is made; a sweet fragrant pear. **muscadine,** *n.* one of several varieties of grape with a musky flavour or odour; †the wine muscadel. [OF, from MIt. *moscadello, -tello,* dim. of *moscato,* from *musco,* MUSK]

muscardine, *n.* a disease fatal to silkworms, caused by a fungoid or parasitic growth. [F *muscardine, muscadin,* It. *moscardino,* nutmeg, musk-lozenge, as prec.]

Muscat, *n.* (Arabic **Masqat**) capital of Oman, E Arabia, adjoining the port of Matrah, which has a deep-water harbour; combined population (1982) 80,000. It produces natural gas and chemicals.

Muschelkalk, *n.* a series of German shelly limestone beds of Middle Triassic age, absent in Britain. [G (*Muschel,* mussel, *Kalk,* lime)]

Musci, *n.pl.* the true mosses. **musciform,** *a.* [L]

muscle, *n.* an organ consisting of a band or bundle of contractile fibrous tissue serving to effect movement of some part of the animal body; the tissue of which this is composed; muscular strength; power or influence. **to muscle in,** to force one's way in; to interfere. **muscle-bound,** *a.* stiff and inflexible as a result of over-developed muscles. **muscle-man,** *n.* a man with very developed muscles, often used to intimidate. **muscled,** *a.* (*usu. in comb.*) having muscles, as *brawny-muscled.* **muscleless,** *a.* [F, from L *musculus, -um,* dim. of *mus,* MOUSE]

muscoid, *a.* resembling moss. *n.* a moss-like plant. **muscology,** *n.* the science of mosses, bryology. **muscologist,** *n.* **muscose,** *a.* †**muscosity,** *n.* [L *musc-,* see MUSCI, -OID]

muscovado, *n.* moist, dark-coloured, unrefined sugar left after evaporation from cane-juice and draining off from the molasses. [Sp. *mascabado,* unrefined]

Muscovite, *n.* a native of Muscovy (an old name for Russia); a native or inhabitant of Moscow; common mica, formerly called Muscovy glass. *a.* of Muscovy or Moscow. **Muscovy duck,** *n.* the musk-duck, *Cairina moschata.* [from F *Muscovie,* Russ. *Moskva,* Moscow]

muscular, *a.* pertaining to, consisting of or performed by the muscles; having well-developed muscles; strong, brawny. **muscular Christianity,** *n.* the combination of full physical, moral and religious development inculcated by Charles Kingsley, Thomas Hughes etc. **muscular dystrophy,** *n.* a genetic disease causing progressive deterioration of the muscles. **muscularity,** *n.* **muscularly,** *adv.* **musculature,** *n.* the arrangement or disposition of the muscles in the body or an organ. **musculo-,** *comb.form.* †**musculous,** *a.* [L *musculus,* MUSCLE]

Muse¹, *n.* in Greek mythology, one of nine goddesses, daughters of Zeus and Mnemosyne, who presided over the liberal arts: Clio was the muse of history; Euterpe, of lyric poetry; Thalia, of comedy and idyllic poetry; Melpomene, of tragedy; Terpsichore, of music and dancing; Erato, of amatory poetry; Calliope, of epic poetry; Urania, of astronomy; and Polyhymnia, of singing and harmony; the inspiring power of poetry, poetical genius; a person, esp. a woman, who inspires or influences a poet or poem; †a poet. †**museless,** *a.* [F, from L *Mūsa,* Gr. *Mousa*]

muse², *v.i.* to ponder, to meditate (upon); to study or reflect (upon) in silence; to dream, to engage in reverie; †to wonder. *v.t.* to meditate on; to think or say meditatively. *n.* abstraction of mind; reverie; †wonder, surprise. †**museful,** *a.* †**musefully,** *adv.* **muser,** *n.* **musingly,** *adv.* [F *muser,* prob. from OF *muse,* mouth, snout, whence *musel, museau,* MUZZLE]

†**muset,** *n.* a gap in a hedge, a meuse. [OF *mucette, musette,* dim. of *muce, musse,* MEUSE]

musette, *n.* a small bagpipe formerly used in France; a soft pastoral melody imitating the sound of the bagpipe; a reed-stop on the organ; †a rustic dance. [F, dim. of OF *muse,* bagpipe]

museum, *n.* a room or building for the preservation or exhibition of objects illustrating antiquities, art, natural science etc. **museum-piece,** *n.* an object so splendid or old-fashioned that it should be on display in a museum. **museography,** *n.* the art of describing or cataloguing museums. **museographer,** *n.* **museology,** *n.* the science of organizing and managing museums. **museologist,** *n.* [L, from Gr. *mouseion,* a temple of the Muses (see MUSE¹)]

Museveni, *n.* **Yoweri Kaguta** (1945–), Ugandan general and politician, president from 1986. He led the opposition to Idi Amin's regime (1971–78) and was minister of defence (1979–80) but, unhappy with Milton Obote's autocratic leadership, formed the National Resistance Army (NRA), which helped to remove him. Museveni leads a broad-based coalition government.

mush, *n.* a mash; a soft pulp, pulpy mass; (*N Am.*) porridge made of maize-meal boiled; (*sl.*) sentimental nonsense. **mushy,** *a.* [prob. var. of MASH¹]

mushroom, *n.* a quick-growing edible fungus, esp. *Agaricus campestris,* the common or meadow mushroom; an upstart. *a.* pertaining to or made from mushrooms; (*fig.*) ephemeral, upstart. *v.i.* to gather mushrooms; of bullets, to expand and flatten out; to grow or increase quickly. **mushroom cloud,** *n.* a cloud shaped like a mushroom, esp. that produced by a nuclear explosion. [F *mousseron,* prob. from OF *mousse,* moss]

music, *n.* the art of combining vocal and instrumental tones in a rhythmic form for the expression of emotion under the laws of beauty; such an artistic combination of tones; any pleasant combination of sounds; melody, harmony; musical taste; a musical score; †a band, an orchestra. **music to one's ears,** something that one is pleased to hear. **set to music,** of a poem or other composition, furnished with music to which it can be sung. **to face the music** FACE. **music-book,** *n.* **music-case, -folio, -holder,** *n.* a cover for sheet-music. **music centre,** *n.* a unit incorporating several devices for sound reproduction, e.g. a turntable, tape-deck. **music-hall,** *n.* a theatre devoted to variety entertainments. **music-master, -mistress,** *n.* one who teaches music. **music-stand,** *n.* a light frame for supporting a sheet of music. **music-stool,** *n.* a stool with a revolving adjustable seat. **musical,** *a.* of or pertaining to music; fond of or skilled in music; harmonious, melodious. *n.* a stage show, film etc. with much singing and dancing. **musical-box,** *n.* a box with a barrel-organ mechanism for playing different tunes. **musical chairs,** *n. sing.* a parlour game. **musical-clock,** *n.* a clock that plays tunes at the hours. **musical-glasses,** *n.pl.* a musical instrument consisting of a series of glass vessels or tubes of varying pitch. **musicality, musicalness,** *n.* **musically,** *adv.* **musician,** *n.* one skilled in music, esp. in playing an instrument. **musicianship,** *n.* **musicology,** *n.* the science of musical lore and history. **musicologist,** *n.* a writer on this. [F *musique,* L *mūsica,* Gr. *mousikē technē,* the art of the Muses (see MUSE[1])]

musk, *n.* an odoriferous, resinous substance obtained from a sac in the male musk-deer; the odour of this; similar perfumes; the muskplant, *Mimulus moschatus;* the musk-cranesbill, *Erodium moschatum;* applied to other plants. **musk-bag,** *n.* the bag or sac containing musk in various animals, esp. the musk-deer. **musk-beaver,** *n.* the musk-rat. †**musk-cat,** *n.* a civet; a dandy. **musk-deer,** *n.* a small hornless deer, *Moschus moschiferus,* of Central Asia, from which musk is obtained. **musk-duck,** *n.* a tropical American duck, *Cairina moschata,* erroneously called the Muscovy or Barbary duck; an Australian duck, *Biziura lobata.* **musk melon,** *n.* the melon, *Cucumis melo.* **musk-ox,** *n.* an Arctic-American bovine ruminant, *Ovibos moschatus.* **musk-pear,** *n.* a pear with a musky smell. **musk-rat,** *n.* any of several rodents emitting a musky odour, esp. the musquash, *Fiber zibethicus;* applied also to Indian shrews, *Crocidura caerulea* and *C. murina.* **musk-rose,** *n.* a rambling rose with large white flowers and a musky odour. **musk-tree, -wood,** *n.* a Jamaica tree, *Moschoxylum swartzii,* and various Oceanic and Australian trees and shrubs with musky odour. **musky,** *a.* **muskiness,** *n.* [F *musc,* late L *muscus -cum,* late Gr. *moschos,* Pers. *musk,* perh. from Sansk. *muska,* testicle]

musket, *n.* the old fire-arm of the infantry now superseded by the rifle; any old-fashioned smooth-bore gun; †the male of the sparrow-hawk. **musket-proof,** *a.* **musket-shot,** *n.* the distance a musket will carry; a ball or shot from a musket. **musketeer,** *n.* a soldier armed with a musket. †**musketoon,** *n.* a short musket or carbine with a large bore; a soldier armed with this. **musketry,** *n.* muskets collectively; the art of using the musket; fire from small-arms. [F *mousquet,* It. *mosquetto,* orig. a sparrowhawk, perh. from L MUSCA]

Muslim, *n.* a person of the Islamic faith. *a.* of or pertaining to the Islamic faith, culture etc. **Muslim Brotherhood,** *n.* a religious movement founded in 1929 for the purpose of influencing social and political action by a return to strict Islamic faith. **Muslimism,** *n.* **Muslimize, -ise,** *v.t.* [Arab. *muslim,* pres.p. of *aslama,* to be safe or at rest, whence ISLAM]

Muslim Brotherhood, *n.* movement founded by members of the Sunni branch of Islam in Egypt in 1928. It aims at the establishment of a theocratic Islamic state and is headed by a 'supreme guide'. It is also active in Jordan, Sudan and Syria.

muslin, *n.* a fine, thin, cotton fabric used for dresses, curtains etc.; a dress made of this; (*N Am.*) calico. *a.* made of muslin. **muslin-de-laine,** MOUSSELINE-DE-LAINE. **muslined,** *a.* **muslinet,** *n.* a coarse kind of muslin. [F *mousseline,* It. *mussolina, -ino,* dim. of *Mussolo,* Mosul in Mesopotamia where it was formerly made]

musmon, *n.* the mouflon. [L *mūsimon,* late Gr. *mousmōn*]

musquash, *n.* a N American aquatic rodent, *Fiber zibethicus,* yielding a valuable fur and secreting a musky substance in a large gland, also called the musk-rat. [Algonkin *musk-wessu*]

muss, *n.* a state of confusion or disorder, a mess. *v.t.* to disarrange, to throw into disorder. **mussy,** *a.* untidy; disordered. **mussiness,** *n.* [var. of MESS]

mussel, *n.* any mollusc of the bivalve genus *Mytilus,* esp. the edible *M. edulis.* [OE *mūscelle, muxle,* late L *muscula,* as MUSCLE]

mussitation, *n.* a muttering or mumbling; a movement of the lips as in mumbling. [late L *mussitātio,* from L *mussitāre,* freq. of *mussāre,* to mutter]

Mussolini, *n.* **Benito** (1883–1945), Italian dictator, 1925–43. As founder of the Fascist Movement, 1919, and prime minister from 1922, he became known as *Il Duce* 'the leader'. He invaded Ethiopia (1935–36), intervened in the Spanish Civil War (1936–39) in support of Franco, and conquered Albania in 1939. In June 1940 Italy entered World War II supporting Hitler. Forced by military and domestic setbacks to resign 1943, Mussolini established a breakaway government in N Italy (1944–45), but was killed trying to flee the country.

Mussorgsky, *n.* **Modest Petrovich** (1839–81), Russian composer, who was largely self-taught. His opera *Boris Godunov* was completed in 1869, although not produced in St Petersburg until 1874. Some of his works were 'revised' by Rimsky-Korsakov, and only recently has their harsh and primitive beauty been recognized.

Mussulman, *n.* (*pl.* **-mans**) formerly used for a Muslim. [Pers. *musulmān,* that is a true believer, from Arab. MUSLIM]

mussy etc. MUSS.

must[1], *n.* new wine, the expressed juice of the grape before fermentation; mustiness, mould. *v.t.* to make mouldy. *v.i.* to grow mouldy. [OE from L *mustum,* neut. of *mustus,* fresh, new]

must[2], *n.* mustiness, mould. [prob. from MUSTY (Skeat identifies with prec.)]

must[3], *aux. v.* to be obliged to, to be under a necessity to; to be requisite, to be virtually or logically necessary to; to be certain to; (used also with p.p. as a kind of historic present). *n.* a thing that must not be missed; an essential thing. [OE *mōste,* past of *mōt,* may, be free to (infin. *mōtan,* not found)]

must[4], *a.* of male elephants and camels, in a dangerous state of frenzy. *n.* this state which recurs irregularly. [Hind. and Pers. *mast,* intoxicated]

†**mustache** MOUSTACHE.

mustachio, *n.* a moustache, esp. a large one. **mustachioed,** *a.* [MOUSTACHE]

Mustafa Kemal, *n.* Turkish leader, who assumed the name of ATATÜRK.

mustang, *n.* the wild horse of the American prairies. **mustang grape,** *n.* a small red Texan grape, *Vitis candicans.* **mustanger,** *n.* one who lassoes mustangs for the market. [Sp. *mestengo* (now *mesteño*), prob. from *mesta* (rel. to L *mixta,* see MIX), a company of graziers, confused with *mostrenco,* astray, rel. to L *monstrāre,* to show, to point out]

mustard, *n.* the seeds of *Sinapis alba* and *S. nigra* ground and used as a condiment and as a rubefacient; any plant of the Linnaean cruciferous genus *Sinapis,* now included in *Brassica;* a brownish-yellow colour; (*N Am., coll.*) zest. *a.* brownish-yellow. **keen as mustard,** (*coll.*) very keen. **mustard and cress,** white mustard, *Sinapis alba,* and cress, *Lepidium sativum,* used in the seed-leaf as salad herbs. **mustard gas,** *n.* an irritant poison gas. **mustard-oil,** *n.* oil expressed from black mustard. **mustard plaster,** *n.* a mixture of powdered mustard seeds applied to the skin as a stimulant, counter-irritant etc. **mustard-pot,** *n.* a pot or cruet for holding mustard at table. **mustard-tree,** *n.* (*Bibl.*) the white mustard, *Sinapis alba* or some shrub or small tree. [OF *mostarde* (F *moutarde*), from Rom. *mosto,* MUST[1]]

mustee, *n.* the offspring of a white person and a quadroon. [Sp. MESTIZO]

Mustela, *n.* a genus of small Carnivora containing the weasels or martens. **musteline,** *n., a.* **mustelinous,** *a.* **musteloid,** *n., a.* [L, weasel, from *mūs,* MOUSE]

muster, *n.* the assembling of troops for parade or review; a register of forces mustered; a collection, a gathering; a collection of peacocks; †a pattern, a show. *v.t.* to collect or assemble for review, checking of rolls etc.; (*N Am.*) to enrol in the army; to bring together;

to summon (up strength, courage etc.). *v.i.* to meet in one place. **to muster out,** (*N Am.*) to discharge (a soldier) from the army. **to pass muster,** to pass inspection without censure; to be accepted as satisfactory. **muster-book,** *n.* a book in which military forces are registered. †**muster-master,** *n.* one who takes account of troops and their equipment. **muster-roll,** *n.* a roll or register of troops, a ship's company etc. [OF *mostre,* It. *mostra,* a show, a display, from L *monstrāre,* to show (see MONSTER)]

musth MUST[4].

mustn't, contr. form of *must not.*

musty, *a.* mouldy; sour, stale; vapid, antiquated, spiritless. **mustily,** *adv.* **mustiness,** *n.* [etym. doubtful, see MUST[2]]

mutable, *a.* liable to change; inconstant, fickle, unstable. **mutability,** †**mutableness,** *n.* **mutably,** *adv.* [L *mūtābilis,* from *mūtāre,* to change]

mutage, *n.* the process of checking fermentation of must[1]. [F, from *muter,* from L *mūtus,* dumb]

mutagen, *n.* a substance that causes or assists genetic mutation. **mutagenesis,** *n.* [*muta*te, -GEN]

mutant, *n.* an organism that has undergone mutation.

mutate[1], *v.i.* to change; to be transmuted; (*Biol.*) to sport. *v.t.* to change or modify (a sound), esp. by umlaut. **mutation,** *n.* the act or process of changing; umlaut; the change of an initial consonant in Celtic languages; a permanent variation in organisms giving rise to a new species; a species so produced. **mutative, mutatory,** *a.*

mutate[2], *a.* (*Bot.*) changed. *n.* (*Gram.*) a form having a mutated vowel. [as prec.]

mutatis mutandis, the necessary changes being made. [L]

mutch, *n.* (*Sc.*) a woman's cap or coif. [MDut. *mutse* (Dut. *muts*), prob. from *amutse* or *almutse,* cp. AMICE[2] and MOZETTA]

mutchkin, *n.* (*Sc.*) a measure of about three-quarters of a pint (426 ml). [MDut. *mudseken,* dim. of *mudde, mud,* L *modius,* a corn-measure]

mute[1], *a.* silent, uttering no sound, speechless; not having the power of speech, dumb; of hounds, not giving tongue; not spoken; (*Phon.*) not sounded, unpronounced; produced by complete closure of the organs of the mouth or interruption of the passage of breath (as *h, p, ph, d, t, th, k* and *g*). *n.* one who is silent or speechless; a dumb person; a hired attendant at a funeral; a dumb porter or janitor in Eastern countries; an actor in dumb show or whose part is speechless; a contrivance for deadening sound (as in a piano); (*Philol.*) a letter which is not pronounced; a consonant that stops the sound entirely. *v.t.* to deaden or muffle the sound of. **to stand mute,** to refuse or be unable to speak; (*Law*) to refuse to plead (usu. from malice). **mute swan,** *n.* a Eurasian swan, *Cygnus olor,* with white plumage and an orange bill. **muted,** *a.* unassertive, subdued. **mutely,** *adv.* **muteness,** *n.* **mutism,** *n.* muteness; silence; inability to hear, dumbness. [ME and OF *muet,* pop. L *mūtettus,* dim. of *mūtus,* assim. later to L]

mute[2], *v.i.* of birds, to excrete. *v.t.* to void (as excrement). *n.* muting. [OF *mutir, muetir, esmeutir, esmaltir,* perh. from Teut]

mutilate, *v.t.* to cut off a limb or an essential part of; to maim, to mangle; to disfigure; to injure (literary and other work) by excision. **mutilation,** *n.* **mutilator,** *n.* [L *mutilātus,* p.p. of *mutilāre,* from *mutilus,* maimed (perh. rel. to Gr. *mutilos, mutulos,* hornless)]

mutineer, *n.* one who mutinies. *v.t.* to mutiny. †**mutine,** *n.* a mutineer. *v.i.* to mutiny. **mutinous,** *a.* given to mutiny; rebellious. **mutinously,** *adv.* †**mutinousness,** *n.* **mutiny,** *n.* open resistance to or revolt against constituted authority, esp. by sailors or soldiers against their officers. *v.i.* to rise or rebel against authority (esp. in the army or navy). **Mutiny Act,** *n.* an act formerly passed every year for the maintenance of discipline in the army and navy, now embodied in the annual Army Act of 1881. [F *mutinier,* from *mutin,* mutinous, pop. L *movita,* a movement, commotion, from L *movēre,* to MOVE]

mutism MUTE[1].

mutograph, *n.* an early type of kinetograph for photographing moving objects. *v.t.* to photograph with this. **mutoscope,** *n.* an apparatus for displaying such photographic pictures by means of rapidly revolving wheels. **mutoscopic,** *a.* [*mūto-,* from L *mūtāre,* to change]

Mutsuhito, *n.* (1852–1912), emperor of Japan from 1867, when he took the title *meiji tennō* ('enlightened sovereign'). During his reign Japan became a world military and naval power. He abolished the feudal system and discrimination against the lowest caste, established state schools, and introduced conscription, the Western calendar, and other measures in an attempt to modernize Japan, including a constitution (1889).

mutt, *n.* (*sl.*) a fool, a silly ass; a dog, esp. a mongrel. [etym. doubtful]

mutter, *v.i.* to speak, in a low voice or with compressed lips; to grumble, to murmur (at or against); to make a low, rumbling noise. *v.t.* to utter in a low or indistinct voice; to say in secret. *n.* a low or indistinct utterance; a low rumbling sound; a murmur, a grumble. **mutterer,** *n.* **mutteringly,** *adv.* [prob. imit.]

mutton, *n.* the flesh of sheep used as food; (*facet.*) a sheep; (*sl.*) a loose woman. **mutton dressed (up) as lamb,** (*coll.*) an old woman dressed or made up to look younger. **mutton-chop,** *n.* a rib or other small piece of mutton for broiling; a side whisker of this shape. **mutton-fist,** *n.* (*sl.*) a large, coarse, red hand. **mutton-ham,** *n.* a leg of mutton salted and cured. **mutton-head,** *n.* (*coll.*) a stupid person. **mutton-headed,** *a.* **muttony,** *a.* [OF *moton* (F *mouton*), med. L *multo -ōnem,* prob. from Celt. (cp. OIr. *molt,* Gael. *mult,* W *mollt*)]

mutual, *a.* reciprocal, reciprocally given and received; possessed, done, felt etc. by each of two persons, parties etc., to or towards the other; shared by or common to two or more persons, as *mutual friend.* **mutual accounts,** *n. pl.* accounts in which each of two parties submit charges against the other. **mutual conductance,** *n.* a measure of a radio valve's efficiency. **mutual inductance,** *n.* the coupling of two electrical circuits in such a way that an alteration of current in one effects an electromotive force in the other. **mutual insurance,** *n.* a system of insurance in which parties agree to indemnify each other for specified losses; insurance under a company granting a certain share of the profits to policy-holders. **mutualism,** *n.* the doctrine that true welfare is based on mutual dependence; symbiosis in which organisms are associated without detriment to either. **mutualist,** *n.* **mutuality,** *n.* **mutualize, -ise,** *v.t., v.i.* **mutually,** *adv.* [F *mutuel,* L *mūtuus,* reciprocal, from *mūtāre,* to change]

mutule, *n.* a modillion, or one of the projecting blocks under the corona of a Doric cornice. [F, from L *mūtulus*]

†**mutuum,** *n.* a contract under which goods are lent for consumption, to be repaid in property of the same kind and quantity. [L, neut. of *mūtuus,* borrowed]

Muybridge, *n.* **Eadweard** (adopted name of Edward James Muggeridge) (1830–1904), British photographer. He made a series of animal locomotion photographs in the US in the 1870s and proved that, when a horse trots, there are times when all its feet are off the ground. He also explored motion in birds and humans.

Muzak®, *n.* a type of recorded background music played in shops, restaurants etc.

muzhik, *n.* a Russian peasant; a serf. [Rus.]

Muzorewa, *n.* **Abel (Tendekayi)** (1925–), Zimbabwean politician and Methodist bishop. He was president of the African National Council (1971–85), and was prime minister of Rhodesia/Zimbabwe, 1979. He was detained for a year in 1983–84. He is leader of the minority United Africa National Council (UANC).

muzzle, *n.* the projecting mouth and nose of an animal, as of a horse, dog etc.; the snout; the mouth of a gun or cannon; a guard put over an animal's muzzle to prevent biting. *v.t.* to put a muzzle on; to silence. **muzzle-loader,** *n.* a gun loaded at the muzzle. **muzzle velocity,** *n.* the velocity of a projectile as it leaves the muzzle. [OF *musel* (F *museau*), prob. from med. L *mūsellum,* dim. of *mūsus -um,* etym. doubtful]

muzzy, *a.* muddled, dazed; dull; fuddled, tipsy. **muzzily,** *adv.* **muzziness,** *n.* [etym. doubtful]

MV, (*abbr.*) megavolt.

MVD, *n.* Soviet Ministry of Internal Affairs, name of the secret police (1946–53; now the KGB).

MW, (*abbr.*) megawatt; medium wave.

Mwiiny, *n.* **Ali Hassan** (1925–), Tanzanian socialist politician, president from 1985, when he succeeded Nyerere. He began a revival of private enterprise and control of state involvement and spending.

Mx, (*chem. symbol*) maxwell.

my, *poss. a.* (*absol.* **mine**) belonging to me; used as a vocative in some forms of address (as *my boy, my dear*). *int.* a mild ejaculation of surprise. **my word!** used to express surprise, admiration etc. [ME *mī, mīn,* MINE]

my- MY(O)-.

Mya, *n.* (*pl.* **Myae,Myas**) a genus of bivalves containing the soft clams. **Myaria**, *n.pl.* an old name for the family comprising these, now called **Myidae**. **myarian**, *n., a.* [mod. L, prob. from Gr. *mūs,* MUSSEL]

myalgia, *n.* a morbid state of the muscles characterized by pain and cramp. **myalgic,** *a.* **myalgic encephalomyelitis,** *n.* a viral disease affecting the nervous system and characterized by excessive fatigue, general malaise, lack of coordination, depression etc. [Gr. *mūs,* MUSCLE, *-algia, algos,* pain]

myalism, *n.* a species of witchcraft practised in the W Indies. [*myal,* prob. from native W African, -ISM]

myall, *n.* one of two Australian acacias, *Acacia pendula* and *A. homalophylla,* yielding scented wood used in making tobacco-pipes. **myall-tree, myall-wood,** *n.* [Abor. *maiāl*]

Myanma, Union of, *n.* (formerly **Burma**) Socialist Republic of the Union of (*Pyidaungsu Socialist Thammada Myanma Naingngandaw*), a country in SE Asia, bordered by India to the NW, China to the NE, Laos and Thailand to the SE and the Bay of Bengal to the SW. **area** 676,577 sq km/261,159 sq miles. **capital** and chief port Yangon (formerly Rangoon). **towns** Mandalay, Karbe. **physical** over half is forested; rivers Irrawaddy and Chindwin; mountains in N, W, and E. **exports** rice, rubber, jute, teak, jade, rubies, sapphires. **population** (1989) 39,893,000; annual growth rate 1.9%. **language** Burmese. **religion** Hinayana Buddhist; religious centre Pagan.

myasthenia, *n.* loss of muscle power. **myasthenic,** *a.*

mycelium, *n.* (*pl.* **-lia**) the vegetative parts of fungi, mushroom spawn. **mycelial,** *a.* [Gr. *mukēs,* mushroom, *-l,* -IUM]

Mycenae, *n.* an ancient Greek city in the E Peloponnese, which gave its name to the Mycenaean (Bronze Age) civilization. Its peak was 1400–1200 BC, when the Cyclopean walls (using close-fitting stones) were erected. The city ceased to be inhabited after about 1120 BC. **Mycenaean,** *a.*

Mycenaean civilization, *n.* a Bronze Age civilization that flourished in Crete, Cyprus, Greece, the Aegean Islands and W Anatolia about 4000–1000 BC. During this period, magnificent architecture and sophisticated artefacts were produced.

mycete-, *comb. form.* fungus. **myceto-, myco-,** *comb. form.* fungus. [Gr. *mukētes,* pl. of *mukēs,* mushroom]

mycetology MYCOLOGY.

mycetoma, *n.* a fungoid disease affecting the bones of the feet or hand. **mycetomatous,** *a.*

Mycetozoa, *n.pl.* a group of fungoid organisms now usu. regarded as protophytes and included in the division Myxomycetes.

myco- MYCETE-.

Mycoderma, *n.* a genus of fermentation fungi including those that form the mother of vinegar.

mycology, *n.* the science of fungi; a treatise on fungi. **mycological**, *a.* **mycologically,** *adv.* **mycologist,** *n.*

mycophagy, *n.* eating of fungi. **mycophagist,** *n.* **mycophagous**, *a.*

mycorrhiza, *n.* a fungoid growth supplying the roots of a plant with material from humus. [Gr. *rhiza,* a root]

mycose, *n.* a kind of sugar obtained from certain lichens and fungi.

mycosis, *n.* the presence of parasitic fungi in the body. **mycotic,** *a.*

mycotoxin, *n.* a poisonous substance produced by a fungus.

mydriasis, *n.* an abnormal dilatation of the pupil of the eye. **mydriatic**, *a.* of mydriasis. *n.* a drug that causes the pupils to dilate. [late L, from Gr. *mudriāsis*]

myel- MYEL(O)-.

myelasthenia, *n.* spinal debility.

myelatrophia, *n.* atrophy of the spinal cord.

myelin, *n.* a soft, white, fatty tissue forming a sheath round certain nerve fibres. **myelinated,** *a.* having a myelin sheath.

myelitis, *n.* inflammation of the spinal cord. **myelitic,** *a.* [Gr. *muelon,* var. of *muelos,* marrow]

myel(o)-, *comb.form* spinal cord. [Gr. *muelos,* marrow]

myelomalacia, *n.* softening of the spinal marrow.

myelomeningitis, *n.* spinal meningitis.

myelon, *n.* the spinal cord. **myelonal**, *a.* **myelonic**, *a.*

Mygale, *n.* a genus of large hairy S American spiders. [Gr., field-mouse]

My Lai massacre, the killing of 109 civilians in My Lai, a village in South Vietnam, by US troops in Mar. 1968. An investigation in 1969 was followed by the conviction of Lt. William Calley, commander of the platoon.

Mylodon, *n.* a genus of gigantic fossil sloth-like edentates. **mylodont,** *n., a.* [Gr. *mulē,* mill, *odous odontos,* tooth]

mylohyoid, *a.* of or pertaining to the molar teeth and the hyoid bone. **mylohyoidean**, *n., a.* [as prec., HYOID]

myna, mynah MINA².

Mynheer, *n.* a Dutchman. [Dut. *mijnheer,* Mr, Sir (*mijn,* my, *heer,* lord, master, cp. HERR)]

my(o)-, *comb.form* pertaining to muscles. [Gr. *mūs muos,* muscle]

myocarditis, *n.* inflammation of the myocardium. **myocardium**, *n.* the muscular substance of the heart.

myodynamics, *n. sing.* the science of muscular contraction.

myography, *n.* a description of the muscles. **myographic, -ical**, *a.* **myographist,** *n.*

myology, *n.* the science dealing with the muscles; a treatise on the muscles. **myologic, -ical**, *a.* **myologist,** *n.*

myomancy, *n.* divination by the movements of mice. **myomantic**, *a.* [Gr. *mūs,* MOUSE]

myope, *n.* a short-sighted person. **myopia, myopy,** *n.* short-sightedness. **myopic**, *a.* [F, from late L *myōps myōpis,* Gr. *muōps muōpos* (*muein,* to shut, *ōps,* eye)]

myosin, *n.* an albuminous compound in the contractile muscular tissue.

myosis, *n.* contraction of the eye-pupil. [Gr. *muein,* to shut]

myositis, *n.* inflammation of a muscle.

myosotis, *n.* a genus of hardy plants comprising the forget-me-not. **myosote**, *n.* the forget-me-not. [L, from Gr. *muosōtis* (*mūs muos,* MOUSE, *ous ōtos,* ear)]

myotomy, *n.* dissection of muscles.

myriad, *a.* innumerable, countless. *n.* ten thousand; a very great number. [med. L *myrias -adis,* Gr. *mūrias -ados* (from *mūrios,* countless, *mūrioi,* ten thousand)]

myriapod, *a.* having numerous legs. *n.* one of the Myriapoda. **Myriapoda**, *n.pl.* a class of Arthropoda, comprising the centipedes and millipedes, characterized by a very large indeterminate number of jointed feet. [Gr. *pous podos,* foot]

Myrica, *n.* the tamarisk; a Linnaean genus of plants comprising the bog-myrtle or sweet-gale. **myricin,** *n.* the part of beeswax insoluble in boiling alcohol. [L,

from Gr. *murikē*]
myriophyllous, *a.* having many leaves. [Gr. *mūrios,* see MYRIAD, *phullon,* leaf]
myriorama, *n.* a kind of landscape kaleidoscope in which separate sections of views are combined in various ways. [as prec., Gr. *horama,* view]
myrioscope, *n.* a variety of kaleidoscope giving multiple reflections, esp. a form used to show by means of a small piece how a whole carpet would look on a floor.
myristic, *a.* applied to a fatty acid obtained from nutmeg oil and other vegetable and animal sources. **myristicin,** *n.* a colourless crystalline compound contained in oil of nutmeg. [med. L *myristica,* nutmeg, from Gr. *murizein,* to anoint]
myrmec(o)-, *comb. form* ant. [Gr. *myrmēx,* ant]
myrmecology, *n.* the study of ants. **myrmecological,** *a.* **myrmecologist,** *n.*
myrmecophile, *n.* an organism living in a symbiotic relationship with ants.
Myrmidon, *n.* one of a warlike people of Thessaly, ruled over by Achilles, and led by him to the siege of Troy; a faithful follower, esp. an unscrupulous underling. †**Myrmidonian,** *a.* [L, from Gr. *Murmidones*]
myrobalan, *n.* the dried plum-like fruit of species of *Terminalia,* used in calico-printing, and for dyeing and tanning; a variety of plum-tree largely used as a stock for budding. [F, from L *myrobalanum,* Gr. *murobalanos* (*muron,* unguent, *balanos,* acorn)]
Myron, *n.* (*c.* 500–440 BC), Greek sculptor. His *Discobolus/Discus-Thrower* and *Athene and Marsyas,* much admired in his time, are known through Roman copies. They confirm his ancient reputation for brilliant composition and naturalism.
myrrh1, *n.* a gum resin from *Balsamodendron myrrha* or other trees growing in Arabia and Abyssinia, used in the manufacture of incense, perfumes etc. **myrrhic, myrrhy,** *a.* [OE *myrre* or OF *mirre,* L *myrrha,* Gr. *murra,* from Semitic (cp. Arab. *murr,* Heb. *mōr*)]
myrrh2, *n.* an umbelliferous plant, *Myrrhis odorata,* also called sweet cicely. [late L *myrrhis,* Gr. *murris*]
myrrhine MURRHINE.
myrtle, *n.* a tree or shrub of the genus *Myrtus,* esp. *M. communis,* a tall shrub with glossy evergreen leaves and sweet-scented white or rose-coloured flowers, anciently sacred to Venus. **myrtle-berry,** *n.* **myrtle-wax,** *n.* a vegetable wax, from *Myrica cerifera,* also called bay-berry tallow. **myrtaceous,** *a.* [OF *myrtille,* L *myrtus,* Gr. *murtos*]
myself, *pron.* used in the nominative after 'I', to express emphasis; in the objective reflexively.
mysophobia, *n.* fear of contamination; mania for cleanness. [Gr. *musos,* uncleanness, *phobos,* fear of, flight from]
mystagogue, *n.* one who interprets or initiates into divine mysteries, esp. an initiator into the Eleusinian and other ancient Greek mysteries. **mystagogic, -ical,** *a.* **mystagogy,** *n.* [L *mystagōgus,* Gr. *mustagōgos* (*mustēs,* from *muein,* to close the eyes or lips, *agein,* to lead)]
mystery1, *n.* something beyond human comprehension; a secret or obscure matter; secrecy, obscurity; a form of mediaeval drama the characters and events of which were drawn from sacred history, a miracle-play; a divine truth partially revealed; (*pl.*) secret rites and ceremonies known to and practised only by the initiated; the esoteric rites practised by the ancient Greeks, Romans etc.; the Eucharist. **mystery tour,** *n.* an excursion to a destination that is kept secret until it is reached. †**mysterial,** *a.* †**mysteriarch,** *n.* one presiding over mysteries. **mysterious,** *a.* not plain to the understanding; obscure, mystic, occult; fond of mystery. **mysteriously,** *adv.* **mysteriousness,** *n.* [prob. through an A-F *misterie,* OF *mistere* (F *mystère*), L *mystērium,* Gr. *mustērion,* as prec.]
†**mystery**2, *n.* a handicraft, trade or occupation. [ME *mistere,* med. L *misterium, ministerium,* MINISTRY]
mystic, *a.* pertaining to or involving mystery or mysticism; occult, esoteric; allegorical, emblematical. *n.* one addicted to mysticism; a supporter of the doctrine of mysticism. **mystical,** *a.* **mystically,** *adv.* †**mysticalness,** *n.* **mysticism,** *n.* the doctrine that man may by self-surrender and spiritual apprehension attain to direct communion with and absorption in God, or that truth may be apprehended directly by the soul without the intervention of the senses and intellect. **mysticize, -ise,** *v.t.* [OF *mystique,* L *mysticus,* Gr. *mustikos,* as MYSTERY1]
mystify, *v.t.* to involve in mystery; to bewilder, to puzzle, to hoax. **mystification,** *n.* **mystifyingly,** *adv.* [F *mystifier* (as prec., -FY)]
mystique, *n.* professional skill or technique that impresses the layman; the mystery surrounding some creeds, professions etc.; any mysterious aura surrounding a person or thing. [MYSTIC]
mytacism, *n.* the wrong use or too frequent repetition of the letter *m,* esp. in Latin composition before words beginning with a vowel. [med. L *mytacismus,* Gr. *mutakismos* (*mû,* μ, *m,* -ISM)]
myth, *n.* a fictitious legend or tradition, accepted as historical, usu. embodying the beliefs of a people on the creation, the gods, the universe etc.; a parable, an allegorical story; a fictitious event, person, thing etc. **mythic, -ical,** *a.* of myths; legendary; imaginary, untrue. **mythically,** *adv.* **mythicism,** *n.* **mythicist,** *n.* **mythicize, -ise,** *v.t.* **mythicizer, -iser,** *n.* [Gr. *muthos,* fable]
mythico-, mytho-, *comb. form* myth; mythical.
mythogenesis, *n.* the creation or production of myths.
mythogony, *n.* the study of the origin of myths.
mythography, *n.* the writing or narration of myths, fables etc. **mythographer, -phist,** *n.*
mythology, *n.* a system of myths in which are embodied the beliefs of a people concerning their origin, deities, heroes etc.; the science of myths, a treatise on myths. **mythologer, -gist,** *n.* **mythologic, -ical,** *a.* **mythologically,** *adv.* **mythologize, -ise,** *v.t.* to make the basis of a myth. *v.i.* to invent myths; to study or interpret myths. [F *mythologie,* late L *mythologia,* Gr. *mūthologia* (MYTHO-, -LOGY)]
mythomania, *n.* an abnormal tendency to lie or exaggerate.
mythometer, *n.* a standard for judging myths by.
†**mythoplasm,** *n.* a fabulous narration.
mythopoeic, mythopoetic, *a.* myth-making; pertaining to a stage of culture when myths were developed. **mythopoeia,** *n.* **mythopoeist,** *n.* [Gr. *mūthopoios* (*poieein,* to make)]
mythus, MYTH.
Mytilus, *n.* a genus of bivalves containing the marine mussels. **mytilite,** *n.* a fossil mussel. **mytiloid,** *n., a.* [L]
myx(o)-, *comb.form* pertaining to or living in slime; pertaining to or consisting of mucus. [Gr. *muxa,* slime, mucus]
myxoedema, (*esp. N Am.*) **myxedema,** *n.* a cretinous disease characterized by atrophy of the thyroid gland and conversion of the connective tissue throughout the body into gelatinous matter. **myxoedematous,** *a.*
myxoma, *n.* (*pl.* **-mata**), a tumour composed of mucous tissue. **myxomatous,** *a.*
myxomatosis, *n.* a contagious and fatal virus disease in rabbits.
Myxomycetes, *n.pl.* the slime moulds or fungi, a group of organisms by some regarded as belonging to the Mycetozoa, by others as related to the fungi.
myxopod, *n.* a protozoan having pseudopodia.
myxosarcoma, *n.* a tumour consisting of myxomatous and sarcomatous tissue.
myxovirus, *n.* any of a group of viruses causing such illnesses as influenza, mumps etc.
Myzontes, *n.pl.* a class of vertebrates characterized by an incomplete cartilaginous skull, no lower jaw, and pouch-like gills, comprising the lampreys and hags. [Gr. *muzontes,* pl. pres.p. of *muzein,* to suck]

N

N¹, *n* the 14th letter and 11th consonant (*pl.* **Ns, N's, Ens**) is a dentilingual nasal, and its ordinary sound is heard in *not, ton,* but before *g* or *k* it often is a sound almost equivalent to *ng,* as in *sink, link;* (*Print.*) **n, en,** a unit of measurement; an indefinite number.
N², (*chem. symbol*) nitrogen.
N³, (*abbr.*) north; newton.
na NO¹.
NA, (*abbr.*) National Academy; Nautical Almanac; North America.
n/a, (*abbr.*) in banking, no advice; no account; non-acceptance.
Na, (*chem. symbol*) sodium.
NAACP, (*abbr.*) National Association for the Advancement of Colored People, a US civil-rights organization.
Naafi, *n.* an organization for supplying the Services with canteens. [acronym for the *N*avy, *A*rmy and *A*ir *F*orce *I*nstitutes]
nab¹, *v.t.* (*sl.*) (*past, p.p.* **nabbed**) to catch, to seize, to apprehend. [cp. Norw. and Swed. *nappa,* Dan. *nappe*]
nab², *n.* (*chiefly North. and Sc.*) a rocky or projecting hill or part of a hill; a projection on the bolt of a lock or the keeper into which the bolt catches. [Icel. *nabbr, nabbi,* Norw. *dial. nabb, nabbe,* Swed. *nabb*]
Nabis, les, *n.pl.* a group of French artists, active in the 1890s in Paris, united in their admiration of Gauguin – the mystic content of his work, the surface pattern and intense colour. In practice their work was decorative. Bonnard and Vuillard were members.
nabob, *n.* a deputy-governor or prince under the Mogul empire in India; a very rich man, esp. one who amassed wealth in India. [NAWAB]
Nabokov, *n.* **Vladimir** (1899–1977), US writer who left his native Russia in 1917, and began writing in English in the 1940s. His principal book is *Lolita* (1955), the story of the infatuation of middle-aged Humbert Humbert with a precocious child of 12. His other books include *The Real Life of Sebastian Knight* (1945) and *Pnin* (1957).
nacarat, *n.* a pale-red colour tinged with orange; a fine linen or crape dyed this colour. [F, from Sp. and Port. *nacarado,* from *nacar,* NACRE]
nacelle, *n.* the basket suspended from a balloon; a small, streamlined body on an aircraft, distinct from the fuselage, housing engines, crew etc. [F, from late L *nāvicella,* dim. of *nāvis,* ship]
nache NATCH.
Nachingwea, *n.* a military training base in Tanzania, about 360 km/225 miles south of Dar-es-Salaam. It was used by the guerrillas of Frelimo (Mozambique) (1964–75) and the African National Congress (Zimbabwe) (1975–80).
nacho, *n.* a crisp corn chip used as an appetizer in Mexican cuisine, often served with melted cheese and/or a chilli dip.
nachtmusik, *n.* a piece of music of a serenade-like character. [G, lit. night music]
nacket, *n.* (*Sc., North.*) a snack, a light luncheon; a small cake. [var. of *nocket,* etym. doubtful]
nacre, *n.* the pinna, sea-pen or other fish yielding mother-of-pearl; mother-of-pearl. **nacreous, nacrous,** *a.* **nacrite,** *n.* a pearly variety of mica. [F, from Sp. and Port. *nacar* (cp. Arab. *naqrah,* a cavity)]
Nadar, *n.* (adopted name of Gaspard-Félix Tournachon) (1820–1910), French portrait photographer and caricaturist. He took the first aerial photographs (from a balloon, 1858) and was the first to use artificial light.
Nader, *n.* **Ralph** (1934–), US lawyer. The 'scourge of corporate morality', he has led many consumer campaigns. His book *Unsafe at Any Speed* (1965) led to US car-safety legislation.
nadir, *n.* the point of the heavens directly opposite to the zenith or directly under our feet; the lowest point or stage (of decline, degradation etc.). [Arab., opposite to (the zenith)]
Nadir, *n.* **Shah (Khan)** (*c.* 1880–1933), king of Afghanistan from 1929. Nadir played a key role in the 1919 Afghan War, but was subsequently forced into exile in France. He returned to Kabul in 1929 to seize the throne and embarked on an ambitious modernization programme. This alienated the Muslim clergy and in 1933 he was assassinated by fundamentalists. His successor as king was his son Zahir Shah.
naevus, *n.* (*pl.* **-vi**) a congenital discoloration of the skin, a birth-mark. †**naeve,** *n.* **naevoid, naevose, naevous,** *a.* [L]
Nafud, *n.* a desert area in Saudi Arabia to the south of the Syrian Desert.
nag¹, *n.* a small horse or pony for riding; (*coll.*) a horse. [ME *nagge,* akin to D *negge,* a small horse]
nag², *v.i.,* (*past, p.p.* **nagged**) to be continually finding fault; to scold (at). *v.t.* to find fault with or scold continually; to be continually pestering with complaints or fault-finding. **nagger,** *n.* **naggish, naggy,** *a.* [perh. from Scand. (cp. Norw. and Swed. *nagga,* Dan. *nage,* Icel. *gnaga,* to gnaw)]
Nagaland, *n.* a state of NE India, bordering Burma on the east. **area** 16,721 sq km/6,456 sq miles. **capital** Kohima. **products** rice, tea, coffee, paper, sugar. **population** (1981) 775,000.
Nagari DEVANAGARI.
Nagasaki, *n.* an industrial port (coal, iron, shipbuilding) on Kyushu island, Japan; population (1987) 447,000. An atom bomb was dropped on it 9 Aug. 1945.
nagor, *n.* a small brown antelope from Senegal. [arbitrary name, by Buffon]
Nagorno-Karabakh, *n.* an autonomous region (*oblast*) of the Soviet republic of Azerbaijan; population (1987) 180,000 (76% Armenian, 23% Azerbaijani), the Christian Armenians forming an enclave within the predominantly Shi'ite Muslim Azerbaijan. Since Feb. 1988 the region has been the site of ethnic conflicts between the two groups and the subject of violent disputes between Azerbaijan and the neighbouring republic of Armenia.
Nagoya, *n.* an industrial seaport (cars, textiles, clocks) on Honshu island, Japan; population (1987) 2,091,000.
Nagpur, *n.* an industrial city (textiles, metals) in Maharashtra, India; population (1981) 1,298,000.
Nagy, *n.* **Imre** (1895–1958), Hungarian politician, prime minister (1953–55 and 1956). He led the Hungarian revolt against Soviet domination in 1956, for which he was executed.
Nahayan, *n.* **Sheikh Zayed bin Sultan al-** (1918–), emir of Abu Dhabi from 1969, when he deposed his brother, Sheikh Shakhbut. He was elected president of the supreme council of the United Arab Emirates (UAE) in 1971. Before 1969 he was governor of the eastern province of Abu Dhabi, one of seven Trucial States in the Persian Gulf and Gulf of Oman, which were under British protection. He was unanimously re-elected emir in 1986.
Nahua, *n.* an indigenous people of Central Mexico. The Nahua language, in the Uto-Aztecan family, is spoken

by over a million people today.

Nahuatl, *n.* the language of the Aztecs.

naiad, *n.* (*pl.* **-ads**) a water-nymph. **naiades,** *n.pl.* water-nymphs; an order of aquatic plants; a family of freshwater shellfish. [L and Gr. *naiad-,* nom. *naias,* from *naiein,* to flow]

naiant, *a.* (*Her.*) swimming, natant. [prob. through an A-F *naiant* (OF *noiant,* pres.p. of *noier*), L *natāre,* to swim]

naif NAÏVE.

nail, *n.* the horny substance at the tip of the human fingers and toes; a claw, a talon; a horny plate on the soft bill of certain birds; a measure of 2¼ in. (5·7 cm); a pointed spike, usu. of metal, with a head, for hammering into wood or other material to fasten things together, or for use as a peg etc. *v.t.* to fasten or secure with nails; to stud with nails; to hold, to fix; to seize, to catch; to engage (attention); to clinch (a bargain); (*sl.*) to nab, to steal; †to spike (a gun). **hard as nails,** (*coll.*) in a hard state of training; callous, unsympathetic. **on the nail,** on the spot; at once. **right as nails,** (*coll.*) perfectly right. **to hit the nail on the head,** to hit upon the true facts of a case; to do exactly the right thing. **to nail to the counter** or **barn-door,** to expose, to brand as spurious. **to nail up,** to close or fasten up by nailing; to fix at a height with nails. **nail-biting,** *n.* chewing off the ends of one's finger-nails. *a.* of an event or experience, which creates an amount of tension (likely to induce this activity). **nail-brush,** *n.* a small brush for cleaning the finger-nails. **nail-head,** *n.* the head of a nail; (*Arch.*) an ornament on late Norman and Early English mouldings, shaped like the head of a nail. **nail-headed,** *a.* **nail polish** NAIL VARNISH. **nail varnish,** *n.* a type of varnish, often coloured, for putting on finger-nails or toenails. **nailrod,** *n.* (*Austral.*) a coarse tobacco. **nailed,** *a.* (*usu. in comb.,* as *long-nailed, nailed-on*). **nailer,** *n.* a maker of nails; (*dated sl.*) a fine specimen, one who is first-rate (at). **nailery,** *n.* **nailing,** *a.* (*dated sl.*) first-rate. [OE *nægel* (cp. Dut. and G *Nagel,* Icel. *nagl*), cogn. with L *unguis,* Gr. *onux*]

nain, *a.* one's own. **nainsell,** *n.* one's own self. [Sc., corr. of MINE OWN]

nainsook, *n.* a thick muslin or jaconet, formerly made in India. [Hind. *nainsukh* (*nain,* eye, *sukh,* pleasure)]

Naipaul, *n.* **V(idiadhar) S(urajprasad)** (1932–), British writer, born in Trinidad of Hindu parents. His novels include *A House for Mr Biswas* (1961), *The Mimic Men* (1967), and *A Bend in the River* (1979). His brother **Shiva(dhar) Naipaul** (1940–85) was also a novelist (*Fireflies*, 1970) and journalist.

Nairobi, *n.* the capital of Kenya, in the central highlands at 1660 m/5450 ft; population (1985) 1,100,000. It has light industry and food processing, and is the headquarters of the United Nations Environment Programme (UNEP).

naissant, *a.* (*Her.*) rising or coming forth, as from a fesse or other ordinary. [F, pres.p. of *naître,* ult. from L *nascī,* to be born]

naïve, *a.* artless, ingenuous, simple, unaffected. **naïvely,** *adv.* **naïveté,** *n.* [F, fem. of *naïf,* L *nātīvus,* NATIVE]

naja, *n.* a genus of venomous snakes comprising the Indian and the African cobra. [mod. L from Hind. *nāg*]

Najaf, *n.* a holy city near the Euphrates in Iraq, 144 km/90 miles south of Baghdad.

Najibullah, *n.* **Ahmadzai** (1947–), Afghan communist politician, a member of the Politburo from 1981, and leader of the ruling People's Democratic Party of Afghanistan (PDPA) from 1986, later entitled state president. His attempts to broaden the support of the PDPA regime had little success, but his government survived the following withdrawal of Soviet troops in Feb. 1989.

Nakasone, *n.* **Yasuhiro** (1917–), Japanese conservative politician, leader of the Liberal Democratic Party (LDP) and prime minister (1982–87). He stepped up military spending and increased Japanese participation in international affairs, with closer ties to the US. His reputation was tarnished by his involvement in the Recruit insider-trading scandal.

naked, *a.* destitute of clothing, uncovered, nude; without natural covering, as leaves, hair, shell etc.; not sheathed; exposed, unsheltered, defenceless, unarmed, stripped, destitute, devoid (of); unfurnished; not ornamented; bare, plain, undisguised; unsupported, uncorroborated, unconfirmed; unassisted, as without a telescope (of the eye). **the naked eye,** *n.* the eye unassisted by any optical instrument. †**naked-bed,** *n.* a bed the occupant of which is naked. **naked lady,** *n.* the meadow saffron, *Colchicum autumnale.* **nakedly,** *adv.* **nakedness,** *n.* [OE *nacod* (cp. Dut. *naakt,* G *nackt,* Swed. *naken,* Dan. *nögen*), cogn. with L *nūdus*]

†**naker,** *n.* a kind of kettle-drum. [OF *nacre, nacaire,* Arab. *naqārah*]

Nakhichevan, *n.* autonomous republic in S USSR, bordering Iran, peopled mainly by Azeri Muslims. Although geographically situated within the republic of Armenia, administratively it forms part of Azerbaijan. Nakhichevan has been affected by the Armenia–Azerbaijan conflict; many Azeris have fled to Azerbaijan, and in Jan. 1990 frontier posts and border fences with Iran were destroyed.

Nakuru, Lake, *n.* a salt lake in the Great Rift Valley, Kenya.

NALGO, (*acronym*) National *and* Local Government Officers' Association.

†**namable** NAMEABLE, see NAME.

namby-pamby, *a.* weakly and insipidly sentimental; affectedly pretty or simple. *n.* namby-pamby talk or writing. **namby-pambyism,** *n.* [from *Ambrose* Philips, 1671–1749, a sentimental, pastoral poet]

name, *n.* a word denoting any object of thought, esp. that by which a person, animal, place or thing is known, spoken of or addressed; a mere term as distinct from substance, sound or appearance, as opp. to reality; reputation, honourable character, fame, glory; authority, countenance; †a race, a family; †a noun. *v.t.* to give a name to, to call, to style; to call by name; to nominate, to appoint; to mention, to specify, to cite. **by name,** called. **give it a name,** mention what you will have (to drink, as a present etc.). **in the name of,** by the authority of; in reliance upon (esp. as an invocation); under the designation of. **no names, no pack-drill,** (*coll.*) mention no names, then no-one gets into trouble. **the name of the game,** (*coll.*) the central or important thing; what it is all about. **to call names** CALL[1]. **to name names,** to mention people by name usu. in order to accuse or blame them. **to name the day,** (*coll.*) to fix the date for a wedding. **to take a name in vain,** to use it profanely. **name-child,** *n.* a child or person named after one. **name-day,** *n.* the day sacred to a saint after whom one is named. **name-dropper,** *n.* one who tries to impress by mentioning the names of important or famous people as if they were close friends. **name-drop,** *v.i.* **namesake,** *n.* a person or thing having the same name as or named after another. **nameable,** *a.* **nameless,** *a.* having no name; anonymous; illegitimate, unknown, obscure, inglorious; inexpressible, indefinable; unfit to be named, abominable, detestable. **namelessly,** *adv.* **namely,** *adv.* that is to say. **namer,** *n.* [OE *nama* (cp. Dut. *naam,* G *Name,* Icel. *nafn,* Sansk. *nāman,* L *nōmen,* Gr. *onoma*), whence OE *genamian, nemnan*]

Namib Desert, *n.* a coastal desert region in Namibia, SW Africa. Its sand dunes are amongst the tallest in the world, reaching heights of 370 m/1200 ft.

Namibia, *n.* (formerly South West Africa), a country in SW Africa, bounded on the N by Angola and Zambia, on the E by Botswana and South Africa and on the W by the Atlantic Ocean. **area** 824,300 sq km/318,262 sq miles. **capital** Windhoek. **physical** mainly desert; includes the enclave of Walvis Bay (area 1120 sq km/432 sq miles) currently administered by South Africa. **exports** diamonds, uranium. **population** (1988) 1,288,000 (85% black African, 6% European). There are 300,000 displaced families, 50,000 refugees, and 75,000 in SWAPO camps in exile. **language** Afrikaans, German, English. **religion** 51% Lutheran, 19% Roman Catholic, 6% Dutch Reformed Church, 6% Anglican.

namma hole, *n.* a native well. [Austral. Abor.]

nan, *n.* a type of slightly leavened bread as baked in India or Pakistan. [Hind.]

Nanak, *n.* (1469–*c.* 1539), Indian guru and founder of Sikhism, a religion based on the unity of God and the equality of all human beings. He was strongly opposed to caste divisions.

Nana Sahib, *n.* (popular name for Dandhu Panth) (1820–*c.* 1859), adopted son of a former *peshwa* (chief minister) of the Mahrattas in central India. He joined the rebels in the Indian Mutiny (1857–58), and was responsible for the massacre at Kanpur when safe conducts given to British civilians were broken and many women and children massacred. After the failure of the mutiny he took refuge in Nepal.

Nancarrow, *n.* **Conlon** (1912–), US composer who settled in Mexico in 1940. Using a player-piano as a form of synthesizer, punching the rolls by hand, he experimented with complicated combinations of rhythm and tempo, producing a series of studies that anticipated minimalism and brought him recognition in the 1970s.

Nanchang, *n.* industrial (textiles, glass, porcelain, soap) capital of Jiangxi province, China, about 260 km/160 miles SE of Wuhan; population (1986) 1,120,000.

nancy, *n.* an effeminate young man; a homosexual. [from the girl's name]

nandine, *n.* a small W African cat-like animal. [prob. local name]

nanism, *n.* dwarfishness; being stunted. **nanization,** *n.* [F *nanisme* (L *nānus*, Gr. *nānos*, dwarf)]

Nanjing, *n.* (formerly **Nanking**) capital of Jiangsu province, China, 270 km/165 miles NW of Shanghai; centre of industry (engineering, shipbuilding, oil refining), commerce and communications; population (1986) 2,250,000. The bridge 1968 over the Chang Jiang river is the longest in China at 6705 m/22,000 ft.

nankeen, *n.* a cotton fabric, usu. of a buff or yellow colour, exported from Nankin; a fabric made in imitation of this; (*pl.*) clothes, esp. trousers, made of this. [*Nankin*, capital of province of Kiangsu, China]

nanna, nana, *n.* a child's word for grandmother.

Nanning, *n.* industrial river port, capital of Guangxi autonomous region, China, on the You Jiang; population (1982) 866,000. It was an important supply town during the Vietnam war and the Sino-Vietnamese confrontation 1979.

nanny, *n.* a children's nurse. **nanny-goat,** *n. fem.* a she-goat. [dim. of Anne]

nannygai, *n.* an edible red fish found in Australian rivers. [Austral. Abor.]

nano-, *comb. form.* one thousand millionth, as in **nanogram, nanosecond**. [Gr. *nānos*, a dwarf]

Nansen, *n.* **Fridtjof** (1861–1930), Norwegian explorer and scientist. In 1893, he sailed to the Arctic in the *Fram*, which was deliberately allowed to drift N with an iceflow. Nansen, accompanied by F. J. Johansen, continued N on foot and reached 86° 14′ N, the highest latitude then attained. After World War I, Nansen became League of Nations high commissioner for refugees; Nobel Peace Prize 1923.

Nantes, Edict of, a decree by which Henry IV of France granted religious freedom to the Huguenots (1598). It was revoked 1685 by Louis XIV.

nap[1], *v.i.* to sleep lightly or briefly, to doze; to be careless or unprepared. *n.* a short sleep, a doze, esp. in the day-time. **to catch napping,** to take unawares; to catch unprepared or at a disadvantage. [OE *hnæppian* (cp. OHG *hnaffezan*)]

nap[2], *n.* the smooth and even surface produced on cloth or other fabric by cutting and smoothing the fibre or pile; a smooth, woolly, downy or hairy growth on a surface. *v.t.* to put a nap on. **napless,** *a.* [prob. from MDut. or MLG *noppe* (cp. Dut. *nop,* Dan. *noppe,* Norw. *napp*)]

nap[3], *n.* a card-game in which five cards are dealt to each player, the one engaging to take the highest number of tricks playing against the others; (*Racing*) a tip claimed to be a certainty. **to go nap,** to offer to take all five tricks. [short for NAPOLEON]

nap[4] NAB[1].

napalm, *n.* a highly inflammable petroleum jelly which is produced from naphthalene and coconut palm oil, largely used for bombs.

nape, *n.* the back of the neck. [etym. doubtful]

napery, *n.* linen, esp. table-linen; †linen underclothing. †**naperer,** *n.* [OF *naperie, napperie,* from *nape, nappe,* L *mappa,* NAPKIN]

naphtha, *n.* an inflammable oil produced by dry distillation of organic substances, as bituminous shale or coal. **naphthalic,** *a.* **naphthaline,** *n.* a white crystalline product of the dry distillation of coal-tar, used as a disinfectant and in the manufacture of dyes and explosives. **naphthalize, -ise,** *v.t.* **naphthene,** *n.* a liquid hydrocarbon obtained from Caucasian naphtha. **naphthol,** *n.* either of two phenols derived from naphthaline. [L and Gr.]

Napier, *n.* **John** (1550–1617), Scottish mathematician who invented logarithms (1614), and 'Napier's bones'. **Napier's bones,** *n.pl.* a contrivance invented by Napier for facilitating the multiplication and division of high numbers by means of slips of bone or other material divided into compartments. **Naperian,** *a.*

napiform, *a.* (*Bot.*) turnip-shaped. [L *nāpus*, turnip, -FORM]

napkin, *n.* a small cloth usu. of linen, esp. one used at table to wipe the hands etc., protect the clothes, or serve fish etc., on; a serviette; a baby's nappy; a small towel; a handkerchief. **table-napkin,** *n.* a napkin used to wipe the hands etc. at table, a serviette. **napkin-ring,** *n.* a ring used to enclose a table-napkin and indicate the owner. [ME *nappekyn* (F. *nappe,* see NAPERY)]

Naples[1], *n.* (Italian **Napoli**) industrial port (shipbuilding, cars, textiles, paper, food processing) and capital of Campania, Italy, on the Tyrrhenian Sea; population (1988) 1,201,000. To the south is the Isle of Capri, and behind the city is Mount Vesuvius, with the ruins of Pompeii at its foot.

Naples[2], **Kingdom of,** *n.* the southern part of Italy, alternately independent and united with Sicily in the Kingdom of the Two Sicilies.

napless NAP[2].

Naples yellow, *n.* a yellow pigment made from antimony; the colour of this. [*Naples*, city in S Italy]

napoleon, *n.* a French gold coin of 20 francs issued by Napoleon I; a variety of top-boot; a card-game, see NAP[3].

Napoleon I, *n.* **Bonaparte** (1769–1821), emperor of the French (1804–14) and (1814–15). A general from 1796 in the Revolutionary Wars, in 1799 he overthrew the Directory and made himself dictator. From 1803 he conquered most of Europe, and installed his brothers as puppet kings. After the Peninsular War and retreat from Moscow 1812, he was forced to abdicate, 1814, and was banished to Elba. In Mar. 1815 he reassumed power but was defeated at the Waterloo and exiled to the island of St Helena. His internal administrative reforms are still evident in France.

Napoleon II, *n.* (1811–32), title given by the Bonapartists to the son of Napoleon I and Marie Louise; until 1814 he was known as the king of Rome, and after 1818 as the duke of Reichstadt. After his father's abdication 1814 he was taken to the Austrian court, where he spent the rest of his life.

Napoleon III, *n.* (1808–73), emperor of the French (1852–70), known as **Louis-Napoleon**. After two attempted coups (1836 and 1840) he was jailed and went into exile, returning for the revolution of 1848, when he became president of the Second Republic, but soon turned authoritarian. In 1870 he was manoeuvred by the German chancellor Bismarck into war with Prussia; he was forced to surrender at Sedan, NE France, and the empire collapsed.

Napoleonic, *a.* resembling Napoleon I; dominating,

masterful; spectacular. **Napoleonically,** *adv.* **Napoleonism,** *n.* belief in the hereditary claims of the Napoleonic dynasty; belief in autocracy. **Napoleonist,** *n.* **Napoleonize, -ise,** *v.t.*

Napoleonic Wars, *n.pl.* (1803–15) a series of European wars which followed the Revolutionary Wars.

nappy[1] NAP.

nappy[2], *a.* foaming, strong, heady (of ale or beer). *n.* ale, liquor. [prob. from NAP[1]]

nappy[3] *n.* a square of towelling etc., placed between a baby's legs and kept in place by a fastening at the waist, to absorb urine and faeces. **nappy-rash,** *n.* a rash on a baby's body created by its nappy, especially by ammonia from its urine. [NAPKIN]

narceine, *n.* a bitter crystalline alkaloid contained in opium after the extraction of morphine, also called **narceia**. [F *narcéine,* Gr. *narkē,* numbness, torpor, -INE]

narcissism, *n.* a state of self-love present at an early stage of development when one's own body rather than an outside love-object furnishes sensual gratification. [NARCISSUS].

narcissus, *n.* (*pl.* **-es, -i**) a genus of ornamental bulbous plants, containing the daffodils and jonquils; a plant of this genus, esp. the white *Narcissus poeticus.* [L, from Gr. *Narkissos,* perh. rel. to prec.]

Narcissus, *n.* (*Gr. Myth.*) a beautiful youth, who rejected the love of the nymph Echo, and was condemned to fall in love with his own reflection in a pool. He pined away and in the place where he died a flower sprang up, which was named after him.

narco-, *comb. form.* pertaining to torpor or narcotics. [Gr. *narkē,* torpor]

narcolepsy, *n.* a nervous disease characterized by fits of irresistible drowsiness. [Gr. *-lepsy* (see EPILEPSY)]

narcomania, *n.* an abnormal craving for, or insanity resulting from, narcotics.

narcosis, *n.* narcotic poisoning, the effect of continuous use of narcotics; a state of stupor.

narcotic, *a.* producing torpor or coma; soporific; causing sleep or dullness. *n.* a substance that allays pain by inducing sleep or torpor; any of a group of addictive drugs such as opium and morphine that induce numbness and stupor. **narcotically,** *adv.* **narcoticism,** **narcotism,** *n.* **narcotist,** *n.* **narcotize, -ise,** *v.t.* **narcotization, -isation,** *n.* **narcotherapy,** *n.* the treatment of mental disorder by drug-induced sleep.

nard, *n.* an unguent or balsam used by the ancients, prepared from an aromatic plant, spikenard. †**nardine,** *a.* [F, from L *nardus,* Gr. *nardos,* of Oriental orig. (cp. Heb. *nēr'd,* Sansk. *narada, nalada*)]

nardoo, *n.* an Australian plant, *Marsilea drummondii,* the spore-case of which is pounded and eaten by the Aborigines. [Abor. Austral.]

nares, *n.pl.* the nostrils. [L]

narghile, *n.* a hookah or tobacco-pipe in which the smoke is drawn through water. [Pers. *nārgīleh,* from *nārgīl,* coco-nut]

nark, *n.* (*sl.*) a police spy, a decoy. [Romany *nak,* nose]

Narmada River, *n.* a river that rises in the Maikala range in Madhya Pradesh state, central India and flows 1245 km/778 miles WSW to the Gulf of Khambat, an inlet of the Arabian Sea. Forming the traditional boundary between Hindustan and Deccan, the Narmada is a holy river of the Hindus. India's Narmada Valley Project is one of the largest and most controversial river development projects in the world. Between 1990 and 2040 it is planned to build 30 major dams, 135 medium-sized dams and 3000 smaller dams in a scheme that will involve moving 1 million of the valley's population of 20 million people.

Narodnik, *n.* a member of a secret Russian political movement, active 1873–76 before its suppression by the tsarist authorities. Narodniks were largely university students, and their main purpose was to convert the peasantry to socialism.

narrate, *v.t.* to tell, to relate, to give an account of the successive particulars of in speech or writing. **narration,** *n.* **narrative,** *a.* in the form of narration; relating to an event or story. *n.* a recital of a series of events; a tale, a story. **narratively,** *adv.* **narrator,** *n.* **narratress,** *n. fem.* [L *narrātus,* p.p. of *narrāre* (prob. cogn. with *gnārus,* aware, and Eng. KNOW)]

narrow, *a.* of little breadth or extent from side to side; constricted, limited, restricted, of limited scope; illiberal in views or sentiments; prejudiced, bigoted; selfish, niggardly; straitened, impoverished; close, near, within a small distance, with little margin; precise, accurate. *v.t.* to make narrow or narrower; to contract in range, views or sentiments; to confine, to limit, to restrict. *v.i.* to become narrow or narrower; to take too little ground (said of a horse). *n.* (*usu. pl.*) a strait; a narrow mountain-pass; the contracted part of an ocean current. **a narrow escape,** *n.* an escape only just managed. **a narrow squeak,** *n.* (*coll.*) a narrow escape. **narrow-boat,** *n.* a canal boat. **narrow circumstances,** *n.* poverty. **narrow cloth,** cloth, esp. woollen, under 52 in. (1·3 m) in width. **narrow gauge,** *n.* a railway gauge of less than 4 ft. 8½ in. (1·43 m). **narrow goods,** *n.* braid, ribbons. **narrow-minded,** *a.* illiberal, bigoted. **narrow-mindedness,** *n.* **narrowly,** *adv.* **narrowness,** *n.* [OE *nearu* (cp. Dut. *naar,* dismal)]

Narses, *n.* (*c.* 478–*c.* 573), Byzantine general. Originally a eunuch slave, he later became an official in the imperial treasury. He was joint commander with the Roman general Belisarius in Italy (538–39), and in 552 destroyed the Ostrogoths at Taginae in the Apennines.

narthex, *n.* a vestibule or porch across the west end in early Christian churches, to which catechumens, women and penitents were admitted. [Gr. *narthēx,* a plant]

nartjie, *n.* a small sweet orange like a mandarin. [Afrikaans]

narwhal, *n.* an Arctic delphinoid cetacean, *Monodon monoceros,* with a long tusk (or tusks) developed from one (or both) of its teeth. [Dan. or Swed. *narhval* (cp. Icel. *nāhvalr*)]

nary, (*dial.*) *a.* not one single. [alt. of *ne'er a*]

NASA, the US space exploration authority [acronym for *N*ational *A*eronautics and *S*pace *A*dministration].

nasal, *a.* of or pertaining to the nose; sounded or produced with the nasal passage open; pronounced through or as if through the nose. *n.* a letter or sound produced with the nasal passage open; a nose-guard. **nasality,** *n.* **nasalize, -ise,** *v.t.* **nasalization, -isation,** *n.* **nasally,** *adv.* [F, from med. L *nāsālis* (*nāsus,* nose)]

Nasalis, *n.* the genus comprising *Semnopithecus nasalis,* the proboscis monkey.

nascent, *a.* coming into being; beginning to develop; immature. **nascency,** *n.* [L *nascens -ntis,* pres.p. of *nascī,* to be born]

naseberry, *n.* the sapodilla. [Sp. or Port. *nespera,* L *mespila,* Gr. *mespilē,* MEDLAR]

Naseby, Battle of, decisive battle of the English Civil War, 14 June 1645, when the Royalists led by Prince Rupert were defeated by Oliver Cromwell and Gen. Fairfax. Named after the nearby village of Naseby, 20 km/12 miles NW of Northampton.

Nash[1], *n.* **John** (1752–1835), English architect. He laid out Regent's Park, London, and its approaches. From 1813–1820 he planned Regent Street (later rebuilt), repaired and enlarged Buckingham Palace (for which he designed Marble Arch), and rebuilt Brighton Pavilion in flamboyant oriental style.

Nash[2], *n.* **Ogden** (1902–1971), US poet. He published numerous volumes of humorous verse characterized by its puns, light epigrams and unorthodox rhymes.

Nash[3], *n.* **Paul** (1889–1946), English painter, an official war artist in World Wars I and II. In the 1930s he was one of a group of artists promoting avant-garde styles in the UK. Two of his most celebrated works are *Totes Meer/Dead Sea* (Tate Gallery, London) and *The Battle of Britain* (Imperial War Museum, London).

Nash[4], *n.* **(Richard) 'Beau'** (1674–1762), British dandy. As master of ceremonies at Bath from 1705, he made the town the most fashionable watering-place in England, and introduced a polished code of manners into general use.

Nash[5], *n.* **Walter** (1882–1968), New Zealand Labour politician. He was born in England, and emigrated to New Zealand in 1909. He held ministerial posts (1935–49), was prime minister (1957–60), and leader of the Labour Party until 1963.

Nash(e), *n.* **Thomas** (1567–1601), born in Suffolk, he settled in London about 1588, where he was rapidly drawn into the Martin Marprelate controversy (a pamphleteering attack on the clergy of the Church of England by Puritans), and wrote at least three attacks on the Martinists. Among his later works are the satirical *Pierce Pennilesse* (1592); the religious *Christes Teares over Jerusalem* (1593); and the comedy *Summer's Last Will and Testament* (1592).

Nashville, *n.* port on the Cumberland river and capital of Tennessee, US; population (1986) 931,000. It is a banking and commercial centre, and has large printing, music-publishing, and recording industries.

nasicorn, *a.* having a horn or horns on the nose (as the rhinoceros).

nas(o)-, *comb. form.* pertaining to the nose. [L *nāsus,* nose]

naso-bronchial, *a.* pertaining to or involving the nasal and the bronchial tubes.

naso-frontal, *a.* pertaining to the nose and frontal bone.

naso-labial, *a.* pertaining to the nose and the lips. [LABIAL]

naso-lachrymal, *a.* pertaining to the nose and tears. [LACHRYMAL]

nasorbital, *a.* of or pertaining to the nose and the ocular orbit.

Nassan agreement, *n.* signed 18 Dec. 1962, whereby the US provided Britain with Polaris missiles marking a strengthening in Anglo-American relations.

Nassau, *n.* capital and port of the Bahamas, on New Providence island; population (1980) 135,000. English settlers founded it 1629.

Nasser, *n.* **Gamal Abdel** (1918–1970), Egyptian politician, prime minister (1954–56) and from 1956 president of Egypt (the United Arab Republic, 1958–71). In 1952 he was the driving power behind the Neguib coup, which ended the monarchy. His nationalization of the Suez Canal in 1956 and his ambitions for an Egyptian-led Arab union led to disquiet in the Middle East (and in the West).

nastic, *a.* of movement, not related to the direction of the stimulus. [Gr. *nastos,* close-pressed]

nasturtium, *n.* (*pl.* **-ums**) a genus of Cruciferae containing the watercress; a trailing plant of the genus *Tropaeolum* with vivid orange flowers, also called Indian cress. [L (*nās-us, tort-,* stem of *torquēre,* to TORMENT)]

nasty, *a.* dirty, foul, filthy to a repulsive degree; indecent, obscene; repellent to taste, smell etc., nauseous; objectionable, annoying, vexatious; spiteful, odious, vicious, unpleasant, awkward, trying. **nastily,** *adv.* **nastiness,** *n.* [cp. Dut. *nestig,* Swed. dial. *naskug*]

natal[1], *a.* of, from or pertaining to one's birth. †**natalitial**, *a.* **natality,** *n.* [F, from L *nātālis,* from *nātus,* p.p. of *nascī,* to be born]

†**natal**[2], *a.* pertaining to the buttocks. [NATES]

Natal, *n.* province of South Africa, NE of Cape Province, bounded on the E by the Indian Ocean. **area** 91,785 sq km/35,429 sq miles. **capital** Pietermaritzburg. **towns** Durban. **physical** slopes from the Drakensberg to a fertile subtropical coastal plain. **products** sugar cane, black wattle (*Acacia mollissima*), maize, fruits, vegetables, tobacco, coal. **population** (1985) 2,145,000.

natant, *a.* swimming; (*Bot.*) floating; (*Her.*) applied to fish represented as swimming. †**natantly,** *adv.* **natation,** *n.* **Natatores,** *n.pl.* (*Zool.*) an order of birds containing the gulls, divers, ducks etc. **natatorial, natatory,** *a.* [L *natans -ntem,* pres.p. of *natāre,* freq. of *nāre,* to swim]

Nataraja, *n.* 'Lord of the Dance' in Hinduism, a title of Siva.

natch[1], *n.* the part of an ox between the loins, the rump. [var. of *nache,* see AITCHBONE]

natch[2], *int.* (*sl.*) of course. [short for *naturally*]

Natchez, *n.* a member of a North American Indian people of the Mississippi area, one of the Mound-builder group of peoples. They had a highly developed caste system, headed by a ruler priest (the 'Great Sun'), unusual in North America. This lasted until the near genocide of the Natchez by the French in 1731; only a few survive in Oklahoma.

nates, *n.pl.* the buttocks; the anterior pair of lobes in the brain, connected with the optic tracts. **natiform,** *a.* having the form of buttocks. [L]

†**natheless,** †**nathless** NEVERTHELESS.

nation, *n.* a people under the same government and inhabiting the same country; a people belonging to the same ethnological family and speaking the same language; (*Aberdeen, Glasgow and mediaev. univs.*) a body of students from the same country or district; †a family; a kingdom or country. **nation-wide,** *a.* covering the whole nation. **national,** *a.* of or pertaining to the nation, esp. to the whole nation; public, general, as opp. to local; peculiar to a nation; attached to one's country. *n.* a member or subject of a particular nation; one's fellow-countryman. **National Defence Contribution,** a tax introduced in 1937 to help to finance the cost of rearmament. **National Health Service,** in Britain, the system of state-provided medical service, established 1948. **national anthem,** *n.* a hymn or song embodying the patriotic sentiments of a nation, as the Eng. 'God Save the King', the French 'La Marseillaise' etc. **National Assembly** CONSTITUENT ASSEMBLY. **national grid,** *n.* a country-wide network of high-voltage electric power-lines linking major power-stations; the coordinate system in Ordnance Survey maps. **National Guard,** *n.* a force which took part in the French Revolution, first formed in 1789; organized militia of individual states in the US. **national insurance,** *n.* a system of compulsory insurance paid for weekly by the employer and employee and yielding benefits to the sick, retired or unemployed. **National Park,** *n.* an area owned by the nation and set aside to preserve beauty, wildlife etc. **national service,** *n.* compulsory service in the armed forces. **National Socialism,** *n.* the political doctrine of the National Socialist German Workers' Party, which came into power in Germany under Adolf Hitler in 1933, with prominent among its teachings the superiority of the German race, hatred of Jews and a need for world-expansion. **National Trust,** *n.* an organization in the UK concerned with the preservation of historic buildings and areas of countryside of great beauty. **nationalism,** *n.* devotion to the nation, esp. the whole nation as opp. to sectionalism; nationalization of industry; the policy of national independence, esp. in Ireland; patriotic effort, sentiment etc. **nationality,** †**nationalness,** *n.* **nationalize, -ise,** *v.t.* to make national; to naturalize; to bring (an industry etc) under state control. **nationalization, -isation,** *n.* **nationally,** *adv.* **nationhood,** *n.* [F, from L *nātiōnem,* nom. *-tio,* from *nāt-,* see NATAL[1]]

National Association for the Advancement of Colored People, (NAACP) a US civil-rights organization, dedicated to ending black inequality and segregation through non-violent protest. Founded in 1910, its first aim was to eradicate lynching. The NAACP campaigned to end segregation in state schools; it funded test cases which eventually led to the Supreme Court decision of 1954 outlawing school segregation, although it was only through the Civil Rights movement of the 1960s that de-segregation was achieved. In 1987 it had about 500,000 members, black and white.

National Book League, former name of the BOOK TRUST.

National Country Party, former name for the AUSTRALIAN NATIONAL PARTY.

National Curriculum, *n.* a scheme set up by the UK government in 1987 to establish a single course of study in ten subjects common to all primary and secondary state schools. The national curriculum is divided into three core subjects – English, maths and science – and seven foundation subjects – geography, history, technology, a foreign language (for secondary school pupils), art, music and physical education. There are four key stages, on completion of which the pupil's work is assessed. The stages are for ages 5–7, 7–11, 11–14 and 14–16.

National Dock Labour Scheme, in the UK a scheme that guaranteed continued employment and pay for dockworkers, even if there was no work to be done; some 9000 dockworkers were registered under the scheme, which operated from 1947 until its abolition by the Thatcher government in 1989.

National Economic Development Council, known as '*Neddy*', the UK forum for economic consultation between government, management, and trade unions. Established in 1962, it examines the country's economic and industrial performance, in both the public and private sectors, and seeks agreement on ways to improve efficiency. Its role has diminished under the Thatcher administration.

National Front, *n.* a British extreme right-wing political party founded in 1967. It was formed from a merger of the League of Empire Loyalists and the British National Party. In 1980 dissension arose and splinter groups formed. Electoral support in the 1983 and 1987 general elections was minimal. Some of its members had links with the National Socialist Movement of the 1960s.

National Guard, *n.* a militia force recruited by each state of the US.

National Health Service, UK government medical scheme.

National Insurance Act, an act of Parliament (1911), introduced by Lloyd George, Liberal chancellor, which first provided insurance for workers against ill-health and unemployment.

National Liberal Foundation, the central organization of the British Liberal party, established 1877 in Birmingham. The first president was Joseph Chamberlain.

National Party, Australian, an Australian political party representing the interests of the farmers and people of the smaller towns. It developed from about 1860 as the National Country Party, and holds the power balance between Liberals and Labour. It gained strength following the introduction of proportional representation in 1918, and has been in coalition with the Liberals since 1949.

National Research Development Council, UK corporation exploiting inventions derived from public or private sources, usually jointly with industrial firms. It was set up 1967 under the Development of Inventions Acts 1948–65.

National Rivers Authority, a British environmental agency launched Sept. 1989. It is responsible for managing water resources, investigating pollution controls, and taking over flood controls and land drainage from the former 10 regional water authorities of England and Wales.

National Socialism, *n.* official name for the Nazi movement in Germany.

National Sound Archive, a department of the British Library. It now has over 750,000 disks and over 40,000 hours of tapes, ranging from birdsong to grand opera.

National Theatre, *n.* the British national theatre company established in 1963, and the complex, opened 1976, that houses it on London's South Bank. The national theatre of France is the Comédie Française, founded 1680.

National Trust, *n.* a British trust founded 1895 for the preservation of land and buildings of historic interest or beauty, incorporated by act of Parliament 1907. It is the largest private landowner in Britain. The National Trust for Scotland was established 1931.

native, *a.* pertaining to a place or country by birth, indigenous not exotic; belonging to a person, animal or thing, by nature; inborn, innate, natural not acquired; pertaining to the time or place of one's birth; †rightful, hereditary; natural (to); plain, simple, unaffected; occurring in a pure or uncombined state (of metals); raised in British waters (of oysters); of or pertaining to the natives of a place or region. *n.* one born in a place; a produce of a place or country; a plant or animal indigenous to a district or country; a member of an indigenous people of a country; (*Austral.*) a white born in Australia; (*offensive*) a coloured person; an oyster raised in British waters, esp. in an artificial bed; †natural source. **natively,** *adv.* **nativeness,** *n.* **nativism,** *n.* (*US*) advocacy of the rights of natives as opp. to naturalized Americans; (*Phil.*) the doctrine of innate ideas. [L *nātīvus,* as prec.]

nativity, *n.* birth, esp. that of Jesus Christ, the Virgin or St John the Baptist; a festival in commemoration of this; a picture of the birth of Christ; a horoscope. [as prec.]

NATO, (*abbr.*) North Atlantic Treaty Organization.

natron, *n.* native sesquicarbonate of soda. †**natrium,** *n.* sodium. **natrolite,** *n.* (*Min.*) a hydrated silicate of aluminium containing much soda. [F and Sp., from Arab. *natrūn, nitrūn,* Gr. *nitron,* NITRE]

Natron, Lake, *n.* a salt and soda lake in the Great Rift Valley, Kenya.

natter, *v.i.* (*coll.*) to find fault, to be peevish; to chatter idly; to chat, exchange gossip. *n.* idle chatter; a chat, gossip. **nattered,** *a.* **natteredness,** *n.* [etym. doubtful]

natterjack, *n.* a European toad, *Bufo calamita,* with a yellow stripe down the back. [etym. doutbful]

natty, *a.* (*coll.*) neat, tidy, spruce. **nattily,** *adv.* **nattiness,** *n.* [etym. doubtful]

natural, *a.* of, pertaining to, produced or constituted by nature; innate, inherent, uncultivated, not artificial; inborn, instinctive; in conformity with the ordinary course of nature, normal, not irregular, exceptional or supernatural; pertaining to physical things, animal, not spiritual; true to life; unaffected, not forced or exaggerated; undisguised; ordinary, to be expected, not surprising; coming by nature, easy (to); related by nature only, illegitimate; concerned with nature; concerned with animal life; (*Mus.*) applied to the diatonic scale of c; (*Theol.*) unregenerate. *adv.* naturally. *n.* an idiot; (*Mus.*) a sign cancelling the effect of a preceding sharp or flat; a certainty, something by its very nature certain. **natural childbirth,** *n.* a method of childbirth involving breathing and relaxation exercise with no anaesthetic. **natural death,** *n.* death owing to disease or old age, not violence or accident. **natural gas,** *n.* gas from the earth's crust, specif. a combination of methane and other hydrocarbons used mainly as a fuel and as raw material in industry. **natural history,** *n.* the science or study of animal life, zoology; the study or description of the earth and its productions, loosely applied to botany, zoology, geology and mineralogy. **natural law,** *n.* the sense of right and wrong implanted by nature; a law governing the operations of physical life etc. **natural numbers,** *n.* the whole numbers starting at one upwards. **natural order,** *n.* an order of plants in a system of classification based on the nature of their sexual organs or their natural affinities. **natural philosophy,** *n.* the study of natural phenomena; physics. **natural religion,** *n.* religion not depending upon revelation. **natural resources,** *n.pl.* features or properties of the land such as minerals, water, timber etc. that occur naturally and can be exploited by man. **natural scale,** *n.* a scale without sharps or flats. **natural science,** *n.* the science of physical things as distinguished from mental and moral science; natural history. **natural selection,** *n.* the process by which plants and animals best fitted for the conditions in which they are placed survive and reproduce, while the less fitted leave fewer or no descendants. **natural theology,** *n.* theology based on principles established by reason, not derived from revelation. **naturalness,** *n.* **naturally,** *adv.* according to nature; spontaneously; as might be expected, of course. [L *nātūrālis* (NATURE, -AL)]

Natural Bridge, *n.* a village in Virginia, US, 185 km/

115 miles W of Richmond. The nearby Cedar Creek is straddled by an arch of limestone 66 m/215 ft high and 27 m/90 ft wide.

Natural Environment Research Council, a British organization established by royal charter 1965 to undertake and support research in the earth sciences, to give advice both on exploiting natural resources and on protecting the environment, and to support education and training of scientists in these fields of study. Research areas include geothermal energy, industrial pollution, waste disposal, satellite surveying, acid rain, biotechnology, atmospheric circulation and climate. Research is carried out principally within the UK but also in Antarctica and in many developing countries. It comprises 13 research bodies.

naturalism, *n.* a mere state of nature; condition or action based on natural instincts; a philosophical or theological system that explains the universe as produced and governed entirely by physical laws; strict adherence to nature in literature and art, realism.

naturalist, *n.* one versed in natural history; a believer in naturalism; a realist as distinct from an idealist. **naturalistic**, *a.* in accordance with nature; realistic, not conventional or ideal; of or pertaining to natural history. **naturalistically,** *adv.*

naturalize, -ise, *v.t.* to make natural; to adopt; to acclimatize; to confer the rights and privileges of a natural-born subject on; to explain by natural laws, to free from the miraculous. *v.i.* to become naturalized; to explain phenomena by naturalistic reasoning; to study natural history. **naturalization, -isation,** *n.* [as prec.]

nature, *n.* the essential qualities of anything; the physical or psychical constitution of a person or animal; natural character or disposition; kind, sort, class; the inherent energy or impulse determining these; vital or animal force; the whole sum of things, forces, activities and laws constituting the physical universe; the physical power that produces the phenomena of the material world; this personified; the sum of physical things and forces regarded as distinct from man; the material universe regarded as distinct from the supernatural or from a creator; the natural condition of man preceding social organization; the undomesticated condition of animals or plants; unregenerate condition as opp. to a state of grace; nakedness; fidelity to nature in art. **by nature,** innately. **from nature,** directly from the living model or natural landscape. **in nature,** in actual existence; anywhere, at all; in the sphere of possibility. **state of nature,** nudity. **nature-myth,** *n.* a myth symbolizing some natural phenomenon. **nature-printing,** *n.* a process by which impressions are produced from natural objects such as leaves, feathers etc. on a metal plate from which prints may then be made. **nature-worship,** *n.* worship of natural objects or phenomena or of the powers of nature. **natured,** *a.* (*usu. in comb.* as *ill-natured.*) **naturism,** *n.* nature-worship; naturalism in religion; nudism; belief in the curative work of nature. **naturist,** *n.* **naturistic**, *a.* †**naturize, -ise,** *v.t.* [F, from L *nātūra,* from *nāt-*, p.p. stem of *nascī,* to be born]

Nature Conservancy Council, a British government agency established by act of Parliament 1973 (Nature Conservancy created by royal charter 1949). It is responsible for designating and managing national nature reserves and other conservation areas, advising government ministers on policies, providing advice and information, and commissioning or undertaking relevant scientific research.

naught, *n.* nothing; a cipher. *a.* worthless; †bad, wicked; †lost, ruined. *adv.* in no degree. **to set at naught,** to disregard. [OE *nāwiht* (*nā,* NO, *wiht,* WHIT)]

naughty, *a.* perverse, mischievous; disobedient, ill-behaved; disagreeable; mildly indecent; †worthless; †wicked. **naughtily,** *adv.* **naughtiness,** *n.* [prec.]

Naukratis, *n.* a city of Greek traders in ancient Egypt, in the Nile delta, rediscovered by the British archaeologist William Petrie in 1884.

naumachia, naumachy, *n.* a naval combat, esp. a mock battle shown as a spectacle; an artificial basin for the production of this. [L and Gr. *naumachia* (*naus,* ship, *machē,* a battle)]

nauplius, *n.* (*pl.* **-plii**) a larval stage of development in certain of the lower crustaceans. **nauplial, naupliiform**, **nauplioid**, *a.* [L, from Gr. *Nauplios,* son of Poseidon]

Nauru, *n.* Republic of, an island country in the SW Pacific, in Polynesia, W of Kiribati. **area** 21 sq km/8 sq miles. **capital** Yaren. **physical** island country in W Pacific. **exports** phosphates. **population** (1989) 8,100 (mainly Polynesian; Chinese 8%, European 8%); annual growth rate 3.1%. **language** Nauruan (official), English. **religion** Protestant 45%.

nausea, *n.* a feeling of sickness, with a propensity to vomit; loathing; sea-sickness. †**nauseant,** *a., n.* **nauseate,** *v.i.* to feel nausea; to turn away in disgust (at). *v.t.* to cause to feel nausea; to reject with loathing. **nauseating,** *a.* causing nausea. **nauseation,** *n.* **nauseous,** *a.* causing nausea; disgusting, distasteful. **nauseously,** *adv.* **nauseousness,** *n.* [L, from Gr. *naus,* ship]

nautch, *n.* an E Indian exhibition of dancing by girls. **nautch-girl,** *n. fem.* [Hind. *nach*]

nautical, *a.* pertaining to ships, navigation or sailors; naval. **Nautical Almanac,** *n.* an astronomical ephemeris published in advance, for use by navigators and astronomers. **nautical mile** MILE. **nautically,** *adv.* [L *nauticus,* Gr. *nautikos,* from *nautēs,* sailor, from *naus,* ship]

nautilus, *n.* (*pl.* **-li**) a genus of cephalopods comprising the pearly nautilus, with a many-chambered shell (the outermost and last-formed of which is occupied by the living animal), and the paper nautilus or argonaut; a diving-bell requiring no suspension. **nautilite,** *n.* **nautiloid,** *a., n.* [L, from Gr. *nautilos,* a seaman, as prec.]

Navajo, *n.* a North American Indian people, related to the Apache; population about 200,000. They were defeated by Kit Carson and US troops 1864, and were rounded up and exiled. Their reservation, created 1868, is the largest in the US (65,000 sq km/25,000 sq miles), and is mainly in NE Arizona, but extends into NW New Mexico and SE Utah. They earn an income from uranium, natural gas, tourism, rugs and blankets, and silver and turquoise jewellery. They use sand painting to make temporary altars.

naval, *a.* consisting of or pertaining to ships or a navy; fought or won by war-ships or navies. **navally,** *a.* [F, from L *nāvālis,* from *nāvis,* a ship]

Navarino, Battle of, a decisive naval action, 20 Oct. 1827, off Pylos in the Greek war of liberation that was won by the combined fleets of the English, French and Russians under Vice-Admiral Edward Codrington (1770–1851) over the Turkish and Egyptian fleets. Navarino is the Italian and historic name of Pylos Bay, Greece, on the SW coast of the Peloponnese.

Navarre[1], *n.* (Spanish **Navarra**) autonomous mountain region of N Spain. **area** 10,400 sq km/4,014 sq miles. **capital** Pamplona. **population** (1986) 513,000.

Navarre[2], **Kingdom of,** a former kingdom comprising the Spanish province of Navarre and part of the French *département* of Basses-Pyrénées. It resisted the Moorish conquest, and was independent until it became French (1284) on the marriage of Philip IV to the heiress of Navarre. In 1479 Ferdinand of Aragon annexed Spanish Navarre, with French Navarre going to Catherine of Foix (1483–1512), who kept the royal title. Her grandson became Henry IV of France, and Navarre was absorbed in the French crown lands (1620).

nave[1], *n.* the central block of a wheel in which the axle and spokes are inserted, the hub; †the navel. [OE *nafu* (cp. Dut. *naaf,* G *Nabe,* Icel. *nöf,* Dan. *nav,* Swed. *naf*), cp. NAVEL]

nave[2], *n.* the body of a church, extending from the main doorway to the choir or chancel, distinct, and usually separated by pillars, from the aisles. [L *nāvis,* ship (cp. Gr. *naus*)]

navel, *n.* the cicatrix of the umbilical cord, forming a depression on the surface of the abdomen. **navel**

orange, *n.* a variety of orange with a navel-like depression and a smaller orange enclosed. **navel-string,** *n.* the umbilical cord. **navelwort,** *n.* applied to the marsh pennywort, *Cotyledon umbilicus,* and other plants. [OE *nafela* (cp. Dut. *navel,* G *Nabel,* Icel. *nafli,* Dan. *navle*), cogn. with NAVE[1], cp. Sansk. *nābhīla,* Gr. *omphalos,* L *umbilicus*]

navew, *n.* the wild turnip or rape, *Brassica campestris.* [MF *naveau,* L *nāpellum, -lus,* dim. of *nāpus,* turnip]

navicert, *n.* a certificate authorizing the passage in war-time of approved seaborne merchandise to neutral ports.

navicular, *a.* pertaining to small ships or boats; shaped like a boat; pertaining to the navicular bone. *n.* the navicular bone; inflammation of the navicular bone in horses. **navicular bone,** *n.* the scaphoid bone of the foot or (rarely) the hand. **naviculoid,** *a.* [late L *nāviculāris,* from *nāvicula,* dim. of *nāvis,* ship]

navigate, *v.i.* to sail, to pass from place to place by water or air; to direct and plot the route or position of (a ship, aircraft etc.); to manage a ship; to be in charge of plotting and pointing out a route to the driver of a car. *v.t.* to pass over or up or down, in a ship etc.; to manage, to conduct (a ship, flying-machine etc.). **navigable,** *a.* **navigability,** *n.* **navigableness,** *n.* **navigably,** *adv.* **navigation,** *n.* the act, art or science of navigating; (*prov.*) a canal or waterway. **navigator,** *n.* one who navigates; one skilled in navigation; an explorer by sea; a navvy. [L *nāvigātus,* p.p. of *nāvigāre* (*nāvis,* ship, *agere,* to drive)]

Navigation Acts, *n.pl.* a series of acts passed from 1381 to protect English shipping from foreign competition, and to ensure monopoly trading between Britain and its colonies. The last was repealed 1849. The Navigation Acts helped to establish England as a major sea power. They ruined the Dutch merchant fleet in the 17th cent., and were one of the causes of the War of American Independence.

Navratilova, *n.* **Martina** (1956–), Czechoslovakian tennis player, who became a naturalized US citizen in 1981. The most outstanding woman player of the 1980s, she has 52 Grand Slam victories, including 17 singles titles. She has won the Wimbledon singles title eight times, including six in succession (1982–87).

navvy, *n.* (*pl.* **-vvies**) orig. a labourer employed on making canals; now a labourer in any kind of excavating work, as the construction of railways etc. **steam navvy,** *n.* a mechanical excavator. [short for NAVIGATOR]

navy, *n.* (*poet.*) a fleet; the shipping of a country; the warships of a nation; their officers, men, dockyards etc. **navy blue,** the dark-blue colour used for naval uniforms. **navy-blue,** *a.* **Navy List,** *n.* an official list of naval officers. **navy-yard,** *n.* a naval dockyard. [OF *navie,* L. *nāvis,* ship]

nawab, *n.* an Indian governor or nobleman; a nabob. [Hind. *nawwāb*]

Naxalite, *n.* a member of an Indian extremist communist movement named after the town of Naxalbari, W Bengal, where a peasant rising was suppressed 1967. The movement was founded by Charu Mazumdar (1915–72).

nay, *adv.* no; a word expressing negation or refusal; not only so, not this alone, more than that, and even. *n.* the word 'nay'; a denial, a refusal. *v.t.* to deny, to refuse. *v.i.* to make refusal or denial. †**nayward,** *adv.* †**nayword,** *n.* a byword; a watchword; a refusal. [Icel. *nei* (*ne,* not, *ei,* AYE[1]), cp. Swed. and Dan. *nei*]

Nazarene, *n.* a native or inhabitant of Nazareth; a name applied in reproach to Christ and the early Christians; an early Judaizing sect of Christians. *a.* of or belonging to this sect; of or pertaining to Nazareth. [L *Nazarēnus,* Gr. *Nazarēnos,* from *Nazaret,* Nazareth]

Nazareth, *n.* town in Galilee, N Israel, SE of Haifa; population (1981) 64,000. According to the New Testament, it was the boyhood home of Jesus.

Nazarite, *n.* a Hebrew who had taken certain vows of abstinence set forth in Numbers vi. **Nazaritism,** *n.* [Heb. *nāzar,* to separate oneself, -ITE]

naze, *n.* a promontory, a headland. [OE *næs,* NESS]

Nazi, *n.* a member of the Nazi Party. *a.* pertaining to that party. [abbr. of G *National Sozialist*]

Nazi Party, *n.* German fascist political party. It was formed from the German Workers' Party (founded 1919), and led by Adolf Hitler, 1921–45. The ideology was based on racism, nationalism, and the supremacy of the state over the individual. During the 1930s, many similar parties were created throughout Europe, although only those of Austria and Sudetenland were of any major importance. These parties collaborated with the German occupation of Europe (1939–45). After the Nazi atrocities of World War II, the party was banned in Germany, but there are parties with Nazi or neo-Nazi ideologies in many countries.

nazir, *n.* a native official formerly employed in Anglo-Indian courts; a title of various Muslim officials. [Hind.]

Nazi-Soviet pact HITLER-STALIN PACT.

NB, (*abbr.*) note well. [L *nota bene*]

Nb, (*chem. symbol*) niobium.

NBS, (*abbr.*) National Bureau of Standards, the US Federal standards organization, to whose technical standards all US government procurement is based.

NCB, (*abbr.*) National Coal Board.

NCO, (*abbr.*) Non-Commissioned Officer.

Nd, (*chem. symbol*) neodymium.

N'djamena, *n.* the capital of Chad, at the confluence of the Chari and Logone rivers, on the Cameroon border; population (1985) 511,700.

Ndola, *n.* mining centre and chief city of the Copperbelt province of central Zambia; population (1987) 418,000.

NE, (*abbr.*) North-East.

†**ne,** *adv.* not; never. *conj.* nor. [OE, cp. OHG *ni,* Icel. *nē,* L and Gr. *nē*]

Neagh, Lough, *n.* a lake in Northern Ireland, 25 km/15 miles W of Belfast; area 396 sq km/153 sq miles. It is the largest lake in the British Isles.

nealogy, *n.* the study or description of the early adolescent stages in the development of an animal. [Gr. *neos,* new, -LOGY]

Neanderthal[1], *a.* of a Palaeolithic species of man whose remains were first found in the Neanderthal valley (see below); (*coll.*) extremely old-fashioned, reactionary; (*coll.*) boorish. **Neanderthal man,** *n.* **Neanderthaloid,** *a.*

Neanderthal[2], *n.* a hominid of the Palaeolithic period named from a skeleton found in Neanderthal valley near Dusseldorf, West Germany, in 1956. *Homo sapiens neanderthalensis* lived from about 100,000 to 40,000 years ago and was very similar to present-day people, being slightly smaller, stockier and heavier-featured with prominent brow ridges and a strong jaw. They looked after their disabled and buried their dead carefully. They were replaced throughout Europe by, or possibly interbred with, modern *Homo sapiens sapiens.*

neap, *a.* low or lowest (applied to the tides which happen in the middle of the second and fourth quarters of the moon, when the rise and fall are least). *n.* a neap tide. *v.i.* to diminish towards the neap (of the tides); to reach the flood (of a neap tide); to be left aground by a neap tide (of a vessel). [OE *nēp,* in *nēp flōd,* etym. doubtful]

Neapolitan, *a.* pertaining to or distinctive of Naples or its inhabitants. *n.* an inhabitant of Naples. **Neapolitan ice,** ice-cream made of different ices in distinct layers; a sweetmeat resembling this. **Neapolitan violet,** *n.* a double, sweet-scented viola. [L *Neāpolitānus,* from *Neāpolītēs,* from L and Gr. *Neāpolis,* Naples]

near, *adv.* at or to a short distance, at hand, nigh; not far off, not remote in place, time or degree; nearly, almost; closely; carefully, sparingly, parsimoniously. *prep.* close to in place, time, condition etc. *a.* nigh, close at hand, not distant in place, time or degree; closely resembling, almost; closely related; familiar, intimate; literal, not free or loose (of a likeness, translation etc.); close, narrow; direct, short, straight (of roads etc.); on the left (of horses, parts or sides of vehicles etc.); parsimonious, niggardly. *v.t.* to approach, to draw nigh to. *v.i.* to draw nigh. **a near thing,** a narrow escape. **as near as dammit,** (*coll.*) very nearly. **near-,** *comb. form.* close; almost, as in *near-white.* **near beer,** *n.* comprehensive term for all the malt liquors permitted in US in the era of Prohibition. **nearby,** *adv.* close at hand. **near-miss,** *n.* a miss that is almost a hit. **nearside,** *n., a.* (of) the left side of a horse etc; (of) the side of a vehicle nearer the kerb. **near-sighted,** *a.* short-sighted. **near-sightedness,** *n.* **nearish,** *a.* **nearly,** *adv.* almost; intimately; in a parsimonious manner. **nearness,** *n.* [OE *nēar* (compar. of *nēah,* NIGH), blended with Icel. *nær* (compar. of *nā,* nigh, also used as positive)]

Nearctic, *a.* of or pertaining to the northern (Arctic and temperate) part of North America. [Gr. *neos,* new]

neat[1]**,** *n.* cattle of the bovine kind; an animal of this kind. *a.* pertaining to animals of this kind. **neat-herd,** *n.* a cowherd. **neat-house,** *n.* **neats-foot-oil,** *n.* [OE *nēat* (cp. Icel. *naut,* Swed. *nöt,* Dan. *nōd*), cogn. with *nēotan,* to use, to enjoy]

neat[2]**,** *a.* tidy, trim; simply but becomingly ordered; nicely proportioned, well made; elegantly and concisely phrased; adroit, dexterous, clever; of e.g. alcoholic drink, undiluted, pure; †net. (*N Am.*) excellent, admirable. **neat-handed,** *a.* clever, dexterous, deft. **neatly,** *adv.* **neatness,** *n.* [A-F *neit,* F *net,* L *nitidum,* nom. *-dus,* from *nitēre,* to shine]

'neath *prep.* (*poet.*) beneath. [BENEATH]

NEB, (*abbr.*) New English Bible; National Enterprise Board.

neb, *n.* a beak or bill; a nose or snout; the tip or point of anything; a spout; a nib; (*Sc.*) the face, the mouth. [OE *nebb,* cp. Dut. *nebbe, neb,* Icel. *nef,* Dan. *næb*]

nebbuk, *n.* a thorny shrub, *Zizyphus spina-christi,* supposed to have furnished the thorns for Christ's crown. [Arab. *nebq*]

Nebraska, *n.* a plains state of the central US; nickname Cornhusker State. **area** 200,400 sq km/77,354 sq miles. **capital** Lincoln. **towns** Omaha, Grand Island, North Platte. **products** cereals, livestock, processed foods, fertilizers, oil, natural gas. **population** (1987) 1,594,000.

Nebuchadnezzar, Nebuchadrezzar II, *n.* king of Babylonia from 604 BC. Shortly before his accession he defeated the Egyptians at Carchemish and brought Palestine and Syria into his empire. Judah revolted, with Egyptian assistance, 596 and 587–586 BC; on both occasions he captured Jerusalem and carried many Jews into captivity. He largely rebuilt Babylon and constructed the hanging gardens.

nebula, *n.* (*pl.* **-lae**) a cloudy patch of light in the heavens produced by groups of stars or by a mass of gaseous or stellar matter; a speck on the cornea causing defective vision. **nebular,** *a.* of or pertaining to nebulae. **nebular hypothesis,** *n.* that the bodies composing the solar and stellar systems once existed in the form of nebulae. †**nebule,** *n.* a cloud, a mist; a nebula. **nebulé** NEBULY. **nebulous,** *a.* cloudy; turbid; hazy, vague, indistinct, obscure, uncertain; muddled, bewildered; (*Astron.*) belonging to or resembling a nebula. **nebulosity, nebulousness,** *n.* [L, mist (cp. Gr. *nephelē,* G *Nebel,* Dut. *nevel,* Icel. *nifl*)]

nebulium, *n.* a hypothetical element which was thought to give the lines in the spectra of gaseous nebulae now known to be due to ionized oxygen.

nebuly, *a.* (*Her.*) represented by, shaped in or ornamented with wavy lines; (*Arch.*) undulating (of mouldings). [F *nebulé,* med. L *nebulātus,* p.p. of *nebulāre,* to cloud, as prec.]

necessary, *a.* needful, requisite, indispensable, requiring to be done; such as cannot be avoided, inevitable; happening or existing by necessity; resulting from external causes or determinism; determined by natural laws; not voluntary, not of free will, compulsory; resulting from the constitution of the mind, intuitive, conclusive. *n.* that which is indispensably requisite; (*pl.*) things that are essentially requisite, esp. to life; that which must be as opposed to the contingent; (*sl.*) money; †a privy. **necessarian,** etc. NECESSITARIAN. **necessarily,** *adv.* of necessity; inevitably. †**necessariness,** *n.* **necessitarian,** *n.* one believing in the doctrine that man's will is not free, but that actions and volitions are determined by antecedent causes. **necessitarianism,** *n.* **necessitate,** *v.t.* to make necessary or unavoidable; to constrain, to compel; to entail as an unavoidable condition, result etc. **necessitation,** *n.* **necessity,** *n.* the quality of being necessary; inevitableness; absolute need, indispensability; constraint, compulsion; the compelling force of circumstances, the external conditions that compel one to act in a certain way; that which is necessary, an essential requisite (*often in pl.*); want, poverty. †**necessitied,** *a.* **necessitous,** *a.* needy, destitute, in poverty. †**necessitously,** *adv.* [L *necessārius,* from *necesse,* unavoidable]

neck, *n.* the narrow portion of the body connecting the trunk with the head; this part of an animal used for food; anything resembling this, as an isthmus, a narrow passage or strait; the slender part of a bottle near the mouth; the lower part of a capital; the part of a garment that is close to the neck. *v.t.* (*sl.*) to hug, to fondle. **a stiff neck,** obstinacy, esp. in sin; a disorder of the neck which makes it sore and difficult to move. **neck and crop** CROP. **neck and neck,** equal, very close (in a race). **neck or nothing,** at all risks; desperately. **to get it in the neck,** (*coll.*) to be hard hit; to be reprimanded severely. †**to harden the neck,** to grow obstinate. **neck-band,** *n.* a part of a garment fitting round the neck. **neck-cloth,** *n.* a cravat or neck-tie. **neckerchief,** *n.* a kerchief worn round the neck. **necklace,** *n.* a string of beads or gems worn round the neck; in S Africa, a tyre soaked in petrol, put round a person's neck and set alight in order to kill by burning. *v.t.* in S Africa, to kill a person by means of a burning necklace. **necklaced,** *a.* **necklacing,** *n.* **neck-mould, -moulding,** *n.* a moulding surrounding a column at the junction of the shaft and capital. **neck-tie,** *n.* a strip of silk or other material encircling or worn as if encircling the neck and collar and tied in front. †**neck-verse,** *n.* a Latin verse printed in black-letter placed before a prisoner claiming benefit of clergy, by reading which he might save his neck. **necking,** *n.* the hollow part of a column between the shaft and the capital; (*sl.*) fondling, cuddling. **necklet,** *n.* a small fur boa for the neck; an ornament for the neck. [OE *hnecca* (cp. Dut. *nek,* G *Nacken,* Icel. *nakki*]

Necker, *n.* **Jacques** (1732–1804), French politician. As finance minister (1776–81), he attempted reforms, and was dismissed through Queen Marie Antoinette's influence. Recalled 1788, he persuaded Louis XVI to summon the States General (parliament), which earned him the hatred of the court, and in July 1789 he was banished. The outbreak of the French Revolution with the storming of the Bastille forced his reinstatement, but he resigned, Sept. 1790.

necro-, *comb. form.* pertaining to dead bodies or the dead. [Gr. *nekros,* a dead body]

necrobiosis, *n.* decay of living tissue, as in old age. **necrobiotic,** *a.* [Gr. *bios,* life]

necrogenic, *a.* of or derived from contact with dead bodies.

necrolatry, *n.* worship of the dead, esp. ancestors.

necrology, *n.* a register of deaths, a death-roll; an account of the dead. **necrological,** *a.* **necrologist,** *n.*

necromancy, *n.* the art of revealing future events by communication with the dead; enchantment, magic. **necromancer,** *n.* **necromantic,** *a.* †**necromantically,** *adv.* [ME and OF *nigromancie,* med L *nigromantia,* L *necromantia,* Gr. *nekromanteia,* -MANCY]

necron, *n.* dead plant material not yet rotted into humus.

necronite, *n.* a variety of orthoclase emitting a fetid odour when struck.

necrophagous, *a.* eating or feeding on carrion.

necrophilia, *n.* an obsession with, and usu. an erotic interest in, corpses. **necrophiliac,** *a.*

necrophobia, *n.* revulsion from or fear of anything to do with the dead. **necrophobic,** *a.*

necropolis, *n.* a cemetery, esp. one on a large scale. [Gr.]

necropsy, *n.* an examination of a dead body, an autopsy; a post-mortem examination. **necroscopy,** *n.* necropsy. **necroscopic,** *a.* [Gr. *opsis,* sight]

necrosis, *n.* the mortification of part of the body, esp. of bone. **necrotic,** *a.* **necrotize, -ise,** *v.i.*

nectar, *n.* the drink of the gods; any delicious drink; the honey or sweet fluid secretion of plants. **nectarean,** †**-eal, nectareous, nectarous,** *a.* **nectared,** *a.* imbued or filled with nectar. **nectarial,** *a.* of the nature of a nectary. **nectariferous,** *a.* **nectarine,** *a.* nectarean. *n.* a smooth-skinned and firm variety of the peach. **nectary,** *n.* the organ or part of a plant or flower secreting honey. [L, from Gr. *nektar,* etym. doubtful]

nectocalyx, *n.* (*pl.* **-lyces**) the bell-shaped swimming-organ in the Hydrozoa. **nectocalycine,** *a.* [Gr. *nēktos,* swimming, from *nēchein,* to swim]

NEDC, (*abbr.*) National Economic Development Council (also known as **Neddy**).

Neddy[1], *n.* a donkey; (**neddy**) a fool. [fam. form of *Edward*]

Neddy[2] NEDC.

née, *a.* born (used with the maiden name of a married woman as in *neé Smith*). [F, fem. p.p. of *naître,* to be born]

need, *n.* a state of urgently requiring something; lack of something; a state requiring relief, urgent want; indigence, destitution; a difficult, critical or perilous situation; emergency; that which is wanted, requirement. *v.i.* (*3rd sing.* **need** or **needs**) to be wanting or necessary, to require, to be bound, to be under necessity or obligation to; to be in want. *v.t.* to be in want of, to require. **in need,** poor or in distress. **needfire,** *n.* a fire produced by friction, from dry wood; a signal-fire. †**needer,** *n.* **needful,** *a.* **the needful,** (*coll.*) that which is required, esp. money. **needfully,** *adv.* **needfulness,** *n.* **needless,** *a.* unnecessary, not required; useless, superfluous; †not in want. **needlessly,** *adv.* **needlessness,** *n.* †**needly,** *adv.* **needs,** *adv.* of necessity, necessarily, indispensably (*usu. with* must). **needy,** *a.* in need; necessitous, indigent; †needful. **needily,** *adv.* †**neediness,** *n.* [OE *nied, nēad, nēod* (cp. Dut. *nood,* G *noth,* Icel. *nauth*), whence *nēadian,* to need]

Needham, *n.* **Joseph** (1900–), British biochemist and sinologist known for his work on the history of Chinese science. He worked first as a biochemist concentrating mainly on problems in embryology. In the 1930s he learnt Chinese and began to collect material. The first volume of his *Science and civilisation in China* was published in 1954 and by 1989 15 volumes had appeared.

needle, *n.* a small, thin, rod-shaped, pointed steel instrument with an eye for carrying a thread, used in sewing; analogous instruments of metal, bone, wood etc., used in knitting, crocheting etc.; a piece of magnetized steel used as indicator in a mariner's compass, a telegraphic receiver etc.; applied to pointed instruments used in surgery, assaying, etching etc., and in machinery, firearms etc.; a beam, esp. one used as a temporary support in underpinning etc.; a pointed peak or pinnacle of rock; an obelisk; a needle-like leaf of a pine-tree; a needle-shaped crystal; a pointed piece of metal, fibre etc., used to receive or transmit the vibrations in the groove of a revolving gramophone record. *v.t.* to make or sew with the needle; to work upon with the needle; to penetrate; to thread (one's way) through or between; to shore up or underpin with needle-beams. *v.i.* to form needle-like crystals; to thread one's way; to work with the needle; (*coll.*) to irritate; to force into action. **look for a needle in a haystack,** to engage in a hopeless search. **needle-bath,** *n.* a variety of shower-bath in which the water is emitted in thin needle-like jets. **needle-beam,** *n.* a cross-beam in the flooring of a bridge etc. **needle-book, -case,** *n.* a case, usu. with flannel leaves, for sticking needles in. **needle-cord,** *n.* a cotton material with closer ribs and flatter pile than corduroy. **needle-exchange,** *n.* a place where drug addicts may exchange their used hypodermic needles for new. **needle-fish,** *n.* a long, slender fish of the family Belonidae. **needle-gun,** *n.* a breech-loading gun in which a cartridge is exploded by the prick of a needle. **needle-lace,** *n.* lace made with needles, not with bobbins. **needle-point,** *n.* any fine sharp point; point-lace. **needle-woman,** *n.* a seamstress. **needlework,** *n.* **needleful,** *n.* **needly,** *a.* [AS *nædl* (cp. Dut. *neald,* G *Nadel,* Icel. *nāl,* Dan. *naal*), prob. cogn. with Gr. *neein,* L *nēre,* to spin]

needless etc. NEED.

neep, *n.* (*Sc.*) a turnip. [OE *næp,* L *nāpus*]

ne'er, *adv.* (*poet.*) never. **n'er-do-well,** *a.* good for nothing. *n.* a good-for-nothing. [contr. of NEVER]

†**neeze,** *v.i.* to sneeze. *n.* a sneeze. [prob. from Icel. *hnōjsa* (cp. Dan. *nyse,* Dut. *niezen,* G *niesen*)]

nef, *n.* an ornamental piece of plate shaped like a boat or ship formerly used for holding the salt-cellars, table-napkins etc. of persons of great distinction; an incense-boat; a sanctuary lamp in the shape of a ship; †the nave of a church. [F, ship]

nefandous, *a.* unspeakable, atrocious. [L *nefandus* (*ne,* not, *fandus,* ger. of *fārī,* to speak)]

nefarious, *a.* wicked, abominable, infamous. **nefariously,** *adv.* **nefariousness,** *n.* [L *nefārius,* from *nefas* (*ne,* not, *fas,* right, divine justice)]

Nefertiti, Nofretète, *n.* (14th cent. BC), queen of Egypt, who ruled *c.* 1372–1350 BC. She was the wife of the pharoah Ikhnaton.

neg., (*abbr.*) negative.

negate, *v.t.* to render negative, to nullify; to be the negation of; to deny, to affirm the non-existence of. **negation,** *n.* denial; a declaration of falsity; refusal, contradiction; the absence or the opposite of certain qualities, nullity, voidness; (*Log.*) negative statement, affirmation of absence or exclusion. **negationist,** *n.* one who denies, esp. one who holds merely negative views in religion. **negative,** *a.* containing, declaring or implying negation; denying, contradicting, prohibiting, refusing; lacking positive qualities such as optimism or enthusiasm; (*Log.*) denoting difference or discrepancy; denoting the opposite to positive, denoting that which is to be subtracted (expressed by the minus sign −); denoting the kind of electricity produced by friction on resin, opp. to positive, produced on glass; showing the lights dark and the shadows light. *n.* a proposition, reply, word etc., expressing negation; the right of veto; a veto; the side of a question that denies; a negative quality, lack or absence of something; an image or plate bearing an image in which the lights and shades of the object are reversed; negative electricity, or the negative plates in a voltaic cell; a negative or minus sign or quantity. *v.t.* to veto, to reject, to refuse to accept, sanction or enact; to reprove; to contradict; to reverse (a positive statement or sentence); to neutralize. **in the negative,** indicating dissent or refusal. **negative feed-back,** *n.* interconnexion of input and output terminals of an amplifier in such a manner that the output opposes the input. This decreases the gain but increases the stability and the fidelity of the amplifier. **negative pole,** *n.* the pole of a freely swinging magnet that swings to the south. **negative quantity,** *n.* a minus quantity, nothing. **negatively,** *adv.* **negativeness, negativity,** *n.* **negativism,** *n.* the quality of being negative; the doctrine of a negationist. **negativist,** *n.* **negatory,** *a.* [from L *negāre,* to deny]

Negev, *n.* a desert in S Israel which tapers to the port of Eilat. It is fertile under irrigation, and minerals include oil and copper.

neglect, *v.t.* to treat carelessly; to slight, to disregard; to pass over; to leave undone; to omit (to do or doing). *n.* disregard (of); omission to do anything that should be done; carelessness, negligence; the state of being neglected. †**neglectable** NEGLIGIBLE. †**neglectedness,** *n.* **neglecter, -or,** *n.* **neglectful,** *a.* **neglectfully,** *adv.* **neglectfulness,** *n.* †**neglectingly,** *adv.* **neglection,** *n.* [L *neglectus,* p.p. of *negligere* (*neg-,*

not, *legere,* to pick up)]
negligé, *n.* a state of undress or free-and-easy attire. **negligée,** *n.* a lady's loose gown worn in the 18th cent., a woman's loose dressing gown of flimsy material; a long necklace of irregular beads or coral. [F]
negligence, negligency, *n.* disregard of appearances, conventions etc., in conduct, literature etc.; (*Law*) failure to exercise proper care and precaution. **negligent,** *a.* careless, neglectful. **negligently,** *adv.* **negligible,** *a.* that can be ignored, not worth notice.
negotiate, *v.i.* to treat (with another) in order to make a bargain, agreement, compromise etc.; to traffic. *v.t.* to arrange, bring about or procure by negotiating; to carry on negotiations concerning; to transfer (a bill, note etc.) for value received; to obtain or give value for; to accomplish, to get over successfully. **negotiable,** *a.* **negotiability,** *n.* **negotiant,** *n.* a negotiator; †a merchant, a trader. **negotiation,** *n.* **negotiator,** *n.* **negotiatory,** *a.* **negotiatress, -trix,** *n. fem.* [L *negōtiātus,* p.p. of *negōtiārī,* from *negōtium,* business (*neg-,* not, *ōtium,* leisure)]
Negress NEGRO.
Negrilo, *n.* one of a black people of small stature in central and southern Africa. **Negrito,** *n.* one of a black people in some islands of the Malay Archipelago etc. **Negriloid,** *a.* [Sp., dim. of NEGRO]
Negro, *n.* (*pl.* **-oes,** *fem.* **Negress**) a person belonging to, or descended from, one of the black-skinned African peoples. *a.* of or pertaining to these peoples; black or dark-skinned. **negro-corn,** *n.* Indian millet, durra. **Negro-head,** *n.* strong, black, plug tobacco soaked in molasses. **Negroid, negroidal,** *a.* of Negro type; having the physical characteristics associated with the Negro peoples. [Sp. from L *nigrum,* nom. *niger,* black]
negus¹, *n.* a beverage of wine, hot water, sugar and spices. [Col. Francis *Negus,* d. 1732, its inventor]
negus², *n.* the sovereign of Ethiopia. [Amharic]
Nehemiah, *n.* (5th cent. BC), Jewish governor of Judaea under Persian rule. He rebuilt Jerusalem's walls 444 BC, and made religious and social reforms.
Nehru, *n.* **Jawaharlal** (1889–1964), Indian nationalist politician, prime minister from 1947. Before partition he led the socialist wing of the Congress Party, and was second in influence only to Mahatma Gandhi. He was imprisoned nine times (1921–45) for political activities. As prime minister from the creation of the dominion (later republic) of India Aug. 1947, he originated the idea of nonalignment. His daughter was Indira Gandhi. He was born in Allahabad and educated at a UK public school and Cambridge University.
neigh, *v.i.* to utter the cry of a horse; to whinny. *n.* the cry of a horse. [OE *hnægan* (cp. LG *neigen,* MHG *nêgen*), imit. in orig.]
neighbour, *n.* one who lives near, one in the same street, village, community etc.; a person or thing standing or happening to be next or near another; one having the claims of a fellow-man etc.; (*fig.*) an inhabitant of an adjoining town, district or country; †a confidant. *a.* near, adjoining, neighbouring. *v.t.* to adjoin; to lie near to; †to associate with familiarly. *v.i.* to border (upon). **neighbourhood,** *n.* the state of being neighbours; neighbourliness; the locality round or near; the vicinity; nearness; (*collect.*) those who live near, neighbours. **in the neighbourhood of,** approximately. **neighbouring,** *a.* situated or living near. **neighbourly,** *a., adv.* **neighbourliness,** *n.* **neighbourless,** *a.* **neighbourship,** *n.* [OE *nēahgebūr* (NIGH, BOOR)]
neinei, *n.* an ornamental shrub found in New Zealand. [Maori]
neither, *a.* not either. *pron.* not the one nor the other. *conj.* not either, not on the one hand (usu. preceding one of two alternatives and correlative with *nor* preceding the other); nor, nor yet. *adv.* (*coll., at end of sentence*) either, any more than another person or thing. [OE *nawther, nāhwæther* (*nā,* not, WHETHER), assim. to EITHER]
Nekrasov, *n.* **Nikolai Alekseevich** (1821–77), Russian poet and publisher. He espoused the cause of the freeing of the serfs, and identified himself with the peasants in such poems as 'Who Can Live Happy in Russia?' (1876).
nekton, *n.* term for all forms of organic life found in various depths of salt and fresh water. [Gr. *nēchein,* to swim]
nelli, *n.* a large petrel, *Ossifraga gigantea.* [prob. *Nelly,* fam. form of *Ellen*]
nelly, nellie, *n.* **not on your nelly,** *int.* (*sl.*) not likely, certainly not. [perh. from *not on your Nelly Duff* with Duff being rhyming slang for puff meaning life]
nelson, *n.* (**full nelson**) a wrestling hold in which the arms are passed under both the opponent's arms from behind, and the hands joined so that pressure can be exerted with the palms on the back of his neck. **half nelson,** *n.* such a hold applied from one side only. [from the proper name]
Nelson¹, *n.* **Azumah** (1958–), Ghanaian featherweight boxer, world champion from 1984.
Nelson², *n.* **Horatio, Viscount Nelson** (1758–1805), English admiral. He joined the navy, 1770. In the Revolutionary Wars against France he lost the sight in his right eye (1794), and his right arm (1797). He became a national hero, and rear-admiral, after the victory off Cape St Vincent, Portugal. In 1798 he tracked the French fleet to Aboukir Bay, and almost entirely destroyed it in the Battle of the Nile. In 1801 he won a decisive victory over Denmark at Copenhagen, and in 1805, after two years of blockading Toulon, another over the Franco-Spanish fleet at Trafalgar, near Gibraltar.
nelumbo, nelumbium, *n.* a genus of water-beans belonging to the family Nymphaeaceae, comprising *Nelumbo speciosum,* the sacred lotus. [Sinhalese *nelumbu*]
nemalite, *n.* the fibrous variety of brucite, or native hydrate of magnesium. [Gr. *nema,* a thread; *lithos,* a stone]
nemathecium, *n.* a wart-like elevation on the thallus of certain algae containing tetraspores or other generative bodies. **nemathecial,** *a.* [mod. L (Gr. *nēma,* thread, *thēkē,* box)]
nemathelminth, *n.* (*Zool.*) a thread-worm or nematode. **nemathelminthic,** *a.* [*nēma matos,* as foll., *helmins -nthos,* worm]
nemato-, *comb. form.* thread-like; filamentous. [Gr. *nēma nēmatos,* thread]
nematocerous, *a.* having filiform antennae. [Gr. *keras,* horn]
nematocide, *a.* a substance that destroys nematodes.
nematocyst, *n.* a thread-cell in jelly-fish and other coelenterates from which the stinging thread is projected.
nematode, nematoid, *a.* thread-like; pertaining to the Nematoidea, a class of worms comprising the parasitic round-worm, thread-worm etc. *n.* a nematode worm.
Nembutal®, *n.* proprietary name for sodium ethyl methylbutyl barbiturate, used as a sedative, hypnotic and anti-spasmodic.
nem. con., (*abbr.*) NEMINE CONTRADICENTE.
Nemean, *a.* of or pertaining to Nemea. **Nemean games,** *n.pl.* one of the great Hellenic festivals held at Nemea in the second and fourth of each Olympiad. [L *Nemeæus, Nemæus, Nemeus,* Gr. *Nemeæos, Nemeios, Nemeos,* from *Nemea,* in Argolis]
Nemerov, *n.* **Howard** (1920–), US poet, critic, and novelist. He published his poetry collection *Guide to the Ruins* (1950), a short story collection *A Commodity of Dreams* (1959), and in 1977 his *Collected Poems* won both the National Book Award and the Pulitzer Prize.
nemertean, -tine, *a.* belonging to the Nemertea, a division of flat- or ribbon-worms, chiefly marine. *n.* a worm of this class. [Gr. *Nēmertēs,* a sea-nymph]
Nemesis, *n.* the Greek goddess of retribution; retributive justice. [Gr., from *nemein,* to allot]
nemine contradicente, without opposition; no-one speaking in opposition (often abbr. nem. con.). [L]
nemocerous, *a.* belonging to the Nemocera, an order of dipterous insects, with filamentous antennae. **ne-**

moceran, *a., n.* [Gr. *nēma,* thread, *keras,* horn]
nemophila, *n.* an annual trailing plant with blue and white flowers. [Gr. *nemos,* a glade, wooded pasture, *phileein,* to love]
†**nemoral,** *a.* pertaining to a wood. †**nemorous,** *a.* [L *nemorālis,* from *nemus,* grove]
Nennius, *n.* (*c.* 800), Welsh historian, believed to be the author of a Latin *Historia Britonum*, which contains the earliest reference to King Arthur's wars against the Saxons.
nenuphar, *n.* the white water-lily, *Nymphaea alba.* [F, from Pers. *nīnūfar,* Sansk. *nīlōtpala* (*nīla,* blue, *utpala,* lotus)]
neo-, *comb. form.* new, recent, modern, later, fresh. [Gr. *neos*]
neo-Catholic, *a.* of or pertaining to the Puseyite school in the Church of England, or to the school of Liberal Catholicism headed by Lamennais and Lacordaire in the Church of France.
neo-Christian, *a.* of or pertaining to neo-Christianity or rationalism.
neo-classicism, *n.* movement in art and architecture in Europe and North America about 1750–1850, a revival of classical art, which superseded the Rococo style. It was partly inspired by the excavation of the Roman cities of Pompeii and Herculaneum. The architect Piranesi was an early neo-classicist; in sculpture Canova and in painting David were exponents. **neo-classic, -ical,** *a.* **neo-classicist,** *n.*
neocolonialism, *n.* the policy of a strong nation gaining control over a weaker through economic pressure etc.
Neocomian, *a.* of or pertaining to the lower division of the Cretaceous strata typically exhibited near Neuchâtel in Switzerland. [F *Néocomien,* from *Neocomium* (NEO-, Gr. *kōmē,* village), latinized from *Neuchâtel*]
neocosmic, *a.* pertaining to the later or existing stage of development of the universe; pertaining to mankind in the historical period.
neocracy, *n.* government by new or upstart persons.
neo-Darwinism, *n.* Darwinism as modified by later investigators, esp. those who accept the theory of natural selection but not that of the inheritance of acquired characters. **neo-Darwinian,** *a., n.*
neodox, *a.* holding new views. **neodoxy,** *n.*
neodymium, *n.* a metallic element, at. no. 60; chem. symbol Nd; of the cerium group of rare earth elements. [Gr. *neos,* new, *didymos,* twins]
neofascism, *n.* a movement attempting to reinstate the policies of fascism. **neofascist,** *n.*
†**neogamist,** *n.* a person who has recently married. [Gr. *neogamos,* from *gamos,* marriage]
neo-Gothic, *n., a.* the Gothic revival of the mid-19th cent., or pertaining to this.
neogrammarian, *n.* one of a modern school of grammarians who insist upon the invariability of the laws governing phonetic change. **neogrammatical,** *a.*
neo-Hellenism, *n.* the revival of Greek ideals in art and literature, as in the Italian Renaissance.
neo-impressionism, *n.* a movement in French painting in the 1880s, an extension of the impressionists' technique of placing small strokes of different colour side by side. Seurat was the chief exponent; his minute technique became known as **pointillism**. Signac and Pissarro practised the same style for a few years.
neo-Kantian, *a.* pertaining to the teaching of Kant as modified by recent interpreters. *n.* an adherent of neo-Kantianism. **neo-Kantianism,** *n.*
neo-Lamarckian, *a.* the teaching of Lamarck on organic evolution as revived in a modified form by those who believe in the inheritance of acquired characters.
neolite, *n.* a dark-green hydrous silicate of aluminium and magnesium.
Neolithic, *n., a.* (pertaining to the) last period of the Stone Age, characterized by developed communities based on agriculture, and identified by sophisticated stone tools. In W Asia the earliest neolithic communities appeared about 9,000 BC. In Europe farming began in about 6,500 BC in the Balkans and Aegean. **neolith,** *n.* a weapon, implement or person belonging to this period. [Gr. *lithos,* stone]
neology, *n.* the introduction or use of new words; a neologism; the adoption of or the tendency towards rationalistic views in theology. **neologian,** *a., n.* **neological,** *a.* **neologically,** *adv.* **neologism,** *n.* a new word or phrase, or a new sense for an old one; the use of new words; neology. **neologist,** *n.* **neologistic,** *a.* **neologize, -ise,** *v.i.* [F *néologie*]
neomycin, *n.* an antibiotic effective against some infections that resist ordinary antibiotics. [Gr. *mykes,* fungus]
neon, *n.* a gaseous element, at. no. 10; chem. symbol Ne; existing in minute quantities in the air, isolated from argon in 1898. **neon lamp,** *n.* a lamp possessing two electrodes and containing an atmosphere of rarefied neon gas. [neut. of Gr. *neos,* new]
neonatal, *a.* pertaining to the first few weeks of life in human babies. **neonate,** *n.* a baby at this stage in its development.
neonomous, *a.* modified in accordance with recent conditions of environment. [NEO-, *nomos,* law]
neontology, *n.* the study of living as distinguished from extinct species.
neo-paganism, *n.* a revived form of paganism. **neo-pagan,** *n., a.* **neo-paganize, -ise,** *v.t.* **neophron,** *n.* the white Egyptian vulture. [Gr.]
neophyte, *n.* one newly converted or newly baptized; one newly admitted to a monastery or to the priesthood; a beginner, a novice, a tyro. *a.* newly entered. **neophytic,** *a.* **neophytism,** *n.* [late L *neophytus,* Gr. *neophutos* (*phutos,* grown, from *phuein,* to plant)]
neoplasm, *n.* an abnormal growth of new tissue in some part of the body, a cancer. [Gr. *plasma,* from *plassein,* to form]
neoplasty, *n.* restoration of a part by granulation, adhesive inflammation etc. **neoplastic,** *a.*
Neoplatonism, *n.* a system of philosophy combining the Platonic ideas with the theosophy of the East, originating in Alexandria in the 3rd cent. AD. **Neoplatonic,** *a.* **Neoplatonist,** *n.*
Neo-Realism, *n.* a movement in Italian cinema that emerged in the 1940s. It is characterized by its naturalism, its social themes, and the visual authenticity achieved through location filming. Exponents included the directors de Sica, Visconti and Rossellini.
neoteric, *a.* new; of recent origin. *n.* one of modern times. **neoterically,** *adv.* **neoterism,** *n.* **neoterist,** *n.* **neoterize, -ise,** *v.t.* [Gr. *neoteros,* newer]
neotropical, *a.* of, pertaining to or characteristic of tropical and S America.
Neozoic, *a.* belonging to the later or post-Palaeozoic period, including both Mesozoic and Cainozoic, or corresponding to Cainozoic.
nep, *n.* a bunch or knot in cotton-fibre. [etym. doubtful]
Nepal, *n.* (*Sri Nepala Sarkar*), a landlocked country in the Himalayan mountain range, bounded to the N by Tibet, to the E by Sikkim, and to the S and W by India. **area** 147,181 sq km/56,812 sq miles. **capital** Katmandu. **physical** descends from the Himalaya mountain range in the north to the river Ganges plain in the south. **exports** jute, rice, timber. **population** (1989) 18,760,000 (mainly known by the name of the predominant clan, the Gurkhas; the Sherpas are a Buddhist minority of NE Nepal); annual growth rate 2.3%. **language** Nepali. **religion** Hindu, with Buddhist minority.
nepenthe, -thes, *n.* a drug or potion that drives away sorrow or grief; a drug that relieves pain; a genus of plants containing the pitcher plant. [L and Gr. *nēpenthes* (*nē-,* not, *penthos,* grief)]
nephalism, *n.* total abstinence from intoxicants, teetotalism. [late Gr. *nēphalismos,* from *nēphalios,* sober]
nepheline, -lite, *n.* a vitreous silicate of aluminium and sodium found in volcanic rocks. [F *nephéline,* as foll.]
nephel(o)-, *comb. form.* pertaining to clouds. [Gr. *nephelē,* cloud]
nepheloid, *a.* clouded, turbid.
nephelology *n.* the scientific study of clouds. [-LOGY]

nephelometer, *n.* an instrument for measuring cloudiness esp. in liquids.
nephelosphere, *n.* an atmosphere of cloud enveloping a planet or other heavenly body.
nephew, *n.* the son of a brother or sister; extended to the son of a brother- or sister-in-law, also to a grandnephew; †(*euphem.*) an illegitimate son; †a descendant, a cousin. [OF *neveu,* L *nepōtem,* nom. *-pos,* grandson, nephew (cp. OE *nefa,* Dut. *neef,* G *Neffe*)]
nephoscope, *n.* an instrument for observing the elevation, direction and velocity of clouds.
nephralgia, *n.* pain or disease in the kidneys. [NEPHR(O)-, *-algia,* from *algos,* pain]
nephrectomy, *n.* removal of a kidney by surgical means.
nephr(i)- *comb. form.* pertaining to the kidney. [NEPHR(O)-]
nephric, *a.* pertaining to the kidney.
nephrite, *n.* jade, formerly believed to cure kidney-disease. [Gr. *nephrit*]
nephritic, †-ical, *a.* pertaining to the kidneys; suffering from kidney disease; relieving disorders of the kidney. *n.* a medicine for relieving kidney diseases. **nephritis,** *n.* a disease or disorder of the kidneys.
nephr(o)-, *comb. form.* pertaining to the kidneys. [Gr. *nephros,* kidney]
nephrocele, *n.* hernia of the kidneys. [-CELE]
nephroid, *a.* pertaining to the kidneys.
nephrology, *n.* the study of the kidneys.
nephrotomy, *n.* incision of the kidney, esp. for the extraction of a stone. [-TOMY]
ne plus ultra, the most perfect or uttermost point. [L]
nepotism, *n.* favouritism (as in bestowing patronage) towards one's relations (originally applied to the patronage of a Pope's illegitimate sons, euphem. called 'nephews'). **neopotal,** *a.* **nepotic,** *a.* **nepotist,** *n.* [It. *nepotismo* (*nepote,* see NEPHEW, -ISM)]
Neptune[1], *n.* the Roman god of the sea; (*fig.*) the sea; one of the sun's planets. **Neptunian,** *a.* pertaining to Neptune or the sea; deposited by the sea or produced by the agency of water. *n.* a Neptunist. **Neptunist,** *n.* one asserting the aqueous origin of certain rocks. **neptunium,** *n.* a radio-active element, at. no. 93, chem. symbol Np, obtained by the bombardment of uranium with neutrons. [L *Neptūnus*]
Neptune[2], *n.* in astronomy, the eighth planet in average distance from the Sun. Neptune orbits the Sun every 164.8 years at an average distance of 4,497,000,000 km/2,794,000,000 miles. It is a giant gas (hydrogen, helium, methane) planet with a diameter of 48,600 km/30,200 miles and a mass 17.2 times that of Earth. It has three narrow rings enclosed in a disk of dust which may reach down to the Neptunian cloud tops. Its rotation period is 16 hours 3 minutes. Neptune has two named moons (Nereid and Triton), and six more discovered by Voyager 2 probes.
NERC, (*abbr.*) Natural Environment Research Council.
nerd, *n.* (*sl.*) an ineffectual person, a fool. **nerdish,** *a.* [etym. doubtful]
nereid, *n.* (*pl.* **-ids**) a sea-nymph; a sea-worm or marine centipede of the genus *Nereis.* **nereidian,** *a., n.* **nereidous,** *a.* [L and Gr. *Nēreid-,* stem of *Nēreis,* daughter of Nereus, a sea-god]
Nergal, *n.* the Babylonian god of the sun, war and pestilence, ruler of the underworld, symbolized by a winged lion.
nerine, *n.* a S African amaryllid genus with scarlet or rose coloured flowers, including the Guernsey Lily. [L *nērinē,* a nereid]
nerite, *n.* a gasteropod mollusc of the genus *Nerita.* **neritine,** *a.* [L *nerīta,* from Gr. *nēritēs, nēreitēs,* sea-mussel]
Nernst, *n.* **Hermann** (1864–1941), German physical chemist. Nernst's investigations, for which he won the 1920 Nobel Chemistry Prize, were concerned with heat changes in chemical reactions. He proposed in 1906 the principle known variously as the Nernst heat theorem and the third law of thermodynamics. The law states that chemical changes at absolute zero involve no change of entropy.
Nero, *n.* (37–68 AD), Roman emperor from 54. He is said to have murdered his stepfather Claudius' son Britannicus, his own mother, his wives Octavia and Poppaea, and many others. After the great fire of Rome 64, he persecuted the Christians, who were suspected of causing it. Military revolt followed in 68; the Senate condemned Nero to death, and he committed suicide.
neroli, *n.* an essential oil distilled from the flowers of the bitter or Seville orange, used as a perfume. [name of Italian princess said to have discovered it]
Neronian, *a.* of, pertaining to or like the emperor Nero; cruel, tyrannical, debauched. [L *Nerōniānus* from C. Claudius *Nero,* Roman emperor]
Neruda, *n.* **Pablo** (pen name of Neftalí Ricardo Reyes y Basualto) (1904–73), Chilean poet, diplomat and communist leader. His work includes lyrics and the epic of the American continent *Canto General* (1950). He was consul and ambassador to many countries as well as a senator (1945–48).
Nerva, *n.* **Marcus Cocceius Nerva** (*c.* 35–98 AD), Roman emperor. He was proclaimed emperor on Domitian's death 96 AD, and introduced state loans for farmers, family allowances and allotments of land to poor citizens.
Nerval, *n.* **Gérard de** (pen name of Gérard Labrunie) (1808–55), French writer and poet, precursor of French symbolism and surrealism. His writings include the travelogue *Voyage en Orient* (1851); short stories, including the collection *Les Filles du feu* (1854); poetry; a novel *Aurélia* (1855), contains episodes of visionary psychosis and drama. He lived a wandering life, with periodic insanity, and committed suicide.
nerve, *n.* one of the fibres or bundles of fibres conveying sensations and impulses to and from the brain or other organ; a tendon or sinew; strength, coolness, resolution, pluck; one of the ribs or fibrovascular bundles in a leaf; (*pl.*) the nervous system, esp. as regards its state of health or the state of interaction between it and the other parts of the organism; also, an excited or disordered condition of the nerves, nervousness; a non-porous kind of cork; (*coll.*) impudence, cheek, audacity. *v.t.* to give strength or firmness to. **bundle of nerves,** (*coll.*) a very timid, anxious person. **get on one's nerves,** (*coll.*) to become oppressively irritating. **lose one's nerve,** to lose confidence; to become afraid. **nerve cell,** *n.* any cell forming part of the nervous system. **nerve-centre,** *n.* an aggregation of nerve cells from which nerves branch out; the central or most important part of a business, organization etc. **nerve gas,** *n.* any one of a number of gases which have a paralysing and possibly fatal effect on the nervous system, used in warfare etc. **nervate,** *a.* having nerves or ribs. **nervation,** *n.* **nerved,** *a.* (*usu. in comb.,* as *strong-nerved*). **nerveless,** *a.* destitute of strength, energy or vigour; without nerves; without nervures; (*fig.*) feeble, flabby. **nervelessly,** *adv.* **nervelessness,** *n.* **nervelet,** *n.* **nervi-, nervo-,** *comb. form.* **nervine,** *a.* capable of acting upon the nerves. *n.* a medicine that acts on the nerves. **nervose,** *a.* nerved; having nervures. **nervous,** *a.* pertaining to or composed of nerves; abounding in nervous energy; having weak or sensitive nerves, excitable, highly strung, timid; sinewy, muscular; vigorous in sentiment or style. **nervous breakdown,** *n.* a loose term for a mental illness or disorder which prevents a person from functioning normally, often characterized by depression, agitation or excessive anxiety. **nervous system,** *n.* a network of nerve cells, including the spinal cord and brain, which collectively controls the body. **nervously,** *adv.* **nervousness,** *n.* **nervule,** *n.* a small nerve or nervure. **nervular, nervulose,** *a.* **nervure,** *n.* the principal vein of a leaf; the ribs supporting the membranous wings of insects. **nervuration,** *n.* **nervy,** *a.* nervous, jerky, jumpy; strong, muscular, sinewy; full of nerve, cool, confident. [L *nervus* (cp. Gr. *neuron*))]
Nervi, *n.* **Pier Luigi** (1891–1979), Italian architect, who

used soft steel mesh within concrete to give it flowing form, for example Turin exhibition hall (1949), the UNESCO building in Paris (1952), and the cathedral at New Norcia, near Perth, Australia (1960).

nescient, *a.* ignorant, having no knowledge (of); agnostic. *n.* an agnostic. **nescience,** *n.* [L *nesciens -ntem,* pres.p. of *nescīre* (*ne-,* not, *scīre,* to know)]

nesh, *a.* soft, friable; tender, succulent; delicate, poor-spirited. **neshen,** *v.t.* (*prov.*). **neshness,** *n.* [OE *hnesce* (cp. Dut. *nesch, nisch,* Goth. *hnasqus*), etym. unknown]

nesiote, *a.* insular, inhabiting an island. [Gr. *nesiotes,* an islander]

ness, *n.* a promontory, a cape. [OE *næs* (cp. Icel. *nes*), rel. to *nasu,* NOSE]

-ness, *suf.* forming abstract nouns denoting state or quality, as *goodness, holiness, wilderness.* [OE *-nes, -ness, -nis, -niss* (cp. Dut. *-nis,* G *-niss,* OHG *-nessi, -nassi, -nissi,* Goth. *-nassus,* orig. *-assus*)]

nest, *n.* the bed or shelter constructed or prepared by a bird for laying its eggs and rearing its young; any place used by animals or insects for similar purposes; a snug place of abode, shelter or retreat; a haunt (as of robbers); a series or set, esp. a number of boxes each inside the next larger. *v.t.* to put, lodge or establish in or as in a nest; to pack one inside another. *v.i.* to build and occupy a nest; to hunt for or take birds' nests. **nest-egg,** *n.* a real or artificial egg left in a nest to prevent a hen from forsaking it; something laid by, as a sum of money, as a nucleus for saving or a reserve. **nestful,** *n.* **nestlike,** *a.* **nestling,** *n.* a bird too young to leave the nest; (*fig.*) a young child; †a little nest. [OE (cp. Dut. and G *nest,* and OIr. *net,* W *nyth,* also L *nīdus,* from *ni-,* down, and the root *sed-,* to sit)]

nestitherapy, *n.* hunger cure, treatment by fasting. [Gr. *nestis,* fasting, *therapeutikos,* cure]

nestle, *v.i.* to nest; to be close or snug; to settle oneself (down, in or among); to press closely (up to). *v.t.* to put or shelter in or as in a nest; to settle down snugly; to cuddle, to cherish. **nestler,** *n.* [OE *nestlian,* from prec.]

Nestle, *n.* **Henri** (1814–90), Swiss industrialist who established a milk-based baby food factory in Vevey, Switzerland (1867), Farine Lactée Henri Nestle. He abandoned all his interest in the business in 1875. After various amalgamations and takeovers, the company once more took the name of Nestle in 1947.

nestling NEST.

Nestor, *n.* a wise counsellor; a sage; a venerable senior. [Gr. *Nestōr,* king of Pylus, character in Homer]

Nestorian, *a.* pertaining to Nestorius or his doctrines. *n.* a follower of Nestorius, patriarch of Constantinople (5th cent.), who held that there were two distinct persons and two natures, divine and human, in Christ. **Nestorianism,** *n.* [L *Nestoriānus* (*Nestorius,* -AN)]

net¹, *n.* a fabric of twine, cord etc., knotted into meshes, for catching fish, birds, or other animals, or for covering, protecting, carrying etc.; a snare; network. *v.t.* (*past, p.p.* **netted**) to make into a net or netting; to make or form in a network; to make network of, to reticulate; to cover, hold or confine with a net; to catch in a net; to fish with nets or set nets in (a stream, pond etc.); to catch as in a net, to ensnare. *v.i.* to make netting or network; to make nets; to fish with a net or nets. **net-ball,** *n.* a game in which a ball has to be thrown into a suspended net. **net-veined,** *a.* having a reticulated series of veins or nervules (as the wings of insects, leaves etc.). **net-winged,** *a.* having net-veined wings. **network,** *n.* an open-work fabric, netting; a system of intersecting lines, a reticulation, a ramification; a system of stations for simultaneous broadcasting; any system of lines, roads etc., resembling this; (*Comput.*) a system of communication between different computers, terminals, circuits etc.; a system of units related in some way, e.g. part of a business organization; a group of people who are useful to each other because of the similarity of their aims, background etc. as in *old boy network. v.t., v.i.* to connect; to broadcast (a television or radio programme) throughout the country rather than in one region; to form or be part of a network, e.g. through business contact. (*Comput.*) to create or use a system of communication between computers, circuits etc. **netted,** *a.* reticulated. **netting,** *n.* **netting-needle,** *n.* †**netty,** *a.* [OE (cp. Dut., Icel. and Dan. *net,* G *Netz*), cogn. with L *nassa,* creel]

net², *a.* free from all deductions; obtained or left after all deductions; not subject to discount; unadulterated, pure; †clean, spotless. *v.t.* to yield or realize as clear profit. [F, NEAT²]

Ne Temere, *n.* a papal decree declaring that marriage between Roman Catholics and members of other faiths is not valid unless the ceremony is performed by a Roman Catholic bishop or a priest deputed by him. [L *ne,* not, *temere,* rashly]

nether, *a.* lower; belonging to the region below the heavens or the earth. **nether garments,** trousers. **nether regions** or **world,** Hell; (*rare*) the earth. †**netherstock,** *n.* a stocking. †**nethermore,** *a.* lower. **nethermost,** *a.* †**netherward, -wards,** *adv.* [OE *neothera* (cp. Dut. *neder,* G *nieder,* Icel. *nethri*)]

Netherlander, *n.* a native or inhabitant of the Netherlands; †a native or inhabitant of Flanders or Belgium. **Netherlandish,** *a.* [Dut. *Nederlander,* from *Nederland,* Netherlands]

Netherlands, *n.* Kingdom of the (*Koninkrijk der Nederlanden*), popularly referred to as **Holland**, a country in W Europe on the North Sea, bounded to the E by West Germany and to the S by Belgium. **area** 41,900 sq km/16,178 sq miles. **capital** Amsterdam. **towns** The Hague (seat of government); chief port Rotterdam. **physical** almost completely flat; rivers Rhine, Schelde (*Scheldt*), Maas; Frisian Islands. **territories** Aruba, Netherlands Antilles. **exports** dairy products, flower bulbs, vegetables, petrochemicals, electronics. **population** (1988) 14,715,000 (including 300,000 of Dutch-Indonesian origin absorbed (1949–64) from former colonial possessions); annual growth rate 0.5%. **language** Dutch. **religion** Roman Catholic 35%, Protestant 28%.

Netherlands Antilles, *n.pl.* two groups of Caribbean islands, part of the Netherlands with full internal autonomy, comprising Curaçao and Bonaire off the coast of Venezuela (Aruba is considered separately), and St Eustatius, Saba and the S part of St Maarten in the Leeward Islands, 800 km/500 miles NE. **area** 797 sq km/308 sq miles. **capital** Willemstad on Curaçao. **products** oil from Venezuela is refined here; tourism. **language** Dutch (official), Papiamento, English. **population** (1983) 193,000.

netsuke, *n.* a small piece of carved wood or ivory worn or attached to various articles, as a toggle or button, by the Japanese. [Jap.]

nett NET².

netting NET¹.

nettle, *n.* a plant of the genus *Urtica,* with two European species, the great or common and the small nettle, with inconspicuous flowers and minute stinging hairs; applied to various plants bearing some resemblance to these. *v.t.* to sting; to irritate, to provoke; to sting with nettles. **to grasp the nettle,** to take decisive or bold action. **dead-nettle** DEAD. **nettle-rash,** *n.* an eruption on the skin resembling the sting of a nettle. †**nettler,** *n.* [OE *netele* (cp. Dut. *netel,* G *Nessel,* Dan. *nelde,* Swed. *nässla*)]

nettling, *n.* the joining of two ropes by twisting the loosened ends together; the tying of yarns together in pairs to prevent entangling. [*nettle,* var. of *knittle,* from KNIT, -ING]

network NET¹.

Neufchâtel, *n.* a soft white cheese similar to cream cheese but with less fat. [from *Neufchâtel,* a town in France]

Neumann¹, *n.* **Balthasar** (1687–1753), German Rococo architect and military engineer, whose work includes the bishop's palace in Würzburg.

Neumann², *n.* **Johann von** (1903–57), Hungarian-born US scientist and mathematician, known for his pioneering work on computer design. He invented his celebrated 'rings of operators' (called von Neumann algebras) in the late 1930s, and also contributed to set theory, games theory, cybernetics (with his theory of self-reproducing automata) and the development of the atomic and hydrogen bombs.

neume, *n.* (*Mus.*) a sequence of notes to be sung to one syllable in plainsong. [F, from med. L *neuma,* Gr. *pneuma,* breath]

neur- NEUR(O)-.

neural, *a.* of or pertaining to the nerves or the nervous system. [NEUR(O)-]

neuralgia, *n.* an acute pain in a nerve or series of nerves, esp. in the head or face. **neuralgic,** *a.* [Gr. *algos,* pain]

neurasthenia, *n.* weakness of the nervous system, nervous debility. **neurasthenic,** *a.*

neuration, *n.* the arrangement of the nervures, as in insects' wings.

neurectomy, *n.* excision of a nerve, or part of it.

neuric, *a.* of or pertaining to the nerves. **neuricity,** *n.*

neurilemma, *n.* the membranous sheath encasing a nerve. [Gr. *eilema,* covering]

neurility, *n.* the power of a nerve to convey stimuli.

neurin, *n.* nerve energy, the force or stimulus produced in or conveyed to neurons.

neurine, *n.* the matter of which nerves are composed, nerve fibre or tissue; a poisonous ptomaine derived from putrefying organic matter.

neuritis, *n.* inflammation of a nerve.

neur(o)-, *comb. form.* pertaining to a nerve cell; pertaining to nerves; pertaining to the nervous system. [Gr. *neuron,* a nerve]

neurochemistry, *n.* the biochemistry of the transmission of impulses down nerves.

neurohypnology, *n.* the study of sleep and its hygiene; the study of hypnotism. **neurohypnologist,** *n.* **neurohypnotism,** *n.* nervous sleep induced by hypnotic means. **neurohypnotic,** *a.*

neurology, *n.* the scientific study of the anatomy, physiology and pathology of nerves. **neurological,** *a.* **neurologist,** *n.*

neuroma, *n.* (*pl.* **neuromata**) a tumour consisting of nerve tissue.

neuron, *n.* a nerve cell with its processes and ramifications, one of the structural units of the nervous system; †the cerebro-spinal axis comprising the spinal cord and brain.

neuropath, *n.* a person suffering from a nervous disorder or having abnormal nervous sensibility; a physician who regards nervous conditions as the main factor in pathology. **neuropathic,** *a.* relating to or suffering from a nervous disease. **neuropathology,** *n.* the pathology of the nervous system. **neuropathy,** *n.* any nervous disease. **neuropathist,** *n.*

neurophysiology, *n.* the physiology of the nervous system.

neuropnology NEUROHYPNOLOGY.

neuropod, *n.* an annulose or invertebrate animal whose limbs are in the neural aspect of its body.

neuropsychic, *a.* relating to the nervous and psychic functions and phenomena.

neuropsychology, *n.* psychology based upon the study of the nervous system.

neuroptera, *n.pl.* (*Ent.*) an order of insects with four reticulated membranous wings. **neuropteral, -oid, -ous,** *a.* **neuropteran,** *a., n.* [NEURO-, Gr. *pteron,* wing]

neuroradiology, *n.* a method of diagnosis of such conditions as cerebral tumours, aneurysms etc. by X-ray examination.

neurose, *a.* having numerous nervures; neurotic.

neurosis, *n.* functional disorder of the nervous system; (*loosely*) a mild mental disorder, usu. with symptoms of anxiety; the change in the nerve cells or neurons, or the discharge of nerve energy, forming the physical basis of psychic activity. **neurotic,** *a.* pertaining to or situated in the nerves; acting on the nerves; suffering from neurosis. *n.* a substance acting upon the nerves; a person suffering from neurosis; a person of abnormal nervous excitability.

neurosurgery, *n.* the branch of surgery dealing with the nervous system. **neurosurgical,** *a.*

neurotomy, *n.* dissection of the nerves; an incision in a nerve, usu. to produce sensory paralysis. **neurotomical,** *a.* **neurotomist,** *a.*

neurotonic, *a.* strengthening the nervous system. *n.* a medicine for this purpose.

neurotransmitter, *n.* a chemical substance by means of which nerve cells communicate with each other.

neuter, *a.* neither masculine, nor feminine; (of verbs) intransitive; neither male nor female, without pistil or stamen; undeveloped sexually, sterile; †neutral, taking neither side. *n.* a neuter noun, adjective or verb; the neuter gender; a flower having neither stamens nor pistils; a sterile female insect, as a working bee; a castrated animal; a neutral. [L, neither (*ne-,* not, *uter,* either)]

Neutra, *n.* **Richard Joseph** (1892–1970), Austrian architect, who became a US citizen in 1929. His works, often in impressive landscape settings, include Lovell Health House, Los Angeles, and Mathematics Park, Princeton.

neutral, *a.* taking no part with either side, esp. not assisting either of two belligerents; belonging to a state that takes no part in hostilities; indifferent, impartial; having no distinct or determinate character, colour etc.; neither good nor bad, indefinite, indeterminate; the position of parts in gear mechanism when no power is transmitted; neither acid nor alkaline; neither positive nor negative; neuter, asexual. *n.* a state or person that stands aloof from a contest; a subject of a neutral state. **neutral-tinted,** *a.* **neutrality,** *n.* **neutralize, -ise,** *v.t.* to render neutral; to render inoperative or ineffective, to counteract; to declare (a state or territory) neutral either permanently or during hostilities. **neutralization, -isation,** *n.* **neutralizer, -iser,** *n.* **neutrally,** *adv.* [L *neutrālis,* as prec.]

neutrino, *n.* a sub-atomic particle with almost zero mass, zero charge but specified spin.

neutrodyne, *n.* (*Radio*) the protected trade name of an apparatus for neutralizing capacity between plate and grid in a valve. [L *neuter,* neither, Gr. *dunamos,* power]

neutron, *n.* a particle that is neutral electrically with approximately the same mass as a proton.

Nevada, *n.* a state of the western US; nickname Sagebrush, Silver or Battleborn State. **area** 286,400 sq km/ 110,550 sq miles. **capital** Carson City. **towns** Las Vegas, Reno. **physical** Mojave Desert, Lake Tahoe, mountains and plateaus alternating with valleys. **products** mercury, barite, gold, copper, oil, gaming machines. **population** (1987) 1,053,000.

névé, *n.* consolidated snow above the glaciers, in process of being converted into ice. [F ult. from L *nivem,* nom. *nix,* snow]

never, *adv.* not ever, at no time; on no occasion; not at all; none; (*ellipt. in exclamations*) surely not. **never a one,** not a single person etc., none. **never more,** at no future time; never again. **never-never land,** an imaginary place with conditions too ideal to exist in real life. **never-never system, the never-never,** (*coll.*) the hire-purchase system. **never so,** (*loosely* **ever so**) to an unlimited extent; exceedingly. **The Never-never,** term applied to areas in North and West Queensland. **never-ending, -failing,** *a.* **nevertheless,** *conj.* but for all that; notwithstanding; all the same. [OE *næfre* (*ne,* not, *æfre,* ever)]

new, *a.* not formerly in existence; lately made, invented or introduced; not before known; recently entered upon or begun; never before used, not worn or exhausted; fresh, unfamiliar, unaccustomed; (of bread) newly baked; fresh (from), not yet accustomed (to). *adv.* newly, recently (*in comb.,* as *new-blown, newborn*); anew, fresh. †**New Red Sandstone,** the sandstone strata between the Carboniferous and the Jurassic systems. **New Year's day,** the first day of the year. **the New World,** the Western Hemisphere. **New**

Australian, *n.* a non-British immigrant to Australia. **new-blown,** *a.* having just come into bloom. **new-born,** *a.* just born; regenerate. **new chum,** *n.* (*Austral. coll.*) an immigrant. **new-come,** *a.* modern, new-fangled; beginning afresh, recurring; changed, different, another. **new-comer,** *n.* a person who has recently arrived in a place or who has just begun to take part in something. **new-create,** *v.t.* **new-fashioned,** *a.* **new-fledged,** *a.* **new learning,** *n.* the Renaissance. **new look,** *n.* an up-to-date appearance. **new man,** *n.* one in sympathy with the Women's Liberation Movement and who undertakes tasks traditionally associated with women, such as housework. **new-made,** *a.* **new-model,** *v.t.* to give a fresh form to. **New Order,** *n.* a scheme for the organization and government of Europe devised by Adolf Hitler, its principal basis being the hegemony of the German nation. **newspeak,** *n.* a form of language, often used by officials and bureaucrats, which is ambiguous, misleading and verbose, coined by George Orwell in his novel *Nineteen Eighty-Four*. **new town,** *n.* a town planned by the government to aid housing development in nearby large cities, stimulate development etc. **new woman,** *n.* a term formerly applied to a woman of advanced ideas, esp. one who claimed equality with men in the social, economic and political spheres. **newish,** *a.* **newly,** *adv.* recently (*usu. in comb.*). **newness,** *n.* [OE *nīve* (cp. Dut. *nieuw*, G *neu*, Icel. *nȳr*, Gr. *neos*, L *novus*)]

New Age, *n.* a type of instrumental pop music of the 1980s, often semi-acoustic or electronic; less insistent than rock.

New Brunswick, *n.* a maritime province of E Canada. **area** 73,400 sq km/28,332 sq miles. **capital** Fredericton. **towns** Saint John, Moncton. **products** cereals; wood, paper; fish; lead, zinc, copper, oil and natural gas. **population** (1986) 710,000, 37% French-speaking.

New Caledonia, *n.* an island group in the S Pacific, a French overseas territory between Australia and the Fiji Islands. **area** 18,576 sq km/7,170 sq miles. **capital** Nouméa. **physical** fertile, surrounded by a barrier reef. **products** nickel (the world's third largest producer), chrome, iron. **population** (1983) 145,300, 43% Kanak (Melanesian), 37% European, 8% Wallisian, 5% Vietnamese and Indonesian, 4% Polynesian. **language** French (official). **religion** Roman Catholic 60%, Protestant 30%.

Newcastle disease, *n.* an acute highly contagious disease of chickens and other birds, first recorded in *Newcastle* upon Tyne in 1926. Also called **fowl pest**.

Newcastle-upon-Tyne, *n.* an industrial port (coal, shipbuilding, marine and electrical engineering, chemicals, metals), commercial and cultural centre, in Tyne and Wear, NE England, administrative headquarters of Tyne and Wear and Northumberland; population (1981) 278,000.

New Deal, *n.* (*US Hist.*) a programme introduced by President F. D. Roosevelt (1933) to counter the Depression of 1929, including employment on public works, farm loans at low rates, and social reforms such as old-age and unemployment insurance, prevention of child labour, protection of employees against unfair practices by employers, and loans to local authorities for slum clearance. Many of its provisions were declared unconstitutional by the Supreme Court (1935–36), and full employment did not come until World War II.

New Delhi, *n.* a city in the Union Territory of Delhi, designed by Lutyens; capital of India since 1912; population (1981) 273,000.

New Democratic Party, a Canadian political party, moderately socialist, formed 1961 by a merger of the Labour Congress and the Cooperative Commonwealth Federation. Its leader from 1975, **Edward Broadbent** (1936–), resigned 1989.

New Economic Policy, an economic policy of the USSR (1921–29) devised by the Soviet leader Lenin. Rather than requisitioning all agricultural produce above a stated subsistence allowance, the state requisitioned only a fixed proportion of the surplus; the rest could be traded freely by the peasant. The NEP thus reinstated a limited form of free-market trading. The state retained complete control of major industries.

newel, *n.* the central column from which the steps of a winding stair radiate; the hollow or well of a winding stair; an upright post at the top or bottom of a stair supporting the hand-rail. [OF *nuel* (F *noyau*), kernel, from late L *nucāle,* from *nux nucis,* nut]

New England, *n.* a region of NE US, comprising the states of Maine, New Hampshire, Vermont, Massachusetts, Rhode Island and Connecticut, originally settled by Pilgrims and Puritans from England.

†**newfangle,** *v.t.* to change by introducing novelties. **newfangled,** *a.* new-fashioned; different from the accepted fashion; fond of novelties, inconstant. **newfangledly,** *adv.* **newfangledness,** *n.* [ME *fangel,* from OE *fang-,* p.p, *fōn,* to take (see FANG)]

Newfoundland, *n.* a breed of dog, said to have originated in Newfoundland. Males can grow to 70 cm/2.3 ft tall, and weigh 65 kg/145 lbs, the females slightly smaller. They are gentle in temperament, and their fur is dense, flat and usually dull black.

Newfoundland and Labrador, a Canadian province on the Atlantic Ocean. **area** 405,700 sq km/156,600 sq miles. **capital** St John's. **towns** Corner Brook, Gander. **physical** Newfoundland island and Labrador on the mainland on the other side of the Straits of Belle Isle; rocky. **products** newsprint, fish products, hydroelectric power, iron, copper, zinc, uranium, offshore oil. **population** (1986) 568,000.

Newgate, *n.* a London prison, demolished in 1902. **Newgate Calendar,** *n.* a list of prisoners in Newgate with accounts of their careers and crimes. **Newgate frill** or **fringe,** *n.* a beard under the chin and jaw (with alln. to the hangman's noose). **Newgate knocker,** *n.* a lock of hair twisted over the ear. [from the new gate of the City of London near which it was built in 1218]

New Guinea, *n.* an island in the SW Pacific, N of Australia, comprising Papua New Guinea and Irian Jaya (administered by Indonesia); area 775,213 sq km/229,232 sq miles; population (1980) 1,174,000. Part of the Dutch East Indies from 1828, it was ceded by the UN to Indonesia in 1963. Its tropical rainforest is under threat from logging companies and resettlement schemes.

New Hampshire, *n.* a state of the NE US; nickname Granite State. **area** 24,000 sq km/9,264 sq miles. **capital** Concord. **towns** Manchester, Nashua. **products** electrical machinery, gravel, apples, maple syrup, livestock. **population** (1987) 1,057,000.

New Hebrides, *n.* former name (until 1980) of VANUATU.

Ne Win, *n.* **Maung Shu Maung,** 'Brilliant Sun' (1911–), Burmese politician, ruler from 1962 to 1974, president 1984–81.

New Ireland Forum, a meeting between politicians of the Irish Republic and Northern Ireland in May 1983. It offered three potential solutions to the Northern Irish problem, but all were rejected by the UK the following year.

New Jersey, *n.* a state of NE US; nickname Garden State. **area** 20,200 sq km/7,797 sq miles. **capital** Trenton. **towns** Newark, Jersey City, Paterson, Elizabeth. **products** asparagus, fruit, potatoes, tomatoes, poultry, chemicals, metal goods, electrical machinery, clothing. **population** (1985) 7,562,000.

Newman[1], *n.* **John Henry** (1801–90), English Roman Catholic theologian. While still an Anglican, he wrote a series of *Tracts for the Times*, which gave their name to the Tractarian Movement (subsequently called the Oxford Movement). He became a Catholic 1845 and was made a cardinal 1879. In 1864 his autobiography, *Apologia pro vita sua*, was published.

Newman[2], *n.* **Paul** (1925–), US actor and director, Hollywood's leading male star of the 1960s and 1970s. His films include *The Hustler* (1962), *Butch Cassidy and the Sundance Kid* (1969), *The Sting* (1973), and

The Color of Money (1986) (for which he won an Academy Award).

Newmarket[1], *n.* a Newmarket coat; a card game. **Newmarket coat,** *n.* a close-fitting overcoat, orig. for riding, worn by men or women. [see foll.]

Newmarket[2], *n.* British racecourse. Situated in Cambridgeshire, it has been the home of racing since the days of Charles II and the straight mile is nicknamed, after him, Rowley Mile. Amongst others, Newmarket stages two classics each year, the One Thousand and Two Thousand Guineas, and the Autumn Double of the Cambridgeshire and Cesarwitch. The national stud is situated in Newmarket.

New Mexico, *n.* a state of the SW US; nickname Land of Enchantment. **area** 315,000 sq km/121,590 sq miles. **capital** Santa Fé. **towns** Albuquerque, Las Cruces, Roswell. **physical** more than 75% of the area is over 1200 m/3900 ft above sea level; plains, mountains, caverns. **products** uranium, oil, natural gas, cotton, cereals, vegetables. **population** (1987) 1,500,000.

New Model Army, the army created in 1645 by Oliver Cromwell to support the cause of Parliament during the English Civil War. It was characterized by organization and discipline. Thomas Fairfax was its first commander.

New Orleans, *n.* a commercial and industrial city (banking, oil refining, rockets) and Mississippi river port in Louisiana, US; population (1980) 557,500. It is the traditional birthplace of jazz.

New Rochelle, *n.* a residential suburb of New York on Long Island Sound; population (1980) 70,800.

news, *n.pl.* (*usu. as sing.*) recent or fresh information, tidings; a regular radio or television broadcast of up-to-date information on current affairs; †a newspaper. **news-agency,** *n.* an organization for supplying information to newspapers etc. **newsagent,** *n.* a dealer in newspapers and other periodicals. **news-boy, -girl,** *n.* one who delivers or sells newspapers in the street. **newscaster,** *n.* a news broadcaster. **news editor,** *n.* a newspaper editor specially engaged with the editing and display of news. **newsflash,** *n.* a short important news item, esp. one which interrupts a television or radio programme. **newshound,** (*coll.*) *n.* a reporter in search of news. **news-letter,** *n.* a weekly letter in the 17th cent. circulating news; any news sent out regularly to a particular group. **newsmonger,** *n.* one who makes it his business to spread news, usu. false; a busybody in news. **newspaper,** *n.* a printed publication, usu. issued daily or weekly, containing news usu. with leaders expressing opinions on questions of the hour, articles on special topics, advertisements and often reviews of literature, plays etc. **newspaper- man, -woman,** *n.* a journalist. **newsprint,** *n.* the cheap-quality paper upon which newspapers are printed. **newsreel,** *n.* a film giving the day's news. **news-room,** *n.* a room for reading newspapers etc.; a room where news is edited. **news-sheet,** *n.* a printed sheet of news, an early form of newspaper. **news stand,** *n.* a newspaper kiosk. **news-vendor,** *n.* a seller of newspapers. †**news-writer,** *n.* **newsless,** *a.* **newsy,** *a.* **newsiness,** *n.* [pl. of NEW (cp. F *novelles,* L *nova,* pl. of *novus,* new)]

New South Wales, state of SE Australia. **area** 801,600 sq km/309,418 sq miles. **capital** Sydney. **towns** Newcastle, Wollongong, Broken Hill. **physical** Great Dividing Range (including Blue Mountains) and part of the Australian Alps (including Snowy Mountains and Mount Kosciusko); Murray, Darling, Murrumbidgee river system irrigates the Riverina district. **products** cereals, fruit, sugar, tobacco, wool, meat, hides and skins, gold, silver, copper, tin, zinc, coal; hydroelectric power from the Snowy river. **population** (1987) 5,570,000; 60% living in Sydney.

newt, *n.* a small tailed amphibian like the salamander, an eft. [ME *ewte* (*a newt,* from *an ewt*), AS *efeta,* EFT]

New Testament, *n.* the second part of the Bible, recognized by the Christian church from the 4th cent. as sacred doctrine. The New Testament includes the Gospels, which tell of the life and teachings of Jesus, the history of the early church, teachings of St Paul, and mystical writings. It was written in Greek during the 1st and 2nd cents. AD, and the individual sections have been ascribed to various authors.

newton, *n.* a unit of force equal to 100,000 dynes.

Newton, *n.* **Isaac** (1642–1727), English physicist and mathematician, who discovered the law of gravity, created calculus, discovered that white light is composed of many colours, and developed the three standard laws of motion still in use today. During 1665–66, he discovered the binomial theorem, differential and integral calculus, and also began to investigate the phenomenon of gravitation. In 1685, he expounded his universal law of gravitation. His greatest work, *Philosophiae Naturalis Principia Mathematica,* was published in three volumes (1686–87), with the aid of Edmund Halley.

Newtonian, *a.* of or pertaining to Newton or his theories; discovered or invented by Newton. *n.* a follower of Newton; a Newtonian telescope. [see prec.]

Newton's laws of motion, (*Phys.*) three laws that form the basis of Newtonian mechanics. (1) Unless acted upon by a net force, a body at rest stays at rest, and a moving body continues moving at the same speed in the same straight line. (2) A net force applied to a body gives it a rate of change of momentum proportional to the force and in the direction of the force. (3) When a body A exerts a force on a body B, B exerts an equal and opposite force on A, that is, to every action there is an equal and opposite reaction.

Newton's rings, *n.pl.* (*Opt.*) an interference phenomenon seen (using white light) as concentric rings of spectral colours where light passes through a thin film of transparent medium, such as the wedge of air between a large-radius convex lens and a flat glass plate. With monochromatic light (light of a single wavelength), the rings take the form of alternate light and dark bands. They are caused by interference (interaction) between light rays reflected from the plate and those reflected from the curved surface of the lens.

New Wave[1], *n.* (French **nouvelle vague**) a French literary movement of the 1950s, a cross-fertilization of the novel (Marguerite Duras, Alain Robbe-Grillet, Nathalie Sarraute) and film (directors Jean-Luc Godard, Alain Resnais and François Truffaut).

New Wave[2], *n.* in pop music, a style that evolved parallel to punk in the second half of the 1970s. It shared the urban aggressive spirit but was musically and lyrically more sophisticated; examples are the early work of Elvis Costello in the UK and Talking Heads in the US.

New World, *n.* the Americas, so called by Europeans who reached them later than other continents. The term is used as an adjective to describe animals and plants that live in the western hemisphere.

New York[1], *n.* a state of the NE US; nickname Empire State. **area** 127,200 sq km/49,099 sq miles. **capital** Albany. **towns** New York, Buffalo, Rochester, Yonkers, Syracuse. **physical** Adirondack and Catskill mountains; Lake Placid; bordering on lakes Erie and Ontario; Hudson river; Niagara Falls; Long Island. **products** clothing, printing, Steuben glass, titanium concentrate, cereals, apples, maple syrup, poultry, meat, dairy products, wine. **population** (1985) 17,783,000.

New York[2], *n.* the largest city in US, industrial port (printing, publishing, clothing), cultural and commercial centre in New York State, at the junction of the Hudson and East rivers; comprises the boroughs of the Bronx, Brooklyn, Manhattan, Queens and Staten Island; population (1980) 9,081,000.

New Zealand, *n.* a country in the S Pacific, SE of Australia. **area** 268,000 sq km/103,448 sq miles. **capital** Wellington. **towns** Hamilton, Palmerston North, Christchurch, Dunedin; ports Wellington, Auckland. **physical** comprises North Island, South Island, Stewart Island, Chatham Islands and minor islands; mainly mountainous. **overseas territories** Tokelau (three atolls transferred 1926 from the former Gilbert and

Ellice Islands colony); Niue Island (one of the Cook Islands, but separately administered from 1903: chief town Alafi); Cook Islands are internally self-governing, but share common citizenship with New Zealand; Ross Dependency is in Antarctica. **exports** lamb, beef, wool, leather, dairy products and other processed foods; kiwi fruit became a major export crop in the 1980s; seeds and breeding stock; timber, paper, pulp, light aircraft. **population** (1989) 3,397,000 (including 270,000 Maoris and 60,000 other Polynesians; the whites are chiefly of British descent); annual growth rate 0.9%. **language** English (official); Maori (the Lange government pledged to give it official status). **religion** Protestant 50%, Roman Catholic 15%.

next, *a.* nearest in place, time or degree; nearest in order or succession, immediately following. *adv.* nearest or immediately after; in the next place or degree. *prep.* nearest to. *n.* the next person or thing. **next best,** second best. **next but one,** the one next to that immediately preceding or following. **next door to,** in or at the house adjoining. **next, please,** let the next person come. **next to,** almost; all but. **next to nothing,** scarcely anything. **what next?** *int.* can anything exceed or surpass this? [OE *nēahst* (NIGH, -EST)]

nexus, *n.* (*pl.* **nexus**) a link, a connection. [L, from *nec-*, stem of *nectere,* to bind]

Ney, *n.* **Michael, Duke of Elchingen, Prince of Ney** (1769–1815), marshal of France under Napoleon I, who commanded the rearguard of the French army during the retreat from Moscow, and for his personal courage was called 'the bravest of the brave'. When Napoleon returned from Elba, Ney was sent to arrest him, but instead deserted to him and fought at Waterloo. He was subsequently shot for treason.

NFU, (*abbr.*) National Farmers' Union.

ngaio, *n.* a New Zealand tree noted for its fine white wood. [Maori]

Ngorongoro Crater, *n.* a crater in the Tanzanian section of the African Great Rift Valley noted for its large numbers of wildebeests, gazelle and zebra.

Ngugi wa Thiong'o, *n.* (1938–), Kenyan writer of essays, plays, short stories, and novels. He was imprisoned after the performance of the play *Ngaahika Ndeenda/I Will Marry When I Want* (1977), and lived in exile from 1982. His novels, written in English and Gikuyu, include *The River Between*, *Petals of Blood*, and *Caitaani Mutharaba-ini/Devil on the Cross*, and deal with colonial and post-independence oppression.

Nguyen Van Linh, *n.* (1914–), Vietnamese communist politician, member of the Politburo (1976–81) and from 1985; party leader from 1986. He began economic liberalization and troop withdrawal from Cambodia and Laos.

NHS, (*abbr.*) National Health Service.

NI, (*abbr.*) National Insurance; Northern Ireland.

Ni, (*chem. symbol*) nickel.

niacin, *n.* nicotinic acid.

Niagara Falls, *n.pl.* two waterfalls on the Niagara river, on the Canada-US border, separated by Goat Island. The **American Falls** are 51 m/167 ft high, 330 m/1080 ft wide; **Horseshoe Falls**, in Canada, are 49 m/160 ft high, 790 m/2600 ft across.

Niamey, *n.* a river port and capital of Niger; population (1983) 399,000. It produces textiles, chemicals, pharmaceuticals and foodstuffs.

†**nias** EYAS.

nib, *n.* the point of a pen; a pen-point for insertion in a pen-holder; the point of a tool etc.; the beak of a bird; one of the handles projecting from the shaft of a scythe; (*pl.*) crushed cocoa-seeds. *v.t.* (*past, p.p.* **nibbed**) to put a nib into (a pen); to sharpen the nib of (a quill-pen). **his nibs,** (*sl.*) a burlesque title; (*coll.*) an important or self-important person. [prob. var. of NEB]

nibble, *v.t.* to bite little by little; to bite little bits off; to bite at cautiously (as a fish at a bait); (*sl.*) to nab, to catch. *v.i.* to take small bites or to bite cautiously (at); (*fig.*) to criticize carpingly, to cavil. *n.* the act of nibbling; a little bite; a bit which is nibbled off. **nibbler,** *n.* **nibblingly,** *adv.* [etym. doubtful, cp. LG *nibbelen,* Dut. *knibbelen*]

Nibelungenlied, *n.* an anonymous 12th-cent. German epic poem, *Song of the Nibelungs*, derived from older sources. The composer Richard Wagner made use of the legends in his *Ring* cycle.

niblick, *n.* (*Golf*) a club with a small cup-shaped iron head. [etym. doubtful]

NIC, (*abbr.*) newly industrializing country.

Nicaea, Council of, Christian church council held in Nicaea (modern Iznik, Turkey) in 325, called by the Roman emperor Constantine. It upheld the doctrine of the Trinity in the Nicene Creed.

Nicaragua, *n.* Republic of (*República de Nicaragua*), a country in Central America, between the Pacific Ocean and the Caribbean, bounded N by Honduras and S by Costa Rica. **area** 127,849 sq km/49,350 sq miles. **capital** Managua. **towns** chief port Corinto. **physical** volcanic mountain ranges; lakes Nicaragua and Managua. **exports** coffee, cotton, sugar. **population** (1989) 3,692,000 (70% mestizo, 15% Spanish descent, 10% Indian or black); annual growth rate 3.3%. **language** Spanish (official). **religion** Roman Catholic.

Nicaraguan Revolution, *n.* the revolt (1978–79) in Nicaragua, led by the socialist **Sandinistas** against the US-supported right-wing dictatorship established by Anastasio Somoza. His son, President Anastasio (Debayle) Somoza, was forced into exile and assassinated in Paraguay (1980). The Sandinista National Liberation Front (FSLN) is named after Augusto César Sandino, a guerrilla leader killed by the US-trained National Guard in 1934.

niccolite, *n.* native arsenide of nickel.

nice, *a.* fastidious, over-particular, hard to please, dainty, punctilious, scrupulous; acute, discerning, discriminating, sensitive to minute differences; requiring delicate discrimination or tact, delicate, subtle, minute; pleasing or agreeable; satisfactory; delightful, attractive, friendly, kind; †trivial; †ignorant, silly, foolish. **niceish,** *adv.* rather nice, rather pleasant. **nicely,** *adv.* **niceness,** *n.* **nicety,** *n.* exactness, precision; a minute point, a delicate distinction; a small detail; †a delicacy, a dainty. **to a nicety,** exactly, with precision. [OF, from L *nescium,* nom. *-us,* ignorant (see NESCIENT)]

Nice, *n.* a city on the French Riviera; population (1982) 449,500. Founded in the 3rd cent. BC, it repeatedly changed hands between France and the Duchy of Savoy from the 14th–19th cents. In 1860 it was finally transferred to France.

Nicene, *a.* of or pertaining to Nicaea. **Nicene councils,** *n.pl.* two councils held at Nicaea (the first in AD 325 to settle the Arian controversy, the second in 787 on the question of images and the iconoclasts). **Nicene creed,** *n.* a statement of Christian belief formulated by the first council of Nicaea. [late L *Nicēnus,* from *Nīcaea,* Gr. *Nikaia,* a town in Asia Minor]

niche, *n.* a recess in a wall for a statue, vase etc.; one's proper place or natural position. *v.t.* to put in a niche; to settle (oneself) in a comfortable place. [F, from It. *nicchia,* etym. doubtful]

Nichiren, *n.* (1222–82), Japanese Buddhist monk, founder of the sect that bears his name. It bases its beliefs on the *Lotus Sūtra*, which Nichiren held to be the only true revelation of the teachings of Buddha, and stresses the need for personal effort to attain enlightenment.

Nicholas, *n.* two tsars of Russia:

Nicholas I, *n.* (1796–1855), tsar of Russia from 1825. His Balkan ambitions led to war with Turkey (1827–29) and the Crimean War (1853–56).

Nicholas II, *n.* (1868-1918), tsar of Russia (1894–1917). He was dominated by his wife, Princess Alix of Hessen, who was under the influence of Rasputin. His mismanagement of the Russo-Japanese War and of internal affairs led to the revolution of 1905, which he suppressed, although he was forced to grant limited constitutional reforms. He took Russia into World War I (1914), was forced to abdicate (1917), and was shot with his family by the Bolsheviks at Ekaterinburg July 1918.

Nicholas, St, *n.* also known as **Santa Claus** (4th cent.), in the Christian church, patron saint of Russia, children, merchants and sailors; bishop of Myra (now in Turkey). His legendary gifts of dowries to poor girls led to the custom of giving gifts to children on the eve of his feast day, 6 Dec., still retained in some countries, such as the Netherlands, although elsewhere now transferred to Christmas Day. His emblem is three balls.

Nicholson[1], *n.* **Ben** (1894–1982), English abstract artist. After early experiments influenced by Cubism and de Stijl, he developed a style of geometrical reliefs, notably a series of white reliefs (from 1933).

Nicholson[2], *n.* **Jack** (1937–), US film actor, who captured in the late 1960s the mood of non-conformist, uncertain young Americans in such films as *Easy Rider* (1969) and *Five Easy Pieces* (1970). He subsequently became a mainstream Hollywood star, appearing in *Chinatown* (1974), *One Flew over the Cuckoo's Nest* (1975), and *Batman* (1989).

Nichrome®, *n.* a nickel chromium alloy with high electrical resistance and an ability to withstand high temperature.

Nick, *n.* the devil, also Old Nick. [short for *Nicholas*]

nick, *n.* a small notch, cut or dent, esp. used as a guide, a tally or score for keeping account; the critical moment; a winning throw at dice; the exact point or moment; (*sl.*) prison, police cell. *v.t.* to cut or make a nick or nicks in; to snip, to cut; to hit upon, to hit luckily or at the lucky moment; to catch at the exact moment; to make (a lucky throw), as at dice; †to cheat; (*sl.*) to steal. *v.i.* to fit in exactly; (*Stock-breeding*) to mingle well, to produce offspring of good quality; to make a lucky throw, as at dice; to cut (in), to make a short cut (in, at or past), as in a race. **in good nick,** (*coll.*) in good condition. **in the nick of time,** only just in time. **to nick a horse** or **a horse's tail,** to make an incision at the root of the tail, in order to make him carry it higher. **nick-eared,** *a.* crop-eared. [etym. doubtful]

nickel, *n.* a lustrous silvery-white ductile metallic element, at. no. 28; chem. symbol Ni; usu. found in association with cobalt, used in manufacture of German silver and in other alloys; a US 5-cent piece (formerly a 1-cent piece). *v.t.* to coat with nickel. **nickel-plate,** *v.t.* to cover with nickel. **nickel-plating,** *n.* **nickel-silver,** *n.* an alloy like German silver but containing more nickel. **nickel-steel,** *n.* an alloy of nickel and steel. **nickelage,** *n.* the process of nickeling. **nickelic,** *a.* **nickeliferous,** *a.* **nickeline, -lite,** *n.* niccolite. **nickelize, -ise,** *v.t.* [Swed., abbrev. from G *Kupfernickel* (*Kupfer,* copper, *Nickel,* a demon, cp. OE *nicol*), so called from disgust at its not yielding copper]

nickelodeon, *n.* an early form of juke-box, especially one operated by a 5-cent piece. [NICKEL, (MEL)ODEON]

nicker[1], *v.i.* to neigh; (*fig.*) to guffaw. *n.* a neigh; a guffaw. [Sc., North., imit.]

nicker[2], *n.* (*sl.*) a pound (money), £1.

Nicklaus, *n.* **Jack (William)** (1940–), US golfer, nicknamed 'the Golden Bear'. He won a record 20 major titles, including 18 professional 'majors' (1962–86).

nicknack, KNICK-KNACK.

nickname, *n.* a name given in derision or familiarity. *v.t.* to give a nickname to; to call by a nickname. [ME *nekename,* corr. of *ekename,* from *an ekename* (EKE[1], NAME)]

Nicobar Islands, *n.* a group of Indian islands, part of the Union Territory of Andaman and Nicobar Islands.

nicol, *n.* a crystal of calcium carbonate so cut and cemented as to transmit only the extraordinary ray, used for polarizing light. [Scottish inventor William *Nicol,* c. 1768–1851]

Nicolle, *n.* **Charles** (1866–1936), French bacteriologist whose discovery in 1909 that typhus is transmitted by the body louse made the armies of World War I introduce delousing as a compulsory part of the military routine.

Nicosia, *n.* the capital of Cyprus, with leather, textile and pottery industries; population (1987) 165,000.

nicotine, *n.* an acrid, poisonous alkaloid contained in tobacco. **nicotinism,** *n.* (*Path.*) a morbid condition caused by over-indulgence in tobacco. **nicotinize, -ise,** *v.t.* **nicotian,** *a.* of or pertaining to tobacco. *n.* one who uses tobacco; †tobacco. **nicotianin,** *n.* a camphorous oil obtained from tobacco. [F Jean *Nicot,* 1530–1600, who introduced tobacco into France]

nictate, nictitate, *v.i.* to wink, esp. to open and shut the eyes rapidly. **nictation, nictitation,** *n.* **nictitating membrane,** a third or inner eyelid possessed by birds, fishes and many animals. [L *nictātus,* p.p. of *nictāre,* to wink (freq. *nictitāre*)]

nidamental, *a.* serving as a receptacle or protection for ova, eggs or young. [L *nīdōmentum,* from *nīdus,* nest]

niddle-noddle, *v.i.* to wag the head. *v.t.* to wag (the head). *a.* vacillating.

nide, *n.* a nest, esp. of young pheasants; a collection of pheasants. [L *nidus,* a nest]

nidge, *v.t.* to dress the face of stone with a pointed hammer. [from NICK[2]]

nidificate, nidify, *v.i.* to build a nest or nests. **nidification,** *n.* †**nidulation,** etc. NIDUS, *n.* [L *nīdificātus,* p.p. of *nīdificāre* (*nīdus, -ficāre, facere,* to make)]

nid-nod, *v.i.* to keep nodding, as if sleepy. [redupl. from NOD]

†**nidor,** *n.* the smell of cooked meat; any strong odour. †**nidorose, nidorous,** *a.* [L]

nidus, *n.* (*pl.* **-di**) a nest, a place for the deposit of eggs laid by birds, insects etc.; a place in which spores develop; a place in an organism where germs develop, a centre of infection; a group of eggs, tubercles etc.; (*fig.*) a source or origin, a place of development. †**nidulate,** *v.i.* to build a nest. †**nidulation,** *n.* nidification. [L]

Niebuhr, *n.* **Reinhold** (1892–1971), US Protestant Christian theologian. His *Moral Man and Immoral Society* (1932) reflected liberalism for biblical theology and attacked depersonalized industrial society.

niece, *n.* the daughter of one's brother or sister, or one's brother-in-law or sister-in-law; orig. a granddaughter. [OF *nièce,* pop. L *neptia,* L *neptis,* rel. to *nepos,* NEPHEW]

Niederösterreich, *n.* German name for the federal state of Lower Austria.

niello, *n.* (*pl.* **-li**) a black alloy used to fill the lines of incised designs on metal plates; an example of this work. **niellist,** *n.* [It., from L *nigellum,* neut. of *nigellus,* dim. of *niger,* black]

Nielsen, *n.* **Carl (August)** (1865–1931), Danish composer. His works show a progressive tonality, as in his opera *Saul and David* (1902) and six symphonies.

Niemeyer, *n.* **Oscar** (1907–), Brazilian architect, joint designer of the United Nations headquarters in New York, and of many buildings in Brasilia.

Niemöller, *n.* **Martin** (1892–1984), German Christian Protestant pastor. He was imprisoned in a concentration camp (1938–45) for campaigning against Nazism in the German church. and was president of the World Council of Churches (1961–68).

Niepce, *n.* **Joseph Nicéphore** (1765–1833), French pioneer of photography.

Niersteiner, *n.* a white Rhenish hock. [*Nierstein,* near Hesse, Germany]

Nietzsche, *n.* **Friedrich Wilhelm** (1844–1900), German philosopher who rejected the accepted absolute moral values and the 'slave morality' of Christianity. He argued that 'God is dead' and therefore people were free to create their own values. His ideal was the *Übermensch*, or 'Superman', who would impose his will on the weak and worthless. Nietzsche claimed that knowledge is never objective, but always serves some interest or unconscious purpose. **Nietzschean,** *n., a.*

niff, *n.* (*sl.*) a stink, a bad smell. **niffy** [perh. from SNIFF]

niffer, *v.t.* (*Sc., North.*) to exchange, to barter. *v.i.* to make an exchange; to haggle, to bargain. *n.* an exchange. [etym. doubtful (perh. rel. to NIEVE)]

nifty, *a.* (*coll.*) smart, stylish; quick, slick.

nigella, *n.* a genus of ranunculaceous plants comprising love-in-a-mist. [L fem. of *nīgellus,* dim. of *niger,* black]

Niger¹, *n.* Republic of (*République du Niger*) a landlocked country in W Africa, bounded to the N by Algeria and Libya, to the E by Chad, to the S by Nigeria and Benin, and to the W by Burkina Faso and Mali. **area** 1,186,408 sq km/457,953 sq miles. **capital** Niamey. **physical** mountains in centre; arid except in S (savanna) and SW (river Niger). **exports** groundnuts, livestock, gum arabic, tin, uranium. **population** (1989) 7,444,000; annual growth rate 2.8%. **language** French (official), Hausa, Djerma. **religion** Sunni Muslim 85%, animist 15%.

Niger², *n.* the third longest river in Africa, 4185 km/ 2600 miles from the highlands bordering Sierra Leone and Guinea NE through Mali, then SE through Niger and Nigeria to an inland delta on the Gulf of Guinea. Its flow has been badly affected by the expansion of the Sahara Desert.

Nigeria, *n.* Federal Republic of, a country in W Africa on the Gulf of Guinea, bounded to the N by Niger, to the E by Chad and Cameroon, and to the W by Benin. **area** 923,773 sq km/356,576 sq miles. **capital** Abuja; chief port Lagos. **towns** administrative headquarters Abuja; Ibadan, Ogbomosho, Kano; ports Port Harcourt, Warri, Calabar. **physical** the arid north becomes savanna and farther south tropical rainforest, with mangrove swamps along the coast; river Niger. **exports** petroleum (richest African country in oil resources), cocoa, groundnuts, palm oil, cotton, rubber, tin. **population** (1989) 115,152,000 (of three main ethnic groups, Yoruba in the W, Ibo in the E, and Hausa-Fulani in the N); annual growth rate 3.3%. **language** English (official), Hausa, Ibo, Yoruba. **religion** Sunni Muslim in the north, Christian in the south.

niggard, *n.* a stingy person, a miser; one who is grudging (of). *a.* miserly, mean, parsimonious. †*v.t.* to begrudge, to stint. †*v.i.* to be stingy. †**niggardish,** *a.* **niggardly,** *a.* and *adv.* **niggardliness,** *n.* [etym. obscure (Skeat compares Icel. *hnöggr,* Swed. *nugg,* Swed. dial. *nugger,* also OE *hnēaw,* sparing)]

nigger, *n.* (*offensive*) a negro; (*offensive*) one of any dark-skinned people; the black caterpillar of the turnip saw-fly. **the nigger in the woodpile,** a person or thing that spoils something good. **to work like a nigger,** (*offensive*) to work hard. [F *nègre,* Sp. NEGRO]

niggle, *v.i.* to busy oneself with petty details; to fiddle, to trifle. †*v.t.* to trick. *n.* small, cramped handwriting. **niggler,** *n.* **niggling,** *a., n.* [cp. Norw. *nigla*]

nigh, *adv.* near; almost. *a.* near; closely related, *prep.* near, close to. †*v.t., v.i.* to approach. †**nighly,** *adv.* †**nighness,** *n.* [OE *nēah* (cp. Dut. *na,* G *nah,* Icel. *na-*), cp. NEAR, NEXT]

night, *n.* the time of darkness from sunset to sunrise; the darkness of this period; the end of daylight, nightfall; a period of state of darkness; (*fig.*) ignorance; intellectual and moral darkness; death; old age; a period of grief or mourning. **a night out,** an evening spent in festivity; the evening on which a servant is allowed out. **to make a night of it,** to spend an evening in festivity. **night-bell,** *n.* a bell for use at night, as a physician's. **night-bird,** *n.* the owl or nightingale; (*fig.*) a person who goes about at night or routinely stays up late. **night-blindness,** *n.* nyctalopia. **nightcap,** *n.* a cap worn in bed; an alcoholic drink taken at bed-time. **night-cart,** *n.* (*Hist.*) a cart for removing refuse, esp. excrement. **night-chair** NIGHT-STOOL. **night-clothes,** *n.* clothes worn in bed. **night-club,** *n.* a club open late at night and in the early hours of the morning. †**night-crow,** *n.* a bird croaking at night, and supposed to be of ill omen. **night-dog,** *n.* a watch-dog. **night-dress, -gown,** *n.* a woman's or child's night attire. **night-effect,** *n.* transmission phenomena which are produced after sunset. **nightfall,** *n.* the beginning of night, the coming of darkness; dusk. **night-faring,** *a.* travelling by night. **night-fire,** *n.* a fire burning at night; an ignis fatuus. **night-fly.** *n.* a moth or other insect that flies by night; an angler's artificial fly for use after dark. **night-flower,** *n.* a flower that opens at night and shuts in the day. **night-foundered,** *a.* wrecked by night. **night-glass,** *n.* a telescope enabling one to see objects at night. **night-gear** NIGHT-CLOTHES. **night-gown** NIGHT-DRESS. †**night-hag,** *n.* a witch riding the air at night; a nightmare. **night-hawk,** *n.* the night-jar; an American bird, *Chordeiles virginianus.* **night-jar,** *n.* the goatsucker. **night-light,** *n.* a short, thick candle for keeping alight at night; the light of the moon or stars. **night-life,** *n.* late evening entertainment or social life. **night-line,** *n.* a line with baited hooks left in the water at night to catch fish. **night-long,** *a.* lasting through a night. *adv.* all night. **nightman,** *n.* one who removes night-soil. **nightmare,** *n.* a terrifying dream often accompanied with pressure on the chest and a feeling of powerlessness; orig. a monster supposed to sit upon a sleeper, an incubus; (*fig.*) a haunting sense of dread or anything inspiring such a feeling. **nightmarish,** *a.* **night-owl,** *n.* an exclusively nocturnal owl; a person who habitually stays up late. **night-piece,** *n.* a picture or description representing a night scene; a picture best seen by artificial light. **night-raven,** *n.* a bird of ill-omen supposed to cry at night. **night-school,** *n.* an evening school for those at work during the day. **night-season,** *n.* night-time. **night-shirt,** *n.* a long shirt worn in bed by men or boys. **night-soil,** (*formerly*) the contents of lavatories and cesspools removed at night. **night-stick,** (*N Am.*) a truncheon. **night-stool, -chair,** *n.* a bedroom commode. **night-time,** *n.* **night-terrors,** *n.pl.* a nightmare of childhood, *pavor nocturnus.* †**night-waking,** *n.* **night-walker,** *n.* a somnambulist; one who prowls about at night for evil purposes; a prostitute. **night-walking,** *n.* **night-wanderer,** *n.* †**night-wandering,** *a.* †**night-warbling,** *a.* singing at night. **night-watch,** *n.* a watch or guard on duty at night; one of the periods into which the Jews and Romans divided the night. **night-watcher,** *n.* **nightwatchman,** *n.* a person who keeps watch on a public building, factory etc. at night, a night security guard. **night-work,** *n.* †**nighted,** *a.* darkened; benighted. **nightless,** *a.* **nightly,** *a.* **nightward,** *a., adv.* **nightwards,** *adv.* **nighty,** *a.* (*coll.*) a night-gown. [OE *niht* (cp. Dut. *nacht* and G *Nacht,* Icel. *nätt, nött,* L *nox,* Gr. *nux,* Sansk. *nekta*)]

nightingale¹, *n.* a small migratory bird, *Daulias luscinia,* singing at night as well as by day. [OE *nihtegale* (NIGHT, *galan,* to sing)]

nightingale², *n.* a jacket or wrap worn by invalids sitting up in bed. [Florence *Nightingale,* see below]

Nightingale, *n.* **Florence** (1820–1910), English nurse, the founder of nursing as a profession. She took a team of nurses to Scutari (now Üsküdar, Turkey) in 1854 and reduced the Crimean War hospital death rate from 42% to 2%. In 1856 she founded the Nightingale School and Home for Nurses in London.

Night Journey, *n.* or **al-Miraj** (Arabic 'the ascent') in Islam, the journey of the prophet Mohammed, guided by the archangel Gabriel, from Mecca to Jerusalem, where he met the earlier prophets, including Adam, Moses and Jesus; he then ascended to paradise, where he experienced the majesty of Allah, and was also shown hell.

nightmare NIGHT.

nightshade, *n.* one of several plants of the genus *Solanum,* esp. the black nightshade, *S. nigrum,* with white flowers and poisonous black berries, and the woody nightshade, *S. dulcamara,* a trailing plant with purple flowers and brilliant red berries; also the deadly nightshade, *Atropa belladonna.*

nigrescent, *a.* growing black; blackish. **nigrescence,** *n.* [*nigrere,* to grow black, from *niger,* black]

nigrify, *v.t.* to blacken. **nigrification,** *n.*

nigrine, *n.* a ferriferous variety of rutile.

nigritude, *n.* blackness.

nigr(o)-, *comb. form.* black.

nigrosine, *n.* a blue-black dye-stuff obtained from aniline hydrochlorates.

nihil, *n.* nothing; †a return of no effects to a writ of distraint. **nihil obstat,** in the Roman Catholic Church, phrase denoting no objection to a publication (L, nothing hinders). **nihilism**, *n.* any theological, philosophical or political doctrine of a negative kind; denial of all existence, or of the knowledge of all existence; (*Hist.*) a Russian form of anarchism aiming at the subversion of all existing institutions. **nihilist**, *n.* **nihilistic**, *a.* **nihility**, *n.* the state of being nothing, of nothingness; (*fig.*) a mere nothing. [L]

Nihilist, *n.* member of a group of Russian revolutionaries in the reign of Alexander II 1855–81. The name, popularized by the writer Turgenev, means one who approves of nothing (Latin *nihil*) belonging to the existing order. In 1878 the Nihilists launched a guerrilla campaign leading to the murder of the tsar 1881.

Nijinsky, *n.* **Vaslav** (1890–1950), Russian dancer and choreographer. Noted for his powerful but graceful technique, he was a legendary member of Diaghilev's Ballets Russes, for whom he choreographed Debussy's *L'Après-midi d'un faune* (1912) and *Jeux* (1913), and Stravinsky's *The Rite of Spring* (1913).

Nijmegen, Treaties of, peace treaties (1678–79) between France on the one hand and the Netherlands, Spain and the Holy Roman Empire on the other, ending the Third Dutch War.

-nik *comb. form.* a person who practices something, e.g. *beatnik, kibbutznik, peacenik*. [from Russ. suffix from Yiddish suffix denoting an agent]

nikau, *n.* the New Zealand palm. [Maori]

nil, *n.* nothing; zero.

Nile, *n.* a river in Africa, the world's longest, 6695 km/4160 miles. The Blue Nile rises in Lake Tana, Ethiopia, the White Nile at Lake Victoria, and they join at Khartoum, Sudan. It enters the Mediterranean at a vast delta in N Egypt.

nilgai, *n.* a large Indian antelope. [Pers. and Hind. *nil*, blue, Hind. *gai*, Pers. *gaw*, cow.]

nilghau NYLGHAU.

nill, *v.i.* to be unwilling (now only in 3rd sing. in phrase *will he, nill he* or *willing, nilling* or *willy-nilly*). [OE *nyllan* (NE, WILL¹)]

Nilometer, *n.* an instrument for measuring the rise of the Nile during its floods. **Nilotic**, *a.* pertaining to the Nile etc.

nim¹, *n.* an ancient game for two players in which a number of counters are used. [per. OE *niman*, to take]

†**nim²,** *v.t.* to steal, to filch. *v.i.* to steal, to pilfer. [OE *niman* (cp. MDut. *nemen*, OHG *neman*, Icel. *nema*), prob. cogn. with Gr. *nemein*, to deal out]

nimble, *a.* light and quick in motion; agile, swift, dexterous; alert, clever, brisk, lively, versatile. **nimble-fingered,** *a.* **nimble-footed,** *a.* †**nimble-witted,** *a.* **nimbleness,** *n.* **nimbly,** *adv.* [OE *numol* (root of prec., -LE)]

nimbus, *n.* (*pl.* **-buses**) a halo or glory surrounding the heads of divine or sacred personages in paintings etc.; (*Meteor.*) a rain-cloud, a dark mass of cloud, usu. with ragged edges, from which rain is falling or likely to fall. **nimbused,** *a.* †**nimbiferous**, *a.* bringing storms. †**nimbose**, *a.* stormy. [L, cloud]

nimby, *a.* an expression indicating the views of those who support the dumping of nuclear waste, the construction of ugly buildings etc. as long as they or their property are not affected. **nimbyism,** *n.* [acronym for *n*ot *i*n *m*y *b*ack *y*ard]

†**nimiety,** *n.* excess, redundancy. [late L *nimietas*, from *nimis*]

niminy-piminy, *a.* affecting niceness or delicacy; mincing; affected. [imit. of affected pronun.]

Nimrod, *n.* a great hunter; military jet aircraft equipped with radar. [the mighty hunter of Gen. x.8–9]

nincompoop, *n.* a noodle, a blockhead, a fool. [etym. unknown]

nine, *n.* the number or figure 9; the age of 9. **nine days' wonder,** an event, person or thing that is a novelty for the moment but is soon forgotten. **nine times out of ten,** usually, generally. **the Nine,** the Muses. **to the nines,** to perfection, elaborately. **nine-pins,** *n.* a game with nine skittles set up to be bowled at. **nine-tenths,** *n.* (*coll.*) nearly all. **ninefold,** *a.* nine times repeated. **nineteen**, *n.* the number or figure 19; the age of 19. *a.* 19 in number; aged 19. **nineteen to the dozen,** volubly. **nineteenth**, *n.* one of nineteen equal parts. *n., a.* (the) last of 19 (people, things etc.); the next after the eighteenth. **nineteenth hole,** *n.* (*colloq. Golf*) the clubhouse bar. **ninety**, *n.* the number or figure 90; the age of 90; (*pl.*) the period of time between one's ninetieth and one hundredth birthdays; the range of temperature between ninety and one hundred degrees; the period of time between the ninetieth and final years of a century. **ninetieth**, *n.* one of ninety equal parts. *n., a.* (the) last of ninety (people, things etc.); the next after the eighty-ninth. [OE *nigon* (cp. Dut. *negen*, G *neun*, Icel. *nīu*, L *novem*, Gr. *ennea*, Sansk. *navan*]

Nineteen Propositions, *n.pl.* demands presented by the English Parliament to Charles I, 1642. They were designed to limit the powers of the crown, and their rejection represented the final breakdown of peaceful negotiations and the beginning of the Civil War.

Nineveh, *n.* capital of the Assyrian Empire from the 8th century BC until its destruction by the Medes under King Cyaxares in 612 BC, as forecast by the Old Testament prophet Nahum. It was situated on the Tigris (opposite the modern city of Mosul, Iraq) and was adorned with splendid palaces.

Ningxia (Hui), *n.* autonomous region (formerly Ninghsia-Hui) of NW China. **area** 170,000 sq km/65,620 sq miles. **capital** Yinchuan. **physical** desert plateau. **products** cereals and rice under irrigation; coal. **population** (1986) 4,240,000, including many Muslims, and nomadic herdsmen.

ninjutsu, *n.* a martial art based on the killing techniques of the Ninjas, members of an ancient Japanese society of assassins. [*Ninja*, ju-*jutsu*]

ninny, *n.* a fool, a simpleton. [perh. imit., cp. Sp. *niño*, It. *ninno*, child]

ninon, *n.* a semi-diaphanous light silk material. [F]

ninth *n.* one of nine equal parts; an interval of an octave and a second. *n., a.* (the) last of nine (people, things etc.); the next after the eighth. **ninthly,** *adv.* [NINE, -TH]

niobium, *n.* a metallic element, at. no. 41; chem. symbol Nb; occurring in tantalite etc. **niobic,** *a.* **niobite**, *n.* a niobic salt; a variety of tantalite. [*Niobe*, daughter of Tantalus, -IUM]

Nip NIPPON.

nip¹, *v.t.* (*past, p.p.* **nipped**) to pinch, to squeeze or compress sharply; to cut or pinch off the end or point of; to bite; to sting, to pain; to check the growth of; to blast, to wither; to benumb; †to slander. *v.i.* to cause pain; (*coll.*) to move, go, or step quickly (in, out, etc.). *n.* a pinch, a sharp squeeze or compression; a bite; a check to vegetation, esp. by frost; a sharp saying, a sarcasm. **nip-cheese,** *n.* (*Naut. slang*) a purser. **nipper,** *n.* one who or that which nips; a device for seizing and holding; a horse's fore-tooth or incisor; a chela or great claw of a crab or other crustacean; a fish of various kinds; (*sl.*) a boy, a lad; (*pl.*) a pair of pincers, forceps or pliers; a pair of pince-nez. **nippingly,** *adv.* keenly. **nippy,** *a.* cold; active; agile; sharp in temper; quick, alert. [cp. Dut. *nўpen*, G *kneifen*]

nip² *n.* a small drink, esp. of spirits *v.i.* to take a nip or nips. *v.t.* to take a nip of. **nipperkin,** *n.* (*now chiefly Sc.*) a small cup or the quantity held in this; orig. a measure of capacity less than half a pint (0·25 l). [etym. doubtful]

nipa, *n.* a palm tree of tropical SE Asia and the islands of the Indian Ocean, with feathery leaves used in thatching, basket-weaving etc., and packing bunches of fruit; an intoxicating beverage made from the sap of this. [Malay *nīpah*]

nipper etc. NIP¹.

nipple, *n.* the small prominence in the breast of female mammals, esp. women, by which milk is sucked or drawn, a teat; a similar contrivance attached to a baby's feeding bottle; a nipple-shield; a nipple-shaped perforated projection, as on a gun-breach for holding a percussion-cap; a nipple-shaped prominence on the surface of metal or glass; a pap-shaped elevation on a mountain etc. **nipple-shield,** *n.* a protection worn over the nipple by nursing mothers. **nipplewort,** *n.* a slender weed, *Lapsana communis,* with small yellow flowers. [a dim. of *neb* or *nib*]

Nippon, *n.* the Japanese name for Japan. **Nip,** *n.* (*offensive*) a Japanese.

nippy NIP[1].

Nirvana, *n.* absorption of individuality into the divine spirit with extinction of personal desires and passions, the Buddhist state of beatitude; (*coll.*) bliss, heaven. [Sansk., from *nirvā,* to blow]

nis[1], *n.* (*Scand. folklore*) a brownie or hobgoblin. [from Dan. or Swed. *nisse*]

†**nis**[2] *v.i.* is not. [NE, IS]

Nisei, *n.* a person of Japanese descent born in the US and loyal to that country. [Jap.]

nisi, *conj.* (*Law*) unless, if not. **decree, order,** or **rule nisi,** one that takes effect, or is made absolute, after a certain period, unless cause is shown for rescinding it. **nisi prius,** orig. a writ commanding a sheriff to empanel a jury; an authority to judges of assize to try causes; applied to trial of civil causes before judges of assize. [L]

nissen, *n.* a long hut of corrugated iron with semicircular roof. [from Col. P. N. *Nissen,* 1871–1930, British engineer]

nisus, *n.* an effort, a conatus. [L, from *nītī,* to endeavour]

nit[1], *n.* the egg of a louse or other small, esp. parasitic, insect. **nit-picking,** *n.* (*coll.*) petty criticism of minor details. **nit-pick,** *v.i.* **nitter,** *n.* a fly that deposits nits on horses; the bot-fly. **nitty,** *a.* [OE *hnitu* (cp. Dut. *neet,* G *Niss,* Icel. *nitr*)]

nit[2], *n.* (*coll.*) a fool. [perh. from NITWIT]

nit[3] *n.* the unit of luminance, one candela per square metre. [L *nitor,* brightness]

nit[4], *n.* a unit of information in computing (1·44 bits) also **nepit**. [*Naperian digit*]

Niterci, *n.* a resort city on the E shore of Guanabara Bay opposite Rio de Janeiro; population (1980) 382,700.

†**nither,** *v.t.* to bring low; to humiliate, to abase. [OE *nitherian,* from *nither,* NETHER]

nitid, *a.* shining; bright, gay. [L *nitidus,* from *nitēre,* to shine]

niton, *n.* gaseous radioactive element. [L *nitere,* to shine]

nitrate, *a.* a salt of nitric acid; sodium or potassium nitrate. *v.t.* to treat or combine with nitric acid. **nitration,** *n.*

nitre, *n.* saltpetre, potassium nitrate, occurring as an orthorhombic mineral. **nitriferous,** *a.* **nitrify,** *v.t.* to turn into nitre; to make nitrous. *v.i.* to become nitrous. **nitrification,** *n.* **nitrite,** *n.* [F, from *L nitrum,* Gr. *nitron,* perh. of Oriental orig. (cp. Heb. *nether*)]

nitric, *a.* pertaining to nitre. **nitric acid,** *n.* a colourless, corrosive acid liquid based on the ingredients of nitre, aqua fortis.

nitride, *n.* a compound of nitrogen with phosphorus, boron, silicon etc.

nitro-, *comb. form.* nitric.

nitrobenzene, nitrobenzol, *n.* an oily compound of benzene with nitric acid, having an odour of oil of bitter almonds, used for flavouring perfumes and confectionery.

nitro-compound, *n.* a compound obtained by treatment with nitric acid.

nitroexplosive, *n.* one of a class of explosives which is prepared by treatment with nitric acid.

nitrogen, *n.* a colourless, tasteless, gaseous element, at. no. 7; chem. symbol N; forming 80% of the atmosphere, the basis of nitre and nitric acid. **nitrogenize, -ise,** *v.t.* **nitrogenic, nitrogenous,** *a.* [F *nitrogène*]

nitroglucose, *n.* a compound obtained from powdered cane-sugar treated with nitrosulphuric acid.

nitroglycerine , *n.* a highly explosive colourless oil, obtained by adding glycerine to a mixture of nitric and sulphuric acids.

nitroleum, *n.* nitroglycerine.

nitromagnesite, *n.* a white, bitter magnesium nitrate found as an efflorescent mineral in limestone caves.

nitrometer, *n.* an instrument for determining nitrogen in some of its combinations.

nitromuriatic, *a.* nitrohydrochloric.

nitronaphthalene, *n.* a substance that is obtained by mixing naphthalene with nitric acid.

nitro-powder, *n.* an explosive prepared from an organic compound by treatment with nitric acid.

nitrous, *a.* obtained from, impregnated with, or resembling nitre. **nitrous oxide,** *n.* nitrogen monoxide used as an anaesthetic, laughing-gas.

nitroxyl, *n.* a radical composed of one atom of nitrogen in chemical combination with two of oxygen.

nitter, nitty NIT[1].

nitty gritty, *n.* the basic facts, the realities of a situation. [etym. doubtful]

nitwit, *n.* (*coll.*) a foolish or stupid person.

†**nival,** *a.* growing in or under snow; niveous. **nivation,** *n.* erosion due to the action of snow. **niveous,** *a.* resembling snow; snowy. **nivosity,** *n.* [L *nivālis,* from *nivem,* nom. *nix,* snow]

nix[1], *n.* (*sl.*) nothing, nobody. [G, colloq. for *nichts*]

nix[2], *int.* look out! **keeping nix,** keeping watch.

nix[3], **nixie,** *n.* a water-sprite. [G *Nix,* fem. *Nixe* (cogn. with OE *nicor,* Icel. *nykr,* prob. rel. to Gr. *nizein, niptein,* to wash)]

Nixon, *n.* **Richard (Milhous)** (1913–), 37th president of the US, 1969–74, a Republican. He attracted attention as a member of the Un-American Activities Committee (1948), and was vice-president to Eisenhower (1953–61). As president he was responsible for US withdrawal from Vietnam, and forged new links with China, but at home his culpability in the cover-up of the Watergate scandal and the existence of a 'slush fund' for political machinations during his re-election campaign 1972 led to his resignation 1974 after being threatened with impeachment.

nizam, *n.* (*pl.* **nizam**) a man in the Turkish regular army; the title of the ruler of Hyderabad. [Hind. from Arab. *nidhām,* order, government]

Nkomati Accord, *n.* a non-aggression treaty between South Africa and Mozambique concluded 1984, under which they agreed not to give material aid to opposition movements in each other's countries, which in effect meant that South Africa pledged itself not to support the Mozambique National Resistance (Renamo), while Mozambique was committed not to help the outlawed African National Congress (ANC).

Nkomo, *n.* **Joshua** (1917–), Zimbabwean politician, president of ZAPU (Zimbabwe African People's Union) from 1961, and a leader of the black nationalist movement against the white Rhodesian regime. He was a member of Robert Mugabe's cabinet (1980–82) and from 1987.

Nkrumah, *n.* **Kwame** (1909–72), Ghanaian nationalist politician, prime minister of the Gold Coast (1952–57) and of independent Ghana (1957–60), and Ghana's first president (1960–66). His policy of 'African socialism' led to links with the communist bloc.

NKVD, *n.* the Soviet secret police, 1934–38, replaced by the KGB. The NKVD was reponsible for Stalin's infamous purges.

NNE, (*abbr.*) north north-east.

NNW, (*abbr.*) north north-west.

No, (*chem. symbol*) nobelium.

no, no. No (*abbr.*) number.

n.o., (*abbr.*) not out.

no[1], *adv.* a word of denial or refusal, the categorical negative; not; (*with comp.*) not at all, by no amount. *n.* (*pl.* **noes**) the word 'no'; a negative reply, a denial, a refusal; (*pl.*) voters against a motion. **no less,** *adv.* as much, as much as. **no more,** *adv.* not any more; nothing further; no longer; dead, gone; never again; just as little as. [OE *nā* (NE, ever)]

no[2] *a.* not any; not one, not a; quite other, quite opposite or the reverse; not the least; hardly any; absent, lacking; expressing opposition, objection, or rejection (as *no popery*). *adv.* not (usu. at end of sentence with *or*). **no-claims bonus,** *n.* a reduction in the price of an insurance policy because no claims have been made on it. **no-man's-land,** waste or unclaimed land; the contested land between two opposing forces. **no ball,** (*Cricket*) a ball not delivered according to the rules, counting for one to the other side. **no-ball,** *v.t.* to declare (a ball) to be no-ball; to declare (a bowler) to have bowled this. **no go** GO². **nohow,** *adv.* in no way, not by any means. **no man,** no one, no person, nobody. **no one,** *pron.* nobody, no person. **no thoroughfare,** a notice that a road, path etc. is closed or has no exit or through way. **no trump,** *int.* in bridge, the call for the playing of a hand without any trump suit. **noway, †noways, nowise,** *adv.* in no way, not at all. **nowhence,** *adv.* **nowhither,** *adv.* **no whit,** *adv.* not at all, not in the least. [NONE¹]

Nō, Noh, *n.* the classical, aristocratic Japanese drama, which developed in the 14th–16th cents. and is still performed. There is a repertory of some 250 pieces, of which five, one from each of the several classes devoted to different subjects, may be put on in a performance lasting a whole day. Dance, mime, music and chanting develop the mythical or historical themes. All the actors are men, some of whom wear masks and elaborate costumes; scenery is limited. Nō influenced kabuki drama.

Noachian, Noachic, *a.* pertaining to Noah or his times. **Noah's ark** ARK.

Noah, *n.* in the Old Testament or Hebrew Bible, the son of Lamech and father of Shem, Ham and Japheth, who built an ark so that he and his family and specimens of all existing animals might survive the Flood; there is also a Babylonian version of the tale.

nob¹, *n.* (*sl.*) the head; (*Cribbage*) a point scored for holding the knave of the same suit as the turn-up. *v.t.* (*Boxing*) to hit on the head. [prob. var. of KNOB]

nob² *n.* a person of rank or distinction; a swell. **nobby,** *a.* smart, elegant. [etym. doubtful]

nobble, *v.t.* (*coll.*) to dose, lame or otherwise tamper with (a horse) to prevent its winning a race; to circumvent, to over-reach; to get round, to square; to get hold of dishonestly; to catch, to nab; to nob, to hit on the head; to buttonhole (a person); to persuade or win over by dishonest means. to influence (e.g. a member of a jury) esp. by bribery or threats. **nobbler,** *n.* [perhaps *nab*]

nobbut, (*dial*) no more than; only. [ME *no but* from *no* (adv) + *but*]

Nobel, *n.* **Alfred Bernhard** (1833–96), Swedish chemist and engineer. He invented dynamite (1867) and ballistite, a smokeless gunpower, 1889. He amassed a large fortune from the manufacture of explosives and the exploitation of the Baku oilfields in Russia. He left this fortune in trust for the endowment of five Nobel prizes.

nobelium, *n.* an artificially produced radioactive element, at. no. 102; chem. symbol No. [from its production at the Nobel Institute, Stockholm]

Nobel prize, *n.* annual international prize, first awarded in 1901 under the will of Alfred Nobel. The interest on the Nobel fund is divided annually among the persons who have made the greatest contributions in the fields of physics, chemistry, medicine, literature and world peace.

nobility, *n.* the quality of being noble; magnanimity, greatness, dignity; nobleness of birth or family; (*collect.*) the nobles, the peerage. **nobiliary,** *a.* **†nobilitate,** *v.t.* **†nobilitation,** *n.* [F *nobilité,* L *nōbilitātem,* nom. *-tas,* as foll.]

noble, *a.* lofty or illustrious in character, worth or dignity; magnanimous, high-minded, morally elevated; of high rank, of ancient or illustrious lineage; belonging to the nobility; magnificent, grand, stately, splendid, imposing; excellent, fine, admirable; valuable, pure (of metals). *n.* a nobleman, a peer, an obsolete gold coin worth usu. 6s. 8d. **nobleman,** *n.* a peer. **noble metals,** *n.pl.* metals such as gold, silver, platinum, which are not affected by air or water, and not easily by acids. **noble-minded,** *a.* **noble-mindedness,** *n.* **noble-woman,** *n. fem.* **nobleness,** *n.* **noblesse,** *n.* the nobility (of a foreign country); †noblemen, nobility. **noblesse oblige,** rank imposes obligations. **nobly,** *adv.* [F, from L *nōbilis,* from base of *noscere,* to KNOW]

Noble Savage, the, an influential Enlightenment idea of the virtuous innocence of 'savage' peoples, often embodied in the American Indian, and celebrated by the writers J. J. Rousseau, Chateaubriand (in *Atala,* 1801), and James Fenimore Cooper.

nobody, *n.* no one, no person; a person of no importance. **like nobody's business,** very energetically or intensively.

†nocent, *a.* hurtful, mischievous; criminal, guilty. *n.* a guilty person. [L *nocens -ntem,* pres.p. of *nocēre,* to injure]

nock, *n.* a notched tip of horn etc. at the butt-end of an arrow; the notch in this; †the notched tip at each end of a bow; the upper fore corner of a sail. *v.t.* to fit (an arrow) to the bowstring. [ME *nokke,* prob. from Dut. or LG *nokk*]

noctambulant, *a.* night-walking. **noctambulation,** *n.* somnambulism, *n.* **noctambulism,** *n.* **noctambulist,** *n.* **noctambulous,** *a.* [L *ambulare,* to walk]

noct(i)- *comb. form* nocturnal, by night. [L *nox, noctis,* night]

noctiflorous, *a.* night-flowering.

noctilionine, *a.* belonging to the genus of bats *Noctilio.*

noctiluca, *n.* a phosphorescent marine animalcule.

noctilucent, *a.* shining by night.

noctivagant, *a.* wandering by night. **noctivagation,** *n.* **noctivagous,** *a.*

noctograph, *n.* a writing-frame for the blind; a nocturnograph; a noctuary.

Noctua *n.* a genus of moths typical of the Noctuidae, the largest family of Lepidoptera. **noctuid,** *a.* and *n.* [L night-owl]

noctuary, *n.* an account of nightly events, experiences etc.

noctule, *n.* the great bat *Vesperugo noctula.*

nocturn, *n.* in the Roman Catholic Church, one of the divisions of matins.

Nocturnae, *n.pl.* the owls.

nocturnal, *a.* relating to or occurring, performed, or active, by night. **nocturnally,** *adv.*

nocturne, *n.* a painting or drawing of a night scene; a dreamy piece of music suited to the night or evening.

nocturnograph, *n.* an instrument for recording work done at night in factories, mines etc.

nocuous, *a.* hurtful, noxious; poisonous, venomous. **nocuously,** *adv.* [L *nocuus,* from *nocēre,* to injure]

nod, *v.i.* (*past, p.p.* **nodded**) to incline the head with a slight, quick motion in token of assent, command, indication, or salutation; to incline, to totter (of a building); to let the head fall forward; to be drowsy, to sleep; to make a careless mistake, *v.t.* to bend or incline (the head etc.); to signify by a nod. *n.* a quick bend of the head; a bending downwards; (*fig.*) command. **Land of Nod,** sleep. **to nod off,** (*coll.*) to fall asleep. **to nod through,** in Parliament, to allow to vote by proxy; to pass (a motion etc.) without formal discussion, voting etc. **nodder,** *n.* **nodding,** *n., a.* **nodding acquaintance,** *n.* a slight acquaintance. [ME *nidde,* not known in OE]

nodal NODE.

noddle¹, *n.* (*sl.*) the head. [etym. doubtful]

noddle², *v.t., v.i.* to nod frequently, to wag.

noddy, *n.* a simpleton, a fool; a tropical sea-bird, *Anous stolida,* from its being easily caught; †a light two-wheeled hackney-vehicle; an inverted pendulum used to indicate vibration. [prob. rel. to NOD]

node, *n.* a knot, a knob; the point of a stem from which leaves arise; a thickening or swelling e.g. of a joint of the body; the point at which the orbit of a planet intersects the ecliptic, or in which two great circles of the celestial sphere intersect; the point at which a curve crosses itself and at which more than one tangent can be drawn; a similar point on a surface; a point of rest in a vibrating body; the plot of a story, play or poem. **nodal,** *a.* **nodal lines,** *n.pl.* lines on the surface of an elastic body which remain at rest when the body is made to vibrate. **nodal points,** *n.pl.* the points in a string extended between two fixed objects which remain at rest when the string is made to vibrate. **nodical,** *a.* relating to the nodes. **nodose,** *a.* knotty; having nodes. **nodosity,** *n.* **nodule,** *n.* a small knot, node or lump; a rounded lump or mass of irregularly rounded shape; a small node; a small knot or tumour. **nodular, nodulated, noduled, nodulose, nodulous,** *a.* **nodulation,** *n.* **nodus,** *n.* a knotty point, a complication, a difficulty; a node. [L *nodus,* a knot]

Noel, *n.* Christmas. [F]

noesis, *n.* pure thought; an intellectual view of the world. **noetic, -al** *a.* relating to the intellect; performed by or originating in the intellect. †**noematic, -al,** *a.* [Gr. *noēsis,* mental perception, from *noein,* to perceive (*noos,* mind, thought)]

Noetian, *n.* a follower of Noetus of Smyrna (2nd cent. AD), who taught that there was only one person in the Godhead, and that Christ was a mode of manifestation of the Father. *a.* of or pertaining to Noetus or Noetianism. **Noetianism,** *n.*

†**nog**[1], *n.* a strong ale, brewed in East Anglia; an eggnog. [etym. doubtful]

nog[2] *n.* a pin, tree-nail or peg; a wooden block shaped like a brick, built into a wall to take nails; a snag or stump. *v.t.* to fix or secure with a nog or nogs; to build with nogging. [etym. doubtful]

noggin, *n.* a small mug; a measure, usu. a gill (125 ml); the contents of such a measure. [etym. doubtful]

nogging, *n.* a wall of scantling filled with bricks. [NOG[2], -ING]

nohow NO[2].

noil, *n.* (*often in pl.*) tangles and knots of wool removed by the comb. [etym. doubtful]

noise, *n.* a sound of any kind, esp. a loud, discordant, harsh or disagreeable one; clamour, din, loud or continuous talk; evil report, scandal; †rumour; a band of musicians. †*v.i.* to make a noise. *v.t.* to make public, to spread (about or abroad). **big noise,** *n.* (*coll.*) a person of importance. †**noiseful,** *a.* **noiseless,** *a.* **noiselessly,** *adv.* **noiselessness,** *n.* **noisy,** *a.* causing noise; making much noise; (*fig.*) glaring, violent, loud (of colours, dress, style etc.). **noisily,** *adv.* **noisiness,** *n.* [F, *noise,* quarrel]

noisette[1], *n.* a variety of rose, a cross between the China rose and the musk-rose. [Philippe *Noisette,* US horticulturalist]

noisette[2], *n.* (*pl.*) small pieces of mutton, veal, etc., cooked for the table in a special way; a nutlike or nut flavoured sweet. [F, hazel nut, dim. of *noix*]

noisome, *a.* hurtful, noxious; unwholesome, offensive, disgusting (especially of smells). **noisomely,** *adv.* **noisomeness,** *n.* [ME *noy,* ANNOY, SOME]

Nolan, *n.* **Sidney** (1917–), Australian artist, who created atmospheric paintings of the outback, exploring themes from Australian history such as the life of the outlaw Ned Kelly and the folk heroine Mrs Fraser.

Nolde, *n.* **Emil** (adopted name of Emil Hansen) (1867–1956), German Expressionist painter. He studied in Paris and Dachau, joined the group of artists known as *die Brücke* (1906–07), and visited Polynesia 1913; he then became almost a recluse in NE Germany. Many of his themes were religious.

nolens volens, *adv.* willing or unwilling, willy-nilly, perforce. [*nōlens,* pres.p. of *nolle,* to be unwilling, *volens,* pres.p. of *velle,* to be willing]

noli-me-tangere, *n.* a plant of the genus *Impatiens,* esp. *I. noli-me-tangere,* the yellow balsam; an ulcerous disease of the skin, lupus. [L, touch me not]

noll, *n.* the head. [OE *hnol* (cp. OHG *hnol,* top)]

Nollekens, *n.* **Joseph** (1737–1823), English sculptor, specializing in portrait busts and memorials.

nolle prosequi, the record of a decision to proceed no further with part of a prosecution. [L]

nolo contendere, I will not contest it, a plea which accepts conviction without admitting guilt. [L]

Nom, *n.* Chinese-style characters used in writing the Vietnamese language. Nom characters were used from the 13th cent. for Vietnamese literature, but were replaced in the 19th cent. by a romanized script known as Quoc Ngu.

noma, *n.* a destructive ulceration of the cheek, esp. that affecting debilitated children. [L *nomē,* ulcer, Gr. *nemein,* to consume]

nomad, *n.* one of a people that wanders about seeking pasture for their flocks, a wanderer. *a.* wandering. **nomadic,** *a.* **nomadically,** *adv.* **nomadism,** *n.* **nomadize, -ise,** *v.i.* [L and Gr. *nomad-,* nom. *nomas,* from *nemein,* to allot, to pasture]

no-man's land NO[2].

nomarch, *n.* a ruler or governor of an Egyptian nome or Greek nomarchy. **nomarchy,** *n.* a province of modern Greece. [Gr. *nomarchēs* or *nomarchos* (*nomos,* NOME, *archein,* to govern)]

nombril, *n.* (*Her.*) the point of an escutcheon between the fesse-point and the base-point. [F, the navel]

nom de guerre, *n.* an assumed name, a pseudonym (F, war-name). **nom de plume** (ploom) *n.* a pen-name. [incorrect F]

nome, *n.* a province of a country, esp. in modern Greece and Egypt. [Gr. *nomos,* from *nemein,* to divide]

nomenclator, *n.* one who gives names to things, esp. in classification of natural history etc.; (*Rom. Ant.*) a servant or attendant, esp. on a candidate for office, whose duty it was to name or introduce persons met; an officer who assigned places at banquets. **nomenclative,** †**nomenclatory,** *a.* **nomenclatress,** *n.* **nomenclature,** *n.* a system of names for the objects of study in any branch of science; a system of terminology; a vocabulary, a glossary; †a name. **nomenclatural,** *a.* [L (*nōmen,* name, *calāre,* to call)]

†**nomial,** *n.* (*Alg.*) a single term or name. [from BINOMIAL]

nomic, *a.* ordinary, customary (of spelling). *n.* the usual spelling. [Gr. *nomikos,* from *nomos,* law]

nominal, *a.* existing in name only; opp. to real; trivial, inconsiderable; of, pertaining to or consisting of a name or names; containing names; of or pertaining to a noun, substantival. **nominalism,** *n.* the doctrine that general or abstract concepts have no existence but as names or words. cp. REALISM. **nominalist,** *n.* **nominalistic,** *a.* **nominally,** *adv.* in name only. [L *nōminālis,* from *nōmen -inis,* name]

nominate, *v.t.* to name, to designate; to mention by name; to appoint to an office or duty; to propose as a candidate; to call, to denominate. †**nominately,** *adv.* **nomination,** *n.* **nominative,** *a.* applied to the case of the subject. *n.* the case of the subject; the subject of the verb. **nominatival,** *a.* **nominator,** *n.* **nominee,** *n.* person named or appointed by name. **nomineeism,** *n.* [L *nōminātus,* p.p. of *nōmināre,* as prec.]

nomistic, *a.* of or based upon law.

nom(o)- *comb. form.* of or pertaining to law. [Gr. *nomos,* law]

nomocracy, *n.* a system of government according to a code of laws.

nomogeny, *n.* origination of life according to natural law, not by miracle. **nomogram,** *n.* a chart with scales of quantities arranged side by side, which can be used to carry out rapid calculations. **nomography,** *n.* the art of drafting laws or a treatise on this. **nomographer,** *n.*

nomology, *n.* the science of law. **nomologist,** *n.*

nomothetical, *a.* legislative. [Gr. *nomothetikos,* from *nomothetēs,* lawgiver (*tithenai,* to put or set)]

non-, *pref.* freely prefixed to indicate a negative; only a selection of such words is given below. **non-ability,** *n.* a want of ability. **non-abstainer,** *n.* one who is not a total abstainer from intoxicating liquors. **non-acceptance,** *n.* **non-access,** *n.* (*Law*) absence of opportunity for sexual intercourse, a plea in questions of paternity. **non-acquaintance,** *n.* lack of acquaintance (with). **non-acquiescence,** *n.* refusal of acquiescence. **non-aggression pact,** *n.* an agreement between two states to settle differences by negotiation rather than by force. **non-alcoholic,** *a.* not containing alcohol. **non-aligned,** *a.* not taking any side in international politics, esp. not belonging to the Warsaw Pact or NATO. **non-appearance,** *n.* default of appearance, esp. in court. **non-attendance,** *n.* **non-belligerent,** *n.* a neutral; a country that remains neutral in name only, supporting a belligerent country with everything save armed force. **non-claim,** *n.* failure to make a claim within the legal time. **non-collegiate,** *a.* not belonging to a college (of a student); not having colleges (of a university). **non-combatant,** *a.* not in the fighting line. *n.* a civilian, esp. a surgeon, chaplain etc. attached to troops. **non-com.**, *n.* (*sl.*) a non-commissioned officer. **non-commissioned,** *a.* not holding a commission, applied to military officers below the rank of 2nd lieutenant. **non-committal,** *n.* refusal to commit or pledge oneself; the state of not being committed to either side. *a.* not committing one, impartial. **non-communicant**, *n.* one who fails to attend Holy Communion. **non-compliance,** *n.* (*Law*) failure to comply. **non-complying,** *a.* **non-concurrence,** *n.* **non-conducting,** *a.* not conducting heat or electricity. **non-conductor,** *n.* a substance or medium that offers resistance to heat or electricity. **non-conductibility,** *n.* **nonconformist,** *n.* see separate article below. **nonconforming,** *a.* **nonconformity,** *n.* **non-contagious,** *a.* not contagious. **non-content,** *n.* (*House of Lords*) one who votes in the negative. **non-cooperation,** *n.* refusal to cooperate; inactive opposition; refusal, by non-payment of taxes, to cooperate with the government of a country. **non-delivery,** *n.* **non-development,** *n.* **non-discovery,** *n.* **non-effective,** *a.* not qualified for active service. **non-ego,** *n.* (*Phil.*) the external or objective in perception or thought. [L, not I] **non-egoistical,** *a.* **non-elect,** *a.* not elected. *n.* one not elected; one not predestined for salvation. **non-election,** *n.* †**non-electric,** *a.* not electric; conducting electricity. *n.* a non-electric substance. **non-emphatic,** *a.* without emphasis. **non-episcopal,** *a.* not belonging to the Episcopalian Church. **non-episcopalian,** *n.* **non-essential,** *a.*, n. **non-execution,** *n.* **non-existence,** *n.* **non-existent,** *a.* **non-exportation,** *n.* **non-feasance,** *n.* failure to perform an act that is legally incumbent on one. **non-ferrous,** *a.* containing no iron. **non-fiction,** *n., a.* (of) a literary work, containing no deliberate fictitious element. **non-flammable,** *a.* not capable of supporting flame, though combustible, difficult or impossible to set alight. **non-forfeiting,** *a.* applied to policies which are not forfeited upon non-payment of premiums. **non-fulfilment**, *n.* **non-human,** *a.* not belonging to the human race. **non-importation,** *n.* **non-importing,** *a.* **non-interference, non-intervention,** *n.* the principle or policy of keeping aloof from the disputes of other nations. **non-intrusion,** *n.* in the Church of Scotland, the principle that a patron should not impose an unacceptable minister on a congregation. **non-intrusionist**, *n.* **non-joinder,** *n.* failure to join with another as party to a suit. **non-juring,** *a.* not swearing allegiance; pertaining to the Non-jurors. **Non-juror,** *n.* see separate entry. **non-jury,** *a.* tried without jury. **non-manufacturing,** *a.* **non-member,** *n.* one who is not a member. **non-membership,** *n.* **non-metallic,** *a.* **non-moral,** *a.* not involving ethical considerations. **non-natural,** †(*Med.*) *a.* not natural; not part of the nature of man but essential to his existence, as air, food, sleep etc. **non-nuclear,** *a.* not having, or using, nuclear power or weapons. **non-obedience,** *n.* **non-observance,** *n.* **non-party,** *a.* not concerned with questions of party. **non-payment,** *n.* **non-performance,** *n.* **non-placental,** *a.* not having a placenta. **non-ponderous,** *a.* having no weight. **non-production,** *n.* **non-professional,** *a.* not professional, amateur; unskilled. **non-proficient,** *a., n.* **non-provided,** *a.* denoting schools which are not provided by the Education Authority, e.g. Church Schools. **non-regardance,** *n.* want of due regard. **non-residence,** *n.* the state of not residing in a place, on one's estate, at one's office etc. **non-resident,** *a., n.* **non-resistance,** *n.* passive obedience or submission even to power unjustly exercised. †**non-resistant,** *a., n.* **non-resisting,** *a.* **non-returnable,** *a., n.* a bottle jar or other container on which a returnable deposit has not been paid. **non-sexual,** *a.* asexual, sexless. **non-skid,** *n., a.* (a tyre) designed to prevent skidding. **non-smoker,** *n.* someone who does not smoke; a part of a train etc. in which it is not permitted to smoke. **non-society** NON-UNION. **non-solvent,** *a.* insolvent. *n.* an insolvent. **non-solvency,** *n.* **non-starter,** *n.* in a race, a horse which is entered but does not start; (*coll.*) an idea or person with no chance whatsoever of success. **non-stick,** *a.* of a cooking pan, treated so that food will not stick to it. **non-stop,** *a.* without a pause; not stopping at certain stations. **non-submissive,** *a.* **non-union,** *a.* not connected with a society or trade union. **non-unionist,** *n.* **non-user,** *n.* neglect to use a right by which it may become void. **non-violence,** *n.* the practice of refraining from violence on principle. **non-white,** *n.* a member of any race other than the white race. [L, not]

nonage, *n.* the state of being under age; minority; a period of immaturity. [OF (NON-, AGE)]

nonagenarian, *a.* ninety years old. *n.* a person 90 years old, or between 90 and 100. [L *nōnāgēnārius,* from *nōnāgēnī,* ninety each]

nonagesimal, *a.* pertaining to 90 or to a nonagesimal. *n.* (*Astron.*) the point of the ecliptic highest above the horizon. [L *nōnāgēsimus,* from *nōnāginta,* ninety]

nonagon, *n.* a figure having nine sides and nine angles. [from L *nōnus,* ninth, after DECAGON, etc.]

nonary, *a.* based on the number nine (of a scale of notation). *n.* a group of nine; a tertian fever recurring on the ninth day. [L *nōnārius,* from *nōnus,* ninth]

nonce, *n.* the present time, occasion, purpose, etc. **nonce-word,** *n.* a word coined for the occasion. [*for then once,* read as *for the nonce* (ONCE)]

nonchalant, *a.* careless, cool, unmoved, indifferent. **nonchalance,** *n.* **nonchalantly,** *adv.* [F pres.p. of OF *nonchaloir* (L *calere,* to glow)]

Nonconformist, *n.* in religion, originally a member of the Puritan section of the Church of England clergy who, in the Elizabethan age, refused to conform to certain practices, for example the wearing of the surplice and kneeling to receive Holy Communion. After 1662 the term was confined to those who left the church rather than conform to the Act of Uniformity requiring the use of the Prayer Book in all churches. It is now applied mainly to members of the Free churches.

nondescript, *a.* not easily described or classified; neither one thing nor another; hybrid. *n.* such a person or thing that is odd or abnormal. [L *descriptus,* p.p. of *descrībere,* to DESCRIBE]

none[1], *pron.* no one, no person; (*coll.*) no persons; not any, not any portion (of). *a.* no, not any. *adv.* in no respect; by no amount; not at all. **none-so-pretty**, *n.* the London Pride, *Saxifraga umbrosa.* †**nonesparing,** *a.* all-destroying. [OE *nān* (NE, ONE)]

none[2] NONES.

nonentity *n.* non-existence; a thing not existing, a mere figment, an imaginary thing; (*fig.*) an unimportant person or thing. [NON-, ENTITY]

nones, *n.pl.* (*Rom. Ant.*) the ninth day before the ides; in the Roman Catholic Church, the office for the ninth hour after sunrise, or 3 p.m. [F, from L *nōnas,* nom. *nōnæ,* fem. pl. of *nōnus,* ninth (or pl. of obs. *none* L *nōna,* NOON]

nonesuch, *n.* one who or that which is without an equal, a paragon, a nonpareil; black medick; †the scarlet lychnis; a variety of apple.

nonet, *n.* musical composition for nine players or singers. [It. *nonetto,* ninth]

non-feasance, etc. NON-.

nonillion, *n.* a million raised to the ninth power, denoted by a unit with 54 ciphers annexed; (*esp. F and N Am.*) the tenth power of a thousand, denoted by a unit with 30 ciphers. **nonillionth**, *a., n.* [from L *nōnus,* ninth, after BILLION]

nonius, *n.* a contrivance for the graduation of mathematical instruments, now superseded by the vernier. [mod L, from Pedro *Nuñez,* 1492–1577, Portuguese mathematician]

non-joinder etc. NON.

Non-jurors, *n.pl.* priests of the Church of England who after the revolution of 1688 refused to take the oaths of allegiance to William and Mary. They continued to exist as a rival church for over a century, and consecrated their own bishops, the last of whom died in 1805. Thomas Ken (1637–1711), William Law (1686–1761) and Jeremy Collier were Nonjurors.

nonny, *n.* a refrain in old ballads etc., often covering indecent allusions; also **hey nonny, nonny-no, nonny-nonny.** [meaningless sound]

Nono, *n.* **Luigi** (1924–), Italian composer. His early vocal compositions have something of the spatial character of Gabrieli, for example *Il Canto Sospeso* (1955–56). After the opera *Intolleranza* (1960) his style became increasingly expressionistic. His music is frequently polemical in subject matter and a number of works incorporate tape-recorded elements.

nonpareil, *a.* having no equal; peerless, unrivalled, unique. *n.* a paragon, a thing of unequalled excellence; a variety of apple, bird, wheat etc.; (*Print.*), a size of type [as this]. [F *pareil,* med. L *pariculus,* dim. of *par,* equal]

non placet, *n.* the formula used in university and ecclesiastical assemblies in giving a negative vote (L, it does not please). **non-possumus,** *n.* a plea of inability (L, we cannot). **non sequitur,** *n.* an inference not warrantable from the premises (L, it does not follow).

nonplus, *n.* a state of perplexity; a puzzle, a quandary, *v.t.* (*past, p.p.* **nonplussed**) to puzzle, to confound, to bewilder. [L *nōn plūs,* no more]

non-residence etc. NON-.

nonsense, *n.* unmeaning words, ideas etc.; foolish or extravagant talk, conduct etc.; foolery, absurdity; rubbish, worthless stuff, trifles. **nonsense book,** *n.* a book containing amusing absurdities. **nonsense name,** *n.* a name or term arbitrarily made up for mnemonic or other purposes. **nonsense verses,** *n.pl.* verses having no meaning, used for mnemonic purposes; verses intentionally absurd written to amuse. **nonsensical,** *a.* **nonsensicality, nonsensicalness,** *n.* **nonsensically,** *adv.*

nonsuch NONESUCH.

nonsuit, *n.* the stoppage of a suit during trial through insufficient evidence or non-appearance of the plaintiff. *v.t.* to subject to a nonsuit.

non-union etc. NON-.

noodle[1], *n.* a simpleton, a fool. **noodledom, noodleism,** *n.* [etym. doubtful]

noodle[2], *n.* a strip or ball of dried dough made of wheat-flour and eggs, served with soup etc. [G *Nudel,* etym. doubtful]

nook, *n.* a corner; a cosy place, as in an angle; a secluded retreat. [ME *nōk,* prob. Scand.]

noology, *n.* the science of the understanding. **noological,** *a.* **noologist,** *n.* [Gr. *noos,* mind]

noon, *n.* the middle of the day, 12 o'clock; (*fig.*) the culmination or height. *a.* pertaining to noon. **noonday,** *n., a.* **noontide,** *n.* **noontide prick,** (*Shak.*) the point of noon. †**nooning,** *n.* a rest or a meal at noon. [OE *nōn* (in *nōn-tīd*), from L *nōna hōra,* ninth hour]

noose, *n.* a loop with a running knot binding the closer the more it is pulled, as in a snare, a hangman's halter etc.; (*fig.*) a tie, a bond, a snare. *v.t.* to catch in a noose; to entrap; to tie a noose on; to tie in a noose. **to put one's head in a noose,** to put oneself into a dangerous or exposed situation. [perh. from OF or Prov. *nous,* L nodus]

nopal, *n.* an American genus of cacti resembling *Opuntia,* grown for the support of the cochineal insect. **nopalry,** *n.* a plantation of these. [Sp.]

nope, (*sl; orig. N Am.*) an emphatic form of no.

nor, *conj.* and not (a word marking the second or subsequent part of a negative proposition); occasionally used without the correlative. †*adv.* neither. [prob. short for ME *nother,* OE *nāwaether* (*nā,* NO[2], WHETHER)]

nor' NORTH.

noradrenaline, *n.* an amine related to adrenalin, used as a heart resuscitant. [fr. *nor* + *adrenalin, adrenaline*]

noraghe, *n.* (*pl.* **noraghi**) a prehistoric stone structure common in Sardinia. [It.]

Nordenfelt, *n.* a machine-gun invented by Nordenfeld. [I. V. *Nordenfeld,* b. 1842, Swedish inventor]

Nordenskjöld, *n.* **Nils Adolf Erik** (1832–1901), Swedish explorer. He made voyages to the Arctic with the geologist Torell and in 1878–79 discovered the North-east Passage. He published the results of his voyages in a series of books, including *Voyage of the Vega round Asia and Europe* (1881).

Nordic, *n.* (*Ethn.*) a tall, blond dolichocephalic racial type inhabiting Scandinavia, parts of Scotland and other parts of N Europe. [Scand. *nord.* north]

Nord-Pas-de-Calais, *n.* a region of N France; area 12,400 sq km/4786 sq miles; population (1986) 3,923,000. Its capital is Lille, and consists of the *départements* of Calvados, Manche and Orne.

Norfolk[1], *n.* (*coll.*) a Norfolk jacket. **Norfolk dumpling,** *n.* a dumpling made in Norfolk; (*fig.*) a native or inhabitant of Norfolk. **Norfolk jacket,** *n.* a man's loose-jacket with vertical pleats in the back and front and a waist-band. [from foll.]

Norfolk[2], *n.* county on E coast of England. **area** 5360 sq km/2069 sq miles. **towns** administrative headquarters Norwich; King's Lynn, and resorts Great Yarmouth, Cromer and Hunstanton. **physical** rivers Ouse, Yare, Bure, Waveney; the Broads; Halvergate Marshes wildlife area. **products** cereals, turnips, sugar beet, turkeys, geese, offshore natural gas. **population** (1987) 736,000.

noria, *n.* an endless chain of buckets on a wheel for raising water from a stream or similar. [Spl., from Arab. *nā' ūrah*]

Noriega, *n.* **Manuel Antonio Morena** (1940–), Panamanian soldier and politician, effective ruler of Panama from 1982 until arrested by the US in 1989 and detained for trial on drugs-trafficking charges.

norland, (*Sc.*) NORTHLAND.

norm, *n.* a standard, model, pattern or type; a typical structure etc. [L *norma,* carpenter's square]

normal, *a.* according to rule, standard, or established law; regular, typical, usual; perpendicular. *n.* the usual state, quality, quantity etc.; a perpendicular line; the average or mean value of observed quantities; the mean temperature, volume etc. **normal school,** *n.* (*formerly*) a school where teachers were trained. **normality,** *n.* **normalize, -ise,** *v.t.* to make normal; to cause to conform to normal standards etc. **normalization, -isation,** *n.* **normally,** *adv.* [as prec.]

Norman[1], *a.* of or pertaining to Normandy or the Normans. **Norman architecture,** see separate entry. **Norman conquest,** *n.* the conquest of England by Duke William of Normandy in 1066. **Norman-English,** *n.* English mixed with Norman-French forms as spoken in England after the Norman Conquest. **Norman-French,** see separate entry. **Normanesque,** *a.* **Normanism,** *n.* **Normanize, -ise,** *v.t.* **Normanization, -isation,** *n.* [OF *Normans,* pl. of *Normant* (F *Normand*), from Teut. NORTHMAN]

Norman[2], *n.* descendant of the Norsemen, to whose chief, Rollo, Normandy was granted by Charles III of France 911, and who adopted French language and culture. In the 11th–12th centuries they conquered England (under William the Conqueror), parts of Wales and Ireland, S Italy, Sicily, and Malta, settled in Scotland, and took a prominent part in the Crusades.

Norman[3], *n.* **Greg** (1955–), Australian golfer, nickname 'the Great White Shark'. After many wins in his home country, he enjoyed success on the European PGA Tour before joining the US Tour. He has won the world match-play title three times.

norman, *n.* a bar inserted in a capstan or bitt for fastening the cable. [perh. ident. with NORMAN[1] (cp. Dut.

noorman, G *Normann*, Dan. *normand*)]

Norman architecture, *n.* English term for Romanesque, the style of architecture used in England 11th–12th cents. Norman buildings are massive, with round arches (although trefoil arches are sometimes used for small openings). Buttresses are of slight projection, and roofs are barrel-vaulted. Examples in England include the Keep of the Tower of London, and parts of the cathedrals of Chichester, Gloucester, and Ely.

Normandy, *n.* two regions of NW France: Haute-Normandie and Basse-Normandie. Its main towns are Alençon, Bayeux, Dieppe, Deauville, Lisieux, Le Havre and Cherbourg. It was named after the Viking Northmen (Normans) people, who conquered the area in the 9th cent. As a French duchy it reached its peak under William the Conqueror and was noted for its centres of learning established by Lanfranc and St Anselm. Normandy was united with England (1100–35). England and France fought over it during the Hundred Years' War, England finally losing it (1449) to Charles VII. The Normandy beaches were the site of the Allied invasion on D-day, 6 June 1944. Features of Normandy include the painter Monet's restored home and garden at Giverny, Mont St Michel, Château Miromesnil, the birthplace of de Maupassant, Victor Hugo's house at Villequier and Calvados apple brandy.

Norman French, *n.* the form of French used by the Normans in Normandy from the 10th cent., and by the Norman ruling class in England after the Conquest. It remained the language of the court until the 15th cent., the official language of the law courts until the 17th cent., and is still used in the Channel Islands.

Norn, *n.* in Scandinavian mythology, any of three goddesses of fate - the goddess of the past (Urd), the goddess of the present (Verdandi), and the goddess of the future (Skuld). [Icel.]

Norris, *n.* **Frank** (1870–1902), US novelist. An influential naturalist writer, he wrote *McTeague* (1899), about a brutish San Francisco dentist and the love of gold. He completed only two parts of his projected trilogy, the *Epic of Wheat*: *The Octopus* (1901), dealing with the struggles between wheat farmers, and *The Pit* (1903), describing the gamble of the Chicago wheat exchange.

Norroy, *n.* the third King-of-Arms, having jurisdiction north of the Trent. [A-F *nor*, NORTH, *roy*, king]

Norse, *a.* pertaining to Norway or its inhabitants, Norwegian. *n.* the Norwegian language; the language of Norway and its colonies (till the 14th cent.); (*loosely*) the Scandinavian languages, including early Swedish and Danish. **Norseman,** *n.* early inhabitant of Norway. The term Norsemen is also applied to Scandinavian Vikings who during the 8th–11th centuries raided and settled in Britain, Ireland, France, Russia, Iceland, and Greenland. [prob. from Dut. *noorsch, noordsch* (*noord* NORTH, -ISH)]

North[1], nor', *n.* one of the four cardinal points, that to the right of a person facing the setting sun at the equinox; a region or part north of any given point; the northern part (of any country); the portion of the US to the north of the former slave-holding States; the north wind. *a.* situated in or towards the north; belonging or pertaining to the north, northern. *adv.* towards or in the north. *v.i.* to change or veer towards the north. *v.t.* to steer to the north of (a place). **north and south,** along a line running to and from north and south. **North Britain,** *n.* Scotland. (*esp. formerly*) **north by east, west,** one point east, west of north. **north of,** *a.* farther north than. **north-cock,** *n.* the snow-bunting. **north country,** *n.* the part of a country to the north, esp. northern England or the northern part of Great Britain; of, pertaining to or characteristic of this. **north-countryman,** *n.* **north-east, -west,** *n.* the point midway between the north and east, or north and west, a region lying in this quarter. *a.* pertaining to or proceeding from the north-east etc. **north-easter,** *n.* a north-east wind. **north-easterly** *a.* towards or from the north-east. **north-eastern,** *a.* in or towards this. **north-eastward,** *a.* **north-eastwardly,** *a.* and *adv.* **northland,** *n.* (*poet*) countries in the north; the northern part of a country. **north latitude,** *n.* latitude north of the equator. **north-light** NORTHERN LIGHTS. **northman,** *n.* an inhabitant of the north of Europe, esp. of Scandinavia. **north pole** POLE. **north-star,** *n.* the pole-star. **north-west, -wester, -westerly, -western, -westward, -westwardly** NORTH-EAST. **northerly**, *a., adv,.* **northerliness,** *n.* **northern**, *a.* pertaining to, situated or living in, or proceeding from the north; of the northern States of the US; towards the north. *n.* a northerner. **northern lights,** *n.pl.* the aurora borealis. **northerner,** *n.* a native or inhabitant of the north. **northernmost, †northmost,** *a.* **northing,** *n.* the distance or progress in a northward direction. **northward**, *a., adv., n.* **northwardly,** *a., adv.* **northwards**, *adv., n.* **nor'-wester,** *n.* a wind from the north-west; a glass of strong liquor; a sou'-wester hat. [OE (cp. Dut. *noord*, G, Dan., and Swed. *nord*, Icel. *northr*)]

North[2], *n.* Oliver (1943–), US Marine lieutenant-colonel. In 1981 he was inducted into the National Security Council (NSC), where he supervised the mining of Nicaraguan harbours (1983), an air-force bombing raid on Libya (1986), and an arms-for-hostages deal with Iran (1985) which, when uncovered in 1986 (Irangate), forced his dismissal and conviction on charges of obstructing Congress, mutilating government documents, and taking an illegal gratuity; he was fined $150,000.

North[3], *n.* Thomas (1535–1601), English translator, whose version of Plutarch's *Lives* (1579) was the source for Shakespeare's Roman plays.

North America, *n.* third largest of the continents (including Central America), and over twice the size of Europe. **area** 24,000,000 sq km/9,500,000 sq miles. **largest cities** (population over 1 million) Mexico City, New York, Chicago, Toronto, Los Angeles, Montreal, Guadalajara, Monterrey, Philadelphia, Houston, Guatemala City, Vancouver, Detroit. **physical** mountain belts to the E (Appalachians) and W (see Cordilleras), the latter including the Rocky Mountains and the Sierra Madre; coastal plain on the Gulf of Mexico, into which the Mississippi river system drains from the central Great Plains; the St Lawrence and the Great Lakes form a rough crescent (with the Great Bear and Great Slave lakes, and lakes Athabasca and Winnipeg) around the exposed rock of the great Canadian/Laurentian Shield, into which Hudson Bay breaks from the north. **population** (1981) 345 million; the aboriginal American Indian, Inuit, and Aleut peoples are now a minority within a population predominantly of European immigrant origin. Many Africans were brought in as part of the slave trade. **language** predominantly English, Spanish, French.

North American Indian, an indigenous inhabitant of North America. Many prefer to describe themselves as 'Native Americans' rather than 'American Indians', the latter term having arisen because Columbus believed he had reached the East Indies.

Northamptonshire, *n.* a county in central England. **area** 2367 sq km/914 sq miles. **towns** administrative headquarters Northampton; Kettering. **products** cereals, cattle. **population** (1986) 554,000. **famous people** John Dryden.

North Atlantic Drift, a warm ocean current in the N Atlantic Ocean; the continuation of the Gulf Stream. It flows E across the Atlantic and has a mellowing effect on the climate of W Europe, particularly the British Isles and Scandinavia.

North Atlantic Treaty, an agreement signed 4 Apr. 1949 by Belgium, Canada, Denmark, France, Iceland, Italy, Luxembourg, Netherlands, Norway, Portugal, UK, US; Greece, Turkey 1952; West Germany 1955; Spain 1982. They agreed that 'an armed attack against one or more of them in Europe or North America shall be considered an attack against them all'. The North Atlantic Treaty Organization (Nato) is based on this treaty.

North Atlantic Treaty Organization, an association set up in 1949 to provide for the collective defence of the major W European and North American states against the perceived threat from the USSR. Its chief body is the Council of Foreign Ministers (who have representatives in permanent session), and there is an international secretariat in Brussels, Belgium, and also the Military Committee consisting of the Chiefs of Staff. The military headquarters SHAPE (Supreme Headquarters Allied Powers, Europe) is in Chièvres, near Mons, Belgium. US dominance and nuclear weapons have caused controversy.

North Brabant, *n.* (Dutch **Noord-Brabant**) southern province of the Netherlands, lying between the Maas (Meuse) and Belgium; area 4940 sq km/1907 sq miles; population (1988) 2,156,000. The capital is 's-Hertogenbosch. Former heathland is now under mixed farming. Towns such as Breda, Tilburg and Eindhoven are centres of brewing, engineering, microelectronics, and textile manufacture.

North Cape, *n.* (Norwegian **Nordkapp**) a cape in the Norwegian county of Finnmark; the most northerly point of Europe.

North Carolina, *n.* a state of the US; nickname Tar Heel or Old North State. **area** 136,400 sq km/52,650 sq miles. **capital** Raleigh. **towns** Charlotte, Greensboro, Winston-Salem. **products** tobacco, maize, soybeans, livestock, poultry, dairy products, textiles, clothing, furniture, computers, mica, feldspar, bricks. **population** (1986) 6,331,000.

Northcliffe, *n.* **Alfred Charles William Harmsworth, 1st Viscount Northcliffe** (1865–1922), British newspaper proprietor born in Dublin. Founding the *Daily Mail* (1896), he revolutionized popular journalism, and with the *Daily Mirror* (1903) originated the picture paper. In 1908 he also obtained control of *The Times*.

North Dakota, *n.* a prairie state of the northern US; nickname Sioux or Flickertail State. **area** 183,100 sq km/70,677 sq miles. **capital** Bismarck. **towns** Fargo, Grand Forks, Minot, **products** cereals, meat products, farm equipment, oil, coal. **population** (1984) 686,000.

North-East India, *n.* an area of India (Meghalaya, Assam, Mizoram, Tripura, Manipur, Nagaland and the union territory of Arunachal Pradesh) linked with the rest of India only by a narrow corridor. There is opposition to immigration from Bangladesh and the rest of India, and demands for secession.

North-East Passage, *n.* a sea-route from the N Atlantic to the N Pacific, pioneered by Nordenskjold (1878–79) and developed by the USSR in settling N Siberia from 1935. The USSR owns offshore islands, and claims it as an internal waterway. The US claims that it is international.

Northern Rhodesia, *n.* former name (until 1964) of ZAMBIA.

Northern Territory, *n.* a territory of Australia. **area** 1,356,165 sq km/523,620 sq miles. **capital and chief port** Darwin. **town** Alice Springs. **exports** beef cattle; prawns; bauxite (Gove), gold and copper (Tennant Creek), uranium (Ranger). **population** (1984) 158,400.

North Holland, *n.* (Dutch **Noord-Holland**) low-lying coastal province of the Netherlands occupying the peninsula jutting northwards between the North Sea and the Ijsselmeer; area 2670 sq km/1031 sq miles; population (1988) 2,353,000. Most of it is below sea-level, protected from the sea by a series of sand dunes and artificial dykes. The capital is Haarlem; other towns are Amsterdam, Hilversum, Den Helder and the cheese centres Alkmaar and Edam. Famous for its bulbfields, the province also produces grain and vegetables.

North Korea KOREA, NORTH.

North Pole POLE.

North Rhine-Westphalia, *n.* (German **Nordrhein-Westfalen**) administrative *Land* of West Germany. **area** 34,100 sq km/13,163 sq miles. **capital** Düsseldorf. **towns** Cologne, Essen, Dortmund, Duisburg, Bochum, Wuppertal, Bielefeld, Bonn, Gelsenkirchen, Münster, Mönchengladbach. **products** iron, steel, coal, lignite, electrical goods, fertilizers, synthetic textiles. **population** (1988) 16,700,000. **religion** Roman Catholic 53%, Protestant 42%.

Northrop, *n.* **John** (1891–1987), US chemist. In the 1930s he crystallized a number of enzymes, including pepsin and trypsin, showing conclusively that they were proteins. He shared the 1946 Nobel Chemistry Prize with Wendell Stanley and James Sumner.

North Sea, *n.* a sea to the E of Britain and bounded by the coasts of Belgium, the Netherlands, Germany, Denmark and Norway; area 523,000 sq km/202,000 sq miles; average depth 55 m/180 ft, greatest depth 660 m/2165 ft. In the northeast it joins the Norwegian Sea, and in the south it meets the Strait of Dover. It has fisheries, oil and gas.

Northumberland[1]**,** *n.* a county in N England. **area** 5030 sq km/1942 sq miles. **towns** administrative headquarters Newcastle-upon-Tyne; Berwick-upon-Tweed, Hexham. **products** sheep. **population** (1986) 301,000.

Northumberland[2]**,** *n.* **John Dudley, Duke of Northumberland** (*c.* (1502–53), English politician, son of the privy councillor Edmund Dudley (beheaded 1510), raised to a dukedom in 1551, and chief minister until Edward VI's death 1553. He tried to place his daughter-in-law Lady Jane Grey on the throne, and was executed on Mary's accession.

Northumbria, *n.* an Anglo-Saxon kingdom which covered NE England and SE Scotland, comprising the 6th-cent. kingdoms of Bernicia (Forth–Tees) and Deira (Tees–Humber), united in the 7th cent. It accepted the supremacy of Wessex in 827, and was conquered by the Danes in the later 9th cent.

Northumbrian, *n.* a native or inhabitant of ancient Northumbria (England north of the Humber) or of Northumberland; the old English dialect of Northumbria. *a.* of or pertaining to one of these districts. [OE *Northhymbre* (NORTH, *Humber*)]

northward etc. NORTH.

North-West Passage, *n.* an Atlantic-Pacific sea route round the north of Canada. Canada, which owns offshore islands, claims it as an internal waterway; the US insists that it is an international waterway, and sent an icebreaker through without permission in 1985.

Northwest Territories, *n.pl.* a territory of Canada. **area** 3,426,300 sq km/1,322,552 sq miles. **capital** Yellowknife. **physical** extends to the North Pole, to Hudson's Bay in the east, and in the west to the edge of the Canadian Shield. **products** oil and natural gas, zinc, lead, gold, tungsten, silver. **population** (1986) 52,000, over 50% native peoples (Indian, Inuit).

North Yorkshire, *n.* a county in NE England. **area** 8320 sq km/3212 sq miles. **towns** administrative headquarters Northallerton; York, and the resorts of Harrogate, Scarborough and Whitby. **products** cereals, wool and meat from sheep, dairy products, coal, electrical goods. **population** (1987) 706,000.

Norway, *n.* Kingdom of (*Kongeriket Norge*) a country in NW Europe, on the Scandinavian peninsula, bounded E by Sweden, and NE by Finland and the USSR. **area** 387,000 sq km/149,421 sq miles (includes Svalbard and Jan Mayen). **capital** Oslo. **towns** Bergen, Trondheim. **physical** mountainous; forests cover 25%; extends north of Arctic Circle. **territories** dependencies in the Arctic (Svalbard and Jan Mayen) and in Antarctica (Bouvet and Peter I Island, and Queen Maud Land). **exports** petrochemicals from North Sea oil and gas, paper, wood pulp, furniture, iron ore and other minerals, high-tech goods, sports goods, fish. **population** (1989) 4,204,000; annual growth rate 0.3%. **language** Riksmal (formal Dano-Norwegian) and Landsmal (based on the local dialects of Norway). **religion** Evangelical Lutheran (endowed by state). **Norwegian**, *a.* pertaining to Norway or its inhabitants. *n.* a native or inhabitant of Norway; the language of the Norwegians. [med. L *Norvegia*]

Norwich, *n.* a cathedral city in Norfolk, E England; population (1986) 121,600. Industries include shoes, clothing, chemicals, confectionery, engineering and printing.

nose, *n.* the projecting part or the face between the forehead and mouth, containing the nostrils and the organ of smell; the power of smelling; odour, scent; aroma esp. the bouquet of wine; (*fig.*) sagacity; a part of thing resembling a nose, as the nozzle of a pipe, tube, bellows etc., a beak, point, prow etc. *v.t.* to perceive, trace or detect by smelling; (*fig.*) to find out; to rub or push with the nose; to push (one's way). *v.i.* to smell, to sniff (about, after, at etc.); (*fig.*) to search, to pry; to push one's way, to push ahead. **nose of wax,** one who or that which is easily influenced or moulded. **to count** or **tell noses,** to reckon the number of persons present; to count votes, supporters etc. **to follow one's nose,** to go straight ahead. **to lead by the nose,** to cause to follow blindly. **to pay through the nose,** to be charged an exorbitant price. **to put one's nose out of joint** JOINT. **to thrust** or **put one's nose into,** to meddle officiously. **to turn up the nose,** to show contempt (at). **under one's nose,** in one's actual presence or sight. **nose-bag,** *n.* a bag containing provender for hanging over a horse's head; (*sl.*) a bag of provisions. **nose-band,** *n.* the part of a bridle passing over the nose and attached to the cheek-straps. **nose bleed,** *n.* bleeding from the nose. **nose-dive,** *n.* of an aircraft, a sudden plunge towards the earth. *v.i.* to make this plunge. **nose-leaf,** *n.* a membranous process on the nose of certain bats, constituting an organ of touch. **nose-piece,** *n.* a nozzle; a nose-band; the end-piece of a microscope to which the object-glass is fastened. **nose-pipe,** *n.* a piece of pipe used as a nozzle. **nose-rag,** *n.* (*sl.*) a handkerchief. **nose-ring,** *n.* a ring worn in the nose as ornament; a leading-ring for a bull etc. **nosed,** *a.* (*usu. in comb.*, as *red-nosed*). **noseless,** *a.* **noser,** *n.* (*coll.*) a wind in one's face, a head wind; a fall on the nose. **nosing,** *n.* the prominent edge of a moulding, step etc. **nosy,** *a.* having a large or prominent nose; strong- or evil-smelling; fragrant; sensitive to bad odours; (*coll.*) very inquisitive. [OE *nosu* (cp. Dut. *neus,* Icel. *nōs*)]

nosegay, *n.* a bunch of flowers, especially fragrant flowers.

nosh, *n.* (*sl.*) food; a meal. *v.i.* to eat. **nosh-up,** *n.* (*sl.*) a large meal, a feast. [Yiddish]

noso- *comb. form.* pertaining to diseases. [Gr. *nosos,* disease]

nosocomial, *a.* pertaining to hospitals. [Gr. *nosokomeion,* a hospital]

nosography, *n.* the scientific description of diseases.

nosology, *n.* a systematic classification of diseases; the branch of medical science treating of such a classification. **nosological,** *a.* **nosologist,** *n.*

nosonomy, *n.* the nomenclature of diseases.

nosophobia, *n.* morbid fear of disease.

nostalgia, *n.* morbid longing for home; home-sickness; a yearning for the past. **nostalgic,** *a.* [Gr. *nostos,* return, *-algia* from *algos,* pain]

nost(o)-, *comb. form.* pertaining to a return. [Gr. *nostos,* return]

nostoc, *n.* a genus of gelatinous freshwater algae, also called star-jelly or witches' butter. [G *Nostoch,* a term invented by Paracelsus]

nostology, *n.* the scientific study of senility and second childhood. [Gr. *nostos,* return, -LOGY]

nostomania, *n.* an abnormal anxiety to go back to a familiar place.

nostophobia, *n.* an abnormal fear of going back thus.

Nostradamus, *n.* (latinized name of Michel de Nôtredame) (1503–66), French physician and astrologer who was consulted by Catherine de' Medici and was physician to Charles IX. His book of prophecies in rhyme, *Centuries* (1555), has had a number of interpretations.

nostril, *n.* one of the apertures of the nose. [OE *nosthyrl* (NOSE, *thyrel,* hole, cogn. with THRILL)]

nostrum, *n.* (*pl.* **-ums**) a medicine based on a secret formula; a quack remedy. [L, neut. of *noster,* our]

nosy NOSE.

not, *adv.* (*enclitically* **n't**) a particle expressing negation, denial, prohibition or refusal. **not but what,** or **not but that,** nevertheless. **not a few** FEW. **not in it,** (*coll.*) not aware of (a secret); not participating in (an advantage); not in the running. **not in the running,** standing no chance, not worth considering. **not once or twice,** many times, often. **not on,** *n.* (*sl.*) not possible; not morally, socially etc. acceptable. **not out,** *a.* having reached the end of a cricket innings or of play for the day without being dismissed. **not that,** *conj.* it is not meant however that. **not well, not too well,** *a.* feeling rather unwell. [NAUGHT]

nota bene, mark well; take notice; often abbreviated to **NB.** [L]

notable, *a.* worthy of note; remarkable, memorable, distinguished; notorious; eminent, conspicuous; excellent, capable. *n.* a person or thing of note or distinction; (*Fr. Hist., pl.*) persons summoned by the king to a council of State or temporary parliament, at times of emergency in France prior to 1789. **notabilia,** *n.pl.* notable things. **notability,** *n.* †**notableness,** *n.* **notably,** *adv.* [F, from L *notābilis,* from *notāre,* to note]

notalgia, *n.* pain in the back. **notalgic,** *a.* [Gr. *notos,* back, *-algia, algos,* pain]

notandum, *n.* (*pl.* **-da**) something to be noted, a memorandum. [L, ger. of *notāre,* to NOTE]

notary, *n.* a public official (chiefly in foreign countries) appointed to attest deeds, contracts etc., administer oaths etc., frequently called a **notary public**. **notarial,** *a.* **notarially,** *adv.* [A-F *notarie* (F *notaire*), L *notārium,* nom. *-us,* from *notāre,* to NOTE]

notation, *n.* the act or process of representing by signs, figures etc.; a system of signs, figures etc., employed in any science or art. **notate,** *a.* marked with spots etc. of a different colour. [L *notātio,* as prec.]

notch, *n.* a nick, a cut, a V-shaped indentation; a tally-point; †(*Cricket*) a run scored; (*N Am.*) an opening, narrow pass or short defile. *v.t.* to cut a notch or noches in; to score by notches; to get (a number of runs); to fix (stairs etc.) by means of notches. **notch-wing,** *n.* applied to various moths. **notched, notchy,** *a.* [F *oche* (now *hoche*) through *an oche* (cp. NEWT)]

note, *n.* a sign, mark or token; a distinctive feature, a characteristic, a mark of identity, genuineness, quality etc.; a mark of interrogation, exclamation etc.; a stigma; a brief record, a memorandum, a short or informal letter; a diplomatic communication; a bank-note or piece of paper money; a written promise to pay a certain sum of money; note-paper; an annotation, a comment, explanation, or gloss, appended to a passage in a book etc.; notice, attention, observation; distinction, repute, importance; a sign representing the pitch and duration of a sound; a musical sound; a significant sound, tone or mode of expression; a key in a musical instrument; †notice, information. *v.t.* to observe, to take notice of; to show respect to; to pay attention to; to make a memorandum of; to set down or record as worth remembering; to annotate; (*in p.p.*) to celebrate. **note of hand,** a promissory note. **of note,** distinguished. **to compare notes** COMPARE. **to strike the right (strong) note,** to act, behave etc. in an appropriate (inappropriate), or suitable (unsuitable) manner. **notebook,** *n.* a book for entering memoranda in. **note-case,** *n.* a pocket wallet for holding paper money. **note-paper,** *n.* a small size of paper for letters, esp. private correspondence. **noted,** *a.* eminent, remarkable. †**notedly,** *adv.* **noteless,** *a.* not note-worthy; unmusical, discordant. **noter,** *n.* **noteworthy,** *a.* outstanding, famous; worth attention. [OF, from L *nota,* a mark (whence *notāre,* to mark, OF *noter*)]

nothing, *n.* no thing that exists; not anything, naught; no amount, a cipher, a naught; nothingness, non-existence; an insignificant or unimportant thing, a trifle. *adv.* in no degree, in no way, not at all. **mere nothings,** trifling, unimportant things, events etc. **next to nothing,** almost nothing. **nothing doing,** (*sl.*) nothing happening; a refusal to do something. **nothing else than** or **but,** merely, only, no more than (this or that). **nothing for it but,** no alternative but. **nothing**

to you, not your business. **sweet nothings,** words of endearment. **to come to nothing,** to turn out a failure; to result in no amount or naught. **to make nothing of,** to fail to understand or deal with. **to stop at nothing,** to be totally ruthless. †**nothing-gift,** *n.* a worthless gift. **nothingarian,** *a.* believing nothing; having no creed, purpose etc. **nothingarianism,** *n.* **nothingism,** *n.* nihilism. **nothingness,** *n.*

notice, *n.* intelligence, information, warning; a written or printed paper giving information or directions; an intimation or instruction; intimation of the termination of an agreement, contract of employment etc., at a specified date; an account of something in a newspaper etc., esp. a review of a book, play etc.; observation, regard, attention; the act of noting. *v.t.* to take notice of, to perceive; to remark upon; to pay respect to; to serve a notice upon; to give notice to. **at short notice,** with little advance warning. **to give notice,** to intimate the termination of an agreement, particularly a contract of employment. **to take no notice of,** to pay no attention to; to ignore. **notice board,** *n.* a board exposed to public view on which notices are posted. **noticeable,** *a.* **noticeably,** *adv.* [F, from L *nōtitia,* from *nōtus,* p.p. of *noscere,* to know]

notify, *v.t.* to make known, to accounce, to declare, to publish; to give notice to, to inform (of or that). **notifiable,** *a.* to be notified (esp. of cases of disease that must be reported to the sanitary authorities). **notification,** *n.* [F *notifier,* L *nōtificāre* (*nōtus* known, *-ficāre, facere,* to make)]

notion, *n.* an idea, a conception; an opinion, a view; a theory, a scheme, a device; (*coll.*) an inclination, desire, intention or whim; (*N Am.*) a small ingenious device or useful article; (*pl., N Am.*) fancy goods, haberdashery, novelties etc.; a knick-knack; a general concept or idea. **notional,** *a.* pertaining to notions or concepts; abstract, imaginary, hypothetical; speculative, ideal; given to notions or whims, fanciful. **notionist,** *n.* **notionally,** *adv.* [F, from L *notio, nōtiōnem,* acc. as prec.]

notitia, *n.* a list, register, or catalogue. [L]

noto- *comb. form* pertaining to the back. [Gr. *notos,* back]

notobranchiate, *a.* having dorsal branchiae or gills.

notochord, *n.* the elastic cartilaginous band constituting a rudimentary form of the spinal column in the embryo and some primitive fishes.

Notogaea, *n.* a zoological division of the earth embracing Australia, New Zealand and the neotropical regions. [Gr. *notos,* south, *gaiā,* land]

notonecta, *n.* a boat-fly or back-swimmer, a species of water-beetle. **notonectal, -toid,** *a.* [Gr. *nēktēs,* swimmer]

notopodium, *n.* the dorsal or upper part of the parapodium of an annelid. **notopodial,** *a.* [Gr. *podion,* dim. of *pous podos,* foot]

notorious, *a.* widely or publicly or commonly known (now used only in a bad sense); manifest, evident, patent; †notable. **notoriety, notoriousness,** *n.* **notoriously,** *adv.* [med. L *nōtōrius,* from *nōtus,* known]

notornis, *n.* a gigantic New Zealand coot, *Notornis mantelli,* now very rare. [Gr. *ornis,* bird]

nototherium, *n.* an extinct Australian family of gigantic marsupials. [Gr. *thērion,* beast]

Nottingham, *n.* an industrial city (engineering, coalmining, cycles, textiles, knitwear, pharmaceuticals, tobacco, lace, electronics) and administrative headquarters of Nottinghamshire, England; population (1981) 217,080.

Nottinghamshire, *n.* a county in central England. **area** 2,160 sq km/834 sq miles. **towns** administrative headquarters Nottingham; Mansfield, Worksop. **products** cereals, cattle, sheep, light engineering, footwear, limestone, ironstone, oil. **population** (1987) 1,008,000.

notturno, *n.* a title given by some 18th cent. composers to music written for evening performance; another word for *nocturne.* [It. lit. night piece.]

notum, *n.* (*pl.* **-ta**) the back of the thorax in insects. [mod. L, from Gr. *noton, notos,* back]

Notus, *n.* the south wind. [L, from Gr. *Notos*]

notwithstanding, *prep.* in spite of, despite. *adv.* nevertheless; in spite of this. *conj.* although; in spite of the fact (that).

nougat, *n.* a confection of almonds or other nuts and sugar. [F, from Sp. *nogado,* from L *nucem,* nom. *nux*]

nought NAUGHT.

noumenon, *n.* (*pl.* **-mena**) the substance underlying a phenomenon; an object or the conception of an object as it is in itself, or as it appears to pure thought. **noumenal,** *a.* **noumenally,** *adv.* [Gr. *nooumenon,* neut. pres.p. of *noein,* to apprehend]

noun, *n.* a word used as the name of anything, a substantive; †the name of a thing or of an attribute, called noun substantive or noun adjective. †**nounal,** *a.* [A-F, from OF *nun, num,* L *nōmen,* NAME, rel. to *noscere,* to KNOW]

nourish, *v.t.* to feed, to sustain, to support; to maintain, to educate; to foster, to cherish, to nurse. *v.i.* to promote growth. †**nourice,** NURSE. †**nourishable,** *a.* **nourisher,** *n.* **nourishing,** *a.* **nourishment,** *n.* the act of nourishing; the state of being nourished; that which nourishes, food, sustenance. **nouriture,** *n.* nourishment, sustenance; nurture, education. [OF *noris-,* stem of *norir* (F *nourrir*), from L *nutrīre*]

nous, *n.* mind, intellect; (*coll.*) sense, wit, intelligence. [Gr.]

nouveau, *fem.* **nouvelle**, new. **nouveau riche**, *a.* of a person who has recently acquired wealth but who has not acquired good taste or manners. **nouvelle cuisine**, *n.* a style of simple French cooking which does not involve rich food, creamy sauces etc. and relies largely on artistic presentation. **Nouvelle Vague**, *n.* a movement in the French cinema, dating from just before 1960, which aimed at imaginative quality in films. [F]

nova, *n.* a star; a star that flares up to great brightness and subsides after a time. [L *novus,* new]

novachord, *n.* an electrically-operated musical instrument with keys and pedals, the sound being produced by the oscillation of radio valves and the power obtained from low-frequency alternating current. The sound effects are precussive, as of a piano, and sustained, as of an organ. [L *novus,* new, CHORD]

novaculite, *n.* a fine-grained slate used for hones; a hone, a whetstone. [L *novacula,* razor, -ITE]

Novak, *n.* **(Marilyn Pauline) Kim** (1933–), US film actress who starred in the mid-1950s and early 1960s in such films as *Pal Joey* (1957), *Vertigo* (1958), *Kiss Me Stupid* (1964), and *The Legend of Lyla Clare* (1968).

novalia, *n.pl.* (*Sc. Law*) waste lands newly brought into cultivation. [L, pl. of *novāle,* neut. sing., from *novus,* new]

Novalis, *n.* (pen name of Freiherr von Hardenburg) (1772–1801), pioneer German Romantic poet, who wrote *Hymnen an die Nacht/Hymns to the Night* (1800), prompted by the death of his fiancée Sophie von Kühn. He left two unfinished romances, *Die Lehrlinge zu Sais/The Novices of Sais* and *Heinrich von Ofterdingen*.

Nova Scotia, *n.* a province of E Canada. **area** 55,490 sq km/21,065 sq miles. **capital** and chief port Halifax. **towns** Dartmouth. **products** coal, gypsum; dairy products, poultry, fruit; forest products; fish products incl. scallop and lobster. **population** (1986) 873,000.

Novatian, *n.* a follower of Novatianus (3rd cent.), who taught that the Church had no power to absolve the lapsed or to admit them to the Eucharist. *a.* of or pertaining to Novatianus or the Novatians. **Novatianism,** *n.* **Novatianist,** *n.*

novation, *n.* the substitution of a new obligation or debt for an old one. **novate,** *v.t.* to replace by a new obligation, debt etc. [L *novātio,* from *novāre,* to make new, from *novus,* new]

novel, *a.* new, recent, fresh; unusual, strange. *n.* a fictitious narrative in prose, usu. of sufficient length to fill a volume, portraying characters and actions from real life; this type of literature; a new or supplementary decree or constitution; †(*pl.*) news. **novelese**, (*often derog.*) *n.* the language or style considered appropriate for novels. **novellette**, *n.* a short novel, usu. of a sentimental nature; (*Mus.*) a kind of romance dealing freely with several themes. **novelettish,** *a.* cheaply sentimental. **novelish,** *a.* **novelism,** *n.* **novelist,** *n.* a writer of novels. **novelistic,** *a.* **novelize, -ise,** *v.t.* to make (a play, facts etc.) into a novel. **novelization, -isation,** *n.* **novella**, *n.* a tale, a short story; a short novel. **novelty,** *n.* newness, freshness; something new. [OF *novelle* (F *nouvelle*) or It. *novella,* L *novella,* neut. pl. of *novellus,* dim. of *novus,* new]

Novello, *n.* **Ivor** (adopted name of Ivor Novello Davies) (1893–1951), Welsh composer and actor-manager. He wrote popular songs, such as 'Keep the Home Fires Burning', in World War I, and musicals in which he often appeared as the romantic lead, including *Glamorous Night* (1925), *The Dancing Years* (1939), and *Gay's the Word* (1951).

November, *n.* the 11th month of the year, the ninth of the Roman year; code word for the letter **n**. [L, from *novem,* nine (cp. DECEMBER)]

November criminals, *n.pl.* a name given by right-wing nationalists in post-1918 Germany to the socialist politicians who had taken over the government after the abdication of Kaiser Wilhelm II and had signed the armistice with the Western Allies, Nov. 1918.

novena, *n.* in the Roman Catholic Church, a devotion consisting of a prayer or service repeated on nine successive days. [med. L, from *novem,* nine]

novenary, *n.* nine collectively; a group or set of nine; a novena. †*a.* pertaining to or consisting of the number nine. †**novene**, *a.* proceeding by nines. **novennial**, *a.* happening every ninth year. [L *novēnārius,* as prec.]

novercal, *a.* pertaining or suitable to a stepmother. [L *novercālis,* from *noverca,* stepmother]

Noverre, *n.* **Jean-Georges** (1727–1810), French choreographer, writer and ballet reformer. He promoted *ballet d'action* and simple, free movement, and is often considered the creator of modern Classical ballet. *Les Petits Riens* (1778) was one of his works.

Novgorod, *n.* industrial (chemicals, engineering, clothing, brewing) city on the Volkhov River, NW USSR, a major trading city in mediaeval times; population (1987) 228,000. **Novgorod school,** *n.* a Russian school of icon and mural painters, active from the late 14th to the 16th cent. in Novgorod. They were inspired by the work of the refugee Byzantine artist Theophanes the Greek. Russian artists imitated his linear style, but this became increasingly stilted and mannered.

Novial, *n.* an artificial language invented by Otto Jespersen.

novice, *n.* one entering a religious house on probation before taking the vows; a new convert; one who is new to any business, an inexperienced person, a beginner. †*a.* inexperienced. [OF, from L *novīcius,* from *novus,* new]

novilunar, *a.* pertaining to the new moon. [late L *novilūnium* (*novus,* new, LUNAR)]

Novi Sad, *n.* industrial and commercial (pottery and cotton) city, capital of the autonomous province of Vojvodina, Yugoslavia on the river Danube; population (1981) 257,700. Products include leather, textiles, and tobacco.

novitiate, *n.* the term of probation passed by a novice; the part of a religious house allotted to novices; (*fig.*) a period of probation or apprenticeship.

Novocaine®, *n.* a synthetic produce derived from coal tar, used as a local anaesthetic, known as procaine. [L *novus,* new; COCAINE]

Novosibirsk, *n.* an industrial city (engineering, textiles, chemicals, food processing) in W Siberia, USSR, on the river Ob; population (1987) 1,423,000. Winter lasts eight months here.

novum, *n.* an old game with dice, the principal throws at which were five and nine. [prob. L, neut. sing. of *novus,* new]

now, *adv.* at the present time; at once, forthwith, immediately; very recently; at this point or time, then (in narrative); in these circumstances; used as an expletive in explaining, remonstrating, conciliating, threatening etc. *conj.* since, seeing that, this being the case (that). *n.* the present time. *a.* (*coll.*) present, existing. **just now,** a little time or a moment ago. **now and then** or **again,** from time to time; occasionally. **now or never,** at this moment or the chance is gone for ever. **nowaday,** *a.* of the present time. **nowadays,** *adv.* at the present time; in these days. *n.* the present time. [OE *nu* (cp. Dut. *nu,* G *nun,* Icel. *nū,* Dan. and Swed. *nu,* Gr. *nūn,* L. *nunc,* Sansk. *nu*)]

Nowa Huta, *n.* an industrial suburb of Krakow, on the Vistula River. The centre of Poland's steel industry.

noway, -ways NO[1].

nowel, *int.* a shout of joy in Christmas carols. [OF *noel,* Prov. *nadal,* L *nātalem,* nom. *-lis,* NATAL]

nowhere, *adv.* not in, at, or to any place or state. **nowhere near,** not at all near. **to be** or **come in nowhere,** (*coll.*) to be badly defeated (esp. in a race or other contest).

nowhither, nowise NO[2].

†**nowt[1]**, *n.* (*Sc.*) cattle, a bovine animal; (*fig.*) a coarse stupid or ungainly man. [from Icel. *naut* (cp. OE *nēat,* NEAT[2])]

nowt[2], *n.* (*dial.*) nothing. [from *naught*]

nowy, *a.* having a convex projection in the middle (of a line etc., on a shield). [OF *noé* (F *noué*), p.p. of *noer,* L *nōdāre,* to tie, from *nōdus,* knot]

noxious, *a.* hurtful, harmful, unwholesome; pernicious, destructive. **noxiously,** *adv.* **noxiousness,** *n.* [L *noxius,* from *noxa,* harm, rel. to *nocēre,* to injure]

noyade, *n.* a mode of executing political prisoners by drowning, esp. wholesale, as during the Reign of Terror in France in 1794. [F, from *noyer,* to drown, L *necāre,* to kill]

noyau, *n.* brandy cordial flavoured with bitter almonds etc. [F, from L *nucāle,* from *nucem,* nom. *nux,* nut]

†**noyous,** *a.* vexatious, troublesome. [earlier *anoyous,* from ANNOY]

nozzle, *n.* a spout, projecting mouthpiece, or end of pipe or hose. [NOSE]

NP, (*abbr.*) Notary Public.

n.p. (*abbr.*) new paragraph.

NPA, (*abbr.*) New People's Army (Philippines).

NPL, (*abbr.*) National Physical Laboratory.

NSPCC, (*abbr.*) National Society for the Prevention of Cruelty to Children.

NSU, (*abbr.*) Non-specific urethritis.

NSW, (*abbr.*) New South Wales.

NT, (*abbr.*) National Trust; New Testament.

NTP, *n.* (*abbr.*) *N*ormal *T*emperature and *P*ressure, former name for STP (*S*tandard *T*emperature and *P*ressure).

NTS, (*abbr.*) National Trust for Scotland.

nu, *n.* the 13th letter of the Greek alphabet. [Gr. *nȳ*]

nuance, *n.* a delicate gradation in colour or tone; a fine distinction between things, feelings, opinions etc. [F, from *nuer,* to shade, from *nue,* L *nūbes,* cloud]

nub, *n.* a small lump, as of coal; a tangle, a knot, a snarl; the pith or gist (of). **nubble**, *n.* a nub. **nubbly** (*prov.*), **nubby,** *adv.* [var. of KNOB]

Nuba, *n.* the peoples of the Nuba mountains, W of the White Nile, Sudan. Their languages belong to the Nubian branch of the Chari-Nile family.

nubecula, *n.* (*pl.* **-lae**) a cloudy appearance in the urine; a film on the eye; one of the two southern nebulae called the Magellanic clouds. [L, dim. of *nūbes,* cloud]

nubiferous, *a.* producing or bringing clouds. †**nubigenous**, *a.* †**nubilose**, †**nubilous,** *a.* cloudy. [L *nūbifer* (*nūbes,* see prec., -FEROUS)]

nubile, *a.* marriageable (usu. of women); sexually mature; sexually attractive. **nubility**, *n.* [L *nūbilis,* from *nūbere,* to marry]

nucellus, *n.* the nucleus of an ovule. [mod. L dim. of NUCLEUS]

nuchal, *a.* pertaining to the nape of the neck. [med. L *nucha,* Arab. *nukhā',* spinal cord, -AL]

nuci-, *comb.form* pertaining to nuts. [L *nux,* nut]

nuciferous, *a.* bearing nuts. **nuciform**, *a.* nut-shaped.
nucifrage, *n.* (*Ornith.*) the nut-cracker. **nucifragous**.
nucivorous, *a.* eating or feeding on nuts.
nuclear, *a.* relating to atomic nuclei; pertaining to the nucleus of a biological cell; of or using nuclear power or weapons. **nuclear charge,** *n.* the positive electric charge in the nucleus of an atom. **nuclear disarmament,** *n.* the reduction or giving up of a country's nuclear weapons. **nuclear energy,** *n.* energy released during a nuclear reaction, whether by nuclear fission or nuclear fusion. **nuclear family,** *n.* the basic family unit consisting of a mother and father and their children. **nuclear fission,** *n.* the breaking up of a heavy atom, as of uranium, into atoms of smaller mass, thus causing a great release of energy. **nuclear fuel,** *n.* uranium, plutonium and other metals consumed to produce nuclear energy. **nuclear fusion,** *n.* the creation of a new nucleus by merging two lighter ones, with release of energy. **nuclear physics,** *n.pl.* the study of atomic nuclei. **nuclear power,** *n.* power obtained from a controlled nuclear reaction. **nuclear reaction,** *n.* reaction in which the nuclei of atoms are transformed into isotopes of the element itself, or atoms of a different element. **nuclear reactor,** *n.* a structure of fissile material such as uranium, with a moderator such as carbon or heavy water, so arranged that nuclear energy is continuously released under control. Also called an atomic pile. **nuclear warfare,** *n.* the use of atomic or hydrogen bombs in warfare. **nuclear winter,** *n.* a period of coldness and darkness predicted as likely to follow a nuclear war. [NUCLEUS]
nucleate, *v.t.* to form into a nucleus; *v.i.* to form a nucleus., *a.* having a nucleus, nucleated. **nucleation,** *n.*
nucleic acids, *n.pl.* complex organic acids forming part of nucleo proteins.
nuclein, *n.* the protein forming the chief constituent of cell-nuclei.
nucle(o)- *comb. form.* pertaining to a nucleus. [L from *nucula,* dim. of *nux nucis,* a nut.]
nucleobranch, *a.* belonging to the Nucleobranchiata, a family of molluscs having the gills in a tuft. *n.* one of the Nucleobranchiata, a heteropod. [Gr. *branchia,* gills]
nucleolus, *n.* (*pl.* **-li**) a nucleus of or within another nucleus. **nucleolar, nucleolated**, *a.*
nucleonics, *n.sing.* the science of the nucleus of the atom.
nucleus, *n.* (*pl.* **-clei**) a central part about which aggregation, accretion or growth goes on; a kernel; the charged centre of an atom consisting of protons and neutrons; the central body in an ovule, seed, cell etc., constituting the organ of vitality, growth, or other functions; (*fig.*) a centre of growth, development, activity etc.; the brightest part of the head of a comet. **nucleal, nuclear, nucleary,** *a.* [L, from *nucula,* dim. of *nux nucis,* nut]
nucule, *n.* a small nut or nut-like fruit or seed; the female productive organ in the cryptogamic genus *Chara*. [F, from L *nucula,* see prec.]
nude, *a.* bare, naked, uncovered, unclothed, undraped; (*Law*) made without any consideration and consequently void. *n.* an undraped figure in painting or sculpture. **the nude,** the undraped human figure or the state of being undraped. **nudely,** *adv.* **nudeness, nudity,** *n.* **nudism,** the cult of nude; belief in the physical and spiritual benefit of being nude. **nudist,** *n.* a member of the cult of the nude. **nudist colony,** *n.* an open-air camp inhabited by nudists. [L *nūdus*]
nudge, *v.t.* to push gently, as with the elbow; to draw attention or give a hint with, or as with such a push. *n.* such a push. **nudge-nudge,** *int.* (*coll.*) suggesting some secret or underhand behaviour, esp. sexual. [etym. doubtful]
nudi- *comb.form* bare, naked. [L *nudus,* nude]
nudibranch, *n.* a mollusc of the order Nudibranchiata characterized by naked gills or the absence of a shell. **nudibranchial, nudibranchian**, *a.* **nudibranchiate**, *a., n.* [Gr. *branchia,* gills]
nudifolious, *a.* having smooth or bare leaves.
nudirostrate, *a.* having a naked beak.
nudism, nudist, nudity NUDE.
Nuffield, *n.* **William Richard Morris, Viscount Nuffield** (1877–1963), English manufacturer and philanthropist. Starting with a small cycle-repairing business, in 1910 he designed a car that could be produced cheaply, and built up Morris Motors Ltd at Cowley, Oxford.
nugae, *n.pl.* trifles, esp. literary compositions of a trifling and fugitive kind. **nugatory**, *a.* trifling, insignificant; futile, ineffective, inoperative. [L]
nugger, *n.* a broad, strongly built boat used on the upper Nile. [Arab. *nuggar*]
nugget, *n.* a lump of native metal, esp. of gold; something small but valuable. [etym. doubtful]
nuisance, *n.* anything that annoys, irritates or troubles; an offensive or disagreeable person, action, experience etc.; (*Law*) anything causing annoyance, inconvenience or injury to another. **nuisance value,** *n.* the capacity to cause irritation, obstruction etc. [OF, from *nuire,* L *nocēre,* to injure]
Nujoma, *n.* **Sam** (1929–), Namibian left-wing politician, leader of SWAPO from 1959. He was exiled 1960 after founding SWAPO in 1959 and controlled guerrillas from Angolan bases until the first free elections were held (1989), making Nujoma president designate.
nuke, *n.* (*sl.*) a nuclear weapon *v.t.* to attack with nuclear weapons; (*fig.*) to destroy completely, ruin. [from *nuclear*]
Nukua'lofa, *n.* capital and port of Tonga on Tongatapu; population (1986) 29,000.
null, *a.* void, having no legal force or validity; (*fig.*) without character, expression, or individuality; (*Math., Log.*) amounting to nothing, equal to zero, nil. †*v.t.* to nullify. [OF *nul, nulle,* L *nullum,* nom. *-lus* (*ne,* not, *ullus,* any)]
nullah, *n.* a ravine, gully or water-course. [Hind. *nāla*]
nulla-nulla, *n.* a club-shaped weapon of hard wood used by the Australian Aborigines. [Austral. Abor.]
nullifidian, *a.* of no religion. *n.* an unbeliever. [L *nulli-,* NULLUS, (see NULL) *fidēs,* faith]
nullify, *v.t.* to make void; to cancel; to annul, to invalidate; to efface, to destroy. **nullification**, *n.* **nullifier,** *n.* [late L *nullificāre* (L *nulli-, nullus, -ficāre, facere,* to make)]
nullipara, *n.* a woman who has never given birth to a child. **nulliparous,** *a.* [*parēre,* to bring forth]
nullipore, *n.* a seaweed with calcareous fronds, a coralline. [NULLUS (see NULL), PORE[1]]
nullity, *n.* invalidity; an invalid act, instrument, etc.; nothingness, non-existence; a nonentity, a mere cipher.
NUM (*abbr.*) National Union of Mineworkers.
numb, *a.* deprived of sensation and motion; torpid, stupefied, dulled; †causing numbness. *v.t.* to benumb, to paralyse. **numb-fish,** *n.* the electric ray or torpedo. **numb-hand,** *n.* a clumsy person. **numbly,** *adv.* **numbness,** *n.* [earlier, *num,* OE *numen,* p.p. of *niman,* to take (*b* excrescent, cp. NIMBLE)]
number, *n.* a measure of discrete quantity; a name or symbol representing any such quantity, a numeral; a sum or aggregate of persons, things or abstract units; one of a numbered series; a single issue of a periodical, one of the parts of a literary or other work so issued, a division of an opera etc.; numerical reckoning, arithmetic; poetical measure, verse, rhythm (*often in pl.*); plurality, multitude, numerical preponderance (*usu. in pl.*); the distinctive form of a word according as it denotes unity or plurality; a song or piece of music forming part of a popular musician's act or repertoire; (*sl.*) a position or job, esp. an advantageous or lucrative one. *v.t.* to count, to reckon; to ascertain the number of; to amount to; to assign a number to, to distinguish with a number; to include, to comprise (among etc.); to have lived (a specified amount of years). **Numbers,** *n.* the fourth book of the Old Testament, giving an account of the two censuses of the Israelites. **by numbers,** performed in simple stages

esp. orig. with each one numbered. **his/her number is up,** he/she is going to die. **to have someone's number,** (*coll.*) to understand someone's intentions, motives or character. **without number,** *n.* innumerable. **number-crunching,** *n.* the large-scale processing of numbered information esp. by computer. **number one,** *n.* (*coll.*) the first in a series; the most senior person in an organization; (*coll.*) oneself; the product which is at the top of a sales chart esp. a pop record. **number plate,** *n.* the plate on a motor vehicle showing its registration number. **Number Ten,** *n.* 10 Downing Street, the British Prime Minister's residence. **number two,** *n.* a deputy. **numberer,** *n.* **numberless,** *a.* [OF *nombre, numbre,* L *numerum,* nom. *-rus,* cogn. with Gr. *nemein,* to distribute]

numbles, *n.pl.* certain inward parts of a deer used as food, cp. *umble.* [OF *nombles,* prob. var. of *lombles,* L *lumbulus,* dim. of *lumbus,* loin]

numdah, *n.* an embroidered felt rug found in India. [Hind. *namdā*]

numeral, *a.* pertaining to, consisting of, or denoting number. *n.* a word, symbol or group of symbols denoting number; Roman figures, e.g. I, III, V, X, C. **numerable,** *a.* **numerableness,** *n.* **numerally,** *adv.* **numerary,** *a.* **numerical,** *a.* **numerically,** *adv.* [late L *numerālis*]

numerate, *v.t.* to reckon, to number. *a.* able to count; competent in mathematics. **numeration,** *n.* **numerator,** *n.* one who numbers; the part of a vulgar fraction written above the line indicating how many fractional parts are taken.

numeric, *n.* the numerical part of an expression.

numérotage, *n.* the numbering of yarns so as to denote their fineness. [F, from *numéroter,* to number, from It. *numero,* NUMBER]

numerous, *a.* many in number; consisting of a great number of individuals; rhythmical, musical, harmonious; †thronged. **numerously,** *adv.* **numerousness,** *n.* **numerology,** *n.* the study of the alleged significance of numbers.

numinous, *a.* pertaining to divinity; feeling awe of the divine. [L *numen,* divinity]

numismatic, *a.* pertaining to coins or coinage. **numismatically,** *adv.* **numismatics, numismatology,** *n.* the science or study of coins and medals. **numismatist, numismatologist,** *n.* [F *numismatique,* L *numismat-,* stem of *numisma,* Gr. *nomisma,* from *nomizein,* to practise, to have in current use]

nummary, *a.* of or pertaining to money. **nummular, -lary,** *a.* pertaining to or resembling coins. **nummulated,** *a.* coin-shaped. [L *nummārius,* from *nummus,* coin]

nummulation, *n.* the arrangement of the blood corpuscles like piles of coins.

nummulite, *n.* a fossil foraminifer resembling a coin. **nummuline, nummulitic,** *a.*

numnah, *n.* a fabric or sheepskin pad placed under a saddle to prevent chafing. [Hind. *namda*]

numskull, *n.* a blockhead, a dunce; the head of a doll, a thick head. **numskulled,** *a.*

nun, *n.* a woman devoted to a religious life and living in a convent under certain vows, usu. of poverty, chastity and obedience; a variety of pigeon; the smew; the blue titmouse. **nun's cloth,** *n.* a variety of bunting used as material for dresses etc. **nun's thread,** *n.* fine thread used in lace-making. **nun's veiling,** *n.* a soft, thin, woollen dress-stuff. **nunhood, nunship,** *n.* **nunlike,** *a., adv.* **nunnery,** *n.* a religious home for women. **nunnish,** *a.* [OE *nunne,* late L *nonna,* fem. of *nonnus,* monk, orig. a title of address to old people]

nunatak, *n.* a mountain peak which projects through an ice sheet. [Eskimo]

nun-buoy, *n.* a buoy shaped like two cones united at the base. [obsolete *nun* (perh. from prec.), a spinning-top, BUOY]

Nunc dimittis, *n.* the canticle 'Lord, now lettest thou thy servant depart in peace' (Luke ii.29); (*fig.*) a peaceful death. [L, now lettest thou depart]

†**nuncheon,** *n.* luncheon. [ME *noneschenh* (*none,* L *nōna,* NOON, *schench,* OE *scenc,* cup, draught)]

nuncio, *n.* (*pl.* **-ios**) a papal envoy to a foreign Catholic power. **nunciature,** *n.* [It., from L *nuncius,* messenger]

†**nuncle,** *n.* uncle. [UNCLE (through *mine uncle,* cp. NEWT, NONCE)]

nuncupate, *v.t.* to declare (a will, vow etc.) orally, as dist. from in writing. **nuncupation,** *n.* **nuncupative,** †**-tory,** *a.* oral, not written; designative, nominal. **nuncupative will** or **legacy,** *n.* a will or legacy made orally. [L *nuncupātus,* p.p. of *nuncupāre* (*nōmen,* name, *capere,* to take)]

nundinal, *a.* relating to fairs or markets. †**nundinary,** *a.* [L *nundinālis,* from *nundinae,* pl., a market-day (*novem,* nine, *dies,* day)]

nunhood, nunnery etc. NUN.

Nunn, *n.* **Trevor** (1940–), British stage director, linked with the Royal Shakespeare Company from 1968. He received a Tony award (with John Caird) for his production of *Nicholas Nickleby* (1982) and for *Les Miserables* (1987).

nunnation, *n.* the addition of final *n.* to words, in the declension of Arabic nouns etc. †**unnated,** *a.* [Arab. *nun,* the letter *n,* -ATION]

Nupe, *n.* (*pl.* **Nupes,** esp. collectively **Nupe**) a member, or the Kwa language, of a Negro people of West Central Nigeria.

NUPE, (*abbr.*) National Union of Public Employees.

nuphar *n.* the yellow water-lily. [NENUPHAR]

nuptial, *a.* pertaining to, done at, or constituting a wedding. *n.pl.* a wedding. **nuptial flight,** *n.* the flight of a virgin queen-bee, during which she is impregnated. **nuptial plumage,** *n.* the brightly coloured plumage developed by many male birds prior to the start of the breeding season. [F, from L *nuptiālis,* from *nuptiæ,* wedding, from *nubere* (p.p. *nuptus*), to marry]

NUR, (*abbr.*) National Union of Railwaymen.

Nuremberg, *n.* (German **Nürnberg**) an industrial city (electrical and other machinery, precision instruments, textiles, toys) in Bavaria, West Germany; population (1988) 467,000. From 1933 the Nuremberg rallies were held here, and in 1945 the Nuremberg trials of war criminals. **Nuremberg rallies,** *n.pl.* the annual meetings of the German Nazi Party. They were characterized by extensive marches in party formations and mass rallies addressed by Nazi leaders such as Hitler and Goebbels. **Nuremberg trials,** *n.pl.* after World War II, the trials of the 24 chief Nazi war criminals, Nov. 1945–Oct. 1946, by an international military tribunal consisting of four judges and four prosecutors: one of each from the UK, US, USSR and France. An appendix accused the German cabinet, general staff, high command, Nazi leadership corps, SS, Sturm Abteilung and Gestapo of criminal responsibility.

Nureyev, *n.* **Rudolf** (1938–), Soviet dancer and choreographer. A soloist with the Kirov Ballet, He defected to the West (1961), where he was mainly associated with the Royal Ballet, and was Margot Fonteyn's principal partner.

nurl KNURL.

†**nurr** KNUR.

nurse, *n.* a woman employed to suckle the child of another, usu. called a wet-nurse, or to have the care of young children, also called a dry-nurse; one who tends the sick, wounded or infirm; one who or that which fosters or promotes; the condition of being nursed; a tree planted to protect another or others during growth; a sexually imperfect bee, ant etc., which tends the young brood; an individual in a sexual stage of metagenesis; one of various sharks or dogfish. *v.t.* to suckle; to give suck to or feed (an infant); to hold or clasp, esp. on one's knees or lap; to rear, to nurture; to foster, to tend, to promote growth in; to tend in sickness; to manage with care; to cherish, to brood over; to economize, to husband; (*Billiards*) to keep (the balls) in a good position for cannons. *v.i.* to act as nurse; to suckle a baby. **wet nurse,** a woman able to breast-feed a baby as well as, or in place of, her own. **nursemaid,** *n.* a woman or girl in charge of young children.

nurser, *n.* **nursing,** *n.* the act of nursing, the profession of being a nurse. *a.* **nursing chair,** *n.* a lower chair without arms, used when feeding a baby. **nursing home,** *n.* a (usu.) private hospital or home where care is provided for the elderly or chronically sick. **nursing officer,** *n.* any of several grades of nurse having administrative duties. **nursling,** *n.* an infant, esp. in relation to the one who nurses it. [ME and OF *norice,* late L *nūtricia,* fem. of *nūtricius,* from *nūtrix -īcis,* from *nūtrīre,* to nourish]

nursery, *n.* a room set apart for young children; a day-care establishment for young children; a place or garden for rearing plants; a place or atmosphere conducive to development; the place, sphere or condition in which persons, qualities etc. are bred or fostered; an establishment for rearing fish; a place where animal life is developed; a handicap or race for two-year-old horses. **nursery-governess,** *n.* a woman or girl in charge of young children, usu. combining the duties of a nurse and a teacher. **nursery-maid,** *n.* a person who looks after a children's nursery. **nurseryman, -woman,** *n.* one who raises plants in a nursery. **nursery rhyme,** *n.* a traditional rhyme known to children. **nursery school,** *n.* a school for young children aged two to five. **nursery slopes,** ski slopes set apart for novices; (*fig.*) the easiest early stages of anything.

nurture, *n.* the act of bringing up, training, fostering; nourishment; education, breeding. *v.t.* to nourish, to rear, to train, to educate. [AF, from OF *nourture, nourriture,* L *nūtrītūra,* from *nūtrīre,* to NOURISH]

NUS, (*abbr.*) National Union of Seamen; National Union of Students.

NUT, (*abbr.*) National Union of Teachers.

nut, *n.* the indehiscent fruit of certain trees, containing a kernel in a hard shell; a metal block with a hole for screwing on and securing a bolt, screw etc.; a projection on a spindle engaging with a cogwheel; various parts of machinery, usu. in which a screw works; a projection on the shank of an anchor; (*sl.*) the head; (*sl.*) a crazy person, a fanatic; a masher, a dude, a swell; (*pl.*) small lumps of coal; (*pl., sl.*) testicles; (*fig.*) a person, thing or problem that is hard to deal with. *v.i.* (*past, p.p.* **nutted**) to gather nuts. **a hard nut to crack,** a difficult problem to solve. **can't do it for nuts,** (*sl.*) can't succeed in doing it even in the most favourable circumstances. **nuts and bolts,** the basic essential facts. **off his nut,** (*sl.*) mad; drunk. **to be nuts** or **dead nuts on,** (*sl.*) to delight in; to be very fond of; to be skilled at. **nut-brown,** *a.* brown as a hazel-nut long kept. **nut-butter,** *n.* a substitute for butter, extracted from the oil of nuts. **nutcase,** (*sl.*) a crazy person. **nutcracker,** *n.* (*usu. pl.*) an instrument for cracking nuts; (*fig.*) a nose and chin that tend to meet; a European bird of the genus *Nucifraga.* **nut cutlet,** *n.* a preparation of crushed nuts etc., eaten by vegetarians as a substitute for meat. **nut-gall,** *n.* an oak-gall. **nut-hatch,** *n.* a small bird of the genus *Sitta,* allied to the woodpecker, esp. *S. Europaea.* **nut-hook,** *n.* a hooked stick to pull down boughs in nutting; †a bailiff. **nut-oil,** *n.* oil expressed from hazel-nuts or walnuts, used in paints and varnishes. **nut-palm,** *n.* an Australian tree bearing edible nuts. **nut-pine,** *n.* one of various pines bearing nut-like edible seeds. **nutshell,** *n.* the hard shell enclosing the kernel of a nut; (*fig.*) something holding, containing or sheltering in a very small compass. **to be** or **lie in a nutshell,** to be contained or expressed in a very concise statement. **nut-tree,** *n.* a tree bearing nuts, esp. the hazel. **nut-weevil,** *n.* a beetle infesting nuts, esp. one laying eggs in green hazel-nuts etc. **nut-wrench,** *n.* a spanner. **nutlet,** *n.* **nuts,** *a.* (*sl.*) crazy. **nutter,** *n.* (*sl.*) a mad person. **nutty,** *a.* abounding in nuts; tasting like nuts; (*sl.*) sweet (on); spicy; smart; (*sl.*) crazy. [OE *hnutu* (cp. Dut. *noot,* G *Nuss,* Icel. *hnot*)]

nutate, *v.i.* to nod, to bend forward, to droop. **nutant,** *a.* drooping, hanging with the apex downwards. **nutation,** *n.* a nodding or oscillation; a movement of the tips of growing plants, usu. towards the sun; a periodical oscillation of the earth's axis due to the attractive influence of the sun and moon on the greater mass round the equator; (*Path.*) morbid oscillation of the head. [L *nūtātus,* p.p. of *nūtāre,* freq. of *nuere* (in *abnuere*), to nod]

nutmeg, *n.* the hard aromatic seed of the fruit of species of *Myristica,* esp. *M. fragrans,* the nutmeg-tree, used for flavouring and in medicine. **nutmeg-apple,** *n.* the pear-shaped drupaceous fruit of the nutmeg tree. **nutmeg-liver,** *n.* a diseased condition of the liver, due to excessive drinking. **nutmeggy,** *a.* [ME *notemuge* (NUT, OF *muge, mugue,* in *noix mugue* or *muguede,* med. L *nux muscāta,* musk-like nut)]

nutria, *n.* a S American beaver, *Myopotamus coypus;* its skin, formerly much used in hat-making. [Sp., from L *lutra,* otter]

nutrient, *a.* nourishing; serving as or conveying nourishment. *n.* a nutritious substance. **nutriment,** *n.* that which nourishes or promotes growth, esp. food. **nutrimental,** *a.* **nutrition,** *n.* the function or process of promoting the growth of organic bodies; nourishment, food. **nutritional,** *a.* **nutritious,** *a.* affording nourishment, efficient as food. **nutritiously,** *adv.* **nutritiousness,** *n.* **nutritive,** *a., n.* **nutritively,** *adv.* **nutritiveness,** *n.* [L *nūtriens -ntem,* pres.p. of *nūtrīre,* to nourish]

nutshell, nutty NUT.

Nuuk, *n.* Greenlandic for GODTHAAB, capital of Greenland.

nux vomica, *n.* the seed of an East Indian tree, *Strychnos nux-vomica,* which yields strychnine. [med. L *nux,* nut, *vomere,* to VOMIT]

nuzzle¹, *v.t.* to rub or press the nose against; to fondle; to root up with the nose. *v.i.* to root about with the nose; to nestle, to hide the head, as a child in its mother's bosom. [NOSE, -LE]

†**nuzzle²,** *v.t.* to bring (up), to nurse, to nourish, to nurture; (*fig.*) to cherish, to foster. [etym. doubtful]

NW, (*abbr.*) North-West.

NY, (*abbr.*) New York.

Nyasa, *n.* former name for Lake MALAWI.

Nyasaland, *n.* former name (until 1964) for MALAWI.

NYC, (*abbr.*) New York City.

nyct(a)-, (o)-, *etc. comb. form.* pertaining to night. [Gr. *nukti-, nux,* night]

nyctalopia, nyctalopy, *n.* a disease of the eyes in which vision is worse in shade or twilight than in daylight, night-blindness. **nyctalops,** *n.* a person affected with this. [late L *nyctalopia,* from Gr. *nuktalōps* (*nukti-, nux,* night, *alaos,* blind, *ōps,* eye)]

nyctitropic, *a.* changing position or direction at night (of leaves). **nyctitropism,** *n.* [Gr. *tropos,* turn,]

nyctophobia, *n.* a morbid fear of darkness.

nycturia, *n.* nocturnal incontinence of urine, bed-wetting.

Nyerere, *n.* **Julius (Kambarage)** (1922–), Tanzanian socialist politician, president (1964–85). Orig. a teacher, he devoted himself from 1954 to the formation of the Tanganyika African National Union and subsequent campaigning for independence. He became chief minister (1960), was prime minister of Tanganyika (1961–62), president of the newly formed Tanganyika Republic (1962–64), first president of Tanzania (1964–85), and head of the Organization of African Unity (1984).

Nyers, *n.* **Rezso** (1923–), Hungarian socialist leader. As secretary of the ruling Hungarian Socialist Worker's Party's (HSWP) central committee (1962–74) and a member of its politburo (1966–74), he was the architect of Hungary's liberalizing economic reforms in 1968.

Nykvist, *n.* **Sven** (1922–), Swedish director of photography, associated with the film director Ingmar Bergman. He worked frequently in the US from the mid-1970s onwards. His films include *The Virgin Spring* (1960, for Bergman), *Pretty Baby* (1978, for Louis Malle), and *Fanny and Alexander* (1982, for Bergman).

nylghau, *n.* a large, short-horned Indian antelope, the male of which is slate-coloured. [Pers. *nīlgāw,* blue ox]

nylon, *n.* name applied to a group of thermoplastics, used largely for hosiery, shirts, dress fabrics, imitation furs, ropes, brushes etc.

nymph, *n.* one of a class of youthful female divinities inhabiting groves, springs, mountains, the sea etc.; a beautiful or attractive young woman; a nympha. **nymphean**, †**nymphal,** *a.* **nymphet**, *n.* a young girl who is very sexually attractive and precocious. †**nymphical, nymphish, nymphlike,** *a.* †**nymphly,** *adv.* [F *nymphe,* L *nympha,* Gr. *numphē,* bride]

nympha, *n.* (*pl.* **-phae**) a pupa or chrysalis, **nymphiparous**, *a.* producing nymphae or pupae. [as prec.]

nymphaea, *n.* a genus of aquatic plants, containing the white water-lily. [Gr. *numphaia,* fem. of *numphaios* (see NYMPH), sacred to the nymphs]

nymph(o)-, *comb. form.* pertaining to a nymph or young girl. [NYMPH]

nympholepsy, *n.* a state of ecstasy or frenzy supposed to befall one who has gazed on a nymph; (*fig.*) a wild desire for the unattainable. **nympholept,** *n.* **nympholeptic**, *a.*

nymphomania, *n.* excessive sexual desire in woman. **nymphomaniac**, *n.* **nymphomaniacal**, *a.*

nystagmus, *n.* a spasmodic movement of the eyeballs, a condition affecting miners and others working in a dim light. [Gr. *nustagmos,* a nodding, from *nustazein,* to nod, to be sleepy]

NZ, (*abbr.*) New Zealand.

O

O[1], **o**, the 15th letter, and the fourth vowel (*pl.* **Os, O's, Oes**), has three distinct sounds: (1) as in *pot* (o); (2) this lengthened by a following *r* as in *or* (aw); (3) as in *go* (ō); there is also the unstressed sound (ə). *n.* an O-shaped mark; a circle, oval, or any round or nearly round shape; a naught, nothing, zero. **O-grade,** *n.* (a pass in) an examination in the Scottish Certificate of Education corresponding to O-level. **O-level,** *n.* (a pass in) an examination at the ordinary level of the General Certificate of Education in England and Wales (superseded by the GCSE in 1988).

O[2], (*chem. symbol*) oxygen.

O[3], **o,** (*abbr.*) ocean; octavo; old; Ohio; ohm; only; order; ordinary.

O[4], **oh,** *int.* an exclamation of earnest or solemn address, entreaty, invocation, pain, surprise, wonder etc. [prob. from L]

o-, *pref.* (*Chem.*) ortho-.

-o, *suf.* to *n.*, *a.* (*coll.*) serving as a diminutive; as in *cheapo, wino;* (*coll.*) forming an interjection; as in *cheerio, righto*.

O', *pref.* descendant of, in Irish surnames. [Ir. *ó, ua,* descendant]

o', *prep.* (*coll.* or *dial.*) short for OF, ON.

oaf, *n.* (*pl.* **oafs**) orig. a silly child left by fairies in place of one taken by them; a deformed child; a silly, stupid person, a lout. **oafish,** *a.* **oafishly,** *adv.* **oafishness,** *n.* [var. of obs. *auf,* Icel. *ālfr,* ELF]

oak, *n.* any tree or shrub of the genus *Quercus,* esp. *Q. robur,* a forest tree much valued for its timber; the wood of this; any tree of the Australian genus *Casuarina;* applied to various trees and plants bearing a real or fancied resemblance to the oak; one of various species of moth. **Oak-apple Day,** 29 May, the anniversary of the escape of Charles II at Boscobel in 1651. **the Oaks,** a race for three-year-old fillies, named after an estate at Epsom. **oak-apple, -gall, -nut,** *n.* a gall or excrescence of various kinds produced on oaks by various gall-flies. **oak-fern,** *n.* a slender, three-branched polypody, *Thelypteris dryopteris*. **oak-leather,** *n.* a tough fungus growing on old oaks; **oaken,** *a.* **oakling,** *n.* a young oak. **oaky,** *a.* full of oaks; like oak. [OE *āc* (cp. Dut. and Icel. *eik,* G *Eiche*)]

Oakley, *n.* **Annie (Phoebe Annie Oakley Mozee)** (1860–1926), US sharpshooter, member of Buffalo Bill's Wild West Show.

Oaks, *n.* a horse race, one of the English classics, run at Epsom racecourse in June (normally two days after the Derby), for three-year-old fillies only. The race is named after the Epsom home of the 12th Earl of Derby.

oakum, *n.* old rope, untwisted and pulled into loose fibres, used for caulking seams, stopping leaks etc. in ships. [OE *ācumba,* tow, lit. combings (*ā-, æ-,* off, *cemban,* to comb)]

OAP, (*abbr.*) old age pension, pensioner.

oar, *n.* a long pole with a flattened blade, for rowing, sculling or steering a boat; an oarsman; anything resembling an oar in form or function, as a fin, wing or arm used in swimming etc. *v.i.* to row. *v.t.* to propel by or as by rowing. **to lie, rest on one's oars,** to cease rowing without shipping the oars; to stop for rest, to cease working. **to put, stick one's oar in,** to intrude into conversation; to interfere, esp. with unasked-for advice. **oarfish,** *n.* any of various long ribbonfish. **oarlock,** *n.* (*N Am.*) a rowlock. **oarsman, -woman,** *n.* a (skilled) rower. **oarsmanship,** *n.* **oarage,** *n.* (*poet.*). **oared,** *a.* having oars. **oarless,** *a.* **oar-like,** *a.* **oary,** *a.* [OE *ār,* (cp. Icel. *-ār,* Dan. *aare*), perh. rel. to Gr. *eretēs* rower]

OAS, (*abbr.*) on active service; Organization of American States; *Organisation de l'Armée Secrète* (violently opposed to Algerian independence).

oasis, *n.* (*pl.* **oases**) a fertile spot in a waste or desert; a thing or place offering peace, pleasure, refuge etc.; (**Oasis**®) in flower arranging, a soft, porous material into which cut flowers, foliage etc. are inserted. [L and Gr., prob. from Egyptian (cp. Copt. *ouahe,* from *ouīh,* to dwell)]

oast, *n.* a kiln for drying hops. **oast-house,** *n.* [OE *āst* (cp. Dut. *eest*), rel. to L *aestus,* heat, *aedes,* house, Gr. *aithos,* heat]

Oastler, *n.* **Richard** (1789–1861), English social reformer. He opposed child labour and the Poor Law 1834, and was largely responsible for securing the Factory Act 1833 and the Ten Hours Act 1847. He was born in Leeds, and was known as the 'Factory King'.

oat, *n.* (*usu. in pl.*) a cereal plant of the genus *Avena,* esp. *A. sativa;* (*pl.*) the grain of this, used for food; a musical pipe made from an oat-stem; hence, pastoral bucolic poetry or song. **to feel one's oats,** to feel vitality or be full of self-esteem. **to get one's oats,** (*sl.*) to have regular sexual intercourse. **to sow one's wild oats,** to indulge in youthful (esp. sexual) excess. **wild oats,** a tall grass of the same genus as the oat-plant; youthful dissipation. **oatcake,** *n.* a flat cake or biscuit made from oatmeal. **oat-grass,** *n.* wild oat. **oatmeal,** *n.* oats ground into meal, used chiefly for making porridge or oatcake; a fawny-grey colour (of porridge). **oaten,** *a.* [OE *āte*]

Oates, *n.* **Titus** (1649–1705), British conspirator. A priest, he entered the Jesuit colleges at Valladolid, Spain, and St Omer, France, as a spy in 1677–78, and on his return to England announced he had discovered a 'Popish Plot' to murder Charles II and re-establish Catholicism. Although this story was almost entirely false, many innocent Roman Catholics were executed during 1678–80 on Oates's evidence. In 1685 he was flogged, pilloried and imprisoned for perjury. He was pardoned and granted a pension after the revolution of 1688.

oath, *n.* (*pl.* **oaths**) a solemn appeal to God or some holy or revered person or thing in witness of the truth of a statement or of the binding nature of a promise, esp. in a court of law; the form of an oath; a profane imprecation or expletive, a curse; a swear word. **on, under, upon oath,** sworn to attesting the truth; pledged or attested by oath; having taken an oath. **to take an oath,** to swear formally to the truth of one's attestations. **oath-breaking,** *n.* **oathable,** *a.* [OE *āth* (cp. Dut. *eed,* G *Eid,* Icel. *eithr,* OHG *Eit*)]

oatmeal OAT.

OAU, (*abbr.*) Organization of African Unity.

Oaxaca, *n.* capital of a state of the same name in the Sierra Madre del Sur mountain range, central Mexico; population (1980) 157,300; former home town of presidents Benito Juárez and Porfirio Diaz; industries include food processing, textiles, and handicrafts.

OB, (*abbr.*) old boy; outside broadcast.

Ob, *n.* a river in Asiatic USSR, flowing 3380 km/2100 miles from the Altai mountains through the W Siberian Plain to the Gulf of Ob in the Arctic Ocean. With its main tributary, the Irtysh, it is 5600 km/3480 miles.

ob., (*abbr.*) *obiit,* he/she died; *obiter,* incidentally, in passing; oboe.

ob-, *pref.* toward, to, meeting, in, facing; against,

opposing, hindering, resisting, hostile; reversely, obversely, contrary to the normal; as in *object, objurgate, oblique, obovate*. [L, in the way of, against]

Obad., (*abbr.*) Obadiah.

obang, *n.* an oblong gold coin formerly current in Japan. [Jap. *ôban,* great sheet]

obbligato, *a.* (*Mus.*) not to be omitted; indispensable to the whole. *n.* an instrumental part or accompaniment that forms an integral part of the composition or is independently important (usu. by a single instrument). [It., from L *obligātus,* p.p. of *obligāre,* to OBLIGE]

obconic(al), *a.* (*Bot.*) inversely conical.

obcordate, *a.* inversely heart-shaped.

obdurate, *a.* hardened in heart, esp. against moral influence; stubborn; impenitent. *v.t.* to make obdurate. **obduracy, †obdurateness,** *n.* **obdurately,** *adv.* **†obdure,** *v.t.* to obdurate. **obduration,** *n.* [L *obdūrātus,* p.p. of *obdūrāre* (OB-, *dūrāre,* to harden, from *dūrus,* hard)]

OBE, (*abbr.*) Officer of (the Order of) the British Empire.

obeah, obi, *n.* a form of sorcery practised by Negroes, esp. in the W Indies; a magical charm. **obiman, obiwoman,** *n.* an expert practitioner in obeah. [W Afr.]

obedience, *n.* the act or practice of obeying; dutiful submission to authority; compliance with law, command or direction; the authority of a Church or other body; (*collect.*) those subject to such authority (e.g. a monastic order); a written command or instruction from a religious superior. **passive obedience,** submission to the authority of a person or body without participation, unquestioning submission to laws or commands whatever their nature. **obedient,** *a.* **†obediential,** *a.* **obedientiary,** *n.* a member of, esp. a holder of office in, a monastery or convent, subject to obedience to the superior. **obediently,** *adv.* [OF, from L *obēdientia,* from *obēdīre,* to OBEY]

obeisance, *n.* a bow, a curtsy, or any gesture signifying deference, submission, respect or salutation; homage; †obedience. **obeisant,** *a.* **obeisantly,** *adv.* [F *obéissance,* orig. obedience]

obelion, *n.* the part of the skull between the two parietal foramina where the sagittal suture becomes simple.

obelisk, *n.* a quadrangular stone shaft, usually monolithic and tapering, with a pyramidal apex; an obelus. **obeliscal, obeliscoid,** *a.*

obelus, *n.* (*pl.* **-li**) a mark (–, ÷, or †), used to mark spurious or doubtful passages in ancient MSS; in printing, a dagger symbol (†) indicating a cross-reference, footnote or death date. Also **double obelisk** (‡). **obelize, -ise,** *v.t.* [L, from Gr. *obelos,* a spit; dim. *obeliskos*]

Oberammergau, *n.* village in Bavaria, West Germany, where a Christian passion play has been performed every ten years (except during the world wars) since 1634 to commemorate the ending of the plague.

Oberon¹, *n.* king of the elves or fairies, and, according to a 13th-cent. French romance *Huon of Bordeaux*, an illegitimate son of Julius Caesar. Shakespeare used the character in *A Midsummer Night's Dream*.

Oberon², *n.* **Merle** (stage name of Estelle Merle O'Brien Thompson) (1911–79), Tasmanian-born British actress who starred in several Alexander Korda films, including *The Scarlet Pimpernel* (1935), and was briefly married to him. She played Cathy to Laurence Olivier's Heathcliff in *Wuthering Heights* (1939), and after 1940 worked successfully in the US.

Oberösterreich, *n.* German name for the federal state of Upper Austria.

obese, *a.* excessively fat, fleshy, corpulent. **obeseness, obesity,** *n.* [L *obēsus,* p.p. of *obedere* (OB-, *edere,* to eat)]

obex, *n.* (*Anat.*) a band of white matter in the *medulla oblongata;* †an obstacle, an impediment. [L, cogn. with *obicere* (OB-, *jacere,* to cast)]

obey, *v.t.* to perform or carry out (a command, instruction or direction); to be obedient to; to yield to the direction or control of, to act according to. *v.i.* to do what one is directed or commanded. **obeyer,** *n.* **obeyingly,** *adv.* [F *obéir,* L *obēdīre* (OB-, *audīre,* to hear)]

obfuscate, *v.t.* to darken, to obscure; to bewilder, to confuse. **obfuscation,** *n.* **obfuscatory,** *a.* [L *obfuscātus,* p.p. of *obfuscāre* (OB-, *fuscāre,* from *fuscus,* dark)]

obi¹, *n.* (*pl.* **obi, obis**) a coloured sash worn around a Japanese kimono. [Jap.]

obi² OBEAH.

obit, *n.* a memorial service or commemoration of a death; (*coll.*) short for obituary. **obitual,** *n., a.* **obituarily,** *adv.* **obituarist,** *n.* **obituary,** *a.* relating to or recording a death or deaths. *n.* a notice of a death, usu. in the form of a short biography of the deceased; a register or list of deaths. [OF, from L *obitus,* p.p. of *obīre,* to set, to die]

obiter, *adv.* incidentally, by the way. **obiter dictum,** (*pl.* **obiter dicta**), a passing remark. [L]

object¹, *v.t.* to oppose; to offer or adduce in opposition, to allege (a fact, usu. with *that*) in criticism, disapproval, or condemnation; †to propose. *v.i.* to make objections; to dislike, to disapprove. [L *objectāre,* freq. of *objicere* (OB-, *jacere,* to throw)]

object², *n.* anything presented to the senses or the mind, esp. anything visible or tangible; a material thing; that to which an action or feeling is directed; aim, end, ultimate purpose; a person or thing of pitiable or ridiculous appearance; a noun, or word, phrase or sentence equivalent to a noun, governed by a transitive verb or preposition; a thing or idea regarded as external to, distinct from, or independent of the subjective consciousness. **no object,** no obstacle; no deterrent. **object-ball,** *n.* in billiards etc., the ball at which a player aims with his/her cueball. **object code, program,** *n.* a computer program which has been translated from a high-level language (source code) into machine code by an assembler or compiler program. **object-finder,** *n.* an eye-piece on a microscope for enabling one to locate the object on a slide; an analogous instrument on a large telescope. **object-glass,** *n.* the lens or combination of lenses at the end of an optical instrument nearest the object. **object language,** *n.* a language which is described by another language. **object-lesson,** *n.* a lesson in which the actual object described or a representation of it is used for illustration; a practical illustration. **object-soul,** *n.* a primitive belief in the presence of a soul in inanimate objects. **objectification,** *n.* **objectify,** *v.t.* to render objective; to present to the mind as a concrete or sensible reality. **objection,** *n.* the act of objecting; an adverse argument, reason or statement; disapproval, dislike, or the expression of this. **objectionability,** *n.* **objectionable,** *a.* liable to objection, reprehensible; offensive, unpleasant. **objectionableness,** *n.* **objectionably,** *adv.* **objective,** *a.* proceeding from the object of knowledge or thought as dist. from the perceiving or thinking subject; external, actual, real, self-existent, substantive; pertaining to or concerned with outward things as dist. from the subjective, uninfluenced by emotion, impulse, prejudice etc.; denoting the case of the object of a transitive verb or preposition. *n.* an objective point, e.g. of military operations; an aim, goal or target; the objective case; an object-glass. **objective case,** *n.* the case governed in English by a transitive verb or a preposition. **objectival,** *a.* **objectively,** *adv.* **objectiveness,** *n.* **objectivism,** *n.* the tendency to give priority to what is objective; the theory that stresses objective reality. **objectivist,** *n.* **objectivistic,** *a.* **objectivity,** *n.* **objectivize, -ise,** *v.t., v.i.* **objectless,** *a.* **objector,** *n.* one who objects. **conscientious objector** CONSCIENTIOUS

object-oriented programming, (OOP), *n.* a type of computer programming based on 'objects', in which data are closely linked to the procedures that operate on them. For example, a circle on the screen might be an object; it has data, such as a centre point and a radius, as well as procedures for moving it, erasing it, changing its size, and so on.

objet, *n.* (*pl.* **objets**) an object. **objet d'art,** *n.* (*pl.* **objets d'art**) an art object. **objet trouvé,** *n.* (*pl.* **objets trouvés**) a found object. [F]

objurgate, *v.t.*, *v.i.* to chide, to reprove. **objurgation,** *n.* **objurgator,** *n.* **objurgatory,** *a.* [L *objurgātus,* p.p. of *objurgāre* (OB-, *jurgāre,* to chide)]

oblanceolate, *a.* (*Bot.*) inversely lanceolate.

oblast, *n.* (*pl.* **-lasts, -lasti**) an administrative district or province in the USSR. [Rus.]

oblate[1], *a.* flattened at the poles, opp. to *prolate.* **oblate spheroid,** *n.* such a sphere as is produced by the revolution of an ellipse about its shorter axis. **oblately,** *adv.* **oblateness**, *n.* [L *oblātus* (OB-, *lātus,* p.p. of *ferre,* to carry)]

oblate[2], *n.* one not under vows but dedicated to monastic or religious life or work, esp. one of a congregation of secular priests or sisters who live in community. **oblation,** *n.* the act of offering or anything offered in worship; a sacrifice; the presentation of the elements in the Eucharist; a sacrifice; a sacrificial victim; a gift or donation to the Church. **oblational, oblatory,** *a.* [as prec.]

obligation, *n.* the binding power of a promise, contract, vow, duty, law etc.; a duty, responsibility, commitment; (*Law*) a binding agreement, esp. one with a penal condition annexed. **under an obligation,** indebted for some benefit, favour or kindness. **obligate,** *v.t.* to place under an obligation, legal or moral; to compel. *a.*, (*Bot.*) compelled, limited to a single mode of life. †**obligable**, *a.* **obligant**, *n.*, *a.* **obligatory,** *a.* mandatory. [OF, from L *obligātiōnem,* nom. *-tio,* from *obligāre,* to oblige]

obligato OBBLIGATO.

oblige, *v.t.* to bind or constrain by legal, moral or physical force; to be binding on; to place under a debt of gratitude by a favour or kindness; to do a favour to, to gratify; (*p.p.*) to put under an obligation (for). *v.i.* to perform a favour or task. **obligately,** *adv.* **obligee,** *n.* (*Law*) one to whom another is obligated; a conferred favour. †**obligement,** *n.* **obliger**, *n.* **obliging**, *a.* kind, complaisant; helpful, accommodating. **obligingly,** *adv.* **obligingness,** *n.* **obligor**, *n.* (*Law*) one who binds him or herself to another.

oblique, *a.* slanting, deviating from the vertical or horizontal; deviating from the straight or direct line, indirect, roundabout; evasive, not to the point; inclined at an angle other than a right angle; differing from a right angle, *n.* acute or obtuse; (*Anat.*) slanting, neither parallel nor vertical to the longer axis of the body or limb (of muscles etc.); (*Bot.*) unequal-sided (of leaves); of or pertaining to any grammatical cases other than the nominative or vocative. *n.* that which is at an angle, slanting, esp. a geometric figure, military advance; solidus etc. *v.i.* (*Mil.*) to move forwards obliquely; to slant. **oblique angle,** an angle greater or less than a right angle. **oblique case,** *n.* in grammar, any case other than the nominative or vocative. **oblique narration, speech,** *n.* indirect speech. **obliquely,** *adv.* **obliqueness,** *n.* **obliquity**, *n.* obliqueness; (an instance of) mental or moral deviation.

obliterate, *v.t.* to efface, to erase; to wear out, to destroy; to reduce to an illegible or imperceptible state. **obliteration,** *n.* **obliterative,** *a.* **obliterator,** *n.* [L *obliterātus,* p.p. of *obliterāre* (OB-, *litera,* LETTER]

oblivion, *n.* forgetfulness, unawareness; the state of being forgotten; an amnesty or pardon. **oblivious,** *a.* forgetful, unaware (of); lost in thought or abstraction; causing forgetfulness. **obliviously,** *adv.* **obliviousness,** *n.* [OF, from L *oblīviōnem,* nom. *-vio,* from *oblīviscī* (OB-, *līviscī,* to forget, perh. rel. to *līvēre,* to be livid or black and blue)]

oblong, *a.* longer than broad, of greater breadth than height esp. of rectangles with adjoining sides unequal; elliptical (of leaves). *n.* an oblong figure or object. [L *oblongus* (OB-, *longus,* LONG[1])]

obloquy, *n.* censorious language; discredit, disgrace, infamy. [late L *obloquium,* from *obloquī,* to speak against (OB-, *loquī,* to speak)]

obmutescence, *n.* loss of speech; obstinate silence or taciturnity. **obmutescent**, *a.* [L *obmūtescere* (*mūtescere,* incept., from *mūtus,* MUTE)]

obnoxious, *a.* liable or exposed (to injury, attack, criticism etc.); offensive, objectionable, hateful, odious. **obnoxiously,** *adv.* **obnoxiousness,** *n.* [L *obnoxius* (*noxa,* harm)]

†**obnubilate,** *v.t.* to cloud, to obscure. **obnubilation,** *n.* [L *obnūbilātus,* p.p. of *obnūbilāre* (*nūbilus,* cloudy)]

oboe, *n.* a woodwind instrument with a double reed, usu. of soprano pitch; one who plays this instrument in an orchestra; a reed organ-stop of similar tone. **oboist,** *n.* [It., from F *hautbois,* HAUTBOY]

obol, obolus, *n.* (*pl.* **-li**) a small coin of ancient Greece weighing and worth one sixth of a drachma. **obole,** *n.* a small French coin (10th–15th cent.), worth half a denier.

Obote, *n.* **(Apollo) Milton** (1924–), Ugandan politician who led the independence movement from 1961. He became prime minister (1962) and was president (1966–71 and 1980–85), being overthrown by first Idi Amin and then Brig. Tito Okello.

obovate, *a.* (*Bot.*) inversely ovate. **obovately,** *adv.* **obovoid,** *a.*

Obrenovich, *n.* a Serbian dynasty which ruled (1816–42 and 1859–1903). The dynasty engaged in a feud with the rival house of Karageorgevich, which obtained the throne by the murder of the last Obrenovich in 1903.

obreption, *n.* acquisition or attempted acquisition of gifts etc. by falsehood. **obreptitious**, *a.* [F, from L *obreptiōnem,* nom. *-tio* (*repere,* to creep)]

O'Brien[1], *n.* **Angela Maxine ('Margaret')** (1937–), US child actress, a star of the 1940s. She received a special Academy Award in 1944, but her career, including leading parts in *Lost Angel* (1943), *Meet Me in St Louis* (1944), and *The Secret Garden* (1949), did not survive into adolescence.

O'Brien[2], *n.* **Willis H.** (1886–1962), US film animator and special effects man, responsible for one of the cinema's most memorable monsters, *King Kong* (1933).

obs., (*abbr.*) obsolete.

obscene, *a.* repulsive, disgusting, indecent, lewd; in law, that which is liable to corrupt or deprave (of publications etc.). **obscenely,** *adv.* †**obsceneness, obscenity,** *n.* [L *obscēnus* (*scēnus,* etym. doubtful)]

obscurant, *n.* an opponent of intellectual progress. **obscurantism,** *n.* **obscurantist,** *n.*, *a.* [OBSCURE]

obscure, *a.* dark, dim; not clear, indefinite, indistinct; abstruse; difficult to understand; unexplained, doubtful; hidden, secluded, remote from public observation; unknown, lowly, humble; dull, dingy; †gloomy, murky. *v.t.* to make dark, to cloud; to make less intelligible, visible or legible; to dim, to throw into the shade, to outshine; to conceal; †to degrade, to disparage. *v.i.* to darken, to conceal. *n.* obscurity; indistinctness. **obscuration**, *n.* **obscurely,** *adv.* †**obscurement,** †**obscureness,** *n.* †**obscurer,** *n.* **obscurity,** *n.* the quality or state of being obscure; an obscure person or thing. [OF *obscur,* L *obscurus* (*scurus,* from *scu-*, Sansk. *sku-*, to cover, cp. *scūtum,* shield)]

obsecration, *n.* the act of imploring, entreaty; a clause in the Litany beginning with 'by'. †**obsecrate**, *v.t.* to implore, to supplicate. [L *obsecrātio,* from *obsecrāre,* to beseech (*sacrāre,* to make sacred, from *sacer,* SACRED)]

obsequent, *a.* of a stream which flows in the opposite direction to the original slope of the land. [L *sequi,* to follow]

obsequies, *n.pl.* funeral rites. **obsequial**, *a.* [pl. of obs. *obsequy,* A-F *obsequie* (OF *obsèque,* med. L *obsequiae* (L *exsequiae,* acc. to OED conf. with *obsequium,* see foll.)]

obsequious, *a.* servile, cringing, fawning, over-ready to comply with the desires of others; †obedient, submissive, yielding. **obsequiously,** *adv.* **obsequiousness,** *n.* [L *obsequiōsus,* from *obsequium,* from *obsequī,* to comply (*sequī,* to follow)]

observe, *v.t.* to regard attentively, to note, to take notice of, to perceive; to watch, to scrutinize; to examine and note scientifically; to follow attentively, to heed; to perform duly; to comply with; to celebrate; to remark, to express as an opinion. *v.i.* to make a remark or remarks (upon); †to take notice. **observable,** *a.*, *n.*

observableness, *n.* **observably,** *adv.* **observance,** *n.* the act of observing, complying with, keeping, following, performing etc.; a customary rite, form or ceremony; a rule or practice, esp. in a religious order; †observation, heed; †respectful attention, compliance or submission, deference. †**observancy,** *n.* **observant,** *a.* watchful, attentive; quick or strict in observing, esp. rules etc.; †obedient. *n.* an Observantine; †one who observes carefully; an obsequious attendant. **Observantine,** *n.* one of a branch of the Franciscan order observing the stricter rule, also called Observant Friars. **observantly,** *adv.* **observation,** *n.* the act, habit or faculty of observing; scientific watching and noting of phenomena as they occur, as dist. from experiment; the result of such a scrutiny, a fact scientifically noted or taken from an instrument; experience and knowledge gained by systematic observing; a remark, an incidental comment or expression of opinion or reflection; †observance. **observational,** *a.* deriving from observation (rather than experiment); containing or consisting of comment or observation. **observationally,** *adv.* **observation car,** *n.* (*N Am.*) a railway carriage designed so that one can view passing scenery. **observation-post,** *n.* (*Mil.*) a post from which an observer can watch the effect of artillery fire; a position from which one observes. **under observation,** in a state of being watched carefully, undergoing scrutiny. **observatory,** *n.* an institution, building, room etc. for observation of astronomical or meteorological phenomena. **observer,** *n.* one who observes; an official looker-on at a proceeding; formerly, the member of an aircraft's crew employed on reconnaissance, the flying officer. **observing,** *a.* **observingly,** *adv.* **observatorial,** *a.* **observedly,** *adv.* [OF *observer,* L *observāre* (*servāre,* to keep, to heed)]

obsess, *v.t.* to haunt, to beset, to trouble (as an evil spirit); to preoccupy the mind of (as a fixed idea). **obsession,** *n.* (the condition of having) an unhealthily deep-rooted or persistent fixation. **obsessional,** *a.* **obsessionally,** *adv.* **obsessionist,** *n.* an obsessive (person). **obsessive,** *a., n.* **obsessively,** *adv.* **obsessiveness,** *n.* [L *obsessus,* p.p. of *obsidēre,* to besiege (*sedēre,* to sit)]

obsidian, *n.* a black or dark-coloured vitreous lava. [L *Obsidiānus,* from *Obsidius,* erron. for *Obsius,* personal name]

obsidional, *a.* pertaining to a siege. [L *obsidiōnālis,* from *obsidio -ōnis,* siege]

†**obsign, obsignate,** *v.t.* to seal, to ratify. †**obsignation,** *n.* [L *obsignātus,* p.p. of *obsignāre, signāre,* to SIGN)]

obsolescent, *a.* becoming obsolete; gradually disappearing, going out of use; outmoded. **obsolescence,** *n.* **built in, planned obsolescence,** the prearranged demise of a commodity through deterioration or supersedence by a newer model. **obsolete,** *a.* passed out of use, no longer practised, current or accepted; discarded, bygone, out-of-date; imperfectly developed, atrophied. **obsoletely,** *adv.* **obsoleteness,** †**obsoletion, obsoletism,** *n.* [L *obsolescens -ntem,* pres.p. of *obsolescere,* incept. of *obsolēre* (*solēre,* to be accustomed)]

obstacle, *n.* an impediment, an obstruction. †*a.* obstinate. **obstacle-race,** *n.* a race in which the competitors have to surmount or avoid a series of natural or artificial obstacles. [OF, from L *obstāculum* (*stāre,* to stand)]

obstetric, -ical, *a.* of or pertaining to childbirth or obstetrics; (*pl.*) the branch of medical science dealing with childbirth and ante- and postnatal care of women. **obstetrically,** *adv.* **obstetrician,** *n.* [L *obstetrīcius,* from *obstetrix,* midwife (*stāre,* as prec.)]

obstinate, *a.* pertinaciously adhering to one's opinion or purpose, stubborn, refractory; not easily remedied, persistent. **obstinacy, obstinateness,** *n.* **obstinately,** *adv.* [L *obstinātus,* p.p. of *obstināre* (*stanāre,* from *stāre,* to stand)]

obstipation, *n.* extreme constipation. [L *stīpāre,* to cram, to pack]

obstreperous, *a.* noisy, clamorous; boisterous, unruly. **obstreperously,** *adv.* **obstreperousness,** *n.* [L *obstreperus* (*strepere,* to make a noise)]

†**obstriction,** *n.* the state of being legally constrained; an obligation. [med. L *obstrictio,* from *stringere,* to tie]

obstruct, *v.t.* to block up, to close by means of obstacles; to hinder, to impede; to hamper, to check, to retard, to stop. *v.i.* to practise obstruction, esp. in Parliament. **obstructer,** *n.* **obstruction,** *n.* **obstructional,** *a.* **obstructionism,** *n.* deliberate obstruction of (legislative) business, procedure etc. **obstructionist,** *n.* **obstructionistic,** *a.* **obstructive,** *a.* causing or tending to cause obstruction; intended to retard progress, esp. of parliamentary business. *n.* one who causes obstruction, esp. in Parliament; a hindrance. **obstructively,** *adv.* **obstructiveness,** *n.* **obstructor,** *n.* [L *obstructus,* p.p. of *obstruere* (*struere,* to build)]

obtain, *v.t.* to gain, to acquire, to secure; to procure, to get; to attain, to reach. *v.i.* to be prevalent or accepted; to be in common use. **obtainable,** *a.* **obtainability,** *n.* **obtainer,** *n.* **obtainment,** *n.* [F *obtenir,* L *obtinēre* (*tenēre,* to hold)]

obtect, obtected, *a.* of the pupae of some insects, protected, encased by a chitinous covering. [L *obtectus,* p.p. of *obtegere* (*tegere,* to cover)]

obtest, *v.t.* to beseech, to supplicate, to adjure; to beg for. *v.i.* to protest. **obtestation,** *n.* [L *obtestārī* (*testārī,* to bear witness)]

obtrude, *v.t.* to thrust out, forward or upon; to introduce or thrust in without warrant or invitation. *v.i.* to enter without right, to thrust oneself forward. **obtruder,** *n.* **obtrusion,** *n.* **obtrusive,** *a.* **obtrusively,** *adv.* **obtrusiveness,** *n.* a thrusting forward, a desire to be noticed; undue prominence. [L *obtrūdere* (*trūdere,* to thrust, p.p. *trūsus*)]

†**obtruncate,** *v.t.* to lop, to cut the head off, to decapitate. [L *obtruncātus,* p.p. of *obtruncāre* (*truncāre,* to cut off)]

obtund, *v.t.* to blunt, to deaden. **obtundent,** *a., n.* [L *obtundere* (OB-, *tundere,* to beat)]

obturate, *v.t.* to stop up or close, esp. the breech of a gun. **obturation,** *n.* **obturator,** *n.* that which closes an aperture, cavity etc.; (*Anat.*) one of two muscles of the gluteal region; in gunnery, a device for closing the aperture of the breech and preventing the escape of gas. [L *obturātus,* p.p. of *obturāre,* to close]

obtuse, *a.* blunt or rounded, not pointed or acute; denoting an angle greater than a right angle; dull, stupid, slow of apprehension. **obtuse-angular, -angled,** *a.* **obtusely,** *adv.* **obtuseness,** *n.* [L *obtūsus,* p.p. of *obtundere,* to OBTUND]

†**obumbrate,** *v.t.* to overshadow, to darken. [L *obumbrātus,* p.p. of *obumbrāre* (*umbrāre,* to shade)]

obverse, *a.* turned towards one; of leaves, having a base narrower than the apex, forming a counterstatement, complemental. *n.* the face or front; the side of a coin or medal bearing the main device; the counterpart or complementary side or aspect of a statement, fact etc. **obversely,** *adv.* **obversion,** *n.* in logic, a method of immediate inference by reversing the predicate and changing the quality of a proposition. **obvert,** *v.t.* to turn the front towards one; in logic, to infer the obverse of (a proposition). [L *obversus,* p.p. of *obvertere* (*vertere,* to turn)]

obviate, *v.t.* to clear away, to remove, to overcome, counteract or neutralize (as dangers, difficulties etc.); to anticipate, to forestall. **obviation,** *n.* [L *obviātus,* p.p. of *obviāre* (*via,* way)]

obvious, *a.* plain to the eye, perfectly manifest, immediately evident; unsubtle; †standing or situated in the way. *n.* what is obvious, needing no explanation. **obviously,** *adv.* **obviousness,** *n.* [L *obvius* (*ob viam,* in the way)]

obvolute, -ted, *a.* folded together so that the alternate margins are respectively exposed or covered. **obvolution,** *n.* **obvolutive, obvolvent,** *a.* [L *obvolūtus,* p.p. of *obvolvere* (*volvere,* to roll)]

Oc., (*abbr.*) Ocean.

OC, (*abbr.*) Officer Commanding.

oc-, *pref.* OB- (before *c*).
ocarina, *n.* a musical instrument of terracotta with finger-notes and mouthpiece, giving a mellow whistling sound. [It. *oca,* goose]
O'Casey, *n.* **Sean** (adopted name of John Casey) (1884–1964), Irish dramatist. His early plays are tragicomedies, blending realism with symbolism and poetic with vernacular speech: *The Shadow of a Gunman* (1922), *Juno and the Paycock* (1925), and *The Plough and the Stars* (1926). Later plays include *Red Roses for Me* (1946) and *The Drums of Father Ned* (1960).
Occamism, Ockhamism, *n.* the doctrines of William of Occam or Ockham (*c.* 1270– *c.* 1349) the English scholastic philosopher and teacher of nominalism. **Occam's, Ockham's razor,** *n.* the philosophic principle that interpretations should include as few assumptions as possible. **Occamist, Ockhamist,** *n.*
†**occamy,** *n.* an alloy imitating silver. [corr. of ALCHEMY]
occas., (*abbr.*) occasional(ly).
occasion, *n.* an event, circumstance or position of affairs, giving an opportunity, reason, or motive for doing something; motive, ground, reason need; an opportunity; an incidental or immediate cause or condition; a time or occurrence, esp. of special interest or importance; †(*Sc.*) a communion service. *v.t.* to cause directly or indirectly; to be the occasion or incidental cause of; to induce, to influence. **on occasion,** now and then. **as the occasion arises,** when needful, when circumstances demand. **to rise to the occasion,** to be equal to a demanding event or situation. **to take the occasion to,** to take the opportunity of. **occasional,** *a.* happening, made, employed or done as opportunity arises; irregular, infrequent, incidental, casual; of or made for a special occasion. **occasional table,** *n.* a small moveable table (used as occasion demands). **occasionalism,** *n.* the doctrine of certain Cartesians that body and mind form a dualism of heterogeneous entities, and that there is no real interaction, the corresponding phenomena of sensation and volition being due to the simultaneous action of God. **occasionalist**, *n.* **occasionality**, *n.* **occasionally**, *adv.* [F, from L *occāsiōnem,* nom. *-sio,* from *occidere* (*cadere,* to fall)]
Occident, occident, *n.* the west; western Europe, Europe and America; the western hemisphere; sunset. **Occidental**, *a.* western; characteristic of western culture, thoughts etc.; applied to gems of inferior quality or worth, the best supposedly coming from the East. *n.* a westerner. **occidentalism,** *n.* **occidentalist,** *n.* **occidentalize, -ise,** *v.t.* **occidentally,** *adv.* [F, from L *occidentem,* nom. *-dens,* pres.p. of *occidere* (oc-, *cadere,* to fall)]
occiput, *n.* the back part of the head. **occipital**, *n.* short for **occipital bone,** the bone forming the back and part of the base of the skull. **occipitally,** *adv.* [L *occiput* (oc-, *caput,* head)]
occlude, *v.t.* to shut or stop up; to close, to bring together (the eyelids, the teeth); to form or cause to form an occlusion; of metals etc., to absorb (a gas). **occluded front,** *n.* an occlusion. **occludent,** *a., n.* **occlusal**, *a.*, relating to dental occlusion. **occlusion**, *n.* a shutting or stopping up; in meteorology, the closing of a cold front upon a warm one, which is narrowed and raised up, an occluded front; absorption; the manner in which teeth come together, the bite; (*Phon.*) closure of the breath passage prior to articulating a sound. **occlusive**, *n., a.* (*Phon.*) (of) a sound made when the breath passage is completely closed. **occlusor**, *n.* [L *occlūdere* (oc-, *claudere,* to shut), p.p. *occlūsus*]
occult, *a.* concealed, kept secret, esoteric; mysterious, recondite, beyond the range of ordinary knowledge or perception; supernatural, magical, mystical. *v.t.* to hide, to conceal, to cover or cut off from view (esp. during a planetary eclipse). *v.i.* to become temporarily hidden or eclipsed. **the occult,** that which is hidden, mysterious, magical; the supernatural. **occultation**, *n.* **occulted, occulting,** *a.* of a lighthouse beacon, temporarily shut off, becoming invisible at regular intervals. **occultism,** *n.* **occultist,** *n.* **occultly,** *adv.* **occultness,** *n.* [L *occultus,* p.p. of *occulere* (oc-, *-celere,* rel. to *celāre,* to hide, cp. HELE)]
occupant, *n.* one who occupies; one who resides or is in a place; a tenant in possession as dist. from an owner; one who establishes a claim by taking possession. **occupancy,** *n.* **occupation**, *n.* the act of occupying or taking possession (e.g. of a country by a foreign army); the state of being occupied; occupancy, tenure; the state of being employed or engaged in some way; pursuit, employment, business, trade, calling, job. **occupational,** *a.* caused by or related to employment. **occupational disease, hazard,** *n.* a disease, injury, risk etc. resulting directly from or common to an occupation. **occupational therapy,** *n.* treatment of various illnesses by providing a creative occupation or hobby. **occupational therapist,** *n.* **occupationally,** *adv.* †**occupative,** *a.* **occupier,** *n.* an occupant of a house etc.
occupy, *v.t.* to take possession of; to hold in possession, to be the tenant of; to reside in, to be in; to take up, to fill; to give occupation to; to employ, to engage (oneself, or in p.p.); [F *occuper,* L *occupāre* (oc-, *capere,* to take)]
occur, *v.i.* (*past, p.p.* **occurred**) to happen, to take place; to be met with, to be found, to exist; to present itself to the mind. **occurrence**, *n.* an event, an incident; the happening or taking place of anything. †**occurrent,** *a.* [MF *occurrer,* L *occurrere* (oc-, *currere,* to run)]
ocean, *n.* the vast body of water covering about two-thirds of the surface of the globe; any one of its principal divisions, the Antarctic, Atlantic, Arctic, Indian and Pacific Oceans; the sea; an immense expanse or quantity. *a.* pertaining to the ocean. **ocean-basin,** *n.* the depression of the earth's surface containing an ocean. **ocean-going,** *a.* (suitable for) travelling on the ocean. **oceanarium,** *n.* an aquarium for specimens of deep-sea animal life. **oceanic,** *a.* of, pertaining to, occurring in, or (expansive) like the ocean; pertaining to Oceania. **Oceanid,** *n.* (*pl.* **-nids, -nides** an ocean-nymph of Gr. mythology; (*pl.* **-anides**) marine as dist. from freshwater molluscs. **oceano-,** *comb. form.* **oceanographer,** *n.* **oceanographic, -ical**, *a.* **oceanography**, *n.* the branch of science concerned with oceans and their biological, geographic, chemical features etc. **oceanology**, *n.* the study of the sea esp. concerned with the distribution of its economic resources, oceanography. [OF, from L *ōceanum,* nom. *-us,* Gr. *ōkeanos*]
Oceania, *n.* the islands of the S Pacific (Micronesia, Melanesia, Polynesia). The term is sometimes taken to include Australasia and the Malay archipelago, in which case it is considered as one of the seven continents. **Oceanian,** *a.*
Oceanus, *n.* in Greek mythology, the god (one of the Titans) of a river supposed to encircle the earth. He was the progenitor of other river gods, and the nymphs of the seas and rivers.
ocellus, *n.* (*pl.* **-lli**) a simple eye, as opposed to the compound eye of insects; a part or facet of a compound eye; an eyespot or spot of colour surrounded by a ring or rings of other colour, as on feathers, wings etc. **ocellar, ocellate**, **-ted,** *a.* **ocellation,** *n.* **ocelli-,** *comb. form.* [L, dim. of *oculus,* eye]
ocelot, *n.* a small American feline, *Felis pardalis,* the tiger-cat or leopard-cat; its fur. [F, from Nahuatl *ocelotl*]
och, *int.* expressing impatience, contempt, regret, surprise etc. [Ir. and Sc.]
oche, *n.* in darts, the line or mark behind which a player must stand when throwing at the dartboard. [etym. doubtful, prob. from ME *oche,* groove, notch, from MF]
ochlocracy, *n.* mob rule. **ochlocrat**, *n.* **ochlocratic, -ical,** *a.* **ochlocratically,** *adv.* **ochlophobia**, *n.* fear of crowds. [F *ochlocratie,* Gr. *ochlokratia* (*ochlos,* crowd, -CRACY)]

Ochoa, *n.* **Severo** (1905–), US biochemist. He discovered an enzyme able to assemble units of the nucleic acid RNA in 1955, whilst working at New York University. For his work towards the synthesis of RNA Ochoa shared the 1959 Nobel Physiology or Medicine Prize with Arthur Kornberg.

ochone OHONE.

ochre, *n.* a native earth consisting of hydrated peroxide of iron with clay in various proportions, used as a red or yellow pigment; a yellow colour; (*sl.*) money (from the yellow colour of gold). **ochraceous**, **ochreous**, **ochroid**, **ochrous, ochreish**, **ochry,** *a.* **ochreo-,** *comb. form.* [OF *ocre,* L and Gr. *ōchra,* from *ōchros,* yellow]

-ock, *suf.* indicating smallness or youngness, as in *bullock, hillock.* [OE *-oc, -uc*]

ocker, *n.* (*Austral. sl.*) a boorish, chauvinistic Australian. *a.* characteristic of such a person. [after a Australian television character]

Ockhamism, Ockham's razor OCCAMISM.

o'clock CLOCK[1].

O'Connell, *n.* **Daniel** (1775–1847), Irish politician, called 'the Liberator'. In 1823 he founded the Catholic Association to press Roman Catholic claims. Although ineligible as a Roman Catholic to take his seat, he was elected MP for County Clare (1828), and so forced the government to grant Catholic emancipation. In Parliament he cooperated with the Whigs in the hope of obtaining concessions until 1841, when he launched his campaign for repeal of the union.

O'Connor[1], *n.* **Feargus** (1794–1855), Irish parliamentary follower of Daniel O'Connell. He sat in parliament (1832–35), and as editor of the *Northern Star* became an influential figure of the Chartist movement.

O'Connor[2], *n.* **Flannery** (1925–64), US novelist and story writer. Her works have a great sense of evil and sin, and often explore the religious sensibility of the Deep South. Her short stories include *A Good Man Is Hard to Find* (1955) and *Everything That Rises Must Converge* (1965).

OCR, (*abbr.*) optical character reader, recognition.

ocrea, *n.* (*pl.* **-eae**) (*Bot.*) a sheath formed by the union of two stipules round a stem; a sheath round the foot or leg of a bird. **ocreaceous**, **ocreate**, *a.*

Oct., (*abbr.*) October.

oct., (*abbr.*) octavo.

oct(a)-, octo-, *comb. form* having eight; consisting of eight. [Gr. *oktō,* eight]

octachord, *n.* a musical instrument with eight strings; a system of eight sounds, as the diatonic scale.

octad, *n.* a group or series of eight. **octadic**, *a.* [Gr. *oktas, oktō,* eight]

octagon, *n.* a plane figure of eight sides and angles; any object or building of this shape. **octagonal**, *a.* **octagonally,** *adv.* [L *octā-, octōgōnos,* Gr. *oktagōnos, gōnia,* corner]

octahedron, *n.* (*pl.* **-dra, -drons**) a solid figure contained by eight plane faces. **regular octahedron**, one contained by eight equal equilateral triangles. **octahedral,** *a.* **octahedrite**, *n.* native titanic dioxide. [Gr. *hedra,* seat, base]

octal, *a.* referring to or based on the number eight. [Gr. *oktō,* eight]

octamerous, *a.* having parts in eights or in series of eight.

octameter, *n.* a line of eight metrical feet.

Octandria, *n.pl.* a Linnaean class of plants having flowers with eight stamens. **octandrous,** *a.* having eight stamens. [Gr. *anēr andros,* male]

octane, *n.* a colourless liquid hydrocarbon of the alkane series that occurs in petroleum. **octane number, rating,** *n.* a percentage measure of the anti-knock quality of a liquid motor fuel.

octangular, *a.* having eight angles.

Octans, *n.* a constellation in the southern hemisphere containing the southern celestial pole.

octant, *n.* an arc comprising the eighth part of a circle's circumference; an eighth of the area of a circle contained within two radii and an arc; one of the eight parts into which a space is divided by three planes (usu. at right angles) intersecting at one point; the position of a celestial body when it is 45° distant from another or from a particular point; an instrument similar to a sextant for measuring angles, having a graduated arc of 45°.

octapodic, *a.* containing eight metrical feet. **octapody**, *n.*

octaroon OCTOROON.

octastich, *n.* a strophe, stanza or series of eight lines of verse. **octastichous**, *a.* [Gr. *stichos,* a row]

octastrophic, *a.* consisting of eight strophes.

octastyle, octostyle, *n., a.* (a building) having eight columns in front.

octateuch, *n.* the first eight books of the Old Testament. [Gr. *teuchos,* book]

octave, *n.* the eighth day after a church festival; a festival day and the seven days following it; the interval between any musical note and that produced by twice or half as many vibrations per second (lying eight notes away inclusively); a note at this interval above or below another; two notes separated by this interval; the scale of notes filling this interval; any group of eight, as the first eight lines of a sonnet or a stanza of eight lines; a cask containing one-eighth of a pipe of wine or $13\frac{1}{2}$ gallons (about 60 l); this volume; a low thrust towards the right side of the opponent; the eighth basic position in fencing.

Octavian, *n.* original name of AUGUSTUS, the first Roman emperor.

octavo, *n.* (*pl.* **-vos**) a book in which a sheet is folded into 8 leaves or 16 pages; the size of such a book or paper (written 8vo). *a.* of this size, having this number of leaves per sheet.

octennial, *a.* recurring every eighth year; lasting eight years. **octennially,** *adv.* **octet**, *n.* a musical composition of eight parts or for eight instruments or singers; a group of eight, esp. musicians or singers; an octave (of verse). [L *octennium* (OCT-, *annus,* year), -AL]

octile, *n.* an eighth part.

octillion, *n.* the number produced by raising a million to the eighth power of a thousand, represented by 1 followed by 48 ciphers; (*N Am.* and *Fr.*) the eighth power of a thousand, 1 followed by 27 ciphers. **octillionth,** *a., n.*

octingenary, octingentenary, *n.* an 800th anniversary.

oct(o)-, OCT(A)-.

October, *n.* the 10th month of the year (the eighth of the Roman year); †ale or cider brewed in October, hence, good ale. **Octobrist,** *n.* a member of a moderate reforming party in Czarist Russia (after the Czar's liberal manifesto pubd. Oct. 1905). [L, from prec.]

October Revolution, *n.* the second stage of the Russian Revolution of 1917.

octobrachiate, *a.* having eight limbs, arms or rays.

octocentenary, *n.* an 800th anniversary. **octocentennial**, *n.*

octodecimo, *n.* (*pl.* **-mos**) a book having 18 leaves to the sheet; the size of such a book (written 18mo). *a.* having 18 leaves to the sheet. [L *octodecimus,* eighteenth (*decimus,* tenth), after OCTAVO]

octodentate, *a.* having eight teeth.

octofid, *a.* having eight segments.

octogenarian, *n.* one who is 80, or between 80 and 90, years old. **octogenary**, *a.* [L *octogēnārius* (*octōgēni,* eighty each)]

octogynous, *a.* having eight pistils. [Gr. *gunē,* woman]

octohedron OCTAHEDRON.

octonary, *a.* relating to, computing or proceeding by the number eight. *n.* a group of eight, a stanza or group of eight lines. **octonarian**, *a.* consisting of eight metrical feet. *n.* a line of eight metrical feet. †**octonocular**, *a.* having eight eyes. [L *octōni,* eight each]

octoped, *n.* an eight-footed animal. **octopetalous**, *a.* having eight petals. [L *pes pedis,* foot]

octopod, *a.* having eight feet. *n.* an animal with eight feet. **octopodous**, *a.* [Gr. *oktōpod-,* stem of *oktōpous,* see foll.]

octopus, *n.* (*pl.* **octopuses**) one of a genus of cephalopods, having eight arms furnished with suckers, a cuttlefish; (*fig.*) an organization or influence having far-extending powers (for harm). [Gr. *oktōpous* (*pous podos,* foot)]

octoroon, octaroon, *n.* the offspring of a quadroon and a white person (having one-eighth Negro ancestry).

octosepalous, *a.* having eight sepals.

octospermous, *a.* having eight seeds.

octosporous, *a.* eight-spored.

octosyllabic, *a.* having eight syllables; a line of eight syllables. **octosyllable**, *n.* a word of eight syllables.

octroi, *n.* a tax levied at the gates of some Continental, esp. French, towns on goods brought in; the barrier or place where this is levied; the body of officials collecting it; a road toll for cars. [F, from *octroyer,* from late L *auctorizāre,* to AUTHORISE]

octuple, *a.* eightfold. *n.* the product of multiplication by eight. *v.t., v.i.* to multiply by eight. **octuplet**, *n.* one of eight offspring produced at one birth. [L *octuplus*]

octyl, *n.* the hypothetical organic radical of a hydrocarbon series. **octylene**, *n.* an oily hydrocarbon obtained by heating octylic alcohol with sulphuric acid. **octylic**, *a.*

ocular, *a.* of, pertaining to, by or with the eye or eyes, visual; known from actual sight. *n.* an eye piece. **ocularist,** *n.* a maker of artificial eyes. **ocularly,** *adv.* **oculate**, **-ated**, *a.* having eye-like spots; †having eyes or sight. **oculist,** *n.* a former name for an ophthalmologist or optician. **oculo-,** *comb. form.* [L *oculus,* eye]

Ocussi Ambeno, *n.* until 1975, an exclave of the Portuguese colony of East Timor, on the N coast of Indonesian West Timor. The port is an outlet for rice, copra and sandalwood.

OD[1], (*abbr.*) Officer of the Day; Old Dutch; ordinance data, datum; outside diameter.

OD[2], *n.* (*coll.*) an overdose of a drug. *v.i.* (*pres.p.* **OD'ing**, *past, p.p.* **OD'd**) to take an overdose of a drug. [over dose]

O/D, o/d, (*abbr.*) on demand; overdrawn.

od, odyl(e), *n.* a natural force supposed by Baron von Reichenbach (1788–1869) to pervade the universe and to produce the phenomena of magnetism, crystallization, hypnotism etc. **odic**[1], *a.* **odism,** *n.* [arbitrary]

†**'od,** *int., n.* a minced form of 'God' used as an expletive or asseveration. †**'od's bodikins** BODIKIN. †**'od's life,** God's life.

ODA, (*abbr.*) Overseas Development Administration.

odal UDAL.

odalisque, odalisk, *n.* an Oriental female slave or concubine, esp. in a harem. [F, from Turk. *ōdalïq,* chambermaid, from *ōdah,* chamber]

odd, *a.* remaining after a number or quantity has been divided into pairs; not even; not divisible by two; bearing such a number; wanting a match or pair; singular, strange, eccentric, queer; occasional, casual; indefinite, incalculable; (*ellipt.*) and more, with others thrown in (added to a round number in enumeration as *two hundred odd*); †at variance. *n.* a handicap stroke in golf; a stroke more than one's opponents score; in whist, one trick above book. **odd man out,** one who is left when a number pair off; one who is at variance with, excluded from, or stands out as dissimilar to a group etc. **oddball,** *n., a.* (one who is) eccentric or peculiar. **oddjob,** *n.* a casual, irregular or occasional piece of work, esp. a domestic repair. **oddjobber, oddjobman, -woman,** *n.* **odd pricing,** *n.* the practice of pricing commodities in such a way as to suggest a bargain (e.g. £9.99 instead of £10). **odd trick,** *n.* in bridge, every trick after six won by the declarer's side. **Odd Fellow,** *n.* a member of an 18th-cent. Friendly Society known as the Order of Odd Fellows. **odd-looking,** *a.* **oddish,** *a.* **oddity,** *n.* oddness; a peculiar feature or trait; an odd person or thing. **oddly,** *adv.* **oddment,** *n.* a remnant. *n.pl.* odds and ends. **oddness,** *n.* **odds,** *n.pl.* (*usu. as sing.*) inequality, difference; balance of superiority, advantage; the chances in favour of a given event; an allowance to the weaker of two competitors; the ratio by which the amount staked by one party to a bet exceeds that by the other; variance, strife, dispute. **at odds,** at variance. **odds and ends,** miscellaneous remnants, trifles, scraps etc. **to make no odds,** to make no difference, not matter. **to shout the odds,** (*coll.*) to talk loudly, stridently, vehemently etc. **over the odds,** higher, more than is acceptable, necessary, usual etc. **what's the odds?** (*coll.*) what difference does it make? **odds-on,** *a.* having a better than even chance of happening, winning, succeeding etc. [Icel. *odda-* (in *oddamathr,* odd man, *oddalala,* odd number), cogn. with OE *ord,* point, tip]

ode, *n.* formerly, a lyric poem meant to be sung; a lyric poem in an elevated style, rhymed or unrhymed, of varied and often irregular metre, usu. in the form of an address or invocation. **odic**[2], *a.* †**odist,** *n.* [F, from late L *ōda,* Gr. *ōdē, aoidē,* from *aeidein,* to sing]

-ode[1], *suf.* denoting a thing resembling or of the nature of, as *geode, sarcode* [Gr. *-ōdēs* (*-o-, eidēs,* like, cogn. with *eidos,* form)]

-ode[2], *suf.* denoting a path or way, as *anode, cathode.* [Gr. *hodos,* way]

odeon, odeum, *n.* (*pl.* **odea**) in ancient Greece or Rome, a theatre in which poets and musicians contended for prizes; hence, a concert-hall, a theatre used for musical performances; a cinema. [Gr. *odeion,* as ODE]

Odessa, *n.* a seaport in the Ukraine, USSR, on the Black Sea, capital of Odessa region; population (1987) 1,141,000. Products include chemicals, pharmaceuticals and machinery. Odessa was founded by Catherine II (1795) near the site of an ancient Greek settlement.

odic[1], **odism** OD[2].

odic[2], †**odist** ODE.

Odin, *n.* the chief god of Scandinavian mythology, the **Woden** or **Wotan** of the Germanic peoples. A sky god, he is resident in Asgard, at the top of the world-tree, and receives the souls of heroic slain warriors from the Valkyries (the 'divine maidens') feasting with them in his great hall, Valhalla. The wife of Odin is Freya, or Frigga, and Thor is their son. Wednesday is named after him.

odious, *a.* hateful, repulsive; offensive. **odiously,** *adv.* **odiousness,** *n.* **odium**, *n.* general dislike, reprobation; repulsion. [L *odiōsus,* from *odium,* hatred, cogn. with *ōdī,* I hate]

Odoacer, *n.* (433–493), king of Italy from 476, when he deposed Romulus Augustulus, the last Roman emperor. He was a leader of the barbarian mercenaries employed by Rome. He was overthrown and killed by Theodoric the Great, king of the Ostrogoths.

odometer, *n.* an instrument attached to a vehicle for measuring and recording the distance travelled. **odometry,** *n.* [Gr. *hodos,* way, -METER]

-odont, *comb. form* -toothed. [Gr. *odous odontos,* tooth]

odontalgia, odontalgy, *n.* toothache. **odontalgic**, *a., n.* [Gr. *algos,* pain]

odontiasis, *n.* cutting of teeth; dentition.

odontic, *a.* dental.

odont(o)-, *comb. form* having teeth or processes resembling teeth. [Gr. *odous odontos,* tooth]

odontoblast, *n.* a cell producing dentine.

odontocete, *n.* one of the Odontoceti or toothed whales.

odontogeny, *n.* the origin and development of teeth. **odontogenic**, *a.*

Odontoglossum, *n.* a genus of tropical American epiphytal orchids with finely coloured flowers. [Gr. *glōssa,* a tongue]

odontography, *n.* the description of teeth.

odontoid, *a.* toothlike; of or relating to an odontoid process. **odontoid process,** *n.* a toothlike projection from the axis or second cervical vertebra in certain mammals and birds.

odontology, *n.* the science dealing with the structure and development of teeth. **odontologic, -ical**, *a.* **odontologist**, *n.*

odontoma, *n.* a small tumour or excrescence composed

of dentine. **odontomatous**, *a.*
odontophore, *n.* a ribbon-like organ covered with teeth used for mastication by certain molluscs. **odontophoral**, *a.* **odontophorous**, *a.*
odontorhyncus, *a.* having toothlike serrations in the bill or beak.
odontotherapia, *n.* the treatment and care of the teeth, dental hygiene or therapeutics.
odontotoxia, *n.* unevenness of the teeth.
odontotrypy, *n.* the operation of perforating a tooth to draw off pus from an abscess in the internal cavity.
odour, (*N Am.*) **odor**, *n.* a smell, whether pleasant or unpleasant; scent, fragrance; (*coll.*) a bad smell; (*fig.*) repute, esteem; †(*usu. in pl.*) substances exhaling fragrance, perfumes. **in bad odour,** in bad repute; out of favour. **in good odour,** in favour. **odour of sanctity,** a reputation for holiness; (*facet.*) the odour of an unwashed body; sanctimoniousness. **odorant, odoriferous**, *a.* diffusing fragrance; (*coll.*) smelly. **odoriferously,** *adv.* **odoriferousness,** *n.* **odorizer, -iser,** *n.* **odorous,** *a.* having a sweet scent, fragrant. **odorously**, *adv.* **odorousness,** *n.* **odoured, odourless,** *a.* [OF *odor,* L *odōrem,* nom. *odor*]
Odysseus, *n.* the chief character of Homer's *Odyssey*, mentioned also in the *Iliad* as one of the foremost leaders of the Greek forces at the siege of Troy, noted for his courage and ingenuity. He is said to have been the ruler of the island of Ithaca.
Odyssey, *n.* an epic poem attributed to Homer, describing the wanderings of Odysseus (Ulysses) after the fall of Troy (prob. written before 700 BC); (a story of) a long journey containing a series of adventures and vicissitudes. **Odyssean**, *a.* [L *Odyssēa,* Gr. *Odusseia,* from *Odusseus,* Odysseus, Ulysses]
OE, (*abbr.*) Old English.
Oe, (*symbol*) oersted.
OECD, (*abbr.*) Organization for Economic Cooperation and Development.
oecology ECOLOGY.
oecumenical ECUMENICAL.
OED, (*abbr.*) Oxford English Dictionary.
oedema, (*esp. N Am.*) **edema**, *n.* (*Path.*) swelling due to accumulation of serous fluid in the cellular tissue; dropsy; in plants, swelling due to water accumulation in the tissues. **oedematose, -tous, edematose, -tous,** *a.* **oedematously,** *adv.* [Gr. *oidēma -matos,* from *oidein,* to swell]
Oedipus, *n.* in Greek legend, king of Thebes. Left to die at birth because his father Laius had been warned by an oracle that his son would kill him, he was saved and brought up by the king of Corinth. Oedipus killed Laius in a quarrel (without recognizing him) and married his mother Jocasta. After four children had been born, the truth was discovered. Jocasta hanged herself, Oedipus blinded himself, and as an exiled wanderer was guided by his daughter, Antigone.
Oedipus complex, *n.* a psychical impulse in offspring comprising excessive love or sexual desire for the parent of the opposite sex and hatred for the parent of the same sex. **oedipal, oedipean**, *a.* [Oedipus, king of Thebes, COMPLEX]
Oedipus Tyrannus, *n.* (or **Oedipus the King**) (409 BC) and **Oedipus at Colonus** (401 BC), two tragedies by Sophocles based on the legend of Oedipus, King of Thebes.
oenanthic, enanthic, *a.* possessing a vinous odour. [L *oenanthē,* Gr. *oinanthē* (*oinē,* vine, *anthē,* bloom), -IC]
oen(o)-, oin(o)-, (*esp. N Am.*) **en(o)-,** *comb. form.* wine. [Gr. *oinos,* wine]
oenology, (*esp. N Am.*) **enology**, *n.* the science or study of wines. **oenological, enological,** *a.* **oenologist, enologist,** *n.*
oenomancy, *n.* divination from the appearance of wine poured out in libations.
oenomania, *n.* dipsomania; mania due to intoxication. **oenomaniac**, *n.*
oenomel, *n.* wine mingled with honey, a beverage used by the ancient Greeks. [Gr. *meli,* honey)]
oenometer, *n.* an instrument for testing the alcoholic strength of wines.
oenophil(e), oenophilist, *n.* a wine connoisseur. **oenophily**, *n.* love or knowledge of wines.
Oenothera, *n.* a genus of plants containing the evening primrose. [L, from Gr. *oinothēras* (*oinos,* wine, *-thēras,* catcher, from *thēraein,* to hunt)]
o'er, *prep., adv.* (*poet.*) short for OVER.
Oersted, *n.* **Hans Christian** (1777–1851), Danish physicist who founded the science of electromagnetism. In 1820 he discovered the magnetic field associated with an electric current.
oersted, *n.* the cgs electromagnetic unit of magnetic field or magnetizing force. [H. C. *Oersted,* see prec.]
oesophagalgia, *n.* pain, esp. neuralgia, in the oesophagus.
oesophagectomy, *n.* excision of part of the oesophagus.
oesophagitis, *n.* inflammation of the oesophagus.
oesophag(o)-, (*esp. N Am.*) **esophag(o)-,** *comb. form* oesophagus.
oesophagocele, *n.* hernia of the mucous membrane of the oesophagus.
oesophagopathy, *n.* disease of the oesophagus.
oesophagoplegia, *n.* paralysis of the oesophagus.
oesophagorrhagia, *n.* haemorrhage of the oesophagus.
oesophagospasmus, *n.* spasm of the oesophagus.
oesophagotome, *n.* a cutting-instrument for use in oesophagotomy. **oesophagotomy**, *n.* the operation of opening the oesophagus.
oesophagus, (*esp. N Am.*) **esophagus**, *n.* (*pl.* **-gi**) the gullet, the canal by which food passes to the stomach. **oesophageal, esophageal**, *a.* [late L, from Gr. *oisophagos,* etym. unknown]
oestradiol, *n.* the major oestrogenic hormone in human females (used to treat breast cancer and oestrogen deficiency).
oestriol, *n.* an oestrogenic hormone often used to treat menopausal symptoms.
oestrogen, (*esp. N Am.*) **estrogen**, *n.* any of the female sex hormones which induce oestrus and encourage the growth of female secondary sexual characteristics. **oestrogenic**, *a.* **oestrogenically,** *adv.* [L *oestrus,* gadfly; -GEN]
oestrone, *n.* an oestrogenic hormone derived from oestradiol.
oestrus, (*esp. N Am.*) **estrus**, **-trum**, *n.* a violent impulse, a raging desire or passion, esp. the sexual impulse in animals; the period when this regularly occurs; heat. **oestral,** *a.* **oestrous,** *a.* **oestr(o)us cycle**, *n.* the hormonal changes occurring in a female mammal from one oestrus to the next. [L *oestrus,* Gr. *oistros*]
OF, (*abbr.*) Old French.
of, *prep.* denoting connection with or relation to, in situation, point of departure, separation, origin, motive or cause, agency, substance or material, possession, inclusion, partition, equivalence or identity, reference, respect, direction, distance, quality, condition, objectivity; †during; †among; †from. [OE (cp. Dut. *af,* G *ab,* Icel., Swed. and Dan. *af,* L *ab,* Gr. *apo*)]
of-, *pref.* OB- (before *f,* as in offence).
off, *adv.* away, at a distance or to a distance in space or time (expressing removal, separation, suspension, discontinuance, decay or termination); to the end, utterly, completely; (*Naut.*) away from the wind. *prep.* from (denoting deviation, separation, distance, disjunction, removal etc.). *a.* more distant, farther, opp. to near; right, opp. to left; removed or aside from the main street etc., divergent, subsidiary; (*coll.*) unacceptable, unfair; contingent, possible; not occupied, disengaged, on bad form (as an *off day*); applied to that part of a cricket-field to the left side of the bowler when the batsman is right-handed. *n.* the off side of a cricket-field; the beginning, start. *v.i.* (*coll.*) to go off, to put off, to withdraw; (*Naut.*) to go away from the land. *int.* away, begone. **off and on,** intermittently, now and again. **off-the-cuff,** spontaneous, impromptu. **off-the-peg,** ready made. **off-the-record,** unofficial,

confidential. **off-the-wall,** new, eccentric, unexpected. **to be off,** to leave. **to be off one's head,** to lose one's reason. **to come off** COME. **to go off** GO[1]. **to take off,** to divest oneself of; to mimic; of a plane, to leave the ground. **badly off,** in bad circumstances; poor. **well off** WELL[1]. **offbeat,** *a.* (*coll.*) unconventional, unusual. **off Broadway,** *n.*, *a.* situated outside the Broadway theatrical area of New York (of a theatre); relating to New York fringe theatre, experimental, low-cost, non-commercial etc. **off-off Broadway,** *n.*, *a.* **off-chance,** *n.* a remote possibility. **on the off chance,** in the slim hope that, just in case. **off colour** COLOUR[1]. **off-cut,** *n.* a section cut off the main piece of a material (of fabric, meat, paper, wood etc.). **off day,** *n.* day when one is on bad form. **off-drive,** *v.t.* in cricket, to drive (the ball) off. **off-hand,** *adv.* without consideration, preparation, or warning; casually, summarily, curtly, or brusquely. *a.* impromptu; casual; summary, curt or brusque. **off-handed,** *a.* **off-handedly,** *adv.* **off-handedness,** *n.* **off-licence,** *n.* a licence to sell intoxicating liquors to be consumed off the premises; the premises operating under such a licence. **off-limits,** *a. adv.* out of bounds; forbidden. **off-line,** *a.* of a computer peripheral, switched off, not under the control of a central processor. **off-load,** *v.i.*, *v.t.* to unload; to get rid of something (on to someone else). **off-peak,** *a.* of a service, during a period of low demand. **off-print,** *n.* a reprint of an article or separate part of a periodical etc. **off-putting,** *a.* disconcerting; displeasing, unattractive. **off-screen,** *adv.*, *a.* (appearing or happening) out of sight of the viewer of a film, television programme etc. **off-season,** *a.*, *adv.* out of season. *n.* a period of low (business) activity. **off-set,** *n.* a lateral shoot or branch that takes root or is caused to take root and is used for propagation, an off-shoot, a scion; a spur or branch of a mountain range; anything allowed as a counterbalance, equivalent, or compensation; an amount set off (against); a short course measured perpendicularly to the main line; a part where the thickness of a wall is diminished, usu. towards the top; a bend or fitting bringing a pipe past an obstacle. **offset printing,** a (lithographic) printing process in which the image is first transferred from a plate on to a cylinder before it is printed on to paper. *v.t.* to balance by an equivalent; to counterbalance, to compensate. **offshoot,** *n.* a branch or shoot from a main stem; a side-issue. **offspring,** *n.* issue, progeny; (*collect.*) children, descendants; a child; a production or result of any kind; †origin, descent. **off-shore,** *a. adv.* blowing off the land; situated a short way from the land. **offside,** *n.* in football etc., the field between the ball and the opponents' goal. **to be offside,** for a player, to be in a position to kick a goal when no defender is between him and the goal-keeper. **offsider,** *n.* (*Austral. coll.*) a friend, partner. **off-stage,** *a. adv.* out of sight of the theatre audience. **off-white,** *a.* not quite white. **offing,** *n.* that portion of the sea beyond the half-way line between the coast and the horizon. **in the offing,** likely to occur soon. **offish,** *a.* inclined to be distant, reserved or stiff in manner. **offishly,** *adv.* **offishness,** *n.* [stressed form of OF]

Offa, *n.* (d. 796), king of Mercia, England, from 757. He conquered Essex, Kent, Sussex and Surrey, defeated the Welsh and the West Saxons, and established Mercian supremacy over all England south of the Humber.

offal, *n.* parts of the carcass of an animal, including the head, tail, kidneys, heart, liver etc. (used as food); refuse, rubbish, waste. [OFF, FALL]

Offaly, *n.* a county of the Republic of Ireland, in the province of Leinster, between Galway on the west and Kildare on the east; area 2000 sq km/772 sq miles; population (1986) 60,000.

Offa's Dyke, *n.* a defensive earthwork along the Welsh border, of which there are remains from the mouth of the river Dee to that of the river Severn. It represents the boundary secured by Offa's wars with Wales.

Offenbach, *n.* **Jacques** (1819–80), French composer. He wrote light opera, initially for presentation at the Bouffes Parisiens. Among his works are *Orphée aux enfers/Orpheus in the Underworld* (1858), *La Belle Hélène* (1864), and *Les Contes d'Hoffmann/The Tales of Hoffmann* (1881).

offend , *v.t.* to wound the feelings of, to hurt; to make angry, to cause displeasure or disgust in, to outrage, to annoy, to transgress; †to tempt to go astray; †to attack, to assail. *v.i.* to transgress or violate any human or divine law; to cause anger, disgust etc., to scandalize. **offence,** *n.* the act of offending, an aggressive act; an affront, an insult; the state or a sense of being hurt, annoyed, or affronted, umbrage; a breach of custom, a transgression, a sin; a misdeed; an illegal act. **to give offence,** to cause umbrage, to affront or insult. **to take offence,** to be offended, to feel a grievance. **offenceless,** *a.* **offendedly,** *adv.* **offender,** *n.* †**offendress,** *n. fem.* **offense,** *n.* (*chiefly N Am.*) offence. **offensive,** *a.* pertaining to or used for attack, aggressive; causing or meant to cause offence; irritating, vexing, annoying; disgusting; disagreeable, repulsive. *n.* the attitude, method or act of attacking; (*Mil.*) a strategic attack. **offensively,** *adv.* **offensiveness,** *n.* [OF *offendre,* L *offendere,* p.p. offensus]

offer, *v.t.* to present as an act of worship; to sacrifice, to immolate; to present, to put forward, to tender for acceptance or refusal; to propose; to bid (as a price); to evince readiness (to do something); to essay, to attempt; to proffer to show (e.g. for sale); to show an intention (to); *v.i.* to present or show itself, to appear, to occur; to make an attempt (at). *n.* an act of offering; an expression of willingness or readiness (to); a tender, proffer, or proposal, to be accepted or refused; a price or sum bid; an attempt, an essay. **on offer,** presented for sale, consumption etc., esp. at a bargain price. **special offer,** an article or service proffered at a bargain price. **under offer,** provisionally sold prior to and subject to the signing of a contract. †**offerable,** *a.* **offerer,** *n.* **offering,** *n.* **offertory,** *n.* that part of the Mass or liturgical service during which offerings or oblations are made; in the Church of England, an anthem sung or the text spoken while these are being made; the offering of these oblations; the gifts offered; any collection made at a religious service. [OE *offrian,* to bring an offering, to sacrifice]

office, *n.* duty, charge, function, the task or service attaching to a particular post or station; a post of service, trust or authority, esp. under a public body; a particular task, service or duty; an act of worship of prescribed form, an act of help, kindness or duty; (*often in pl.*) a service; a room, building or other place where business is carried on (*collect.*) persons charged with such business, the official staff or organization as a whole; a government department or agency; (*pl.*) the rooms or places in which the domestic duties of a house are discharged; (*coll.*) a lavatory. **divine office** DIVINE[2]. **Holy Office** HOLY. **the office,** a hint, a private signal. **last offices,** *n.pl.* rites due to the dead. **office-bearer,** *n.* one who holds office; one who performs an appointed duty. **office-block,** *n.* a large building containing offices. **office boy, girl,** *n.* one employed to perform minor tasks in an office. **officer,** *n.* one holding a post or position of authority, esp. a government functionary, one elected to perform certain duties by a society, committee etc., or appointed to a command in the armed services or merchant navy; a policeman. *v.t.* to furnish with officers; to act as commander of. **officer of arms,** *n.* an officer of the College of Arms responsible for creating and granting heraldic arms. **officer of the day,** *n.* an army officer responsible for security on a particular day. **official,** *a.* of or pertaining to an office or public duty; holding an office, employed in public duties; derived from or executed under proper authority; duly authorized; characteristic of persons in office; authorized by the pharmacopoeia, officinal. *n.* one who holds a public office; a judge or presiding officer in an ecclesiastical court. **Official Receiver,** *n.* an officer appointed by a receiving order to administer a bankrupt's estate. **officialdom, -ism,** *n.* **officialese,** *n.* official jargon. †**officiality,** †**offici-**

alty, *n.* **officially,** *adv.* **officiant,** *n.* **officiate,** *v.i.* to perform official duties, to act in an official capacity; to perform a prescribed function or duty; to conduct public worship. **officiation,** *n.* **officiator,** *n.* [OF, from L *officium* (OF-, *facere,* to make or do)]

Official Secrets Act, a British act of Parliament (1989), making disclosure of confidential material from government sources by employees subject to disciplinary procedures; it replaced Section 2 of an act of 1911, which had long been accused of being too wide-ranging. It remains an absolute offence for a member or former member of the security and intelligence services (or those working closely with them) to disclose information about their work. There is no public-interest defence, and disclosure of information already in the public domain is still a crime. Journalists who repeat disclosures may also be prosecuted.

officinal, *a.* ready-prepared, available (of a pharmaceutical product); authorized by the pharmacopoeia, now OFFICIAL; used in medicine; medicinal; †used in or pertaining to a shop. *n.* an officinal preparation or plant. **officinally,** *adv.*

officious, *a.* forward in doing or offering unwanted kindness, meddling, intrusive; in diplomacy, informally related to official concerns or objects, †official; †observant, attentive, obliging. **officiously,** *adv.* **officiousness,** *n.*

off-print, offshore, offside OFF.

O'Flaherty, *n.* **Liam** (1897–1984), Irish author whose novels of Fenian activities in county Mayo include *The Neighbour's Wife* (1923), *The Informer* (1925), and *Land* (1946).

OFT, (*abbr.*) Office of Fair Trading.

oft, often, *adv.* frequently, many times; in many instances. †*a.* frequent, repeated. **(as) more often than not,** (quite) frequently. **†oftenness,** *n.* **†oft(en)times,** *adv.* frequently. **oft-recurring,** *a.* frequently recurring. [OE, cp. Icel. and G *oft,* Dan. *ofte,* Swed. *ofta*]

Oftel, *n.* the Government body which monitors British Telecom. [*Of*fice of *Tel*ecommunications]

Ogallala Aquifer, *n.* the largest source of groundwater in the US, stretching from southern South Dakota to NW Texas. The over-exploitation of this water resource has resulted in the loss of over 18% of the irrigated farmland of Oklahoma and Texas in the period 1940-90.

ogam OG(H)AM.

Ogbomosho, *n.* a city and commercial centre in W Nigeria, 80 km/50 miles NE of Ibadan; population (1981) 590,600.

Ogden, *n.* **C(harles) K(ay)** (1889–1957), English writer and scholar. With I.A. Richards he developed the simplified form of English known as Basic English. Together they wrote *Foundations of Aesthetics* (1921) and *The Meaning of Meaning* (1923).

ogee, *n.* a wave-like moulding having an inner and outer curve like the letter S, a talon; short for **ogee arch,** a pointed arch each side of which is formed of a concave and a convex curve. *a.* having such a double curve (of arches, windows etc.). [prob. from F OGIVE, this moulding being commonly used for ribs in groining]

Ogen melon, *n.* a variety of small sweet melon resembling a cantaloupe. [after the Kibbutz in Israel where it was developed]

og(h)am, *n.* an ancient Celtic system of writing consisting of an alphabet of twenty characters derived from the runes; any character in this; an inscription in this. **og(h)amic,** *a.* [OIr. *ogam, ogum,* said to be from the inventor *Ogam*]

ogive, *n.* a diagonal rib of a vault; a pointed or Gothic arch. **ogival,** *a.* [F, earlier *augive,* perh. from Sp. *auge,* Arab. *āwj,* the summit, vertex, highest point]

ogle, *v.t.* to look or stare at with admiration, wonder etc., esp. amorously; to gape. *v.i.* to cast amorous or lewd glances. *n.* an amorous glance, look; a lewd stare. **ogler,** *n.* [cp. LG *äegeln,* G *hugeln,* freq. of *augen,* to look, from *Auge,* eye]

Oglethorpe, *n.* **James Edward** (1696–1785), English soldier. He joined the Guards, and in 1732 obtained a charter for the colony of Georgia, intended as a refuge for debtors and for European Protestants.

OGPU, *n.* former name (1923–34) of the Soviet secret police, the KGB.

ogre, *n.* a fairytale giant living on human flesh; a monster, a barbarously cruel person. **ogr(e)ish,** *a.* **ogress,** *n. fem.* [F, first used by Charles Perrault in his *Contes,* 1697]

Ogun, *n.* a state of SW Nigeria; population (1982) 2,473,300; area 16,762 sq km/6474 sq miles; capital Abeokuta.

Ogygian, *a.* pertaining to Ogyges, a legendary king of Attica or Boeotia; of great or obscure antiquity, primeval. [L *Ogygius,* Gr. *Ōgugios,* from *Ōgugos* or *Ōugēs*]

oh, O[2].

OHG, (*abbr.*) Old High German.

O'Higgins, *n.* **Bernardo** (1778–1842), Chilean revolutionary, known as 'the Liberator of Chile'. He was a leader of the struggle for independence from Spanish rule (1810–17) and head of the first permanent national government (1817–23).

Ohio, *n.* a state of the midwest US; nickname Buckeye State. **area** 107,100 sq km/41,341 sq miles. **capital** Columbus. **towns** Cleveland, Cincinnati, Dayton, Akron, Toledo, Youngstown, Canton. **products** coal, cereals, livestock, machinery, chemicals, steel. **population** (1986) 10,752,000.

Ohm, *n.* **Georg Simon** (1787–1854), German physicist who studied electricity and discovered the fundamental law that bears his name. The SI unit of electrical resistance is named after him, and the unit of conductance (the reverse of resistance) is called the mho, which is Ohm spelt backwards.

ohm, *n.* the unit of electrical resistance, being the resistance between two points on a conductor when a potential difference of one volt produces a current of one amp. **Ohm's law,** *n.* **ohmage,** *n.* **ohmic,** *a.* **ohmically,** *adv.* **ohmmeter,** *n.* [Georg S. *Ohm,* see prec.]

OHMS, (*abbr.*) On Her/His Majesty's Service.

Ohm's law, *n.* law proposed by Georg Ohm in 1827 that states that the steady electrical current in a metallic circuit is directly proportional to the constant total electromotive force in the circuit.

oho, *int.* expressing surprise, irony, or exultation. [O[2], HO]

ohone, *int.* and *n.* a Scottish and Irish cry of lamentation. [Gael. and Ir. *ochōin*]

Ohrid, Lake, *n.* a lake on the frontier between Albania and Yugoslavia; area 350 sq km/135 sq miles.

oi, *int.* used to give warning, attract attention etc. *n.*, *a.* (of) an aggressive type of early 1980s music which often expressed racist sentiments.

-oid, -oidal, *comb. form* denoting resemblance, as in *colloid, cycloid, rhomboid.* [mod. L *-oïdes,* Gr. *-oeidēs* (*-eidēs,* like, rel. to *eidos,* form)]

-oidea, *comb. form* denoting zoological classes or families. [L *-oīdēs,* -oid]

Oidium, *n.* a former genus of fungi containing the mildews etc. **oidium,** *n.* (*pl.* **-dia**) any of various fungal spores; a powdery mildew. [mod. L, from Gr. *ōon,* egg, *-idion,* dim. suf.]

oik, *n.* (*coll.*) a stupid or inferior person; a fool, a cad. [etym. doubtful]

oil, *n.* an unctuous liquid, insoluble in water, soluble in ether and usually in alcohol, obtained from various animal and vegetable substances; (*pl.*) oil-colours, paints. *v.t.* to smear, anoint, rub, soak, treat or impregnate with oil; to lubricate with or as with oil. *v.i.* to turn into oil; to take oil aboard as fuel; to become oily. **essential, fixed, mineral oils,** ESSENTIAL, FIX, MINERAL. **oil of vitriol,** sulphuric acid. **to burn the midnight oil,** to study or work far into the night. **to oil the wheels,** to facilitate matters, to help things go smoothly. **to oil someone's palm,** to bribe someone. **to strike oil** STRIKE. **oil bird,** *n.* a nocturnal S American bird, the fat of whose young yields edible oil. **oilcake,** *n.* the refuse after oil is pressed or extracted from linseed etc., used as fodder. **oil-can,** *n.* a can for holding oil, esp. one used for oiling machinery. **oil-**

cloth, *n.* a fabric coated with white lead ground in oil; an oilskin. **oil-colour,** *n.* oil-paint. **oil-engine,** *n.* an internal-combustion engine which burns vaporized oil. **oil-fired,** *a.* burning oil as fuel. **oil-gas,** *n.* gas obtained from oil by distillation. **oil-field,** *n.* a region where mineral oil is obtained. **oil-gauge,** *n.* an instrument showing the level of oil in a tank etc. **oil-gland,** *n.* a gland secreting oil. **oil-hole,** *n.* a hole through which lubricating oil is applied to parts of machinery. **oilman,** *n.* one whose business is oils; one who works in the oil industry; one who owns an oil well. **oil-meal,** *n.* oilcake ground into meal. **oil-mill,** *n.* an oil-press; a factory where oil is expressed. **oil-nut,** *n.* any of various oil-yielding nuts including the butternut and buffalo-nut. **oil-paint, -colour,** *n.* a paint made by grinding a pigment in oil. **oil-painting,** *n.* the art of painting with oil-paints; a painting in oil-paints. **oil palm,** *n.* a palm tree bearing fruits yielding palm-oil. **oil platform,** *n.* a floating or fixed off-shore structure which supports an oil rig. **oil-press,** *n.* a machine for pressing the oil from seeds, nuts etc. **oil rig,** *n.* an installation for drilling and extracting oil and natural gas. **oil seed,** *n.* any of various oil-yielding seeds including sesame and sunflower seeds. **oil shale,** *n.* a shale from which mineral oils can be distilled. **oil-shark,** *n.* a species of shark that yields oil. **oilskin,** *n.* cloth rendered waterproof by treatment with oil; a garment of this cloth; (*pl.*) a suit of such garments. **oil slick,** *n.* a patch of floating oil, usu. pollutive. **oil-stock,** *n.* a vessel for holding Holy Oil. **oil-stone,** *n.* a fine-grained whetstone lubricated with oil before use. **oil tanker,** *n.* a large vessel for transporting oil. **oil-tree,** *n.* any bush or tree which yields oil, e.g. the castor-oil plant. **oil-well,** *n.* a boring made for petroleum. **oiled,** *a.* greased with, lubricated by, saturated or preserved in oil; (*coll.*) drunk. **well oiled,** (*coll.*) very drunk. **oiler,** *n.* one who or that which oils; an oil-can for lubricating machinery etc. **oilily,** *adv.* **oilless,** *a.* **oily,** *a.* consisting of, containing, covered with, or like oil; unctuous, smooth, insinuating. **oiliness,** *n.* [ME, OF *oile* , L *oleum,* from *olea,* olive]

oink, *n.* the grunt of a pig. *v.i.* to make such a sound. [imit.]

ointment, *n.* a soft unctuous preparation applied to diseased or injured parts or used as a cosmetic, an unguent. [ME *oinement,* OF *oignement,* L *unguentum,* UNGUENT]

Oireachtas, *n.* the national parliament of the Republic of Ireland. [Ir.]

Ojibwa, -way, *n.* (*pl.* **-wa(s), -way(s)**) a member of a N American people living in the westerly region of the Great Lakes; their language. [*ojib-ubway,* a type of moccasin]

OK, okay, (*coll.*) *a.*, *int.*, *adv.* quite correct, all right. *v.t.* (*past, p.p.* **OK'd, OKed, okayed**) to authorize, to endorse, to approve. *n.* approval, sanction, agreement. **okeydoke(y)**, (*coll.*) *int.* a casual or amiable form of assent or agreement. [said to be short for *orl korrect*]

okapi, *n.* a deer-like animal related to and partially marked like a giraffe. [W Afr. word]

O'Keeffe, *n.* **Georgia** (1887–1986), US painter, based mainly in New York and New Mexico, known for her large, semi-abstract studies of flowers and skulls.

Okhotsk, Sea of, an arm of the N Pacific between the Kamchatka Peninsula and Sakhalin, and bordered southward by the Kuril Islands; area 937,000 sq km/ 361,700 sq miles. Free of ice only in summer, it is often fogbound.

Okinawa, *n.* the largest of the Japanese Ryukyu Islands in the W Pacific. **area** 2250 sq km/869 sq miles. **capital** Naha. **population** (1986) 1,190,000.

Oklahoma, *n.* a state of the south central US; nickname Sooner State. **area** 181,100 sq km/69,905 sq miles. **capital** Oklahoma City. **towns** Tulsa, Lawton, Norman, Enid. **products** cereals, peanuts, cotton, livestock, oil, natural gas, helium, machinery and other metal products. **population** (1986) 3,305,000.

Oklahoma City, *n.* an industrial city (oil refining, machinery, aircraft, telephone equipment), capital of Oklahoma, US, on the Canadian river; population (1984) 443,500.

okra, *n.* an African plant cultivated for its green pods used in curries, soups, stews etc.; gumbo; lady-finger. [W Indian word]

Okrana, *n.* the Russian secret police in Czarist days. [Rus., guard, police]

Okubo, *n.* **Toshimichi** (1831–78), Japanese samurai leader whose opposition to the Tokugawa shogunate made him a leader in the Meiji restoration (1866–68).

Okuma, *n.* **Shigenobu** (1838–1922), Japanese politician and prime minister. He helped to found the Jiyuto (Liberal Party) 1881, and became prime minister briefly in (1898) and again in 1914, when he presided over Japanese pressure for territorial concessions in China, before retiring in 1916.

-ol, *suf.* denoting a chemical compound containing an alcohol, or (loosely) an oil, as *benzol, menthol, phenol.* [L *oleum,* OIL]

Olaf, *n.* five kings of Norway, including:

Olaf I Tryggvesson, *n.* (969–1000), king of Norway from his election in 995. He began the conversion of Norway to Christianity, and was killed in a sea battle against the Danes and Swedes.

Olaf II Haraldsson, *n.* (995–1030), king of Norway from 1015. He offended his subjects by his centralizing policy and zeal for Christianity, and was killed in battle by Norwegian rebel chiefs backed by Canute of Denmark. He was declared the patron saint of Norway 1164.

Olaf V, *n.* (1903–), king of Norway from 1957, when he succeeded his father Haakon VII.

Olazabal, *n.* **Jose Maria** (1966–), Spanish golfer, one of the leading players on the European circuit. After a distinguished amateur career he turned professional 1986. He was a member of the European Ryder Cup teams in 1987 and 1989.

Olbrich, *n.* **Joseph Maria** (1867–1908), Viennese architect who worked under Otto Wagner and was opposed to the over-ornamentation of Art Nouveau. His major buildings, however, remain Art Nouveau in spirit: the Vienna Sezession (1897–98), the Hochzeitsturm (1907), and the Tietz department store in Düsseldorf, Germany.

old, *a.* (*comp.* **older,** *superl.* **oldest,** cp. ELDER[1], -EST) advanced in years or long in existence; not young, fresh, new or recent; like an old person, experienced, thoughtful; crafty, cunning, practised (at), confirmed (in); decayed by process of time, worn, dilapidated; stale, trite; customary, wonted; obsolete, effete, out-of-date, antiquated, matured; of any specified duration; belonging to a former period, made or established long ago, ancient, bygone, long cultivated or worked; early, previous, former, quondam; of a language, denoting the earliest known form; (*coll.*) expressing familiarity or endearment; (*coll.*) used to emphasize (as in e.g. *high old time*). **of old,** in or from ancient times; long ago, formerly. **of old standing,** long established. **the good old days,** better or happier former times; the past viewed nostalgically. **the Old Bill,** the police. **the Old Country,** the country of origin of an immigrant or his/her ancestors. **the Old Dart,** (*Austral. sl.*) Britain; England. **old age,** the latter part of life. **old age pension,** in the UK, a weekly state pension paid to a man at 65 and a woman at 60 years of age. **old age pensioner,** *n.* **Old Bailey,** *n.* the Central Criminal Court of the City of London. **Old Boy, Old Girl,** *n.* a former pupil of a school; (*coll.*) a friendly form of address; an elderly man or woman. **Old Boy, Girl network** NETWORK. **old dear,** *n.* (*coll.*) an elderly person, esp. a woman. **Old English** ENGLISH. **Old English Sheepdog,** a large English breed of sheepdog with a bob tail and a shaggy coat. **old-fashioned,** *a.* out-of-date, outmoded; quaint. **old fogy,** *n.* (*derog.*) an older person with conservative, eccentric or old-fashioned ideas or ways. **Old Glory,** *n.* (*N Am.*) the US flag. **old gold** GOLD. **old guard,** *n.* the old or conservative members of a party etc. **old hand,** *n.* one who is skilled or practised at a trade, craft or practice of any kind; one of the early convicts. **old hat** HAT. **old lady, man,** *n.* (*coll.*) a sexual partner, a husband or wife; a father or mother; a friendly form of address; an elderly man or woman. **old maid,** *n.* (*derog.*) an unmarried woman of advanced years or unlikely ever to marry; a card game; a precise, prudish, fidgety person of either sex. **old-maidish,** *a.* **old man's beard,** a kind of moss; wild clematis. **old master,** *n.* a painter or painting of the 16th–18th cents. **Old Nick, Gentleman, One,** *n.* (*coll.*) the devil. **old penny,** *n.* a former unit of British money of which there were 240 to the £. **old school,** *a., n.* (of) those who adhere to past traditions or principles. **old school tie,** a tie sporting a public school's colours worn by its old boys; a symbol of the mutual allegiance of a group of (esp. privileged or upper class) people. **Old Style** STYLE. **Old Testament** see separate article below. **old-time,** *a.* old, ancient; old-fashioned. **old-timer,** *n.* (*coll.*) an old man; a veteran; a person who has remained in a situation for a long time. **old woman,** *n.* (*coll.*) a wife or mother; a timid, fidgety or fussy man. **old-womanish,** *adj.* **old-womanishness,** *n.* **Old World,** *n.* the eastern hemisphere; **old(e) world(e),** *a.* (emphatically) old-fashioned and quaint. **old year,** *n.* the year just ended or on the point of ending. **olden,** *a.* old, ancient, bygone. **oldie,** *n.* (*coll.*) an old thing or person (e.g. an old song, film). **oldish,** *a.* **oldness,** *n.* **oldster,** *n.* an old or oldish person. [OE *eald, ald* (cp. Dut. *oud,* G *alt,* L *ultus,* in *adultus*), from the root *al-*, to nourish, as in L *alere,* to feed]

Old Catholic, *n.* one of various breakaway groups from Roman Catholicism, including those in Holland (such as the Church of Utrecht, who separated from Rome in 1724 after accusations of Jansenism) and groups in Austria, Czechoslovakia, Germany and Switzerland, who rejected the proclamation of papal infallibility of 1870. Old Catholic clergy are not celibate.

Oldenbarnevelt, *n.* **Johan van** (1547–1619), Dutch politician, a leading figure in the Netherlands' struggle for independence from Spain, who helped William I negotiate the Union of Utrecht (1579).

Oldenburg[1], *n.* **Claes** (1929–), US pop artist, known for *soft sculptures*, gigantic replicas of everyday objects and foods, made of stuffed canvas or vinyl.

Oldenburg[2], *n.* **Henry** (1615–77), German official who founded and edited the first-ever scientific periodical *Philosophical Transactions* and through his extensive correspondence, acted as a clearing house for the science of the day. He was born in Bremen and first appeared in London in 1652 working as a Bremen agent and then a tutor. In 1663 he was appointed to the new post of Secretary to the Royal Society, a position he held until his death.

Oldfield, *n.* **Bruce** (1950–), English fashion designer, who set up his own business in 1975. His evening wear has been worn by the British royal family and other personalities.

Old Man of the Sea, in the *Arabian Nights*, a man who compels strangers to carry him until they drop, encountered by Sinbad the Sailor on his fifth voyage. Sinbad escapes by getting him drunk. The term is also used in Greek mythology to describe Proteus, an attendant of the sea god Poseidon.

Old Moore's Almanac, an annual publication in the UK containing prophecies of the events of the following year. It was first published in 1700 under the title *Vox Stellarum/Voices of the Stars*, by Francis Moore (1657–*c.* 1715).

Old Pretender, *n.* nickname of James Edward Stuart, the son of James II of England.

Old Testament, *n.* a Christian term for the Hebrew Bible, which is the first part of the Christian Bible. It contains 39 (according to Christians) or 24 (according to Jews) books, which include the history of the Jews and their covenant with God, prophetical writings, and religious poetry. The first five books are traditionally ascribed to Moses and known as the Pentateuch (by Christians) or the Torah (by Jews).

Old Trafford, *n.* two sporting centres in Britain, both situated in Manchester. The **Old Trafford football ground** is the home of Manchester United FC and was opened in 1910. The record attendance is 76,692, its capacity now reduced to 56,385. It is one of the most modern grounds in Britain. During the war it was heavily bombed and the team had to play at neighbouring Manchester City's Maine Road Ground. It was used for the 1966 World Cup competition and has also hosted the FA Cup Final and replays. The **Old Trafford cricket ground** was opened in 1857 and has staged test matches regularly since 1884. The ground capacity is 40,000.

Olduvai Gorge, *n.* a deep cleft in the Serengeti steppe, Tanzania, where the Leakeys found prehistoric stone tools in the 1930s. They discovered (1958–59) Pleistocene remains of prehumans and gigantic animals. The gorge has given its name to the **Olduvai culture**, a simple stone-tool culture of prehistoric hominids, dating from 2 to 0.5 million years ago.

Old Vic, *n.* a theatre in S London, England, former home of the National Theatre (1963–76).

olé, *int.* expressing approval or victory at a bull fight. [Sp., Arab. *wa,* and, *allah,* God]

ole-, OLE(O)-.

oleaginous, *a.* oily, greasy, unctuous. **oleaginously,** *adv.* **oleaginousness,** *n.* [through F *oléagineux* or directly from L *oleāginus,* from *oleum,* oil]

oleander, *n.* a poisonous evergreen shrub of the genus *Nerium,* esp. *N. oleander* and *N. odorosum,* with lanceolate leaves and pink or white flowers. [med. L, perh. var. of *lōrandrum,* corr. of *rhododendrum,* RHODODENDRON, or *lauridendrum* (L *laurus,* LAUREL, Gr. *dendron,* tree)]

oleaster, *n.* any shrub or tree of the genus *Elaeagnus,* called the wild olive, the true wild olive. *Olea oleaster*. [L (*olea,* olive, -ASTER)]

oleate, *n.* a salt or ester of oleic acid.

olefin, -fine, *n.* any one of a group of hydrocarbons containing two atoms of hydrogen to one of carbon. **olefinic,** *a.*

oleic, *a.* pertaining to or derived from oil. **oleic acid,** *n.* an unsaturated liquid fatty acid that occurs as a glyceride in many fats and oils. **oleiferous,** *a.*

olein, *n.* an oily compound, chief constituent of fatty oils, triolene; a liquid oil occurring in most natural oils or fats.

olent, *a.* smelling, yielding fragrance. [L *olens -ntem,* pres.p. of *olēre,* to smell]

oleo, *n.* (*pl.* **oleos**) short for OLEOMARGARINE or OLEOGRAPH.

ole(o)-, *comb. form* oil. [L *oleum,* oil.]

oleograph, *n.* a picture printed in oil-colours to resemble a painting. **oleographic,** *a.* **oleography,** *n.*

oleomargarine, *n.* (*chiefly N Am.*) margarine.

oleometer, *n.* an instrument for determining the relative densities of oil.

oleon, *n.* an oily liquid obtained by the dry distillation of oleic acid with lime.

oleoresin, *n.* a mixture of an essential oil and a resin.

oleum, *n.* fuming sulphuric acid.

oleraceous, *a.* of the nature of a pot-herb; edible; esculent. [L *oleraceus* (*olus oleris,* pot-herb, -ACEOUS)]

O-level, O.

olfactory, *a.* pertaining to or used in smelling. *n.* (*usu.* pl.) an organ of smell. **olfaction,** *n.* the sense or process of smelling. **olfactive,** *a.* [L *olfacere (olēre,* to smell, *facere,* to make)]

OLG, (*abbr.*) Old Low German.

olibanum, †oliban, *n.* a gum-resin from certain species of *Boswellia,* formerly used in medicine, now as incense, frankincense. [med. L, from late L and Gr. *libanos,* incense]

olid, *a.* rank, stinking. [L *olidus,* from *olēre,* to smell]

oligarch, *n.* a member of an oligarchy. **oligarchal, oligarchic, -ical,** *a.* **oligarchically,** *adv.* **oligarchist,** *n.* **oligarchy,** *n.* a form of government in which power is vested in the hands of a small exclusive class; the members of such a class; a state so governed. [Gr. *oligarchēs* (OLIGO-, *archein,* to govern)]

olig(o)-, *comb. form* denoting few, small. [Gr. *oligos*, small, *oligoi*, few]
oligocarpous, *a.* having few fruits.
Oligocene, *n.*, *a.* tertiary, (of) the age or strata between the Eocene and Miocene (38–25 million years ago). [OLIGO-, Gr. *kainos*, new]
oligochaete, *n.*, *a.* (of) any of various fresh-water or land worms having (few) bristles along its length for locomotion.
oligochrome, *a.* painted or decorated in few colours.
oligoclase, *n.* a soda-lime feldspar resembling albite.
oligopod, *a.* (*Zool.*) having few legs or feet.
oligopoly, *n.* a situation in the market in which a few producers control the supply of a product. **oligopolist**, *n.* **oligopolistic**, *a.*
oligopsony, *n.* a situation in the market in which purchase is in the hands of a small number of buyers. **oligopsonist**, *n.* **oligopsonistic**, *a.*
oligotrophic, *a.* of lakes etc. in rocky terrain, being nutritionally poor, sparsely vegetated, but rich in oxygen.
olio, *n.* (*pl.* **olios**) a mixed dish; a mixture, a medley, a variety, a potpourri. [Sp. *olla*, stew, L, a pot]
†**oliphant**, *n.* a horn or trumpet of ivory. [ELEPHANT]
†**olitory**, *a.* pertaining to a kitchen-garden. *n.* a kitchen-garden. [L *olitōrius*, from *olitor*, kitchen-gardener, from *olus oleris*, pot-herb]
Olivares, *n.* **Count-Duke of** (born Gaspar de Guzmán) (1587–1645), Spanish prime minister (1621–43). He overstretched Spain in foreign affairs, and unsuccessfully attempted domestic reform. He committed Spain to recapturing the Netherlands and to involvement in the Thirty Years' War (1618–48), and his efforts to centralize power led to revolts in Catalonia and Portugal, which brought about his downfall.
olive, *n.* an evergreen tree, *Olea europaea*, with narrow leathery leaves and clusters of oval drupes yielding oil when ripe and eaten unripe as a relish; the fruit of this tree; its wood; the colour of the unripe olive a dull, yellowish green or brown; an oval bar or button fitting into a loop, for fastening a garment; (*pl.*) slices of beef or veal rolled with onions etc., stewed. *a.* of an olive, colour. **olive-branch**, *n.* a branch of the olive-tree as an emblem of peace; that which indicates a desire for peace (e.g. a goodwill gesture, an offer of reconciliation). **olive-crown**, *n.* a garland of olive-leaves as a symbol of victory. **olive drab**, *n.* (*N Am.*) a dull olive-green colour; a fabric or garment of this colour, esp. a US army uniform. **olive-green**, *a.* of a dull yellowish green colour. **olive-oil**, *n.* **olive-yard**, *n.* a piece of ground on which olives are cultivated. **olivaceous**, *a.* olive-coloured. **olivary**, *a.* olive-shaped, oval. **olivet**, *n.* an olive-shaped button; a kind of mock pearl, used as a trading bead. **olivine**, *n.* a mineral silicate of magnesium and iron. **olivinic, olivinitic**, *a.* [F, from L *olīva*]
oliver, *n.* a small trip-hammer worked by the foot, used in making nails etc. [etym. doubtful, prob. from the proper name]
Oliver, *n.* **Isaac** (*c.* 1556–1617), British painter of miniatures, originally a Huguenot refugee, who studied under Nicholas Hilliard. He became a court artist in the reign of James I. Famous sitters include the poet John Donne.
Oliverian, *a.* of or pertaining to the Protector Oliver Cromwell (1599–1658). *n.* a partisan or adherent of Cromwell.
Olives, Mount of, a range of hills E of Jerusalem, important in the Christian religion: a former chapel (now a mosque) marks the traditional site of Jesus' ascension to heaven, and the Garden of Gethsemane was at its foot.
olivet OLIVE.
Olivier, *n.* **Laurence (Kerr), Baron Olivier** (1907–89), English actor and director. For many years associated with the Old Vic, he was director of the National Theatre company (1962–73). His stage roles include Henry V, Hamlet, Richard III and Archie Rice in Osborne's *The Entertainer*. His acting and direction of filmed versions of Shakespeare's plays received critical acclaim, for example *Henry V* (1944) and *Hamlet* (1948).
olla, *n.* an olio; an olla podrida. **olla podrida**, *n.* a favourite Spanish dish, consisting of meat chopped fine, stewed with vegetables; a multifarious or incongruous mixture. [Sp.]
ollamh, ollav, *n.* a learned man, a doctor, a scholar, among the ancient Irish. [Ir.]
olm, *n.* a blind, cave-dwelling type of European salamander. [G]
Olmos, *n.* a small town on the edge of the Sechura Desert, NW Peru. It gives its name to the large scale Olmos Project which began in 1926 in an attempt to irrigate the desert plain and increase cotton and sugar cane production.
ology, *n.* a science; one of the sciences whose names end thus.
-ology -LOGY.
oloroso, *n.* a medium-sweet golden sherry. [Sp., fragrant]
Olympia, *n.* a sanctuary in the W Peloponnese, ancient Greece, with a temple of Zeus, and the stadium (for foot races, boxing, wrestling) and hippodrome (for chariot and horse races), where the original Olympic games were held.
olympiad, *n.* a period of four years, being the interval between the celebrations of the Olympic Games; a method of chronology used from 776 BC to AD 394; (a staging of) an international contest, esp. the modern Olympic games. **Olympian**, *a.* pertaining to Mt Olympus, the home of the gods, celestial; magnificent, lofty, superb; †Olympic. *n.* a dweller in Olympus; one of the Greek gods; (*chiefly N Am.*) a contestant in the Olympic games. **Olympic**, *a.* pertaining to Olympia or the Olympic Games; †Olympian. **Olympic flame**, *n.* the flame which burns throughout the Olympic Games, lit by the Olympic torch. **Olympic Games**, see separate article below. **Olympic torch**, *n.* the lighted torch brought by a runner from Olympia to light the Olympic flame. **the Olympics**, *n.pl.* the Olympic Games. [F *olympiade*, L *olympias -adis*, Gr. *olumpias -ados*, from *Olumpios*, pertaining to *Olumpos*]
Olympic Games, *n.pl.* sporting contests orig. held in Olympia, ancient Greece, every four years during a sacred truce; records were kept from 776 BC. Women were forbidden to be present and the male contestants were naked. The ancient games were abolished AD 394. The modern games have been held every four years since 1896. Since 1924 there has been a separate winter games programme. From 1994 the winter and summer games will be held two years apart.
Olympus, *n.* (Greek **Olimbos**) several mountains in Greece and elsewhere, the most famous being **Mount Olympus** in N Thessaly, Greece, 2918 m/9577 ft high. In ancient Greece it was considered the home of the gods.
O&M, (*abbr.*) organization and method(s).
OM, *n.* abbreviation for Order of Merit.
Om, *n.* sacred word in Hinduism, used to begin prayers and placed at the beginning and end of books. It is composed of three syllables, symbolic of the Hindu Trimurti, or trinity of gods.
-oma, *comb. form* (*pl.* **-omas, -omata**) denoting a tumour or growth. [Gr. *oma*, tumour]
omadhaun, *n.* a fool, a simpleton. [Ir. *amedan*]
Oman, *n.* Sultanate of, a country on the Arabian peninsula, bounded to the W by the United Arab Emirates, Saudi Arabia and South Yemen. **area** 272,000 sq km/105,000 sq miles. **capital** Muscat. **towns** Salalah. **physical** mountains and a high arid plateau; fertile coastal strip. **exports** oil, dates, silverware. **population** (1989) 1,389,000; annual growth rate 4.7%. **language** Arabic. **religion** Sunni Muslim.
Omar, *n.* (581–644), adviser of the prophet Mohammed. In 634 he succeeded Abu Bakr as caliph (civic and religious leader of Islam), and conquered Syria, Palestine, Egypt and Persia. He was assassinated by a slave. The Mosque of Omar in Jerusalem is attributed to him.
Omar Khayyam, *n.* (*c.* 1050–1123), Persian astrono-

mer and poet. Born in Nishapur, he founded a school of astronomical research and assisted in reforming the calendar. The result of his observations was the *Jalālī* era, begun 1079. In the West, Omar Khayyam is chiefly known as a poet through Fitzgerald's version of *The Rubaiyat of Omar Khayyam* (1859).

omasum, *n.* (*pl.* **-sa**) the third stomach of a ruminant. [L]

Omayyad dynasty, *n.* an Arabian dynasty of the Islamic empire who reigned as caliphs 661–750. They were overthrown by Abbasids, but a member of the family escaped to Spain and in 756 assumed the title of emir of Córdoba. His dynasty, which took the title of caliph 929, ruled in Córdoba until the early 11th cent.

ombre, *n.* a game of cards, for two, three or five players, popular in the 17th and 18th cents. [Sp. *hombre,* L *homo hominem,* man]

ombro-, *comb. form* denoting rain. [Gr. *ombros*]

ombrology, *n.* the branch of meteorology concerned with rainfall. **ombrometer,** *n.* a rain-gauge.

Ombudsman, *n.* (*pl.* **-men**) an official investigator of complaints against government bodies or employees; a Parliamentary Commissioner. **Ombudswoman,** *n. fem.* [Swed.]

Omdurman, *n.* a city in Sudan, on the White Nile, a suburb of Khartoum; population (1983) 526,000.

-ome, *comb. form* denoting a mass or part. [var. of -OMA]

omega, *n.* the last letter of the Greek alphabet, Ω, ω, $\bar{o}$; the last of a series; the conclusion, the end, the last stage or phase. [Gr. *ō mega,* the great *o*]

omelet, -lette, *n.* a flat dish made with beaten eggs cooked in fat, eaten plain or seasoned and filled with herbs, cheese etc. [F *omelette,* earlier *amelette,* corr. of *alemette,* var. of *alemelle,* a thin plate, acc. to Littré prob. from L LAMELLA]

omen, *n.* an incident, object or appearance taken as indicating a good or evil event, issue, fortune, a portent etc.; prognostication or prophetic signification. *v.t.* to prognosticate, to portend. **ill-omened,** *a.* attended by bad portents; portending bad fortune etc. [L, earlier *osmen,* perh. for *ausmen* (cogn. with *audīre,* to hear)]

omentum, *n.* (*pl.* **-ta**) a fold of the peritoneum connecting the viscera with each other. **omental,** *a.* [L]

†**omer,** *n.* a Hebrew measure of capacity, the tenth part of an ephah or $5\frac{1}{16}$ pts (about 2·8 l). [Heb.]

omertà, *n.* a conspiracy of silence, part of the Mafia code of honour. [It.]

omicron, *n.* the 15th letter of the Greek alphabet, the short o. [Gr. *o mikron,* the small *o*]

ominous, *a.* portending evil; of evil omen, inauspicious. **ominously,** *adv.* **ominousness,** *n.* [L *ōminōsus* (OMEN, -OUS)]

omit, *v.t.* to leave out; not to include, insert, or mention; to neglect; to leave undone. **omissible,** *a.* **omission,** *n.* †**omissive,** *a.* †**omittance,** *n.* **omitter,** *n.* [L *omittere* (*o-,* OB-, *mittere,* to send), p.p. *omissus*]

ommateum, *n.* (*pl.* **-tea**) a compound eye. **ommatidium,** *n.* (*pl.* **-dia**) any of the elements of a compound eye. [Gr. *omma -atos,* an eye]

omni-, *comb. form* universally, in all ways, of all things. [L *omnis,* all]

omnibus, *n.* a large passenger vehicle for transporting members of the public, hotel guests, employees etc., a bus; a volume containing reprints of a number of works, usually by the same author. *a.* inclusive, embracing several or various items, objects etc. **omnibus Bill, clause, resolution,** *n.* one dealing with several subjects. [L, dat. pl. of *omnis* (see prec.), for all]

omnicompetence,, *n.* competence in all areas or matters. **omnicompetent,** *a.*

omnidirectional, *a,* (capable of) moving, sending or receiving in every direction (of radio waves, a radio transmitter or receiver).

omnifarious, *a.* of all kinds. **omnifariously,** *adv.* **omnifariousness,** *n.* [L *omnifarius*]

omnipotent, *a.* almighty; having unlimited power. **omnipotence, omnipotency,** *n.* **The Omnipotent,** God. **omnipotently,** *adv.*

omnipresent, *a.* present in every place at the same time. **omnipresence,** *n.*

omniscience, *n.* infinite knowledge. **omniscient,** *a.* **omnisciently,** *adv.*

omnium, *n.* a Stock Exchange term used to express the aggregate value of the different stocks in which a loan is funded. **omnium gatherum,** a miscellaneous collection or assemblage, a medley. [L, of all (things, kinds etc.), as prec.]

omnivore, *n.* a creature that eats any type of available food (i.e. vegetable matter and meat). **omnivorous,** *a.* all-devouring; feeding on anything available; (*fig.*) reading anything and everything. **omnivorously,** *adv.* **omnivorousness,** *n.*

omo-, *comb. form* pertaining to the shoulder. [Gr. *omos,* shoulder]

omohyoid, *a.* of or pertaining to the shoulder-blade and the hyoid bone. *n.* the muscle between these.

omophagic, omophagous, *a.* eating raw flesh. [Gr. *ōmophagos* (*ōmos,* raw, *phagein,* to eat)]

omoplate, *n.* the shoulder-blade.

omosternum, *n.* an ossified process at the anterior extremity of the sternum, in certain animals.

omphacite, *n.* a green variety of pyroxene. [G *omphazit* (Gr. *omphax,* unripe, -ITE)]

omphalos, *n.* the boss of an ancient Greek shield; a stone in the temple of Apollo at Delphi, believed to be the middle point or navel of the earth; a central point, a hub. **omphalic, omphaloid,** *a.* pertaining to or resembling the navel.

Omsk, *n.* an industrial city (agricultural and other machinery, food processing, sawmills, oil refining) in the USSR, capital of Omsk region, W Siberia; population (1987) 1,134,000. The refineries are linked with Tuimazy in Bashkiria by a 1600 km/1000 mile pipeline.

ON, (*abbr.*) Old Norse.

on, *prep.* in or as in contact with, esp. as supported by, covering, environing or suspended from, the upper surface or level of; into contact with the upper surface of, or in contact with from above; in the direction of, tending toward, arrived at, against; exactly at, next in order to, beside, immediately after, close to; about, concerning, in the act of, in the making, performance, support, interest, process etc., of; attached to; present on; carried with; taking (e.g. a drug); at the expense of; at the date, time or occasion of; in a condition or state of; sustained by; by means of; on the basis of; in the manner of. *adv.* so as to be in contact with and supported by, covering, environing, suspended from or adhering to something; in advance, forward, in operation, action, movement, progress, persistence (*coll.*), or continuance of action or movement; (*coll.*) drunk; nearly drunk; taking place; arranged; planned. *a.* denoting the side of a cricket field to the left of the batsman; operating; (*coll.*) wagered; performing, broadcasting, playing (e.g. of a batsman); definitely happening as arranged; acceptable, possible, tolerable. *n.* (*Cricket*) the on side. **... and so on,** etcetera. **off and on, on and off,** intermittently. **on and on,** ceaselessly, continuously. **on time,** *adv.* punctually. **to be on to,** to be aware of, to have twigged on to, tumbled to. **to get on** GET. **to go on at someone,** to nag at a person. **to go on to,** to advance, progress, move or travel to a further level, position or place. **oncome,** *n.* (*Sc.*) something that comes on one, as a disease; a fall of rain or snow. **oncoming,** *n.* the coming on, advance or approach (of). **oncost,** *n.* a supplementary or additional expense, an overhead. **onfall,** *n.* an attack, an onset; (*Sc.*) a fall of rain or snow. **onflow,** *n.* onward flow. **ongoing,** *n.* procedure, progress; (*pl.*) goings-on, misbehaviour; proceedings. *a.* unceasing, continuous; in progress. **on licence,** *n.* a licence to sell intoxicating liquor for consumption on the premises. **on-line,** *a.* of a computer peripheral, under the control of the central processor. **onlooker,** *n.* a spectator, one who looks on. **onlooking,** *a.* **onrush,** *n.* a rushing on, an attack, an onset. **onset,** *n.* an attack, an assault, an onslaught; the outset, beginning. **onsetter, onsetting,** *n.* **onslaught,** *n.* a furious attack or onset. **on-stream,**

a., *adv.* of a manufacturing plant, industrial installation etc., in operation. **onward,** *adv.* toward the front or a point in advance, forward, on. *a.* moving, tending or directed forward; advancing, progressive. **onwards,** *adv.* **on to, onto,** *prep.* (*coll.*) to and upon, to a position on or upon. [OE *on, an,* cp. Dut. *aan,* G *an,* Icel. *ā,* Dan. *an,* Gr. *ana*]

-on, *comb. form* denoting a chemical compound, as in *interferon;* denoting an elementary particle, as in *electron, neutron;* denoting a quantum, as in *photon;* denoting an inert gas, as in *neon.* [from Gr. *ion,* going, from *ienai,* to go]

onager, *n.* the wild ass, esp. the *Equus onager* of the Asiatic deserts; an ancient and mediaeval war machine resembling a large catapult for hurling rocks at the enemy. [L, from Gr. *onagros* (*onos,* ass, *agrios,* wild)]

onanism, *n.* masturbation; the withdrawal of the penis from the vagina prior to ejaculation. **onanist,** *n.* **onanistic,** *a.* [*Onan* (Gen. xxxviii.9), -ISM]

Onassis, *n.* **Aristotle (Socrates)** (1906–75), Turkish-born Greek shipowner. During the 1950s he was one of the first shipbuilders to build supertankers. In 1968 he married Jacqueline Kennedy, widow of US president John F. Kennedy.

ONC, (*abbr.*) Ordinary National Certificate.

once, *adv.* one time; one time only; at one time, formerly, at some past time; at any time, ever, at all; as soon as; at some future time, some time or other. *conj.* as soon as. *n.* one time. *a.* former. **all at once,** all together, simultaneously, suddenly. **at once,** immediately, without delay; simultaneously; **for once,** for one time or occasion only. **once (and) for all,** finally; definitively. **once in a way** or **while,** very seldom. **once or twice,** a few times. **once upon a time,** at some past date or period, usu. beginning a fairytale. **once-over,** *n.* a look of appraisal. **oncer,** *n.* (*coll.*) a £1 note.

onco-, *comb. form.* denoting a tumour. [Gr. *onkos*]

oncogene, *n.* any of several genes capable of causing cancer. **oncogenic**, **oncogenous**, *a.* causing tumours. **oncogenicity**, **oncogenesis,** *n.*

oncology, *n.* the study of tumours and cancers. **oncologist,** *n.* **oncological**, **oncologic**, *a.*

oncotomy, *n.* the opening of an abscess or the excision of a tumour.

OND, (*abbr.*) Ordinary National Diploma.

ondes Martenot, *n.* an electronic musical instrument invented by Maurice Martenot and first demonstrated in 1928. A melody of considerable range and voice-like timbre is produced by sliding a contact along a conductive ribbon, the left hand controlling the tone colour. In addition to inspiring works from Messiaen, Varkse, Jolivet and others, it has been in regular demand among composers of film and radio incidental music.

on dit, *n.* (*pl.* **on dits**) hearsay, gossip; a bit of gossip. [F, they say]

-one, *suf.* denoting certain chemical compounds, esp. hydrocarbons, as in *acetone, ketone, ozone.* [Gr. *ōnē,* fem. patronymic]

one, *a.* single, undivided; being a unit and integral; a or an; single in kind, the only, the same; this, some, any, a certain. *pron.* a person or thing of the kind implied, someone or something, anyone or anything; a person unspecified; (*coll.*) any person, esp. the speaker; (*incorr.*) I. *n.* a single unit, unity; the number 1, a thing or person so numbered; a single thing or person; (*coll.*) a joke or story; a blow, a setback; a drink. †*v.t.* to make one. **all in one,** combined. **all one** ALL. **at one,** in accord or agreement. **many a one,** many people. **never a one,** none. **one and all,** jointly and severally. **one and only,** unique. **one-armed bandit,** a fruit machine operated by a single lever. **one by one,** singly, individually, successively. **one-man-band, -show,** a sole musician playing a variety of instruments simultaneously; a company, enterprise etc., consisting of, or run by, a single person. **one or two,** a few. **one-, single-parent family,** a family living together having only one parent present to tend the child or children. **one way and another,** altogether, on balance. **one with another,** on the average, in general. **to be one for,** to be an enthusiast for. **one another,** *pron.* each other. **one-armed,** *a.* having or executed by one arm. **one-dimensional,** *a.* superficial, shallow, flat. **one-eyed,** *a.* **one-fold,** *a.* having only one member or constituent; single; single-minded, simple in character. **one-handed,** *a.* single-handed, done with one hand; having only one hand. **one-horse,** *a.* drawn by a single horse; (*sl.*) of meagre capacity, resources or efficiency; insignificant, petty. **one-legged,** *a.* **one-liner,** *n.* a short punchy joke or witticism. **one-man,** *a.* employing, worked by, or consisting of one man. **one-night stand,** a single performance at one venue; (*coll.*) a sexual encounter or relationship lasting one evening or night; a person engaging in such an encounter. **one-off,** *a.*, *n.* (of) a unique object, product, event etc. **one-piece,** *a.*, *n.* (of) a garment consisting of one piece of material (e.g. a one-piece swimsuit). **one-sided,** *a.* having or happening on one side only; partial, unfair, favouring one side of an argument, topic etc.; more developed on one side than another. **one-sidedly,** *adv.* **one-sidedness,** *n.* **one-step,** *n.* form of a quick-stepping type of ballroom dancing. **one-time,** *a.* former; sometime in the past. **one-to-one,** corresponding, esp. in mathematics, pairing each element of a set with only one of another; of one person to or with another, as in a *one-to-one relationship*. **one-track,** *a.* single-track; (*coll.*) capable of, or obsessed by, only one idea at a time. **one-two,** *n.* in boxing, two successive blows rapidly delivered; a type of football pass. **one-up,** *a.* (*coll.*) having, or in, a position of advantage. **one-upmanship,** *n.* the art of gaining or keeping an advantage over someone. **one-way,** *a.* denoting a traffic system which allows vehicles to go in one direction only through certain streets; unilateral. *n.*, *a.* (of) a single ticket, fare (e.g. for a bus, train, aeroplane etc.). **oneness,** *n.* singleness; singularity, uniqueness; unity, union, agreement, harmony; sameness. **oner**, *n.* (*sl.*) a striking, extraordinary or pre-eminent person or thing; an expert, an adept; a heavy blow; a big lie; (*Cricket*) a hit for one run. **oneself,** *pron.* the reflexive form of one. **to be oneself,** to be alone. **to be oneself,** to behave naturally, without constraint, pretension, artifice etc. [OE *ān* (cp. Dut. *een,* G *ein,* Icel. *einn*), cogn. with L *ūnus,* Gr. *oinē,* ace]

Onega, Lake, *n.* the second largest lake in Europe, NE of Leningrad, partly in Karelia, USSR; area 9600 sq km/3710 sq miles. The **Onega canal**, along its south shore, is part of the Mariinsk system linking Leningrad with the river Volga.

O'Neill[1], *n.* **Eugene (Gladstone)** (1888–1953), US playwright, often regarded as the leading US dramatist between World Wars I and II. His plays include *Anna Christie* (1922), *Desire under the Elms* (1924), *The Iceman Cometh* (1946), and the posthumously produced autobiographical drama *Long Day's Journey into Night* (1956, written 1940). Nobel prize 1936.

O'Neill[2], *n.* **Terence, Baron O'Neill of the Maine** (1914–90), Northern Irish Unionist politician. In the Ulster government he was minister of finance (1956–63), prime minister (1963–69). He resigned when opposed by his party on measures to extend rights to Roman Catholics, including a universal franchise.

on(e)iric, *a.* of or pertaining to dreams.

oneir(o)-, *comb. form* pertaining to dreams. [Gr. *oneiros,* dream]

oneirodynia, *n.* nightmare, disturbed sleep. [Gr. *odunē,* pain]

oneirology, *n.* the science of dreams. **oneirologist,** *n.*

oneiromancy, *n.* divination by dreams. **oneiromancer,** *n.*

onerous, *a.* burdensome, heavy, weighty, troublesome. **onerously,** *adv.* **onerousness,** *n.* [OF *onereus,* L *onerōsus,* from *onus oneris,* burden]

oneself ONE.

onfall, onflow, ongoing etc. ON.

onion, *n.* a plant, *Allium cepa,* with an underground bulb of several coats and a pungent smell and flavour, much used in cookery; other species of the genus *Allium*. **to know one's onions,** (*coll.*) to be knowledgeable in one's subject or competent in one's job. **onionskin,** *n.* a thin glazed paper. **oniony,** *a.* [F *oignon,* L *ūniōnem,* nom. *ūnio,* a large pearl, a kind of onion]

onkus, *a.* (*Austral. sl.*) bad, no good. [etym. doubtful]

on-line, onlooker ON.

only, *a.* solitary, single or alone in its or their kind; the single, the sole; †mere, *adv.* solely, merely, exclusively, alone; with no other, singly; wholly; not otherwise than; not earlier than. *conj.* except that; but; were it not (that). **if only,** expressing a desire or wish. **only too willing,** more than willing. **only too true,** regrettably true. **only-begotten,** *a.* begotten as the sole issue. **only child,** *n.* one without brothers or sisters. **onliness,** *n.* [OE *ānlic* (ONE, -LY)]

Onnes, *n.* **Kamerlingh** (1853–1926), Dutch physicist who worked mainly in the field of low temperature physics and in 1911 discovered the phenomenon of superconductivity, for which work he was awarded the 1913 Nobel physics prize.

o.n.o., (*abbr.*) or nearest offer.

onomastic, *a.* pertaining to a name. **onomasticon,** *n.* a dictionary of proper names. **onomastics,** *n. sing.* the study of proper names. [ONOMA(TO)-]

onoma(to)-, *comb. form* pertaining to a name or word. [Gr. *onoma-matos,* name]

onomatopoeia, *n.* the formation of words in imitation of the sounds associated with or suggested by the things signified; the rhetorical use of a word so formed. **onomatopoeic, -poetic,** *a.* **onomatopoeically, -poetically,** *adv.* **onomatopoesis, -poiesis,** *n.* [L, from Gr. *onomatopoiia* (as prec., *-poios,* making, from *poieein,* to make)]

onrush ON.

Ontario, *n.* a province of central Canada. **area** 1,068,600 sq km/412,480 sq miles. **capital** Toronto. **towns** Hamilton, Ottawa (federal capital), London, Windsor, Kitchener, St Catharines, Oshawa, Thunder Bay, Sudbury. **products** nickel, iron, gold, forest products, motor vehicles, iron, steel, paper, chemicals, copper, uranium. **population** (1986) 9,114,000.

Ontario, Lake, *n.* smallest and easternmost of the Great Lakes, on the US-Canadian border; area 19,200 sq km/7400 sq miles. It is connected to Lake Erie by the Welland Canal and the Niagara River, and drains into the St Lawrence River. Its main port is Toronto.

onto-, *comb. form* being. [Gr. *ōn ontos,* being]

ontogenesis, *n.* the origin and development of the individual organism. **ontogenetic, -genic,** *a.* **ontogenetically, -genically,** *adv.*

ontogeny, *n.* ontogenesis; the history or science of this, embryology.

ontology, *n.* the branch of metaphysics dealing with the theory of pure being or reality. **ontologic, -ical,** *a.* **ontologically,** *adv.* **ontologist,** *n.*

onus, *n.* a burden; a duty, obligation or responsibility. [L]

onychia, *n.* inflammation of or near the nail, a whitlow. **onychitis,** *n.* [mod. L, from Gr. *onux onuchos,* nail]

-onym, *comb. form* denoting a name or word, as in *pseudonym, antonym.* **onymous,** *a.* having or bearing a name or signature, opp. to anonymous. [from Doric variant *onuma* of Gr. *onoma -atos,* name]

onyx, *n.* a variety of quartz resembling agate, with variously-coloured layers. **onyx marble,** *n.* a calcium carbonite mineral resembling marble. [Gr. *onux,* a nail, onyx]

oo-, *comb. form* pertaining to ova, or an egg. [Gr. *ōon,* egg]

oocyte, *n.* the unfertilized ovum or egg cell.

oodles, (*coll.*) *n. pl.* a great quantity, superabundance. [etym. doubtful]

ooecium, *n.* a sac-like receptacle in which ova are received and fertilized, as in certain Polyzoa. **ooecial,** *a.* [Gr. *oikion,* dim. of *oikos,* house]

oogamous, *a.* reproducing by the union of male and female cells. **oogamete,** *n.* one of such cells. **oogamy,** *n.* [Gr. *gamos,* marriage]

oogenesis, oogeny, *n.* the origin and development of an ovum. **oogenetic,** *a.*

ooh, *int.* expressing delight, surprise, pain, admiration etc. *v.i.* to say 'ooh'.

Oolite, *n.* a limestone composed of grains or particles of sand like the roe of a fish; the upper portion of the Jurassic strata in England, composed in great part of oolitic limestone. **oolitic,** *a.*

oology, *n.* the study of birds' eggs. **oological,** *a.* **oologically,** *adv.* **oologist,** *n.*

oolong, *n.* a kind of China tea. [Chin. *wu,* black, *lung,* dragon]

oomiak, oomiac UMIAK.

oompah, *n.* an imitation or representation of the sound of a large brass musical instrument. *v.i.,* to make such a sound.

oomph, *n.* (*coll.*) vigour, energy. [etym. doubtful]

oopak, *n.* a variety of black tea. [Chin. *u-pak, Hu-peh,* province in central China]

oops, *int.* expressing surprise, dismay, apology, esp. having dropped something.

Oort, *n.* **Jan Hendrik** (1900–), Dutch astronomer. In 1927, he calculated the mass and size of the Galaxy, and the Sun's distance from its centre, from the observed movements of stars around the Galaxy's centre. In 1950 Oort proposed that comets exist in a vast swarm, now called the **Oort Cloud,** at the edge of the Solar System.

oose, *n.* (*Sc.*) fluff. **oosy,** *a.*

oosperm, *n.* a fertilized egg.

oospore, *n.* a fertilized ovum.

ooze, *n.* wet mud, slime; a slimy deposit consisting of foraminiferal remains found on ocean-beds; the liquor of a tan-vat, consisting of an infusion of bark etc.; a gentle, sluggish flow, an exudation; †seaweed. *v.i.* to flow, pass gently; to percolate (through the pores of a body etc.) *v.t.* to emit or exude. **oozily,** *adv.* **ooziness,** *n.* **oozy,** *a.*

o.p., (*abbr.*) out of print.

op. (*abbr.*) opera; operation; operator; optical; opposite; opus.

op-, *pref.* OB- (before P).

opacity OPAQUE.

opah, *n.* a rare Atlantic fish, *Lampris guttatus,* of the mackerel family, famous for its brilliant colours. [Ibo *úbá*]

opal, *n.* an amorphous, transparent, vitreous form of hydrous silica, several kinds of which are characterized by a play of iridescent colours and used as gems; the colour of opal. *a.* opal-like, of opal. **opaled,** *a.* **opalescence,** *n.* **opalescent,** *a.* **opaline,** *a.* pertaining to or like opal. *n.* a translucent variety of glass; a yellow chalcedony. [F *opale,* L *opalus,* Sansk. *upala*]

opaque, *a.* impervious to rays of light; not transparent or translucent; impenetrable to sight; obscure, unintelligible; †dark. *n.* opacity; darkness. **opaquely,** *adv.* **opaqueness, opacity,** *n.* [F, from L *opācum,* nom. *-cus,* shady]

op art, *n.* movement in modern art, especially popular in the 1960s. It uses scientifically based optical effects that confuse the spectator's eye. Precisely painted lines or dots are arranged in carefully regulated patterns that create an illusion of surface movement. Exponents include Victor Vasarely and Bridget Riley.

op. cit., (*abbr.*) *opere citato,* in the work cited.

ope, *a., v.t., v.i.* (*poet.*) (to) open. [OPEN]

OPEC, (*abbr.*) Organization of Petroleum-Exporting Countries.

opeidoscope, *n.* an instrument for exhibiting sound-vibrations by means of reflections of light. [Gr. *ōps,* voice, *eidos,* form, -SCOPE]

open, *a.* not closed, obstructed or enclosed; affording entrance, passage, access or view; unclosed, unshut, having any barrier, gate, cover etc. removed, withdrawn or unfastened; uncovered, bare, unsheltered, exposed; unconcealed, undisguised, manifest; unrestricted, not exclusive or limited; ready to admit, receive or be affected; liable, subject (to); unoccupied, vacant; disengaged, free; unobstructed, clear, affording wide views; widely spaced; loosely woven, or latticed, or having frequent gaps or spaces; free, generous, liberal; frank, candid; not closed or decided, debatable, moot; (of weather) not frosty; (*Mus.*) not stopped, or produced from an unstopped pipe, string etc.; enunciated with the vocal organs comparatively unclosed; (of a vowel or syllable) not ended by a consonant. *n.* unenclosed space or ground; public view; (*Sport*) a tournament open to any class of player. *v.t.* to make open; to unclose; to unfasten, unlock; to remove the covering from; to unfold, spread out, expand; to free from obstruction or restriction, to make free of access; to reveal, to make manifest or public; to announce open; to widen, to enlarge, to develop; to make a start in, to begin. to set going; in law, to state a case before calling evidence. *v.i.* to become unclosed or unfastened; to crack, to fissure, to gape; to unfold, to expand; to develop; to make a start, to begin. **to bring into the open,** to disclose what was hitherto hidden or secret. **to open fire,** to begin firing ammunition. **to open out,** to unfold; to develop; to reveal; to become communicative; (*Naut.*) to bring into full view; to accelerate. **to open someone's eyes,** to undeceive. **to open up,** to make accessible; to reveal; to discover, to explore, to colonize, to make ready for trade. **open air,** *n., a.* outdoor(s). **open-and-shut,** needing little deliberation, easily solved, simple. **open-armed,** *a.* ready to receive with cordiality. **open-bill,** *n.* a bird of the Anastomus family, akin to the stork, native to Africa and Asia. **open book,** *n.* someone or thing easily understood. **open-cast,** *n., a.* in mining, (of) a surface excavation *adv.* **open circuit,** *n.* an electrical circuit that has been broken so that no current can flow; **open court,** *n.* a court to which the public are admitted. **open day,** *n.* a day when an institution (e.g. a school or university) is open to the public. **open door,** *n.* free admission or unrestricted access; a policy of equal trading with all nations. **open-ended,** *a.* having no set limit or restriction on duration, time, amount etc. **open-faced,** *a.* innocent-looking, having a candid expression. **open-eyed,** *a.* watchful, vigilant, aware; astonished, surprised. **open field,** *n.* undivided arable land; **open-handed,** *a.* generous, liberal. **open-handedly,** *adv.* **open-handedness,** *n.* **open-heart surgery,** *n.* surgery performed on a heart while its functions are temporarily performed by a heart-lung machine. **open-hearted,** *a.* frank, ingenuous, sincere, candid, unsuspicious. **open-heartedly,** *adv.* **open-heartedness,** *n.* **open-hearth,** *a.* of, made by or used in an open-hearth furnace or process. **open-hearth furnace,** *n.* a reverberatory furnace for producing steel from pig iron. **open-hearth process,** *n.* the process of making steel in such a furnace. **open-house,** *n.* hospitality proffered to all comers. **open letter,** *n.* a letter addressed to an individual but published in a newspaper. **open market,** *n.* a market situation of unrestricted commerce and free competition. **open mind,** *n.* **open-minded,** *a.* accessible to ideas, unprejudiced, candid, unreserved. **open-mindedly,** *adv.* **open-mindedness,** *n.* **open-mouthed,** *a.* gaping with voracity, stupidity, surprise etc.; greedy, ravenous; clamorous. **open-plan,** *a.* having no, or few, dividing partitions or walls. **open prison,** *n.* one allowing greater freedom of movement. **open question,** *n.* one that is undecided. **open sandwich,** *n.* a sandwich without an upper slice of bread, exposing its filling. **open sea,** *n.* sea not enclosed or obstructed by land. **open season,** *n.* a period during which it is legal to hunt or angle for various species of game or fish; (*fig.*) an unrestricted period in which to attack, attempt, take etc. **open secret,** *n.* an apparently undivulged secret which is however generally known. **open sesame** SESAME. **open shop,** *n.* an establishment where union membership is not a condition of employment. **Open University,** see separate entry. **open verdict,** *n.* a verdict which names no criminal or records no cause of death. **open-work,** *n.* ornamental work showing openings. **openable,** *a.* **opener,** *n.* **opening,** *a.* that opens; beginning, first in order, initial. *n.* the act of making or becoming open; a gap, a breach, an aperture; a beginning, a commencement, the first part or stage, a prelude; in law, a counsel's statement of a case before evidence is called; in chess etc., a series of moves beginning a game; a vacancy, an opportunity; the two facing pages of an open book. **opening time,** *n.* the time at which bars and public houses can legally begin selling alcohol. **openly,** *adv.* **openness,** *n.* [OE (cp. Dut. *open,* G *offen,* Icel. *opinn*), rel. to UP]

Open College, *n.* in the UK, an initiative launched by the Manpower Services Commission (now the Training Commission) to enable people to gain and update technical and vocational skills by means of distance teaching, such as correspondence, radio and television.

Open University, *n.* an institution established in the UK (1969) to enable mature students without qualifications to study to degree level without regular attendance. Open University teaching is based on a mixture of correspondence courses, TV and radio lectures and demonstrations, personal tuition organized on a regional basis, and summer schools.

opera[1], *n.* a dramatic entertainment in which music forms an essential part; a composition comprising words and music for this; the branch of the musical and dramatic arts concerned with this; the theatre in which it is performed; the company which performs it; this form of dramatic art; a libretto, a score; **comic opera** COMIC. **light opera,** operetta. **grand opera,** a type of opera having large or tragic dramatic themes, and without spoken dialogue. **opera bouffe**, **buffa**, *n.* a farcical variety of opera. **opéra comique**, *n.* a type of opera having some spoken dialogue; comic opera. **opera-glasses,** *n. pl.* small binoculars for use in theatres. **opera-hat,** *n.* a collapsible tall hat for men. **opera-house,** *n.* **opera seria**, *n.* a serious type of opera having a heroic or mythical plot. **operatic**, *a.* **operatically,** *adv.* **operetta**, *n.* a short opera of a light character. **operettist,** *n.* [It., from L, work]

opera[2], *pl.* OPUS.

operate, *v.i.* to (cause to) work, to act; to produce effect; to exert power, force, strength, influence etc.; (*Med.*) to produce a certain effect on the human system; to perform a surgical operation; (*Mil.*) to carry out strategic movements; to deal in stocks; to trade, to carry on a business. *v.t.* to work or control the working of; to control, manage, run (a business, an organization etc.). **operable**, *a.* suitable or capable of being operated (on); practicable. **operability**, *n.* **operand**, *n.* that which is operated on, esp. a quantity in mathematics. †**operant,** *a., n.* **operating table,** *n.* a table on which a patient lies during a surgical operation. **operating theatre,** *n.* a specially-fitted room where surgery is performed. **operation,** *n.* the act or process of operating; working, action, mode of working; activity, performance of function; effect; a planned campaign or series of military or naval movements; a surgical act performed with or without instruments upon the body, to remove diseased parts, extract foreign matter, remedy infirmities etc.; in mathematics, the act of altering the value or form of a number or quantity by such a process as multiplication or division; a commercial or financial transaction; a procedure, a process. **operational,** *a.* ready for or capable of action or use; working, in operation; of or pertaining to military operations. **operational**, **operations research,** *n.* the application of mathematical techniques to problems of military or naval strategy, industrial planning, economic organization etc. **operations room,** *n.* a room from where (esp. military) operations are controlled or directed. **operative,** *a.* acting, exerting force; producing the proper result; efficacious, effective; relevant, significant; of or pertaining to a surgical operation, practical, as distinguished from theoretical or contemplative. *n.* a (skilled) workman, an operator; (*N Am.*) a private detective. **operatively,** *adv.* **operativeness,** *n.* **operator,** *n.* one who runs or operates a machine, a telephone switchboard, a business etc.; in mathematics or logic, a symbol etc. representing a function to be performed; a financial speculator; (*coll.*) a skilled manipulator. [L *operātus*, p.p. of *operārī*, from *opus*, work]

operculum, *n.* (*pl.* **-la**) a lid or cover as of the pitcher in Nepenthes, or of the spore-vessel in mosses; the gill-cover in fishes; the plate closing the mouth of many univalve shells. **opercular, -late, -lated,** *a.* **operculiferous,** *a.* [L, from *operīre*, to cover, rel. to *aperīre*, see APERIENT]

opere citato, in the work cited. [L]

†**operose,** *a.* done with or requiring much labour, laborious, wearisome. †**operosely,** *adv.* **operoseness,** *n.* [L *operōsus*, from *opus operis*, work]

operetta OPERA[1].

ophicleide, *n.* a musical wind-instrument, consisting of a wide conical tube with usu. eleven finger-levers and a bass or alto pitch.

Ophidia, *n.* the suborder of reptiles comprising the snakes. **ophidian,** *a.* of or pertaining to the Ophidia; snake-like. *n.* any individual of the Ophidia. **ophidiarium,** *n.* a place where snakes are kept.

ophi(o)-, *comb. form.* pertaining to a serpent. [Gr. *ophis*, serpent]

ophiolatry, *n.* serpent-worship. **ophiolater,** *n.*

ophiology, *n.* the study of snakes. **ophiologic, -ical,** *a.* **ophiologist,** *n.*

ophiophagous, *a.* feeding on serpents.

Ophite, *n.* a member of a gnostic sect who regarded the serpent as an embodiment of divine wisdom. **Ophitic,** *a.*

ophite, *n.* serpentine, serpentine marble. **ophitic,** *a.*

Ophiuchus, *n.* a large constellation of the equatorial region of the sky, known as the serpent-bearer. The Sun passes through Ophiuchus each Dec., although the constellation is not part of the zodiac. Ophiuchus contains Barnard's Star.

ophiuran, *a.* belonging to the genus *Ophiura* or the class Ophiuroidea of echinoderms, comprising the sand-stars. *n.* a starfish of this genus. **ophiurid, ophiuroid,** *a.*, *n.* [Gr. *ophis*, snake]

ophthalmia, *n.* inflammation of the eye.

ophthalmic, *a.* pertaining to the eye. **ophthalmic optician,** *n.* an optician qualified to test eyesight and prescribe and dispense glasses or lenses.

ophthalmitis, *n.* ophthalmia, esp. inflammation involving all the structures of the eye.

ophthalm(o)-, *comb. form* pertaining to the eye. [Gr. *ophthalmos*, eye]

ophthalmology, *n.* the science of the eye, its structure, functions and diseases. **ophthalmologic, -ical,** *a.* **ophthalmologically,** *adv.* **ophthalmologist,** *n.*

ophthalmoscope, *n.* an instrument for examining the inner structure of the eye. **ophthalmoscopic, -ical,** *a.* **ophthalmoscopy,** *n.*

Ophüls, *n.* **Max** (adopted name of Max Oppenheimer) (1902–57), German film director. He moved to cinema from the theatre, and his work used intricate camera movements. He worked in Europe and the US, attracting much critical praise for films such as *Letter from an Unknown Woman* (1948) and *Lola Montes* (1955).

-opia, *comb. form* denoting a condition or defect of the eye, as in *myopia, diplopia*. [Gr. *ōps*, eye]

opiate, *n.* a medicine compounded with opium; a narcotic; anything serving to dull sensation, relieve uneasiness, or induce sleep. †*a.* soporific, narcotic, soothing; consisting of or containing opium. *v.t.* to treat with opium; to dull the sensibility of. [med. L *opiātus*, from L OPIUM]

opine, *v.i.*, *v.t.* to think, to suppose; to express an opinion. [L *opīnārī*]

opinion, *n.* a judgment, conviction, or belief falling short of positive knowledge; a view regarded as probable; views, sentiments, esp. those generally prevailing; one's judgment, belief or conviction with regard to a particular subject; the formal statement of a judge, counsel, physician or other expert on a question submitted to him; estimation, reputation; †opinionativeness. **a matter of opinion,** a matter open to debate or question. **opinion poll** POLL[1]. **opinionated, opinionative,** *a.* stiff or obstinate in one's opinions; dogmatic, stubborn. **opinionatedly, opinionatively,** *adv.* **opinionatedness, opinionativeness,** *n.* †**opinionist,** *n.* **opinionless,** *a.* [F, from L *opīniōnem*, nom. *-nio*, as prec.]

opistho-, *comb. form* behind. [Gr. *opisthen*, behind]

opisthobranchiate, *a.* belonging to the Opisthobranchiata, an order of gasteropods having the gills behind the heart. *n.* a gasteropod of this order. **opisthobranchism,** *n.* [Gr. *branchia*, gills]

opisthocoelian, *a.* hollow behind (of vertebrae). *n.* an opisthocoelian animal. **opisthocoelous,** *a.* [Gr. *koilos*, hollow]

opisthodomos, *n.* (*Gr. Ant.*) a chamber at the back of an ancient Greek temple. [Gr. *domos*, house]

opisthodont, *a.* having back teeth only. [Gr. *odous odontos*, tooth]

opisthogastric, *a.* (*Anat.*) situated behind the stomach.

opisthognathous, *a.* having retreating jaws or teeth.

opisthograph, *n.* (*Class. Ant.*) a manuscript having writing on the back as well as the front. **opisthographic,** *a.*

opium, *n.* a narcotic drug prepared from the dried exudation of the unripe capsules of the poppy, esp. the dried juice obtained from *Papaver somniferum*. **opium-den,** *n.* a place where opium is smoked. **opium-eater, -smoker,** *n.* one who habitually eats or smokes opium as a stimulant or narcotic. [L, from Gr. *opion*, dim. of *opos*, juice]

Opium Wars, *n.pl.* wars waged in the mid-19th cent. by the UK against China to enforce the opening of Chinese ports to trade in opium. Opium from British India paid for Britain's imports from China, such as porcelain, silk and, above all, tea, then obtainable in bulk only from China.

opoponax, *n.* the resinous juice from the root of *Opoponax chironium*, formerly used as a stimulant and in medicine; a gum-resin used in perfumery. [L and Gr. (*opos*, juice, *panax*, all-heal, cp. PANACEA)]

Oporto, *n.* alternative form of Porto in Portugal.

opossum, *n.* (*pl.* **-ssums, -ssum**) an American marsupial quadruped with a prehensile tail and a thumb on the hind-foot, most species of which are arboreal and one aquatic; applied to small marsupials of Australia and Tasmania.

opotherapy, *n.* the treatment of diseases with prepared extracts of glands or organs. [Gr. *opokos*, juice, *therapeia*, medical treatment]

Oppenheimer, *n.* **J(ulius) Robert** (1904–67), US physicist. As director of the Los Alamos Science Laboratory (1943–45), he was in charge of the development of the atomic bomb (the Manhattan Project). He objected to the development of the hydrogen bomb, and was declared a security risk (1953) by the US Atomic Energy Commission (AEG)

oppidan, *n.* at Eton College, a student not on the foundation who boards in the town; †a townsman. [L *oppidānus*, from *oppīdum*, town]

oppilate, *v.t.* (*Med.*) to block up, to obstruct. **oppilation,** *n.* [L *oppīlātus*, p.p. of *oppilāre* (OP-, *pīlāre*, to ram, from *pīlum*, pestle)]

opponent, *n.* one who opposes, esp. in a debate, argument or contest; an adversary, an antagonist. *a.* opposing, , *n.* [L *oppōnens -ntem*, pres.p. of *oppōnere* (OP-, *pōnere*, to put)]

opportune, *a.* situated, occurring, done etc. at a favourable moment, seasonable, timely, well-timed; fit, suitable. **opportunely,** *adv.* **opportuneness, opportunism,** *n.* utilizing circumstances or opportunities to gain one's ends, esp. the act or practice of shaping policy according to the needs or circumstances of the moment; acceptance of what may be realized as a partial advance towards an ideal; adaptation to circumstances, compromise; sacrifice of principle to expediency; political time-serving. **opportunist,** *n.* **opportunity,** *n.* an opportune or convenient time or occasion; a chance, an opening; a favourable circumstance.

oppose, *v.t.* to set against, to place or bring forward as an obstacle, adverse force, counterpoise, contrast or refutation (to); to set oneself against or act against, to resist, withstand, obstruct; to object to, to dispute; (*in p.p.*) opposite, contrasted. *v.i.* to offer resistance or objection. **opposable,** *a.* **opposability**, *n.* **opposeless**, *a.* (*poet.*). **opposer,** *n.* [F *opposer* (OP-, *poser,* to POSE[1])]

opposite, *a.* situated in front of or contrary in position (to); fronting, facing; antagonistic, adverse, contrary, diametrically different (to or from); (*Bot.*) placed in pairs on contrary sides on the same horizontal plane (of leaves on a stem). *n.* one who or that which is opposite; an opponent, an adversary; a contrary thing or term; (*Log.*) a contradictory; (*coll.*) a person facing one. *adv.* in an opposite place or direction. *prep.* opposite to; as a co-star with (in a play, film etc.). **opposite number,** *n.* a person in the corresponding position on another side; a counterpart. **oppositely,** *adv.* **oppositeness,** *n.*

opposition, *n.* the act or state of opposing; antagonism, resistance, hostility; the state of being opposite; antithesis, contrast, contrariety; an obstacle, a hindrance; the chief parliamentary party opposed to the party in office; (*Astron.*) the situation of two heavenly bodies when their longitudes differ by 180°; (*Log.*) difference of quantity or quality, or of both, in propositions having the same subject and predicate. **oppositional,** *a.* **oppositionist,** *a.*; *n.*

Opposition, Leader of His/Her Majesty's, in UK politics, official title (from 1937) of the leader of the largest opposition party in the House of Commons.

oppress, *v.t.* to overburden; to lie heavy on; to weigh down; to inflict hardships, cruelties, or exactions upon, to govern cruelly or unjustly; to tyrannize over; †to ravish. **oppression**, *n.* **oppressive,** *a.* overbearing, exacting, tyrannous; (of the weather) close, muggy, sultry. **oppressively,** *adv.* **oppressiveness,** *n.* **oppressor,** *n.* [OF *oppresser,* med. L *oppressāre* (OP-, *pressāre,* to PRESS[1])]

opprobrium, *n.* disgrace, infamy, ignominy, obloquy. **opprobrious,** *a.* abusive, vituperative, scornful. **opprobriously,** *adv.* **opprobriousness** [through OF *opprobrieux* or directly from late L *opprobriōsus,* from *opprobrium* (OP-, *probrum,* infamous act)]

oppugn, *v.t.* to oppose, to dispute, to call in question; †to fight against, to oppose, to resist. †**oppugnant,** *a.* †**oppugnancy,** †**oppugnation,** *n.* †**oppugner,** *n.* [F *oppugner,* L *oppugnāre* (OP-, *pugnāre,* to fight)]

†**opsimath,** *n.* one who acquires education late in life. **opsimathy**, *n.* [Gr. *opsimathēs* (*opse,* late, *manthanein,* to learn)]

opsomania, *n.* an abnormal craving for some special kind of food; morbid daintiness of the appetite. [Gr. *opson,* food; MANIA]

opsonin, *n.* an antibody in the blood which renders germs more vulnerable to destruction by phagocytes. **opsonic,** *a.* [Gr. *opsōnion,* victuals]

opt, *v.i.* to choose, to make a choice between. **to opt out,** to choose not to be involved in something; of a school, hospital etc., no longer to be under the control or management of a local authority. [OPTION]

opt., (*abbr.*) optative; optical; optician; optimum; optional.

optative, *a.* (*Gram.*) expressing a wish or desire. *n.* the optative mood; a verbal form expressing this. **optatively,** *adv.* [F *optatif,* late L *optātivus,* from *optāre,* to choose, opt]

optic, *a.* pertaining to vision or the eye. *n.* (*now facet.*) an eye; a glass device fixed to the neck of a bottle to measure out spirits. **optical character reader,** a device which scans and reads printed characters optically, translating them into binary code which can then be processed by a computer. **optical activity,** *n.* the ability (of some substances and their solutions) to rotate the plane of vibration of polarized light. **optical disk,** *n.* a small disk which can be read by a laser beam and can hold large quantities of information in digital form, used as a mass storage medium for computers. **optical fibre,** *n.* a thin glass fibre which can transmit light, used in communications and in fibre optics. **optical glass,** *n.* a high-quality glass used for making lenses. **optical microscope, telescope,** *n.* one used to view objects by the light they emit, as opposed to an electron microscope or radio telescope. **optic nerve,** *n.* a nerve of sight connecting the retina with the brain. **optically,** *adv.* **optician**, *n.* one who prescribes or dispenses spectacles and contact lenses to correct eye defects. **optics,** *n.sing.* the science of the nature, propagation, behaviour and function of light. [F *optique,* med. L *opticus,* Gr. *optikos,* from *optos,* seen, from *op-,* stem of *opsomai,* I shall see]

optimal OPTIMISM.

optimates, *n.pl.* the Roman patricians; any aristocracy or nobility. [L, from *optimus,* best]

optime, *n.* at Cambridge Univ., one of those ranked in the mathematical tripos immediately below the wranglers (the **senior optimes** in the second, and the **junior** in the third class). [L, very well, as prec.]

optimism, *n.* the view that the existing state of things is the best possible, orig. set forth by Leibnitz from the postulate of the omnipotence of God; the view that the universe is tending towards a better state and that good must ultimately prevail; a sanguine temperament, disposition to take a hopeful view of things. **optimal,** *a.* optimum. **optimally,** *adv.* **optimize, -ise,** *v.t.* to make the most of; to organize or execute with maximum efficiency; to write or restructure (a computer program) to achieve maximum efficiency. **optimist,** *n.* **optimistic,** *a.* **optimistically,** *adv.* **optimum,** *n.* (*pl.* **-ma**, **-mums**) the most favourable condition. [F *optimisme* (L *optimus,* best)]

option, *n.* the right, power or liberty of choosing; choice, preference; the thing chosen or preferred; the purchased right to deliver or call for the delivery of securities, land, commodities etc. at a specified rate within a specified time. **soft option,** an easy choice between alternatives. **to keep, leave one's options open,** to refrain from committing oneself. **local option** LOCAL. **optional,** *a.* open to choice; not compulsory. **optionally,** *adv.* [F, from L *optiōnem,* nom. *-tio,* rel. to *optāre,* to choose]

opt(o)-, *comb. form* pertaining to sight or optics. [Gr. *optos,* seen]

optometer, *n.* an instrument for ascertaining the range of vision and other powers of the eye. **optometry,** *n.*

optophone, *n.* a device for enabling the blind to read by sound.

opulent, *a.* rich, wealthy, affluent; abounding (in); abundant, profuse, copious. **opulence,** †**-cy,** *n.* **opulently,** *adv.* [L *opulentus,* from *ops opem,* pl. *opēs,* power, wealth]

opuntia, *n.* a genus of cactus plants comprising the prickly pear or Indian fig. [L, from *Opus,* a city of Locris, an ancient region of Greece]

opus, *n.* (*pl.* **opera**, **opuses**) a work, esp. a musical composition (*usu. written* **op.,** *pl.* **opp.**), esp. one numbered in order of publication. **opuscule, opusculum,** *n.* (*pl.* **-cules**, **-cula**) a minor literary or musical work.

Opus Dei, *n.* a Roman Catholic institution aiming at the dissemination of the ideals of Christian perfection, particularly in intellectual and influential circles. Founded in Madrid in 1928, and still powerful in Spain, it is now international. Its members may be of either sex, and lay or clerical.

OR, (*abbr.*) operational research; other ranks.

or[1], *conj.* a disjunctive particle introducing an alternative; used also to connect synonyms, words explaining, correcting etc. [contr. of obs. *other,* prob. from OE *oththe,* or]

†**or[2],** *adv.* ere, before; sooner than. [OE *ār,* early, with sense of the compar. *ær,* ERE]

or[3], *n.* (*Her.*) gold. [F, from L *aurum*]

-or, *suf.* denoting agency or condition as in *actor, author, creator, equator, favour, vigour.* [(1) through OF *-or, -ur,* or F *-eur,* or directly from L *-or, -ōrem,* denoting agency; (2) through OF *-eor, -eur,* from L *-ātor, -ētor,*

-itor, or *-ītor*, denoting agency; (3) A-F *-our*, OF *-or*, *-ur* (F *-eur*), L *-or -ōrem*, denoting nouns of conditions (in Eng. usu. *-our*, N Am. always *-or*)]

orache, orach, *n.* a plant of the goosefoot family used as a vegetable like spinach. [previously *arache*, F *arroche*, L *atriplicem*, nom. *atriplex*, Gr. *atraphaxus*]

oracle, *n.* the answer of a god or inspired priest to a request for advice or prophecy; the agency or medium giving such responses; the seat of the worship of a deity where these were sought; the sanctuary or holy of holies in the Jewish Temple; a person of profound wisdom, knowledge, or infallible judgment; an utterance regarded as profoundly wise, authoritative or infallible; a mysterious, ambiguous or obscure utterance; a divine messenger, a prophet. *v.i.* to speak as an oracle. †*v.t.* to utter as an oracle. **to work the oracle,** to secure a desired answer from the mouthpiece of an oracle by craft; to obtain some object by secret influence; to gain one's point by stratagem. **oracular, †-ulous,** *a.* **oracularly,** *adv.* **oracularity,** *n.* [F, from L *ōrāculum*, from *ōrāre*, to speak, to pray]

Oracle®, *n.* the teletext service of British Independent Television [acronym for *O*ptional *R*eception of *A*nnouncements by *C*oded *L*ine *E*lectronics]

oral, *a.* spoken, not written, by word of mouth; of, at or near the mouth; pertaining to the early stage of infantile sexual development when gratification is obtained from eating and sucking. *n.* an oral examination. **oracy,** *n.* skill in spoken communication and self-expression. **oral contraceptive,** *n.* a contraceptive pill. **oral history,** *n.* interviews with living people about past events, recorded and written down as historical evidence. **orally,** *adv.* [L *ōs ōris*, mouth, -AL]

Oran, *n.* (Arabic **Wahran**) a seaport in Algeria; population (1984) 663,500. Products include iron, textiles, footwear and processed food. It was part of the Ottoman Empire except 1509–1708 and 1732–91 under Spanish rule.

orange, *n.* the large roundish cellular pulpy fruit of *Citrus aurantium;* the evergreen tree, *C. aurantium;* the colour of the fruit, reddish-yellow. *a.* of the colour of an orange. **orangeade,** *n.* a drink made from orange-juice. **orange-blossom,** *n.* the blossom of the orange-tree (commonly worn in wreaths by brides). **orange-lily,** *n.* *Lilium croceum* or *L. bulbiferum*, var. *aurantium*, with large reddish or orange flowers. **orange-marmalade,** *n.* marmalade made from oranges. **orange-peel,** *n.* the rind of an orange; a pitted effect on porcelain. **orange squash,** *n.* a concentrated orange drink. **orange-stick,** *n.* a thin piece of orange-tree wood used for manicure purposes. **orange-tawny,** *a.* **orange-tip,** *n.* a variety of butterfly. **orangery,** *n.* a building designed for the cultivation of orange trees in a cool climate. [ME and OF *orenge*, *orange*, It. *narancia* (now *arancia*), Arab. *nāranj*]

Orange, *a.* pertaining to the Irish extreme-Protestant party or to the Society of Orangemen formed 1795 to uphold the Protestant ascendancy in Ireland. See ORANGEMAN. **Orangeism,** *n.* [town in department of Vaucluse, France, formerly seat of the principality of Orange, whence the Princes of Orange, including William III, King of England, took their title]

Orange, House of, the royal family of the Netherlands. The title is derived from the small principality of Orange, in S France, held by the family from the 8th cent. to 1713. They held considerable possessions in the Netherlands, to which, after 1530, was added the German county of Nassau.

Orange, Project, *n.* a plan (1980) for a white South African 'homeland' (Projek Oranje) to be established on the border between Orange Free State and the Northern Cape. No black person would be allowed to live or work there.

Orange Free State, *n.* a province of the Republic of South Africa. **area** 127,993 sq km/49,405 sq miles. **capital** Bloemfontein. **products** grain, wool, cattle, gold, oil from coal, cement, pharmaceuticals. **population** (1987) 1,863,000 (1,525,000 ethnic Africans).

Orangeman, *n.* a member of the Ulster Protestant **Orange Society,** established 1795 in opposition to the United Irishmen and the Roman Catholic secret societies. It was a revival of the Orange Institution (1688), formed in support of William (III) of Orange, the anniversary of whose victory over the Catholic James II at the Battle of the Boyne (1690) is commemorated by Protestants in parades on 12 July.

orang-utan, -outang, *n.* a large, red-haired, arboreal anthropoid ape, *Pongo pygmaeus*, of Borneo and Sumatra. [Malay *ōrang ūtan*, wild man of the woods]

orarium, *n.* a linen napkin or neck-cloth, a stole; a scarf sometimes wound round the handle of the mediaeval crozier. **orarion,** *n.* in the Greek church, a deacon's stole, wider than the orarium. [L, from *ōs ōris*, mouth, face]

Orasul Stalin, *n.* name (1948–56) of the Romanian town Braşov.

orate ORATION.

oration, *n.* a formal speech, treating of some important subject in elevated language; (*Gram.*) language, discourse. **oblique oration** OBLIQUE. **orate,** *v.i.* to make an oration; to talk at length. **orator,** *n.* one who delivers an oration; an eloquent speaker; an officer at a University who acts as public speaker on ceremonial occasions; †(*Law*) a petitioner or complainant. **†oratorial,** *a.* oratorical; pertaining to an oratorio. **oratorian** ORATORY[2]. **oratorical,** *a.* **oratorically,** *adv.* **oratorize, -ise,** *v.i.* **oratress, -trix,** *n. fem.* **oratory[1],** *n.* the art of public speaking, rhetoric; eloquence; rhetorical language. [L *ōrātio*, from *ōrāre*, to speak]

oratorio, *n.* (*pl.* **-ios**) a musical composition for voices and instruments, usually semi-dramatic in character, and treating of a scriptural theme. [It., from L *ōrātōrium*, ORATORY[2]]

oratory[1] ORATION.

oratory[2], *n.* a small chapel, esp. one for private devotions; (*usu. cap.*) one of several congregations of Roman Catholic priests living in community without vows, the first of which was established at Rome by St Philip Neri in 1564 to preach and hold services among the people. **Oratorian,** *a.* belonging to any congregation of the Oratory. *n.* a member of any congregation of the Oratory. [L *ōrātōrium*, neut. of *ōrātōrius*, from *ōrāre*, to pray]

orb, *n.* a sphere, a globe; a heavenly body; an eye or eyeball; a circle, ring or orbit; anything circular; the globe forming part of the regalia; (*fig.*) a round or complete whole. *v.t.* to form into a circle; to surround, encircle or enclose in an orb. *v.i.* to become round or like an orb. **orbicular,** *a.* **orbicularity,** *n.* **orbicularly,** *adv.* **orbiculate,** *a.* **†orbiculation,** *n.* **†orby,** *a.* **orbless,** *a.* **orblet,** *n.* [L *orbis*, ring]

Orbison, *n.* **Roy** (1936–88), US pop singer and songwriter, noted for his operatic ballad style on songs like 'Only The Lonely' (1960) and 'Running Scared' (1961).

orbit, *n.* (*Anat., Zool., etc.*) the bony cavity of the eye; the ring or border round the eye in insects, birds etc.; the path of a celestial body around another; a course or sphere of action, a career; the path of an electron around the nucleus of an atom. *v.t.* to move in a curved path around; to circle (a planet etc.) in space; to send into an orbit. *v.i.* to revolve in an orbit. **orbital,** *a.* **orbiter,** *n.* a spacecraft designed to orbit a planet etc. [L *orbita*, a track, as prec.]

orc, *n.* a whale of the genus *Orca*, esp. *O. gladiator*, a grampus; a marine animal, a sea-monster, an ogre. [F *orque*, L *orca*]

Orcadian, *a.* pertaining to the Orkney Islands. *n.* a native or inhabitant of these. [L *Orcades*, Orkney Islands]

orcein, *n.* the colouring principle of archil and cudbear.

orchard, *n.* an enclosure containing fruit trees, or a plantation of these. **orchard-house,** *n.* a glass-house for fruit trees. **orchardman, orchardist,** *n.* **orcharding,** *n.* [OE *orceard*, *ortgeard* (L *hortus*, garden)]

orchestra, *n.* in an ancient Greek theatre, the semicircular space between the stage and the seats for the spectators, where the chorus danced and sang; the place for the band, or band and chorus, in modern concert-rooms, theatres etc.; the body of musicians in a theatre or concert-room; the music performed by them. **orchesis**, *n.* the art of dancing. **orchestic**, *a.* **orchestics,** *n.* orchesis. **orchestra stalls,** *n.pl.* seats just behind the orchestra in a theatre. **orchestral**, *a.* **orchestrate,** *v.t.* to compose or arrange (music) for an orchestra. **orchestration,** *n.* **orchestrina**, **orchestrion**, **orchestrionette**, *n.* a mechanical musical instrument designed on the principle of the barrel-organ to give the effect of an orchestra. [L and Gr. *orchēstra,* from *orcheesthai,* to dance]

orchid, *n.* one of a large order of mono-cotyledonous plants, the Orchidaceae, of which the genus *Orchis* is the type, characterized by tuberous roots and flowers usually of a fantastic shape and brilliant colours in which the pistils and stamens are united with the floral axis. **orchidaceous**, **orchidean**, **orchideous,** *a.* **orchidist,** *n.* **orchido-,** *comb. form* **orchidology**, *n.* **orchidomania**, *n.* **orchis**, *n.* the typical genus of the Orchidaceae, comprising those belonging to temperate regions; a plant of this genus; (*loosely*) an orchid. [from L and Gr. *orchisios,* testicle, an orchis, from the shape of the tubers]

orchidectomy, orchiectomy, *n.* the surgical removal of one or both testicles.

orchil, orchilla, *n.* a violet, purple or red colouring-matter obtained from various lichens, esp. *Roccella tinctoria;* this and other species of lichen yielding such colouring-matter. [OF *orchel,* etym. doubtful (cp. ARCHIL)]

orchis ORCHID.

orchitis, *n.* inflammation of the testicles. **orchitic**, *a.* [Gr. *orchis,* a testicle; -ITIS]

orcin, *n.* a colourless crystalline compound obtained from several species of lichens, yielding colours used for dyeing on treatment with various reagents. [as prec.]

Orczy, *n.* **Baroness Emmusca** (1865–1947), Hungarian-born British novelist, who wrote the historical adventure *The Scarlet Pimpernel* (1905). The foppish Sir Percy Blakeney, the bold rescuer of victims of the French Revolution, appeared in many sequels.

ord., (*abbr.*) ordained; ordinal; ordinance; ordinary.

ordain, *v.t.* to set apart for an office or duty, to appoint and consecrate, to confer Holy Orders on; to decree, to establish, to destine. **ordainable,** *a.* **ordainer,** *n.* **ordainment,** *n.* [OF *ordener* (F *ordonner*), L *ordināre,* from *ordo -dinis,* ORDER]

ordeal, *n.* the ancient practice of referring disputed questions of criminality to supernatural decision, by subjecting a suspected person to physical tests by fire, boiling water, battle etc.; an experience testing endurance, patience, courage etc. [OE *ordēl, ordāl* (cp. Dut. *oordeel,* G *Urteil*), rel. to *dǣlan,* to DEAL[1], *adǣlan,* to divide, to allot, to judge]

order, *n.* regular or methodical disposition or arrangement; sequence, succession, esp. as regulated by a system or principle; normal, proper or right condition; a state of efficiency, a condition suitable for working; tidiness, absence of confusion or disturbance; established state of things, general constitution of the world; customary mode of procedure, esp. the rules and regulations governing an assembly or meeting; a rule, regulation; a mandate, an injunction, an authoritative direction; a direction to supply specified commodities or to carry out specified work; a signed document instructing a person or persons to pay money or deliver property; a tier; a social class, rank or degree; kind, sort, quality; a class or body of persons united by some common purpose; a fraternity of monks or friars, or formerly of knights, bound by the same rule of life; a grade of the Christian ministry; (*pl.*) the clerical office or status; a body usu. instituted by a sovereign, organized in grades like the mediaeval orders of knights, to which distinguished persons are admitted as an honour; the insignia worn by members of this; any of the nine grades of angels and archangels; a system of parts, ornaments and proportions of columns etc., distinguishing styles of architecture, esp. Classical, as the Doric, Ionic, Corinthian, Tuscan and Composite; in the Roman Catholic Church, a sacrament bestowing grace for the performance of sacred duties conferred on those entering any of the seven grades or orders of priestly office; (*Math.*) degree of complexity; (*Biol.*) a division below that of class and above that of family and genus. *v.t.* to put in order; to regulate; to manage; to ordain; to direct, to command; to arrange beforehand; to instruct (a person, firm etc.) to supply goods or perform work; to direct the supplying, doing or making of. *v.i.* to give orders. **by order,** according to direction by proper authority. **Holy Orders,** the different ranks of the Christian ministry; the clerical office. **a tall, large order,** a difficult or demanding task. **in order,** properly or systematically arranged; in due sequence. **in, of the order of,** approximately the size or quantity specified. **in order to,** to the end that; so as to. **on order,** having been ordered but not yet arrived. **order of battle,** the disposition of troops for attack or defence. **Order of Merit,** an order conferred on British servicemen or civilians for eminence in any field. **order of the day,** business arranged beforehand, esp. the programme of business in a legislative assembly; the prevailing state of things. **out of order,** disarranged; untidy; not consecutive; not systematically arranged; not fit for working or using. **to order,** according to, or in compliance with, an order. **to order about,** to send from one place to another; to domineer over. **to order arms,** (*Mil.*) to bring rifles vertically against the right side with the butts resting on the ground. **to take orders,** to be ordained. **order-book,** *n.* a book, usu. with counterfoils and detachable leaves, on which orders for goods, work etc. are written; a book in which motions to be submitted to the House of Commons must be entered. **order-clerk,** *n.* one appointed to enter orders. **order form,** *n.* a printed paper with blanks for a customer to enter goods to be supplied. **order paper,** *n.* a paper on which the order of business, esp. in Parliament, is written or printed. **orderer,** *n.* **ordering,** *n.* arrangement, disposition; ordination of priests etc. †**orderless**, *a.* **orderly**[1], *a.* in order; methodical, regular; keeping or disposed to keep order, free from disorder or confusion; pertaining to orders and their execution. *adv.* duly, regularly. **orderly-bin,** *n.* a box for street-refuse. **orderliness,** *n.* [ME and OF *ordre,* L *ordinem,* nom. *ordo*]

orderly[2], *n.* a soldier who attends on an officer to carry orders, messages etc.; a male hospital attendant. **orderly book,** *n.* a book for regimental orders. **orderly officer,** *n.* the officer of the day. **orderly-room,** *n.* a room in barracks used as the office for company or regimental business.

ordinaire, *n.* wine of ordinary grade, *vin ordinaire.* [F, ordinary]

ordinal, *a.* denoting order or position in a series. *n.* a number denoting this, e.g. first, second; a book containing orders, rules, rubrics etc., esp. forms for ordination in the Church of England. [late L *ordinālis,* as prec.]

ordinance, *n.* an order, decree or regulation laid down by a constituted authority; an established rule, rite or ceremony etc. **ordinant,** *a.* ordaining, regulating, directing. *n.* one who confers orders. **ordinand**, *n.* one preparing for Holy Orders. [OF *ordenance* (F *ordonnance*), med. L *ordinantia,* from *ordināre,* to ORDAIN]

ordinand ORDAIN.

ordinary, *a.* usual, habitual, customary, regular, normal, not exceptional or unusual; commonplace; mediocre; having immediate or ex officio jurisdiction; ill-looking, plain. *n.* a rule or order, as of the Mass; a tavern or inn meal prepared at a fixed rate for all comers; hence, an eating-house; (*Her.*) one of the simplest and commonest charges, esp. the chief, pale, fesse, bend, bar, chevron, cross and saltire; (*Sc. Law*) a judge of the Court of Session; a bishop or his deputy, esp. sitting as ecclesiastical judge; the ordinary run of humanity, course of life, procedure etc. **in ordinary,** in actual and constant service. **out of the ordinary,** exceptional. **ordinary level** o. **ordinary seaman,** *n.* a sailor not fully qualified as able seaman. **ordinary shares,** *n.pl.* shares in a company which pay dividends according to profit only after the claims of preference shares have been met, cp. PREFERENCE SHARES. **ordinarily,** *adv.* **ordinariness,** *n.* **ordinaryship,** *n.* [L *ordinārius,* from *ordo -dinis,* ORDER]

ordinate, *a.* arranged in a row or rows; ordinary, regular, proper. *n.* a line drawn from a point parallel to one of a pair of reference lines, called the coordinate axes, and meeting the other. **ordination,** *n.* the act of ordaining; the state of being ordained or appointed; arrangement in order, classification; appointment, ordainment. †**ordinative,** *a.* †**ordinator,** *n.* **ordinee,** *n.* one newly ordained. [L *ordinātus,* p.p. of *ordināre,* to ORDAIN]

ordnance, *n.* heavy guns, cannon, artillery; the department of the public service dealing with military stores and equipment, except those pertaining to the quartermaster's department. **Ordnance datum,** *n.* the level taken as the basis for the Ordnance Survey, since 1921 the mean sea level at Newlyn, Cornwall. **Ordnance Survey,** *n.* the (Government map-making body responsible for the) survey of Great Britain and Northern Ireland. [var. of ORDINANCE]

Ordovician, *n.* the middle period of the lower Palaeozoic era (505–438 million years ago), which followed the Cambrian period and during which animal life was confined to the sea. [*Ordovices,* ancient British people]

ordure, *n.* excrement, dung, filth. [F, from OF *ord,* foul, L *horridus,* see HORRID]

ore, *n.* a natural mineral substance from which metal may be profitably extracted; (*poet.*) precious metal. [OE *ār,* brass (cp. Icel. *eir,* Goth. *aiz,* L. *aes aeris*), confused with *ōra,* unwrought metal (cp. Dut. *oer*)]

öre, *n.* (*pl.* **öre**) a monetary unit in Sweden and (**øre**) Norway and Denmark.

oread, *n.* a mountain nymph. [L *orēas -ados,* Gr. *oreias,* from *oros,* mountain]

orectic, *a.* of or pertaining to appetite or desire; appetitive. **orexis,** *n.* [Gr. *orektikos,* from *orektos,* stretched out, from *oregein,* to stretch out, to grasp after, to desire]

oregano, *n.* a plant of the genus *Origanum,* a genus of aromatic labiate herbs and shrubs comprising the wild marjoram. [N Am. Sp. *orégano,* wild marjoram, from L *origanum,* Gr. *origanon*]

Oregon, *n.* a state of the northwestern US, on the Pacific; nickname Beaver State. **area** 251,500 sq km/97,079 sq miles. **capital** Salem. **towns** Portland, Eugene. **products** wheat, livestock, timber, gold, silver, nickel, electronics. **population** (1987) 2,690,000.

Orestes, *n.* in Greek legend, the son of Agamemnon and Clytemnestra.

orfe, *n.* a small semi-domesticated yellow or golden-coloured fish of the carp family. [Gr. *orphos,* a sea-perch]

Orff, *n.* **Carl** (1895–1982), German composer, an individual stylist whose work is characterized by sharp dissonances and percussion. Among his compositions are the scenic cantata *Carmina Burana* (1937) and the opera *Antigone* (1949).

Orford, 1st Earl of, *n.* title of the British politician Robert Walpole.

organ, *n.* a musical wind-instrument composed of an assemblage of pipes sounded by means of a bellows and played by keys; a wind-instrument having some resemblance to this, played by keys or other mechanism; an instrument; a medium or agent of communication etc., as a newspaper or other periodical; a mental faculty regarded as an instrument; the human voice with regard to its musical quality, power etc.; a part of an animal or vegetable body performing some definite vital function. **great organ,** the principal organ of a large composite organ, comprising the main flue-work and having a separate keyboard. **mouth-organ** MOUTH. **organ-blower,** *n.* **organ-builder,** *n.* **organ-grinder,** *n.* a player on a barrel-organ. **organ-loft,** *n.* **organ-piano,** *n.* a piano with a series of small hammers for striking the strings repeatedly and giving a sustained organ-like sound. **organ-pipe,** *n.* one of the sounding-pipes of a pipe-organ. **organ-screen,** *n.* a screen or partition, usu. between the nave and the choir, on which the organ is placed in a large church. **organ-stop,** *n.* the handle by which a set of pipes in an organ is put in or out of action; the set of pipes or reeds of a certain quality controlled by this. **organelle,** *n.* a unit in a cell having a particular structure and function. **organist,** *n.* one who plays a church or other organ. [ME and OF *organe* (F *orgue*), L *organa,* pl. treated as sing. of *organum,* Gr. *organon,* rel. to *ergon,* work]

organdie, *n.* a stiff, light transparent muslin. **organza,** *n.* a thin transparent fabric of silk, rayon or nylon. [F *organdi,* etym. doubtful]

organic, *a.* of or pertaining to a bodily organ or organs; of, pertaining to, or of the nature of organisms or plants or animals; pertaining to or affecting an organ or organs (of diseases etc.); (*Chem.*) existing as parts of or derived from organisms; hence, of hydrocarbons and their derivatives whether of natural or artificial origin; of or pertaining to an organized system; organized, systematic, coordinated; structural, fundamental, inherent, not accidental; vital, not mechanical; of vegetables etc., grown without artificial fertilizers, pesticides etc. **organic chemistry,** *n.* see separate article below. **organic compounds,** *n. pl.* chemical compounds containing carbon combined with oxygen and other elements. †**organical,** *a.* organic; instrumental; performed on an organ (of music). **organically,** *adv.* †**organicalness,** *n.* **organicism,** *n.* (*Biol.*) the theory that all things in nature have an organic basis. [L *organicus,* Gr. *organikos* (ORGAN, -IC)]

organic chemistry, *n.* the chemistry of carbon compounds, particularly the more complex carbon compounds. The basis of organic chemistry is the ability of carbon to form long chains of atoms, branching chains, rings and other complex structures. In a typical organic compound, each carbon atom forms a bond with each of its neighbouring carbon atoms in the chain or ring, and two more with hydrogen atoms (carbon has a valency of four). Other atoms that may be involved in organic molecules include oxygen and nitrogen. Compounds containing only carbon and hydrogen are known as hydrocarbons.

organism, *n.* an organized body consisting of mutually dependent parts fulfilling functions necessary to the life of the whole; an animal, a plant; organic structure; a whole having mutually related parts analogous to those of a living body.

organist ORGAN.

Organization for Economic Cooperation and Development, Paris-based international organization of 24 industrialized countries which coordinates member states' economic policy strategies. The OECD's subsidiary bodies include the International Energy Agency (1974), set up in the face of a world oil crisis.

Organization of African Unity, an association established 1963 to eradicate colonialism and improve economic, cultural and political cooperation in Africa; headquarters Addis Ababa, Ethiopia. The secretary-general is Salim Ahmed Salim (deputy prime minister of Tanzania). The French-speaking **Joint African and Mauritian Organization** (*Organisation Commune Africaine et Mauritienne*) (1962) works within the framework of the OAU for African solidarity; headquarters Yaoundé, Cameroon.

Organization of American States, an association founded 1948 by a charter signed by representatives of 30 North, Central and South American states. Canada held observer status from 1972 and became a full member 1989. It aims to maintain peace and solidarity within the hemisphere, and is also concerned with the social and economic development of Latin America. Its headquarters are in Washington, DC, US. It is based on the International Union of American Republics (1890–1910) and Pan-American Union (1910–48), set up to encourage friendly relations between countries of North and South America.

Organization of Central American States, (*Organizacion de Estados Centro Americanos*) international association promoting common economic, political, educational and military aims in Central America. The first organization, est. 1951, was superseded in 1962. Its members are Costa Rica, El Salvador, Guatemala, Honduras and Nicaragua, provision being made for Panama to join at a later date. The permanent headquarters is in Guatemala City.

Organization of the Petroleum Exporting Countries, a body established 1960 to coordinate price and supply policies of oil-producing states, and also to improve the position of Third World states by forcing Western states to open their markets to the resultant products. Its concerted action in raising prices in the 1970s triggered worldwide recession but also lessened demand so that its influence was reduced by the mid-1980s. OPEC members in 1986 were: Algeria, Ecuador, Gabon, Indonesia, Iran, Iraq, Kuwait, Libya, Nigeria, Qatar, Saudi Arabia, United Arab Emirates and Venezuela.

organize, -ise, *v.t.* to form or furnish with organs; to make organic, to make into an organism, to make into a living part, structure or being; to correlate the parts of and make into an organic whole; to put into proper working order; to arrange or dispose things or a body of people in order to carry out some purpose effectively; (*Mus.*) to render or sing in parts. *v.i.* to become organic; to unite into an organic whole. **organizable, -isable,** *a.* **organization, -isation,** *n.* the act of organizing; the state of being organized; an organized system, body or society. **organizational, -isational,** *a.* **organizer, -iser,** *n.*

organo-, *comb. form* organ; organic.

organogenesis, organogeny, *n.* the development of organs in animals and plants.

organography, *n.* a description of the organs of plants and animals. **organographist,** *n.*

organoleptic, *a.* affecting the bodily or sense organs; relating to substances that stimulate the senses (e.g. taste and smell).

organology, *n.* the branch of biology or physiology treating of the organs of the body. **organological,** *a.* **organologist,** *n.*

organometallic, *a.* of, being or relating to a compound containing linked carbon and metal atoms.

organon, *n.* a system of principles and rules of investigation, deduction and demonstration regarded as an instrument of knowledge.

organotherapy, *n.* the treatment of disease by the administration of one or more hormones in which the body is deficient.

organza ORGANDIE.

organzine, *n.* silk thread made of several threads twisted together in a direction contrary to that of the strands, thrown silk; a fabric made therefrom. [F *organsin,* It. *organzino,* etym. unknown]

orgasm, *n.* immoderate excitement; a paroxysm of excitement or passion; violent excitation and turgescence of an organ, as in sexual coition; the culminating excitement in the sexual act. **orgasmic, orgastic,** *a.* [Gr. *orgaein,* to swell (for *-sm* cp. SPASM]

orgeat, *n.* a liquor made from barley or sweet almonds and orange-flower water. [F, from *orge,* L *hordeum,* barley]

†orgulous, *a.* proud, haughty. [OF *orguillus* (F *orgueilleux*), from *orgueil,* pride, prob. from Teut.]

orgy, *n.* (*pl.* **-gies**) secret and licentious rites, the worship of Dionysus or Bacchus etc.; a wild revel, a drunken carouse; (*fig.*) a bout of indulgence; (*pl.*) revelry, debauchery. **orgiastic, †orgiastical,** *a.* [orig. in pl. only, F *orgeis,* L and Gr. *orgia*]

oribi, *n.* (*pl.* **-bis**) a small fawn-coloured antelope of S and E Africa. [Afrikaans]

oriel, *n.* a projecting polygonal recess with a window or windows, usu. built out from an upper storey and supported on corbels or a pier. **oriel window,** *n.* the window of such a structure. [OF *oriol,* etym. doubtful]

orient, *n.* the East, the countries east of S Europe and the Mediterranean; (*poet.*) the eastern sky; the peculiar lustre of a pearl of the finest quality; an orient pearl. *a.* (*poet.*) rising, ascending, as the sun; (*poet.*) eastern, Oriental; bright, shining; lustrous, perfect, without a flaw (of pearls). *v.t.* to orientate. **oriency,** *n.* **Oriental,** *a.* situated in or pertaining to the East or the (esp. Asiatic) countries east of S Europe and the Mediterranean; derived from or characteristic of the civilization etc. of the East; (*poet.*) easterly, orient; excellent, precious (of pearls). *n.* a native or inhabitant of the East. **Orientalism,** *n.* an idiom or custom peculiar to the East; knowledge of Oriental languages and literature. **Orientalist,** *n.* **Orientality,** *n.* **orientalize, -ise,** *v.t., v.i.* **orientalization, -isation,** *n.* **Orientally,** *adv.* [F, from L *orientem,* nom. *-ens,* pres.p. of *orīrī,* to rise]

orientate, *v.t.* to orient; to place (a church) so that the chancel points due east; to bury (a body) with feet towards the east; to determine the position of, with reference to the east and accordingly to all points of the compass; to find the bearings of; to find or correct one's mental relations and principles. *v.i.* to turn or face towards the east. **orientation,** *n.* the act of orientating oneself; the determination of one's position, mental or physical, with regard to the surroundings; (*Psych.*) awareness of one's temporal, social and physical situation. **orientator,** *n.* an instrument for orientating. **orienteer,** *v.i.* to take part in orienteering. *n.* one who orienteers. **orienteering,** *n.* a sport in which the contestants race cross-country following checkpoints located by a map and compass.

orifice, *n.* an opening or aperture, as of a tube etc.; a perforation, a mouth, a vent. [F, from late L *orificium* (*ōs ōris,* mouth, *facere,* to make)]

oriflamme, *n.* the ancient royal banner of France, orig. the red silk banderole of the Abbey of St Denis handed to the early kings in setting out for war; (*fig.*) a symbol of lofty endeavour; a bright or glorious object. [F (*or,* L *aurum,* gold, *flamme,* FLAME)]

orig., (*abbr.*) origin; original(ly).

origami, *n.* the (traditionally Japanese) art of paper folding. [Jap. *ori,* a fold, *kami,* paper]

origan, origanum OREGANO.

Origen, *n.* (*c.* 185–*c.* 254), Christian theologian, born in Alexandria, who produced a fancifully allegorical interpretation of the Bible. He castrated himself to ensure his celibacy.

origin, *n.* beginning, commencement or rise (of anything); derivation, source; extraction, ancestry; ground, foundation, occasion; (*Math.*) the point where coordinate axes intersect; (*Anat.*) the point of attachment of a muscle, opposite to its insertion. **originable,** *a.* **original,** *a.* of or pertaining to the origin, beginning, or first stage; first, primary, primitive; initial, innate; not copied or imitated, not produced by translation; fresh, novel; able to devise, produce, think or act for oneself; inventive, creative. *n.* the pattern, the archetype, the first copy; that from which a work is copied or translated; the language in which a work is written; an eccentric person; †origin, derivation, cause, primitive stock, ancestry. **original sin,** the sin of Adam in eating the forbidden fruit; the innate depravity of man. **originality,** *n.* **originally,** *adv.* **originate,** *v.t.* to be the origin of; to cause to begin, to bring into existence. *v.i.* to rise, to begin; to have origin (in, from or with). **origination,** *n.* **originative,** *a.* **originator,** *n.* [F *origine,* L *orīginem,* nom. *orīgo;* rel. to *orīrī,* to rise]

orinasal, *a.* of or pertaining to or sounded by the mouth and nose. *n.* a vowel sounded both by mouth and nose, as the nasal vowels in French. [L *ōri-, ōs,* mouth, NASAL]

Orinoco, *n.* a river in N South America, flowing for about 2400 km/1500 miles through Venezuela and forming for about 320 km/200 miles the boundary with Colombia; tributaries include the Guaviare, Meta, Apure, Ventuari, Caura and Caroni. It is navigable by large steamers for 1125 km/700 miles from its Atlantic delta; rapids obstruct the upper river.

oriole, *n.* a bird of the European genus *Oriolus,* esp. *O. galbula,* with bright-yellow and black plumage; a bird of the American genus *Icterus,* a hangbird. [med. L *oriolus,* L *aureolus,* from *aureus,* golden, from *aurum,* gold]

Orion[1], *n.* (*Astron.*) a very prominent constellation in the equatorial region of the sky, representing the hunter of Greek mythology. It contains the bright stars Betelgeuse and Rigel, as well as a distinctive row of three stars that make up Orion's belt. Beneath the belt, marking the sword of Orion, is the Orion nebula; nearby is one of the most distinctive dark nebulae, the Horsehead. **Orion's hound,** *n.* the star Sirius. [L and Gr., a giant in Gr. myth.]

Orion[2], *n.* in Greek mythology, a giant of Boeotia, famed as a hunter.

Orion nebula, *n.* a luminous cloud of gas and dust 1500 light years away, in the constellation Orion, from which stars are forming. It is about 15 light years in diameter, and contains enough gas to make a cluster of thousands of stars. At the nebula's centre is a group of hot young stars, called the Trapezium, which make the surrounding gas glow. It is visible to the naked eye as a misty patch below the belt of Orion.

orismology, *n.* the branch of science concerned with definitions and the explanation of technical terms. **orismologic, -ical,** *a.* [Gr. *horismos,* definition, from *horizein,* to define, from *horos,* boundary]

orison, *n.* a prayer, a supplication. [OF (F *oraison*), from L *ōrātiōnem,* nom. *-tio,* from *ōrāre,* to pray]

Orissa, *n.* a state of NE India. **area** 155,800 sq km/ 60,139 sq miles. **capital** Bhubaneswar. **towns** Cuttack, Rourkela. **products** rice, wheat, oilseed, sugar, timber, chromite, dolomite, graphite, iron. **population** (1981) 26,272,000. **language** Oriya (official). **religion** Hindu 90%.

Oriya, *n.* a member of a people living in Orissa in India; the language of Orissa.

Orkney Causeway, *n.* a construction in N Scotland put up in World War I, completed 1943, joining four of the Orkney Islands, built to protect the British fleet from intrusion through the eastern entrances to Scapa Flow.

Orkney Islands, *n.* a island group off the NE coast of Scotland. **area** 970 sq km/375 sq miles. **towns** administrative headquarters Kirkwall, on Mainland (Pomona). **products** fishing and farming, wind power (Burgar Hill has the world's most productive wind generator; blades 60 m/197 ft diameter). **population** (1987) 19,000.

Orlando, *n.* **Vittorio Emanuele** (1860–1952), Italian politician, prime minister (1917–19). He attended the Paris Peace Conference after World War I, but dissatisfaction with his handling of the Adriatic settlement led to his resignation. He initially supported Mussolini, but was in retirement (1925–46), when he returned to the assembly and then the senate.

Orlando Furioso, *n.* a poem by the Italian Renaissance writer Ariosto, published 1532 as a sequel to Boiardo's *Orlando Innamorato* (1441–94). The poem describes the unrequited love of Orlando for Angelica, set against the war between Saracens (Arabs) and Christians during Charlemagne's reign. It influenced Shakespeare, Byron and Milton, and is considered to be the perfect poetic expression of the Italian Renaissance.

orle, *n.* (*Her.*) a bearing in the form of a narrow band round the edge of a shield; †(*Arch.*) a fillet under the ovolo of a capital. [F, from med. L *orla,* dim. of *ora,* border]

Orleans, *n.* a cloth of cotton and wool used for women's dresses; a kind of plum. **Orleanist,** *n.* an adherent of the branch of the French royal family descended from the Duke of Orleans, younger brother of Louis XIV, one of whom, Louis Philippe, reigned as King of the French (1830–48). *a.* of or pertaining to this house. **Orleanism,** *n.* **Orleanistic,** *a.* [city in France]

Orlon®, *n.* (a fabric made from) acrylic fibre.

orlop, orlop deck, *n.* the lowest deck of a vessel having three or more decks. [Dut. *overloop,* a covering, rel. to *overloopen* (OVER, *loopen,* to run, see LEAP]

Orly, *n.* a suburb of Paris in the *département* of Val-de-Marne; population (1982) 17,000. There is an international airport.

ormer, *n.* a sea-ear or ear-shell, esp. *Haliotis tuberculata,* an edible gasteropod mollusc. [Channel Is. var. of F *ormier* (*oreille-de-mer,* sea-ear)]

ormolu, *n.* orig. leaf-gold ground and used as a pigment for decorating furniture etc.; a gold-coloured alloy of copper, zinc and tin, used for cheap jewellery; metallic ware, furniture etc. decorated with this. [F *ormoulu* (*or,* gold, *moulu,* p.p. of *moudre,* to grind)]

Ormuzd, *n.* the good principle in the Zoroastrian religious dualism, opp. to Ahriman. [Pers. *Ahuramazdah,* the wise lord]

ornament, *n.* a thing or part that adorns; an embellishment, a decoration; ornamentation; a person, possession or quality that reflects honour or credit; a mark of distinction, a badge; †furniture or accessories, esp. such as pertain to a church or worship; (*Mus.*) decorations such as trills, mordents etc. to be improvised. *v.t.*, to adorn, to decorate, to embellish. **ornaments rubric,** *n.* the short rubric respecting the ornaments to be used in church immediately preceding the order for Morning and Evening Prayer in the Prayer Book. **ornamental,** *a.* **ornamentalism,** *n.* **ornamentalist,** *n.* **ornamentally,** *adv.* **ornamentation,** *n.* **ornamenter,** *n.* [OF *ornement,* L *ornāmentum,* from *ornāre,* to equip]

ornate, *a.* adorned, ornamented, richly embellished; florid, elaborately finished (of literary style etc.). **ornately,** *adv.* **ornateness,** *n.* [L *ornātus,* p.p. of *ornāre,* see prec.]

ornery, *a.* (*N Am., coll.*) mean, low. [corr. of ORDINARY]

ornith- ORNITH(O)-.

Ornithodelphia, *n.pl.* (*Zool.*) a sub-class of oviparous mammals comprising the Monotremata. **ornithodelphian, ornithodelphic, ornithodelphid, ornithodelphous,** *a.* [Gr. *delphus,* womb]

ornithology, *n.* the branch of zoology dealing with birds. **ornithological,** *a.* **ornithologist,** *n.*

ornithopter, *n.* an aeroplane driven by power supplied by the aviator and not by an engine.

Ornithorhyncus, *n.* a genus of monotremes containing the duck-billed platypus; the duck-billed platypus, an Australian aquatic oviparous mammal. [Gr. *rhunchos,* a bill]

ornith(o)-, *comb. form* pertaining to birds. [Gr *ornis -ithos,* bird]

ornithoscopy, *n.* observation of birds for purposes of divination.

oro-, *comb. form* pertaining to mountains. [Gr. *oros,* a mountain]

orogenesis, orogeny, *n.* the process of forming mountains. **orogenetic, orogenic,** *a.*

orography, *n.* the branch of physical geography treating of mountains and mountain systems. **orographic,** *a.*

orohippus, *n.* (*Palaeont.*) a fossil quadruped considered to be the ancestor of the horse. [Gr. *hippos,* a horse]

oroide, *n.* an alloy of copper and zinc, resembling gold in appearance, used for cheap jewellery. [F or L *aurum,* gold, -OID]

orometer, *n.* an instrument for measuring the height of mountains.

oropesa float, *n.* a float used in mine-sweeping to support the sweeping wire between two trawlers.

orotund, *a.* characterized by fullness and resonance; rich and musical (said of the voice and utterance); pompous, magniloquent, inflated. *n.* orotund quality of voice. [L *ore rotundo,* lit. with round mouth]

Orozco, *n.* **José Clemente** (1883–1949), Mexican painter, known for his murals inspired by the Mexican revolution of 1910, such as the series in the Palace of Government, Guadalajara, 1949.

orphan, *n.* a child bereft of one parent, or of both. *a.* bereft of one parent, or of both. **orphanage,** *n.*

orphan condition; an institution for bringing up orphans. **orphaned,** *a.* **orphanhood, orphanism,** *n.* **orphanize, -ise,** *v.t.* [late L *orphanus,* Gr. *orphanos,* destitute, bereaved, from *orphus* (cp. L *orbus*)]

Orphean, *a.* pertaining to Orpheus, melodious, enchanting. **Orphic,** *a.* pertaining to Orpheus or the mysteries supposed to be founded by him; oracular, mysterious. **Orphism,** *n.* [L *Orphēus,* Gr. *Orpheios*]

Orpheus, *n.* mythical Greek poet and musician. The son of Apollo and a muse, he married Eurydice, who died from the bite of a snake. Orpheus went down to Hades to bring her back and her return to life was granted on condition that he walked ahead of her without looking back. He broke this condition, and Eurydice was irretrievably lost. In his grief, he despised the Maenad women of Thrace, and was torn in pieces by them.

Orphic, Orphism ORPHEAN.

orphrey, *n.* a band of gold and silver embroidery decorating an ecclesiastical vestment. [ME and OF *orfreis,* med. L *aurifrisium,* L *auriphrygium* (*aurum,* gold, *Phrygium,* Phrygian)]

orpiment, *n.* native yellow trisulphide of arsenic, used as a pigment and a dyestuff. [OF from L *auripigmentum* (*aurum,* gold, PIGMENT)]

orpine, orpin, *n.* a fleshy-leaved plant, *Sedum telephium,* of the stone-crop family, with purple flowers; orpiment. [F *orpin,* corr. of prec.]

Orpington, *n.* a variety of domestic fowl. [village in W Kent]

Orr, *n.* **Robert 'Bobby'** (1948–), Canadian hockey player, who played for the Boston Bruins (1967–76) and the Chicago Blackhawks (1976–79) of the National Hockey League. He was voted the best defence every year 1967–75, and was Most Valuable Player 1970–72. He was the first defence to score 100 points in a season, and won the scoring leader 1970 and 1975.

orra, *a.* (*Sc.*) odd, extra, left over; incidental; disreputable, low. [etym. unknown]

orrery, *n.* a mechanical model for illustrating the motions, magnitudes and positions of the planetary system. [4th Earl of *Orrery,* 1676–1731, for whom one of the first was made]

orris[1], *n.* a kind of iris. **orris-root,** *n.* the root of one of three species of iris, used as a perfume and in medicine. **orris-powder,** *n.* [prob. corr. of IRIS]

orris[2], *n.* varieties of gold and silver lace. [contr. of ORPHREY]

Orsini, *n.* **Felice** (1819–58), Italian political activist, a member of the Carbonari secret revolutionary group, who attempted unsuccessfully to assassinate Napoleon III in Paris Jan. 1858. He was subsequently executed, but the Orsini affair awakened Napoleon's interest in Italy and led to a secret alliance with Piedmont at Plombières (1858), directed against Italy.

ort, *n.* (*usu. in pl.*) refuse, fragments, odds and ends, leavings. [late ME *ortes,* pl., cp. Dut. *oor-aete* (*oor-,* not, *etan,* to eat, cogn. with OE *ǣt,* food)]

Ortega (Saavedra), *n.* **Daniel** (1945–), Nicaraguan socialist politician, head of state from 1981. He was a member of the Sandinista Liberation Front (FSLN) which overthrew the regime of Anastasio Somoza 1979. US-sponsored Contra guerrillas opposed his government from 1982.

ortho-, *comb. form* straight; upright; perpendicular; correct; denoting an organic compound having substituted atoms attached to two adjacent carbon atoms in a benzene ring (cp. META-, PARA-); denoting an oxyacid derived from an acid anhydride by combination with the largest number of water molecules. [Gr. *orthos,* straight]

orthocephalic, *a.* having a breadth of skull from 70 to 75 per cent of the length, between brachycephalic and dolichocephalic.

orthochromatic, *a.* giving the correct values of colours in relations of light and shade.

orthoclase, *n.* common or potash feldspar having a rectangular cleavage. [Gr. *klasis,* cleavage]

orthodontia, orthodontics, *n.sing.* dentistry dealing with the correction of irregularities of the teeth. **orthodontic,** *a.* **orthodontist,** *n.* [Gr. *odous odontos,* tooth]

orthodox, *a.* holding right or accepted views, esp. in matters of faith and religious doctrine; in accordance with sound or accepted doctrine; approved, accepted, conventional, not heretical, heterodox or original. **Orthodox Church,** *n.* see separate article below. †**orthodoxal,** †**orthodoxical,** *a.* **orthodoxly,** †**orthodoxically,** *adv.* **orthodoxy,** †**orthodoxness,** *n.* [Gr. *doxa,* opinion]

Orthodox Church, *n.* (or **Eastern Orthodox Church** or **Greek Orthodox Church**) a federation of self-governing Christian churches mainly found in E Europe and parts of Asia. The centre of worship is the Eucharist. There is a married clergy, except for bishops; the Immaculate Conception is not accepted. The highest rank in the church is that of Ecumenical Patriarch, or Bishop of Istanbul. There are approximately 130 million adherents.

orthodromic, *a.* pertaining to orthodromics. **orthodromics, orthodromy,** *n.* the art of sailing in the arc of some great circle the shortest distance between any two points on the surface of the globe. [Gr. *dromos,* course]

orthoepy, *n.* the branch of grammar dealing with pronunciation, phonology; correct speech or pronunciation. **orthoepic, -ical,** *a.* **orthoepically,** *adv.* **orthoepist,** *n.* [Gr. *epos,* a word]

orthogenesis, *n.* a theory of evolution that postulates that variation is determined by the action of environment. **orthogenetic,** *a.*

orthognathous, *a.* (*Craniology*) straight-jawed, having little forward projection of the jaws. **orthognathic,** *a.* **orthognathism,** *n.*

orthogon, *n.* a rectangular figure; a right-angled triangle. **orthogonal,** *a.* **orthogonally,** *adv.* [Gr. *gōnia,* corner, angle]

orthography, *n.* correct spelling; that part of grammar which deals with letters and spelling; mode of spelling as regards correctness and incorrectness; the art of drawing plans, elevations etc., in accurate projection, as if the object were seen from an infinite distance. **orthographer, -phist,** *n.* **orthographic, -ical,** *a.* **orthographically,** *adv.* [OF *ortographie,* L and Gr. *orthographia* (ORTHO-, -GRAPHY)]

orthometry, *n.* the art of correct versification. **orthometric,** *a.*

orthopaedic, -ical, (*esp. N Am.*) **orthopedic, -ical** *a.* **orthopaedics, orthopedics,**, *n.* the act or art of curing muscular or skeletal deformities by surgery, esp. in children. **orthopaedist, -pedist,** *n.* [Gr. *pais paidos,* child]

orthopnoea, *n.* (*Path.*) difficulty of breathing except in an upright posture, a form of asthma. **orthopnoic,** *a.* [L, from Gr. *orthopnoia* (*pnoē,* breathing)]

orthopraxy, *n.* orthodox procedure or behaviour, correct practice. [Gr. *praxis,* doing]

Orthoptera, *n.pl.* an order of insects with two pairs of wings, the hind wings membranous and those in front coriaceous and usually straight. **orthopteral, -ous,** *a.* **orthopteran,** *n., a.* [Gr. *pteron,* wing]

orthoptic, *a.* relating to correct vision with both eyes; (*Math.*) referring to tangents that intersect at right angles. *n.* a perforated disk on the backsight of a firearm, used in aiming. **orthoptics,** *n.* the correction of defective eyesight, e.g. by exercising weak eye muscles. **orthoptist,** *n.*

orthorhombic, *a.* having three planes of dissimilar symmetry at right angles to each other.

orthoscope, *n.* an instrument for examining the interior of the eye, the refraction of the cornea being corrected by a body of water. **orthoscopic,** *a.* having or giving correct vision, normal proportions, or a flat field of view.

orthotone, *a.* (*Gr. grammar*) having its own accent, independently accented. *n.* an orthotone word. **orthotonic,** *a.*

orthotropal, orthotropous, *a.* turned or growing straight (of ovules, embryos etc.). **orthotropic,** *a.*

growing vertically upwards or downwards. **orthotropism**, *n*. [Gr. *tropos*, turning]

orthotypous, *a*. having a perpendicular cleavage.

ortolan, *n*. a small bunting, *Emberiza hortulana*, the garden bunting or ortolan bunting, esteemed as a delicacy; applied to several W Indian and American birds. [F, from It. *ortolano*, earlier *hortolano*, gardener, L *hortulānus*, from *hortulus*, dim. of *hortus*, garden]

Orton, *n*. **Joe** (1933–67), English dramatist of black comedies in which surreal and violent action takes place in genteel and unlikely settings. Plays include *Entertaining Mr Sloane* (1964), *Loot* (1966), and *What the Butler Saw* (1968). His diaries deal frankly with his personal life. He was murdered by his lover Kenneth Halliwell.

†**Orvietan,** *n*. a compound of treacle formerly used as an antidote to poison. [*Orvieto* in Italy, -AN]

Orwell, *n*. **George** (pen name of Eric Arthur Blair) (1903–50), English author. His books include the satire *Animal Farm* (1945) which included such sayings as 'All animals are equal, but some are more equal than others', and the prophetic *Nineteen Eighty-Four* (1949), portraying state control of existence carried to the ultimate extent. Other works include *Down and Out in Paris and London* (1933) and *Homage to Catalonia* (1938).

-ory¹, *comb. form* denoting place where or instrument, as in *dormitory, lavatory, refectory*. [A-F *-orie*, L *-ōrium*, from adjectives in *-ōrius*]

-ory², *comb. form* forming adjectives, as *amatory, admonitory, illusory*. [ONorth.F *-ori, -orie*, L *-ōrius*, *-ōria, -ōrium*]

oryx, *n*. (*pl*. **-yxes, -yx**) a genus of straight-horned African antelopes. [L, from Gr. *orux*]

oryza, *n*. a tropical genus of grasses comprising *Oryza sativa*, rice. [Gr. *oruza*, rice]

OS, (*abbr*.) Old Style; Ordinary Seaman; Ordnance Survey; outsize.

Os, (*chem. symbol*) osmium.

os, *n*. (*pl*. **ossa**) a bone. [L]

OS/2, *n*. (*Comput*.) a single-user operating system for use on large microcomputers. Its main features are multi-tasking and the ability to access large amounts of internal memory.

Osaka, *n*. an industrial port (iron, steel, shipbuilding, chemicals, textiles) on Honshu island; population (1987) 2,546,000, metropolitan area 8,000,000. It is the oldest city of Japan, and was at times the seat of government in the 4th–8th cent.

Osborne, *n*. **John (James)** (1929–), English dramatist. He was one of the first Angry Young Men of British theatre with his debut play, *Look Back in Anger* (1956). Other plays include *The Entertainer* (1957), *Luther* (1960), and *Watch It Come Down* (1976).

Oscan, *n*. one of an ancient Italian people; their language. *a*. pertaining to this people or their language. [L *Oscī*, -AN]

Oscar, *n*. a gold-plated statuette awarded by the American Academy of Motion Picture Arts and Sciences to the actor, director, film-writer etc. whose work is adjudged the best of the year. [etym. doubtful]

oscillate, *v.i.* to swing, to move like a pendulum; to vibrate; to fluctuate, to vacillate, to vary. **oscillation,** *n*. the movement of oscillation; the regular variation in an alternating current; a single cycle (of something oscillating) from one extreme to the other. **oscillative, -tory,** *a*. **oscillator,** *n*. someone or something that oscillates; a device for producing alternating current. **oscillograph**, *n*. a device for giving a visible representation of the oscillations of an electric current. **oscillogram**, *n*. **oscillometer**, *n*. an instrument for measuring the roll of a ship at sea. **oscilloscope**, *n*. an instrument which registers the oscillations of an alternating current or the fluorescent screen of a cathode-ray tube; an instrument to facilitate the detection of vibrations and other faults in machinery. [L *oscillātus*, p.p. of *oscillāre*, from *oscillum*, a swing, orig. a little mask of Bacchus suspended from a tree, dim. of *osculum*, dim. of *ōs*, mouth]

oscine, *a*. of, pertaining to or being the suborder Oscines of passerine birds that includes most of the songbirds. [L *oscen*, singing bird]

†**oscitant,** *a*. yawning, sleepy; dull, negligent. †**oscitancy,** *n*. †**oscitantly,** *adv*. †**oscitate,** *v.i.* †**oscitation,** *n*. [L *oscitans -ntem*, pres.p. of *oscitāre*, to gape, *ōs*, mouth, *citāre*, to move)]

osculate, *v.t.* †to kiss; (*Geom*.) to touch by osculation. *v.i.* to kiss; (*Geom*.) to touch each other by osculation; (*Biol*.) to come into contact with through having characters in common or through an intermediate species etc. **osculant,** *a*. **osculation,** *n*. **osculatory**, *a*. kissing; (*Geom*.) osculating. *n*. a tablet or board on which a sacred picture is painted, to be kissed by the priest and people during Mass. **oscule**, *n*. a small mouth or bilabiate opening. **osculum**, *n*. (*pl*. **-la**). [L *osculātus*, p.p. of *osculāri*, to kiss, from *osculum*, dim. of *ōs*, mouth]

-ose¹, *comb. form* denoting fulness, abundance, as in *grandiose, jocose, verbose*. [L *-ōsus*]

-ose², *comb. form* denoting the carbohydrates and isomeric compounds. [after GLUCOSE]

Oshima, *n*. **Nagisa** (1932–), Japanese film director, whose violent and sexually explicit *In the Realm of the Senses/Ai No Corrida* (1977) has been one of cinema's most controversial films. His other work includes *Death by Hanging* (1968) and *Merry Christmas Mr Lawrence* (1983), which starred the singer David Bowie.

Oshogbo, *n*. a city and trading centre on the river Niger, in W Nigeria, 200 km/125 miles NE of Lagos; population (1986) 405,000. Industries include cotton and brewing.

osier, *n*. a species of willow, *Salix viminalis*, the pliable shoots of which are used for basket-making. **osier-bed, -holt,** *n*. †**osiered,** *a*. [F, from L *ausāria, ōsāria*, willow-bed]

Osiris, *n*. an ancient Egyptian god, the embodiment of goodness, ruled the underworld, after being killed by Set. The sister-wife of Osiris was Isis or Hathor and their son Horus captured his father's murderer.

-osis, *comb. form* denoting condition, esp. morbid states, as *chlorosis necrosis*. [Gr. *-ōsis*, suf. forming nouns from verbs in *-oein*]

-osity, *comb. form* forming nouns from adjectives in -OSE or -OUS, as *grandiosity, luminosity*. [F *-osité*, L *-ōsitātem*, nom. *-ōsitas* (-OSE, -OUS, -TY)]

Oslo, *n*. capital and industrial port (textiles, engineering, timber) of Norway; population (1988) 454,000. The first recorded settlement was made by Harald III, but after a fire (1624), it was entirely replanned by Christian IV and renamed Christiania (1624–1924).

Osman (or **Othman**) I, *n*. (1259–1326), Turkish ruler from 1299. He began his career in the service of the Seljuk Turks, but in 1299 he set up a kingdom of his own in Bithynia, NW Asia, and assumed the title of sultan. He conquered a great part of Anatolia, so founding a Turkish empire. His successors were known as 'sons of Osman', from which the term **Ottoman** is derived.

Osmanli, *a*. of or pertaining to the Ottoman Empire, the W branch of the Turkish peoples or their language. *n*. a member of the Ottoman dynasty; a Turk. [Turk. *osmānli*, from *Osman* or Othman I, 1259–1326, founder of the Turkish empire]

osmazome, *n*. (*Chem*.) the portion of the aqueous product of meat in which are found those constituents of the flesh which decide its taste and smell. [Gr. *osmē*, a smell; *zomos*, broth]

osmiridium, *n*. a very hard natural alloy of osmium and iridium used esp. in pen nibs. [(OSM)IUM + IRIDIUM]

osmium, *n*. the heaviest known metallic element, at. no. 76; chem. symbol Os, usu. found in association with platinum. **osmic,** *a*. [Gr. *osmē*, smell (from the disagreeable smell of the oxide), -IUM]

osmosis, *n*. the diffusion of a solvent through a semipermeable membrane into a more concentrated solution. **osmose,** *v.t., v.i.* to (cause to) diffuse by osmosis. **osmograph**, **osmometer**, *n*. an instrument for measuring osmotic pressures. **osmotic**, *a*. **osmotic pressure,** *n*. the pressure required to prevent osmosis into a solution through a semipermeable membrane separating the solution and the pure solvent. **osmotically,** *adv*. [Gr. *ōsmos,* push, thrust, from *ōthein,* to push]

osmund, osmunda, *n*. the flowering fern, *Osmunda regalis,* also called the royal fern or the king fern. [A-F *osmunde,* OF *osmonde,* etym. unknown]

osnaburg, *n*. a coarse kind of linen. [*Osnabrück,* in Germany]

osprey, *n*. a large bird, *Pandion haliaetus,* preying on fish, also known as the sea-eagle or sea-hawk; an egret plume used for trimming hats and bonnets (a term used erroneously by milliners). [ult. from L *ossifraga* (*os ossis,* bone, *frag-,* stem of *frangere,* to break)]

Ossa, Mount, *n*. the highest peak on the island of Tasmania, Australia; height 1617 m/5250 ft.

ossein, *n*. the gelatinous tissue left when mineral matter is eliminated from a bone.

osselet, *n*. an ossicle; the cuttle-bone of cephalopods.

osseous, *a*. of the nature of or like bone, bony; consisting of bone, ossified; containing or abounding in fossil bones; the protein which forms the organic basis of bone. [L *osseus,* from *os ossis,* bone]

Ossetia, *n*. a region of SW USSR, in the Caucasus, on the border of the republic of Georgia. It is inhabited mainly by the Ossets (a people of Iranian origin), and has been the scene of Osset-Georgian inter-ethnic conflict from 1989.

Ossian, *n*. (Celtic **Oisin**) legendary Irish hero, invented by the Scottish writer James Macpherson. He is sometimes represented as the son of Finn Mac Cumhaill (*c*. 250), and as having lived to tell the tales of Finn and the Ulster heroes to St Patrick, about 400. The publication (1760) of Macpherson's poems, attributed to Ossian, made Ossian's name familiar throughout Europe. **Ossianic**, *a*.

ossicle, *n*. a small bone; a bony calcareous, or chitinous part or process in various animals.

ossiferous, *a*. containing or yielding bones (of cave deposits etc.). **ossification**, *n*.

ossifrage OSPREY.

ossify, *v.t.* to turn into bone. *v.i.* to become bone; to become inflexible in attitudes, habits etc.

ossuary, *n*. a charnel-house; a bone-urn; a deposit of bones (as in a cave).

oste- OSTE(O)-.

osteal, *a*. osseous, bony, sounding like bone (of sounds made by percussion of bones).

ostealgia, *n*. pain in a bone.

ostein, *n*. ossein.

osteitis, *n*. inflammation of bone. **osteitic, ostitic,** *a*.

ostensible, *a*. put forward for show or to hide the reality; professed, pretended, seeming. **ostensibly,** *adv*. **ostension,** *n*. in the Roman Catholic Church, the uplifting or holding forth of the Host for public adoration. **ostensive,** *a*. exhibiting, showing; ostensible; (*Log.*) setting forth a general principle obviously including the proposition to be proved. **ostensively,** *adv*. **ostensory**, *n*. in the Roman Catholic Church, a monstrance. †**ostent**, *n*. show, manifestation, appearance; a portent, a prodigy. **ostentation**, *n*. pretentious or ambitious display; parade, pomp; †a show, a pageant. **ostentatious,** *a*. **ostentatiously,** *adv*. **ostentatiousness,** *n*. [F, from L *ostens-,* p.p. stem of *ostendere,* to show (*os-,* OB-, *tendere,* to stretch)]

oste(o)-, *comb. form* bone. [Gr. *osteon,* bone]

osteoarthritis *n*. degenerative arthritis, esp. of the weight-bearing joints of the spine, hips and knees. **osteoarthritic**, *a*.

osteoblast, *n*. a cell concerned in the development of bone. [Gr. *blastos,* bud]

osteoclasis, *n*. the operation of breaking a bone to remedy a deformity etc. **osteoclast,** *n*.

osteocolla, *n*. an incrustation of carbonate of lime on the roots and stems of plants growing in sandy ground; an inferior kind of glue obtained from bones. [Gr. *kolla,* glue]

osteoid, *a*. like bone.

osteology, *n*. the branch of anatomy treating of bones, osseous tissue etc.; the bony structure of an animal. **osteologic, -ical,** *a*. **osteologist,** *n*.

osteomalacia, *n*. softening of the bones. [Gr. *malakia,* softness]

osteomyelitis, *n*. inflammation of the marrow of the bones.

osteopathy, *n*. a method of treating diseases by eliminating structural derangement by manipulation, mainly of the spinal column. **osteopathist, osteopath**, *n*. a practitioner of oestopathy.

osteoplasty, *n*. transplantation of bone with its periosteum. **osteoplastic**, *a*.

osteoporosis, *n*. development of porous or brittle bones due to lack of calcium in the bone matrix.

osteosarcoma, *n*. a disease of the bones due to the growth of medullary or cartilaginous matter within them.

osteotome, *n*. an instrument used in the dissection of bones. **osteotomy**, *n*.

Ostia, *n*. ancient Roman town near the mouth of the Tiber. Founded about 330 BC, it was the port of Rome and had become a major commercial centre by the 2nd cent. AD. It was abandoned in the 9th cent.

ostinato, *n*. (*pl*. **-tos**) a musical figure continuously reiterated throughout a composition. [It., from L *obstinatus,* OBSTINATE]

ostium, *n*. (*pl*. **-tia**) (*Anat.*) the mouth or opening of a passage; the mouth of a river. **ostiole**, *n*. a small opening in the perithecia of fungi etc. **ostial,** *a*. [L]

ostler, hostler, *n*. a man who looks after horses at an inn, a stableman; †an inn-keeper. [orig. *hostler* (HOSTEL, -ER)]

ostmark, *n*. the standard unit of currency in East Germany (until 1990). [lit. east mark]

Ostpolitik, *n*. West German chancellor Brandt's policy of reconciliation with the communist bloc from 1971, pursued to a modified extent by his successors Schmidt and Kohl.

ostracean, *n*. any mollusc of the family Ostracea, a family of bivalves containing the oysters. *a*. pertaining to the Ostracea. **ostraceous**, *a*. **ostracite**, *n*. a fossil shell of a species related to the oyster. [Gr. *ostrakeos,* from *ostrakon,* tile, potsherd, oyster-shell]

ostracize, -ise, *v.t.* (*Gr. Ant.*) in ancient Greece, to banish by a popular vote recorded on a potsherd or shell; to exclude from society, to ban, to send to Coventry. **ostracism,** *n*. [Gr. *ostrakizein,* as prec.]

Ostrava, *n*. an industrial city (iron works, furnaces, coal, chemicals) in Czechoslovakia, capital of Severomoravsky region, NE of Brno; population (1984) 324,000.

ostre-, ostre(o)- *comb. form* oyster. [L *ostrea, ostreum,* Gr. *ostreon,* oyster]

ostreiculture, *n*. the artificial breeding of oysters.

ostreophagous, *a*. eating or feeding on oysters.

ostrich, *n*. a large African bird, *Struthio camelus,* having rudimentary wings, but capable of running with great speed, and greatly valued for its feathers, which are used as plumes; one who refuses to recognize unpleasant facts. **ostrich-farm,** *n*. **ostrich-tip,** *n*. the end of an ostrich-feather. [ME *ostrice,* OF *ostruce,* pop. L *avis strūthio* (*avis,* bird, late L *strūthio,* Gr. *strouthiōn,* from *strouthos*)]

Ostrogoth, *n*. an eastern Goth, one of the division of the Gothic peoples who conquered Italy in the 5th cent. **ostrogothic**, *a*. [late L *Ostrogothī,* pl. (cp. OS *ōstar,* eastward, GOTH)]

Ostrovsky, *n*. **Alexander Nikolaevich** (1823–86), Russian playwright, founder of the modern Russian theatre. He dealt satirically with the manners of the middle class in numerous plays, for example *A Family Affair* (1850). His fairy-tale play *The Snow Maiden* (1873) inspired the composers Tchaikovsky and Rimsky-Korsakov.

Ostwald, *n*. **Wilhelm** (1853–1932), German chemist whose work on catalysts laid the foundations of the petrochemical and other industries. Nobel prize 1909.

Oswald, St, *n.* (*c.* 605–642), king of Northumbria from 634, after killing the Welsh king Cadwallon. Oswald had become a Christian convert during exile on the Scottish island of Iona. With the help of St Aidan he furthered the spread of Christianity until he was defeated and killed by King Penda of Mercia. Feast day 9 Aug.

OT, (*abbr.*) occupational therapy; Old Testament; overtime.

†**otacoustic,** *a.* assisting the sense of hearing. *n.* an instrument to assist the hearing. †**otacousticon,** *n.*

Otago, *n.* a peninsula and coastal plain on South Island, New Zealand, constituting a district; area 64,230 sq km/ 25,220 sq miles; chief cities include Dunedin and Invercargill.

otalgia, *n.* earache. [Gr. *algos,* pain]

otarian, *a.* of or pertaining to the Otariidae, a family of pinnipeds with external ears, including the fur-seals and sea-lions. **otariid,** *n.* **otaroid, otarine,** *a.* [Gr. *ōtaros,* large-eared]

Othello, *n.* a tragedy by William Shakespeare, first performed 1604–05. Othello, a commander in the Venetian army, is persuaded by Iago that his wife Desdemona is having an affair with his friend Cassio. Othello murders Desdemona; on discovering her innocence, he kills himself.

other, *a.* not the same as one specified or implied; different, distinct in kind; alternative, additional; extra; second, only remaining (of two alternatives); opposite, contrary. *n., pron.* an or the other person, thing, example, instance etc. *adv.* otherwise. **every other,** every alternate (day, week etc.). **someone, something or other,** an unspecified person or thing. **the other·day** etc., on a day etc. recently. **other-directed,** *a.* influenced in thought and action by values derived from external sources. †**othergates, otherguess,** *adv.* otherwise. *a.* of another kind. †**otherguise,** *a.* other. *adv.* otherwise. **otherness,** *n.* **otherwhence,** *adv.* from elsewhere. **otherwhere, -wheres,** *adv.* (*poet.*) elsewhere. **other-while, -whiles,** *adv.* **otherwise,** *adv.* in a different way or manner; in other respects; by or from other causes; in quite a different state. †*conj.* else, or; but for this. **other world,** *n.* the future life; a world existing outside of or in a different mode from this; fairy-land. **otherworld,** *a.* interested or concerned only with the future life, or the imaginative world as opp. to material being. **other-worldly,** *a.* **other-worldliness,** *n.* [OE *ōther* (cp. Dut. and G *ander,* Icel. *annarr,* Swed. *andra,* Sansk. *anatras,* L *alter*)]

Othman, *n.* (*c.* 574–656), Arabian caliph (leader of the Islamic empire) from 644, when he was elected; he was a son-in-law of the prophet Mohammed. Under his rule the Arabs became a naval power and captured Cyprus, but Othman's personal weaknesses led to his assassination. He was responsible for the final editing of the Koran, the sacred book of Islam.

Othman I, *n.* another name for the Turkish sultan OSMAN I.

Otho I, *n.* (1815–67), king of Greece 1832–62. As the 17-year-old son of King Ludwig I of Bavaria, he was selected by the European powers as the first king of independent Greece. He was overthrown by a popular revolt.

otic, *a.* pertaining to the ear. **otorhinolaryngology,** *n.* ear, nose and throat medicine. Also **otolaryngology,** *n.* [Gr. *ōtikos,* from *ous ōtos,* ear]

-otic, *comb. form* forming adjectives corresponding to nouns in -OSIS, as *neurotic, osmotic.* [Gr. *-ōtikos,* formed on the same stems as -OSIS]

otiose, *a.* not wanted, useless, superfluous; futile, sterile; †at leisure, unemployed, lazy. **otiosely,** *adv.* **otioseness,** *n.* [L *ōtiōsus,* from *ōtium,* leisure]

Otis, *n.* **Elisha Graves** (1811–61), US engineer, who developed a lift that incorporated a safety device, making it acceptable for passenger use in the first skyscrapers. The device, invented 1852, consisted of vertical ratchets on the sides of the lift shaft into which spring-loaded catches would engage and 'lock' the lift in position in the event of cable failure.

otitis, *n.* inflammation of the ear.

ot(o)-, *comb. form* pertaining to the ear. [Gr. *ous ōtos,* ear]

otolith, *n.* an ear-stone or calcareous concretion found in the inner ear of vertebrates and some invertebrates.

otology, *n.* the science of the ear or of diseases of the ear; anatomy of the ear; a treatise on the ear. **otologist,** *n.*

O'Toole, *n.* **Peter** (1932–), British actor who made his name as *Lawrence of Arabia* (1962), and remained a star in films such as *Beckett* (1964) and *The Lion in Winter* (1968) until the early 1970s. Subsequent appearances were few and poorly received by critics until *The Stuntman* (1978).

otorrhoea, *n.* purulent discharge from the ear.

otoscope, *n.* an instrument for inspecting the ear and ear-drum.

ottava rima, *n.* a form of versification consisting of stanzas of eight lines, of which the first six rhyme alternately, and the last two form a couplet (as in Byron's *Don Juan*). [It., octave rhyme]

Ottawa, *n.* the capital of Canada, in E Ontario, on the hills overlooking the Ottawa river, and divided by the Rideau Canal into the Upper (western) and Lower (eastern) Town; population (1986) 301,000, metropolitan area (with adjoining Hull, Québec) 819,000. Industries include timber, pulp and paper, engineering, food processing and publishing. It was founded 1826–32 as Bytown, in honour of John By (1781–1836) whose army engineers were building the Rideau Canal. It was renamed (1854) after the Outaouac Indians.

otter, *n.* a furred, web-footed aquatic mammal of the genus *Lutra* esp. *L. vulgaris,* a European animal feeding exclusively on fish; the fur of this; the sea-otter; a device for catching fish consisting usu. of a float armed with hooks. **otter-dog, -hound,** *n.* a variety of dog used for hunting otters. [OE *oter, ottor* (cp. Dut. and G *Otter,* Icel. *otr*), cogn. with Gr. *hudra,* water-snake, *hudōr,* water]

otto ATTAR.

Otto, *n.* four Holy Roman emperors, including:

Otto I, *n.* (912–973), Holy Roman emperor from 936. He restored the power of the empire, asserted his authority over the pope and the nobles, ended the Magyar menace by his victory at the Lechfeld 955, and refounded the East Mark, or Austria, as a barrier against them.

Otto IV, *n.* (*c.* 1182–1218), Holy Roman emperor, elected 1198. He engaged in controversy with Pope Innocent III, and was defeated by the Pope's ally, Philip of France, at Bouvines (1214).

Otto cycle, *n.* the correct name for the four-stroke cycle, introduced by the German engineer Nikolaus Otto (1832–91) in 1876. It improved upon existing engine cycles by compressing the fuel mixture before it was ignited.

Ottoman, *a.* of or pertaining to the dynasty of Othman or Osman I; pertaining to the Turks. *n.* a Turk. †**Ottomite,** *n.* [F, ult. from Arab. *Othmān,* Turk. *Osmān,* see OSMANLI]

ottoman, *n.* a cushioned seat or sofa without back or arms, introduced from Turkey. [F, *ottomane,* as prec.]

Ottoman Empire, *n.* the Muslim empire of the Turks 1300–1920, the successor of the Seljuk Empire. It was founded by Osman I and reached its height with Suleiman in the 16th cent. Its capital was Istanbul (formerly Constantinople). At its greatest extent its bounds were Europe as far as Hungary, part of S Russia, Iran, the Palestinian coastline, Egypt and N Africa. From the 17th cent. it was in decline. There was an attempted revival and reform under the Young Turk party (1908), but the regime crumbled when Turkey took the German side in World War I. The sultanate was abolished by Atatürk (1922); the last sultan was Mohammed VI.

Otway, *n.* **Thomas** (1652–85), English dramatist. His plays include the tragedies *Alcibiades* (1675), *Don Carlos* (1676), *The Orphan* (1680), and *Venice Preserv'd* (1682).

Otztal Alps, *n.pl.* a range of the Alps in Italy and Austria, rising to 3774 m/12,382 ft at Wildspitze, Austria's second highest peak.
OU, (*abbr.*) Open University; Oxford University.
Ouagadougou, *n.* capital and industrial centre of Burkina Faso; population (1985) 442,000. Products include textiles, vegetable oil and soap.
oubit, woobut, *n.* a hairy caterpillar. [perh. from OE *wibba,* beetle, or *wull,* WOOL]
oubliette, *n.* an underground dungeon in which persons condemned to perpetual imprisonment or secret death were confined. [F, from *oublier,* to forget]
†**ouch**[1], *n.* a clasp or buckle; a clasped necklace etc., the setting of a gem. [OF *nouche* (cp. ADDER[2], APRON), late L *nusca,* OHG *nusche,* prob. of Celtic orig.]
ouch[2], *int.* used to express sudden pain. [etym. doubtful]
ought[1], *v.aux.* to be found in duty or rightness, to be necessary, fit or proper; to behove. *n.* duty, obligation. **oughtness,** *n.* (*rare*). [OE *āhte,* past of *āgan,* to possess, to OWE]
ought[2], NAUGHT.
Ouija®, *n.* a board inscribed with the letters of the alphabet, used for receiving messages etc. in spiritualistic manifestations. [F *oui,* yes; G *ja,* yes]
ouistiti WISTITI.
Oujda, *n.* industrial and commercial city (lead and coalmining) in N Morocco, near the border with Algeria; population (1982) 471,000. It trades in wool, grain and fruit.
ounce[1], *n.* a unit of weight; the 12th part of a pound troy, and 16th part of a pound avoir-dupois (about 28 g); a small quantity. [OF *unce* (F *once*), L *uncia* (cp. INCH[1])]
ounce[2], *n.* a lynx or other leopard-like animal; the mountain-panther, *Felis uncia,* of S and Central Asia, also called the snow leopard. [OF *once* (*l'once*), *lonce,* It. *lonza,* L *lyncea,* LYNX (cp. ADDER, APRON)]
our, *a.* of, pertaining to or belonging to us; used instead of 'my' by royalty, editors, reviewers etc. **ours,** *a.* belonging to us. *n.* that or those belonging to us; our regiment or corps. **ourself,** *pron.* (*pl.* **-selves,** or **-self** when a sovereign) myself (used in regal or formal style); (*pl.*) we, not others, we alone (usu. in apposition with *we*); (*reflex.*) the persons previously alluded to as we. [OE *ūre,* orig. gen. pl. of *ūs,* US (cp. G *unser,* Goth. *unsar*)]
-our, *comb. form* forming nouns, as *amour, ardour, clamour.* [-OR]
ourang-outang, ORANG-UTAN.
ouranography etc. URANO-.
ourie, *a.* (*Sc.*) shivering, chilly; dreary, depressed, dejected. [cp. Icel. *ūrig,* from *ūr,* drizzle]
ourology etc. URINO-.
-ous, *comb. form* full of, abounding in; (*Chem.*) denoting a compound having more of the element indicated in the stem than those whose names end in -IC; as *dubious, glorious, nitrous, sulphurous.* [OF *-ous, -os, -us* (F *-eux*), L *-ōsus* (cp. -OSE)]
ousel OUZEL.
Ousmane, *n.* **Sembene** (1923–), Senegalese writer and film director. His novels, written in French, include *Le Docker Noir* (1956), about his experiences as a union leader in Marseille, *Les bouts de bois/ God's Bits of Wood* (1960), *Le Mandat/The Money Order,* and *Xala,* the last two of which he made into films.
oust, *v.t.* to eject, to expel, to turn out (from); to dispossess, to deprive (of); †to take away, to deprive. **ouster,** *n.* (*Law*) ejectment, dispossession; one who ousts. [OF *oster* (F *ôter*), to take away, etym. doubtful]
out, *adv.* from the inside or within; not in, not within; from among; forth or away; not at home, not in office; not engaged or employed; on strike; not batting; dismissed from the wicket; (*Boxing*) denoting defeat through inability to rise within the ten seconds allowed after being knocked down; not in fashion; not in practice; in error, wrong; at a loss; at odds, not in agreement; not to be thought of; so as to be visible, audible, revealed, published etc.; introduced to society; exhausted or extinguished; clearly; forcibly; at full extent; no longer conscious; to an end or conclusion, completely, thoroughly. *prep.* (*coll.*) from inside of. *n.* (*usu.* pl.) those out of office, the opposition; an outing; (*Print.*) an omission, matter omitted. *a.* external; outlying, remote, distant; played away from the home ground. *int.* (*ellipt.*) begone! away! an expression of impatience, anger or abhorrence. *v.t.* †to turn out, to expel; to knock out, to disable. **all out,** striving to the uttermost. **from out,** out of. **murder will out,** the guilt will be disclosed; the secret is bound to be revealed. **out and about,** able to get up and go outside. **out and away** AWAY. **out and out,** completely, unreservedly. **out-and-outer,** *n.* a thoroughgoing person. **out at elbows** ELBOW. **out of date** DATE[1]. **out-of-door,** outdoor. **out of hand** HAND. **out of it,** not included, neglected; at a loss; in error, mistaken. **out of one's head,** delirious. **out of one's time,** having served one's apprenticeship. **out of pocket** POCKET. **out of print,** not on sale by the publisher (of books). **out of sorts,** indisposed, unwell. **out of temper,** irritated, vexed. **out of the way,** unusual; remote. **out of trim,** not in good order. **out for,** *a.* striving for. **out of,** *adv.* from the inside of; from among; beyond the reach of; from (material, source, condition etc.); born of; without; denoting deprivation or want. **outer,** *a.* being on the exterior side, external; farther from the centre or the inside; objective, material, not subjective or psychical. *n.* the part of a target outside the rings round the bull's-eye. **outer man,** *n.* external appearance, attire. **outer space,** *n.* the vast, immeasurable region beyond the earth. **outer world,** *n.* the world beyond one's familiar sphere, people in general. **outermost,** *a.* **outing,** *n.* an excursion, a pleasure-trip, an airing. **outness,** *n.* externality, objectivity, separateness from the perceiving mind. [OE *ūt,* whence *ūte,* away, abroad, *ūtan,* from outside (cp. Dut. *uit,* Icel. *ūt,* G *aus*)]
out-, *pref.* out, towards the outside, external; from within, forth; separate, detached, at a distance; denoting issue or result; expressing excess, exaggeration, superiority, surpassing, defeating, enduring, getting through or beyond. **outact,** *v.t.* to exceed in action, to excel, to outdo. **outask,** *v.t.* (*prov.*) to publish the banns of for the last time. **outback,** *n., a., adv.* (*Austral.*) the hinterland, the bush, the interior. **outbalance,** *v.t.* to outweigh, to exceed. **outbargain,** *v.t.* to get the better of in a bargain. **outbid,** *v.t.* (*past* **-bad, -bade,** *p.p.* **-bidden**) to bid more than; to outdo by offering more. **outbluster,** *v.t.* to silence, worst or get the better of by blustering. **outboard,** *a.* situated on or directed towards the outside of a ship; having an engine and propeller outside the boat. *adv.* out from a ship's side or away from the centre. **outbound,** *v.t.* to leap farther than, to overleap. **out-bound,** *a.* outward bound. †**out-bounds,** *n.pl.* the outer bounds (the utmost limits). **out-brag,** *v.t.* to outdo in bragging; †to excel, to surpass. **outbrave,** *v.t.* to surpass in bravery, beauty, splendour etc.; to stand up against defiantly. **outbreak, -breaking,** *n.* a sudden bursting forth, an eruption; a riot or insurrection. **outbreaker,** *n.* a breaker far from the shore. **out-breathe,** *v.t.* to breathe out; to exhaust, to wear out. *v.i.* to be exhaled. **outbreed,** *v.t.* **outbreeding,** *n.* interbreeding of unrelated plants or animals. **outbudding,** *n.* a budding out, a bursting forth. **out-building,** *n.* a detached building, an outhouse. **outburn,** *v.i.* to burn out, to be consumed. *v.t.* to burn longer than. **outburst,** *n.* an outbreak, an explosion; an outcry. **outby, -bye,** *adv.* (*Sc.*) outside, abroad; to the outside. **outcast,** *a.* rejected, cast out; exiled. *n.* a castaway, a vagabond; an exile. **outclass,** *v.t.* to be of a superior class, kind or qualifications than; to surpass as a competitor. **out-clearing,** *n.* the sending out of cheques, bills etc., drawn on other banks to the clearing house; the total amount thus standing to the account of a bank. **outcome,** *n.* issue, result, consequence, effect. **out-craft,** *v.t.* to excel in cunning. **out-crop,** *n.* (*Geol.*) the exposure of a stratum at the surface. *v.i.* to crop out at the surface. **out-**

cry, *n.* a vehement or loud cry; noise, clamour; †a public auction. *v.t.* to cry louder than. **outdare,** *v.t.* to exceed in daring; to defy. **outdated,** *a.* obsolete, out of date. **outdistance,** *v.t.* to outstrip. **outdo,** *v.t.* to excel, to surpass. **outdoor**, *a.* living, existing, being, happening etc. out of doors or in the open air. **outdoors,** *adv.* in the open air, out of the house. †**outdwell,** *v.t.* to stay beyond one's time. **outdweller**, *n.* one who lives outside of or beyond certain limits. **outface,** *v.t.* to brave; to confront boldly; to stare down. **outfall**, *n.* the point of discharge of a river, drain etc.; an outlet; †a sortie; †a falling out. †**outfangthief**, (OE *ūtfangenne thēof* (OUT, *fangen,* p.p. of *fōn,* to seize, THIEF)). *n.* (*OE Law*) the right of a lord to try a thief who was his own man in his own court. **outfield**, *n.* (*Sc.*) the outlying land of a farm formerly cropped but not manured; (*Cricket, Baseball*) the part of the field at a distance from the batsman; †the players occupying this. **outfielder,** *n.* **outfit**, *n.* the act of equipping for a journey, expedition etc.; the tools and equipment required for a trade, profession etc.; a set of (esp. selected) clothes; (*coll.*) a set or group of people who work as a team. *v.t.* to fit out, to provide with an outfit. **outfitter,** *n.* one who deals in outfits for journeys, athletic sports, ceremonies, schools etc. **outflank,** *v.t.* to extend beyond or turn the flank of; to get the better of. **outflow**, *n.* the process of flowing out; that which flows out; a place of flowing out, an outlet. **outfly,** *v.t.* to fly faster than; to outstrip. **outfoot,** *v.t.* to outstrip, to outrun, outpace etc. **outfox,** *v.t.* to outwit; to surpass in cunning. **outfrown,** *v.t.* to frown down. †**outgate**, (GATE[2]) *n.* a passage out; an outlet. **outgeneral,** *v.t.* to surpass in generalship; to manoeuvre so as to get the better of. **outgive,** *v.t.* to give more than; to surpass in giving. *v.i.* (*poet.*) to give out, to come to an end. **outgo**, *n.* that which goes out; expenditure, outlay, cost, outflow, issue. *v.t.*, to surpass, to go beyond, to excel. **outgoer**, *n.* **outgoing**, *a.* leaving. *n.* a going out, departure, termination; (*usu. in pl.*) outlay, expenditure. **outgrow,** *v.t.* to surpass in growth; to grow too much or too great for; to grow out of. **outgrowth**, *n.* something, or the process of, growing out from a main body; a result or by-product. **outguard**, *n.* a guard at a distance from the main body; an outpost. **outgun,** *v.t.* to defeat with superior weaponry; (*fig.*) to surpass. **out-Herod,** *v.t.* to outdo, to exaggerate, to overact; to surpass any kind of excess. (*Herod,* Tetrarch of Galilee, represented in the old miracle-plays as a swaggering tyrant) **outhouse**, *n.* a smaller building away from the main building. **outjest,** *v.t.* to jest or laugh away. **outjet**, *n.* a projection. **outjut, outjutting,** *n.* **outland**, *n.* a foreign land; †the outlying part of an estate; land beyond the domain lands, let to tenants. *a.* foreign, alien; outlying. **outlander,** *n.* a foreigner, a stranger; an alien settler. **outlandish**, *a.* foreign-looking, strange, extraordinary; foreign, alien; bizarre, unconventional. **outlast,** *v.t.* to last longer than; to surpass in duration, endurance etc. (LAST[4]). **outlaw**, *n.* one deprived of the protection of the law; a lawless person; †an exile, a fugitive; (*Austral.*) an untamable horse. *v.t.* to deprive of the protection of the law. **outlawry,** *n.* **outlay**, *n.* expenditure. *v.t.* to expend, to lay out; †to display. **outleap,** *v.t.* to surpass in leaping, to leap farther than. *n.*, a leaping out. **outlet**, *n.* a passage outwards; a vent; a means of egress. **outlier**, *n.* one who lodges or resides away from his office or business; (*Geol.*) a portion of a bed detached from the main mass by denudation of the intervening parts. **outline**, *n.* the line or lines enclosing and defining a figure; a drawing of such lines without shading; the first general sketch, rough draft or summary; (*pl.*) general features, facts, principles etc. *v.t.* to draw the outline of; to sketch. **outlive,** *v.t.* to survive; to outlast. *v.i.* to survive. **outliver,** *n.* **outlook,** *v.t.* to stare down; †to look out, to select. *n.*, prospect, general appearance of things, esp. as regards the future; a view, a prospect; looking out, watch, vigilance. †**outlustre,** *v.t.* to shine more brightly than. **outlying**, *a.* situated at a distance, or on the exterior frontier. **outmanoeuvre,** *v.t.* to get the better of by manoeuvring. **outmarch,** *v.t.* to march faster than, outstrip by marching. **outmoded,** *a.* out of fashion. **outnumber,** *v.t.* to exceed in number. **outpace,** *v.t.* to walk faster than. **out-paramour,** *v.t.* to surpass in number of mistresses. **out-part**, *n.* an outer or exterior part. **outpatient**, *n.* a patient receiving treatment at a hospital without being a resident. †**outpeer,** *v.t.* to outmatch, to excel. **out-perform,** *v.t.* to do much better than. **outplay,** *v.t.* to play better than or defeat an opponent in a game. **outpoint,** *v.t.* to score more points than. **outport**, *n.* a seaport outside a chief town or chief seat of trade. **outpost**, *n.* a post or station at a distance from the main body. (POST[3]). **outpour,** *v.t.* to pour out, to discharge. *v.i.* to flow forth. *n.*, a pouring out; an overflow. **outpouring**, *n.* †**outpray,** *v.t.* to exceed in entreaty. †**outprise,** *v.t.* to exceed in value. **output**, *n.* the produce of a factory, mine etc.; the aggregate amount produced; the data produced by a computer; the signal delivered by an electronic system or device; the terminal for the output of a computer etc. *v.t.* to produce output (PUT[1]). †**outquench,** *v.t.* to extinguish. **outrange,** *v.t.* (of artillery) to have a longer range than. **outrank,** *v.t.* to excel in rank. **outreach,** *v.t.* to exceed in reach, to surpass; to overreach, to reach out. *v.i.* to extend. **outredden,** *v.t.* (*poet.*) to grow redder than. **outreign,** *v.t.* to reign longer than; to reign throughout (a long period). **out-relief**, *n.* aid given out of the rates to the poor who are not inmates of an institution. **outride,** *v.t.* to ride faster than. **outrider**, *n.* an escort who rides ahead of or beside a carriage; one sent in advance as a scout, or to discover a safe route etc. **outrigger**, *n.* a projecting spar, boom, beam or framework extended from the sides of a ship for various purposes; a bracket carrying a rowlock projecting from the sides of a boat to give increased leverage in rowing; a boat with these; a projecting beam or framework used in building etc.; a projection from the shafts for attaching an extra horse to a vehicle; the horse so attached. **outrigged,** *a.* **outright,** *adv.* completely, entirely; at once, once for all; openly. *a.*, downright, positive; unrestrained, thorough. **outrightness**, *n.* **outrival,** *v.t.* to surpass as a rival. †**outroad,** *n.* an excursion, a foray. **outroar,** *v.t.* to roar louder than. **outrun,** *v.t.* to run faster or farther than, to outstrip; to escape by running. *n.*, (*Austral.*) a distant sheep-run. **out-runner**, *n.* **outscold,** *v.t.* to scold louder than. **outscorn,** *v.t.* to bear down with contempt. **outscouring** *n.* (*usu. in pl.*) anything scoured or washed out, refuse. **outsell,** *v.t.* to exceed in price or value; to sell more or faster than. **outset,** *n.* commencement, beginning, start. **outshine,** *v.i.* to shine forth. *v.t.* to excel in lustre; to surpass in splendour. **outsight**, *n.* perception of external things, observation; †outlook, prospect; (*Sc., pl.*) movable goods, also called **outsight plenishing**. **outsit,** *v.t.* to sit beyond the time of; to sit longer than. **outsize,** *n., a.* (a person or thing) abnormally large; (a ready-made garment) larger than the standard size. **outskirt**, *n.* (*usu. in pl.*) the outer border. †*v.t.* to be the outskirt of; to pass along the outskirts of. **outsleep,** *v.t.* to sleep beyond (a particular time); to sleep longer than. **outsmart,** *v.t.* (*coll.*) to outwit; to get the better of. **outsoar,** *v.t.* to soar beyond or higher than. **out-sole**, *n.* the outside or lower sole, which comes in contact with the ground. **outspan,** *v.t.* (*S Afr.*) to unyoke or unharness. *v.i.* to unyoke or unharness animals. *n.*, the act or the place of this (Dut. *uitspannen* (SPAN)). **outspoken,** *a.* open, candid, frank in speech. **outspokenly,** *adv.* **outspokenness,** *n.* **outsport,** *v.t.* to outdo in sport. **outspread,** *v.t.* to spread out. *a.*, spread out. **outstand,** *v.t.* to stand out against, to withstand; †to outstay. **outstanding,** *a.* remaining unpaid; projecting outward; salient, conspicuous, prominent; superior, excellent. †**outstare,** *v.t.* to outface, to abash by staring. **out-station**, *n.* (*Austral.*) a distant station. **outstay,** *v.t.* to stay longer than (a specified time or another person). **outstep,** *v.t.* to overstep. **outstretch,** *v.t.* to extend, to expand; to stretch out; to stretch or strain to the utmost. **outstrike,** *v.t.* to strike faster or heavier blows than. **outstrip,** *v.t.* to outrun, to leave behind; to escape by running; to surpass in progress (STRIP, in obs. sense to run fast). **outswear,** *v.t.* to bear down by swearing. †**outsweeten,** *v.t.* to exceed in sweetness. †**outswell,** *v.t.* to exceed in swelling, to swell more than. **out-take,** *n.* an unreleased piece of recorded music, film or television. **out-talk,** *v.t.* to outdo in talking; to talk down. †**out-throw,** *v.t.* to cast out. **out-thrust,** *n.* outward thrust or pressure. *a.* thrust or projected forward. *v.t.* to thrust forth or forward. †**out-tongue,** *v.t.* to out-talk. **out-tray,** *n.* a tray in an office for outgoing documents, correspondence etc. †**outvalue,** *v.t.* to exceed in value. †**outvenom,** *v.t.* to exceed in venom. †**outvie,** *v.t.* to exceed, to surpass, in rivalry, emulation etc. †**outvillain,** *v.t.* to surpass in villainy. †**outvoice,** *v.t.* to sound louder than. **outvote,** *v.t.* to out-number in voting; to cast more votes than. **outwalk,** *v.t.* to outdo or outstrip in walking. †**outwall,** *n.* the outside, the exterior; (*fig.*) the body. **outwatch,** *v.t.* to watch longer than; to watch throughout (a specified time). **outwear,** *v.t.* to wear out; to exhaust, to weary out; to last longer than. †**outweed,** *v.t.* to root out. **outweigh,** *v.t.* to weigh more than; to be too heavy for; to be of more value, importance etc. than. **outwell,** *v.i.* to pour or flow forth; †*v.t.* to pour out. **outwick,** *n.* (*Curling*) a shot striking another stone so as to drive it nearer the tee. †**outwin,** *v.t.* to get out of. †**outwind,** *v.t.* to disentangle. †**outwing,** *v.t.* to outstrip in flying; to outflank. **outwit,** *v.t.* to defeat by superior ingenuity or cunning; to overreach, to cheat. **outwork,** *n.* a work included in the defence of a place, but outside the parapet. *v.t.* (*poet.*) to work out, to complete; to work faster than. **outworker,** *n.* one who works outside (a factory, shop etc.). **outworn,** *a.* worn out; obsolete. **out-worth,** *v.t.* to exceed in value. †**outwrest,** *v.t.* to extort. [as prec.]

outer, outing OUT.

outmost OUTERMOST under OUT.

outrage, *n.* wanton injury to or violation of the rights of others; a gross offence against order or decency; a flagrant insult; †violence, excess, extravagance; †a furious outbreak. *v.t.* commit an outrage on; to injure or insult in a flagrant manner; to violate, to commit a rape upon; to transgress, flagrantly. †*v.i.* to act outrageously. **outrageous,** *a.* flagrant, heinous, atrocious, extravagant; excessive, shocking; violent, furious; grossly offensive or abusive. **outrageously,** *adv.* **outrageousness,** *n.* [OF *ultrage, oultrage* (L *ultrā,* beyond, -AGE)]

outré, *a.* extravagant, exaggerated, eccentric; outraging convention or decorum. [F, p.p. of *outrer* (from L *ultrā,* beyond)]

outside, *n.* the external part or surface, the exterior; external appearance, superficial aspect; that which is without; external space, region, position etc.; the utmost limit, the extreme; (*formerly*) an outside passenger on a horse-drawn coach etc.; (*pl.*) outer sheets of a ream of paper. *a.* pertaining to, situated on, near, or nearer to the outside, outer; external, superficial; highest or greatest possible, extreme; remote, most unlikely. *adv.* to or on the outside; without, not within; (*sl.*) not in prison. *prep.* at, on, to, or of the exterior of; without, out from, forth from; beyond the limits of. **outside in,** having the outer side turned in, and vice versa. **outside of,** *prep.* outside. **outside broadcast,** *n.* a radio or television broadcast from outside the studio. **outside edge,** *n.* (*Skating*) a stroke on the outer edge of the skate. **outside-left, -right,** *n.* (*Football, Hockey*) a member of a team who plays on the extreme left or right. **outside seat,** *n.* one at the end of a row. **outsider,** *n.* one who is not a member of a profession, party, circle, coterie etc.; one not acquainted with or interested in something that is going on; one not admissible to decent society; (*Racing etc.*) a horse or competitor not included among the favourites.

Outsider, The, *n.* (French **L'Etranger**) a novel by Albert Camus, published 1942. A man is sentenced to death, ostensibly for murder, but as much for his failure to conform to the values of a hypocritical society.

outward, *a.* exterior, outer; tending or directed toward the outside; external, visible, apparent, superficial; material, worldly, corporeal, not spiritual; extraneous, extrinsic; †foreign. *adv.* outwards. *n.* outward or external appearance; (*pl.*) externals. **to outward seeming,** apparently. **outward bound,** *a.* going away from home. **outward form,** *n.* appearance. **outward man,** *n.* the carnal man as opp. to the spiritual or the soul. **outward things,** *n.pl.* visible or sensible things; things of this world. **outwardly,** *adv.* **outwardness,** *n.* **outwards,** *adv.* [OE *ūteweard* (OUT, -WARD)]

ouzel, ousel, *n.* one of various thrush-like birds, including the dipper or water-ouzel. **ouzel-cock,** *n.* (*Shak.*) the blackbird. [OE *ōsle* (cp. G *Amsel,* OHG *amsala*)]

ouzo, *n.* (*pl.* **ouzos**) an aniseed-flavoured spirit from Greece. [mod. Gr. *ouzon*]

ova OVUM.

oval, *a.* egg-shaped, roughly elliptical. *n.* a closed convex curve with one axis longer than the other; an egg-shaped figure or thing, e.g. a sports field. **ovally,** *adv.* **ovalness,** *n.* [med. L *ovalis,* from L *ovum,* egg]

Oval, the, a cricket ground in Kennington, London, England, the home of Surrey County Cricket Club. It was the venue for the first test match between England and Australia, 1880.

Ovamboland, *n.* a region of N Namibia stretching along the Namibia-Angola frontier; the scene of conflict between SWAPO guerrillas and South African forces in the 1970s and 1980s.

ovary, *n.* one of the organs (two in number in the higher vertebrates) in a female in which the ova are produced; (*Bot.*) the portion of the pistil in which the ovules are contained. **ovarian,** *a.* **ovariectomy,** *n.* the removal of the ovary by excision, or of a tumour from the ovary. **ovaritis,** *n.* inflammation of the ovary. **ovate,** *a.* egg-shaped. [OVUM, -ARY]

ovation, *n.* in ancient Rome, a minor triumph; a display of popular favour, an enthusiastic reception. [L *ovātio,* from *ovāre,* to rejoice]

oven, *n.* a close chamber in which substances are baked etc.; a furnace or kiln for assaying, annealing etc. **Dutch oven** DUTCH. **oven-bird, -builder,** *n.* the long-tailed titmouse and other birds making oven-shaped nests. **oven glove,** *n.* a thick glove for handling hot dishes. **oven-ready,** *a.* of food, already prepared for immediate cooking in an oven. **ovenware,** *n.* heat-resistant dishes used for cooking and serving food. [OE *ofn* (cp. Dut. *oven,* G *Ofen,* Icel. *ofn,* cogn. with Gr. *ipnos*]

over, (*poet.*) **o'er,** *prep.* above, in a higher position than, above or superior to in excellence, dignity or value; more than, in excess of; in charge of, concerned or engaged with; across from side to side of; through the extent or duration of; having recovered from the effect of. *adv.* so as to pass from side to side or across some space, barrier etc.; in width, in distance across; on the opposite side; from one side to another; so as to be turned down or upside down from an erect position; so as to be across or down from a brink, brim etc.; so as to traverse a space etc.; from end to end, throughout; at an end; in excess, in addition; excessively, with repetition, again. *a.* upper, outer, covering, excessive. *int.* in radio signalling etc., indicating that a reply is expected. *n.* (*Cricket*) the interval between the times when the umpire calls 'over'; the number of balls (6 or 8) delivered by one bowler during this. **all over,** completely, everywhere; most characteristic of him, or her; finished. **over again,** *adv.* afresh, anew. **over against,** *prep.* opposite; in front of; in contrast with. **over and above,** in addition to; besides. **over and over,** so as to turn completely round several times; repeatedly. **over head and ears** HEAD. **over one's head,** beyond one's comprehension. **oversea,** *a.* denoting dominions etc., across the sea. **to give over** GIVE. **to turn over** TURN. [OE *ofer* (cp. Dut. *over,* G *über, ober,* Icel. *yfir, ofr*), cogn. with Gr. *huper,* Sansk. *upari*]

over-, *pref.* above; across; outer, upper; as a covering; past, beyond; extra; excessively, too much, too great. **overabound,** *v.i.* to be superabundant; to abound too much (with or on). **overact,** *v.t.* to overdo; to act (a part) in an exaggerated way. *v.i.* to act more than is necessary. **overall,** *a.* from end to end, total. **overalls**, *n.pl.* trousers or other garments worn over others as a protection against dirt etc. †**overall,** *adv.* everywhere, in all parts or directions. **overarch,** *v.t.* to form an arch over. *v.i.* to form an arch overhead. **overarm**, *a.* in sports, esp. cricket, bowled or thrown with the arm raised above the shoulder. *adv.* the arm raised above the shoulder. **overawe,** *v.t.* to keep in awe; to control or restrain by awe. **overbalance,** *v.t.* to outweigh; to destroy the equilibrium of; to upset. *v.i.* to lose one's equilibrium; to topple over. *n.* excess of value or amount; that which exceeds an equivalent. **overbear,** *v.t.* to bear down, to overpower. **overbearing,** *a.* arrogant, haughty, imperious. **overbearingly,** *adv.* **overbid,** *v.t.*, *v.i.* to outbid; to bid more than the value of (one's hand of cards). *n.* a higher bid. **overblow,** *v.i.*, *v.t.* to blow over. **overblown[1],** *a.* inflated, pretentious. **overblown[2],** *a.* more than full blown. **overboard,** *adv.* over the side of a ship; out of a ship. **to go overboard about, for,** (*coll.*) to go to extremes of enthusiasm about, for. **overbold,** *a.* bold to excess. **overboldly,** *adv.* **overboldness,** *n.* **overbook,** *v.t.*, *v.i.* to make bookings for more places than are available. (e.g. in a hotel, plane, ship etc.) **overbuild,** *v.t.* to build more than is required. to build too much upon (land etc.). †**overbulk,** *v.t.* to surpass in bulk; to overtop. **overburden,** *v.t.* to overload, to overweigh. **overbuy,** *v.i.* to buy more than is required. *v.t.* to pay too much for. **overby** *adv.* (*Sc.*) a little way across; over the way. **overcall,** *v.t.* to bid higher than a previous bid or player at bridge. *n.*, a higher bid than the preceding one. **overcanopy,** *v.t.* to cover with or as with a canopy. **over- capitalize, -ise,** *v.t.* to rate or fix the nominal value of the capital of (a company etc.) at too high a figure. **overcareful,** *a.* careful to excess. **overcast,** *v.t.* to darken, to cloud; to render gloomy or depressed; to sew (an edge etc.) with long stitches to prevent unravelling etc., or as embroidering; to cast off (an illness, etc.); †to rate too high. *a.* clouded all over (of the sky); sewn or embroidered by overcasting; in excess of the proper amount. *n.* something thrown over; a cloud covering the sky; overcast needlework. **overcasting,** *n.* †**overcatch,** *v.t.* to overtake; to outwit. **overcaution,** *n.* excess of caution. **overcautious,** *a.* **overcautiously,** *adv.* **overcharge,** *v.t.* to charge with more than is properly due; to overburden, to overload; to load (a firearm) with an excessive charge; to saturate; to exaggerate. *n.* an excessive charge, load or burden. **overcloud,** *v.t.* to cloud over; to depress, to deject. *v.i.* to become overcast (of the sky). **overcloy,** *v.t.* to surfeit, to satiate. **overcoat,** *n.* a great-coat, a top-coat. **overcoated,** *a.* **overcoating,** *n.* material for overcoats. **overcome,** *v.t.* to overpower, to vanquish, to conquer. **overcomer,** *n.* **overcompensate,** *v.t.* to provide too much in compensation; to react excessively to feelings of inferiority or inadequacy etc. **overcompensation,** *n.* **overconfidence,** *n.* excessive confidence. **over-confident,** *a.* **over-confidently,** *adv.* †**overcount,** *v.t.* to rate above the true value. †**over-cover,** *v.t.* to cover completely over. **overcredulous,** *a.* too credulous. **overcredulously,** *adv.* **overcredulity,** *n.* **overcrop,** *v.t.* to crop (land) to excess; to exhaust by continual cropping. **overcrow,** *v.t.* to crow or triumph over. **overcrowd,** *v.t.*, *v.i.* to crowd to excess. **overcrust,** *v.t.* to cover with a crust. **overcunning,** *a.* too cunning. **overcurious,** *a.* too curious. **overdevelop,** *v.t.* to develop a photographic negative too much so that the image is too dense. †**overdight,** *a.* overspread; decked all over. **overdo,** *v.t.* (*past* **-did,** *p.p.* **-done**) to do to excess; to exaggerate; to overact; to excel; to cook to excess; to fatigue, to wear out. **overdose,** *n.* an excessive dose. *v.t.* to give too large a dose to. **overdraft,** *n.* a withdrawal of money from a bank in excess of the amount to one's credit. **overdraw,** *v.t.* (*past* **-drew,** *p.p.* **-drawn**) to exaggerate; to draw upon for a larger sum than stands to one's credit. **overdress,** *v.t.*, *v.i.* to dress too formally or ostentatiously. *n.* a dress worn over other clothes. **overdrive,** *v.t.* (*past* **-drove,** *p.p.* **-driven**) to drive too far or too hard. *n.* an extra high gear in a motor car which drives the propeller shaft at a higher speed than the engine crankshaft. **overdue,** *a.* remaining unpaid after the date on which it is due; not arrived at the time it was due. *n.* a debt or account that is overdue. (DUE[1]) †**overdye,** *v.t.* to dye too deeply or with a second colour. **overearnest,** *a.* too earnest. **overeat,** *v.i.* to eat to excess. (*reflex.*) to injure (oneself) by eating to excess. *v.t.* to eat or nibble all over. **overestimate,** *v.t.* to give too high a value to. **overexpose,** *v.t.* (*Phot.*) to expose (a film) to light too long so as to make the negative defective. **overexposure,** *n.* †**over-exquisite,** *a.* too nice or exact. **overfall,** *n.* a turbulent race or current with choppy waves caused by shoals, the meeting of cross-currents etc.; a structure for the overflow of water from a canal etc. **overfeed,** *v.t.* to surfeit with food. *v.i.* to eat to excess. †**overflourish,** *v.t.* to adorn superficially; to cover with flowers and verdure. **overflow,** *v.t.* to flow over, to flood, to inundate; to cover as with a liquid. *v.i.* to run over; to abound; to overflow the banks (of a stream). *n.* a flood, an inundation; a superabundance, a profusion; any outlet for surplus liquid. **overflowing,** *a.* **overflowingly,** *adv.* **overfold,** *n.* (*Geol.*) a fold of strata in which the lower part has been pushed over the upper, a reflexed or inverted fold. *v.t.* (*usu. in p.p.*). to push or fold (strata) over in this manner **overfond,** *a.* too fond; doting. **overfondly,** *adv.* †**overfraught,** *a.* overladen. †**overfreight,** *v.t.* to overload, to freight too heavily. **overfull,** *a.* too full; surfeited. †**overgive,** *v.t.* to give over, to surrender. †**overglance,** *v.t.* to glance over. †**overgo,** *v.t.* to go beyond; to pass over; to overcome. *v.i.* to go by; to pass away. †**overgorge,** *v.i.* to gorge to excess. †**overgrassed,** *a.* overgrown with grass. **over-greedy,** *a.* excessively greedy. †**overgreen,** *v.t.* to cover with green, to embellish. **overground,** *a.* situated or running above ground, opp. to underground. **overgrow,** *v.t.* (*past* **-grew,** *p.p.* **-grown**) to cover with vegetation; to outgrow (one's strength etc.). *v.i.* to grow too large. **overgrowth,** *n.* **overhand,** *a.* thrown or done with the hand raised above the level of the shoulder or elbow (of a ball, bowling etc.). *adv.* in this manner. **overhanded,** *a.* with the hand over the object grasped; having too many hands or workers employed. †**overhandle,** *v.t.* to handle or mention too much. **overhang,** *v.i.* (*past, p.p.* **-hung**) to hang over, to jut out. *v.t.* to hang or impend over; to threaten. *n*the act of overhanging; the part or thing that overhangs. **overhappy,** *a.* too happy. **overhaul,** *v.t.* to turn over thoroughly for examination; to examine thoroughly; to overtake, to gain upon. *n.* inspection, thorough examination. **overhead,** *adv.* above the head, aloft; in the zenith, ceiling, roof etc. *a.* situated overhead; (*Mach.*) working from above downwards; (*fig.*) all round, average, general. *n.* a stroke in racket games made above head height; (*pl.*) expenses of administration etc. **overhead projector,** *n.* a device that projects an enlarged image of a transparency on to a screen behind the operator. **overhear,** *v.t.* to hear (words not meant for one) by accident or stratagem; †to hear over again. **overheat,** *v.t.* to heat to excess; to stimulate or agitate. *v.i.* to become overheated. †**overhent,** *v.t.* to overtake. †**overhold,** *v.t.* to value too highly. **overindulge,** *v.t.* (*often reflex.*) to indulge to excess. **overindulgence,** *n.* **overindulgent,** *a.* **overindulgently,** *adv.* **overissue,** *v.t.* to issue in excess (as bank-notes, etc.). *n.* an issue in excess. **overjoy,** *v.t.* to transport with joy. **overjoyed,** *a.* **overjump,** *v.t.* to jump over; to jump beyond; to injure (oneself) by too great a jump. **overkill,** *n.* destructive capability, esp. in nuclear weapons, in excess of military requirements; something applied in excess of what is suitable or required. **overknee,** *a.* reaching above the knee. **overla-**

bour, *v.t.* to harass with labour; to work upon excessively, to elaborate too much. †**overlade,** *v.t.* (*p.p.* **-laden**) to overburden. **overlaid** OVERLAY. **overland,** *a.* lying, going, made or performed by land. *adv.* across the land. *v.t.* (*Austral.*) to take stock across country. **overlander,** *n.* (*Austral.*) one who takes his stock a great distance for sale or to a new station. **overlap,** *v.t.* to lap or fold over; to extend so as to lie or rest upon. *n.* an act, case, or the extent of overlapping; the part that overlaps something else. **overlavish,** *a.* lavish to excess. **overlay,** *v.t.* (*past, p.p.* **-laid**) to cover or spread over the surface of; to cover with a layer; to overcast, to cloud; (*Print.*) to put overlays on; †to weigh down. *n.* something laid over (as a covering, layer etc.); (*Print.*) paper pasted on the tympan to produce a heavier impression. **overlaying,** *n.* a covering. **overleaf,** *adv.* on the other side of the leaf (of a book etc.). **overleap,** *v.t.* to leap over; to leap beyond; to leap too far; (*fig.*) to omit. **to overleap oneself,** to miss one's aim by leaping too far or too high. †**overleather,** *n.* the upper leather of a boot or shoe. **overlie,** *v.t.* (*past* **-lay**) to lie above or upon; to smother by lying on. †**over-light,** *a.* too light. **over-lighted,** *a.* **overload,** *v.t.* to load too heavily; to overcharge. *n.* an excessive load. **overlook,** *v.t.* to view from a high place; to be situated so as to command a view of from above; to superintend, to oversee; to inspect or peruse, esp. in a cursory way; to look over, to pass over with indulgence, to disregard, to slight; to bewitch, to look at with an evil eye. **overlooker,** *n.* **overlord,** *n.* a superior lord, one who is lord over other lords; one who is supreme over another or others. *v.t.* to lord it over; to rule as an overlord. **overlordship,** *n.* †**overlusty,** *a.* too lusty or merry. **overly,** *adv.* excessively, too. **overman,** *n.* a superman; an overseer or foreman. **overman,** *v.t.* to furnish with too many men. **overmantel,** *n.* ornamental woodwork placed over a mantelpiece. **overmany,** *a.* too many. †**overmaster,** *v.t.* to overcome, to subdue. **overmasteringly,** *adv.* **overmasterful,** *a.* **overmasterfulness,** *n.* **overmatch,** *v.t.* to be more than a match for. *n.* a person or thing that is superior in power, skill etc. †**overmeasure,** *v.t.* to estimate too largely. *n.* measure above what is sufficient or due. †**overmount,** *v.t.* to rise above. *v.i.* to mount too high. *n.* a mount for a picture etc. **overmuch,** *a.* too much, more than is sufficient or necessary. *adv.* in or to too great a degree. *n.* more than enough. †**overmultitude,** *v.t.* to out-number. †**overname,** *v.t.* to name in order. **overnice,** *a.* too nice, scrupulous, or fastidious. **overnicely,** *adv.* **overnight,** *a.* done or happening the night before. *adv.* in the course of the night or evening; in or on the evening before; during or through the night †**overoffice,** *v.t.* to lord over in virtue of one's office. **overofficious,** *a.* too officious. **overofficiously,** *adv.* **overofficiousness,** *n.* **overpass,** *v.t.* (*past, p.p.* **-passed, -past**) to pass or go over; to overlook; to pass or go beyond. *n.* a flyover. **overpay,** *v.t., v.i.* to pay more than is sufficient; to pay in excess. **overpayment,** *n.* **overpeer,** *v.t.* to look or peer over; to rise above, to crow over. **overpeople,** *v.t.* to overstock with people. **overpersuade,** *v.t.* to persuade against one's inclination or judgment. **overpicture,** *v.t.* to represent in an exaggerated manner. **overplay,** *v.t.* to exaggerate the importance of; to overemphasize. **to overplay one's hand,** to overestimate one's capabilities. **overplus,** *n.* surplus, excess; an amount left over. **overply,** *v.t.* to ply or exercise to excess. †**overpoise,** *v.t.* to outweigh; to cause to outweigh. *n.*, preponderant weight. †**overpost,** *v.t.* to get over quickly and easily. **overpower,** *v.t.* to be too strong or powerful for; to overcome, conquer, vanquish; to overcome the feelings or judgment of, to overwhelm. **overpoweringly,** *adv.* **overpraise,** *v.t.* to praise too highly. **overpraising,** *n.* excessive eulogy. **overpress,** *v.t.* to overwhelm, to crush, to overpower. **overprint,** *n.* printed matter added to a previously printed surface, esp. a postage stamp. **overprint,** *v.t.* **overprize,** *v.t.* to overvalue; to exceed in value. **overproduction,** *n.* production in excess of demand. **overproduce,** *v.t., v.i.* **overproof,** *a.* above proof, containing a larger proportion of alcohol than is contained in proof-spirit. **overproud,** *a.* excessively proud. †**overrake,** *v.t.* (*Naut.*) to sweep over or through (of shot or waves). **overrate,** *v.t.* to rate too highly. **overreach,** *v.t.* to reach or extend beyond; to get the better of, to outwit, to cheat; †to overtake. *v.i.* to bring the hind feet too far forwards so as to strike the fore foot (of horses). **overread,** *v.t.* to injure (oneself) by too much reading; †to peruse. **overrefine,** *v.t.* to refine too much, to be oversubtle. **overrefinement,** *n.* **override,** *v.t.* (*past* **-rode,** *p.p.* **-ridden**) to ride over; to trample as if underfoot, to disregard, to set aside, to supersede; to fatigue or exhaust by excessive riding; to outride, to overtake; to take manual control of an automatic system. *n.* a device used to override automatic control. **overrider,** *n.* an attachment to the bumper of a motor vehicle to prevent it becoming interlocked with the bumper of another vehicle. **overriding,** *a.* dominant, taking precedence. **overripe,** *a.* ripe to excess. **overripen,** *v.i., v.t.* **overroast,** *v.t.* to roast too much. **overrule,** *v.t.* to control by superior power or authority; to set aside; to reject, to disallow. *v.i.* †to bear sway. **overrun,** *v.t.* to run or spread over; to grow over; to invade or harass by hostile incursions; to extend over; to run beyond, to outrun; (*Print.*) to carry over and change the arrangement of (type set up). *v.i.* to overflow; to extend beyond the proper limits. **overrunner,** *n.* †**over-scutched,** *a.* (*Shak.*), prob. worn out in service. **oversea,** *a.* beyond the sea, foreign. *adv.* from beyond sea. **overseas,** *adv.* **oversee,** *v.t.* to overlook, to superintend; to overlook, to disregard, to neglect. **overseer,** *n.* a superintendent, an inspector; a parish officer charged with the care of the poor. **overseership,** *n.* **oversell,** *v.t.* to sell more than; to sell more of (stocks etc.) than one can deliver; to exaggerate the merits (of a commodity); to use aggressive sales methods. **overset,** *v.t.* to upset; to overthrow; (*Print.*) to set up too much type for (a page etc.). *v.i.* to upset, to be turned over. **oversew,** *v.t.* to sew (two pieces or edges) together by passing the needle through from one side only so that the thread between the stitches lies over the edges. **oversexed,** *a.* obsessed with sexual activity; having an abnormally active sex life. **overshade,** *v.t.* to cover with shade. **overshadow,** *v.t.* to throw a shadow over, to shade over, to obscure with or as with cloud; to shelter, to protect; to tower high above, to exceed in importance. **overshine,** *v.t.* to shine upon. **overshoe,** *n.* a shoe worn over another.

Overijssel, *n.* a province of the E central Netherlands; capital Zwolle; area 3340 sq km/1289 sq miles; population (1988) 1,010,000. It is generally flat, and contains the rivers Ijssel and Vecht. Products include sheep, cattle and dairy products.

Overlord, Operation, *n.* the Allied invasion of Normandy, 6 June 1944, during World War II.

Overseas Development Administration, a British official body that deals with development assistance to overseas countries, including financial aid on concessionary terms and technical assistance, usu. in the form of sending specialists abroad and giving training in the UK.

overt, *a.* open, plain, public, apparent; (*Her.*) spread open (of wings). **overtly,** *adv.* [OF, p.p. of *ovrir* (F *ouvrir*), L *operīre,* to open]

overture, *n.* (*usu. in pl.*) a preliminary proposal, an offer to negotiate, or of suggested terms; an exordium of a poem etc.; (*Mus.*) an introductory piece for instruments, a prelude to an opera or oratorio; a single-movement orchestral piece. *v.t.* to bring forward, introduce or transmit as an overture. [OF (OVERT, -URE)]

ov(i)-¹, ovo-, *comb. form* pertaining to an egg or ovum. [L *ovum,* egg]

ov(i)-², *comb. form* pertaining to sheep. [L *ovis,* sheep]

ovibovine, *a.* belonging to the Ovibovinae, a subfamily of the Bovinae having characters intermediate between those of sheep and oxen. *n.* an animal of this subfamily, a musk-ox. [L *ovis,* sheep, *bōs bovis,* ox]

Ovid, *n.* (full name **Publius Ovidius Naso**) (43–17 BC), Roman poet. His poetry deals mainly with the themes of love (*Amores*, *Ars amatoria*), mythology (*Metamorphoses*), and exile (*Tristia*). **Ovidian**, *a.* of or in the manner of Ovid.

oviduct, *n.* a passage through which ova pass from the ovary, esp. in oviparous animals. **oviducal**, **oviductal**, *a.*

oviferous, *a.* egg-bearing; applied to the receptacle for ova in certain crustaceans.

oviform, *a.* egg-shaped.

ovigerous, *a.* egg-bearing, carrying eggs.

ovine, *a.* of, pertaining to, or like sheep. [L *ovis,* sheep]

oviparous, *a.* producing young by means of eggs that are expelled and hatched outside the body. **oviparity**, *n.* **oviparously,** *adv.* **oviparousness,** *n.*

oviposit, *v.i.* to deposit eggs, esp. with an ovipositor. **oviposition**, *n.* **ovipositor,** *n.* a tubular organ in many insects serving to deposit the eggs.

ovisac, *n.* a closed receptacle in the ovary in which ova are developed.

ovoid, *a.* egg-shaped, oval with one end larger than the other; ovate. *n.* an ovoid body or figure. **ovoidal**, *a.*

ovolo, *n.* (*pl.* **-li**) (*Arch.*) a convex moulding, in Roman architecture a quarter-circle in outline, in Greek, elliptical with the greatest curve at the top. [It. (now *uovolo,*), dim. of *ovo,* egg, L *ōvum*]

ovoviviparous, *a.* producing young by ova hatched within the body of the parent.

ovule, *n.* the rudimentary seed; the body in the ovary which develops into the seed after fertilization; the ovum or germ-cell in an animal, esp. before fertilization. **ovular,** *a.* **ovulate,** *v.i.* **ovulation,** *n.* the periodical discharge of the ovum or egg-cell from the ovary. **ovulite**, *n.* a fossil egg. [F, from mod. L *ōvulum,* dim. of *ovum*]

ovum, *n.* (*pl.* **ova**) the female egg cell, or gamete, produced within the ovary and capable, usu. after fertilization by the male, of developing into a new individual; applied to the eggs of oviparous animals when small; (*Bot.*) an ovule; (*Arch.*) an egg-shaped ornament. [L *ōvum,* an egg]

owe, *v.t.* to be indebted to for a specified amount; to be under obligation to pay or repay (a specified amount); to be obliged or indebted for; to have to thank for (a service, a grudge etc.). *v.i.* to be indebted or in debt. **owing,** *a.* due as a debt; attributable, ascribable, resulting from, on account of. [OE *āgan* (cp. Icel. *eiga,* Dan. *eie,* OHG *aigan*)]

Owen[1], *n.* **David** (1938–), British politician, originally a doctor. He entered Parliament in 1966, and was Labour foreign secretary (1977–79). In 1981 he was one of the founders of the Social Democratic Party (SDP), and in 1983 became its leader. Opposed to the decision of the majority of the party to merge with the Liberals (1987), Owen stood down, but emerged (1988) as leader of a rump SDP.

Owen[2], *n.* **Richard** (1804–92), British anatomist and palaeontologist. He attacked the theory of natural selection and in 1860 published an anonymous and damaging review of Charles Darwin's work. He was Director of the Natural History Museum, London, 1856–83 and was responsible for the first public exhibition of dinosaurs.

Owen[3], *n.* **Robert** (1771–1858), British socialist, born in Wales. In 1800 he became manager of a mill at New Lanark, Scotland, where by improving working and housing conditions and providing schools he created a model community. His ideas stimulated the cooperative movement.

Owen[4], *n.* **Wilfred** (1893–1918), English poet. His verse, owing much to the encouragement of Siegfried Sassoon, expresses his hatred of war, for example *Anthem for Doomed Youth*, published 1921.

Owenism, *n.* the principles of humanitarian and communistic cooperation taught by Robert Owen (see above). †**Owenian**, **Owenist, -ite,** *n.*

Owens, *n.* **(James Cleveland) 'Jesse'** (1913–80), US track and field athlete, who excelled in the sprints, hurdles and long jump. At the 1936 Olympics he won four gold medals.

ower, owercome etc. (*Sc.* OVER, OVER-).

owl, *n.* a nocturnal raptorial bird with large head, short neck and short hooked beak, of various species belonging to the family Strigidae, akin to the night-jars; a fancy breed of domestic pigeons; a solemn-looking person. **owl-light,** *n.* imperfect light, dusk, twilight. **owl-like,** *a., adv.* **owlery,** *n.* **owlet,** *n.* a young owl. **owlish,** *a.* **owlishly,** *adv.* [OE *ūle* (cp. Dut. *uil,* G *Eule,* Icel. *ugla*), cp. L *ulula,* owl]

own[1], *a.* belonging or proper to, particular, individual, not anyone else's (usu. appended as an intensive to the poss. pronoun, adjective etc.); (*ellipt.*) in the closest degree, by both parents (of a brother or sister). **on one's own,** without aid from other people, independently. **to come into one's own,** to gain what one is due; to have one's talents or potential acknowledged. **to get one's own back,** to be even with. **to hold one's own** HOLD. [OE *āgen,* p.p. of *āgan,* OWE]

own[2], *v.t.* to possess; to have as property by right; to acknowledge as one's own; to recognize the authorship, paternity etc. of; to admit, to concede as true or existent. *v.i.* to confess (to). **to own up,** to confess, to make a clean breast (of). **own brand,** *a.* denoting goods on sale which display the name or label of the retailer rather than the producer. **own goal,** *n.* in soccer, a goal scored by a player against his own side by accident; (*coll.*) any action which results in disadvantage to the person taking it. **owner,** *n.* a lawful proprietor. **owner-occupier,** *n.* someone who owns the house he or she lives in. **ownerless**, *a.* **ownership,** *n.* [OE *āgnian,* from *āgen,* OWN[1]]

ox, *n.* (*pl.* **oxen**) the castrated male of the domesticated *Bos taurus;* any bovine animal, esp. of domesticated species of the taurine group, large cloven-hoofed ruminants, usu. horned. **ox-bot, -fly,** *n.* a bot-fly, *Oestrus bovis,* or its larva. **ox-bow**, *n.* the bow-shaped piece of wood in an ox-yoke; a bend in a river. **ox-eye,** *n.* the great titmouse; applied to other birds; the moon-daisy, *Chrysanthemum leucanthemum,* and other composite plants. **ox-eyed,** *a.* having large, full eyes. **ox-fly** OX-BOT. **ox-gall,** *n.* the gall of the ox, used as a cleansing agent in water-colour drawing. **ox-head,** *n.* a dolt, a blockhead. **ox-hide,** *n.* the skin of an ox; ox-skin. **oxlip,** *n.* a cross between the cowslip and primrose. **ox-tail,** *n.* the tail of an ox, esp. when used for making soup. **ox-tongue,** *n.* the alkanet and other plants with tongue-like leaves. [OE *oxa* (cp. Dut. *os,* G *Ochse,* Icel. *uxe, oxe,* Sansk. *ukshan,* pl.)]

Oxalis, *n.* a genus of plants containing the wood-sorrel. **oxalic,** *a.* belonging to or derived from oxalis. **oxalic acid,** *n.* a sour, highly-poisonous acid found in numerous plants. **oxalate,** *n.* a salt or ester of oxalic acid. [L and Gr., from *oxus,* sour]

Oxbridge, *n., a.* (of) the Universities of Oxford and Cambridge, esp. seen as elitist educational establishments conferring unfair social, economic and political advantages. [*Ox*ford and *Cam*bridge]

oxen OX.

Oxfam, *n.* a charity established in the UK 1942 by Canon Theodore Richard Milford (1896–1987), initially to assist the starving people of Greece and subsequently to relieve poverty and famine worldwide. [acronym for *Ox*ford Committee for *Fam*ine Relief]

Oxford, *a.* of, pertaining to, or derived from Oxford. **Oxford bags,** *n.pl.* trousers very wide at the ankles. **Oxford blue,** *n.* a dark shade of blue. **Oxford clay,** *n.* a stiff blue clay underlying the coral rag in the Midland counties, the most characteristic bed of the Middle Oolite series. **Oxford grey,** *n.* a very dark grey. **Oxford Group,** *n.* the religious sect of BUCHMANITES. **Oxford mixture,** *n.* a dark-grey cloth. **Oxford Movement,** *n.* a movement in the Church of England against a tendency toward liberalism, rationalism and Erastianism, originating in the Univ. of Oxford (1833–41) under the leadership of J. H. Newman. **Oxford ochre,** *n.* a yellow ochre found near Oxford. **Oxford ragwort,**

n. a kind of ragwort, *Senecio squalidus*. **Oxford School,** *n.* the school of thought represented by the Oxford Movement. **Oxford shoe,** *n.* a low shoe laced over the instep. [university city in England]

Oxford and Asquith, Earl of, title of British Liberal politician Herbert Henry ASQUITH.

Oxfordshire, *n.* a county in S central England. **area** 2610 sq km/1007 sq miles. **towns** administrative headquarters Oxford; Abingdon, Banbury, Henley-on-Thames, Witney, Woodstock. **products** cereals, cars, paper, bricks, cement. **population** (1987) 578,000.

oxide, *n.* a binary compound of oxygen with another element or an organic radical. **oxidant,** *n.* a substance used as an oxidizing agent. **oxidation,** *n.* the process of oxidizing. **oxidize, -ise,** *v.t.* to combine with oxygen; to cover with a coating of oxide, to make rusty. *v.i.* to enter into chemical combination with oxygen; to rust. **oxidizable, -isable,** *a.* **oxidization, -isation,** *n.* **oxidizer, -iser,** *n.* [OXYGEN, -IDE)]

oxlip etc. OX.

Oxon, (*abbr.*) Oxfordshire (L *Oxonia*); of Oxford (used for degrees etc.) (L *Oxoniensis*).

Oxonian, *n.* a student or graduate of Oxford Univ. *a.* belonging to Oxford. [mod. L *Oxonia,* Oxford, -AN]

oxter, *n.* (*Sc.*) the armpit. [OE *ōxta,* cogn. with *ōxn,* cogn. with L *axilla*]

oxy-, *comb. form* sharp, keen; denoting the presence of oxygen or its acids or of an atom of hydroxyl substituted for one of hydrogen. [Gr. *oxus,* sharp, biting, acid]

oxyacetylene, *a.* yielding a very hot blowpipe flame from the combustion of oxygen and acetylene, used for welding metals etc.

oxyacid, *n.* an acid containing oxygen as distinguished from one formed with hydrogen; (*pl.*) one of the groups of acids derived from the fatty or aromatic series by the substitution of an atom of hydroxyl for one of hydrogen.

oxycarpous, *a.* having pointed fruit. [Gr. *karpos,* fruit]

oxygen, *n.* a colourless, tasteless, odourless divalent element (at. no. 8; chem. symbol O) existing in a free state in the atmosphere, combined with hydrogen in water, and with other elements in most mineral and organic substances. **oxygen mask,** *n.* an apparatus for supplying oxygen in rarefied atmospheres to aviators etc. **oxygen tent,** *n.* an oxygen-filled tent placed over a patient to assist breathing. **oxygenate,** *v.t.* to treat or impregnate with oxygen; to oxidize. **oxygenation,** *n.* **oxygenator,** *n.* **oxygenous,** *a.* **oxygenize, -ise,** *v.t.* [F *oxygène* (OXY-, -GEN), from the belief that it was the essential element in all acids]

oxyhydrogen, *a.* consisting of a mixture of oxygen and hydrogen, applied to a mixture used to create an intense flame for welding. [OXY-, HYDROGEN]

oxymoron, *n.* a rhetorical figure in which an epithet of a quite contrary signification is added to a word for the sake of point or emphasis, e.g. a clever fool, a cheerful pessimist. [Gr. *oxumōron* (OXY-, *mōros,* stupid)]

oxytocin, *n.* a hormone secreted by the pituitary gland that stimulates uterine muscle contraction during childbirth. [OXY-, Gr. *tokos,* birth]

oxytone, *a.* having an acute accent on the last syllable. *n.* an oxytone word. [Gr. *oxutonos* (OXY-, *tonos,* TONE)]

oyer, *n.* (*Law*) a hearing or trial of causes under writ of oyer and terminer. **oyer and terminer,** a commission formerly issued to two or more of the judges of assize, empowering them to hear and determine specified offences. [A-F, in *oyer et terminer,* hear and determine (L *audīre,* to hear, *termināre,* to TERMINATE)]

oyez, oyes, *int.* thrice repeated as introduction to any proclamation made by an officer of a court of law or public crier. [OF, hear ye, pl. imper. of *oir* (F *ouïr*), L *audīre,* to hear]

oyster, *n.* an edible bivalve mollusc of the genus *Ostrea,* found in salt or brackish water, eaten as food; an oyster-shaped morsel of meat in the hollow on either side of a fowl's back. **oyster-bank, -bed,** *n.* a part of a shallow sea-bottom forming a breeding-place for oysters. **oyster-catcher,** *n.* a wading-bird, *Haematopus ostralegus,* the sea-pie; also the American *H. palliatus*. **oyster-farm, -field, -park,** *n.* a part of the sea-bottom used for breeding oysters. **oyster-knife,** *n.* a knife specially shaped for opening oysters. **oyster-patty,** *n.* a small pie made from oysters. [OF *oistre* (F *huître,* L *ostrea,* Gr. *ostreon*]

oz, (*abbr.*) ounce. [It. *onza*]

Oz, *n.* (*Austral. sl.*) Australia.

Ozark Mountains, *n.pl.* an area in the US (shared by Arkansas, Illinois, Kansas, Mississippi and Oklahoma) of ridges, valleys and streams, the highest point only 700 m/2300 ft.; area 130,000 sq km/50,000 sq miles.

ozocerite , ozokerite , *n.* a fossil resin like spermaceti in appearance, used for making candles, insulators etc. [G *Ozokerit* (Gr. *ozō,* I smell, *kēros,* wax[1], -ITE)]

ozone, *n.* an allotropic form of oxygen, having three atoms to the molecule, with a slightly pungent odour, found in the atmosphere, probably as the result of electrical action. **ozonic, ozoniferous,** *a.* **ozonize, -ise,** *v.t.* to charge with ozone. **ozonizer, -iser,** *n.* **ozonosphere, ozone layer,** *n.* a layer of ozone in the stratosphere which protects the earth from the sun's ultraviolet rays. **ozone-friendly,** *a.* of sprays etc., not damaging the ozone layer, not containing chlorofluorocarbon (cfc). [F (Gr. *ozein,* to smell, -ONE)]

P

P¹, p¹, the 16th letter, and the 12th consonant (*pl.* **Pees, P's, Ps**), is a voiceless labial mute, having the sound heard in *pull, cap,* except when in combination with *h* it forms the digraph *ph*, sounded as *f*. **to mind one's Ps and Qs,** to be careful over details, esp. in behaviour.

P², (*chem. symbol*) phosphorus.

P³, (*abbr.*) parking; in chess, pawn; Portugal.

p², (*abbr.*) page; penny, pence; (*Mus.*) piano, used as an instruction to play softly; pint; power; pressure.

PA, (*abbr.*) Panama; personal assistant; Press Association; public address (system).

Pa¹, (*abbr.*) Pennsylvania.

Pa², (*chem. symbol*) protactinium.

pa¹, *n.* a child's name for father. [short for PAPA]

pa² PAH².

p.a., (*abbr.*) per annum.

pabulum, *n.* food; nourishment; nutriment of a physical, mental or spiritual kind. **pabular,** *a.* [L *pabulum,* cogn. with *pascere,* to feed]

PABX, (*abbr.*) private automatic branch (telephone) exchange.

paca, *n.* a large Central and South American semi-nocturnal rodent, *Coelogenys paca,* and others of the same genus. [Tupí-Guaraní]

pacable, *a.* able to be pacified or appeased, placable. **†pacation,** *n.* [L *pācābilis,* from *pācāre,* to appease, from *pax pācis,* PEACE]

pace¹, *n.* a step, the space between the feet in stepping (about 30 in., 76 cm); in ancient Rome, the space between the point where the heel left the ground and that where the same heel descended in the next stride (about 60 in., 152 cm); gait, manner of going, either in walking or running; the carriage and action of a horse etc.; an amble, rate of speed or progress. *v.i.* to walk with slow or regular steps; to walk with even strides or in a slow, deliberate manner; to amble. *v.t.* to measure by carefully regulated steps; to traverse in slow and measured steps; to set the pace for. **to be put through one's paces,** to be examined closely, to be tested. **to force the pace,** to try to increase the speed or tempo of any activity. **to go the pace,** to go very fast; to lead a life of dissipation or recklessness. **to keep pace with,** to go or progress at equal rate with. **to set, make the pace,** to fix the rate of going in a race or any other activity. **pacemaker,** *n.* a rider or runner who sets the pace in a race; a person who sets the pace in any form of activity; a small device, usu. implanted in the chest, that corrects irregularities in the heartbeat. **pace-setter,** *n.* a pacemaker. **paced,** *a.* having a particular pace or gait (*in comb.*, as *thorough-paced*). **pacer,** *n.* one who paces; a horse trained in pacing. **pacey, pacy,** *a.* (*coll.*) of a story, film etc., moving at a fast, exciting pace. [ME and OF *pas,* L *passum,* nom. *-sus,* p.p. of *pandere,* to stretch]

pace², *prep.* with the permission of; with due respect to (someone who disagrees). [L, abl. of PAX]

pacha, etc. PASHA.

pachisi, *n.* an Indian game played on a board with cowries for dice, named after the highest throw. [Hindi, lit. 25]

pachy-, *comb.form* denoting thickness. [Gr. *pachus,* thick, large]

pachydactyl, *n.* an animal having thick toes.

pachyderm, *n.* any individual of the Pachydermata, an order of mammals containing hoofed non-ruminant animals with thick integuments; a thick-skinned person. **pachydermatoid, -tous, pachydermoid,** *a.* **pachydermia,** *n.* abnormal thickening of the skin.

pachyhaemia, *n.* thickness of the blood. [Gr. *haima,* blood]

pachymeter, *n.* an instrument for determining the thickness of glass, paper etc.

pacific, *a.* inclined or tending to peace, conciliatory; tranquil, quiet, peaceful; of the Pacific Ocean. **the Pacific,** the Pacific Ocean. **Pacific Islands,** *n. pl.* a United Nations trust territory in the W Pacific comprising over 2000 islands and atolls, under Japanese mandate 1919–47, and administered by the US 1947–80, when all its members, the Carolines, Marianas (except Guam), and Marshall islands, became independent. **Pacific Ocean,** *n.* the world's largest ocean, so named by Magellan, extending from Antarctica to the Bering Strait; area 166,242,500 sq km/64,170,000 sq miles; average depth 4188m/13,745 ft. **†pacifical,** *a.* **pacifically,** *adv.* **pacification,** *n.* the act of pacifying. **pacificator,** *n.* **pacificatory,** *a.* **pacifier,** *n.* one who or that which pacifies; (*N Am.*) a baby's dummy or similar object for sucking. **pacifism,** *n.* the doctrine of non-resistance to hostilities and of total non-cooperation with any form of warfare. **pacifist,** *n.* one who practises pacifism. *a.* of pacifism. **pacify,** *v.t.* to appease, to calm, to quiet; to restore peace to. [F *pacifique,* L *pacificus* (*pax pācis, -ficāre, facere,* to make)]

Pacific Security Treaty, military alliance agreement between Australia, New Zealand and US, signed 1951.

Pacific War, *n.* a war (1879–83) by an alliance of Bolivia and Peru against Chile. Chile seized Antofagasta and the coast between the mouths of the rivers Loa and Paposo, rendering Bolivia completely landlocked.

pack¹, *n.* a bundle of things tied or wrapped together for carrying; a parcel, a burden, a load; a quantity going in such a bundle or parcel taken as a measure, varying with different commodities; a small packet, e.g. of cigarettes; a set, a crew, a gang; a set of playing-cards; a number of dogs kept together; a number of wolves or other beasts or birds, esp. grouse, going together; a quantity of broken ice floating in the sea; a quantity of fish packed for the market; in rugby, the forwards of a team. *v.t.* to put together into a pack or packs; to stow into a bundle, box, barrel, bag, tin etc., for keeping, carrying etc.; to crowd closely together, to compress; to fill completely; to cram (with); to wrap tightly, to cover or surround with some material to prevent leakage, loss of heat etc.; to load with a pack; to arrange (cards) in a pack; to manipulate (cards) so as to win unfairly; to select or bring together (a jury etc.) so as to obtain some unfair advantage; to send off or dismiss without ceremony. *v.i.* to put things in a pack, bag, trunk etc., for sending away, carrying or keeping; of animals, to crowd together, to form a pack; to leave with one's belongings; to depart hurriedly. **to pack a punch,** (*coll.*) to be able to punch hard; to be strong or forceful. **to pack in, up,** (*sl.*) to stop doing (something); to stop going out with (someone). **to pack on all sail,** (*Naut.*) to put all sail on. **to pack up,** (*sl.*) to stop functioning; to break down. **to send packing,** to dismiss summarily. **packdrill,** *n.* a form of military punishment consisting of high-speed drill in full kit. **packhorse,** *n.* a horse employed in carrying goods. **pack-ice,** *n.* large pieces of ice floating in the polar seas. **packman,** *n.* a pedlar. **pack rat,** *n.* a rat of western N America, with a long tail that is furry in some species. **packsaddle,** *n.* one for supporting packs. **packstaff,** *n.* a pedlar's staff for slinging his pack on. **packthread,** *n.* strong thread for sewing or tying up parcels. **package**, *n.* a parcel, a bundle; the packing of goods, the manner in which they are packed; the container, wrapper etc. in which a thing is packed; a number of items offered together. *v.t.* to place in a packet; to bring (a number of items) together as a single unit. **package deal,** *n.* a deal in which a number of items are offered, and all must be accepted. **package holiday,** *n.* a holiday where travel, accommodation, meals etc. are all included in the price. **packaging,** *n.* the container etc. in which something is packaged; the presentation of a person or thing to the public in a particular, esp. favourable, way. **packer,** *n.* one who packs, esp. one employed to pack meat, fish, fruit etc. for the market; a machine for doing this. **packing,** *n.* that which is used for packing; material closing a joint or helping to lubricate a journal. **packing-case,** *n.* a large box made of unplaned wood. **packing-needle,** *n.* a long curved needle, used for sewing up bales etc. **packing-ring,** *n.* the piston-ring in an internal-combustion engine. **packing-sheet,** *n.* a large sheet for packing; a wet sheet for wrapping a patient, in hydropathic treatment. [cp. Dut. *pak,* Icel. *pakki,* G *Pack*]

pack[2], *a.* (*Sc.*) intimate, closely confederate, confidential. [etym. doubtful]

packet, *n.* a small package; a packet-boat; (*sl.*) a large sum of money. *v.t.* to make up in a packet. **packet-boat,** *n.* a vessel conveying mails, goods and passengers at regular intervals. [PACK[1]]

paco, *n.* (*pl.* **-cos**) the alpaca; a native brown, earthy, iron oxide. [Sp. and Quichua]

pact, *n.* an agreement, a compact. [OF, from L *pactum,* agreement, orig. neut. p.p. of *paciscere,* cogn. with PAX]

pacy PACE[1].

pad[1], *n.* the road, the way; a footpad; highway robbery; an easy-paced horse. *v.i.* to travel on foot; to trudge. *v.t.* to tramp or travel over; to tread. **knight, squire of the pad,** a knight of the road, a highwayman. **to pad the hoof,** to tramp on foot. **pad-groom,** *n.* a groom of light weight who rides a second horse for his master when hunting. †**pad-nag,** *n.* an ambling nag. [Dut., PATH]

pad[2], *n.* a soft cushion; a bundle or mass of soft stuff of the nature of a cushion; a soft saddle without a tree; a cushion-like package, cap, guard etc., for stuffing, filling out, protecting parts of the body etc.; sanitary towel; a quantity of blotting-paper or soft material for writing on; a number of sheets of paper fastened together at the edge for writing upon and then detaching; a rocket-launching platform; an area for take-off and landing, esp. for helicopters; the cushion-like sole of the foot, or the soft cushion-like paw of certain animals; (*coll.*) one's home or room. *v.t.* (*past, p.p.* **padded**) to stuff or line with padding; to furnish with a pad or padding; to fill out (a sentence, article etc.) with unnecessary words; to impregnate with a mordant. **padsaw,** *n.* a small narrow saw for cutting curves. **padded cell, room,** *n.* a room with padded walls for confining violent patients. **padding,** *n.* material used for stuffing a saddle, cushion etc.; unnecessary matter inserted to fill out an article, magazine or book. [etym. doubtful]

paddle[1], *n.* a broad short oar used without a rowlock; the blade of this or of an oar; a paddle-board; a paddle-wheel; a spell of paddling; a spade-like implement used for cleaning a plough-share of earth, digging up weeds etc.; a similar implement used in washing clothes; a table-tennis bat; a creature's broad, flat limb for swimming, a flipper. *v.t.* to propel by means of paddles; (*N Am.*) to spank. *v.i.* to ply a paddle; to move along by means of a paddle; to row gently; to swim with short, downward strokes. **paddle-board,** *n.* one of the floats or blades of a paddle-wheel. **paddle-box,** *n.* the casing over the upper part of a paddle-wheel. **paddle-wheel,** *n.* a wheel with floats or boards projecting from the periphery for pressing against the water and propelling a vessel. [etym. doubtful]

paddle[2], *v.i.* to dabble in the water with the hands or, more usually, the feet; to move the fingers in a fondling way (in, upon or about); to toddle. [etym. doubtful]

paddock[1], *n.* a small field or enclosure, usu. under pasture and near a stable; a turfed enclosure attached to a stud-farm; (*Austral.*) any pasture land enclosed by a fence; a turfed enclosure adjoining a racecourse where horses are kept before racing; an area beside a motor-racing circuit where cars are parked, repaired etc. [prob. corr. of OE *pearruc,* cp. PARK]

paddock[2], *n.* (*Sc.*) a frog; a toad; †a repulsive person. **paddock-stool,** *n.* a toadstool. [ME *padde* (cp. Icel. *padda,* Dut. *padde*), -OCK]

Paddy, *n.* (*sometimes derog.*) an Irishman. **Paddy's lucerne,** *n.* (*Austral.*) a Queensland weed. [short for *Padraig,* St *Patrick,* the patron of Ireland]

paddy[1], *n.* rice in the straw or in the husk; a paddy-field. **paddy-field,** *n.* a field planted with rice. [Malay *paddi*]

paddy[2], *n.* (*coll.*) a rage, temper.

paddymelon, *n.* (*Austral.*) a small bush kangaroo or wallaby. [corr. of Abor. name]

padella, *n.* a shallow vessel containing oil etc. in which a wick is set, used esp. in Italy for illuminations. [It., from L PATELLA]

padishah, *n.* the title of the Shah of Iran, also formerly in India of the British sovereign and of the Great Mogul. [Turk., from Pers. *pādshāh* (Sansk. *pati,* master, lord, SHAH)]

padkos, *n.* food for a journey. [South African]

padlock, *n.* a detachable lock with a bow or loop for fastening to a staple etc. *v.t.* to fasten with this. [*pad,* etym. doubtful, LOCK[1]]

padre, *n.* used in addressing a priest in Italy, Spain and Spanish America; a chaplain in the armed forces. [Port., Sp. and It., father or priest]

padrone, *n.* a master, an Italian employer or house-owner; the proprietor of an inn in Italy; the master of a small trading-vessel in the Mediterranean. [It., from med. L *patrōnem,* nom. *patro,* L *patrōnus,* PATRON]

padsaw PAD[2].

Padua, *n.* (Italian **Padova**), city in N Italy, 45 km/25 miles W of Venice; population (1986) 226,000. The astronomer Galileo taught at the university (founded 1222).

paduasoy, *n.* a kind of silk stuff, much worn in the 18th cent.; a garment of this. [F *pou-de-soie,* corr. by association with *Padua,* a city in Italy]

paean, *n.* a choral song addressed to Apollo or some other deity; a song of triumph or rejoicing. [L, from Gr. *Paian,* a name of Apollo]

paed- PAED(O)-.

paedagogy, etc. PEDAGOGY.

paederast, PEDERAST.

paedeutics, *n. sing.* the science of education. [Gr. *paideutikos,* from *paideuein,* to bring up a child, from *pais paidos,* a child]

paediatrics, (*esp. N Am.*) **pediatrics**, *n. sing.* the branch of medicine dealing with children's diseases. **paediatric,** *a.* **paediatrician**, *n.* a specialist in paediatrics.

paed(o)-, *comb. form* relating to children. [Gr. *pais paidos,* boy, child]

paedobaptism, *n.* infant as opposed to adult baptism. **paedobaptist,** *n.* [BAPTISM]

paella, *n.* a Spanish dish of rice, seafood, meat and vegetables, flavoured with saffron. [Sp., lit. pan, from L PATELLA]

paeon, *n.* a metrical foot of four syllables, one long, the others short in different order. [L, from Gr. *paiōn,* Attic form of *paian,* PAEAN]

paeony, PEONY.

pagan, *n.* a heathen; a barbarous or unenlightened person; a person who has no religion or disregards Christian beliefs. *a.* heathen, heathenish; unenlightened; irreligious. **pagandom**, **paganism,** *n.* **paganish,** *a.* **paganize, -ise,** *v.t., v.i.* [L *pāgānus* (from *pāgus,* the country), a countryman, hence a non-militant (opp. to *miles Christi,* a soldier of Christ)]

Pagan, *n.* archaeological site in Burma with the ruins of the former capital (founded 847), including Buddhist temples with wall paintings of 11th-13th cents.

Paganini, *n.* **Niccolò** (1782–1840), Italian violinist, a soloist from the age of nine. He composed works for the violin which exploit all the instrument's potentials.

page[1], *n.* a young male attendant on persons of rank; hence, a title of various functionaries attached to the royal household; a boy acting as an attendant at a wedding; a boy in livery employed to go on errands, attend to the door etc.; †a youth in training for knighthood attached to a knight's retinue. †*v.t.* to attend on as a page; to summon a person (in a hotel etc.) by calling the name aloud; to summon by transmitting an audible signal on an electronic device. **page boy,** *n.* a page; a (woman's) medium-length hairstyle, with the ends curled under. **pagehood, pageship,** *n.* [OF, etym. doubtful]

page[2], *n.* (one side of) a leaf of a book; a record, a book; an episode; a subdivision of a computer memory. *v.t.* to put numbers on the pages of (a book). **paginal,** †**paginary,** *a.* **paginate,** *v.t.* **pagination,** *n.* **paging,** *n.* [F, from L *pāgina,* from *pāg-,* stem of *pangere,* to fasten]

Page[1], *n.* **Earle (Christmas Grafton)** (1880–1961), Australian politician who served in the British war cabinet 1941–42 and as minister of health 1949–55.

Page[2], *n.* **Frederick Handley** (1885–1962), British aircraft engineer, founder of an aircraft manufacturing company in 1909 and designer of long-range civil aeroplanes and multi-engined bombers in both World Wars.

pageant, *n.* a brilliant display or spectacle, esp. a parade or procession of an elaborate kind; a theatrical exhibition, usu. representing well-known historical events, and illustrating costumes, buildings, manners etc.; a tableau or allegorical design, usu. mounted on a car in a procession; empty and specious show. †*v.t.* to exhibit in a show. **pageantry,** *n.* [perh. as prec.]

paginate, pagination PAGE[2].

pagoda, *n.* a sacred temple, usu. in the form of a pyramidal tower in many receding storeys, all elaborately decorated, in India, China and other Eastern countries; a building imitating this; a gold coin formerly current in India. **pagoda-tree,** *n.* the name of several kinds of Indian and Chinese trees shaped more or less like pagodas. **pagodite,** *n.* a soft limestone which the Chinese carve into figures. [Port. *pagode,* corr. of Indian name]

pagurian, paguroid, *a.* of or pertaining to the Paguridae or decapod crustaceans. *n.* a member of this family, a hermit crab. [L *pagūrus,* Gr. *pagouros*]

pah[1], *int.* an exclamation of disgust etc.

pah[2], pa[2], *n.* a native settlement. [Maori]

Pahlavi, *n.* the characters used for the sacred writings of the Iranians; the literary language of Iran under the Sassanian kings, old Persian. **Pahlavi dynasty,** *n.* Iranian dynasty founded by Riza Khan (1877–1944), an army officer who seized control of the government in 1921 and was proclaimed shah in 1925. During World War II Britain and the USSR compelled him to abdicate in favour of his son Mohammed Riza, who was deposed in the Islamic Revolution (1979). [Pers., from *Pahlav,* a district in Parthia]

paid, PAY[1].

paideutics, PAEDEUTICS.

paigle, *n.* (*dial.*) the cowslip; applied to the oxlip, buttercup etc. [etym. doubtful]

paik, *v.t.* (*Sc.*) to hit, to beat. *n.* a hard blow, a beating. [etym. doubtful]

pail, *n.* an open vessel, usu. round, of metal or wood, for carrying liquids; a pailful. **pailful,** *n.* (*pl.* **-fuls**). [cp. OE *pægel,* Dut. *pegel,* G *Pegel* a small measure of liquid]

paillette, *n.* a small piece of metal or foil used in enamel-painting; a spangle. [F, dim. of *paille,* L *palea,* straw, chaff]

paillon, *n.* a bright metal backing for enamel or painting in translucent colours.

pain, *n.* bodily or mental suffering; a disagreeable sensation in animal bodies; (*pl.*) labour, trouble; (*coll.*) a nuisance; †punishment, penalty. *v.t.* to inflict pain upon, to afflict or distress bodily or mentally; †to torture, to punish. **a pain in the neck,** (*coll.*) a nuisance. **on pain of, under pain of,** subject to the penalty of. **to take pains,** to take trouble, to labour hard or be exceedingly careful. **painkiller,** *n.* a drug that alleviates pain. **painkilling,** *a.* **painstaker,** *n.* one who takes pains, a laborious worker. **painstaking,** *n., a.* **pained,** *a.* having or showing distress, embarrassment etc. **painful,** *a.* attended with or causing mental or physical pain; laborious, toilsome, difficult. **painfully,** *adv.* **painfulness,** *n.* **painless,** *a.* **painlessly,** *adv.* **painlessness,** *n.* [OF *peine,* L *paena,* Gr. *poinē,* penalty]

Paine, *n.* **Thomas** (1737–1809), British left-wing political writer, active in the American and French revolutions. His pamphlets include *Common Sense* (1776), *The Rights of Man* (1791), and *The Age of Reason* (1793). He advocated republicanism, deism, abolition of slavery, and the emancipation of women.

paint, *v.t.* to cover or coat with paint; to give a specified colour to with paint; to tinge; to portray or represent in colours; to adorn with painting; to depict vividly in words. *v.i.* to practise painting; to rouge. *n.* a solid colouring-substance or pigment, usu. dissolved in a liquid vehicle, used to give a coloured coating to surfaces; colouring-matter used as a cosmetic, rouge. **to paint out,** to efface by painting over. **to paint the town red,** (*sl.*) to go out on a noisy spree. **paint-box,** *n.* a box in which oil- or water-colours are kept in compartments. **paint-brush,** *n.* **painted lady,** *n.* an orange-red butterfly spotted with black and white; the sweet pea. **painter[1],** *n.* one whose occupation is to colour walls, woodwork etc. with paint; an artist who paints pictures. **painter's colic,** *n.* a kind of lead-poisoning to which painters are subject. **painterly,** *a.* pertaining to or having the qualities of painting. **painting,** *n.* the act, art or occupation of laying on colours or producing representations in colours; a picture. **painty,** *a.* (*coll.*) like paint in smell etc.; covered in paint. [OF *peint,* p.p. of *peindre,* L *pingere*]

painter[2], *n.* a bow-rope for fastening a boat to a ring, stake etc. [perh. from OF *pentoir,* med. L *penditōrium,* from *pendēre,* to hang; or from A-F *panter* (F *pantière*), a snare]

pair[1], *n.* two things of a kind, similar in form, or applied to the same purpose or use; a set of two, a couple, usu. corresponding to each other; an implement or article having two corresponding and mutually dependent parts, as scissors, spectacles; two playing-cards of the same value; an engaged or married couple; a flight (of stairs); (*Parl.*) two members of opposite views abstaining from voting by mutual agreement. *v.t.* to make or arrange in pairs or couples; to cause to mate. *v.i.* to be arranged in pairs; to mate; to unite in love; (*coll.*) to marry; (*Parl.*) to make a pair (with). **to pair off,** to separate into couples; to go off in pairs; (*Parl.*) to make a pair (with). **pair-bond,** *n.* a lasting, exclusive relationship between a male and a female. **pair-horse,** *a.* of harness etc., for a pair of horses. **pairing-time,** *n.* the time when birds mate. **pair-oar,** *n.* a boat rowed by two men each with one oar. †**pair royal,** *n.* three cards of the same denomination in certain games. [F *paire,* L *paria,* neut. pl. of *par,* equal]

†**pair[2],** *v.t.* to impair. [from obs. *appair empeirer,* IMPAIR]

paisley, *n.* (a fabric bearing) a colourful pattern of small intricate curves, a shawl made of this fabric. *a.* of or concerning this fabric or pattern. [*Paisley,* town in Scotland]

pajamas, PYJAMAS.

pake, *n.* a Maori mat or cloak. [Maori]

pakeha, *n.* a white man in New Zealand. **Pakeha Maori,** *n.* a European who lives as a Maori with them. [Maori]

Pakhtoonistan, *n.* independent state desired by the Pathan people.

Paki, *n.* (*sl.*, *offensive*) a Pakistani.

Pakistan, *n.* Islamic Republic of, country of S Asia, stretching from the Himalayas to the Arabian Sea, bounded to the W by Iran, to the NW by Afghanistan, to the NE by China, and to the E by India. **area** 796,100 sq km/307,295 sq miles; one-third of Kashmir is under Pakistani control. **capital** Islamabad. **towns** Karachi (largest city and port), Lahore. **physical** fertile plains; Indus river; Himalaya mountains in the north. **exports** cotton textiles, rice, leather, carpets. **population** (1989) 110,358,000 (66% Punjabi, 13% Sindhi); annual growth rate 3.1%. **language** Urdu and English (official); Punjabi. **religion** Sunni Muslim 75%, Shi'ite Muslim 20%, Hindu 4%.

Pakistani, *a.* pertaining to Pakistan. *n.* a native or inhabitant of Pakistan.

pakora, *n.* an Indian dish of pieces of chicken, vegetable etc. dipped in spiced batter and deep-fried. [Hind.]

paktong, *n.* a Chinese alloy of zinc, nickel and copper, like silver. [Cantonese for Chin. *peh t'ung* (*peh,* white, *t'ung,* copper)]

PAL, (*acronym*) *p*hase *a*lternation *l*ine, a system of colour television broadcasting used in Europe.

pal, *n.* (*coll.*) a friend, chum or mate. **to pal up with,** (*coll.*) to become friendly with. **pally,** *a.* (*coll.*) friendly. [Gipsy]

palace, *n.* the official residence of an emperor, king, bishop or other distinguished personage; a splendid mansion; a large building for entertainments, a music-hall, cinema, theatre, showy drinking-saloon etc. **palace-car,** *n.* a luxuriously-appointed railway car. [OF *palais,* L *palātium,* orig. a house built by Augustus on the Palatine Hill at Rome]

paladin, *n.* one of Charlemagne's 12 peers; a knight-errant. [F, from L *palātīnus,* PALATINE²]

palae- PALAE(O)-.

palaearctic, *a.* pertaining to the northern parts of the Old World, including Europe, N Africa, and Asia north of the Himalayas, esp. as a zoogeographical region.

palaeichthyology, *n.* the branch of palaeontology concerned with extinct fishes.

palae(o)-, (*esp. N Am.*), **pale(o)-,** *comb.form* pertaining to or existing in the earliest times. [Gr. *palaios,* old, ancient]

palaeobotany, *n.* the botany of extinct or fossil plants. **palaeobotanical,** *a.* **palaeobotanist,** *n.*

Palaeocene, *n., a.* (of) the oldest epoch of the Tertiary period, 65–55 million years ago. Many types of mammal spread rapidly after the disappearance of the great reptiles of the Mesozoic.

palaeoclimatology, *n.* the science of the climates of the geological past.

palaeogean, *a.* pertaining to the early conditions of the earth's surface; pertaining to the Old World as a zoogeographical region. [Gr. *gaia, gē,* the earth]

palaeography, *n.* the art or science of deciphering ancient inscriptions or manuscripts; ancient inscriptions or manuscripts collectively. **palaeograph,** *n.* **palaeographer,** *n.* **palaeographic,** *a.*

palaeolithic, *a.* pertaining to the earlier Stone Age. **palaeolith,** *n.* a stone implement of this period. [Gr. *lithos,* a stone]

palaeology, *n.* the science of antiquities, archaeology. **palaeologist,** *n.*

palaeomagnetism, *n.* the study of the magnetic properties of rocks.

palaeont., (*abbr.*) palaeontology.

palaeontology, *n.* the science or the branch of biology or geology dealing with fossil animals and plants. **palaeontological,** *a.* **palaeontologist,** *n.*

palaeothere, palaeotherium, *n.* an extinct genus of pachydermatous mammals chiefly from the Eocene strata. [Gr. *thērion,* beast]

Palaeozoic, *a., n.* (denoting) the era of geological time 590–248 million years ago, extending from the Cambrian to the Permian periods and marked by the lowest fossiliferous strata and the earliest forms of life.

palaestra, *n.* in ancient Greece, a place where athletic exercises were taught and practised; a gymnasium or wrestling-school. **palaestral, -tric,** *a.* [Gr. *palaistra,* from *palaiein,* to wrestle]

palafitte, *n.* a prehistoric house built on piles, a lake-dwelling. [F, from It. *palafitta* (*palo,* PALE¹, *fitto,* fixed)]

palais (de danse), *n.* (*coll.*) a public dance-hall. [F]

palama, *n.* the webbing of the feet in aquatic birds. [Gr. *palamē,* palm of the hand]

palampore, *n.* a decorated chintz counterpane, formerly made in India. [etym. doubtful]

palankeen, palanquin *n.* a couch or litter borne by four or six men on their shoulders. [Port. *palanquim,* Hindi *pālakī* or *palang,* Sansk. *palyaṅka, paryaṅka,* couch, bed]

palatable, *a.* pleasing to the taste; agreeable, acceptable. **palatability, palatableness,** *n.* **palatably,** *adv.* [PALATE, -ABLE]

palate, *n.* the roof of the mouth; the sense of taste; liking, fancy. *v.t.* to try with the taste; to relish. **hard, bony palate,** the anterior or bony part of the palate. **soft palate,** the posterior part consisting of muscular tissue and mucous membrane terminating in the uvula. **palatal,** *a.* pertaining to or uttered by the aid of the palate. *n.* a sound produced with the palate, esp. the hard palate, as *k, g, ch, y, s, n.* **palatalize, -ise, palatize, -ise,** *v.t.* **palatic,** *a.* **palatine,** *a.* of or pertaining to the palate. *n.pl.* (also **palatine bones**) the two bones forming the hard palate. [L *palātum*]

palatial, *a.* pertaining to or befitting a palace; magnificent, splendid. **palatially,** *adv.* [L *palātium,* PALACE, -AL]

palatine¹ PALATE.

palatine², *a.* pertaining to or connected with a palace, orig. the palace of the Caesars, later of the German Emperors; palatial; possessing or exercising royal privileges (as the counties of Chester, Durham and Lancaster); of or pertaining to a count palatine. *n.* one invested with royal privileges; a count or earl palatine; a woman's fur tippet worn over the shoulders. **The Palatine,** the territory of the Count Palatine of the Rhine, an elector of the Holy Roman Empire. **palatinate,** *n.* the office or territory of a palatine. [F *palatin, -tine,* L *palātīnus,* from *palātium,* PALACE]

palaver, *n.* a discussion, a conference, a parley; talk, chatter; cajolery, flattery; tedious activity. *v.t.* to talk over, to flatter. *v.i.* to confer; to talk idly and profusely. **palaverer,** *n.* [Port. (Sp. *palabra*), from L *parabola,* PARABLE]

palay, *n.* a small Indian tree, *Wrightia,* of the dogbane family, with hard, close-grained wood used for turnery. [Tamil]

palberry, *n.* a type of currant. [Austral. Abor. *palbri*]

pale¹, *n.* a pointed stake; a narrow board used in fencing; a limit or boundary; a region, a district, a territory, a sphere; (*Her.*) a vertical band down the middle of a shield. *v.t.* to enclose with or as with pales. **beyond the pale,** unacceptable. **the Pale,** formerly, the part of Ireland in which English authority was recognized. †**paled,** *a.* fenced in; †striped. **paling,** *n.* a fence made with pales; material for making fences. [F *pal,* L *pālus*]

pale², *a.* whitish, ashen, wanting in colour, not ruddy; of colours or light, dim, faint; poor, feeble, inadequate. *v.t.* to make pale. *v.i.* to turn pale, to be pale, dim or poor in comparison. **pale ale,** *n.* light-coloured ale. **pale-eyed,** *a.* **paleface,** *n.* a name supposed to be given by N American Indians to white persons. **pale-faced,** *a.* †**pale-hearted,** *a.* fearful, timid. **pale-visaged,** *a.* **palely,** *adv.* **paleness,** *n.* **palish, paly²,** *a.* [OF *pale, palle,* L *pallidus,* from *pallēre,* to be pale]

palea, *n.* a bract or scale resembling chaff, at the base of the florets in composite flowers, enclosing the stamens and pistil in grass-flowers, or on the stems of ferns. **paleaceous,** *a.* [L, chaff]

pale(o)- PALAE(O)-.

Palermo, *n.* capital and seaport of Sicily; population (1986) 724,000. Industries include shipbuilding, steel, glass, and chemicals. It was founded by the Phoenicians in the 8th cent. BC.

Palestine, *n.* the area between the Mediterranean and the river Jordan, with Lebanon to the N and Sinai to the S. Also called the Holy Land because of its links with Judaism, Christianity and Islam. In ancient times it was dominated in turn by Egypt, Assyria, Babylonia, Persia, Macedonia, the Ptolemies, the Seleucids, and the Roman and Byzantine empires. Today it forms part of Israel. The Palestinian people (about 500,000 in the West Bank, E Jerusalem, and the Gaza Strip; 1,200,000 in Jordan; 1,200,000 in Israel; 300,000 in Lebanon; 100,000 in US) are descendants of the people of Canaan. **Palestine Liberation Organization,** an organization founded in 1964 to bring about an independent state of Palestine. It is formed of several distinct groupings, chief of which is al-Fatah, led by Yassir Arafat, president of the PLO since 1969. To achieve its ends it has pursued diplomatic initiatives, but also operates as a guerrilla army. In 1988, the Palestine National Council voted to create a state of Palestine whilst recognizing Israel's right to exist. **Palestinian,** *a.* pertaining to Palestine. *n.* a native of Palestine or a descendant of such.

palestra, PALAESTRA.

paletot, *n.* a loose overcoat for men or women. [F, etym. doubtful (perh. *palle,* L *palla,* cloak, TOQUE)]

palette, *n.* a flat board used by artists for mixing colours on; the colours or arrangement of colours used for a particular picture or by a particular artist; the range of colours a computer can reproduce on a visual display unit. **palette-knife,** *n.* a thin, flexible knife for mixing and sometimes for putting on colours. [F, dim. of *pale,* L *pāla,* shovel]

palfrey, *n.* a small saddle-horse, esp. for a woman. [OF *palefrei* (F *palefroi*), low L *palafrēdus, paraverēdus* (PARA-, *verēdus,* post-horse, prob. of Celt. orig.)]

Pali, *n.* the canonical language of Buddhist literature, akin to Sanskrit. [Hind., line (of letters), canon]

†palification, *n.* the driving of piles for a foundation etc. **paliform,** *a.* having the form of a palus. [med. L *pālificātio,* from *pālificāre* (*pālus,* PALE[1], *-ficāre, facere,* to make)]

palimony, *n.* (*chiefly N Am.*) alimony paid to an unmarried partner after the end of a long-term relationship. [*pal,* al*imony*]

palimpsest, *n.* a manuscript on parchment or other material from which the original writing has been erased to make room for another record. *a.* treated in this manner. *v.t.* to write on (parchment etc.) from which a previous record has been erased. [L *palimpsēstus,* Gr. *palimpsēstos* (*palin,* again, *psēstos,* scraped, from *psaein,* Ionic *pseen,* to scrape or rub)]

palin-, *comb. form* again, back. [Gr. *palin*]

palinal, *a.* moving backward.

palindrome, *n.* a word, verse, or sentence that reads the same backwards or forwards, e.g. 'Madam I'm Adam' (Adam's alleged self-introduction to Eve). **palindromic,** *a.* **palindromist,** *n.* [Gr. *palindromos* (*dromos,* from *dromein,* to run)]

paling PALE[1].

palingenesia, -genesy, *n.* a new birth, a regeneration.

palingenesis, *n.* palingenesy; the form of ontogeny in which the development of the ancestors is exactly reproduced; the repetition of historical events in the same order in an infinite number of cycles, or the theory of such repetition. **palingenetic,** *a.* **palingenetically,** *adv.*

palinode, *n.* a poem in which a previous poem, usu. satirical, is retracted; a recantation. *v.t.* to retract. **palinodial, -dic,** *a.* **palinodist,** *n.* **†palinody,** *n.* [from L and Gr. *palinōdia*]

palisade, *n.* a fence or fortification of stakes, timbers, or iron railings. *v.t.* to enclose or to fortify with stakes. **palisade cells,** *n.pl.* a layer of cells rich in chloroplasts situated beneath the epidermis of leaves. **†palisado,** *n., v.t.* [F *palissade,* from *palisser,* to enclose with poles, from *palis,* PALE[1]]

palish PALE[2].

pall[1], *n.* a large cloth, usu. of black, purple or white cloth, velvet etc., thrown over a coffin, hearse or tomb; a pallium; anything that covers or shrouds; an oppressive atmosphere. †*v.t.* to cover with or as with a pall, to shroud. **pall-bearer, †-holder,** *n.* one who attends the coffin at a funeral, or who holds up the funeral pall. [OE *pæll,* L *pallium,* cloak]

pall[2], *v.i.* to become vapid or insipid; to become boring. *v.t.* to make vapid, insipid or spiritless; to cloy, to dull. [prob. from APPAL]

Palladian, *a.* of or according to the architect Andrea Palladio or his school of architecture; pertaining to the free and ornate classical style modelled on the teaching of Vitruvius. **Palladianism,** *n.* **Palladianize, -ise,** *v.t.*

Palladio, *n.* **Andrea** (1518–80), Italian architect. His country houses (e.g. Malcontenta, and the Villa Rotonda near Vicenza) were designed from 1540 for patrician families of the Venetian Republic.

palladium[1], *n.* a statue of Pallas (Athena) on the preservation of which, according to tradition, the safety of Troy depended; a defence, a safeguard. **palladian,** *a.* [L, from Gr. *palladion*]

palladium[2], *n.* a greyish-white metallic element of the platinum group, at. no. 46; chem. symbol Pd, used as an alloy with gold and other metals. [Gr. *Pallas -ados,* Greek goddess of wisdom, the second asteroid]

pallescent, *a.* growing pale. **pallescence,** *n.* [L *pallescens -ntem,* pres.p. of *pallescere,* incept. of *pallēre,* to pale]

pallet[1], *n.* a palette; a tool, usu. consisting of a flat blade and handle, used for mixing and shaping clay in pottery-making, or for taking up gold-leaf and for gilding or lettering in bookbinding; a pawl or projection on a part of a machine, for converting reciprocating into rotary motion or vice versa; a valve regulating the admission of air from the wind-chest to an organ-pipe; a flat wooden structure on which boxes, crates etc. are stacked or transported. **palletize, -ise,** *v.t., v.i.* to use pallets for storing and transporting (goods). **palletization, -isation,** *n.* [PALETTE]

pallet[2], *n.* a small rude bed; a straw mattress. [ME and prov. F *paillet,* from *paille,* L *pālea,* straw]

pallial, *a.* pertaining to the pallium or mantle of molluscs.

†palliament, *n.* a robe. [med. L *palliāmentum*]

palliasse, *n.* a mattress or under-bed of straw or other material. [F *paillasse,* from *paille,* L *pālea,* straw]

palliate, *v.t.* to cover with excuses; to extenuate; to mitigate, to alleviate (a disease etc.) without entirely curing. **palliation,** *n.* **palliative,** *n., a.* (a substance) serving to alleviate a disease etc. without curing it. **palliatively,** *adv.* **†palliatory,** *a.* [L *palliātus,* p.p. of *palliāre,* to cloak, from PALLIUM]

pallid, *a.* pale, wan; feeble, insipid. **pallidly,** *adv.* **pallidness,** *n.* [L *pallidus*]

pallium, *n.* (*pl.* **-llia**) a man's square woollen cloak, worn esp. by the ancient Greeks; a scarf-like vestment of white wool with red crosses, worn by the Pope and certain metropolitans and archbishops; the mantle of a bivalve. **pallial,** *a.* [L]

pall-mall, *n.* an old game in which a ball was driven with a mallet through an iron ring; an alley or long space in which this was played, whence the name of the London thoroughfare Pall Mall. [MF *pallemaille,* It. *pallamaglio* (*palla,* ball, *maglio,* L *malleus,* MAUL[1])]

pallone, *n.* an Italian game like tennis, in which the ball is struck with the arm protected by a wooden guard. [It., from *palla,* ball]

pallor, *n.* paleness, want of healthy colour. [L, from *pallēre,* to be pale]

pally PAL.

palm[1], *n.* a tree or shrub belonging to the Palmae, a family of tropical or subtropical endogens, usu. with a tall branched stem and head of large fan-shaped leaves; a palm-branch or leaf as a symbol of victory or triumph; victory, triumph, the prize, the pre-eminence; applied to the sallow and other trees, or their branches carried instead of palms in northern countries on Palm Sunday. **to bear the palm,** to have the pre-eminence. **palm-cabbage,** *n.* the edible terminal bud of some palms. **palm-cat, -civet,** *n.* the paradoxure. **palm-house,** *n.* a glass-house for palms and other tropical plants. **palm-oil,** *n.* an oil obtained from the fruit of certain kinds of palm; (*coll.*) a tip, a bribe. **Palm Sunday,** *n.* the Sunday immediately preceding Easter, commemorating the triumphal entry of Christ into Jerusalem. **palmaceous,** *a.* **palmary,** *a.* bearing or worthy of the palm; pre-eminent, chief, noblest. **palmy,** *a.* abounding in palms; victorious, flourishing. [OE, from L *palma*]

palm[2]**,** *n.* the inner part of the hand; the part of a glove etc. covering this; a measure of breadth (3–4 ins., 7·5–10 cm) or of length (8–8½ ins., 20–21·5 cm); the under part of the foot; the broad flat part of an oar, tie, strut, antler etc.; the fluke of an anchor. *v.t.* to conceal (dice etc.) in the palm; hence, to pass (off) fraudulently; to touch with the palm, to handle; (*sl.*) to bribe. **in the palm of one's hand,** under one's control; in one's power. **to palm off,** to foist. **palmar,** *a.* of, pertaining to, in or connected with the palm. *n.* a palmar muscle or nerve; a brachial plate or joint in crinoids. **palmate, -ated,** *a.* (*Bot., Zool.*) resembling a hand with the fingers spread out; of the foot of a bird, webbed. **palmately,** *adv.* **palmed,** *a.* having a palm or palms (*usu. in comb.*, as *full-palmed*). **palmistry,** *n.* fortune-telling by the lines and marks on the palm of the hand. **palmist, †palmister,** *n.* [ME and F *paume,* L *palma,* cp. Gr. *palamē*]

Palma, *n.* (Spanish **Palma de Mallorca**), industrial port (textiles, cement, paper, pottery), resort, and capital of the Balearic Islands, Spain, on Majorca; population (1981) 304,500. Palma was founded in 276 BC as a Roman colony.

palmar PALM[2].

palmary PALM[1].

Palmas, Las, LAS PALMAS.

palmate PALM[2].

palmati-, *comb. form* palmate. **palmatifid,** *a.* palmately cleft or divided. **palmatiform,** *a.* (*Bot.*)

palmer, *n.* a pilgrim who carried a palm-branch in token of his having been to the Holy Land; a pilgrim, devotee, itinerant monk etc.; a palmer-worm; an angler's imitation of this. **palmer-worm,** *n.* a hairy caterpillar. [A-F *palmer,* OF *palmier,* med. L *palmārius,* PALMARY]

Palmer, *n.* **Samuel** (1805–81), British painter and etcher. He lived 1826–35 in Shoreham, Kent, with a group of artists, followers of William Blake, who called themselves the Ancients.

Palmerston, *n.* **Henry John Temple, 3rd Viscount Palmerston** (1784–1865), British politician. Initially a Tory and secretary-at-war (1809–28), he broke with the Tories in 1830, sitting as Whig foreign secretary 1830–34, 1835–41, and 1846–51. He was prime minister 1855–58 and 1859–65.

palmette, *n.* a carved or painted ornament in the form of a palm-leaf. [F, dim. of *palme,* PALM[1]]

palmetto, *n.* a small variety of palm, esp. *Sabal palmetto,* a fan-palm of the Southern United States; the dwarf fan-palm and other species of *Chamaerops.* [Sp. *palmito,* dim. of *palma,* PALM[1]]

palmi-, *comb. form* palm. [L *palma,* PALM[1], [2]]

†palmiferous, *a.* producing or carrying palms.

palmification, *n.* a method, employed by the Babylonians, of artificially fecundating the female flowers of the date palm by suspending clusters of male flowers of the wild date above them. [cp. CAPRIFICATION]

palmigrade PLANTIGRADE.

palmiped, *a.* of a bird, having palmate or webbed feet. *n.* a web-footed bird. [L *palmipēs* (*pes pedis,* foot)]

palmitic, *a.* of or derived from palm-oil. **palmitate,** *n.* a salt or ester of palmitic acid. **palmitin,** *n.* a natural fatty compound contained in palm-oil etc. [F *palmitique* (*palmite,* palm-pith, from L *palma*)]

palmy PALM[1].

palmyra, *n.* an E Indian palm, *Borassus flabelliformis,* with fan-shaped leaves used for mat-making. [Port. *palmeira,* as PALMARY, assim. to *Palmyra,* see foll.]

Palmyra, *n.* ancient city and oasis in the Syrian desert, about 240 km/150 miles NE of Damascus. Palmyra (the biblical Tadmor) was flourishing by *c.* 300 BC. It was destroyed in AD 272, extensive temple ruins remain.

Palomar, Mount, *n.* a mountain 80 km/50 miles NE of San Diego, California, the site of an observatory with a 5m/200 in. diameter reflecting telescope, the Hale.

palomino, *n.* (*pl.* **-nos**) a cream, yellow or gold horse with a white mane and tail. [Sp., like a dove]

palp, palpus, *n.* (*usu. pl.* **palps, palpi**) jointed sense-organs developed from the lower jaws of insects etc., feelers. **palpal, palped,** *a.* **palpiferous,** *a.* bearing palpi, esp. maxillary palpi. **palpiform,** *a.* [L *palpus*]

palpable, *a.* perceptible to the touch; easily perceived, plain, obvious. **†palpableness, palpability,** *n.* **palpably,** *adv.* [late L *palpābilis,* from L *palpāre,* to feel]

palpate, *v.t.* to feel, to handle, to examine by feeling. **palpation,** *n.* [see prec.]

palpebral, *a.* pertaining to the eyelid. **†palpebrate,** *a.* [F *palpébral,* L *palpebrālis,* from *palpebra,* eyelid]

palpi PALP.

palpifer, *n.* in insects, the feeler-bearer, or the sclerite bearing the maxillary palpi. [L *palpi-,* PALPUS, *-fer,* bearing]

palpiform, palpiferous PALP.

palpiger, *n.* the part of the labium bearing the labial palpi. **palpigerous,** *a.*

palpitate, *v.i.* to throb, to pulsate; to flutter; of the heart, to beat rapidly. **palpitation,** *n.* [L *palpitātus,* p.p. of *palpitāre,* freq. of *palpāre,* to PALPATE]

palpus PALP.

palsgrave, *n.* a count palatine, orig. one who had the superintendence of a prince's palace. **palsgravine,** *n. fem.* [Dut. *paltsgrave* (now *paltsgraaf*), cp. G *Pfalzgraf,* OHG *pfalenzgrâvo* (*pfalenza,* PALACE, *grâvo,* COUNT[2])]

palstave, *n.* a bronze celt shaped like an axe-head, made to fit into a handle instead of being socketed. [Dan. *paalstav,* from Icel. *pālstafr* (*pāll,* hoe, STAVE)]

palsy, *n.* paralysis; infirmity, inefficiency, helplessness. *v.t.* to paralyse. **palsied,** *a.* [ME *palesy,* OF *paralisie,* PARALYSIS]

palter, *v.i.* to equivocate, to shuffle, to act trickily (with); to haggle; to trifle; †to chatter. **†palterer,** *n.* [etym. unknown]

paltry, *a.* mean, petty, despicable; trivial. **paltrily,** *adv.* **paltriness,** *n.* [cp. dial. *paltry,* rubbish, trash, ME *palter,* pl., rags (cp. Swed. *paltor,* Dan. *pjalter,* rags, LG *palte,* MDut. and Fris. *palt*)]

paludal, -udic, -ludine, -udinal, -udinous, *a.* pertaining to marshes or fens, marshy; malarial. **paludism,** *n.* the morbid conditions produced by living among marshes. **paludous, -udose,** *a.* growing or living in or among or produced by marshes. [L *palus palūdis,* marsh]

paludament, *n.* a cloak or mantle worn by a Roman general and his chief officers. [L *palūdāmentum*]

Paludrine®, *n.* a synthetic quinine substitute for the treatment of malaria.

palus, *n.* (*pl.* **-li**) one of the upright calcareous laminae or septa in corals. [L, PALE[1]]

paly[1]**,** *a.* (*Her.*) divided into several equal parts by perpendicular lines. [PALE[1], -Y]

paly[2] PALE[2].

palynology, *n.* the study of pollen grains and other spores. **palynological,** *a.* **palynologist,** *n.* [Gr. *palunein,* to sprinkle]

pam, *n.* the knave of clubs, esp. in fivecard loo, where this is the highest trump; a nickname of Lord Palmerston. [F *pamphile,* prob. from L *Pamphilus,* Gr. *Pamphilos,* personal name, beloved of all]

Pamirs, *n. pl.* central Asian plateau, mainly in the USSR but extending into China and Afghanistan, traversed by mountain ranges. Its highest peak is Mt Communism (Kommunizma Pik 7495 m/24,600 ft) in the Akademiya Nauk range, the highest mountain in the USSR.

pampas, *n.pl.* (*sing.* **pampa**) the open, far-extending, treeless plains in S America, south of the Amazon. The E pampas contain large cattle ranches and the flax- and grain-growing area of Argentina; the W pampas are arid. **pampas-grass**, *n.* a lofty grass, *Gynerium argenteum,* originally from the pampas. **pampean**, *a.* [Sp., pl. of *pampa,* Quichua *bamba,* a plain, a steppe]

pamper, *v.t.* to feed (a person, oneself etc.) luxuriously; to indulge (a person, oneself), often excessively; to gratify (tastes etc.) to excess. **pamperedness,** *n.* **pamperer,** *n.* [prob. freq. of obs. *pamp,* LG *pampen,* to gorge oneself]

pampero, *n.* (*pl.* **-ros**) a violent westerly or southwesterly wind blowing over the pampas. [Sp.]

pamphlet, *n.* a small book of a few sheets, stitched, but not bound, usu. on some subject of temporary interest. **pamphleteer,** *v.i.* to write pamphlets, esp. controversial ones. *n.* a writer of pamphlets. **pamphleteering,** *n.* [OF *Pamphilet,* fem. form of *Pamphile,* L *Pamphilus,* title of a Latin erotic poem of the 12th cent.]

pamphysical, *a.* of or pertaining to material nature regarded as originating and embracing all things. [Gr. *pam-,* PAN-, PHYSICAL]

pampiniform, *a.* curling like a vine-tendril. **pampiniform plexus,** *n.* a convoluted plexus of veins carrying blood from the genital gland. [L *pampinus,* vine-shoot]

pamplegia, *n.* general paralysis. [Gr. *pam-,* PAN-, *plēgē,* stroke, blow]

Pan, *n.* the chief rural divinity of the Greeks, represented as horned and with the hindquarters of a goat. **Pan-pipes,** *n.* (*pl.*) a musical instrument made of a number of pipes or reeds, a mouth-organ. [Gr.]

pan[1], *n.* a broad shallow vessel of metal or earthenware, usu. for domestic uses; a panful; a vessel for boiling, evaporating etc., used in manufacturing etc.; a hollow in the ground for evaporating brine in salt-making; a sheet-iron dish used for separating gold from gravel etc., by shaking in water; the part of a flint-lock that holds the priming; hardpan; a lavatory bowl; either of the two shallow receptacles of a balance; the act or process of panning a camera; (*coll.*) the face; †the skull, the brain-pan. *v.t.* (*past, p.p.* **panned**) (usu. with *out*) to wash (gold-bearing earth or gravel) in a pan; (*coll.*) to criticize severely; to move (a camera) in panning. *v.i.* to move the camera while taking the picture of a moving object. **to pan out,** to yield gold; to yield a specified result (esp. well or badly). **pancake,** *n.* a thin flat cake of batter fried in a frying-pan. *v.i.* to alight from a low altitude at a large angle of incidence, remaining on an even keel. **Pancake Day** SHROVE TUESDAY. **panful,** *n.* [OE *panne* (cp. Dut. *pan,* G *Pfanne,* Icel. *panna*)]

pan[2], *n.* a betel leaf; such a leaf wrapped around sliced betel-nut mixed with spices, used for chewing. [Hind. *pan,* from Sansk. *parna,* wing, leaf]

pan-, *comb. form* all. [Gr. *pas pantos,* all]

panacea, *n.* a universal remedy; †a plant of healing virtue. **panaceist,** *n.* [L, from Gr. *panakeia* (*ak-,* root of *akeomai,* I heal)]

panache, *n.* a tuft or plume, esp. on a head-dress or helmet; show, swagger, bounce; style; airs. [F, from It. *pennacchio*]

panada, †panade, *n.* bread boiled to a pulp, sweetened and flavoured. [Sp. *panada* (F *panade*), ult. from L *pānis,* bread]

panaesthesia, *n.* the whole sum of perceptions by an individual at any given time. **panaesthetic,** *a.* [Gr. *panaisthēsia* (PAN-, *aisthēsis,* perception, *aisthanesthai,* to perceive)]

Pan-African, *a.* of the whole of the African continent; of Pan-Africanism. **Pan-Africanism,** *n.* the advocacy of cooperation between or unification of all the African nations. **Pan-Africanist Congress,** a militant South African nationalist group which broke from the ANC in 1959. More radical than the ANC, it holds a black-only policy for Africa. Its military wing is called Poqo ('we alone').

Panama, *n.* Republic of (*República de Panamá*), country in Central America, on a narrow isthmus between the Caribbean and the Pacific Ocean, bounded to the W by Costa Rica and to the E by Colombia. **area** 77,100 sq km/29,768 sq miles. **capital** Panama City. **towns** Cristóbal, Balboa, Colón. **physical** mountain ranges; tropical rainforest. **exports** bananas, petroleum products, copper from one of the world's largest deposits, shrimps. **population** (1989) 2,370,000; annual growth rate 2.2%. **language** Spanish. **religion** Roman Catholic.

Panama Canal, *n.* a canal across the Panama isthmus in Central America, connecting the Pacific and Atlantic oceans; length 80 km/50 miles, with 12 locks. Built by the US 1904–14 after an unsuccessful attempt by the French, it was formally opened in 1920. The **Panama Canal Zone** comprising land about 5 km/3 miles on either side of the canal was acquired by the US in 1903. It passed to Panama in 1979 but the US retains control of the management and defence of the canal itself until 1999.

Panama City, *n.* capital of Panama, near the Pacific end of the Panama Canal; population (1980) 386,000. Products include chemicals, plastics, and clothing.

panama (hat), *n.* a hat made from the undeveloped leaves of the S American screw-pine, *Carludovica palmata.* [*Panama* City, see prec.]

Pan-American, *a.* of or pertaining to the whole of both N and S America; of Pan-Americanism. **Pan-American Union**, former name (1910–48) of the Organization of American States. **Pan-Americanism,** *n.* the advocacy of cooperation between the nations of N and S America.

Pan-Anglican, *a.* of, including or representing all members of the Anglican and allied Churches.

Pan-Arab(ic), *a.* relating to the movement for political unity between the Arab nations. **Pan-Arabism,** *n.*

panarthritis, *n.* inflammation involving the whole structure of a joint.

panatella, *n.* a type of long slender cigar. [Am. Sp., long thin biscuit, from It. *panatella,* small loaf]

Panathenaea, *n.pl.* the chief annual festival of the Athenians, celebrating with games and processions the union of Attica under Theseus. [Gr. *panathēnaia*]

pancake PAN[2].

†panch, PAUNCH.

Panchen Lama, *n.* (10th incarnation 1935–1989), Tibetan spiritual leader, second in importance to the Dalai Lama.

pancheon, *n.* a large earthenware pan, used for standing milk in etc.

Pan-Christian, *a.* pertaining to all Christians.

panchromatic, *a.* uniformly sensitive to all colours.

panclastite, *n.* an explosive produced by mixing together nitrogen tetroxide and certain carbon preparations. [Gr. *klastos,* broken, from *klaiein,* to break]

pancratium, *n.* in ancient Greece, an athletic contest including both boxing and wrestling. **pancratiast, -cratist,** *n.* **pancratic,** *a.* pertaining to the pancratium; excellent in athletic exercises; of lenses, capable of adjustment to many degrees of power. [L, from Gr. *pankration* (PAN-, *kratos,* strength)]

pancreas, *n.* a gland near the stomach secreting a fluid that aids digestive action, the sweetbread. **pancreatic,** *a.* **pancreatic juice,** *n.* the fluid secreted by the pancreas into the duodenum to aid the digestive process. **pancreatin,** *n.* a protein compound found in the pancreas and the pancreatic juice. **pancreatitis,** *n.* inflammation of the pancreas. [L and Gr. (PAN-, *kreas -atos,* flesh)]

pand, *n.* (*Sc.*) a narrow bed-curtain, a valance. [prob. from OF *pandre,* L *pendēre,* to hang]

panda, *n.* a small racoon-like animal, *Aelurus fulgens,* from the SE Himalayas and Tibet; a giant panda. **giant panda,** the *Ailuropus melanoleucus,* linking the panda with the bears. **panda car,** *n.* a police patrol car, usu. painted with a dark stripe on a light background. [native name]

Pandanus, *n.* a genus of trees or bushes containing the screw-pines. [mod. L, from Malay *pandan*]

Pandean, *a.* pertaining to the god Pan. **Pandean pipes,** *n.pl.* Pan-pipes.

pandect, *n.* (*usu. pl.*) the digest of the Roman civil law made by direction of the emperor Justinian in the 6th cent.; any complete system or body of laws; †a comprehensive treatise or digest. [F *pandecte,* L *pandecta,* Gr. *pandektēs* (PAN-, *dechesthai,* to receive)]

pandemic, *a.* widely epidemic, affecting a whole country or the whole world. *n.* a pandemic disease. [Gr. *pandēmos* (PAN-, *dēmos,* people)]

pandemonium, *n.* (*pl.* **-niums**) the abode of all demons or evil spirits; a place or state of lawlessness, confusion or uproar; confusion, uproar. [coined by Milton (PAN-, DEMON)]

pander, *n.* a procurer, a pimp, a go-between in an amorous intrigue; one who ministers to base or evil passions, prejudices etc. *v.t.* to act as pander to; to minister to the gratification of. *v.i.* to act as an agent (to) for the gratification of evil passions, desires, lusts etc. **panderess,** *n. fem.* **panderism, †panderage,** *n.* [*Pandare* (L *Pandarus*), who procured for Troilus the favour of Criseyde, in Chaucer's *Troilus and Criseyde*]

pandiculation, *n.* a stretching of the body and limbs in drowsiness or in certain nervous disorders; yawning. [L *pandiculārī,* to stretch oneself, from *pandere,* to stretch]

pandit, PUNDIT.

Pandora, *n.* in Greek mythology, the first woman. **Pandora's box,** *n.* a box containing all human ills and blessings, which Pandora brought with her from heaven. On its being opened by her husband, Epimetheus, all escaped except Hope. [Gr. (*dōra,* pl. of *dōron,* gift)]

pandora, pandore, *n.* a lute-like musical instrument, a bandore. [It. *pandora, pandura* (F *pandore*), L *pandūra,* Gr. *pandoura,* etym. unknown]

pandour, -door, *n.* one of a body of foot-soldiers, noted for their ferocity, raised by Baron von der Trenck in 1741, and subsequently enrolled in the Austrian army; hence, a rapacious and brutal soldier. [F *Pandour,* Serbo-Croatian *pàndūr, bàndūr,* med. L *bandērius,* from *bandum,* see BANNER]

pandowdy, *n.* (*N Am.*) a deep-dish dessert of sweetened apple slices topped with a cake crust. [etym. unknown]

panduriform, *a.* fiddle-shaped. [L *pandūra,* PANDORA[2]]

pandy, *n.* (*Sc.*) a stroke on the palm with a cane, ferule etc. *v.t.* to strike on the palm. [said to be from L *pande,* stretch out]

pane, *n.* a sheet of glass in a window etc.; one square of the pattern in a plaid etc.; †a piece, part or division, †a side, face or surface. *v.t.* to make up (a garment etc.) with panes or strips of different colours; to put panes in (a window). **paned,** *a.* **paneless,** *a.* [F *pan,* L *pannum,* nom. *-nus,* piece of cloth]

panegyric, *n.* a eulogy written or spoken in praise of some person, act or thing; an elaborate encomium. †*a.* panegyrical. **panegyrical,** *a.* **panegyrically,** *adv.* **panegyrism,** *n.* **panegyrist,** *n.* **panegyrize, -ise,** *v.t., v.i.* [F *panégyrique,* L *panēgyricus,* Gr. *panēgurikos* (PAN-, AGORA)]

panel, *n.* a rectangular piece (orig. of cloth); a rectangular piece of wood or other material inserted in or as in a frame, forming a compartment of a door, wainscot etc.; a thin board on which a picture is painted; a picture, photograph etc., the height of which is much greater than the width; a flat section of metal, plastic etc. into which switches and instruments are set; a control panel; a piece of stuff of a different colour let in lengthwise in a woman's dress; a cloth placed under a saddle to prevent chafing; a kind of saddle; (*Law*) a list of persons summoned by the sheriff as jurors; a jury; the team in a quiz game, brains trust etc.; an official list of persons; (*formerly*) persons receiving medical treatment under the National Insurance Act; (*Sc. Law*) a prisoner or the prisoners at the bar. *v.t.* (*past, p.p.* **panelled**) to fit or furnish (a door, wall etc.) with panels; to decorate (a dress) with panels; to put a panel on (a horse etc.). **panel beater,** *n.* a person who repairs the damaged body panels of motor vehicles. **panel-doctor,** *n.* (*formerly*) a doctor on the official list of those undertaking duty in connection with the National Insurance Act. **panel-game,** *n.* a quiz game in which a panel of experts etc. answer questions from an audience or a chairman. **†panel-house,** *n.* a house of ill-fame into which persons were enticed and robbed by means of panels in the walls. **panel pin,** *n.* a short, slender nail with a small head. **panel-plane, -saw,** *n.* a plane or saw used in panel-making. **panel-strip,** *n.* a strip of wood for covering the joint between a panel and a post or between two panels. **panel truck,** *n.* (*N Am.*) a delivery van. **panel-work, panelling,** *n.* **panellist,** *n.* a member of a team in a quiz-game, brains trust etc. [OF, from med. L *pannellus,* dim. of *pannus,* PANE]

paneless PANE.

panful PAN[2].

pang[1], *n.* a sudden paroxysm of extreme pain, physical or mental; a throe, agony. †*v.t.* to torture; to torment. **pangless,** *a.* [etym. doubtful]

pang[2], *v.i.* (*Sc., North.*) to cram, to stuff. [etym. doubtful]

pangenesis, *n.* reproduction from every unit of the organism, a theory of heredity provisionally suggested by Darwin. **pangenetic,** *a.*

Pan-German, *a.* relating to Germans collectively or to Pan-Germanism. **Pan-Germanism,** *n.* the movement to unite all Teutonic peoples into one nation.

pangolin, *n.* a scaly ant-eater, of various species belonging to the genus *Manis.* [Malay *pang-gōling,* a roller (from its habit of rolling itself up)]

panhandle, *n.* (*N Am.*) a strip of territory belonging to one political division extending between two others. *v.i.* (*N Am., coll.*) to beg. **panhandler,** *n.*

panharmonic, *a.* universally harmonic. **panharmonicon,** *n.* a mechanical musical instrument.

Pan-Hellenic, *a.* of, characteristic of, including, or representing all Greeks. **Pan-Hellenism,** *n.*

panic[1], *n.* sudden, overpowering, unreasoning fear, esp. when many persons are affected; a general alarm about financial concerns causing ill-considered action; (*coll.*) a very amusing person or thing. *a.* sudden, extreme, unreasoning; caused by fear. *v.t., v.i.* (*past, p.p.* **panicked**) to affect or be affected with panic. **panic button,** *n.* button, switch etc. operated to signal an emergency. **panic buying,** *n.* buying goods in panic, e.g. in anticipation of shortage. **panic-monger,** *n.* **panic stations,** *n.pl.* a state of alarm or panic. **panic-stricken, -struck,** *a.* struck with sudden fear. **panicky,** *a.* [F *panique,* Gr. *panikos,* from PAN[1]]

panic[2], *n.* a common name for several species of the genus *Panicum,* esp. the Italian millet. **panic-grass,** *n.* [L *pānicum*]

panicky PANIC[1].

panicle, *n.* a loose and irregular compound flower-cluster. **panicled, paniculate,** *a.* **paniculately,** *adv.* [L *pānicula,* dim. of *pānus,* a swelling, ear of millet]

Panicum, *n.* a genus of grasses with numerous species, some (as the millet) valuable for food. [L, PANIC[2]]

panification, *n.* the process of making or converting into bread. [F, from *panifier,* to make into bread, from L *pānis,* bread]

Pan-Islam, *n.* the whole of Islam; a union of the Muslim peoples. **Pan-Islamic,** *a.* **Pan-Islamism,** *n.*

panjandrum, *n.* a mock title for a self-important or arrogant person; a high and mighty functionary or pompous pretender. [humorous coinage by Samuel Foote]

Pankhurst *n.* **Emmeline** (born Goulden) (1858–1928), British suffragette. Founder of the Women's Social and Political Union in 1903, she launched the militant suffragette campaign in 1905. In 1926 she joined the Conservative Party and was a prospective parliamentary candidate.

panlogism, *n.* the doctrine that the universe is the outward manifestation of the inward idea or logos. [Gr. *logos,* word, reason]

panmixia, *n.* fortuitous mingling of hereditary characters due to the cessation of the influence of natural selection in regard to organs that have become useless. [Gr. *-mixia, mixis,* mixing, from *mignunai,* to MIX]

†**pannade,** *n.* the curvet of a horse. [obs. F, from *panader,* to strut, to curvet]

pannage, *n.* the feeding or the right of feeding swine in a forest, or the payment for this; mast picked up by swine in a forest. [A-F *panage,* OF *pasnage,* late L *pastionāticum,* from *pastio,* grazing, from *pascere,* to feed]

panne, *n.* a soft, long-napped fabric. [F]

pannier¹, *n.* a large basket, esp. one of a pair slung over the back of a beast of burden; one of a pair of bags fixed on either side of the wheel of a bicycle, motorcycle etc.; a covered basket for drugs and surgical instruments for a military ambulance; a framework, usu. of whalebone, formerly used for distending a woman's skirt at the hips; (*Arch.*) a sculptured basket, a corbel. **panniered,** *a.* [ME and F *panier,* L *pānārium,* bread-basket, from *pānis,* bread]

pannier², *n.* one of the robed waiters in the dining-hall at Inns of Court. [etym. doubtful]

pannikin, *n.* a small drinking-cup of metal; that contained in it; (*N Am.*) a dipper, a small saucepan. **pannikin boss,** *n.* (*Austral.*) a sub-overseer on a station. [PAN², -KIN]

pannose, *a.* (*Bot.*) like cloth in texture. [as foll.]

pannus, *n.* an opaque vascular state of the cornea; a tent for a wound; a birthmark. **pannous,** *a.* of the nature of pannus. [prob. L *pannus,* cloth, see PANE]

panoistic, *a.* of the ovaries of some insects, producing ova only, as distinct from *meroistic.* [Gr. *ōon,* egg]

panophobia, *n.* excessive fear (literally of everything).

panoply, *n.* a complete suit of armour; complete defence; a full, impressive array. **panoplied,** *a.* [Gr. *panoplia* (PAN-, *hopla,* arms, pl. of *hoplon,* tool, implement)]

panopticon, *n.* a prison constructed on a circular plan with a central well for the warders so that the prisoners would be always under observation; an exhibition-room for novelties etc. **panoptic,** *a.* viewing all aspects; all-embracing, comprehensive. [Gr. *optikon,* neut. of *-kos,* of sight, OPTIC]

panorama, *n.* a continuous picture of a complete scene on a sheet unrolled before the spectator or on the inside of a large cylindrical surface viewed from the centre; complete view in all directions; a general survey. **panorama sight,** *n.* a gun sight that can be rotated, giving a wide field of view. **panoramic,** *a.* **panoramically,** *adv.* [Gr. *horama,* view, from *horaein,* to see]

panotitis, *n.* inflammation of both the middle and internal ear. [Gr. *ous ōtos,* ear]

panotrope, *n.* an electrical reproducer of disc gramophone records operating one or more loudspeakers. [Gr. *tropos,* a turn]

Pan-pipe(s) PAN.

Pan-Presbyterian, *a.* of or pertaining to all Presbyterians.

pansclerosis, *n.* complete induration of the interstitial tissue of a part.

Pan-Slavism, *n.* a movement for the union of all the Slavic races. **Pan-Slavic,** *a.* **Pan-Slavist,** *n.* **Pan-Slavistic,** *a.* †**Pan-Slavonian, -vonic,** *a.*

pansophy, *n.* universal knowledge; a scheme of universal knowledge; pretence of universal wisdom. **pansophic, -ical,** *a.* **pansophically,** *adv.* [Gr. *sophia,* wisdom]

panspermia, -spermatism, -spermism, -spermy, *n.* the theory that the atmosphere is pervaded by invisible germs which develop on finding a suitable environment. **panspermatist,** *n.* **panspermic,** *a.* [Gr. *sperma,* seed]

pansy, *n.* a species of viola, with large flowers of various colours in the cultivated varieties, the heartsease; (*coll.*) an effeminate man or boy. **pansied,** *a.* [F *pensée,* thought, orig. fem. p.p. of *penser,* to think, L *pensāre,* freq. of *pendere,* to weigh]

pant, *v.i.* to breathe quickly; to gasp for breath; to throb, to palpitate; to long, to yearn (after, for etc.). *v.t.* to utter gaspingly or convulsively. *n.* a gasp; a throb, a palpitation. **panting,** *n.* the bulging in and out of the plating of a ship under the stress of heavy seas. [cp. A-F *pantoiser,* OF *pantaisier* (F *panteler*), pop. L *phantasiāre,* to dream, to have a nightmare, L *phantasiārī,* see PHANTASM]

pant- PANT(O)-.

pantagamy, *n.* a system of communistic marriage in which all the men are married to all the women, as practised in the Oneida Community in Idaho, from 1838 onwards. [*panta-,* irreg. for PANT(O)-, *-gamia, gamos,* marriage]

pantagogue, *n.* a medicine supposed to be capable of expelling all morbid matter. [Gr. *agōgos,* leading, driving out]

pantagraph, PANTOGRAPH.

Pantagruelism, *n.* coarse and boisterous burlesque and buffoonery, esp. with a serious purpose, like that of Pantagruel. **Pantagruelian,** *a.* **Pantagruelist,** *n.* [*Pantagruel,* character in Rabelais]

pantalets, -lettes, *n.pl.* loose drawers extending below the skirts, with frills at the bottom, worn by children and women in the early 19th cent.; detachable frilled legs for these; drawers, cycling knickerbockers etc. for women.

pantaloon, *n.* a character in pantomime, the butt of the clowns' jokes; (*pl.*) tight trousers fastened below the shoe, as worn in the Regency period; trousers, esp. loose-fitting ones. [F *pantalon,* It. *pantalone* (Venetian character on the Italian stage, prob. from San *Pantaleone,* a popular saint in Venice)]

pantechnicon, *n.* a storehouse for furniture; a place where all sorts of manufactured articles are exposed for sale; a pantechnicon van. **pantechnicon van,** *n.* a large van for removing furniture. [Gr. *technikon* (*technē,* art)]

pantheism, *n.* the doctrine that God and the universe are identical; the heathen worship of all the gods. **pantheist,** *n.* **pantheistic, -ical,** *a.* **pantheistically,** *adv.*

Pantheon, *n.* a famous temple with a circular dome at Rome, built about 27 BC, and dedicated to all the gods; (*collect.*) the divinities of a nation; a treatise on all the gods; a building dedicated to the illustrious dead, esp. a building at Paris, orig. a church, so dedicated in 1791; applied to buildings for public entertainment, after the one opened in London in 1772. [L, from Gr. *pantheion* (PAN-, *theios,* divine, from *theos,* god)]

panther, *n.* the leopard; (*N Am.*) the puma. [ME and OF *pantere,* L *panthēra,* Gr. *panthēr*]

panties, *n.pl.* (*coll.*) women's or children's short knickers.

pantihose, *n.pl.* (*esp. N Am.*) tights.

pantile, *n.* a tile curved transversely to an ogee shape.

pantisocracy, *n.* a Utopian scheme of communism in which all are equal in rank, and all are ruled by all. **pantisocrat,** *n.* **pantisocratic,** *a.* [Gr. *isokratia*]

†**pantler,** *n.* the officer who has charge of the bread or the pantry in large establishments. [corr. of ME *paneter,* OF *panetier,* med. L *pānetārius,* from *pānis,* bread]

panto, *n.* (*coll.*) short for PANTOMIME.

pant(o)-, *comb. form* all. [Gr. *pas pantos,* all]

†**pantochronometer,** *n.* a combination of compass, sundial and universal sundial.

†**pantofle,** *n.* a slipper. [F *pantoufle*]

pantograph, *n.* an instrument used to enlarge, copy or reduce plans etc.; a framework similar in appearance attached to the roof of an electrically-driven vehicle, for collecting electrical power from an overhead cable. **pantographic, -ical,** *a.* **pantography,** *n.*

pantology, *n.* universal knowledge; a work of universal information. **pantologic, -ical,** *a.*

pantometer, *n.* an instrument for measuring angles and determining elevations, distances etc.

pantomime, *n.* in ancient Rome, one who performed in dumb show; representation in dumb show; a theatrical entertainment, usu. produced at Christmas-time, consisting largely of farce and burlesque; a muddled or farcical situation. *v.t.* to express or represent by dumb

show. *v.i.* to express oneself by dumb show. **pantomimic, -ical**, *a.* **pantomimically,** *adv.* **pantomimist,** *n.* [L *pantomīmus,* Gr. *pantomimos*]
pantomorphic, *a.* assuming all or any shapes.
panton, *n.* (*Sc.*) a slipper; a kind of horseshoe. [etym. doubtful, prob. rel. to PANTOFLE]
pantophagist, *n.* a person or animal that eats all kinds of food. **pantophagous**, *a.* **pantophagy,** *n.* [Gr. *pantophagos* (PANTO-, *phagein,* to eat)]
pantoscope, *n.* a panoramic camera; a lens with a very wide angle. **pantoscopic**, *a.* having great breadth of vision.
pantothenic acid, *n.* an oily acid, a member of the vitamin B complex. [Gr. *pantothen,* from all sides]
pantry, *n.* a room or closet in which bread and other provisions are kept. **pantryman,** *n.* a butler or his assistant. [OF *paneterie,* med. L *pānetāria,* a place where bread is made etc., from L *pānis,* bread]
pants, *n.pl.* drawers for men and boys; (*N Am.*) men's or women's trousers; women's knickers. **with one's pants down,** in an embarrassing or ill-prepared position. **pants suit,** *n.* (*N Am.*) a trouser suit for women. [PANTALOONS]
panty hose, *n.pl.* tights.
panurgic, *a.* able to do any kind of work. [late Gr. *panourgikos,* from *panourgos* (*ergon,* work)]
panzer, *a.* term applied to armoured bodies, esp. an armoured division, in the German army; a vehicle in such a division, esp. a tank. [G, armour, armour-plating]
panzoism, *n.* according to Herbert Spencer, the sum of the elements making up vital force. [Gr. *zoē,* life]
Paolozzi, *n.* **Eduardo** (1924–), British sculptor, a major force in the pop art movement in London in the 1950s. He typically uses bronze casts of pieces of machinery to crate robot-like structures.
pap¹, *n.* soft or semi-liquid food for infants etc.; pulp; trivial or insubstantial ideas, talk etc. **pappy,** *a.* [prob. imit.]
pap², *n.* a teat, a nipple; a conical hill or small peak. [imit., cp. prec.]
papa¹, *n.* a dated children's word for father. [F, from L *pāpa,* imit. in orig. (cp. Gr. *pappas*)]
papa², *n.* the Pope; a parish priest or one of the inferior clergy of the Greek Church. [med. L, from Gr. *pappas,* see prec.]
papa³, *n.* a blue clay found in New Zealand. [Maori]
papacy, *n.* the office, dignity or tenure of office of the Pope; the papal system of government; the Popes collectively. **papal,** *a.* pertaining to the Pope or his office, or to the Roman Catholic Church. **papal cross,** *n.* a cross with three horizontal shafts. **Papal States,** *n. pl.* an area of central Italy in which the Pope was temporal ruler 756–1870, when Italy became a united state. **papalism,** *n.* †**papalist,** *n.* †**papalize, -ise,** *v.t., v.i.* **papalization, -isation,** *n.* **papally,** *adv.* †**papaphobia**, *n.* **paparchy**, *n.* [med. L *pāpātia,* from prec.]
papain, *n.* a protein compound found in the milky juice of the papaya. [Sp. *papaya*]
Papandreou, *n.* **Andreas** (1919–), Greek socialist politician, founder of the Pan-Hellenic Socialist Movement (PASOK), and prime minister from 1981.
paparazzo, *n.* (*pl.* **-zzi**) a freelance professional photographer who specializes in photographing celebrities at private moments, usu. without their consent. [It.]
papaverous, *a.* resembling or allied to the poppy. **papaveraceous**, *a.* [L *papāver,* poppy, -OUS]
papaw, pawpaw, *n.* a N American tree, *Asimina triloba,* the milky juice of which, obtained from the stem, leaves or fruit, makes meat tender; its fruit. [from foll.]
papaya, *n.* a tropical American tree, *Carica papaya,* yielding papain that bears large oblong edible yellow fruit; its fruit. [Sp. *papaya,* Carib *abābai*]
Papeete, *n.* capital and port of French Polynesia on Tahiti; population (1983) 79,000. Products include vanilla, copra, and mother of pearl.
Papen, *n.* **Franz von** (1879–1969), German right-wing politician. As chancellor (1932), he negotiated the Nazi-Conservative alliance which made Hitler chancellor in 1933. Although acquitted at the Nuremburg trials, he was imprisoned by a German denazification court for three years.
paper, *n.* a thin flexible substance made of rags, wood-fibre, grass or similar materials, used for writing and printing on, wrapping etc.; a piece, sheet or leaf of this; a written or printed document; an essay, a dissertation; a lecture; a newspaper; a set of questions for an examination; negotiable instruments, as bills of exchange; paper money; paper-hangings; (*sl.*) free passes, also persons admitted to a theatre etc. by such passes; (*pl.*) documents establishing identity etc.; a ship's documents. *a.* made of paper; like paper; stated only on paper, having no real existence. *v.t.* to cover with or decorate with paper; to wrap or fold up in paper; to rub with sandpaper; to furnish with paper; (*sl.*) to admit a large number to (a theatre etc.) by free passes. **on paper,** theoretically, rather than in reality. **to commit to paper,** to write down; to record. **to paper over,** to disguise, cover up (dispute, mistake etc.). **to send in one's papers,** to resign. **paperback,** *n.* a book with a soft cover of flexible card. *a.* being or relating to a paperback or paperbacks. **paper-boy, -girl,** *n.* a boy or girl who delivers newspapers. **paper-chase,** *n.* a game in which one or more persons (called the hares) drop pieces of paper as scent for pursuers (called the hounds) to track them by. **paper-clip,** *n.* a small clip of looped wire used to fasten pieces of paper together. **paper credit,** *n.* credit allowed on the score of bills, promissory notes etc., showing that money is due to the person borrowing. **paper-currency** PAPER-MONEY. **paper-cutter, -knife,** *n.* a flat piece of wood, ivory etc., for cutting open the pages of a book, opening letters etc. **paper-girl** PAPER-BOY. **paper-hanger,** *n.* a person whose occupation is hanging wallpaper; (*N Am.*) a person who passes false cheques. **paper-hangings,** *n.pl.* paper ornamented or prepared for covering the walls of rooms, etc. **paper-knife** PAPER-CUTTER. **paper-making,** *n.* **paper-mill,** *n.* a mill in which paper is manufactured. **paper-money,** *n.* banknotes or bills used as currency, opp. to coin. **paper-profits,** *n.pl.* hypothetical profits shown on a company's prospectus etc. **paper-stainer,** *n.* a manufacturer of paper-hangings. **paper tiger,** *n.* a person or thing that is apparently threatening or powerful, but is not so in reality. **paper-weight,** *n.* a weight for keeping loose papers from being displaced. †**paper-white,** *a.* **paper-work,** *n.* clerical work, e.g. writing letters; documents, letters etc. **papery,** *a.* **paperiness,** *n.* [OF *papier,* L PAPYRUS]
papeterie, *n.* an ornamental case for writing materials. [F, from *papetier,* a paper-factory, paper-maker, med. L *papeterius,* as prec.]
Paphian, *a.* pertaining to Paphos, a city of Cyprus sacred to Venus; pertaining to Venus or her worship. *n.* a native of Paphos; a courtesan.
papier mâché, *n.* a material made from pulped paper, moulded into trays, boxes etc., and usu. japanned. *a.* made of papier mâché. [F, chewed paper]
papilionaceous, *a.* resembling a butterfly; used of plants with butterfly-shaped flowers, as the pea. [L *papilio -ōnis,* butterfly]
papilla, *n.* (*pl.* **-llae**) a small pap, nipple or similar process; a small protuberance on an organ or part of the body or on plants. **papillary, -llate, -llose,** †**-llous,** *a.* **papilliferous**, *a.* **papilliform**, *a.* **papillitis**, *n.* inflammation of the optic papilla. **papilloma**, *n.* (*pl.* **mas, -mata**) a tumour formed by the growth of a papilla or group of papillae, as a wart, corn etc. **papillomatous,** *a.* **papilloso-**, *comb. form.*, pertaining to papilla(e). [L, dim. of PAPULA]
papillon, *n.* a breed of toy spaniel with large butterfly-shaped ears. [L *papilio -ōnis,* butterfly]
†**papillote,** *n.* a curl-paper. [F, perh. from *papillon,* L *papilio -ōnis,* butterfly]
papist, *n.* (*chiefly derog.*) a Roman Catholic. **papism, papistry,** *n.* **papistic, -ical**, *a.* [F *papiste* (PAPA², -IST)]
papoose, *n.* a young child. [N Am. Ind.]
pappus, *n.* (*pl.* **pappi**) the calyx of composite plants,

consisting of a tuft of down or fine hairs or similar agent for dispersing the seed; the first hair of the chin. **pappous, pappose,** *a.* downy. [mod. L, from Gr. *pappos*]

pappy PAP¹.

paprika, *n.* a powdered condiment made from a sweet variety of red pepper. [Hung.]

Pap smear, test, *n.* a test for the early diagnosis of cancer in which cells are scraped from a bodily organ esp. the cervix, and examined under a microscope. [George N. *Pap*anicolaou, 1883–1962, US anatomist]

Papuan, *a.* of or pertaining to Papua New Guinea. *n.* a member of the black peoples native to the Melanesian archipelago.

Papua New Guinea, country in the SW Pacific, comprising the E part of the island of New Guinea, the New Guinea islands, the Admiralty islands, and part of the Solomon islands. **area** 462,840 sq km/178,656 sq miles. **capital** Port Moresby (on E New Guinea). **physical** mountains in centre; thickly forested. **exports** copra, coconut oil, palm oil, tea, copper. **population** (1989) 3,613,000 (including Papuans, Melanesians, Pygmies, and various minorities); annual growth rate 2.6%. **language** English (official); pidgin English. **religion** Protestant 33%, Roman Catholic 18%, local faiths.

papula, *n.* (*pl.* **-lae**) a pimple; a small fleshy projection on a plant. **papular, -lose, -lous,** *a.* **papulation,** *n.* **papule,** *n.* **papuliferous,** *a.* [L, a pustule, dim. from *pap-*, to swell]

papyro-, *comb. form* papyrus; paper.

papyrograph, *n.* an apparatus for multiplying copies of a document, esp. by the use of a paper stencil. **papyrographic,** *a.* **papyrography,** *n.* printing or copying by means of a papyrograph; papyrotype.

papyrotype, *n.* a form of photo-lithography in which the writing or drawing is executed on paper before transfer to the zinc plate for printing.

papyrus, *n.* (*pl.* **-ri, -ruses**) a rush-like plant of the genus *Cypereae,* common formerly on the Nile and still found in Ethiopia, Syria etc.; a writing-material made from this by the Egyptians and other ancient peoples; a manuscript written on this material. **papyraceous,** *a.* made of or of the nature of papyrus; of the consistence of paper, papery. **papyral, papyrian, papyriferous, papyrine,** *a.* [L, from Gr. *papuros,* of Egyptian orig.]

par¹, *n.* state of equality, parity; equal value, esp. equality between the selling value and the nominal value expressed on share certificates and other scrip; average or normal condition, rate etc.; in golf, the number of shots which a good player is expected to play in order to complete a hole. **above par,** at a price above the face value, at a premium. **below par,** at a discount; out of sorts. **on a par with,** of equal value, degree etc. to. **par for the course,** what is to be expected or usual. **up to par,** of the required standard. [L, equal, equally]

par², PARR.

par³, (*abbr.*) paragraph; parallel; parish.

par- PAR(A)-.

par excellence, *adv.* above all others, pre-eminently. [F]

para¹, (*abbr.*) paragraph.

para², *n.* (*coll.*) short for PARATROOPER.

par(a)-, *comb. form* denoting closeness of position, correspondence of parts, situation on the other side, wrongness, irregularity, alteration etc.; (*Chem.*) denoting substitution or attachment at carbon atoms directly opposite in a benzene ring. [Gr. *para,* by the side of, beyond]

parabaptism, *n.* irregular or uncanonical baptism. [late Gr. *parabaptisma*]

parabasis, *n.* (*pl.* **-bases**) a choral part in ancient Greek comedy in which the chorus addressed the audience, in the name of the poet, on personal or public topics. [Gr., from *parabainein* (*bainein,* to go)]

parabiosis, *n.* the anatomical union of two organisms with shared physiological processes. **parabiotic,** *a.*

parablast, *n.* the peripheral nutritive yolk of an ovum, or a germ-layer supposed to be developed from this and to produce the blood etc. **parablastic,** *a.* [Gr. *blastos,* sprout]

parable, *n.* an allegorical narrative of real or fictitious events from which a moral is drawn; an allegory, esp. of a religious kind; a cryptic or oracular saying. †*v.t.* to represent in a parable. [OF *parabole,* as foll.]

parabola, *n.* a plane curve formed by the intersection of the surface of a cone with a plane parallel to one of its sides. †**parabole,** *n.* a parable; comparison, similitude. **parabolic, -ical,** *a.* pertaining to or of the form of a parabola; pertaining to or of the nature of a parable; allegorical, figurative. **parabolically,** *adv.* **paraboliform,** *a.* **parabolist,** *n.* **parabolize, -ise,** *v.t.* **paraboloid,** *n.* a solid of which all the plane sections parallel to a certain line are parabolas, esp. that generated by the revolution of a parabola about its axis. **paraboloidal,** *a.* [L, from Gr. *parabolē* (*ballein,* to throw)]

Paracelsus, *n.* (original name Theophrastus Bombastus von Hohenheim) (1493–1541), Swiss physician, alchemist, and scientist. He developed the idea that minerals and chemicals might have medical uses. He introduced the use of laudanum (which he named) for pain-killing purposes. His rejection of the ancients and insistence on the value of experimentation make him an important figure in early science. **Paracelsian,** *a.* pertaining to or characteristic of the philosophical teaching or medical practice of Paracelsus *n.* a follower of Paracelsus, esp. as distinguished from *Galenist.*

paracentesis, *n.* the operation of perforating a cavity of the body, or tapping, for the removal of fluid etc. [L, from Gr. *parakentēsis* (*kentein,* to pierce)]

paracentral, *a.* situated beside or near the centre.

paracetamol, *n.* a mild painkilling drug. [*para-acetam*idophen*ol*]

parachordal, *a.* (*Embryol.*) situated near the notochord. *n.* parachordal cartilage.

parachromatism, *n.* colour-blindness.

parachronism, *n.* an error in chronology, esp. post-dating of an event. [Gr. *chronos,* time]

parachute, *n.* an umbrella-shaped contrivance by which a descent is made from a height, esp. from an aircraft; a part of an animal or an appendage to a fruit or seed serving for descent or dispersion by the wind. *v.t., v.i.* (to cause) to land by means of a parachute. **parachute flare,** *n.* a pyrotechnic flare which can be dropped from an aeroplane to illuminate the ground below. **parachutism,** *n.* **parachutist,** *n.* [F (It. *para,* imper. of *parare,* to ward off, F *chute,* fall)]

paraclete, *n.* an advocate, esp. as a title of the Holy Ghost, the Comforter. [F *paraclet,* L *paraclētus,* Gr. *paraklētos* (*kalein,* to call)]

paracme, *n.* (*Biol.*) a point past the acme or highest development; a point past the crisis (of a fever etc.). [Gr. (ACME)]

paracolpitis, *n.* inflammation of the external coat of the vagina. [Gr. *kolpos,* womb]

paracorolla, *n.* a crown or appendage of a corolla, esp. one forming a nectary.

paracrostic, *n.* a poetic composition in which the first verse contains, in order, all the letters which commence the remaining verses.

paracyanogen, *n.* a porous brown substance obtained from cyanide of mercury when heated.

paracyesis, *n.* extra-uterine pregnancy. [Gr. *kuēsis,* conception]

paradactyl, *n.* the side of a digit or toe of a bird.

parade, *n.* show, ostentatious display; a muster of troops for inspection etc.; ground where soldiers are paraded, drilled etc.; a public promenade; a row of shops. *v.t.* to make display of; to assemble and marshal (troops) in military order for or as for review. *v.i.* to be marshalled in military order for display or review; to show oneself or walk about ostentatiously. **parade-ground,** *n.* an area where soldiers parade. [F, from Sp. *parada,* It. *parata,* from L *parāre,* to get ready]

paradigm, *n.* an example, a pattern; an example of a word in its grammatical inflections. **paradigmatic,** *a.* **paradigmatically,** *adv.* [F *paradigme,* L *paradigma,*

Gr. *paradeigma* (*deiknunai,* to show)]

paradise, *n.* the garden of Eden; a place or state of bliss; heaven; a place or condition of perfect bliss; a park or pleasure-ground, esp. one in which animals are kept, a preserve. **paradise-fish,** *n.* an E Indian fish, *Macropodus viridiauratus,* which is sometimes kept in aquariums for its brilliant colouring. **paradisaic, -ical,** †**paradisiac,** †**-iacal, paradisial, -ian, paradisic -ical,** *a.* [F *paradis,* L *paradīsus,* Gr. *paradeisos,* OPers. *paradaeza* (*pairi,* PERI-, *diz,* to mould)]

parados, *n.* (*Mil.*) a rampart or earthwork to protect against fire from the rear. [F]

paradox, *n.* a statement, view or doctrine contrary to received opinion; an assertion seemingly absurd but really correct; a self-contradictory or essentially false and absurd statement; a person, thing or phenomenon at variance with normal ideas of what is probable, natural or possible. **paradoxer, -doxist,** *n.* **paradoxical,** *a.* **paradoxical sleep,** *n.* sleep that is apparently deep but is marked by rapid eye movement, increased brain activity etc. **paradoxicality, -calness, paradoxy,** *n.* **paradoxically,** *adv.* [F *paradoxe,* L *paradoxum,* Gr. *paradoxon* (*doxa,* opinion)]

paradoxure, *n.* a civet-like animal with a long, curving tail, the palm-cat of S Asia and Malaysia. **paradoxurine,** *n., a.* [PARADOX, Gr. *oura,* tail]

paraenetic, -ical, *a.* exhorting, persuasive, advisory. **paraenesis,** *n.* [med. L *paraeneticus,* Gr. *parainetikos,* from *parainein* (*ainein,* to speak of, to praise)]

paraesthesia, (*esp. N Am.*) **paresthesia,** *n.* disordered perception or hallucination. [Gr. *aisthēsis,* perception]

paraffin, *n.* an alkane; a mixture of liquid paraffins used as a lubricant or fuel; kerosene. **liquid paraffin** LIQUID. **paraffin wax,** *n.* a colourless, tasteless, odourless, fatty substance consisting primarily of a mixture of paraffins, and obtained from distillation of coal, bituminous shale, petroleum, peat etc., used for making candles, waterproofing etc.; (*N Am.*) white wax. [F *paraffine,* from L *parum,* little, *affinis,* akin, so called from the small affinity with other bodies]

paragastric, *a.* situated near the gastric cavity; pertaining to the gastric cavity of a sponge.

†**parage,** *n.* lineage, descent; in feudal law, equality of condition, as among brothers holding part of a fief as coheirs. [F, from med. L *parāticum,* from PAR[1]]

paragenesis, *n.* the production in an organism of characteristics of two different species; hybridism in which the individuals of one generation are sterile among themselves but those of the next fertile. **paragenetic, paragenic** (-jen'ik), *a.*

paragliding, *n.* the sport of gliding while attached to a device like a parachute, in which one is pulled by an aircraft, then allowed to drift to the ground.

paraglobulin, *n.* the globulin of blood-serum.

paraglossa, *n.* (*pl.* **-ssae**) either of the two appendages of the ligula in insects. [Gr. *glōssa,* tongue]

paragoge, *n.* the addition of a letter or syllable to a word. [Gr., leading past]

paragon, *n.* a pattern of perfection; a model, an exemplar; a person or thing of supreme excellence; a diamond of 100 carats or more; †a match, an equal, a companion; emulation, rivalry; in printing, a size of type, now usu. called two-line long primer. *v.t.* to compare; to rival, to equal. [F, from It. *paragone,* etym. doubtful]

†**paragram,** *n.* a play upon words; a pun. †**paragrammatist,** *n.*

paragraph, *n.* a distinct portion of a discourse or writing marked by a break in the lines; a reference mark [¶]; a mark used to denote a division in the text; an item of news in a newspaper etc. *v.t.* to form into paragraphs; to mention or write about in a paragraph. **paragrapher, -phist,** *n.* **paragraphic, -ical,** *a.* **paragraphy,** *n.* [F *paragraphe,* late L *paragraphus,* Gr. *paragraphos*]

paragraphia, *n.* the habitual writing of words or letters other than those intended, often a sign of brain disorder. [Gr. *graphein,* to write]

Paraguay, *n.* Republic of (*República del Paraguay*), landlocked country in S America bounded to the NE by Brazil, to the S by Argentina, and to the NW by Bolivia. **area** 406,752 sq km/157,006 sq miles. **capital** Asunción. **town** port Concepción. **physical** mostly flat; divided by river Paraguay; river Paraná in the south. **exports** cotton, soya beans, timber, tung oil, maté. **population** (1989) 4,518,000 (95% of mixed Guaraní Indian-Spanish descent); annual growth rate 3.0%. **language** Spanish (official), spoken by 6%; Guaraní 40%; remainder bilingual. **religion** Roman Catholic.

Paraguay (tea), *n.* an infusion of the leaves of *Ilex paraguayensis,* maté.

Paraguay Reservations, *n.* a Jesuit colony that existed in Paraguay (1608–1750).

paraheliotropic, *a.* of leaves, turning so that the surfaces are parallel to the rays of sunlight. **paraheliotropism,** *n.*

para-influenza virus, any of various viruses causing influenza-like symptoms.

parakeet, *n.* a popular name for any of the smaller long-tailed parrots. [OF *paroquet* (F *perroquet*), perh. from It. *parrochetto,* dim. of *parroco,* a parson, or of *parrucca,* PERUKE]

parakite, *n.* a series of kites connected together for the purpose of raising a person; a tailless kite used for scientific purposes. [from KITE, after PARACHUTE]

paraldehyde, *n.* a hypnotic used in asthma, respiratory and cardiac diseases, and epilepsy.

paralipomena, *n.pl.* things omitted in a work; †(*Bibl.* **paralipomenon,** *gen. pl.*) the Books of Chronicles as giving particulars omitted in the Books of Kings. [L, from Gr. *paraleipomena,* see prec.]

paralipsis, *n.* a rhetorical figure by which a speaker pretends to omit mention of what at the same time he really calls attention to. [Gr. *paraleipsis* (*leipein,* to leave)]

parallax, *n.* apparent change in the position of an object due to change in the position of the observer; angular measurement of the difference between the position of a heavenly body as viewed from different places on the earth's surface or from the earth at different positions in its orbit round the sun. **parallactic,** *a.* [F *parallaxe,* Gr. *parallaxis,* alternation, change (*allassein,* to change)]

parallel, *a.* of lines etc., having the same direction and everywhere equidistant; having the same tendency, similar, corresponding. *n.* a line which throughout its whole length is everywhere equidistant from another; any one of the parallel circles on a map or globe marking degrees of latitude on the earth's surface; direction parallel to that of another line; a trench parallel to the front of a place that is being attacked; a comparison; a person or thing corresponding to or analogous with another, a counterpart; in printing, a reference mark (‖) calling attention to a note etc. *v.t.* (*past, p.p.* **paralleled**) to be parallel to, to match, to rival, to equal; to put in comparison with; to find a match for; to compare. **parallel bars,** *n.pl.* a pair of horizontal bars used for various exercises in gymnastics. **parallel connection,** *n.* the arrangement of pieces of electrical apparatus across a common voltage supply. **parallel rule,** *n.* a draughtsman's instrument consisting of two rulers movable about hinged joints, but always remaining parallel. **parallelism,** *n.* the state of being parallel, correspondence, esp. of successive paragraphs, as in Hebrew poetry, a comparison, a parallel. [ME *parallele,* L *parallēlus,* Gr. *parallēlos* (*allēlos,* one another)]

parallelepiped, -pipedon, *n.* a regular solid bounded by six parallelograms, the opposite pairs of which are parallel. [Gr. *parallēlepipedon* (PARALLEL, *epipedon,* a level, a plane, from *epi,* upon, and *pedon,* the ground)]

parallelogram, *n.* a four-sided rectilinear figure whose opposite sides are parallel and equal; (*pop.*) any quadrilateral figure of greater length than breadth. **parallelogram rule,** *n.* a rule for finding the resultant of two vectors, by constructing a parallelogram in which two sides represent the vectors, and the diagonal originating at their point of intersection represents the resultant. **parallelogrammatic, -ical, parallelogrammic, -ical**, *a.* [F *parallèlogramme,* L *parallēlogrammum,* Gr. *parallēlogrammon* (PARALLEL, *grammē,* line)]

paralogism, *n.* a fallacious argument, esp. one of which the reasoner is unconscious. †**paralogize, -ise,** *v.i.* †**paralogy,** *n.* [F *paralogisme,* L *paralogismus,* Gr. *paralogismos,* from *paralogizesthai* (*logizesthai,* to reason, from *logos,* reason)]

paralyse, (*esp. N Am.*) **paralyze**, *v.t.* to affect with paralysis; to render powerless or ineffective; to render immobile or unable to function. **paralysation,** *n.* [F *paralyser,* as foll.]

paralysis, *n.* total or partial loss of the power of muscular contraction or of sensation in the whole or part of the body; palsy; complete helplessness or inability to act; inability to move or function properly. **paralytic,** *a.* of paralysis; characterized by paralysis; afflicted with paralysis; (*sl.*) very drunk. *n.* a paralysed or paralytic person. **paralytically,** *adv.* [L, from Gr. *paralusis* (*lusis,* from *luein,* to loosen)]

paramagnetic, *a.* having the property of being attracted by the poles of a magnet, magnetic, distinguished from *diamagnetic*. **paramagnetism,** *n.*

Paramaribo, *n.* port and capital of Surinam, S America, 24 km/15 miles from the sea on the river Surinam; population (1980) 68,000. Products include coffee, fruit, timber, and bauxite. It was founded by the French in 1540 and placed under Dutch rule in 1816.

paramastoid, *a.* situated near the mastoid process of the temporal bone. *n.* a paramastoid process.

paramatta PARRAMATTA.

paramecium, paramoecium, *n.* (*pl.* **-cia**) one of a genus (*Paramecium*) of Protozoa, a slipper-animalcule. [mod. L, from Gr. *paramēkēs* (*mēkos,* length)]

paramedical, -medic, *a.* auxiliary to the work of medical doctors. *n.* a paramedical worker.

paramenia, *n.pl.* disordered menses.

paramere, *n.* one of a series of radiating parts, as in starfish; either of the symmetrical halves of a bilateral animal or somite. **parameric,** *a.* [Gr. *meros,* part]

parameter, *n.* (*Math.*) a quantity remaining constant for a particular case, esp. a constant quantity entering into the equation of a curve etc.; (*coll.*) a limiting factor, a constraint.

paramilitary, *a.* having a similar nature or structure to military forces. *n.* a member of a paramilitary force.

paramnesia, DÉJÀ VU.

paramoecium PARAMECIUM.

paramorph, *n.* (*Min.*) a pseudomorph having the same chemical composition but differing in molecular structure. **paramorphic, -phous,** *a.* **paramorphism, -phosis,,** *n.* [Gr. *morphē,* form]

paramount, *a.* supreme above all others, pre-eminent; superior (to). *n.* the highest in rank or authority; a lord paramount. **paramountcy,** *n.* **paramountly,** *adv.* [A-F *paramount,* OF *par amont,* at the top (*par,* by, AMOUNT)]

paramour, *n.* a lover, usu. an illicit one. [OF *par amour,* L *per amōrem,* by love]

Paraná, *n.* river in S America, formed by the confluence of the Rio Grande and Paranaiba; the Paraguay joins it at Corrientes, and it flows into the Rio de la Plata with the Uruguay; length 4500 km/2800 miles.

parang, *n.* a heavy sheath-knife. [Malay]

paranoia, paranoea, *n.* mental derangement, esp. in a chronic form characterized by delusions etc.; (*coll.*) a sense of being persecuted. **paranoiac,** *n., a.* **paranoic,** *a.* [Gr. *paranoia* (*nous,* mind)]

†**paranomasia,** †**paranomasy** PARONOMASIA.

paranormal, *a.* not rationally explicable. *n.* paranormal events.

paranthelion, *n.* a diffuse image of the sun at the same altitude and at an angular distance of 120° due to reflection from ice-spicules in the air. [Gr. *anth'*, ANTI-, *hēlios,* sun]

paranucleus, *n.* (*pl.* **-lei**) a subsidiary nucleus in some Protozoa. **paranuclear, -leate,** *a.* **paranucleolus,** *n.* a mass of substance extruded from the mother-cell in pollen-grains and spores.

paranymph, *n.* in ancient Greece, a friend of the bridegroom who went with the bridegroom to fetch the bride, or the maiden who conducted the bride to the bridegroom; a 'best man', a bridesman or a bridesmaid; †an advocate or a spokesman for another. [L *paranymphus,* Gr. *paranumphos* (*numphē,* bride)]

parapet, *n.* a low or breast-high wall at the edge of a roof, bridge etc.; a breast-high wall or rampart for covering troops from observation and attack. **parapeted,** *a.* [F, from It. *parapetto* (*parare,* to defend, *petto,* L *pectus,* breast)]

paraph, *n.* a flourish after a signature, orig. intended as a protection against forgery. *v.t.* to sign; to initial. [F *paraphe,* med. L *paraphus, paragraphus,* PARAGRAPH]

paraphernalia, *n.pl.* (*Law*) personal property allowed to a wife over and above her dower, including her personal apparel, ornaments etc.; miscellaneous belongings, ornaments, trappings, equipments. **paraphernal,** *a.* [neut. pl. of L *paraphernālis,* from Gr. *parapherna,* neut. pl. (Gr. *phernē,* a dowry, from *pherein,* to bring)]

paraphimosis, *n.* permanent retraction of the prepuce.

paraphrase, *n.* a free translation or rendering of a passage; a restatement of a passage in different terms; any one of a series of hymns, used in the Church of Scotland etc., consisting of poetical versions of passages of Scripture. *v.t.* to express or interpret in other words. *v.i.* to make a paraphrase. **paraphrast,** *n.* one who paraphrases. **paraphrastic,** †**-ical,** *a.* **paraphrastically,** *adv.* [F, from L and Gr. *paraphrasis* (*phrazein,* to tell)]

paraphrenia, *n.* a type of schizophrenia characterized by ideas of persecution, grandeur etc.

paraphyllum, *n.* (*pl.* **-lla**) a small foliaceous or hair-like organ in certain mosses; a stipule. [Gr. *phullon,* leaf]

paraphysis, *n.* (*pl.* **-physes**) a sterile filament accompanying sexual organs in some cryptogams. [Gr. *phusis,* growth]

paraplegia, *n.* paralysis of the lower limbs and the lower part of the body. **paraplegic,** *n., a.* [Gr. *paraplēgia* (*plēssein,* to strike)]

parapleuritis, *n.* pleurodynia, or a mild form of pleurisy.

parapleurum, *n.* one of the sternal side-pieces in a beetle. [Gr. *pleuron,* rib]

parapodium, *n.* one of the jointless lateral locomotory organs of an annelid. [Gr. *pous podos,* foot]

parapophysis, *n.* a process on the side of a vertebra, usu. serving as the point of articulation of a rib. [Gr. *apophusis,* an off-shoot (APO-, *phusis,* growth)]

parapsychical, *a.* denoting phenomena such as hypnotism or telepathy which appear to be beyond explanation by the ascertained laws of science.

Paraquat®, *n.* a very poisonous weedkiller. [PAR(A)-, *quat*ernary (referring to its chemical composition)]

†**paraquet** PARAKEET.

parasang, *n.* an ancient Persian measure of length, about $3\frac{1}{4}$ miles (5·25 km). [L *parasanga,* Gr. *parasangēs,* from Pers.]

parascending, *n.* a sport in which a parachutist is towed at ground level until he or she ascends, then descends by parachute. [*para*chute, *ascending*]

parasceve, *n.* the day of preparation for the Jewish Sabbath. [L *parascēvē,* Gr. *paraskeuē* (*skeuē,* outfit)]

paraselene, *n.* (*pl.* **-nae**) a mock moon appearing in a lunar halo. **paraselenic,** *a.* [Gr. *selēnē,* moon]

parasite, *n.* one who frequents the tables of the rich, earning a welcome by flattery; a hanger-on, a sponger; an animal or plant subsisting at the expense of another organism; (*loosely*) a plant that lives on another without deriving its nutriment from it, a commensal; (*pop.*) a plant that climbs about another. **parasitic, -ical,** *a.* **parasitically,** *adv.* †**parasiticalness,** *n.* **parasiticide,** *n.* a preparation for destroying parasites. **parasitism,** *n.* **parasitize, -ise,** *v.t.* **parasitology,** *n.* **parasitologist,** *n.* [L *parasītus,* Gr. *parasitos* (*sitos,* food)]

parasol, *n.* a small umbrella used to give shelter from the sun; a sunshade. **parasolette,** *n.* [F, from It. *parasole* (*para,* imper. of *parare,* to ward off, *sole,* L *sol,* sun)]

parasympathetic, *a.* of that part of the autonomic nervous system that slows the heartbeat, stimulates the smooth muscles of the digestive tract, constricts the bronchi of the lungs etc. and thus counteracts the sympathetic nervous system.

parasynthesis, *n.* the principle or process of forming derivatives from compound words. **parasynthetic,** *a.* **parasyntheton,** *n.* (*pl.* **-ta**) a word so formed.

parataxis, *n.* an arrangement of clauses, sentences etc., without connectives indicating subordination etc. **paratactic,** *a.* **paratactically,** *adv.* [Gr. *parataxis* (*tassein,* to arrange)]

parathesis, *n.* juxtaposition of primary elements etc. equivalent in relation or meaning, as the monosyllabic roots in Chinese; apposition; a parenthetical notice; matter contained between brackets. [Gr. *tithenai,* to place]

parathion, *n.* a highly toxic insecticide. [PAR(A)-, *thio-*phosphate]

parathyroid, *n.* a small endocrine gland, one of which is situated on each side of the thyroid.

paratonic, *a.* of plant-movements etc., due to external stimuli; of the effect of light in certain cases, retarding growth; pertaining to overstrain. **paratonically,** *adv.*

paratrooper, *n.* a soldier belonging to a unit borne in aeroplanes and gliders and dropped by parachute, with full equipment, usu. behind enemy lines. **paratroops,** *n.pl.*

paratyphoid, *n.* an infectious fever of the enteric group, similar in symptoms to typhoid but of milder character.

paravane, *n.* a mine-sweeping appliance for severing the moorings of submerged mines.

†**paravant,** †**-vaunt,** *adv., prep.* before, in front. [OF *paravant* (*par,* by, *avant,* before)]

par avion, *adv.* by air mail. [F, by aeroplane]

parazoan, *n.* a member of the *Parazoa,* multicellular invertebrates, such as sponges. [Gr. *zōon,* animal]

parbake, *v.t.* to bake partially. [F *par-,* see prec.]

†**parbreak,** *v.t., v.i.* to vomit. *n.* vomit, spewing. [F *par-,* see PARBOIL, BREAK[1]]

parboil, *v.t.* to boil partially; †to boil thoroughly. [OF *parboillir,* from late L *perbullīre,* to boil thoroughly (PER-, *bullīre,* to BOIL[1]), conf. with PART]

parbuckle, *n.* a double sling usu. made by passing the two ends of a rope through a bight for hoisting or lowering a cask or gun. *v.t.* to hoist or lower by a parbuckle. [etym. unknown]

Parcae, *n.pl.* The Fates, in Roman mythology. [L, those who spare]

parcel, *n.* †a portion or part, an item; a number or quantity of things dealt with as a separate lot; a distinct portion, as of land; a quantity of things wrapped up together; a bundle, a package. †*adv.* partly. *v.t.* (*past, p.p.* **parcelled**) to divide (*usu.* out) into parts or lots; to wrap (a rope) with strips of canvas, or cover (a seam) with strips of canvas and pitch; to make into a parcel; †to detail, to enumerate, to specify. †**parcel-bearded, -blind, -drunk, -gilt,** *a.* partly bearded, blind, drunk or gilt. **parcel-office,** *n.* an office for the receipt or dispatch of parcels. **parcel-post,** *n.* a branch of the postal service for the delivery of parcels. **parcelling,** *n.* a wrapping of tarred canvas to prevent chafing of a rope etc. [F *parcelle,* late L *particella,* dim. of *particula,* PARTICLE]

parcenary, *n.* coheirship, coparcenary. **parcener,** *n.* [A-F *parcenarie,* OF *parçonerie,* from *parçonier, parcener,* med. L *partiōnārius* (PARTITION, -ER)]

parch, *v.t.* to scorch or roast partially dry, to dry up. *v.i.* to become hot or dry. **parched,** *a.* dried up; (*coll.*) very thirsty. †**parchedly,** *adv.* †**parchedness,** *n.* [etym. unknown]

Parcheesi®, *n.* a modern board game based on pachisi.

parchment, *n.* the skin of calves, sheep, goats etc., prepared for writing upon, painting etc.; a manuscript on this, esp. a deed; a tough skin, as the husk of the coffee-berry. *a.* made of or resembling parchment. **parchmenty,** *a.* [F *parchemin,* L *pergamēna,* orig. fem. of *Pergamēnus,* pertaining to *Pergamum,* city of Mysia]

parcimony, PARSIMONY.

parclose, *n.* a screen or railing enclosing an altar, tomb etc. in a church. [ME and OF *parclos, -close,* p.p. of *parclore* (PER-, *claudere,* to CLOSE)]

†**pard[1]**, †**pardal,** *n.* a panther, a leopard. [OF *pard,* L *pardus,* Gr. *pardos,* earlier *pardalis,* of Eastern orig.]

pard[2], *n.* (*N Am. sl.*) a partner. [coll. abbr. of PARTNER]

pardie, †**parde,** *int., adv.* certainly, assuredly; of a truth. [OF *par dé* (F *par dieu*), by God]

pardner PARD[2].

pardon, *v.t.* to forgive, to absolve from; to remit the penalty of; to refrain from exacting; to excuse, to make allowance for. *n.* the act of pardoning; a complete or partial remission of the legal consequences of crime; an official warrant of a penalty remitted; a papal indulgence; a religious festival when this is granted; courteous forbearance; †permission. **I beg your pardon, pardon me,** excuse me, a polite apology for an action, contradiction or failure to hear or understand what is said. **pardon my French** FRENCH. **pardonable,** *a.* **pardonableness,** *n.* **pardonably,** *adv.* **pardoner,** *n.* one who pardons; a person licensed to sell papal pardons or indulgences. [OF *pardoner, perduner,* late L *perdōnāre* (PER-, *dōnāre,* to give, from *dōnum,* gift)]

pare, *v.t.* to cut or shave (away or off); to cut away or remove the rind etc. of (fruit etc.); to trim by cutting the edges or irregularities of; to diminish by degrees. **parer,** *n.* **paring,** *n.* the act of cutting off, pruning or trimming; that which is pared off; a shaving, rind etc. [F *parer,* L *parāre,* to prepare]

Paré, *n.* **Ambroise** (1509–90), French surgeon who introduced modern principles into wound treatment and amputations, abandoning cauterization in favour of soothing balms and the use of ligatures to tie off blood vessels.

†**paregal,** *a.* equal, fully equal. *n.* an equal or peer. [OF *parigal* (PER-, EQUAL)]

paregoric, *a.* assuaging or soothing pain. *n.* a camphorated tincture of opium for assuaging pain. [late L *parēgoricus,* Gr. *parēgorikos,* soothing, from *parēgoros,* addressing, exhorting (PAR(A)-, AGORA, assembly)]

pareira, *n.* a drug used in urinary disorders, obtained from the root of *Chondrodendron tomentosum* or *Cissampelos pareira,* a Brazilian climbing plant. [Port. *parreira*]

parella, *n.* a crustaceous lichen, *Lecanora parella,* from which litmus and orchil are obtained. **parellic,** *a.* [mod. L, from F *parelle,* med. L *paratella*]

parembole, *n.* an insertion, usu. more intimately related to the subject of the sentence than a parenthesis. [Gr. PAR(A)-, *embolē,* insertion]

parenchyma, *n.* the soft cellular tissue of glands and other organs, distinguished from connective tissue etc.; thin cellular tissue in the softer part of plants, pith, fruit pulp etc. **parenchymal, -matous, -mous,** *a.* [Gr. *parenchuma* (PAR(A)-, *enchuma,* infusion, from *encheein,* to pour in)]

parent, *n.* a father or mother; a forefather; an organism from which others are produced; a source, origin, cause, or occasion. *v.t.* to be a parent or the parent of. **parent–teacher association,** an association formed by the parents and teachers of a school, esp. for social and fund-raising purposes. **parent company,** *n.* a company having control of one or more subsidiaries. **parentage,** *n.* birth, extraction, lineage, origin; †a parent or parents collectively. **parental,** *a.* **parentally,** *adv.* **parenthood,** *n.* **parenticide,** *n.* one who kills a parent; the killing of parents. **parenting,** *n.* the skills or activity of being a parent. **parentless,** *a.* [F, from L *parentem,* nom. *-ens* from *parēre,* to produce, to beget]

parenteral, *a.* situated or occurring outside the digestive tract, esp. being the means of administering a drug other than via the digestive tract. [Gr. *enteron,* intestine]

parenthesis, *n.* (*pl.* **-theses**) a word, phrase or sentence inserted in a sentence that is grammatically complete without it, usu. marked off by brackets, dashes or commas; (*pl.*) round brackets () to include such words; an interval, interlude, incident etc. **parenthesize, -ise,** *v.t.* to insert as a parenthesis; to place (a clause etc.) between parentheses. **parenthetic, -ical,** *a.* **parenthetically,** *adv.* [med. L and Gr., from *parentithenai* (PAR(A)-, EN-, *tithenai,* to put)]

parergon, *n.* (*pl.* **-ga**) a subsidiary work, a by-work. [L and Gr. (*ergon,* work)]

paresis, *n.* incomplete paralysis, affecting muscular movement but not sensation. **paretic,** *a.* [Gr., from *parienai* (*hienai,* to let go)]

paresthesia, PARAESTHESIA.

Pareto, *n.* **Vilfredo** (1848–1923), Italian economist and political philosopher, born in Paris. Vigorously opposed to socialism and liberalism, he justified income inequality on the grounds that income distribution remained constant whatever efforts were made to change it (**Pareto's Law**).

parfait, *n.* a rich, cold dessert made with whipped cream, eggs, fruit etc. [F, perfect]

†**parfilage,** *n.* the unravelling of woven fabrics, or of gold and silver thread from laces, an amusement among women in the 18th cent. [F, from *parfiler,* to unravel (*par,* by, *filer,* from *fil,* thread)]

parfleche, *n.* a hide, usu. of buffalo, stripped of hair and dried on a stretcher; a tent, wallet or other article made of this. [Canadian F, from N Am. Ind.]

pargasite, *n.* a greenish variety of hornblende. [G *Pargasit,* from *Pargas,* Finland]

parget, *v.t.* to plaster over; to paint (the face etc.). *n.* plaster; †pargeting; †paint, esp. for the face. **pargeter,** *n.* **pargeting,** *n.* plasterwork, esp. decorative plasterwork. †**pargework,** *n.* [OF *pargeter, porgeter,* L *prōjectāre* (PRO-, *jactāre,* freq. of *jacere,* to throw)]

parhelion, *n.* (*pl.* **-lia**) a mock-sun or bright spot in a solar halo, due to ice-crystals in the atmosphere. **parheliacal, parhelic,** *a.* **parhelic circle,** *n.* a circle of light parallel to the horizon at the altitude of the sun, caused by the reflection of sunlight by ice-crystals in the atmosphere. [L and Gr. (PAR(A)-, *hēlios,* sun)]

pariah, *n.* one of a people of very low caste in S India and Burma; one of low caste or without caste; a social outcast. **pariah-dog,** *n.* a vagabond mongrel dog, esp. in India. [Tamil *paraiyar,* pl. of *paraiyan,* a drummer, from *parai,* drum]

Parian, *a.* pertaining to the island of Paros, celebrated for its white marble. *n.* a white variety of porcelain, used for statuettes etc.

paridigitate, *a.* having an even number of toes or digits on each foot. [L *pari-, pār,* equal, DIGITATE]

parietal, *a.* pertaining to a wall or walls, esp. those of the body and its cavities; (*Bot.*) pertaining to or attached to the wall of a structure, esp. of placentae or ovaries; (*N Am.*) pertaining to residence within the walls of a college. **parietal bone,** *n.* either of the two bones forming part of the top and sides of the skull. **parieto-,** *comb. form* (*Anat.*). [F *pariétal,* L *parietālis,* from *paries -etis,* wall]

pari mutuel, *n.* a system of betting in which the winners divide the losers' stakes less a percentage for management. [F]

paring PARE.

pari passu, *adv.* (esp. in legal contexts) with equal pace, in a similar degree, equally. [L]

paripinnate, *a.* equally pinnate, without a terminal leaflet. [L *pari-, pār,* equal, PINNATE]

Paris[1], *n.* port and capital of France, on the River Seine; department in the Île de France region; area 105 sq km/40.5 sq miles; population (1982, metropolitan area) 8,707,000. Products include metal, leather and luxury goods, chemicals, glass, and tobacco. Notable features include the Champs-Elysées leading to the Arc de Triomphe, the Place de la Concorde, and the Eiffel Tower. *a.* used attributively of things derived from Paris, capital of France. **plaster of Paris** PLASTER. **paris blue,** *n.* a bright Prussian blue; a bright-blue colouring-matter obtained from aniline. **paris doll,** *n.* a lay-figure used by dressmakers as a model. **paris green,** *n.* a light-green pigment obtained from arsenite of copper. **paris white,** *n.* a fine grade of whiting used for polishing.

Paris[2], *n.* in Greek legend, a prince of Troy whose abduction of Helen, wife of king Menelaus of Sparta, caused the Trojan war.

Paris Commune, *n.* two periods of government in France: **The Paris municipal government** (1789–94), was established after the storming of the Bastille and remained powerful until after the fall of Robespierre. **The provisional national government** (18 Mar.–May 1871), often considered the first socialist government in history. Elected after the right-wing National Assembly at Versailles tried to disarm the National Guard, it fell when the Versailles troops captured Paris and massacred about 20,000 people (21–28 May).

Paris, Treaty of, any of various peace treaties signed in Paris, including 1763, ending the Seven Years' War; 1783, recognizing American Independence; 1856, ending the Crimean War; 1898, ending the Spanish-American War; 1946, after World War II the peace treaties between the Allies and Italy, Romania, Hungary, Bulgaria, and Finland; 1973, concluding the Vietnam War.

parish, *n.* an ecclesiastical district with its own church and clergyman; a subdivision of a county; a civil district for purposes of local government etc.; the people living in a parish. *a.* pertaining to or maintained by a parish. **on the parish,** (*formerly*) being financially supported by the parish. **parish clerk,** *n.* a subordinate lay official in the church, formerly leading the congregation in the responses. **parish council,** *n.* a local administrative body elected by the parishioners in rural districts. **parish pump,** *a.* (*coll.*) of local interest; parochial. **parish register,** *n.* a register of christenings, marriages, burials etc., kept at a parish church. **parishioner,** *n.* one who belongs to a parish. [A-F *parosse, paroche* (F *paroisse*), late L *parochia,* Gr. *paroikia* (PAR(A)-, *oikos,* dwelling)]

parisyllabic, *a.* of Greek and Latin nouns, having the same number of syllables, esp. in all the cases.

parity, *n.* equality of rank, condition, value etc., esp. of rank among ministers as in a non-prelatical church; parallelism, analogy; the amount of a foreign currency equal to a specific sum of domestic currency; equivalence of a commodity price as expressed in one currency to its price expressed in another; (*Math.*) the property of being odd or even. **parity check,** *n.* a check of computer data which uses the state of oddness or evenness of the number of bits in a unit of information as a means of detecting errors. [F *parité,* L *paritātem,* nom. *-tas,* from *pār,* equal]

park, *n.* a piece of land, usu. for ornament, pleasure or recreation, with trees, pasture etc., surrounding or adjoining a mansion; a piece of ground, ornamentally laid out, enclosed for public recreation; a large tract or region, usu. with interesting physical features, preserved in its natural state for public enjoyment; (*Mil.*) a space occupied by the artillery, stores etc. in an encampment; the train of artillery, with stores and equipment, pertaining to a field army; (*coll.*) a soccer pitch; (*N Am.*) a sports stadium or arena. *v.t.* to enclose in or as in a park; to mass (artillery) in a park; to leave (a vehicle) in a place allotted for the purpose; to leave temporarily. *v.i.* to leave a vehicle in a place allotted for the purpose. **parking lot,** *n.* (*N Am.*) a car-park. **parking-meter,** *n.* a coin-operated appliance on a kerb that charges for the time cars are parked there. **parking ticket,** *n.* a document issued for a parking offence requiring payment of a fine or appearance in court. **park-keeper,** *n.* **parkish,** *a.* [OF *parc* (cp. Dut. *perk,* Swed. and Dan. *park,* G *Pferch*), from Teut., cp. OE *pearruc,* PADDOCK[1]]

Park, *n.* **Mungo** (1771–1806), Scottish surgeon and explorer. He traced the course of the Niger (1795–97) and probably drowned during a second expedition (1805–06). He published *Travels in the Interior of Africa* (1799).

parka, *n.* a hooded jacket often edged or lined with fur. [Aleutian, skin]

Park Chung Hee, *n.* (1917–79), president of South Korea (1963–79). Under his rule South Korea had the world's fastest-growing economy and the wealth was widely distributed, but recession and his increasing authoritarianism led to his assassination 1979.

Parker[1], *n.* **Charles ('Charlie') Christopher ('Bird', 'Yardbird')** (1920–55), US alto saxophonist and jazz composer, associated with the trumpeter Dizzy Gillespie in developing the bebop style. His mastery of improvisation inspired performers on all jazz instruments.

Parker[2], *n.* **Dorothy** (born Rothschild) (1893–1967), US writer and wit. She reviewed for the magazines *Vanity Fair* and the *New Yorker*, and wrote wittily ironic verses, collected in several volumes including *Not So Deep As a Well* (1940), and short stories.

Parkes[1], *n.* the site in New South Wales of the Australian National Radio Astronomy Observatory, featuring a radio telescope of 210 ft. (64 m) aperture, run by the Commonwealth Scientific and Industrial Research Organization.

Parkes[2], *n.* **Henry** (1815–96), Australian politician, born in the UK. He promoted education and the cause of federation, and suggested the official name 'Commonwealth of Australia'. He was five times premier of New South Wales (1872–91).

parkin, *n.* a cake made of gingerbread or oatmeal and treacle. [etym. unknown]

Parkinson, *n.* **Cecil (Edward)** (1931–), British Conservative politician. He was chair of the party 1981–83, and became minister for trade and industry, but resigned Oct. 1984 following disclosure of an affair with his secretary. In 1987 he rejoined the cabinet as secretary of state for energy, and in 1989 became the transport secretary.

Parkinson's disease, parkinsonism, *n.* a chronic disorder of the central nervous system causing loss of muscle coordination and tremor. [James *Parkinson,* 1755–1824, British surgeon who first described it]

Parkinson's Law, *n.* the principle in office management etc. that work expands to fill the time available for its completion. [adumbrated facetiously by C. Northcote Parkinson, 1909–88, British historian]

Parkman, *n.* **Francis** (1823–93), US historian and traveller, whose work chronicles the European exploration and conquest of North America, in such books as *The California and Oregon Trail* (1849) and *La Salle and the Discovery of the Great West* (1879). Parkman viewed the defeat by England of the French at Québec 1759 (described in his *Montcalm and Wolfe*, 1884) as the turning point of North American history, insofar as it swung the balance of power in North America towards the British colonies which would form the US.

parky, *a.* (*coll.*) chilly, uncomfortable. [etym. doubtful]

parl., (*abbr.*) parliament(ary).

parlance, *n.* way of speaking, idiom; †conversation, a conference, a parley. †**parle,** *n., v.i.* [OF, as foll.]

parley, *v.i.* to confer with an enemy with pacific intentions; to talk, to dispute. *v.t.* to converse in, to speak (esp. a foreign language). *n.* a conference for discussing terms, esp. between enemies. [F *parler* or OF *parlee,* fem. p.p. of *parler,* pop. L *parabolāre,* from *parabola,* PARABLE]

parleyvoo, *n.* (*dated sl.*) French; a Frenchman. *v.i.* to speak French. [F *parlez-vous français,* do you speak French?]

parliament, *n.* a deliberative assembly; a legislative body, esp. the British legislature, consisting of the Houses of Lords and Commons, together with the sovereign. **parliament-cake,** *n.* a thin crisp gingerbread cake. **parliamentarian,** *n.* one versed in parliamentary rules and usages or in parliamentary debate; a member of parliament; (*Hist.*) one who supported the Parliament against Charles I in the time of the Great Civil War. *a.* parliamentary. **parliamentary,** *a.* of, pertaining to or enacted by (a) parliament according to the rules of (a) parliament; esp. of language, admissible in (a) parliament, civil. **parliamentary private secretary,** an ordinary member of the British parliament appointed to assist a Minister. **parliamentary agent,** *n.* a person employed by a private person or persons to draft bills or manage the business of private legislation. **Parliamentary Commissioner,** (in Britain) the official designation of an ombudsman. **parliamentary train,** *n.* (*Hist.*) a train carrying passengers at a rate not exceeding one old penny per mile which by Act of Parliament (repealed 1883) every railway was obliged to run daily each way over its system. [ME and OF *parlement* (PARLEY, -MENT)]

Parliament, European, EUROPEAN PARLIAMENT.

Parliament, Houses of, the building where the UK legislative assembly meets. The present Houses of Parliament in London, designed in Gothic Revival style by the architects Charles Barry and A.W. Pugin, were built 1840–60, the previous building having burned down in 1834. It incorporates portions of the mediaeval Palace of Westminster.

parlour, *n.* orig. a room in a convent for conversation; the family sitting-room in a private house; any of various commercial establishments, e.g. a beauty-parlour; a building used for milking cows. **parlour-boarder,** *n.* a pupil at a boarding-school living with the principal's family. **parlour-car,** *n.* (*N Am.*) a luxuriously fitted railway-carriage, a drawing-room car. **parlour-maid,** *n.* a maid-servant waiting at table. [OF *parleor,* med. L *parlātōrium,* from *parlāre, parabolāre,* to speak, see PARLEY]

parlous, *a.* perilous, awkward, trying; shrewd, clever, venturesome. *adv.* extremely. [var. of PERILOUS]

Parmesan, *n.* a kind of hard, dry cheese made at Parma and elsewhere in N Italy, used grated as a topping for pasta dishes.

Parnassus, *n.* a mountain in central Greece; height 2457 m/8064 ft, revered as the abode of Apollo and the Muses. Delphi lies on its southern flank; poetry, literature.

Parnell, *n.* **Charles Stewart** (1846–91), Irish nationalist politician. He supported a policy of obstruction and violence to attain Home Rule, and became the president of the Nationalist Party (1877). In 1879 he approved the Land League, and his attitude led to his imprisonment (1881). His career was ruined (1890) when he was cited as co-respondent in a divorce case. **Parnellism,** *n.* the political views and tactics of Parnell.

parochial, *a.* relating to a parish; petty, narrow. **parochialism, -ality,** *n.* **parochialize, -ise,** *v.t.* **parochially,** *adv.* [OF, from late L *parochiālis,* from *parochia,* PARISH]

parody, *n.* a literary composition imitating an author's work for the purpose of ridicule; a poor imitation, a mere travesty. *v.t.* to turn into a parody, to burlesque. **parodic,** †**-ical,** *a.* **parodist,** *n.* [L and Gr. *parōdia* (PAR(A)-, ODE)]

parole, *n.* a word of honour, esp. a promise by, e.g. a prisoner of war that he/she will not attempt to escape, that he/she will return to custody on a certain day if released, or will not take up arms against his/her captors unless exchanged; the release of a prisoner under certain conditions; the daily password used by officers etc., as distinguished from the countersign; actual speech, by contrast with language as an abstract system (cp. *performance*). *v.t.* to put or release on parole. **on parole,** of a prisoner, released under certain conditions. [F, from late L *parabola,* PARABLE]

paronomasia, †**paranomasia,** *n.* a play upon words, a pun. **paronomasial, -ian, paronomastic, -ical,** *a.* †**paranomasy,** *n.* [L and Gr. (*onomazein,* to name, from *onoma,* name)]

paronym, *n.* a paronymous word. **paronymous,** *a.* having the same root, cognate; alike in sound, but differing in origin, spelling and meaning. **paronymy,** *n.* [Gr. *parōnumos,* paronymous (*onoma,* name)]

parotid, *a.* situated near the ear. *n.* a parotis; †a parotid tumour. **parotid duct,** *n.* a duct from the parotid gland by which saliva is conveyed to the mouth. **parotid gland** PAROTIS. **parotic, parotideal, -dean,** *a.* **parotiditis, parotitis,** *n.* inflammation of the parotid gland, mumps. **parotis,** *n.* one of a pair of salivary glands situated on either side of the cheek in front of the ear, with a duct to the mouth; †a tumour on one of these glands. [F *parotide,* from L and Gr. *parōtis -tidos* (*ous ōtos,* ear)]

-parous, *comb. form* producing, bringing forth. [L *-parus,* from *parere,* to bring forth]

parousia, *n.* Christ's second coming, to judge the world. [Gr., presence]

paroxysm, *n.* a sudden and violent fit; the exacerbation of a disease at periodic times; a fit of laughter or other emotion. **paroxysmal, -mic,** *a.* **paroxysmally,** *adv.* [F *paroxysme,* L *paroxysmus,* Gr. *paroxusmos* (*oxunein,* to sharpen, from *oxus,* sharp)]

paroxytone, *a.* in classical Greek, applied to a word having an acute accent on the penultimate syllable. *n.* a word having such an accent. **paroxytonic,** *a.* [Gr. *paroxutonos*]

parpen, *n.* a bond-stone. [OF *parpain* (F *parpaing*), etym. doubtful]

parquet, *n.* a flooring of parquetry; (*N Am.*) the part of the floor of a theatre between the orchestra and the row immediately under the front of the gallery. *v.t.* to floor a room with parquetry. **parquetry,** *n.* inlaid woodwork for floors. [F, a floor, orig. a compartment, dim. of *parc,* PARK]

parr, *n.* a young salmon. [etym. doubtful]

Parr, *n.* **Catherine** (1512–48), sixth wife of Henry VIII of England. She had already lost two husbands when in 1543 she married Henry VIII. She survived him, and in 1547 married Lord Seymour of Sudeley (1508–49).

parrakeet, PARAKEET.

par(r)amatta, *n.* a light twilled dress-fabric of merino wool and cotton, orig. from Parramatta in New South Wales.

parrhesia, *n.* freedom or boldness in speaking. [late L and Gr. (*rhēsis,* speech)]

parricide, *n.* one who murders, or the murder of, a parent or a revered person; treason or one guilty of treason against his country. **parricidal,** *a.* [F, from L *parricīda* or *parricīdium*]

parrot, *n.* one of a group of tropical birds with brilliant plumage, esp. the genus *Psittacus,* remarkable for their faculty of imitating the human voice; one who repeats words or imitates actions mechanically or unintelligently; a chatterbox. *v.t.* to repeat mechanically or by rote. *v.i.* to repeat words or to chatter as a parrot. **parrot-fashion,** *adv.* by rote. **parrot-fish,** *n.* a fish of the genus *Scarus,* or some allied genera, from their brilliant coloration, and the beak-like projection of the jaws. **parroter,** *n.* **parrotism,** *n.* **parrotry,** *n.* [etym. doubtful, perh. from *periquito,* dim. of *perico,* cp. PARAKEET]

parry, *v.t.* to ward off (a blow or thrust); to evade; to shirk. *n.* a defensive movement in fencing, the warding off of a blow etc. [F *parer,* to parry, L *parāre,* see PARADE]

Parry, *n.* **William Edward** (1790–1855), English admiral and Arctic explorer. He made detailed charts during explorations of the Northwest Passage (1819–20, 1821–23, and 1824–25).

parse, *v.t.* to describe or classify (a word) grammatically, its inflectional forms, relations in the sentence etc.; to analyse (a sentence) and describe its component words and their relations grammatically. *v.i.* of a word or sentence, to be conformable to grammatical rules. [L *pars,* PART]

parsec, *n.* a unit of length in calculating the distance of the stars, being $1{\cdot}9 \times 10^{13}$ miles (3×10^{13} km) or 3·26 light years. [*par*allax *sec*ond]

Parsee, Parsi, *n.* a Zoroastrian, a descendant of the Persians who fled to India from the Muslim persecution in the 7th and 8th cents.; the language of the Persians under the Sassanian kings, before it was corrupted by Arabic. **Parseeism, Parsiism,** *n.* the Parsee religion, Zoroastrianism. [Pers. *Pārsī,* Persian from *Pārs,* Persia]

Parsifal, *n.* in Germanic legend, the father of Lohengrin and one of the knights who sought the Holy Grail.

parsimonious, *a.* sparing in the expenditure of money; frugal, niggardly, stingy. **parsimoniously,** *adv.* **parsimoniousness, parsimony,** *n.* [L *parsi-, parci-mōnia,* from *parcere,* to spare]

parsley, *n.* an umbelliferous herb, *Petroselinum sativum,* cultivated for its aromatic leaves used for seasoning and garnishing dishes. [ME *percil,* OF *peresil* (F *persil*), late L *petrosillum,* L *petroselīnum,* Gr. *petroselīnon* (*petro-, petros,* stone, *selīnon,* parsley)]

parsnip, *n.* an umbelliferous plant, *Pastinaca sativa,* with an edible root used as a culinary vegetable. [ME *pasnep,* OF *pastenaque,* L *pastināca,* from *pastinum,* a fork for digging].

parson, *n.* a rector, vicar or other clergyman holding a benefice; (*coll.*) a clergyman. **parson-bird,** *n.* the poe-bird. **parson's nose,** *n.* the rump of a fowl. **parsonage,** *n.* the dwelling-house of a parson; the benefice of a parish. **parsonic, -ical, parsonish,** *a.* [ME *persone,* PERSON]

Parsons, *n.* **Charles Algernon** (1854–1931), English engineer who invented the Parsons steam turbine (1884), a landmark in marine engineering and later universally used in electricity generation (to drive an alternator).

part, *n.* a portion, piece or amount of a thing or number of things; a portion separate from the rest or considered as separate; a member, an organ; a proportional quantity; one of several equal portions, quantities or numbers into which a thing is divided, or of which it is composed; a section of a book, periodical etc., as issued at one time; a share, a lot; interest, concern; share of work etc., act, duty; side, party; the role, character, words etc. allotted to an actor; a copy of the words so allotted; a person's allotted duty or responsibility; (*pl.*) qualities, accomplishments, talents; quarters; (*pl.*) region, district; one of the constituent melodies of a harmony; a melody allotted to a particular voice or instrument; (*N Am.*) a parting in the hair. *v.t.* to divide into portions, shares, pieces, etc.; to separate; to brush (the hair) with a division along the head. *v.i.* to divide; to separate (from); to resign; of a cable etc., to give way. *adv.* partly. *a.* partial. **for my part,** so far as I am concerned. **for the most part** MOST. **in good part,** with good temper, without offence. **in ill part** ILL. **in part,** partly. **on the part of,** done by or proceeding from. **part and parcel,** an essential part or element. **part of speech,** a grammatical class of words of a particular character, comprising noun, pronoun, adjective, verb, adverb, preposition, conjunction, interjection. **to part company,** to separate. **to part with,** to relinquish, to give up. **to play a part,** to assist or be involved; to act deceitfully. **to take part,** to assist; to participate. **to take the part of,** to back up or support the cause of. **part-exchange,** *n.* a form of purchase in which one item is offered as partial payment for another, the balance being paid as money. *v.t.* to offer in part-exchange. **part-owner,** *n.* one who has a share in property with others. **part-song,** *n.* a composition for at least three voices in harmony, usu. without accompaniment. **part-time,** *a.* working or done for less than the usual number of hours. **part-time,** *a., adv.* **part-timer,** *n.* a part-time worker, student etc. **partway,** *adv.* (*esp. N Am.*) to some extent; partially. **partwork,** *n.* a magazine etc. issued in instalments intended to be bound to form a complete book or course of study. [OE, from L *partem,* nom. *pars,* whence *partīre,* F *partir,* to divide]

part., (*abbr.*) participle.

partake, *v.t.* to take or have a part or share in common with others; †to distribute; †to share with. *v.i., v.i.* to take or have a part or share (of or in, with another or others); to have something of the nature (of); to eat and drink (of). **partaker,** *n.*

partan, *n.* (*Sc.*) a crab, esp. the edible sea-crab. [prob. from Gael.]

parterre, *n.* an ornamental arrangement of flower-beds, with intervening walks; the ground-floor of a theatre or the part of this behind the orchestra; (*N Am.*) the part under the galleries. [F *par terre,* on the ground]

parthenogenesis, *n.* generation without sexual union. **parthenogenetic,** *a.* **parthenogenetically,** *adv.* [Gr. *parthenos,* virgin]

Parthenon, *n.* the temple of Athena Parthenos ('the Virgin') on the Acropolis at Athens; built 447–438 BC under the supervision of Phidias, and the most perfect example of Doric architecture (by Callicrates and Ictinus). In turn a Christian church and Turkish mosque, it was then used as a gunpowder store, and reduced to ruins when the Venetians bombarded the Acropolis 1687. Greek sculptures from the Parthenon were removed by Lord Elgin in the early 19th cent.; popularly known as the Elgin marbles.

Parthia, *n.* ancient country in W Asia in what is now NE Iran, capital Ctesiphon. Originating about 248 BC, it reached the peak of its power under Mithridates I in the 2nd cent. BC, and was annexed to Persia under the Sassanids 226 AD. **Parthian,** *a.* of or pertaining to Parthia, an ancient kingdom in W Asia. **Parthian arrow, glance, shaft, shot,** *n.* a look, word etc. delivered as a parting blow, like the arrows shot by the Parthians in the act of fleeing.

parti, *n.* a person regarded as eligible matrimonially. [F]

partial, *a.* affecting a part only, incomplete; biased in favour of one side or party, unfair; having a preference for. **partiality,** *n.* †**partialize, -ise,** *v.t., v.i.* **partially,** *adv.* [F, from L *partiālis,* from *pars partis,* PART]

†**partible,** *a.* divisible; separable. **partibility,** *n.* [L *partibilis,* from *partīrī,* to divide, as prec.]

participate, *v.i.* to have or enjoy a share, to partake (in); to have something (of the nature of). *v.t.* to have a part or share in (with). **participating policy,** *n.* an insurance policy entitling the holder to a share in the surplus profits of the business. **participating stock,** *n.* a type of preferred capital stock which in addition to dividends at a fixed rate is entitled to share in any surplus earnings. **participable,** *a.* **participant,** *n., a.* **participation,** *n.* **participative,** *a.* **participator,** *n.* [L *participātus,* p.p. of *participāre* (PART, *capere,* to take)]

participle, *n.* a word partaking of the nature of a verb and of an adjective, a verbal adjective qualifying a substantive. **participial,** *a.* **participially,** *adv.* [OF (F *participe*), L *participium,* as prec.]

particle, *n.* a minute part or portion; an atom; a word not inflected, or not used except in combination. **elementary particle** *n.* one so-called because thought indivisible. **particle accelerator,** *n.* a device for accelerating elementary particles, used in high-energy physics. **particulate,** *a.* [L *particula,* dim. of *pars,* PART]

†**parti-coated,** *a.* having a parti-coloured coat; dressed in motley.

†**parti-coloured,** *a.* partly of one colour, partly of another; variegated.

particular, *a.* pertaining to a single person or thing as distinguished from others; special, peculiar, characteristic; private, personal; single, separate, individual; minute, circumstantial; fastidious, exact, precise; remarkable, noteworthy; †intimate, specially attentive. *n.* an item, a detail, an instance; (*pl.*) a detailed account; †personal interest or concern; †personal character, idiosyncrasy. **in particular,** particularly. **Particular Baptists,** *n.pl.* a sect holding the doctrines of particular election and redemption (see PARTICULARISM). **particularism,** *n.* devotion to private interests or those of a party, sect etc.; the policy of allowing political independence to the separate states of an empire, confederation etc.; (*Theol.*) the doctrine of the election or redemption of particular individuals of the human race. **particularist,** *n.* **particularistic,** *a.* **particularity,** *n.* the quality of being particular; circumstantiality; †a minute point or instance; †a peculiarity; †a particular or private interest. **particularize, -ise,** *v.t.* to mention individually; to specify; to give the particulars of. *v.t.* to be attentive to particulars or details. **particularization, -isation,** *n.* **particularly,** *adv.* **particularness,** *n.* [ME and OF *particuler,* L *particulāris,* from *particula,* PARTICLE]

particulate PARTICLE.

partim, *adv.* partly. [L, from *pars partis,* PART]

parting, *a.* serving to part; departing; given or bestowed on departure or separation. *n.* separation, division; a point of separation or departure; a dividing-line, esp. between sections of hair combed or falling in opposite directions; a departure; leave-taking.

parti pris, *n.* preconceived view, bias, prejudice. [F, side taken]

partisan[1], *n.* an adherent of a party, faction, cause etc., esp. one showing unreasoning devotion; one of a body of irregular troops carrying out special enterprises, such as raids. *a.* pertaining or attached to a party. **partisanship,** *n.* [It. *partigiano*]

partisan[2], **partizan,** *n.* a pike or long-handled spear like a halberd; a quarter-staff, a truncheon or baton. [F *partizane* (now *pertuisane*), It. *partesana, partegiana,* perh. rel. to prec., or from Teut. (cp. OHG *parta,* halberd)]

partita, *n.* a suite of music. [It., cp. PART]

partite, *a.* (*Bot., Ent. etc.*) divided nearly to the base. [L *partītus*]

partition, *n.* division into parts, distribution; a separate part; that which separates into parts, esp. a wall or other barrier; (*Law*) division of property among joint-owners etc. *v.t.* to separate (off); to divide into parts or shares. **partitioned,** *a.* **partitive,** *a.* denoting a part. *n.* a word denoting partition, as *some, any* etc. **partitively,** *adv.* [F, from L *partītiōnem,* nom. *-tio,* from L *partīrī,* to PART]

†**partlet**[1], *n.* a neck-covering worn by women; a ruff. [ME *patelet,* OF *patelette,* perh. dim. of *patte* paw]

†**partlet**[2], *n.* a hen; a woman. [OF *Pertelote,* a female name]

partly, *adv.* in part; to some extent; not wholly.

partner, *n.* one who shares with another, esp. one associated with others in business; an associate; one of two persons who dance together; one of two playing on the same side in a game; a husband or a wife; (*pl.*) (*Naut.*) timber framing round a mast, pump etc., relieving the strain on the deck-timbers. *v.t.* to join in partnership, to be a partner (of). **partnerless,** *a.* **partnership,** *n.* the state of being a partner or partners; a contractual relationship between a number of people involved in a business enterprise. [var. of PARCENER]

parton, *n.* an elementary particle postulated as a constituent of neutrons and protons.

partridge, *n.* a gallinaceous bird of the genus *Perdix,* esp. *P. cinerea,* preserved for game. [ME *pertriche,* OF *perdiz, pertuz,* L *perdīcem,* nom. *perdix,* Gr. *perdix -dikos*]

part-song PART.

†**parture,** DEPARTURE.

parturient, *a.* about to bring forth young; of the mind etc., learned, fertile. **parturition,** *n.* the act of bringing forth. †**parturitive,** *a.* [L *parturiens -ntem,* pres.p. of *parturīre,* to be in labour, from *parere,* to produce]

party[1], *n.* a number of persons united together for a particular purpose; the principle or practice of taking sides on questions of public policy; a number of persons gathered together for some purpose, esp. of persons invited to a house for social entertainment; each of the actual or fictitious personages on either side in a legal action, contract etc.; an accessory, one concerned in any affair; (*coll.*) a person; †a game, a match. *v.i.* to attend parties, entertainments etc. **the party's over,** (*coll.*) something enjoyable, pleasant etc. is at an end. †**party-coated** PARTI-COATED. †**party-coloured** PARTI-COLOURED. **party line,** *n.* a telephone exchange line used by a number of subscribers; the policy laid down by a political party. **party-spirit,** *n.* zeal for a party. **party-spirited,** *a.* **party-verdict,** *n.* a joint verdict. **party-wall,** *n.* a wall separating two buildings etc., the joint-property of the respective owners. †**partyism,** *n.* [F *partie,* L *partīta,* fem. p.p. of *partīrī,* to divide, from *pars partis,* PART]

party², *a.* of a shield, divided into compartments distinguished by different tinctures. [F *parti,* as prec.]

parure, *n.* a set of jewels or other personal ornaments. [F, from *parer,* L *parāre,* to adorn]

parvanimity, *n.* littleness of mind; mean-spiritedness. [L *parvus,* petty, *animus,* mind, after MAGNANIMITY]

Parvati, *n.* in Hindu mythology, the consort of Siva in one of her gentler manifestations, and the mother of Ganesa; she is said to be the daughter of the Himalayas.

parvenu, *n.* a person who has risen socially or financially, an upstart. **parvenue,** *n. fem.* [F, p.p. of *parvenir,* L *pervenīre,* to arrive (PER, *venīre,* to come)]

parvis, *n.* the name given in the Middle Ages to the vacant space before a church where the mysteries were performed. [F, from L *paradīsus,* PARADISE]

parvovirus, *n.* one of a group of viruses each of which affects a particular species, as *canine parvovirus.* [L *parvus,* small]

pas, *n.* precedence. **to have the pas,** to take precedence (of). [F, step, from L *passus,* PACE]

PASCAL, *n.* a high-level computer-programming language. Designed by Niklaus Wirth (1934–) in the 1960s as an aid to teaching programming, it is still widely used as such in universities, but is also recognized as a good general-purpose programming language. [Blaise *Pascal*]

Pascal, *n.* **Blaise** (1623–62), French philosopher and mathematician. He contributed to the development of hydraulics, the calculus, and the mathematical theory of probability.

pascal, *n.* a unit of pressure, 1 newton per square metre. [Blaise *Pascal*]

paschal, *a.* pertaining to the Passover or to Easter. †**pasch,** *n.* the Passover; Easter. **pasch-egg,** *n.* an Easter-egg. [F *pascal,* L *paschālis,* from L and Gr. *pascha,* Heb. *pasakh,* the Passover, from *pāskh,* be passed over]

pas de deux, (*pl.* **pas de deux**) a dance performed by two people, esp. in ballet. [F, dance of two]

†**pash¹,** *n.* the face, the head. [etym. doubtful]

†**pash²,** *v.t.* to strike violently, esp. so as to smash. *v.i.* of waves etc., to beat. *n.* a blow. [prob. onomat.]

pash³, *n.* (*coll.*) a violent infatuation; a crush. [PASSION]

pasha, *n.* a Turkish title of honour, usu. conferred on officers of high rank, governors etc. **pashalic,** *n.* the jurisdiction of a pasha. [Turk.]

Pashto, *n.* a language spoken in Afghanistan and NW India. *a.* of or using this language.

pasigraphy, *n.* a universal system of writing, by means of signs representing ideas not words. **pasigraphic, -ical,** *a.* [Gr. *pasi,* for all, pl. dat. of *pan,* PAN-, -GRAPHY]

Pasiphae, *n.* in Greek mythology, the wife of Minos and mother of Phaedra and of the Minotaur, the offspring of her sexual union with a bull sent from the sea by the god Poseidon.

paso doble, *n.* (the music for) a Latin-American ballroom dance in fast 2/4 time, based on a march step. [Sp., double step]

Pasolini, *n.* **Pier Paolo** (1922–75), Italian poet, novelist, and film director, an influential figure of the post-war years. His writings (making much use of first Friulan and later Roman dialect) include the novels *Ragazzi di vita/The Ragazzi* (1955) and *Una vita violenta/A Violent Life* (1959). Among his films are *Il vangelo secondo Mateo/The Gospel According to St Matthew* (1964) and *I racconti de Canterbury/The Canterbury Tales* (1972).

pasque-flower, *n.* a species of anemone, *Anemone pulsatilla,* with bell-shaped purple flowers. [formerly *passe-flower,* F *passefleur* (*pasque,* Easter, FLOWER), assim. to PASCH]

pasquinade, *n.* a lampoon, a satire. *v.t.* to lampoon, to satirize. †**pasquin**, †**pasquil**, *n., v.t.* †**pasquillant,** †**-ller,** *n.* [*Pasquino,* or *Pasquillo,* popular name of a piece of ancient statuary at Rome on which in the 15th cent. Latin verses were displayed, said to be so named after a satirical cobbler]

pass, *v.i.* to move from one place to another, to proceed, to go (along, on, swiftly etc.); to overtake a vehicle; to circulate, to be current; to be changed from one state to another; to change gradually; to change hands; to be transferred; to disappear, to vanish; to die; to go by, to elapse; to go through, to be accepted without censure or challenge; to be enacted (as a bill before parliament); to receive current recognition; to be approved by examining; to take place, to happen, to occur; (*Cards*) to give up one's option of playing, making trumps etc.; to choose not to do something, esp. to answer a question; (*Fencing*) to lunge or thrust; (*Law*) to be transferred or handed on; †to exceed all bounds; †to give heed, to care for; †to be tolerably well off. *v.t.* to go by, beyond, over, or through; to transfer, to hand round, to circulate, to give currency to, to spend (time etc.); to endure; to admit, to approve, to enact; to satisfy the requirements of (an examination etc.); to outstrip, to surpass; to move, to cause to move; to cause to go by; to allow to go through (as a bill, a candidate etc.) after examination; to pledge (one's word etc.); to pronounce, to utter; to void, to discharge; to overlook, to disregard, to reject; (*N Am.*) to omit; †to make (a thrust). *n.* the act of passing; a passage, avenue or opening, esp. a narrow or difficult way; a narrow passage through mountains, a defile; a navigable passage, as at the mouth of a river; a written or printed permission to pass; a ticket authorizing one to travel (on a railway etc.) or to be admitted (to a theatre etc.) free; a critical state or condition of things; the act of passing an examination, esp. without special merit or honours; a thrust; a sexual advance; a passing of hands over anything (as in mesmerism); a juggling trick; the act of passing a ball etc. in various games. **to bring to pass** BRING. **to come to pass** COME. **to make a pass at,** to attempt to seduce. **to pass away,** to die, to come to an end. **to pass by,** to omit, to disregard. **to pass for,** to be taken for. **to pass off,** to proceed (without a hitch etc.); to disappear gradually; to circulate as genuine, to palm off. **to pass out,** (*coll.*) to faint; of an officer cadet, to complete training at a military academy. **to pass over,** to go across; to allow to go by without notice, to overlook; to omit; to die. **to pass the time of day,** to exchange greetings. **to pass through,** to undergo, to experience. **to pass up,** to renounce. **to sell the pass** SELL. **pass-book,** *n.* a book that passes between a tradesman and a customer, in which purchases on credit are entered; a bank-book. **pass degree,** *n.* a bachelor's degree without honours. **pass-key,** *n.* a master-key; a key for passing in when a gate etc. is locked. **pass laws,** *n.pl.* in South Africa, laws, repealed in 1986, that restricted blacks' freedom of movement. **passman,** *n.* a candidate in an examination obtaining only a pass not honours. **passout,** *n.* any permission to leave temporarily. **password,** *n.* a word by which to distinguish friends from strangers, a watchword. **passable,** *a.* that may be passed; acceptable, allowable, tolerable, fairly good. **passably,** *adv.* **passer,** *n.* one who passes. **passer-by,** *n.* (*pl.* **passers-by**) one who passes by or near, esp. casually. [F *passer,* from L *passus,* PACE¹]

pass., (*abbr.*) passive.

†**passade,** *n.* a turn or course of a horse backwards or forwards on the same spot; a passado. †**passado,** *n.* (*pl.* **does, -dos**) a thrust in fencing. [F, from Prov. *passada* or It. *passata,* p.p. of *passare,* to PASS]

passage, *n.* the act of passing; movement from one place to another, transit, migration; transition from one state to another; a journey, a voyage, a crossing; a way by which one passes, a way of entrance or exit; a corridor or gallery giving admission to different rooms in a building; right or liberty of passing; a separate portion of a discourse etc., esp. in a book; the passing of a bill etc., into law; (*pl.*) events etc. that pass between persons, incidents, episodes; reception, currency. **bird of passage** BIRD. **passage of, at arms,** a fight; a contest or encounter. **to work one's passage,** to work as a sailor etc., receiving a free passage in lieu of wages;

to work one's way without help from influence etc. **passageway,** *n.* a corridor. [F, from *passer,* to PASS]

passant, *a.* (*Her.*) walking and looking towards the dexter side with the dexter fore-paw raised. [F, pres.p. of *passer,* to PASS]

Passchendaele, *n.* village in W Flanders, Belgium, near Ypres. The Passchendaele ridge before Ypres was the object of a costly and unsuccessful British offensive in World War I, July–Nov. 1917; British casualties numbered nearly 400,000.

passé, *a.* (*fem.* **-sée**) past the prime, faded; old-fashioned, behind the times. [F, p.p. of *passer,* to PASS]

†**passemeasure,** *n.* an Italian variety of pavan. [corr. of It. *passemezzo* (prob. *passo e mezzo,* a step and a half)]

passementerie, *n.* trimming for dresses, esp. gold and silver lace. [F, from *passement,* gold or silver lace]

passenger, *n.* one who travels on a public conveyance; (*coll.*) a person who benefits from something without contributing to it; †a traveller, a wayfarer. **passenger-pigeon,** *n.* an extinct N American migratory pigeon. [ME and OF *passager*]

passepartout, *n.* a paper frame for a picture, photograph etc.; a master-key; †a safe-conduct. [F, pass everywhere]

passer, passer-by PASS.

passerine, *a.* pertaining to the order Passeriformes or suborder Passeres or perchers, which contains the great mass of the smaller birds; like a sparrow, esp. in size. *n.* a passerine bird. [L *passer,* sparrow]

Passfield, *n.* **Baron Passfield,** title of the Fabian socialist Sidney Webb.

passible, *a.* capable of feeling or suffering; susceptible to impressions from external agents. **passibility,** †**-ibleness,** *n.* [OF, from late L *passibilis,* from *patī,* to suffer]

Passiflora, *n.* a genus of plants containing the passion-flower. [L *passi-, passio,* PASSION, *-florus,* flowering]

passim, *adv.* here and there, throughout (indicating the occurrence of a word, allusions etc. in a cited work). [L, from *passus,* p.p. of *pandere,* to scatter]

passimeter, *n.* an automatic ticket-issuing machine.

passing, *a.* going by, occurring; incidental, casual, cursory; transient, fleeting; †surpassing, egregious, notable. †*adv.* surpassingly; exceedingly. *n.* passage, transit, lapse. **in passing,** casually, without making direct reference. **passing-bell,** *n.* a bell tolled at the hour of a person's death to invite prayers on his or her behalf. **passing-note,** *n.* (*Mus.*) a note forming a transition between two others, but not an essential part of the harmony. **passing shot,** *n.* a stroke in tennis that wins the point by passing an opponent beyond his or her reach.

passion, *n.* intense emotion, a deep and overpowering affection of the mind, as grief, anger, hatred etc.; violent anger; sexual love; zeal, ardent enthusiasm (for); the object of this; the last agonies of Christ; an artistic representation of this; a musical setting of the Gospel narrative of the Passion. *v.i.* (*poet.*) to be affected with passion. **passion-flower,** *n.* a plant of the genus *Passiflora,* chiefly consisting of climbers, with flowers bearing a fancied resemblance to the instruments of the Passion. **passion fruit,** *n.* the edible fruit of a passion-flower; a granadilla. **passion-play,** *n.* a mystery-play representing the Passion. **Passion Sunday,** *n.* the fifth Sunday in Lent. **Passiontide,** *n.* the last two weeks of Lent. **Passion Week,** *n.* the week following Passion Sunday; (*loosely*) Holy Week. **passional, passionary,** *n.* a book describing the sufferings of saints and martyrs. **passionate,** *a.* easily moved to strong feeling, esp. anger; excited, vehement, warm, intense; †sorrowful; compassionate. **passionately,** *adv.* **passionateness,** *n.* **passioned,** *a.* impassioned. **Passionist,** *n.* a member of a religious order in the Roman Catholic Church devoted to the commemoration of Christ's passion. **passionless,** *a.* **passionlessly,** *adv.* **passionlessness,** *n.* [OF, from L *passiōnem,* nom. *-sio,* from *patī,* to suffer]

passive, *a.* suffering, acted upon, not acting; capable of receiving impressions; of a verb form, expressing an action done to the subject of a sentence; esp. of a metal, not chemically reactive; inactive, inert, submissive, not opposing. *n.* the passive voice of a verb. **passive resistance,** *n.* inert resistance, without active opposition. **passive smoking,** *n.* the inhalation of others' cigarette smoke by non-smokers. **passive voice,** *n.* the form of a transitive verb representing the subject as the object of the action. **passively,** *adv.* **passiveness, passivity,** *n.* [L *passīvus,* as prec.]

pass laws, passman, passout PASS.

Passover, *n.* a Jewish feast, on the 14th day of the month Nisan, commemorating the destruction of the first-born of the Egyptians and the 'passing over' of the Israelites by the destroying angel (Exod. xii); Christ, the paschal lamb.

passport, *n.* an official document authorizing a person to travel in a foreign country and entitling him or her to legal protection; anything ensuring admission (to society etc.). [F *passe-port*]

password PASS.

Passy, *n.* **Frédéric** (1822–1912), French economist, who shared the first Nobel peace prize (1901) with J. H. Dunant. He founded the International League for Permanent Peace (1867), and was co-founder, with the English politician William R. Cremer (1828–1908), of the Inter-Parliamentary Conferences on Peace and on Arbitration (1889).

past, *a.* gone by, neither present nor future; just elapsed; in grammar, denoting action or state belonging to the past; former. *n.* past times; one's past career or the history of this, esp. a disreputable one; the past tense of a verb. *adv.* so as to go by. *prep.* beyond in time or place; after, beyond the influence or range of; more than. **past it,** (*coll.*) no longer young and vigorous. **pastmaster,** *n.* one who has been master of a Freemasons' lodge, a guild etc.; a thorough master (of a subject etc.). **past participle,** *n.* a participle derived from the past tense of a verb, with a past or passive meaning. **past perfect** PLUPERFECT. [p.p. of PASS]

pasta, *n.* a flour and water dough, often shaped and eaten fresh or in processed form, e.g. as spaghetti. [It., paste]

paste, *n.* a mixture of flour and water, usu. with butter, lard etc., kneaded and used for making pastry etc.; sweetmeats of similar consistency; a relish of pounded meat or fish; an adhesive compound of flour, water, starch etc. boiled; any doughy or plastic mixture, esp. of solid substances with liquid; a vitreous composition used for making imitations of gems. *v.t.* to fasten or stick with paste; to stick (up) with paste; (*sl.*) to thrash. **scissors and paste** SCISSORS. **pasteboard,** *n.* a board made of sheets of paper pasted together or of compressed paper pulp; (*N Am.*) cardboard; a card, as a visiting-card, railway-ticket or playing-card; a board on which dough is rolled. *a.* made of pasteboard; thin, flimsy, sham. **paste-up,** *n.* a sheet of paper on to which proofs, drawings etc. are pasted prior to being photographed for a printing process. **pasting,** *n.* (*coll.*) a thrashing. [OF (F *pâte*), Prov., It. and Sp. *pasta,* perh. from Gr. *pastē,* fem. of *pastos,* sprinkled]

pastel, *n.* woad; a dry paste composed of a pigment mixed with gum-water; a coloured crayon made from this; a picture drawn with such crayons; the art of drawing with these; a subdued colour. *a.* of pastel colour. **pastellist,** *n.* [F, from It. *pastello,* dim. of *pasta,* PASTE]

pastern, *n.* the part of a horse's leg between the fetlock and the hoof. **pastern-joint,** *n.* [OF *pasturon* (F *paturon*), from *pasture,* a shackle, prob. ident. with PASTURE]

Pasternak, *n.* **Boris Leonidovich** (1890–1960), Russian poet and novelist. His volumes of lyric poems include *A Twin Cloud* (1914), and *On Early Trains* (1943), and he translated Shakespeare's tragedies. His novel *Dr Zhivago* (1957), was followed by a Nobel prize (which he declined).

Pasteur, *n.* **Louis** (1822–95), French chemist and microbiologist who discovered that fermentation was caused by microorganisms. He also developed a vaccine for rabies, which led to the foundation of the Institut Pasteur in Paris in 1888.

Pasteurism, *n.* a method of preventing or curing certain diseases, esp. hydrophobia, by progressive inoculation. **pasteurize, -ise,** *v.t.* **pasteurized milk,** *n.* milk subjected to treatment by heat in order to destroy the organisms which may be present. **pasteurization, -isation,** *n.* [Louis *Pasteur*]

pastiche, pasticcio, *n.* a medley, a musical work, painting etc. composed of elements drawn from other works or which imitates the style of a previous work. [F *pastiche,* It. *pasticcio,* from *pasta,* PASTE]

pastille, *n.* a roll, cone or pellet of aromatic paste for burning as a fumigator or disinfectant; an aromatic lozenge. [F, from L *pastillum,* nom. *-lus,* etym. doubtful]

pastime, *n.* that which serves to make time pass agreeably; a game, a recreation; sport, diversion. [PASS, TIME]

pasting PASTE.

pastis, *n.* an aniseed-flavoured alcoholic drink. [F]

pastor, *n.* †a shepherd; a minister having charge of a church and congregation; one acting as a spiritual guide; the crested starling. **pastorate,** *n.* **pastorless,** *a.* †**pastorly,** *a.* **pastorship,** *n.* [ME and OF *pastour,* OF *pastor,* L *pastōrem,* nom. *-or,* from *pascere,* to feed]

pastoral, *a.* pertaining to shepherds; of land, used for pasture; of poetry etc., treating of country life; rural, rustic; relating to the cure of souls or the duties of a pastor; befitting a pastor. *n.* a poem, romance, play, picture etc. descriptive of the life and manners of shepherds or rustics; a letter or address from a pastor, esp. from a bishop to his diocese; a pastorale. **pastoralism,** *n.* **pastoralist,** *n.* (*Austral.*) a sheep- or cattle-raiser as distinct from an agriculturist. **pastorality,** *n.* **pastorally,** *adv.*

pastorale, *n.* a simple rustic melody; a cantata on a pastoral theme; a symphony dealing with a pastoral subject. [It.]

pastrami, *n.* a highly seasoned smoked beef, esp. cut from the shoulder. [Yiddish, from Romanian *pastramă,* from *păstra,* to serve]

pastry, *n.* articles of food made with a crust of baked flour-paste. **pastry-cook,** *n.*

pasture, *n.* ground fit for the grazing of cattle; grass for grazing. *v.t.* to put (cattle etc.) on land to graze; of sheep, to eat down (grass-land), to feed by grazing. *v.i.* to graze. **pasturable,** *a.* **pasturage,** *n.* **pastureless,** *a.* [F *pâture,* from late L *pastūra,* as PASTOR]

pasty[1], *a.* of or like paste; pale, unhealthy-looking. **pasty-faced,** *a.* having a pale, dull complexion. **pastiness,** *n.*

pasty[2], *n.* a small pie, usu. of meat, baked without a dish. [ME and OF *pastee* (F *pâte*), from *pasta,* PASTE]

Pat, *n.* an Irishman. **on one's Pat,** (*Austral.*) on one's own, all alone. [short for *Patrick*]

pat, *n.* a light quick blow with the hand; a tap, a stroke; a small mass or lump (of butter etc.) moulded by patting; the sound of a light blow with something flat. *v.t.* (*past, p.p.* **patted**) to strike gently and quickly with something flat, esp. the fingers or hand; to tap, to stroke gently. *v.i.* to strike gently; to run with light steps. *a.* exactly suitable or fitting; opportune, apposite, apt; facile. *adv.* aptly, opportunely; facilely. **patly,** *adv.* **patness,** *n.* [prob. onomat.]

pat., (*abbr.*) patent(ed).

patagium, *n.* (*pl.* **-gia**) the wing membrane of a bat, flying-lemur etc. [L, from Gr. *patageion,* a gold border]

Patagonia, *n.* geographic area of South America, south of latitude 40° S, with sheep farming, and coal and oil resources. Sighted by Magellan (1520), it was claimed by both Argentina and Chile until divided between them in 1881.

pataurist, *n.* a genus of arboreal marsupials or flying phalangers. [Gr. *petauristēs,* a performer on the *petauron* or spring-board]

patch, *n.* a piece of cloth, metal or other material put on to mend anything; anything similar; a piece put on to strengthen a fabric etc.; a piece of cloth worn over an injured eye; a piece of court-plaster etc. covering a wound etc.; a small piece of black silk or court-plaster worn (esp. in the 17th and 18th cents.) to conceal a blemish or to set off the complexion; a differently coloured part of a surface; a small piece of ground, a plot; a scrap, a shred; †a clown, a fool. *v.t.* to put a patch or patches on; to mend with a patch or patches (usu. with *up*); to mend clumsily; to make (up) of or as of shreds or patches; to put together or arrange hastily; to serve as a patch for; to show as a patch or patches on. **a bad, good** etc. **patch,** (*coll.*) a sequence of bad, good etc. experiences or achievements. **not a patch on,** (*sl.*) not to be compared with. **to patch up,** to mend. **to patch up a quarrel,** to be reconciled temporarily. **patchboard,** *n.* a board with a number of electrical sockets used for making temporary circuits. **patch pocket,** *n.* one consisting of a flat piece of cloth sown to the outside of a garment. **patchwork,** *n.* work composed of pieces of different colours, sizes etc., sewn together; clumsy work. **patcher,** *n.* **patchery,** *n.* **patchy,** *a.* of inconsistent quality, frequency etc.; covered with patches; appearing in patches. **patchily,** *adv.* **patchiness,** *n.* [etym. doubtful]

patchouli, *n.* an Indian plant, *Pogostemon patchouli,* yielding a fragrant oil; a perfume prepared from this. [F, from Ind. native name]

pate, *n.* the head, esp. the top of the head. **pated,** *a.* (*usu. in comb.*). [etym. doubtful]

pâté, *n.* a pie, a patty; a paste made of cooked, diced meat, fish or vegetables blended with herbs etc. **pâté de foie gras**, pâté made of fatted goose liver. [F]

†**patefaction,** *n.* disclosure; open manifestation. [L *patefactio,* from *patefacere* (*patēre,* to be open, *facere* to make)]

Patel, *n.* **Vallabhbhai Jhaverbhai** (1875–1950), Indian nationalist politician. A fervent follower of Gandhi, he participated in the Satyagraha at Kaira in 1918, and later became home minister in Nehru's first government after independence.

patella, *n.* the knee-cap; †a small dish or pan; (**Patella**) a genus of molluscs containing the limpets. **patellar, patellate, patelliform,** *a.* **patellite,** *n.* a fossil limpet. [L, dim. of *patina,* PATEN]

paten, *n.* a plate or shallow dish for receiving the eucharistic bread; †a circular metal plate. [OF *patene,* L *patena, patina*]

Patenier, Joachim PATINI(E)R.

patent, *a.* open to the perusal of all; protected or conferred by letters patent; plain, obvious, manifest; (*Bot. etc.*) expanded, spreading. *n.* a grant from the Crown by letters patent of a title of nobility, or of the exclusive right to make or sell a new invention; an invention so protected; anything serving as a sign or certificate (of quality etc.). *v.t.* to secure by patent. **letters patent,** an open document from the sovereign or an officer of the Crown conferring a title, right, privilege etc., esp. the exclusive right to make or sell a new invention. **patent-leather,** *n.* a leather with a japanned or varnished surface. **patent medicine,** *n.* a medicine sold under a licence with a registered name and trade mark. **patent office,** *n.* a government department responsible for granting patents. **patent rolls,** *n.pl.* the rolls or register of patents granted by the Crown since 1201. **patency,** *n.* **patentable,** *a.* **patentee,** *n.* a person granted a right or privilege by patent. **patently,** *adv.* [OF, from L *patentem,* nom. *-tens,* pres.p. of *patēre,* to lie open]

pater, *n.* a paternoster; (*coll.*) father. [L, father]

Pater, *n.* **Walter Horatio** (1839–94), English critic. A stylist and supporter of 'art for art's sake', he published *Studies in the History of the Renaissance* (1873), *Marius the Epicurean* (1885), *Imaginary Portraits* (1887), and other works.

patera, *n.* (*pl.* **-rae**) a round dish used for libations in ancient Rome; a flat round ornament on a frieze or in bas-reliefs. [L, from *patēre,* to be open]

paterfamilias, *n.* the head or father of a family or

household. [L]

paternal, *a.* of or pertaining to a father; fatherly; connected or related through the father. **paternalism,** *n.* the exercise of benign, overprotective authority, esp. in a form of government, often seen as interference with individual rights. **paternalistic,** *a.* **paternally,** *adv.* **paternity,** *n.* fatherhood; ancestry or origin on the male side, descent from a father; authorship, source. **paternity leave,** *n.* official leave from work granted to a man when his wife is in childbirth or recovering from it. [F *paternel,* late L *paternālis,* from *paternus,* fatherly, from PATER]

paternoster, *n.* the Lord's Prayer, esp. in Latin; every 11th bead of a rosary, indicating that the Lord's Prayer is to be repeated; hence, a rosary; a fishing-line with a weight at the end and short lines with hooks extending at intervals. [L, our Father]

Paterson, *n.* **Andrew Barton** (1864–1941), Australian journalist, known as 'Banjo' Paterson, author of volumes of light verse and 'Waltzing Matilda', adapted from a traditional song.

path, *n.* a footway, esp. one beaten only by feet; a course or track; course of life, action etc. †*v.t.* to walk on. †*v.i.* to go, as in a path. **cinder path** CINDER. **pathfinder,** *n.* an explorer or pioneer; a radar device used for navigational purposes or for targeting missiles. **pathless,** *a.* **pathway,** *n.* [OE *pæth* (cp. Dut. *pad,* G *Pfad*)]

path- PATH(O)-.

-path, *comb. form* a person suffering from a pathological disorder; a medical practitioner. **-pathy,** *comb. form* suffering, feeling; disease, treatment of this, as in *sympathy, homoeopathy*. [Gr. *-patheia,* PATHOS, suffering]

Pathan, *n.* a member of a Muslim people of NW Pakistan and Afghanistan. The Pakistani Pathans now claim independence, with the Afghani Pathans, in their own state of Pakhtoonistan. [prob. Afghan, rel. to *Pushtu, Pukhtu,* the Afghan language, cp. Gr. *Paktues* (Herodotus)]

Pathé, *n.* **Charles** (1863–1957), French film pioneer, who began his career selling projectors in 1896 and with the profits formed Pathé Frères with his brothers. In 1901 he embarked on film production and by 1908 had become the world's biggest producer, with branches worldwide. He also developed an early colour process and established a weekly newsreel, *Pathé Journal*. World War I disrupted his enterprises and by 1918 he was gradually forced out of business by foreign competition.

pathetic, *a.* affecting or moving the feelings, esp. those of pity and sorrow; (*coll.*) poor, mean or contemptible; †passionate. *n.* that which is pathetic; (*pl.*) the display of pathos or sentiment; (*pl.*) the study of pathetic emotions. **pathetic fallacy,** *n.* in literature, the attribution of human feelings to objects associated with nature such as trees. †**pathetical,** *a.* **pathetically,** *adv.* †**patheticalness,** *n.* [late L *pathēticus,* Gr. *pathētikos,* from PATHOS]

pathfinder, pathless PATH.

pathic, *n.* a catamite. [Gr. *pathikos,* passive]

path(o)-, *comb. form* disease. [Gr. *pathos,* suffering]

pathogen, *n.* any disease-producing substance or micro-organism. **pathogenic,** *a.* **pathogenically,** *adv.* **pathogenicity,** *n.*

pathogenesis, *n.* the origin and development of disease. **pathogenetic, -genic, -genous,** *a.* **pathogeny,** *n.*

pathognomy, *n.* expression of the passions; the science of their signs. **pathognomic,** *a.*

pathology, *n.* the science of diseases, esp. of the human body; the changes which characterize disease. **pathologic, -ical,** *a.* pertaining to pathology; caused by or involving disease; (*coll.*) driven or motivated by compulsion rather than reason. **pathologically,** *adv.* **pathologist,** *n.*

pathophobia, *n.* a morbid fear of disease.

pathos, *n.* (a quality or element in events or expression that excites) emotion, esp. pity or sorrow. [Gr., suffering, from *path-,* root of *paschein,* to suffer]

pathway PATH.

-pathy -PATH.

†**patibulary,** *a.* belonging to or shaped like a gallows. [L *patibulum,* gibbet, from *patēre,* to lie open]

patience, *n.* the quality of being patient; calm endurance of pain, provocation or other evils, fortitude; a card-game, usu. played by one person. **out of patience with,** unable to endure or put up with. **to have no patience with,** to be unable to stand or put up with; to be irritated by. [OF, from L *patientia,* from *patī,* to suffer]

patient, *a.* capable of bearing pain, suffering etc. without fretfulness; not easily provoked, indulgent; persevering, diligent. *n.* one who suffers; a person under medical treatment. †*v.t.* to compose, to calm. **patiently,** *adv.*

patiki, *n.* the New Zealand sole or flounder. [Maori]

patina, *n.* the green incrustation that covers ancient bronzes; †a Roman dish or pan, a paten. **patinated, patinous,** *a.* covered with patina. **patination,** *n.* [L *patina, patena,* a shallow dish, or F *patine,* perh. from this]

Patini(e)r, *n.* (*c.* 1485–*c.* 1524), Flemish painter, active in Antwerp, whose inspired landscape backgrounds dominated his religious subjects. He is known to have worked with Matsys and to have painted landscape backgrounds for other artists' works.

patio, *n.* (*pl.* **-tios**) the open inner court of a Spanish or Spanish-American residence; a paved area beside a house, used for outdoor meals, sunbathing etc. [Sp.]

patisserie, *n.* a pastry-cook's shop; (a) pastry. [F]

Patna rice, *n.* a variety of long-grain rice used for savoury dishes. [*Patna,* a city in NE India]

patois, *n.* a non-standard dialect of a district; broken language. [F, etym. doubtful]

Paton, *n.* **Alan** (1903–88), South African writer. His novel *Cry, the Beloved Country* (1948) focused on the racial inequality in South Africa. Later books include the study *Land and People of South Africa* (1956), *The Long View* (1968), and his autobiography *Towards the Mountain* (1980).

patonce, *a.* applied to a cross the four arms of which expand in curves from the centre and have floriated ends. [etym. doubtful]

Patras, *n.* (Greek **Patrai**) industrial city (hydroelectric installations; textiles and paper) in the NW Peloponnese, Greece, on the Gulf of Patras; population (1981) 141,500. The ancient *Patrae,* it is the only one of the 12 cities of Achaea to survive.

patr(i)-, patro-, *comb. form* father. [L *pater,* father]

patrial, *a.* of or pertaining to one's native land; (*Gram.*) derived from the name of a country. *n.* (*Gram.*) a patrial noun; a person legally entitled to reside in the UK.

patriarch, *n.* the head of a family or tribe, ruling by paternal right; in the Bible, applied to Abraham, Isaac and Jacob, their forefathers, and the sons of Jacob; the highest grade in the hierarchy of the Roman Catholic Church; in the Eastern and early Churches, a bishop, esp. of Alexandria, Antioch, Constantinople, Jerusalem and some other sees; the founder of a religion, science etc.; a venerable old man, the oldest living person (in an assembly, order etc.). **patriarchal,** †**-ical,** *a.* **patriarchate,** *n.* **patriarchism, patriarchy,** *n.* a patriarchal system of government or social organization, esp. as distinguished from matriarchy. [OF *patriarche,* L *patriarcha,* Gr. *patriarchēs* (*patria,* family *archein,* to rule)]

patrician, *a.* in ancient Rome, senatorial, not plebeian; noble, aristocratic. *n.* a member of the Roman aristocracy; a member of ancient or later orders established by the Western and the Byzantine emperors, esp. a chief magistrate of a Roman province in Italy or Africa; a noble, an aristocrat, a member of the highest class of society. **patricianship,** *n.* **patriciate,** *n.* [L *patricius,* from *pater,* father, *patrēs,* senators, nobles]

patricide, *n.* (the act of) one who kills his or her father. **patricidal,** *a.*

Patrick, St, *n.* (389–*c.* 461), patron saint of Ireland. Born in Britain, probably in S Wales, he was carried off by pirates to six years' slavery in Antrim before escaping either to Britain or Gaul – his poor Latin suggests the former – to train as a missionary. He is variously said to have landed again in Ireland in 432 or 456, and his work was a vital factor in the spread of Christian influence there. His symbols are snakes and shamrocks; feast day 17 Mar.

patrilineal, *a.* by descent through the father.

patrimony, *n.* an estate or right inherited from one's father or ancestors; a church estate or endowment; a heritage. **patrimonial,** *a.* **patrimonially,** *adv.* [F *patrimoine,* L *patrimōnium*]

patriot, *n.* one who loves his or her country and is devoted to its interests, esp. its freedom and independence. **patriotic,** *a.* **patriotically,** *adv.* **patriotism,** *n.* [F *patriote,* late L *patriōta,* Gr. *patriōtēs,* from *patrios,* of one's fathers, from *patēr -tros,* father]

patristic, -ical, *a.* pertaining to the ancient Fathers of the Church or their writings. *n.pl.* (*sing. in constr.*) the study of patristic writings. [F *patristique* (L *patri-, pater,* father)]

patro- PATR(I)-.

patrol, *v.i.* (*past, p.p.* **patrolled**) to go on a patrol. *v.t.* to go round. *n.* the action of moving around an area, esp. at night, for the maintenance of order and for security; the detachment of soldiers, police, firemen etc., or the soldier, constable etc., doing this; a detachment of troops, sent out to reconnoitre; (*Aviat.*) a routine operational flight. **patrol car,** *n.* a car in which police officers patrol an area. **patrolman,** *n.* (*N Am.*) a police officer. **patrol wagon,** *n.* (*N Am.*) a black Maria. [F *patrouiller, patouiller,* to dabble in the mud (cp. OF *patouil,* a pool)]

patron[1], *n.* one who supports, fosters or protects a person, cause, art etc.; a tutelary saint; one who holds the gift of a benefice; (*coll.*) a regular customer (at a shop etc.); (*Rom. Ant.*) the former owner of a manumitted slave; a guardian or protector of a client; an advocate or defender in a court of law. **patron saint,** *n.* a saint regarded as the patron of a particular group, country etc. **patronage,** *n.* support, fostering, encouragement, or protection; the right of presentation to a benefice or office; the act of patronizing; support by customers (of a shop etc.). **patronal,** *a.* **patroness,** *n. fem.* **patronize, -ise,** *v.t.* to act as a patron towards; to assume the air of a patron towards, to treat in a condescending way; to frequent as a customer. **patronizer, -iser,** *n.* **patronizingly, -isingly,** *adv.* [OF, from L *patrōnum,* nom. *-us,* from *pater patris,* father]

patron[2], *n.* the proprietor of a hotel, restaurant etc. in France. [F, as prec.]

patronymic, *a.* derived (as a name) from a father or ancestor. *n.* a name so derived; a family name. †**patronymical,** *a.* **patronymically,** *adv.* [L *patrōnymicus,* Gr. *patrōnumikos,* from *patrōnumos* (*onoma,* Aeolic *onuma,* name)]

patroon, *n.* (*N Am.*) a proprietor of land with manorial privileges and right of entail under a Dutch grant, esp. in New York and New Jersey (abolished 1850). [var. of PATRON]

patsy, *n.* (*chiefly N Am., coll.*) a person who is easily deceived, cheated etc.; a sucker; a scapegoat. [etym. unknown]

patten, *n.* a clog or overshoe mounted on an iron ring etc., for keeping the shoes out of the mud or wet; (*Arch.*) a sole for the foundation of a wall; the base-ring of a column. [F *patin,* perh. from OF *patte,* paw]

Patten, *n.* **Chris(topher Francis)** (1944–), British Conservative politician, environment secretary from 1989.

patter[1], *v.i.* to strike, as rain, with a quick succession of light, sharp sounds; to move with short, quick steps. *v.t.* to cause (water etc.) to patter. *n.* a quick succession of sharp, light sounds or taps. [freq. of PAT[1]]

patter[2], *v.t.* to say (one's prayers) in a mechanical, sing-song way. *v.i.* to pray in this manner; to talk glibly. *n.* the patois or slangy lingo of a particular class; glib talk, chattering, gossip; rapid speech introduced impromptu into a song, comedy etc. [ME *pateren,* from PATERNOSTER]

pattern, *n.* a model or original to be copied or serving as a guide in making something; a shape used to make a mould into which molten metal is poured to make a casting; a model, an exemplar; a sample or specimen (of cloth etc.); a decorative design for a carpet, wallpaper, frieze etc.; hence type, style; the marks made by shot on a target. *v.t.* to copy, to model (after, from or upon); to decorate with a pattern; †to match, equal. **pattern-box,** *n.* a box at either side of a weaving loom from which a shuttle is sent along as required for the pattern. **pattern-maker,** *n.* a maker of patterns for the moulders in a foundry. **pattern-shop,** *n.* a room or shop in a foundry etc., where patterns are made. [ME *patron,* as PATRON]

Patterson, *n.* **Harry** (1929–), English nóvelist, born in Newcastle. He has written many thrillers under his own name, including *Dillinger* (1983), as well as under the pseudonym Jack Higgins, including *The Eagle Has Landed* (1975).

Patti, *n.* **Adelina** (1843–1919), Anglo-Italian soprano renowned for her performances of Lucia in *Lucia di Lammermoor* and Amina in *La sonnambula.* At the age of 62 she was persuaded out of retirement to make a number of gramophone recordings, one of the first opera singers to be recorded.

pattle, *n.* an implement used for cleaning the earth from a ploughshare.

Patton, *n.* **George (Smith)** (1885–1945), US general in World War II, known as 'Blood and Guts'. He commanded the 2nd Armoured Division in 1940, and in 1942 led the Western Task Force that landed at Casablanca, Morocco. After commanding the 7th Army, he led the 3rd Army across France and into Germany, and in 1945 took over the 15th Army.

patty, *n.* a little pie; a small, flat cake of minced food. [F PÂTÉ]

patulous, *a.* open, having a wide aperture; of boughs etc., spreading, expanding. **patulously,** *adv.* **patulousness,** *n.* [L *patulus,* cogn. with *patēre,* to be open]

paua, *n.* the New Zealand mutton-fish; a handsome iridescent shell; a fish-hook. [Maori]

paucity, *n.* fewness in number; scarcity. [F *paucité,* L *paucitātem,* nom. *-tas,* from *paucus,* few]

†**paul,** PAWL.

Paul[1], *n.* six popes, including:

Paul VI, *n.* Giovanni Battista Montini (1897–1978), pope from 1963. His encyclical *Humanae Vitae/Of Human Life* (1968) reaffirmed the church's traditional teaching on birth control, thus following the minority report of the commission originally appointed by Pope John, rather than the majority view.

Paul[2], *n.* (1901–64), king of the Hellenes from 1947, when he succeeded his brother George II. He was the son of Constantine I. He married in 1938 Princess Frederika (1917–), daughter of the Duke of Brunswick, whose involvement in politics brought her under attack.

Paul[3], *n.* **Les** (adopted name of Lester Polfuss) (1915–), US inventor of the solid-body electric guitar in the early 1940s, and a pioneer of recording techniques including overdubbing and electronic echo. The **Gibson Les Paul guitar** was first marketed in 1952 (the first commercial solid-body guitar was made by Leo Fender). As a guitarist in the late 1940s and the 1950s he recorded with the singer Mary Ford (1928–77).

Paul I, *n.* (1754–1801), czar of Russia from 1796, in succession to his mother Catherine II. Mentally unstable, he pursued an erratic foreign policy, and was assassinated.

Pauli, *n.* **Wolfgang** (1900–58), Austrian physicist, who originated **Pauli's exclusion principle**: in a given system no two electrons, protons, neutrons, or other elementary particles of half-integrated spin can be characterized by the same set of quantum numbers. He also predicted the existence of neutrinos. He won the

Nobel prize 1945 for his work on atomic structure.

Pauline, *a.* of or pertaining to St Paul or his writings. *n.* a scholar of St Paul's School, London. **Paulinism,** *n.* the theological doctrine taught by or ascribed to the apostle Paul.

Pauling, *n.* **Linus Carl** (1901–), US chemist, noted for his fundamental work on the nature of the chemical bond and on the discovery of the helical structure of many proteins. Nobel Prize for Chemistry 1954. An outspoken opponent of nuclear testing, he also received the Nobel Peace Prize in 1962.

Paulinus, *n.* (d. 644), Roman missionary to Britain who joined St Augustine in Kent in 601, converted the Northumbrians in 625, and became the first archbishop of York. Excavations (1978) revealed a church he built in Lincoln.

paulo-post-future, *n.* the future-perfect tense in classical Greek. [L *paulo post futurum,* future after a little]

Paul, St, *n.* (*c.* AD 3–*c.* AD 68), Christian missionary and martyr; in the New Testament, one of the apostles and author of 13 epistles. He is said to have been converted by a vision on the road to Damascus. His emblems are a sword and a book; feast day 29 June.

Paulus, *n.* **Friedrich von** (1890–1957), German field marshal in World War II, commander of the forces that besieged Stalingrad (now Volgograd) in the USSR (1942–43); he was captured and gave evidence at the Nuremberg trials before settling in East Germany.

paunch, *n.* the belly, the abdomen; (*coll.*) a fat or protruding belly; the first and largest stomach in ruminants; (*Naut.*) a thick mat or wooden shield fastened on a mast etc., to prevent chafing. *v.t.* to rip open the belly of, to disembowel; to stab in the belly; to stuff with food. **paunchy,** *a.* **paunchiness,** *n.* [ONorthF *panch,* L *panticem,* nom. *pantex*]

pauper, *n.* one without means of support, a destitute person, a beggar; one entitled to public assistance; one permitted to sue in forma pauperis. **in forma pauperis,** (*Law*) allowed on account of poverty to sue without paying costs. **pauperdom, pauperism,** *n.* **pauperize, -ise,** *v.t.* **pauperization, -isation,** *n.* [L, poor]

Pausanias, *n.* (2nd cent. AD), Greek geographer, author of a valuably accurate description of Greece compiled from his own travels, *Description of Greece*, also translated as *Itinerary of Greece*.

pause, *n.* a cessation or intermission of action, speaking etc.; a break in reading, speaking, music etc., for the sake of emphasis; hesitation a mark to denote a break or pause; (*Mus.*) a mark ⌒ or ◡ over a note etc., indicating that it is to be prolonged. *v.i.* to make a pause or short stop; to wait; to linger (upon or over). †*v.t.* to repose oneself. **to give pause,** to cause to hesitate, esp. for reconsideration. †**pausingly,** *adv.* [F, from L *pausa,* Gr. *pausis,* from *pauein,* to cease]

pavan, pavane, *n.* a slow and stately dance, usu. in elaborate dress, in vogue in the 16th and 17th cents.; music for this. [F *pavane,* It. or Sp. *pavana,* etym. doubtful]

Pavarotti, *n.* **Luciano** (1935–), Italian tenor, whose operatic roles have included Rodolfo in *La Bohème*, Cavaradossi in *Tosca*, the Duke of Mantua in *Rigoletto*, and Nemorino in *L'Elisir d'amore*.

pave, *v.t.* to make a hard, level surface upon, with stone, bricks etc.; to cover with or as with a pavement. **to pave a way for, to,** to prepare for. †**pavage,** *n.* **pavé,** *n.* pavement; a stone-paved road in France. **pavement,** *n.* that with which anything is paved; a hard level covering of stones, bricks, tiles, wood-blocks etc.; a paved footway at the side of a street or road; (*N Am.*) the paved surface of a road; (*Zool. etc.*) a close, level structure or formation (as of teeth) resembling a pavement. **pavement artist,** *n.* a person drawing figures etc. on a pavement in order to obtain money from passers-by. **paver, paviour,** *n.* one who lays pavements; a rammer for driving paving-stones; a paving-stone, block etc. **paving,** *n.* **paving-stone,** *n.* [OF *paver,* L *pavīre,* to ram]

†**pavid,** *a.* timid. [L *pavidus*]

pavilion, *n.* a tent, esp. a large one, of conical shape; a temporary or movable structure for entertainment, shelter etc.; an ornamental building, usu. of light construction, for amusements etc., esp. one for spectators and players on a cricket-ground etc.; a belvedere, projecting turret or other portion of a building, usu. of ornamental design; †a flag; a heraldic bearing in the form of a tent. †*v.t.* to furnish with or shelter in a pavilion. [F *pavillon,* L *pāpiliōnem,* nom. *-lio,* butterfly]

paving, paviour PAVE.

†**pavis,** †**pavise,** *n.* a convex shield for the whole body. *v.t.* to shelter or defend with this. [OF *pavais* (F *pavois*), It. *pavese,* prob. from *Pavia,* town in Italy]

Pavlov, *n.* **Ivan Petrovich** (1849–1936), Russian physiologist who studied conditioned reflexes in animals. His work greatly influenced behavioural theory and learning theory. **Pavlovian,** *a.* of or relating to conditioned reflexes.

pavlova, *n.* a dessert consisting of a meringue base topped with fruit and whipped cream. [Anna *Pavlova*]

Pavlova, *n.* **Anna** (1881–1931), Russian dancer. Prima ballerina of the Imperial Ballet from 1906, she left Russia in 1913, and went on to become the world's most famous classical ballerina. With London as her home, she toured extensively with her own company, influencing dancers worldwide with roles such as Fokine's *The Dying Swan* solo 1905.

Pavlovian PAVLOV.

pavonazzo, *a.* brilliantly coloured like a peacock. *n.* a variety of marble with brilliant markings like the colours of a peacock. [It., from L *pāvōnāceum,* as foll.]

pavonine, *a.* pertaining to or resembling a peacock; resembling the tail of a peacock; iridescent. *n.* a pavonine lustre or tarnish on certain ores and metals. †**pavone,** *n.* a peacock. **pavonian,** *a.* [L *pāvōnīnus,* from *pāvo-ōnis,* peacock]

paw, *n.* the foot of a quadruped having claws, as dist. from a hoof; (*sl.*) the hand or handwriting. *v.t.* to scrape or strike with the forefoot; of a horse, to strike the ground with the hoofs; (*coll.*) to handle roughly, familiarly, sexually or clumsily. †**pawed,** *a.* [OF *powe,* prob. from Frankish (cp. Dut. *poot,* G *Pfote*)]

pawky, *a.* (*chiefly Sc., North.*) sly, shrewd; humorous, arch. **pawkily,** *adv.* **pawkiness,** *n.* [obs. *pawk,* a trick]

pawl, *n.* a hinged piece of metal or lever engaging with the teeth of a wheel etc., to prevent it from running back etc.; (*Naut.*) a bar for preventing the recoil of a windlass etc. *v.t.* to stop from recoiling with this. [prob. from OF *paul* (F *pal*), L *pālum,* nom. *-lus,* stake, PALE[1]]

pawn[1], *n.* a piece of the lowest value in chess; an insignificant person used in the plans of a cleverer one. [ME and A-F *poun,* OF *paon, peon* (F *pion*), med. L *pedōnem,* nom. *pedo,* foot-soldier, from *pes pedis,* foot]

pawn[2], *n.* something deposited as security for a debt or loan, a pledge; the state of being held as a pledge. *v.t.* to deliver or deposit as a pledge for the repayment of a debt or loan, or the performance of a promise; to stake, to wager, to risk. **in pawn, at pawn,** deposited as a pledge or security. **pawnbroker,** *n.* one who lends money on the security of goods pawned. **pawnbroking,** *n.* **pawnshop,** *n.* the place where this is carried on. **pawnee,** *n.* **pawner,** *n.* [OF *pan,* prob. from Teut. (cp. OFris. and Dut. *pand,* G *Pfand*)]

pawpaw, PAPAW.

Pax, *n.* Roman goddess of peace; Greek counterpart Irene; (**pax**) a tablet or plaque bearing a representation of the Crucifixion or other sacred subject which was formerly kissed by the priest and congregation at Mass, an osculatory. *int.* calling for a truce. **Pax Romana,** *n.* peace imposed by the Roman Empire. [L, PEACE]

Paxton, *n.* **Joseph** (1801–65), English architect, garden superintendent to the Duke of Devonshire from 1826 and designer of the Great Exhibition building (Crystal Palace) in 1851, revolutionary in its structural use of glass and iron.

paxwax, *n.* a strong, stiff tendon from the dorsal vertebrae to the occiput in many mammals and, in a modified form, in humans. [formerly *faxwax* (OE *feax,* hair, *weaxan,* to grow, to WAX²)]

pay¹, *v.t.* (*past, p.p.* **paid**) to hand over what is due in discharge of a debt or for services or goods; to discharge (a bill, claim, obligation etc.); to deliver as due; to deliver the amount, defray the cost or expense of; to expend (away); to compensate, to recompense, to requite; to be remunerative or worthwhile to; to bestow, to tender (a compliment, visit etc.). *v.i.* to make payment; to discharge a debt; to make an adequate return (to); to be remunerative or worthwhile. *n.* payment, compensation, recompense; wages, salary. **pay as you earn,** a method of collecting income tax by deducting it before payment of the earnings. **to pay away,** to hand out (money, a fund etc.) in wages etc.; to let a rope run out by slackening it. **to pay back,** to repay; to return (a favour etc.); to take revenge on. **to pay for,** to make a payment for; to suffer as a result of. **to pay off,** to pay the full amount of, to pay in full and discharge; (*Naut.*) to fall to leeward; to be profitable or rewarding. **to pay one's way,** to keep out of debt. **to pay out,** to punish; to disburse; to cause (a rope) to run out. **to pay the piper,** to bear the cost. **to pay through the nose,** to pay an exorbitant price. **pay bed,** *n.* a bed for a private patient in a National Health Service hospital. **pay-bill,** *n.* a bill stating the amounts due as wages to workers, soldiers etc. **pay-day,** *n.* (*Stock Exch.*) the day on which transfers of stock are to be paid for. **pay-dirt,** *n.* a deposit containing enough gold to make mining worth while; anything profitable or useful. **paying guest,** *n.* a lodger who lives with the family. **payload,** *n.* the part of a transport vehicle's load that brings profit; the passengers, cargo or weaponry carried by an aircraft; the explosive capacity of a bomb, missile warhead etc.; that which a spacecraft carries as the purpose of its mission, contrasted with those things necessary for its operation. **paymaster,** *n.* one who pays, esp. one who regularly pays wages etc.; (*Mil., Nav.*) an officer whose duty it is to pay the wages. **Paymaster-General,** *n.* the officer at the head of the treasury department concerned with the payment of civil salaries and other expenses. **pay-off,** *n.* (*coll.*) the final result or outcome; the final payment of a bill etc.; the conclusion of a story, joke etc. **pay-office,** *n.* a place where payment is made of wages, debts etc. **pay-packet,** *n.* an envelope containing a person's wages. **pay-phone,** *n.* a public telephone operated by coins. **pay-roll,** *n.* alist of employees. **payslip,** *n.* a slip of paper giving details of one's pay, income tax deductions etc. **payable,** *a.* that can or must be paid. **payee,** *n.* person to whom money is paid. **payer,** *n.* **payment,** *n.* [OF *paier* (F *payer*), L *pācāre,* to appease, from *pax pācem,* peace]

pay², *v.t.* (*past, p.p.* **payed**) (*Naut.*) to coat, cover or fill with hot pitch for waterproofing. [ONorthF *peier,* L *picāre,* from *pix picis,* PITCH¹]

PAYE (*abbr.*) pay as you earn.

†**paynim,** *n.* a pagan, a heathen; a Muslim. [A-F *paienime,* late L *pāgānismus*]

paynize, -ise, *v.t.* to inject calcium or barium sulphide, followed by calcium sulphate, into wood in order to preserve it. [*Payne,* inventor]

payola, *n.* (*sl.*) clandestine reward paid for illicit promotion of a commercial product, e.g. of a record by a disc jockey. [PAY¹, *-ola,* perh. from *victrola,* a make of gramophone]

Paysandú, *n.* city in Uruguay, capital of Paysandú department, on the River Uruguay; population (1985) 74,000. Tinned meat is the main product. The city dates from 1772, and is linked by bridge (since 1976) with Puerto Colón in Argentina.

Pays de la Loire, agricultural region of W France, comprising the departments of Loire-Atlantique, Maine-et-Loire, Mayenne, Sarthe, and Vendée; capital Nantes; area 32,100 sq km/12,391 sq miles; population (1986) 3,018,000. Industries include shipbuilding and wine.

Paz¹, *n.* **(Estenssoro) Victor** (1907–), president of Bolivia 1952–56, 1960–64, and from 1985. He founded and led the **Movimiento Nacionalista Revolucionario** which seized power in 1952. His regime extended the vote to Indians, nationalized the country's largest tin mines, and embarked on a major programme of agrarian reform.

Paz², *n.* **Octavio** (1914–), Mexican poet, whose *Sun Stone* (1957) is a personal statement taking the Aztec Calendar Stone as its basic symbol.

Pb, (*chem. symbol*) lead. [L *plumbum*]

PC, (*abbr.*) parish council; personal computer; police constable.

pc, (*abbr.*) per cent; personal computer; postcard.

PCB, (*abbr.*) polychlorinated biphenyl; printed circuit board.

PD, (*abbr.*) (*N Am.*) police department.

pdq, (*abbr.*) (*coll.*) pretty damn quick.

PDSA, (*abbr.*) People's Dispensary for Sick Animals.

PE, (*abbr.*) physical education.

pea, *n.* a leguminous plant, *Pisum sativum,* the seeds of which are used as food; the seed of this. **pea-cod** PEASECOD. **pea-crab,** *n.* a small crab living in the shell of a mollusc. **pea-flour,** *n.* pease-meal. **pea-green,** *n., a.* (of) a colour like that of fresh green peas. **pea-maggot,** *n.* a caterpillar infesting peas. **pea-pod,** *n.* the pericarp of the pea. **pea-rigger,** *n.* (*sl.*) a thimble-rigger. **peashooter,** *n.* a tube through which dried peas are shot, usu. from the mouth. **peasoup,** *n.* soup made with peas, esp. dried and split peas. **peasouper,** *n.* (*coll.*) a dense yellowish fog. **peasoupy,** *a.* **pea-stone,** *n.* pisolite. [from PEASE, taken as pl.]

peace, *n.* a state of quiet or tranquillity; absence of civil disturbance or agitation; freedom from or cessation of war or hostilities; a treaty reconciling two hostile nations; a state of friendliness; calmness of mind. **at peace,** in a state of harmony or tranquillity. **Justice of the Peace** JUSTICE. **king's, queen's peace,** the state of tranquillity, order and absence of strife throughout the realm, for which the sovereign is responsible. **peace be with you,** a solemn formula of leave-taking. **to hold one's peace,** to be silent. **to keep the peace,** to abstain from strife; to prevent a conflict. **to make peace,** to reconcile or be reconciled (with); to bring about a treaty of peace. **peace-breaker,** *n.* **Peace Corps,** *n.* a US government body that sends volunteers to help developing countries, especially in the fields of teaching and health, and with agricultural and other projects. **peacekeeper,** *n.* a law officer; one who preserves peace between hostile parties. **peacekeeing,** *n.* **peacemaker,** *n.* one who reconciles. **peace-offering,** *n.* an offering to God as a token of thanksgiving etc.; a gift to procure peace or reconciliation. **peace-officer,** *n.* a civil officer whose duty it is to preserve the public peace. **peace pipe,** *n.* a pipe smoked by N American Indians as a sign of peace. **peacetime,** *n.* a time when there is no war. **peaceable,** *a.* peaceful, quiet; disposed to peace. **peaceableness,** *n.* **peaceably,** *adv.* **peaceful,** *a.* in a state of peace; free from noise or disturbance; quiet, pacific, mild. **peacefully,** *adv.* **peacefulness,** *n.* **peaceless,** *a.* [ME and OF *pais,* L *pācem,* nom. *pax*]

peach¹, *n.* the fleshy, downy fruit of *Amygdalus persica,* or the tree; (*coll.*) a pretty girl, anything superlatively good or pretty; a pinkish-yellow colour. *a.* pinkish-yellow. **peach-bloom,** *n.* the delicate powder on a ripe peach; a soft, pink colour on the cheeks. **peach-blossom,** *n.* peach-flower; a delicate purplish pink; a moth with spots of rosy white on its wings. **peach-blow,** *n.* a light purple or pink glaze on porcelain. **peach-brandy,** *n.* a spirit distilled from peach-juice. **peach-colour,** *n.* **peach-coloured,** *a.* of the colour of peach-blossom. **peachwort,** *n.* persicaria. **peach-yellows,** *n.* a disease attacking peach-trees in the Eastern US. **peachy,** *a.* soft and downy like a peach; having the colour of a peach; (*coll.*) excellent, good. **peachiness,** *n.* [OF *pesche,* L *persicum,* Persian (apple)]

peach², *v.i.* to turn informer against an accomplice; to inform (against or upon). †*v.t.* to impeach or inform against. [ME *apechen,* as IMPEACH]

peacock, *n.* any individual, esp. the male, of the genus *Pavo* or peafowl, esp. *Pavo cristatus,* a bird with gorgeous plumage and long tail capable of expanding like a fan; a vainglorious person. *v.t.* to display or plume (oneself). *v.i.* to strut about ostentatiously. **peacock-butterfly,** *n.* one of various butterflies with ocellated wings. **peacock-fish,** *n.* a brilliantly variegated fish, *Crenilabrus pavo.* **peacockery,** *n.* **peacockish, peacocklike,** *a.* [OE *pēa, pāwe,* L *pāvo,* COCK[1]]

Peacock, *n.* **Thomas Love** (1785–1866), English satirical novelist and poet. His works include *Headlong Hall* (1816), *Nightmare Abbey* (1818), *Crotchet Castle* (1831), and *Gryll Grange* (1860).

peafowl, *n.* a pheasant of the genus *Pavo,* of which the peacock is the male. **pea-chick,** *n.* the young of the peafowl. **peahen,** *n.* the female peafowl.

pea-jacket, *n.* a coarse, thick, loose overcoat worn by seamen etc. [prob. after Dut. *pij-jakker* (*pij,* pea-jacket)]

peak[1], *n.* a sharp point or top, esp. of a mountain; the projecting brim in front of a cap; the upper after-corner of a sail extended by a gaff; the upper end of a gaff; (*Elec.*) the culminating point of a load curve during a specified period, and the maximum load of electricity required; the point of greatest activity, use, demand etc. *v.i.* to reach a peak. *a.* of or relating to the point of greatest activity, use, demand etc. **peak value, voltage,** *n.* (*Elec.*) the highest value of an alternating quantity. **peaked, peaky,** *a.* [var. of PIKE[1]]

peak[2], *v.i.* to look sickly; to pine away; (*in p.p.*) to look sharp-featured or emaciated. **peaky,** *a.* [etym. doubtful]

peak[3], *v.t.* (*Naut.*) to raise (a gaff or yard) more nearly vertical; to raise the oars apeak. *v.i.* of an aircraft, to dive vertically so as to raise the tail into the air. [from APEAK]

Peake, *n.* **Mervyn (Lawrence)** (1911–68), English writer and illustrator, born in China. His novels include the grotesque fantasy trilogy *Titus Groan* (1946), *Gormenghast* (1950), and *Titus Alone* (1959).

peal[1], *n.* a loud, esp. a prolonged or repercussive sound, as of thunder, bells etc.; a set of bells tuned to each other; a series of changes rung on these. *v.i.* to sound a peal; to resound. *v.t.* to cause to give out loud and solemn sounds; to utter or give forth sonorously; †to celebrate; †to assail with noise. [prob. from APPEAL]

peal[2], *n.* (*dial.*) a grilse or young salmon, usu. under 2 lb (0·9 kg); a sea-trout. [etym. unknown]

Peale, *n.* **Charles Willson** (1741–1827), American artist, head of a large family of painters. His portraits of leading figures in the War of Independence include the earliest known portrait of Washington (1772).

pean, *n.* a heraldic fur, represented by sable with or (golden) spots. [etym. doubtful]

peanut, *n.* a plant of the bean family with pods ripening underground which are edible and are used for their oil; a monkey-nut; (*pl.*) (*sl.*) an insignificant sum of money. **peanut butter,** *n.* a paste made from ground peanuts.

pear, *n.* the fleshy obovoid fruit of *Pyrus communis;* the fruit of the pear-tree. **pear-shaped,** *a.* **pear-tree,** *n.* [OE *pere,* late L *pira,* L *pirum*]

pearl[1], *n.* a smooth, white or bluish-grey lustrous and iridescent calcareous concretion, found in several bivalves, the best in the pearl-oyster, prized as a gem; mother-of-pearl; something round and clear and resembling a pearl, as a dewdrop, tooth etc.; pearl-eye; anything exceedingly valuable, or the finest specimen of its kind; (*Print.*) a small size of type [AS THIS]. *a.* pertaining to, containing or made of pearls. *v.t.* to set or embroider with pearls; to sprinkle with pearly drops; to rub and strip barley into pearly grains. *v.i.* to form pearly drops or fragments; to fish for pearls. **pearl-ash,** *n.* crude carbonate of potash. **pearl-barley** BARLEY. **pearl-button,** *n.* a button made of mother-of-pearl. **pearl-diver,** *n.* one who dives for pearl-oysters. **pearl-eye,** *n.* a pearl-coloured film or speck on the eye, causing cataract. **pearl-eyed,** *a.* **pearl-fisher,** *n.* one who fishes for pearls. **pearl-fishing,** *n.* **pearl millet,** *n.* a tall grass, *Pennisetum glaucum,* grown esp. as fodder in Africa, India and the southern US. **pearl-oyster,** *n.* **pearl-powder** PEARL-WHITE. **pearl-shell,** *n.* mother-of-pearl in its natural state. **pearl-sinter,** *n.* fiorite. **pearl-spar,** *n.* a variety of dolomite. **pearl-stone,** *n.* perlite. **pearl-studded,** *a.* **pearl-white,** *n.* oxychloride of bismuth, used as a cosmetic for whitening the skin. **pearlaceous,** PERLACEOUS. **pearled,** *a.* **pearlies,** *n.pl.* costermonger's festal dress covered with pearl buttons. **pearliness,** *n.* **pearling,** *n.* the process of removing the outer coat of barley etc. **pearly,** *a.* **pearly gates,** *n.pl.* (*coll., facet.*) the entrance to heaven. **pearly king, queen,** *n.* a costermonger wearing pearlies. [F *perle,* etym. doubtful]

pearl[2], *n.* a fine loop, a row of which forms an ornamental edging on various fabrics. *v.t.* to knit this. **pearl-edge,** *n.* a border or edging made of this. **pearled,** *a.* **pearling,** *n.* [prob. var. of PURL[1]]

Pearl Harbor, *n.* US Pacific naval base in Oahu, Hawaii, US, the scene of a Japanese attack on 7 Dec. 1941, which brought the US into World War II. It took place while Japanese envoys were holding so-called peace talks in Washington. More than 2000 US servicemen were killed, and a large part of the US Pacific fleet was destroyed or damaged during the attack.

pearmain, *n.* a kind of apple. [F *per*main]

Pearse, *n.* **Patrick Henry** (1879–1916), Irish poet prominent in the Gaelic revival, a leader of the Easter Rising (1916). Proclaimed president of the provisional government, he was court-martialled and shot after its suppression.

Pearson[1], *n.* **Karl** (1857–1936), British statistician, who followed Galton in introducing statistics and probability into genetics, and developed the concept of eugenics. He introduced the term standard deviation into statistics.

Pearson[2], *n.* **Lester Bowles** (1897–1972), Canadian politician, leader of the Liberal Party from 1958, prime minister 1963–68. As foreign minister (1948–57), he effectively represented Canada at the United Nations. Nobel Peace Prize 1957.

Peary, *n.* **Robert Edwin** (1856–1920), US polar explorer who, after several unsuccessful attempts, became the first person to reach the North Pole on 6 Apr. 1909. In 1988 an astronomer claimed Peary's measurements were incorrect.

peasant, *n.* a countryman; a rustic labourer; (*coll.*) a rough, uncouth person. *a.* rustic, rural; †base. **peasantlike,** *a.* **peasantry,** *n.* [OF *paisant* (F *paysan*), L *pāgensem,* nom. *-sis,* of or pertaining to a *pāgus* or village]

Peasants' Revolt, *n.* the rising of the English peasantry in June 1381. Following the Black Death, there was a shortage of agricultural workers, which led to higher wages. The Statute of Labourers was enacted in 1351, attempting to return wages to pre-plague levels. When a poll tax was enforced in 1379, riots broke out all over England, especially in Essex and Kent. Led by Wat Tyler and John Ball, the rebels sacked Canterbury, and marched to London, where they burnt John of Gaunt's palace at the Savoy, took the prisons at Newgate and Fleet, took the Tower of London, and murdered Archbishop Sudbury and Sir Robert Hales. Wat Tyler was stabbed to death by Sir William Walworth, the Lord Mayor of London. The king, Richard II, made concessions to the rebels, and they dispersed, but the concessions were revoked immediately.

pease, *n.* (*pl. or collect. sing.*) peas. **peasecod,** *n.* a pea-pod. **peasecod-bellied,** *a.* applied to a 16th-cent. doublet with the lower part padded and quilted. **peascod-doublet,** *n.* †**peasecod-time,** *n.* the season for peas. **pease-meal,** *n.* meal obtained by grinding peas. **pease-porridge, -pudding,** *n.* porridge or pudding made of peas. [OE *pise,* pea, pl. *pisan,* late L *pisa,* L *pisum,* Gr. *pison* (cp. PEA[1])]

peat, *n.* decayed and partly carbonized vegetable-matter found in boggy places and used as fuel. **peat-bog, -moss,** *n.* a bog containing peat. **peat-hag** MOSS-HAG.

peat-reek, *n.* smoke from a peat-fire; (*sl.*) whisky distilled over this, whisky illicitly distilled, mountain-dew. **peatery,** *n.* a place where peat is cut and prepared for use. **peaty,** *a.* [ME *pete,* etym. doubtful]

pebble, *n.* a small stone rounded by the action of water; an agate; a transparent rock-crystal, used for spectacles etc.; a lens made of this. *v.t.* to pelt with pebbles; to pave with pebbles; to impart a rough indented surface or grain to (leather). **pebble-crystal,** *n.* a crystal in the rough state in the form of a pebble. **pebble-dash,** *n.* a coating for external walls consisting of small stones imbedded in mortar. **pebble-stone,** *n.* **pebble-ware,** *n.* a variety of Wedgwood ware having different coloured clays worked into the paste. **pebbled, pebbly,** *a.* [OE *papol-stān,* pebble-stone, etym. doubtful]

pebrine, *n.* an epidemic disease characterized by black spots, attacking silkworms. [F, from Port. *pebrino,* from *pebre,* PEPPER]

pecan, *n.* a N American hickory, *Carya olivaeformis,* or its fruit or nut. **pecan pie,** *n.* a pie made with pecan nuts. [F *pacane,* Sp. *pacana,* from native name]

peccable, *a.* liable to sin. **peccability**, *n.* [med. L *peccābilis,* from *peccāre,* to sin]

peccadillo, *n.* (*pl.* **-lloes, -llos**) a slight fault or offence. [Sp., dim. of *pecado,* L *peccātum,* sin, as prec.]

peccant, *a.* sinful; guilty; informal, wrong; morbid, inducing or indicating disease. †*n.* an offender. **peccancy**, *n.* [F, from L *peccantem,* nom. *-cans,* pres.p. of *peccāre,* to sin]

peccary, *n.* one of two small American species of pig-like mammals, *Dicotyles torquatus* and *D. labiatus.* [Carib. *pakira*]

peccavi, *int.* expressing contrition or error. *n.* a confession of error. [L, I have sinned]

pech, *v.i.* (*Sc., North.*) to breathe hard, to pant. *n.* a pant, a puff. [perh. onomat.]

peck¹, *n.* a measure of capacity for dry goods, 2 gallons (about 9 l); the fourth part of a bushel; a vessel used for measuring this; a large quantity. [A-F and OF *pek,* etym. doubtful]

peck², *v.t.* to strike with a beak or a pointed instrument; to pick up with or as with the beak; to break, open, eat etc. thus; to break (up or down) with a pointed implement; (*coll.*) to eat, esp. in small amounts. *v.i.* to strike or aim with a beak or pointed implement. *n.* a sharp stroke with or as with a beak; a mark made by this; a sharp kiss. **pecker,** *n.* one who or that which pecks; a woodpecker; a kind of hoe; (*sl.*) the mouth, the appetite; spirits, courage; (*N Am., taboo sl.*) the penis. **keep your pecker up,** keep cheerful. **pecking order,** *n.* the hierarchical order of importance in any social group. **peckish,** *a.* (*coll.*) hungry. [var. of PICK¹]

Peck, *n.* **Eldred Gregory** (1916–), US actor. One of Hollywood's most enduring stars, he was often cast as a decent man of great moral and physical strength, as in *The Old Gringo* (1989). His other films include *Spellbound* (1945) and *To Kill a Mockingbird* (1962).

Peckinpah, *n.* **Sam** (1925–85), US film director, often of westerns, usually associated with slow-motion, blood-spurting violence. His best films, such as *The Wild Bunch* (1969), exhibit a thoughtful, if depressing, view of the world.

Pecksniff, *n.* a unctuous, canting hypocrite. **Pecksniffian**, *a.* [character in Dickens's *Martin Chuzzlewit*]

Pécs, *n.* city in SW Hungary, the centre of a coalmining area on the Yugoslavia frontier; population (1988) 182,000. Industries include metal, leather, and wine. The town dates from Roman times, and was under Turkish rule 1543–1686.

pecten, *n.* a comb-like process forming a membrane in the eyes of birds and some reptiles; an appendage behind the posterior legs in scorpions, and various other parts or organs; a genus of Ostreidae containing the scallops. [L *pecten -tinis,* comb, from *pectere,* to comb (cp. Gr. *pektein*)]

pectic, *a.* derived from or containing pectin. **pectin,** *n.* a white, amorphous compound found in fruits and certain fleshy roots, formed from pectose by the process of ripening. **pectinate, -nated,** *a.* having projections like the teeth of a comb. **pectination,** *n.* **pectose,** *n.* an insoluble compound allied to cellulose found in unripe fruits and other vegetable tissue. [Gr. *pēktos,* from *pēg-,* stem of *pēgnuein,* to make firm or solid]

pectinato-, pectini-, *comb. form* comb-like.

pectoral, *a.* pertaining to or for the breast; good for diseases of the breast. *n.* an ornament worn on the breast, esp. the breast-plate of the Jewish high priest; a pectoral fin; a medicine to relieve chest complaints; the pectoral muscle. **pectoral muscle,** *n.* either of the two muscles at the top of the chest on each side, controlling certain arm and shoulder movements. **pectoriloquism**, **-quy**, *n.* the transmission of the sound of the voice through the walls of the chest, as heard with the stethoscope, a symptom of certain chest disorders. [F, from L *pectorālis,* from *pectus -toris,* breast]

pectose PECTIC.

peculate, *v.t., v.i.* to appropriate to one's own use (money or goods entrusted to one's care). **peculation,** *n.* **peculator,** *n.* [L *pecūlātus,* p.p. of *pecūlārī,* as foll.]

peculiar, *a.* belonging particularly and exclusively (to); one's own, private, not general; pertaining to the individual; particular, special; singular, strange, odd. *n.* exclusive property, right or privilege; a parish or church exempt from diocesan jurisdiction; one of the Peculiar People. **Peculiar People,** *n.pl.* a Christian sect, founded 1838, having no ministry or regular organization and believing in the cure of diseases by prayer. **peculiarity**, *n.* the quality of being peculiar; a characteristic; an idiosyncrasy. **peculiarize, -ise,** *v.t.* **peculiarly,** *adv.* [L *pecūliāris,* from *pecūlium,* private property, from *pecū,* cattle]

pecuniary, *a.* relating to or consisting of money. **pecuniarily,** *adv.* †**pecunious,** *a.* having plenty of money. [L *pecūniārius,* from *pecūnia,* as prec.]

ped- PAED(O)-.

-ped -PED(E).

pedagogue, *n.* a teacher of young children, a schoolmaster (usu. in contempt, implying conceit or pedantry). †*v.t.* to teach; to instruct superciliously. **pedagogic, -ical**, *a.* **pedagogics,** *n. sing.* the science of teaching. **pedagogism, -goguism,** *n.* the occupation, manners or character of a pedagogue. **pedagogy**, *n.* pedagogics; pedagogism. [MF, from L *paedagōgus,* Gr. *paidagōgos* (*pais paidos,* boy, *agein,* to lead)]

pedal, *n.* a lever acted on by the foot; in an organ, a wooden key moved by the feet, or a foot-lever for working several stops at once, for opening and shutting the swell-box etc.; a foot-lever for lifting the damper of a piano, for muffing the notes, and other purposes; (*Mus.*) a sustained note, usu. in the bass. *v.t.* (*past, p.p.* **pedalled**) to work (a bicycle, sewing-machine etc.) by pedals; to play on (an organ) by pedals. *v.i.* to play an organ or work a bicycle etc. by pedals. *a.* of or pertaining to a foot or foot-like part (esp. of molluscs). **pedal-note,** *n.* a tonic or dominant note sustained through various harmonics. **pedal-pipe,** *n.* an organ pipe acted on by a pedal. **pedal-pushers,** *n.pl.* women's calf-length trousers, usu. close-fitting below the knee. **pedalist,** *n.* one expert in the use of pedals; a cyclist. **pedalo,** *n.* (*pl.* **-loes, -los**) a small boat propelled by paddles operated with pedals. [prob. through F *pédale,* It. *pedale,* L *pedālem,* nom. *-lis,* from *pes pedis,* foot]

pedant, *n.* one who makes a pretentious show of book-learning, or lays undue stress on rules and formulas; one with more book-learning than practical experience or common sense; †a schoolmaster. **pedantic,** †**-ical**, *a.* **pedantically,** *adv.* †**pedantize, -ise,** *v.i.* **pedantocracy**, *n.* **pedantry,** *n.* [F *pédant,* It. *pedante,* a schoolmaster, prob. cogn. with PEDAGOGUE]

pedate, *a.* having feet; (*Bot.*) palmately divided with the two lateral lobes divided into smaller segments like digits or toes. **pedately,** *adv.* [L *pedātus,* from *pes* *pedis*, foot]

peddle, *v.i.* to travel about the country selling small wares; to busy oneself about trifles. *v.t.* to hawk; to sell in small quantities, to retail. **peddler,** *n.* one who sells illegal drugs; (*chiefly N Am.*) a pedlar. **peddling,** *a.* trifling, insignificant. [etym. doubtful; in first sense prob. from PEDLAR]

-ped(e), *comb. form* foot. [L *pes*, foot]

pederast, *n.* one who practises sodomy, esp. with a boy. **pederastic,** *a.* **pederasty,** *n.* [Gr. *paiderastēs* (*pais paidos*, boy, *eraein*, to love)]

pedestal, *n.* an insulated base for a column, statue etc.; either of the supports of a knee-hole desk; a base, foundation or support; a movable cupboard for a chamber-pot; the china pan of a water-closet. *v.t.* to set on a pedestal; to serve as a pedestal for. **on a pedestal,** in a position of (excessive) respect or devotion. [G *Pedestal* or F *piédestal*, It. *piedestallo* (*piè*, L *pes pedis*, foot, *di*, of, *stallo*, STALL[1])]

pedestrian, *a.* going or performed on foot; pertaining to walking; prosaic, dull, commonplace. *n.* one who journeys on foot; an expert walker; one who races on foot. **pedestrian crossing,** *n.* a marked strip across a road where vehicles must stop to allow pedestrians to cross. **pedestrial,** *a.* **pedestrianism,** *n.* **pedestrianize, -ise,** *v.t.* to convert (a road etc.) so that it may only be used by pedestrians. [L *pedester -tris*, from *pes pedis*, foot]

pedi-, *comb. form* foot. [L *pes pedis*, foot]

pediatric, PAEDIATRIC.

pedicel, *n.* (*Bot.*, *Zool.*) the stalk supporting a single flower etc.; any small foot-stalk or stalk-like structure. **pedicellate,** *a.* **pedicle,** *n.* a pedicel or peduncle. **pediculate,** *a.* [mod. L *pedicellus*, dim. of *pedīculus*, dim. of *pes pedis*, foot]

pedicular, -ulous, *a.* lousy. **Pedicularis,** *n.* a genus of Scrophulariaceae containing the betony. †**pediculation, pediculosis,** *n.* (*Path.*) lousiness, phthiriasis. [L *pedīculāris*, *-lōsus*, from *pedīculus*, louse]

pedicure, *n.* the surgical treatment of the feet; cosmetic care of the feet; a chiropodist. [F *pédicure* (L *pes pedis*, foot, *curāre*, to CURE)]

pediferous, pedigerous, *a.* having feet or foot-like parts. [L *pes pedis*, foot, -FEROUS, -GEROUS]

pedigree, *n.* genealogy, lineage, esp. ancient lineage; a genealogical table or tree; derivation, etymology. *a.* of cattle, dogs etc., pure-bred, having a known ancestry. **pedigreed,** *a.* [formerly *pedegru*, OF *pee de grue*, F *pié de grue* (L *pes pedis*, foot, *de*, of, *grue*, L *gruem*, nom. *grus*, crane)]

pedimanous, *a.* of lemurs, opossums etc., having the feet shaped like hands. **pedimane,** *n.* [L *pes pedis*, foot, *manus*, hand]

pediment, *n.* the triangular part surmounting a portico, in buildings in the Grecian style; a similar member crowning doorways, windows etc. in buildings in classical Renaissance styles. **pedimental,** *a.* **pedimented,** *a.* [formerly *periment*, perh. corr. of L *operīmentum*, from *operīre*, to cover, or of PYRAMID]

pedipalp, *n.* an arachnid of the order Pedipalpi, characterized by pincer-like feelers, comprising the true scorpions. **pedipalpal, -palpous,** *a.* [L *pes pedis*, foot, *palpus*, PALP]

pedlar, (*esp. N Am.*) **peddler,** *n.* a travelling (on foot) hawker of small wares, usu. carried in a pack; one who retails (gossip etc.). **pedlar's pony, horse, pad,** *n.* (*sl.*) a walking-stick. **pedlary,** *n.* [etym. doubtful, prob. cogn. with obs. *ped*, basket]

ped(o)- PAED(O)-.

pedology, *n.* the science of soils. **pedological,** *a.* **pedologist,** *n.* [Gr. *pedon*, ground]

pedometer, *n.* an instrument for measuring the distance covered on foot by registering the number of the steps taken. **pedomotive,** *a.* moved or propelled by the feet. *n.* a velocipede. **pedomotor,** *n.* a contrivance for using the feet as motive power; a vehicle so propelled, a velocipede. [F *pédomètre* (L *pes pedis*, foot)]

pedrail, *n.* a contrivance for enabling a traction-engine to move over rough ground; the traction-engine so equipped.

Pedro, *n.* two emperors of Brazil:

Pedro I, *n.* (1798–1834), emperor of Brazil 1822–31. The son of John VI of Portugal, he escaped to Brazil on Napoleon's invasion, and was appointed regent in 1821. He proclaimed Brazil independent (1822) and was crowned emperor, but abdicated (1831) and returned to Portugal.

Pedro II, *n.* (1825–91), emperor of Brazil 1831–89. He proved an enlightened ruler, but his antislavery measures alienated the landowners, who compelled him to abdicate.

peduncle, *n.* a flower-stalk, esp. of a solitary flower or one bearing the subsidiary stalks of a cluster; a stalk-like process for the attachment of an organ or an organism. **peduncular, -culate, -lated,** *a.* [L *pes pedis*, foot, -UNCLE]

pee, *v.i.* (*coll. euphem.*) to urinate. *n.* an act of urinating; urine. [initial letter of taboo PISS]

Peeblesshire, *n.* former county of S Scotland, included from 1975 in Borders region; Peebles was the county town.

peek, *v.i.* to peer, to peep, to pry. *n.* a peep. **peekaboo,** *n.* a game used for amusing babies, in which the face is hidden, then suddenly revealed. [etym. doubtful]

peel[1], *v.t.* to strip the skin, bark or rind off; to strip (rind etc. off); to pillage, to plunder. *v.i.* to lose the skin or rind, to become bare; of paint etc., to flake off; (*sl.*) to undress. *n.* skin or rind. **to peel off,** (*coll.*) to undress; to leave and move away from (e.g. a column of marchers). **peeler**[1], *n.* **peeling,** *n.* the skin of a fruit etc. that has been peeled off. [var. of PILL[2], perh. influ. by F *peler*, to peel]

peel[2], *n.* a wooden shovel used by bakers; the blade of an oar. [OF *pele* (F *pelle*), L *pāla*]

peel[3], **pele,** *n.* a square fortified tower, esp. those built about the 16th cent. in the border counties of Scotland and England for defence against raids. [ME and OF *pel*, a palisade, L *pālum*, nom. *-lus*, stake, PALE[1]]

Peel, *n.* **Robert** (1788–1850), British Conservative politician. As home secretary 1822–27 and 1828–30, he founded the modern police force and in 1829 introduced Roman Catholic emancipation. He was prime minister 1834–35 and 1841–46, when his repeal of the Corn Laws caused him and his followers to break with the party.

peeler[1] PEEL[1].

peeler[2], *n.* (*dated sl.*) a policeman, orig. a constable in the police organized by Sir Robert Peel in 1828.

peeling PEEL[1].

Peelite, *n.* a adherent of Sir Robert Peel esp. a Conservative supporting his measure for the repeal of the Corn Laws.

peen, *n.* (*dial.*, *N Am.*) the point of a mason's hammer, opposite to the face. *v.t.* to hammer. [etym. doubtful]

Peenemünde, *n.* fishing village in East Germany, used from 1937 by the Germans to develop the V2 rockets used in World War II.

peep[1], *v.i.* to cry, chirp or squeak, as a young bird, a mouse etc. *n.* a chirp, squeak etc.; (*coll.*) any spoken sound. **peeper,** *n.* a chicken just out of the shell. [perh. from OF *pipier*, L *pīpāre*, of imit. orig., or var. of PIPE[1]]

peep[2], *v.i.* to look through a crevice or narrow opening; to look slyly or furtively; to show oneself or appear partially or cautiously, to come (out) gradually into view. *n.* a furtive look, a hasty glance, a glimpse; the first appearance. **Peep-o'-day boys,** a secret society of Protestants in Ireland, founded in 1784, from their early visits to the houses of Roman Catholics in search of arms. **peep-hole,** *n.* **peeping Tom,** *n.* one guilty of prurient curiosity. **peep-show,** *n.* an exhibition of pictures etc., shown through a small aperture containing a lens; a sex show seen by customers in separate compartments fitted with a small window. **peep-sight,** *n.* a movable disc on the breech of a firearm pierced with a small hole through which aim can be taken with accuracy. **peeper,** *n.* one who peeps; (*sl.*) an eye.

[perh. rel. to PEEK]

peer[1], *n.* one of the same rank; an equal in any respect; a noble, esp. a member of a hereditary legislative body; in the UK, a member of one of the degrees of nobility, comprising dukes, marquesses, earls, viscounts and barons. *v.t.* to equal, to rank with; to make a peer. *v.i.* to be equal. **peers of Ireland,** Irish peers of whom 28 representatives are elected for life; **peers of Scotland,** of whom 16 representatives are elected to each Parliament. **peers of the United Kingdom, of the realm,** those British peers all of whom are entitled to sit in the House of Lords. **peer group,** *n.* a group of people equal in status, age etc. **peerage,** *n.* the rank of a peer; the body of peers, the nobility, the aristocracy; a book containing particulars of the nobility. **peeress,** *n. fem.* **peerless,** *a.* without an equal. **peerlessly,** *adv.* **peerlessness,** *n.* [OF *per,* L *parem,* nom. *par,* equal]

peer[2], *v.i.* to peep, to pry (at, into etc.); to peep out; to appear, to come into sight. [etym. doubtful]

peerless PEER[1].

peesweep, *n.* (*Sc.*) the pewit. [imit. of the bird's cry]

peevers, *n.* (*Sc.*) the game of hopscotch.

peevish, *a.* fretful, irritable, petulant; expressing discontent; †childish. **peeved,** *a.* (*sl.*) irritated, annoyed. **peevishly,** *adv.* **peevishness,** *n.* [etym. doubtful]

peewit, PEWIT.

peg, *n.* a pin or bolt, usu. of wood, for holding parts of a structure or fastening articles together, hanging things on, supporting, holding, marking etc.; a step, a degree; an occasion, pretext, excuse, or topic for discourse etc.; (*coll.*) a drink. *v.t.* (*past, p.p.* **pegged**) to fix or fasten (down, in, out etc.) with a peg or pegs; to mark (a score) with pegs on a cribbage-board; to mark (out) boundaries; (*coll.*) to fix (esp. prices) at an agreed level. **a square peg in a round hole, a round peg in a square hole,** person in an unsuitable job, function etc. **off the peg,** ready-made. **to peg away,** to work at or struggle persistently. **to peg down,** to fasten down with pegs; to restrict (to rules etc.). **to peg out,** (*Croquet*) to go out by hitting the final peg; (*Cribbage*) to win by attaining the final hole in the cribbage-board; to mark out a claim; (*sl.*) to die; to fail, to be done for. **to take someone down a peg,** to humiliate, to degrade. **pegboard,** *n.* a board with holes into which pegs can be fixed, used for scoring in games, or placed on a wall and used for hanging things. **peg-leg,** *n.* a crude wooden leg; a person who has a wooden leg. **peg-top,** *n.* a spinning-top with a metal peg, usu. spun by means of string which unwinds rapidly when the top is thrown from the hand; (*pl.*) trousers very wide at the top and narrowing towards the ankles. [ME *pegge* (cp. Dut. dial. *peg,* Swed. dial. *pegg*)]

Pegasus, *n.* in Greek mythology, a winged steed that sprang from the blood of Medusa and with a blow of its hoofs produced the fountain Hippocrene or Halicon, whence poets were fabled to draw their inspiration; poetic inspiration or genius; a genus of fishes with broad pectoral fins, typical of the family *Pegasidae*; a constellation of the northern hemisphere, near Cygnus. [L, from Gr. *Pēgasos,* from *pēgē,* fountain]

pegmatite, *n.* a coarse-grained variety of granite, with a little mica. **pegmatitic,** *a.* [L and Gr. *pēgma,* from *pēgnuein,* to fasten, -ITE]

Pegu, *n.* city in S Burma, on the river Pegu, NE of Rangoon; population (1983) 254,762. It was founded AD 573 and is noted for the Shwemawdaw pagoda.

Péguy, *n.* **Charles** (1873–1914), French Catholic socialist, who established a socialist publishing house in Paris. From 1900 he published on political topics *Les Cahiers de la Quinzaine/Fortnightly Notebooks* and poetry, including *Le Mystère de la charité de Jeanne d'Arc/The Mystery of the Charity of Joan of Arc* (1897).

Pehlevi, PAHLAVI.

Pei, *n.* **Ieoh Ming** (1917–), Chinese Modernist/high-tech architect, who became a US citizen in 1948. His buildings include Dallas City Hall, Texas; East Building, National Gallery of Art, Washington DC, (1978); John F. Kennedy Library Complex and the John Hancock tower, Boston (1979); the Bank of China Tower, Hong Kong (1987); and a glass pyramid in front of the Louvre, Paris (1989).

peignoir, *n.* a loose robe or dressing-gown worn by women. [F, from *peigner,* to comb]

peirameter, *n.* an instrument for measuring the resistance of road surfaces to traction. [Gr. *peiraein,* to try, -METER]

†**peise,** *v.t.* to weigh, to balance; to poise; to weight, to burden. *v.i.* to press down. *n.* heaviness, weight; a weight; a heavy impact, a blow. [A-F *peiser,* OF *peser,* L *pensāre,* freq. of *pendere,* to weigh]

peishwa, PESHWA.

pejorative, *a.* depreciatory. *n.* a word or form expressing depreciation. **pejorate,** *v.t.* **pejoration,** *n.* **pejoratively,** *adv.* [L *pējōrātus,* p.p. of *pējōrāre,* to make worse, from *pējor,* worse, -ATIVE]

pekan, *n.* a N American carnivorous animal, *Mustela pennanti,* of the weasel family, prized for its fur. [Canadian F, from Algonkin *pékané*]

pekin, *n.* a fabric of silk or satin, usu. with stripes running the way of the warp; a civilian (orig. used by the soldiers of Napoleon I). **Peke, Pekinese, Pekingese,** *n.* a rough-coated variety of Chinese pug. **Pekinese, Pekingese,** *a.* of or pertaining to Peking. [F *pékin,* Chin. *Pe-king,* lit. northern capital]

Peking, *n.* former name of **Beijing**, capital of China. **Peking man,** *n.* early type of human, *Homo erectus,* first found SW of Peking in 1929. Carbon dating indicates that they lived between 500,000 and 1,500,000 years ago. [see prec.]

pekoe, *n.* a fine black tea. [Chin. *pek-ho* (*pek,* white, *ho,* down)]

pelage, *n.* the coat or hair of an animal, esp. of fur. [F, from OF *pel,* ult. from L *pilus,* hair]

Pelagian, *n.* a follower of Pelagius. **Pelagianism,** *n.*

pelagian, pelagic, *a.* of or inhabiting the deep sea. *n.* a pelagian animal. [L *pelagius,* Gr. *pelagios,* from *pelagos,* sea]

Pelagius, *n.* (360–420), British theologian. He went to Rome about 400, and taught that every person possesses free will, denying Augustine's doctrines of predestination and original sin. Cleared of heresy by a synod in Jerusalem in 415, he was later condemned by the pope and the emperor.

pelargonium, *n.* a large genus of ornamental plants of the family Geraniaceae, popularly called geraniums. [Gr. *pelargos,* stork]

Pelasgic, *a.* of or pertaining to the Pelasgi, a widely-diffused prehistoric race inhibiting the coasts and islands of the eastern Mediterranean and the Aegean.

pele PEEL[3].

Pelé, *n.* (adopted name of Edson Arantes do Nascimento) (1940–), Brazilian footballer, a prolific goal scorer. He appeared in four World Cup competitions (1958–70) and won three winner's medals.

pelecoid, *n.* a figure enclosed by a semicircle and two concave quadrants meeting in a point. [Gr. *pelekoeides,* axe-like]

pelerine, *n.* a lady's long narrow fur cape. [F *pèlerine,* fem. of *pèlerin,* L. *peregrīnus,* PILGRIM]

pelf, *n.* money, wealth, gain. [ME *pelfe,* OF *pelfre,* etym. doubtful]

Pelham, *n.* **Henry** (1696–1754), British Whig politician. He held a succession of offices in Walpole's cabinet 1721–42, and was prime minister 1743–54.

pelican, *n.* a large piscivorous water-fowl of the genus *Pelecanus,* esp. *P. onocrotalus,* with an enormous pouch beneath the mandibles for storing fish when caught. **pelican crossing,** *n.* a type of pedestrian crossing controlled by pedestrian-operated traffic lights. [F, from late L *pelicānus,* Gr. *pelekan,* prob. rel. to *pelekus,* axe]

Pelion, *n.* mountain in Thessaly, Greece, near Mount Ossa; height 1548 m/5079 ft. In Greek mythology it was the home of the centaurs.

pelisse, *n.* a woman's long cloak or mantle; a garment worn over other clothes by a child. [F, from L *pellicia,* fem. of *pellicius,* of skin, from *pellis,* skin]

†**pell,** *n.* a skin, a hide; a roll of parchment. †**pellage,** *n.* [OF *pel* (F *peau*), L *pellem,* nom. *-lis,* skin]

pellagra, *n.* a virulent disease attacking the skin and causing nervous disorders and mania, caused by deficiency of vitamins B. [prob. from It. *pelle agra,* rough skin]

pellet, *n.* a little ball, esp. of bread, paper or something easily moulded; a small pill; a small shot, a rounded boss or prominence. *v.t.* to form into pellets; to hit with pellets. [OF *pelote,* med. L *pelōta,* dim. of L *pila,* ball]

pellicle, *n.* a thin skin; a membrane or film. **pellicular,** *a.* [F *pellicule,* from L *pellicula,* dim. of *pellis,* skin]

pellitory, *n.* a herb of the genus *Parietaria,* esp. the wall-pellitory, *P. officinalis;* also applied to a herb of the aster family, *Anacyclus pyrethrum,* or pellitory of Spain. [obs. *pelleter,* A-F *peletre,* L *piretārum,* Gr. *purethron,* feverfew, coalescing with obs. *parietary,* A-F *paritarie,* L *parietāria,* from *paries parietis,* wall]

pell-mell, *adv.* in a confused or disorderly manner, anyhow; in disorderly haste. *a.* confused, disorderly; hasty. *n.* disorder, confusion; a medley. [F *pêle-mêle,* prob. a redup. of *mêle,* from *mêler,* late L *misculāre,* L *miscēre,* to mix]

pellucid, *a.* clear, limpid, transparent; clear in thought, expression or style. **pellucidity,** *n.* **pellucidly,** *adv.* **pellucidness,** *n.* [F *pellucide,* L *pellūcidus,* from *pel-, perlūcēre* (PER-, *lūcēre,* to shine)]

pelmet, *n.* a canopy, built-in or detachable, which conceals the fittings from which curtains hang; a valance.

Peloponnese, *n.* (Greek **Peloponnesos**) peninsula forming the S part of Greece; area 21,549 sq km/8318 sq miles; population (1981) 1,012,500. It is joined to the mainland by the narrow isthmus of Corinth, and is divided into the nomes of Argolis, Arcadia, Achaea, Elis, Corinth, Lakonia, and Messenia, representing its seven ancient states.

Peloponnesian War, *n.* conflict between Athens and Sparta and their allies, 431–404 BC, originating in suspicions about the 'empire-building' ambitions of Pericles. It was ended by Lysander's destruction of the political power of Athens.

peloria, *n.* symmetry or regularity in flowers that are normally irregular. [mod. L, from Gr. *pelōros,* monstrous, from *pelōr,* prodigy]

pelorus, *n.* a sighting device on a ship's compass.

pelota, *n.* a game somewhat like squash played with a ball and a curved racket fitting upon the hand, popular in Spain and the Basque country. [Sp., from *pella,* L *pila,* ball]

pelotherapy, *n.* treatment of disease by the application of mud. [Gr. *pelos,* mud, *therapeuein,* to heal]

pelt¹, *n.* a hide or skin with the hair on, esp. of a sheep or goat; an undressed fur-skin; a raw skin stripped of hair or wool; (*facet.*) the human skin. **pelt-monger,** *n.* **pelt-wool,** *n.* wool from a dead sheep or lamb. **peltry,** *n.* pelts. [ME, rel. to PELL]

pelt², *v.t.* to strike or assail by throwing missiles; to throw; to strike repeatedly. *v.i.* to throw missiles; to keep on throwing, firing etc. (at); of rain etc., to beat heavily; (*sl.*) to hurry (along). *n.* a blow from something thrown. **full pelt,** at full speed, with violent impetus. **pelter,** *n.* **pelting**¹, *a.* [etym. doubtful]

pelta, *n.* a small light shield or target used by the ancient Greeks and Romans; (*Bot.*) a structure or part like a shield in form or function. **peltate, -tated,** *a.* (*Bot.*) of leaves etc., shield-shaped and fixed to the stalk at the centre. **peltation,** *n.* **peltati-, peltato-,** *comb. form* (*Bot.*). [L, from Gr. *peltē,* perh. rel. to *pella,* hide]

Peltier effect, *n.* in physics, a change in temperature at the junction of two different metals produced when an electric current flows through them. The extent of the change depends on what the conducting metals are, and the nature of change (rise or fall in temperature) depends on the direction of current flow. It is the reverse of the Seebeck effect. [French physicist Jean Charles *Peltier* (1785–1845) who discovered it 1834]

pelting¹ PELT².

†**pelting**², *a.* petty, mean, paltry, contemptible. †**peltingly,** *adv.* [prob. rel. to PALTRY]

peltry PELT¹.

pelvis, *n.* the lower portion of the great abdominal cavity; the bony walls of this cavity; the interior cavity of the kidney. **pelvic,** *a.* **pelvic girdle, arch,** *n.* the arrangement of bones which supports the hind-limbs of vertebrates, the lower limbs in humans. **pelviform,** *a.* **pelvimeter,** *n.* an instrument for measuring the diameter of the pelvis. **pelvimetry,** *n.* [L, basin]

Pembrokeshire, *n.* former extreme SW county of Wales, which became part of Dyfed in 1974; the county town was Haverfordwest.

pemmican, *n.* dried meat, pounded, mixed with a large proportion of melted fat and pressed into cakes; a similar preparation of beef with currants; digested or condensed information. [Cree *pimikan*]

pemphigus, *n.* a disease characterized by the eruption of watery vesicles on the skin. [Gr. *pemphix,* a bubble]

PEN, (*abbr.*) International Association of Poets, Playwrights, Essayists and Novelists.

pen¹, *n.* a small enclosure for cattle, sheep, poultry etc.; (*W Indies*) a country-house, a farm etc.; (*N Am., sl*) prison. *v.t.* (*past, p.p.* **penned**) to enclose, to confine; to shut or coop (up or in); to confine (water) with a dam etc. [OE *penn,* whence prob. *pennian* (found only in *onpennad,* unpenned)]

pen², *n.* a quill; an instrument for writing with ink; writing, style of writing; a writer; a penman; †a feather, a wing; a female swan. *v.t.* (*past, p.p.* **penned**) to write, to compose and write. **pen and ink,** instruments for writing; writing. **pen-and-ink,** *a.* written or drawn with these. **pen-case,** *n.* **pencraft,** *n.* penmanship, authorship. **pen-feather,** *n.* a quill feather; a pin-feather. **pen-feathered,** *a.* half-fledged. **pen-fish,** *n.* a squid or calamary. **pen-friend, -pal,** *n.* a person, usu. living abroad, whom one has not usu. met and with whom one corresponds. **penholder,** *n.* a rod of wood or other material forming a handle for a pen. **penknife,** *n.* a small knife (orig. for cutting quill pens), usu. carried in the pocket. **penman,** *n.* **penmanship,** *n.* the art of writing; style of writing. **pen-name,** *n.* a nom-de-guerre, a literary pseudonym. **pen-point,** *n.* (*N Am.*) a nib. **pen-pusher,** *n.* (*coll.*) a person doing dull, routine, clerical work. **penwiper,** *n.* **penwoman,** *n. fem.* **penful,** *n.* [ME and OF *penne,* L *penna,* a feather]

pen., (*abbr.*) peninsula.

penal, *a.* enacting, inflicting or pertaining to punishment; of the nature of punishment; punishable, esp. by law. **penal servitude,** *n.* imprisonment with hard labour. **penalize, -ise,** *v.t.* to make or declare penal; (*Sport*) to subject to a penalty or handicap; to put under an unfair disadvantage. **penalization, -isation,** *n.* **penally,** *adv.* [F *pénal,* L *pēnālis,* from *poena,* penalty, Gr. *poinē,* fine]

penalty, *n.* legal punishment for a crime, offence or misdemeanour; a sum of money to be forfeited for non-performance or breach of conditions; a fine, a forfeit; (*Sport*) a handicap imposed for a breach of rules or on the winner in a previous contest. **penalty area,** *n.* a rectangular area in front of the goal in soccer, where a foul against the attacking team results in a penalty and where the goal-keeper may handle the ball. **penalty box,** *n.* the penalty area; an area to which penalized players are confined in ice hockey. **penalty kick,** *n.* in football, a kick allowed to the opposite side when a penalty has been incurred (a goal thus scored is a **penalty goal.**) [F *pénalité,* med. L *pœnālitas,* as prec.]

penance, *n.* sorrow for sin evinced by acts of self-mortification etc.; in the Roman Catholic and Greek Churches, a sacrament consisting of contrition, confession and satisfaction, with absolution by the priest; an act of self-mortification undertaken as a satisfaction for sin, esp. one imposed by a priest before giving absolution. *v.t.* to inflict penance on. [OF *penance, peneance,* L *poenitentia,* PENITENCE]

Penang, *n.* (Malay **Pulau Pinang**) state in W Peninsular Malaysia, formed of Penang Island, Province Wellesley, and the Dindings on the mainland; area 1030 sq km/398 sq miles; capital Penang (George Town); population (1980) 955,000. Penang Island was bought by Britain from the ruler of Kedah in 1785; Province Wellesley was acquired in 1800.

penannular, *a.* nearly annular, almost a complete ring. [L *paene,* nearly]

Penates, *n.pl.* the Roman household gods, orig. of the store-room and kitchen. [L, rel. to *penes,* within]

pence, *n.pl.* PENNY.

penchant, *n.* a strong inclination or liking; a bias. [F, orig. pres.p. of *pencher,* to lean, ult. from L *pendēre,* to hang]

pencil, *n.* a cylinder or slip of graphite, crayon etc., usu. enclosed in a casing of wood, used for writing, drawing etc.; a small brush used by painters and by Chinese writers; skill or style in painting, the art of painting; (*Opt.*) a system of rays diverging from or converging to a point; (*Math.*) the figure formed by a series of straight lines meeting at a point; applied to various appliances in the form of a small stick; anything long and slim. *v.t.* (*past, p.p.* **pencilled**) to paint, draw, write or mark with or as with a pencil; to jot (down); to mark or shade in delicate lines; to enter (a racehorse's name) in a betting-book. **pencil-case,** *n.* a case for holding pencils; a holder or hollow handle for a pencil. **pencilled,** *a.* painted, drawn or marked with or as with a pencil; radiating; (*Bot.*) marked with fine lines. **pencilling,** *n.* [OF *pincel* (F *pinceau*), L *pēnicillum, -lus,* dim. of *pēniculus,* brush, dim. of PENIS]

pencraft PEN².

Penda, *n.* (*c.* 577–654), king of Mercia from about 632. He raised Mercia to a powerful kingdom, and defeated and killed two Northumbrian kings, Edwin (632) and Oswald (641). He was killed in battle by Oswy, king of Northumbria.

pendant, *n.* anything hanging down or suspended by way of ornament etc., as an earring, a locket, a tassel etc.; a pendant chandelier, gaselier or electrolier; a boss hanging from a ceiling or roof; the shank and ring of a watch-case; (*Naut.*) a short rope hanging from a mast-head etc., a tapering flag or pennant; (*sometimes pron.* pē'dã) a companionpiece, a counterpart, a match. [F, orig. pres.p. of *pendre,* L *pendēre,* to hang]

pendent, *a.* hanging; overhanging; pending, undetermined; (*Gram.*) incomplete in construction, having the sense suspended. **pendency,** *n.* **pendentive,** *n.* one of the triangular pieces of vaulting resting on piers or arches and forming segments of a dome. **pendently,** *adv.* **pending,** *a.* depending, awaiting settlement, undecided. *prep.* until; during. [as PENDANT]

Penderecki, *n.* **Krzysztof** (1933–), Polish composer of expressionist works, such as the *Threnody for the Victims of Hiroshima* for strings, employing cluster and percussion effects, later turning to religious subjects and a more orthodox style, as in the *Magnificat* (1974) and the *Polish Requiem* (1980–83).

pendulous, *a.* hanging, suspended; swinging, oscillating. **pendulate,** *v.i.* to swing as a pendulum; to waver, to hesitate. **penduline,** *a.* hanging (as a nest); of birds, building a hanging nest. **pendulously,** *adv.* **pendulousness,** *n.* [L *pendulus,* see hanging, from *pendēre,* to hang]

pendulum, *n.* (*pl.* **-lums**) a body suspended from a fixed point and oscillating freely by the force of gravity, as the weighted rod regulating the movement of the works in a clock. **the swing of the pendulum,** (the regular pattern of) change in public opinion, political power etc. [L, neut. of *pendulus,* see prec.]

Penelope, *n.* in Greek legend, wife of Odysseus. During his absence after the siege of Troy she kept her many suitors at bay by asking them to wait until she had woven a shroud for her father-in-law, but undid her work nightly. When Odysseus returned, he killed her suitors; a chaste wife. **penelopize, -ise,** *v.t.* to undo a piece of work. [Gr. *Pēnelopē*]

peneplain, *n.* an area of flat land produced by erosion. [L *paene, pene,* almost, PLAIN]

penetralia, *n.pl.* the inner part of a house, palace, temple or shrine; secrets, mysteries. [L, pl. of *penetrāle,* as foll.]

penetrate, *v.t.* to enter, to pass into or through; to pierce; to permeate; to saturate or imbue (with); to move or affect the feelings of; to reach or discern by the senses or intellect. *v.i.* to make way, to pass (into, through, to etc.). **penetrable,** *a.* capable of being penetrated; impressible, susceptible. **penetrability,** *n.* †**penetrance,** †**-trancy,** *n.* **penetrant,** *a.* **penetrating,** *a.* sharp, piercing; subtle, discerning. **penetratingly,** *adv.* **penetration,** *n.* penetrating or being penetrated; acuity, discernment. **penetrative,** *a.* **penetratively,** *adv.* **penetrativeness,** *n.* [L *penetrātus,* p.p. of *penetrāre,* rel. to *penitus,* within]

penfold PINFOLD.

penful etc. PEN².

penguin, *n.* a bird of the family Sphoeniscidae, belonging to the southern hemisphere, consisting of swimming-birds with rudimentary wings or paddles and scale-like feathers, a great auk. **penguinery,** *n.* a place where penguins breed. [etym. doubtful]

penholder PEN².

penial, PENIS.

penicil, *n.* (*Nat. Hist.*) a small tuft of hairs, like a hair-pencil; (*Surg.*) a tent or pledget. **penicillate,** *a.* (*Nat. Hist.*) furnished with, forming or consisting of a bundle of short close hairs or fibres; having delicate markings, pencilled. **penicillately,** *adv.* **penicillation,** *n.* **penicilliform,** *a.* [L *pēnicillus,* PENCIL]

penicillin, *n.* a ether-soluble substance produced from the mould *Penicillium* and having an intense growth-inhibiting action against various bacteria, esp. in wounds etc.

peninsula, *n.* a piece of land almost surrounded by water, usu. connected with the mainland by an isthmus. **the Peninsula,** Spain and Portugal. **peninsular,** *a.* of, pertaining to or resembling a peninsula. *n.* an inhabitant of a peninsula; a soldier in the Peninsular War. **Peninsular War,** *n.* the war in Spain and Portugal (1808–14), caused by Napoleon's invasion, between the British (in support of the native insurrection) and the French. The results were inconclusive, and the war was ended by Napoleon's abdication. **peninsularity,** *n.* **peninsulate,** *v.t.* to form or convert into a peninsula. [L *paeninsula* (*poene,* almost, *insula,* island)]

penis, *n.* (*pl.* **penises, penes**) the copulatory and urethral organ of a male mammal. **penis envy,** *n.* in Freudian theory, the female's subconscious desire to be male. **penial, penile,** *a.* [L, tail]

penitent, *a.* contrite, repentant, sorry; †doing penance. *n.* one who is penitent; a contrite sinner; one submitting to penance under the direction of a confessor; one belonging to any of various Roman Catholic orders devoted to the practice of penance and mutual discipline. **penitence,** *n.* **penitential,** *a.* pertaining to or expressing penitence; relating to or of the nature of penance. *n.* a book containing rules relating to penitence. **penitentially, penitently,** *adv.* **penitentiary,** *a.* penitential; pertaining to the reformatory treatment of criminals etc. *n.* a reformatory prison, a house of correction; (*N Am.*) a prison; an asylum for prostitutes seeking reformation; in the Roman Catholic Church, a papal court granting dispensations and dealing with matters relating to confessions. **Grand Penitentiary,** the president of this court. [OF, from L *poenitentem,* nom. *-tens,* pres.p. of *poenitēre,* rel. to *punīre,* to PUNISH]

penknife, penman etc. PEN².

Penn¹, *n.* **Irving** (1917–), US fashion, advertising, portrait, editorial, and fine art photographer. In 1948 he took the first of many journeys to Africa and the Far East, resulting in a series of portrait photographs of local people, avoiding sophisticated technique. He was associated for many years with *Vogue* magazine in the US.

Penn², *n.* **William** (1644–1718), English Quaker, born in London. He joined the Quakers in 1667, and in 1681 obtained a grant of land in America, in settlement of a debt owed by the king to his father, on which he established the colony of Pennsylvania as a refuge for the persecuted Quakers.

Penn(a), (*abbr.*) Pennsylvania.

pennant, *n.* a pennon; (*Naut.*) a long narrow streamer borne at the mast-head of a ship of war, a pendant; (*N Am.*) a flag indicating championship, e.g. in baseball. [conf. of PENNON and PENDANT]

pennate, -nated PINNATE.

†**penner,** *n.* a pen-case, formerly carried at the girdle. [med. L *pennārium,* from *penna,* PEN²]

Penney, *n.* **William** (1909–), British scientist. He worked at Los Alamos (1944–45), designed the first British atomic bomb, and developed the advanced gas-cooled nuclear reactor used in some power stations.

penniform, *a.* (*Nat. Hist.*) having the form of a feather. **penniferous, pennigerous,** *a.* [L *penna,* feather, -FORM]

penniless, *a.* without money; destitute. **pennilessness,** *n.*

pennill, *n.* (*pl.* **pennillion**) a short stanza of improvised verse sung to the harp at eisteddfods etc. [W, from *pen,* head]

Pennines, *n.* mountain system, 'the backbone of England', broken by a gap through which the river Aire flows to the E and the Ribble to the W; length (Scottish border to the Peaks in Derbyshire) 400 km/ 250 miles.

pennon, *n.* a small pointed or swallow-tailed flag, formerly borne on the spears of knights and later as the ensign of a regiment of lancers; a long streamer carried by a ship. **pennoned,** *a.* [ME and OF *penon,* prob. from L *penna,* feather, see PEN²]

Pennsylvania, *n.* state of NE USA; nickname Keystone State. **area** 117,400 sq km/45,316 sq miles. **capital** Harrisburg. **towns** Philadelphia, Pittsburgh, Erie, Allentown, Scranton. **products** mushrooms, fruit, flowers, cereals, tobacco, meat, poultry, dairy products, anthracite, electrical equipment. **population** (1986) 11,889,000. One of the original Thirteen States, it was founded and named by William Penn (1682), following a land grant by Charles II.

penny, *n.* (*pl.* **pennies,** denoting the number of coins; **pence,** denoting the amount) a bronze coin, a 100th part of a pound sterling, formerly a 12th part of a shilling; (*N Am.*) a one-cent piece; (*Bibl.*) a denarius; †money, a small sum of money. **a pretty penny,** a good round sum; considerable cost or expense. **penny-a-line,** *a.* cheap, shoddy, superficial. **penny-a-liner,** one who writes for newspapers at a low rate of pay; a hack writer. **penny-in-the-slot,** *a.* applied to automatic machines for giving out small articles, tickets etc. in return for a coin inserted in a slot. **Peter's pence** PETER¹. **the penny drops,** (*coll.*) the truth is realized; something is made clear. **to turn an honest penny,** to earn money by honest work. **penny dreadful,** *n.* a cheap crime-story, shocker. **penny-farthing,** *n.* an early type of bicycle with a large front wheel and small back wheel. **penny-pinch,** *v.i.* to save money by being nigarrdly. **penny-pinching,** *a.* miserly, niggardly. **penny post,** *n.* (*Hist.*) a post for conveying letters at the ordinary rate of a penny. **penny-wedding,** *n.* (*Sc.*) a wedding where the guests contribute towards the expenses. **pennyweight,** *n.* 24 grains or one-twentieth of an ounce troy (1·5 g). **penny-wise,** *a.* saving small sums at the risk of larger ones. **pennywort,** *n.* one of several plants with round peltate leaves. **pennyworth,** *n.* as much as can be bought for a penny; anything bought or sold; a good (or bad) bargain; a small amount, a trifle. [OE *pening* (cp. Dut., Dan. and Swed. *penning,* G *Pfennig*)]

pennyroyal, *n.* a kind of mint, *Mentha pulegium,* formerly and still popularly used for medicinal purposes. [prob. a corr. of *puliol ryale* (OF *puliol, poliol,* prob. from a dim. of *pūlēgium,* thyme, ROYAL)]

penology, *n.* the science of punishment and prison management. **penological,** *a.* **penologist,** *n.* [Gr. *poinē,* fine, PENALTY, -LOGY]

pen-pusher PEN².

pensile, *a.* hanging, suspended, pendulous; of birds, constructing a pendent nest. †**pensileness,** *n.* [L *pensilis,* from *pensus,* p.p. of *pendēre,* to hang]

pension¹, *n.* a periodical allowance for past services paid by the government or employers; a similar allowance to a person for good will, to secure services when required etc., or to literary people, scientists etc., to enable them to carry on their work; money paid to a clergyman in lieu of tithes; a consultative assembly of the members of Gray's Inn. *v.t.* to grant a pension to; to pay a pension to for the retention of services. **to pension off,** to cease to employ and to give a pension to; to discard as useless, worn etc. **pensionable,** *a.* **pensionary,** *n., a.* **pensioner,** *n.* one in receipt of a pension; a dependant; a hireling; a Cambridge undergraduate who is not a scholar on the foundation or a sizar. **Grand Pensioner,** the President of the States-General of Holland and Zeeland (1618–1791). [F, from L *pensiōnem,* nom. *-sio,* payment, from *pendere,* to pay]

pension², *n.* a boarding-house; a boarding-school. **en pension,** as a boarder. [F]

pensive, *a.* thoughtful; serious, anxious, melancholy; expressing sad thoughtfulness. †*v.t.* to make pensive. **pensively,** *adv.* **pensiveness,** *n.* [F *pensif, -sive,* from *penser,* to think, L *pensāre,* freq. of *pendere,* to weigh]

penstemon, PENTSTEMON.

penstock, *n.* a conduit, usu. in the form of a wooden trough, conveying water to a water-wheel; a flood-gate. [PEN¹, STOCK¹]

pent, *a.* penned in or confined; shut (up or in). **pent-up,** *a.* not openly expressed; suppressed. [for *penned,* p.p. of PEN¹]

pent(a)-, *comb.form* five. [Gr. *pente,* five]

pentacapsular, *a.* (*Bot.*) having five seed-vessels.

pentachord, *n.* a scale of five notes; a musical instrument with five strings.

pentacle, *n.* a figure like a star with five points formed by producing the sides of a pentagon in both directions to their points of intersection; a pentagram, used as a symbol by the mystics and astrologers of the Middle Ages. [med. L *pentaculum* (prob. PENT(A)-, -CULE)]

pentacoccous, *a.* (*Bot.*) having five seeds, or five cells with a seed in each. [Gr. *kokkos,* grain]

pentacrostic, *a.* containing five acrostics on the same name.

pentad, *n.* the number five; a group of five; a chemical element or radical having a valency of five. [Gr. *pentas -ados,* from *pente,* five]

pentadactyl, *a.* having five fingers or toes. *n.* a person or animal having five digits on each limb. **pentadactylic,** *a.* **pentadactylism,** *n.* [Gr. *daktulos,* toe]

pentadelphous, *a.* having the stamens united in five sets. [Gr. *adelphos,* brother]

pentaglot, *a.* in five languages. *n.* a work in five languages. [Gr. *glōtta,* tongue]

pentagon, *n.* a plane (usu. rectilineal) figure having five sides and five angles. **the Pentagon,** the headquarters of the US Department of Defense, Arlington, Virginia; the US military defence establishment. **pentagonal,** *a.* [L *pentagōnus,* Gr. *pentagōnos* (*gōnia,* angle)]

pentagram, *n.* a pentacle. [Gr. *pentegrammon*]

pentagraph, PANTOGRAPH.

Pentagynia, *n.pl.* a Linnaean order containing plants with five pistils. **pentagynian, pentagynous,** *a.* [Gr. *gunē,* woman, female]

pentahedron, *n.* a figure having five sides, esp. equal sides. **pentahedral,** *a.* [Gr. *hedra,* base]

pentahexahedral, *a.* having five ranges of faces, one above another, each with six faces. **pentahexahedron,** *n.*

pentalpha, *n.* a pentagram or pentacle. [Gr. ALPHA, the letter *a*]

pentamerous, *a.* of a flower-whorl, composed of five parts; (*Zool.*) five-jointed. [Gr. *meros,* part]

pentameter, *n.* a verse of five feet; (*Gr. and L Pros.*) a dactylic verse consisting of two halves each containing two feet (dactyls or spondees in the first half, dactyls in the second, and one long syllable), used principally with alternate hexameters in elegiacs; (*Eng. Pros.*) the iambic verse of ten syllables.

Pentandria, *n.pl.* a Linnaean class containing plants with five stamens. **pentandrian, pentandrous,** *a.* [Gr. *anēr andros,* man, male]

pentane, *n.* a volatile fluid paraffin hydrocarbon contained in petroleum etc.

pentangle, *n.* a pentagram. **pentangular,** *a.* having five angles.

pentapetalous, *a.* having five petals.

pentaphyllous, *a.* having five leaves. [Gr. *phullon,* leaf]

pentapody, *n.* a verse or sequence of five natural feet. [Gr. *pentapous* (*pous podos,* foot)]

pentapolis, *n.* a group or confederacy of five towns. **pentapolitan,** *a.* of or pertaining to a pentapolis, esp. that of Cyrenaica. [Gr. *polis,* city]

pentaprism, *n.* a five-sided prism used in reflex cameras to invert the image by deflecting light from any direction through 90°.

pentarchy, *n.* government by five rulers; a group of five kingdoms. [Gr. *archia,* from *archein,* to rule]

pentasepalous, *a.* having five sepals.

pentaspermous, *a.* having five seeds.

pentastich, *n.* a stanza or group of five lines of verse. **pentastichous,** *a.* [Gr. *pentastichos* (*stichos,* row)]

pentastyle, *a.* of a building, having five columns at the front or end. *n.* a pentastyle building or portico. [Gr. *stulos,* pillar]

Pentateuch, *n.* the first five books of the Old Testament, usu. ascribed to Moses. [L *Pentateuchus,* Gr. *Pentateuchos* (PENT(A)-, *teuchos,* tool, book)]

pentathlon, *n.* in ancient Greece, an athletic contest comprising leaping, running, wrestling, throwing the discus and hurling the spear; a modern athletics event based on this. **pentathlete,** *n.* [Gr. *athlon,* contest]

pentatomic, *a.* containing five atoms in the molecule, esp. five replaceable atoms of hydrogen.

pentatonic, *a.* (*Mus.*) consisting of five tones.

pentavalent, *a.* having a valency of five.

Pentecost, *n.* a solemn Jewish festival at the close of harvest, held on the 50th day from the second day of the Passover; †Whit-sunday. **Pentecostal,** *a.* of Pentecost; of or relating to any of various fundamentalist Christian sects which stress the powers of the Holy Spirit, e.g. in healing. **Pentecostalism,** *n.* **Pentecostalist,** *n.* [L *pentēcostē,* Gr. *pentēkostē,* 50th (day), from *pentēkonta,* 50]

penthemimer, *n.* (*Gr. Pros.*) a group of two and a half metrical feet, as a half of a pentameter. **penthemimeral,** *a.* [Gr. *penthēmimerēs* (*hēmimerēs,* halved)]

penthouse, †pentice, *n.* a roof or shed standing aslope against a main wall or building; a shed-like structure against a wall, a canopy, a protection over a window or door etc.; (*N Am.*) a subsidiary roof construction, a small dwelling-house built on the roof of a larger block of flats, offices etc. *v.t.* to furnish with or as with a penthouse. *a.* overhanging. [ME *pentice, pentis,* prob. from OF *apentis,* late L *appendicium,* from *appendere,* to APPEND]

pentimento, *n.* (*pl.* **-menti**) (a part of) a painting that has been painted over and later becomes visible. [It., correction]

pentode, *n.* a five-electrode thermionic valve.

pentose, *n.* any of various sugars containing five carbon atoms in the molecule.

pent-roof, *n.* a lean-to roof. [PENTHOUSE]

pentstemon, *n.* a genus of scrophulariaceous plants with showy tubular flowers. [Gr. *stēmōn,* erron. for STAMEN]

penult, †penultima, *n.* the last syllable but one of a word. **penultimate,** *n., a.* (the) last but one. [L *paenultima,* fem. a. (*paene,* almost, *ultimus,* last)]

penumbra, *n.* (*pl.* **-bras**) the partly-shaded zone around the total shadow caused by an opaque body intercepting the light from a luminous body, esp. round that of the earth or moon in an eclipse; the lighter fringe of a sun-spot; the blending or boundary of light and shade in a painting etc. **penumbral,** *a.* [L *paene,* almost, *umbra,* shadow]

penury, *n.* extreme poverty, destitution; lack or scarcity (of). **penurious,** *a.* niggardly, stingy; poor, scanty. **penuriously,** *adv.* **penuriousness,** *n.* [F *pénurie,* L *pēnūria,* cogn. with Gr. *peina,* hunger, *penia,* poverty]

peon, *n.* in India, a foot-soldier, a native constable, an attendant; a Mexican labourer, formerly a bondman serving his creditor in order to work off a debt; in Spanish America, a day-labourer etc. **peonage,** *n.* [Sp., from L *pedōnem,* nom. *pedo,* foot-soldier, see PAWN[1]]

peony, *n.* a plant of the genus *Paeonia,* with large globular terminal flowers, usu. double in cultivation. [OE *peonie,* L *paeōnia,* Gr. *paiōnia* from *Paiōn,* god of healing]

people, *n.* (*collect. sing. with pl.* **peoples**) the persons composing a nation, community or race; any body of persons, as those belonging to a place, a class, a congregation or company of any sort etc.; persons generally or indefinitely; one's family, kindred or tribe; followers, retinue, servants, workpeople etc. *v.t.* to stock with inhabitants, to populate; to occupy, inhabit. **the people,** the commonalty, the populace, as dist. from the self-styled higher orders. **people mover,** *n.* any of various methods of moving many people over short distances, e.g. moving pavements, driverless shuttles etc. **People's Charter,** *n.* the key document of Chartism, a movement for reform of the British political system in the 1830s. Drawn up in Feb. 1837, it was used to mobilize working-class support following the restricted extension of the franchise specified by the 1832 Reform Act. [A-F *people, poeple,* OF *pople* (F *peuple*), L *populum,* nom. *populus*]

PEP, (*abbr.*) personal equity plan.

pep, *n.* (*coll.*) vigour, spirit, energy. **to pep up,** to give energy, vigour etc. to; to cheer up. **pep pill,** *n.* (*coll.*) a tablet containing a stimulant. **pep-talk,** *n.* (*coll.*) a talk intended to encourage or stimulate. **peppy,** *a.* (*coll.*) full of vitality, energetic; fast. [PEPPER]

peperino, *n.* a porous volcanic tuff, composed of sand, cinders etc. cemented together. [It., from *pepere,* PEPPER]

Pepin the Short, (*c.* 714–*c.* 768), king of the Franks from 751. The son of Charles Martel, he acted as mayor of the palace to the last Merovingian king, Childeric III, deposed him and assumed the royal title himself, founding the Carolingian line.

peplum, peplus, *n.* (*pl.* **-lums, -la**) an outer robe or gown worn by women in ancient Greece; an over-skirt supposed to resemble the ancient peplum; a flared extension attached to the waist of a tight-fitting jacket or bodice. [L *peplum,* Gr. *peplos*]

pepo, *n.* (*pl.* **-pos**) any of various fruits of the gourd family, e.g. cucumber, melon, with a hard rind, watery pulp, and many seeds. [Gr. *pepōn,* ripe, from *peptein,* to ripen]

pepper, *n.* a pungent aromatic condiment made from the dried berries of *Piper nigrum* or other species of *Piper* used whole or ground into powder; the pepper-plant, *P. nigrum,* or other species; applied also to plants of the genus *Capsicum,* or to various strong spices, e.g. cayenne pepper, prepared from the fruit of capsicums; rough treatment, pungent criticism or sarcasm etc. *v.t.* to sprinkle or season with pepper; to besprinkle; to season with pungent remarks; to pelt with missiles; to beat severely; to sprinkle. **black pepper,** *Piper nigrum,* the common pepper. **cayenne pepper** CAYENNE. **pepper-and-salt,** *n.* a cloth of grey and black or black and white closely intermingled and having a speckled appearance. *a.* of hair, black mingled with grey. **white pepper,** pepper made by removing the skin by rubbing etc. before grinding. **pepper-box,** *n.* a small round box with a perforated top for sprinkling pepper on food. **pepper-cake,** *n.* a kind of gingerbread or spiced cake. **pepper-caster, -castor** PEPPER-BOX. **peppercorn,** *n.* the dried fruit of the pepper-tree; anything of little value. **peppercorn rent,** *n.* a nominal rent. **pepper-gingerbread,** *n.* hot-spiced gingerbread. **pepper-grass,** *n.* the pillwort, *Pilularia globulifera;* a garden herb, *Lepidium sativum,* with a pungent taste. **peppermill,** *n.* a small hand-operated device for grinding peppercorns. **pepper-pot,** *n.* a pepper-box; a W Indian dish of meat or fish with okra, chillies etc., flavoured with cassareep. **pepper-tree,** *n.* (*Austral.*) a shrub with leaves and bark having a biting taste like pepper. †**pepperwater,** *n.* a liquor prepared from powdered black pepper, used in microscopical observations. **pepperwort,** *n.* the dittany, *Lepidium latifolium.* **peppery,** *a.* having the qualities of pepper; pungent; choleric, hot-tempered; irascible, hasty. [OE *pipor,* L *piper,* Gr. *peperi,* of Oriental orig. (cp. Sansk. *pippalī*)]

peppermint, *n.* a pungent aromatic herb, *Mentha piperita;* an essential oil distilled from this plant; a lozenge flavoured with this. **peppermint tree,** *n.* (*Austral.*) a eucalyptus with fragrant leaves.

peppy PEP.

pepsin, *n.* a protein-digesting enzyme contained in gastric juice. **peptic,** *n.* promoting digestion; pertaining to digestion; having good digestive powers. *n.* a medicine that promotes digestion; (*pl.*) (*facet.*) the digestive organs. **pepticity,** *n.* **peptide,** *n.* a group of two or more amino acids, in which the carbon of one amino acid is linked to the nitrogen of another. [F *pepsine* (Gr. *pepsis,* digestion, cogn. with *peptein,* to cook)].

peptogen, *n.* a substance promoting the formation of pepsin. **peptogenic,** *a.*

peptone, *n.* any of the soluble compounds into which the proteins in food are converted by the action of pepsin. **peptonize, -ise,** *v.t.* **peptonization, -isation,** *n.* **peptonoid,** *n.*

Pepusch, *n.* **Johann Christoph** (1667–1752), German composer who settled in England about 1700. He contributed to John Gay's ballad operas *The Beggar's Opera* and *Polly.*

Pepys, *n.* **Samuel** (1633–1703), English diarist. His diary, written 1659–69 (when his sight failed) in shorthand, was a unique record of both the daily life of the period and the intimate feelings of the man. It was not deciphered until 1825.

per, *prep.* by; through, by means of; according to. [L]

PER, (*abbr.*) Professional Employment Register.

per-, *comb. form* through, completely; very, exceedingly, to the extreme; denoting the highest degree of combination or of valency in similar chemical compounds. [PER]

per-acute, *a.* (*Path.*) very acute or violent.

peradventure, *adv.* perhaps, perchance. *n.* uncertainty; doubt, conjecture. [ME *peraventure,* OF *par aventure*]

perambulate, *v.t.* to walk over or through, esp. for the purpose of surveying or inspecting; to walk along the boundaries of (a parish etc.) in order to survey or preserve them. *v.i.* to walk about. **perambulation,** *n.* **perambulator,** *n.* an instrument for measuring distances travelled, a hodometer, a pedometer; a pram. **perambulatory,** *a.* [L *perambulātus,* p.p. of *perambulāre* (*ambulāre,* to walk)]

per annum, *adv.* yearly, by the year. [L]

per ardua ad astra, through difficulties to the stars (motto of the Royal Air Force). [L]

percale , *n.* a closely woven cotton cambric. **percaline,** *n.* a glossy cotton cloth. [F, etym. doubtful]

per capita, *adv.* by the head, for each person. [L]

†**perceant,** *a.* piercing, sharp, penetrating. [F *perçant,* pres.p. of *percer,* to PIERCE]

perceive, *v.t.* to apprehend with the mind; to discern, to understand; to have cognizance of by the senses. **perceivable,** *a.* **perceiver,** *n.* [OF *perceiv-,* stem of *perceivre, perçoivre* (F *percevoir*), L *percipere* (*capere,* to take)]

per cent, *a.* calculated in terms of 100 parts of a whole. *n.* a percentage. **percentage,** *n.* a proportion expressed as a per cent figure; allowance, commission, duty; (*coll.*) advantage, profit.

percept, *n.* that which is perceived, the mental product of perception. **perceptible,** *a.* that may be perceived by the senses or intellect. **perceptibility,** *n.* **perceptibly,** *adv.* **perceptive,** *a.* having the faculty of perceiving; discerning, astute. **perceptively,** *adv.* **perceptiveness, perceptivity,** *n.* [L *perceptum,* neut. p.p. of *percipere,* to PERCEIVE]

perception, *n.* the act, process or faculty of perceiving; the mental action of knowing external things through the medium of sense presentations; intuitive apprehension, insight or discernment; (*Law*) collection or receipt of rents.

Perceval, *n.* **Spencer** (1762–1812), British Tory politician. He became chancellor of the Exchequer (1807) and prime minister in 1809. He was shot in the lobby of the House of Commons in 1812 by a merchant who blamed government measures for his bankruptcy.

perch[1], *n.* a striped spiny-finned freshwater fish, *Perca fluviatilis,* also *P. flavescens,* the yellow perch of the US. **percoid,** *n., a.* [F *perche,* L *perca,* Gr. *perkē*]

perch[2], *n.* a pole or bar used as a rest or roost for birds; anything serving this purpose; an elevated seat or position; the centre-pole connecting the front and back gear of a spring-carriage; a land measure of $5\frac{1}{2}$ yd. (5·03 m). *v.i.* to alight or rest as a bird; to alight or settle on or as on a perch. *v.t.* to set or place on or as on a perch. **percher,** *n.* one who or that which perches; one of the Insessores or perching-birds. [ME and OF *perche,* L *pertica,* pole]

perchance, *adv.* perhaps, by chance. [ME and OF *par chance* (*par,* by, CHANCE)]

percheron, *n.* one of a breed of heavy and powerful horses from the district of le Perche. [F]

perchlorate, *n.* a salt of perchloric acid. **perchloric,** *a.* pertaining to a compound of chlorine containing oxygen in the highest possible proportion. **perchloride,** *n.*

percipient, *a.* perceiving, apprehending, conscious. *n.* one who or that which perceives, esp. one receiving a supposed telepathic message. **percipience,** †**-ency,** *n.* [L *percipiens -ntem,* pres.p. of *percipere,* to PERCEIVE]

percoct, *a.* overdone, hackneyed. [L *percoctus,* p.p. of *percoquere* (*coquere,* to COOK)]

percoid PERCH[1].

percolate, *v.i.* to pass through small interstices, to filter (through). *v.t.* to ooze through, to permeate; †to strain, to filter; to make (coffee) in a percolator. **percolation,** *n.* **percolator,** *n.* one who or that which strains or filters; a filter; a coffee-pot in which the boiling water filters through the coffee. [L *percōlātus,* p.p. of *percōlāre* (*cōlum,* strainer)]

per contra, *adv.* on the contrary. [L]

†**percurrent,** *a.* (*Bot.*) going through the entire length (as the midrib of a leaf). †**percursory,** *a.* cursory, slight; running swiftly. [L *percurrens -ntem,* pres.p. of *percurrere* (*currere,* to run)]

percuss, *v.t.* to strike quickly or tap forcibly, esp. (*Med.*) to test or diagnose by percussion. **percussant,** *a.* (*Her.*) beating or lashing (of the tail of a lion etc.). [L *percussus,* p.p. of *percutere* (*quatere,* to shake)]

percussion, *n.* forcible striking or collision; the shock of such collision; the effect of the sound of a collision on the ear; medical examination by gently striking some part of the body with the fingers or an instrument; the production of sound by striking on an instrument; musical instruments struck in this way. **percussion-cap,** *n.* a small copper cap containing fulminating powder, used in a percussion-lock. **percussion-lock,** *n.* a gunlock in which the hammer strikes a cap to explode the charge in a firearm. **percussionist,** *n.* a person who plays a percussion instrument. **percussive,** †**percutient,** *a.* [L *percussio,* as prec.]

percutaneous, *a.* acting or done through the skin. **percutaneously,** *adv.*

†**perdie,** PARDIE.

Percy[1], *n.* **Henry 'Hotspur'** (1364–1403), English soldier, son of the 1st Earl of Northumberland. In repelling a border raid, he defeated the Scots at Homildon Hill in Durham in 1402, and was killed at the battle of Shrewsbury while in revolt against Henry IV.

Percy[2], *n.* **Thomas** (1729–1811), English scholar and bishop of Dromore from 1782. He discovered a manuscript collection of songs, ballads, and romances, from which he published a selection as *Reliques of Ancient English Poetry* (1765), influential in the Romantic revival.

per diem, *a., adv.* by the day, for each day. [L]

perdition, *n.* utter destruction, entire ruin; the loss of the soul or of happiness in a future state, damnation. [ME and OF *perdiciun,* L *perditiōnem,* nom. *-tio,* from *perdere,* to destroy (*dare,* to give)]

†**perdu,** *a.* (*fem.* **perdue**) hidden, concealed; (*Mil.*) forlorn, exposed, desperate, in ambush. *n.* one in ambush; one of a forlorn hope; one employed in a desperate enterprise or in a hopeless case. **to lie perdu,** to lie in ambush; to be hidden or out of sight; to be in a hazardous situation. [F, p.p. of *perdre,* to lose, as prec.]

perdurable, *a.* very lasting or durable; permanent, everlasting. **perdurability,** *n.* **perdurably,** *adv.* †**perdurance,** †**perduration,** *n.* [OF, from late L *perdūrābilis*]

†**peregal,** PAREGAL.

peregrination, *n.* a travelling about; a sojourning in foreign countries. †**peregrinate,** *v.i.* **peregrinator,** *n.* [F *pérégrination,* L *peregrīnātiōnem,* nom. *-tio,* from *peregrīnārī,* from *peregrīnus,* foreign, as foll.]

peregrine, *a.* †foreign, outlandish; migratory, travelling abroad. *n.* a peregrine falcon. **peregrine falcon,** *n.* a widely-distributed species of falcon, *Falco peregrinus,* used for hawking. [L *peregrīnus,* from *peregre,* abroad (PER, *ager,* field)]

pereion, *n.* the thorax in Crustacea. [Gr. *peraiōn,* pres.p. of *peraioein,* to transport (in mistake for *periienai,* to walk about)]

peremptory, *a.* precluding question or hesitation; absolute, positive, decisive, determined; imperious, dogmatic, dictatorial; (*Law*) final, determinate. **peremptorily,** *adv.* **peremptoriness,** *n.* [A-F *peremptorie,* L *peremptōrius,* destructive, from *perimere* (*emere,* to take, to buy)]

perennial, *a.* lasting throughout the year; unfailing, unceasing, lasting long, never ceasing; of plants, living for more than two years. *n.* a perennial plant. **perenniality,** *n.* **perennially,** *adv.* [L *perennis* (*annus,* year)]

perennibranchiate, *a.* belonging to the Perennibranchiata, a division of amphibians retaining their gills through life. *n.* an animal of this division. [as prec., BRANCHIATE]

Peres, *n.* **Shimon** (1923–), Israeli socialist politician, prime minister 1984–86. Peres emigrated from Poland to Palestine in 1934, but was educated in the US. In 1959 he was elected to the Knesset (Israeli parliament). He became leader of the Labour Party in 1977. Peres was prime minister under a power-sharing agreement with the leader of the Consolidation Party (Likud), Yitzhak Shamir.

perestroika, *n.* the policy of restructuring and reforming Soviet institutions initiated by Mikhail Gorbachev. [Rus.]

Pérez de Cuélar, Javier (1920–), Peruvian diplomat. A delegate to the first United Nations general assembly 1946–47, he held several ambassadorial posts and was appointed secretary-general of the UN 1982.

perf., (*abbr.*) perfect; perforated.

perfect[1], *a.* complete in all its parts, qualities etc., without defect or fault; finished, thoroughly versed, trained, skilled etc.; of a lesson, thoroughly learned; of the best, highest and most complete kind; entire, complete, unqualified; of a flower, having all the essential parts; (*Gram.*) expressing action completed. *n.* a perfect tense of a verb. **future perfect** FUTURE. **perfect number,** *n.* an integer, e.g. 6, that is equal to the sum of all its possible factors, excluding itself. **perfection,** *n.* the act of making or the state of being perfect; supreme excellence; complete development; faultlessness; a perfect person or thing; the highest degree, the extreme (of); an excellent quality or acquirement. **to perfection,** completely, perfectly. **perfectionism,** *n.* **perfectionist,** *n.* one believing in the possibility of attaining (moral or religious) perfection; a member of a communistic community founded by J. H. Noyes in 1838 at Oneida Creek, in Madison County, New York State; a person who tolerates no fault or imperfection. †**perfectionment,** *n.* **perfective,** *a.* tending to make perfect; (*Gram.*) expressing completed action (cp. *imperfective*). **perfectly,** *adv.* **perfectness,** *n.* [ME and OF *perfit,* L *perfectus* (*factus,* p.p. of *facere,* to make)]

perfect[2], *v.t.* to finish or complete, to bring to perfection; to render thoroughly versed or skilled (in). **perfecter,** *n.* **perfectible,** *a.* **perfectibilian, -bilist,** *n.* one believing that it is possible for humanity to attain moral and social perfection, a perfectionist. **perfectibility,** *n.*

perfecto, *n.* (*pl.* **-tos**) a large cigar that tapers at both ends. [Sp., perfect]

perfervid, *a.* very fervid. **perfervidness, perfervour,** *n.*

†**perficient,** *a.* effectual, efficient; actual. *n.* one who perfects. [L *perficiens -ntem,* pres.p. of *perficere* (*facere,* to make)]

perfidy, *n.* violation of faith, allegiance or confidence. **perfidious,** *a.* treacherous, faithless, deceitful, false. **perfidiously,** *adv.* **perfidiousness,** *n.* [F *perfidie,* L *perfidia,* from *perfidus,* treacherous (*fides,* faith)]

perfoliate, *a.* applied to leaves so surrounding the stem as to appear as if perforated by it. [L *folium,* leaf]

perforate, *v.t.* to bore through, to pierce; to make a hole or holes through by boring; to pass or reach through. *v.i.* to penetrate (into or through). *a.,* perforated; (*Bot.*) pierced with small holes or having small transparent dots like holes. **perforation,** *n.* a perforating or being perforated; a hole made by piercing, e.g. one of many made in paper so that it is easy to tear. **perforative,** *a.* **perforator,** *n.* [L *perforātus,* p.p. of *perforāre* (*forāre,* to bore)]

perforce, *adv.* of necessity; compulsorily. [earlier *parforce,* OF *par force,* by FORCE[1]]

perform, *v.t.* to carry through, to execute, to accomplish; to discharge, to fulful; to represent, as on the stage; to play, to render (music etc.). *v.i.* to act a part; to play a musical instrument etc.; to do what is to be done. **performable,** *a.* **performance,** *n.* execution, carrying out, completion; a thing done, an action; a feat, a notable deed; a literary work; the performing of a play, display of feats etc.; an entertainment; the capacity (as of a vehicle) to function (well); language as manifested in actual use in speech or writing; (*coll.*) elaborate or laborious action. **performer,** *n.* one who performs, esp. an actor, musician, gymnast etc. **performing,** *a.* **performing art,** *n.* an art form requiring performance before an audience. [ME *perfourmer,* prob. var. (assim. to FORM) of ME and OF *perfournir* (*fournir,* to FURNISH)]

perfume, *v.t.* to fill or impregnate with a scent or sweet odour; to scent. *n.,* a substance emitting a sweet odour; fragrance, scent; fumes of something burning, cooking etc. **perfumatory,** *a.* **perfumeless,** *a.* **perfumer,** *n.* one who or that which perfumes; one who makes or sells perfumes. **perfumery,** *n.* (the preparation of) perfumes; a place where perfumes are sold. [F *parfumer* (*par-,* PER-, L *fūmāre,* to smoke, from *fūmus,* smoke)]

perfunctory, *a.* done merely for the sake of having done with, done in a half-hearted or careless manner; careless, negligent, superficial, mechanical. **perfunctorily,** *adv.* **perfunctoriness,** *n.* [late L *perfunctōrius,* from *perfunctus,* p.p. of *perfungī* (*fungī,* to perform)]

perfuse, *v.t.* to besprinkle; to spread over, to suffuse (with), to pour (water etc.) over or through. **perfusion,** *n.* **perfusive,** *a.* [L *perfūsus,* p.p. of *perfundere* (*fundere,* to pour)]

Perga, *n.* ruined city of Pamphylia, 16 km/10 miles NE of Adalia, Turkey, noted for its local cult of Artemis. It was visited by the apostle St Paul.

pergameneous, *a.* of skin etc., of the texture of parchment. **pergamentaceous,** *a.* [from L *pergamēna*, PARCHMENT]
pergola, *n.* a covered walk or arbour with climbing plants trained over posts, trellis-work etc. [It., from L *pergula,* projecting roof, balcony etc., from *pergere,* to proceed]
perh., (*abbr.*) perhaps.
perhaps, *adv.* it may be, by chance, possibly. [PER, HAP]
peri, *n.* a being represented as a descendant of fallen angels, excluded from paradise until some penance is accomplished; a beautiful being, a fairy. [Pers. *parī*]
Peri, *n.* **Jacopo** (1561–1633), Italian composer, who served the Medici family. His experimental melodic opera *Euridice* (1600) established the opera form and influenced Monteverdi. His first opera, *Dafne* (1597), is now lost.
peri-, *pref.* around, near. [Gr., around, about]
perianth, *n.* a floral envelope. [Gr. *anthos,* flower]
periapt, *n.* something worn about the person, as an amulet or charm. [F *périapte,* Gr. *periapton* (*haptein,* to fasten)]
periaxial, *a.* surrounding an axis.
periblast, *n.* the protoplasm around a cell-nucleus. **periblastic,** *a.*
pericardium, *n.* the membrane enveloping the heart. **pericardiac, -dial, -dic,** *a.* **pericarditis,** *n.* inflammation of the pericardium. [Gr. *perikardion* (*kardia,* heart)]
pericarp, *n.* the seed-vessel or wall of the developed ovary of a plant. **pericarpial,** *a.* [Gr. *perikarpion* (*karpos* fruit)]
pericentre, *n.* the point in the orbit of a body where it passes nearest to the centre. **pericentral, -tric,** *a.*
perichondrium, *n.* the membrane investing the cartilages except at joints. [Gr. *chondros,* cartilage]
periclase, *n.* a greenish mineral composed of magnesia and protoxide of iron, from Vesuvius. [Gr. PERI-, very, *klasis,* fracture]
Pericles, *n.* (*c.* 490–429 BC), Athenian politician, who dominated the city's affairs from 461 BC (as leader of the democratic party), and under whom Greek culture reached its height. He created a confederation of cities under the leadership of Athens, but the disasters of the Peloponnesian War led to his overthrow in 430 BC. Although quickly reinstated, he died soon after.
periclinal, *a.* of geological strata, sloping from a common centre. [Gr. *periklinēs* (*klinein,* to lean)]
pericope, *n.* an extract, a quotation, esp. a selection from the Gospels or Epistles read in public worship. [late L, from Gr. *perikopē* (*kopein,* to cut)]
pericranium, *n.* the membrane investing the skull; (*facet.*) the skull, the brain. **pericranial,** *a.* **pericranially,** *adv.*
pericycle, *n.* a thin layer of cells surrounding the vascular tissue in roots and stems. [Gr. *kuklos,* spherical]
pericynthion, PERILUNE.
pericystic, *a.* around the bladder. **pericystitis,** *n.* inflammation of the tissue around the bladder. [Gr. *kustis,* bladder]
periderm, *n.* the hard integument of certain Hydrozoa; the outer bark; the whole of the tissues comprising this and the cork-cambium.
peridesmium, *n.* the sheath of a ligament. [Gr. *desmos,* band]
peridium, *n.* (*pl.* **-dia**) the outer envelope of certain fungi enclosing the spores. **peridial,** *a.* **peridiole, peridiolum,** *n.* a secondary or inner peridium. [Gr. *pēridion,* dim. of *pēra,* bag, wallet]
peridot, *n.* a yellowish-green chrysolite; olivine. **peridotic,** *a.* **peridotite,** *n.* a mineral composed chiefly of olivine. [F *péridot,* etym. doubtful]
peridrome, *n.* the open space between the columns and the wall in ancient temples etc. [Gr. *peridromos* (*dromos,* course)]
periegesis, *n.* a travelling round, a perambulation; a description of this. [Gr. *periegēsis* (*agein* to lead)]
perienteron, *n.* the primitive perivisceral cavity. **perienteric,** *a.* [Gr. *enteron,* intestine]
perifibrum, *n.* the membranous envelope surrounding the fibres etc. of sponges. **perifibral,** *a.*
periganglionic, *a.* surrounding a ganglion.
perigastric, *a.* surrounding the alimentary canal.
perigee, *n.* the nearest point to the earth in the orbit of the moon, one of the planets or an artificial satellite. **perigeal, -gean,** *a.* [F *périgée,* late L *perigēum, perigaeum,* Gr. *perigeion* (*gē,* earth)]
perigenesis, *n.* reproduction through rhythmic vibrations of protoplasmic molecules.
periglottis, *n.* the epithelium or skin of the tongue. **periglottic,** *a.* [Gr. *glōtta,* tongue]
perigone, *n.* the perianth; the walls of a spore-sac in a hydroid. **perigonial,** *a.* (*Bot.*). [F *périgone* (Gr. *gonos,* offspring, seed)]
perigynous, *a.* of stamens, growing upon some part surrounding the ovary. **perigynium,** *n.* [Gr. *gunē,* female]
perihelion, *n.* the part of the orbit of a planet, comet etc. nearest the sun. [Gr. *hēlios,* sun]
perihepatic, *a.* surrounding the liver. [Gr. *hēpas hēpatos,* liver]
peril, *n.* danger, risk, hazard, jeopardy; exposure to injury, loss or destruction. *v.t.* (*past, p.p.* **perilled**) to risk, to endanger. †*v.i.* to be in danger. **perilous,** *a.* **perilously,** *adv.* **perilousness,** *n.* [OF *péril,* L *perīclum, perīculum,* rel. to *perīrī,* to try]
perilune, *n.* the point in the orbit of a body round the moon where the body is closest to the centre of the moon. [F *lune,* L *luna,* moon]
perilymph, *n.* the clear fluid surrounding the membranous labyrinth in the ear.
perimeter, *n.* the bounding line of a plane figure; the length of this, the circumference; an instrument for measuring the field of vision; the boundary of a camp etc. **perimetrical,** *a.* [L and Gr. *perimetros* (*metron,* measure)]
perimorph, *n.* a mineral enclosing another. **perimorphic, -phous,** *a.* **perimorphism,** *n.* [Gr. *morphē,* form]
perimysium, *n.* (*pl.* **-sia**) the fibrous connective tissue surrounding muscle fibres. [Gr. *mūs, muos,* muscle]
perinatal, *a.* occurring at or relating to the period shortly before and after birth.
perineum, *n.* the part of the body between the genital organs and the anus. **perineal,** *a.* [late L *perinēum -naeum,* Gr. *peri-, pērinaion,* from *pēris -inos,* scrotum]
period, *n.* a portion of time marked off by some recurring event, esp. an astronomical phenomenon; the time taken up by the revolution of a planet round the sun; any specified portion of time; a definite or indefinite portion of time, an age, an era, a cycle; length of duration, existence or performance; a complete sentence, esp. a complex one in which the predicate is not fully stated till the end; a pause; a full stop (.) marking this; an end, a limit; the menses; the interval between the recurrences of equal values in a periodic function. *a.* descriptive of a picture, object etc. characteristic of a certain period, belonging to a historical period. †*v.t.* to put an end to. **the period,** the present day. **period piece,** *n.* an objet d'art, piece of furniture etc. belonging to a historical period, esp. one of value; a person of outdated views, dress etc. **periodic,** *a.* pertaining to a period or periods; performed in a regular revolution; happening or appearing at fixed intervals; constituting a complete sentence. **periodic table,** *n.* a table showing the chemical elements in order of their atomic number, and arranged to show the periodic nature of their properties. **periodical,** *a.* periodic; appearing at regular intervals (as a magazine etc.). *n.* a magazine or other publication published at regular intervals, as monthly, quarterly etc. †**periodicalist,** *n.* one who writes for a periodical. **periodically,** *adv.* **periodicity,** *n.* [F *période,* L *periodus,* Gr. *periodos* (*hodos,* way)]
periodontal, *a.* of tissues, around a tooth. **periodontics,** *n. sing.* the treatment of periodontal disorders.

[ODONT(O)-]

perioeci, *n.pl.* the inhabitants of the same latitudes on the opposite sides of the globe; (*Gr. Hist.*) the dwellers in the surrounding country, in relation to a town or city. **perioecian,** *n.* **perioecic,** *a.* [Gr. *perioikoi* (*oikeein,* to dwell)]

periorbital, *a.* around the orbit of the eye.

periosteum, *n.* a dense membrane covering the bones. **periosteal, †-teous,** *a.* **periostitis,** *n.* inflammation of the periosteum. **periostitic,** *a.* [Gr. *periosteon* (*osteon,* bone)]

periotic, *a.* surrounding the inner ear. *n.* a periotic bone. [Gr. *ous ōtos,* ear]

peripatetic, *a.* walking about, itinerant; pertaining to the philosophy of Aristotle (from his habit of walking about whilst teaching in the Lyceum). *n.* one who walks about; one who cannot afford to ride; a follower of Aristotle. **peripatetically,** *adv.* **peripateticism,** *n.* [F *péripatétique,* L *peripatēticus,* Gr. *peripatētikos* (*patein,* to walk)]

Peripatus, *n.* a genus of worm-like arthropods living in damp places in the southern hemisphere, and believed to represent an ancestral type of both insects and myriapods. [mod. L, from Gr. *peripatos,* walking about, as prec.]

peripeteia, *n.* a reversal of circumstances or sudden change of fortune in a play or in life. [Gr. *pet-,* stem of *piptein,* to fall]

periphery, *n.* the outer surface; the perimeter or circumference of a figure or surface. **peripheral,** *a.* of a periphery; being an additional or auxiliary device, esp. in computing. *n.* a device, e.g. a printer, a VDU, connected to a computer for input/output, storage etc. [ME and OF *periferie,* late L *peripherīa,* Gr. *periphereia,* circumference (*pherein,* to bear)]

periphractic, *a.* (*Geom.*) enclosing round, as the surface of a ring or a globe with an internal cavity. [Gr. *periphraktos,* fenced round (*phrassein,* to fence)]

periphrasis, *n.* (*pl.* **-phrases**) roundabout speaking or expression, circumlocution; a roundabout phrase. **†periphrase,** *v.t.* to express by circumlocution. *v.i.* to use circumlocution. *n.* periphrasis. **periphrastic,** *a.* of or using periphrasis; using two words instead of an inflected form of one word. **periphrastically,** *adv.* [L and Gr. (*phrasis,* a speech, a PHRASE)]

periplast, *n.* the main substance of a cell as distinguished from the external coating of the nucleus; a cell-wall or cell-envelope; †intercellular substance. **periplastic,** *a.* [Gr. *plastos,* formed, moulded]

periplus, *n.* (*pl.* **-pli**) circumnavigation. [L *periplūs,* Gr. *periplous* (*-plous,* voyage)]

peripteral, *a.* surrounded by a single row of columns. **peripterous,** *a.* (*Ornith.*) feathered on all sides; peripteral. **periptery,** *n.* a peripteral building. [Gr. *peripteron* (*pteron,* wing)]

Perique, *n.* a strong, dark-coloured variety of tobacco grown and manufactured in Louisiana, used chiefly in mixtures. [etym. doubtful]

perirhinal, *a.* around the nose. [Gr. *rhis rhinos,* nose]

periscope, *n.* an apparatus enabling persons inside a submarine, trench etc. to look about above the surface of the water etc.; a look round, a general view. **periscopic, -ical,** *a.*

perish, *v.i.* to be destroyed, to come to naught; to die, to lose life or vitality in any way; to decay, to wither; to be lost eternally. †*v.t.* to destroy, to ruin. **perishable,** *a.* liable to perish; subject to rapid decay. *n.pl.* foodstuffs and other things liable to rapid decay or deterioration. **perishability, -bleness,** *n.* **perishably,** *adv.* **perished,** *a.* (*coll.*) of a person, very cold; of rubber etc., in poor condition due to age, damp etc. **perisher,** *n.* (*coll.*) an irritating person, esp. a child. **perishing,** *a.* that perishes; deadly, extreme; (*sl.*) infernal, damned; (*coll.*) freezing cold. **perishingly,** *adv.* [OF, stem of *perir,* L *perīre* (PER-, *īre,* to go)]

perisperm, *n.* the testa of a seed; the mass of albumen outside the embryo-sac in certain seeds. [F *périsperme*]

†perispheric, *a.* globular.

perispome, perispomenon, *a.* having a circumflex accent on the last syllable. *n.* a word with this. [Gr. *perispōmenon,* neut. p.p. of *perispaein* (*spaein,* to draw)]

perissad, *n.* a chemical element or radical whose valency is represented by an odd number; a perissodactyl. [Gr. *perissos,* uneven, -AD]

perissodactyl, *a.* of or belonging to the Perissodactyla, a division of Ungulata in which all the feet are oddtoed. *n.* any individual of the Perissodactyla. [Gr. *perissos,* uneven, *daktulos,* digit]

peristalith, *n.* a group of stones standing round a burial-mound etc. [Gr. *peristatos* (*statos,* standing), -LITH]

peristalsis, *n.* the automatic vermicular contractile motion of the alimentary canal and similar organs by which the contents are propelled along. **peristaltic,** *a.* **peristaltically,** *adv.* [Gr. *stellein,* to send]

peristeronic, *a.* of or pertaining to pigeons. [Gr. *peristerōn,* dovecot, from *peristera,* pigeon]

peristeropod, *a.* pigeon-footed. *n.* a member of the Peristeropodes, a group of gallinaceous birds in which the hind toe is on a level with the other toes. [as prec.; Gr. *pous podos,* foot]

peristome, *n.* the fringe round the mouth of the capsule in mosses; the margin of the aperture of a mollusc, the oval opening in insects, Crustacea, Infusoria etc. **peristomal, -mial,** *a.* [F *péristome* (Gr. *stoma,* mouth)]

peristyle, *n.* a row of columns about a building, court etc.; a court etc. with a colonnade around it. [F *péristyle,* L *peristylum,* Gr. *peristulon* (*stulos,* pillar)]

perisystole, *n.* the interval between the systole and diastole of the heart.

perithoracic, *a.* around the thorax.

peritomous, *a.* (*Min.*) having the faces similar and cleaving in more directions than one parallel to the axis. [Gr. *tomos,* cut]

peritoneum, *n.* a serous membrane lining the abdominal cavity and enveloping all the abdominal viscera. **peritoneal,** *a.* **peritonitis,** *n.* inflammation of the peritoneum. [L *peritonaeum,* Gr. *peritonaion* (*ton-,* stem of *teinein,* to stretch)]

perityphlitis, *n.* inflammation of the connective tissue surrounding the caecum or blind gut. [Gr. *tuphlon,* the caecum, neut. of *tuphlos,* blind]

perivascular, *a.* surrounding a vessel.

perivisceral, *a.* surrounding the viscera.

periwig, *n.* a peruke, a wig. [earlier *perwigge, perwicke,* F *perruque,* PERUKE]

periwinkle¹, *n.* a small univalve mollusc, *Littorina littorea.* [OE *pine-wincle, wine- wincle*]

periwinkle², *n.* a plant of the genus *Vinca,* comprising trailing evergreen shrubs with blue or white flowers. [OE *perwince, pervince,* L *pervinca*]

perjink, *a.* (*Sc.*) precise, prim. [etym. unknown]

perjure, *v.t.* (*reflex.*) to forswear (oneself); †to cause to swear falsely. †*v.i.* to swear falsely. †*n.* a perjurer. **perjured,** *a.* forsworn. **perjurer,** *n.* **perjurious,** *a.* [OF *parjurer,* L *perjūrāre* (*jūrāre,* to swear)]

perjury, *n.* the act of swearing falsely, the violating of an oath; the act of wilfully giving false evidence.

perk¹, *v.t.* to make smart or trim; to hold or prick up; to thrust (oneself) forward. *v.i.* to bear oneself saucily or jauntily; to be jaunty, self-assertive or impudent. *a.* pert, brisk, smart, trim. **to perk up,** (*coll.*) (to cause) to be more cheerful, lively etc. **perky,** *a.* lively; cheerful, jaunty. **perkily,** *adv.* **perkiness,** *n.* [etym. doubtful]

perk², *v.i.* (*dial.*) to perch. *v.t.* (*reflex.*) to perch (oneself) on an elevated spot. [var. of PERCH²]

perk³, *n.* a benefit enjoyed by an employee over and above his or her salary. [from PERQUISITE]

perlaceous, *a.* like pearl, pearly, nacreous.

perlite, *n.* a glassy igneous rock characterized by spheroidal cracks formed by contractile tension in cooling, pearlstone. **perlitic,** *a.* [F *perlite* (*perle*)]

perlustration, *n.* the act of inspecting thoroughly or viewing all over. [from L *perlustrāre* (*lustrāre,* to traverse, to inspect)]

Perm, *n.* industrial city (shipbuilding, oil refining, aircraft, chemicals, sawmills), capital of Perm region, USSR, on the Kama near the Ural mountains; population (1987) 1,075,000. It was called Molotov 1940–57.

perm¹, *n.* a hairstyle in which hair is shaped and then set by chemicals, heat etc. *v.t.* to put a perm in (hair). [short for *permanent wave*]

perm², *n.* a forecast of a number of football match results selected from a larger number of matches. [short for *permutation*]

permafrost, *n.* a layer of permanently frozen earth in very cold regions. [*perma*nent *frost*]

permalloy, *n.* an alloy with high magnetic permeability.

permanent, *a.* lasting, remaining or intended to remain in the same state, place or condition. **permanent press,** *n., a.* (fabric) subjected to treatment with chemicals or heat to give resistance to creasing and often to impart permanent creases or pleats. **permanent wave** PERM¹. **permanent way,** *n.* the finished roadbed of a railway. **permanence, -ency,** *n.* **permanently,** *adv.* [F, from L *permanentem,* nom. *-nens,* pres.p. of *permanēre* (*manēre,* to remain)]

permanganate, *n.* a salt of permanganic acid. **permanganic,** *a.* of or containing manganese in its highest valency.

permeate, *v.t.* to pass through the pores or interstices of; to penetrate and pass through; to pervade, to saturate. *v.i.* to be diffused (in, through etc.). **permeability,** *n.* being permeable; the degree to which a magnetizable medium affects the magnetic field surrounding it. **permeable,** *a.* yielding passage to fluids; penetrable. **permeably,** *adv.* **permeance, permeation,** *n.* **permeant,** *a.* **permeative,** *a.* [L *permeātus,* p.p. of *permeāre* (*meāre,* to run, to pass)]

Permian, *n., a.* (applied to) the period of geological time 286–248 million years ago, the last period of the Palaeozoic era, or the uppermost strata of the Palaeozoic series of rocks, consisting chiefly of red sandstone and magnesian limestone. The end of the Permian was marked by a significant change in marine life, including the extinction of many corals and trilobites. Deserts were widespread, and terrestrial amphibians and mammal-like reptiles flourished. Cone-bearing plants (gymnosperms) came to prominence. [*Perm,* USSR]

†**permiscible,** *a.* capable of being mixed. [L *permiscēre* (*miscēre,* to MIX)]

permit¹, *v.t.* (*past, p.p.* **permitted**) to allow by consent, to suffer; to give permission to or for, to authorize; †to resign, to leave. *v.i.* to allow, to admit (of). **permissible,** *a.* **permissibly,** *adv.* **permission,** *n.* the act of permitting; leave or licence given. **permissive,** *a.* permitting, allowing; granting liberty, leave or permission; not hindering or forbidding; allowing great licence in social and sexual conduct. **permissively,** *adv.* **permissiveness,** *n.* †**permittance,** *n.* **permitter,** *n.* **permittivity,** *n.* a measure of a substance's ability to store potential energy in an electric field. [L *permittere* (*mittere,* to send, p.p. *missus*)]

permit², *n.* an order to permit, a permission or warrant, esp. a written authority to land or remove dutiable goods.

permutation, *n.* (*Math.*) change of the order of a series of quantities; each of the different arrangements, as regards order, that can be made in this; alteration, transmutation; PERM²; †exchange of one thing for another, exchange, barter. **permutant,** *n.* (*Math.*) [ME and OF *permutacion,* L *permūtātiōnem,* nom. *-tio,* as foll.]

permute, *v.t.* to change thoroughly; (*Math.*) to subject to permutation; †to interchange, to barter. **permutable,** *a.* interchangeable. **permutableness,** *n.* **permutably,** *adv.* [L *permūtāre* (*mūtāre,* to change)]

pern, *n.* a bird of the genus *Pernis,* a honey-buzzard. [mod. L *pernis,* erron. from Gr. *pternis*]

pernicious, *a.* destructive, ruinous, deadly, noxious, hurtful; †malicious, wicked. **pernicious anaemia,** *n.* a very severe, sometimes fatal, form of anaemia. **perniciously,** *adv.* **perniciousness,** *n.* [F *pernicieux,* L *perniciōsus,* from *pernicies,* destruction (*nex necis,* death)]

pernickety, (*esp. N Am.*) **persnickety,** *a.* (*coll.*) fastidious, fussy, over-particular, awkward to handle, ticklish. [etym. doubtful]

pernoctation, *n.* a remaining out or watching all night. [L *pernoctātio,* from *pernoctāre* (*nox noctis,* night)]

Perón¹, *n.* **(María Estela) Isabel** (born Martínez) (1931–), president of Argentina 1974–76, and third wife of Juan Perón. She succeeded him after he died in office, but labour unrest, inflation, and political violence pushed the country to the brink of chaos. Accused of corruption, she was held under house arrest for five years. She went into exile in Spain.

Perón², *n.* **(Maria) Eva** ('Evita') (born Duarte) (1919–52), Argentinian populist leader, born in Buenos Aires. A successful radio actress, in 1945 she married Juan Perón. After he became president she virtually ran the health and labour ministries, and did a lot of charitable work. In 1951 she stood for the post of vice president, but was opposed by the army and withdrew; she died of cancer soon afterwards.

Perón³, *n.* **Juan (Domingo)** (1895–1974), Argentine politician, dictator 1946–55 and from 1973 until his death. He took part in the military coup of 1943, and his popularity with the *descamisados* ('shirtless ones') led to his election as president in 1946. He instituted social reforms, but encountered economic difficulties. After the death of his second wife Eva Perón he lost popularity, and was deposed in a military coup in 1955. He returned from exile to the presidency in 1973, but died in office in 1974, and was was succeeded by his third wife Isabel Perón.

perone, *n.* the fibula or small bone of the leg. **peroneal,** *a.* **peroneo-,** *comb. form.* [Gr. *peronē,* pin, the fibula]

perorate, *v.i.* to deliver an oration; (*coll.*) to speechify. *v.t.* to declaim. **peroration,** *n.* (the concluding part or winding up of) an oration. [L *perōrātus,* p.p. of *perōrāre* (*ōrāre,* to speak)]

Perotin, the Great (*c.* 1160–*c.* 1220), French composer. His church music has a timeless quality and introduced new concepts of harmony and part-writing to traditional organum.

peroxide, *n.* the oxide of a given base that contains the greatest quantity of oxygen; peroxide of hydrogen. *v.t.* (*coll.*) to bleach (hair) with peroxide of hydrogen. **peroxide of hydrogen,** a bleaching compound, used mainly for lightening the hair and as an antiseptic. **peroxidation,** *n.* **peroxidize, -ise,** *v.t., v.i.*

perp., (*abbr.*) perpendicular (style).

perpend, *v.t.* to consider carefully. *v.i.* to take thought. [L *perpendere* (*pendere,* to weigh)]

perpendicular, *a.* at right angles to the plane of the horizon; perfectly upright or vertical; of a hill, road etc., nearly vertical, extremely steep; at right angles to a given line or surface. *n.* a perpendicular line; perpendicular attitude or condition; a plumb-rule, plumb-level or other instrument for determining the vertical; (*dated sl.*) a meal or entertainment at which the guests stand; a period or style of English Gothic architecture lasting from the end of the 14th cent. to the mid-16th cent., characterized by window tracery consisting chiefly of vertical members, two or four arc arches, lavishly decorated vaults and use of traceried panels. Examples include the choir and cloister of Gloucester Cathedral, and King's College Chapel, Cambridge. **perpendicularity,** *n.* **perpendicularly,** *adv.* [ME and OF *perpendiculer,* L *perpendiculāris,* from *perpendiculum,* plummet, as prec.]

perpetrate, *v.t.* to perform, to commit; to be guilty of. **perpetrable,** *a.* **perpetration,** *n.* **perpetrator,** *n.* [L *perpetrātus,* p.p. of *perpetrāre* (*patrāre,* to effect)]

perpetual, *a.* unending, eternal; always continuing, persistent, continual, constant; of a plant, blooming continually throughout the season. **perpetual calendar,** *n.* a calendar adjustable to any year. **perpetual curate,** *n.* (*formerly*) a clergyman in charge of an ecclesiastical district forming part of an ancient parish (perpetual curates are now called vicars). **perpetually,**

adv. **perpetuity**, *n.* the number of years' purchase to be given for an annuity; a perpetual annuity. **for, in perpetuity,** for ever. [F *perpétuel,* L *perpetuālis,* from *perpetuus* (*pet-,* rel. to *petere,* to seek)]

perpetuate, *v.t.* to make perpetual; to preserve from extinction or oblivion. **perpetuable,** *a.* **perpetuance, perpetuation**, *n.* **perpetuator,** *n.*

perplex, *v.t.* to puzzle, to bewilder, to embarrass, to make anxious; to complicate, confuse or involve; to make difficult to understand or to unravel; to entangle. **perplexedly**, *adv.* **perplexedness**, *n.* **perplexing,** *a.* **perplexity,** *n.* †**perplexly,** *adv.* [from obs. *perplex,* perplexed, confused, L *perplexus,* p.p. of *perplectere* (*plectere,* to plait)]

per pro, (*abbr.*) on behalf of. [L *per procurationem*]

perquisite, *n.* gain, profit or emolument, over and above regular wages or salary; anything to which a servant etc. has a prescriptive right after it has served its purpose; (*coll.*) a gratuity, a tip; (*Law*) profit accruing to a lord of a manor over and above the ordinary revenue. [L *perquīsītum,* neut. p.p. of *perquīrere* (*quaerere,* to seek)]

†**perquisition,** *n.* a thorough search or enquiry. [F, from L *perquīsītio,* as prec.]

perradial, *a.* pertaining to or constituting a primary ray (in Hydrozoa etc.). **perradiate,** *v.t.* to radiate through. **perradius**, *n.* (*pl.* **-dii**) a perradial ray or primary ray (in certain coelenterates).

Perrault, *n.* **Charles** (1628–1703), French author of the fairy tales *Contes de ma mère l'oye/ Mother Goose's Fairy Tales* (1697), including 'Sleeping Beauty', 'Red Riding Hood', 'Blue Beard', 'Puss in Boots', and 'Cinderella'.

Perrin, *n.* **Jean** (1870–1942), French physicist who produced the crucial evidence that finally established the atomic nature of matter. Assuming the atomic hypothesis, Perrin demonstrated how the phenomenon of Brownian movement could be used to derive precise values of Avogadro's number. He won the 1926 Nobel physics prize.

perron, *n.* a platform with steps in front of a large building. [F, from It. *petrone,* L *petra,* stone]

perruque, etc. PERUKE.

perry, *n.* a fermented liquor made from the juice of pears. [OF *peré,* from *peire* (F *poire*), PEAR]

Perry, *n.* **Matthew Calbraith** (1794–1858), US naval officer, commander of the expedition of 1853 that reopened communication between Japan and the outside world after 250 years' isolation. Evident military superiority enabled him to negotiate the Treaty of Kanagawa 1854 giving the US trading rights with Japan.

†**perscrutation,** *n.* a minute scrutiny. [MF, from L *perscrūtātiōnem,* nom. *-tio,* from *perscrūtāre* (*scrūtāre,* to search closely)]

†**perse,** *a.* bluish-grey. *n.* a bluish-grey colour; a kind of cloth of this colour. [OF *pers, perse,* late L *persus,* etym. doubtful]

per se, *adv.* by itself, in itself. [L]

persecute, *v.t.* to pursue in a hostile, envious or malicious way; to afflict with suffering or loss of life or property, esp. for adherence to a particular opinion or creed; to harass, to worry, to importune. **persecution,** *n.* **persecution complex,** *n.* an irrational conviction that others are conspiring against one. †**persecutive, -cutory,** *a.* **persecutor,** *n.* **persecutrix,** *n. fem.* [F *persécuter,* L *persecūtus,* p.p. of *persequī* (*sequī,* to follow)]

Perseid PERSEUS.

Persephone, *n.* Greek goddess, the daughter of Zeus and Demeter. She was carried off to the underworld by Pluto, who later agreed that she should spend six months of the year with her mother. The myth symbolizes the growth and decay of vegetation.

Persepolis, *n.* ancient capital of the Persian Empire, 65 km/40 miles NE of Shiraz. It was burned down after its capture in 331 BC by Alexander the Great.

Perseus, *n.* in Greek mythology, son of Zeus and Danaë. He slew Medusa, the Gorgon; rescued Andromeda; and became king of Tiryns; a constellation of the northern hemisphere, near Cassiopeia. **Perseid,** *n.* one of a group of meteors appearing about 12 Aug. having their radiating point in this constellation.

persevere, *v.i.* to persist in or with any undertaking, design or course. **perseverance,** *n.* persistence in any design or undertaking; sedulous endeavour; (*Theol.*) continuance in a state of grace. **perseverant,** *a.* persevering. **perseveringly,** *adv.* [F *persévérer,* L *persevērāre* (*sevērus,* SEVERE)]

Persia, ancient, *n.* kingdom in SW Asia. The early Persians were a nomadic Aryan people that migrated through the Caucasus to the Iranian plateau.

Persian, *a.* pertaining to Persia, now Iran, its inhabitants or language. *n.* a native of Persia; the Persian language; a Persian cat; a kind of thin silk; (*Arch.*) a figure in Persian dress forming a pillar or pilaster supporting an entablature etc. **Persian insect powder,** a preparation from the flowers of *Pyrethrum roseum* used as an insecticide. †**Persian apple,** *n.* the peach. **Persian blind** PERSIENNE. **Persian carpet,** *n.* a carpet made of knotted twine etc., finely decorated, from Persia. **Persian cat,** *n.* a variety of cat with long silky hair. **Persian Gulf,** *n.* a large shallow inlet of the Arabian Sea; area 233,000 sq km/90,000 sq miles, dividing the Arabian peninsula from Iran, and linked by the Strait of Hormuz and the Gulf of Oman to the Arabian Sea. **Persian morocco,** *n.* a variety of morocco leather made from the skin of a hairy sheep called the Persian goat. **Persian Wars,** *n.pl.* a series of conflicts between the Greeks and the Persians 499–449 BC. The eventual victory of Greece marked the end of Persian domination of the ancient world and the beginning of Greek supremacy. **Persian wheel,** *n.* a wheel with buckets on the rim used for raising water, a noria.

persicaria, *n.* a weed, *Polygonum persicaria,* also called peachwort. [med. L, from L *persicum,* peach, neut. of *Persicus,* Persian]

persicot, *n.* a cordial made from peaches, nectarines etc. macerated in spirit and flavoured with their kernels. [F *persico* (now *persicot*), It. *persico,* L *persicum,* PEACH[1]]

persienne, *n.* an Oriental cambric or muslin; (*pl.*) window blinds or shutters like Venetian blinds. [F, Persian]

persiflage, *n.* banter, raillery; frivolous treatment of any subject. **persifleur,** *n.* [F, from *persiffler,* to jeer (*siffler,* L *sībilāre,* to whistle, to hiss)]

persimmon, *n.* the plum-like fruit of *Diospyros virginiana,* the American date-plum. [corr. of Algonquian name]

persist, *v.i.* to continue steadfast in the pursuit of any design; to remain, to continue, to endure. **persistence, -ency,** *n.* **persistence of vision,** the ability of the eye to retain perception for a brief period after the stimulus has been removed, as in the illusion of a continuous picture formed from the number of still pictures in a cinematograph film. **persistent,** *a.* persisting, persevering; lasting, enduring; of leaves etc., not falling off; of a chemical, slow to break down. **persistently, persistingly,** *adv.* †**persistive,** *a.* [F *persister,* L *persistere* (*sistere,* causal of *stāre,* to stand)]

persnickety PERNICKETY.

person, *n.* a human being, an individual; a being possessed of personality; a human being as distinguished from one of the lower animals or an inanimate object; the living body of a human being; a human being or body corporate having legal rights and duties; one of the three individualities in the Godhead, Father, Son or Holy Spirit; one of the three relations of the subject or object of a verb, as speaking, spoken to or spoken of; an individual in a compound organism or a hydrozoan colony; the penis; †a part or character (on the stage); †a parson; a personage. **in person,** by oneself; not by deputy. **personable,** *a.* handsome, pleasing, attractive. **personableness,** *n.* **personage,** *n.* a person of rank, distinction or importance; a person; a character in a play, story etc.; †external appearance. **personal,** *a.* pertaining to a person as distinct from a thing; relating to or affecting an indivual; individual, private; of criticism etc. reflecting on an individual, esp. disparaging, hostile; hence, making or prone to make such remarks; relating to the physical person, bodily, corporeal; transacted or done in person; (*Law*) appertaining to the person (applied to all property except land or heritable interests in land); (*Gram.*) denoting or indicating one of the three persons. *n.* (*Law*) a movable article of property, a chattel. **personal equity plan,** a scheme under which individuals may invest a fixed sum each year in UK shares without paying tax on capital gains or dividend income. **personal column,** *n.* a newspaper column in the classified advertisement section containing personal messages, requests for donations to charity etc. **personal computer,** *n.* a small computer designed for business or home use, e.g. for keeping records, word processing etc. **personal effects,** *n.pl.* articles of property intimately related to the owner. **personal equation** EQUATION. **personal estate, property,** *n.* personalty, as distinguished from real property. **personal organizer,** *n.* a portable personal filing system, usu. in the form of a small loose-leafed book, containing details of appointments telephone numbers, memoranda etc.; **personal pronoun,** *n.* a pronoun, e.g. *I, you, we* etc., used to refer to a person or thing. **personal stereo,** *n.* a very small, portable stereo set with headphones, designed to be attached to a belt or held in the hand. **personality,** *n.* the quality or state of being a person; individual existence or identity; the sum of qualities and characteristics that constitute individuality; a distinctive personal character; an important or famous person, a celebrity; personal application (of remarks etc.); (*pl.*) disparaging personal remarks; †(*Law*) personalty. **multiple personality,** (*Psych.*) the existence of more than one personality in one individual. **personality cult,** *n.* the excessive adulation and boosting of political leaders. **personality disorder,** *n.* any of various psychological disorders marked by a tendency to do harm to oneself or others. **personalize, -ise,** *v.t.* to make personal; to cater for the needs of a particular person; to take as referring to a particular person; to mark (something) so that it is identifiable as belonging to a particular person; to inscribe with a person's name, initials etc.; to personify. **personalization, -isation,** *n.* **personally,** *adv.* in person; particularly, individually; as regards oneself. [ME and OF *persone,* L *persōna,* a mask, a character, a personage, perh. rel. to *personāre* (*sonāre,* to sound)]

persona, *n.* (*pl.* **-nae**) (*often pl.*) a character in a play, novel etc.; (*pl. also* **-nas**) a person's social façade. **persona non grata,** an unacceptable person, esp. in diplomatic parlance. **persona grata,** *n.* acceptable person. [L]

personalty, *n.* personal estate, movable property as distinguished from real property.

personate, *v.t.* to assume the character or to act the part of; to impersonate, esp. for the purpose of voting without being entitled to do so, or for any other fraudulent purpose; †to counterfeit, to feign; †to represent, to describe; †to typify, to symbolize. *a.*, masklike (applied to a two-lipped corolla in which the mouth is closed by an upward projection of the lower part, as in the snapdragon). **personation,** *n.* **personator,** *n.* [L *personātus,* p.p. of *personāre,* from *persōna,* mask, see PERSON]

personify, *v.t.* to regard or represent (an abstraction) as possessing the attributes of a living being; to symbolize by a human figure; to embody, to exemplify, to typify, in one's own person. **personification,** *n.* [F *personnifier* (PERSON, -FY)]

personnel, *n.* the body of persons engaged in some service, esp. a public institution, military or naval enterprise etc.; the staff of a business firm etc.; the department of a business firm etc. that deals with the welfare, appointment and records of personnel. [F, orig. personal]

perspective, *n.* the art of representing solid objects on a plane exactly as regards position, shape and dimensions, as the objects themselves appear to the eye at a particular point; the apparent relation of visible objects as regards position and distance; a representation of objects in perspective; the relation of facts or other matters as viewed by the mind; a view, a vista, a prospect; a point of view from which something is considered. *a.* of or pertaining to perspective; in perspective; †optical. **in perspective,** according to the laws of perspective; in due proportion. **perspectively,** *adv.* **perspectograph,** *n.* an instrument for mechanically drawing objects in perspective. **perspectography,** *n.* [F, from med. L *perspectīva* (*ars*), perspective (art), from L *perspectus,* p.p. of *perspicere* (*specere,* to look)]

Perspex®, *n.* a transparent plastic, very tough and of great clarity, widely used for watch glasses, advertising signs, domestic baths, motorboat windshields and protective shields.

perspicacious, *a.* quick-sighted; mentally penetrating or discerning. **perspicaciously,** *adv.* **perspicacity, perspicaciousness,** *n.* [L *perspicax -cācis* (*specere,* to see)]

perspicuous, *a.* free from obscurity or ambiguity, clearly expressed, lucid. **perspicuity, perspicuousness,** *n.* **perspicuously,** *adv.* [L *perspicuus,* as prec.]

perspire, *v.i.* to sweat. *v.t.* to give out (the excretions of the body) through the pores of the skin, to sweat; †to breathe or blow gently through. **perspirable,** *a.* that may be perspired or excreted by perspiration; liable to perspire. †**perspirability,** *n.* **perspiration,** *n.* **perspiratory,** *a.* [L *perspīrāre* (*spīrāre,* to breathe)]

perstringe, *v.t.* to criticize; †to touch upon. **perstriction,** *n.* †**perstrictive,** *a.* [L *perstringere* (*stringere,* to tie, to bind, p.p. *strictus*)]

persuade, *v.t.* to influence or convince by argument, advice, entreaty, or expostulation; to induce; to try to influence, to advise; †to recommend. **persuadable** PERSUASIBLE. **persuader,** *n.* one who or that which persuades; (*sl.*) a pistol, a firearm, a weapon, a burglar's tool. **persuasible,** *a.* capable of being persuaded. **persuasibility,** †**-ibleness,** *n.* **persuasion,** *n.* the act of persuading; power to persuade, persuasiveness; the state of being persuaded, a settled conviction; creed, belief, esp. in religious matters; a religious sect or denomination; (*coll.*) a sort, a kind. **persuasive,** *a.* able or tending to persuade; winning. *n.* that which persuades, a motive, an inducement. **persuasively,** *adv.* **persuasiveness,** *n.* †**persuasory,** *a.* persuasive. [F *persuader,* L *persuādēre* (*suādēre,* to advise)]

persue[1], *n.* the track of a wounded deer etc. [prob. from F *percée,* piercing, n. of action from *percer,* to pierce, conf. with PURSUE]

†**persue**[2] PURSUIT.

persulphate, *n.* a sulphate containing the greatest relative quantity of acid.

pert, *a.* sprightly, lively; saucy, forward; †open, evident, plain. **pertly,** *adv.* **pertness,** *n.* [corr. of obs. *apert,* OF from L *apertus* (p.p. of *aperīre,* to open), confused with *expertus,* EXPERT]

pertain, *v.i.* to belong (to) as attribute, appendage, part etc.; to relate, to apply, to have reference (to). [OF *partenir,* L *pertinēre* (*tenēre,* to hold)]

Perth, *n.* capital of Western Australia, with its port at nearby Fremantle on the Swan river; population (1986) 1,025,300. Products include textiles, cement, furniture, and vehicles. It was founded 1829, and is the commercial and cultural centre of the state.

Perthshire, *n.* former inland county of central Scotland, of which the major part was included in Tayside 1975, the SW being included in Central region; Perth was the administrative headquarters.

pertinacious, *a.* obstinate; stubborn, persistent; †incessant, constant. **pertinaciously,** *adv.* **pertinaciousness, pertinacity,** *n.* [L *pertinax -ācis* (*tenax,* TENACIOUS)]

pertinent, *a.* related to the matter in hand; relevant, apposite; fit, suitable. *n.pl.* (*Sc.*) belongings, appurtenances. **pertinence, -ency,** *n.* **pertinently,** *adv.* [F, from L *pertinentem,* nom. *-ens,* pres.p. of *pertinēre,* to PERTAIN]

perturb, *v.t.* to disturb; to disquiet, to agitate; to throw into confusion or physical disorder; to cause (a planet, electron etc.) to deviate from a regular path. **perturbate,** *v.t.* to perturb. **perturbation, perturbment,** *n.* [L *perturbāre* (*turbāre,* to disturb, from *turba,* crowd)]

pertuse, -tused, *a.* esp. of leaves, punched, pierced with holes). †**pertusion,** *n.* [L *pertūsus,* p.p. of *pertundere* (*tundere,* to beat)]

pertussis, *n.* whooping-cough. **pertussal,** *a.*

Peru, *n.* Republic of (*República del Perú*) country in S America, on the Pacific, bounded to the N by Ecuador and Colombia, to the E by Brazil and Bolivia, and to the S by Chile. **area** 1,285,200 sq km/496,216 sq miles. **capital** Lima, including port of Callao. **towns** Arequipa, Iquitos, Chiclayo. **physical** Andes mountains N–S cover 27%; Amazon river-basin jungle in NE. **exports** coffee, alpaca, llama and vicuna wool, fish meal, lead, copper, iron, oil. **population** (1989) 21,792,000 (46% American Indian, mainly Quechua and Aymara; 43% of mixed Spanish-American Indian descent); annual growth rate 2.6%. **language** Spanish 68%, Quechua 27% (both official), Aymará 3%. **religion** Roman Catholic.

Peru Current, *n.* (formerly **Humboldt Current**) a cold ocean current flowing north from the Antarctic along the W coast of South America to S Ecuador, then west.

Perugino, *n.* **Pietro** (assumed name of Pietro Vannucci) (*c.* 1445–1523), Italian painter, active chiefly in Perugia, the teacher of Raphael, who absorbed his soft and graceful figure style. Perugino produced paintings for the lower walls of the Sistine Chapel (1481), and in 1500 decorated the Sala del Cambio in Perugia.

peruke, *n.* a wig, a periwig. [F *perruque,* It. *parrucca* (cp. Sardinian *pilucca*), prob. ult. from L *pilus,* hair]

peruse, *v.t.* to read with attention; to read; to observe or examine carefully. **perusal,** *n.* **peruser,** *n.* [USE (earlier, to use up)]

Perutz, *n.* **Max** (1914–), British biochemist, who shared the Nobel chemistry prize in 1962 with John Kendrew for work on the structure of the haemoglobin molecule.

Peruvian, *a.* pertaining to Peru. *n.* a native of Peru. **Peruvian balsam,** *n.* balsam obtained from *Myroxylon pereirae.* **Peruvian bark,** *n.* the bark of several species of cinchona, used as a tonic in debility and intermittent fevers. **peruvin,** *n.* an alcohol distilled from Peruvian balsam.

pervade, *v.t.* to pass through; to permeate, to saturate; to be diffused throughout. **pervasion,** *n.* **pervasive,** *a.* **pervasively,** *adv.* **pervasiveness,** *n.* [L *pervādere* (*vādere,* to go)]

perverse, *a.* wilfully or obstinately wrong; turned against what is reasonable or fitting; unreasonable, perverted, intractable; petulant, peevish; †unlucky, unpropitious. **perversely,** *adv.* **perverseness, perversity,** *n.* [F *pervers,* L *perversus,* p.p. of *pervertere,* see PERVERT[1]]

perversion, *n.* the act of perverting; a misinterpretation, misapplication or corruption; the act of forsaking one's religion; abnormal sexual proclivity.

pervert[1], *v.t.* to turn aside from the proper use; to put to improper use; to misapply, to misinterpret; to lead astray, to mislead, to corrupt. **perversive,** *a.* **perverted,** *a.* marked by (esp. sexual) perversion. **perverter,** *n.* **pervertible,** *a.* [F *pervertir,* L *pervertere* (*vertere,* to turn)]

pervert[2], *n.* one who has been perverted, esp. one who has forsaken his or her religion; a person with abnormal sexual proclivities.

†**perveyaunce** PURVEYANCE.

pervicacious, *a.* very obstinate, wilfully perverse. †**pervicaciousness,** †**pervicacity,** *n.* [L *pervicax -cācis,* -OUS]

pervious, *a.* allowing passage (to); permeable; intelligible; accessible (to facts, ideas etc.); †pervasive. **perviousness,** *n.* [L *pervius* (*via,* way)]

Pesach, *n.* the Jewish festival of Passover.

pesade, *n.* the motion of a horse when raising the forequarters without advancing. [F, earlier *posade,* It. *posata,* from *posare,* to PAUSE]

peseta, *n.* the monetary unit in Spain. [Sp., dim. of *pesa,* weight, cp. POISE]

pesewa, *n.* a Ghanaian unit of currency, 100th of a cedi. [native name]

Peshawar, *n.* capital of North-West Frontier Province, Pakistan, 18 km/11 miles E of the Khyber Pass; population (1981) 555,000. Products include textiles, leather, and copper.

Peshito, *n.* the Syriac version of the Holy Scriptures. [Syriac *p'shītâ, p'shītô,* the simple orphan]

peshwa, *n.* the hereditary ruler of the Mahrattas; earlier, the chief minister. [Pers., chief]

pesky, *a.* (*coll.*) annoying; plaguy, troublesome. *adv.* peskily. **peskily,** *adv.* [etym. doubtful, perh. from PEST]

peso, *n.* (*pl.* **-sos**) a silver coin worth 5 pesetas, used in the S American republics, known as the Spanish dollar. [Sp., weight, L *pensus,* p.p. of *pendere,* to weigh]

pessary, *n.* a device introduced into the vagina to prevent or remedy prolapse of the uterus or as a contraceptive; a medicated plug or suppository introduced into the vagina. [med. L *pessārium,* from L *pessum,* Gr. *pessos,* an oval pebble used in games]

pessimism, *n.* the habit of taking a gloomy and despondent view of things; the doctrine that pain and evil predominate enormously over good, or that there is a predominant tendency towards evil throughout the universe. **pessimist,** *n., a.* **pessimistic,** *a.* **pessimistically,** *adv.* [L *pessimus,* worst, superl. of *malus,* bad]

pest, *n.* one who or that which is extremely destructive, hurtful or annoying; any plant or animal that harms crops, livestock or humans; †plague, pestilence. **pesthouse,** *n.* a hospital for contagious diseases. **pesticide,** *n.* a chemical used to kill pests that damage crops etc. **pestology,** *n.* the study of pests, esp. insects, and methods of dealing with them. [F *peste,* L *pestem,* nom. *-tis,* plague]

pester, *v.t.* to bother, to worry, to annoy; †to overload, to cram. **pesterer,** *n.* [prob. short for earlier *empester,* F *empestrer* (now *empêtrer*)]

pesticide PEST.

pestiferous, *a.* pestilential; hurtful or noxious in any way; bearing social or moral contagion. **pestiferously,** *adv.* [L *pestifer*]

pestilence, *n.* any contagious disease that is epidemic and deadly, esp. bubonic plague, formerly called the Black Death. **pestilent,** *a.* noxious to health or life, deadly; fatal to morality or society; vexatious, troublesome, mischievous. **pestilential,** *a.* **pestilentially, pestilently,** *adv.* [F, from L *pestilentia,* from *pestis,* PEST]

pestle, *n.* an implement used in pounding substances in a mortar; any appliance used for pounding or crushing things. *v.t.* to pound or pulverize with a pestle. *v.i.* to use a pestle. [ME and OF *pestel,* L *pistillum,* from *pinsere,* to pound, p.p. *pistus*]

pestology PEST.

pet[1], *n.* an animal brought up by hand or kept in the house as a favourite; a fondling, a darling, a favourite. *a.* petted, indulged, favourite. *v.t.* (*past, p.p.* **petted**) to make a pet of; to fondle; to pamper. *v.i.* to engage in amorous fondling. **pet aversion, hate,** *n.* a thing especially disliked. [etym. doubtful]

pet[2], *n.* a fit of peevishness or ill temper. **pettish,** *a.* peevish, fretful; inclined to ill-temper. **pettishly,** *adv.* **pettishness,** *n.* [etym. doubtful]

Pétain, *n.* **Henri Philippe** (1856–1951), French general and right-wing politician. His defence of Verdun (1916) during World War I made him a national hero. In World War II he became prime minister (June 1940) and signed an armistice with Germany. Removing the seat of government to Vichy, he established an authoritarian regime. He was imprisoned after the war.

petal, *n.* one of the divisions of a corolla of a flower, consisting of several pieces. **petal-shaped,** *a.* **petaline**, †**petaliform**, *a.* **petalled,** *a.* (*usu. in comb.*, as *fine-petalled*). **petaloid,** *a.* **petalous,** *a.* having petals. [Gr. *petalon,* a thin plate or leaf (of metal etc.)]

petalite, *n.* a vitreous silicate of lithium and aluminium.

petalon, *n.* a leaf of gold worn on the linen mitre of the Jewish High Priest.

pétanque, *n.* a Provençal word for the French game of boules.

petard, *n.* a conical case or box of iron etc., formerly used for blowing open gates or barriers; a firework in the form of a bomb or cracker. **hoist with one's own petard,** caught in one's own trap. [F *pétard,* from *péter,* L *pēdere,* to break wind]

petasus, *n.* a broad-brimmed low-crowned hat worn by the ancient Greeks; the winged cap of Hermes or Mercury. [L, from Gr. *petasos*]

petechiae, *n.pl.* spots on the skin formed by extravasated blood etc., in malignant fevers etc. **petechial, petechoid**, *a.* [mod. L, from It. *petecchia,* etym. doubtful]

peter, *v.i.* of a lode or vein in mining, to thin or give (out); to come to an end, to die (out). [sl., etym. unknown]

Peter¹, *n.* †a kind of cosmetic; (*sl.*) a portmanteau, a cloak-bag. **blue Peter** BLUE. **Peter Pan collar,** a collar on a round-necked garment having two rounded ends meeting at the front. **to rob Peter to pay Paul,** to take away from one person in order to give to another; to pay off one debt by incurring a new one. **Peterman,** *n.* a fisherman; (*sl.*) a thief who steals peters or portmanteaus; (*sl.*) a safe-cracker. **Peter-penny, Peter's penny,** *n.* (*pl.* **(-)pence**) an annual tax of a penny from each householder formerly paid to the pope; (since 1860) voluntary contributions to the pope from Roman Catholics. **Peter's fish,** *n.* the haddock (from marks supposed to have been made by St Peter's thumb). [L, from Gr. *Petros,* a masculine name, orig. a stone]

Peter², *n.* three czars of Russia:

Peter I, *n.* **the Great** (1672–1725), czar of Russia from 1682 on the death of his brother Czar Feodor, he assumed control of the government 1689. He attempted to reorganize the country on Western lines; the army was modernized, a fleet was built, the administrative and legal systems were remodelled, education was encouraged, and the church was brought under state control. On the Baltic coast, where he had conquered territory from Sweden, Peter built his new capital, St Petersburg (now Leningrad).

Peter II, *n.* (1715–30), czar of Russia from 1727. Son of Peter the Great, he had been passed over in favour of Catherine I 1725, but succeeded her 1727. He died of smallpox.

Peter III, *n.* (1728–62), czar of Russia 1762. Weak-minded son of Peter I's eldest daughter, Anne, he was adopted 1741 by his aunt Elizabeth and at her command married the future Catherine II in 1745. He was deposed in favour of his wife, and probably murdered by her lover Alexius Orlov.

Peter Lombard, *n.* (1100–60), Italian Christian theologian whose *Sententiarum libri quatuor* considerably influenced Roman Catholic doctrine.

Peterloo massacre, *n.* name given, in analogy with the Battle of Waterloo, to the events in St Peter's Fields, Manchester, England, 16 Aug. 1819, when an open-air meeting in support of parliamentary reform was charged by yeomanry and hussars. Eleven people were killed and 500 wounded.

petersham, *n.* a heavy overcoat, also shooting or riding breeches; a heavy woollen cloth used for these; a thick corded-silk ribbon used for belts, hatbands etc. [Viscount *Petersham,* one of the 'dandies', died 1851]

Peter, St, *n.* (d. AD 64), Christian martyr, the author of two epistles in the New Testament and leader of the apostles. Tradition has it that he later settled in Rome; he is regarded as the first bishop of Rome, whose mantle the pope inherits. His emblem is two keys; feast day 29 June.

Peter the Hermit, (1050–1115), French priest whose eloquent preaching of the First Crusade sent thousands of peasants marching against the Turks, who massacred them in Asia Minor. Peter escaped and accompanied the main body of crusaders to Jerusalem.

pethidine, *n.* a synthetic analgesic drug with sedative effects similar to but less powerful than morphine. [perh. from *piperidine, ethyl*]

pething-pole, *n.* (*Austral.*) a sharp-pointed spear for killing cattle by piercing the spinal cord.

pétillant, *a.* of wine, slightly sparkling. [F *pétiller,* to effervesce]

petiole, *n.* the leaf-stalk of a plant; a small stalk. **petiolar, -late, -lated,** *a.* **petiolule,** *n.* a small petiole. [F *pétiole,* L *petiolus,* perh. dim. of *pes pedis,* foot]

petit, *a.* (*fem.* **-tite**) small, petty; inconsiderable, inferior. **petit bourgeois**, *n.*, *a.* (a member) of the petite bourgeoisie. **petite bourgeoisie**, *n.* the lower middle class. **petit four** , *n.* (*pl.* **petits fours, petit fours**) a small fancy cake or biscuit. **petit-maître**, *n.* a spruce fellow who affects the society of women; a fop, a coxcomb. **petit mal**, *n.* a mild form of epilepsy. **petit point**, *n.* a kind of fine embroidery. **petits pois**, *n.pl.* small, sweet green peas. [F]

Petit, *n.* **Alexis** (1791–1820), French physicist, co-discoverer of **Dulong and Petit's law**, which states that the specific heat capacity of an element is inversely proportional to its atomic mass.

petite, *a.* of a woman, slight, dainty, graceful. [as prec.]

petition, *n.* an entreaty, a request, a supplication, a prayer; a single article in a prayer; a formal written supplication to persons in authority, esp. to the sovereign, Parliament etc.; the paper containing such supplication; (*Law*) a formal written application to a court, as for a writ of habeas corpus, in bankruptcy etc. *v.t.* to solicit, to ask humbly (for etc.); to address a formal supplication to. **Petition of Right,** the declaration of the rights and liberties of the people made by Parliament to Charles I and assented to in 1628. **petitionary,** *a.* **petitioner,** *n.* **petitory**, *a.* petitioning, begging, supplicating; (*Law*) claiming title or right of ownership. [F *pétition,* L *petitiōnem,* nom. *-tio,* from *petere,* to seek]

Petöfi, *n.* **Sándor** (1823–49), Hungarian nationalist poet. He published his first volume of poems in 1844. He expressed his revolutionary ideas in the semi-autobiographical poem 'The Apostle', and died fighting the Austrians in the battle of Segesvár.

Petra, *n.* (Arabic **Wadi Musa**) ruined city carved out of the red rock at a site in modern Jordan, on the eastern slopes of the Wadi el Araba, 90 km/56 miles S of the Dead Sea. An Edomite stronghold and capital of the Nabataeans in the 2nd cent., it was captured by the Roman emperor Trajan in AD 106 and wrecked by the Arabs in the 7th cent. It was forgotten in Europe until 1812 when the Swiss traveller J.L. Burckhardt came across it.

Petrarch, *n.* (Italian **Petrarca**), **Francesco** (1304–74), Italian poet, born in Arezzo, a devotee of the classical tradition. His *Il Canzoniere* were sonnets in praise of his idealized love 'Laura', whom he first saw in 1327. She was a married woman, who refused to become his mistress and died of plague in 1348.

petre, SALTPETRE.

†**petrean,** *a.* of or pertaining to rock or stone; rocky. [L *petraeus,* Gr. *petraios,* from *petra,* rock]

petrel, *n.* any individual of the genus *Procellaria* or the family Procellariidae, small dusky sea-birds, with long wings and great power of flight. [F *pétrel* (prob. dim. of *Pêtre,* PETER)]

petri- PETR(O)-.

Petri dish, *n.* a shallow, circular, flat-bottomed dish used for cultures of microorganisms. [Julius *Petri,* 1852–1921, German bacteriologist]

Petrie, *n.* **(William Matthew) Flinders** (1853–1942), English archaeologist, who excavated sites in Egypt (the pyramids at Giza, the temple at Tanis, the Greek city of Naucratis in the Nile delta, Tell el Amarna, Naquada, Abydos, and Memphis) and Palestine from

1880. He was a grandson of the explorer Matthew Flinders.

petrify, *v.t.* to convert into stone or stony substance; to stupefy, as with fear, astonishment etc.; to make hard, callous, benumbed or stiffened. *v.i.* to be converted into stone or a stony substance; to become stiffened, benumbed, callous etc. †**petrescent**, *a.* changing into stone; petrifactive. †**petrescence,** *n.* **petrifaction,** *n.* **petrifactive,** †**petrific**, *a.* having the power to petrify. †**petrification**, *n.* petrifaction. [F *pétrifier,* It. *petrificare* (L *petra,* stone, -FY)]

Petrine, *a.* of, relating to or derived from the apostle Peter. **Petrinism**, *n.* the theological doctrine of or attributed to St Peter, esp. as distinguished from Paulinism.

petr(o)-, petri-, *comb. form* stone; petrol. [Gr. *petra,* stone, rock]

petrochemical, *n., a.* (a chemical) obtained from petroleum; relating to such chemicals.

petrocurrency, *n.* the currency of a country which exports significant quantities of petroleum.

petrodollar, *n.* a dollar earned from the exporting of petroleum.

petroglyph, *n.* a rock carving. **petroglyphic**, *a.* **petroglyphy**, *n.* [F *pétroglyphe* (Gr. *gluphē,* carving)]

Petrograd, *n.* name 1914–24 of Leningrad, city in the USSR.

petrograph, *n.* a writing or inscription on rock. **petrography**, *n.* descriptive petrology. **petrographer**, *n.* **petrographic**, **-ical,** *a.*

petrol, *n.* a refined form of petroleum used in motorcars etc.; motive power. *v.t.* to supply (a motor etc.) with petrol. **petrol bomb,** *n.* a bottle or other container full of petrol, used as an incendiary. **petrol-lighter,** *n.* a cigarette-lighter with a petrol-soaked wick. **petrol station,** *n.* a retail outlet for the sale of petrol to motorists. **petrolatum**, *n.* a fatty compound of paraffin hydrocarbons obtained by refining the residue from petroleum after distillation, pure petroleum jelly. [F *pétrole,* med. L PETROLEUM]

petroleum, *n.* an inflammable oily liquid exuding from rocks or pumped from wells, used for lighting, heating and the generation of mechanical power. **petroleum jelly,** *n.* a product of petroleum used in pharmacy as a lubricant. **pétroleur**, *n.* an arsonist who uses petroleum. **pétroleuse**, *n. fem.* **petrolic**, *a.* of or pertaining to petroleum or petrol. **petroliferous**, *a.* **petrolin**, *n.* a solid mixture of hydrocarbons obtained by distilling Rangoon petroleum. [med. L *petroleum* (PETR(O)-, *oleum,* OIL)]

petrology, *n.* the study of the origin, structure and mineralogical and chemical composition of rocks. **petrologic**, **-ical,** *a.* **petrologically,** *adv.* **petrologist,** *n.*

Petronius, *n.* **Gaius,** (known as Petronius Arbiter), Roman author of a licentious romance *Satyricon.* He was a companion of the emperor Nero, and supervisor of his pleasures.

Petropavlovsk-Kamchatskiy, *n.* Pacific seaport and Soviet naval base on the E coast of the Kamchatka peninsula, USSR; population (1987) 252,000.

petrosal, *a.* (*Anat.*) of great hardness, like stone. *n.* the petrosal bone, the petrous portion of the temporal bone. [L *petrōsus,* PETROUS, -AL]

petrosilex, *n.* felsite. **petrosiliceous**, *a.*

petrous, *a.* like stone, stony; applied to the hard part of the temporal bone. [L *petrōsus,* from L and Gr. *petra,* rock]

petitchaps, *n.* the garden warbler, *Sylvia hortensis.* [PETTY, CHAP²]

petticoat, *n.* a loose under-skirt, falling from the waist; one who wears this, a woman, a girl; (*pl.*) skirts; (*fig., pl.*) the female sex. *a.* feminine; (*coll., facet., often derog.*) of or by women. **petticoat-government,** *n.* government by women, esp. in domestic affairs. **petticoat tails,** *n.pl.* (*esp. Sc.*) small cakes of shortbread (with a frilled edge). **petticoated,** *a.* **petticoatless,** *a.* [PETTY, COAT]

pettifog, *v.i.* to do legal business in a mean or tricky way, to practise chicanery; to act in a mean, quibbling or shifty way. **pettifogger,** *n.* a petty, second-rate lawyer, esp. one given to sharp practices; a petty, second-rate or shuffling practitioner in any profession. **pettifoggery,** *n.* **pettifogging,** *n., a.* petty, trivial, quibbling (activity or speech). [PETTY, *-fog* (perh. from *-fogger*), etym. doubtful]

pettily etc. PETTY.

pettish PET².

pettitoes, *n.pl.* the feet of a pig as food, pig's trotters. [etym. doubtful, perh. from F *petite oie,* little goose, giblets]

pettle, *v.t.* to pet, to indulge.

petto, *n.* the breast. **in petto,** in secret, in reserve. [It., from L *pectus*]

petty, *a.* little, trifling, insignificant; minor, inferior, subordinate, on a small scale; small-minded, mean. **petty average** AVERAGE. **petty bag,** *n.* a court formerly attached to the Court of Chancery, dealing with cases involving solicitors and officers of that court. **petty cash,** *n.* minor items of receipt and expenditure. **petty jury,** *n.* a jury in criminal cases who try the bills found by the grand jury. **petty larceny,** *n.* in the US and formerly in the UK, the theft of property worth less than a specified figure. **petty officer,** *n.* a naval officer corresponding in rank to a non-commissioned officer. **petty sessions,** *n.pl.* court of two or more justices of the peace for trying minor offences. **pettily,** *adv.* **pettiness,** *n.* [ME and F *petit,* etym. doubtful]

petulant, *a.* given to fits of ill temper; peevish, irritable; †saucy, forward, capricious. *n.* a petulant person. **petulance, -ancy,** *n.* **petulantly,** *adv.* [F *pétulant,* L *petulantem,* nom. *-lans,* prob. from *petere,* to seek, to aim at, through a dim. form *petulāre*]

petunia, *n.* one of a genus (*Petunia*) of S American plants, allied to the tobacco, cultivated in gardens for their showy funnel-shaped flowers. [mod. L from F *pétun,* Tupí-Guaraní *petў* (pron. *petun*), tobacco]

petuntse, *n.* a fusible substance of feldspathic nature used for the manufacture of porcelain. [Chin. *pai-tun-tzu*]

pew, *n.* a box-like enclosed seat in a church for a family etc.; a long bench with a back, for worshippers in church; (*coll.*) a seat, a chair. *v.t.* to furnish with pews; to enclose in a pew. **to take a pew,** (*coll.*) to sit down. **pew-rent,** *n.* rent paid for a pew or for sittings in a church. **pewage,** *n.* **pewless,** *a.* [ME *puwe,* OF *puie,* a stage or platform, L *podia,* pl. of *podium,* Gr. *podion,* pedestal, from *pous podos,* foot]

pewit, *n.* the lapwing; its cry; the pewit-gull or black-headed gull, *Larus ridibundus.* [imit. of the cry]

pewter, *n.* an alloy usu. of tin and lead, sometimes of tin with other metals; vessels or utensils made of this; a pewter tankard or pot; (*dated sl.*) a prize tankard, prize-money. *a.* made of pewter. **pewterer,** *n.* **pewtery,** *n., a.* [OF *peutre,* It. *peltro,* etym. doubtful]

peyote, *n.* a Mexican intoxicant made from cactus tops. [Nahuàtl *peyotl*]

P.F., (*abbr.*) Procurator Fiscal.

Pfalz, *n.* German name of the historic division of Germany, the Palatinate.

Pfennig, *n.* (*pl.* **-ige**) a small copper coin of Germany, worth the hundredth part of a mark. [G, cogn. with PENNY]

PFLP, (*abbr.*) Popular Front for the Liberation of Palestine.

PG, (*abbr.*) paying guest; parental guidance (used to classify the content of cinema films).

pH, *n.* a measure of the acidity or alkalinity of a solution on a scale from 0 to 14, with 7 representing neutrality, and figures below it denoting acidity, those above it alkalinity. [G *potenz,* power, and *H,* the symbol for hydrogen]

Phaedra, *n.* in Greek mythology, a Cretan, daughter of Minos and Pasiphae, married to Theseus of Athens. Her adulterous passion for her stepson Hippolytus leads to her death in plays by Euripides and Seneca, adapted by Racine.

phaenogam, etc. PHANEROGAM.

phaenomenon, PHENOMENON.

Phaethon, *n.* (*Gr. Myth.*) the son of Helios, who was allowed for one day to drive the chariot of the Sun. Losing control of the horses, he almost set the Earth on fire, and was killed by Zeus with a thunderbolt.

phaeton, *n.* a light four-wheeled open carriage, usu. drawn by two horses. [F *phaéton,* L and Gr. *Phaethōn,* shining, see prec.]

-phage, *comb.form* eater. **-phagia, -phagy**, *comb. form* eating. [PHAG(O)-]

phag(o)-, *comb.form* eating. [Gr. *phagein,* to eat]

phagocyte, *n.* a leucocyte that absorbs microbes etc., protecting the system against infection. **phagocytal, phagocytic**, *a.* **phagocytism,** *n.* **phagocytosis**, *n.* the destruction of microbes etc. by phagocytes.

-phagous, *comb. form* eating, devouring, as in *anthropophagous, sarcophagous*. [Gr. *phagos,* from *phagein,* see PHAG(O)-]

-phagy -PHAGE.

Phalaena, *n.* a moth. **phalaenian, phalaenoid**, *n., a.* [Gr. *phalaina*]

phalange PHALANX.

phalanger, *n.* any individual of the sub-family Phalangistinae, small Australian woolly-coated arboreal marsupials, comprising the flying squirrel and flying-opossum. [F, from Gr. *phalangion,* spider's web]

phalangial etc. PHALANX.

Phalangist, *n.* a member of a right-wing Lebanese military organization, since 1958 the political and military force of the Maronite Church in Lebanon.

phalanx, *n.* (*pl.* **-xes**, *Anat.*, *Bot.* **-ges**) the close order in which the heavy-armed troops of a Greek army were drawn up, esp. a compact body of Macedonian infantry; hence, any compact body of troops or close organization of persons; (also **phalange**) each of the small bones of the fingers and toes; one of the bundles of stamens in polyadelphous flowers. **phalangeal, -gian**, *a.* **phalangiform**, *a.* [L and Gr. *phalanx -angos*]

Phalaris, *n.* (570–554 BC), tyrant of the Greek colony of Acragas (Argrigento) in Sicily. He is said to have built a hollow bronze bull in which his victims were roasted alive. He was killed in a people's revolt.

phalarope, *n.* a small wading bird of the family Phalaropodidae, related to the snipes. [F (Gr. *phalaris,* coot, *pous,* foot)]

phallus, *n.* (*pl.* **-lli**) a figure of the male organ of generation, venerated as a symbol of the fertilizing power in nature; a penis; a genus of fungi containing the stink-horn. **phallic,** *a.* **phallicism**, **phallism,** *n.* the worship of the phallus. [Gr. *phallos*]

phanariot, *n.* a resident in the Greek or Phanar quarter of Constantinople (now Istanbul); (*Hist.*) one of the class of Greek officials under Turkey. [mod. Gr. *phanariōtēs,* from *phanari,* Gr. *phanarion,* lighthouse, dim. of *phanos,* lamp]

phanerogam, *n.* a plant having pistils and stamens, a flowering plant. **phanerogamic**, **-gamous**, *a.* [F *phanérogame* (Gr. *phaneros,* visible, *gamos,* marriage)]

Phanerozoic, *n.* an eon in Earth history, consisting of the most recent 590 million years. It comprises the Palaeozoic, Mesozoic, and Cainozoic eras. The vast majority of fossils come from this eon, owing to the evolution of hard shells and internal skeletons. The name means 'interval of well-displayed life'.

phantascope, *n.* an instrument used to illustrate some phenomena of binocular vision; a phenakistoscope. [Gr. *phantos,* visible]

Phantasiast, *n.* one of those among the Docetae, who believed that Christ's body was not material but mere appearance. [Gr. *Phantasiastēs,* from *phantasia,* FANTASY]

phantasm, *n.* a phantom; an optical illusion; a deception, a figment, an unreal likeness or presentation (of); an imaginary idea of a fantastic kind; a fancy, a fantasy; (*Psych.*) a mental representation of an object; a vision or image of an absent or deceased person. **phantasmal, -mic**, *a.* **phantasmally,** *adv.* [ME and OF *fantosme, L and Gr. phantasma,* from *phantazein,* to display, from *phan-,* stem of *phainein,* to show]

phantasmagoria, phantasmagory, *n.* an exhibition of dissolving views and optical illusions produced by a magic lantern, produced in London in 1802; a series of phantasms, fantastic appearances or illusions appearing to the mind as in nightmare, frenzy etc. **phantasmagorial, -goric**, *a.* [Gr. AGORA, assembly]

phantasy, FANTASY.

phantom, *n.* an apparition, a ghost, a spectre; a vision, in illusion, an imaginary appearance; an empty show or mere image (of); in angling, an artificial bait that expands in the water and resembles a live fish. *a.* seeming, apparent; illusory, imaginary, fictitious. **phantomatic**, **phantomic**, *a.* **phantomically,** *adv.* [ME and OF *fantosme,* as PHANTASM]

Pharaoh, *n.* any one of the ancient Egyptian kings; a tyrant, a despotic task-master; †the game of faro. **Pharaoh ant,** *n.* a small reddish-yellow ant of tropical regions which has spread to other countries and infests heated buildings etc. **Pharaoh's serpent,** *n.* a chemical toy consisting of sulphocyanide of mercury, which fuses into a serpentine shape when lighted. **Pharaonic**, *a.* [L and Gr., from Egypt. *pr-'o,* great house]

phare, *n.* a lighthouse. [F, from L *pharus,* Gr. PHAROS]

Pharisee, *n.* one of an ancient Jewish sect who rigidly observed the rites and ceremonies prescribed by the written law, and were marked by their exclusiveness towards the rest of the people; a self-righteous person, a formalist, an unctuous hypocrite. **pharisaic, -ical,** *a.* **pharisaically,** *adv.* †**pharisaicalness, pharisaism**, *n.* the doctrines of the Pharisees as a sect; hypocrisy in religion, self-righteousness. [OF, from L *pharisaeus, -seus,* Gr. *pharisaios,* ult. from Heb. *parush,* separated]

pharm., (*abbr.*) pharmaceutical; pharmacy.

pharmaceutical, *a.* of, pertaining to or engaged in pharmacy. *n.* a medicinal preparation. **pharmaceutically,** *adv.* **pharmaceutics,** *n. sing.* pharmacy. **pharmaceutist, pharmacist,** *n.* one trained in pharmacy; one legally entitled to sell drugs and poisons. [L *pharmaceuticus,* Gr. *pharmakeutikos,* from *pharmakeutēs,* druggist, from *pharmakon,* drug]

pharmaco-, *comb. form* pertaining to chemistry or to drugs. [Gr. *pharmakon,* drug]

pharmacography, *n.* a description of drugs and their properties.

pharmacology, *n.* the science of drugs and medicines. **pharmacological**, *a.* **pharmacologically,** *adv.* **pharmacologist,** *n.* .FS enc.p31

pharmacopoeia, *n.* a book, esp. an official publication containing a list of drugs, formulas, doses etc.; a collection of drugs; (*collect.*) the drugs available for use. **pharmacopoeial,** *a.* †**pharmacopolist**, *n.* one who sells drugs; an apothecary. [Gr. *pharmakopoiia,* from *pharmakopoios,* a preparer of drugs (*-poios,* from *poieein,* to make)]

pharmacy, *n.* the art or practice of preparing, compounding and dispensing drugs, esp. for medicinal purposes; a chemist's shop; a dispensary. [OF *farmacie,* late L *pharmacīa,* Gr. *pharmakeia,* as prec.]

pharos, *n.* a lighthouse, a beacon. **pharology**, *n.* the art of directing ships by light-signals from the shore. [L and Gr., name of a small island in the bay of Alexandria, on which a beacon was erected]

pharyngal, -geal, pharyngitis PHARYNX.

pharyng(o)-, *comb. form* pertaining to the pharynx.

pharyngo-glossal, *a.* of or pertaining to the pharynx and the tongue. [Gr. *glōssa,* tongue]

pharyngo-laryngeal, *a.* of or pertaining to the pharynx and the larynx.

pharyngoscope, *n.* an instrument for inspecting the throat. **pharyngoscopy**, *n.*

pharyngotomy, *n.* the surgical operation of cutting the pharynx. **pharyngotome**, *n.* an instrument used in this.

pharynx, *n.* (*pl.* **-ringes**) the canal or cavity opening from the mouth into the oesophagus and communicating with the air passages of the nose. **pharyngal, -geal**, *a.* **pharyngitis**, *n.* inflammation of the pharynx. **pharyngitic**, *a.* [Gr. *pharunx -ngos*]

phase, †**phasis**, *n.* (*pl.* **-ses**) a particular aspect or appearance; the form under which anything presents itself to the mind; a stage of change or development; a particular aspect of the illuminated surface of the moon or a planet, applied esp. to the successive quarters etc. of the moon; the relationship in time between the peaks of two alternating voltages etc.; a distinct, mechanically separable, homogeneous portion of matter that is part of a physical-chemical system. *v.t.* to carry out in phases; to organize in phases (*see* SINGLE PHASE, THREE-PHASE). **phase-contrast microscope,** a microscope used for examining colourless, transparent objects, which operates by changing differences in the phase of light transmitted, reflected or refracted by the object into differences in the intensity of the image. **to phase in,** to introduce gradually. **to phase out,** to discontinue gradually. **phasic**, *a.* **phaseless,** *a.* [late L and Gr. *phasis,* from the stem *pha-,* to shine]

-phasia, *comb. form* speech disorder. [Gr. *phasis,* utterance, from *phanai,* to speak]

Phasma, *n.* a genus of orthopterous insects comprising the walking-leaves etc. [L and Gr., a spectre]

phatic, *a.* of speech, used to express feelings, sociability etc., rather than to express meaning. [Gr. *phatos,* spoken]

Ph.D., (*abbr.*) Doctor of Philosophy. [L *Philosophiae Doctor*]

pheasant, *n.* a game bird, *Phasianus colchicus,* naturalized in Britain and Europe, noted for its brilliant plumage and its delicate flesh. **pheasantry,** *n.* [A-F *fesant* (F *faisan*), L *phāsiānus, Gr. Phasianos,* of or pertaining to the *Phasis,* a river of Colchis]

†**pheeze,** *v.t.* to do for; to beat, to drive off. *v.i.* (*N Am.*) to fret, to be uneasy. *n.* a state of fretfulness. [OE *fēsian* (cp. Norw. *föysa,* Swed. *fösa*)]

phellem, *n.* a layer of cork cells formed by phellogen.

phello-, *comb. form* cork. [Gr. *phellos*, cork]

phelloderm, *n.* a layer of parenchymatous tissue containing chlorophyll, and sometimes formed on the inner side of a layer of phellogen. **phellodermal**, *a.*

phellogen, *n.* the layer of meristematic cells from which the cork-tissue is formed, cork-tissue. **phellogenetic**, **-genic**, *a.*

phelloplastic, *n.* a figure carved or modelled in cork; (*pl., sing. in constr.*) the art of making such figures.

phen- PHEN(O)-.

phenacetin, *n.* a white crystalline compound used as an antipyretic.

phenakistoscope, *n.* a scientific toy in which a disc bearing figures in successive attitudes of motion is rapidly revolved so as to convey to the observer, by means of a mirror or a series of slits, the impression of continuous movement. [Gr. *phenakistēs,* an impostor, from *phenakizein,* to cheat, -SCOPE]

phen(o)-, *comb. form* applied to substances derived from coal-tar, orig. in the production of coal-gas for illuminating. [Gr. *phainos,* shining, from *phainein,* to show]

phenobarbitone, *n.* a white, crystalline powder used as a sedative or hypnotic drug.

phenol, *n.* carbolic acid; any of various weakly acidic compounds derived from benzene, and containing a hydroxyl group. **phenolic**, *a.*

phenology, *n.* the study of the times of recurrence of natural phenomena, esp. of the influence of climate on plants and animals. **phenological**, *a.* [contr. of PHENOMENOLOGY, after G *phänologisch*]

phenomenon, (*esp. formerly*) **phaenomenon**, *n.* (*pl.* **-na**) that which appears or is perceived by observation or experiment, esp. a thing or occurrence the law or agency causing which is in question; (*coll.*) a remarkable or unusual appearance; that which is apprehended by the mind, as distinguished from real existence. **phenomenal,** *a.* of or pertaining to phenomena, esp. as distinguished from underlying realities or causes; of the nature of a phenomenon, perceptible, cognizable by the senses; (*coll.*) extraordinary, prodigious. **phenomenalism, phenomenism,** *n.* the doctrine that phenomena are the sole material of knowledge, and that underlying realities and causes are unknowable. **phenomenalist, phenomenist,** *n.* **phenomenalistic, -menistic**, *a.* **phenomenalize, -ise,** *v.t.* to treat or conceive as phenomenal. **phenomenally,** *adv.* **phenomenize, -ise,** *v.t.* to make phenomenal; to phenomenalize. **phenomenology**, *n.* the science of phenomena, opp. to *ontology;* the division of any inductive science treating of the phenomena forming its basis. **phenomenological**, *a.* **phenomenologically,** *adv.* [L *phænomenon,* Gr. *phainomenon,* neut. pres.p. of *phainein,* to show]

phenotype, *n.* the observable characteristics of an organism produced by the interaction of the genotype and the environment. [Gr. *phainein,* to show, TYPE]

phenyl, *n.* the organic radical found in benzene, phenol, aniline etc. **phenylbutazone**, *n.* an analgesic drug used for treating rheumatic disorders.

pheon, *n.* in heraldry, the barbed head of a dart, arrow or javelin, a broad arrow. [etym. doubtful]

pheromone, *n.* any chemical substance secreted by an animal that stimulates responses from others of its species. [Gr. *pherein,* to bear, hor*mone*]

phew, *int.* expressing surprise, disgust, impatience etc. [onomat.]

phi, *n.* the 21st letter of the Greek alphabet. [Gr. *phei*]

phial, *n.* a small glass vessel or bottle, esp. for medicine or perfume. *v.t.* to put or keep in or as in a phial. [ME and OF *fiole,* L *phiala,* Gr. *phialē*]

Phi Beta Kappa, the oldest of the American college fraternities. [initials of Gr. *Philosophia Biou Kubernētēs,* Philosophy is the guide of life]

Phidias, *n.* (mid-5th century BC), Greek sculptor, one of the most influential of classical times. He supervised the sculptural programme for the Parthenon (most of it preserved in the British Museum, London, and known as the Elgin marbles). He also executed the colossal statue of Zeus at Olympia, one of the Seven Wonders of the World.

phil., (*abbr.*) philosophy.

phil- PHIL(O)-.

†**-phil** -PHILE.

Philadelphia, *n.* industrial city and port on the Delaware river in Pennsylvania, US; population (1980) 1,688,000, metropolitan area 3,700,000. Products include refined oil, chemicals, textiles, processed food, printing and publishing. Founded 1682 as the 'city of brotherly love', it was the first capital of the US (1790–1800).

philander, *v.i.* to make love in a trifling way; to flirt. **philanderer**, *n.* a man who does this. [Gr. *philandros* (*anēr andros,* man, perh. after a character in Beaumont and Fletcher's *Laws of Candy*, or from a lover in Ariosto's *Orlando Furioso*)]

philanthropy, *n.* love of mankind; active benevolence towards one's fellow-humans. **philanthrope,** *n.* **philanthropic, -ical**, *a.* **philanthropically,** *adv.* **philanthropism,** *n.* **philanthropist,** *n.* **philanthropize, -ise,** *v.t.*, *v.i.* [late L and Gr. *philanthrōpia* (*anthrōpos,* human being)]

philately, *n.* the collecting of postage stamps. **philatelic**, *a.* **philatelist,** *n.* **philatelistic**, *a.* [F *philatélie* (Gr. *ateleia,* freedom from toll, from *a-,* not, *telos,* toll, tax)]

Philby, *n.* **(Harold) 'Kim'** (1912–88), British intelligence officer from 1940 and Soviet agent from 1933. He was liaison officer in Washington 1949–51, when he was asked to resign. Named in 1963 as having warned Guy Burgess and Donald Maclean (similarly double agents) that their activities were known, he fled to the USSR, and became a Soviet citizen and general in the KGB. A fourth member of the ring was Anthony Blunt.

-phile, *comb. form* a lover or friend of; loving, as in *bibliophile, gastrophile, Germanophile*. **-philic, -philous,** *a.* [Gr. *philos,* loving, dear, friendly, from *philein,* to love]

philharmonic, *a.* loving music. *n.* a person fond of music; a musical society. [F *philharmonique*]

Philhellene, *n.* a friend or lover of the Greeks or a supporter of Greek independence. *a.* friendly to Greece or supporting Greek independence. **Philhelle-**

nic, *a.* **Philhellenism,** *n.* **Philhellenist,** *n.*

-philia, *comb. form* love of. **-philiac,** *n., a.* [-PHILE]

philibeg, FILIBEG.

-philic -PHILE.

Philip[1], *n.* six kings of France, including:

Philip II, *n.* (Philip Augustus) (1165–1223), king of France from 1180. He waged war in turn against the English kings Henry II, Richard I (with whom he also went on the Third Crusade), and John (against whom he won the decisive battle of Bouvines in Flanders 1214) to evict them from their French possessions, and establish a strong monarchy.

Philip IV, *n.* **the Fair** (1268–1314), king of France from 1285. He engaged in a feud with Pope Boniface VIII, and made him a prisoner in 1303. Clement V (1264–1314), elected pope through Philip's influence, moved to Avignon, and collaborated with Philip to suppress the Templars, a powerful order of knights. Philip allied with the Scots against England, and invaded Flanders.

Philip VI, *n.* (1293–1350), king of France from 1328, first of the house of Valois, elected by the barons on the death of his cousin, Charles IV. His claim was challenged by Edward III of England, who defeated him at Crécy in 1346.

Philip II of Macedon, (382–336 BC), king of Macedonia from 359 BC. He seized the throne from his nephew, for whom he was regent, conquered the Greek city states, and formed them into a league whose forces could be united against Persia. He was assassinated while he was planning this expedition, and was succeeded by his son Alexander the Great. His tomb was discovered at Vergina, N Greece, in 1978.

Philip[2], *n.* five kings of Spain, including:

Philip I, *n.* **the Handsome** (1478–1506), king of Castile from 1504, through his marriage (1496) to Joanna the Mad (1479–1555). He was the son of the Holy Roman emperor Maximilian I.

Philip II, *n.* (1527–98), king of Spain from 1556. He was born at Valladolid, the son of the Habsburg emperor Charles V, and in 1554 married Queen Mary of England. On his father's abdication (1556) he inherited Spain, the Netherlands, and the Spanish possessions in Italy and the Americas, and in 1580 annexed Portugal. His intolerance and lack of understanding of the Netherlanders drove them into revolt. Political and religious reasons combined to involve him in war with England and, after 1589, with France. The defeat of the Spanish Armada marked the beginning of the decline of Spanish power.

Philip V, *n.* (1683–1746), king of Spain from 1700. A grandson of Louis XIV of France, he was the first Bourbon king of Spain. He was not recognized by the major European powers until 1713. See SPANISH SUCCESSION.

Philip[3], *n.* **Duke of Edinburgh** (1921–), prince of the UK, husband of Elizabeth II, and a grandson of George I of Greece and a great-great-grandson of Queen Victoria. He was born in Corfu, raised in England, and educated at Gordonstoun and Dartmouth Naval College. During World War II he served in the Mediterranean, taking part in the battle of Matapan, and in the Pacific.

Philip, St, *n.* (1st cent. AD), in the New Testament, one of the 12 apostles. He was an inhabitant of Bethsaida (N Israel), and is said to have worked as a missionary in Anatolia. Feast day 3 May.

Philip Neri, St, (1515–95), Italian Roman Catholic priest who organized the Congregation of the Oratory (see ORATORIAN). He built the oratory over the church of St Jerome, Rome, where prayer meetings were held and scenes from the Bible performed with music, originating the musical form oratorio. Feast day 26 May.

Philip the Good, (1396–1467), duke of Burgundy from 1419. He engaged in the Hundred Years' War as an ally of England until he made peace with the French at the Council of Arras in 1435. He made the Netherlands a centre of art and learning.

Philippi, *n.* ancient city of Macedonia founded by Philip of Macedon in 358 BC. Near Philippi, Mark Antony and Augustus defeated Brutus and Cassius in 42 BC. It was the first European town where St Paul preached (about 53 AD), founding the congregation to which he addressed the Epistle to the Philippians.

philippic, *n.* one of three orations of Demosthenes against Philip of Macedon; applied also to Cicero's orations against Antony; any speech or declamation full of acrimonious invective. †**philippize, -ise,** *v.i.* to take the part of Philip of Macedon; hence, to act or speak as if under corrupt influence; (*erron.*) to write or deliver a philippic. [L *Philippicus,* Gr. *philippikos,* from *Philippos,* Philip]

philippina, PHILOPENA.

Philippines, *n.* Republic of the (*Republika ng Pilipinas*), country on an archipelago between the Pacific Ocean to the E and the South China Sea to the W. **area** 300,000 sq km/115,800 sq miles. **capital** Manila (on Luzon). **towns** Quezon City. **ports** Cebu, Davao (on Mindanao) and Iloilu. **physical** comprises over 7000 islands, with volcanic mountain ranges traversing the main chain N–S, and 50% of the area still forested. The largest islands are Luzon 108,172 sq km/41,754 sq miles and Mindanao 94,227 sq km/36,372 sq miles; others include Samar, Negros, Palawan, Panay, Mindoro, Leyte, Cebu, and the Sulu group. **exports** sugar, copra and coconut oil, timber, iron ore and copper concentrates. **population** (1989) 61,971,000 (93% Malaysian); annual growth rate 2.4%. **language** Filipino (based on the Malay dialect Tagalog), but English and Spanish are in common use. **religion** Roman Catholic 84%, Protestant 9%, Muslim 5%.

Philistine, *n.* a member of a people of non-Semitic origin (possibly from Asia Minor) who founded city states on the Palestinian coastal plain in the 12th century BC, adopting a Semitic language and religion. They were at war with the Israelites in the 11th–10th centuries BC; a person of narrow or materialistic views or ideas; one deficient in liberal culture; (after G *Philister*) applied by German students to a non-university man. *a.* pertaining to the Philistines; commonplace, uncultured, prosaic. **Philistinism,** *n.* [F *Philistin,* late L *Philistīnus,* Gr. *Philistīnoi,* pl., Assyrian *Palastu, Pilistu*]

†**phill horse** THILL.

Phillip, *n.* **Arthur** (1738–1814), British vice admiral, founder and governor of the convict settlement at Sydney, Australia (1788–1792), and hence founder of New South Wales.

Phillips, *n.* **Anton** (1874–1951), Dutch industrialist and founder of electronics firm. The Philips Bulb and Radio Works was founded by Gerard Philips at Eindhoven in 1891. Anton, his brother, served as chairman of the company (1921–51), during which time the firm became the largest producer of electrical goods outside the US.

Phillips curve, *n.* a graph showing the relationship between percentage changes in wages and unemployment, and indicating that wages rise faster during periods of low unemployment as employers compete for labour. The implication is that the dual objectives of low unemployment and low inflation are inconsistent. The concept has been widely questioned since the early 1960s because of the apparent instability of the wages/unemployment relationship. It was developed by the British economist A(lban) W(illiam) Phillips (1914–75), who plotted graphically wage and unemployment changes between 1861 and 1957.

phillipsite, *n.* a monoclinic hydrous silicate of aluminium, potassium and calcium. [J. W. *Phillips,* 1800–74, British mineralogist]

phillumeny, *n.* the collecting of matchboxes or matchbox labels. **phillumenist,** *n.* [L *lumen,* light]

phil(o)-, *comb. form* fond of, affecting, inhabiting. [Gr. *philos,* loving, from *philein,* to love, cp. -PHILE]

philobiblic, *a.* fond of books or literature. **philobiblian,** *a.* **philobiblical,** *a.* philobiblic; devoted to the study of the Bible. **philobiblist,** *n.* [Gr. *biblos,* book]

philodendron, *n.* (*pl.* **-drons, -dra**) any of various plants of the arum family, cultivated for their showy foliage. [Gr. *dendron,* a tree]

philogynist, *n.* one devoted to women. **philogynous,** *a.* **philogyny**, *n.* [Gr. *philogunia,* love of woman (*gunē,* woman)]

philology, *n.* the historical or comparative study of language; †love of learning or literature. **philologer, -logian**, **-logist,** *n.* **philological**, *a.* **philologically,** *adv.* [L and Gr. *philologia* (*logos,* word, discourse)]

philomath, *n.* a lover of learning, esp. of mathematics, a scholar. **philomathic, -ical**, *a.* **philomathy**, *n.* [Gr. *philomathēs* (*math-*, stem of *manthanein,* to learn)]

Philomela, *n.* (*poet.*) a nightingale. **philomel**, *n.* [F *philomèle,* L and Gr. *Philomēla,* daughter of Pandion, king of Athens, changed by the gods into a nightingale]

philopena, *n.* a game in which two persons at dessert share the double kernel of a nut, esp. an almond, the first being entitled to a forfeit, under certain conditions, on the next meeting with the other sharer; the kernel so shared; the forfeit or present. [corr. of G *Vielliebchen,* dim. of *viellieb* (*viel,* much, *lieb,* dear)]

philopolemic, -ical, *a.* fond of war or controversy. [Gr. *philopolemos* (*polemos,* war)]

philoprogenitive, *a.* characterized by love of offspring; prolific. **philoprogenitiveness,** *n.* [L *progenit-,* stem of *progignere,* to beget]

philosopher, *n.* a lover of wisdom; one who studies or devotes him- or herself to natural or moral philosophy or to the investigation of the principles of being or of knowledge; one who regulates conduct and actions by the principles of philosophy; one of philosophic temper. **philosopher's stone,** *n.* an imaginary stone, sought for by the alchemists in the belief that it would transmute the baser metals into gold or silver. **philosophe**, *n.* a philosophist or pretender to philosophy; †a philosopher. **philosophical**, *a.* pertaining or according to philosophy; devoted to or skilled in philosophy; wise, calm, temperate, unimpassioned. **philosophically,** *adv.* **philosophism,** *n.* affectation of philosophy (applied esp. to the French Encyclopaedists); sophistry. **philosophist,** *n.* **philosophistic, †-ical**, *a.* **philosophize, -ise**, *v.t.*, *v.i.* **philosophizer, -iser,** *n.* [A-F *philosofre,* F *philosophe,* L *philosophus,* Gr. *philosophos* (*sophos,* wise)]

philosophy, *n.* love of wisdom; the knowledge or investigation of ultimate reality or of general principles of knowledge or existence; a particular system of philosophic principles; the fundamental principles of a science etc.; practical wisdom; calmness and coolness of temper; serenity, resignation; †reasoning, argumentation.

philotechnic, *a.* fond of the arts, esp. the industrial arts. [Gr. *philotechnos* (*technē,* art)]

-philous PHILE.

philozoic, *a.* fond of or kind to animals. **philozoist,** *n.* [Gr. *zōon,* animal]

philtre, (*esp. N Am.*) **philter**, *n.* a love-potion, a love-charm. *v.t.* to charm or excite with a love-potion. [F, from L *philtrum,* Gr. *philtron,* from *philein,* to love]

phimosis, *n.* constriction of the opening of the prepuce. **phimosed,** *a.* [Gr., from *phimoein,* to muzzle]

phiz, phizog, *n.* (*sl.*) the face, the visage; the expression, the countenance. [short for obs. *phisnomy,* PHYSIOGNOMY]

Phiz, *n.* pseudonym of Hablot Knight Browne (1815–82), British artist. He illustrated the greater part of the *Pickwick Papers* and other works by Dickens, as well as novels by C. J. Lever and Harrison Ainsworth (1805–82).

phleb- PHLEB(O)-.

phlebitis, *n.* inflammation of the inner membrane of a vein. **phlebitic**, *a.*

phleb(o)-, *comb. form* vein. [Gr. *phleps phlebos,* vein]

phlebolite, -lith, *n.* a calculus in a vein. **phlebolitic**, **-lithic**, *a.*

phlebology, *n.* the department of physiology or anatomy dealing with the veins; a treatise on the veins.

phlebotomy, *n.* the opening of a vein, blood-letting. **phlebotomist,** *n.* **phlebotomize, -ise,** *v.t.* to let blood from. *v.i.* to practise phlebotomy. [OF *flebothomie* (F *phlébotomie*), L and Gr. *phlebotomia*]

phlegm, *n.* viscid mucus secreted in the air passages or stomach, esp. as a morbid product and discharged by coughing etc.; watery matter forming one of the four humours of the body; self-possession; coolness, sluggishness, apathy. **†phlegmagogue**, *n.* a medicine for expelling phlegm, an expectorant. **phlegmagogic**, *n.*, *a.* **phlegmasia**, *n.* inflammation, esp. with fever. **phlegmatic, -ical**, *a.* cool, sluggish, apathetic, unemotional. **phlegmatically,** *adv.* **phlegmy**, *a.* abounding in or of the nature of phlegm. [ME and OF *fleume* (F *phlegme*), L and Gr. *phlegma,* from *phlegein,* to burn]

phlegmon, *n.* a tumour or inflammation of the cellular tissue. **phlegmonic**, **-monous,** *a.* [ME *flegmon,* L *phlegmon, -mona,* Gr. *phlegmonē,* as prec.]

phloem, *n.* the softer cellular portion of fibrovascular tissue in plants, the bark and the tissues closely connected with it. [Gr. *phloos,* bark]

phlogiston, *n.* the principle of inflammability formerly supposed to be a necessary constituent of combustible bodies. **phlogistic,** *a.* of phlogiston; (*Med.*) inflammatory. **phlogisticate,** *v.t.* **†phlogosis**, *n.* inflammation. [Gr., neut. of *phlogistos,* burnt up, from *phlogizein,* to set on fire, cogn. with *phlegein,* to burn]

phlorizin, *n.* a bitter substance found in the root-bark of the apple, pear and other trees. [Gr. *phloos,* bark, *rhiza,* root]

phlox, *n.* a plant of a genus (*Phlox*) of N American plants of the family Polemoniaceae, with clusters of showy flowers. [Gr., flame, name of a plant]

phlyctaena, *n.* a vesicle, pimple or blister, esp. on the eyeball. **phlyctenar, -tenous, -tenoid**, *a.* [Gr. *phluktaina,* from *phluein,* to swell]

Phnom Penh, *n.* capital of Cambodia, on the Mekong, 210 km/130 miles NW of Saigon; population (1981) 400,000. Industries include textiles and food-processing.

-phobe, *comb. form* fearing, as in *Anglophobe, Gallophobe;* one who fears or hates. **-phobia,** *comb. form* fear, morbid dislike, as in *Anglophobia, hydrophobia*. **-phobic,** *a.* [F, as foll.]

phobia, *n.* an irrational fear or hatred. **phobic,** *a.* [from L and Gr. *-phobos,* from *phobos,* fear]

Phobos, *n.* one of the two moons of Mars, discovered in 1877 by the US astronomer Asaph Hall. It is an irregularly shaped lump of rock, cratered by meteorite impacts. Phobos is 27 × 21 × 19 km/17 × 13 × 12 miles across, and orbits Mars every 0.32 days at a height of 9400 km/5840 miles. It is thought to be an asteroid captured by Mars' gravity.

phoca, *n.* (*Zool.*) a seal; **(Phoca)** a genus of pinniped mammals containing the true seals. **phocacean**, *n.*, *a.* **phocaceous**, **phocal, phocine**, *a.* [L, from Gr. *phōkē,* seal]

Phoebus, *n.* Apollo as the sun-god; the sun. [L, from Gr. *phoibos,* bright, shining]

Phoenicia, *n.* ancient Greek name for N Canaan on the E coast of the Mediterranean. The Phoenicians lived about 1200–332 BC, were seafaring traders and artisans, and are said to have circumnavigated Africa and established colonies in Cyprus, N Africa (for example Carthage), Malta, Sicily, and Spain. Their cities (Tyre, Sidon, and Byblos were the main ones) were independent states ruled by hereditary kings but dominated by merchant ruling classes. The fall of Tyre to Alexander the Great ended the separate history of Phoenicia. **Phoenician**, *a.* of or pertaining to Phoenicia, or to its colonies, Punic, Carthaginian. *n.* a native or inhabitant of Phoenicia or its colonies.

phoenix, *n.* a fabulous Arabian bird, the only one of its kind, said to live for 500 or 600 years in the desert and to immolate itself on a funeral pyre, whence it rose again in renewed youth; a person or thing of extreme rarity or excellence, a paragon. [L, from Gr. *phoinix,* phoenix, also purple, Carthaginian]

Phoenix, *n.* capital of Arizona, US; industrial city (steel, aluminium, electrical goods, food processing) and tourist centre on the Salt river; population (1986)

882,000.

Phoenix Park Murders, the murder of several prominent members of the British government in Phoenix Park, Dublin on 6 May 1882. It threatened the co-operation between the Liberal government and the Irish nationalist members at Westminster which had been secured by the Kilmainham Treaty.

pholas, *n.* (*pl.* **-lades**) a genus of stone-boring bivalves, a piddock. **pholad,** *n.* **pholadean, pholadid,** *n.* **pholadoid,** *a.* [Gr.]

phon, *n.* the unit of loudness. **phonmeter,** *n.* an instrument for estimating loudness of sound. [Gr. *phōnē,* voice]

phon., (*abbr.*) phonetics; phonology.

phon- PHON(O)-.

phonate, *v.i.* to make a vocal sound. *v.t.* to utter vocally. **phonation,** *n.* **phonatory,** *a.*

phonautograph, *n.* an apparatus for recording the vibrations of sounds. **phonautographic,** *a.* **phonautographically,** *adv.*

phone[1], *v.t., v.i.* to telephone. *n.* a telephone; a headphone. **phone book** TELEPHONE DIRECTORY. **phonecard,** *n.* a plastic card inserted into a slot in a public telephone, which cancels out the prepaid units on the card as the call is made. **phone freak, phreak,** *n.* one who makes obscene calls or otherwise misuses the telephone system. **phone-in,** *n.* a radio or TV programme in which members of the audience at home telephone to make comments, ask questions etc., as part of a live broadcast. [by shortening]

phone[2], *n.* an articulate sound, as a simple vowel or consonant sound. [Gr. *phōnē,* voice]

-phone, *comb. form* sound; voice; a device producing sound; (a person) speaking a specified language, as in *Francophone*. [Gr. *phōnē,* sound, voice]

phoneme, *n.* the smallest distinctive group of phones in a language. **phonemic,** *a.* **phonemically,** *adv.* **phonemics,** *n. sing.* the study of phonemes. [Gr. *phōnēma,* a sound]

phonendoscope, *n.* a variety of stethoscope for enabling small sounds, esp. within the human body, to be distinctly heard. [Gr. *endon,* within, -SCOPE]

phonetic, *a.* pertaining to the voice or vocal sounds; representing sounds, esp. by means of a distinct letter or character for each. **phonetically,** *adv.* **phonetician,** *n.* **phoneticism,** *n.* phonetic writing, phonetic representation of language. **phoneticist,** *n.* **phoneticize, -ise,** *v.t.* **phoneticization, -isation,** *n.* **phonetics,** *n.sing.* the science of articulate sounds, phonology. **phonetist,** *n.* one versed in phonetics, a phonologist; an advocate of phonetic writing, a phoneticist.

phoney, (*esp. N Am.*) **phony,** *a.* (*coll.*) bogus, false; fraudulent, counterfeit; of a person, pretentious. *n.* a phoney person or thing. [etym. doubtful]

phonic, *a.* pertaining to sounds, acoustic; pertaining to vocal sounds. **phonics,** *n. sing.* phonetics; acoustics; a method of teaching people to read by associating sounds with their phonetic values.

phonogram, *n.* a written character indicating a particular spoken sound, as in Pitman's system of phonography; a sound-record made by a phonograph. **phonograph,** *n.* an instrument for automatically recording and reproducing sounds; (*N Am.*) a gramophone; †a phonogram; †a phonautograph. *v.t.* to record by means of phonography; to reproduce by means of a phonograph. **phonographer, -graphist,** *n.* one skilled in phonography. **phonographic,** *a.* **phonographically,** *adv.* **phonography,** *n.* a system of shorthand invented by Sir Isaac Pitman (1813–97), in which each sound is represented by a distinct character; automatic recording and reproduction of sounds, as by the phonograph; the art of using the phonograph.

phonolite, *n.* clinkstone.

phonology, *n.* the science of vocal sounds; the sounds and combinations of sounds in a particular language. **phonologic, -ical,** *a.* **phonologist, †-ger,** *n.*

phonometer, *n.* an instrument for recording the number and intensity of vibrations, esp. of sound-waves.

phonon, *n.* a quantum of vibrational energy in a crystal lattice.

phonopore, *n.* a device attached to a telegraph wire for allowing telephonic messages to be sent over the line at the same time as telegraphic messages, without interference from the current transmitting the latter. **phonoporic,** *a.* [Gr. *poros,* passage]

phonoscope, *n.* an instrument for testing the quality of musical strings; an instrument of various kinds for translating sound vibrations into visible figures; a phenakistoscope representing a person speaking.

phonotype, *n.* a character used in phonetic printing. **phonotypic, -ical,** *a.* **phonotypy,** *n.* phonetic printing.

phony PHONEY.

phooey, *int.* used to express contempt, disbelief etc.

-phore, *comb. form* bearer, as in *gonophore, gynophore, semaphore*. **-phorous,** *comb. form* bearing, -ferous, as in *electrophorous, galactophorous*. [Gr. *phoros,* bearing]

-phoresis, *comb. form* transmission. [Gr. *phorēsis,* carrying]

phosgene, *n.* gaseous carbon oxychloride, used as a poison gas. **phosgenite,** *n.* a mineral consisting of carbonate and chloride of lead in nearly equal proportions. [F *phosgène* (Gr. *phōs,* light, -GEN)]

phosph- PHOSPH(O)-.

phosphate, *n.* a salt of phosphoric acid; (*pl.*) phosphates of calcium, iron and alumina etc., used as fertilizing agents. **phosphatic,** *a.*

phosphene, *n.* a luminous image produced by pressure on the eyeball, caused by irritation of the retina. [Gr. *phōs,* light, *phainein,* to show]

phosphide, *n.* a combination of phosphorus with another element or radical. **phosphite,** *n.* a salt of phosphorous acid.

phosph(o)-, phosphor(o)-, *comb. form* phosphorus.

phosphor, *n.* (often **Phosphor,**) the morning-star, Lucifer; phosphorus; a substance that exhibits phosphorescence. **phosphor-bronze, -copper, -tin** etc., *n.* a combination of phosphorus with the metal named. **phosphoresce,** *v.i.* to give out a light unaccompanied by perceptible heat or without combustion. **phosphorescence,** *n.* the emission of or the property of emitting light under such conditions; such emission of light caused by radiation bombardment, and continuing after the radiation has ceased. **phosphorescent,** *a.* [L PHOSPHORUS]

phosphorate, phosphoric etc. PHOSPHORUS.

phosphor(o)- PHOSPH(O)-.

phosphorogenic, *a.* causing phosphorescence.

phosphorograph, *n.* a luminous image produced on a phosphorescent surface. **phosphorographic,** *a.* **phosphorography,** *n.*

phosphoroscope, *n.* an apparatus for measuring the duration of phosphorescence.

phosphorus, *n.* a non-metallic element, at.no. 15; chem. symbol P, occurring in two allotropic forms. White phosphorus is waxy, poisonous, spontaneously combustible at room temperature and appears luminous. Red phosphorus is non-poisonous and ignites only when heated. **phosphorus necrosis,** *n.* gangrene of the jaw caused by the fumes of phosphorus, esp. in the manufacture of matches. **phosphorate,** *v.i.* to combine, impregnate with phosphorus. **phosphoric,** *a.* pertaining to phosphorus in its higher valency; phosphorescent. **phosphorism,** *n.* phosphorus necrosis. **phosphorite,** *n.* a massive variety of phosphate of lime. **phosphorous,** *a.* pertaining to, of the nature of or obtained from phosphorus, esp. in its lower valency. [L, the morning star, from Gr. *phōsphoros,* bringing light]

†phosphuret, *n.* phosphide. **phosphuretted,** *a.*

phossy jaw, *n.* (*coll.*) phosphorus necrosis.

phot, *n.* the unit of illumination, one lumen per square centimetre. [Gr. *phōs, phōtos,* light]

phot., (*abbr.*) photographic; photography.

phot- PHOT(O)-.

photic, *a.* pertaining to light; accessible to the sun's light; pertaining to the upper layers of the sea that receive the sun's light. **photically,** *adv.*

photism, *n.* a hallucinatory sensation of colour accompanying some other sensation. [Gr. *phōtismos,* from *phōtizein,* to shine, from *phōs phōtos,* light]

photo, *n.* (*pl.* **-tos**) a photograph. *v.t.* to photograph. *a.* photographic. **photo-finish,** *n.* a close finish of a race etc., in which a photograph enables a judge to decide the winner. [short for PHOTOGRAPH]

phot(o)-, *comb. form* pertaining to light or to photography. [Gr. *phōs phōtos,* light]

photocall, *n.* an occasion when someone is photographed by arrangement for publicity purposes.

photocell, *n.* a photoelectric cell.

photochemical, *a.* of, pertaining to or produced by the chemical action of light. **photochemically,** *adv.* **photochemistry,** *n.*

photochromatic, *a.* of, pertaining to or produced by the chromatic action of light. **photochrome,** *n.* a coloured photograph. **photochromic,** *a.* changing colour in response to the incidence of radiant energy. **photochromism,** *n.* **photochromotype,** *n.* a picture in colours printed from plates prepared by a photorelief process. *v.t.* to reproduce by this process. **photochromy,** *n.* colour photography.

photochronograph, *n.* an instrument for taking a series of photographs, as of moving objects, at regular intervals of time; a photograph so taken; an instrument for making a photographic record of an astronomical event. **photochronographic,** *a.* **photochronographically,** *adv.* **photochronography,** *n.*

photocomposition, *n.* the composition of print etc. directly on film or photosensitive paper for reproduction.

photoconductivity, *n.* electrical conductivity that varies with the incidence of radiation, esp. light.

photocopy, *n.* a photographic reproduction of matter that is written, printed etc. *v.t.* to make a photocopy of. **photocopier,** *n.* a device for making photocopies.

photoelectric, *a.* of or pertaining to photoelectricity, or to the combined action of light and electricity. **photoelectric cell,** *n.* a device for measuring light by a change of electrical resistance when light falls upon a cell, or by the generation of a voltage. **photoelectricity,** *n.* electricity produced or affected by light.

photoelectron, *n.* an electron emitted during photoemission.

photoemission, *n.* the emission of electrons from a substance on which radiation falls.

photo-engraving, *n.* any process for producing printing-blocks by means of photography.

photo-finish PHOTO.

Photo-fit®, *n.* (a method of composing) a likeness of someone's face consisting of photographs of parts of faces, used for the identification of criminal suspects.

photogen, *n.* a light hydrocarbon obtained by distilling coal, shale, peat etc., used for burning in lamps.

photogenic, *a.* produced by the action of light; producing light, phosphorescent; descriptive of one who comes out well in photographs or in a cinematograph film.

photoglyph, *n.* a photogravure.

photogrammetry, *n.* the technique of taking measurements from photographs, e.g. making maps from aerial photographs.

photograph, *n.* a picture etc. taken by means of photography. *v.t.* to take a picture of by photography. *v.i.* to practise photography; to appear in a photograph (well or badly). **photographer,** *n.* **photographic,** *a.* **photographically,** *adv.* **photography,** *n.* the process or art of producing images or pictures of objects by the chemical action of light on certain sensitive substances.

photogravure, *n.* the process of producing an intaglio plate for printing by the transfer of a photographic negative to the plate and subsequent etching; a picture so produced. *v.t.* to reproduce by this process. [F (GRAVURE)]

photolithography, *n.* a mode of producing by photography designs upon stones etc., from which impressions may be taken at a lithographic press. **photolithograph,** *n.*

†**photology,** *n.* the science of light. **photologic, -ical,** *a.* **photologist,** *n.*

photolysis, *n.* decomposition resulting from the incidence of radiation. **photolytic,** *a.*

photomechanical, *a.* of or pertaining to a process by which photographic images are reproduced or employed in printing by mechanical means.

photometer, *n.* a contrivance for measuring the relative intensity of light. **photometric, -ical,** *a.* **photometry,** *n.*

photomicrography, *n.* the process of making magnified photographs of microscopic objects. **photomicrograph,** *n.* **photomicrographer,** *n.* **photomicrographic,** *a.*

photomontage, *n.* a means of producing pictures by the montage of many photographic images; the picture thus produced.

photon, *n.* the unit of light intensity; quantum of radiant energy.

photo-offset, *n.* offset printing from photolithographic plates.

photophobia, *n.* abnormal shrinking from or intolerance of light. **photophobic,** *a.*

photophone, *n.* an instrument for transmitting sounds by the agency of light.

photophore, *n.* an organ that emits light.

photopia, *n.* vision in normal daylight. **photopic,** *a.*

photoprocess, *n.* any photomechanical process.

photopsia, photopsy, *n.* an affection of the eye causing the patient to see lines, flashes of light etc.

photoreceptor, *n.* a nerve-ending receptive to light.

photorelief, *n.* an image in relief produced by a photographic process. *a.* pertaining to any process of producing such reliefs.

photosensitive, *a.* sensitive to the action of light. **photosensitivity,** *n.* **photosensitize, -ise,** *v.t.* to make photosensitive. **photosensitization, -isation,** *n.*

photosetting, *n.* photocomposition. **photoset,** *v.t.*

photosphere, *n.* the luminous envelope of the sun or a star. **photospheric,** *a.*

Photostat®, *n.* a camera to photograph prints, documents etc.; a photograph so produced.

photosynthesis, *n.* the process by which carbohydrates are produced from carbon dioxide and water through the agency of light; esp. this process occurring in green plants. **photosynthesize, -ise,** *v.t.* **photosynthesization, -isation,** *n.* **photosynthetic,** *a.* **photosynthetically,** *adv.*

phototherapy, *n.* the treatment of skin diseases by means of certain kinds of light rays.

phototropism, *n.* tropism due to the influence of light.

phototype, *n.* a printing-plate produced by photoengraving; a print from this. **phototypy,** *n.* **phototypography,** *n.* a photomechanical process of engraving in relief for reproduction with type in an ordinary printing-press. **phototypesetting,** *n.* photocomposition.

photoxylography, *n.* engraving on wood from photographs printed on the block.

photozincography, *n.* the process of producing an engraving on zinc by photomechanical means for printing in a manner analogous to photolithography. **photozincograph,** *n.*

phrase, *n.* an expression denoting a single idea or forming a distinct part of a sentence; a brief or concise expression; mode, manner or style of expression, diction; idiomatic expression; a small group of words equivalent grammatically to a single word, esp. to an adjective, adverb or noun; (*pl.*) mere words; (*Mus.*) a short, distinct passage forming part of a melody. *v.t.* to express in words or phrases. **phrase-book,** *n.* a handbook of phrases or idioms in a foreign language. **phrase-monger,** *n.* one who uses mere phrases; one addicted to extravagant phrases. **phrasal,** *a.* †**phraseless,** *a.* indescribable. **phraser,** *n.* **phrasing,** *n.* the way in which a speech etc. is phrased, phraseology; the manner or result of grouping phrases in music. [F,

from L and Gr. *phrasis*, from *phrazein*, to speak]
phraseo-, *comb. form* pertaining to a phrase or phrases.
phraseogram, phraseograph, *n.* a character standing for a whole phrase, as in shorthand.
phraseology, *n.* choice or arrangement of words; manner of expression, diction; †a phrase-book. **phraseological**, *a.* **phraseologically**, *adv.* **phraseologist**, *n.*
phratry, *n.* in ancient Greece, a division of the people for political or religious purposes; one of the three subdivisions of a tribe in Athens; any tribal subdivision among primitive races. **phratric**, *a.* [F *phratrie*, Gr. *phratria*, from *phratēr*, a clansman, cogn. with L *frāter*, Eng. BROTHER]
phreak PHONE-FREAK under PHONE.
phren- PHREN(O)-.
phrenetic, FRENETIC.
phrenic, *a.* of or pertaining to the diaphragm. *n.* the phrenic nerve; †(*pl.*) psychology.
phrenitis, *n.* inflammation of the brain or its membranes, attended with delirium; brain-fever. **phrenitic**, *a.*
phren(o)-, mind; diaphragm. [Gr. *phrēn phrenos*]
phrenograph, *n.* an instrument for registering the movements of a diaphragm in breathing; a phrenological chart of a person's mental characteristics. **phrenography**, *n.* the description of phenomena as the first stage in comparative psychology.
phrenology, *n.* the theory that the mental faculties and affections are located in distinct parts of the brain denoted by prominences on the skull. **phrenological**, *a.* **phrenologically**, *adv.* **phrenologist**, *n.*
phrontistery, *n.* a place for thought or study, a thinking-shop. [Gr. *phrontistērion*, from *phrontizein*, to think, from *phrontis*, thought]
Phrygia, *n.* former kingdom of W Asia covering the Anatolian tableland. It was inhabited in ancient times by an Indo-European people, and achieved great prosperity in the 8th cent. BC under a line of kings bearing in turn the names Gordius and Midas, but then fell under Lydian rule. From Phrygia the cult of Cybele was introduced into Greece and Rome. **Phrygian**, *a.* pertaining to Phrygia. *n.* a native or inhabitant of Phrygia. **Phrygian cap**, *n.* a conical cap worn by the ancient Phrygians, since adopted as an emblem of liberty. **Phrygian mode**, *n.* (*Mus.*) one of the four ancient Greek modes, having a warlike character.
phthalic, *a.* of, pertaining to or derived from naphthalene. **phthalein**, *n.* one of a series of organic compounds, largely used for dyeing, produced by the combination of phthalic anhydride with the phenols. **phthalin**, *n.* a colourless crystalline substance obtained from phthalein. [short for NAPHTHALIC]
phthiriasis, *n.* a morbid condition in which lice multiply on the skin. [L, from Gr. *phtheiriasis*, from *phtheiriaein*, to be lousy]
†**phthisic**, *n.* phthisis; one suffering from phthisis. **phthisical, phthisicky**, *a.* [ME and OF *tisike*, L *phthisicus*, Gr. *phthisikos*]
phthisis, *n.* a wasting disease, esp. pulmonary consumption. **phthisiology**, *n.* [Gr., from *phthiein*, to decay]
phut, to go phut, to collapse, to stop. [Hind. *phatna*, to burst]
phycology, *n.* the botany of seaweeds or algae. **phycologist**, *n.* **phycography**, *n.* descriptive phycology. [Gr. *phukos*, seaweed]
phyl- PHYL(O)-.
phyla PHYLUM.
phylactery, *n.* a charm, spell or amulet worn as a preservative against disease or danger; a small leather box in which are enclosed slips of vellum inscribed with passages from the Pentateuch, worn on the head and left arm by Jews during morning prayer, except on the Sabbath. **phylacteric**, *a.* **phylacteried**, *a.* [L *phylactērium*, Gr. *phulaktērion*, from *phulaktēr*, a guard, from *phulassein*, to guard]
phylarch, *n.* the chief or commander of a tribe or clan, esp. in ancient Greece. **phylarchic, -ical**, *a.* **phylarchy**, *n.* [L *phȳlarchus*, Gr. *phūlarchos* (*phūlē*, tribe, *archein*, to rule)]
phyletic, *a.* pertaining to a phylum, racial. [Gr. *phūletikos*, from *phūletēs*, tribesman, as prec.]
phyll- PHYLL(O)-.
-phyll, *comb. form* leaf, as in *chlorophyll, xanthophyll.* [Gr. *phullon*]
phyllite, *n.* an argillaceous schist or slate.
phyllitis SCOLOPENDRIUM.
phyll(o)-, *comb. form* leaf. [Gr. *phullon*, leaf]
phyllobranchia, *n.* (*pl.* **-chiae**) a gill of a leaf-like or lamellar structure, as in certain crustaceans. [Gr. *branchia*, gills]
phyllode, phyllodium, *n.* (*pl.* **-odes, -odia**) a petiole having the appearance and functions of a leaf. **phylloid**, *a.* [F *phyllode*, mod. L *phyllōdium*, from Gr. *phyllōdēs*]
phyllomania, *n.* abnormal production of leaves.
phyllome, *n.* a leaf or organ analogous to a leaf; foliage. **phyllomic**, *a.*
phyllophagan, *n.* an animal feeding on leaves, as a group of lamellicorn beetles including the chafers, or one of the Phyllophaga, a group of Hymenoptera containing the saw-flies. **phyllophagous**, *a.*
phyllophorous, *a.* leaf-bearing.
phyllopod, *n.* any individual of the Phyllopoda, a group of entomostracous Crustacea with never less than four pairs of leaf-like feet. **phyllopodiform**, *a.* **phyllopodous**, *a.* [Gr. *pous podos*, foot]
phyllorhine, *a.* having a leaf-like appendage to the nose. *n.* a leaf-nosed bat. [Gr. *rhis rhīnos*, nose]
phyllostome, *n.* a bat of the genus *Phyllostoma*, characterized by a nose-leaf. **phyllostomatous, phylostomine, -moid, -mous**, *a.* [Gr. *stoma -atos*, mouth]
phyllotaxis, phyllotaxy, *n.* the arrangement of the leaves etc. on the stem or axis of a plant.
phylloxera, *n.* an aphid or plant-louse, orig. from America, very destructive to grape-vines. [Gr. *xēros*, dry]
phyl(o)-, *comb. form* tribe, race. [Gr. *phūlon, phūlē*, tribe]
phylogeny, -genesis, *n.* the evolution of a group, species or type of plant or animal life; the history of this. **phylogenetic, -ical, -genic**, *a.*
phylum, *n.* (*pl.* **phyla**) a primary group consisting of related organisms descended from a common form.
phyma, *n.* (*pl.* **-ata**) an external tubercle or imperfectly suppurating tumour. [L, from Gr. *phūma -atos*]
phys., (*abbr.*) physical; physics.
Physalia, *n.* a genus of large oceanic Hydrozoa comprising the Portuguese man-of-war. [mod. L, from Gr. *phusaleos*, inflated]
physalite, *n.* a greenish-white variety of topaz. [see PYROPHYSALITE]
Physeter, *n.* a genus of Cetacea, containing the sperm-whales; a filter working by air-pressure. [L, from Gr. *phūsētēr*, a blower, a whale, from *phūsaein*, to blow]
physi- PHYSI(O)-.
physic, *n.* the science or art of healing; the medical profession; medicine, esp. a purge or cathartic; †a physician. *v.t.* (*past, p.p.* **physicked**) to administer physic to, to dose; to purge. [ME *fisike*, OF *fisique*, L *physica*, Gr. *phusikē*, of nature, from *phusis*, nature, from *phuein*, to produce]
physical, *a.* of or pertaining to matter; obvious to or cognizable by the senses; pertaining to physics, esp. as opposed to chemical; material, bodily, corporeal, as opposed to spiritual; medicinal; †curative; †purgative. *n.* an examination to ascertain physical fitness. **physical geography**, *n.* the study of the earth's natural features. **physical jerks**, *n.pl.* (*coll.*) physical exercises to promote fitness. **physicality**, *n.* excessive concern with physical matters. **physically**, *adv.*
physician, *n.* one versed in or practising the art of healing, including medicine and surgery; a legally qualified practitioner who prescribes remedies for diseases; (*fig.*) a healer; †a physicist.
physicist, *n.* one versed in physics; a natural philosopher; one who believes in the physical and chemical

origin of vital phenomena, opposed to *vitalist*. **physicism,** *n.*
physico- *comb. form* physical.
physico-theology, *n.* theology based on natural philosophy, natural theology.
physics, *n. sing.* the science dealing with the phenomena of matter, esp. as affected by energy, and the laws governing these, excluding biology and chemistry.
physio, *n.* (*coll.*) short for PHYSIOTHERAPIST.
physi(o)-, *comb. form* pertaining to nature; physical. [Gr. *phusis,* nature]
physiocracy, *n.* government according to a natural order, taught by François Quesnay (1694–1774) founder of the physiocrats, to be inherent in society. **physiocrat,** *n.* **physiocratic,** *a.* **physiocratism,** *n.*
physiogeny, *n.* the genesis or evolution of vital functions; the history of this. **physiogenic,** *a.*
physiognomy, *n.* the art of reading character from features of the face or the form of the body; the face or countenance as an index of character; cast of features; (*coll.*) the face; the lineaments or external features (of a landscape etc.); aspect, appearance, look (of a situation, event etc.). **physiognomic, -ical,** *a.* **physiognomically,** *adv.* **physiognomist,** *n.* [ME *fisnomie,* OF *phisonomie,* med. L *phisonomia,* Gr. *phusiognōmonia* (*gnōmōn,* interpreter)]
physiography, *n.* the scientific description of the physical features of the earth, and the causes by which they have been modified; physical geography. **physiographer,** *n.* **physiographic, -ical,** *a.*
physiol., (*abbr.*) physiologist; physiology.
physiolatry, *n.* nature-worship.
physiology, *n.* the science of the vital phenomena and the organic functions of animals and plants. **physiologic, -ical,** *a.* **physiologically,** *adv.* **physiologist,** *n.* one versed in physiology. [L and Gr. *physiologia*]
physiotherapy, *n.* a form of medical treatment in which physical agents such as movement of limbs, massage, electricity etc. are used in place of drugs or surgery. **physiotherapeutic,** *a.* **physiotherapist,** *n.* a practitioner of this.
physique, *n.* physical structure or constitution of a person. [F, as PHYSIC]
physitheism, *n.* deification of natural forces or phenomena.
physiurgic, *a.* produced or affected solely by natural causes. [Gr. *ergon,* work, -IC]
physo-, *comb. form* relating to the bladder. [Gr. *phūsa,* bellows, bladder, cogn. with *phūsaein,* to blow]
physoclist, *a.* belonging to the Physoclisti, a division of teleostean fishes having the air-bladder closed and not connected with the intestine. **physoclistous,** *a.* [Gr. *kleistos,* shut]
physograde, *n.* any individual of the Physograda, containing siphonophores with a vesicular organ which renders them buoyant. [L *-gradus,* going]
physopod, *n.* a mollusc with suckers on the feet. [Gr. *pous podos,* foot]
Physostigma, *n.* a genus of W African climbing plants of the bean family containing the highly poisonous Calabar bean; this bean or its extract. **physostigmine,** *n.* a toxic alkaloid constituting the active principle of the Calabar bean.
physostome, *a.* belonging to the Physostomi, a division of teleostean fishes having the air-bladder connected by a duct with the intestinal canal. *n.* a fish of this division. **physostomous,** *a.* [Gr. *stoma,* mouth]
-phyte, *comb. form* denoting a vegetable organism, as in *lithophyte, zoophyte*. **-phytic,** *a.* [Gr. *phuton,* plant]
phyto-, *comb. form* plant. [Gr. *phuton,* plant]
phytobranchiate, *a.* of certain crustaceans, having leaf-like gills.
phytochemistry, *n.* the chemistry of plants. **phytochemical,** *a.*
phytogenesis, phytogeny, *n.* the origin, generation or evolution of plants.
phytogeography, *n.* the geographical distribution of plants.
phytography, *n.* the systematic description and naming of plants.
phytoid, *a.* plant-like. *n.* a plant-bud.
†**phytology,** *n.* botany. †**phytologist,** *n.*
phytomer, *n.* a phyton. [Gr. *meros,* part]
phyton, *n.* a plant-unit.
phytonomy, *n.* the science of plant growth.
phytopathology, *n.* the science of the diseases of plants; the pathology of diseases due to vegetable organisms. **phytopathological,** *a.* **phytopathologist,** *n.*
phytophagous, *a.* plant-eating.
phytoplankton, *n.* plant life as a constituent of plankton.
phytotomy, *n.* dissection of plants, vegetable anatomy.
phytotoxic, *a.* poisonous to plants.
phytozoon, *n.* (*pl.* **-zoa**) a plant-like animal, a zoophyte. [Gr. *zōon,* animal]
PI, (*abbr.*) petrol injection.
pi[1], *n.* the Greek letter π, p, the symbol representing the ratio of the circumference of a circle to the diameter, i.e. 3·14159265. [Gr. *pi*]
pi[2], PIE[3].
pi[3], *a.* (*coll.*) short for PIOUS.
pia, *n.* a Polynesian herb of the genus *Tacca,* esp. *T. pinnatifida,* yielding a variety of arrow-root. [Hawaiian]
piacular, *a.* expiatory; requiring expiation; atrociously bad. [L *piāculāris,* from *piāculum,* expiation, from *piāre,* to propitiate]
Piaf, *n.* **Edith,** stage name of Edith Gassion (1915–63), French Parisian singer and songwriter, best known for her defiant song 'Je ne regrette rien/I Regret Nothing'.
piaffe, *v.i.*, of a horse to move at a piaffer. *n.* an act of piaffing. **piaffer,** *n.* a movement like a trot but slower. [F *piaffer,* etym. doubtful]
Piaget, *n.* **Jean** (1896–1980), Swiss psychologist noted for his studies of the development of thought, concepts of space and movement, logic and reasoning in children.
pia mater, *n.* a delicate membrane, the innermost of the three meninges investing the brain and spinal cord; the brain. [med. L version of Arab. *umm raqīqan,* tender mother]
pianette, pianino, *n.* a small piano. [It., dim. of PIANO[2]]
pianissimo, *adv.* (*Mus.*) very softly. *a.* very soft. *n.* a passage so rendered. [It., superl. of PIANO[1]]
piano[1], *adv.* (*Mus.*) softly. *a.* played softly. *n.* a passage so rendered. [It., from L *plānus,* even, flat, late L, soft, low]
piano[2], **pianoforte,** *n.* (*pl.* **-nos**) a musical instrument the sounds of which are produced by blows on the wire strings from hammers acted upon by levers set in motion by keys. **piano accordion,** *n.* an accordion equipped with a keyboard resembling that of a piano. **piano-organ,** *n.* a mechanical organ worked on similar principles to those of the barrel-organ. **piano-player,** *n.* a pianist; a device for playing a piano mechanically. **pianism,** *n.* piano-playing; the technique of this. **pianist,** *n.* a performer on the pianoforte. **pianiste,** *n. fem.* **pianola**®, *n.* a type of piano-player. [It., earlier *piano e forte,* L *plānus et fortis,* soft and strong]
piassava, *n.* a coarse stiff fibre obtained from Brazilian palms, used esp. to make ropes and brushes. [Port., from Tupi *piaçaba*]
piastre, (*esp. N Am.*) **piaster,** *n.* the Spanish dollar or silver peso; a small coin of Turkey and several former dependencies. [F, from It. *piastra,* plate or leaf of metal, as PLASTER]
piazza, *n.* a square open space, public square, or market-place, esp. in Italian towns; applied to any open space surrounded by buildings or colonnades; improperly applied to a colonnade, or an arcaded or colonnaded walk, and (*N Am.*) to a verandah about a house. [It., from pop. L *plattia,* L *platea,* Gr. *plateia* broad, see PLACE]
pibroch, *n.* a series of variations, chiefly martial, played on a bagpipe; (*erron.*) the bagpipe. [Gael. *piobaireachd* (*piobair,* piper, from *piob,* from PIPE)]

pic, *n.* (*pl.* **pics, pix**) (*coll.*) a photograph.

Pica[1], *n.* a genus of Corvidae containing the magpie; a vitiated appetite causing the person affected to crave for things unfit for food, as coal, chalk etc. [L, magpie]

pica[2], *n.* a size of type, the standard of measurement in printing. [med. L, an ordinal giving rules for movable feasts, perh. ident. with foll.]

picador, *n.* in Spanish bullfights, a horseman with a lance who rouses the bull. [Sp., from *picar,* to prick]

picamar, *n.* an oily compound, one of the products of the distillation of wood-tar. [L *pix picis,* PITCH[1] *amarus,* bitter]

Picardie, *n.* (English **Picardy**) region of N France, including Aisne, Oise, and Somme departments; area 19,400 sq km/7488 sq miles; population (1986) 1,774,000. Industries include chemicals and metals. It was a major battlefield in World War I.

picaresque, *a.* describing the exploits and adventures of picaroons; being or relating to a style of fiction describing the episodic adventures of a usu. errant rogue. [see foll.]

picaroon, *n.* a rogue, a vagabond; a cheat; a thief, a robber; a pirate, a corsair; a pirate-ship. [Sp. *picaron,* from *picaro,* perh. rel. to *picar,* to prick]

Picasso, *n.* **Pablo** (1881–1973), Spanish artist, active chiefly in France, one of the most inventive and prolific talents in 20th cent. art. His Blue Period (1901–04) and Rose Period (1905–06) preceded the revolutionary *Les Demoiselles d'Avignon* (1907; Metropolitan Museum of Art, New York), which paved the way for Cubism. In the early 1920s he was considered a leader of the Surrealist movement. In the 1930s his work included metal sculpture, book illustration, and the mural *Guernica* (1937; Casón del Buen Retiro, Madrid), a comment on the bombing of civilians in the Spanish Civil War. He continued to paint into his 80s.

picayune, *n.* (*N Am.*) a small Spanish coin, value 6¼ cents, now obsolete; applied to the 5-cent piece and other small coins; hence something of small value. *a.* of little value; petty, trifling. [Louisiana, from Prov. *picaioun* (F *picaillon*), etym. doubtful]

piccadil, piccadilly, *n.* a high collar or ruff, usu. with a laced or perforated edging, worn in the 17th cent. [F *picadille, piccadille,* Sp. dim. of *picado,* pricked, slashed, p.p. of *picar,* to prick]

piccalilli, *n.* a pickle of various chopped vegetables with pungent spices. [etym. doubtful]

piccaninny, *n.* (*offensive*) a little child. esp. of blacks or Australian Aborigines. *a.* tiny, baby. [W Ind., from Sp. *pequeño* or Port. *pequeno,* small, rel. to foll.]

Piccard, *n.* **August** (1884–1962), Swiss scientist. In 1931–32, he and his twin brother, Jean Félix, made ascents to 16,800 m/55,000 ft in a balloon of his own design, resulting in important discoveries concerning stratospheric phenomena such as cosmic rays. He also built and used, with his son Jacques Ernest, bathyscaphes for research under the sea.

piccolo, *n.* (*pl.* **-los**) a small flute, with the notes one octave higher than the ordinary flute. **piccoloist,** *n.* [It., small, a small flute]

pice, *n.* an Indian copper coin the quarter of an anna. [Hindi *paisa*]

piceous, *a.* pitch-black, brownish or reddish black; inflammable. [L *piceus,* from *pix picis,* PITCH[1]]

pichiciago, *n.* a small S American armadillo. [Sp. *pichiciego* (prob. Tupi-Guarani *pichey,* Sp. *ciego,* L *caecus,* blind)]

pick[1], *v.t.* to break, pierce, or indent with a pointed instrument; to make (a hole) or to open thus; to strike at with something pointed; to remove extraneous matter from (the teeth etc.) thus; to clean by removing that which adheres with the teeth, fingers etc.; to pluck, to gather; to take up with a beak etc.; to eat in little bits; to choose, to cull, to select carefully; to make (one's way) carefully on foot; to find an occasion for (a quarrel etc.); to steal the contents of; to open (a lock) with an implement other than the key; to pluck, to pull apart; to twitch the strings of, to play (a banjo); †to strike with the bill, to puncture. *v.i.* to strike at with a pointed implement; to eat in little bits; to make a careful choice; to pilfer. *n.* choice, selection; the best (of). **to pick and choose,** to make a fastidious selection. **to pick at,** to criticize in a cavilling way; to eat sparingly. **to pick off,** to gather or detach (fruit, etc.) from the tree etc.; to shoot with careful aim one by one. **to pick on,** to single out, to select; to single out for unpleasant treatment; to bully. **to pick out,** to select; to distinguish (with the eye) from surroundings; to relieve or variegate with or as with distinctive colours; to gather (the meaning of a passage etc.); to gather by ear and play (a tune) on the piano etc. **to pick someone's brains,** to consult someone with special expertise or experience. **to pick to pieces,** to analyse or criticize spitefully. **to pick up,** to take up with the beak, fingers etc.; to gather or acquire here and there or little by little; to collect; to accept and pay (a bill); to detain (a suspect etc.); to receive (an electronic signal etc.) to come across, to fall in with; to make acquaintance (with); to regain or recover (health etc.); to recover one's health. **pick-lock,** *n.* an instrument for opening a lock without the key; one who picks locks; a thief. **pick-me-up,** *n.* a drink or medicine taken to restore the tone of the system. **pickpocket,** *n.* one who steals from pockets. †**pickpurse,** *n., a.* †**pickthank,** *n.* an officious person; a toady. †**picktooth,** *n.* a toothpick. **pick-up,** *n.* the act of picking up, esp. at cricket; a person or thing picked up; a casual acquaintance, esp. one made for the purpose of having sexual intercourse; the act of making such an acquaintance; a vehicle with a driver's cab at the front, and an open back with sides and a tailboard. a device holding a needle which follows the track of a gramophone record and converts the resulting mechanical vibrations into acoustic or electrical vibrations. **picked,** *a.* gathered, culled; chosen, selected, choice. **picker,** *n.* **pickings,** *n.pl.* gleanings, odds-and-ends; profit or reward, esp. when obtained dishonestly. **picky,** *a.* (*coll.*) excessively fastidious, choosy. [ME *pikken, piken,* perh. rel. to foll. and to F *piquer,* to prick]

pick[2], *n.* a tool with a long iron head, usu. pointed at one end and pointed or having a chisel-edge at the other, fitted in the middle on a wooden shaft, used for breaking ground etc.; one of various implements used for picking. **picked**, *a.* having a point or spike, pointed, sharp; †peaked, tapering. †**picked- ness,** *n.* [prob. var. of PIKE[1]]

pick-a-back, *adv.* on the back or shoulders, like a pack. *v.t.* to carry (a person) pick-a-back *n.* an act of carrying a person pick-a-back. [etym. doubtful]

pickaxe, *n.* an instrument for breaking ground etc., a pick. *v.t.* to break up with a pickaxe. *v.i.* to use a pickaxe. [ME pikois, OF *picois,* rel. to OF *pic,* see PIKE[1]]

pickeer, *v.i.* to maraud; to skirmish; to reconnoitre. [etym. doubtful]

picker PICK[1].

pickerel, *n.* a young or small pike.

picket, *n.* a pointed stake, post, or peg, forming part of a palisade or paling, for tethering a horse to etc.; a small body of troops posted on the outskirts of a camp etc., as a guard, sent out to look for the enemy, or kept in camp for immediate service; a guard sent out to bring in men who have exceeded their leave; a person or group of people set by a trade-union to watch a shop, factory etc., during labour disputes; a person or group posted in a certain place as part of a protest or demonstration; †a military punishment of making an offender stand with one foot on a pointed stake. *v.t.* to fortify or protect with stakes etc., to fence in; to tether to a picket; to post as a picket; to set a picket or pickets at (the gates of a factory etc.). *v.i.* to act as a picket. **picket-line,** *n.* a group of people picketing a factory etc. [F *piquet,* from *piquer,* to prick]

Pickford, *n.* **Mary,** adopted name of Gladys Smith (1893–1979), American silent film actress, born in Toronto, Canada. As a child she toured with various road companies, started her film career 1909, and in 1919 formed United Artists with Charlie Chaplin, D. W. Griffith, and her second husband (1920–36) Douglas

Fairbanks. She often appeared as a young girl, even when she was well into her twenties. The public did not like her talking films, and she retired 1933. She was known as 'America's Sweetheart'.

pickle[1], *n.* a liquid, as brine, vinegar etc., for preserving fish, meat, vegetables etc.; (*often pl.*) vegetables or other food preserved in pickle; diluted acid used for cleaning etc.; a disagreeable or embarrassing position; a troublesome child. *v.t.* to preserve in pickle; to treat with pickle; †to rub (a person's back after flogging) with salt and water; to imbue thoroughly with any quality. **to have a rod in pickle,** to have a beating or scolding in store (for). †**pickle-herring,** *n.* a pickled herring; a merry-andrew, a buffoon. **pickled** *a.* (*coll.*) drunk. [cp. Dut. and LG *pekel,* etym. doubtful]

pickle[2], *v.t.* (*chiefly Sc.*) to nibble, to eat sparingly; to pilfer. *n.* (*Sc.*) a small quantity, a little. [freq. of PICK[1]]

picklock, pickpocket etc. PICK[1].

picksome, *a.* fastidious, select. [PICK[1], -SOME[1]]

Pickwickian, *a.* relating to or characteristic of Mr Pickwick; (*facet.*) of the sense of words, merely technical or hypothetical. [Mr *Pickwick,* in Dickens's *Pickwick Papers*]

picky PICK[1].

picnic, *n.* originally an entertainment to which each guest contributed his or her share; an outdoor pleasure-party the members of which carry with them provisions on an excursion into the country etc.; an informal meal, esp. one eaten outside. (*Austral.*) a mess, a confusion; (*often in neg; coll.*) an easy or pleasant undertaking. *v.i.* (*past, p.p.* **picnicked**) to go on a picnic. **picnicker,** *n.* **picnicky,** *a.* [F *pique-nique,* etym. doubtful]

pico-, *comb.form* one millionth of a millionth part (10^{-12}). [Sp. *pico,* a small amount].

picot, *n.* a small loop of thread forming part of an ornamental edging. **picot-edge,** *n.* machined stitching for a garment; bisected hem-stitching. [F, dim. of *pic,* a peak, see PIKE[1]]

picotee, *n.* a hardy garden variety of the carnation, with a spotted or dark-coloured margin. [F *picoté,* p.p. of *picoter,* from *piquer,* to prick, as prec.]

picotite, *n.* a variety of spinel containing chromium oxide. [*Picot,* Baron de la Peyrouse, 1744–1818]

picric, *a.* having an intensely bitter taste; applied to an acid obtained by the action of nitric acid on phenol etc., used in dyeing and in certain explosives. **picrate,** *n.* a salt of this. **picrite,** *n.* a blackish-green rock, composed largely of chrysolite. [Gr. *pikros,* bitter, -IC]

picr(o)-, *comb. form.* bitter.

picrotoxin, *n.* a bitter crystalline compound constituting the bitter principle of *Cocculus indicus.*

Pict, *n.* one of a people who anciently inhabited parts of northern Britain. Of pre-Celtic origin, and speaking a non-Celtic language, the Picts were united with the Celtic Scots under the rule of Kenneth MacAlpin in 844. **Pictish,** *a.* of the Picts. *n.* their language. [late L *Pictī,* perh. from native name, assim. to *pictus,* p.p. of *pingere,* to paint]

pictograph, *n.* a picture standing for an idea, a pictorial character or symbol; a record or primitive writing consisting of these; a diagram showing statistical data in pictorial form. **pictogram,** *n.* a pictograph. **pictographic,** *a.* **pictography,** *n.* [L *pictus,* p.p. of *pingere,* to paint, -GRAPH]

pictorial, *a.* pertaining to, containing, expressed, or illustrated by pictures. *n.* an illustrated journal etc. **pictorially,** *adv.* [late L *pictōrius,* from *pictor,* painter, as prec.]

picture, *n.* a painting or drawing representing a person, natural scenery, or other objects; a photograph, engraving, or other representation on a plane surface; an image, copy; a vivid description; a perfect example; a beautiful object; a scene, a subject suitable for pictorial representation; a motion picture, a film; the image on a television screen. *v.t.* to represent by painting; to depict vividly; to form a mental likeness of, to imagine vividly. **in the picture,** having all the relevant information. **the pictures,** *n.pl.* (*coll.*) a cinematograph entertainment. **to get the picture,** to understand the situation. **picture-book,** *n.* an illustrated book, esp. one full of illustrations for children. **picture-card,** *n.* a court card. **picture-gallery,** *n.* a gallery or large room in which pictures are exhibited. **picture-hat,** *n.* a lady's hat with wide drooping brim, like those often seen in Reynolds's and Gainsborough's pictures. **picture-house,** *n.* a cinema. **picture postcard,** *n.* a postcard with a picture on the back. *a.* picturesque. **picture window,** *n.* a large window, usu. with a single pane, framing an attractive view. **picture-writing,** *n.* a primitive method of recording events etc., by means of pictorial symbols, as in hieroglyphics, pictography. **pictural,** *a.* [L *pictūra,* from *pictus,* p.p. of *pingere,* to paint]

picturesque, *a.* having those qualities that characterize a good picture, natural or artificial; of language, graphic, vivid. *n.* that which is picturesque. **picturesquely,** *adv.* **picturesqueness,** *n.* [It. *pittoresco*]

piddle, *v.i.* to trifle; to work, act, behave etc., in a trifling way; to urinate. *n.* an act of urinating; urine. **piddler,** *n.* **piddling,** *a.* trifling; squeamish. [etym. doubtful]

piddock, *n.* a bivalve mollusc of the burrowing genus *Pholas* of which *P. dactylus* is largely used for bait. [etym. doubtful]

pidgin, *n.* a language that is a combination of two or more languages, used esp. for trading between people of different native languages. **not my pidgin,** PIGEON. **pidgin English,** *n.* pidgin in which one of the languages is English, orig. a trade jargon or contact language between the British and the Chinese in the 19th cent. [Chin. (corr. of BUSINESS)]

pie[1], *n.* a magpie; applied to other pied birds, as the spotted woodpecker, the oyster-catcher etc. **pied,** *a.* black-and-white. [OF, from L *pīca*]

pie[2], *n.* meat, fruit etc., baked with a pastry top. **pie in the sky,** an unrealistic aspiration. **to have a finger in every pie** FINGER. **pie chart,** *n.* a pictorial representation of relative quantities, in which the quantities are represented by sectors of a circle. **pie-eyed,** *a.* (*coll.*) drunk.

pie[3], *n.* †a set of rules in use before the Reformation relating to the services for movable festivals etc.; a confused mass of printers' type; a jumble, disorder, confusion. *v.t.* to mix or confuse (type). †**by cock and pie,** a minced oath–by God and the old Roman Catholic service-book. [perh. from PIE[1], from the appearance of the black-letter type on white paper]

pie[4] *n.* an Indian copper coin one-twelfth of the anna. [Hindi *pa'i,* prob. cogn. with PICE]

piebald, *a.* of a horse or other animal, having patches of two different colours, usu. black and white; particoloured, mottled; motley, mongrel. *n.* a piebald horse or other animal.

piece, *n.* a distinct part of anything; a detached portion, a fragment (of); a division, a section; a plot or enclosed portion (of land); a definite quantity or portion in which commercial products are made up or sold; a cask (of wine etc.) of varying capacity; an example, an instance; an artistic or literary composition or performance, usu. short; a coin; a gun, a firearm; a man at chess, draughts etc.; (*offensive sl.*) a woman; (*Sc.*) a thick slice of bread with butter, jam, or cheese. *v.t.* to add pieces to, to mend, to patch; to put together so as to form a whole; to join together, to reunite; to fit (on). *v.i.* to come together, to fit (well or ill). **a piece of cake,** something very easy. **a piece of the action,** (*coll.*) active involvement. **by the piece,** of wages, according to the amount of work done. **in pieces,** broken. **of a piece,** of the same sort, uniform. **piece of eight,** old Spanish dollar of eight *reals,* worth about 22½p. **to go to pieces,** to collapse. **to piece on,** to fit on (to). **to piece out,** to complete by adding one or more pieces to; to eke out. **to piece up,** to patch up. **to say one's piece,** to express one's opinion. **piece goods,** *n.pl.* work paid for by the piece or job. **piecemeal,** *adv.* piece by piece, part at a time; in pieces. *a.* made up of pieces; done by the piece; fragmentary.

piece-work, *n.* work paid for by the piece or job. **pieceless,** *a.* whole, entire. **piecer,** *n.* [OF *pece* (cp. Prov. *peza, pessa,* It. *pezza, pezzo,* Sp. *pieza*), etym. doubtful]

pièce de résistance, an outstanding item; the main dish of a meal. [F, piece of resistance]

pie chart PIE².

Pieck, *n.* **Wilhelm** (1876–1960), German communist politician. He was a leader of the 1919 Spartacist revolt and a founder of the Socialist Unity Party (1946). From 1949 he was president of East Germany; the office was abolished on his death.

pied, *a.* parti-coloured, variegated, spotted. **piedness,** *n.* [PIE¹, -ED]

pied-à-terre, *n.* a footing, a temporary lodging, e.g. a city apartment for a country dweller. [Fr., foot on the ground]

Piedmont, *n.* (Italian **Piemonte**) region of N Italy, bordering Switzerland on the north and France on the west, and surrounded, except on the east, by the Alps and the Apennines; area 25,400 sq km/9804 sq miles; population (1988) 4,377,000. Its capital is Turin, and towns include Alessandria, Asti, Vercelli, and Novara. It also includes the fertile Po river valley. Products include fruit, grain, cattle, cars, and textiles. The movement for the unification of Italy started in the 19th century in Piedmont, under the house of Savoy.

pie-eyed PIE².

†**piepowder,** *n.* a traveller, a wayfarer. **Piepowder Court,** *n.* a summary court of record formerly held in fairs and markets by the steward for dealing with disputes arising there. [OF *pied pouldré* (F *pied-poudreux*), dusty foot]

pier, *n.* a mass of masonry supporting an arch, the superstructure of a bridge, or other building; a pillar, a column; a solid portion of masonry between windows etc.; a buttress; a breakwater, mole, jetty; a structure projecting into the sea etc., used as a landing-stage, promenade etc. **pier-glass,** *n.* a looking-glass orig. placed between windows; a large ornamental mirror. **pier-table,** *n.* a low table placed between windows. **pierage,** *n.* toll for using a pier or jetty. [ME and AF *pere,* OF *piere* (F *pierre*), L *petra,* stone]

pierce, *v.t.* to penetrate or transfix with or as with a pointed instrument; of such an instrument, to penetrate, to transfix, to prick; to make a hole in; to move or affect deeply; to force a way into, to explore; of light, to shine through; of sound, to break (a silence etc.). *v.i.* to penetrate (into, through etc.). **pierceable,** *a.* **piercer,** *n.* **piercing,** *a.* penetrating; affecting deeply. **piercingly,** *adv.* **piercingness,** *n.* [OF *percer, percier,* etym. doubtful]

Pierian, *a.* pertaining to Pieria, in Thessaly, or to the Pierides or Muses.

Piero della Francesca, (*c.* 1420–92), Italian painter, active in Arezzo and Urbino. His work has a solemn stillness and unusually solid figures, luminous colour and compositional harmony. It includes a fresco series, *The Legend of the True Cross* (S Francesco, Arezzo), begun about 1452. Piero wrote two treatises, one on mathematics, one on the laws of perspective in painting.

Piero di Cosimo, (*c.* 1462–1521), Italian painter, noted for inventive pictures of mythological subjects, often featuring fauns and centaurs. He also painted portraits.

pierrot, *n.* a buffoon or itinerant minstrel, orig. French and usu. dressed in loose white costume and with the face whitened. **pierrette,** *n. fem.* [F, dim. of *Pierre,* PETER]

piet, *n.* a magpie. [ME *piot,* from PIE¹]

pietà, *n.* a pictorial or sculptured representation of the Virgin and the dead Christ. [It., from L *pietas,* PIETY]

Pietism, *n.* a religious movement within Lutheranism in the 17th cent. which emphasized spiritual and devotional Christianity. The movement was led by P. J. Spener (1635–1705), who cultivated personal godliness to the disregard of dogma and the services of the church. **Pietist,** *n.* one who makes a display of strong religious feelings; an adherent of Pietism. **pietistic, -ical,** *a.*

piety, *n.* the quality of being pious; reverence towards God; †filial reverence or devotion. [F *piété,* L *pietas*]

piezo-, *comb. form.* pressure. [Gr. *piezein,* to press]

piezochemistry, *n.* the study of the effect of high pressures on chemical reactions.

piezoelectricity, piezoelectric effect, *n.* a property possessed by some crystals, e.g. those used in gramophone crystal pick-ups, of generating surface electric charges when mechanically strained. they also expand along one axis and contract along another when subjected to an electric field.

piezometer, *n.* an instrument for determining the compressibility of liquids or other forms of pressure. [Gr. *piezein,* to press]

piffero, *n.* (*pl* **-ros**) a small flute like an oboe; an organ-stop with a similar tone. **pifferaro,** *n.* an itinerant player on the **piffero**. [It., from Teut. (cp. FIFE)]

piffle, *v.i.* to talk or act in a feeble, ineffective, or trifling way. *n.* trash, rubbish, twaddle. **piffler,** *n.*

pig, *n.* a swine, a hog, esp. when small or young; the flesh of this, pork; (*coll.*) a greedy, gluttonous, filthy, obstinate, or annoying person; an oblong mass of metal (esp. iron or lead) as run from the furnace. (*sl.*) a police officer; (*sl.*) a very difficult or unpleasant thing; *v.i.* to bring forth pigs; to be huddled together like pigs. *v.t.* (*past, p.p.* **pigged**) to bring forth (pigs); to overindulge oneself in eating. **a pig in a poke,** goods purchased without being seen beforehand. **to make a pig's ear of,** (*sl.*) to make a mess of, to botch. **to pig it,** (*sl.*) to live in squalor; to behave in an unmannerly way. **pig-eyed,** *a.* having small sunken eyes. **pig-fish,** *n.* any of various kinds of fish that make a grunting noise. **pigheaded,** *a.* having a large, ill-shaped head; stupid; stupidly obstinate or perverse. **pigheadedly,** *adv.* **pigheadedness,** *n.* **pig-iron,** *n.* iron in pigs. **pig-jump,** *v.i.* (*Austral. sl.*) of a horse, to jump with all four legs without bringing them together. **pignut,** *n.* an earth-nut. **pigroot,** *v.i.* (*Austral. sl.*) of a horse to kick out with the back legs while the fore legs are firmly planted on the ground. **pigskin,** *n.* the skin of a pig; leather made from this; (*sl.*) a saddle; *a.* made of this leather. **pigsticking,** *n.* the sport of hunting wild boars with a spear; pig-killing. **pigsticker,** *n.* **pigsty,** *n.* a sty or pen for pigs; a dirty place, a hovel. **pig's wash,** *n.* swill or refuse from kitchens, etc., for feeding pigs. **pig-tail,** *n.* the tail of a pig; the hair of the head tied in a long queue like a pig's tail; tobacco prepared in a long twist. **pigtailed,** *a.* **pigwash** PIG'S WASH. **pigweed,** *n.* the goosefoot or other herb eaten by pigs. **piggery,** *n.* **piggish,** *a.* like a pig, esp. in greed. **piggishly,** *adv.* **piggishness,** *n.* **piggy,** *n.* a little pig; the game of tipcat. **piggy-bank,** *n.* a container for saved coins, usu. in the shape of a pig. **piggy-wiggy,** *n.* a little pig; a term of endearment applied to children. **piglet, pigling,** *n.* **piglike,** *a.* [ME *pigge,* etym. doubtful]

Pigalle, *n.* **Jean Baptiste** (1714–85), French sculptor. In 1744 he made the marble *Mercury* (Louvre, Paris), a lively, naturalistic work. His subjects ranged from the intimate to the formal, and included portraits.

pigeon, *n.* a bird of the order Columbae, a dove; a greenhorn, a gull, a simpleton. *v.t.* to fleece, to swindle, esp. by tricks in gambling. **not my pigeon,** (*coll.*) not my business, not concerning me. **pigeon-breast,** *n.* a deformity in which the breast is constricted and the sternum thrust forward. **pigeon-breasted,** *a.* **pigeon-English** PIDGIN-ENGLISH under PIDGIN. **pigeon-gram,** *n.* a message carried by a pigeon. †**pigeon-hearted,** *a.* timid, easily frightened. **pigeonhole,** *n.* a hole in a dove-cot, by which the pigeons pass in or out; a nesting compartment for pigeons; a compartment in a cabinet etc., for papers, etc.; a category, esp. an over-simplified one. *v.t.* to put away in this; to defer for future consideration, to shelve; to give a definite place to in the mind, to label, to classify. †**pigeon-livered,** *a.* **pigeon-pea,** *n.* the pea-like seed of an Indian shrub, *Cajanus indicus*. **pigeon-post,** *n.* the conveyance of letters etc., by homing pigeons. **pigeon's milk,** *n.* a milky substance consisting of half-digested food with which pigeons feed their young; a sham object for which fools are sent. **pigeon-toed,** *a.* having the toes turned in. **pigeon-wing,** *n.* the hair at the side of the head dressed like a pigeon's wing, or a wig of this form, fashionable among men in the 18th cent.; (*N Am.*) a fancy dance-step, a fancy-figure in skating. **pigeonry,** *n.* [ME *pyjon,* OF *pijon* (F *pigeon*), late L *pīpiōnem,* nom. *pīpio,* from *pīpīre,* to chirp]

piggery etc. PIG.

piggin, *n.* a small pail or vessel, usu. of wood, with a handle formed by one of the staves, for holding liquids. [etym. doubtful]

Piggott, *n.* **Lester** (1935–), English jockey. He was regarded as a brilliant tactician and adopted a unique high riding style. A champion jockey 11 times 1960–82, he rode a record nine Derby winners.

piggy-back, PICK-A-BACK.

pightle, *n.* a small enclosure of land, a croft. [etym. doubtful]

pigment, *n.* colouring-matter used as paint or dye; a substance giving colour to animal or vegetable tissues. **pigmental**, **pigmentary,** *a.* **pigmentation,** *n.* [L *pigmentum,* cogn. with *pingere,* to paint]

†**pignoration,** *n.* the act of pledging or pawning. †**pignorative**, *a.* [L *pignerātio,* from *pignerāre,* from *pignus -neris,* pledge]

pignut, pigroot PIG.

†**pigsney,** *n.* a term of endearment. [ME *pigges neyge* (*neyge,* var. of EYE prob. from *a neye,* an eye]

pigsty, pigtail PIG.

pika, *n.* a small burrowing mammal of the Ochotonidae family, related to the rabbit, a native of Asia and N America. [Tungus, *piika*]

pike¹, *n.* a military weapon, consisting of a narrow, elongated lance-head fixed to a pole; a pickaxe, a spike; a peak, a peaked or pointed hill, esp. in the English Lake District; (prob. short for *pike-fish*) a large slender voracious freshwater fish of the genus *Esox,* with a long pointed snout; a diving position in which the legs are straight, the hips bent, and the hands clasp the feet or knees. *v.t.* to run through or kill with a pike. **pikeman** *n.* a miner working with a pick-axe; a soldier armed with a pike. **pikestaff,** *n.* the wooden shaft of a pike; a pointed stick carried by pilgrims etc. **plain as a pikestaff** [earlier PACKSTAFF] perfectly clear or obvious. **piked,** *a.* pointed, peaked. [F *pique,* in first sense, cogn. with *piquer,* to pierce, *pic,* pick-axe, others prob. from cogn. OE *pīc*]

pike², *n.* a toll-bar; a turnpike road. **pikeman** a turnpike-man. **piker,** *n.* a tramp; (*N Am. sl.*) a poor sport; a timid gambler; (*Austral.*) a wild bullock; a trickster, a sharp fellow. [short for TURNPIKE]

pikelet, *n.* a small round teacake or crumpet. [short for obs. *bara-piklet,* W *bara-pyglyd,* pitchy bread]

pikeman PIKE¹,².

piker PIKE².

pikestaff PIKE¹.

pilaf(f), PILAU.

pilar, *a.* of or pertaining to hair. **pilary,** *a.* [L *pilus*, hair, -AR]

pilaster, *n.* a rectangular column engaged in a wall or pier. **pilastered,** *a.* [F *pilastre,* It. *pilastro* (*pila,* L *pīla,* pillar, -ASTER)]

Pilate, *n.* **Pontius** (early 1st cent. AD), Roman procurator of Judaea 26–36 AD. Unsympathetic to the Jews, his actions several times provoked riots, and in 36 AD he was recalled to Rome after brutal suppression of a Samaritan uprising. The New Testament Gospels describe his reluctant ordering of Jesus' crucifixion, but there has been considerable debate about his actual role in it; many believe that pressure was put on him by Jewish conservative priests. The Greek historian Eusebius says he committed suicide, but Coptic tradition says he was martyred as a Christian.

pilau, pilaw, *n.* an Oriental mixed dish consisting of rice boiled with meat, fowl, or fish, together with raisins, spices etc. [Pers. *pilāw* (cp. Hind. *pilāo, palāo*)]

pilch, *n.* a flannel wrapper for an infant; †a garment of fur or skin, a coarse outer garment. †**pilcher,** *n.* (*Shak.*) a scabbard. [OE *plyce,* med. L *pellicea,* PELISSE]

pilchard, *n.* a small sea-fish, *Clupea pilchardus,* allied to the herring, and an important food-fish. [etym. doubtful]

pile¹, *n.* a heap, a mass of things heaped together; a funeral pyre, a heap of combustibles for burning a dead body; a very large, massive, or lofty building; an accumulation; (*coll.*) a great quantity or sum, a fortune; a series of plates of different metals arranged alternately so as to produce an electrical current; an atomic pile; †the reverse of a coin (from the mark left by the pillar or pile of the minting apparatus). *v.t.* to collect or heap up or together, to accumulate; to load; to stack (rifles) with butts on the ground and muzzles together. *v.i.* to move in a crowd. **to pile it on,** (*coll.*) to exaggerate. **to pile up,** to accumulate; to be involved in a pile up. **to pile up the agony** AGONY. **pile-up,** (*coll.*) *n.* a crash involving several vehicles. **piler,** *n.* [F, from L *pīla,* pillar]

pile², *n.* a sharp stake or post; a heavy timber driven into the ground, esp. under water, to form a foundation. *v.t.* to drive piles into; to furnish or strengthen with piles. **pile-driver, -engine,** *n.* a device for driving piles into the ground. **pile-worm,** *n.* a worm attacking piles. [OE *pīl,* L *pīlum,* javelin]

pile³, *n.* soft hair, fur, down, wool; the nap of velvet, plush, or other cloth, or of a carpet. [L *pilus,* hair]

pile⁴, *n.* (*usu. pl.*) small tumours formed by the dilatation of the veins about the anus, haemorrhoids. **pilewort,** *n.* the lesser celandine or figwort, *Ranunculus ficaria,* supposed to be a remedy for this. [L *pīla,* ball]

pileate, -ated, *a.* having a pileus or cap. [L *pīleātus,* from PILEUS]

pileum, *n.* the top of the head, from the base of the bill to the nape, in a bird. [L, var. of foll.]

pileus, *n.* (*pl.* **-lei**) in classical antiquity, a brimless felt cap; the cap of a mushroom; the pileum. [L *pīleus, pilleus* (cp. Gr. *pīlos*)]

pilfer, *v.t.* to steal in small quantities. **pilferage**, *n.* **pilferer,** *n.* **pilfering,** *n.* **pilferingly,** *adv.* [OF *pelfrer,* from *pelfre* PELF]

†**pilgarlick,** *n.* a bald head, one who has lost his hair by disease; a sneaking fellow. [*pilled,* see PILL², pealed, *garlick*]

pilgrim, *n.* one who travels to a distance to visit some holy place, in performance of a vow etc.; a traveller, a wanderer. *v.i.* to go on a pilgrimage; to wander as a pilgrim. **Pilgrim Fathers,** *n.pl.* the English Puritan colonists who sailed in the *Mayflower* to N America, and founded Plymouth, Massachusetts in 1620. **Pilgrims' Way,** *n.* track running from Winchester to Canterbury, England, which was the route of mediaeval pilgrims visiting the shrine of Thomas à Becket. Some 195 km/120 miles long, the Pilgrims' Way can still be traced for most of its of its length. **pilgrimage,** *n.* a pilgrim's journey to some holy place; the journey of human life. *v.i.* to go on a pilgrimage. **pilgrimize, -ise,** *v.i.* to play the pilgrim. [ME *pelegrim,* prob. through an OF *pelegrin* (cp. F *pèlerin,* It. *pellegrino*), L *peregrīnus,* stranger, see PEREGRINE]

Pilgrimage of Grace, a rebellion against Henry VIII of England 1536–37, originating in Yorkshire and Lincolnshire. The rising, headed by Robert Aske (died 1537), was directed against the policies of the monarch (such as the dissolution of the monasteries and the effects of enclosure).

Pilgrim's Progress, *n.* an allegory by John Bunyan, published 1678–84, which describes a man's journey through life to the Celestial City. On his way through the Slough of Despond, the House Beautiful, Vanity Fair, Doubting Castle, and other landmarks, Christian meets a number of allegorical figures.

piliferous, *a.* bearing hairs. **piliform**, *a.* **piligerous**, *a.* having a covering of hair. [L *pilus,* hair.]

pill¹, *n.* a little ball or capsule of some medicinal substance to be swallowed whole; something unpleasant which has to be accepted or put up with; (*sl.*) a black balloting-ball; (*pl.*) billiard balls. *v.i.* †to dose with pills; (*sl.*) to blackball, to reject. **the pill,** (*coll.*) the contraceptive pill, based on female hormones. **to gild, sugar, sweeten the pill,** to make something unpleasant more acceptable. **pill-box,** *n.* a small box for holding pills; a small carriage or building; a concrete blockhouse, used as a machine-gun emplacement or for other defensive purposes; small round brimless hat, formerly part of some military uniforms, now worn esp. by women. **pill-milliped, -worm,** *n.* a milliped that rolls up into a ball. **pillwort,** *n.* a cryptogamous aquatic plant of the genus *Pillularia*. [L *pilula,* dim. of *pila,* ball]

†**pill**[2], *v.t.* to pillage, to plunder, to rob; (*dial.*) to peel. *v.i.* (*dial.*) to strip, to peel. †*n.* peel, skin. †**piller,** *n.* [F *piller,* prob. from L *pilare,* from *pilus,* hair (cp. PEEL[1])]

pillage, *n.* the act of plundering; plunder, esp. the property of enemies taken in war. *v.t.* to strip of money or goods by open force; to lay waste. *v.i.* to rob, to ravage, to plunder. **pillager,** *n.* [F, from *piller,* as prec.]

pillar, *n.* an upright structure of masonry, iron, timber etc., of considerable height in proportion to thickness, used for support, ornament, or as a memorial; a column, a post, a pedestal; an upright mass of anything analogous in form or function; a mass of coal, stone etc., left to support the roof in a mine or quarry; person or body of persons acting as chief support of an institution, movement etc. *v.t.* to support with or as with pillars; to furnish or adorn with pillars. **from pillar to post,** from one place to another; from one difficult situation to another. **Pillars of Hercules,** two rocks on either side of the Straits of Gibraltar beyond which the ancients thought it a feat of daring to sail. **pillar-box,** *n.* a short hollow pillar in which letters may be placed for collection by the post office. **pillar-box red,** *n., a.* vivid red. **pillared,** *a.* **pillaret,** *n.* [ME and OF *piler,* pop. L *pīlāre,* from *pīla*]

pillau, PILAU.

†**piller** PILL[2].

pillion, *n.* a low light saddle for a woman; a cushion for a person, usu. a woman, to ride on behind a person on horseback; a passenger-seat on a motorcycle. *a., adv.* (riding) on a pillion. **pillion-rider,** *n.* **pillion-seat,** *n.* [prob. through Celt. (cp. Gael. *pillean, pillin*), from L *pellis,* skin]

pilliwinks, *n.pl.* a mediaeval instrument of torture which crushes the fingers. [etym. unknown]

pillock, *n.* (*coll.*) a stupid or feeble person.

pillory, *n.* a wooden frame supported on a pillar and furnished with holes through which the head and hands of a person were put, so as to expose him or her to public derision (abolished in 1837). *v.t.* to set in the pillory; to hold up to ridicule or execration. **pillorize, -ise,** *v.t.* [ME *pillori,* OF *pellori* (F *pilori*), etym. unknown]

pillow, *n.* a cushion filled with feathers or other soft material, used as a rest for the head of a person reclining, esp. in bed; a block used as a cushion or support on a machine; the block on which the inner end of the bowsprit of a ship rests; anything resembling a pillow in form or function. *v.t.* to lay or rest on a pillow; to prop up with a pillow or pillows. *v.i.* to rest on a pillow. †**pillow-bere,** *n.* a pillow-case. **pillow-block,** *n.* a metal block or case supporting the end of a revolving shaft, with a movable cover for allowing adjustment of the bearings. **pillow-case, -slip,** *n.* a washable cover of linen etc., for drawing over a pillow. **pillow fight,** *n.* a game in which the participants strike each other with pillows. **pillow talk,** *n.* intimate conversation in bed. **pillowy,** *a.* [OE *pyle, pylu* (cp. Dut. *peluw,* G *Pfühl*), L *pulvīnus*]

pill-worm, pillwort PILL[1].

Pilobolous Dance Theater, US troupe whimsically named after a light-sensitive fungus. Its members collectively choreograph surreal body-sculptures with a mixture of dance, gymnastics and mime.

Pilocarpus, *n.* a genus of tropical American shrubs comprising the jaborandi. **pilocarpene,** *n.* a volatile oil obtained from this. **pilocarpine,** *n.* a white crystalline or amorphous alkaloid from the same source. [Gr. *pilos,* wool, *karpos,* fruit]

pilose, -lous, *a.* covered with or consisting of hairs. **pilosity,** *n.* [L *pilōsus*]

pilot, *n.* a steersman, esp. one qualified to conduct ships into or out of harbour or along particular coasts, channels etc.; a person directing the course of an aeroplane, spacecraft etc.; a guide, a director, esp. in difficult or dangerous circumstances; a radio or TV programme made to test its suitability to be extended into a series. *a.* serving as a preliminary test or trial. *v.t.* to act as pilot or to direct the course of (esp. a ship, aircraft etc.) **pilot balloon,** *n.* a small, free hydrogen-filled balloon sent up to obtain the direction and velocity of the upper winds. **pilot-bird,** *n.* a bird found in the vicinity of the Caribbean Islands whose appearance indicates to sailors that they are near land; (*Austral.*) a sweet-toned scrub bird. **pilot-boat,** *n.* a boat in which pilots cruise off the shore to meet incoming ships. **pilot-cloth,** *n.* a heavy blue woollen cloth for sailors' wear. **pilot-engine,** *n.* a locomotive sent in advance to clear the line for a train. **pilot-fish,** *n.* a small sea-fish, *Naucrates ductor,* said to act as a guide to sharks. **pilot-jacket,** *n.* a pea-jacket. **pilot-jet,** *n.* an auxiliary jet in a carburettor for starting and slow-going. **pilot-light,** *n.* a small jet of gas kept burning in order to light a cooker, geyser etc.; a small light on the dial of a wireless that goes on when the current is switched on. **pilot officer,** *n.* a junior commissioned rank in the RAF corresponding to second lieutenant in the Army. **pilotage,** *n.* **pilotism, pilotry,** *n.* **pilotless,** *a.* [F *pillotte* (now *pilote*), It. *pilota,* perh. corr. of *pedota,* prob. from Gr. *pēdon,* rudder]

pilous PILOSE.

Pilsen, *n.* German form of Czechoslovakian town of Plzeň.

pilsner, *n.* a pale beer with a strong flavour of hops. [named after the town of *Pilsen* in Czechoslovakia, where it was first brewed]

Piltdown man, *n.* an early hominid postulated on the basis of fossil bones found in a gravel pit at Piltdown, E Sussex in 1912, but later found to be a hoax.

pilular PILULE.

pilularia, *n.* a genus of aquatic plants growing near the margins of lakes and pools, the pillworts. [mod. L, as foll.]

pilule, *n.* a pill, esp. a small pill. **pilular, pilulous,** *a.* [L *pilula*]

pilum, *n.* (*pl.* **-la**) the heavy javelin used by the ancient Roman infantry. [L]

pimelode, *n.* a catfish of the genus *Pimelodus*. [Gr. *pīmelōdēs,* from *pīmelē,* fat]

†**piment,** *n.* a drink made of wine mixed with spice or honey. [OF, as PIGMENT]

pimento, *n.* the dried unripe aromatic berries of a W Indian tree, allspice; the tree itself. [Port. *pimenta* (cp. Sp. *pimienta*), L *pigmentum,* as prec.]

pimp, *n.* a man who finds customers for a prostitute or lives from her earnings. *v.i.* to act as a pimp. [etym. doubtful, cp. F *pimpant,* spruce, attractive, seductive]

pimpernel, *n.* a plant of the genus *Anagallis* belonging to the family *Primulaceae,* esp. the common red pimpernel, a small annual found in sandy fields etc., with scarlet flowers that close in dark or rainy weather. [OF *pimprenele* (F *pimprenelle*), med. L *pipinella,* perh. corr. of *bipinnela,* dim. of *bipennula,* dim. of *bipennis* (*penna,* feather)]

pimping, *a.* small, puny; feeble, sickly. [etym. doubtful]

pimple, *n.* a small pustule, or inflamed swelling on the skin. **pimpled, pimply,** *a.* [etym. doubtful]

pin, *n.* a short, slender, pointed piece of wood, metal etc., used for fastening parts of clothing, papers etc., together; a peg or bolt of metal or wood used for various purposes, as the bolt of a lock, a thole, a peg to which the strings of a musical instrument are fastened, a hairpin, a ninepin etc.; an ornamental device with a pin used as a fastening etc., or as a decoration for the person; a keg or small cask of 4½ gall. (about 20.5 l); (*pl.*) (*sl.*) legs; anything of slight value; a badge pinned to clothing. *v.t.* (*past, p.p.* **pinned**) to fasten (to, on, up etc.) with or as with a pin; to pierce, to transfix; to seize, to make fast, to secure; to enclose; to bind (down) to a promise of obligation; to place (the blame) (on). **not to care a pin,** not to care in the slightest. **on one's pins, on one's legs;** in good condition. **pins and needles,** a tingling sensation when a limb has been immobile for a long time. **to pin one's faith to, on,** to place full reliance upon. **pinball,** *n.* a game played on a machine with a sloping board down which a ball runs, striking targets and thus accumulating points. **pinball machine,** *n.* a machine for playing this. **pin-case,** *n.* **pincushion,** *n.* a small cushion for sticking pins into. **pin-dust,** *n.* small particles of metal rubbed off in pointing pins. **pin-feather,** *n.* an incipient feather. **pin-feathered,** *a.* **pin-fire,** *n.* a mechanism for discharging firearms by driving a pin into the fulminate in a cartridge. *a.* fired or exploded with this. **pin-footed** FIN-FOOTED. **pin-head,** *n.* the head of a pin; a very small object; (*coll.*) a very stupid person. **pinhole,** *n.* a very small aperture; a hole into which a pin or peg fits. **pinhole camera,** *n.* a camera with a pinhole instead of a lens. **pin-maker,** *n.* **pin-money,** *n.* an allowance of money for dress or other private expenses; money earned or saved, esp. by a woman, for personal expenditure. **pinpoint,** *n.* the point of a pin; anything sharp, painful, or critical; *v.t.* to locate accurately and precisely. **pin-prick,** *n.* a prick or minute puncture with or as with a pin; a petty annoyance. *v.t.* to prick with or as with a pin; to molest with petty insults or annoyances. **pin-stripe,** *n.* (a cloth with) a very narrow stripe. **pin-stripe(d),** *a.* **pin-table** PINBALL MACHINE. **pintail,** *n.* a duck, *Dafila acuta,* with a pointed tail; applied also to some species of grouse. **pintail-duck,** *n.* **pin-up,** *n.* a person, esp. a girl, whose face or figure is considered sufficiently attractive for his or her photograph to be pinned on the wall. **pinwheel,** *n.* a wheel with pins set in the face instead of cogs in the rim; a small catherine-wheel. **pin-worm,** *n.* a small threadworm. [OE *pinn* (cp. Dut. and G *Pin, Pinne,* Icel. *pinni,* Norw. and Swed. *Pinne*)]

piña, *n.* a pineapple; pina-cloth. **pina-cloth, -muslin,** *n.* a delicate cloth made in the Philippines from the fibres of the pineapple leaf. [Sp. from L *pīnea,* pine-cone]

pinafore, *n.* a sleeveless apron worn to protect the front of clothes. **pinafore dress,** *n.* a sleeveless dress usu. worn over a blouse or sweater. **pinafored,** *a.* [PIN, AFORE]

pinaster, *n.* a pine, *Pinus pinaster,* indigenous to the Mediterranean regions of Europe. [L, wild pine]

pinatype process, *n.* a colour process in which prints are made on glass coated with bichromated gelatine.

pince-nez, *n.* a pair of eye-glasses held in place by a spring clipping the nose. [F, pinch-nose, see PINCH]

pincers, *n.pl.* a tool with two limbs working on a pivot as levers to a pair of jaws, for gripping, crushing, extracting nails etc.; a nipping or grasping organ, as in crustaceans. **pincer movement,** *n.* a military manoeuvre in which one army encloses another on two side at once. [ME *pynsors, pinsours*]

pincette, *n.* a pair of tweezers or forceps. [F dim. of *pince,* pincers, see PINCH]

pinch, *v.t.* to nip or squeeze, to press so as to cause pain or inconvenience; of animals, to grip, to bite; to take off or remove by nipping or squeezing; to afflict, to distress, esp. with cold, hunger etc.; to straiten, to stint; to extort, to squeeze (from or out of); to urge (a horse); to steer (a ship) close-hauled; (*coll.*) to steal, to rob; (*coll.*) to arrest, to take into custody. *v.i.* to nip or squeeze anything; to be niggardly; to be straitened; to cavil. *n.* a sharp nip or squeeze, as with the ends of the fingers; as much as can be taken up between the finger and thumb; a pain, a pang; distress, straits, a dilemma, stress, pressure. **at a pinch,** in an urgent case; if hard pressed. **with a pinch of salt,** SALT. **pinch-commons, -fist, -penny,** *n.* a niggard; one who stints his or her own and other people's allowances. **pincher,** *n.* **pinchers** PINCERS. **pinchingly,** *adv.* sparingly, stingily. [O.North.F *pinchier* (F *pincer*), etym. doubtful]

pinchbeck, *n.* an alloy of copper, zinc, etc., formerly used for cheap jewellery. *a.* specious and spurious. [Christopher *Pinchbeck, c.* 1670–1732, inventor]

Pincus, *n.* **Gregory Goodwin** (1903–67), US biologist who devised the contraceptive pill in the 1950s.

pincushion PIN.

Pindar, *n.* (*c.* 552–442 BC), Greek poet, born near Thebes. He is noted for his choral lyrics, 'Pindaric Odes', written in honour of victors of athletic games. **Pindaric,** *a.* pertaining to or in the style of Pindar. *n.* (*usu. pl.*) applied to odes, metres etc., of an irregular kind, more or less resembling the style of Pindar. **pindarism,** *n.*

Pindari, *n.* a mounted marauder employed as an irregular soldier by native princes in Central India during the 17th and 18th cents. [Hind.]

†**pinder,** *n.* a pound-keeper, an officer appointed by a parish etc., to impound stray beasts. [obs. *pind,* OE *pyndan,* to shut up (cp. POUND²), -ER]

Pindling, *n.* **Lynden (Oscar)** (1930–), Bahamian prime minister from 1967. After studying law in London, he returned to the island to join the newly formed Progressive Liberal Party, and then became the first black prime minister of the Bahamas.

pine¹, *n.* any tree of the coniferous genus *Pinus,* consisting of evergreen trees with needle-shaped leaves; timber from various coniferous trees; a pineapple. *a.* of pines or pine-timber. **pineapple,** *n.* the large multiple fruit of the ananas, so-called from its resemblance to a pine-cone; (*sl.*) a hand-grenade. **pine-barren,** *n.* a tract of sandy land producing only pines. **pine-beauty, -carpet,** *n.* moths destructive to Scotch firs. **pine-beetle, -chafer,** *n.* a beetle feeding on pine-leaves. **pine-clad, -covered,** *a.* **pine-marten,** *n.* a European marten, *Mustela martes.* **pine-needle,** *n.* the needle-shaped leaf of the pine. **pine-oil,** *n.* **pinery,** *n.* a hothouse in which pineapples are grown; a plantation of pine-trees. **pinetum,** *n.* (*pl.* **-ta**) a plantation of pine-trees. **piny,** *a.* [OE *pīn,* L *pīnus*]

pine² *v.i.* to languish, waste away; to long or yearn (for etc.); †to starve, to waste away from hunger. *v.t.* to spend (time etc,) in pining; †to afflict with suffering; to torment. †*n.* pain, suffering; famine, want. [OE *pīnian,* to torture, from *pīn,* torment, pain]

pineal, *a.* shaped like a pine-cone. **pineal eye,** *n.* a rudimentary eye, perhaps orig. connected with the pineal gland, found between the brain and the parietal foramen in many lizards. **pineal gland,** *n.* a dark-grey conical structure situated behind the third ventricle of the brain that secretes melatonin into the blood stream, thought by Descartes to be the seat of the soul. [F *pinéal* (L *pīnea,* pine-cone, -AL)]

pineapple, pinery etc. PINE¹.

pin-feather etc. PIN.

pinfold, *n.* a pound in which stray cattle are shut up; a narrow enclosure. *v.t.* to shut up in a pound. [OE *punfald* (POUND², FOLD¹)]

ping, *n.* a sharp ringing sound as of a bullet flying through the air. *v.i.* to make such a sound; to fly with such a sound. [imit.]

pingao, *n.* a New Zealand plant with a stem like thick cord. [Maori]

pingle, *v.t.* (*Sc., North.*) to worry, to trouble. *v.i.* to dally, to dawdle; to nibble, to eat with feeble appetite. [etym. doubtful]

Ping-pong®, *n.* table tennis.

Pinguicula, *n.* a genus of bog-plants, the butterworts. [as foll.]

pinguid, *a.* fat, oily, greasy, unctuous. †**pinguefy,** *v.t.* to make fat. †**pinguescent,** *a.* growing fat. †**pinguescence,** *n.* **pinguidity, pinguitude,** *n.* [L *pinguis,* fat]

pinguin, *n.* a W Indian plant of the pineapple family with a fleshy fruit. [etym. unknown]

pinion¹, *n.* a wing-feather; a wing; the joint of a bird's wing remotest from the body. *v.t.* to cut off the first joint of the wing to prevent flight; to shackle, to fetter the arms of; to bind (the arms etc.); to bind fast (to). [OF *pignon,* L *penna,* var. *pinna,* feather, wing]

pinion², *n.* the smaller of two cog-wheels in gear with each other; a cogged spindle or arbor engaging with a wheel. [F *pignon,* OF *pinon, penon,* L *pinna,* pinnacle, gable, cp. prec.]

pink¹, *n.* a plant or flower of the genus *Dianthus,* largely cultivated in gardens; applied to several allied or similar plants; a pale rose colour or pale red slightly inclining towards purple, from the garden pink; the supreme excellence, the very height (of); a fox-hunter's scarlet coat; a fox-hunter. *a.* of the colour of the garden pink, pale red or rose; (*coll.*) moderately left-wing. **in the pink,** in fine condition. **tickled pink** TICKLE. **pink elephants,** *n.pl.* hallucinations induced by intoxication with alcohol. **pink-eye,** *n.* a contagious influenza among horses, cattle and sheep, characterized by inflammation of the conjunctiva; a form of conjunctivitis in humans; the herb *Spigelia marilandica* and other N American plants. **pink gin,** *n.* gin mixed with angostura bitters. **pink slip,** *n.* (*N Am.*) a note given to an employee, terminating employment. **pinkwood,** *n.* (*Austral.*) a Tasmanian tree with wood of that colour. **pinkiness,** *n.* **pinkish,** *a.* **pinkness,** *n.* **pinko,** *n.* (*pl.* **-kos, -koes**) (*usu. derog.*) a person with (moderately) left-wing views. **pinky¹,** *a.* [etym. doubtful]

pink², *v.t.* to pierce, to stab; to make small round holes in for ornament; to decorate in this manner. **pinking-iron,** *n.* a tool for pinking. **pinking shears,** *n.pl.* a pair of shears with zig-zag cutting edges, used to cut cloth to prevent fraying. [ME *pinken* (cp. LG *pinken,* also PICK¹ F *piquer*)]

†**pink³,** *n.* a sailing-ship with a very narrow stern, used chiefly in the Mediterranean. [MDut. *pinke* (now *pink*), etym. doubtful]

pink⁴, *n.* a yellow pigment obtained from quercitron bark or other vegetable sources. **Dutch, French, Italian pink,** various yellow pigments. [etym unknown]

†**pink⁵,** *a.* small; winking, half-shut. †**pink-eyed,** *a.* [etym. doubtful, cp. Dut. *pink ooghen,* pink eye]

pink⁶, *v.i.* of an internal combustion engine, to detonate prematurely, making a series of popping sounds. [imit.]

Pinkerton, *n.* **Allan** (1819–84), US detective, born in Glasgow. In 1852 he founded **Pinkerton's National Detective Agency**, and built up the federal secret service from the espionage system he developed during the US Civil War.

Pink Floyd, *n.* British psychedelic rock group, formed 1965. The original members were Syd Barrett (1946–), Roger Waters (1944–), Richard Wright (1945–), and Nick Mason (1945–). Their albums include *The Dark Side of the Moon* (1973) and *The Wall* (1979), with its spin-off film starring Bob Geldof.

pinkie, pinky², *n.* (*coll.*) the little finger.

pinna, *n.* (*pl.* **-nae, -nas**) a leaflet of a pinnate leaf; a wing a fin, or analogous structure; the projecting upper part of the external ear. [L, feather, wing, fin]

pinnace, *n.* a man-of-war's boat with six or eight oars; †a small schooner-rigged vessel provided with sweeps. [F *pinasse,* prob. ult. from L *pīnus,* PINE¹]

pinnacle, *n.* a turret, usu. pointed or tapering, placed as an ornament on the top of a buttress etc., or as a termination on an angle or gable; a pointed summit; the apex, the culmination (of). *v.t.* to furnish with pinnacles; to set on or as on a pinnacle; to surmount as a pinnacle. [OF *pinacle,* late L *pinnāculum,* dim. of PINNA]

pinnate, -ated, *a.* having leaflets arranged featherwise along the stem; divided into leaflets; (*Zool.*) having lateral processes along an axis. **pinnately,** *adv.* **pinnatifid,** *a.* (*Bot.*) divided into lobes nearly to the midrib. **pinnatiped,** *a.* fin-footed, having the toes bordered by membranes. **pinnatisect,** *a.* having the lobes of a pinnate leaf cleft to the midrib. **pinnato-,** *comb.form* [L *pinnātus,* from PINNA]

pinner, *n.* one who pins; a cap or coif with the lappets or laps pinned on; a pin-maker; (*dial.*) a pinafore. [PIN, -ER]

pinnigrade, *a.* walking by means of fins or flippers. *n.* a pinnigrade animal. [L *pinni-* PINNA, *-gradus,* walking]

pinniped, *a.* having feet like fins. *n.* any individual of the Pinnipedia, a group of marine carnivores containing the seals, sea-lions and walruses. [L *pes pedis,* foot]

pinnock, *n.* (*dial.*) a hedge-sparrow; a titmouse. [etym. doubtful]

pinnule, *n.* one of the smaller or ultimate divisions of a pinnate leaf; a small fin, fin-ray, wing, barb of a feather etc. **pinnulate, -lated,** *a.* **pinnulet,** *n.* [L *pinnula,* dim. of PINNA]

pinny, (*coll*) PINAFORE.

Pinochet (Ugarte), *n.* **Augusto** (1915–), military ruler of Chile from 1973, when a CIA-backed coup ousted and killed president Salvador Allende. Pinochet took over the presidency and ruled ruthlessly, crushing all opposition. He was voted out of power when general elections were held in 1989 but remains head of the armed forces until 1997.

pinochle, pinocle, penuchle, *n.* a card-game similar to bezique, played with a 48-card pack by two or four players. [etym. unknown]

pinole, *n.* (*N Am.*) meal made from maize, mesquite beans etc., a common article of food in California and Mexico. [Am. Sp., from Aztec *pinolli*]

piñon, *n.* any of various low-growing pines of the west of N America; its edible seed. [from Sp., pine nut, see PINEAL]

pinpoint PIN.

pint, *n.* a measure of capacity, the eighth part of a gallon (0.568 l). **pint-size(d),** *n.* (*coll.*) small. [F *pinte,* perh. through Sp. *pinta,* from late L *pincta,* picta, fem. p.p. of *pingere,* to paint]

pin-table PIN.

pintado, *n.* (*pl.* **-dos, -does**) a species of petrel; a guinea-fowl; †chintz. **pintado-bird,** *n.* the pintado petrel. [Port. or Sp., p.p. of *pintar,* ult. from L *pingere* (p.p. *pinctus, pictus*), to PAINT]

pintail PIN.

Pinter, *n.* **Harold** (1930–), English writer, orig. an actor. He specializes in the tragicomedy of the breakdown of communication, broadly in the tradition of the theatre of the absurd, for example *The Birthday Party* (1958) and *The Caretaker* (1960). Later plays include *The Homecoming* (1965), *Old Times* (1971), *Betrayal* (1978), and *Mountain Language* (1988).

pintle, *n.* a pin or bolt, esp. one used as a pivot; one of the pins on which a rudder swings. [OE *pintel* penis, etym. doubtful]

pinto, *n.* (*pl.* **-tos, -toes**) a horse or pony with patches of white and another colour. [Am. Sp., spotted, cp. PINTADO]

†**Pinturicchio, Pintoricchio,** *n.* pseudonym of Bernadino di Betti (*c.* 1454–1513), Italian painter, active in Rome, Perugia, and Siena. His chief works are the frescoes in the Borgia Apartments in the Vatican, (1490s) and in the Piccolomini Library of Siena Cathedral (1503–08).

pin-up PIN.

pin-wheel etc. PIN.

pinxit, *v.t.* (he or she) painted it (in the signature to a picture). [L]

piny PIN.

Pinyin, *n.* the Chinese phonetic alphabet approved 1956, and used from 1979 in transcribing all names of people and places from the Chinese language into foreign languages using the Roman alphabet. For example, Chou En-lai becomes Zhou Enlai, Hua Kuo-feng becomes Hua Guofeng, Teng Hsiao-ping becomes Deng Xiaoping, Peking becomes Beijing.

piolet, *n.* a climber's ice-axe. [F Savoy dial., dim. of *piolo,* prob. rel. to *pioche,* from *pic,* see PIKE¹]

pion, *n.* a meson with positive or negative or no charge, chiefly responsible for nuclear force. [*pi -meson*]

pioned, *a.* (*Shak.*) dug, trenched (?).

pioneer, *n.* one of a body of soldiers whose duty it is to clear and repair roads, bridges etc., for troops on the march; one who goes before to prepare or clear the way; an explorer; an early leader. *v.t.* to prepare the way for; to act as pioneer to; to lead, to conduct. [F *pionnier,* from *pion,* PAWN[1]]

Pioneer probes, *n.pl.* a series of US space probes 1958–78. Pioneer 5, launched 1960, was the first of a series to study the solar wind between the planets. Pioneer 10, launched Mar. 1972, was the first probe to reach Jupiter (Dec. 1973) and to leave the solar system 1983. Pioneer 11, launched Apr. 1973, passed Jupiter Dec. 1974, and was the first probe to reach Saturn (Sept. 1979), before also leaving the solar system. Pioneers 10 and 11 carry plaques containing messages from Earth in case they are found by other civilizations among the stars. Pioneer Venus probes were launched May and Aug. 1978. One orbited Venus, and the other dropped three probes onto the surface. In early 1990 Pioneer 10 was 7.1 billion km from the Sun. Both it and Pioneer 11 were still returning data-measurements of starlight intensity to Earth.

piopio, *n.* the New Zealand thrush. [Maori]

pious, *a.* reverencing God; religious, devout; feeling or exhibiting filial affection; dutiful; sanctimonious. **pious fraud,** *n.* a deception in the interests of religion or of the person deceived; a sanctimonious hypocrite. **piously,** *adv.* [L *pius,* orig. dutiful]

pip¹, *n.* a disease in poultry etc., consisting a secretion of thick mucus in the throat; applied facetiously to various human disorders. **to have, get the pip,** (*sl.*) to be out of sorts or dejected. [prob. from MDut. *pippe,* ult. from pop. L. *pipita,* corr. of *pītuīta*]

pip², *n.* the seed of an apple, orange etc. *v.t.* to remove the pips from (fruit). **pipless,** *a.* [prob. from PIPPIN]

pip³, *n.* a spot on a playing-card, domino, die etc.; one of the segments on the rind of a pineapple; a small flower in a clustered inflorescence etc.; a star on an officer's uniform indicating rank. [formerly *peep,* etym. doubtful]

pip⁴, *v.t.* (*past, p.p.* **pipped**) (*sl.*) to blackball; to beat; to hit with a shot; to get the better of. **to pip at the post,** to beat, outdo etc. at the last moment, e.g. in a race or contest. [perh. from PIP²]

pip⁵, *v.i.* to chirp, as a bird. *v.t.* to break through (the shell) in hatching. *n.* a short, high-pitched sound. [perh. var. of PEEP¹, or imit.]

pip⁶, *n.* signallers' name for letter P. **pipemma,** *n.* pm, afternoon.

pipe, *n.* a long hollow tube or lines of tubes, esp. for conveying liquids, gas etc.; a musical wind-instrument formed of a tube; a boatswain's whistle; a signal on this; a tube producing a note of a particular tone in an organ; a tubular organ, vessel, passage etc., in an animal body; the windpipe; the voice, esp. in singing; a shrill note or cry of a bird etc.; a tube with a bowl for smoking tobacco; a pipeful (of tobacco); a large cask for wine; this used as a measure of capacity, usu. 150 gall (682 l); a vein containing ore or extraneous matter penetrating rock; †the Pipe-office in the Exchequer; (*pl.*) a bagpipe. *v.t.* to play or execute on a pipe; to whistle; to utter in a shrill tone; to lead or bring (along or to) by playing or whistling on a pipe; to call or direct by a boatswain's pipe or whistle; to furnish with pipes; to propagate (pinks) by slips from the parent stem; to trim or decorate with piping; to convey or transmit along a pipe or wire. *v.i.* to play on a pipe; to whistle, to make a shrill high-pitched sound; (*sl*) to smoke the drug crack. **pipe of peace,** a pipe smoked in token of peace, a calumet. **to pipe down,** to fall silent. **to pipe one's eye,** (*dated sl.*) to weep. **to pipe up,** to begin to sing; to sing the first notes of; (*coll.*) to begin to speak. **pipe-clay,** *n.* a fine, white, plastic clay used for making tobacco-pipes, and for cleaning military accoutrements etc.; excessive regard for correctness of dress, drill etc. *v.t.* to whiten with pipe-clay. **piped music,** *n.* music recorded for playing in shops, restaurants, etc as background music. **pipe-dream,** *n.* a fantastic notion, a castle in the air. **pipe-fish,** *n.* a fish of the family Syngnathidae, from their elongated form. **pipe-light,** *n.* a spill for lighting tobacco-pipes. **pipe-line,** *n.* a long pipe or conduit laid down from an oil-well, or oil region, to convey the petroleum to a port etc. **in the pipeline,** under preparation, soon to be supplied, produced etc. **pipe-major,** *n.* a non-commissioned officer in charge of pipers. †**Pipe-office,** *n.* the office of the Exchequer which dealt with the Pipe-roll. **pipe-rack,** *n.* a stand for tobacco-pipes. **Pipe-roll,** *n.* the great roll of the Exchequer containing the pipes or annual accounts of sheriffs and other officers. **pipe-stone,** *n.* a hard stone used by the N American Indians for making tobacco-pipes. **pipe-tree,** *n.* the syringa; the lilac. †**pipe-wine,** *n.* wine from the pipe or cask. **pipeful,** *n.* **pipeless,** *a.* **piper,** *n.* one who plays upon a pipe, esp. a strolling player or a performer on the bagpipes; a broken-winded horse; a dog used to lure birds into a decoy-pipe. **to pay the piper** [PAY¹]. **pipy,** *a.* [OE *pipe* (cp. Dut. *pijp,* G *Pfeife,* Icel. *pīpa*), late L *pīpa,* from *pīpāre,* to chirp]

Piper, *n.* **John** (1903–), British painter and designer. He painted mostly traditional romantic views of landscape and architecture. As an official war artist he painted damaged buildings in a melancholy vein. He also designed theatre sets and stained-glass windows (Coventry Cathedral; Catholic Cathedral, Liverpool).

piperaceous, piperic, *a.* pertaining to or derived from pepper. **piperine,** *n.* an alkaloid obtained from black pepper. [L *piper,* PEPPER, -ACEOUS]

pipette, *n.* a fine tube for removing quantities of a fluid, esp. in chemical investigations. [F, dim. of PIPE]

pipi, *n.* a tropical American plant, *Caesalpinia pipai,* with astringent pods used for tanning; (*also* **pipipod**) the pod. [Tupi-Guarani *pipai*]

piping, *n.* the action of one who pipes; a shrill whistling or wailing sound; a fluting; a covered cord for trimming dresses; a cord-like decoration of sugar etc., on a cake; a quantity, series, or system of pipes. *a.* playing upon a pipe; shrill, whistling. **piping hot,** *a.* hissing hot; fresh, newly out. **piping times,** *n.pl.* merry, prosperous times.

pipistrelle, , *n.* a small, reddish-brown bat, *Vesperugo pipistrellus,* the commonest British kind. [F, from It. *pipistrello,* ult. from L *vespertilio,* from *vesper,* evening]

pipit, *n.* a lark-like bird belonging to the genus *Anthus.* [prob. imit. of the cry]

pipkin, *n.* a small earthen pot, pan, or jar. [etym. doubtful]

pippin, *n.* a name for several varieties of apples. [OF *pepin,* pip or seed etym. doubtful]

pip-pip, *int.* (*dated sl.*) goodbye.

pippy¹, *a.* full of pips; (*sl.*) esp. of the prices of stocks, shaky, unsteady. [PIP²,¹ -Y]

pippy², *n.* a small New Zealand shellfish; a sand-worm. [Maori]

pipsqueak, *n.* (*coll.*) a small, contemptible or insignificant person.

pipy PIPE.

piquant, *a.* having an agreeably sharp, pungent taste; interesting, stimulating, racy, lively, sparkling. **piquancy,** *n.* **piquantly,** *adv.* [F, as foll]

pique¹, *v.t.* to irritate; to touch the envy, jealousy, or pride of; to stimulate or excite (curiosity etc.); to plume or value (oneself on). *n.* ill-feeling, irritation, resentment. [F *piquer,* to prick, see PIKE¹]

pique², *n.* in the game of piquet, the scoring of 30 points before one's opponent begins to count, entitling one to 30 more points. *v.t.* to score this against. *v.i.* to score a pique. [F *pic,* etym. doubtful]

piqué, *n.* a heavy cotton fabric with a corded surface, quilting. [F, p.p. of *piquer,* see PIQUE¹]

piquet¹, *n.* a game of cards for two persons, with a pack of cards from which all below the seven have been withdrawn. [F, etym. doubtful]

†**piquet²,** PICKET.

piracy, *n.* the crime of a pirate; robbery on the high seas; unauthorized publication; infringement of copyright.

piragua, *n.* a long narrow boat or canoe made from one or two trunks hollowed out, a dug-out; a pirogue. [Sp., from Carib., dug-out]

Piran, St, *n.* (*c.* 500 AD), Christian missionary sent to Cornwall by St Patrick. There are remains of his oratory at Perranzabuloe, and he is the patron saint of Cornwall and its nationalist movement; feast day 5 Mar.

Pirandello, *n.* **Luigi** (1867–1936), Italian writer. The novel *Il fu Mattia Pascal/The Late Mattia Pascal* (1904) was highly acclaimed, along with many short stories. His plays include *La Morsa/The Vice* (1912), *Sei personaggi in cerca d'autore/Six Characters in Search of an Author* (1921), and *Enrico IV/Henry IV* (1922). The theme and treatment of his plays anticipated the work of Brecht, O'Neill, Anouilh, and Genet. Nobel Prize for Literature 1934.

piranha, *n.* a small, voracious, flesh-eating S American tropical fish, *Serrasalmo piraya,* that can attack and wound people and large animals. [Port., from Tupi *pira,* fish, *sainha,* tooth]

pirate, *n.* a robber on the high seas; a piratical ship; a marauder; one who infringes the copyright of another; (*coll.*) an omnibus that runs on the recognized routes of others or overcharges passengers; an unauthorized radio station. *v.i.* to practise piracy. *v.t.* to plunder; to publish (literary or other matter belonging to others) without permission or compensation. **piratic, -ical,** *a.* **piratically,** *adv.* [F, from L *pīrāta,* Gr. *peiratēs,* from *peiran,* to attempt]

piraya, PIRANHA.

piriform, PYRIFORM.

Pirithous, *n.* in Greek mythology king of the Lapiths, and friend of Theseus. His marriage with Hippodamia was the occasion of a battle between the Lapiths and their guests, the Centaurs, which is a recurrent subject of Greek art.

pirn, *n.* (*Sc.*) a bobbin, reel, or spool; as much as a pirn will take (of yarn etc.). **pirnie,** *n.* a woollen nightcap, usu. striped. [etym. doubtful]

pirogue, *n.* a large canoe formed of a hollowed trunk of a tree; a large flat-bottomed boat or barge for shallow water, usu. with two masts rigged fore-and-aft. [F, as PIRAGUA]

pirouette, *n.* a rapid whirling round on the point of one foot, in dancing; a sudden short turn of a horse. *v.i.* to dance or perform a pirouette. [F, a whirligig, a top (cp. It. *piruolo,* top)]

Pisa, *n.* city in Tuscany, Italy; population (1988) 104,000. The Leaning Tower is 55 m/180 ft high and about 5 m/16.5 ft out of perpendicular.

pis aller, *n.* a makeshift. [F]

Pisanello, *n.* nickname of Antonio Pisano (*c.* (1395–1455/56), Italian artist active in Verona, Venice, Naples, Rome, and elsewhere. His panel paintings reveal a rich international gothic style; his frescoes are largely lost. He was also an outstanding portrait medallist.

Pisano[1], *n.* family of Italian sculptors, father and son, Nicola (died ?1284) and his son Giovanni (died after 1314). They made decorated marble pulpits in churches in Pisa, Siena, and Pistoia. Giovanni also created figures for Pisa's baptistery and designed the façade of Siena Cathedral.

Pisano[2], *n.* **Andrea** (*c.* (1290–1348), Italian sculptor, who made the earliest bronze doors for the Baptistery of Florence Cathedral, completed 1336.

pisc- PISC(I)-.

piscary, *n.* (*Law.*) right of fishing. **common of piscary,** the right of fishing in another person's waters, in common with the owner and sometimes with others.

piscatory, *a.* pertaining to fishers or fishing. **piscatorial,** *a.* piscatory; fond of or pertaining to angling. [L *piscātōrius,* from *piscātor,* fisher]

Pisces, *n.* a faint constellation mainly in the northern hemisphere near Pegasus, represented by two fish tied together by their tails; (*Astrol*) the Fishes, the 12th sign of the zodiac. [L, pl. of *piscis,* fish]

pisc(i)-, *comb.form* fish. [L *piscis,* fish]

pisciculture, *n.* the artificial breeding, rearing, and preserving of fish. **piscicultural,** *a.* **pisciculturist,** *n.*

pisciform *a.* like a fish in form.

piscina, *n.* (*pl.* **-nas, -nae**) a stone basin with outlet beside the altar in some churches to receive the water used in purifying the chalice etc.; in Roman antiquity, a fish-pond; a bathing pond. †**piscinal,** *a.*

piscine, *a.* of or pertaining to fish.

Piscis Austrinus, *n.* a constellation of the southern hemisphere whose brightest star is Fomalhaut.

piscivorous, *a.* living on fish.

pisé, *n.* a mode of forming walls of rammed clay; rammed clay forming a wall. [F, p.p. of *piser,* L *pīnsāre,* to pound]

pish, *int.* an exclamation expressing contempt, disgust etc., pshaw. *v.i.* to express contempt by saying 'pish'. [instinctive sound]

pishogue, *n.* sorcery, witchery or enchantment of a sinister kind. [Ir. *píseog*]

pisiform, *a.* pea-shaped. [L *pisum,* pea, -FORM]

Pisistratus, *n.* (*c.* 605–527 BC), Athenian politician. Although of noble family, he assumed the leadership of the peasant party, and seized power in 561 BC. He was twice expelled, but recovered power from 541 BC until his death. Ruling as a dictator under constitutional forms, he was the first to have the Homeric poems written down, and founded Greek drama by introducing the Dionysiac peasant festivals into Athens.

pisky, PIXY.

pismire, *n.* an ant, an emmet. [PISS (with alln. to smell of an ant-hill), obs. *mire,* ant (cp. Dut. *mier,* E Fris. *mīre*)]

pisolite, *n.* a variety of calcite made up of pea-like concretions. **pisolitic,** *a.* [Gr. *pisos,* pea, -LITE]

piss, *n.* (*taboo sl.*) urine. *v.i.* to discharge urine. *v.t.* to discharge in the urine; to wet with urine. **piss artist,** *n.* (*sl.*) a habitual heavy drinker; a drunk. **to piss down,** (*sl.*) to rain heavily. **to piss off,** (*sl.*) to go away; to annoy; to bore, to make discontented. **to take the piss,** (*sl.*) to make fun of someone, to tease. **pissabed,** *n.* (*dial.*) the dandelion. **piss-up,** *n.* (*sl.*) a bout of drinking. **pissed,** (*sl.*) drunk. [OF *pissier* (F *pisser*), prob. imit.]

Pissarro, *n.* **Camille** (1831–1903), French impressionist painter, born in the West Indies. He went to Paris in 1855, met Corot, then Monet, and soon became a leading member of the impressionist group. He experimented with various styles, including pointillism, in the 1880s.

pissasphalt, *n.* mineral tar. [L *pissasphaltus,* Gr. *pissaphaltos* (*pissa,* pitch, ASPHALT)]

pissoir, *n.* a public urinal. [Fr., from *pisser,* to urinate]

pistachio, *n.* the nut of a W Asiatic tree, *Pistacia vera,* with a pale greenish kernel; the flavour of this. **pistachio-nut,** *n.* [It. *pistacchio* or Sp. *pistacho,* L *pistācium,* Gr. *pistakion*]

pistareen, *n.* (*N Am., W Ind.*) a former Spanish silver coin. *a.* petty, paltry. [from PESETA]

piste, *n.* a slope prepared for skiing; a rectangular area on which a fencing contest is held. [F, from OI. *pista* from *pistare,* to tread down]

pistil, *n.* the female organ in flowering plants, comprising the ovary and stigma, usu. with a style supporting the latter. †**pistillaceous, -llary, -llate,** *a.* **pistilliferous, -lline,** *a.* [L *pistillum,* PESTLE]

pistol, *n.* a small firearm for use with one hand. *v.t.* (*past, p.p.*) **pistolled**) to shoot with a pistol. **pistol-shot,** *n.* the range of this. **pistol-whip,** *v.t.* to strike with a pistol. **pistoleer,** †**-ier,** *n.* **pistolet,** *n.* **pistolgraph** *n.* a photographic apparatus operated like a pistol, for instantaneous work. [F *pistole,* from *pistolet,* pistol, orig. dagger, It. *pistolese,* dagger, from *Pistoja,* where made]

†**pistole,** *n.* a foreign gold coin formerly current, esp. a 16th- and 17th-cent. Spanish coin. [F, prob. from *pistolet,* perh. as prec.]

piston, *n.* a device fitted to occupy the sectional area of a tube and be driven to and fro by alternating pressure on its faces, so as to impart or receive motion, as in a steam-engine or a pump; a valve in a musical wind-instrument; in an internal combustion engine, a plunger which passes on the working pressure of the burning gases via the connecting rod to the crankshaft. **piston-ring,** *n.* a split ring encircling the piston in a groove. **piston-rod,** *n.* a rod attaching a piston to machinery. **piston-slap,** *n.* a noise caused by the piston fitting too loosely in the cylinder. [F, from It. *pistone,* var. of *pestone,* pestle, cogn. with *pestare,* from late L *pistāre,* freq. of *pinsere,* to pound, see PESTLE]

Piston, *n.* **Walter (Hamor)** (1894–1976), US composer and teacher. He wrote a number of textbooks, including *Harmony* (1941) and *Orchestration* (1955). His neo-classical works include eight symphonies, a number of concertos, chamber music, the orchestral suite *Three New England Sketches* (1959), and the ballet *The Incredible Flautist* (1938).

pit[1], *n.* a natural or artificial hole in the ground, esp. one of considerable depth in proportion to its width; one made in order to obtain minerals or for industrial or agricultural operations; a coal mine; a hole dug and covered over as a trap for wild animals or enemies; an abyss; hell; a hollow or depression in the surface of the ground, of the body etc.; a hollow scar, esp. one left by smallpox; the ground floor of the auditorium in a theatre, esp. behind the stalls; the part of an audience occupying this; (*pl.*) an area on a motor-racing course where cars are repaired, their tyres are changed etc.; an area for cock-fighting, a cockpit; a trap, a snare. *v.t.* (*past, p.p.*) **pitted**) to put into a pit, esp. for storage; to mark with pits or hollow scars, as with smallpox (*usu. in p.p.*); to match (against) in a pit; to match, to set in competition (against). **the pit,** the grave; hell; the wheat market at Chicago. **the pits,** (*sl.*) a very unpleasant person, thing, place or situation. **pit-coal,** *n.* mineral coal. **pitfall,** *n.* a pit slightly covered so that animals may fall in; a trap; (*fig.*) a hidden danger. **pit-head,** *n.* (the area or buildings near) the top of a mine-shaft. **pit-hole,** *n.* a pit-like cavity, a pit; the grave. **pit-man,** *n.* one who works in a pit, a collier. **pit-saw,** *n.* a large saw worked in a sawpit by two men. **pit-sawyer,** *n.* the sawyer who works in the pit, opposed to *top-sawyer*. **pit-stop,** *n.* a stop by a racing car in the pits for tyre-changes etc. **pit-viper,** *n.* any of various N American snakes with a heat-sensitive pit on each side of the head. **pitting,** *n.* the uneven wearing of valve-seatings and other surfaces in an internal combustion engine. [OE *pytt* (cp. Dut. *put,* G *Pfütze*), L *puteus,* well]

pit[2], *n.* (*N Am.*) the stone of a fruit. *v.t.* to remove the pit from (fruit). [PITH]

pita (bread) PITTA.

pit-a-pat, *n.* a tapping, a flutter, a palpitation. *adv.* with this sound, palpitatingly, falteringly. [imit.]

pitau, *n.* a tree-fern of New Zealand. [Maori]

Pitcairn Islands, *n.* British colony in Polynesia, 5300 km/3300 miles NE of New Zealand **area** 27 sq km/10 sq miles. **capital** Adamstown. **exports** fruit and souvenirs to passing ships. **population** (1982) 54. **language** English. The islands were first settled by nine mutineers from the *Bounty* together with some Tahitians, their occupation remaining unknown until 1808.

pitch[1], *n.* a dark-brown or black resinous substance obtained from tar, turpentine, and some oils, used for caulking, paving roads etc. *v.t.* to cover, coat, line, or smear with pitch. **pitch-black,** *a.* brownish black; as dark as pitch. **pitchblende,** *n.* native oxide of uranium, the chief source of radium. **pitch-cap,** *n.* a cap lined with pitch, used as an instrument of torture. **pitch-dark,** *a.* as dark as pitch, very dark. **pitch-darkness,** *n.* **pitchpine,** *n.* a highly resinous pine, *Abies picea,* much used for woodwork. **pitchstone,** *n.* a brittle vitreous volcanic rock almost identical with obsidian. [OE *pic,* from L *pix picis* (cp. Dut. *pek,* G *Pech,* Icel. *bik*)]

pitch[2], *v.t.* to fix or plant in the ground; to fix; to set in orderly arrangement, to fix in position; to throw, to fling, esp. with an upward heave or underhand swing; to toss (hay) with a fork; to pave with cobbles or setts; to expose for sale; to set to a particular pitch or keynote; (*coll.*) to put or relate in a particular way; (*Baseball etc.*) to deliver or throw (the ball) to the batsman; (*Golf*) to strike (the ball) with a lofted club. *v.i.* to encamp; to light, to settle; to plunge, to fall; of a ball, esp in cricket, to bounce; to fall headlong; to plunge at the bow or stern, as opposed to *rolling*. *n.* the act of pitching; mode of pitching; the delivery of the ball in various games; height, degree, intensity; extreme height, extreme point; point or degree of elevation or depression; degree of inclination or steepness; degree of slope in a roof; the place or station taken up by a person for buying and selling, residence etc.; an attempt at persuasion, usu. to induce someone to buy something; (*Cricket*) the place in which the wickets are placed or the distance between them; (*Cricket*) the point at which a bowled ball bounces; any area marked out for playing sports, e.g. football; the lineal distance between points etc., arranged in series, as between teeth on the pitchline of a cog-wheel, between floats on a paddle-wheel, between successive convolutions of the thread of a screw etc.; (*Mus.*) the degree of acuteness or gravity of a tone. †**pitch and pay,** cash down. **to pitch in,** to begin or set to vigorously; (*coll.*) to participate or contribute. **to pitch into,** (*coll.*) to assail with blows, abuse, etc.; to attack vigorously. **to pitch upon,** to select, to decide upon; to happen upon. **to queer the pitch,** to spoil a plan, to thwart. **pitch-and-toss,** *n.* a game in which coins are pitched at a mark, the player getting nearest having the right to toss all the others' coins into the air and take those that come down with heads up. **pitch-circle, -line,** *n.* the circle of contact of a cog-wheel in gear. **pitched battle,** *n.* a battle for which both sides have made deliberate preparations. **pitch-farthing** CHUCK-FARTHING. **pitch-fork,** *n.* a large fork, usu. with two prongs, with a long handle, used for lifting hay sheaves of corn etc. *v.t.* to lift or throw with or as with a pitch-fork; to place unexpectedly or unwillingly in a certain situation. **pitch-pipe,** *n.* a small pipe for sounding with the mouth to set the pitch for singing or tuning. **pitch-wheel,** *n.* a gear-wheel. [ME *pichen, pykken,* etym. doubtful, perh. rel. to PICK[1]]

pitchblende, pitch-cap etc. PITCH[1].

pitcher[1], *n.* one who or that which pitches; a player delivering the ball in baseball and other games; a street performer, costermonger etc., who pitches a tent or stall in a particular place; a block of stone used for paving.

pitcher[2], *n.* a large vessel, usu. of earthenware, with a handle and a spout, for holding liquids; (*N Am.*) a jug; a pitcher-shaped leaf, usu. closed with an operculum. **pitcher-plant,** *n.* one of various plants with such leaves, esp. the E Indian genus *Nepenthes.* and the N American genus *Sarracenia,* **pitcherful,** *n.* [ME and OF *picher,* med. L *picārium, bicārium,* BEAKER]

pitch-farthing, pitchfork etc. PITCH[2].

pitchi, *n.* a wooden pitcher, a wooden receptacle. [Austral. Abor.]

pitchpine PITCH[1].

pitchy, *a.* of the nature of or like pitch; dark, dismal. **pitchiness,** *n.*

piteous, *a.* exciting or deserving pity; lamentable, sad, mournful; †compassionate; †mean, pitiful. **piteously,** *adv.* **piteousness,** *n.*

pitfall PIT[1].

pith, *n.* a cellular spongy substance occupying the middle of a stem or shoot in dicotyledonous plants; the soft, white tissue under the skin of a lemon, grapefruit etc.; the spinal cord; the essence, the essential part, the main substance; strength, vigour, energy; cogency, point; importance. *v.t.* to remove the pith of; to sever the spinal cord of; to kill in this way. **pith hat, helmet,** *n.* a lightweight sun-hat made of pith. **pithless,** *a.* destitute of strength; weak, feeble. **pithy,** *a.* consisting of, like, or abounding in pith; forcible, energetic; condensed, sententious. **pithily,** *adv.* **pithiness,** *n.* [OE *pitha* (cp. Dut. and Dan. *pit*)]

pithead PIT[1].

pithecanthrope, *n.* former name for *Homo erectus,* an extinct human species of which remains have been found in Java and elsewhere. **pithecanthropic, -thropoid,** *a.* **pithecoid,** *a.* ape-like. [Gr. *pithekos,* ape, *anthrōpos,* man]

pithless, pithy, PITH.

pitiable, pitiful, pitiless, etc. PITY.

Pitman, *n.* **Isaac** (1813–97), English teacher and inventor of Pitman's shorthand. He studied Samuel Taylor's scheme for shorthand writing, and in 1837 published his own system, *Stenographic Soundhand,* fast and accurate, and adapted for use in many languages.

pit-mirk, *a.* (*Sc.*) as dark as a pit, very dark indeed.

piton, *n.* a bar, staff, or stanchion used for fixing ropes on precipitous mountain-sides etc.; a peak, a cone. [F, etym. unknown]

Pitot tube *n.* a right-angled tube open at both ends used with a manometer to measure pressure in a flow of liquid or gas. [Henri *Pitot,* 1696–1771, French physicist]

pitpan, *n.* a narrow, long, flat-bottomed dug-out canoe, used in Central America. [etym. doubtful]

Pitt[1], *n.* **William, the Elder, 1st Earl of Chatham** (1708–78), British Whig politician, 'the Great Commoner'. As paymaster of the forces 1746–55, he broke with tradition by refusing to enrich himself; he was dismissed for attacking Newcastle, the prime minister. He served effectively as prime minister in coalition governments in 1756–61 (successfully conducting the Seven Years' War) and 1766–68.

Pitt[2], *n.* **William, the Younger** (1759–1806), British Tory prime minister 1783–1801 and 1804–06. He raised the importance of the House of Commons and clamped down on corruption, carried out fiscal reforms and union with Ireland. He attempted to keep Britain at peace but underestimated the importance of the French Revolution and became embroiled in wars with France from 1793; he died on hearing of Napoleon's victory at Austerlitz.

Pitta, *n.* the typical genus of Pittidae including most of the Old World ant-thrushes. [Telugu]

pitta (bread), pita, *n.* a flat, round, slightly leavened bread, hollow inside so that it can be filled with food.

pittacal, *n.* a blue substance with a bronze-like lustre obtained from wood-tar, used in dyeing. [G (Gr. *pitta,* pitch, *kalos,* beautiful)]

pittance, *n.* orig. a gift or bequest to a religious house for food etc.; a dole, an allowance, esp. of a meagre amount. [OF *pitance,* etym. doubtful, perh. from L *pietas,* PIETY]

pitted PIT[2].

pitter-patter, PIT-A-PAT.

†**pittikins,** PITIKINS under PITY.

pittite, *n.* one who occupies a place in the pit of a theatre.

Pittsburgh, *n.* industrial city (machinery and chemicals) and inland port, where the Allegheny and Monongahela join to form the Ohio River in Pennsylvania, US; population (1980) 423,940, metropolitan area 2,264,000. Established by the French as Fort Duquesne 1750, the site was taken by the British 1758 and renamed Fort Pitt.

pituitary, *a.* containing or secreting phlegm, mucus; of the pituitary gland. **pituitary body, gland,** *n.* a small structure attached by a pedicle to the base of the brain, secreting hormones which regulate growth, the production of other hormones etc. †**pituita,** †**pituite,** *n.* phlegm, mucus. **pituitous,** *a.* **Pituitrin®,** *n.* a compound hormone extract from the posterior lobe of the pituitary gland. [L *pītuītārius,* from *pītuīta,* phlegm]

pituri, *n.* a plant of the solanaceous genus *Duboisa* of shrubs and trees, the leaves of which are used medicinally and as a narcotic. [Austral. Abor.]

pit-viper PIT[1].

pity, *n.* a feeling of grief or tenderness aroused by the sufferings or distress of others, compassion; a subject for pity, a cause of regret, an unfortunate fact. *v.t.* to feel pity for. *v.i.* to be compassionate. **more's the pity,** it is unfortunate. **to take pity on,** to be compassionate; to act compassionately towards. **what a pity,** how unfortunate! **pitiable,** *a.* deserving or calling for pity; piteous. **pitiableness,** *n.* **pitiably,** *adv.* **pitiful,** *a.* full of pity, compassionate; calling for pity; pitiable, contemptible. **pitifully,** *adv.* **pitifulness,** *n.* †**pitikins,** *n., int.* pity, esp. God's pity, used in oaths and imprecations. **pitiless,** *a.* destitute of pity; merciless, unfeeling, hard-hearted. **pitilessly,** *adv.* **pitilessness,** *n.* **pityingly,** *adv.* [OF *pitet,* L *pietātem,* nom. *-tas,* PIETY]

pityriasis, *n.* squamous inflammation of the skin, dandruff. [Gr. *pituriasis,* from *pituron,* bran]

piu *adv.* (*Mus.*) more. [It., from L *plūs*]

Pius, *n.* twelve popes, including:

Pius IV, *n.* (1499–1565), pope from 1559, of the Medici family. He reassembled the Council of Trent (see COUNTER-REFORMATION) and completed its work 1563.

Pius V, *n.* (1504–72), pope from 1566, who excommunicated Elizabeth I of England, and organized the expedition against the Turks that won the victory of Lepanto.

Pius VI, *n.* (Giovanni Angelo Braschi) (1717–99), pope from 1775. He strongly opposed the French Revolution, and died a prisoner in French hands.

Pius VII, *n.* (1742–1823), pope from 1800. He concluded a concordat with France in 1801 and took part in Napoleon's coronation, but relations became strained. Napoleon annexed the Papal States, and Pius was imprisoned (1809–14). After his return to Rome (1814) he revived the Jesuit order.

Pius IX, *n.* (1792–1878), pope from 1846. He never accepted the incorporation of the Papal States and of Rome in the kingdom of Italy, and proclaimed the dogmas of the Immaculate Conception of the Virgin (1854) and papal infallibility (1870); his pontificate was the longest in history.

Pius XI, *n.* (Achille Ratti) (1857–1939), pope from 1922, he signed the concordat with Mussolini 1929.

Pius XII, *n.* (Eugenio Pacelli) (1876–1958), pope from 1939. He proclaimed the dogma of the bodily assumption of the Virgin Mary in 1950 and in 1951 restated the doctrine (strongly criticized by many) that the life of an infant must not be sacrificed to save a mother in labour. He was also widely criticized for failing to speak out against atrocities committed by the Germans during World War II.

pivot, *n.* a pin, shaft, or bearing on which anything turns or oscillates; of a body of troops, a soldier at the flank on whom a company wheels; a thing or event on which an important issue depends. *v.i.* to turn on or as on a pivot; to hinge (upon) *v.t.* to place on or provide with a pivot. **pivotal,** *a.* of a pivot; of crucial importance, critical. [F, perh. from It. *piva,* L *pīpa,* PIPE]

piwakawaka, *n.* (*New Zealand*) the pied fantail pigeon. [Maori]

pix PIC.

pixel, *n.* one of the minute units which together form an image, e.g. on a cathode ray tube. [*pix,* pictures, *el*ement]

pixilated, pixillated, *a.* (*N Am.*) mentally unbalanced; eccentric. [perh. from earlier *pixy-led*]

pixy, *n.* a supernatural being akin to a fairy or elf. [etym. doubtful]

Pizarro, *n.* **Francisco** (*c.* 1475–1541), Spanish conquistador who took part in the expeditions of Balboa and others. In 1526–27 he explored the NW coast of South America, and conquered Peru (1531) with 180 followers. The Inca king Atahualpa was seized and murdered. In 1535 Pizarro founded Lima. Internal feuding led to Pizarro's assassination.

pizza, *n.* a flat, round piece of baked dough covered usu. with cheese and tomatoes, and also often with anchovies, mushrooms, slices of sausage etc. **pizzeria,** *n.* a place where pizzas are made or sold. [It., prob. from fem. of L *pinceus,* of pitch]

pizzazz, pizazz, *n.* (*esp. N Am., coll.*) vigour, élan, panache, glamour. [etym. unknown]

pizzicato, *a.* (*Mus.*) played by plucking the strings (of a violin etc.) with the fingers. *adv.* in this manner. *n.* a passage or work so played. [It., p.p. of *pizzicare,* to twitch, to twang]

pizzle, *n.* the penis of some quadrupeds, esp. a bull, used as a whip for flogging. [cp. Flem. *pēzel,* LG *Pesel,* Dut. *pees,* sinew]

pl., (*abbr.*) plural.

Plaatje, *n.* **Solomon** (1876–1932), pioneer South African writer and nationalist who was the first secretary-general and founder of the African National Congress in 1912.

placable, *a.* that may be appeased; ready to forgive, mild, complacent. **placability, -ableness,** *n.* **placably,** *adv.* [F, from L *plācābilis,* from *plācāre,* to PLACATE]

placard, *n.* a written or printed paper or bill posted up in a public place, a poster. *v.t.* to post placards on; to announce or advertise by placards; to display as a placard. [OF *placard, plaquard,* from *plaquier,* Dut. *plakken,* to paste, to glue]

placate, *v.t.* to appease, to pacify, to conciliate. **placatory,** *a.* tending to placate. [L *plācātus,* p.p. of *plācāre*]

place, *n.* a particular portion of space; a spot, a locality; a city, a town, a village; a residence, an abode; a building, esp. as devoted to some particular purpose; a residence with its surroundings, esp. in the country; a fortified post; an open space in a town; a passage in a book etc.; position in a definite order, as of a figure in a relation to others in a series or group; a stage or step in an argument, statement etc.; a suitable juncture; stead, lieu; space, room for a person; rank, station in life, official position; situation, employment, appointment, esp. under government; a vacancy, e.g. for a student at a university; duty, sphere, province; a position among the competitors that have been placed. *v.t.* to put or set in a particular place; to put, to set, to fix; to arrange in proper places; to identify; to assign to class; to put in office, to appoint to a post; to find an appointment, situation, or living for; to put out at interest, to invest, to lend; to dispose of (goods) to a customer; to arrange (esp. a bet); to set or fix (confidence etc., in or on); the assign a definite date, position etc., to, to locate; in racing, to indicate the position of (a horse etc.), usu. among the first three passing the winning-post; to get a goal by a place-kick. **in place,** suitable, appropriate. **in place of,** instead of. **out of place** unsuitable, inappropriate. **to give place to,** to give precedence, to give way to; to make room for; to be succeeded by. **to go places,** to be successful. **to put in one's place,** to humiliate someone who is (regarded as) arrogant, presumptious etc. **to take place,** to come to pass, to occur. **to take the place of,** to be substituted for. **place-brick,** a brick imperfectly burnt through being on the windward side of the clamp. **place-hunter,** *n.* one seeking an appointment, esp. under government. **place-kick,** *n.* (*Football*) a kick after the ball has been placed for the purpose by another player. **placemen,** *n.* one holding an appointment, esp. under government. **place-mat,** a table-mat. **place-name,** *n.* the name of a place, esp. as distinguished from a personal name. **place setting,** *n.* the plate, knife, fork etc. set for one person at a table. **placer,** *n.* one who places or sets; one who arranges the sheets of a book etc. for binding; one who puts ceramic ware into the kiln for burning. [F, from L *platea,* Gr. *plateia,* a broad way, a street, orig. fem. of *platus,* flat, wide]

Place, *n.* **Francis** (1771–1854), English Radical. He showed great powers as a political organizer, and made Westminster a centre of Radicalism. He secured the repeal of the anti-union Combination Acts in 1824.

placebo, *n.* (*pl.* **-bos, -boes**) in the Roman Catholic Church, the first antiphon in the vespers for the dead; a medicine having no physiological action, given to humour the patient or to provide psychological comfort, or as a control during experiments to test the efficacy of a genuine medicine. [L, I shall please, 1st sing. fut. of *placēre,* to please]

placenta, *n.* (*pl.* **-tas, -tae**) the organ by which the foetus is nourished in the higher mammals; the part of the ovary to which the ovules are attached. **placental** *n.*, *a.* **placentalian, placentary,** *a., n.* **placentate,** *a.* **placentation,** *n.* (*Zool., Bot.*) the formation, arrangement, or mode of attachment of the placenta. **placentiferous,** *a.* **placentitis,** *n.* inflammation of the placenta. [L, from Gr. *plakous plakounta,* contr. of *-oenta,* flat cake, from *plax,* flat plate]

placer[1] PLACE.

placer[2], *n.* a place where deposits are washed for minerals; an alluvial or other deposit containing valuable minerals; any mineral deposits not classed as veins. [Am. Sp., from *plaza,* PLACE]

placet, *n.* permission, assent, sanction. [L, it pleases, 3rd sing. pres. of *placēre,* to PLEASE]

placid, *a.* gentle, quiet; calm, peaceful, serene, unruffled. **placidity, placidness,** *n.* **placidly,** *adv.* [F *placide,* L *placidus,* as prec.]

†**placitum,** *n.* a decree, judgment, or decision, esp. in a court of justice or a state assembly. †**placitory,** *a.* [L, orig. p.p. of *placēre,* to PLEASE]

†**plack,** *n.* a small copper coin formerly current in Scotland; anything of slight value. **plackless,** *a.* penniless. [Sc., prob. from Flem. *placke* (perh. through F *plaque*), a coin of the Netherlands]

placket, *n.* the opening or slit in a petticoat or skirt; a woman's pocket; a petticoat; a woman. **placket-hole,** *n.* [var. of PLACARD]

placoderm, *a.* belonging to the Placodermi, a Palaeozoic division of fishes having the head and pectoral region covered with large bony plates. *n.* a fish of this division. [as foll., DERM]

placoid, *a.* of fish scales, plate-shaped, *n.* one of the Placoidei, a group of fish with plate-like scales. [Gr. *plax plakos,* flat plate, -OID]

plafond, *n.* a ceiling, esp. one of a richly decorated kind. [F (*plat,* flat, *fond,* bottom)]

plagal, *a.* of the Gregorian modes, having the principal notes between the dominant and its octave; denoting the cadence formed when a subdominant chord immediately precedes the final tonic chord. [med. L *plagālis,* from *plaga,* perh. from med. Gr. *plagios,* orig. oblique, slanting, from Gr. *plagios,* side]

plage, *n.* beach, shore at a seaside resort; a light or dark spot on a spectroheliogram, associated with hot or cool gas on the earth's surface. [F]

plagiarize, -ise, *v.t.* to appropriate and give out as one's own (the writings, inventions, or ideas of another). **plagiarism,** *n.* **plagiarist,** *n.* **plagiary** *n.* one who appropriates the writings or ideas of another and passes them off as his or her own; literary theft, plagiarizing. *a.* practising literary theft. [L *plagiārius,* from *plagiāre,* to kidnap]

plagio- *comb. form.* slanting, oblique. [Gr. *plagios*]

plagiocephalic, *a.* having the skull developed more on one side than the other. **plagiocephaly,** *n.*

plagioclastic, *a.* (*Min.*) having the cleavage oblique, opp. to *orthoclastic.* **plagioclase,** *n.* a plagioclastic feldspar.

plagiostome, *n.* a fish with the mouth placed transversely beneath the snout, as a shark or ray. **plagiostomatous, plagiostomous,** *a.*

plagiotropic, *a.* obliquely geotropic, the two halves (of plants, organs etc.) reacting differently to external influences. **plagiotropically,** *adv.* **plagiotropism,** *n.*

plagium, *n.* (*Law*) kidnapping, man-stealing. [L, kidnapping, from *plagiāre,* see PLAGIARY]

plague, *n.* a blow, a calamity, an affliction; a pestilence, an intensely malignant epidemic, esp. the bubonic or pneumonic forms of infection by *Pasteurella pestis;* a nuisance, a trouble. *v.t.* to visit with plague; to afflict with any calamity or evil; to vex, to tease; to annoy. **plague spot,** *n.* a centre of infection. †**plagueful,** *a.* **plagueless,** *a.* **plaguesome,** *a.* (*coll.*) **plaguer,** *n.* **plaguy,** *a.* vexatious, annoying. **plaguily,** *adv.* [OF *plage, plague,* L *plāga,* a stroke, cogn. with *plangere* to beat (cp. Gr. *plēgē,* blow, *plēssein,* to strike)]

plaice, *n.* a flat-fish, *Pleuronectes platessa,* much used for food. [OF *plïis,* late L *platessa,* prob. from Gr. *platus,* broad]

plaid, *n.* a long rectangular outer garment of woollen cloth, usu. with a checkered or tartan pattern, worn by Scottish Highlanders; plaiding. *a.* like a plaid in pattern. **plaided,** *a.* wearing a plaid; made of plaid cloth. **plaiding,** *n.* cloth for making plaids. [Gael. *plaide,* cp. Ir. *ploid*]

Plaid Cymru, *n.* Welsh nationalist political party established 1925, dedicated to an independent Wales. In 1966 the first Plaid Cymru Member of Parliament was elected.

plain[1], *a.* clear, evident, manifest; simple, free from difficulties; easily seen, easy to understand; not intricate; of knitting, consisting of plain stitches; devoid of ornament; unvariegated, uncoloured; not luxurious, not seasoned highly; of flour, having no raising agent; homely, unaffected, unsophisticated; straightforward, sincere, frank; direct, outspoken; ugly. *adv.* plainly; totally, utterly. *n.* a tract of level country. **plain-chant** PLAINSONG. **plain chocolate,** *n.* dark chocolate with a slightly bitter flavour. **plain clothes,** *n.pl.* private clothes, as opp. to uniform, mufti. **plain-clothes,** *a.* wearing such clothes. **plain-dealer,** *n.* one who speaks his or her mind plainly; †a simpleton. **plain-dealing,** *n., a.* **plain-hearted,** *a.* sincere; free from hypocrisy. **plain Jane,** *n.* (*coll.*) an unattractive woman or girl. **plain sailing** [cp. **plane sailing** under PLANE[3]], *n.* a simple course of action. **Plains Indian**, *n.* any of the North American Indians of the High Plains, which run over 3000 km/2000 miles from Alberta to Texas. The various groups are Blackfoot, Cheyenne, Comanche, Pawnee, and the Dakota or Sioux. **plainsman, plainswoman,** *n.* a dweller on a plain. **plainsong,** *n.* a variety of vocal music according to the ecclesiastical modes of the Middle Ages, governed as to time not by metre but by word-accent, and sung in unison. **plain-spoken,** *a.* speaking or said plainly and without reserve. **plain stitch,** *n.* a simple stitch in knitting, in which a loop is made by passing wool round the right-hand needle and pulling it through a loop on the left-hand needle. **plain-wanderer,** *n.* the turkey quail. **plainwork,** *n.* plain needle-work, as dist. from embroidery etc. **plainly,** *adv.* **plainness,** *n.* [OF, from L *plānum,* nom. *plānus,* flat]

plain[2], *v.i.* to mourn, to lament, to complain; to make a mournful sound. [OF *plaign-,* stem of *plaindre,* L *plangere,* to beat (the breast)]

plaint, *n.* an accusation, a charge; (*poet.*) a lamentation, a mournful song. †**plaintful,** *a.* [OF, from L *planctus,* lamentation (with which OF *plainte,* from L *plancta,* fem. p.p. of *plangere,* see prec., has been assim.)]

plaintiff, *n.* one who brings a suit against another, a complainant, a prosecutor.

plaintive, *a.* expressive of sorrow or grief. **plaintively,** *adv.* †**plaintiveness,** *n.* **plaintless,** *a.* [OF *plaintif,* -tive (as prec., -IVE)]

plaister, PLASTER.

plait, *n.* a braid of several strands of hair, straw, twine etc., esp. a braided tress of hair; a flat fold, a doubling over, as of cloth, a pleat. *v.t.* to braid, to form into a plait or plaits; to fold. **plaiter,** *n.* [OF *ploit, pleit,* L *plicitum,* p.p. of *plicāre,* to fold]

plan, *n.* a delineation of a building, machine etc., by projection on a plane surface, usu. showing the relative positions of the parts on one floor or level; a map of a town, estate, on a large scale; a scheme; a project, a design; an outline of a discourse, sermon etc.; method of procedure; habitual method, way, custom; one of the ideal planes, perpendicular to the line of vision, passing through the objects in a picture, in which these appear of diminishing size according to the distance. *v.t.* to draw a plan of; to design; to contrive, to scheme, to devise. *v.i.* to make plans. **planform,** *n.* the outline of an object, e.g. an aircraft, seen from above. **planless,** *a.* **planner,** *n.* **planning,** *n.* the making of plans, esp. the laying down of economic, social etc. goals and the means of achieving them, or the allocation of land for specific purposes. **planning blight,** *n.* the reduction in property values caused by uncertainty with regard to possible future building development. **planning permission,** *n.* official permission from a local authority etc. to erect or convert a building or change its use. [F, var. of PLAIN[1]]

planar PLANE[3].

planarian, *a.* belonging to the genus *Planaria* of the suborder Planarida, minute, flat, aquatic worms found in salt or fresh water and in moist places. *n.* a flatworm. **planaridan,** *n., a.* **planariform, planarioid,** *a.* [L *plānārius,* flat]

planch, *n.* a slab of metal, fire-brick etc., used in enamelling; †a plank. †*v.t.* to plank, to board. [F *planche,* PLANK]

planchet, *n.* a disk of metal for making into a coin. [dim. of prec.]

planchette, *n.* a small, usu. heart-shaped, board resting on two castors, and a pencil which makes marks as the board moves under the hands of the person resting upon it. believed by spiritualists to be a mode of communicating with the unseen world. [F, dim. of *planche,* PLANK]

Planck, *n.* **Max** (1858–1947), German physicist who framed the quantum theory 1900. **Planck's constant,** *n.* a constant (*h*) which expresses the ratio of a quantum of energy to its frequency, 6.626196×10^{-34} joule seconds.

plane[1], *n.* a tree of various species of the genus *Platanus,* consisting of large spreading branches with broad angular leaves palmately lobed. **plane-tree,** *n.* [F, from L *platanum,* nom. *-nus,* Gr. *platanos,* from *platus,* broad]

plane[2], *n.* a tool for smoothing boards and other surfaces. *v.t.* to smooth or dress with a plane; to make flat and even; to remove (away) or pare (down) irregularities. **planer,** *n.* **planing-machine,** *n.* a machine for planing wood or metal. [F, from late L *plāna,* as foll., whence *plānāre,* to plane, and F. *planer*]

plane[3], *a.* level, flat, without depressions or elevations; lying or extending in a plane. *n.* a surface such that a straight line joining any two points in it lies wholly within it; such a surface imagined to extend to an indefinite distance, forming the locus for certain points or lines; a level surface; an even surface extending uniformly in some direction; one of the natural faces of a crystal; a main road in a mine; an imaginary surface for determining points in a drawing; level (of thought, existence etc.). *v.i.* to glide, to soar; to skim across water. **plane figure,** *n.* a figure all the points in which lie in one plane. **plane geometry,** *n.* the geometry of plane figures. **plane sailing,** *n.* the art of determining a ship's position on the supposition that she is moving on a plane; plain sailing, a simple course of action. **plane-table,** *n.* a surveying instrument marked off into degrees from the centre for measuring angles in mapping. *v.t.* to survey with this. **planar**, *a.* [L *plānus,* flat, level (cp. PLAIN[1] in use in this sense till 17th cent.)]

plane[4], *n.* an aeroplane; one of the thin horizontal structures used as wings to sustain an aeroplane in flight.

planet, *n.* a heavenly body revolving round the sun, either as a primary planet in a nearly circular orbit or as a secondary planet or satellite revolving round a primary; in ancient astronomy, one of the major planets, Mercury, Venus, Mars, Jupiter, Saturn, together with the sun and moon, distinguished from other heavenly bodies as having an apparent motion of its own. **planet-gear, -gearing,** *n.* a system of gearing in which planet-wheels are employed. †**planet-struck, -stricken,** *a.* affected by planetary influence, blasted; panic-stricken, confounded. **planet-wheel,** *n.* a cogged wheel revolving round a wheel with which it engages. **planetarium**, *n.* an apparatus for exhibiting the motions of the planets, an orrery; a building in which this is exhibited on a large scale. **planetary,** *a.* pertaining to the planets or the planetary system. **planetesimal**, *n.* a small body of matter in solar orbit existing at an earlier stage in the formation of the solar system. **planetoid**, *n., a.* **planetoidal,** *a.* †**planetule,** *n.* [OF *planete,* late L *planēta,* Gr. *planētēs,* from *planan,* to lead astray, *planasthai*, to wander]

plane-table PLANE3.

plane-tree PLANE1.

planform PLAN.

plangent, *a.* sounding noisily; resounding sorrowfully. **plangency,** *a.* [L *plangens -ntem,* pres.p. of *plangere,* see PLAINT]

plani-, *comb.form* level, flat, smooth. [L *plānus,* PLANE3]

planigraph, *n.* an instrument for reproducing drawings on a different scale. [F *planigraphe* (-GRAPH)]

planimeter, *n.* an instrument for measuring the area of an irregular plane surface. **planimetric, -ical,** *a.* **planimetry,** *n.* the mensuration of plane surfaces.

planipetalous, *a.* having flat petals.

planish, *v.t.* to flatten, smooth, or toughen (metal) by hammering or similar means; to reduce in thickness by rolling; to polish (metal plates, photographs etc.) by rolling; to polish by hammering. **planisher,** *n.* one who planishes; a planishing tool or machine. [F *planiss-,* stem of *planir* (now *aplanir*), from *plan,* level, PLANE3]

planisphere, *n.* a plane projection of a sphere, esp. of part of the celestial sphere. **planispheric,** *a.*

plank, *n.* a long piece of sawn timber thicker than a board, usu. from $1\frac{1}{2}$ to $4\frac{1}{2}$ in. (about 4–12 cm) thick and 6 to 12 in. (15–30 cm) wide; an article or principle of a political programme. *v.t.* to cover or lay with planks; (*coll.*) to lay down (money, etc.) as if on a board or table. **to walk the plank,** to be compelled to walk blindfold along a plank thrust over a ship's side (a pirates' mode of putting to death). **plank-bed,** *n.* a bed of boards without a mattress (a form of prison discipline). **planking,** *n.* [ONorth.F *planke,* late L *planca,* prob. cogn. with Gr. *plax plakos,* flat plate]

plankton, *n.* Pelagic fauna and flora, esp. minute animals and plants or those of low organization, floating at any level. **planktology,** *n.* [G, from Gr. *plankton,* neut. of *planktos,* wandering, from *plazesthai,* to wander)

planless, planner, planning PLAN.

plano-, *comb.form* flat, level. PLANE3.

plano-concave, *a.* plane on one side and concave on the other.

plano-convex, *a.* plane on one side and convex on the other.

plano-horizontal, *a.* having a level horizontal surface or position.

planometer, *n.* a plane plate used as a gauge for plane surfaces.

plano-subulate , *a.* smooth and awl-shaped.

plant, *n.* any vegetable organism, usu. one of the smaller plants distinguished from shrubs and trees; a sapling; †a shoot, a slip, a cutting; a scion, an offshoot, a descendant; a growth or crop of something planted; the tools, machinery, apparatus, and fixtures used in an industrial concern; mobile mechanical equipment used for earth-moving, road-building etc.; a factory; any place where an industrial process is carried on; a person or thing used to entrap another, esp. an article secretly left so as to be found in a person's possession and provide incriminating evidence. *v.t.* to set in the ground for growth; to put (young fish, spawn etc.) into a river etc.; to furnish or lay out with plants; to fix firmly, to station; to settle, to found, to introduce, to establish; to implant (an idea etc.); to aim and deliver (a blow etc.); to put into position secretly in order to observe, deceive or entrap. *v.i.* to sow seed; to perform the act of planting. **to plant out,** to transplant (seedlings) from pots etc. to open ground. **plant-canes,** *n.pl.* the crop of the sugar-cane of the first growth. **plant-louse,** *n.* an insect infesting plants, esp. the aphis. †**plantable,** *a.* †**plantage,** *n.* **plantation,** *n.* a large quantity of trees or growing plants that have been planted; a growing wood, a grove; a large estate for the cultivation of sugar, cotton, coffe, etc.; the act of planting; †a colony or settlement, settling of colonists, colonization. **planter,** *n.* one who plants; an implement or machine for planting; one who owns or works a plantation; a settler in a colony; an English or Scottish settler in forfeited lands in Ireland in the 17th cent.; (*19th cent.*) a person settled in a holding from which another has been evicted; an ornamental pot for plants; (*sl.*) a well-directed blow. **plantership,** *n.* **plantlet,** *n.* **plantless,** *a.* **plantlike,** *a.* [OE *plante,* L *planta,* a sucker, shoot or slip, also OE *plantian v.i.* L *plantare*]

Plantagenet, *n.* English royal house, reigning 1154–1399, whose name comes from the nickname of Geoffrey, Count of Anjou (1113–51), father of Henry II, who often wore a sprig of broom, in his hat. In the 1450s, Richard, duke of York, revived it as a surname to emphasize his superior claim to the throne over Henry VI. [OF from L *planta,* sprig, *genista,* broom]

plantain1, *n.* any plant of the genus *Plantago,* esp. *P. major,* a low perennial weed with broad flat leaves and a spike of dull green flowers. [OF, from L *plantāginem,* nom. *-go,* prob. from *planta,* foot-sole, from the prostrate leaves]

plantain2, *n.* a tropical American herbaceous tree, *Musa paradisiaca,* closely akin to the banana, and bearing similar fruit; its fruit. [Sp. *plantano, platano,* L *platanus,* PLANE1]

plantar, *a.* pertaining to the sole of the foot. [L *plantāris,* from *planta,* foot-sole]

plantation, planter PLANT.

plantigrade, *a.* walking on the sole of the foot; of or pertaining to the Plantigrada, a section of the Carnivora embracing the bears, badgers etc. *n.* a plantigrade animal. [F (L *planta,* sole, *-gradus,* walking)]

planula, *n.* the locomotory embryo of coelenterates. **planular, -late, -loid,** *a.* **planuliform,** *a.* [dim. of L *plānus,* PLANE3]

planuria, *n.* discharge of urine through an abnormal channel. [Gr. *planos,* wandering, Gr. *ouron,* urine]

planxty, *n.* (*Ir.*) a melody of a sportive and animated character for the harp. [etym. unknown]

plap, *v.i.* to fall with a flat impact. *n.* the sound of this. [onomat.]

plaque, *n.* a plate, slab, or tablet, of metal, porcelain, ivory etc., usu. of an artistic or ornamental character; a small plate worn as a badge or personal ornament; a patch or spot on the surface of the body; a filmy deposit on the surface of the teeth consisting of mucus and bacteria. **plaquette,** *n.* [F, see PLACK]

plash1, *n.* a large puddle, a marshy pool, a pond. **plashy** *a.* marshy, watery. [OE *ploesc* (cp. Dut. and LG *plas*) prob. cogn. with foll.]

plash2, *v.t.* to cause (water) to splash; to dabble in; to sprinkle colouring-matter on (walls), in imitation of granite, etc. *v.i.* to dabble in water; to make a splash. *n.* a splash, a plunge; the sound made by this. **plashy,** *a.* marked as if with splashes of colour etc. [prob. imit., cp. Dut. *plassen,* G *platschen,* Swed. *plaska*]

plash3, *v.t.* to bend down or cut partly and intertwine the branches of (to form a hedge); to make or repair (a hedge) in this way. *n.* a branch partly cut and interwoven with other branches. [OF *plessier, plaissier,* to PLEACH]

-plasia, *comb.form* growth, development. [NL *-plasia* from Gr. *plasis,* a moulding from *plassein,* to mould]

plasm, *n.* †a mould or matrix, in which anything is cast or formed; plasma. **plasma,** *n.* the viscous living matter of a cell, protoplasm; the fluid part of the blood, lymph, or milk; sterilized blood plasma used for transfusions; a hot, ionized gas containing approximately equal numbers of positive ions and electrons; †a mould or matrix; a green variety of quartz allied to chalcedony. **plasma torch,** *n.* a device in which gas is converted to a plasma by being heated electrically and which is used for melting metals etc. **plasmatic, plasmic** *a.* **plasmid,** *n.* a small circle of DNA found esp. in bacteria, which exists and replicates itself independently of the main bacterial chromosome. *a.* **plasmin,** *n.* an enzyme in blood plasma that dissolves fibrin. [late L and Gr. *plasma,* from *plassein,* to mould]

plasmo-, *comb. form.* plasm.

plasmodium, *n.* (*pl.* **-dia**) a mass of mobile, naked protoplasm resulting from the fusion or aggregation of numerous amoeboid cells, as in the vegetative stage of Myxomycetes and Mycetozoa; a genus of Protozoa found in the blood in malaria and quartan and tertian ague. **plasmodial, -modic, -modiate,** *a.*

plasmogen, *n.* true or formative protoplasm.

plamogeny, -gony, *n.* the spontaneous generation of individualized organisms.

plasmology, *n.* the science of the ultimate corpuscles of living matter.

plasmolysis, *n.* the contraction of the protoplasm in active cells under the influence of a reagent or of disease. **plasmolyse,** (*esp. N Am.*) **-lyze,** *v.t.* **plasmolytic,** *a.*

-plast, *comb. form.* a living cell or subcellular particle. [Gr. *plastos,* moulded, from *plassein* to mould]

plaster, *n.* a mixture of lime, sand etc., for coating walls etc.; calcined gypsum or sulphate of lime, used, when mixed with water, for coating or for moulding into ornaments, figures etc.; an adhesive application of some curative substance, usu. spread on linen, muslin, or a similar fabric, placed on parts of the body; a strip of sticking plaster; a surgical plaster cast. *a.* made of plaster. *v.t.* to cover or overlay with plaster or other adhesive substance; to apply a plaster to (a wound etc.); to daub, to smear over, to smooth over; to cause to lie flat or adhere to; to cover with excessive quantities of, to use excessively and/or tastelessly; to stick (on) as with plaster; to treat (wine) with gypsum to cure acidity; (*coll.*) to inflict heavy damage, injury, or casualties on. **plaster of Paris,** gypsum, esp. calcined gypsum used for making casts of statuary etc. **plasterboard,** *n.* (a thin, rigid board consisting of) a layer of plaster compressed between sheets of fibreboard, used in making partition walls, ceilings etc. **plaster cast,** *n.* a plaster copy, made from a mould, of any object, esp. a statue; a covering of plaster of Paris used to immobilize and protect e.g. a broken limb. **plaster-stone,** *n.* raw gypsum. **plastered,** *a.* (*coll.*) drunk. **plasterer,** *n.* **plastering,** *n.* the act of coating or treating with plaster; a covering or coat of plaster. **plastery,** *a.* [OE, from L *emplastrum,* Gr. *emplastron, emplaston,* from *emplassein,* to daub on (EM-, *plassein,* to mould)]

plastic, *a.* having the power of giving form or fashion; capable of being modelled or moulded; pertaining to or produced by modelling or moulding; continuously extensible or pliable without rupturing; capable of adapting to varying conditions; formative, causing growth; forming living tissue; made of plastic; (*coll., derog.*) outwardly and conventionally attractive but lacking substance or reality; synthetic, insincere. *n.* any of a group of usu. synthetic, polymeric substances which, though stable in use at ordinary temperatures, are plastic at some stage in their manufacture and can be shaped by the application of heat and pressure; (*coll.*) a credit card, or credit cards collectively. **extruded plastic,** plastic formed into strips, rods etc., by extrusion through a die. **plastic art,** *n.* art which is concerned with moulding or shaping or representation in three dimensions; any visual art. **plastic bullet,** *n.* a cylinder of plastic approximately 4 in. (10 cm) long, less lethal than an ordinary bullet, used mainly for riot control. **plastic explosive,** *n.* an adhesive, jelly-like explosive substance. **plastic money,** *n.* credit cards used instead of money. **plastic surgery,** *n.* the branch of surgery concerned with the restoration of lost, deformed, or disfigured parts of the body or with the cosmetic improvement of any feature. **plastically,** *adv.* **plasticate,** *v.t.* (*esp. in p.p.*) to treat or cover with plastic. **plasticity,** *n.* the state of being plastic; (apparent) three-dimensionality. **plasticize, -ise,** *v.t.* **plasticizer, -iser,** *n.* a substance which renders rubber, plastic, etc. more flexible. [L *plasticus,* Gr. *plastikos,* as prec.]

Plasticine ®, *n.* a modelling substance for the use of children.

plastid, , *n.* a small particle in the cells of plants and some animals containing pigment, starch, protein etc. [Gr *plastis -idos,* modeller]

plastin, *n.* a viscous substance found in the nuclei of cells.

plastron, *n.* a padded leather shield worn by fencers to protect the breast; an ornamental front to a woman's dress; a shirtfront; the under part of the buckler of a tortoise or turtle, an analogous part in other animals; †a breast-plate, usu. worn under a coat of mail. **plastral,** *a.* [F, from It. *piastrone,* from *piastria,* breast-plate, see PIASTRE]

-plasty, *comb.form.* formation or replacement by plastic surgery. [F *-plastie* from Gr. *-plastia,* moulding, from *plassein*]

-plasy -PLASIA.

plat[1], *n.* a small plot, patch, or piece of ground; a small bed (of flowering-plants etc.); a map, a chart. *v.t.* (*past, p.p.* **platted**) to make a plan of; (*N Am.*) to lay out in plats or plots. [var. of PLOT]

plat[2] PLAIT.

Plataea, Battle of, a battle of 479 BC held at Plataea, an ancient city in S Boeotia, in which the Greeks defeated the Persians during the Persian Wars.

platan, *n.* a plane-tree. **plataneous, platanine,** *a.* [L *platanus,* PLANE[1]]

platband, *n.* a border or strip (of flowers, turf etc.); a flat, rectangular, slightly-projecting moulding; a fillet between the flutings of pillars; a square lintel; a plain impost. [F *plateband* (*plate,* flat, as foll., BAND[2])]

plate, *n.* a flat, thin piece of metal etc., usu. rigid and uniform in thickness; a very thin coating of one metal upon another; a flat, rigid layer of bone, horn etc. forming part of an animal's body or shell; a huge plate-like section of the earth's crust; a piece of metal with an inscription for attaching to an object; a piece of metal used for engraving; a print taken from this; a sheet of glass or other material coated with a sensitized film for photography; an electro-type or stereotype cast of a page of type, to be used for printing; a whole-page illustration separately inserted into book and often on different paper from the text; a device for straightening teeth; the plastic base of a denture, fitting the gums and holding the artificial teeth; a horizontal timber laid on a wall as base for framing; a small shallow vessel, now usu. of crockery, for eating from; a plateful; the contents of a plate, a portion served on a plate; any shallow receptable esp. for taking a collection in church; (*collect.*) domestic utensils, as spoons, forks, knives, cups, dishes etc., of gold, silver, or other metal; plated ware; a cup or other article of gold or silver offered as a prize in a race etc.; a race for such a prize; †a piece of silver money. *v.t.* to cover or overlay with plates of metal for defence, ornament, etc.; to coat with a layer of metal, esp. gold, silver, or tin; to beat into thin plates; to make an electrotype or stereotype from (type). **half-plate,** (*Phot.*) a photographic plate $6\frac{1}{2} \times 4\frac{3}{4}$ in. (16.5 × 12 cm) **quarter-plate,** *n.* $4\frac{1}{4} \times 3\frac{1}{4}$ in. (10.75 × 8.25 cm) **whole-plate,** *n.* $8\frac{1}{2} \times 6\frac{1}{2}$ in. (21.5 × 16.5 cm) **handed to one on a plate,** (*coll.*) obtained without effort. **to have on one's plate,** (*coll.*) to have waiting to be done, to be burdened with. **plate-armour,** *n.* armour composed of heavy plates of metal with which ships, forts etc., are covered to protect them against artillery fire; defensive armour formerly worn by knights and men-at-arms, distinguished from chain or mail armour. **plate-basket,** *n.* a receptable for spoons, forks etc. **plate-fleet,** *n.* a fleet of vessels carrying bullion, esp. from America to Spain in the 16th cent. **plate-glass,** *n.* a superior kind of glass made in thick sheets, used for mirrors, large windows etc. **plate-layer,** *n.* one who fixes or repairs railway metals. **plate-paper,** *n.* fine quality paper for taking engravings etc. **plate-powder,** *n.* powder for cleaning domestic plate. **plate-rack,** *n.* a frame for holding plates and dishes. **plate-rail,** *n.* a flat rail formerly used on railways. **plate-ship** PLATE-FLEET. **plate tectonics,** *n. sing.* (the study of the earth's crust based on) the theory that the lithosphere is made up of a number of continually moving and interacting plates. **plate-tracery,** *n.* tracery, esp. in Early English and Decorated windows, giving the appearance of solid surfaces pierced with ornamental patterns. **plateful,** *n.* **plateless,** *a.* **platelet,** *n.* a minute blood particle involved in clotting. **plater,** *n.* one who plates articles with silver, etc.; one who works upon plates; one who fits plates in shipbuilding; an inferior race-horse that runs chiefly in selling plates. **plating,** *n.* the act, art, or process of covering articles with a coating of metal; a coating of gold, silver, or other metal; (*collect.*) the plates covering a ship, fort etc.; (*Racing*) competing for plates. [OF, fem. of *plat,* flat, perh. from Gr. *platus,* broad]

plateau, *n.* (*pl.* **-teaus, -teaux**) a table-land, an elevated plain; a large ornamental centre dish; an ornamental plaque; a woman's level-topped hat; a period of stability after or during an upward progression, a levelling-off. [F, dim. of *plat,* a platter, a dish, orig. flat. as prec.]

platen, *n.* the part of a printing-press that presses the paper against the type to give the impression; the roller in a typewriter serving the same purpose. [ME *plateyne,* OF *platine,* from *plat,* flat, as prec.]

plater PLATE.

Plate, River, *n.* English name of Río de la Plata, estuary in South America.

platform, *n.* any flat or horizontal surface raised above some adjoining level; a stage or raised flooring in a hall etc., for speaking from etc.; a landing-stage; a raised pavement etc., beside the line at a railway station etc.; a vehicle or emplacement on which weapons are mounted and fired; a raised metal structure moored to the sea-bed and used for off-shore drilling. marine exploration etc.; the small floor by which one enters or alights from a bus; (a shoe with) a thick sole; platform oratory; a political programme; the principles forming the basis of a party; (*N Am.*) a declaration of principles and policy issued by a party before an election. *v.t.* to place on or as on a platform. *v.i.* to speak from a platform. [F *plateforme,* a model, a ground plan (*plat,* flat, see PLATE, FORM)]

Plath, *n.* **Sylvia** (1932–63), US poet and novelist. Plath's powerful, highly personal poems, often expressing a sense of desolation, are distinguished by their intensity and sharp imagery. Collections include *The Colossus* (1960), *Ariel* (1965), published after her death, and *Collected Poems* (1982). Her autobiographical novel, *The Bell Jar* (1961), deals with the events surrounding a young woman's emotional breakdown.

plating PLATE.

platinum, *n.* a heavy, ductile and malleable metallic element of a silver colour, fusing only at extremely high temperatures, immune to attack by most chemical reagents. **platinum-black,** *n.* finely divided platinum in the form of a black powder, obtained by the reduction of platinum salts. **platinum blonde,** *n.* (*coll.*) a woman with hair so fair as to be almost white. **platinum metals,** *n.pl.* the platinoids. **platinic,** *a.* of or containing (tetravalent) platinum. **platiniferous,** *a.* **platinize, -ise,** *v.t.* to coat with platinum. **platinode,** *n.* the cathode or negative pole or plate of a voltaic cell, frequently of platinum, opp. to *zincode.* **platinoid,** *a.* like platinum. *n.* a name for certain metals found associated with platinum; an alloy of German silver etc. **platinotype,** *n.* a photographic printing process in which a deposit of platinum black gives a positive; a print with this. **platinous,** *a.* of or containing (bivalent) platinum. [formerly *platina,* from Sp., dim. of *plata,* silver, PLATE]

platitude, *n.* flatness, commonplaceness, insipidity, triteness; a trite remark, esp. of a didactic kind. **platitudinize, -ise,** *v.i.* **platitudinous,** *a.* **platitudinously,** *adv.* **platitudinarian,** *n., a.* [F, from *plat,* flat, see PLATE]

Plato, *n.* (*c.* 428–347 BC), Greek philosopher, pupil of Socrates, teacher of Aristotle, and founder of the Academy. He was the author of philosophical dialogues on such topics as metaphysics, ethics, and politics. Central to his teachings is the notion of forms, which are located outside the everyday world, timeless, motionless, and absolutely real. **Platonic,** *a.* of or pertaining to Plato, or to his philosophy or school; (*usu.* **platonic**) not involving sexual desire or activity. **Platonically,** *adv.* **Platonism,** *n.* **Platonist,** *n.*

platoon, *n.* a subdivision, usu. half, of a company, formerly a tactical unit under a lieutenant; a volley fired by this; a body or set of people. [corr. of F *peloton,* dim. of *pelote,* PELLET]

platter, *n.* a large shallow dish or plate. [ME and A-F *plater,* from *plat,* PLATE]

platting, *n.* slips of bark, cane, straw etc., woven or plaited, for making hats etc.

platy-, *comb.form.* broad, flat.

platycephalic, -cephalous, *a.* of skulls, flat and broad relatively to length.

platypus, *n.* a small, aquatic, egg-laying mammal of E Australia having a broad bill and tail, thick fur and webbed feet. [Gr. *platus,* broad]

platyrrhine, *n.* of monkeys, broad-nosed. [Gr. *rhis rhinos,* nose]

plaudit, *n.* (*usu. pl.*) an expression of applause; praise or approval. **plauditory,** *a.* [L *plaudite,* imper. of *plaudere,* to applaud (with suppression of final vowel)]

plausible, *a.* apparently right, reasonable, or probable; specious; apparently trustworthy; ingratiating. †**plausibleness, plausibility,** *n.* **plausibly,** *adv.* †**plausive,** *a.* applauding; ingratiating. [L *plausibilis,* from *plaus-,* p.p. stem of *plaudere,* see prec.]

plaustral, *a.* of or pertaining to a wagon. [L *plaustrum,* wagon, -AL]

Plautus, *n.* (*c.* 254–184 BC), Roman dramatist, born in Umbria, who settled in Rome and worked in a bakery before achieving success as a dramatist. He wrote at least 56 comedies, freely adapted from Greek originals, of which 20 survive. Shakespeare based *The Comedy of Errors* on his *Menaechmi.*

play, *n.* free, light, aimless movement or activity; freedom of movement or action; space or scope for this; a state of activity; a series of actions engaged in for pleasure or amusement; sport, exercise, amusement, fun; playing in a game; manner or style of this; the period during which a game is in progress; (*esp. N Am.*) a manoeuvre, esp. in a game; style of execution, playing (as on an instrument); exercise in any contest; gaming, gambling; a dramatic composition or performance, a drama; conduct or dealing towards others (esp. as fair or unfair). *v.i.* to move about in a lively, light, or aimless manner, to dance, frisk, shimmer etc.; to act or move freely; of instruments, machinery, guns etc. to perform a regular operation; of a part of a machine etc., to move loosely or irregularly; to be discharged or directed onto something, as water, light etc.; to sport, to frolic; to do something as an amusement; to toy, to trifle; to take part in a game; to take one's turn at performing an action specific to a game; to perform in a specified position or manner in a game; to perform on a musical instrument; to emit or reproduce sound; to take part in a game of chance; to game, to gamble; to behave, to act, to conduct oneself in regard to others; to personate a character; to act a part (esp. on a stage); of a drama, show etc., to be in performance; of an actor or company, to be performing. *v.t.* to engage in (a game or sport); to execute (a stroke, a shot etc.); to proceed through (a game, a rubber etc.); to oppose, to compete against; to make use of (as a player or an implement) in a game; to bring (as a card) into operation in a game; to cause (a ball etc) to move in a certain direction by striking, kicking etc.; (*coll.*) to gamble on; to perform (a trick etc.) esp. in jest or mockery; to give a performance or performances of (a musical or dramatic work, the works of a specified composer or author); to perform music on; to emit or reproduce sounds, esp. music; to act the role of; to act, or stage a play, in (a specified theatre or town); to pretend to be; to handle, to deal with, to manage; to give (a fish) freedom to exhaust itself; to discharge (as guns, a hose) continuously (on or upon); to cause to move lightly or aimlessly over; †to exercise, to ply. **play on words,** punning, a pun. **play-or-pay bet,** one that holds good whether the horse runs or not. **to bring, call into play,** to make operative. **to make a play for,** (*coll.*) to try to get. **to make great play with,** to make much of, to parade, to flourish ostentatiously. **to play about, around,** to act in a frivolous or irresponsible manner; to have casual sexual relationships. **to play along (with),** to (seem to) agree or cooperate (with). **to play at,** to engage (in a game); to perform or execute in a frivolous or half-hearted way. **to play back,** to replay something just recorded. **to play ball,** to cooperate, to comply. **to play down,** to treat as unimportant, not to stress. **to play false,** to betray. **to play fast and loose,** to be fickle; to act recklessly. **to play God,** to (seek to) control other people's destinies, to affect omnipotence. **to play hard to get,** (*coll.*) to act coyly, esp. as a come-on. **to play into the hands of,** to play or act so as to give the advantage to one's partner or opponent. **to play it by ear,** not to plan one's actions in advance, to improvise a response as situations develop. **to play it cool,** not to get excited. **to play (it) safe,** to take no risks. **to play off,** to pass (a thing) off as something else; to oppose (one person) against another, esp. for one's own advantage; to show off; to tee off; to take part in a play-off. **to play on,** to perform upon; to play the ball on to one's own wicket; (also **upon**) to exploit. **to play the field** FIELD. **to play the game,** to play according to the rules of a game and accept defeat without complaint; to act honestly and courageously in any undertaking. **to play up,** to cause trouble or suffering to; to misbehave; to malfunction or function erratically; to give prominence to; to play more vigorously. **to play up to,** to humour, to draw out. **to play with,** to amuse oneself or sport with; to treat with levity. **play-act,** *v.i.* to make believe; to behave insincerely or overdramatically. **play-acting,** *n.* **playback,** *n.* a reproduction, esp. immediately after the recording has been made, of recorded sound or vision; a device for producing the above. **play-bill,** *n.* a bill or programme announcing or giving the cast of a play. **play-book,** *n.* a book of dramatic compositions; a book of games for children. **playboy, playgirl,** *n.* a young man or woman who lives for pleasure, a social parasite. **play-club,** *n.* (*Golf*) a driver. **play-day,** *n.* a holiday; a day on which miners do not work. **play-debt,** *n.* a gambling debt. **playfellow,** *n.* a companion in play. **playgoer,** *n.* one who frequents theatres. **playgoing,** *a.* **playground,** *n.* a piece of ground used for games, esp. one attached to a school; a favourite district for tourists, mountain-climbers etc. **playgroup,** *n.* a group of pre-school children who meet regularly for supervised and usu. creative play. **playhouse,** *n.* a theatre. **playmate,** *n.* a playfellow. **play-off,** *n.* a game to decide the final winner of a competition, esp. an extra game when two competitors are tied. **playpen,** *n.* a portable wooden framework inside which young children can play in safety. **playschool,** *n.* a nursery school or playgroup. **plaything,** *n.* a toy; a person or article used for one's amusement. **playtime,** *n.* time allotted for play. **playwright, play-writer,** *n.* a dramatist. **playable,** *a.* able to be played or performed (on); (*Cricket*) able to be struck by the batsman. **played-out,** *a.* tired out; worn out, used up. **player,** *n.* one who plays; one engaged in a game; a person skilled in a particular game; a professional player, esp. a professional cricketer; an actor; a performer on a musical instrument; an automatic device for playing a musical instrument; a gambler; (*Billiards, Croquet, etc.*) the ball coming next into play. **playful,** *a.* frolicsome, sportive; sprightly, humourous, jocular, amusing. **playfully,** *adv.* **playfulness,** *n.* **playing,** *n.* **playing-cards,** *n.pl.* cards used for games. **playing field,** *n.* a field or open space used for sports. †**playsome,** *a.* †**playsomeness,** *n.* [OE *plega,* cogn. with *plegian, plagian, plœgian* (cp. Dut. *plegen,* G *pflegen,* to have the care of, *Pflege,* care)]

plaza, *n.* a public square or open paved area; (*chiefly N Am.*) a shopping centre. [Sp. from L *platea* see PLACE]

PLC, plc (*abbr.*) public limited company.

plea, *n.* the accused's answer to an indictment; something alleged by a party to legal proceedings in support of a claim or defence; an excuse; an urgent entreaty. **plea-bargaining,** *n.* (*chiefly N Am.*) the practice of arranging more lenient treatment by the court in return for an admission of guilt by the accused. [A-F *plee,* OF *plai, plaid,* L PLACITUM]

pleach, *v.t.* to interlace, to intertwine, to plash. [ME *plechen,* OF *plessier, plaisser,* late L *plectiāre* (not extant), L *plectere,* to PLAIT (cp. PLASH³)]

plead, *v.i.* (*past, p.p.* **pleaded**) to speak or argue in support of a claim, or in defence against a claim; to urge arguments for or against a claim; to urge arguments for or against; to supplicate earnestly; to put forward a plea or allegation, to address a court on behalf of; to answer to an indictment. *v.t.* to discuss, maintain, or defend by arguments; to allege in pleading or argument; to offer in excuse, to allege in defence. **to plead guilty, not guilty,** to admit or deny guilt or liability. **to plead with,** to entreat or supplicate (for, against etc.). **pleadable,** *a.* **pleader,** *n.* one who pleads in a court of law; one who offers reasons for or against; one who draws up pleas. **pleading,** *n.* the act of making a plea; entreating, imploring; a written statement of a party in a suit at law; the art or practice of drawing up such statements. *a.* imploring, appealing. **special pleading** SPECIAL. **pleadingly,** *adv.* [OF *plaidier,* from *plaid,* PLEA]

†**pleasance,** *n.* pleasure, gaiety, pleasantness; a pleasure-ground, esp. a park or garden attached to a mansion. [OF *plaisance,* as foll.]

Pleasance, *n.* **Donald** (1919–), English actor. He has been acclaimed for roles in Pirandello's *The Rules of the Game*, in Pinter's *The Caretaker*, and also in the title role of the film *Dr Crippen* (1962), conveying the sinister aspect of the outcast from society. Other films include *THX 1138* (1971) and *The Eagle has Landed* (1976).

pleasant, *a.* pleasing, agreeable, affording gratification to the mind or senses; affable, friendly; good-humoured; †cheerful, gay, jocular, merry. **pleasantly,** *adv.* **pleasantness,** *n.* **pleasantry,** *n.* jocularity, facetiousness; a jest, a joke, an amusing trick; an agreeable remark, made esp. for the sake of politeness. †pleasure, pleasantness. [ME and OF *plaisant* (PLEASE, -ANT)]

please, *v.t.* to afford pleasure to; to be agreeable to; to satisfy; to win approval from. *v.i.* to afford gratification; to like, to think fit, to prefer; a polite formula used in making requests or expressing acceptance. **if you please,** if it is agreeable to you; with your permission; (*iron*) expressing sarcasm or protest. **please yourself** *int.* do as you wish. **pleased,** *a.* gratified; delighted. **pleasedly,** *adv.* **pleasedness,** *n.* **pleaser,** *n.* **pleasing,** *a.* **pleasingly,** *adv.* **pleasingness,** *n.* [ME *plese,* plaise, OF *plesir, plaisir* (F *plaire*), L *placēre*]

pleasure, *n.* the gratification of the mind or senses; enjoyment, gratification, delight; sensual gratification; a source of gratification; choice, wish, desire. *v.t.* to give pleasure to. *v.i.* to take pleasure (in). **pleasure-boat,** *n.* a boat for pleasure excursions. **pleasure-ground,** *n.* a park or garden (usu. public) used for outdoor entertainments. **pleasure-trip,** *n.* **pleasurable,** *a.* affording pleasure; pleasant, gratifying, †seeking pleasure. **pleasurableness,** *n.* **pleasurably,** *adv.* [ME and OF *plesir, plaisir,* to PLEASE, used as noun]

pleat, *v.t.* to fold or double over, to crease. *n.* a flattened fold, a crease. [var. of PLAIT]

pleb, *n.* short for PLEBEIAN; (*derog.*) a common, vulgar person.

plebeian, *a.* pertaining to the ancient Roman commoners; pertaining to the common people; common, vulgar, low. *n.* a commoner in ancient Rome; one of the common people. **plebianism, plebeianness,** *n.* **plebeianize, -ise,** *v.t.* **plebeianly,** *adv.* [F *plébéien,* L *plēbēius,* from *plebs,* earlier *plēbes,* the common people]

plebiscite, *n.* a law enacted by a vote of the commonalty in an assembly presided over by a tribune of the people; a direct vote of the whole body of citizens in a state on a definite question, a referendum; an expression of opinion by the whole community. **plebiscitary**, *a.* [F *plébiscite,* L *plēbiscītum* (*plebs plēbis, scītum,* decree, p.p. of *sciscere,* to vote, incept. of *scīre,* to know)]

plectognath, *a.* of the Plectognathi, an order of teleostean fishes having the cheek-bones united with the jaws. *n.* a fish of this order. **plectognathic**, **-gnathous**, *a.* [Gr. *plektos,* plaited, *gnathos,* jaw]

plectrum, *n.* (*pl.* **-tra**, **-trums**) a small implement of ivory, etc., with which players pluck the strings of the guitar, harp, lyre etc. [L, from Gr. *plēktron,* cogn. with *plēssein,* to strike]

pled, (*Sc.*) p.p. of PLEAD.

pledge, *n.* anything given or handed over by way or guarantee of security for the repayment of money borrowed, or for the performance of some obligation; a thing put in pawn; an earnest, a token; a gage of battle; (*fig.*) one's child; an agreement, promise, or binding engagement; the state of being pledged; a health, a toast; †a person standing surety or bail. *v.t.* to give as a pledge or security; to deposit in pawn; to engage solemnly; to drink a health to. **to take the pledge,** to pledge oneself to abstain from alcoholic drink. **pledgeable,** *a.* †**pledgee**, *n.* **pledgeless,** *a.* **pledger,** *n.* [ME and OF *plege* (F *pleige*), prob. rel. to *plevir,* to warrant, to engage, from Teut. (cp. PLIGHT[1])]

pledget, *n.* a compress of lint for laying over an ulcer, wound etc. [etym. doubtful]

-plegia, *comb.form* paralysis. [Gr. *plēgē* stroke from *plēssein* to strike]

Pleiad, *n.* a cluster of brilliant persons, esp. seven. **La Pléiade,** a group of seven poets in 16th-cent. France led by Pierre Ronsard, who were inspired by classical models to improve French verse. **Pleiades**, *n.pl.* a star cluster about 400 light years away in the constellation Taurus. Its brightest stars (highly luminous, very young blue-white giants only a few million years old) are visible to the naked eye, but there are many fainter ones; in Greek mythology, seven daughters of Atlas, who asked to be changed to a cluster of stars to escape the pursuit of Orion. [L *Plēias -adis,* Gr. *Pleias -ados*]

plein air, *a.* (done) out of doors, esp. in relation to the principles and practice of the Impressionist school of painting. [F]

pleio- PLIO-.

Pleiocene, PLIOCENE.

Pleistocene, *a., n.* (pertaining to) the strata or first epoch of the Quaternary period of geological time, beginning 1.8 million years ago and ending 10,000 years ago. Glaciers were abundant during the Ice Age, and humans, evolved into modern *Homo sapiens*, appeared about 100,000 years ago. [Gr. *pleistos,* most, *kainos,* new]

Plekhanov, *n.* **Georgi Valentinovich** (1857–1918), Russian Marxist revolutionary and theorist, founder of the Menshevik party. He led the first populist demonstration in St Petersburg, and left for exile in 1880. He became a Marxist and, with Lenin, edited the newspaper *Iskra* ('spark'). In 1903 his opposition to Lenin led to the Bolshevik-Menshevik split. In 1917 he returned to Russia.

plenary, *a.* full, complete, entire, absolute; attended by all members. **plenary indulgence,** in the Roman Catholic Church, an indulgence remitting all the temporal penalties due to sin. **plenary inspiration,** *n.* full inspiration, with complete freedom from error. **plenarily,** *adv.* †**plenariness,** *n.* [late L *plēnārius,* from *plēnus,* full]

pleni-, *comb.form.* full. [L *plēnus*]

plenicorn, *a.* having solid horns. [L *cornu* horn]

plenilune, *n.* the time of full moon; a full moon. **plenilunal, plenilunar, -nary**, *a.* [L *plēnilūnium* (*lūna,* moon)]

plenipotentiary, *a.* invested with full powers; full, absolute. *n.* an ambassador or envoy to a foreign court, with full powers. [med. L *plēnipotentiārius,* (*potentia*)]

plenish, *v.t.* (*chiefly Sc.*) to fill up, to replenish, to stock, to furnish (esp. a farm). **plenishing, plenishment,** *n.* [OF *pleniss-,* stem of *plenir,* as foll.]

plenist, *n.* one who maintains that all space is full of matter. [PLEN-UM, -IST]

plenitude, *n.* fullness; completeness, abundance; †repletion. [OF, from L *plēnitūdo,* from *plēnus,* full]

plenty, *n.* abundance, copiousness; fruitfulness; (*sing or pl in constr.*) a large quantity or number, an ample supply, lots. *a.* (*coll.*) plentiful, abundant. *adv.* (*coll.*) quite, abundantly. **horn of plenty,** a cornucopia. **plenteous**, *a.* (*poet.*) **plenteously,** *adv.* **plenteousness,** *n.* **plentiful,** *a.* existing in abundance; yielding abundance, copious. **plentifully,** *adv.* **plentifulness,** *n.* [OF *plentet,* L *plēnitātem,* nom. *-tas,* from *plēnus,* full]

plenum, *n.* (*pl.* **-nums, -na**) space, as considered to be full of matter, oposed to vacuum; an enclosure containing gas at a higher pressure than the surrounding environment; a condition of fullness, plethora; a full meeting. [L, neut of *plēnus,* full]

pleo- PLIO.

pleomorphism, *n.* the occurrence of more than one different form in the life cycle of a plant or animal; polymorphism.

pleonasm, *n.* redundancy of expression in speaking or writing. **pleonastic**, *a.* **pleonastically,** *adv.* [L *pleonasmus,* Gr. *pleonasmos,* from *pleonazein,* to abound or be redundant, from *pleon,* full]

pleroma, *n.* fullness, abundance; the divine being filling the universe and including all the aeons emanating from it. [Gr. *plērōma,* from *plêroun,* to make full, from *plērēs,* full]

plesiomorphous, -morphic, *a.* (*Cryst.*) nearly alike in form. **plesiomorphism,** *n.* [Gr. *plēsios,* near, *morphē,* form, -OUS]

plesiosaur, *n.* any of a genus, *Plesiosaurus,* of extinct marine saurians with long necks, small heads and four paddles. [Gr. *plēsios,* near, *sauros,* lizard]

plethora, *n.* superabundance; excessive fullness of blood. †**plethoretic, -ical**, **plethoric**, *a.* having an excess of blood in the body; superabundant. [med. L, from Gr. *plēthōrē,* fullness, from *plēthein,* to become full]

pleur- PLEUR(O)-.

pleura, *n.* (*pl.* **-rae, -ras**) a thin membrane covering the interior of the thorax and investing the lungs; a part of the body-wall in arthropods; a part to which the secondary wings are attached in insects; a part on each side of the rachis of the lingual ribbon in molluscs. **pleural,** *a.* **pleurisy,** *n.* (*Path.*) inflammation of the pleura, usu. attended by fever, pain in the chest or side, etc. **pleuritic**, *a.* [med. L and Gr., side]

pleurenchyma, *n.* the woody tissue of plants. [Gr. *enchuma,* infusion]

pleur(o)-, *comb.form.* pertaining to the side or ribs; pertaining to the pleura. [Gr. *pleuron,* side, rib]

pleurocarpous, *a.* bearing the fructification laterally on the branches. [Gr. *karpos,* fruit]

pleurodynia, *n.* pain in the side due to chronic rheumatism of the walls of the chest.

pleuronectid, *n.* a fish of the family Pleuronectidae, or the flat-fishes or flounders; a flat-fish. [Gr. *nēktēs,* swimmer]

pleuropneumonia, *n.* inflammation of the lungs and pleura, esp. as contagious disease among cattle.

plexal, plexiform PLEXUS.

Plexiglass®, *n.* a transparent plastic.

pleximeter, *n.* a plate employed in examining the chest by mediate percussion. **pleximetric**, *a.* **pleximetry,** *n.* the art of using the pleximeter. **plexor**, *n.* an instrument used as a hammer in this process. [Gr. *plēxis,* stroke, cogn. with *plēssein,* to strike]

plexus, *n.* (*pl,* **plexuses, plexus**) a network of veins, fibres, or nerves; a network, a complication. **plexal,** *a.* **plexiform**, *a.* [L, from *plectere,* to PLAIT p.p. *plexus*]

pliable, *a.* easily bent; flexible, pliant; supple, limber; yielding readily to influence or arguments. **pliableness, pliability**, *n.* **pliably,** *adv.* **pliant,** *a.* pliable, flexible; yielding, compliant. **pliancy,** †**pliantness,** *n.*

pliantly, *adv.* [F, from *plier,* L *plicāre,* to bend (see PLY[1])]

plica, *n.* a fold of membrane etc.; a skin disease, Plica Polonica, once endemic in Poland, in which the hair becomes matted and filthy; undue development of small twigs which form an entangled mass. [med. L, from *plicāre,* to fold]

plicate, -cated, *a.* plaited; folded like a fan. **plication,** †**plicature,** *n.* [L *plicātus,* p.p. of *plicāre* to fold]

plié, *n.* a ballet movement in which the knees are bent outwards while the back remains straight. [F, p.p. of *plier,* to bend]

pliers, *n.pl.* small pincers with long jaws for bending wire etc. [obs. *ply,* F *plier,* see PLIABLE, -ER]

plight[1], *v.t.* to pledge, to promise, to engage (oneself, one's faith etc.). *n.* a engagement, a promise. **to plight one's troth,** to become engaged to be married. [OE *plihtan,* from *pliht,* danger (cp. Dut. *plight,* G. *Pflicht,* duty, obligation, OHG *plegan,* to engage)]

plight[2], *n.* condition, state, case, esp. one of distress or disgrace; †a plait; †attire, dress. †*v.t.* to fold, to plait. [ME and A-F *plit,* OF *ploit,* PLAIT]

plim, *v.i.* to fill out, to become plump. *v.t.* to cause to swell or expand. [dial., perh. rel. to PLUMP[1]]

plimsoll, *n.* a rubber-soled canvas shoe worn for sports etc. [from the resemblance of the upper edge of the sole to a Plimsoll line]

Plimsoll, *n.* **Samuel** (1824–98), English social reformer, born in Bristol. He sat in Parliament as a Radical (1868–80), and through his efforts the Merchant Shipping Act was passed in 1876, providing for Board of Trade inspection of ships, and the compulsory painting of a Plimsoll line. **Plimsoll line, mark,** *n.* a line, required to be placed on every British ship, marking the level to which the authorized amount of cargo submerges her.

plinth, *n.* a square member forming the lower division of a column etc.; a block serving as a pedestal; the plain projecting face at the bottom of a wall. [L *plinthus,* from Gr. *plinthos,* brick]

Pliny the Elder, (Gaius Plinius Secundus) (*c.* AD 23–79), Roman scientist and historian; only his works on astronomy, geography, and natural history survive. He was killed in an eruption of Vesuvius.

Pliny the Younger, (Gaius Plinius Caecilius Secundus) (*c.* AD 61–113), Roman administrator, nephew of Pliny the Elder, whose correspondence is of great interest. Among his surviving letters are those describing the eruption of Vesuvius, his uncle's death, and his correspondence with the emperor Trajan.

plio- *comb.form.* more. [Gr. *pleiōn* or *pleōn,* more]

Pliocene, *n., a.* (pertaining to) the most modern epoch of the Tertiary period of geological time, 5–1.8 million years ago. Human-like apes ('australopithecines') evolved in Africa. [Gr. *pleiōn,* more, *kainos,* new]

Plisetskaya, *n.* **Maya** (1925–), Soviet ballerina and actress. She attended the Moscow Bolshoi Ballet School and succeeded Ulanova as prima ballerina of the Bolshoi Ballet.

plisky, *a.* (*Sc. North.*) a mischievous prank; an awkward plight. [etym. unknown]

plissé, *n.* (a fabric having) a wrinkled finish. [F p.p. of *plisser* to pleat]

PLO, (*abbr.*) Palestine Liberation Organization.

plod, *v.i.* (*past, p.p.* **plodded**) to walk painfully, slowly, and laboriously; to trudge; to toil, to drudge; to study with steady diligence. *v.t.* to make (one's way) thus. *n.* a laborious walk, a trudge; a wearisome piece of work. **plodder,** *n.* **plodding,** *a.* **ploddingly,** *adv.* [prob. onomat]

plonge, †**plongee,** *n.* the superior slope of the parapet of a fortification. [F *plongée,* p.p. of *plonger,* PLUNGE]

plonk[1], *v.t., v.i.* to (be) put down or drop heavily, forcefully or with a plonk. *n.* a heavy, hollow sound. **plonker,** *n.* (*sl.*) a (big and) stupid person. **plonking,** *a.* (*sl.*) large, unwielding. [imit.]

plonk[2], *n.* (*coll.*) cheap (and inferior) wine. [perh. from F *blanc,* as in *vin blanc,* white wine]

plop, *n.* the sound of something falling heavily into water. *adv.* suddenly; heavily, with the sound 'plop'. *v.i.* (*past, p.p.* **plopped**) to fall thus into water. [imit.]

plosive, *n. a.* (*Phon.*) explosive.

plot[1], *n.* a small piece of ground; a plan of a field, farm, estate etc.; a complicated plan, scheme, or stratagem; a conspiracy; the plan or skeleton of the story in a play, novel etc.; a graphic representation. *v.t.* (*past, p.p.* **plotted**) to make a plan, map, or diagram of; to mark on a map (as the course of a ship or aircraft); to locate and mark on a graph by means of coordinates; to draw a curve through points so marked; to lay out in plots; to plan, to devise, to contrive secretly. *v.i.* to form schemes or plots against another; to conspire. **plotter,** *n.* [OE *plot,* a patch of ground, perhaps influ. by F *complot,* a conspiracy]

plot[2], *v.t.* (*past, p.p.* **plotted**) (*Sc.*) to scald; to steep in boiling water. [etym. doubtful]

plotty, *n.* a hot drink made of wine, water, spices etc.

plough, (*esp N Am.*) **plow,** *n.* an implement for cutting, furrowing, and turning over land for tillage; tillage, agriculture; arable land; an implement or machine resembling a plough in form or function, a machine for cutting paper, a grooving-plane, a snow-plough etc.; (**Plough**) the seven brightest stars in Ursa Major, also called Charles's Wain; (*sl.*) failure or rejection in an examination. *v.t.* to turn up (ground) with a plough; to make (a furrow) with a plough; to furrow, groove, or scratch, with or as with a plough; to wrinkle; (*sl.*) to reject at an examination; (*sl.*) to fail in an examination subject. *v.i.* to advance laboriously. **to follow the plough,** to be a ploughman or peasant. **to plough back profits,** to reinvest profits. **to plough in,** to bury or cover with earth by ploughing. **to plough into,** to collide with violently. **to plough out,** to root out or remove by ploughing. **to plough the sands,** to labour uselessly. **to plough through,** to smash a way through; to work or read through laboriously. **to plough up,** to break up by ploughing. **to put one's hand to the plough,** to begin a task or undertaking (Luke ix.62). †**plough-beam,** *n.* the central beam of a plough-frame. †**plough-bote,** *n.* timber formerly allowed to a tenant for the repair of instruments of husbandry. **plough-boy,** *n.* a boy leading the horses drawing the plough. **plough-land,** *n.* land fit for tillage; arable land, a carucate. **ploughman,** *n.* one who ploughs; a husbandman, a rustic. **ploughman's lunch,** *n.* a cold snack of bread and cheese with pickle, served esp. in a pub. †**Plough Monday,** *n.* the Monday after Epiphany. **plough-shoe,** *n.* an appliance attached to a ploughshare in traversing highways etc., to protect it. **ploughshare,** *n.* the blade of a plough. **plough-staff,** *n.* a spade-shaped appliance for cleaning the coulter etc., of earth, weeds etc. **plough-tail,** *n.* the rear part or the handle of the plough; a ploughman, a farm-labourer. **plough-wright,** *n.* one who makes or repairs ploughs. **ploughable,** *a.* **plougher,** *n.* [late OE *plōh* (cp. Dut. *ploeg,* G *Pflug,* Icel. *plōgr,* Swed. *plog,* Dan. *plov*)]

plout, *v.i.* (*Sc.*) to splash or paddle about. *n.* a heavy fall of rain. **plouter,** *v.i.* to dabble, to paddle, to flounder; to potter (about). *n.* a floundering, a splashing. [prob. onomat.]

Plovdiv, *n.* industrial city (textiles, chemicals, leather, tobacco) in Bulgaria, on the Maritsa; population (1987) 357,000. Conquered by Philip of Macedon in the 4th cent. BC, it was known as Philippopolis (Philip's city).

plover, *n.* the common English name for several grallatorial birds, esp. the golden, yellow or green plover, *Charadrius pluvialis.* [OF *pluvier,* prob. from a late L *pluvārius,* from *pluvia,* rain]

plow etc. PLOUGH.

ploy, *n.* employment, an undertaking; a game, a pastime; a prank; a manoeuvre, a tactic, a stratagem. [etym. doubtful]

PLP, (*abbr.*) Parliamentary Labour Party.

PLR, (*abbr.*) Public Lending Right.

pluck, *v.t.* to pull off or out, to pick; to pull, to twitch; to pull, to drag (away etc.); to strip by pulling out feathers; to fleece, to swindle; (*sl.*) to reject (as a candidate for a degree etc.). *v.i.* to pull, drag, or snatch (at). *n.* the act of plucking; a pull, a twitch; the heart, lights and liver of an animal; courage, spirit. **a crow to pluck** CROW[1]. **to pluck up courage** COURAGE. **plucked,** *a.* (*usu. in comb., as well-plucked*). **plucker,** *n.* **pluckless,** *a.* **plucky,** *a.* having pluck, spirit, or courage. **pluckily,** *adv.* **pluckiness,** *n.* [OE *pluccian* (cp. Dut. *plukken,* G *pflücken,* Icel. *plokke,* Dan. *plukke*)]

pluff, *n.* (*Sc.*) a puff, a burst. *v.t.* (*Sc.*) to emit in a puff or puffs; to shoot. *v.i.* to become swollen. **pluffy,** *a.* [imit.]

plug, *n.* a piece of wood or other substance used to stop a hole; a stopper, a peg, a wedge; anything wedged in or stopping up a pipe, or used to block the outlet to a waste-pipe; a piece of wood etc. inserted into masonry to take a nail or screw; a mass of volcanic rock stopping a vent; (a cake, stick, or small piece of) compressed tobacco; a sparking-plug; a fire-plug; a device with a non-conducting case, having usu. three pins, which is attached to an electric cable to make an electrical connection with a suitable socket; (*coll.*) an electrical socket; (*coll.*) a piece of favourable publicity, esp. one inserted into other material. *v.t.* (*past & p.p.* **plugged**) to stop with a plug; to insert as a plug; (*sl.*) to shoot; (*N Am. sl*) to strike with the fist; (*coll.*) to give favourable publicity to; (*coll.*) to allude to repeatedly, esp. as a form of publicity. **to plug away at,** to work at doggedly and persistently. **to plug in,** to establish an electrical connection (with). **to pull the plug on,** (*coll.*) to bring to an (abrupt) end. **plughole,** *n.* the outlet for waste water in a sink, bath etc. which can be closed with a plug. **plug-in coil,** *n.* (*Radio.*) an inductance coil equipped with a plug for quick changing. **plug-ugly,** *n.* (*N Am. sl.*) a hooligan, a rowdy. **plugging,** *n.* [prob. from MDut. *plugge* (Dut. *plug,* cp. G *Pflock*)]

plum, *n.* the fleshy drupaceous fruit of *Prunus domestica* or other trees of the same genus; a tree bearing this; applied to other fruits, esp. to the raisin used in cakes, puddings etc.; plum-colour; the best part of anything, the choicest thing of a set, any handsome perquisite, windfall etc.; (*sl.*) £100,000 sterling, a fortune. *a.* plum-coloured; choice, cushy. **plum-cake,** *n.* a cake containing raisins, currants etc. **plum-colour,** *n.* dark purple. **plum-duff,** *n.* a plain boiled flour pudding with raisins etc. **plum-porridge,** *n.* porridge with raisins or currants. **plum-pudding,** *n.* a pudding containing raisins, currants, etc., esp. a rich one with spices etc., eaten at Christmas. **plum-pudding dog,** *n.* a Dalmatian dog. **plum-pudding stone,** *n.* pudding-stone, a variety of conglomerate. **plummy,** *a.* full of or rich in plums; luscious, inviting; desirable; of the voice, rich and round to the point of affectation. [OE *plūme,* late L *prūna,* L *prūmum,* late Gr. *prounon,* Gr. *proumnon*]

plumage, plumassier PLUME.

plumb, *n.* a weight, usu. of lead, attached to a line, used to test perpendicularity; a position parallel to this, the vertical; a sounding-lead, a plummet. *a.* perpendicular, vertical; downright, sheer, perfect, complete; (*Cricket*) level. *adv.* vertically; exactly, correctly, right; completely. *v.t.* to adjust by a plumline; to make vertical or perpendicular; to sound with a plummet, to measure the depth of; to fathom, to understand. **out of plumb,** not exactly vertical. **to plumb (in),** to connect to a water main and/or drainage system. **plumb-bob,** *n.* a conical weight used in a plum-rule or on a plumb-line. **plumb-line,** *n.* the cord by which a plumb is suspended for testing perpendicularity; a vertical line. **plumb-rule,** *n.* a mason's or carpenter's rule with a plumb-line attached. **plumbean,, -beous** *a.* consisting of or resembling lead; glazed with lead; †(*fig.*) dull, heavy, stupid. **plumbic,** *a.* pertaining to, derived from, or combined with lead; due to the presence of lead. **plumbiferous,** *a.* **plumbless,** *a.* fathomless. [F *plomb,* L *plumbum,* lead]

plumbago, *n.* a form of carbon used for making pencils etc., blacklead, graphite; a genus of perennial herbs, with blue, rose, or violet flowers. **plumbaginous,** *a.* [L *plumbāgo -ginis,* from *plumbum,* lead]

plumber, *n.* orig. one who worked in lead; an artisan who fits and repairs cisterns, pipes, drains, gas fittings etc.; in buildings. **plumber-block** PLUMMER-BLOCK. **plumbing,** *n.* the work of a plumber; the arrangement of water-pipes, gas installations etc. in a building; (*euphem.*) the lavatory or lavatories. [OF *plummier* (F. *plumbier*), L. *plumbārius,* as prec.]

plume, *n.* a feather, esp. a large or conspicuous feather; a feather-bunch or tuft of feathers, or anything resembling this worn as an ornament; (*Zool.*) a feather-like part or form; a feathery appendage to a seed etc.; †(*fig.*) a token of honour. *v.t.* to trim, dress, or arrange (feathers), to preen; to adorn with or as with feathers, esp. in borrowed plumage; to pride (oneself on); to strip of feathers. **borrowed plumes,** decorations or honours to which one is not entitled, as the peacock's feathers worn by the jackdaw in the fable. **plumage,,** *n.* a bird's entire covering of feathers. **plumassier,,** *n.* a worker or dealer in feathers for clothing. **plumeless,** *a.* **plumelet,** *n.* **plumelike,** *a.* †**plumiform,** *a.* †**plumigerous,** *a.* feathered. †**plumiped,** *a.* having feathered feet. **plumose, plumous** *a.* resembling a feather or feathers, feathery. **plumosity,** *n.* **plumy,** *a.* covered with feathers; adorned with plumes; feathery. [OF, from L *plūma*]

plummer-block, *n.* a pillow-block. [etym. doubtful]

plummet, *n.* a weight attached to a line used for sounding; a ball of lead for a plumb-line; (*fig.*) a weight, an encumbrance; †a solid lead pencil formerly used to rule paper. *v.i.* to fall sharply or rapidly. [OF *plommet,* dim. of *plomb,* PLUMB]

plummy PLUM.

plump[1]**,** *a.* well-rounded, fat, fleshy, filled out, chubby; of a purse etc, well-filled; rich, abundant. *v.t.* to make plump; to fatten, to distend. *v.i.* to grow plump; to swell (out or up). **to plump up,** to make (pillows, cushions) rounded and soft by shaking. **plumper,** *n.* a dish, ball, or pad carried in the mouth to distend hollow cheeks. **plumply,** *adv.* **plumpiness,** *n.* **plumpy,** *a.* [cp. LG and EFris. *plump,* Dut. *plomp,* rude, blunt, Swed., Dan., and G *plump,* coarse, rude]

plump[2]**,** *v.i.* to plunge or fall suddenly and heavily; to vote for one candidate when more might be voted for; to give all one's votes to a single candidate. *v.t.* to fling or drop suddenly and heavily. *n.* a sudden plunge, a heavy fall; the sound of this. *adv.* suddenly and heavily; directly, straight down; flatly, bluntly. *a.* downright, plain, blunt. **to plump for,** to decide in favour of, to choose. **plumper,** *n.* one who or that which plumps; a vote given to a single candidate when more than one has to be elected; voter who plumps; (*sl.*) a downright lie. **plumply** *adv.* bluntly, flatly, plainly. [cp. LG *plumpen,* Dut. *plompen*]

plumpness, plumpy PLUMP[1].

Plumularia, *n.* a genus of plume-like hydroids. **plumularian,** *n., a.* [as foll]

plumule, *n.* the rudimentary stem in an embryo; a little feather, one of the down feathers; a downy scale on the wings of butterflies, etc. **plumulaceous, plumular** [L *plūmula,* dim. of *plūma,* PLUME]

plumy PLUME.

plunder, *v.t.* to pillage, to rob, to strip; to take by force, to steal, to embezzle. *n.* forcible or systematic robbery; spoil, booty; (*sl.*) profit, gain; (*N Am.*) luggage, personal belongings. **plunderage,,** *n.* pillage, esp. the embezzlement of goods on board ship; the booty so obtained. **plunderer,** *n.* [G *plündern,* to plunder, orig. household stuff, from *Plunder,* bed-clothes, etc.]

plunge, *v.t.* to force or thrust into water or other fluid; to immerse; to force, to drive (into a condition, action etc.); to sink (a flower-pot) in the ground. *v.i.* to throw oneself, to dive (into); to rush or enter impetuously (into a place, condition, etc.); to fall or descend very steeply or suddenly; of a horse, to throw the body forward and the hind legs up; of a ship, to pitch; (*coll.*) to gamble or bet recklessly, to spend money or get into debt heavily. *n.* the act of plunging; a dive; a sudden and violent movement; a risky or critical step. **to take the plunge,** (*coll.*) to commit oneself after hesitating. **plunger,** *n.* one who plunges; (*coll.*) a reckless gambler, speculator, or spendthrift; a cavalry man; a part of a machine working with a plunging motion, as the long solid cylinder used as a piston in a force-pump; a rubber suction cup on a handle, used to unblock drains, etc. **plunging,** *a.* [OF *plunjer* (F *plonger*), prob. from late L, *plumbicāre* (not extant), from L *plumbum,* lead]

plunk, *v.t.* to pluck the strings of (a banjo etc.); to emit a plunk; to plonk. *v.i.* to plonk. *n.* a dull, metallic sound.

plup., (*abbr.*) pluperfect.

pluperfect, *a.* (*Gram.*) expressing action or time prior to some other past time. *n.* the pluperfect tense; a pluperfect form. [L *plūs quam perfectum,* more than perfect]

plural, *a.* denoting more than one; consisting of more than one. *n.* the form of a word which expresses more than one, or (in languages having a dual number) more than two. **plural voter,** *n.* an elector with a vote in more than one constituency. **pluralism,** *n.* the state of being plural; the holding of more than one office, esp. an ecclesiastical benefice, at the same time; (*Phil.*) the doctrine that there is more than one ultimate principle in the universe, opp. to monism; a social system in which members of diverse ethnic, cultural etc. groups coexist, preserving their own customs and lifestyle but having equal access to power. **pluralist,** *n.* **pluralistic,** *a.* **plurality,** *n.* a number consisting of two or more; a majority, or the excess of (votes etc.) over the next highest number; pluralism; a benefice or other office held by a pluralist. **pluralize, -ise,** *v.t.* **pluralization, -isation,** *n.* **plurally,** *adv.* [OF *plurel,* L *plūrālis* from *plūs plūris,* more]

pluri-, *comb. form.* several, more, more than one. [L *plūs plūris,* more]

pluriliteral, *a.* containing more than the usual number of letters, i.e. more than three. *n.* a word of more than three letters.

plurilocular, *a.* multiocular.

pluriparous, *a.* bringing forth more than one at a birth. **pluripara,** *n.* a woman who has borne more than one child.

†**pluripresence,** *n.* presence in more places than one.

plus, *n.* a character (+) used as the sign of addition; an addition; a positive quantity; an advantage, a positive feature; a surplus. *prep.* with the addition of. *a.* above zero, positive; additional, extra, esp. additional and advantageous electrified positively. **plus fours,** *n.pl.* long, baggy knickerbockers. [L, more]

plush, *n.* a cloth of various materials with a pile or nap longer than that of velvet; (*pl.*) breeches of this, worn by footmen. *a.* of plush; (also **plushy**) rich, luxurious, lavishly appointed. [F *pluche,* contr. form of *peluche* (cp. Sp. *pelusa,* It. *peluzza*), prob. from a late L. *pilūceus,* hairy, from *pilus,* hair]

Plutarch, *n.* (*c.* AD 46–120), Greek biographer, born at Chaeronea. He lectured on philosophy at Rome, and was appointed procurator of Greece by Hadrian. His *Parallel Lives* comprise biographies of pairs of Greek and Roman soldiers and politicians, followed by comparisons between the two. Thomas North's 1579 translation inspired Shakespeare's Roman plays.

plutarchy, *n.* plutocracy. [Gr. *plutos,* wealth, *archein,* to rule]

pluteus, *n.* (*pl.* **-tei**) a barrier or light wall closing intervals between columns; a free-swimming larva of an echinoid or ophiuroid. [L]

Pluto, *n.* in Roman mythology, the lord of Hades, the underworld, and the brother of Jupiter and Neptune; the ninth planet in the solar system in order of distance from the sun, from which it is distant 3666 million miles (5902 million km). It was located by Clyde Tombaugh in 1930. It orbits the Sun every 248.5 years and has a diameter of about 2000 miles (3000 km) and a mass about 0.005 that of Earth. It is of low density, composed of rock and ice, with frozen methane on its surface. Charon, Pluto's moon, was discovered in 1978; the operation name in World War II of a system of pipelines under the English Channel to carry petrol from England to the armies in France. **Plutonian,** *a.* pertaining to Pluto or the lower regions; infernal, subterranean, dark; igneous. *n.* a plutonist. **Plutonic,** *a.* plutonian; (*Geol.*) igneous; pertaining to the Plutonic theory. **Plutonic rocks,** *n.pl.* igneous rocks, as granite, basalt etc. **Plutonic theory,** *n.* the theory that most geological changes have been caused by igneous agency. **Plutonism,** *n.* **Plutonist,** *n.* an adherent of the Plutonic theory. [L *Plūtōnius,* Gr. *Ploutōnios,* from *Ploutōn,* god of the infernal regions]

pluto-, *comb. form* pertaining to wealth. [see foll.]

plutocracy, *n.* the rule of wealth or the rich; a ruling class of rich people; (*coll.*) the wealthy class. **plutocrat,** *n.* **plutocratic,** *a.* [Gr. *ploutokratia* (*ploutos*), wealth]

pluto-democracy, *n.* a democracy dominated by wealth.

plutolatry, *n.* worship of wealth.

plutonium, *n.* a radioactive element, at no. 94; chem. symbol Pu; formed by the radioactive decay of neptunium.

plutonomy, *n.* political economy. **plutonomic,** *a.* [Gr. *ploutos,* wealth, *-nomia,* arrangement, cogn. with *nemein,* to deal out]

pluvial, *a.* of or pertaining to rain; rainy; humid; (*Geol.*) due to the action of rain. **pluviograph,** *n.* a self-recording rain-gauge. **pluviometer,** *n.* a rain-gauge. **pluviometrical,** *a.* **pluvioscope,** *n.* a variety of rain-gauge. **pluvious,** *a.* **pluvius insurance, policy,** *n.* an insurance policy to cover damage sustained through bad weather. [F, from L *pluviālis,* from *pluvia,* rain]

ply[1], *n.* a fold, a plait, a twist, a strand (of a rope, twine etc.); a thickness, a layer; a bent, a bias. **two-, three-, four-ply,** (of) wool etc., twisted in so many strands. **plywood,** *n.* board consisting of three or more thin layers of wood glued together in such a manner that the grain of each is at right-angles to that of its neighbour. [F *pli,* fold, OF *ploy,* from *ployer* (F *plier*), L *plicāre,* to bend]

ply[2], *v.t.* (*pres. p.* **plying,** *past, p.p.* **plied**) to use (a tool) vigorously or busily; to work at, to employ oneself in; to pursue, to press, to urge; to supply (with) or subject (to) repeatedly; to travel regularly along. *v.i.* to go to and fro, to travel or sail regularly; to be busy, to be employed; to stand or wait for custom; (*Naut.*) to work to windward. [from ME *applier,* to APPLY]

plyers, PLIERS.

Plymouth, *n.* city and seaport in Devon, England, at the mouth of the river Plym, with dockyard, barracks, and naval base at Devonport; population (1981) 244,000.

Plymouth Brethren, *n.pl.* a fundamentalist Christian Protestant sect characterized by extreme simplicity of belief, founded in Dublin about 1827 by the Reverend John Nelson Darby (1800–82). An assembly was held in Plymouth 1831 to celebrate its arrival in England, but by 1848 the movement had split into 'Open' and 'Close' Brethren. The latter refuse communion with all those not of their persuasion. The Plymouth Brethren are mainly found in the fishing villages of NE Scotland. **Plymouthism,** *n.* **Plymouthist, Plymouthite,** *n.*

Plymouth Rock, *n.* a breed of domestic fowl.

plywood PLY[1].

Plzeň, *n.* (German **Pilsen**) industrial city (heavy machinery, cars, beer) in W Czechoslovakia, capital of Západočeský region; 84 km/52 miles SW of Prague; population (1984) 174,000.

PM[1], (*abbr.*) Prime Minister; Provost Marshal.

PM[2], pm[1], (*abbr.*) post meridiem (after noon); post-mortem.

Pm, (*chem. symbol*) promethium.

pm[2], (*abbr.*) premium.

PMBX, (*abbr.*) private manual branch exchange.
PMG, (*abbr.*) Paymaster General; Postmaster General.
PMT, (*abbr.*) pre-menstrual tension.
pn, (*abbr.*) promissory note.
PNdB, (*abbr.*) perceived noise decibel.
pneuma, *n.* breath, spirit, soul. [Gr., wind, spirit, see foll.]
pneumatic, *a.* pertaining to or consisting of air; gaseous; containing or filled with air; actuated by means of compressed air or a vacuum; having air-filled cavities. †spiritual. *n.* a pneumatic tyre; a cycle fitted with such tyres; **pneumatic brake,** *n.* (*Rail.*) a braking system in which air-pressure is applied simultaneously to brake-cylinders throughout the length of the train. **pneumatic dispatch,** *n.* transmission of parcels, messages etc., through tubes by means of compression or exhaustion of air. **pneumatic drill,** *n.* (*Eng.*) a rock drill in which compressed air reciprocates a loose piston which hammers a steel bit. **pneumatic railway,** *n.* a railway worked by air-pressure. **pneumatic trough,** *n.* a trough containing mercury or water used for the collection of gases in inverted vessels slightly immersed. **pneumatic tyre,** *n.* a rubber tube inflated with air under pressure, used as a tyre for cycles, motor-cars etc. **pneumatically,** *adv.* **pneumaticity,** *n.* the condition of having air-filled cavities. **pneumatics,** *n. sing.* the science treating of the mechanical properties of air and other gases. [L *pneumaticus,* Gr. *pneumatikos,* from *pneuma -matos,* wind, cogn. with *pneein,* to breathe]
pneumato-, *comb.form.* air; breath; spirit, soul. [PNEUMA]
pneumatocyst, *n.* an air-sac or swim-bladder in a bird, hydrozoon etc.
pneumatology, *n.* the science of spiritual existence; the doctrine of the Holy Spirit; †psychology. **pneumatological,** *a.* **pneumatologist,** *n.*
pneumatometer, *n.* an instrument for measuring the air exhaled at one expiration.
pneumatophore, *n.* the pneumatocyst or other air-cavity of a compound hydrozoon; a respiratory organ in the roots of some tropical trees growing in mud; an apparatus for enabling respiration to be carried on in a mine pervaded by poisonous fumes, as after an explosion of fire-damp.
pneumo-, *comb.form.* pertaining to the lungs. [Gr, *pneumōn -monos,* lung]
pneumococcus, *n.* (*pl.* **-cocci**) a bacterium which causes pneumonia.
pneumoconiosis, *n.* any disease of the lungs or bronchi caused by habitually inhaling metallic or mineral dust. [Gr. *konis,* dust]
pneumogastric, *n.* of or pertaining to the lungs and the stomach.
pneumonia, *n.* acute inflammation of a lung or the lungs. **pneumonic,** *a.* **pneumonitis,** *n.* **pneumonitic,** *a.* [Gr. *pneumōn -monos,* lung]
pneumothorax, *n.* accumulation of air in the pleural cavity, usu. associated with pleurisy.
PNG, (*abbr.*) Papua New Guinea.
Pnom Penh, PHNOM PENH.
P&O, (*abbr.*) Peninsular and Oriental (Steam Navigation Company).
PO, (*abbr.*) Personnel Officer; Petty Officer; Pilot Officer; postal order; Post Office.
Po, (*chem. symbol*) polonium.
po, *n.* (*pl.* **pos**) (*coll.*) chamber pot. [prob. euphem. F pronunciation of *pot*]
POA, (*abbr.*) Prison Officers' Association.
Poa, *n.* a genus of grasses; meadow grass. [Gr., grass]
poach[1], *v.t.* to cook (as an egg, fish) in simmering liquid. **poacher,** *n.* a vessel for poaching eggs in. [OF *pochier* (F *pocher*), from *poche,* pocket, see POKE[1]]
poach[2], *v.i.* to encroach or trespass on another's lands), esp. to take game etc.; to take game, fish etc. by illegal or unsportsmanlike methods; to intrude or enroach upon another's rights, area of responsibility etc.; to take an advantage unfairly, as in a race or game; of ground, to become soft, swampy, or miry; (*Lawn Tennis*) to hit the ball when in the court of one's partner. *v.t.* to take (game, fish etc.) from another's preserves or by illegitimate methods; to take game from (another's preserves); to trample, to tread into mire; †to thrust, push, or drive (into); †to stab, to spear. **poacher,** *n.* **poachy,** *a.* wet and soft; swampy; easily trodden into holes by cattle. **poachiness,** *n.* [prob. from OF *pocher,* to thrust into, to encroach, prob. rel. to POKE[2]]
poaka, *n.* the New Zealand white-headed stilt-bird. [Maori]
pochard, *n.* a European diving sea-duck, *Aethyia* or *Fuligula ferina;* other ducks of the same genus. [etym. doubtful]
Po Chu-i, *n.* former transliteration of Bo Zhu Yi, Chinese poet.
pock, *n.* a pustule in an eruptive disease, as in smallpox. **pockmark,** *n.* the pit or scar left by a pock; any similar mark or indentation. **pockmarked, pock-pitted, †-fretten,** pocky, *a.* **pockiness,** *n.* **pock-pudding** POKE-PUDDING under POKE[1]. [OE *poc* (*cp. Dut. pok,* G *Pocke*), whence POX]
pocket, *n.* a small bag, sack, or pouch, esp. a small bag inserted in the clothing, to contain articles carried about the person; pecuniary means; a small netted bag in billiards or snooker to receive the balls; a measure for hops, wool, ginger etc.; (*Geol.*) a cavity in rock containing foreign matter; (*Mining*) a cavity containing gold or other ore; an isolated area or patch; an air pocket. *a.* for the pocket; small. *v.t.* to put into a pocket; to keep in or as in the pocket; to hem in (a horse etc.) in a race; to appropriate, esp. illegitimately; to put up with; to repress or conceal (one's feelings); in billiards or snooker, to drive (a ball) into a pocket. **in, out of pocket,** the richer, the poorer. **out-of-pocket,** of expenses etc, unbudgeted and paid for in cash. **to have in one's pocket,** to have complete control over; to be assured of winning. **to line one's pockets,** (to abuse a position of trust in order) to enrich oneself. **to pocket an affront, insult, wrong** etc.: to receive or submit to it without showing resentment. **to pocket one's pride, to put one's pride in one's pocket,** not to stand on one's dignity, to adopt an amenable attitude. **to put one's hand in one's pocket,** to spend or give money. **pocket battleship,** *n.* a small battleship, esp. one built by Germany before World War II in apparent compliance with limitations imposed by the Treaty of Versailles. **pocket-book,** *n.* a note-book or book or case for carrying papers etc., in the pocket; (*N Am.*) a handbag. **pocket-borough** BOROUGH. **pocket-edition,** *n.* a pocket-size edition of a book; a smaller version of anything. **pocket-glass,** *n.* a portable looking-glass. **pocket-handkerchief,** *n.* **pocket-knife,** *n.* a knife with blades shutting into the handle, for carrying in the pocket. **pocket-money,** *n.* money for occasional expenses or amusements; a small, regular allowance given to a child. **pocket-piece,** *n.* a coin kept in the pocket as a memento or for luck. **pocket-pistol,** *n.* a small pistol for carrying in the pocket; (*facet.*) a small spirit-flask for the pocket. **pocket-size, -sized,** *a.* small, supposedly small enough to fit into a pocket. **pocketable,** *a.* **pocketful,** *n.* **pocketless,** *a.* **pockety,** *a.* (*Mining, Aviat.*) characterized by pockets. [ME *poket,* Ang. -Norman *pokete,* dim. of O.North.F *poque,* as F *poche,* POKE[1]]
pockmanteau, (*Sc.*) PORTMANTEAU.
pockmark, pocky POCK.
pococurante, *n.* a careless or apathetic person, a trifler. *a.* indifferent. **pococurantism,** *n.* [It., little-caring]
poculiform, *a.* cup-shaped. [L *pōculum,* cup]
pod[1], *n.* a long capsule or seed-vessel, esp. of leguminous plants; applied to similar receptacles, as the case enclosing the eggs of a locust, a silk-worm cocoon, a narrow-necked eel-net etc.; the socket into which the bit enters in a brace; the channel or grove in an auger etc.; a streamlined container, housing an engine, fuel, armaments etc., attached to the outside of an aircraft; any protective (external) housing; a detachable

compartment on a spacecraft. *v.i.* (*past, p.p.* **podded**) to produce pods; to swell into pods. *v.t.* to shell (peas etc.). **podded,** *a.* bearing pods; pod-bearing, leguminous; (*fig.*) snug, rich. [etym. unknown]

pod², *n.* a flock, bunch, or small herd, esp. of whales, seals etc. *v.t.* to drive (seals, etc.) into a pod. [etym. doubtful]

pod- POD(O)-.

-pod, *comb. form* foot. [Gr. *pous podos,* foot]

podagra, *n.* gout, esp. in the foot. **podagral, -gric, -grous,** *a.* [L and Gr. (*pous podos,* foot, *agra,* catching)]

podal, *n.* of or pertaining to the feet. [Gr. *pous podos,* foot]

poddy, *n.* (*Austral.*) a hand-fed calf or foal. **poddy-dodger,** *n.* a station-hand, a dairyman.

podestà, (*It.*) *n.* a subordinate municipal judge in an Italian city. [from L *potestatem,* nom. *-tas,* power, authority]

podge, *n.* a short and stout person. **podgy,** *a.* [var. of PUDGE]

podium, *n.* (*pl.* **-diums, -dia**) a low projecting wall or basement supporting a building; a platform encircling the arena in an amphitheatre; a continuous structural bench round a hall etc.; a small raised platform (for a conductor, lecturer etc.). **podial,** *a.* [L, from Gr. *podion,* from *pous podos,* foot]

pod(o)-, *comb.form.* foot. [Gr. *pous podos* foot.]

podocarp, *n.* a foot-stalk supporting a fruit. **podocarpous,** *a.* of or pertaining to the genus *Podocarpus,* consisting of evergreen coniferous trees of tropical Asia and New Zealand, the black pines. [Gr. *pous podos,* foot, *karpos,* fruit]

podophthalmate, *a.* stalk-eyed. **podophthalmian,** *n.* a stalk-eyed crustacean. *a.* belonging to this class. [Gr. *ophthalmos,* eye]

podophyllum, *n.* a genus of plants, containing the may-apple. **podophyllic,** *a.* **podophyllin,** *n.* a purgative resin extracted from the root of *Podophyllum peltatum.* **podophyllous,** *a.* (*Ent.*) having the organs of locomotion so compressed as to resemble leaves. [Gr. *phullon,* leaf]

Podura, *n.* a genus of apterous insects comprising the springtails. [Gr. *pous podos,* foot, *oura,* tail]

Poe, *n.* **Edgar Allan** (1809–49), US writer and poet. His short stories are renowned for their horrific atmosphere (as in 'The Fall of the House of Usher', 1839) and acute reasoning (for example, 'The Gold Bug' (1843) and 'The Murders in the Rue Morgue' (1841), in which the investigators Legrand and Dupin anticipate Conan Doyle's Sherlock Holmes). His poems include 'The Raven' (1844). His novel, *The Narrative of Arthur Gordon Pym of Nantucket* (1838), has attracted critical attention recently.

poe-bird, *n.* a New Zealand bird, *Prosthemadera novaeseelandiae,* larger than a thrush, with dark metallic plumage and a tuft of white feathers on the neck, also called the parson-bird or tui. [prob. *arbitrary*]

poem, *n.* a metrical composition, esp. of an impassioned and imaginative kind; an artistic and imaginative composition in verse or prose; anything supremely beautiful, well-executed or satisfying. [F *poème,* L *poēma,* Gr. *poiēma,* from *poiein,* to make]

poenology, PENOLOGY.

poephagous, *a.* (*Zool.*) subsisting on grass. [Gr. *poēphagos* (*poa,* grass, -PHAGOUS)]

poesy, *n.* the art of poetry; (*collect.*) metrical compositions; †a posy. [ME and OF *poesie,* L *poēsis,* Gr. *poiēsis,* as prec.]

poet, *n.* a writer of poems or metrical compositions, esp. one possessing high powers of imagination and rhythmical expression; one possessed of high imaginative or creative power. **Poet Laureate,** *n.* an officer of the British royal household whose nominal duty is to compose an ode every year for the sovereign's birthday, for any great national victory, etc. **poetaster,** *n.* an inferior or petty poet; a pitiful versifier. **poetess,** *n. fem.* **poetic, -ical,** *a.* pertaining to or suitable for poetry; expressed in poetry, written in poetry; having the finer qualities of poetry; fit to be expressed in poetry. **poetic justice,** *n.* punishment or reward ideally (often ironically) fitted to deserving. **poetic licence,** *n.* the latitude in grammar etc., allowed to poets. **poetically,** *adv.* **poeticize, -ise,** *v.t.* **poetics,** *n. sing.* the theory or principles of poetry. **poeticule,** *n.* a poetaster. **poetize, -ise,** *v.i.* to compose verses, to write poetry. *v.t.* to poeticize. **poetry,** *n.* the art or work of the poet; that one of the fine arts which expressed the imagination and feelings in sensuous and rhythmical language, usu. in metrical forms; imaginative, impassioned, and rhythmical expression whether in verse or prose; imaginative or creative power; a quality in anything that powerfully stirs the imagination or the aesthetic sense; (*collect.*) metrical compositions, verse, poems. [OF *poete,* L *poēta,* Gr. *poiētes,* maker, poet, as prec.]

po-faced, *a.* (*coll.*) deadpan; humourless, stolid; stupidly solemn. [etym. doubtful]

pogo stick, *n.* a toy consisting of a strong pole attached to a spring and having a handle at the top and a crossbar on which one stands to bounce along.

pogrom, *n.* an organized attack, usu. with pillage and massacre, upon a class of the population, esp. Jews. [Rus., destruction]

poh, *int.* expressing contempt or disgust. [instinctive sound]

pohutakawa, *n.* (*New Zealand*) the Christmas bush, a tree which has red flowers during the summer. [Maori]

poi¹, *n.* a ball of flax used by Maori women in a ceremonial dance. [Maori]

poi², *n.* a paste of fermented taro root. [Hawaiian]

poignant, *a.* sharp; stimulating to the palate, pungent; keen, piercing; bitter, painful. **poignancy,** *n.* **poignantly,** *adv.* [OF, pres.p. of *poindre,* L. *pungere,* to prick]

poikilothermal, -thermic, *a.* having a body temperature which varies with the surrounding temperature. **poikilothermism, poikilothermy,** *n.*

Poincaré¹, *n.* **Jules Henri** (1854–1912), French mathematician, who developed the theory of differential equations and was a pioneer in relativity theory. He also published the first paper devoted entirely to topology.

Poincaré², *n.* **Raymond Nicolas Landry** (1860–1934), French politician, prime minister 1912–13, president 1913–20, and again prime minister 1922–24 (when he ordered the occupation of the Ruhr, Germany) and 1926–29. He was a cousin of the mathematician Jules Henri Poincaré.

poind, *v.t.* (*Sc.*) to distrain upon; to seize and sell (a debtor's goods); to impound. *n.* the act of poinding, distraint. [OE *pyndan,* to impound, cogn. with POUND², PINFOLD]

Poindexter, *n.* **John Marlan** (1936–), US rear admiral and Republican government official. In 1981 he joined the Reagan administration's National Security Council (NSC) and became national security adviser in 1985. As a result of the Irangate scandal, Poindexter was forced to resign in 1986, along with his assistant, Oliver North.

poinsettia, *n.* a genus of S American and Mexican plants with gorgeous red leaf-like bracts and small greenish-yellow flowerheads. [J.R. *Poinsett* 1779–1853, US politician, the discoverer]

point, *n.* a mark made by the end of anything sharp, a dot; a dot used as a mark of punctuation, to indicate vowels etc.; (*Print.*) a full stop, or decimal mark to separate integral from fractional digits in decimal numbers, etc.; a particular item, a detail; a particular place or position; a specific position or stage in a development or on a scale; a state or condition; a particular moment; the precise moment for an event, action, etc., the instant; the verge; a step or stage in an argument, discourse etc.; a unit used in measuring or counting, in assessing superiority etc., in appraising qualities of an exhibit in a show, a racehorse etc., in reckoning odds given to an opponent in a game, in betting, or in scoring in games; a salient quality, a trait, a characteristic;

the essential element, the exact object (of a discussion, joke etc.), the main purport, the gist; the aim, the purpose; a conclusion; a suggestion, a tip; the sharp end of a tool, weapon etc., the tip; a nib; a cape, a promontory (esp. in place-names); point-lace; a sharp-pointed tool, as an etcher's needle, glass-cutter's diamond, various implements or parts of machinery used in the industrial arts etc.; a tapering rail moving on a pivot for switching a train from one line to another; hence, (*pl.*) a railway switch; (*pl.*) the contact-breakers in the distributor of an internal-combustion engine; a power point; a tine of a deer's horn; pungency, effectiveness, force; (*Geom.*) that which has position but not magnitude; the unit of measurement for printing type-bodies, approx. 1/72 in. (0·351 mm); a position on a shield; a fielder or position on the off-side square of, and close in to, the batsman in cricket; (*Hunting*) a spot to which a straight run is made; a musical passage or subject to which special importance is drawn; the leading party of an advanced guard; (*pl.*) the extremities of a horse; (*Ballet*) pointe; a unit of increase or decrease in the price of stocks or the value of currencies; the act of pointing by a setter etc.; (*Fencing*) a twist; a point of the compass; a short cord for reefing sails; a buckling-strap on harness; †a tagged lace for lacing bodices, doublets etc.; †a signal on a musical instrument in war or the chase; †the pommel of a saddle. *v.t.* to sharpen; to mark with points, to punctuate; to mark off (as a psalm) in groups of syllables for singing; to give force or point to; to fill (the joints of masonry) with mortar or cement pressed in with a trowel; to indicate, to show; to direct (a finger etc., at); to turn in a particular direction, to aim; to give effect or pungency to (a remark, jest etc.); to indicate the meaning or point of by a gesture; to turn in (manure etc.) with the point of a spade; †to prick or pierce. *v.i.* to direct attention to; of a pointer or setter, to draw attention to game by standing rigidly and looking at it; to aim (at or towards); to face or be directed (towards); to sail close to the wind. **at all points,** in every part or direction; completely, perfectly. †**at point,** in readiness. **at** or **on the point,** on the verge (of). **beside the point,** irrelevant. **in point,** apposite, relevant. **in point of fact** FACT. **not to put too fine a point on it,** to speak bluntly. **point of distance** DISTANCE. **point of honour,** a matter of punctilio, a matter involving personal honour, involving a demand for satisfaction by a duel etc. **point of no return,** the point in a flight where shortage of fuel makes it necessary to go on as return is impossible; critical point (at which one must commit oneself irrevocably to a course of action). **point of order,** a question of procedure. **point of sale,** the place, esp. a retail shop, where the sale of an article physically takes place. **point of the compass,** one of the 32 angular divisions of the compass; the angle of 11° 15′ between two such points. **point of view,** the position from which a thing is looked at; way of regarding a matter. **to carry one's point,** to prevail in an argument or dispute. **to make a point,** to score a point; to establish a point in argument. **to make a point of,** to attach special importance to; to take special care to. **to point out,** to indicate. **to point up,** to emphasize, to highlight. **to score points off,** to score off. **to stretch a point,** STRETCH. **to the point,** appropriate, apposite, pertinent. **point-blank,** *a.* fired horizontally; aimed directly at the mark making no allowance for the downward curve of the trajectory; hence very close (permitting such aim to be taken); direct, blunt. *adv.* horizontally, with direct aim; directly, bluntly. *n.* a point-blank shot. †**point-device,** *a.* correct, precise, finical, neat. *adv.* correctly, precisely, to a nicety. **point-duty,** *n.* the work of a constable stationed at a junction of streets or other point to regulate traffic. **point-lace,** *n.* lace made with the point of a needle. **pointsman,** *n.* a constable on point-duty; a person in charge of the switches on a railway. **point system,** *n.* a standard system for measuring type bodies. **point-to-point,** *a.* denoting a steeplechase or other race in a direct line from one point of a course to another. **pointed,** *a.* having a sharp point; having point, penetrating, cutting; referring to some particular person or thing; emphasized, made obvious. **pointedly,** *adv.* with special meaning. **pointedness,** *n.* **pointer,** *n.* one who or that which points; the index-hand of a clock etc.; a rod used for pointing on a blackboard etc.; an indication, a hint, a tip; a dog trained to point at game; (*pl.*) two stars of the Plough a line drawn through which points nearly to the pole-star; (*Austral.*) a trickster, a swindler; (*Austral.*) one of the bullocks next to the pole in a team. **pointing,** *n.* the act of indicating, directing, sharpening etc.; punctuation; division into groups of words or syllables for singing; the act of finishing or renewing a mortar-joint in a wall. **pointless,** *a.* having no point; purposeless, futile. **pointlessly,** *adv.* **pointlessness,** *n.* [partly through F. *point,* a dot, a point, *pointe,* a sharp end. L. *punctum,* orig. neut. p.p. L. *puncta,* piercing; and *pointer,* to point, med. L. *punctāre,* all from L. *punct-,* p.p. stem of *pungere,* to prick]

pointe, *n.* (*Ballet*) the extreme tip of the toe; a position in which the dancer balances on this. [F]

Pointe-Noire, *n.* chief port of the Congo, formerly (1950–58) the capital; population (1984) 297,000. Industries include oil refining and shipbuilding.

pointillism, *n.* (*Art*) delineation by means of dots of various colours which merge into a whole. The technique was developed in the 1880s by the neo-impressionist Seurat who used small dabs of pure colour laid side by side to create an impression of shimmering light when viewed from a distance. **pointillist,** *n., a.* [F *pointiller,* draw in points]

poise, *v.t.* to balance to hold or carry in equilibrium; to place in a carefully balanced position; to counterpoise; to ponder. *v.i.* to be balanced or in equilibrium; to hang (in the air) over, to hover. *n.* equipoise, equilibrium; a counterpoise; a state of suspense, indecision etc.; composure, assurance, self-possession; physical balance. **poised,** *a.* balanced; having or showing composure etc.; in a state of readiness (to), all set (to). [ME and OF *poise,* ind. of *peser,* ult. from L *pensāre,* freq. of *pendere,* to weigh]

poison, *n.* a substance that injures or kills an organism into which it is absorbed; anything noxious or destructive to health or morality; a substance which retards catalytic activity or a chemical reaction, or, by absorbing neutrons, the course of a nuclear reaction; (*sl.*) liquor, drink. *v.t.* to put poison in or on; to infect with poison; to administer poison; to kill or injure by this means; to taint, to corrupt, to vitiate, to pervert. **poison gas,** *n.* (*Mil.*) poisonous or stupefying gas or liquid used in war. **poison ivy,** *n.* any of various N American shrubs or climbing plants which cause an intensely itching skin rash. **poison-pen letter,** *n.* one written maliciously and usu. anonymously, to abuse or frighten the recipient. **poisonable,** *a.* **poisoner,** *n.* **poisonous,** *a.* **poisonously,** *adv.* [F *poison,* as POTION]

Poisson, *n.* **Siméon Denis** (1781–1840), French applied mathematician. In probability theory he formulated the **Poisson distribution** which is widely used in probability calculations. He published four notable treatises and several papers on aspects of physics, including mechanics, heat, electricity and magnetism, elasticity and astronomy.

Poitier, *n.* **Sidney** (1924–), US actor and film director, the first black actor to become a star in Hollywood. His films as an actor included *In the Heat of the Night* (1967), and as director *Stir Crazy* (1980).

Poitou-Charentes, *n.* region of W central France, comprising the departments of Charente, Charente-Maritime, Deux-Sèvres, and Vienne; capital Poitiers; area 25,800 sq km/9959 sq miles; population (1986) 1,584,000. The region is noted for the celebrated brandy produced at Cognac.

†**poitrel,** *n.* armour for the breast of a horse. [OF *poitral,* L *pectorāle,* PECTORAL]

poke[1], *n.* (*esp. Sc.*) a bag, a sack. **a pig in a poke** PIG. [cp. O.North.F *poque,* F *poche,* Icel. *poki,* perh. rel.

to OE *pohha*]

poke², *v.t.* to thrust, to push (in, out, through etc.) with the end of something; to jab, to prod; to stir (a fire) with a poker; to cause to protrude; to put, move etc. by poking; to make (a hole etc.) by poking; (*coll.*) to punch; (*sl.*) to have sexual intercourse with *v.i.* to thrust, to jab; to protrude; (*coll.*) to pry, to search; to dawdle, to busy oneself without any definite object. *n.* a poking, a push, a thrust, a prod, a nudge; a collar with a drag attached to prevent animals from breaking through fences, etc.; (*coll.*) a punch; (*sl.*) an act of sexual intercourse. **to poke fun at**, FUN. **to poke one's nose into**, NOSE. **pokeweed**, *n.* a N American herb, *Phytolacca decandra*, †**poking-stick, -iron**, *n.* a rod for stiffening the plaits of ruffs. **poky**, *a.* of a room etc., cramped, confined, stuffy; (*coll.*) shabby; petty, dull. [cp. Dut. and LG *poken*, to thrust, *Poke*, dagger, G. *pochen*, also POACH²]

poke³, *n.* a projecting front on a woman's hat or bonnet, formerly a detachable rim. **poke-bonnet**, *n.* **poke-bonneted**, *n.* [perh. ident. with POKE¹ or ²]

poker¹, *n.* a iron rod used to stir a fire; an instrument employed in poker-work; (*Univ. sl.*) one of the bedells carrying a mace before the Vice-Chancellor at Oxford or Cambridge. *v.t.* to adorn with poker-work. *v.i.* to carry out (a design) in this. **red-hot poker**, *n.* popular name of plant of the genus *Tritoma*, or flame-flower. **poker-work**, *n.* the production of decorative designs on wood by burning or scorching with a heated instrument.

poker², *n.* a cardgame in which the players bet on the value in their hands. **poker-face**, *n.* an expressionless face. [etym. doubtful]

poker³, *n.* a bugbear, a hobgoblin. [N Am. cp. Dan. *pokker*, Swed. *pokcer*, the devil]

poky POKE².

Pol., (*abbr.*) Poland; Polish.

pol., (*abbr.*) political; politics.

pol, *n.* (*sl.*) a politician. [POLITICIAN]

polacca, polacre, *n.* a three-masted vessel used in the Mediterranean. [F *polacre*, It. *polacca*, etym. doubtful]

Polack, *n.* (*now offensive*) a Pole. [Pol. *Polak*]

Poland, *n.* Polish Republic, country in E Europe, bounded to the E by the USSR, to the S by Czechoslovakia, and to the W by East Germany. **area** 312,700 sq km/120,733 sq miles. **capital** Warsaw. **towns** Lódź, Kraków, Wroclaw, Poznań, Katowice, Bydgoszcz, Lublin; ports Gdánsk, Szczecin, Gdynia. **physical** comprises part of the great plain of Europe; Vistula, Oder, and Neisse rivers; Sudeten, Tatra, and Carpathian mountains. **exports** coal, softwood timber, chemicals, machinery, ships **population** (1989) 38,389,000; annual growth rate 0.9%. **language** Polish, a member of the western branch of the Slavonic family. **religion** Roman Catholic 93%.

Polanski, *n.* **Roman** (1933–), Polish film director, born in Paris. He suffered a traumatic childhood in Nazi-occupied Poland, and later his wife, actress Sharon Tate, was the victim of murder by the Charles Manson 'family'. His tragic personal life is reflected in a fascination with horror and violence in his work. His films include *Repulsion* (1965), *Cul de Sac* (1966), *Rosemary's Baby* (1968), *Tess* (1979), *Frantic* (1988).

polar, *a.* pertaining to or situated near the poles of the earth or the celestial sphere; coming from the regions near the poles; pertaining to a magnetic pole, having polarity, magnetic; having two opposite elements or tendencies, esp. positive and negative electricity; pertaining to the poles of a cell; relating to or of the nature of a polar; remote or opposite as the poles; resembling the polestar, attracting, guiding. *n.* a plane curve having a particular relation to another and to a point called the pole; the line connecting the points of contact of two tangents drawn to a given curve from the pole. **polar angle**, *n.* the angles formed by two meridians at a pole. **polar bear**, *n.* a white arctic bear, *Ursus maritimus*. **polar caps**, *n.pl.* two white regions round the poles of the planet Mars. **polar circles** CIRCLE. **polar distance**, *n.* the angular distance of a point from the nearest pole. [med. L *polāris*, from L. *polus*, POLE²]

polar(i)-, *comb.form.* pertaining to poles or polarized light.

polarimeter, *n.* an instrument for measuring the polarization of light **polarimetric**, *a.* **polarimetry** *n.*

Polaris, *n.* the pole-star.

polariscope, *n.* an instrument for showing the phenomena of polarized light. **polariscopic**, *a.*

polarity, *n.* the state of having two opposite poles, or of having different or opposing properties in opposite parts or directions; the quality (in electricity) of being attracted to one pole and repelled from the other; the disposition in a body to place its mathematical axis in a particular direction; diametric opposition.

polarization, -isation, *n.* the collecting of hydrogen on the positive electrode of a battery causing a counter electromotive force; the act of polarizing; the state of being polarized; (*Opt.*) modification of the rays of light or heat by reflection or transmission so that they exhibit different properties in different planes parallel to the direction of propagation. **polarize, -ise**, *v.t.*, *v.i.* to (cause to) acquire electrical or magnetic polarity; to divide into sharply opposed groups or factions; of opinions etc., to (cause to) become more sharply opposed or more radically different. **polarizable, -isable**, *a.* **polarizer, -iser**, *n.*

Polaroid®, *n.* a light-polarizing material used esp. in sunglasses; a type of camera which produces a finished print from inside itself within seconds of the picture's being taken, invented by Edwin Land in the US in 1947.

polatouche, *n.* a small flying squirrel of Europe and Siberia. [F, from Rus. *poletuchii*]

polder, *n.* a tract of land below sea or river level, that has been drained and cultivated. [Dut.]

pole¹, *n.* a long slender piece of wood or metal, usu. rounded and tapering, esp. fixed upright in the ground as a flagstaff, support for a tent, telegraph wires etc.; the shaft of a large vehicle; an instrument for measuring; a measure of length, a rod or perch, $5\frac{1}{2}$ yd. (5 m); a mast. *v.t.* to furnish or support with, to convey or impel by poles. **bare poles**, masts without sails. **up the pole**, (*sl.*) crazy, mad; mistaken, wrong. **pole position**, *n.* the most advantageous position at the start of a race, esp. a motor or horse race. **poler**, *n.* (*Austral.*) the bullock next to the pole in a team; (*Austral. sl.*) a sponger. **poling**, *n.* [OE *pāl*, L. *pālus*, PALE¹]

pole², *n.* one of the extremities of the axis on which a sphere or spheroid, esp. the earth, revolves; one of the points where the projection of the axis of the earth pierces the celestial sphere and round which the stars appear to revolve; a point from which a pencil of rays radiates, a fixed point of reference; one of the two points in a body where the attractive or repelling force is greatest, as in a magnet; a terminal of an electric cell, battery etc.; the extremity of the axis of a cell nucleus, etc.; either of the polar regions; either of two opposite extremes; (*poet.*) the sky, the firmament. **magnetic pole** MAGNETIC. **poles apart**, as far apart as possible; having widely divergent views, attitudes etc. **pole-star**, *n.* a bright star, Polaris, in Ursa Minor, within a degree and a quarter of the northern celestial pole; a guiding principle, a lodestar. **pole vault**, *n.* a field event in which the competitor attempts to clear a very high bar with the aid of a long flexible pol. **pole-vault**, *v.i.* **pole-vaulter**, *n.* **poleward**, *a.*, *adv.* **polewards**, *adv.* [through OF *pole*, or directly from L *polus*, Gr. *polos*, pivot, axis]

Pole¹, *n.* a native of Poland or one of Polish race.

Pole², *n.* **Reginald** (1500–58), English cardinal from 1536, who returned from Rome as papal legate on the accession of Mary in order to readmit England to the Catholic church. He succeeded Cranmer as archbishop of Canterbury in 1556.

poleaxe, *n.* a form of battle-axe consisting of an axe set on a long handle; such a weapon with a hook formerly used by sailors in boarding etc.; a long-handled butcher's axe with a hammer at the back, used for slaughtering cattle. *v.t.* to strike kill or destroy (as if) with a poleaxe. [ME *pollax* (POLL[1], AXE)]

polecat, *n.* a small carnivorous European weasel-like mammal, *Putorious foetidus,* with two glands emitting an offensive smell. [ME *polcat* (perh. from *poule,* chicken, CAT[1])]

polemarch, *n.* the third archon, orig. a military commander-in-chief; a civil magistrate with varying functions. [Gr. *polemarchos* (*polemos,* war, *archein,* to rule)]

polemic, *n.* a controversy or controversial discussion; a controversialist; (*pl.*) the art or practice of controversial discussion, esp. in theology; an aggressive attack on, or rebuttal of, another's conduct or views. **polemical,** *a.* pertaining to controversy; controversial, disputatious. **polemically,** *adv.* **polemicize, -ise, polemize, -ise,** *v.i.* **polemicist,** *n.* [Gr. *polemikos,* from *polemos,* war]

polemoniaceous, *a.* of or belonging to the Polemoniaceae, a family of plants containing the phloxes, and typified by *Polemonium caeruleum,* the Greek valerian or Jacob's ladder. [mod. L *Polemoniaceae,* from Gr. *polemōnion,* Greek valerian]

polemoscope, *n.* a telescope or other perspective glass with a mirror set at an angle for viewing objects obliquely. [F *polémoscope* (Gr. *polemos,* war. -SCOPE)]

polenta, *n.* a kind of porridge made of maize-meal or chestnut-meal, a common food in Italy; a similar food made of barley-meal. [It.]

pole-star POLE[2].

poley, *a.* (*dial.*) of cattle, without horns. [POLL[2], -Y]

Polianthes, *n.* a genus of Amaryllidaceae, containing the tuberose. [Gr. *polios,* white, *anthos,* flower]

police, *n.* the executive administration concerned in the preservation and enforcement of public order; the government department responsible for this; a civil force organized for the maintenance of order, the detection of crime, and the apprehension of offenders; (*pl.*) constables etc., belonging to this force. *v.t.* to control by the use of police; to supervise, to regulate, to discipline. **Police Complaints Authority** in the UK, a statutory body, set up in 1984, which supervises the investigation of complaints against the police and can order disciplinary action to be taken against police officers. **police constable** CONSTABLE. **police-court,** *n.* a court of summary jurisdiction dealing with minor charges, esp. those preferred by the police. **police dog,** *n.* a dog trained to assist police. **police force,** *n.* a separately organized body of police. **police magistrate,** *n.* a magistrate presiding over a police court. **policeman,** *n.* any (male) member of a police force, esp. a constable. **police office,** *n.* the headquarters of a police force in a town or district. **police officer,** *n.* a policeman or policewoman. **police state,** *n.* a totalitarian state maintained by the use of political police. **police station,** *n.* the headquarters of a local section of the police. **police trap,** *n.* an ambush by police to trap offenders against road regulations. **policewoman,** *n.* a female member of the police force. [F, from med. L *pōlīta,* L *polītīa,* POLICY[1]]

policlinic, *n.* a clinic in a private house instead of a hospital; the dispensary or out-patients' department of a hospital. [G *poliklinik* (Gr. *polis,* city, CLINIC)]

policy[1], *n.* prudence, foresight, or sagacity in managing or conducting, esp. state affairs; conduct governed by material or selfish interests; prudent conduct; a course of action or administration recommended or adopted by a party, government, firm, organization or individual. [OF *policie,* L *polītīa,* Gr. *politeia,* from *polītēs,* citizen, from *polis,* city]

policy[2], *n.* a document containing a contract of insurance; a warrant, voucher etc.; (*N Am.*) a method of gambling by betting on numbers drawn in a lottery. **policy-shop,** *n.* (*N Am.*) an office where drawings take place in connection with such lotteries. [F *police,* prob. from med. L *apodissa -dixa,* Gr. *apodeixis,* demonstration, proof, from *apodeiknunai* (APO-, *deiknunai,* to show)]

policy[3], *n.* (*often pl.*) (*Sc.*) the pleasure-grounds about a country-house; †the improvement or the improvements and embellishments of an estate. [prob. from L *polītus,* improved, see POLITE, conf. with POLICY[1]]

Policy Research, Institute for, British left-wing think-tank established in 1988 with Baroness Blackstone as chair of the board of trustees. It was designed to set the agenda for a future Labour government and challenge the conservative government's belief in the advantages of the free market economy.

poligar, *n.* a subordinate feudal chieftain in S India; a follower of such a chieftain. **poligar-dog,** *n.* a large hairless variety of dog from S India. **poligarship,** *n.* [Marathi *pālegār*]

poling POLE[1].

poliomyelitis, polio, *n.* inflammation of the grey matter of the spinal cord; infantile paralysis. [Gr. *polios,* grey, *muelos,* marrow]

polis, *n.* (*pl.* **poleis**) a Greek city-state. **-polis,** *comb. form.* city. [Gr.]

Polish, *a.* pertaining to Poland or its inhabitants. *n.* the language of the Poles, a member of the Slavonic branch of the Indo-European language family. Its standard form is based on the dialect of Poznań in W Poland; (*collect.*) the Polish people. **Polish Corridor,** *n.* a strip of land, designated under the Treaty of Versailles 1919 to give Poland access to the Baltic. It cut off East Prussia from the rest of Germany. It was absorbed when Poland took over the southern part of East Prussia in 1945.

polish, *v.t.* to make smooth or glossy, usu. by friction; to refine, to free from rudeness or coarseness; to bring to a fully finished state. *v.i.* to take a polish. *n.* a smooth glossy surface, esp. produced by friction; friction applied for this purpose; a substance applied to impart a polish; refinement, elegance of manners. **to polish off,** (*coll.*) to finish speedily; to get rid of. **to polish up,** to give a polish to; to improve, or refresh, (one's knowledge of something) by study. **polishable,** *a.* **polished,** *a.* accomplished; impeccably executed. **polisher,** *n.* **polishing,** *n.* **polishing-paste, -powder, -slate,** *n.* substances applied in polishing the surface of various materials. †**polishment,** *n.* [F *poliss-,* stem of *polir,* L *polīre*]

Politburo, *n.* the Political Bureau of the Central Committee of the Communist Party of the USSR. It consists of 12 voting and 6 candidate (non-voting) members. [Rus.]

polite, *a.* refined in manners; courteous; well-bred; cultivated; of literature, elegant, refined. **politely,** *adv.* **politeness,** *n.* [L *polītus,* p.p. of *polīre,* to POLISH]

politesse, *n.* formal politeness. [F]

Politian, *n.* (Italian **Angelo Poliziano**) pen name of Angelo Ambrogini (1454–94), Italian poet, playwright, and exponent of humanist ideals; he was tutor to Lorenzo de Medici's children, professor at the University of Florence, and wrote commentaries and essays on classical authors.

politic, *a.* prudent and sagacious; prudently devised, judicious, expedient; crafty, scheming, artful; specious; consisting of citizens. **body politic** BODY. **politicly,** *adv.* artfully, cunningly. [F *politique,* L *polīticus,* Gr. *politikos,* as POLICY[1]]

political, *a.* relating to civil government and its administration; of or relating to politics, esp. party politics; interested or involved in politics; having an established system of government. *n.* a civil officer, an administrator, as dist. from a military officer etc. **political agent, resident,** *n.* in British India, a government official appointed to advise a native ruler. **political economy** ECONOMY. **political geography** GEOGRAPHY. **political prisoner,** *n.* a person imprisoned for his or her political beliefs or activities. **politically,** *adv.* †**politicaster,** *n.*

politician, *n.* a person versed in politics, a statesman; one engaged in or devoted to party politics, usually as a career; (*N Am.*) one who makes use of politics for private ends, a spoilsman.

politicize, -ise, *v.t.* to give a political tone or scope to; to make politically aware. *v.i.* to engage in or discuss politics. **politicization, -isation,** *n.*

politicking, *n.* political activity, esp. vote-getting. **politick,** *v.i.*

politico, *n.* (*pl.* **-cos, -coes**) (*coll.*) a politician **politico-** *comb. form.* political and.

politics, *n. sing.* the art or science of civil government; the profession of politics; (*sing. or pl. in constr.*) political affairs; (*pl.*) the political dimension to any action or activity; (*pl.*) any activities concerned with the acquisition, apportionment or exercise of power within an organization, manoeuvring, intrigue; (*pl.*) a person's political views of sympathies.

polity, *n.* the form, system, or constitution of the civil government of a State; the State; an organized community, a body politic; the form of organization of an institution, etc.; †policy.

Polk, *n.* **James Knox** (1795–1849), 11th president of the US from 1845, a Democrat, born in North Carolina. He admitted Texas to the Union, and forced the war on Mexico that resulted in the annexation of California and New Mexico.

polka, *n.* a lively round dance of Bohemian origin; a piece of music in duple time for this; a woman's tight-fitting jacket, usu. made of knitted wool. *v.i.* to dance a polka. **polka dots,** *n.pl.* small dots arranged in a regular pattern esp. as a textile design. **polka-dot,** *a.* [etym. doubtful, perh. from Pol. *Polka,* fem. of *Polak,* POLACK]

poll¹, *n.* a human head; the part of the head on which the hair grows; a register or enumeration of heads or persons, esp. of persons entitled to vote at elections; the voting at an election, the number of votes polled, or the counting of these; the time or place of election; an attempt to ascertain public opinion by questioning a few individuals; the butt-end of an axe or other tool. *v.t.* to remove the top of (trees etc.); to crop the hair of; to cut off the horns of; to clip, to shear; to take the votes of; to receive (a specified number of votes); to give (one's vote); to question in a poll; (*Comput.*) to interrogate (computer terminals) in sequence to ascertain whether they have any data on them for use; †to plunder. *v.i.* to give one's vote. **deed-poll** DEED¹. **to poll a jury,** (*N Am.*) to examine each juror as to his or her concurrence in a verdict. **poll-tax,** *n.* a capitation tax or one levied on every person. **pollable,** *a.* **poller,** *n.* **polling,** *n.* **polling booth,** *n.* a semi-enclosed structure in which a voter marks his or her ballot paper. **polling station,** *n.* a building designated as a place where voters should go to cast their votes. **pollster,** *n.* one who conducts an opinion poll. [ME and MDut. *polle,* head or pate (cp. Dan. *puld*)]

poll², *a.* polled; hornless. **poll-beast, -cow, -ox,** *n.* a polled beast, esp. one of a breed of hornless cattle. [short for dial. *pold,* for *polled,* p.p. of prec.]

poll³, *n.* a familiar name for a parrot. [var. of *Moll,* see MOLL]

poll⁴, *n.* (*sl.*) at Cambridge Univ., the people who take a degree without honours. **poll-man,** *n.* [prob. short for POLLOI]

pollack, *n.* a sea-fish, *Gadus pollachius,* allied to the cod. [etym. doubtful]

Pollaiuolo, *n.* **Antonio** (*c.* 1432–98) and **Piero** (*c.* 1441–96), Italian artists, active in Florence. Both brothers were painters, sculptors, goldsmiths, engravers, and designers. Antonio is said to have been the first Renaissance artist to make a serious study of anatomy. The *Martyrdom of St Sebastian* (1475; National Gallery, London) is considered a joint work.

pollan, *n.* a herring-like Irish freshwater fish, *Coregonus pollan.* [rel. to Gael. *pollag* or Ir. *pollôg,* perh. from Gael. *poll, phuill,* pool, pit]

pollard, *n.* a tree with its top cut off so as to have a dense head of young branches; a stag or other animal that has cast its horns; a polled or hornless ox, sheep or other animal; the chub; a mixture of fine bran with a small quantity of flour, orig. bran sifted from flour. *v.t.* to lop the top of (a tree). **pollarded,** *a.* lopped, cropped; wanting horns. [POLL¹, -ARD]

pollen, *n.* the fertilizing powder discharged from the anthers of flowers and causing germination in the ovules. **pollen count,** *n.* a measure of the pollen present in the air, published to assist hay-fever sufferers etc. **pollenless,** *a.* **pollinar, pollinarious, pollinary, pollinic,** *a.* **pollinate,** *v.t.* to sprinkle with pollen so as to cause fertilization. **pollination,** *n.* **polliniferous, pollinoid, pollinose,** *a.* [L, fine flour]

pollicitation, *n.* a voluntary promise or engagement, or a paper containing such engagement; (*Law*) a promise not yet accepted, an offer. [L *pollicitātio,* from *pollicitārī,* to promise]

pollinar, pollination etc. POLLEN.

polling booth, polling station POLL¹.

polliwog, *n.* a tadpole. [ME, *polwygle* (POLL¹, WIGGLE)]

pollock, POLLACK.

Pollock, *n.* **Jackson** (1912–56), US painter, a pioneer of abstract expressionism and the foremost exponent of the dripping and splashing technique of action painting, a style he developed around 1946.

polloi, *n.pl.* the mob, the rabble, the majority. [Gr. *hoi polloi,* the many]

pollster POLL¹.

pollute, *v.t.* to make foul or unclean; to contaminate (an environment), esp. with man-made waste; to defile; to corrupt the moral purity of; to dishonour, to ravish; to profane. †*a.* polluted. **pollutedly,** *adv.* **pollutedness,** *n.* **polluter,** *n.* **pollution,** *n.* [L *pollūtus,* p.p. of *polluere* (*pol-,* earlier *por-, pro-,* forth, *luere,* to wash)]

Pollux, *n.* in Greek mythology, the twin brother of Castor; the brightest star in the constellation Gemini, and the 17th brightest star in the sky. Pollux is a yellowish star with a true luminosity 35 times that of the sun. It is 35 light years away.

polo, *n.* a game of Asian origin resembling hockey but played on horseback. **polo-jumper,** *n.* a knitted jumper with a fold-over collar. **polo neck,** *n.* (a jumper with) close-fitting, doubled-over collar. [Tibetan *pulu,* ball]

Polo, *n.* **Marco** (1254–1324), Venetian traveller and writer. He travelled overland to China (1271–75), and served under the emperor Kublai Khan until he returned to Europe by sea (1292–95). He was then captured while fighting for Venice against Genoa, and in prison wrote an account of his travels.

polonaise, *n.* an article of dress for women, consisting of a bodice and short skirt in one piece; a similar garment for men worn early in the 19th cent.; a slow dance of Polish origin; a piece of music in 3/4 time for this. [F, fem. of *polonais,* Polish]

polonium, *n.* a radioactive element, at. no. 84; chem. symbol Po.

polony, *n.* a sausage of partly-cooked pork. [prob. corr. of BOLOGNA]

Pol Pot, *n.* (1925–), Cambodian politician and communist leader in power 1975–79, also known as Saloth Sar, Tol Saut, and Pol Porth. He became a member of the anti-French resistance under Ho Chi Minh in the 1940s and a member of the communist party. As leader of the Khmer Rouge, he overthrew the government of General Lon Nol in 1975 and proclaimed a republic of Democratic Kampuchea with himself as prime minister. The policies of the Pol Pot government were to evacuate cities and put people to work in the countryside. The Khmer Rouge also carried out a systematic extermination of the educated and middle classes before the regime was overthrown by a Vietnamese invasion in 1979. Since then, Pol Pot has led a resistance group against the Vietnamese although he has been tried and convicted, in absentia, of genocide.

†**polt,** *n.* a blow; †a club or pestle. **polt-foot,** *n.* a club-foot. [etym. doubtful]

poltergeist, *n.* an alleged spirit which makes its presence known by noises and violence. [G, noisy ghost]

poltroon, *n.* an arrant coward; a dastard. †*a.* cowardly, base, contemptible. **poltroonery,** *n.* [F *poltron,* It. *poltrone,* from *poltro,* sluggard, orig. bed, perh. cogn.

with BOLSTER]

†**polverine,** *n.* the calcined ashes of a plant from the Levant, used in glass-making. [It. *polverino,* from *polvere,* L *pulverem,* nom. *pulvus,* dust]

poly, *n.* (*pl.* **polys**) short for POLYTECHNIC; short for POLYTHENE, as in *poly bag.*

poly-, *comb. form.* several, many; excessive, abnormal; denoting a polymer. [Gr. *polus,* many]

polyacoustic, *a.* capable of multiplying or increasing sound. *n.* an instrument for doing this.

polyact, *a.* having several rays, as a sponge spicule.

polyad, *n.* an element whose valency is greater than two.

Polyadelphia, *n.pl.* a Linnaean class of plants having the stamens in three or more bundles. **polyadelphian, -phous,** *a.* [Gr. *adelphos,* brother]

polyamide, *n.* a synthetic, polymeric material such as nylon.

Polyandria, *n.pl.* a Linnaean class of plants having stamens hypogynous and free. **polyandrian, -drous,** *a.* having numerous stamens; pertaining to or practising polyandry. **polyandrist,** *n.* a woman having several husbands. **polyandry,** *n.* the practice or condition of a woman having more than one husband at once; plurality of husbands. [Gr. *anēr andros,* man]

polyanthus, *n.* (*pl.* **-thuses**) a garden variety of primula, prob. a development from the cowslip or oxlip. [Gr. *poluanthos* (*anthos,* flower)]

polyarchy, *n.* government by many. [Gr. *archia,* government, from *archein,* to rule]

polyatomic, *a.* applied to elements having more than one atom in their molecules, esp. replaceable atoms of hydrogen.

†**polyautography,** *n.* the process of multiplying copies of handwriting, drawings etc., an early name for lithography.

polybasic, *a.* of acids etc., having two or more equivalents of a base.

polybasite, *n.* an iron-black orthorhombic mineral.

Polybius, *n.* (*c.* 201–120 BC), Greek politician and historian. He was involved with the Achaean League against the Romans and, following the defeat of the Macedonians at Pydna in 168 BC, he was taken as a political hostage to Rome. He returned to Greece in 151 and was present at the capture of Carthage by his friend Scipio in 146. His history of Rome in 40 books, covering the years 220–146, has largely disappeared.

polycarpellary, -carpous, *a.* composed of several carpels.

polychaete, *a.* belonging to the Polychaeta, a class of worms with setae, mostly marine. *n.* a polychaete worm. **polychaetan, -tous,** *a.*

polychord, *a.* having many chords. *n.* a ten-stringed musical instrument resembling the double bass without a neck; (*Organ*) an apparatus coupling two octave notes.

polychroite, *n.* the yellow colouring-matter of saffron.

polychromatic, *a.* exhibiting many colours or a play of colours. **polychrome,** *n.* a work of art executed in several colours, esp. a statue. *a.* having or executed in many colours. **polychromic, -chromous,** *a.* **polychromy,** *n.* the art of decorating (pottery, statuary or buildings) in many colours.

polyclinic, *n.* a clinic dealing with various diseases; a general hospital.

polycotyledon, *n.* a plant with seeds having more than two cotyledons. **polycotyledonous,** *a.*

polydactyl, *a.* having more than the normal number of fingers or toes. *n.* a polydactyl animal. **polydactylism,** *n.* **polydactylous,** *a.*

polydaemonism, *n.* belief in numerous demons or spirits controlling the operations of nature.

polydipsia, *n.* insatiable thirst.

polyester, *n.* any of a group of synthetic polymers made up of esters, used esp. in making fibres for cloth, plastics, and resins.

polyethylene, POLYTHENE.

Polygamia, *n.pl.* a Linnaean class of plants, bearing hermaphrodite and unisexual (male or female) flowers on the same plant. **polygamian,** *n., a.* [Gr. *gamos,* marriage]

polygamy, *n.* the practice or condition of having a plurality of wives or husbands at the same time; the state of having more than one mate; the state of being polygamian. **polygamist,** *n.* **polygamous,** *a.*

polygastric, *a.* having many stomachs. **polygastrian,** *n., a.*

polygenesis, *n.* the doctrine that living beings originate not in one but in several different cells or embryos. **polygenetic,** *a.* **polygenic,** *a.* forming more than one compound with hydrogen; (*Geol.*) polygenous. **polygenism,** *n.* the doctrine that the different races of mankind are descended from different original ancestors, and therefore represent different species. **polygenist,** *n.* **polygenistic,** *a.* **polygenous,** *a.* (*Geol.*) consisting of many kinds of material; (*Chem.*) polygenic.

polyglot, *a.* expressed in or speaking many languages. *n.* a book, esp. the Bible, written or set forth in many languages. **polyglottal, -ttic,** *a.* **polyglottism,** *n.* [Gr. *poluglōttos,* (*glōtta,* tongue)]

polygon, *n.* a closed plane figure, usu. rectilinear and of more than four angles or sides. **polygonal,** †**-gonous,** *a.* **polygonally,** *adv.* [L *polygōnum,* Gr. *polugōnon* (*gōnia,* corner, angle)]

Polygonum, *n.* a genus of plants comprising the snakeweed, knot-grass etc., belonging to the family Polygonaceae. [Gr. *polugōnon* (*gonu,* knee)]

polygram, *n.* a figure consisting of many lines. **polygraph,** *n.* an apparatus for multiplying copies of writing, drawings etc.; a writer of multifarious works; a collection of different works; an instrument which registers several small physiological changes simultaneously, e.g. in pulse rate, body temperature, often used as a lie detector. **polygraphic,** *a.* **polygraphy,** *n.*

Polygynia, *n.pl.* a Linnaean class of plants containing those having flowers with many styles. †**polygynian, -gynic,** *a.* **polygynous,** *a.* pertaining to or practising polygyny. **polygyny,** *n.* plurality of wives. [Gr. *gunē,* woman]

polyhedron, *n.* (*pl.* **-drons, -dra**) a solid bounded by many (usu. more than four) plane sides. **polyhedral, -dric, -drous,** *a.* having many sides. [Gr. *poluedron* (*hedra,* a base)]

polyhistor, *n.* a polymath. [Gr. *poluistōr* (*histōr,* learned, see HISTORY)]

polyhybrid, *n.* a cross between parents of differing heritable characters.

Polykleitos, *n.* (5th century BC), Greek sculptor, whose *Spear Carrier* (450–40 BC) (Roman copies survive) exemplifies the naturalism and harmonious proportions of his work. He created the legendary colossal statue of *Hera* in Argos, in ivory and gold.

polymath, *n.* a person of great and varied learning. **polymathic,** *a.* **polymathist,** *n.* **polymathy,** *n.* wide and multifarious learning. [Gr. *polumathēs* POLY-, *manthanein,* to learn]

polymer, *n.* a chemical compound, formed by polymerization, which has large molecules made up of many comparatively simple repeated units. **polymeric,** *a.* of or constituting a polymer. **polymerization, -isation,** *n.* a chemical reaction in which two or more small molecules combine as repeating units in a much larger molecule. **polymerize, -ise,** *v.t.* to render polymerous or polymeric. *v.i.* to become polymeric. **polymerous,** *a.* (*Nat. Hist.*) consisting of many parts; polymeric. [Gr. *polumerēs* (POLY-, *meros,* portion)]

polymignite, *n.* an orthorhombic brilliant black mineral composed of the cerium metals with iron and calcium. [Gr. *mignunai,* to mix, -ITE]

polymorphic, -morphous, *a.* having, assuming, or occurring in many forms. **polymorph,** *n.* **polymorphism,** *n.* [Gr. *morphē,* form]

polyneme, *n.* any fish belonging to the genus *Polynemus,* consisting of tropical spiny sea-fishes having the pectoral fin divided into free rays. [Gr. *nēma,* thread]

Polynesia, *n.* a collective name for the islands of the central and southern Pacific, including Hawaii, Kiribati, Tuvalu, Fiji, Tonga, Tokelau, Samoa, Cook Islands, and French Polynesia. **Polynesian,** *a.* pertaining to Polynesia. *n.* a native or inhabitant of Polynesia. [Gr. *nēsos,* island]

polyneuritis, *n.* simultaneous inflammation of many nerves.

polynia, polynya,, *n.* an open place in water that is for the most part frozen over, esp. in the Arctic. [Rus. *poluinya*]

polynomial, *a.* (*Alg.*) multinomial. *n.* a multinomial. **polynomialism,** *n.* **polynomialist,** *n.* **polynomic,** *a.* [L *nōmen,* name]

polyonymous, *a.* having many different names. **polyonym,** *n.* **polyonymic,** *a.* **polyonymist,** *n.* **polyonymy,** *n.* [Gr. *onoma,* a name]

polyopia, *n.* double or multiple vision. **polyoptrum, -tron,** *n.* a lens giving a number of diminished images of an object.

polyorama, *n.* a view of many objects; an optical apparatus presenting many views, a panorama.

polyp, *n.* one of various aquatic animals of low organization, as the hydra, the sea-anemone etc., an individual in a compound organism of various kinds; a polypus. **polypary,** *n.* the calcareous or chitonous structure supporting a colony of polyps. [F *polype,* L POLYPUS]

polypeptide, *n.* any of a group of polymers made up of long amino-acid chains.

polypetalous, *a.* having many or separate petals.

polyphagous, *a.* feeding on various kinds of food; voracious.

polypharmacy, *n.* the prescribing of too many medicines; a prescription composed of many ingredients.

polyphase, *a.* having two or more alternating voltages of equal frequency, the phases of which are cyclically displaced by fractions of a period.

polyphone, *n.* (*Philol.*) a character or sign standing for more than one sound. **polyphonic, -phonous,** *a.* representing different sounds; contrapuntal; having several sounds or voices, many-voiced. **polyphony, -phonism,** *n.* the state of being polyphonic; composition in parts, each part having an independent melody of its own, counterpoint. **polyphonist,** *n.* a contrapuntist. [Gr. *poluphōnos* (*phōnē,* voice, sound)]

polyphyletic, *a.* polygenetic.

polyphyllous, *a.* having many leaves.

polypidom, *n.* a polypary. **polypite,** *n.* an individual polyp. [POLYPUS, L *domus,* Gr. *domos,* house]

polyplastic, *a.* having or assuming many forms.

polyploid, *a.* having more than twice the basic (haploid) number of chromosomes. **polyploidy,** *n.* [by analogy with *haploid, diploid*]

polypod, *a.* having numerous feet. *n.* a millipede, e.g. a wood-louse. [F *polypode* (Gr. *pous podos,* foot)]

polypody, *n.* a fern of the genus *Polypodium,* esp. *P. vulgaris,* the common polypody, growing on rocks, walls, trees etc. **polypodiaceous,** *a.* [L *polypodium,* Gr. *polupodion* (*podion,* dim. of *pous podos,* foot)]

polypoid, *a.* like a polyp or polypus. **polypose, -pous,** *a.*

polyporous, *a.* having many pores.

Polyporus, *n.* a genus of hymenomycetous fungi growing on the decaying parts of trees, the spores of which are borne on the inner surface of pores or tubes. **polyporaceous,** *a.* **polyporoid,** *a.* [Gr. *poluporos*]

polypropylene, *n.* any of various plastics or fibres that are polymers of propylene.

polypus, *n.* (*pl.* **-pi**) a tumour with ramifications growing in a mucous cavity; a polyp. [L, from Gr. *polupous* (*pous podos,* foot)]

polyrhizous, *a.* having many roots. [Gr. *rhiza,* root]

polyscope, *n.* a multiplying-glass; an instrument for lighting the cavities of the body for surgical examination.

polysemous, *a.* having several meanings. **polysemy,** *n.* [Gr. *sema,* a sign]

polysepalous, *a.* having the sepals distinct.

polyspermal, -mous, *a.* having many seeds.

polyspore, *n.* a compound spore; a spore-case containing many spores. **polysporous,** *a.*

polystigmous, *a.* having several carpels each bearing a stigma.

polystome, *a.* having many mouths. *n.* an animal with many mouths or suckers. **polystomatous, -stomous,** *a.*

polystyle, *a.* having or supported on many columns. **polystylous,** *a.* [Gr. *stulos,* column]

polystyrene, *n.* a polymer of styrene used esp. as a transparent plastic for moulded products or in expanded form, as a rigid white foam, for packaging and insulation.

polysyllabic, *a.* consisting of many syllables; characterized by polysyllables. **polysyllable,** *n.* [L *polysyllabus,* Gr. *polusullabos*]

polysyndeton, *n.* a figure in which the conjunction or copulative is repeated several times. [Gr. *sundetos,* from *sundeein* (SYN-, *deein,* to bind)]

polysynthetic, *a.* compounded of several elements; combining several words (as verbs and adverbs, complements etc.) into one. **polysynthesis,** *n.* **polysynthetically,** *adv.* **polysyntheticism, -thetism,** *n.*

polytechnic, *a.* connected with, pertaining to, or giving instruction in many subjects, esp. technical ones. *n.* a college where degree and other advanced courses are given in technical, vocational, and academic subjects. [F *polytechnique,* Gr. *polutechnos* (*technē,* art), -IC]

polytetrafluoroethylene, PTFE, *n.* a tough, translucent plastic used esp. for moulded articles and as a non-stick coating.

polythalamous, *a.* (*Nat. Hist.*) having many cells or chambers.

polytheism, *n.* the doctrine or worship of a plurality of gods. **polytheist,** *n.* **polytheistic, †-ical,** *a.* [F *polythéisme,* Gr. *polutheos* (*theos,* god), -ISM]

polythene, *n.* any of various thermoplastics that are polymers of ethylene.

polytocous, *a.* multiparous, producing several at a birth. [Gr. *polutokos* (*tokos,* a bringing forth, cogn. with *tiktein,* to bring forth)]

polytomous, *a.* pinnate, the divisions not articulated with a common petiole.

polytype, *a.* a form of stereotype obtained by pressing wood-engravings etc. into semifluid metal; a print obtained in this way. **polytypage,** *n.* **polytypic,** *a.* having or existing in many forms.

polyunsaturated, *a.* of certain animal and vegetable fats, having long carbon chains with many double bonds.

polyurethane, *n.* any of a class of polymeric resins used esp. as foam for insulation and packing.

polyvalent, MULTIVALENT.

polyvinyl, *n., a.* (of or being) a polymerized vinyl compound. **polyvinyl chloride,** *n.* a plastic used esp. as a rubber substitute, e.g. for coating wires and cables and as a dress and furnishing fabric.

Polyzoa, *n.pl.* (*sing.* **-zoon**, a class of invertebrate animals, mostly marine, produced by gemmation, existing in coral-like or plant-like compound colonies. **polyzoal,** *a.* **polyzoan,** *n., a.* **polyzoary,** *n.* the polypidom of a polyzoic colony. **polyzoarial,** *a.* **polyzoic, polyzooid,** *a.* [Gr. *zōon,* animal]

polyzonal, *a.* of lighthouse lenses, composed of many zones or annular segments.

pom, (*Austral., New Zealand, derog. sl.*) POMMY.

pomace, *n.* the mashed pulp of apples crushed in a cider-mill, esp. the refuse after the juice has been pressed out. **pomaceous,** *a.* of the nature of a pome or of trees producing pomes, as the apple, pear, quince etc. [history obscure, from F *pomme* or L *pōmum,* apple]

pomade, *n.* pomatum. *v.t.* to apply this to (the hair etc.). [F *pommade,* from *pomme,* apple]

pomander, *n.* a perfumed ball or powder kept in a box, bag etc., used as a scent and formerly carried about the person to prevent infection; the perforated box or hollow ball, in which this is kept or carried. [altered from *pomamber,* OF *pomme d'ambre* (*pomme,* apple, *ambre,* AMBER)]

Pomard, *n.* a red Burgundy wine. [village in Côte d'Or, France]

pomatum, *n.* a perfumed ointment (said to have been prepared partly from apple-pulp) for dressing the hair. *v.t.* to apply pomatum to. [mod. L, from L *pōmum,* apple, -ATE]

pome, *n.* a compound fleshy fruit, composed of the walls of an adnate inferior calyx enclosing carpels containing the seeds, as the apple, pear, quince etc.; (*poet.*) an apple; a ball, a globe; a metal ball filled with hot water, with which priests warmed their hands at the altar. †**pomecitron**, *n.* a citron. †**pomeroy, -royal**, *n.* a variety of apple. **pome-water,** *n.* a large sweet juicy apple. **pomiculture**, *n.* fruit-growing. **pomiferous**, *a.* bearing apples or pomes. **pomiform**, *a.* shaped like a pome or apple. **pomology**, *n.* the art or science of the cultivation of fruit. **pomological**, *a.* **pomologist** *n.* [OF *pome* (F *pomme*), L *pōmum*]

pomegranate, *n.* the fruit of a N African and W Asiatic tree, *Punica granatum,* resembling an orange, with a thick, tough rind and acid red pulp enveloping numerous seeds; the tree bearing this fruit. [OF *pome grenate* (POME, *grenate,* L *grānāta,* seeded, from *grānum,* seed)]

Pomeranian, *a.* of or pertaining to Pomerania. *n.* a native or inhabitant of Pomerania; a Pomeranian dog, esp. a dog about the size of a spaniel, with a fox-like pointed muzzle and long, silky hair.

†**pomeroy** POME.

Pomfret-cake, *n.* a flat cake of liquorice made in Pomfret. [*Pomfret,* now *Pontefract,* town in Yorkshire, CAKE]

pomiculture POME.

pommel, *n.* a round ball or knob, esp. on the hilt of a sword; the upward projection at the front of a saddle; either of the two handles on top of a gymnastics horse. *v.t.* to pummel. [ME and OF *pomel* (F *pommeau*), dim. of L *pōmum,* POME]

pommy, *n.* (*Austral., New Zealand, derog. sl.*) a British person, esp. an immigrant to Australia or New Zealand. *a.* British. [etym. doubtful, perh. from *pomegranate,* alluding to immigrants' red cheeks]

pomology POME.

pomp, *n.* a pageant; state, splendour; ostentatious display or parade. [F *pompe,* L *pompa,* Gr. *pompē,* sending, procession, cogn. with *pempein,* to send]

pompadour, *n., a.* applied to methods of wearing the hair brushed up from the forehead or (in women) turned back in a roll from the forehead, to a style of corsage with low square neck, to a shade of crimson or pink or a fabric of this tint, a pattern on cloth for dresses, a walking-stick with a silver handle etc.; a Brazilian bird with gorgeous plumage. [Marquise de *Pompadour*]

Pompadour, *n.* **Jeanne Antoinette Poisson, Marquise de Pompadour** (1721–64), mistress of Louis XV of France from 1744, born in Paris. She largely dictated the government's ill-fated policy of reversing France's anti-Austrian policy for an anti-Prussian one. She acted as the patron of the Enlightenment philosophers Voltaire and Diderot.

pompano, *n.* a W Indian food-fish of various species belonging to the genus *Trachinotus*. [Sp. *pámpano*]

Pompeii, *n.* ancient city in Italy, near Vesuvius, 21 km/13 miles SE of Naples. In AD 63 an earthquake destroyed much of the city, which had been a Roman port and pleasure resort; it was completely buried beneath volcanic ash when Vesuvius erupted in AD 79. Over 2000 people were killed. Pompeii was rediscovered 1748 and the systematic excavation begun 1763 still continues. **Pompeian,** *a.*

Pompey, *n.* **the Great** (Gnaeus Pompeius Magnus) (106–48 BC), Roman soldier and politician. Originally a supporter of Sulla and the aristocratic party, he joined the democrats when he became consul with Crassus in 70 BC. He defeated Mithridates VI of Pontus, and annexed Syria and Palestine. In 60 BC he formed the First Triumvirate with Julius Caesar (whose daughter Julia he married) and Crassus, and when it broke down after 53 BC he returned to the aristocratic party. On the outbreak of civil war in 49 BC he withdrew to Greece, was defeated by Caesar at Pharsalus in 48 BC, and was murdered in Egypt.

Pompidou, *n.* **Georges** (1911–74), French conservative politician, president from 1969. An adviser on Gen. de Gaulle's staff (1944–46), he held administrative posts until he became director-general of the French House of Rothschild in 1954, and even then continued in close association with de Gaulle. In 1962 he became prime minister, but resigned after the Gaullist victory in the elections of 1968, and was elected to the presidency on de Gaulle's resignation.

pompier, *n.* a fireman. **pompier ladder,** *n.* a fireman's scaling-ladder, consisting of a hooked pole with cross-pieces. [F, fireman, from *pompe,* PUMP[1]]

†**pompion,** *n.* a pumpkin. **pompion-berry,** *n.* (*N Am.*) the hackberry, *Celtis occidentalis*. [MF *pompon,* a form of *popon,* L *pepōnem,* nom. *pepo,* Gr. *pepōn*]

pom-pom, *n.* an automatic quick-firing gun, usu. mounted for anti-aircraft defence. [imit.]

pompom, pompon, *n.* an ornament in the form of a tuft or ball of feathers, ribbon etc. worn on women's and children's hats, shoes etc., on the front of a soldier's shako, on a French sailor's cap etc.; a small compact chrysanthemum. [F *pompon,* etym. doubtful]

pompous, *a.* displaying pomp; grand, magnificent; ostentatious, pretentious; exaggeratedly solemn or portentous, self-important. **pomposo**, *adv.* (*Mus.*) in a stately or dignified manner. **pompously,** *adv.* **pomposity**, **pompousness,** *n.* [F *pompeux,* late L *pompōsus*]

ponce, *n.* (*sl.*) a prostitute's pimp; an effeminate man. *v.i.* to pimp. **to ponce about, around,** (*sl.*) to act in an ostentatious or effeminate manner; to fool about, to waste time. **poncy,** *a.* (*sl.*) [perh. from POUNCE[1]]

Ponce de León, *n.* **Juan** (*c.* 1460–1521), Spanish soldier and explorer. He is believed to have sailed with Columbus in 1493, and served (1502–04) in Hispaniola. He conquered Puerto Rico in 1508, and was made governor in 1509. In 1513 he was the first European to reach Florida.

Poncelet, *n.* **Jean** (1788–1867), French mathematician, who worked on projective geometry. His book, started in 1814 and completed 1822, deals with the properties of plane figures unchanged when projected.

poncho, *n.* a woollen cloak, worn in S America, with a slit through which the head passes; a cycling-cape of this pattern. [S Am. Sp., from Araucanian]

pond, *n.* a body of still water, often artificial, smaller than a lake; (*facet.*) the sea, esp. the Atlantic. *v.t.* to dam back; to make into a pond. *v.i.* to form a pool or pond (of water). **pond-lily,** *n.* a water-lily, esp. the yellow *Nuphar lutea*. **pond-weed,** *n.* an aquatic plant growing on stagnant water, esp. species of *Potamogeton*. **pondage**, *n.* **pondlet**, *n.* [prob. var. of POUND[2]]

ponder, *v.t.* to weigh carefully in the mind; to think over, to consider deeply, to reflect upon; †to examine carefully, to value, to estimate. *v.i.* to think, to deliberate, to muse (on, over etc.). †*n.* meditation. **ponderable,** *a.* capable of being weighed, having appreciable weight, opp. to *imponderable*. **ponderability**, **-ableness,** *n.* **ponderal,** *a.* **ponderance,** *n.* weight; gravity, importance. **ponderation,** *n.* (*lit.* or *fig.*) the act of weighing. **ponderer,** *n.* **ponderingly,** *adv.* **ponderous,** *a.* very heavy or weighty; bulky, unwieldy; dull, tedious; pompous, self-important. **ponderously,** *adv.* **ponderosity**, **ponderousness,** *n.* [OF *ponderer,* L *ponderāre,* from *pondus -deris,* weight]

Pondicherry, *n.* Union Territory of SE India; area 480 sq km/185 sq miles; population (1981) 604,000. Its capital is Pondicherry, and products include rice, groundnuts, cotton, and sugar. Pondicherry was founded by France 1674 and changed hands several times between French, Dutch, and British before being returned to France 1814 at the close of the Napoleonic wars. Together with Karaikal, Yanam, and Mahé (on the Malabar Coast) it formed a French colony until 1954 when all were transferred to the government of India; since 1962 they have formed the Union Territory of Pondicherry. Languages spoken include French, English, Tamil, Telugu, and Malayalam.

pone[1], *n.* a kind of bread made by the N American Indians of maize-meal; similar bread made with eggs, milk etc.; a loaf of this. [Algonquin]

pone[2], *n.* the player to the dealer's right who cuts the cards. [from L *pone,* imper. of *ponere,* to put]

ponent, *a.* west, western. [It. *ponente,* L *pōnens -ntem,* setting, sunset, orig. p.p. of *pōnere,* to put, to set]

pong, *n.* (*coll.*) a bad smell, a stink. *v.i.* to stink. [prob. Romany *pan,* to stink]

pongee, *n.* a soft unbleached kind of Chinese silk. [perh. from N Chin. *pun-chī,* own loom]

pongo, *n.* (*pl.* **-gos,** (*Austral.*) **-goes**) a large African anthropoid ape; erroneously applied to the orang-outan etc.; (*Austral. Abor.*) the flying-squirrel. [Kongo *mpogni*]

poniard, *n.* a dagger. *v.t.* to stab with a poniard. [F *poignard,* from *poing,* L *pugnus,* fist]

pons, *n.* a bridge; (*Anat.*) a connecting part, esp. the pons Varolii. **pons asinorum,** *n.* the asses' bridge, see ASS; any severe test for a beginner. **pons Varolii,** *n.* a band of fibres connecting the two hemispheres of the cerebellum. **pontal, pontic**[2]**, pontile, pontine,** *a.* [L *pons pontis*]

†**pontage,** *n.* a toll for the maintenance of a bridge or bridges. [OF, from med. L *pontāticum,* from *pons pontis,* bridge]

Pontiac[1], *n.* a motor-manufacturing city in Michigan, US, 38 km/24 miles NW of Detroit; population (1980) 76,700.

Pontiac[2], *n.* (*c.* 1720–69), North American Indian, chief of the Ottawa from 1755. In 1763–64 he led the 'Conspiracy of Pontiac' in an attempt to stop British encroachment on Indian lands. He achieved remarkable success against overwhelming odds, but eventually signed a peace treaty 1766, and was murdered by an Illinois Indian at the instigation of a British trader.

Pontic, *a.* pertaining to the Black Sea. [L *ponticus,* Gr. *Pontikos,* from *pontos,* sea, esp. the Black Sea]

pontic PONS.

pontifex, *n.* (*pl.* **-tifices**) a member of the highest of the ancient Roman colleges of priests. **Pontifex Maximus,** *n.* the president of this; the Pope. [L (*pons pontis,* bridge, or Oscan-Umbrian *puntis,* sacrifice, *-fex, -fic,* from *facere,* to make)]

pontiff, *n.* the Pope; a pontifex, a high priest. **pontifical,** †**pontific,** *a.* of, pertaining to, or befitting a pontiff, high priest or pope; papal, popish; with an assumption of authority. *n.* a book containing the forms for rites and ceremonies to be performed by bishops; (*pl.*) the vestments and insignia of a pontiff or bishop. **pontifically,** *adv.* **pontificate,** *n. v.t.,* to celebrate (Mass etc.) as a bishop. *v.i.* to officiate as a pontiff or bishop, esp. at Mass; to speak or behave in a pompous and dogmatic manner. †**pontifice,** *n.* the erection or structure of a bridge. †**pontificial,** †**pontifician,** *a.* **pontify,** *v.i.* to act in the style of a pontiff, esp. to claim infallibility. [F *pontife, pontif,* from prec.]

pontil, *n.* an iron rod used for handling, twisting or carrying glass in process of manufacture. [F, prob. from It. *pontello, puntello,* dim. of *punto,* POINT]

pontile PONS.

pont-levis, *n.* a drawbridge; the repeated rearing of a horse on its hind legs. [F (*pont,* L *pons pontis,* bridge, OF *leveïs,* movable, ult. from L *levāre,* to raise)]

pontonier, *n.* a soldier in charge of a pontoon, or who constructs pontoon bridges. [F *pontonnier* (as foll.)]

pontoon[1], VINGT-ET-UN.

pontoon[2], *n.* a flat-bottomed boat, cylinder, or other buoyant structure supporting a floating bridge; a caisson; a barge or lighter; a pontoon-bridge; *v.t.* to bridge with pontoons. **pontoon-bridge,** *n.* a platform or roadway laid across pontoons. [F *ponton,* L. *pontōnem,* nom. *-to,* from *pons pontis,* bridge]

Pontormo, *n.* **Jacopo Carucci** (1494–1557), Italian painter, active in Florence. He developed a dramatic mannerist style, with lurid colours.

Pontus, *n.* kingdom of NE Asia Minor on the Black Sea from about 300–65 BC when its greatest ruler, Mithridates VI, was defeated by Pompey.

pony, *n.* a small horse, esp. one of a small breed; a small glass; (*sl.*) 25 pounds sterling; (*N Am., sl.*) a crib used in getting up lessons. **Jerusalem pony,** a donkey. **pony-engine,** *n.* a small locomotive for shunting. **pony express,** *n.* a postal and delivery system across the western US (1860–61), using relays of horses and riders. **pony-tail,** *n.* a woman's hair style in which the hair is gathered at the back and hangs down over the nape of the neck like a tail. **pony trekking,** *n.* cross-country pony-riding in groups as a pastime. [Lowland Sc. *powney,* OF *poulenet,* dim. of *poulain,* late L *pullānus,* L *pullus,* foal]

pooch, *n.* (*sl.*) a dog, esp. a mongrel.

pood, *n.* a Russian weight of about 36 lb. (16 kg). [Rus. *pudu,* from LG or Norse *Pund,* POUND]

poodle, *n.* a breed of pet dog with long woolly hair, often clipped in a fanciful style; a servile follower. *v.t.* to clip the hair of (a dog) thus. [G *Pudel, Pudelhund,* from *pudeln,* to waddle or to splash (cp. PUDDLE)]

poof, pooftah, poofter, poove, pouf, *n.* (*sl., offensive*) a male homosexual. [perh. from F *pouffe,* puff]

pooh, *int.* an exclamation of contempt or impatience. **pooh-pooh,** *v.t.* to laugh or sneer at; to make light of. [imit. of instinctive action of blowing away]

Pooh-bah, *n.* (*facet.*) a person holding many offices. [character in *The Mikado*]

pooka, *n.* a hobgoblin, usu. represented in the form of a horse. [Ir. *púca*]

pool[1], *n.* a small body of water, still or nearly still; a deep, still part of a stream; a puddle; a pond, natural or ornamental; a swimming pool; an underground accumulation of oil or gas. *v.t.* (*Quarrying*) to sink (a hole) for a wedge; (*Mining*) to undercut and bring down. [OE *pōl* (cp. Dut. *poel,* G *Pfuhl*)]

pool[2], *n.* the receptacle for the stakes in certain games of cards; the collective amount of stakes, forfeits etc.; a game on a billiard-table in which the players aim to drive different balls into the pockets in a certain order; the collective stakes in a betting arrangement; (*pl.*) football pools; a combination of persons, companies etc., for manipulating prices and suppressing competition; any common stock or fund; a group of people or things which can be called upon when required. *v.t.* to put (funds, risks etc.) into a common fund or pool. **poolroom,** *n.* (*N Am.*) a billiards saloon. [prob. from F *poule,* hen]

poon, *n.* an Indian tree of the genus *Calophyllum.* **poon-oil,** *n.* a bitter oil obtained from the seeds of this, used in medicine and as an illuminant. **poon-wood,** *n.* [Sinhalese *pūna*]

Poona, PUNE.

poop[1], *n.* the stern of a ship; a deck over the after part of a spar-deck. *v.t.* of waves, to break heavily over the poop of; to take (a wave) over the stern (of a ship). **pooped,** *a.* having a poop (*usu. in comb.*) struck on the poop. [ME and OF *pupe* (F *poupe*), late L *puppa,* L *puppis*]

poop[2], *v.t.* (*coll.*) to make out of breath, to exhaust. *v.i.* to become exhausted. **to poop out,** to poop; to give up.

poor, *a.* wanting means of subsistence, needy, indigent; badly supplied, lacking (in); barren, unproductive; scanty, meagre, inadequate in quantity or quality, unsatisfactory; lean, thin, wasted; unhealthy; uncomfortable; inferior, sorry, paltry, miserable, contemptible; insignificant, humble, meek; unfortunate, pitiable, used as a term of slight contempt, pity or endearment. **the poor,** those who are needy or indigent, esp. those who depend on charity or parochial relief. **poor-box,** *n.* a money-box, esp. in a church for charitable contributions. **Poor Clare,** *n.* a member of an austere order of nuns founded by St Clare in 1212. **poorhouse,** *n.* a workhouse. †**poor-john,** *n.* a coarse kind of fish, salted and dried. **poor-law,** *n.* the body of laws formerly relating to the maintenance of paupers. **poorman's weather-glass,** *n.* the pimpernel. **poor-rate,** *n.* a rate levied for the support of paupers. **poor relation,** *n.* a person or thing looked down on, considered inferior, or shabbily treated in comparison to others. **poor-spirited,** *a.* timid, cowardly; mean, base. **poor-spiritedness,** *n.* **poor white,** *n.* (*usu. derog.*) a member of a class of poverty-stricken and socially inferior white people in the southern US or S Africa. **poorly,** *adv.* with poor results, with little success; defectively, imperfectly; meanly, despicably; in delicate health; unwell, indisposed. **poorliness,** *n.* **poorness,** *n.* **poortith,** *n.* (*Sc.*) poverty. [ME and OF *povre, poure* (F *pauvre*), L)]

poove POOF.

pop[1], *v.i.* (*past, p.p.* **popped**) to make a short, sharp, explosive noise as of the drawing of a cork; to burst open with such a sound; esp. of the eyes, to protrude as with amazement; to enter or issue forth with a quick, sudden motion; to dart; to move quickly; to shoot (at) with a gun, pistol etc. *v.t.* to push or thrust (in, out, up) suddenly; to put (down etc.) quickly or hastily; to fire off (a gun etc.); to cause (a thing) to pop by breaking etc.; (*sl.*) to pawn; (*sl.*) to take (drugs) orally or by injection; (*sl.*) to consume habitually. *adv.* with a pop; suddenly. *n.* a short, sharp, explosive noise; a dot, spot or other mark, esp. used in marking sheep etc.; (*coll.*) an effervescing drink, esp. ginger-beer or champagne; (*sl.*) the act of pawning. **in pop,** (*sl.*) in pawn. **to go pop,** to make, or burst with, a popping sound. **to pop off,** (*coll.*) to leave hastily; to die. **to pop the question,** (*coll.*) to propose marriage. **to pop up,** to appear suddenly. **popcorn,** *n.* maize kernels burst and puffed up by heating; the kind of maize suitable for this. **pop-eyed,** *a.* with bulging eyes. **pop-gun,** *n.* a small toy gun used by children, shooting a pellet or cork with air compressed by a piston; a poor or defective fire-arm. **pop-shop,** *n.* (*sl.*) a pawnshop. **pop socks,** *n.pl.* knee-length nylon stockings. **pop-up,** *a.* of books, having illustrations etc. which stand up off the page when the book is opened to give a quasi-three-dimensional effect; having a device which causes the contents to spring up; (*Comput.*) of or being a computer facility which can be accessed during the running of a program. **popper,** *n.* something that pops; (*coll.*) a press-stud. **popping-crease,** *n.* (*Cricket*) a line four feet in front of the stumps parallel with the bowling crease. [imit.]

pop[2], *n.* pop music; (*coll.*) a popular piece of (usu. light) classical music. *a.* popular. **top of the pops,** (a record, singer etc.) currently (among) the most popular in terms of sales; one who or that which is currently enjoying great popularity. **pop art,** *n.* a movement of young artists in the mid-1950s and 1960s, reacting against the elitism of abstract art. Pop art used popular imagery drawn from advertising, comic strips, film, and television. It originated in the UK in 1956 with Richard Hamilton, Peter Blake (1932–), and others, and broke through in the US with the paintings of flags and numbers by Jasper Johns 1958 and Andy Warhol's first series of soup cans 1962. **pop concert,** *n.* a concert at which pop music is played. **pop festival,** *n.* **pop group,** *n.* a (usu. small) group of musicians who play pop music. **pop music,** *n.* modern popular music, post 1950, esp. as characterized by a simple, heavy rhythmic beat and electronic amplification. **pop record,** *n.* **pop singer,** *n.* **popster,** *n.* (*sl.*) one who is engaged in or interested in pop music. [short for POPULAR]

pop[3], *n.* (*coll.*) father; a familiar form of address to an old man.

pop., (*abbr.*) popular(ly); population.

Pop, *n.* **Iggy** (stage name of James Osterberg) (1947–), US rock singer and songwriter, initially known as Iggy Stooge with a seminal garage band called the Stooges (1967–74), noted for his self-destructive proto-punk performances. David Bowie contributed as producer and composer to *The Idiot* (1977), *Lust for Life* (1977), and *Blah, Blah, Blah* (1986).

popadum, POPPADOM.

pope, *n.* the bishop of Rome as the head of the Roman Catholic Church; (*fig.*) a person claiming or credited with infallibility; a priest in the Orthodox Church, esp. in Russia; a small freshwater fish, *Acerina cernua,* akin to the perch, the ruff. **pope-Joan,** *n.* a game at cards named after a legendary female pope. **pope's eye,** *n.* the gland surrounded with fat in the middle of the thigh of an ox or sheep. **pope's head,** *n.* a round broom with a long handle; a W Indian and S American cactus, *Melocactus communis.* **pope's nose** PARSON'S NOSE. **popedom,** *n.* **popeless,** *a.* †**popeling,** *n.* **popery,** *n.* (*derog.*) the religion or ecclesiastical system of the Church of Rome. **popish,** *a.* (*often derog.*) of or pertaining to the Pope; (*derog.*) pertaining to popery, papistical. **Popish Plot,** *n.* a supposed plot to murder Charles II; see under TITUS OATES. **popishly,** *adv.* [OE *pāpa* as PAPA[2]]

Pope, *n.* **Alexander** (1688–1744), English poet and satirist. He established his reputation with the precocious *Pastorals* (1709) and *Essay on Criticism* (1711), which were followed by a parody of the heroic epic *The Rape of the Lock* (1712–14), and 'Eloisa to Abelard' (1717). Other works include a highly neo-classical translation of Homer's *Iliad* and *Odyssey* (1715–26).

†**popinjay,** *n.* a parrot; a mark like a parrot set up on a pole to be shot at by archers etc.; a conceited chattering fop; (*dial.*) a woodpecker, esp. the green woodpecker. [ME *popingay,* OF *papingay* (cp. It. *papagallo,* med. L *papagallus,* med. Gr. *papagallos, papagas,* Arab. *babaghā,* prob. of imit. orig.)]

†**popjoy,** *v.i.* to enjoy or amuse oneself. [etym. doubtful]

poplar, *n.* a large tree of the genus *Populus,* of rapid growth, and having a soft, light wood. [OF *poplier* (F *peuplier,* L *pōpulus*]

poplin, *n.* a silk and worsted fabric with a ribbed surface, a cotton or other imitation of the above; (*N Am.*) broadcloth. [F *popeline,* earlier *papeline,* It. *papalina,* PAPAL, because made at Avignon]

popliteal, poplitic, *a.* pertaining to the ham or hollow behind the knee-joint. [L *popliteus,* from *poples poplitem,* ham, hough]

Popocatépetl, *n.* volcano in central Mexico, 50 km/30 miles SE of Mexico City; 5340 m/17,526 ft. It last erupted in 1920. [Aztec, smoking mountain]

Popov, *n.* **Alexander** (1859–1905), Russian physicist who devised the first aerial, in advance of Marconi (although he did not use it for radio communication), and a detector for radio waves.

poppa, *n.* (*N Am., coll.*) father. [var. of *papa*]

poppadom, -dum, *n.* a crisp, thin Indian bread, fried or roasted and served with curry. [Tamil, Malayalam, *poppatam*]

popper POP[1].

Popper, *n.* **Karl (Raimund)** (1902–), Austrian philosopher of science. His theory of falsificationism says that although scientific generalizations cannot be conclusively verified, they can be conclusively falsified by a counterinstance, and therefore science is not certain knowledge, but a series of 'conjectures and refutations', approaching, though never reaching, a definitive truth. For Popper, psychoanalysis and Marxism are unfalsifiable and therefore unscientific.

poppet, *n.* a framework bearing the hoisting-gear at a pithead; (*Naut.*) a piece of wood used for various purposes; one of the timbers on which a vessel rests in launching; a puppet, a marionette; a darling, a term of endearment. **poppet-head,** *n.* (*Mining*) a poppet; †(*Mech.*) a lathe-head. **poppet-valve,** *n.* [early form of PUPPET]

popple, *v.i.* of floating bodies or water, to bob up and down, to toss, to heave. *n.* a tossing or rippling; the sound of this. [prob. imit.]

poppy, *n.* a plant or flower of the genus *Papaver,* containing plants with large showy flowers chiefly of scarlet colour, with a milky juice having narcotic properties; (*Arch.*) a poppy-head. **opium-poppy,** *n.* the species, *P. somniferum,* from which opium is collected. **poppycock,** *n.* (*sl.*) nonsense, balderdash. **Poppy Day,** *n.* **remembrance Sunday**. **poppy-head,** *n.* the seed-capsule of a poppy; a finial of foliage or other ornamental top to ecclesiastical woodwork, esp. a bench-end. **poppied,** *a.* [OE *popig, popæg,* L *papāver*]

popsy, *n.* (*dated sl., often derog.*) an attractive young woman. [perh. from *pop,* short for POPPET]

populace, *n.* the common people; the masses. [F, from It. *popolaccio, popolazzo,* from *popolo,* L *populus,* PEOPLE]

popular, *a.* pleasing to or esteemed by the general public or a specific group or an individual; pertaining to, or carried on by, or prevailing, among the general public or the common people; suitable to or easy to be understood by ordinary people, not expensive, not abstruse, not esoteric; democratic; †courting the favour of the people; †crowded. **popular front,** *n.* a coalition of socialist and other parties in a common front against dictatorship. **popularity**, *n.* **popularize, -ise,** *v.t.* to make popular; to treat (a subject etc.) in a popular style; to spread (knowledge etc.) among the people; to extend (the suffrage etc.) to the common people. **popularization, -isation,** *n.* **popularly,** *adv.* [through OF *populeir* (F *populaire*) or directly from L *populāris,* as prec.]

populate, *v.t.* to furnish with inhabitants, to people; to form the population of, to inhabit. **population,** *n.* the inhabitants of a country etc., collectively; the number of such inhabitants; the (number of) people of a certain class and/or in a specified area; (*Statistics*) the aggregate of individuals or items from which a sample is taken; the group of organisms, or of members of a particular species, in a particular area; the act of populating. [late L *populātus,* p.p. of *populāre,* as prec.]

populin, *n.* a crystalline substance obtained from the aspen. [F *populine* (L *pōpul-us,* POPLAR, -INE)]

Populism, *n.* in US history, a late 19th-cent. political movement that developed out of farmers' protests against economic hardship. The Populist, or People's, Party was founded in 1892 and fielded several presidential candidates. It failed, however, to reverse increasing industrialization and the relative decline of agriculture in the US.

populist, *n.* a person claiming to represent the interests of the common people; a person who believes in the rights, virtues, or wisdom of the common people. **populism,** *n.* **populist, -istic**, *a.*

populous, *a.* full of people; thickly populated; †popular; †numerous. **populously,** *adv.* **populousness,** *n.* [F *populeux,* L *populōsus,* as prec.]

poral PORE[1].

porbeagle, *n.* a shark of the genus *Lamna,* a mackerel-shark. [Cornish dial., etym. unknown]

porcate, -cated, *a.* formed in ridges. [L *porca,* ridge, -ATE]

porcelain, *n.* a fine kind of earthenware, white, thin, and semi-transparent; ware made of this. *a.* pertaining to or composed of porcelain; fragile, delicate. **porcelainize, -ise,** *v.t.* **porcelainous**, **porcellaneous**, **-llanic**, **-llanous**, *a.* **porcellanite**, *n.* a rock composed of hard metamorphosed clay. [F *porcelaine,* It. *porcellana,* the sea-snail, porcelain, dim. of *porco,* L *porcus,* hog, prob. from the resemblance of the shell to a hog's back]

porch, *n.* a covered structure before or extending from the entrance to a building; a covered approach to a doorway; (*N Am.*) a verandah; †a covered walk or portico. **the Porch,** the school or philosophy of the Stoics (from the painted portico at Athens in which Zeno and his disciples held their discussions). **porched,** *a.* **porchless**, *a.* [F *porche,* L *porticum,* nom. *-cus,* PORTICO]

porcine, *a.* pertaining to or resembling a pig. [F *porcin, -cine,* L *porcīnus,* from *porcus,* hog]

porcupine, *n.* any individual of the genus *Hystrix,* rodent quadrupeds covered with erectile, quill-like spines; one of various appliances or machines armed with pins, knives, teeth etc. **porcupine-fish,** *n.* a tropical fish, *Diodon hystrix,* covered with spines. **porcupine grass,** *n.* a coarse, spiky, tussocky grass, *Triodia,* that covers many areas in Australia, also known as spinifex. **porcupinish, porcupiny,** *a.* [ME *porkepyn,* OF *porc espin,* L *porcus,* hog, *spina,* thorn, SPINE]

pore[1], *n.* a minute opening, esp. a hole in the skin for absorption, perspiration etc.; one of the stomata or other apertures in the cuticle of a plant; a minute interstice between the molecules of a body. **poral,** *a.* **poriferous**, *a.* **poriform**, *a.* **porous,** *a.* having (many) pores; permeable to liquids etc. **porosity**, *n.* **porously,** *adv.* **porousness,** *n.* **pory,** *a.* †**poriness,** *n.* [F, from L *porus,* Gr. *poros,* passage]

pore[2], *v.i.* to look with steady, continued attention and application (at); to meditate or study patiently and persistently (over, upon etc.). *v.t.* to fatigue (the eyes) by persistent reading. **porer,** *n.* [ME *pouren, pūren,* etym. doubtful]

porge, *v.t.* in the Jewish faith, to extract the sinews of (slaughtered animals) in order that they may be ceremonially clean. **porger,** *n.* [prob. var. of PURGE]

porgy, *n.* the name of a number of N American sea-fishes, including various species of *Calemus* and *Sparus*. [etym. doubtful]

Porgy and Bess, classic US folk opera (1935) by George and Ira Gershwin, based on the novel *Porgy* (1925) by DuBose Heyward, a story of the black residents of Catfish Row in Charleston, South Carolina.

Porifera, *n.pl.* the sponges; the Foraminifera. **poriferal,** *a.* **poriferan,** *n., a.* [L *porus,* PORE[1], *-fer,* bearing]

porism, *n.* a proposition dealing with the conditions rendering certain problems indeterminate or capable of innumerable solutions; a corollary. **porismatic,** **poristic, -ical**, *a.* [L and Gr., *porisma,* from *porizein,* to deduce, from *poros,* way]

pork, *n.* the flesh of pigs, esp. fresh, as food; †(*fig.*) a stupid, obstinate person. **pork-butcher,** *n.* one who kills pigs for sale. †**pork-eater,** *n.* a Christian, as distinguished from a Jew. **pork-pie,** *n.* a pie made of minced pork, usu. round with vertical sides. **pork-pie hat,** *n.* a round hat with flat crown and rolled-up brim. **porker, porklet,**, *n.* a pig raised for killing, esp. a young fattened pig. **porkling**, *n.* **porky,** *a.* like pork; (*coll.*) fat, fleshy. [F *porc,* L *porcus,* hog]

porn(o), *n.* (*coll.*) short for PORNOGRAPHY, PORNOGRAPHIC.

pornocracy, *n.* the rule or domination of harlots, as in the government of Rome during the 10th cent. [Gr. *pornē,* harlot]

pornography, *n.* the obscene and exploitive depiction of erotic acts; written, graphic etc. material consisting of or containing the above. **pornographer,** *n.* **pornographic**, *a.* **pornographically,** *adv.* [as prec.]

poro-, *comb. form.* pertaining to pores.

poromeric, *a.* permeable to water vapour, as certain synthetic leathers. *n.* a substance having this characteristic.

poroplastic, *a.* of a felt used in dressing fractures etc., both porous and plastic.

poroporo, *n.* a New Zealand shrub bearing edible fruit like plums. [Maori]

porotype, *n.* a copy made from an engraving, writing etc., by subjecting it to a gas that penetrates the paper where it is not protected by the ink.

porphyria, *n.* one of a group of inborn metabolic disorders characterized by an abnormal pigment in the urine, severe pain, photosensitivity, and periods of mental confusion. [Gr. *porphuros,* purple]

porphyrogenitism, *n.* succession to the throne of a younger son born while his father was actually monarch in preference to an older son born before his father's accession. †**porphyrogenite**, *n.* one born after his father's accession to a throne, one born in the purple; orig. one born of the imperial family of Constantinople. **porphyrogeniture**, *n.* [med. L *porphyrogenitus,* late Gr. *porphurogennētos* (*porphuros,* purple, *gennētos,* born, from *gennaein,* to beget)]

porphyry, *n.* an igneous rock consisting of a felsitic or crypto-crystalline groundmass full of feldspar or quartz crystals; a rock quarried in Egypt having a purple groundmass with enclosed crystals of feldspar. **porphyry-shell,** *n.* a shell of the genus *Murex,* esp. any species yielding a purple dye. **porphyrite**, *n.* porphyry. **porphyritic, †-ical**, *a.* **poryphyrize, -ise,** *v.t.* [through OF or L from Gr. *porphuros,* purple]

porpoise, *n.* any individual of the genus *Phocaena,* esp. *P. communis,* a gregarious delphinine cetacean, about 5 ft. (1.5 m) long, with a blunt snout. [ME *porpays,* OF *porpeis* (L *porcum,* nom. *-cus,* hog, *piscem,* nom. *-cis,* fish)]

porraceous, *a.* greenish, leek-green. [L *porrāceus,* from *porrum,* leek]

porrect, *v.t.* to stretch forth horizontally (esp. a part of the body, as the palpi of moths); (*Eccles. Law*) to tender or submit. *a.* stretched forth horizontally. [L *porrectus,* p.p. of *porrigere* (*por-,* PRO-, *regere,* to stretch, direct)]

porret, *n.* (*dial.*) a leek or small onion. [OF *poret,* L *porrum,* leek]

porridge, *n.* a soft or semi-liquid food made by boiling meal etc. in water or milk till it thickens; a broth or stew of vegetables or meal; (*sl.*) a term of imprisonment. [var. of POTTAGE]

porrigo, *n.* a skin-disease affecting the scalp. **porriginous,** *a.* [L]

porringer, *n.* a small basin or bowl out of which soup etc. is eaten by children; †a hat shaped like this. [corr. of earlier *potager,* as PORRIDGE]

Porritt, *n.* **Jonathon** (1950–), British environmental campaigner, director of Friends of the Earth from 1984. He has stood for election in both British and European elections as an Ecology (Green) Party candidate.

Porsche, *n.* **Ferdinand** (1875–1951), German car designer. Among his designs were the Volkswagen (German 'people's car'), marketed after World War II, and Porsche sports cars.

port¹, *n.* a harbour, a sheltered piece of water into which vessels can enter and remain in safety; a town or other place having a harbour, esp. where goods are imported or exported under the customs authorities. **free port** FREE. **Port Jackson shark,** a shark found off the eastern shores of Australia. **port of call,** a port at which a ship stops during a voyage; any stopping place on an itinerary. **port of entry,** an airport, harbour etc. having customs facilities through which goods or persons may enter or leave a country. **port-admiral,** *n.* the admiral commanding at a naval port. **port-bar¹,** *n.* a bar at the mouth of a harbour; a boom across a port to prevent entrance or egress. **port-charges, -dues** HARBOUR-DUES. [OE, from L *portus*]

port², *n.* a gate, an entrance, esp. to a walled town, fortress etc.; a porthole; an aperture in a wall or the side of an armoured vehicle for firing through; (*Mach.*) an opening for the passage of steam, gas, water etc; a connector on a computer into which a peripheral can be plugged. **port-bar,** *n.* a bar to secure the ports of a ship in a gale. **porthole,** *n.* (*Naut.*) an aperture in a ship's side for light, air etc., formerly for discharging guns through; a small window in the side of a ship or aircraft; (*Mach.*) a passage for steam, gas etc., in a cylinder. **port-lanyard, -rope,** *n.* a rope for drawing up a port-lid. **port-lid,** *n.* [F *porte,* L *porta*]

port³, *n.* carriage, mien, deportment; †state. *v.t.* to carry or hold (a rifle etc.) in a slanting position across the body in front. **port-crayon,** *n.* a pencil-case; a handle to hold a crayon. [F *porter,* L *portāre,* to carry]

port⁴, *n.* a fortified dessert wine (usu. dark-red or tawny) made in Portugal. [contr. from *Oporto,* in Portugal]

port⁵, *n.* the larboard or left-hand side of a ship as one looks forward. *a.* towards or on the left. *v.t.* to turn or put (the helm) to the left side of a ship. *v.i.* to turn to port (of a ship). [etym. doubtful, perh. from PORT¹]

Port., (*abbr.*) Portugal; Portuguese.

porta, *n.* the portal or aperture where veins, ducts etc. enter an organ, esp. the transverse fissure of the liver. [L, gate]

portable, *a.* capable of being easily carried, esp. about the person; not bulky or heavy; of a pension, transferable as the holder changes jobs; †endurable. *n.* a portable version of anything. **portability,** **†-ableness,** *n.* [F, from L *portābilis,* from *portāre,* to carry]

portage¹, *n.* the act of carrying, carriage; the cost of carriage; a break in a line of water-communication over which boats, goods etc. have to be carried; transportation of boats etc. over this. *v.t.* to carry over a portage. *v.i.* to make a portage. [F, from *porter,* PORT³]

†portage², *n.* an opening, a porthole. [PORT², -AGE]

Portakabin®, *n.* a portable building delivered intact to, or speedily erected on, a site as temporary offices etc.

portal¹, *n.* a door, a gate, a gateway, an entrance, esp. one of an ornamental or imposing kind. [OF, from med. L *portāle,* neut. of *portālis,* from L *porta,* gate, PORT²]

portal², *a.* of or connected with the porta. **portal vein,** *n.* the large vein conveying blood to the liver. [med. L *portālis,* see prec.]

portamento, *n.* (*pl.* **-menti**), a smooth, continuous glide from one note to another across intervening tones.

†portance, *n.* air, mien, carriage; demeanour. [F, from *porter,* to carry, see PORT³]

Port Arthur, *n.* former name (until 1905) of the port and naval base of Lushun in NE China. Scene of a naval engagement between Japan and Russia in 1904.

portative, *a.* pertaining to or capable of carrying or supporting; †portable. [F *portatif, -tive,* as prec.]

Port-au-Prince, *n.* capital and industrial port (sugar, rum, textiles, plastics) of Haiti; population (1982) 763,000.

port-crayon PORT³.

portcullis, *n.* a strong timber or iron grating, sliding in vertical grooves over a gateway, and let down to close the passage in case of assault. **portcullised,** *a.* [ME *porte-colys,* OF *porte coleïce* (*porte,* L *porta,* door, PORT², COULISSE)]

Porte, *n.* the old Imperial Turkish Government. [F *Sublime Porte,* sublime gate (see PORT²), translation of Turkish name of the chief government office, the high gate, orig. the gate of the palace where justice was administered]

porte-cochère, *n.* a carriage-entrance leading into a courtyard; a roof extending from the entrance of a building over a drive to shelter people entering or alighting from vehicles. [F (PORT², *cochère,* from *coche,* COACH)]

Port Elizabeth, *n.* industrial port (engineering, steel, food processing) in Cape province, South Africa, about 710 km/440 miles E of Cape Town on Algoa Bay; population (1980) 492,140.

portend, *v.t.* to indicate by previous signs, to presage, to foreshadow; to be an omen of. **portent,** *n.* that which portends; an omen, esp. of evil; prophetic significance; a prodigy, a marvel. **portentous,** *a.* ominous; impressive; solemn; self-consciously solemn or meaningful. **portentously,** *adv.* **portentousness,** *n.* [L *portendere* (*por-,* PRO-, *tendere,* to stretch]

porter¹, *n.* a person employed to carry loads, esp. parcels, luggage etc. at a railway station, airport or hotel, or goods in a market; a person who transports patients and does other manual labour in a hospital; a dark-brown beer made from charred or chemically-coloured malt etc. (perh. so called from having been made specially for London porters). **porter-house,** *n.* a tavern at which porter etc. is sold; an eating-house, a chop-house. **porter-house steak,** *n.* a choice cut of beef-steak next to the sirloin, and including part of the tenderloin. **porter's knot,** *n.* a pad worn on the shoulders by porters when carrying heavy loads. **porterage,** *n.* **porterly,** *a.* [ME and OF *portour* (F *porteur*), from *porter,* to carry, see PORT³]

porter², *n.* a gatekeeper, a door-keeper esp. of a large building, who usu. regulates entry and answers enquiries. **porter's lodge,** *n.* a room, apartment or house beside a door or gateway for the porter's use. **porteress, portress**, *n. fem.* [OF *portier,* L *portārtus,* from *porta,* PORT[2]]

Porter[1], *n.* **Cole (Albert)** (1892–1964), US composer and lyricist of musical comedies. His shows, many of which were made into films, include *The Gay Divorcee* (1932) and *Kiss Me Kate* (1948).

Porter[2], *n.* **Edwin Stanton** (1869–1941), US director of silent films, a pioneer of his time. His 1903 film *The Great Train Robbery* lasted 12 minutes, which for the period was extremely long, and contained an early use of the close-up. More concerned with the technical than the artistic side of his films, which include *The Teddy Bears* (1907) and *The Final Pardon* (1912), Porter abandoned film-making in 1916.

Porter[3], *n.* **Eric** (1928–), English actor. His numerous classical roles include title parts in *Uncle Vanya, Volpone*, and *King Lear*; on television he played Soames in *The Forsyte Saga*.

Porter[4], *n.* **Rodney Robert** (1917–85), British biochemist, Nobel prizewinner (with G. M. Edelmann) 1972 for pioneering work on the chemical structure of antibodies.

portfire, *n.* a slow match, formerly used for firing guns, now chiefly in mining etc. [F *porte-feu* (assim. to FIRE)]

portfolio, *n.* a portable case for holding papers, drawings etc.; a collection of such papers; the office and duties of a minister of state; the investments made, or securities held, by an investor. [It. *portafogli* (*porta,* imper. of *portare,* L *portāre,* to carry, *fogli,* leaves, from L *folium*)]

porthole PORT[2].

portico, *n.* (*pl.* **-coes, -cos**) a colonnade, a roof supported by columns; a porch with columns. [It., from L *porticus,* from *porta,* gate]

portière, *n.* a door-curtain; a portress. [F, from L *portāria*]

portion, *n.* a part; a share, a part assigned, an allotment; a helping; a wife's fortune, a dowry; the part of an estate descending to an heir; one's lot. *v.t.* to divide, to distribute; to allot, to endow. **portioner,** *n.* one who portions; (*Eccles.*) a portionist. **portionist,** *n.* at Merton College, Oxford, one of the scholars on the foundation; (*Eccles.*) a joint incumbent of a benefice. **portionless**, *a.* [F, from L *portiōnem,* nom. *-tio,* cogn. with *pars,* PART]

Portland[1], *a.* of or derived from Portland. **Portland cement,** *n.* a cement having the colour of Portland stone. **Portland stone,** *n.* a yellowish-white freestone, quarried in Portland, much used for building. [peninsula in Dorset]

Portland[2], *n.* **William Henry Cavendish Bentinck, 3rd Duke of Portland** (1738–1809), British politician, originally a Whig, who in 1783 became nominal prime minister in the Fox–North coalition government. During the French Revolution he joined the Tories, and was prime minister 1807–09.

Port Louis, *n.* capital of Mauritius, on the island's NW coast; population (1987) 139,000. Exports include sugar, textiles, watches, and electronic goods.

portly, *a.* dignified or stately in mien or appearance; stout, corpulent. **portliness,** *n.* [PORT[3], -LY]

portmanteau, *n.* (*pl.* **-teaus, -teaux**) a long leather trunk or case for carrying apparel etc., in travelling. *a.* combining several uses or qualities. **portmanteau word,** *n.* an artificial word combining two distinct words as *chortle,* from *chuckle* and *snort,* coined by Lewis Carroll. [F *portemanteau*]

Port Moresby, *n.* capital and port of Papua New Guinea on the S coast of New Guinea; population (1987) 152,000.

Porto, *n.* (English **Oporto**) industrial city (textiles, leather, pottery) in Portugal, on the Douro, 5 km/3 miles from its mouth; population (1984) 327,000. It exports port.

Pôrto Alegre, *n.* port and capital of Rio Grande do Sul state, S Brazil; population (1986) 2,705,000. It is a freshwater port for ocean-going vessels, and is Brazil's major commercial centre.

Port-of-Spain, *n.* port and capital of Trinidad and Tobago, on Trinidad; population (1988) 58,000.

Porton Down, *n.* site of the Chemical Defence Establishment (CDE) of the Ministry of Defence in Wiltshire, SW England. Its prime role is to conduct research into means of protection from chemical attack.

Porto Novo, *n.* capital of Benin, W Africa; population (1982) 208,258. It was a former Portuguese centre for the slave and tobacco trade with Brazil, and became a French protectorate 1863.

portrait, *n.* a likeness or representation of a person or animal, esp. from life; a vivid description; a type, a similitude. **portrait-gallery,** *n.* **portrait-painter, portraitist,** *n.* one whose occupation is to paint portraits. **portraiture**, *n.* a portrait; portraits collectively; the art of painting portraits; vivid description. **portray**, *v.t.* to make a portrait of; to describe; to play the role of; to present (as). **portrayal,** *n.* **portrayer,** *n.* [OF *pourtraict,* p.p. of *pourtraire,* to portray]

Port Rashid, *n.* port serving Dubai in the United Arab Emirates.

†**portreeve,** *n.* †the chief magistrate of a town or borough; now, an officer in certain towns subordinate to the mayor, a bailiff. [OE *port-gerēfa* (PORT[2], REEVE)]

portress PORTER[2].

Port Said, *n.* port in Egypt, on reclaimed land at the N end of the Suez Canal; population (1983) 364,000. During the 1967 Arab-Israel war the city was damaged and the canal was blocked; Port Said was evacuated by 1969, but by 1975 had been largely reconstructed.

Portsmouth, *n.* city and naval port in Hampshire, England, opposite the Isle of Wight; population (1981) 179,500.

Portugal, *n.* Republic of (*República Portuguesa*), country in SW Europe, on the Atlantic, bounded to the N and E by Spain. **area** 92,000 sq km/35,521 sq miles (including Azores and Madeira). **capital** Lisbon. **towns** Coimbra, ports Porto, Setúbal. **physical** mountainous in the north, plains in the south. **exports** port wine, olive oil, resin, cork, sardines, textiles, pottery, pulpwood. **population** (1989) 10,240,000; annual growth rate 0.7%. **language** Portuguese, one of the Romance languages, ultimately derived from Latin, but considerably influenced later by Arabic. **religion** Roman Catholic.

Portuguese, *a.* of or pertaining to Portugal. *n.* (*pl.* **Portuguese**) a native or inhabitant of Portugal; the Portuguese language, a member of the Romance branch of the Indo-European language family, closely related to Spanish and strongly influenced by Arabic. **Portuguese East Africa,** former name of Mozambique. **Portuguese Guinea,** former name of Guinea-Bissau. **Portuguese man-of-war,** *n.* a jellyfish of the genus *Physalia*. **Portuguese West Africa,** former name of Angola.

portulaca, *n.* a genus of low succulent herbs with flowers opening only in direct sunshine, comprising the purslane. [L]

posada, *n.* a Spanish inn. [Sp., from *posar,* to lodge]

posaune, *n.* (*Organ*) a rich and powerful reed-stop. [G, a trombone]

pose[1], *v.t.* to place, to cause to take a certain attitude; to affirm, to lay down; to put forward, to ask; to present, to be the cause of. *v.i.* to assume an attitude or character; to attempt to impress by affecting an attitude or style, to behave affectedly; to appear or set up (as). *n.* a bodily or mental attitude or position, esp. one put on for effect; (*Dominoes*) the first play. **posé**, *a.* (*Her.*) applied to a lion, horse etc., standing still, with all its feet on the ground. **poser,** *n.* one who poses; a poseur. **poseur**, *n.* an affected person. [F *poser,* L *pausāre,* to PAUSE, late L to rest, to set (conf. with *pōnere,* to put)]

pose[2], *v.t.* to puzzle, to cause to be at a loss. **poser,** *n.* one who or that which puzzles; a puzzling question or proposition. **posingly,** *adv.* [short for OPPOSE]

Poseidon, *n.* a Greek god (Roman Neptune), the brother of Zeus and Pluto. The brothers dethroned their father, Kronos, and divided his realm, Poseidon taking the sea; he was also worshipped as god of earthquakes. His son was Triton.

posh, *a.* (*coll.*) smart, elegant, fashionable; (*sometimes derog.*) genteel, upper-class. [unlikely, alas, to be an acronym for *p*ort *o*ut *s*tarboard *h*ome, the most desirable shipboard accommodation for imperial travellers to and from the Orient, more likely from obs. sl. *posh,* a dandy]

posit, *v.t.* to place, to set in position; to lay down as a fact or principle, to assume, to postulate. [L *positus,* p.p. of *pōnere,* to put]

position, *n.* a location, the place occupied by a person or thing; the place belonging or assigned to a person or thing; (*Mil.*) an occupied and defended or a defensible point or area; (*Sport*) a player's place in a team formation or usual area of operation on the field of play; a posture; arrangement, disposition; a point of view, a stance; a situation, a state of affairs; situation relative to other persons or things; social rank; an office, a post, an appointment; status, rank, condition; a principle laid down, a proposition; the act of positing. *v.t.* to place in position; to locate. **in a position to,** able to. **positional,** *a.* [L *positiōnem,* nom. *-tio,* as prec.]

positive, *a.* definitely, explicitly, or formally laid down or affirmed; explicit, express, definite; intrinsic, inherent, absolute, not relative; existing, real, actual; authoritatively laid down, prescribed by artificial enactment as distinguished from natural; incontestable, certain, undoubted; fully convinced; confident, cocksure, dogmatic; (*coll.*) downright, thorough; tending to emphasize the good or laudable aspects; constructive, helpful; (*Gram.*) simple, not comparative or superlative; (*Phil.*) practical, positivist; (*Phys.*) denoting the presence of some quality, not negative; having the same polarity as the charge of a proton; having relatively higher electrical potential; denoting the north-seeking pole of a magnet or the south pole of the earth; (*Math.*) denoting increase or progress, additive, greater than zero; (*Med.*) indicating the presence of a suspected condition or organism; (*Phot.*) exhibiting lights and shades in the same relations as in nature. *n.* that which may be affirmed; (*Gram.*) the positive degree, a positive adjective; (*Math.*) a positive quantity; a photograph in which the lights and shades are shown as in nature. **positive discrimination** DISCRIMINATION. **positive organ,** *n.* an organ used as a choir organ, orig. not portative, not carried in procession. **positive philosophy,** *n.* positivism. **positive sign,** *n.* the sign +, denoting addition. **positive vetting,** *n.* active investigation of a person's background etc. to check whether he or she is suitable for work involving national security. **positively,** *adv.* **positiveness, positivity,** *n.* **positivism,** *n.* the philosophical system of Auguste Comte (1798–1857), which recognizes only observed phenomena and rejects speculation or metaphysics; the religious system based on this, professing to be a synthesis of all human conceptions of the external order of the universe, and to secure the victory of social feeling over self-love. **positivist,** *n.* **positivistic,** *a.* [ME and F *positif,* L *positīvus* (POSIT, -IVE)]

positron, *n.* a positive electron.

posnet, *n.* a small basin or pot used for boiling. [OF *poçonet,* dim. of *poçon,* pot]

posology, *n.* the art or science treating of doses or the quantities to be administered; the science of quantity, mathematics. **posological,** *a.* [F *posologie* (Gr. *posos,* how much, -LOGY)]

posse, *n.* a body or force (of persons); a posse comitatus; (*Law*) possibility. **in posse,** within possibility, possible. **posse comitatus,** *n.* a force which the sheriff of a county is empowered to raise in case of riot etc. [L, to be able]

possess, *v.t.* to have the ownership of, to own as property, to have full power over, to control (oneself, one's mind etc.); to occupy, to dominate; to imbue, to impress (with); to acquire; to gain, to hold; to inhabit; †to attain; to accomplish. **to be possessed of,** to own. **to possess oneself of,** to acquire, to obtain as one's own. **possessed,** *a.* owned; owning; dominated (by an idea etc.); controlled (as by a devil), mad. [OF *possesser,* L *possess-,* p.p. stem of *possidēre* (*port-,* towards, *sedēre,* to sit)]

possession, *n.* the act or state of possessing; holding or occupancy as owner; the exercise of such control as attaches to ownership, actual detention, or occupancy; that which is possessed; territory, esp. a subject dependency in a foreign country; (*pl.*) property, goods, wealth; self-possession; the state of being possessed or under physical or supernatural influence; †conviction, certainty. **in possession,** in actual occupancy, possessed (of); holding, possessing; position of a bailiff in a house. **to give possession,** to put another in possession. **to take possession of,** to enter on; to seize. **writ of possession,** an order directing a sheriff to put a person in possession. †**possessionary,** *a.* **possessor,** *n.* **possessory,** *a.*

possessive, *a.* of or pertaining to possession; showing a strong urge to possess or dominate, unwilling to share, unwilling to allow another to be independent of oneself; (*Gram.*) denoting possession, genitive. *n.* the possessive case; a word in this case. **possessively,** *adv.* **possessiveness,** *n.*

posset, *n.* a drink made of hot milk curdled with ale, wine etc. †*v.t.* to curdle. [ME *possyt, poshote,* etym. doubtful]

possible, *a.* that may happen, be done, or exist; not contrary to the nature of things; feasible, practicable; having a specified potential use or quality; that may be dealt with or put up with, tolerable, reasonable. *n.* that which is possible; a possibility; (*Shooting*) the highest score that can be made. **possibilist,** *n.* a member of a political party, esp. a Spanish constitutional republican or a French Socialist, aiming only at reforms that are actually practicable. **possibility,** *n.* the state of being possible; a possible thing; a contingency; one who or that which has an outside to moderate chance of success, selection etc.; (*usu. pl.*) potential. **possibly,** *adv.* by any possible means; perhaps; by remote chance. [F, from L *possibilis* (*posse,* to be able, -BLE)]

possum, *n.* (*coll.*) an opossum. **to play possum,** to feign, to dissemble (in alln. to the opossum's feigning death on the approach of danger). [short for OPOSSUM]

post[1]**,** *n.* a piece of timber, metal etc., set upright, and intended as a support to something; a stake, a stout pole; a starting or winning post; an upright forming part of various structures, machines etc.; a pillar or vertical mass of coal or ore left as a support in a mine. *v.t.* to fix (*usu.* up) on a post or in a public place; to fasten bills etc., upon (a wall etc.); to advertise, to make known; to enter (a name) in a list posted up of defaulters etc., esp. of students failing at an examination; to publish (the name of a ship) as overdue or missing. [OE, from L *postis,* prob. rel. to *pōnere* (p.p. *positus*), to set, to fix]

post[2]**,** *n.* a fixed place, position, or station; a military station; the troops at such station; a fort; a place established for trading purposes, esp. among uncivilized peoples; a situation, an appointment; an established system of letter-conveyance and delivery; orig. one of a series of men stationed at points along a road whose duty was to ride forward to the next man with letters; a courier, a messenger; a mail-cart; a post-office; a postal letter-box; a dispatch of mails; (*collect.*) the letters, packages etc., taken from a post-office or letter-box at one time; the letters delivered at a house at one time; a relay of horses; a size of writing-paper, about $18\frac{3}{4}$ in. (47.6 cm) by $15\frac{1}{4}$ in. (38.7 cm); a bugle-call announcing the time of retiring for the night etc. *adv.* in relays of horses; express, with speed. *v.t.* to station, to place in a particular position; to transfer to another unit or location; to transmit by post; to put into a postal letter-box for transmission; to send by or as by post-horses; to send with speed; to transfer (accounts) to a ledger, to enter in this from a day-book etc.; †to postpone, to delay. *v.i.* to travel with post-horses; to travel rapidly, to hurry. **first, last post,** (*Mil.*) the first or second of two bugle-calls announcing the time for retiring for the night. **to keep someone posted,** to keep someone supplied with up-to-date information. **to post up,** to complete (a ledger) with entries of accounts from a day-book etc.; to supply with full information. **to ride post,** to ride with post-horses; hence, to ride in haste. **post-bag,** *n.* a mail-bag; mail received (esp. by a public figure, magazine, radio show etc.). **post-bill,** *n.* a post-office way-bill of letters etc., transmitted by mail. **post-boat,** *n.* a boat employed in postal work, a mail-boat, or one conveying passengers, a stage-boat. **post-boy, -rider,** *n.* a boy who carries the post; a boy who rides a post-horse, a postilion. †**post-captain,** *n.* a full naval captain, usu. of three years' standing. **postcard,** *n.* a card for sending by post unenclosed. **post-chaise,** †**-coach,** *n.* a vehicle for travelling by post. **postcode,** *n.* a code of letters and numbers denoting a particular subsection of a postal area, used to help in sorting mail. **post-free,** *a.* carried free of charge for postage. **post-haste,** *adv.* with all speed. **post-horn,** *n.* a long straight horn formerly blown to signalize the arrival of a mail-coach. **post-horse,** *n.* a horse kept as a relay at an inn etc., for post or for travellers. **post-house,** *n.* a house where post-horses were kept for relays. **postman, -woman,** *n.* one who delivers letters brought by post; †a courier or post. **postman's knock,** *n.* a children's game in which a kiss is the reward for delivering an imaginary letter. **post-mark,** *n.* a mark stamped by the post-office officials on letters etc., usu. stating place, date, and hour of dispatch, and serving to deface the postage-stamp. *v.t.* to stamp (an envelope etc.) with this. **postmaster,** *n.* the superintendent of a post-office; †one who lets out post-horses. **postmaster general,** *n.* the executive head of a national post office. **postmastership,** *n.* **postmistress,** *n. fem.* **Post Office,** *n.* the public postal authority. **post-office,** *n.* a place for the receipt and delivery of letters etc. **post-office box,** *n.* a private numbered box at a post-office in which the holder's mail is deposited awaiting collection. **post-paid,** *a.* having the postage prepaid. **post-rider** POST-BOY. **post-road,** *n.* a road on which relays of horses were available for posting. **post-town,** *n.* a town in which a head post-office is established; †a town in which post-horses were kept for travellers. **postwoman,** *n. fem.* POSTMAN. [F *poste,* It. and late L *posta,* from L *posita,* fem. p.p. of *pōnere,* to set, to place]

post-, *pref.* after; behind. [L *post*]

postage, *n.* the fee for conveyance of a letter etc. by post. **postage-stamp,** *n.* an embossed or printed stamp or an adhesive label to indicate that postage has been paid.

postal, *a.* pertaining to the mail service; carried on by post. **postal code** POSTCODE under POST[2]. **postal order,** *n.* an order for a sum of money (specified on the document) issued at one post-office for payment at another. **postal vote,** *n.* a vote submitted by post.

post-boy etc. POST[2].

post-classical, *a.* later than the classical writers, artists etc., esp. those of Greece and Rome.

post-communion, *n.* that part of the eucharistic service which follows after the act of communion.

post-costal, *a.* behind a rib.

post-date, *v.t.* to assign or mark with a date later than the actual one. *n.* a date later than the actual one.

postdiluvial, *a.* being or happening after the Flood. **postdiluvian,** *n., a.*

post-doctoral, *a.* pertaining to studies, research etc. carried out after obtaining a doctorate.

poste-haste etc. POST[2].

post-entry, *n.* an additional or subsequent entry; a late entry (for a race etc.).

poster[1], *n.* a large placard or advertising bill; one who posts this. **poster paint, colour,** *n.* an opaque, gum-based watercolour paint.

†**poster**[2], *n.* one who travels post; a courier, a messenger; a post-horse; one who posts a letter.

poste restante, *n.* a department in a post-office where letters are kept until called for. [F, remaining post]

posterior, *a.* coming or happening after; later; hinder. *n.* the buttocks. **posteriority,** *n.* **posteriorly,** *adv.* [L, comp. of *posterus,* from *post,* after]

posterity, *n.* those proceeding in the future from any person, descendants; succeeding generations. [F *postérité,* L *posteritātem*]

postern, *n.* a small doorway or gateway at the side or back; a private entrance, esp. to a castle, town etc.; a way of escape. [OF *posterne, posterle* (F *poterne*), late L *posterula*]

poster paint POSTER[1].

post-exilian, -exilic, *a.* later than the Babylonian exile.

post-feminist, *a.* occurring after the rise of the feminist movement.

post-fix, *v.t.* to append (a letter etc.) at the end of a word. *n.*, a suffix.

post-glacial, *a.* later than glacial.

postgraduate, *a.* carried on or awarded after graduation; working for a postgraduate qualification. *n.* a graduate who pursues a further course of study.

posthumous, *a.* born after the death of the father; happening after one's decease; published after the death of the author or composer. **posthumously,** *adv.* [L *postumus,* superl. of *post,* after (late L *posthumus,* as if *post humum,* after the ground)]

posthypnotic suggestion, *n.* giving instructions to a hypnotic subject which the latter will act on after emerging from the trance.

postiche, *a.* artificial, superadded (applied to superfluous ornament). *n.* an imitation, a sham; a hairpiece. [F, from It. *posticcio,* from L *postus, positus,* p.p. of *pōnere,* to place]

posticous, *a.* (*Bot.*) on the hinder side; turned away from the axis, extrorse. [L *postīcus,* from *post,* after, behind]

†**postil,** *n.* a marginal note in a Bible; hence, any explanatory note, esp. one in the margin; a commentary; a homily on the Gospel or Epistle for the day. *v.i.* to write comments. *v.t.* to write marginal notes on. †**postillate,** *v.i., v.t.* †**postillation,** *n.* †**postillator,** †**postiller,** *n.* [ME and F *postille,* med. L *postilla* (prob. *post illa,* after these)]

postilion, postillion, *n.* one who rides on the near horse of the leaders or of a pair drawing a carriage. [F *postillon,* from *posta,* POST[2]]

post-impressionism, *n.* the doctrines and methods of a school of (esp. French) painters of the late 19th cent. who rejected the naturalism and momentary effects of impression in favour of a use of pure colour for more formal or subjective ends. **post-impressionist,** *n., a.*

postliminy, *n.* (*Rom. Law*) the right of resumption of former rights and privileges by an exile or captive returning to his own country; (*Inter. Law*) the right of restoration of things taken in war to their former civil status or ownership on their coming back into the power of the nation to which they belonged. [L *postliminium* (*limen liminis,* threshold)]

postlude, *n.* (*Mus.*) a closing piece or voluntary.

postman, -mark, -master etc. POST[2].

postmeridian, *a.* of or belonging to the afternoon; late. **post meridiem,** after midday (applied to the hours from noon to midnight, usu. abbr. *p.m.).* [L *postmeridiānus*]

post-millennial, *a.* of to a period after the millennium. **post-millennialism,** *n.* the doctrine that the second advent of Christ will follow the millennium. **post-millennialist,** *n.*

postmodernism, *n.* a late 20th-cent. movement in the arts which rejects the preoccupation of modernism with form and technique rather than content. In the visual arts, and in architecture, it uses an amalgam of styles from the past, such as the classical and the baroque, whose slightly off-key familiarity has a more immediate appeal than the austerities of modernism. **post-modernist,** *n., a.*

post-mortem, *adv.* after death. *a.* made or occurring after death. *n.* an examination of a dead body; a subsequent analysis or review, esp. after defeat or failure. [L, after death]

post-nasal, *a.* behind the nose.

post-natal, *a.* happening after birth.
post-nuptial, *a.* after marriage.
post-obit, *a.* taking effect after death; post-mortem. *n.* a bond securing payment of a sum of money to a lender on the death of a specified person from whose estate the borrower has expectations. [L *post obitum* (*post,* after, *obitus,* decease, from *obīre,* to die)]
post-office etc. POST².
post-operative, *a.* pertaining to the period just after a surgical operation.
post-oral, *a.* behind the mouth.
post-orbital, *a.* behind the orbit of the eye.
post-partum, *a., adv.* after childbirth.
post-Pliocene, *a.* (*Geol.*) pertaining to the formation immediately above the Pliocene.
postpone, *v.t.* to put off, to defer, to delay; to regard as of minor importance to something else. *v.i.* (*Path.*) to be late in recurring. **postponement,** *n.* **postponer,** *n.* [L *postpōnere* (*pōnere,* to put)]
postposition, *n.* the act of placing after; the state of being placed after or behind; a word or particle placed after a word, esp. an enclitic. **postpositional,** *a.* **postpositive,** *a.* (*Gram.*) placed after something else. *n.* a postpositive word or particle.
postprandial, *a.* after dinner.
post-rider, post-road POST².
postscenium, *n.* (*Class. Ant.*) the back part of a theatre behind the scenes. [L *postscaenium* (*scaena,* Gr. *skēnē,* stage, SCENE)]
postscript, *n.* a paragraph added to a letter after the writer's signature; any supplement added on to the end of a book, document, talk etc.; (later) additional information. **postscriptal,** *a.* [L *postscriptum,* (*scriptum,* neut. p.p. of *scrībere,* to write)]
post-Tertiary, *a.* pertaining to formations later than the Tertiary.
postulant, *n.* a candidate for entry into a religious order or for an eccelesiastical office; one who demands.
postulate¹, *n.* a position assumed without proof as being self-evident; a fundamental assumption; a necessary condition, an indispensable preliminary; a statement of the possibility of a simple operation such as a geometrical construction. [L *postulatum,* neut. p.p. of *postulāre,* to demand]
postulate², *v.t.* to demand, to claim; to assume without proof, to take as self-evident; to stipulate; (*Eccles. Law*) to nominate subject to sanction by superior authority. **postulation,** *n.* **postulator,** *n.* †**postulatory,** *a.*
posture, *n.* a pose, attitude or arrangement of the parts of the body; the manner of holding the body; a mental attitude; situation, condition, state (of affairs etc.); †situation, location. *v.t.* to arrange the body and limbs of in a particular posture. *v.i.* to assume a posture, to pose; to endeavour to look or sound impressive. **postural,** *a.* **posturer,** *n.* [F, from L *positūra,* from *posit,* p.p. stem of *pōnere,* to put]
post-viral syndrome, *n.* a medical condition occurring after a viral infection, characterized by fatigue, muscular pain, depression etc.
posy, *n.* a motto or short inscription, esp. in a ring; orig. one in verse; a bunch of flowers, a nosegay. [contr. of POESY]
pot, *n.* a round vessel of earthenware or metal, usu. deep relatively to breadth, for holding liquids etc.; a vessel of this kind used for cooking; a large drinking-cup of earthenware, pewter etc.; the quantity this holds; (*loosely*) a quart (0.95 l); a vessel used for various domestic or industrial purposes; a chamber-pot, a coffee-pot, a flower-pot, a teapot etc.; a chimney-pot; a wicker trap for catching lobsters etc.; (*Racing etc.*) a cup offered as a prize; (*often pl., coll.*) a large sum; a heavy sum staked on a horse etc.; the money or stakes in the pool in gambling games; a potbelly; (*sl.*) marijuana. *v.t.* (*past, p.p.* **potted**) to put into a pot or pots; to plant in pots; to season and preserve in pots etc.; (*Billiards*) to pocket; (*coll.*) to bring down, esp. with a pot-shot; to bag, to secure; to sit (a young child) on a potty; to shape clay as a potter. *v.i.* (*coll.*) to shoot (at). **big pot** BIG¹. **to go to pot,** (*sl.*) to be ruined or done for, to degenerate. **to keep the pot boiling** KEEP¹. **pot-ale,** *n.* fermented grain as refuse from a distillery. **potbelly,** *n.* a protuberant belly; a pot-bellied person. **potbellied,** *a.* **pot-boiler,** *n.* a work of art or literature produced merely for money; one who produces this. **pot-bound,** *a.* of a plant, filling the pot with its roots, not having room to grow. **pot-boy, -man,** *n.* one employed in a public-house to clean pots etc. **pot-companion,** *n.* a companion in drinking. **pot-hanger,** †**-hangle,** *n.* a pot-hook. **pot-herb,** *n.* a culinary herb. **pothole,** *n.* a cauldron-shaped cavity in the rocky bed of a stream; a pit-like cavity in mountain limestone etc., usu. produced by a combination of faulting and water-action; a cavity in a roadway caused by wear or weathering. **potholer,** *n.* **potholing,** *n.* the exploration of underground caverns as a sport. **pot-hook,** *n.* an S-shaped hook for suspending a pot or kettle over a fire; a letter like a pot-hook, esp. in clumsy handwriting. **pot-house,** *n.* a low public-house. **pot-hunter,** *n.* one who kills game, fish etc., for food or profit rather than sport; one who competes merely to win prizes. **pot-hunting,** *n.* **pot-lead,** *n.* blacklead, esp. as used on the hulls of racing yachts to reduce friction. **pot-lid,** *n.* **pot-luck,** *n.* whatever food may be available without special preparation; whatever luck or chance may offer. **pot-man** POT-BOY. **pot-metal,** *n.* a cheap alloy of copper and lead used for making pots; stained glass coloured throughout while in a state of fusion. **pot-roast,** *n.* a piece of meat stewed in a closed receptacle. **pot-shot,** *n.* a shot at game etc. that happens to be within easy range; a random shot; a shot for filling the pot, esp. one of an unsportsmanlike kind. **potstone,** *n.* a granular variety of steatite; a large mass of flint found in chalk. **pot-valiant,** *a.* made courageous by drink. †**pot-walloper** *n.* a man having a parliamentary vote because he had boiled his pot; at his own fireside, a qualification in some English boroughs previous to 1832. **potful,** *n.* **potted,** *a.* put in a pot; preserved in the form of a paste; condensed, abridged; of music, recorded for reproduction by gramophone etc.; (*coll.*) drunk. [OE *pott* (cp. Dut. *pot,* G *Pott,* Icel. *pottr,* F *pot*), perh. cogn. with L *pōtus,* drunk, Gr. *potos,* a drinking]
potable, *a.* drinkable. *n.* (*usu. pl.*) anything drinkable. **potableness,** *n.* [F, from late L *pōtābilis,* from L *pōtāre,* to drink]
potage, *n.* thick soup. [F]
potamic, *a.* of or pertaining to rivers. **potamology,** *n.* [Gr. *potamos,* river]
potash, †**potass,** *n.* a powerful alkali, consisting of potassium carbonate in a crude form, orig. obtained from the ashes of plants; caustic potash; potassium or a potassium compound. **potash-water,** *n.* an artificial mineral water containing bicarbonate of potash and charged with carbon dioxide. [POT, ASH¹ (perh. after Dut. *potasch*)]
potassa, *n.* potassium monoxide.
potassium, *n.* a bluish or pinkish white metallic element, at. no. 19; chem. symbol K. **potassium hydroxide** CAUSTIC POTASH under CAUSTIC. **potassic,** *a.*
potation, *n.* the act of drinking; a draught; a beverage; (*usu. pl.*) tippling. †**potator,** *n.* **potatory,** *a.* [ME and OF *potacion,* L *pōtātiōnem,* nom. *-tio,* from *pōtāre,* to drink]
potato, *n.* (*pl.* **-toes**) a plant, *Solanum tuberosum,* with edible farinaceous tubers; a tuber of this. **hot potato,** a controversial issue, something difficult or dangerous to deal with. **small potatoes,** (*sl.*) something very inferior and contemptible. **to drop like a hot potato,** to cease to have anything to do with (a person or subject which suddenly becomes risky or controversial). **potato-beetle, -bug,** *n.* the Colorado beetle. **potato-bogle,** *n.* (*Sc.*) a scarecrow. **potato-box, -trap,** *n.* (*sl.*) the mouth. **potato chip,** *n.* a long slice of potato fried in deep fat; (*N Am., S Afr.*) potato crisp. **potato crisp,** *n.* a flake of potato thus fried. **potato fern,** *n.* (*Austral.*) a fern with edible tubers, also called the na-

tive potato. **potato-ring,** *n.* a ring or hoop formerly used, esp. in Ireland, for standing dishes on. [Sp. *patata,* Haitian *batata*]

poteen, *n.* Irish whiskey illicitly distilled. [Ir. *poitin,* dim. of *poite,* POT]

Potemkin, *n.* **Grigory Aleksandrovich, Prince Potemkin** (1739–91), Russian politician. He entered the army and attracted the notice of Catherine II, whose friendship he kept throughout his life. He was an active administrator who reformed the army, built the Black Sea Fleet, conquered the Crimea, developed S Russia, and founded the Kherson arsenal 1788 (the first Russian naval base on the Black Sea).

potence[1], *n.* (*Her.*) a cross with ends resembling the head of a crutch or a T; (*Eng.*) a T-shaped framework; (*Watchmaking*) a stud or support for a bearing, esp. the lower pivot of a verge; †a cross or gibbet. **potent**[1], *n.* †a support, a crutch; (*Her.*) having the arms (of a cross) terminating in cross-pieces or crutch-heads. **potented, potentée,** *a.* (*Her.*) [F, a crutch, as foll.]

potent[2], *a.* powerful, mighty; having great force or influence; cogent; strong, intoxicating; of a male, capable of having sexual intercourse. †*n.* a potentate. **potency, potence**[2], *n.* **potently,** *adv.* †**potentness,** *n.* **potentate,** *n.* one who possesses great power; a monarch, a ruler. **potential,** *a.* of energy, existing but not in action, latent; existing in possibility not in actuality; (*Gram.*) expressing possibility; †having force or power, potent. *n.* anything that may be possible; a possibility; as yet undeveloped value, resources or ability; (*Gram.*) the potential mood; the voltage of a point above zero or earth; the work done in transferring a unit (of mass, electricity etc.) from infinity to a given point. **potential difference,** *n.* the work required to move an electrical charge between two points, measured in volts. **potential energy,** *n.* energy possessed by a body as a result of its position. **potential function,** *n.* (*Math.*) a quantity by the differentiation of which the value of the force at any point in space arising from any system of bodies can be obtained. **potentiality,** *n.* **potentialize, -ise,** *v.t.* to transform into a potential condition. **potentially,** *adv.* **potentiate,** *v.t.* esp. of drugs, to make potent; to make more effective. **potentiation,** *n.* **potentiator,** *n.* **potentiometer,** *n.* an instrument for measuring electromotive force or potential difference. [L *potens -ntem,* pres.p. of *posse,* to be able]

Potentilla, *n.* a genus of Rosaceae, comprising the cinquefoil, tormentil etc. [med. L, dim. from L *potens -ntem,* POTENT]

pother, *n.* bustle, confusion; †a cloud of dust or smoke. *v.i.* to make a bustle or stir; to make a fuss. *v.t.* to harass. [etym. doubtful]

pothole, pot-hook, pot-hunter etc. POT.

potichomania, *n.* a craze for coating glass-ware with varnished paper etc., to intimate painted ware or china. [F *potichomaine* (*potiche,* an Oriental pot or vase)]

potin, *n.* a composition of copper, lead, tin, and silver, of which Roman coins were made; pot-metal. [F, from POT]

potion, *n.* a drink, a draught; a liquid mixture intended as a medicine, poison, or a magic charm. †*v.t.* to drug. [ME and OF *pocion,* L *pōtiōnem,* nom. *-tio,* from *pōtus,* drunk]

potlatch, *n.* a ceremonial feast of Indians of the northwestern US involving emulation in the giving of extravagant gifts. [Chinook]

potoroo, *n.* (*pl.* **-roos**) the marsupial kangaroo-rat. [Austral. Abor.]

potpourri, *n.* a mixture of dried flower-petals and spices, usu. kept in a bowl for perfuming a room; a literary miscellany, a musical medley etc. [F, rotten pot]

Potsdam Conference, *n.* a conference held at Potsdam, E Germany, in July 1945 between representatives of the US, the UK, and the USSR. They established the political and economic principles governing the treatment of Germany in the initial period of Allied control at the end of World War II, and sent an ultimatum to Japan demanding unconditional surrender on pain of utter destruction.

potsherd, *n.* a broken piece of earthenware. [POT, SHERD]

pott, *n.* a size of printing or writing paper, usu. $15\frac{1}{2} \times 12\frac{1}{2}$ in. (39.3×31.75 cm). **pott-folio, pott-octavo, pott-quarto,** *n.* sizes of books. [POT]

pottage, *n.* a kind of soup; porridge. [F *potage* (POT, -AGE)]

potter[1], *n.* a maker of pottery. **potter's asthma, bronchitis, consumption,** *n.* an acute form of bronchitis caused by dust in pottery-manufacture. **potter's clay,** *n.* a tenacious clay containing kaolin, used for pottery. **potter's field,** *n.* (*N Am.*) a public burying-place for the poor or strangers. **potter's lathe,** *n.* a machine for moulding clay. **potter's wheel,** *n.* a horizontal wheel used in this. **pottern,** *a.* pertaining to potters or pottery. **pottern-ore,** *n.* an ore vitrifying with heat, used by potters to glaze their ware. **pottery** *n.* earthenware; a place where this is manufactured, a potter's workshop; the making of earthenware. [late OE *pottere* (POT, -ER)]

potter[2], *v.i.* to busy oneself in a desultory but generally agreeable way; to proceed in a leisurely and often random fashion. *v.t.* to waste or pass (time away) in a desultory way. [perh. freq. of obs. *pote,* OE *potian,* to prod, to push, etym. doubtful]

Potter[1], *n.* **Beatrix** (1866–1943), English writer and illustrator of children's books, beginning with *Peter Rabbit* (1900); her diaries, written in a secret code, were translated and published in 1966. Her Lake District home is a museum.

Potter[2], *n.* **Paulus** (1625–54), Dutch painter, active in Delft, The Hague, and Amsterdam. He is known for paintings of animals, such as *The Young Bull* (1647; Mauritshuis, The Hague).

Potteries, the, *n.pl.* the centre of the china and earthenware industry in England, lying in the upper Trent basin of N Staffordshire. Wedgwood and Minton are factory names associated with the Potteries, which cover the area around Stoke-on-Trent, and include the formerly separate towns of Burslem, Hanley, Longton, Fenton, and Tunstall.

pottery POTTER[1].

pottle, *n.* a liquid measure of 4 pt. (2.3 l); a large tankard; a vessel or basket for holding fruit. †**pottle-deep,** *adv.* to the bottom of the tankard. **pottle-pot,** *n.* a 4 pt. (2.3 l) pot or tankard. [ME and OF *potel,* dim. of POT)]

potto, *n.* (*pl.* **-ttos**) a W African lemuroid, *Perodicticus potto.* [W African]

potty[1], *a.* insignificant; crazy, foolish. [etym. doubtful]

potty[2], *n.* (*coll.*) a chamber pot, esp. one for use by small children.

pouch, *n.* a small bag; a purse, a detachable pocket; a leather bag for holding cartridges etc.; the bag-like part in which marsupials carry their young; a pouch-like sac in plants. *v.t.* to put into a pouch; to pocket; to cause (a bodice etc.) to hang like a pouch; to swallow; (*fig.*) to put up with; (*sl.*) to supply the pocket of, to tip. *v.i.* of a dress, to hang like a pouch. **pouched, pouchy,** *a.* [ME and ONorth.F *pouche,* OF *poche,* POKE[1]]

†**pou-de-soy** PADUASOY.

poudrette, *n.* a dry manure made of night-soil with charcoal, gypsum etc. [F, dim of *poudre,* POWDER]

pouf[1], **pouffe,** *n.* a part of a woman's dress gathered into a kind of knot or bunch; a mode of dressing women's hair fashionable in the 18th cent.; a large, solid cushion used as a seat. [F]

pouf[2] **pouffe** POUF[1] POOF.

Poujadist, *n., a.* a follower of, or characteristic of this champion of the small man and tax reduction. [Pierre *Poujade,* F politician]

Poulenc, *n.* **Francis (Jean Marcel)** (1899–1963), French composer and pianist. A self-taught composer of witty and irreverent music, he was a member of the group of French composers known as Les Six. Among his many works are the operas *Les Mamelles de Tirésias* (1947), and *Dialogues des Carmélites* (1957), and the ballet *Les Biches* (1923).

poulpe, *n.* an octopus or cuttle-fish, esp. *Octopus vulgaris*. [F, POLYPUS]

Poulsen, *n.* **Valdemar** (1869–1942), Danish engineer who in 1900 was the first to demonstrate that sound could be recorded magnetically – originally on a moving steel wire or tape; this was the forerunner of the tape recorder.

poult, *n.* a young pullet, partridge, turkey etc. **poulterer, †poulter,** *n.* one who deals in poultry for the table. **poultry,** *n.* domestic fowls, including barn-door fowls, geese, ducks, turkeys etc. **poultry-house, poultry-yard,** *n.* [F *poulet,* dim. of *poule,* see PULLET]

poultice, *n.* a usu. heated, soft composition, as of bread, meal etc., for applying to sores or inflamed parts of the body to reduce inflammation, a cataplasm. *v.t.* to apply a poultice to. [L *puls pultis,* PULSE[2]]

pounamu, *n.* nephrite, green-stone. [Maori]

pounce[1], *n.* the claw of a bird of prey; a pouncing, an abrupt swoop, spring etc. *v.i.* to sweep down or spring upon and seize prey with the claws; to sieze (upon), to dart or dash (upon) suddenly; to speak abruptly. †*v.t.* to seize in the claws; to perforate. **†pounced,** *a.* (*Her.*) furnished with claws. [etym. doubtful, perh. rel. to PUNCH, and PUNCHEON[1]]

pounce[2], *n.* a fine powder formerly used to dry up ink on manuscript; a powder used for sprinkling over a perforated pattern in order to transfer the design. *v.t.* to smooth with pounce or pumice; to mark out (a pattern) by means of pounce. **pounce-box,** *n.* a box out of which pounce is sprinkled. **pouncet-box,** *n.* a box with a perforated lid for holding perfumes. [F *ponce,* L *pūmicem,* nom. *pūmex,* PUMICE]

pound[1], *n.* an avoirdupois unit of weight divided into 16 ounces and equal to approx. 0.454 kg; a troy unit of weight divided into 12 ounces and equal to approx. 0.373 kg; the basic monetary unit of the UK, divided into 100 (new) pence (formerly 20 shillings); the standard monetary unit of various other countries. *v.t.* to test the weight of (coins). **pound of flesh,** the exact amount owing to one, esp. when recovering it involves one's debtor in considerable suffering or trouble. **pound-cake,** *n.* a rich sweet cake, from the ingredients being pound for pound of each. **pound-foolish,** *a.* neglecting the care of large sums, esp. through trying to make small economies. **pound Scots,** *n.* (*Hist.*) 1s. 8d. **poundage[1],** *n.* an allowance, fee, commission etc., of so much in the pound; a percentage of the aggregate earnings of an industrial concern paid as or added to wages; a payment or charge per pound weight; the charge on a postal order; (*Eng. Hist.*) a subsidy to the Crown raised by an impost on each pound exported or imported. †*v.t.* to impose poundage on. **pounder,** *n.* (*usu. in comb.*) a gun firing a shot of a specified number of pounds weight; a person worth or possessing a specified sum in pounds sterling; something weighing a pound, or a specified number of pounds, as a fish. [OE *pund* (cp. Dut. *pond,* G *Pfund*), L *pondo,* rel. to *pendere,* to weigh, *pendēre,* to hang]

pound[2], *n.* an enclosure for confining stray cattle etc.; an enclosure, a pen; a trap, a prison; a place whence there is no escape, esp. in hunting; a pond, a part between locks on a canal. *v.t.* to confine in or as in a pound; (*usu. in p.p.*) to shut in, to enclose in front and behind. **pound-keeper,** *n.* **pound-net,** *n.* a series of nets, set in shoal water, to form a trap. **poundage[2],** *n.* confinement in a pound; a charge upon cattle impounded. [OE *pund,* enclosure]

pound[3], *v.t.* to crush, to pulverize, to comminute; to beat, to strike heavily; to thump, to pommel. *v.i.* to strike heavy blows, to hammer (at, upon etc.); to fire heavy shot (at); to walk or go heavily along. **pounder,** *n.* one who or that which pounds, esp. a pestle. [OE *pūnian*]

Pound, *n.* **Ezra** (1885–1972), US poet, who lived in London from 1908. His verse *Personae* and *Exultations* (1909) established the principles of the imagist movement. His largest modern work was the series of *Cantos* (1925–1969) (intended to number 100), which attempted a massive reappraisal of history.

poundage POUND[1], POUND[2].

pounder POUND[1], POUND[3].

pour, *v.t.* to cause (liquids etc.) to flow; to discharge, to emit copiously; to send (forth or out) in a stream; or great numbers; to shed freely; to utter, to give vent to. *v.i.* to flow in a stream of rain, to fall copiously; to rush in great numbers; to come in a constant stream. *n.* a heavy fall, a downpour; the amount of molten material poured at one time. **to pour oil on troubled waters,** to exercise a soothing, calming or conciliatory influence. **pourer,** *n.* [ME *pouren,* etym. doubtful]

pourboire, *n.* a gratuity, a tip. [F, for drinking]

pour-parler, *n.* a preliminary discussion with a view to formal negotiation. [F, to discuss (*pour,* for, before, *parler,* to speak)]

poussette, *v.i.* to swing partners with hands joined as in a country dance. *n.* this figure. [F, dim. of *pousse,* PUSH]

Poussin, *n.* **Nicolas** (1594–1665), French painter, active chiefly in Rome; court painter to Louis XIII 1640–43. He was one of France's foremost landscape painters in the 17th cent. He painted mythological and literary scenes in a strongly classical style, for example *Rape of the Sabine Women* (about 1636–37; Metropolitan Museum of Art, New York).

pout[1], *n.* one of various fishes that have a pouting appearance (see EEL-POUT, WHITING-POUT). [OE *-pūta,* in *æle-pūtan,* eel-pouts (cp. Dut. *puit,* G. *-putte*), cogn. with foll.]

pout[2], *v.i.* to thrust out the lips in sullenness, displeasure, or contempt; of lips, to be protruded or prominent. *v.t.* to thrust out. *n.* a protrusion of the lips; a fit of sullenness. **in the pouts,** sullen. **pouter,** *n.* one who pouts; a variety of pigeon, from its way of inflating its crop. **poutingly,** *adv.* [ME *pouten* (cp. Swed. *puta,* pad, Dan. *pude,* pillow)]

poverty, *n.* the state of being poor; want, destitution, indigence; scarcity, meagreness, dearth (of); deficiency (in); inferiority. **poverty-stricken,** *a.* poor; inferior, mean. **poverty trap,** *n.* a situation in which any increase in one's earned income is immediately offset by a decrease in one's entitlement to state benefit, thus making it impossible to raise one's standard of living. [ME and OF *poverte,* L *paupertātem,* nom. *-tas,* from PAUPER]

POW, (*abbr.*) prisoner of war.

pow, *int.* an exclamation imitating the sound of an impact, blow etc.

powan, *n.* a freshwater fish, *Coregonus clupeoides,* found in Loch Lomond etc. [Sc. POLLAN]

powder, *n.* any dry comminuted substance or fine particles; dust; a cosmetic in the form of fine dust; a medicine in the form of powder; gun-powder. *v.t.* to reduce to powder; to put powder on; to sprinkle or cover with powder; to sprinkle with fine spots or figures for decoration. *v.i.* to become powder or like powder; to powder one's hair. **powder-blue,** *n.* pulverized smalt, esp. for use in a laundry; the colour of this. *a.* having the colour of smalt. **powder-box,** *n.* a box for cosmetic powder etc. **powder-cart,** *n.* a cart for conveying ammunition for artillery. **powder-closet,** *n.* a small room where women's hair used to be powdered. **powder-down,** *n.* a peculiar kind of down-feathers disintegrating into fine powder, occurring in definite patches on herons etc. **powder-flask, -horn,** *n.* a case or horn fitted to hold gunpowder. **powder keg,** *n.* a small barrel to hold gunpowder; a potentially explosive place or situation. **powder-magazine,** *n.* a storing-place for gunpowder. **powder-mill,** *n.* works in which gunpowder is made. **powder-monkey,** *n.* (*Naut.*) a boy formerly employed to bring powder from the magazine to the guns. **powder-puff,** *n.* a soft pad or brush for applying powder to the skin. **powder-room,** *n.* the apartment in a ship where gunpowder is kept; (*coll.*) a ladies' cloakroom. **powdering-tub,** *n.* a tub in which meat is salted or pickled; (*Shak.*) †a tub in which an infected lecher was sweated. **powderiness,** *n.* **powdery,** *a.* [F *poudre,* OF *poldre, polre,* L *pulver*]

Powell[1], *n.* **Anthony (Dymoke)** (1905–), English novelist, who wrote the monumental series of 12 volumes *A Dance to the Music of Time* (1951–75), which begins shortly after World War I and chronicles a period of 50 years in the lives of Nicholas Jenkins and his circle of upper-class friends.

Powell[2], *n.* **Cecil Frank** (1903–69), English physicist, awarded a Nobel prize in 1950 for his use of photographic emulsion as a method of tracking charged nuclear particles.

Powell[3], *n.* **(John) Enoch** (1912–), British Conservative politician. He was minister of health 1960–63, and contested the party leadership in 1965. In 1968 he made a speech against immigration that led to his dismissal from the shadow cabinet. He resigned from the party in 1974, and was Official Unionist Party member for South Down, Northern Ireland 1974–87.

Powell[4], *n.* **Michael** (1905–90), English film director, who collaborated with screenwriter Emeric Pressburger (1902–88). Their work, often criticized for extravagance, is richly imaginative, and includes the films *A Matter of Life and Death* (1946), and *Black Narcissus* (1947).

Powell[5], *n.* **William** (1892–1984), US film actor who co-starred with Myrna Loy in the *Thin Man* series of films (1934–1947). He also played leading roles in *My Man Godfrey* (1936), *Life with Father* (1947), and *Mister Roberts* (1955). He retired 1955.

power, *n.* ability to do or act so as to effect something; a mental or bodily faculty, or potential capacity; strength, force, energy, esp. as actually exerted; influence, dominion, authority (over); right or ability to control; legal authority or authorization; political ascendancy; a person or body invested with authority; a state having influence on other states; (*coll.*) a great deal; the product obtained by multiplication of a quantity or number into itself; the index showing the number of times a factor is multiplied by itself; mechanical energy as distinguished from hand labour; electricity; the capacity (of a machine etc.) for performing mechanical work; the rate at which energy is emitted or transferred, esp. the rate of doing work, measured in watts (joules per second), foot-pounds per second, or ergs per second; the magnifying capacity of a lens etc.; †the sixth order of angels; †a naval or military force; †a supernatural being having sway over some part of creation, a deity. *a.* concerned with power; worked by mechanical power; involving a high degree of physical strength or skill. *v.t.* to supply with esp. motive power. *v.t.*, *v.i.* (*coll.*) to (cause to) move with great force or speed. **in power,** in office. **in someone's power,** within the limits of a person's capabilities or authority; under someone's control, at someone's mercy. **more power to your elbow,** (*coll.*) a way of showing one's approval of someone's efforts by urging that person to continue and even intensify them. **power behind the throne,** a person with no official position in government who exercises a strong personal influence on a ruler. **power of attorney** ATTORNEY[2]. **the powers that be,** (*often facet.*) established authority. **power amplifier,** *n.* a low-frequency amplifier for powerful loudspeakers. **powerboat,** *n.* a boat propelled by a motor, esp. a speedboat. **power component,** *n.* that part of an alternating current which is in phase with the voltage. **power cut,** *n.* an interruption or reduction in the supply of electricity. **power dive,** *n.* (*Aviat.*) a steep dive under engine power. **power-dive,** *v.i.* **power drill, lathe, loom etc.,** *n.* a drill, lathe, loom etc. worked by mechanical or electrical power. **power factor,** *n.* that fraction which is less than unity by which the produce of amperes and volts in an alternating-current circuit has to be multiplied in order to estimate the true power. **powerhouse,** *n.* a power station; (*coll.*) a very forceful and dynamic person or thing. **power pack,** *n.* a unit for converting a power supply to the voltage required by an electronic circuit. **power plant,** *n.* a power station; the machinery etc. used to generate power; the engine and related parts which power a car, aircraft etc. **power point,** *n.* an electrical socket by which an appliance can be connected to the mains. **power politics,** *n.* diplomacy backed by armed force or the threat of it. **power-rail,** *n.* an insulated rail conveying current to the motors on electric railways of certain kinds. **power-station,** *n.* a building for the generation of power, esp. electrical power. **power steering,** *n.* a system in which the torque applied to a vehicle's steering wheel is augmented by engine power. **power transmission,** *n.* the transmission of electrical power from the generating system to the point of application. **powerful,** *a.* having great strength or energy; mighty, potent; impressing the mind, forcible, efficacious; producing great effects; (*coll.*) great, numerous, extreme. **powerfully,** *adv.* **powerfulness,** *n.* **powerless,** *a.* **powerlessly,** *adv.* **powerlessness,** *n.* [ME and OF *poër* (F *pouvoir*), late L *potēre,* from L *pot-*, stem of *posse,* to be able]

powwow, *n.* a N American Indian medicine-man or wizard; magic rites for the cure of diseases; a meeting, talk or conference. *v.i.* to practise sorcery, esp. for healing the sick; to hold a powwow; (*N Am.*) to talk about, to discuss. *v.t.* to treat with sorcery, esp. with a view to healing. [N Am. Ind.]

Powys[1], *n.* county in central Wales. **area** 5080 sq km/1961 sq miles. **towns** administrative headquarters Llandrindod Wells. **products** agriculture, dairy cattle, sheep. **population** (1987) 113,000. **language** 20% Welsh, English.

Powys[2], *n.* **John Cowper** (1872–1963), English novelist. His mystic and erotic books include *Wolf Solent* (1929) and *A Glastonbury Romance* (1933). He was one of three brothers (**Theodore Francis Powys** (1875–1953) and **Llewelyn Powys** (1884–1939)), all writers.

pox, *n.* any disease characterized by the formation of pustules; syphilis; †smallpox; †a mild imprecation. **poxy,** *a.* syphilitic; (*sl.*) bloody. [pl. of POCK]

Poznań, *n.* (German **Posen**) industrial city (machinery, aircraft, beer) in W Poland; population (1985) 553,000. Settled by German immigrants in 1253, it passed to Prussia in 1793, but was restored to Poland in 1919.

Pozsgay, *n.* **Imre** (1933–), Hungarian socialist politician, presidential candidate for the Hungarian Socialist Party from 1989. Influential in the democratization of Hungary 1988–89, he was rejected by the electorate in the parliamentary elections of Mar. 1990, coming a poor third in his constituency.

pozzolana, pozzuolana, *n.* a volcanic ash used in hydraulic cements. [It., from *Pozzuoli,* near Naples]

p&p, (*abbr.*) postage and packing.

PP, (*abbr.*) Parish Priest; past President.

pp, (*abbr.*) pages; for and on behalf of, by proxy; pianissimo. [L *per procurationem*]

p.p., (*abbr.*) past participle.

ppd, (*abbr.*) post-paid; prepaid.

PPE, (*abbr.*) Philosophy, Politics and Economics.

PPS, (*abbr.*) Parliamentary Private Secretary; further postscript. [L *post-postscriptum*].

PQ, (*abbr.*) Parti Québecois; Province of Quebec.

PR, (*abbr.*) proportional representation; public relations; Puerto Rico.

Pr[1], (*chem. symbol*) praseodymium.

Pr[2], (*abbr.*) priest; prince.

pr, (*abbr.*) pair; present; price.

praam, PRAM[1].

prabble, *n.* a squabble, a quarrel. *v.i.* to chatter. [var. of BRABBLE]

†practic, *a.* practical; practised, skilful, cunning, treacherous. *n.* practice; (*usu. pl.*) a deed, a doing, a practice; deceit, a trick, a deception. [OF *practique* (F *pratique*), late L *practicus,* Gr. *praktikos,* from *prassein,* to do]

practicable, *a.* capable of being done, feasible; of roads etc., usable, passable; of stage properties, functioning, real, not simulated; (*sl.*) easily taken in, gullible. **practicability, -ableness,** *n.* **practicably,** *adv.* [F *practicable,* from *practiquer,* to PRACTISE, assim. to foll.]

practical, *a.* of, pertaining to, or governed by practice; derived from practice, experienced; capable of being used, available, serving, or suitable for use; pertaining to action not theory or speculation; realistic, down-to-earth; such in effect, virtual. **practical joke,** *n.* a joke or trick entailing some action and intended to make the victim look foolish. **practicality**, †**practicalness,** *n.* **practically,** *adv.* in a practical manner; virtually, in effect, as regards results.

practice[1], *n.* habitual or customary action or procedure; habit, custom; the continued or systematic exercise of any profession, art, craft etc.; business, professional connection; actual performance, doing or execution, as opposed to theory or intention; conduct, dealings; regular, repeated exercise in order to gain proficiency in something; a rule for multiplying quantities of various denominations; legal procedure, the rules governing this; (*usu. pl.*) †scheming, artifice, contrivance; †skill, dexterity acquired by experience. **in practice,** in the sphere of action; in training, in condition for working, acting, playing etc., effectively. **out of practice,** out of training. **practician**, *n.* one who works or practises, a practitioner. [prob. from PRACTISE]

practice[2] PRACTISE.

practise, (*esp. N Am.*) **practice**, *v.t.* to do or perform habitually; to carry out; (to exercise a profession etc.); to exercise oneself in or on; to instruct, to exercise, to drill (in a subject, art etc.); to accustom; †to plot, to scheme. *v.i.* to exercise oneself; to exercise a profession or art; to do a thing or perform an act habitually; †to scheme, to plot, to use stratagems; to use influence, to impose (upon). **practisant,** *n.* an agent, a plotter. **practised,** *a.* **practiser,** *n.* [OF *practiser* (F *pratiquer*), med. L *practicāre,* from *practicus*]

practitioner, *n.* one who regularly practices any profession, esp. of medicine; †a plotter. **general practitioner,** one practising both medicine and surgery; a physician not a specialist.

prad, *n.* a horse. [sl., from Dut. *paard*]

prae-, *pref.* pre. [L *prae,* before]

praecipe, *n.* a writ requiring something to be done, or a reason for its non-performance. [L, imper. of *praecipere,* to enjoin; *capere,* to take]

praecocial, PRECOCIAL.

praecognitum, *n.* (*pl.* **-nita**) something known before, esp. a science or branch of knowledge necessary in order to understand something else. [L (*cognitum,* p.p. of *cognoscere,* to know)]

praecordia, *n.pl.* the chest and the parts it contains, the region about the heart. [L (*cor cordis,* heart)]

praemunire, *n.* (*Law*) a writ or process against a person charged with obeying or maintaining the papal authority in England; an offence against the Statute of Praemunire (1393) on which this is based; the penalty incurred by it. [L, to defend, conf. with *praemonēre,* to forewarn (PRAE-, *monēre,* to warn)]

praenomen, PRENOMEN.

praesidium, PRESIDIUM.

praetexta, *n.* (*Rom. Ant.*) a long white Roman toga or robe with a purple border. [L *toga praetexta,* bordered toga (PRAE-, *texta,* from p.p. of *texere,* to weave)]

praetor, (*esp. N Am.*) **pretor**, *n.* (*Rom. Hist.*) a Roman magistrate; orig. a consul as leader of the army; later a curule magistrate elected yearly to perform various judicial and consular duties. **praetorial**, *a.* **praetorian,** *a.* of or pertaining to a praetor; pertaining to the body-guard of a Roman general or emperor, esp. the imperial body-guard established by Augustus. *n.* a soldier in this body-guard; a man of praetorian rank. **praetorian gate,** *n.* the gate of a Roman camp in front of the general's quarters towards the enemy. **praetorium**, *n.* the general's tent or official quarters in a Roman camp; a Roman governor's official residence or court. [L, for *praeitor,* from *praeīre* (PRAE-, *īre,* to go)]

pragmatic, *a.* pertaining to the affairs of a state; concerned with the causes and effects and the practical lessons of history; concerned with practicalities or expediency rather than principles; pragmatical. *n.* one busy in affairs; a busybody; a sovereign decree. **pragmatic sanction,** *n.* ordinance made by a sovereign and constituting a fundamental law, esp. that of the Emperor Charles VI settling the succession to the throne of Austria. **pragmatical,** *a.* busy, diligent, officious, given to interfering in the affairs of others; dogmatic; relating to pragmatism; pragmatic. **pragmaticality**, **pragmaticalness,** *n.* **pragmatically,** *adv.* **pragmatism**, *n.* pragmaticalness, officiousness; treatment of things, esp. in history, with regard to causes and effects; a practical approach to problems and affairs; (*Phil.*) the doctrine that our only test of the truth of human cognitions or philosophical principles is their practical results. **pragmatist,** *n.* **pragmatistic**, *a.* **pragmatize, -ise,** *v.t.* to represent (an imaginary thing) as real. [F *pragmatique,* L *pragmaticus,* Gr. *pragmatikos,* from *pragma pragmatos,* deed, from *prassein,* to do]

Prague, *n.* (Czech **Praha**) city and capital of Czechoslovakia on the river Vltava; population (1985) 1,190,000. Industries include cars and aircraft, chemicals, paper and printing, clothing, brewing, and food processing. It became capital in 1918.

Praia, *n.* port and capital of the Republic of Cape Verde, on the island of São Tiago (Santiago); population (1980) 37,500. Industries include fishing and shipping.

prairie, *n.* an extensive tract of level or rolling grassland, usu. destitute of trees, esp. in the western US. **prairie-chicken, -hen,** *n.* a N American grouse, *Tetrao cupido*. **prairie-dog,** *n.* a small rodent of the genus *Cynomys,* esp. *C. ludovicianus,* living in large communities on the prairies. **prairie oyster,** *n.* a pick-me-up of egg, Worcester Sauce etc. **prairie-schooner,** *n.* (*N Am.*) an emigrants' name for the covered wagons used in crossing the western plains. **prairie-squirrel,** *n.* a N American ground-squirrel of the genus *Spermophilus*. **prairie value,** *n.* the value of land before labour has been expended on it. **prairie-wolf,** *n.* the coyote, *Canis latrans*. [F, through a pop. L *prātāria,* from L *prātum,* meadow]

praise, *v.t.* to express approval and commendation of, to applaud; to extol, to glorify. *n.* praising, approbation, encomium; glorifying, extolling; an object of praise. **praisable,** *a.* **praiser,** *n.* **praiseful,** *a.* laudable, commendable. **praisefulness,** *n.* **praiseless**, *a.* **praiseworthy,** *a.* deserving of praise; laudable, commendable. **praiseworthily,** *adv.* **praiseworthiness,** *n.* [ME *preiser,* OF *preisier,* late L *pretiāre,* from L.*pretium,* price, value, cp. PRICE]

Prakrit, *n.* a general name for any of the ancient Indo-European dialects of N India, contrasted with the sacred classical language Sanskrit. The Prakrits are considered to be the ancestors of such modern N Indian languages as Hindi, Punjabi, and Bengali. [Sansk. *prākrta,* natural, vulgar]

praline, *n.* a confection of almond or other nut with a brown coating of sugar. [F]

pram[1], *n.* a flat-bottomed barge or lighter used in Holland and the Baltic; a similar boat formerly used as a floating battery. [Dut.]

pram[2], *n.* a usu. four-wheeled carriage for a baby, with a box-like body in which the child can lie down.

prance, *v.i.* to spring or caper on the hind legs, as a horse in high mettle; to walk or strut in a pompous or swaggering style. *n.* the act of prancing. **prancer,** *n.* [etym. doubtful, perh. rel. to PRANK[2]]

prandial, *a.* (*facet.*) relating to dinner. [L *prandium,* breakfast]

prang, *v.t.* (*sl.*) to bomb heavily; to strike; to crash. *n.* a bombing raid; a crash. [onomat.]

prank[1], *v.t.* to dress up in a showy fashion; to deck (out); to adorn (with). *v.i.* to make a show. [ME *pranken,* cp. G *prangen,* to make a show, Dut. *pronken,* G *prunken,* to make a show of; also Eng. PRINK]

prank[2], *n.* a wild frolic; a trick, a playful act, a practical joke; a gambol, a capricious action. **prankful, prank-**

ish, pranky, *a.* **prankishness,** *n.* [etym. unknown]
Prasad, *n.* **Rajendra** (1884–1963), Bihari lawyer, politician, and follower of Mohandas Gandhi in Bihar. Prior to World War II, he succeeded Subhas Chandra Bose as national president of the Indian National Congress. He went on to become India's first president after independence.
prase, *n.* a dull leek-green translucent quartz. **prasinous,** †**prasine**, *a.* of a light-green colour. [F, from L *prasius,* Gr. *prasios*]
praseodymium, *n.* a rare metallic element, at. no. 59; chem. symbol Pr, occurring in certain rare-earth minerals. [Gr. *prasinos,* leek-green]
prat, *n.* a stupid or contemptible person. [perh. from *prat,* (*sl.*) buttocks]
prate, *v.i.* to chatter; to talk much and without purpose or reason; to babble, to cackle. *v.t.* to utter foolishly; to boast idly about. *n.* idle or silly talk; unmeaning loquacity. **prater,** *n.* **prating,** *n., a.* **pratingly,** *adv.* [ME *praten,* cp. Dut. *praten,* Dan. *prate,* Swed. *prata*]
pratfall, *n.* (*esp. N Am.*) a fall on one's buttocks; a humiliating blunder or mishap. [*prat,* buttocks, FALL]
pratique, *n.* licence to a ship to hold communication with a port after quarantine, or upon certification that the vessel has not come from an infected place. [F, PRACTICE[1]]
prattle, *v.i.* to talk in a childish or foolish manner. *v.t.* to utter or divulge thus. *n.* childish or idle talk; a babbling sound, as of running water. **prattler,** *n.* [freq. of PRATE]
Pravda, *n.* the official newspaper of the Central Committee of the Communist Party in the USSR. [Rus., truth]
pravity, *n.* depravity; corruption. [L *prāvitas,* from *prāvus,* perverse, bad]
prawn, *n.* a small crustacean, *Palaemon serratus,* like a large shrimp. [ME *prane, prayne,* etym. doubtful]
praxinoscope, *n.* an optical toy in which successive positions of moving figures are blended in a rotating cylinder etc., so as to give reflections in a series of mirrors as of objects in motion. [F PRAXIS, -SCOPE]
praxis, *n.* use, practice, application as distinguished from theory; (*Gram.*) a collection of examples for practice. [Gr., rel. to *prassein,* to do]
Praxiteles, *n.* (mid-4th cent. BC), Greek sculptor, active in Athens. His *Aphrodite of Knidos* (about 350 BC), known through Roman copies, is thought to have initiated the tradition of life-size freestanding female nudes in Greek sculpture.
pray, *v.t.* to ask for with earnestness or submission; to beseech, to entreat, to supplicate; to petition for, to beg; to address devoutly and earnestly. *v.i.* to address God with adoration or earnest entreaty; to make supplication, to beseech or petition (for). *int.* (*often iron.*) may I ask, I ask you. **prayer[1]**, *n.* one who prays. **praying mantis** MANTIS. **prayingly,** *adv.* [OF *preier* (F *prier*), late L *precāre,* L *precārī,* from *prex precis,* prayer]
prayer[2], *n.* the act of praying; a solemn petition addressed to God or any object of worship; the practice of praying, a formula for praying; a prescribed formula of divine worship; a liturgy; (*often pl.*) a religious service; an entreaty; a memorial or petition; that part of a petition which specifies the thing desired; a petition to the Queen to annul an Order in Council. **not to have a prayer,** (*coll.*) to have not the slightest chance or hope. **prayer-book,** *n.* a book containing prayers and forms of devotion, esp. the Anglican Book of Common Prayer. **prayer-meeting,** *n.* a meeting for divine worship in which prayer is offered by several persons. **prayer rug,** *n.* a small carpet on which a Muslim kneels and prostrates himself while praying. **prayer-wheel, praying-machine,** *n.* a revolving wheel or cylinder on which written prayers are inscribed or fastened by Tibetan Buddhists. **prayerful,** *a.* given to prayer; devotional, devout. **prayerfully,** *adv.* **prayerfulness,** *n.* **prayerless**, *a.* **prayerlessly,** *adv.* [ME and OF *preiere,* med. L *precāria,* as PRECARIOUS]
PRB, (*abbr.*) Pre-Raphaelite Brotherhood.
pre, *prep.* (*coll.*) before.
pre-, *pref.* before, earlier than; in advance; in front of, anterior to; surpassingly. [OF and med. L *pre-,* L PRAE-, before]
preach, *v.i.* to deliver a sermon or public discourse on some religious subject; to give earnest religious or moral advice, esp. in an obtrusive or persistent way. *v.t.* to proclaim, to expound in a common or public discourse; to deliver (a sermon); to teach or advocate in this manner. *n.* (*coll.*) a preaching, a sermon. **to preach down,** to denounce or disparage by preaching; to preach against. **preachable,** *a.* **preacher,** *n.* **preachership,** *n.* **preachify,** *v.i.* to hold forth in a sermon, esp. tediously; to sermonize. **preachification,** *n.* **preachment,** *n.* (*usu. derog.*) a discourse or sermon. **preachy,** *a.* fond of preaching or sermonizing, disposed to preach. **preachiness,** *n.* [OF *prechier,* L *praedicāre* (PRAE-, *dicāre,* to proclaim, rel. to *dīcere,* to say)]
preacquaint, *v.t.* to acquaint beforehand. **preacquaintance,** *n.*
pre-Adamite, *n.* an inhabitant of this world before Adam; one who holds that there were persons in existence before Adam. *a.* existing before Adam; pertaining to the pre-Adamites. **pre-Adamic, pre-Adamitic**, *a.*
preamble, *n.* an introductory statement, esp. the introductory portion of a statute setting forth succinctly its reasons and intentions; a preliminary event, fact etc. *v.i.* to make a preamble. **preambulary,,** *a.* **preambulate,** *v.i.* to make a preamble. †**preambulation,** *n.* **preambulatory,** *a.* [OF *preambule,* med. L *praeambulum,* from L *praeambulus,* going before (PRAE-, *ambulāre,* to walk)]
preamplifier, *n.* an amplifier used to boost a low-level signal and often to equalize it before feeding it to the main amplifier.
preapprehension, *n.* a preconceived opinion; a foreboding.
prearrange, *v.t.* to arrange in advance. **prearranged,** *a.* **prearrangement,** *n.*
preaudience, *n.* (*Law*) the right of being heard before another, precedence at the bar.
prebend, *n.* the stipend or maintenance granted to a canon of a cathedral or collegiate church out of its revenue; the land or tithe yielding this; a prebendary; a prebendaryship. **prebendal,** *a.* **prebendal stall, prebendary stall,** *n.* a prebendary's stall in a cathedral or his benefice. **prebendary,** *n.* the holder of a prebend. **prebendaryship,** *n.* [OF *prebende,* med. L *praebenda,* payment, pension, orig. neut. pl. ger. of L *praebēre,* to grant (PRAE-, *habēre,* to have)]
prec., (*abbr.*) preceding.
Precambrian, *n., a.* (of or pertaining to) the earliest geological era, the time from the formation of Earth (4.6 billion years ago) up to 590 million years ago. Its boundary with the succeeding Cambrian period marks the time when animals first developed exoskeletons and so left abundant fossil remains. It comprises about 85% of geological time and is divided into two periods: the Archaean and the Proterozoic.
precancel, *v.t.* to cancel (a postage stamp) before use.
precarious, *a.* depending on the will or pleasure of another; held by a doubtful tenure; not well-established, insecure, unstable; doubtful, dependent on chance, uncertain, hazardous. **precariously,** *adv.* **precariousness,** *n.* [L *precārius,* obtained by prayer, from *precārī,* to PRAY]
precast, *a.* of concrete blocks, panels etc., cast before being put in position.
precative, *a.* (*Gram.*) expressing a wish or entreaty. **precatory,** *a.* of the nature of or expressing a wish or recommendation. [late L *precativus, precatorius,* from *precatus,* p.p. of *precārī*]
precaution, *n.* previous caution, prudent foresight; a measure taken beforehand to guard against or bring about something. *v.t.* to caution or warn beforehand. **precautionary,** †**-cautional,** *a.* **precautiously,** *adv.* [F *précaution,* med. L *praecautiōnem,* nom. *-tio,* from

L *praecavēre* (PRAE-, *cavēre,* to beware)]

precede, *v.t.* to go before in time, order, rank or importance; to walk in front of; to exist before; to cause to come before, to preface or prelude. *v.i.* to go or come before; to have precedence. **precedence, †-ency**, *n.* the act or state of preceding; priority; superiority; the right to a higher position or a place in advance of others at public ceremonies, social functions etc. **precedent,** *n.* something done or said which may serve as an example to be followed in a similar case, esp. a legal decision, usage etc.; a necessary antecedent. *a.* going before in time, order, rank etc.; antecedent. **precedented,** *a.* having or warranted by a precedent. **precedential,** *a.* **precedently,** *adv.* **preceding,** *a.* going before in time, order etc; previous; immediately before. [F *précéder,* L *praecēdere* (PRAE-, *cēdere,* to go)]

precentor, *n.* a cleric who directs choral services in a cathedral; a person who leads the singing of choir or congregation; in pre-Reformation cathedrals, a member of the chapter ranking next below the dean; in those of new foundation, a minor canon or chaplain; in Presbyterian churches, the leader of the psalmody. **precent,** *v.i.* to act as precentor. *v.t.* to lead the singing of (psalms etc.). **precentorship,** *n.* **presentress**, **precentrix,** *n. fem.* [late L *praecentor* (PRAE-, *cantor,* from *cantāre,* freq. of *canere,* to sing)]

precept, *n.* a command, a mandate; an injunction respecting conduct; a maxim; a writ, a warrant; a sheriff's order to hold an election; an order for the levying or collection of a rate. **preceptive**, **†preceptial**, **preceptual**, *a.* of the nature of a precept; containing or giving moral instruction; didactic. **preceptor,**, *n.* a teacher, an instructor; the head of a preceptory among the Knights Templars. **†preceptorial**, *a.* **preceptorship,** *n.* **preceptory**, *n.* a subordinate house or community of the Knights Templars; the estate, manor etc., pertaining to this. *†a.* preceptive. **preceptress**, *n. fem.* [OF (F *précepte*), L *praeceptum,* neut. p.p. of *praecipere* (PRAE-, *capere,* to take)]

preces, *n.pl.* the short petitions said alternately by the minister and the congregation. [L, pl. of *prex precis,* prayer]

precession, *n.* precedence in time or order. **precession of the equinoxes,** (*Astron.*) a slow but continual shifting of the equinoctial points from east to west, occasioned by the earth's axis slowly revolving in a small circle about the pole of the ecliptic, causing an earlier occurrence of the equinoxes in successive sidereal years. **precessional,** *a.* [late L *praecessio,* from *praecēdere,* to PRECEDE]

pre-Christian, *a.* of or pertaining to the times before Christ or before Christianity.

precinct, *n.* the space enclosed by the walls or boundaries of a place, esp. a church; a boundary, a limit; a pedestrianized area of a town set aside for a particular activity, usu. shopping; (*N Am.*) a municipal police district; (*N Am.*) a polling district; (*pl.*) the environs or immediate surroundings (of). [med. L *praecinctum,* orig. neut. p.p. of L *praecingere* (PRAE-, *cingere,* to gird)]

precious, *a.* of great price or value; very costly; highly esteemed, dear, beloved; affected, over-refined in manner, style, workmanship etc.; (*iron.*) worthless, rascally. *adv.* very, extremely. **preciosity**, *n.* overfastidiousness or affected delicacy in the use of language, in workmanship etc. **precious metals,** *n.pl.* gold, silver, and (sometimes) platinum. **precious stone,** *n.* a gem. **preciously,** *adv.* **preciousness,** *n.* [OF *precios* (F *précieux*), L *pretiōsus,* from *pretium,* PRICE]

precipice, *n.* a vertical or very steep cliff; the edge of a cliff, hence a situation of extreme danger. [F *précipice,* L *praecipitium,* a falling headlong, precipice, from *praeceps,* headlong (PRAE-, *caput,* head)]

precipitate, *v.t.* to throw headlong; to urge on with eager haste or violence; to hasten; to bring on, esp. prematurely; (*Chem.*) to cause (a substance) to be deposited at the bottom of a vessel, as from a solution; to cause (moisture) to condense and be deposited, as from vapour; to cause to fall as rain, snow etc. *v.i.* of a substance in solution, to fall to the bottom of a vessel; of vapour, to condense and be deposited in drops; to fall as rain, snow etc. *a.*, headlong; flowing or rushing with haste and violence; hasty, rash, inconsiderate; adopted without due deliberation. *n.* a solid substance deposited from a state of solution. **†red precipitate,** red oxide of mercury. **white precipitate,** ammoniated chloride of mercury. **precipitable,** *a.* capable of being precipitated, as a substance in solution. **precipitability,** *n.* **precipitant,** *a.* falling or rushing headlong; headlong, precipitate. *n.* any substance that, being added to a solution, causes precipitation. **†precipitantly, precipitately,** *adv.* **precipitance, -ancy, precipitateness,** *n.* **precipitation,** *n.* the act of precipitating, the state of being precipitated; violent speed; rash haste; (the amount of) rain, snow, sleet etc. **precipitator,** *n.* [L *praecipitātus,* p.p. of *praecipitāre*]

precipitous, *a.* like or of the nature of a precipice, very steep; †headlong, precipitate, hasty, rash. **precipitously,** *adv.* **precipitousness,** *n.* [MF *precipiteux,* as PRECIPICE]

précis, *n.* an abstract, a summary; the act or practice of drawing up such abstracts. *v.t.* to make a précis of. [F, as foll.]

precise, *a.* definite, sharply defined or stated; accurate, exact; strictly observant of rule, punctilious, over-nice, over-scrupulous; particular, identical. **precisely,** *adv.* in a precise manner; exactly, quite so. **preciseness,** *n.* **precisian**, *n.* a punctilious person; one rigidly observant of rules etc., a formalist, a stickler. *a.* precise, punctilious; formal. **precisianism,** *n.* **precision**, *n.* accuracy, exactness. *a.* characterized by great accuracy in execution; intended for very accurate measurement or operation. **precisionist,** *n.* **precisionize, -ise,** *v.t.* **precisive,** *a.* [F *précis, -ise,* L *praecīsus,* p.p. of *praecīdere* (PRAE-, *caedere,* to cut)]

preclude, *v.t.* to shut out, to exclude; to hinder, to prevent; to render inoperative; to neutralize. **preclusion**, *n.* **preclusive**, *a.* **preclusively,** *adv.* [L *praeclūdere* (PRAE-, *claudere,* to shut), *p.p. praeclūsus*]

precocial, *a.* (having young which are) hatched with a complete covering of down and capable of leaving the nest within a very short time. **precocious,** *a.* developing or ripe before the normal time; prematurely developed intellectually; characteristic of such development; forward, pert. **precociously,** *adv.* **precociousness, precosity**, *n.* [L *praecox -cōcis,* from *praecoquere* (PRAE-, *coquere,* to COOK[1])]

precognition, *n.* foreknowledge; clairvoyance; (*Sc. Law*) preliminary examination of witnesses with a view to determining whether there is ground for a prosecution. **precognosce**, *v.t.* [late L *praecognitio,* from *praecognoscere* (PRAE-, *cognoscere,* to COGNOSCE]

preconceive, *v.t.* to conceive or form an opinion of beforehand. **preconceit**, **preconception,** *n.*

preconcert, *v.t.* to contrive or agree on by previous arrangement. *n.*, an arrangement previously made. **preconcertedly,** *adv.* **preconcertedness,** *n.*

precondition, *n.* a necessary preliminary condition. *v.t.* to prepare beforehand, to put into a desired condition or frame of mind beforehand.

preconize, -ise, *v.t.* to proclaim publicly; to cite or summon publicly; of the Pope to confirm publicly (an appointment or one nominated). **preconization, -isation,** *n.* [med. L *praecōnīzāre,* from *praeco -cōnis,* herald]

pre-Conquest, *n.* before the time of the Norman Conquest (1066).

preconscious, *a.* pertaining to a state antecedent to consciousness.

precontract, *n.* a previous contract. *v.i., v.t.*, to contract beforehand.

precook, *v.t.* to cook beforehand.

precordia, PRAECORDIA.

precostal, *a.* in front of the ribs.

precourse, *v.t.* to run before, to herald. [L *praecursus,* p.p. of *praecurrere* (*currere,* to run)]

precritical, *a.* preceding the critical treatment of a subject, esp. preceding the critical philosophy of Kant.

precurrent, *a.* occurring beforehand, precursory. †**precurrer,** *n.* †**precurse,** *n.* a forerunning, a heralding. **precursive,** *a.* precursory. **precursor,** *n.* a forerunner, a harbinger; one who or that which precedes the approach of anything, esp. John the Baptist; a predecessor in office etc. **precursory,** *a.* preceding and indicating as a forerunner or harbinger; preliminary, introductory. [L *praecurrens -ntens,* pres.p. *praecursus,* p.p., of *praecurrere* (PRAE-, *currere,* to run)]

pred., (*abbr.*) predicate.

predaceous, -acious, *a.* living by prey, predatory; pertaining to animals living by prey. **predacean,** *n.* **predacity,** *n.* †**predal,** *a.* practising plunder; predatory. **predation,** *n.* the way of life of a predator, the relationship between a predator and its prey; depredation. **predator,** *n.* a predatory animal. **predatory,** *a.* habitually hunting and killing other animals for food; living by plunder; pertaining to or characterized by plunder or pillage; rapacious, exploitive. [from L *praeda,* booty]

pre-Darwinian, *a.* preceding the doctrines of evolution etc. propounded by Charles Darwin in 1859.

predate, *v.t.* to antedate.

predecease, *n.* the death of a person before some other. *v.t.* to die before (a particular person).

predecessor, *n.* one who precedes another in any position, office etc.; a thing preceding another thing; a forefather, an ancestor. [F *prédécesseur,* late L *praedēcessor* (PRAE-, *dēcessor,* from *dēcēdere,* to go away, see DECEASE]

†**predeclare,** *v.t.* to declare beforehand.

predefine, *v.t.* to define, limit or settle beforehand. **predefinition,** *n.*

predella, *n.* (*pl.* **predelle**) the platform on which an altar stands or the highest of a series of altar-steps; a painting on the face of this; a painting on a step- or shelf-like appendage, usu. at the back of the altar, a gradine. [It., stool, dim. prob. from OHG *Pret,* board]

predesignate, *v.t.* to designate or indicate beforehand; (*Log.*) to designate by a sign or word denoting quantity, as *only, sole, some; a.* (*Log.*) having such a sign prefixed. **predesignation,** *n.*

predestinate, *v.t.* to predestine. *a.*, ordained or appointed beforehand. **predestinarian,** *a.* pertaining to predestination. *n.* a believer in predestination. **predestination,** *n.* the act of predestining, esp. the act of God in foreordaining some to salvation and some to perdition. **predestinator,** *n.* **predestine,** *v.t.* to appoint beforehand by irreversible decree; to preordain (to salvation, to do a certain deed etc.); to predetermine. †**predestiny,** *n.* [L *praedestinātus* p.p. of *praedestināre* (PRAE-, *destināre,* to DESTINE)]

predetermine, *v.t.* to determine or settle beforehand; to foreordain; to predestine. *v.i.* to determine beforehand. **predeterminable,** *a.* **predeterminate,** *a.* **predetermination,** *n.* [late L *praedetermināre*]

predial, *a.* consisting of lands or farms; attached to lands or farms; arising from or produced by land. [F *prédial,* med. L *praediālis,* from L *praedium,* farm]

predicable, *a.* capable of being predicated or affirmed of something. *n.* anything that may be predicated of something; (*Log.*) one of Aristotle's five classes of predicates–genus, species, difference, property, accident. **predicability,** *n.* [F *prédicable,* L *praedicābilis,* from *praedicāre,* to PREDICATE]

predicament, *n.* that which is predicted, a category; a particular state, condition or position, esp. a critical or unpleasant one. **predicamental,** *a.* [late L *praedicāmentum,* as prec.]

predicant, *n.* a preaching friar, esp. a Dominican; a predikant. *a.* engaged in preaching. [L *praedicans -ntem,* pres.p. of *praedicāre,* see foll.]

predicate, *v.t.* to affirm, to assert as a property etc; (*Log.*) to assert about the subject of a proposition; (*N Am.*) to found, to base (an argument etc. on). *v.i.* to make an affirmation. *n.*, (*Log.*) that which is predicated, that which is affirmed or denied of the subject; (*Gram.*) the entire statement made about the subject, including the copula as well as the logical predicate; an inherent quality. **predication,** *n.* **predicative,** *a.* **predicatively,** *adv.* [L *praedicātus,* p.p. of *praedicāre* (PRAE-, *dicāre,* to proclaim), see PREACH]

predicatory, *a.* of or pertaining to a preacher or to preaching. [late L *praedicātōrius,* from *praedicātor,* a proclaimer, a preacher, as prec.]

predict, *v.t.* to forecast; to foretell, to prophesy. †*n.* a prediction. †*a.* predicted. **predictable,** *a.* able to be forecast or foretold; (occurring or apt to behave in a manner which is) easily foreseen. **predictability,** *n.* **prediction,** *n.* **predictive,** *a.* **predictively,** *adv.* **predictor,** *n.* one who predicts; a range-finding and radar device for anti-aircraft use. [L *praedictus,* p.p. of *praedīcere* (PRAE-, *dīcere,* to say)]

predigest, *v.t.* to digest partially before introducing into the stomach; to render more easily digestible. **predigested,** *a.* **predigestion,** *n.*

predikant, *n.* a minister of the Dutch Reformed Church, esp. in S Africa. [Dut., as PREDICANT]

predilection, *n.* a prepossession in favour of something, a preference, a partiality. [F *prédilection* (L *dīlectio,* from *dīligere,* see DILIGENT)]

predispose, *v.t.* to dispose or incline beforehand; to make susceptible or liable to. **predisponent,** *n.*, *a.* **predisposition,** *n.* [F *prédisposer*]

predominate, *v.i.* to be superior in strength, influence or authority; to prevail, to have the ascendancy (over); to have control (over); to preponderate. †*v.t.* to dominate over. **predominance, -ancy,** *n.* **predominant,** *a.* predominating (over); superior, overruling, controlling. **predominantly,** *adv.* **predominatingly,** *adv.* †**predomination** *n.* [through F *prédominer*]

pre-eclampsia, *n.* a serious toxic condition occurring in late pregnancy, characterized by high blood pressure and oedema.

pre-elect, *v.t.* to elect beforehand. †*a.* chosen beforehand or in preference to others. **pre-election,** *n.* previous election. *a.* occurring or done before an election.

pre-embryo, *n.* the developing embryo during the first 14 days after fertilization of the ovum.

pre-eminent, *a.* eminent beyond others; superior to or surpassing all others, paramount, outstanding. **pre-eminence,** *n.* **pre-eminently,** *adv.* [F *prééminent,* L *praeēminentem,* nom. *-ens,* pres.p. of *praeēminēre* (PRAE-, *ēminēre,* see EMINENT)]

pre-empt, *v.t.* to secure by pre-emption; to seize on to the exclusion of others; to act before another (in order to thwart), to anticipate. *v.i.* (*Bridge*) to make a pre-emptive bid. **pre-emption,** *n.* the act or right of buying before others; a government's right to seize the property of subjects of another state while in transit, esp. in wartime; anticipating, forestalling. **pre-emptive,** *a.* **pre-emptive bid,** *n.* (Bridge) an unusually high bid intended to shut out opposition. **pre-emptive strike,** *n.* an attack on enemy installations intended to forestall a suspected attack on oneself.

preen[1], *v.t.*, *v.i.* to clean and arrange (feathers) using the beak; to take great trouble with, or an excessive interest in (one's appearance); to pride or congratulate oneself (on). [prob. var. of PRUNE[2], conf. with foll.]

preen[2], *n.* (*Sc.*) a pin, a brooch; a trifle. *v.t.* to fasten, to pin. [OE *prēon* (cp. LG *Preen, Preem,* Dut. *priem,* G *Pfriem,* Icel. *prjōnn*)]

pre-engage, *v.t.* to engage by previous contract or pledge; to preoccupy; to engage in conflict beforehand. **pre-engagement,** *n.*

pre-establish, *v.t.* to establish beforehand. **pre-established harmony** HARMONY. †**pre-establishment,** *n.*

pre-exilian, *a.* before the period of exile, esp. of the Jewish exile in Babylon. **pre-exilic,** *a.*

pre-exist, *v.i.* to exist previously, esp. of the soul before its union with the body. **pre-existence,** *n.* **pre-existent,** *a.*

pref., (*abbr.*) preface; preference; preferred; prefix.

prefab, *n.* (*coll.*) a prefabricated building, esp. a small house.

prefabricate, *v.t.* to manufacture (the component parts of a structure) in advance for rapid on-site assembly. **prefabrication,** *n.*

preface, *n.* something spoken or written as introductory to a discourse or book; an introduction; an exordium, a preamble, a prelude; the thanksgiving etc. forming the prelude to the consecration of the Eucharist. *v.t.* to furnish with a preface; to introduce (with preliminary remarks etc.). *v.i.* to make introductory remarks. **prefacer,** *n.* **prefatorial**, **prefatory**, *a.* **prefatorily,** *adv.* [OF, med. L *praefātia, praefātio,* from *praefārī* (PRAE-, *fārī,* to speak)]

prefect, *n.* (*Rom. Ant.*) a commander, a governor, a chief magistrate; the civil governor of a department in France, or of a province in Italy; in some schools, a senior pupil with limited disciplinary powers over others. **prefectoral**, **-torial**, *a.* †**prefectship,** *n.* **prefecture**, *n.* the office, jurisdiction, official residence, or the term of office of a prefect. **prefectural**, *a.* [OF (F *préfet*), L. *praefectus,* an overseer, orig. p.p. of *praeficere* (PRAE-, *facere,* to make)]

prefer, *v.t.* (*past, p.p.* **preferred**) to set before, to hold in higher estimation, to like better; to bring forward, to submit; to promote; to recommend, to favour. **preferred debt,** *n.* one having priority of payment. **preferred shares, stock** etc., *n.pl.* preference shares etc. **preferable**, *a.* **preferability**, †**-ableness,** *n.* **preferably,** *adv.* **preference**, *n.* the act of preferring one thing to another; liking for one thing more than another, predilection; right or liberty of choice; that which is preferred; favour displayed towards a person or country before others, esp. in commercial relations; (*Law*) priority of right to payment, esp. of debts. **preference-bonds, -shares, stock,** *n.pl.* those entitled to a dividend before ordinary shares. **preferential**, *a.* giving, receiving or constituting preference; favouring certain countries, as in the commercial relations between Great Britain and the rest of the Commonwealth. **preferentialism,** *n.* **preferentialist,** *n.* **preferentially,** *adv.* **preferment,** *n.* advancement, promotion; a superior office or dignity, esp. in the church. [F *préférer,* L *praeferre* (PRAE-, *ferre,* to bear)]

prefigure, *v.t.* to represent by antecedent figures, types or similitudes; to foreshadow; to picture to oneself beforehand. †**prefigurate**, *v.t.* **prefiguration,** †**prefigurement,** *n.* **prefigurative,** *a.* [late L *praefigurāre*]

prefix, *v.t.* to put, place or set in front of; to attach at the beginning (as an introduction, prefix etc.); †to determine beforehand, to prearrange. *n.*, a letter, syllable or word put at the beginning of a word to modify the meaning; a title prefixed to a name. †**prefixion,** **prefixture**, *n.* [OF *prefixer*]

prefloration, *n.* (*Bot.*) aestivation. [F *préfloraison* (PRE-, PRAE-, L *flos flōris,* flower)]

preform, *v.t.* to form beforehand. **preformation,** *n.* the act of preforming. **theory of preformation,** the theory (prevalent in the 18th cent.) that the organism exists in all its parts in the germ and is merely developed. **preformative,** *a.* forming beforehand. *n.* a formative letter or other element prefixed to a word.

prefrontal, *a.* situated in front of the frontal bone or the frontal region of the skull. *n.* a prefrontal bone, esp. in reptiles and fishes.

preggers, *a.* (*coll.*) pregnant.

pre-glacial, *a.* belonging to the period before the glacial epoch.

pregnable, *a.* capable of being taken by force. [late ME and F *prenable,* as IMPREGNABLE]

pregnant[1], *a.* being with child or young, gravid; fruitful, big (with consequences etc.); inventive, imaginative; full of meaning or suggestion, significant; portentous, fraught; (*Gram. etc.*) implying more than is expressed. **pregnancy,** †**pregnance,** *n.* **pregnantly,** *adv.* [L *praegnans -ntis* (PRAE-, *gna-* root of *gnāscī,* to be born)]

†**pregnant**[2], *a.* pressing, urgent, cogent. [OF *preignant,* pres.p. of *preindre,* L *premere,* to PRESS[1]]

prehallux, *n.* a rudimentary digit or toe found in certain mammals, reptiles etc.

preheat, *v.t.* to heat beforehand.

prehensile, *a.* seizing, grasping; adapted to seizing or grasping, as the tails of monkeys. †**prehensible,** *a.* **prehensility**, *n.* **prehension**, *n.* the act of taking hold of or seizing; apprehension. **prehensive,** †**-sory,** *a.* **prehensor,** *n.* [F *préhensile,* from L *prehens-,* p.p. stem of *prehendere* (PRE-, *hendere,* cogn. with Gr. *chandanein,* to seize)]

prehistoric, *a.* of or pertaining to the time prior to that known to history. **prehistorically,** *adv.* **prehistory**, *n.*

pre-ignition, *n.* premature ignition of the explosive mixture in the cylinder of an internal-combustion engine.

prejudge, *v.t.* to judge before a case has been fully heard, to condemn in advance; to form a premature opinion about. **prejudgment, prejudication**, *n.* †**prejudicant**, *a.* prejudging. †**prejudicate**, *v.t.* to prejudge; to prejudice. *a.*, judged beforehand; preconceived; prejudiced. [F *préjuger,* L *praejūdicāre*]

prejudice, *n.* opinion, bias or judgment formed without due consideration of facts or arguments; intolerance or hostility toward a particular group, race etc.; mischief, damage or detriment arising from unfair judgment or action. *v.t.* to prepossess with prejudice, to bias; to affect injuriously, esp. to impair the validity of a right etc. **without prejudice,** (*Law*) without impairing any pre-existing right, detracting from any subsequent claim, or admitting any liability. **prejudiced,** *a.* prepossessed, biased. **prejudicial**, *a.* causing prejudice or injury; mischievous, detrimental; †influenced by prejudice, biased. **prejudicially,** *adv.* †**prejudicialness,** *n.* [OF, from L *praejūdicium* (PRAE-, *jūdicium,* from *jūdex,* JUDGE)]

prelate, *n.* an ecclesiastical dignitary of the highest order, as an archbishop, bishop etc., formerly including abbot and prior. **prelacy,** *n.* the office, dignity or see of a prelate; (*collect.*) prelates; episcopacy (in a hostile sense). **prelateship,** *n.* **prelatess**, *n.* an abbess or prioress; (*facet.*) the wife of a prelate. **prelatic, -ical**, *a.* **prelatically,** *adv.* †**prelatish,** *a.* †**prelatism,** *n.* prelacy, episcopacy; adherence to or partisanship of this. **prelatist,** *n.* **prelatize, -ise,** *v.i.* to support or encourage prelacy. *v.t.* to bring under the influence of the prelacy. †**prelature**, †**-try,** †**-ty,** *n.* prelacy. [OF *prelat,* L *praelātus* (PRAE-, *lātus,* p.p. of *ferre,* to bear)]

prelect, *v.i.* to read a lecture or discourse in public. **prelection,** *n.* **prelector,** *n.* [L *praelectus,* p.p. of *praelegere* (PRAE-, *legere,* to choose, to read)]

prelibation, *n.* a foretaste; a libation previous to tasting. [late L *praelībātio* (PRAE-, *lībātio,* from *lībāre,* to taste)]

preliminary, *a.* introductory; previous to the main business or discourse. *n.* something introductory; (*pl.*) introductory or preparatory arrangements, etc. **preliminarily,** *adv.* **prelims**, *n.pl.* preliminary matter of a book; preliminary examinations at university. [*līmen -minis,* threshold]

prelingual, *a.* preceding the acquisition or development of language.

prelude, *n.* something done, happening etc., introductory or preparatory to that which follows; a harbinger, a precursor; (*Mus.*) a short introductory strain preceding the principal movement, a piece played as introduction to a suite. *v.t.* to perform or serve as a prelude to; to introduce with a prelude; to usher in, to foreshadow. *v.i.* to serve as a prelude (to); to begin with a prelude; (*Mus.*) to play a prelude. †**preluder,** *n.* **prelusive**, †**preludial**, †**-dious,** *a.* **preludize, -ise,** *v.i.* **prelusively,** *adv.* **prelusory,** *a.* [F *prélude,* late L *praelūdium* (PRAE-, *lūdere,* to play)]

Premadasa, *n.* **Ranasinghe** (1924–), Sri Lankan politician, a United National Party member of parliament from 1960, prime minister from 1978, and president from 1988, having gained popularity through overseeing a major housebuilding and poverty-alleviation programme.

premarital, *a.* occurring before marriage.

premature, *a.* ripe or mature too soon; happening, arriving, existing or performed before the proper time; born after a gestation period of less than 37 weeks. *n.*

(*Mil.*) the premature explosion of a shell. **prematurely**, *adv.* **prematureness, prematurity**, *n.* [L *praemātūrus* (PRAE-, *mātūrus*, ripe)]

premaxillary, *a.* situated in front of the maxilla or upper jaw. *n.* the premaxillary bone.

premedical, *a.* of or pertaining to a course of study undertaken before medical studies. *n.* a premedical student; premedical studies. **premedicate,** *v.t.* **premedication,** *n.* drugs administered to sedate and to prepare a patient for general anaesthesia.

premeditate, *v.t.* to meditate on beforehand; to plan and contrive beforehand. *v.i.* to deliberate previously. †*a.* meditated beforehand; deliberate. **premeditatedly,** *adv.* **premeditation,** *n.* [L *praemeditātus*, p.p. of *praemeditārī* (PRAE-, *meditārī*)]

premenstrual, *a.* preceding menstruation. **premenstrual tension,** *n.* nervous tension caused by the hormonal changes which precede menstruation.

premier, *a.* first, chief, principal. *n.* a prime or chief minister. **premiership,** *n.* [F, from L *prīmārius*, PRIMARY]

première, *n.* a first performance of a play or film. [F, fem. of *premier*, see prec.]

premillennial, *a.* previous to the millennium. **premillenarian,** *n.* one believing that the Second Advent will precede the millennium. **premillenarianism, premillennialism,** *n.*

Preminger, *n.* **Otto (Ludwig)** (1906–86), US film producer, director, and actor. Born in Vienna, he went to the US in 1935. He directed *Margin for Error* (1942), *Laura* (1944), *The Moon is Blue* (1953), *The Man With the Golden Arm* (1955), *Anatomy of a Murder* (1959), *Skidoo!* (1968), and *Rosebud* (1974). His films are characterized by an intricate technique of story-telling, and a masterly use of the wide screen and the travelling camera.

premise, *n.* a proposition laid down, assumed or proved from which another is inferred; (*Log.*) one of the two propositions of a syllogism from which the conclusion is drawn (see MAJOR, MINOR); *v.t.*, to put forward as preparatory to what is to follow; to lay down as an antecedent proposition or condition. *v.i.* to lay down antecedent propositions. [F *prémisse*, L *praemissa*, (*propositio* or *sententia*), fem. p.p. of *praemittere* (PRAE-, *mittere*, to send)]

premises, *n.pl.* (*Law*) matters previously set forth (in a deed or conveyance), esp. the aforesaid house or lands etc; hence a piece of land and the buildings upon it, esp. considered as a place of business.

premiss, PREMISE.

premium, *n.* a reward, a recompense, a prize; a sum paid in addition to interest, wages etc., a bonus; a fee for instruction in a craft, profession etc.; a payment (usu. periodical) made for insurance; the rate at which shares, money etc., are selling above their nominal value. **at a premium,** above their nominal value, above par; in great esteem or demand. **to put a premium on,** to render more than usually valuable or advantageous. **Premium Bond,** *n.* a British government bond bearing no interest but subject to a monthly draw for money prizes. [L *praemium* (PRAE-, *emere*, to buy, to take)]

premolar, *n.* one of the teeth situated in front of the molars. *a.* in front of the molars.

premonition, *n.* previous warning or notice; a foreboding, a presentiment. †**premonish**, *v.t.* **premonitor**, *n.* **premonitory,** *a.* [F, from late L *praemonitio*, from *praemonēre* (PRAE-, *monēre*, to warn)]

Premonstratensian, *n.* a member of a Roman Catholic order of regular canons, founded by St Norbert (*c.* 1080–1134), at Prémontré, near Laon, France, in 1119, or of the corresponding order of nuns. *a.* belonging to the Premonstratensians. **Premonstrant**, *n.* [med. L *Praemonstrātensis*, from *Praemonstrātus*, Prémontré]

premorse, *a.* (*Ent.*) abruptly truncate as if bitten off. [L *praemorsus*, p.p. of *praemordere* (PRAE-, *mordere*, to bite)]

Prempeh I, *n.* chief of the Ashanti people in W Africa. He became king in 1888, and later opposed British attempts to take over the region. He was deported and in 1900 the Ashanti were defeated. He returned to Kumasi (capital of the Ashanti region) in 1924 as chief of the people.

premunire, PRAEMUNIRE.

†**premunition,** *n.* the act of guarding beforehand, as against objections. [late L *praemūnītio*, from *praemūnīre* (*emūnīre*, to defend)]

prenatal, *a.* anterior to birth. **prenatally,** *adv.* [NATAL[1]]

prenomen, *n.* (*Rom. Ant.*) a personal name, first name, corresponding to the modern Christian name. [PRAE-, L *nomen*, name]

†**prenominate,** *v.t.* to name or mention beforehand. *a.*, named beforehand. [late L *praenōminātus*, p.p. of *praenōmināre*]

prenti, *n.* the lizard of Central Australia. [Austral. Abor.]

†**prentice** etc. APPRENTICE.

preoccupy, *v.t.* to take possession of beforehand or before another; to prepossess; to pre-engage, to engross (the mind etc.). **preoccupancy,** *n.* the act or right of taking possession before others. **preoccupation,** *n.* prepossession, prejudice; prior occupation; the state of being preoccupied or engrossed (with); that which preoccupies, as a business affair etc.; †preoccupancy. **preoccupiedly,** *adv.* [L *praeoccupāre* (PRAE-, *occupāre*, to OCCUPY)]

preordain, *v.t.* to ordain beforehand. **preordainment, preordination**, *n.* †**preordinance**, *n.* previous decree or ordinance. †**preordinate**, *a.*

preordinance PREORDAIN.

prep, *n.* (*School sl.*) preparation or private study; (*chiefly N Am.*) a preparatory school. **prep school,** *n.* a preparatory school. **preppy,** *a.* (*N Am.*) denoting a young but classic look in clothes, clean-cut, conventionally smart; holding (middle-class) values associated with students at preparatory schools. *n.* (*N Am.*) a student at a preparatory school; a person who dresses in a preppy fashion. [short for PREPARATION]

prep., (*abbr.*) preparation; preparatory; preposition.

prepaid, *a.* paid in advance (as postage etc.).

prepare, *v.t.* to make ready; to bring into a suitable condition, to fit for a certain purpose; to make ready or fit (to do, to receive etc.); to produce; to construct, to put together, to draw up; to get (work, a speech, a part etc.) ready by practice, study etc.; (*Mus.*) to lead up to (a discord) by sounding the dominant note in a consonance. *v.i.* to get everything ready; to take the measures necessary (for); to make oneself ready. †*n.* preparation. **preparation**, *n.* the act of preparing; the state of being prepared; (*often pl.*) a preparatory act or measure; anything prepared by a special process, as food, a medicine, a part of a body for anatomical study etc.; the preparing of lessons or school-work; (*Mus.*) the introduction of a note to be continued in a subsequent discord; †a military or naval force; ceremonious introduction; †accomplishment. **preparative**, *a.* preparatory. *n.* that which tends or serves to prepare; an act of preparation; (*Mil., Nav.*) a signal to make ready. **preparatively,** *adv.* **preparatory,** *a.* tending or serving to prepare; introductory (to). **preparatory school,** *n.* a private school for pupils usu. aged 6–13, which prepares them for entry to a public school; (*N Am.*) a private secondary school which prepares students for college. **preparatorily,** *adv.* **prepared,** *a.* **to be prepared,** to be ready; to be willing (to). **preparedly**, *adv.* **preparedness**, *n.* **preparer,** *n.* [F *préparer*, L *praeparare* (PRAE-, *parāre*, to make ready)]

prepay, *v.t.* to pay beforehand; to pay in advance, esp. by affixing a postage stamp to (a telegram etc.). **prepayable,** *a.* **prepayment,** *n.*

prepense, *a.* premeditated, deliberate. *v.t.* to premeditate. **malice prepense,** intentional malice. †**prepensely,** *adv.* †**prepensive,** *a.* [formerly *prepensed*, p.p. of *prepense*, *purpense*, OF *purpenser* (*pur-*, *pour-*, L *prō*, forth, OF *penser*, to think)]

preperception, *n.* previous perception; (*Psychol.*) an impress forming the material of a percept.

†**prepollent,** *a.* having superior power or influence; predominating. †**prepollence,** †**-ency,** *n.* [L *prae-*

pollens -ntem, pres.p. of *praepollēre* (PRAE-, *pollēre,* to be strong)]

preponderate, *v.i.* to be heavier; to be superior or to outweigh in number, power, influence etc.; to sink (as the scale of a balance). †*v.t.* to overweigh, to overpower by superior force or influence. **preponderance, †-ancy,** *n.* **preponderant,** *a.* **preponderantly, preponderatingly,** *adv.* **†preponderation,** *n.* [L *praeponderātus,* p.p. of *praeponderāre* (PRAE-, *ponderāre,* to PONDER)]

preposition, *n.* a word or group of words, e.g. *at, by, in front of,* used to relate the noun or pronoun it is placed in front of to other constituent parts of the sentence. **prepositional,** *a.* **prepositionally,** *adv.* **prepositive,** *a.* prefixed, intended to be placed before (a word). *n.* a prepositive word or particle. [L *praepositio,* from *praepōnere* (PRAE-, *pōnere,* to put, p.p. *positus*)]

prepositor, *n.* a scholar appointed to the charge of others; a prefect, a monitor. [L *praepositor,* as prec.]

prepossess, *v.t.* to occupy beforehand; to imbue (with an idea, feeling etc.); to bias (esp. favourably); of an idea etc., to preoccupy. **prepossessing,** *a.* biasing; tending to win favour, attractive. **prepossessingly,** *adv.* **prepossession,**, *n.*

preposterous, *a.* contrary to nature, reason or common sense; obviously wrong, foolish, absurd. **preposterously,** *adv.* **preposterousness,** *n.* [L *praeposterus* (*prae,* before, *posterus,* coming after)]

prepotent, *a.* very powerful; possessing superior force or influence; overbearing; (*Biol.*) possessing superior fertilizing influence. **prepotence, -ency,** *n.* **prepotential,** *a.* **prepotently,** *adv.* [L *praepotens -ntem,* pres.p. of *praeposse* (PRE-, *posse,* to be able)]

preppy PREP.

pre-prandial, *a.* done, happening etc., before dinner.

pre-preference, *a.* ranking before preference shares etc.

prepuce, *n.* the foreskin, the loose covering of the glans penis; a similar fold of skin over the clitoris. **preputial,** *a.* [L *praepūtium*]

Pre-Raphaelite, *n.* an artist who aimed at reviving the spirit and technique that characterized painting before the time of Raphael. *a.* having the characteristics of Pre-Raphaelitism. **Pre-Raphaelite Brotherhood,** *n.* a small group of painters formed in London in 1848, including Holman Hunt, Millais and D. G. Rossetti, to cultivate the spirit and methods of the early Italian painters, esp. in respect to truth to nature and vividness of colour. Their subjects were mainly biblical and literary, painted with obsessive naturalism. **Pre-Raphaelitism,** *n.*

preremote, *a.* occurring, done etc., still more remotely in the past.

prerequisite, *a.* required beforehand. *n.* a requirement that must be satisfied in advance, a precondition.

prerogative, *n.* an exclusive right or privilege vested in a particular person or body of persons, esp. a sovereign, in virtue of his or her position or relationship; any peculiar right, option, privilege, natural advantage etc.; †precedence. *a.* of, pertaining to or having a prerogative; (*Rom. Hist.*) having the right of voting first; †having precedence. **prerogatived,** *a.* [F *prérogative,* L *praerogatīva,* a previous choice, privilege, fem. of *praerogatīvus* (PRE-, *rogātīvus,* rel. to *rogātus,* p.p. of *rogāre,* to ask)]

Pres., (*abbr.*) President.

pres., (*abbr.*) present.

presage, *n.* something that foretells a future event, an omen, a prognostic; foreboding, presentiment. *v.t.* (*also* prisāj′) to foreshadow, to betoken; to indicate by natural signs etc.; to forebode, to foretell. †*v.i.* (*also* prisāj′), to prophesy. **presageful,** *a.* **†presagement,** *n.* **†presager,** *n.* [F *présage,* L *praesāgium* (PRE-, *sāgīre,* to perceive quickly)]

presbyopia, *n.* a form of long-sightedness with indistinct vision of near objects, caused by alteration in the refractive power of the eyes with age. **presbyope, †presbyte,** *n.* one affected with this. **presbyopic,** *a.* [Gr. *presbus,* old man, *ōpia,* from *ōps ōpos,* eye]

presbyter, *n.* an elder who had authority in the early Church; in the Episcopal Church, a minister of the second order, a priest; in the Presbyterian Church, a minister of a presbytery, an elder. **presbyteral, -terial,** *a.* **presbyterate, presbytership,** *n.* **Presbyterian,** *n.* any adherent of Presbyterianism; a member of a Presbyterian Church. *a.* pertaining to Church government by presbyters; governed by presbyters. **Presbyterian Church,** *n.* a Church governed by elders, including ministers, all equal in rank. **United Presbyterian Church,** the Church formed by the union of the United Secession and Relief Churches in 1847, united in 1900 with the Free Church of Scotland. **Presbyterianism,** *n.* a system of Christian Protestant church government, expounded during the Reformation by John Calvin, which gives its name to the established Church of Scotland, and is also practised in England, Ireland, Switzerland, North America, and elsewhere. There is no compulsory form of worship and each congregation is governed by presbyters or elders (clerical or lay), who are of equal rank. Congregations are grouped in presbyteries, synods, and general assemblies. **presbytery,** *n.* a body of elders in the early Church; a court consisting of the pastors and ruling elders of the Presbyterian churches of a given district, ranking above the kirk-session and below the synod; the district represented by a presbytery; the eastern portion of a chancel beyond the choir in a cathedral or other large church, the sanctuary; in the Roman Catholic Church, a priest's residence. [late L, from Gr. *presbuteros,* elder, comp. of *presbus,* see prec.]

preschool, *a.* (for children who are) under school age.

prescient, *a.* foreknowing, far-seeing. **prescience,** *n.* **prescientific,** *a.* pertaining to the period before the rise of science or of scientific method; †pertaining to prescience. **presciently,** *adv.* [F, from L *praescientem,* nom. *-ens,* pres.p. of *praescīre* (PRAE-, *scīre,* to know)]

prescind, *v.t.* to cut off; to abstract, to consider independently. *v.i.* to separate one's consideration (from). [L *praescindere* (PRAE-, *scindere,* to cut)]

Prescott, *n.* **John Leslie** (1938–), British Labour Party politician, a member of the Kinnock shadow cabinet.

prescribe, *v.t.* to lay down with authority; to appoint (a rule of conduct etc.); to direct to be used as a remedy. *v.i.* to write directions for medical treatment; (*Law*) to assert a prescriptive title (to or for). **prescriber,** *n.* **prescript,** *n.* a direction, a command, a law; †(*Med.*) a prescription. *a.* prescribed, directed. **†prescriptible,** *a.* **prescription,** *n.* the act of prescribing; that which is prescribed, esp. a written direction for the preparation of medical remedies, and the manner of using them; the medication etc. prescribed; (*Law*) long-continued or immemorial use or possession without interruption, as giving right or title; right or title founded on this; ancient or long-continued custom, esp. when regarded as authoritative; a claim based on long use. **prescriptive,** *a.* acquired or authorized by long use; based on long use or prescription; laying down rules. **prescriptively,** *adv.* [L *praescrībere* (PRAE-, *scrībere,* to write), p.p. *praescriptus*]

preselector, *n.* a system whereby a gear can be selected before it is engaged.

presence, *n.* the quality or state of being present; the immediate vicinity of a person; the immediate vicinity of a person of high rank; (a person with) an imposing or dignified bearing; personal magnetism, the ability to grasp and hold an audience's attention; a group or force representing one's interests or exercising an influence on one's behalf; an influence as of a being invisibly present; †a presence-chamber. **presence of mind,** a calm, collected state of mind, esp. in danger or emergency. **real presence,** the actual existence of the body and blood of Christ in the Eucharist. **presence-chamber, -room,** *n.* the room in which a great personage receives company. [OF, from L *praesentia,* as PRESENT[2]]

presensation, *n.* sensation, feeling, or consciousness

of something before it exists. †**presension**, *n.*

present1, *a.* being in a place referred to; being in view or at hand; found or existing in the thing referred to; being under discussion, consideration etc.; now existing, occurring, going on etc.; (*Law*) instant, immediate; (*Gram.*) expressing what is actually going on; ready at hand, assisting in emergency, †attentive, propitious. *n.* the present time; the present tense; (*pl.*) these writings, a term used in documents to express the document itself. **at present,** at the present time, now. **by these presents,** (*Law*) by this document. **for the present,** for the time being; just now; so far as the time being is concerned. **present-day,** *a.* contemporary, of the current time. **present tense,** *n.* the form of the verb expressing being or action at the present time. [OF, from L *praesentem,* nom. *-ens,* pres.p. of *praeesse* (PRAE-, *esse,* to be)]

present2, *v.t.* to introduce to the acquaintance or presence of, esp. to introduce formally; to introduce to a sovereign at Court; to submit (oneself) as a candidate, applicant etc.; to offer (a clergyman) to a bishop for institution (to a benefice); to exhibit, to show, to offer to the sight; to hold in position or point (a gun etc.); to offer or suggest (itself) to the attention; to offer for consideration, to submit; to exhibit (an actor, a play etc.) on the stage; to act as the presenter of (as a television programme); to portray, to depict, to represent; to offer, to give, to bestow, esp. in a ceremonious way; to invest or endow (with a gift); to tender, to deliver. *v.i.* to come forward as a patient (with); of a foetus, to be in a specified position during labour with respect to the mouth of the uterus. *n.*, that which is presented, a gift; (*Mil.*), position for or act of aiming a firearm. **to present arms,** to hold a rifle etc., in a perpendicular position in front of the body to salute a superior officer. **presentable,** *a.* fit to be presented; of suitable appearance for company etc.; fit to be shown or exhibited; suitable for offering as a gift; suitable for presentation to a living. **presentably,** *adv.* **presentability**, *n.* [OF *presenter,* L *praesentāre,* as prec.]

presentation, *n.* the act of presenting; a formal offering or proffering; a present, a gift; an exhibition, a theatrical representation; a verbal report on, or exposé of, a subject, often with illustrative material; the manner of presenting, esp. the appearance, arrangement, neatness etc. of material submitted; an introduction, esp. a formal introduction to a superior personage; a formal introduction to the sovereign at Court; (*Law*) the act or right of presenting to a benefice; (*Obstetrics*) the particular position of the foetus at birth; (*Psych.*) the process by which an object becomes present to consciousness, or the modification of consciousness involved in the perception of an object. **presentation copy,** *n.* a book presented gratis by an author or publisher. **presentational,** *a.* **presentationism,** *n.* the doctrine that the mind has immediate cognition of objects of perception, or of elemental categories such as space, time etc. **presentationalist, -tionist,** *n.* **presentative**, *a.* pertaining to or of the nature of mental presentation; subserving mental presentation; of a benefice, admitting of the presentation of an incumbent.

presentee, *n.* one presented to a benefice; one recommended for office; one presented at Court; one receiving a present.

presenter, *n.* one who presents; a broadcaster who introduces and comperes, or provides a linking commentary for, a radio or television programme.

presentient, *a.* feeling or perceiving beforehand. [L *praesentiens -ntem,* pres.p. of *praesentīre* (PRAE-, *sentīre,* to feel)]

presentiment, *n.* apprehension or anticipation, more or less vague, of an impending event, esp. of evil, a foreboding.

presentive, *a.* presenting an object or conception directly to the mind, opp. to symbolic; presentative. **presentiveness,** *n.*

presently, *adv.* soon, shortly; †at once, immediately; (*chiefly N Am., Sc.*) at the present time.

presentment, *n.* the act of presenting; a theatrical representation, a portrait, likeness, a semblance; a statement, an account, a description; the act or mode of presentation to the mind; a report by a grand jury respecting an offence, from their own knowledge; formal information by parish authorities respecting a charge to a bishop or archdeacon at his visitation; a formal accusation or indictment. [OF *presentement*]

preserve, *v.t.* to keep safe, to guard, to protect; to save, to rescue; to maintain in a good or the same condition; to retain, to keep intact; to keep from decay or decomposition by chemical treatment, boiling, pickling etc.; to keep (a stream, covert, game etc.) for private use by preventing poaching etc. *v.i.* to make preserves; to maintain protection for game in preserves. *n.* fruit prepared with sugar or preservative substances, jam; a place where game is preserved; water where fish are preserved; a special domain, something reserved for certain people only; *pl.* goggles worn as a protection against dust, sunlight etc. **preservable,** *a.* **preservation**, *n.* **preservationist,** *n.* one who is interested in preserving traditional and historic things. **preservative, †-atory,** *a.* having the power of preserving from injury, decay or corruption; tending to preserve. *n.* that which preserves, esp. a chemical substance used to prevent decomposition in foodstuffs. **preservatize, -ise,** *v.t.* **preserver,** *n.* **preserving pan,** *n.* a large pan used for making jams and preserves. [F *préserver,* late L *praeservāre* (PRAE-, *servāre,* to keep)]

preses, *n.* (*Sc.*) a chairman, a president. [L *praeses,* cogn. with foll.]

preside, *v.i.* to be set in authority over others; to sit at the head of a table; to act as director, controller, chairman or president; to lead, to superintend; to officiate (at the organ, piano etc.). **presidency**, *n.* the office, jurisdiction or term of office of a president; the territory administered by a president, esp. one of the three former great divisions of the East India Company's territory, Bombay (now Gujarat and Maharashtra), Bengal, Madras (now Tamil Nadu). **president**, *n.* one (usu. elected) presiding over a temporary or permanent body of persons; the chief magistrate or elective head of the government in a modern republic; one presiding over the meetings of a society; the chief officer of certain colleges and universities, esp. in the US; (*N Am.*) the permanent chairman and chief executive officer of a railway, banking or other corporation, board of trustees, government department etc. **Lord President of the Council,** a member of the House of Lords who acts as president of the Privy Council. **presidential**, *a.* **presidentially,** *adv.* **presidentship,** *n.* **presider,** *n.* [F *présider,* L *praesidēre* (PRAE-, *sedēre,* to sit)]

presidial, -ary, *a.* pertaining to a garrison; having or serving as a garrison. [F *présidial,* late L *praesidiālis,* from *praeses -idis,* PRESES]

presidio, *n.* (*pl.* **-dios**) a fort or fortified settlement; a Spanish penal colony. [Sp.]

presidium, *n.* (*pl.* **-diums, -dia**) a permanent executive committee in a Communist country.

presignify, *v.t.* to signify or intimate beforehand. [MF *presignifier,* L *praesignificare*]

Presley, *n.* **Elvis (Aaron)** (1935–77), US singer and guitarist, born in Tupelo, Mississippi. With his recordings for Sun Records in Memphis, Tennessee (1954–55), and early hits such as 'Heartbreak Hotel' (1956), 'Hound Dog' (1956), and 'Love Me Tender' (1956), he created an individual vocal style, influenced by Southern blues, gospel music, country music, and rhythm and blues.

press1, *v.t.* to act steadily upon with a force or weight; to push (something up, down, against etc.) with steady force; to put or hold (upon etc.) with force; to squeeze, to crush, to compress; to extract juice from; to make by pressing in a mould; esp. to make (a gramophone record) from a matrix; to clasp, to embrace, to hug; to crowd upon; to urge, to ply hard, to bear heavily on; to invite with persistent warmth; to put forward vigorously and persistently; to weigh down, to distress; to straiten, to constrain; to enforce strictly, to impress; to force (upon); to make smooth by pressure (as cloth or paper). *v.i.* to exert pressure; to bear heavily, or weigh heavily; to be urgent; to throng,to crowd, to encroach, to intrude; to strive eagerly, to hasten, to strain, to push one's way. *n.* the act of pressing, urging or crowding; a crowd, a throng; urgency, pressure, hurry; an upright case, cupboard or closet, for storing things, esp. linen; a book-case; cabinet-work made by pressing successive cross-gained veneers together while hot; an instrument or machine for compressing any body or substance, forcing it into a more compact form, shaping, extracting juice etc.; a machine for printing; a printing-establishment; the process or practice of printing; the reaction of newspapers etc. to a person, event etc. **freedom of the press,** the right to print and publish statements, opinions etc., without censorship. **in the press,** being printed; on the eve of publication. **press of sail,** as much sail as the wind will let a ship carry. **the press,** the news media collectively, esp. newspapers and periodicals; journalists. **to go to press,** to start printing, to begin to be printed. **to press on, ahead, forward,** to continue (determinedly) on one's way; to proceed, esp. in spite of difficulties or opposition. **press agent,** *n.* a person employed to handle relations with the press, esp. to ensure good publicity for an actor, organization etc. **press-bed,** *n.* a bed that may be folded and shut up in a case. **press-box,** *n.* a shelter for reporters on a cricket-field etc. **press conference,** *n.* a meeting of a statesman etc. with journalists to announce a policy or answer their questions. **Press Council,** *n.* in the UK, organization (established 1953) that aims to preserve the freedom of the press, to maintain standards, consider complaints, and report on monopoly developments. **press-cutting,** *n.* a clipping from a newspaper. **press-gallery,** *n.* a gallery set aside for reporters, esp. in the Houses of Parliament. **pressman,** *n.* one who manages a printing-press; a journalist. **press-mark,** *n.* a number, symbol or other mark indicating the place of a book on the shelves of a library. **press release,** *n.* an official statement or report given to the press. **press-room,** *n.* the room in a printing-office where the presses are. **press-stud,** *n.* a fastener consisting of two small round buttons, one of which has a small raised knob which snaps into a hole in the other. **press-up,** *n.* a gymnastic exercise in which the body is held rigid in a prone position and raised and lowered by bending and straightening the arms. **press-work,** *n.* the work or management of a printing-press; journalistic work. **presser,** *n.* **pressing,** *a.* urgent, importunate, insistent. *n.* the gramophone records made from a single matrix at one time. **pressingly,** *adv.* **pression,** *n.* the act of pressing; pressure. [F *presser,* L *pressāre,* freq. of *premere*]

press², *v.t.* to force into naval or military service. *v.i.* to impress soldiers or sailors. *n.* a compulsory enlisting of men into naval or military service; a commission to force men into service. **press-gang,** *n.* a detachment of men employed to impress men, usu. into the navy. **press-money,** *n.* prest-money. [from PREST]

Pressburger, *n.* **Emeric** (1902–88), Hungarian director, producer, and screenwriter, known for his partnership with Michael Powell.

pressiroster, *n.* any individual of the Pressirostres, a group of wading birds with a compressed beak. **pressirostral,** *a.* [F *pressirostre* (L *pressus,* PRESS¹, *rostrum,* beak)]

pressure, *n.* the act of pressing; the state of being pressed; a force steadily exerted upon or against a body by another in contact with it; the amount of this, usu. measured in units of weight upon a unit of area; constraining force, compulsion; moral force; persistent attack; stress, urgency; trouble, affliction, oppression. *v.t.* to apply pressure to; to constrain, to subject to compelling moral force against one's will. **high pressure** HIGH. **pressure-cabin,** *n.* (*Aviat.*) a pressurized cabin in an aircraft. **pressure-cook,** *v.t.* to cook in a pressure-cooker. **pressure-cooker,** *n.* an apparatus for cooking at a high temperature under high pressure. **pressure group,** *n.* a group or small party exerting pressure on government etc. for its own ends. **pressure point,** *n.* any of various points on the body where a blood vessel may be pressed against a bone to check bleeding. **pressure-suit,** *n.* an airman's suit that inflates automatically if there is a failure in the pressure-cabin. **pressurize, -ise,** *v.t.* to fit an aircraft cabin with a device that maintains normal atmospheric pressure at high altitudes; to (seek to) coerce. **pressurized-water reactor,** a type of nuclear reactor used in nuclear power stations in many countries and in nuclear-powered submarines, that uses water under pressure as coolant and moderator. [OF, from L *pressūra,* from PRESS¹]

†**prest,** *n.* an advance, a loan; earnest-money paid to a sailor or soldier on enlistment. *a.* ready, prepared. **prest-money,** *n.* money paid to men who enlist. †**prestation,** *n.* a payment of money as a toll; performance, purveyance. [OF (F *prêt*), from *prester,* L *praestāre* (PRAE-, *stāre,* to come forward, to stand)]

Prestel®, *n.* the British Telecom viewdata system, pioneered 1975, which provides information on the television screen via the telephone network.

Prester John, *n.* a mythical Christian sovereign and priest, supposed in the Middle Ages to rule in Abyssinia or somewhere in the interior of Asia.

presternum, *n.* the front part of the sternum; (*Ent.*) the prosternum.

prestidigitation, *n.* sleight of hand, conjuring. **prestidigitator,** *n.* [F *preste,* It. PRESTO, L *digitus,* finger, -ATION]

prestige, *n.* influence or weight derived from former fame, excellence, achievements etc.; †an illusion, a trick, an imposture. *a.* having or conferring prestige; superior, very high-quality, very stylish etc. **prestigious,** *a.* having or conferring prestige. [F, from L *praestigium,* a trick, illusion, glamour, from *praestringere* (PRAE-, *stringere,* to bind)]

presto¹, *adv.* (*Mus.*) quickly. *a.* quick. *n.* a quick movement. **prestissimo,** *adv.* very fast indeed. *a.* very fast. *n.* a very fast movement. [It., from late L *praestus,* from L *praesto* (PRAE-, *situ,* abl. of *situs,* SITUATION)]

presto², hey presto, *adv., int.* immediately (to indicate the speed with which e.g. a conjuring trick is performed). [from prec.]

prestressed, *a.* of concrete, reinforced with stretched steel wires or rods.

presume, *v.t.* to venture on without leave; to take for granted or assume without previous inquiry or examination. *v.i.* to venture without previous leave; to form over-confident or arrogant opinions; to behave with assurance or arrogance. **to presume on,** to rely on, to depend on; to take unfair advantage of. **presumable,** *a.* **presumably, presumedly,** *adv.* **presumer,** *n.* **presuming,** *a.* presumptuous. **presumingly,** *adv.* **presumption,** *n.* the act of presuming; assumption of the truth or existence of something without direct proof; that which is taken for granted; the ground for presuming; over-confidence, arrogance, impudence, effrontery. **presumption of fact,** an inference as to a fact from facts actually known. **presumption of law,** assumption of the truth of a proposition until the contrary is proved; an inference established by law as universally applicable to particular circumstances. **presumptive,** *a.* giving grounds for or based on presumption; †presumptuous. **heir presumptive,** an heir whose actual succession may be prevented by the birth of one nearer akin to the present holder of a title, estate etc. **presumptive evidence,** *n.* evidence derived from circumstances which necessarily or usually attend a fact. **presumptively,** *adv.* **presumptuous,** *a.* full of presumption; arrogant, forward; rash, venturesome. **presumptuously,** *adv.* **presumptuousness,** *n.* [OF *presumer,* L *praesūmere* (PRAE-, *sūmere,* to take)]

presuppose, *v.t.* to assume beforehand; to imply as a necessary antecedent. †**presupposal, presupposition,** *n.* the act of presupposing; a supposition adopted beforehand. [F *présupposer*]

pretend, *v.t.* to assume the appearance of; to feign to be; to simulate, to counterfeit; to allege or put forward falsely; to put forward, to assert, to claim; †to aim at, to aspire to; †to intend to design. *v.i.* to feign, to make believe; to put forward a claim (to); †to aim, to attempt. *a.* make-believe. **pretence,** (*esp. N Am.*) **pretense**, *n.* a claim (true or false); a false profession; an excuse, a pretext; display, show, ostentation; (an act of) pretending or feigning; (a) semblance; †a purpose, plan or design. **pretendedly,** *adv.* **pretender,** *n.* one who makes a claim, esp. a claim that cannot be substantiated; a claimant, esp. a claimant to a throne held by another branch of the same family. **Old Pretender,** James Stuart, 1688–1766, son of James II. **Young Pretender,** Charles Edward Stuart, 1720–88, son of Old Pretender. **pretendership,** *n.* **pretendingly,** *adv.* **pretension**, *n.* (*often pl.*) a claim; (*often pl.*) an aspiration; a pretext; pretentiousness; †a pretence, a deception. **pretentious**, *a.* full of pretension; making specious claims to excellence etc.; ostentatious, arrogant, conceited. **pretentiously,** *adv.* **pretentiousness,** *n.* [F *prétendre,* L. *praetendere* (PRAE-, *tendere,* to stretch), p.p. *praetensus*]

preter-, *pref.* beyond; beyond the range of; more than. **preterhuman**, *a.* more than human, superhuman. †**preterimperfect**, *a.* applied to the imperfect tense as expressing a past action that is described as still going on. [L *praeter,* past, beyond, comp. of *prae,* before]

preterist, *n.* one whose chief interest is in the past; one who holds that the prophecies in the Apocalypse have already been fulfilled. [see foll.]

preterite, (*esp. N Am.*) **preterit**, *a.* (*Gram.*) denoting completed action or existence in past time; past, gone by. *n.* the preterite tense; †the past. **preteriteness,** *n.* **preteritial**, *a.* (*Biol.*) having ceased from activity. **pretention**, *n.* the act of passing over or omitting; the state of being passed over; (*Rhet.*) the summary mention of a thing while one pretends to pass it over; (*Theol.*) the passing over of the non-elect, opp. to *election*. **preteritive**, *a.* [OF, from L *praeteritus,* p.p. of *praeterīre* (PRETER-, *īre,* to go)]

pretermit, *v.t.* to pass by or over, to neglect, to omit (to mention, to do etc.); to discontinue. **pretermission**, *n.* [L *praetermittere* (PRETER-, *mittere,* to send, to let go)]

preternatural, *a.* beyond what is natural; out of the regular course of nature. **preternaturalism,** *n.* the state of being preternatural; a preternatural occurrence, thing etc.; belief in or doctrine of the preternatural. **preternaturalist,** *n.* **prenaturally,** *adv.* **preternaturalness,** *n.*

†**preterperfect,** *a.* the past perfect tense; more than perfect. †**preterpluperfect**.

pretext, *n.* an excuse; an ostensible reason or motive. *v.t.*, to allege as pretext or motive. [F *prétexte,* L *praetextus,* p.p. of *praetexere* (PRAE-, *texere,* to weave)]

pretone, *n.* the vowel or syllable preceding the accented syllable. **pretonic**, *a.* [TONE]

pretor etc. PRAETOR.

Pretoria, *n.* administrative capital of the Republic of South Africa from 1910 and capital of Transvaal province from 1860; population (1985) 741,300. Industries include engineering, chemicals, iron, and steel. Founded 1855, it was named after Boer leader Andries Pretorius (1799–1853).

pretty, *a.* good-looking, attractive, appealing (though without the striking qualities or perfect proportions of beauty); aesthetically pleasing (with the same qualification); superficially or conventionally attractive; (*coll., derog.*) of a man, effeminate-looking; (*chiefly iron.*) nice, fine; considerable, large; †commendable. *adv.* moderately, fairly; very. *n.* a pretty thing or person. **a pretty penny** PENNY. **pretty much, well,** nearly, almost. **to be sitting pretty** SIT. **to pretty up,** to prettify, to adorn. **pretty-pretty,** *a.* affectedly pretty, over-pretty. *n.pl.* knick-knacks, gewgaws. **pretty-spoken,** *a.* speaking in a pleasing manner. **prettify**, *v.t.* to make pretty; to put or depict in a pretty way. **prettily,** *adv.* in a pretty manner; daintily, with taste and elegance; pleasingly to the eye, ear etc. **prettiness,** *n.* **prettyish,** *n.* **prettyism,** *n.* [OE *prætig, prættig,* from *præt, prætt,* trick, trickery (cp. Dut. *part,* Norw. *pretta*)]

pretypify, *v.t.* to prefigure.

pretzel, *n.* a crisp biscuit of wheaten flour flavoured with salt, usu. in the shape of a stick or a knot and eaten as a relish with beer. [G]

prevail, *v.i.* to have the mastery or victory (over, against etc.); to predominate; to be in force, to be current or in vogue; to be customary; **to prevail on, upon,** to succeed in persuading, to induce. **prevailing,** *a.* predominant, most frequent; current, generally accepted; **prevailingly,** *adv.* †**prevailment,** *n.* **prevalence**, †**-ency,** *n.* the act of prevailing; a superiority, predominance; frequency, vogue, currency. **prevalent,** *a.* **prevalently,** *adv.* [L *praevalēre* (PRAE-, *valēre,* to be strong)]

prevaricate, *v.i.* to shuffle, to quibble; to act or speak evasively; to equivocate. **prevarication,** *n.* **prevaricator,** *n.* [L *praevārīcātus,* p.p. of *praevārīcārī* (PRAE-, *vārīcus*, straddling, from *vārus,* bent)]

prevenance, †**-ancy** *n.* anticipation of the wants or wishes of others. [F *prévenance,* from *prévenir,* L *praevenīre,* as foll.]

prevenient, *a.* going before, preceding, previous; preventive (of). **prevenient grace,** *n.* grace preceding repentance and predisposing to conversion. **prevenience,** *n.* [L *praeveniens -ntem,* pres.p. of *praevenīre,* to precede, to anticipate, to prevent (PRAE-, *venīre,* to come)]

prevent, *v.t.* to keep from happening; to hinder, to thwart, to stop; †to anticipate; to go before, to precede, to be earlier than. **preventable, -ible,** *a.* capable of prevention. **preventative** PREVENTIVE. **preventer,** *n.* one who or that which prevents or hinders; (*Naut.*) a supplementary rope, chain, spar, stay etc., to support another. **preventingly,** *adv.* **prevention,** *n.* the act of preventing; hindrance, obstruction; †the act of going before, anticipation; †precaution; †prejudice. †**preventional,** *a.* **preventive,** (*loosely*) **preventative,** *a.* tending to hinder or prevent; prophylactic; of or belonging to the coastguard or customs and excise service. *n.* that which prevents; a medicine or precaution to ward off disease; a contraceptive. **preventive detention,** *n.* a system for dealing with a habitual criminal by detention for a definite period after the completion of the sentence for a specific crime. **preventive service,** *n.* the coastguard or customs and excise service. **preventively,** *adv.* [L *praeventus,* p.p. of *praevenīre,* as prec.]

preview, *n.* an advance view, a foretaste; an advance showing of a play, film, art exhibition etc. before its general presentation to the public; (also, *esp. N Am.* **prevue**) a television or cinema trailer. *v.t.* to view or show in advance.

Previn, *n.* **André (George)** (1929–), US conductor and composer, born in Berlin. After a period working as a composer and arranger in the US film industry, he concentrated on conducting. He was principal conductor of the London Symphony Orchestra 1968–79. He was appointed music director of Britain's Royal Philharmonic Orchestra in 1985 (a post he relinquished the following year, staying on as principal conductor), and of the Los Angeles Philharmonic in 1986.

previous, *a.* going before, antecedent; prior (to); (*sl.*) premature, hasty. *adv.* before, previously (to). **Previous Examination,** *n.* (*Camb. Univ.*) *n.* the Little-go or first examination for the degree of BA. **previous question,** *n.* in the House of Commons, a motion 'that the question be not now put', which, if carried, has the effect of delaying a vote; in the House of Lords and US legislature, a motion to proceed to a vote immediately; in public meetings, a motion to proceed with the next business. **previously,** *adv.* **previousness,** *n.* [L *praevius* (PRAE-, *via,* way)]

previse, *v.t.* to know beforehand, to foresee; to forewarn. **prevision**, *n.* **previsional,** *a.* **previsionally,**

adv. [L *praevīsus,* p.p. of *praevidēre* (PRAE-, *vidēre,* to see)]

Prévost d'Exiles, *n.* **Antoine François** (1697–1763), French novelist, known as Abbé Prévost, who sandwiched a military career into his life as a monk. His *Manon Lescaut* (1731) inspired operas by Massenet and Puccini.

prey, *n.* that which is or may be seized to be devoured by carnivorous animals; booty, spoil, plunder; a victim; (*Bibl.*) that which is brought away safe (from a battle etc.); †ravage, depredation. *v.i.* to take booty or plunder; to take food by violence. **beast, bird of prey,** a carnivorous beast or bird. **to prey on,** to rob, to plunder; to chase and seize as food; to make a victim of, to subject to robbery, extortion etc.; to have a depressing or obsessive effect on. **preyer,** *n.* **†preyful,** *a.* [OF *praie, preia,* L *praeda,* booty]

Priam, *n.* in Greek mythology, the last king of Troy. He was killed by Pyrrhus, son of Achilles, when Greeks entered the city of Troy concealed in a wooden horse.

Priapus, *n.* Greek god of garden fertility and procreation, son of Dionysus and Aphrodite, represented as grotesquely ugly, with an exaggerated phallus; (**priapus**) a phallus; (**priapus**) the penis. **priapean, priapic,** *a.* **priapism,** *n.* lasciviousness; continuous erection of the penis without sexual excitement. [L, from Gr. *Priapos*]

pribble, *n.* empty chatter. [var. of PRABBLE]

price, *n.* the amount asked for a thing or for which it is sold; the cost of a thing; the amount needed to bribe somebody; that which must be expended, sacrificed, done etc., to secure a thing; (*Betting sl.*) the odds; estimation, value, preciousness; †a prize. *v.t.* to fix the price of, to value, to appraise; to ask the price of; †to pay for. **above, beyond, without price,** priceless. **a price on one's head,** the reward offered for one's killing or capture. **at a price,** for a lot of money etc. **not at any price,** under no circumstances. **to price oneself out of the market,** to lose trade by charging too high prices. **what price?,** (*iron.*) what about? **price control,** *n.* the fixing by government of maximum prices for goods and services. **price-fixing,** *n.* the setting of prices by agreement between producers and distributors; price control. **price list,** *n.* a table of the current prices of merchandise, stocks etc. **price ring,** *n.* a group of manufacturers or traders who cooperate to maintain prices at an agreed, high level. **price tag,** *n.* the label attached to an object showing its price; price, cost. **priceless** *a.* invaluable, inestimable; †of no value, unsaleable; (*sl.*) very funny. **pricelessness,** *n.* **pricey,** *a.* (*comp.* **pricier,** *superl.* **priciest**) expensive. [ME and OF *pris* (F *prix*), L *pretium,* cp. PRAISE, PRIZE[1]]

Price, *n.* **Vincent** (1911–), US actor, star of horror films including *House of Wax* (1953) and *House of Usher* (1960).

prick, *n.* the act of pricking; the state or the sensation of being pricked; a puncture; a dot, point or small mark made by or as by pricking; a pointed instrument, a goad, a spur; a sharp, stinging pain; (*Naut.*) a small roll (of tobacco); (*sl.*) the penis; (*sl.*) an obnoxious or inept man. *v.t.* to pierce slightly, to puncture; to make by puncturing; to mark off (names etc.) with a prick, hence, to select; to cause (the ears) to point upwards; to goad, to rouse, to incite. *v.i.* to ride rapidly, to spur; to point upward; to feel as if pricked. **to kick against the pricks,** to hurt oneself in unavailing struggle against something. **to prick off, out,** to mark a pattern out with dots; to plant seedlings more widely apart with a view to transplanting later to their permanent quarters. **to prick up the ears,** of dogs etc., to raise the ears as if listening; to become very attentive. **prick-eared,** *a.* of dogs etc., having erect or pointed ears; priggish (applied to the Roundheads by the Cavaliers). **prick-ears,** *n.pl.* **†pricklouse, †prick-the-louse, †prick-the-clout,** *n.* a tailor. **prick-song,** *n.* music sung from notes pricked down, written music. **pricker,** *n.* a sharp-pointed instrument, a bradawl; †a light-horseman. [OE *prica* (cp. Dan. *prik,* Swed. *prick*), cogn. with *prician,* to prick (cp. Dan. *prikke,* Dut. *prikken*)]

pricket, *n.* a buck in its second year; a sharp point for sticking a candle on. **pricket's sister,** *n.* the female fallow deer in the second year. [from prec., in alln. to the straight unbranched horns]

prickle[1], *n.* a small, sharp point; a thorn-like growth capable of being peeled off with the skin or bark, opp. to thorn or spine; (*loosely*) a small thorn, spine etc. *v.t.* to prick slightly; to give a pricking or tingling sensation to. *v.i.* to have such a sensation. **prickle-back,** *n.* the stickleback. **prickly,** *a.* full of or armed with prickles. **prickly heat,** *n.* a skin condition characterized by itching and stinging sensations, prevalent in hot countries. **prickly pear,** *n.* (the pear-shaped fruit of) any cactus of the genus *Opuntia,* usu. covered with prickles. **prickliness,** *n.* [OE *pricel,* cogn. with prec.]

prickle[2], *n.* a variety of wicker basket; a measure of weight of about 50 lb (22.7 kg). [etym. unknown]

pride, *n.* inordinate self-esteem, unreasonable conceit of one's own superiority; insolence, arrogance; sense of dignity, self-respect, proper self-esteem; generous elation or satisfaction arising out of some accomplishment, possession or relationship; a source of such elation; the acme, the highest point, the best condition; a collection of lions. **pride of place,** the highest, most prominent or most important position. **to pride oneself on,** to be proud of oneself for. **prideful,** *a.* (*chiefly Sc.*). **pridefully,** *adv.* **pridefulness,** *n.* **prideless,** *a.* [OE *prȳto, prȳte,* cogn. with *prūt,* PROUD]

Pride and Prejudice, a novel by Jane Austen, published in the UK in 1813. Mr and Mrs Bennet, whose property is due to pass to a male cousin, William Collins, are anxious to secure good marriage settlements for their five daughters. Central to the story is the romance between the witty Elizabeth Bennet and the proud Mr Darcy.

Pride's purge, *n.* the removal of about 100 Royalists and Presbyterians of the English House of Commons from Parliament by a detachment of soldiers led by Col. Thomas Pride (died 1658) in 1648. They were accused of negotiating with Charles I and were seen as unreliable by the army. The remaining members were termed the Rump and voted in favour of the king's trial.

prie-Dieu, *n.* a kneeling desk for prayers. **prie-Dieu chair,** *n.* a chair with a tall sloping back, esp. for praying. [F, pray God]

prier, *n.* one who pries. [PRY[1], -ER]

priest, *n.* one who officiates in sacred rites, esp. by offering sacrifice; a minister of the second order, below a bishop and above a deacon, esp. as having authority to administer the sacraments and pronounce absolution; (*coll.*) a clergyman, a minister (esp. in a hostile sense); a small mallet or club for killing fish when caught. **priest-craft,** *n.* priestly policy based on material interests. **priest-in-the-pulpit,** PRIEST'S HOOD. **priest-ridden,** *a.* (*derog.*) dominated or swayed by priests. **priest's hole,** *n.* a hiding-place for fugitive priests, esp. in England under the penal laws. **priest's hood,** *n.* the wild arum. **priest-vicar,** *n.* a minor canon in certain cathedrals. **priestess,** *n. fem.* **priest-hood,** *n.* **priestless,** *a.* **priestlike,** *a.* **priestling,**, *n.* **priestly,** *a.* of, pertaining to, or befitting a priest or the priesthood; sacerdotal. **priestliness,** *n.* [OE *prēost,* PRESBYTER]

Priestley, *n.* **J(ohn) B(oynton)** (1894–1984), English novelist and playwright. His first success was a novel about travelling theatre, *The Good Companions* (1929). He followed it with a realist novel about London life, *Angel Pavement* (1930); later books include *Lost Empires* (1965) and *The Image Men* (1968). As a playwright he was often preoccupied with theories of time, as in *An Inspector Calls* (1945), but had also a gift for family comedy, for example, *When We Are Married* (1938).

prig, *n.* a conceited, formal or moralistic person; †(*sl.*) a thief. *v.t.* †(*sl.*) to filch, to steal. **priggery,** *n.* **priggish,** *a.* conceited, affectedly precise, formal, moralistic. **priggishly,** *adv.* **priggishness,** *n.* [prob. var. of PRICK]

Prigogine, *n.* **Ilya** (1917–), Russian-born Belgian chemist who, as a highly original theoretician, has made major contributions to the field of thermodynamics for which work he was awarded the Nobel physics prize 1977. Earlier theories had considered systems at or about equilibrium. Prigogine began to study 'dissapative' or non-equilibrium structures frequently found in biological and chemical reactions.

prill, *n.* (*Mining*) one of the better portions of copper ore; a button of metal from an assay. [Cornish dial.]

prim, *a.* formal, affectedly proper, demure. *v.t.* (*past, p.p.* **primmed**) to put (the lips, mouth etc.) into a prim expression; to deck with great nicety or preciseness. *v.i.* to make oneself look prim. **primly,** *adv.* **primness,** *n.* [prob. 17th cent. sl.]

prima, *a.* first, chief, principal. **prima ballerina,** *n.* the leading female ballet dancer. **prima buffa**, a chief comic singer or actress. **prima donna,** *n.* (*pl.* **prime donne**) a chief female singer in an opera; a person who is temperamental, hard to please, and given to histrionics. [It., fem. of *primo,* L *prīmus,* first]

primacy, *n.* the dignity or office of a primate; pre-eminence. [OF *primacie,* med. L *prīmātia,* L *prīmātus,* from *prīmus,* PRIME[1]]

primaeval, PRIMEVAL.

prima facie, *adv.* at first sight, on the first impression. **prima facie case,** (*Law*) a case apparently established by the evidence. [L, abl. of *prīma facies,* first face]

primage, *n.* a percentage on the freight paid to the owner of a ship for care in loading or unloading cargo. [med. L *primāgium,* etym. doubtful]

primal, *a.* primary, original, primitive; fundamental, chief. **primally,** *adv.* [L *prīmālis,* from *prīmus,* PRIME[1]]

primary, *a.* first in time, order or origin; original, radical, firsthand; primitive, fundamental; first in rank or importance, chief; first or lowest in development, elementary; of or being an industry that produces raw materials; of or being the inducing current or its circuit in an induction coil or transformer; pertaining to the lowest series of strata, Palaeozoic. *n.* that which stands first in order, rank, or importance; a planet as distinguished from its satellites; a celestial body round which other members of a system orbit; a meeting or election for the selection of party candidates by voters of a state or region, esp. in the US; one of the large quill-feathers of a bird's wing; a primary colour; a primary school. **primary cell,** *n.* a battery in which an irreversible chemical action is converted into electrical energy (cp. SECONDARY CELL). **primary colours** COLOUR. **primary consumer,** *n.* a herbivore. **primary education,** *n.* education in primary, junior, and infant schools. **primary feather,** *n.* a primary. **primary school,** *n.* a school for children aged under 11 (England and Wales) or under 12 (Scotland). **primary winding,** *n.* the winding of a transformer which is on the input side; the input winding on the stator of an induction motor. **primarily**, *adv.* **primariness,** *n.* [L *prīmārius,* from *prīmus,* PRIME[1]]

primate, *n.* the chief prelate in a national episcopal church, an archbishop; a member of the order Primates. **Primate of all England,** the archbishop of Canterbury. **Primate of England,** the archbishop of York. **primates**, *n.pl.* the highest group of mammals, comprising humans, apes, monkeys and lemurs. **primateship,** *n.* **primatial**, *a.* **primatology**, *n.* the study of primates. **primatologist,** *n.* [late L *prīmas -ātis,* from L *prīmus,* PRIME[1]]

prime[1], *a.* first in time, rank, excellence or importance; esp. of meat and provisions, chief; first-rate, excellent; original, primary, fundamental; in the vigour of maturity, blooming; divisible by no integral factors except itself and unity (as 2, 3, 5, 7, 11, 13). *n.* the period or state of highest perfection; the best part (of anything); the first canonical hour of the day, beginning at 6 am or at sunrise; in the Roman Catholic Church, the office for this hour; the first stage, the beginning (of anything); dawn, spring, youth; a prime number; (*Fencing*) the first of the eight parries or a thrust in this position; (*Calendar*) the golden number. **prime cost,** *n.* the cost of material and labour in the production of an article. **prime-meridian** MERIDIAN. **prime minister,** *n.* the first Minister of State, esp. in the UK. **prime mover,** *n.* one who or that which originates a movement or an action, esp. the force putting a machine in motion; God. **prime number,** *n.* a number that is divisible by no integral factors except itself and unity. **prime rate,** *n.* the lowest commercial rate of interest charged by a bank at a particular time. **prime time,** *n.* peak viewing or listening time for television or radio audiences, for which advertising rates are highest. **prime vertical,** *n.* a great circle of the heavens passing through the east and west points of the horizon and the zenith. **primely,** *adv.* **primeness,** *n.* [F, from L *prīmus,* first]

prime[2], *v.t.* to prepare (a gun) for firing; to supply (with information); to coach; to fill (with liquor); to fill (a pump) with fluid to expel the air before starting; to inject fuel into the float chamber of (a carburettor); to lay the first coat of paint, plaster or oil on. *v.i.* of a boiler, to carry over water with the steam to the cylinder; of a tide, to come before the mean time. **primer[1],** *n.* a person or thing that primes; a priming-wire; a detonator; (a type of) paint used as a sealant and a base for subsequent coats. **priming,** *n.* the act of preparing a firearm for discharge; the powder placed in the pan of a flint gun; a train of powder connecting a blasting-charge with the fuse; fluid introduced before starting a pump; a first layer of paint etc.; a mixture used as a preparatory coat; water carried from the boiler into the cylinder of a steam-engine; hasty instruction, cramming. **priming-iron, -wire,** *n.* a wire for piercing a cartridge when home, or for clearing the vent of a gun etc; the shortening of the interval between tides (from neap to spring tides), opp. to *lagging*. [etym. doubtful]

primer[2], *n.* an elementary reading-book for children; a short introductory book; †a prayer-book or book of religious instruction for the laity, orig. a book for prime; one of two sizes of type, great primer and long primer. [OF, from med. L *prīmārius,* PRIMARY]

primero, *n.* a game of cards fashionable in the 16th and 17th cents., the original of poker. [Sp. *primera,* fem. of *primero,* as prec.]

primeval, primaeval, *a.* belonging to the earliest ages, ancient, original, primitive. **primevally, primaevally,** *adv.* [L *prīmaevus* (*prīm-us,* PRIME[1], *aevum,* age)]

†**primigenial,** †**primigenious,** *a.* first formed or generated; original, primary. [L *prīmigenius* (*prīmi-, prīmus* PRIME[1], *gen-,* stem of *gignere,* to produce)]

priming PRIME[2].

primiparous, *a.* bringing forth a child for the first time. [L *prīmus,* PRIME[1], *-parous,* from *parere,* to bring forth]

primitiae, *n.pl.* first fruits, annates; the discharge of fluid from the uterus before parturition. [L, from *prīmus* PRIME[2]]

primitive, *a.* pertaining to the beginning or the earliest periods; early, ancient, original, primary, primordial; (*Gram.*) radical, not derivative; rude, simple, plain, old-fashioned; crude, uncivilized; of a culture or society, not advanced, lacking a written language and all but basic technical skills; (*Geol.*) belonging to the lowest strata or the earliest period; (*Biol.*) pertaining to an early stage of development; (*Art.*) belonging to the period before the Renaissance not conforming to the traditional standards of Western painting; painting in a naive, childlike, or apparently untaught manner. *n.* a primitive painter; a picture by such a painter; a primitive word; a Primitive Methodist. **primitive colours,** *n.pl.* primary colours. **Primitive Methodism,** *n.* a connection or sect aiming at a preponderance of lay control in church government, established in 1810 by secession from the Methodist Church. Inspired by American example, open-air sermons were accompanied by prayers and hymn singing. In 1932 the Primitive Methodists became a constituent of a unified Methodist church. **Primitive Methodist,** *n.* a member of this connection. **primitive rocks,** *n.pl.* primary rocks. **primitively,** *adv.* **primitiveness,** *n.* [F *primitif, -tive,* L *prīmitīvus,* as prec.]

primo, *n.* (*pl.* **-mos**) the first part (in a duet etc.). **primo basso,** *n.* the chief bass singer. [It., as PRIME[1]]

Primo de Rivera, Miguel (1870–1930), Spanish soldier and politician, dictator from 1923 as well as premier from 1925. He was captain-general of Catalonia when he led a coup against the ineffective monarchy and became virtual dictator of Spain with the support of Alfonso XIII. He resigned in 1930.

†**primogenial, -nious** PRIMIGENIAL.

primogeniture, *n.* seniority by birth amongst children of the same parents; the right, system or rule under which, in cases of intestacy, the eldest son succeeds to the real estate of his father. **primogenital, -ary,** *a.* **primogenitive,** *a., n.* **primogenitor,** *n.* the first father or ancestor; an ancestor. †**primogenitureship,** *n.* [F *primogéniture,* med. L *prīmogenitūra* (L *prīmō,* PRIME[1], GENITURE)]

primordial, *a.* first in order, primary, original, primitive; existing at or from the beginning; first-formed. *n.* an origin; a first principle or element. **primordiality, primordialism,** *n.* **primordially,** *adv.* [F, from late L *prīmordiālis,* from *prīmordium,* origin (*prīmus,* PRIME[1], *ordīrī,* to begin)]

Primorye, *n.* territory of the Russian Soviet Federal Socialist Republic in SE Siberia on the Sea of Japan; area 165,900 sq km/64,079 sq miles; population (1985) 2,136,000. Capital is Vladivostock. Timber and coal are produced.

primp, *v.t.* to make prim; to prink. *v.i.* to prink oneself; to preen; to behave primly or put on affected airs.

primrose, *n.* *Primula vulgaris,* a common British wild plant, flowering in early spring; any plant of the genus *Primula;* a pale yellow colour; †the best, the chief, the most excellent. *a.* like a primrose; of a pale yellow colour; †gay as with flowers; flowery. **Primrose dame, knight,** *n.* a member of the Primrose League. **Primrose Day,** *n.* the anniversary of the death of Lord Beaconsfield, 19 Apr. 1881, commemorated by the wearing of primroses (said to have been his favourite flower). **Primrose League,** *n.* a conservative league formed in memory of Benjamin Disraeli, Earl of Beaconsfield, having for its objects 'the maintenance of religion, of the estates of the realm, and of the imperial ascendancy of the British Empire'. **primrose path,** *n.* the path of ease and pleasure, esp. as leading to perdition. [ME and OF *primerose* (med. L *prīma rōsa,* early rose), corr. of ME and OF *primerole,* ult. from L *prīmula,* dim. from *prīmus,* PRIME[1]]

primsie, *a.* (*Burns*) prim, demure. [PRIM]

Primula, *n.* a genus of herbaceous plants belonging to the family Primulaceae, comprising the primrose, cowslip etc.; **primula** a plant of this genus. [L]

primum mobile, *n.* in the Ptolemaic system, an imaginary sphere believed to revolve from east to west in 24 hours, carrying the heavenly bodies with it; the first source of motion, the mainspring of any action. [L, first moving thing]

primus, *a.* first, eldest (of the name, among boys in a school). *n.* the presiding bishop in the Scottish Episcopal Church. **Primus**®, *n.* a portable paraffin cooking stove used esp. by campers. [L, first]

prince, *n.* (*now rhet.*) a sovereign, a monarch; the ruler of a principality or small state, usu. feudatory to a king or emperor; a male member of a royal family, esp. the son or grandson of a monarch; a member of a foreign order of nobility usu. ranking next below a duke; in parliamentary writs, a duke, marquess or earl; a chief, leader or foremost representative. **Prince of Darkness,** the Devil. **Prince of Peace,** the Messiah, Christ. **prince of the Church,** a cardinal. **Prince of Wales,** the title customarily conferred on the heir-apparent to the British throne. **Prince Rupert's drop,** a pear-shaped lump of glass formed by falling in a molten state into water, bursting to dust when the thin end is nipped off. **prince-bishop,** *n.* a bishop whose see is a principality. **Prince Charming,** *n.* an ideal suitor. **Prince Consort,** *n.* a prince who is the husband of a reigning female sovereign. **Prince Regent,** *n.* a prince acting as regent. **prince royal,** *n.* the eldest son of a sovereign. **prince's feather,** *n.* a popular name for several plants, esp. the Mexican *Amaranthus hypochondriacus.* **prince's metal,** *n.* an alloy of copper and zinc. **princedom,** †**princehood,** *n.* **princekin, princelet, princeling,** *n.* **prince-like,** *a.* **princely,** *a.* pertaining to or befitting a prince; having the rank of a prince; stately, dignified; generous, lavish. *adv.* as becomes a prince. **princeliness,** *n.* **princeship,** *n.* **princess,** *n.* †a female sovereign; the daughter or granddaughter of a sovereign; the wife of a prince; a princesse. **Princess Regent,** *n.* a princess acting as regent; the wife of a Prince Regent. **princess royal,** *n.* title conferrable for life on the eldest daughter of a reigning sovereign. [F, from L *principem,* nom. *-ceps* (*prin-, prīm-us,* PRIME[1], *capere,* to take)]

Prince, *n.* stage name of Prince Rogers Nelson (1960–), US pop musician, who composes, arranges, and produces his own records, and often plays all the instruments. His albums, including *1999* (1982) and *Purple Rain* (1984), contain elements of rock, funk, and jazz.

Prince Edward Island, province of E Canada. **area** 5700 sq km/2200 sq miles. **capital** Charlottetown. **products** potatoes, dairy products, lobsters, oysters, farm vehicles. **population** (1986) 127,000. **history** first recorded visit by Cartier 1534, who called it Isle St-Jean; settled by French; taken by British 1758; annexed to Nova Scotia 1763; separate colony 1769; settled by Scottish 1803; joined Confederation 1873.

princeps, *a.* (*pl.* **-cipes**) first. *n.* a chief or head man; the title of the Roman emperor as constitutional head of the state. **editio princeps,** (*pl.* **editiones, principes**) the original edition of a book. **facile, princeps,** easily first, beyond question the chief or most important. [L, first, chief, see prec.]

princesse, princess, *n., a.* (a dress) having a close-fitting bodice and flared skirt cut in one piece. [F, as PRINCESS]

Prince William Sound, a sound of the Gulf of Alaska, extending 200 km/125 mi NW from Kayak Island. In March 1989 the oil tanker Exxon Valdez ran aground here, spilling 12 million gallons of crude oil in what was reckoned to be the world's greatest oil pollution disaster.

principal, *a.* chief, leading, main; first in rank, authority, importance, influence or degree; constituting the capital sum invested. *n.* a chief or head; a president, a governor, the head of a college etc.; a leader or chief actor in any transaction, the chief party, the person ultimately liable; a person employing another as agent; the actual perpetrator of a crime, the principal in the first degree, or one aiding and abetting, principal in the second degree; a performer who takes a leading role; a capital sum invested or lent, as distinguished from income; a main rafter, esp. one extending to the ridge-pole; an organ-stop of the open diapason family, usu. sounding an octave above standard pitch. **principal boy,** *n.* the leading male role in a pantomime, usu. taken by a woman. **principal parts,** *n.pl.* those inflected forms of a verb from which all other inflections can be derived. **principally,** *adv.* chiefly, mainly, for the most part. †**principalness,** *n.* **principalship,** *n.* [F, from L *principālis,* from *princeps -cipis,* see PRINCE]

principality, *n.* the territory or jurisdiction of a prince; the country from which a prince derives his title; †sovereignty, royal state or condition, superiority; (*pl.*) the name given to one order of angels. **the Principality,** Wales.

principate, *n.* (*Rom. Hist.*) the form of government under the early emperors when some republican features were retained; a principality.

principia, *n.pl.* beginnings, origins, elements, first principles. †**principial,** †**principiant,** *a.* [L, pl. of *principium,* see foll.]

principle, *n.* a source, an origin; a fundamental cause or element; a comprehensive truth or proposition from which others are derived; a general truth forming a basis for reasoning or action; a fundamental doctrine or tenet; a rule of action or conduct deliberately adopted, as distinguished from impulse; the habitual regulation of conduct by moral law; a law of nature by virtue of which a given mechanism etc. brings about certain results; the mechanical contrivance, combination of parts, or mode of operation, forming the basis of a machine, instrument, process etc.; (*Chem.*) the constituent that gives specific character to a substance; †a beginning. *v.t.* to establish in certain principles. **in principle,** as far as the basic idea or theory is concerned. **on principle,** because of the fundamental (moral) issue involved; in order to assert a principle. **principled,** *a.* guided by principle; based on a principle. [F *principe,* L *principium,* beginning, from *princeps -cipis,* see PRINCE]

princock, *n.* a pert young fellow; a coxcomb. [etym. doubtful]

prink, *v.i.* to dress for show; to make oneself smart, esp. excessively so. *v.t.* to prank or dress up. **prinker,** *n.* [rel. to PRANK[2]]

print, *n.* an indentation or other mark made by pressure, an imprint, an impression; an impression from type, an engraved plate etc.; printed lettering; printed matter; a printed publication, esp. a newspaper; an engraving, lithograph etc.; a reproduction of a work of art made by a photographic process; printed cotton cloth; an article made of such material; a fingerprint; (*Phot.*) a positive image produced from a negative. *v.t.* to impress, to mark by pressure; to take an impression of, to stamp; to impress or make copies of by pressure, as from inked types, plates or blocks, on paper, cloth etc.; to cause (a book etc.) to be so impressed or copied, to issue from the press, to publish; to reproduce a design, writing etc. by any transfer process; to mark with a design etc. by stamping; to imprint, to form (letters etc.) in imitation of printing; to impress (on the memory etc.) as if by printing; (*Phot.*) to produce (a positive image) from a negative. *v.i.* to practise the art of printing; to publish books etc.; to form letters etc. in imitation of printing. **in print,** in a printed form; on sale (of a printed book etc.). **out of print,** no longer obtainable from the publisher. **to print out,** to product a print-out (of). **to rush into print,** to write to a newspaper or publish a book without adequate justification. **print-out,** *n.* (a) printed copy automatically produced by a computer. **print run,** *n.* (the number of copies produced in) a single printing of a book etc. **print-seller,** *n.* one who deals in engravings. **print-shop,** *n.* a place where printing is carried out; a place where engravings etc. are sold. **print-works,** *n.* an establishment for printing cotton fabrics. **printable,** *a.* able to be printed or printed on or from; fit to appear in print. **printed circuit,** *n.* an electronic circuit consisting of conductive material etched or electrode deposited onto an isulating base. **printless,** *a.* **printer,** *n.* one engaged in printing books, pamphlets, newspapers etc.: a typesetter, a compositor; one who carries on a printing business; one who prints calico etc.; a machine or instrument for printing copies, designs etc.; a device for producing print-out. **printer's devil,** *n.* a boy of all work in a printing-office. **printer's ink** *n.* a viscous mixture of black pigment and oil or varnish used as ink in printing. **printer's mark,** *n.* an engraved design used as a device or trade-mark by a printer or publisher, an imprint. **printer's pie** PIE[3]. **printing,** *n.* the act, process, or practice of impressing letters, characters, or figures on paper, cloth or other material; the business of a printer; typography. **printing-ink,** *n.* printer's ink. **printing machine,** *n.* a machine for taking impressions from type etc. esp. a power-operated one. **printing-office,** *n.* an establishment where printing is carried on. **printing-paper,** *n.* paper suitable for printing. **printing out paper,** *n.* sensitized paper for daylight printing. **printing-press,** *n.* a printing-machine; a hand-press for printing. [OF *preinte,* from *preint,* p.p. of *preindre,* L *premere,* to PRESS]

prior[1], *a.* former, preceding; earlier, antecedent; taking precedence. *adv.* previously, antecedently (to). [L, comp. of obs. *pri,* before]

prior[2], *n.* a superior of a monastic house or order next in rank below an abbot; (*Hist.*) a chief magistrate in certain Italian republics, a head of a guild at Florence etc. **claustral prior,** a prior acting as assistant to an abbot. **priorate, priorship,** *n.* **prioress**, *n. fem.* **priory,** *n.* a religious house governed by a prior or prioress. [late OE, as prec.]

priority, *n.* going before, antecedence; precedence, a superior claim or entitlement; something given or meriting special attention; the right to proceed while other vehicles wait *a.* having or entitling to priority.

†**prisage,** *n.* an obsolete customs duty on wine. [obs. *prise,* OF *prise,* a taking or seizure, from *pris, prise,* p.p. of *prendre,* to take, -AGE]

prise, *n.* leverge; †a lever. *v.t.* to wrench; to force open with or as with a lever; to extract with difficulty. [PRIZE[2]]

prism, *n.* a solid having similar, equal and parallel plane bases or ends, its sides forming similar parallelograms; a transparent solid of this form, usu. triangular, with two refracting surfaces set at an acute angle to each other, used as an optical instrument; a spectrum produced by refraction through this; any medium acting on light etc. in a similar manner. **prismal, prismatic,** †**-al**, *a.* pertaining to or resembling a prism; formed, refracted or distributed by a prism; (*Cryst.*) orthorhombic. **prismatic binoculars,** *n.pl.* binoculars shortened by the insertion of prisms. **prismatic colours** [COLOURS]. **prismatic compass,** *n.* a hand-compass with an attached prism by which the dial can be read while taking the sight. **prismatic powder,** *n.* gunpowder, the grains of which are hexagonal prisms. **prismatically,** *adv.* **prismatoid**, *n.* a solid with parallel polygonal bases connected by triangular faces. **prismatoidal**, *a.* **prismoid**, *n.* **prismoidal,** *a.* **prismy**, *a.* [late L *prisma,* from Gr. *prisma -matos,* from *prizein,* to saw]

prison, *n.* a place of confinement, esp. a public building for the confinement of criminals, persons awaiting trial etc.; confinement, captivity. *v.t.* (*poet.*) to imprison; to confine, to restrain. †**prison-base** [PRISONER'S BASE]. **prison-bird** [JAIL-BIRD]. **prison-breaker,** *n.* one who escapes from legal imprisonment. **prison-breaking,** *n.* **prison-house,** *n.* (*poet.*) a prison. **prison officer,** *n.* a person who guards and supervises prisoners in a prison. **prisoner,** *n.* one confined in a prison; one under arrest; a captive. **prisoner at the bar,** a person in custody or on trial upon a criminal charge. **prisoner of conscience,** a person whose political, religious etc. beliefs have led to imprisonment. **prisoner of war,** a person captured in war. **to take prisoner,** to capture; to arrest and hold in custody. **prisoner's-base,** †**-bars,** *n.* a game played by two sides occupying opposite goals or bases, the object being to touch and capture a player away from his base. [OF *prison, prisun,* L *prensiōnem,* nom. *prensio, prehensio,* from *prehendere,* to seize]

pristine, *a.* pertaining to an early state or time; ancient, primitive; pure, unadulterated, uncorrupted; as new. [L *pristinus,* cogn. with *priscus,* see PRISCAN]

Pritchett, *n.* **V(ictor) S(awdon)** (1900–), English short story writer, novelist, and critic, with an often witty and satirical style. His critical works include *The Living Novel* (1946) and a biography of the French novelist Balzac.

†**prithee,** *int.* pray, please. [corr. of PRAY THEE]

privacy PRIVATE.

privatdozent, *n.* (*G. Univ.*) a recognized teacher or lecturer not on the regular staff. [G, private teacher (as foll. L *docens -ntem* pres.p. of *docēre,* to teach)]

private, *a.* not public; kept or withdrawn from publicity or observation; retired, secluded; secret, confidential; not holding a public position, not administered or provided by the state not part of, or being treated under, the National Health Service; not official; personal, not pertaining to the community; one's own; secretive, reticent. *n.* a soldier of the lowest rank; (*pl.*) the private parts; †a private matter; †privacy. **in private,** privately, confidentially; in private life. **private act** or **bill,** *n.* one affecting a private person or persons and not the general public. **private company,** *n.* a company with a restricted number of shareholders, whose shares are not offered for sale to the general public. **private detective** DETECTIVE. **private enterprise,** *n.* economic activity undertaken by private individuals or organizations. **private eye,** *n.* (*coll.*) a private detective. **private investigator,** *n.* a private detective. **private judgment,** *n.* one's individual judgment, esp. as applied to a religious doctrine or passage of Scripture. **private member's bill,** *n.* one introduced and sponsored by a member of Parliament who is not a government minister. **private parts,** *n.pl.* the genitals. **private school,** *n.* one run independently by an individual or group esp. for profit. **private secretary,** *n.* one entrusted with personal and confidential matters; a civil servant acting as an aide to a minister or senior government official. **private sector,** *n.* the economy which is not state owned or controlled. **private soldier,** *n.* a private. **private view,** *n.* occasion when only those invited to an exhibition are admitted. **privacy** , *n.* **privately,** *adv.* **privateness,** *n.* **privatize, -ise,** *v.t.* to denationalize, to take back into the private sector, to return to private ownership. **privatization, -isation,** *n.* [L *prīvātus,* p.p. of *prīvāre,* to bereave, to set apart]

privateer, *n.* an armed ship owned and officered by private persons commissioned by Government by letters of marque to engage in war against a hostile nation, esp. to capture merchant shipping; one who engages in privateering; an officer or one of the crew of such a ship. *v.i.* to cruise or engage in hostilities in a privateer. **privateering,** *n.* **privateersman,** *n.* [prec., -EER]

privation, *n.* deprivation or lack of what is necessary; want, destitution; absence, loss, negation (of). **privative,** *a.* causing privation; consisting in the absence of something; expressing privation or absence of a quality etc. negative. *n.* that which depends on or of which the essence is the absence of something; a prefix or suffix (as *un-* or *-less*) giving a negative meaning to a word. **privatively,** *adv.*

privet, *n.* an evergreen, white-flowered shrub of the genus *Ligustrum,* esp. *L vulgare,* largely used for hedges. [etym. doubtful]

privilege, *n.* a benefit, right, advantage or immunity pertaining to a person, class, office etc.; favoured status, the possession of privileges, a special advantage; (*Law*) a particular right or power conferred by a special law; an exemption pertaining to an office; a right of priority or precedence in any respect. *v.t.* to invest with a privilege; to license, to authorize (to do); to exempt (from). **bill of privilege,** a peer's petition to be tried by his peers. **breach of privilege,** infringement of rights belonging to Parliament. **privilege of clergy,** benefit of clergy. **writ of privilege,** a writ to deliver a privileged person from custody when arrested in a civil suit. **privileged,** *a.* **privileged communication,** *n.* (*Law*) a communication which there is no compulsion to disclose in evidence. [OF, from L *prīvilēgium* (*prīvi-, prīvus,* private, *lex lēgis,* law), whence med. L *prīvilēgiāre* and F *privilegier,* to privilege]

privy, *a.* secluded, hidden, secret, clandestine, private; cognizant of something secret with another, privately knowing (with *to*). *n.* a latrine; (*Law*) a person having an interest in any action or thing. **privy chamber,** *n.* a private apartment in a royal residence. **Privy Council,** *n.* the private council of the British sovereign (the functions of which are now largely exercised by the Cabinet and committees), consisting of the princes of the blood, certain high officers of State, and members appointed by the Crown. **Privy Councillor,** *n.* **privy purse,** *n.* an allowance of money for the personal use of the sovereign; the officer in charge of this. **Privy Seal,** *n.* the seal appended to grants etc. which have not to pass the Great Seal. **Lord Privy Seal,** the officer of State entrusted with the Privy Seal. **privily,** *adv.* secretly, privately. **privity,** *n.* the state of being privy to (certain facts, intentions etc.); (*Law*) any relationship to another party involving participation in interest, reciprocal liabilities etc.; †privacy, secrecy. [F *privé,* L *prīvātus,* PRIVATE]

Prix Goncourt, *n.* a French literary prize for fiction, given by the Académie Goncourt from 1903.

prize[1], *n.* that which is offered or won as the reward of merit or superiority in any competition, contest, exhibition etc.; a sum of money or other object offered for competition in a lottery etc.; a well-paid appointment, a; fortune, or other desirable object of perseverance, enterprise etc. *a.* offered or gained as a prize; gaining or worthy of a prize, first-class, of superlative merit. *v.t.* to value highly, to esteem. **prize-fellow,** *n.* one who holds a fellowship awarded for pre-eminence in an examination. **prize-fellowship,** *n.* **prize-fight,** *n.* a boxing-match for stakes. **prize-fighter,** *n.* **prize-fighting,** *n.* **prizeman,** *n.* the winner of a prize. **prize-money,** *n.* money offered as a prize. **prize-ring,** *n.* the roped space (now usu. square) for a prize-fight; prize-fighting. **prize-winner,** *n.* **prize-winning,** *a.* **prizeless,** *a.* †**prizer,** *n.* a prize-fighter; a valuer, an appraiser. [ME and OF *pris,* PRICE; v. from OF *preisier* (F *priser*), to PRAISE]

prize[2], *n.* that which is taken from an enemy in war, esp. a ship or other property captured at sea. *v.t.* to make a prize of. **to become prize of,** to capture (a ship, cargo etc.). **prize-court,** *n.* a court adjudicating on cases of prizes captured at sea, in England and US a department of the courts of Admiralty. **prize-money,** *n.* the proceeds of the sale of a captured vessel etc. [F *prise,* a taking, a seizure, booty, orig. fem. of *pris,* p.p. of *prendre, prehendere,* to take]

prize[3], PRISE.

PRO, (*abbr.*) Public Records Office; public relations officer.

pro[1], *prep.* for; in favour of. *adv.* in favour. [L] **pro and con,** for and against; on both sides. **pros and cons,** reasons or arguments for and against. **pro bono publico**, for the public good. **pro forma**, as a matter of form; of invoice etc. made out to show the market price of goods. **pro rata**, in proportion, proportionally; proportional. **pro tempore**, for the time being; temporary. [L *pro et contra*]

pro[2], *n.* (*coll.*) a professional football player, cricketer, actor etc.; (*sl.*) a prostitute. [short for PROFESSIONAL]

pro-[1], *pref.* in favour of; replacing, substituting for; (in existing latinate compounds) onward, forward, before. [L *pro* for]

pro-[2], *pref.* before (in time or position); earlier than projecting, forward; rudimentary. [G *pro* before]

proa, *n.* a long, narrow, swift Malayan canoe, usu. equipped with both sails and oars. [Malay *prāū, prāhū*]

proactive, *a.* energetic, enterprising, taking the initiative.

pro-am, *a.* involving both professionals and amateurs.

prob., (*abbr.*) probably.

probabiliorism, *n.* in Roman Catholic theology, the doctrine that in cases of doubt among several courses of conduct it is proper to choose that which appears to have the most likelihood of being right; the teaching that a law is to be obeyed unless a very probable opinion is opposed to it. **probabiliorist,** *n.* [Latin *probābilior,* comp. of *probābilis,* PROBABLE, -ISM]

probabilism, *n.* in Roman Catholic theology, the doctrine that, in matters of conscience about which there is disagreement or doubt, it is lawful to adopt any course, at any rate if this has the support of any recognized authority. **probabilist,** *n.* [F *probabilisme*]

probability, *n.* the quality of being probable; that which is or appears probable; (*Math.*) likelihood of an event measured by the ratio of the favourable chances to the whole number of chances. **in all probability,** most likely. [F *probabilité,* L *probābilitātem,* nom. *-tas*]

probable, *a.* likely to prove true, having more evidence for than against, likely; †capable of being proved. *n.* a person likely to be chosen for a team, post etc. **prob-**

ably, *adv.* [F, from L *probābilem,* nom. *-lis* (*probāre,* to PROVE, -ABLE]

probang, *n.* a slender whalebone rod with a piece of sponge, a button or ball at the end, for introducing into or removing obstructions in the throat. [orig. *provang,* name given by the inventor]

probate, *n.* the official proving of a will; a certified copy of a proved will; the right or jurisdiction of proving wills. **probate duty,** *n.* a tax charged upon the personal property of deceased persons, now merged in estate duty. [L *probātum,* neut. of *-tus,* p.p. of *probāre,* to PROVE]

probation, *n.* a proving or testing of character, ability etc. esp. of a candidate for a religious ministry etc. by employment for a fixed period; a moral trial, esp. the discipline undergone in this life as a means to salvation; a method of dealing with criminals by allowing them to go at large under supervision during their good behaviour; the act of proving; evidence, proof. **on probation,** being tested for suitability etc.; under the supervision of a probation officer. **probation officer,** *n.* a court official whose duty it is to supervise and assist offenders who are on probation. **probational,** *a.* serving for or pertaining to probation or trial. **probationary,** *a.* probational; undergoing probation. *n.* a probationer. **probationer,** *n.* one on probation or trial; a divinity student licensed to preach and eligible for a charge; a nurse in training; an offender under probation. **probationership,** *n.* [ME and OF *probacion,* L *probātiōnem,* nom. *-tio,* as prec.]

probative, *a.* proving or tending to prove; serving as proof, evidential; †probational. **probator,** *n.* an examiner; an approver. †**probatory,** *a.* probative. [L *probātīvus*]

probe, *n.* a surgical instrument, usu. a silver rod with a blunt end, for exploring cavities of the body, wounds etc.; (*Elec.*) a lead containing or connected to a monitoring circuit; a docking device esp. a projecting pipe which connects with the drogue of a tanker aircraft to permit in-flight refuelling; an unmanned vehicle used to send back information from exploratory missions in space; an exploratory survey; a thorough investigation, as by a newspaper of e.g. alleged corruption. *v.t.* to search or examine (a wound, ulcer etc.) with, or as with, a probe; to scrutinize thoroughly. *v.i.* to make a tentative or exploratory investigation. **probe-scissors,** *n.pl.* scissors with the points tipped with buttons, used to open wounds. [late L *proba,* PROOF]

probity, *n.* tried honesty, sincerity or integrity; high principle, rectitude. [F, *probité,* L *probitātem,* nom. *-tas,* from *probus,* good]

problem, *n.* a question proposed for solution; a matter, situation or person that is difficult to deal with or understand; a source of perplexity or distress; (*Geom.*) a proposition requiring something to be done; (*Phys. etc.*) an investigation starting from certain conditions for the determination or illustration of a law etc.; an arrangement of pieces on a chess-board from which a certain result has to be attained, usu. in a specified number of moves. **no problem,** it's all right; it doesn't matter. **to have a problem, problems,** to have difficulty (with); to be in trouble. **problem child,** *n.* one whose character presents parents, teachers etc. with exceptional difficulties. **problem play, picture,** *n.* play or picture dealing with a social problem or with tricky moral questions. **problematic, -al,** *a.* doubtful, questionable, uncertain; (*Log.*) propounding or supporting that which is possible or probable but not necessarily true, contingent. **problematically,** *adv.* **problemist, problematist,** *n.* one who studies or composes (chess) problems. †**problematize, -ise,** *v.i.* [ME and OF *probleme,* L *problēma -atis,* Gr. *problēma -matos* (PRO-, *ballein,* to cast)]

pro-Boer, *n.* one who favoured the Boers in the S African war of 1899–1902. *a.* favouring the Boers.

proboscis, *n.* (*pl.* **-ides**) the trunk of an elephant or the elongated snout of a tapir etc.; the elongated mouth of some insects; the suctorial organ of some worms etc.; (*facet.*) the human nose. **proboscis monkey,** *n.* a monkey of Borneo with a long, flexible nose. **proboscidean,** *a.* having a proboscis; pertaining to the Proboscidea, an order of mammals containing the elephants, the extinct mastodon etc. *n.* any individual of the Proboscidea. **proboscidiferous,** *a.* [L *proboscis -cidis,* Gr. *proboskis -kidos* (*boskein,* to feed)]

proc., (*abbr.*) proceedings.

procacious, *a.* forward, pert, petulant. [L *procax -cācis,* OUS]

procaine, *n.* a crystalline substance used as a local anaesthetic. [PRO-[1], *cocaine*]

pro-cathedral, *n.* a church or other building used as a substitute for a cathedral.

proceed, *v.i.* to go (in a specified direction or to a specified place); to go on; to go forward, to advance, to continue to progress; to carry on a series of actions, to go on (with or in); to take steps; to act in accordance with a method or procedure; to be carried on; to issue or come forth, to originate, to take a degree; to take or carry on legal proceedings. **procedure,** *n.* the act or manner of proceeding; the (customary or established) mode of conducting business etc. esp. in a court or at a meeting; a course of action; an action, a step in a sequence of actions. **procedural,** *a.* **proceeder,** *n.* one who proceeds, esp. to a university degree. **proceeding,** *n.* progress, advancement; a line of conduct; a transaction; (*pl.*) events, what was going on; (*pl.*) steps in the prosecution of an action at law; (*pl.*) the records of a learned society. **proceeds,** *n.pl.* produce, material results, profits, as the amount realized by the sale of goods. [F *procéder,* L *prōcēdere* (*cēdere,* to go), p.p. *prōcessus*]

proceleusmatic, *a.* (*Pros.*) denoting a metrical foot of four short syllables; †inciting, animating. *n.* such a foot; (*pl.*) verse in this metre. [late L *proceleusmaticus,* Gr. *prokeleusmatikos,* from *prokeleusma,* incitement, from *prokeleuin* (*keleuein,* to urge)]

procellarian, *a.* (*Zool.*) belonging to the genus *Procellaria* or the Procellaridae, a family of Tubinares containing the petrels. *n.* a bird of this genus. [mod. L *Procellāria,* from L *procella,* storm]

procephalic, *a.* of or pertaining to the anterior part of the head, esp. in invertebrates. [Gr. *kęphalē, head)*]

procerebrum, *n.* the prosencephalon. **procerebral,** *a.* [CEREBRUM]

†**procerity,** *n.* tallness, height. †**procerous,** *a.* [MF *procerité,* L *prōcēritātem,* nom. *-tas,* from *prōcērus,* high, tall]

process[1], (*esp. N Am.*), *n.* a course or method of proceeding or doing, esp. a method of operation in manufacture, scientific research etc.; a natural series of continuous actions, changes etc.; a progressive movement or state of activity, progress, course; the course of proceedings in an action at law; a writ or order commencing this; a method of producing a printing surface by photography and mechanical or chemical means; (*Anat., Zool. etc.*) an out-growth, an enlargement, a protuberance of a bone etc. *v.t.* to institute legal proceedings against; to serve a writ on; to treat (food etc.) by a preservative or other process; to subject to routine procedure, to deal with; (*Comput.*) to perform operations on (data); to reproduce by a photo-mechanical process. **in the process,** during the carrying-out (of a specified operation). **in the process of,** engaged in; undergoing. **process block,** *n.* a printing block produced by photo-mechanical means. **process-server,** *n.* a sheriff's officer who serves processes or summonses. **processor,** *n.* a person or thing that processes; a device or program that processes data; a central processing unit. [OF *proces,* L *prōcessus,* see PROCEED]

process[2], *v.i.* to go in procession. [from foll.]

procession, *n.* a train of persons, vehicles, etc. proceeding in regular order for a ceremony, display, demonstration etc.; the movement of such a train; the act or state of proceeding or issuing forth, emanation (as of the Holy Ghost from the Father). *v.i.* to go in procession. *v.t.* to go round in procession; to perambulate the bounds of. **processional,** *a.* pertaining to or used in processions. *n.* a service-book giving the ritual of or the hymns sung in religious processions; a processional hymn. †**processionally,** *adv.* **processionary, processive,** *a.* **processionist,** *n.* one who takes part in a procession. **processionize, -ise,** *v.i.* [F, from L *prōcessiōnem,* nom. *-sio,* from *prōcēdere,* to PROCEED]

procès-verbal, *n.* (*pl.* **-baux**), (*F. Law*) a written statement of particulars relating to a charge; an official record of proceedings, minutes. [F, verbal process]

prochain, *a.* (*Law*) nearest, next. **prochain ami** or **amy,** [F *ami,* friend] the nearest friend, who is entitled to sue etc. on behalf of an infant. [F, from *proche,* L *propius,* comp. of *prope,* near]

prochronism, *n.* an error in chronology dating an event before its actual occurrence.

procidence, *n.* a slipping from the normal position, a prolapsus. **procident,** †**prociduous,** *a.* [F, from L *prōcidentia* (PRO-, *cadere,* to fall)]

procinct, *a.* prepared, ready. †**in procinct,** ready, prepared; at hand, close. [L *prōcinctus,* p.p. of *procingere* (*cingere,* to gird)]

proclaim, *v.t.* to announce publicly, to promulgate; to declare publicly or openly, to publish; to declare (war etc.); to announce the accession of; to outlaw by public proclamation; to put (a district etc.) under certain legal restrictions by public proclamation. **proclaimer,** *n.* **proclamation,** *n.* **proclamatory,** *a.* [F *proclamer,* L *prōclāmāre* (*clāmāre,* to cry out)]

proclitic, *a.* (*Gr. Gram*) attached to and depending in accent upon a following word. *n.* a monosyllable attached to a following word and having no separate accent. [after ENCLITIC]

proclivity, *n.* tendency, bent, propensity. **proclivitous,** *a.* steep, abrupt. **proclivous,** *a.* inclined or sloping forward (of teeth). [L *prōclīvitas,* from *prōclīvus* (PRO-, *clīvus,* slope)]

proconsul, *n.* a Roman magistrate, usu. an ex-consul, exercising consular power as governor of a province or commander of an army; a governor or viceroy of a modern dependency etc. **proconsular,** *a.* **proconsulate, proconsulship,** *n.*

Proconsul, *n.* the prehistoric ape whose skull was found on Rusinga Island in Lake Victoria (Nyanza), E Africa, by Mary Leakey. It is believed to be 20 million years old.

procrastinate, *v.i.* to put off action; to be dilatory. *v.t.* to put off, to defer. **procrastinatingly,** *adv.* **procrastination,** *n.* **procrastinative, -tory,** *a.* **procrastinator,** *n.* [L *procrastinātus,* p.p. of *procrastināre* (*crastinus,* pertaining to to-morrow)]

procreate, *v.t.* to generate, to beget. **procreant,** *a.* **procreation,** *n.* **procreative,** *a.* **procreativeness,** *n.* **procreator,** *n.* [L *prōcreātus,* p.p. of *prōcreāre* (*creāre,* to CREATE)]

Procrustean, *a.* reducing to strict conformity by violent measures. [Gr. *Prokroustēs* (from *prokrouein,* to hammer out), a mythical robber of Attica, who stretched or mutilated his victims till their length was exactly that of his couch]

proctalgia, *n.* pain in the anus.

proctectomy, *n.* excision of the rectum or anus.

proctitis, *n.* inflammation of the anus or rectum.

proct(o)-, *comb. form* pertaining to the anus. [Gr. *prōktos,* anus, *algos,* pain]

proctor, *n.* a University official (usu. one of two elected annually) charged with the maintenance of order and discipline; a person employed to manage another's cause, esp. in an ecclesiastical court. **Queen's** or **King's Proctor,** an officer of the Crown who intervenes in probate, divorce or nullity cases when collusion or other irregularity is alleged. **proctorage,** *n.* management by a proctor. **proctorial,** *a.* **proctorship,** *n.* **proctorize, -ise,** *v.t.* to deal with (an undergraduate) in the capacity of proctor. **proctorization, -isation,** *n.* [a form of PROCURATOR]

procumbent, *a.* lying down on the face, prone; (*Bot.*) lying or trailing along the surface of the ground. [L *prōcumbens -ntem,* pres.p. of *prōcumbere* (*cumbere,* to lie, to lay oneself)]

†**procuracy** PROCURATOR

procuration, *n.* the act of procuring or obtaining; action on behalf of another, function of attorney, a proxy; a document authorizing one person to act for another; entertainment formerly provided, or the fee now paid in commutation of this, by the clergy for the bishop, archdeacon etc. at their visitations; procuring of girls for unlawful purposes. [F, from L *prōcūrātiōnem,* nom. *-tio,* from *prōcūrāre,* to PROCURE]

procurator, *n.* one who manages another's affairs, esp. those of a legal nature, an agent, a proxy, an attorney; a chief magistrate in some Italian cities; (*Mediaeval and Sc. Univ.*) an elective officer having financial, electoral and disciplinary functions, a proctor; (*Rom. Hist.*) a fiscal officer in an imperial province having certain administrative powers. **procurator fiscal,** *n.* (*Sc.*) the public prosecutor in a county or district. **procuracy, procuratorship,** *n.* **procuratorial,** *a.* **procuratory,** *n.* the instrument appointing a procurator; a power of attorney. **procuratrix,** *n. fem.* one of the superiors managing the temporal affairs in a nunnery. [L]

procure, *v.t.* to obtain, to get by some means or effort; to acquire, to gain; to obtain as a pimp; †to bring about. *v.i.* to act as procurer or procuress, to pimp. **procurable,** *a.* **procural, procurance, procurement,** *n.* **procurer,** *n.* one who procures or obtains, esp. one who procures a woman to gratify a person's lust, a pimp, pander. **procuress,** *n. fem.* [F *procurer,* L *prōcūrāre* (PRO-, *cūrāre,* to see to, from *cūra,* care)]

procureur, *n.* a procurator. **procureur général,** *n.* a public prosecutor acting in a court of appeal or of cassation. [F, as PROCURATOR]

Procyon, *n.* the eighth-brightest star in the sky, and the brightest in the constellation Canis Minor. Procyon is a white star 11.3 light years away, with a mass of 1.7 Suns. It has a white dwarf companion that orbits it every 40 years; a genus of mammals containing the racoons. [L, from Gr. *Prokuōn* (PRO-, *kuōn, dog*)]

prod, *n.* a pointed instrument, a goad, a poke with or as with this. *v.t.* (*past, p.p.* **prodded**) to poke with or as with such an instrument; to goad, to incite. **prodder,** *n.* [etym. doubtful]

prod-, *pref.* PRO-, before vowels.

prodelision, *n.* (*Pros.*) elision of the initial vowel (of a word etc.)

prodigal, *a.* given to extravagant expenditure; wasteful, lavish (of). *n.* a prodigal person, a spendthrift. †*adv.* prodigally. **prodigality,** *n.* extravagance, profusion; lavishness, waste. **prodigalize, -ise,** *v.t.* to spend prodigally. **prodigally,** *adv.* [F (now *prodigue*), from L *prōdigus* (PROD-, *agere,* to drive)]

prodigy, *n.* something wonderful or extraordinary; a wonderful example (of); a person, esp. a child, or thing with extraordinary gifts or qualities; something out of the ordinary course of nature, a monstrosity. **prodigious,** *a.* wonderful, astounding; enormous in size, quality, extent etc. **prodigiously,** *adv.* **prodigiousness,** *n.* [L *prōdigium,* portent (PROD-, *agium,* cp. ADAGE)]

prodrome, prodromus, *n.* (*pl.* **-dromes, -dromi**) an introductory book or treatise; (*Med.*) a symptom of aproaching disease. **prodromal, prodromatic,** *a.* [Gr. *prodromos* (*dromos,* running]

produce, *v.t.* to bring into view, to bring forward; to publish, to exhibit; to bring into existence, to bring forth; to bear, to yield, to manufacture; to make; to bring about, to cause; to extend, to continue (a line) in the same direction (*Theat., Cinema, TV*) to act as producer of. *n.,* that which is produced or yielded; the result (of labour, skill etc.); (*collect.*) natural or agricultural products of a country etc.; (*Assaying*) the percentage of copper or other metal yielded by a given amount of ore; (*Ordnance*) materials produced from the breaking up of condemned military and naval stores. **producer,** *n.* one who produces, esp. a cultivator, manufacturer etc. as distinguished from a consumer; a furnace used for the manufacture of carbon monoxide gas; (*Theat, TV*) (*dated*) a director; (*Theat.,*

Cinema, TV) a person who exercises general administrative and financial control over a play, film or broadcast. **producer gas,** *n.* gas produced in a producer. **producible,** *a.* **producibility**, †**producibleness,** *n.* **product**, *n.* that which is produced by natural processes, labour, art or mental application; effect, result; the quantity obtained by multiplying two or more quantities together; (*Chem.*) a compound not previously existing in a substance but produced by its decomposition. **product placement,** *n.* an oblique form of advertising in which a product is used or displayed incidentally in a film or TV programme. **productile**, *a.* capable of being produced or extended. **production**, *n.* the act of producing, esp. as opposed to consumption; a thing produced, a product; the amount produced, the ouput; (*Econ.*) the creation of goods and services with exchange value; a play, film, broadcast etc. esp. relation to its producers; the work of a film etc. producer; (preparation for) the public presentation of a stage work. **production line,** *n.* a system of stage-by-stage manufacture in which a product undergoes various processes or operations as it passes along a conveyor belt. **production model,** *n.* a standard mass-produced model of esp. a car. **productive**, *a.* producing or tending to produce; yielding in abundance, fertile; (*Econ.*) producing commodities having exchangeable value. **productively,** *adv.* **productiveness, productivity**, *n.* yield in abundance; efficiency of production. **productivity deal,** *n.* an agreement making wage increases dependent on increased efficiency and output. **productor**, *n.* **productress**, *n. fem.* [L *prōdūcere* (*dūcere,* to lead)]

pro-educational, *a.* in favour of education.

proem, *n.* a preface, a preamble, an introduction, a prelude. **proemial**, *a.* [OF *proëme* (F *proème*), L *prooemium,* Gr. *prooimion* (PRO-, *oimos,* way, or *oimē,* song)]

proembryo, *n.* a cellular structure of various forms in plants from which the embryo is developed. **proembryonic**, *a.*

proemptosis, *n.* the occurrence of a natural event before the calculated date; hence, the addition of a day to a calendar to correct an error so arising esp. in connection with the date of a new moon. [Gr. *emptōsis* (EM-, *piptein,* to fall)]

Prof., (*abbr.*) Professor.

prof, *n.* (*coll.*) short for PROFESSOR.

profane, *a.* not sacred, not inspired, not initiated into sacred or esoteric rites or knowledge; secular; irreverent towards holy things; irreverent, impious, blasphemous; heathenish; common, vulgar. *v.t.* to treat with irreverence; to desecrate, to violate, to pollute. **profanation**, *n.* **profanely,** *adv.* **profaneness, profanity**, *n.* **profaner,** *n.* [F, from L *prōfānus* (PRO-, *fānum,* temple, see FANE, whence *prōfānāre,* to profane]

profess, *v.t.* to make open or public declaration of, to avow publicly; to affirm one's belief in or allegiance to; to affirm one's skill or proficiency in; to undertake the teaching or practice of (an art, science etc.); to teach (a subject) as a professor; to lay claim to, to make a show of, to pretend (to be or do). *v.i.* to act as a professor; to make protestations or show of. **professed,** *a.* avowed, declared, acknowledged; pretending to be qualified (as a teacher practitioner etc.); in the Roman Catholic Church, of a religious person who has taken vows. **professedly**, *adv.* by profession; avowedly; pretendedly, ostensibly. **profession**, *n.* the act of professing; a declaration, an avowal; a protestation, a pretence; an open acknowledgment of sentiments, religious belief etc.; a vow binding oneself to, or the state of being a member of a religious order; a calling, a vocation, esp. an occupation involving high educational or technical qualifications; the body of persons engaged in such a vocation. **the profession,** (*coll.*) actors. **the three professions,** divinity, law, medicine. **professional,** *a.* of or pertaining to a profession; engaging in an activity as a means of livelihood, esp. as opposed to amateur; characterized by or conforming to the technical or ethical standards of a profession; competent, conscientious. *n.* a member of a profession; one who makes his living by some art, sport etc. as distinguished from one who engages in it for pleasure; a person who shows great skill and competence in any activity. **professionalism,** *n.* the qualities, stamp or spirit of a professional; participation by professionals, esp. in sports. **professionalize, -ise,** *v.t.* **professionally,** *adv.* **professionless,** *a.* **professor,** *n.* one who makes profession, esp. of a religious faith; a public teacher of the highest rank, esp. in a university. **professoriate**, †**professorate**, *n.* **professoress**, *n.* **professorship,** *n.* **professorial**, *a.* pertaining to or characteristic of professors. **professorially,** *adv.* [L *prōfessus,* p.p. of *prōfitērī* (PRO-, *fatēri,* to confess)]

proffer, *v.t.* to offer or tender for acceptance; †to attempt. *n.* an offer, a tender; †an attempt. **profferer,** *n.* [OF *proffrir* (PRO-, *offrir,* L. *offerre,* to OFFER)]

proficient, *a.* well versed or skilled in any art, science etc. expert, competent. *n.* one who is proficient, an adept, an expert. **proficiency,** †**-cience,** *n.* **proficiently,** *adv.* [L *proficiens -ntem,* pres.p. of *prōficere,* see PROFIT]

profile, *n.* an outline, a contour; a side view, esp. of the human face; a drawing, silhouette, or other representation of this; the outline of a vertical section of a building, the contour of architectural detail etc.; a vertical section of soil or rock showing the various layers; a vertical section of a fort, rampart etc.; hence, the relative thickness of a rampart etc.; a wooden framework used as a guide in forming an earthwork; a short biographical sketch. *v.t.* to draw in profile or in vertical section; to shape (stone, wood, metal etc.) to a given profile; to write a profile of. **high, low profile,** *n.* a position, attitude or behaviour calculated (not to call attention to oneself; extensive, limited involvement. **to keep a low profile,** to avoid calling attention to oneself. **high-profile,** *a.* **low-profile,** *a.* **profilist,** *n.* one who draws profiles. [It. *profilo* (now *proffilo*), from *profilare,* to draw in outline (late L. *filāre,* to spin, from *fīlum,* thread)]

profit, *n.* any advantage or benefit, esp. one resulting from labour or exertion; excess of receipts or returns over outlay, gain (*often in pl.*); (*Econ.*) the portion of the gains of an industry received by the capitalist or the investors. *v.t.* to benefit, to be of advantage to. *v.i.* to be of advantage (to); to receive benefit or advantage (by or from). **profit and loss,** (*Accountancy*) gains credited and losses debited in an account so as to show the net loss or profit; (*Arith.*) the rule by which such gain or loss is calculated. **profit motive,** *n.* (*Econ.*) the incentive of private profit for the production and distribution of goods. **profit-sharing,** *n.* a system of remuneration by which the workers in an industrial concern are apportioned a percentage of the profits in order to give them an interest in the business. **profitable,** *a.* yielding or bringing profit or gain, lucrative; advantageous, beneficial, useful. **profitableness,** *n.* **profitably,** *adv.* **profiteer,** *v.i.* to make undue profits at the expense of the public, esp. in a time of national stress. *n.* one guilty of this social crime. **profiteering,** *n.* **profitless,** *a.* **profitlessly,** *adv.* **profitlessness,** *n.* [OF, from L *prōfectum,* nom. *prōfectus,* p.p. of *prōficere, facere,* to do)]

profiterole, *n.* a small, hollow ball of choux pastry with a sweet or savoury filling [F from *profiter* to profit]

profligate, *a.* abandoned to vice, licentious, dissolute; wildly extravagant. *n.* a profligate person. **profligacy, profligateness,** *n.* **profligately,** *adv.* [L *prōflīgātus,* p.p. of *prōflīgāre,* to cast down, *flīgere,* to strike)]

†**profluent,** *a.* flowing forward or forth. †**profluence,** *n.* [L *prōfluens -ntem,* pres.p. of *prōfluere* (PRO-, *fluere,* to flow)]

pro forma PRO.

profound, *a.* having great intellectual penetration or insight; having great knowledge; requiring great study or research, abstruse, recondite; deep, intense; deep-seated, far below the surface; reaching to or extending from a great depth; coming from a great depth, deep-drawn; thorough-going, extensive; very low (as an obeisance). *n.* a vast depth, an abyss; the deep, the ocean; chaos. **profoundly,** *adv.* **profoundness, profundity**, *n.* [OF *profund* (F *profond*), L *profundus, fundus,* bottom)]

Profumo, *n.* **John (Dennis)** (1915–), British Conservative politician, secretary of state for war from 1960 to June 1963, when he resigned on the disclosure of his involvement with Christine Keeler, mistress also of a Soviet naval attaché. In 1982 Profumo became administrator of the social and educational settlement Toynbee Hall in London.

profunda, *n.* one of various deep-seated veins or arteries. [L, fem. of *profūndus,* as prec.]

profundity PROFOUND.

profuse, *a.* poured forth lavishly, exuberant, copious, super-abundant; liberal to excess, prodigal, extravagant. **profusely,** *adv.* **profuseness, profusion**, *n.* [L *profūsus,* p.p. of *prōfundere (fundere,* to pour)]

Prog, (*abbr.*) (*coll.; sometimes offensive*) progressive.

prog¹, *v.i.* to poke about (esp. for food); to forage, to beg. *n.* (*sl.*) victuals, provender, food. [etym. doubtful]

prog², *n.* (*Oxf. and Camb. sl.*) a proctor. *v.t.* to proctorize. **proggins**, *n.* a prog. [short for PROCTOR]

progenitor, *n.* an ancestor in the direct line, a forefather, a parent; a predecessor, an original. †**progenerate,** *v.t.* **progenitorial**, *a.* **progenitress**, **-trix**, *n. fem.* **progenitorship,** *n.* **progeniture**, *n.* begetting, generation; offspring. [MF *progeniteur,* L *prōgenitōrem,* nom. *-tor,* from *prōgignere* (PRO-, *gignere,* to beget)]

progeny, *n.* offspring of human beings, animals or plants; children, descendants; issue, results, consequences; †descent, lineage. [OF *progenie,* L *progeniem,* nom. *-ies,* as prec.]

progeria, *n.* premature old age. [PRO-, Gr. *geras,* old age]

progesterone, *n.* a female steroid hormone that prepares and maintains the uterus for pregnancy. [*ges*tation + *ster*ol + *one*]

progestogen, *n.* any of a range of hormones of the progesterone type, synthetic progestogens being used in oral contraceptives. [*ges*tation + *eron*]

proggins PROG².

proglottis, *n.* (*pl.* **-ides**) a segment of a tapeworm forming a distinct animal with genital organs. **proglottic,** *a.* [Gr. (*glōtta,* tongue)]

prognathic, prognathous, *a.* having the jaws projecting; projecting (of the jaws). **prognathism**, *n.* [Gr. *gnathos,* jaw]

prognosis, *n.* (*pl.* **-noses**) an opinion as to the probable course or result of an illness; a forecast, a prediction. [L and Gr., from *progignōskein (gignōskein,* to know)]

prognostic, *n.* a sign or indication of a future event; an omen, a token; a prediction, a forecast; a symptom; †a prognosis. *a.* prognosis. *a.* foreshowing; indicative of something future by signs or symptoms. **prognosticable,** *a.* **prognosticate,** *v.t.* to foretell from present signs; to foreshadow, to presage, to betoken. **prognostication,** *n.* **prognosticative,** *a.* **prognosticator,** *n.* [ME and OF *pronostique,* med. L *prognōsticon,* Gr. *prognōstikon,* as prec.]

programme, (*esp. N Am., Comput.*) **program**, *n.* (a paper, booklet etc. giving) a list of the successive items of any entertainment, public ceremony, conference, course of study etc. plus other relevant information; the items on such a list; a broadcast presented at a scheduled time; (*Comput.*) a sequence of instructions which, when fed into a computer, enable it to process data in specified ways; material for programmed instruction; a plan or outline of proceedings or actions to be carried out. *v.t.* to arrange a programme for; to enter in a programme; to cause to conform to a certain pattern, esp. of thought, behaviour; (usu. **program, -gramming, -grammed**) to prepare as a program for, to feed a program into, a computer. **programme music,** *n.* music intended to suggest a definite series of scenes, incidents etc. **programmable**, *a.* (*Comput.*) capable of being programmed for processing by a computer. **programmability**, *n.* **programmatic**, *a.* of or having a programme; of, or of the nature of, programme music. **programmed,** *a.* **programmed instruction, learning,** *n.* a teaching method involving the breaking down of the subject matter into small items in a logical sequence on which students can check themselves as they proceed. **programmer,** *n.* (*Comput.*) **programming,** *n.* **programming language,** *n.* any of various code systems used in writing computer programs and giving instructions to computers. [F, from L and Gr. *programma* (*graphein,* to write)]

progress, *n.* a moving or going forward; movement onward, advance; advance towards completion, fruition, a higher state; increased proficiency; growth development; †a journey of state. *v.i.*, to move forward, to advance; to be carried on, to proceed; to advance, to develop; to make improvement; †to travel in state. **in progress,** going on, proceeding. **progression**, *n.* progress, motion onward; movement in successive stages; a regular succession of notes or chords in melody or harmony; regular or proportional advance by increase or decrease of numbers. **arithmetical progression** ARITHMETIC. **geometrical progression** GEOMETRY. **progressional,** *a.* **progressionist,** *n.* a believer in or advocate of social and political progress; one who believes in the perfectibility of man and society; one who believes that organisms have advanced from lower to higher forms, an evolutionist. **progressionism,** *n.* **progressist**, *a.* advocating progress, esp. in politics. *n.* a progressive, a reformer. **progressive**, *a.* moving forward or onward; advancing; improving; of a disease, increasing in extent or severity; in a state of progression, proceeding step by step, successive; continuously increasing; believing in or advocating social and political reform; denoting an educational system which allows flexibility and takes the needs and abilities of the individual child as its determinant; denoting a verb form which expresses action in progress. *n.* a progressive person; (*usu.* **Progressive**) an adherent of a party called progressive; an adherent of Progressivism; the progressive form of a verb. **progressive whist** or **bridge,** *n.* whist or bridge played by a number of sets of players at different tables, each winning player moving to another table at the end of each hand or series of hands. **progressively,** *adv.* **progressiveness,** *n.* **progressivism,** *n.* the principles of a progressive or reformer; (**Progressivism**) in US history, a reform movement and a political party, active in the two decades before World War I. Mainly middle-class and urban-based, Progressives secured legislation at national, state, and local levels to improve the democratic system, working conditions, and welfare provision.

Progymnasium, *n.* (*pl.* **-sia**) a school in Germany preparatory to the Gymnasia. [G]

prohibit, *v.t.* to forbid authoritatively, to interdict; to hinder, to prevent. **prohibiter, prohibitor,** *n.* **prohibition**, *n.* the act of prohibiting; an order or edict prohibiting; the forbidding by law of the manufacture and the sale of intoxicating liquors for consumption as beverages; (**Prohibition**) in US history, the period 1920–33 when alcohol was illegal, and which represented the culmination of a long campaign by church and women's organizations, temperance societies, and the Anti-Saloon League. This led to bootlegging, to the financial advantage of organized crime, and public opinion insisted on repeal 1933. **prohibitionist,** *n.* one in favour of prohibiting the sale of intoxicating liquors; **prohibitive, -itory,** *a.* tending to prohibit or preclude; (of costs, prices etc.) such as to debar purchase, use etc. **prohibitively,** *adv.* **prohibitiveness,** *n.* [L *prōhibitus,* p.p. of *prōhibēre, habēre,* to have)]

project, *n.* a plan, a scheme, a design; an (esp. large-scale) undertaking; a piece of work undertaken by a pupil or group of pupils to supplement and apply classroom studies. *v.t.*, to throw or shoot forward; to cause to extend forward or jut out; to cast (light, shadow, an image) on to a surface or into space; to enable (one's voice) to be heard at a distance; to transport in the imagination; to make a prediction based on known data; to impute (something in one's own mind) to another person, group or entity; to contrive, to plan; to make (an idea etc.) objective; (*Geom.*) to draw straight lines from a given centre through every point of (a figure) so as to form a corresponding figure on a surface; to produce (such a projection); to make a projection of. *v.i.* to jut out, to protrude; to make oneself audible at a distance; to communicate effectively. **projectment**, *n.* a scheme, a design, a contrivance. **projector**, *n.* one who forms schemes; a promoter, esp. of bubble companies; an instrument or apparatus for projecting rays of light, images etc. †**projecture**, *n.* a projecting or jutting out; a projection, a prominence. **projectile**, *n.* a body projected or thrown forward with force; a self-propelling missile, esp. one adapted for discharge from a heavy gun. *a.* impelling forward; adapted to be forcibly projected, esp. from a gun. **projection**, *n.* the act or state of projecting, protruding, throwing or impelling; a part or thing that projects, a prominence; the act of planning; the process of externalizing an idea or making it objective; a mental image viewed as an external object; the showing of films or slides by projecting images from them onto a screen; a prediction based on known data; the geometrical projecting of a figure; the representation of the terrestrial or celestial sphere, or a part of it, on a plane surface; (*Alch.*) the casting of a substance into a crucible; hence, the transmutation of metals; †a project, a scheme; the process whereby one ascribes to others mental factors and attributes really in ourselves. **Mercator's projection**, a projection of the surface of the earth upon a plane so that the lines of latitude are represented by horizontal lines and the meridians by parallel lines at right angles to them. **projectionist**, *n.* one who operates a film projector. **projective**, *a.* pertaining to or derived by projection; (*Geom.*) such that they may be derived from one another by projection (of two plane figures); externalizing or making objective. **projective property**, *n.* a property that remains unchanged after projection. **projectively**, *adv.* [MF (F *projet*), L *prōjectum*, neut. p.p. of *prōicere*, *jacere*, to throw)]

prokaryote, *n.* an organism whose cells have no distinct nucleus, their genetic material being carried in a single filament of DNA. [Gr. *karyon*, a kernel]

Prokhorov, *n.* **Aleksandr** (1916–), Russian physicist whose fundamental work on microwaves in 1955 led to the construction of the first practical maser by Townes for which they shared the 1964 Nobel physics prize.

Prokofiev, *n.* **Sergey (Sergeyevich)** (1891–1953), Soviet composer. His music includes operas such as *The Love of Three Oranges* (1921); ballets for Diaghilev, including *Romeo and Juliet* (1935); seven symphonies including the *Classical Symphony* (1916–17); music for films; piano and violin concertos; songs and cantatas (for example, that composed for the 30th anniversary of the October Revolution); and *Peter and the Wolf* (1936).

prolapse, *n.* prolapsus. *v.i.* to fall down or out. **prolapsus**, *n.* a falling down or slipping out of place of an organ or part, as the uterus or rectum. [late L *prōlapsus*, from L *prōlaps-*, p.p. stem of *prōlābī* (*lābī*, to slip)]

prolate, *a.* extended in the direction of the longer axis, elongated in the polar diameter, opposed to oblate. **prolately**, *adv.* **prolateness**, *n.* **prolation**, *n.* (*Mediaeval Music*) the time of music measured by the division of semibreves into minims. **prolative**, *a.* (*Gram.*) extending or completing the predicate. [L *prōlātus*, *lātus*, p.p. of *ferre*, to bear)]

prole, *n.*, *a.* (*derog.*, *offensive*) short for PROLETARIAN.

proleg, *n.* one of the soft, fleshy appendages or limbs of caterpillars etc. distinct from the true legs.

prolegomenon, *n.* (*usu. in pl.* **-ena**) an introductory or preliminary discourse prefixed to a book etc. **prolegomenary, -enous**, *a.* [Gr., neut. p.p. of *prolegein* (*legein*, to say)]

prolepsis, *n.* anticipation; (*Rhet.*) a figure by which objections are anticipated or prevented; the anticipatory use of a word as attributive instead of a predicate, as in *their murdered man* for *the man they intended to murder;* a prochronism. **proleptic, -al**, *a.* **proleptically**, *adv.* [L and Gr. *prolēpsis* (*lambanein*, to take)]

proletaire, *n.* a proletarian. **proletairism**, *n.* [F *prolétaire*]

proletarian, *a.* of or pertaining to the common people. *n.* a member of the proletariat. **proletarianism**, *n.* **proletariat**, *n.* the class of the community without property, the wage-earners, the unprivileged classes. **proletary**, *a.* and *n.* [L *prōlētārius*, one of the lowest class of citizens, one whose only property is his children, from *prōles*, offspring]

prolicide, *n.* the crime of killing one's offspring, esp. before or immediately after birth. **prolicidal**, *a.* [L *prōles*, offspring]

pro-life, *a.* favouring greater restrictions on the availability of legal abortions and/or a ban on the use of human embryos for experimental purposes. **pro-lifer**, *n.*

proliferate, *v.i.* to grow or reproduce itself by budding or multiplication of parts; to grow or increase rapidly and abundantly; to become more widespread. *v.t.* to produce by proliferation. **proliferation**, *n.* **proliferative**, *a.* **proliferous**, *a.* producing buds, shoots etc. from leaves, flowers etc.; producing new individuals from buds, parts etc.; multiplying by proliferation. **proliferously**, *adv.* [med. L *prōlifer* (*prōles*, -fer, bearing)]

prolific, *a.* bearing offspring, esp. abundantly; fruitful, productive, fertile; abounding (in); very productive (of); (*Bot.*) bearing fertile seed. **prolificacy, prolificity, prolificness**, *n.* **prolifically**, *adv.* **prolification**, *n.* the generation of animals or plants; (*Bot.*) the production of buds from leaves etc., the development of an abnormal number of parts. [F *prolifique*, L *prōlificus* (*prōles*, offspring, -FIC)]

prolix, *a.* long and wordy; tedious, tiresome, diffuse. †**prolixious**, *a.* **prolixity**, **prolixness**, *n.* **prolixly**, *adv.* [F *prolixe*, L *prōlixus*, *-lixus*, p.p. of *liquēre*, to flow)]

prolocutor, *n.* a chairman or speaker, esp. of the Lower House of Convocation in the Church of England. **prolocutorship**, *n.* [L, from *prōloquī* (PRO-, *loquī*, to speak, p.p. *locūtus*)]

Prolog, *n.* a computer programming language based on logic and used mainly for artificial intelligence programming.

prologue (*esp. N Am.*) **prolog**, *n.* an introductory discourse, esp. lines introducing a play; an act or event forming an introduction to some proceeding or occurrence; the speaker of a prologue. †**prologist**, *n.* **prologize, -ise**, *v.t.* to introduce, to preface. [F, from L *prologus*, Gr. *prologus*, *logus*, speech)]

prolong, *v.t.* to extend in duration; to lengthen, to extend in space or distance; to lengthen the pronunciation of. **prolongable**, *a.* †**prolongate**, *v.t.* **prolongation**, *n.* the act of lengthening or extending; a lengthening in time or space; the part by which anything is lengthened. **prolonger**, *n.* [F *prolonger*, late L *prōlongāre* (*longāre*, from *longus*, LONG[1])]

prolonge, *n.* a rope in three pieces connected by rings with a hook at one end and a toggle at the other, used for moving a gun etc. [F, as prec.]

prolusion, *n.* a prelude; a preliminary essay, exercise or attempt. **prolusory**, *a.* [L *prōlūsio*, from *prōlūdere* (*lūdere*, to play)]

PROM, *n.* (*Comput.*) a memory device in the form of a silicon chip that can be programmed to hold information permanently. PROM chips are empty of information when manufactured, unlike ROM chips, which have their memories built into them. [acronym for Programmable Read Only Memory]

prom, *n.* short for (sea-front) PROMENADE, PROMENADE CONCERT, PERFORMANCE.

promenade, *n.* a walk, drive or ride for pleasure, exercise or display; a place for promenading, esp. a paved terrace on a sea-front; a processional sequence in a square or country dance; (*N Am.*) a dance at college, school, unit or association. *v.i.* to take a walk etc. for pleasure, exercise, or show; (*Dancing*) to perform a promenade. *v.t.* to take a promenade along, about or through; to lead (a person) about, esp. for display. **promenade concert, performance**, *n.* a concert or performance at which the floor of the hall is left bare for the audience to stand when there is no room to walk about. **promenade deck,** *n.* an upper deck on a ship where passengers may stroll. **promenader,** *n.* a standing member of the audience at a promenade concert or performance. [F, from *promener,* to walk, late L *prōmināre,* to drive (*mināre,* to threaten)]

Promerops, *n.* a S African genus of birds, comprising the Cape promerops, *P. cafer,* with a slender, curved bill and a long tail. [Gr. *merops,* bee-eater]

Prometheus, *n.* in Greek mythology, a Titan who stole fire from heaven for the human race. In revenge, Zeus had him chained to a rock with an eagle preying on his liver, until he was rescued by Hercules. **Promethean**, *a.* of, pertaining to or like Prometheus; original, creative. †*n.* a small glass tube, containing sulphuric acid, surrounded by an inflammable mixture, which is ignited on being crushed, used before the introduction of matches for getting a light quickly. **promethium**, *n.* a metallic element, at. no. 61; chem. symbol Pm, obtained as a fission product of uranium. [Gr. *Promētheus*]

prominent, *a.* standing out, jutting, projecting, protuberant; conspicuous; distinguished. **prominence, -nency,** the state of being prominent; a prominent point or thing, a projection; an eruption of incandescent gas from the surface of the sun. *n.* **prominently,** *adv.* [F, from L *prōminentem,* nom. *-ens,* pres.p. of *prōminēre,* to project (*minēre,* from *minae,* projections, threats)]

promiscuous, *a.* mixed together in a disorderly manner; of different kinds mingled confusedly together; not restricted to a particular person, kind etc.; indulging in indiscriminate sexual intercourse; fortuitous, accidental, casual. **promiscuity**, *n.* sexual promiscuousness; hetaerism or communal marriage. **promiscuously,** *adv.* **promiscuousness,** *n.* [L *prōmiscuus* (*miscēre,* to MIX)]

promise, *n.* a verbal or written engagement to do or forbear from doing some specific act; that which is promised; ground or basis of expectation, esp. of success, improvement or excellence. *v.t.* to engage to do or not do; to engage to give or procure; to make a promise of something to; to give good grounds for expecting. *v.i.* to bind oneself by a promise; to give grounds for favourable expectations; †to become surety (for). **breach of promise** [BREACH]. **land of promise** or **promised land,** the land of Canaan promised to Abraham and his seed; heaven; any place of expected happiness or prosperity. **to promise well** or **ill,** to hold out favourable or unfavourable prospects. **promise-breaker,** *n.* one who violates his promises. **promisee,** *n.* (*Law*) one to whom a promise is made. **promiser,** *n.* **promising,** *a.* giving grounds for expectation or hope; hopeful, favourable. **promisingly,** *adv.* **promisor,** *n.* one who enters into a covenant. †**promisorily,** *adv.* **promissory,** *a.* containing or of the nature of a promise, esp. a promise to pay money. **promissory note,** *n.* a signed engagement to pay a sum of money to a specified person or the bearer at a stated date or on demand. [L *prōmissum,* neut. p.p. of *prōmittere* (*mittere,* to send)]

promo, *n.* (*pl.* **-mos**), (*coll.*) something used to promote a product, esp. a pop video.

promontory, *n.* a headland; a point of high land projecting into the sea; a rounded protuberance. **promontoried,** *a.* [L *prōmontōrium, mons montis,* MOUNT)]

promote, *v.t.* to forward, to advance, to contribute to the growth, increase or advancement of; to support, to foster, to encourage; to raise to a higher rank or position, to exalt, to prefer; to bring to the notice of the public, to encourage the sale of by advertising; to organize and float (a joint-stock company etc.); (*Chess*) to raise (a pawn) to the rank of queen. **promoter,** *n.* one who or that which promotes or furthers; one who promotes a joint-stock company (usu. in an unfavourable sense); one who organizes a sporting event, esp. a boxing match; the plaintiff in an ecclesiastical suit. **promoterism,** *n.* the practice of floating joint-stock companies. **promotion,** *n.* advancement in position; furtherance, encouragement, a venture, esp. in show business; (an advertising campaign, special offer etc. intended as a means of) bringing a product, person to public notice. **on promotion,** awaiting, expecting or preparing oneself for promotion; on one's good behaviour. **promotive,** *a.* [L *prōmōtus,* p.p. of *prōmovēre, movēre,* to MOVE)]

prompt, *a.* acting quickly or ready to act as occasion demands; done, made or said with alacrity; †inclined, disposed. *n.* time allowed for payment of a debt as stated in a prompt-note; the act of prompting, or the thing said to prompt an actor etc. *v.t.* to urge or incite (to action or to do); to instigate; to suggest to the mind, to inspire, to excite (thoughts, feelings etc.); to assist (a speaker, actor etc.) when at a loss, by suggesting the words forgotten. **prompt-book,** *n.* a copy of the play for the use of the prompter at a theatre. **prompt-note,** *n.* a note reminding a purchaser of a sum due and the date of payment. **prompt-side,** *n.* the side of a stage on which the prompter stands, usu. to the left of the actor. **prompter,** *n.* one who prompts, esp. one employed at a theatre to prompt actors. **promptitude, promptness,** *n.* **promptly,** *adv.* †**promptuary**, *n.* a storehouse, a repository; a note-book, a digest. †**prompture,** *n.* [F, from L *promptum,* nom. *-tus,* p.p. of *prōmere (emere,* to take)]

promulgate, *v.t.* to make known to the public; to publish abroad, to disseminate; to announce publicly. **promulgation,** *n.* **promulgator,** *n.* †**promulge**, *v.t.* †**promulger,** *n.* [L *prōmulgātus), p.p. of prōmulgāre,* etym. doubtful, perh. corr. of *prōvulgāre* (*vulgus,* the crowd)]

promuscis, *n.* the proboscis of the Hemiptera and some other insects. [L, var. of PROBOSCIS]

pron., (*abbr.*) pronoun; pronounced; pronunciation.

pronaos, *n.* (*Gr. and Roman Ant.*) the area immediately before a temple enclosed by the portico; the vestibule. [L and Gr. (PRO-, *naos,* temple)]

pronate, *v.t.* to lay (a hand or forelimb) prone so as to have the palm downwards. **pronation**, *n.* **pronator**, *n.* (*Anat.*) a muscle of the forearm employed to turn the palm downwards. [late L *prōnātus,* p.p. of *prōnāre,* from *prōnus,* PRONE]

prone, *a.* leaning or bent forward or downward; lying with the face downward, opp. to supine; lying flat, prostrate; sloping downwards, descending steeply or vertically; disposed, inclined, apt. **pronely,** *adv.* **proneness,** *n.* [L *prōnus*]

prong, *n.* a forked instrument; one of the spikes of a fork; a sharp-pointed instrument or spike-like projection. *v.t.* to pierce, stab or prick with a prong. **prongbuck, pronghorn** or **prong-horned antelope,** *n.* a N American ruminant, *Antilocapra americana.* **prong-hoe,** *n.* a kind of hoe with prongs to break clods. **pronged,** *a.* [etym. doubtful]

pronograde, *a.* carrying the body horizontally, as quadrupeds. [L *prōnus,* PRONE. *gradī,* to walk]

pronominal, *a.* pertaining to or of the nature of a pronoun. **pronominally,** *adv.* [late L *prōnōminālis,* from *prōnōmen, -minis,* pronoun]

prononcé, *a.* (*fem.* **-cée**) pronounced, emphatic, obvious. [F, p.p. of *prononcer,* to PRONOUNCE]

pronotary PROTHONOTARY.

pronotum, *n.* the dorsal part of the prothorax of an insect. [mod. L (PRO-, Gr. *nōton,* back)]

pronoun, *n.* a word used in place of a noun to denote a person or thing already mentioned or implied. [after L *prōnōmen* or F *pronom*]

pronounce, *v.t.* to utter articulately, to say correctly; to utter formally, officially or rhetorically; to declare, to affirm. *v.i.* to articulate; to declare one's opinion (on, for, against etc) †*n.* pronouncement. **pronounceable,** *a.* **pronounced,** *a.* strongly marked, emphatic, decided; conspicuous, obvious. **pronouncedly,** *adv.* **pronouncement,** *n.* a statement. **pronouncer,** *n.* **pronouncing,** *a.* pertaining to, indicating or teaching pronunciation. **pronunciation,** *n.* the act or mode of pronouncing words etc.; the correct pronouncing of words etc.; the art or act of speaking in public with propriety and grace. **pronunciability,** *n.* **pronuncial,** *a.* †**pronunciative, -tory,** *a.* declarative, dogmatical. [ME *pronunce,* OF *pronuncier,* late L *prōnuntiāre* (*nuntiāre,* to announce, from *nuntius,* messenger)]

pronto, *adv.* (*coll.*) without delay; quickly. [Sp. from L *promptus* quick]

pronunciamento, *n.* (*pl.* **-tos**) a manifesto, a proclamation, esp. one issued by revolutionaries in Spanish-speaking countries. [Sp.]

pronunciation PRONOUNCE.

prooemium, PROEM.

proof, *n.* the act of proving, a test, a trial; testing, assaying, experiment; demonstration; a sequence of steps establishing the correctness of a mathematical or logical proposition; convincing evidence of the truth or falsity of a statement, charge etc. esp. oral or written evidence submitted in the trial of a cause; (*Sc. Law*) evidence taken before a judge, or a trial before a judge instead of by jury; the state or quality of having been proved or tested; proved impenetrability, esp. of armour; a standard degree of strength in spirit; a trial impression from type for correction; an impression of an engraving taken with special care before the ordinary issue is printed; a first or early impression of a photograph, coin, medal etc.; rough edges left in a book to show it has not been cut down; †experience. *a.* proved or tested as to strength, firmness etc.; impenetrable; able to resist physically or morally; used in testing, verifying etc.; of a certain degree of alcoholic strength. *v.t.* to make proof, esp. waterproof. **armour of proof,** armour proved impenetrable to ordinary weapons, missiles etc. **proof before letters,** a proof taken of an engraving etc. before the inscription is appended. **proof-plane,** *n.* a disk-shaped conductor with insulating handle used in measuring the electrification of a body. **proofread,** *v.t.* to read and correct (printer's proofs). **proof-reader,** *n.* **proof-reading,** *n.* **proof-sheet,** *n.* a sheet of printer's proof. **proof spirit,** *n.* a mixture of alcohol and water containing a standard amount of alcohol, in Britain 57.1% by volume. **proofless,** *a.* [ME *preove, preve,* OF *prueve,* late L *proba,* from *proba,* from *probāre,* to PROVE]

-proof, *comb. form* (to make) resistant, impervious, immune to.

pro-ostracum, *n.* (*Palaeont.*) the anterior prolongation of the guard or rostrum of a belemnite or other cephalopod. [Gr. *ostrakon,* potsherd, shell]

pro-otic, OTIC, *a.* in front of the ear. *n.* one of three pro-otic bones usually found in the skulls of lower vertebrates.

prop¹, *n.* a support, esp. a loose or temporary one; a buttress, a pillar, a stay; a person supporting a cause etc; a prop forward. *v.t.* (*past, p.p.* **propped**) to support or hold (up) with or as with a prop; to support, to hold up (of a prop). **to prop up,** to support in an upright position; to keep going with financial etc. help. **prop forward,** *n.* (*Rugby*) either of the two forwards supporting the hooker in the front row of the scrum. [ME *proppe,* cp. Dut. *proppe,* etym. doubtful]

prop², *n.* (*Theat.*) a stage property. **props,** *n.pl.* stage properties; *n. sing.* (also **props man, -mistress** etc.) PROPERTY-MAN

prop³, *n.* an aeroplane propeller. **propfan,** *n.* (an aircraft with) a jet engine having turbine-driven, rear-mounted, propellors. **propjet,** TURBOPROP under TURBO-.

prop⁴, *v.i.* of a horse, to come to a sudden halt, to pull up sharply. [Austral. (*coll.*)]

propaedeutic, *a.* pertaining to or of the nature of introductory or preparatory study. *n.pl.* preliminary learning or instruction introductory to any art or science. [G *propaideuein (paideuein,* to teach, from *pais paidos,* child), -IC]

propaganda, *n.* information, ideas, opinions etc. propagated as a means of winning support for, or fomenting opposition to, a government, cause, institution etc.; an organization, scheme or other means of propagating such information etc. **Propaganda,** *n.* in the Roman Catholic Church, a congregation of cardinals charged with all matters connected with foreign missions. **College of the Propaganda,** the college in Rome where missionary priests are trained. **propagandism,** *n.* **propagandist,** *n.* one devoted to or engaged in propaganda. *a.* propagandistic. **propagandistic,** *a.* **propagandize, -ise,** *v.t.* and *i.* to spread (by) propaganda; to subject to propaganda. [PROPAGATE]

propagate, *v.t.* to cause to multiply by natural generation or other means; to reproduce; to cause to spread or extend; to diffuse, to disseminate; to impel forward, to transmit, to cause to extend in space. *v.i.* to be reproduced or multiplied by natural generation or other means; to have offspring. **propagable,** *a.* **propagation,** *n.* the act of propagating; dissemination, diffusing; extension or transmission through space. **propagative,** *a.* **propagator,** *n.* a person or thing that propagates; a heated, covered box for growing plants from seed or cuttings. [L *prōpāgātus,* p.p. of *prōpāgāre,* to propagate by layers (PRO-, *pāg-,* stem of *pangere,* to set, to fix)]

propale, *v.t.* (*chiefly Sc.*) to publish; to reveal, to disclose. [late L *prōpalāre,* from *prōpalam* (PRO-, *palam,* openly)]

propane, *n.* a flammable, gaseous alkane used as fuel.

proparoxytone, *a.* (*Gr. Gram.*) having an acute accent on the antepenultimate syllable. *n.* a proparoxytone word. [Gr. *proparoxutonos*]

propedutic, PROPAEDEUTIC.

propel, *v.t.* (*past, p.p.* **propelled**) to drive forward; to cause to move forward or onward. **propellant,** *a.* that propels. *n.* that which propels, esp. the fuel mixture used by a rocket engine or the gas in an aerosol. **propeller,** *n.* one who or that which propels; a rotating device, usu. consisting of two to four blades set at an angle and twisted like the thread of a screw, at the end of a shaft driven by steam, electricity etc. for propelling a vessel through the water or an aeroplane or airship through air. (*also known as screw-propeller*) **propelling pencil,** *n.* one having a metal or plastic casing which, when turned, extends or retracts a replaceable lead. **propelment,** *n.* [L *prōpellere, pellere,* to drive)]

propensity, *n.* bent, natural tendency, inclination. †**propense,** *a.* inclined, disposed. †**propensely,** *adv.* †**propension,** †**propenseness,** *n.* propensity. [L *prōpensus,* propense, p.p. of *prōpendēre,* as prec., -ITY]

proper, *a.* †own; belonging or pertaining exclusively or peculiarly (to); correct, just; suitable, appropriate; fit, becoming; decent, respectable; strictly decorous; real, genuine, according to strict definition (*usu. following its noun*); well-made, good-looking; (*coll.*) thorough, complete (*Her.*) in the natural colours. *n.* that part of the mass which varies according to the liturgical calendar. **proper fraction,** *n.* a fraction less than unity. **proper name, noun,** *n.* one designating an individual person, animal, place etc. **properly,** *adv.* in a proper manner, fitly, suitably; rightly, justly, correctly, accurately; (*coll.*) thoroughly, quite. **properness,** *n.* [ME and OF *propre,* L *proprium,* nom. *proprius,* one's own]

properispomenon, *a.* (*Gr. Gram.*) having the circumflex accent on the penultimate syllable. *n.* a properispomenon word. [Gr. *properispōmenon*]

properly, etc. PROPER.

Propertius, *n.* **Sextus** (*c.* 47–15 BC), Roman elegiac poet, a member of Maecenas' circle, who wrote of his love for his mistress 'Cynthia'.

property, *n.* peculiar or inherent quality; character, nature; that which is owned; a possession, possessions, a piece of real estate; exclusive right of possession, ownership; (*pl.*) articles required for the production of a play on the stage. †*v.t.* to appropriate; to make a property of, to exploit, to use as one's tool; to endow with properties or qualities. **property-man, -master, -mistress, -woman,** *n.* the man or woman in charge of theatrical properties. **property qualification,** *n.* a qualification for voting, holding an office etc. derived from the possession of property. **property-tax,** *n.* a direct tax on property. **propertied,** *a.* [ME *proprete,* OF *propriété,* L *proprietātem,* nom. *-tas,* from *proprius,* PROPER]

propfan, PROP[3].

prop-forward, PROP[1].

prophasis, *n.* prognosis. [Gr. (PRO-, *phasis,* PHASE)]

prophecy, *n.* a prediction, esp. one divinely inspired; the prediction of future events; the gift or faculty of prophesying; (*Bibl.*) a book of prophecies; †the public interpretation of Scripture. [OF *profecie* (F *prophétie*), late L *prophētīa,* Gr. *prophēteia,* as foll.]

prophesy, *v.t.* to predict, to foretell; to herald. *v.i.* to utter prophecies; †to interpret Scripture, to preach. **prophesier,** *n.* [OF *profecier, -phecier, -phesier,* as prec.]

prophet, *n.* one who foretells future events, esp. under divine inspiration; a revealer or interpreter of the divine will; a religious leader, a founder of a religion; a preacher or teacher of a cause etc.; †an interpreter. **major prophets,** Isaiah, Jeremiah, Ezekiel, Daniel. **minor prophets,** the prophets in the Old Testament from Hosea to Malachi. **prophet of doom,** a person who is continually predicting ruin and disaster. **the Prophet,** Mohammed. **the prophets,** the prophetic writers of the Old Testament; the books written by them. **prophetess,** *n. fem.* **prophethood, prophetship,** *n.* **prophetic, -al,** *a.* of, pertaining to, or containing prophecy; predictive, anticipative. **prophetically,** *adv.* †**propheticalness,** *n.* **propheticism,** *n.* [ME and OF *prophete,* L *prophēta,* Gr. *prophētēs* (*phē-,* stem of *phanai,* to speak)]

prophylactic, *a.* protecting against disease; preventive. *n.* a preventive medicine; (*esp. N Am.*) a condom. **prophylaxis,** *n.* [F *prophylactique,* Gr. *prophulaktikos,* from *prophulassein* (*phulassein,* to guard)]

†**propine,** *v.t.* to drink (health, fortune etc.) to; to present, to propose; to reward. *n.* a present, a gift. [L *propīnāre,* Gr. *propinein* (*pinein,* to drink)]

propinquity, *n.* nearness in time, space, or relationship; similarity. **propinquate,** *v.i.* to approach. [OF *propinquité,* L *propinquitātem,* nom. *-tas,* from *propinquus,* near, from *prope,* near]

propionic acid, *n.* a fatty acid used esp. in making flavourings and perfumes. [PRO + Gr. *piōn,* fat]

propitiate, *v.t.* to appease, to conciliate; to render favourable. †*v.i.* to atone. **propitiable,** *a.* **propitiation,** *n.* the act of propitiating; atonement, esp. that of Christ; †a propitiatory gift. **propitiator,** *n.* **propitiatory,** *a.* intended or serving to propitiate. *n.* a propitiation; the mercy-seat, esp. as symbolizing Christ. **propitious,** *a.* favourable; disposed to be kind or gracious; auspicious, suitable (for etc.). **propitiously,** *adv.* **propitiousness,** *n.* [L *propitiātus,* p.p. of *propitiāre,* from *propitius,* propitious, perh. a term in augury (*petere,* to fly)]

propjet, PROP[3].

proplasm, *n.* a mould, a matrix. †**proplastic,** *n.* the art of making moulds for casting. [L and Gr. *proplasma* (PRO-, PLASM)]

propodium, *n.* the anterior of the three lobes of the foot in some molluscs. **propodial,** *a.* **propodite,** *n.* the penultimate joint of the typical limb of a crustacean. **propoditic,** *a.* [mod. L (Gr. *pous podos,* foot)]

propolis, *n.* a resinous substance obtained by bees from buds etc. and used to cement their combs, stop up crevices etc., bee-glue. [Gr., a suburb, bee-glue (*polis,* city)]

proponent, *a.* proposing. *n.* one who makes a proposal or proposition; one who argues for, an advocate. [L *prōpōnens -ntem,* pres.p. of *prōpōnere,* to PROPOSE]

proportion, *n.* the comparative relation of one part or thing to another with respect to magnitude, number or degree; ratio; due relation, suitable adaptation of one part or thing to others; a proportional part, a share; (*pl.*) dimensions; equality of ratios between pairs of quantities; a series of such quantities; the rule by which from three given quantities a fourth may be found bearing the same ratio to the third as the second bears to the first, the rule of three. *v.t.* to adjust in suitable proportion; to make proportionate (to); to apportion. **geometrical, harmonic proportion** [GEOMETRY, HARMONIC]. **in, out of proportion (to),** (not) in due relation as to magnitude, number etc.; (not) consistent with the real importance of the matter in hand. **proportionable,** *a.* †capable of being made proportional; being in proportion, corresponding, proportional; †well-proportioned, symmetrical. **proportionableness,** *n.* **proportionably,** *adv.* **proportional,** *a.* having due proportion; pertaining to proportion; (*Math.*) having a constant ratio. *n.* a quantity in proportion with others, one of the terms of a ratio. **proportional representation,** *n.* an electoral system in which the representation of parties in an elected body is as nearly as possible proportional to their voting strength. (*Polit.*) **proportionalist,** *n.* one who makes designs according to the laws of proportion; an advocate of proportional representation. **proportionalism,** *n.* **proportionality,** *n.* **proportionally,** *adv.* **proportionate,** *a.* in due or a certain proportion (to). *v.t.,* to make proportionate or proportional. **proportionately,** *adv.* **proportinateness,** *n.* **proportioned,** *a.* (*usu. in comb., as well-proportioned*). **proportionless,** *a.* without proportion; unsymmetrical, shapeless. **proportionment,** *n.* [F, from L *proportiōnem,* nom. *-tio* (PRO-, PORTION)]

propose, *v.t.* to put forward, to offer, to present, for consideration etc.; to nominate for election; to put forward as a design, to purpose, to intend. *v.i.* to put forward a plan or intention; to make an offer, esp. of marriage. **proposal,** *n.* the act of proposing; something proposed; an offer of marriage; an application for insurance. **proposer,** *n.* [F *proposer*]

proposition, *n.* that which is propounded; a statement, an assertion; (*Log.*) a sentence in which something is affirmed or denied; (*Math.*) a formal statement of a theorem or problem, sometimes with the demonstration; a proposal, a scheme proposed for consideration or adoption; an invitation to have sexual intercourse; (*coll.*) a person or thing that has to be dealt with. *v.t.* to make a proposition to, esp. to invite to have sexual intercourse. **propositional,** *a.* [F, from L *prō- positiōnem,* nom. *-tio,* as foll.]

propound, *v.t.* to state or set forth for consideration, to propose; to bring forward (a will etc.) for probate. **propounder,** *n.* [from obs. *propone,* L *prōpōnere* (*pōnere,* to put), p.p. *prōpositus*]

propraetor, *n.* a praetor who at the expiration of his term of office was made governor of a province. [L, orig. *pro praetore,* (acting) for a praetor]

proprietor, *n.* an owner, one who has the exclusive legal right or title to anything, whether in possession or not, a possessor in his own right. **proprietary,** *n.* a body of proprietors collectively; proprietorship; †a proprietor, esp. (US) a grantee of a proprietary colony, as of Maryland. *a.* of or pertaining to a proprietor or proprietorship; owned as property; made and marketed under a patent, trademark etc. **proprietorial,** *a.* **proprietorially,** *adv.* **proprietorship,** *n.* **proprietress, -trix,** *n. fem.* [formerly *proprietary,* late L *proprietārius,* from *proprietas,* PROPERTY]

propriety, *n.* the quality of being conformable to an acknowledged or correct standard or rule; fitness, correctness, rightness; correctness of behaviour, becomingness; †exclusive ownership, property; †individuality, particular nature, particularity, idiosyncrasy. [F *propriété*]

proprioception, *n.* reception of or activation by, stimuli from within the organism. **proprioceptive,** *a.* **proprioceptor,** *n.* any reptor which receives such stimuli. [L *proprius,* own + *reception*]

proprium, *n.* (*pl.* **-pria**) a distinctive attribute, essential nature; (*Log.*) a property. [L, neut. of *proprius,* own]
proproctor, *n.* one acting for or under a proctor.
props PROP[2].
propterygium, *n.* (*pl.* **-gia**) the anterior basal portion of a pectoral fin. **propterygial,** *a.*
†**propugnation,** *n.* defence, vindication. **propugnator, propugner,** *n.* a defender, a champion. [L *prōpugnātio,* from *prōpugnāre* (*pugnāre,* to fight)]
propulsion, *n.* the act of propelling, a driving forward; that which propels, a driving force. **propulsive,** †**-sory,** *a.* [F, from L *prōpellere,* to PROPEL]
propyl, *n.* a hydrocarbon radical derived from propane. **propylene,** *n.* a colourless, gaseous alkene obtained from petroleum. [*prop*rionic acid + YL]
propylaeum, *n.* (*pl.* **-laea**) a gateway or entrance, esp. one of imposing architectural character, to a temple etc. **the Propylaea,** the entrance to the Athenian Acropolis. [L, from Gr. *propuleion, pulē,* a gate)]
propylon, *n.* (*pl.* **-lons, -la**), a propylaeum, esp. before an Egyptian temple.
pro rata PRO[1].
prorate, *v.t.* (*N Am.*) to distribute proportionally. **prorateable,** *a.* [L *pro rata,* for the rate, in proportion]
prorector, *n.* the deputy of a rector or president, esp. in a German university.
prorogue, *v.t.* to put an end to the meetings of Parliament without disolving it. *v.t.* to be prorogued. **prorogate,** *v.t.* (*chiefly Sc.*) to prorogue. **prorogation,** *n.* [F *proroger,* L *prōrogāre,* to extend, to defer (*rogāre,* to ask)]
pros-, *pref.* to, towards; before, in addition. [Gr., *pros,* prep.]
prosaic, *a.* pertaining to or resembling prose; unpoetic, unimaginative; dull, commonplace. **prosaically,** *adv.* **prosaicness, prosaism, prosaicism,** *n.* **prosaist,** *n.* a writer of prose; a prosaic person. [med. L *prōsaicus,* from *prōsa,* PROSE]
proscenium, *n.* (*pl.* **-nia**) the part of a stage between the curtain or drop-scene and the orchestra; (*Ant.*) the space in front of the scenery, the stage. **proscenium (arch),** *n.* the frame through which the audience views the traditional type of stage. [L, from Gr. *proskēnion* (*skēnē,* SCENE)]
proscribe, *v.t.* to publish the name of, as doomed to death, forfeiture of property etc. to outlaw; to banish, to exile; to denounce as dangerous; to interdict, to forbid. **proscriber,** *n.* **proscription,** *n.* **proscriptive,** *a.* [L *prōscrībere* (*scrībere,* to write)]
prose, *n.* ordinary written or spoken language not in metre, as opposed to verse; a passage for translation into a foreign language; commonplaceness; a tedious or unimaginative discourse. *a.* written in or consisting of prose; dull, commonplace, prosaic. *v.i.* to write or talk in a dull, tedious manner. *v.t.* to write or utter in prose; to turn into prose. **prose poem,** *n.* a piece of prose that has some of the characteristics of poetry. **proser,** *n.* **prosification,** *n.*, **prosifier,** *n.* **prosify,** *v.t., v.i.,* **prosing,** *n.* speaking or writing in a prosy way. **prosy,** *a.* dull, tedious, long-winded. **prosily,** *adv.* **prosiness,** *n.* [F, from L *prōsa,* from *prōsa* (*prorsa*) *ōrātio,* straightforward discourse, masc. *prorsus* (*versus,* p.p. of *vertere,* to turn)]
prosector, *n.* a dissector, esp. one who dissects bodies in preparation for lectures, demonstrations etc. †**prosect,** *v.t.,* and *v.i.* **prosection,** *n.* **prosectorial,** *a.* **prosectorium,** *n.* (*pl.* **-ria** ( ) a building or laboratory where prosection is performed. **prosectorship,** *n.* [late L *prōsector* (PRO-, SECTOR)]
prosecute, *v.t.* to pursue or follow up with a view to attain or accomplish; to carry on (work, trade etc.); to take legal proceedings against; to seek to obtain by legal process. *v.i.* to act as a prosecutor. **prosecutable,** *a.* **prosecution,** *n.* the act of prosecuting; the exhibition of a charge against an accused person before a court; the instituting and carrying on of a civil or criminal suit; the prosecutor or prosecutors collectively. **prosecutor,** *n.* **public prosecutor,** an officer conducting criminal proceedings on behalf of the public. **prosecutrix,** *n.* [L *prosecūtus,* p.p. of *prosequī* (*sequī,* to follow)]
Prosecution Service, Crown, body established by the Prosecution of Offences Act 1985, responsible for prosecuting all criminal offences in England and Wales. It is headed by the Director of Public Prosecutions (DPP), and brings England and Wales in line with Scotland (see PROCURATOR FISCAL) in having a prosecution service independent of the police.
proselyte, *n.* a new convert to some religion, party of system, esp. a gentile convert to Judaism. †*v.t.* to proselytize. **proselytism,** *n.* **proselytize, -ise,** *v.t.* and *i.* **proselytizer, -iser,** *n.* [ME and OF *proselite,* late L *prosēlytus,* Gr. *prosēlutos,* from *prosēluth-,* aorist stem of *proserchesthai* (PRO-, *erchesthai,* to come)]
prosencephalon, *n.* (*pl.* **-la**) the anterior part of the brain comprising the cerebral hemispheres etc. and sometimes including the olfactory lobes. **prosencephalic,** *a.*
prosenchyma, *n.* tissue composed of elongated thick-walled cells closely interpenetrating, esp. fibrovascular tissue. **prosenchymatous,** *a.* [Gr. *enchuma,* infusion, after PARENCHYMA]
Proserpina, *n.* Roman equivalent of Persephone, goddess of the underworld.
prosify, etc. PROSE.
prosimian, *a., n.* (of or being) one of a primitive sub-order of primates which includes lemurs, lorises and tarsiers. [PRO + L *simia,* ape]
prosit, *int.* may it benefit you, success, used in (German) drinking toasts. [L, may it be to your good]
prosobranch, *n.* a prosobranchiate. *a.* prosobranchiate. **prosobranchiate,** *a.* having the gills anterior to the heart. *n.* one of the Prosobranchiata, an order of aquatic gasteropods with the gills anterior to the heart. [Gr. *prosō,* forward, *branchia,* gills]
prosody, *n.* the science of versification, formerly a branch of grammar. **prosodiacal, prosodial, prosodic,** *a.* **prosodian, prosodist,** *n.* [L and Gr. *prosōdia*]
prosopopoeia, *n.* a rhetorical figure by which abstract things are represented as persons, or absent persons as speaking. [L, from Gr. *prosōpopoiia* (*prosōpon,* person, *poiein,* to make)]
prospect[1], *n.* an extensive view; the way a house etc. fronts or looks; a scene; a pictorial representation of a view; a mental picture of what is to come; expectation, ground of expectation; an indication of the presence of ore, a sample of ore for testing, the mineral obtained by testing; (*pl.*) expectation of money to come or of an advancement in career; a prospective customer. [L PROSPECTUS]
prospect[2], *v.i.* to search, to explore, esp. for minerals; to promise well or ill (of a mine). *v.t.* to search or explore (a region) for minerals; to promise (a good or poor yield); †to look over, to survey. †**prospection,** *n.* **prospective,** *a.* pertaining to the future; anticipated, expected, probable, characterized by foresight. *n.* prospect, view, anticipation; †a field-glass, a telescope. †**prospective glass,** *n.* a magic crystal in which future events were supposed to be visible; a field-glass, a telescope. **prospectively,** *adv.* **prospectiveness,** *n.* **prospectless,** *a.* **prospector,** *n.* one who searches for minerals or mining sites.
prospectus, *n.* a descriptive circular announcing the main objects and plans of a commercial scheme, institution, literary work etc. [L, a look-out, a prospect, from *prōspicere, specere,* to look)]
prosper, *v.t.* to make successful or fortunate. *v.i.* to succeed; to thrive. **prosperity,** *n.* the condition of being prosperous; success, wealth. **prosperous,** *a.* successful, thriving, making progress, or advancement; favourable, fortunate, auspicious. †**prosperousness,** *n.* **prosperously,** *adv.* [F *prospérer,* L *prosperāre,* to cause to succeed, from *prosper,* favourable, fortunate]
†**prospicience,** *n.* the act of looking forward, foresight. [L *prōspiciens -ntem,* pres.p. of *prōspicere,* see PROSPECT[2]]
prost PROSIT.
Prost, *n.* **Alain** (1955–), French motor racing driver.

He won 39 races from 153 starts, and was world champion 1985, 1986, and 1989.

prostaglandin, *n.* any of a group of hormone-like substances which have wide-ranging effects on body processes, e.g. muscle contraction. [from *prostate gland,* a major source of these]

prostate, *n.* the prostate gland. *a.* situated in front. **prostate gland,** *n.* a gland situated before the neck of the bladder in male mammals. **prostatectomy**, *n.* surgical removal of the prostate gland. **prostatic**, *a.* **prostatic body** or **gland,** *n.* the prostate. **prostatitis**, *n.* inflammation of the prostate. [med. L *prostata,* Gr. *prostatēs,* one who stands before (PRO-, *sta-*, stem of *histanai,* to stand)]

prosternum, *n.* the ventral segment of the thorax of an insect.

prosthesis, *n.* (*Gram.*) the addition of one or more letters to the beginning of a word; (*Surg.*) the addition of an artificial part to supply a defect; an artificial part thus supplied. **prosthetic**, *a.* **prosthetically,** *adv.* **prosthetics,** *n. sing.* the branch of surgery or dentistry concerned with prosthesis. **prosthetist,** *n.* [L and Gr. (*thesis,* a thing laid down, from *tithenai,* to put)]

prostitute, *v.t.* to hire (oneself, another) out for sexual purposes; to offer or sell for base or unworthy purposes; to devote to base uses. *a.* prostituted. *n.* a person (esp. a woman or homosexual man) who engages in sexual intercourse for money; a base hireling. **prostitution,** *n.* **prostitutor,** *n.* [L *prostitūtus,* p.p. of *prostituere* (*statuere,* to place, to set)]

prostrate, *a.* lying flat or prone; lying in a horizontal position, procumbent, lying in a posture of humility or at mercy; overcome, exhausted. *v.t.*, to lay flat; to cast (oneself) down; esp. in reverence or adoration (before); to throw down, to overthrow, to overcome, to demolish; to reduce to physical exhaustion. **prostration,** *n.* [L *prostrātus,* p.p. of *prosternere* (*sternere,* to lay flat)]

prostyle, *a.* having a row of columns, usu. four, entirely in front of the building. *n.* a portico supported on columns entirely in front of the building, opp. to those having antae at the sides. [F, from L *prostylos,* Gr. *prostulos* (PRO-, *stulos,* STYLE[2])]

prosy PROSE.

prosyllogism, *n.* (*Log.*) a syllogism so connected with another that the conclusion of the first is the major or the minor premise of the second. [L *prosyllogismus,* Gr. *prosyllogismos*]

Prot., (*abbr.*) Protectorate; Protestant.

prot- PROTO-.

protactinium, *n.* a radioactive element, yielding actinium on disintegration, at. no. 91; chem. symbol Pa, [*proto* + *actinium*]

protagon, *n.* a fatty nitrogenous compound containing phosphorus, found in brain and nerve tissue. [G (Gr. *agon,* neut. pres.p. of *agein,* to lead)]

protagonist, *n.* the leading character or actor in a Greek play; a leading character, advocate, champion etc. [Gr. *prōtagōnistēs* (*agōnistēs,* actor, see AGONISTIC)]

protasis, *n.* (*pl.* **-ases**) a clause containing the antecedent, esp. in a conditional sentence; the first part of a classic drama, in which the characters are introduced and the argument explained; †a proposition, a maxim. **protatic**, *a.* [late L and Gr., *tasis,* from *teinein,* to stretch)]

protean, *a.* readily assuming different shapes or aspects; variable, changeable. **proteiform**, *a.* [PROTEUS]

protect, *v.t.* to shield, defend or keep safe (from or against injury, danger etc.); to support (industries) against foreign competition by imposing duties on imports; to provide funds so as to guarantee payment of (bills etc.). **protectingly,** *adv.* **protection,** *n.* the act of protecting; the state of being protected; that which protects, a covering, shield or defence; a passport, a safe conduct; protection money; freedom from injury, molestation etc. purchased by protection money; (*N Am.*) a certificate of citizenship of the US issued to seamen by the customs authorities; †a document granting exemption from arrest in civil suits; the promotion of home industries by bounties or by duties on imports. **protection money,** *n.* a bribe extorted by gangsters from shopkeepers etc. by threats of damage to property, personal assault etc. **protection racket,** *n.* an organized system of extortion whereby gangsters leave shopkeepers etc. and their property unscathed in return for regular pay-offs. **protectionism,** *n.* the doctrine or system of protecting home industries against foreign competition. **protectionist,** *n.* and *a.* **protective,** *a.* affording protection; intended to protect; (of person) desirous of shielding another from harm or distress. *n.* something that protects; a condom. **protective coloration, colouring,** *n.* colouring that enables animals to escape detection by blending with their surroundings, camouflage. **protective custody,** *n.* detention before trial in order to ensure an accused's personal safety. **protective detention,** (*Law*) *n.* detention of a criminal to protect Society from his further activities. **protectively,** *adv.* **protectiveness,** *n.* [L *prōtectus,* p.p. of *prōtegre* (*tegere,* to cover)]

protector, *n.* one who protects against injury or evil etc.; a protective device, a guard; one in charge of the kingdom during the minority, incapacity etc. of the sovereign; title of Oliver Cromwell, Lord Protector of the Commonwealth (1653–8), and his son Richard Cromwell (1658–9). **protectoral,** †**protectorial**, *a.* **protectorate**, *n.* protection, usu. combined with partial control, of a weak State by a more powerful one; territory under such protection; the office of protector of a kingdom; the period of this, esp. that of Oliver and Richard Cromwell. **protectorless,** *a.* **protectorship,** *n.* **protectory,** *n.* in the Roman Catholic Church, an institution for the care of destitute or vicious children. **protectress**, **-trix**, *n.* [ME and OF *protectour* (F. *protecteur*), L *prōtectōrem,* nom. *-tor*]

protégé, *n.* (*fem.* **-gée,**) one under the protection, care, or patronage of another. [F, p.p. of *protéger,* to PROTECT)]

proteid, *n.* a name applied to the amorphous organic substances now usually called proteins.

proteiform PROTEAN.

protein, *n.* a complex and unstable organic compound, containing carbon, oxygen, hydrogen and nitrogen, usu. with some sulphur, found in all organic bodies and forming an essential constituent of animal foods; orig. applied to a nitrogenous compound supposed to form the basic material of all organisms; the essential principal of food, obtained from albumen, fibrin or casein. **proteinaceous**, **proteinic**, **proteinous**, *a.* [F *protéine* or G *protēin* (Gr. *prōteios,* from *prōtos,* first, -IN)]

pro tem, (*abbr.*) pro tempore under PRO.

protend, *v.t.* to hold out; to stretch forth; to extend. †**protense,** †**protension**, **protensity,** *n.* †**protensive,** *a.* [L *protendere (tendere,* to stretch)]

proteolysis, *n.* (*Chem.*) the resolution or splitting up of the proteins by the process of digestion or the application of ferments. **proteolytic**, *a.* [PROTE-IN, Gr. *lusis,* loosening, resolving, from *luein,* to loosen]

proter-, protero-, *comb. form* former, anterior. [Gr. *proteros,* comp. of *pro,* before]

proterandrous, *a.* having the stamens mature before the pistil; having the male organs or individuals in a zooid colony mature before the female. **proterandrousness, proterandry**, *n.* [Gr. *anēr andros,* man]

proterogynous, *a.* having the pistil mature before the stamens. **proterogyny**, *n.* [Gr. *guné,* woman]

Proterozoic, *a.*, *n.* (pertaining to) the period of geological time, 2.5 billion to 590 million years ago, the second division of the Precambrian era. It is defined as the time of simple life, since many rocks dating from this eon show traces of biological activity, and some contain the fossils of bacteria and algae. [Gr. *proteros,* former, earlier and ZOIC]

protest[1], *v.i.* to make a solemn affirmation; to express dissent or objection. *v.t.* to affirm or declare formally or earnestly; to object (that); (*esp. N Am.*) to express one's disapproval of or objection to; to make a formal declaration, usu. by a notary public, that payment (of a bill) has been demanded and refused; †to appeal to; †to proclaim, to publish. [F *protester*. L *prōtestārī* (*testārī*, to declare, to witness, from *testis*, witness)]

protest[2], *n.* the act of protesting; a solemn or formal declaration of opinion, usu. of dissent or remonstrance; an expression or demonstration of dissent, disapproval etc.; a formal declaration by the holder of the non-payment of a bill; a written declaration by the master of a ship, usu. before a magistrate, consul etc. stating the circumstances attending an injury or loss of a ship or cargo. *a.* expressing or intended to express objection, dissent.

Protestant, *n.* one of the party adhering to Luther at the Reformation, who at the second Diet of Spires (1529) protested against the decree of the majority involving submission to the authority of the Roman Catholic Church; a member of a Church upholding the principles of the Reformation, or (loosely) of any Church not within the Roman communion; one who makes a protest. *a.* pertaining to the Protestants, or to Protestantism; making a protest. **Protestantism,** *n.* one of the main divisions of Christianity, which emerged from Roman Catholicism at the Reformation. The chief sects are the Anglican Communion, Baptists, Christian Scientists, Lutherans, Methodists, Pentecostal Movement, Presbyterians, and Unitarians, with a total membership of about 320 million. **Protestantize, -ise,** *v.t., v.i.* (to cause) to become Protestant. [F, pres.p. of *protester*, to PROTEST]

protestation, *n.* a solemn affirmation or declaration; a solemn declaration of dissent, a protest; a vow or promise; a declaration in pleading. †**protestator, protester,** *n.* **protestingly,** *adv.*

Proteus, *n.* in Greek mythology an old man, the warden of the sea beasts of Poseidon, who possessed the gift of prophecy, but could transform himself to any form he chose to evade questioning; a changeable, shifty or fickle person or thing; a genus of amphibians, resembling a salamander, found in Austrian caves; a group of bacteria; †an amoeba. **proteus animalcule,** *n.* an amoeba. [L and Gr.]

protevangelium, *n.* the first announcement of the Gospel; an apocryphal gospel attributed to St James the Less. **protevangelist**, *n.* [PROT-, L *evangelium*, EVANGEL]

prothalamion,, -mium, *n.* a song in honour of the bride and bridegroom before the wedding. [coined by Spenser (EPITHALAMIUM)]

prothallium, *n.* (*Bot.*) a cellular structure bearing the sexual organs in vascular cryptogams. [Gr. *thallion*, dim. of *thallos*, THALLUS]

prothesis, *n.* the placing of the elements in readiness for use in the Eucharist; hence, a credence-table, or the part of a church in which this stands; (*Gram.*) prosthesis. **prothetic**, *a.* [Gr. (*thesis*, a thing laid down, from *tithenai*, to put)]

prothonotary, *n.* a chief clerk or notary; the chief clerk or registrar of a court, now chiefly in some American and foreign courts, and formerly of the Courts of Chancery, Common Pleas and King's Bench; a member of the Roman Catholic College of Prothonotaries Apostolic who register the papal acts. **prothonotariat**, *n.* **prothonotarial,** *a.* **prothonotaryship,** *n.* [obs. F *prothonotaire*, late L *prōtonotārius*, Gr. *prōtonotarios* (L *notārius*, NOTARY)]

prothorax, *n.* the anterior segment of the thorax in insects. **prothoracic**, *a.*

prothysteron HYSTERON-PROTERON.

Protista, *n.pl.* a name proposed by Haeckel for a kingdom including microscopic organisms whose position (as animals or plants) was doubtful. **protist**, *n.* any individual of the Protista. [Gr., neut. pl. of *prōtistos*, superl. of *prōtos*, first]

protium, *n.* (*Chem.*) ordinary hydrogen of atomic weight 1 (as opposed to deuterium, tritium). [Gr. *protos*, first]

proto- *comb. form* chief; earliest, original, primitive; denoting that chemical compound in a series in which the distinctive element or radical combines in the lowest proportion with another element. [Gr. *prōtos*, first]

proto-Arabic, -Celtic, -Egyptian, -Semitic, etc., *a.* denoting the primitive or original tribes, languages, arts etc. of the Arabs etc.

Protococcus, *n.* (*pl.* **-cocci**) (*Bot.*) a genus of unicellular algae such as form the familiar green layers on damp stones, trees, timber etc. [Gr. *kokkos*, grain, seed]

protocol, *n.* the original draft of an official document or transaction, esp. minutes or a rough draft of a diplomatic instrument or treaty, signed by the parties to a negotiation; the formal etiquette and procedure governing diplomatic and ceremonial functions; the official formulas used in diplomatic instruments, charters, wills etc. *v.i.* to draft protocols. *v.t.* to reduce to or record in a protocol. **protocolist,** *n.* [OF *prothocole* (F *protocole*), med. L *prōtocollum*, Gr. *protokollon*, orig. the first leaf glued to a MS. (*kolla*, glue)]

Protocols of Zion, a forged document containing supposed plans for Jewish world conquest alleged to have been submitted by Herzl to the first Zionist Congress at Basel in 1897, and published in Russia in 1905. They were proved to be a forgery by *The Times* in 1921, but were used by Hitler in his anti-Semitic campaign.

protogenic, protogenetic, *a.* primitive, of primitive or earliest origin or production. [Gr. *protogenes* (*gen-*, root of *gignesthai*, to be born)]

protogine, *n.* a variety of granite forming the central mass of Mont Blanc and other mountains in the Alps, having a foliated structure due to dynamic action.

protohippus, *n.* an extinct quadruped about the size of a sheep, from the lower Pliocene in America, probably an ancestor of the horse. [Gr. *hippos*, horse]

protomartyr, *n.* a first martyr (applied esp. to St Stephen); the first who suffers in any cause. [med. L (MARTYR)]

proton, *n.* a particle occurring in atomic nuclei and identical with the nucleus of the hydrogen atom, having an electric charge equal and opposite to that of the electron, and a mass 1840 times as great. **Proton rocket,** *n.* a Soviet space rocket introduced 1965, used to launch heavy satellites, space probes, and the Salyut and Mir space stations. [Gr. *protos*, first]

protonotary, PROTHONOTARY.

Protophyta, *n.pl.* a primary division of the vegetable kingdom comprising plants of the lowest organization, usu. microscopic in size and unicellular. **protophyte**, *n.* [Gr. *phuta*, plants, sing. *phuton*]

protoplasm, *n.* the viscid semifluid substance composed of oxygen, hydrogen, carbon and nitrogen, constituting the living matter from which all living organisms are developed. **protoplasmatic, protoplasmic**, *a.* [Gr. *prōtoplasma* (Gr. *plasma*, a moulded thing, from *plassein*, to mould)]

protoplast, *n.* the first individual, esp. the first-created man; the original, the archetype, the model; (*Biol.*) a unit of protoplasm, a bioplast, a unicellular organism. **protoplastic**, *a.* [F *protoplaste*, late L *prōtoplastus*, Gr. *protoplastos* (*plastos*, moulded, as prec.)]

protosalt, *n.* a salt corresponding to the protoxide of a metal. [PROTO-, SALT]

protosulphide, *n.* one of a series of sulphides containing the lowest proportion of sulphur.

Prototheria, *n.pl.* Huxley's name for the lowest division of mammals comprising the Monotremata and their ancestors. **prototherе**, *n.* **prototherian,** *a.* and *n.* [Gr. *thēria*, beasts]

prototype, *n.* an original or primary type or model, an exemplar, an archetype; a pre-production model on which tests can be carried out to trace design faults, indicate possible improvements etc. **prototypal, prototypic, -al**, *a.* [F, from Gr. *prototupon*]

protoxide, *n.* (*Chem.*) a compound of oxygen and an element containing the lowest proportion of oxygen. **protoxydize, -ise**, *v.t.*

Protozoa, *n.pl.* (*sing.* **-zoon**) the lowest division of the animal kingdom, comprising those consisting of a single cell or a group of cells not differentiated into two or more tissues. **protozoal,** *a.* of or pertaining to the Protozoa; caused by the agency of Protozoa (of diseases). **protozoan,** *a.* and *n.* **protozoic** *a.* (*Geol.*, *Palaeont.*) belonging to the strata in which the earliest traces of life are found; protozoal. **protozoology**, *n.* the branch of zoology dealing with the Protozoa. [Gr. *zōa,* animals, sing. *zōon*]

protract, *v.t.* to extend in duration, to prolong; to draw (a map, plan etc.) to scale, esp. with a scale and protractor. **protractedly,** *adv.* **protracter,** *n.* **protractile,** *a.* capable of extension (of the organ etc. of an animal). **protraction,** *n.* **protractor,** *n.* an instrument, usu. in the form of a graduated arc, for laying down angles on paper etc.; a muscle that protracts or extends a limb; an instrument for drawing extraneous bodies out of a wound. [L *prōtractus,* p.p. of *prōtrahere* (*trahere,* to draw)]

protrude, *v.t.* to thrust forward or out; to cause to project or issue; to obtrude. *v.i.* to project, to be thrust forward. **protrudent,** *a.* **protrusible,** *a.* **protrusile,** *a.* **protrusion**, *n.* **protrusive,** *a.* **protrusively,** *adv.* [L *prōtrūdere* (*trūdere,* to thrust, p.p. *trūsus*)]

protuberant, *a.* swelling, bulging out, prominent. **protuberance,** *n.* a swelling, a prominence, a knob, a bump. **protuberantly,** *adv.* †**protuberate,** *v.i.* †**protuberation,** *n.* [L *prōtūberans -ntem,* pres.p. of *prōtūberāre*]

protyle, *n.* a word introduced by Sir William Crookes (1886) to express the idea of the original primal matter existing before the differentiation of the chemical elements.

proud, *a.* having high or inordinate self esteem; haughty, arrogant; having a due sense of dignity; elated, exultant, feeling honoured, pleased, gratified; grand, imposing; stately, inspired by pride (of words, looks etc.); inspiring pride, noble, grand (of deeds etc.); projecting, standing out above a plane surface; swollen, in flood (of a stream). **proud flesh,** *n.* swollen flesh growing about a healing wound. **proudly,** *adv.* †**proudness,** *n.* [OE *prūt,* perh. from OF *prud* (*F preux*), prob. ult. from L *prōdesse,* to be of use]

Proudhon, *n.* **Pierre Joseph** (1809–65), French anarchist, born in Besançon. He sat in the Constituent Assembly of 1848, was imprisoned for three years, and had to go into exile in Brussels. He published *Qu'est-ce que la propriété/What is Property?* (1840) and *Philosophie de la misère/Philosophy of Poverty* (1846). His most noted dictum is 'property is theft'.

Proust, *n.* **Marcel** (1871–1922), French novelist and critic. The autobiographical novel *À la recherche du temps perdu/Remembrance of Things Past* (1913) is the expression of his childhood memories coaxed from his subconscious; it is also a precise reflection of life in provincial France at the end of the 19th cent.

Prout, *n.* **William** (1785–1850), British chemist. In 1815 Prout, a London physician, published his hypothesis that the atomic weight of every atom was an exact and integral multiple of the hydrogen atom. The discovery of isotopes in the 20th cent. established Prout's Hypothesis.

Prov., (*abbr.*) Provençal, Provence; Proverbs; Province; Provost.

prove, *v.t.* (*p.p.* **proved, proven**) †to test, to try by experiment, to make trial of; to put to a test, to try by a standard; to have experience of; to take a proof impression from; to show to be true; to establish or demonstrate by argument, reasoning or testimony; to establish the authenticity or validity of, esp. to obtain probate of (a will); to show or ascertain the correctness of, as by a further calculation. *v.i.* to be found by experience or trial; to turn out to be; to turn out (to be); †to make a trial or attempt; (of dough) to rise and become aerated before baking. **not proven**, (*Sc. Law*) not proved (a verdict given when there is not sufficient evidence to convict). **provable,** *a.* **provableness,** *n.* **provably,** *adv.* **prover,** *n.* one who or that which proves or tests; one employed in printing proof impressions; (*Law*) an approver. **proving,** *a.*, *n.* **proving ground,** *n.* a place where something, esp. a vehicle is subjected to trials and scientific tests; any testing experience or situation. [OF *prover* (F *prouver*), L *probāre,* to test, to approve]

provection, *n.* the mutation of voice consonants to breath consonants, esp. in Celtic languages; the carrying on of a terminal letter to the first syllable of the succeeding word (as in *nickname* from *an eke-name*). [late L *prōvectio,* from *provehere* (*vehere,* to carry)]

proveditor, provedore, *n.* a commissioner, inspector, governor or other officer of the Venetian republic; a purveyor, a caterer. [It. *proveditore* (now *provveditore*), ult. from L *prōvidēre,* to PROVIDE]

proven PROVE.

provenance, *n.* origin source. [F, from *provenant,* pres.p. of *provenir,* L *prōvenīre* (*venīre,* to come)]

Provençal, *n.* a native or inhabitant of Provence, SE France; the language of Provence, a member of the Romance branch of the Indo-European language family. *a.* pertaining to Provence, its language, or inhabitants. [F]

Provence-Alpes-Côte d'Azur, a region of SE France, comprising the departments of Alpes-de-Haute-Provence, Hautes-Alpes, Alpes-Maritimes, Bouches-du-Rhône, Var, and Vaucluse; area 31,400 sq km/ 12,120 sq miles; capital Marseille; population (1986) 4,059,000. The Côte d'Azur, on the Mediterranean, is a tourist centre. Provence was an independent kingdom in the 10th century, and the area still has its own language, Provençal.

provend, *n.* food, provisions, provender; orig. a prebend, or the allowance of food to each inmate of a monastery. **provender,** *n.* dry food for beasts, fodder; (*facet.*) provisions, food; †provend. [OF *provende,* corr. of med. L *praebenda,* PREBEND]

provenience, PROVENANCE.

prover PROVE.

proverb, *n.* a short, pithy sentence, containing some truth or wise reflection proved by experience or observation; a maxim, a saw, an adage; a typical example, a byword; a short dramatic composition illustrating some well-known popular saying; (*pl.*) a round game played on well-known sayings. *v.t.* to speak of in a proverb, to make a byword of; to provide with a proverb. **Proverbs,** a collection of maxims forming a book of the Old Testament. **proverbial**, *a.* **proverbiality**, *n.* **proverbialism,** *n.* **proverbialist,** *n.* a writer, composer or collector of proverbs. **proverbialize, -ise,** *v.t.* and *i.* **proverbially,** *adv.* [F *proverbe,* L *prōverbium* (*verbum,* word)]

proviant, *n.* provisions, esp. for an army. [G, from It. *provianda,* PROVEND]

provide, *v.t.* to procure or prepare beforehand; to furnish, to supply; to equip (with); to lay down as a preliminary condition, to stipulate; (*Eccles.*) to appoint (to a benefice); (of the Pope) to grant the right to be appointed (to a benefice not yet vacant). *v.i.* to make preparation or provision (for or against); to furnish means of subsistence (for). **provided,** *a.* supplied, furnished; provided in readiness; laid down, stipulated. *conj.* on the understanding or condition (that). **provider,** *n.* **providing,** *n.* the action of supplying, furnishing, or preparing beforehand. *pres.p., conj.* provided. [L *prōvidēre* (*vidēre,* to see)]

providence, *n.* foresight, timely care or preparation; frugality, economy, prudence; the beneficent care or control of God over His creatures; God or nature regarded as exercising such care; a manifestation of such care. **provident,** *a.* making provision for the future, thrifty; showing foresight, prudent. **provident society,** FRIENDLY SOCIEY **providential**, *a.* due to or effected by divine providence; lucky, fortunate, opportune. **providentially,** *adv.* **providently,** *adv.* †**providentness,** *n.* [F, from L *prōvidentia,* as prec.]

province, *n.* (*Rom. Hist.*) a country or territory beyond the confines of Italy under a Roman governor; a large administrative division of a kingdom, country or state; the territory under the authority of an archbishop or metropolitan; (*pl.*) all parts of a country except the metropolis; proper sphere of action, business, knowledge etc. **provincial**, *a.* pertaining to a province; constituting a province; of, pertaining to, or characteristic of the provinces; narrow, rustic, rude, unpolished. *n.* one who belongs to a province or the provinces; (*Eccles.*) the superior of an order etc., in a province. **provincialism,** *n.* the quality of being provincial; a mode of speech, thought, behaviour etc. or a word or expression, peculiar to a province or the provinces; use of such peculiarities as an offence against style etc. **provincialist,** *n.* **provinciality**, *n.* **provincialize, -ise,** *v.t.* to render provincial. **provincially,** *adv.* [F, from L *prōvincia,* business or duty, province, etym. doubtful]

proving PROVE.

provision, *n.* the act of providing; previous preparation; a precautionary measure; a stipulation or condition providing for something; a supply of food etc.; (*pl.*) victuals, eatables etc.; †(*Eccles.*) appointment to a benefice not yet vacant. *v.t.* to provide with provisions. **provisional,** *a.* provided for present need; temporary, not permanent; requiring future confirmation. **Provisional,** *n., a.* (a member) of the militant breakaway faction of the IRA or Sinn Fein. **provisionality**, **provisionalness,** *n.* **provisionally,** *adv.* †**provisionary,** *a.* **provisionment,** *n.* [F, from L *prōvīsiōnem,* from *prōvidēre,* to PROVIDE]

proviso, *n.* (*pl.* **-sos, -soes**) a provisional condition, a stipulation; a clause in a covenant or other document rendering its operation conditional. [L, being provided that, see PROVIDE]

provisor, *n.* one appointed, esp. by the Pope, to a benefice before the death of the incumbent; the purveyor, steward or treasurer of a religious house; a vicar-general. [ME and A-F *provisour* (F *proviseur*), L *prōvīsōrem,* nom. *-sor,* as prec.]

provisory, *a.* conditional; provisional. **provisorily,** *adv.*

Provo, *n.* short for PROVISIONAL

provocation PROVOKE.

provoke, *v.t.* to rouse; to incite or stimulate to action, anger etc.; to irritate, to incense, to exasperate; to instigate, to call forth, to cause. **provocation,** *n.* **provocative**, *a.* tending to provoke; irritating, annoying, esp. with the intention to excite anger or rouse to action. *n.* a provocative action, thing, word etc. **provocatively,** *adv.* **provocativeness,** *n.* †**provokable,** *a.* †**provokement,** *n.* **provoker,** *n.* **provoking,** *a.* tending to provoke, annoying, exasperating. **provokingly,** *adv.* [OF *provoker* (F *provoquer*) L *prōvocāre* (*vocāre,* to call)]

provost, *n.* one appointed to superintend or hold authority; the head of a college; the head of a chapter, a prior, a dignitary in a cathedral corresponding to a dean; in Germany, a Protestant clergyman in charge of the principal church; (*Sc.*) the chief magistrate in a municipal corporation or burgh; (*Hist.*) an officer in charge of a body of men, establishment etc. a steward, a provost-marshal. **Lord Provost,** *n.* the chief magistrate of Edinburgh, Glasgow, Aberdeen, Perth and Dundee. **provost-marshal**, *n.* a commissioned officer, the head of the military police in a camp or in the field; (*Nav.*) an officer in charge of prisoners awaiting court-martial; (*W Indies*) a chief of police; (*Hist.*) a French semi-military public officer. **provostship, provostry,** *n.* [OE *prōfost, prāfost,* L *praepositus*]

prow[1], *n.* the fore part of a vessel, the bow. [F *proue,* prob. from L and Gr. *prōra,* rel. to *pro,* before]

†**prow**[2], *a.* brave, valiant, worthy. [OF *prou* (OF *preux*), prob. from L *prōdesse,* see PROUD]

prowess, *n.* valour, bravery, gallantry; outstanding ability or skill. [OF *prouesse, from prou,* see prec.]

prowl, *v.i.* to rove (about) stealthily as if in search of prey. *v.t.* to go through or about in this way. *n.* the act or an instance of **prowling. prowler,** *n.* **prowlingly,** *adv.* [ME *prollen,* etym. doubtful]

Proxima Centauri, *n.* the closest star to the Sun, 4.3 light years away. It is a faint red dwarf, visible only with a telescope, and is a member of the Alpha Centauri triple star system.

proximal, *a.* nearest the centre of the body or the point of attachment, opposed to distal. **proximally,** *adv.* [L *proximus,* superl. of *prope,* near]

proximate, *a.* nearest, next; immediately preceding or following; approximate. **proximate cause,** that which immediately precedes and produces the effect. **proximately,** *adv.* **proximity**, *n.* immediate nearness in place, time, relation, etc. esp. of kinship. **proximo**, *a.* in or of the month succeeding the present. [late L *proximātus,* p.p. of *proximāre,* as prec.]

proxy, *n.* the agency of a substitute for a principal; one deputed to act for another, esp. in voting; a document authorizing one person to act or vote for another; a vote given under his authority. *a.* done, made etc. by proxy. **proxyship,** *n.* [contr. from PROCURACY]

Prozymite, *n.* (*Eccles. Hist.*) one of those using leavened bread in the Eucharist, opposed to Azymite. [Gr. *prozumitēs,* from *prozumion,* leaven (PRO-, *zumē,* leaven)]

prude, *n.* a person who affects great modesty or propriety, esp. in regard to sexual matters **prudery**, **prudishness,** *n.* **prudish,** *a.* **prudishly,** *adv.* [F, *n.*, and *a.* from OF *prude* (fem. of *prou, prod,* PROW[2], or from *prudefemme,* cp. *prud'homme*)]

prudent, *a.* cautious, discreet, circumspect; worldly-wise, careful of consequences; showing good judgement, foresight; †correct, decorous. **prudence,** *n.* **prudential**, *a.* actuated or characterized by prudence; worldly-wise, mercenary. *n.pl.* prudential considerations, matters of practical wisdom; prudential maxims or precepts. **prudentialism, prudentiality**, *n.* **prudentialist,** *n.* **prudentially,** *adv.* **prudently,** *adv.* [F, from L *prūdentem,* nom. *-dens, prōvidens,* PROVIDENT]

prudery PRUDE.

prudhomme, *n.* (*Hist.*) a trusty man; a member of a French board composed of masters and workmen, for arbitration in trade disputes. [F, from OF *prodhomme* (PROW [2], *homme,* man)]

Prud'hon, *n.* **Pierre** (1758–1823), French painter who worked in a soft, romantic style. He became drawing instructor and court painter to the Emperor Napoleon's wives.

pruinose, *a.* (*Nat. Hist.*) covered with a powdery substance or bloom, frosted. **pruinescence**, *n.* †**pruinous,** *a.* [L *pruīnōsus,* frosty, from *pruīna,* hoar-frost]

prune [1], *n.* the dried fruit of various kinds of *Prunus domestica,* the common plum; a plum; a dark purple colour; (*coll.*) a stupid or uninteresting person. **pruniferous**, *a.* [F, from L *prūnum,* Gr. *prounon*]

prune [2], *v.t.* to cut or lop off the superfluous branches etc. from; to cut or lop (off, away etc.); to free from anything superfluous; †to dress or trim, to preen. **pruner,** *n.* **pruning-hook, -knife, -shears,** *n.* instruments of various forms for pruning trees etc. [OF *proignier,* etym. doubtful]

prunella[1], *n.* a throat disorder, quinsy, angina; a genus of labiate plants, with purplish, bluish or white flowers, comprising the common self-heal. [var. of med. L *brunella,* dim. of *brūnus,* brown]

prunella[2], *n.* a smooth dark woollen stuff, used for making the uppers of shoes and gaiters, and formerly for clergymen's and barristers' gowns. [etym. doubtful (cp. F *prunelle,* perh. plum-colour, rel. to PRUNE[1])]

prunello, *n.* a superior variety of prune, usu. made from greengages. [It.]

pruniferous PRUNE[1].

prunt, *n.* a piece of ornamental glass laid on to or impressed on a glass vase or other object; a tool for making prunts. [perh. dial. var. of PRINT]

Prunus, *n.* a genus of trees, family Rosaceae, producing fruit with a fleshy, edible pericarp. The genus includes plums, peaches, apricots, almonds, and cherries.

prurient, *a.* disposed to, characterized by or arousing an unhealthy interest in sexual matters; characterized by a morbid curiosity. **prurience, -ency,** *n.* **pruriently,** *adv.* [L *prūriens -ntem,* pres.p. of *prūrīre,* to itch]

prurigo, *n.* a papular disease of the skin attended with intolerable itching. **pruriginous**, *a.* **pruritus**, *n.* itching.

Prussia, *n.* a N German state 1618–1945. It was an independent kingdom until 1867 when it became a dominant part of the North German Confederation and part of the German Empire in 1871 under the Prussian King Wilhelm I. West Prussia became part of Poland under the Versailles Treaty and East Prussia was largely incorporated into the USSR after 1945. **Prussian,** *a.* of or pertaining to Prussia; over-bearing; militaristic. *n.* a native or inhabitant of Prussia. **Prussian blue,** *n.* a deep-blue pigment obtained from ferrocyanide or iron. **Prussian carp,** *n.* a small variety of the common carp. **Prussianism,** *n.* practices or policies (e.g. the imposition of rigid discipline, militaristic organization) held to be typically Prussian. **Prussianize, -ise,** *v.t.* **Prussianizer, -iser,** *n.* **prussiate,** *n.* (*Chem.*) **prussic,** *a.* of or derived from Prussian blue. **prussic acid,** hydrocyanic acid, first obtained from Prussian blue. [med. L *Prussiānus* (*Pruzzi, Borussi,* -AN)]

Prut, *n.* a river that rises in the Carpathian Mountains of SW Ukraine and flows 900 km/565 miles to meet the Danube at Reni. For part of its course it follows the E frontier of Romania.

pry[1], *v.i.* to look closely or inquisitively; to peep, to peer; to search or inquire curiously or impertinently (into) *v.t.* to search or find (out) inquisitively or impertinently *n.* the act of prying. **prying,** *a.* **pryingly,** *adv.* [ME *prien,* etym. doubtful]

pry[2], *v.t.* PRISE[1] **pryse,** PRICE, PRIZE[1]

prytaneum, *n.* (*Gr. Ant.*) the public hall, esp. at Athens, in which the duties of hospitality were exercised towards ambassadors and citizens honoured with special distinction. [L, from Gr. *prutaneion,* from *prutanis,* president]

Przewalski, Przhevalsky, *n.* **Nikolai Mikhailovitch** (1839–88), Russian explorer and soldier. In 1870 he crossed the Gobi Desert to Beijing and then went on to the upper reaches of the Chang Jiang River. His attempts to penetrate Tibet as far as Lhasa failed on three occasions, but he continued to explore the mountain regions between Tibet and Mongolia, where he made collections of plants and animals, including a wild camel and a wild horse. **Przewalski's horse,** *n.* a primitive, wild horse of central Asia, having an erect mane and no forelock.

PS, (*abbr.*) Police Sergeant; postscript; private secretary; (*Theat.*) prompt side.

PSA, (*abbr.*) Property Services Agency; Public Services Authority.

psalm, *n.* a sacred song or hymn. **the Psalms,** a book of the Old Testament consisting of sacred songs, many of which are ascribed to David. **psalmist,** *n.* **the psalmist,** David or the composer of any of the Psalms. **psalmody,** *n.* the act, art or practice of singing psalms, esp. in divine worship; psalms collectively. **psalmodic,** *a.* **psalmodist,** *n.* a composer or singer of psalms. **psalmodize, -ise,** *v.i.* **psalmographer,** †**psalmographist,** *n.* a writer of psalms. **psalmography,** *n.* **psalter,** *n.* The Book of Psalms; a book containing the Psalms for use in divine service, esp. the version of the Psalms in the Prayer Book or the Latin collection used in the Roman Catholic Church. [L *psalmus,* Gr. *psalmos,* from *psallein,* to twang, to sing to the harp]

psalterium, *n.* the third stomach of a ruminant, the manyplies. [as foll.]

psaltery, *n.* a mediaeval stringed instrument somewhat resembling the dulcimer, but played by plucking the strings. **psalterian,** *a.* **psaltress,** *n.* a female player on the psaltery. [OF *psalterie,* L *psaltērium,* Gr. *psaltērion,* cp. prec.]

psammite, *n.* (*Min.*) sandstone. **psammitic,** *a.* [F, from Gr. *psammos,* sand]

PSBR, (*abbr.*) public sector borrowing requirement.

pschent, *n.* (*Egyptol.*) the double crown of ancient Egypt, combining the white pointed mitre of Upper Egypt and the red crown with square front of Lower Egypt. [Gr. *pschent,* Egypt. *p-skhent* (*p,* the, *skhent, sekhent*)]

psellism, *n.* any defect in speech, such as stammering, lisping etc. **psellismology,** *n.* [Gr. *psellismos,* from *psellos,* stammering]

psephology, *n.* the statistical and sociological study of elections **psephological,,** *a.* **psephologist,** *n.* [Gr. *psēphos,* a pebble (as used for voting in the Athenian assembly) + -LOGY]

pseud, *n.* (*coll.*) an affected or pretentious person, a pretender, a sham. *a.* pseudo. **pseudery,** *n.* (*coll.*) pretentiousness; falseness. **pseudo,** *a.* a false, sham, spurious; affected, pretentious.

pseud-, pseudo-, *comb. form* false, counterfeit, spurious; closely resembling, as in *pseudoclassical, pseudo-Gothic, pseudohistorical.* [Gr., from *pseudēs,* false]

pseudaesthesia, *n.* imaginary sense of feeling in organs that have been removed. [cp. ANAETHESIA]

Pseudechis, *n.* a genus of highly venomous snakes. **pseudechic,** *a.* [Gr. *echis,* viper]

pseudepigrapha, *n.pl.* spurious writings, esp. uncanonical writings ascribed to Scriptural authors etc. **pseudepigraphal, pseudepigraphical,** *a.* **pseudepigraphy,** *n.* the ascription of false names of authors to books. [neut. pl. or Gr. *pseudepigraphos* (*epigraphein,* to inscribe, see EPIGRAPH)]

pseudoblepsia, *n.* deceptive vision. [Gr. *blepsis,* looking]

pseudocarp, *n.* a fruit composed of other parts besides the ovary. [Gr. *karpos,* fruit]

pseudo-dipteral. DIPTERAL, *a.* having a single peristyle placed at the same distance from the walls as the outer row of columns in a dipteral temple.

pseudograph, *n.* a spurious writing, a literary forgery. **pseudography,** *n.* [Gr. *pseudographia*]

pseudologer, -gist, -LOGER, *n.* one who makes false statements, a liar. **pseudological,** *a.* **pseudology,** *n.* untruthful speaking; the art of lying.

pseudomorph, *n.* a mineral having the crystalline form of another. **pseudomorphic, -ous,** *a.* **pseudomorphism,** *n.* **pseudomorphosis,** *n.* [Gr. *morphē,* form]

pseudonym, *n.* a fictitious name, esp. a *nom de plume.* **pseudonymity,** *n.* **pseudonymous,** *a.* **pseudonymously,** *adv.* [Gr. *pseudōnumos* (*onoma, Aeolic onuma,* name)]

pseudopodium, *n.* (*pl.* **-podia**) a process formed by the protrusion of the protoplasm of a cell or a unicellular animal serving for locomotion, ingestion of food etc.; a false pedicel in mosses etc. **pseudopodial,** *a.* [Gr. *podion,* dim. of *pous podos,* foot]

pseudoscope. -SCOPE, *n.* a stereoscopic instrument for producing an apparent reversion of relief, making convex objects appear concave and vice versa. **pseudoscopic,** *a.* **pseudoscopically,** *adv.* **pseudoscopy,** *n.*

pseudostome, *n.* (*Zool.*) the mouth of the larva of an echinoderm; the opening of a secondary canal in a sponge to the exterior. **pseudostomosis,** *n.* **pseudostomotic, pseudostomous,** *a.* [Gr. *pseudostoma* (*stoma,* mouth)]

PSFD, (*abbr.*) public sector financial deficit.

pshaw, *int.* an exclamation of contempt, impatience, disdain or dislike. *a.* this exclamation. *v.i.* to say 'pshaw' (at). *v.t.* to express contempt for thus. [an instinctive sound]

psi[1], *n.* the twenty-third letter of the Greek alphabet, equivalent to *ps;* paranormal or psychic phenomena collectively. **psi particle,** *n.* an elementary particle formed by electron-positron collision.

psi[2], (*abbr.*) pounds per square inch.

psilanthropism, *n.* the doctrine that Christ was a mere man. **psilanthropic,** *a.* **psilanthropist,** *n.* [Gr. *psilanthrōpos* (*psilos,* bare, mere, *anthrōpos,* man), -ISM]

psilocybin, *n.* a hallucogenic drug obtained from Mexican mushrooms (*Psilocybe mexicana*). [Gr. *psilos,* bare + *kybe,* head]

psilosis, *n.* (*Path.*) sprue; shedding of the hair. [Gr. *psilos,* bare]

psittaceous, psittacine, *a.* belonging or allied to the parrots; parrot-like. **psittacosis,** *n.* a disease of parrots communicable to man, with a high mortality. [L *psittacus,* parrot]

psoas, *n.* either of the two large hip-muscles. **psoatic,**

a. [Gr., acc. pl. of *psoa,* mistaken for the sing.]

psora, *n.* (*Path.*) the itch or an analogous skin-disease. **psoriasis**, *n.* a dry, scaly skin disease. **psoriatic**, *a.* **psoriatiform,** *a.* **psoric,** *a.* pertaining to or suffering from itch *n.* a remedy for the itch. [L and Gr.]

Ps., Psa., (*abbr.*) Psalm; Psalms.

PST, (*abbr.*) Pacific Standard Time.

PSV, (*abbr.*) public service vehicle.

psych, psyche, *v.t.* (*coll.*) to psychoanalyse. **to psych (out),** (*N Am.*) to work out, to divine, to anticipate correctly; to intimidate or defeat by psychological means. **to psych up,** to prepare or stimulate psychologically as a preliminary to action.

psych- *comb. form.* PSYCH(O)-.

Psyche, *n.* (*Gr. Ant.*) a Greek nymph, the personification of the soul, beloved of Eros or Cupid; (**psyche**) the soul, the spirit, the mind; (**psyche**) the principles of emotional and mental life; (*Ent.*) a genus of day-flying moths; (*Astron.*) one of the asteroids. [Gr. *psuchē,* breath, life, soul]

psychedelic, *a.* pertaining to new, altered or heightened states of consciousness and sensory awareness as induced by the use of certain hallucinatory drugs; (of drugs) capable of producing such states; having an effect on the mind similar to that of psychedelic drugs; resembling the phenomena of psychedelic experience; (of colours) unnaturally vivid, fluorescent. [Gr. PSYCHE + dē]

psychiatry, *n.* the study and treatment of mental disorders. **psychiatric**, *a.* **psychiatrist,** *n.*

psychic, *a.* pertaining to the human soul, spirit, or mind; of or pertaining to phenomena that appear to be outside the domain of physical law, paranormal, extra-sensory; sensitive to non-physical or paranormal forces and influences. *n.* one having psychic powers; a medium; (*pl.*) psychology. **psychic force,** *n.* a non-physical force supposed to be the agent in spiritualistic phenomena. **psychical,** *a.* Psychic. **psychically,** *adv.* **psychicism,** *n.* **psychicist,** *n.* [Gr. *psuchikos*]

psycho, *n., a.* (*coll.*) short for PSYCHOPATH(IC), PSYCHOTIC.

psych(o)-, *comb. form.* mental; psychical. PSYCHE.

psychoactive, *a.* (of drugs) capable of affecting the mind or behaviour.

psychoanalysis, *n.* a method devised by Sigmund Freud for exploring and bringing to light concepts, experience etc. hidden in the unconscious mind as a form of treatment for functional nervous diseases or mental illness. **psychoanalyse**, *v.t.* to subject to, or treat by, psychoanalysis, **psychoanalyst**, *n.* **psychoanalytic, -al**, *a.*

psychodrama, *n.* an improvised dramatization of events from a patient's past life, used as a form of mental theory. **psychodramatic**, *a.*

psychodynamics, *n. sing.* the study of mental and emotional forces and their effect on behaviour. **psychodynamic,** *a.*

psychogenesis, *n.* (the study of) the origin or development of the mind: orgination in the mind. **psychogenetic**, *a.*

psychogenic, *a.* of mental, as opposed to physical, origin.

psychokinesis, *n.* apparent movement or alteration in physical objects produced by mind power. **psychokinetic**, *a.*

psycholinguistics, *n. sing.* the study of the psychology of language, its acquisition, development, use etc. **psycholinguist**, *n.* **psycholinguistic,** *a.*

psychology, *n.* the science of the human mind or soul; a system or theory of mental laws and phenomena; a treatise on this; (characteristic) mentality or motivation; (*coll.*) skill in understanding or motivating people. **psychological**, *a.* pertaining or relating to psychology; relating to or affecting the mind; existing only in the mind. **psychological moment,** *n.* the critical moment, the exact time for action etc. **psychological warfare,** *n.* the use of propaganda to reduce enemy morale. **psychologically,** *adv.* **psychologist,** *n.* **psychologize, -ise,** *v.t., v.i.* [PSYCHO-, -LOGY]

psychomancy, *n.* divination by means of communication with spirits; †necromancy.

psychometer, *n.* an instrument for measuring times of reactions etc.; one who measures mental processes; one who has the power of psychometry. **psychometrics**, *n. sing.* the branch of psychology dealing with the measurement of mental capacities and attributes, esp. by the use of psychological tests and statistical methods. **psychometry,** *n.* psychometrics; the occult faculty of divining by touching a physical object, the character, surroundings, experiences etc. of persons who have touched it. **psychometric, -ical,** *a.* **psychometrically,** *adv.* **psychometrist,** *n.*

psychomotor, *a.* pertaining to muscular action proceeding from mental activity.

psychoneurosis, *n.* (*pl.* **-roses**), a neurosis, esp. one due to emotional conflict. **psychoneurotic**, *a.*

psychopath, *n.* one suffering from a severe personality disorder characterized by anti-social behaviour and a tendency to commit acts of violence. **psychopathic**, *a.* **psychopathological,** *a.* **psychopathologist,** *n.* **psychopathology**, *n.* (the branch of psychology dealing with) mental and behavioural aberrance.

psychophysics, *n.* the science of the relations between mind and body, esp. between physical stimuli and psychological sensation. **psychophysicist**, *n.*

psychophysiology, *n.* the branch of physiology treating of mental phenomena.

psychosexual, *a.* pertaining to the psychological aspects of sex.

psychosis, *n.* (*pl.* **-ses**), *n.* a mental derangement, not due to organic lesion, characterized by a severe distortion of the sufferer's concept of reality. **psychotic,** *a., n.*

psychosomatic, *a.* denoting a physical disorder caused by or influenced by the patient's emotional condition.

psychotherapeutic, *a.* treating disease by psychological methods **psychotherapeutics,** *n. sing.* **psychotherapy**, *n.* the treatment of disease by psychological or hypnotic means.

psychotic PSYCHOSIS.

psychrometer, *n.* the wet-and-dry bulb hygrometer for measuring the humidity of the atmosphere.

PT, (*abbr.*) Pacific time; physical training.

Pt, (*chem. symbol*) platinum. (*abbr.*) point; port.

pt, (*abbr.*) part; pint(s); (*Math.*) point.

PTA, (*abbr.*) Parent-Teacher Association; Public Transport Authority.

ptarmic, *a.* exciting sneezing *n.* a ptarmic medicine. [L *ptarmicûs,* Gr. *ptarmikos,* from *ptarmos,* sneeze]

ptarmigan, *n.* a bird, *Lagopus mutus,* allied to the grouse, having grey or brown plumage in the summer and white in the winter. [Gael. *tarmachan,* etym. doubtful]

Pte, (*abbr.*) (*Mil.*) Private.

pter-, pteri-, ptero-, *comb. form* winged; having processes resembling wings. **-ptera,** *comb. form.* organisms having a certain number or type of wings. **-pteran, -pterous,** *a. comb. form* [Gr. *pteron,* feather, a wing]

pteranodon, *n.* a toothless flying reptile of the Cretaceous period with a horn-like crest. [Gr. *pteron,* wing, *an;* without, *odous, odontos,* tooth]

ptere, *n.* a wing-like organ. [F *ptere,* as prec.]

pteridology, *n.* the science of ferns. **pteridological**, *a.* **pteridologist,** *n.* [Gr. *pteris -idos,* fern, from *pteron,* feather, -LOGY]

pterion, *n.* (*Anat.*) the H-shaped suture where the frontal, parietal and sphenoid bones of the skull meet. [dim., from Gr. *pteron,* wing]

pterodactyl, *n.* an extinct winged reptile from the Mesozoic strata. [Gr. *daktulos,* finger]

pterography, [-GRAPHY], *n.* the science of feathers or plumage. **pterographer,** *n.* **pterographic, -al,** *a.*

pterology, *n.* (*Ent.*) the branch of entomology treating of insects' wings. **pterological**, *a.*

Pteromys, *n.* a genus of rodents, comprising the flying squirrels. [Gr. *mus,* mouse]

pteropod, *n.* (*Zool.*) any individual of the Pteropoda.

Pteropoda, *n.pl.* a sub-class of Mollusca in which the foot is expanded into wing-like lobes or paddles. [Gr. *pous podos,* foot]

pteropus, *n.* (*pl.* **-pi**) a genus of tropical and subtropical bats comprising the flying-foxes.

pterosaur, *n.* any individual of the Pterosauria. **Pterosauria**, *n.pl.* an order of flying reptiles of the Mesozoic age. [Gr. *sauros,* lizard]

pterygium, *n.* a varicose excrescence of the conjunctiva of the eye. **pterygial,** *a.* [Gr. *pterugion,* dim. as foll.]

pterygoid, *a.* (*Anat.*) wing-shaped; of or connected with the pterygoid processes *n.* a pterygoid bone or process. **pterygoid process,** *n.* either of the wing-like processes descending from the great wings of the sphenoid bone of the skull. **pterygo-,** *comb. form* [Gr. *pterugoeides* (*pteruxugos,* wing, -OID)]

pteryla, *n.* (*pl.* **-lae**) one of the tracts or patches of feathers on the skin of a bird. **pterylography**, *n.* the science of or a treatise on pterylosis. **pterylographic, -al**, *a.* **pterylographically,** *adv.* **pterylosis**, *n.* the arrangement of the feather tracts on the skin of birds. [mod. L, from Gr. *pteron,* feather]

PTFE, (*abbr.*) polytetrafluorethylene.

ptisan, *n.* barley-water or other mucilaginous decoction used as a nourishing beverage. [F *tisane,* L *ptisana,* Gr. *ptisanē,* peeled barley, from *ptissein,* to peel]

PTO, (*abbr.*) please turn over.

ptochocracy, *n.* government by paupers, opposed to plutocracy. **ptochogony**, *n.* the production of beggars. [Gr. *ptōchos,* poor,]

Ptolemaic, *a.* pertaining to the astronomer Ptolemy; pertaining to the Ptolemies, kings of Egypt. **Ptolemaic system,** *n.* Ptolemy's conception of the universe.

Ptolemy¹, *n.* (Claudius Ptolemaeus) (*c.* 100–170 AD), Egyptian astronomer and geographer, who worked in Alexandria. The *Almagest* developed the theory that earth is the centre of the universe, with the sun, moon, and stars revolving around it. In 1543 Copernicus disproved the Ptolemaic system. Ptolemy's *Geography* was also a standard source of information until the 16th cent.

Ptolemy², *n.* dynasty of kings of Macedonian origin who ruled Egypt over a period of 300 years; they included:

Ptolemy I, *n.* (*c.* 367–283 BC), ruler of Egypt from 323 BC, king from 304. He was one of Alexander the Great's generals, and possibly his half-brother (see also THAÏS). He established the library at Alexandria.

Ptolemy XIII, *n.* (63–47 BC), joint ruler of Egypt with his sister-wife Cleopatra; she put him to death.

ptomaine, *n.* one of a class of sometimes poisonous amines derived from decaying animal and vegetable matter. **ptomaine poisoning,** *n.* food poisoning – formerly, and erroneously, thought to be due to ptomaines. **ptomaic,** *a.* [It. *ptomaina,* from Gr. *ptōma,* corpse, cogn. with *piptein,* to fall]

ptosis, *n.* a drooping of the upper eyelid from paralysis of the muscle raising it. [Gr., falling, as prec.]

ptyalin, *n.* (*Physiol.*) an enzyme or ferment contained in saliva, which converts starch into dextrin. **ptyalize, -ise,** *v.t.* to salivate. **ptyalism,** *n.* salivation. **ptyalose**, *n.* (*Chem.*) sugar formed by the action of ptyalin or starch. [Gr. *ptūalon,* spittle, from *ptūein,* to spit]

Pu, (*chem. symbol*) plutonium.

pub, *n.* a public house *v.i.* to visit public houses (esp. in **go pubbing**). **pub-crawl,** *n.* (*coll.*) a drinking tour of a number of pubs.

pub., (*abbr.*) public; published; publisher; publishing.

puberty, *n.* the period of life at which persons become capable of begetting or bearing children; the age at which a plant begins to flower. **age of puberty,** (*Law*) in boys 14, in girls 12. **pubertal,** *a.* **puberulent**, *a.* pubescent, downy. **pubes**, *n.* the hypogastric region which in the adult becomes covered with hair; the hair of the pubic region; the pubis. **pubescence**, *n.* the state or age of puberty; †soft, hairy down on plants or parts of animals, esp. insects, downiness, hairiness. **pubescent,** *a.* arrived at the age of puberty; covered with soft hairy down. **pubic,** *a.* of or pertaining to the pubes or pubis. **pubis**, *n.* a bone forming the anterior part of the pelvis. **pubo-,** *comb. form* [F *puberté,* L *pūbertātem,* nom. *-tas,* from *pūber,* youth, or *pūbes,* hair]

public, *a.* pertaining to or affecting the people as a whole, opp. to personal or private; open to the use or enjoyment of all, not restricted to any class; done, existing or such as may be observed by all, not concealed or clandestine; open, notorious; well-known, prominent; of or pertaining to the affairs or service of the people. *n.* the people in general; any particular section of the people; (*coll.*) a public house. **in public,** openly, publicly. **Public Against Violence,** (Slovak *Verejnosť Proti Násil'u*) the Slovak half of the Czechoslovak democratic movement, counterpart of the Czech organization Civic Forum. **to go public,** to become a public company; to make publicly known. **public-address system,** *n.* a system of microphones, amplifiers, loudspeakers etc. used for addressing a large audience. **public bar,** *n.* a bar in a public house, usu. less well appointed, and serving drinks at cheaper prices than a saloon bar. **public company,** *n.* one whose shares can be purchased on the stock exchange by members of the public. **public convenience,** *n.* a public lavatory. **public corporation,** *n.* an organization set up by government to run a nationalized service or industry. **public domain,** *n.* the status in law of a published work on which the copyright has expired. **public enemy,** *n.* somebody, esp. a notorious criminal, considered to be a menace to the community. **public health,** *n.* the field of responsibility for the general health of the community covering e.g,. sanitation, food-handling in shops and restaurants, hygiene in public places. **Public Health Acts,** 1848, 1872, 1875 in the UK, legislation enacted by parliament to deal with squalor and disease and to establish a code of sanitary law. The first act established a central board of health with three members who were responsible to parliament to impose local boards of health in districts where the death rate was above the national average and made provision for other local boards of health to be established by petition. The 1872 act made it obligatory for every local authority to appoint a medical officer of health. The 1875 act consolidated previous acts and provided a comprehensive code for public health. **public house,** *n.* a house licensed for the retail of intoxicating liquors, an inn, a tavern. **public law,** *n.* international law. **public lending right,** the right of authors to royalties when their books are borrowed from public libraries. **public nuisance,** *n.* (*Law*) an illegal act affecting the whole community rather than an individual; (*coll.*) a generally objectionable person. **public opinion,** *n.* the views of the general public or the electorate on political and social issues. **public opinion poll,** an assessment of public opinion on an issue based on the responses of a scientifically selected sample of the community to certain questions. **public orator,** *n.* the official spokesperson for a university. **public prosecutor,** *n.* an official who conducts criminal prosecutions on behalf of the state. **Public Record Office,** a government office containing the English national records since the Norman Conquest, brought together from courts of law and government departments, including the Domesday Book, the Gunpowder Plot papers, and the log of HMS *Victory* at Trafalgar. It was established 1838 in Chancery Lane, London; records from the 18th century onwards have been housed at Kew, London, since 1976. **public relations,** *n.* (*sing. or pl. in construction*) the relationship between an organization and the public; (a department entrusted with) the maintenance of goodwill towards, and a favourable image of, an organization in the mind of the public. **public school,** *n.* a school under the control of a publicly elected body; a school whose headmaster is a member of the Headmasters' Conference, usu. endowed school providing a liberal education for such as can afford it. **public sector,** *n.* the state-owned part of the economy. **public servant,** *n.* a government employee. **public spirit,** *n.* interest in or devotion to the community. **public-spirited,** *a.* **public-spiritedly,** *adv.* **public-spiritedness,** *n.* **public utility,** *n.* an enterprise concerned with the provision of an essential service, e.g. gas, water electricity, to the public. **public works,** *n.pl.* roads, buildings etc. constructed for public use by or on behalf of the government. **publicness,** *n.* **publicly,** *adv.* [F, from L *pūblicus,* contr. of *populicus,* from *populus,* people]

publican, *n.* (*Rom. Hist.*) a collector or farmer of the revenues, taxes etc.; a keeper of a public house.

publication, *n.* the act of making publicly known; the act of publishing a book, periodical, musical composition etc.; a work printed and published.

publicist, *n.* a writer or authority on international law; a writer on current social or political topics, esp. a journalist, one who publicizes, esp. a press or publicity agent. **publicism,** *n.* **publicistic,** *a.*

publicity, *n.* the quality of being public; public attention or interest; the process of attracting public attention to a product, person etc; anything calculated to arouse public interest, as a newsworthy event or information, advertising etc. **publicity agent,** *n.* a person employed to keep before the public the name of a product, film etc. **publicity stunt,** *n.* an unusual or attention-grabbing event engineered specifically for purposes of publicity.

publicize, -ise, *v.t.* to make known to the public; to advertise.

publish, *v.t.* to make public, to promulgate, to announce publicly; to ask (the banns of marriage); to issue or print and offer for sale to the public; to issue the works of (an author); to put into circulation (counterfeit money etc.) *v.i.* to print and offer for sale. **publishable,** *a.* **publisher,** *n.* one who publishes, esp. books and other literary productions. **publishing,** *n.* [ME *publischen,* F *publier,* L *publicāre,* as prec.]

pubo- PUBERTY.

Puccini, *n.* **Giacomo (Antonio Domenico Michele Secondo Maria)** (1858–1924), Italian opera composer whose music shows a strong gift for melody and dramatic effect. His realist works include *Manon Lescaut* (1893), *La Bohème* (1896), *Tosca* (1900), *Madame Butterfly* (1904), and the unfinished *Turandot* (1926).

puccoon, *n.* one of various N American plants yielding a red or yellow dye. [NAm. Ind.]

puce, *a.* brownish purple. [F, from L *pūlicem,* nom. *pūlex,* flea]

pucelage, *n.* a state of virginity. [F, from *pucelle,* a young girl]

Puck, *n.* a mischievous sprite, elf or fairy, esp. the fairy celebrated by Shakespeare in *Midsummer Night's Dream;* **puckish,** *a.* [OE *pūca,* cogn. with Icel. *pūki,* Ir. *púca,* POOKA]

puck, *n.* a vulcanized rubber disk used instead of a ball in ice hockey.

pucka, pukka, *a.* (*Ang.-Ind.*) of full weight; durable, substantial; genuine; superior. [Hind., cooked, ripe]

pucker, *v.t.* to gather into small folds or wrinkles. *v.i.* to become wrinkled or gathered into small folds etc. *n.* a fold, a wrinkle, a bulge. **puckery,** *a.* [prob. rel. to POKE¹]

pud¹, *n.* (*Childish*) a hand; the forepaw of some animals. [etym. doubtful, cp. Dut. *poot*]

pud², *n.* (*coll.*) short for PUDDING.

puddening, *n.* (*Naut.*) a pad of rope etc. used as a fender. [corr. of PUDDING]

pudding, *n.* a mixture of animal or vegetable ingredients, usu. with flour or other farinaceous basis, of a soft or moderately hard consistency, baked or boiled, and eaten either as a main dish or as a sweet; meat or fruit cooked in a flour-based casing; dessert; a skin or intestine stuffed with minced meat etc., a large sausage; food, victuals, material reward; (*sl.*) poisoned liver used by burglars to silence house-dogs; (*Naut.*) a puddening. **pudding-ball,** *n.* (*Austral.*) a fish resembling the mullet. **pudding-face,** *n.* a fat, round, smooth face. **pudding-faced,** *a.* **pudding-head,** *n.* (*coll.*) a stupid person. **pudding-heart,** *n.* (*coll.*) a spiritless person. **pudding-pie,** *n.* a pudding with meat baked in it; a tart made with pie-crust and custard. **pudding-sleeve,** *n.* a full sleeve as in a clerical gown. **pudding-stone,** *n.* a conglomerate of pebbles in a siliceous matrix. †**pudding-time,** *n.* the time for pudding; a lucky or favourable time. **puddingy,** *a.* [ME, etym. doubtful]

puddle, *n.* a small pool, esp. of rainwater; clay and sand worked together to form a watertight lining for a pond, canal etc.; a muddle; a bungler, an awkward person. *v.i.* to dabble (in mud, water etc.); to mess, to muddle (about). *v.t.* to make dirty or muddy; to work (clay etc.) into puddle; to line or render watertight with puddle; to stir up (molten iron) in a furnace so as to convert it into wrought-iron. **puddler,** *n.* one who puddles, esp. a workman employed in puddling iron. **puddling,** *n.* **puddly,** *a.* [ME *podel,* dim. from OE *pudd,* a ditch]

puddock, PADDOCK².

pudency, *n.* modesty, shamefacedness. **pudendum,** *n.* (*often pl.* **pudenda,** the privy parts, the genitals. **pudendal, pudic,** †**-al,** *a.* pertaining to the pudenda. †**pudicity,** *n.* modesty, chastity. [late L *pudentia,* from L *pudens -ntis,* pres.p. of *pudēre,* to make or be ashamed]

pudge, *n.* a short, thick or fat person or figure. **pudgy,** *a.* [cp. PODGE]

pudic PUDENCY.

Pudovkin, *n.* **Vsevolod Illationovich** (1893–1953), Russian film director, whose films include the silent *Mother* (1926), *The End of St Petersburg* (1927), and *Storm over Asia* (1928); and the sound films *Deserter* (1933) and *Suvorov* (1941).

pudsy, *a.* (*coll., dial.*) plump. [etym. doubtful, perh. rel. to PUDGY]

Pueblo, *n.* generic name for North American Indians of SW North America including the Hopi; (**pueblo**) a village, town or settlement, esp. of the Indians of New Mexico etc. **pueblan,** *a.* [Sp.]

puerile, *a.* childish, silly, inane. **puerilely,** *adv.* †**puerileness, puerility,** *n.* [L *puerīlis,* from *puer,* boy]

puerperal, *a.* pertaining to or resulting from childbirth. **puerperal fever,** *n.* a fever, caused by infection of the genital tract, attacking women after childbirth. **puerperalism,** *n.* (*Path.*) [L *puerperus* (*puer,* boy, *-parus,* bringing forth, from *parere,* to bring forth)]

Puerto Rico, *n.* an autonomous commonwealth. **area** 9000 sq km/3475 sq miles. **capital** San Juan. **towns** ports Mayagüez, Ponce. **exports** sugar, tobacco, rum, pineapples, textiles, plastics, chemicals, processed foods. **population** (1980) 3,197,000, 67% urban. **language** Spanish and English (official). **religion** Roman Catholic. It was visited in 1493 by Columbus; annexed by Spain 1509; ceded to the US after the Spanish-American War 1898; achieved commonwealth status with local self-government 1952.

Puerto Sandino, *n.* a major port on the Pacific W coast of Nicaragua, known as Puerto Somoza until 1979.

puff, *v.i.* to breathe, to blow, to emit or expel air, steam etc. in short, sudden blasts; to move or go while puffing; to breathe hard; to come (out) in a short, sudden blast; to become inflated or distended. *v.t.* to emit, to blow out, with a short sudden blast or blasts; to blow or drive (away) thus; to draw at (a cigarette, pipe); to utter pantingly; to inflate, to blow (up or out); to blow (away etc.); to bid at an auction in order to inflate the price; to cause to be out of breath; to praise or advertise in an exaggerated or misleading way. *n.* a short, sudden blast of breath, smoke, steam etc., a whiff, a gust; the sound made by this; a small amount of breath, smoke etc., emitted at one puff; a light, puffy thing or small mass of any material; a cake, tart etc. of light or spongy consistency; a light wad, pad or tuft for applying powder to the skin; an exaggerated or misleading advertisement, review etc. **puffed (out),** (*coll.*) out of breath. **puffed up,** inflated; swollen up with conceit or self-importance. **puff-adder,** *n.* a highly venomous African snake, *Clotho arietans,* which inflates part of its body when aroused. **puff-ball,** *n.* a fungus of the genus *Lycoperdon,* the roundish spore-case of which emits dry, dust-like spores. **puff-bird,** *n.* a bird of the family Bucconidae, so called from their habits of puffing out their plumage. **puff-box,** *n.* a toilet-box for holding powder and puff. **puff-paste, -pastry** *n.* (a rich dough used to make) a light, flaky pastry etc. **puffer,** *n.* a person or thing that puffs, esp. a steamboat, steam engine etc.; a globefish. **puffily,** *adv.* **puffing,** *a.* and *n.* **puffingly,** *adv.* **puffy,** *a.* puffing, blowing or breathing in puffs; short-winded; swollen, distended; tumid, turgid, bombastic. **puffiness,** *n.* [ME *puffen,* imit.]

puffin, *n.* a sea-bird of the genus *Fratercula,* esp. the N Atlantic *F. arctica.* [etym. doubtful]

puffing, puffy, etc. PUFF.

pufftaloonies, *n.pl.* (*Austral.*) fried cakes eaten hot with jam, honey, syrup etc.

pug[1], *n.* a pug-dog; a proper name for a fox; a pug-engine; (among servants) an upper servant; †an imp, an elf; †a monkey. **pug-dog,** *n.* a small, short-haired dog with wrinkled face, up-turned nose and tightly curled tail. **pug-engine,** *n.* a small locomotive for shunting etc. **pug-faced,** *a.* **pug-nose,** *n.* a short squat nose. **pug-nosed,** *a.* [etym. unknown]

pug[2], *n.* clay and other material mixed and prepared for making into bricks. *v.t.* (*past, p.p.* **pugged**) to grind (clay etc.) and render plastic for brick-making; to puddle with clay; to pack (a wall, floor etc.) with sawdust etc. to deaden sound. **pug-mill,** *n.* a mill in which clay is made into pug. **pugging,** *n.* [etym. doubtful]

pug[3], *n.* (*Ang.-Ind.*) the footprint or trail of an animal. *v.i.* to track game etc. [Hindi *pag*]

pugaree, puggree, *n.* an Indian light turban; a long piece of muslin wound round a hat or helmet in hot climates to protect from the sun. **pugareed,** *a.* [Hind. *pagrī*]

Puget, *n.* **Pierre** (1620–94), French baroque sculptor who developed a powerful and expressive style. He created a muscular statue of the tyrant *Milo of Croton* (1672–82; Louvre, Paris) for the garden of the palace of Versailles.

Puget Sound, *n.* an inlet of the Pacific Ocean on the W coast of Washington state, US.

pugging PUG[2].

†pugh, POOH.

pugil, *n.* a pinch, as much as can be taken up between the thumb and first two fingers. [L *pugillus,* a handful, from *pug-,* root of *pugnus,* fist (cp. Gr. *pugmē*)]

pugilist, *n.* a boxer, a prize-fighter; (*fig.*) a fighter, a pugnacious controversialist etc. **pugilism,** *n.* **pugilistic,** *a.* [L *pugil,* boxer, as prec.]

Pugin, *n.* **Augustus Welby Northmore** (1812–52), English architect, collaborator with Barry in the detailed design of the Houses of Parliament. He did much to revive Gothic architecture in England.

Puglia, *n.* (English **Apulia**) region of Italy, the south-eastern 'heel'; area 19,300 sq km/7450 sq miles; capital Bari, population (1988) 4,043,000. Products include wheat, grapes, almonds, olives, and vegetables. The main industrial centre is Taranto.

pugnacious, *a.* inclined to fight; quarrelsome. **pugnaciously,** *adv.* **pugnacity**, **pugnaciousness,** *n.* [L *pugnax -ācis,* from *pugnāre,* to fight, as prec.]

puisne, *a.* junior or inferior in rank (applied to judges); (*Law*) later, more recent. *n.* a puisne judge. [OF *puis,* L *postea,* from *post,* after, *né,* L *nātus,* born]

puissant, *a.* powerful, strong, mighty. **puissance,** *n.* power, strength;, a showjumping event that tests a horse's power to jump high obstacles. **puissantly,** *adv.* [F, cp. It. *possente;* both prob. from a low L *possens -ntem,* pres.p. of L *posse,* to be able]

puke[1], *v.t., v.i.* (*sl.*) to vomit. *n.* vomit; the act of vomiting. **†puker,** *n.* [etym. doubtful]

puke[2], *n.* a kind of woollen cloth; a dark colour formerly used for woollens. [prob. from M Dut. *puyck*]

pukka PUCKA.

puku, *n.* a red African antelope, *Cobuis vardoni.* [Zulu *mpuku*]

pulchritude, *n.* beauty. **pulchritudinous,**, *a.* [L *pulchritūdo,* from *pulcher,* beautiful]

pule, *v.i.* to cry plaintively or querulously, to whine, to whimper; to pipe, to chirp. *v.t.* to utter in a querulous, whining tone. **puling,** *a.* and *n.* **pulingly,** *adv.* [perh. from *F piaulir* or imit.]

Pulex, *n.* a genus of fleas; the flea. [L, flea]

Pulitzer, *n.* **Joseph** (1847–1911), US newspaper proprietor, born in Hungary. He acquired the *New York World* in 1883 and in 1903 founded the school of journalism at Columbia University, which awards the annual Pulitzer prizes in journalism and letters.

pulka, *n.* a travelling sleigh with a prow like a canoe, used by Laplanders. [Finnish *pulkka*]

pull, *v.t.* to draw towards one by force; to drag, to haul, to tug; to draw (up, along, nearer etc.); to move (a vehicle) in a particular direction; to pluck; to remove by plucking, to pick; to strip of feathers; to draw the entrails from (a fowl); to bring out (a weapon); to strain (a muscle or tendon); to row (a boat); to take (a person in a boat) by rowing; (*coll.*) to attract (a crowd); (*sl.*) to carry out esp. with daring and imagination or with deceptive intent; (*sl.*) to seduce; (*sl.*) to make a raid upon (a gambling-house), to arrest, (*Print.*) to take (an impression) by a hand-press, to take (a proof); (*Cricket*) to strike (a ball) from the off to the on side; (*Golf*) to strike a ball to the left; (*Racing*) to rein in a horse, esp. so as to lose a race. *v.i.* to give a pull; to tug, to haul; to move in a motor vehicle in a particular direction; to strain against the bit (of a horse); to draw, to suck (at a pipe); to pluck, to tear (at). *n.* the act of pulling, a tug; that which is pulled; a handle by which beer is drawn, a door opened, a bell rung etc.; a quantity of beer etc. drawn; a draught, a swig; an impression from a hand-press, a proof; (*Cricket*) a stroke by which a ball is sent from the off to the on side; (*Golf*) a stroke sending a ball to the left; the checking of a horse by its rider, esp. to secure defeat; a spell of rowing; (*coll.*) a hold, unfair or illegitimate influence; (*coll.*) a spell of hard exertion. **to pull about,** to pull to and fro, to handle roughly. **to pull a fast one,** FAST. **to pull apart,** to pull asunder or into pieces; to become separated or severed; to pull to pieces. **to pull back,** to retreat; to withdraw. **to pull down,** to demolish; to degrade, to humble; to weaken, to cause (prices etc.) to be reduced. **to pull faces,** FACE; **to pull in,** to retract, to make tighter; (of train) to enter a station; (of vehicle, driver) to stop (at), to pull over; (*coll.*) to attract (audiences etc.); (*sl.*) to arrest; to earn. **to pull off,** to accomplish (something difficult or risky). **to pull oneself together,** to regain one's composure or self-control. **to pull one's, somebody's leg,** LEG. **to pull one's weight,** WEIGHT. **to pull out,** to leave, to depart; to withdraw; to cease to participate in; to move out from the side of the road or from behind another vehicle; (of aircraft) to level off after a dive. **to pull over,** to draw in to the side of the road (and stop). **to pull round,** to (cause to) recover. **to pull through,** to (cause to) survive, recover or not fail against the odds. **to pull together,** to cooperate. **to pull to pieces,** to tear (a thing) up; to criticize, to abuse. **to pull up,** to drag up forcibly; to pluck up; to cause to stop; to come to a stop; to rebuke; to gain on, to draw level with, **pull-back,** *n.* a drawback, a restraint, hindrance; a device for holding back and keeping in parts of a woman's skirt; a retreat, a withdrawal. **pull-down,** *a.* (*Comput.*) of or being a menu which can be accessed during the running of the program and which brings a list of options down over the screen. **pull-in,** *n.* a stopping place; a transport café. **pull-on,** *n., a.* (a garment) without fastenings, requiring simply to be pulled on. **pull-out,** *n.* a removable section of a magazine; a large fold-out leaf in a book. **pullover,** *n.* a jersey which is pulled over the head. **pull-through,** *n.* a cord with a rag attached, used for cleaning the barrel of a firearm. **pulled,** *a.* plucked, stripped (as fowls, skins etc.); depressed in health, spirits etc., dragged (down). **puller,** *n.* one who or that which pulls; an implement, machine etc. for pulling; a horse that pulls against the bit, a hard-mouthed or high-spirited horse. †**puller-down,** *n.* [OE *pullian,* etym. doubtful]

pullet, *n.* a young fowl, esp. a hen before the first moult. †**pullet-sperm,** *n.* the sperm of an egg. [ME and OF *polete* (F *poulet*), dim. of *poule,* late L *pulla,* hen, fem. of L *pullus,* a young animal, cogn. with FOAL]

pulley, *n.* a wheel with a grooved rim, or a combination of such wheels, mounted in a block for changing the direction or for increasing the effect of a force; a wheel used to transmit power or motion by means of a belt, chain etc. passing over its rim. *v.t.* to lift or hoist with a pulley; to furnish or fit with pulleys. **fast and loose pulley,** a pair of pulleys on a shaft, one fixed and revolving with the shaft, the other loose, for throwing the shaft into or out of gear by means of a belt running round the one or the other. [OF *polie* (F. *poulie*), prob. ult. from a late Gr. *polidion,* dim. of *polos,* POLE[2]]

pullicat, *n.* a kind of coloured checked handkerchief, orig. made at Pulicat; the material of which this is made. [*Pulicat,* on the coast of Madras]

Pullman[1], *n.* a Pullman car; a train made up of these. **Pullman car,** *n.* a luxurious railway saloon or sleeping-car originally built at the Pullman works. Illinois. [see foll.]

Pullman[2], *n.* **George** (1831–1901), US engineer who developed the Pullman railway car. In an attempt to improve the standard of comfort of rail travel, he built his first Pioneer Sleeping Car in 1863. He formed the Pullman Palace Car Company in 1867 and in 1881 the town of Pullman, Illinois, was built for his workers.

pullulate, *v.i.* to shoot, to bud; to germinate, to breed; to swarm; to develop, to string up. **pullulant,** *a.* **pullulation,** *n.* [L *pullulātus,* p.p. of *pullulāre,* to sprout, from *pullulus,* dim. of *pullus,* see PULLET]

pulmo-, *comb. form* pertaining to the lungs. [Latin *pulmo -mōnis,* lung]

pulmobranchiate, *a.* having the branchiae adapted to breathe air, as in some molluscs etc.

pulmometer, *n.* an instrument for measuring the capacity of the lungs. **pulmometry,** *n.*

pulmonary, *a.* pertaining to the lungs. **pulmonary artery,** *n.* the artery carrying blood from the heart to the lungs. **pulmonary disease,** *n.* lung disease, esp. consumption. **pulmonic,** *a.* pulmonary; affected with or subject to disease of the lungs. *n.* one having diseased lungs; a medicine for lung-diseases.

pulmonate, *a.* (*Zool.*) furnished with lungs. *n.* a pulmonate mollusc.

pulp, *n.* any soft, moist, coherent mass; the fleshy or succulent portion of a fruit; the soft tissue of an animal body or in an organ or part, as in the internal cavity of a tooth; the soft mixture of rags, wood etc. from which paper is made; a magazine or book printed on cheap paper and sentimental or sensational in content; (*Mining*) pulverized ore mixed with water. *v.t.* to convert into pulp; to extract the pulp from. *v.i.* to become pulpy. **pulper,** *n.* **pulpify,** *v.t.* **pulpless,** *a.* **pulplike,** *a.* **pulpous, pulpy,** *a.* **pulpiness,** *n.* [L *pulpa*]

pulpit, *n.* an elevated enclosed stand from which a preacher delivers his sermon. *a.* pertaining to the pulpit or to preaching. *v.t.* to provide with a pulpit or pulpits. *v.i.* to preach. **the pulpit,** preachers generally; preaching. **pulpitarian,** *a.* and *n.* **pulpiteer,** *n.* (*contempt.*) a preacher. **pulpiteering,** *n.* **pulpiter,** *n.* [L *pulpitum*]

pulplike, pulpous, pulpy etc. PULP.

pulque, *n.* a Mexican vinous beverage made by fermenting the sap of species of agave. **pulque brandy,** a liquor distilled from this. [Mex. Sp.]

pulsar, *n.* an interstellar source of regularly pulsating radio waves, prob. a swiftly rotating neutron star. [*puls*ating st*ar*]

pulsate, *v.i.* to move, esp. to expand and contract, with rhythmical alternation, to beat, to throb; to vibrate, to thrill. *v.t.* to agitate with a pulsator. **pulsatile,** *a.* pulsatory; (*Mus.*) played by beating, percussive. **pulsation,** *n.* the action of pulsating; the movement of the pulse. **pulsatory,** †**pulsative,** *a.* of or pertaining to pulsation; actuated by or having the property of pulsation. **pulsator,** *n.* a machine for separating diamonds from earth, a jigging-machine; part of a milking-machine; a pulsometer. [L *pulsātus,* p.p. of *pulsāre,* freq. of *pellere,* to drive, p.p. *pulsus*]

pulsatilla, *n.* the pasque-flower, *Anemone pulsatilla.* [med. L, dim. of *pulsāta,* beaten, as prec.]

pulse[1], *n.* the rhythmic beating of the arteries caused by the propulsion of blood along them from the heart; a beat of the arteries or the heart; a pulsation, a vibration; a short-lived variation in some normally constant value in a system, as in voltage etc.; an electromagnetic or sound wave of brief duration; a quick, regular stroke or recurrence of strokes (as of oars); a throb, a thrill. *v.i.* to pulsate. *v.t.* to send (forth, out etc.) by or as by rhythmic beats. **to feel one's pulse,** to gauge the rate or regularity of one's pulse as a sign of health etc.; to sound one's intentions, views etc. **to keep one's finger on the pulse of,** to keep up to date with developments in. **pulse-rate,** *n.* the number of pulse beats per minute. **pulseless,** *a.* **pulselessness,** *n.* †**pulsific,** *a.* causing pulsation; pulsatory. **pulsimeter,** *n.* an instrument for measuring the rate, force, regularity etc. of the pulse. **pulsometer,** *n.* a pumping device operated by the admission and condensation of steam in alternate chambers; a pulsimeter. [ME and OF *pous,* L *pulsum,* nom. *-sus,* as prec.]

pulse[2], *n.* the seeds of leguminous plants; a plant producing such seeds. [ME and OF *pols,* L *puls pultis,* pottage of meal etc.]

†**pultaceous,** *a.* pulplike, macerated, softened. [L *puls pultis,* PULSE[2], -ACEOUS]

pulu, *n.* a vegetable silk or wool obtained from certain Hawaiian tree-ferns, used for stuffing mattresses etc. [Hawaiian]

pulverize, -ise, *v.t.* to reduce to fine powder or dust; to demolish, to smash, to defeat utterly. *v.i.* to be reduced to powder. **pulverate,** *v.t.* **pulverable,** *a.* **pulverizable, -isable,** *a.* **pulverization, -isation,** *n.* **pulverizer, -iser,** *n.* one who or that which pulverizes; a machine for reducing a liquid to fine spray; a machine for pulverizing earth. **pulverous,** *a.* **pulverulent,** *a.* consisting of fine powder; covered with powder, powdery; liable to disintegrate into fine powder. **pulverulence,** *n.* [late L *pulverīzāre,* from L *pulvus, -veris,* dust]

†**pulvil,** *n.* a scented powder formerly used as a cosmetic. *v.t.* to sprinkle with pulvil. [It. *polviglio,* from *polve,* as prec.]

pulvillus, *n.* the pad or cushion of an insect's foot. **pulvillar, pulvilliform,** *a.* [L, contr. for *pulvīnulus,* dim. of *pulvīnus,* a pillow]

pulvinar, *n.* (*Anat.*) a cushion-like prominence at the end of the optic thalamus of the brain. **pulvinate,** *a.* (*Nat. Hist.*) cushion-shaped, pad-like. **pulvinated,** *a.* having a convex face (as a frieze). [L, a couch]

puma, *n.* the cougar, *Felis concolor,* a large feline carnivore of the Americas. [Peruv.]

pumice, *n.* a light, porous or cellular kind of lava, used as a cleansing and polishing material. *v.t.* to rub, polish or clean with this. **pumice-stone,** *n.* pumice. **pumicate,** *v.t.* **pumiceous,** *a.* †**pumiciform,** *a.* [OF *pomis,* late L *pumicem,* L *pūmicem,* nom. *-ex*]

pummace, POMACE.

pummel, *v.t.* (*past, p.p.* **pummelled**) to strike or pound repeatedly, esp. with the fists. *n.* POMMEL.

pump[1], *n.* a device or engine usu. in the form of a cylinder and piston, for raising water or other liquid; a machine for exhausting or compressing air, an air-pump; the act of pumping, a stroke of a pump; an attempt at extracting information from a person; one good at this. *v.t.* to raise or remove with a pump; to free from water or make dry with a pump; to propel, to pour, with or as with a pump; to move up and down as if working a pump-handle; to put out of breath (*usu. in p.p.*); to elicit information from by artful interrogations. *v.i.* to work a pump; to raise water etc., with a pump; to move up and down in the manner of a pump-handle. **to pump iron,** to do weight-lifting exercises. **to pump up,** to inflate (a pneumatic tyre); to inflate the tyres of (a cycle etc.). **pump-action,** *a.* (of a shotgun) requiring a pump-like movement to bring a shell into the chamber. **pump-brake,** *n.* the handle of a ship's pump. **pump-handle,** *n.* the handle by which a pump is worked; (*coll.*) the hand or arm. **pump-head,** *n.* the casing at the head of a chain pump for directing the water into the discharge-spout. **pump-priming,** *n.* introducing fluid into a pump to expel the air before operation; investing money to stimulate commercial activity esp. in stagnant or depressed areas. **pump-room,** *n.* a room where a pump is worked; a room at a spa where the waters from the medicinal spring are dispensed. **pumpage**, *n.* **pumper,** *n.* [ME *pumpe,* Dut. *pomp,* G *pumpe,* F *pompe*]

pump[2], *n.* a light low-heeled, slipper-like shoe, usu. of patent leather, worn with evening dress and for dancing; a plimsoll. [etym. doubtful]

pumpernickel, *n.* German whole-meal rye bread. [G, etym. doubtful]

pumpkin, *n.* the large globular fruit of *Cucurbita pepo;* the trailing, annual plant bearing this fruit. [earlier *pumpion,* POMPION]

pun[1], *n.* the playful use of a word in two different senses or of words similar in sound but different in meaning. *v.i.* (*past, p.p.* **punned**) to make a pun. **punnage**, punning, *n.* **punningly,** *adv.* **punster,** *n.* one who makes puns; one addicted to pun-making. [etym. doubtful]

pun[2], *v.t.* to pound, to crush, to consolidate by ramming; to work (up clay etc.) with a punner. [dial. form of POUND[3]]

puna, *n.* a cold high plateau between the two ranges of the Cordilleras; the cold wind prevalent there; mountain-sickness. [Peruv.]

Punch, *n.* the chief character in the popular puppet-show of Punch and Judy, represented as a grotesque humped-backed man. **as pleased as Punch,** highly delighted. [short for PUNCHINELLO]

punch[1], *n.* a tool, usu. consisting of a short cylindrical piece of steel tapering to a sharp or blunt end, for making holes, indenting, forcing bolts out of holes etc.; a machine in which a similar tool is used, esp. one for making holes in paper or cardboard; a tool or machine for stamping a die or impressing a design; a blow with the fist; vigour, forcefulness; striking power. *v.t.* to stamp or perforate with a punch; to make (a hole or indentation) thus; to drive (out etc.) with a punch; to strike, esp. with the fist; to press in vigorously, as a key or button; to record by pressing a key. **to pull one's punches** (*usu. in neg.*) to strike or criticize with less than full force. **punchbag,** *n.* a heavy, stuffed bag struck with the fists as exercise or by boxers in training; an unresisting victim. **punchball,** *n.* a ball usu. suspended or on an elastic stand used for punching practice. **punch-card, punched card,** *n.* a card in which data are represented by perforations, used in computers. **punch-drunk,** *a.* suffering a form of cerebral concussion from having taken repeated blows to the head; dazed. **punchline,** *n.* the conclusion of a joke, story that shows the point of it, produces the laugh or reveals an unexpected twist. **punch-up,** *n.* (*coll.*) a brawl, a fist-fight. **puncher,** *n.* **punchy,** *a.* (*coll.*) forceful, incisive; punch-drunk. [prob. from PUNCHEON[1]]

punch[2], *n.* a beverage compounded of wine or spirit, water or milk, lemons, sugar, spice etc. **punch-bowl,** *n.* [perh. from Hind. *panch,* five, from its consisting originally of five ingredients, or from PUNCHEON[2]]

punch[3], *n.* a short, fat fellow; a stout-built cart-horse. **punchy,** *a.* [etym. doubtful]

puncheon[1], *n.* a short upright timber, used for supporting the roof in a mine or as an upright in the framework of a roof; †a perforating or stamping tool, a punch. [ONorth. F *punchon,* OF *poinçon,* L *punctiōnem,* nom. *-tio,* a pricking, from *pungere,* to prick, p.p. *punctus*]

puncheon[2], *n.* a large cask holding from 72 to 120 gallons (324–540 l). [perh. ident. with prec.]

punchinello, *n.* a buffoon, a Punch, a grotesque person. [It. *polichinello, Pulcinello,* a character in Neapolitan low comedy]

punchline, punch-up, punchy PUNCH[1].

punctate, *a.* covered with points, dots, spots etc. **punctation,** *n.* **punctiform,** *a.* like a point or dot; punctate. [L PUNCTUM, -ATE]

punctilio, *n.* (*pl.* **-tilios**) a nice point in conduct, ceremony or honour; precision in form or etiquette. **punctilious,** *a.* precise or exacting in punctilio; strictly observant of ceremony or etiquette. **punctiliously,** *adv.* **punctiliousness,** *n.* [Sp. *puntillo,* or It. *puntiglio,* dim. of *punto,* POINT, as prec.]

punctual, *a.* observant and exact in matters of time; done, made, or occurring exactly at the proper time; (*Geom.*) of or pertaining to a point; †exact, punctilious. **punctualist,** *n.* One who is very exact in observing forms and ceremonies. **punctuality**, *n.* **punctually,** *adv.* [med. L *punctuālis,* from *punctus,* a POINT]

punctuate, *v.t.* to mark with stops, to divide into sentences, clauses etc. with stops; to interrupt or intersperse; (*coll.*) to emphasize, to accentuate; to enforce (with). **punctuation** *n.* **punctuation mark,** *n.* **punctuative,** *a.* [med. L *punctuātus,* p.p. of *punctuāre,* as prec.]

punctum, *n.* (*pl.* **-ta**) a point, a speck, a dot, a minute spot of colour etc. **punctule**, *n.* a minute point, speck or pit. **punctulate**, *a.* **punctulation,** *n.* a point. [L, orig. neut. of *punctus,* POINT]

puncture, *n.* a small hole made with something pointed, a prick; the act of pricking or perforating. *v.t.* to make a puncture in; to pierce or prick with something pointed. *v.t.* to sustain a puncture (of a tyre, balloon etc.). [L *punctūra,* as prec.]

pundit, *n.* a Hindu learned in the Sanskrit language and the science, laws and religion of India; a learned person; a pretender to learning. [Hind. *pandit,* from Sansk. *pandita,* learned]

Pune, *n.* (formerly **Poona**), a city in Maharashtra, India; population (1985) 1,685,000. Products include chemicals, rice, sugar, cotton, paper, and jewellery.

pung, *n.* a low sled for one horse; a toboggan. [N Am. Ind. *tom-pung*]

punga, *n.* a New Zealand tree-fern, the pith of which is edible. [Maori]

pungent, *a.* sharply affecting the senses, esp. those of small or taste; pricking or stinging to the sense of touch; acrid, keen, caustic, biting; piquant, stimulating; (*Nat. Hist.*) sharp-pointed, adapted for pricking or piercing. **pungency,** †**-gence,** *n.* **pungently,** *adv.* [L *pungens -ntem,* pres.p. of *pungere,* to prick]

Punic, *a.* pertaining to Carthage, ancient city in N Africa founded by the Phoenicians, or to the Carthaginians, Carthaginian; (*fig.*) treacherous, faithless. *n.* the language of the Carthaginians. **Punic Wars,** *n.* three wars between Rome and Carthage: **First** (264–241 BC), resulted in the defeat of the Carthaginians under Hamilcar Barca and the cession of Sicily to Rome. **Second** (218–201 BC), Hannibal invaded Italy, defeated the Romans under Fabius Maximus at Cannae, but was finally defeated by Scipio at Zama (now in Algeria). **Third** (149–146 BC), ended in the destruction of Carthage, and her possessions becoming the Roman province of Africa. [L *Pūnicus, Poenicus,* from *Poenus,* Gr. *Phoinix,* Phoenician]

puniceous, *a.* bright-red, purple. [L *pūniceus,* as prec.]

punier, puniness etc. PUNY.

punish, *v.t.* to inflict a penalty on for an offence; to visit judicially with pain, loss, confinement or other penalty, to chastise; to inflict a penalty for (an offence); to inflict pain or injury on, to handle severely, to maul; to give great trouble to (opponents in a game, race etc.); (*coll.*) to consume large quantities of (food etc.). **punishable,** *a.* **punishability**, **punishableness,** *n.* **punishably,** *adv.* **punisher,** *n.* **punishing,** *a.* severe, wearing. **punishment,** *n.* **punitive**, **punitory**, *a.* awarding or inflicting punishment; retributive. [F *puniss-*, pres. part. stem of *punir,* L *pūnire,* from *poena*. Gr. *poinē,* fine, PENALTY]

Punjab[1], *n.* Sanskrit name meaning 'five rivers' (the Indus tributaries Jhelum, Chnab, Ravi, Beas, and Sutlej). It was a former state of British India, now divided between India and Pakistan. Punjab was annexed by Britain in 1849, after the Sikh Wars (1845–46 and 1848–49), and formed into a province with its capital at Lahore. Under the British, W Punjab was extensively irrigated, and land was granted to Indians who had served in the British army.

Punjab[2], *n.* state of NW India. **area** 50,400 sq km/ 19,454 sq miles. **capital** Chandigarh. **towns** Amritsar. **population** (1981) 16,670,000. **language** Punjabi. **religion** Sikhism 60%, Hinduism 30%; there is friction between the two groups.

Punjab[3], *n.* state of NE Pakistan. **area** 205,344 sq km/ 79,263 sq miles. **capital** Lahore. **population** (1981) 47,292,000. **language** Punjabi, Urdu. **religion** Muslim.

Punjabi, *n.* a member of the people of the Punjab; the language spoken in the Punjab provinces of India and Pakistan, a member of the Indo-Iranian branch of the Indo-European language family, considered by some to be a variety of Hindi, by others to be a distinct language.

punk[1], *n.* (*Am.*) wood decayed through the growth of a fungus, touch-wood; amadou, a composition for igniting fireworks. [etym. doubtful]

punk[2], *n.* worthless articles; (a follower of) a youth movement of the late 1970s and 1980s, characterized by a violent rejection of established society, outlandish (often multi-coloured) hairstyles, and the use of worthless articles such as safety pins, razor blades, as decoration; punk rock; (*esp. N Am.*) a novice; (*esp N Am.*) a petty criminal; †a prostitute; †a catamite. *a.* associated with the punk movement or punk rock; (*N Am.*) inferior. **punk rock,** *n.* a style of popular music associated with the punk movement and characterized by a driving beat, crude or obscene lyrics and an aggressive performing style. **punk rocker,** *n.* [etym. unknown]

punkah, *n.* a large portable fan; a large screen-like fan suspended from the ceiling and worked by a cord. [Hind. *pankhā*]

punner, *n.* a tool used for ramming earth, in a hole etc. [PUN[2], -ER]

punnet, *n.* a small, shallow basket for fruit, flowers etc. [etym. doubtful]

punster PUN[1].

punt[1], *n.* a shallow, flat-bottomed, square-ended boat, usu. propelled by pushing against the bottom of the stream with a pole. *v.t.* to propel (a punt etc.) thus; to convey in a punt. *v.i.* to propel about thus; to go (about) in a punt. **punter, puntist, puntsman,** *n.* [OE, *from L ponto,* prob. from Gallic]

punt[2], *v.i.* (*Basset, Faro, Ombre etc.*) to stake against the bank; (*sl.*) to bet on a horse etc. *n.* (*Faro*) a point in the game; the act of playing basset, faro etc.; †a punter. **punter,** *n.* a petty backer of horses; a small gambler to the Stock Exchange; a prostitute's client; (*coll.*) any customer or client. [F *ponter,* etym. unknown]

punt[3], *v.t.* (*Football*) to kick the ball after dropping it from the hand and before it touches the ground. *n.* such a kick. [etym. doubtful]

punt[4], *n.* the Irish pound.

punter, etc. PUNT[1, 2].

punto, *n.* a thrust or pass in fencing. †**punto dritto,** a direct thrust. **punto riverso,** a backhanded thrust. [It. or Sp., as POINT]

punty, *n.* a pontil; a round ornamental mark on a glass article, like the hollow left by the end of a pontil. [PONTIL]

puny, *a.* (*comp.* **punier,** *superl.* **puniest**) small and feeble, tiny, undersized, weak, poorly developed; petty, trivial; †puisne. *n.* a junior, a freshman. **puniness,** *n.* [PUISNE]

pup, *n.* a puppy. *v.t.* to bring forth (pups). *v.i.* to bring forth pups, to whelp, to litter. **in pup,** pregnant. **to sell a pup to,** (*sl.*) to trick into buying something worthless; to swindle. **pup tent,** *n.* a very small and basic shelter tent. [PUPPY]

pupa, *n.* (*pl.* **-pae**, **-pas**) an insect at the immobile, metamorphic stage between larva and imago. **pupal,** *a.* **puparium**, *n.* a coarctate pupa. **puparial,** *a.* **pupate**, *v.i.* to become a pupa. **pupation,** *n.* **pupigerous**, *a.* forming a puparium. **Pupipara**, *n.pl.* a division of Diptera in which the young are developed as pupae within the body of the mother. **pupiparous,** *a.* **pupivorous**, *a.* feeding on the pupae of other insects. **pupoid**, *a.* [L, a girl, a puppet]

pupil[1], *n.* a young person of either sex under the care of a teacher; one who is being, or has been, taught by a particular person; (*Law*) a boy or girl under the age of puberty and under the care of a guardian, a ward. **pupil-teacher,** *n.* formerly one in apprenticeship as a teacher and receiving general education at the same time. †**pupillage**, pupilship. *n.* the state or period of being a pupil. **pupillarity**, *n.* (*Sc. Law*) the period before puberty. **pupillary,** *a.* **pupilize, -ise,** *v.t.* to take charge of or teach (pupils). *v.i.* to take pupils. [F *pupille,* L *pūpillum,* nom. *-lus,* dim. of *pūpus,* boy]

pupil[2], *n.* the circular opening of the iris through which rays of light pass to the retina. **pupillary**, *a.* **pupillate**, **pupilled,** *a.* having a central spot like a pupil (of ocelli). **pupillometer**, *n.* an instrument for measuring the pupil of the eye or the distance between the eyes. **pupillometry,** *n.* [F *pupille,* L *pūpilla,* fem. of *pūpillus,* see prec.]

Pupipara, etc. PUPA.

puppet, *n.* an articulated toy figure moved by strings, wires or rods, a marionette; a small figure with a hollow head and cloth body into which the operator's hand is inserted; one whose actions are under another's control; a mere tool. **puppet-clack** PUPPET-VALVE. **puppet-play, -show,** *n.* a play with puppets as dramatis personae. **puppet-theatre,** *n.* **puppet-valve,** *n.* a disk on a stem with vertical motion to and from its seat. **puppeteer**, *n.* one who manipulates puppets. **puppetry,** *n.* the art of making and manipulating puppets and presenting puppet shows. [OF *poupette,* dim. from L *puppa, pūpa,* see PUPA]

puppy, *n.* a young dog; (*fig.*) a silly young fellow, a coxcomb, a fop. **puppy-dog,** *n.* a puppy. **puppy fat,** *n.* temporary plumpness in children or adolescents. **puppy-headed,** *a.* **puppy love,** *n.* temporary infatuation in adolescence. **puppydom**, **puppyhood**, *n.* the state of being a puppy. **puppyish,** *a.* **puppyism,** *n.* [prob. from F *poupée,* doll, irreg. as prec.]

purana, *n.* any of a great division of Sanskrit poems comprising the whole body of Hindu mythology and dating from the 4th cent. AD onwards. The 18 main texts include the *Vishnu Purāna* and *Bhāgavata*, which encourage devotion to Vishnu, especially in his incarnation as Krishna. **puranic,** *a.* [Sansk., from *para,* formerly]

Purbeck, *n.* Purbeck stone. **Purbeck marble,** *n.* one of the finer varieties of Purbeck stone, used for shafts etc. in architecture. **Purbeck limestone,** *n.* a hard limestone from Purbeck. [Isle of *Purbeck,* a peninsula in Dorset]

purblind, *a.* partially blind, near-sighted; dim-sighted. **purblindly,** *adv.* **purblindness,** *n.* [orig. totally blind (perh. PURE or PUR-, BLIND)]

Purcell, *n.* **Henry** (1659–95), English baroque composer. His work can be highly expressive, for example, the opera *Dido and Aeneas* (1689) and music for Dryden's *King Arthur* (1691) and for *The Fairy Queen* (1692). He wrote more than 500 works, ranging from secular operas and incidental music for plays to cantatas and church music.

purchase, *v.t.* to obtain by payment of an equivalent; to buy; to acquire at the expense of some sacrifice, exertion, danger etc.; to haul up, hoist, or draw in by means of a pulley, lever, capstan etc. *n.* the act of purchasing or buying; that which is purchased; annual value, annual return, esp. from land; the acquisition of property by payment of a price or value, any mode of acquiring property other than by inheritance; advantage gained by the application of any mechanical power, leverage; an appliance furnishing this, as a rope, pulley etc.; an effective hold or position for leverage, a grasp, a foothold; the system of buying commissions in the army, abolished in 1871. **purchase-money,** *n.* the price paid or contracted to be paid for anything purchased. **purchase tax,** *n.* formerly a differential tax on certain goods sold to the public. **purchasable,** *a.* **purchaser,** *n.* [ME *purchasen,* A-F *purchacer,* OF *pur-, pourchacier,* to procure (PURCHASE[1])]

purdah, *n.* a curtain or screen, esp. one keeping women from the view of strangers; the custom in India and elsewhere of secluding women; a cotton cloth for making curtains. [Hind. and Pers. **pardah**]

pure, *a.* unmixed, unadulterated; free from anything foul or polluting, clear, clean; of unmixed descent, free from admixture with any other breed; mere, sheer, absolute; free from moral defilement, innocent, guiltless; unsullied, chaste; free from discordance, harshness etc., perfectly correct in tone-intervals; having a single sound or tone, not combined with another; (of sciences) entirely theoretical, not applied. †*n.* purity. †*adv.* purely. †*v.t.* to purify, to cleanse. **purebred,** *a.* of a pure strain through many generations of controlled breeding. **pure science,** *n.* science based on self-evident truths, as logic, mathematics etc. **purely,** *adv.* **pureness,** *n.* [OF *pur,* fem. *pure,* L *pūrum,* nom. *-us*]

purée, *n.* a smooth thick pulp of fruit, vegetables etc. obtained by liquidizing, sieving etc; a thick soup made by boiling meat or vegetables to a pulp and straining it. *v.t.* to reduce to a purée. [F, etym. doubtful]

Pure Land Buddhism, the dominant form of Buddhism in China and Japan. It emphasizes faith in and love of Buddha, in particular Amitābha (Amida in Japan, Amituofo in China), the ideal 'Buddha of boundless light', who has vowed that all believers who call on his name will be reborn in his Pure Land, or Western Paradise. This also applies to women, who had been debarred from attaining salvation through monastic life. There are over 16 million Pure Land Buddhists in Japan.

purfle, *n.* †to decorate with a wrought or ornamental border, to border; to adorn, to beautify; to give a border of fur etc. to; to ornament the edge of a canopy etc. with knobs, crockets etc. *n.* a border or edging of embroidered work. **purfling,** *n.* ornamental bordering; the ornamental border on the backs and bellies of stringed instruments. [OF, *porfiler,* as PROFILE]

purgation, *n.* the act of purging, purification; cleansing of the bowels by the use of purgatives; (*Hist.*) the act of clearing oneself from an imputed crime by oath or ordeal; in the Roman Catholic Church, the process of spiritual purification of souls in purgatory. **purgative,** *a.* having the quality of cleansing, esp. evacuating the intestines, aperient. *n.* an aperient or cathartic. **purgatively,** *adv.* [ME and OF *purgacion,* L *purgātiōnem,* nom. *-tio,* from *purgāre,* to PURGE]

purgatory, *n.* a place or state of spiritual purging, esp. a place or state succeeding the present life in which, according to the Roman Catholic Church, the souls of the faithful are purified from venial sins by suffering; any place of temporary suffering or tribulation; (*coll.*) an acutely uncomfortable experience. *a.* cleansing, purifying. **purgatorial**, †**purgatorious,** *a.* **purgatorian,** *a.* and *n.* [ME and A-F *purgatorie* (OF *purgatoire*), med. L *purgātōrium*]

purge, *v.t.* to cleanse or purify; to free (of or from impurity, sin etc.); to remove (off or away) by cleansing; to clear (of an accusation, suspicion etc.); to get rid of persons actively in opposition; to atone for, expiate or annul (guilt, spiritual defilement etc.); to cleanse the bowels by cathartic action; †to clear (itself) by defecation (of a liquid). †*v.i.* to grow pure by clarification. *n.* a purgative medicine; an act of purging. **purger,** *n.* **purging,** *a.* and *n.* [OF *purger,* L *purgāre*]

puri, *n.* an unleavened whole-wheat bread, deep-fried and sometimes containing a spicy vegetable etc. mixture [Hind.]

purification etc. PURIFY.

puriform, *a.* in the form of pus; like pus. [L *pūs pūris,* PUS, -FORM]

purify, *v.t.* to make pure, to cleanse; to free from sin, guilt, pollution etc.; to make ceremonially clean; to clear of or from foreign elements, corruptions etc. **purification**, *n.* the act of physical or spiritual purifying; the act or process of cleansing ceremonially, esp. of women after child-birth. **purificator**, *n.* a piece of linen used to wipe the chalice and paten at the Eucharist. **purificatory,** *a.* having power to purify; tending to purify. **purifier,** *n.* [F *purifier,* late L *pūrificāre,* (*pūrus,* PURE, *-ficāre, facere,* to make)]

Purim, *n.* a Jewish festival instituted in commemoration of the deliverance of the Jews from the destruction threatened by Haman's plot (Esther ix.20–32). [Heb. *pūrīm,* pl. of *pūr,* prob. lot]

purin, purine, *n.* a crystalline solid derivable from uric acid, of which caffeine, xanthine etc. are derivatives. [G. *purin* from L *purus,* pure + NL *uricus,* uric]

puriri, *n.* the New Zealand oak or teak. [Maori]

purist, *n.* one advocating or affecting purity, esp. in the choice of words; a rigorous critic of literary style. **purism,** *n.* **puristic, -al**, *a.* [F *puriste*]

Puritan, *n.* one of a party or school of English Protestants of the 16th and 17th cents., who aimed at purifying religious worship from all ceremonies etc. not authorized by Scripture, and at the strictest purity of conduct. The Puritans were identified with the parliamentary opposition under James I and Charles I, and after the Restoration were driven from the church, and more usually known as Dissenters or Nonconformists; any person practising or advocating extreme strictness in conduct or religion (usu. applied in a depreciatory sense). *a.* pertaining to the Puritans; excessively strict in religion or morals. **puritanic, -ical**, *a.* **puritanically,** *adv.* **Puritanism,** *n.* **puritanize, -ise,** *v.t.*, *v.i.*

purity, *n.* the state of being pure, cleanness; freedom from pollution, adulteration or admixture of foreign elements; moral cleanness, innocence, chastity. [F *pureté*]

purl[1], *n.* an edging or fringe of twisted gold or silver wire; the thread or cord of which this is made; a small loop on the edges of pillow lace; a series of such loops as an ornamental hem or edging; an inversion of the stitches in knitting. *v.t.* to border or decorate with purl or purls; to knit with an inverted stitch. [perh. from obs. *pirl,* to twist]

purl[2], *n.* beer or ale with an infusion of wormwood; hot spiced gin and beer. [etym. doubtful]

purl[3], *v.i.* the flow with a soft, bubbling, gurgling or murmuring sound. *n.* a gentle bubbling, gurgling or murmuring sound. [cp. Norw. *purla,* Swed. *porla,* to bubble up]

purl[4], *v.t.* and *i.* to upset, to overturn. *n.* a heavy fall, an overturn. **purler,** *n.* (*coll.*) a heavy fall or throw, a cropper, a spill; a knockdown blow. [prob. from *pirl,* PURL[1]]

purlieu, *n.* (*usu. pl.*) the bounds or limits within which one ranges; *pl.* outlying parts, outskirts, environs; (*Hist.*) the borders or outskirts of a forest, esp. a tract of land, once included in forest but entirely or partially disafforested. [A-F *puralé,* OF *puralee* (PUR-, *aley,* see ALLEY[1]), assim. to LIEU]

purlin, *n.* a horizontal timber resting on the principal rafters and supporting the common rafters or boards on which the roof is laid. [etym. doubtful]

purloin, *v.t.* to steal, to take by theft; †to rob. *v.i.* to practise theft; to pilfer. **purloiner,** *n.* [A-F and OF *purloigner* (*loign, loin,* L *longe,* FAR)]

purple, *a.* of the colour of red and blue blended, the former predominating; (*Rom. Ant.*) of the colour obtained from the mollusca, purpura and murex, prob. crimson; dyed with or as with blood; imperial, regal; (of literary style) florid, highly rhetorical. *n.* this colour; a purple pigment or dye; a purple dress or robe, esp. of an emperor, king, Roman consul or a bishop; (*fig.*) imperial or regal power; the cardinalate; *pl.* swine fever; †purpura. *v.t.* to make or dye purple *v.i.* to become purple. **born in the purple,** of high and wealthy, esp. royal or imperial, family [see PORPHYROGENITE]. **royal purple,** *n.* a deep violet tending to blue. **purple emperor,** *n.* a variety of butterfly. **purple heart,** *n.* a mauve, heart-shaped, amphetamine tablet taken as a stimulant; (*with caps.*) a US decoration for wounds received on active service. **purple passage, patch,** *n.* a passage of obtrusively elevated or ornate writing. **purplish, purply,** *a.* [ME *purpre,* OE *purpure,* L PURPURA]

purport, *v.t.* to convey as the meaning, to imply, to signify; to profess, to be meant to appear (to). *n.*, meaning, tenor, import; object, purpose; †pretext, disguise. **purportless**, *a.* [A-F and OF *purporter* (PUR-, *porter,* L *portāre,* to carry)]

purpose, *n.* an end in view, an object, an aim; the reason why something exists; effect, result, consequence; determination, resolution. *v.t.* to intend, to design. *v.i.* to have an intention or design; †to be bound (for a place). **on purpose,** intentionally, designedly, not by accident; in order (that). **to the purpose,** with close relation to the matter in hand, relevantly; usefully. **purpose-built,** *a.* constructed to serve a specific purpose. **purposeful,** *a.* having a definite end in view; determined. **purposefully,** *adv.* **purposefulness,** *n.* **purposeless,** *a.* **purposelessly,** *adv.* **purposelessness,** *n.* **purposelike,** *a.* **purposely,** *adv.* of set purpose, intentionally, not by accident. **purposive,** *a.* having or serving a purpose; purposeful. **purposiveness,** *n.* [ME and OF *pourpos,* L *prōpositum,* p.p. of *prōpōnere,* to propose, see PROPOUND]

purpresture, *n.* (*Law.*) an illegal enclosure or encroachment (now on the property of the public). [OF *pourpresture,* from *pourprendre* (PUR-, *pendre,* L *prendere,* to seize, to take)]

Purpura, *n.* a genus of gasteropods, many species of which secrete a fluid from which the ancients obtained their purple dye; **purpura,** a morbid condition of the blood or blood-vessels characterized by livid spots on the skin. **purpure,** *n.* (*Her.*) purple, represented in engraving by diagonal lines from left to right. **purpureal**, *a.* (*Poet.*) purple. **purpurescent**, *a.* purplish. **purpuric,** *a.* of or pertaining to the disease purpura; of or pertaining to a purple colour. **purpurin**, *n.* a red colouring matter used in dyeing, orig. obtained from madder. [L, from Gr. *porphura*]

purr, *n.* a soft vibratory murmuring as of a cat when pleased. *v.i.* to make this sound. *v.t.* to signify, express or utter thus. **purring,** *a.* and *n.* **purringly,** *adv.* [imit.]

purse, *n.* a small bag or pouch for money, usu. carried in the pocket; (*N Am.*) a woman's handbag; money, funds, resources, a treasury; a sum of money subscribed or collected or offered as a gift, prize etc.; a definite sum (varying in different Eastern countries); a bag-like receptable, a pouch, a cyst. *v.t.* to wrinkle, to pucker; †to put into one's purse. *v.i.* to become wrinkled or puckered. **a light purse, an empty purse,** poverty, want of resources. **a long purse, a heavy purse,** wealth, riches. **privy purse** PRIVY. **public purse,** *n.* the national treasury. **purse-bearer,** *n.* one who has charge of the purse of another person or of a company etc., a purser; an officer who carried the Great Seal in a purse before the Lord Chancellor. **purse-net,** *n.* a net the mouth of which can be drawn together with cords like an old-fashioned purse. **purse-proud,** *a.* proud of one's wealth. **purse-seine,** *n.* a large purse-net for sea-fishing. **purse-strings,** *n.* strings for drawing together the mouth of an old-fashioned purse; (*fig.*) control of expenditure. †**purse-taking,** *n.* thieving. **purseful,** *n.* **purseless,** *a.* [OE *purs,* late L *bursa,* Gr. *bursa,* hide, leather]

purser, *n.* an officer on board ship in charge of the provisions, clothing, pay and general business. **pursership,** *n.*

purslane, *n.* a succulent herb, *Portulaca oleracea,* used as a salad and pot-herb. [OF *porcelaine,* L *porcilāca,* PORTULACA, assim. to PORCELAIN]

pursue, *v.t.* to follow with intent to seize, kill etc.; to try persistently to gain or obtain, to seek; to proceed in accordance with; to apply oneself to, to practise continuously; to attend persistently, to haunt (of consequences etc.); to continue to discuss, to follow up; †to attend, to accompany. *v.i.* to follow, to seek (after); to go in pursuit; to go on, to proceed, to continue. **pursuable,** *a.* **pursuance,** *n.* carrying out, performance; implementation. **pursuant,** *a.* in accordance, consonant, conformable (to). *adv.* in accordance or conformably (to). **pursuantly,** *adv.* **pursuer,** *n.* One who pursues; (*Sc. Law*) a plaintiff, a prosecutor. **pursuit,** *n.* the act of pursuing, a following; a prosecution, an endeavour to attain some end; an employment, occupation, business or recreation that one follows persistently. [A-F *pursuer,* OF *porsievre* (F *poursuivre*), late L *prōsequere* (PRO-, *sequere, sequī,* to follow)]

pursuivant, *n.* (*Her.*) an attendant on a herald, an officer of the College of Arms of lower rank than a herald; (*poet.*) a follower, an attendant. [OF *porsivant* (F *poursuivant*), pres.p., as prec.]

pursy[1], *a.* short-winded, asthmatical; fat, corpulent. **pursiness,** *n.* [formerly *pursive,* A-F *prosif,* OF *polsif* (F *poussif*), from *polser* (F *pousser*), to breathe with labour, from L *pulsāre,* to PULSE[1]]

pursy[2], *a.* like a purse, puckered up like a purse-mouth; moneyed, purse-proud. [PURSE, -Y]

purtenance, APPURTENANCE.

purulent, *a.* consisting of or discharging pus or matter. **purulence, -lency,** *n.* **purulently,** *adv.* [F, from L *pūrulentus,* from *pūs pūris,* PUS]

purvey, *v.t.* to provide, to supply, esp. provisions; to procure; †to foresee. *v.i.* to make provision; to act as purveyor; to pimp, to pander. **purveyance,** *n.* the purveying or providing of provisions; provisions supplied; (*Hist.*) the old royal prerogative of buying up provisions, impressing horses etc. **purveyor,** *n.* one who purveys provisions etc., a caterer, esp. on a large scale; †a procurer, a pimp. [A-F *purveier* (F *pourvoir*), to PROVIDE]

purview, *n.* extent, range, scope, intention; range of vision, knowledge etc.; (*Law*) the body of a statute consisting of the enacting clauses. [A-F *purveu* (F *pourvu*), p.p. of *purveier,* see prec.]

pus, *n.* the matter secreted from inflamed tissues, the produce of suppuration. [L]

Pusan, Busan, *n.* chief industrial port of South Korea (textiles, rubber, salt, fishing); population (1985) 3,517,000. It was invaded by the Japanese in 1592, and opened to foreign trade in 1883.

Puseyism, *n.* the High Church tenets of the Oxford School of which Dr Edward Pusey (1800–82) was a prominent member. Tractarianism. **Puseyite,** *a., n.*

push, *v.t.* to press against with force, tending to urge forward; to move (a body along, up, down etc.) thus; to make (one's way) vigorously; to impel, to drive; to put pressure on (a person); to develop or carry, as a point, an argument, esp. to extremes; (with a number) to approach; to seek to promote, esp. to promote the sale of; to peddle (drugs). *v.i.* to exert pressure (against, upon etc.); to press forward, to make one's way vigorously, to hasten forward energetically; to thrust or butt (against); to be urgent and persistent; (*Billiards*) to make a push-stroke. *n.* the act of pushing, a thrust, a shove; a vigorous effort, an attempt, an onset; pressure; an exigency, a crisis, an extremity; persevering energy, self-assertion; (*Mil.*) an offensive; (*Billiards*) a stroke in which the ball is pushed, not struck; (*Austral.*) a gang of larrikins, a clique or party. **at a push, if it comes to the push,** if really necessary. **to get, give the push,** (*sl.*) to dismiss, be dismissed, esp. from a job. **to push around,** (*coll.*) to bully, to treat with contempt. **to push for,** (*coll.*) to advocate vigorously, to make strenuous efforts to achieve. **to push in,** (*coll.*) to force one's way into (esp. a queue) ahead of others. **to push off,** to push against the bank with an oar so as to move a boat off; (*coll.*) to go away. **to push on,** to press forward; to hasten; to urge or drive on. **to push one's luck,** (*coll.*) to take risks, esp. by overplaying an existing advantage. **to push through,** to secure the acceptance of speedily or by compulsion. **to push up the daisies,** (*coll.*) to be dead and buried. **push-cart,** *n.* (*N Am.*) a barrow. **push-bike, -bicycle,** *n.* one worked by the rider as distinguished from a motor-bicycle. **pushbutton,** *n.* (*Elec.*) a device for opening or closing an electric circuit by the pressure of the finger on a button. **push-button,** *a.* operated by means of a push button. **pushchair,** *n.* a light, folding chair on wheels for a child. **pushover,** *n.* (*coll.*) something easy; a person, team etc. easy to defeat. **push-pin,** *n.* a child's game. **push-pull,** *a.* of any piece of apparatus in which electrical or electronic devices, e.g. two transistors in an amplifier, act in opposition to each other. **push-start,** *v.t.* to set a vehicle in motion by pushing, then engage a gear thus starting the engine. **push-stroke,** *n.* (*Billiards*) a push. **pusher,** *n.* a person or thing that pushes, esp. a device used in conjunction with a spoon for feeding very young children; a pushful person; a drug peddler. **pusher aeroplane,** *n.* (*Aviat.*) an aeroplane with its propeller at the rear. **pushful,** *a.* (*coll.*) self-assertive, energetic, vigorous or persistent in advancing oneself. **pushfulness,** *n.* **pushing,** *n.* enterprising, energetic. **pushingly,** *adv.* **pushy,** *a.* (*coll.*) pushful. [OF *pousser,* L *pulsāre,* to PULSATE]

Pushkin, *n.* **Aleksandr** (1799–1837), Russian poet and writer. He was exiled in 1820 for his political verse, and in 1824 was in trouble for his atheistic opinions. He wrote ballads such as *The Gypsies* (1827), and the novel in verse *Eugene Onegin* (1823–31). Other works include the tragic drama *Boris Godunov* (1825) and the prose pieces *The Captain's Daughter* (1836) and *The Queen of Spades* (1834). Pushkin's range was enormous, and his willingness to experiment freed later Russian writers from many of the archaic conventions of the literature of his time.

Pushtoo, Pushtu, Pushto, PASHTO.

pusillanimous, *a.* destitute of courage, firmness or strength of mind, fainthearted. **pusillanimity,** *n.* **pusillanimousness, pusillanimously,** *adv.* [eccles. L *pusillanimis* (*pusillus,* small, petty, *animus,* soul)]

puss, *n.* a pet name for a cat, esp. in calling; a hare; (*coll.*) a child, a girl. **Puss in Boots,** a fairy tale, included in Charles Perrault's collection. The youngest son of a poor miller inherits nothing from his father but a talking cat. By ingenuity and occasional magic the cat enables the hero to become rich, noble, and the husband of a princess. **puss-moth,** *n.* a large bombycid moth, *Cerura vinula.* **pussy,** *n.* (*Childish*) puss; (*taboo sl.*) the female pudenda. **pussy-cat,** *n.* a cat; anything woolly or fuzzy, as a willow catkin. **pussyfoot,** *v.i.* to move stealthily or warily; to avoid committing oneself. **pussy-willow,** *n.* a small American willow, *Salix discolor.* [cp. Dut. *poes,* LG *Puus,* Norw. *puse,* Swed. dial. *pus;* prob. imit.]

pustule, *n.* a small vesicle containing pus, a pimple; a small excrescence, a wart, a blister. **pustular,** *a.* **pustulate,** *v.t.* and *i.* to form into pustules. *a.*, covered with pustules or excrescences. **pustulation,** *n.* **pustulous,** *a.* [F, from L *pustula,* prob. conn. with Gr. *phusalis, phuskē,* a bladder, *phusan,* to blow]

put[1], *v.t.* (*pres. p.* **putting,** *past, p.p.* **put**) to move so as to place in some position; to set, lay, place or deposit; to bring into some particular state or condition; to append, to affix; to connect, to add; to assign; to express, to state; to render, to translate (into); to apply, to set, to impose; to stake (money on); to invest; to inflict; to subject, to commit (to or upon); to advance, to propose (for consideration etc.), to submit (to a vote); to constrain, to incite, to force, to make (a person do etc.); to make (one) appear in the right, wrong etc.; to repose, as trust, confidence etc.; to estimate; to hurl, to cast, to throw; to thrust, to stab with. *v.i.* (*Naut.*) to go, to proceed, to steer one's course (in a specified direction). *n.* the act of putting; a cast, a throw (of a weight etc.); an agreement to sell or deliver (stock, goods etc.) at a stipulated price within a specified time; a thrust; †a game or cards. **not to put it past somebody,** to consider a person capable of. **to put about,** to inconvenience; (*Naut.*) to go about, to change the course of to the opposite tack; (*coll.*) to make public, to spread abroad. **to put across,** to communicate effectively. **to put away,** to remove; to return to its proper place; to lay by; to divorce; to imprison; (*coll.*) to consume. **to put back,** to retard, to check the forward motion of; to postpone; to move the hands of (a clock) back; to replace; (*Naut.*) to return (to land etc.). **to put by,** to put, set or lay aside; to evade; to put off with evasion; to desist from. **to put down,** to suppress, to crush; to take down, to snub, to degrade; to confute, to silence; to reduce, to diminish; to write down, to enter, to subscribe; to reckon, to consider, to attribute; to put (a baby) to bed; to kill, esp. an old or ill animal; to pay (as a deposit); (of an aircraft) to land. **to put forth,** to present to notice; to publish, to put into circulation; to extend; to shoot out; to exert; to sprout, to bud. **to put forward,** to set forth, to advance, to propose; to thrust (oneself) into prominence; to move the hands of (a clock) onwards. **to put in,** to introduce, to interject, to interpose; to insert, to enter; to install in office etc.; to present, to submit, as an application, request etc.; to enter a harbour; (*coll.*) to spend, to pass (time). **to put in mind,** to remind. **to put it across someone,** (*coll.*) to defeat someone by ingenuity; **to put it on,** to pretend (to be ill etc.); to exaggerate. **to put off,** to lay aside, to discard, to take off; to postpone; to disappoint, to evade; to hinder, to distract the attention of; to dissuade (from); to cause aversion to; to foist, to palm off (with). **to put on,** to take on; to clothe oneself with; to assume; to add, to affix, to apply; to come to have an increased amount of; to bring into play, to exert; to cause to operate; to stage, to produce; to appoint; to move the hands of (a clock) forward. **to put one over on,** to deceive into believing or accepting. **to put out,** to invest, to place (at interest); to eject; to extinguish; to disconcert; to annoy, to irritate; to inconvenience; to exert; to dislocate; to publish, to broadcast; to give out (work) to be done at different premises; to render unconscious. **to put over,** to put across. **to put to it,** to distress; to press hard. **to put up,** to raise; to offer, to present, as for sale, acution; to give, to show, as a fight, resistance etc.; to provide (money, a prize); to offer (oneself) as a candidate; to present as a candidate; to publish (banns etc.); to pack up; to place in a safe place; to lay aside; to sheathe; to erect, to build; to lodge and entertain; to take lodgings. **to put upon,** to impose upon; to take undue advantage of. **to put up to,** to incite to; to make conversant with. **to put up with,** to tolerate, to submit to. **to put upon,** to victimize. **to stay put,** STAY. **put-down,** *n.* a snub; an action or remark intended to humiliate. **put-off,** *n.* an evasion, an excuse. **put-on,** *n.* an attempt to deceive or mislead. **put-up job,** *n.* something secretly prearranged for purposes of deception. **putter,** *n.* one who puts; a shot-putter. **putting (the shot),** *n.* the act or sport of throwing a heavy weight from the shoulder by an outward thrust of the arm. [late OE *putian* (in *putung*), *potian,* to put, *pȳtan,* to put or thrust out]

put[2], *n.* a silly fellow, a lout, a bumpkin. [(*coll.*)]

put[3], PUTT.

putamen, *n.* the hard bony stone or endocarp of a drupe; the membrane of skin of an egg; (*Anat.*) the outer zone of the lenticular nucleus of the brain. [L, from *putāre,* to prune]

putative, *a.* reputed, supposed; commonly regarded as. **putatively,** *adv.* [F *putatif,* fem. *-tive,* late L *putātīvus,* from *putāre,* to think]

†**pute,** *a.* clean, pure. **pure and pute** or **pure pute,** pure, mere. [L *putus*]

puteal, *n.* the stone kerb round the opening of a well. [L *puteāle,* neut. of *puteālis,* from *puteus,* well]

putid, *a.* foul, mean, low, worthless. **putidness,** *n.* [L *pūtidus,* from *pūtēre,* to stink]

putlog, *n.* a short horizontal piece of timber for the floor of a scaffold to rest on. [etym. doubtful]

putrefy, *v.t.* to make putrid; to cause to rot or decay; to make carious or gangrenous; to corrupt. *v.i.* to become putrid, to rot, to decay; to fester, to suppurate. † **putredinous**, *a.* **putrefaction**, *n.* **putrefactive,** *a.* **putrescent**, *a.* **putrescence,** *n.* **putrescible,** *a.* **putrescin**, *n.* (*Chem.*) a poisonous alkaloid contained in decaying animal matter. **putrid**, *a.* in a state of putrefaction, decomposition, or decay; tainted, foul, noxious; (*fig.*) corrupt. **putrid fever,** *n.* typhus or jail-fever. **putrid sore throat,** *n.* a gangrenous form of laryngitis or diphtheria. **putridity**, **putridness,** *n.* **putridly,** *adv.* [F *putréfier,* L *putrefacere* (*putre-,* as in *putrēre,* to be rotten, *facere,* to make)]

putsch, *n.* a rising, revolt. [G]

putt, *v.i.* (*Golf*) to strike the ball with a putter. *v.t.* to strike (the ball) gently with a putter so as to get it into the hole on the putting-green. *n.* this stroke. **putter,** *n.* a short, stiff golf-club, used for striking the ball on the putting-green; a person who putts. **putting-green,** *n.* the piece of ground around each hole on a golf-course, usu. kept rolled, closely mown and clear of obstacles; an area of smooth grass with several holes for putting games. [var. of PUT[1]]

puttee, *n.* a long strip of cloth wound spirally round the leg, usu. from ankle to knee, as a form of gaiter. [Hind. *patti,* bandage]

putter, putting-green etc. PUTT.

puttier PUTTY.

Puttnam, *n.* **David Terence** (1941–), English film producer, influential in reviving the British film industry internationally. Films include *Chariots of Fire* (1981) and *The Killing Fields* (1984).

putto, *n.* (*pl.* **putti**) a figure of a small boy, cherub or cupid in Renaissance and Baroque art. [It.]

puttock, *n.* a kite or buzzard. [ME *puttocke,* etym. doubtful]

putty, *n.* calcined tin or lead used by jewellers as polishing-powder for glass, metal etc.; whiting and linseed-oil beaten up into a tenacious cement, used in glazing; fine lime-mortar used by plasterers for filling cracks etc. *v.i.* to fix, cement, fill up, or cover with putty. **up to putty,** (*Austral. sl.*) no good, valueless, of bad quality. **putty-faced,** *a.* having a smooth, colourless face like putty. **putty-powder,** *n.* jewellers' putty in the form of powder, used for polishing. **putty-root,** *n.* an American orchid, *Aplectrum hyemale,* the root of which contains glutinous matter used as cement. **puttier,** *n.* a worker with putty, a glazier. [F *potée,* orig. potful, see POT]

puy, *n.* a conical hill of volcanic origin, esp. in Auvergne. [F, ult. from L *podium,* elevation, height]

Pu-Yi, *n.* former name of the last Chinese emperor Henry P'u-i.

puzzle, *n.* a state of bewilderment or perplexity; a perplexing problem, question or enigma; a toy, riddle or other contrivance for exercising ingenuity or patience. *v.t.* to perplex, to embarrass, to mystify; †to make intricate. *v.i.* to be bewildered or perplexed. **to puzzle out,** to discover, or work out by mental labour. **puzzle-headed,** *a.* having the head full of confused notions. **puzzle-peg,** *n.* a piece of wood fastened under the jaw of a dog so as to keep his nose from the ground. **puzzledom**, *n.* **puzzlement,** *n.* **puzzler,** *n.* **puzzlingly,** *adv.* [etym. doubtful]

puzzolana, POZZOLANA.

PVC, (*abbr.*) polyvinyl chloride.

PW, (*abbr.*) policewoman.

p.w., (*abbr.*) per week.

PWA, (*abbr.*) person with Aids.

PWR, (*abbr.*) pressurized water reactor.

pyaemia, *n.* (*Path.*) blood-poisoning, due to the absorption of putrid matter into the system causing multiple abcesses. **pyaemic,** *a.* [Gr. *puon,* pus, *haima,* blood]

pyalla, *v.i.* to shout, to yell. [Austral. Abor.]

pycnidium, *n.* (*pl.* **-dia**) a receptacle bearing pycnidiospores or stylospores in certain fungi. **pycnid**, *n.* **pycnidiospore**, *n.* a stylospore developed in a pycnidium. [Gr. *puknos,* thick, *-idion,* dim. suf.]

pycnite, *n.* a columnar variety of topaz. [Gr. *puknos,* see foll., -ITE]

pycno-, *comb. form* thick, dense. [Gr. *puknos,* thick, dense]

pycnodont, *n.* any individual of the Pycnodontidae, a family of extinct ganoid fishes. *a.* pertaining to or having the characteristics of the Pycnodontidae [Gr. *odous odontos,* tooth]

pycnogonid, *n.* (*Zool.*) a marine arthropod belonging to the group Pycnogonida, comprising the sea-spiders. **pycnogonoid**, *a.* and *n.* [Gr. *gonu,* knee]

pycnometer, *n.* a bottle or flask used in measuring the specific gravity of fluids.

pycnospore, PYCNIDIOSPORE.

pycnostyle, *a.* having an intercolumniation of one diameter and a half. *n.* a pycnostyle building. [Gr. *stulos,* column]

pye, PIE[1].

†**pyebald,** PIEBALD.

pye-dog, *n.* a pariah dog, a cur. [Hind.]

pyelitis, *n.* (*Path.*) inflammation of the pelvis of the kidney. **pyelitic**, *a.* [mod. L (Gr. *puelos,* trough]

pyelo-, *comb. form* pertaining to the kidneys.

pyelonephritis, *n.* inflammation of the kidney and of the renal pelvis. **pyelonephritic**, *a.*

pyemia, PYAEMIA.

pygal, *a.* of, pertaining to, or near the rump or hind quarters. *n.* the pygal shield or plate of the carapace of a turtle. [Gr. *pug-ē,* rump, -AL]

pygarg, *n.* the osprey; an antelope mentioned by Herodotus and Pliny. [L *pygargus,* Gr. *pugargus* (*pugē,* rump, *argos,* white)]

Pygmalion, *n.* in Greek legend, a king of Cyprus who fell in love with an ivory statue he had carved, and when Aphrodite brought it to life as Galatea, he married her.

pygmy, pigmy, *n.* one of a race of dwarfish people mentioned by Herodotus and other ancient historians as living in Africa and India; one of various dwarf races living in Malaysia and Central Africa, esp. the Akka, Batwa and Obongo of equatorial Africa; a dwarf, a small person, anything very diminutive; a pixy, a fairy; one having a certain faculty or quality in relatively a very small degree; †the chimpanzee. *a.* diminutive, dwarf; small and insignificant. **pygmaean**, *a.* [L *pygmaeus,* Gr. *pugmaios,* dwarfish, from *pugmē,* fist, the length from elbow to knuckles]

pygo-, *comb. form a.* diminutive, dwarf; small and insignificant. [Gr. *pugo-, pugē,* rump]

pygopod, *a.* of or pertaining to the Pygopedes, an order of aquatic birds; of or belonging to the Pygopodidae, a family of Australian lizards. *n.* one of the Pygopodidae.

pygostyle, *n.* the vomer or ploughshare bone forming the end of the vertebral column in most birds. **pygostyled,** *a.* [Gr. *pous podos,* foot]

pyjamas, (*N Am.*), **pajamas**, *n.pl.* loose trousers of silk, cotton etc. worn by both sexes among Muslims in India and Pakistan; a sleeping-suit consisting of a loose jacket and trousers. [Pers. and Hind. *pāejāmah* (*pāe,* by, *jāmah,* clothing, garment)]

pylon, *n.* a gateway of imposing form or dimensions, esp. the monumental gateway of an Egyptian temple; a stake marking out the course in an aerodrome; a structure, usu. of steel, supporting an electric cable; a rigid, streamlined support (for an engine etc.) on the outside of an aircraft. [Gr. *pulōn,* from *pulē,* gate]

pylorus, *n.* the contracted end of the stomach leading into the small intestine; the adjoining part of the stomach. **pyloric**, *a.* [late L, from Gr. *pulōros,* gatekeeper (*pulē,* gate, *ouros,* keeper, watcher)]

Pym, *n.* **John** (1584–1643), English parliamentarian, largely responsible for the Petition of Right (1628). As leader of the Puritan opposition in the Long Parliament from 1640, he moved the impeachment of Charles I's advisers Strafford and Laud, drew up the Grand Remonstrance, and was the chief of five Members of Parliament Charles I wanted arrested in 1642. The five took refuge in the City, from which they emerged triumphant when the king left London.

Pynchon, *n.* **Thomas** (1937–), US novelist, who creates a bizarre, labyrinthine world in his books, which include *V* (1963), *The Crying of Lot 49* (1966), *Gravity's Rainbow* (1973), and *Vineland* (1989).

pyo-, *comb. form*, pus. [Gr. *puon,* pus]

pyogenesis, *n.* the formation of pus, suppuration. **pyogenetic**, **pyogenic,** *a.*

pyoid, *a.* of the nature of pus.

pyonephritis, *n.* suppurative inflammation of the kidney.

Pyongyang, *n.* capital and industrial city (coal, iron, steel, textiles, chemicals) of North Korea; population (1984) 2,640,000.

pyonoma, *n.* a suppurating sore.

pyopoiesis PYOGENESIS.

pyoptysis, *n.* expectoration of pus, as in consumption.

pyorrhoea, *n.* discharge of pus; inflammation of the teeth sockets.

pyosis, *n.* suppuration.

pyr- PYRO-.

pyracanth, *n.* an evergreen thorny shrub, *Crataegus pyracantha,* with white flowers and coral-red berries, also called the evergreen thorn, commonly trained against walls as an ornamental climber. [L *pyracantha,* Gr. *puracantha* (see ACANTHUS)]

pyrallolite, *n.* (*Min.*) an altered pyroxene from Finland. [Gr. *allos,* other, -LITE]

pyramid, *n.* a monumental structure of masonry, with a square base and triangular sloping sides meeting at the apex; a similar solid body, with a triangular or polygonal but usu. square base; a pile or heap of this shape; a tree trained in this form; a game of pool played with fifteen coloured balls and a cue-ball. **the Pyramids,** the great pyramids of ancient Egypt. **pyramid selling,** *n.* a fraudulent system of selling whereby batches of goods are sold to agents who sell smaller batches at increased prices to sub-agents and so on down. **pyramidal**, †**pyramidic, -al**, *a.* **pyramidally, pyramidically,** *adv.* **pyramidist,** *n.* a student or investigator of the origin, structure etc. of ancient pyramids, esp. those of Egypt. **pyramidalism,** *n.* **pyramidize, -ise,** *v.t.* **pyramidoid**, †**pyramoid**, *n.* a solid resembling a pyramid; (*erron.*) a parabolic spindle. **pyramidwise,** *adv.* **pyramidon**, [after ACCORDION], *n.* (*Organ*) a stop having stopped pipes like inverted pyramids, producing very deep tones. [L *pyramis -idis,* Gr. *puramis -idos,* prob. of Egypt. orig.]

Pyramus and Thisbe, legendary Babylonian lovers whose story was retold by Ovid. Pursued by a lioness, Thisbe lost her veil, and when Pyramus arrived at their meeting-place, he found it bloodstained. Assuming Thisbe was dead, he stabbed himself, and she, on finding his body, killed herself. In *A Midsummer Night's Dream*, the 'rude mechanicals' perform the story as a farce for the nobles.

pyrargyrite, *n.* (*Min.*) a native sulphide of silver and antimony. [PYR-, Gr. *arguros,* silver]

pyre, *n.* a funeral pile for burning a dead body; any pile of combustibles. [L *pyra,* Gr. *pura,* cogn. with *pur,* fire]

pyrene[1], *n.* the stone of a drupe, a putamen. [Gr. *purēn*]

pyrene[2], *n.* one of the hydrocarbons obtained in the dry distillation of coal. [Gr. *pur,* fire]

Pyrenees, *n.* (French **Pyrénées**; Spanish **Pirineos**) mountain range in SW Europe between France and Spain; length about 435 km/270 miles; highest peak Aneto (French *Néthon*) 3404 m/11,172 ft. Andorra is entirely within the range. Hydroelectric power has encouraged industrial development in the foothills.

pyrethrum, *n.* a genus of compositous plants (usu. regarded as a sub-division of *Chrysanthemum*), comprising the feverfew; an insecticide made from the dried heads of these. **pyrethrin**, *n.* either of two oily, insecticidal compounds found in pyrethrum flowers. [L, from Gr. *purethron,* as prec.]

pyretic, *a.* of, relating to, or producing fever; remedial in fever. *n.* a pyretic medicine. [Gr. *puretos,* fever]

Pyrex®, *a., n.* (made of) heat-resistant glass containing oxide of boron.

pyrexia, *n.* fever, feverish condition. **pyrexial, -ical,** *a.*

pyrheliometer, *n.* an instrument for measuring the amount of solar radiation. **pyrheliometric**, *a.* [PYR-, HELIOMETER]

pyridine, *n.* a liquid alkaloid obtained from bone-oil, coal-tar naphtha etc., used as a remedy for asthma. [PYR-, -ID, -INE]

pyriform, *a.* pear-shaped. [med. L *pyrum,* L *pirum,* PEAR]

pyrites, *n.* a native sulphide of iron, one of two common sulphides, chalcopyrite, yellow or copper pyrites, or marcasite, usu. called iron pyrites. **pyretaceous**, **pyritic, -al**, **pyritous**, *a.* **pyritiferous**, *a.* **pyritize, -ise**, *v.t.* **pyritoid**, *a.* **pyritology**, -LOGY, *n.* [L, from Gr. *puritēs,* orig. pertaining to fire, from *pur,* fire]

pyro, *n.* pyrogallic acid. [short for PYROGALLIC]

pyro-, *comb. form* fire, heat; obtained (as if) by heating. [Gr. *pur puros,* fire]

pyroacetic, *a.* of or derived from acetic acid by heat.

pyroclastic, *a.* formed from or consisting of the fragments broken up or ejected by volcanic action. [Gr. *klastos,* broken]

pyroelectric, *a.* becoming electropolar on heating (of some minerals). **pyroelectricity,** *n.*

pyrogallic, *a.* produced from gallic acid by heat. **pyrogallol**, *n.* pyrogallic acid, used as a developing agent in photography.

pyrogen, *n.* a substance, such as ptomaine, that produces fever on being introduced into the body; †electricity. **pyrogenetic**, **pyrogenic**, *a.* producing heat; producing feverishness; pyrogenous. **pyrogenous**, *a.* produced by fire, igneous.

pyrognomic, GNOMIC, *a.* having the property of becoming incandescent when heated.

pyrognostic, *a.* of or pertaining to those properties of a mineral that are determinable by heat.

pyrography, *n.* the art of making designs in wood by means of fire, poker-work. **pyrograph**, *v.i.* **pyrographer, -phist,** *n.* **pyrographic**, *a.* **pyrogravure,** *n.* pyrography; a picture produced by this means.

Pyrola, *n.* a genus of low evergreen plants of the family Ericaceae, which comprises the winter-greens. [dim., from med. L *pyrus,* L *pirus,* PEAR]

pyrolatry, *n.* fire-worship. [PYRO-, -LATRY]

pyroligneous, *a.* derived from wood by heat. **pyrolignite**, *n.* a salt of pyroligneous acid.

pyrology, *n.* the science of fire or heat, esp. the branch of chemistry dealing with the application of heat, blow-pipe analysis etc. **pyrological**, *a.* **pyrologist**, *n.*

pyrolusite, *n.* (*Min.*) native manganese dioxide, one of the most important of the ores of manganese. [G *pyrolusit* (Gr. *lousis,* washing)]

pyrolysis, *n.* the decomposition of a substance by heat. **pyrolyse,** (*N Am.*) **-lyze**, *v.t.* to subject to this process. **pyrolytic**, *a.* LYSIS.

pyromagnetic, *a.* of or pertaining to the alterations of magnetic intensity due to changes in temperature. **pyromagnetic generator,** *n.* a dynamo for generating electricity by induction through changes in the temperature of the field-magnets.

pyromancy, *n.* divination by fire. †**pyromantic**, *a.* [OF *pyromancie,* late L. *pyromantīa,* Gr. *puromanteia*]

pyromania, *n.* insanity manifested in an irresistible desire to destroy by fire. **pyromaniac**, *n.* **pyromaniacal**, *a.* [-MANIA]

pyrometer, *n.* an instrument for measuring high temperatures; an instrument for measuring the expansion of bodies by heat. **pyrometric, -al**, *a.* **pyrometrically,** *adv.* **pyrometry,** *n.* [PYRO-, -METER[1]]

pyromorphous, *a.* crystallizing after fusion by heat.

†**pyronomics**, *n.* the science of heat. [Gr. *morphē,* from, -OUS]

pyrope, *n.* a deep-red garnet. [OF *pirope,* L *pyrōpus,* Gr. *purpos* (*pur,* fire, *ōps,* face, eye)]

pyrophane, *n.* a variety of opal that absorbs melted wax and becomes translucent when heated and opaque again on cooling. **pyrophanous**, *a.* [PYRO-, Gr. *-phanēs,* appearing]

pyrophone, *n.* a musical instrument the notes of which are produced in glass tubes each containing two hydrogen flames.

pyrophoric, *a.* igniting spontaneously on contact with air; (of an alloy) emitting sparks when struck. [NL *pyrophorus,* from Gr. *purophoros,* fire-bearing]

pyrophosphoric, *a.* derived by heat from phosphoric acid.

pyrophotograph, *n.* a photographic picture fixed on glass or porcelain by firing. **pyrophotographic**, *a.* **pyro-photography**, *n.*

pyrophysalite, *n.* a coarse, nearly opaque variety of topaz which swells on being heated. [Gr. *phusallis,* bubble]

pyroscope, *n.* an instrument for measuring the intensity of radiant heat.

pyrosis, *n.* heartburn, water-brash. [Gr. *purōsis,* from *puroun,* to set on fire]

pyrosome, *n.* an animal of the genus *Pyrosoma,* consisting of highly phosphorescent compound ascidians united in free-swimming cylindrical colonies, mostly belonging to tropical seas. [PYRO-, Gr. *sōma,* body]

pyrotartaric, *a.* obtained by the dry distillation of tartaric acid. **pyrotartrate**, *n.* a salt of pyrotartaric acid. [TARTARIC]

pyrotechnic, *a.* pertaining to fireworks or their manufacture; of the nature of fireworks; (*fig.*) resembling a firework show, brilliant, dazzling. **pyrotechnics,** *n. sing.* the art of making fireworks; (*sing. or pl.*) a display of fireworks; (*sing. or pl.*) a dazzling or virtuoso display. **pyrotechnical,** *a.* **pyrotechnically,** *adv.* **pyrotechnist,** *n.* **pyrotechny**, *n.* [Gr. *technē,* art]

pyrotic, *a.* caustic. *n.* a caustic substance. [Gr. *purōtikos,* from *puroun,* to burn]

pyroxene, *n.* a name used for a group of silicates of lime, magnesium or manganese, of various forms and origin. **pyroxenic**, *a.* [PYRO-, Gr. *xenos,* stranger]

pyroxyle, pyroxylin, *n.* any explosive, including guncotton, obtained by immersing vegetable fibre in nitric or nitrosulphuric acid, and then drying it. **pyroxylic**, *a.* denoting the crude spirit obtained by the distillation of wood in closed vessels. [F *pyroxyline* (Gr. *xulon,* wood)]

Pyrrhic, *a.* of or pertaining to Pyrrhus. **Pyrrhic victory,** *n.* a victory that is as costly as a defeat, like that of Pyrrhus.

pyrrhic, *n.* a warlike dance among the ancient Greeks; a metrical foot of two short syllables. *a.* of or pertaining to such dance; consisting of two short syllables. [L *pyrrhica,* Gr. *purrhichē,* from *Purrhichos,* the inventor]

Pyrrho, *n.* (*c.* 360–270 BC), Greek philosopher, founder of Scepticism, who maintained that since certainty was impossible, peace of mind lay in renouncing all claims to knowledge. **Pyrrhonism,** *n.* the sceptical philosophy taught by Pyrrho; universal doubt, philosophic nescience. **Pyrrhonian**, **Pyrrhonic**, *a.* **Pyrrhonist,** *n.*

Pyrrhus, *n.* (*c.* 318–272 BC), king of Epirus from 307, who invaded Italy in 280, as an ally of the Tarentines against Rome. He twice defeated the Romans but with heavy losses. He returned to Greece 275 after his defeat at Beneventum, and was killed in a riot in Argos.

Pyrus, *n.* a genus of Rosaceae comprising the apple and pear. **Pyrus Japonica**, *n.* a small tree or shrub of this genus bearing bright scarlet flowers. [med. L, from L *pirus,* PEAR]

Pythagoras, *n.* (*c.* 580–500 BC), Greek mathematician and philosopher, who formulated Pythagoras' theorem. **Pythagoras's theorem,** *n.* the theorem that the square on the hypotenuse of a right-angled triangle is equal to the sum of the squares on the other two sides. **Pythagorean,** *n.* a follower of Pythagoras. *a.* pertaining to Pythagoras or his philosophy. **Pythagoreanism,** †**Pythagorism,** *n.*

Pythian, *a.* pertaining to Delphi, to Apollo, or to his priestess who delivered oracles at Delphi. *n.* Apollo or his priestess at Delphi. **Pythic,** *a.* **Pythian** or **Pythic games,** *n., pl.* one of the four great Panhellenic festivals, celebrated once every four years near Delphi. [L *Phythius,* Gr. *Puthios,* from *Puthō,* former name of Delphi]

pythogenic, *a.* produced by filth or putrid matter. **pythogenesis**, *n.* generation from or through filth. [Gr. *puthein,* to rot. Gr. *-gen,* root of *gennaein,* to produce]

python[1], *n.* (*Gr. Myth.*) a gigantic serpent slain by Apollo near Delphi; a large non-venomous serpent that crushes its prey. [L, from Gr. *Puthōn,* prob. from *Puthō,* see PYTHIAN]

python[2], *n.* a familiar spirit or demon; one possessed by this, a soothsayer, a diviner. **pythoness**, *n.* a woman possessed by a familiar spirit or having the gift of prophecy, a witch; applied esp. to the priestess of the temple of Apollo at Delphi who delivered the oracles. **pythonic**, *a.* inspired, oracular, prophetic. **pythonism,** *n.* [late L *pytho -ōnem,* or late Gr. *puthōn,* prob. rel. to prec. but history obscure]

pyuria, *n.* the presence of pus in the urine. [Gr. *puon,* pus; *ouron,* urine]

pyx, *n.* (*Eccles.*) the covered vessel, usu. of precious metal, in which the host is kept; a box at the Royal Mint in which sample coins are placed for testing at the annual trial by a jury of the Goldsmiths' Company. *v.t.* to test (a coin) by weighing and assaying. **pyxidium**, *n.* (*pl.* **-dia**) (*Bot.*) a capsule or seed-vessel dehiscing by a transverse suture, as in the pimpernel. **pyxis**, *n.* a box, a casket; (*Bot.*) a pyxidium; (*Anat.*) the acetabulum of the hip-bone. [L *pyxis,* Gr. *puxis,* a box, from *puxos,* box-tree]

pzazz, PIZZAZZ.

Q

Q, q, the 17th letter and the 13th consonant (*pl.* **Ques, Q's, Qs**), is always followed by *u,* the combination *qu* having the sound of *kw.* **to mind one's p's and q's** P[1]. **Q-boat,** *n.* an armed vessel disguised as a merchantman, employed to lure and surprise hostile submarines. **Q factor,** *n.* the difference between stored energy and the rate at which energy is being expended; the heat released in a nuclear explosion. [*Q*uality *factor*] **Q fever,** *n.* an acute fever whose symptoms include fever and pneumonia. [*Q*uery *fever,* the cause being originally unknown] **Q-ship,** *n.* a ship with concealed guns which acts as a decoy. [*Q*uery *-ship*]

Q., (*abbr.*) heat; queen; question.

q., (*abbr.*) quart; quarter; quarterly; query; quire; question.

Qaboos bin Said (1940–), sultan of Oman. The 14th descendant of the Albusaid family, opposed to the conservative views of his father, in 1970 he overthrew him, in a bloodless coup, and assumed the sultanship. Since then he has followed more liberal and expansionist policies, while maintaining his country's position of international non-alignment.

Qaddafi KHADDHAFI.

Qadisiya, Battle of, battle fought in S Iraq in 637. A Muslim Arab force defeated a larger Zoroastrian Persian army and ended the Sassanian Empire. The defeat is still resented in Iran, where modern Muslim Arab nationalism threatens to break up the Iranian state.

QANTAS, *n.* the national airline of Australia. [acronym for *Q*ueensland *and N*orthern *T*erritory *A*ir *S*ervices]

QARANC, (*abbr.*) Queen Alexandra's Royal Nursing Corps.

Qatar, *n.* (*Dawlat Qatar*), country in the Middle East, occupying Qatar peninsula in the Arabian Gulf, bounded to the SW by Saudi Arabia and to the S by the United Arab Emirates. **area** 11,400 sq km/4402 sq miles. **capital** and chief port Doha. **towns** Dukhan, centre of oil production. **physical** mostly flat desert. **exports** oil, natural gas, petrochemicals, fertilizers, iron, steel. **population** (1989) 342,000 (half in Doha); annual growth rate 6.8%. **language** Arabic. **religion** Sunni Muslim.

QB, (*abbr.*) Queen's Bench.

QC, (*abbr.*) Queen's Counsel.

QED, (*abbr.*) quod erat demonstrandum, which was to be proved.

Qin dynasty, *n.* Chinese imperial dynasty 221–206 BC. Shi Huangdi was its most noted emperor.

Qinghai, *n.* (formerly **Tsinghai**), province of NW China. **area** 721,000 sq km/278,306 sq miles. **capital** Xining. **products** oil, livestock, medical products. **population** (1986) 4,120,000, including many Tibetans and other minorities.

Qisarya, *n.* Mediterranean port north of Tel Aviv-Jaffa, Israel; there are underwater remains of Herod the Great's port of Caesarea.

QM, (*abbr.*) quarter-master.

Qom, Qum, *n.* holy city of Shi'ite Muslims, in central Iran, 145 km/90 miles south of Tehran; population (1986) 551,000.

QSO, (*abbr.*) quasi-stellar object, a quasar.

qt, (*abbr.*) quantity; quart, quarts; quiet. **on the qt,** (*coll.*) secretly, on the sly.

qua, *conj.* in the character of, by virtue of being, as. [L, abl. fem. sing. of *qui,* rel. pron.]

quack[1], *v.i.* to make a harsh cry like that of a duck; (*fig.*) to chatter loudly, to brag. *n.* the cry of a duck; a noisy outcry. **quack-quack,** *n.* (*childish*) a duck. [imit., cp. Dut. *kwakken,* G *quacken,* Icel. *kvaka,* also L *coaxāre,* Gr. *koax,* a croak]

quack[2], *n.* a mere pretender to knowledge or skill, esp. one in medicine offering pretentious remedies and nostrums; an ignorant practitioner, an empiric, a charlatan. *a.* pertaining to quacks or quackery. **quackery, quackism,** *n.* **quackish,** *a.* [short for QUACKSALVER]

†**quackle,** *v.i.* to quack; to choke. *v.t.* to choke. [freq. of QUACK[1]]

†**quacksalver,** *n.* one who brags of his medicines or salves; a quack. [Dut. *kwakzalver,* earlier *quacksalver*]

quad[1], *n.* a quadrangle or court, as of a college etc. [short for QUADRANGLE]

quad[2], *n.* (*Print.*) a quadrat. *v.i.* to insert quadrats (in a line of type). [short for QUADRAT]

quad[3] QUOD.

quad[4], *n.* (*coll.*) one child (of quadruplets). [QUADRUPLET]

quad[5] QUADRAPHONIC.

quadr- *comb.form.* QUADR(I)-.

quadra, *n.* (*pl.* **-rae**) a socle or plinth of a podium; one of the fillets of an Ionic base. [L, a square]

quadrable QUADRATE.

quadragenarian, *a.* 40 years old. *n.* one 40 years old. †**quadragene,** *n.* a papal indulgence for 40 days. [L *quadrāgēnārius,* from *quadrāgēnī,* distrib. of *quadrāginta,* 40 (*quadrus,* cogn. with *quatuor,* four, *-ginta,* prob. for *dekinta,* tenth, from *decem,* ten)]

Quadragesima, *n.* the first Sunday in Lent, also called Quadragesima Sunday; †Lent, so called because it consists of 40 days. **quadragesimal,** *a.* lasting 40 days (of a fast); pertaining to or used in Lent, Lenten. *n.pl.* Offerings formerly made to the mother church of a diocese on Mid-Lent Sunday. [med. L, fem. of *quadrāgēsimus,* 40th, as prec.]

quadrangle, *n.* a plane figure having four angles and four sides, esp. a square or rectangle; an open square or four-sided court surrounded by buildings; such a court together with the surrounding buildings. **quadrangular,** *a.* **quadrangularly,** *adv.* [F, from L *quadrangulum*]

quadrant, *n.* the fourth part of the circumference of a circle, an arc of 90°; a plane figure contained by two radii of a circle at right angles to each other and the arc between them; a quarter of a sphere; an instrument shaped like a quarter-circle graduated for taking angular measurements; (*Naut.*) such an instrument formerly used for taking the altitude of the sun, now superseded by the sextant. **quadrantal,** *a.* [L *quadrans -ntis,* as QUADRI-]

quadraphonics, quadrophonics, *n.* a system of recording and reproducing sound using four independent sound signals or speakers. **quadraphonic, quadrophonic,** *a.* **quadraphony, quadrophony,** *n.*

quadrat, *n.* a block of type-metal lower than the type, used for spacing out lines etc.; †an instrument formerly used in taking altitudes; a square of vegetation taped off for intensive study. [var. of foll.]

quadrate, *a.* square, rectangular; †square, raised to the second power. *n.* the quadrate bone; a quadrate muscle; †a square, cubical or rectangular object; †(*Astron.*) an aspect of the heavenly bodies, in which they are distant from each other 90°; (*Elec.*) the position when there is a phase difference of one quarter of a cycle between two alternating currents. †*v.t.,* to square; to make conformable. *v.i.* to square, to agree, to match, to correspond. **quadrate bone,** *n.* in birds and reptiles, a bone by means of which the jaws are articulated with the skull. **quadrate muscle,** *n.* a square-shaped muscle in the hip, forearm etc. **quadrable,** *a.* capable of quadrature; capable of being squared or of being represented by a finite number of algebraic terms. **quadratic,** *a.* involving the second and no higher power of the variable or unknown quantity; †square. *n.* a quadratic equation; (*pl.*) the part of algebra dealing with quadratic equations. **quadratrix,** *n.* (*pl.* **-trices**) a curve by means of which straight lines can be found equal to the circumference of circles or other curves and their several parts. **quadrature,** *n.* the act of squaring or finding a square equal in area to a given curved figure; the position of a heavenly body with respect to another 90° distant. [L *quadrātus,* p.p. of *quadrāre,* to square, from *quadrus,* square]

quadrel, *n.* a square block; a brick or kind of artificial stone, used in Italy, made of chalky earth dried in the sun. [It. *quadrello,* dim. of *quadro,* square, as QUADR(I)-]

quadrella, *n.* (*Austral.*) a form of betting where the person making the bet must pick the winners of four races.

quadrennial, *a.* comprising or lasting four years; recurring every four years. **quadrennially,** *adv.* **quadrennium,** *n.* a period of four years. [L *quadriennium* (QUADRI-, *annus,* year)]

quadri- *comb.form.* four. **quadric,** *a.* of the second degree; quadratic. *n.* a quantic, curve or surface of the second degree. [L, rel. to *quatuor,* four]

quadricapsular, *a.* having four capsules.

quadricentennial, *n.* the 400th anniversary of an event. *a.* pertaining to a period of 400 years.

quadriceps, *n.* a four-headed muscle acting as extensor to the leg. **quadricipital,** *a.*

quadricone, *n.* a quadric cone.

quadricorn, *n.* any animal having four horns or antennae. *a.* Quadricornous. **quadricornous,** *a.*

quadricycle, *n.* a cycle having four wheels.

quadridentate, *a.* having four indentations or serrations.

quadrifid, *a.* cleft into four parts, segments or lobes.

quadrifoliate, *a.* four-leaved; having four leaflets.

quadriga, *n.* (*pl.* **-gae**) an ancient Roman two-wheeled chariot drawn by four horses abreast. [L, orig. in pl. form. *quadrīgae* for *quadrijugae* (*jugum,* yoke)]

quadrigeminal, -nous, *n.* pertaining to four medullary tubercles situated at the base of the brain. **quadrigeminate,** *a.* fourfold; occurring in fours. **quadrigenarious,** *a.* consisting of 400. **quadrijugate, -gous,** *a.* pinnate with four pairs of leaflets. [GEMINOUS, see GEMINI]

quadrilateral, *a.* having four sides and four angles. *n.* a quadrangular figure or area. **the Quadrilateral,** the district in N Italy defended by the fortresses of Mantua, Verona, Peschiera and Legnano. **quadrilaterality, quadrilateralness,** *n.* [L *quadrilaterus*]

quadrilingual, *a.* speaking or written in four languages. **quadriliteral,** *a.* consisting of four letters. *n.* a quadrilateral word, esp. a Semitic root containing four consonants. [LINGUAL]

quadrille, *n.* a dance consisting of five figures executed by four sets of couples; a piece of music for such a dance; a game of cards played by four persons with 40 cards, fashionable in the 18th cent. *v.i.* to dance a quadrille; to play music for a quadrille. [F, from Sp. *cuadrillo,* a squadron, a band, dim. of *cuadra,* square, as QUADRI-]

quadrillion, *n.* the number produced by raising a million to its fourth power, represented by 1 followed by 24 ciphers; (*N Am., F.*) the fifth power of 1000, 1 followed by 15 ciphers. [F (MILLION, cp. BILLION)]

quadrilobate, *a.* having four lobes.

quadrilocular, *a.* having four cells or chambers.

†**quadrimanous** QUADRUMANOUS.

quadrinomial, *a.* consisting of four terms. *n.* a quantity consisting of four algebraic terms.

quadripartite, *a.* divided into or consisting of four parts; affecting or shared by four parties. **quadripartitely,** *adv.* **quadripartition,** *n.* division by four or into four parts.

quadripennate, *a.* having four functional wings. *n.* a quadripennate insect.

quadriphyllous, *a.* having four leaves.

quadriplegia, *n.* paralysis of all four limbs. **quadriplegic,** *n., a.*

†**quadrireme,** *n.* (*Gr., Rom. Ant.*) a galley having four banks of oars. [L *quadrirēmis* (*rēmus,* oar)]

quadrisection, *n.* division into four equal parts.

quadrisyllabic, *a.* consisting of four syllables. **quadrisyllable,** *n.*

quadrivalent, *a.* having a valency or combining power of four. **quadrivalence,** *n.* **quadrivalency,** *n.*

quadrivalve, *n.* a plant with a quadrivalvular seed-pod; a door or shutter in four parts or leaves. *a.* quadrivalvular.

quadrivalvular, *a.* opening by four valves.

quadrivium, *n.* in the Middle Ages, an educational course consisting of arithmetic, music, geometry, and astronomy. †**quadrivial,** *a.* having four ways meeting in a point; pertaining to the quadrivium. *n.pl.* the sciences comprised in this. [L (*via,* way)]

quadroon, *n.* a person of quarter Negro and three-quarters white blood; applied to similarly proportioned hybrids in human, animal and vegetable stocks. [Sp. *cuarteron*]

Quadrumana, *n.pl.* an order of mammals in which the hind as well as the fore feet have an opposable digit and are used as hands, containing the monkeys, apes, baboons and lemurs. **quadrumane,** *n.* **quadrumanous,** *a.* [L *quadru-,* QUADRI,- *manus,* hand]

quadruped, *n.* a four-footed animal, esp. a mammal. *a.* having four legs and feet. **quadrupedal,** *a.* [L *quadrupes -pedis* (*quadru-,* QUADRI-, *pes pedis,* foot)]

quadruple, *a.* fourfold; consisting of four parts; involving four members, units etc.; multiplied by four; equal to four times the number or quantity of. *n.* a number or quantity four times as great as another; four times as much or as many. *v.i.* to become fourfold as much; to increase fourfold. *v.t.* to make four times as much; to multiply fourfold. **quadruplet,** *n.* a compound or combination of four things working together; a bicycle for four; (*pl.*) four children born of the same mother at one birth; four notes to be played in a time value of three. **quadruplex,** *a.* fourfold; used four times over (of a telegraphic wire). *n.* an electrical apparatus by means of which four messages may be sent simultaneously over one telegraphic wire. *v.t.* to arrange (a wire etc.) for quadruplex working. **quadruplicate,** *a.* fourfold; four times as many or as much; four times copied. *n.* one of four copies or similar things; quadruplicity. *v.t.*, to make fourfold, to quadruple. **quadruplication,** *n.* **quadruplicity,** *n.* **quadruply,** *adv.* [F, from L *quadruplus,* acc. *-plum* (*quadru-,* QUADRI-, *-plus,* fold)]

Quadruple Alliance, *n.* in European history, three military alliances of four nations: **the Quadruple Alliance 1718** of Austria, Britain, France, and the United Provinces (Netherlands), to prevent Spain from annexing Sardinia and Sicily; **the Quadruple Alliance 1813** of Austria, Britain, Prussia, and Russia, aimed at defeating the French emperor Napoleon; renewed 1815 and 1818. See CONGRESS OF VIENNA. **the Quadruple Alliance 1834** of Britain, France, Portugal, and Spain, guaranteeing the constitutional monarchies of Spain and Portugal against rebels in the Carlist War.

quadrupole, *n.* a system where the two dipoles are of equal length but opposing direction. **quadrupolar,** *a.*

quaere, *v.t.* ask, inquire, it is a question. *n.* a question, a query. **quaesitum,** *n.* (*pl.* **-ta**) a query. [L, imp. of *quaerere,* to ask, to INQUIRE]

quaestor, *n.* a magistrate having charge of public funds, a public treasurer, paymaster etc. **quaestorial,** *a.* **quaestorship,** *n.* [L, for *quaesītor,* from *quaerere,* see prec., p.p. *quaesitus*]

†**quaestuary,** *a.* seeking profit, studious of gain. *n.* one

employed to collect profits; a questor. [L *quaestuārius,* from *quaestus,* gain, as prec.]

quaff, *v.t.* to drink in large draughts. *v.i.* to drink copiously. *n.* a copious draught. **quaffer,** *n.* [etym. doubtful]

quag, *n.* a piece of marshy or boggy ground. **quagginess,** *n.* **quaggy,** *a.* **quagmire,** *n.* a quaking bog, a marsh, a slough. [onomat.]

quagga, *n.* a S African quadruped, *Equus quagga,* intermediate between the ass and the zebra, now extinct; Burchell's zebra, *Equus burchellii.* [prob. orig. Bantu, imit. of its cry]

quaggy, quagmire QUAG.

quahaug, quahog, *n.* the common round or hard clam, *Venus mercenaria,* of the Atlantic coast of N America. [Narraganset *poquauhock*]

quaich, quaigh, *n.* (*Sc.*) a shallow drinking-vessel, usu. of wood. [Gael. *cuach,* prob. from L *caucus,* Gr. *kauka*]

Quai d'Orsay, *n.* term for the French Foreign Office, from its location on the Quai d'Orsay, on the S bank of the Seine in Paris. [F]

quail[1], *v.i.* to shrink, to be cowed, to lose heart; to give way (before or to); †to wither, to decline, †to slacken. †*v.t.* to cast down, to cow, to daunt; to defeat, to conquer. [etym. doubtful]

quail[2], *n.* a small migratory bird of the genus *Coturnix,* allied to the partridge, esp. *C. coturnix;* one of various allied gallinaceous birds; †a courtesan. **quail-call,** *n.* **quail-hawk,** *n.* the New Zealand sparrow-hawk. **quail-pipe,** *n.* a whistle imitating the cry of the quail for enticing them to the net; †(*fig.*) the human throat. [OF *quaille* (F *caille*), prob. from Teut. (cp. Dut. *kwakkel,* OHG *quatala*), prob. of imit. orig.]

quaint, *a.* †wise, cunning, crafty; old-fashioned and odd, pleasing by virtue of strangeness, oddity or fancifulness; odd, whimsical, singular. **quaintish,** *a.* **quaintly,** *adv.* **quaintness,** *n.* [ME and OF *cointe,* L *cognitus,* acc. *-tum,* p.p. of *cognoscere,* to know, to learn]

†**quair** QUIRE[1].

quake, *v.i.* to shake, to tremble, to quiver, to rock, to vibrate. †*v.t.* to cause to quake. *n.* a tremulous motion, a shudder. **quaking,** *a.* trembling; unstable. **quaking ash,** *n.* the aspen. **quaking-grass,** *n.* grass of the genus *Briza,* the spikelets of which have a tremulous motion. **quaky,** *a.* **quakiness,** *n.* [OE *cwacian,* prob. of imit. orig., cp. QUAG]

Quaker, *n.* a member of the Society of Friends, founded by George Fox (1624–91). *a.* pertaining to Quakers or Quakerism. **quaker-bird,** *n.* the sooty albatross. **quaker-gun,** *n.* a wooden gun mounted to deceive the enemy. **Quakerdom,** *n.* **Quakeress,** *n. fem.* **Quakerish,** *a.* **Quakerism,** *n.* **Quakerly,** *a.* like a Quaker. [prec., -ER, orig. applied in derision, 1650]

qualify, *v.t.* to invest or furnish with the requisite qualities; to make competent, fit, or legally capable (to be or do, or for any action, place, office or occupation); to modify, to limit, to narrow the scope, force etc. of (a statement, opinion or word); to moderate, to mitigate, to temper; to reduce the strength or flavour of (spirit etc.) with water, to dilute; to attribute a quality to, to describe or characterize as; †to ease, to soothe. *v.i.* to become qualified or fit; to make oneself competent, suitable or eligible (for). **qualifiable, qualification,** *n.* the act of qualifying or the state of being qualified; modification, restriction or limitation of meaning, exception or partial negation restricting completeness or absoluteness; any natural or acquired quality fitting a person or thing (for an office, employment etc.); a condition that must be fulfiiled for the exercise of a privilege etc. **qualificative, -tory,** *n. a.* **qualified,** *a.* **qualifier,** *n.* **qualifying,** *n., a.* **qualifying round,** *n.* a preliminary round in a competition. **qualifyingly,** *adv.* [F *qualifier,* med. L *quālificāre* (L *quālis,* such, *-ficāre, facere,* to make)]

qualitative QUALITY.

quality, *n.* relative nature or kind, distinguishing character; a distinctive property or attribute, that which gives individuality; a mental or moral trait or characteristic; particular capacity, value, or function; particular efficacy, degree of excellence, relative goodness; the affirmative or negative nature of a proposition; that which distinguishes sounds of the same pitch and intensity, timbre; †an accomplishment. †**the quality,** persons of high rank, the upper classes. **quality control,** *n.* the testing of manufactured products to ensure they are up to standard. **qualitative,** *a.* of or pertaining to quality, opp. to quantitative. **qualitative analysis,** *n.* the detection of the constituents of a compound body. **qualitatively,** *adv.* **qualitied,** *a.* [F *qualité,* L *quālitas* acc. *-tātem,* from *quālis,* as prec]

qualm, *n.* a sensation of nausea, a feeling of sickness; a sensation of fear or uneasiness; a misgiving, a scruple, compunction. **qualmish,** *a.* **qualmishly,** *adv.* **qualmishness,** *n.* **qualmy,** *a.* [perh. from OE *cwealm,* pestilence; or rel. to G *Qualm,* vapour, dial. swoon, Dut. *kwalm,* Dan. *kvalm,* Swed. *qvalm,* vapour, closeness]

qualy, *n.* a method of measuring the quality of length of the life given to a patient and medical treatment, used to assess the cost-effectiveness of treatment, and to compare different, expensive, treatments. [acronym for *qu*ality-*a*djusted *l*ife *y*ear]

quamash, *n.* the bulb of a liliaceous plant, *Camassia esculenta,* eaten by various N American peoples. [N Am. Ind.]

quandary, *n.* a state of difficulty or perplexity; an awkward predicament, a dilemma. [etym. doubtful]

quandong, *n.* a small Australian tree, *Fusanus acuminatus,* with edible drupaceous fruit. [Austral. Abor.]

quango, *n.* a board set up by central government to supervise activity in a specific field, e.g. the Race Relations Board. [*acronym* for *qu*asi-*a*utonomous *n*on-governmental *o*rganization]

quant, *n.* a punting-pole with a flange at the end to prevent its sinking in the mud. *v.t.* to propel with this. *v.i.* to propel a boat with this. [perh. from L *contus,* Gr. *kontos*]

Quant, *n.* **Mary** (1934–), British fashion designer. Her Chelsea boutique, Bazaar, achieved a revolution in women's clothing and make-up, which epitomized the 'swinging London' of the 1960s.

quantic, *n.* a rational integrally homogeneous function of two or more variables. **quantical,** *a.* [L *quantus,* how much]

quantify, *v.t.* to determine the quantity of, to measure as to quantity; to express the quantity of; to define the application of as regards quantity. **quantifiable,** *a.* **quantification,** *n.* **quantifier,** *n.* that which indicates quantity. [med. L *quantificāre* (*quantus,* as prec., *-ficāre, facere,* to make)]

quantitative, quantitive, *a.* pertaining to or concerned with quantity, opp. to *qualitative;* relating to or based on the quantity of vowels (as accent, verse etc.). **quantitative analysis,** the determination of the amounts and proportions of the constituents of a compound body. **quantitatively, quantitively,** *adv* [QUANTITY]

quantity, *n.* that property in virtue of which anything may be measured; extent, measure, size, greatness, volume, amount or number; a sum, a number; a certain or a large number, amount or portion; (*pl.*) large quantities, abundance; the duration of a syllable; the extent to which a predicate is asserted of the subject of a proposition; a thing having such relations, of number or extension, as can be expressed by symbols, a symbol representing this; †a small part, an insignificant thing; †proportion. **unknown quantity,** a person, thing or number whose importance or value is unknown. **quantity-mark,** *n.* a mark placed over a vowel to indicate quantity. **quantity-surveyor,** *n.* one employed to estimate the quantities of materials used in erecting a building. [OF *quantité,* L *quantitas,* from *quantus,* as prec.]

quantivalence, *n.* valency. **quantivalent,** *a.* [L *quanti-, quantus,* how much, *-valence,* as in EQUIVALENCE]

quantize, -ise, *v.t.* to restrict or limit to a set of fixed values; to express in terms of quantum theory. **quantization, -isation,** *n.* [etym. doubtful, perh. from *quantus*]

Quantrill, *n.* **William Clarke** (1837–65), US criminal, who became leader of a guerrilla unit on the Confederate side in the Civil War. Frank and Jesse James were among his aides.

quantum, *n.* (*pl.* **-ta**) a quantity, an amount; a portion, a proportion, a share; an amount required, allowed or sufficient. **quantum sufficit,** a sufficient amount (usu. **quant. suf.** in prescriptions). **quantum jump, leap,** *n.* (*coll.*) a sudden transition; unexpected and spectacular progress. **quantum mechanics,** *n.sing.* a branch of mechanics based on quantum theory, applied to elementary particles and atoms which do not behave according to Newtonian mechanics. **quantum mechanical,** *a.* **quantum mechanically,** *adv.* **quantum number,** *n.* a set of integers or half-integers which serve to describe the energy states of a particle or system of particles. **quantum theory,** *n.* the theory that energy transferences occur in bursts of a minimum quantity. [L, neut. of *quantus,* how much, so much]

quaquaversal, *a.* pointing in every direction; inclined outwards and downwards in all directions (of dip). **quaquaversally,** *adv.* [late L *quāquāversus* (*quāquā,* whithersoever, *versus,* towards)]

quarantine, *n.* the prescribed period of isolation (usu. 40 days) imposed on persons or ships coming from places infected with contagious disease; the enforced isolation of such persons, ships, goods etc. or of persons or houses so infected; a place where quarantine is enforced; †any period of 40 days, esp. the period of 40 days during which a widow was entitled to remain in the mansion-house of her deceased husband. *v.t.* to isolate or put in quarantine. **quarantine flag,** *n.* the yellow flag flown from ships to show infectious disease aboard. [from OF *quarantine* (F *quarantaine*), or from It. *quarantina,* from *quaranta,* L. *quadrāginta,* 40, see QUADRAGENARIAN]

quarant' ore, *n.* in the Roman Catholic Church, 40 hours' exposition of the blessed Sacrament. [It., 40 hours]

quarenden, -der, *n.* a large red variety of apple, common in Devon and Somerset. [etym. doubtful]

quark, *n.* any of several hypothetical particles thought to be the fundamental units of other subatomic particles. [From a word coined by James Joyce in *Finnegan's Wake*, 1939]

quarl1, *n.* a curved segment of fire-clay or fire-brick used to make a support for melting-pots, retort-covers etc. [var. of QUARREL1]

quarl2, *n.* a jelly-fish or medusa. [prob. rel. to G *Qualle,* Dut. *kwal*]

quarrel1, *n.* a short, heavy bolt or arrow with a square head, formerly used for shooting from cross-bows or arbalests; †a square or diamond-shaped pane of glass used in lattice-windows. [ME and OF *quarel* (F *carreau*), It. *quadrello,* dim. of *quadro,* med. L *quadrus,* square, cp. QUADREL]

quarrel2, *n.* a falling-out or breach of friendship; a noisy or violent contention or dispute, an altercation, a brawl, a petty fight; a ground or cause of complaint or dispute, a reason for strife or contention. *v.i.* (*past, p.p,* **quarrelled**) to fall out, to break off friendly relations (with); to dispute violently, to wrangle, to squabble; to cavil, to take exception, to find fault (with); (*fig.*) to be at variance, to be discordant or incongruous (of colours or other qualities etc.). †*v.t.* to dispute, to call in question, to find fault with. **quarreller,** *n.* **quarrelling,** *a.* †**quarrellous, quarrelsome**, *a.* inclined or apt to quarrel, contentious; irascible, choleric, easily provoked. **quarrelsomely,** *adv.* **quarrelsomeness,** *n.* [ME and OF *querele,* L *querēla,* complaint, from *querī,* to complain]

quarrian, -rrion, *n.* a cockatiel found in inland Australia. [Austral. Abor.]

quarry1, *n.* a place whence building-stone, slates etc. are dug, cut, blasted etc; (*fig.*) a source whence information is extracted. *v.t.* to dig or take from or as from a quarry. **quarryman, -woman,** *n.* a person employed in a quarry. **quarrymaster,** *n.* the owner of a quarry. **quarriable,** *a.* **quarrier,** *n.* [med. L *quareia, quareria, quadrāria,* from L. *quadrāre,* to square, as QUADRATE]

quarry2, *n.* †a part of the entrails etc. of a deer placed on a skin and given to the hounds; any animal pursued by hounds, hunters, a bird of prey etc.; game, prey; (*fig.*) any object of pursuit. †*v.i.* to prey or feed (as a vulture or hawk). †*v.t.* to hunt down. [ME *quirre,* OF *cuirée,* from *cuir,* L *corium,* skin]

quarry3, *n.* a square or diamond-shaped pane of glass, a quarrel; a square stone or tile. *v.t.* to glaze with quarries; to pave with quarries. **quarry-tile,** *n.* an unglazed floor tile. [later form of QUARREL1]

quart1, *n.* a measure of capacity, the fourth part of a gallon, two pints (1·136 l); a measure, bottle or other vessel containing such quantity; (*coll.*) a quart of beer. [F *quarte,* fem. of *quart,* L *quarta,* fem. of *quartus,* fourth]

quart2, *n.* a sequence of four cards in piquet etc.

quartan, *a.* occurring or recurring every fourth day. *n.* quartan ague or fever. **quartan ague, fever,** one recurring every third or, inclusively, every fourth day. [F *quartaine,* L *quartāna* (*febris*), fem. of *quartānus,* fourth, from *quartus,* see QUART1]

quartation, *n.* the addition of silver, usu. in the proportion of 3:1, in the process of separating gold from its impurities by means of nitric acid. [L *quartus,* fourth]

quarte CARTE2.

quarter, *n.* a fourth part, one of four equal parts; the fourth part of a year, three calendar months; the fourth part of a cwt. (28 lb., 12·7 kg); a grain measure of 8 bushels (2·91 hl); the fourth of a fathom; the fourth part of a dollar, 25 cents; one of four parts, each comprising a limb, into which the carcase of an animal or bird may be divided; (*pl.*) the similar parts into which the body of a criminal or traitor was formerly divided after execution; a haunch; one of the divisions of a shield when this is divided by horizontal and perpendicular lines meeting in the fesse point; either side of a ship between the main chains and the stern; the fourth part of a period of the moon; one of the four phases of increase or decrease of the moon's face during a lunation; a point of time 15 minutes before or after the hour; one of the four chief points of the compass; one of the main divisions of the globe corresponding to this; a particular direction, region, or locality; place of origin or supply, source; a division of a town, esp. one assigned to or occupied by a particular class; (*usu. in pl.*) allotted position, proper place or station, esp. for troops; (*pl.*) place of lodging or abode, esp. a station or encampment occupied by troops; (*pl.*) appointed stations of a crew at exercise or in action; exception from death allowed in war to a surrendered enemy; mercy, clemency; †friendship, peace, concord. *v.t.* to divide into four equal parts; to cut the body of (a traitor) into quarters; to bear or arrange (charges or coats of arms) quarterly on a shield etc., to add (other arms) to those of one's family, to divide (a shield) into quarters by vertical and horizontal lines; to put into quarters, to assign quarters to, to provide (esp. soldiers) with lodgings and food; to range over (a field) in all directions (of a hound). †*v.i.* to be stationed or lodged; to range in search of game; of the wind, to blow on a ship's quarter. **at close quarters,** close at hand. **quarter of an hour,** a period of 15 minutes. **a bad quarter of an hour,** a short disagreeable experience. **quarter-back,** *n.* a player in American football who directs the attacking play of his team. **quarter-bell,** *n.* a bell sounding the quarter-hours. **quarter-bill,** *n.* (*Nav.*) a list of the stations, posts and duties of a vessel, with names of officers and men. **quarter-binding,** *n.* leather or cloth on the back only of a book, with none at the corners. **quarter-bound,** *a.* **quarter-boy,** *n.* an automaton used for striking the quarter-hours. **quarter-bred,** *a.* having one-fourth pure blood (of horses or cattle). **quarter-butt,** *n.* (*Billiards*) a long cue, shorter than a half-butt.

quarter-day, *n.* the day beginning each quarter of the year (Lady Day, 25 Mar., Midsummer Day, 24 June, Michaelmas Day, 29 Sept. and Christmas Day, 25 Dec.) on which tenancies etc. begin and end, payments are due etc. **quarter-deck,** *n.* the upper deck extending from the stern to the mainmast, usu. assigned for the use of officers and cabin passengers. **quarter-final,** *n.* the round before the semi-final, in a knockout competition. **quarter-finalist,** *n.* **quarterfoil** QUATREFOIL. **quarter-horse,** *n.* (*N Am.*) a horse capable of running short distances at great speed. **quarter-hour,** *n.* a quarter of an hour; the point of time 15, 30 or 45 minutes before or after the hour. **quarter-hourly,** *adv.* **quarter-jack** QUARTER-BOY. **quarter light,** *n.* the small window in the front door of a car, often for ventilation. **quarter-line,** *n.* a position of ships such that the bow of one is abaft the beam of the one in front; a line fastened to the lower edge of a seine net to help in hauling it in. **quartermaster,** *n.* a regimental officer appointed to provide and assign quarters, lay out camps, and issue rations, clothing, ammunition etc.; a petty officer, having charge of the steering, signals, stowage etc. **quartermaster-general,** *n.* a staff-officer in charge of the department dealing with quartering, encamping, moving, or embarking troops. **quartermaster-sergeant,** *n.* a sergeant assisting the quartermaster. **quarter-miler,** *n.* an athlete who specializes in the quarter-mile race. **quarter note,** *n.* (*N Am.*) a crotchet. **quarter-plate,** *n.* a photographic plate measuring $4\frac{1}{4} \times 3\frac{1}{4}$ in. ($10{\cdot}8 \times 8{\cdot}3$ cm); a picture produced from this. **quarter-round,** *n.* a convex moulding having the contour of a quarter-circle, an ovolo, an echinus. **quarter-sessions,** *n.pl.* a general court of limited criminal and civil jurisdiction held by the Justices of the Peace in every county (and in boroughs where there is a Recorder). **quarter-staff,** *n.* an iron-shod pole about $6\frac{1}{2}$ ft. (2 m) long, formerly used as a weapon of offence or defence, usu. grasped by one hand in the middle and by the other between the middle and one end. **quarter-tone,** *n.* an interval of half a semitone. **quarterage,** *n.* a quarterly payment, wages, allowance etc. **quartered,** *a.* **quartering,** *n.* a dividing into quarters or fourth parts; the assignment of quarters or lodgings; a length of square-section timber with side from 2 to 6 in. (5 to 15 cm); the grouping of several coats of arms on a shield; one of the coats so quartered. **quarterly,** *a.* containing a quarter; occurring or done every quarter of a year. *adv.* once in each quarter of the year; in quarters, arranged in the four quarters of the shield. *n.* a periodical published every quarter. [OF, from L *quartārius,* a fourth part, from *quartus,* fourth]

quartern, *n.* a quarter or fourth part of various measures, esp. of a loaf; a pint, peck or pound. **quartern-loaf,** *n.* a loaf of the weight of 4 lb. (1·8 kg). [OF *quarteron,* from *quarte,* fourth]

quarteroon QUADROON.

quartet, quartette, *n.* a musical composition for four voices or four instruments; a group or set of four similar things. [F *quartette,* It. *quartetto,* from *quarto,* L *quartus,* fourth]

quartic, *a.* pertaining to the fourth degree; *n.* a curve of the fourth degree. [L *quartus,* fourth]

quartile, *a.* denoting the aspect of two heavenly bodies when distant from each other a quarter of a circle. *n.* a quartile aspect; a quarter of the individuals studied in a statistical survey, whose characteristics lie within stated limits. [med. L *quartīlis,* from L *quartus,* fourth]

quarto, *n.* a size obtained by folding a sheet twice, making four leaves or eight pages (usu. written 4to); a book, pamphlet etc., having pages of this size. *a.* having the sheet folded into four leaves. [L *in quarto* (abl. of *quartus,* fourth), in a fourth part]

quartz, *n.* a mineral consisting of pure silica or silicon dioxide, either massive or crystallizing hexagonally. **quartz clock,** *n.* a synchronous electric clock of high accuracy in which the alternating current frequency is determined by the mechanical resonance of a quartz crystal. The mechanical strain of the crystal is translated into an electrical signal by the piezoelectric effect. **quartz crystal,** *n.* a piece of piezoelectric quartz cut and ground so that it vibrates at a natural frequency. **quartz glass,** *n.* glass made of almost pure silica, transparent to ultraviolet radiation and resistant to high temperatures. **quartz iodine lamp,** *n.* a light source, based on iodine vapour, used for high-intensity lighting in car-lamps and cine projectors. **quartziferous,** *a.* **quartzite,** *n.* a massive or schistose metamorphic rock consisting of sandstone with a deposition of quartz about each grain. **quartzitic,** *a.* **quartzose, quartzy,** *a.* [G *Quarz,* etym. unknown]

quas KVASS.

quasar, *n.* any of a group of unusually bright, star-like objects outside our galaxy, with large red-shifts. They are a powerful source of radio waves and other energy sources. [from *qua*si-*s*tellar *r*adio source]

quash, *v.t.* to anul or make void; to put an end to, esp. by legal procedure; to suppress, to extinguish; †to crush, to dash, to quell. [OF *quasser,* L *quassāre*]

Quashie, *n.* (*offensive*) a Negro, a black, a simple-minded one. [Ashanti *Kwasi,* boy born on Sunday]

quasi, *conj.* as if. **quasi-,** *comb. form* apparent, seeming, not real; practical, half, not quite. **quasi-crime,** *n.* **quasi-historical, quasi-public, quasi-sovereign,** *a.* **quasi-stellar object,** *n.* any of various classes of very distant celestial bodies, including quasars. [L, as if]

Quasimodo[1], *n.* the first Sunday after Easter. [from first words of the introit for that day. L *quasi modo geniti infantes,* as new-born babes]

Quasimodo[2], *n.* a grotesque, hunch-backed character in Victor Hugo's novel *Notre Dame de Paris* (1831).

Quasimodo[3], *n.* **Salvatore** (1901–68), Italian poet. His first book *Acque e terre/Waters and Land* appeared in 1930. Later books, including *Nuove poesie/New Poetry* (1942), and *Il falso e vero verde/The False and True Green* (1956), reflect a growing preoccupation with contemporary political and social problems. Nobel Prize 1959.

†**quassation,** *n.* the act of shaking; concussion; the state of being shaken. †**quassative,** *a.* [L *quassātio -tiōnem,* from *quassāre,* to QUASH]

Quassia, *n.* a genus of S American and W Indian (esp. Surinam) trees, the bitter wood, bark and oil of which yield a tonic. **quassic,** *a.* **quassin,** *n.* the bitter principle of quassia. [named by Linnaeus after *Quassi* (QUASHIE), a W African slave who discovered its curative properties]

†**quat,** *n.* a pustule, a pimple; (*fig.*) a diminutive or insignificant person. [etym. unknown]

†**quatch,** *a.* (*Shak.*) squat, flat (?). [etym. unknown]

quater-centenary, *n.* a 400th anniversary. **quater-centennial,** *n., a.* [L *quater,* four times, CENTENARY]

quater-cousin CATER-COUSIN.

quaterfoil QUATREFOIL.

quaternary, *a.* consisting of four, having four parts, esp. composed of four elements or radicals arranged in fours; fourth in order; (**Quaternary**) pertaining to the Quaternary or the most recent strata of rock. *n.* a set of four; the number four; (**Quaternary**) the period of geological time that began 1.8 million years ago and is still in process. It is divided into the Pleistocene and Holocene epochs. †**quatern,** *a.* quaternal, quaternate, fourfold, arranged in or composed of four or fours. **quaternity,** *n.* a set of four. [L *quaternārius,* from *quaternī,* four at a time, distrib. of *quater,* four times]

quaternion, *n.* a set, group or system of four; a quire of four sheets once folded; an operator that changes one vector into another, so called as depending upon four irreducible geometrical elements; (*pl.*) the form of the calculus of vectors employing this. *v.t.* to divide into or arrange in quaternions, files or companies.

quatorzain, *n.* a poem or stanza of 14 lines, esp. a sonnet of an irregular form. †**quatorze,** *n.* a set of four aces, kings, queens, knaves or tens. [F *quatorzaine,* from *quatorze,* L *quātuordecim* (*quator,* four, *decem,* ten), 14]

quatrain, *n.* a stanza of four lines, usu. rhyming alternately. [F, from *quatre,* L *quātuor,* four]

quatre CATER².

Quatre Bras, Battle of, a battle fought on 16 June 1815 during the Napoleonic Wars, in which the British commander Wellington defeated French forces under Marshal Ney. It is named after a hamlet in Brabant, Belgium, 32 km/20 miles SE of Brussels.

quatrefoil, quaterfoil, *n.* an opening, panel or other figure in ornamental tracery, divided by cusps into four foils; a leaf or flower composed of four divisions or lobes. [OF *quatre,* L *quātuor,* four, FOIL¹]

Quattrocento, *n.* the 15th cent., regarded as a distinctive period in Italian art and literature. **quattrocentism,** *n.* **quattrocentist,** *n.* [It., lit. 400 (L *quātuor,* four, *centum,* hundred), usu. 1400]

quaver, *v.i.* to quiver, to tremble, to vibrate; to sing or play with tremulous modulations or trills. *v.t.* to sing or utter with a tremulous sound. *n.* a shake or rapid vibration of the voice, a trill; a quiver or shakiness in speaking; a note equal in duration to half a crotchet or one-eighth of a semibreve. **quaverer,** *n.* **quavering,** *a.* **quaveringly,** *adv.* **quavery,** *a.* [freq. of obs. *quave,* ME *quaven,* rel. to QUAKE]

quay, *n.* a landing-place or wharf, usu. of masonry and stretching along the side of or projecting into a harbour, for loading or unloading ships. *v.t.* to furnish with a quay or quays. **quayage,** *n.* a system of quays; a charge imposed for the use of a quay. **quayside,** *n.* the edge of a quay. [ME *key,* A-F *kaie,* OF *kay* (F *quai*), prob. Celt. (cp. W *cae,* Bret. *kaé,* hedge, enclosure)]

Quayle, *n.* **(J.) Dan(forth)** (1947–), US Republican politician, an Indiana congressman from 1977, senator from 1981, vice president from 1989.

quean, *n.* a slut, a hussy, a jade, a strumpet; (*Sc.*) a young or unmarried woman, a lass. [OE *cwene,* woman (cp. Dut. *kween,* barren cow, OHG *quena,* Gr. *gunē,* woman, Eng. QUEEN)]

queasy, *a.* sick at the stomach, affected with nausea; causing or tending to cause nausea; unsettling the stomach; easily nauseated; (*fig.*) fastidious, squeamish. **queasily,** *adv.* **queasiness,** *n.* [formerly *queisy, coisy,* perh. from OF *coisié, p.p. of coisir,* to hurt]

Québec¹, *n.* capital and industrial port (textiles, leather, timber, paper, printing and publishing) of Québec province, on the St Lawrence river, Canada; population (1986) 165,000, metropolitan area 603,000. It was founded in 1608.

Québec², *n.* province of E Canada. **area** 1,540,700 sq km/594,710 sq miles. **capital** Québec. **towns** Montreal, Laval, Sherbrooke, Verdun, Hull, Trois-Rivières. **products** iron, copper, gold, zinc, cereals, potatoes, paper, textiles, fish, maple syrup (70% of world's output). **population** (1986) 6,540,000. **language** French is the only official language since 1974, although 17% speak English. Language laws 1989 prohibit the use of English on street signs.

Québec Conference, *n.* two conferences of Allied leaders in the city of Québec during World War II. The first conference (1943) approved the British admiral Mountbatten as supreme Allied commander in SE Asia and made plans for the invasion of France. The second conference (Sept. 1944) adopted plans for intensified air attacks on Germany, created a unified strategy against Japan, and established a postwar policy for a defeated Germany.

Québecker, Québecer, *n.* a native or inhabitant of Québec. **Québecois,** *n.* a French-speaking inhabitant of Québec.

quebracho, *n.* one of several N American trees producing a medicinal bark, used esp. in cases of fever. [Sp., contr. of *quebrahacha* (*quebrar,* to break, *hacha,* axe)]

Quechua, *n.* a member of any of various groups of South American Indian peoples, including the Incas; their language, the second official language of Peru. **Quechuan,** *a.* [Sp. Quechua, Quichua]

queen, *n.* the wife of a king; a queen-dowager; a female sovereign of a kingdom; a court-card bearing a conventional figure of a queen; the most powerful piece in chess; a queen-bee; (*fig.*) a woman of majestic presence; one masquerading as a sovereign or presiding at some festivity; a city, nation or other thing regarded as the supreme example of its class; a female cat; (*sl., derog.*) an effeminate male homosexual, often an aging one. *v.t.* to make (a woman) queen; (*Chess*) to make (a pawn) into a queen. *v.i.* to act the queen; to act in a superior or arrogant way; to become a queen. **Queen Anne is dead,** stale news. **Queen Anne's bounty** BOUNTY. **Queen Anne's lace,** the wild carrot. **Queen Anne** *or* **Anne's style,** the architectural style prevalent in the reign of Queen Anne (*c.* 1700–20), characterized by plain and unpretentious design with classic details; also applied to a style of decorative art typified by Chippendale furniture. **queen-apple,** *n.* a variety of apple. **queen-bee,** *n.* a fully-developed female bee; a woman in a dominating position, socially or in business. **queen-cake,** *n.* a small, soft, usu. heart-shaped currant cake. **queen-consort** CONSORT¹. **queen-dowager,** *n.* the widow of a king. **queen-mother,** *n.* a queen-dowager who is also the mother of the reigning sovereign. **queen olive,** *n.* a type of large, fleshy olive which can be used for pickling. **queen-post** *n.* one of two suspending or supporting posts between the tie-beam and rafters in a roof. **Queen regent,** *n.* a queen who reigns as regent. **Queen regnant,** *n.* a reigning queen. **Queen's Bench** BENCH. **Queen's Counsel** COUNSEL. **Queen's English,** *n.* southern British English when taken as the standard. **Queen's flight,** a unit of the RAF reserved for the use of the royal family, established as King's Flight in 1936. **Queen's Guide, Scout,** *n.* a guide or scout who has passed the highest tests of proficiency and ability. **queen's-metal,** *n.* an alloy of tin, antimony, lead and bismuth. **queen substance,** *n.* a secretion of the queen bee fed to worker bees to stop the development of their ovaries. **queen truss,** *n.* a truss in a roof, framed with queen posts. **queen's-ware,** *n.* glazed Wedgewood earthenware of a creamy colour. **queencraft,** *n.* **queendom, queenhood, queenship,** *n.* **queening,** *n.* a queen-apple. **queenless, queenlike, queenly,** *a.* **queenliness,** *n.* [OE *cwēn,* cogn. with QUEAN]

Queen Maud Land, *n.* a region of Antarctica W of Enderby Land, claimed by Norway since 1939.

Queens, *n.* a borough and county at the W end of Long Island, New York City, US; population (1980) 1,891,300.

Queensberry, *n.* **John Sholto Douglas, 8th Marquess of Queensberry** (1844–1900), British patron of boxing. In 1867 he formulated the **Queensberry Rules** which form the basis of modern-day boxing rules.

Queensland, *n.* state in NE Australia, part of New South Wales until 1859, then self-governing. **area** 1,727,200 sq km/666,699 sq miles. **capital** Brisbane. **towns** Gold Coast-Tweed, Townsville, Sunshine Coast, Toowoomba, Cairns. **exports** sugar, pineapples, beef, cotton, wool, tobacco, copper, gold, silver, lead, zinc, coal, nickel, bauxite, uranium, natural gas. **population** (1987) 2,650,000. **Queensland nut,** *n.* a proteaceous tree of Queensland and New South Wales; its edible nut. **Queensland sore,** *n.* a festering sore.

queer, *a.* strange, odd; singular, droll; curious, questionable, suspicious; out of sorts; unfavourable; (*coll.*) in a bad way, in trouble or disgrace; (*coll., perh. another word*) bad, worthless, counterfeit. *n., a.* (*sl., derog.*) homosexual. *v.t.* (*coll.*) to spoil, to put out of order. **in Queer Street,** (*coll.*) in trouble, esp. financial; off colour; under a cloud. **to queer one's pitch,** to spoil one's chances. **queer fish,** *n.* (*coll.*) a strange person. **queerish,** *a.* **queerly,** *adv.* **queerness,** *n.* [prob. from LG, cp. G *quer,* crosswise]

quell, *v.t.* to suppress, to put down, to subdue; to crush; to cause to subside; to calm, to allay, to quiet; †to kill. †*v.i.* to be abated. †*n.* slaughter, murder; power or means of quelling or subduing, a weapon. **queller,** *n.* [OE *cwellan,* to kill (cp. Dut. *kwellen,* G *kwälen*)]

quench, *v.t.* to extinguish, to put out, esp. with water; to cool (heat or a heated thing) with water; to allay, to slake; to suppress, to subdue. †*v.i.* to be extinguished.

quenchable, *a.* **quencher,** *n.* one who or that which quenches; (*coll.*) a draught that allays thirst. **quenching,** *a.* **quenchless**, *a.* that cannot be quenched; inextinguishable. **quenchlessly,** *adv.* **quenchlessness,** *n.* [OE *cwencan,* found in *acwencan,* causal of *cwincan,* to go out (cp. Fris. *kwinka*)]

quenelle, *n.* a ball of savoury paste made of meat or fish, usu. served as an entrée. [F, etym. doubtful]

quercitron, *n.* The N American black or dyer's oak, *Quercus tinctoria;* the bark of this, or a yellow dye made from it. **quercitin**, *n.* a yellow crystalline substance obtained from quercitrin etc. **quercitrin**, *n.* the yellow crystalline colouring-matter contained in the bark of *Q. tinctoria*. [L *querci-, quercus,* oak, CITRON]

quercus, *n.* a genus of trees containing the oaks, most of the species valuable for their timber. **quercetum**, *n.* a collection of living oaks, an arboretum of oak-trees. [L]

†**querent**[1], *n.* one who inquires, esp. of an astrologer etc. [L *quaerens -ntem,* pres.p. of *quaerere,* see QUAERE]

querent[2], *n.* a complainant, a plaintiff, *a.* complaining. [L *querens -ntem,* pres.p. of *querī,* to complain]

querimonious, *a.* complaining, querulous, discontented. **querimoniously,** *adv.* **querimoniousness,** *n.* [late L *queri-mōniōsus,* from L *querimōnia,* from *querī*, to complain]

querist, *n.* one who asks questions, an inquirer. [L *quaerere,* see QUAERE]

querl, *n.* a twirl, a curl, a twist, a coil. *v.t.* to twirl, to turn or wind round, to coil.

quern, *n.* a simple hand-mill for grinding corn, usu. consisting of two stones resting one on the other; a small hand-mill for grinding spices. **quernstone,** *n.* [OE *cweorn* (cp. Dut. *kweern,* Icel. *kvern*)]

querquedule, *n.* a pin-tail duck; any species of *Querquedula,* a genus of ducks containing the teals. [L *querquedula*]

querulous, *a.* complaining; discontented, peevish, fretful; of the nature of complaint; †quarrelsome. **querulously,** *adv.* **querulousness,** *n.* [late L *querulōsus,* L *querulus,* from *querī*, to complain]

query, *n.* a question (often used absolutely as preface to a question); a point or objection to be answered; a mark of interrogation (?). *v.i.* to put a question; to express a doubt or question. *v.t.* to question, to call in question; to express doubt concerning; to mark with a query. **querying,** *n., a.* **queryingly,** *adv.* [var. of QUAERE]

quesadilla, *n.* a tortilla filled, fried and topped with cheese. [Sp.]

quest, *n.* the act of seeking, a search; an expedition or venture in search or pursuit of some object, esp. in the days of chivalry; the object of such an enterprise; an official inquiry; a jury or inquest. *v.t.* to seek for or after. *v.i.* to make quest or search; to go (about) in search of something. **quester**, *n.* **questful,** *a.* **questing,** *a.* **questingly,** *adv.* [OF *queste* (F *quête*), pop. L *questa,* L *quaesīta,* p.p. of *quaerere,* to seek]

question, *n.* the act of asking or inquiring, interrogation, inquiry; a sentence requiring an answer, an interrogative sentence; a subject for inquiry, a problem requiring solution; a subject under discussion; a proposition or subject to be debated and voted on, esp. in a deliberative assembly; a subject of dispute, a difference, doubt, uncertainty, objection; †examination under torture. *v.t.* to ask a question or questions of, to interrogate, to examine by asking questions; to study (phenomena etc.) with a view to acquiring information; to call in question, to treat as doubtful or unreliable, to raise objections to. *v.i.* to ask a question or questions; to doubt, to be uncertain. **a burning question,** a subject causing intense interest. **beyond all, past question,** undoubtedly, unquestionably. **indirect, oblique question,** one expressed in a dependent clause. **in question,** referred to, under discussion, **leading question**. LEAD[2]. **open question,** a question that remains in doubt or unsettled. †**out of question,** doubtless. **out of the question,** not worth discussing, impossible. **previous question** PREVIOUS. **question!** an exclamation recalling a speaker who is wandering from the subject, or expressing incredulity. **to beg the question** BEG. **to call in question** CALL[1]. **to pop the question** POP[1]. **to put the question,** to put to the vote, to divide the meeting or House upon. **question-mark, -stop,** *n.* a mark of interrogation. **question master,** *n.* a person who puts questions, e.g. the person who asks the questions in a quiz or game. **question time,** *n.* time set aside each day in Parliament where ordinary members may question ministers. **questionable,** *a.* open to doubt or suspicion; disputable; †capable of being questioned. **questionability**, **questionableness,** *n.* **questionably,** *adv.* **questionary,** *a.* questioning, inquiring. *n.* a series of questions for the compilation of statistics, etc; †a questor, an intinerant pedlar of indulgences or relics. **questioner, -ist,** *n.* **questioningly,** *adv.* **questionless,**, *adv.* beyond all question or doubt. **questionnaire,** *n.* a series of questions designed to collect information. [OF, from L *quaestio* acc. *-ōnem,* as prec.]

questor[1], *n.* a pardoner; a treasurer of the French National Assembly; an Italian commissary of police. [med. L, as QUAESTOR]

questor[2], etc. QUAESTOR.

Quetelet, *n.* **Lambert Adolphe Jacques** (1796–1874), Belgian statistician, a pioneer of modern statistical methods. He developed tests for the validity of statistical information, and gathered statistical data of many kinds. From his work on sociological data comes the concept of the 'average person'.

quetzal, *n.* a brilliant Guatemalan trogon, *Pheromacrus mocinno*. [Sp., from Nahuatl *quetzalli*]

Quetzalcoatl, *n.* feathered serpent god of air and water in the pre-Columbian Aztec and Toltec cultures of Central America. In legendary human form, he was said to have been fair-skinned and bearded, and to have reigned on Earth during a golden age. He disappeared across the sea, with a promise to return.

queue, *n.* a plaited tail hanging at the back of the head, either of the natural hair or a wig, a pigtail; a file of persons, vehicles etc. waiting their turn. *v.t.* to dress (the hair etc.) in a queue. *v.i.* to form into a waiting queue. **queue-jumping,** *n.* going to the beginning of the queue instead of to the end. **queue-jumper,** *n.* [F, from L *cauda,* tail]

quey, *n.* (*Sc., North.*) a young cow that has not yet had a calf, a heifer. [from Icel. *kvīga,* prob. cogn, with COW[1])]

queyn, quine, *n.* (*Sc. dial.*) a girl. [QUEAN]

†**quhilk,** (*Sc.*) WHICH.

Quezon City, *n.* former capital of the Philippines 1948–76, NE part of metropolitan Manila, on Luzon Island; population (1980) 1,166,000. It was named after the Philippines' first president, Manuel Luis Quezon (1878–1944).

†**quib** QUIP.

quibble, *n.* an evasion of the point, an equivocation; a trivial or sophistical argument or distinction, esp. one exploiting a verbal ambiguity; a play upon words; a pun. *v.i.* to evade the point in question; to employ quibbles; to pun. **quibbler,** *n.* **quibbling,** *a.* **quibblingly,** *adv.* [prob. freq. of obs. *quip,* L *quibus,* dat. of *quī*, who, which]

quiche, *n.* a savoury pastry shell filled with egg custard, and usually cheese, bacon, onion or other vegetables. [Fr. from G *Kuche,* cake]

quick, *a.* alive, living; pregnant, with child, esp. when movement is perceptible; lively, vigorous, ready, alert, acutely sensitive or responsive, prompt to feel or act, intelligent; irritable, hasty; rash, precipitate; rapid in movement, acting swiftly, swift, nimble; done or happening in a short time, speedy, expeditious; quickset; †sharp, caustic (of words spoken); †keen, bracing. *adv.* in a short space, at a rapid rate; quickly. *n.* living persons; living flesh, esp. the sensitive flesh under the nails; (*fig.*) the feelings, the seat of the feelings. *v.t., v.i.* to quicken. **the quick and the dead,** the living and the dead. **to be quick on the draw,** to be a fast shooter. **to have a quick one,** (*coll.*) to have a quick (alcoholic) drink. **quick-answered,** *a.* quick in reply. **quickbeam,** *n.* the quicken, *Pyrus aucuparia,* or mountain-ash or rowan. **quick-change,** *a.* making rapid changes of costume or appearance (of actors etc.). **quick-change artist,** *n.* a performer who executes quick changes; someone who frequently changes their opinions. **quick-eared,** *a.* having acute hearing; quick to hear. **quick-eyed,** *a.* having sharp sight. **quick-fence,** *n.* a fence of growing shrubs (as opp. to palings). **quick-firer,** *n.* a gun with a mechanism for firing shots in rapid succession. **quick-firing,** *a.* **quick-freeze,** *n.* very rapid freezing to retain the natural qualities of food; a receptacle in which such food is kept frozen. **quick march,** *n.* a march in quick time; the music for such a march. **quick-match,** *n.* quick-burning match for firing cannon etc. usu. made of cotton wick soaked in a mixture of alcohol, salt-petre etc. **quick-sighted,** *a.* having acute sight; quick to see or understand. **quick-sightedness,** *n.* **quick step,** *n.* the step used in marching at quick time; a fast foxtrot. **quick-tempered,** *a.* easily irritated, irascible. **quick-thorn,** *n.* the hawthorn, esp. when planted as a hedge. **quick time,** *n.* the ordinary rate of marching in the British Army, usu. reckoned at 128 paces of 33 in. to the minute or 4 miles an hour. **quick-trick,** *n.* a card that should win a trick during the opening rounds of play. **quick-witted,** *a.* having a keen and alert mind; having a ready wit. **quick-wittedly,** *adv.* **quick-wittedness,** *n.* **quickie**, *n.* (*coll.*) something that is done rapidly; a swiftly consumed (alcoholic) drink; a swift act of sexual intercourse. **quickly,** *adv.* **quickness,** *n.* [OE *cwic, cwicu* (cp. Dut. *kwik,* G. *keck,* Icel. *kvikr,* Swed. *quick,* also L *vīvus,* lively, Gr. *bios,* life)]

quicken, *v.t.* to give or restore life or animation to; to stimulate, to rouse, to inspire, to kindle; to cheer, to refresh; to accelerate. *v.i.* to receive life; to come to life; to move with increased rapidity; to be in that state of pregnancy in which the child gives signs of life; to give signs of life in the womb. *n.* the rowan or mountain-ash, the quickbeam; the service tree. **quicken-tree,** *n.* the quickbeam. **quickener,** *n.* **quickening,** *a.*

quicklime, *n.* burned lime not yet slaked.

quicksand, *n.* loose wet sand easily yielding to pressure and engulfing persons, animals etc.; a bed of such sand.

quickset, *a.* of a hedge, composed of living plants, esp. hawthorn bushes. *n.* slips of plants, esp. hawthorn, put in the ground to form a quickset hedge; a quickset hedge.

quicksilver, *n.* mercury; (*fig.*) an unpredictable temperament. *v.t.* to coat the glass of a mirror with an amalgam of quicksilver and tin-foil. *a.* **quicksilvered,** *a.* **quicksilvering,** *n.* **quicksilverish,** *a.* **quicksilvery,** *a.*

quid[1], *n.* a piece of tobacco for chewing. [var. of CUD]

quid[2], *n.* (*pl.* **quid**) (*sl.*) a pound (sterling). **quids in** (*sl.*) in a profitable position. [etym. doubtful]

quid[3], *n.* something. **quid pro quo,** something in return (for something), an equivalent; †the substitution of one thing for another, or a mistake or blunder consisting in this. [L, what, anything, neut. of *quis,* who]

†**quidam,** *n.* somebody; a person unknown. [L]

quiddity, *n.* the essence of a thing; a quibble, a trifling or captious subtlety. **quiddative, quidditative,** *a.* [med. L *quidditas,* from QUID[3]]

quiddle, *v.i.* (*chiefly N Am.*) to waste time in trifling or useless employments. *n.* a quiddler. **quiddler,** *n.* [etym. doubtful]

quidnunc, *n.* one who is curious to know or pretends to know everything that goes on; a newsmonger, a gossip. [L, what now?]

quiescent, *a.* at rest, still, not moving, inert, dormant; tranquil, calm, free from anxiety, agitation or emotion; not sounded. *n.* a silent letter. **quiesce,** *v.i.* to become silent. **quiescence, -cy,** *n.* **quiescently,** *adv.* [L *quiescens -ntem,* pres.p. of *quiescere,* from *quies,* QUIET]

quiet, *a.* in a state of rest, motionless; calm, unruffled, placid, tranquil, peaceful, undisturbed; making no noise, silent, hushed; gentle, mild, peaceable; unobtrusive, not glaring or showy; not overt, private; retired, secluded. *n.* a state of rest or repose; freedom from disturbance, tranquillity; silence, stillness, peace, calmness; peace of mind, calm, patience, placidness. *v.t.* to bring to a state of rest; to soothe, to calm, to appease. *v.i.* to become quiet. **at quiet,** at peace, peaceful. **on the quiet,** secretly. †**quietage,** *n.* **quieten,** *v.t., v.i.* to quiet. to make, or become, calm, quiet. **quieter,** *n.* **quietly,** *adv.* **quietness, quietude,** *n.* †**quietsome,** *a.* [L *quiētus,* p.p. of *quiescere,* to rest, from *quies -ētis,* rest]

Quietism, *n.* a form of religious mysticism based on the doctrine that the essence of religion consists in the withdrawal of the soul from external objects and in fixing it upon the contemplation of God; a state of calmness and placidity. **Quietist,** *a.* quietistic. *n.* an adherent of Quietism. **quietistic,** *a.*

quietus, *n.* a final discharge or settlement; release from life, death. [med. L *quiētus est,* he is QUIT]

quiff, *n.* a curl lying flat on the forehead. [Fr. *coiffure,* hairdressing]

quill, *n.* the hollow stem or barrel of a feather; one of the large strong feathers of a bird's wing or tail; a pen made from such a feather, a pen; also, a plectrum, tooth-pick, angler's float etc. made from this; a spine of a porcupine; a tube or hollow stem on which weavers wind their thread, a bobbin, a spool; a musical pipe made from a hollow cane, reed etc.; a strip of cinnamon or cinchona bark rolled into a tube; a fluted fold. *v.t.* to form into rounded folds, flutes etc., to goffer; to wind on a quill or quills. *v.i.* to wind thread on a quill or quills. **quill-driver,** *n.* (*contemp.*) a writer, an author, a clerk. **quill-feather,** *n.* a large wing or tail feather. **quilled,** *a.* (*usu. in comb.*, as *long-quilled*). **quilling,** *n.* lace, tulle or ribbon, gathered into small round plaits resembling quills. [etym. doubtful, cp. G *Kiel*]

quillet, *n.* a quibble, a quirk. [perh. from obs. *quillity,* var. of QUIDDITY]

quillon, *n.* one of the arms forming the cross-guard of a sword. [F, from *quille,* ninepin]

quilt, *n.* a bed-cover or coverlet made by stitching one cloth over another with some soft warm material as padding between them, a counterpane. *v.t.* to pad or cover with padded material; to stitch together, esp. with crossing lines of stitching, (two pieces of cloth) with soft material between them; to stitch in crossing lines or ornamental figures, like the stitching in a quilt; to sew up, as in a quilt; †(*fig.*) to put together (literary extracts etc.) as in a quilt; (*sl.*) to beat, to thrash. **continental quilt,** a quilt or duvet stuffed with down. **quilted,** *a.* **quilter,** *n.* **quilting,** *n.* the process of making quilted work; material for making quilts; quilted work. [OF *cuilte,* L *culcita,* cushion]

Quimby, *n.* **Fred(erick)** (1886–1965), US film producer, in charge of MGM's short films department 1926–56. Among the cartoons produced by this department were the *Tom and Jerry* series and those directed by Tex Avery.

quin[1], *n.* a variety of pecten or scallop. [etym. doubtful]

quin[2] *n.* one child (of quintuplets). [QUINTUPLET]

quina QUINIA.

quinary, *a.* consisting of or arranged in fives. **quinate,** *a.* composed of five leaflets (of a leaf). [L *quīnārius,* from *quīnī,* five each, distrib. of *quinque,* five]

quince, *n.* the hard, acid, yellowish fruit of a shrub or small tree, *Pyrus cydonia,* used in cookery for flavouring and for preserves etc. [orig. pl. of obs. *quine,* ME *coine,* OF *cooing,* L *cotōneum,* var. of *cydōnium,* from *Cydōnia,* in Crete]

quincentenary QUINGENTENARY.

quincunx, *n.* an arrangement of five things in a square or rectangle, one at each corner and one in the middle, esp. such an arrangement of trees in a plantation. **quincuncial,** *a.* **quincuncially,** *adv.* [L *quinque,* five, *uncia,* OUNCE[1]]

quindecagon, *n.* a plane figure having 15 sides and 15 angles. [from L *quindecim,* see foll., after DODECAGON]

quindecemvir, *n.* (*pl.* **-viri**) (*Rom. Ant.*) one of a body of 15 men, esp. one of a college of 15 priests who had the charge of the Sibylline books. [L *quindecim* (*quinque,* five, *decem,* ten), 15, *vir,* man]

quinella, *n.* (*Austral.*) a form of betting where the person placing the bet must pick the first- and second-placed winners. [Am. Sp. *quiniela*]

quingentenary, *n.* a 500th anniversary; its celebration. [L *quingentī,* 500]

quinia, *n.* quinine. [Sp. *quina,* from Quechua, *kina,* bark, cp. QUINQUINA]

quinine, *n.* a bitter alkaloid obtained from cinchona barks, used as a febrifuge, tonic etc.; sulphate of quinine (the form in which it is usually employed as a medicine). **quinic,** *a.* **quinicine,** *n.* a yellow resinous amorphous alkaloid compound obtained from quinidine or quinine. **quinidine,** *n.* an alkaloid, isomeric with quinine, contained in some cinchona barks. **quinism,** †**quininism,** *n.* **quinize, -ise,** *v.t.* **quinology,** *n.* **quinologist,** *n.* [F]

Quinn, *n.* **Anthony** (1915–), Mexican actor, in films from 1935. Famous for the title role in *Zorba the Greek* (1964), he later often played variations on this larger-than-life character.

quinnal, *n.* the king-salmon of the Pacific coast of N America. [N Am. Ind.]

quinoa, *n.* an annual herb. *Chenopodium quinoa,* the ground farinaceous seeds of which are made into cakes in Chile and Peru. [Sp., from Quechua, *kinua*]

quinol, *n.* hydroquinone. **quinotic,** *a.* [QUIN-A, -OL]

quinoline, *n.* a colourless, pungent, liquid compound, obtained by the dry distillation of bones, coal and various alkaloids, forming the basis of many dyes and medicinal compounds. **quinology,** etc. [QUININE]

quinone, *n.* (*Chem.*) a yellow crystalline compound, usu. produced by the oxidation of quinic acid; any of a series of similar compounds derived from the benzene hydrocarbons by the substitution of two oxygen atoms for two of hydrogen. [as prec., -ONE]

quinquagenarian, *n.* a person 50 years old. *a.* 50 years old. **quinquagenary,** *a.* quinquagenarian. *n.* a quinquagenarian; a 50th anniversary. [L *quinquāgēnārius,* from *quinquāgēnī,* 50 each, distrib. of *quinquāginta,* 50 (*quinque,* five, *-ginta,* see QUADRAGENARIAN)]

quinquagesima, *n.* Quinquagesima Sunday; †the period from the Sunday before Lent to Easter Sunday, or the first week of this. **Quinquagesima Sunday,** the Sunday next before Lent, about 50 days before Easter. **quinquagesimal,** *a.* pertaining to the number 50; pertaining to 50 days. [L, 50th, as prec.]

quinquangular, *a.* having five angles.

quinquarticular, *a.* relating to or consisting of five articles (applied to the controversy between the Arminians and Calvinists).

quinque-, quinqui-, *comb. form.* relating to five. [L *quinque,* five]

quinquecostate, *a.* having five ribs.

quinquedentate, *a.* having five teeth or indentations.

quinquefarious, *a.* arranged in five parts or rows. **quinquefoliate,** *a.* having five leaves or leaflets.

quinquelateral, *a.* having five sides. *n.* a five-sided thing.

quinqueliteral, *a.* consisting of five letters. *n.* a word (esp. a Hebrew root-word) of five letters.

quinquenniad, *n.* a quinquennium. **quiquennium,** *n.* (*pl.* **-nia**) a period of five years. **quinquennial,** *a.* recurring once in five years; lasting five years. **quinquennially,** *adv.* [L *annus,* year, -AD]

quinquepartite, *a.* divided into five parts.

quinquereme, *n.* a galley having five banks of rowers. [cp. QUADRIREME]

quinquevalve, -valvular *a.* opening by five valves, as the pericarp of flax.

quinquifid, *a.* cleft into five divisions.

quinquina, *n.* Peruvian bark, cinchona. [Quechua, *kinkina,* redupl. of *kina,* QUINIA]

quinquivalent, *a.* having a valency or combining power of five. **quinquivalence,** *n.*

quinsy, *n.* inflammatory sore throat, esp. with suppuration of one tonsil or of both. **quinsied,** *a.* [OF *quinancie,* med. L *quinancia,* Gr. *kunanche* (*kun-, kuōn,* dog, *anchein,* to throttle)]

quint[1], *n.* a sequence of five cards of the same suit; a fifth; a stop giving tones a fifth above the normal. **quint major,** the cards from ten to ace. **quint minor,** those from seven to knave. [F *quinte,* L *quinta,* fem. of *quintus,* fifth, from *quinque,* five]

quint[2], *n.* (*N Am., Can.*) a quin. [from quintuplet]

quinta, *n.* a country-house or villa, in Portugal, Madeira and Spain. [Sp. and Port. (from being orig. let at a fifth of the produce)]

quintad PENTAD.

quintain, *n.* a post, or a figure or other object set up on a post, in the Middle Ages, to be tilted at, often fitted with a sandbag, sword or other weapon that swung round and struck a tilter who was too slow; the exercise of tilting at this. [OF *quintaine,* perh. from L *quintāna,* as QUINTAN, the fifth street of a camp]

quintal, *n.* a weight of 100 or 112 lb. (45.36 or 50.8 kg); 100 kg or 220½ lb. [OF, Sp., and Port., from Arab. *qintār,* L *centum,* 100]

quintan, *a.* recurring every fourth (or inclusively fifth) day. *n.* an intermittent fever or ague the paroxysms of which return every fourth day. [L *quintāna* (*febris*), fifth-day fever (*quintāna,* fem. of *quintānus,* from *quintus,* fifth, from *quinque,* five)]

quinte, *n.* the fifth of the thrusts or parries. [F, as QUINT]

Quintero, *n.* **Serafin Alvárez** and **Joaquin Alvárez** ALVÁREZ QUINTERO.

quintessence, *n.* the fifth, last or highest essence, apart from the four elements of earth, air, fire and water, forming the substance of the heavenly bodies and latent in all things; the pure and concentrated essence of any substance, a refined extract; the essential principle or pure embodiment (of a quality, class of things etc.). **quintessential,** *a.* **quintessentially,** *adv.* [F, from L *quinta essentia,* fifth ESSENCE]

quintet, quintette, *n.* a musical composition for five voices or instruments; a party, set or group of five persons or things. [F *quintette,* It. *quintetto,* from *quinto,* L. *quintus,* fifth]

quintic, *a.* (*Math.*) of the fifth degree. *n.* a quantic of the fifth degree. [L *quintus,* fifth, -IC]

quintile, *n.* (*Astrol.*) the aspect of planets when distant from each other one-fifth of a circle or 72°.

Quintilian, *n.* (Marcus Fabius Quintilianus) (*c.* AD 35–95), Roman rhetorician. He was born at Calgurris, Spain, taught rhetoric in Rome from AD 68, and composed the *Institutio Oratorio/The Education of an Orator*, in which he advocated a simple and sincere style of public speaking.

quintillion, *n.* the fifth power of a million, represented by 1 followed by 30 ciphers; (*F, N Am.*) the sixth power of a thousand, 1 followed by 18 ciphers. **quintillionth,** *n., a.* [from L *quintus,* after BILLION]

quintroon, *n.* one-fifth (inclusively) in descent from a Negro, the offspring of a white and an octoroon. [Sp. *quinteron,* from *quinto,* L *quintus,* fifth]

quintuple, *a.* fivefold. *n.* a fivefold thing, group or amount. *v.t.* to multiply fivefold. *v.i.* to increase fivefold. **quintuplet,** *n.* a set of five things; (*pl.*) five children at a birth; five notes played in the time of four. **quintuplicate,** *a.* consisting of five things (parts) etc. *n.* a set of five; one of five similar things. *v.t.* to multiply by five. **quintuplication,** *n.* [F, from L *quintus,* fifth, after QUADRUPLE]

quinzaine, *n.* a poem or stanza of five verses; a fortnightly event, meeting etc. [F, from foll.]

quinze, *n.* a card-game of chance analogous to vingt-et-un, the object being to score nearest to 15 points without exceeding it. [F, from L *quindecim* (*quinque,* five, *decem,* ten), 15]

quip, *n.* a sarcastic jest or sally; a witty retort; a smart saying; a quibble. †*v.t.* (*past, p.p.* **quipped**) to utter quips, to sneer at. *v.i.* to make quips, to scoff. **quippish, quipsome**, *a.* **quipster**, *n.* someone who makes witty remarks. [var. of obs. *quippy*, L *quippe*, forsooth]

quipu, *n.* a contrivance of coloured threads and knots used by the ancient Peruvians in place of writing. [Quechua, knot]

quire[1]**,** *n.* 24 sheets of paper; orig. a set of four sheets of paper or parchment folded into 8 leaves, as in mediaeval manuscripts; †a small book, pamphlet etc. [ME, OF *quaer* (F *cahier*), L *quaternī*, four each, a set of four, from *quātuor*, four]

†**quire**[2] CHOIR.

Quirinal, *n.* one of the seven hills on which ancient Rome was built. Its summit is occupied by a palace built in 1574 as a summer residence for the pope and occupied 1870–1946 by the kings of Italy. [*Quirinus*, local god of the Sabines]

†**quirister** CHORISTER.

Quirites, *n.pl.* a name applied to the Roman citizens in their civil capacity. **quiritary, quiritarian**, *a.* (*Law*) held in accordance with the Roman or old civil law, legal as distinguished from equitable. [L, pl. of *Quiris -rītis*, inhabitant of the Sabine town *Cures*]

quirk, *n.* an artful trick, evasion or subterfuge, a shift; a quibble, a quip, a twist or flourish in drawing or writing; a fantastic turn or flourish in music; a mannerism; an acute recess between the moulding proper and the fillet or soffit. **quirk-moulding,** *n.* **quirkish, quirksome**, *a.* **quirky,** *a.* **quirkiness,** *n.* [etym. doubtful]

quirt, *n.* a riding-whip with a short handle and a long, braided leather lash. *v.t.* to strike with a quirt. [Sp. *cuerda*, CORD]

Quisling, *n.* **Vidkun** (1887–1945), Norwegian politician. Leader from 1933 of the Norwegian Fascist Party, he aided the Nazi invasion of 1940 by delaying mobilization and urging non-resistance. He was made premier by Hitler in 1942, and was arrested and shot as a traitor by the Norwegians in 1945; (**quisling**) a traitor; one who openly allies himself with his nation's enemy.

quit, *v.t.* (*past, p.p.* **quitted,** †**quit**) to rid (oneself) of: to give up, to renounce, to abandon; to leave, to depart from; to cease, to desist from; to free, to liberate; †to acquit, to behave, to conduct (one, them etc., usu. without 'self'); †to acquit; †to remit; to pay off a debt. *v.i.* to leave, to depart; †to part (with or from). *a.* clear, absolved; rid (of). **quits,** even, left on even terms, so that neither has the advantage. **double or quits** DOUBLE[2]. **to be, to cry quits,** to declare things to be even, to agree not to go on with a contest, quarrel etc., to make it a draw. †**to quit cost,** to pay or balance the cost. **to quit scores,** to balance or make even. **quitclaim,** *n.* a renunciation of right or claim; †a deed of release. *v.t.* to renounce claim or title (to); †to release, to discharge. **quit-rent,** *n.* a rent (usu. small) paid by a freeholder or copyholder in discharge of other services. †**quittal,** *n.* requital, quittance. **quittance,** *n.* a discharge or release from a debt or obligation; a receipt, an acquittance; †repayment, requital. †*v.t.* to repay, to requite. **quitter**[1]**,** *n.* one who quits; a shirker, a coward. [OF *quiter* (F *quitter*), as QUIET]

qui tam, *n.* an action brought by an informer under a penal statute. [L, who as well (first words of clause in the statute)]

quitch, *n.* couch-grass, *Triticum repens.* **quitch-grass,** *n.* [OE *cwic*, QUICK]

quite[1]**,** *adv.* completely, entirely, altogether, to the fullest extent, absolutely, perfectly; (*coll.*) very considerably. **quite so,** *int.* certainly, decidedly (a form of affirmation). **quite something,** *n.* someone or something remarkable. **quite the thing,** quite proper or fashionable. [from foll. a.]

†**quite**[2]**,** *a., v.* QUIT.

Quito, *n.* capital and industrial city (textiles, chemicals, leather, gold, silver) of Ecuador, about 3000 m/9850 ft above sea level; population (1982) 1,110,250. It was an ancient settlement, taken by the Incas about 1470 and by the Spanish in 1534. It has a temperate climate all year round.

quittance QUIT.

quitter[1] QUIT.

quitter[2]**,** *n.* an ulcer or suppurating sore on the quarter of a horse's hoof. [etym. doubtful]

quiver[1]**,** *n.* a portable case for arrows. **quivered,** *a.* **quiverful,** *n.* **to have one's quiver full,** to have many children. [OF *cuivre*, prob. from Teut. (cp. OE *cocor*, G *Köcher*)]

quiver[2]**,** *v.i.* to tremble or be agitated with a rapid tremulous motion; to shake, to shiver. *v.t.* to cause (wings etc.) to quiver. *n.* a quivering motion. †*a.* nimble, active. **quivering,** *a.* **quiveringly,** *adv.* **quiverish,** *a.* **quivery,** *a.* [prob. imit., perh. rel. to QUAVER]

qui vive, *n.* a sentry's challenge. **on the qui vive,** on the look-out, alert, expectant. [F, who lives, who goes there?]

quixotic, *a.* extravagantly romantic, visionary; aiming at lofty but impracticable ideals. **quixotically,** *adv.* **quixotism -try,** *n.* **quixotize, -ise,** *v.t., vi.* [after the hero of Cervantes' Don *Quixote*]

quiz, *n.* something designed to puzzle or turn one into ridicule, a hoax; a question; a test of knowledge; a radio or television game based on this; a quizzer; an odd-looking or eccentric person. *v.t.* (*past, p.p.* **quizzed**) to banter, to chaff, to make fun of, to look at in a mocking or offensively curious way. *v.i.* to behave in a bantering or mocking way. **quizzable,** *a.* **quizzer,** *n.* one given to quizzing. **quizzery, quizzism,** *n.* **quizzical,** *a.* questioning, mocking. **quizzically,** *adv.* **quizzify,** *v.t.* **quizzing,** *n., a.* **quizzing-glass,** *n.* a small eye-glass, a monocle. **quizzingly,** *adv.* [etym. doubtful]

Qum, *n.* a holy city of the Shia Muslims in Iran, 145 km/90 miles S of Tehran.

Qumran, *n.* ruined site, excavated from 1951, in the foothills on NW shores of the Dead Sea in Jordan. Originally an Iron Age fort (6th cent. BC) it was occupied in the late 2nd cent. BC by a monastic community, the Essenes, until the buildings were burned down AD 68. The monastery library contained the Dead Sea Scrolls, discovered 1947; the scrolls had been hidden for safekeeping and never reclaimed.

quod, *n.* (*sl.*) prison, jail. [etym. doubtful]

quod erat demonstrandum, which was to be proved. [L]

quod erat faciendum, which was to be done. [L]

quodlibet, *n.* a fantasia, a medley; †a scholastic discussion or argument; a knotty point, a subtlety. †**quodlibetarian,** *n.* one fond of quodlibets or subtle arguments. †**quodlibetic, -ical,** *a.* [L, what you please]

quoin, *n.* a large stone, brick etc. at the external angle of a wall, a corner-stone; the external angle of a building; an internal angle, a corner; a wedge-shaped block of wood used by printers etc. for various purposes, as locking up type in a form, raising the level of a gun etc. *v.t.* to raise or secure with a quoin or wedge. **quoining,** *n.* [var. of COIN]

quoit, *n.* a flattish circular ring of iron for throwing at a mark; (*pl.*) a game of throwing such rings. †*v.t.* to throw or pitch as a quoit. **quoiter,** *n.* [etym. doubtful]

quokka, *n.* a variety of bandicoot with short ears. [Austral. Abor.]

quondam, *a.* having formerly been, sometime, former. [L, formerly]

Quonset hut®**,** *n.* (*N Am.*) a hut similar to a Nissen hut.

Quorn®**,** *n.* a high-protein, low-calorie vegetable foodstuff based on a tiny plant of the mushroom family.

quorum, *n.* (*pl.* **-ums**) the minimum number of officers or members of a society, committee etc. that must be present to transact business. **quorate,** *a.* being or consisting of a quorum. [L, of whom, gen. pl. of *qui*, who]

quota, *n.* a proportional share, part, or contribution; a prescribed number, e.g. of students to be admitted to a given college at the beginning of each year. [L *quota* (*pars*), how great (a part), fem. of *quotus*, from *quot*, how many]

quote, *v.t.* to adduce or cite from (an author, book

etc.); to repeat or copy out the words of (a passage in a book etc.); to name the current price of. *v.i.* to cite or adduce a passage (from). **quote–unquote,** an expression used to show the beginning and end of a quotation. **quotable,** *a.* worth quoting. **quotability**, **quotableness,** *n.* **quotably,** *adv.* **quotation** *n.* the act of quoting; a passage quoted; a price quoted or current; (*Print.*) a quadrat for filling up blanks etc. **quotation-marks,** *n.pl.* punctuation marks (in Eng. usu. double or single inverted commas) at the beginning and end of a passage quoted. **quoted,** *a.* **quoted company,** *n.* a company whose shares are quoted on the Stock Exchange. **quoter,** *n.* **quoteworthy,** *a.* [orig. to mark the number of (chapters etc.), from med. L *quotāre,* from QUOTA]

quoth, *v.t.* (*1st and 3rd pers.*) said, spoke. †**quotha**, for QUOTH HE, *int.* forsooth, indeed. [past of obs. *quethe,* OE *cwœth,* from *cwethan,* to speak (cp. Icel. *kvetha,* OHG *quedan*)]

quotidian, *a.* daily; (*Path.*) recurring every day; (*fig.*) commonplace, everyday. *n.* a fever or ague of which the paroxysms return every day. [L *quotīdiānus,* from *quotīdiē,* daily (QUOTA, *dies,* day)]

quotient, *n.* the result obtained by dividing one quantity by another. **quotiety**, *n.* relative frequency. †**quotity,** *n.* a certain number (of people). [F, irreg. from L *quotiens,* how many times, as QUOTA]

quotum QUOTA.

quo vadis?, whither goest thou? [L]

quo warranto, *n.* (*Law*) a writ requiring a person or body to show the authority by which some office or franchise is claimed or exercised. [med. L, by what warrant?]

Qurán, Qur'an KORAN.

qv (*abbr.*) quod vide, which see (*imp.*), an instruction to look up a cross-reference. [L]

QwaQwa, *n.* a black homeland of South Africa which achieved self-governing status in 1974; population (1985) 181,600.

qwerty, *n.* the standard English typewriter or keyboard layout. [from the first six letters of the top line of keys]

R

R, r, the 18th letter, and the 14th consonant of the English alphabet (*pl.* **Ars, R's** or **Rs**), has two sounds; the first when it precedes a vowel, as in *ran, morose*; the second, at the end of syllables and when it is followed by a consonant, as in *Her, martyr, heard*. **R months,** *n.pl.* those months with an 'r' in the spelling, when oysters are in season. **the three Rs,** reading, writing and arithmetic, the fundamental elements of primary education.

RA, (*abbr.*) Royal Academy of Art.

Ra, (*chem. symbol*) radium.

Rabat, *n.* capital of Morocco, industrial port (cotton textiles, carpets, leather goods) on the Atlantic coast, 177 km/110 miles W of Fez; population (1982) 519,000, Rabat-Salé 842,000. It is named after its original *ribat* or fortified monastery.

rabat, *n.* a neck-band with flaps, worn by French ecclesiastics; a turned-down collar; †a stiff collar worn by both sexes in the early 17th cent.; †a similar collar supporting a ruff. [F, rel. to *rabattre* (RE-, *abattre,* see ABATE)]

rabbet, *v.t.* to cut a groove or slot along the edge of (a board) so that it may receive the edge of another piece cut to fit it; to unite or fix in this way. *n.* such a groove or slot made in the edge of a board that it may join with another; a joint so made; a rabbet-plane; a spring-pole. **rabbet-plane,** *n.* a plane for cutting rabbets. [OF *rabat,* from *rabattre,*]

rabbi, *n.* (*pl.* **-bbis**) a Jewish doctor or teacher of the law, esp. one ordained and having certain juridical and ritual functions. **rabbin**, *n.* a rabbi, esp. one of the great scholars and authorities on Jewish law and doctrine flourishing in the Middle Ages. **rabbinate**, *n.* the office of rabbi; rabbis collectively. **rabbinic**, *n.* the language or dialect of the rabbins, later Hebrew. *a.* rabbinical. **rabbinical**, *a.* pertaining to the rabbins, their opinions, learning or language. **rabbinically,** *adv.* **rabbinism,** *n.* **rabbinist,** *n.* **rabbinistic**, *a.* **rabbinite**, *n.* a person who follows the traditions of the rabbis and the Talmud. [L, from Gr. *rhabbi,* Heb. *rabbī,* my master (*rabh,* master, *ī,* my)]

rabbit, *n.* a burrowing rodent, *Lepus cuniculus,* allied to the hare, killed for its flesh and fur; (*sl.*) a bungling player at an outdoor game. *v.i.* to hunt rabbits; (*often with* **on**) to talk at length, often aimlessly. **rabbit fever,** *n.* tularaemia. **rabbit-hutch,** *n.* a cage for rearing tame rabbits in. **rabbit punch,** *n.* a sharp blow to the back of the neck that can cause unconsciousness or death. †**rabbit-sucker,** *n.* a sucking rabbit. **rabbit-warren, rabbitry,** *n.* a piece of ground where rabbits are allowed to live and breed. **rabbiter,** *n.* **rabbity,** *a.* [perh. from Walloon *robett* from Flem. *robbe,*]

rabble[1], *n.* a noisy crowd of people, a mob; the common people, the mob, the lower orders; †a string of meaningless words, a rigmarole. *v.t.* to mob; †to utter in an incoherent manner. †*v.i.* to gabble. **rabble-rouser,** *n.* someone who stirs up the common people, who manipulates mass anger or violence; a demagogue. **rabble-rousing,** *n., a.* **rabblement,** *n.* [ME *rabel,* prob. rel. to Dut. *rabbelen,* to speak in a confused, indistinct way (cp. LG *rabbeln*)]

rabble[2], *n.* an iron tool consisting of a bar with the end sharply bent, used for stirring molten metal. [F *râble,* ult. from L *rutābulum,* fire-shovel, from *ruere,* to cast, to rake up]

rabdomancy RHABDOMANCY.

Rabelais, *n.* **François** (1495–1553), French satirist, monk, and physician, whose name has become synonymous with bawdy humour. He was educated in the Renaissance humanist tradition and was the author of satirical allegories, *La Vie inestimable de Gargantua/The Inestimable Life of Gargantua* (1535) and *Faits et dits héroïques du grand Pantagruel/Deeds and Sayings of the Great Pantagruel* (1533), the story of two giants (father and son) Gargantua and Pantagruel. **Rabelaisian**, *a.* of, pertaining to or characteristic of the French satirical humorist François Rabelais; extravagant, grotesque, coarsely and boisterously satirical. *n.* a student or admirer of Rabelais. **Rabelaisianism,** *n.*

rabi, *n.* the grain crop reaped in the spring, the chief of the three Indian crops. [Hind., from Arab. *rabī',* spring]

Rabi, *n.* **Isidor Issac** (1898–1988), US physicist who developed techniques to measure the strength of weak magnetic fields with astonishing accuracy. These fields are generated when charged elementary particles, such as the electron, spin about their axis. The work won for him the Nobel physics prize in 1944. Born in Russia, Rabi was taken to the US at the age of one.

rabic RABIES.

rabid, *a.* mad, raging, furious, violent; fanatical, headstrong, excessively zealous or enthusiastic, unreasoning; affected with rabies. **rabidity**, **rabidness,** *n.* **rabidly,** *adv.* [L *rabidus,* from *rabēre,* to rage]

rabies, *n.* a disease of the nervous system arising from the bite of a rabid animal, characterized by hydrophobia. **rabic**, **rabietic**, **rabific**, *a.* [L, as prec.]

Rabin, *n.* **Itzhak** (1922–), Israeli prime minister who succeeded Golda Meir 1974–77.

rabot, *n.* a block of hard wood used for polishing marble. [F, a plane, from *raboter,* to plane, var. of *rebouter* (RE-, *bouter,* to set, to thrust)]

RAC, (*abbr.*) Royal Armoured Corps; Royal Automobile Club.

raccahout, *n.* a starch or meal prepared from the acorns of the Barbary oak, *Quercus ballota*. [F, *racahout,* Arab. *rāqaout*]

raccoon, *n.* a furry ring-tailed N American carnivore of the genus *Procyon,* allied to the bears, esp. *P. lotor*. [Algonquin]

race[1], *n.* a rapid movement, a swift rush; a rapid current of water, esp. in the sea or a tidal river; a channel of a stream, esp. an artificial one; a contest of speed between horses, runners, ships, motor-vehicles etc.; (*fig.*) any competitive contest depending chiefly on speed; a course or career; a channel or groove along which a piece of mechanism, as a shuttle, glides to and fro; (*Austral.*) a fenced passage in a sheep-fold; (*pl.*) a series of racing contests for horses. *v.i.* to run or move swiftly; to go at full speed; to go at a violent pace owing to diminished resistance (as a propeller when lifted out of the water); to contend in speed or in a race (with); to attend races. *v.t.* to cause to contend in a race; to contend against in speed; to cause (a horse) to run in a race; (*fig.*) to get rid of (one's property) on horse-racing. **race-ball,** *n.* a ball held in connection with a race-meeting. **race-card,** *n.* a programme of a race-meeting with particulars of the horses, prizes etc. **racecourse, -track,** *n.* a piece of ground on which horse-races are run; a mill-race. **race-goer,** *n.* someone who frequently goes to race-meetings. **race-going,** *n.* **race-ground,** *n.* a racecourse. **race-horse,** *n.* a blood-horse bred for racing. **race-meeting,** *n.* a meeting for horse-racing. **raceway,** *a.* (*N Am.*) a channel or passage for water, as a mill-race; (*Mach.*) a groove for the passage of a shuttle etc.; (*Elec.*) a conduit or subway for wires or a cable. **racer,** *n.* one who races or contends in a race; a race-horse; a yacht, cycle, motor-car etc. built for racing. **racing,** *n.* **racing-car,** *n.* a car specially built to go at high speeds in competition. **racy,** *a.* RACY. [Icel. *rās* or OE *rǣs*]

race[2], *n.* a group or division of persons, animals or plants sprung from a common stock; a particular ethnic stock; a subdivision of this, a tribe, nation or group of peoples, distinguished by less important differences; a clan, a family, a house; a genus, species, stock, strain or variety, of plants or animals, persisting through several generations; (*fig.*) lineage, pedigree, descent; a class of persons or animals differentiated from others by some common characteristic; †a peculiar quality, a strong flavour, as of wine; natural disposition. **race-hatred,** *n.* hatred of other people on grounds of race. **race relations,** *n.pl.* the relations between people of different races within a single community; the study of such relations. **race riot,** *n.* a riot caused by a feeling of being discriminated against on grounds of race. **racial,** *a.* pertaining to race or lineage. **racially,** *adv.* **racism, racialism,** *n.* antagonism between different races; a tendency towards this; a belief in the superiority of one race over another; discrimination based on this belief. **racist, racialist,** *n.* [F *race, rasse,* It. *razza,* etym. unknown]

race[3], *n.* a root (of ginger). **race-ginger,** *n.* ginger in the root, not pulverized. [OF *raïs,* L *rādīcem,* nom. *-dix,* root]

†**race[4],** *v.t.* to tear or snatch (away) out etc. [from obs. *arace,* F *arracher,* L *eradicāre,* to ERADICATE]

raceme, *n.* a centripetal inflorescence in which the flowers are attached separately by nearly equal stalks along a common axis. **racemate,** *n.* a racemic compound. **racemed,** *a.* **racemic,** *a.* pertaining to or obtained from grape-juice. **racemiferous,** *a.* **racemism,** *n.* the quality of being racemic. **racemize, -ise,** *v.t., v.i.* to change into a racemic form. **racemization, -isation,** *n.* **racemose, -mous,** *a.* **racemose gland,** *n.* a gland consisting of branching ducts. **racemule,** *n.* a small raceme. **racemulose,** *a.* [F *racème,* L *racēmus,* bunch of grapes]

racer, raceway etc. RACE[1].

†**rach,** *n.* a dog that hunted by scent. [OE *ræcc,* cp. Icel. *rakki,* dog]

rachel, *n.* a type of face powder. [French actress Mme *Rachel,* 1821–58]

rachialgia, *n.* pain in the spine; †painters'-colic. **rachialgic,** *a.*

rachidial, rachidian, *a.* vertebral, spinal.

rachilla, *n.* the zig-zag axis on which the florets are arranged in the spikelets of grasses.

rachiomyelitis, *n.* inflammation of the spinal marrow.

rachi-, rachio-, *comb. form* pertaining to the spine. [Gr. *rachis,* spine]

rachis, *n.* (*pl.* **-ides**) the axis of an inflorescence; the axis of a pinnate leaf or frond; the spinal column; the shaft of a feather, esp. the part bearing the barbs. [Gr. *rachis,* spine]

rachitis, *n.* rickets. **rachitic,** *a.*

rachitome, *n.* an instrument used for cutting open the vertebral canal.

Rachmaninov, *n.* **Sergei (Vasilevich)** (1873–1943), Russian composer, conductor, and pianist. After the 1917 Revolution he went to the US. His dramatically emotional Romantic music has a strong melodic basis and includes operas, such as *Francesca da Rimini* (1906), three symphonies, four piano concertos, piano pieces, and songs. Among his other works are the *Prelude in C-sharp Minor* (1892) and *Rhapsody on a Theme of Paganini* (1934) for piano and orchestra.

Rachmanism, *n.* the conduct of an unscrupulous landlord who exploits his tenants and charges extortionate rents for slum property. [P. *Rachman,* 1920–62, such a landlord]

racial RACE[2].

racily etc. RACY.

Racine, *n.* **Jean** (1639–99), French dramatist and exponent of the classical tragedy in French drama. Most of his tragedies have women in the title role, for example *Andromaque* (1667), *Iphigénie* (1674), and *Phèdre* (1677). After the contemporary failure of the latter he no longer wrote for the secular stage, but, influenced by Madame de Maintenon, wrote two religious dramas, *Esther* (1689) and *Athalie* (1691), which achieved posthumous success.

rack[1], *v.t.* to stretch or strain, esp. on the rack; to torture, to cause intense pain or anguish to; to strain, tear, shake violently or injure; (*fig.*) to strain, to puzzle (one's brains etc.); to wrest, to exaggerate (a meaning etc.); to extort or exact (rent) in excess or to the utmost possible extent; to harass (tenants) by such exaction of rent. *n.* an apparatus for torture consisting of a framework on which the victim was laid, his wrists and ankles being tied to rollers which were turned so as to stretch him, to the extent sometimes of dislocating the joints. **on the rack,** under torture; under great stress. **to rack one's brains,** to use great mental effort. **rack-rent,** *n.* an exorbitant rent, approaching the value of the land. *v.t.* to extort such a rent from (a tenant, land etc.). **rack-renter,** *n.* a landlord extorting such a rent; a tenant paying it. **racking[1],** *a.* [prob. from MDut. or MLG *recken* (Dut. *rekken,* G *recken*), cp Icel. *rekja,* OE *reccan*]

rack[2], *n.* an open framework or set of rails, bars, woven wire etc. for placing articles on; a grating or framework of metal or wooden rails or bars for holding fodder for cattle etc.; a bar or rail with teeth or cogs for engaging with a gear-wheel, pinion or worm. *v.t.* to place on or in a rack; to fill (a rack) for a horse; to fasten (up) at a rack. *v.i.* to fill (up) a stable rack for a horse. **rack and pinion,** *n.* a device for converting rotary motion into linear motion and vice versa, with a gearwheel which engages in a rack; a type of steering gear found in some vehicles. **rack-railway,** *n.* a railway (usu. on a steep incline) with a cogged rail between the bearing rails. **rack-wheel,** *n.* a cog-wheel. [prob. rel. to prec., cp. Dut. *rek, rekke,* Dan. *række,* Swed. *räck*]

rack[3], *n.* light vapoury clouds, cloud-drift; (perh. var. of WRACK) destruction, wreck. *v.i.* to fly, as cloud or vapour before the wind. **to go to rack and ruin,** to fall completely into ruin. [perh. from Scand., cp. Norw., Swed. dial. *rak,* wreckage, Icel. *rek,* drift, *reka,* to drive, rel. to WREAK[1]]

rack[4] ARRACK.

rack[5], *v.t.* to draw off (wine etc.) from the lees. **racking-can, -cock, -engine, -faucet, -pump,** *n.* kinds of vessel, tap, pump etc. used in racking off wine. [OProv. *arracar,* from *raca,* the stems, husks, dregs]

rack[6], *n.* a horse's mode of going in which both hoofs of one side are lifted from the ground almost or quite simultaneously, all four legs being off the ground entirely at times. *v.i.* to go in this manner (of a horse). **racker,** *n.* a horse that goes at a racking pace. **racking[2],** *a.* [etym. doubtful]

rack[7], *n.* (*dial.*) the neck and spine of a forequarter of veal or mutton. [etym. unknown]

rackarock, *n.* an explosive composed of chlorate of potassium and nitro-benzol. [RACK[1, 2], ROCK[1]]

racket[1], racquet, *n.* a kind of bat, with a network of catgut instead of a blade, with which players at tennis, squash, badminton or rackets strike the ball; a snow-shoe resembling this; (*pl.*) a game of ball resembling tennis, played against a wall in a four-walled court. *v.t.* to strike with or as with a racket. **racket-court, -ground,** *n.* a four-walled court where rackets is played. **racket-press,** *n.* a press for keeping the strings of a racket taut. **racket tail,** *n.* a type of humming-bird which has two long, racket-shaped tail feathers. **racket-tailed,** *a.* [F *raquette,* perh. dim. from low L *racha,* Arab. *rāha,* palm of the hand]

racket[2], *n.* a clamour, a confused noise, a din; a commotion, a disturbance, a fuss; a frolic, a spree, uproarious gaiety, excitement or dissipation; (*sl.*) a scheme, a dodge, an underhand plan; an underhand combination; an organized illegal or unethical activity; (*sl.*) business; a mediaeval instrument of the woodwind family, with a deep bass pitch, like a bassoon. *v.i.* to make a noise or din; to frolic, to revel, to live a gay life, to knock about. **to stand the racket,** to stand the expenses, to pay the score; to put up with the consequences; to get through without mishap. **racketer,** *n.* **racketing,** *n.* confused, tumultuous mirth. **rackety,** *a.* **racketeer,** *n.* a member of a gang engaged in systematic blackmail, extortion or other illegal activities for profit. *v.t.* to operate an illegal business or enterprise for profit. **racketeering,** *n.* [prob. imit.]

racking[1,2] RACK[1,6].

racking-can etc. RACK[5].

rackle, *a.* (*Sc., North.*) hasty, rash; rough, vigorous, esp. in old age. [etym. doubtful]

rack-rent RACK[1].

racloir, *n.* (*Archaeol.*) a flint implement used for scraping sideways. [F *racler,* to scrape]

racon, *n.* a radar beacon. [acronym for *ra*dar bea*con*]

raconteur, *n.* a (good, skilful etc.) storyteller. **raconteuse,** *n. fem.* **raconteuring,** *n.* [F, from *raconter,* to RECOUNT[1]]

racoon RACCOON.

racquet RACKET[1].

racy, *a.* having the characteristic qualities in high degree; strongly flavoured; smacking of the race, type or origin, tasting of the soil; lively, pungent, piquant, spirited; (*coll.*) suggestive, bordering on the indecent, risqué. **racily,** *adv.* **raciness,** *n.* [RACE[2]]

rad[1], (*abbr.*) radical (in politics); radius.

rad[2], *n.* a unit measuring the dosage of ionized radiation absorbed, equivalent to 100 ergs of energy per gram of mass of irradiated material. [*rad*iation]

rad[3], (*chem. symbol*) radian.

RADA, (*abbr.*) Royal Academy of Dramatic Art.

radar, *n.* the employment of reflected or retransmitted radio waves to locate the presence of objects and to determine their angular position and range; the equipment used for this. **radar beacon,** *n.* a fixed radio transmitter which sends out signals which allow an aircraft or ship to determine its own position. **radar gun,** *n.* a device like a gun, which, when 'fired' at a moving car, uses radar to record the car's speed, used by the police. **radarscope,** *n.* a cathode-ray oscilloscope capable of showing radar signals. **radar trap,** *n.* a device which uses radar to allow the police to identify vehicles exceeding the speed limit. [acronym for *ra*dio *d*etection *a*nd *r*anging]

Radcliffe, *n.* **Anne** (born Ward) (1764–1823), English novelist, a chief exponent of the gothic novel or 'romance of terror', for example, *The Mysteries of Udolpho* (1794).

raddle[1], *n.* a lath, stick or branch interwoven with others to form a fence, usu. plastered over with clay etc.; a hurdle or hedge of twisted branches. *v.t.* to interweave, to twist (sticks etc.) together. [A-F *reidele,* OF *reddalle* (F *ridelle*), a pole, the back rail of a cart]

raddle[2], *n.* ruddle. *v.t.* to paint or colour with red ochre; to apply rouge (to the face) excessively or badly. **raddled,** *a.* dilapidated; unkempt; haggard-looking due to age or debauchery. [var. of RUDDLE[2]]

Radha, *n.* in the Hindu epic *Mahābhārata,* the wife of a cowherd who leaves her husband for love of Krishna (an incarnation of the god Vishnu). Her devotion to Krishna is seen by the mystical *bhakti* movement as the ideal of the love between humans and God.

radial, *a.* of, pertaining to or resembling a ray, rays or radii; extending or directed from a centre as rays or radii, divergent; having radiating parts, lines etc.; of or pertaining to radium; of or pertaining to the radius of the forearm. *n.* a radiating part, bone, nerve, artery etc. **radial artery,** *n.* artery of the forearm, felt at the wrist when taking the pulse. **radial axle,** *n.* an axle so arranged as to take the position of a radius to a curve it is traversing on a railway line etc. **radial axle-box,** *n.* an axle-box on a locomotive etc. adapted for such motion. **radial engine,** *n.* an internal-combustion engine which has its cylinders arranged radially. **radial-ply,** *n.* a motor tyre which has the fabric in the outer casing placed radially to the centre for increased flexibility. **radial symmetry,** *n.* the state of having several planes arranged symmetrically around a common axis. **radially symmetrical,** *a.* **radial velocity,** *n.* the component of velocity of an object along the line of sight between the observer and the object. **radiality,** *n.* radial symmetry. **radialize, -ise,** *v.t.* to cause to radiate as from a centre. **radialization, -isation,** *n.* **radially,** *adv.* **radian,** *n.* an arc equal in length to the radius of its circle; the angle subtending such an arc, 57·296°. [RADIUS or RADIUM, -AL]

radiant, *a.* emitting rays of light or heat; issuing in rays; (*fig.*) shining, beaming (with joy, love etc.); splendid, brilliant; radiating, radiate. *n.* the point from which a star-shower seems to proceed; the point from which light or heat radiates; a straight line proceeding from a fixed pole about which it is conceived as revolving. **radiant energy,** *n.* energy given out in the form of electromagnetic waves. **radiant flux,** *n.* the rate at which radiant energy is emitted or transmitted. **radiant heat,** *n.* heat by radiation, employed therapeutically in rheumatism by the use of electric lamps. **radiant point,** *n.* a radiant. **radiance, †-ancy,** *n.* **radiantly,** *adv.* [L *radians -ntem,* pres.p. of *radiāre,* as prec.]

Radiata, *n.pl.* Cuvier's name for one of the great divisions of animals in which the organs are arranged round a central axis, as in the sea-anemone and the star-fish. [L, neut. pl. of *radiātus,* see foll.]

radiata pine, *n.* a pine tree grown in Australia and New Zealand for timber. [L, fem. of *radiātus,* see foll.]

radiate, *v.i.* to emit rays of light or heat; to send out rays from or as from a centre; to issue and proceed in rays from a central point. *v.t.* to send out as rays or from a central point; to send forth in all directions, to disseminate. *a.* having rays or parts diverging from a centre, radiating; radially arranged, marked etc., radially symmetrical; belonging to the Radiata. **radiate flower,** *n.* composite flower in which the florets of the disk are radial and usu. ligulate. **radiately,** *adv.* **radiatiform,** *a.* **radiation,** *n.* the act of radiating or emitting rays; the transmission of heat, light etc. in the form of electromagnetic waves, from one body to another without raising the temperature of the intervening medium; a travelling outwards, as radii, to the periphery; a group of rays of the same wave-length; the gamma rays emitted in nuclear decay. **radiation sickness,** *n.* illness caused by too great absorption of radiation in the body, whose symptoms include fatigue, nausea, vomiting, internal bleeding, loss of hair and teeth, and in extreme cases, leukaemia. **radiational,** *a.* **radiative,** *a.* **radiato-,** *comb. form.* **radiator,** *n.* that which radiates; a vessel, chamber or coil of pipes charged with hot air, water, steam etc. for radiating heat in a building; a device for dissipating the heat absorbed by the cooling-water of an engine jacket; the part of an aerial which radiates electromagnetic waves. **radiatory,** *a.* [L *radiātus,* p.p. of *radiāre,* from RADIUS]

Radić, *n.* **Stjepan** (1871–1928), Yugoslav nationalist politician, born near Fiume. He led the Croat national movement within the Austro-Hungarian Empire, and supported union with Serbia 1919. His opposition to Serbian supremacy within Yugoslavia led to his murder in the parliament house.

Radical, *n.* in Britain, a supporter of parliamentary reform before the Reform Bill 1832. As a group the Radicals later became the progressive wing of the Liberal Party. During the 1860s (led by Cobden, Bright, and J. S. Mill) they campaigned for extension of the franchise, free trade, and *laissez-faire*, but after 1870, under the leadership of J. Chamberlain and Dilke, they adopted a republican and semi-socialist programme. With the growth of socialism in the later 19th cent., Radicalism ceased to exist as an organized movement.

radical, *a.* pertaining to the root, source or origin; inherent, fundamental; original, basic, primary; going to the root, thorough-going, extreme; belonging, pertaining or according to radical politics, favouring extreme changes; arising from or close to the root; of or pertaining to the root of a number or quantity; pertaining to a root, primary, underived. *n.* one promoting extreme measures or holding advanced views on either side of the political spectrum; a root; a quantity that is, or is expressed as, the root of another; the radical sign (√, ∛ etc.); an element, atom or group of atoms forming the base of a compound and not decomposed by the reactions that normally alter the compound. **radical chic,** *n.* (*derog.*) superficial, dilettantish left-wing radicalism. **radical mastectomy** MASTECTOMY. **radical sign,** *n.* the symbol √ placed before a number to show that the square root, or some higher root as shown by a superscript number (e.g. ∛), is to be calculated. **radicalism,** *n.* the principles of radical politics. **radicalistic,** *a.* **radicalistically,** *adv.* **radicality, radicalness,** *n.* **radicalize, -ise,** *v.t., v.i.* **radicalization, -isation,** *n.* **radically,** *adv.* thoroughly, fundamentally, essentially. [F, from late L *rādīcālis,* from *rādix -īcis,* root]

radicand, *n.* a number from which a root is to be extracted, usually preceded by a radical sign, e.g. three is the radicand of √ 3. [Lat. *rādīcandum,* that which is to be rooted]

radicate, *a.* having a root, rooted; having root-like organs of attachment (as some molluscs). †*v.t.*, to root, to plant firmly. †*v.i.* to take root. **radicant,** *a.* producing roots from the stem. **radication,** *n.* **radicel,** *n.* a rootlet. **radici-,** *comb. form* **radicicolous,** *a.* infesting roots (as a variety of phylloxera). **radiciflorous,** *a.* flowering from the root. **radiciform,** *a.* **radicivorous,** *a.* feeding on roots. [L *rādīcātus,* p.p. of *rādīcāre,* as prec.]

radicchio, *n.* (*pl.* **-chios**) a type of chicory from Italy with purple and white leaves eaten raw in salads. [It.]

radices RADIX.

radicle, *n.* the part of an embryo that develops into the primary root; a small root, a rootlet; a root-like part of a nerve, vein etc.; a radical. **radicular,** *a.* [L *rādīcula,* dim. of *rādix*]

radii RADIUS.

radio, *n.* electromagnetic waves used in two-way broadcasting; any device which can send signals through space using electromagnetic waves; a wireless capable of demodulating and transmitting a signal sent using electromagnetic waves; a wireless receiving set; broadcasting; the programmes broadcast on the radio. *v.t., v.i.* to communicate by wireless. [L *rādius,* a ray, a spoke]

radio-¹, *comb. form.* pertaining to radio, radio frequency or broadcasting; pertaining to radiation or radioactivity.

radio-², *comb. form.* radiate; pertaining to the outer bone of the forearm. **radiocarpal,** *a.* pertaining to the radius and the wrist. **radiolarian,** *a.* of or pertaining to the Radiolaria, a class of marine rhizopod Protozoa emitting radiate filamentous pseudopodia, abounding in warm seas. *n.* an individual of the Radiolaria. **radiolite,** *n.* a fossil bivalve from the chalk; a variety of natrolite. **radio-ulna,** *n.* a bone in the forelimb of amphibians, equal to the radius and ulna of more advanced vertebrates. [RADIUS]

radioactive, *a.* having the property of emitting invisible rays that penetrate bodies opaque to light, affecting the electrometer, photographic plates etc. **Radioactive Incident Monitoring Network** (RIMNET), a monitoring network at 46 (to be raised to about 90) Meteorological Office sites throughout the UK. It feeds into a central computer, and was installed in 1989 to record contamination levels from nuclear incidents such as the Chernobyl disaster. **radioactive decay,** *n.* the disintegration of a nucleus as a result of electron capture. **radioactive series,** *n.* a series of nuclides which each undergo radioactive decay, finally creating a stable element, usually lead. **radioactively,** *adv.* **radioactivity,** *n.*

radio-astronomy, *n.* the study of radio waves received from celestial objects.

radio beacon, *n.* a transmitting station which sends out signals to aid navigators.

radiobiology, *n.* the study of the effects of radiation on the body using radioactive tracers. **radiobiological,** *a.* **radiobiologically,** *adv.* **radiobiologist,** *n.*

radiocarbon, *n.* carbon-14, a radioactive carbon isotope. **radiocarbon dating,** *n.* a method of dating organic material by measuring the carbon-14 levels.

radiocarpal RADIO-².

radiochemistry, *n.* the chemistry of radioactive elements.

radiocompass, *n.* a device for navigation which can determine the direction of incoming radio waves from a beacon.

radio control, *n.* remote control using radio signals. **radio-controlled,** *a.*

radiodramatist, *n.* one who writes dramas for broadcasting.

radioelement, *n.* a chemical element with radioactive powers.

radio frequency, *n.* frequency which is within the range for radio transmission. **radio-frequency amplifier,** a high-frequency amplifier. **radio-frequency choke,** a coil presenting a high impedance to high-frequency alternating currents. **radio-frequency transformer,** a high- frequency transformer.

radiogenic, *a.* produced by radioactivity; suitable for radio broadcasting.

radiogoniometer, *n.* apparatus for the adjustment of coils linking aerials in the Bellini-Tosi direction-finding system.

radiogram, *n.* a radio and record player; an X-ray; a radiotelegraphic message.

radiograph, *n.* an actinograph; a negative produced by X-rays; a print from this. *v.t.* to obtain a negative of by means of such rays. **radiographer,** *n.* one who takes X-ray pictures of parts of the body. **radiographic,** *a.* **radiographically,** *adv.* **radiography,** *n.*

radio-immuno-assay, *n.* an immunological assay which uses radioactive labelling of various levels, such as hormone levels.

radioisotope, *n.* a radioactive isotope, produced in an atomic pile or in an atomic bomb explosion. **radioisotopic,** *a.* **radioisotopically,** *adv.*

radiolarian RADIO-².

radiolite RADIO-².

radiolocation, *n.* the employment of a radio pulse and the time-delay of its reflection to ascertain the relative position in space of a reflecting object such as an aeroplane.

radiology, *n.* the branch of medical science concerned with radioactivity, X-rays and other diagnostic or therapeutic radiations. **radiologic, radiological,** *a.* **radiologically,** *adv.* **radiologist,** *n.* a medical practitioner trained in radiology, such as one who interprets X-ray pictures of parts of the body.

radioluminescence, *n.* that luminous radiation which is emitted by radioactive material.

radiometer, *n.* an instrument for illustrating the conversion of radiant light and heat into mechanical energy. **radiometric,** *a.*

radiomicrometer, *n.* an instrument for measuring minute variations of heat etc.

radiomimetic, *a.* pertaining to a chemical or substance which affects living tissue in a similar way to ionizing radiation.

radio-opaque, *a.* not allowing X-rays or other radiation to pass through.

radiopaging, *n.* a system for alerting a person, using a small device which emits a sound in response to a signal at a distance.

radiophone, *n.* an instrument for the production of sound by means of radiant energy. **radiophonic,** *a.* pertaining to music produced electronically. **radiophonics,** *n.* the art of producing music electronically. **radiophonically,** *adv.* **radiophony,** *n.*

radioscopy, *n.* examination of bodies by means of X-rays.

radiosensitive, *a.* liable to injury from radiation.

radiosonde, *n.* a miniature radio transmitter sent up in a balloon and dropped by parachute, for sending information on pressures, temperatures etc.

radio source, *n.* any celestial object, e.g. a quasar, which emits radio waves.

radio spectrum, *n.* that range of electromagnetic frequencies, between 10 kHz and 300,000 MHz, used in radio transmissions.

radio star, *n.* a radio source.

radiotelegram, *n.* a message sent by wireless telegraphy.

radiotelegraphy, *n.* telegraphy which transmits messages using radio waves. **radio telegraph,** *n.* **radiotelegraphic,** *a.*

radiotelephone, *n.* apparatus for sending telephone messages using radio waves. *v.t.* to telephone using radiotelephone. **radiotelephonic,** *a.* **radiotelephony,** *n.* wireless telephony.

radio telescope, *n.* an apparatus for collecting radio waves from outer space.

radioteletype, *n.* a teleprinter which can transmit or receive messages using radio waves; a network of teleprinters used to communicate news and messages.

radiotherapy, *n.* the treatment of disease by means of radiation; actinotherapy. **radiotherapist,** *n.*

radio-ulna RADIO-².

radio wave, *n.* an electromagnetic wave of radio frequency.

radish, *n.* a cruciferous plant, *Raphanus sativus,* cultivated for its root, which is eaten as a salad. [F *radis,* from L *rādix, -īcem,* see RADIX]

radium, *n.* a highly radioactive metallic element resembling barium, at. no. 88; chem. symbol Ra, obtained from pitchblende, discovered by Pierre and Marie Curie and G. Bémont in 1898. **radium therapy,** *n.* treatment of disease, esp. cancer, using radiation from radium. [as foll., -IUM]

radius, *n.* (*pl.* **-dii**) the shorter of the two long bones of the forearm; the corresponding bone in animals and birds; the straight line from the centre of a circle or sphere to any point in the circumference; the length of this, half the diameter; a radiating line, part, object etc., as a spoke; a circular area measured by its radius; the outer zone of a composite flower; a floret in this; a branch of an umbel. **the radius, the four-mile radius,** an area extending four miles in all directions from Charing Cross, London, beyond which cab-fares are higher. **radius vector,** *n.* (*pl.* **radii vectores**) the distance from a fixed point to a curve; a line drawn from the centre of a heavenly body to that of another revolving round it. [L, rod, spoke, ray]

radix, *n.* (*pl.* **radices**) a quantity or symbol taken as the base of a system of enumeration, logarithms etc.; a source or origin; a root. **radix point,** *n.* any point which separates the integral part from the fractional part of a number, such as a decimal point. [L, root]

Radnorshire, *n.* former border county of Wales, merged with Powys 1974. Presteign was the county town.

radome, *n.* a protective covering for radar antennae, through which radio waves can pass. [*ra*dar, *dome*]

radon, *n.* a gaseous radioactive element emitted by radium, at. no. 86; chem. symbol Rn.

radula, *n.* (*pl.* **-lae**) the odontophore or lingual ribbon of some molluscs. **radular,** *a.* [L, scraper, from *rādere,* to scrape, see RAZE]

Raeburn, *n.* **Henry** (1756–1823), Scottish portrait painter, active mainly in Edinburgh. He developed a technique of painting with broad brushstrokes directly on the canvas without preparatory drawing. He was appointed painter to George IV in 1823.

RAF, (*abbr.*) Royal Air Force.

Rafelson, *n.* **'Bob' (Robert)** (1934–), US film director who gained critical acclaim for his second film, *Five Easy Pieces* (1971). His other films include *Head* (1968), *The Postman Always Rings Twice* (1981), and *Black Widow* (1987).

raff, *n.* sweepings, refuse; the rabble, the ruck, the lowest class; a person of this class, a rowdy. **raff-merchant,** *n.* a dealer in lumber etc. **raffish,** *a.* disreputable, disorderly, dissipated-looking. **raffishly,** *adv.* **raffishness,** *n.* [prob. from RIFF-RAFF]

Raffaelesque, etc. RAPHAELESQUE.

raffia, raphia, *n.* a Madagascar palm with a short stem and gigantic pinnate leaves; fibre prepared from these used for tying, ornamental work etc. [Malagasy]

raffish RAFF.

raffle¹, *n.* a kind of lottery in which an article is put up to be disposed of by lot among a number of persons each subscribing a like sum. *v.t.* to dispose of by means of a raffle. *v.i.* to engage in a raffle (for). **raffler,** *n.* [ME and F *rafle,* a game with dice]

raffle², *n.* rubbish, lumber; a tangle of cordage, gear etc. [OF *rafle* (in *rifle ou rafle*), prob. rel. to RAFF]

Raffles, *n.* **Thomas Stamford** (1781–1826), British colonial administrator, born in Jamaica. He served in the East India Company, took part in the capture of Java from the Dutch (1811), and while governor of Sumatra (1818–23) was responsible for the acquisition and foundation of Singapore in 1819. He was a founder and first president of the Zoological Society, London. **Rafflesia,** *n.* a genus of very large stemless parasitic plants from Java and Sumatra named after Sir Stamford Raffles.

Rafsanjani, *n.* **Hojatoleslam Ali Akbar Hashemi** (1934–), Iranian cleric and politician. After training as a mullah under Ayatollah Khomeini at the holy city of Qom, he acquired considerable wealth through his construction business but kept in touch with his exiled mentor. When the Ayatollah returned after the revolution of 1979–80 Rafsanjani became the eminent speaker of the Iranian parliament and, after Khomeini's death in 1989, state president and effective political leader.

raft¹, *n.* a number of logs, planks etc. fastened together for transport by floating; a flat floating framework of planks or other material used for supporting or carrying persons, goods etc., esp. as a substitute for a boat in a shipwreck etc.; a floating accumulation of driftwood, ice etc. in a river. *v.t.* to transport on or as on a raft; to fasten together with a raft. *v.i.* to travel on a raft; to work on a raft; **rafter², raftsman,** *n.* one who manages or works on a raft. [Icel. *raptr* (cp. Swed. *raft,* Dan. *rafte*)]

raft², *n.* (*N Am., coll.*) a large number, a crowd, a lot. [var. of RAFF]

Raft, *n.* **George** (stage name of George Ranft) (1895–1980), US film actor, usually cast as a gangster (as in *Scarface*, 1932). His later work included *Some Like it Hot* (1959).

rafter¹, *n.* a sloping piece of timber supporting a roof, or the framework on which the tiles etc. of the roof are laid. *v.t.* to furnish with rafters; to plough with ridges by turning a strip over on the unploughed adjoining strip, to half-plough. **raftering,** *n.* [OE *ræfter,* cp. RAFT¹]

rafter², raftsman RAFT¹.

rafty, *a.* (*prov.*) damp, foggy; musty, stale, rancid. [etym. doubtful]

rag¹, *n.* a fragment of cloth, esp. an irregular piece detached from a fabric by wear and tear; (*pl.*) tattered or shabby clothes; (*fig.*) a remnant, a scrap, the smallest piece (of anything); (*collect.*) torn fragments of cloth, linen etc., used as material for paper, stuffing etc.; a handkerchief; (*contemptuous*) a flag, sail, drop-curtain, a newspaper etc.; ragtime music. **ragamuffin,** *n.* a ragged, beggarly fellow. **ragamuffinly,** *adv.* **rag-and-bone man,** an itinerant dealer in household refuse. **ragbag,** *n.* a bag for scraps of cloth; (*coll.*) a carelessly-dressed woman. **rag-bolt,** *n.* a bolt with jags on the shank to prevent its being easily withdrawn. *v.t.* to fasten with these. **rag-book,** *n.* a book for a child made out of cloth instead of paper. **rag-doll,** *n.* a doll made from cloth. **rag-fair,** *n.* a market for or sale of old clothes. **ragman¹, -woman,** *n.* one who collects or deals in rags. **rag-paper,** *n.* paper made from rags. **rag-picker,** *n.* someone who collects rags from rubbish bins etc. **ragtag** or **ragtag and bobtail,** the riff-raff, the rabble. **rag-time,** *n.* irregular syncopated time in music, played esp. on the piano. **rag-trade,** *n.* (*coll.*) the clothing industry. **rag-weed,** *n.* ragwort. **rag-**

wheel, *n.* a wheel with a notched margin, a sprocket-wheel. **rag worm,** *n.* any of several burrowing marine worms used as bait in fishing. **ragwort,** *n.* a yellow-flowered plant of the genus *Senecio*. **ragged**, *a.* rough, shaggy; broken, jagged, or uneven in outline or surface; disjointed, irregular, imperfect; lacking in uniformity, finish etc.; harsh, dissonant; worn into rags, rent, tattered; wearing tattered clothes; shabby, poor, miserable in appearance. **ragged robin,** *n.* a crimson-flowered plant, *Lychnis floscuculi,* the petals of which have a tattered appearance. **ragged school,** *n.* (*Hist.*) a free school for the education of poor children. **ragged staff,** *n.* a stick with branch stubs. **raggedly,** *adv.* **raggedness,** *n.* **raggedy,** *a.* tattered. [cp Icel. *rögg,* Norw., Swed. *ragg,* rough hair]

rag², *n.* a hard, coarse, rough stone, usu. breaking up into thick slabs; a large roofing-slate with a rough surface on one side (also called **ragstone**). **rag work,** *n.* thick slabs of masonry. [etym. doubtful]

rag³, *v.t.* (*past, p.p.* **ragged**) to tease, irritate or play rough practical jokes on; to rate, to reprove, to talk to severely. *n.* the act of ragging; a piece of boisterous and disorderly conduct. **to lose one's rag,** (*sl.*) to lose one's temper. **rag-day, -week,** *n.* in British universities, a day or week devoted to fund-raising and other charity work. **ragging,** *n.* **raggy,** *a.* (*sl.*) angry. [cp. BALLYRAG]

raga, *n.* in traditional Hindi music, a form or a mode which forms the basis for improvisation; a composition composed following such a pattern. [Sansk. *rāga,* tone, colour]

ragamuffin, rag-bolt RAG¹.

rage, *n.* violent anger, fury; a fit of passionate anger; (*fig.*) extreme violence, vehemence or intensity (of); a violent desire or enthusiasm (for); intense emotion, passion or ardour; (*coll.*) an object of temporary pursuit, enthusiasm or devotion. *v.i.* to storm, to rave, to be furious with anger; to be violently incensed or agitated; to express anger or passion violently; to be violent, to be at the highest state of vehemence, intensity or activity. *v.t.* †to enrage. **all the rage,** an object of general desire, quite the fashion. **rageful,** *a.* **ragefully,** *adv.* **rager,** *n.* (*Austral.*) a fierce old cow or bullock. **raging,** *a.* acting with violence; angry, furious, frantic, vehement. *n.* violence; fury. **ragingly,** *adv.* [F, late L *rabia,* RABIES]

ragged RAG¹.

raggle-taggle, *a.* untidy. [RAG¹, TAG]

ragi, raggee, raggy, *n.* an Indian food-grain, *Eleusine coracana*. [Hind.]

Raglan, *n.* **FitzRoy James Henry Somerset, 1st Baron Raglan** (1788–1855), English general. He took part in the Peninsular War under Wellington, and lost his right arm at Waterloo. He commanded the British forces in the Crimean War from 1854. The **raglan sleeve**, cut right up to the neckline with no shoulder seam, is named after him.

ragman¹ RAG¹.

†ragman², *n.* a document or sealed instrument, especially the Ragman roll. **Ragman, Ragman's roll,** *n.* the list of the deeds by which the Scottish king (Balliol) and nobles vowed allegiance to Edward I in 1296. [etym. doubtful]

Ragnarök, *n.* in Norse mythology, the ultimate cataclysmic battle between gods and forces of evil from which a new order will come.

ragout, *n.* a stewed dish of small pieces of meat and vegetables, highly seasoned. *v.t.* to make into a ragout. [F *ragoût,* from *ragoûter,* (to bring, to awaken or stimulate the appetite), (RE-, *goût,* GUST²)]

ragstone RAG².

raguly, †raguled, *a.* obliquely indented (of a bearing), having projections like lopped branches at the sides. [prob. rel. to RAG¹]

rag-wheel, ragwort RAG¹.

rah, *int.* a short form of HURRAH.

Rahman, *n.* **Tunku Abdul** (1903–), Malaysian politician, first prime minister of independent Malaya (1957–63) and of Malaysia (1963–70).

Rai, rai, *n.* a form of dance music originating in Algeria and combining a traditional vocal line with a modern pop-style backing.

raid, *n.* a hostile or predatory incursion, esp. of mounted men moving with rapidity in order to surprise, a foray; a sudden invasion or descent, esp. of police or custom-house officers; an air raid. *v.t.* to make a raid upon. *v.i.* to make a raid. **to raid the market,** artificially to upset stock market prices for future gain. **raider,** *n.* [Sc., from OE *rād,* ROAD]

Raikes, *n.* **Robert** (1735–1811), English printer who started the first Sunday school (for religious purposes) in Gloucester in 1780 and who stimulated the growth of weekday voluntary 'ragged schools' for poor children.

rail¹, *n.* a bar of wood or metal or series of such bars resting on posts or other supports, forming part of a fence, banisters etc.; one of a continuous line of iron or steel bars, resting on sleepers etc. laid on the ground, usu. forming one of a pair of such lines constituting the track of a railway or tramway; one of a similar pair of lines serving as track for part of a machine; the railway as a means of travel or transportation; a bar fixed on a wall on which to hang things; a horizontal structural support in a door; the railway in general; (*pl.*) railway shares. *v.t.* to enclose with rails; to furnish or fill with rails; to lay down rails upon; to send by rail. *v.i.* to travel by rail. **to go off the rails,** to go awry; to go mad. **rail-car,** *n.* a motor-driven vehicle on railway lines. **rail card,** *n.* an identity card issued to certain people (e.g. pensioners and students) allowing the holder cheap rail fares. **rail-chair,** *n.* an iron socket or holder, fixed on a sleeper, to which a rail is fastened. **rail-fence,** *n.* a fence made of rails. **railhead,** *n.* a terminus; the farthest point to which rails have been laid. **railman, -woman,** *n.* a railway worker. **railroad,** *n.* (*chiefly N Am.*) a railway. *v.t.* to force hurriedly to a conclusion. **railroader,** *n.* a person employed on a railway. **railer¹,** *n.* one who makes or fits rails. **railing¹,** *n.* a fence made of wooden or other rails; materials for railings; the laying of rails. **railless**, *a.* [OF *reille,* L *rēgula,* RULE]

rail², *v.i.* to use abusive or derisive language; to scoff (at or against). †*v.t.* to effect by raillery. **railer²,** *n.* one who rails or scoffs. **railing²,** *n., a.* **railingly,** *adv.* **raillery,** *n.* good-humoured ridicule or pleasantry, banter. [F *railler,* etym. doubtful]

rail³, *n.* a bird of the family Rallidae, esp. of the genus *Rallus,* comprising *R. aquaticus,* the water-rail, and the corncrake or landrail, *Crex pratensis*. [F *râle,* etym. doubtful]

†rail⁴, *v.i.* to flow, to gush (down). [etym. doubtful]

railer, railing etc. RAIL¹·².

raillery RAIL².

railway, *n.* a road laid with a track formed of rails of iron or steel along which trains and vehicles are driven, usu. by locomotives; a track laid with rails for the passage of heavy horse-vehicles, travelling-cranes, trucks etc.; a system of tracks, stations, rolling-stock and other apparatus worked by one company or organization. *v.i.* to make railways; to travel by rail. **British Railways,** the unification for nationalization of the principal railway systems in Great Britain under the Transport Act of 1947, which came into force 1 Jan. 1948 (and changed its name to **British Rail** in 1965). **Railway Bill,** *n.* a proposed Act of Parliament for constructing a new railway or conferring further powers on a railway company. **railway company,** *n.* a joint-stock company owning and managing a railway. **railway-carriage,** *n.* a railway vehicle for passengers. **railway-crossing,** *n.* a crossing of two railway lines, or a road and a railway. **railwayman, -woman,** *n.* a railway worker. **railway novel,** *n.* a light novel for reading on a journey by rail. **railway sub-office,** *n.* a place on a railway with a post-office subordinate to another office. **railway-ize, -ise,** *v.t.* **railwayless**, *a.* [RAIL¹]

raiment, *n.* dress, apparel, clothes. [short for obs. *arrayment* (ARRAY, -MENT)]

rain, *n.* the condensed moisture of the atmosphere falling in drops; a fall of such drops; a similar fall or shower of liquid, dust or bodies; a large quantity of anything falling quickly; (*pl.*) the rainy season in a tropical country; a rainy region of the Atlantic, 4–20° N lat. *v.i.* (*usu. impers*); to fall in drops of water from the clouds to fall in showers like rain. *v.t.* to pour down (rain); to send down in showers like rain. **come rain, come shine,** whatever the weather, whatever the circumstances. **right as rain,** perfectly all right. **to be rained off, out,** to be cancelled or postponed due to rain or bad weather. **to rain cats and dogs** CAT[1]. **rain-bird,** *n.* one of various birds supposed to foretell rain, esp. the green woodpecker. **rainbow,** *n.* a luminous arc showing the prismatic colours, appearing opposite the sun during rain, caused by the reflection, double refraction and dispersion of the sun's rays passing through the drops. *a.* coloured like the rainbow; many-coloured. **rainbow-coloured,** *a.* **rainbow-tinted,** *a.* **rainbow trout,** *n.* a brightly-coloured Californian trout, *Salmo irideus.* **rainbowy,** *a.* **rain-box,** *n.* a device imitating the noise of rain. **raincheck,** *n.* (*esp. N Am.*) a ticket for a sports event which allows readmission on another day if rain stops play; the postponing of a decision. **to take a raincheck,** to postpone accepting an invitation till a later date. **rain-cloud,** *n.* a cloud producing rain, a nimbus. **raincoat,** *n.* a waterproof coat or cloak for wearing in wet weather; a mackintosh. **rain-doctor,** *n.* a wizard professing to cause rain by incantations. **raindrop,** *n.* a particle of rain. **rainfall,** *n.* the amount of rain which falls in a particular district in a given period; a shower of rain. **rain forest,** *n.* a dense tropical forest of mostly evergreen trees with a very heavy rainfall. **rain-gauge,** *n.* an instrument for measuring the amount of rain falling on a given surface. **rain-glass,** *n.* (*coll.*) a barometer. **rain-maker** RAIN-DOCTOR. **rainproof, -tight,** *a.* impervious to rain. *v.t.* to make something impervious to rain. **rain shadow,** *n.* the leeward side of hills, which has a relatively light rainfall compared to the windward side. **rainstorm,** *n.* a storm with very heavy rain. **rain-wash,** *n.* the movement of soil and stones effected by rain. **rainwater,** *n.* water that has fallen in the form of rain. **rainless,** *a.* **rainy,** *a.* characterized by much rain; showery, wet. **rainy day,** a time of misfortune or distress, esp. pecuniary need. **rainily,** *adv.* **raininess,** *n.* [OE *regn, rēn* (cp. Dut. and G *Regen,* Icel., Swed. and Dan. *regn*), whence *regnian,* to rain, *rēnig,* rainy]

Raine, *n.* **Kathleen** (1908–), English poet. Her volumes of poetry include *Stone and Flower* (1943) and *The Lost Country* (1971), and reflect both the Northumberland landscape of her upbringing and the religious feeling which led her to the Roman Catholic Church in 1944.

Rainier III, *n.* (1923–), Prince of Monaco from 1949. He was married to the US film actress Grace Kelly.

Rais, *n.* **Gilles de** (1404–40), French marshal who fought alongside Joan of Arc. In 1440 he was hanged for the torture and murder of 140 children, but the court proceedings were irregular. He is the historical basis of the Bluebeard character.

raise, *v.t.* to cause to rise, to elevate; to cause to stand up, to set upright; to restore to life, to rouse, to excite, to stir up (against, upon etc.); to erect, to build, to construct; to rear, to cause to grow, to breed; to produce, to create, to cause; to collect, to procure, to levy (money etc.); to bid more money at cards; to occasion; to set up, to suggest (a point etc.); to advance, to promote, to heighten, to make higher or nobler, to cause to ascend; to make tender; to increase the amount of; to come in sight of (land etc.); to establish radio links with; to multiply a number by itself a specified number of times. *n.* (*N Am.*) a rise in salary. **to raise a blockade, siege,** to relinquish the attempt to take a place by blockade or siege. **to raise a hand to,** to hit. **to raise Cain,** to create a disturbance. **to raise cloth,** to put a nap on cloth. **to raise hell,** (*coll.*) to make a lot of trouble. **to raise money on,** to sell or pawn something to make money. **to raise one's eyebrows,** to look surprised or bemused; to look disapproving. **to raise one's eyes,** to look upwards (to). **to raise one's glass (to),** to drink a toast (to). **to raise the hat to** HAT. **to raise the wind,** (*sl.*) to make a disturbance or commotion; to get hold of cash. **raised beach** BEACH. **raiser,** *n.* **raising agent,** *n.* a natural or chemical substance which causes dough or cakes to rise. **raising-gig,** *n.* a machine for raising a nap on cloth. **raising-piece,** *n.* a piece of timber laid on a brick wall or frame to carry a beam or beams. **raising-plate,** *n.* a horizontal timber for carrying the heels of rafters. [Icel. *reisa,* (cp. Dan. *reise,* Swed. *resa*)]

raisin, *n.* a dried grape, the partially dried fruit of various species of vine. [OF *raizin* (F *raisin*), pop. L *racīmum,* L *racēmum,* RACEME]

raison d'être, *n.* the reason for a thing's existence. [F, reason of being]

raisonné, *a.* arranged systematically (of a catalogue). [F, p.p. of *raisonner,* to REASON]

raj, *n.* the British rule of India before 1947. [Hind.]

Rajah, -ja, *n.* an Indian king, prince or tribal chief, a title of a dignitary or noble; a Malayan or Javanese chief. **Rajahship,** *n.* [Hind., from Sansk. *rāj,* to reign, rel. to L *rex,* king]

Rajasthan, *n.* state of NW India. **area** 342,200 sq km/ 132,089 sq miles. **capital** Jaipur. **population** (1981) 34,103,000. **products** oilseed, cotton, sugar, asbestos, copper, textiles, cement, glass. **language** Rajasthani, Hindi. **religion** Hindu 90%, Muslim 3%. **history** formed 1948, enlarged 1956.

Rajneesh meditation, *n.* a form of meditation based on the teachings of the Indian Shree Rajneesh (born Chaadra Mohan Jain), established in the early 1970s. Until 1989 he called himself Bhagwan (Hindi 'God'). His followers, who number about half a million worldwide, regard themselves as Sannyas, or Hindu ascetics; they wear orange robes and carry a string of prayer beads. They are not expected to observe any specific prohibitions but to be guided by their instincts.

Rajpoot, -put, *n.* one of an Indian warrior caste who claim descent from the Kshatriyas; one of a Hindu aristocratic class. [Hind. *rajpūt* (Sansk. *rāja,* see prec., *putra,* son)]

rake[1], *n.* an implement having a long handle with a cross-bar set with teeth, used for drawing loose material together, smoothing soil etc.; a two-wheeled implement drawn by a horse for gathering hay together etc.; a similar implement for collecting light articles. *v.t.* to collect or gather (up or together) with a rake; to scrape, scratch, smooth, clean etc. (soil) with a rake; to search with or as with a rake, to scour, to ransack; to fire along the length of, to enfilade; to sweep (a ship, deck, line of soldiers etc.) from end to end; to pass (of shot) from end to end of; (*fig.*) to command from end to end with the eye. *v.i.* to use or work with a rake; to search (about etc.) with or as with a rake. **to rake in,** (*sl.*) to accumulate, usu. money. **to rake off,** (*coll.*) to receive a share of the profits from an illegal job. **to rake up,** (*sl.*) to revive something, such as a quarrel, the past etc. †**rake-hell,** *n.* an utterly abandoned scoundrel, a RAKE[2]. †**rake-helly,** *a.* **rake-off,** *n.* (*sl.*) commission on a job; more or less illicit profits from a job. **raker,** *n.* **raking,** *n.* the act of using or working with a rake; the amount of ground or quantity of material raked; (*usu. in pl*). that which is raked together [OE *raca* (cp. Dut. *raak,* G *Rechen,* Icel. *reka*)]

rake[2], *n.* a dissolute or immoral man, a debauchee, a libertine. †*v.i.* to lead a dissolute life. **rakery,** *n.* dissoluteness. **rakish[1],** *a.* **rakishly[1],** *adv.* **rakishness,** *n.* [short for RAKE-HELL, see prec.]

rake[3], *n.* inclination, slope, esp. backward slope; projection of the stem or stern of a vessel beyond the extremities of the keel; the slope of a mast or funnel towards the stern; the slope of the stage, an auditorium. *v.i.* to slope backwards from the perpendicular. *v.t.* to give such an inclination to. **raker,** *n.* a sloping shore or support. **rakish[2],** *a.* with masts sharply inclined; apparently built for speed; smart-looking with a suggestion of the pirate or smuggler (prob. with alln. to RAKE[2]). **rakishly[2],** *adv.*

[etym. doubtful]

raki, -kee, *n.* an aromatic liquor made from spirit or grape-juice, usu. flavoured with mastic, used in the E Mediterranean region. [Turk, *rāqī,* brandy, spirit]

rakish etc. RAKE[2,3].

râle, *n.* a rattling sound in addition to that of respiration, heard with the stethoscope in lungs affected by disease. [F, from *râler,* etym. doubtful]

Raleigh or **Ralegh,** *n.* **Walter** (*c.* 1552–1618), English adventurer. He made colonizing and exploring voyages to N America (1584–87) and S America (1595), and naval attacks on Spanish ports. He was imprisoned by James I (1603–16) and executed on his return from an unsuccessful final expedition to S America.

rallentando, *adv.* (*Mus.*) gradually slower. [It., p.p. of *rallentare,* as RELENT]

rallier RALLY[2].

ralline, *a.* of or pertaining to the Rallidae or rails. [mod. L *rallus,* RAIL[3]]

rally[1], *v.t.* to reunite, to bring (disordered troops) together again; to restore, to reanimate, to revive, to pull together. *v.i.* to reassemble, to come together again after a reverse or rout; to regain strength, to recover tone or spirit, to return to a state of health, vigour or courage. *n.* the act of rallying or recovering order, strength, health, energy etc.; an assembly, a reunion; (*Lawn tennis etc.*) rapid return of strokes; a sharp increase in trade on the Stock Exchange after a period of decline; a type of motor race which tests the driver's skill or the quality of the vehicle. **to rally round,** to come to (someone's) aid morally or financially. **rally-cross,** *n.* a motor race in which specially adapted saloon cars race over a course with a rough, uneven surface. **rallying-point,** *n.* a spot or moment for making a rally. [F *rallier* (RE-, *allier,* to ALLY)]

rally[2], *v.t.* to attack with raillery; to banter, to chaff. *n.* banter, raillery. **rallier,** *n.* **rallyingly,** *adv.* [F *railler,* to RAIL[2]]

RAM, *n.* in computing, a form of storage frequently used for the internal memory of microcomputers. It is made up of a collection of integrated circuits (chips). Unlike ROM, RAM can be both read from and written to by the computer, but its contents are lost when the power is switched off. Today's microcomputers have up to eight megabytes of RAM. [acronym for *r*andom-*a*ccess *m*emory]

ram[1], *n.* a male sheep, a tup; a battering-ram; a battleship armed with a beak of steel at the bow for cutting into a hostile vessel; such a beak; the drop-weight of a pile-driver or steam-hammer; a hydraulic engine for raising water, lifting etc.; a rammer; the compressing piston of a hydrostatic press; the plunger of a force-pump; a spar for driving planks etc. by impact. *v.t.* (*past, p.p.* **rammed**) to beat, drive, press or force (down, in, into etc.) by heavy blows; to stuff, to compress, to force (into) with pressure; to make firm by ramming; to strike (a ship) with a ram; to drive or impel (a thing against, into etc.) with violence. *v.i.* to beat, to pound or hammer with or as with a rammer. **the Ram,** the constellation or zodiacal sign Aries. **to ram something down someone's throat,** to force someone to accept an idea, for example, by arguing aggressively or forcefully. **ram-jet, ram-jet engine,** *n.* a form of aero-engine where the compressed air produced by the forward movement of the aircraft is used to burn the fuel; an aircraft powered by such an engine. **ramrod,** *n.* a rod for forcing down the charge of a muzzle-loading gun. **ramroddy,** *a.* stiff as a ramrod, uncompromising, formal. **ramrodism,** *n.* **ram's-horn,** *n.* a horn of a male sheep; a scroll-ornament like a ram's skull and horns; a semicircular work commanding a ditch; †an ammonite. **rammer,** *n.* one who or that which rams; an instrument for pounding, driving etc.; a ramrod. [OE (cp. Dut. and OHG *ram,* G *Ramme,* prob. rel. to Icel. *ramr,* strong)]

ram[2], *n.* length of a boat over all. **ram-line,** *n.* a small rope used for striking the centre-line of a vessel, as a guide in setting the frames etc. [etym. doubtful]

Rama, *n.* incarnation of Vishnu, the supreme spirit of Hinduism. He is the hero of the epic poem, the *Ramamayana,* and he is regarded as an example of morality and virtue.

Ramadan, *n.* in the Muslim calendar, the ninth month of the Muslim year. Throughout Ramadan a strict fast is observed during the hours of daylight; Muslims are encouraged to read the whole Koran as a commemoration of the Night of Power, which falls during the month, and is when Muslims believe Muhammad first received his revelations from the angel Gabriel. [Arab. (cp. Pers. and Turk. *ramazan*), from *ramada,* to be hot]

Ramakrishna, *n.* (1834–86), Hindu sage, teacher, and mystic (one dedicated to achieving oneness with or a direct experience of God or some force beyond the normal world). Ramakrishna claimed that mystical experience was the ultimate aim of religions, and that all religions which led to this goal were equally valid.

ramal, *a.* of, pertaining to or growing on a branch. †**ramage,** *n.* (*collect.*) branches. *a.* having left the nest, hence wild, shy, untamed (of hawks). [L *rāmus,* branch, -AL]

Raman effect, *n.* the change in wavelength which light undergoes when it passes through a transparent medium. **Raman spectroscopy,** *n.* the study of the properties of molecules using the Raman effect. [Sir Chandrasekhara *Raman,* 1888–1970, Indian physicist]

rama-rama, *n.* a widely spread New Zealand shrub. [Maori]

Ramayana, *n.* Sanskrit epic *c.* 300 BC, in which Rama (an incarnation of the god Vishnu) and his friend Hanuman (the monkey chieftain) strive to recover Rama's wife, Sita, abducted by demon king Ravana.

Rambert, *n.* **Marie** (adopted name of Cyvia Rambam) (1888–1982), British ballet dancer and teacher born in Warsaw, Poland, who became a British citizen in 1918. One of the major innovative and influential figures in modern ballet, she was with the Diaghilev ballet (1912–13), opened the Rambert School (1920), and in 1926 founded the Ballet Rambert which she directed (renamed Rambert Dance Company 1987).

ramble, *v.i.* to walk or move about freely or aimlessly, to rove; to wander or be incoherent in speech, writing etc. *n.* a roaming about; a walk for pleasure or without a definite object, a stroll. **rambler,** *n.* one who rambles about; especially a person who takes long walks in the countryside; a variety of climbing-rose. **rambling,** *a.* wandering about; desultory, disconnected, irregular, straggling. **ramblingly,** *adv.* [ME *ramblen,* poss. from MDut. *rammelen,* to ROAM]

Ramboesque, Rambo, *a.* pertaining to the fictional film character Rambo, looking or behaving like him, i.e. with mindless violence and aggression. **Ramboism,** *n.* [*Rambo, First Blood II,* film released in Britain in 1985]

rambunctious, *a.* unruly, boisterous, exuberant. **rambunctiously,** *adv.* [perh. from Icel. *ram, bunctious* from BUMPTIOUS]

rambustious RUMBUSTIOUS.

rambutan, *n.* the red, hairy, pulpy fruit of a Malaysian tree, *Nephelium lappaceum.* [Malay, from *rambut,* hair]

RAMC, (*abbr.*) Royal Army Medical Corps.

Ram Das, *n.* (1534–81), Indian religious leader, fourth guru (teacher) of Sikhism (1574–81), who founded the Sikh holy city of Amritsar.

ramé, *a.* attired. [F, branched, from *rame,* L *rāmus,* branch]

rameal RAMAL.

Rameau, *n.* **Jean-Philippe** (1683–1764), French organist and composer. He wrote *Treatise on Harmony* (1722) and his varied works include keyboard and vocal music and many operas, such as *Castor and Pollux* (1737).

ramee RAMIE.

ramekin, *n.* a dish of cheese, eggs, breadcrumbs etc., baked in a small dish or mould; the mould itself. [F *ramequin,* etym. doubtful]

ramentum, *n.* (*usu. pl.*, **-ta**) thin membranous scales formed on leaves, stems etc.; debris of organic tissue discharged in some diseases. **ramentaceous**, *a*. [L, from *rādere,* to RAZE]

rameous, *a*. of or belonging to branches. [L *rāmus,* branch, -EOUS]

rami (*pl.*) RAMUS.

ramicorn, *a*. (*Ent.*) having ramified antennae. *n*. the horny sheath of the rami of the lower mandible in birds. [L *rāmus,* branch, *cornu,* horn]

ramie, *n*. a bushy Chinese and E Indian plant, *Boehmeria nivea,* of the nettle family; the fine fibre of this woven as a substitute for cotton. [Malay *rāmī*]

ramify, *v.i.* to divide into branches or subdivisions, to branch out, to send out offshoots; to develop a usually complicated consequence. *v.t.* to cause to divide into branches etc. **ramification**, *n*. the act of ramifying; a subdivision in a complex system, structure etc.; the production of figures like branches; the arrangement of branches; a consequence. [F *ramifier,* med. L *rāmificāre* (L *rāmus,* branch, *-ficāre, facere,* to make)]

Ramillies, Battle of, battle in which the British commander Marlborough defeated the French 23 May 1706, during the War of the Spanish Succession, at a village in Brabant, Belgium, 21 km/13 miles N of Namur.

ram-line RAM².

rammer RAM¹.

rammish, †rammy, *a*. strong-smelling; rank. **rammishness,** *n*. [RAM¹]

Ram Mohun Roy, *n*. (1774–1833), Indian religious reformer, founder in 1830 of Brahma Samaj, a mystic cult.

ramollissement, *n*. a morbid softening of some organ or tissue, esp. of the brain. [F, from *ramollir* (RE-, *amollir,* from *mou,* L *mollis,* soft, cp. MOLLIFY)]

ramose, †ramous, *a*. branching; branched; full of branches. **ramosely, -mously,** *adv*. **ramosity**, *n*. [L *rāmōsus,* from *rāmus,* branch]

ramp¹, *v.i.* of a heraldic lion, to rear or stand up on the hind-legs, with the forelegs raised; to dash about, to rage, to storm; to act in a violent or aggressive manner; to ascend or descend to another level (of a wall). *v.t.* to build or provide with ramps. *n*. a slope or inclined plane or way leading from one level to another, esp. in the interior of a fortification; a moveable stairway for boarding a plane; a hump in the road designed to slow traffic down; a difference in level between the abutments of a rampart arch; a sloping part in the top of a hand-rail, wall, coping etc.; †the act of ramping; †a vulgar, badly-behaved woman. **to ramp and rage,** to act in a violent manner. [OF *ramper,* to creep, crawl, climb, etym. doubtful]

ramp², *v.t.* (*sl.*) to rob with violence; to force (one) to pay a bet etc.; to swindle. *n*. (*sl.*) a swindle, esp. one involving exhorbitant price increases. **ramper, rampman,** *n*. a swindler; a robber, a footpad. [etym. doubtful]

rampage, *v.i.* to dash about, to storm, to rage, to behave violently or boisterously. *n*., boisterous, excited or violent behaviour. **on the rampage,** violently excited; on a drunken spree. **rampageous**, *a*. **rampageously,** *adv*. **rampageousness,** *n*. **rampager,** *n*. [etym. doubtful]

†rampallion, *n*. a rapscallion, a ruffian. [etym. doubtful]

rampant, *a*. standing upright on the hind legs, ramping (of the heraldic lion); unrestrained, aggressive, wild, violent; rank, luxuriant (of weeds etc.); springing from different levels (of an arch). **rampant gardant,** *a*. rampant, with the animal looking full-faced. **rampant passant,** *a*. in the attitude of walking with the dexter forepaw raised. **rampant regardant,** *a* rampant with the head looking backward. **rampancy,** *n*. **rampantly,** *adv*. [F, pres.p. of *ramper,* to RAMP¹]

rampart, *n*. an embankment, usu. surmounted by a parapet, round a fortified place, or such an embankment together with the parapet; (*fig.*) a defence. *v.t.* to fortify or defend with or as with a rampart. [F *rempart,* from *remparer,* to fortify (RE-, EM-, *parer,* L *parāre,* see PARRY]

ramper RAMP².

Ramphal, *n*. **Shridath Surendranath ('Sonny')** (1928–), Guyanese politician. He was minister of foreign affairs and justice (1972–75), and became secretary-general of the British Commonwealth (1975). He studied at the University of London and Harvard Law School.

rampick, rampike, *n*. (*dial., N Am.*) a dead or partly-decayed tree, a stump. **rampicked, -piked,** *a*. [etym. doubtful]

rampion, *n*. a bell-flower, *Campanula rapunculus,* with red, purple or blue blossoms. [prob. rel. to F *raiponce* or It. *raperonzolo*]

†rampire RAMPART.

Rampling, *n*. **Charlotte** (1945–), British actress, whose sometimes controversial films include *Georgy Girl* (1966), *The Night Porter/ Il Portiere di Notti* (1974), and *Farewell My Lovely* (1975).

ramplor, *n*. (*Sc.*) a happy wanderer. [prob. from RAMP¹]

ramrod etc. RAM¹.

Ramsay¹, *n*. **Allan** (1686–1758), Scottish poet, born in Lanarkshire. He became a wig-maker and then a bookseller in Edinburgh. He published *The Tea-Table Miscellany* (1724–37), and *The Evergreen* (1724), collections of ancient and modern Scottish song including revivals of the work of such poets as Dunbar and Henryson.

Ramsay², *n*. **Allan** (1713–84), Scottish portrait painter. After studying in Edinburgh and Italy, he established himself as a portraitist in London, and became painter to George III in 1760. He was the son of the poet Allan Ramsay.

Ramsay³, *n*. **William** (1852–1916), Scottish chemist who, with Lord Rayleigh, discovered argon in 1894. In 1895 Ramsay manufactured helium, and in 1898, in cooperation with Morris Travers, identified neon, krypton, and xenon. In 1903 with Frederick Soddy, he noted the transmutation of radium into helium, which led to the discovery of the density and atomic weight of radium. Nobel prize 1904.

Ramses II or **Rameses II,** *n*. king of Egypt about 1304–1236 BC, the son of Seti I. He campaigned successfully against the Hittites, and built two rock temples at Abu Simbel in Upper Egypt.

Ramses III or **Rameses III,** *n*. king of Egypt about 1200–1168 BC. He won a naval victory over the Philistines and other peoples, and asserted his suzerainty over Palestine.

ramshackle, *a*. in a crazy state, shaky, tumble-down, rickety. *v.t.* to construct in a ramshackle way. **ramshackly,** *a*. in bad repair. [var. of obs. *ramshackled,* prob. from *ransackle,* freq. of RANSACK]

ram's-horn RAM¹.

ramskin RAMEKIN.

ramson, *n*. (*usu. in pl.*) the broad-leaved garlic, *Allium ursinum,* or its bulbous root, eaten as a relish. [OE *hramsan,* pl. of *hramsa* (cp. G, Dan., Swed. *rams,* also Gr. *kromuon*)]

ram-stam, *a*. reckless, precipitate, headstrong, forward. *adv*. headlong, rashly, precipitately. *n*. a headstrong or hasty person. [Sc. (perh. RAM¹, *stam,* dial. var. of STAMP]

ramulose, -ulous, *a*. having many small branches. **ramuliferous,** *a*. **ramulus,** *n*. (*pl.* **-li**), a small branch or ramus. [L *rāmulōsus,* from *rāmulus,* dim. of *rāmus*]

ramus, *n*. (*pl.* **rami**) a branched or forked part or structure; (*Zool.*) the barb of a feather. [L *rāmus,* a branch]

ramuscule, *n*. a small branch.

ran¹, *n*. a length of 20 cords of twine. [etym. unknown]

ran², (*past*) RUN.

Rana, *n*. a genus of batrachians comprising the frogs and toads. [L, frog.]

rance¹, *n*. a variegated kind of marble. [etym. doubtful]

rance², *n*. a rod, bar or prop. [prob. from F *ranche*]

†rancescent, *a*. becoming sour or rancid. [L *rancescens -ntem,* pres.p. of *rancescere,* cogn. with *rancidus,* RANCID]

ranch, rancho, *n.* (*N Am.*) a farm for rearing cattle and horses; a house belonging to such a farm; any large farm devoted to a particular crop. *v.t.* to manage or work on a ranch. **ranchman, rancher, ranchero,** *n.* **rancheria,** *n.* a house or hut of a ranchero or rancheros; a cluster of Indian huts. [Sp. *rancho,* mess, a party eating together, prob. rel. to RANK[1]]

rancherie, *n.* any settlement of N American Indians in British Columbia, Canada. [Sp. *rancheria*]

rancid, *a.* having the taste or smell of stale oil or fat; rank; stale. **rancidify,** *v.t., v.i.* **rancidity, rancidness,** *n.* **rancidly,** *adv.* [L *rancidus*]

rancour, *n.* inveterate spite, resentment or enmity, malignancy, deep-seated malice; (*fig.*) corruption, poison. **rancorous,** *a.* **rancorously,** *adv.* [OF, from L *rancōrem,* nom. *-cor*]

rand, *n.* orig. a border, edge or margin; a strip of leather between the sole and heel-piece of a boot or shoe; a thin inner sole; (*S Afr.*) the highlands bordering a river-valley; the standard monetary unit of S Africa. **the Rand,** abbr. for Witwatersrand, the gold and diamond country in S Africa of which Johannesburg is the centre. [OE, also Dut. and G, Swed. and Dan., cp. Icel. *rönd*]

randan[1], *n.* a boat worked by three rowers, the one amidships using two oars; this method of rowing a boat. [etym. doubtful]

randan[2], *n.* (*sl.*) a spree. [perh. rel. to RANDOM]

R and B, (*abbr.*) rhythm and blues.

R and D, (*abbr.*) research and development.

randem, *a.* having three horses harnessed tandem. *adv.* in this fashion. *n.* a team or carriage driven thus. [from RANDOM after TANDEM]

randle-balk, -tree RANNEL-TREE.

random, *n.* great speed or impetuosity. *a.* done, made etc. without calculation or method; left to chance; of a statistical value which cannot be determined, only defined in terms of probability. **at random,** at haphazard; without direction or definite purpose; †at great speed. **random access,** *n.* direct access to specific data in a larger store of computer data. **random shot,** *n.* a shot discharged without direct aim; orig. a shot fired at the extreme range attainable by elevating the muzzle of a gun. **randomize, -ise,** *v.t.* to set up (e.g. a survey) in a deliberately random way to make any results more viable statistically. **randomization, -isation,** *n.* **randomizer, -iser,** *n.* **randomly,** *adv.* **randomwise,** *adv.* [F *randon*]

R and R, (*abbr.*) rock and roll.

randy, *a.* lustful; sexually aroused; (*chiefly Sc.*) loud-tongued, boisterous; disorderly, riotous; lustful, on heat. *n.* a sturdy beggar, a vagrant; a scold, a virago. **randily,** *adv.* **randiness,** *n.* [*rand* (RANT), -Y]

ranee, -ni, *n.* a Hindu queen; the consort of a rajah. [Hind. *rānī,* Sansk. *rājnī,* fem. of *rājā,* RAJAH]

rang, (*past*) RING[2].

rangatira, *n.* a Maori chief of either sex. [Maori]

range, *v.t.* to set in a row or rows; to arrange in definite order, place, company etc., to classify, to array; to rank; to roam or pass over, along or through; to sail along or about. *v.i.* to lie, extend or reach; (*Ordnance*) to carry (a specified distance) in a particular direction; to rank, to be in place (among, with etc.); to vary (from one specified point to another); to roam, to wander, to rove, to sail (along etc.); (*Ordnance*) to go or be thrown (of a projectile); to straighten. *n.* a row, rank, line, chain or series; a stretch, a tract, esp. of grazing or hunting-ground; the area, extent, scope, compass or sphere of power, activity, variation, voice-pitch etc.; a set of coils; the extreme horizontal distance attainable by a gun and the object aimed at; a piece of ground with targets etc. for firing practice; a cooking-stove or fireplace, usu. containing a boiler, oven or ovens, hotplate etc.; the set of values of a dependent variable in statistics. **to range oneself,** to adopt a more settled course of life, to settle down (as by marrying). **range-finder,** *n.* an instrument for measuring the distance of an object from the observer, used in shooting a gun or focusing a camera. **rangé,** *a.* set in order (of a number of charges). **ranger,** *n.* one who ranges, a rover, a wanderer; the superintendent of a royal forest or park; (*chiefly N Am.*) one who patrols a national park or forest; a dog used to scour over ground; a Girl Guide of 16 and upwards; (*N Am.*) a commando in the US army; (*pl.*) a body of mounted troops. **rangership,** *n.* **ranging rod,** *n.* a usually red and white striped rod used in surveying. **rangy,** *a.* tall, wiry, strong; (*Austral.*) mountainous. **rangily,** *adv.* **ranginess,** *n.* [OF *ranger,* from *rang,* RANK[1]]

rangiora, *n.* a broad-leaved shrub found in New Zealand. [Maori]

Rangoon, *n.* former name (until 1989) of YANGON.

rani RANEE.

ranine, *a.* of or pertaining to the underside of the tip of the tongue, where ranula occurs; †pertaining to or like frogs. **raniform,** *a.* frog-shaped. **ranivorous,** *a.* frog-eating. [RANA]

Ranjit Singh, *n.* (1780–1839), Indian maharajah. He succeeded his father as a minor Sikh leader in 1792, and created a Sikh army that conquered Kashmir and the Punjab. In alliance with the British, he established himself as 'Lion of the Punjab', ruler of the strongest of the independent Indian states.

rank[1], *n.* a row, a line, a row of soldiers ranged side by side, opp. to file; order, array; a row of taxis for hire; relative position, degree, standing, station, class; high station, dignity, eminence; relative degree of excellence etc.; a line of squares stretching across a board from side to side. *v.t.* to draw up or marshal in rank; to classify, to estimate, to give a (specified) rank to. *v.i.* to hold a (specified) rank; to have a place or position (among, with etc.); to have a place on the list of claims on a bankrupt's estate; (*N Am.*) to take precedence (over). **rank and fashion,** people of high society. **rank and file,** common soldiers; (*fig.*) ordinary people. **the ranks,** ordinary unpromoted soldiers collectively. **to close ranks,** to maintain solidarity. **to pull rank,** to take precedence by virtue of higher rank, sometimes unfairly. **to take rank with,** to be placed on a level or be ranked with. **ranker,** *n.* one who arranges in ranks; a commissioned officer promoted from the ranks. **ranking,** *a.* (*N Am., Can.*) highly placed; prominent; (*Carib. sl.*) stylish; exciting. *n.* a position on a scale of excellence. [F *ranc* (now *rang*)]

rank[2], *a.* luxuriant in growth, over-fertile, over-abundant; coarse, gross; rich, fertile; rancid, offensive, strong, evil-smelling; strongly marked, thorough, flagrant, arrant, utter; indecent, obscene; complete, total (e.g. a rank outsider). †*adv.* rankly. **rankly,** *adv.* **rankness,** *n.* [OE *ranc*]

Rank, *n.* **Joseph Arthur** (1888–1972), British film magnate. Having entered films in 1933 to promote the Methodist cause, he proceeded to gain control of much of the industry through takeovers and forming new businesses.

ranker RANK[1].

rankle, *v.i.* to be inflamed, to fester (of a wound etc.); to be inflamed, to irritate, to cause pain (of resentment etc.), anger or bitterness. [OF *rancler,* from *rancle, drancle,* an eruption or sore, med. L *dracunculus,* dim. of *draco,* DRAGON]

rankly RANK[2].

rankness RANK[2].

rannel-tree, *n.* (*Sc., North.*) a horizontal beam or bar, esp. one fixed across an open chimney for hanging cooking-utensils etc. on, also called **rannel-balk.** [etym. doubtful, perh. Scand.]

ransack, *v.t.* to search thoroughly, to rummage; to pillage, to plunder; †to ravish. **ransacker,** *n.* [Icel. *rannsaka,* (*rann,* house, *sækja,* to seek, cogn. with OE *sēcan,* SEEK)]

ransom, *n.* release from captivity in return for a payment; a sum of money paid for such release or for goods captured by an enemy; (*euphem.*) blackmail; †a fine or sum paid for the pardon of some offence. *v.t.* to redeem from captivity or obtain the restoration of (property) by paying a sum of money; to demand or exact a ransom for, to hold to ransom; to release in return for a ransom; to redeem from sin, to atone for. **a king's ransom,** a very large sum of money or amount of valuables. **to hold to ransom,** to keep in confinement until a ransom is paid. **ransomable,** *a.* **ransomer,** *n.* **ransomless,** *a.* [OF *ranson* (F *rançon*), L *redemptiōnem,* nom. *-tio,* REDEMPTION]

Ransome, *n.* **Arthur** (1884–1967), English journalist (correspondent in Russia for the *Daily News* during World War I and the Revolution) and writer of adventure stories for children, such as *Swallows and Amazons* (1930) and *Peter Duck* (1932).

rant, *v.i.* to use loud, bombastic or violent language; to declaim or preach in a theatrical or noisy fashion. *n.* bombastic or violent declamation; a tirade, a noisy declamation; inflated talk. **ranter,** *n.* one who rants; a declamatory preacher; (*pl.*) a nickname given to the Primitive Methodists. **ranterism,** *n.* **ranting,** *a.* **rantingly,** *adv.* **rantipole,** *n.* a wild, harum-scarum or romping person; a scold, a termagant. *a.* wild, harum-scarum, rakish. *v.i.* to behave or go about in a boisterous or extravagant fashion. †**rantism,** *n.* ranterism. [MDut. *randten, ranten*]

ranula, *n.* a cystic tumour under the tongue, sometimes called frog-tongue. **ranular,** *a.* [L *rānula,* dim. of *rāna,* frog]

ranunculus, *n.* (*pl.* **-luses, -li**) a genus of plants including the buttercup. **ranunculaceous,** *a.* pertaining to or belonging to this genus of plants. [L, dim. of *rāna,* frog]

ranz-des-vaches, *n.* a melody or flourish blown on their horns by Swiss herdsmen to call their cattle. [F (Swiss) *ranz,* etym. doubtful, *des vaches,* of the cows]

Rao, *n.* **Raja** (1909–), Indian writer, born at Hassan, Karnataka. He studied at Montpellier and the Sorbonne in France. He wrote about Indian independence from the perspective of a village in S India in *Kanthapura* (1938) and later, in *The Serpent and the Rope* (1960), about a young cosmopolitan intellectual seeking enlightenment.

Raoult, *n.* **Francois** (1830–1901), French chemist. In 1882, while working at the University of Grenoble, Raoult formulated one of the basic laws of chemistry. **Raoult's law** enabled the molecular weight of a substance to be determined by noting how much of the substance was required to depress the freezing point of a solvent by a certain amount.

rap[1], *v.t.* (*past, p.p.* **rapped**) to strike with a slight, sharp blow; to strike smartly; (*fig.*) to utter in a quick, abrupt way; to rebuke. *v.i.* to strike a sharp, quick blow, esp. at a door; to make a sharp, quick sound like a light blow; (*sl.*) to talk freely and informally; (*sl.*) to perform a rap. *n.* a slight, sharp blow; a sound like the blow from a knocker, the knuckles etc. on a door; a similar sound made by some agency as a means of communicating messages at a spiritualistic séance; a sharp rebuke; (*sl.*) a fast monologue spoken, often impromptu, over music. **to beat the rap,** (*N Am., Can. sl.*) to be acquitted of a crime, to escape punishment. **to rap on the knuckles,** to reprove, reprimand. **to take the rap,** (*coll.*) to take the blame for another. **rapper,** *n.* one who raps; a spirit-rapper; a door-knocker. **rapping,** *n.* the art of performing rhythmic monologues to music. [prob. imit., cp. G *rappeln,* to rattle]

rap[2], *n.* a counterfeit Irish coin, passing for a halfpenny in the time of George I; (*fig.*) a thing of no value. **not worth a rap,** worthless. [etym. doubtful]

†**rap**[3], *v.t.* to snatch away, to seize by violence; to transport, to carry out of oneself. [prob. rel. to Dan. *rappe,* Swed. *rappa,* G *rappen;* prob. in later sense a back-formation from RAPT]

rap[4], *n.* (*coll.*) an informal talk, chat. *v.t.* to get along well. [from *rapport,* etym. doubtful]

rapacious, *a.* grasping, extortionate; given to plundering or seizing by force, predatory; living on food seized by force (of animals). **rapaciously,** *adv.* †**rapaciousness, rapacity,** *n.* [L *rapax -pācis,* from *rapere,* to seize, see RAPE[1]]

Rapa Nui, *n.* another name for EASTER ISLAND.

rape[1], *v.t.* to ravish, to force (a woman) to have sexual intercourse against her will; to despoil, to violate; †to seize, to carry off. *n.* penetrative sexual intercourse of someone (usu. a woman) against the person's will; seizing or carrying off by force; violation, despoiling (e.g. of the countryside). **rapist,** *n.* [prob. from L *rapere,* to seize]

rape[2], *n.* one of six divisions of the county of Sussex. [prob. from OE, etym. doubtful]

rape[3], *n.* a plant, *Brassica napus,* allied to the turnip, grown as food for sheep; a plant, *B. campestris oleifera,* grown for its seed which yields oil, cole-seed. **wild rape,** charlock. **rape-cake,** *n.* the compressed seeds and husks of rape after the oil has been expressed, used for feeding cattle and as manure. **rape-oil,** *n.* oil obtained from the seed of *B. napus.* **rape-seed,** *n.* the seed of *B. napus.* [L *rāpum, rāpa,* turnip]

rape[4], *n.* the refuse stems and skins of grapes after the wine has been expressed, used to make vinegar; a large vessel used in making vinegar. [F *râpe,* med. L *raspa*]

rap-full, *a.* full of wind (of a sail when close-hauled). [etym. doubtful]

Raphael, *n.* **(Raffaello Sanzio)** (1483–1520), Italian painter, one of the greatest of the High Renaissance, active in Perugia, Florence, and Rome (from 1508), where he painted frescoes in the Vatican and for secular patrons. His harmoniously composed religious and mythological scenes were enormously influential; his portraits enhance his sitter's character and express dignity. Many of his designs were engraved. Much of his later work was the product of his studio. **Raphaelesque,** *a.* after the style of the Italian painter Raphael. **Raphaelism,** *n.* the idealistic principles of Raphael in painting. **Raphaelite,** *n.* [cp. PRERAPHAELITE]

raphanus, *n.* a genus of cruciferous plants typified by the radish. **raphania** , *n.* a form of ergotism supposed to be due to the use of grain containing seeds of species of raphanus. [L, from Gr. *raphanos,* radish]

raphe, *n.* a seam-like suture or line of union; a suture or line of junction, a median line or rib, a fibrovascular cord connecting the hilum of an ovule with the base of the nucleus. [mod. L and Gr.]

raphia RAFFIA.

raphilite, *n.* a tremolite. [as foll., -LITE]

raphis, *n.* (*usu. in pl.* **raphides**) needle-shaped transparent crystals, usu. of calcium oxalate, found in the cells of plants. [Gr. *raphis -idos,* needle]

rapid, *a.* very swift, quick, speedy; done, acting, moving or completed in a very short time; descending steeply. *n.* (*usu. pl.*) a sudden descent in a stream, with a swift current. **Rapid Deployment Force,** *n.* former name (until 1983) of US Central Command, a military strike force. **rapid eye movement** (*abbr.* **REM**), *n.* the rapid eye movement which usu. occurs during the dreaming phase of sleep. **rapid-fire,** *a.* quick-firing (of guns). **rapid-firer,** *n.* **rapid transit,** *n.* (*N Am.*) fast passenger transport, usually by underground, in urban areas. **rapidity,** †**rapidness,** *n.* **rapidly,** *adv.* [L *rapidus,* from *rapere,* to seize, see RAPE[1]]

rapier, *n.* a light, narrow sword, used only in thrusting, a small-sword. **rapier-fish,** *n.* a sword-fish. [F *rapière,* etym. doubtful]

rapine, *n.* the act of plundering or carrying off by force; plunder, spoliation, robbery. [F *rapine,* L *rapīna,* from *rapere,* to seize]

raploch, *n.* (*Sc.*) coarse homespun. *a.* coarse, homely. [etym. unknown]

rapparee, *n.* an Irish freebooter or robber, esp. during the late 17th and the 18th cents. [Ir. *repaire,* a noisy fellow, a robber]

rappee, *n.* a coarse kind of snuff. [F *râpé,* from *râper,* to RASP]

rappel, *n.* the beat of a drum calling soldiers to arms; abseiling. *v.i.* to abseil. [F, from *rappeler,* to recall, as REPEAL]

rapport, *n.* correspondence, sympathetic relationship, agreement, harmony. **rapporteur,** *n.* a person responsible for carrying out an investigation and presenting a report on it to a higher committee. [F, from *rapporter* (RE-, AP-, *porter,* L *portāre,* to carry)]

rapprochement, *n.* reconciliation, re-establishment of friendly relations, esp. between nations. [F, from *rapprocher*]

rapscallion, *n.* a rascal, a scamp, a good-for-nothing. *a.* rascally. [RASCALLION]

rapt, *a.* transported, carried away by one's thoughts or emotions, enraptured, absorbed, engrossed. **raptly,** *adv.* **raptness,** *n.* **raptor,** *n.* †a ravisher; one of the Raptores, birds of prey. [L *raptus,* p.p. of *rapere,* to seize, see RAPE[1]]

Raptores, *n.* an order of birds of prey containing the eagles, hawks and owls. **raptorial,** *n., a.* (pertaining to a) bird of prey; (of) its talons, adapted for seizing. **raptorious,** *a.* [L, pl. of *raptor,* as prec.]

rapture, *n.* ecstasy, transport, ecstatic joy; (*pl.*) a fit or transport of delight; †vehemence or violence of passion etc.; †a fit, a paroxysm. **raptured, rapturous,** *a.* **rapturist,** *n.* an enthusiast. **rapturously,** *adv.* [RAPT, -URE]

rara avis, *n.* a rarity, something very rarely met with. [L, rare bird]

rare[1], *a.* of sparse, tenuous, thin or porous substance, not dense; exceptional, seldom existing or occurring, not often met with, unusual, scarce, uncommon; especially excellent, singularly good, choice, first-rate. **rare earth metals,** a group of rare metals (in many of their properties resembling aluminium) which occur in some rare minerals. **rare gas,** *n.* an inert gas. **rarely,** *adv.* seldom; exceptionally; remarkably well. **rareness,** *n.* [L *rārus*]

rare[2], *a.* of eggs, soft; half-cooked, underdone. **rarebit,** WELSH RABBIT. [var. of *rear,* OE *hrēr*]

raree-show, *n.* a show carried about in a box, a peep-show. [corr. of RARE[1], SHOW]

rarefy, *v.t.* to make rare, thin, porous or less dense and solid; to expand without adding to the substance of; (*fig.*) to purify, to refine, to make less gross. *v.i.* to become less dense. **rarefaction, rarefication,** *n.* **rarefactive,** *a.* †**rarefiable,** *a.* **rarefied,** *a.* thin; exalted. [obs. F *raréfier,* L *rārēfacere* (*rārus,* RARE[1], *facere,* to make)]

rareripe, *a.* (*N Am.*) early ripe. *n.* an early fruit, esp. a variety of peach or an onion that ripens early. [var. of RATHE-RIPE]

raring, *a.* ready; eager. **raring to go,** eager to get started. [REAR[1]]

rarity, *n.* rareness; tenuity; unusual excellence; a rare thing; a thing of exceptional value through being rare. [F *rarité,* L *rāritātem,* nom. *-tas,* from *rārus,* RARE[1]]

ras, *n.* an Ethiopian governor or administrator. [Arab.]

rasbora, *n.* any of the small, brightly coloured cyprinid fishes from tropical Asia and E Africa, popular for aquariums. [etym. doubtful]

rascal, *n.* a mean rogue, a tricky, dishonest or contemptible fellow, a knave, a scamp; applied playfully to a child or animal etc. *a.* worthless, low, mean. **rascaldom, rascalism, rascality,** *n.* **rascallion,** *n.* a rascal. **rascally,** *a.* dishonest, contemptible. *adv.* in a dishonest manner. [OF *rascaille, rescaille* (F *racaille*), rabble, dregs, outcasts]

raschel, *n.* a type of knitted fabric, often with open patterns. [G *Raschelmaschine,* from Elisa Félix *Rachel,* 1821–58, French actress]

rase RAZE.

rash[1], *a.* hasty, precipitate, impetuous, venturesome; reckless, thoughtless, acting or done without reflection. **rashling,** *n.* a rash person. **rashly,** *adv.* **rashness,** *n.* [cp. Dan. and Swed. *rask,* Dut. and G *rasch,* quick, vigorous]

rash[2], *n.* an eruption of spots or patches on the skin; a series of unwelcome, unexpected events. [perh. from MF *rasche* (F *rache*)]

†**rash[3],** *v.i.* to snatch, to tear (away), to pull (down, out etc.). [form of obs. *arrache,* F *arracher* see RACE[4]]

Rashdun, *n.* the 'rightly guided ones', the first four caliphs (heads) of Islam: Abu Bakr, Umar, Uthman, and Ali.

rasher, *n.* a thin slice of bacon or ham for frying. [from obs. *rash,* to cut, var. of RAZE, or rel. to RASH[1], with the sense rashly or hastily cooked]

rashling, rashly, rashness RASH[1].

raskolnik, *n.* a dissenter from the Orthodox or Greek Church in Russia. [Rus., a schismatic]

Rasores, *n.pl.* an order of birds usu. called the Gallinae of which the common fowl is the type, characterized by the toes ending in strong claws for scratching up seeds etc. **rasorial,** *a.* [L, pl. of *rāsor,* from *rādere,* to scrape, see RAZE[1]]

rasp, *v.t.* to rub down, scrape or grate with a coarse, rough implement; to file with a rasp; (*fig.*) to irritate. *v.i.* to rub, to grate; to make a grating sound; (*fig.*) to grate (upon feelings etc.); to utter in a harsh tone. *n.* an instrument like a coarse file with projections or raised teeth for scraping away surface material; a harsh, grating noise. **raspatory,** *n.* a rasp for scraping the outer membrane from bones etc. **rasper,** *n.* a rasp, scraper, a rasping-machine; (*sl.*) an unpleasant sort of person; an extraordinary person or thing; (*coll.*) a difficult fence in hunting. **rasping,** *a.* **raspingly,** *adv.* [OF *rasper* (F *râper*), from Teut.]

raspberry, *n.* the fruit of various species of *Rubus,* esp. *R. idaeus,* consisting of red or sometimes white or yellow drupes set on a conical receptacle; (*coll.*) a rude derisive sound with the lips. **raspberry-cane,** *n.* a long woody shoot of the raspberry plant. **raspberry-vinegar,** *n.* a syrup prepared from raspberry juice. [obs. *rasp, raspis,* perh. rel. to RAPE[4]]

Rasputin, (Russian **'dissolute'**), *n.* **Gregory Efimovich** (1871–1916), Siberian wandering 'holy man', the illiterate son of a peasant. He acquired influence over the tsarina Alexandra, wife of Nicholas II, because of her faith in his power to cure her son of his haemophilia, and he was able to make political and ecclesiastical appointments. His abuse of power and his notorious debauchery (reputedly including the tsarina) led to his being murdered by a group of nobles, who (when poison had no effect) dumped him in the river Neva after shooting him.

rasse, *n.* a feline carnivore allied to the civet, inhabiting the E Indies and S China. [Jav. *rase*]

Rastafarian, Rasta, *n.* a member of the religious and political cult of Rastafarianism. *a.* pertaining to Rastafarians or Rastafarianism. **Rastafarianism,** *n.* religion originating in the West Indies, based on the ideas of Marcus Garvey, who preached that the only way for black people to escape their poverty and oppression was to return to Africa. When Haile Selassie (Ras Tafari, the Lion of Judah) was crowned emperor of Ethiopia in 1930, this was seen as a fulfilment of prophecy and Rastafarians acknowledged him as the Messiah, the incarnation of God (Jah). The use of ganja (marijuana) is a sacrament. There are no churches. **Rastaman,** *n.* a Rastafarian. [*Ras Tafari*]

raster, *n.* the scanning lines which appear as a patch of light on a television screen and which reproduce the image. [L *rastrum,* rake]

†**rasure,** *n.* the art of scraping or shaving; erasure. [F, from L *rāsūra,* from *rādere,* to RAZE[1]]

rat, *n.* one of the large rodents of the mouse family, esp. the black rat, *Mus rattus,* and *M. decumanus,* the grey, brown or Norway rat; one who deserts his party or his friends, a turncoat; (*coll.*) a worker who works for less than the trade-union rate of wages or who works during a strike, a blackleg; a despicable person. *v.i.* (*past, p.p.* **ratted**) to hunt or kill rats (esp. of dogs); (*coll.*) to play the rat in politics, in a strike etc. **like a drowned rat,** soaked to the skin. **rats!** (*sl.*) an exclamation of incredulity or derision. **to rat on,** to betray, to divulge secret information, to inform against. **to smell a rat,** to be suspicious. **ratbag,** *n.* (*sl.*) a despicable or unreliable person. **rat-catcher,** *n.* one who gets his living by catching rats. **rat kangaroo,** *n.* a kangaroo-like marsupial about the size of a rabbit. **rat race,** *n.* the continual competitive scramble of everyday life. **rat- run,** a minor road regularly used as a short-cut by drivers to avoid busy sign-posted routes. **ratsbane,** *n.* poison for rats. **rat-snake,** *n.* an Indian snake, *Zamenis mucosus,* which preys on rats. **rat's-tail,** *n.* (*pl.* **rat-tails**) a thing, esp. a file, like the tail of a rat. **rat-tail,** *n.* an excrescence growing from the pastern to the middle of the shank of a horse; a disease in horses in which the hair of the tail is lost; a tail like a rat's. **rat-tailed,** *a.* **rat-trap,** *n.* a trap for catching rats; a rat-trap pedal. *a.* applied to a cycle-pedal consisting of two parallel notched or toothed steel plates. **ratter,** *n.* someone or something, such as a dog, who or which catches rats. **ratting,** *n., a.* **ratty,** *a.* infested with or characteristic of rats; (*sl.*) annoyed, ill-tempered. [OE *ræt*]

rata, *n.* a large New Zealand forest tree of two species belonging to the myrtle family, having beautiful crimson flowers and yielding hard red timber. [Maori]

ratable, RATEABLE under RATE[1].

ratafia, *n.* a liqueur or cordial flavoured with the kernels of cherry, peach, almond or other kinds of fruit; a sweet biscuit eaten with this. [F]

ratal RATE[1].

ratan RATTAN[1].

ratany RHATANY.

rataplan, *n.* a noise like the rapid beating of a drum. *v.t.* to beat (a drum). *v.i.* to make a rataplan on a drum. **rat-a-tat** RAT-TAT. [F, imit.]

ratatouille, *n.* a vegetable casserole from Provence, France, made with aubergines, tomatoes, peppers etc., stewed slowly in olive oil. [F *touiller,* to stir]

ratch, *n.* a ratchet or ratchet-wheel. **ratchet,** *n.* a wheel or bar with inclined angular teeth, between which a pawl drops, permitting motion in one direction only; the pawl or detent that drops between the teeth of a ratchet-wheel. **ratchet-bar,** *n.* a bar with teeth into which a pawl drops to prevent motion in more than one direction. **ratchet-brace, -coupling, -drill, -jack, -lever, -punch, -wrench,** *n.* various tools or mechanical applicances working on the principle of the ratchet-bar or wheel with a pawl. **ratch-, ratchet-wheel,** *n.* a wheel with toothed edge. [etym. doubtful, cp. G *Ratsche,* also F *rochet,* whence prob. the form *ratchet*]

ratchel, *n.* (*prov.*) fragments of stone lying above bed-rock; hard pan. [etym. doubtful]

rate[1], *n.* the proportional measure of something in relation to some other thing, ratio, comparative amount, degree etc.; a standard by which any quantity or value is fixed; valuation, price, value, relative speed etc.; a sum levied upon property for local purposes, distinguished from taxes which are for national purposes (*N Am.* local tax); †rank or class, esp. of a ship of war. *v.t.* to estimate the value, relative worth, rank etc. of; to fix the rank of (a seaman etc.); to assess for local rates; to subject to payment of local rates; (*coll.*) to consider, to regard as. *v.i.* to be rated or ranked (as). **at any rate,** in any case; even so. **at that rate,** if that is so. **to rate up,** to subject to a higher rate or premium in order to cover increased risks. **rate-book,** *n.* a book of rates or prices; a record of local valuations for assessment of rates. **rate-cap,** *v.t.* to restrict the amount of money a local authority may levy in rates. **rate-capping,** *n.* **ratepayer,** *n.* one who is liable to pay rates. **rate support grant,** *n.* the money given to local authorities by central government to supplement the amount it raises in rates. **ratal,** *n.* the amount on which local rates are assessed. **rateable,** *a.* liable to be rated, subject to assessment for municipal rates; †capable of being rated or valued; proportional, estimated proportionally. **rateable value,** *n.* the estimated value of a property, used annually to assess the rates chargeable on the property. **rateability,** *n.* **rateably,** *adv.* **rater,** *n.* one who rates or assesses. **-rater,** *n.* (*in comb.*) a ship or boat, esp. a yacht, of a specified rate. [OF from med. L *rata,* fem. of L *ratus,* p.p. of *rērī,* to think, to judge]

rate[2], *v.t.* to chide angrily, to scold. *v.i.* to chide, to storm (at). [etym. doubtful]

ratel, *n.* a nocturnal carnivore of the genus *Mellivora,* allied to the badger, with two species, *M. indicus,* from India, and *M. capensis,* the honey-badger of W and S Africa. [Afrikaans, etym. doubtful]

ratepayer, rater etc. RATE[1].

ratfink, *n.* (*derog.*) a despicable person. *a.* mean, despicable. [etym. doubtful]

rath[1], *n.* a prehistoric Irish hill-fort or earthwork. [Ir.]

rath[2], †rathe[1], *adv.* early, soon, quickly. *a.* coming, appearing, ripening etc. early or before the usual time; quick, speedy; pertaining to early morning. **rath-, rathe-ripe,** *a.* ripening early. *n.* an early kind of apple, pea etc. [OE *hrathe,* adv. from *hræd,* a., quick]

Rathaus, *n.* a town-hall in Germany. [G *Rät,* counsellor, cp. OE *ræd,* counsel, *haus,* HOUSE]

Rathbone, *n.* **(Philip St John) Basil** (1892–1967), South African-born British character actor, one of the cinema's great villains; he also played Sherlock Holmes (the fictional detective created by Arthur Conan Doyle) in several films. He worked mainly in Hollywood, in films such as *The Adventures of Robin Hood* (1938) and *The Hound of the Baskervilles* (1939).

rathe[1] RATH[2].

rathe[2] RAVE[2].

Rathenau, *n.* **Walther** (1867–1922), German politician. He was a leading industrialist, and was appointed economic director during World War I, developing a system of economic planning in combination with capitalism. After the war he founded the Democratic Party, and became foreign minister in 1922. The same year he signed the Rapallo Treaty of Friendship with the USSR, cancelling German and Soviet counterclaims for indemnities for World War I, and soon after was murdered by right-wing fanatics.

rather, *adv.* sooner, more readily or willingly, preferably, for choice; with more reason, more properly, rightly, or truly, more accurately; in a greater degree, to a greater extent; to a certain extent; slightly, somewhat; (*coll.*) very much, assuredly; yes, certainly. **the rather,** by so much the more. **ratherish,** *adv.* (*N Am.*). **ratherly,** *adv.* (*Sc.*). [comp. of RATH[2]]

ratify, *v.t.* to confirm, to establish or make valid (by formal consent or approval). **ratifiable,** *a.* **ratification,** *n.* **ratifier,** *n.* [F *ratifier,* med. L *ratificāre* (*ratus,* RATE[1], *-ficāre, facere,* to make)]

rating[1], *n.* the act of assessing, judging, renting etc.; the amount fixed as a local rate; the class or grade of a seaman as stated in the ship's books; (*collect. pl.*) persons of a particular rating; a ship's crew; an evaluation of the popularity of radio or television programmes.

rating[2], *n.* a scolding, a harsh reprimand.

rating[3], *n.* a limit on the conditions under which a device, equipment, apparatus etc. will operate satisfactorily.

ratio, *n.* the relation of one quantity or magnitude to another of the same kind, measured by the number of times one is contained by the other, either integrally or fractionally; the relation existing between speeds of driving and driven gears, pulleys etc. **turns ratio,** the ratio of the number of turns of wire in the primary winding of a transformer to the number in the secondary. [L, as RATE[1]]

ratiocinate, *v.i.* to reason or argue; to deduce consequences from premises or by means of syllogisms. **ratiocination,** *n.* **ratiocinative,** *a.* **ratiocinator,** *n.* **ratiocinatory,** *a.* [L *ratiōcinātus,* p.p. of *ratiōcinārī,* as prec.]

ration, *n.* a fixed allowance of food served out for a given time; a portion of provisions etc. allowed to one individual; (*pl.*) provisions, esp. food. *v.t.* to supply with rations; to put on fixed rations. **ration book,** *n.* a book issued periodically containing coupons etc. authorizing the holder to draw rations. [F, from L RATIO]

rational[1], *a.* having the faculty of reasoning, endowed with mental faculties; agreeable to reasoning, reasonable, sensible, not foolish, not extravagant; based on or conforming to what can be tested by reason; of a number which can be expressed as the ratio of two integers, quantities. **rational dress,** *n.* a dress regarded as more sensible than the conventional one for women.

rational number, *n.* a number expressed as the ratio of two integers. †**rationable,** *a.* **rationally,** *adv.* **rationale,** *n.* a statement or exposition of reasons or principles; the logical basis or fundamental reason (of anything). **rationalism,** *n.* the determination of all questions of belief, esp. in religious matters, by the reason, rejecting supernatural revelation; the doctrine that reason supplies certain principles for the interpretation of phenomena that cannot be derived from experience alone. **rationalist,** *n.* **rationalistic,** *a.* **rationalistically,** *adv.* **rationality,** †**rationalness,** *n.* the quality of being rational; the power of reasoning; reasonableness. **rationalize, -ise,** *v.t.* to convert to rationalism; to interpret as a rationalist; to render rational or reasonable; to clear (an equation etc.) of radical signs; to reorganize so as to make more efficient and economic. *v.i.* to think or act as a rationalist. **rationalization, -isation,** *n.* the act of rationalizing; the attempt to supply a conscious reason for an unconscious motivation in the explanation of behaviour. **rationalization of industry,** the systematic organization of industries, co-operation between employers and employees, and the extension of scientific methods to all phases of production. **rationalizer, -iser,** *n.* [L *ratiōnālis,* as prec.]

rational[2]**,** *n.* a pectoral formerly worn by bishops in celebrating Mass; †the breastplate of the Jewish high priest. [L *ratiōnāle,* neut. of *ratiōnālis,* as prec., translating Heb. *hōshen,* after Gr. *logeion,* oracle]

ratite, *n.* of or belonging to the group Ratitae or birds with a keelless sternum and abortive wings, comprising the ostrich, emu, cassowary, kiwi, moa etc. **ratitous,** †**ratitate,** *a.* [L *ratis,* raft, -ITE]

ratline, ratling, *n.* one of the small ropes extended across the shrouds on each side of a mast, forming steps or rungs. [etym. doubtful, perh. rel. to OF *raalingue,* small cords strengthening a sail etc.]

ratoon, rattoon, *n.* a sprout from the root of a sugarcane that has been cut down. *v.t.* to cut down so as to encourage growth. [Sp. *retoño,* shoot, sprout]

ratsbane RAT.

rattan[1]**,** *n.* the long, thin, pliable stem of various species of E Indian climbing palms of the genus *Calamus;* a switch or walking-stick of this material; (*collect.*) such stems used for wickerwork etc. [Malay *rōtan,* from *rāut,* to pare]

rattan[2]**,** *n.* the beat of a drum, a rataplan.

rat-tat, *n.* a rapid knocking sound as of a knocker on a door. [imit.]

ratteen, *n.* a thick quilted or twilled woollen stuff. [F *ratine,* etym. doubtful]

ratten, *v.t.* to annoy or molest by destroying, injuring or taking away the tools or machinery of (a worker or employer) in a trade-union dispute etc. *v.i.* to practise this method of persecution. **rattener,** *n.* [etym. doubtful, perh. var. of obs. *ratton,* OF *raton,* RAT]

ratter RAT[1].

Rattigan, *n.* **Terence** (1911–77), English playwright. His play *Ross* (1960) was based on T.E. Lawrence (Lawrence of Arabia).

†**rattinet,** *n.* a woollen stuff thinner than ratteen. [RATTEEN, -ET]

rattle, *v.i.* to make a rapid succession of sharp noises, as of things clattered together or shaken in a hollow vessel; to talk rapidly, noisily or foolishly; to move, go or act with a rattling noise; to run, ride or drive rapidly. *v.t.* to cause to make a rattling noise, to make (a window, door etc.) rattle; to utter, recite, play etc. (off, away etc.) rapidly; to stir (up); to cause to move quickly with noise, to drive fast; to scold. *n.* a rapid succession of sharp noises; an instrument, esp. a child's toy, with which such sounds are made; a rattling noise in the throat; rapid, noisy or empty talk, chatter; an incessant chatterer; noise, bustle, racket, boisterous gaiety; the horny articulated rings in the tail of the rattlesnake, which make a rattling noise; a plant (**red rattle, yellow rattle**) having seeds that rattle in their cases. **rattle-bag, -box,** *n.* a bag or box with loose things inside for rattling. **rattle-brain, -head, -pate,** *n.* **rattle-brained, -headed, -pated,** *a.* giddy, wild, empty-headed. **rattlesnake,** *n.* a snake of the American genus *Crotalus,* the tail of which is furnished with a rattle. **rattletrap,** *n.* a rickety object, esp. a vehicle; (*pl.*) valueless articles, rubbishy curios. *a.* rickety, rubbishy. **rattlewort,** *n.* a plant of the genus *Crotalaria.* **rattler,** *n.* one who or that which rattles; (*sl.*) a first-rate specimen. **rattling,** *a.* making a rapid succession of sharp noises; (*coll.*) brisk, vigorous; (*sl.*) first-rate, excellent. [ME *ratelen* (cp. Dut. *ratelen,* G *rasseln*)]

Rau, *n.* **Johannes** (1931–), West German socialist politician, member of the Social Democratic Party (SPD).

raucous, *a.* hoarse, rough or harsh in sound. **raucity,** *n.* **raucously,** *adv.* **raucousness,** *n.* [L *raucus*]

†**raught,** (*past, p.p.*) REACH[1].

raunchy, *a.* (*sl.*) earthy; smutty; slovenly. **raunchily,** *a.* **raunchiness,** *n.* [etym. unknown]

Raunkiaer system of classification, *n.* a scheme devised by the Danish ecologist Christen Raunkiaer (1860–1938) whereby plants are divided into groups according to the position of their perennating buds in relation to the soil surface. For example, plants in cold areas, such as the tundra, generally have their buds protected below ground, whereas in hot, tropical areas they are above ground and freely exposed. This method of plant classification is useful for comparing vegetation types in different parts of the world.

raupo, *n.* the giant bulrush of New Zealand. [Maori]

Rauschenberg, *n.* **Robert** (1925–), US pop artist, a creator of happenings (art in live performance) and incongruous multimedia works such as *Monogram* (1959, Moderna Muséet, Stockholm), a car tyre around the body of a stuffed goat daubed with paint.

rauwolfia, *n.* a tropical flowering shrub from SE Asia; the root of this plant, which yields a drug. [Leonhard *Rauwolf,* d. 1596, G botanist]

ravage, *n.* devastation, ruin, havoc, waste; (*pl.*) devastating effects. *v.t.* to devastate; to spoil, to pillage. *v.i.* to make havoc. **ravager,** *n.* [F, from *ravir,* to RAVISH]

Ravana, *n.* in the Hindu epic *Ramamayana,* the demon king of Lankā (Sri Lanka) who abducted Sita, the wife of Rama.

rave[1]**,** *v.i.* to wander in mind, to be delirious, to talk wildly, incoherently or irrationally; to speak in a furious way (against, at etc.); to act, move or dash furiously, to rage; to be excited, to go into raptures (about etc.); (*sl.*) to enjoy oneself wildly. *v.t.* to utter in a wild, incoherent or furious manner. *n.* the act of raving; a raving sound; extravagant enthusiasm; infatuation. **rave-up,** *n.* (*sl.*) a very lively party. **raver,** *n.* **raving,** *a.* frenzied; marked. *n.pl.* extravagant, irrational utterances. **ravingly,** *adv.* [prob. from OF *raver,* var. of *rêver,* to dream (cp. REVERIE)]

rave[2]**,** †**rathe**[2]**,** *n.* a cart-rail, esp. (*pl.*) a framework added to enable a larger load to be carried; (*N Am.*) a vertical sidepiece in a wagon, sleigh etc. [etym. doubtful]

ravel, *v.t.* (*past, p.p.* **ravelled**) to entangle, to confuse, to complicate, to involve; to untwist, to disentangle, to separate the component threads of; to fray. *v.i.* to become tangled; to become untwisted, unravelled or unwoven; to fray (out); †to busy oneself with intricacies. **raveller,** *n.* **ravelling,** *n.* the act of entangling, confusing etc.; the act of unravelling; anything, as a thread, separated in the process of unravelling. †**ravelly,** *a.* **ravelment,** *n.* [prob. from MDut. *ravelen*]

Ravel, *n.* **(Joseph) Maurice** (1875–1937), French composer. His work is characterized by its sensuousness, unresolved dissonances, and 'tone colour'. Examples are the piano pieces *Pavane pour une infante défunte* (1899) and *Jeux d'eau* (1901), and the ballets *Daphnis et Chloë* (1912) and *Boléro* (1928).

ravelin, *n.* (*Fort.*) a detached work with a parapet and ditch forming a salient angle in front of the curtain of a larger work. [F, from It. *rivellino,* earlier *ravellino*]

raven[1]**,** *n.* a large, black, omnivorous bird, *Corvus cor-*

ax, of the crow family. *a.* resembling a raven in colour, glossy black. [OE *hræfn* (cp. Dut. *raaf,* G *Rabe,* Icel. *hragn,* Dan. *ravn*]

raven[2], *v.t.* to devour with voracity; †to ravage, to plunder. *v.i.* to plunder; to go about ravaging; to prowl after prey; to be ravenous. †*n.* ravin. †**ravener,** *n.* **ravening,** *n., a* **raveningly,** *adv.* [OF *raviner,* from L *rapīna,* RAPINE]

ravenous, *a.* voracious, hungry, famished; furiously rapacious, eager for gratification. **ravenously,** *adv.* **ravenousness,** *n.* [OF *ravineux,* as prec.]

†**ravin,** *n.* plundering, rapine, spoliation, ravaging; prey. **beast of ravin,** a beast of prey. †**ravined[1],** *a.* ravenous. [OF *ravine,* L *rapīna,* RAPINE]

ravine, *n.* a long, deep hollow caused by a torrent, a gorge, a narrow gully or cleft. **ravined[2],** *a.* [F, orig. a torrent, as prec.]

ravingly RAVE[1].

ravioli, *n.* small pasta cases with a savoury filling. [It. dial. *raviolo,* little turnip]

ravish, *v.t.* to carry away, to enrapture, to transport (with pleasure etc.); to violate, to rape; †to snatch away or carry off by force. **ravisher,** *n.* one who ravishes, rapes or carries off by force. **ravishing,** *a.* enchanting, charming, entrancing, transporting, filling one with rapture. **ravishingly,** *adv.* **ravishment,** *n.* [F *raviss-,* pres.p. stem of *ravir,* L *rapere,* to seize, to snatch]

raw, *a.* uncooked; in the natural state; not wrought, not manufactured, requiring further industrial treatment; unhemmed; untrained, unskilled, inexperienced, undisciplined, immature, fresh; crude, untempered; having the skin off, having the flesh exposed, galled, inflamed, sore; cold and damp, bleak (of weather). *n.* a raw place on the body, a sore, a gall. **in the raw,** in its natural state; naked. **to touch on the raw,** to wound in a sensitive spot. **raw-boned,** *a.* having bones scarcely covered with flesh, gaunt. **raw deal,** *n.* (*coll.*) unfair treatment. **raw-head,** *n.* a spectre or goblin. **raw-head and bloody-bones,** a death's-head and cross-bones. *a.* applied to blood-and-thunder fiction etc. **rawhide,** *n.* untanned leather; a whip made of this. *v.t.* to whip with this. **raw material,** *n.* the material of any manufacturing process. **raw silk,** *n.* natural and untreated silk fibre; material made from untreated silk fibres. **raw umber,** *n.* umber that has not been calcined; the colour of this. **rawish,** *a.* †**rawly,** *adv.* **rawness,** *n.* [OE *hrēaw* (cp. Dut. *raauw,* G *roh,* Icel. *hrār,* also L *crūdus, cruor,* blood, Gr. *kreas,* raw flesh)]

Rawalpindi, *n.* city in Punjab province, Pakistan, in the foothills of the Himalayas; population (1981) 928,400. Industries include oil refining, iron, chemicals, and furniture.

rawinsonde, *n.* a hydrogen balloon which carries meteorological instruments to measure wind velocity. [*ra*dar, *win*d, radio*sonde*]

Rawlinson, *n.* **Henry Creswicke** (1810–95), English orientalist and political agent in Baghdad in the Ottoman Empire from 1844. He deciphered the Babylonian and Old Persian scripts of Darius I's trilingual inscription at Behistun, Persia, continued the excavation work of A.H. Layard, and published a *History of Assyria* (1852).

Rawls, *n.* **John** (1921–), US philosopher. In *A Theory of Justice* (1971), he revived the concept of the 'social contract', and its enforcement by civil disobedience.

rax, *v.i.* (*Sc., North.*) to stretch or reach (out or up). *v.t.* to stretch or strain (oneself); to stretch (the hand) out. [OE *raxan,* etym. doubtful]

ray[1], *n.* a line or beam of light proceeding from a radiant point; a straight line along which radiant energy, esp. light or heat, is propagated; (*fig.*) a gleam, a vestige or slight manifestation (of hope, enlightenment etc.); one of a series of radiating lines or parts; the outer whorl of florets in a composite flower; one of the bony rods supporting the fin of a fish, one of the radial parts of a starfish or other radials. *v.t.* to shoot out (rays), to radiate; to adorn with rays. *v.i.* to issue or shine forth in rays. **Becquerel rays** BECQUEREL. **Röntgen rays** RÖNTGEN. **ray flower, floret,** *n.* any of the small strap-shaped flowers in the flower head of some composite plants, such as the daisy. **ray fungus,** *n.* the Actinomyces bacterium which forms radiating threads. **ray-gun,** *n.* in science fiction, a gun which sends out rays to kill or stun. **rayed,** *a.* **rayless,** *a.* **raylet,** *n.* a small ray. [OF *rai, ray,* nom. *rais,* L RADIUS]

ray[2], *n.* any of several large cartilaginous fish allied to the sharks, with a flat disk-like body and a long, slender tail. [ME and OF *raye* (F *raie*) L *raia*]

ray[3], *n.* the second note in the tonic sol-fa notation.

Ray[1], *n.* **John** (1627–1705), English naturalist who devised a classification system accounting for nearly 18,000 plant species. It was the first system to divide flowering plants into monocotyledons and dicotyledons, with additional divisions made on the basis of leaf and flower characters and fruit types.

Ray[2], *n.* **Man** (adopted name of Emmanuel Rudnitsky) (1890–1976), US photographer, painter, and sculptor, active mainly in France; associated with the DADA movement. His pictures often showed surrealist images like the photograph *Le Violon d'Ingres* (1924).

Ray[3], *n.* **Nicholas** (adopted name of Raymond Nicholas Kienzle) (1911–79), US film director, critically acclaimed for his socially aware dramas such as *Rebel Without a Cause* (1955). His later epics, such as *King of Kings* (1961), were less successful.

Ray[4], *n.* **Satyajit** (1921–), Indian film director, renowned for his trilogy of life in his native Bengal: *Pather Panchali*, *Unvanquished*, and *The World of Apu* (1955–59). Later films include *The Chess Players* (1977) and *The Home and the World* (1984).

Rayah, *n.* a non-Muslim subject in Turkey. [Arab. *ra'ūjah,* flock, from *ra'ā,* to feed]

rayed, rayless RAY[1].

†**rayle** RAIL[2].

Raynaud's disease, *n.* a condition in which the blood supply to the extremities is reduced by periodic spasm of the blood vessels on exposure to cold. It is most often seen in young women.

rayon, *n.* a radius, an area measured from a central point; artificial silk made from cellulose; †a ray, a beam. †**rayonnance,** *n.* radiance. **rayonné,** *a.* having radiating points or alternate projections and depressions. [F, from *rai,* RAY[1]]

razee, *n.* a vessel cut down to a less number of decks. *v.t.* to reduce (a ship) in height thus. [F *rasée,* p.p. of prec.]

raze[1], rase, *v.t.* †to graze or shave; (*usu. fig.*) to wound slightly; to scratch (out); to erase, to obliterate; to demolish, to level with the ground, to destroy. **razed, rased,** *a.* **razer, raser,** *n.* [F *raser,* pop. L *rāsāre,* freq. of L *rādere* (p.p. *rāsus*), to scrape]

†**raze[2]** RACE[3], RAISE.

razoo, *n.* (*Austral. sl.*) a farthing. **not a brass razoo,** not a farthing. [etym. unknown]

razor, *n.* a cutting instrument for shaving off the hair of the beard or head. *v.t.* to shave with a razor; to shave; to cut (down) close. **razor-back,** *n.* a sharp back like a razor; (*Austral.*) a skinny bullock. *a.* having a sharp back or ridge like a razor. **razor-backed,** *a.* **razor-bill,** *n.* a bird with a bill like a razor, esp. the razor-billed auk, *Alca torda.* **razor-billed,** *a.* **razor-blade,** *n.* a blade used in a razor, for cutting or shaving. **razor-edge,** *n.* the edge of a razor; a keen edge; (*fig.*) a sharp crest or ridge, as of a mountain; a critical situation, a crisis; a sharp line of demarcation, esp. between parties or opinions. **razor-fish,** *n.* a fish of the Labridae, *Xyrichthis novacula* or *X. lineatus.* **razor-shell,** *n.* a bivalve mollusc with a shell like a razor. **razor-strop,** *n.* a leather pad on which a razor is sharpened. **razor wire,** *n.* strong wire set across with pieces of sharp metal. †**razorable,** *a.* fit to be shaved. [OF *rasor* (F *rasoir*), late L *rāsōrium,* from *rādere,* to RAZE]

†**razure** RASURE.

razz, *n.* (*sl.*) a sound of contempt, a raspberry. *v.t.* (*N Am., Can.*) to jeer at, to heckle.

razzamatazz, *n.* colourful, noisy, lively atmosphere or activities.

razzia, *n.* a foray or incursion for the purpose of capturing slaves etc., as practised by African Muslims. [F, from Algerian *ghāzīah,* var. of Arab. *ghazwah,* from *ghazw,* making war]

razzle-dazzle, *n.* (*coll.*) bewilderment, excitement, stir, bustle; intoxication. *v.t.* to dazzle, to daze; to bamboozle; to intoxicate. **on the razzle-dazzle,** on the spree. [DAZZLE]

Rb, (*chem. symbol*) rubidium.

RC, (*abbr.*) Red Cross; Roman Catholic.

RCA, (*abbr.*) Royal College of Art.

RCN, (*abbr.*) Royal Canadian Navy; Royal College of Nursing.

RCP, (*abbr.*) Royal College of Physicians.

RCS, (*abbr.*) Royal College of Surgeons; Royal Corps of Signals.

RCVS, (*abbr.*) Royal College of Veterinary Surgeons.

rd, (*abbr.*) road; rod.

RDC, (*abbr.*) (*formerly*) Rural District Council.

RE, (*abbr.*) religious education; Royal Engineers.

Re, (*chem. symbol*) rhenium.

re[1]**,** *n.* the second note of a major scale; the second note of the scale of C major, D. [It., see GAMUT]

re[2]**,** *prep.* in the matter of; (*coll.*) as regards, about. [L, abl. of *rēs,* thing, matter, affair]

re-, *pref.* back, backward, back again; after, behind; un-; in return, mutually; again, again and again, afresh, anew, repeatedly; against, in opposition; off, away, down. [L, back, again]

reabsorb, *v.t.* to absorb anew or again. **reabsorption,** *n.* **reaccommodate,** *v.t.* to accommodate or adjust afresh or again. **reaccuse,** *v.t.* to accuse again.

reach, *v.t.* to stretch out; to extend; to extend towards so as to touch, to extend as far as, to attain to, to arrive at, to hit, to affect; to hand, to deliver, to pass. *v.i.* to reach out, to extend; to reach or stretch out the hand; to make a reaching effort, to put forth one's powers, to be extended so as to touch, to have extent in time, space etc.; to attain (to). *n.* the act or power of reaching; extent, range, compass, power, attainment; an unbroken stretch of water, as between two bends; the direction travelled by a vessel on a tack. **reach-me-down,** *a.* cheap ready-made or second-hand (of clothes). *n.pl.* ready-made or second-hand clothes. **reachable,** *a.* **reacher,** *n.* **reaching,** *a.* [OE *rǣcan* (cp. Dut. *reiken,* G *reichen*]

reacquire, *v.t.* to acquire anew.

react, *v.i.* to act in response (to a stimulus etc.); to have a reciprocal effect, to act upon the agent; to act or tend in an opposite manner, direction etc.; to exert an equal and opposite force to that exerted by another body; to exert chemical action (upon). *v.t.*, to act again. **reaction,** *n.* reciprocal action; the response of an organ etc. to stimulation; the chemical action of one substance upon another; the equal and opposite force exerted upon the agent by a body acted upon; contrary action or condition following the first effects of an action; action in an opposite direction, esp. in politics after a reform movement, revolution etc.; a phenomenon obtained from a three-electrode valve whereby a small voltage on the grid is strengthened by the amplified currents flowing in the anode circuit. **reaction engine, -motor,** *n.* an engine or motor which develops thrust by expelling gas at high speed. **reaction turbine,** *n.* a turbine where the working fluid is accelerated through expansion in the static nozzles and the rotor blades. **reactionary,** *a.* involving or tending towards reaction, esp. in politics, retrograde, conservative. *n.* a reactionary person. **reactionism,** *n.* **reactionist,** *n.* **reactivate,** *v.t.* to restore to a state of activity. **reactivation,** *n.* **reactive,** *a.* **reactively,** *adv.* **reactivity**, †**reactiveness,** *n.* **reactor,** *n.* a substance which undergoes a reaction; a vessel in which reaction takes place; a nuclear reactor; a person sensitive to a given drug or medication.

read, *v.t.* (*past, p.p.* **read**), to perceive and understand the meaning of (printed, written or other characters, signs, symbols, significant features etc.), to peruse; to reproduce mentally or vocally or instrumentally (words, notes etc. conveyed by symbols etc.); to discover by observation, to interpret, to explain; to assume as implied in a statement etc.; to see through; to learn or ascertain by reading; to study by reading; to bring into a specified condition by reading; to study for an examination; to indicate or register (of a meteorological instrument etc.). *v.i.* to follow or interpret the meaning of a book etc.; to pronounce (written or printed matter) aloud; to render written music vocally or instrumentally (well, easily etc.); to acquire information (about); to study by reading; to mean or be capable of interpretation (in a certain way etc.); to sound or affect (well, ill etc.) when perused or uttered. *n.* an act of reading, a perusal. **to read a lesson, lecture, to someone,** to scold, to reprimand someone. **to read between the lines** LINE[1]. **to read into,** to extract a meaning not explicit. **to read off,** to take a reading, or information, from an instrument, e.g. a thermometer. **to read oneself in,** to enter upon an incumbency by the public reading of the Thirty-nine Articles. **to read out,** to read aloud; †to read through or to the end. **to read out of,** to expel from by the formal reading of a sentence or proclamation. **to read someone's mind,** to make an accurate guess as to what someone is thinking. **to take as read** TAKE. **read-out,** *n.* the data retrieved from a computer; the act of retrieving data from computer storage facilities for display on screen or as print-out. **read-write head,** *n.* the electromagnetic head in a computer disk-drive which reads or writes data on magnetic tape or disk. **readable,** *a.* worth reading, interesting, legible. **readableness, readability**, *n.* **readably,** *adv.* **reader,** *n.* one who reads; one who reads much; a person employed by a publisher to read and report upon manuscripts etc. offered for publication; a corrector of the press; a person appointed to read aloud, esp. parts of the church service; a professional elocutionist; a lecturer in some universities, Inns of Court etc.; a text-book, a book of selections for translation, a reading-book for schools. **readership,** *n.* the post of university reader; a body of readers, especially of a particular author or publication. **reading,** *a.* addicted to reading, studious. *n.* the act, practice or art of reading; the study or knowledge of books, literary research, scholarship, a public recital or entertainment at which selections etc. are read to the audience; the form of a passage given by a text, editor etc.; the way in which a passage reads, an interpretation, a rendering, an observation made by examining an instrument; the recital of the whole or part of a Bill as a formal introduction or measure of approval in a legislative assembly. **first reading,** the formal introduction of a Bill. **second reading,** a general approval of the principles of a Bill. **third reading,** the final acceptance of a Bill together with the amendments passed in committee. **reading-book,** *n.* a book of selections to be used as exercises in reading. **reading-desk,** *n.* a stand for books etc. for the use of a reader, esp. in church, a lectern. **reading-glass,** *n.* a hand magnifying-glass. **reading-lamp,** *n.* a lamp for reading by. **reading-room,** *n.* a room in a library, club etc. furnished with books, papers etc. for the use of readers. [OE *rǣdan* (cp. Dut. *raden,* G *rathen,* Icel. *ratha,* Goth. *rēdan,* rel. to Sansk. *rāth,* to succeed)]

readapt, *v.t.* **readaptation,** *n.* [RE-ADAPT]

readdress, *v.t.* to put a new (esp. a corrected) address upon. [RE-, ADDRESS]

reader, reading READ.

readily, readiness READY.

readjourn, *v.t.* to adjourn again. **readjournment,** *n.* **readjust,** *v.t.* to arrange or adjust afresh. **readjustment,** *n.* **readmit,** *v.t.* to admit again. **readmission, readmittance,** *n.* **readopt,** *v.t.* to adopt again. **readoption,** *n.* **readorn,** *v.t.* to adorn afresh. **readvertise,** *v.t.*, *v.i.* to advertise again.

ready, *a.* in a state of preparedness, fit for use or action; willing, apt, disposed, about (to); quick, prompt; able, expert, facile; at hand, within reach, handy, quickly available; held in the position preparatory to presenting and aiming (of a firearm). *adv.* (*usu. in comb. with p.p.*) in a state of preparedness, beforehand *n.* the position in which a firearm is held before presenting and aiming; (*sl.*) ready money. *v.t.* †to make ready, to prepare; (*sl.*) to pull (a horse) with a view to a handicap for another race. **ready, steady, go!** words used to start a race. **ready to hand,** nearby. **ready-to-wear,** *a.* off-the-peg. *n.* off-the-peg clothing. **to make ready,** to prepare; to prepare a forme before printing. **to ready up,** (*Austral. coll.*) to swindle. **to the ready,** prepared for use. **ready-made,** *a.* made beforehand, not made to order (esp. of clothing in standard sizes); selling ready-made articles (of a shop etc.). **ready-mix,** *n.* a food or concrete mix which only needs liquid to be added to make it ready for use. **ready money,** *n.* actual cash, ready to be paid down. **ready-money,** *a.* conducted on the principle of payment on delivery. **ready-reckoner,** *n.* a book with tables of interest etc. for facilitating business calculations. **ready-witted,** *a.* quick of apprehension. **readily,** *adv.* without trouble or difficulty, easily; willingly, without reluctance. **readiness,** *n.* the state of being ready, preparedness; willingness, prompt compliance; facility, ease, aptitude, quickness in acting. [ME *redi, rædi,* prob. from OE *geræde* (cp. OHG *bireiti,* G *bereit,* Dut. *bereid*) -Y, from conf. with OE *-ig*]

reaffirm, *v.t.* to affirm again. **reaffirmation,** *n.* **reafforest,** *v.t.* to convert again into forest. **reafforestation,** *n.*

Reagan, *n.* **Ronald Wilson** (1911–), US Republican politician, governor of California (1966–74), president (1981–89). A former Hollywood actor, Reagan was a hawkish and popular president. He introduced deregulation of domestic markets and withstood criticism of his interventionist foreign policy, but failed to confront a mounting trade deficit. He was succeeded by George Bush. He unsuccessfully contested the Republican presidential nomination in 1968 and 1976, and defeated Carter in the 1980 election, and Mondale in 1984. He adopted an aggressive policy in Central America, attempting to overthrow the government of Nicaragua, and invading Grenada (1983). In 1987, *Irangate* was investigated by the Tower Commission; Reagan regretted that US/Iran negotiations had become an 'arms for hostages deal', but denied knowledge of resultant funds being illegally sent to the Contras in Nicaragua. He increased spending on defence (increasing the national budget deficit to record levels), cut social programs, introduced deregulation of domestic markets, and cut taxes. His Strategic Defense Initiative, announced in 1983, has proven controversial due to the cost and unfeasibility. **Reaganism**, *n.* the political, economic etc. policy and philosophy associated with Ronald Reagan. **Reaganomics**, *n.* the economic policies of Reagan's administration, e.g. major tax-cutting.

reagent, *n.* a substance used to detect the presence of other substances by means of their reaction; a force etc. that reacts. **reagency,** *n.* reciprocal action. **reaggravation,** *n.* in the Roman Catholic Church, the last admonition, to be followed by excommunication.

†**reaks,** *n.pl.* pranks, tricks, freaks. [etym. doubtful, cp. FREAK]

real[1], *a.* actually existing; not fictitious, affected, imaginary, apparent, theoretical or nominal; true, genuine; not counterfeit, not spurious; having substantial existence, objective; consisting of fixed or permanent things, as lands or houses, opp. to personal; having an absolute and independent existence, opp. to nominal or phenomenal. **for real,** (*sl.*) in reality; in earnest. **the real,** that which is actual, esp. as opposed to the ideal; the genuine thing. **the real McCoy,** the genuine article; the best. **the real thing,** the genuine article and not a substitute. **real ale,** *n.* beer which is allowed to ferment and mature in the cask and is not pumped up from the keg with carbon dioxide. **real estate,** *n.* landed property. **real life,** *n.* actual human life, as opposed to fictional representation of human life. **real number,** *n.* any rational or irrational number. **realpolitik**, *n.* politics based on practical reality rather than moral or intellectual ideals. **real presence,** *n.* the actual presence of the body and blood of Christ in the Eucharist. **real property,** *n.* immovable property such as freehold land. **real-time,** *a.* pertaining to the processing of data by a computer as it is generated. **really,** *adv.* in fact, in reality; (*coll.*) positively, I assure you; is that so? [late L *reālis,* from *rēs,* thing]

real[2], *n.* (*pl.* **reales**) a Spanish silver coin or money of account. [Sp., from L *rēgālis,* REGAL]

real[3], *a.* royal. **real tennis,** *n.* royal tennis, played in a walled indoor court. [L *rēgālis,* royal]

realgar, *n.* native disulphide of arsenic, also called red arsenic or red orpiment, used as a pigment and in the manufacture of fireworks. [med. L or F *réalgar,* Arab. *rehj alghār,* powder of the mine or cave]

realign, *v.t.* to align again; to group together on a new basis. **realignment,** *n.*

realism, *n.* the scholastic doctrine that every universal or general idea has objective existence, opp. to *nominalism* and *conceptualism;* the doctrine that the objects of perception have real existence, opp. to *idealism;* the doctrine that in perception there is an immediate cognition of the external object; the practice of representing objects, persons, scenes etc. as they are or as they appear to the painter, novelist etc., opp. to *idealism* and *romanticism*. **realist,** *n.* a believer in realism; a practical person. **realistic**, *a.* pertaining to realism; matter-of-fact, common-sense. **realistically,** *adv.* [REAL[1], -ISM]

reality, *n.* the quality of being real, actuality, actual existence, being, that which underlies appearances; truth, fact; that which is real and not counterfeit, imaginary, suppositious etc.; the real nature (of); (*Law*) the permanent quality of real estate. **in reality,** in fact. [F *réalité,* med. L *realitātem,* nom. *-tas.*]

realize, ise, *v.t.* to perceive as a reality; to apprehend clearly and vividly; to bring into actual existence, to give reality to; to present as real, to impress on the mind as real, to become aware of, to make realistic; to convert into money; to sell; to bring in, as a price. **realizable, -isable,** *a.* **realization, -isation,** *n.* **realizer, -iser,** *n.*

reallege, *v.t.* to allege again.

reallocate, *v.t.* **reallocation,** *n.* **reallot,** *v.t.* **reallotment,** *n.*

really etc. REAL[1].

realm, *n.* a kingdom; (*fig.*) domain, region, sphere, field of interest. [OF *realme, reaume* (F *royaume*), prob. through pop. L *rēgālimen,* from L *rēgālis,* REGAL[1]]

realtor, *n.* (*N Am.*) estate agent, esp. a member of the National Association of Real Estate Boards; a dealer in land for development. **realty,** *n.* real property; †reality.

ream[1], *n.* 480 sheets or 20 quires of paper (often 500 or more sheets to allow for waste). **printer's ream,** *n.* 516 sheets. [ME *rēm, rīm,* through OF *rayme,* or Dut. *riem,* from Arab. *rizmah,* bundle]

ream[2], *v.t.* to enlarge (a hole in metal); to turn the edge of (a cartridge-case) over; to open (a seam) for caulking. **reamer,** *n.* an instrument or tool used in reaming. [OE *ryman,* cogn. with *rūm,* ROOM[2]]

ream[3], *n.* cream; froth or scum. **reamy,** *a.* [OE *rēam,* cp. Dut. *room,* G *Rahm,* Icel. *rjōmi*]

reanalyse, *v.t.* to analyse again. **reanalysis,** *n.*

reanimate, *v.t.* to restore to life; to revive, to encourage, to give new spirit to. **reanimation,** *n.* **reannex,** *v.t.* to annex anew; to reunite. **reannexation,** *n.* †**reanswer,** *v.t.* to be equivalent to.

reap, *v.t.* to cut with a scythe, sickle or reaping-machine; to gather in (a harvest etc.); to cut the harvest off (ground etc.); (*fig.*) to obtain as return for labour, deeds etc. *v.i.* to perform the act of reaping; to receive the consequences of labour, deeds etc. **reaper,** *n.* one who reaps; a reaping-machine. **the grim reaper,** death. **reaping-hook,** *n.* a sickle. **reaping-machine,** *n.* [OE *rīpan*]

reapparel, *v.t.* to clothe again. **reappear,** *v.i.* to appear again. **reappearance,** *n.* **reapply,** *v.t.* to apply again.

reapplier, *n.* **reapplication,** *n.* **reappoint,** *v.t.* to appoint again. **reappointment,** *n.* **reapportion,** *v.t.* to share out again. **reapportionment,** *n.* **reappraise,** *v.t.* to revalue. **reappraisal,** *n.* **reapproach,** *v.t.* to approach again.

rear[1], *v.t.* to raise, to set up, to elevate to an upright position; to build, to erect, to uplift, to place or hold on high; to bring up, to breed, to educate; to raise, to cultivate, to grow; to raise from a prostrate position; †to rouse, to reanimate. *v.i.* to stand on the hind legs (of a horse). **rearer,** *n.* [OE *rǣran,* cogn. with RAISE, which has largely superseded it]

rear[2], *n.* the back or hindmost part, esp. the hindmost division of a military or naval force; the back (of); a place or position at the back; (*coll.*) a water closet, a latrine; (*euphem.*) the buttocks. *a.* pertaining to the rear. **in the rear,** at the back. **to bring up the rear,** to come last. **rear-admiral,** *n.* a naval officer next below the rank of vice-admiral. **rear-arch,** *n.* an inner arch of a doorway or window-opening differing in size or form from the outer arch. **rear-end,** *n.* the back part of anything; (*coll.*) the buttocks. *v.t.* to crash into the rear of (a vehicle). **rear-guard,** *n.* a body of troops protecting the rear of an army. **rear-lamp, -light,** *n.* a red light at the back of a bicycle or motor vehicle. **rear-rank, -line,** *n.* the rank or line of a body of troops in the rear. **rear-view mirror,** *n.* a small mirror in a motor vehicle which allows the driver to observe the traffic behind him. **rearmost,** *a.* coming or situated last of all. **rearward,** *n.* †the rear-guard; (*fig.*) those coming last; the rear. *a.* situated in or towards the rear. *adv.* rearwards. **rearwards,** *adv.* towards the rear. [shortened from ARREAR]

reargue, *v.t.* to argue or debate afresh. **rearguement,** *n.* **rearm,** *v.t.* to arm afresh, esp. with more modern weapons. **rearmament,** *n.*

†**rearmouse,** *n.* a bat. [OE *hrēremūs* (*hrēre,* etym. doubtful, MOUSE)]

rearrange, *v.t.* to arrange in a new order. **rearrangement,** *n.* **rearrest,** *v.t.* to arrest again. *n.* a second arrest. **reascend,** *v.t., v.i.* to ascend again. **reascension,** *n.* **reascent,** *n.*

reason, *n.* that which is adduced to support or justify, or serves as a ground or motive for an act, opinion etc.; that which accounts for anything, a final cause; the premise of an argument, esp. the minor premise when stated after the conclusion; the intellectual faculties, esp. the group of faculties distinguishing man from animals; the intuitive faculty which furnishes a priori principles, categories etc.; the power of consecutive thinking, the logical faculty; good sense, judgment, sanity; sensible conduct; moderation; the exercise of the rational powers. *v.i.* to use the faculty of reason; to argue, esp. to employ argument (with) as a means of persuasion; to reach conclusions by way of inferences from premises. *v.t.* to debate, discuss or examine by means of the reason or reasons and inferences; to assume, conclude or prove by way of argument; to persuade or dissuade by argument; to set forth in orderly argumentative form. **by reason of,** because, on account of, in consequence of. **in, within reason** within moderation; according to good sense. **pure reason,** reason without the benefit of experience. **reasons of state,** politics or state security used to justify immoral acts. **to listen to reason,** to allow oneself to be persuaded. **to stand to reason,** to follow logically. **reasonable,** *a.* endowed with reason; rational, reasoning, governed by reason; conformable to reason, sensible, proper; not extravagant, moderate, esp. in price, fair, not extortionate. **reasonableness,** *n.* **reasonably,** *adv.* **reasoned,** *a.* well-thought-out or well-argued. **reasoner,** *n.* **reasoning,** *n.* the act of drawing conclusions from premises or using the reason; argumentation; a statement of the reasons justifying a course, opinion, conclusion etc. **reasonless,** *a.* [OF *raisun* (F *raison*), L *ratiōnem,* nom. *-tio,* see RATIO]

reassemble, *v.t., v.i.* to assemble or collect together again. **reassembly,** *n.* **reassert,** *v.t.* to assert anew. **reassertion,** *n.* **reassess,** *v.t.* to make a new assessment of. **reassessment,** *n.* **reassign,** *v.t.* to assign again; to transfer back or to another what has been already assigned. **reassignment,** *n.* **reassume,** *v.t.* to take up again; to revoke; to take upon oneself again; to resume. **reassumption,** *n.* **reassure,** *v.t.* to assure or confirm again; to restore to confidence, to give fresh courage to; to reinsure. **reassurance,** *n.* **reassurer,** *n.* **reassuring,** *a.* **reassuringly,** *adv.*

reata, *n.* a lariat. [Sp., from *reatar,* to tie again (RE-, L *aptāre,* to apply, see APT)]

reattach, *v.t.* to attach afresh. **reattachment,** *n.* **reattain,** *v.t.* to attain again. **reattainment,** *n.* **reattempt,** *v.t.* to attempt afresh. *n.* a new attempt.

Réaumur, *a.* applied to the thermometer invented by the French physicist R. A. F. de *Réaumur* (1683–1757), or to his thermometric scale, the zero of which corresponds to freezing-point and 80° to boiling-point.

reavouch, *v.t.* to avouch again. **reawake,** *v.t., v.i.* to awake again. **reawaken,** *v.t., v.i.* **rebaptize, -ise,** *v.t.* to baptize again. **rebaptizer, -iser,** *n.* **rebaptism, rebaptization, -isation,** *n.* **rebaptist,** *n.* **rebarbarize, -ise,** *v.t.* to reduce to barbarism again. **rebarbarization, -isation,** *n.*

rebarbative, *a.* repellent, grim, forbidding; surly; uncooperative. [F *barbe,* a beard]

rebate[1], *v.t.* to make a deduction from, to abate; to reduce, to diminish; to refund a part of the amount payable; to make blunt, to dull; to remove a portion of (a charge). *n.* a deduction, a drawback, a discount. **rebatable, rebateable,** *a.* **rebatement,** *n.* **rebater,** *n.* [OF *rabattre* (RE-, *abattre,* to ABATE]

rebate[2], *n.* (*prov.*) a kind of hard freestone. [etym. doubtful]

rebate[3], RABBET.

rebato RABAT.

Rebeccaite, *n.* a member of an anti-turnpike association formed in Wales in 1843–4, who attempted to carry out their objects by violence. **Rebeccaism,** *n.* [*Rebecca* (the leader and his followers being called 'Rebecca and her daughters', from a misapplication of Gen. XXIV.60)]

rebeck, rebec, *n.* a mediaeval three-stringed musical instrument played with a bow. [OF *rebec,* var. of *rebebe,* Arab. *rebāb*]

rebel, *a.* rebellious; pertaining to rebellion or to rebels. *n.* one who forcibly resists the established government or renounces allegiance thereto; one who resists authority or control. *v.i.* (*past, p.p.* **rebelled**) to engage in rebellion (against); to revolt (against any authority or control); (*fig.*) to feel or show repugnance (against). **rebel-like,** *a.* †**rebeller,** *n.* **rebellion,** *n.* organized resistance by force of arms to the established government; opposition to any authority. **rebellious,** *a.* engaged in rebellion; defying or opposing lawful authority; disposed to rebel, refractory, insubordinate, difficult to manage or control. **rebelliously,** *adv.* **rebelliousness,** *n.* [F *rebelle,* L *rebellem,* nom. *-llis,* rebellious (RE-, *bellum,* war)]

rebellow, *v.i.* to bellow in return; to echo back loudly. *v.t.* to re-echo loudly. **rebid,** *v.t., v.i.* to bid again, usu. in bridge, to bid on the same suit as the previous bid. **rebind,** *v.t.* (*past, p.p.* **rebound**[1]) to bind again; to give a new binding to. **rebirth,** *n.* a second birth, esp. an entrance into a new sphere of existence, as in reincarnation. **reborn,** *a.* **rebite,** *v.t.* to bite again, to apply acid etc. again to an etched plate.

reboant, *a.* rebellowing, loudly resounding or reechoing. [L *reboans -ntem,* pres.p. of *reboāre* (*boāre,* to bellow)]

reboil, *v.i.* to boil again. **reborn,** *a.* born again (esp. of spiritual life). **rebore,** *v.t.* to bore again, e.g. a cylinder, so as to clear it.

rebound[1], *past, p.p.* REBIND.

rebound[2], *v.i.* to bound back, to recoil (from a blow etc.); to react, to recoil (upon); †to re-echo. †*v.t.* to cause to rebound, to return (blows etc.). *n.* the act of rebounding, a recoil; reaction (of feeling etc.). **on the rebound,** in the act of bouncing back; as a reaction to a disappointment. **rebounder,** *n.* a small trampoline used for performing jumping exercises on. **rebounding,** *n.* the act of rebounding; a form of exercise involving jumping up and down on a rebounder. **rebrace,** *v.t.* to brace again. **rebreathe,** *v.t.* to breathe again. **rebroadcast,** *v.t.* to broadcast again. *a.* broadcast again. *n.* a second broadcast. [OF *rebondir*]

rebuff, *n.* a rejection, a check (to an offer or to one who makes advances etc.); a curt denial, a snub; a defeat, a sudden or unexpected repulse. *v.t.* (*past, p.p.* **rebuffed**) to give a rebuff to, to repel. [obs. F *rebuffe,* It. *re-, ribuffo* (*buffo,* puff, imit. in orig.)]

rebuild, *v.t.* (*past, p.p.* **rebuilt**) to build again, to reconstruct.

rebuke, *v.t.* to reprove, to reprimand, to chide; to censure, to reprehend (a fault etc.); †to repress, to repulse. *n.* the act of rebuking; a reproof. **rebukable,** *a.* **rebukeful,** *a.* **rebukefully,** *adv.* **rebukefulness,** *n.* **rebuker,** *n.* **rebukingly,** *adv.* [A-F and ONorth.F *rebuker,* OF *rebuchier* (RE-, *bucher,* to beat, perh. orig. to lop, from *busche,* F *bûche,* a log)]

rebury, *v.t.* to bury again. **reburial,** *n.*

rebus, *n.* a picture or figure representing enigmatically a word, name or phrase, usu. by objects suggesting words or syllables; (*Her.*) a device representing a proper name or motto in this way. [L, abl. pl. of *rēs,* thing, etym. doubtful]

rebut, *v.t.* (*past, p.p.* **rebutted**) to thrust back, to check, to repel; to contradict or refute by plea, argument or countervailing proof. **rebuttable,** *a.* **rebutment, rebuttal,** *n.* **rebutter,** *n.* one who rebuts; the answer of a defendant to a plaintiff's surrejoinder. [A-F *reboter,* OF *rebouter, -boter* (RE-, *boter,* to BUTT[4])]

rec., (*abbr.*) receipt; recipe; record, recorded, recorder.

recalcitrant, *a.* refractory, obstinately refusing submission. *n.* a recalcitrant person. **recalcitrance, -cy,** *n.* **recalcitrate,** *v.i.* to kick (against or at a proposal etc.); to refuse compliance, to show resistance, to be refractory. **recalcitration,** *n.* [F *récalcitrant* or L *recalcitrans -ntem,* pres.p. of *recalcitrāre* (RE-, *calcitrāre,* to strike with the heel, from *calx calcis,* heel)]

recalculate, *v.t.* to calculate again. **recalculation,** *n.*

recalesce, *v.i.* to grow hot again (esp. of iron or steel which glows more brightly when certain temperatures are reached in the process of cooling). **recalescence,** *n.* **recalescent,** *a.* [L *recalescere* (RE-, *calescere* to grow hot, incept. of *calēre,* to be warm)]

recall, *v.t.* to call back; to summon to return; to bring back to mind, to recollect; to renew, to revive, to resuscitate; to revoke, to annul, to take back. *n.*, a calling back; a summons to return; a signal calling back soldiers, a ship etc.; the power of recalling, remembering, revoking or annulling; (*N Am.*) the right of electors to dismiss an elected official by popular vote. **total recall,** the ability to remember in great detail. **recallable,** *a.* **recallment,** *n.*

recant, *v.t.* to retract, to renounce, to abjure; to disavow. *v.i.* to disavow or abjure opinions or beliefs formerly avowed, esp. with a formal acknowledgment of error. **recantation,** *n.* **recanter,** *n.* [L *recantāre* (RE-, *cantāre* freq. of *canere,* to sing)]

recap, *v.t.* to recapitulate.

recapitulate, *v.t.* to repeat in brief (as the principal heads of a discourse), to sum up, to summarize. **recapitulation,** *n.* the act of recapitulating, e.g. at the end of a speech; the apparent repetition of the evolutionary stages of a species in the embryonic development of a member of that species; the repeating of earlier themes in a piece of music. **recapitulative, recapitulatory,** *a.*

recaption, *n.* recovery of goods, wife, child etc. from one unlawfully withholding them; a writ for the recovery of damages by one who has been distrained twice. **recaptor,** *n.* **recapture,** *n.* the act of recapturing; that which is recaptured. *v.t.* to capture again, to recover (a prize from the captor). **recarburize, -ise,** *v.t.* to carburize (steel) after decarbonization. **recarburizer, -iser,** *n.* **recarburization, -isation,** *n.* **recarry,** *v.t.* to carry back or again. **recarriage,** *n.* **recarrier,** *n.* **recast,** *v.t.* to cast, found or mould again; to fashion again, to remodel; to compute or add up again. *n.* that which has been recast; the process or result of recasting. **recaster,** *n.*

recce, *n.* (*pl.* **recces**) reconnaissance. *v.t., v.i.* to reconnoitre.

recd, (*abbr.*) received.

recede¹, *v.i.* to go back or away (from); to be gradually lost to view by distance; to incline, slope or trend backwards or away; to retreat, to withdraw (from); (*fig.*) to decline, to retrograde; of hair, to cease to grow at the temples; to draw back, e.g. from a promise. [L *recēdere* (RE-, *cēdere,* to go, see CEDE)]

recede², *v.t.* to cede again, to restore to a former possessor.

receipt, *n.* the act or fact of receiving or being received; (*usu. in pl.*); that which is received, esp. money; a written acknowledgment of money or goods received; a recipe; †a place for officially receiving money; †the act of admitting, reception (as of guests); †a receptacle; †capacity, power of receiving. *v.t.* to give a receipt for; to write an acknowledgment of receipt on (a bill etc.). [ME *receit,* A-F *receite,* OF *recete, reçoite,* L *recepta,* fem. p.p. of *recipere* to RECEIVE]

receive, *v.t.* to obtain, get or take as a thing due, offered, sent, paid or given; to be given, to be furnished or supplied with, to acquire; to accept with approval or consent, to admit, as proper or true; to admit to one's presence, to welcome, to entertain as guest, to encounter, to take or stand the onset of; to be a receptacle for; to understand, to regard (in a particular light); to accept (stolen goods) from a thief; to convert incoming electrical signals into sounds or pictures by means of a receiver; to return the service in tennis or squash. *v.i.* to hold a reception of visitors or callers. **receivable,** *a.* **receivability, receivableness,** *n.* **received,** *a.* generally accepted or believed. **Received (Standard) English,** *n.* English spoken by educated British people, taken as the standard of the language. **Received Pronunciation,** *n.* the non-localized pronunciation of British English, taken as the standard. **receiver,** *n.* one who receives; one who receives stolen goods, a fence; a receptacle, as a part of a telephonic or telegraphic apparatus for receiving messages or current; a vessel for receiving the products of distillation or for collecting gas; the bell-glass of an air-pump etc.; an officer appointed to administer property under litigation, esp. that of bankrupts; an apparatus for the reception of radio, television or telephone signals; someone who receives stolen goods. **official receiver,** a person appointed by a bankruptcy court to receive the sums due to and administer the property of a bankrupt. **receiver-general,** *n.* an officer appointed to receive public revenues, now applied to an officer of the Duchy of Lancaster. **receiving-house, -office, -room** etc., *n.* places for the receipt of parcels, money, recruits etc. **receiving-order,** *n.* an order from a bankruptcy court staying separate action against a debtor and placing his affairs in the hands of an official receiver. **receivership,** *n.* the office of receiver; the state of being administered by the receiver. [A-F *receivre* (OF *reçoivre*), L *recipere* (RE-, *capere,* to take)]

re-celebrate, *v.t.* to celebrate again.

recency RECENT.

recension, *n.* the act of revising; a critical revision of a text, a revised edition. **recensor,** *n.* [L *recensio,* from *recensēre* (RE-, *censēre* to review)]

recent, *a.* of or pertaining to the present or time not long past; that happened, existed or came into existence lately; late (of existence); modern, fresh, newly begun or established; pertaining to the existing epoch, Post-Pliocene, Quaternary. **recency, recentness,** *n.* **recently,** *adv.* [F *récent,* L *recentem,* nom. *-cens,* etym. unknown]

receptacle, *n.* that which receives, holds or contains; a vessel, space or place of deposit; a part forming a support, as the portion of a flower on which the sexual organs are set, the axis of a flower cluster etc. **receptacular,** *a.* [F, from L *receptāculum,* from *recept-,* p.p. stem of *recipere,* to RECEIVE]

†**receptible,** *a.* receivable. **receptibility**, *n.* [L *receptibilis,* as foll.]

reception, *n.* the act of receiving; the state of being received; receipt, acceptance, admission; the receiving, admitting or accommodating of persons, esp. guests, new members of a society etc.; a formal welcome; an occasion of formal or ceremonious receiving of visitors; the act or process of receiving (ideas or impressions) into the mind; mental acceptance, admission or recognition (of a theory etc.); the quality of received radio or television signals. **reception centre,** *n.* a place where people can receive immediate assistance for problems, such as drugs or homelessness. **reception order,** *n.* the official order required for detention in a mental hospital. **reception-room,** *n.* a room for receptions; (*coll.*) a room to which visitors are admitted, opp. to bedrooms, kitchen etc. **receptionist,** *n.* person at a hotel or elsewhere, whose duty it is to receive and look after visitors. **receptor,** *n.* any of various devices which receive signals or information; an organ adapted for receiving stimuli; a sensory nerve ending which changes stimuli into nerve impulses. [F, from L *receptiōnem,* nom. *-tio,* from *recipere,* to RECEIVE, p.p. *receptus*]

receptive, *a.* having ability or capacity to receive; quick to receive impressions, ideas etc. **receptively,** *adv.* **receptiveness, receptivity**, *n.*

recess, *n.* cessation or suspension of public or other business, a vacation; a part that recedes, a depression, indentation, hollow, niche or alcove; a secluded or secret place, a nook; †the act of withdrawing or receding; a depression, cavity, indentation or fold. *v.t.* to put into a recess; to build a recess in a wall. *v.i.* to adjourn. **recessed,** *a.* **recessed arch,** *n.* an arch set within another. [L *recessus,* p.p. of *recēdere,* to RECEDE[1]]

recession[1], *n.* the act of receding, withdrawal, retirement; a receding part or object; a slump, esp. in trade or economic activity; the withdrawal of the clergy and choir after a church service. **recessional,** *a.* pertaining to the recession of the clergy and choir from the chancel. *n.* a hymn sung during this ceremony. **recessive,** *a.* tending to recede; of a stress accent, tending to move towards the beginning of a word. **recessive gene,** *n.* one that must be inherited from both mother and father in order to show its effect in the individual. **recessively,** *adv.* **recessiveness, recessivity**, *n.*

recession[2], *n.* the act of giving back to a former owner. [RECEDE]

Rechabite, *n.* orig. one of the descendants of Jonadab, son of Rechab, who bound themselves to abstain from wine; a member of a society of total abstainers called the Independent Order of Rechabites. **Rechabitism,** *n.*

recharge, *v.t.* to charge again; to put a new charge into; to make a new charge against; to charge or attack again or in return; to restore the vitality, e.g. of batteries. *n.* a new charge or a charge in return. **rechargeable,** *a.* **recharter,** *v.t.* to charter again; to give a new charter to.

réchauffé, *n.* a dish warmed up again; (*fig.*) a rehash. [F, p.p. of *réchauffer,* to warm up again (RE-, *chauffer,* to CHAFE]

recheat, *v.i.* to blow a recheat. *n.* a call on the horn to rally the hounds in a deer hunt. [prob. from OF *rachater,* to rally]

recheck, *v.t.* to check again. *n.* the act of checking something again.

recherché, *a.* (*fem.* **-chée**) out of the common; rare, choice. [F, p.p. of *rechercher* (RE-, *chercher,* to SEARCH)]

rechristen, *v.t.* to christen again; (*fig.*) to give a new name to.

recidivist, *n.* a relapsed or inveterate criminal, usu. one serving or who has served a second term of imprisonment. **recidivation, recidivism,** *n.* a habitual relapse into crime. **recidivistic**, *a.* [F *récidiviste,* L *recidīvus,* from *recidere* (RE-, *cadere,* to fall)]

Recife, *n.* industrial seaport (cotton textiles, sugar refining, fruit canning, flour milling) and naval base in Brazil, capital of Pernambuco state, at the mouth of the river Capibaribe; population (1980) 1,184,215. It was founded in 1504.

recipe, *n.* a formula or prescription for compounding medical or other mixtures, a receipt; directions for preparing a dish; a remedy, expedient, device or means for effecting some result. [L, imper. of *recipere,* to RECEIVE]

recipient, *a.* receiving; receptive. *n.* one who receives, a receiver. **recipience, recipiency,** *n.* [L *recipiens -entem,* pres.p. of *recipere,* to RECEIVE]

reciprocal, *a.* acting, done or given in return, mutual; mutually interchangeable, inversely correspondent, complementary; expressing mutual action or relation; †reflexive. *n.* the quotient resulting from dividing unity by a quantity. **reciprocal pronoun,** *n.* a pronoun which expresses a mutual action or relationship. **reciprocal ratio,** *n.* the ratio between the reciprocals of two quantities. **reciprocal terms,** *n.* terms having the same signification and therefore interchangeable. †**reciprocality**, *n.* reciprocity. **reciprocally,** *adv.* **reciprocant,** *n.* a different invariant. [L *reciprocus* (prob. RE-, back, *pro,* forward)]

reciprocate, *v.i.* to alternate, to move backwards and forwards; to return an equivalent, to make a return in kind. *v.t.* to give alternating or backward-and-forward motion to; to give and take mutually, to interchange; to give in return. **reciprocating engine,** *n.* an engine performing work with a part having reciprocating, not rotatory, motion. **reciprocating motion,** *n.* backward-and-forward or up-and-down motion, as of a piston. **reciprocation,** *n.* the act of reciprocating; giving and returning; reciprocal motion. † **reciprocative,** *a.* **reciprocator,** *n.* **reciprocatory,** *a.* reciprocating, opp. to rotatory.

reciprocity, *n.* the state of being reciprocal, reciprocation of rights or obligations; mutual action or the principle of give-and-take, esp. interchange of commercial privileges between two nations.

recirculate, *v.t.* to pass or go round again. **recirculation,** *n.*

†**recision,** *n.* the act of cutting back, pruning; an annulment. [L *recīsio,* from *recīdere* (RE-, *caedere,* to cut)]

recital, *n.* the act of reciting; an enumeration or narrative of facts or particulars, a story; the part of a document formally stating facts, reasons, grounds etc:; a public entertainment consisting of recitations; a musical performance, esp. by one person or of the works of one person. **recitalist,** *n.*

recitation, *n.* the recital of prose or poetry, esp. the delivery of a composition committed to memory; a composition intended for recital.

recitative, *n.* a style of rendering vocal passages intermediate between singing and ordinary speaking, as in oratorio and opera; a piece or part to be sung in recitative. *a.*, pertaining or suitable for recitative; pertaining to a recital. *v.t.* to render in recitative. **recitatively,** *adv.*

recite, *v.t.* to repeat aloud or declaim from memory, esp. before an audience; to narrate, to rehearse (esp. facts etc. in a legal document); to quote, to cite; to enumerate. *v.i.* to give a recitation. **recitable,** *a.* **reciter,** *n.* one who recites; a book of selections etc. for reciting. **reciting note,** *n.* in Gregorian chant, that note on which most of a verse is sung. [F *réciter,* L *recitāre* (RE-, *citāre,* to CITE)]

recivilize, -ise, *v.t.* to civilize again. **recivilization, -isation,** *n.* [RE-, CIVILIZE]

reck, *v.t.* (*chiefly poet.*) to care, to heed. *v.i.* to have a care or thought (of); to trouble oneself, to be concerned, to be heedful. **reckless**, *a.* careless, heedless; rash, venturesome; regardless, indifferent, neglectful, heedless of the consequences. **recklessly,** *adv.* **recklessness,** *n.* [OE *reccan* (cp. OHG *ruohhen,* MHG *ruochen,* Icel. *rækja*)]

reckon, *v.t.* to count, to add (up), calculate or compute; to count or include (in or among), to regard (as), to account, to esteem, to consider (to be); to be of the opinion, to calculate, to guess (that). *v.i.* to compute, to calculate, to settle accounts with; to rely, to count, to place dependence (upon); to suppose, to believe, to guess, to calculate. **to reckon on,** to rely upon, to expect. **to reckon with, without,** to take, or fail to take, into account. **to reckon without one's host,** to underestimate. **reckoner,** *n.* any of several devices or tables for quick calculations. **reckoning,** *n.* the act of calculating or counting; a statement of accounts or charges, a bill, esp. for liquor at a tavern, a score; a settling of accounts; an estimate or calculation of a ship's position. **day of reckoning,** the day of settling accounts; (*fig.*) the Day of Judgment. **dead reckoning** DEAD. **out of one's reckoning,** mistaken in one's judgment or expectation. [OE *gerecenian* (cp. MDut. *rekenen,* G *rechnen,* Icel. *reikna*), cogn. with prec.]

reclaim, *v.t.* to bring back from error, vice, wildness etc.; to reform, to tame, to civilize, to bring under cultivation; to demand back, to claim the restoration of; †to call back, to recall; †to bring back (a hawk) to the wrist; to recover usable substances from waste products. †*v.i.* to cry out, to exclaim or protest; †to reform; to draw back. *n.* the act of reclaiming or being reclaimed, reclamation. **reclaimable,** *a.* **reclaimably,** *adv.* †**reclaimant,** *n.* one who remonstrates against anything. **reclaimer,** *n.* **reclaiming,** *a.* appealing from a judgment. **reclamation,** *n.* the act of reclaiming; the state of being reclaimed; the cultivation of waste land; the recovery of usable substances from waste products. [OF *reclamer,* L *reclāmāre,* to cry out against (RE-, *clāmāre,* to shout)]

réclame, *n.* notoriety; puffing, self-advertisement. [F, from *réclamer,* see prec.]

reclasp, *v.t.* to clasp again.

reclassify, *v.t.* to classify again or elsewhere. **reclassification,** *n.*

recline, *v.t.* to lay or lean (one's body, head, limbs etc.) back, esp. in a horizontal or nearly horizontal position. *v.i.* to assume or be in a leaning or recumbent posture, to lie down or lean back upon cushions or other supports; (*fig.*) to rely (upon). †*a.* reclining, recumbent. **reclinable,** *a.* **reclinate,** *a.* of plants, inclined from an erect position, bending downwards. **reclination,** *n.* **recliner,** *n.* someone who or something which, reclines; a type of armchair which can be adjusted to recline backwards. [L *reclīnāre* (RE-, *clīnāre,* to lean), see DECLINE]

reclose, *v.t., v.i.* to shut again. **reclothe,** *v.t.* to clothe again.

recluse, *a.* retired from the world; solitary, secluded, retired, sequestered. *n.* one who lives retired from the world, esp. a religious devotee who lives in a solitary cell and practises austerity and self-discipline, a hermit, an anchorite or anchoress. †**reclusely,** *adv.* †**recluseness,** *n.* **reclusery** RECLUSORY. **reclusion,** *n.* **reclusive,** *a.* **reclusory,** *n.* a hermitage. [OF *reclus -cluse,* p.p. of *reclure,* L *reclūdere* (RE-, *claudere,* to shut)]

recoal, *v.t.* to furnish with a fresh supply of coal. *v.i.* to take in a fresh supply of coal (of a steamship). **recoat,** *v.t.* to coat again (with paint etc.).

recognition, *n.* act of recognizing; state of being recognized; acknowledgment, notice taken; a perceiving as being known. †**recognitor,** *n.* one of a jury at an assize or inquest. **recognitive, recognitory,** *a.* [L *recognitio,* from *recognit-,* p.p. stem of *recognoscere,* to RECOGNIZE]

recognizance, *n.* (*Law*) a bond or obligation entered into in a court or before a magistrate to perform a specified act, fulfil a condition etc. (as to keep the peace or appear when called upon); a sum deposited as pledge for the fulfilment of this; †recognition, avowal; †a badge or token. [A-F *reconisaunce,* OF *recoignisance,* as foll.]

recognize, -ise, *v.t.* to know again; to recall the identity of; to acknowledge, to admit the truth, validity, existence etc. of; to reward, to thank; to show appreciation of. *v.i.* (*N Am.*) to enter into recognizances. **recognizable, -isable,** *a.* **recognizability, -isability,** *n.* **recognizably, -isably,** *adv.* **recognizant, -isant,** *a.* **recognizer, -iser,** *n.* [OF *reconoistre* (F *reconnaître*), L *recognoscere* (RE-, *cognoscere,* to COGNOSCE)]

recoil, *v.i.* to start or spring back; to rebound; to shrink back, as in fear or disgust; to be driven back; to retreat; to go wrong and harm the perpetrator. †*v.t.* to drive back. *n.* the act of recoiling; a rebound; the act or feeling of shrinking back, as in fear or disgust; the backward kick of a gun when fired; the change in motion of an atom caused by emission of a particle. **recoil escapement,** *n.* a clock escapement in which after each beat the escape-wheel recoils slightly. **recoiler,** *n.* **recoilingly,** *adv.* **recoilment,** *n.* [OF *reculer* (RE-, *cul,* L *culum,* nom. *-lus,* the posterior)]

recoin, *v.t.* to coin over again. **recoinage,** *n.* **recoiner,** *n.*

recollect[1], *v.t.* to gather together again; to collect or compose (one's ideas, thoughts or feelings); to summon up, to rally, to recover (one's strength, spirit etc.). *v.i.* to come together again.

recollect[2], *v.t.* to recall to memory, to remember, to succeed in recalling the memory of. *v.i.* to succeed in remembering. **recollection,** *n.* the act or power of recollecting; a memory, a reminiscence; the period of past time over which one's memory extends. **recollective,** *a.* **recollectively,** *adv.* [L *recollectus,* p.p. of *recolligere,* after F *récolliger*]

Recollect[3], *n.* a member of an Observantine branch of the Franciscan order, founded in Spain in 1500, characterized by strictness of rule and devotional contemplation or recollection. [as prec. or from F *récollet*]

recolonize, -ise, *v.t.* to colonize afresh. **recolonization, -isation,** *n.* **recolour,** *v.t.* to colour again. **recombine,** *v.t.* to combine again. **recombinant,** *n., a.* **recombinant DNA,** *n.* DNA prepared in the laboratory by combining DNA molecules from different individuals or species. **recombination,** *n.* the process of combining genetic material from different sources. **recomfort,** *v.i.* to comfort or console again; to give new strength to. †**recomforture,** *n.* **recommence,** *v.t., v.i.* to begin again. **recommencement,** *n.*

recommend, *v.t.* to commend to another's notice, use or favour, esp. to represent as suitable for an office or employment; to advise (a certain course of action etc.), to counsel; to render acceptable or serviceable (of qualities etc.); †to give or commend (one's soul, a person etc.) in charge (to God etc.). **recommendable,** *a.* **recommendableness, recommendability,** *n.* **recommendably,** *adv.* **recommendation,** *n.* the act of recommending; a quality or feature that tends to procure a favourable reception, a ground of approbation; a letter recommending a person for an appointment etc. **recommendatory,** *a.* **recommender,** *n.* [from F *recommender,* var. of *recommander,* or med. L *recommendāre* (RE-, *commendāre,* to COMMEND)]

recommission, *v.t.* to commission anew. **recommit,** *v.t.* to commit again; to refer back (to a committee etc.). **recommitment, recommittal,** *n.* **recommunicate,** *v.t.* to communicate anew. **recompact,** *v.t.* to join together again.

recompense, *v.t.* to make a return or give an equivalent for, to requite, to repay (a person, a service, an injury etc.); to indemnify, to compensate (for), to make up (for); †to atone for. *n.* that which is given as a reward, compensation, requital or satisfaction (for a service, injury etc.). **recompensable,** *a.* **recompensation,** *n.* (*Sc. Law*) a counter-plea of compensation to a defender's plea of compensation from the pursuer. **recompenser,** *n.* **recompensive,** *a.* [OF *recompenser,* late L *recompensāre* (RE-, *compensāre,* to COMPENSATE)]

recompile, *v.t.* to compile again. **recompilation,** *n.* **recompose,** *v.t.* to compose or put together again; to rearrange; to restore the composure of, to tranquillize again. **recomposition,** *n.* **recompound,** *v.t.* to compound afresh.

reconcile, *v.t.* to restore to friendship after an

estrangement; to make content, acquiescent or submissive (to); to harmonize, to make consistent or compatible (with); to adjust, to settle (differences etc.); in the Roman Catholic Church, to purify or restore (a desecrated church etc.) to sacred uses, to reconsecrate. **reconcilable,** *a.* **reconcilability,** †**reconcilableness,** *n.* **reconcilably,** *adv.* **reconcilement, reconciliaton,** *n.* **reconciler,** *n.* **reconciliatory,** *a.* [F *réconcilier,* L *reconciliāre* (RE-, *conciliāre,* to conciliate)]

recondense, *v.t., v.i.* to condense again. **recondensation,** *n.*

recondite, *a.* out of the way, abstruse, little known, obscure; pertaining to abstruse or special knowledge, profound; hidden, secret. **reconditely,** *adv.* **reconditeness,** *n.* †**reconditory,** *n.* a repository. [L *reconditus,* p.p. of *recondere* (RE-, *condere,* to hide, see CONDIMENT)]

recondition, *v.t.* to repair, to make as new. **reconditioned,** *a.*

reconduct, *v.t.* to conduct back again. **reconfirm,** *v.t.* to confirm or ratify again. **reconjoin,** *v.t.* to join together again.

reconnaissance, *n.* the act of reconnoitring, a preliminary examination or survey, esp. of a tract of country or a coast-line in war-time to ascertain the position of the enemy, the strategic features etc.; a detachment of soldiers or sailors performing this duty. **reconnaissance in force,** a reconnaissance by a large body of troops or vessels of war. [F, from *reconnaître,* late form of foll.]

reconnoitre, *v.t.* to make a reconnaissance of; to make a preliminary examination or survey of. *v.i.* to make a reconnaissance. *n.* a reconnaissance. **reconnoitrer,** *n.* [F, now *reconnaître,* L *recognoscere,* to RECOGNIZE]

reconquer, *v.t.* to conquer again; to regain. **reconquest,** *n.* **reconsecrate,** *v.t.* to consecrate afresh. **reconsecration,** *n.* **reconsider,** *v.t.* to consider again (esp. with a view to rescinding); to review, to revise. **reconsideration,** *n.* **reconsolidate,** *v.t., v.i.* to consolidate again. **reconsolidation,** *n.* **reconstitute,** *v.t.* to constitute again; to give a new constitution to. **reconstituent,** *n. a.* **reconstitution,** *n.* **reconstruct,** *v.t.* to construct again; to rebuild; to build up a picture of something from the available evidence, e.g. of a crime. **reconstructible,** *a.* **reconstruction,** *n.* the act or process of reconstruction; (*N Am. Hist.*) the process by which the southern States which had seceded from the Union were restored to Federal rights and privileges after the Civil War of 1861–5. **reconstructional,** *a.* **reconstructionary,** *a.* **reconstructive,** *a.* **reconstructively,** *a.* **reconstructor,** *n.* **reconvalescent,** *a.* becoming convalescent or healthy again. **reconvalescence,** *n.* **reconvene,** *v.t., v.i.* to convene or assemble again. **reconvention,** *n.* a counter-action brought by the defendant in a suit against the plaintiff. **reconvert,** *v.t.* to convert again, back to its previous state, religion etc. **reconversion,** *n.* **reconvey,** *v.t.* to convey back; to restore to a former owner. **reconveyance,** *n.*

record[1], *v.t.* to register, to write an account of, to set down permanent evidence of, to imprint deeply on the mind; to make a recording (on disk, tape, video tape etc.) of for subsequent reproduction; to go over, to rehearse; †of birds, to sing over (a tune); to bear witness to; to indicate, to register; to celebrate. †*v.i.* of birds, to sing or warble a tune. **recordable,** *a.* **recorded,** *a.* **recorded delivery,** *n.* a postal service where an official record of posting and delivery is kept. **recording,** *a.* registering waveforms arising from sound sources, or the readings of meteorological and other instruments making a record automatically. *n.* a record of sound or image on record, tape or film; the record, tape or film so produced; a radio or television programme which has been recorded. **Recording Angel,** *n.* an angel supposed to keep a record of every person's good and bad deeds. [OF *recorder,* L *recordāre -dari*(RE-, *cor cordis,* heart)]

record[2], *n.* a written or other permanent account or statement of a fact or facts; a register, a report, a minute or minutes of proceedings, a series of marks made by a recording instrument; a thin plastic disk on to which sound is recorded; an official report of proceedings, judgment etc. to be kept as authentic legal evidence, or an official memorial of particulars, pleadings etc. to be submitted as a case for decision by a court; the state of being recorded, testimony, attestation; the past history of a person's career, esp. as an index of character and abilities; a list of crimes which a person has committed; the authentic register of performances in any sport; hence, the best performance or the most striking event of its kind recorded; a portrait, monument or other memento of a person, event etc. **court of record,** a court whose proceedings are officially recorded and preserved as evidence. **for the record,** for the sake of accuracy. **off the record,** in confidence, not said officially. **on record,** recorded, esp. with legal authentication. **to beat, break, the record,** to surpass all former achievements or events of the kind. **to go on record,** to state one's beliefs publicly. **to have a record,** to be a known, previously convicted criminal. **to put, set, the record straight,** to correct an error or false impression. **record-breaker,** *n.* **record-breaking,** *n., a.* **Record Office,** *n.* an official repository for state papers. **record-player,** *n.* a machine for playing and reproducing sounds on a record. **recordable,** *a.* †**recordation,** *n.* remembrance. **records,** *n.pl.* **public records,** official statements of public deeds or acts.

recorder, *n.* one who or that which records; a magistrate having a limited criminal and civil jurisdiction in a city or borough and presiding over quarter-sessions; a machine for recording sound on to tape; a vertical form of flageolet or flute with a fipple. **recordership,** *n.*

recount[1], *v.t.* to relate in detail, to narrate. **recountal,** †**recountment,** *n.* [OF *reconter*]

recount[2], *v.t.* to count over again, esp. of votes at an election. *n.* a new count.

recoup, *v.t.* to reimburse, to indemnify (oneself) for a loss or expenditure; to compensate, to make up for (a loss, expenditure etc.); (*Law*) to keep back (a part of something due). *v.i.* (*Law*) to make such a deduction. **recoupable,** *a.* **recoupé, recouped,** *a.* (*Her.*) couped, clean-cut. **recouper,** *n.* **recoupment,** *n.* [F *recouper* (RE-, *couper,* to cut, see COUP[1])]

recourse, *n.* resorting or applying (to) as for help; a source of help, that which is resorted to; †recurrence, flowing back; the right to demand payment. **to have recourse to,** to go to for advice, help etc., esp. in emergency. †*v.i.* to go back, to return (to). **without recourse,** a qualified endorsement of a bill or negotiable instrument which shows that the endorser takes no responsibility for non-payment. †**recourseful,** *a.* [F *recours,* L *recursum,* nom. *-sus* (RE-, *cursus,* COURSE)]

recover, *v.t.* to regain, to repossess oneself of, to win back; to make up for, to retrieve; to save (the by-products of an industrial process); to bring (a weapon) back after a thrust etc.; to obtain by legal process; †to bring back to health, consciousness, life etc. *v.i.* to regain a former state, esp. after sickness, misfortune etc.; to come back to consciousness, life, health etc.; to be successful in a suit; to come back to a posture of defence. *n.* the position of a weapon or the body after a thrust etc.; the act of coming back to this. **recoverable,** *a.* **recoverableness,** *n.* **recoverability,** *n.* †**recoveree,** *n.* the person against whom a judgment is obtained in recovery. **recoverer,** *n.* the person who obtains such a judgment. **recovery,** *n.* the act of recovering or the state of having recovered; restoration to health after sickness etc.; the obtaining of the right to something by the judgment of a court; a golf stroke played on to the fairway or green from a bunker or the rough; the retrieval of by-products from an industrial process. [OF *recovrer* (F *recouvrer*), L *recuperāre,* to RECUPERATE]

re-cover, *v.t.* to cover again, to put a new covering on.

recreant, *a.* craven, cowardly; disloyal. *n.* one who has yielded in combat, one who has begged for mercy, a coward, a mean-spirited wretch, an apostate, a deserter. **recreance,** *n.* **recreancy,** *n.* **recreantly,** *adv.* [OF, pres.p. of *recroire,* to yield in trial by combat (RE-, *croire,* L *crēdere,* to believe, to entrust)]

recreate, *v.t.* to refresh after toil; to divert, to entertain, to amuse. *v.i.* to take recreation. **recreation,** *n.* the act of refreshing oneself or renewing one's strength after toil; amusement, diversion; an amusing or entertaining exercise or employment. **recreation ground,** *n.* a communal open space in an urban area. **recreational, recreative,** *a.* refreshing, reinvigorating. **recreatively,** *adv.* **recreativeness,** *n.* [L *recreātus,* p.p. of *recreāre*]

re-create, *v.t.* to create anew. *a.* re-created. **re-creation,** *n.* **re-creator,** *n.* **re-creative** etc. [RECREATE[1]]

recrement, *n.* useless matter separated from that which is useful, refuse; fluid separated from the blood and absorbed into it again, as gastric juice, saliva etc. **recremental, -mentitial, -titious,** *a.* [F *récrément,* L *recrēmentum,* from *recernere* (RE-, *cernere,* to sift)]

recriminate, *v.i.* to retort an accusation, to bring counter-charges against. *v.t.* to accuse in return. **recrimination,** *n.* the act of bringing a counter-charge, of accusing in return; a counter-charge. **recriminative, recriminatory,** *a.* **recriminator,** *n.* [med. L *recrīminātus,* p.p. of *recrīminārī* (RE-, *crīminārī,* to CRIMINATE)]

recross, *v.t., v.i.* to cross or pass over again. **recrucify,** *v.t.* to crucify again.

recrudesce, *v.i.* to open, break out or become raw or sore again. **recrudescence,** *n.* the state of becoming sore again; a relapse, a breaking-out again; the production of a young shoot from a ripened spike etc.; (*loosely*) a renewal, a reappearance. **recrudescent,** *a.* [L *recrūdescere* (RE-, *crūdescere,* to become raw, from *crūdus,* raw)]

recruit, *v.t.* to enlist (persons, esp. soldiers, sailors or airmen); to supply (an army, regiment, crew etc.) with recruits, to enrol members, to replenish with fresh supplies, to fill up gaps etc.; to restore to health, to refresh, to reinvigorate. *v.i.* to gain new supplies; to seek to recover health; to act as a recruiting-officer etc. *n.* a service man or woman newly enlisted; (*fig.*) one who has newly joined a society etc.; †a new supply, a recruitment. **recruitable,** *a.* **recruital, recruitment,** *n.* **recruiter,** *n.* one who recruits. **recruiting ground,** *n.* any source of, or place from which, recruits may be gained. **recruiting-officer, -party, -sergeant,** *n.* persons engaged in enlisting recruits. [F *recruter,* from obs. *recrute,* a recruit, prov. form of *recrue,* fem. p.p. of *recroître* (RE-, *croître,* OF *creistre,* L *crescere,* to grow, to INCREASE)]

Recruit scandal, *n.* a scandal in post-war Japanese history. The Recruit company was accused in July 1988 of illegal stock trading, but the affair widened as increasing numbers of senior government politicians were implicated, for example, Prime Minister Noboru Takeshita was accused in 1989 of receiving 'political donations', as well as bribery and fraud.

recrystallize, -ise, *v.t., v.i.* to crystallize again. **recrystallization, -isation,** *n.*

rectal RECTUM.

rectangle, *n.* a plane rectilinear quadrilateral figure with four right-angles. **rectangled,** *a.* having an angle or angles of 90°. **rectangular,** *a.* shaped like a rectangle; rectangled; placed or having parts placed at right-angles. **rectangular coordinates,** *n.pl.* in a cartesian system, coordinates which have axes perpendicular to each other. **rectangular hyperbola,** *n.* a hyperbola with asymptotes at right-angles. **rectangularity,** *n.* **rectangularly,** *adv.* [F, from late L *rectangulus* (*rectus,* straight, *angulus,* ANGLE[2])]

rect(i)-, *comb. form* straight; right. [L *rectus*]

rectify, *v.t.* to set right, to correct, to amend, to adjust; to reform, to supersede by what is right or just, to abolish; to refine or purify (spirit etc.) by repeated distillations and other processes; to determine the length of (an arc etc.); to transform (an alternating current) into a continuous one. **rectifiable,** *a.* **rectification,** *n.* rectifying in all its senses; (*Radio*) the conversion of an alternating current into a direct current. **rectifier,** *n.* person or thing that rectifies. [F *rectifier,* late L *rectificāre* (**recti-,** *-ficāre facere,* to make)]

rectigrade, *a.* (*Ent.*) walking in a straight line; belonging to the Rectigrada, a class of spiders that walk straight forward. [L *recti-, rectus,* straight, *gradus,* GRADE]

rectilineal, rectilinear, *a.* consisting of, lying or proceeding in a straight line; straight; bounded by straight lines. **rectilineally, rectilinearly,** *adv.* **rectilinearity,** *n.* [late L *rectilīneus* (as prec., *līnea,* LINE[1])]

rectiserial, *a.* arranged in a straight line, esp. in vertical ranks (of leaves). [L *recti-, rectus,* straight, SERIAL]

rectitis, *n.* inflammation of the rectum. **rectitic,** *a.*

rectitude, *n.* uprightness, rightness of moral principle, conformity to truth and justice; †freedom from error, correctness. [F, from late L *rectitūdo,* from L *rectus,* right]

recto, *n.* the right-hand page of an open book (usu. that odd numbered), opp to *verso.* [L *recto* (*folio*), on the right (leaf)]

recto- RECTUM.

rector, *n.* a parson or incumbent of a Church of England parish whose tithes are not impropriate; the head of a religious institution, university, incorporated school etc.; a clergyman in charge of a parish in the Episcopalian Church; †a director, a ruler. **Lord Rector** LORD. **rectorate,** *n.* a rector's term of office. **rectorial,** *a.* pertaining to rector; the election of a Lord Rector. **rectorship,** *n.* **rectory,** *n.* the benefice or living of a rector with all its rights, property etc.; the house of a rector. **rectress,** *n. fem.* a female ruler or governor. [L, ruler, from *regere* (p.p. *rectus*), to rule]

rectoscope, recto-uterine etc. RECTUM.

rectrix, *n.* (*pl.* **rectrices**) a rectress; the quill-feathers in a bird's tail which guide its flight. [L, fem. of RECTOR]

rectum, *n.* (*pl.* **-ta**) the lowest portion of the large intestine extending to the anus. **rectal,** *a.* **rectally,** *adv.* **recto-,** *comb. form.* **rectocele,** *n.* prolapse of the anus with protrusion. **rectoscope,** *n.* a speculum for examining the rectum. **recto-uterine,** *a.* of or pertaining to the rectum and the uterus. **rectovaginal,** *a.* of or pertaining to the rectum and the vagina. [L, neut. of *rectus,* straight]

rectus, *n.* (*pl.* **-ti**) one of various straight muscles, esp. of the abdomen, thigh, neck and eyes. [L, straight]

recultivate, *v.t.* to cultivate afresh. **recultivation,** *n.*

recumbent, *a.* lying down, reclining; (*fig.*) inactive, idle. **recumbence, recumbency,** *n.* **recumbently,** *adv.* [L *recumbens -ntem,* pres.p. of *recumbere* (RE-, *cumbere,* to lie)]

recuperate, *v.t.* to recover, to regain (health, strength etc.); to restore to health. *v.i.* to recover (from sickness, loss of power etc.). †**recuperable,** *a.* **recuperation,** *n.* **recuperative,** †**recuperatory,** *a.* **recuperator,** *n.* [L *recuperātus,* p.p. of *recuperāre,* var. of *reciperāre,* form of *recipere,* to RECEIVE]

recur, *v.i.* (*past, p.p.* **recurred**) to return, to go back to in thought etc.; to come back to one's mind; to happen again, to happen repeatedly; to be repeated indefinitely. **recurrence,** †**recurrency,** *n.* **recurring,** *a.* happening or being repeated. **recurring fever,** *n.* a relapsing fever. **recurring decimals,** *n.* figures in a decimal fraction that recur over and over again in the same order. **recursion,** *n.* the act of returning; the computation of a sequence from a preceding mathematical value. **recursive,** *a.* **recursively,** *adv.* [L *recurrere* (RE-, *currere,* to run)]

†**recure,** *v.t.* to cure, to heal; to recover, to retrieve. *n.* recovery. [L *recūrāre*]

recurrent, *a.* returning, recurring, esp. at regular intervals; turning in the opposite direction (of veins, nerves etc.), running in an opposite course to those from which they branch. *n.* a recurrent nerve or artery, esp. one of the laryngeal nerves. **recurrently,** *adv.*

recurve, *v.t., v.i.* to bend backwards. **recurvate,** *a.* recurved, reflexed. †*v.t.,* to bend back. **recurvation, recurvature,** *n.* **recurviroster,** *n.* a bird with the beak bent upwards, as the avocet. **recurvirostral,** *a.* †**recurvity,** *n.* **recurvo-,** *comb. form.* **recurvous,** *a.* [L *recurvāre*]

recusant, *a.* obstinately refusing to conform, esp. (*Eng. Hist.*) to attend the services of the Established Church. *n.* one who refuses to submit or comply, esp. one who refused to attend the services of the Established Church. **recusance, -cy,** *n.* †**recusation,** *n.* the act of objecting against a judge on the score of prejudice etc. **recusative,** *a.* †**recuse,** *v.t.* to object against, to renounce, esp. to object against a judge. [L *recusans -antem,* pres.p. of *recusāre,* to refuse, to object (RE-, *causa,* CAUSE)]

recut, *v.t.* to cut again.

recycle, *v.t.* to pass again through a system of treatment or series of changes, esp. a waste product (e.g. paper, glass), so as to make it reusable. *v.i.* to return to the original position so the operation can begin again, esp. of electronic devices. *n.* the repetition of a sequence of events. **recyclable,** *a.* **recycler,** *n.*

red-, *pref.* RE- (before vowels in words of L orig.).

red[1], *a.* of a bright warm colour, as blood, usually including crimson, scarlet, vermilion etc., of the colour at the least refracted end of the spectrum or that farthest from the violet; (*fig.*) flushed, stained with blood; revolutionary, anarchistic; (*fig.*) a sign of danger. *n.* a red colour or a shade of this; the red colour in roulette etc.; the red ball at billiards; a red pigment; red clothes; (*fig.*) a revolutionary, an extreme radical, an anarchist; †one of the three former divisions of the British fleet (the others being the white and the blue). **to be in the red,** to be overdrawn at the bank. **to be on red alert,** to be in a state of readiness for a crisis or disaster. **to paint the town red,** to have a riotous time. **to put out the red carpet,** to give an impressive welcome. **to see red,** to become enraged. **red admiral** ADMIRAL. **red algae,** *n.pl.* one family of seaweeds, the Rhodophyceae, with red pigment as well as chlorophyll. **red-and-black,** *n.* rouge-et-noir. **Red Army,** *n.* former name of the army of the USSR. It developed from the Red Guards, volunteers who carried out the Bolshevik revolution, and received its name because it fought under the red flag. It was officially renamed the Soviet Army 1946. The Chinese revolutionary army was also called the Red Army. **red-backed,** *a.* **red-backed shrike,** *n.* the butcher-bird, *Lanius collurio.* **red-backed spider,** *n.* (*Austral.*) a venomous spider with red spots on its back. **red bark,** *n.* a variety of cinchona. **red-bearded, -bellied, -berried, -billed,** *a.* having a red beard, belly, berries etc. **red biddy,** *n.* red wine mixed with methylated spirits. **red-blind,** *a.* colour-blind with regard to red. **red-blindness,** *n.* **red blood cell,** *n.* any blood cell containing haemoglobin, which carries oxygen to the tissues. **red-blooded,** *a.* vigorous, virile, crude. **red-bloodedness,** *n.* **red book,** *n.* a book, orig. bound in red, containing a list of the peerage, civil servants etc. **redbreast,** *n.* the robin, *Erythacus rubecula.* **red-breasted,** *a.* **redbrick university,** *n.* one of the pre-1939 provincial universities in Britain. **Red Brigades,** *n.pl.* (**Italian** *Brigate rosse*) extreme left-wing guerrilla groups active in Italy during the 1970s and early 1980s. They were implicated in many kidnappings and killings, including that of Christian Democrat leader Aldo Moro 1978. **redbud,** *n.* the Judas-tree, *Cercis canadensis.* **red cabbage,** *n.* a reddish-purple cabbage, used for pickling. **red campion,** *n.* a Eurasian plant of the pink family, with red flowers. **red-cap,** *n.* a popular name for any small bird with a red head, esp. the goldfinch. **red card,** *n.* a piece of red cardboard shown by a soccer referee to a player to indicate that he has been sent off. **red carpet,** *n.* a strip of red carpet put out for a celebrity or important person to walk on; deferential treatment. **red cedar,** *n.* any of various species of cedar, esp. a juniper with fragrant, red wood; the timber from such a tree. **red cent,** *n.* (*N Am. coll.*) a trifle of money. **Red Centre,** *n.* (*Austral.*) the interior of the continent. **red-chalk,** *n.* ruddle. **red-cheeked,** *a.* **red-coat,** *n.* a British soldier, so called from the scarlet tunics worn by line regiments. **red-coated,** *a.* **red coral,** *n.* any of several pinkish red corals used to make ornaments and jewellery. **red corpuscle,** *n.* a red blood cell. **Red Crescent,** *n.* the Red Cross Society in Muslim countries. **red cross,** *n.* St George's Cross, the English national emblem. **Red Cross Society,** *n.* an international society or organization having a red cross as emblem, for the provision of ambulance and hospital service for the wounded in time of war, and to assist in severe epidemics and national disasters in peace time, in accordance with the Geneva Convention of 1864. **redcurrant,** *n.* the small, red, edible berry from a shrub of the gooseberry family. **red deer,** *n.* a large species of deer with reddish coat and branching antlers *Cervus elaphus,* still wild in the Scottish Highlands, Exmoor etc.; the Virginia deer, *Cariacus virginianus.* **red-drum,** *n.* the red-fish, *Sciaena ocellata.* **red duster,** *n.* (*sl.*) the red ensign. **red dwarf,** *n.* a star with a relatively small mass and low luminosity. **red earth,** *n.* soil coloured red by iron compounds, found in tropical savanna. **red ensign,** *n.* a red flag with the Union Jack in one corner, used as the ensign of the British Merchant Navy. **red-eye,** *n.* an animal, bird etc. with a red iris; the name of several American fishes, also of the European *Leuciscus erythrophthalmus,* with scarlet lower fins; (*Austral.*) a black cicada with red eyes; low quality whisky. **red-eyed,** *a.* **red eyes,** *n.pl.* bloodshot eyes, with lids red and inflamed with weeping. **red-faced,** *a.* flushed with embarrassment; with a red, florid complexion. **redfin,** *n.* any of several small fish with red fins. **red-fish,** *n.* the name of various American fishes, including the red-drum, the blue-back salmon, *Oncorhyncus nerka* etc.; a male salmon in the spawning season. **red flag,** *n.* the symbol of revolution or of communism; (*fig.*) a danger signal. **red fox,** *n.* the common European fox, *Vulpes vulpes.* **red giant,** *n.* a giant red star with high luminosity. **red grouse** GROUSE[1]. **Red Guards,** *n.pl.* armed workers who took part in the Russian Revolution of 1917. The name was also given to the school and college students, wearing red arm-bands, active in the Cultural Revolution in China (1966–68). **red-gum,** *n.* an eruption of red pimples in infants, caused by dentition; an Australian eucalyptus of various species yielding reddish resin. **red-haired,** *a.* having red hair. **red-handed,** †**red-hand,** *a.* having hands red with blood; (caught) in the very act (originally of homicide). **red hat,** *n.* a cardinal's hat; a staff officer. **redhead,** *n.* any person with red hair. **redheaded,** *a.* **red-heat,** *n.* the temperature at which a thing is red-hot; the state of being red-hot. **red herring,** *n.* herring dried and smoked; (*fig.*) anything which diverts attention from the real issue or line of enquiry. **to draw a red herring across the track,** (*fig.*) to distract attention by starting an irrelevant discussion. **red-hot,** *a.* heated to redness; (*fig.*) excited, furious, wildly enthusiastic. **red-hot poker,** *n.* the flame-flower. **Red Indian,** *n.* (*offensive*) a N American Indian. **red lattice,** *n.* a lattice window painted red, formerly the sign of a tavern. **red-lattice phrases,** *n.pl.* pot-house talk. **red lead,** *n.* red oxide of lead used as a pigment. **red-legged,** *a.* having red legs (of birds). **red-legs,** *n.* a name for various red-legged birds; the bistort. **red-letter,** *a.* marked with red letters. **red-letter day,** *n.* an auspicious or memorable day, because saints' days were so marked in the calendar. **red light,** *n.* any signal to stop; a danger signal. **red-light area, district,** *n.* an area or district in a town where there is a collection of brothels etc. **red man** REDSKIN. **red meat,** *n.* beef and mutton. **red mullet,** *n.* an edible fish found in European waters. **redneck,** *n.* (*N Am., derog.*) a poor white farm labourer in the South; a reactionary person or institution. *a.* reactionary. **red ochre,** *n.* any of several red earths, used as pigments. **red pepper,** *n.* any of various pepper plants cultivated for their hot red fruits; the fruit of such a plant; cayenne pepper; the red fruit of the sweet pepper. **Red Planet,** *n.* Mars. **redpole, -poll,** *n.* a popular name for two species of birds of the Fringillidae family, from the red hue of their heads, esp. the greater redpole, the male linnet; (*pl.*) red-haired polled cattle. **red rag,** *n.* (*fig.*) anything that excites rage as a red object is supposed to enrage a bull. **red rattle** RATTLE. **red ribbon,** *n.* the ribbon worn by members of the Order of the Bath, hence, membership of this. **Red River cart,** *n.* (*Can.*) a strong, two-wheeled, horse- or ox-drawn cart from W Canada. **red rose,** *n.* the emblem of the House of Lancaster during the Wars of the Roses (1455–85). **red-rumped,** *a.* **red salmon,** *n.* any salmon with red flesh, especially the sockeye salmon. **red sanders,** *n.* red sandalwood. **Red Scare,** *n.* in US history, a campaign against radicals and dissenters that took place in the aftermath of World War I and the Russian revolution, and during a period of labour disorders and violence in the US. Mainly middle-class and urban-based, progressives secured legislation at national, state, and local levels to improve the democratic system, working conditions, and welfare provision. †**red-sear,** *v.i.* to crack when too hot, as iron under the hammer. **redshank,** *n.* the red-legged sand-piper, *Tringa totanus;* †(*pl.*) a Celtic Highlander of Scotland, also applied to the native Irish (from their going bare-legged). **red shift,** *n.* the shift of lines in the spectrum towards the red, caused by a receding light source. **red-shirt,** *n.* a follower of Garibaldi (1807–82); a revolutionary. **red-short,** *a.* hot-short. **red-shouldered,** *a.* **Redskin,** *n.* (*offensive*) a N American Indian. **red snapper,** *n.* any of several edible fish of the snapper family. **red snow,** *n.* snow reddened by a minute alga, *Protococcus nivalis,* frequent in Arctic and Alpine regions. **red spider,** *n.* a mite infesting vines and other hot- house plants. **Red Spot,** *n.* a reddish spot, oval in shape and about 48,000 km long which drifts around the southern hemisphere of Jupiter. **red squirrel,** *n.* a reddish squirrel found in Europe and some parts of Asia. **redstart,** *n.* a red-tailed migratory song-bird, *Phoenicurus phoenicurus* (OE *steort,* tail). **red-streak,** *n.* a kind of cider apple. **red-tape,** *n.* extreme adherence to official routine and formality (from the red tape used in tying up official documents). *a.* characterized by this. **red-tapery, red-tapism,** *n.* **red-tapist,** *n.* **Red Terror,** *n.* term used by opponents to describe the Bolshevik seizure and retention of power in Russia after Oct 1917. **red tide,** *n.* the sea, when discoloured and made toxic by red protozoans. **red-top,** *n.* (*N Am.*) a kind of bent grass. **Red Triangle,** *n.* the emblem of the YMCA. **red underwing,** *n.* a large moth with red and black hind wings. **red-water,** *n.* haematuria in cattle and sheep, the most marked symptom of which is the red urine. **red weed,** *n.* the corn poppy; herb Robert and other plants. **red wine,** *n.* wine coloured by grape skins. **redwing,** *n.* a variety of thrush, *Turdus musicus,* with red on the wings. **redwood,** *n.* a name of various trees and their timber, esp. the gigantic Californian *Sequoia sempervirens*. **redden,** *v.t.* to make red. *v.i.* to become red, esp. to blush. **reddish, reddy,** *a.* **reddishness,** *n.* **redly,** *adv.* **redness,** *n.* [OE *read* (cp. Dut. *rood,* G *roth,* Icel. *rauthr,* also L *rufus, ruber,* Gr. *eruthros,* Sansk. *rudhira-*)]

red[2], REDD.

†**red**[3], (*past*) READ.

-red, *suf.* condition, as in *hatred, kindred*. [OE *rǣdan*]

redaction, *n.* reduction to order, esp. revising, rearranging and editing a literary work; a revised or rearranged edition. **redact,** *v.t.* to reduce to a certain form, esp. a literary form, to edit, to prepare for publication. **redacteur,** *n.* **redactional,** *a.* **redactor,** *n.* one who redacts, an editor. **redactorial,** *a.* [F *rédaction,* late L *redactiōnem,* nom. *-tio,* from *redigere* (RED-, *agere,* to bring), p.p. *redactus*]

redan, *n.* (*Fort.*) a work having two faces forming a salient towards the enemy. [F, for *redent* (RE-, DENT, tooth)]

†**redargue,** *v.t.* (*Sc.*) to refute, to disprove. †**redargution,** *n.* [F *rédarguer,* L *redarguere* (RED-, ARGUE)]

redbreast etc. RED[1].

redd, *v.t.* (*Sc.*) to clear, to make clear; to clean out, to get rid of; to adjust, to clear up, to put in order, to tidy, to make ready; to interfere between, to separate (combatants etc.), to settle (a quarrel). **to redd up,** to put in order. **redder,** *n.* **redding-blow, -stroke,** *n.* a blow received by one interfering in a quarrel. **redding-comb,** *n.* a hair-comb. [etym. doubtful, cp. Dut. *redden*]

redden etc. RED[1].

Redding, *n.* **Otis** (1941–67), US soul singer and songwriter. He had a number of hits in the mid-1960s such as 'My Girl' (1965), 'Respect' (1967), and 'Sittin' on the Dock of the Bay' (1968), released after his death in a plane crash.

†**reddition,** *n.* restitution; surrender; translation, version, explanation. †**redditive,** *a.* [F *reddition,* or L *redditio,* from *reddere,* to RENDER]

reddle, *var. of* RUDDLE[2].

†**rede,** *n.* counsel, advice; resolve, intention, plan; a tale, a story; a saying, a motto. *v.t.* to counsel, to advise; to read or interpret (a riddle etc.). **redeless,** *a.* without counsel or advice. [OE *rǣd,* from *rǣdan,* see READ]

redecorate, *v.t.* to decorate afresh. **redecoration,** *n.* **rededicate,** *v.t.* to dedicate anew. **rededication,** *n.* **rededicatory,** *a.*

redeem, *v.t.* to buy back, to recover by paying a price; to recover (mortgaged property), to discharge (a mortgage), to buy off (an obligation etc.); to perform (a promise); to recover from captivity by purchase, to ransom; to deliver, to save, to rescue, to reclaim; to deliver from sin and its penalty; to atone for, to make amends for; to make good. **redeemability, redeemableness,** *n.* **redeemable,** *a.* **redeemer,** *n.* one who redeems, esp. Christ, the Saviour of the world. **redeeming,** *a.* compensating for faults. [F *redimer,* L *redimere* (RED-, *emere,* to buy), p.p. *redemptus*]

redefine, *v.t.* to define again or afresh.

redeliver, *v.t.* to deliver back, to restore, to free again; to repeat, to report. **redeliverance, redelivery,** *n.* **redemand,** *v.t.* to demand again or back. **redemise,** *v.t.* (*Law*) to transfer (an estate etc.) back. *n.* a retransfer.

redemption, *n.* the act of redeeming or the state of being redeemed, esp. salvation from sin and damnation by the atonement of Christ; release by purchase, ransom; reclamation (of land etc.); purchase (of admission to a society etc.); (*fig.*) that which redeems. **redemptioner,** *n.* (*N Am. Hist.*) an emigrant to the US who sold his services for a certain time to pay his passage-money etc. †**Redemptionist,** *n.* a member of an order devoted to the redemption of Christian slaves in the hands of the Infidels. **redemptive,** †**redemptory,** *a.* †**redemptor,** *n.* a redeemer. **Redemptorist,** *n.* a member of a Roman Catholic congregation of missionary priests founded at Naples in 1732 by St Alfonso Liguori. [F, from L *redemptiōnem,* nom. *-tio,* from *redimere,* to REDEEM]

redeploy, *v.t.* to transfer (troops, labour force) from one area to another; to assign a new task to. **redeployment,** *n.* improved internal arrangements in a factory etc. as a means to improving output.

redescend, *v.t., v.i.* to descend again. **redescribe,** *v.t.* to describe again. **redescription,** *n.* **redesign,** *v.t.* to make a new design of something, incorporating improvements. **redetermine,** *v.t., v.i.* to determine again. **redetermination,** *n.* **redevelop,** *v.t.* to develop again; to renovate and build in a depressed urban area. **redevelopment,** *n.* **redevelopment area,** *n.* an urban area where existing buildings are either demolished and rebuilt or renovated.

Redford, *n.* **(Charles) Robert** (1937–), US actor and film director. His first starring role was in *Butch Cassidy and the Sundance Kid* (1969), and his other films as an actor include *All the President's Men* (1976) and *Out of Africa* (1985). He directed *Ordinary People* (1980) and *The Milagro Beanfield War* (1988).

Redgrave[1], *n.* **Michael** (1908–85), British actor. His stage roles included Hamlet and Lear (Shakespeare), Uncle Vanya (Chekhov), and the schoolmaster in Rattigan's *The Browning Version*. He also appeared in films. He was the father of Vanessa and Lynn Redgrave, both actresses.

Redgrave[2], *n.* **Vanessa** (1937–), British actress. She has played Shakespeare's Lady Macbeth and Cleopatra on the stage, and the title role in the film *Julia* (1976) (Academy Award). She is active in left-wing politics. Daughter of Michael Redgrave.

redia, *n.* (*pl.* **rediae**) an asexual stage in certain trematode worms such as the liver-fluke. [mod. L, after Francesco *Redi,* 1626–95, It. naturalist]

redid REDO.

redif, *n.* the first Turkish reserve; a soldier in this. [Turk. and Arab.]

redigest, *v.t.* to digest again. **redigestion,** *n.*

redingote, *n.* a woman's long double-breasted coat; orig. a similar coat worn by men. [F, corr. of RIDING-COAT]

redintegrate, *v.t.* to restore to completeness, make united or perfect again; to renew, to re-establish. †*a.* redintegrated. **redintegration,** *n.* **redintegrative,** *a.* [L *redintegrātus,* p.p. of *redintegrāre*]

redirect, *v.t.* to direct again; to re-address. **redirection,** *n.* †**redisburse,** *v.t., v.i.* to pay back again, to refund. †**redisbursement,** *n.* **rediscover,** *v.t.* to discover afresh. **rediscovery,** *n.* **redispose,** *v.t.* to dispose again. **redisposition,** *n.* **redisseisin,** *n.* (*Law*) a writ to recover seisin of lands or tenements, a second disseisin. **redisseisor,** *n.* **redissolve,** *v.t., v.i.* to dissolve again. **redissoluble, redissolvable,** *a.* **redissolution,** *n.* **redistribute,** *v.t.* to distribute again. **redistribution,** *n.* the act of distributing again; the reallocation of seats in the Canadian House of Commons to each province according to population, carried out every 10 years from a census. **redivide,** *v.t.* to divide again. **redivision,** *n.*

†**redivivous,** *a.* revived, or tending to revive; come to life again. [L *redivīvus* (*redi-,* RED-, *vīvus,* living)]

Redmond, *n.* **John Edward** (1856–1918), Irish politician, Parnell's successor as leader of the Nationalist Party (1890–1916). The 1910 elections saw him holding the balance of power in the House of Commons, and he secured the introduction of a Home Rule bill, hotly opposed by Protestant Ulster.

redo, *v.t.* (*past* **redid,** *p.p.* **redone**) to do again; to redecorate.

redolent, *a.* giving out a strong smell; (*fig.*) suggestive, reminding one (of); esp. of †fragrant odours. **redolence, -cy,** *n.* **redolently,** *adv.* [OF, L *redolentem,* nom. *-lens,* pres.p. of *redolēre* (RED-, *olēre,* to smell)]

Redon, *n.* **Odilon** (1840–1916), French Symbolist painter. He used fantastic symbols and images, sometimes mythological. From the 1890s he also produced still lifes and landscapes. His work was much admired by the Surrealists.

redondilla, *n.* a Spanish stanza in trochaics, the first and fourth and the second and third lines of which rhymed with each other. [Sp., dim. of *redonda,* fem. of *redondo,* round]

redouble, *v.t.* to double again; to increase by repeated additions, to intensify, to multiply; to fold back; to double an opponent's double, in bridge. *v.i.* to become increased by repeated additions, to grow more intense, numerous etc.; to be repeated, to re-echo. *n.* the act of redoubling. **redoublement,** *n.* [F *redoubler*]

redoubt, *n.* a detached outwork or field-work enclosed by a parapet without flanking defences. [F *redoute,* It. *redotto,* L *reductus,* retired (later, a secret place, a refuge), p.p. of *redūcere,* to REDUCE]

Redoubt, Mount, an active volcanic peak rising to 3140 m/10,197 ft. W of Cook inlet in S Alaska, US. There have been recent eruptions in 1966 and 1989.

redoubtable, *a.* formidable; valiant. **redoubtableness,** *n.* **redoubtably,** *a.* †**redoubted,** *a.* dreaded. [OF *redoutable,* from *redouter,* to fear]

redound, *v.i.* to have effect, to conduce or contribute (to one's credit etc.); to result (to), to act in return or recoil (upon); †to be in excess, to be redundant. [F *rédonder,* L *redundāre,* to overflow (RED-, *undāre,* from *unda,* wave)]

redowa, *n.* a Bohemian round dance of two forms, one resembling a waltz, the other a polka. [F and G, from Boh. *reydovák,* from *reydovati,* to whirl round]

redox, *a.* pertaining to a chemical reaction where one agent is reduced and another oxidized. [*red*uction *ox*idation]

redpole etc. RED[1].

redraft, *v.t.* to draft or draw up a second time. *n.* a second draft. **redraw,** *v.t.* to draw again. *v.i.* to draw a fresh bill of exchange to cover a protested one. **redrawer,** *n.*

redress[1], *v.t., v.i.* to dress again.

redress[2], *v.t.* to set straight or right again, to readjust, to rectify; to remedy, to amend, to make reparation for; †to repair, to mend; †to re-erect, to set upright again. *n.* redressing of wrongs or oppression; reparation; rectification. **redressable,** *a.* capable of being redressed. **redresser,** *n.* †**redressive,** *a.* **redressment,** *n.*

Red Riding Hood, *n.* traditional European fairy story. Little Red Riding Hood is on her way to visit her sick grandmother when she meets a wolf. After discovering where she is going he gets there before her, and eats and impersonates the grandmother. In Charles Perrault's version (1697) Red Riding Hood is eaten too, but later writers introduced a woodcutter to rescue her.

Red Sea, *n.* submerged section of the Great Rift Valley (2000 km/1200 miles long and up to 320 km/200 miles wide). Egypt, Sudan, and Ethiopia (in Africa) and Saudi Arabia (Asia) are on its shores.

redshank etc. RED[1].

reduce, *v.t.* to bring to an original or a specified condition; to bring back (to); to modify (so as to bring into another form, a certain class etc.), to make conformable (to a rule, formula etc.); to bring by force (to a specified condition, action etc.), to subdue, to conquer; to bring down, to lower, degrade, to diminish, to weaken; to change from one denomination to another; to set aside or annul by judicial action; to cause a chemical reaction with hydrogen; to remove oxygen atoms; to bring about an increase in the number of electrons; to lessen the density of a photographic print or negative. *v.i.* to resolve itself; to lessen. **to reduce to the ranks,** to degrade to the rank of private soldier. **reduced,** *a.* **in reduced circumstances,** poor, hard-up. **reducement,** *n.* **reducent,** *n., a.* **reducer,** *n.* one who or that which reduces; a piece of pipe for connecting two other pieces of different diameter. **reducible,** *a.* **reducibility, reducibleness,** *n.* **reducibly,** *adv.* **reducing,** *a.* **reducing agent,** *n.* a substance which reduces another in a chemical process. **reducing glass,** *n.* a lens or mirror which reflects an image smaller than the actual object observed. †**reduct,** *v.t.* to reduce or bring (to or into). **reductase,** *n.* any enzyme which reduces organic compounds. **reductive,** *a.* [L *redūcere* (RE- *dūcere,* to bring), p.p. *reductus*]

reduction, *n.* the act of reducing; the state of being reduced; a conquest; a decrease, a diminution; a reduced copy of anything; the process of making this; the process of finding an equivalent expression in terms of a different denomination; the process of reducing the opacity of a negative etc.; a term applied to any process whereby an electron is added to an atom. **reductio ad absurdum** , reduction to absurdity; proof of the truth of a proposition by showing that its contrary has absurd consequences; (*coll.*) an absurd conclusion. **reductionism,** *n.* the explaining of complex data or phenomena in simpler terms. **reductionist,** *n., a.* **reductionistic,** *adv.*

redundant, *a.* superfluous, excessive, superabundant; deprived of one's job as one is no longer necessary; using more words than are necessary, pleonastic, tautological; exuberant, copious, luxuriant. **redundance, -cy,** *n.* **redundantly,** *adv.* [L *redundans -antem,* pres.p. of *redundāre,* to REDOUND]

reduplicate, *v.t.* to redouble, to repeat; to repeat a letter or syllable to form a tense. *a.* doubled, repeated; of petals or sepals, with edges turned out. *n.* a duplicate. **reduplication,** *n.* the act of doubling or repeating; the repetition of a syllable or other part of a word; the part so repeated; the doubling or folding back of a part or organ. **reduplicative,** *a.* [med. L *reduplicātus,* p.p. of *reduplicāre* (RE-, *duplicāre,* to DUPLICATE]

reduviid, *a.* belonging to the Reduviidae, a family of predaceous bugs. *n.* a bug of this family. **reduvioid,** *n., a.* [mod. L *Reduvius,* -ID]

redwing, redwood etc. RED[1].

re-dye, *v.t.* to dye again.

ree[1], *n.* the female ruff. [var. of REEVE[3]]

ree[2], *a.* (*Sc.*) excited, wild, esp. with drink; delirious. [etym. doubtful]

ree[3] REIS[1].

reebok, *n.* (*S Afr.*) a small S African antelope, *Pelea capreola.* [Afrikaans, ROEBUCK]

re-echo, *v.t.* to echo again; to return the sound, to resound. *v.i.* to echo again; to reverberate.

†**reechy,** *a.* smoky; dirty, foul; rancid. [var. of REEKY]

reed, *n.* the long straight stem of certain water or marsh plants belonging to the genera *Phragmites, Arundo* or *Ammophila;* (*collect.*) these as material for thatching etc.; a musical pipe made of this, a shepherd's pipe; (*fig.*) pastoral poetry; a thin strip of metal or wood inserted in an opening in a musical instrument, set in vibration by a current of air to produce the sound; hence, a musical instrument or organ-pipe constructed with this (*usu. in pl.*); an implement or part of a loom for separating the threads of the warp and beating up the weft; a semicircular moulding, usu. in parallel series (*usu. in pl.*). *v.t.* to thatch with reed; to fit (an organ-pipe etc.) with a reed; to decorate with reeds. **broken reed,** *n.* an unreliable person. **reed-babbler, -warbler, -wren,** *n.* a common European bird, *Acrocephalus scirpaceus.* **reed-band,** *n.* a consort of reed instruments. **reed-bird,** *n.* the bobolink. **reedbuck,** *n.* an antelope with a buff-coloured coat, found south of the Sahara in Africa. **reed-bunting,** *n.* a common European bunting with a black head, *Emberiza schoeniclus.* **reed-grass,** *n.* any of the reeds or any grasses of similar habit. **reed-instrument,** *n.* a woodwind instrument with a reed, such as an oboe. **reed-mace,** *n.* the bulrush. **reed-organ,** *n.* a musical instrument with a keyboard, the sounds of which are produced by reeds of the organ type. **reed-pheasant,** *n.* the bearded titmouse. **reed-pipe,** *n.* a reeded organ-pipe; a musical pipe made of a reed. **reed-stop,** *n.* an organ-stop controlling a set of reed-pipes. †**reeden,** *a.* consisting or made of reeds. **reeding,** *n.* a semi-cylindrical moulding or series of these; milling on the edge of a coin. **reedless,** *a.* **reedling,** *n.* the bearded titmouse. **reedy,** *a.* abounding in reeds; like a reed; sounding like a reed, thin, sharp in tone; thin, frail in form. **reediness,** *n.* [OE *hrēod* (cp. Dut. and G *reet*)]

Reed[1], *n.* **Lou** (1942–), US rock singer, songwriter, and former member (1965–70) of the seminal New York garage band the Velvet Underground. His solo work deals largely with urban alienation and angst, and includes the albums *Berlin* (1973), *Street Hassle* (1978), and *New York* (1989).

Reed[2], *n.* **Oliver** (1938–), British actor, nephew of the director Carol Reed. He became a star through such films as *Oliver!* (1968), *Women in Love* (1969), *The Devils* (1971), and *Castaway* (1987).

re-edify, *v.t.* to rebuild; (*fig.*) to reconstruct, to re-establish. **re-edification,** *n.*

re-edit, *v.t.* to edit afresh.

re-educate, *v.t.* to educate again; to teach new skills to. **re-education,** *n.*

reef[1], *n.* a ridge of rock, coral sand etc. in the sea at or near the surface of the water; a lode or vein of auriferous quartz, or the bed-rock left after the removal of the diamantiferous portion. **reefy,** *a.* abounding in reefs. [prob. from Dut. *rif,* Icel. *rif,* perh. cogn. with RIB]

reef[2], *n.* one of the horizontal portions across the top of a square sail or the bottom of a fore-and-aft sail, which can be rolled up or wrapped and secured in order to shorten sail. *v.t.* to reduce the extent of a sail by taking in a reef or reefs; to take in a part of (a bowsprit, topmast etc.) in order to shorten it. **to take in a reef,** to reef a sail; (*fig.*) to proceed with caution or in moderation. **reef-knot,** *n.* a square or symmetrical double knot. **reef-line,** *n.* a small rope passing through eyelet-holes for reefing a sail. **reef-point,** *n.* a short length of rope stitched to a sail, for attaching a reef. **reefer[1],** *n.* one who reefs; a reef-knot; a reefing-jacket; (*Naut. sl.*) a midshipman. **reefing-jacket,** *n.* a stout, close-fitting double-breasted jacket. [Icel. *rif,* see prec.]

reefer[2], *n.* a marijuana cigarette.

reek, *n.* smoke; vapour, steam, fume; a foul, stale or disagreeable odour, a foul atmosphere. *v.i.* to emit smoke, vapour or steam; to smoke, to steam, to emit fumes; to give off a disagreeable odour; to be steamy, sweaty or smeared with foul moisture. **Auld Reekie,** *n.* Edinburgh. **reeking, reeky,** *a.* smoky; filthy, dirty. [OE *rēc* (cp. Dut. *rook,* G *Rauch,* Icel. *reykr*), whence *rēocan,* Dut. *rieken,* G *rauchen,* to smoke]

reel[1], *n.* a rotatory frame, cylinder or other device on which thread, cord, wire, paper etc. can be wound, either in the process of manufacture or for winding and unwinding as required; a quantity of material wound on a reel; a bobbin; the spool on which a film is wound; a portion of film, usually 1000 ft. (about 300 m); (*coll.*) the film itself. *v.t.* to wind on a reel; to unwind or take (off) a reel. **to reel in, up,** to wind (thread, a line etc.) on a reel; to draw (a fish etc.) towards one by using a reel. **to reel off,** to unwind or pay out from a reel; (*fig.*) to tell (a story) fluently and without a hitch. **to reel up,** to wind up entirely on a reel. **reel-check,** *n.* a contrivance for checking the motion of a fishing-line pulled off the reel by a fish etc. **reel-cotton,** *n.* sewing-cotton or thread wound on reels or spools. **reel-fed,** *a.* pertaining to printing on a web of paper. **reel-line,** *n.* an angler's line wound on a reel, esp. the back part as distinguished from the casting-line. **reelman,** *n.* (*Austral., New Zealand*) the person who controls the reel with the rescue line on, in a beach life-saving team. **reel-plate,** *n.* a metal plate on an angler's reel fitting into a groove etc. on a fishing-rod. **reel-to-reel,** *a.* of magnetic tape, wound from one reel to another; using such tape. **reelable,** *n.* **reeler,** *n.* **reeling,** *n., a.* **reeling-machine,** *n.* a machine used for winding up thread, cotton etc. **reelingly,** *adv.* [OE *hrēol*]

reel[2], *v.i.* to stagger, to sway; to go (along) unsteadily; to have a whirling sensation, to be dizzy, to swim; to be staggered, to rock, to give way. *n.* a staggering or swaying motion or sensation. **reeling,** *n., a.* **reelingly,** *adv.* [perh. rel. to prec.]

reel[3], *n.* a lively Scottish dance in which the couples face each other and describe figures-of-eight; a piece of music for this. *v.i.* to dance a reel. **reel of three,** a manoeuvre in which three dancers go round each other in a figure-of-eight. **Virginia reel,** an American country dance. [perh. from REEL[2]]

re-elect, *v.t.* to elect again. **re-election,** *n.* **re-elevate,** *v.t.* to elevate again. **re-elevation,** *n.* **re-eligible,** *a.* capable of being re-elected to the same position. **re-eligibility,** *n.* **re-embark,** *v.t., v.i.* to embark again. **re-embarkation,** *n.* **re-embattle,** *v.t.* to array again for battle. **re-embody,** *v.t.* to embody again. **re-embodiment,** *n.* **re-embrace,** *v.t.* to embrace again. *n.* a second embrace. **re-emerge,** *v.i.* to emerge again. **re-emergence, re-emersion,** *n.* **re-emergent,** *a.* **re-enable,** *v.t.* to make able again. **re-emphasize, -ise,** *v.t.* to emphasize again. **re-enact,** *v.t.* to enact again. **re-enactment,** *n.* **re-endow,** *v.t.* to endow again. **re-enforce,** *v.t.* to give fresh or additional force or strength to; to strengthen a part, esp. a support; to reinforce. *n.* a reinforce. **re-engage,** *v.t., v.i.* to engage again. **re-engagement,** *n.* **re-engine,** *v.t.* to furnish with new engines. **re-enlist,** *v.t., v.i.* to enlist again. **re-enter,** *v.t., v.i.* to enter again. **re-entrance,** *n.* **re-entrant,** *a.* re-entering, pointing inward. *n.* a re-entrant angle, esp. in fortification, opp. to *salient.* **re-entry,** *n.* the act of re-entering; a new entry in a book etc.; re-entering upon possession; the re-entry of a spacecraft into the earth's atmosphere. **re-equip,** *v.t.* to equip again. **re-erect,** *v.t.* to erect again. **re-erection,** *n.*

Rees-Mogg, *n.* **Lord William** (1928–), British journalist, editor of *The Times* (1967–81), chairman of the Arts Council (1982–89), and from 1988 chairman of the Broadcasting Standards Council.

reest[1], *v.t.* (*Sc., North.*) to dry or smoke (bacon, fish etc.), to cure. *v.t.* to become smoke-dried. [etym. doubtful]

reest[2], *v.i.* (*Sc., North.*) to stop, to refuse to go on, to balk (of a horse etc.). **reesty,** *a.* [prob. var. of REST[1] or a form of Sc. *arreest,* ARREST]

re-establish, *v.t.* to establish anew, to restore. **re-establisher,** *n.* **re-establishment,** *n.* **re-evaluate,** *v.t.* to evaluate again. **re-evaluation,** *n.*

reeve[1], *n.* a chief officer or magistrate of a town or district, holding office usually under the king but sometimes by election; (*Can.*) the presiding officer of a township or village council; †a bailiff, a steward. [OE *gerēfa,* etym. doubtful]

reeve[2], *v.t.* (*past, p.p.* **rove, reeved**) to pass (the end of a rope, a rod etc.) through a ring, a hole in a block etc.; to fasten (a rope etc.) round some object by this means. [prob. from Dut. *reven,* to REEF[2]]

reeve[3], *n.* the female of the ruff. [etym. obscure, cp. RUFF[2]]

Reeves, *n.* **William Pember** (1857–1932), New Zealand politician and writer. He was New Zealand minister of education (1891–96), and director of the London School of Economics (1908–19). He wrote poetry and the classic description of New Zealand, *Long White Cloud* (1898).

re-examine, *v.t.* to examine again. **re-examination,** *n.* **re-exchange,** *v.t.* to exchange again. *n.* (*Comm.*) a renewed exchange; the difference in the value of a bill of exchange occasioned by its being dishonoured in a foreign country where it was payable. **re-exhibit,** *v.t.* to exhibit again. **re-exist,** *v.i.* to exist again. **re-existence,** *n.* **re-existent,** *a.* **re-export,** *v.t.* to export again; to export after having been imported; to export imported goods after processing. *n.* a commodity re-exported. **re-exportation,** *n.* **re-exporter,** *n.* **reface,** *v.t.* to put a new face or surface on. **refacing,** *n.* **refashion,** *v.t.* to fashion anew. **refashioner,** *n.* **refashionment,** *n.* **refasten,** *v.t.* to fasten again.

ref[1], (*abbr.*) referee; reference; reformed; reformer.

ref[2], *v.t., v.i* to referee.

refection, *n.* refreshment by food; a light meal, a repast. **refect,** *v.t.* to refresh with food; to restore after fatigue. **refective,** *n., a.* **refectory,** *n.* a room or hall where meals are taken in religious houses etc. **refectory table,** *n.* a long narrow dining table, esp. on two trestles. [F *réfection,* L *refectiōnem,* nom. *-tio*]

refer, *v.t.* (*past, p.p.* **referred**) to trace back, to assign (to a certain cause, source, class, place etc.); to hand over (for consideration and decision); to send or direct (a person) for information etc.; to commit (oneself) to another's favour, etc.; to fail an examinee. *v.i.* to apply for information; to appeal, to have recourse; to cite, to allude, to direct attention (to); to be concerned with, to have relation (to). **referable,** *a.* **referrable,** *a.* **referent,** *n.* that to which a word or phrase refers. **referential,** *a.* **referentially,** *adv.* †**referment,** *n.* **referral,** *n.* the act of referring or being referred. **referred,** *a.* **referred sensation,** *n.* pain or other sensation localized at a different point from the part actually causing it. **referrible** REFERABLE. [OF *referer,* L *referre* (RE-, *ferre,* to bear)]

referee, *n.* one to whom a point or question is referred; a person to whom a matter in dispute is referred for settlement or decision, an arbitrator, an umpire; a person who is prepared to testify to the abilities and character of someone, and who furnishes testimonials. *v.i.* to act as a referee (in football etc.).

reference, *n.* the act of referring; relation, respect, correspondence; allusion, directing of attention (to); a note or mark referring from a book to another work or from the text to a commentary, diagram etc.; that which is referred to; a person referred to for information, evidence of character etc., a referee; a testimonial. *v.t.* (*usu. in p.p.*) to furnish (a work) with cross-references, references to authorities etc. **cross-reference** CROSS[1]. **in, with reference to,** with regard to, as regards, concerning. **terms of reference,** the specific limits of the scope of an investigation or piece of work. **without reference to,** irrespective of, regardless of. **reference Bible,** *n.* a Bible with cross-references in the margin. **reference, book, work,** *n.* an encyclopaedia, dictionary or the like, consulted when occasion requires, not for continuous reading. **reference library,** *n.* a library where books may be consulted but not borrowed. †**referendary,** *n.* a referee; an adviser, an assessor; an officer in a papal, royal or imperial Court who formerly delivered answers to petitions etc.

referendum, *n.* (*pl.* **-da, -dums**) the submission of a political question to the whole electorate for a direct decision by general vote.

reffo, *n.* (*Austral. coll.*) a political refugee from Europe. [REFUGEE]

†**refigure,** *v.t.* to figure or represent anew. **refill,** *v.t.* to fill again. *n.* (rē′-), that which is used to refill; a fresh fill (as of lead for a pocket-pencil, tobacco for a pipe etc.). **refillable,** *a.* **refind,** *v.t.* to find again.

refine, *v.t.* to clear from impurities, defects etc., to purify, to clarify; to free from coarseness, to educate, to polish, to cultivate the taste, manners etc. of; to make (a statement, idea etc.) more subtle, complex or abstract; to transform or modify into a subtler or more abstract form. *v.i.* to become pure or clear; to become polished or more highly cultivated in talk, manners etc.; to affect subtlety of thought or language; to draw subtle distinctions (upon). **refinable,** *a.* **refined,** *a.* freed from impurities; highly cultivated, polished, elegant. **refinedly,** *adv.* **refinedness,** *n.* **refinement,** *n.* the act or process of refining; the state of being refined; elegance of taste, manners, language etc.; high culture, polish; elaboration (of luxury etc.); affected subtlety; a subtle distinction or piece of reasoning. **refiner,** *n.* one who refines, esp. a person whose business it is to refine metals etc.; an apparatus for purifying coal-gas etc.; one who invents superfluous subtleties or distinctions. **refinery,** *n.* a place for refining raw materials, such as sugar and oil. [RE-, FINE[2]]

refit, *v.t.* to make fit for use again, to repair, to fit out anew (esp. a ship). *v.i.* to repair damages (of ships). *n.*, the repairing or renewing of what is damaged or worn out, esp. the repairing of a ship. **refitment,** *n.*

refl., (*abbr.*) reflection, reflective, reflectively; reflex, reflexive, reflexively.

reflate, *v.t.* to inflate again. **reflation,** *n.* an increase in economic activity, esp. through an increase in the supply of money and credit. **reflationary,** *a.*

reflect, *v.t.* to turn or throw (light, heat, sound, an electric body etc.) back, esp. in accordance with certain physical laws; to mirror, to throw back an image of; (*fig.*) to reproduce exactly, to correspond in features or effects; to cause to accrue or to cast (honour, disgrace etc.) upon; †to bend, fold or turn back; to show, to give an idea of. *v.i.* to throw back light, heat, sound etc.; to turn the thoughts back, to think, to ponder, to meditate; to remind oneself (that); to bring shame or discredit (upon). **to reflect on,** to cast censure or blame upon. **reflectance,** *n.* the amount of light or radiation reflected by a surface. **reflectible,** *a.* **reflecting,** *a.* **reflecting factor,** *n.* reflectance. **reflecting microscope,** *n.* a microscope with a series of mirrors instead of lenses. **reflecting telescope,** *n.* a telescope in which the object glass is replaced by a polished reflector, from which the image is magnified by an eyepiece. **reflectingly,** *adv.* casting censure or reflections (upon); reproachfully. **reflection,** †**reflexion,** *n.* the act of reflecting; the state of being reflected; that which is reflected; rays of light, heat etc. or an image thrown back from a reflecting surface; reconsideration; the act or process by which the mind takes cognizance of its own operations; continued consideration, thought, meditation; a thought, idea, comment or opinion resulting from deliberation; censure, reproach (brought or cast upon etc.); that which entails censure or reproach (upon); reflex action. **reflectional,** *a.* **reflectionless**, *a.* **reflective,** *a.* throwing back an image, rays of light, heat etc.; pertaining to or concerned with thought or reflection; meditative, thoughtful; taking cognizance of mental operations; †reflexive; †reflected; †reflex, reciprocal. **reflectively,** *adv.* **reflectiveness,** *n.* **reflectivity**, *n.* the ability to reflect radiation. **reflector,** *n.* one who or that which reflects, esp. a reflecting surface that throws back rays of light, heat etc., usu. a polished, concave surface, as in a lamp, lighthouse, telescope, surgical or other instrument etc.; (*fig.*) a person or thing that reflects or reproduces impressions, feelings etc. **reflet**, *n.* a metallic lustre or glow. [L *reflectere* (RE-, *flectere,* to bend), p.p. *reflexus*]

reflex, *a.* turned backward; introspective; reactive, turned back upon itself or the source, agent etc.; bent back, recurved; reflected, lighted by reflected light; involuntary, produced independently of the will under stimulus from impressions on the sensory nerves; reflexive. *n.* a reflection; a reflected image, reproduction or secondary manifestation; a reflex action; reflected light, colour etc.; a part of a picture represented as lit by the reflected light or colour of other parts. *v.t.* to bend or fold back, to recurve; †to reflect. **conditioned reflex,** a behaviouristic mechanism or reaction by which the emotions may be organized in the education of an individual. **reflex anal dilatation,** involuntary widening of the anus on physical examination, used as a diagnostic procedure to detect repeated anal penetration, esp. in cases involving suspected sexual abuse in children. **reflex action,** *n.* the involuntary contraction of a muscle in response to stimulus from without the body. **reflex arc,** *n.* the nervous pathway which nerve impulses travel along to produce a reflex action. **reflex camera,** *n.* a camera in which the main lens is used as a viewfinder. **reflexed,** *a.* bent backwards or downwards. **reflexible,** *a.* **reflexibility**, *n.* †**reflexity,** *n.* **reflexive,** *a.* denoting action upon the agent; implying action by the subject upon itself, himself or referring back to the grammatical subject; reflective. **reflexive verb,** *n.* a verb that has for its direct object a pronoun which stands for the agent or subject. **reflexively,** *adv.* **reflexiveness,** *n.* **reflexivity**, *n.* **reflexly,** *adv.* **reflexology**, *n.* a form of alternative medical therapy where the soles of the feet are massaged to stimulate the circulation and nerves, and so release tension. **reflexologist,** *n.* [L *reflexus,* p.p. of *reflectere,* to reflect (whence late L *reflexus -ūs,* a reflex)]

reflexion REFLECT.

refloat, *v.t., v.i.* to float again. **reflorescence,** *n.* a second florescence. **reflorescent,** *a.* **reflourish,** *v.i.* to flourish anew. **reflow,** *v.i.* to flow back; to ebb. *n.* a reflowing, a reflux; the ebb (of the tide). **reflower,** *v.i.* to flower again.

refluent, *a.* flowing back; ebbing. **refluence,** *n.* **reflux,** *n.* a flowing back; a return, an ebb; the boiling of liquid in a flask fitted with a condenser, so that the vapour condenses and flows back into the flask. [L *refluens -entem,* pres.p. of *refluere* (RE-, *fluere,* to flow)]

refold, *v.t.* to fold again. **refoot,** *v.t.* to put a new foot to (a stocking, etc.). **reforest,** *v.t.* to reafforest. **reforestation,** *n.* **reforge,** *v.t.* to forge over again; to refashion.

re-form, *v.t.* to form again or anew. **re-formation,** *n.* **re-former,** *n.*

reform, *v.t.* to change from worse to better by removing faults, imperfections, abuses etc.; to improve, to amend, to redress, to cure, to remedy. *v.i.* to amend one's habits, morals, conduct etc.; to abandon evil habits etc. *n.* the act of reforming; an alteration for the better, amendment, improvement, reformation, correction of abuses etc., esp. in parliamentary representation. **Reform Acts,** *n.pl.* Acts passed in 1832, 1867, and 1884 for enlarging the electorate and reforming the constitution of the House of Commons. **Reform Judaism,** *n.* a form of Judaism which adapts Jewish Law to contemporary life. **reform school,** *n.* a reformatory. **reformable,** *a.* **reformability**, *n.* [F *reformer,* L *reformāre*]

†**reformado,** †**reformade**, *n.* an officer deprived of his command by the disbanding or re-forming of his company, but retaining his rank and usu. his pay; a volunteer serving without a commission but with the rank of officer. [Sp., from L *reformātus,* p.p. of *reformāre,* to REFORM¹]

reformation, *n.* the act of reforming; the state of being reformed; redress of grievances or abuses, esp. a thorough change or reconstruction in politics, society or religion. **the Reformation,** *n.* the great religious revolution in the 16th cent. which resulted in the establishment of the Protestant Churches. **reformational,** *a.* **reformationist,** *n.* **reformative**, *a.* tending to produce reformation. **reformatory**, *a.* reformative. *n.* an institution for the detention and reformation of juvenile offenders. [F, from L *reformātiō,* acc. *-ōnem,* from *reformāre,* to REFORM]

reformed, *a.* corrected, amended, purged of errors and abuses. **Reformed Church,** *n.* one of the Protestant Churches that adopted Calvinistic doctrines and polity, distinguished from Lutheran Churches.

reformer, *n.* one who effects a reformation; one who favours political reform; one who took a leading part in the Reformation of the 16th cent. **reformism,** *n.* any policy advocating religious or political reform. †**reformist,** *n., a.*

reformulate, *v.t.* to formulate again. **reformulation,** *n.*

refortify, *v.t.* to fortify anew. **refound,** *v.t.* to found anew, to recast.

refract, *v.t.* to deflect or turn (a ray of light etc.) from its direct course (of water, glass or other medium differing in density from that through which the ray has passed). **refractable,** *a.* **refracted,** *a.* deflected from a direct course, as a ray of light or heat; bent back at an acute angle. **refracting,** *a.* **refracting telescope,** *n.* the earliest form of telescope, in which the image of an object is received direct through a converging lens and magnified by an eye-piece. **refraction,** *n.* the deflection that takes place when a ray of light, heat etc. passes at any other angle than a right angle from the surface of one medium into another medium of different density; the amount of deflection which takes place. **astronomical refraction,** the deflection of a luminous ray proceeding from a heavenly body not in the zenith to the eye of a spectator on the earth, due to the refracting power of the atmosphere. **double refraction,** the splitting of a ray of light, heat etc. into two polarized rays which may be deflected differently on entering certain materials, e.g. most crystals. **refractional, refractive,** *a.* **refractive index,** *n.* the amount by which a medium refracts light; the ratio of the speed of radiation or light in free space to its speed in any other medium. **refractivity**, *n.* **refractometer**, *n.* any instrument which measures the refractive index of a medium. **refractometric**, *a.* **refractometry**, *n.* **refractor,** *n.* a refracting medium, lens or telescope. [L *refractus,* p.p. of *refringere* (RE-, *frangere,* to break)]

refractory, *a.* perverse, contumacious, obstinate in opposition or disobedience, unmanageable; not amenable to ordinary treatment; not easily fused or reduced, not easily worked; fire-resistant; tardily responsive to stimulus (of nerves etc.). *n.* a piece of refractory ware used in a kiln with a flux for glazing pottery; †a refractory person. **refractorily,** *adv.* **refractoriness,** *n.* [L *refractārius,* as prec.]

refracture, *v.t.* to fracture again.

†**refragable,** *a.* refutable. †**refragability**, *n.* [med. L *refragābilis* from L *refragārī,* see IRREFRAGABLE]

refrain¹, *n.* the burden of a song, a phrase or line usu. repeated at the end of every stanza. [OF, from *refraindre,* pop. L *refrangere,* L *refringere,* to REFRACT]

refrain², *v.i.* to hold back, to restrain, to curb (oneself, one's tears etc.). *v.i.* to forbear; to abstain (from an act or doing). **refrainer,** †**refrainment,** *n.* [OF *refrener,* L *refrēnāre* (RE-, *frēnum,* bit, curb)]

reframe, *v.t.* to frame again, to fashion anew.

refrangible, *a.* capable of being refracted. **refrangibility**, †**refrangibleness,** *n.* [pop. L *refrangibilis*, from *refrangere*, see REFRAIN[1]]

refreeze, *v.t.* to freeze again.

refresh, *v.t.* to make fresh again; to reanimate, to reinvigorate; to revive or restore after depression, fatigue etc.; to freshen up (one's memory); to restore, to repair; (*coll.*) to give (esp. liquid) refreshments to; †to give a sensation of coolness to; to pour cold water over blanched food. *v.i.* (*coll.*) to take (esp. liquid) refreshment. **refresher,** *n.* one who or that which refreshes; an extra fee paid to counsel when a case is adjourned or continued from one term or sitting to another; (*coll.*) a drink. **refresher course,** *n.* a course to bring up to date knowledge of a particular subject. **refreshing,** *a.* reinvigorating, reanimating. **refreshingly,** *adv.* **refreshingness,** *n.* **refreshment,** *n.* the act of refreshing; the state of being refreshed; that which refreshes, esp. (*pl.*) food or drink. **refreshment room,** *n.* a room at a railway station etc. for the supply of refreshments. [OF *refreschir*]

refrigerate, *v.t.* to make cool or cold; to freeze or keep at a very low temperature in a refrigerator so as to preserve in a fresh condition. **refrigerant,** *a.* cooling, allaying heat. *n.* that which cools or refreshes; a medicine for allaying fever or inflammation. **refrigeration,** *n.* **refrigerative,** *n., a.* [L *refrīgerātus*, p.p. of *refrīgerāre* (RE- *frīgus -goris*, cold)]

refrigerator, *n.* an apparatus for keeping meat and other provisions in a frozen state or at a very low temperature, in order to preserve their freshness. **refrigeratory,** *a.* cooling. *n.* a vessel attached to a still for condensing vapour; a refrigerator.

refringent, *a.* refractive. **refringence, refringency**, *n.* [L *refringens -entem,* pres.p. of *refringere*, to REFRACT]

reft, (*past, p.p.*) REAVE.

refuel, *v.t.* to provide with fresh fuel. *v.i.* to take on fresh fuel.

refuge, *n.* shelter or protection from danger or distress; a place, thing, person or course of action that shelters or protects from danger, distress or calamity; a stronghold, retreat, sanctuary, a house of refuge; an expedient, a subterfuge; a raised area in the middle of a road forming a safe place for crossers to halt at. *v.t.* to give refuge to. *v.i.* to take refuge. **city of refuge,** one of six cities in the Holy Land appointed as places of refuge to one who had unintentionally committed manslaughter. **house of refuge,** a charitable institution for the destitute and homeless. **refugee**, *n.* one who flees to a place of refuge, esp. one who takes refuge in a foreign country in time of war or persecution or political commotion. **refugeeism,** *n.* **refugium**, *n.* (*pl.* **-gia**) a geographical region which has not been changed by geographical or climatic conditions and so becomes a haven for relict varieties of flora and fauna. [F, from L *refugium* (RE-, *fugium,* from *fugere,* to flee)]

refulgent, *a.* shining brightly, brilliant, radiant, splendid. †**refulgence,** †**-gency,** *n.* **refulgently,** *adv.* [L *refulgens -ntem,* pres.p. of *refulgēre* (RE-, *fulgēre,* to shine)]

refund, *v.t.* to pay back, to repay, to restore; to reimburse. *v.i.* to make repayment. *n.* the money reimbursed. **refundable,** *a.* **refunder,** *n.* **refundment,** *n.* [L *refundere,* to pour back (RE-, *fundere,* see FOUND[1])]

re-fund, *v.t.* to pay off an old debt by borrowing more money.

refurbish, *v.t.* to furbish up anew.

refurnish, *v.t.* to furnish anew; to supply with new furniture.

refusal, *n.* the act of refusing; denial of anything solicited, demanded or offered; the choice or option of taking or refusing something before it is offered to others.

refuse[1]**,** *v.t.* to decline to do, yield, grant etc.; to deny the request of; to decline to jump over (a ditch etc.); to fail to take, to repel (a dye etc.); †to disown. *v.i.* to decline to comply; to fail to jump (of a horse); to be unable to follow suit; †**refusable,** *a.* **refusenik, refusnik,** *n.* a Soviet Jew who has been refused permission to emigrate; (*coll.*) a person who refuses to cooperate in some way. **refuser,** *n.* [OF *refuser,* prob. through a pop. L *refūsāre,* from L *refundere,* see REFUND, p.p. *refūsus*]

refuse[2]**,** *a.* refused, rejected; valueless. *n.* that which is refused or rejected as worthless; waste or useless matter. **refuse tip,** *n.* a place where refuse is heaped or disposed of. [prob. OF *refus, refuse,* p.p. of prec.]

re-fuse, *v.t.* to fuse or melt again. **re-fusion,** *n.*

refusenik, refusnik REFUSE[1].

refute, *v.t.* to prove (a statement, argument etc.) false or erroneous, to disprove; to prove wrong, to rebut in argument, to confute. **refutable,** *a.* **refutably,** *adv.* **refutal, refutation**, *n.* **refutatory, refuter,** *n.* [F *refuter,* L *refūtāre,* see CONFUTE]

reg., (*abbr.*) regent; regiment; register, registrar; registry; regular, regularly; regulation.

regain, *v.t.* to recover possession of; to reach again; to gain anew, to recover. **regainable,** *a.* **regainer,** *n.* **regainment,** *n.* [F *regagner* (RE-, GAIN[1])]

regal[1]**,** *a.* pertaining to or fit for a king or kings. *n.* kingly, royal, magnificent. **regally,** *adv.* [L *rēgālis,* from *rex rēgis,* king]

†**regal**[2]**,** *n.* a small portable reed-organ held in the hands, in use in the 16th and 17th cents. (*often in pl. form,* as *a pair of regals*). [F *régale,* perh. from prec.]

regale, *v.t.* to entertain sumptuously; to delight, to gratify (with something rich or choice). *v.i.* to feast, to fare sumptuously (on). †*n.* a choice repast, a feast, a sumptuous entertainment. **regalement,** *n.* **regaler,** *n.* [F *régaler,* It. *regalare,* etym. doubtful]

regalia[1]**,** *n.pl.* †the prerogatives and rights of a sovereign; the insignia of royalty, esp. the emblems worn or displayed in coronation ceremonies etc.; finery in general. [L, neut. pl. of *rēgālis,* REGAL[1]]

regalia[2]**,** *n.* a Cuban cigar of superior quality. [Sp., royal privilege, as prec.]

regalism, *n.* the doctrine of the royal supremacy in ecclesiastical affairs. **regality**, *n.* royalty, kingship; sovereign jurisdiction; an attribute of royalty; (*Sc.*) a territorial distinction formerly conferred on a noble by the king; a monarchical state, a kingdom.

regally REGAL[1].

regalvanize, -ise, *v.t.* to galvanize again.

Regan, *n.* **Donald** (1918–), US Republican political adviser to Ronald Reagan. He was secretary of the Treasury (1981–85), and chief of White House staff (1985–87), when he was forced to resign because of widespread belief of his complicity in the Irangate scandal.

regard, *v.t.* to look at, to observe, to notice; to give heed to, to pay attention to, to take into account; to value, to pay honour to, to esteem; to look upon or view in a specified way or with fear, reverence etc., to consider (as); to concern; to affect, to relate to. *v.i.* to look; to pay attention. *n.* a look, a gaze; observant attention, heed, care, consideration; esteem, kindly or respectful feeling; reference; relation; (*pl.*) compliments, good wishes. **as regards,** regarding. **in, with regard to,** regarding; as touching. **in this regard,** on this point. **with kind regards,** with good wishes. †**regardable,** *a.* **regardant,** *a.* looking backward; observant, watchful. **regarder,** *n.* **regardful,** *a.* showing regard, respect or consideration. **regardfully,** *adv.* **regardfulness,** *n.* **regarding,** *prep.* respecting, concerning. **regardless**, *a.* heedless, careless, negligent. *adv.* (*coll.*) regardless of expense, lavishly dressed; in spite of. **regardlessly,** *adv.* **regardlessness,** *n.* [F *regarder*]

regather, *v.t., v.i.* to gather or collect again.

regatta, *n.* a race-meeting at which yachts or boats contend for prizes. [It., orig. contention]

regelate, *v.i.* to freeze together again; to unite into a mass by freezing together (of fragments of ice, snow etc.) with moist surfaces in contact at a temperature not lower than 32° F (0° C). **regelation,** *n.* [RE-, L *gelātus,* p.p. of *gelāre,* to freeze]

regency, *n.* †rule, government, control; the office, commission or government of a regent; a body entrusted with the office or duties of a regent; the period of office of a regent or a body so acting. *a.* of the style of architecture popular in England during the late 18th and early 19th cents. characterized by its restrained simplicity and its imitation of ancient classical architecture, especially Greek. Architects of this period include Decimus Burton (1800–81), Henry Holland (1746–1806), and John Nash. **the Regency,** *n.* the period (1810–20) when George, Prince of Wales, was regent for George III. **regent,** *a.* exercising the authority of regent; †governing, ruling, controlling. *n.* a person appointed to govern a kingdom during the minority, absence or disability of a sovereign; †(*Oxf. and Camb. Univs.*) a Master of Arts presiding over deputations etc.; (*N Am.*) a member of the governing body of a State university; †a ruler, a governor. **regentess,** *n. fem.* **regent bird, oriole,** *n.* an Australian bower-bird, *Sericulus melinus,* having beautiful plumage. **regentship,** *n.* [F, from L *regentem,* nom. *-gens,* pres.p. of *regere,* to rule]

regenerate, *v.t.* to change fundamentally and reform the moral and spiritual nature of; to impart fresh vigour or higher life to; to generate anew, to give new existence to; (*Theol.*) to cause to be born again, to renew the heart of by the infusion of divine grace; to convert. *a.* regenerated, renewed; reformed, converted. **regeneracy, regenerateness, regeneration,** *n.* **baptismal regeneration,** (*Theol.*) spiritual regeneration or new birth as the consequence of baptism. **regenerative, regeneratory,** *a.* **regeneratively,** *adv.* [L *regenerātus,* p.p. of *regenerāre* (RE-, *generāre,* to GENERATE)]

regenerator, *n.* one who or that which regenerates; a device in furnaces, hot-air engines and gas-burners, by which the waste heat is applied to the incoming current of air or combustible gas. **regeneratrix,** *n. fem.*

regenesis, *n.* the state of being born again or reproduced.

Reger, *n.* **(Johann Baptist Joseph) Max(imilian)** (1873–1916), German composer and pianist. He taught at Munich (1905–07), was professor at the Leipzig Conservatoire from 1907, and was conductor of the Meiningen ducal orchestra from 1911–14. His works include organ and piano music, chamber music, and songs.

regerminate, *v.i.* to germinate anew. **regermination,** *n.*

†**regest,** *n.* a register. [late L *regesta,* neut. pl. p.p. of *regerere* (RE-, *gerere,* to carry on)]

reggae, *n.* a form of rhythmical W Indian rock music in 4/4 time. [W Indian word]

regicide, *n.* the killing or one who takes part in the killing of a king. **the Regicides,** *n.pl.* those taking part in the trial and execution of Charles I (1649). **regicidal,** *a.* [F *régicide* (L *rex rēgis,* king, -CIDE)]

Régie, *n.* the revenue department in some European countries having sole control of the importation of tobacco and sometimes of salt. [F, from *régir,* L *regere,* see REGENT]

regild, *v.t.* to gild again.

regime, régime, *n.* mode, conduct or prevailing system of government or management; the prevailing social system or general state of things. **ancien régime,** the system of government and society prevailing in France before the Revolution of 1789. [F *régime,* L REGIMEN]

regimen, *n.* the systematic management of food, drink, exercise etc. for the preservation or restoration of health; †rule, orderly government; the syntactical dependence of one word on another; government, †a regime, a prevailing system of government. **regiminal,** *a.* [L, from *regere,* to rule]

regiment, *n.* a body of soldiers forming the largest permanent unit of the army, usu. divided into two battalions comprising several companies or troops, and commanded by a colonel; †rule, government; †regimen. *v.t.* to form into a regiment or regiments; to organize into a system of bodies or groups; to discipline, especially harshly. **regimental,** *a.* of or pertaining to a regiment. *n.pl.* military uniform. **regimentally,** *adv.* **regimentation,** *n.* organization into a regiment or a system of groups etc. [F, from L *regimentum,* as prec.]

Regina, *n.* industrial city (oil refining, cement, steel, farm machinery, fertilizers), capital of Saskatchewan, Canada; population (1986) 175,000.

regina, *n. fem.* a reigning queen. **reginal,** *a.* [L, fem. of *rex rēgis,* king]

region, *n.* a tract of land, sea, space etc. of large but indefinite extent having certain prevailing characteristics, as of fauna or flora; a part of the world or the physical or spiritual universe (*often in pl.*); a district, a sphere, a realm; a civil division of a town or district; one of the strata into which the atmosphere or the sea may be divided; a part of the body surrounding an organ etc. **in the region of,** near; approximately. **the infernal, lower, nether regions,** hell, Hades, the realm of the dead. **upper regions,** the higher strata of the atmosphere or the sea; the sky; heaven. **regional,** *a.* **Regional Crime Squad,** *n.* in the UK, a local police force that deals with serious crime. **regionalism,** *n.* sectionalism on a regional basis; loyalty to one's region. **regionalist,** *n.* **regionalistic,** *a.* **regionalize, -ise,** *v.t.* to organize into administrative regions. **regionalization, -isation,** *n.* **regionally,** *adv.* **regionary,** *a.* regional. *n.* an account of the regions of Rome. **regioned, regionic,** [A-F *regiun,* L *regiōnem,* nom. *-gio,* from *regere,* to rule, to direct]

régisseur, *n.* an official in a dance company whose responsibilities include directing. **régisseuse,** *n. fem.* [F *régir,* to manage]

register, *n.* an official written record; a book, roll or other document in which such record is kept; an official or authoritative list of names, facts etc., as of births, marriage, deaths, persons entitled to vote at elections, shipping etc.; an entry in such a record or list; registration; a mechanical device for registering automatically the number of persons entering a public building or the movements of a gauge or other instrument, a recording indicator; a contrivance for regulating the admission of air or heat to a room, ventilator, fireplace etc.; the range or compass of a voice or instrument; a particular portion of this; a form of language used in a particular situation; a sliding device in an organ for controlling a set of pipes; (*Print.*) precise correspondence of lines etc. on one side of the paper to those on the other; (*Colour print.*) exact overlaying of the different colours used; (*Phot.*) correspondence of the surface of a sensitized film to that of the focusing-screen; a computer device which can store small amounts of data. *v.t.* to enter in a register; to record as in a register; to cause to be entered in a register, esp. (a letter etc.) at a post office for special care in transmission and delivery; to record, to indicate (of an instrument); (*Print., Phot. etc.*) to cause to correspond precisely. *v.i.* to enter one's name in or as in a register; to express an emotion facially; to make an impression; (*Print. etc.*) to be in register; (*Artill.*) to carry out experimental shots in order to ascertain the exact range. **in register,** exactly corresponding (of printed matter, photographic and colour plates etc.). **parish register** PARISH. **ship's register** SHIP. **register office,** *n.* an office at which a register is kept. **register ton,** *n.* a unit used to measure the internal capacity of a ship, of 100 cu. ft. (about 3 m^3). **registered,** *a.* **Registered General Nurse,** *n.* a nurse who has passed the General Nursing Council for Scotland's examination. **registered post,** *n.* a Post Office service where a registration fee is paid for mail and compensation paid in case of loss; mail sent by this service. **registered trademark,** *n.* a trademark which is legally registered and protected. **registrable,** *a.* **registrant,** *n.* one registering, esp. a trademark etc. [F *registre,* or med. L *registrum,* var. of *regestrum,* late L *regesta,* pl. REGEST]

registrar, *n.* an official keeper of a register or record; an official charged with keeping registers of births, deaths and marriages; a hospital doctor between the grades of houseman and consultant. **Registrar-General,** *n.* a public officer who superintends the registration of births, deaths and marriages. **registrarship,**

n. **registrary**, *n.* the registrar of Cambridge Univ. **registration,** *n.* the act of registering; the state of being registered; an entry in a register; a group of people all registered at a single time; (*Austral.*) a tax paid by anyone who owns a motor vehicle. **registration document,** *n.* a document which shows the official details of a motor vehicle. **registration number,** *n.* a combination of letters and numbers, displayed by every motor-vehicle, showing place and year of registration.

registry, *n.* an office or other place where a register is kept; registration; a register; the place where a ship is registered. **registry office,** *n.* an employment agency for domestic servants; a registrar's office where marriages etc. are performed.

regium donum, an annual grant of public money formerly made in favour of the income of the Presbyterian clergy in Ireland (commuted 1860); a similar grant made at various dates to other Nonconformist clergy. [L, royal gift]

regius, *a.* royal; appointed by the sovereign. **Regius Professor,** *n.* one of several professors at Oxford and Cambridge Univs. whose chairs were founded by Henry VIII, or in Scottish Univs. whose chairs were founded by the Crown. [L, royal from *rex rēgis,* king]

reglaze, *v.t.* to glaze again. **reglazing,** *n.*

reglet, *n.* a strip of wood, less than type high, used for separating pages, filling blank spaces etc.; a flat, narrow band separating moulding etc. [F *réglet,* dim. of *règle,* L *rēgula,* RULE]

regma, *n.* (*pl.* **-mata**) a dry fruit made up of several cells that dehisce when ripe. **regmacarp,** *n.* a dry dehiscent fruit. [Gr. *rhēgma,* fracture]

regnal, *a.* of or pertaining to a reign. **regnal day,** *n.* the anniversary of a sovereign's accession. **regnal year,** *n.* the year of a reign dating from the sovereign's accession (used in dating some documents). **regnant,** *a.* reigning, ruling, exercising regal authority; predominant, prevalent. **regnancy,** *n.* [med. L *regnālis,* from *regnum,* see REIGN]

regorge, *v.t.* to disgorge, to vomit up; to swallow back again. *v.i.* to gush or flow back (from a river etc.). †**regrade,** *v.i.* to go back, to retire (L *gradī,* to go). **regraft,** *v.t.* to graft again. **regrant,** *v.t.* to grant anew. *n.* a renewed or fresh grant.

regrate, *v.t.* to buy up (corn, provision etc.) and sell again in the same or a neighbouring market so as to raise the prices. **regrater,** *n.* [OF *regrater* (F *regratter*), prob. RE-, *gratter,* to GRATE[2])]

regrede, *v.i.* to go back, to retrograde. [L *regredī* (RE-, *gradī,* to go), cp. REGRADE]

regress, *n.* passage back, return, regression. *v.i.* to move back, to return. **regression,** *n.* retrogradation; reversion to type; return to an earlier form of behaviour; the turning back of a curve upon itself; the statistical analysis between dependent and independent variables. **regressive,** *a.* **regressively,** *adv.* **regressiveness,** *n.* **regressivity,** *n.* **regressor,** *n.* [L *regressus,* p.p. of *regredī,* to REGREDE]

regret, *n.* distress or sorrow for a disappointment, loss or want; grief, repentance or remorse for a wrong-doing, fault or omission (esp. in offering an apology); vexation, annoyance, disappointment. *v.t.* (*past, p.p.* **regretted**) to be distressed or sorry for (a disappointment, loss etc.); to regard (a fact, action etc.) with sorrow or remorse. **regretful,** *a.* sorry for past action. **regretfully,** *adv.* **regretfulness,** *n.* **regrettable,** *a.* to be regretted. **regrettably,** *adv.* [F, from *regretter,* OF *regrater,* etym. doubtful]

regroup, *v.t.* to group again. **regrow,** *v.t., v.i.* to grow again. **regrowth,** *n.*

Regt, (*abbr.*) regent, regiment.

reguerdon, *v.t.* to reward, to recompense. *n.* reward, recompense.

regulable REGULATE.

regular, *a.* conforming to or governed by rule, law, type or principle; systematic, methodical, consistent, symmetrical, unvarying, harmonious, normal; acting, done or happening in an orderly, uniform, constant or habitual manner, not casual, fortuitous or capricious; conforming to custom, etiquette etc., not infringing conventions; duly authorized, properly qualified; (*N Am., Can.*) popular, likeable; conforming to the normal type of inflection; governed throughout by the same law, following consistently the same process; having the sides and angles equal; belonging to the standing army, opp. to territorials, yeomanry etc.; belonging to a religious or monastic order; complete, thorough, out-and-out, unmistakable. *n.* a soldier belonging to a permanent army; one of the regular clergy; (*coll.*) a person permanently employed or constantly attending (as a customer etc.). **regularity,** *n.* **regularize, -ise,** *v.t.* **regularization, -isation,** *n.* **regularly,** *adv.* [OF *reguler* (F *régulier*), L *rēgulāris,* from *rēgula,* rule]

regulate, *v.t.* to adjust, control or order by rule; to subject to restrictions; to adjust to requirements, to put or keep in good order; to reduce to order. **regulable,** *a.* **regulation,** *n.* the act of regulating; the state of being regulated; a prescribed rule, order or direction. *a.* (*coll.*) prescribed by regulation; formal, normal, accepted, ordinary, usual. **regulative,** *a.* **regulator,** *n.* one who or that which regulates; a clock keeping accurate time, used for regulating other timepieces; the lever of a watch or other contrivance for regulating or equalizing motion. **regulator valve,** *n.* a valve in a locomotive which controls the supply of steam to the cylinders. **regulatory,** *a.* [late L *regulātus,* p.p. of *regulāre,* as prec.]

regulo, *n.* the temperature of a gas oven, given by numbers. [from Regulo®, trademark for a type of thermostat on gas ovens]

regulus, *n.* (*pl.* **-luses** or **-li**), the purer mass of a metal that sinks to the bottom when ore is being smelted, an intermediate product retaining to a greater or less extent the impurities of the ore; (**Regulus**) a genus of warblers containing the crested wren; (**Regulus**) brightest star in the constellation Leo, and the 21st-brightest star in the sky. Regulus has a true luminosity 160 times that of the Sun, and is 85 light years away. **reguline,** *a.* [L, dim. of *rex rēgis,* king, prob. applied to antimony on account of its readiness to combine with gold]

regurgitate, *v.t.* to throw or pour back again; to bring back (partially digested food) into the mouth after swallowing. *v.i.* to gush or be poured back. **regurgitant,** *a.* **regurgitation,** *n.* [med. L *regurgitātus,* p.p. of *regurgitāre* (RE-, L *gurges -gitis,* eddy, whirlpool)]

rehabilitate, *v.t.* to restore to a former rank, position, office or privilege, to reinstate; to re-establish one's character or reputation; to make fit after disablement, imprisonment etc. for making a living or playing a part in the life of society; to restore a building to good condition. **rehabilitation,** *n.* re-establishment of character or reputation; the branch of occupational therapy which deals with the restoration of the maimed or unfit to a place in society. **rehabilitative,** *a.*

rehandle, *v.t.* to handle or deal with again. **rehang,** *v.t.* to hang again (e.g. curtains). **reharness,** *v.t.* to harness again. **rehash,** *v.t.* to work over again; to remodel, esp. in a perfunctory or ineffective manner. *n.*, something stated or presented under a new form.

rehear, *v.t.* to hear a second time; to try over again. **rehearing,** *n.* a second hearing; a retrial.

rehearse, *v.t.* to repeat, to recite; to relate, to recount, to enumerate; to recite or practise (a play, musical performance, part etc.) before public performance. *v.i.* to take part in a rehearsal. **rehearsal,** *n.* the act of rehearsing; a preparatory performance of a play etc. **rehearser,** *n.* **rehearsing,** *n.* [OF *rehercer,* to harrow over again (RE-, HEARSE)]

reheat, *v.t.* to heat again; to inject fuel into a jet aircraft's exhaust gases, to produce more thrust. *n.* the process by which thrust is produced in an aircraft by the ignition of fuel added to exhaust gases. **reheater,** *n.* an apparatus for reheating, esp. in an industrial process. **reheel,** *v.t.* to heel (a shoe etc.) again. **rehire,** *v.t.* to hire again (usu. after dismissal). **rehouse,** *v.t.* to house anew. **rehumanize, -ise,** *v.t.* to humanize again. **rehypothecate,** *v.t.* to hypothecate again; to pledge again. **rehypothecation,** *n.*

Rehnquist, *n.* **William** (1924–), chief justice of the US Supreme Court. Active within the Republican Party, he was appointed head of the office of legal counsel by President Nixon in 1969 and controversially defended such measures as pre-trial detention and wiretapping.

Rehoboam, *n.* King of Judah about 932–915 BC, son of Solomon. Under his rule the Jewish nation split into the two kingdoms of Israel and Judah. Ten of the tribes revolted against him and took Jeroboam as their ruler, leaving him only the tribes of Judah and Benjamin.

rehoboam, *n.* a wine bottle (especially a champagne bottle) which holds six times the amount of a standard bottle, approximately 156 fl. oz. (about 4·6 l). [*Rehoboam,* son of King Solomon, and King of Israel]

Rehoboth Gebeit, *n.* a district of Namibia to the south of Windhoek; area c.32,168 sq km/ 12,420 sq miles; chief town Rehoboth. The area is occupied by the Basters, a mixed race of European-Nama descent.

rei REIS[1].

Reich[1], *n.* three periods in history. The First Reich was the Holy Roman Empire (962–1806), the Second Reich the German Empire (1871–1918), and the Third Reich Nazi Germany (1933–45).

Reich[2], *n.* the standard monetary unit of Germany between 1924 and 1948. **Reichsrat,** *n.* the old Austrian parliament. [G, kingdom]

Reich[3], *n.* **Steve** (1936–), US composer. His Minimalist music consists of simple patterns carefully superimposed and modified to highlight constantly changing melodies and rhythms; examples are *Phase Patterns* for four electronic organs (1970), *Music for Mallet Instruments, Voices, and Organ* (1973), and *Music for Percussion and Keyboards* (1984).

Reich[4], *n.* **Wilhelm** (1897–1957), Austrian doctor, who emigrated to the US in 1939. He combined Marxism and psychoanalysis to advocate sexual freedom, for example in *Die Sexuelle Revolution/The Sexual Revolution* (1936–45), and *Die Funktion des Orgasmus/The Function of the Orgasm* (1948). Reich died in prison following committal for contempt of court.

Reichstadt, Duke of, *n.* title of Napoleon II, son of Napoleon I.

Reichstag, *n.* German parliament building and lower legislative house during the German Empire (1871–1918) and Weimar Republic (1919–33). **Reichstag Fire,** *n.* the burning of the German parliament building in Berlin 27 Feb. 1933, less than a month after the Nazi leader Hitler became chancellor. The fire was used as a justification for the suspension of many constitutional guarantees, and also as an excuse to attack the communists. There is still debate over Nazi involvement in the crime, not least because they were the main beneficiaries.

Reichstein, *n.* **Tadeus** (1897–), Swiss biochemist who investigated the chemical activity of the adrenal glands. By 1946 Reichstein had identified a large number of steroids secreted by the adrenal cortex, some of which would later be used in the treatment of Addison's disease. Reichstein shared the 1950 Nobel physiology or medicine prize with Edward Kendall and Philip Hench (1896–1965).

reify, *v.t.* to make (an abstract idea) concrete, to treat as real. **reification,** *n.* **reificatory,** *a.* **reifier,** *n.* [L *rēs rēi,* thing, -FY]

reign, *n.* supreme power, sovereignty, dominion; rule, sway, control, influence; the period during which a sovereign reigns; †a kingdom, realm, sphere. *v.i.* to exercise sovereign authority, to be a king or queen; to predominate, to prevail. [ME and OF *regne,* L *regnum,* from *regere,* to rule]

reignite, *v.t.* to ignite again. **reillume, reillumine,** *v.t.* to light up again, to illumine again. **reillumination,** *n.* **reimburse,** *v.t.* to repay (one who has spent money); to refund (expenses etc.). **reimbursable,** *a.* **reimbursement,** *n.* **reimburser,** *n.* **reimplant,** *v.t.* to implant again. **reimplantation,** *n.* **reimport,** *v.t.* to import again after exportation; to import goods made from exported raw materials. **reimportation,** *n.* **reimpose,** *v.t.* to impose again. **reimposition,** *n.* **reimpress,** *v.t.* to impress anew. **reimpression,** *n.* **reimprint,** *v.t.* to imprint again; to reprint. **reimprison,** *v.t.* to imprison again. **reimprisonment,** *n.*

Reims, *n.* (English **Rheims**) capital of Champagne-Ardenne region, France; population (1982) 199,000. It is the centre of the champagne industry, and has textile industries. It was known in Roman times as *Durocorturum.* From AD 987 all but six French kings were crowned here. Ceded to England in 1420 under the Treaty of Troyes, it was retaken by Joan of Arc, who had Charles VII consecrated in the 13th-cent. cathedral.

rein, *n.* a long narrow strip, usu. of leather, attached at each end to a bit for guiding and controlling a horse or other animal in riding or driving; a similar device for controlling a young child; (*fig.*) means of restraint or control (*often in pl.*). *v.t.* to check, to control, to manage with reins; to pull (in or up) with reins; (*fig.*) to govern, to curb, to restrain. *v.i.* to obey the reins. **to draw rein,** to pull up. **to give rein, the reins to,** to leave unrestrained; to allow (a horse) to go its own way. **to keep on a tight rein,** to control carefully. **to rein in,** to cause a horse to stop by pulling on the reins. **to take the reins,** to assume guidance, direction, office etc. **reinsman,** *n.* (*N Am.*) a driver. [OF *rene, reine, resne* (F *rêne*), prob. through late L *retina,* from L *retinēre* (RE-, *tenere,* to hold)]

reinaugurate, *v.t.* to inaugurate anew. **reincarnate,** *v.t.* to incarnate anew; to cause to be born again. *a.* born again in a new body. **reincarnation,** *n.* metempsychosis. **reincarnationism,** *n.* the belief in the reincarnation of the soul. **reincarnationist,** *n.* **reincense,** *v.t.* to incense anew. **reincite,** *v.t.* to incite anew. **reincorporate,** *v.t.* to incorporate again. **reincorporation,** *n.* †**reincrease,** *v.t., v.i.* to increase again. **reincur,** *v.t.* to incur again.

reindeer, *n.* a deer, *Rangifer tarandus,* now inhabiting the sub-arctic parts of the northern hemisphere, domesticated for the sake of its milk and as a draught animal. **reindeer-lichen, -moss,** *n.* a lichen, *Cladonia rangiferina,* which forms the winter food of the reindeer. [Icel. *hreinn* (in *hreindȳri*), DEER]

reinduce, *v.t.* to induce again. **reinduction,** *n.*

reinfect, *v.t.* to infect again. **reinfection,** *n.*

reinforce, *v.t.* to add new strength to; to strengthen or support with additional troops, ships etc.; to strengthen by adding to the size, thickness etc., to add a strengthening part; to enforce again. *n.* the thicker part of a gun, that next the breech; a reinforcing or strengthening part, band etc. **reinforceable,** *a.* **reinforced concrete,** *n.* concrete given great tensile strength by the incorporation of rods etc. of iron etc., ferro-concrete. **reinforcement,** *n.* the act of reinforcing; the state of being reinforced; anything that reinforces; additional troops, ships etc. (*usu. in pl.*). **reinforcer,** *n.*

reinform, *v.t.* to inform again; to invest with form again. **reinfuse,** *v.t.* to infuse again. **reingratiate,** *v.t.* to ingratiate (oneself) again. **reinhabit,** *v.t.* to inhabit again. **re-ink,** *v.t.* to ink again.

Reinhardt[1], *n.* **'Django' (Jean Baptiste)** (1910–53), Belgian jazz guitarist and composer, who was coleader, with Stephane Grappelli, of Quintet de Hot Club de France (1934–39).

Reinhardt[2], *n.* **Max** (1873–1943), Austrian producer and director, whose expressionist style was widely influential in German theatre and film during the 1920s and 1930s. Directors such as Murnau and Lubitsch and actors such as Dietrich worked with him. He codirected the US film *A Midsummer Night's Dream* (1935).

reinoculate, *v.t.* to inoculate again. **reinoculation,** *n.*

†**reins,** *n.pl.* the kidneys; the loins (formerly supposed to be the seat of the affections and passions). [OF,

from L *rēnēs*]

reinscribe, *v.t.* to inscribe again. **reinsert,** *v.t.* to insert again. **reinsertion,** *n.*

reinsman REIN.

reinspect, *v.t.* to inspect again. **reinspection,** *n.* **reinspire,** *v.t.* to inspire again. **reinstall,** *v.t.* to install again. **reinstalment,** *n.* **reinstate,** *v.t.* to restore, to replace (in a former position, state etc.); to replace, to repair (property damaged by fire etc.). **reinstatement, reinstation,** *n.* **reinstruct,** *v.t.* to instruct again or in turn. **reinstruction,** *n.* **reinsure,** *v.t.* to insure against insurance risks. **reinsurance,** *n.* **reinsurer,** *n.* **reintegrate,** *v.t.* to redintegrate. **reintegration,** *n.* **reinter,** *v.t.* to inter or bury again. **reinterment,** *n.* **reinterpret,** *v.t.* to interpret again, or differently. **reinterpretation,** *n.* **reinterrogate,** *v.t.* to interrogate again. **reinterrogation,** *n.* †**reinthrone,** *v.t.* to enthrone again, to replace on a throne. **reintroduce,** *v.t.* to introduce or bring back into again. **reintroduction,** *n.* **reinvade,** *v.t.* to invade again. **reinvasion,** *n.* **reinvent,** *v.t.* to invent again. **reinvention,** *n.* **reinvest,** *v.t., v.i.* to invest again. **reinvestment,** *n.* **reinvestigate,** *v.t.* to investigate again. **reinvestigation,** *n.* **reinvigorate,** *v.t.* to reanimate; to give fresh vigour to. **reinvigoration,** *n.* **reinvite,** *v.t.* to invite again. **reinvolve,** *v.t.* to involve again.

Reis, *n.* a head, a chief, a governor; a captain of a boat etc. **Reis Effendi,** *n.* the title of a former Turkish state officer acting as chancellor and minister of foreign affairs. [Arab., from *rās,* head]

reis, *n.pl.* a Portuguese and Brazilian money of account, the thousandth part of a milreis. [Port., sing. *ree rei,* correctly REAL²]

reissue, *v.t., v.i.* to issue again. *n.* a second issue. **reissuable,** *a.*

Reisz, *n.* **Karel** (1926–), Czechoslovak film director who lived in Britain from 1938, originally a writer and film critic. His first feature film, *Saturday Night and Sunday Morning* (1960), was a critical and commercial success. His other work includes *Morgan* (1966), *The French Lieutenant's Woman* (1981), and *Sweet Dreams* (1986).

†**reiter,** *n.* a German trooper or cavalry soldier, esp. in the religious wars of the 16th and 17th cents. [G, from *reiten,* to RIDE]

reiterate, *v.t.* to repeat again and again. **reiteratedly,** *adv.* **reiteration,** *n.* **reiterative,** *a.* expressing or characterized by reiteration. *n.* a word or part of a word repeated so as to form a reduplicated word. **reiteratively,** *adv.*

†**reive, reiver** REAVE.

reject, *v.t.* to put aside, to discard, to cast off; to refuse to accept (e.g. an implanted organ), receive, grant etc., to deny (a request etc.); to repel, to cast up again, to vomit. *n.* something that has been rejected; something which is not perfect, substandard and offered for sale at a discount. **rejectable,** *a.* **rejectamenta,** *n.pl.* matter rejected, refuse, excrements. **rejecter, -tor,** *n.* **rejection,** *n.* **rejective,** *a.* †**rejectment,** *n.* [from F *rejecter* (now *rejeter*) or L *rējectus,* p.p. of *rēicere* (RE-, *jacere,* to throw)]

rejig, *v.t.* to rearrange or re-equip, sometimes in an unethical way. *n.* the act of rejigging. **rejigger,** *n.*

rejoice, *v.t.* to make joyful, to gladden. *v.i.* to feel joy or gladness in a high degree; to be glad (that or to); to delight or exult (in); to express joy or gladness; to make merry. **to rejoice in,** to be glad because of; to have. **rejoiceful,** *a.* **rejoicer,** *n.* **rejoicing,** *n.* joyfulness; the expression of joyfulness, making merry, celebrating a joyful event (*usu. in pl.*). **rejoicingly,** *adv.* [OF *rejoiss-,* pres.p. stem of *rejoir* (F *rejouir*)]

rejoin, *v.t.* to join again; to join together again, to reunite after separation. *v.i.* to come together again; to answer to a reply, to retort; to answer a charge or pleading, esp. as the defendant to the plantiff's replication. **rejoinder,** *n.* an answer to a reply, a retort; a reply or answer in general; the answer of a defendant to the plaintiff's replication. †**rejoindure,** *n.* [F *rejoin-,* stem of *rejoindre*]

rejoint, *v.t.* to reunite the joints of; to fill up the joints of (stone-, brickwork etc.) with new mortar, to point.

†**rejourn,** *v.t.* to adjourn.

rejudge, *v.t.* to judge again; to re-examine.

rejuvenate, *v.t.* to make young again; to restore to vitality or a previous condition. *v.i.* to become young again. **rejuvenation,** *n.* **rejuvenator,** *n.* **rejuvenesce,** *v.i.* to grow young again; (*Biol.*) to acquire fresh vitality (of cells). *v.t.* to give fresh vitality to. **rejuvenescence,** *n.* **rejuvenescent,** *a.* **rejuvenize, -ise,** *v.t., v.i.* [L *juvenis,* young, -ATE]

rekindle, *v.t.* to kindle again; (*fig.*) to inflame or rouse anew. *v.i.* (*lit., fig.*) to take fire again.

rel., (*abbr.*) relative, relatively; religion, religious; relics.

relabel, *v.t.* to label again. **relaid,** *past, p.p.* RELAY².

relais, *n.* (*Fort.*) a narrow space between a rampart and the ditch, for keeping earth from falling into the latter. [F]

Rélamur, *n.* **Réné de** (1683–1757), French metallurgist and entymologist who wrote a definitive work on the early steel industry as well as the first books on entomology. His work, published in 1722, described how to convert iron into steel and laid the foundations of the modern steel industry. He produced a six-volume work between 1734 and 1742 on the natural history of insects.

reland, *v.t., v.i.* to land again.

relapse, *v.i.* to fall or slip back (into a former bad or vicious state or practice), esp. into illness after partial recovery; to fall away after moral improvement, conversion or recantation. *n.* a falling or sliding back into a former bad state, esp. in a patient's state of health after partial recovery. **relapser,** *n.* **relapsing fever,** *n.* an epidemic infectious fever characterized by frequent relapses. [L *relapsus,* p.p. of *relābi* (*lābi,* to slip)]

relate, *v.t.* to tell, to narrate, to recount; to bring into relation or connection (with); to ascribe to as source or cause, to show a relation (with). *v.i.* to have relation or regard (to); to refer (to); to get on well with. **relatable,** *a.* **related,** *a.* narrated; connected; connected or allied by blood or marriage. **relatedness,** *n.* **relater,** *n.* [F *relater,* med. L *relātāre,* from *relātus,* p.p. of *referre,* see REFER]

relation, *n.* the act of relating; that which is related; a narrative, an account, a story; respect; the condition of being related or connected; the way in which a thing stands or is conceived in regard to another as dependence, independence, similarity, difference, correspondence, contrast etc.; connection by blood or marriage, kinship; a person so connected, a relative, a kinsman or kinswoman; (*Law*) the laying of an information before the Attorney-General by a person bringing an action; (*pl.*) dealings, affairs with; (*euphem.*) sexual intercourse. **relational,** *a.* having, pertaining to or indicating relation; having kinship. **relationally,** *adv.* **relationless**, *a.* **relationship,** *n.* the state of being related; connection by blood etc., kinship; mutual connection between people or things; an emotional or sexual affair.

relative, *a.* being in relation to something, involving or implying relation, correlative; resulting from relation, proportioned to something else, comparative; not absolute but depending on relation to something else; having mutual relation, corresponding, related; relevant, pertinent, closely related (to); having reference, relating; referring or relating to another word, sentence or clause, called the antecedent; (*Mus.*) having the same key signature. *n.* a person connected by blood or marriage, a kinsman or kinswoman, a relation; a relative word, esp. a pronoun; something relating to or considered in relation to another thing, a relative term. **relative aperture,** *n.* the ratio of the diameter of a lens to its focal length, in a camera. **relative atomic mass,** *n.* atomic weight. **relative density,** *n.* the density of a substance as compared to the density of a standard substance under the same, or special, conditions. **relative frequency,** *n.* in statistics, the actual number of favourable events as compared to the number of total possible events. **relative humidity,** *n.* the amount of water vapour present in the air as compared to the same amount of saturated air at the same temperature. **relative majority,** *n.* the majority held by the winner of an election where no candidate has won more than 50% of the vote. **relative molecular mass,** *n.* molecular weight. **relative permeability,** *n.* the permeability of any medium as compared to that of free space. **relatival,** *a.* **relatively,** *adv.* in relation to something else; comparatively. **relativeness,** *n.* **relativism,** *n.* the doctrine that existence is not absolute but relative to the thinking mind, relatively of knowledge. **relativist,** *n.* **relativistic,** *a.* **relativity,** *n.* **relativity of knowledge,** the doctrine that knowledge is of and through relations only. **relativity theory,** *n.* a theory enunciated by Albert Einstein founded on the postulate that velocity is relative, and developing the Newtonian conception of space, time, motion and gravitation. [F *relatif -tive,* L *relatīvus,* as prec.]

relator, *n.* an informer, a complainant, esp. one who institutes proceedings by way of a relation or information to the Attorney-General; a relater, a narrator.

relatum, *n* (*pl.* **-ta**), in logic, one of two or more objects between which a relationship is said to exist. [late L]

relax, *v.t.* to slacken, to loosen; to allow to become less tense or rigid; to enervate, to enfeeble, to make languid; to make less strict or severe, to abate, to mitigate; to relieve from constipation; to relieve from strain or effort. *v.i.* to become less tense, rigid, stern or severe; to grow less energetic; to take relaxation. †**relaxable,** *a.* **relaxant,** *a.* relaxing. *n.* a relaxing medicine. **relaxation,** *n.* the act of relaxing; the state of being relaxed; a diminution of tension, severity, application or attention; cessation from work, indulgence in recreation, amusement; remission of a penalty etc. **relaxative,** *a.* **relaxed,** *a.* informal. **relaxedly,** *adv.* **relaxer,** *n.* **relaxin,** *n.* a hormone found in pregnant mammals which relaxes the pelvic ligaments and so makes childbirth easier; a preparation of this hormone used in childbirth. **relaxing,** *a.* [L *relaxāre* (*laxus,* LAX)]

relay¹, *n.* a supply of fresh horses, workers, hounds etc. to relieve others when tired; a supply of anything to be ready when required; a contrivance for strengthening a current by means of a local battery in transmitting messages over an unusually long distance; the passing along of something by stages. *v.t.,* to spread information by relays; to broadcast signals or a programme received from another station. *v.i.* to obtain or operate by relays. **relay race,** *n.* a race between teams each member of which runs a certain distance. [OF *relais,* from *relayer,* to relay]

relay², *v.t.* to lay again.

release¹, *v.t.* to set free from restraint, to liberate; to deliver from pain, care, trouble, grief or other evil; to free from obligation or penalty; to make information public; (*Law*) to surrender, to quit, to remit (a right, debt, claim etc.). *n.* liberation from restraint, pain, care, obligation or penalty; a discharge from liability, responsibility etc.; (*Law.*) surrender or conveyance of property or right to another; the instrument by which this is carried out; a handle, catch or other device by which a piece of mechanism is released; anything newly issued for sale or to the public; a news item available for broadcasting. †**releasable,** *a.* **releasee,** *n.* a person to whom property is released. †**releasement,** *n.* **releaser,** *n.* **releasor,** *n.* (*Law*) one releasing property or a claim to another. [OF *relesser, relaisser,* var. of *relâcher,* L *relaxāre,* to RELAX]

release², *v.t.* to give a new lease to.

relegate, *v.t.* to send away, to banish; to consign or dismiss (usu. to some inferior position etc., such as a football team to a lower division); to refer, commit, or hand over (to). **relegable,** *a.* **relegation,** *n.* [L *relegātus,* p.p. of *relegāre* (*legāre,* to send)]

relent, *v.i.* to become less harsh, severe or obdurate; to give way to compassion, to yield. †*v.t.* to abate, to give up, to relinquish; to cause to relent; to repent. *n.* relenting; slackening or remission of speed. **relenting,** *n., a.* **relentingly,** *adv.* **relentless,** *a.* merciless, pitiless; unrelenting. **relentlessly,** *adv.* **relentlessness,** *n.* [etym. doubtful, perh. through F *ralentir,* to slacken; ult. from RE-, L *lentus,* soft]

relet, *v.t.* to let again.

relevant, *a.* pertinent, applicable, bearing on the matter in hand, apposite; (*Sc. Law*) legally sufficient. **relevance, -cy,** *n.* **relevantly,** *adv.* [med. L *relevans -ntem,* orig. pres.p. of L *relevāre* (*levāre,* to raise)]

reliable, reliant RELY.

relic, *n.* some part or thing remaining after loss or decay of the rest, a remnant, a fragment, a scrap, a survival, a trace; any ancient object of historical interest; something remaining or kept in remembrance of a person, esp. a part of the body or other object religiously cherished from its having belonged to some saint; a keepsake a souvenir, a memento; (*pl.*) a dead body, a corpse, remains. **relic-monger,** *n.* one who trades in relics. [OF *relique,* L *reliquiae,* pl., remains, as foll.]

relict, *n.* a widow; †a survivor (esp. a plant or animal which is a remnant of a formerly widely distributed group), a survival, a relic; a geological or geographical feature, such as a mountain, which is a remnant of an earlier formation. *a.* surviving. †**relicted,** *a.* (*Law*) left uncovered by the recession of water (of land). †**reliction,** *n.* [OF *relicte* or L *relicta,* p.p. of *relinquere* (*linquere,* to leave)]

relief¹, *n.* alleviation of pain, grief, discomfort etc.; that which alleviates; assistance given to people in poverty or distress, esp. under the Poor Law; redress of a grievance etc., esp. by legal remedy or compensation; release from a post or duty by a person or persons acting as substitute; such a substitute; assistance in time of stress or danger, raising of the siege of a besieged town; an army or detachment carrying this out; (*fig.*) anything that breaks monotony or relaxes tension. **comic relief,** dialogue, incidents or scenes of a comic nature alleviating the stress in a tragic play or story. **indoor, outdoor relief,** poor-relief given in the workhouse or at home. **relief works,** *n.pl.* public works organized for the unemployed, refugees etc. [OF *relef,* from *relever,* to RELIEVE]

relief², *n.* the projecting of carved or moulded figures or designs from a surface in approximate proportion to the objects represented; a piece of sculpture, moulding etc. with the figures etc. projecting; apparent projection of forms and figures due to drawing, colouring and shading; distinctness of contour, clearness, vividness. **relief map,** *n.* one in which hills and valleys are shown by prominences and depressions (usu. in exaggerated proportion) instead of contour-lines. **relief printing,** *n.* printing by letterpress of blocks, as dist. from lithography. [It. *rilievo,* from *rilevare,* L *relevāre,* to RELIEVE, assim. to prec.]

relieve, *v.t.* to alleviate, to mitigate, to relax, to lighten; to free wholly or partially from pain, grief, discomfort etc.; to remove a grievance from, esp. by course of law or by legislation; to release from a post, duty, responsibility etc., esp. to take turn on guard; to raise the siege of; (*coll.*) to take away, to deprive one of; to break or mitigate monotony, dullness etc.; to give relief or prominence to, to bring out or make conspicuous by contrast. **to relieve nature, oneself,** to defecate or urinate. **to relieve someone of something,** to take something without the owner's approval, to steal. **relievable,** *a.* **relieved,** *a.* experiencing relief, especially from worry or emotion. **relievedly,** *adv.* **reliever,** *n.* **relieving,** *n., a.* **relieving arch,** *n.* one constructed in a wall to take the weight off a part underneath. **relieving-officer,** *n.* an officer appointed by the guardians to superintend the relief of the poor in a parish or union. **relievo** RILIEVO. [OF *relever,* L *relevāre* (*levāre,* to raise, from *levis,* light)]

relight, *v.t.* to light, kindle or illumine afresh. *v.i.* to take fire again.

religieuse, *n.* a nun. **religieux,** *n.* a monk. [F, RELIGIOUS]

religion, *n.* belief in a superhuman being or beings, esp.

a personal god, controlling the universe and entitled to worship and obedience; the feelings, effects on conduct and the practices resulting from such belief; a system of faith, doctrine and worship; (*coll.*) spiritual awakening, conversion; (*fig.*) devotion, sense of obligation; the monastic state, the state of being bound by religious vows; anything of great personal importance. **to get religion,** to be converted. †**religionary,** *a.* **religioner,** *n.* a member of an order. **religionism,** *n.* a profession or affectation of religion, the outward practice of religion; excessive or exaggerated religious zeal. **religionist,** *n., a.* **religionize, -ise,** *v.t.* to make religious, to imbue with religion. *v.i.* to profess or display religion. **religionless,** *a.* **religiose,** *a.* morbidly affected with religious emotion; pious, sanctimonious. **religiosely,** *adv.* **religiosity**, *n.* religious sentimentality or emotionalism. **religious,** *a.* pertaining to, or imbued with, religion; pious, devout; of or pertaining to religion; bound by vows to a monastic life, belonging to a monastic order; (*fig.*) conscientious, rigid, strict. *n.* one bound by monastic vows. **religious house,** *n.* a house for monks or nuns, a monastery, a convent. **religiously,** *adv.* in a religious manner; (*coll.*) scrupulously. **religiousness,** *n.* [A-F *religiun* (F *religion*), L *religiōnem,* nom. *-gio,* perh. rel. to *religāre,* to bind (perh. from *religens,* fearing the gods, opp. to *negligens,* NEGLIGENT)]

reline, *v.t.* to line again, to give a new lining to.

relinquish, *v.t.* to forsake, to abandon, to resign; to quit, to desist from; to give up a claim to, to surrender; to let go. **relinquent,** *n., a.* **relinquisher,** *n.* **relinquishment,** *n.* [OF *relinquiss-,* pres.p. stem of *relinquir,* L *relinquere* (*linquere,* to leave)]

reliquary, *n.* a depository for relics, a casket for keeping a relic or relics in. **reliquaire,**, *n.* a reliquary. †**relique** , *n.* relic. [F *reliquaire,* from *relique*]

reliquiae, *n.pl.* remains; fossil remains of organisms; withered leaves remaining on plants. [L]

relish, *n.* the effect of anything on the palate, taste, distinctive flavour, esp. a pleasing taste or flavour; something taken with food to give a flavour, a condiment; enjoyment of food etc., gusto, appetite, zest, fondness, liking; a slight admixture or flavouring, a smack, a trace (of); pleasing anticipation. *v.t.* to give agreeable flavour to, to make piquant etc.; to partake of with pleasure, to like; to be gratified by, to enjoy; to look forward to with pleasure. *v.i.* to have a pleasing taste; to have a flavour, to taste or smack (of); to affect the taste (well etc.). **relishable,** *a.* [ME and OF *reles,* var. of *relais,* that left behind, from *relesser,* see RELEASE[1]]

relisten, *v.i.* to listen again. **relive,** *v.i.* to live again, to revive. *v.t.* to live over again, esp. in the imagination; †to animate, to revive. **relivable,** *a.* **reload,** *v.t.* to load again. *v.i.* to load a firearm again. **relocate,** *v.t., v.i.* to locate again; to move (e.g. a factory, workers, business) to a new location. **relocation,** *n.* the act of relocating; (*Sc. Law*) renewal of a lease without a fresh agreement.

†**relucent,** *a.* refulgent, bright, shining. [L *relūcens -ntem* (LUCENT)]

reluctant, *a.* struggling or resisting, unwilling, averse, disinclined (to); doing, done or granted unwillingly. **reluct,** *v.i.* to be disinclined; to show reluctance or resistance (at or against). **reluctance,** †**-ancy,** *n.* unwillingness; the ratio of the opposition between a magnetic substance and the magnetic flux. **reluctantly,** *adv.* **reluctate,** *v.i.* to reluct. **reluctation**, *n.* **reluctivity**, *n.* the reluctance of a magnetic substance. [L *reluctans -antem,* pres.p. of *reluctārī* (*luctārī,* to struggle)]

relume, relumine, *v.t.* to light again, to rekindle; to make bright or light up again.

rely, *v.i.* to trust or depend (upon) with confidence. **reliable**, *a.* that may be relied on; trustworthy. **reliability**, **reliableness,** *n.* **reliably,** *adv.* **reliance,** *n.* confident dependence (upon), trust; a ground of confidence. **reliant,** *a.* **reliantly,** *adv.* [OF *relier,* L *religāre* (*ligāre,* to bind)]

REM, (*abbr.*) rapid eye movement. **REM sleep,** *n.* a phase of sleep that recurs several times nightly in humans and is associated with dreaming. The eyes flicker quickly beneath closed lids.

rem[1] (*abbr.*) remark(s).

rem[2], *n.* a unit of radiation dosage which has the same biological effect as 1 rad of X-ray or gamma radiation. [*r*öntgen *e*quivalent *m*an or *m*ammal]

remain, *v.i.* to stay behind or be left over after use, separation, destruction etc.; to survive; to continue in a place or state; to last, to abide, to continue, to endure; to continue (to be); to be still to be done or dealt with. *n.* (*usu. pl.*) that which remains behind; a dead body, a corpse; literary productions published after one's death; ruins, relics. **remainder**, *n.* anything left over after a part has been taken away, the rest, the residue; the quantity left over after subtraction, the excess remaining after division; an interest in an estate limited to take effect and be enjoyed after a prior estate is determined; copies of an edition left unsold after the demand has ceased and offered at a reduced price. *v.t.* to offer such copies at a reduced price. **remainder-man,** *n.* one to whom an estate in remainder is devised. **remaining,** *a.* [OF *remaindre,* L *remanēre* (*manēre,* to stay)]

remake, *v.t.* to make again or anew. *n.*, anything made again from the original materials; a new version of an old film, record etc. **reman,** *v.t.* to man (a ship, gun etc.) again; to equip with a new complement of men.

remanation, *n.* flowing back, reabsorption (as of a soul in the universal spirit). [L *remānāre* (*mānāre,* to flow)]

remand, *v.t.* to send back (to); to recommit in custody after a partial hearing. *n.* the act of remanding; the state of being remanded. **to be on remand,** to be in custody awaiting trial. **remand centre,** *n.* a place of detention for people awaiting trial. **remand home,** *n.* (*formerly*) a place where children aged 8–14 years were detained as punishment for criminal offences. **remandment,** *n.* [OF *remander,* late L *remandāre* (*mandāre,* to commit)]

remanent, *a.* remaining, left behind, surviving; (*Sc.*) remaining over, additional. **remanence,** *n.* the ability of any magnetized substance to remain magnetic when the magnetizing force becomes zero. **remanet**, *n.* a remainder; a case postponed to another term; a Bill deferred to another session. [from L *remanens- ntem,* pres.p. of *remanēre,* to REMAIN]

remargin, *v.t.* to give a fresh margin to (a page etc.).

re-mark, *v.t.* to mark again.

remark, *v.t.* to take notice of, to observe with particular attention, to perceive; to utter by way of comment, to comment (upon); †to distinguish. *v.i.* to make a comment or observation on. *n.* the act of noticing, observation; an observation, a comment; (*coll., usu. pl.*) anything said, conversation; (*Engraving,* also **remarque**) a distinguishing mark indicating the particular state of an engraved plate, usu. as a marginal sketch. **remark-proof,** *n.* a proof bearing such a mark. **remarkable,** *a.* worthy of special observation or notice, notable; unusual, extraordinary, striking. **remarkableness,** *n.* **remarkably,** *adv.* **remarked,** *a.* conspicuous; with a remark etched on. **remarker,** *n.* [F *remarquer* (*marquer,* to MARK[1])]

remarque REMARK.

Remarque, *n.* **Erich Maria** (1898–1970), German novelist, a soldier in World War I, whose *All Quiet on the Western Front* (1929) led to his being deprived of German nationality. He lived in Switzerland (1929–39), and then in the US.

remarry, *v.t., v.i.* to marry again. **remarriage,** *n.* **remast,** *v.t.* to furnish with a new mast or masts. **remaster,** *v.t.* to make a new, master recording from an older original to improve the sound quality. **remasticate,** *v.t.* to chew over again. **remastication,** *n.*

remblai, *n.* the material used to form a rampart or embankment. [F, from *remblayer,* to embank]

Rembrandt, *n.* **Harmensz van Rijn** (1606–69), Dutch painter and etcher, one of the most prolific and influential artists in Europe of the 17th cent. Between 1629 and 1669 he painted some 60 penetrating self-portraits. He also painted religious subjects, and produced about 300 etchings and over 1000 drawings. His group portraits include *The Anatomy Lesson of Dr Tulp*, 1632 (Mauritshuis, The Hague) and *The Night Watch*, 1642 (Rijksmuseum, Amsterdam). **Rembrandtesque**, *a.* in the style or resembling the effects of Rembrandt van Rijn, esp. in chiaroscuro. **Rembrandtish**, *a.*

REME, (*abbr.*) Royal Electrical and Mechanical Engineers.

remeant, *a.* coming back, returning. [L *remeans -ntem*, pres.p. of *remeāre* (RE-, *meāre,* to pass)]

remeasure, *v.t.* to measure again. **remeasurement,** *n.*

remedy, *n.* that which cures a disease; medicine, healing treatment; that which serves to remove, counteract or repair any evil; redress, reparation; the tolerated variation in the standard weight of coins. *v.t.* to cure, to heal; to repair, to rectify, to redress. **remediable**, *a.* **remediableness,** *n.* **remediably,** *adv.* **remedial**, *a.* affording, containing or intended for a remedy; pertaining to the teaching of slow learners, and people with special needs, such as the disabled. **remedially,** *adv.* †**remediate**, *a.* **remediless**, *a.* **remedilessly,** *adv.* **remedilessness,** *n.* [A-F *remedie* (F *remède*), L *remedium* (*mederī,* to heal)]

remelt, *v.t.* to melt again.

remember, *v.t.* to bear or keep in mind, not to forget, to know by heart; to recall to mind, to recollect; to keep in mind with gratitude, reverence or respect; (*coll.*) to convey a greeting from; to be good to, to make a present to, to tip; †to remind; to recall to the memory of someone else; to commemorate (e.g. the dead). *v.i.* to have the power of, and exercise the, memory. **to remember oneself,** to bethink oneself (of). **rememberable,** *a.* **rememberability**, *n.* **rememberably,** *adv.* †**rememberer,** *n.* **remembrance**, *n.* the act of remembering; memory; the time over which memory extends; the state of being remembered; a recollection, a memory; that which serves to recall to or preserve in memory; a keepsake, a memento, a memorial; (*pl.*) regards, greetings; †admonition. **Remembrance Day, Sunday,** *n.* the Sunday nearest to 11 Nov., when the fallen in the two World Wars are remembered, also called Armistice Day. **remembrancer,** *n.* one who or that which puts in mind; a reminder, a memento. **City Remembrancer,** an officer of the City of London representing the City Corporation before parliamentary committees etc. **Queen's, King's Remembrancer,** an officer of the Court of Exchequer whose business is to collect debts due to the sovereign. [OF *remembrer,* late L *rememorārī* (*memor,* mindful)]

remerge, *v.t.* to merge again.

remex, *n.* (*pl.* **remiges**) one of the quill feathers of a bird's wings. **remiform**, *a.* oar-shaped. **remigate,** *v.i.* to row. **remigation,** *n.* **remigial**, *a.* [L, rower, from *rēmus,* oar]

remigrate, *v.i.* to migrate back again, to return to a former place or state. **remigrant** , *n.* an aphid that returns to the tree that was its former host. **remigration,** *n.* [L *remigrātus,* p.p. of *remigrāre* (MIGRATE)]

remind, *v.t.* to put in mind (of); to cause to remember (to do etc.). **reminder,** *n.* a person who, or thing which, reminds. †**remindful,** *a.* serving to remind, reminiscent; mindful.

Remington[1], *n.* **Frederic** (1861–1909), US sculptor, painter, and illustrator. His exploratory trips to the American West inspired lively images of cowboys and horses, such as his sculpture *Off the Range* (Corcoran Gallery of Art, Washington DC).

Remington[2], *n.* **Philo** (1816–89), US inventor of the typewriter and breech-loading rifle that bear his name. He began manufacturing typewriters in 1873, using the patent of Christopher Sholes (1819–1890), and made improvements that resulted five years later in the first machine with a shift key, thus providing lower-case letters as well as capital letters. The Remington rifle and carbine, which had a falling block breech and a tubular magazine, were developed in collaboration with his father.

reminiscence, *n.* the act or power of remembering or recalling past knowledge; that which is remembered; (*pl.*) a collection of personal recollections of past events; (*fig.*) something reminding or suggestive (of); the philosophical doctrine that the human mind has seen everything before in an earlier, disembodied, existence. **reminisce,** *v.i.* to talk, think or write about past experiences. **reminiscent,** *a.* recalling past events to mind; of the nature of or pertaining to reminiscence; reminding or suggestive (of). *n.* one who records reminiscences. **reminiscential**, **reminiscitory,** *a.* **reminiscently,** *adv.* [late L *reminiscentia,* from *reminiscī* (*men-*, stem of *meminī,* I remember, cogn. with MIND)]

remint, *v.t.* to mint over again.

remiped, *a.* having oar-like feet. *n.* a small crustacean or aquatic insect with oar-like feet. [F *rémipède* (L *rēmi-*, *rēmus,* oar, *pes pedis,* foot)]

remise, *n.* a release of property; a surrender of a claim; †a coach-house;, †a carriage from a livery-stable; (*Fencing*), a thrust following up one that misses before the opponent has time to recover. *v.t.*, to surrender, to release or grant back;, to make a remise. [F, from *remettre,* to REMIT]

remiss, *a.* careless or lax in the performance of duty or business; heedless, negligent; slow, slack, languid. †**remissful,** *a.* **remissible,** *a.* that may be remitted, admitting of remission. **remissibility**, *n.* **remissly,** *adv.* **remissness,** *n.* [L *remissus,* p.p. of *remittere,* to REMIT]

remission, *n.* the act of remitting; the remitting or discharge of a debt, penalty etc.; forgiveness, pardon; abatement (e.g. in the symptoms of a disease), diminution, reduction (e.g. of a prison sentence), relaxation; remittance (of money etc.). **remissive,** *a.* **remissively,** *adv.* **remissly, remissness** REMISS. **remissory,** *a.* remitting, relieving, abating; forgiving. [OF, from L *remissiōnem,* nom. *-sio,* as prec.]

remit, *v.t.* (*past, p.p.* **remitted**) to send or put back; to transmit (cash, bills etc.); to refer or submit, to send back for consideration, to refer to a lower court; to defer, to put off; to relax, to slacken, to mitigate, to desist from partially or entirely; to refrain from exacting etc., to forgo, to discharge from (a fine, penalty etc.); to pardon, to forgive. *v.i.* to become less intense, to abate. **remitment,** *n.* remittance (of money). **remittal,** *n.* a giving up, a surrender; remission from one court to another; remission (for offences etc.). **remittance,** *n.* the act of remitting money, bills or the like, in payment for goods etc.; the sum so remitted; †a consignment of goods. **remittance-man,** *n.* an emigrant depending on remittances from home for his living. **remittee,** *n.* one receiving a remittance. **remittence,** *n.* **remittent,** *a.* of an illness, having alternate increase and decrease of intensity. *n.* a malarial fever marked by alternate increase and decrease of intensity. **remittently,** *adv.* [L *remittere* (*mittere,* to send), p.p. *remissus*]

remitter, *n.* (*Law*) remission to the more valid of two titles to an estate in favour of the holder entering in possession by the inferior title; remission to another court. **remittitur**, *n.* an order sending back a case to an inferior court; a surrender of damages in order to avert further litigation on appeal. [OF, as prec.]

remix, *v.t.* to change the balance of a recording. *n.* a remixed version of a recording.

remnant, *n.* that which is left after a larger part has been separated, lost or destroyed; the part surviving after destruction; the remainder; the last part of a piece of cloth etc., esp. a portion offered at a reduced price; a scrap, a fragment, a surviving trace. *a.* surviving; remaining. [ME and OF *remenant,* pres.p. of *remenoir, manoir,* to REMAIN]

remodel, *v.t.* (*past, p.p.* **remodelled**) to model again; to refashion. **remodify,** *v.t.* to modify again. **remodification,** *n.* †**remollient**, *a.* mollifying, softening. *n.* an emollient. †**remolten,** *p.p.* REMELT. **remonetize, -ise,** *v.t.* to reinstate (a metal etc.) as legal currency. **remonetization, -isation,** *n.*

remonstrance, *n.* the act of remonstrating; an expostulation, a protest; a formal representation or protest against public grievances etc. **the Grand Remonstrance,** *n.* the statement of grievances presented by Parliament to Charles I in 1641. **remonstrant,** *a.* containing or of the nature of remonstrance, expostulatory; †pertaining to the Arminian party in the Dutch Church. *n.* one who remonstrates; †(*pl.*) the Dutch Arminians who in 1610 presented to the States of Holland a remonstrance formulating their points of departure from Calvinism. **remonstrantly,** *adv.* **remonstrate**, *v.t.* to say or state in remonstrance. *v.i.* to make a remonstrance. **remonstratingly,** *adv.* **remonstration,** *n.* **remonstrative**, **remonstratory**, *a.* **remonstrator,** *n.* [OF, from med. L *remonstrāre* (L *monstrāre,* to show)]

remontant, *a.* blooming more than once in the season (of roses). *n.* a rose blooming more than once in the season. [F, pres.p. of *remonter,* to REMOUNT]

remora, *n.* a sucking-fish, *Echeneis remora,* having a suctorial disk for attaching itself to sharks, sword-fishes etc. and believed by the ancients to have the power of stopping ships in this way. [L, orig. hindrance, impediment (*mora,* delay)]

remorse, *n.* the pain caused by a sense of guilt, bitter repentance; compunction, reluctance to commit a wrong or to act cruelly. † **remord**, *v.t.* to cause remorse to. †**remordency,** *n.* **remordent,** *a.* **remorseful,** *a.* feeling remorse; penitent. **remorsefully,** *adv.* **remorsefulness,** *n.* **remorseless**, *a.* without remorse; cruel. **remorselessly,** *adv.* **remorselessness,** *n.* [OF *remors,* late L *remorsus,* from *remordere* (*mordere,* to bite, p.p. *morsus*)]

remote, *a.* far off, distant in time or space; not closely connected or related, separated, diferent, alien, foreign; out-of-the-way, retired, sequestered; slight, inconsiderable, least (*usu. in superl.*). **remote control,** *n.* electric or radio control of apparatus etc. from a distance. **remote-controlled,** *a.* **remotely,** *adv.* **remoteness,** *n.* †**remotion,** *n.* [L *remōtus,* p.p. of *removēre,* REMOVE]

rémoulade, *n.* a sauce, often made with mayonnaise, flavoured with herbs, mustard and capers and served with fish, cold meat, salads etc. [F dial. *ramolas,* horseradish, from L *armoracea*]

remould, *v.t.* to mould, fashion or shape anew. *n.* a used tyre which has had a new tread bonded into the casing and the walls coated with rubber. **remount,** *v.t.* to mount again, to reascend; to mount or set up (a gun, jewellery, a picture etc.) again; to supply (a regiment etc.) with fresh horses. *v.i.* to mount a horse again; to make a fresh ascent; to go back (to a date, source etc.). *n.* a fresh horse for riding on; a fresh mount or setting.

remove, *v.t.* to move from a place; to move to another place; to take away, to get rid of; to transfer to another post or office; to dismiss. *v.i.* to go away (from), esp. to change one's place or abode. *n.* a degree of difference or gradation; a dish removed to give place to another, or the dish brought on in its place; a class or form (in some public schools); removal, change of place or position, departure; †distance, esp. between stopping-places on a stage-road. **removable,** *a.* able to be moved; liable to removal. *n.* a removable official, esp. formerly in Ireland holding office during the pleasure of the Government. **removability**, *n.* **removal,** *n.* the act of removing or displacing; change of place, site or abode; dismissal; (*euphem.*) murder. **removalist,** *n.* (*Austral.*) a person or company responsible for moving furniture etc. to a new home. **removed,** *a.* distant in space or time; distant in relationship. **once, twice removed,** separated by one or two intervals of relationship. †**removedness**, *n.* the state of being removed or estranged. **remover,** *n.* one who removes, esp. one whose business is to remove furniture from one house to another. [OF *remouvoir, -movoir,* L *removēre* (*movēre,* to MOVE)]

remunerate, *v.t.* to reward, to recompense, to pay for a service etc.; to serve as recompense or equivalent (for or to). †**remunerable,** *a.* †**remunerability**, *n.* **remuneration,** *n.* **remunerative, remuneratory,** *a.* producing a due return for outlay; paying, profitable. **remuneratively,** *adv.* **remunerativeness,** *n.* [L *remūnerātus,* p.p. of *remūnerāre, -erārī* (*mūnus,* gift)]

remurmur, *v.t.* to utter back in murmurs. *v.i.* to return a murmuring echo (L *remurmurāre*). †**remutation,** *n.* the act of changing back again.

Renaissance, *n.* the period and intellectual movement in European cultural history that is traditionally seen as ending the Middle Ages and beginning modern times. The Renaissance started in Italy in the 14th cent. and flourished in W Europe until about the 17th cent. The aim of Renaissance education was to produce the 'complete human being' **Renaissance man**, conversant in the humanities, mathematics and science (including their application in war), the arts and crafts, and athletics and sport; to enlarge the bounds of learning and geographical knowledge; to encourage the growth of scepticism and free-thought, and the study and imitation of Greek and Latin literature and art. **Renaissance art,** *n.* movement in European art of the 15th and 16th cents. It began in Florence, Italy, with the rise of a spirit of humanism and a new appreciation of the classical past. In painting and sculpture this led to greater naturalism and interest in anatomy and perspective. Renaissance art peaked around 1500 with the careers of Leonardo da Vinci, Raphael, Michelangelo, and Titian in Italy and Dürer in Germany.

renal, *a.* pertaining to the kidneys. **renal pelvis,** *n.* the cavity joining the kidney and the ureter. [late L *rēnālis,* from *rēn,* kidney]

rename, *v.i.* to name anew, to give a new name to.

renascent, *a.* coming into being again; pertaining to the Renaissance. **renascence,** *n.* rebirth, renewal, a springing into fresh life; the Renaissance. †**renascible**, *a.* [L *renascens -ntem,* pres.p. of *renascī* (*nascī,* to be born)]

Renault, *n.* **Mary** (pen name of Mary Challans) (1905–83), English novelist who recreated the world of ancient Greece, with a trilogy on Theseus and two novels on Alexander: *Fire from Heaven* (1970) and *The Persian Boy* (1972).

rencounter, rencontre, *n.* a hostile meeting or collision, an encounter, a combat, a duel, a skirmish; an unexpected meeting or encounter. †*v.t.* to fall in with unexpectedly; to meet in combat. *v.i.* to come together, to clash; to meet an enemy unexpectedly. [F *rencontre,* from *rencontrer* (ENCOUNTER)]

rend, *v.t.* (*past, p.p.* **rent**[1]) to tear, pull or wrench (off, away, apart, asunder etc.); to split or separate with violence; to make (laths) by splitting wood; (*fig.*) to lacerate, to cause anguish to; to pierce, disturb, with sound. *v.i.* to be or become torn or pulled apart. **render**[1], *n.* [OE *rendan,* cp. OFris. *renda*]

Rendell, *n.* **Ruth** (1930–), English novelist and short-story writer, author of a detective series featuring Chief Inspector Wexford; her psychological crime novels explore the minds of people who commit murder, often through obsession or social inadequacy, as in *A Demon in my View* (1976) and *Heartstones* (1987).

render[2], *v.t.* to give in return; to pay or give back; to give up, to surrender; to bestow, to give, to pay, to furnish; to present, to submit, to hand in; to reproduce, to express, to represent, to interpret, to translate, to perform, to execute; to make, to cause to be; to boil down, to melt and clarify (fat); to give the first coat of plaster to. *n.* a return, a payment in return; the first coat of plaster on a wall etc.; †a surrender; †a statement, a declaration. **renderset,** *v.t.* to coat (a wall) with two coats of plaster. *a.* consisting of two such coats. *n.* the laying on of two such coats. **renderable,** *a.* **renderer,** *n.* **rendering,** *n.* a return; a translation, a version; interpretation, execution (of a piece of music, a dramatic part etc.); the first coat of plaster on brickwork etc. **rendition,** *n.* surrender, giving up; translation, interpretation; execution, performance, rendering (of music etc.). [OF *rendre,* pop. L *rendere,* var. of L *reddere* (*dare,* to give)]

rendezvous, *n.* (*pl. unchanged*) a place appointed

for assembling, esp. of troops or warships; a place agreed upon for meeting; a place of common resort; †a resort, a shift; †a refuge, a retreat. *v.i.* to meet or assemble at a rendezvous. [F *rendez-vous,* render or betake yourselves]

rendition RENDER.

René, *n.* **France-Albert** (1935–), Seychelles politician, president from 1987.

renegade, †**renegado**, *n.* an apostate, esp. from Christianity; a deserter; a turncoat. *v.i.* to turn renegade. **renegation,** *n.* **renegue, renege**, *v.i.* to fail to follow suit, to revoke; †to make denial; to go back on one's commitments or promise. †*v.t.* to deny, to renounce, to refuse, to decline. **reneguer, reneger,** *n.* [Sp. *renegado,* med. L *renegātus,* p.p. of *renegāre* (*negāre,* to deny)]

renerve, *v.t.* to put fresh nerve or vigour into.

renew, *v.t.* to make new again or as good as new, to renovate; to restore to the original or a sound condition; to make fresh or vigorous again, to reanimate, to revivify, to regenerate; to repair, to patch up, to replace (old or worn-out with new); to make, do or say over again, to recommence, to repeat; to grant a further period of (a lease, patent, mortgage etc.); to obtain such a grant. *v.i.* to become young or new again; to grow again; to begin again. **renewable,** *a.* **renewability**, *n.* **renewal,** *n.* the act of renewing; the state of being renewed; revival, regeneration; a fee paid for continuance of anything. †**renewedly**, *adv.* †**renewedness,** *n.* **renewer,** *n.* **renewing,** *n.*

†**renfierce,** *v.t.* to render fierce.

†**renforce,** *v.t.* to reinforce; to force (to do). [F *renforcer* (ENFORCE)]

reni-, *comb.form* pertaining to the kidney. [L *rēnēs*]

renidify, *v.i.* to build another nest. **renidification,** *n.*

reniform, *a.* kidney-shaped. [L *rēn rēnis,* kidney, -FORM]

renin, *n.* a protein enzyme secreted by the kidneys, which helps to maintain blood pressure. [L *rēnēs*]

†**renitence ,** †**renitency** *n.* resistance, esp. of a body to pressure; moral resistance, reluctance, disinclination. †**renitent,** *a.* [obs. F *rénitence,* from *rénitent,* L *renitentem,* nom. *-tens,* pres.p. of *renītī* (*nītī,* to struggle)]

Rennes, *n.* industrial city (oil refining, chemicals, electronics, cars) and capital of Ille-et-Vilaine *département*, W France, at the confluence of the Ille and Vilaine, 56 km/35 miles SE of St Malo; population (1982) 234,000. It was the old capital of Britanny.

rennet¹, *n.* curdled milk from the stomach of an unweaned calf etc. or an aqueous infusion of the stomach-membrane of the calf, used to coagulate milk; a similar preparation from seeds or other vegetable sources. **rennin**, *n.* an enzyme with the power of coagulating the protein in milk. [ME, from *renne,* to RUN]

rennet², *n.* a name for several varieties of apple, esp. pippins. [F *reinette,* prob. dim. of *reine,* queen (perh. from F *rainette,* dim. of *raine,* frog, see RANA, with alln. to the speckled skin)]

Rennie, *n.* **John** (1761–1821), Scottish engineer who built the old Waterloo Bridge and old London Bridge (reconstructed in Arizona, US).

Renoir¹, *n.* **Jean** (1894–1979), French film director, son of the painter Auguste Renoir, whose films include *La Grande Illusion/Grand Illusion* (1937), and *Règle du Jeu/The Rules of the Game* (1939).

Renoir², *n.* **Pierre-Auguste** (1841–1919), French impressionist painter. He met Monet and Sisley in the early 1860s and together they formed the nucleus of the impressionist movement. He developed a lively, colourful painting style with feathery brushwork and painted many voluptuous female nudes, such as *The Bathers* about 1884–87 (Philadelphia Museum of Art, US). In his later years he turned to sculpture.

renominate, *v.t.* to nominate again. **renomination,** *n.*

renounce, *v.t.* to declare against, to reject or cast off formally, to repudiate, to disclaim, to disown; to forsake, to abandon; to forswear, to abjure; to give up, to withdraw from; (*Law*) to decline or resign a right or trust; to fail to follow suit through having none left of that suit. *v.i.* to fail to follow suit. *n.* such failure to follow suit. **renouncement, renouncer,** *n.* [F *renoncer,* L *renuntiāre* (*nuntiāre,* from *nuntius,* messenger, see NUNCIO]

renovate, *v.t.* to make new again; to restore to a state of soundness or vigour; to repair. **renovation,** *n.* **renovative,** *a.* **renovator,** *n.* [L *renovātus,* p.p. of *renovāre* (*novus,* new)]

renown, *n.* exalted reputation, fame, celebrity. *v.t.* to make renowned or famous. **renowned,** *a.* famous, celebrated. **renownedly**, *adv.* †**renowner,** *n.* a braggart, a boaster. †**renownless**, *a.* inglorious. [ME and A-F *renoun,* OF *renon* (F *renommée*), from *renoumer, renomer,* L *renomināre,* see RENOMINATE]

rent¹, (*past, p.p.*) REND.

rent², *n.* a tear, slit or breach, an opening made by rending or tearing asunder; a cleft, a fissure, a chasm; (*fig.*) a schism, a separation brought about by violent means. [from obs. v. *rent,* var. of REND]

rent³, *n.* a sum of money payable periodically for the use of lands, tenements etc.; payment for the use of any kind of property; the return from cultivated land after production costs have been subtracted. *v.t.* to occupy, hold in tenancy or use in return for rent; to let for rent; to impose rent upon; to hire. *v.i.* to be let (at a certain rent); to hire. **for rent,** available for use on payment of a rent. **rent-a-,** *comb.form* rented or hired, e.g. *rent-a-crowd, rent-a-mob.* **rent boy,** *n.* a young male homosexual prostitute. **rent-charge,** *n.* a periodical charge on land etc. granted by deed to some person other than the owner. **rent collector,** *n.* person who collects rents. **rent-day,** *n.* the day on which rent is due. **rent-free,** *a.* exempted from the payment of rent. *adv.* without payment of rent. **rent-restriction,** *n.* restrictions on a landlord's powers to charge rent. **rent-roll,** *n.* a schedule of a person's property and rents; a person's total income from this source. **rent strike,** *n.* the refusal by tenants to pay their rent. **rentable,** *a.* **rental,** *n.* the total income from rents of an estate; a rent-roll; (*Sc.*) a favourable rent or lease to a 'kindly' tenant; property available for rent. *v.t.* (*Sc.*) to let or hold (land) on a rental. **rentaller,** *n.* **renter¹,** *n.* one who holds an estate or tenement by paying rent; a tenant; the proprietor of a seat in a theatre. **rentless**, *a.* [OF *rente,* prob. through pop. L *rendita,* var. of *reddita,* fem. p.p. of *reddere,* to RENDER²]

rente, *n.* income, revenue; (*pl.*) interest or annuities from French government stocks; the stocks themselves. **rentier**, *n.* a person drawing his income from rentes or investments. [F]

Rentenmark, *n.* currency introduced in Germany at the end of 1923 by the president of the Reichsbank, Hjalmar Schacht (1877–1970), to replace old Reichsmarks which had been rendered worthless by inflation.

renter¹ RENT³.

renter², *v.t.* to fine-draw; to sew together the edges of two pieces of cloth without doubling them, so that the seam is scarcely visible. **renterer,** *n.* [F *rentrer,* var. of *rentraire*]

renuent, *a.* throwing back the head (applied to muscles which perform this function). [L *renuens -ntem,* pres.p. of *renuere* (*nuere,* to nod)]

renule, *n.* a renal lobule or small kidney (as in some animals). [dim. of L *rēn,* kidney, see RENIFORM]

renumber, *v.t.* to number again.

renunciation, *n.* the act of renouncing; a declaration or document expressing this; self-denial, self-sacrifice, self-resignation. †**renunciance,** *n.* **renunciant,** *n., a.* **renunciative, -tory,** *a.* [L *renuntiātio,* from *renuntiāre,* to RENOUNCE]

renverse, *v.t.* to reverse, to turn the other way; to overthrow, to upset. **renversé, renverse,** *a.* inverted, reversed. [OF *renverser* (RE-, *enverser,* from *envers,* L *inversus,* see INVERSE)]

reobtain, *v.t.* to obtain again. **reobtainable,** *a.* **reoccupy,** *v.t.* to occupy again. **reoccupation,** *n.* **reoffer,** *v.t.* to offer for public sale. **reopen,** *v.t., v.i.* to open again. **reopening clause,** *n.* in collective bargaining, a clause in a contract which allows an issue to be reconsidered before the expiry date of the contract. **reordain,** *v.t.* to ordain again; to appoint or enact again. **reordination,** *n.* **reorder,** *v.t.* to put in order again, to rearrange; to order or command again. **reorganize, -ise,** *v.t.* to organize anew. **reorganizer, -iser,** *n.* **reorganization, -isation,** *n.* **reorient,** *a.* (*poet.*) rising again. *v.t.* to orient again. **reorientate,** *v.t.* to restore the normal outlook of.

rep., (*abbr.*) report, reporter; republic, republican.

rep[1], short for REPRESENTATIVE.

rep[2], *n.* a textile fabric of wool, cotton or silk, with a finely-corded surface. **repped,** *a.* having a surface like rep. [F *reps,* etym. unknown]

rep[3] REPERTORY THEATRE.

repacify, *v.t.* to pacify again. **repack,** *v.t.* to pack again. **repacker,** *n.* **repaganize, -ise,** *v.t.* to make pagan again. *v.i.* to become pagan again. **repaid,** (*past, p.p.*) REPAY. **repaint,** *v.i.* to paint again.

repair[1], *v.i.* to go, to betake oneself, to resort (to). *n.* a place to which one goes often or which is frequented by many people. [OF *repairer,* late L *repatriāre* (RE-, *patria,* one's native land)]

repair[2], *v.t.* to restore to a good or sound state after dilapidation or wear; to make good the damaged or dilapidated parts of, to renovate, to mend; to remedy, to set right, to make amends for; †to revive, to recreate. *n.* restoration to a sound state; good or comparative condition. **in repair** or **in good repair,** in sound working condition. **in bad repair** or **out of repair,** in a dilapidated condition, needing repair. **repairable** REPARABLE. **repairer,** *n.* †**repairment,** *n.* [OF *reparer,* L *reparāre* (RE-, *parāre,* to make ready)]

repand, *a.* (*Bot.*) having an uneven, wavy or sinuous margin. **repandly,** *adv.* †**repandous,** *a.* [L *repandus* (*pandus,* bent)]

repaper, *v.t.* to paper (walls etc.) again.

reparable, *a.* capable of being made good, put in a sound state, or repaired. **reparation,** *n.* the act of repairing or restoring; the state of being repaired; satisfaction for wrong or damage, amends, compensation; (*pl.*) repairs. **reparative,** *a.* **reparatory,** *a.* [F, from L *reparābilis,* from *reparāre,* to REPAIR[2]]

repartee, *n.* a smart or witty rejoinder, a witty retort. †*v.i.* to make repartees. [F *repartie,* fem. p.p. of *repartir,* to start again (*partir,* to PART)]

repartition, *n.* distribution, allotment; a fresh distribution or allotment.

repass, *v.t.* to pass again; to go past again; to recross. *v.i.* to pass in the opposite direction; to pass again (into, through etc.). **repassage,** *n.*

repast, *n.* a meal; food, victuals; the act of taking food; †repose. *v.i.* to feed, to feast (upon etc.). †**repasture,** *n.* food, a repast. [OF, from *repaistre* (F *repaître*) (RE-, L *pascere,* to feed, see PASTURE)]

repatriate, *v.t.* to restore to one's country. *v.i.* to return to one's country. *n.* a person who has been repatriated. **repatriation,** *n.* [late L *repatriātus,* p.p. of *repatriāre* (*patria,* one's country)]

repay, *v.t.* (*past, p.p.* **repaid**) to pay back, to refund; to return, to deal (a blow etc.) in retaliation or recompense; to pay (a creditor etc.), to make recompense for, to requite. *v.i.* to make a repayment or requital. **repayable,** *a.* **repayment,** *n.* [OF *repayer*]

repeal, *v.t.* to revoke, to rescind, to annul; †to recall, to summon back; to recall or retract. *n.* abrogation, revocation, annulment. **repealable,** *a.* †**repealability,** †**repealableness,** *n.* **repealer,** *n.* one who repeals; one who advocates repeal, esp. one who advocated a repeal of the Union between Great Britain and Ireland in the time of O'Connell. **repealist,** *n.* [A-F *repeler,* OF *rapeler* (*apeler,* to APPEAL)]

repeat, *v.t.* to do, make or say over again; to reiterate; to rehearse; to reproduce, to imitate. *v.i.* to do something over again; to recur, to happen again; to strike over again the last hour or quarter-hour struck (of a watch etc.); to rise to the mouth, to be tasted again (of food). *n.* repetition, esp. of a song or other item on a programme; (*Mus.*) a passage to be repeated, a sign indicating this; a supply of goods corresponding to the last; the order for this; a radio or television programme broadcast for the second time or more. **repeatable,** *a.* **repeatedly,** *adv.* **repeater,** *n.* one who repeats; a repeating firearm; a watch or clock striking the hours and parts of hours when required; a repeating signal etc.; an indeterminate decimal in which the same figures continually recur in the same order. **repeating decimal** RECURRING. **repeating rifle,** *n.* one constructed usu. with a magazine, to fire several shots without reloading. [F *repeter,* L *repetere* (*petere,* to seek)]

repechage, *n.* a heat, esp. in rowing or fencing, where contestants beaten in earlier rounds get another chance to qualify for the final. [F *repêchage,* fishing out again]

repel, *v.t.* (*past, p.p.* **repelled**) to drive or force back; to check the advance of; to repulse, to ward off; to keep at a distance; (of fluids etc.) to refuse to mix with (each other); to tend to drive back, to be repulsive or antagonistic to. **repellence, -ency,** *n.* **repellent,** *a.* repelling or tending to repel; repulsive. *n.* that which repels. **repellently,** *adv.* **repeller,** *n.* [L *repeller* (*peller,* to drive, p.p. *pulsus*)]

repent[1], *a.* of a plant, creeping, esp. along the ground and rooting. [L *rēpens, -ntem,* pres.p. of *rēpere,* to creep]

repent[2], *v.i.* to feel sorrow, regret, or pain for something done or left undone, esp. to feel such sorrow for sin as leads to amendment, to be penitent or contrite; to be sorry; †to grieve, to mourn. *v.t.* to feel contrition or remorse for, to regret; to affect (oneself) with penitence. **repentance,** *n.* **repentant,** *a.* **repentantly, repentingly,** *adv.* **repenter,** *n.* [F *repentir* (RE- L *paenitēre,* to make contrite, see PENITENT)]

repercussion, *n.* the act of driving or forcing back; recoil; echo, reverberation; (*Mus.*) frequent repetition of the same subject, note, chord etc. †**repercuss,** *v.t.* **repercussive,** *a.* driving back, repellent; causing reverberation; driven back; reverberated. [F *répercussion* or L *repercussiōnem,* nom. *-sio,* from *repercutere* (*percutere,* to PERCUSS)]

repertoire, *n.* a stock of musical pieces, songs etc., that a person or company is ready to perform. [F *répertoire,* as foll.]

repertory, *n.* a place in which things are so disposed that they can be readily found; a storehouse, a collection, a magazine, esp. of information, statistics etc.; a repertoire. **repertory theatre,** *n.* a theatre served by a stock or permanent company prepared to present a number of different plays, called a **repertory company.** [L *repertōrium,* from *reperīre* (p.p. *repertus*), to find (OL *parīre,* L *parere,* to produce)]

reperuse, *v.t.* to peruse again. **reperusal,** *n.*

repetend, *n.* something repeated, a recurring word or phrase; a refrain; that part of a repeating decimal which keeps recurring. [L *repetendum,* ger. of *repetere,* to REPEAT]

répétiteur, *n.* a person who coaches opera singers. [F, see REPEAT]

repetition, *n.* the act of repeating, iteration; recital from memory; that which is repeated, a piece set to be learnt by heart; a copy, a reproduction, a replica; (*Mus.*) the ability of a musical instrument to repeat a note in rapid succession. **repetitional, -ary, repetitious, repetitive,** *a.* **repetitive strain injury,** a condition in which the joints and tendons of usu. the hands become inflamed, typically as the result of repeated use of (usu. industrial) apparatus or machinery. **repetitiously,** *adv.* **repetitiousness, repetitiveness,** *n.* [OF *repeticion* (F *répétition*), L *repetitiōnem,* nom. *-tio,* as prec.]

repiece, *v.t.* to piece together again.

repine, *v.i.* to fret oneself, to be discontented (at); to murmur; to complain, to grumble. †*n.* repining. **repiner,** *n.* **repiningly,** *adv.*

repique, *n.* (*Piquet*) the scoring of 30 points on cards alone before playing. *v.t.* to make a repique against. *v.i.* to make a repique. [F *repic*]

replace, *v.t.* to put back again in place; to take the place of, to succeed; to be a substitute for; to supersede, to displace; to put a substitute in place of, to fill the place of (with or by); to put in a fresh place; †to repay, to refund. **replaceable,** *a.* **replacer,** *n.* **replacement,** *n.* one that replaces; a substitute.

replant, *v.t.* to plant (a tree etc.) again; to re-establish, to resettle; to plant (ground) again. **replantation,** *n.*

repleader, *n.* (*Law*) a second pleading; the right of pleading again (F *replaider*). †**repledge,** *v.t.* (*Sc. Law*) to take (a prisoner or cause) from the jurisdiction of the court to that of another on the pledge that justice shall be done (OF *repleger*). **replay,** *v.t.* to play again (a record, game etc.). *n.* a second game between two contestants; also called **action replay,** the playing again of part of a broadcast match or game, often in slow motion.

replenish, *v.t.* to fill up again; to fill completely; to stock abundantly; †to occupy completely; †to finish, to perfect. †*v.i.* to become filled. **replenisher,** *n.* **replenishment,** *n.* [OF *repleniss-*, pres.p. stem of *replenir* (RE-, L *plēnus,* full)]

replete, *a.* completely filled; abundantly supplied or stocked (with); filled to excess, sated, gorged (with). **repletion,** *n.* the state of being replete; eating and drinking to satiety; surfeit; fullness of blood, a plethoric condition. †**repletive, repletory,** *a.* **repletively,** *adv.* [F *replet, -plète,* L *replētus,* p.p. of *replēre* (RE-, *plēre,* to fill)]

replevy, *v.t.* (*Law*) to recover possession of (distrained goods) upon giving security to submit the matter to a court and to surrender the goods if required. *n.* a replevin. **repleviable, replevisable,** *a.* **replevin,** *n.* an action for replevying; the writ by which goods are replevied. [A-F and OF *replevir* (*plevir,* etym. doubtful, cp. PLEDGE)]

replica, *n.* a duplicate of a picture, sculpture etc. by the artist who executed the original; an exact copy, a facsimile (sometimes on a smaller scale). [It., from *replicare,* to REPLY]

replicate, *a.* folded back on itself. *n.* a tone one or more octaves above or below a given tone. *v.t.* to fold back on itself; to add a replicate to (a tone); †to reproduce, to make a replica of; †to repeat; †to reply. **replicatile,** *a.* capable of being folded back (of a wing). **replication,** *n.* a reply, a rejoinder; (*Law*) the reply of a plaintiff to the defendant's plea; an echo, a repetition, †a copy, an imitation; (*Mus.*) a replicate. **replicative,** *a.* [L *replicātus,* p.p. of *replicāre* (*plicāre,* to fold)]

replum, *n.* (*pl.* **-pla**) the central process or placenta remaining after the valves of a dehiscent fruit have fallen away. [L, a bolt]

replume, *v.t.* to preen or rearrange.

replunge, *v.t., v.i.* to plunge again. *n.* the act of plunging again. **replunger,** *n.*

reply, *v.i.* (*pres.p.* **replying,** *past, p.p.* **replied**) to answer, to respond, to make answer orally, in writing, or by action; (*Law*) to plead in answer to a defendant's plea. *v.t.* to return as in answer; to answer (that etc.). *n.* the act of replying; that which is said, written, or done in answer, a response. **replier,** *n.* [OF *replier,* L *replicāre* (*plicāre,* to fold, cp. REPLICATE)]

repoint, *v.t.* to repair the joints of brickwork etc. with new cement or mortar. **repopulate,** *v.t.* to populate again.

report, *v.t.* to bring back as an answer; to give an account of, to describe or to narrate, esp. as an eyewitness; to state as a fact or as news; to prepare a record of, esp. for official use or for publication; to take down in full or to summarize (a speech, sermon etc.); to announce, to make a formal or official statement about, to certify; to give information against. *v.i.* to make or tender a report; to act as a reporter; to report oneself (at a certain place etc.); to be responsible to an employer or supervisor. *n.* that which is reported, esp. the formal statement of the result of an investigation, trial etc.; a detailed account of a speech, meeting etc., esp. for publication in a newspaper; common talk, popular rumour; fame, repute, accepted character; end-of-term statement of a pupil's work and behaviour at school; a loud noise, esp. of an explosive kind. **report stage,** *n.* the stage of progress with a Bill in the House of Commons when a committee has reported. **reportable,** *a.* **reportage,** *n.* the art of reporting news; writing in a factual or journalistic style; a type of film journalism using no words. **reported speech,** *n.* indirect speech. **reporter,** *n.* one who reports; one who draws up official statements of law proceedings and decisions of legislative debates; one who gathers news etc., for a newspaper or broadcasting company. **reporterism, reportership,** *n.* †**reportingly,** *adv.* **reportorial,** *a.* [OF *reporter,* L *reportāre* (*portāre,* to bring)]

repose[1], *v.t.* to place, to put (confidence etc. in). **reposal,** *n.* [L *repos-*, p.p. stem of *repōnere* (*pōnere,* to place, p.p. *positum*)]

repose[2], *v.t.* to lay (oneself etc.) to rest, to rest; to refresh with rest; to place at rest or recline. *v.t.* to rest; to lie at rest; to be laid or be in a recumbent position, esp. in sleep or death; to rest or be supported (on). *n.* the act of resting or being at rest; rest, cessation of activity, excitement, toil etc.; sleep, quiet, tranquillity, calmness, composure, ease of manner etc.; (*Art.*) restful effect; quietude, moderation and harmony of colour and treatment. **reposedness,** *n.* **reposeful,** *a.* **reposefully,** *adv.* **reposefulness,** *n.* [F *reposer,* late L *repausāre* (*pausāre,* to PAUSE, conf. with L *pōnere,* see prec.)]

reposit, *v.t.* to lay up; to deposit, as in a place of safety. **reposition,** *n.* **repositor,** *n.* (*Surg.*) an instrument for replacing (used for prolapsus). **repository,** *n.* a place where things are deposited for safety or preservation; a depository, a museum, a store, a magazine, a shop, a warehouse, a vault, a sepulchre; a person to whom a secret etc. is confided. [L *repositus,* p.p. of *repōnere,* to put back, lay aside]

repossess, *v.t.* to possess again. **repossession,** *n.*

repot, *v.t.* to put (a plant) into a fresh pot.

repoussé, *a.* formed in relief by hammering from behind (of ornamental metal work). *n.* metal work ornamented in this way. **repoussage,** *n.* [F, p.p. of *repousser* (RE-, *pousser,* to PUSH)]

repp, repped REP[1].

reprehend, *v.t.* to find fault with; to censure, to blame; †to convict of fallacy. **reprehender,** *n.* **reprehensible,** *a.* open to censure or blame. **reprehensibleness,** *n.* **reprehensibly,** *adv.* **reprehension,** *n.* †**reprehensive,** †**-sory,** *a.* [L *reprehendere* (RE-, *prehendere,* to seize, cp. COMPREHEND), p.p. *reprehensus*]

represent, *v.t.* to present to or bring before the mind by describing, portraying, imitating etc.; to serve as a likeness of, to depict (of a picture etc.); to set forth, to state (that), to describe (as), to make out (to be); to enact (a play etc.) on the stage, to personate, to play the part of; to serve as symbol for, to stand for, to be an example or specimen of; to take the place of as deputy, substitute etc.; to act as agent or spokesman for, esp. in a representative chamber; to bring a mental image of (an event, object etc.) before the mind. **representable,** *a.* **representation,** *n.* the act of representing; a dramatic performance; a statement of arguments etc.; the system of representing bodies of people in a legislative assembly; the rights, status or functions of a representative; representatives collectively. **proportional representation,** *n.* an electoral system by which minorities are represented in proportion to their numbers. **Representation of the People Acts** (1918), in the UK, a series of laws that extended voting rights, creating universal suffrage in 1928. **representational,** *a.* **representationism,** *n.* the doctrine that the immediate object in perception is only an idea, image, or other representation of the external thing. **representationist,** *n.* **representative,** *a.* serving to represent or symbolize, able or fitted to represent, typical; presenting the general characters of; similar or corresponding to other species etc. living elsewhere; acting as agent, delegate, deputy etc.; consisting of delegates etc.; based on representation by delegates; presenting images or ideas to the mind. *n.* one who or that which represents; an example, a specimen, a typical instance or embodiment; an agent, deputy, or substitute, esp. a person chosen by a body of electors; a travelling salesperson, a sales representative; (*Law*) one who stands in the place of another as heir etc. **House of Representatives,** the lower house of the US Congress. **representative government,** *n.* system of government by representatives elected by the people. **representatively,** *adv.* **representativeness,** *n.* **representer,** *n.* [OF *representer,* L *repraesentāre*]

re-present, *v.t.* to present again. **re-presentation,** *n.*

repress, *v.t.* to restrain, to keep under restraint; to put down, to suppress, to quell; to prevent from breaking out etc.; to banish (unpleasant thoughts etc.) to the unconscious. †**represser,** *n.* **repressible,** *a.* **repression,** *n.* the act of repressing; unconscious exclusion from the conscious mind of thoughts and memories which are in conflict with conventional behaviour. **repressive,** *a.* **repressively,** *adv.* [L *repressus,* p.p. of *reprimere* (*premere,* to PRESS[1])]

re-press, *v.t.* to press again.

reprieve, *v.t.* to suspend the execution of for a time; to grant a respite to; to rescue, to save (from); †to set free, to acquit. *n.* the temporary suspension of a sentence on a prisoner; the warrant authorizing this; a respite. †**reprieval,** *n.* [from obs. *repry,* to remand, A-F and OF *repris,* p.p. of *reprendre* (RE-, L *prehendere,* to seize, see COMPREHEND)]

reprimand, *n.* a severe reproof, a rebuke, esp. a public or official one. *v.t.* to reprove severely, to rebuke, esp. publicly or officially. [F *réprimande, reprimende,* from *reprimer,* to REPRESS]

reprint, *v.t.* to print (a book etc.) again; to print (letterpress etc.) over again; †to renew the impression of (a word, mark etc.). *n.* a new edition or impression of a printed work without considerable alteration of the contents.

reprisal, *n.* the act of seizing from an enemy by way of indemnification or retaliation; that which is so taken; any act of retaliation. [OF *reprisaille* (cp. F *représaille,* It. *ripresaglia*), from foll.]

reprise, *n.* (*Law*) a yearly rent-charge or other payment out of a manor and lands (*usu. in pl.*); (*Mus.*) a refrain, a repeated phrase etc.; †a resumption or renewal of action; †a reprisal. [F, fem. of *repris,* p.p. of *reprendre,* see REPRIEVE]

reprize, *v.t.* to prize anew.

repro, *n.* (*pl.* **-pros**) short for REPRODUCTION.

reproach, *v.t.* to censure in opprobrious terms, to upbraid; to find fault with (something done); †to disgrace. *n.* censure mingled with opprobrium or grief; a rebuke, a censure; shame, infamy, disgrace; an object or cause of scorn or derision. **above, beyond reproach,** blameless, pure. **reproachable,** *a.* †**reproachableness,** *n.* **reproachably,** *adv.* **reproacher,** *n.* **reproachful,** *a.* containing or expressing reproach; upbraiding, opprobrious, abusive; shameful, infamous, base. **reproachfully,** *adv.* **reproachfulness,** *n.* **reproachingly,** *adv.* **reproachless,** *a.* **reproachlessness,** *n.* [F *reprocher,* etym. doubtful (perh. from a pop. L *repropriāre,* from L *prope,* near, cp. as APPROACH, or from L as APPROVE)]

reprobate, *a.* abandoned to sin, lost to virtue or grace; depraved. *n.* one who is abandoned to sin; a wicked, depraved wretch. *v.t.* to express disapproval and detestation of, to condemn severely; to abandon to wickedness and eternal punishment; †to disallow, to reject. †**reprobacy,** †**reprobance,** †**reprobateness,** *n.* †**reprobater,** *n.* **reprobation,** *n.* †**reprobationer,** *n.* (*Theol.*) one who believes in the doctrine of the nonelect. **reprobative, reprobatory,** *a.* [L *reprobātus,* p.p. of *reprobāre,* see REPROVE]

reprocess, *v.t.* to process again; to treat a substance or material in order to make it reusable in a new form. **reprocessing,** *n., a.*

reproduce, *v.t.* to produce again; to copy; to produce new life through sexual or asexual processes. *v.i.* to produce offspring; to come out (well, badly etc.) as a copy. **reproducer,** *n.* **reproducible,** *a.* **reproduction,** *n.* the act of reproducing; any of the sexual or asexual processes by which animals or plants produce offspring; a copy, imitation. **reproductive, -tory,** *a.* **reproductively,** *adv.* **reproductiveness, reproductivity,** *n.*

reprography, *n.* the art or process of reproducing printed matter (e.g. by photocopying). **reprographic,** *a.* **reprographically,** *adv.*

reproof, *n.* an expression of blame; censure, blame, reprehension; disproof. †**reproval,** *n.* **reprove,** *v.t.* to rebuke, to censure, esp. to one's face, to chide; †to convict; †to disprove. †to refute. **reprovable,** *a.* **reprover,** *n.* **reprovingly,** *adv.* [OF *reprove,* from *reprover,* L *reprobāre,* to disapprove (RE-, *probāre,* to PROVE)]

reprovision, *v.t.* to provision (a ship etc.) afresh. **reprune,** *v.t.* to prune again.

reps, var. of REP[1].

reptant, *a.* (*Biol.*) creeping. **reptation,** *n.* **reptatory,** *a.* [L *reptans -ntem,* pres.p. of *reptāre,* freq. of *rēpere,* to creep]

reptile, *a.* creeping, crawling, moving on the belly or on small, short legs; grovelling, servile, mean, base. *n.* a crawling animal; one of the Reptilia, a class of animals comprising the snakes, lizards, turtles, crocodiles etc.; a grovelling, mean, base person. **reptilian,** *n., a.* **reptiliferous,** *a.* containing fossil reptiles. **reptiliform, reptilious, reptiloid,** *a.* **reptilivorous,** *a.* devouring reptiles. [F, from late L *reptilis,* from *rēpere,* to creep, p.p. *reptus*]

republic, *n.* a state or a form of political constitution in which the supreme power is vested in the people or their elected representatives, a commonwealth. **republic of letters** LETTER. **republican,** *a.* pertaining to or consisting of a republic; characteristic of the principles of a republic; believing in or advocating these. *n.* (*also* **Republican**) one who favours or advocates a republican form of government; a member of the Republican party in the US; a supporter of republicanism in N Ireland. **Republican Party,** *n.* one of the US's two main political parties, formed 1854 by a coalition of slavery opponents, who elected their first president, Abraham Lincoln, in 1860. The early Republican Party supported protective tariffs and favoured genuine settlers (homesteaders) over land speculators. Towards the end of the century the Republican Party was identified with US imperialism and industrial expansion. With few intermissions, the Republican Party controlled the legislature from the 1860s until defeated by the New Deal Democrats 1932. After an isolationist period before World War II, the Republican Party adopted an active foreign policy under Nixon and Ford, but the latter was defeated by Carter in the presidential election 1976. However, the party enjoyed landslide presidential victories for Reagan and also carried the Senate 1980–86. Bush won the 1988 election, but faced the prospect of a Democratic Senate and Congress. **republicanism,** *n.* **republicanize, -ise,** *v.t.* [F *république,* L *rēspublica* (*rēs,* thing, concern, PUBLIC)]

republish, *v.t.* to publish again; to print a new edition of. †**republisher,** *n.* **republication,** *n.*

repudiate, *v.t.* to refuse to acknowledge, to disown, to disclaim (a debt etc.); to disavow, to reject, to refuse to admit, accept, recognize etc.; to cast off, to put away, to divorce (one's wife). *v.i.* to repudiate a public debt (of a state). †**repudiable,** *a.* **repudiation,** *n.* **repudiator,** *n.* [L *repudiātus,* p.p. of *repudiāre,* from *repudium,* divorce (RE-, *pud-,* stem of *pudēre,* to feel shame)]

repugn, *v.i.* to oppose, to resist, to strive (against); †(*fig.*) to be repugnant (to) or inconsistent (with). *v.t.* to combat, to oppose, to strive against. **repugnance, repugnancy,** *n.* antipathy, dislike, distaste, aversion; inconsistency, incompatibility, or opposition, of mind, disposition, statements, ideas etc. **repugnant,** *a.* **repugnantly,** *adv.* [F *répugner,* L *repugnāre* (RE-, *pugnāre,* to fight)]

repullulate, *v.i.* to sprout, shoot, or bud again; to break out again, to recur, to reappear (of a disease or morbid growth). **repullulation,** *n.* **repullulescent,** *a.* [L *repullulāre*]

repulse, *v.t.* to repel, to beat or drive back, esp. by force of arms; to reject, esp. in a rude manner, to rebuff, to snub; to defeat in argument. *n.* the act of repulsing; the state of being repulsed; a rebuff, a refusal, a failure, a disappointment. **repulser,** *n.* **repulsion,** *n.* the act of repulsing; the state of being repulsed; (*Phys.*) the tendency of certain bodies to repel each other, opp. to attraction; dislike, repugnance, aversion. **repulsive,** *a.* acting so as to repel; unsympathetic, forbidding; repellent, loathsome, disgusting; (*Phys.*) acting by repulsion. **repulsively,** *adv.* **repulsiveness,** *n.* [L *repulsus,* p.p. of *repellere* (RE-, *pellere,* to drive)]

repurchase, *v.t.* to purchase back or again. *n.* the act of buying again; that which is so bought.

reputable, *a.* being in good repute; respectable, creditable. **reputableness,** *n.* **reputably,** *adv.*

reputation, *n.* the estimation in which one is generally held, repute; good estimation, good fame, credit, esteem, respectability; †estimation, consideration; character or repute; the repute, honour, or credit derived from favourable public opinion or esteem. **reputative,** *a.* putative. †**reputatively,** *adv.* [L *reputātio,* from *reputāre,* to REPUTE]

repute, *v.t.* to think, to account, to reckon; (*chiefly in p.p.*) to consider, to report, to regard (as). *n.* reputation, fame; character attributed by public report. **reputed,** *a.* generally regarded (usu. with implication of doubt etc.). **reputedly,** *adv.* †**reputeless,** *a.* [F *réputer,* L *reputāre* (RE-, *putāre,* to think)]

request, *n.* an expression of desire or the act of asking for something to be granted or done; a petition; that which is asked for; the state of being demanded or sought after; †an inquiry. *v.t.* to ask (that); to address a request to. **on request,** if, or when asked for. **request stop,** *n.* a stop on a route where a bus etc. will stop only if signalled to do so. †**requestant, requester,** *n.* [OF *requeste* (RE-, QUEST)]

requicken, *v.t.* to quicken again, to reanimate.

requiem, *n.* a mass for the repose of the soul of a person deceased; the musical setting of this, a dirge; †repose, rest, quiet. [L, rest (the first word of the introit *Requiem aeternam dona eis, Domine*)]

requiescat, *n.* a wish or prayer for the repose of the dead. [L *requiescat in pace,* let him (or her) rest in peace]

require, *v.t.* to ask or claim as a right or by authority, to order; to demand (something of a person), to insist (on having, that etc.); to have need of, to call for imperatively, to depend upon for completion etc. *v.i.* to be necessary. **requirable,** *a.* **requirement,** *n.* that which is required; an essential condition; †the act of requiring, a requisition. †**requirer,** *n.* [OF *requerre* (F *requérir*), assim. to L *requīrere* (RE-, *quaerere,* to seek)]

requisite, *a.* required by the nature of things, necessary for completion etc., indispensable. *n.* that which is required; a necessary part or quality. †**requisitely,** *adv.* **requisiteness,** *n.* [L *requīsītus,* p.p. of *requīrere,* as prec.]

requisition, *n.* the act of requiring or demanding; application made as of right; a formal and usu. written demand or request for the performance of a duty etc.; an authoritative order for the supply of provisions etc., esp. a military order to a town etc.; the state of being called upon or put in use. *v.t.* to make a formal or authoritative demand for, esp. for military purposes; to make such a demand upon (a town etc.); to take upon requisition, to call in for use. **requisitionist,** *n.* one who makes a requisition. †**requisitive,** *n., a.* †**requisitory,** *a.* [F *réquisition,* L *requīsītiōnem,* nom. *-tio,* as prec.]

requite, *v.t.* to repay, to make return to, to recompense; to give or deal in return; to make return for; to reward, to avenge. **requital,** *n.* **requiter,** *n.* [RE-, *quite,* var. of QUIT]

rerail, *v.t.* to put (rolling stock) on the rails again. **reread,** *v.t.* to read or peruse again.

reredos, *n.* (*pl.* **-doses**) the ornamental screen at the back of an altar; the back of an open hearth, a fire-back. [ME *rere,* REAR[2], F *dos,* L *dorsum,* back]

rerun, *v.t.* to run (a race etc.) again; to show a film or television programme again. *n.* a repeated film etc.; a race run a second time.

res, *n.* (*pl.* **res**) a thing, property; subject matter of a court action. [L]

res., (*abbr.*) research; reserve; residence; resides; resigned; resolution.

resaddle, *v.t., v.i.* to saddle again. **resail,** *v.t.* to sail (a race etc.) again. *v.i.* to sail back again. **resale,** *n.* a second sale; a sale at second hand. †**resalute,** *v.t.* to salute again; to salute in return.

rescind, *v.t.* to annul, to cancel, to revoke, to abrogate; †to cut off or away. **rescission,** *n.* **rescissory,** *a.* [F *rescinder,* L *rescindere* (RE-, *scindere,* to cut, p.p. *scissus*)]

rescript, *n.* the answer or decision of a Roman emperor to a question or appeal, esp. on a point of jurisprudence; a Pope's written reply to a question of canon law, morality etc.; an edict, a decree, an order, or official announcement; something rewritten, the act of rewriting; a palimpsest. †**rescription,** *n.* †**rescriptive,**, *a.* †**rescriptively,** *adv.* [L *rescriptum,* neut. p.p. of prec.]

rescue, *v.t.* to deliver from confinement, danger, evil, or injury; (*Law*) to liberate by unlawful means from custody, to recover (property etc.) by force. *n.* deliverance from confinement, danger, evil or injury; forcible seizure (of a person, property etc.) from the custody of the law. **rescuable,** *a.* **rescuer,** *n.* [OF *rescoure,* ult. L *exutere* (EX-, *cutere, quatere,* to shake)]

research, *n.* diligent and careful inquiry or investigation; systematic study of phenomena etc., a course of critical investigation. *v.i.* to make researches. *v.t.* to make careful and systematic investigation into. **researcher,** *n.* [F *recerche* (now *recherche*)]

reseat, *v.t.* to seat again; to replace (a person) in a seat; to furnish (a church etc.) with new seats; to provide (a chair, pair of trousers etc.) with a new seat.

resect, *v.t.* (*Surg.*) to excise a section of an organ or part; to cut or pare down, esp. the articular extremity of a bone. **resection,** *n.* [L *resectus,* p.p. of *resecāre* (RE-, *secāre,* to cut)]

reseda, *n.* a genus of plants containing the mignonette and dyer's weed; a pale or greyish green (usu. in F form **réséda**). [L, prob. imper. of *resedāre,* to assuage (first word of a charm for allaying tumours)]

reseek, *v.t.* to seek again; **reseize,** *v.t.* to seize again; to take possession of (disseized lands and tenements); †to reinstate. †**reseizer,** *n.* †**reseizure,** *n.* (OF *resaisir* (F *ressaisir*)). **resell,** *v.t.* to sell again.

resemble, *v.t.* to be like, to be similar to; to have features, nature etc., like those of; †to liken, to compare, †to imitate, to counterfeit. †*v.i.* to be similar (to). †**resemblable,** *a.* **resemblance,** *n.* similarity; appearance. **resemblant,** *a.* [OF *resembler* (F *ressembler*) (RE-, *sembler,* L *similāre, simulāre,* from *similis,* SIMILAR)]

resend, *v.t.* to send back or again.

resent, *v.t.* to regard as an injury or insult; to feel or show displeasure or indignation at; to cherish bitter feelings about; †to perceive by the senses, to be sensibly affected by. *v.i.* to feel indignant. **resenter,** *n.* **resentful,** *a.* **resentfully,** *adv.* **resentfulness,** *n.* **resentingly,** *adv.* †**resentive,** *a.* **resentment,** *n.* [F *ressentir* (RE-, *sentir,* L *sentire,* to feel)]

reserpine, *n.* an alkaloid extracted from *Rauwolfia serpentina* used to treat high blood pressure and as a sedative. [G *Reserpin,* prob. from the L name of the plant]

reservation, *n.* the act of reserving; that which is reserved; the booking of accommodation in a hotel, train, ship etc.; (*N Am.*) a tract of land reserved for native Indian tribes or for public use; in the Roman Catholic church, the reserving of the right of nomination to benefices, of the power of absolution, or of a portion of the consecrated elements of the Eucharist; an expressed or tacit limitation, exception, or qualification; a strip of land separating a dual carriageway.

mental reservation, an unexpressed qualification or exception radically affecting or altering the meaning of a statement, oath etc.

reserve, *v.t.* to keep back for future use, enjoyment, treatment etc., to hold over, to postpone, to keep in store; to retain for oneself or another, esp. as an exception from something granted; to book, keep or set apart; to retain the right of nomination to a benefice for the Pope; to set apart (a case) for absolution by the Pope, a bishop etc.; to retain a portion of the consecrated elements of the Eucharist; (*in p.p.*) to set apart for a certain fate, to destine; †to preserve. *n.* that which is reserved; a sum of money or a fund reserved, esp. by bankers, to meet any demand; a reservation of land for a special use; troops kept for any emergency, such as to act as reinforcements or cover a retreat; a part of the military or naval forces not embodied in the regular army and navy, but liable to be called up in case of emergency; a member of these forces, a reservist; the state of being reserved or kept back for a special purpose; (*Sport*) a substitute; mental reservation, exception or qualification; a limitation attached to a price etc.; an award to an exhibit entitling it to a prize if another should be disqualified; reticence, self-restraint, caution in speaking or action. **in reserve,** reserved from and ready for use in emergency. **without reserve,** fully, without reservation; (offered for sale) to the highest bidder without the condition of a reserve price. **reserve currency,** *n.* a foreign currency acceptable as a medium of international banking transactions and held in reserve by many countries. **reserve price,** *n.* a price below which no offer will be accepted. †**reservative,** *a.* †**reservatory,** *n.* a receptacle, a reservoir. **reserved,** *a.* reticent, backward in communicating one's thoughts or feelings, undemonstrative, distant; retained for a particular use, person etc. **reserved list,** *n.* a list of naval officers not on active service but liable to be called up in emergency. **reserved occupation,** *n.* vital employment which exempts one from military service in the event of war. **reserved sacrament,** *n.* portion of the consecrated elements reserved after communion, for adoration. **reservedly**, *adv.* **reservedness**, *n.* **reservist,** *n.* a member of the military or naval reserve. [OF *reserver,* L *reservāre* (*servāre,* to keep)]

reservoir, *n.* a receptacle in which a quantity of anything, esp. fluid, may be kept in store; a receptacle of earthwork or masonry for the storage of water in large quantity; a part of an implement, machine, animal or vegetable organ etc., acting as a receptacle for fluid; a reserve supply or store of anything. *v.t.* to collect or store in a reservoir. [F *réservoir,* late L *reservātorium,* as prec.]

reset[1], *v.t.* to set (type, a jewel etc.) again. *n.* (*Print.*) matter set up again. **resettable,** *a.* [RE-, SET[1]]

reset[2], *n.* the receiving of stolen goods; (*Sc. Law*) the act of harbouring an outlaw or criminal. *v.t.* (*Sc. Law*) to receive (stolen goods); †to harbour (an outlaw etc.). *v.i.* to receive stolen goods. **resetter,** *n.* [OF *recet,* L *receptum,* p.p. of *recipere,* to RECEIVE]

resettle, *v.t.* and *i.* to settle again. **resettlement,** *n.* **res gestae,** *n.pl.* achievements; exploits; (*Law*) relevant facts or circumstances admissible in evidence. **reshape,** *v.t.* to shape again. **reshuffle,** *v.t.* to shuffle again; to rearrange, or reorganize, esp. cabinet or government department. *n.* the act of reshuffling.

†**resiant,** *a.* residing, resident. *n.* a resident. †**resiance,** *n.* [OF *reseant,* pres.p. of *reseoir,* L *residēre,* to RESIDE]

reside, *v.i.* to dwell permanently or for a considerable length of time, to have one's home (at); to be in official residence; (of qualities, rights etc.) to inhere, to be vested (in), †to be precipitated, to sink. **residence**, *n.* the act or state of residing in a place; the act of living or remaining where one's duties lie; the place where one dwells, one's abode; a house of some size or pretensions. **in residence,** actually resident; of an artist, writer etc., acting in a regular capacity for a limited period at a gallery, university etc. **residency,** *n.* formerly the official residence of a resident or governor of a British protectorate in India; a period of specialized training undertaken by a doctor following internship. **resident**, *a.* residing; having a residence, esp. official quarters in connection with one's duties; non-migratory; inherent; †fixed, firm. *n.* one who dwells permanently in a place as dist. from a visitor; a representative of the British government in a British protectorate; a junior doctor who lives and works in a hospital to gain specialized experience; a non-migratory bird or animal. **residenter,** *n.* (*Sc.*) a resident. **residential**, *a.* suitable for residence or for residences; pertaining to residence. **residentiary**, *a.* maintaining or bound to an official residence. *n.* an ecclesiastic bound to an official residence. [F *résider,* L *residēre* (RE-, *sedēre,* to sit)]

residue, *n.* that which is left or remains over; the rest, remainder; that which remains of an estate after payment of all charges, debts, and particular bequests; residuum. **residual**, *a.* of the nature of a residue or residuum; remaining after a part has been taken away; (*Math.*) left by a process of subtraction; remaining unexplained or uneliminated. *n.* a residual quantity, a remainder; the difference between the computed and the observed value of a quantity at any given moment, a residual error; a payment to an artist for reuse of a film, recording etc. **residuary**, *a.* pertaining to or forming a residue, residual, remaining; pertaining to the residue of an estate. **residuum**, *n.* (*pl.* **-dua**) that which is left after any process of separation or purification, esp. after combustion, evaporation etc.; the remainder left by subtraction or division, a residual error; the lowest classes, the dregs of society. [A-F (F *résidu*), L *residuum,* nom. *-duus,* remaining, as prec.]

resign[1], *v.t.* to sign again.

resign[2], *v.t.* to give up, to surrender, to relinquish; to hand over (to or unto); to renounce, to abandon; to yield, to submit, to reconcile (oneself, one's mind etc. to). *v.i.* to give up office, to retire (from). **resignation**, *n.* the act of resigning, esp. an office; a document announcing this; the state of being resigned, patience, acquiescence, submission. **resigned,** *a.* submissive, patiently acquiescent or enduring; surrendered, given up. **resignedly**, *adv.* †**resignee**, **resigner,** *n.* †**resignment,** *n.* [OF *resigner,* L *resignare,* to unseal (RE-, *signāre,* to seal, see SIGN)]

resile, *v.i.* to spring back, to rebound, to recoil; to resume the original shape after compression, stretching etc.; to show elasticity. **resilience, -cy,** *n.* elasticity; (of a person) an ability to recover quickly from physical illness, misfortune etc. **resilient,** *a.* †**resilition**, *n.* [obs. F *resiler,* L *resilēre* (RE-, *salīre,* to leap)]

resin, *n.* an amorphous inflammable vegetable substance secreted by plants and usu. obtained by exudation, esp. from the fir and pine; a similar substance obtained by the chemical synthesis of various organic materials, used esp. in making plastics. *v.t.* to treat with resin. †**resinaceous**, *a.* **resiniferous**, **resiniform**, *a.* **resinify**, *v.t.*, *v.i.* **resinification**, *n.* **resinoid**, *n.*, *a.* **resinolic**, *a.* **resinous,** *a.* pertaining to or resembling resin; obtained from resin; (*Elec.*) negative. **resinously,** *adv.* **resinousness,** *n.* **resiny,** *a.* [F *résine,* L *rēsīna,* rel. to Gr. *rhētinē*]

resipiscence, *n.* wisdom after the fact; recognition of error etc. **resipiscent,** *a.* [L *resipiscentia,* from *resipiscere* (RE-, *sapere,* to be wise, see SAPIENT)]

resist, *v.t.* to stand or strive against, to act in opposition to, to endeavour to frustrate; to oppose successfully, to withstand, to stop, to repel, to frustrate, to be proof against; to be disagreeable to. *v.i.* to offer resistance. *n.* a substance applied to a surface etc. to prevent the action of a chemical agent, such as the mordant used in dyeing calico. **resistant,** *n.* someone or something that resists. *a.* offering resistance. **resistance,** *n.* the act or power of resisting; opposition, refusal to comply; that which hinders or retards, esp. the opposition exerted by a fluid to the passage of a body; the opposition exerted by a substance to the passage of electric current, heat etc. through it; the body's natural power to withstand disease; a resistance-coil etc. **line of least**

resistance, the easiest course of action. **resistance-coil,** *n.* a coil of insulated wire used to offer resistance to a current. **Resistance Movement,** *n.* an underground organization of civilians and others in an enemy-occupied country directed to sabotaging the invaders' plans and rendering their position as difficult as possible. **resistance thermometer,** *n.* a type of thermometer which accurately measures high temperatures from the change in resistance of a wire coil or semiconductor as the temperature varies. **passive resister** PASSIVE. **resistor,** *n.* an electronic component with a specified resistance. **resistible,** *a.* **resistibility**, **resistibleness,** *n.* **resistibly, resistingly,** *adv.* **resistive,** *a.* **resistivity**, *n.* (formerly called **specific resistance**) the electrical resistance of a conducting material of unit cross-sectional area and unit length. **resistless**, *a.* **resistlessly,** *adv.* **resistlessness,** *n.* [OF *resister*, L *resistere* (*sistere*, redupl. of *stare*, to stand)]

resit, *v.t.*, *v.i.* to sit (an examination) again after failing. *n.* an examination which one must sit again. **res judicata,** *n.* (*Law*) an issue that has already been settled in court and cannot be raised again.

Resnais, *n.* **Alain** (1922–), French film director, whose work is characterized by the themes of memory and unconventional concepts of time. His films include *Hiroshima mon amour* (1959), *L'Année Dernière à Marienbad/Last Year at Marienbad* (1961) and *Providence* (1977).

resoluble, *a.* capable of being dissolved, resolved or analysed. **resolute**, *a.* having a fixed purpose, determined, constant in pursuing an object, firm, decided, unflinching, bold. †*n.* a determined person, a desperado. **resolutely,** *adv.* **resoluteness,** *n.* **resolution,** *n.* the act or process of resolving or separating anything into the component parts, decomposition, analysis; analysis of a force into two or more jointly equivalent, as in a parallelogram of forces; the disappearance of inflammation without production of pus; (*Mus.*) the conversion of a discord into a concord; the substitution of two short syllables for a long one; the definition of a television or film image; mental analysis, solution of a problem etc.; a formal proposition, statement of opinion, or decision by a legislative or corporate body or public meeting; a proposition put forward for discussion and approval; a resolve, a settled purpose; resoluteness, determination, firmness and boldness in adhering to one's purpose. **resolutionist,** *n.* one who makes or supports a resolution. **resolutive,** *a.* having the power or tending to resolve, dissolve, or relax; a drug or application for reducing inflammation. †**resolutory,** *a.* [L *resolūtus*, p.p. of *resolvere*, see foll.]

resolve, *v.t.* to separate into the component parts; to dissolve, to analyse, to disintegrate, to dissipate; to reduce to the constituent parts or elements; to analyse mentally, to solve, to explain, to clear up, to answer; to convert (into) by analysis; (*Med.*) to cause to disperse or pass away without suppuration; (*Mus.*) to convert (a discord) into concord; to make up one's mind, to decide, to determine on; to pass by vote a resolution that; to cause (a person) to decide or determine; †to relax. *v.i.* to separate into the component parts, to dissolve, to break up, to be analysed; (*Med.*) to pass away without suppuration; (*Mus.*) to be converted from discord into concord; to make one's mind up, to decide or determine (upon); to pass a resolution. *n.* a resolution, a firm decision or determination; resoluteness, firmness of purpose; (*N Am.*) a resolution by a deliberative assembly. **resolvable,** *a.* **resolvability**, †**resolvableness,** *n.* **resolved,** *a.* determined, resolute. **resolvedly**, *adv.* †**resolvedness**, *n.* **resolvent,** *a.* having the power of resolving, dissolving, or disintegrating. *n.* that which has the power of resolving, esp. a chemical substance, drug, or medical application, a discutient. **resolver,** *n.* **resolving power,** *n.* the ability of a microscope or telescope to distinguish or produce separable images of small adjacent objects; the ability of a photographic emulsion to produce fine detailed images. [L *resolvere* (RE-, *solvere*, to loosen, see SOLVE)]

resonant, *a.* capable of returning sound; re-echoing, resounding; having the property of prolonging or reinforcing sound, esp. by vibration; (of sounds) prolonged or reinforced by vibration or reverberation. **resonance,** *n.* the quality or state of being resonant; sympathetic vibration; (*Eng., Elec.*) the specially large vibration of a body or system when subjected to a small periodic force of the same frequency as the natural frequency of the system; the amplification of human speech by sympathetic vibration in the bone structure of the head and chest resounding in the vocal tract; (*Chem.*) the description of the electronic structure of a molecule in certain compounds in terms of different arrangements of two or more bonds. **resonantly,** *adv.* **resonate,** *v.i.* to resound; reverberate. **resonator,** *n.* a body or system that detects and responds to certain frequencies; a device for enriching or amplifying sound. [L *resonans -ntem*, pres.p. of *resonāre* (RE-, *sonāre*, to SOUND[2])]

resorb, *v.t.* to absorb again. **resorbence,** *n.* **resorbent,** *a.* **resorption**, *n.* **resorptive,** *a.* [L *resorbēre* (*sorbēre*, to drink in, p.p. *sorptus*)]

resorcin, resorcinol, *n.* a crystalline phenol, $C_6H_4(OH)_2$, used as a dye-stuff in resins, adhesives, and in medicine. [RESIN, ORCIN]

resorption, resorptive RESORB.

resort[1], *v.i.* to go, to repair, to betake oneself; to have recourse, to apply, to turn to (for aid etc.). *n.* the act of frequenting a place; the state of being frequented; the place frequented, esp. a place popular with holiday makers; recourse; that to which one has recourse, an expedient; a concourse, a company, a meeting. **last resort,** that to which one comes for aid or relief when all else has failed; the final tribunal; a final attempt. **resorter,** *n.* [OF *resortir* (F *ressortir*), to come out, etym. doubtful]

resort[2], *v.t.* to sort again.

resound, *v.i.* to ring, to re-echo, to reverberate (with); to be filled with sound (of a place); to be re-echoed, to be repeated, reinforced, or prolonged (of sounds, instruments etc.); to be noised abroad, to make a sensation (of news, events etc.). *v.t.* to sound again; to return the sound of; to spread the fame of. †*n.* an echo, a resonance. **resounding,** *a.* clear, decisive; ringing, resonant. **resoundingly,** *adv.* [SOUND[2], after F *resonner*, cp. RESONANT]

resource, *n.* a means of aid, support, or safety; an expedient, a device; (*pl.*) means of support and defence, esp. of a country; capacity for finding or devising means; fertility in expedients, practical ingenuity; †possibility of being aided. **resourceful,** *a.* ingenious, clever, full of expedients. **resourcefully,** *adv.* **resourcefulness,** *n.* **resourceless**, *a.* **resourcelessness,** *n.* [F *ressource*, from OF *ressourdre*, from L *resurgere* (RE-, *surgere*, to rise)]

re-speak, *v.t.* to speak again; to echo back.

respect, *n.* relation, regard, reference; attention, heed (to), regard (to or of); particular, aspect, point; esteem, deferential regard, demeanour, or attention; (*pl.*) expressions of esteem sent as a complimentary message. *v.t.* to esteem, to regard with deference; to treat with consideration, to spare from insult, injury, interference etc.; to relate or have reference to; †to heed, to regard. †**in respect of,** in comparison with. **in respect to,** with regard to. **to pay one's respects,** to send a message of esteem or compliment. **respectable,** *a.* worthy of respect, of good repute; of fair social standing, honest, decent, not disreputable; fairly good, tolerable, passable; not mean, not inconsiderable, above the average in number, quantity, merit etc. **respectability**, **respectableness,** *n.* the quality or character of being respectable; one who is respectable. **respectably,** *adv.* **respecter,** *n.* **respecter of persons,** one who pays undue consideration to and is biased by wealth and station. **respectful,** *a.* showing respect. **respectfully,** *adv.* **respectfulness,** *n.* **respecting,** *prep.* in regard to, in respect of. **respective,**

a. relating severally to each of those in question, several, comparative, relative. **respectively,** *adv.* †**respectless**, *a.* disrespectful; regardless, heedless; impartial. [F, from L *respectus,* p.p. of *respicere* (*specere,* to look)]

respell, *v.t.* to spell again.

Respighi, *n.* **Ottorino** (1879–1936), Italian composer, a student of Rimsky-Korsakov, whose works include the symphonic poems *The Fountains of Rome* (1917) and *The Pines of Rome* (1924) (incorporating the recorded song of a nightingale), operas, and chamber music.

respire, *v.i.* to breathe; to inhale or take air into and exhale it from the lungs; to recover breath; (*fig.*) to recover hope, spirit etc.; (*fig.*) to be alive; †to take rest, as after toil. *v.t.* to inhale and exhale, to breathe out, to emit (perfume etc.). **respirable**, *a.* capable of being respired; fit to be breathed; †that can respire. **respirability**, **respirableness,** *n.* **respiration**, *n.* the act or process of breathing; one act of inhaling and exhaling; the absorption of oxygen and emission of carbon dioxide by living organisms. **respirator**, *n.* an appliance worn over the mouth or mouth and nose to exclude poisonous gases, fumes etc., or to protect the lungs from the sudden inspiration of cold air; a gas-mask. **respiratory,** *a.* **respiratory disease,** *n.* any disease involving an organ concerned in respiration. **respiratory quotient,** *n.* (*Biol.*) the ratio of carbon dioxide expired to the volume of oxygen consumed by an organism or tissue in a given period. **respirometer**, *n.* an instrument for measuring respiration; an apparatus for supplying a diver with air for breathing. [F *respirer,* L *respīrāre* (RE-, *spīrāre,* to breathe)]

respite, *n.* a temporary intermission of labour, effort, suffering etc., esp. a delay in the execution of a sentence; an interval of rest or relief, a reprieve. *v.t.* to relieve by a temporary cessation of labour, suffering etc.; to grant a respite to, to reprieve; to suspend the execution of (a sentence); to postpone, to defer, to delay; (*Mil.*) to suspend from pay, to keep back (pay); †to save or prolong (one's life). **respiteless,** *a.* [OF *respit,* from L, as RESPECT]

resplendent, *a.* shining with brilliant lustre; vividly or gloriously bright. **resplendence, -cy,** *n.* **resplendently,** *adv.* [L *resplendens -ntem,* pres.p. of *resplendēre* (RE-, *splendēre,* to shine, to glitter)]

respond, *v.i.* to answer, to make reply (esp. of a congregation returning set answers to a priest); to perform an act or show an effect in answer or correspondence to; to react (to an external irritation or stimulus); to be responsive, to show sympathy or sensitiveness (to); †to correspond, to suit, to be analogous. *v.t.* to answer, to say in response. *n.* an anthem or versicle sung in response, a responsory; (*Arch.*) a half-column or half-pier in a wall supporting the impost of an arch. †**respondence,** †**-cy,** *n.* **respondent,** *a.* giving response, answering; responsive (to); in the position of defendant. *n.* one who answers; one who maintains a thesis in reply; one who answers in a suit at law, a defendant, esp. in a divorce case. **respondentia**, *n.* a loan upon a cargo repayable provided that the goods arrive safely. [OF *respondre* (F *répondre*), L *respondēre* (RE-, *spondēre,* to pledge, p.p. *sponsus*)]

response, *n.* the act of answering; that which is answered in word or act, an answer, a reply, a retort; a versicle or other portion of a liturgy said or sung in answer to the priest, a responsory; the ratio of the output to the input level on an electrical transmission system at any particular frequency; the reaction of an organism to stimulation. †**responsal,** *n.* a response; a responsory; a reaction, feeling, movement etc., called forth by an external stimulus, influence etc. **responsible,** *a.* answerable, liable, accountable (to or for); morally accountable for one's actions, able to discriminate between right and wrong; respectable, trustworthy; involving responsibility. **responsibility**, †**responsibleness,** *n.* the state of being responsible, as for a person, trust etc.; ability to act according to the laws of right and wrong; that for which one is responsible. **responsibly,** *adv.* **responsion**, *n.* a response; *pl.* formerly, the first of three examinations for the degree of BA at Oxford Univ. **responsive,** *a.* answering or inclined to answer; of the nature of an answer; reacting to stimulus; responding readily, sympathetic, impressionable. **responsively,** *adv.* **responsiveness,** *n.* **responsory,** *n.* an anthem said or sung alternately by the soloist and a choir after one of the lessons. *a.* of, pertaining to or of the nature of a response. [OF, from L *responsum,* neut. p.p. of *respondēre,* to RESPOND]

ressaldar, risaldar, *n.* the captain of a troop in Indian cavalry. [Hind.]

rest[1]**,** *n.* cessation from bodily or mental exertion or activity, repose, sleep; freedom from care, disturbance, or molestation, peace, tranquillity; a period of such cessation or freedom, esp. a brief pause or interval; a place of quiet and repose; a stopping-place, a place for lodging; a shelter for cabmen, sailors etc.; that on which anything stands or is supported, a prop, a support, a device for steadying a rifle on in taking aim, for supporting the cutting-tool in a lathe etc.; a long cue with a cross-piece at one end used as a support for a billiard cue in playing; (*Mus.*) an interval of silence, the sign indicating this; a pause in a verse, a caesura; death; †stay, abode, residence. *v.i.* to cease from exertion, motion, or activity; to be relieved from toil or exertion, to repose; to lie in sleep or death, to lie buried; to be still, to be without motion; to be free from care, disturbance, or molestation, to be tranquil, to be at peace; to be allowed to lie fallow (of land); to lie; to be spread out; to be supported or fixed, to be based, to lean, to recline, to stand (on); to depend, to rely (upon); to trust or put one's confidence (in God etc.); (of eyes) to be fixed, to be directed steadily (upon); to remain; (*US*) (of an attorney) to call no more evidence. *v.t.* to cause to cease from exertion; to give repose to, to lay at rest; (*in p.p.*) to refresh by resting; to give (oneself) rest; to place for support, to base, to establish, to lean, to lay, to support. **at rest,** reposing; not in motion; still; not disturbed, agitated, or troubled; (*euphem.*) dead, in the grave. **to lay to rest,** to bury. **to rest with,** to be left in the hands of. **rest-balk,** *n.* a ridge left unploughed between furrows. *v.t.* to plough so as to leave these. **rest-cure,** *n.* seclusion and repose (usu. in bed) as a method of treatment for nervous disorders. **rest-day,** *n.* a day of rest, esp. from marching; Sunday. **rest-house,** *n.* a place where travellers can rest. **rest mass,** *n.* the mass of an object at rest. **rest room,** *n.* (*N Am.*) a room with toilet facilities etc. in a public building. **restful,** *a.* inducing rest, soothing, free from disturbance; at rest, quiet. **restfully,** *adv.* **restfulness,** *n.* **resting-place,** *n.* a place for rest; the grave. **restless**, *a.* not resting, never still, agitated, uneasy, fidgety, unsettled, turbulent; not affording sleep, sleepless. **restlessly,** *adv.* **restlessness,** *n.* [OE *rest, ræst* (cp. Dut. *rust,* G *Raste,* Icel. *röst*), whence *ræstan,* to rest (cp. Dut. *rusten,* G *rasten*)]

rest[2]**,** *n.* that which is left, the remaining part or parts, the residue, the remainder; the others; a reserve fund, a balance or surplus fund for contingencies; a balancing, a stock-taking and balancing; (*Tennis*) a continuous series of quick returns of the ball. *v.i.* to remain, to stay, to continue (in a specified state); †to be left, to remain over. **all the rest,** all that remains, all the others. **for the rest** or **as for the rest,** as regards the remaining persons, matters, or things, as regards anything else. [F *reste,* from *rester,* L *restāre* (RE-, *stāre,* to stand)]

restamp, *v.t.* to stamp again.

restart, *v.t.*, *v.i.* to start afresh.

restate, *v.t.*, *v.i.* to state again or express differently.

restaurant, *n.* a place for refreshment; an eating house. **restaurant car,** *n.* a dining-car. **restaurateur**, *n.* the keeper of a restaurant. †**restauration**, *n.* restoration, reinstatement. [F, from *restaurer,* to RESTORE]

†**restem,** *v.t.* to stem again.

restful etc. REST[1].

rest-harrow, *n.* a shrubby pink-flowered plant, *Ononis* *arvensis,* also called cammock, with a tough woody root, arresting the prongs of the harrow, whence the name. [REST[3], HARROW[1]]

restiform, *a.* (*Anat.*) rope- or cord-like (applied to two bundles of fibrous matter connecting the medulla oblongata with the cerebellum). **restiform body,** *n.* either of these bundles. [L *restis,* cord, -FORM]

resting-place REST[1].

restitution, *n.* the act of restoring something taken away or lost; making good, reparation, indemnification; restoration to a former state or position; the resumption of its former shape by an elastic body. **restitutive, -ory,** *a.* [OF, from L *restitutiōnem,* nom. *-tio,* from *restituere* (RE-, *statuere,* to set up)]

restive, *a.* unwilling to go forward, standing still, halting, unruly, refractory; restless, fidgety, impatient of control, unmanageable. **restively,** *adv.* **restiveness,** *n.* [formerly *restiff,* OF *restif,* from *rester,* to REST[3]]

restock, *v.t.* to stock again.

restoration, restorative RESTORE.

restore, *v.t.* to bring back to a former state, to repair, to reconstruct; to put back, to replace, to return; to bring back to health, to cure; to bring back to a former position, to reinstate; to bring into existence or use again, to re-establish, to renew; to reproduce (a text or part of a text) by emendation, conjecture etc.; to represent (an extinct animal, mutilated picture, ruin etc.) as it is supposed to have been originally; to give back, to make restitution of. **restorable,** *a.* **restoration,** *n.* the act of restoring; a building etc., restored to its supposed original state; a skeleton of an extinct animal built up of its remains; a drawing, model, or other representation of a building, extinct animal etc., in its supposed original form. **the Restoration,** the return of Charles II in 1660 and the re-establishment of the monarchy after the Commonwealth; the return of the Bourbons to France in 1814. **Restoration comedy,** *n.* style of English theatre, dating from the Restoration. It witnessed the first appearance of women on the English stage, most notably in the 'breeches part', specially created in order to costume the actress in male attire, thus revealing her figure to its best advantage. The genre placed much emphasis on sexual antics. Examples include Wycherley's *The Country Wife* (1675), Congreve's *The Way of the World* (1700), and Farquhar's *The Beaux' Strategem* (1707). **restorationism,** *n.* the doctrine of the final restoration of all men to happiness and sinlessness in the future life. **restorationist,** *n.* **restorative,** *a.* tending to restore health, strength etc. *n.* food, drink, a medicine etc., for restoring strength, vigour etc., a stimulant, a tonic. **restoratively,** *adv.* **restorer,** *n.* [OF *restorer,* L *restaurāre* (RE-, *sta-,* root of *stāre,* to stand, cp. Gr. *stauros,* stake)]

restrain[1], *v.t.* to strain again.

restrain[2], *v.t.* to hold back, to check, to curb; to keep under control, to repress, to hold in check, to restrict; to confine, to imprison; †to forbear. **restrainable,** *a.* **restrainedly,** *adv.* **restrainer,** *n.* †**restrainment,** *n.* **restraint,** *n.* the act of restraining; the state of being restrained; check, repression, control, self-repression, avoidance of excess; constraint, reserve; restriction, limitation; abridgment of liberty, confinement. **restraint of trade,** interference with free competition in business. [OF *restraign-,* pres.p. stem of *restraindre* (F *restreindre*), L *restringere* (RE-, *stringere,* to draw tight, p.p. *strictus*)]

restrengthen, *v.t.* to strengthen anew.

restrict, *v.t.* to limit, to confine, to keep within certain bounds. **restricted,** *a.* limited, confined; out of bounds to the general public; denoting a zone where a speed limit or waiting restrictions apply for vehicles. **restriction,** *n.* something that restricts; a restrictive law or regulation; restricting or being restricted. **restrictive,** *a.* restricting or tending to restrict; (*Gram.*) describing a relative clause or phrase which restricts the application of the verb to the subject. **restrictive practice,** *n.* a trading agreement contrary to the public interest; a practice by a trade union, e.g. the closed shop, regarded as limiting managerial flexibility. **restrictedly, restrictively,** *adv.* [L *restrictus,* see RESTRAIN[2]]

restrike, *v.t.* to strike again.

†**restringe,** *v.t.* to restrict; to affect with costiveness; to astringe. †**restringent,** *a.* astringent. *n.* an astringent medicine. [L *restringere,* see RESTRAIN[2]]

restuff, *v.t.* to stuff anew.

†**resty,** *a.* restive; indolent, lazy. [var. of RESTIVE]

result, *v.i.* to be the actual or follow as the logical consequence, to ensue; to have an issue, to terminate or end (in). *n.* consequence, issue, outcome, effect; a quantity, value, or formula obtained from a calculation; a final score in a game or contest. **resultance,** *n.* **resultant,** *a.* resulting; following as a result; resulting from the combination of two factors, agents etc. *n.* that which results; the force resulting from the combination of two or more forces acting in different directions at the same point, ascertained by a parallelogram of forces. **resultful,** *a.* **resulting,** *a.* **resultless,** *a.* [F *résulter,* L *resultāre* (RE-, *saltāre,* freq. of *salīre,* to leap)]

resume, *v.t.* to take back, to take again, to reoccupy, to recover; to begin again, to recommence, to go on with after interruption; to sum up, to recapitulate, to make a résumé of. *v.i.* to continue after interruption, to recommence. **resumable,** *a.* [OF *resumer,* L *resūmere* (RE-, *sūmere,* to take, p.p. *sumptus*)]

résumé, *n.* a summary, a recapitulation, a condensed statement, an abstract; (*esp. N Am.*) a CURRICULUM VITAE. [F, p.p. of *résumer,* to RESUME]

resummon, *v.t.* to summon again; to convene again. **resummons,** *n.*

resumption, *n.* the act of resuming. **resumptive,** *a.* [L *resumptio,* from *resūmere,* to RESUME]

resupinate, *a.* (*Bot.*) inverted, apparently upside-down. **resupination,** *n.* †**resupine,** *a.* lying on the back, supine. [L *resupīnātus,* p.p. of *resupīnāre* (RE-, *supināre,* to make SUPINE)]

resurge, *v.i.* to rise again. **resurgence,** *n.* **resurgent,** *a.* rising again, rising from the dead. *n.* one who rises from the dead. [L *resurgere* (RE-, *surgere,* to rise)]

resurrect, *v.t.* to bring back to life; to bring again into vogue or currency, to revive; to exhume. **resurrection,** *n.* a rising again from the dead, esp. the rising of Christ from the dead, and the rising of all the dead at the Last Day; the state of being risen again; the future state; a springing again into life, vigour, vogue, or prosperity; exhumation, resurrecting, body-snatching. **resurrectionism,** *n.* belief in the Christian doctrine of resurrection. **resurrection-man, resurrectionist,** *n.* a body-snatcher. **resurrection plant,** *n.* a desert plant which curls into a tight ball in drought and unfolds when moistened. **resurrectional,** *a.* [OF, from late L *resurrectiōnem,* nom. *-tio,* from *resurgere,* to RESURGE]

resurvey, *v.t.* to survey again; to read and examine again. *n.* a renewed survey.

resuscitate, *v.t.* to revive, to restore from apparent death; to revivify, to restore to vigour, animation, usage etc. *v.i.* to revive, to come to life again. †*a.* restored to life. †**resusitable,** *a.* **resuscitant,** *n., a.* **resuscitation,** *n.* **resuscitative,** *a.* **resuscitator,** *n.* [L *resuscitātus,* p.p. of *resuscitāre* (RE-, SUS-, *citāre,* to CITE)]

ret, *v.t.* (*past, p.p.* **retted**) to subject (flax etc.) to the action of retting. *v.i.* to be spoilt by wet (of hay). **rettery,** *n.* **retting,** *n.* the act or process of steeping flax or hemp to loosen the fibre from the woody portions. [etym. obscure, cp. Dut. *reten,* Swed. *röta,* Norw. *röyta,* rel. to ROT]

ret., (*abbr.*) retain; retired; return(ed).

retable, *n.* a shelf, ledge or panelled frame above the back of an altar for supporting ornaments. [F *rétable,* after med. L *retrotabulum*]

retail, *n.* the sale of commodities in small quantities; a dealing out in small portions. *a.* pertaining to selling by retail. *v.t.* to sell in small quantities; to tell (a story etc.) in detail, to recount, to retell, to spread about. *v.i.* to be sold by retail (at or for a specified price). **retail price index,** an index of the cost of living, based on average retail prices of selected goods, usu. updated monthly. **retailer,** *n.* †**retailment,** *n.* [OF *retail, retaille,* from *retailler,* to cut off a piece (RE-, *tailler,* see TAILOR)]

retain, *v.t.* to hold or keep possession of, to keep; to continue to have, to maintain, to preserve; to hire, to engage the services of (esp. counsel) by paying a preliminary fee; to hold back, to keep in place; to remember. **retainable,** *a.* **retainer,** *n.* one who or that which retains; an attendant, a follower, esp. of a feudal chieftain; (*Law*) an agreement by which an attorney acts in a case; a preliminary fee paid (esp. to a counsel) to secure his services. **retaining fee,** *n.* a retainer. **retaining force,** *n.* a body of troops stationed to keep part of an enemy from interfering with large movements. **retaining wall,** *n.* a massive wall built to support and hold back the earth of an embankment, a mass of water etc. [OF *retenir,* L *retinēre* (RE-, *tenēre,* to hold)]

retake, *v.t.* (*pres.p.* **-taking,** *past* **-took,** *p.p.* **-taken**) to take again; to recapture; to shoot a film (scene) again; to record (a performance) again. *n.* a second photographing (of a scene); a rerecording.

retaliate, *v.t.* to return like for like, esp. evil for evil, to return or retort in kind. *v.i.* to return like for like, to make reprisals. **retaliation,** *n.* the act of retaliating; the imposition of import duties by one country against another which imposes duties on imports from the country first mentioned. **retaliative, -tory,** *a.* [L *retāliātus,* p.p. of *retāliāre* (RE-, *tāliāre,* from *tālis,* such, cp. *tālio,* retaliation)]

retard, *v.t.* to cause to move more slowly; to hinder, to impede, to check, restrain or delay the growth, advance, arrival or occurrence of. *v.i.* to be delayed; to happen or arrive abnormally late. *n.* delay, retardation. **retardant,** *n.* a substance that slows down a chemical reaction. *a.* serving to delay or slow down. **retardation,** *n.* **retardative, -tory,** *a.* **retarded,** *a.* underdeveloped intellectually or emotionally; subnormal in learning ability. **retarder,** *n.* someone or something that retards; a retardant, esp. an additive that delays cement setting. **retardment,** *n.* [F *retarder,* L *retardāre* (RE-, *tardus,* slow)]

retch, *v.i.* to make an effort to vomit; to strain, as in vomiting. *n.* the act or sound of retching. [OE *hrǣcan,* from *hrāca,* spittle (cp. Icel. *hrœkja,* from *hrāki,* spittle)]

retd, (*abbr.*) retained; retired; returned.

rete, *n.* (*pl.* **retia**) a network of nerves or blood-vessels. **retial,** *a.* [L *rēte,* a net]

retell, *v.t.* (*past, p.p.* **retold**) to tell again.

retention, *n.* the act of retaining; the state of being retained; confinement; the power of retaining, esp. ideas in the mind; (*Med.*) failure to evacuate urine etc., power of retaining food etc. †**retent,** *n.* that which is retained. **retentive,** *a.* **retentively,** *adv.* **retentiveness,** *n.* [OF from L *retentiōnem,* nom. *-tio,* from *retinēre,* to RETAIN]

rethink, *v.t.* to think again, to reconsider (a plan, decision etc.) and take an alternative view.

retiarius, *n.* (*pl.* **-arii**) a gladiator armed with a net and trident. [L *rētiārius,* from *rēte,* net]

reticent, *a.* reserved in speech; not disposed to communicate one's thoughts or feelings; keeping back something; inclined to keep one's own counsel; silent, taciturn. **reticence,** †**-cy,** *n.* **reticently,** *adv.* [L *reticens -ntem,* pres.p. of *reticēre* (RE-, *tacēre,* to be silent)]

reticle, *n.* a network of fine lines, etc., drawn across the focal plane of an optical instrument. **reticular,** *a.* having the form of a net or network; formed with interstices, retiform. **reticularly,** *adv.* †**reticulary,** *a.* **reticulate,** *v.t.* to make or divide into or arrange in a network, to mark with fine intersecting lines. *v.i.* to be divided into or arranged in a network. *a.*, formed of or resembling network. **reticulately,** *adv.* **reticulation,** *n.* **reticule,** *n.* a kind of bag, orig. of network; a lady's handbag; a reticle. **reticulum,** *n.* (*pl.* **reticula**) (*Anat.*) the second stomach of ruminants; a net-like or reticulated structure, membrane etc. [L *rēticulum,* dim. of *rēte,* net]

retiform, *a.* reticulated. [L *rēte,* net]

retina, *n.* (*pl.* **-nas, -nae**) a net-like layer of sensitive nerve-fibres and cells behind the eyeball in which the optic nerve terminates. **retinal,** *a.* [med. L, prob. from L *rēte,* net]

retinaculum, *n.* (*pl.* **-la**) (*Anat.*) a connecting band or cord; an apparatus in some insects controlling the sting; an apparatus by which the wings of insects are interlocked in flight. [L, from *retinēre,* to RETAIN]

retinalite, *n.* (*Min.*) a variety of serpentine with a resinous lustre. **retinite,** *n.* pitch-stone. †**retinoid,** *a.* **retinol,** *n.* a liquid hydrocarbon obtained from resin, used in pharmacy etc. [Gr. *rhētinē,* RESIN, -LITE]

retinitis, *n.* inflammation of the retina.

retin(o)-, *comb. form* pertaining to the retina. [RETINA]

†**retinoid, retinol** RETINALITE.

retinoscopy, *n.* examination of the eye using an instrument that throws a shadow onto the retina. **retinoscopic,** *a.* **retinoscopically,** *adv.*

retinue, *n.* the attendants on a distinguished person. [ME and OF *retenue,* p.p. of *retenir,* to RETAIN]

retire, *v.i.* to withdraw, to go away, to fall back, to retreat, to recede; to withdraw from business to a private life; to resign one's office or appointment, to cease from or withdraw from active service; to go to or as to bed; to go into privacy or seclusion. *v.t.* to cause to retire or resign; to order (troops) to retire; to withdraw (a bill or note) from circulation or operation. *n.* a signal (to troops) to retire; †retirement, seclusion. **retired,** *a.* private, withdrawn from society; given to privacy or seclusion; secluded, sequestered; having given up business etc. **retired list,** *n.* a list of retired officers, etc., usually on half-pay. †**retiredly,** *adv.* **retiredness,** *n.* **retirement,** *n.* **retiring,** *a.* unobtrusive, not forward, unsociable. **retiringly,** *adv.* **retiringness,** *n.* [OF *retirer* (RE-,*tirer,* to draw, from Teut.)]

retold, *past, p.p.* RETELL.

retool, *v.t., v.i.* to replace or re-equip (a factory etc.) with new tools. *v.t.* to reorganize, remake.

†**retorsion,** var. of RETORTION.

retort[1], *n.* a vessel with a bulb-like receptacle and a long neck bent downwards used for distillation of liquids etc.; a large receptacle of fire-clay, iron etc. of analogous shape, used for the production of coal-gas. *v.t.* to purify (mercury etc.) by treatment in a retort. [F *retorte,* as foll.]

retort[2], *v.t.* to turn or throw back; to turn (an argument, accusation, etc.) on or against the author; to pay back (an attack, injury etc.) in kind; to say, make, or do, by way of repartee etc. *v.i.* to turn an argument or charge against the originator or aggressor. *n.* the turning of a charge, taunt, attack etc. against the author or aggressor; a sharp rejoinder, a repartee. †**retorted,** *a.* recurved, bent or twisted back. **retorter,** *n.* **retortion,** *n.* bending, turning, or twisting back; the act of retorting; retaliation by a state on the subjects of another without actual war. †**retortive,** *a.* [L *retortus,* p.p. of *retorquēre* (*torquēre,* to twist)]

retouch, *v.t.* to touch again; to improve (a photograph, picture etc.) by new touches. *n.* a second touch given to a picture etc.; a photograph, painting etc. that has been retouched. **retoucher,** *n.* **retouchment,** *n.* **retrace,** *v.t.* to trace back to the beginning, source etc.; to go over (one's course or track) again; (*fig.*) to go over again in memory, to try to recollect; to trace (an outline) again. **retraceable,** *a.*

retract, *v.t.* to draw back or in; to take back, to revoke, to recall, to recant, to disavow, to acknowledge to be false or erroneous. *v.i.* to withdraw, to shrink back; to withdraw or recall a declaration, promise, concession etc. **retractable, retractile,** *a.* capable of being retracted. **retractability, retractility,** *n.* **retractation,** *n.* the act of retracting, disavowing, or recanting. **retraction,** *n.* the act or process of drawing in; the act of retracting; retractation. **retractive,** *a.* serving to retract or draw in. **retractor,** *n.* a muscle used for drawing back; an instrument or bandage for holding back parts in the way of a surgeon; a contrivance for withdrawing cartridge-cases from the breech. [L *retractus,* p.p. of *retrahere* (*trahere,* to draw), later senses from *retractāre,* to revoke, freq. of *retrahere*]

†**retrait,** *n.* a picture, a portrait. [It. *ritratto,* as prec.]

retral, *a.* situated at the back, posterior, hinder; bending backward. [RETRO-, -AL]

retransfer, *v.t.* to transfer again. *n.* an act of retransferring. **retransform,** *v.t.* to transform anew. **retransformation,** *n.* **retranslate,** *v.t.* to translate again; to translate back again to the original language. **retranslation,** *n.* **retraxit,** *n.* (*Law*) the voluntary withdrawing of a suit by the plaintiff (L, he withdrew, as RETRACT). **retread,** *v.t.* (*past* **retrod,** *p.p.* **-trodden**) to tread again; to remould a tyre. *n.* (*Austral.*) a re-enlisting soldier; a retired man who re-enters his employment; a used tyre which has had its worn tread replaced.

retreat, *n.* the act of withdrawing or retiring, esp. the retiring of an army before an enemy; a signal for such retirement; a drum-beat at sunset; a state of retirement or seclusion; a period of retirement; a place of retirement, security, privacy, or seclusion; a lurking-place, a lair, a refuge, as asylum for lunatics, inebriates, aged persons etc.; retirement for meditation, prayer etc. *v.i.* to move back, to retire, esp. before an enemy or from an advanced position; to withdraw to a place of privacy, seclusion, or security; to recede. *v.t.* to cause to retire; (*Chess*) to move (a piece) back. [OF *retret, -trete* (F *retraite*), p.p. of *retraire,* L *retrahere,* to RETRACT]

retrench, *v.t.* to cut down, to reduce, to curtail, to diminish; to shorten, to abridge, to cut out or pare down; (*Mil.*) to furnish with a retrenchment. *v.t.* to curtail expenses, to make economies. **retrenchment,** *n.* the act of retrenching; a work constructed with or behind another to prolong a defence. [F *retrencher,* obs. var. of *retrancher* (TRENCH)]

retrial, *n.* a new trial.

retribution, *n.* recompense, a suitable return, esp. for evil; requital, vengeance; the distribution of rewards and punishments in the future life. †**retribute,** *v.t.* **retributive, -tory,** *a.* **retributor,** *n.* [OF *retribucion, -tion,* L *retributio,* acc. *-ōnem,* from *retribuere* (*tribuere,* to assign)]

retrieve, *v.t.* to find and bring in (esp. of a dog bringing in game or a stick, ball etc.); to recover by searching or recollecting, recall to mind; to regain (that which has been lost, impaired etc.); to rescue (from); to restore, to re-establish (one's fortunes etc.); to remedy, to make good, to repair; in tennis etc., to return a difficult ball successfully; to recover data stored in a computer system. *v.i.* to fetch (of a dog). **retrievable,** *a.* **retrievably,** *adv.* †**retrieval,** *n.* †**retrievement,** *n.* **retriever,** *n.* a dog usu. of a special breed, trained to fetch in game that has been shot. [OF *retroev-,* a stem of *retrover* (*trouver,* to find, see TROVER and CONTRIVE[1])]

retrim, *v.t.* to trim again. [RE-, TRIM]

retro-, *pref.* backwards, back; in return; (*Anat. etc.*) behind. [L, behind, backwards]

retroact, *v.i.* to act backwards or in return; to act retrospectively, to react. **retroaction, retroactivity,** *n.* **retroactive,** *a.* (of laws etc.) applying to the past; operating backward. **retroactively,** *adv.* [L *retroactus,* p.p. of *retroagere* (ACT)]

retrocede, *v.t.* to cede back again, to restore (territory etc.). *v.i.* to move backward; to recede. **retrocedent, retrocessive,** *a.* **retrocession,** *n.* [L *retrōcēdere* (*cēdere,* to yield, to go back, see CEDE)]

retrochoir, *n.* a part of a cathedral or other large church east of or beyond the high altar.

retrofit, *v.t.* (*pres.p.* **-fitting,** *past, p.p.* **-fitted**) to equip or modify (an aircraft, car etc.) with new parts or safety equipment after manufacture.

retroflected, retroflex, -flexed, *a.* turned or curved backward; (of vowels or consonants) articulated with the tip of the tongue bent upwards and backwards. **retroflexion, retroflection,** *n.* [med. L *retroflexus,* p.p. of *retroflectere* (*flectere,* to bend)]

retrofract, -fracted, *a.* (*Bot.*) bent back so as to look as if broken. [cp. REFRACT]

retrograde, *a.* going, moving, bending or directed backwards; inverted, reversed; declining, degenerating, deteriorating; (*Astron.*) applied to the motion of a planet relatively to the fixed stars when it is apparently from east to west; †opposite, contrary. *n.* a backward movement or tendency, deterioration, decline; a degenerate person. *v.i.* to move backward; to decline, to deteriorate, to revert, to recede; (*Astron.*) to move or appear to move from east to west relatively to the fixed stars. †*v.t.* to turn back, to cause to go backward. **retrogradation,** *n.* retrogression; (*Astron.*) backward or apparently backward motion of a planet in the zodiac or relatively to the fixed stars. [L *retrōgradus,* from *retrōgradī,* to go backward (*gradī,* to go)]

retrogress, *v.i.* to go backward, to retrograde; to degenerate. **retrogression,** *n.* **retrogressive,** *a.* **retrogressively,** *adv.* [L *retrōgressus,* p.p. of *retrōgradī,* as prec.]

retromingent, *a.* discharging the urine backwards. *n.* an animal that discharges the urine backwards. [L *mingens -ntem,* pres.p. of *mingere,* to make water]

retropulsion, *n.* shifting of a disease from an external to an internal part; a locomotory disease characterized by a tendency to make the patient walk backwards. **retropulsive,** *a.*

retrorocket, *n.* a small rocket on a spacecraft, satellite etc. which produces thrust in the opposite direction to flight for deceleration or manoeuvring.

retrorse, *a.* turned or bent backwards, reverted. **retrorsely,** *adv.* [L *retrorsus* (*versus,* p.p. of *vertere,* to turn)]

retrospect, *n.* a looking back on things past; view of, regard to, or consideration of previous conditions etc.; a review of past events. *v.i.* to look or refer back (to). *v.t.* to view or consider retrospectively. **retrospection,** *n.* **retrospective,** *a.* in retrospection; viewing the past; applicable to what has happened; licensing, condoning, or condemning a past action. *n.* an exhibition of an artist's life work. **retrospectively,** *adv.* [L *retrospectus,* p.p. of *retrospicere* (RETRO-, *specere,* to look)]

retroussé, *a.* turned up at the end (of the nose). [F, p.p. of *retrousser*]

retrovert, *v.t.* to turn back, esp. of the womb. **retroversion,** *n.* [late L *retrovertere* (RETRO-, *vertere,* to turn, p.p. *versus*)]

retrovirus, *n.* any of a group of viruses that uses RNA to synthesize DNA, reversing the normal process of cellular transcription of DNA into RNA. Many cause cancer in animals and one is the cause of Aids in humans.

retry, *v.t.* to try again.

retsina, *n.* a resin-flavoured white wine from Greece. [mod. Gr. from It. *resina,* resin]

rettery, retting RET.

returf, *v.t.* to turf again.

return, *v.i.* to come or go back, esp. to the same place or state; to revert, to happen again, to recur; †to answer, to retort. *v.t.* to bring, carry, or convey back; to give, render, to send back; to repay, to put or send back or in return, to requite; to say in reply, to retort; to report officially; to elect; to play a card of the same suit as another player has led. *n.* the act of coming or going back; the act of giving, paying, putting, or sending back; that which is returned; an official account or report; a sheriff's report on a writ or a returning officer's announcement of a candidate's election; the act of electing or returning; the state of being elected; the proceeds or profits on labour, investments etc. (*often in pl.*); a return bend in a pipe etc.; (*Arch.*) a receding part of a façade etc., a part of a hood-moulding etc. bending in another direction; (*Games, Fencing etc.*) a stroke, thrust etc. in return; a return match or game; (*Law*) the rendering back or delivery of a writ, precept, or execution to the proper officer or court; (*pl.*) a mild kind of tobacco, orig. refuse of tobacco. **by return (of post),** by the next post back to the sender. **in return,** in reply or response; in requital; sent, given etc. back. **many happy returns,** a birthday greeting.

to return a lead, (*Cards*) to lead from the same suit. **to return thanks,** to offer thanks; to answer a toast. **return-day,** *n.* (*Law*) the day on which the defendant is to appear in court, or the sheriff is to return his writ. **return game** or **match,** *n.* a second meeting of the same clubs or teams. **return ticket,** *n.* a ticket for a journey to a place and back again; the return-half of such a ticket. **returnable,** *a.* **returner,** *n.* **returning officer,** *n.* the presiding officer at an election. **returnable, returnless,** *a.* [OF *returner* (F *retourner*)]

retuse, *a.* having a round end with a depression in the centre. [L *retūsus,* p.p. of *retundere* (RE-, *tundere,* to beat)]

Retz, *n.* **Jean François Paul de Gondi, Cardinal de Retz** (1614–79), French politician. A priest with political ambitions, he stirred up and largely led the insurrection of the Fronde. After a period of imprisonment and exile he was restored to favour in 1662 and created abbot of St Denis.

Réunion, *n.* French island of the Mascarenes group, in the Indian Ocean, 650 km/400 miles E of Madagascar, and 180 km/110 miles SW of Mauritius. **area** 2512 sq km/970 sq miles. **capital** St Denis. **physical** forested, rising in Piton de Neiges to 3069 m/10,072 ft. **population** (1987) 565,000. **products** sugar, maize, vanilla, tobacco, rum.

reunion, *n.* the act of reuniting; the state of being reunited; a meeting or social gathering, esp. of friends, associates, or partisans. **reunite,** *v.t.* to join again after separation; to reconcile after variance. *v.i.* to become united again. †**reunition,** *n.* †**reunitive,** *a.* [F *réunion* (UNION)]

Reus, *n.* industrial city with an international airport in Catalonia, E Spain, 10 km/6 miles NW of Tarragona.

reuse, *v.t.* to use again. *n.* the act of using again.

Reuter, *n.* **Paul Julius, Baron de Reuter** (1816–99), German founder of Reuters international news agency. He began a continental pigeon post 1849, and in 1851 he set up a news agency in London. In 1858 he persuaded the press to use his news telegrams, and the service became worldwide.

Rev., (*abbr.*) Revelation (of St John the Divine); Reverend.

rev, *n.* a revolution in an engine. *v.t., v.i.* (*pres.p.* **revving,** *past, p.p.* **revved**) to run an engine quickly by increasing the speed of revolution. **rev counter,** *n.* (*coll.*) TACHOMETER. [abbr. of REVOLUTION]

rev., (*abbr.*) revenue; reverse(d); review; revise(d); revision; revolution; revolving.

revalenta, *n.* a lentil meal. [altered from *ervalenta,* from L *ervum lens,* LENTIL]

revalorization, *n.* (*Econ.*) restoration of the value of currency.

revalue, *v.t.* to adjust the exchange rate of a currency, usu. upwards; to reappraise. **revaluation,** *n.*

revamp, *v.t.* to renovate, to restore the appearance of. *n.* something renovated or revamped; the act or process of revamping.

revanche, *n.* a policy directed towards restoring lost territory or possessions. **revanchism,** *n.* **revanchist,** *n., a.* [F]

Revd, (*abbr.*) Reverend.

reveal[1], *v.t.* to make known by supernatural or divine means; to disclose, to divulge (something secret, private or unknown), to betray; to allow to appear. *n.* †revelation. **revealable,** *a.* **revealer,** *n.* **revealing,** *a.* significant; exposing more of the body than is usual (of a dress etc.). **revealingly,** *adv.* **revealment,** *n.* [OF *reveler,* L *revēlāre* (*vēlāre,* from *vēlum,* VEIL)]

reveal[2], *n.* the depth of a wall as revealed in the side of an aperture, doorway or window. [earlier *revale,* from OF *revaler* (RE-, *valer, avaler,* to VAIL[1])]

réveillé, *n.* a morning signal by drum or bugle to awaken soldiers or sailors. [F *réveillez,* awake, pl. imper. of *réveiller* (RE-, *veiller,* L *vigilāre,* to watch, see VIGIL)]

revel, *v.i.* (*pres.p.* **revelling,** *past, p.p.* **revelled**) to make merry, to feast, to carouse; to be boisterously festive; to take unrestrained enjoyment (in). *v.t.* to spend or waste in revelry. *n.* an act of revelling, a carouse, a merry-making. **revel-rout,** *n.* tumultuous festivity; a band of revellers. **reveller,** *n.* †**revelment, revelry,** *n.* [OF *reveler,* L *revellāre,* to revel]

revelation, *n.* the act of revealing, a disclosing of knowledge or information; that which is revealed, esp. by God to man; an astonishing disclosure. **Revelation,** *n.* last book of the New Testament, traditionally attributed to the author of the Gospel of St John but now generally held to be the work of another writer. It describes a vision of the end of the world, of the Last Judgment, and of a new heaven and earth ruled by God from Jerusalem. **revelational,** *a.* **revelationist,** *n.* one who believes in divine revelation; the author of the Apocalypse. **revelative, -tory,** *a.* [ME and OF *revelacion,* L *revēlātiōnem,* nom. *-tio,* from *revēlāre,* to REVEAL[1]]

reveller, †revelment, revelry REVEL.

revenant, *n.* one who returns from the grave or from exile, esp. a ghost. [F, from *revenir,* L *revenīre* (*venīre,* to come)]

revendication, *n.* (*International Law*) a formal claim for the surrender of rights, esp. to territory. **revendicate,** *v.t.* [F]

revenge, *v.t.* to exact satisfaction or retribution for, to requite, to retaliate; to avenge or satisfy (oneself) with such retribution or retaliation; to inflict injury on in a malicious spirit. *v.i.* to exact vengeance. *n.* retaliation, requital, retribution or spiteful return for an injury; a means, mode or act of revenging; the desire to inflict revenge, vindictiveness. **revengeful,** *a.* **revengefully,** *adv.* **revengefulness,** *n.* **revengeless,** *a.* **revengement,** *n.* **revenger,** *n.* **revengingly,** *adv.* [OF *revenger*]

revenue, *n.* income, esp. from a considerable amount of many forms of property (*often in pl.*); the annual income of a state, derived from taxation, customs, excise etc.; the department of the Civil Service collecting this; †return, reward. **inland revenue** INLAND. **revenue-cutter,** *n.* a vessel employed to prevent smuggling. **revenue-officer,** *n.* a customs officer. **revenue-tax,** *n.* one for raising revenue not to affect trade, opp. to protective. [F, fem. p.p. of *revenir,* to return (L *revenīre*)]

reverberate, *v.t.* to send back, to re-echo, to reflect (sound, light, or heat); †to drive or force back, to repulse. *v.i.* to be driven back or to be reflected (of sound, light, heat); to resound, to re-echo; to rebound, to recoil. **reverb,** *n.* an electronic device which creates an artificial echo in recorded music. †**reverb,** *v.t.* †**reverberant,** *a.* †**reverberative,** *a.* **reverberation,** *n.* **reverberator,** *n.* a reflector; a reflecting lamp; a reverberating furnace. **reverberatory,** *a.* producing or acting by reverberation. *n.* a reverberatory-furnace or kiln, in which metal or other material is exposed to the action of flame and heat which are thrown back from a vaulted roof etc. [L *reverberātus,* p.p. of *reverberāre* (*verberāre,* to beat, from *verber,* a scourge)]

revere, *v.t.* to regard with awe mingled with affection, to venerate. **reverence,** *n.* the act of revering, veneration; a feeling of or the capacity for feeling this; †an act or gesture of respect, an obeisance, a bow, a curtsy (*now vulg. or facet.*); a title given to the clergy (in *his reverence* etc.). *v.t.* to regard or treat with reverence, to venerate. †**to do reverence to,** to treat with reverence. **saving your reverence,** (*facet.*) with all respect to you. **reverencer,** *n.* **reverend,** *a.* worthy or entitled to reverence or respect, esp. as a title of respect given to clergymen (a dean is addressed as **Very Reverend,** a bishop as **Right Reverend,** and an archbishop as **Most Reverend**). **reverent,** *a.* feeling or expressing reverence; submissive, humble. **reverential,** *a.* **reverentially,** *adv.* **reverently,** *adv.* [F *révérer,* L *reverērī* (*verērī,* to fear)]

Revere, *n.* **Paul** (1735–1818), American nationalist, a Boston silversmith, who carried the news of the approach of British troops to Lexington and Concord (see AMERICAN INDEPENDENCE, WAR OF) on the night of 18 Apr. 1775. Longfellow's poem 'Paul Revere's Ride' commemorates the event.

reverie, *n.* listless musing; a day-dream, a loose or

irregular train of thought; a dreamy musical composition; †a wild or fantastic conceit, a vision, a delusion. [F *rêverie*, from *rêver*, to dream, etym. doubtful, cp. RAVE[1]]

revers, *n.* (*pl.* **revers**) a part of a coat, esp. a lapel, turned back so as to show the lining. [F as foll.]

reverse, *a.* turned backward, inverted, reversed, upside down; having an opposite direction, contrary. *n.* the contrary, the opposite; the back surface (of a coin etc.), the opposite of obverse; a complete change of affairs for the worse, a check, a defeat; †a back-handed stroke or thrust in fencing. *v.t.* to turn in the contrary direction, to turn the other way round, upside down, or inside out; to invert, to transpose; to cause to have a contrary motion or effect; to revoke, to annul, to nullify; †to remove; †to recall, to bring back (to). *v.i.* to change to a contrary condition, direction etc.; to put a car into the reverse gear; in dancing, to begin to turn in the opposite direction. **to reverse the charges,** to make a telephone call for which the recipient pays. **reverse video,** *n.* (*Comput.*) a technique for highlighting information on a VDU in which the normal colours for text and background are reversed. **reversal,** *n.* **reversed,** *a.* turned in a reverse direction; changed to the contrary; made or declared void; resupinate; applied to the spire of a shell turning from right to left. **reversedly**, *adv.* †**reverseless,** *a.* not to be reversed. **reversely,** *adv.* **reverser,** *n.* one who reverses; (*Sc. Law*) one borrowing on a mortgage of land. **reversi**, *n.* a game played by two persons on a draught-board with pieces differently coloured above and below, which may be reversed; †an obsolete card-game in which the player wins who takes fewest tricks. **reversible,** *a.* **reversibility**, *n.* **reversing,** *n., a.* **reversing light,** *n.* a light on the rear of a motor vehicle which is illuminated when reverse gear is engaged. **reversion**, *n.* return to a former condition, habit etc.; the tendency of an animal or a plant to revert to ancestral type or characters; the returning of an estate to the grantor or his heirs after a particular period is ended; the right of succeeding to an estate after the death of the grantee etc.; a sum payable upon some event, as a death, esp. an annuity or life assurance; the right or expectation of succeeding to an office etc., on relinquishment by the present holder. **reversional, reversionary,** *a.* **reversionally,** *adv.* **reversioner,** *n.* one who holds the reversion to an estate etc. **reverso**, *n.* the left-hand page of an open book, usu. even-numbered. [OF *revers,* L *reversus,* p.p. of *revertere* (*vertere,* to turn)]

revert, *v.t.* to turn (esp. the eyes) back; †to reverse. *v.i.* to return, to go back, to fall back, to return (to a previous condition, habits, type etc., esp. to a wild state); to recur, to turn the attention again (to); (*Law*) to come back by reversion to the possession of the former proprietor. *n.* a return; one who or that which reverts, esp. to a previous faith. **revertant,** *a.* (*Her.*) bent back, esp. like the letter S. **reverter,** *a.* one who or that which reverts; (*Law*) reversion. **revertible,** *a.* †**revertive,** *a.* †**revertively,** *adv.* [OF *revertir,* L *revertere,* as prec.]

†**revest,** *v.t.* to clothe, to attire; to robe; to reinvest. *v.i.* (*Law*) to vest or take effect again, to return to a former owner. †**revestiary, revestry**, *n.* a vestry. [OF *revestir* (F *revêtir*), late L *revestīre*]

revet, *v.t.* (*past, p.p.* **revetted**) to face (a wall, scarp, parapet etc.) with masonry. **revetment,** *n.* a facing of stones, concrete etc. to protect a wall or embankment; a retaining wall. [F *revêtir,* as prec.]

revictual, *v.t.* to victual again.

review, *v.t.* to view again; to look back on, to go over in memory, to revise; to survey, to look over carefully and critically; to write a critical review of; to hold a review of, to inspect. *v.i.* to write reviews. *n.* a repeated examination, a reconsideration, a second view; a retrospective survey; a revision, esp. by a superior court of law; a critical account of a book etc.; a periodical publication containing essays and criticisms; a display or a formal or official inspection of military or naval forces. **court of review,** one to which sentences and decisions are submitted for judicial revision. **review copy,** *n.* a copy of a new book sent to a periodical for review. **review order,** *n.* (*Mil.*) parade uniform and arrangement; full dress, full rig. **reviewable,** *a.* †**reviewage**, **reviewal,** *n.* **reviewer,** *n.* one who reviews, esp. books.

revigorate, *v.t.* to reinvigorate. [F *revigorer,* med. L *revigorāre* (L *vigor,* VIGOUR)]

revile, *v.t.* to address with opprobrious or scandalous language, to abuse, to vilify. *v.i.* to be abusive, to rail. †*n.* abuse. **revilement,** *n.* **reviler,** *n.* **revilingly,** *adv.* [OF *reviler*]

†**revindicate,** *v.t.* to vindicate again; to reclaim, to restore. †**revindication,** *n.*

revise, *v.t.* to look over, to re-examine for correction or emendation; to correct, alter, or amend; to reread course notes etc. for an examination. *n.* a revision; a proof-sheet in which corrections made in rough proof have been embodied; a revised form or version. **revisable,** *a.* **revisal,** *n.* **Revised Version,** *n.* the revision of the Authorized Version of the Bible, made in 1870–84. **reviser, revisor,** *n.* **revisership,** *n.* **revision,** *n.* the act or process of revising; the process of rereading course notes etc. before an exam; a revised version. **revising barrister** BARRISTER. **revisional, -ary, revisory,** *a.* **revisionism,** *n.* **revisionist,** *n.* one in favour of revision; a reviser of the Bible; one who believes in the broadening and evolution of the theories of Marxism; (*derog.*) one who departs from the principles of orthodox Communism. [F *reviser* (*viser,* L *vidēre,* to see, p.p. *vīsus*)]

revisit, *v.t.* to visit again; †to revise. *n.* a further visit. **revisitation,** *n.*

revisor, revisory REVISE.

revitalize, -ise, *v.t.* to vitalize again. **revitalization, -isation,** *n.*

revival REVIVE.

revive, *v.i.* to return to life, consciousness, health, vigour activity, vogue, the stage etc.; to gain new life or vigour; to recover from a state of obscurity, neglect, or depression; to come back to the mind again, to reawaken. *v.t.* to bring back to life, consciousness, vigour, etc.; to reanimate; to resuscitate, to renew, to renovate, to reawaken, to re-establish, to re-encourage; (*Chem.*) to restore or reduce to its natural or metallic state. **revivable,** *a.* **revivably,** *adv.* **revival,** *n.* the act of reviving; the state of being revived; return or recovery of life, consciousness, vigour, activity or vogue; a renaissance; a new production of a dramatic work previously neglected or forgotten; a religious awakening, esp. a movement for the renewal of religious fervour by means of special services etc. **revivalism,** *n.* **revivalist,** *n.* **reviver,** *n.* one who or that which revives; a preparation for renovating leather, cloth etc.; (*sl.*) a drink, a stimulant. **revivingly,** *adv.* [F *revivre,* L *revīvere* (*vīvere,* to live)]

revivify, *v.t.* to restore to life; to reanimate, to reinvigorate, to put new life into; to revive. **revivification,** *n.* **revivingly** REVIVE. [F *revivifier,* late L *revīvificāre*]

reviviscent, *a.* recovering life and strength, reviving. **reviviscence, -cy,** *n.* [L *revīviscens -ntem,* pres.p. of *revīviscere*]

revoke, *v.t.* to annul, to cancel, to repeal, to rescind; †to recall; †to withdraw, to take back. *v.i.* (*Cards*) to fail to follow suit when this is possible. *n.* the act of revoking at cards. **revocable, revokable,** *a.* **revocability, revokability**, **revocableness, revokableness,** *n.* **revocably, revokably,** *adv.* **revocation**, *n.* **revocatory**, *a.* †**revokement,** *n.* [OF *revoquer,* L *revocāre* (RE-, *vocāre,* to call)]

revolt, *v.i.* to renounce allegiance, to rise in rebellion or insurrection, to turn away (from); to be repelled (by), to feel disgust (at), to turn away in loathing (from), to feel repugnance (at); †to desert; †to be faithless. *v.t.* to repel, to nauseate, to disgust; †to turn back. *n.* a renunciation of allegiance and subjection; a rebellion, a rising, an insurrection; a change of sides; †revulsion. **revolter,** *n.* **revolting,** *a.* causing disgust, repulsion, or abhorrence. **revoltingly,** *adv.* [F *révolte,* from *révolter,*

MIt. *revoltare* (It. *rivoltare*) (RE-, L *volutāre,* freq. of *volvere,* to roll, p.p. *volūtus*)]

revolute[1], *a.* (of a leaf) rolled backwards from the edge. [L *revolūtus,* p.p. of *revolvere* (RE-, *volvere,* to roll)]

revolution, *n.* the act or state of revolving; the circular motion of a body on its axis, rotation; the motion of a body round a centre; a complete rotation or movement round a centre; the period of this; a round or cycle or regular recurrence or succession; a radical change or reversal of circumstances, conditions, relations or things; a fundamental change in government, esp. by the forcible overthrow of the existing system and substitution of a new ruler or political system. **revolute**[2], *v.i.* **revolutionary,** *a.* pertaining to or tending to produce a revolution in government; †pertaining to rotation. *n.* an advocate of revolution; one who takes an active part in a revolution. **Revolutionary Wars,** *n.pl.* a series of wars (1791–1802) between France and the combined armies of England, Austria, Prussia, and others, during the period of the French Revolution. **revolutionism,** *n.* **revolutionist,** *n.* (*dated*) a revolutionary. **revolutionize, -ise,** *v.t.* to bring about a revolution in; to cause radical change in. [ME and OF *revolucion* (F *révolution*), L *revolūtiōnem,* nom. *-tio,* from *revolvere,* to REVOLVE]

revolve, *v.t.* to turn round; to move round a centre, to rotate; to move in a circle, orbit, or cycle; to roll along; †to return. *v.t.* to cause to revolve or rotate; to turn over and over in the mind, to meditate on, to ponder over. †**revolvency,** *n.* **revolver,** *n.* one who or that which revolves; a pistol having a revolving breech cylinder by which it can be fired several times without reloading. **revolving,** *a.* **revolving credit,** *n.* credit which allows repeated borrowing of a fixed sum as long as that sum is never exceeded. **revolving door,** *n.* a door, usu. with four leaves at right angles, that rotates about a vertical axis. [L *revolvere* (*volvere,* to roll)]

revue, *n.* a light entertainment with songs, dances etc., representing topical characters, events, fashions etc. [F]

revulsion, *n.* a sudden or violent change or reaction, esp. of feeling; reduction of a disease in one part of the body by treatment of another part, as by counter-irritation; †violent withdrawal from something. **revulsive,** *a.* causing or tending to cause revulsion. *n.* an application causing revulsion, a counter-irritant. **revulsively,** *adv.* [F *révulsion,* L *revulsiōnem,* nom. *-sio,* from *revellere* (*vellere,* to pull, p.p. *vulsus*)]

reward, *v.t.* to repay, to requite, to recompense (a service or offence, a doer or offender). *n.* that which is given in return for good or evil done or received; a recompense, a requital, retribution; a sum of money offered for the detection of a criminal or for the restoration of anything lost. **reward claim,** *n.* (*Austral.*) land awarded to a miner who discovers gold in a new area. **rewardable,** *a.* **rewardableness,** *n.* **rewardably,** *adv.* **rewarder,** *n.* **rewardfulness,** *n.* **rewarding,** *a.* profitable; personally satisfying. **rewardingly,** *adv.* **rewardless,** *a.* [A-F and ONorth. F *rewarder,* OF *reguarder,* to REGARD]

rewind, *v.t.* (*past* **-wound**) to wind (film or tape) on to the original spool. *n.* something rewound. **rewire,** *v.t.* to install new electrical wiring in a house etc. **reword,** *v.t.* to put into words again; to repeat; to re-echo; to put into new words. **rework,** *v.t.* to treat or use again; to revise; to reprocess for renewed use. **rewrite,** *v.t.* to write over again; to revise. *n.* something rewritten or revised.

rex, *n.* a reigning king; the official title used by a king, esp. on documents, coins etc. [L]

Reykjavik, *n.* capital (since 1918) and chief port of Iceland, on the SW coast; population (1988) 93,000. Fish processing is the main industry. Reykjavik is heated by underground mains fed by volcanic springs.

reynard, *n.* a proper name for the fox. [OF *Renart,* name of the fox in the mediaeval *Roman de Renart,* from Teut. (cp. OHG *Reginhart*)]

Reynolds[1], *n.* **Burt** (1936–), US film actor in adventure films and comedies. His films include *Deliverance* (1972), *Hustle* (1975), and *City Heat* (1984).

Reynolds[2], *n.* **Joshua** (1723–92), English portrait painter, active in London from 1752. He became the first president of the Royal Academy in 1768. His portraits display a facility for striking and characterful compositions in a consciously grand manner. He often borrowed classical poses, for example *Mrs Siddons as the Tragic Muse*, 1784 (San Marino, California, US).

Reynolds[3], *n.* **Osborne** (1842–1912), British physicist and engineer who studied fluid flow, and devised the **Reynolds number**, which relates to turbulence in flowing fluids.

RF, (*abbr.*) radio frequency.

RFC, (*abbr.*) Royal Flying Corps; Rugby Football Club.

RFU, (*abbr.*) Rugby Football Union.

RGB, *n.* a method of connecting a colour screen to a computer, involving three separate signals: red, green, and blue. All the colours displayed by the screen can be made up from these three component colours. [acronym for *r*ed-*g*reen-*b*lue]

RGN, (*abbr.*) Registered General Nurse.

RGS, (*abbr.*) Royal Geographical Society.

RH, rh, (*abbr.*) right hand.

Rh[1], (*chem. symbol*) rhodium.

Rh[2], (*abbr.*) rhesus.

RHA, (*abbr.*) Royal Horse Artillery.

rhabdomancy, *n.* divination by a rod, esp. the discovery of minerals, underground streams etc. with the divining-rod. **rhabdomancer,** *n.* **rhabdomantic,** *a.* [Gr. *rhabdos,* rod, *manteia,* divination]

rhachis, rhachitis, etc. RACHIS.

Rhadamanthine, *a.* rigorously just and severe. [L *Rhadamanthus,* judge in Hades]

Rhaetian, *a.* pertaining to the ancient Roman district of Rhaetia, embracing the Grisons and part of Tyrol, or the people inhabiting this. *n.* Rhaeto-Romanic. **Rhaetic,** *a.* (*Geol.*) of or pertaining to the Rhaetian Alps (applied to the group of strata between the Lias and Trias developed there and also in England). *n.* the Rhaetic formation or strata. **Rhaeto-Romanic, -Romansch,** *a.* belonging to the Romance peoples of SE Switzerland and Tyrol or their dialects, esp. Romansch and Ladin. *n.* the Rhaeto-Romanic language.

rhamphoid, *a.* beak-shaped. **ramphorhyncus,** *n.* a pterodactyl of the Jurassic period. **rhamphotheca,** *n.* the horny integument of the beak. [Gr. *rhamphos,* curved beak, *rhunchos,* beak]

rhapontic, *n.* a species of rhubarb, *Rheum rhaponticum.* [mod. L *rhaponticum* (*Rha,* see RHUBARB, PONTIC[1])]

rhapsody, *n.* a high-flown, enthusiastic composition or utterance; (*Mus.*) an irregular and emotional composition, esp. of the nature of an improvisation; in ancient Greece, an epic poem, or a portion of this for recitation at one time by a rhapsodist. **rhapsode,** *n.* an ancient Greek reciter of epic poems, esp. one of a professional school who recited the Homeric poems. **rhapsodic, -al,** *a.* of or pertaining to rhapsody; enthusiastic; irregular, disconnected; high-flown, extravagant. **rhapsodically,** *adv.* **rhapsodize, -ise,** *v.t.* to speak or write with emotion or enthusiasm; *v.i.* to recite or write rhapsodies. **rhapsodist,** *n.* a rhapsode; any professional reciter or improvisor of verses; one who writes or speaks rhapsodically. [Gr. *rhapsōdos* (*rhaptein,* to sew, ODE)]

rhatany, *n.* a Peruvian shrub, *Krameria triandra,* or its root, from which an extract is obtained used in medicine and for adulterating port wine. [Port. *ratanhia* or Sp. *ratania,* Quichua, *rataña*]

Rhea, *n.* in Greek mythology, a fertility goddess, one of the Titans, wife of Kronos and mother of several gods, including Zeus.

rhea[1], *n.* a genus of birds containing the S American tree-toed ostriches; a bird of this genus. [Gr., daughter of Uranos and Gea.

rhea[2], *n.* the ramie plant. [Assamese]

Rhee, *n.* **Syngman** (1875–1965), Korean right-wing politician. A rebel under Chinese and Japanese rule, he became president of South Korea from 1948 until riots forced him to resign and leave the country in 1960.

rheic, *a.* of or derived from rhubarb. **rhein,** *n.* rheic acid, an orange-coloured liquid obtained from rhubarb. [F *rhéique* (RHEUM[2], -IC)]

Rheims, *n.* English version of REIMS.

Rheinland-Pfalz, *n.* German name for the RHINELAND-PALATINATE.

rhematic, *a.* pertaining to the formation of words, esp. verbs. †*n.pl.* the science of propositions. [Gr. *rhēmatikos,* from *rhēma -atos,* word]

Rhemish, *a.* of or pertaining to Rheims (applied esp. to an English translation of the New Testament by Roman Catholic students in 1582).

Rhenish, *a.* pertaining to the Rhine or Rhineland. *n.* Rhine wine, hock.

rhenium, *n.* a metallic element, at. no. 75; chem. symbol Re, occurring in certain platinum and molybdenum ores. [L *Rhenus,* the Rhine]

rheo-, *comb. form* pertaining to a current; flow. **rheology,** *n.* the science dealing with the flow and deformation of matter. **rheologic, -ical,** *a.* **rheologist,** *n.* **rheostat,** *n.* a variable resistance for adjusting and regulating an electric current. **rheostatic,** *a.* **rheotropism,** *n.* the tendency in growing plant-organs exposed to running water to dispose their longer axes either in the direction of or against the current. [Gr. *rheos,* stream, current, rel. to *rheein,* to flow]

rhesus, *n.* one of the macaques, *Macacus rhesus,* an Indian monkey, held sacred in some parts of India. **rhesus (Rh) factor,** *n.* an antigen substance occurring in the red blood corpuscles of most human beings and many mammals (e.g. the rhesus monkey). **Rh positive** or **Rh negative** indicate whether this substance is present or absent. [L, from Gr. *Rhēsos,* a king of Thrace]

Rhetian, Rhetic etc. RHAETIAN.

rhetor, *n.* in ancient Greece, a teacher or professor of rhetoric; a professional orator, a mere orator. **rhetoric,** *n.* the art of effective speaking or writing, the rules of eloquence; a treatise on this; the power of persuading by looks or acts; the use of language for effect or display, esp. affected or exaggerated oratory or declamation. **rhetorical,** *a.* pertaining to or of the nature of rhetoric; designed for effect or display, florid, showy, affected, declamatory. **rhetorical question,** one put merely for the sake of emphasis and requiring no answer. **rhetorically,** *adv.* **rhetorician,** *n.* a teacher of rhetoric; a skilled orator; a flamboyant or affected speaker. †**rhetorize, -ise,** *v.i.* [OF *rethorique* (F *rhétorique*), L *rhētorica,* Gr. *rhētorikē technē,* rhetorical art, *rhētōr,* a public speaker, rel. to *eirein,* to speak, perf. *eirēka*]

rheum[1]**,** *n.* the thin serous fluid secreted by the mucous glands as tears, saliva, or mucus; (*poet.*) tears; †moisture; mucous discharge, catarrh; (*pl. dated*) rheumatic pains. **rheumatic,** *a.* pertaining to, of the nature of, suffering from, or subject to rheumatism. **rheumatically,** *adv.* **rheumatic fever,** *n.* a disease characterized by fever, acute pain in the joints and potential inflammation of the heart and pericardium. **rheumatics,** *n.pl.* (*coll.*) rheumatism. **rheumatism,** *n.* an inflammatory disease affecting muscles and joints of the human body, and attended by swelling and pain. **rheumatismal,** *a.* rheumatic. [OF *reume,* L *rheuma,* Gr. *rheuma -atos,* stream, from *rheu-,* root of *rheein,* to flow; L *rheumaticus,* Gr. *rheumatikos*]

rheum[2]**,** *n.* a genus of plants comprising the rhubarbs. [mod. L, from Gr. *rhēon*]

rheumat(o)-, *comb. form* rheumatic.

rheumatoid, *a.* **rheumatoid arthritis,** *n.* disease of the synovial tissues of the joints.

rheumatology, *n.* the study of rheumatism. **rheumatological,** *a.* **rheumatologist,** *n.*

rheumophthalmia, *n.* rheumatic inflammation of the sclerotic membrane.

rhinal, *n.* of or pertaining to the nose or nostrils. **rhinalgia,** *n.* nasal neuralgia. [RHIN(O)-]

Rhinanthus, *n.* a genus of scrophulariaceous plants containing the yellow-rattle.

rhinarium, *n.* the anterior part of the clypeus in an insect.

Rhine[1]**,** *n.* (German **Rhein,** French **Rhin**) European river rising in Switzerland and reaching the North Sea via West Germany and the Netherlands; length 1320 km/820 miles. Tributaries include the Moselle and the Ruhr. The Rhine is linked with the Mediterranean by the Rhine-Rhône Waterway, and with the Black Sea by the Rhine-Main-Danube Waterway. **Rhine wine,** *n.* a wine made from grapes grown in the neighbourhood of the Rhine.

Rhine[2]**,** *n.* **Joseph Banks** (1895–1980), US parapsychologist. His work at Duke University, North Carolina, involving controlled laboratory experiments in telepathy, clairvoyance, precognition, and psychokinesis, described in *Extra-Sensory Perception* (1934) made ESP a common term.

rhine[1]**,** *n.* (*W of England*) a large ditch or drain. [prob. from OE *ryne,* cogn. with RUN]

rhine[2]**,** *n.* a superior quality of Russian hemp. [formerly *rine hemp,* G *Reinhanf,* clean hemp]

Rhineland-Palatinate, *n.* (German **Rheinland-Pfalz**) administrative region (German *Land*) of West Germany. **area** 19,800 sq km/7643 sq miles. **capital** Mainz. **towns** Ludwigshafen, Koblenz, Trier, Worms. **physical** wooded mountain country, river valleys of Rhine and Moselle. **population** (1988) 3,611,000. **products** wine (75% of German output), tobacco, chemicals, machinery, leather goods, pottery.

rhinencephalon, *n.* the olfactory lobe of the brain. **rhinencephalic, rhinencephalous,** *a.*

rhinestone, *n.* a species of rock crystal; a colourless artificial gem cut to look like a diamond. [from F *caillou du Rhin,* referring to Strasbourg where the gems were made]

rhinitis, *n.* inflammation of the nose. [RHIN(O)-]

rhino[1]**,** *n.* (*sl.*) money, coin. [etym. doubtful]

rhino[2]**,** *n.* (*pl.* **-nos, -no**) a rhinoceros.

rhin(o)-, *comb. form* pertaining to the nose or nostrils. [Gr. *rhis rhinos,* nose]

rhinobatid, *n.* a shark-like ray. [Gr. *batos,* ray]

rhinocaul, *n.* the peduncle of the olfactory bulb of the brain.

rhinoceros, *n.* (*pl.* **-oses**) a large pachydermatous quadruped, now found only in Africa and S Asia, with one or two horns on the nose. **rhinoceros-bird,** *n.* the African beef-eater or ox-pecker, *Buphaga africana.* **rhinocerical, rhinoceroid, rhinocerotic, rhinocerotiform,** *a.* **rhinocerotoid,** *n., a.* [late L, from Gr. *rhīnokerōs* (RHIN(O)-, *kerōs, keras,* horn)]

rhinolith, *n.* nasal calculus. [RHIN(O)-, -LITH]

rhinology, *n.* the branch of science dealing with the nose and nasal diseases. **rhinological,** *a.* **rhinologist,** *n.*

rhinopharyngeal, *a.* pertaining to the nose and the pharynx. **rhinopharyngitis,** *n.* inflammation of the nose and pharynx.

rhinoplasty, *n.* an operation for restoring an injured nose. **rhinoplastic,** *a.*

rhinorrhoea, *n.* discharge of blood from the nose.

rhinoscleroma, *n.* a disease affecting the nose, lips etc. with a tuberculous growth.

rhinoscope, *n.* an instrument for examining the nasal passages. **rhinoscopic,** *a.* **rhinoscopy,** *n.*

rhipid(o)-, *comb. form* having fan-like processes. [Gr. *rhipis rhipidos,* fan]

rhipidoglossal, *a.* belonging to the Rhipidoglossa, a division of gasteropods having an odontophore with several median and many marginal teeth. [Gr. *glōssa,* tongue]

rhipipteran, *a.* fan-winged. *n.* one of the Rhipiptera, an order of insects. **rhipipterous,** *a.* [Gr. *rhipis,* fan, *pteron,* wing]

rhiz(a)-, rhiz(o)-, *comb. form* pertaining to a root; having roots or root-like processes. [Gr. *rhiza,* root]

rhizanth, *n.* a plant flowering or seeming to flower from the root. **rhizanthous,** *a.* [Gr. *anthos,* flower]

rhizic, *a.* of or pertaining to the root of an equation.

rhizocarp, *n.* a plant of the family Rhizocarpeae (now Marsileaceae). **rhizocarpean,** *a.* **rhizocarpic,**

-carpous, *a.* having a perennial root but a stem that withers annually. [Gr. *karpos,* fruit]

rhizocephalan, *n.* one of the Rhizocephala, a sub-order of parasitic crustaceans related to the cirripeds. **rhizocephalous,** *a.* [Gr. *kephalē,* head]

rhizodont, *a.* having teeth rooted and anchylosed with the jaw (as crocodiles). *n.* a rhizodont reptile.

rhizogen, *n.* a plant parasitic on the roots of another plant. **rhizogenic,** †**-genetic,** *a.* root-producing.

rhizoid, *a.* root-like. *n.* a filiform or hair-like organ serving for attachment, in mosses etc.

rhizome, rhizoma, *n.* a prostrate, thickened, root-like stem, sending roots downwards and yearly producing aerial shoots etc. **rhizomatous,** *a.* [Gr. *rhizōma,* from *rhizoun,* to cause to take root, from *rhiza,* root]

rhizomorph, *n.* a root-like mycelial growth by which some fungi attach themselves to higher plants. **rhizomorphoid, -phous,** *a.*

rhizophagous, *a.* feeding on roots; pertaining to the Rhizophaga, a sub-order of marsupials comprising the wombat. **rhizophagan,** *n., a.* [Gr. *phagein,* to eat]

rhizophore, *n.* a root-like structure bearing the roots in species of *Selaginella.* **rhizophorous,** *a.* root-bearing. [-PHORE]

rhizopod, *n.* an animalcule of the class Rhizopoda, division of the Protozoa, comprising those with pseudopodia for locomotion and the ingestion of food; the mycelium of fungi. *a.* of or pertaining to the Rhizopoda. **rhizopodal, rhizopodic, rhizopodous,** *a.* [Gr. *pous podos,* foot]

rho, *n.* (*pl.* **rhos**) the 17th letter of the Greek alphabet (Ρ, ϱ).

rhodamine, *n.* any of a group of fluorescent, usu. red dyestuffs.

rhodanic, *a.* producing a rose-red colour with ferric salts. **rhodanic acid,** *n.* sulphocyanic acid. **rhodanate,** *n.* sulphocyanate. [Gr. *rhodon,* rose, -IC]

Rhode Island, *n.* smallest state of the US, in New England; nickname Little Rhody or the Ocean State. **area** 3100 sq km/1197 sq miles. **capital** Providence. **towns** Cranston, Woonsocket. **population** (1987) 986,000. **products** apples, potatoes, poultry (especially Rhode Island Reds), dairy products, jewellery (30% of the workforce), textiles, silverware, machinery, rubber, plastics, electronics. **Rhode Island Red,** *n.* an American breed of domestic fowl with reddish-brown plumage.

Rhodes[1], *n.* (Greek **Rodhos**) Greek island, largest of the Dodecanese, in the E Aegean Sea. **area** 1412 sq km/545 sq miles. **capital** Rhodes. **population** (1981) 88,000. **products** grapes, olives. **Rhodian,** *a.* pertaining to Rhodes. *n.* a native or inhabitant of Rhodes.

Rhodes[2], *n.* **Cecil (John)** (1853–1902), South African politician, born in the UK, prime minister of Cape Colony (1890–96). Aiming at the formation of a South African federation and of a block of British territory from the Cape to Cairo, he was responsible for the annexation of Bechuanaland (now Botswana) in 1885, and formed the British South Africa Company in 1889, which occupied Mashonaland and Matabeleland, thus forming Rhodesia (now Zambia and Zimbabwe). **Rhodes Scholar,** *n.* a student holding one of the Rhodes scholarships at Oxford founded under the will of Cecil Rhodes for students from the British Commonwealth and the US.

Rhodes[3], *n.* **Wilfred** (1877–1973), English cricketer. He was the game's most prolific wicket-taker, taking 4187 wickets (1898–1930), and also scoring 39,802 first class runs.

Rhodes[4], *n.* **Zandra** (1940–), English fashion designer, known for the extravagant fantasy and luxury of her dress creations.

Rhodesia, *n.* former name of Zambia (Northern Rhodesia) and Zimbabwe (Southern Rhodesia).

rhodinol, *n.* an alcohol occurring in geranium- and rose-oil. [Gr. *rhodinos,* made of roses, as foll., -OL]

rhodium[1], *n.* the Jamaica rosewood; the hard, white, scented wood of either of two shrubby convolvuluses growing in the Canary islands, also called rhodium- or rhodian-wood. **oil of rhodium,** an oil obtained from this. **rhodian,** *a.* [mod. L, neut. of *rhodius,* rose-like, from Gr. *rhodon,* rose]

rhodium[2], *n.* a greyish-white metallic element, at. no. 45; chem. symbol Rh, belonging to the platinum group. **rhodic, rhodous,** *a.* [Gr. *rhodon,* rose, -IUM]

rhod(o)-, *comb. form* rose; rose-like; scented like a rose. [Gr. *rhodon,* rose]

rhodocrinite, *n.* one of the Palaeozoic family of encrinites, the Rhodocrinidae or rose-encrinites. **rhodocrinid, rhodocrinoid,** *n., a.*

rhododendron, *n.* a genus of evergreen shrubs akin to the azaleas, with brilliant flowers; a shrub of this genus. [late L and Gr. (RHOD(O)-, *dendron,* tree)]

rhodolite, *n.* a pale pink or purple garnet used as a gemstone.

rhodonite, *n.* a rose-pink silicate of manganese. [G *Rhodonit* (Gr. *rhodon,* rose)]

Rhodope Mountains, *n.* a range of mountains on the frontier between Greece and Bulgaria, rising to 2925 m/9497 ft. at Musala.

rhodophyl, *n.* the compound pigment giving red algae their colour. **rhodophyllous,** *a.* [RHOD(O)-, Gr. *phullon,* leaf]

rhodopsin, *n.* a purplish pigment found in the retina, visual purple. [Gr. *opsis,* sight]

rhodora, *n.* a N American flowering shrub, *Rhodora canadensis,* belonging to the family Ericaceae, growing in boggy ground. [Gr. *rhodon,* rose]

rhoeadic, *a.* derived from the red poppy, *Papaver rhoeas.* **rhoeadic acid,** *n.* a compound found in the flowers of this, the principle of their colouring-matter. **rhoeadine,** *n.* an alkaloid obtained from the red poppy. [Gr. *rhoias -ados,* a kind of poppy, -IC]

rhomb, *n.* an oblique parallelogram, with equal sides; (*Cryst.*) a rhombohedron. **rhomb-spar,** *n.* a perfectly crystallized variety of dolomite. **rhombic,** *a.* **rhombiform,** *a.* [F *rhombe,* L *rhombus,* Gr. *rhombos*]

rhomb(o)-, *comb. form* pertaining to a rhomb.

rhombohedron, *n.* (*pl.* **-dra**) a solid figure bounded by six equal rhombs. **rhombohedral,** *a.*

rhomboid, *n.* a parallelogram the adjoining sides of which are not equal and which contains no right angle; a rhomboid muscle. *a.* having the shape or nearly the shape of a rhomboid. **rhomboid ligament,** *n.* a ligament connecting the first rib and the end of the clavicle. **rhomboid muscle,** *n.* either of two muscles connecting the vertebral border of the scapula with the spine. **rhomboidal,** *a.* **rhomboidally,** *adv.*

rhomboideum, *n.* (*pl.* **-dea**) a rhomboid ligament.

rhombus, *n.* (*pl.* **-buses, -bi**) a rhomb; a genus of flatfishes containing the turbot, brill etc.

Rhône, *n.* river of S Europe; length 810 km/500 miles. It rises in Switzerland and flows through Lake Geneva to Lyons in France, where at its confluence with the Saône the upper limit of navigation is reached. The river turns due south, passes Vienne and Avignon, and takes in the Isère and other tributaries. Near Arles it divides into the Grand and Petit Rhône, flowing respectively SE and SW into the Mediterranean west of Marseille.

Rhône-Alpes, *n.* region of E France in the upper reaches of the Rhône; area 43,700 sq km/16,868 sq miles; population (1986) 5,154,000. It consists of the *départements* of Ain, Ardèche, Drôme, Isère, Loire, Rhône, Savoie, and Haute-Savoie. The chief town is Lyon. There are several notable wine-producing areas including Chenas, Fleurie, and Beaujolais. Industrial products include chemicals, textiles, and motor vehicles.

rhotacism, *n.* exaggerated or erroneous pronunciation of the letter *r,* burring; (*Philol.*) the change of *s* into *r,* as in Indo-European languages. **rhotacize, -ise,** *v.i.* [Gr. *rhōtakizein,* to rhotacize, from *rhō,* the letter *r,* -ISM]

RHS, (*abbr.*) Royal Historical Society; Royal Horticultural Society; Royal Humane Society.

rhubarb, *n.* any herbaceous plant of the genus *Rheum,* esp. *R. rhaponticum,* the English, French, common or garden rhubarb, the fleshy and juicy leaf-stalks of which are cooked when young as a substitute for fruit; the roots of several central Asian species of *Rheum*, usu. called E Indian, Russia, or Turkey rhubarb, from which purgative medicines are prepared; the sound made by actors to simulate background conversation; nonsense; (*N Am. sl.*) a loud argument, an angry quarrel. **rhubarby,** *a.* [OF *reubarbe* (F *rhubarbe*), med. L *rheubarbum, rheubarbarum,* altered from *rhabarbarum* (*rha barbarum,* foreign *Rha,* the Volga)]

rhumb, *n.* a line cutting all the meridians at the same angle, such as a ship would follow sailing continuously on one course; any one of the 32 principal points of the compass; the angular distance, 11° 15′, between any successive pair of these. **rhumbline,** *n.* [from F *rumb* or Sp. *rhumbo*]

rhumba RUMBA.

rhyme, rime[1], *n.* a correspondence of sound in the final accented syllable or group of syllables of a line of verse with that of another line, consisting of identity of the vowel sounds and of all the consonantal sounds but the first; verse characterized by rhyme (*sing. or pl*); poetry, verse; a word rhyming with another. *v.i.* to make rhymes, to versify; to make a rhyme with another word or verse; to be in accord, to harmonize (with). *v.t.* to put into rhyme; to pass or waste (time etc.) in rhyming. **without rhyme or reason,** inconsiderately, thoughtlessly; unreasonable, purposeless. **rhyme royal,** *n.* a seven-lined decasyllabic stanza rhyming *a b a b b c c,* so called because employed by James I of Scotland in the *King's Quhair*. **rhyme scheme,** *n.* the pattern of rhymes in a stanza, poem etc. **rhymeless**, *a.* **rhymelessness,** *n.* **rhymer, rhymester**, **rhymist,** *n.* a poet, esp. of inferior talent; a poetaster; minstrel. †**rhymic,** *a.* **rhyming slang,** *n.* a form of slang originating among Cockneys in London in which the word to be disguised (often an indecent one) is replaced by a rhyming phrase of which often only the first element is used, so that the rhyme itself disappears (e.g. *Barnet fair* becomes *Barnet* meaning *hair*). [OF *rime*, L *rhythmum,* nom. *-mus,* Gr. *rhuthmos,* RHYTHM, first form assim. to RHYTHM]

rhynch(o)-, *comb. form* having a snout or snout-like process. [Gr. *rhunchos,* snout]

rhynchocephalian, *a.* belonging to the Rhyncocephalia, an almost extinct order of reptiles. *n.* a reptile of this order. [Gr. *kephalē,* head]

rhyncholite, *a.* a fossil beak of a tetrabranchiate cephalopod. [-LITE]

rhynchonella, *n.* a brachiopod of the Rhynchonellidae.

rhynchophore, *n.* one of the Rhynchophora, a division of tetramerous beetles containing the weevils or snout-beetles. **rhyncophoran**, *n., a.* **rhynchophorous**, *a.* [-PHORE]

rhynchosaur, rhynchosauros, *n.* a genus of edentulous saurians from the Devonian strata. [Gr. *sauros,* lizard]

rhyncocoele, *a.* belonging to the Rhynchocoela, an order of turbellarians comprising the nemerteans. [Gr. *koilos,* hollow]

rhyolite, *n.* an igneous rock of structure showing the effect of lava-flow, composed of quartz and feldspar with other minerals. **rhyolitic**, *a.* [G *Rhyolit* (Gr. *rhuax,* stream)]

rhyparographer, *n.* a painter of squalid subjects. **rhyparographic**, *a.* **rhyparography,** *n.* [late L *rhyparographus,* Gr. *rhuparographos* (*rhuparos,* filthy)]

Rhys, *n.* **Jean** (1894–1979), British novelist, born in Dominica. Her works include *Wide Sargasso Sea* (1966), a recreation of the life of Rochester's mad wife in *Jane Eyre* by Charlotte Brontë.

rhysimeter, *n.* an instrument for measuring the velocity of a fluid or the speed of a ship. [Gr. *rhusis,* flowing, rel. to *-rheein,* to flow, -METER]

rhythm, *n.* movement characterized by action and reaction or regular alternation of strong and weak impulse, stress, accent, motion, sound etc.; metrical movement determined by the regular recurrence or harmonious succession of groups of long and short or stressed and unstressed syllables called feet; the flow of words in verse or prose characterized by such movement; the regulated succession of musical notes according to duration; structural system based on this; (*Art*) correlation of parts in a harmonious whole; any alternation of strong and weak states or movements. **rhythm and blues,** a style of popular music integrating elements of folk, rock and roll and blues. **rhythm method,** *n.* a method of contraception requiring sexual abstinence during the period when ovulation is most likely to occur. **rhythm section,** *n.* the section of instruments (usu. piano, double-bass and drums) in a band whose main task is to provide the rhythm. **rhythmic, -al,** *a.* **rhythmically,** *adv.* **rhythmist,** *n.* **rhythmless**, *a.* [F *rithme* (now *rhythme*), L *rhythmus,* Gr. *rhuthmos,* from *rhu-,* root of *rheein,* to flow]

RI, (*abbr.*) refractive index; religious instruction; Royal Institution.

ria, *n.* a long, narrow inlet into the sea-coast. [Sp., river-mouth]

rial, *n.* the unit of currency in Iran, Oman, Saudi Arabia and the Yemen Arab Republic (see also RIYAL). [Arab. *riyal* from Sp. *real,* REAL[2]]

riant, *a.* (*fem.* **riante**) smiling, cheerful, gay. †**riancy,** *n.* [F pres.p. of *rire,* L *ridēre,* to laugh]

rib[1], *n.* one of the bones extending outwards and forwards from the spine, and in man forming the walls of the thorax; a ridge, strip, line etc., analogous in form or function to this; a cut of meat including one or more ribs; a curved timber extending from the keel for supporting the side of a ship etc.; a raised moulding or groin on a ceiling or vaulted roof; a timber or iron beam helping to support a bridge; a hinged rod forming part of an umbrella-frame; a purlin; a ridge for stiffening a casting etc.; a main vein in a leaf; a spur of a mountain; a raised row in a knitted or woven fabric; (*facet.*) a wife, in allusion to Eve. *v.t.* (*past, p.p.* **ribbed**) to furnish with ribs; to mark with ribs or ridges; to enclose with ribs; to rafter or half-plough; to knit alternate plain and purl stitches to form a raised row. **false ribs,** the lower five pairs of ribs. **floating ribs,** the two lowest pairs of ribs. **ribcage,** *n.* the structure of ribs and tissue which forms the enclosing wall of the chest. **rib-grass, -wort,** *n.* the narrow-leaved plantain, *Plantago lanceolata*. **rib-roast,** *v.t.* (*sl.*) to beat soundly, to thrash. **rib-roaster,** *n.* (*sl.*) a heavy blow on the body. **rib-vaulting,** *n.* **ribbed,** *a.* **ribbing,** *n.* a system or arrangement of ribs, as in a vaulted roof etc.; a method of ploughing, raftering or half-ploughing. **ribless**, *a.* [OE *ribb* (cp. Dut. *rib,* G *Rippe,* Icel. *rif,* Norw. *riv*)]

rib[2], *v.t.* (*coll.*) to tease, make fun of. **ribbing,** *n.* [prob. from tickling of the ribs to cause laughter]

RIBA, (*abbr.*) Royal Institute of British Architects.

ribald, *n.* a low, coarse, or indecent fellow, esp. one using scurrilous language. *a.* scurrilous, coarse, licentious, lewd (of language). †**ribaldish,** †**ribaldrous,** *a.* **ribaldry**, *n.* [OF *ribaud* (F *ribaut*), a low ruffian, etym. doubtful]

riband RIBBON.

ribband, *n.* a strip, scantling, or spar temporarily attached lengthwise to the body of a ship to hold the ribs in position; a piece of timber used in launching, as a stop, guide etc., or in the construction of pontoons, gun-platforms etc. [var. of prec. or from RIB, BAND[2]]

Ribbentrop, *n.* **Joachim von** (1893–1946), German Nazi leader, born in the Rhineland. He joined the Nazi Party 1932, acted as Hitler's adviser on foreign affairs, and was German ambassador to Britain (1936–38) and foreign minister (1938–45). He was tried at Nuremberg as a war criminal 1946 and hanged. **Ribbentrop-Molotov pact,** *n.* see HITLER-STALIN PACT.

ribble-rabble, *n.* rabble; a rabble, a mob; meaningless talk, a rigmarole.

ribbon, *n.* a narrow woven strip or band of silk, satin etc., used for ornamenting dress etc.; such a strip or band worn as distinctive mark of an order, college, club etc.; a narrow strip of anything; an ink-impregnated cloth strip used in typewriters etc.; (*pl.*) driving-reins; torn shreds, ragged strips. **Blue Ribbon,** the Order of the Garter; a teetotal badge; the highest distinction for creating a record. **ribbon development,** *n.* urban extension in the form of a single depth of houses along roads radiating from the town. **ribbon-fish,** *n.* a long, narrow, flattish fish of various species. **ribbon-grass,** *n.* an American grass, *Phalaris arundinacea picta,* grown for ornamental purposes in gardens. **ribbon worm,** *n.* a nemertean. **ribboned,** *a.* wearing or adorned with ribbons (*usu. in comb.*). [F *riban* (now *ruban*), etym. doubtful]

Ribera, *n.* **José (Jusepe) de** (1591–1652), Spanish painter, active in Italy from 1616 under the patronage of the viceroys of Naples. His early work shows the impact of Caravaggio, but his colours gradually lightened. He painted many full-length saints and mythological figures, and genre scenes, which he produced without preliminary drawing.

Ribes, *n.* the genus comprising the currant and gooseberry plants. [med. L, from Arab. *rībās*, sorrel]

riboflavin, riboflavine, *n.* a yellow vitamin of the B complex found esp. in milk and liver, which promotes growth in children.

ribonuclease, *n.* any of several enzymes that catalyse the hydrolysis of RNA.

ribonucleic acid, RNA, *n.* any of a group of nucleic acids present in all living cells and playing an essential role in the synthesis of proteins.

ribose, *n.* a pentose sugar occurring in RNA and riboflavin. [from *arabinose,* (gum) arabic]

ribosome, *n.* any of numerous minute granules containing RNA and protein in a cell, which are the site for protein synthesis.

Ribston pippin, *n.* a choice variety of apple first cultivated in England at Ribston Park, Yorkshire.

Ricardian, *a.* of or pertaining to the economist David Ricardo or his opinions. *n.* a follower of Ricardo.

Ricardo, *n.* **David** (1772–1823), English economist, author of *Principles of Political Economy* (1817). Among his discoveries were the principle of comparative advantage (that countries can benefit by specializing in goods they produce efficiently and trading internationally to buy others), and the law of diminishing returns (that continued increments of capital and labour applied to a given quantity of land will eventually show a declining rate of increase in output).

rice, *n.* the white grain or seeds of *Oryza sativa,* an E Indian aquatic grass extensively cultivated in warm climates for food. **rice-bird,** *n.* the Java sparrow; the bobolink. **rice-biscuit,** *n.* **rice milk,** *n.* milk boiled and thickened with rice. **rice-paper,** *n.* a paper made from the pith of the Taiwanese *Aralia papyrifera,* and used by Chinese artists for painting on; a thin edible paper made from rice straw, used in baking. [OF *riz,* It. *riso,* L *oryza,* Gr. *oruza,* prob. from OPers.]

Rice, *n.* **Elmer** (1892–1967), US playwright. His works include *The Adding Machine* (1923) and *Street Scene* (1929), which won a Pulitzer Prize and was made into an opera by Kurt Weill. Many of his plays deal with such economic and political issues as the Depression (*We, the People*, 1933) and racism (*American Landscape*, 1939).

rich, *a.* wealthy, having large possessions, abounding (in resources, productions etc.); abundantly supplied with; producing ample supplies; fertile, abundant, well-filled; valuable, precious, costly; elaborate, splendid; abounding in qualities pleasing to the senses, sweet, luscious, high-flavoured, containing much fat, oil, sugar, spices etc.; vivid, bright; mellow, deep, full, musical (of sounds); comical, funny, full of humorous suggestion. †*v.t.* to enrich. †**richen,** *v.t., v.i.* **riches,** †**richesse,** *n.* (*usu. in pl.*) abundant possessions, wealth, opulence, affluence. **richly,** *adv.* in a rich manner, abundantly, thoroughly. **richness,** *n.* [OE *rīce* (cp. Dut. *rijk,* G *Reich,* Icel. *rīkr*), rel. to L *rex,* king, perh. ult. derived from it]

Rich, *n.* **Adrienne** (1929–), US radical feminist poet, writer, and critic. Her poetry is both subjective and political, concerned with female consciousness, peace, and gay rights. Her works include *The Fact of a Doorframe: Poems Selected and New* (1984) and *On Lies, Secrets and Silence* (1979).

Richard, *n.* **Cliff** (stage name of Harry Roger Webb) (1940–), English pop singer. In the late 1950s he was influenced by Elvis Presley, but became a Christian family entertainer, continuing to have hits in the UK through the 1980s. His original backing group were the Shadows (1958–68 and later re-formed).

Richard I, *n.* **the Lionheart** (French **Coeur-de-Lion**) (1157–99), king of England from 1189. He was the third son of Henry II, against whom he twice rebelled. In the third Crusade (1191–92) he won victories at Cyprus, Acre, and Arsuf (against Saladin), but failed to recover Jerusalem. While returning overland he was captured by the Duke of Austria, who handed him over to the emperor Henry VI, and he was held prisoner until a large ransom was raised. His later years were spent in warfare in France, and he was killed while besieging Châlus. Himself a poet, he became a hero of legends after his death. He was succeeded by his brother John.

Richard II, *n.* (1367–1400), king of England from 1377, effectively from 1389, son of Edward the Black Prince. He reigned in conflict with Parliament; they executed some of his associates in 1388 and then some of the opposing barons in 1397, whereupon he made himself absolute. Two years later, forced to abdicate in favour of Henry IV, he was jailed and probably assassinated.

Richard III, *n.* (1452–85), king of England from 1483. The son of Richard, Duke of York, he was created duke of Gloucester by his brother Edward IV, and distinguished himself in the Wars of the Roses. On Edward's death in 1483 he became protector to his nephew Edward V, and soon secured the crown on the plea that Edward IV's sons were illegitimate. He proved a capable ruler, but the suspicion that he had murdered Edward V and his brother undermined his popularity. In 1485 Henry, Earl of Richmond (later Henry VII), raised a rebellion, and Richard III was defeated and killed at Bosworth. Scholars now tend to minimize the evidence for his crimes as Tudor propaganda.

Richards¹, *n.* **Frank** (pen name of Charles Harold St John Hamilton) (1875–1961), English writer for the children's papers *Magnet* and *Gem*, who invented Greyfriars public school and the fat boy Billy Bunter.

Richards², *n.* **Gordon** (1905–86), English jockey who was champion on the flat a record 26 times from 1925–53.

Richards³, *n.* **Theodore** (1868–1928), US chemist. Working at Harvard University, Boston, for much of his career, Richards concentrated upon determining as accurately as possible the atomic weights of a large number of elements. He was awarded the 1914 Nobel Chemistry Prize.

Richardson¹, *n.* **Dorothy** (1873–1957), experimental novelist whose works were collected under the title *Pilgrimage* (1938). She used the 'stream of conciousness' technique to great effect and has been linked with Virginia Woolf in creating a specifically feminine genre. Woolf credited her as having invented 'the psychological sentence of the feminine gender'.

Richardson², *n.* **Ralph (David)** (1902–83), English actor. He played many stage parts, including Falstaff (Shakespeare), Peer Gynt (Ibsen), and Cyrano de Bergerac (Rostand). He shared the management of the Old Vic theatre with Laurence Olivier (1944–50).

Richardson³, *n.* **Samuel** (1689–1761), English novelist, one of the founders of the modern novel. *Pamela* (1740–41), written in the form of a series of letters, and containing much dramatic conversation, achieved a sensational vogue all across Europe, and was followed by *Clarissa* (1747–48), and *Sir Charles Grandison* (1753–54).

Richardson⁴, *n.* **Tony** (1928–), English director and producer. With George Devine he established the English Stage Company in 1955 at the Royal Court

Theatre, with productions such as *Look Back in Anger* (1956). His films include *Saturday Night and Sunday Morning* (1960), *A Taste of Honey* (1961), *Tom Jones* (1963), *Dead Cert* (1974), and *Joseph Andrews* (1977). He is the father of the actress Natasha Richardson.

Richelieu, *n.* **Armand Jean du Plessis de** (1585–1642), French cardinal and politician, chief minister from 1624. He aimed to make the monarchy absolute; he ruthlessly crushed opposition by the nobility, and destroyed the political power of the Huguenots, while leaving them religious freedom. Abroad he sought to establish French supremacy by breaking the power of the Habsburgs; he therefore supported the Swedish king Gustavus Adolphus and the German Protestant princes against Austria, and in 1635 brought France into the Thirty Years' War.

Richter[1], *n.* **Burton** (1931–), US high energy physicist who, in the 1960s, designed the Stanford Positron Accelerating Ring (SPEAR). In 1974 Richter used SPEAR to produce a new particle, later named the £gw (psi) particle, thought to be formed from the charmed quark postulated by Sheldon Glashow. Richter shared the 1976 Nobel Physics Prize with Samuel Ting.

Richter[2], *n.* **Charles Francis** (1900–85), US seismologist, deviser of the **Richter scale,** a scale based on measurement of seismic waves, used to determine the magnitude of an earthquake at the epicentre. The magnitude of an earthquake differs from the intensity, measured by the Mercalli scale, which is subjective and varies from place to place for the same earthquake.

Richter[3], *n.* **Johann Paul Friedrich** (1763–1825), German author, commonly known as Jean Paul. He created a series of comic eccentrics in works such as the romance *Titan* (1800–03) and *Die Flegeljahre/The Awkward Age* (1804–05).

Richthofen, *n.* **Manfred, Freiherr von** (the 'Red Baron') (1892–1918), German aviator. In World War I he commanded the 11th Chasing Squadron, known as **Richthofen's Flying Circus**, and shot down 80 aircraft before being killed in action.

Ricinus, *n.* a genus of plants comprising the castor-oil plant. **ricinic**, **ricinoleic**, **ricinolic**, *a.* derived from castor-oil. [L]

rick[1], *n.* a stack of corn, hay etc., regularly built and thatched. *v.t.* to make or pile into a rick. **rick-barton, -yard,** *n.* space on a farm reserved for ricks. **rick-stand,** *n.* a platform of short pillars and joists for keeping a rick above the ground. [OE *hrēac* (cp. Dut. *rook,* Icel. *hraukr*)]

rick[2], *v.t.* to wrench or sprain. *n.* a wrench or sprain. [var. of WRICK]

rickets, *n.* a disease of children consisting in the softening of the bones, esp. the spine, bow-legs, emaciation etc., owing to lack of mineral matter in the bones. **rickety,** *a.* affected with or of the nature of rickets; feeble in the joints; shaky, tumble-down, fragile, unsafe. [etym. doubtful]

rickettsia, *n.* (*pl.* **-siae, -sias**) any of a group of micro-organisms found in lice, ticks etc. which when transmitted to man cause serious diseases, e.g. typhus. **rickettsial,** *a.* [after Howard T. *Ricketts,* 1871–1910, US pathologist]

rickshaw, ricksha, *n.* a light two-wheeled hooded carriage drawn by one or two men, or attached to a bicycle etc. [Jap. *jin-riki-sha* (*jin,* man, *riki,* strength, *sha,* vehicle)]

ricochet, *n.* a bounding or skipping of a stone, projectile, or bullet off a hard or flat surface; the act of aiming so as to produce this, or a hit so made. *v.i.* (*past, p.p.* **ricocheted**) to skip or bound in this manner. *v.t.* to aim at or hit thus. [F, etym. doubtful]

ricotta, *n.* a soft white Italian cheese made from sheep's milk. [It. from L *recocta,* fem. p.p. of *recoquĕre,* to cook again]

RICS, (*abbr.*) Royal Institution of Chartered Surveyors.

rictus, *n.* (*pl.* **rictuses, rictus**) the expanse of a person's or animal's open mouth, gape; grimace; the opening of a two-lipped corolla. [L, p.p. of *ringī,* to open the mouth wide]

rid[1], *v.t.* (*past* **ridded, rid,** *p.p.* **rid, †ridded**) to free, to clear, to disencumber (of); †to deliver, to save (from etc.); †to redd; †to drive away; †to destroy by violence. *a.* free, clear. **to be** or **get rid of,** to free oneself or become free from. **riddance,** *n.* clearance; deliverance; relief. **(a) good riddance,** a welcome relief from someone or something undesirable. [Icel. *rythja,* conf. with REDD]

†rid[2], **ridden,** *p.p.* RIDE.

riddle[1], *n.* a question or proposition put in ambiguous language to exercise the ingenuity; a puzzle, conundrum or enigma; any person, thing, or fact of an ambiguous, mysterious, or puzzling nature. *v.i.* to speak in riddles. *v.t.* to solve, to explain (a riddle, problem etc.); to express in a riddle or riddles (*usu. in p.p.*); to be a riddle to. **riddler,** *n.* **riddlingly,** *adv.* [OE *rædels,* from *rædan,* to READ (cp. Dut. *raadsel,* G *Rätsel*)]

riddle[2], *n.* a coarse sieve for sifting gravel, cinders etc., or washing ore. *v.t.* to pass through a riddle, to sift; to perforate with holes, as with shot; to assail with arguments, questions, facts etc. **riddlings,** *n.pl.* screenings, siftings. [OE *hriddel, hridder,* from *hrīd-,* to shake (cp. G *Reiter,* also L *crībrum*)]

riddler, riddlingly RIDDLE[1].

ride, *v.i.* (*past* **rode**, **†rid**, *p.p.* **ridden, †rid**) to sit and be carried along, as on a horse, cycle, public conveyance etc., esp. to go on horseback; to practise horsemanship; to float, to seem to float; to lie at anchor; to be supported, to be on something, esp. in motion; to project, to overlap; to work (up); to serve for riding; to be in a (specified) condition for riding. *v.t.* to sit on and be carried along by (a horse etc.); to traverse on a horse, cycle etc.; to execute or accomplish this; to cause to ride, to give a ride to; to be upborne by, to float over; to oppress, to tyrannize, to domineer (over); (*sl.*) to copulate with. *n.* the act of riding; a journey on horseback or in a public conveyance; a road for riding on, esp. through a wood; a district under an excise-officer; (*sl.*) an act of copulation; (*sl.*) a sexual partner. **to let (something) ride,** to let (something) alone, let (something) continue without interference. **to ride and tie,** to ride and walk alternately (of two persons having only one horse). **to ride down,** to overtake by riding; to trample on in riding. **to ride for a fall,** to go recklessly. **to ride hard,** to pitch violently when at anchor. **to ride out,** to come safely through (a storm etc.); to endure successfully. **to ride to death,** to overdo. **to ride to hounds,** to hunt. **to ride up,** of a skirt etc., to work up out of normal position. **to take for a ride,** to kidnap and murder; to play a trick on. **ridable, rideable,** *a.* **-ridden,** *comb. form* oppressed, dominated by, or excessively concerned with something in particular. **rider,** *n.* one who rides, esp. on a horse; an additional clause to a document, act etc., an opinion, recommendation etc. added to a verdict; a subsidiary problem, a corollary, an obvious supplement; an additional timber or plate for strengthening the framework of a ship (*usu. pl.*); a rope overlying or crossing another; (*Curling*) a stone dislodging another. **riderless**, *a.* **riding**[1], *n.* the act or state of one who rides; a road for riding on, esp. a grassed track through or beside a wood. **riding-crop,** *n.* a whip with a short lash used by riders on horseback. **riding-habit,** *n.* a woman's costume for riding on horseback. **riding-hood,** *n.* a hood formerly worn by women when travelling. **riding light,** *n.* light shown by a ship at anchor. **riding-master,** *n.* one who teaches riding, an officer superintending the instruction of troopers in the riding-school. **riding-school,** *n.* a place where riding is taught. [OE *rīdan* (cp. Dut. *rijdan,* G *reiten,* Icel. *rīthā,* Dan. *ride*)]

rideau, *n.* an eminence commanding a fortified place; a mound or ridge covering a camp from hostile approach. [F, curtain]

rider etc. RIDE.

ridge, *n.* the long horizontal angle formed by the junction of two slopes; an elevation of the earth's surface long in comparison with its breadth; a long and narrow hill-top or mountain-crest; a continuous range of hills or mountains; a strip of ground thrown up by a plough or other implement; the spine of an animal; a tongue of high pressure on a weather map. *v.t.* to break (a field etc.) into ridges; to plant in ridges; to mark or cover with ridges. *v.i.* to gather into or be marked with ridges. **ridge-piece, -plate,** *n.* a horizontal timber along the ridge of a roof. **ridge-pole,** *n.* a ridge-piece; the horizontal pole of a long tent. **ridgeway,** *n.* a road or way along a ridge. **ridgelet,** *n.* **ridgy,** *a.* [OE *hrycg* (cp. Dut. *rug,* G *Rücken,* Icel. *hryggr,* Dan. *ryg*)]

ridicule, *n.* words or actions intended to express contempt and excite laughter; derision, mockery; †ridiculousness. *v.t.* to treat with ridicule; to laugh at; to make fun of; to expose to derision. **ridiculer,** *n.* **ridiculous,** *a.* meriting or exciting ridicule. **ridiculously,** *adv.* **ridiculousness,** *n.* [L *ridiculus,* laughable, from *rīdēre,* to laugh]

riding[1] RIDE.

riding[2], *n.* one of the three former administrative divisions of Yorkshire. [orig. *thriding* (THIRD, -ING)]

Ridley[1], *n.* **Nicholas** (*c.* 1500–55), English Protestant bishop. He became chaplain to Henry VIII 1541, and bishop of London in 1550. He took an active part in the Reformation and supported Lady Jane Grey's claim to the throne. After Mary's accession he was arrested and burned as a heretic.

Ridley[2], *n.* **Nicholas** (1929–), British Conservative politician, and former cabinet minister. After a period in industry he became active as a 'dry' right winger in the Conservative Party: a 'Thatcherite' before Margaret Thatcher had brought the term to public attention. He served under Harold Macmillan, Edward Heath and Alec Douglas-Home, but did not become a member of the cabinet until 1983. His apparent disdain for public opinion caused his transfer, in 1989, from the politically sensitive Department of the Environment to that of Trade and Industry.

ridotto, *n.* an entertainment consisting of singing and dancing, esp. a masked ball. [It., from med. L *reductus,* orig. p.p. of *redūcere,* to REDUCE]

Rie, *n.* **Lucie** (1902–), Austrian-born potter who worked in England from the 1930s. Her pottery, exhibited all over the world, is simple and pure in form, showing a debt to Bernard Leach.

Riefenstahl, *n.* **Leni** (1902–), German film-maker. Her film of the Nazi rallies at Nuremberg *Triumph des Willens/Triumph of the Will* (1934), vividly illustrated Hitler's charismatic appeal but tainted her career. After World War II her work was blacklisted by the Allies until 1952.

Riel, *n.* **Louis** (1844–85), French-Canadian rebel, a champion of the Métis (an Indian-French people); he established a provisional government in Winnipeg in an unsuccessful revolt in 1869–70 and was hanged for treason after leading a second revolt in Saskatchewan in 1885.

riem, *n.* (*S Afr.*) a rawhide strap or thong. **riempie,** *n.* (dim. of *riem*) a long narrow riem used for lacing the backs of chairs etc. [Afrikaans, from Dut.]

Rienzi, *n.* **Cola di** (*c.* 1313–54), Italian political reformer. In 1347, he tried to re-establish the forms of an ancient Roman republic. His second attempt seven years later ended with his assassination.

riesling, *n.* a dry white wine, or the grape that produces it. [G]

Riesman, *n.* **David** (1909–), US sociologist, author of *The Lonely Crowd: A Study of the Changing American Character* (1950).

Rietvelt, *n.* **Gerrit Thomas** (1888–1964), Dutch architect, an exponent of De Stijl. He designed the Schroeder House at Utrecht 1924; he is also well known for colourful, minimalist chair design.

rieve, river REAVE.

rifacimento, *n.* (*pl.* **-ti-**) a recast of a literary work etc. [It., from *rifare* (RE-, L *facere,* to make)]

rife, *a.* occurring in great quantity, number etc., current, prevalent, abundant. †**rifely,** *adv.* **rifeness,** *n.* [late OE *rȳfe* (cp. Icel. *rīfa,* Dut. *rijf*)]

Riff, *n.* Berber people of N Morocco, who under Abd el-Krim long resisted the Spaniards and French.

riff, *n.* a phrase or figure played repeatedly in jazz or rock music, usu as background to an instrument solo. [perh. altered from *refrain*]

riffle[1], *n.* (*Gold-min.*) a groove, channel, slab, block or cleat set in an inclined trough, sluice, or cradle for arresting the particles of auriferous sand etc.; (*N Am.*) a timber or plank forming part of a fish-ladder; an obstruction in a stream; a scour. [etym. doubtful]

riffle[2], *v.t.* to ruffle; to flick through rapidly (the pages of a book etc.); to shuffle playing cards by halving the deck and flicking the corners together using both thumbs. *v.i.* to flick cursorily (with *through*).

riffler, *n.* a file with curved ends for working in shallow depressions etc. [F *rifloir,* from *rifler,* to RIFLE]

riffraff, *n.* worthless people; rabble. [formerly *riff* and *raff,* F *rif et raf,* prob. from Teut. (cp. MDut. *rijf ende raf*)]

rifle, *v.t.* to search and rob; to plunder, to pillage, to strip; to snatch and carry off; to furnish (a firearm or the bore or barrel of a firearm) with spiral grooves in order to give a rotary motion to the projectile. *v.i.* to shoot with a rifle. *n.* a firearm having the barrel spirally grooved so as to give a rotary motion to the projectile; (*pl.*) troops armed with rifles. **rifle-bird,** *n.* an Australian bird (*Ptilorrhis paradisea*) with velvety black plumage. **rifle-brigade,** *n.* a brigade comprising several British regiments of infantry. **rifle-corps,** *n.* **rifle-man,** *n.* **rifle-pit,** *n.* a trench or pit forming a projection for riflemen. **rifle range,** *n.* an area for target practice using rifles. **rifle-shot,** *n.* the distance a rifle will carry; a marksman with the rifle. **rifler,** *n.* a robber, a plunderer. **rifling,** *n.* the spiral grooves in the bore of a firearm which cause the rotation of the projectile fired. [OF *rifler,* to scrape, scratch, strip, plunder (cp. LG *rifeln,* G *riefeln,* Dan. *rifle,* Swed. *reffla*)]

rift, *n.* a cleft, a fissure; a wide crack, rent, or opening, made by riving or splitting; a break in cloud. *v.t.* (*past, p.p.* **riven**) to cleave, to split, to rive. *v.i.* to break open. **rift valley,** *n.* a narrow valley formed by the subsidence of the earth's crust between two faults. **riftless,** *a.* **rifty,** *adv.* [from Scand. (cp. Dan. and Norw. *rift,* Icel. *ript,* from *rīfa,* to RIVE))

Rift Valley, Great, volcanic valley formed 10–20 million years ago by a crack in the Earth's crust, and running about 6400 km/4000 miles from the Jordan valley in Syria through the Red Sea to Mozambique in SE Africa. At some points its traces have been lost by erosion, but elsewhere such as S Kenya, cliffs rise thousands of metres. It is marked by a series of lakes, including Lake Turkana (formerly Lake Rudolph) and volcanoes, such as Mount Kilimanjaro.

rig[1], *v.t.* (*pres.p.* **rigging,** *past, p.p.* **rigged**) to furnish or fit (a ship) with spars, gear, or tackle; to dress, clothe, or fit (up or out); to put together or fit (up) in a hasty or make-shift way. *v.i.* to be rigged. *n.* the way in which the masts and sails of a ship are arranged; (*coll.*) the style or look of a person's clothes etc.; an outfit, a turn-out; (*coll.*) an articulated lorry; an oil rig. **rig-out, -up,** *n.* dress, outfit; appearance or look as regards this. **rigger,** *n.* one who rigs vessels; a band-wheel having a slightly curved rim. **-rigger,** *comb. form* a ship rigged in the specified manner. **rigging,** *n.* the system of tackle, ropes etc. supporting the masts, and controlling the sails etc. of a ship; the adjustment or alignment of the components of an aeroplane. **rigging-loft,** *n.* a large room or gallery where rigging is fitted; a space over the stage in a theatre from which the scenery is worked. [etym. doubtful, Norw. and Swed. *rigga,* may be from Eng.]

rig[2], *n.* a swindling scheme, a corner, a dodge, a trick; a prank, a frolic, a practical joke; †a wanton, a strumpet. *v.t.* to manipulate fraudulently; to hoax, to trick. †*v.i.* to play the wanton. **to rig the market,** to manipulate the market so as to raise or lower prices for underhand purposes. **to run the rig,** to indulge in practical joking.

†**riggish,** *a.* [etym. doubtful]

rig[3], (*Sc.*, *North.*) RIDGE.

Riga, *n.* capital and port of Latvian Republic, USSR; population (1987) 900,000. A member of the Hanseatic League from 1282, Riga has belonged in turn to Poland (1582), Sweden (1621), and Russia (1710). It was the capital of independent Latvia (1918–40), and was occupied by Germany (1941–44), before being annexed by the USSR.

†**rigadoon,** *n.* a lively dance performed by one couple; the music (in duple time) for this. [F *rigaudon, rigodon,* etym. doubtful, perh. from *Rigaud,* name of a dancing-master]

†**rigation,** *n.* irrigation. [L *rigātio,* from *rigāre,* cp. IRRIGATE]

Rigaud, *n.* **Hyacinthe** (1659–1743), French portraitist, court painter to Louis XIV from 1688. His portrait of *Louis XIV*, 1701 (Louvre, Paris) is characteristically majestic, with the elegant figure of the king enveloped in ermine and drapery.

Rigel, *n.* the brightest star in the constellation Orion. It is a blue-white supergiant, with an estimated diameter of over 50 Suns. It is 900 light years away, and is 50,000 times more luminous than our Sun. It is the seventh-brightest star in the sky.

rigescent, *a.* growing stiff, rigid, or numb. **rigescence,** *n.* [L *rigescens -ntem,* pres.p. of *rigescere,* incept. of *rigēre,* to be stiff]

Rigg, *n.* **Diana** (1938–), English actress. Her stage roles include Héloïse in *Abelard and Héloïse* (1970), and television roles include Emma Peel in *The Avengers* (1965–67) and Lady Deadlock in *Bleak House* (1985). She became the hostess for *Mystery Theater* on US public TV 1989.

rigger, rigging etc. RIG[1].

riggish RIG[2].

right, *a.* required by or acting, being, or done in accordance with truth and justice; equitable, just, good, proper, correct, true, fit, suitable, most suitable, the preferable, the more convenient; sound, sane, well; properly done, placed etc., not mistaken, satisfactory; real, genuine, veritable; on or towards the side of the body which is to the south when the face is to the sunrise; straight; direct; formed by lines meeting perpendicularly; not oblique, involving or based on a right-angle or angles (of cones, pyramids, cylinders etc.); politically conservative, right-wing. *adv.* in accordance with truth and justice, justly, equitably, rightly; aright, exactly, correctly, properly; satisfactorily, well; very, quite, to the full; to or towards the right hand; straight; all the way to, completely. *n.* that which is right or just; fair or equitable treatment; the cause or party having justice on its side; just claim or title, esp. a claim enforceable at law, justification; that which one is entitled to; (*pl.*) proper condition, correct or satisfactory state; (*coll.*) the right hand; the right-hand side, part or surface of anything; a thing, part etc. pertaining or corresponding to this; the party sitting on the right of the president in a foreign legislature, usu. the more conservative party. *v.t.* to set in or restore to an upright, straight, correct, or proper position, to correct, make right, to rectify; to do justice to, to vindicate, to rehabilitate; to relieve from wrong or injustice. *v.i.* to resume a vertical position. *int.* expressing approval, compliance, enthusiasm. **all right,** (*coll.*) correct, satisfactory, in good condition, safe etc.; yes. **by right(s),** properly; with justice. **in one's own right,** by right independent of marriage. **in one's right mind,** sane, lucid. **in the right,** correct; in accordance with reason or justice. **right and left,** in all directions; on both sides; with both hands etc. **right away, right off,** *adv.* at once, immediately. **right, left and centre,** on every side. **right of way,** the right established by usage or by dedication to the public to use a track, path, road etc. across a person's land; the right of a vehicle or vessel to take precedence in passing according to law or custom; (*N Am.*) permanent way of a railway. **righto, right oh! right you are,** (*coll.*) forms of assent, approval etc. **to do someone right,** to treat someone justly. **to put** or **set to rights,** to arrange, to put in order. **to right the helm,** to place it amidships. **to serve one right,** to be thoroughly well deserved. **right-about,** *n.* the opposite direction, the reverse to the opposite direction. **right-angle,** *n. adv.* one formed by two lines meeting perpendicularly. **right-angled,** *a.* having a right-angle or angles. **at right-angles,** placed at or forming a right-angle. **right ascension,** *n.* the distance from the first point of Aries, measured along the celestial equator. **right hand,** *n.* the hand on the right side, esp. as the better hand; position on or direction to this side; one's best or most efficient assistant, aid, or support. **right hand,** *a.* situated on or towards the right hand; denoting one whose help is most useful or necessary. **right-hand man,** a soldier placed on this side; one's best assistant, aid etc. **right-handed,** *a.* using the right hand more readily than the left; clever, dexterous; used by or fitted for use by the right hand (of tools etc.); turning to the right (of the thread of a screw etc.). **right-hander,** *n.* a blow with the right hand. **right-handedness,** *n.* **right-hearted,** *a.* **right honourable,** a title given to peers, peeresses, privy councillors etc. **right-minded,** *a.* properly, justly, or equitably disposed. **right-mindedness,** *n.* **rights issue,** *n.* (*Stock Exch.*) an issue of new shares by a company to its existing shareholders on more favourable terms. **right-thinking,** *a.* holding acceptable opinions. **right whale,** *n.* a true whale, one yielding the best whalebone etc. **rightable,** *a.* †**righten,** *v.t.* **righter,** *n.* **rightful,** *a.* just, equitable, fair; entitled, holding, or held by legitimate claim. **rightfully,** *adv.* **rightfulness,** *n.* **rightist,** *n.* a conservative, an adherent of the right in politics. **rightless,** *a.* **rightly,** *adv.* justly, fairly, equitably; honestly, uprightly; correctly, accurately, properly. **rightness,** *n.* **rightward,** *a.*, *adv.* **right wing,** *n.* the conservative section of a party or grouping; the right side of an army, football ground etc. **right-wing,** *a.* of or on the right wing; having or relating to conservative political views. **right-winger,** *n.* [OE *riht* (cp. Dut. *regt,* G *recht,* Icel. *rettr*), cogn. with L *rectus,* rel. to *reg-,* root of *regere,* to rule]

righteous, *a.* just, upright, morally good; equitable, deserved, justifiable, fitting. **righteously,** *adv.* **righteousness,** *n.* [OE *rihtwīs* (RIGHT, WISE[1] or -WISE)]

rightful, rightly etc. RIGHT.

Rights of Man and the Citizen, Declaration of, historic French document. According to the statement of the French National Assembly (1789), it provides for: representation in the legislature; equality before the law; equality of opportunity; freedom from arbitrary imprisonment; freedom of speech and religion; taxation in proportion to ability to pay; and security of property. In 1946 were added equal rights for women; right to work, join a union, and strike; leisure, social security, and support in old age; and free education.

rigid, *a.* stiff, not easily bent, not pliant, unyielding; rigorous, strict, punctilious, inflexible, harsh, stern, austere. **rigid airship,** *n.* an airship in which the envelope is attached to a framework of hoops and girders. **rigidify,** *v.i.* (*pres.p.* **rigidifying**, *past, p.p.* **rigidified**) to make or become rigid. **rigidity**, **rigidness,** *n.* **rigidly,** *adv.* **rigidulous**, *a.* (*Bot.*) rather stiff. [L *rigidus*]

rigmarole, *n.* a long unintelligible story; loose disjointed talk. *a.* incoherent. [prob. corr. of RAGMAN-ROLL under RAGMAN[2]]

†**rigol,** *n.* a circle; a ring. [It. *rigolo,* dim. of *rigo, riga,* OHG *rīga,* line]

rigor, *n.* a feeling of chill, a shivering attended with stiffening etc., premonitory of fever etc.; a state of rigidity assumed by certain animals and commonly known as 'shamming dead'. **rigor mortis**, *n.* the stiffening of the body following death. [L, RIGOUR]

rigour, *n.* strictness, exactness in enforcing rules; stiffness or inflexibility of opinion, doctrine, observance etc., austerity of life; sternness, harshness, asperity; inclemency of the weather etc., hardship, distress; (*pl.*) harsh proceeding, severities. **rigorism,** *n.* **rigorist,** *a.*

and *n.* **rigorous,** *a.* strict, precise, severe, stern, inflexible; logically accurate, precise, stringent; inclement, harsh. **rigorously,** *adv.* **rigorousness,** *n.* [OF, from L *rigōrem,* nom. *-or,* from *rigēre,* to be stiff]

Rigsdag, *n.* the Danish parliament. [Dan. *rige,* kingdom, *dag,* DAY]

Rig-Veda, *n.* the oldest and most original of the Vedas, the chief sacred writings of Hinduism. It consists of hymns to the Aryan gods, such as Indra, and to nature gods. [Sansk. *ric,* praise, *veda,* knowledge]

rigwiddy, *n.* (*Sc.*) a band, orig. of twisted withes, going over a horse's back to support the shafts. *a.* deserving the rope (or gallows). [RIG[3], WITHY]

Riksdag, *n.* the Swedish parliament. [Swed., cp. RIGSDAG]

rile, *v.t.* to make angry, to vex, to irritate. [var. of ROIL]

Riley, *n.* **Bridget (Louise)** (1931–), British Op art painter. In the early 1960s she invented her characteristic style, arranging hard-edged black-and-white dots or lines in regular patterns that created disturbing effects of scintillating light and movement. *Fission,* 1963 (Museum of Modern Art, New York) is an example of this style. She introduced colour in the late 1960s and experimented with silk-screen prints on Plexiglass.

rilievo, *n.* (*pl.* **-vi**) raised or embossed work, relief. [RELIEF[2]]

Rilke, *n.* **Rainer Maria** (1875–1926), Austrian writer, born in Prague. His prose works include the semi-autobiographical *Die Aufzeichnungen des Malte Laurids Brigge/Notebook of Malte Laurids Brigge* (1910), and his poetical works *Die Sonnette an Orpheus/Sonnets to Orpheus* (1923) and *Duisener Elegien/Duino Elegies* (1923). His verse is characterized by a form of mystic pantheism that seeks to achieve a state of ecstasy in which existence can be apprehended as a whole.

rill, *n.* a small brook, a rivulet; a trench or furrow; a rille. *v.i.* to issue or flow in a small stream. **rille,** *n.* a furrow, trench or narrow valley on Mars or the moon. **rillet,** *n.* [cp. LG and G *Rille,* Dut. *ril*]

rim[1], *n.* an outer edge, border or margin, esp. of a vessel or other circular object; a ring or frame; the peripheral part of the framework of a wheel, between the spokes or hub and the tyre; *v.t.* (*past, p.p.* **rimmed**) to form or furnish with a rim; to serve as rim to, to edge, to border. **rim-fire,** *a.* having the detonating fulminate in the rim not the centre (of a cartridge). **rim-brake,** *n.* one acting on the rim not the hub of a wheel. **rimless,** *a.* **rimmed,** *a.* having a rim (*usu. in comb.*). [OE *rima* (cp. Icel. *rime, rimi,* strip, ridge)]

†**rim[2],** *n.* the peritoneum or inner membrane (of the abdomen). [OE *reoma* (cp. Dut. *riem,* G *Riemen,* strap, thong)]

Rimbaud, *n.* **(Jean Nicolas) Arthur** (1854–91), French Symbolist poet. His verse was chiefly written before the age of 20, notably *Les Illuminations* published 1886.

rime[1] RHYME.

rime[2], *n.* hoar-frost; a deposit of ice caused by freezing fog or low temperatures. *v.t.* to cover (as) with rime. **rimy,** *a.* [OE *hrīm* (cp. Dut. *rijm,* Icel. *hrīm,* OF *rime*)]

rimose, -mous, *a.* full of chinks or cracks, as the bark of trees. [L *rīmōsus,* from *rīma,* chink]

rimple, *n.* a wrinkle, a fold. *v.t.* to wrinkle, to pucker, to ripple. *v.i.* to become wrinkled or rippled. [cp. OE *hrimpan,* also RUMPLE]

Rimsky-Korsakov, *n.* **Nikolay Andreyevich** (1844–1908), Russian composer. He used Russian folk idiom and rhythms in his Romantic compositions and published a text on orchestration. His operas include *The Maid of Pskov* (1873), *The Snow Maiden* (1882), *Mozart and Salieri* (1898), and *The Golden Cockerel* (1907), a satirical attack on despotism that was banned until 1909.

rimu, *n.* the red pine of New Zealand. [Maori]

rimy RIME[2].

rind, *n.* the outer coating of trees, fruits etc.; bark, peel, husk, skin. *v.t.* to strip the rind from. **rinded,** *a.* having rind (*in comb.* as *coarse-rinded*). **rindless, rindy,** *a.* [OE, cp. G *Rinde*]

rinderpest, *n.* a malignant contagious disease attacking ruminants, esp. oxen, cattle-plague. [G *Rinder,* pl. of *Rind,* OX, PEST]

ring[1], *n.* a circlet; a circlet of gold etc., worn usu. on a finger or in the ear as an ornament, token etc.; anything in the form of a circle; a line, mark, moulding, space or band round or the rim of a circular or cylindrical object or sphere; a concentric band of wood formed by the annual growth of a tree; a group or concourse of people, things etc. arranged in a circle; a circular space, enclosure or arena for boxing, circus performances etc.; a combination of persons acting in concert, often illegally for commercial or political ends; a closed chain of atoms; in mathematics, a closed set. *v.t.* (*past, p.p.* **ringed**) to put a ring round; to encircle, to enclose, to hem in; to fit with a ring; to cut a ring of bark from (a tree); to put a ring on or in. *v.i.* (*past* **ringed,** *p.p.* **ringed**) to form a ring; to rise in spirals (of a bird). **the ring,** boxing. **to make, run rings round,** to outstrip easily. **to throw one's hat into the ring,** to challenge; to present oneself as a candidate or contestant. **ring-bark,** *v.t.* to cut a ring of bark from a tree in order to check growth, kill it or induce it to fruit. **ring binder,** *n.* a binder consisting of metal rings which hold loose-leaf pages by means of perforations in the paper. **ring-bolt,** *n.* a bolt with a ring or eye at one end. **ring-bone,** *n.* a deposit of bony matter on the pastern-bones of a horse. **ring-dove,** *n.* a wood-pigeon. **ring-fence** FENCE. **ring-finger,** *n.* the third finger, esp. of the left hand, on which the wedding-ring is worn. **ring-leader,** *n.* the leader of a riot, mutiny, piece of mischief etc. **ring main,** *n.* an electrical system in which power points are connected to the supply through a closed circuit. **ringmaster,** *n.* the manager and master of ceremonies of a circus performance. **ring-neck,** *n.* a ring plover; the ring-necked duck; a variety of Australian parakeet. *a.* **ring-necked,** *a.* having a band or bands of colour round the neck. **ring-ouzel,** *n.* a thrush-like bird, *Turdus torquatus,* allied to the blackbird, having a white band on the breast. **ring-pull,** *n.* a metal ring attached to a can of soft drink, beer etc. which opens it when pulled. **ring road,** *n.* a road circumnavigating an urban centre. **ring-side,** *n., a.* (of) the area or seats immediately beside a boxing or wrestling ring or any sporting arena; (of) any position affording a close and unobstructed view. **ring-snake,** *n.* the grass-snake; a harmless American snake. †**ring-streaked,** *a.* streaked with bands of colour. **ring-tail, -tailed,** *a.* having the tail marked with rings or bands of colour. **ring-wall,** *n.* a wall round an estate etc. (cp. RING-FENCE). **ringworm,** *n.* a contagious skin-disease, tinea tonsurans, caused by a white fungus. **ringed,** *a.* having, encircled by or marked with a ring or rings (*often in comb.*); annular. **ringer[1],** *n.* a quoit falling round the pin; a quoit so thrown or a throw resulting in this; one who rings; (*Austral.*) the fastest shearer in a shearing-shed. **ringless,** *a.* **ringlet,** *n.* a small ring or circle; a curl, a curly lock of hair; a satyrid butterfly, *Hipparchia hyperanthus.* **ringleted,** *a.* **ring-like,** *a.* [OE *hring* (cp. Dut. and G *Ring,* Icel. *hringr*)]

ring[2], *v.i.* (*past* **rang,** *p.p.* **rung**) to give a clear vibrating sound, as a sonorous metallic body when struck; to re-echo, to resound, to reverberate, to continue to sound; to have a sensation as of vibrating metal, to tingle (of the ears); to give a summons or signal by ringing. *v.t.* to cause to ring; to sound (a knell, peal etc.) on a bell or bells; to utter, to repeat; to summon, signal, announce, proclaim, celebrate etc., by ringing; (*coll.*) to telephone; to usher (in or out). *n.* the sound of a bell or other resonant body; the act of ringing a bell; a set of bells tuned harmonically; a ringing sound, a continued or reverberated sound; the quality of resonance; (*coll.*) a telephone call; the characteristic sound of a voice, statement etc. **to ring a bell,** to sound familiar, to cause to remember. **to ring down, up,** to lower or raise the curtain in a theatre. **to ring false** or

true, to appear genuine or insincere. **to ring in,** to report in by telephone. **to ring off,** to end a telephone call; to hang up (the receiver). **to ring the changes** CHANGE. **to ring up,** to call on the telephone; **ringer²,** *n.* one who rings, e.g. church bells; a device for ringing a bell-pull; a horse, athlete etc. racing under the name of another; (*coll.*) a person or thing almost identical to another, as in a **dead ringer**. **ringing,** *a.* sounding like a bell; sonorous, resonant. *n.* a sound of or as a bell. **ringing-tone,** *n.* the tone heard on a telephone after an unengaged number is dialled. **ringingly,** *adv.* [OE *hringan* prob. imit.]

ringent, *a.* irregular and gaping (of a flower or corolla). [L *ringens -ntem,* pres.p. of *ringere,* to gape]

ringgit, *n.* the unit of currency of Malaysia, the Malaysian dollar, equal to 100 cents. [Malay]

ringhals, rinkhals, *n.* (*pl.* **-hals, -halses**) a venom-spitting snake of southern Africa, *Haemachatus haemachatus.* [Afrikaans, ring neck]

rink, *n.* a strip of ice or of a green marked off for playing bowls or curling; a division of a side so playing; a prepared floor for roller-skating or an area of usu. artificially-formed ice for ice-skating; the building or structure housing a skating-rink. [prob. rel. to RANK¹ or RING¹]

rinse, *v.t.* to wash, to cleanse with an application of clean water; to remove soap by rinsing. *n.* the act of rinsing; a hair tint. **rinser,** *n.* [F *rincer,* etym. doubtful]

Rinzai, *n.* (Chinese **Lin-ch'i**) a school of Zen Buddhism introduced to Japan from China in the 12th cent. by the monk Eisai and others. It emphasizes rigorous monastic discipline and sudden enlightenment by meditation on a *kōan* (paradoxical question).

Río de Janeiro, *n.* port and resort in Brazil; population (1980) 5,091,000, metropolitan area 10,217,000. The name commemorates the arrival of Portuguese explorers 1 Jan. 1502, but there is in fact no river. Sugar Loaf Mountain stands at the entrance to the harbour. It was the capital of Brazil (1822–1960).

Río Grande, *n.* river rising in the Rockies in S Colorado, US, and flowing south to the Gulf of Mexico, where it is reduced to a trickle by irrigation demands on its upper reaches; length 3050 km/1900 miles. Its last 2400 km/1500 miles form the US-Mexican border.

Rioja, *n.* a type of Spanish table wine. [a region in N Spain]

Riom, *n.* town on the river Ambène, in the Puy-de-Dôme *département* of central France. In World War II, it was the scene Feb.–Apr. 1942 of the 'war guilt' trials of several prominent Frenchmen by the Vichy government. The accused included the former prime ministers Blum and Daladier, and Gen Gamelin. The occasion turned into a wrangle over the reasons for French unpreparedness for war, and at the German dictator Hitler's instigation, the court was dissolved. The defendants remained in prison until released by the Allies 1945.

Río Muni, *n.* the mainland portion of EQUATORIAL GUINEA.

Riopelle, *n.* **Jean Paul** (1923–), Canadian artist, active in Paris from 1946. In the 1950s he developed an abstract expressionist style and produced colourful impasto (with paint applied in a thick mass) paintings and sculptures. *Encounter*, 1956 (Wallraf-Richartz Museum, Cologne, W Germany) is a typically rough-textured canvas.

riot, *n.* a disturbance, an outbreak of lawlessness, a tumult, an uproar; wanton or unrestrained conduct, loose living, profligacy, revelry; unrestrained indulgence in something; luxuriant growth, lavish display; in law, a tumultuous disturbance of the peace by three or more persons; (*coll.*) a person or thing which is hilariously funny. *v.i.* to take part in a riot; to revel, to behave or live licentiously. **to run riot,** to act without control or restraint; to grow luxuriantly. **Riot Act,** *n.* in the UK, an act passed 1714 to suppress the Jacobite disorders enjoining riotous persons to disperse within an hour of the Act being read by a magistrate after which they might be dispersed by force. It was superseded by the 1986 Public Order Act. **to read the riot act,** to give a severe warning that something must cease; to reprimand severely. **riot gun,** *n.* a type of gun used to disperse rioters. **riot police,** *n.* police specially trained and equipped to deal with rioters. **riot shield,** *n.* a large transparent shield used as protection by riot police. **rioter,** *n.* **riotous,** *a.* **riotously,** *adv.* **riotousness, †riotry,** *n.* [OF *riote,* whence, *rioter,* to riot (cp. It. *riotta*), etym. doubtful]

RIP, (*abbr.*) *requiescat, requiescant in pace,* may he, she, they rest in peace. [L]

rip¹, *v.t.* (*past, p.p.* **ripped**) to tear or cut forcibly (out, off, up etc.); to rend, to split; to saw (wood) with the grain; to take out or away by cutting or tearing; to make a long tear or rent in; to undo the seams of; to open (up) for examination or disclosure; to make (a passage, opening etc.) by ripping; to utter (an oath etc.) with violence. *v.i.* to come or be torn forcibly apart, to tear; to go (along) at a great pace. *n.* a rent made by ripping, a tear. **to let it rip,** (*coll.*) to allow to proceed without restraint. **to let rip,** (*coll.*) to speak, act or proceed without restraint. **to rip off,** to steal (from); to cheat. **rip cord,** *n.* a cord which when pulled, releases a parachute from its pack or opens the gas-bag of a balloon allowing it to descend. **rip-off,** *n.* (*sl.*). a theft; a cheat; an exploitative imitation. **rip-roaring,** *a.* (*coll.*) noisy, unrestrained, exuberant. **rip-saw,** *n.* one for sawing along the grain. **ripper,** *n.* one who rips or tears; a rip-saw; a murderer who mutilates the victim's body; (*sl.*) an excellent person or thing. **ripping,** *a.* (*sl.*) excellent, fine, splendid. **rippingly,** *adv.* (*sl.*) [prob. from Scand.]

rip², *n.* disreputable person, a scamp; a cheat; a worthless horse. [etym. doubtful, perh. var. of *rep,* short for REPROBATE]

rip³, *n.* an eddy, an overfall, a stretch of broken water; a riptide. **rip current, riptide,** *n.* a rip caused by tidal currents flowing away from the land. [etym. doubtful, perh. from RIP¹]

riparian, *a.* pertaining to or dwelling on the banks of a river. *n.* an owner of property on the banks of a river. **riparial,** *a.* [L *rīpārius,* from *rīpa,* bank]

ripe, *a.* ready for reaping or gathering; mature, come to perfection in growth, fully developed, mellow, fit for use, ready or in a fit state (for); resembling ripe fruit, rosy, rounded, luscious. *v.t., v.i.* to ripen. **ripely,** *adv.* **ripen,** *v.t., v.i.* **ripener,** *n.* **ripeness,** *n.* [OE *rīpe* (cp. Dut. *rijp,* G *reif*), whence *rīpian,* to ripen]

ripieno, *a.* (*Mus.*) additional, supplemental. *n.* a ripieno player or instrument. **ripienist,** *n.* [It. (*ri-,* RE-, *pieno,* L *plēnus,* full)]

riposte, *n.* in fencing, a quick lunge or return thrust; a quick reply, a retort, a repartee; a counterstroke. *v.i.* to reply with a riposte. [F *riposte,* It. *risposta,* repartee]

ripper, ripping etc. RIP¹.

ripple¹, *n.* a large comb for removing the seeds from flax. *v.t.* to clean or remove seeds with a ripple. [cp. Dut. *repel* (v. *repelen*), G *Riffel* (v. *riffeln*)]

ripple², *v.i.* to run in small waves or undulations; to sound as water running over a rough surface. *v.t.* to agitate or cover with small waves or undulations. *n.* the ruffling of the surface of water; a wavelet; an undulation (of water, hair etc.); a sound as of rippling water. **ripple-mark,** *n.* a mark as of ripples or wavelets on sand, mud, rock etc. **ripple-marked,** *a.* **ripplet,** *n.* **rippling,** *n., a.* **ripplingly,** *adv.* **ripply,** *a.* [etym. doubtful]

riprap, *n.* (*N Am.*) a foundation of loose stones, as in deep water or on a soft bottom; a firework giving a succession of loud reports. *v.t.* to give such a foundation. [redupl. of RAP¹]

rip-saw RIP¹.

Ripuarian, *a.* of or pertaining to the ancient Franks dwelling near the Rhine; applied to their code of laws. *n.* a Ripuarian Frank. [med. L *Ripuārius,* perh. from L *rīpa,* bank]

Rip Van Winkle, *n.* legendary US character invented by Washington Irving in his 1819 tale of a man who falls into a magical 20-year sleep, and wakes to find he has slumbered through the War of Independence.

riro-riro, *n.* the grey warbler of New Zealand, the New Zealand wren. [Maori]

RISC, *n.* in computing, a kind of processor on a single silicon chip that is faster and more powerful than others in common use today. By reducing the range of operations the processor can carry out, the chips are able to optimise those operations to execute more quickly. Computers based on RISC chips became commercially available in the late 1980s but are less widespread than traditional processors. [acronym for *r*educed *i*nstruction-*s*et *c*omputer]

rise, *v.i.* (*past* **rose**, *p.p.* **risen**) to move upwards, to ascend, to leave the ground, to mount, to soar; to get up from a lying, kneeling, or sitting position, or out of bed, to become erect, to stand up; to adjourn, to end a session; to come to life again; to swell or project upwards; to increase, to become lofty or tall; to be promoted, to thrive; to increase in confidence, cheerfulness, energy, force, intensity, value, price etc.; to slope up; to arise, to come into existence, to originate; to come to the surface, to come into sight; to become audible; to become higher in pitch; to respond esp. with annoyance; to become equal to; to break into insurrection, to revolt, to rebel (against). *n.* the act of rising; ascent, elevation; an upward slope, the degree of this; a hill, a knoll; source, origin, start; increase or advance in price, value, power, rank, age, prosperity, height, amount, salary etc.; promotion, upward progress in social position, advancement; the rising of a feeding fish to the surface; the vertical part of an arch, step etc.; appearance above the horizon, rising (of the sun etc.). **to give rise to,** to cause. **to rise and shine,** to rise from bed in the morning. **to rise to the occasion,** to become equal to the demands of an occurrence, event etc. **to take a rise out of someone,** to provoke a person to anger, by teasing. **riser,** *n.* one who or that which rises; the vertical part of a step etc. **rising,** *n.* a mounting up or ascending; a resurrection; a revolt, an insurrection; a protuberance, a tumour, a knoll; the agent causing dough to rise. *a.* increasing; growing. *adv.* (*coll.*) approaching, nearing. **rising damp,** *n.* the absorption of ground moisture into the fabric of a building. [OE *rīsan,* cp. Dut. *rijzen,* G *reisen,* Icel. *rīsa,* OHG *rīsan*]

rishi, *n.* a seer, a saint, an inspired poet, esp. one of the seven sages said to have communicated the Vedas to mankind. [Sansk.]

risible, *a.* inclined to laugh; exciting laughter; pertaining to laughter. **risibility,** *n.* [F, from late L *rīsibilis,* from *rīdēre,* to laugh]

rising RISE.

risk, *n.* hazard, chance of harm, injury, loss etc.; a person or thing liable to cause a hazard or loss. *v.t.* to expose to risk or hazard; to venture on, to take the chances of. **at risk,** in danger (of); vulnerable (to). **to run a risk,** to incur a hazard; to encounter danger. †**risker,** *n.* **riskful,** *a.* **riskily,** *adv.* **riskiness,** *n.* **riskless,** *a.* **risky,** *a.* dangerous, hazardous; venturesome, daring; **risqué,** *a.* (F) suggestive of indecency, indelicate. [F *risque,* It. *risco*]

Risorgimento, *n.* (*pl.* **-tos**) movement for Italian national unity and independence from 1815. Uprisings failed in 1848–49, but with French help, a war against Austria, including the Battle of Solferino (1859), led to the foundation of an Italian kingdom (1861). Unification was finally completed with the addition of Venetia (1866) and the Papal States (1870). Leading figures in the movement included Cavour, Mazzini, and Garibaldi. **risorgimento,** *n.* a rebirth, renewal, revival. [It., RESURRECTION]

risotto, *n.* an Italian dish of rice cooked in butter and stock or broth, with onions, cheese, chicken, ham etc. [It.]

risqué RISK.

rissole, *n.* a ball or flat cake of minced meat, fish etc., fried with breadcrumbs etc. [F, from OF *roussole,* perh. from L *russeolus,* reddish, from *russus,* red]

rit., (*abbr.*) ritardando; ritenuto.

ritardando, *adv., a.* (*Mus. direction*) slower, slowing. *n.* (*pl.* **-dos**) a slowing down; a musical passage played in this way. [It., from *ritardare,* to RETARD]

rite, *n.* a religious or solemn prescribed act, ceremony or observance; (*pl.*) the prescribed acts, ceremonies or forms of worship of any religion. **rite of passage,** a ceremony marking an individual's change of status, esp. into adulthood or matrimony (also **rite de passage,** [F]). [L *rītus*]

ritenuto, *a., adv.* (*Mus.*) restrained, held back. *n.* (*pl.* **-tos**) a passage played in this way. [It., from L *ritenēre,* to hold back]

ritornello, *n.* (*pl.* **-lli**, **-llos**) (*Mus.*) a brief prelude, interlude or refrain. [F *ritournelle,* It. *ritornello,* dim. of *ritorno,* RETURN]

Ritter, *n.* **(Woodward Maurice) 'Tex'** (1905–74), US singer and actor, popular as a singing cowboy in 'B' films in the 1930s and 1940s. He sang the title song to *High Noon* (1952), and his other films include *Sing Cowboy Sing* (1937) and *Arizona Trail* (1943).

†**ritter** REITER.

ritual, *a.* pertaining to, consisting of or involving rites. *n.* a prescribed manner of performing divine service; performance of rites and ceremonies, esp. in an elaborate or excessive way; a book setting forth the rites and ceremonies of a particular Church; any formal or customary act or series of acts consistently followed; (*pl.*) ritual observances. **ritualism,** *n.* punctilious or exaggerated observance of ritual. **ritualist,** *n.* **ritualistic,** *a.* **ritualistically,** *adv.* **ritualization, -isation,** *n.* **ritualize, -ise,** *v.t., v.i.* **ritually,** *adv.* [F, from L *rītuālis,* from *rītus,* RITE]

ritzy, *a.* (*coll.*) elegant, showy, luxurious, rich. **ritzily,** *adv.* **ritziness,** *n.* [after the *Ritz* hotels estab. by César Ritz, 1850–1918]

†**rivage,** *n.* a bank, a shore, a coast. [F, from *rive,* L *rīpa,* bank]

rival, *n.* one's competitor for something; a person or thing considered as equal to another; one striving to surpass another in a quality, pursuit etc., an emulator. *a.* being a rival, having the same claims or pretensions, emulous; in competition. *v.t.* (*past, p.p.* **rivalled**) to vie with, to emulate, to strive to equal or surpass; to be, or almost be, the equal of. **rivalry, rivalship,** *n.* [F, from L *rīvālis,* orig. on the same stream, from *rīvus,* stream]

rive, *v.t.* (*p.p.* **riven**, †**rived**) to tear, split, cleave or rend asunder; to wrench or rend (away, from, off etc.). *v.i.* to split, to cause to split. [Icel. *rīfa,* cp. Dan. *rive,* Swed. *rifva*]

†**rivel,** *v.t., v.i.* to wrinkle, to pucker; to shrivel (up). **rivelled,** *a.* [OE *ge-riflian,* extant only in *rifelede,* wrinkled, etym. doubtful]

riven RIVE.

river, *n.* a large stream of water flowing in a channel over a portion of the earth's surface and discharging itself into the sea, a lake, a marsh or another river; a large and abundant stream, a copious flow. *a.* of, or dwelling in or beside, a river or rivers. **to sell down the river,** to let down, to betray. **river-bed, -channel,** *n.* the channel in which a river flows. **river-crab,** *n.* a freshwater crab belonging to the genus *Thelphusa.* **river-craft,** *n. pl.* small craft plying only on rivers. **river-god,** *n.* a deity presiding over or personifying a river. **river-hog,** *n.* an African wild hog of the genus *Potamochoerus,* inhabiting river banks etc. **river-horse,** *n.* the hippopotamus. **river novel** ROMAN FLEUVE. **river-side,** *n.* the ground along the bank of a river. *a.* built on or pertaining to this. **riverain,** *a.* of or pertaining to a river; living on or near a river. *n.* one who lives on or near a river. **rivered,** *a.* having a river or rivers (*usu. in comb.*). **riverine,** *a.* of, pertaining to, resembling or produced by a river; riparian. **riverless,** *a.* **rivery,** *a.* like a river; having many rivers. [A-F *rivere,* OF *riviere,* pop. L *rīpāria,* from *rīpa,* bank (cp. RIPARIAN)]

Rivera[1], **Primo de** PRIMO DE RIVERA.

Rivera[2], *n.* **Diego** (1886–1957), Mexican painter, active in Europe until 1921. He received many public commissions for murals exalting the Mexican revolution. A vast cycle on historical themes (National Palace, Mexico City) was begun in 1929. In the 1930s he visited the US and produced murals in the Rockefeller Center, New York (later overpainted because he included a portrait of Lenin).

rivet, *n.* a short bolt, pin or nail, usu. with a flat head at one end, the other end being flattened out and clinched by hammering, used for fastening metal plates together, ornamenting denim jeans etc. *v.t.* (*past, p.p.* **riveted**) to join or fasten together with a rivet or rivets; to clinch; to fasten firmly; to fix (attention, eyes etc. upon); to engross the attention of. **riveter,** *n.* **riveting,** *n., a.* [F, from *river,* to clinch, etym. doubtful]

Riviera, *n.* the Mediterranean coast of France and Italy from Marseille to La Spezia.

riviera, *n.* a coastal strip reminiscent of the French and Italian Rivieras on the Mediterranean. [It., shore]

rivière, *n.* a necklace of gems, usu. of several strings. [F, RIVER]

rivulet, *n.* a small stream; one of the Geometridae, a family of moths. [perh. through L *rīvulus,* dim. from *rīvus,* stream]

Rix, *n.* **Brian** (1924–), British actor and manager. He became known for his series of farces at London's Whitehall Theatre, notably *Dry Rot* (1954–58). He made several films for cinema and television, including *A Roof Over My Head* (1977), and is responsible for promoting charities for the mentally handicapped.

Riyadh, *n.* (Arabic **Ar Riyad**) capital of Saudi Arabia and of the Central Province, formerly the sultanate of Nejd, in an oasis, connected by rail with Damman on the Arabian Gulf; population (1986) 1,500,000.

riyal, *n.* the unit of currency of Dubai, Qatar, Saudi Arabia and the Yemen (also **rial**). [Arab., from Sp. *real,* REAL[2]]

rizzar, *v.t.* to dry (haddocks etc.) in the sun. *n.* a rizzared haddock. [Sc., from obs. F *ressoré,* rizzared (*sorer,* to dry, to make red)]

Rizzio, *n.* **David** (1533–66), Italian adventurer at the court of Mary, Queen of Scots. After her marriage to Darnley, Rizzio's influence over her incited her husband's jealousy, and he was murdered by Darnley and his friends.

RKO (Radio Keith Orpheum), *n.* US film production and distribution company, formed 1928 as a result of a series of mergers and acquisitions. It was the most financially unstable of the major Hollywood studios, despite the success of many of its films, including *King Kong* (1933) and the series of musicals starring Fred Astaire and Ginger Rogers. In 1948, Howard Hughes bought the studio and accelerated its decline through poor management. The company ceased production 1953.

RL, (*abbr.*) Rugby League.

Rly, (*abbr.*) railway.

RM, (*abbr.*) Royal Mail; Royal Marines.

rm, (*abbr.*) ream; room.

RMA, (*abbr.*) Royal Marine Artillery; Royal Military Academy.

RN, (*abbr.*) Registered Nurse; Royal Navy.

Rn, (*chem. symbol*) radon.

RNA, *n.* RIBONUCLEIC ACID [*ribo*nucleic *a*cid]

RNIB, (*abbr.*) Royal National Institute for the Blind.

RNLI, (*abbr.*) Royal National Lifeboat Institution.

roa, *n.* the large, brown kiwi. [Maori]

roach[1], *n.* a freshwater fish, *Leuciscus rutilus,* allied to the carp. [OF *roche, roce,* perh. from Teut. (cp. G *Roche,* OE *reohhe*)]

roach[2], *n.* the upward curve in the foot of a square sail. [etym. doubtful]

roach[3], *n.* (*N Am.*) short for COCKROACH; (*sl.*) the butt or filter of a cannabis cigarette.

Roach, *n.* **Hal** (1892–), US film producer, usually of comedies, active from the 1910s to the 1940s. He worked with Laurel and Hardy, and also produced films for Harold Lloyd and Charley Chase. His work includes *The Music Box* (1932), *Way Out West* (1936), and *Of Mice and Men* (1939).

road, *n.* a track or way for travelling on, esp. a broad strip of ground suitable for motor-vehicles, forming a public line of communication between places, a highway; way of going anywhere, route, course; a roadstead. **one for the road,** (*coll.*) a last drink before leaving. **on the road,** passing through, travelling, touring (often as a way of life). **rule of the road,** a regulation governing the methods of passing each other for vehicles on the road, vessels on the water etc. **to get in, out (of) someone's, the road,** (*esp. Sc.*) to get in or out of the way. **to hit the road,** to leave, to begin travelling. **to take (to) the road,** to set out on a journey; to become an itinerant. **road bed,** *n.* the foundation upon which a railway track or highway is laid. **roadblock,** *n.* a road obstructed by the army or police checking for escaped criminals, terrorists etc. **road-book,** *n.* a guide-book describing roads, distances etc. **road-hog,** *n.* a selfish motorist or cyclist paying no regard to the convenience of other people using the road. **road film, movie,** *n.* a film or genre of film that has a central plot involving a journey. **road house,** *n.* a public house, restaurant etc. on a highway which caters for motorists. **road-man,** *n.* one who keeps roads in repair. **road-metal,** *n.* broken stones for road-making. **road roller,** *n.* a vehicle with a large metal roller for compacting the surface of a newly-laid (section of) road. **road-sense,** *n.* the instinct of a road-user which enables him or her to cope with a traffic emergency, avoid an accident etc. **road-show,** *n.* a touring group of performers; a musical or theatrical performance by such a group; a live or prerecorded outside broadcast by a touring radio or television unit. **roadside,** *n.* the border of a road. *a.* pertaining to this, situated or growing there. **roadstead,** *n.* an anchorage for ships some distance from the shore. **road test,** *n.* a test for roadworthiness. *v.t.* **roadway,** *n.* the central part of a highway, used by vehicles, horses etc.; the part of a bridge, railway etc., used for traffic. **roadwork,** *n.* physical training comprising running or jogging along roads. *n.pl.* repairs to or under a section of road. **roadworthiness,** *n.* **roadworthy,** *a.* fit for use or travel. **roadie,** *n.* (*sl.*) a person employed to transport, set up and dismantle the instruments and equipment of a touring band or pop group. **roadless,** *a.* **roadster,** *n.* a horse, cycle or motor-car suitable for the road, opposed to a racer; (*N Am. dated*) a two-seater automobile. [OE *rād,* from *rīdan,* RIDE]

roadway, roadworthy ROAD.

roam, *v.i.* to wander about without any definite purpose, to rove, to ramble. *v.t.* to range, to wander, to rove over. **roamer,** *n.* [etym. doubtful]

roan[1], *a.* of a bay, sorrel or dark colour, with spots of grey or white thickly interspersed; of a mixed colour having a decided shade of red. *n.* a roan colour, a roan animal, esp. a horse. [OF (cp. It. and Sp. *roano,* Port. *ruão*), etym. unknown]

roan[2], *n., a.* (of) a soft flexible leather made of sheepskin tanned with sumach. [perh. from *Rouen,* France]

roan[3], ROWAN.

roar, *v.i.* to make a loud, deep, hoarse, continued sound, as a lion; to make a confused din like this (of a person in rage, distress or loud laughter, the sea, thunder, guns, a conflagration etc.); to make a noise in breathing (of a diseased horse); to resound, to re-echo, to be full of din (of a place). *v.t.* to shout, say, sing or utter with a roaring voice. *n.* a loud, deep, hoarse, continued sound as of a lion etc.; a confused din resembling this; a burst of mirth or laughter; a loud engine noise. **roarer,** *n.* one who roars; a broken-winded horse. **roaring,** *a.* shouting, noisy, boisterous, stormy; brisk, active. *n.* a loud, continued or confused noise; a peculiar sound emitted during respiration by some horses, due to disease in the air-passages. *adv.* extremely, boisterously. **roaring drunk,** extremely and noisily drunk. **roaring trade,** *n.* thriving and profitable business. **the roaring forties** FORTY. **roaringly,** *adv.* [OE *rārian* (cp. G *raren,* MDut. *reeren,* G *rehren*), prob. imit.]

roast, *v.t.* to cook by exposure to the direct action of radiant heat, esp. at an open fire or (incorrectly) to bake in an oven; to dry and parch (coffee beans etc.) by exposure to heat; to heat excessively or violently; to heat highly (ore etc.) without fusing, to drive out impurities; (*coll.*) to banter, quiz or criticize strongly. *v.i.* to dress meat by roasting; to be roasted. *a.* roasted. *n.* the act or operation of roasting; that which is roasted, roast meat or a dish of this, a roast joint. **to rule the roast,** to take the lead or mastery. **roaster,** *n.* one who or that which roasts; a contrivance for roasting coffee, a kind of oven for roasting; a furnace for roasting ore; a pig or other animal or vegetable etc. suitable for roasting. **roasting,** *n., a.* [OF *rostir* (F *rôtir*), from Teut. (cp. OHG *rōsten,* from *Rōst,* grate, grid-iron)]

rob, *v.t.* (*past, p.p.* **robbed**) to despoil of anything by unlawful violence or secret theft; to plunder, to pillage, to deprive, to strip (of); †to steal. *v.i.* to commit robbery. **robber,** *n.* **robber-baron,** *n.* a mediaeval baron exacting tribute by oppressive means. **robber-crab,** *n.* one of the hermit-crabs. **robber-gull,** *n.* the skua. **robbery,** *n.* the act or practice of robbing; the felonious taking of goods or money from the person of another by violence or threat. **daylight robbery,** flagrant extortion or overpricing. [OF *robber, rober,* rel. to REAVE]

Robbe-Grillet, *n.* **Alain** (1922–), French writer, the leading theorist of *le nouveau roman ('the new novel'),* for example his own *Les Gommes/The Erasers* (1953), *La Jalousie/Jealousy* (1957), and *Dans le labyrinthe/In the Labyrinth* (1959), which concentrates on detailed description of physical objects. He also wrote the script for the film *L'Année dernière à Marienbad/Last Year in Marienbad* (1961).

Robben Island, *n.* a notorious prison island in Table Bay, Cape Town, South Africa.

Robbia, della, *n.* Italian family of sculptors and architects, active in Florence. **Luca della Robbia** (1400–82) created a number of important works in Florence, notably the marble *cantoria* (singing gallery) in the cathedral (1431–38) (Museo del Duomo), with lively groups of choristers. Luca also developed a characteristic style of glazed terracotta work.

Robbins, *n.* **Jerome** (1918–), US dancer and choreographer. He choreographed the musicals *The King and I* (1951), *West Side Story* (1957), and *Fiddler on the Roof* (1964). Robbins was ballet master of the New York City Ballet (1969–83), when he became joint ballet master-in-chief.

robe, *n.* a loose outer garment; a dress, gown or vestment of state, rank or office (*often in pl.*); a dressing-gown; a bathrobe. *v.t.* to invest with a robe or robes; to clothe, to dress. *v.i.* to put on a robe or dress. **robe de chambre**, a dressing-gown or morning-dress. **robing,** *n.* [OF, cogn. with ROB, cp. OE *rēaf,* spoil, clothing, G *Raub,* Icel. *rauf,* booty]

Robert I[1], *n.* **Robert the Bruce** (1274–1329), king of Scotland from 1306, and grandson of Robert de Bruce. He shared in the national uprising led by William Wallace, and, after Wallace's execution in 1305, rose once more against Edward I of England, and was crowned at Scone in 1306. He defeated Edward II at Bannockburn in 1314. In 1328 the treaty of Northampton recognized Scotland's independence and Robert as king.

Robert I[2], *n.* **the Devil**. Duke of Normandy from 1028. He was the father of William the Conqueror, and is the hero of several romances; he was legendary for his cruelty.

Robert II[1], *n.* (1316–90), king of Scotland from 1371. He was the son of Walter (1293–1326), steward of Scotland, who married Marjory, daughter of Robert I. He was the first king of the house of Stuart.

Robert II[2], *n.* (*c.* 1054–1134), eldest son of William I (the Conqueror), succeeding him as duke of Normandy (but not on the English throne) in 1087. His brother William II ascended the English throne, and they warred until 1096, allowing Robert to take part in the First Crusade. When his other brother Henry I claimed the English throne in 1100, Robert contested the claim and invaded England unsuccessfully in 1101. Henry invaded Normandy in 1106, and captured Robert, who remained a prisoner in England until his death.

Robert III, *n.* (*c.* 1340–1406), king of Scotland from 1390, son of Robert II. He was unable to control the nobles, and the government fell largely into the hands of his brother, Robert, duke of Albany (*c.* 1340–1420).

Roberts[1], *n.* **David** (1796–1864), Scottish painter whose oriental paintings were the result of several trips to the Middle East.

Roberts[2], *n.* **Frederick Sleigh, 1st Earl Roberts** (1832–1914), British field marshal, known as 'Bobs'. During the Afghan War of 1878–80 he occupied Kabul, and during the Second South African War (1899-1902) he made possible the annexation of the Transvaal and Orange Free State.

Roberts[3], *n.* **'Tom' (Thomas William)** (1856–1931), Australian painter, born in England, founder of the Heidelberg School which introduced impressionism to Australia. He painted scenes of pioneering life.

Robertson, *n.* **Thomas William** (1829–71), English dramatist. Initially an actor, he had his first success as a dramatist with *David Garrick* (1864), which set a new, realistic trend in English drama of the time; later plays included *Society* (1865) and *Caste* (1867).

Robeson, *n.* **Paul** (1898–1976), US bass singer and actor. He graduated from Columbia University as a lawyer, but limited opportunities for blacks led him instead to the stage. He appeared in *The Emperor Jones* (1924) and *Showboat* (1928), in which he sang 'Ol' Man River'. He played *Othello* in (1930), and his films include *Sanders of the River* (1935) and *King Solomon's Mines* (1937). An ardent advocate of black rights, he had his passport withdrawn (1950–58) because of his association with left-wing movements. He then left the US to live in England.

Robespierre, *n.* **Maximilien François Marie Isidore de** (1758–94), French politician in the French Revolution. As leader of the Jacobins in the National Convention he supported the execution of Louis XVI and the overthrow of the Girondins, and in Jul. 1793 was elected to the Committee of Public Safety. A year later he was guillotined; many believe that he was a scapegoat for the Reign of Terror since he only ordered 72 executions personally.

robin, *n.* a small warbler, the redbreast, also called robin redbreast; a N American red-breasted thrush. **Robin Goodfellow,** *n.* a merry domestic fairy, famous for mischievous pranks. **Robin Hood,** *n.* legendary English outlaw and champion of the poor against the rich. He is said to have lived in Sherwood Forest, Nottinghamshire, during the reign of Richard I (King of England, 1189–99). He feuded with the Sheriff of Nottingham, accompanied by Maid Marian and a band of followers, known as his 'merry men'. He appears in ballads from the 13th cent., but his first datable appearance is in Langland's *Piers Plowman* about 1377. **robin-run-in-the-hedge,** *n.* ground-ivy, bindweed and other trailers or climbers. [OF, fam. for ROBERT]

robinia, *n.* a genus of leguminous shrubs or trees including the false acacia, *Robinia pseudacacia.* [from Jean *Robin*, 1550–1629, French botanist]

Robinson[1], *n.* **Edward G.** (stage name of Emanuel Goldenberg) (1893–1973), US film actor, born in Romania, he emigrated with his family to the US 1903. He was noted for his gangster roles, such as *Little Caesar* (1930). Other films include *Dr Ehrlich's Magic Bullet* (1940), *Double Indemnity* (1944), *The Ten Commandments* (1956), and *Soylent Green* (1973).

Robinson[2], *n.* **Henry Crabb** (1775–1867), English writer, whose diaries, journals, and letters are a valuable source of information on his friends Lamb, Coleridge, Wordsworth, and Southey.

Robinson[3], *n.* **'Sugar' Ray** (assumed name of Walker Smith) (1920–89), US boxer, world welterweight champion (1945–51), defending his title five times. He defeated Jake LaMotta in 1951 to take the middleweight title. He lost the title six times and won it seven times. He had 202 fights, and fought until the age of 45.

Robinson[4], *n.* **W(illiam) Heath** (1872–1944), British cartoonist and illustrator, known for his humorous drawings of bizarre machinery for performing simple tasks, such as raising one's hat. Clumsy designs are often described as a 'Heath Robinson' contraption.

Robinson Crusoe, *n. The Life and strange and surprising Adventures of Robinson Crusoe*, a novel by Daniel Defoe, published in 1719, in which the hero is shipwrecked on an island and survives for years by his own ingenuity until rescued; based on the adventures of Alexander Selkirk. The book had many imitators and is the first major English novel.

roble, *n.* the Californian white-oak, *Quercus lobata;* a W Indian catalpa; a Chilean beech, *Fagus obliqua*. [Sp. and Port., from L *rōbur,* oak]

roborant, *a.* strengthening, of a medicine, tonic etc. *n.* a strengthening medicine. [L *rōborans -ntem,* pres.p. of *rōborāre,* to strengthen, from *rōbur -boris,* strength]

robot, *n.* a man-like machine capable of acting and speaking in a human manner; a humanoid; an automaton; a brutal, mechanically efficient person who is devoid of sensibility; (*S Afr.*) traffic lights. **robot-like,** *a.* **robotic,** *a.* **robotic dancing,** *n.* a style of dancing with robot-like mechanical movements. **robotics,** *n.pl.* the branch of technology concerned with the design, construction, maintenance and application of robots. **robotize, -ise,** *v.t.* to cause (work etc.) to be done by a robot. **robotization, -isation,** *n.* [from Karel Capek's play *R.U.R.*, 1923]

Robson, *n.* **Flora** (1902–84), English actress. Her successes included Queen Elizabeth in the film *Fire Over England* (1931) and Mrs Alving in Ibsen's *Ghosts* (1959).

robust, *a.* strong, hardy, vigorous, capable of endurance, having excellent health and physique; sturdy, hardy (of plants); full-bodied (of wine); requiring muscular strength, invigorating (of exercise, sports, discipline etc.); sinewy, muscular; mentally vigorous, firm, self-reliant. **robustious,** *a.* boisterous, rough, noisy. **robustiously, robustly,** *adv.* **robustness,** *n.* [F *robuste,* L *rōbustus*, strong]

ROC, (*abbr.*) Royal Observer Corps.

roc, *n.* a fabulous bird of immense size and strength. [F *rock,* Arab. *rokh, rukh*]

rocaille, *n.* a decorative work of rock, shell or a similar material. [F]

rocambole, *n.* a plant related to the leek, *Allium scorodoprasum,* Spanish garlic. [F, etym. doubtful]

Rocard, *n.* **Michel** (1930–), French socialist politician. A former radical, he joined the Socialist Party (PS) in 1973, emerging as leader of its moderate social-democratic wing. He held ministerial office under Mitterrand (1981–85), and was appointed prime minister in 1988.

Roccella, *n.* a genus of shrubby lichens containing the orchil. [mod. L, from OF *orchel,* ORCHIL]

Roche, *n.* **Stephen** (1959–), Irish cyclist. One of the outstanding riders on the continent in the 1980s, he was the first British winner of the Tour de France in 1987 and the first English-speaking winner of the Tour of Italy the same year, as well as the 1987 world professional road race champion.

Rochelle-powder, *n.* Seidlitz powder. **Rochelle-salt,** *n.* a tartrate of soda and potash, used as Epsom salt.

roche moutonnée, *n.* (*pl.* **roches moutonnées**) rock ground down by glacial action so as to present a rounded appearance on the side from which the flow came. [F, rocks rounded like the backs of sheep]

Rochester, *n.* **John Wilmot, 2nd Earl of Rochester** (1647–80), English poet and courtier. He fought gallantly at sea against the Dutch, but chiefly led a debauched life at the court of Charles II. He wrote graceful (but often obscene) lyrics, and his *A Satire against Mankind* (1675) rivals Swift. He was patron of John Dryden.

rochet[1], *n.* an open-sided vestment with tight sleeves, resembling a surplice worn by bishops and abbots. [OF *rochet, roket,* from Teut. (cp. Dut. *rok,* G *Rock,* OE *rocc*)]

rochet[2], *n.* the red gurnard. [OF *rouget,* from *rouge,* red]

rock[1], *n.* the solid matter constituting the earth's crust or any portion of this; any solid, indurated or stony part of this, a mass of it, esp. forming a hill, promontory, islet, cliff etc.; a detached block of stone, a boulder; a stone, a pebble; (*sl.*) a diamond or other precious or large gem; a hard sweet often in the form of a stick; (*fig.*) anything on which one may come to grief; a person or thing providing refuge, stability, supportiveness etc. **on the rocks,** poor, hard up; at an end, destroyed (e.g. of a marriage); of a drink, served with ice. **rock English,** the mixed patois spoken at Gibraltar. **Rock of Ages,** Christ. **the Rock,** Gibraltar. **the Rockies,** the Rocky Mts. **rock-basin,** *n.* a hollow occupied by a lake etc., in rock, usually attributed to glacial action. **rock-bird,** *n.* any of various cliff-dwelling birds (e.g. the gannet, the puffin). **rock-bottom,** *n.* the lowest stratum reached in excavating, mining etc.; the lowest point (e.g. of despair). *a.* lowest possible (of prices). **rock-bound,** *a.* hemmed in by rocks. **rock-cake,** *n.* a bun with a hard rough surface. **rock-candy,** *n.* candy in hard crystals. **rock-climber,** *n.* a mountaineer who scales rock-faces. **rock-climbing,** *n.* **rock-cod,** *n.* a gadoid fish allied to the cod; a cod caught on a rocky bottom. **rock-cork,** *n.* a cork-like variety of asbestos. **rock-crystal,** *n.* the finest and most transparent kind of quartz, usu. found in hexagonal prisms. **rock-dove, rock-pigeon,** *n.* the European wild pigeon, *Columba livia,* supposed to be the ancestor of the domesticated varieties. **rock-face,** *n.* the surface of a vertical or nearly vertical cliff or mountain-side. **rock-fish,** *n.* the black goby; a name for several wrasses etc. **rock garden,** *n.* a rockery; a garden containing a rockery or rockeries. **rock-goat,** *n.* the ibex. **rock-hewn,** *a.* hewn or quarried from the rock. **rock-hopper,** *n.* the crested penguin. **rock lily,** *n.* a long-leaved plant of the genus *Arthropodium* (family Liliaceae), native to Australia and New Zealand. **rock-oil,** *n.* petroleum. **rock-pigeon** ROCK-DOVE. **rock-plant,** *n.* any of various plants dwelling among rocks, esp. an alpine. **rock-rabbit,** *n.* a hyrax, esp. *Hyrax capensis.* **rock-rose,** *n.* the cistus. **rock salmon,** *n.* dogfish or other coarse fish disguised for the market. **rock-salt,** *n.* salt found in stratified beds, halite. **rock-shelter,** *n.* a cave etc. used as a shelter by early man. **rock-snake,** *n.* any species of the genus *Python* or the Australian genus *Morelia.* **rock tripe,** *n.* any of various types of edible lichen. **rock-tar,** *n.* petroleum. **rock wool,** *n.* mineral wool. **rock-work,** *n.* a rockery; rock-climbing; masonry made to resemble rock. **rockery,** *n.* a mound or slope of rocks, stones and earth, for growing alpine and other plants; a display of rocks. **rockiness,** *n.* **rockless,** *a.* **rocklike,** *a.* **rockling,** *n.* a small gadoid fish, esp. the sea-loach. **rocky**[1], *a.* full of or abounding with rocks; consisting of or resembling rock; solid; rugged, hard, stony, obdurate, difficult. [OF *roke, roque, roche,* etym. doubtful]

rock[2], *v.t.* to move backwards and forwards; to cause a cradle to move to and fro; hence, to soothe, to lull to sleep; to shake, to cause to sway or reel; to work a gold-miner's cradle or other rocking apparatus; to shake or sift in a cradle. *n.* an act or spell of rocking; rocking motion; rock music. *a.* pertaining to rock music. *v.i.* to move backwards and forwards; to sway, to reel; to dance to rock or rock and roll music. **off one's rocker,** crazy. **rockabilly**, *n.* a quick-paced type of Southern American rock and country music originating in the 1950s. **rock and roll, rock'n'roll,** a type of music popular from the 1950s which combines jazz and country and western music; the type of dancing executed to this music. *a.* pertaining to this type of music or style of dancing. *v.i.* to dance in the rock-and-roll style. **rock and roller, rock'n'roller,** *n.* **rock music,** *n.* a type of popular music characterized by a strong persistent beat which developed out of rock and roll.

rockshaft, *n.* a shaft rocking, instead of revolving, on its bearings, usu. for conveying horizontal motion. **Rocker,** *n.* one of a teenage band of leather-clad motorcyclists of the 1960s. **rocker,** *n.* one who or that which rocks; a rocking-chair; a curved piece of wood on which a cradle, rocking-chair etc., rocks; a gold-miner's cradle; a low skate with a curved blade; the curve of this blade; of machinery, applied to various devices and fittings having a rocking motion. **rockily,** *adv.* unsteadily. **rockiness,** *n.* **rocking,** *n., a.* **rocky**[2], *a.* (*coll.*) unsteady, tottering, fragile. **rocking-chair,** *n.* a chair mounted on rockers. **rocking-horse,** *n.* a large toy horse mounted on rockers. **rocking-stone,** *n.* a stone so balanced on a natural pedestal that it can be rocked. **rocking-tool,** *n.* an instrument used in mezzotinting to give the plate a burr. [OE *roccian,* cp. G *rücken*]

rock-basin, -bottom, -bound, -candy, -cork etc. ROCK[1].

Rockefeller, *n.* **John D(avison)** (1839–1937), US millionaire, founder of Standard Oil in 1870 (which achieved control of 90% of US refineries by 1882). The activities of the Standard Oil Trusts led to an outcry against monopolies and the passing of the Sherman Anti-Trust Act of 1890. A lawsuit of 1892 prompted the dissolution of the Trust, only for it to be refounded in 1899 as a holding company. In 1911, this was also declared illegal by the Supreme Court. He founded the philanthropic **Rockefeller Foundation** in 1913, to which his son John D(avison) Rockefeller Jr. (1874–1960) devoted his life.

rocket[1], *n.* a name for some species of *Hesperis, Brassica* and other Cruciferae, some used for salads etc. and others as garden flowers. [F *roquette,* It. *ruchetta,* dim. of *ruca,* L *ērūca*]

rocket[2], *n.* a firework consisting of a cylindrical case of metal or paper filled with a mixture of explosives and combustibles, used for display, signalling, conveying a line to stranded vessels and in warfare; a device with a warhead containing high explosive and propelled by the mechanical thrust developed by gases generated through the use of chemical fuels; (*coll.*) a severe scolding, a telling off. *v.t.* to propel by means of a rocket. *v.i.* to fly straight up or to fly fast and high (as a flushed pheasant); to rise rapidly (e.g. of prices); to advance to a high position speedily (e.g. of a promoted person). **rocket range,** *n.* a place for testing rocket projectiles. **rocketeer,** *n.* **rocketer,** *n.* a pheasant etc. that flies straight up in the air when flushed. **rocketry,** *n.* the scientific study of rockets. [F *roquet,* It. *rocchetta,* dim. of *rocca,* ROCK[3]]

rock-fish, -goat etc. ROCK[1].

Rockwell, *n.* **Norman** (1894–1978), US painter and illustrator, noted for magazine covers and cartoons portraying American life. His folksy view of the nation earned him huge popularity.

Rocky Mountains, *n.pl.* largest North American mountain system. They extend from the junction with the Mexican plateau, northward through the west central states of the US, through Canada to the Alaskan border. The highest mountain is Mount McKinley (6194 m/20,320 ft.).

rococo, *n.* a florid style of ornamentation (in architecture, furniture etc.) flourishing under Louis XV in the 18th cent. and becoming widespread in Europe especially in the churches and palaces of S Germany and Austria; design or ornament of an eccentric and over-elaborate kind. *a.* in this style. [F, prob. coined from *rocaille,* ROCKERY]

rod, *n.* a straight, slender piece of wood, a stick, a wand; this or a bundle of twigs etc. as an instrument of punishment; punishment; a baton, a sceptre; a fishing-rod; an enchanter's wand; a slender bar of metal, esp. forming part of machinery etc.; a unit of lineal measure, equal to 5½ yards (about 5 m); (*N Am. sl.*) a revolver; a rod-like body or structure in the retina of the eye. **Napier's rods** NAPIER'S BONES. **rodless,** *a.* **rodlike,** *a.* **rod(s)man, rodster,** *n.* an angler. [OE *rodd,* cp. Icel. *rudda,* rel. to ROOD]

Roddick, *n.* **Anita** (1943–), British entrepreneur, founder of the Body Shop, which now has branches worldwide. Roddick started with one shop in Brighton, England in 1976, only selling natural products in refillable plastic containers.

rode[1], *past* RIDE.

rode[2], *v.i.* to fly in the evening, as woodcocks. **ro(a)ding,** *n.* [etym. unknown]

rodent, *n.* any animal of the order Rodentia, having two (or sometimes four) strong incisors and no canine teeth, comprising the squirrel, beaver, rat etc. *a.* gnawing; pertaining to the Rodentia. **Rodentia,** *n.* an order of small mammals. **rodenticide,** *n.* an agent that kills rodents. [L *rōdens -ntem,* pres.p. of *rōdere,* to gnaw]

rodeo, *n.* a driving together or rounding-up of cattle; a place they are rounded up in; an outdoor entertainment or contest exhibiting the skills involved in this (extended to other contests suggestive of this). [Sp., from *rodear,* to go round]

Rodgers, *n.* **Richard (Charles)** (1902–79), US composer. He collaborated with librettist Lorenz Hart (1895–1943) on songs such as 'Blue Moon' (1934), and musicals such as *On Your Toes* (1936); and with Oscar Hammerstein II (1895–1960) in musicals such as *Oklahoma!* (1943), *South Pacific* (1949), *The King and I* (1951), and *The Sound of Music* (1959).

Rodhos, *n.* Greek name for the island of RHODES.

Rodin, *n.* **Auguste** (1840–1917), French sculptor, considered the greatest of his time. Through his work he freed sculpture from the current idealizing conventions by its realistic treatment of the human figure, introducing a new boldness of style and expression. Examples are *Le Penseur/The Thinker* (1880), *Le Baiser/The Kiss* (1886) (marble version in the Louvre, Paris), and *Les Bourgeois de Calais/The Burghers of Calais* (1885–95) (copy in Embankment Gardens, Westminster, London).

rodless, rodlike, rodman ROD.

Rodnina, *n.* **Irina** (1949–), Soviet ice skater. From 1969–1980 she won 23 world, Olympic, and European gold medals in pairs competitions. Her partners were Alexei Ulanov and then Alexsandr Zaitsev, who became her husband in 1975.

rodomontade, *n.* brag, bluster, rant. *v.i.* to boast, to bluster, to rant. *a.* bragging, boastful. **rodomontader,** *n.* a vain boaster. [F, from *Rodomont, Rodomonte,* leader of the Saracens in Ariosto's *Orlando Furioso*]

roe[1], *n.* a small species of deer, *Capreolus capraea.* **roebuck,** *n.* the male roe. **roedeer,** *n.* the roe. [OE *rāha,* cp. Icel. *rā,* Dut. *ree,* G *Reh*]

roe[2], *n.* the mass of eggs forming the spawn of fishes, amphibians etc., called the hard roe; the sperm or milt, called the soft roe. **roe-stone,** *n.* oolite. **roed,** *a.* containing roe. [cp. MDut. and MLG *Roge,* OHG *Rogo*]

Roeg, *n.* **Nicolas** (1928–), English film director. His work is noted for its stylish visual appeal and imaginative, often off-beat, treatment of subjects. His films include *Performance* (1970), *Walkabout* (1971), *Don't Look Now* (1973), *The Man Who Fell to Earth* (1976), *Insignificance* (1984), and *Track 29* (1988).

Roentgen (Röntgen), *n.* **Wilhelm Konrad** (1845–1923), German physicist who discovered X-rays in 1895. While investigating the passage of electricity through gases, he noticed the fluorescence of a barium platinocyanide screen. This radiation passed through some substances opaque to light, and affected photographic plates. Developments from this discovery have revolutionized medical diagnosis. **roentgen, röntgen,** *n.* the international unit of quantity of X- or gamma-rays. **röntgen rays,** *n.pl.* a form of radiant energy penetrating most substances opaque to ordinary light, employed for photographing hidden objects and for therapeutic treatment of lupus, cancer etc., also known as X-rays.

Roethke, *n.* **Theodore** (1908–63), US poet. His father owned a large nursery business, and the greenhouses and plants of his childhood provide the detail and imagery of much of his lyrical, personal, and visionary poetry. Collections include *Open House* (1941), *The*

Lost Son (1948), *The Waking* (1953) (Pulitzer Prize), and the posthumous *Collected Poems* (1968).

rogation, *n.* (*usu. in pl.*) a solemn supplication, esp. that chanted in procession on Rogation Days. **Rogation Days,** *n.pl.* the Monday, Tuesday and Wednesday preceding Ascension Day marked by prayers, processions, supplications now only rarely observed. **Rogation Sunday,** *n.* that preceding Ascension Day. **Rogation Week,** *n.* the week comprising these. **rogatory,** *a.* [L *rogātio,* from *rogāre,* to ask]

roger, in radio communications etc., an expression meaning 'received and understood'; an expression of agreement or acquiescence. *v.t.* (*sl.*) used of a man, to have sexual intercourse with. **jolly Roger** JOLLY. [OF, a personal name, prob. from Teut.]

Rogers[1], *n.* **Carl** (1902–87), US psychologist who developed the client-centred approach to counselling and psychotherapy. This stressed the importance of clients making their own decisions and developing their own potential (self-actualization).

Rogers[2], *n.* **Ginger** (stage name of Virginia Katherine McMath) (1911–), US actress, dancer and singer. She worked from the 1930s to the 1950s, often starring with Fred Astaire in such films as *Top Hat* (1935) and *Swing Time* (1936). Her later work includes *Bachelor Mother* (1939) and *Kitty Foyle* (1940).

Rogers[3], *n.* **Richard** (1933–), British architect. His works include the Centre Pompidou in Paris (1977) (jointly with Renzo Piano) and the Lloyd's building in London (1986).

Rogers[4], *n.* **Roy** (stage name of Leonard Slye) (1912–), US actor who moved to the cinema from radio. He was one of the original singing cowboys of the 1930s and 1940s. Confined to 'B' films for most of his career, he appeared opposite Bob Hope and Jane Russell in *Son of Paleface* (1952). His other films include *The Big Show* (1936) and *My Pal Trigger* (1946).

Roget, *n.* **Peter Mark** (1779–1869), English physician, one of the founders of the University of London, and author of a *Thesaurus of English Words and Phrases* (1852), a text constantly republished and still in use.

rogue, *n.* a rascal, a scamp, a trickster, a swindler; a playful term of endearment for a child or mischievous person; a vicious wild animal cast out or separate from the herd, esp. an elephant; a shirking or vicious racehorse or hunter; an inferior or intrusive plant among seedlings; a variation from the standard type or variety; †a vagrant. *a.* roguish. *v.t.* to weed out (inferior plants) from among seedlings, a crop etc. **rogues' gallery,** *n.* a collection of photographic portraits kept in police records for identification of criminals. **rogue-buffalo, elephant** etc., *n.* a solitary savage animal. **roguery,** *n.* **roguish,** *a.* mischievous, high-spirited, saucy. **roguishly,** *adv.* **roguishness,** *n.* [16th cent. cant]

Röhm, *n.* **Ernst** (1887–1934), German leader of the Nazi 'Brownshirts', the SA (Sturmabteilung). On the pretext of an intended SA *Putsch* (uprising) some hundred of them, including Röhm, were killed 29–30 June 1934, known as 'the Night of the Long Knives'.

Rohmer[1], *n.* **Eric** (adopted name of Jean-Marie Maurice Sherer) (1920–), French film director and writer, formerly a critic and television director. Part of the French new wave, his films are concerned with exploring the minds of his characters. They include *My Night at Maud's/Ma Nuit chez Maud* (1969), *Claire's Knee/Le Genou de Claire* (1970), and *The Marquise of O/La Marquise d'O/Die Marquise von O* (1976).

Rohmer[2], *n.* **Sax** (pen name of Arthur Sarsfield Ward) (1886–1959), English crime writer who created the sinister Chinese character Fu Manchu.

Roh Tae-woo, *n.* (1932–), South Korean right-wing politician and general. He held ministerial office from 1981 under President Chun, and became chairman of the ruling Democratic Justice Party in 1985. He was elected president in 1987, amid allegations of fraud and despite being connected with the massacre of about 2000 anti-government demonstrators in 1980.

roil, *v.t.* to render turbid, as by stirring or shaking up sediment; to make angry, to irritate, to rile. [perh. from obs. F *ruiler,* to mix up mortar, cp. RILE]

†roinish, roynish, *a.* scabby, scurvy, paltry, vile. [obs. *roin,* F *rogne,* scab, scurf, etym. unknown, -ISH]

roister, *v.i.* to behave uproariously, to revel boisterously; to swagger. †*n.* a roisterer. **roisterer,** *n.* one who roisters, a swaggering, noisy reveller. **roisterous,** *adv.* [F *rustre,* a ruffian, var. of *ruste,* L *rusticus,* RUSTIC]

†rokelay, rocklay, *n.* a woman's short cloak, worn in the 18th cent. [F *roquelaire,* var. of ROQUELAURE]

Roland, *n.* French hero of many romances, including the 11th-cent. *Chanson de Roland* and Ariosto's *Orlando Furioso.* Roland was a soldier, killed AD 778 with his friend Oliver and the twelve peers of France, at Roncesvalles (in the Pyrenees) by the Basques. He headed the rearguard during Charlemagne's retreat from his invasion of Spain. **a Roland for an Oliver,** a blow for a blow, an effective retort, a story capping another.

Roland de la Platière, *n.* **Jeanne Manon** (born **Philipon**) (1754–93), French intellectual politician, whose salon from 1789 was a focus of democratic discussion. Her ideas were influential after her husband Jean Marie Roland de la Platière (1734–93) became minister of the interior in 1792. As a supporter of the Girondin party, opposed to Robespierre and Danton, she was condemned to the guillotine in 1793, without being allowed to speak in her own defence. Her last words were 'O liberty! What crimes are committed in thy name!' While in prison she wrote *Mémoires.*

role, rôle, *n.* a part or character taken by an actor; any part or function one is called upon to perform. **role-play, -playing,** *n.* an enactment of a possible situation or playing of an imaginary role as therapy, training etc. [F, ROLL]

Rolfe, *n.* **Frederick** (1860–1913), English writer, who called himself Baron Corvo. A Roman Catholic convert, frustrated in his desire to enter the priesthood, he wrote the novel *Hadrian VII* (1904), in which the character of the title rose from being a poor writer to become pope. In *Desire and Pursuit of the Whole* (1934) he wrote about his homosexual fantasies and friends, earning the poet Auden's description of him as 'a master of vituperation'.

roll, *n.* anything rolled up, a cylinder of any flexible material formed by or as by rolling or folding over on itself; a small loaf of bread; a pastry or cake rolled round a filling; a document, an official record, a register, a list, esp. of names, as of solicitors, soldiers, schoolboys etc.; a cylindrical or semi-cylindrical mass of anything; a fold, a turned-back edge, a convex moulding, a volute; a roller; a rolling motion or gait; a resounding peal of thunder etc.; a continuous beating of a drum with rapid strokes; (*N Am.*) a wad of money. *v.t.* to send, push or cause to move along by turning over and over on its axis; to cause to rotate; to cause to revolve between two surfaces; to knead, press, flatten or level with or as with a roller or rollers; to enwrap (in), to wrap (up in); to form into a cylindrical shape by wrapping round and round or turning over and over; to carry or impel forward with a sweeping motion; to carry (oneself along) with a swinging gait; to convey in a wheeled vehicle; to utter with a prolonged, deep, vibrating sound. *v.i.* to move along by turning over and over and round and round; to revolve; to operate or cause to operate; to move along on wheels; to be conveyed (along) in a wheeled vehicle; (*coll.*) to progress; to move or slip about with a rotary motion (of eyes etc.); to wallow about; to sway, to reel, to go from side to side; to move along with such a motion; of a ship, to turn back and forth on her longitudinal axis; of an aircraft, to make a full corkscrew revolution about the longitudinal axis; to undulate or sweep along; to be formed into a cylindrical shape by turning over upon itself; to grow into a cylindrical or spherical shape by turning over and over; to spread (out) under a roller. **all rolled into one,** combined together. **a roll in the hay,** (*coll.*) sexual intercourse; a period of love-play. **heads will roll,** persons will be severely punished. **Master of the Rolls,** the head of the Record Office, an ex-officio judge of the Court of Appeal and member of the Judicial Committee. **to roll along,** to move or push along by rolling; to walk in a casual manner or with an undulating gait; to have a casual or unambitious approach to life. **to roll in,** to come in quantities or numbers; to arrive in a casual manner; to wind in; to push in by rolling. **to roll up,** to wind up (e.g. a car window); to make a cigarette by hand; to wind into a cylinder; to assemble, to come up. **to strike off the roll(s),** to remove from the official list of qualified solicitors; to debar, expel. **rollbar,** *n.* a metal strengthening bar which reinforces the frame of a (racing) vehicle which may overturn. **roll-call,** *n.* the act of calling a list of names to check attendance. **rollmop,** *n.* a rolled-up fillet of herring pickled in vinegar and usu. garnished with onion. **roll-neck,** *a., n.* (of) an upper garment usu. a jumper with a high neck folded over. **roll on!** *int.* hurry along, come quickly (of a day, date, event). **roll-on,** *n.* a step-in elastic corset that fits by stretching; a deodorant applied by a plastic rolling ball in the neck of its container. **roll-on roll-off,** *a., n.* (of) a vessel carrying motor vehicles which drive on and off when embarking and disembarking. **roll-top,** *a.* **roll-top desk,** *n.* a desk with a flexible cover sliding in grooves. **roll up,** *n.* (*coll.*) a hand-made cigarette made with tobacco and a cigarette paper; (*Austral.*) an assemblage. **rollable,** *a.* suitable for rolling; capable of being rolled. **rolled,** *a.* **rolled gold,** *n.* metal covered by a thin coating of gold. **roller,** *n.* one who or that which rolls; a cylindrical body turning on its axis, employed alone or forming part of a machine, used for inking, printing, smoothing, spreading out, crushing etc.; a long, heavy, swelling wave; a long, broad bandage, rolled up for convenience; any bird of the genus *Coracias,* remarkable for their habit of turning somersaults in the air; a tumbler pigeon; a small cylinder for curling the hair, a curler. **rollerball,** *n.* a type of pen with a nib consisting of a rolling ball which controls the flow of ink. **roller-bearing,** *n.* a bearing comprised of strong steel rollers for giving a point of contact. **roller-coaster,** *n.* a switchback railway at an amusement park, carnival, fair etc. **roller derby,** *n.* a (often boisterous) roller-skating race. **roller-skate,** *n.* a skate mounted on wheels or rollers for skating on asphalt etc. *v.i.* to skate on these. **roller-skater,** *n.* **roller-skating,** *n.* **roller-towel,** *n.* a continuous towel hung on a roller. **rolling,** *a., n., adv.* **a rolling stone,** a person who cannot settle down in one place. **to be rolling in it,** to be extremely wealthy. **rolling-mill,** *n.* a factory in which metal is rolled out by machinery into plates, sheets, bars etc. **rolling-pin,** *n.* a hard wooden roller for rolling out dough, pastry etc. **rolling-stock,** *n.* the carriages, vans, locomotives etc. of a railway. [OF *roler, roller,* It. *rololare,* from L *rotula,* dim. of *rota,* wheel]

rollick, *v.i.* to behave in a careless, merry fashion; to frolic, to revel, to be merry or enjoy life in a boisterous fashion. *n.* a frolic, a spree, an escapade. **rollicking,** *a.* boisterous, carefree. *n.* (*coll.*) a scolding. [etym. doubtful]

Rolling Stones, the, British band formed in 1962, once notorious as the 'bad boys' of rock. Original members were Mick Jagger (1943–), Keith Richard (1943–), Brian Jones (1942–69), Bill Wyman (1936–), Charlie Watts (1941–), and the pianist Ian Stewart (1938–85). In the 1970s they became a rock-and-roll institution and by the late 1980s Jagger and Richard were working separately.

Rollo, *n.* **1st Duke of Normandy** (*c.* 860–932), Viking leader. He left Norway about AD 875, and marauded, sailing up the Seine to Rouen. He besieged Paris AD 886, and in AD 912 was baptized and granted the province of Normandy by Charles III of France. He was its duke until his retirement to a monastery AD 927. He was an ancestor of William the Conqueror.

rollock ROWLOCK.

Rolls, *n.* **Charles** (1877–1910), British engineer who joined with Royce in 1905 to design and produce their own cars. He trained as a mechanical engineer at Cambridge where he also developed a passion for engines of all kinds. After working initially at the railway works in Crewe, he set up a business in 1902 as a motor dealer. Rolls was the first to fly nonstop across the English Channel and back in 1910, but died shortly afterwards before the business could flourish.

Rolls-Royce, *n.* industrial company manufacturing cars and aeroplane engines, founded 1906 by Henry Royce and Charles Stewart Rolls. In 1906, the 'Silver Ghost' was designed, and produced until 1925, when the 'Phantom' was produced. In 1914, Royce designed the Eagle aircraft engine, used extensively in World War I. Royce also designed the Merlin engine, used in Spitfires and Hurricanes in World War II. Jet engines followed, and became an important part of the company.

roly-poly, *a.* round, plump, podgy. *n.* a pudding made of a sheet of suet paste, spread over with jam, rolled up and baked or boiled; a plump or dumpy person, esp. a child; †a name for various ball-games. *a.* plump, dumpy. [prob. a redupl. of ROLL]

ROM, *n.* a data-storage device in computers which retains information permanently in an unalterable state. [*r*ead *o*nly *m*emory]

ROM., (*abbr.*) Roman; Romance (language); Rumania(n); Romans.

rom, *n.* (*pl.* **roma(s)**) a male gipsy, a Romany. [Romany, man]

rom., (*abbr.*) roman (type).

Romaic, *n.* the vernacular language of modern Greece. *a.* of, pertaining to or expressed in modern Greek. [Gr. *Rōmaikos,* from *Rōmē,* L *Rōma,* Rome]

Romains, *n.* **Jules** (pen name of Louis Farigoule) (1885–1972), French novelist, playwright and poet. His plays include the farce *Knock, ou le triomphe de la médecine/Dr Knock* (1923) and *Donogoo* (1930), and his novels include *Mort de quelqu'un/Death of a Nobody* (1911), *Les Copains/The Boys in the Back Room* (1913), *Les Hommes de bonne volonté/Men of Good Will* (27 volumes) (1932–47).

romal, rumal, *n.* an East Indian silk or cotton fabric; orig. a handkerchief worn as a head-dress etc. [Hind. and Pers. *rūmāl*]

Roman, *a.* pertaining to the modern or ancient city of Rome or its territory or people; denoting numerals expressed in letters, not in figures; belonging to the Roman alphabet; of or pertaining to the Roman Catholic Church, papal. *n.* an inhabitant or citizen of Rome; a Roman Catholic; a letter of the Roman alphabet. *n.pl.* an epistolary book in the New Testament written by St Paul to the Christians of Rome. **roman,** *a.* denoting ordinary upright characters used in print as distinct from italic or gothic. *n.* roman type. **Roman architecture,** *n.* a style of architecture in which the Greek orders are combined with the use of the arch, distinguished by its massive character and abundance of ornament. **Roman art,** *n.* sculpture and painting of ancient Rome, from the 4th cent. BC onwards to the fall of the empire. Much Roman art was intended for public education, notably the sculpted triumphal arches and giant columns, such as Trajan's Column AD 106–113 and portrait sculptures of soldiers, politicians, and emperors. Surviving mural paintings (in Pompeii, Rome, and Ostia) and mosaic decorations show Greek influence. Roman art was to prove a lasting inspiration in the West. **Roman candle** CANDLE. **Roman Catholic,** *a.* of or pertaining to the Church of Rome. *n.* a member of this Church. **Roman Catholicism,** *n.* one of the main divisions of the Christian religion, separate from the Eastern Orthodox Church from 1054, and headed by the pope. Membership is about 585 million worldwide, concentrated in S Europe, Latin America, the Philippines. **Roman Empire,** *n.* the empire established by Augustus, 27 BC, divided in AD 395 into the Western or Latin and Eastern or Greek Empires. **Roman holiday,** *n.* an entertainment or enjoyment which depends on others suffering. **Roman law,** *n.* the system of law evolved by the ancient Romans which forms the basis of many modern legal codes. **Roman nose,** *n.* one with a high bridge, an aquiline nose. **Roman numerals,** *n. pl.* the ancient Roman system of numbering consisting of letters representing cardinal numbers, occasionally still in use. The seven key symbols in Roman numerals as represented today (originally they were a little different) are I (= 1), V (= 5), X (= 10), L (= 50), C (= 100), D (= 500) and M (= 1000). There is no zero. **Roman religion,** *n.* a religious system that retained early elements of animism, with reverence to stones and trees, and totemism; and had a strong domestic base in the lares and penates, the cult of Janus and Vesta. It also had a main pantheon of gods derivative of the ancient Greek, which included Jupiter and Juno, Mars and Venus, Minerva, Diana, Ceres, and many lesser deities. **Romanic,** *a.* derived from Latin; Romance (of languages or dialects), derived or descended from the Romans. *n.* Romance. **Romanish,** *a.* of, pertaining to or characteristic of the Church of Rome. **Romanism,** *n.* **Romanist,** *n.* **Romanistic,** *a.* **Romanity,** *n.* the spirit or influence of Roman civilization and institutions. **romanize, -ise,** *v.t.* to make Roman in character; to subject to the authority of ancient Rome; to Latinize; to convert to the Roman Catholic religion. *v.i.* to use Latin words or idioms; to conform to Roman Catholic opinions. **romanization, -isation,** *n.* **romanizer, -iser,** *n.* **Romano-,** *comb.form* Roman. [L *Rōmānus*]

roman à clef, *n.* 'novel with a key', a novel in which a knowing reader is expected to identify real people under fictitious names or actual events disguised as fictitious. [F]

Roman Britain, *n.* the period in British history from the mid-1st cent. BC to the mid-4th cent. AD. Roman relations with Britain began with Caesar's invasions of 55 and 54 BC, but the actual conquest was not begun until AD 43. England was rapidly Romanized, but N of York fewer remains of Roman civilization have been found. After several unsuccessful attempts to conquer Scotland the N frontier was fixed at Hadrian's Wall. During the 4th cent. Britain was raided by the Saxons, Picts, and Scots. The Roman armies were withdrawn AD 407 but there were partial re-occupations AD 417–*c.* 427 and *c.* AD 450. Roman towns include London, York, Chester, St Albans, Colchester, Lincoln, Gloucester, and Bath. The most permanent remains of the occupation were the system of military roads radiating from London.

Romance, *n.* one of a group of Indo-European languages derived from 'vulgar' Latin, e.g. French, Spanish, Romanian. *a.* of or pertaining to this group of languages. **romance,** *n.* a mediaeval tale, usu. in verse, orig. in early French or Provençal, describing the adventures of a hero of chivalry; a story, usu. in prose, rarely in verse, with characters, scenery and incidents more or less remote from ordinary life; fiction of this character; a modern literary genre of sentimental love-stories, romantic fiction; the spirit or atmosphere of imaginary adventure, chivalrous or idealized love, strangeness and mystery; an episode, love-affair or series of facts having this character; a fabrication, a fiction, a falsehood; a short musical composition of simple character, usu. suggestive of a love-song. *v.i.* to imagine or tell romantic or extravagant stories; to make false, exaggerated or imaginary statements. **romancer,** *n.* a writer or composer of romances; one who romances or exaggerates. **romancing,** *n., a.*

Romanes ROMANY.

Romanesque, *n.* style of W European architecture of the 8th to 12th cents., marked by rounded arches, solid volumes, and emphasis on perpendicular elements. In England the style is called Norman. *a.* of this style of architecture. **Romanesque art,** *n.* a style of medieval art.

roman fleuve, *n.* 'a river novel', a novel sequence or saga chronicling a family history, and thereby a social period. [F]

Romania, Socialist Republic of (*Republica Socialistă România*). **area** 237,500 sq km/91,699 sq miles. **capital** Bucharest. **towns** Brasov, Timisoara, Cluj, Iasi; ports Galati, Constanta, Sulina. **physical** mountains surrounding a plateau, with river plains south and east. **population** (1989) 23,155,000, including 2,000,000 Hungarians, 1,000,000 Gypsies, 250,000 Germans, and 30,000 Jews; annual growth rate 0.7%. **exports** petroleum products and oilfield equipment, electrical goods, cars (largely to communist countries). **language** Romanian. **religion** Romanian Orthodox (linked with Greek Orthodox). **Romanian,** *a.* of or pertaining to the country of Romania, its people or language. *n.* the Romanian language; a native or inhabitant of Romania. **Romanian language,** *n.* a member of the Romance branch of the Indo-European language family, spoken in Romania, Macedonia, Albania, and parts of N Greece. It has been strongly influenced by the Slavonic languages and by Greek. The Cyrillic alphabet was used until the 19th cent., when a variant of the Roman alphabet was adopted.

Romano, Giulio GIULIO ROMANO.

Romanov, *n.* dynasty that ruled Russia from 1613 to the Russian Revolution in 1917. Under the Romanovs, Russia developed into an absolutist empire. The last Csar, Nicholas II, abdicated Mar. 1917.

Romansch, *n.* a member of the Romance branch of the Indo-European language family, spoken by some 50,000 people in the eastern cantons of Switzerland. It was accorded official status in 1937 alongside French, German, and Italian. It is also known among scholars as Rhaeto-Romanic.

romantic, *a.* pertaining to, of the nature of or given to romance; imaginative, visionary, poetic, extravagant, fanciful; fantastic, unpractical, chimerical, quixotic, sentimental (of conduct etc.); wild, picturesque, suggestive of romance (of scenery etc.); pertaining to the movement in literature and art tending away from the moderation, harmonious proportion and sanity of classicism towards the unfettered expression of ideal beauty and grandeur. *n.* a romantic poet, novelist etc., a romanticist; a romantic person; a person given to sentimental thoughts or acts of love. **romantically,** *adv.* **romanticism,** *n.* the quality or state of being romantic in literature, music, and art, a style that emphasizes the imagination, emotions, and creativity of the individual artist. The term is often used to characterize the culture of 19th-cent. Europe, as contrasted with 18th-cent. Classicism. Inspired by social change and revolution (US, French) and reacting against the classical restraint of the Augustan age and Enlightenment, the romantics asserted the importance of how the individual feels about the world, natural and supernatural. The French painter Delacroix is often cited as the quintessential romantic artist. Many of the later romantics were strong nationalists, for example Pushkin, Wagner, Verdi, Chopin. The **Romantic Movement** or **Romantic Revival**. **romanticist,** *n.* **romanticize, -ise,** *v.t., v.i.* **romanticization, -isation,** *n.* [F *romantique,* from OF *romant,* ROMAUNT]

Romany, *n.* (a member of) a nomadic people, also called **gypsy** (a corruption of 'Egyptian', since they were erroneously thought to come from Egypt), who in the 14th cent. settled in the Balkan peninsula, spread over Germany, Italy, and France, and arrived in England about 1500; the Romany language, a member of the Indo-European family.

†**romaunt,** *n.* a romance, a tale of chivalry in verse. [OF *romant,* var. of *romanz,* ROMANCE]

Rome, *n.* (Italian **Roma**), capital of Italy and Lazio, on the Tiber, 27 km/17 miles from the Tyrrhenian Sea; population (1988) 2,817,000. Rome has few industries but is an important cultural, road, and rail centre. Remains of the ancient city include the Forum, Colosseum, and Pantheon. After the deposition of the last emperor Romulus Augustus AD 476, the papacy became the real ruler of Rome, and from the 8th cent. was recognized as such. In 1870 Rome became the capital of Italy, the pope retiring into the Vatican until 1929 when the Vatican City was recognized as a sovereign state. **Rome was not built in a day,** accomplishments of any lasting worth require time and patience. **Sack of Rome,** *n.* (AD 410), the invasion and capture of the city of Rome by the Goths, generally accepted as marking the effective end of the Roman Empire. **Treaties of Rome,** *n.* treaties establishing and regulating the European Community. **Romish,** *a.* (*derog.*) belonging to or tending towards Roman Catholicism. [L *Rōma*]

Romeo, *n.* the love-lorn hero of Shakespeare's *Romeo and Juliet;* hence, a man who is an ardent lover.

Rommel, *n.* **Erwin** (1891–1944), German field marshal. He served in World War I, and in World War II he played an important part in the invasions of central Europe and France. He was commander of the N African offensive from 1941 (when he was nicknamed 'Desert Fox') until defeated in the Battles of El Alamein. He was commander-in-chief for a short time against the Allies in Europe (1944) but (as a sympathizer with the Stauffenberg plot) was forced to commit suicide.

Romney, *n.* **George** (1734–1802), English portrait painter, active in London from 1762. He painted several portraits of Lady Hamilton, Admiral Nelson's mistress.

romp, *v.i.* to play or frolic roughly or boisterously; to go rapidly (along, past etc.) with ease. *n.* a child or girl fond of romping; rough or boisterous play; a swift run; an easy win. **to romp home,** to win easily. **romper,** *n.* one who romps. *n.pl.* a one-piece play-suit for infants, a **romper suit. rompish,** *a.* [var. of RAMP[1]]

Romulus, *n.* in Roman mythology, the legendary founder and first king of Rome, the son of Mars by Rhea Silvia, daughter of Numitor, king of Alba Longa. He and his twin brother Remus were thrown into the Tiber by their great-uncle Amulius, who had deposed Numitor, but were suckled by a she-wolf and rescued by a shepherd. On reaching adulthood they killed Amulius and founded Rome.

Romulus Augustulus (born *c.* AD 461), last Roman emperor in the West. He was made emperor by his soldier-father Orestes about AD 475 but was compelled to abdicate AD 476 by Odoacer, leader of the barbarian mercenaries, who nicknamed him Augustulus. Orestes was executed and Romulus Augustulus confined to a Neapolitan villa.

rondavel, *n.* a round hut or building in S Africa. [Afrikaans *rondawel*]

ronde, *n.* an upright angular form of type imitating handwriting. [F, fem. of *rond,* ROUND[2]]

rondeau, *n.* (*pl.* **-deaux**) a poem in iambic verse of eight or ten syllables and ten or thirteen lines, with only two rhymes, the opening words coming twice as a refrain; a rondo. **rondel,** *n.* a particular form of rondeau, usu. of thirteen or fourteen lines with only two rhymes throughout; †a round tower; a rondelle. **rondelet,** *n.* a poem of seven lines with a refrain, usu. repeating words from the opening. **rondelle,** *n.* a circular piece, disk, pane of glass etc.; a rondel. **rondo,** *n.* (*pl.* **-dos**) a musical composition having a principal theme which is repeated after each subordinate theme, often forming part of a symphony etc. [F from *rond,* ROUND[2]]

Rondônia, *n.* a state in NW Brazil; known as the Federal Territory of Guaporé until 1956, it became a state in 1981; the centre of Amazonian tin and gold mining and of experiments in agricultural colonization; area 243,044 sq km/93,876 sq miles; population (1986) 776,000.

rone, rone-pipe, *n.* (*Sc.*) a gutter, a pipe for channelling rainwater from a roof.

Roneo®, *n.* (*pl.* **-neos**) a duplicating machine using stencils. *v.t.* to make duplicate copies with this machine.

Ronsard, *n.* **Pierre de** (1524–85), French poet, leader of the Pléiade group of poets. Under the patronage of Charles IX, he published original verse in a lightly sensitive style, including odes and love sonnets, for example *Odes* (1550), *Les Amours/Lovers* (1552–53), and the 'Marie' cycle, *Continuation des amours/Lovers Continued* (1555–56).

Röntgen, röntgen ROENTGEN.

roo, *n.* (*Austral. coll.*) a kangaroo.

rood, *n.* the cross of Christ, a crucifix, esp. one set on a rood-beam or screen; a measure of land, usu. the fourth part of an acre (about 0·1 ha). **rood-beam,** *n.* a beam across the arch opening into a choir, supporting the rood. **rood-loft,** *n.* a gallery over the rood-screen. **rood-screen,** *n.* a stone or wood screen between the nave and choir, usu. elaborately designed and decorated with carving etc., orig. supporting the rood. [OE *rōd*]

roof, *n.* (*pl.* **roofs**) the upper covering of a house or other building; the covering or top of a vehicle etc.; any analogous part, as of a furnace, oven etc.; the palate; (*fig.*) the top of a mountain or plateau; a covering, a canopy; a house, shelter etc.; an upper limit, a ceiling. *v.t.* to cover with or as with a roof; to be the roof of; to shelter. **roof garden,** *n.* a garden of plants and shrubs growing in soil-filled receptacles on a flat roof. **roof rack,** *n.* a detachable rack on the roof of a motor vehicle for holding luggage etc. **rooftop,** *n.* the outside surface of a roof. **roof-tree,** *n.* the ridge-pole of a roof. **roofage,** *n.* **roofed,** *a.* **roofer,** *n.* **roofing,** *n., a.* **roofless,** *a.* **roof-like,** *a.* **roofy,** *a.* [OE *hrōf,* cp. Dut. *roef,* Icel. *hrōf*]

rooinek, *n.* (*S Afr.*) a nickname for an Englishman. [Afrik., red neck]

rook[1], *n.* a gregarious bird, *Corvus frugilegus,* of the crow family with glossy black plumage; a cheat, a swindler, a sharper, esp. at cards, dice etc. *v.t.* to cheat, to swindle; to charge extortionately. **rookery,** *n.* a wood or clump of trees where rooks nest; a colony of rooks; a place frequented by seabirds or seals for breeding; a colony of seals etc.; an old tenement or poor, densely-populated neighbourhood. **rookish,** *a.* **rooky,** *a.* [OE *hrōc* (cp. Dut. *roek,* G *Ruch,* Icel. *hrōkr*), prob. imit., cp. Gr. *krōzein,* to caw]

rook[2], *n.* the castle in chess. [OF *roc, rock,* ult. from Pers. *rukh*]

rookie, rooky, *n.* (*sl.*) a raw recruit or beginner. [from RECRUIT]

room[1], *n.* a deep blue dye, from a plant of the genus *Ruellia.* [Assamese]

room[2], *n.* space regarded as occupied or available for occupation, accommodation, capacity, vacant space or standing-ground; opportunity, scope; a portion of space in a building enclosed by walls, floor and ceiling; those present in a room; (*pl.*) apartments, lodgings, accommodation for a person or family. *v.i.* to occupy rooms, to lodge. *v.t.* to accommodate, to lodge (guests). **to give, leave, make room,** to withdraw so as to leave space for other people. **room mate,** *n.* one with whom a person shares a room or lodgings. **room service,** *n.* in a hotel, the serving of food and drink to guests in their rooms. **roomed,** *a.* having rooms (*usu. in comb.* as *six-roomed*). **roomer,** *n.* (*N Am.*) a lodger. **roomette,** *n.* (*N Am.*) a sleeping compartment in a train. **roomful,** *n.* (*pl.* **-fuls**). **roomily,** *adv.* **roominess,** *n.* **rooming,** *a., n.* **rooming-house,** *n.* (*N Am.*) a lodging-house. **roomy,** *a.* having ample room; spacious, extensive. [OE *rūm* (cp. G *Raum,* Dan. and Swed. *rum,* also Dut. *ruim* and Icel. *rūmr,* spacious)]

roon, *n.* (*Sc.*) a rim, a strip, a shred. [etym. doubtful]

Roon, *n.* **Albrecht Theodor Emil, Count von Roon** (1803–79), Prussian field marshal. As war minister from 1859, he reorganized the army and made possible the victories over Austria (1866) and in the Franco-Prussian War (1870–71).

Rooney, *n.* **Mickey** (stage name of Joe Yule), (1920–), US actor, who began his career aged two in his parents' stage act. He played Andy Hardy in the Hardy Family series of 'B' films (1936–46) and starred opposite Judy Garland in several musicals, including *Babes in Arms* (1939). He also played Puck in *A Midsummer Night's Dream* (1935), and starred in *Boy's Town* (1938).

roop ROUP[1].

Roosevelt[1], *n.* **(Anna) Eleanor** (1884–1962), US social worker and lecturer; her newspaper column 'My Day' was widely syndicated, she was a delegate to the UN general assembly, and later chair of the UN commission on human rights (1946–51). Within the Democratic Party she formed the left-wing Americans for Democratic Action group in 1947. She was married to President Franklin Roosevelt.

Roosevelt[2], *n.* **Franklin Delano** (1882–1945), 32nd president of the US (1933–45), a Democrat. He served as governor of New York (1929–33). Becoming president amid the Depression, he launched the NEW DEAL economic and social reform programme, which made him popular with the people. After the outbreak of World War II he introduced lend-lease for the supply of war materials to the Allies and drew up the Atlantic Charter of solidarity, and once the US had entered the war in 1941 he spent much time in meetings with Allied leaders.

Roosevelt[3], *n.* **Theodore** (1858–1919), 26th president of the US (1901–09), a Republican. After serving as governor of New York (1898–1900) he became vice president to McKinley, whom he succeeded as president on McKinley's assassination in 1901. He campaigned against the great trusts (combines that reduce competition), while carrying on a jingoist foreign policy designed to enforce US supremacy over Latin America. Alienated after his retirement by the conservatism of his successor Taft, Roosevelt formed the Progressive or 'Bull Moose' Party. As their candidate he unsuccessfully ran for the presidency in 1912.

roost[1], *n.* a pole or perch for birds to rest on; a place for fowls to sleep in at night; a resting-place, a room, esp. a bedroom. *v.i.* to perch on or occupy a roost, to sleep on a roost. *v.t.* to provide with a roost or a resting-place. **rooster,** *n.* the domestic cock. [OE *hrōst,* cp. Dut. *roest*]

roost[2], *n.* a powerful tidal current, esp. off the Orkney and Shetland Islands. [Icel. *rost*]

root[1], *n.* the descending part of a plant which fixes itself in the earth and draws nourishment therefrom; (*pl.*) the ramifying parts, rootlets or fibres into which this divides, or the analogous part of an epiphyte etc.; a young plant for transplanting; an esculent root; the part of an organ or structure that is embedded; the basis, the bottom, the fundamental part or that which supplies origin, sustenance, means of development etc.; (*pl.*) one's ancestry, origins, place of origin or belonging; the elementary, unanalysable part of a word as distinguished from its inflexional forms and derivatives; the fundamental note of a chord; in mathematics, the quantity or number that, multiplied by itself a specified number of times, yields a given quantity. *v.i.* to take root. *v.t.* to cause to take root; to fix or implant firmly (to the spot); to pull or dig (up) by the roots. **root and branch,** utterly, radically. **to root out,** to uproot; to extirpate. **to take, strike root,** to become planted and send out living roots or rootlets; to become immovable or established. **root-bound,** *a.* fixed to the earth by roots; immovable. **root-cap,** *a.* a protective covering of cells on the tip of a root. **root-crop,** *n.* a crop of plants with esculent roots. **root-leaf,** *n.* a leaf apparently growing immediately from the root, but really from a part of the stem underground. **root-stock,** *n.* a rhizome; the original source or primary form of anything. **root vegetable,** *n.* a vegetable that is or has an esculent root. **rootage,** *n.* **rooted,** *a.* **rootedly,** *adv.* **rootedness,** *n.* **rooter,** *n.* **rootery,** *n.* a pile of roots and stumps for growing plants in. **rootiness,** *n.* **rootless,** *a.* **rootlet,** *n.* a small root, a radicle. **rootlike,** *a.* **rooty,** *a.* [late OE and Icel. *rōt,* rel. to L *rādix* and WORT]

root[2], *v.t.* to dig, turn or grub (up) with the snout, beak, etc. *v.i.* to turn up the ground in this manner in search of food; to hunt (up or out), to rummage (about, in etc.); **rooter,** *n.* **rootle,** *v.t., v.i.* [OE *wrōtan,* from *rōt,* ROOT[1]]

root[3], *v.i.* (*coll.*) to cheer, to shout encouragements to, to support. **rooter,** *n.* one who roots, cheers, supports. [perh. var. of ROUT]

rooti, roti, ruti, *n.* bread, food. [Hind.]

rope, *n.* a stout cord of twisted fibres of hemp, flax, cotton etc., or wire; a general name for cordage, over one inch in circumference; a series of things strung together in a line e.g. of garlic, onions, pearls; a halter for hanging a person; a slimy or gelatinous formation in beer etc. *v.t.* to tie, fasten or secure with a rope; to enclose or close (in) with rope; to pull (a horse) so as to avoid winning a race; to fasten (persons) together or to tie (a person on) with a rope when climbing. *v.i.* to form threads or filaments (of glutinous matter in liquid) into a rope; to put a rope on for climbing. **rope of sand,** a feeble or delusive bond. **the rope,** a hangman's noose; death by hanging. **to give (someone) enough** (or **plenty of**) **rope to hang himself, herself,** to allow someone enough freedom of speech or action to commit a blunder or cause his or her own downfall. **to know the ropes,** to be well acquainted with the circumstances, methods and opportunities in any sphere. **to rope in,** to capture or pull in a steer, horse etc. with a rope, to lasso; (*coll.*) to enlist or persuade someone to join a group or enter into an activity. **rope-dancer,** *n.* one who performs feats on the tight-rope. **rope-dancing,** *n.* **rope-ladder,** *n.* a ladder made of two ropes connected by rungs usu. of wood. **rope's-end,** *n.* a short piece of rope formerly used for flogging, esp. on shipboard. **rope-walk,** *n.* a long piece of usu. covered ground where ropes are twisted. **rope-walker,** *n.* a tight-rope artist. **rop(e)able,** *a.* (*Austral. coll.*) wild, intractable; angry, out of temper, irascible; capable of being roped. **roped,** *a.* **roper,** *n.* **ropiness,** *n.* **roping,** *n., a.* **roping-pole,** *n.* (*Austral.*) a pole with a noose attached, for catching cattle. **rop(e)y,** *a.* resembling a rope; glutinous, viscid; (*coll.*) inferior, shoddy; (*coll.*) unwell. **ropily,** *adv.* [OE *rāp* (cp. Dut. *reep,* G *Reif,* Icel. and Norw. *reip,* Swed. *rep*)]

Roquefort, *n.* French cheese made from goats' and ewes' milk. [orig. made at *Roquefort*]

roquelaure, *n.* a short cloak for men worn in the 18th cent. [Duc de *Roquelaure*]

roquet, *v.t.* in croquet, to make one's ball strike another; to strike another ball (of one's ball). *v.i.* to make this stroke. *n.* this stroke or a hit with it. [from CROQUET]

†**roral,** †**-ric,** *a.* pertaining to or like dew; dewy. †**roriferous,** *a.* producing dew or moisture. [L *rōs rōris,* dew, -AL, -IC]

ro-ro, (*abbr.*) roll-on roll-off.

rorqual, *n.* a whale with dorsal fins, one of the genus *Balaenoptera,* the finback. [F, from Norw. *röyrkval* (*reythr,* red, *kval,* whale)]

Rorschach test, *n.* in psychiatry, a method of diagnosis involving the use of ink-blot patterns which subjects are asked to interpret, to help indicate personality type, degree of intelligence, and emotional stability. It was invented by the Swiss psychiatrist Hermann Rorschach (1884–1922).

rort, *n.* (*Austral. sl.*) a party or boisterous celebration; a noise; a deception. **rorter,** *n.* **rorty,** *a.* rowdy, noisy. [etym. doubtful, perh. from *rorty,* fine, excellent]

Rosa, *n.* **Salvator** (1615–73), Italian painter, etcher, poet, and musician, active in Florence (1640–49) and subsequently in Rome. He created wild, romantic, and sometimes macabre landscapes, seascapes, and battle scenes. He also wrote verse satires.

rosace, *n.* a rose-shaped centre-piece or other ornament, a rosette; a rose-window. **rosacea,** *n.* a chronic skin-disease characterized by redness of the skin. **rosaceous,** *a.* pertaining to the Rosaceae family of plants to which the rose belongs; rose-like, rose-coloured. **rosaniline,** *n.* a compound having powerful basic properties derived from aniline; a salt of this used as a dye-stuff under the names aniline red, magenta etc. **rosarian,** *n.* a rose-fancier, a cultivator of roses. **rosarium,** *n.* a rose-garden. **rosary,** *n.* a rose-garden, a rose-plot; a form of prayer in the Roman Catholic

Church in which three sets of five decades of aves, each decade preceded by a paternoster and followed by a gloria, are repeated; this series of prayers; a string of beads by means of which account is kept of the prayers uttered; †a chaplet, a garland. [F, from ROSE[1]]

†**roscid,** *a.* dewy. [L *rōscidus,* from *rōs,* dew]

Roscius Gallus, *n.* **Quintus** (*c.* 126–62 BC), Roman actor, originally a slave, so gifted that his name became proverbial for a great actor. **Roscian,** *a.* of or after the manner of Roscius Gallus.

Roscoff, *n.* a port on the Brittany coast of France with a ferry link to Plymouth in England; population (1982) 4000.

Roscommon, *n.* county of the Republic of Ireland in the province of Connacht. **area** 2460 sq km/950 sq miles. **towns** county town Roscommon. **physical** bounded on the east by the river Shannon; lakes Gara, Key, Allen; rich pastures. **population** (1986) 55,000.

rose[1], *n.* any plant or flower of the genus *Rosa,* consisting of prickly bushes or climbing and trailing shrubs bearing single or double flowers, usu. scented, of all shades of colour from white and yellow to dark crimson; one of various other flowers or plants (with distinctive adjective or phrase) having some resemblance to the rose; a light crimson or pink colour; a complexion of this colour (*often in pl.*); a device, rosette, knot, ornament or other object shaped like a rose; a perforated nozzle for a hose or watering-pot; a rose-window; a rose-shaped ornament on a ceiling; a circular card, disk or diagram with radiating lines, used in a mariner's compass etc.; erysipelas. *a.* coloured like a rose, pink or pale red. *v.t.* (*chiefly in p.p.*) to make rosy. **a bed of roses,** a luxurious situation, ease. **all roses, roses all the way,** completely pleasant, unproblematic or easy. **everything is coming up roses,** everything is turning out successfully. **rose of Jericho,** a small annual cruciferous plant of N Africa and the Levant, having fronds that expand with moisture, also called the resurrection plant. **rose of May,** the white narcissus. **rose of Sharon,** an Eastern plant sometimes identified with the meadow saffron, the cystus and the polyanthus narcissus; a species of St John's wort. **under the rose,** in secret; privately, confidentially, sub-rosa. **Wars of the Roses,** the civil wars (1455–85) between the Houses of Lancaster and York, who respectively took a red and a white rose as their emblems. **rose-acacia,** *n.* the locust tree, *Robinia hispida.* **rose-apple,** *n.* a tropical tree of various species of the genus *Eugenia* cultivated for its foliage, flowers and fruit. **rose-bay,** *n.* the great willow-herb, *Epilobium angustifolium;* the azalea; the oleander; the rhododendron. **rose bowl,** *n.* a bowl-shaped ornamental vase for roses. **rose-bud,** *n.* a flower-bud of a rose; a young girl. *a.* like a rose-bud (of a mouth). **rose-bug,** *n.* an American beetle destructive to roses. **rose-campion,** *n.* a garden plant with crimson flowers of the genus *Agrostemma.* **rose-chafer, beetle,** *n.* a European beetle, *Cetonia aurata,* infesting roses. **rose-colour,** *n.* a deep pink. **rose-coloured,** *a.* attractive, encouraging; sanguine, optimistic; of a rose-colour. **rose-cut,** *a.* cut with a flat surface below and a hemispherical or pyramidal part above covered with facets (of diamonds etc.). **rose-diamond,** *n.* a diamond so cut. **rose-gall,** *n.* a gall on the dog-rose, produced by an insect. **rosehip,** *n.* a red berry, the fruit of the rose plant. **rose-hued,** *a.* **rose-leaf,** *n.* a petal (or leaf) of a rose. **rose-mallow,** *n.* the hollyhock, a plant of the genus *Hibiscus.* †**rose-noble,** *n.* an old English gold coin, with the impression of a rose. **rose-pink,** *n.* a pigment composed of whiting dyed with Brazil-wood. *a.* **rose-quartz,** *n.* a rose-red variety of quartz. **rose-rash** ROSEOLA. **rose-red,** *a.* the red of a rose; blushing. **rose-root,** *n.* a species of stonecrop, *Sedum rhodiola,* with a fragrant root. **rose-water,** *n.* scented water distilled from rose leaves. *a.* affectedly delicate, fine or sentimental. **rose-window,** *n.* a circular window filled with tracery branching from the centre, usu. with mullions arranged like the spokes of a wheel. **rosewood,** *n.* a hard close-grained fragrant wood of a dark-red colour obtained chiefly from various species of *Dalbergia.* **rosewood oil,** *n.* oil obtained from a species of rosewood. **roseal,** *a.* **roseate,** *a.*, rose-coloured, rosy; smiling, promising, optimistic. **roseless,** *a.* **roselike,** *a.* **rosery,** *n.* a place where roses grow, a rose-plot, a rosarium. **rosily,** *adv.* **rosiness,** *n.* **rosy,** *a.* resembling a rose; blooming; favourable, auspicious. **rosy-cheeked,** *a.* having a healthy bloom, pink cheeks. [OE *rose,* L *rosa,* prob. ult. from Gr. *rhodea, rhodon*]

rose[2], *past* RISE.

rosé, *a., n.* (of) a pink-coloured wine made from red grapes with their skins removed or combined from red and white wines. [F, pink]

Roseau (formerly **Charlotte Town**), *n.* capital of Dominica, West Indies; population (1981) 20,000.

rose-bud, rose-leaf etc. ROSE[1].

Roseirks, *n.* a port at the head of navigation of the Blue Nile in Sudan. A hydro-electric scheme here provides the country with 70% of its electrical power.

rosella, *n.* (*Austral.*) a variety of brightly-coloured parakeet. [from *Rose Hill,* a district near Sydney where it was first observed]

roselle, *n.* the E Indian hibiscus, called in the W Indies red sorrel.

rosemary, *n.* an evergreen fragrant shrub, *Rosmarinus officinalis,* of the mint family, leaves of which yield a perfume and oil and are used in cooking etc.; †a funeral emblem signifying remembrance. [orig. *rosmarine,* OF *rosmarin* (F *romarin*), late L *rōsmarīnum* (*rōs,* dew, *marīnus,* MARINE)]

Rosenberg[1], *n.* **Alfred** (1893–1946), German politician, born in Tallinn, Estonia. He became the chief Nazi ideologist, and was Reich minister for eastern occupied territories (1941–44). He was tried at Nuremberg 1946 as a war criminal and hanged.

Rosenberg[2], *n.* **Isaac** (1890–1918), English poet of the World War I period. Trained as an artist at the Slade school in London, Rosenberg enlisted in the army in 1915. He wrote about the horror of life on the front line, as in 'Break of Day in the Trenches'.

Rosenberg[3], *n.* **Julius** (1918–53) and **Ethel** (1915–53), US married couple, accused of being leaders of a nuclear-espionage ring passing information to the USSR; both were executed.

roseola, *n.* a non-contagious febrile disease with rose-coloured spots, German measles; a rash occurring in measles etc. **roseolar,** *a.* [dim. of ROSE[1]]

Roses, Wars of the, name given in the 19th cent. by novelist Walter Scott to civil wars in England (1455–85) between the houses of Lancaster (badge, red rose) and York (badge, white rose): **1455** Opened with battle of St Albans 22 May, a Yorkist victory (Henry VI made prisoner). **1459–61** War renewed until Edward IV, having become king, confirmed his position by a victory at Towton 29 Mar. 1461. **1470** Warwick (who had helped Edward to the throne) allied instead with Henry VI's widow, Margaret of Anjou, but was defeated by Edward at Barnet 14 Apr. and by Margaret at Tewkesbury 4 May. **1485** Yorkist regime ended with the defeat of Richard III by the future Henry VII at Bosworth 22 Aug.

roset, (*Sc.*) var. of ROSIN.

Rose Theatre, *n.* former London theatre near Southark Bridge where many of Shakespeare's plays were performed. The excavation and preservation of the remains of the theatre, discovered in 1989, caused controversy between government bodies and archaeologists.

Rosetta Stone, *n.* a slab of basalt with inscriptions from 197 BC, found near the town of Rosetta, Egypt, 1799. It has the same text in Greek as in the hieroglyphic and demotic scripts, and was the key to deciphering other Egyptian inscriptions.

rosette, *n.* a rose-shaped ornament, knot or badge; a bunch of ribbons, worsted, strips of leather etc., arranged concentrically more or less as the petals of a rose (usu. worn as a badge or given as a prize); a carved or painted ornament in the conventional form of a rose; a circular group of leaves usu. round the base of a stem. **rosetted,** *a.* [F]

rosewood etc. ROSE[1].

Rosh Hashanah, *n.* the two-day holiday that marks the start of the Jewish New Year (first new moon after the autumn equinox), traditionally announced by blowing a ram's horn. [Heb., head of the year]

Rosicrucian, *n.* a member of a secret religious society devoted to the study of occult science, which became known to the public early in the 17th cent., and was alleged to have been founded by a German noble, Christian Rosenkreuz, in 1484. *a.* of or pertaining to Rosenkreuz, this society or its members. **Rosicrucianism,** *n.* [from L *rŏsa,* rose, *crux,* cross]

rosily ROSE[1].

rosin, *n.* resin, esp. the solid residue left after the oil has been distilled from crude turpentine, colophony. *v.t.* to rub, smear etc. with rosin, esp. to apply it to a violin etc. bow. **rosined,** *a.* **rosiny,** *a.* [var. of RESIN]

rosinante, *n.* a worn-out horse, a nag. [horse in Cervantes' *Don Quixote*]

rosiness ROSE[1].

†**rosmarine**[1], *n.* rosemary; sea-dew, sea-spray. [see ROSEMARY]

†**rosmarine**[2], *n.* the walrus. [Dan. *rosmar*]

rosolio, *n.* a cordial made from raisins, spirit etc., in Italy and S Europe; a Maltese red wine. [It. (L *rōs,* dew, *sōlis,* gen. of *sōl,* sun)]

ROSPA, (*abbr.*) Royal Society for the Prevention of Accidents.

ross, *n.* (*N Am.*) the rough scaly surface of the bark of certain trees; (*Sc.*) refuse of plants, loppings from trees etc. *v.t.* to strip the ross from; to cut (bark) up for tanning. [prob. from Scand. (cp. Norw. dial. *ros, rus*)]

Ross[1], *n.* **Martin** (pen name of Violet Florence Martin), Irish novelist.

Ross[2], *n.* **James Clark** (1800–62), English explorer who discovered the magnetic North Pole in 1831. He also went to the Antarctic in 1839; Ross Island, Ross Sea, and Ross Dependency are named after him.

Ross[3], *n.* **Ronald** (1857–1932), British physician and bacteriologist, born in India. From 1881-99, he served in the Indian medical service, and in 1895–98 identified the *Anopheles* mosquito as being responsible for the spread of malaria. Nobel prize 1902.

Ross Dependency, *n.* all the Antarctic islands and territories between 160° E and 150° W longitude and south of 60° S latitude; it includes Edward VII Land, Ross Sea and its islands, and parts of Victoria Land.

Rossellini, *n.* **Roberto** (1906–77), Italian film director. His World War II theme trilogy of films, *Roma Città aperta/Rome, Open City* (1945), *Paisà/Paisan* (1946), and *Germania Anno Zero/Germany Year Zero* (1947) are considered landmarks in postwar European cinema.

Rossetti[1], *n.* **Christina Georgina** (1830–94), English poet, sister of Dante Rossetti, and a devout High Anglican. Her verse includes *Goblin Market and Other Poems* (1862) and expresses unfulfilled spiritual yearning and frustrated love. She was a skilful technician and made use of irregular rhyme and line length.

Rossetti[2], *n.* **Dante Gabriel** (1828–82), British painter and poet, a founder member of the PRE-RAPHAELITE BROTHERHOOD (PRB) in 1848. Apart from romantic medieval scenes, he produced dozens of idealized portraits of women. His verse includes 'The Blessed Damozel' (1850). His sister was the poet Christina Rossetti.

Rossini, *n.* **Gioachino (Antonio)** (1792–1868), Italian composer. His first success was the opera *Tancredi* (1813). In 1816 his 'opera buffa' *Il barbiere di Siviglia/The Barber of Seville* was produced in Rome. During his fertile composition period (1815–23), he produced 20 operas, and created (with Donizetti and Bellini) the 19th-cent. Italian operatic style. After *Guillaume Tell/William Tell* (1829) he gave up writing opera and his later years were spent in Bologna and Paris.

Rostand, *n.* **Edmond** (1869–1918), French dramatist, who wrote *Cyrano de Bergerac* (1897) and *L'Aiglon* (1900) (based on the life of Napoleon III), in which Sarah Bernhardt played a leading role.

rostellum, *n.* (*pl.* **-la**) an elevated portion of the stigma in orchids; any small beak-like part or process, as the protruding fore part of the head in tapeworms, the mouth-part of lice etc.; that part of the seed which descends and forms the root, a radicle. **rostellar, rostellate,** *a.* [L, dim. of ROSTRUM]

roster, *n.* a list showing the order of rotation in which employees, officers, members etc. are to perform their turns of duty. *v.t.* to put on a roster. [Dut. *rooster,* list, orig. grid-iron, from *roosten,* to ROAST]

rostrum, *n.* (*pl.* **-stra**) the beak or prow of a Roman war-galley; a platform (decorated with beaks of captured galleys) in the Roman forum from which public orations etc. were delivered; hence, a platform, a pulpit; a beak, bill, beak-like snout, part or process. **rostral,** *a.* pertaining to, situated on or resembling a rostrum or beak; (*Rom. Ant.*) decorated with the beaks of war-galleys or representations of these (of columns etc.). **rostrate, -strated,** *a.* furnished with or ending in a part resembling a bird's beak; (*Rom. Ant.*) rostral. [L, beak, cogn. with *rōdere,* to gnaw, cp. RODENT]

rosula, *n.* a rosette of leaves. **rosulate,** *a.* with leaves making a small rosette. [ROSE[1]]

rot, *v.i.* (*past, p.p.* **rotted**) to decay, to decompose by natural change, to putrefy; to be affected with sheep-rot or other decaying disease; to become morally corrupt, to pine away. *v.t.* to cause to rot, to decompose, to make putrid. *n.* putrefaction, rottenness; dry-rot, wet-rot; a malignant liver-disease in sheep etc.; (*coll.*) nonsense, rubbish. *int.* expressing disbelief or disagreement. **rotgut,** *n.* an alcoholic drink of inferior quality. [OE *rotian* (cp. Dut. *rotten,* Icel. *rotna*)]

rota, *n.* a list of names, duties etc., a roster; **(Rota)** in the Roman Catholic Church, the supreme court deciding on ecclesiastical and secular causes. **rotaplane** GYROPLANE. **rotable,** *a.* **rotal,** *a.* **rotary,** *a.* rotating on its axis; acting or characterized by rotation. *n.* a rotary machine. **Rotary Club, the Rotary,** *n.* a local business club for mutual benefit and service. **rotary cultivator,** *n.* a horticultural machine with revolving blades or claws for tilling. **rotary machine,** *n.* a printing press in which the printing surface is a revolving cylinder. **rotary pump,** *n.* a pump in which the liquid is delivered at low pressure by means of shaped rotating members. **Rotarian,** *n., a.* (a member) of a Rotary Club. **Rotarianism,** *n.* [L, wheel]

rotate, *v.i.* to revolve round an axis or centre; to act in rotation. *v.t.* to cause (a wheel etc.) to revolve; to arrange (crops etc.) in rotation. *a.* wheel-shaped (of a calyx, corolla etc.). **rotatable,** *a.* **rotation,** *n.* the act of rotating, rotary motion; alternation, recurrence, regular succession. **rotational,** *a.* **rotative,** *a.* **rotator,** *n.* that which moves in or gives a circular motion; a muscle imparting rotatory motion. **rotatory,** *a.* **rotovate,** *v.i.* **Rotovator**®, *n.* a rotary cultivator.

rote[1], *n.* mere repetition of words, phrases etc. without understanding; mechanical, routine memory or knowledge. *v.t.* to repeat from memory; †to learn by rote. [etym. doubtful, said to be rel. to ROUTE]

†**rote**[2], *n.* a mediaeval musical instrument like a fiddle. [OF, prob. from Celt., cp. CROWD[2]]

Roth, *n.* **Philip** (1933–), US novelist, noted for his portrayals of modern Jewish-American life. His books include *Goodbye Columbus* (1959); *Portnoy's Complaint* (1969); and a series of novels about a writer, Nathan Zuckerman, including *The Ghost Writer* (1979), *Zuckerman Unbound* (1981), and *The Anatomy Lesson* (1984).

Rothamsted, *n.* an agricultural research centre in Hertfordshire, England, NW of St Albans.

Rothko, *n.* **Mark** (1903–70), US painter, born in Russia, an abstract expressionist and a pioneer of Colour Field painting (abstract, dominated by areas of unmodulated, strong colour).

Rothschild, *n.* a European family, noted for its activity in the financial world for two centuries. Mayer Anselm

(1744–1812) set up as a moneylender in Frankfurt-am-Main, Germany, and important business houses were established throughout Europe by his ten children.

roti ROOTI.

rotifer, *n.* (*pl.* **-fers**) one of the Rotifera. **Rotifera,** *n.* the wheel-animalcules, a phylum of minute aquatic animals with swimming organs appearing to have a rotary movement. **rotiferal, rotiferous,** *a.* [ROTA, L *-fer,* -FEROUS]

rotisserie, *n.* a device with a spit on which food esp. meat is roasted or barbecued; a restaurant specializing in meat cooked in this way. [F, cookshop]

rotogravure, *n.* a process of photogravure-printing on a rotary machine; a print produced by this process. [L *rota,* a wheel, F *gravure,* engraving]

rotor, *n.* name given to any system of revolving blades that produce lift in aircraft; the rotating part of an electric machine. [short for ROTATOR]

rotten, *a.* decomposed, decayed, decaying, tainted, putrid, fetid; unsound, liable to break, tear etc.; morally corrupt, unhealthy, untrustworthy, defective; affected with sheep-rot; (*coll.*) poor or contemptible in quality; disagreeable, annoying, unpleasant, distressed. **rotten borough** BOROUGH. **rottenstone,** *n.* a friable siliceous limestone used for polishing. **rottenly,** *adv.* **rottenness,** *n.* **rotter,** *n.* (*sl.*) a good-for-nothing or detestable person. [prob. from Icel. *rotinn* (cp. Swed. *rutten*), cogn. with ROT and RET]

Rotterdam, *n.* industrial port (brewing, distilling, shipbuilding, sugar and petroleum refining, margarine, tobacco) in the Netherlands and one of the foremost ocean cargo ports in the world, in the Rhine-Maas delta, linked by canal (1866–90) with the North Sea; population (1988) 1,036,000.

Rottweiler, *n.* breed of guard dog originating from Rottweil in S Germany. Large and powerful, it needs regular exercise, and has not proved successful as a pet.

rotula, *n.* (*pl.* **-lae**) the knee-cap or patella; one of the radial parts of the oral skeleton of a sea-urchin. [L, dim. of ROTA]

rotund, *a.* rounded, circular or spherical; orotund, sonorous, magniloquent (of speech or language); plump, well-rounded. **rotunda,** *n.* a circular building, hall etc., esp. with a dome. **rotundate,** *a.* **rotundity,** *n.* **rotundly,** *adv.* [L *rotundus,* ROUND²]

roturier, *n.* a plebeian. [F, from *roture,* prob. from L *ruptūra,* RUPTURE]

Rouault, *n.* **Georges** (1871–1958), French painter, etcher, illustrator, and designer. Early in his career he was associated with the Fauves, but created his own style using heavy, dark colours and bold brushwork. His subjects included sad clowns, prostitutes, and evil lawyers; from about 1940 he painted mainly religious works.

Roubiliac (or **Roubillac**), *n.* **Louis François** (*c.* 1705–62), French sculptor, a Huguenot who fled religious persecution to settle in England in 1732. He became a leading sculptor of the day, creating a statue of Handel for Vauxhall Gardens (1737, Victoria and Albert Museum, London) and teaching at St Martin's Lane Academy from 1745.

rouble, ruble, *n.* the Russian monetary unit, equal to 100 kopecks. [Rus. *rubl'*]

roué, *n.* a rake, a debauchee. [F, p.p. of *rouer,* to break on the wheel, L *rotāre,* to ROTATE]

rouge, *n.* a cosmetic prepared from safflower, *Carthamus tinctorius,* used esp. to colour the cheeks red; red oxide of iron used for polishing metal, glass etc. †*a.* red. *v.t.* to colour with rouge. *v.i.* to colour (one's cheeks etc.) with rouge. **Rouge Croix, Rouge Dragon,** *n.* the titles of two pursuivants in the English College of Arms. **rouge et noir,** a gambling card-game played by a 'banker' and a number of persons on a table marked with four diamonds, two red and two black. [F, from L *rubeus* (cp. *ruber, rufus,* also RED)]

rough, *a.* having an uneven, broken or irregular surface, having prominences or inequalities, not smooth, level or polished; shaggy, hairy, of coarse texture; rugged, hilly, hummocky; harsh to the senses, astringent, discordant, severe; violent, boisterous, tempestuous; turbulent, disorderly; harsh or rugged in temper or manners; cruel, unfeeling; rude, unpolished; lacking finish or completeness, not completely wrought, crude; approximate, not precise or exact, general; difficult, hard (to bear). *adv.* roughly, in a rough manner. *n.* a rough or unfinished state; rough ground; the ground to right and left of a golf fairway; a rough person, a rowdy; a spike put in a horseshoe to prevent slipping; a draft, a rough drawing; (*collect.*) rough or harsh experiences, hardships. *v.t.* to make rough, to roughen; to furnish (a horse or horseshoe) with roughs or spikes; to plan or shape (out) roughly or broadly. **the rough side of one's tongue,** (*coll.*) a scolding, a rebuke. **to cut up rough,** to be upset, to grow quarrelsome. **to rough in,** to outline, to draw roughly. **to rough it,** to put up with hardships; to live without the ordinary conveniences. **to rough up,** (*sl.*) to beat up, to injure during a beating. **to sleep rough,** to sleep out-of-doors. **to take the rough with the smooth,** to be subject to unpleasantness or difficulty as well as ease, happiness etc. **rough-and-ready,** *a.* hastily prepared, without finish or elaboration; provisional, makeshift. **rough-and-tumble,** *a.* disorderly, irregular, boisterous, haphazard. *n.* an irregular fight, contest, scuffle etc. *adv.* **rough-cast,** *v.t.* to form or compose roughly; to coat (a wall) with coarse plaster. *n.* a rough model or outline; a coarse plastering, usu. containing gravel, for outside walls etc. *a.* formed roughly, without revision or polish; coated with rough-cast. *n.* **rough-cut,** *n.* the first assembly of a film by an editor from the selected takes which are joined in scripted order. **rough diamond,** *n.* a person of rough exterior or manners but with a genuine or warm character. **rough draft,** *v.t., n.* (to make) a rough sketch. **rough-draw,** *v.t.* to draw roughly. **rough-dry,** *v.t., a.* to dry without smoothing or ironing. **rough-hew,** *v.t.* to hew out roughly; to give the first crude form to. **rough-hewn,** *a.* rugged, rough, unpolished. **rough-hound,** *n.* a species of dog-fish. **rough house,** *n.* (*coll.*) horse-play, brawling. **rough justice,** *n.* justice appropriate to a crime but not strictly legal; a sentence or verdict hastily reached and executed. **rough-neck,** *n.* (*N Am. coll.*) a rowdy, a hooligan; an oil-worker employed to handle drilling equipment on a rig. **rough-rider,** *n.* a horse-breaker; a bold skilful horseman able to ride unbroken horses; an irregular horse-soldier. **rough-shod,** *a.* shod with roughened shoes. **to ride rough-shod over,** to treat in a domineering and inconsiderate way. **rough shooting,** *n.* game-shooting without the use of beaters, on rough ground or moorland. **rough-spoken,** *a.* having coarse speech. **rough stuff,** *n.* (*sl.*) violence, violent behaviour. **rough trade,** *n.* (*sl.*) a usu. casual homosexual partner who is uncultivated or aggressive. **rough-wrought,** *a.* worked only as regards the initial stages. **roughage,** *n.* food materials containing a considerable quantity of cellulose, which resist digestion and promote peristalsis. **roughed-up,** *a.* beaten-up. **roughen,** *v.t., v.i.* **rougher,** *n.* one who works in the rough or in the rougher stages of a process etc. **roughish,** *a.* **roughly,** *adv.* **roughness,** *n.* [OE *rūh* (cp. Dut. *ruig,* G *rauh,* Dan. *ru*)]

roulade, *n.* (*Mus.*) a run of notes on one syllable, a flourish; a rolled piece of veal or pork; a thin slice of meat spread with a stuffing and rolled into a sausage. [F, from *rouler,* to ROLL]

rouleau, *n.* (*pl.* **-leaux**) a small roll, esp. a pile of coins done up in paper; a trimming of decorative piping. [F, from ROLE]

roulette, *n.* a game of chance played with a ball on a table with a revolving disk; a wheel with points for making dotted lines, used in engraving, for perforating etc.; in geometry, a curve that is the locus of a point rolling on a curve. [F, dim. of *rouelle,* dim. of *roue,* L *rota,* wheel]

Roumanian ROMANIAN.

rounce, *n.* in hand-printing, the handle by which the

bed of a printing-press is run in and out under the platen. [Dut. *ronse, ronds*]

†**round**[1], *v.i., v.t.* to whisper (to). [OE *rūnian,* from *rūn,* mystery, cogn. with RUNE]

round[2], *a.* spherical, circular, cylindrical or approximately so; convexly curved in contour or surface, full, plump, not hollow, corpulent; going and returning to the same point, with circular or roughly circular course or motion; continuous, unbroken; plain, open, frank, candid, fair; quick, smart, brisk (of pace etc.); full-toned, resonant; articulated with lips formed into a circle (of sounds); liberal, ample, large, considerable; composed of tens, hundreds etc., esp. evenly divisible by ten, approximate, without fractions. *n.* a round object, piece, slice etc.; a ladder-rung, a circle, coil, sphere or globe; a thick cut from a joint (of beef); that which goes round, circumference, extent; a circular course, a circuit, a heat, a cycle, a recurrent series, a bout, a session, a spell, an allowance, a series of actions etc.; an order of drinks for several people, each of whom is buying drinks for the group in turn; a burst of applause; a single shot or volley fired from a firearm or gun; ammunition for this; the state of being completely carved out in the solid, opp. to relief; a circuit of inspection, the circuit so made; a piece of music sung by several voices each taking it up in succession. *adv.* on all sides so as to encircle; so as to come back to the same point; to or at all points on the circumference or all members of a party etc.; by a circuitous route; with rotating motion. *prep.* on all sides of; so as to encircle; to or at all parts of the circumference of; in all directions from (in the relation of a body to its axis or centre); revolving round. *v.t.* to make round or curved; to pass, go or travel round; to collect together, to gather (up); to fill out, to complete; to pronounce fully and smoothly; †to surround. *v.i.* to grow or become round; to go the rounds, as a guard; (*chiefly Naut.*) to turn round. **in round numbers,** approximately; to the nearest large number. **in the round,** able to be viewed from every side. **round the bend, twist,** mad, crazy. **to bring someone round,** to resuscitate someone; to persuade someone to accept an idea, a situation etc. **to come round,** to revive; to begin to accept an idea, situation etc. **to get round someone,** to take advantage of by flattery or deception. **to round down,** to lower a number to avoid fractions or reach a convenient figure. **to round off,** to shape (angles etc.) to a round or less sharp form; to finish off, complete, perfect. **to round on,** to turn upon, to attack. **to round to,** to turn the prow of a ship toward the wind, in order to heave to. **to round out,** to fill out, become more plump. **to round up,** to raise a number to avoid fractions or reach a convenient figure. **round about,** *prep., adv.* in or as in a circle round, all round; circuitously, indirectly; approximately; in an opposite direction. **roundabout,** *a.* circuitous, indirect, loose; encircling; plump, stout; †ample, extensive. *n.* a merry-go-round; a circuitous or indirect journey, way, course etc.; a device at a cross-roads whereby traffic circulates in one direction only; a circumlocution. **roundaboutness,** *n.* **round arm,** *a.* with a swing in which the arm turns at shoulder level. **round-backed,** *a.* having a round or curved back. **round bracket,** *n.* parenthesis. **round-dance,** *n.* a dance in which the performers are ranged or move in a circle, esp. a waltz. **round-eyed,** *a.* **round-faced,** *a.* **round game,** *n.* one in which there are a number of players but no sides or partners. **round-hand,** *n.* writing in which the letters are round and full; a style of bowling (at cricket) with the arm swung more or less horizontally. **Roundhead,** *n.* a term applied by the Cavaliers during the Civil War to the Parliamentarians, from their wearing their hair short. *a.* pertaining to the Parliamentarians. **round-house,** *n.* †a lock-up; a cabin on the after part of the quarterdeck, esp. on sailing ships; this part of the deck; (*N Am.*) a circular building containing a turntable for servicing railway locomotives. **round robin,** *n.* (*coll.*) a petition with the signatures placed in a circle so that no name heads the list; a tournament in which each contestant plays every other contestant. **round-shouldered,** *a.* bent forward so that the back is rounded. **roundsman,** *n.* one who makes calls to collect orders, deliver goods etc.; (*N Am.*) a policeman making a round of inspection. **round table,** *n.* a conference or meeting at which all parties are on an equal footing. **round-the-clock,** *a.* continuous; lasting 24 hours a day. **round-top,** *n.* a platform at the top of a mast. **round tower,** *n.* a high narrow tower, tapering from the base upwards, usu. with a conical top (frequent in Ireland, esp. near an ancient church or monastery. **round trip,** *n.* a return journey to a place and back. *a.* (*N Am.*) a return. **round-up,** *v.t.* to gather (horses, cattle etc.) together. *n.* a gathering together of cattle etc.; a similar gathering of people, objects, news, facts etc. (e.g. a news round-up). **roundworm,** *n.* a parasitic elongated worm, a nematode. **rounded,** *a.* **roundedness,** *n.* **roundel,** *n.* †a circle, anything of a round shape; a round disk, panel, heraldic circular charge etc.; a rondel or rondeau; †a round dance. **roundelay,** *n.* a simple song, usu. with a refrain; a bird's song; a round dance. **rounder,** *n.* one who or that which rounds, esp. a tool used in bookbinding, a wheelwright's plane etc.; a complete run through all the bases in rounders; (*pl.*) a game with a short bat and a ball, between two sides, with four bases to which a player hitting the ball has to run without being hit by it. **rounding,** *a.* becoming round, nearly round. *n.* the act of making or turning round; material wrapped round a rope to save chafing. **roundish,** *a.* **roundly,** *adv.* in a round or roundish form; bluntly, straightforwardly, plainly, emphatically. **roundness,** *n.* [OF *rund, rond, round* (F *rond*), L *rotundus,* from *rota,* wheel]

roundel, roundelay ROUND[2].

roup[1], *n.* a respiratory disease of poultry caused by a virus. **roupy,** *a.* [etym. doubtful]

roup[2], *v.t.* (*Sc., North.*) to sell by auction. *n.* a sale by auction. [cp. Icel. *raupa*]

rouse[1], *v.t.* to raise or startle (game) from a covert; to wake; to excite to thought or action; to provoke, to stir (up), to agitate; (*Naut.*) to haul (in) with vigour. *v.i.* to wake or be wakened; to start up; to be excited or stirred (up) to activity etc. *n.* reveille. **to rouse on,** (*Austral.*) to scold, to tell off. **rouseabout,** *n.* (*Austral.*) an odd-job man in a shearing-shed or on a station. **rouser,** *n.* one who or that which rouses; anything that excites or startles. **rousing,** *a.* having power to awaken, excite or rouse. **rousingly,** *adv.* **roust,** *v.t.* to rouse, to rout (out). **roustabout,** *n.* (*N Am.*) a labourer on wharves; (*N Am., Austral*) a casual labourer; a rouse about; an unskilled worker on an oil rig. [etym. doubtful, perh. rel. to RUSH[2]]

†**rouse**[2], *n.* a draught of liquor, a bumper; a carouse. [prob. from CAROUSE]

Rousseau[1], *n.* **Henri 'Le Douanier'** (1844–1910), French painter, a self-taught naive artist. His subjects included scenes of the Parisian suburbs and exotic junglescapes, painted with painstaking detail, for example *Surprised! Tropical Storm with a Tiger*, 1891 (National Gallery, London).

Rousseau[2], *n.* **Jean-Jacques** (1712–78), French social philosopher and writer, born in Geneva. *Discourses on the Origins of Inequality* (1754) made him famous, denouncing civilized society and postulating the paradox of the superiority of the 'noble savage'. *Social Contract* (1762) emphasized the rights of the people over those of the government, and stated that a government could be legitimately overthrown if it failed to express the general will of the people. It was a significant influence on the French Revolution. In the novel *Emile* (1762) he outlined a new theory of education, based on natural development and the power of example, to elicit the unspoiled nature and abilities of children. *Confessions*, published posthumously 1782, was a frank account of his occasionally immoral life, and was a founding work of autobiography. **Rousseauism,** *n.* the views or teaching of Jean Jacques Rousseau on education, ethics, politics, religion etc. **Rousseauan, Rousseauesque**.

Roussillon, *n.* a red wine from the south of France. [the former province of *Roussillon,* France]

roust, roustabout ROUSE[1].

rout[1], *n.* a crowd, a miscellaneous or disorderly concourse; in law, an assembly and attempt of three or more people to do an unlawful act upon a common quarrel; a riot, a brawl, an uproar, a disturbance; an utter defeat and overthrow; a disorderly and confused retreat of a defeated army etc.; †a large evening party. *v.t.* to defeat utterly and put to flight. †**rout-cake,** *n.* a rich cake orig. for use at routs. †**rout-seat,** *n.* a long, light seat hired out for use at receptions etc. **routable,** *a.* †**routous,** *a.* [OF *route,* a troop, company etc.]

rout[2], *v.t.* to root (up or out); to turn, fetch, drive out etc. (of bed, house etc.); to gouge, to scoop, to tear (out etc.). *v.i.* to root (about), to search. **router,** *n.* a plane, a saw or any of various other tools for hollowing out or cutting grooves; one who or that which routs; a plane used in cutting grooves, mouldings etc. [var. of ROOT[2]]

rout[3], *v.i.* (*dial.*) to bellow, to roar (of cattle etc.); to make a loud noise (of the sea etc.). [from Scand. (cp. Icel. *rauta,* Norw. *ruta*), rel. to prec.]

route, *n.* the course, way or road(s) travelled or to be travelled. *v.t.* to send by a certain route; to arrange or plan the route of. **en route**, on the way. **routeman,** *n.* (*N Am.*) a roundsman. **route-march,** *n.* an arduous military-training march; (*coll.*) a long tiring walk. **route-step,** *n.* an irregular step allowed in long marching. [F, from L *rupta,* broken (way), fem. p.p. of *rumpere,* to break]

routh, *n.* (*Sc.*) plenty. *a.* abundant, plentiful. [etym. doubtful]

routine, *n.* a course of procedure, business or official duties etc., regularly pursued; any regular or mechanical habit or practice; a sequence of jokes, movements, steps etc. regularly performed by a comedian, dancer, skater, stripper etc.; (*coll.*) tiresome or insincere speech or behaviour; a computer program or part of one which performs a particular task. *a.* tiresome, repetitive, commonplace; of or pertaining to a set procedure. **routinely,** *a.* **routinism,** *a.* **routinist,** *n.* [F]

roux, *n.* a sauce base, the thickening element in a sauce made from fat and flour cooked together. [F, brown]

rove[1], *past* REEVE[2].

rove[2], *v.i.* to wander, to ramble, to roam; to troll with live-bait; †in archery, to shoot at a chance mark or for distance etc. *v.t.* to wander over, through etc. *n.* the act of roving; a ramble. **rove-beetle,** *n.* a beetle also called the devil's coach-horse. **Rover, Rover Scout,** *n.* (*formerly*) a member of the Rovers or Rover Scouts. **rover,** *n.* a pirate, a buccaneer, a freebooter; a wanderer; a fickle person; in croquet, a ball that has gone through all the hoops but not pegged out; the person playing this; in archery, a mark chosen at random, a mark for long-distance shooting. **Rovers, Rover Scouts,** *n.pl.* (*formerly*) a branch of the Scouts for boys over 16 years old. **roving,** *n., a.* **roving commission,** *n.* a commission without a rigidly defined area of authority. **roving eye,** *n.* a promiscuous sexual interest. **rovingly,** *adv.* **roving-shot,** *n.* [etym. doubtful, perh. rel. to Icel. *rāfa* or to Dut. *rooven,* to rob]

rove[3], *v.t.* to draw out and slightly twist slivers of wool, cotton etc., before spinning into thread; fibres prepared in this way. *n.* a slightly-twisted sliver of wool, cotton etc. **roving,** *n.* rove. [etym. doubtful]

rovingly ROVE[2].

row[1], *n.* a series of persons or things in a straight or nearly straight line; a line, a rank (of seats, vegetables etc.); a street usu. of identical houses. **in a row,** (placed) one after the other, (ordered) in succession. [OE *rāw,* cp. Dut. *rij,* G *Reihe*]

row[2], *v.t.* to propel by oars; to convey by rowing. *v.i.* to row a boat; to labour with an oar; to be impelled by oars. *n.* a spell at rowing; an excursion in a row-boat. **to row down,** to overtake by rowing, esp. in a bumping race. **row-, rowing-boat,** *n.* a boat propelled by rowing. **rowlock, rollock**, *n.* a crotch, notch or other device on the gunwale of a boat serving as a fulcrum for an oar. **row-port,** *n.* a small port hole, cut near the water's edge for the use of oars in a small vessel. **rowable,** *a.* **rower,** *n.* **rowing,** *n., a.* **rowing-machine,** *n.* an exercise machine fitted with oars and a sliding seat. [OE *rōwan* (cp. Dut. *roeijen,* Icel. *rōa,* MHG *rüejen,* also L *rēmus,* Gr. *eretmon,* oar)]

row[3], *n.* a noisy disturbance, a noise, a din, a commotion, a tumult, a quarrel; a scolding. *v.t.* to berate, to scold, to reprimand. *v.i.* to make a row, to quarrel. **row-de-dow, rowdydow**, *n.* a hubbub, a din. [etym. doubtful, prob. orig. slang]

rowan, *n.* the mountain-ash, *Pyrus aucuparia.* **rowan-berry,** *n.* the small red fruit of the rowan. **rowan-tree,** *n.* [Sc. and ONorth.F, from Scand. (cp. Swed. *röun,* Dan. *rön,* Icel. *reynir*)]

Rowbotham, *n.* **Sheila** (1943–), British socialist feminist, historian, lecturer, and writer. Her pamphlet *Women's Liberation and the New Politics*, 1970 laid down fundamental approaches and demands of the emerging British women's movement.

rowdy, *n.* (*pl.* **-dies**) a noisy, rough or disorderly person. *a.* rough, riotous. **rowdily,** *adv.* **rowdiness, rowdyism,** *n.* **rowdyish,** *a.*

Rowe, *n.* **Nicholas** (1674–1718), English playwright and poet, whose dramas include *The Fair Penitent* (1702) and *Jane Shore* (1714), in which Mrs Siddons played. He edited Shakespeare, and was Poet Laureate from 1715.

rowel, *n.* a spiked disk or wheel on a spur; a roll or disk of various materials with a hole in the centre for placing under a horse's skin to discharge purulent matter. *v.t.* to insert a rowel in (a horse etc.); to prick or goad with a rowel. **rowel-spur,** *n.* a spur with a rowel. [OF *rouel,* dim. of *roue,* L *rota,* wheel]

rower, rowlock ROW[2].

Rowlandson, *n.* **Thomas** (1756–1827), English painter and illustrator, a caricaturist of Georgian social life. His *Tour of Dr Syntax in Search of the Picturesque* (1809) and its two sequels (1812–21) proved very popular.

Rowley, *n.* **William** (*c.* 1585–*c.* 1642), English actor and dramatist, collaborator with Middleton in *The Changeling* (1621) and with Dekker and Ford in *The Witch of Edmonton* (1658).

Rowling, *n.* **Wallace 'Bill'** (1927–), New Zealand Labour politician, party leader (1969–75), prime minister (1974–75).

Rowntree, *n.* **Benjamin Seebohm** (1871–1954), British entrepreneur and philanthropist. Much of the money he acquired as chairman (1925–41) of the family firm of confectioners, H.I. Rowntree, he used to fund investigations into social conditions. His writings include *Poverty* (1900). The three Rowntree Trusts, which were founded by his father Joseph Rowntree (1836–1925) in 1904, fund research into housing, social care and social policy, support projects relating to social justice, and give grants to pressure groups working in these areas.

Rowse, *n.* **A(lfred) L(eslie)** (1903–), English popular historian. He published a biography of Shakespeare in 1963, and in 1973 controversially identified the 'Dark Lady' of Shakespeare's sonnets as Emilia Lanier, half-Italian daughter of a court musician, with whom the Bard is alleged to have had an affair (1593–95).

roxburghe, *n.* a style of bookbinding comprising plain leather back, usu. gilt-lettered, cloth or paper sides, gilt top and the other edges untrimmed. [Duke of *Roxburghe,* 1740–1804]

Roy[1], *n.* **Manabendra Nakh** (1887–1954), founder of the Indian Communist Party in exile in Tashkent (1920). Expelled from the Comintern (1929), he returned to India and was imprisoned for five years. A steadfast communist, he finally became disillusioned after World War II and developed his ideas on practical humanism.

Roy[2], *n.* **Rajah Ram Rohan** (1770–1833), Bengali religious and social reformer. He was founder of the Brahma Samaj sect, which formulated the creed of neo-Hinduism akin to Christian Unitarianism. He died in England (1833) as emissary of the Great Mogul, who was still nominal sovereign in India.

royal, *a.* of, pertaining to, suitable to or befitting a king or queen; under the patronage or in the service of a king or queen; regal, kingly, princely; noble, magnificent, majestic; surpassingly fine, on a great scale, splendid, first-rate. *n.* a royal stag; a royal mast or sail next above the topgallant; a royal personage; royal paper. **blood royal,** the royal family. **Burgh Royal** BURGH. **rhyme royal** RHYME. **the Royals,** the royal family; (*formerly*) the first regiment of foot in the British service, the Royal Scots. **the royal we,** the customary use of the 1st person plural by a sovereign referring to him- or herself. **Royal Academy,** *n.* an academy of fine arts in London (est. 1768). **Royal Academy of Dramatic Art (RADA),** *n.* British college founded by Herbert Beerbohm Tree 1904 to train young actors. **Royal Aeronautical Society,** *n.* the oldest British aviation body, formed 1866. Its members discussed and explored the possibilities of flight long before its successful achievement. **Royal Air Force,** *n.* the air-force of Great Britain. **royal assent** ASSENT. **Royal Ballet,** *n.* title under which the British Sadler's Wells Ballet (at Covent Garden), Sadler's Wells Theatre Ballet, and the Sadler's Wells Ballet School were incorporated 1956. **royal blue,** *a., n.* (of) a deep blue. **Royal Botanic Gardens,** *n.* botanic gardens in Richmond, Surrey, popularly known as Kew Gardens. **Royal British Legion,** *n.* full name of the British Legion, a nonpolitical body promoting the welfare of war veterans and their dependants. **Royal Canadian Mounted Police (RCMP),** *n.* Canadian national police force, known as the Mounties. **Royal Commission** COMMISSION. **royal fern,** *n.* the flowering fern, *Osmunda regalis*. **royal flush** FLUSH. **Royal Greenwich Observatory,** *n.* the national astronomical observatory of the UK, founded 1675 at Greenwich, E London, England, to provide navigational information for seamen. After World War II, it was moved to Herstmonceux Castle, Sussex; in 1990 it was transferred to Cambridge. It also operates telescopes on La Palma in the Canary Islands, including the 4.2 m/165 in. William Herschel Telescope, commissioned 1987. **royal icing,** *n.* a hard icing on wedding cakes, fruit cakes etc. **Royal Institution of Great Britain,** *n.* organization for the promotion, diffusion, and extension of science and knowledge, founded in London 1799 by the Anglo-American physicist Count Rumford (1753–1814). Faraday and Davy were among its directors. **royal jelly,** *n.* the food secreted and fed by worker-bees to developing queen-bees; a health preparation of this substance. **Royal Marines,** *n.pl.* corps specializing in commando and amphibious operations. **royal mast,** *n.* the topmost part of a mast above the topgallant. **Royal Military Academy,** *n.* officer training college popularly known as Sandhurst. **Royal Opera House,** *n.* the leading British opera house, Covent Garden, London; the original theatre opened in 1732 and the present building dates from 1858. **royal palm,** *n.* a tall palm of tropical America. **royal paper,** *n.* a size of paper 20×25 in. (about 50×63 cm) for printing, 19×24 in. (about 48×61 cm) for writing. **royal prerogative,** *n.* the constitutional authority and privilege invested in a sovereign. **royal road,** *n.* an easy way or direct route (to a goal etc.). **Royal Shakespeare Company (RSC),** *n.* British professional theatre company that performs Shakespearean and other plays. It was founded 1961 from the company at the Shakespeare Memorial Theatre 1932 (now the Royal Shakespeare Theatre) in Stratford-upon-Avon, Warwickshire, England. **Royal Society,** *n.* the oldest and premier scientific society in Britain, originating 1645 and chartered 1660; Christopher Wren and Isaac Newton were prominent early members. Its Scottish equivalent is the Royal Society of Edinburgh 1783. **Royal Society for the Prevention of Cruelty to Animals (RSPCA),** *n.* British organization formed 1824 to safeguard the welfare of animals; it promotes legislation, has an inspectorate to secure enforcement of existing laws, and runs clinics. **royal stag,** *n.* a stag with antlers having 12 or more points. **royal standard,** *n.* flag with the royal arms. **royal tennis,** *n.* real tennis, court tennis. **royal warrant,** *n.* one authorizing the supply of goods to a royal household. †**royalet**, *n.* a petty king. **royalism,** *n.* **royalist,** *n.* an adherent or supporter of royalism or of monarchical government, esp. a supporter of the royal cause in the Civil War. *a.* supporting monarchical government; belonging to the Royalists. **royally,** *adv.* **royalty,** *n.* (*pl.* **-ties**) the office or dignity of a king or queen, sovereignty; royal rank birth or lineage; kingliness, queenliness; a royal person or persons; a member of a reigning family; a right or prerogative of a sovereign; (*usu. pl.*) a share of profits paid to a landowner for the right to work a mine, to a patentee for the use of an invention, to an author on copies of books sold etc. [OF *roial,* L *rēgālis,* REGAL]

†**royne** ROUND[2].

†**roynish** ROINISH.

Royce, *n.* **(Frederick) Henry** (1863–1933), British engineer, who so impressed Charles Stewart Rolls (1877–1910) by the car he built for his own personal use (1904) that Rolls-Royce Ltd was formed in 1906 to produce cars and engines.

royster, etc. ROISTER.

rozzer, *n.* (*sl.*) a policeman. [etym. unknown]

RP, (*abbr.*) Reformed Presbyterian, Regius Professor; Received Pronunciation.

RPI, (*abbr.*) retail price index.

rpm, (*abbr.*) resale price maintenance; revolutions per minute.

RR, (*abbr.*) Right Reverend.

-rrhagia, *comb. form* abnormal discharge, excessive flow, as in *menorrhagia.* [L from Gr., a bursting forth, from *rhēgnunai,* to break, to burst]

-rrhoea, -rrhea, *comb. form* a discharge, a flow, as in *diarrhoea.* [L from Gr. *-rrhoia,* from *rheein,* to flow]

RS, (*abbr.*) Royal Society.

RSA, (*abbr.*) Republic of South Africa; Royal Scottish Academy or Academician; Royal Society of Arts.

RSFSR, (*abbr.*) Russian Soviet Federated Socialist Republic.

RSM, (*abbr.*) Regimental Sergeant-Major; Royal Society of Medicine.

RSPB, (*abbr.*) Royal Society for the Protection of Birds.

RSPCA, (*abbr.*) Royal Society for the Prevention of Cruelty to Animals.

RSV, (*abbr.*) Revised Standard Version (of the Bible).

RSVP, (*abbr.*) *répondez s'il vous plaît,* reply, if you please. [F]

RTE, (*abbr.*) *Radio Telefis Eireann,* Irish radio and television.

Rt. Hon., (*abbr.*) Right Honourable.

RU, (*abbr.*) Rugby Union.

Ru (*chem. symbol*) ruthenium.

Ruanda, *n.* alternative spelling of RWANDA.

rub, *v.t.* (*past, p.p.* **rubbed**) to apply friction to, to move one's hand or other object over the surface of; to polish, to clean, to scrape, to graze; to slide or pass (a hand or other object) along, over or against something; to take an impression of (a design) with chalk and graphite on paper laid over it; to remove by rubbing; to affect (a person or feelings etc.) as by rubbing; to spread on or mix into by rubbing. *v.i.* to move or slide along the surface of, to grate, to graze, to chafe (against, on etc.); to get (along, on, through etc.) with difficulty; to meet with a hindrance (of bowls). *n.* the act or a spell of rubbing; a hindrance, an obstruction, a difficulty; †a sarcasm, a jibe, a criticism. **to rub along,** to manage, just to succeed; to cope despite difficulties; to keep on friendly terms. **to rub down,** to bring to smaller dimensions or a lower level by rubbing; to clean or dry by rubbing. **to rub in,** to force in by friction; to enforce or emphasize (a grievance etc.). **to rub noses,** to do this as an Eskimo greeting. **to rub off onto (someone),** to pass on by example or close association. **to rub one's hands,** to express expectation, glee, satisfaction etc. in this manner. **to rub shoulders,** to associate or mix (with). **to rub someone's nose in it,** to refer to or remind someone of an error, indiscretion or misfortune. **to rub (up) the wrong way,** to irritate. **to rub out,** to remove or erase by friction, to kill. **to rub up,** to polish, to burnish; to mix into a paste etc. by rubbing; to freshen (one's recollection of something). **rubdown,** *n.* the act of rubbing down. **rubbed,** *a.* **rubber**[1], *n.* one who or that which rubs; an instrument used for rubbing; a rubstone; a part of a machine that rubs, grinds, polishes etc.; a masseur or masseuse; india-rubber or caoutchouc; a piece of india-rubber for erasing pencil marks etc.; (*N Am.*) a condom; (*pl.*) galoshes, rubber over-shoes. *a.* made of, yielding or relating to india-rubber. **rubber band,** *n.* a continuous band of rubber of varying widths and thicknesses, for securing the hair, packages etc. **rubber cement,** *n.* an adhesive containing rubber. **rubberneck, -necker,** *n.* (*esp. N Am.*) a sightseer; one who gapes out of curiosity. *v.i.* (*esp. N Am.*) to sightsee; to gape foolishly. **rubber plant,** *n.* a plant, *Ficus elastica,* common to Asia and related to the fig, with large shiny leaves, in dwarf form grown as a popular house-plant. **rubber stamp,** *n.* a routine seal of approval, an automatic endorsement; a device with a rubber pad for marking or imprinting; a person who makes routine authorizations, a cipher. *v.t.* to imprint with a rubber stamp; to approve or endorse as a matter of routine. **rubber tree,** *n.* a tropical tree native to S America from which latex (the chief constituent of rubber) is obtained. **rubberize, -ise,** *v.t.* **rubbery,** *a.* **rubbing,** *n.* an impression made on paper laid over an image and rubbed with chalk, wax etc. [ME *rubben* (cp. LG *rubben*), etym. doubtful]

rub-a-dub, -dub, *n.* the sound of a rapid drum-beat. *v.i.* to make this sound. [imit.]

rubaiyat, *n.* (*Pers.*) a verse form consisting of quatrains.

rubato, *n.* (*pl.* **-ti**, **-tos**) flexibility of rhythm, fluctuation of tempo within a musical piece. *a.*, *adv.* (to be) performed in this manner. [It. stolen, *tempo rubato,* stolen time, from *rubare,* to rob]

rubber[2], *n.* a series of three games at whist, bridge, back-gammon etc.; two games out of three or the game that decides the contest. [etym. doubtful]

rubbish, *n.* waste, broken or rejected matter, refuse, junk, garbage, litter, trash, nonsense. *a.* (*coll.*) bad, useless, distasteful etc. *v.t.* (*coll.*) to criticize, to reject as rubbish. **on the rubbish heap,** (*coll.*) discarded as ineffective or worthless. **rubbishing, rubbishy,** *a.* [ME *robows,* A-F *robeux,* prob. pl. of foll.]

rubble, *n.* rough, broken fragments of stone, brick etc.; (*Geol.*) disintegrated rock, water-worn stones; rubble-work. **rubble-stone,** *n.* the upper fragmentary and decomposed portion of a mass of rock. **rubble-work,** *n.* masonry composed of irregular fragments of stone, or in which these are used for filling in. **rubbly,** *a.* [prob. from Scand. (cp. Icel. *rubb rubbr,* Norw. *rubl*)]

Rubbra, *n.* **Edmund** (1901–86), British composer. He studied under Holst and was a master of contrapuntal writing, as exemplified in his study *Counterpoint* (1960). His compositions include 11 symphonies, chamber music, and songs.

rube, *n.* (*N Am. sl.*) an unsophisticated country-dweller, a country bumpkin. [*Reuben*]

rubefy, *v.t.* to make red. **rubefacient**, *a.* making red. *n.* an external application causing redness of the skin. **rubefaction**, *n.* [F *rubéfier,* L *rubefacere* (*rubēre,* to be red, *facere,* to make)]

rubella, *n.* German measles. **rubellite** *n.* a pinky-red tourmaline. **rubeola**, *n.* †measles. [dim. of L *rubellus,* reddish]

Rubens, *n.* **Peter Paul** (1577–1640), Flemish painter, who became court painter to the archduke Albert and his wife Isabella in Antwerp. After a few years in Italy, he brought the exuberance of Italian baroque to N Europe, creating, with an army of assistants, innumerable religious and allegorical paintings for churches and palaces. These show mastery of drama in large compositions, and love of rich colour and fleshy nudes. He also painted portraits and, in his last years, landscapes.

Rubicon, *n.* ancient name of the small river flowing into the Adriatic which, under the Roman Republic, marked the boundary between Italy proper and Cisalpine Gaul. When Caesar led his army across it in 49 BC he therefore declared war on the republic; hence to 'cross the Rubicon' means to take an irrevocable step. It is believed to be the present-day Fiumicino, which rises in the Etruscan Apennines 16 km/10 miles WNW of San Marino and enters the Adriatic 16 km/10 miles NW of Rimini. **rubicon,** *n.* in piquet, the winning of the game before one's opponent has scored 100 points. *v.t.* to defeat (one's opponent) thus. **to cross the Rubicon,** to take a decisive step.

rubicund, *a.* ruddy, rosy, red-faced. **rubicundity,** *n.* [F *rubicond,* L *rubicundus,* from *rubēre,* to be red]

rubidium, *n.* a silvery-white metallic element, at. no. 37; chem. symbol Rb, belonging to the potassium group. **rubidic,** *a.* [L *rubidus,* red, as prec., -IUM]

rubied RUBY.

rubify RUBEFY.

rubiginous, *a.* rusty or brownish-red in colour. [L *rūbigo -gīnis,* rust]

Rubik, *n.* **Erno** (1944–), Hungarian architect, who invented the **Rubik('s) cube**®, a multicoloured puzzle consisting of a cube each face of which is divided into nine coloured segments which can be manipulated and rearranged in only one correct way, to obtain the same colour on each face but about 43 trillion wrong ones. Intended to help his students understand three-dimensional design, it became a world craze.

Rubinstein, *n.* **Helena** (1882–1965), Polish tycoon, who emigrated to Australia in 1902, where she started up a face-cream business. She moved to Europe in 1904, and later to the US, opening salons in London, Paris, and New York.

ruble ROUBLE.

Rublev (Rublyov), *n.* (*c.* 1370–1430), Russian icon painter. Only one documented work survives, the *Holy Trinity* about 1411 (Tretyakov Gallery, Moscow). This shows a basically Byzantine style, but with a gentler expression.

rubric, *n.* a title, chapter-heading, entry, set of rules, commentary or direction, orig. printed in red or distinctive lettering, esp. a liturgical direction in the Prayer Book etc.; †such an entry of a saint's name in a calendar, hence, a calendar of saints. *a.* red, marked with red; pertaining to or enjoined by the rubrics. **rubrical,** *a.* **rubrically,** *adv.* **rubricate,** *v.t.* to mark, distinguish, print or illuminate with red; to furnish with a rubric or rubrics. **rubrication,** *n.* **rubricator,** *n.* **rubrician**, †**rubricist**, *n.* one versed in or adhering strictly to liturgical rubric. [F *rubrique,* L *rubrīca,* from *ruber,* red]

Rubus, *n.* a genus of rosaceous shrubs comprising the blackberry, raspberry etc. [L, a bramble bush]

ruby, *n.* a precious stone of a red colour, a variety of corundum; the colour of ruby, esp. a purplish red; something of this colour; a size of type between nonpareil and pearl. *a.* of the colour of a ruby; made of, containing or resembling a ruby or rubies; marking a 40th anniversary. **ruby-coloured, ruby-red,** *a.* of the deep red colour of a ruby. **ruby-tail,** *n.* a brilliant fly with bluish-green back and red abdomen, also called the golden wasp. **ruby wedding,** *n.* a 40th wedding anniversary. **rubied,** *a.* †**rubious,** *a.* ruby-coloured. [OF *rubi, rubis,* ult. from L *rub-,* stem of *rubeus,* red]

RUC, (*abbr.*) Royal Ulster Constabulary.

ruche, *n.* a quilled or pleated strip of gauze, lace, silk or the like used as a frill or trimming. *v.t.* to trim with ruche. **ruched,** *a.* **ruching,** *n.* [F, bee-hive]

ruck[1], *n.* a heap, a rick, a pile; a multitude, a crowd, esp. the mass of horses left behind by the leaders in a race; the common run of people or things; in Rugby, a gathering of players round the ball when it is on the ground. *v.i.* to form a ruck in Rugby. [prob. cogn. with RICK[1]]

ruck[2], *n.* a crease, a wrinkle, a fold, a pleat. *v.i.*, *v.t.* to wrinkle, to crease. **ruckle**[1], *n.*, *v.t.*, *v.i.* [Icel. *hrukka*, cp. Norw. *rukka*]

ruckle[2], *v.i.* to make a rattling or gurgling noise. *n.* a rattling or gurgling noise, esp. in the throat, a death-rattle. [prob. from Scand. (cp. Norw. *rukla*)]

rucksack, *n.* a bag carried on the back by means of straps by campers, hikers, climbers etc. [G (*Rücken*, back, SACK[1])]

ruckus, *n.* (*chiefly N Am.*) a row, a disturbance, an uproar. [prob. combination of RUCTION and RUMPUS]

ruction, *n.* (*coll.*) a commotion, a disturbance, a row.

Rudbeckia, *n.* a genus of N American plants of the aster family, also called the cone-flowers. **rudbeckia,** *n.* a plant of this genus. [Olaus *Rudbeck*, 1630–1702, Swedish botanist]

rudd, *n.* a fish, *Leuciscus erythrophthalmus,* akin to the roach, also called the red-eye. [prob. from obs. *rud*, OE *rudu,* cogn. with RED]

rudder, *n.* a flat wooden or metal framework or solid piece hinged to the stern-post of a boat or ship and serving as a means of steering; a vertical moving surface in the tail of an aeroplane for providing directional control and stability; any steering device; a principle etc., which guides, governs or directs the course of anything. **rudder-band, -brace, -case, -chain, -head, -hole, -post, -tackle, -wheel,** *n.* parts of the rudder, its supports or the apparatus controlling it. **rudderless,** *a.* [OE *rōther* (cp. Dut. *roer*, G *Ruder*, Swed. *roder*), cogn. with ROW[2]]

ruddily, ruddiness RUDDY.

ruddle[1], var. of RADDLE[1].

ruddle[2], **raddle, reddle,** *n.* a variety of red ochre used for marking sheep. *v.t.* to colour or mark with ruddle. [as RUDD]

ruddock, *n.* the robin redbreast. [OE *rudduc,* rel. to RUDD]

ruddy, *a.* of a red or reddish colour; of a healthy complexion, fresh-coloured; (*euphem.*) bloody. *v.t.* to make ruddy. *v.i.* to grow red. **ruddily,** *adv.* **ruddiness,** *n.* [OE *rudig* (cp. Icel. *rothi*), from *rudu*, cogn. with *rēad*, RED[1]]

rude, *a.* simple, primitive, crude, uncultivated, uncivilized, unsophisticated, unrefined; coarse, rough, rugged; unformed, unfinished; coarse in manners, uncouth; impolite, uncivil, insolent, offensive, insulting; violent, boisterous, abrupt, ungentle, tempestuous; hearty, robust, strong. †**rude-growing,** *a.* rough, wild. **rudely,** *adv.* **rudeness,** *n.* **rudery,** *n.* **rudish,** *a.* [F, from L *rudem*, nom. *-dis*]

†**ruderal,** *n.*, *a.* (of) a plant growing on rubbish. [L *rūdera*, pl. of *rūdus*, broken stones]

Rude, *n.* **François** (1784–1855), French romantic sculptor. He produced the low-relief scene on the Arc de Triomphe, Paris, showing the capped figure of Liberty leading the revolutionaries (1833, known as *The Volunteers of 1792* or *The Marseillaise*).

rudiment, *n.* (*often pl.*) an elementary or first principle of knowledge etc.; (*often pl.*) the undeveloped or imperfect form of something, a beginning, a germ; a partially-developed, aborted or stunted organ, structure etc., a vestige. **rudimental, rudimentary,** *a.* **rudimentarily,** *adv.* **rudimentariness,** *n.* [F, from L *rudīmentum*, from *rudis*, RUDE]

rudish RUDE.

Rudolf, *n.* former name of Lake TURKANA.

Rudolph, *n.* (1858–89), crown prince of Austria, the only son of Emperor Franz Joseph. From an early age he showed progressive views which brought him into conflict with his father. He conceived and helped to write a history of the Austro-Hungarian empire. In 1889 he and his mistress, Baroness Marie Vetsera, were found shot in his hunting lodge at Mayerling, near Vienna. The official verdict was suicide, although there were rumours that it was perpetrated by Jesuits, Hungarian nobles, or the baroness's husband. In 1881, he married Princess Stephanie of Belgium, and they had one daughter, Elizabeth.

Rudolph I, *n.* (1218–91), Holy Roman emperor from 1273. Originally count of Habsburg, he was the first Habsburg emperor, and expanded his dynasty by investing his sons with the duchies of Austria and Styria.

Rudolph II, *n.* (1552–1612), Holy Roman emperor from 1576, when he succeeded his father Maximilian II. His policies led to unrest in Hungary and Bohemia, which led to the surrender of Hungary to his brother Matthias (1608), and religious freedom for Bohemia.

Rudra, *n.* early Hindu storm god, most of whose attributes were later taken over by Siva.

rue[1], *n.* a plant of the genus *Ruta,* esp. *R. graveolens,* a shrubby evergreen plant, of rank smell and acrid taste, formerly used as a stimulant etc. in medicine. [F, from L *rūta*, Gr. *rhutē*]

rue[2], *v.t.* (*pres. p.* **rueing, ruing**) to grieve or be sorry for, to regret, to repent of. †*v.i.* to be sorry, to be penitent or regretful. †*n.* sorrow, regret, repentance, compassion. **rueful,** *a.* **ruefully,** *adv.* **ruefulness,** *n.* [OE *hrēowan* (cp. Dut. *rouwen*, G *reuen*), rel. to Icel. *hryggr*, grieved]

rufescent, *a.* reddish; tinged with red. [L *rūfescens* -*ntem*, pres.p. of *rūfescere*, from *rūfus*, reddish]

ruff[1], *n.* †an old card-game; an act of trumping when one cannot follow suit. *v.t.*, *v.i.* to trump. [OF *roffle*, *roufle*, perh. corr. of *triomphe*, cp. TRUMP[2]]

ruff[2], *n.* a broad plaited or fluted collar or frill of linen or muslin worn by both sexes, esp. in the 16th cent.; anything similarly puckered or plaited, as the top of a loose boot turned over; a growth like a ruff, as the ring of feathers round the necks of some birds; a bird, *Philomachus pugnax,* of the sandpiper family (perh. from the conspicuous ruff in the male in the breeding season); a breed of pigeons related to the jacobin. **ruffed,** *a.* having a ruff. **ruff-like,** *a.* [prob. shortened from RUFFLE]

ruff[3], **ruffe,** *n.* a small freshwater fish, *Acerina cernua,* related to and resembling the perch. [prob. from ROUGH]

ruffian, *n.* a low, lawless, brutal person, a bully, a violent hoodlum, a robber, a murderer. *a.* ruffianly, brutal. **ruffianish,** *a.* **ruffianism,** *n.* **ruffian-like, ruffianly,** *a.* [OF, cp. It. *ruffiano*, etym. doubtful]

ruffle[1], *v.t.* to disorder, to disturb the smoothness or order of, to rumple, to disarrange; to annoy, to disturb, to upset, to discompose. *v.i.* to grow rough or turbulent, to play or toss about loosely, to flutter; †to contend, to fight. *n.* a strip or frill of fine plaited or goffered lace etc., attached to some part of a garment, esp. at the neck or wrist; a ruff; a ripple on water; a low, vibrating beat of the drum; †a disturbance, a commotion, a dispute. †**rufflement,** *n.* **ruffled,** *a.* **ruffler**[1], *n.* an attachment to a sewing-machine for making ruffles. **ruffling,** *n.*, *a.* [ME *ruffelen*, etym. doubtful, cp. Dut. *roffelen*, LG *ruffelen*]

ruffle[2], *v.i.* to swagger, to bluster. **ruffler**[2], *n.* a bully, a swaggerer. [etym. doubtful]

rufous, *a.* of a brownish or yellowish red. [L *rūfus*]

rug, *n.* a thick, heavy wrap, coverlet etc., usu. woollen with a thick nap or of skin with the hair or wool left on; a carpet or floor-mat of similar material; (*N Am.*) a carpet; (*coll.*) a false hairpiece, a wig. **to pull the rug (out) from under,** to put (someone) in a defenceless or discomposed state, to undermine someone. **rugging,** *n.* material for making rugs. [prob. from Scand. (cp. Norw. dial. *rugga*, Swed. *rugg*, tangled hair, Icel. *rögg*, cp. RAG[1])]

ruga, *n.* (*pl.* **-gae**) (*Anat.*) a wrinkle, crease, fold or ridge. **rugose,** *a.* wrinkled, ridged, corrugated. **rugosely,** *adv.* **rugosity,** *n.* [L]

Rugby, rugby, Rugby football, *n.*, *a.* a game of football in which players are allowed to use their hands in carrying and passing the ball and tackling their opponents. **Rugby League,** *n.* the professional form of Rugby football founded in England (1895) as the Northern Union, when a dispute about pay caused northern clubs to break away from the Rugby Football Union. The game is similar to Rugby Union but the number of players was reduced from 15 to 13 in 1906, and the scrum now plays a less important role as rule changes have made the game more open and fast-moving. **Rugby Union,** *n.* the amateur form of Rugby football, in which there are 15 players on each side. 'Tries' are scored by 'touching down' the ball beyond the goal-line or by kicking goals from penalties. The Rugby Football Union was formed in 1871 and has its headquarters at Twickenham, Middlesex. The first World Cup was held in Australia and New Zealand in 1987, and was won by New Zealand. **rugger,** *n.* (*coll.*) rugby. [Warwickshire town with public school]

rugged, *a.* having a surface full of inequalities, extremely uneven, broken and irregular; rocky, craggy, of abrupt contour; ragged, shaggy, unkempt; strongly marked (of features); harsh, grating (of sounds); rough in temper, stern, unbending, severe; rude, unpolished; tempestuous, turbulent (of weather, waves etc.); strenuous, hard; hardy, sturdy. **ruggedly,** *adv.* **ruggedness,** *n.* [prob. from Scand., cp. RUG and ROUGH]

rugose, rugosity RUGA.

Ruhr, *n.* river in West Germany; it rises in the Rothaargebirge and flows west to join the Rhine at Duisburg. The **Ruhr valley** (228 km/142 miles), a metropolitan industrial area (petrochemicals, cars; iron and steel at Duisburg and Dortmund) was formerly a coalmining centre.

ruin, *n.* a disastrous change or state of wreck or disaster, overthrow, downfall; bankruptcy; a cause of destruction, downfall or disaster, havoc, bane; the state of being ruined or destroyed; the remains of a structure, building, city etc. that has become demolished or decayed (*often in pl.*); a person who has suffered a downfall, e.g. a bankrupt. *v.t.* to bring to ruin; to reduce to ruin, dilapidate; to destroy, to overthrow, to subvert; to harm, spoil, disfigure; to bankrupt. †*v.i.* to fall violently; to fall into ruins; to come to ruin. **ruinable,** *a.* †**ruinate,** *v.t., a., v.i.* **ruination,** *n.* **ruined,** *a.* **ruiner,** *n.* **ruining,** *a., n.* **ruinous,** *a.* fallen into ruin, dilapidated; causing ruin, baneful, destructive, pernicious. **ruinously,** *adv.* **ruinousness,** *n.* [F *ruine,* L *ruīna,* from *ruere,* to fall]

Ruisdael (or **Ruysdael**), *n.* **Jacob van** (*c.* 1628–82), Dutch landscape painter, active in Amsterdam from about 1655. He painted rural scenes near his native town of Haarlem and in Germany, and excelled in depicting gnarled and weatherbeaten trees. The few figures in his pictures were painted by other artists.

rule, *n.* the act of ruling or the state or period of being ruled, government, authority, sway, direction, control; that which is established as a principle, standard or guide of action or procedure; a line of conduct, a regular practice, an established custom, canon or maxim; method, regularity; an authoritative form, direction or regulation, a body of laws or regulations, to be observed by an association, religious order etc. and its individual members; a strip of wood, plastic, metal etc. usu. graduated in inches or centimetres and fractions of an inch or millimetres, used for linear measurement or guidance; a prescribed formula, method etc. for solving a mathematical problem of a given kind; an order, direction or decision by a judge or court, usu. with reference to a particular case only; in printing, a thin metal strip for separating columns, headings etc.; the line printed with this; the general way of things; (*pl.*) Australian football. *v.t.* to govern, to manage, to control; to curb, to restrain; to be the rulers, governors or sovereign of; to lay down as a rule or as an authoritative decision; to mark (paper etc.) with straight lines. *v.i.* to exercise supreme power (usu. over); to decide, make a decision; to stand at or maintain a certain level (of prices); to dominate, to be prevalent. **as a rule,** usually, generally. **rule of the road** ROAD. **rule of three,** (*Arith.*) simple proportion. **rule of thumb,** practical experience, as dist. from theory, as a guide in doing anything. **to rule out,** to exclude, to eliminate (as a possibility). **to rule the roast,** to be the leader, to be dominant. **rulable,** *a.* capable of being ruled; (*N Am.*) permissible, allowable. **ruleless,** *a.* **ruler,** *n.* one who rules or governs; an instrument with straight edges or sides, used as a guide in drawing straight lines, a rule. **rulership,** *n.* **ruling,** *n.* a authoritative decision, esp. with regard to a special legal case; a ruled line or lines. *a.* having or exercising authority or control; predominant, pre-eminent. [A-F *reule,* OF *riule* (F *règle*), L *rēgula,* whence *rēgulāre,* to rule, to REGULATE]

rullion, *n.* (*Sc.*) a shoe of undressed hide; a virago. [var. of obs. *rilling, riveling,* OE *rifeling*]

rum¹, *n.* a spirit distilled from fermented molasses or cane-juice. **rum baba** BABA. **rum-butter,** *n.* butter mixed with sugar and flavoured with rum. **rum-punch, -toddy,** *n.* a punch or toddy made with rum. **rum-runner,** *n.* a smuggler of rum esp. during the Prohibition era in the US. **rum-running,** *n.* **rummy¹,** *a.* [formerly *rumbo, rumbullion* (now, in Devon dial., a great tumult)]

rum², *a.* (*sl.*) strange, singular, odd, queer. **rumly, rummily,** *adv.* **rumminess, rumness,** *n.* **rummy²,** *a.* [perh. ident. with 16th cent. cant, *rum,* a fine treat]

Rumanian ROMANIAN.

rumb RHUMB.

rumba, rhumba, *n.* a complex and rhythmic Cuban dance; a ballroom dance developed from this; a piece of music for this dance. [Sp.]

rumble, *v.i.* to make a low, heavy, continuous sound, as of thunder, heavy vehicles etc.; to move (along) with such a sound; to mutter, to grumble. *v.t.* to cause to move with a rumbling noise; to utter with such a sound; (*sl.*) to be undeceived about; to see through. *n.* a rumbling sound; (*N. Am*) a gang fight; a seat or place for luggage behind the body of a carriage; a rumble-seat. **rumble-seat,** *n.* (*N Am.*) a dicky; an outside folding-seat on some early motor vehicles. **rumble-tumble,** *n.* a rumbling vehicle; a commotion. **rumbler,** *n.* **rumbling,** *a., n.* **rumblingly,** *adv.* **rumbly,** *a.* [ME *romblen* (cp. Dut. *rommelen,* G *rummeln,* Dan. *rumle*), prob. of imit. orig.]

†**rumbullion** RUM¹.

†**rumbo** RUM¹.

rumbustious, *a.* (*coll.*) boisterous, turbulent, rampageous. **rumbustiously,** *adv.* **rumbustiouness,** *n.* [prob. corr. of ROBUSTIOUS]

rumen, *n.* (*pl.* **-mens, -mina**) the first cavity of the complex stomach of a ruminant. [from L, gullet]

rumgumption, *n.* (*chiefly Sc.*) common sense. [GUMPTION]

ruminant, *n.* any member of the division of cud-chewing animals with a complex stomach comprising the ox, sheep, deer etc.; any other cud-chewing animal (e.g. the camel). **ruminantly,** *adv.* **ruminate,** *v.i.* to chew over the cud; to muse, to meditate. *v.t.* to chew over again (what has been regurgitated); to ponder over. **rumination,** *n.* **ruminative,** *a.* **ruminatively,** *adv.* **ruminator,** *n.* [L *rūminans -ntem,* pres.p. of *rūminārī,* to ruminate, from RUMEN]

rummage, *v.t.* †to stow, to arrange (goods in a ship); to make a careful search in or through, to ransack, esp. by throwing the contents about; to find (out) or uncover by such searching; †to disarrange or throw into disorder by searching. *v.i.* to make careful search. *n.* the act of rummaging, a search; miscellaneous articles, odds and ends (got by rummaging) **rummage sale,** *n.* (*chiefly N Am.*) a sale of miscellaneous articles, esp. in aid of charity, a jumble sale. **rummager,** *n.* [F *arrumage* (now *arrimage*), from *arrumer* (*arrimer*), etym. doubtful]

rummer, *n.* a large drinking-glass. [W Flem. *rummer, rommer,* cp. Dut. *romer,* G *Römer*]

rummy¹,² RUM¹,².

rummy³, *n.* any of several card-games in which the object is to collect combinations and sequences of cards. [etym. doubtful]

rumness RUM².

rumour, (*N Am.*) **rumor,** *n.* †a confused noise; popular report, hearsay, common talk; a current story without any known authority. *v.t.* to report or circulate as a rumour. **rumourmonger,** *n.* (*coll.*) one who spreads rumours. **rumorous,** *a.* **rumourer,** *n.* [A-F, from L *rūmōrem,* nom. *-mor*]

rump, *n.* the end of the backbone with the adjacent parts, the posterior, the buttocks (usu. of beasts or contemptuously of human beings); in birds, the uropygium; the fag- or tail-end of anything. **the Rump,** English parliament formed between Dec. 1648 and Nov. 1653 after Pride's Purge of the Long Parliament to ensure a majority in favour of trying Charles I. It was dismissed in 1653 by Cromwell, who replaced it with the Barebones Parliament. Reinstated after the Protectorate ended in 1659 and the full membership of the Long Parliament restored by Monk in 1660, it dissolved itself shortly afterwards and was replaced by the Convention Parliament which brought about the restoration of the monarchy. **rump-bone,** *n.* the coccyx. **rump steak,** *n.* a beef-steak cut from the rump. **rumpless**, *a.* [prob. from Scand. (cp. Icel. *rumpr,* Swed. and Norw. *rumpa,* Dan. *rumpe*)]

rumple, *v.t.* to wrinkle, to make uneven, to crease, to disorder. *n.* a fold, a crease, a wrinkle. **rumply,** *a.* [Dut. *rompelen;* rel to A-Sax. *gerumpen,* wrinkled]

rumpus, *n.* a disturbance, an uproar, a row. **rumpus room,** *n.* (*chiefly N Am.*) a play or games room esp. for children. [etym. doubtful]

run, *v.i.* (*past* **ran**, *p.p.* **run**) to move or pass over the ground by using the legs more quickly than in walking, esp. with a springing motion, so that both feet are never on the ground at once; to hasten; to amble, trot, or canter (of horses etc.); to flee, to try to escape; to make a run at cricket; to compete in a race; to complete a race in a specific position; to seek election etc.; to move or travel rapidly; to make a quick or casual trip or visit; to be carried along violently; to move along on or as on wheels; to revolve; to be in continuous motion, to be in action or operation; to go smoothly; to glide, to elapse; to flow; to fuse, to melt, to dissolve and spread; to flow (with), to be wet, to drip, to emit liquid, mucus etc.; to go, to ply; to spread or circulate rapidly or in profusion; of a shoal of fish, to migrate, esp. upstream for spawning; to range; to move from point to point; to rove; to extend, to take a certain course, to proceed, to go on, to continue (for a certain distance or duration); to pass or develop (into etc.); to play, feature, print or publish; to tend, to incline; to be current, valid, in force or effect; to occur inherently, persistently or repeatedly; to pass freely or casually; to occur in sequence; to perform, execute quickly or in sequence; to be allowed to wander unrestrainedly or grow (wild); to pass into a certain condition or reach a specific state; to elapse; of a loan, debt etc., to accumulate; to ladder, to unravel; to sail before the wind. *v.t.* to cause to run or go; to cause or allow to pass, penetrate etc., to thrust with; to drive, to propel; to track, to pursue, to chase, to hunt; to press (hard) in a race, competition etc.; to accomplish (as if) by running, to perform or execute (a race, an errand etc.), to follow or pursue (a course etc.); to cause to ply; to bring to a specific state (as if) by running; to keep going, to manage, to conduct, to carry on, to work, to operate; to enter or enrol (as a contender); to introduce or promote the election of (a candidate); to get past or through (e.g. a blockade); to cross, to traverse; to cause to extend or continue; to discharge, to flow with; to cause to pour or flow from; to fill (a bath) from a flowing tap; to convey in a motor vehicle, to give a lift; to pass through a process, routine or treatment; to be affected by or subjected to; to sail with the wind; to graze animals (in open pasture); in billiards, cricket etc., to hit or score a successful sequence of shots, runs etc.; to sew quickly; to have or keep current; to publish; to cast, to found, to mould; to deal in; to smuggle; to incur, to expose oneself to, to hazard; to allow a bill etc. to accumulate before paying. *n.* an act or spell of running; the distance or duration of a run or journey; a trip, a short excursion; the running of two batsmen from one wicket to the other in cricket without either's being put out; a unit of score in cricket; the distance a golf ball rolls along the ground; a complete circuit of the bases by a player in baseball etc.; a continuous course, a sustained period of operation or performance; a sequence series, stretch or succession (e.g. of cards, luck etc.); a succession of demands (on a bank etc.); a pipe or course for flowing liquid; the ordinary succession, trend or general direction, the way things tend to move; a ladder or rip in a stocking, jumper, pair of tights etc.; general nature, character, class or type; a batch, flock, drove or shoal of animals, fish etc. in natural migration; a periodical passage or migration; an inclined course esp. for winter sports; a habitual course or circuit; a regular track (of certain animals), a burrow; a grazing-ground; an enclosure for fowls; free use or access, unrestricted enjoyment; an attempt; a mission involving travel (e.g. a smuggling operation, a bombing run); (*Mus.*) a roulade. **at a run,** running, in haste. **in the long run,** eventually. **in the short run,** in the short term. **on the run,** in flight, fugitive. **to run across,** to traverse at a run; to encounter by chance, to discover by accident. **to run after,** to pursue with attentions; to cultivate, to devote oneself to; to chase. **to run along,** to leave, to go away. **to run at,** to rush at, to attack. **to run a temperature,** to have an abnormally high body temperature. **to run away,** to flee, to abscond, to elope. **to run away with,** to win an easy victory. **to run down,** to stop through not being wound up, recharged etc.; to become enfeebled by overwork etc.; to pursue and overtake; to search for and discover; to disparage, to abuse; to run against or over and sink or collide with. **to run dry,** to stop flowing; to end (of a supply). **to run for it,** to make an escape attempt, to run away. **to run foul of** FOUL. **to run in,** to drive (cattle etc.) in; to call, to drop in; to arrest, to take into custody; to break in (e.g. a motor vehicle, machine) by running or operating; to insert (e.g. printed matter); to approach. **to run in the blood, family,** to be hereditary. **to run into,** to incur, to fall into; to collide with; to reach (a specified number, amount etc.); to meet by chance. **to run into the ground,** to exhaust or wear out with overwork. **to run off,** to print; to cause to pour or flow out. **to run off with,** to elope with; to steal, remove. **to run on,** to talk volubly or incessantly; to be absorbed by (of the mind); to continue without a break. **to run out,** to come to an end; to leak. **to run out on,** to abandon. **to run over,** to review or examine cursorily; to recapitulate; to overflow; to pass, ride or drive over. **to run rings around** RING. **to run riot** RIOT. **to run short** SHORT. **to run the show,** to manage; to have control of something in one's own hands. **to run through,** to go through or examine rapidly; to take, deal with, spend etc. one after another, to squander; to pervade; to transfix; to pierce with a weapon; to strike out by drawing a line through. **to run to,** to extend to. **to run to earth, ground,** to track down, to find after hard or prolonged searching. **to run together,** to fuse, blend, mix. **to run to seed** SEED. **to run upon,** to dwell on, to be absorbed by; to meet suddenly and accidentally. **to run up,** to grow rapidly; to increase quickly; to accumulate (a debt etc.); to force up (prices etc.); to build, make or sew in a hasty manner; to raise or hoist. **runabout,** *n.* a light motor-car or aeroplane; **run-around,** *n.* evasive and deceitful treatment. **runaway,** *n.* one who flies from danger, restraint or service; a deserter, a fugitive; a bolting horse; an escape, a flight. *a.* breaking from restraint; out of control; prodigious, decisive (e.g. of a success); easily won; accomplished by flight; fleeing as a runaway. **run-down,** *a.* exhausted, worn out; dilapidated. **run-down,** *a.* exhausted, worn out; dilapidated. *n.* a brief or rapid resumé; a reduction in number, speed, power etc. **run-in,** *n.* (*coll.*) an argument, a row, a contention; an approach; an insertion of printed matter within a paragraph. **run-off,** *n.* overflow or liquid drained off; an additional tie-breaking contest, race etc. **run-of-the-mill,** *a.* undistinguished, ordinary, mediocre. **run-on,** *n.* continuous printed matter; an additional word, quantity, expense etc. **run through,** a quick examination, perusal or rehearsal. **run-up,** *n.* an approach; a period preceding an event etc., e.g. a general election. **runway,** *n.* a landing-strip for aircraft; a ramp, passageway or chute. **runlet,** *n.* a small stream, a runnel. **runnable,** *a.* that can be run, esp. of a stag fit for the chase. **runner,** *n.* one who runs; a racer, a messenger, a scout, a spy; one who solicits custom etc., an agent, a collector, a tout; a smuggler; †a police officer, a detective; a substitute batsman in cricket; that on which anything runs, revolves, slides etc.; the blade of a skate; a piece of wood or metal on which a sleigh runs; a groove, rod, roller etc. on which a part slides or runs, esp. in machinery; a sliding ring, loop etc. on a strap, rod etc.; a rope run through a single block with one end attached to a tackle-block and the other armed with a hook; a revolving millstone; a creeping stem thrown out by a plant, such as a strawberry, tending to take root; a twining or climbing plant, esp. a kidney bean; a cursorial bird, esp. the water-rail; a longer strip of carpet for a passage etc., or cloth for a table etc. **to do a runner,** (*sl.*) to abscond, to leave clandestinely or quickly. **runner bean,** *n.* a trailing bean also called scarlet runner. **runner-up,** *n.* (*pl.* **runners-up**) the unsuccessful competitor in a final who takes second place. **running,** *n.* the act of one who or that which runs; smuggling; management, control, operation; maintenance, working order; competition, chance of winning a race etc.; discharge from a sore. *a.* moving at a run; cursive (of handwriting); flowing; continuous, uninterrupted; discharging matter; following in succession, repeated; trailing (of plants); current, done at, or accomplished with, a run. *adv.* in succession. **take a running jump,** under no circumstances; go away. **in** or **out of the running,** having or not having a chance of winning. **to make the running,** to set the pace. **running battle,** *n.* a battle between pursuers and pursued; a continuous or long-running argument. **running-board,** *n.* the footboard of an (early) motor-car. **running commentary,** *n.* an oral description, usu. by broadcasting, of an event in progress, e.g. a race. **running gear,** *n.* the wheels, axles or other working parts of a vehicle etc. **running head, title,** *n.* the title of a book used as a head-line throughout. **running knot,** *n.* a knot which slips along the rope, line etc. **running lights,** *n.pl.* lights visible on moving vehicles, vessels or aircraft at night. **running mate,** *n.* a horse teamed or paired with another; a subordinate candidate, one standing for the less important of two linked offices in a US election, esp. the vice-presidency. **running repairs,** *n.pl.* repairs carried out while a machine etc. is in operation, minor repairs. **running stitch,** *n.* a simple continuous stitch used for gathering or tacking. **runningly,** *adv.* **runny,** *a.* [ME *rinnen, rennen,* OE *rinnan* (also *iernan*), perh. affected by Icel. *rinna* (cp. Dut. and G *rennen*)]

runcible, runcible spoon, *n.* a three-pronged fork hollowed out like a spoon and with one of the prongs having a cutting edge. [nonsense word invented by Edward Lear]

Runcie, *n.* **Robert (Alexander Kennedy)** (1921–), English cleric, archbishop of Canterbury from 1980, the first to be appointed on the suggestion of the Church Crown Appointments Commission (formed 1977) rather than by political consultation. He favours ecclesiastical remarriage for the divorced and the eventual introduction of the ordination of women. He announced his retirement in 1990.

Rundstedt, *n.* **Karl Rudolf Gerd von** (1875–1953), German field marshal in World War II. Largely responsible for the German breakthrough in France (1940), he was defeated on the Ukrainian front (1941). As commander-in-chief in France from 1942, he resisted the Allied invasion (1944), and in Dec. launched the temporarily successful Ardennes offensive. He was captured, but in 1949 war-crime charges were dropped owing to his ill-health.

rune, *n.* a letter or character of the earliest Teutonic alphabet or futhorc, formed from the Greek alphabet by modifying the shape to suit carving, used chiefly by the Scandinavians and Anglo-Saxons; any mysterious mark or symbol; a canto or division in Finnish poetry. **runic,** *a.* of, pertaining to, consisting of, written or cut in runes. [Icel. *rūn,* cogn. with OE *rūn,* secret]

rung¹, *n.* a stick or bar forming a step in a ladder; a rail or spoke in a chair etc.; a level, a stage, a position. **rungless,** *a.* [OE *hrung,* cp. Dut. *hronge,* LG *runge*]

rung², *past, p.p.* RING².

Runge, *n.* **Philipp Otto** (1770–1810), German romantic painter, whose portraits, particularly of children, have a remarkable clarity and openness. He also illustrated fairy tales by the brothers Grimm.

runic RUNE.

runnel, *n.* a rivulet, a little brook; a gutter. [OE *rynel,* dim. of RUN]

runt, *n.* the smallest or feeblest animal in a litter esp. a piglet; an ox or bullock of a small breed, esp. Welsh or Highland; a large variety of domestic pigeon; any animal or person who is stunted in growth, deficient or inferior. **runtiness,** *n.* **runtish, runty,** *a.* [etym. doubtful]

Runyon, *n.* **Damon** (1884–1946), US sports and crime reporter in New York, whose short stories *Guys and Dolls* (1932) deal wryly with the seamier side of the city's life in his own invented jargon.

rupee, *n.* the standard monetary unit of various Asian countries including India, Pakistan, Sri Lanka, Nepal, Bhutan, the Maldives, Mauritius and the Seychelles. [Hind. *rūpiyah,* from Sansk. *rūpya,* wrought silver]

Rupert, *n.* **Prince** (1619–82), English Royalist general and admiral, born in Prague, son of the Elector Palatine Frederick V (1596–1632) and James I's daughter Elizabeth. Defeated by Cromwell at Marston Moor and Naseby in the Civil War, he commanded a privateering fleet (1649–52), until routed by Admiral Robert Blake, and, returning after the Restoration, was a distinguished admiral in the Dutch Wars. He founded the Hudson's Bay Company.

rupiah, *n.* (*pl.* **-ah, -ahs**) the standard monetary unit of Indonesia. [Hind. RUPEE]

rupture, *n.* the act of breaking or the state of being broken or violently parted, a break, a breach; a breach or interruption of concord or friendly relations; hernia. *v.t.* to burst, to break, to separate by violence; to sever (a friendship etc.); to affect with hernia. *v.i.* to suffer a breach or disruption. **rupturable,** *a.* [F, from L *ruptūra,* from *rumpere,* to break, p.p. *ruptus*]

rural, *a.* pertaining to the country as distinguished from town; pastoral, agricultural; suiting or resembling the country, rustic. **rural dean,** *n.* a clergyman, ranking below an archdeacon, charged with the inspection of a district. **ruralism, ruralist,** *n.* **rurality, ruralness,** *n.* **ruralize, -ise,** *v.i., v.t.* **ruralization, -isation,** *n.* **rurally,** *adv.* **ruridecanal,** *a.* pertaining to a rural dean or deanery. [F, from L *rūrālis,* from *rus rūris,* the country]

Ruritania, *n.* a fictitious state in SE Europe, scene of great adventures invented by Anthony Hope in *The Prisoner of Zenda;* an imaginary kingdom. **Ruritanian,** *n., a.*

ruru, *n.* the New Zealand morepork. [Maori]

rusa, *n.* a large E Indian deer, a sambar. [Malay]

Ruscus, *n.* a genus of shrubby evergreen plants containing the butcher's broom. **ruscus,** *n.* any plant of this genus. [L *ruscum*]

ruse, *n.* a stratagem, artifice, trick or wile. **ruse de guerre,** a war stratagem. **rusé,** *a.* (*fem.* **-sée**) wily, sly, cunning. [F, from *ruser,* perh. rel. to RUSH²]

rush¹, *n.* a plant with long thin stems or leaves, of the family Juncaceae, growing mostly on wet ground, used for making baskets, mats, seats for chairs etc., and formerly for strewing floors; a stem of this plant; applied to various other similar plants, e.g. the bulrush; a rush-light; something of little or no worth. *a.* (made) of rush or rushes. **rush-bearing,** *n.* a northern country festival when rushes and garlands are carried to strew the floor of a church. **rush-bottomed,** *a.* having a seat made of rushes. **rush-candle, -light,** *n.* a small candle made of the pith of a rush dipped in tallow; any weak flickering light. **rush-lily,** *n.* a plant of the genus *Sisyrinchium* with rushy leaves and blue flowers. **rushiness,** *n.* **rushlike,** *a.* **rushy,** *a.* [OE *risc, rysc,* cp. G *Rusch*]

rush², *v.t.* to drive, urge, force, move or push with violence and haste, to hurry; to perform or complete quickly; to take by sudden assault; to surmount, to pass, to seize and occupy, with dash or suddenness; (*coll.*) to cheat, to swindle; (*coll.*) to overcharge. *v.i.* to move or run impetuously or precipitately; to enter or go (into) with undue eagerness or lack of consideration; to run, flow or roll with violence and impetuosity. *n.* the act of rushing; a violent or impetuous movement, advance, dash or onslaught; a sudden onset of activity, movement or thronging of people (to a gold-field etc.); (*usu. pl.*) the first print from a film; a violent demand (for) or run (on) a commodity etc.; (*sl.*) a surge of euphoria induced by a drug. *a.* characterized by or requiring much activity, speed or urgency. **to rush one's fences,** to act too hastily or precipitously. **rush hour,** *n.* a period when traffic is very congested owing to people going to or leaving work. **rusher,** *n.* [A-F *russher*, OF *reusser, ruser*, perh. from a pop. L *refūsāre*, see REFUSE[1]]

Rushdie, *n.* **(Ahmed) Salman** (1947–), British writer, born in India of a Muslim family. His novel *The Satanic Verses* (1988) (the title refers to verses deleted from the Koran) offended many Muslims with alleged blasphemy. In 1989 the Ayatollah Khomeini of Iran called for Rushdie and his publishers to be killed.

rushy RUSH[1].

rusk, *n.* a piece of bread or cake crisped and browned in the oven; a light cake or sweetened biscuit. [Sp. or Port. *rosca*, twist or roll of bread]

Rusk, *n.* **Dean** (1909–), US Democratic politician. He was secretary of state to presidents Kennedy and Johnson (1961–69), and became unpopular through his involvement with the Vietnam War.

Ruskin, *n.* **John** (1819–1900), British art critic and social critic. He published five volumes of *Modern Painters* (1843–60), *The Seven Lamps of Architecture* (1849), in which he stated his philosophy of art, and *The Stones of Venice* (1851–53), in which he drew moral lessons from architectural history. His writings hastened the appreciation of painters considered unorthodox at the time, such as Turner and the Pre-Raphaelite Brotherhood. His later writings were concerned with social and economic problems.

Russ, *n.* a Russian; the Russian language.

Russ., (*abbr.*) Russia; Russian.

russel, *n.* a twilled woollen or cotton fabric or rep, also called **russel-cord.** [etym. doubtful]

Russell[1], *n.* **Bertrand (Arthur William), 3rd Earl** (1872–1970), English philosopher and mathematician, who contributed to the development of modern mathematical logic, and wrote about social issues. His works include *Principia Mathematica*, 1910–13 (with A.N. Whitehead), in which he attempted to show that mathematics could be reduced to a branch of logic; *The Problems of Philosophy* (1912); and *A History of Western Philosophy* (1946). He was an outspoken liberal pacifist.

Russell[2], *n.* **John, 1st Earl Russell** (1792–1878), British Liberal politician, son of the sixth Duke of Bedford. He entered the House of Commons in 1813, and supported Catholic emancipation and the Reform Bill. He held cabinet posts (1830–41), became prime minister (1846–52), and was again a cabinet minister until becoming prime minister again (1865–66). He retired after the defeat of his Reform Bill in 1866.

Russell[3], *n.* **Charles Taze** (1852–1916), US religious figure, founder of the Jehovah's Witness sect in 1872.

Russell[4], *n.* **George William** (1867–1935), Irish poet and essayist. An ardent nationalist, he helped found the Irish national theatre, and his poetry, published under the pseudonym 'A.E.', includes *Gods of War* (1915), and reflects his interest in mysticism and theosophy.

Russell[5], *n.* **Jane** (1921–), US actress who was discovered by producer Howard Hughes. Her first film, *The Outlaw* (1943), was not properly released for several years owing to censorship problems. Her other films include *The Paleface* (1948), *Gentlemen Prefer Blondes* (1953), and *The Revolt of Mamie Stover* (1957). She retired in 1970.

Russell[6], *n.* **Ken** (1927–), English film director, whose films include *Women in Love* (1969), *Altered States* (1979), and *Salome's Last Dance* (1988).

Russell[7], *n.* **Lord William** (1639–83), British Whig politician. Son of the first Duke of Bedford, he was among the founders of the Whig Party, and actively supported attempts in Parliament to exclude the Roman Catholic James II from succeeding to the throne. In 1683 he was accused, on dubious evidence, of complicity in the Rye House Plot to murder Charles II, and was executed.

russet, *a.* of a reddish-brown colour; †coarse, homespun, rustic, homely, simple. *n.* †a coarse homespun cloth worn by peasants; a reddish-brown colour; a rough-skinned reddish-brown variety of apple. **russety,** *a.* [OF *rousset*, dim. of *rous* (F *roux*), L *russus*, red]

Russia, *n.* originally the name of the pre-revolutionary Russian Empire (until 1917), and now accurately restricted to the Russian Soviet Federal Socialist Republic only. It is incorrectly used to refer to the whole of the present Union of Soviet Socialist Republics. **russia leather,** *n.* a soft leather made from hides prepared with birch-bark oil, used in book-binding etc. **Russian**, *a.* of or pertaining to Russia or its people. *n.* a native or inhabitant of Russia; the Russian language. **Russian art,** *n.* from the 10th to the 17th cents. Russian art was dominated by the Eastern Orthodox Church and much influenced by various styles of Byzantine art. Painters such as Andrei Rublev produced icons, images of holy figures which were often considered precious. By the 17th cent. European influence had grown strong and in the 18th cent. the tsars imported European sculptors and painters. Early Russian modernism (1910–30) anticipated Western trends but was then suppressed in favour of art geared to the sentimental glorification of workers. **Russian language,** *n.* a member of the Slavonic branch of the Indo-European language family. The people of Russia proper refer to it as 'Great Russian', in contrast with Ukrainian (which they call 'Little Russian') and the language of Byelorussia ('White Russian'). It is written in the Cyrillic alphabet and is the standard means of communication throughout the USSR. **Russian Revolution,** *n.* the two revolutions of Feb. and Oct. 1917 (Julian calendar) which began with the overthrow of the Romanov dynasty and ended with the establishment of a Soviet state. **Russian roulette,** *n.* a test of mettle or act of bravado involving firing a revolver loaded with a single bullet at one's own head after spinning the chamber. **Russian salad,** *n.* a salad of pickles and diced vegetables in mayonnaise dressing. **Russianism,** *n.* **Russianist,** *n.* **Russianization, -isation,** *n.* **Russianize, -ise,** *v.t.* **Russification**, *n.* **Russify**, *v.t.* **Russki, Russky**, *n.*, *a.* (*offensive*) Russian.

Russian Soviet Federal Socialist Republic, *n.* (Russian **Rossiyskaya**) (**RSFSR**), *n.* constituent republic of the USSR. **area** 17,075,000 sq km/6,592,658 sq miles. **capital** Moscow. **towns** Leningrad, Gorky, Rostov-on-Don, Volgograd. **physical** largest of the Soviet republics, it occupies about three-quarters of the USSR, and includes the fertile Black Earth district; extensive forests; the Ural Mountains with large mineral resources. **population** (1987) 145,311,000; 83% Russian. **products** three-quarters of the agricultural and industrial output of the USSR. **language** Great Russian. **religion** traditionally Russian Orthodox. **Autonomous Soviet Socialist Republics** (capitals in brackets): Bashkir (Ufa); Buryat (Ulan-Udé); Checheno-Ingush (Grozny); Chuvash (Cheboksary); Dagestan (Makhachkala); Kabardino-Balkar (Nalchik); Kalmyk (Elista); Karelia (Petrozavodsk); Komi (Syktyvkar); Mari (Yoshkar-Ola); Mordovia (Saransk); North Ossetia (Ordzhonikidze); Tatar (Kazan); Tuva (Kizyl); Udmurt (Izhevsk); Yakut (Yakutsk).

Russo-, *comb. form.* Russia; Russian.

Russo-Japanese War, *n.* war between Russia and Japan 1904–05, which arose from conflicting ambitions in

Korea and Manchuria, especially the Russian occupation of Port Arthur (modern Lüda) (1896) and of the Amur province (1900). Japan successfully besieged Port Arthur May 1904–Jan. 1905, took Mukden 29 Feb.–10 Mar., and on 27 May defeated the Russian Baltic fleet, which had sailed halfway around the world to Tsushima Strait. A peace was signed in Portsmouth, New Hampshire, US, 23 Aug. 1905. Russia surrendered its lease on Port Arthur, ceded S Sakhalin to Japan, evacuated Manchuria, and recognized Japan's interests in Korea.

Russophil(e), *n.* a friend or admirer of Russia or the Russians. *a.* friendly to Russia. **Russophilism,** *n.* **Russophobe,** *n.* one who fears or is an opponent of Russia or the Russians. *a.* hating or fearing Russia or the Russians. **Russophobia,** *n.*

rust, *n.* the red incrustation on iron or steel caused by its oxidation when exposed to air and moisture; any similar incrustation on metals; any corrosive or injurious accretion or influence; a dull or impaired condition due to idleness etc.; a plant disease caused by parasitic fungi of the order Uredinales, blight; any of these fungi; the colour of rust, an orangey-red shade of brown. *a.* rust-coloured. *v.i.* to contract rust; to be oxidated; to be attacked by blight; to degenerate through idleness or disuse. *v.t.* to affect with rust, to corrode; to impair by idleness, disuse etc. **rust-coloured,** *a.* **rust-proof,** *a.* impervious to corrosion. **rust-proofing,** *n.* treatment against rusting. **rusted,** *a.* **rustily,** *adv.* **rustiness,** *n.* **rusting,** *n., a.* **rustless,** *a.* **rusty,** *a.* covered or affected with or as with rust; rust-coloured; faded, discoloured by age; antiquated in appearance; harsh, husky (of the voice); impaired by disuse, inaction, neglect etc. [OE *rūst* (cp. Dut. *roest,* G and Swed. *rost,* Dan. *rust*) rel. to RED]

Rust, *n.* **Mathias** (1968–), West German aviator, who in May 1987 piloted a light Cessna 172 turboprop plane from Finland to Moscow, landing in Red Square. Found guilty of 'malicious hooliganism', he served 14 months of a four-year prison sentence.

rustic, *a.* pertaining to the country, rural; like or characteristic of country life or people, unsophisticated, simple, artless; rude, unpolished; awkward, uncouth, clownish; of rough workmanship, coarse, plain; rusticated. *n.* a country person or dweller; an artless, unsophisticated, uncouth or clownish person; rustic work. **rustic work,** *n.* woodwork made of roughly-trimmed trunks, branches etc.; masonry with a rough surface and chamfered joints. **rustically, †rusticly,** *adv.* **rusticate,** *v.i.* to retire or to dwell in the country; to become rustic. *v.t.* to suspend for a time from residence at a university or exile to the country, as a punishment; to make rustic in style, finish etc.; (*in p.p.*) to countrify; to give a rough surface and chamfered joints to (masonry). **rusticated,** *a.* **rusticating,** *a.* **rustication,** *n.* **rusticator,** *n.* **rusticity,** *n.* **rusticize, -ise,** *v.t., v.i.* [L *rusticus,* from *rus,* the country]

rustle, *v.i.* to make a quick succession of small sounds like the rubbing of silk or dry leaves; to move or go along with this sound; (*N Am.*) to bustle, to move quickly and energetically; (*N Am.*) to steal cattle. **to rustle up,** to gather up, to put together; to prepare or make quickly, or without preparation or prior notice. *v.t.* to cause to make this sound; to acquire by rustling. *n.* a rustling. **rustler,** *n.* one who or that which rustles; (*N Am.*) a pushing, bustling person; (*N Am.*) a cattle thief. **rustling,** *n., a.* **rustlingly,** *adv.* [imit. cp. Dut. dial. and LG *russeln*]

rut[1], *n.* the sexual excitement or heat of deer and some other animals; the noise made by the males at this time. *v.i.* (*past, p.p.* **rutted**) to be in a period of this. **rutting,** *n., a.* **ruttish,** *a.* lustful, libidinous, lewd. **ruttishness,** *n.* [OF *rut, ruit,* ult. from L *rugītus,* from *rugīre,* to roar]

rut[2], *n.* a sunken track made by wheels or vehicles; a hollow; a groove; a settled habit or course. *v.t.* (*past, p.p.* **rutted**) to make ruts in. **to be in a rut,** to be stuck in tedious routine. **rutted,** *a.* **ruttily,** *adv.* **ruttiness,** *n.* **rutty,** *a.* [etym. doubtful]

rutabaga, *n.* (*N Am.*) the Swedish turnip, the swede. [F, prob. from Swed.]

Ruth, *n.* in the Old Testament or Hebrew Bible, Moabite (see Moab) ancestress of David (king of Israel) by her second marriage to Boaz. When her first husband died, she preferred to stay with her mother-in-law, Naomi, rather than return to her own people.

ruth, *n.* mercy, pity, compassion, tenderness; remorse, sorrow; penitence. **†ruthful,** *a.* **ruthfully,** *adv.* **ruthless,** *a.* pitiless, merciless, cruel, barbarous. **ruthlessly,** *adv.* **ruthlessness,** *n.* [RUE[1], -TH]

Ruthenia, (Carpathian Ukraine), *n.* region of central Europe, on the south slopes of the Carpathian mountains, home of the Ruthenes or Russniaks. Dominated by Hungary from 10th cent., it was part of Austria-Hungary until World War I. Divided among Czechoslovakia, Poland, and Romania (1918), it was independent for a single day in 1938, immediately occupied by Hungary, captured by the USSR (1944), and from 1945–47 was incorporated into Ukraine Republic, USSR.

ruthenium, *n.* a white, spongy metallic element of the platinum group, at. no. 44; chem. symbol Ru. **ruthenic, ruthenious,** *a.* [*Ruthenia,* Czechoslovakia]

Rutherford[1], *n.* **Ernest** (1871–1937), New Zealand physicist, a pioneer of modern atomic science. His main research was in the field of radioactivity, and he discovered alpha, beta, and gamma rays. He was the first to recognize the nuclear nature of the atom, and named the nucleus.

Rutherford[2], *n.* **Margaret** (1892–1972), British film and theatre actress who specialized in playing formidable yet jovially eccentric roles. She played Agatha Christie's Miss Marple in four films in the early 1960s and won an Academy Award for her role in *The VIPs* (1963).

rutile, *n.* red dioxide of titanium. [F, from L *rutilus,* red]

Rutland, *n.* formerly the smallest English county, now part of Leicestershire.

Ruwenzori, *n.* a mountain range on the frontier between Zaire and Uganda, rising to 5119 m/16,794 ft. at Mt Stanley.

Ruyter, *n.* **Michael Adrianszoon de** (1607–76), Dutch admiral, who led his country's fleet in the wars against England. On 1–4 June 1666 he forced the British fleet under Rupert and Albemarle to retire into the Thames, but on 25 July was heavily defeated off the North Foreland, Kent. In 1667 he sailed up the Medway to burn three men-of-war at Chatham, and captured others.

Ruzicka, *n.* **Leopold Stephen** (1887–1976), Swiss chemist. Born in Yugoslavia, Ruzicka settled in Switzerland in 1929. He began research on such natural compounds as musk and civet. In the 1930s he investigated sex hormones, and in 1934 succeeded in extracting the male hormone androsterone from 31,815 l/56,000 pt of urine and in synthesizing it. Ruzicka, along with Butenandt, shared the 1939 Nobel Chemistry Prize.

RV, (*abbr.*) Revised Version (of the Bible).

Rwanda, Republic of (*Republika y'u Rwanda*), *n.* landlocked country in central Africa, bounded to the N by Uganda, to the E by Tanzania, to the S by Burundi, and to the W by Zaire. **area** 26,300 sq km/10,154 sq miles. **capital** Kigali. **physical** high savanna and hills, with volcanic mountains in NW. **population** (1989) 7,276,000 (Hutu 90%, Tutsi 9%); annual growth rate 3.3%. **exports** coffee, tea, pyrethrum, tin, tungsten. **language** Kinyarwanda (a Bantu language), French. **religion** Christian (mainly Catholic) 54%, animist 45%, Muslim 1%.

-ry, *suf.* shortened form of -ERY, as in *Englishry, poultry, yeomanry.*

Ryan, *n.* **Robert** (1909–73), US theatre and film actor, equally impressive in leading and character roles. His films include *Woman on the Beach* (1947), *The Set-Up* (1949), and *The Wild Bunch* (1969).

Rybinsk, *n.* port and industrial city (engineering) on the Volga, NE of Moscow in the Russian Soviet

Federal Socialist Republic. Between 1984 and 1988 it was named Andropov after a president of the Soviet Union; population(1987) 254,000.

Rydberg constant, *n.* in physics, a constant that relates atomic spectra to the spectrum of hydrogen. Its value is 1.0977 '3 10^7 per metre.

Ryder Cup, *n.* golf tournament for professional men's teams from the US and Europe. It is played every two years and the match is made up of a series of singles, foursomes, and fourballs played over three days.

rye, *n.* the seeds or grain of *Secale cereale,* a cereal allied to wheat, used to make (black) bread, whisky etc.; the plant bearing this; rye whisky; (*N Am.*) rye bread. *a.* of rye. **rye bread,** *n.* bread (white or dark) made from rye flour. **rye flour,** *n.* flour made from rye grain. **rye-grass,** *n.* one of various grasses of the genus *Lolium,* cultivated for fodder grass. **rye whisky,** *n.* whisky distilled from rye grain. [OE *ryge* (cp. Icel. *rūgr,* Dan. *rug,* also Dut. *rogge,* G *Roggen*)]

ry(e)peck, ripeck, *n.* an ironshod pole used for driving into the bed of a stream to moor a punt etc. [etym. doubtful]

Ryle, *n.* **Martin** (1918–84), English radioastronomer. At the Mullard Radio Astronomy Observatory, Cambridge, he developed the technique of sky-mapping using 'aperture synthesis', combining smaller dish aerials to give the characteristics of one large one.

ryot, *n.* an Indian peasant or cultivator of the soil. [Hind. *rāiyat,* as RAYAH]

Ryukyu Islands, *n.* southernmost island group of Japan, stretching towards Taiwan and including Okinawa, Miyako, and Ishigaki. **area** 2254 sq km/870 sq miles. **capital** Naha on Okinawa. **population** (1985) 1,179,000. **products** sugar, pineapples, fish.

Ryzhkov, *n.* **Nikolai Ivanovich** (1929–), Soviet communist politician. He held governmental and party posts from 1975 before being brought into the Politburo and made prime minister in 1985 by Gorbachev. A low-profile technocrat, Ryzhkov is viewed as a more cautious and centralist reformer than Gorbachev.

S

S[1], **s**[1], the 19th letter of the English alphabet (*pl.* **Ss, S's, Esses**) is a voiceless sibilant, with a hard sound, as in *sin, so,* the sound of *z,* as in *music, muse* etc., of *sh* in *sugar, mission,* and of *zh* in *measure, vision;* an S-shaped object or curve. **collar of SS** COLLAR.

S[2], (*abbr.*) Sabbath; Saint; Saxon; siemens; Signor; society; South, Southern; sun.

S[3], (*chem. symbol*) sulphur.

s[2], (*abbr.*) second; shilling; singular; snow; son; succeeded.

-s[1], *suf.* forming plurals of most nouns. [OE *-as,* nom. and acc. pl. endings of various masculine nouns]

-s[2], *suf.* forming third pers. sing. pres. tense of most verbs. [OE *-es, -as,* second pers. sing. ending]

-'s[1], *suf.* forming possessives of sing. nouns and pl. nouns not ending in *s.* [OE *-es*]

-'s[2], *suf.* short for is, has; us.

SA, (*abbr.*) Salvation Army; sex appeal; limited liability company [F *société anonyme*]; South Africa; South America; South Australia.

s.a., (*abbr.*) without date. [L *sine anno*]

SAARC, *n.* (*abbr.*) South Asian Association for Regional Cooperation.

Saarinen[1], *n.* **Eero** (1910–61), Finnish-born US architect. His works include the US embassy, London, the TWA terminal, New York, and Dulles Airport, Washington DC. He collaborated on a number of projects with his father, Eliel Saarinen.

Saarinen[2], *n.* **Eliel** (1873–1950), Finnish architect and town planner, founder of the Finnish Romantic school. In 1923 he emigrated to the US, where he contributed to US skyscraper design by his work in Chicago, and later turned to functionalism.

Saarland, *n.* (French **Sarre**) *Land* (state) of West Germany, crossed NW–S by the river Saar. Saarland is one-third forest. **area** 2570 sq km/992 sq miles. **capital** Saarbrücken. **population** (1988) 1,034,000. **products** former flourishing coal and steel industries survive only by government subsidy; cereals and other crops; cattle, pigs, poultry.

sabadilla, *n.* a Mexican and Central American liliaceous plant yielding acrid seeds from which veratrine is obtained; the barley-like seeds of this. [Sp. *cebadilla,* dim. of *cebada,* barley]

Sabaean, Sabean, *n.* one of the ancient people of Yemen. *a.* of or pertaining to this people. [L *Sabaeus,* Gr. *Sabaios,* from Arab. *Saba',* Sheba]

Sabaism, *n.* the worship of the stars or the host of heaven. **Sabaistic,** *a.* [Heb. *çābā,* host, -ISM]

Sabaoth, *n.* (*Bibl.*) hosts, armies (in the title 'Lord God of Sabaoth'). [Heb. *çabāōth,* pl. of *çābā,* army]

Sabatier, *n.* **Paul** (1854–1951), French chemist. He found in 1897 that if a mixture of ethylene and hydrogen was passed over a column of heated nickel, the ethylene changed into ethane. Further work revealed that nickel could be used to catalyze numerous chemical reactions. Sabatier shared the 1912 Nobel Chemistry Prize with François Grignard.

Sabatini, *n.* **Gabriela** (1970–), Argentine tennis player who in 1986 became the youngest Wimbledon semifinalist for 99 years. She was ranked number three in the world behind Steffi Graf and Martina Navratilova in 1989 after capturing the Italian Open title.

sabbat, SABBATH.

Sabbatarian, *n.* a Jew who strictly observes the seventh day of the week; a Christian who observes Sunday as a Sabbath, or who is specially strict in its observance. *a.* observing or inculcating the observance of the Sabbath or Sunday. **Sabbatarianism,** *n.* [L *Sabbatārius,* as foll.]

Sabbath, *n.* the seventh day of the week, Saturday, set apart, esp. by the Jews, for rest and divine worship; the Christian Sunday observed as a day of rest and worship; a time of rest. (**sabbath, witches' Sabbath, sabbat**) midnight assembly of witches, wizards and demons, supposed to be convoked by the devil. **Sabbath-breaker,** *n.* one who profanes the Sabbath. **Sabbath-breaking,** *n.* **Sabbath Day,** *n.* the Jewish Sabbath (Saturday); Sunday. **Sabbathless,** *a.* **Sabbatic, -ical,** *a.* pertaining to or befitting the Sabbath. **sabbatical,** *n.* an extended period of leave from one's work. **Sabbatical year,** *n.* every seventh year, during which the Hebrews were not to sow their fields or prune their vineyards, and were to liberate slaves and debtors; a year's leave of absence orig. granted every seven years esp. to university teachers. **Sabbatically,** *adv.* †**Sabbatine,** *a.* **Sabbatism,** *n.* **Sabbatismal,** *a.* **Sabbatize, -ise,** *v.t.* to keep as or turn into a Sabbath. *v.i.* to keep the Sabbath. [L *Sabbatum,* from Gr. *Sabbaton,* Heb. *shabbāth,* from *shābath,* to rest]

Sabean etc. SABAEAN.

Sabellian, *a.* pertaining to Sabellianism. *n.* a follower of Sabellius, an African priest of the 3rd cent., who taught that the persons of the Trinity are only different manifestations of one divine person. **Sabellianism,** *n.* the doctrines of Sabellius. [late L *Sabelliānus* (*Sabellius,* -AN)]

sabelline, *a.* pertaining to the sable; coloured like its fur. [med. L *sabellīnus,* from *sabellum,* SABLE]

saber SABRE.

Sabian, *n.* a member of an ancient sect who are classed in the Koran with Muslims, Jews and Christians as worshippers of the true God; (*erron.*) a star-worshipper. *a.* pertaining to Sabianism. **Sabianism,** *n.* the religion of the Sabians; (*erron.*) Sabaism. [Arab. *çabi',* prob. to baptize]

sabin, *n.* a unit of acoustic absorption. [Wallace C. *Sabine,* 1868–1919, US physicist]

Sabin, *n.* **Albert** (1906–), Polish-born US microbiologist, whose involvement in the anti-polio campaigns led to the development of a new, highly effective live vaccine.

Sabine, *n.* a member of an ancient people of central Italy, conquered by the Romans and amalgamated with them in the 3rd century BC. The so-called rape of the Sabine women – a mythical attempt by Romulus in the early days of Rome to carry off the Sabine women to colonise the new city – is frequently depicted in art. *a.* of or pertaining to this people. [L *Sabīnus*]

sable, *n.* a small Arctic and sub-Arctic carnivorous quadruped, *Mustela zibellina,* allied to the marten, the brown fur of which is very highly valued; its skin or fur; a painter's brush made of its hair; (*Her.*) black; (*poet.*) black, esp. as the colour of mourning; (*pl.*) mourning garments. *a.* black; (*poet.*) dark, gloomy. *v.t.* to make dark or dismal. **sable-coloured,** *a.* black. **sable-stoled, sable-vested,** *a.* clothed in sables. **sabled, sably,** *a.* [OF, from Slav., cp. Rus., Pol. and Czech *sobol*]

sabot, *n.* a wooden shoe, usu. made in one piece, worn by peasantry etc. in France, Belgium etc.; a wooden-soled shoe; a wooden disk fastened to a spherical projectile, or a metal cap on a conical one, to make these fit a gun-bore; (*Mech.*) a cap or shoe for protecting the end of a pile etc. [F, etym. doubtful]

sabotage, *n.* the operation of cutting shoes or sockets for railway-lines; malicious damage to a railway, industrial plant, machinery etc., as a protest by discontented workers, or as a non-military act of warfare; any action designed to hinder or undermine. **saboteur**, *n.* one who commits sabotage.

Sabra, *n.* an Israeli born in Israel. [Heb.]

sabre, (*esp. N Am.*) **saber**, *n.* a cavalry sword having a curved blade; (*pl.*) cavalry; a light fencing sword with a tapering blade. *v.t.* to cut or strike down or kill with the sabre. **sabre-bill, -wing,** *n.* S American birds. **sabre-fish,** *n.* the silver eel, *Trichiurus lepturus*. **sabre-rattling,** *n.* a display of military power or aggression. **sabre-toothed tiger,** *n.* a large extinct feline mammal with long upper canines. **sabreur**, *n.* one who fights with the sabre. [F, earlier *sable,* G *Säbel,* cp. Hung. *szábłya,* Pol. *szabla*]

sabre-tache, *n.* a cavalry officer's leather pocket suspended on the left side from the sword-belt. [F, from G *Säbeltasche* (*Säbel,* sabre, *Tasche,* pocket)]

Sabu, *n.* stage name of Sabu Dastagir (1924–63), Indian child actor, memorable as the hero of *The Thief of Bagdad* (1940). He acted in Britain and the US until the 1950s. His other films include *Elephant Boy* (1937) and *Black Narcissus* (1947).

sabulous, *a.* sandy, gritty; applied to gritty particles in the body, sediment in urine etc. †**sabulosity**, *n.* [L *sabulōsus,* from *sabulum,* sand]

saburra, *n.* foul granular matter accumulated in the stomach through indigestion. **saburral,** *a.* **saburration,** *n.* (*Med.*) the application of hot sand as a bath. [L *saburra,* sand]

sac[1], *n.* a right or privilege, such as that of holding a court, granted to a lord of a manor by the Crown. [OE *sacu,* dispute, lawsuit]

sac[2], *n.* a pouch, a cavity or receptacle in an animal or vegetable; a pouch forming the envelope of a tumour, cyst etc. **saccate**, **sacciform**, *a.* having the form of a pouch. [F, from L *saccus,* SACK]

saccade, *n.* a sudden check of a horse with the reins; a strong pressure of a violin bow against the strings; a jump of the eye between fixation points. [F, a jerk, sudden pull, from *saquer,* to pull]

saccate SAC[2].

saccharine, **saccharin**, *n.* an intensely sweet compound obtained from toluene, a product of coal-tar, used as a sugar substitute in food. *a.* pertaining to sugar; having the qualities of sugar; sickly sweet, sugary; ingratiatingly pleasant or polite. **saccharic**, *a.* pertaining to or obtained from sugar. **saccharide**, *n.* a carbohydrate, esp. a sugar. **sacchariferous**, *a.* producing or containing sugar. **saccharify**, *v.t.* to break down into simple sugars. **saccharimeter**, *n.* an instrument for determining the quantity of sugar in solutions, esp. by means of a polarized light. **saccharimetry**, *n.* **saccharite**, *n.* a white or whitish granular variety of feldspar. †**saccharize, -ise,** *v.t.* to convert into sugar. **saccharoid**, *a.* (*Geol.*) having a granular structure. *n.* a sugar-like substance. **saccharoidal**, *a.* **saccharometer**, *n.* a saccharimeter, esp. a hydrometer for measuring sugar concentration. **saccharose**, *n.* sucrose. **saccharous,** *a.* **Saccharum**, *n.* an invert sugar obtained from cane sugar; a genus of grasses comprising the sugar-cane. [F *saccharin* (L *saccharum,* sugar, -INE)]

sacchar(o)-, *comb. form* sugar. [L *saccharum,* from Gr. *sakcharon,* sugar]

Saccharomyces, *n.* a genus of fungi comprising the yeasts. [L SACCHAR(O)-, *-myces,* fungus]

saccharose, Saccharum SACCHARINE.

sacciform SAC[2].

Sacco-Vanzetti case, murder trial in Massachusetts, US (1920–21). Italian immigrants Nicola Sacco (1891–1927) and Bartolomeo Vanzetti (1888–1927) were convicted of murder during an alleged robbery. The conviction was upheld on appeal, with application for retrial denied. Prolonged controversy delayed execution until 1927. In 1977 the verdict was declared unjust because of the judge's prejudice against the accuseds' anarchist views.

saccule, -ulus, *n.* (*pl.* **-les, -li**) a small sac, esp. the smaller of two cavities in the labyrinth of the inner ear. **saccular, sacculate, -ated,** *a.* **sacculation,** *n.* [L *sacculus,* dim. of *saccus,* SAC[2]]

sacellum, *n.* (*pl.* **-la**) a small, usu. roofless sanctuary containing an altar in an ancient Roman building; a chapel, a shrine. [L dim. of *sacrum,* shrine, neut. of *sacer,* holy]

sacerdotal, *a.* pertaining to priests or the priesthood; priestly; attributing sacrificial power and supernatural or sacred character to priests; claiming or suggesting excessive emphasis on the authority of the priesthood. †**sacerdocy**, *n.* sacerdotalism; the priestly office. **sacerdotage**, *n.* sacerdotalism; devotion to or the devotees of the priesthood. **sacerdotalism,** *n.* **sacerdotalist,** *n.* **sacerdotalize, -ise,** *v.t.* **sacerdotally,** *adv.* [L *sacerdōtālis,* from *sacerdōs -dōtis,* priest (*sacer,* holy, *dōs dōtis,* cogn. with *dare,* to give)]

sachem, *n.* a chief of certain tribes of N American Indians; a magnate, a prominent person; (*US*) one of the governing officers of the Tammany Society in New York City. **sachemship,** *n.* [N Am.Ind.]

Sacher, *n.* **Paul** (1906–), Swiss conductor. In 1926 he founded the Basle Chamber Orchestra, for which he has commissioned a succession of works from contemporary composers including Bartok, Stravinsky, and Britten.

Sacher-Masoch, *n.* **Leopold von** (1836–95), Austrian novelist. His books dealt with the sexual pleasures to be obtained by having pain inflicted on oneself, hence masochism.

sachet, *n.* a small ornamental bag or other receptacle containing perfumed powder for scenting clothes etc.; a small packet of shampoo etc. [F, dim. of SAC[2]]

Sachs, *n.* **Hans** (1494–1576), German poet and composer who worked as a master shoemaker in Nuremberg. He composed 4275 *Meisterlieder/mastersongs*, and figures prominently in Wagner's opera *Die Meistersinger/The Mastersingers*.

sack[1], *n.* a large, usu. oblong bag of strong coarse material, for holding corn, raw cotton, wool etc.; the quantity a sack contains, as a unit of capacity and weight; a sack together with its contents; a loose garment, gown or appendage to a dress, of various kinds, a sacque; a loose-fitting waistless dress; (*coll.*) dismissal from employment; (*sl.*) bed. *v.t.* to put into a sack; to give the sack to. **to give** or **to get the sack,** to dismiss or be dismissed. **to hit the sack,** (*sl.*) to go to bed. **sackcloth,** *n.* sacking; this worn formerly in token of mourning or penitence. †**Sack-Friar,** †**Sacked-Friar,** *n.* a member of an order of 13th-cent. mendicant friars who wore sackcloth. **sack-race,** *n.* a race in which the competitors are tied up to the waist or neck in sacks. **sackful,** *n.* **sacking,** *n.* coarse stuff of which sacks, bags etc. are made. [OE *sacc,* L *saccus,* Gr. *sakkos,* Heb. *saq*]

sack[2], *v.t.* to plunder or pillage (a place taken by storm); to rifle, to ransack, to loot. *n.* the pillaging of a captured place; (*poet.*) plunder, booty. †**sackage**, *n.* **sacker,** *n.* [prob. from prec., cp. F *saccager,* It. *saccheggiare*]

sack[3], *n.* an old name for various white wines, esp. those from Spain and the Canaries. **sack-posset, -whey,** *n.* beverages made of sack, milk etc. [orig. *wyne seck,* F *vin sec,* dry wine]

sackage SACK[2].

sackbut, *n.* a mediaeval bass trumpet with a slide like the modern trombone; (*Bibl.*) an Aramaic musical stringed instrument. [F *saquebote,* prob. conf. with ONorth.F *saqueboute,* a lance with a hook]

sacking SACK[1].

sackless, *a.* †innocent; (*chiefly Sc.*) peaceable, simple, feeble-minded. [OE *sacléas* (SAC[1], -LESS)]

Sackville, *n.* **Thomas, 1st Earl of Dorset** (1536–1608), English poet, collaborator with Thomas Norton on *Gorboduc* (1561), written in blank verse and one of the earliest English tragedies.

sacque, *n.* a loose-fitting woman's gown; a loose-fitting coat hanging from the shoulders. [prob. var. of SACK[1]]

sacra, sacral SACRUM.

sacrament, *n.* a religious rite instituted as an outward and visible sign of an inward and spiritual grace (applied by the Eastern and Roman Catholic Churches to baptism, the Eucharist, confirmation, matrimony, penance, holy orders and anointing of the sick, and by most Protestants to the first two of these); the Lord's Supper, the Eucharist; the consecrated elements of the Eucharist; a sacred token, symbol, influence etc.; in Roman times, a military oath; hence a solemn oath or engagement. *v.t.* (*usu. in p.p.*) to bind by an oath. **sacramental,** *a.* pertaining to or constituting a sacrament; bound by oath, consecrated. *n.* a rite or observance ancillary or analogous to the sacraments. **sacramentalism,** *n.* the doctrine of the spiritual efficacy of the sacraments. **sacramentalist,** *n.* **sacramentality,** *n.* sacramental nature. **sacramentally,** *adv.* **Sacramentarian,** *a.* (*also* **sacramentarian**) relating to the sacraments or the Sacramentarians. *n.* one holding extreme or 'high' doctrines regarding the spiritual efficacy of the sacraments; one of the German reformers of the 16th cent. who opposed the Lutheran view of the sacraments and regarded them as merely signs and symbols. **Sacramentarianism,** *n.* **sacramentary,** *a.* pertaining to a sacrament or to the Sacramentarians. *n.* an ancient book of ritual in the Western Church, containing the rites for Mass and for the administration of the sacraments generally etc.; a Sacramentarian. [F *sacrement,* L *sacrāmentum,* orig. military oath, from *sacrāre,* to make sacred, from *sacer sacris,* SACRED]

sacrarium¹, *n.* (*pl.* **-ria**) a sacred place where sacred things were kept in ancient Rome, esp. the room in the house where the penates were kept, or the adytum of a temple; the sanctuary of a church; in the Roman Catholic Church, a piscina. [L, from *sacer -cris,* SACRED]

sacrarium², *n.* the complex sacrum of a bird. [from SACRUM]

sacred, *a.* dedicated to religious use, consecrated; dedicated or dear to a divinity; set apart, reserved or specially appropriated (to); pertaining to or hallowed by religion or religious service, holy; sanctified by religion, reverence etc., not to be profaned, inviolable. **sacred beetle,** *n.* a scarab. **Sacred College,** *n.* the collegiate body of cardinals in the Roman Catholic Church. **sacred cow,** *n.* an institution, custom, etc. regarded with reverence and as beyond criticism. **sacredly,** *adv.* **sacredness,** *n.* [p.p. of ME *sacren,* OF *sacrer,* L *sacrāre,* to consecrate, from *sacer -cris,* holy]

Sacred Thread ceremony, Hindu initiation ceremony which is a passage to maturity for boys of the upper three castes, usually aged between five and twelve. It is regarded as a second birth; the castes whose males are entitled to undergo the ceremony are called 'twice born'.

sacrifice, *n.* the act of offering an animal, person etc., esp. by ritual slaughter, or the surrender of a valued possession to a deity, as an act of propitiation, atonement or thanksgiving; that which is so offered or given up, a victim, an offering; the Crucifixion as Christ's offering of himself; the Eucharist as a renewal of this or as a thanksgiving; the giving up of anything for the sake of another person, object or interest; the sale of goods at a loss; a great loss or destruction (of life etc.). *v.t.* to offer to a deity as a sacrifice; to surrender for the sake of another person, object etc., to devote; (*coll.*) to sell at a much reduced price. †**sacrifical,** *a.* †**sacrificant, sacrificator,** *n.* one who offers a sacrifice. **sacrificatory,** *a.* **sacrificer,** *n.* **sacrificial,** *a.* **sacrificially,** *adv.* [F, from L *sacrificium* (*sacer -cris,* holy, SACRED, *facere,* to make)]

sacrilege, *n.* the violation or profanation of sacred things, esp. larceny from a consecrated building; †the alienation of Church property to lay uses; irreverence towards something or someone (considered) sacred. **sacrilegious,** *a.* **sacrilegiously,** *adv.* †**sacrilegiousness, sacrilegist,** *n.* [OF, from L *sacrilegium,* from *sacrilegus,* a sacrilegious person (*sacer -cris,* SACRED, *legere,* to gather, to steal)]

sacring, *n.* consecration, esp. of the Eucharistic elements in the Mass, and of bishops, kings etc. **sacring-bell,** *n.* the sanctus bell. [ME *sacren,* see SACRED, -ING]

sacrist, *n.* an officer in charge of the sacristy of a church or religious house with its contents. **sacristan,** *n.* a sacrist; a sexton. **sacristy,** *n.* an apartment in a church in which the vestments, sacred vessels, books etc. are kept. [OF *sacriste,* L *sacrista,* from *sacer -cris,* SACRED]

sacro-, *comb. form* sacrum, sacral. **sacro-costal,** *a.* pertaining to the sacrum and of the nature of a rib. *n.* a sacro-costal part. **sacroiliac,** *a.* pertaining to the sacrum and the ilium. **sacro-pubic,** *a.* pertaining to the sacrum and the pubis.

sacrosanct, *a.* inviolable by reason of sanctity; regarded with extreme respect, revered. **sacrosanctity,** *n.* [L *sacrosanctus* (*sacro- sacer,* SACRED, *sanctus,* see SAINT)]

sacrum, *n.* (*pl.* **-cra**) a composite bone formed by the union of vertebrae at the base of the spinal column, constituting the dorsal part of the pelvis. **sacral,** *a.* [L, neut. of *sacer,* holy]

sad, *a.* (*comp.* **sadder,** *superl.* **saddest**) sorrowful, mournful; expressing sorrow; causing sorrow, unfortunate; lamentable, bad, shocking; of bread, cake etc., heavy, not well raised; †dull, dark-coloured. **sad-eyed, -faced, -hearted,** *a.* (*poet.*) sorrowful or looking sorrowful. **sad-iron,** *n.* a solid smoothing iron. **sadden,** *v.t.* to make sad; to tone down (a colour etc.) by certain chemicals, as in dyeing. *v.i.* to become sad. **saddish,** *a.* **sadly,** *adv.* **sadness,** *n.* [OE *sæd,* sated, cp. Dut. *zat,* G *satt,* also L *satis*]

Sadat, *n.* **Anwar** (1918–81), Egyptian politician. Succeeding Nasser as president in 1970, he restored morale by his handling of the Egyptian campaign in the 1973 war against Israel. In 1974 his plan for economic, social, and political reform to transform Egypt was unanimously adopted in a referendum. In 1977 he visited Israel to reconcile the two countries, and shared the Nobel Peace Prize with Israeli prime minister Menachem Begin in 1978. He was assassinated by Islamic fundamentalists.

saddle, *n.* a seat placed on an animal's back, to support a rider; a similar part of the harness of a draught animal; a seat on a cycle, agricultural machine etc.; an object resembling a saddle; a saddle-shaped marking on an animal's back; the rear part of a male fowl's back; a joint of mutton, venison etc., including the loins; a supporting piece in various machines, suspension-bridges, gun-mountings, tackle etc.; a depressed part of a ridge between two summits, a col; a raised and symmetrical anticlinal fold. *v.t.* to put a saddle on; to load or burden with a duty etc. **saddleback,** *n.* a roof or coping sloping up at both ends or with a gable at each end; a saddlebacked hill; an animal with a marking suggestive of a saddle; the hooded crow; a black pig with a white band across the back. *a.* saddlebacked. **saddlebacked,** *a.* of a horse, having a low back with an elevated neck and head; curving up at each end. **saddle-bag,** *n.* one of a pair of bags connected by straps slung across a horse etc. from the saddle; a bag attached to the back of the saddle of a bicycle etc.; a kind of carpeting woven in imitation of Persian saddle-bags for camels. **saddle-blanket,** *n.* a saddle-cloth. **saddle-bow,** *n.* the pommel. **saddle-cloth,** *n.* a cloth laid on a horse under the saddle. **saddle-corporal, -sergeant,** *n.* a regimental saddler. **saddle horse,** *n.* a horse for riding. **saddle-pillar,** *n.* the saddle support of a cycle. **saddle soap,** *n.* an oily soap for cleaning and preserving leather. **saddle-spring,** *n.* the spring of a cycle saddle. **saddle-tree,** *n.* the frame of a saddle; the tulip-tree. **saddleless,** *a.* **saddler,** *n.* a maker or dealer in saddles and harness; (*Mil.*) a non-commissioned officer in charge of the harness in a cavalry regiment. **saddlery,** *n.* the trade or shop of a saddler; saddles and harnesses collectively. [OE *sadol* (cp. Dut. *zadel,* G *Sattel,* Icel. *söthull*), whence *sadelian* (cp. Dut. *zadelen,* G *satteln*), prob. rel. to SIT]

Sadducee, *n.* one of a sect among the Jews, arising in

the 2nd cent. BC, who adhered to the written law to the exclusion of tradition, and denied the resurrection from the dead, existence of spirits etc. **Sadducean,** *a.* **Sadduceeism,** *n.* [L *Sadducaei,* pl., from Gr. *Saddoukaioi,* prob. from *Zadok,* name of High Priest]

Sade, *n.* **Marquis de** (1740–1814), French soldier and author. He was imprisoned for sexual offences, and finally committed to an asylum. He wrote plays and novels dealing explicitly with a variety of sexual practices, including sadism.

sadhu, saddhu, *n.* a Hindu usu. mendicant holy man. [Sansk.]

S'adi, Saadi, *n.* pen name of Sheikh Moslih Addin (*c.* 1184–c. 1291), Persian poet, author of *Bustan/Tree-garden* and *Gulistan/Flower-garden.*

sad-iron SAD.

sadism, *n.* sexual perversion characterized by a passion for cruelty; pleasure derived from inflicting pain. **sadist,** *n.* **sadistic,** *a.* **sadistically,** *n.* **sadomasochism,** *n.* sadism and masochism combined in one person. **sadomasochist,** *n.* **sadomasochistic,** *a.* [F *sadisme,* from the Marquis de *Sade*]

Sadler's Wells, *n.* a theatre in Islington, N London, England. It was originally a music hall. Lilian Baylis developed a later theatre on the site in 1931 as a northern annexe to the Old Vic. For many years it housed the Sadler's Wells Opera Company, which moved to the London Coliseum in 1969 (renamed English National Opera Company in 1974) and the Sadler's Wells Ballet, which later became the Royal Ballet and moved from London to Birmingham (Hippodrome) in Aug. 1989.

Sadowa, Battle of, (or **Battle of Königgrätz**), Prussian victory over the Austrian army 13 km/8 miles NW of Hradec Kralove (German Königgrätz) on 3 July 1866, ending the Seven Weeks' War. It confirmed Prussian hegemony over the German states, and led to the formation of the North German Confederation in 1867. It is named after the nearby village of Sadowa (Czech *Sadová*) in Czechoslovakia.

sae, (*abbr.*) stamped addressed envelope.

safari, *n.* a hunting or scientific expedition, esp. in E Africa. **safari jacket,** *n.* a light, usu. cotton jacket with breast pockets and a belt. **safari park,** *n.* a park containing uncaged wild animals, such as lions and monkeys. **safari suit,** *n.* a suit having a safari jacket. [Ar *safar,* a journey]

safe, *a.* free or secure from danger, damage or evil; uninjured, unharmed, sound; affording security; not dangerous, hazardous or risky; cautious, prudent, trusty; unfailing, certain, sure; no longer dangerous, secure from escape or from doing harm. *n.* a receptacle for keeping things safe, a steel fire-proof and burglar-proof receptacle for valuables, a strong-box; a cupboard or other receptacle for keeping meat and other provisions. **safe-breaker, -cracker,** *n.* one who opens safes to steal. **safe-breaking, -cracking,** *n.* **safe-conduct,** *n.* an official document or passport ensuring a safe passage, esp. in a foreign country or in time of hostilities. †*v.t.* to conduct safely. **safe-deposit, safety deposit,** *n.* a specially-constructed building or basement with safes for renting. **safeguard,** *n.* one who or that which protects; a proviso, precaution, circumstance etc. that tends to save loss, trouble, danger etc.; a safe-conduct, a passport. *v.t.* to make safe or secure by precaution, stipulation etc. **safeguarding,** *n.* protecting specified home industries against foreign competition by customs duties. **safe-house,** *n.* a place that can be used as a refuge. **safe-keeping,** *n.* the act of keeping or preserving in safety; secure guardianship; custody. **safe period,** *n.* the part of the menstrual cycle when conception is least likely to occur. **safe seat,** *n.* a Parliamentary seat that is certain to be held by the same party as previously. **safely,** *adv.* **safeness,** *n.* [ME and OF *sauf,* L *salvus,* whole, uninjured]

safety, *n.* the state of being safe, freedom from injury, danger or risk; safe-keeping or custody; a safety-catch; (*coll.*) a safety-bicycle. **safety belt,** *n.* a seat-belt; a belt fastening a person to a fixed object to prevent falling. **safety-bicycle,** *n.* a low bicycle with wheels of equal size. **safety-catch, -lock,** *n.* a lock that cannot be picked easily; a device in a firearm to prevent accidental discharge. **safety curtain,** *n.* a fire-proof curtain in a theatre that cuts off the stage from the audience. **safety deposit,** *n.* a safe-deposit. **safety-fuse,** *n.* a fuse that allows an explosive to be fired without danger to the person igniting it. **safety glass,** *n.* glass layered with a sheet of plastic to resist shattering; glass treated to prevent splintering when broken. **safety-lamp,** *n.* a miner's lamp protected by wire or gauze so as not to ignite combustible gas. **safety-match,** *n.* a match that ignites only on a surface treated with a special ingredient. **safety net,** *n.* a net to catch tight-rope and trapeze performers if they should fall; a safeguard, precaution. **safety-pin,** *n.* a pin with a part for keeping it secure and guarding the point. **safety-razor,** *n.* one mounted on a handle with a guard to prevent cutting the skin. **safety-valve,** *n.* a valve on a boiler automatically opening to let steam escape to relieve pressure and prevent explosion; any harmless means of relieving anger, excitement etc.

saffian, *n.* leather prepared from goatskin or sheepskin tanned with sumac and dyed yellow or red. [Rus. *safiyanu*]

Saffir–Simpson damage-potential scale, scale of potential damage from wind and sea when a hurricane is in progress. 1 is minimal damage, 5 is catastrophic.

safflower, *n.* a thistle-like plant, *Carthamus tinctorius,* with orange flowers yielding a red dye, and seeds rich in oil. [Dut. *saffloer,* OF *saffleur,* obs. It. *saffiore*]

saffron, *n.* the dried deep orange stigmas of a crocus, *Crocus sativus,* used for colouring and flavouring food; this plant; the colour deep orange; the meadow saffron, *Colchicum autumnale;* the bastard saffron or safflower. *a.* saffron-coloured, deep yellow. *v.t.* to make yellow; to tinge with saffron. **saffrony,** *a.* **safranin, -ine,** *n.* any of a series of basic compounds used in dyeing. [OF *safran,* Arab. *za'farān*]

sag, *v.i.* (*past, p.p.* **sagged**) to droop, to sink, to yield or give way esp. in the middle, under weight or pressure; to bend, to hang sideways; to lose vigour, to weaken; of prices, esp. of stocks, to decline; (*Naut.*) to drift to leeward. *v.t.* to cause to give way, bend, or curve sideways. *n.* the act or state of sagging or giving way; the amount of this; (*Naut.*) a sideways drift or tendency to leeward. **saggy,** *a.* [prob. of Scand. orig. (cp. Dan. and Norw. *sakke,* Dut. *zakken*)]

saga, *n.* a mediaeval prose narrative recounting family or public events in Iceland or Scandinavia, usu. by contemporary or nearly contemporary native writers; a story of heroic adventure; a series of books relating the history of a family; (*coll.*) a long involved story or account. [Icel., cogn. with SAW[2]]

sagacious, *a.* intellectually keen or quick to understand or discern, intelligent, perspicacious, shrewd, wise; of policy etc., characterized by wisdom and discernment; of an animal, sensible, quick-scented. **sagaciously,** *adv.* **sagaciousness, sagacity,** *n.* [L *sagax -ācis* (rel. to *sagīre,* to perceive)]

sagamore, *n.* a N American Indian chief, a sachem. [N Am.Ind. *sagamo*]

Sagan, *n.* **Françoise** (1935–), French novelist. Her studies of love relationships include *Bonjour Tristesse/Hello Sadness* (1954), *Un Certain Sourire/A Certain Smile* (1956), and *Aimez-vous Brahms?/Do You Like Brahms?* (1959).

sagan, *n.* the deputy of the Jewish high priest. [Heb.]

sagapenum, *n.* a gum resin obtained from *Ferula persica,* formerly used to relieve spasms. [late L, from Gr. *sagapēnon*]

sage[1], *n.* a grey-leaved aromatic plant of the genus *Salvia,* esp. *S. officinalis,* formerly much used in medicine, now employed in cookery. **sage-brush,** *n.* a shrubby plant of the various species of *Artemisia,* abounding in the plains in the W US. **sage-cheese,** *n.* cheese flavoured and coloured with layers of or an infusion of sage. **sage-cock, -grouse,** *n.* the largest of the American grouse, *Centrocercus urophasianus,* frequenting the sage-brush regions. **sage-green,** *n.* a greyish green. **sagy,** *a.* [ME and A-F *sauge,* L *salvia*]

sage², *a.* wise, discreet, prudent; judicious, well-considered; grave, serious- or solemn-looking. *n.* a person of great wisdom, esp. one of past times with a traditional reputation for wisdom. **sagely,** *adv.* **sageness,** *n.* **sageship,** *n.* [F, ult. from pop. L *sapius,* from *sapere,* to be wise]

sagene¹, *n.* a fishing-net. [L *sagēna,* Gr. *sagēnē,* cp. SEINE]

sagene², *n.* a Russian measure of length, about 7 ft (2 m). [Rus.]

saggar, *n.* a vessel of fireproof pottery in which delicate porcelain is enclosed while in a kiln. **saggar-house,** *n.* [perh. corr. of SAFEGUARD]

saggy SAG.

Sagitta, *n.* (*Geom.*) the versed sine of an arc; a genus of small transparent pelagic worms; a northern constellation. **sagittal,** *a.* pertaining to or resembling an arrow; of or pertaining to the join between the two parietal bones forming the sides and top of the skull; in or parallel to the mid-plane of the body. **Sagittarius**, see separate entry. **sagittary**, *n.* a centaur; †Sagittarius; (*Shak.*) perh. the arsenal at Venice. †*a.* pertaining to arrows. **sagittate**, *a.* esp. of a leaf, shaped like an arrow-head. **sagittiferous**, *a.* **sagittilingual**, *a.* having an arrow-like tongue. [L, arrow]

Sagittarius, *n.* zodiac constellation representing a centaur aiming a bow and arrow at neighbouring Scorpius. The Sun passes through Sagittarius from mid-Dec. to mid-Jan., including the winter solstice, when it is farthest south of the equator. The constellation contains many nebulae and globular clusters, and open star clusters. The centre of the Galaxy is marked by the radio source Sagittarius A. In astrology, the dates for Sagittarius are between about 22 Nov. and 21 Dec. (see PRECESSION).

sago, *n.* (*pl.* **-gos**) a starchy substance obtained from the soft inner portion of the trunk of several palms or cycads and used as food. **sago-palm,** *n.* [Malay *sāgu*]

saguaro, , *n.* (*pl.* **-ros**) a large Central American cactus, *Carnegeia gigantea,* with edible fruit. [Mex. Sp.]

sagum, *n.* (*pl.* **-ga**) the military cloak worn by ancient Roman soldiers. [L]

sagy SAGE¹.

Sahara, *n.* the largest desert in the world, occupying 5,500,000 sq km/2,123,000 sq miles of N Africa from the Atlantic to the Nile, covering W Egypt, part of W Sudan, large parts of Mauritania, Mali, Niger, and Chad, and southern parts of Morocco, Algeria, Tunisia, and Libya. Small areas in Algeria and Tunisia are below sea level, but it is mainly a plateau with a central mountain system, including the Ahaggar Mountains in Algeria, the Aïr Massif in Niger and the Tibesti Massif in Chad, of which the highest peak is Emi Koussi 3415 m/11,208 ft. The area of the Sahara has expanded by 650,000 sq km/251,000 sq miles in the last half century, but reafforestation is being attempted in certain areas.

sahib, *n.* the title used in colonial India in addressing a European man or a man of rank. [Hind. from Arab. *sāhib,* friend, companion]

sahlite, *n.* a green variety of pyroxene. [from *Sahla,* in Sweden]

sai, *n.* a S American monkey, *Cimia capucina.* [Tupi-Guarani *çahy*]

saic, *n.* a Levantine sailing-vessel. [F *saïque,* Turk. *shāīqā*]

said, *past, p.p.* SAY¹.

saiga, *n.* an antelope, *Saiga tartarica,* of the steppes of E Europe and W Asia. [Rus.]

Saigon HO CHI MINH CITY.

Saigon, Battle of, during the Vietnam War, battle from 29 Jan.–23 Feb. 1968, when 5000 Vietcong were expelled by South Vietnamese and US forces. The city was finally taken by North Vietnamese forces on 30 Apr. 1975, after South Vietnamese withdrawal from the central highlands.

sail, *n.* a piece of canvas or other fabric spread on rigging to catch the wind, and cause a ship or boat to move in the water; some or all of a ship's sails; a ship or vessel with sails; a specified number of ships in a squadron etc.; an excursion by sail or (*loosely*) by water; anything like a sail in form or function; the arm of a windmill; the dorsal fin of some fish; a wing. *v.i.* to move or be driven forward by the action of the wind upon sails; to be conveyed in a vessel by water; to set sail; to handle or make journeys in a vessel equipped with sails as a sport or hobby; to pass gently (along), to float (as a bird), to glide; to go along in a stately manner. *v.t.* to pass over in a ship, to navigate; to perform by sailing; to manage the navigation of (a ship); to cause to sail, to set afloat. **full sail,** with all sails set and a fair wind. **to make sail,** to set sail; to extend an additional quantity of sail. **to sail close to the wind** WIND¹. **to sail into,** to attack vigorously. **to set sail,** to begin a voyage. **to shorten sail,** to reduce the amount of sail spread. **to strike sail,** to lower sails suddenly; to give way, to submit. **under sail,** with sails spread. **sail-arm,** *n.* an arm of a windmill. **sailboard,** *n.* a moulded board with a single mast and sail, used in windsurfing. **sailboarding,** *n.* **sailcloth,** *n.* canvas etc. for making sails; a kind of dress-material. **sail-fish,** *n.* a fish with a large dorsal fin, as the basking shark. **sail-loft,** *n.* a large apartment where sails are cut out and made. **sailplane,** *n.* a glider that rises in an upward air current. **sailplane,** *v.i.* **sail-room,** *n.* an apartment on board ship where spare sails are stowed. **sail-yard,** *n.* a horizontal spar on which sails are extended. †**sailable,** *a.* **sailer,** *n.* a ship (with reference to her power or manner of sailing). **sailing,** *n.* **sailing-boat, -ship,** *n.* a boat or ship with sails. **sailing-master,** *n.* an officer whose duty it is to navigate a yacht etc. **sailless,** *a.* [OE *segel, segl* (cp. Dut. *zeil,* G *Segel,* Icel. *segl*)]

sailor, *n.* a seaman, a mariner, esp. one of the crew as distinguished from an officer. **good, bad sailor,** *n.* one who is not, or who is, liable to be seasick. **sailor-hat,** *n.* a flat-crowned narrow-brimmed straw hat worn by women, or one with a turned-up brim for children. **sailor-man,** *n.* (*coll.*) a seaman. **sailor's-knot,** *n.* a kind of reef-knot used in tying a neck-tie. **sailor-like, sailorly,** *a.* **sailoring,** *n.* **sailorless,** *a.*

†**sain¹,** *v.t.* to make the sign of the cross on; to bless, to guard from evil by divine or supernatural power. [OE *segnian,* L *signāre,* to SIGN]

†**sain²,** *p.p.* SAY¹.

sainfoin, *n.* a leguminous herb, *Onobrychis sativa,* resembling clover, grown for fodder. [F *sainfoin,* L *sānum,* SANE, *foenum,* hay]

saint, *n.* a person eminent for piety and virtue, a holy person; one of the blessed in heaven; one canonized or recognized by the Church as pre-eminently holy and deserving of veneration; (*pl.*) the name used by the Mormons and members of some other sects in speaking of themselves. *v.t.* to canonize; to regard or address as a saint. *v.i.* to act as a saint. **cross of St Anthony, St Andrew's cross, St George's cross** CROSS. **Saint Andrews, Saint Bernard (dog), Saint Elmo's fire** etc. see under ST. **saint's-bell,** *n.* the sanctus-bell. **saint's day,** *n.* a day dedicated to the commemoration of a particular saint, esp. the patron saint of a church, school etc. **saintdom, sainthood**, *n.* **sainted,** *a.* canonized; gone to heaven; holy, pious. **sainting,** *n.* **saint-like, saintly,** *a.* **saintliness,** *n.* **saintship,** *n.* [OF, from L *sanctus,* p.p. of *sancīre,* to make holy, rel. to *sacer,* SACRED]

Sainte-Beuve, *n.* **Charles Augustin** (1804–69), French critic. He contributed to the *Revue des deux mondes/Review of the Two Worlds* from 1831. His articles on French literature appeared as *Causeries du lundi/Monday Chats* (1851–62), and his *Port Royal* (1840–59) is a study of Jansenism.

Saint-Exupéry, *n.* **Antoine de** (1900–44), French author, who wrote the autobiographical *Vol de nuit/Night Flight* (1931) and *Terre des hommes/Wind, Sand, and Stars* (1939). His *Le petit prince/The Little Prince* (1943), a children's book, is also an adult allegory.

Saint-Gaudens, *n.* **Augustus** (1848–1907), US sculptor born in Ireland. His monuments include the granite and bronze *Adams memorial* (1891; Rock Creek Cemetery, Washington DC); he also sculpted portraits.

Saint-Just, *n.* **Louis Antoine Léon Florelle de** (1767–1794), French revolutionary. A close associate of Robespierre, he became a member of the Committee of Public Safety of 1793, and was guillotined.

Saint-Laurent, *n.* **Yves (Henri Donat Mathieu)** (1936–), French couturier, partner to Dior from 1954 and his successor in 1957. He opened his own fashion house in 1962.

Saint-Saëns, *n.* **(Charles) Camille** (1835–1921), French composer, pianist and organist. Among his many lyrical Romantic pieces are concertos, the symphonic poem *Danse macabre* (1875), the opera *Samson et Dalila* (1877), and the orchestral *Carnaval des animaux/Carnival of the Animals* (1886).

Saint-Simon[1], *n.* **Claude Henri, Comte de** (1760–1825), French socialist, who fought in the American War of Independence and was imprisoned during the French Revolution. He advocated an atheist society ruled by technicians and industrialists in *Du Système industrielle/The Industrial System* (1821).

Saint-Simon[2], *n.* **Louis de Rouvroy, Duc de** (1675–1755), French soldier, courtier, and politician, whose *Mémoires* (1691–1723) are unrivalled as a description of the French court.

sair, etc. (*Sc.*) SERVE, SORE.

†**saith,** *3rd sing.* SAY[1].

saithe, *n.* the coal-fish. [Sc., from Icel. *seithr,* cp. Gael. *saigh*]

sajou, *n.* a small S American monkey, one of the sapajous or the capuchin monkeys. [F, also *sajouassu,* Tupi-Guarani *sauiassu*]

sake[1], *n.* end, purpose; desire of obtaining; account, reason, cause. **for God's sake,** a solemn adjuration. **for old sake's** or **time's sake,** in memory of days gone by. **for the sake of, for someone's** or **something's sake,** because of, out of consideration for. [OE *sacu,* SAC[1]]

sake[2], **saké, saki,** *n.* a fermented liquor made from rice. [Jap.]

saker, *n.* a large falcon used in hawking, esp. the female; †a small piece of artillery. **sakeret,** *n.* the male of the saker, which is smaller than the female. [F *sacre,* Sp. and Port. *sacro,* Arab. *çaqr*]

Sakhalin, *n.* (Japanese **Karafuto**) island in the Pacific, north of Japan, which since 1947 forms with the Kurils a region of the USSR. **area** 74,000 sq km/28,564 sq miles. **capital** Yuzhno-Sakhalinsk (Japanese *Toyohara*). **physical** there are two parallel mountain ranges, rising to over 1525 m/5000 ft, which extend throughout its length, 965 km/600 miles. **population** (1981) 650,000, including aboriginal Ainu and Gilyaks. **products** dairy farming, leguminous crops, oats, barley, and sugar beet; in the milder south, there is also timber, rice, wheat, fish, and some oil and coal.

Sakharov, *n.* **Andrei Dmitrievich** (1921–89), Soviet physicist, known both as the 'father of the Soviet H-bomb' and as an outspoken human-rights campaigner. Nobel Peace Prize (1975). He was elected to the Congress of the USSR People's Deputies (CUPD) in 1989, where he emerged as leader of its radical reform grouping.

Saki, *n.* pen name of H(ugh) H(ector) Munro (1870–1916), Burmese-born British writer of ingeniously witty and bizarre short stories, often with surprise endings. He also wrote two novels *The Unbearable Bassington* (1912) and *When William Came* (1913).

saki[1], *n.* any monkey of the S American genera *Pithecia* or *Brachiurus*. [F, prob. from Tupi-Guarani *çahy,* SAI]

saki[2], SAKE[2].

sakieh, *n.* an apparatus used in Egypt for raising water, consisting of a vertical wheel or wheel and chain carrying pots or buckets. [Arab. *sāqiyah,* fem. pres.p. of *saqā,* to irrigate]

Sakti, *n.* the female principle in Hinduism.

Śākyamuni, *n.* the historical Buddha, called Shaka in Japan (because Gautama was of the Śakya clan) see BUDDHA.

sal[1], *n.* (*Chem., Pharm.*) salt (used only with qualifying word). **sal alembroth,** *n.* a compound of corrosive sublimate of mercury and sal-ammoniac. **sal-ammoniac,** *n.* ammonium chloride. †**sal-gem,** *n.* rock salt. **sal-prunella,** *n.* nitrate of potash fused and cast into cakes or balls. **sal-seignette,** *n.* rochelle salt. **sal-soda,** *n.* impure carbonate of soda, washing soda. **sal volatile,** *n.* an aromatic solution of ammonium carbonate. [L]

sal[2], *n.* a large Indian timber tree. [Hind.]

salaam, *n.* a ceremonious salutation or obeisance in Eastern countries. *v.i.* to make a salaam. [Arab. *salam*]

salable SALE.

salacious, *a.* lustful, lecherous; arousing lust, erotic, lewd. **salaciously,** *adv.* **salaciousness, salacity,** *n.* [L *salax -ācis,* cogn. with *salīre,* to leap]

salad, *n.* a dish of (mixed) raw vegetables; a cold dish of precooked vegetables, or of fruit, often mixed with a dressing; any herb or other vegetable suitable for eating raw. **salad-cream,** *n.* a kind of mayonnaise. **salad days,** *n.pl.* the time of youth and inexperience. **salad-dressing,** *n.* a mixture of oil, vinegar, mustard etc., for dressing salads. **salad-oil,** *n.* a vegetable oil suitable for use in salad-dressings. **salading,** *n.* herbs etc. for salads. [OF *salade,* OIt. *salata,* pop. L *salāta,* p.p. of *salāre,* to salt, from SAL[1]]

Saladin, Sala-ud-din (1138–93), sultan of Egypt from 1175, in succession to the Atabeg of Mosul, on whose behalf he conquered Egypt (1164–74). He subsequently conquered Syria (1174–87), and precipitated the third Crusade by his recovery of Jerusalem from the Christians in 1187. Renowned for knightly courtesy, Saladin made peace with Richard I of England in 1192. He was a Kurd.

salal, *n.* an evergreen shrub, *Gaultheria shallon,* of California etc., bearing grape-like edible berries. [Chinook]

Salamanca, Battle of, the British commander Wellington's victory over the French army in the Peninsular War, on 22 July 1812.

salamander, *n.* a lizard-like animal anciently believed to be able to live in fire; a spirit or genie fabled to live in fire; anyone who can stand great heat, a soldier who is unperturbed under fire; any of various implements and utensils used in a heated state; an amphibian of the family *Urodela.* **salamandrian, salamandrine,** *a.* **salamandroid,** *n., a.* [F *salamandre,* L and Gr. *salamandra*]

salami, salame, *n.* (*pl.* **-mis, -mes**) a highly-seasoned Italian sausage. [It.]

Salamis, *n.* ancient city on the E coast of Cyprus, the capital under the early Ptolemies, until its harbour silted up about 200 BC, when it was succeeded by Paphos in the SW.

Salamis, Battle of, naval battle off the coast of the island of Salamis in which the Greeks defeated the Persians 480 BC.

salangane, *n.* a Chinese swift that builds edible nests. [F, from Luzon *salamga*]

Salang Highway, *n.* the main N–S route between Kabul, capital of Afghanistan, and the Soviet frontier; length 422 km/264 miles. The high-altitude Salang Pass and Salang Tunnel cross a natural break in the Hindu Kush mountains about 100 km/60 miles N of Kabul. This supply route was a major target of the Mujaheddin resistance fighters during the Soviet occupation of Aghanistan.

salary, *n.* fixed pay given periodically, usu. monthly, for work not of a manual or mechanical kind. *v.t.* to pay a salary to. **salaried,** *a.* [A-F *salarie* (F *salaire*), L *salārium,* orig. salt-money given to soldiers, from SAL[1]]

Salazar, *n.* **Antonio de Oliveira** (1889–1970), Portuguese prime minister (1932–68), exercising a virtual dictatorship. A corporative constitution on the Italian model was introduced in 1933, and until 1945 Salazar's National Union, founded in 1930, remained the only legal party. Salazar was also foreign minister (1936–47), and during World War II maintained Portuguese neutrality.

salchow, *n.* an ice-skating jump with turns in the air. [Ulrich *Salchow,* 1877–1949, Swed. skater]

sale, *n.* the act of selling; the exchange of a commodity for money or other equivalent; an event at which goods are sold; an auction; a disposal of a shop's remaining goods at reduced prices; demand, market; (*pl.*) quantity of goods sold; (*pl.*) the activities involved in selling goods collectively. **bill of sale** BILL3. **sale of work,** a sale of home-made goods for charitable purposes. **sale or return,** an arrangement by which a retailer may return unsold goods to the wholesaler. **saleroom,** *n.* a room in which goods are sold, an auction-room. **sales-clerk,** *n.* (*chiefly N Am.*) a shop assistant. **salesman, -woman, -person,** *n.* a person employed to sell goods, esp. in a shop; a sales representative. **salesmanship,** *n.* the art of selling, skill in persuading prospective purchasers. **sales representative,** *n.* a person employed to secure orders for a company's products, usu. in an assigned geographical area. **sales resistance,** *n.* opposition of a prospective customer to purchasing a product. **sales talk,** *n.* persuasive or attractive arguments to influence a possible purchaser. **sale-work,** *n.* work made for sale; work done in a perfunctory way. **saleable, salable,** *a.* **saleableness, saleability,** *n.* [OE *sala,* prob. from *Icel. sala,* cogn. with SELL1]

salep, *n.* a farinaceous meal made from the dried roots of *Orchis mascula* and other orchidaceous plants. [F and Turk., from Arab. *tha' leb*]

saleratus, *n.* (*N Am.*) an impure bicarbonate of potash or soda, much used as baking powder. [mod. L *sal aerātus,* aerated salt]

Salian1, *a.* pertaining to the Salii or priests of Mars of ancient Rome. [L *Salii,* from *salīre,* to leap, -AN]

Salian2, *a.* of or pertaining to a Frankish tribe on the lower Rhine to which the ancestors of the Merovingians belonged. *n.* one of this tribe. **Salic,** *a.* Salian. **Salic law** or **code,** *n.* a Frankish law-book written in Latin extant during the Merovingian and Carolingian periods. **Salic law, Salique law,** see separate entry. [late L *Salii,* the tribe, -AN]

salicet, salicional, *n.* organ-stops with notes like those of a willow-pipe. **salicetum,** *n.* (*pl.* **-tums, -ta**) a garden or arboretum of willows. [as foll.]

salicin, *n.* a bitter crystalline compound obtained from the bark of willows and poplars, used medicinally. **salicyl,** *n.* the hypothetical radical of salicylic acid. **salicylate,** *n.* a salt of salicylic acid. *v.t.* to salicylize. **salicylic,** *a.* derived from the willow; belonging to a series of benzene derivatives of salicin; derived from salicylic acid. **salicylic acid,** *n.* an acid whose derivatives, including aspirin, are used to relieve pain and to treat rheumatism. **silicylize, -ise,** *v.t.* to impregnate with salicylic acid. **salicylous,** *a.* [F *salicine* (L *salix -icis,* willow)]

Salic law, *n.* a law adopted in the Middle Ages by several European royal houses, excluding women from succession to the throne. In Sweden 1980 such a provision was abrogated to allow Princess Victoria to become crown princess. The name derives mistakenly from the Salian or northern division of the Franks who were supposed to have practised it.

salient, *a.* leaping, jumping, springing; pointing or projecting outwards; shooting out (of water); conspicuous, prominent, noticeable; (*Her.*) represented in a leaping posture. *n.* a salient angle; a portion of defensive works or of a line of defence projecting towards the enemy. **salience, -ency,** *n.* **saliently,** *adv.* [L *saliens -ntem,* pres.p. of *salīre,* to leap]

Salientia, *n.* an order of Amphibia, including frogs and toads. **salientian,** *n., a.* (a member) of the Salientia.

Salieri, *n.* **Antonio** (1750–1825), Italian composer. He taught Beethoven, Schubert, and Liszt, and was the musical rival of Mozart at the Emperor's court in Vienna.

saliferous, *a.* of rock strata, bearing or producing salt. **saliferous system,** *n.* the Triassic rocks, from the deposits of salt. †**salify,** *v.t., v.i.* to form (into) a salt. **salifiable,** *a.* **salification,** *n.* [L *sal salis,* SAL1, -FEROUS]

Salinas de Gortiari, *n.* **Carlos** (1948–), Mexican politician, president from 1988.

saline, *a.* consisting of or having the characteristics of salt; containing or impregnated with salt or salts. *n.* a salina; a saline substance, esp. a purgative; a saline solution, esp. with the same concentration as body fluids. **salina,** *n.* a salt-marsh, -lake, -spring etc.; salt-works. **saliniferous,** SALIFEROUS. **salinity, salineness,** *n.* **salinometer,** *n.* an instrument for ascertaining the density of brine in the boilers of marine steam-engines. **salinoterrene,** *a.* consisting of a salt and earth. †**salinous,** *a.* [SAL1, -INE]

Salinger, *n.* **J(erome) D(avid)** (1919–), US writer of the novel of adolescence *The Catcher in the Rye* (1951) and stories of a Jewish family, including *Franny and Zooey* (1961).

Salique SALIC under SALIAN2.

Salisbury1 HARARE.

Salisbury2 ROBERT CECIL.

Salisbury3, *n.* **Robert Arthur Talbot Gascoyne-Cecil, 3rd Marquess of Salisbury** (1830–1903), British Conservative politician. He entered the Commons in 1853 and succeeded to his title in 1868. As foreign secretary (1878–80), he took part in the Congress of Berlin, and as prime minister (1885–86, 1886–92, and 1895–1902) gave his main attention to foreign policy, remaining also as foreign secretary for most of this time.

saliva, *n.* an odourless, colourless, somewhat viscid liquid secreted by glands into the mouth where it lubricates ingested food, spittle. †**salival,** *a.* **salivant,** *n., a.* (a medicine) exciting salivation. **salivary,** *a.* of or producing saliva. **salivate,** *v.t.* to excite an unusual secretion and discharge of saliva in, as by the use of mercury. *v.i.* to secrete or discharge saliva in excess. **salivation,** *n.* †**salivous,** *a.* [L]

Salix, *n.* a genus of trees containing the willow. [L]

Salk, *n.* **Jonas Edward** (1914–), US physician and microbiologist. In 1954, he developed the original vaccine which led to virtual eradication of polio in developed countries. He was director of the Salk Institute for Biological Studies, University of California, San Diego from 1963–75. **Salk vaccine,** *n.* a vaccine against poliomyelitis.

sallee, *n.* name given to several kinds of acacia; a species of eucalyptus. [Austral. Abor.]

Sallee-man, Sallee rover, *n.* a Moorish pirate or pirate-ship. [*Sallee,* port in Morocco]

sallenders, *n. sing.* a dry scabby inflammation in the hock-joint of a horse's hind-leg. [F *solandre,* etym. doubtful]

sallet, *n.* a light, hemispherical, crestless helmet with the back curving away, worn by 15th-cent. foot-soldiers. [earlier *salade,* F *salade,* It. *celata,* prob. from L *caelāta,* fem. p.p. of *caelāre,* to engrave or chase (a helmet)]

Sallinen, *n.* **Tyko** (1879–1955), Finnish expressionist painter. Absorbing Fauve influences on visits to France in 1909 and 1914, he created visionary works relating partly to his childhood experiences of religion. He also painted Finnish landscape and peasant life.

sallow1, *n.* a willow-tree, esp. one of the low shrubby varieties; a willow-shoot, an osier; any of various moths feeding on willows. **sallowy,** *a.* [OE *sealh* (cp. Icel. *selja,* OHG *salaha,* also L *salix,* Gr. *helikē*)]

sallow2, *a.* of a sickly-yellowish or pale-brown colour. *v.t.* to make sallow. **sallowish,** *a.* **sallowness,** *n.* [OE *salu* (cp. MDut. *salu,* Icel. *sölr,* OHG *salo*)]

Sallust, *n.* **Gaius Sallustius Crispus** (86–*c.* 34 BC), Roman historian, a supporter of Julius Caesar. He wrote accounts of Catiline's conspiracy and the Jugurthine War in an epigrammatic style.

sally[1], *n.* a sudden rushing out or sortie of troops from a besieged place against besiegers; an issuing forth, an excursion; a sudden or brief outbreak of spirits etc., an outburst; a flight of fancy or wit, a bantering remark etc.; †an act of levity, an escapade. *v.i.* of troops, to rush out suddenly; to go (out or forth) on a journey, excursion etc.; †to leap or come out suddenly. **sally-port,** *n.* a postern or passage for making sallies from. [F *saillie,* from *saillir,* to rush out, L *salīre,* to leap]

sally[2], *n.* the part of a bell-ringer's rope covered with wool for holding; the first movement of a bell when set for ringing. **sally-hole,** *n.* the hole through which the bell-rope is passed. [perh. from prec.]

Sally-lunn, *n.* a sweet tea-cake eaten hot and buttered. [*Sally Lunn,* who hawked them at Bath, *c.* 1800]

salmagundi, *n.* a dish of chopped meat, anchovies, eggs, oil, vinegar etc.; a multifarious mixture, a medley, a miscellany. [F *salmagondis,* etym. doubtful]

salmi, salmis, *n.* (*pl.* **salmis**) a ragout, esp. of game-birds stewed with wine. [F, prob. from SALMAGUNDI]

salmiac, *n.* native sal-ammoniac.

salmis SALMI.

salmon, *n.* (*pl.* in general **salmon;** in particular **salmons**) a larger silvery, pink-fleshed fish of the genus *Salmo,* esp. *S. salar,* an anadromous fish, fished both for food and sport; extended to various fish resembling the salmon. *a.* salmon-coloured. **salmon-colour,** *n.* the colour of salmon flesh, orangey-pink. **salmon-coloured,** *a.* **salmon-ladder, -leap, -pass, -stair, -weir,** *n.* a series of steps, zigzags, or other contrivances to enable salmon to get past a dam or waterfall. **salmon-parr** PARR. **salmon-peal,** *n.* a salmon weighing less than 2 lb (0·9 kg). **salmon-trout,** *n.* an anadromous fish, *Salmo trutta,* resembling the salmon but smaller. †**salmonet**, *n.* a samlet. **salmonoid**, *n., a.* [ME and A-F *saumoun* (OF and F *saumon*), L *salmōnem,* nom. *-mo*]

Salmonella, *n.* a very varied group of bacteria. They can be divided into three broad groups. One of these causes typhoid and paratyphoid fevers, while a second group causes Salmonella food poisoning, which is characterized by stomach pains, vomiting, diarrhoea, and headache. It can be fatal in elderly people, but others recover in a few days without antibiotics. Most cases are caused by contaminated animal products, especially poultry meat. **salmonellosis**, *n.* infection with bacteria of the genus *Salmonella.*

salmonet SALMON.

Salome, *n.* (1st century AD), in the New Testament, granddaughter of the king of Judea, Herod the Great. Rewarded for her skill in dancing, she requested the head of John the Baptist from her stepfather Herod Antipas.

salon, *n.* a reception-room, esp. in a great house in France; a periodical reunion of eminent people in the house of someone socially fashionable, esp. a lady; (*pl.*) fashionable circles; a hall for exhibiting paintings etc.; the business premises of a hairdresser, beautician etc. **the Salon,** an annual exhibition of paintings etc., esp. that held at Paris. [F, from It. *salone*]

saloon, *n.* a large room or hall, esp. one suitable for social receptions, public entertainments etc., or used for a specified purpose; a large room for passengers on board ship; a closed motor-car with no internal partitions; a saloon-carriage; (*esp. N Am.*) a drinking-bar, a public-house. **saloon bar,** *n.* the more reserved bar in a public-house. **saloon-carriage,** *n.* a large railway-carriage without compartments, often arranged as a drawing-room. **saloon-pistol, -rifle,** *n.* firearms suitable for short-range practice in a shooting saloon. [from prec.]

saloop, *n.* an infusion of sassafras etc., formerly used with milk and sugar as a beverage instead of tea or coffee; salep. [var. of SALEP]

salopettes, *n.pl.* thick usu. quilted trousers with shoulder straps, used for skiing. [F]

Salopian, *n.* a native or inhabitant of Shropshire. *a.* pertaining to Shropshire. [*Salop,* Shropshire, from A-F *Sloppesberie,* corr. of OE *Scrobbesbyrig,* Shrewsbury]

salpicon, *n.* a stuffing or thick sauce made with chopped meat and vegetables. [F and Sp., from *salpicar,* to pickle]

salpiglossis, *n.* a genus of S American herbaceous plants with handsome flowers. [Gr. *salpinx -ngos,* trumpet, *glōssa,* tongue]

salpinx, *n.* (*pl.* **salpinges,**) the Eustachian tube; the Fallopian tube. **salpingitis**, *n.* inflammation of the Eustachian or the Fallopian tubes. **salpingitic**, *a.* [Gr. *salpinx -ngos,* trumpet]

salsa, *n.* a Puerto Rican dance or the music for this.

salse, *n.* a mud-volcano. [F, from It. *salsa,* orig. a volcano at Salsuolo, near Modena]

salsify, *n.* a composite plant, *Tragopogon porrifolius,* the long whitish root of which is eaten; this root. [F *salsifis,* etym. doubtful]

salsilla, *n.* the tubers of *Bomarea edulis* and *B. salsilla,* eaten in the W Indies. [Sp., dim. of *salsa,* SAUCE]

Salsola, *n.* a genus of herbs and shrubby plants comprising the saltworts. **salsolaceous**, *a.* [It., dim. of *salso,* SALT, a.]

SALT, (*abbr.*) Strategic Arms Limitation Talks.

salt, *n.* chloride of sodium, used for seasoning and preserving food, obtained from sea-water or brine by evaporation or in crystalline form in beds of various geological age; that which gives flavour; relish, piquancy, pungency, wit, repartee, brilliance in talk etc.; a salt-cellar; (*coll.*) a sailor; a salt-marsh or salting; a compound formed by the union of basic and acid radicals, an acid the hydrogen of which is wholly or partially replaced by a metal; (*pl.*) smelling salts; (*pl.*) any of various mineral salts used as a medicine, esp. as a purgative. *a.* impregnated or flavoured with or tasting of salt, saline; cured with salt; living or growing in salt water; of wit etc., pungent; of grief, bitter; indecent, salacious. *v.t.* to sprinkle or cover with salt; to season with salt; to cure or preserve with salt; to make salt; (*Phot.*) to treat (paper etc.) with a solution of a salt; to add liveliness to (a story, etc.); to misrepresent as valuable by the addition of material, esp. to add pieces of ore etc. to (a mine) so as to represent it as profitable to work. *v.i.* to deposit salt from a saline substance. **above the salt,** at the higher part of a table, above the salt-cellar. **below the salt,** among the less distinguished company. **in salt,** sprinkled with salt or steeped in brine for curing. **(not) worth one's salt,** (not) worth keeping, (not) useful. **salt of lemon,** acid oxalate of potassium. **salt of the earth,** one of the utmost worth. **to eat one's salt,** to accept one's hospitality. **to salt an account** etc., to put down excessively high prices. **to salt away,** to save or hoard (money etc.). **with a grain or pinch of salt,** with doubt or reserve. **salt bath,** *n.* a bath of molten salts used in the hardening or tempering of steel. **salt-box,** *n.* a wooden box for holding salt; (*sl.*) a prison-cell. **salt-bush,** *n.* a shrubby plant of the goosefoot family on which stock feed. **salt-cake,** *n.* crude sulphate of soda, prepared for the use of glass- and soap-makers. **salt-cat,** *n.* a mixture of salt, gravel, cummin seed and stale urine given to pigeons. **salt flat,** *n.* a salt-covered flat area formed by the total evaporation of a body of water. **salt-glaze,** *n.* a glaze produced on pottery by putting salt into the kiln after firing. †**salt-horse, salt-junk,** *n.* dry salt beef for use at sea. **salt-lake,** *n.* an inland body of salt water. **salt-lick,** *n.* a place to which cattle go to lick ground impregnated with salt. **salt-marsh,** *n.* land liable to be overflowed by the sea, esp. used for pasturage or for collecting salt. **salt-mine,** *n.* a mine for rock-salt. **salt-pan,** *n.* a shallow depression in the land in which salt water evaporates to leave salt; a vessel in which brine is evaporated at a salt-works. **salt-pit,** *n.* a pit where salt is obtained. **salt-rheum,** *n.* †a running cold; (*N Am.*) eczema. **salt-water,** *a.* living in or pertaining to salt water, esp. the sea. **salt-works,** *n.* a factory for making salt. **salt-wort,** *n.* any of various plants of the genus *Salsola* or *Salicornia,* growing in salt-marshes and on seashores. **salter,** *n.* one who salts (fish etc.); one who makes or sells salt; a worker at a salt-works. **saltern**, *n.* a salt manufactory; a series of pools for evaporating sea-water. **salting,** *n.* the application of salt for preservation etc.; (*pl.*) salt-lands, a salt-marsh. **saltish,** *a.* **saltishly,** *adv.* **saltishness,** *n.* **saltless,** *a.* **saltness,** *n.* **salty,** *a.* of or containing salt; tasting (strongly) of salt; of the sea or life at sea; witty; earthy, coarse. **saltily,** *adv.* **saltiness,** *n.* [OE *sealt* (cp. Dut. *zout* G *Salz,* Icel., Dan. and Swed. *salt,* also L *sal,* Gr. *halas*)]

saltant, *a.* (*Her.*) salient (used of figures of small animals); leaping. [L *saltans -ntem,* pres.p. of *saltāre,* freq. of *salīre,* to leap]

saltarello, *n.* an Italian or Spanish dance characterized by sudden skips; the music for such a dance. [It., from *saltare,* as prec.]

saltation, *n.* a leaping or bounding; an abrupt transition or variation in the form of an organism. **saltatorial, saltatorian, saltatorious, saltatory,** *a.* [L *saltātio,* from *saltāre,* see SALTANT]

salt-cellar, *n.* a vessel for holding salt at table. [A-F *saler,* OF *saliere* (*salière*), salt-cellar, assim. to CELLAR]

saltigrade, *a.* formed for leaping. *n.* a spider with legs adapted for leaping on its prey. [L *saltus,* leap, from *saltāre,* see SALTANT, *-gradus,* walking]

†**saltimbanco,** *n.* a mountebank, a quack. [It. (*saltare,* as prec., BANCO[2])]

saltire, *n.* (*Her.*) an ordinary in the form of a St Andrew's cross or the letter X. **saltire-wise,** *adv.* [ME *sawtire,* OF *sauteoir, -toir,* a stile, L *saltātōrium,* SALTATORY]

Salt Lake City, capital of Utah, US, on the river Jordan, 18 km/11 miles SE of the Great Salt Lake; population (1982) 164,000. Founded in 1847, it is the headquarters of the Mormon Church. Mining, construction, and other industries are being replaced by high technology.

saltpetre, (*esp. N Am.*) **saltpeter,** *n.* potassium nitrate. **Chile saltpetre,** impure sodium nitrate. **saltpetrous,** *a.* [ME and OF *salpetre,* med. L *salpetra* (L *sal petrae,* salt of the rock), assim. to SALT]

saltus, *n.* a sudden starting aside, breach of continuity or jumping to a conclusion. [L, leap, cp. SALTIGRADE]

salubrious, *a.* of climate etc., promoting health, wholesome; spiritually wholesome, respectable. **salubriously,** *adv.* **salubriousness, salubrity,** *n.* [L *salūbris,* -OUS]

†**salue,** SALUTE.

Saluki, *n.* a Persian greyhound. [Arab.]

salutary, *a.* promoting good effects, beneficial, corrective, profitable; salubrious, wholesome. **salutarily,** *adv.* **salutariness,** *n.* [L *salūtāris, from salus, -ūtis,* health]

salute, *v.t.* to greet with a gesture or words of welcome, respect or recognition; to accost or welcome (as with a bow, kiss, oath, volley etc.); to honour by the discharge of ordnance etc.; to show respect to (a military superior) by a salute; to praise, acknowledge; to meet (the eye etc.); †to hail (as king etc.); †to kiss, esp. at meeting or parting. *v.i.* to perform a salute. *n.* gesture of welcome, homage, recognition etc., a salutation; a prescribed method of doing honour or paying a compliment or respect, as discharge of ordnance, dipping colours, presenting arms etc.; the attitude taken by a soldier, sailor etc. in giving a salute; (*Fencing*) a conventional series of movements performed before engaging; †a kiss. **salutation,** *n.* the act of saluting; that which is said or done in the act of greeting; words of greeting or communicating good wishes or courteous inquiries; a salute. **salutational,** *a.* **salutatorian,** *n.* a student at a N American college who pronounces the salutatory. **salutatory,** *a.* pertaining to or of the nature of a salutation; pertaining to a salutatory. *n.* an oration delivered by a graduating student at the degree-giving ceremony in N American colleges; †an audience-chamber, esp. in a church or monastery. **salutatorily,** *adv.* **saluter,** *n.* [L *salūtāre,* as prec., to wish health to]

salvable, *a.* capable of being saved. **salvableness, salvability,** *n.* **salvably,** *adv.* [L *salvāre,* to SAVE, -ABLE]

Salvador, *n.* port and naval base in Bahia state, NE Brazil, on the inner side of a peninsula separating Todos Santos Bay from the Atlantic; population (1985) 2,126,000. Products include cocoa, tobacco, and sugar. Founded in 1510, it was the capital of Brazil from 1549–1763.

Salvador, El EL SALVADOR.

salvage, *n.* the act of saving a ship, goods etc. from shipwreck, capture, fire etc.; compensation allowed for such saving; property so saved; the saving and recycling of waste or scrap material; material saved for re-use. *v.t.* to save or recover from wreck, capture, fire etc.; to save from ruin or destruction. **salvage-money,** *n.* **salvageable,** *a.* **salvager,** *n.* [OF, from *salver* (F *sauver*), to SAVE]

Salvarsan®, *n.* a compound formerly used for the treatment of syphilis and related bacterial diseases.

salvation, *n.* the act of saving from destruction; deliverance, preservation from danger, evil etc.; deliverance of the soul, or of believers from sin and its consequences; that which delivers, preserves etc. **Salvation Army,** see separate entry. **Salvationism,** *n.* belief in, or the doctrine of, the salvation of the soul; the principles and practices of the Salvation Army. **Salvationist,** *n.* one who advocates Salvationism; a member of the Salvation Army. †**salvatory,** *a.* saving or tending to save or preserve. *n.* a repository, a safe. [ME and OF *sauvacion* (F *salvation*), L *salvātionem,* nom. *-tio,* from *salvāre,* to SAVE]

Salvation Army, *n.* a Christian evangelical, social-service, and social-reform organization, originating in 1865 in London, England, with the work of William Booth. Originally called the Christian Revival Association, it was renamed the East London Christian Mission in 1870 and from 1878 has been known as the Salvation Army, now a worldwide organization. It has military titles for its officials, is renowned for its brass bands, and its weekly journal is the *War Cry*.

salve[1], *n.* a healing ointment; anything that soothes or palliates. *v.t.* to dress or anoint with a salve; to soothe, to ease, to palliate, to make good. [OE *sealf* (cp. Dut. *zalf,* G *Salbe*)]

salve[2], *n.* a Roman Catholic antiphon beginning with the words *Salve Regina,* 'Hail, holy Queen', addressed to the Virgin; music for this. [L, hail, imper. of *salvēre,* to be well]

salve[3], *v.t.* to save from destruction; to salvage; to preserve unhurt. [back formation from SALVAGE]

salver, *n.* a tray, usu. of silver, brass, electro-plate etc., on which refreshments, visiting-cards etc. are presented. **salver-shaped,** *a.* [F *salve,* a tray on which things were presented to a king, from Sp. *salva,* tasting of food before serving, from *salvar,* L *salvāre,* to SAVE]

Salvia, *n.* a genus of labiate plants comprising the common sage and many cultivated species with brilliant flowers. [L, SAGE[1]]

salvo[1], *n.* (*pl.* **-voes, -vos**) a discharge of guns etc. as a salute; a volley of cheers etc.; a concentrated fire of artillery, release of missiles etc. [It. *salva,* salutation, prob. as SALVE[2]]

salvo[2], *n.* (*pl.* **-vos**) a saving clause, a proviso; a mental reservation, an evasion, an excuse; an expedient to save one's reputation etc. [L, abl. of *salvus,* SAFE]

sal volatile SAL[1].

salvor, *n.* a person or ship effecting salvage.

Salyut, *n.* a series of seven space stations launched by the USSR (1971–82). Salyut was cylindrical in shape, 15 m/50 ft long, and weighed 19 tonnes. It housed two or three cosmonauts at a time, for missions lasting up to eight months.

Salzburg[1], *n.* capital of the state of Salzburg, W Austria, on the river Salzach, in W Austria; population (1981) 139,400. The city is dominated by the Hohensalzburg fortress. It is the seat of an archbishopric founded by St Boniface about 700 and has a 17th-century cathedral. Industries include stock rearing, dairy farming, forestry, and tourism.

Salzburg[2], *n.* federal province of Austria. **area** 7200 sq km/2779 sq miles. **capital** Salzburg. **population** (1987) 462,000.

Salzedo, *n.* **Carlos** (1885–1961), French-born harpist and composer. He studied in Paris and moved to New York, where he later co-founded the International Composers' Guild. He did much to promote the harp as a concert instrument, and invented many unusual sounds.

SAM, (*abbr.*) surface-to-air missile.

sam, sammy, *v.t.* (*past, p.p.* **sammed sammied**) to dampen (skins), so as to temper them. [etym. doubtful]

Sam., (*abbr.*) Samuel.

samara, *n.* a one-seeded indehiscent dry fruit with wing-like extensions, produced by the sycamore, ash etc. [L]

Samaria, *n.* region of ancient Israel. The town of Samaria (modern Sebastiyeh) on the W bank of the river Jordan was the capital of Israel 10th–8th centuries BC, renamed Sebarte by Herod the Great. Extensive remains have been excavated.

Samaritan, *a.* pertaining to Samaria; applied to the archaic Hebrew characters in which the Samaritan Pentateuch, a recension of the Hebrew Pentateuch, was written. *n.* a native or inhabitant of Samaria; the language of Samaria; one adhering to the Samaritan religious system; a kind, charitable person, in allusion to the 'good Samaritan' of the parable (Luke x.30–37); a member of the Samaritans voluntary organization.

Samaritans, *n.pl.* a voluntary organization aiding those tempted to suicide or despair, established in 1953 in the UK. Groups of lay people, often consulting with psychiatrists, psychotherapists, and doctors, offer friendship and counselling to those using their emergency telephone numbers, day or night.

samarium, *n.* a silvery-grey metallic chemical element, at. no. 62; chem. symbol Sm, one of the rare-earth metals. [*samarskite,* mineral in which it was observed spectroscopically (Colonel von *Samarski,* 19th-cent. Rus. mine inspector)]

Samarkand, *n.* city in Uzbek Republic, USSR, capital of Samarkand region, near the river Zerafshan, 217 km/135 miles E of Bukhara; population (1987) 388,000. It was the capital of the empire of TAMERLANE, and was once an important city on the SILK ROAD.

Sama-Veda, *n.* the third of the four Vedas, mainly made up of extracts from hymns in the Rig-Veda. [Sansk.]

samba, *n.* a Brazilian dance; a ballroom dance in imitation of this; music for this.

sambar SAMBUR.

sambo, *n.* a person of three-quarters black African descent; (*offensive*) a black person. [Sp. *zambo*]

Sam Browne, *n.* a military officer's belt with a light strap over the right shoulder; a belt of similar design made from a fluorescent material and worn by motorcyclists, cyclists etc. [Sir *Samuel Browne,* 1824–1901]

sambuke, sambuca, *n.* an ancient musical stringed instrument of high-pitched tone. [L *sambuca,* Gr. *sambukē,* cogn. with Aramaic *sabbekā*]

sambur, sambar, *n.* a large deer or elk, *Cervus unicolor,* from the hill-country of India. [Hindi *sābar, sāmbar*]

same, *a.* identical; not other, not different; identical or similar in kind, quality, degree etc.; exactly alike; just mentioned, aforesaid; unchanged, unchanging; uniform, monotonous. *pron.* the same thing; the aforesaid. **all the same,** nevertheless; notwithstanding what is said, done, altered etc. **at the same time,** nevertheless, still. **sameness,** *n.* **samey**, *a.* (*coll.*) monotonous, unvaried. [Icel. *same,* a., or OE *same,* adv. (cp. OHG and Goth. *sama,* also Gr. *homos,* L *similis*), cogn. with Sansk. *sawa*]

Samian, *a.* pertaining to Samos. *n.* a native of Samos. **Samian earth,** *n.* a kind of bole or marl from Samos. **Samian ware,** *n.* red or black pottery made from this or similar earth. [L *Samius,* Gr. *Samios,* from *Samos,* isle in the Aegean]

samiel, *n.* the simoom. [Turk. *samyel,* from *sam,* Arab. *samm,* cp. SIMOOM]

samisen, *n.* a Japanese three-stringed guitar-like instrument played with a plectrum. [Jap., from Chin. *sanhsien* (*san,* three, *hsien,* string)]

samite, *n.* a rich mediaeval silk fabric with a warp, each thread of which was six strands. [OF *samit,* med. L *samitum, examitum,* Gr. *hexamiton* (*hex,* six, *mitos,* a thread)]

samizdat, *n.* the clandestine publishing of banned literature in the USSR. [Rus.]

samlet, *n.* a young salmon.

sammy SAM.

Samnite, *n.* one of an ancient Italian people eventually subjugated by the Romans. *a.* of or pertaining to the Samnites. [L *Samnītes*]

Samoa, *n.* volcanic island chain in the SW Pacific. It is divided into Western Samoa and American Samoa.

Samoa, American, *n.* group of islands 4200 km/2610 miles south of Hawaii, an unincorporated territory of the US. **area** 200 sq km/77 sq miles. **capital** Fagatogo on Tutuila. **population** (1981) 34,000. **exports** canned tuna, handicrafts. **language** Samoan and English. **religion** Christian.

Samoa, Western, *n.* Independent State of (*Samoa i Sisifo*), **area** 2830 sq km/1093 sq miles. **capital** Apia on Upolu. **physical** comprises islands of Savai'i and Upolu, with two smaller islands and islets; mountain ranges on the main islands. **population** (1989) 169,000; annual growth rate 1.1%. **exports** copra, bananas, cocoa; tourism is important. **language** English and Samoan (official). **religion** Christian.

Samoan, *n.* a native or inhabitant or the language of Samoa. *a.* pertaining to Samoa.

samosa, *n.* (*pl.* **samosas, samosa**) an Indian savoury of spiced meat or vegetables in a triangular pastry case. [Hind.]

samovar, *n.* a Russian tea-urn heated by burning charcoal in an inner tube. [Rus. *samovaru,* self-boiler, prob. from Tatar]

Samoyed, *n.* a member of a Mongolian people inhabiting middle Siberia; their language; a breed of white sledge-dog. **Samoyedic**, *a.* pertaining to such a people. *n.* their language. [Rus. *Samoyedu*]

samp, *n.* (*N Am.*) maize coarsely ground or made into porridge. [Algonquin *nasamp*]

sampan, *n.* a Chinese flat-bottomed river boat, frequently used for habitation. [Chin. (*san,* three, *pan,* board)]

samphire, *n.* a herb, *Crithmum maritimum,* growing on sea-cliffs, the aromatic leaves of which are pickled as a condiment; glasswort. [formerly *sampire,* F *herbe de St Pierre,* St Peter's herb]

sample, *n.* a part taken, offered or used as illustrating the whole, a specimen, an example, a pattern, a model. **sample-room,** *n.* a room where samples are shown; (*N Am. sl.*) a grog-shop. *v.t.* to take samples of, to test, to try; to have an experience of; to present samples of. **sampler,** *n.* one who or that which takes samples; a piece of embroidered work done as a specimen of skill. **sampling,** *n.* the act of sampling; the taking of extracts from existing popular songs and putting them together to form a new one. **samplery,** *n.* [orig. *essample,* var. of EXAMPLE]

samsoe, *n.* a firm-textured Danish cheese with a mild flavour. [the island of Samsø]

Samson, *n.* in the Old Testament or Hebrew Bible, a hero of Israel. He was renowned for exploits of strength against the Philistines, which ended when his mistress Delilah cut off his hair, as told in the Old Testament Book of Judges; a man of abnormal strength. **samson's post,** *n.* (*Naut.*) a pillar resting on the kelson and passing through the hold or between decks; an upright in whalers for fastening the harpoon-rope to. [L and Gr. *Sampsōn,* Heb. *Shimshōn*)]

Samsun, *n.* Black Sea port and capital of a province of the same name in N Turkey; situated at the mouth of the Murat river in a tobacco-growing area; site of the ancient city of Amisus; population(1985) 280,000.

Samuel, *n.* in the Old Testament or Hebrew Bible, the last of the judges who ruled the ancient Israelites before their adoption of a monarchy, and the first of the prophets; the two books bearing his name cover the story of Samuel and the reigns of kings Saul and David.

samurai, *n.* (*pl.* **samurai**) a member of the military caste under the Japanese feudal regime, or a military retainer; now, an army officer. [Jap.]

San, *n.* Hottentot name for hunter-gatherers of the Kalahari Desert. Found in Botswana, SW Africa and South Africa, they number approximately 50,000. Their languages belong to the Khoisan family.

San'a, *n.* capital of North Yemen, SW Arabia, 320 km/200 miles north of Aden; population (1986) 427,000. A walled city, with fine mosques and traditional architecture, it is rapidly being modernized.

San Andreas fault, a geological fault line stretching for 1125 km/700 miles in a NW–SE direction through the state of California, US.

San Antonio, *n.* city in S Texas, US; population (1980) 1,070,000. A commercial and financial centre, industries include aircraft maintenance, oil refining, and meat packing. Founded in 1718, it grew up round the site of the Alamo fort.

sanative, *a.* healing, tending to cure, curative. †**sanable,** *a.* †**sanability**, †**sanableness,** *n.* [med. L *sānātīvus,* from *sānāre,* to heal, from *sānus,* SANE]

sanatorium, (*esp. N Am.*) **sanitarium**, *n.* (*pl.* **-riums, -ria,**) an institution for the treatment of chronic diseases, especially pulmonary tuberculosis; a place to which people resort for the sake of their health; an institution for invalids, esp. convalescents; a sick room, esp. in a boarding school. **sanatory** , *a.*

sanbenito, *n.* a penitential garment painted with a red St Andrew's cross worn by heretics who recanted, or painted over with flames and figures of devils, worn at an auto-da-fé by persons condemned by the Inquisition. [Sp. (*San Benito,* St Benedict)]

sancho, *n.* a primitive W African musical instrument like a guitar. [Ashanti *osanku*]

sanctify, *v.t.* to make holy, to consecrate; to set apart or observe as holy; to purify from sin; to give a sacred character to, to sanction, to make inviolable; to render productive of holiness. **sanctification**, *n.* **sanctifier,** *n.* [ME *seintefie,* OF *saintifier* (F *sanctifier*), late L *sanctificāre* (*sanctus,* holy, *-ficāre, facere,* to make)]

sanctimony, *n.* affectation of piety, sanctimoniousness. **sanctimonious**, *a.* making a show of piety or saintliness. **sanctimoniously,** *adv.* **sanctimoniousness,** *n.* [OF *sanctimonie,* L *sanctimōnia,* from *sanctus,* holy]

sanction, *n.* the act of ratifying, ratification, confirmation by superior authority; a provision for enforcing obedience, a penalty or reward; anything that gives binding force to a law, oath etc.; countenance, support, encouragement conferred by usage etc.; that which makes any rule of conduct binding; (*usu. in pl.*) a coercive measure taken by one state against another to force compliance with international law or a change in policy etc. *v.t.* to give sanction to, to authorize, to ratify; to countenance, to approve; to enforce by penalty etc. **sanctionable,** *a.* †**sanctionary,** *a.* **sanctionless,** *a.* [F, from L *sanctiōnem,* nom. *-tio,* from *sancīre,* to render sacred, see SAINT]

sanctity, *n.* the state of being holy, holiness; spiritual purity, saintliness; sacredness, inviolability; (*pl.*) sacred things, feelings etc. **sanctitude,** *n.* holiness, saintliness; sacredness. [OF *saincteté* (F *sainteté*), L *sanctitātem,* nom. *-tas,* from *sanctus,* SAINT]

Sanctorius, *n.* **Sanctorius** (1561–1636), Italian physiologist who pioneered the study of metabolism, and invented the clinical thermometer and a device for measuring pulse rate.

sanctuary, *n.* a holy place; a church, temple or other building or enclosure devoted to sacred uses, esp. an inner shrine or most sacred part of a church etc., as the part of a church where the altar is placed; a church or other consecrated place in which debtors and malefactors were free from arrest; any similar place of immunity, an asylum, a refuge; immunity, protection; a place where deer, birds etc. are left undisturbed. †**sanctuarize, -ise,** *v.t.* [A-F *saintuarie,* OF *sainctuarie* (F *sanctuaire*), L *sanctuārium,* from *sanctus,* saint]

sanctum, *n.* (*pl.* **-tums, -ta,**) a sacred or private place; (*coll.*) a private room, den or retreat. **sanctum sanctorum,** *n.* the holy of holies in the Jewish temple; (*coll.*) one's sanctum. [L, neut. of foll.]

Sanctus, *n.* the liturgical phrase 'Holy, holy, holy', in Latin or English; the music for this. **Sanctus-bell,** *n.* a bell, usu. in a turret or bell-cote over the junction of nave and chancel, rung at the Sanctus before the Canon of the Mass. [L, holy]

sand, *n.* comminuted fragments of rock, esp. of chert, flint and other quartz rocks, reduced almost to powder; a particle of this; (*pl.*) tracts of sand, stretches of beach or shoals or submarine banks of sand; (*pl.*) particles of sand in an hour-glass; (*pl.*) the time one has to live; (*N Am. coll.*) grit, endurance, pluck. *v.t.* to sprinkle or treat with sand; to mix sand with to adulterate; to cover or overlay with or bury under sand; to drive (a ship) on a sand-bank; to smooth or rub with sandpaper or a similar abrasive. **the sands are running out,** the end is approaching. **sandbag,** *n.* a bag or sack filled with sand, used in fortification for making defensive walls, as ballast, for stopping crevices, draughts etc., as a cushion for supporting an engraver's plate, as a weapon for stunning a person etc. *v.t.* to fortify or stop up with sandbags; to strike or fell with a sandbag. **sandbagger,** *n.* **sand-bank,** *n.* a bank or shoal of sand, esp. in the sea, a river etc. **sand-bar,** *n.* a ridge of sand built up by currents in a sea or river. **sand-bath,** *n.* a vessel containing hot sand used for heating, tempering etc. **sand-blast,** *n.* a jet of sand used for engraving and cutting glass, cleaning stone surfaces etc. *v.t.* to cut, clean etc. with a sand-blast. **sand-blight,** *n.* (*Austral.*) an eye inflammation caused by sand. **sand-box,** *n.* a box containing sand carried by a locomotive etc., for sprinkling the rails when slippery; (*Golf*) a box for sand used in teeing; a box with a perforated top formerly used for sprinkling paper with sand to dry up ink; a large open box containing sand for children to play in. †**sand-boy,** *n.* a boy carting or hawking sand. **happy as a sand-boy,** happily engrossed. **sand-castle,** *n.* a model of a castle in sand. **sand-crack,** *n.* a fissure in the hoof of a horse, liable to cause lameness; a crack or flaw in a brick due to defective mixing. **sand-eel,** *n.* an eel-like fish of the genus *Ammodytes*. **sand-flea,** *n.* a sand-hopper. **sand-flood,** *n.* a mass of sand borne along in a desert. **sand-fly,** *n.* a species of midge; an angler's fly. **sand-glass,** *n.* an hour-glass. **Sandgroper,** *n.* (*Austral., derog.*) a Western Australian. **sand-heat,** *n.* heat imparted by warmed sand in chemical operations. **sand-hopper,** *n.* a crustacean, *Talitrus locusta*. **sand-iron,** *n.* a golf club used for lifting the ball from sand. **sandman,** *n.* a being in fairy-lore who makes children sleepy by casting sand in their eyes. **sand-martin,** *n.* a small swallow, *Hirundo riparia,* which makes its nest in sand-banks etc. **sandpaper,** *n.* a paper or thin cloth coated with sand, used for smoothing wood etc. *v.t.* to rub or smooth with this. **sand-pipe,** *n.* (*Geol.*) a deep cylindrical hollow, filled with sand and gravel, penetrating chalk. **sandpiper,** *n.* a popular name for several birds haunting sandy places, chiefly of the genera *Tringa* and *Totanus;* (*Austral.*) the rainbow bird. **sand-pit,** *n.* a container of sand for children to play in, a sand-box. **sand-pump,** *n.* a pump used for extracting wet sand from a drill-hole, caisson etc. **sand-shoe,** *n.* a light shoe, usu. of canvas with a rubber sole, for walking on sands. **sandstone,** *n.* stone composed of an agglutination of grains of sand. **sand-storm,** *n.* a storm of wind carrying along volumes of sand in a desert. **sand-trap,** *n.* (*chiefly N Am., Golf*) a bunker. **sand-worm,** *n.* the lug-worm. **sandwort,** *n.* any plant of the genus *Arenaria,* low herbs growing in sandy soil. **sand-yacht,** *n.* a yacht-like vehicle with wheels and sails for use on sand. **sanded,** *a.* sprinkled with sand; filled, covered or dusted with sand; †of a sandy colour; sand-blind. **sander,** *n.* one who or that which sands, esp. a power tool for smoothing etc. by means of an abrasive belt or disk. **sandy,** *a.* consisting of or abounding in sand; of the colour of sand; of hair, yellowish-red; having hair of this colour; (*N Am. coll.*) plucky, brave, having plenty of grit or sand; shifting, unstable. **sandiness,** *n.* **sandyish,** *a.* [OE, cp. Dut. *zand,* G *Sand,* Icel. *sandr,* Swed. and Dan. *sand*]

Sand, *n.* **George,** pen name of Amandine Aurore Lucie Dupin (1804–76), French author, whose prolific literary output was often autobiographical. After nine years of marriage, she left her husband in 1831, and, while living in Paris as a writer, had love affairs with Alfred de Musset, Chopin, and others. Her first novel *Indiana* (1832) was a plea for women's right to independence.

sandal[1], *n.* a kind of shoe consisting of a sole secured by straps passing over the foot and often round the ankle; a strap for fastening a low shoe. **sandalled,** *a.* wearing sandals; fitted or fastened with a sandal. [F *sandale,* L *sandalium,* Gr. *sandalion*]

sandal[2], *n.* sandalwood. **sandalwood,** *n.* the fragrant wood of various trees of the genus *Santalum,* esp. *S. album,* much used for cabinet work; a tree that yields sandalwood; a similar wood or a tree that yields it. **red sandalwood** RED. [med. L *sandalum,* Gr. *sandalon,* Arab. *sandal,* prob. from Sansk. *chandana*]

sandarac, sandarach, *n.* a whitish-yellow gum-resin obtained from a NW African tree, *Callitris quadrivalvis;* this tree; realgar. [L *sandaraca,* Gr. *sandarakē,* etym. doubtful]

†**sand-blind,** *a.* half-blind, dim-sighted. [prob. corr. of *sam-blind* (OE *sam-,* cogn. with SEMI-, BLIND)]

Sandburg, *n.* **Carl August** (1878–1967), US poet. His poetry celebrates ordinary US life, as in *Chicago Poems* (1916), and *The People, Yes* (1936). *Always the Young Strangers* (1953) is an autobiography. Both his poetry and his biography of Abraham Lincoln won Pulitzer prizes.

Sandemanian, *n.* follower of Robert Sandeman (1718–81), principal exponent of the views of John Glass and leader of the movement founded by him (see GLASSITE).

sanderling, *n.* a small wading bird, *Crocethia alba.* [etym. doubtful]

sanders, sanders-wood SANDALWOOD under SANDAL[2].

Sanders, *n.* **George** (1906–72), Russian-born British actor, usually cast as a smooth-talking cad. Most of his film career was spent in the US where he starred in such films as *Rebecca* (1940), *The Moon and Sixpence* (1942), and *The Picture of Dorian Gray* (1944).

Sandhurst, *n.* popular name for the Royal Military Academy, the British military officer training college near the village of Sandhurst, Berkshire, founded in 1799. Its motto is 'Serve to Lead'.

San Diego, *n.* city and military and naval base in California, US; population (1980) 1,704,000. Industries include bio-medical technology, aircraft missiles, and fish canning. Tijuana adjoins San Diego across the Mexican border.

sandiver, *n.* a saline scum rising to the surface of fused glass in the pot. [prob. corr. of OF *sain de verre* (*suin, suint,* exudation, from *suer,* to sweat, *de verre,* of glass)]

Sandringham House, *n.* private residence of the British sovereign, built in 1863 by the Prince of Wales (afterwards Edward VII, 1869–71)

Sandwich, *n.* **John Montagu, 4th Earl of Sandwich** (1718–92), British politician. He was an inept First Lord of the Admiralty (1771–82) during the American War of Independence, his corrupt practices being held to blame for the British navy's inadequacies.

sandwich, *n.* two thin slices of bread and butter with meat etc. between them; anything resembling a sandwich in layered arrangement. *v.t.* to put, lay or insert between two things of a dissimilar kind. **sandwich course,** *n.* an educational course containing one or more periods of industrial work. **sandwich-man,** *n.* a man carrying two advertisement boards (**sandwich-boards**) hung from his shoulders, one in front and one behind. [after the 4th Earl of *Sandwich,* 1718–92]

Sandwich Islands HAWAII.

Sandy, *n.* (*coll.*) a Scotsman. [Sc., fam. for *Alexander*]

sandy SAND.

Sandys, *n.* **Duncan Edwin** (1908–87), original name of British politician Baron Duncan-Sandys.

†**sandyx,** *n.* a red pigment prepared by calcining carbonate of lead. [L, from Gr. *sandux*]

sane, *a.* sound in mind, not deranged; of views etc., sensible, reasonable; †healthy, sound physically. **sanely,** *adv.* **saneness,** *n.* [L *sānus*]

San Francisco, *n.* chief Pacific port of the US, in California; population (1982) 691,637, metropolitan area of San Francisco-Oakland 3,192,000. The city stands on a peninsula, south of the Golden Gate (1937), the world's second longest single-span bridge, 1280 m/4200 ft. The strait gives access to San Francisco Bay. Industries include meat-packing, fruit canning, printing and publishing, and the manufacture of metal goods.

sang[1], *past* SING[1].

sang[2], (*Sc.*) SONG.

sanga, sangar, *n.* a breastwork or wall of loose stones built for defensive purposes by Indian hill-tribes. [Hind. *sunga*]

sangaree, *n.* wine and water sweetened, spiced and usu. iced. *v.t.* to make (wine) into this. [Sp. SANGRIA]

sang-de-boeuf, *n.* a dark-red colour such as that of some old Chinese porcelain. *a.* of this colour. [F, blood of a bullock]

Sanger, *n.* **Frederick** (1918–), English biochemist, the first to win a Nobel prize for chemistry twice: 1958 for determining the structure of insulin, and 1980 for his work on the chemical structure of genes.

sangfroid, *n.* coolness, calmness, composure in danger etc. [F, cold blood]

Sangha, *n.* in Buddhism, the monastic orders, one of the Three Treasures of Buddhism (the other two are Buddha and the law, or dharma). The term Sangha is sometimes used more generally by Mahāyāna Buddhists to include all believers.

†**sanglier,** *n.* a wild boar. [OF, ult. from L *singulāris,* solitary, see SINGULAR]

sangraal, -greal, GRAIL.

sangrado, *n.* a medical practitioner whose chief resource is blood-letting; a quack. [a physician in Le Sage's *Gil Blas*]

sangria, *n.* a Spanish drink of diluted (red) wine and fruit juices. [Sp., ult. from L *sanguis,* blood]

sanguify, *v.i.* to produce blood. **sanguification,** *n.* the formation of blood. **sanguiferous,** *a.* conveying blood. **sanguifier,** *n.* **sanguifluous,** *a.* running with blood. [L *sanguis,* blood]

sanguinary, *a.* accompanied by bloodshed; delighting in bloodshed, murderous. **sanguinarily,** *adv.* **sanguinariness,** *n.* [L *sanguinārius,* from *sanguis -uinis,* blood]

sanguine, *a.* having the colour of blood; of the complexion, ruddy, florid; formerly said of a temperament supposed to be due to the predominance of blood over the other humours; hopeful, cheerful, confident, optimistic, ardent, enthusiastic; full of blood, plethoric; †composed of blood; †sanguinary. *n.* blood colour, deep red; a crayon of this colour prepared from iron oxide; a drawing with this. *v.t.* to stain with blood; to colour red. **sanguinely,** *adv.* **sanguineness,** *n.* **sanguineous,** *a.* pertaining to, forming or containing blood; sanguinary; of a blood colour; full-blooded, plethoric. **sanguinity,** *n.* sanguineness; consanguinity. **sanguinivorous, sanguivorous,** *a.* feeding on blood. **sanguinolent,** *a.* of blood; bleeding, suffering from haemorrhage. †**sanguinolence,** *n.* **sanguisorb,** *n.* a plant of the rosaceous genus *Sanguisorba,* containing the burnet, formerly used as a styptic. [F *sanguin,* L *sanguineum,* nom. *-us,* as prec.]

Sanhedrin, *n.* the supreme court of justice and council of the Jewish nation, down to AD 425, consisting of 71 priests, elders and scribes. [late Heb., from Gr. *sunedrion* (SYN-, *hedra,* seat)]

sanicle, *n.* a small woodland plant of the umbelliferous genus *Sanicula,* allied to the parsley. [OF, from med. L *sānicula*, from *sānus*, SANE]

sanies, *n.* a thin fetid discharge, usu. stained with blood, from sores or wounds. **sanious,** *a.* [L]

sanify, *v.t.* to make healthy or more sanitary. [L *sānus*, SANE]

sanious SANIES.

sanitary, *a.* relating to or concerned with the preservation of health, pertaining to hygiene; free from dirt, disease-causing organisms etc., hygienic. **sanitary towel** or (*esp. N Am.*) **napkin,** *n.* an absorbent pad used for menstruation. **sanitary wallpaper,** *n.* varnished wallpaper that can be sponged. **sanitary ware,** *n.* ceramic plumbing features, such as sinks, toilet bowls etc. **sanitarian**, *n., a.* **sanitarily,** *adv.* **sanitariness,** *n.* **sanitarist,** *n.* **sanitarium** SANATORIUM. **sanitate,** *v.t.* to improve the sanitary condition of. *v.i.* to carry out sanitary measures. **sanitation,** *n.* **sanitationist,** *n.* **sanitize, -ise,** *v.t.* to make sanitary; to remove offensive language etc. from, make respectable. [cp. F *sanitaire*, from L *sānitas*, see foll.]

sanity, *n.* saneness, mental soundness; reasonableness, moderation. [L *sānitas*, from *sānus*, SANE]

sanjak, *n.* an administrative sub-division of a Turkish vilayet or province. [Turk.]

San José[1], *n.* capital of Costa Rica; population (1984) 245,370. Products include coffee, cocoa, and sugar cane. Founded in 1737, and capital since 1823.

San José[2], *n.* city in Santa Clara Valley, California, US; population (1980) 1,244,000. Industries include aerospace research and development, electronics, flowers, fruit canning, and wine making. It was the first capital of California (1849–51).

San Juan, *n.* capital of Puerto Rico; population (1980) 434,850. It is a port and industrial city. Products include sugar, rum, and cigars.

sank, *past* SINK.

San Luis Potosí, silver-mining city and capital of San Luis Potosí state, central Mexico; population (1986) 602,000. Founded in 1586 as a Franciscan mission, it was the colonial administrative headquarters and has fine buildings of the period.

San Marino, *n.* Most Serene Republic of (*Repubblica di San Marino*), land locked country within N central Italy. **area** 60 sq km/23 sq miles. **capital** San Marino. **physical** on the slope of Mount Titano. **population** (1989) 23,000; annual growth rate 3%. **exports** wine, ceramics, paint, chemicals. **language** Italian. **religion** Roman Catholic.

San Martín, *n.* **José de** (1778–1850), South American nationalist. Born in Argentina, he served in the Spanish army during the Peninsular War, but after 1812 he devoted himself to the South American struggle for independence, playing a large part in the liberation of Argentina, Chile, and Peru from Spanish rule.

San Pedro Sula, main industrial and commercial city in NW Honduras, the second largest city in the country; population (1986) 400,000. It trades in bananas, coffee, sugar, and timber, and manufactures textiles, plastics, furniture, and cement.

sans, *prep.* (*Shak.*) without. **sans-culotte,** *n.* one without breeches; a republican in the French Revolution; a radical extremist, a revolutionary. *a.* republican, revolutionary. **sans-culottic,** *a.* **sans-culottism,** *n.* **sans serif, sanserif,** *n.* a printing type without serifs. [F, from L *sine*, without]

San Salvador, *n.* capital of El Salvador 48 km/30 miles from the Pacific, at the foot of San Salvador volcano 2548 m/8360 ft; population (1984) 453,000. Industries include food processing and textiles. Since its foundation in 1525, it has suffered from several earthquakes.

Sanskrit, *n.* the dominant classical language of the Indian subcontinent, a member of the Indo-Iranian group of the Indo-European language family, and the sacred language of Hinduism. The oldest form of Sanskrit is Vedic, the variety used in the Vedas and Upanishads (*c.* 1500–700 BC). **Sanskritic,** *a.* **Sanskritist,** *n.* [Sansk. *samskrta* (*sam*, together, cp. SAME, *krta*, made)]

Santa Ana, *n.* a periodic warm Californian wind.

Santa Anna, *n.* **Antonio Lopez de** (1795–1876), Mexican revolutionary. A leader in achieving independence from Spain in 1821, he pursued a chequered career of victory and defeat and was in and out of office as president or dictator for the rest of his life; he led the attack on the Alamo in Texas in 1836.

Santa Claus, *n.* a mythical white-bearded old man bringing presents at Christmas and putting them in children's stockings, made popular in Britain in the late 19th cent. [N Am., from Dut. *Sint Klaas*, St Nicholas]

Santa Fé Trail, US trade from route 1821–80 from Independence, Missouri, to Santa Fé, New Mexico.

santal, *n.* sandalwood. **santalin**, *n.* the colouring matter of red sandalwood. [F, from med. L *santalum*, Gr. *santalon*, as SANDAL[2]]

Sant'Elia, *n.* **Antonio** (1888–1916), Italian architect. His drawings convey a futurist vision of a metropolis with skyscrapers, traffic lanes, and streamlined factories.

Santiago, *n.* capital of Chile; population (1987) 4,858,000. Industries include textiles, chemicals, and food processing.

santir, *n.* an Eastern form of dulcimer played with two sticks. [Arab., corr. of Gr. *psālterion*, PSALTERY]

Santo Domingo, *n.* capital and chief sea port of the Dominican Republic; population (1982) 1,600,000. Founded in 1496 by Bartolomeo, brother of Christopher Columbus, it is the oldest colonial city in the Americas.

santolina, *n.* a genus of fragrant shrubby composite plants allied to the camomile. [prob. var. of SANTONICA]

santon, *n.* a Muslim hermit, a dervish. [F or Sp., from *santo*, SAINT]

santonica, *n.* the unexpanded flower-heads of an Oriental species of *Artemisia* or wormwood, containing santonin. **santonin**, *n.* the bitter principle of santonica, used as an anthelmintic. **santoninic,** *a.* [L, fem. adj., pertaining to the *Santones*, a people of Aquitania]

Sānusī, *n.* **Sidi Muhammad ibn 'Ali as-** (1787–1859), Algerian-born Muslim religious reformer. He preached a return to the puritanism of early Islam and met with much success in Libya, where he made Jaghbub his centre and founded the sect called after him.

San Yu, *n.* (1919–.), Burmese politician. A member of the Revolutionary Council which came to power in 1962, he became president in 1981 and was re-elected in 1985. He was forced to resign in July 1988, along with Ne Win, after riots in Rangoon (now Yangon).

Sâo Paulo, *n.* city in Brazil, 72 km/44 miles NW of its port Santos; population (1980) 7,034,000, metropolitan area 15,280,000. It is 900 m/3000 ft above sea level, and 2° S of the Tropic of Capricorn. It is South America's leading industrial city, producing electronics, steel, and chemicals, has meat-packing plants, and is the centre of Brazil's coffee trade.

São Tomé e Principe, Democratic Republic of, country in the Gulf of Guinea, off the coast of W Africa. **area** 1000 sq km/386 sq miles. **capital** São Tomé. **physical** comprises the two main islands and several smaller ones, all of volcanic origin; thickly forested and fertile. **population** (1989) 114,000; annual growth rate 2.5%. **exports** cocoa, copra, coffee, palm oil and kernels. **language** Portuguese. **religion** Roman Catholic.

sap[1], *n.* the watery juice or circulating fluid of living plants; the sapwood of a tree; vital fluid, strength, vigour; (*sl.*) a gullible person, a saphead. *v.t.* (*past, p.p.* **sapped**) to draw off sap; to exhaust the strength or vitality of. **sap-colour,** *n.* an expressed vegetable colour inspissated by evaporation for use by painters. **sap-green,** *n.* a green pigment obtained from the juice of blackthorn berries; the colour of this. *a.* of this colour. **saphead,** *n.* (*sl.*) a softhead, a ninny. **sap-lath,** *n.* a lath of sapwood. **sap-rot,** *n.* dry-rot. **sap-tube,** *n.* a plant vessel conducting sap. **sapwood,** *n.* the soft new wood next to the bark, alburnum. **sapful,** *a.* **sapless,**

a. **sapling**, *n.* a young tree; a youth. **sappy,** *a.* **sappiness,** *n.* [OE *sæp* (cp. Dut. *sap,* G *Saft*), prob. cogn. with L *sapa,* must, new wine]

sap², *v.t.* (*past, p.p.* **sapped**) to undermine; to approach by mines, trenches etc.; to render unstable by wearing away the foundation; to subvert or destroy insidiously. *v.i.* to make an attack or approach by digging trenches or undermining. *n.* the act of sapping; a deep ditch, trench or mine for approach to or attack on a fortification; insidious undermining or subversion of faith etc. **sapper,** *n.* one who saps; (*coll.*) an officer or private of the Royal Engineers. [F *sapper,* from OF *sappe* (F *sape*) or It. *zappa,* late L *sappa,* spade]

sap³, *v.i.* (*past, p.p.* **sapped**) (*sl.*) to be studious, to grind. *n.* (*sl.*) a hard-working student, a plodder; (*sl.*) a tiring piece of work, a grind. [prob. from prec.]

sapajou, *n.* a small S American prehensile-tailed monkey of genus *Cebus*. [F, said to be a Cayenne word]

sapan-wood, sappan-wood, *n.* a brownish-red dyewood obtained from trees of the genus *Caesalpinia,* esp. *C. sappan,* from S Asia and Malaysia. [Dut. *sapan,* Malay *sapang,* wood]

sapele, *n.* a reddish-brown wood resembling mahogany obtained from W African trees of the genus *Entandrophragma;* a tree that yields sapele. [W Afr.]

saphena, *n.* either of two prominent veins of the leg. **saphenal, saphenous,** *a.* [med. L, from Arab. *çāfin*]

sapid, *a.* possessing flavour that can be relished, savoury; not insipid, vapid or uninteresting. **sapidity, sapidness,** *n.* [L *sapidus,* from *sapere,* to taste]

sapient, *a.* wise, sagacious, discerning, sage (often ironical). **sapiently,** *adv.* **sapience,** *n.* **sapiential**, *a.* of or conveying wisdom. **sapiential books,** *n.pl.* (*Bibl.*) Proverbs, Ecclesiastes, Ecclesiasticus, The Book of Wisdom, The Canticles. [L *sapiens -entem,* pres.p. of *sapere,* to be wise, as prec.]

sapi-utan, *n.* the wild ox of Celebes. [Malay, wild ox]

sapling SAP¹.

sapodilla, *n.* the edible fruit of a large evergreen tree, *Achras sapota,* growing in the W Indies and Central America; the tree itself; its durable wood. [Sp. *zapotilla,* dim. of *zapote,* from Nahuatl *zapotl*]

saponaceous, *a.* soapy; resembling, containing or having the qualities of soap. [L *sāpo -pōnis,* soap]

Saponaria, *n.* a genus of plants comprising the soapworts.

saponify, *v.t.* to convert into soap by combination with an alkali. *v.i.* of an oil, fat etc., to become converted into soap. **saponifiable,** *a.* **saponification**, *n.*

saponin, *n.* any of various glucosides obtained from the soapwort, horse-chestnut etc. that produce a soapy foam and are used in detergents.

saponule, *n.* a soap-like compound formed by the action of an alkali on an essential oil.

sapor, *n.* taste; distinctive flavour. **saporific**, *a.* producing taste or savour. **saporous,** *a.* **saporosity**, *n.* [L, from *sapere,* to taste]

sappan-wood SAPAN-WOOD.

sapper SAP².

sapphic, *a.* pertaining to Sappho, a poetess (*c.* 600 BC) from the Greek island of Lesbos; applied to a stanza or metre used by her, esp. a combination of three pentameters followed by a dipody. *n.pl.* sapphic verses or stanzas. **sapphism,** *n.* lesbianism. **sapphist,** *n.* [L *Sapphicus,* Gr. *Sapphikos,* from *Sapphō*]

sapphire, *n.* any transparent blue variety of corundum; an intense and lustrous blue, azure; a S American humming-bird with a blue throat. *a.* sapphire-blue. **sapphirine**, *a.* having the qualities, esp. the colour, of sapphire. *n.* a mineral of a pale blue colour, esp. a silicate of alumina and magnesia or a blue spinel. [F *saphir,* L *saphīrus,* Gr. *sappheiros,* prob. from Semitic (cp. Heb. *sappīr*)]

Sappho, *n.* (*c.* 612–580 BC), Greek lyric poet, friend of the poet Alcaeus, and leader of a female literary coterie at Mytilene (modern *Lesvos*, hence lesbianism); legend says she committed suicide when her love for the boatman Phaon was unrequited. Only fragments of her poems have survived.

Sapporo, *n.* capital of HOKKAIDO, Japan; population (1987) 1,555,000. Industries include rubber and food processing. It is a winter sports centre, and was the site of the 1972 Winter Olympics.

sapraemia, *n.* septic poisoning. **sapraemic,** *a.* [Gr. *haima,* blood]

sapr(o)-, *comb. form* indicating rotting or dead matter. [Gr. *sapros,* rotten]

saprogenic, *a.* producing or produced by putrefaction.

Saprolegnia, *n.* a genus of fungi infesting fishes, and causing a destructive disease. **saprolegnious,** *a.* [Gr. *legnon,* border]

saprophagous, *a.* feeding on decomposing matter. **saprophagan**, *n.* a lamellicorn beetle living on decomposed vegetable matter.

saprophile, *n.* a bacterium feeding on decomposed matter. **saprophilic**, **saprophilous**, *a.*

saprophyte, *n.* a plant, bacterium or fungus that grows on decaying organic matter. **saprophytic**, *a.* **saprophytically,** *adv.* **saprophytism,** *n.*

saprostomus, *n.* foulness of breath. **saprostomous,** *a.* [Gr. *stoma,* mouth]

saprozoic, *a.* saprophagous.

sapsago, *n.* a greenish hard cheese flavoured with melilot, made in Switzerland. [corr. of G *Schabzieger* (*schaben,* to grate, *Zieger,* cheese)]

sapsucker SAP¹.

sapucaya, sapucaia, *n.* a S American tree bearing an edible nut. **sapucaya-nut,** *n.* [Tupi]

sapwood SAP¹.

sar, sargo, *n.* a fish of the genus *Sargus,* comprising the sea-breams. [F, var. of *sargo,* L *sargus*]

saraband, sarabande, *n.* a slow and stately Spanish dance; a piece of music for this in strongly accented triple time. [F *sarabande,* Sp. *zarabanda,* prob. from Arab.]

Saracen, *n.* a nomad Arab of the Syrian-Arabian desert in the times of the later Greeks and Romans; a Muslim or Arab at the time of the Crusades. **Saracenic**, *a.* [late L *Saracēnus,* late Gr. *Sarakēnos,* prob. from Arab.]

Saragossa, *n.* (Spanish **Zaragoza**), industrial city in Aragon, Spain; population (1981) 842,000. It produces iron, steel, chemicals, plastics, canned food, and electrical goods. The medieval city walls and bridges over the Ebro survive, and there is a 15th-century university.

Sarajevo, *n.* capital of Bosnia and Herzegovina, Yugoslavia; population (1982) 449,000. Industries include engineering, brewing, chemicals, carpets, and ceramics. It was the site of the 1984 Winter Olympics.

Saratoga, Saratoga trunk, *n.* a variety of lady's large travelling trunk. [*Saratoga* Springs, New York State]

Saratov, *n.* industrial port (chemicals, oil refining) on the Volga in the European Russian Soviet Socialist Republic; population(1987) 918,000. It was established in the 1590s as a fortress to protect the Volga trade route.

Sarawak, *n.* state of Malaysia, on the NW corner of the island of Borneo. **capital** Kuching. **area** 124,400 sq km/48,018 sq miles. **population** (1986) 1,550,000. **products** timber, oil, rice, pepper, rubber, and coconuts.

sarcasm, *n.* a bitter, taunting, ironical or wounding remark; bitter or contemptuous irony or invective. **sarcast,** *n.* a sarcastic speaker etc. **sarcastic, †-ical**, *a.* containing or characterized by sarcasm; given to using sarcasm. **sarcastically,** *adv.* [late L *sarcasmus,* late Gr. *sarkazmos,* from *sarkazein,* to tear flesh, as SARCO-]

sarcelle, *n.* a teal or an allied long-tailed duck. [OF *cercelle,* ult. from L *querquedula*]

sarcenchyme, *n.* the gelatinous tissue of some higher sponges. **sarcenchymatous**, *a.* [*sarc-,* SARCO-, after PARENCHYMA]

sarcenet, *n.* a thin, fine soft-textured silk used chiefly for linings, ribbons etc. [A-F *sarzinett,* OF *sarcenet,* prob. dim. of *sarzin,* SARACEN]

Sarcina, *n.* a genus of bacteria or schizomycetous fungi in which the cocci break up into cuboidal masses. **sarcinaeform**, **sarcinic**, *a.* [L, bundle, from *sarcīre,* to mend]

sarcine, *n.* a nitrogenous compound existing in the juice of flesh. [G *Sarkin* (*sarc-*, SARCO-, -INE)]

sarco-, *comb. form.* flesh. [Gr. *sarx sarkos*, flesh]

sarcobasis, *n.* (*Bot.*) a fleshy gynobase.

sarcoblast, *n.* a germinating particle of protoplasm. **sarcoblastic,** *a.*

sarcocarp, *n.* the fleshy part of a drupaceous fruit.

sarcocele, *n.* fleshy enlargement of the testicle.

sarcocol, *n.* a gum-resin from Arabia and Iran.

sarcocolla, *n.* sarcocol; a genus of S African shrubs of the family Penaeaceae from which sarcocol was formerly supposed to be obtained.

sarcode, *n.* animal protoplasm. **sarcodal, sarcodic,** *a.*

sarcoderm, *n.* an intermediate fleshy layer in certain seeds.

sarcody, *n.* (*Bot.*) conversion into fleshiness.

sarcoid, *a.* resembling flesh. *n.* a particle of sponge tissue; a swelling, nodule.

sarcolemma, *n.* the tubular membrane sheathing muscular tissue. **sarcolemmic,** *a.*

sarcology, *n.* the branch of anatomy concerned with the soft parts of the body. **sarcological,** *a.* **sarcologist,** *n.*

sarcoma, *n.* (*pl.* **-mas, -mata** -tə) a tumour of connective tissue. **sarcomatosis,** *n.* the formation and spread of sarcomas. **sarcomatous,** *a.* [Gr. *sarkōma*, from *sarkoun*, to become fleshy]

sarcophagous, sarcophagic, *a.* feeding on flesh. **sarcophagon,** *n.* an insect of the order Sarcophaga, a flesh-fly. **sarcophagy,** *n.* the practice of eating flesh. [see foll.]

sarcophagus, *n.* (*pl.* **-gi**) **-guses**) a kind of stone used by the ancient Greeks for coffins, as it was believed to consume the flesh of those buried in it in a few weeks; a stone coffin, esp. one of architectural or decorated design. [L, from Gr. *sarkophagos* (SARCO-, Gr. *phagein*, to eat)]

sarcoplasm, *n.* the substance between the columns of muscle-fibre. **sarcoplasmic,** *a.*

Sarcoptes, *n.* a genus of acaridans comprising the itch-mites; a mite of this genus. **sarcoptic,** *a.* [Gr. *koptein*, to cut]

sarcosis, *n.* (*pl.* **-ses**) a fleshy tumour, a sarcoma. †**sarcotic,** *a.* producing flesh. *n.* a sarcotic medicine. [Gr. *sarkōsis*, from *sarkoun*, as SARCOMA]

sarcotome, *n.* an instrument for cutting through the tissues of the body.

sarcous, *a.* composed of flesh or muscle tissue.

sard, *n.* a precious stone, a variety of cornelian. **sardachate,** *n.* a variety of agate containing layers of cornelian. **sardine**[2], *n.* (*Bibl.*) prob. the sardius. [F *sarde*, L *sarda*, SARDIUS]

sardelle, sardel, *n.* a small Mediterranean clupeoid fish like, and prepared as, the sardine. [It. *sardella*, dim. of *sarda*, SARDINE[1]]

sardine[1], *n.* a fish, *Clupea pilchardus*, caught off Brittany and Sardinia, and cured and preserved in oil; any of various other small fish preserved in the same way. [F, from It. *sardina*, L *sardīna*, late Gr. *sardēnē*, Gr. *sarda*]

sardine[2] SARD.

Sardinia, *n.* (Italian **Sardegna**) mountainous island, special autonomous region of Italy. **area** 24,100 sq km/9303 sq miles. **capital** Cagliari. **physical** the second largest Mediterranean island, and includes Costa Smeralda (Emerald Coast) tourist area in the northeast and *nuraghi* (fortified Bronze Age dwellings). **population** (1988) 1,651,000. **exports** cork and petrochemicals.

Sardinian, *a.* pertaining to the island or the former kingdom of Sardinia. *n.* a native or inhabitant of Sardinia.

sardius, *n.* a precious stone mentioned in Scripture, perhaps the sard or the sardonyx. [L, from Gr. *sardios*, from *Sardeis*, Sardis]

sardonic, *a.* unnatural, forced, affected, insincere; of laughter etc., sneering, malignant, bitterly ironical. **sardonian,** *n., a.* **sardonically,** *adv.* [F *sardonique*, L *Sardonicus*, *Sardonius*, Gr. *Sardonios*, Sardinian (as if in alln. to the effects of a Sardinian plant in contorting the face), for *Sardonios*, etym. doubtful]

sardonyx, *n.* a variety of onyx composed of white chalcedony alternating with layers of sard. [L, from Gr. *sardonux*]

sargasso, *n.* (*pl.* **-sos**) the gulfweed, *Sargassum natans*; a floating mass of this or similar vegetation. **Sargasso Sea,** see separate entry. **sargassum,** *n.* a plant of the genus *Sargassum*, sargasso. [Port. *sargaço*]

Sargasso Sea, *n.* part of the N Atlantic (between 40° and 80° W and 25° and 30° N) left static by circling ocean currents, and covered with floating weed *Sargassum natans*.

sarge, *n.* short for SERGEANT.

Sargent, *n.* **John Singer** (1856–1925), US portrait painter. Born in Florence of American parents, he studied there and in Paris, then settled in London around 1885. He was a prolific and highly fashionable painter.

Sargeson, *n.* **Frank** (1903–82). New Zealand writer of short stories and novels including *The Hangover* (1967) and *Man of England Now* (1972).

sargo SAR.

Sargon I, *n.* king of Akkad (*c.* 2370–2230 BC), and founder of the first Babylonian empire. His story resembles that of Moses in that he was said to have been found floating in a cradle on the river Euphrates.

Sargon II, *n.* (died 705 BC), king of Assyria from 722 BC, who assumed the name of his famous predecessor. To keep conquered peoples from rising against him, he had whole populations moved from their homelands, including the Israelites from Samaria.

sari, saree, *n.* a Hindu woman's dress. [Hind.]

sarigue, *n.* a S American opossum, *Didelphys opossum*. [F, from Port. *sarigué*]

Sark, *n.* one of the Channel Islands, 10 km/6 miles E of Guernsey; area 5 sq km/2 sq miles; there is no town or village. It is divided into Great and Little Sark, linked by an isthmus, and is of great natural beauty. The Seigneurie of Sark was established by Elizabeth I, the ruler being known as Seigneur/Dame, and has its own parliament, the Chief Pleas. There is no income tax and cars are forbidden; immigration is controlled.

sark, *n.* (*Sc.*) a shirt or chemise. *v.t.* to clothe with a sark; to cover (a roof) with sarking. **sarking,** *n.* (*Sc., North*) thin boards for lining, esp. a roof under slates. [OE *serc* or Icel. *serkr*, cp. Swed. *sărk*, Dan. *saerk*]

sarkinite, *n.* a mineral composed of red arsenate of manganese. [Gr. *sarkinos*, fleshy, see SARCINE, -ITE]

sarky, *a.* (*coll.*) sarcastic; bad-tempered.

Sarmatian, *a.* pertaining to ancient Sarmatia, now Poland and part of Russia, or its people; (*poet.*) Polish. *n.* a native or inhabitant of Sarmatia; (*poet.*) a Pole.

sarmentose, -tous, *a.* (*Bot.*) having or producing runners. **sarmentum,** *n.* (*pl.* **-ta, -tums**) a prostrate shoot rooting at the nodes, a runner. [L *sarmentōsus*, from *sarmentum*, twigs, brushwood]

Sarney, *n.* **José** (1930–), president of Brazil (1985–89), member of the Brazilian Democratic Movement (PMDB).

sarong, *n.* a loose, skirt-like garment traditionally worn by men and women in the Malay Archipelago. [Malay *sārung*, from Sansk. *sāranga*, variegated]

saros, *n.* a cycle of 6585⅓ days in which solar and lunar eclipses repeat themselves. [Gr.]

sarothrum, *n.* the pollen brush on the leg of a honey-bee. [Gr. *sarotron*, a broom]

†**sarplier,** *n.* a sack or bale of wool containing 80 tods (1 ton/1·016 tonne); coarse sacking or packing cloth. [A-F *sarpler*, OF *sarpillere*, (F *serpillière*), etym. doubtful]

Sarracenia, *n.* a genus of insectivorous plants with pitcher-shaped leaves. [after Dr D *Sarrazen* of Quebec, *c.* 1700]

†**Sarrasin,** SARACEN.

Sarraute, *n.* **Nathalie** (1920–), Russian-born French novelist whose books include *Portrait d'un inconnu/Portrait of a Man Unknown* (1948), *Les Fruits d'or/The Golden Fruits* (1964), and *Vous les entendez?/Do You Hear Them?* (1972). An exponent of the *nouveau ro-*

man, Sarraute bypasses plot, character, and style for the half-conscious interaction of minds.

sarrusophone, *n.* a brass musical instrument resembling an oboe with a metal tube. [M *Sarrus*, French bandmaster and inventor, *c.* 1860, -PHONE]

sarsaparilla, *n.* the dried roots of various species of *Smilax*, used as a flavouring and formerly in medicine as an alterative and tonic; a plant of this genus; a carbonated drink flavoured with sassafras. [Sp. *zarzaparrilla* (*zarza*, bramble, *-parrilla*, perh. dim. of *parra*, vine)]

sarsen, *n.* a sandstone boulder such as those scattered over the chalk downs of Wiltshire. **sarsen-boulder, -stone,** *n.* [prob. var. of SARACEN]

sarsenet, SARCENET.

sartage, *n.* the clearing of woodland for agricultural purposes. [OF, from *sarter*, to clear ground, from *sart*, med. L *sartum*, neut. p.p. of L *sartīre*, to hoe]

sartorial, *a.* pertaining to a tailor or tailored clothing. [L *sartōrius*, from *sartor*, mender, tailor, from *sarcīre*, to patch]

sartorius, *n.* a muscle of the thigh that helps to flex the knee.

Sartre, *n.* **Jean-Paul** (1905–80), French author and philosopher, one of the leading proponents of existentialism in post-war philosophy. He published his first novel *La Nausée/Nausea* (1937), followed by the trilogy *Les Chemins de la liberté/Roads to Freedom* (1944–45), and many plays, including *Huis Clos/In Camera* (1944). *L'Etre et le néant/Being and Nothingness* (1943), his first major philosophical work, is important for its radical doctrine of human freedom. In the later work *Critique de la raison dialectique/Critique of Dialectical Reason* (1960) he tried to produce a fusion of existentialism and Marxism.

SAS, (*abbr.*) Special Air Service; Scandinavian Airlines System.

sash¹, *n.* an ornamental band or scarf worn round the waist or over the shoulder, frequently as a badge or part of a uniform. **sashed,** *a.* [formerly *shash*, a strip worn as a turban, from Arab. *shāsh*, muslin]

sash², *n.* a frame of wood or metal holding the glass of a window; a sliding light in a greenhouse etc. *v.t.* to furnish with sashes. **sash-cord, -line,** *n.* a stout cord attached to a sash and the sash-weights. **sash-frame,** *n.* the frame in which a sash slides up and down. **sash-pocket,** *n.* the space in which the sash-weights are hung. **sash-weight,** *n.* a weight used to balance a sash and hold it in an open position. **sash-window,** *n.* a window having a movable sash or sashes. **sashed,** *a.* **sashless,** *a.* [corr. of CHASSIS]

sashay, *v.i.* (*chiefly N Am.*) to walk or move in a nonchalant or sauntering manner; to strut, swagger. [alteration of CHASSÉ]

sashimi, *n.* a Japanese dish of thin slices of raw fish. [Jap.]

sasin, *n.* the common Indian antelope, *Antilope cervicapra.* [Nepalese]

sasine, *n.* (*Sc. Law*) the act of giving legal possession of feudal property; the instrument by which this is effected. [var. of SEISIN]

Sask., (*abbr.*) Saskatchewan.

Saskatchewan, *n.* province of W Canada. **area** 652,300 sq km/251,788 sq miles. **capital** Regina. **towns** Saskatoon, Moose Jaw, Prince Albert. **physical** prairies in the south; to the north forests, lakes and subarctic tundra. **population** (1986) 1,010,000. **products** more than 60% of Canada's wheat; oil, natural gas, uranium, zinc, potash (world's largest reserves), copper, the only western reserves of helium outside the US.

Sasquatch, *n.* a hairy humanoid creature reputedly living in W Canada. [Am. Ind.]

sass, *n.* (*N Am., coll.*) impudence, cheek, sauce. *v.t.* to talk impudently to. **sassy,** *a.* (*N Am., coll.*) cheeky, saucy. [var. of SAUCE]

sassaby, *n.* a large S African antelope, *Alcelaphus lunatus*, the bastard hartebeest. [native name]

sassafras, *n.* a tall N American tree, *Sassafras albidum*, of the laurel family; the dried bark of its root used as an aromatic stimulant and flavouring. [Sp. *sasafras*]

Sassanian, *a.* of or pertaining to the Sassanids. *n.* a Sassanian king. **Sassanid,** *n.* one of the descendants of Sasan, ancestor of the last pre-Islamic dynasty of Persia (AD 226–642). *a.* Sassanian. [Pers. *Sāsān*]

Sassanian Empire, *n.* Persian empire founded AD 224 by Ardashir, a chieftain in the area of modern Fars in Iran, who had taken over Parthia; it was named for his grandfather, Sasan. The capital was Ctesiphon, near modern Baghdad. After a rapid period of expansion, when it contested supremacy with Rome, it was destroyed in 637 by Muslim Arabs at the Battle of Qadisiya.

Sassau-Nguesso, *n.* **Denis** (1943–), Congolese socialist politician, president from 1979. He progressively consolidated his position within the ruling left-wing Congolese Labour Party (PCT) and the country, at the same time improving relations with France and the US.

Sassenach , *n.* (*Sc. and Ir., chiefly derog.*) a Saxon, an English person. *a.* English. [Gael. and Ir. *Sassunach*, *Sasanach*, SAXON]

sassoline, *n.* a mineral composed of a native triclinic form of boric acid. [G *Sassolin*]

Sassoon, *n.* **Siegfried** (1886–1967), English writer, author of the autobiography *Memoirs of a Foxhunting Man* (1928). His *War Poems* (1919) express the disillusionment of his generation.

sassy SASS.

sastra, SHASTER under SHASTRA.

Sat., (*abbr.*) Saturday.

sat, *past, p.p.* SIT.

Satan, Satanas, *n.* the arch-fiend, the devil. **satanic, -ical,** *a.* pertaining to, emanating from or having the qualities of Satan; devilish, infernal. **Satanic School,** *n.* Southey's description of Byron, Shelley etc.; applied to other writers charged with deliberate impiety or satanism. **satanically,** *adv.* **satanism,** *n.* a diabolical disposition, doctrine or conduct; the deliberate pursuit of wickedness; Satan-worship; the characteristics of the Satanic School. **satanist,** *n.* **satanize, -ise,** *v.t.* [L and Gr. *Satān*, *Satanās*, Heb. *Sātān*, enemy, adversary]

satano-, *comb. form.* pertaining to Satan. **satanology,** *n.* the study of or a treatise on doctrines relating to the devil.

satanophany, *n.* a visible manifestation of Satan.

satara, *n.* a heavy, horizontally-ribbed woollen or broad-cloth. [town in India]

satay, *n.* a Malaysian and Indonesian dish of cubed meat served with a spicy peanut sauce. [Malay]

SATB, (*abbr.*) soprano, alto, tenor, bass.

satchel, *n.* a small rectangular bag, often suspended by a strap passing over one shoulder, esp. for schoolchildren to carry books etc. in. **satchelled,** *a.* [ME and OF *sachel*, L *saccellum*, nom. *-lus*, dim. of *saccus*, SACK¹]

sate¹, *v.t.* to satisfy (an appetite or desire); to satiate, to surfeit, to glut, to cloy. **sateless,** *a.* (*poet.*). [OF *satier*, to SATIATE, or from OE *sadian*, to make SAD, assim. to this]

†**sate²,** *past* SIT.

sateen, *n.* a glossy woollen or cotton fabric made in imitation of satin. [from SATIN]

satellite, *n.* a secondary planet revolving round a primary one; a man-made device projected into space to orbit the earth, moon etc., used for communications, broadcasting, weather forecasting, surveillance etc.; something dependent on or subordinate to another; an obsequious follower, dependant or henchman. **satellite broadcasting,** *n.* the transmission of broadcast programmes via artificial satellite for reception in the home. **satellite dish,** *n.* a parabolic aerial for reception of programmes transmitted via an artificial satellite. **satellite state,** *n.* a country subservient to a greater power. **satellite town,** *n.* a small town dependent upon a larger town in the vicinity. [F, from L *satellitem*, attendant]

satiate, *v.t.* to satisfy (as a desire or appetite) fully; to sate, to glut, to surfeit. *a.* sated, glutted, cloyed. **satiable,** *a.* **satiation,** *n.* **satiety**, *n.* the state of being sated or glutted; excess of gratification producing disgust; †sufficiency, fullness, overabundance. [L *satiātus*, p.p. of *satiāre*, from *sat*, *satis*, see SATISFY]

Satie, *n.* **Erik (Alfred Leslie)** (1866–1925), French composer. His piano pieces, such as *Gymnopédies* (1888), often combine wit and melancholy. His orchestral works include *Parade* (1917), amongst whose sound effects is a typewriter. He was the mentor of the group of composers known as *Les Six*.

satin, *n.* a silken fabric with an overshot weft and a highly-finished glossy surface on one side only. *a.* made of or resembling this, esp. in smoothness. *v.t.* to give (paper etc.) a glossy surface like satin. **white satin** WHITE. **satin-bird,** *n.* an Australian bower-bird, *Ptilonorhyncus violoceus*. **satin-finish,** *n.* a lustrous polish given to silverware with a metallic brush. **satin-flower,** *n.* honesty; the greater stitchwort. **satin-gypsum,** *n.* a fibrous gypsum used by lapidaries. **satin-paper,** *n.* a fine, glossy writing-paper. **satin-spar,** *n.* a finely fibrous variety of aragonite, calcite, or gypsum. **satin-stitch,** *n.* a stitch in parallel lines giving the appearance of satin. **satin-stone** SATIN-GYPSUM. **satin-wood,** *n.* an ornamental cabinet wood of various species from the E and W Indies. **satiné**, *n.* a variety of satin-wood from Guiana. **satinet, satinette**, *n.* a thin satin; a glossy fabric made to imitate satin. **satining-machine,** *n.* a machine for giving paper etc. a satiny surface. **satinize, -ise,** *v.t.* to satin. **satiny,** *a.* [F, prob. through late L *sētīnus*, silken, from L *sēta*, silk, orig. bristle]

satire, *n.* a composition, orig. a medley in verse, now either in verse or prose, in which wickedness or folly or individual persons are held up to ridicule; ridicule, sarcasm or the use of ridicule, irony and invective ostensibly for the chastisement of vice or folly. **satiric, -ical**, *a.* **satirically,** *adv.* **satiricalness,** *n.* **satirist,** *n.* one who writes or employs satire. **satirize, -ise,** *v.t.* to ridicule by means of satire. *v.i.* to use or write satire. [F, from L *satira*, *satura* (*lanx satura*, full dish, medley), rel. to *satur*, *satis*, see SATISFY]

satisfy, *v.t.* to supply or gratify to the full; to content, to gratify, to please; to pay (a debt etc.); to fulfil, to comply with; to be sufficient for, to meet the desires, expectations or requirements of; (*Math.*, *Log.*) to fulfil the conditions of; to free from doubt; to convince; to meet (a doubt, objection etc.) adequately. *v.i.* to give satisfaction; to make payment, compensation or reparation, to atone. **satisfaction**, *n.* the act of satisfying; the state of being satisfied; gratification, contentment; payment of a debt, fulfilment of an obligation; a source of satisfaction; reparation, compensation, amends; atonement, esp. the atonement for sin achieved by Christ's death; the performance of penance. **satisfactory**, *a.* giving satisfaction, sufficient, adequate, meeting all needs, desires or expectations; relieving the mind from doubt; atoning, making amends. **satisfactorily,** *adv.* **satisfactoriness,** *n.* **satisfiable,** *a.* **satisfier,** *n.* **satisfying,** *a.* **satisfyingly,** *adv.* [OF *satisfier*, L *satisfacere* (*satis*, enough, *facere*, to make, p.p. *factus*)]

Sato, *n.* **Eisaku** (1901–75), Japanese politician. He opposed the policies of Hayato Ikeda (1899–1965) in the Liberal Democratic Party, and succeeded him as prime minister (1964–72), pledged to a more independent foreign policy. He shared a Nobel Peace Prize in 1974 for his rejection of nuclear weapons. His brother Nobosuke Kishi (1896–1987) was prime minister of Japan (1957–60).

satori, *n.* in Zen Buddhism, an intuitive enlightenment. [Jap.]

satrap, *n.* a governor of a province under the ancient Persian empire, a viceroy; a governor, a ruler of a dependency etc., esp. one who affects despotic ways. **satrapal, -pial, satrapic, -ical**, *a.* **satrapess,** *n. fem.* **satrapy,** *n.* the territory, office or period of office of a satrap. [L *satrapa*, *satrapes*, Gr. *satrapēs*, OPers. *khsatrapāvā* (*khsatra*, province, *pa-*, to protect)]

satsuma, , *n.* a seedless type of mandarin orange; a tree that bears such fruit. **Satsuma ware,** *n.* a cream-coloured variety of Japanese pottery. [former Japanese province]

saturate, *v.t.* to soak, impregnate, or imbue thoroughly; to fill or charge (a body, substance, gas, fluid etc.) with another substance, fluid, electricity etc. to the point where no more can be held; to cause (a chemical compound) to combine until no further addition is possible; to overwhelm (a target) with bombs or projectiles. *a.*, of a colour, intense, deep; (*poet.*) saturated. **saturable,** *a.* **saturant,** *a.* saturating. *n.* a substance neutralizing acidity or alkalinity. **saturated,** *a.* of a solution, containing as much dissolved material as possible at a given temperature; full of water, soaked; of an organic compound, containing only single bonds between carbon atoms and not reacting to add further groups to the molecule. **saturated fat,** *n.* a fat containing mostly saturated fatty acids. **saturater,** *n.* **saturation,** *n.* the state of being saturated; the presence in the atmosphere of the maximum amount of water vapour at any particular temperature; the point at which increasing magnetizing force fails to increase any further the flux-density of the magnet; the purity of a colour, freedom from mixture with white. **saturation bombing,** *n.* bombing that completely covers a target area. **saturation current,** *n.* the maximum value of electric current that can be carried. **saturation point,** *n.* the point at which no more can be taken in, held etc. [L *saturātus*, p.p. of *saturāre*, from *satur*, cogn. with *satis*, enough]

Saturday, *n.* the seventh day of the week. [OE *Sæterdæg* (*Sæternes*, L *Saturni*, of SATURN, *dies*, DAY)]

Saturn[1], *n.* in astronomy, the second largest planet in the solar system, sixth from the Sun, and encircled by bright rings. Viewed through a telescope it is white, but appears lemon-coloured when seen at closer range. Saturn orbits the Sun every 29.46 years at an average distance of 1,427,000,000 km/886,700,000 miles. Its equatorial diameter is 120,000 km/75,000 miles, but its polar diameter is 12,000 km/7450 miles smaller, a result of its fast rotation and low density (70% of water, the lowest of any planet). Saturn spins on its axis every 10 hr 14 min at its equator, slowing to 10 hr 40 min at high latitudes. Its mass is 95 times that of Earth, and its magnetic field 1000 times stronger. Saturn is believed to have a small core of rock and iron, encased in ice and topped by a deep layer of liquid hydrogen. There are over 20 known moons, its largest being Titan. The visible rings, made of ice and rock, are 275,000 km/170,000 miles rim to rim, but only 100 m/300 ft thick. The Voyager probes showed that the rings actually consist of thousands of closely spaced ringlets, looking like the grooves in a gramophone record.

Saturn[2], *n.* an ancient Roman god of agriculture, usu. identified with the Greek Kronos, father of Zeus, under whose sway the world was in the golden age; (*Alch.*) lead. **Saturnalia**, *n.pl.* an ancient Roman annual festival held in December in honour of Saturn, regarded as a time of unrestrained licence and merriment; (*often sing.*) a season or occasion of unrestrained revelry. **saturnalian,** *a.* **saturnian**, *a.* pertaining to the god Saturn or the golden age; happy, virtuous, distinguished for purity; of or pertaining to the planet Saturn; denoting the accentual metre of early Latin poetry. *n.* an inhabitant of Saturn; (*pl.*) saturnian verses. **saturnic**, *a.* affected with lead-poisoning. **saturnine**, *a.* born under the influence of the planet Saturn; dull, phlegmatic, gloomy, morose; pertaining to lead or lead-poisoning. **saturninely,** *adv.* **saturnism,** *n.* lead-poisoning. †**saturnist,** *n.* a saturnine person. **saturnite**, *n.* a mineral substance containing lead. [L *Saturnus*, prob. from *sa-* or *se-* (*serere*, to sow)]

Saturn rocket, *n.* a family of large US rockets, developed by Wernher von Braun for the Apollo project.

satyagraha, *n.* non-violent resistance to authority as practised orig. by Mahatma Gandhi. [Sansk. *satya*, faithful, *agraha*, obstinacy]

satyr, *n.* an ancient sylvan Greek deity represented with the legs of a goat, budding horns, and goat-like ears, identified by the Romans with the fauns; a lascivious man; the orang-utan. **satyral,** *n.* (*Her.*) a monster with a human head and parts of various animals. **satyriasis**, *n.* unrestrained sexual appetite in men. **satyric, †-ical**, *a.* **satyric drama,** *n.* a burlesque play with a chorus of satyrs, usu. following a trilogy. [L *satyrus*, Gr. *saturos*]

satyrid, *n.* one of the *Satyridae*, a family of butterflies.

Satyrium, *n.* a genus of tropical orchids with flowers in dense spikes.

sauce, *n.* a preparation, usu. liquid, taken with foods as an accompaniment or to enhance the taste; (*fig.*) anything that gives piquancy or makes palatable; (*coll.*) sauciness, impertinence, impudence, cheek. *v.t.* (*fig.*) to flavour, to make piquant or pungent; (*coll.*) to be saucy or impudent towards; to treat with sauce, to season. **sauce-alone,** *n.* the hedge garlic. **sauce-boat,** *n.* a table-vessel for holding sauce. **sauce-box,** *n.* (*coll.*) an impudent person, esp. a child. **saucepan,** *n.* a metal pan or pot, usu. cylindrical with a long handle, for boiling or stewing; orig. a pan for cooking sauces. **sauceless,** *a.* **saucy,** *a.* pert, impudent, insolent to superiors, cheeky; smart, sprightly; (*dial.*) fastidious, dainty. **saucily,** *adv.* **sauciness,** *n.* [F, from pop. L *salsa*, fem. of *salsus*, salt, from SAL¹]

saucer, *n.* a shallow china vessel for placing a cup on and catching spillings; any small flattish vessel, dish or receptacle of similar use. **saucer-eyes,** *n. pl.* large, round, staring eyes. **saucer-eyed,** *a.* **saucerful,** *n.* (*pl.* **-fuls**). **saucerless,** *a.*

saucisse, saucisson, *n.* a long tube of gunpowder, etc., for firing a charge; a long fascine. [F, SAUSAGE]

Saudi Arabia, *n.* Kingdom of (*al-Mamlaka al-'Arabiya as-Sa'udiya*), a country on the Arabian peninsula, stretching from the Red Sea to the Arabian Gulf, bounded to the N by Jordan, Iraq, and Kuwait, to the E by Qatar and United Arab Emirates, to the SE by Ornan, and to the S by North and South Yemen. **area** 2,200,518 sq km/849,400 sq miles. **capital** Riyadh. **towns** Mecca, Medina; ports Jidda, Dammam. **physical** desert, sloping to the Persian Gulf from a height of 2750 m/9000 ft in the W. **population** (1989) 12,678,000 (16% nomadic); annual growth rate 4.2%. **exports** oil. **language** Arabic. **religion** Sunni Muslim, with a Shi'ite minority in the E.

sauerkraut, *n.* finely chopped cabbage compressed with salt until it ferments. [G]

sauger, *n.* the smaller N American pike-perch, *Stizostedion canadense*. [etym. doubtful]

saugh, sauch, (*Sc.*) SALLOW¹

Saul, *n.* (died *c.* 1010 BC), in the Old Testament or Hebrew Bible, the first king of Israel, who was anointed by Samuel and warred successfully against the Ammonites and Philistines (neighbouring peoples). He turned against Samuel and committed suicide as his mind became unbalanced.

saul¹, SAL².

saul², (*Sc.*) SOUL.

†saulie, *n.* a hired mourner. [Sc., etym. doubtful]

sault, *n.* (*N Am.*) a rapid in a river. [OF, from L *saltus*, from *salīre*, to leap]

sauna, *n.* a Finnish-style steam bath; a building or room used for saunas. [Finnish]

saunders, SANDERS.

saunt, (*Sc.*) SAINT.

saunter, *v.i.* to wander about idly and leisurely; to walk leisurely (along). *n.* a leisurely ramble or stroll; a sauntering gait. **saunterer,** *n.* **saunteringly,** *adv.* [perh. through A-F *sauntrer*, from med. L *exadventūrāre* (EX-, ADVENTURE)]

saurian, *a.* pertaining to or resembling the Sauria, an order of reptiles formerly including the crocodiles and lizards, but now the lizards alone. *n.* a lizard or lizard-like creature, esp. one of the extinct forms as the ichthyosaurus and plesiosaurus. **sauroid,** *n., a.* **†saurus,** *n.* (*pl.* **-ri**) a saurian. [SAUR(O)-, -IAN]

saur(o)-, *comb. form.* lizard. [Gr. *saura*, *sauros*, lizard]

saurodont, *n.* one of the Saurodontidae, an extinct family of fishes of the Cretaceous age. *a.* of or pertaining to this family.

saurognathous, *a.* (*Ornith.*) having a palate similar to that of the lizards. **saurognathism,** *n.* [Gr. *gnathos*, jaw]

saurophagous, *a.* feeding on lizards and other reptiles. [-PHAGOUS]

sauropod, *n.* one of the Sauropoda, an extinct order of gigantic herbivores. **sauropodous,** *a.*

Sauropsida, *n.pl.* one of Huxley's three great primary groups of vertebrates, comprising birds and reptiles. **sauropsidan,** *n., a.* [Gr. *opsis*, appearance]

Saururae, *n.pl.* an extinct sub-class of birds having lizard-like tails. **saururous,** *a.* [Gr. *ouros*, tail]

saury, *n.* a sea-fish, *Scomberesox saurus*, with elongated body ending in a beak. [L *saurus*, lizard]

sausage, *n.* an article of food consisting of pork or other meat minced, seasoned and stuffed into a length of animal's gut or a similar receptacle; anything of similar cylindrical shape. **sausage balloon,** *n.* an observation balloon shaped like an inflated sausage. **sausage-cutter, -filler, -grinder, -machine,** *n.* appliances used in manufacturing sausages. **sausage-dog,** *n.* (*coll.*) a dachshund. **sausage-meat,** *n.* meat used for stuffing sausages, esp. cooked separately as stuffing etc. **sausage-roll,** *n.* sausage-meat enclosed in pastry and baked. [F *saucisse*, late L *salsicia*, from *salsus*, SAUCE]

Saussure, *n.* **Horace de** (1740–99), Swiss geologist who made the earliest detailed and first-hand study of the Alps. He was a physicist at the University of Geneva. The results of his Alpine survey appeared in his classic work *Voyages des Alpes/Travels in the Alps* (1779–86). **saussurite,** *n.* an impure white, grey or green silicate mineral formed by alteration from feldspar. *a.*

saut, (*Sc.*) SALT.

sauté, *a.* lightly fried. *v.t.* (*past, p.p.* **sautéed, sautéd**) to fry lightly. *n.* a dish of this. [F, p.p. of *sauter*, to leap]

Sauternes, *n.* a sweet white Bordeaux wine. [district on the Garonne, France]

sauve qui peut, *n.* a state of panic or chaos [F, save (himself) who can]

savable etc. SAVE.

Savage, *n.* **Michael Joseph** (1872–1940), New Zealand Labour politician. As prime minister (1935–40), he introduced much social security legislation.

savage, *a.* uncultivated, untamed, wild; uncivilized, in a primitive condition; fierce, brutal, cruel, violent, ferocious; (*coll.*) extremely angry, enraged; (*Her.*) nude, unclad. *n.* a human being in a primitive state, esp. a member of a nomadic tribe living by hunting and fishing; a person of extreme brutality or ferocity, a brute, a barbarian. *v.t.* to attack violently, esp. of an animal, to bite, tear or trample; †to make wild or savage. **savagely,** *adv.* **savagedom, savageness, savagery, savagism,** *n.* [OF *salvage*, L *silvāticus*, from *silva*, wood]

savanna, savannah, *n.* an extensive treeless plain covered with low vegetation, esp. in tropical America. **savanna (black)bird,** *n.* the W Indian bird *Crotophaga ani*. **savanna flower,** *n.* an evergreen shrub of various species of *Echites*. [Sp. *sabana*, prob. from Carib.]

savant, *n.* a person of learning, esp. an eminent scientist. [F, orig. p.p. of *savoir*, to know]

savate, *n.* a style of boxing in which the feet are used as well as the hands. [F, from It. *ciabatta*, etym. doubtful]

save, *v.t.* to preserve, rescue or deliver as from danger, destruction or harm of any kind; to deliver from sin, to preserve from damnation; to keep undamaged or untouched; to keep from being spent or lost; to reserve and lay by, to husband, to refrain from spending or using; to spare, to exempt (*with double object*); to obviate, to prevent; to prevent or obviate the need for; to be in time for, to catch. *v.i.* to be economical, to avoid waste or undue expenditure; to set aside money for future use. *prep.* except, saving; leaving out, not including. *conj.* unless. *n.* the act of preventing an opponent from scoring a goal; something saved, an economy. **save-all,** *n.* anything that prevents things from being wasted; a contrivance to hold a candle-end in a candlestick; a strip of canvas laced to a sail to catch a light wind. **save-as-you-earn,** *n.* a government savings scheme in which regular contributions are deducted from earnings. **savable,** *a.* **saver,** *n.* (*usu. in comb.*, as *life-saver*). **saving,** *a.* preserving from danger, loss, waste etc.; economical, frugal; reserving or expressing a reservation, stipulation etc. *n.* the act of economizing; (*usu. pl.*) that which is saved, an economy; (*pl.*) money saved, esp. regularly or over a period of time; an exception, a reservation. *prep.* save, except; with due respect to. **savings bank,** *n.* a bank receiving small deposits and usu. devoting any profits to the payment of interest. **savingly,** *adv.* †**savingness,** *n.* [F *sauver*, L *salvāre*, from *salvus*, SAFE]

saveloy, *n.* a highly-seasoned dried sausage of salted pork (orig. of brains). [corr. of F *cervelas*, It. *cervelatta*, from *cervello*, L CEREBELLUM]

Savery, *n.* **Thomas** (*c.* 1650–1715), British engineer who invented the steam-driven water pump, precursor of the steam engine, in 1696.

Savimbi, *n.* **Jonas** (1934–), Angolan soldier and revolutionary, founder of the National Union for the Total Independence of Angola (UNITA).

savin, savine, *n.* an evergreen bush or low tree, *Juniperus sabina*, with bluish-green fruit, yielding an oil formerly used medicinally. [OE *safine*, OF *savine*, L *sabīna*, SABINE]

saviour, *n.* one who preserves, rescues, or redeems. **our** or **the Saviour,** Christ, the Redeemer of mankind. [OF *saveor*, *salveor*, L *salvātōrem*, nom. *-tor*, from *salvāre*, to SAVE]

savoir faire, *n.* quickness to do the right thing, esp. in social situations, tact, presence of mind. [F, to know what to do]

Savonarola, *n.* **Girolamo** (1452–98), Italian reformer, a Dominican friar. His crusade against political and religious corruption won him huge popularity, and in 1494 he led a revolt in Florence that expelled the ruling Medici family and established a democratic republic. His denunciations of Pope Alexander VI led to his excommunication in 1497, and in 1498 he was arrested, tortured, hanged, and burned for heresy.

savonette, *n.* a toilet preparation of various kinds. **savonette-tree,** *n.* a W Indian tree, the bark of which is used as a substitute for soap. [F (now *savonnette*), dim. of *savon*, L *sāpo*, soap]

savory, *n.* a plant of the aromatic genus *Satureia*, esp. *S. hortensis*, used in cookery. [OF *savereie*, L *saturēia*]

savour, (*esp. N Am.*) **savor,** *n.* (characteristic) flavour, taste, relish; a particular taste or smell; characteristic quality; suggestive quality, smack or admixture (of); †smell, perfume. *v.t.* to give a flavour to; †to have the flavour or to smack of; to perceive, to discern; to relish, to enjoy the savour of. *v.i.* to have a particular smell or flavour, to smack (of); **savourless,** *a.* **savoury,** *a.* having a pleasant savour; palatable, appetizing; free from offensive smells; salty, spicy etc. (as opp. to sweet); respectable, wholesome. *n.* a savoury dish, esp. as served as an appetizer or digestive. **savourily,** *adv.* **savouriness,** *n.* [OF, from L *sapōrem*, nom. *sapor*, from *sapere*, to taste]

Savoy, *n.* area of France between the Alps, Lake Geneva, and the river Rhône. A medieval duchy, it was formed into the *départements* of Savoie and Haute-Savoie, in Rhône-Alpes region.

savoy, *n.* a hardy variety of cabbage with wrinkled leaves. [district in France]

Savoyard, *n.* a native of Savoy; one connected with or a habitué of the Savoy Theatre in the days of the Gilbert and Sullivan operas (1875–96). *a.* of Savoy.

savvy, *v.t., v.i.* (*sl.*) to know, to understand. *n.* understanding, knowingness, cleverness. [corr. of Sp. *sabe*, know, ult. from L *sapere*, to be wise]

saw¹, *n.* a cutting-instrument, usu. of steel, with a toothed edge, worked by hand, or power-driven, as in circular or ribbon form; a tool or implement used as a saw; a serrated body part or organ. *v.t.* (*past* **sawed,** *p.p.* **sawn**) to cut with a saw; to form or make with a saw; to make motions as if sawing; to make cuts in (the back of a book) to receive the threads in sewing. *v.i.* to use a saw; to undergo cutting with a saw; to make motions of one sawing. **saw-bill,** *n.* a tropical or subtropical American bird, the motmot, with serrated mandibles; a duck with a serrated beak. **saw-bones,** *n.* (*sl.*) a surgeon. **saw-doctor,** *n.* a machine for cutting teeth in a saw. **sawdust,** *n.* small fragments of wood produced in sawing, used for packing etc. **saw-fish,** *n.* a fish of the genus *Pristis*, with an elongated, saw-like snout. **saw-fly,** *n.* any of various hymenopterous insects, as of the genus *Tenthredo*, furnished with a saw-like ovipositor. **saw-gin,** *n.* a cotton-gin with saw-teeth. **saw-horse,** *n.* a rack on which wood is laid for sawing. **sawmill,** *n.* a mill with machinery for sawing timber. **sawn-off,** *a.* of a shotgun, having the end of the barrel cut off with or as with a saw. **sawpit,** *n.* a pit over which timber is sawed, one person standing above and the other below the log. **saw-set, -wrest,** *n.* a tool for slanting the teeth of a saw alternately outward. **saw-toothed,** *a.* serrated. **saw-whet,** *n.* a small N American owl, *Nyctale acadica*, with a harsh cry. **sawwort,** *n.* any plant of the genus *Serratula*, having serrated leaves yielding a yellow dye. **sawyer,** *n.* one employed in sawing timber into planks, or wood for fuel; a wood-boring larva; (*N Am.*) a tree fallen into a river and swept along, sawing up and down in the water; (*New Zealand*) a kind of grasshopper, the weta. [OE *saga* (cp. Dut. *zaag*, G *Säge*, Icel. *sög*), cogn. with L *secāre*, to cut]

saw², *n.* a saying, a proverb, a familiar maxim; †a tale, a recital. [OE *sagu*, cogn. with SAY¹]

saw³, *past* SEE¹.

Saw, *n.* **Maung** (1929–), Burmese soldier and politician. Appointed head of the armed forces in 1985 by Ne Win, in 1988 he led a coup to remove Ne Win's successor, Maung Maung, and became leader of an emergency military government.

Sawchuk, *n.* **'Terry' (Terrance Gordon)** (1929–70), Canadian ice-hockey player, often regarded as the greatest goaltender of all time. He played for Detroit, Boston, Toronto, Los Angeles, and New York Rangers (1950–67), and holds the National Hockey League (NHL) record of 103 shut-outs (games in which he did not concede a goal).

sawder, *n.* blarney, flattery. [corr. of SOLDER]

Sawney, *n.* a nickname for a Scotsman. [prob. *Sandy*, corr. of *Alexander*]

sawney, *n.* (*coll.*) a simpleton. [prob. from ZANY]

sawwort, sawyer etc. SAW¹.

sax¹, *n.* a slate-cutter's chopping and trimming tool with a point for making holes. [OE *seax*, knife, cp. Icel. and OHG *sax*]

sax², (*Sc.*) SIX.

sax³, *n.* short for SAXOPHONE.

saxatile, *a.* pertaining to or living among rocks. [F, from L *saxātilis*, from *saxum*, rock]

saxe, *n.* an albumenized photographic paper made in Saxony. **saxe-blue,** *n., a.* (of) a light greyish-blue. [F *Saxe*, Saxony]

Saxe, *n.* **Maurice, Comte de** (1696–1750), soldier, illegitimate son of the Elector of Saxony, who served under Prince Eugène of Savoy and was created marshal of France in 1743 for his exploits in the War of the Austrian Succession.

Saxe-Coburg-Gotha, *n.* Saxon duchy. Albert, the Prince Consort of Queen Victoria, was a son of the 1st Duke (Ernest I 1784–1844), who was succeeded by Albert's elder brother, Ernest II (1818–93). It remained the name of the British royal house until 1917, when it was changed to Windsor.

saxhorn, *n.* a brass musical wind-instrument with a long winding tube, a wide opening and several valves. [Adolphe *Sax*, 1814–94, inventor (*c.* 1845), HORN]

saxicavous, *a.* hollowing out stone; belonging to the *Saxicava*, a genus of rock-boring molluscs. [L *saxi-*, *saxum*, rock, *cavāre*, to hollow]

saxicolous, saxicoline, *a.* inhabiting or growing among rocks, saxatile. [L *saxi-*, *saxum*, rock, *colere*, to inhabit]

saxifrage, *n.* any plant of the genus *Saxifraga* (so called because formerly esteemed good for stone in the bladder), consisting largely of Alpine or rock plants with tufted, mossy or encrusted foliage and small flowers. †**saxifragant, saxifragaceous**, *a.* †**saxifrageous,** *a.* breaking or destroying stone or calculi. *a.*, *n.* [F, from L *saxifraga*, spleenwort (*saxi-*, *saxum*, rock, *frag-*, root of *frangere*, to break)]

Saxon, *n.* one of a Teutonic people from N Germany who conquered England in the 5th and 6th cents.; an Anglo-Saxon; the old Saxon or the Anglo-Saxon language; a native of modern Saxony. *a.* pertaining to the Saxons, their country or language; Anglo-Saxon; pertaining to Saxony or its inhabitants. **Saxon-blue,** *n.* indigo dissolved in sulphuric acid, used by dyers; saxe-blue. **Saxondom**, *n.* **Saxonism,** *n.* **Saxonist,** *n.* **Saxonize, -ise,** *v.t.*, *v.i.* [F, from late L *Saxonēs*, pl., from OE *Seaxan*, from *seax*, see SAX[1], rel. to L *saxum*, rock]

Saxony[1], *n.* (German **Sachsen**), former kingdom in Germany, which is now the modern region of Leipzig, Dresden, and Karl-Marx-Stadt (Chemnitz), East Germany. Saxony lay between Prussia, Bavaria, and Bohemia; Dresden was the capital. The name is derived from its Saxon inhabitants whose territories originally reached as far west as the Rhine.

Saxony[2], *n.* a fine wool or woollen material produced in Saxony. [*Saxony*, in Germany]

Saxony-Anhalt, *n.* former *Land* (administrative region) of East Germany, (1946–52). It consisted of Anhalt, a former duchy and state, and most of the former Prussian province of Saxony.

saxophone, *n.* a brass musical wind-instrument with a single reed used as a powerful substitute for the clarinet. **saxophonist**, *n.* [A *Sax*, see SAXHORN, -PHONE]

saxtuba, *n.* a bass saxhorn. [A *Sax*, see SAXHORN, TUBA]

say[1], *v.t.* (*past*, *p.p.* **said** sed, †*3rd sing. pres.* **saith** seth) to utter in or as words, to speak, to pronounce; to recite, to rehearse, to repeat; to tell, to affirm, to assert, to state; to allege, to report; to promise; to suppose, to assume; to give as an opinion or answer, to decide. *v.i.* to speak, to talk, to answer. *n.* what one says or has to say, an affirmation, a statement; (*coll.*) one's turn to speak; authority, influence. *adv.* approximately, about; for example. **I say,** an exclamation of mild surprise, protest etc. or calling for attention. **it is said** or **they say,** it is generally reported or rumoured. **not to say,** indeed one might say, perhaps even. **that is to say,** in other words. **say-so,** *n.* a dictum; an unfounded assertion; right of decision, authority. **says, sez, you!** *int.* (*sl.*) an expression of incredulity. **saying,** *n.* that which is said; a maxim, an adage, a saw. [OE *secgan*, cp. Icel. *segja*, Dan. *sige*, G *sagen*]

†**say[2],** *n.* a fine thin serge; a kind of silk or satin. [OF *saie*, L *saga*, pl. of *sagum*, Gr. *sagos*, military cloak]

†**say[3],** †**sayer** ASSAY, ASSAYER.

SAYE, (*abbr.*) save-as-you-earn.

Sayers, *n.* **Dorothy L(eigh)** (1893–1957), English writer of crime novels featuring detective Lord Peter Wimsey and heroine Harriet Vane, including *Strong Poison* (1930), *The Nine Tailors* (1934), and *Gaudy Night* (1935). She also wrote religious plays for radio, and translations of Dante.

sayette, *n.* a mixed fabric of silk and wool or silk and cotton. [F, dim. of *saie*, SAY[2]]

Say's law, *n.* in economics, the 'law of markets' enunciated by Jean-Baptiste Say (1767–1832) to the effect that supply creates its own demand and that resources can never be under-used.

sayyid, *n.* a Muslim title of respect; a descendant of certain members of Mohammed's family. [Arab.]

Sb, (*chem. symbol*) antimony. [L *stibnium*]

sbirro, *n.* (*pl.* **-rri,**) an Italian policeman; a police spy. [It.]

†**'sblood,** *int.* an oath or imprecation. [euph. for *God's blood*]

SC, (*abbr.*) South Carolina; Special Constable; Supreme Court.

Sc, (*chem. symbol*) scandium.

sc, (*abbr.*) scene; *scilicet* (namely); *sculpsit* (he/she sculptured it); scruple; small capitals.

s/c, (*abbr.*) self-contained.

scab, *n.* an incrustation formed over a sore etc., in healing; a highly-contagious skin-disease resembling mange, attacking horses, cattle and esp. sheep; one of various fungoid plant-diseases; a despicable scoundrel; a worker who refuses to join in a strike or who takes the place of a striker, a blackleg. *v.i.* (*past*, *p.p.* **scabbed**) to form a scab; to work as a scab or blackleg. **scabmite,** *n.* the itch-mite. **scabbed, scabby,** *a.* **scabbily,** *adv.* **scabbiness,** *n.* [Dan. and Swed. *skabb* (cp. OE *sceab*, *scæb*)]

scabbard, *n.* the sheath of a sword or similar weapon. *v.t.* to put into a scabbard, to sheathe. **scabbard fish,** *n.* a small silver sea-fish (*Lepidopus candatus*) with a blade-like body; any of various related fishes. [ME *scauberc*, A-F *escaubers*, pl., prob. from Teut.]

scabble SCAPPLE.

scaberulous SCABROUS.

scabies, *n.* the itch, a contagious skin-disease. [L, from *scabere*, to scratch]

scabious, *a.* consisting of or covered with scabs; affected with itch. *n.* a plant of the herbaceous genus *Scabiosa*, having involucrate heads of blue, pink and white flowers. [L *scabiōsus*, as prec.]

scabrous, *a.* rough, rugged or uneven; scaly, scurfy; difficult, thorny, awkward to handle; approaching the indecent, indelicate. **scaberulous**, *a.* (*Bot.*) somewhat scabrous. **scabridity, scabrousness,** *n.* [L *scabrōsus*, from *scaber*, cogn. with prec.]

scad[1], *n.* the horse-mackerel. [etym. unknown]

scad[2], *n.* the fry of salmon. [perh. var. of SHAD]

scad[3] (*Sc.*) SCALD[1].

scaff, *n.* (*Sc.*) food. **scaff, scaff-raff**, *n.* the rabble, the riff-raff. [etym. doubtful]

scaffold, *n.* a temporary structure of poles and ties supporting a platform for the use of workers building or repairing a house or other building; a temporary raised platform for the execution of criminals; a platform, or stage for shows or spectators; the bony framework of a structure, esp. one to be covered by developed parts. *v.t.* to furnish with a scaffold; to uphold, to support. †**scaffoldage**, *n.* scaffolding. **scaffolder,** *n.* **scaffolding,** *n.* a scaffold or system of scaffolds for builders, shows, pageants etc.; a framework; materials for scaffolds. [ONorth.F *escafaut*, OF *escadafault* (F *échafaud*), (perh. EX-, It. *catafalco*, CATAFALQUE)]

scaglia, *n.* a red, white or grey Italian limestone corresponding to chalk. **scagliola,** *n.* a hard, polished plaster, coloured in imitation of marble. [It., SCALE[2]]

scaith, (*Sc.***)** SCATHE.

scalable, *a.* that may be scaled.

†**scalade,** †**scalado**, ESCALADE.

scalar, *a.* scalariform; of the nature of a scalar. *n.* a pure number, esp. the term in a quaternion that is not a vector; a quantity having magnitude but no direction (e.g. time). **scalariform**, *a.* of the structure of cells, vessels, veins etc., ladder-shaped. [L *scālāris*, from *scāla*, SCALE[3]]

scalawag SCALLYWAG.

scald[1], *v.t.* to burn with or as with a hot liquid or vapour; to clean (out) with boiling water; to cook briefly in hot water or steam; to raise (milk) nearly to boiling point. *n.* an injury to the skin from hot liquid or vapour. **scalder,** *n.* **scalding,** *n.* **scalding-hot,** hot enough to scald. [ONorth.F *escalder*, OF *eschalder*, L *excaldāre* (EX-, *calidus*, hot)]

scald[2], skald, *n.* an ancient Norse poet or reciter of poems, a bard. **scaldic,** *a.* [Icel. *skald*]

scald[3], *a.* affected with scall. **scald-head,** *n.* a disease of the scalp characterized by a scaly eruption. [orig. *scalled*, see SCALL]

scalder, scalding SCALD[1].

scaldic SCALD[2].

scaldino, *n.* (*pl.* **-ni,**) a small earthenware brazier used for warming the hands etc. [It., from *scaldare*, to warm, from L as SCALD[1]]

scale[1], *n.* one of the thin horny plates forming a protective covering on the skin of fishes, reptiles etc.; a modified leaf, bract, hair, feather, disk, husk or other structure resembling this; a thin flake of dry skin; a scab; a carious coating; an incrustation; a coating deposited on the insides of pipes, kettles etc. by hard water; a small plate or flake of metal etc. *v.t.* to strip the scales off; to remove in scales or layers; to deposit scale on. *v.i.* to form scales; to come off in scales; to become coated with scale; (*Sc.*) to disperse, to scatter; (*Austral.*) to ride on a tram or bus without paying the fare. **scale-armour,** *n.* armour made of small plates overlapping each other like the scales of a fish. **scale-board,** *n.* a thin board for the back of a picture etc. **scale-fern,** *n.* the ceterach. **scale insect,** *n.* an insect, esp. of the family Coccidae, whose female secretes a protective waxy shell and lives attached to a host plant. **scale-winged,** *a.* having the wings covered with scales, lepidopterous. **scale-work,** *n.* an arrangement of overlapping scales, imbricated work. **scaled,** *a.* having scales (*usu. in comb.* as *thick-scaled*). **scaleless,** *a.* **scaly,** *a.* **scaly anteater,** *n.* the pangolin. **scaliness,** *n.* [OF *escale*, OHG *scala* (OE *scealu*, cogn. with foll., G *Schale*)]

scale[2], *n.* the dish of a balance; (*usu. pl.*) a simple balance; (*usu. pl.*) a machine for weighing. *v.t.* to amount to in weight; †to weigh in scales. [OF *escale*, cup, Icel. *skāl*, bowl (cp. Dut. *schaal*), cogn. with prec.]

scale[3], *n.* anything graduated or marked with lines or degrees at regular intervals, as a scheme for classification, gradation etc.; a basis for a numerical system in which the value of a figure depends on its place in the order; a system of correspondence between different magnitudes, relative dimensions etc.; a set of marks or a rule or other instrument marked with these showing exact distances, proportions, values etc., used for measuring, calculating etc.; (*Mus.*) all the tones of a key arranged in ascending or descending order according to pitch. *v.t.* to climb by or as by a ladder; to clamber up; to draw or otherwise represent to scale or proper proportions; to alter the scale of; to arrange, estimate or fix according to a scale; to adjust according to a standard. *v.i.* to have a common scale, to be commensurable. **scaling-ladder,** *n.* a ladder used in storming fortified places. [L *scāla*, ladder, cogn. with *scandere*, to climb]

scalene, *a.* of a triangle, having no two sides equal; of a cone or cylinder, having the axis inclined to the base; pertaining to the scalenus muscles. *n.* a scalene triangle; a scalenus muscle. **scalenohedron**, *n.* a hemihedral form of the hexagonal or the tetragonal crystallographic system with eight similar and equal scalene triangles as faces. **scalenohedral,** *a.* **scalenum**, *n.* a scalene triangle. **scalenus**, *n.* (*pl.* **-ni,**) one of a series of irregularly triangular muscles at the neck. [late L *scalēnus*, Gr. *skalēnos*, prob. rel. to *skolios*, crooked]

scaliness SCALE[1].

scaling-ladder SCALE[3].

†**scall,** *n.* a scabby or scaly eruption, esp. of the scalp. †*a.* mean, scurvy, paltry, low. **scalled-head** SCALD-HEAD, under SCALD[3]. [Icel. *skalli*, cp. Swed. *skallig*, bald]

scallion, *n.* a variety of onion or shallot. [ONorth.F *escalogne*, SHALLOT]

scallop, *n.* a bivalve mollusc of the genus *Pecten* or a related genus, with ridges and flutings radiating from the middle of the hinge and an undulating margin; the large adducter muscle of a scallop eaten as food; a single shell of a scallop worn as a pilgrim's badge; such a shell or a small shallow dish or pan used for cooking and serving oysters etc. in; (*pl.*) an ornamental undulating edging cut like that of a scallop-shell. *v.t.* to cut or indent the edge of thus; to cook in a scallop. **scallop-shell,** *n.* **scalloping,** *n.* **scalloping-tool,** *n.* [OF *escalope*, from Teut. (cp. MDut. *schelpe*), cogn. with SHELL]

scallywag, scalawag, scallawag, *n.* a poor, ill-conditioned or undersized animal (used orig. of Shetland ponies); a scamp, a scape-grace. [corr. of *Scalloway*, Shetland]

scalp, *n.* the top of the head; the skin of this with the hair belonging to it, formerly torn off by N American Indians as a trophy of victory; (*poet.*) a bare hill-top; a whale's head without the lower jaw. *v.t.* to tear or take the scalp from; to cut the top part, layer etc. off (anything); to flay, to lay bare; to criticize or abuse savagely; (*chiefly N Am.*) to buy (cheaply) and resell so as to make a large profit; (*N Am.*) to buy and sell so as to take small quick profits on (stocks etc.). *v.i.* (*N Am.*) to take small profits to minimize risk. **scalp-lock,** *n.* a solitary tuft of hair left on the shaven crown of the head as a challenge by the warriors of some American tribes. **scalper,** *n.* one who scalps; (*chiefly N Am.*) a ticket tout. **scalping,** *n.*, *a.* **scalping-iron,** *n.* a raspatory. **scalping-knife,** *n.* **scalpless,** *a.* [prob. Scand. (cp. MSwed. *skalp*, Icel. *skālpr*, sheath), cogn. with SCALLOP]

scalpel, *n.* a small knife used in surgical operations and anatomical dissections. [L *scalpellum*, dim. of *scalprum*, knife, from *scalpere*, to scrape]

scalper, etc. SCALP.

scalpriform, *a.* chisel-shaped (as the teeth of rodents). [L *scalpri-*, *scalprum*, see SCALPEL, -FORM]

scaly SCALE[1].

†**scamble,** *v.i.* to scramble or struggle (for, after etc.); to get (through or along) somehow. *v.t.* to mangle, to maul; to waste, to squander. *n.* a scramble; a struggle. †**scambler,** *n.* †**scamblingly,** *adv.* [prob. rel. to SHAMBLE and SCRAMBLE]

scammony, *n.* the Asiatic *Convolvulus scammonia;* a purgative gum-resin from the root of this. †**scammoniate**, *a.* **scammonic**, *a.* [OF *scammonie*, L *scammōnia*, Gr. *skammōnia*]

scamp[1], *n.* a worthless person, a knave, a rogue; a mischievous child. **scampish,** *a.* [prob. as SCAMPER]

scamp[2], *v.t.* to do or execute (work etc.) in a careless manner or with bad material. [prob. var. of SCANT]

scamper, *v.i.* to run rapidly, playfully, hastily, or impulsively; †to run away. *n.* a hasty or playful run; a hurried excursion, a hurried tour. [orig. to run away, ONorth.F *escamper* (EX-, L *campus*, field)]

scampi, *n.* (*pl.* **scampi**) large prawns, esp. when fried in breadcrumbs or batter. [It.]

scampish SCAMP[1].

scan, *v.t.* (*past, p.p.* **scanned**) to count, mark or test the metrical feet or the syllables of (a line of verse); to examine closely or intently, to scrutinize; to examine sequentially or systematically; to glance at or read through hastily; to continuously traverse (an area or object) with a beam of laser light, electrons etc. in order to examine or to produce or transmit an image; to observe with a radar beam; to examine and produce an image of (a body part) using ultrasound, X rays etc. †(*Spens.*) to climb. *v.i.* to be metrically correct, to agree with the rules of scansion. *n.* an act of scanning; an image or display produced by scanning. **scanning,** *n.*, *a.* **scanning beam,** *n.* the beam of light or electrons with which an image is scanned for television. **scanning disk,** *n.* a disk with a spiral of holes with or without lenses, used for dividing a transmitted picture into a series of narrow strips. **scanning electron microscope,** *n.* an electron microscope in which a beam of electrons scan an object to produce a three-dimensional image. **scanner,** *n.* one who or that which scans; the aerial of a radar device; an instrument used in scanning the human body, esp. one that takes radiographic photographs from various angles and combines them into a three-dimensional image. [L *scandere*, to climb (*d* prob. conf. with -ED)]

scandal, *n.* indignation, offence or censure at some act or conduct, esp. as expressed in common talk; damage to reputation, reproach, shame, disgrace; malicious gossip, aspersion of character; (*Law*) a defamatory statement, esp. of an irrelevant nature; a disgraceful action, person etc., an affront. †*v.t.* to speak scandal of; to defame, to traduce. **scandal-monger,** *n.* one who disseminates scandal. **scandalize, -ise,** *v.t.* to offend by improper or outrageous conduct, to shock; (*coll.*) to talk scandal about. **scandalous,** *a.* **scandalously,** *adv.* **scandalousness,** *n.* [ME *scandle*, ONorth.F *escandle* (F *scandale*), L *scandalum*, Gr. *skandalon*, snare, stumbling-block]

scandalum magnatum , *n.* (*pl.* **scandala magnatum**) (*Law*) defamation of high personages of the realm. [med. L *magnātum*, gen. pl. of *magnas*, MAGNATE]

scandent, *a.* climbing, as ivy. [L *scandens -ntem*, pres.p. of *scandere*, to climb]

Scandinavia, *n.* peninsula in NW Europe, comprising Norway and Sweden; politically and culturally it also includes Denmark and Finland. **Scandinavian,** *a.* pertaining to Scandinavia, its language or literature. *n.* a native or inhabitant of Scandinavia; the languages of Scandinavia collectively.

scandium, *n.* a rare metallic element, at. no. 21; chem. symbol Sc, discovered in certain Swedish yttrium ores. [obs. *Scandia*, Scandinavia]

scanner, scanner, scanning beam etc. SCAN.

scansion, *n.* the act of scanning verse; a system of scanning. [L *scansio*, from *scandere*, to SCAN]

Scansores, *n.pl.* in former classifications, an order of birds containing the cuckoos, woodpeckers, parrots, trogons etc. with feet adapted for climbing. **scansorial,** *a.* climbing, adapted for climbing; belonging to the Scansores. *n.* any bird of the order Scansores. [mod. L, as prec.]

scant, *a.* not full, large or plentiful; scarcely sufficient, not enough, deficient; short (of); (*chiefly dial. N Am.*) sparing, stingy. *v.t.* to limit, to skimp, to stint; to dole out grudgingly. *v.i.* (*Naut.*) of the wind, to fail, to decrease in force, to become unfavourable. **scantly,** *adv.* **scanty,** *a.* scant, deficient, insufficient; limited or scarcely adequate in extent, size or quantity. **scantily,** *adv.* **scantiness,** *n.* [Icel. *skamt*, short]

scantle, *v.t.* to divide into small pieces, to partition. *n.* a gauge by which slates are cut; a small kind of slate. [perh. from SCANTLING]

scantling, *n.* †a specimen, a sample, a pattern; a small quantity or portion; a rough draft or sketch; a beam less than 5 in. (12·7 cm) in breadth and thickness; the sectional measurement of timber; the measurement of stone in all three dimensions; a set of fixed dimensions, esp. in shipbuilding; a trestle for a cask. [ME *scantilone*, ONorth.F *escantillon* (F *échantillon*), etym. doubtful (perh. EX-, CANTLE)]

scantly, scantiness, scanty SCANT.

scape[1], *n.* the spring or shaft of a column; a leafless radical stem bearing the flower; the basal part of an insect's antenna; the shaft of a feather. **scapeless,** *a.* **scapiferous,** *a.* bearing a scape. **scapiform,** *a.* [L *scapus*, cogn. with SCEPTRE]

†**scape**[2], **scapegoat,** *n.* (*Bibl.*) a goat on whose head the high priest laid the sins of the people and then sent it away into the wilderness; one made to bear blame due to another. **scapegrace,** *n.* a graceless, good-for-nothing person, esp. a child. [ESCAPE]

-scape, *comb. form.* scene, view, as in *seascape, townscape*. [LANDSCAPE]

scapeless SCAPE[1].

scapement, ESCAPEMENT.

scapha, *n.* the boat-shaped depression of the helix of the ear. [L]

†**scaphism,** *n.* an ancient punishment among the Persians in which the victim was confined in a hollow tree, the limbs being smeared with honey to attract insects. [-ISM]

scaphite, *n.* a cephalopod of the fossil genus *Scaphites*.

scaph(o)-, *comb. form.* boat-shaped. [Gr. *skaphē*, boat]

scaphocephalic, *a.* having a boat-shaped skull, owing to premature union of the parietal bones at the sagittal suture. **scaphocephalous,** *a.* **scaphocephalus,** **scaphocephaly,** *n.* [Gr. *kephalē*, head, -IC]

scaphoid, *a.* boat-shaped, navicular. *n.* a scaphoid bone. **scaphoid bone,** *n.* a bone of the carpus or tarsus. [-OID]

scapiform, scapiferous SCAPE[1].

scapinade, *n.* a rascally trick, a piece of roguery. [*Scapin* in Molière's *Les Fourberies de Scapin*]

scapolite, *n.* one of a group of tetragonal silicate minerals of calcium, aluminium and sodium. [G *Skapolith* (Gr. *skapos*, cp. SCAPE[1], -LITE)]

scapple, scabble, *v.t.* to reduce (stone) to a level surface without smoothing. [OF *escapeler*, to dress timber]

scapula, *n.* (*pl.* **-lae, -las**) the shoulder-blade. **scapular,** *a.* pertaining to the scapula or shoulder. *n.* in the Roman Catholic Church, a vestment usu. consisting of two strips of cloth worn by certain monastic orders across the shoulders and hanging down the breast and back; an adaptation of this worn as a badge of affiliation to a religious order; a bandage for the shoulder-blade; any of a series of feathers springing from the base of the humerus in birds, and lying along the side of the back. †**scapulary,** *n.* in the Roman Catholic Church, a scapular. **scapulated,** *a.* having the scapular feathers conspicuous, esp. by their white colour. **scapulimancy,** *n.* divination by a shoulder-blade. **scapulo-,** *comb. form.* **scapulo-humeral,** *a.* pertaining to the scapula and the humerus. **scapulo-ulnar,** *a.* pertaining to the scapula and the ulnus. [late L, sing. of L *scapulae*]

scapus, SCAPE[1].

scar[1], *n.* a mark left by a wound, burn, ulcer etc., a cicatrice; the mark left by the fall of a leaf, stem, seed, deciduous part etc.; the after-effects of emotional distress, a psychological trauma etc. *v.t.* (*past, p.p.* **scarred**) to mark with a scar or scars; to leave with lasting adverse effects. *v.i.* to form a scar, to cicatrize. **scarless,** *a.* **scarry,** *a.* [OF *escare*, L and Gr. *eschara*, hearth, scar of a burn]

scar[2], *n.* a crag, a cliff, a precipitous escarpment. [Icel. *sker*, SKERRY, cogn. with SHEAR]

scar[3], *n.* a parrot-fish.

scarab, *n.* an ancient Egyptian sacred beetle; a seal or gem cut in the shape of a beetle, worn as an amulet by the Egyptians; a scarabaeid. **Scarabaeus,** *n.* a genus of beetles typical of the Scarabaeidae. **scarabaeid,** *a.* of or pertaining to the Scarabaeidae, a family of beetles containing the dung beetles. *n.* a beetle of this family. **scarabaeist,** *n.* **scarabaeoid,** *n., a.* †**scarabee,** *n.* a scarab. [F *scarabée*, L *scarabaeus*]

scaramouch, *n.* a coward and braggart. [It. *Scaramuccia*, a character in old Italian comedy, characterized by great boastfulness and poltroonery]

scarbroite, *n.* a clayey hydrous silicate mineral of alumina found near Scarborough, Yorks. [*Scarbro'*, *Scarborough*]

scarce, *a.* infrequent, seldom met with, rare, uncommon; insufficient, not plentiful, scantily supplied; †parsimonious. *adv.* hardly, scarcely. **to make oneself scarce,** to keep out of the way; to be off, to decamp. **scarcely,** *adv.* hardly, barely, only just; only with difficulty; not quite (used as a polite negative). **scarceness, scarcity,** *n.* deficiency; rareness; a dearth (of); a famine; †parsimoniousness, stinginess. [ONorth.F *escars* (cp. It. *scarso*), perh. from late L *scarpsus*, *excarpsus*, L *excarptus* (EX-, *carptus*, p.p. of *carpere*, to pluck)]

scarcement, *n.* (*Sc., North.*) a set-off in a wall, or a plain flat ledge resulting from this. [etym. doubtful]

scare, *v.t.* to frighten, to alarm, to strike with sudden fear; to drive (away) through fear. *v.i.* to become frightened. *n.* a sudden fright, a panic; a widespread terror of e.g. invasion, epidemic etc. **scarecrow,** *n.* a figure set up to frighten birds away from crops etc.; a bugbear; a shabby or absurd-looking person, a guy. **scaremonger,** *n.* one who causes scares, esp. by circulating unfounded reports etc. **scary,** *a.* [prob. from ME *skerren*, Icel. *skjarr*, shy, timid]

scarf[1], *n.* (*pl.* **scarfs, scarves**) a long strip or square of some material worn round the neck and shoulders or over the head for warmth or decoration; a neckcloth or neck-tie; a stole; a (military or official) sash. *v.t.* to clothe or cover with or as with a scarf; to wrap (around or about) as a scarf; †to blindfold. **scarf-pin, -ring,** *n.* a pin or ring, usu. of gold, used to fasten a neck-tie. **scarf-skin,** *n.* the outer layer of skin, the cuticle. **scarf-wise,** *adv.* used or worn as a scarf, baldric-wise. **scarfed,** *a.* [perh. from Dut. *scherf*, a shred, or ONorth.F *escarpe*, OF *escharpe*, cp. SCRIP and SCRAP[1]]

scarf[2], *v.t.* to join the ends of (timber) by means of a scarf-joint; to cut a scarf in or on; to flench (a whale). *n.* (*pl.* **scarfs**) (**scarf, scarf-joint**) a joint made by bevelling or notching so that the thickness is not increased, and then bolting or strapping together; a bevelled or notched end that forms such a joint; an incision or groove cut along the body of a whale before stripping off the blubber. **scarf-weld,** *n.* a welded joint between two pieces of metal. **scarfing,** *n.* **scarfing-machine,** *n.* [perh. from Swed. *skarfva*, from *scarf*, a seam, cogn. with prec.]

scarf[3], *n.* (*Sc.*) a cormorant. [Icel. *skarfr*, cp. Norw. and Swed. *skarf*]

Scargill, *n.* **Arthur** (1938–), British trade-union leader. Elected president of the National Union of Miners (NUM) in 1981, he embarked on a collision course with the Conservative government of Margaret Thatcher. The damaging strike of 1984–85 split the miners's movement.

scarify, *v.t.* (*Surg.*) to scratch or make slight incisions in; to loosen the surface of (soil); to pain, to torture, to criticize mercilessly. **scarification,** *n.* **scarificator,** *n.* a surgical instrument with lancet-points used in scarifying. **scarifier,** *n.* one who scarifies; a scarificator; an implement or machine for breaking up soil etc. [F *scarifier*, L *scarīficāre*, Gr. *skariphasthai*, from *skariphos*, pencil, style, cogn. with L. *scrībere*, to write]

scarious, -iose, *a.* of bracts etc., membranous and dry. [F *scarieux* (acc. to C.O.D. from L. *scaria*, thorny shrub)]

scarlatina, *n.* (a mild form of) scarlet fever. [It. *scarlattina*]

Scarlatti[1], *n.* **(Giuseppe) Domenico** (1685–1757), Italian composer, eldest son of Alessandro Scarlatti, who lived most of his life in Portugal and Spain in the service of the Queen of Spain. He wrote highly original harpsichord sonatas.

Scarlatti[2], *n.* **(Pietro) Alessandro (Gaspare)** (1660–1725), Italian Baroque composer, Master of the Chapel at the court of Naples, who developed the opera form (arias interspersed with recitative). He composed more than 100 operas, including *Tigrane* (1715), as well as church music and oratorios.

scarless SCAR[1].

scarlet, *n.* a bright red colour tending towards orange; cloth or dress of this colour esp. official robes or uniform. *a.* of a scarlet colour; dressed in scarlet. **scarlet admiral,** *n.* a butterfly, the red admiral. **scarlet-bean** SCARLET RUNNER. **scarlet fever,** *n.* an infectious fever characterized by the eruption of red patches on the skin. **scarlet hat,** *n.* a cardinal's hat; the rank of cardinal. **scarlet rash,** *n.* roseola. **scarlet runner,** *n.* a trailing bean, *Phaseolus multiflorus*, with scarlet flowers. **scarlet woman,** *n.* worldliness or sensuality; pagan or papal Rome (see Rev. xvii.4–5); a prostitute. [OF *escarlate* (F *écarlate*), Pers. *saqalāt*, scarlet cloth]

Scarlet Pimpernel, The, a historical adventure novel by Baroness Orczy published in the UK in 1905. Set in Paris during the Reign of Terror (1793–94), it describes the exploits of a group of Britons, the League of the Scarlet Pimpernel, and particularly their leader, Sir Percy Blakeney, who save aristocrats from the Revolution.

scaroid SCARUS.

scarp[1], *n.* a steep or nearly perpendicular slope; the interior slope of the ditch at the foot of the parapet of a fortification. *v.t.* to cut down so to be steep or nearly perpendicular; (*in p.p.*) precipitous, abrupt. [OF *escarpe*, It. *scarpa*, perh. from OHG *scarpōn*, cp. SHARP]

scarp[2], *n.* (*Her.*) a diminutive of the bend sinister, half its width. [O.North.F *escarpe*, SCARF[1]]

scarper, *v.i.* (*sl.*) to leave in a hurry; to go away without notice or warning. [prob. from It. *scappare*, to escape]

†**scarpines,** *n.pl.* an instrument of torture similar to the boot. [It. *scarpino*, dim. of *scarpa*, shoe]

scart, *v.t.* (*Sc.*) to scratch, to scrape; to scribble. *n.* a scratch; a mark, a dash, a stroke; a puny or miserly person. [var. of SCRAT]

scarus, a genus of sea-fishes containing the parrot-wrasses; a parrot-fish. scaroid, *a., n.* [L, from Gr. *skaros*]

scarves, *pl.* SCARF[1].

scary SCARE.

scat[1], *n.* (*Scand. Hist.*) tax, tribute; a land-tax in Orkney and Shetland from an odaller to the Crown. **scat field, hold** or **land,** *n.* land subject to this. [Icel. *skattr*, cp. OE *sceatt*]

scat[2], *n.* (*dial.*) a blow; the noise of a blow or hit; a brisk shower or squall. **scatty[1],** *a.* showery. [perh. imit.]

scat[3], *int.* go away!, be off! *v.i.* (*past, p.p.* **scatted**) (*coll.*) to depart hastily; (*chiefly N Am., coll.*) to move quickly. [etym. doubtful]

scat[4], *n.* jazz singing in meaningless syllables. *v.i.* (*past, p.p.* **scatted**) to sing in this way. [perh. imit.]

scatch[1], *n.* a stilt. [ONorth.F. *escache* (F. *échasse*), see SKATE[2]]

scatch[2], *n.* a kind of bridle-bit. [It. *scaccia*]

scathe, *n.* †hurt, harm, injury. *v.t.* to hurt, to harm, to injure, esp. by scorching; to attack severely with sarcasm, criticism etc. †**scatheful,** *a.* †**scathefulness,** *n.* **scatheless,** *a.* **scathing,** *a.* hurtful, harmful; of sarcasm etc., very bitter or severe, withering. **scathingly,** *adv.* [Icel. *skatha*, cp. Swed. *skada*, Dan. *skade*, OE *scathan*, G and Dut. *schaden*, also Gr. *askēthēs*, unharmed]

scatology, *n.* the study of fossil excrement or coprolites; the biological study of excrement, esp. to determine diet; interest in or literature characterized by obscenity. **scatological,** *a.* **scatomancy,** *n.* divination by means of faeces. **scatophagous,** *a.* feeding on dung. **scatoscopy,** *n.* diagnosis by means of faeces. [Gr. *skatos*, gen. of *skōr*, dung, -LOGY]

scatter, *v.t.* to throw loosely about, to fling in all directions; to strew, to bestrew; to cause to separate in various directions, to disperse; to dissipate; to diffuse (radiation) or cause to spread out. *v.i.* to disperse; to be dissipated or diffused. *n.* the act of scattering; a small number scattered about; the extent of scattering. **scatter-brain,** *n.* a giddy, heedless person. **scatter-brained,** *a.* **scatter-cushion, -rug,** *n.* a small cushion or rug which can be moved to any position in a room. **scatter-mouch,** SCARAMOUCH. **scattered,** *a.* irregularly situated, not together; widely apart. **scattering,** *n.* the act of dispersing or strewing something; a small amount or number irregularly strewn; the deflecting or spreading out of a beam of radiation in passing through matter. **scatteringly,** *adv.* **scattery,** *a.* [ME *scateren*, freq. of SCAT[3], cogn. with Gr. *skedannunai*, to scatter, Sansk. *skhad*, to cut]

scatty[1] SCAT[2].

scatty[2], *a.* (*coll.*) incapable of prolonged concentration, empty-headed, giddy. [prob. from *scatter-brain*]

†**scaturient,** *a.* gushing out, as from a fountain. [L *scatūriens -ntem*, pres.p. of *scatūrīre*, from *scatere*, to flow]

scaud[1], (*Sc.***)** SCALD[1].

scaud[2], (*Sc.***)** SCOLD.

scaup, scaup-duck, *n.* a sea-duck of the genus *Aythya*, esp. *A. marila*, found in the northern regions. [var. of SCALP]

scauper, *n.* a wood-engraver's gouge-like tool. [prob. var. of SCALPER]

scaur[1], (*Sc.***)** SCAR[2].

scaur[2] *n.* (*Orkney and Shetland*) a young gull. [cp. Norw. *skaare*, Icel. *skāre*]

†**scavage,** *n.* a duty formerly exacted of merchant-

strangers on goods offered for sale in London and other towns. [A-F *scawage*, from *escauwer*, to inspect, Flem. *scauwen*, OE *scēawian*, to SHOW]

scavenger, *n.* a person employed to clean the streets by sweeping, scraping, and carrying away refuse; one who collects waste or discarded objects; a chemical added to remove or neutralize unwanted material; an organism feeding on refuse, carrion etc.; a child employed in a spinning-mill to collect loose cotton; anyone willing to do 'dirty work' or delighting in filthy subjects. **scavenger-beetle, -crab,** *n.* a beetle or crab feeding on carrion. **scavenge,** *v.t.* to clean (streets etc.); to search for or salvage (something usable) from among waste or discarded material; to remove impurities from (molten metal) by causing their chemical combination; to remove (impurities etc.). *v.i.* to act as a scavenger; to search for usable material. **scavengery,** *n.* [orig. *scavager*, collector of scavage, from prec.]

scavenger's daughter, *n.* an instrument of torture for compressing the body, invented by Leonard Skevington or Skeffington, Lieutenant of the Tower, under Henry VIII. [travesty of *Skevington*]

scazon, *n.* a satiric metre of an irregular or faltering character, esp. an iambic trimeter ending with a spondee or trochee, a choliamb. **scazontic,** *a.* [L, from Gr. *skazōn*, orig. pres.p. of *skazein*, to limp]

ScD, (*abbr.*) Doctor of Science.

SCE, (*abbr.*) Scottish Certificate of Education.

†**scelerate,** *n.* a scoundrel, a wretch. [L *scelerātus*, from *scelus -eris*, wickedness (cp. F *scélérat*)]

scelides, *n.pl.* the posterior limbs of a mammal. **scelidate,** *a.* **scelidosaur,** *n.* a dinosaur of the Jurassic genus *Scelidosaurus*. **scelidosaurian,** *n., a.* **scelidosauriform,** *a.* **scelidosauroid,** *n., a.* **scelidothere,** *n.* a S American megatherian edentate mammal. [mod. L, from Gr. *skelos*, leg]

scelp, SKELP.

scena, *n.* (*pl.* **scene,**) a long elaborate solo piece or scene in opera. [It., from L *scēna*, SCENE]

scenario, *n.* (*pl.* **-rios**) a sketch or outline of the scenes and main points of a play etc. the script of a film with dialogue and directions for the producer during the actual shooting; an account or outline of projected, expected or imagined future events. [It.]

scend, (*Naut.*) SEND.

scene, *n.* the stage in a Greek or Roman theatre; hence, the stage, the theatre; the place where anything occurs or is exhibited as on a stage; the place in which the action of a play or story is supposed to take place; one of the painted frames, hangings or other devices used to give an appearance of reality to the action of a play; a division of a play comprising so much as passes without change of locality or break of time, or, in French drama, without intermediate entrances or exits; a single event, situation or incident in a play or film; a film or television sequence; a description of an incident, situation etc. from life; a striking incident, esp. an exhibition of feeling or passion; a landscape, a view, regarded as a piece of scenery; (*coll.*) one's usual or preferred social environment, area of interest etc.; (*coll.*) an area of activity or business. **behind the scenes,** at the back of the stage; in possession of facts etc., not generally known. **change of scene,** change of surroundings by travel. **scene-dock,** *n.* a place near the stage in a theatre for storing scenery. **scene-painter,** *n.* one who paints scenery for theatres. **scene-painting,** *n.* **scene-shifter,** *n.* a person employed in a theatre to move scenery. **scenery,** *n.* the various parts or accessories used on the stage to represent the actual scene of the action; the views presented by natural features, esp. when picturesque. **scenic,** *a.* of or pertaining to the stage; of or pertaining to natural scenery; characterized by beautiful natural scenery, picturesque; arranged for effect, dramatic, theatrical; of a painting etc., depicting a scene or incident. **scenic railway,** *n.* a switchback railway at a fun-fair. [L *scēna*, Gr. *skēnē*, tent, stage]

scenography, *n.* the representation of an object in perspective. **scenograph,** *n.* **scenographer,** *n.* **scenographic,** *a.* **scenographically,** *adv.* [Gr. *skēnographia* (prec., -GRAPHY)]

scent, *v.t.* to perceive by smell; to recognize the odour of; to begin to suspect; to trace or hunt (out) by or as by smelling; to perfume. *v.i.* to exercise sense of smell; †to give forth a smell. *n.* odour, esp. of a pleasant kind; the odour left by an animal forming a trail by which it can be followed (as by hounds); pieces of paper left as a trail in a paper-chase; a trail to be pursued; a clue; a liquid essence containing fragrant extracts from flowers etc., a perfume; the sense of smell, esp. the power of recognizing or tracing things by smelling. **scent-bag,** *n.* an external pouch-like scent-gland, as in the musk-deer; a bag containing aniseed etc., used to leave a track of scent for hounds to follow. **scent-bottle,** *n.* a bottle for holding perfume. **scent-gland,** *n.* a gland secreting an odorous substance, as in the musk-deer, civet etc. **scent-organ,** *n.* **scented,** *a.* having a scent (*usu. in comb.*, as *keen-scented*). †**scentful,** *a.* highly scented; having a quick scent. **scentless,** *a.* [orig. *sent*, F *sentir*, L *sentīre*, to perceive]

sceptic, (*esp. N Am.*) **skeptic,** *n.* one who doubts the truth of a revealed religion; an agnostic; an atheist; a person of a questioning, doubting or incredulous habit of mind; one who casts doubt on any statement, theory etc., esp. in a cynical manner; one who questions or denies the possibility of attaining knowledge of truth; an adherent of philosophic Scepticism, a Pyrrhonist. *a.* sceptical. **scepsis,** *n.* scepticism, sceptical philosophy; the attitude of philosophic doubt. **sceptical,** *a.* pertaining to or characteristic of a sceptic; doubting or denying the truth of revelation, or the possibility of knowledge; given to doubting or questioning, incredulous. **sceptically,** *adv.* †**scepticalness, scepticism,** *n.* **scepticize, -ise,** *v.i.* to act as a sceptic. [F *sceptique*, L *scepticus*, Gr. *skeptikos*, from *skeptesthai*, to examine]

Scepticism, *n.* an ancient philosophical view that absolute knowledge of things is ultimately unobtainable, hence the only proper attitude is to suspend judgement. Its origins lay in the teachings of the Greek philosopher Pyrrho, who maintained that peace of mind lay in renouncing all claims to knowledge.

sceptre, (*esp. N Am.*) **scepter,** *n.* a staff or baton borne by a sovereign as a symbol of authority; royal authority. *v.t.* (*in p.p.*) to invest with a sceptre or with royal authority. **sceptreless,** *a.* [ME and OF *ceptre*, *sceptre*, L *scēptrum*, Gr. *skēptron*, from *skēptein*, to prop]

sch., (*abbr.*) school.

schadenfreude, *n.* pleasure in others' misfortunes. [G *Schaden*, damage, *Freude*, joy]

†**schediasm,** *n.* something done off-hand; an extemporized or hasty writing. [Gr. *schediasma*, from *schediazein*, to do a thing at once, from *schedon*, near]

schedule, *n.* a written or printed table, list, catalogue or inventory (appended to a document); a timetable; a planned programme of events, tasks etc. *v.t.* to enter in a schedule; to make a schedule or list of; to arrange for a particular time. **schedulize, -ise,** *v.t.* [ME and OF *cedule*, from late L *scedula, schedula*, dim. of L *scheda*, strip of papyrus, Gr. *schidē*, splint, from *schizein*, to cleave]

Scheele, *n.* **Karl** (1742–86), Swedish chemist and pharmacist. In the book *Experiments on Air and Fire* (1777), he argued that the atmosphere was composed of two gases. One, which supported combustion (oxygen), he called 'fire air', and the other, which inhibited combustion (nitrogen), he called 'vitiated air'. He thus anticipated Joseph Priestley in his discovery of oxygen by two years.

scheelite, *n.* a vitreous variously-coloured mineral, a tungstate of calcium. [Karl *Scheele*, see prec.]

Scheer, *n.* **Reinhard** (1863–1928), German admiral in World War I, commander of the High Sea Fleet in 1916 at the Battle of Jutland.

Scheherazade, *n.* the storyteller in the *Arabian*

Nights.

scheiner, *n.* term applied to a scale for photographic film speed. [Julius *Scheiner*, 1858–1913, its German inventor]

schema, *n.* (*pl.* **-mata**) a scheme, summary, outline or conspectus; a chart or diagram; the abstract figure of a syllogism; a figure of speech; in Kant's philosophy, the form, type or rule under which the mind applies the categories to the material of knowledge furnished by sense-perception. **schematic**, *a.* having, or in the nature of, a plan or schema. **schematically,** *adv.* **schematize, -ise,** *v.t.* to formulate or express by means of a scheme; to apply the Kantian categories to. **schematism,** *n.* [L, from Gr. *schēma -atos*, from *schē-*, base of *schēsō*, fut. of *echein*, to have]

scheme, *n.* a plan, a project, a proposed method of doing something; a contrivance, an underhand design; a table or schedule of proposed acts, events etc., a syllabus; a systematic statement, representation, diagram or arrangement of facts, objects, principles etc.; a table of classification. *v.t.* to plan, to design to contrive, to plot. *v.i.* to form plans; to plot. **schematist,**, *n.* one given to forming schemes, a projector. **schemer,** *n.* **scheming,** *a.* given to forming schemes. †**schemist,** *n.* [L SCHEMA]

scheme-arch, *n.* an arch of circular form less in extent than a semicircle; the part of a three-centre or elliptical arch having a wider radius. [etym. doubtful]

schepen, *n.* a Dutch alderman or magistrate. [Dut., cp. OHG *sceffin*]

Scherchen, *n.* **Hermann** (1891–1966), German conductor. He collaborated with Schoenberg, and in 1919 founded the journal *Melos* to promote contemporary music. He moved to Switzerland in 1933, and was active as a conductor and teacher. He also wrote two texts, *Handbook of Conducting* and *The Nature of Music*. During the 1950s he founded a music publishing house, Ars Viva Verlag, and an electronic studio at Gravesano.

scherzo, *n.* (*pl.* **-zi**, **-zos**) a light playful movement in music, usu. following a slow one, in a symphony or sonata. **scherzando**, *adv.* (*Mus.*) playfully. [It., from Teut. (cp. G *Scherz*, sport)]

†**schesis,** *n.* (*pl.* **-ses**) relation, condition with regard to other things; disposition or state of the body. †**schetic**, *a.* constitutional; habitual. [Gr. *schesis*, cogn. with SCHEME]

Schiaparelli[1]**,** *n.* **Elsa** (1896–1973), Italian couturier and knitwear designer. Her innovative fashion ideas included padded shoulders, sophisticated colours ('shocking pink'), and the pioneering use of zips and synthetic fabrics.

Schiaparelli[2]**,** *n.* **Giovanni (Virginio)** (1835–1910), Italian astronomer, who discovered the so-called 'Martian canals'. Among his achievements were studies of ancient and medieval astronomy, the discovery of asteroid 69 (Hesperia) Apr. 1861, observation of double stars, and the discovery of the connection between comets and meteors. In 1877 he first drew attention to the linear markings on Mars, which gave rise to the 'Martian canal' controversy. These markings are now known to be optical effects and not real lines.

schiavone, *n.* a 17th-cent. basket-hilted broadsword, so called because the Schiavoni or Slav bodyguards of the Doge were armed with it. [It.]

Schick test, *n.* a test to determine susceptibility to diphtheria by injecting diluted diphtheria toxin into the skin. [Bela *Schick*, 1877–1967, US paediatrician]

Schiedam, *n.* Hollands gin. [town where made]

Schiele, *n.* **Egon** (1890–1918), Austrian expressionist artist. Originally a landscape painter, he was strongly influenced by Art Nouveau and developed a contorted linear style. His subject matter included portraits and nudes. In 1911 he was arrested for alleged obscenity.

Schiller, *n.* **Johann Christoph Friedrich von** (1759–1805), German dramatist, poet, and historian. He wrote *Sturm und Drang* (storm and stress) verse and plays, including the dramatic trilogy *Wallenstein* (1798–99). Much of his work concerns the desire for political freedom and for the avoidance of mediocrity.

schiller, *n.* the peculiar bronze-like sheen or iridescence characteristic of certain minerals. **schiller-spar, schillerite,** *n.* a rock allied to diallage which has undergone schillerization. **schillerization, -isation,** *n.* a process by which minute crystals are deposited in other minerals so as to produce this peculiar sheen. **schillerize, -ise,** *v.t.* [G]

schilling, *n.* the standard monetary unit of Austria. [G]

schindylesis, *n.* (*pl.* **-ses**) an articulation in which a thin part of one bone fits into a groove in another. **schindyletic,** *a.* [Gr. *schindulēsis*]

Schinkel, *n.* **Karl Friedrich** (1781–1841), Prussian neo-classical architect. Major works include the Old Museum, Berlin, (1823–30), the Nikolaikirche in Potsdam (1830–37), and the Roman Bath (1833) in the park of Potsdam.

schipperke, *n.* a small black variety of lapdog. [Dut., little boatman]

schisiophone, *n.* an instrument comprising a hammer and induction-balance for detecting flaws in iron rails. [Gr. *schisis,* schiseōs from *schizein*, to cleave, -PHONE]

schism, *n.* a split or division in a community; division in a Church, esp. secession of a part or separation into two Churches; the sin of causing such division. **schismatic**, *n.*, *a.* **schismatical,** *a.* **schismatically,** *adv.* †**schismaticalness,** *n.* **schismatist,** *n.* **schismatize, -ise,** *v.t.*, *v.i.* **schismless,** *a.* [F *schisme*, late L and Gr. *schisma*, from *schizein*, to split]

schist, *n.* a rock of a more or less foliated or laminar structure, tending to split easily. **schistaceous,** *a.* slate-grey. **schistoid**, **schistose**, **schistous,** *a.* of the nature or structure of schist. [F *schiste*, L and Gr. *schistos*, easily split, as prec.]

schistosoma, *n.* the *Bilharzia* genus of worms. **schistosomiasis**, *n.* a disease caused by infestation with worms of the genus *Schistosoma*.

Schizanthus, *n.* a genus of annual plants from Chile with much-divided leaves and showy flowers. [Gr. *anthos*, flower]

schizo, *n.* (*coll.*) short for SCHIZOPHRENIC.

schiz(o)-, *comb. form.* marked by a cleft or clefts; tending to split. [Gr. *schizein*, to cleave]

schizocarp, *n.* a fruit splitting into several one-seeded portions without dehiscing. **schizocarpic, -pous**, *a.*

schizocoele, *n.* a perivisceral cavity produced by a splitting of the mesoblast of the embryo. **schizocoelous**, *a.* [Gr. *koilos*, hollow]

schizodon, *n.* a genus of S American rodents having a molar with folds meeting in the middle. [Gr. *odous odontos*, tooth]

schizogenesis, *n.* reproduction by fission. **schizogenic, -genetic**, *a.* **schizogenically, -genetically,** *adv.* **schizogony**, *n.* schizogenesis.

schizognathous, *n.* having the bones of the palate cleft from the vomer and each other, as in the gulls, plovers etc. **schizognathism,** *n.* [Gr. *gnathos*, jaw]

schizomycete, *n.* (*Bot.*) one of the Schizomycetes, a class of microscopic organisms comprising bacteria. **schizomycetous**, *a.* [MYCETES]

schizophrenia, *n.* a severe psychological disorder characterized by loss of contact with reality, personality disintegration, hallucinations, delusions etc. **schizophrenic**, *n.*, *a.*

schizopod, *n.* one of the Schizopoda, a sub-order of podophthalmate crustaceans with the feet apparently cleft. **schizopodous**, *a.* [Gr. *pous podos,* foot]

schizothecal, *a.* (*Ornith.*) having the tarsus divided by scutellation or reticulation. [Gr. *thēkē*, case]

schizothymia, *n.* introversion exhibiting elements of schizophrenia but within normal limits. **schizothymic,** *a.* [Gr. *thymos*, mind, spirit]

schläger, *n.* a German student's duelling sword, pointless, but with sharpened edges towards the end. [G, from *schlagen*, to beat]

Schlegel[1]**,** *n.* **August Wilhelm von** (1767–1845), German Romantic author, translator of Shakespeare, whose *Über dramatische Kunst und Literatur/Lectures on Dramatic Art and Literature* (1809–11) broke down the formalism of the old classical criteria of literary composition. Friedrich von Schlegel was his brother.

Schlegel[2], *n.* **Friedrich von** (1772–1829), German critic, who (with his brother August) was a founder of the Romantic movement, and a pioneer in the comparative study of languages.

schlemiel, schlemihl, *n.* (*chiefly N Am., coll.*) a bungling clumsy person who is easily victimized. [Yiddish]

schlepp, , *v.t.* (*chiefly N Am., coll.*) to drag, pull. *n.* an unlucky or incompetent person. [Yiddish]

Schlesinger, *n.* **John** (1926–), British film and television director, responsible for such British films as *Billy Liar* (1963) and *Darling* (1965). His first US film, *Midnight Cowboy* (1969), was a big commercial success and was followed by *Sunday, Bloody Sunday* (1971), *Marathon Man* (1976), and *Yanks* (1979).

Schleswig-Holstein, *n. Land* (state) of West Germany. **area** 15,700 sq km/6,060 sq miles. **capital** Kiel. **towns** Lübeck, Flensburg, Schleswig. **population** (1988) 2,613,000. **products** shipbuilding, mechanical and electrical engineering, food processing. **religion** Protestant 87%; Catholic 6%.

Schlieffen Plan, *n.* military plan produced by chief of the German general staff, Gen. Count Alfred von Schlieffen (1833–1913) Dec. 1905, which formed the basis of German military planning before World War I, and which inspired Hitler's plans for the conquest of W Europe in World War II. It involved a simultaneous attack on Russia and France, the object being to defeat France quickly and then deploy all available resources against the Russians.

Schliemann, *n.* **Heinrich** (1822–90), German archaeologist. He earned a fortune as a businessman, retiring in 1863 to pursue his life-long ambition to discover a historical basis for Homer's Iliad. In 1871 he began excavating at Hissarlik, Turkey, which yielded the ruins of nine consecutive cities and was indeed the site of Troy. His later excavations were at Mycenae (1874–76), where he discovered the ruins of the Mycenaean civilization.

schlieren, *n.* small streaks of different composition in igneous rock; streaks in a transparent fluid caused by regions of differing density and refractive index. [G]

schloss, *n.* a castle (in Germany). [G]

schmaltz, schmalz, *n.* over-sentimentality, esp. in music. **schmaltzy,** *a.* [Yiddish *schmalts*, fat, dripping]

schmelze, *n.* one of various kinds of coloured glass, esp. that coloured red and used to flash white glass. [G *Schmelz*, enamel, cp. SMELT[1]]

Schmidt, *n.* **Helmut** (1918–), West German socialist politician, member of the Social Democratic Party (SPD), chancellor (1974–83). As chancellor, Schmidt introduced social reforms and continued Brandt's policy of Ostpolitik. With the French president Giscard d'Estaing, Schmidt introduced annual world and European economic summits. He was a firm supporter of NATO and of the deployment of US nuclear missiles in West Germany during the early 1980s.

Schmidt-Rottluff, *n.* **Karl** (1884–1974), German expressionist painter and printmaker, a founder member of die Brücke in Dresden in 1905, active in Berlin from 1911. Influenced by van Gogh and the Fauves, he developed a vigorous style of brushwork and a bold palette. He painted portraits and landscapes, and produced numerous woodcuts and lithographs.

schnapps, *n.* Hollands gin. [G, from Dut. *snaps*, mouthful, from *snappen*, to SNAP]

schnauzer, *n.* a wire-haired German terrier. [G *Schnauze*, snout]

Schneider, *n.* **Romy.** stage name of Rosemarie Albach-Retty (1938–82), Austrian film actress who starred in *Boccaccio '70* (1962), *Le Procès/Der Prozess* (1962), and *Ludwig* (1972).

Schneiderian, *a.* applied to the mucous membrane of the nose, first investigated by the anatomist Schneider. [C.V. *Schneider*, 1610–80, German anatomist]

schnitzel, *n.* a veal cutlet. [G]

schnorkel, SNORKEL.

schnozzle, *n.* (*chiefly N Am., coll.*) a nose. [Yiddish *shnoitsl*, G *Schnauze*]

Schoenberg, *n.* **Arnold (Franz Walter)** (1874–1951), Austro-Hungarian composer, a US citizen from 1941. After Romantic early work such as *Verklärte Nacht* (1899) and the *Gurrelieder/Songs of Gurra* (1900–11), he experimented with atonality, producing such works as *Pierrot Lunaire* (1912) before developing the 12-tone system of musical composition. This was further developed by his pupils BERG and WEBERN.

scholar, *n.* a learned person, esp. one with a profound knowledge of literature; an undergraduate on the foundation of a college and receiving assistance from its funds, usu. after a competitive examination; a person acquiring knowledge, a (good or apt) learner; a disciple; a pupil, a student, one attending school. **scholarlike,** *a.* **scholarly,** *a.* befitting a scholar; learned. †*adv.* as befits a scholar. **scholarship,** *n.* high attainments in literature or science; education, instruction; education, usu. with maintenance, free or at reduced fees, granted to a successful candidate after a competitive examination; the emoluments so granted to a scholar. [A-F *escoler* (F *écolier*), cp. OE *scolere* (SCHOOL[2], -ER), assim. to late L *scholāris*]

scholastic, *a.* pertaining to school, schools, universities etc.; educational, academic; pedagogic, pedantic; pertaining to or characteristic of the schoolmen of the Middle Ages; given to precise definitions and logical subtleties. *n.* a schoolman of the Middle Ages; one characterized by the method and subtlety of the schoolman; a mere scholar, an academic person; a Jesuit of the third grade. **scholastically,** *adv.* **scholasticism,** *n.* [L *scholasticus*, Gr. *scholastikos*, from *scholazein*, to be at leisure, see SCHOOL[2]]

scholiast, *n.* a commentator, esp. an ancient grammarian who annotated the classics. **scholiastic,** *a.* **scholium,** *n.* (*pl.* **-lia**) a marginal note, esp. an explanatory comment on the Greek and Latin authors by an early grammarian. [Gr. *scholiastēs*, from *scholiazein*, to write *scholia*]

school[1], *n.* a shoal of fish, porpoises etc. *v.i.* to form a school, swim in a school. **school-fish,** *n.* a fish that usually appears in shoals, esp. the menhaden. **school-whale,** *n.* [Dut., cp. SHOAL[2]]

school[2], *n.* an institution for education or instruction, esp. one for instruction of a more elementary kind than that given at universities; a faculty of a university; an establishment offering specialized teaching; the building or buildings of a school; the body of pupils of a school; a session or time during which teaching is carried on; a lecture-room; a seminary in the Middle Ages for teaching logic, metaphysics and theology; (*pl.*) the mediaeval universities, professors, teaching etc.; scholasticism; any of the branches of study with separate examinations taken by candidates for honours; the hall where such examinations are held; (*pl.*) the final BA examination at Oxford Univ.; the body of disciples or followers of a philosopher, artist etc., or of adherents of a cause, principle, system of thought etc.; (*Mus.*) a book of instruction, a manual; any sphere or circumstances serving to discipline or instruct; (*coll.*) a group of people assembled for a common purpose, as playing poker. *v.t.* to instruct, to educate; to train, to drill; to discipline, to bring under control; to send to school; †to chide, to admonish. **school board,** *n.* a public body (1870–1902) elected to provide for the elementary instruction of children in their district. **school-book,** *n.* a book for use in schools. **schoolboy, -girl,** *n.* a boy or girl attending a school. *a.* pertaining to schoolboys or schoolgirls. **school-dame,** *n.* (*N Am.*) a schoolmistress; the keeper of a dame-school. **school-divine,** *n.* one who adopts scholastic theology. **school-divinity,** *n.* **schoolfellow,** *n.* one who attends the same school. **schoolhouse,** *n.* a building used as a school; the dwelling-house of a schoolmaster or schoolmistress; the head-teacher's house or the chief boarding-house at a public school. **school-ma'am, -marm,** *n.* (*N Am. coll.*) a schoolmistress. **schoolman,** *n.* a teacher or professor in a mediaeval university; one versed in the theology, logic, or metaphysics of the mediaeval schools or the niceties of academic disputation. **schoolmaster, -mistress,** *n.* a head or assistant teacher in a school; a pedagogue; one who or that which trains or disciplines. **schoolmate,** *n.* one attending the same school. **school-miss,** *n.* a schoolgirl; an inexperienced or bashful girl. **schoolroom,** *n.* a room where teaching is given, in a school, house etc. **school-teacher,** *n.* one who teaches in a school. **schoolable,** *a.* **schooling,** *n.* instruction or education at school; training, tuition, coaching, guidance; school fees; discipline; the training of a horse for riding, or in dressage, jumping etc. [A-F *escole*, L *schola*, Gr. *scholē*, rest, leisure, philosophy, lecture-place]

schooner, *n.* a vessel with two or more masts with fore-and-aft rigging; (*N Am.*) a large emigrant-wagon or van; a tall glass for beer or ale; a tall glass for sherry. [Clydesdale *scoon*, *scon*, to skim along, to glide swiftly (rel. to SHUNT), -ER (assim. to Dut. derivative *schooner*)]

Schopenhauer, *n.* **Arthur** (1788–1860), German philosopher, whose *The World as Will and Idea* (1818) expounded an atheistic and pessimistic world view: an irrational will is considered as the inner principle of the world, producing an ever-frustrated cycle of desire, of which the only escape is aesthetic contemplation, or absorption into nothingness.

schorl, *n.* black tourmaline. [F, from G *Schörl*]

schottische, *n.* a dance resembling a polka; the music for it. [G, Scottish]

schout, *n.* a municipal officer in the Netherlands and Dutch colonies. [Dut., cogn. with OE *sculthēta*, *scyldhæta*]

Schreiner, *n.* **Olive** (1862–1920), South African novelist and supporter of women's rights. Her autobiographical *The Story of an African Farm* (1883) describes life on the South African veld.

Schubert, *n.* **Franz (Peter)** (1797–1828), Austrian composer. His eight symphonies include the incomplete eighth in B minor (the 'Unfinished') and the 'Great' in C major (1829). He wrote chamber and piano music, including the 'Trout Quintet', and over 600 *leider* (songs) combining the romantic expression of emotion wih pure melody. They include the cycles *Die schöne Müllerin/The Beautiful Maid of the Mill* (1823) and *Die Winterreise/The Winter Journey* (1827).

Schumacher, *n.* **Ernst Friedrich 'Fritz'** (1911–77), German writer and economist, whose *Small is Beautiful: Economics as if People Mattered* (1973) makes a case for small-scale economic growth without great capital expenditure.

Schuman, *n.* **Robert** (1886–1963), French politician. He was prime minister (1947–48), and as foreign minister (1948–53) he proposed in May 1950 a common market for coal and steel (the Schuman Plan), which was established as the European Coal and Steel Community in 1952, the basis of the European Community.

Schumann, *n.* **Robert Alexander** (1810–56), German Romantic composer. His songs and short piano pieces show simplicity combined with an ability to portray mood and emotion. Among his compositions are four symphonies, a violin concerto, a piano concerto, sonatas, and song cycles, such as *Dichterliebe/Poet's Love* (1840). Mendelssohn championed many of his works.

Schuschnigg, *n.* **Kurt von** (1897–1977), Austrian chancellor in 1934, in succession to Dollfuss. In Feb. 1938 he was forced to accept a Nazi minister of the interior, and a month later Austria was occupied and annexed by Germany. He was imprisoned in Germany until 1945, when he went to the US.

schuss, *n.* a straight fast ski slope; a run made on this. *v.i.* to make such a run. [G, shot]

Schütz, *n.* **Heinrich** (1585–1672), German composer, musical director to the Elector of Saxony from 1614. His works include *The Seven Last Words* (about 1645), *Musicalische Exequien* (1636), and the *Deutsche Magnificat/German Magnificat* (1671).

schwa, *n.* a neutral unstressed vowel sound; the symbol (ə) used to represent this. [G, from Heb. *shĕwā*]

Schwenkfelder, *n.* a member of a Protestant sect founded in Silesia in the 16th cent. by Caspar Schwenkfeld (1496–1561). **Schwenkfeldian,** *n., a.* **Schwenkfeldianism,** *n.*

Schwinger, *n.* **Julian** (1918–), US quantum physicist. His research concerned the behaviour of charged particles in electrical fields. This work, expressed entirely through mathematics, combines elements from quantum theory and relativity theory.

Schwitters, *n.* **Kurt** (1887–1948), German artist, a member of the Dada movement. He moved to Norway in 1937 and to the UK in 1940. From 1918 he developed a variation on collage, using discarded rubbish such as buttons and bus tickets to create pictures and structures.

sci, (*abbr.*) science, scientific. **sci fi** , (*abbr.*) science fiction.

sciagraph, sciamachy, sciametry etc. SKIAGRAPH, SKIAMACHY, SKIAMETRY.

sciatheric, *a.* of or pertaining to a sundial. **sciatherically,** *adv.* [late Gr. *skiathērikos*, from Gr. *skiathēros*, sundial (*skia*, shadow, *thēran*, to catch)]

sciatic, *a.* pertaining to the hip; of or affecting the sciatic nerve; of the nature of or affected by sciatica. **sciatic nerve,** *n.* the nerve that extends from the pelvis down the back of the thigh. **sciatica,** *n.* neuralgia of the hip and thigh; pain in the great sciatic nerve. **sciatically,** *adv.* [F *sciatique*, late L *sciaticus*, L *ischiadicus*, Gr. *ischiadikos*, from *ischias -ados*, pain in the loins, from *ischion*, socket of the thigh-bone]

science, *n.* †knowledge; systematized knowledge; a department of systematized knowledge, a system of facts and principles concerning any subject; a natural science; the pursuit of such knowledge or the principles governing its acquirement; exceptional skill due to knowledge and training, as distinguished from natural ability, esp. in boxing; †a trade or occupation. **science fiction,** *n.* fiction dealing with space travel, life on one of the planets etc. **science park,** *n.* a place where academic scientific research is applied to commercial developments. **sciential,** *a.* of or producing science; having knowledge. **scientially,** *adv.* **scientific,** *a.* pertaining to, used or engaged in science; treating of or devoted to science; made or done according to the principles of science, systematic, exact; of boxing etc., skilful, expert. **scientifically,** *adv.* **scientism,** *n.* scientific methods or attitudes; (belief in) the application of scientific methods to investigate and explain social and psychological phenomena. **scientist,** *n.* one who studies or is expert in a (natural) science. [F, from L *scientia*, from *scīre*, to know]

scienter, *adv.* (*Law.*) with knowledge, wittingly, deliberately. [L]

Scientology®, *n.* an 'applied religious philosophy' based on dianetics, founded in California in 1954 by L. Ron Hubbard as the Church of Scientology. It claims to 'increase man's spiritual awareness', but its methods of recruiting and retaining converts have been criticized. [L *scientia*, *scīre*, to know, -LOGY]

sci fi SCI.

scil., (*abbr.*) scilicet.

scilicet, *adv.* to wit, videlicet, namely. [L (*scīre licet*, it is permitted to know)]

scilla, *n.* a genus of bulbous liliaceous plants containing the squills. **scillitin,** *n.* the chemically active principle of *Scilla maritima*. [L, from Gr. *skilla*]

Scillonian, *n., a.* (a native) of the Scilly Isles.

Scilly Islands, *n.* group of 140 islands and islets lying 40 km/25 miles SW of Land's End, England; administered by the Duchy of Cornwall; area 16 sq km/6.3 sq miles; population (1981) 1850. The five inhabited islands are St Mary's, the largest, on which is Hugh Town, capital of the Scillies; Tresco, the second largest, with sub-tropical gardens; St Martin's, noted for beautiful shells; St Agnes, and Bryher.

scimitar, *n.* a short Oriental sword, single-edged,

curved and broadest towards the point. [orig. OF *cimiterre,* It. *scimitarra,* prob. from Pers. *shimshīr*]

scincoid, *a.* of, pertaining to or resembling the Scincidae or skinks. *n.* a skink-like lizard. **scincoidian,** *n., a.* [L *scincus,* SKINK, -OID]

scintigraphy, *n.* a diagnostic technique that uses the radiation emitted following administration of a radioactive isotope to produce a picture of an internal body organ. **scintigram,** *n.* a picture produced by scintigraphy. [*scinti*llation, -GRAPHY]

scintilla, *n.* a spark; a trace, hint. **scintillate,** *v.i.* to emit sparks; to emit flashes of light when bombarded by electrons, photons etc.; to sparkle, to twinkle; to be brilliantly witty or interesting. **scintillant,** *a.* **scintillation,** *n.* **scintillation counter,** *n.* an instrument for measuring radiation from a source by electronically counting the flashes of light produced by the absorption of radioactive particles by a phosphor. †**scintillescent,** *a.* **scintillometer,** *n.* an instrument attached to a telescope for measuring the amount of scintillation of a star; a scintillation counter. [L]

sciography, SKIAGRAPHY.

sciolist, *n.* one who knows many things superficially, a pretender to knowledge. **sciolism,** *n.* **sciolistic,** †**sciolous,** *a.* [L *sciolus,* smatterer, dim. of *scius,* knowing, from *scīre,* to know]

sciolto, *adv.* (*Mus.*) freely, to one's taste; staccato. [It.]

sciomachy, SKIAMACHY.

sciomancy, *n.* divination through the shades of the dead. **sciomantic,** *a.* [Gr. *skia,* shadow, -MANCY]

scion, *n.* a shoot, esp. for grafting or planting; a descendant, a child. [F, perh. from *scier,* to saw, L *secāre,* to cut]

scioptic, †**-tric,** *a.* pertaining to the camera obscura or its use. †**scioptric ball,** *n.* a ball containing a lens used for producing luminous images in a darkened room. **sciopticon,** *n.* a kind of magic lantern. **scioptics,** *n. sing.* [Gr. *skia,* shadow, -OPTIC, see also CATOPTRIC]

sciotheism, *n.* ghost-worship, esp. of departed ancestors.

sciotheric, SCIATHERIC.

Scipio Africanus Major, (237–*c.* 183 BC), Roman general. He defeated the Carthaginians in Spain (210–206 BC), invaded Africa in 204 BC, and defeated Hannibal at Zama in 202 BC.

Scipio Africanus Minor, (*c.* 185–129 BC), Roman general, the adopted grandson of Scipio Africanus Major, also known as Scipio Aemilianus. He destroyed Carthage in 146 BC, and subdued Spain in 134 BC. He was opposed to his brothers-in-law, the Gracchi (see under GRACCHUS), and his wife is thought to have shared in his murder.

scire facias, *n.* (*Law*) a writ to enforce the execution of or annul judgments etc. [L, make (him) to know]

scirocco, SIROCCO.

scirrhus, *n.* (*pl.* **-rrhi**) a hard (cancerous) tumour. **scirrhoid, scirrhous,** *a.* **scirrhosity,** *n.* [late L, from Gr. *skirros, skīros,* hardened swelling, from *skiros,* hard]

scissel, *n.* metal clippings; the remainder of plates after discs have been punched out in coining. [F *cisaille,* from *ciseler,* to CHISEL]

scissile, *a.* that may be cut. **scission,** *n.* the act of cutting or dividing; a division, separation or split. †**scissure,** *n.* a longitudinal opening made by cutting; a cut, a fissure. [L *scissilis,* from *scindere,* to cut, p.p. *scissus*]

scissors, *n.pl.* (**scissors, pair of scissors**) a cutting instrument consisting of two blades pivoted together that cut objects placed between them; a gymnastic movement in which the legs open and close with a scissor-like action. **scissor,** *v.t.* to cut with scissors; to clip or cut (out) with scissors. **scissor-beak, -bill,** *n.* a skimmer, a bird of the genus *Rhynchops.* **scissor-bird, -tail,** *n.* a N American tyrant-flycatcher. **scissors-and-paste,** *n., a.* (of) compilation, as distinguished from original literary work. **scissors-grinder,** *n.* (*Austral.*) a kind of fly-catcher. **scissors hold,** *n.* a wrestling hold in which the legs lock round the opponent's head or body. **scissors kick,** *n.* a swimming kick in which the legs move in a scissor-like action. **scissor-tooth,** *n.* a tooth working against another like a scissor-blade, in certain carnivores. **scissoring,** *n.* **scissorwise,** *adv.* [ME *sisoures,* OF *cisoires,* L *cīsorium,* from *cīs-, caes-,* p.p. stem of *caedere,* to cut]

sciurine, *a.* pertaining to or resembling the squirrel family. *n.* a squirrel. **sciuroid,** *a.* [L *sciūrus,* Gr. *skiouros,* (*skia,* shadow, *oura,* tail)]

Sclav, Sclavonian etc. SLAV etc.

SCLC, (*abbr.*) Southern Christian Leadership Conference, a US civil-rights organization.

sclera, *n.* the sclerotic. **scleritis,** *n.* sclerotitis.

sclerenchyma, *n.* the strong tissue forming the hard or fibrous parts of plants, such as the walls of nuts and fruit-stones, leaf midribs etc.; the calcareous tissue in coral. **sclerenchymatous,** *a.* [Gr. *enchuma,* infusion, see PARENCHYMA]

scleriasis, *n.* hardening or induration of tissue.

sclerite, *n.* one of the definite component parts of the hard integument of various invertebrates. **scleritic,** *a.*

scler(o)-, *comb. form.* hard, dry; sclerotic. [Gr. *sklēros*]

scleroderm, *n.* a hardened integument or exoskeleton, esp. of corals; a fish of the family Sclerodermi, having hard scales. **scleroderma, -mia,** *n.* a chronic induration of the skin. **sclerodermatous, sclerodermic,** *a.* **sclerodermite,** *n.* one of the hard segments of the body in crustaceans. **sclerodermitic,** *a.*

sclerogen, *n.* the hard matter deposited in the cells of certain plants, as the ivory-nut. **sclerogenous,** *a.*

scleroid, *a.* (*Bot., Zool.*) hard in texture.

scleroma, *n.* (*pl.* **-mata**) hardening of cellular tissue, scleriasis.

scleromeninx, *n.* the dura mater. [MENINX]

scleroprotein, *n.* an insoluble protein, as keratin, forming the skeletal tissues of the body.

sclerosis, *n.* hardening of a plant cell-wall by the deposit of sclerogen; thickening or hardening of a body tissue. **sclerosed,** *a.*

scleroskeleton, *n.* the skeletal parts resulting from ossification of tendons, ligaments etc. **scleroskeletal,** *a.*

sclerotal, *n.* one of the bony plates of the sclerotic coat in some birds and reptiles; the sclerotic. *a.* pertaining to the sclerotal; sclerotic. **sclerotic,** *a.* of the outer coat or tunic of the eye, hard, indurated; of or affected with sclerosis. *n.* the firm white membrane forming the outer coat of the eye, the white of the eye; a medicine hardening the parts to which it is applied. **scleritis, sclerotitis,** *n.* inflammation of the sclerotic.

sclerotium, *n.* a compact tuberous mass formed on the mycelium of certain higher fungi, as ergot; a cyst-like part of a plasmodium in the Mycetozoa. **sclerotioid,** *a.* resembling a sclerotium.

sclerotized, *a.* esp. of the insect exoskeleton, hardened, indurated.

sclerotome, *n.* a knife used in cutting the sclerotic coat of the eye. **sclerotomy,** *n.*

sclerous, *a.* hard, indurated, ossified.

scobby, *n.* (*North.*) the chaffinch. [etym. doubtful]

scobs, *n.* sawdust, scrapings, shavings, filings; dross of metal, ivory, hartshorn or other hard substance. **scobiform,** *a.* [L]

scoff[1]**,** *n.* an expression of contempt, derision, or mockery; a gibe, a taunt; an object of derision, a laughing-stock. *v.i.* to speak in derision or mockery, to mock or jeer (at). †*v.t.* to mock, to ridicule, to deride. **scoffer,** *n.* **scoffingly,** *adv.* [prob. from Scand. (cp. MDan. *skof,* Icel. *skaup,* also OFris. *schof,* MDut. *schobben*), perh. rel. to SHOVE]

scoff[2]**,** *v.t.* (*coll.*) to eat ravenously. *n.* food. [S Afr. Dut.]

Scofield, *n.* **Paul** (1922–), English actor. His wide-ranging lead roles include the drunken priest in Greene's *The Power and the Glory*, Harry in Pinter's *The Homecoming*, and Salieri in Shaffer's *Amadeus*. He appeared as Sir Thomas More in both stage and film versions of *A Man for All Seasons*.

scold, *v.i.* to find fault noisily or angrily; to rail (at). *v.t.* to chide or find fault with noisily or angrily; to chide, to rate, to rail at. *n.* a noisy, railing, nagging woman; a scolding. **scolder,** *n.* **scolding,** *n., a.* **scoldingly,** *adv.* [ME *scolden*, cp. Dut. *schelden*, G *schelten*, OFris. *skelda*]

scolex, *n.* (*pl.* **-lices, -leces**) the larva or embryo in metagenesis; the head of the larval or adult tapeworm. **scoleciform, scolecoid,** *a.* **scolecite,** *n.* the vermiform body formed in the fructification of some fungi; a hydrous silicate mineral of aluminium and calcium. [Gr. *skōlēx*, worm]

scolion, *n.* an impromptu song sung by guests at an ancient Greek banquet. [Gr. *skolion*]

scoliosis, *n.* lateral curvature of the spine. **scoliotic,** *a.* [Gr. *skoliōsis*, from *skolios*, bent]

scollop, SCALLOP.

Scolopax, *n.* a genus of birds containing the woodcock and formerly the snipe and redshank. **scolopaceous, scolopacine, scolopacoid,** *a.* [L and Gr.]

Scolopendra, †**Scolopender,** *n.* a genus of myriapods containing the larger centipedes; a millipede or centipede; †(*Spens.*, **-der**) a fabulous marine animal. **scolopendriform, scolopendrine,** *a.* [L and Gr. *skolopendra*]

Scolopendrium, *n.* a genus of ferns containing the hart's tongue, Phyllitis. [L, from Gr. *skolopendrion*, from a supposed resemblance to prec.]

Scolytus, *n.* a genus of bark-boring beetles. **scolytid,** *n.* **scolytoid,** *a.* [mod. L from Gr. *skoluptein*, to peel, to strip]

Scomber, *n.* a genus of fish containing the mackerel. **scombrid,** *n.* **scombroid,** *a.* of or belonging to the Scombroidea, a suborder of fishes including the mackerels, tunas and swordfishes. *n.* one of the Scombroidea. [L, from Gr. *skombros*]

scomfish, *v.t.* (*Sc.*) to suffocate, to stifle; to discomfit, to disconcert. [*discomfish*, corr. of DISCOMFIT]

scon var. of SCONE.

sconce[1], *n.* a candle-holder fixed to a wall; the socket of a candlestick into which the candle is inserted; †the head, the skull; †brains, sense; †a lantern; [OF *esconse,* hiding-place, concealed light, dark-lantern, L *absconsa*, fem. of *-sus*, var. of *absconditus*, p.p. of *abscondere*, to hide]

sconce[2], *n.* a block-house, a bulwark, a small detached fort; a shelter, a covering, a shed. *v.t.* to fortify with a sconce. [Dut. *schans*]

sconce[3], *n.* a fine at Oxford Univ. for a light offence. *v.t.* to fine. [etym. unknown]

scone, *n.* a soft thin plain cake, usu. in small round or triangular pieces, cooked on a girdle or in an oven. [cp. MDan. *skon-roggen*, muffin of bolted rye-flour (LG *schön*, fine, *Roggen*, rye)]

scoop, *n.* a short-handled shovel-like implement for drawing together, lifting and moving loose material such as coal, grain, sugar, potatoes etc.; a large ladle or dipping-vessel; a gouge-like implement used by grocers, surgeons etc. or for spooning out shaped pieces of ice-cream or other soft food; the bucket of a dredging-machine; a coal-scuttle; the act or movement of scooping; the amount scooped at once; (*coll.*) a large profit made in a speculation or competitive transaction; the publication or broadcasting of a piece of sensational news in advance of rival newspapers etc.; a news item so published; †a basin-like cavity. *v.t.* to ladle or dip (out) or to hollow (out) with a scoop; to lift (up) with a scoop; to scrape, gouge or hollow (out); (*coll.*) to gain (a large profit) by a deal etc.; to forestall (rival newspapers etc.) with a piece of sensational news. **scoop-net,** *n.* a net so formed as to sweep the bottom of a river etc. **scoop-wheel,** *n.* a wheel with buckets round it used to raise water or for dredging. **scooper,** *n.* one who or that which scoops; a tool used by engravers. [perh. through OF *escope*, from Swed. *skopa*, or MDut. *schōpe*, bailing-vessel, or MDut. *schoppe*, (Dut. *schop*), shovel, cp. G *schöpfen*, to draw water]

scoot, *v.i.* (*coll.*) to dart off, bolt, to scurry away. **scooter,** *n.* a two-wheeled toy vehicle on which a child can ride with one foot, propelling with the other; a larger, motorized two-wheeled vehicle with a seat. **scooterist,** *n.* a rider on a scooter. [var. of SHOOT]

scopa, *n.* (*pl.* **-pae**) a brush-like tuft of bristly hairs as on the legs of bees. **scopate,** *a.* brush-shaped; covered with brush-like hairs. **scopiform,** *a.* brush-shaped. **scopiped,** †**scopulipede,** *a.* applied to certain solitary bees with a brush-like contrivance on the hind legs for collecting pollen. **scopula,** *n.* a small brush-like tuft on the legs of bees and spiders, a scopa. **scopulate,** *a.* **scopuliform,** *a.* [L, in pl., twigs]

scope[1], *n.* †a butt or mark; †end, aim, purpose or intention; range of action or observation, outlook, reach, sphere; extent of or room for activity, development etc.; outlet, opportunity, vent; (*Naut.*) length of cable at which a vessel rides; †extent of surface etc. †**scopeful, scopeless,** *a.* [prob. through It. *scopo,* from Gr. *skopos*, a watcher, a mark, rel. to *skeptesthai,* to look out]

scope[2], *n.* short for OSCILLOSCOPE under OSCILLATE, PERISCOPE, TELESCOPE etc.

-scope, *suf.* denoting an instrument of observation etc., as in *microscope*, *spectroscope*. **-scopic,** *suf.* pertaining to this or to observation etc. as in *microscopic, spectroscopic*. **-scopy,** *suf.* observation by the instrument etc., specified, as in *microscopy, spectroscopy*. [Gr. *skopos*, see prec.]

scopelid, *n.* (*Ichthyol.*) a fish of the deep-water, teleostean group Scopelidae. **scopeloid,** *n., a.* [Gr. *skopelos*, -ID]

scopiform, scopiped SCOPA.

scopolamine, *n.* hyoscine hydrobromide, a hypnotic drug used, among other purposes, with morphine for producing twilight sleep.

Scops, *n.* a genus of owls having erect tufts of feathers on the side of the head. **scops-eared,** *a.* **scops-owl,** *n.* [Gr. *skōps*]

scopula, †**scopuliped** etc. SCOPA.

scorbutic, *a.* pertaining to, like or affected with scurvy. *n.* a person affected with scurvy. **scorbutically,** *adv.* [obs. *scorbute* (F *scorbut*), low L *scorbūtus*, scurvy, prob. from LG, cp. SCURF]

scorch, *v.t.* to burn the outside of so as to injure or discolour without consuming, to singe to parch, to dry or shrivel (up); to affect harmfully with or as with heat; †to burn; to criticize or censure severely. *v.i.* to be parched, singed or dried up with or as with heat; (*coll.*) to go at an excessive rate of speed. *n.* a burn or mark caused by scorching; (*coll.*) an act or spell of scorching. **scorched,** *a.* **scorched earth,** a descriptive term for the destruction of everything in a country that might be of service to an invading army. **scorching,** *a.* **scorchingly,** *adv.* **scorcher,** *n.* one who or that which scorches; (*coll.*) an extremely hot day; (*sl.*) a striking or staggering example, a stunner. [OF *escorcher*, late L *excorticāre* (EX-, L *cortex -ticis*, bark)]

scordato, *a.* (*Mus.*) put out of tune. **scordatura,** *n.* an intentional departure from normal tuning to secure special effects. [It., from *scordare*, to be out of tune, for *discordare*, see DISCORD[1]]

scordatura SCORDATO.

score, *n.* a notch or mark on a tally; a reckoning orig. kept on a tally, esp. a running account for liquor marked up against a customer's name at a tavern; an account, a bill, a debt; anything laid up or recorded against one, a grudge; the points made by a player or side at any moment in, or in total in certain games and contests; the record of this; the act of gaining a point in a game or contest; a mark from which a race starts, competitors fire in a shooting-match etc.; a weight of 20 or 21 lb (about 9 or 9·5 kg) used in weighing pigs and cattle; (*Naut.*) a groove in a block etc., for receiving a strap; a line drawn or scratched through writing etc.; a scratch, incision; a copy of a musical work in which all the component parts are shown, either fully or in a compressed form, so called from the line orig. drawn through all the staves; the music for a film, play etc.; the notation for a choreographed work; twenty, a set of twenty; (*pl.*) large numbers; account, category, reason; (*sl.*) a remark etc. in which one scores off another person; (*coll.*) the situation, the facts. *v.t.* to mark with notches, cuts, scratches, lines etc.; to gash, to groove, to furrow; to make or mark (lines etc.); to mark (out) with lines; to mark (up) or enter in a score; to gain (a point, a win etc.) in a game or contest; to arrange in score; to orchestrate; to arrange for an instrument; to prepare the sound-script for (a film). *v.i.* to keep a score; to win points, advantages etc.; (*sl.*) to obtain illegal drugs; (*sl.*) of a man, to successfully seduce someone into having sexual intercourse. **to pay off old scores,** to pay someone out or have revenge for an offence of old standing. **to score off,** (*coll.*) to get the better of; to triumph over in argument, repartee etc. **scoreboard,** *n.* a board on which the score at any point in a game or contest is displayed. **scorer,** *n.* **scoring,** *n.* [OE *scor*, twenty, Icel. *skor*, twenty, notch, cogn. with SHEAR]

scoria, *n.* (*pl.* **-riae**) cellular lava or ashes; the refuse of fused metals, dross. **scoriaceous**, **scoriform**, *a.* **scorify**, *v.t.* to reduce to dross; to assay (metal) by fusing its ore in a scorifier with lead and borax. **scorification**, *n.* **scorifier,** *n.* [L, from Gr. *skōria*, refuse, from *skōr*, dung]

scorn, *n.* contempt, disdain; mockery, derision; a subject or object of extreme contempt. *v.t.* to hold in extreme contempt or disdain, to regard as unworthy, paltry or mean. **to laugh to scorn,** to deride, to mock. †**to take** or **think scorn,** to disdain, to scorn. **scorner,** *n.* **scornful,** *a.* **scornfully,** *adv.* **scornfulness,** *n.* [from ME *scorn*, OF *escorne*, perh. from *escorner*, to deprive of horns (EX-, L *cornu,* horn), or ME *scarn*, OF *escarn*, OHG *Skern,* mockery, sport]

scorodite, *n.* a mineral consisting of a native arsenate of iron. [G *Skorodit*, from Gr. *skorodon*, garlic]

Scorpaena, *n.* a genus of acanthopterygian fishes typical of the family Scorpaenidae. **scorpaenid**, *n.* **scorpaenoid**, *n.*, *a.* [mod. L, from Gr. *skorpaina*, prob. from *skorpios*, SCORPION]

scorper, *n.* a gouging-tool for working in concave surfaces in wood, metal or jewellery. [var. of SCAUPER]

Scorpio SCORPIUS.

scorpioid, *a.* (*Bot.*) curled up like the end of a scorpion's tail and uncurling as the flowers develop. *n.* a scorpioid inflorescence.

scorpion, *n.* one of an order of arachnids, with claws like a lobster and a sting in the jointed tail; (*Bibl.*) a whip armed with points of iron; a form of ballista; the constellation Scorpio. **rock scorpion** ROCK[1]. **scorpion-broom, -thorn,** *n.* a yellow-flowered broom from S Europe, *Genista scorpius*. **scorpion-fish,** *n.* the sea-scorpion. **scorpion-fly,** *n.* a fly of the family Panorpidae, named from the forceps-like point of the abdomen. **scorpion-grass, -wort,** *n.* the myosotis or forget-me-not. **scorpion-plant,** *n.* a Javan orchid with large spider-like flowers; scorpion-broom. **scorpion-, scorpion's-thorn,** *n.* scorpion-broom. [L *scorpiōnem*, nom. *-pio*, Gr. *skorpios*]

Scorpius, Scorpio *n.* zodiac constellation in the southern hemisphere, representing a scorpion. The sun passes briefly through Scorpius in the last week of Nov. The heart of the scorpion is marked by the red supergiant star Antares. Scorpius contains rich Milky Way star fields, plus the strongest X-ray source in the sky, Scorpius X-1. In astrology, the dates for Scorpius are between about 24 Oct. and 21 Nov. (see PRECESSION).

†**scorse,** *v.t.*, *v.i.* to barter, to exchange. *n.* barter, exchange. [etym. doubtful]

Scorsese, *n.* **Martin** (1942–), US director, whose films concentrate on complex characterization and the theme of alienation. His work includes *Taxi Driver* (1976), *Raging Bull* (1979), *After Hours* (1987), and *The Last Temptation of Christ* (1988).

†**scortatory,** *a.* pertaining to or founded in lewdness. [from L *scortātor*, fornicator, from *scortārī*, to be lewd, from *scortum*, whore]

scorza, *n.* an arenaceous variety of epidote. [G, prob. from Wallachian name]

scorzonera, *n.* a genus of herbs the roots of some species of which are used as a vegetable; a plant of this genus, esp. *Scorzonera hispanica.* [It., perh. from *scorzone*, a snake]

Scot, *n.* a native of Scotland; (*pl.*) orig., a Gaelic people migrating to Scotland from Ireland in the 5th or 6th cent. [OE *Scottas*, pl.]

scot, *n.* a payment, an assessment, a tax. **scot and lot,** a town or parish tax levied according to ability to pay. **to pay scot and lot,** to settle outstanding accounts, obligations etc. **scot-free,** *a.* free from payment, untaxed; unpunished; unhurt, safe. [OF *escot*, Icel. *skot,* cp. OE *sceot*, Dut. *schot*, G *Schoss,* SHOT[3]]

Scot., (*abbr.*) Scotland, Scottish.

Scotch, *a.* Scottish. *n.* (a glass of) (Scotch) whisky; the Scots. **Scotch and English,** prisoner's-base. **Scotch-barley,** *n.* pot or husked barley. **Scotch broth,** *n.* a clear broth containing barley and chopped vegetables. **Scotch cap,** *n.* a brimless woollen cap, either a Balmoral or a Glengarry. **Scotch catch** or **snap,** *n.* a short note followed by a long note in two played to the same beat. **Scotch egg,** *n.* a hard-boiled egg encased in sausage-meat and breadcrumbs. **Scotch fir,** *n.* the Scots pine. **Scotch mist,** *n.* a wet dense mist; fine drizzle. **Scotch terrier,** *n.* a breed of dog characterized by short legs and a rough coat. **Scotch thistle,** *n.* one of various thistles regarded as the Scottish national emblem, esp. *Carduus lanceolatus* or *C. nutans*. **Scotch whisky,** *n.* whisky with a flavour of peat-reek, orig. distilled in Scotland. **Scotchman, -woman,** *n.* a Scotsman, -woman. **Scotchman grass,** *n.* (*New Zealand*) a variety of grass with sharp points. **Scotchness,** *n.*

scotch[1], *v.t.* to cut with narrow incisions; to wound slightly, to cripple, to disable. *n.* a slight cut or incision; a mark for hopping from, as in the game of hopscotch. **scotched-collops,** *n.* beef cut into small pieces and stewed in a stew-pan. **scotch-hopper** HOPSCOTCH, under HOP[1]. [ME *scocche,* prob. from SCORE]

scotch[2], *n.* a block for a wheel or other round object. *v.t.* to block, wedge or prop (a wheel, barrel etc.) to prevent rolling; to frustrate (a plan etc.). [etym. doubtful]

scoter, *n.* a large sea-duck of the genus *Melanitta*. [etym. doubtful]

scotia, *n.* a hollow moulding in the base of a column. [Gr. *skotia*, darkness, cp. SCOTO-]

Scotice, *adv.* in a or the Scottish manner.

Scotism, *n.* the scholastic philosophy of Johannes Duns Scotus (d. 1308). **Scotist,** *n.*, *a.*

Scotland, *n.* country in N Europe, part of the British Isles. **area** 78,470 sq km/30,297 sq miles. **capital** Edinburgh. **towns** Glasgow, Dundee, Aberdeen. **population** (1987) 5,113,000. **industry** electronics, aero and marine engines, oil, natural gas, chemicals, textiles, clothing, printing, paper, food processing, tourism. **language** English; Gaelic spoken by 1.3%, mainly in the Highlands. **religion** Presbyterian (Church of Scotland), Roman Catholic.

Scotland Yard, *n.* the headquarters of the London Metropolitan Police; the Criminal Investigation Department of the police; police detectives. [locality in London]

scoto-, *comb. form.* dark, dullness. [Gr. *skotos*]

scotodinia, *n.* dizziness, vertigo, with dimness of vision.

scotograph, *n.* an instrument for writing in the dark or by the blind.

scotoma, *n.* (*pl.* **-mas, -mata**) a blind spot in the field of vision; dizziness or swimming of the head with dimness of sight. **scotomatous,** *a.*

scotoscope, *n.* a night-glass.

Scots, *a.* Scottish (applied to the people, language and law). *n.* the language of Scotland; (*pl.* of SCOT) the people of Scotland. **Scots pine,** *n.* a European pine, *Pinus sylvestris*, prob. indigenous in N Britain. **Scotsman, -woman,** *n.* [ME *Scottis*, Scottish]

Scots language, *n.* the form of the English language as traditionally spoken and written in Scotland, regarded by some scholars as a distinct language.

Scott[1], *n.* **George C(ampbell)** (1927–), US actor who played mostly tough, authoritarian film roles. His work includes *Dr Strangelove* (1964), *Patton* (1970), *The Hospital* (1971), and *Firestarter* (1984).

Scott[2], *n.* **(George) Gilbert** (1811–78), English architect. As the leading practical architect in the mid-19th-century Gothic revival in England, Scott was responsible for the building or restoration of many public buildings, including the Albert Memorial, the Foreign Office, and St Pancras Station, all in London.

Scott[3], *n.* **Giles Gilbert** (1880–1960), English architect, grandson of George Gilbert Scott. He designed Liverpool Anglican Cathedral, Cambridge University Library, and Waterloo Bridge, London (1945). He supervised the rebuilding of the House of Commons after World War II.

Scott[4], *n.* **Peter (Markham)** (1909–89), British naturalist, artist, and explorer, founder of the Wildfowl Trust at Slimbridge, Gloucestershire, England, and a founder of the World Wildlife Fund (now World Wide Fund for Nature).

Scott[5], *n.* **Randolph,** stage name of Randolph Crane (1903–87), US actor. He began his career in romantic films before becoming one of Hollywood's greatest Western stars in the 1930s. His films include *Roberta* (1934), *Jesse James* (1939), and *Ride the High Country* (1962).

Scott[6], *n.* **Robert Falcon** (1868–1912), known as Scott of the Antarctic. English explorer, who commanded two Antarctic expeditions, (1901–04 and 1910–12). On 18 Jan. 1912 he reached the South Pole, shortly after AMUNDSEN, but on the return journey he and his companions died in a blizzard only a few miles from their base camp. His journal was recovered and published in 1913.

Scott[7], *n.* **Walter** (1771–1832), Scottish novelist and poet. His first works were translations of German ballads, followed by poems such as 'The Lady of the Lake' (1810) and 'Lord of the Isles' (1815). He gained a European reputation for his historical novels such as *Heart of Midlothian* (1818), *Ivanhoe* (1819), and *The Fair Maid of Perth* (1828). His last years were marked by frantic writing to pay off his debts. after the bankruptcy of his publishing company in 1826.

Scottish, *a.* pertaining to Scotland, its people, language, dialect or literature. *n.* the Scots language. **Scottish terrier,** *n.* a Scotch terrier. **Scotticism,** *n.* a Scottish idiom. **Scotticize, -ise, Scottify,** *v.t.* to make Scottish. **Scottie, Scotty,** *n.* a nickname for a Scotsman; (*coll.*) a Scotch terrier. **Scottishness,** *n.* [ME *Scottes*]

scoundrel, *n.* an unprincipled person, a rogue, a rascal, a villain. *a.* base, villainous, unprincipled. **scoundreldom, scoundrelism,** *n.* **scoundrelly,** *a.* [etym. unknown]

scoup, *v.i.* (*Sc.*) to bound, trip, caper or scamper. [etym. doubtful]

scour[1], *v.t.* to clean, polish or brighten by friction; to remove or clean (away, off etc.) by rubbing; to flush or clear out; of water etc., to pass swiftly through or over; to purge violently. *v.i.* to clean; to be scoured or cleaned (well, easily etc.); to be purged to excess. *n.* scouring; a swift, deep current; a rapid; the clearing action of this; dysentery in cattle; a cleanser for various fabrics. **scourer,** *n.* [prob. through MDut. *schūren*, OF *escurer*, pop. L *excūrāre* (EX-, *cūrāre*, to CURE[1])]

scour[2], *v.i.* to rove, to range; to skim, to scurry; to search about. *v.t.* to move rapidly over, esp. in search; to search thoroughly. [OF *escourre*, L *excurrere* (EX-, *currere*, to run)]

scourge, *n.* a whip with thongs used as an instrument of punishment; any means of inflicting punishment, vengeance or suffering; a pestilence or plague. *v.t.* to whip with or as with a scourge; to afflict, to harass, to chastise. **scourger,** *n.* [A-F *escorge* (F *écourgée*), ult. from L *excoriāre*, to strip the skin off (EX-, *corium*, hide)]

Scouse, *n.* a native or inhabitant of Liverpool; the dialect of Liverpool. [short for LOBSCOUSE]

scout[1], *n.* one sent out to bring in information, esp. one employed to watch the movements etc. of an enemy; one employed to search for people with talent in a particular field, new sales markets etc.; the act of watching or bringing in such information, a scouting expedition; a member of an organization, established in Great Britain by Lord Baden-Powell in 1908 and now world-wide, intended to train and develop qualities of leadership, responsibility etc. in boys; a college servant at Oxford Univ.; †(*Cricket*) a fielder. *v.t.* to act as a scout. *v.i.* to search for. **Boy Scout,** *n.* the former name for a Scout. **scout-master,** *n.* formerly, the leader of a group of Boy Scouts; a person in charge of a troop of scouts. **Scouter,** *n.* an adult leader of Scouts. **Scouting,** *n.* [OF *éscoute,* eavesdropper, from *escouter* (F *écouter*), to listen, L. *auscultāre*, see AUSCULTATION]

scout[2], *v.t.* to treat with contempt and disdain, to reject contemptuously. [perh. from Scand. (cp. Icel. *skuti*, a taunt, rel. to *skjōta*, to SHOOT)]

scout[3], *n.* (*dial.*) the guillemot; the razor-billed auk. [etym. doubtful]

scow, *n.* a large flat-bottomed, square-ended boat. *v.t.* to transport in a scow. [Dut. *schouw*]

scowl, *v.i.* to frown, to look sullen or ill-tempered; to have a threatening aspect. †*v.t.* to repel, drive or bear (down) by frowning or looking sullen. *n.* an angry frown; a look of sullenness, ill-temper or discontent. **scowlingly,** *adv.* [ME *scoulen*, Dan. *skule*, cp. Icel. *skolla*, to skulk]

scrabble, *v.i.* to make irregular or unmeaning marks; to scrawl, to scribble; to scramble; to scrape, scratch or grope (about) as if to obtain something. *v.t.* to scribble on or over. *n.* a scribble, scrawl; a scratching or scraping; a scramble, struggle; (**Scrabble®**) a word-building board game for two to four players, based on the crossword puzzle, in which 'letter' counters of varying point values are used to form words. [var. of SCRAPPLE]

scrag, *n.* anything thin, lean or shrivelled; a lean or bony person or animal; a lean or bony piece of meat, esp. the lean end of neck of mutton. *v.t.* (*past, p.p.* **scragged**) (*sl.*) to wring the neck of, to throttle; to kill by hanging; (*Football*) to tackle by the neck. **scrag-necked,** *a.* having a long, thin neck. **scragged, scraggy,** *a.* **scraggedness, scragginess,** *n.* **scraggily,** *adv.* [cp. Norw. *skragg*, a poor creature, Dan. *skrog*, carcase, a poor creature, NFris. *skrog*, a lean man]

scraich, scraigh, *v.i.* (*Sc.*) to make a harsh cry, to screech, to scream. *n.* a harsh cry. [imit.]

scram[1], *v.t.* (*dial.*) to benumb, to shram. *a.* small, puny, withered, shrunken. [var. of SHRAM]

scram[2], *int.* (*sl.*) get out of it! go away! [SCRAMBLE]

scram[3] *n.* an emergency shutdown of a nuclear reactor. *v.t.* to shut down (a nuclear reactor) in an emergency. [SCRAM[2]]

scramble, *v.i.* to climb or move along by clambering, crawling, wriggling etc., esp. with the hands and knees; to move with urgent or disorderly haste; to seek or struggle (for, after etc.) in a rough-and-tumble or eager manner; to climb or spread irregularly; of an aircraft or its crew, to take-off immediately. *v.t.* to put or collect together hurriedly or haphazardly; to mix or jumble up; to prepare (eggs) by breaking into a pan and stirring up during cooking; to order (an aircraft or crew) to scramble; to make (a radiotelephonic conversation) unintelligible without a decoding receiver by altering the frequencies. *n.* the act of scrambling; a climb or walk over rocks etc., or in a rough-and-tumble manner; a rough or unceremonious struggle for something; an emergency take-off of fighter aircraft; a motor-cycle race over rough ground. **scrambler,** *n.* one who scrambles; (*Radio.*) an electronic device for scrambling speech transmitted by radio or telephone. [prob. var. of SCRABBLE]

scran, *n.* (*dial.*) (leftover) food; scraps, refuse. *v.t.* (*past, p.p.* **scranned**) to collect or gather up scran. **bad scran to you!,** bad luck to you!. [etym. doubtful]

†**scranch,** *v.t.* to grind with the teeth, to crunch.

[prob. imit.]

†**scrannel,** *a.* of a voice etc., thin, slender, feeble, reedy. **scranky,** (*Sc.*), **scranny** (*dial.*) SCRAWNY. [cp. Norw. and Swed. dial. *skran*]

scrap[1], *n.* a small detached piece, a bit, a fragment; a picture, paragraph etc., cut from a newspaper etc., for preservation; refuse, waste, esp. old pieces of discarded metal collected for melting down etc.; (*pl.*) bits, odds-and-ends, leavings; (*pl.*) leftover fragments of food; (*usu. pl.*) refuse of fat from which the oil has been expressed. *v.t.* (*past, p.p.* **scrapped**) to make scrap of, to consign to the scrap-heap; to condemn and discard as worn out, obsolete etc. **scrapbook,** *n.* a blank book into which pictures, cuttings from newspapers etc. are pasted for preservation. **scrap-cake,** *n.* fish-scrap compressed into cakes. **scrap-heap,** *n.* a heap of scrap metal; a rubbish-heap. **scrap iron** or **metal,** *n.* discarded metal for reprocessing. **scrapyard,** *n.* a place where scrap, esp. scrap metal, is collected or stored. **scrappy,** *a.* consisting or made up of scraps; disconnected. **scrappily,** *adv.* **scrappiness,** *n.* [Icel. *skrap,* SCRAPE]

scrap[2], *n.* (*coll.*) a fight, a scuffle, a dispute. *v.i.* (*past, p.p.* **scrapped**) to engage in a fight. **scrapper,** *n.* **scrapping-match,** *n.* [etym. doubtful]

scrape, *v.t.* to rub the surface of with something rough or sharp; to abrade, smooth or shave (a surface) thus; to remove, to clean (off, out etc.) thus; to erase; to rub or scratch (out); to excavate or hollow (out) by scraping; to rub against with a rasping or grating noise; to draw or rub along something with a scraping noise; to damage or graze by rubbing on a rough surface; to collect or get together by scraping; to save or amass with difficulty or by small amounts. *v.i.* to rub the surface of something with a rough or sharp instrument; to abrade, to smooth, to clean something thus; to rub (against something) with a scraping or rasping noise; to make such a noise; to get through with difficulty or by a close shave; to be saving or parsimonious; to play awkwardly on a violin etc.; to make an awkward bow with a drawing back of the foot. *n.* the act, sound or effect of scraping; an awkward bow with a drawing back of the foot; (*coll.*) an awkward predicament, esp. one due to one's own conduct. **to scrape acquaintance with,** to contrive to make the acquaintance of. **to scrape along** or **by,** (*coll.*) to keep going somehow. **to scrape away,** to abrade, to reduce by scraping. **to scrape down,** to scrape away; to scrape from head to foot or top to bottom; to silence or put down by scraping the feet. **to scrape the barrel** BARREL. **scraper,** *n.* one who scrapes; an instrument for scraping, esp. for cleaning the dirt off one's boots before entering a house; an awkward fiddler; a miser; a prehistoric flint implement used for scraping skins etc. **scraperboard,** *n.* a board with a surface that can be scraped off to form a design; this method of producing designs. **scraping,** *n.* [ME *scrapien*, Icel. *skrapa* (cp. Dan. *skrabe*, Dut. *schrapen*), cogn. with OE *screpan*, to scratch]

scrappy etc SCRAP[1].

†**scrat,** *v.t., v.i.* to scratch. [ME *scratten*]

Scratch, *n.* the Devil, usu. **Old Scratch.** [cp. Icel. *skratte*, OHG *Scrato*, goblin]

scratch, *v.t.* to tear or mark the surface of lightly with something sharp; to wound slightly; to rub or scrape with the nails; to hollow out with the nails or claws; to chafe the surface of; to erase, to obliterate, to score (out, through etc.); to expunge (esp. the name of a horse in a test of entries for a race); to withdraw from a contest; to cancel (a match, game etc.); to form by scratching; to scrape (up or together). *v.i.* to use the nails or claws in tearing, scraping, marking, hollowing out etc.; to rub or scrape one's skin with the nails; to chafe, rub; to scrape the ground as in searching; to make a grating noise; to withdraw one's entry from a contest; to get by or manage with difficulty. *n.* a mark made by scratching; a slight wound; a sound of scratching; an act or spell of scratching; a scratch-wig; a mark from which competitors start in a race, or a line across a prize-ring at which boxers begin; (*pl.*) a horse-disease characterized by scabs or chaps between the heel and pastern-joint. *a.* improvised; put together hastily or haphazardly, multifarious, nondescript; (*Sport*) without handicap. **to be** or **come up to (the) scratch,** to be satisfactory, to fulfil the desired standard or requirements. **to scratch along,** to scrape along. **to start from scratch,** to start from the very beginning, with no advantage. **to toe the scratch,** to be ready when wanted; to stand the test. **scratch-pad,** *n.* (*chiefly N Am.*) a notebook, a scribbling block. **scratch video,** *n.* a collage on video of previously existing pieces of television and cinema film; the technique or genre of making scratch videos. **scratch-wig,** *n.* a wig covering a bald part of the head. **scratcher,** *n.* one who or that which scratches; a bird that scratches for food, one of the Rasores. **scratching,** *n.* a scratchy sound effect produced by manually rotating a (pop) record backwards and forwards, used in some styles of pop music; (*pl.*) refuse strained out of melted lard. **scratchy,** *a.* consisting of or characterized by scratches; tending to scratch or rub, rough; making a noise like scratching; uneven; irregular, heterogeneous. **scratchily,** *adv.* **scratchiness,** *n.* [prob. from prec. and ME *cracchen*, MDut. *kratsen*]

scrattle, *v.i.* (*dial.*) to keep scratching or scraping; to shuffle or scramble (along). [freq. of SCRAT]

scraw, *n.* (*chiefly Ir.*) a turf, a sod. [Ir. and Gael. *sgrath*]

scrawl, *v.t.* to draw, write or mark clumsily, hurriedly or illegibly, to scribble. *v.i.* to scribble, to mark with illegible writing, etc. *n.* a piece of hasty, clumsy or illegible writing. **scrawler,** *n.* **scrawly,** *a.* [perh. var. of SCRABBLE]

scrawny, *a.* excessively lean, thin, bony; meagre.

scray, *n.* the tern or sea-swallow. [W *ysgräen* or *ysgräell*, cp. F *screau*]

screak, *v.i.* (*dial.*) to shriek, to screech; to creak. *n.* a shriek, a screech; a creaking. [Icel. *skraekja*, prob. imit.]

scream, *v.i.* to make a shrill, piercing, prolonged cry as if in extreme pain or terror; to give out a shrill sound, to whistle, hoot or laugh loudly; to speak or write excitedly or violently; to be over-conspicuous or vivid. *v.t.* to utter or say in a screaming tone. *n.* a loud, shrill, prolonged cry, as of one in extreme pain or terror; (*coll.*) something or someone excruciatingly funny. **screamer,** *n.* one who or that which screams, esp. the swift; any bird of the S American semi-aquatic family Palamedeidae, from their harsh cry; (*coll.*) a sensational headline. **screamingly,** *adv.* extremely. **screamy,** *a.* **screamily,** *adv.* **screaminess,** *n.* [cp. Icel. *skraema*, to scare, to terrify]

scree, *n.* loose fragments or debris of rock on a steep slope; a slope covered with this. [Icel. *skritha*, landslip, from *skrītha*, to glide, cp. OE *scrithan*]

screech, *v.i.* to scream out with a sharp, harsh, shrill voice; to make a shrill, strident noise. *v.t.* to utter or say with such a voice. *n.* a shrill, harsh cry as of terror or pain. **screech-hawk,** *n.* (*dial.*) the night-jar. **screech-martin,** *n.* the swift. **screech-owl,** *n.* an owl, *Tyto alba*, that screeches instead of hooting. **screecher,** *n.* **screechy,** *a.* [ME *scriken*, *schriken*, from Icel. as SCREAK]

screed, *n.* a long harangue or tirade; a strip of mortar, wood etc. put on a wall etc. that is to be plastered, as a guide to evenness of surface etc.; a screeding; a piece, a fragment, a strip; a long and tedious piece of writing; (*dial.*) a border, a frill; (*Sc.*) a rent, a tear. **screeding,** *n.* the final rendering of concrete to get a smooth surface. [North. var. of SHRED]

screen, *n.* a partition separating a portion of a room or of a church from the remainder, esp. one between the choir and the nave or ambulatory; a movable piece of furniture, usu. consisting of a light framework covered with paper, cloth etc., used to shelter from excess of heat, draught etc.; anything serving to shelter, protect or conceal; a surface on which images can be projected; a board or structure on which notices etc. can be posted; a coarse sieve or riddle, esp. for sorting coal; a frame containing a mesh placed over a window, door etc. to keep out flies; a body affording a shield against electric or magnetic induction; (*Phot.*) a device for modifying the effect of light passing through a lens; the part of a television set, VDU etc. on which the image appears; the film industry, moving pictures collectively. *v.t.* to shelter or protect from inconvenience, injury, hurt or pain, to shield; to hide, to conceal wholly or partly; to sift, to riddle; to separate with a screen; to test for the presence of disease, weapons etc.; to examine or check thoroughly in order to assess suitability, sort into categories etc.; to project (a film) on a screen; to portray in film. **screening-machine,** *n.* a machine for sifting and assorting coal etc. **screenplay,** *n.* a film script including stage directions and details of characters and sets. **screen printing** or **process** SILK-SCREEN PRINTING under SILK. **screen writer,** *n.* a writer of screenplays. **screenings,** *n.pl.* small stuff or refuse separated by screening. [ME *scren*, OF *escren* (F *écran*), prob. from OHG *skrank*, barrier (cp. G *Schranke*)]

screeve, *v.t.* (*sl.*) to write. *v.i.* to write or draw with coloured chalk etc. on pavements; to write begging letters. [perh. through It. *scrivare*, from L *scrībere*, to write]

screw[1], *n.* a cylinder with a spiral ridge or groove round its outer surface (called a male or exterior screw) or round its inner surface (called a female or internal screw), esp. a male screw used for fastening boards etc. together; a male or female screw forming part of a tool, mechanical appliance or machine and conveying motion to another part or bringing pressure to bear; something resembling a screw in spiral form; a screw-propeller; a screw steamer; a turn of a screw; a sideways motion or tendency like that of a screw, a twist; backspin given to a ball in snooker, billiards etc.; a twisted-up paper (of tobacco etc.); (*sl.*) a stingy person; (*coll.*) salary; (*sl.*) a prison warder; (*sl.*) an act of sexual intercourse. *v.t.* to fasten, secure, tighten, join etc. with a screw or screws; to turn (a screw); to turn round or twist as a screw; to give a spiral thread or groove to; to press hard, to oppress, esp. by exactions, to grind; to extort, to squeeze (money etc.) out of; (*sl.*) to cheat; to twist, to contort, to distort (as the face); (*sl.*) to have sexual intercourse with. *v.i.* to turn as a screw; to twist, to move obliquely or spirally, to swerve; (*sl.*) to have sexual intercourse. **to have a screw at,** (*Austral. coll.*) to take a look at. **to have a screw loose,** to be slightly crazy. **to put the screws on,** (*sl.*) to put pressure on. **to screw up,** to tighten up with or as with a screw; to fasten with a screw or screws; to shut (a person) in thus; to twist; (*sl.*) to bungle, mess up; (*sl.*) to make confused or neurotic, to disturb. **to screw up courage,** to summon up resolution. **screwball,** *a.* (*chiefly N Am. coll.*) eccentric, crazy, zany. *n.* an eccentric person. **screw-coupling,** *n.* a collar with threads for joining pipes etc. together. **screw-cutter,** *n.* a tool for cutting screws. **screwdriver,** *n.* a tool like a blunt chisel for turning screws. **screw-eye,** *n.* a screw with a loop instead of a slotted head, for attaching cords to picture-frames etc. **screw-gear,** *n.* an endless screw or worm for working a cogwheel etc. **screw-jack,** *n.* a lifting-jack with a screw rotating in a nut; a dentist's implement for pressing teeth apart etc. **screw-pile,** *n.* a pile armed with a screw-point, sunk by turning instead of hammering. **screw-pine,** *n.* any tree of the E Indian genus *Pandanus*, with leaves clustered spirally. **screw-press,** *n.* a press worked by means of a screw. **screw-propeller** PROPELLER. **screw steamer,** *n.* a steamer driven by a screw-propeller. **screwtop,** *n.* (a bottle or jar with) a top that opens and closes with a screwing motion. **screw-wrench,** *n.* a tool for gripping the head of a large screw or nut; a wrench with jaws worked by a screw. **screwable,** *a.* **screwed,** *a.* (*sl.*) drunk, tipsy. **screwer,** *n.* [formerly *scrue*, OF *escroue* (F *ecrou*), etym. doubtful]

screw[2], *n.* a broken-down or vicious horse. **screwy,** *a.* of a horse, worn-out, broken down; (*coll.*) eccentric, absurd, zany; (*coll.*) mad, crazy.

Scriabin SKRYABIN.

scribal, scribaceous SCRIBE.

scribble[1], *v.i.* to write hastily, illegibly or without regard to correctness of handwriting or composition; to make random or meaningless marks with a pen, crayon etc.; (*derog.*) to be a journalist or author. *v.t.* to write hastily, carelessly or without regard to correctness. *n.* hasty or careless writing; a scrawl; something written hastily or carelessly. **scribble-scrabble,** *n.* scribble, scrawling; †a scribbler. *v.t.* to scribble. **scribblement,** *n.* **scribbler,** *n.* a minor author. **scribblingly,** *adv.* **scribbling-paper,** *n.* paper for making hasty notes on. [SCRIBE]

scribble[2], *v.t.* to card roughly; to pass through a scribbler. **scribbler, scribbling-machine,** *n.* a carding-machine used for the first rough process in preparing wool, cotton etc. [Swed. *skrubbla*, freq. of *skrubba*, to SCRUB]

scribe, *n.* a writer, a penman; a secretary, a copyist; an ancient Jewish writer or keeper of official records, one of a class of commentators, interpreters and teachers of the sacred law; a pointed instrument for marking lines on wood, bricks etc., a scriber. *v.t.* to mark with a scriber; to mark and fit one piece to the edge of another. **scribal,** *a.* **scribaceous,** *a.* given to (excesses of) writing. **scribedom,** *n.* **scriber, scribing-awl, -iron, -tool,** *n.* a tool used for scoring or marking lines etc. **scribing-compasses,** *n.pl.* compasses used for scoring circles etc. **scribism,** *n.* [L *scrība*, from *scrībere*, to write]

scrieve, *v.i.* (*Sc.*) to stride along swiftly. [prob. from Icel. *skrefa*, to stride]

scriggle, *v.i.* (*chiefly dial.*) to wriggle, to writhe, to squirm. *n.* a wriggling movement. [onomat.]

scrim, *n.* strong cotton or linen cloth used for lining in upholstery and for cleaning. [etym. doubtful]

scrimmage, *n.* a tussle, a confused or rough-and-tumble struggle, a skirmish; in Rugby football, a scrummage; in American football, the period or activity between the ball coming into play and the time it is dead. [var. of SKIRMISH]

scrimp, *v.t.* to make small, scant or short; to limit or straiten, to skimp. *v.i.* to skimp, to be niggardly. *a.* scanty, narrow. *adv.* scarcely, barely. *n.* (*N Am.*) a niggard, a pinching miser. **scrimpy,** *a.* **scrimpily, scrimply,** *adv.* **scrimpiness, scrimpness,** *n.* [cp. Swed. and Dan. *skrumpen*, shrivelled, G *schrumpfen*, cogn. with OE *scrimman*]

scrimshank, *v.i.* (*coll.*) to avoid work, to get out of doing one's duty. [etym. unknown]

scrimshaw, *v.t.* to decorate (ivory, shells etc.) with carvings and coloured designs. *v.i.* to produce decorated work of this kind. *n.* a piece of such work. [prob. a surname]

scrip[1], *n.* orig. a writing, a list, as of names, a schedule; a provisional certificate given to a subscriber for stock of a bank or company; such certificates collectively. **scrip-holder,** *n.* [SCRIPT]

scrip[2], *n.* a small bag, a wallet or satchel. **†scrippage,** *n.* (*Shak.*) that which is contained in a scrip. [OE *scripp*, cp. Icel. *skreppa*, rel. to SCRAP[1]]

script, *n.* a piece of writing; handwriting as dist. from print; printed cursive characters, type in imitation of writing; handwriting in imitation of type; the written text or draft of a film, play or radio or television broadcast as used by the actors or performers; (*Law*) a writing, an original document. *v.t.* to write the script for. **scriptwriter,** *n.* one who writes scripts, esp. for broadcasting or for the cinema. **scription,** *n.* **scriptorium,** *n.* (*pl.* **-riums, -ria**) a writing-room, esp. in a monastery. **scriptorial,** *a.* **†scriptory,** *a.* written, not oral; used for writing. *n.* a scriptorium. [OF *escript* (F *écrit*), L *scriptum*, something written, neut. p.p. of *scrībere*, see SCRIBE]

Script., (*abbr.*) Scripture.

scripture, *n.* a sacred writing or book; the Bible, esp. the books of the Old and New Testament without the

Apocrypha; a passage from the Scriptures; †an inscription. †*v.t.*, *v.i.* to write. **Holy Scripture,** the Bible. **the Scriptures,** the Bible. **Scripture-reader,** *n.* one employed to read the Scriptures publicly. **scriptural,** *a.* pertaining to, derived from, based upon, or contained in the Scriptures. **scripturalism,** *n.* **scripturalist,** †**scripturist,** *n.* **scripturally,** *adv.* **scripturalness,** *n.* [ME from OF *escripture*, L. *scriptūra*, as prec.]

†**scritch,** SCREECH. **scritch-owl** SCREECH-OWL. [imit. cp. SCREECH]

scrive, SCRIBE.

scrivener, *n.* one whose business was to draw up contracts or other documents, a notary; formerly, a financial agent, a broker, a money-lender. [ME *scriveyn*, OF *escrivain* (F *écrivain*), It. *scrivano*, late L *scrībānus*, SCRIBE, -ER]

scrobe, *n.* (*Ent.*) a groove, as that receiving the base of the antenna in a weevil. **scrobicule,** *n.* (*Biol.*) a small pit or depression. **scrobicular**, **scrobiculate**, **-lated**, **scrobiculous**, *a.* **scrobiculus** (*pl.* **-li**) SCROBICULE. [L *scrobis*, trench]

scrofula, *n.* (*dated*) a form of tuberculosis affecting esp. the lymph glands of the neck. **scrofulous,** *a.* **scrofulously,** *adv.* **scrofulousness,** *n.* [L, orig. dim. of *scrōfa*, breeding sow]

scrog, *n.* (*chiefly Sc.*) a stunted bush; brushwood, undergrowth, thicket; (*Her.*) a branch of a tree. **scrogged, scroggy,** *a.* [etym. doubtful]

scroll, *n.* a roll of paper or parchment; an ancient book or volume in this form; †a schedule, a list, a catalogue; a convolved or spiral ornament more or less resembling a scroll of parchment, as a volute, the curved head of a violin etc., a band or ribbon bearing an inscription, a flourish, or tracery consisting of spiral lines; (*Her.*) the ribbon upon which a motto is inscribed. *v.t.* to roll up like a scroll; to decorate with scrolls; to enter in a scroll; (*Comput.*) to move (text) across a screen. *v.i.* to curl up like a scroll; (*Comput.*) to move text upwards, sideways etc. on a screen so as to display the next line or section. **scroll-gear** SCROLL-WHEEL. **scroll-head,** *n.* a volute-shaped timber at a ship's bow. **scroll-saw,** *n.* a fret-saw for cutting scrolls. **scroll-wheel,** *n.* a disk-shaped wheel with cogs arranged spirally on one surface causing variation of speed. **scroll-work,** *n.* ornamental work in spiral lines, esp. cut out with a scroll-saw. [formerly *scrowl*, dim. of ME *scrowe*, *scroue*, OF *escroue*, from Teut. (cp. MDut. *schroode*, OHG *scrōt*, strip) SHRED]

Scrooge, *n.* a miserly person. [Ebenezer *Scrooge*, a character in Dickens's *A Christmas Carol*]

scroop, *v.i.* to make a harsh, grating or creaking noise. *n.* such a noise. [imit.]

scrophularia, *n.* a genus of plants typical of the family Scrophulariaceae, containing the figwort. **scrophulariaceous**, *a.* [mod. L from med. L *scrophula*, SCROFULA]

scrotum, *n.* (*pl.* **-ta -tums**) the pouch enclosing the testes in the higher mammals. **scrotal,** *a.* **scrotiform**, *a.* **scrotitis,** *n.* inflammation of the scrotum. **scrotocele,** *n.* a scrotal hernia. [L]

scrouge, *v.t.* (*dial.*) to press against, to squeeze or crowd (in). **scrouger,** *n.* [etym. doubtful, perh. from SCREW]

scrounge, *v.t.* (*coll.*) to pilfer; to cadge. *v.i.* to forage or hunt around; to cadge things. **scrounger,** *n.* [etym. doubtful]

scrub[1], *v.t.* (*past*, *p.p.* **scrubbed**) to rub hard with something coarse and rough, esp. with soap and water used with a scrubbing-brush for the purpose of cleaning or scouring; to purify (a gas) with a scrubber; (*coll.*) to get rid of, cancel, delete, erase. *v.i.* to clean, scour or brighten things by rubbing hard; to work hard and penuriously, to drudge; to scrub the hands and arms before carrying out surgery. *n.* the act of scrubbing; a worn-out brush or broom; a lotion containing abrasive granules for cleansing the skin. **scrubwoman,** *n.* (*N Am.*) a charwoman. **scrubber,** *n.* one who or that which scrubs; a scrubbing-brush; a gas-purifier for removing tar and ammonia by spraying with water; (*sl.*) a prostitute or promiscuous woman. **scrubbing,** *n.*, *a.* **scrubbing-board,** *n.* a ribbed board used in washing for rubbing clothes on. **scrubbing-brush,** *n.* a stiff brush for scrubbing floors etc. [ME *scrobben*, MDan. *skrubbe* (cp. Swed. *skrubba*, Dut. *schrobben*]

scrub[2], *n.* (a tract of) brushwood, undergrowth or stunted trees; a stunted tree, bush etc.; a paltry, stingy person; *n.* an inferior animal; something mean or despicable; (*N Am.*) a player not of the first team. *a.* mean, paltry, petty, niggardly, contemptible. **the Scrubs,** (*coll.*) Wormwood Scrubs prison. **scrub-bird,** *n.* an Australian passerine bird, *Atrichia clamosa*. **scrub-cattle,** *n.* (*Austral.*) cattle that have run wild and deteriorated. **scrub fowl,** *n.* (*Austral.*) one of the mound-builder birds. **scrub-oak,** *n.* a name for several N American dwarf oaks. **scrub-rider,** *n.* (*Austral.*) one who goes out in search of scrub-cattle. **scrub turkey,** *n.* (*Austral.*) the lowan or mallee mound bird. **scrubber,** *n.* (*Austral.*) a bullock that has run wild. **scrubby,** †**scrubbed,** *a.* mean, stunted, insignificant; covered with brushwood; rough, unshaven. **scrubbiness,** *n.* [SHRUB[2]]

scruff[1], *n.* the nape or back of the neck, esp. as grasped by a person dragging another. [formerly *scuft*, Icel. *skopt* (*skoft*), hair of head]

scruff[2], *n.* (*dial.*) dandruff, scurf; (*coll.*) an unkempt or scruffy person. **scruffy,** *a.* scurvy; untidy, dirty, shabby, down-at-heel. **scruffiness,** *n.* [SCURF]

scrum, scrummage, *n.* a set struggle in rugby between the forwards of both sides grappling in a compact mass with the ball on the ground in the middle; a scuffle. *v.i.* (*past, p.p.* **scrummed**) to form a scrum. **to scrum down,** to scrum. **scrum half,** *n.* the half-back who puts the ball into the scrum. [var. of SCRIMMAGE]

scrump, *v.t.*, *v.i.* (*dial.*) to steal (apples) from an orchard. **scrumpy,** *n.* rough cider. [*scrump*, orig. mean. something withered or shrivelled, a shrivelled apple, from SCRIMP]

scrumptious, *a.* (*coll.*) first-class, stylish; of food, delicious; †fastidious. [perh. orig. mean. stingy, from SCRIMP, perh. var. of SUMPTUOUS]

scrunch, *v.t.* to crunch; to crush, to crumple; to hunch up. *v.i.* to make or move with a crunching sound. *n.* a crunch. **scrunch-dry,** *v.t.* to dry (the hair) with a hair-dryer whilst crushing in the hand, to give body. [var. of CRUNCH]

scruple, *n.* a weight of 20 grains (1·296 g), the third part of a dram (apothecaries' weight); †a small quantity, a tiny fraction, a particle; a doubt, objection or hesitation from conscientious or moral motives. *v.i.* to have scruples, to doubt, to hesitate, to be reluctant (to do etc.). †*v.t.* to doubt, hesitate, or demur, to question the correctness or propriety of. †**scrupler,** †**scrupulist**, *n.* **scrupulous**, *a.* influenced by scruples; careful, cautious, extremely conscientious, punctilious, precise, exact; †captious, inclined to object or demur. **scrupulously,** *adv.* **scrupulousness, scrupulosity**, *n.* [F *scrupule*, L *scrūpulum*, nom. *-lus*, dim. of *scrūpus* sharp stone]

scrutator, *n.* one who scrutinizes, a close inquirer. †**scrutable**, *a.* [L, as foll.]

scrutiny, *n.* close observation or investigation; minute inquiry; critical examination; an official examination of votes given at an election to verify the correctness of a declared result. **scrutineer,** *n.* one who acts as examiner in a scrutiny of votes. **scrutinize, -ise,** *v.t.* to examine narrowly or minutely. **scrutinizer,** *n.* **scrutinizingly,** *adv.* [late L *scrūtinium*, from *scrūtārī*, to search carefully, from *scrūta*, broken pieces, cogn. with SHRED]

scruto, *n.* a trapdoor with springs, made flush with a theatre stage, for rapid disappearances etc. [etym. doubtful]

†**scrutoire,** ESCRITOIRE.

scry, *v.t.* to crystal-gaze; to descry. [DESCRY]

scuba, *n.* an aqualung. **scuba-diving,** *n.* underwater swimming with an aqualung. **scuba-dive,** *v.i.* **scuba-diver,** *n.* [acronym for *s*elf-*c*ontained *u*nderwater *b*reathing *a*pparatus]

scud, *v.i.* (*past*, *p.p.* **scudded**) to run or fly swiftly; (*Naut.*) to run fast before a gale with little or no sail spread. *v.t.* to move swiftly over. *n.* the act or a spell of scudding; loose, vapoury clouds driven swiftly by the wind; a light passing shower. **scudder,** *n.* [Norw. *skudda*, allied to SHOOT]

scudo, *n.* (*pl.* **-di**) an old Italian silver coin and money of account. [It., from L *scūtum*, shield]

Scudamore, *n.* **Peter** (1958–), British National Hunt jockey. He was champion jockey in 1982 (shared with John Francome) and from 1986–89. In the 1988–89 season he became the third jockey to ride 1000 National Hunt winners; in Feb. 1989 he became the first person to ride 150 winners in a season and went on to increase his total to 221.

scuff[1], *v.i.* to drag or scrape with the feet in walking, to shuffle; to become abraded or roughened, esp. by use. *v.t.* to scrape or shuffle (the feet); (*Sc.*) to touch lightly, to graze; to abrade, scratch or roughen the surface of. *n.* the act or noise of scuffing; a mark or roughened place caused by scuffing. **scuffed, scuffy,** *a.* worn, shabby. [etym. doubtful, cp. Swed. *skuffa*, Icel. *skūfa*, to SHOVE, perh. conf. with SCRUFF or SCURF in some senses]

scuff[2], SCRUFF[1].

scuffle, *v.i.* to fight or struggle in a rough-and-tumble way; †to shuffle, to scrape with the feet; to scamper, to scurry. *n.* a confused and disorderly fight or struggle; a soft, shuffling sound. **scuffler,** *n.* [freq. of SCUFF[1]]

sculduddery, *n.* (*chiefly dial.*) lewdness, bawdry, obscenity. [etym. doubtful]

sculduggery, SKULDUGGERY.

sculk, etc. SKULK.

scull, *n.* one of a pair of short oars used by one person for propelling a boat; an oar used with twisting strokes over the stern; one who sculls a boat. *v.t.* to propel (a boat) by a scull or sculls. *v.i.* to propel a boat thus. **sculler,** *n.* one who sculls; a boat rowed thus. [etym. doubtful]

scullery, *n.* a place where dishes and utensils are washed up, vegetables prepared etc. [OF *escuelier*, L *scutellārius*, dish-keeper, from *scutella*, see SCUTTLE[1], -ERY]

†**scullion,** *n.* a servant who cleans pots, dishes etc., a kitchen drudge. †**scullionly,** *a.* [OF *escouillon*, *escouvillon*, Sp. *escobillon,* sponge for a cannon, from *escobilla*, sponge, dim. of *escoba*, L *scōpa*, pl. *scōpae* a besom]

Scullin, *n.* **James Henry** (1876–1953), Australian Labor politician. He was leader of the Federal Parliamentary Labor Party (1928–35), and prime minister and minister of industry (1929–31).

sculp, *v.t.* (*coll.*) to carve, to sculpture. [short for SCULPTURE]

sculp., (*abbr.*) sculptor, sculpture.

sculpin, *n.* a name for various N American seafishes with large spiny heads. [perh. corr. of obs. *scorpene*, SCORPAENA]

sculpture, *n.* the art of cutting, carving, modelling or casting wood, stone, clay, metal etc. into representations of natural objects or designs in round or in relief; carved or sculptured work collectively; a piece of this; raised or sunk markings on a shell, elytrum etc. *v.t.* to represent in or by sculpture; to ornament with sculpture; to shape by or as by carving, moulding etc. **sculpt,** *v.t.*, *v.i.* to sculpture. **sculptor, -tress,** *n.* one who sculptures. **sculptural, sculpturesque,** *a.* **sculpturally,** *adv.* [F, from L *sculptūra*, from *sculpere*, to carve]

scum, *n.* impurities that rise to the surface of liquid, esp. in fermentation or boiling; the scoria of molten metal; froth, foam or any film of floating matter; (*fig.*) refuse, dregs, the vile and worthless part. *v.t.* to clear of scum, to skim. *v.i.* (*past*, *p.p.* **scummed**) to rise as scum, to form a scum; to become covered with scum. **scummer,** *n.* **scummings,** *n.pl.* skimmings. **scummy,** *a.* [Dan. *skum* (cp. Icel. *skūm*, G *Schaum*), rel. to SKIM]

scumble, *v.t.* to cover (an oil-painting) lightly with opaque or semi-opaque colours so as to soften the outlines or colours; to produce a similar effect on (a drawing) by lightly rubbing; to soften (a colour) thus; to prepare (a painted wall) for repainting. *n.* a material for scumbling; the effect produced. [freq. of prec.]

scuncheon, *n.* a bevelling, splay or elbow in a window-opening etc.; arching etc., across the angles of a square tower supporting a spire. [OF *escoinson*]

scunner, *v.t.* (*Sc.*) to disgust to nauseate. *v.i.* to feel loathing, to be sickened. *n.* loathing, disgust an object of loathing. [etym. doubtful]

scupper, *n.* a hole or tube through a ship's side to carry off water from the deck. *v.t.* to sink (a ship); (*coll.*) to ruin, to do for. **scupper-hole,** *n.* **scupper-hose, -shoot,** *n.* a spout hanging from a scupper to carry the water clear of the side. **scupper-nail,** *n.* a short nail with a broad, flat head for nailing on scupper-hose etc. [prob. from OF *escope*, SCOOP]

scuppernong, *n.* (*N Am.*) a variety of the fox-grape, *Vitis vulpina.* [river in N Carolina]

scur, SKIRR.

scurf, *n.* flakes or scales thrown off by the skin, esp. of the head; any loose scaly matter adhering to a surface. **scurfy,** *a.* **scurfiness,** *n.* [OE (cp. Swed. *skorf*, Icel. *skurfur*), rel. to *sceorfan*, to scarify]

scurrilous, †**scurrile,** *a.* using or expressed in low, vulgar, grossly abusive or indecent language. **scurrilously,** *adv.* **scurrilousness, scurrility,** *n.* [L *scurrīlis*, from *scurra*, buffoon]

scurry, *v.i.* to go with great haste, to hurry, to scamper. *n.* an act or the noise of scurrying. [perh. from obs. *scurrier*, a scout, as SCOUR[2], perh. from *hurry-scurry*, reduplication of HURRY]

scurvy, *a.* mean, paltry, base, shabby, contemptible. *n.* a disease caused by lack of vitamin C and characterized by swollen gums, extravasation of blood and general debility, arising orig. esp. among those on shipboard from a deficiency of vegetables. **scurvied,** *a.* **scurvily,** *adv.* **scurviness,** *n.* [SCURFY under SCURF]

scurvy grass, *n.* a plant, *Cochlearia officinalis*, formerly used as a remedy for scurvy. [corr. of CRESS]

scut, *n.* a short tail, as of a hare, rabbit or deer. [cp. Icel. *skott*]

scuta SCUTUM.

scutage, *n.* money paid by a feudal tenant in lieu of personal attendance on his lord in war. [med. L *scūtāgium*, from *scūtum*, shield (cp. OF *escuage*)]

scutal, scutate SCUTUM.

scutch, *v.t.* to dress (cotton, flax etc.) by beating. *n.* a scutcher; coarse tow separated from flax by scutching. **scutch-blade, -rake, scutcher, scutching-sword,** *n.* an implement of various kinds used in scutching flax. [OF *escoucher*, *escousser*, perh. from Scand. (cp. Norw. *skoka*, scutcher)]

scutcheon, *n.* an escutcheon; a cover or frame for a keyhole; a name-plate. **scutcheoned,** *a.* [ESCUTCHEON]

scute SCUTUM.

scutellum, *n.* (*pl.* **-lla**) a small shield, plate, scale or horny segment in or on a plant or animal. **scutellar, scutellate, scutellated,**, *a.* **scutellation,** *n.* **scutelliform,** *a.* shield-shaped. [dim. of SCUTUM]

scutiger, *n.* a centipede of the genus *Scutigera* or the family Scutigeridae. **scutigerous,** *a.* [SCUTUM]

scutiped, *a.* of a bird, having hard scales on the tarsi. [SCUTUM]

scutter, *v.i.* to scurry, scuttle. [SCUTTLE[3]]

scuttle[1], *n.* a metal or other receptacle for carrying or holding coals, esp. for a fire-place, usu. called a coal-scuttle. **scuttleful,** *n.* [OE *scutel*, dish, L *scutella*, salver, dim. of *scutra*, tray, platter]

scuttle[2], *n.* a hole with a movable lid or hatch in a wall or roof or the deck or side of a ship; the lid or hatch covering this. *v.t.* to cut holes through the bottom or sides of (a ship); to sink by cutting such holes. **scuttle-butt, -cask,** *n.* a cask of drinking-water, usu. with a hole for dipping through, kept on the deck of a ship. **scuttler,** *n.* [OF *escoutilles*, pl. hatches (cp. F *ecoutille*), Sp. *escotilla*, from *escotar*, to cut out round the neck, from *escote*, tucker, from Teut. (cp. Dut.

schoot, G *Schoss*, bosom)]

scuttle[3], *v.i.* to hurry along, to scurry; to make off, to bolt. *n.* a hurried run or gait, a hasty flight, a bolt. **scuttler,** *n.* [orig. *scuddle*, freq. of SCUD]

scutum, *n.* (*pl.* **-ta**) the shield of the heavy-armed Roman legionaries; a scute; the kneepan. **scutal, scutate,** *a.* covered with scutes or bony plates; shield-shaped. **scute,** *n.* a shield-like plate, scale or bony or horny segment as of the armour of a crocodile, turtle etc. **scutiform**, *a.* **scutulum**, *n.* (*pl.* **-la**) a shield-shaped scale or scab, esp. in ringworm of the scalp. **scutulate,** *a.* [L, from *sku-*, to cover, cogn. with sky]

scye, *n.* the opening of a coat etc. where the sleeve is inserted. [Sc. dial.]

Scylla, *n.* a rock on the Italian shore of the Straits of Messina, facing Charybdis, described by Homer as a monster devouring sailors. **between Scylla and Charybdis,** caught between alternative risks, escape from one of which entails danger from the other. [L, from Gr. *Skulla*]

†**scymitar,** SCIMITAR.

scyphus, *n.* (*pl.* **-phi**) a bowl-shaped footless Greek cup with two handles; a cup-shaped plant part or organ. **scyphiform**, **scyphose**, *a.* [L, from Gr. *skuphos*]

scytale, *n.* a staff of a special form used by the ancient Greeks for sending dispatches; a method of sending secret messages by writing on a strip of parchment wound about such a staff so that it was legible only when wound about a staff of similar form. [Gr. *skutalē*, staff]

scythe, *n.* a long curved blade with a crooked handle used for mowing or reaping; a curved blade projecting from the axle of an ancient war-chariot. *v.t.* to cut with a scythe. **scytheman,** *n.* one who uses a scythe, a mower; †one of an irregular body of troops armed with scythes. **scythe-stone,** *n.* a whetstone for sharpening scythes. **scythed,** *a.* [OE *sīthe* (cp. Dut. *zeis*, Icel. *sigthr*, LG *Saged*), cogn. with L *secāre*, to cut]

Scythia, *n.* region N of the Black Sea between the Carpathian mountains and the river Don, inhabited by the Scythians 7th–1st centuries BC. From the middle of the 4th century BC the Scythians were slowly superseded by the Sarmatians. They produced ornaments and vases in gold and electrum with animal decoration. **Scythian,** *a.* pertaining to ancient Scythia, or the ancient race inhabiting it. *n.* one of this race; the Scythian language. **Scythic,** *a.* **Scythism,** *n.* **Scytho-,** *comb. form.*

SD, (*abbr.*) Social Democrat; South Dakota; standard deviation.

sd, (*abbr.*) indefinitely. [L *sine die*]

SDA, (*abbr.*) Scottish Development Agency.

S.Dak., (*abbr.*) South Dakota.

†**'sdeath,** *int.* an exclamation of impatience, anger etc. [short for GOD'S DEATH]

SDI, (*abbr.*) Strategic Defence Initiative.

SDLP, (*abbr.*) Social and Democratic Labour Party.

SDP, (*abbr.*) Social Democratic Party.

SDR, (*abbr.*) special discretion required; special drawing rights.

SE, (*abbr.*) south-east, south-eastern.

Se, (*chem. symbol*) selenium.

se-, (*pref.*) as in *secede*, *secure*. [L, away from, apart, without]

sea, *n.* the body of salt water covering the greater part of the earth's surface, the ocean; a definite part of this, or a very large enclosed body of (usu. salt) water; the swell or motion of the sea; a great wave, a billow; the set or direction of the waves; a vast quantity or expanse, an ocean, a flood (of people, troubles etc.). *a.* of, pertaining to, living, growing or used in, on or near the sea, marine, maritime. **at full sea,** at high tide; at the acme or culmination. **at sea,** on the open sea; out of sight of land; perplexed, uncertain, wide of the mark. **brazen** or **molten sea** MOLTEN. **four seas** FOUR. **half-seas-over** HALF. **high seas** HIGH. **over** or **beyond seas,** to or in countries separated by sea. **Seven Seas** SEVEN. **to go to sea, to follow the sea,** to become or to be a sailor. **to put to sea,** to leave port or land. **sea-acorn,** *n.* a barnacle. **sea-anchor** DRAG-ANCHOR under DRAG. **sea-anemone,** *n.* a solitary tentacled polyp of the order Actinaria, an actinia. **sea-angel,** *n.* the angel-fish. **sea-ape** SEA-FOX; SEA-OTTER. **sea-bank,** *n.* the shore; a bank built to keep out the sea. **sea-bar,** *n.* the sea-swallow or tern. **sea-bass** BASS[2]. **sea-bat,** *n.* a flying fish; a fish of the genus *Platax,* from the length of its dorsal and ventral fins. **sea-bear,** *n.* a polar bear; the N Pacific fur-seal. **sea-beat, -beaten,** *a.* beaten by the waves. **seabed,** *n.* the floor of the sea. **sea-bells,** *n. sing.* a species of bindweed growing on the shore. **sea-belt,** *n.* a species of fucus with belt-like fronds. **sea-bird,** *n.* **sea-board,** *n.* land bordering on the sea; the sea-coast; the seashore. *a.* bordering on the sea. **sea-boat,** *n.* a ship (with regard to her sea-going qualities). **seaborne,** *a.* conveyed by sea. **sea-bow,** *n.* a bow like a rainbow produced in sea-spray. **sea-boy,** *n.* a boy employed on board a sea-going vessel. **sea-breach,** *n.* irruption of the sea through an embankment. **sea-bread,** *n.* ship-biscuit. **sea-bream,** *n.* a marine food-fish of the family Sparidae. **sea breeze,** *n.* a breeze blowing from the sea, usu. by day, in alternation with a land-breeze at night. **sea-calf,** *n.* the common seal. **sea-campion,** *n.* a plant of the pink family, *Silene maritima.* **sea-canary,** *n.* the white whale (from its whistling). **sea-cap,** *n.* a cap to be worn on shipboard; the cap of a wave; (*N Am.*) a large basket-shaped sponge. **sea captain,** *n.* the captain of a vessel, as dist. from a military officer; a great commander or admiral. **sea card,** *n.* the card of the mariner's compass; a map or chart. **sea change,** *n.* a transformation or transmutation (produced by the sea). †**sea-coal,** *n.* coal (orig. brought from Newcastle by sea) as distinct from charcoal. **sea-coast,** *n.* a coast. **sea-cob,** *n.* a black-backed sea-gull. **seacock,** *n.* a valve through which the sea can be admitted into the hull of a ship. **sea-colander,** *n.* an olive-coloured seaweed with perforated fronds. **seacow,** *n.* a sirenian; a walrus. **sea-crow, -cormorant, -drake,** *n.* local names for the laughing gull, *Larus ridibundus* and other sea-birds. **sea-cucumber, -gherkin,** *n.* a holothurian such as the trepang. **sea-deity** SEA-GOD. **sea-devil,** *n.* the angler-fish; any holothurian, esp. the bêche-de-mer. **sea dog,** *n.* the common seal; the dogfish; an old sailor, esp. of the Elizabethan era. **sea-dragon,** *n.* applied to various fishes having some resemblance to a dragon. **sea-drake** SEA-CROW. **sea eagle,** *n.* the osprey; any of various fishing-eagles and other large sea-birds. **sea-ear,** *n.* an ormer or mollusc of the genus *Haliotis*. **sea-egg,** *n.* a sea-urchin. **sea-elephant,** *n.* the largest of the seals, *Macrorhinus elephantinus* the male of which has a short proboscis. **sea fan,** *n.* a coral of the genus *Gorgonia* or a related genus, having fan-like branches. **seafarer,** *n.* a sailor. **seafaring,** *a.* travelling by sea; following the occupation of a sailor. *n.* travel by sea; the occupation of a sailor. **sea-fennel,** *n.* samphire. **seafight,** *n.* a naval engagement. **sea-flower,** *n.* the sea-anemone. **sea food,** *n.* edible salt-water fish and crustaceans, esp. shellfish. **sea-fowl,** *n.* **sea-fox,** *n.* the long-tailed shark, *Alopias vulpes*. **seafront,** *n.* the part of a town that faces the sea. **sea-gauge,** *n.* a self-registering apparatus for taking deep-sea soundings; the draught of a ship. **sea-gherkin** SEA-CUCUMBER. **sea-gilliflower,** *n.* the sea-pink. **sea-girt,** *a.* (*poet.*) surrounded by the sea. **sea-god, -deity,** *n.* a deity supposed to preside over the sea. **sea-goddess,** *n. fem.* **seagoing,** *a.* making foreign voyages, as opp. to coasting; seafaring. **sea-gooseberry,** *n.* a ctenophore. †**sea-gown,** *n.* a gown with short sleeves worn at sea. **sea green,** *n., a.* (of) a faint bluish-green. *a.* **sea-gudgeon,** *n.* the black goby, *Gobius niger*. **seagull,** *n.* a gull. **sea-hare,** *n.* a mollusc of the genus *Aplysia* with ear-like tentacles. **sea-hedgehog,** *n.* a sea-urchin. **sea-hog,** *n.* the common porpoise. **sea holly,** *n.* an umbelliferous plant, *Eryngium maritimum,* with spiny leaves. **sea horse,** *n.* †the walrus; the hippocampus or a similar fish; a fabulous animal, half horse and half fish, harnessed to the chariot of a sea-god. **sea-island cotton,** *n.* a fine variety of cotton originally grown on the islands off the coasts of Georgia, S Carolina and Florida. **sea-kale,** *n.* a cruciferous plant, *Crambe maritima,* grown as a culinary vegetable for its young shoots. **sea-king,** *n.* (*poet.*) a viking or piratical Scandinavian chieftain. **sea lane,** *n.* a route for ships at sea. **sea-lark, -laverock,** *n.* the ringed plover; any of various other sea-birds. **sea lavender,** *n.* any species of *Statice,* esp. *S. limonium.* **sea-lawyer,** *n.* a sailor given to arguing and criticizing; a shark. **sea legs,** *n.pl.* ability to walk on the deck of a vessel at sea on a stormy day. **sea-lemon,** *n.* a yellow oval gasteropod of the genus *Doris.* **sea-leopard,** *n.* a spotted seal from the S Pacific and Antarctic. **sea-letter, -pass,** *n.* a document from the custom-house carried by a neutral ship in time of war, specifying the nature of the cargo etc. **sea level,** *n.* a level continuous with that of the surface of the sea at mean tide, taken as a basis for surveying etc. (in Britain at Newlyn, Cornwall). **sea-lily,** *n.* a crinoid. **sea-line,** *n.* the horizon at sea. **sea lion,** *n.* a large-eared seal, esp. of the genus *Otariai;* (*Her.*) a fabulous animal, half lion and half fish. **Sea Lord,** *n.* one of four naval Lords of the Admiralty. **sea-magpie** SEA-PIE[1]. **sea-maid,** *n.* a mermaid, a sea-nymph. **seaman,** *n.* (*pl.* **-men**) a mariner, a sailor, esp. one below the rank of officer; a person able to navigate a ship, a navigator. **seaman-like, seamanly,** *a.* **seamanship,** *n.* **sea-mark,** *n.* an elevated object, such as a lighthouse or beacon, serving as a guide to vessels at sea. **sea-mat,** *n.* a polyzoan forming a flat matted coral. **sea-melon,** *n.* a holothurian, sea-cucumber. **seamew,** *n.* a gull. **sea-mile,** GEOGRAPHICAL MILE under MILE. **sea monster,** *n.* a huge sea-creature, natural or mythical. **sea-moss,** *n.* a moss-like coralline or seaweed; corrageen. **sea mouse,** *n.* an iridescent sea-worm, *Aphrodite aculeata.* **sea-needle,** *n.* the garfish, *Belone vulgaris.* **sea-nettle,** *n.* a jellyfish. **sea-onion,** *n.* the squill. **sea otter,** *n.* a marine otter, *Enhydra marina,* of the shores of the N Pacific. **sea-owl,** *n.* the lump fish. **sea-pad,** *n.* the starfish. **sea-pass** SEA-LETTER. **sea-peach, -pear,** *n.* peach-, or pear-shaped kinds of ascidians. **sea-pen,** *n.* a feather-shaped polyp. **sea-pheasant,** *n.* the pintail duck. **sea-pie[1], -magpie, -pilot,** *n.* the oyster-catcher, *Haematopus ostralegus.* **sea-pie[2],** *n.* a sailors' dish of crust and meat in alternate layers, baked together. **sea-piece,** *n.* a picture representing a scene at sea. **sea-pig,** *n.* a porpoise; a dugong. **sea-pike,** *n.* the garfish; the hake; another fish of a similar kind. **sea-pilot** SEA-PIE[1]. **sea-pink,** *n.* thrift, *Armeria maritima.* **seaplane,** *n.* an aeroplane fitted with floats to enable it to take off from and alight on the water. **seaplane carrier,** *n.* a warship fitted with a deck from which planes can operate. **seaport,** *n.* a town with a harbour on the coast. **sea-pumpkin,** *n.* a sea-melon. **sea-purse,** *n.* the leathery envelope in which sharks and rays deposit their eggs. **sea-rat,** *n.* a pirate. **sea-raven,** *n.* a deep-sea sculpin from the W Atlantic; a cormorant. **sea-risk,** *n.* hazard of injury or loss at sea. **searobber,** *n.* a pirate. **sea-robin,** *n.* the red gurnard. **sea-roll,** *n.* a holothurian. **sea-room,** *n.* room to handle a ship without danger of running ashore or of collision. **sea-rosemary,** *n.* the sea-lavender. **sea-rover,** *n.* a pirate; a piratical vessel. **sea salt,** *n.* salt obtained from sea-water by evaporation. **seascape,** *n.* a sea-piece. **sea scorpion,** *n.* any fish of the genus *Scorpaena;* the sculpin, *Cottus scorpius.* **Sea Scouts,** *n.pl.* a branch of the Scouts specializing in sailing etc. **sea serpent,** *n.* a sea-snake; a creature of immense size and serpentine form, believed by mariners to inhabit the depths of the ocean. **seashell,** *n.* the shell of a marine mollusc. **seashore,** *n.* the shore, coast or margin of the sea; (*Law*) the space between high- and low-water mark; land adjacent to the sea. **seasick,** *a.* suffering from sea-sickness. **seasickness,** *n.* a peculiar functional disturbance characterized by nausea and vomiting, brought on by the motion of a ship. **seaside,** *n.* a place or district close to the sea, esp. a holiday resort. *a.* bordering on the sea. **sea-sleeve,** *n.* a cuttle-fish. **sea-slug,** *n.* a trepang. **sea snail,** *n.* a snail-like marine gasteropod; a slimy fish of the family Liparididae, the unctuous sucker. **sea snake,** *n.* a venomous marine snake of the family Hydrophidae inhabiting the Indian Ocean and other tropical seas; the sea-serpent. **sea-snipe,** *n.* the snipe-fish; the dunlin. **sea squirt,** *n.* an ascidian. **sea-sunflower,** *n.* a sea-anemone. **sea-swallow,** *n.* the tern. **sea-tang, -tangle,** *n.* a seaweed of the genus *Laminaria.* **sea-term,** *n.* a word or phrase peculiar to seamen. **sea-toad,** *n.* the toad-fish; the angler-fish; the sculpin. **sea trout,** *n.* the salmon-trout, bull-trout and some other fishes. **sea unicorn,** *n.* the narwhal. **sea-urchin,** *n.* an echinus. **sea wall,** *n.* a wall or embankment for protecting land against encroachment by the sea. **seaway,** *n.* a ship's progress; a clear way for a ship at sea. **seaweed,** *n.* any alga or other plant growing in the sea. **seaweeded, -weedy,** *a.* **sea-whip,** *n.* a whip-shaped coral. **sea-whipcord,** *n.* a variety of sea-weed. **sea-wife,** *n.* a variety of wrasse. **sea-wolf,** *n.* a viking; a pirate; a large voracious fish, esp. the wolf-fish, *Anarrhicas lupus;* †the sea-elephant. **seaworthy,** *a.* of a ship, in a fit state to go to sea. **sea-worthiness,** *n.* **sea-wrack,** *n.* coarse seaweed, esp. thrown up by the waves. **seaward,** *a.* directed or situated towards the sea. *adv.* towards the sea. *n.* a seaward side or aspect. **seawards,** *adv.* [OE *sǣ,* cp. Dut. *zee,* G *See,* Icel. *saer*]

Seagull, The, *n.* a play by Anton Chekhov, first produced in Russia in 1896. It studies the jealousy between a mother and son, the son's vain search for identity, and his ultimate suicide.

seal[1], *n.* a carnivorous amphibious marine mammal of various species of the family Phocidae, having flipper-like limbs adapted for swimming and thick fur; applied to allied mammals belonging to the family Otariidae, distinguished by having visible external ears, comprising the sea-lions and fur-seals; sealskin. *v.i.* to hunt seals. **seal-fishery,** *n.* **seal-rookery,** *n.* a breeding-place of seals. **sealskin,** *n.* the under-fur of the fur-seal, esp. prepared for use as material for jackets etc.; a sealskin garment. **sealer,** *n.* a ship or person engaged in seal-hunting. [OE *seolh,* cp. Icel. *selr,* Dan. *sæl,* Swed. *säl*]

seal[2], *n.* a die or stamp having a device, usu. in intaglio, for making an impression on wax or other plastic substance; a piece of wax, lead or other material stamped with this and attached to a document as a mark of authenticity etc., or to an envelope, package, box etc. to prevent its being opened without detection etc.; the impression made thus on wax, lead etc.; a stamped wafer- or other mark affixed to a document in lieu of this; any device that must be broken to give access; any act, gift or event regarded as authenticating, ratifying or guaranteeing; a symbolic, significant or characteristic mark or impress; anything used to close a gap, prevent the escape of gas etc.; water in the trap of a drain-pipe preventing the ascent of foul air. *v.t.* to affix a seal to; to stamp with a seal or stamp, esp. as a mark of correctness or authenticity; to fasten with a seal; to close hermetically, to shut up; to close (the lips etc.) lightly; to confine securely; to secure against leaks, draughts etc.; to make (as wood) impermeable to rain, etc. by applying a coating; to fix or fill with plaster etc.; to confirm; to ratify, to certify; to set a mark on, to designate or destine irrevocably. **Fisher's Seal** FISHER. **Great Seal,** the official seal of the United Kingdom used to seal treaties, writs summoning Parliament, and other state documents of great importance. **Privy Seal** PRIVY. **seal-pipe,** *n.* a dip-pipe. **seal ring,** *n.* a finger-ring with a seal. **seal-wort,** *n.* Solomon's seal. **sealed-beam,** *a.* pertaining to electric lights, as car headlights, in which the reflector and bulb are in one sealed unit. †**sealing-day,** *n.* a day for ratification or confirmation. **sealing-wax,** *n.* a composition of shellac and turpentine with a pigment used for sealing letters etc. **sealable,** *a.* **sealant,** *n.* a substance for sealing wood, stopping up gaps etc. [OF *seel* (F *sceau*), L *sigillum,* cogn. with *signum,* SIGN]

seal-pipe, seal-wort SEAL[2].
sealskin SEAL.
sealyham, *n.* a breed of Welsh terrier. [village in Pembrokeshire]
seam[1], *n.* a ridge or other visible line of junction between two parts or things, esp. two pieces of cloth etc. sewn together, planks fitted edge to edge, or sheet-metal lapped over at the edges; (*Anat.*) a suture; a mark of separation, a crack, a fissure; a line on the surface of anything, esp. the face, a wrinkle, a cicatrix, a scar; a thin layer separating two strata of rock; a thin stratum of coal; (*N Am.*) a piece of sewing. *v.t.* to join together with or as with a seam; to mark with a seam, furrow, scar etc. **seam-, seaming-lace,** *n.* galloon, braid etc., used to cover the seams in upholstery. **seam-presser,** *n.* a heavy iron used by tailors for pressing seams; an implement used to flatten down the ridges after ploughing. †**seam-rent,** *n.* a rent along a seam. *a.* ragged. **seamer, seaming-machine,** *n.* a sewing-machine for making seams. **seaming-plough,** *n.* a seam-presser. **seamless,** *a.* †**seamster,** †**sempster,** *n.* one who sews. **seamstress, sempstress,**, *n.* a woman whose occupation is sewing. **seamy,** *a.* showing the seams; disreputable, sordid, unpleasant. [OE (cp. Dut. *zoom,* G *Saum,* Icel. *saumr*), rel. to SEW]
†**seam[2],** *n.* fat, grease; hog's lard. [F *saim,* ult. from L *sagīna,* fattening, fatness]
seam[3], *n.* (*now dial.*) a horse-load measure of 8 bushels (0·06 cu. m) of corn, 6–8 pecks (50–70 l) of sand etc. a cart-load, usu. 3 cwt. (150 kg) of hay or 2 cwt. (100 kg) of straw. [OE *sēam,* OHG *soum,* med. L *sauma,* Gr. *sagma,* pack-saddle]
Seanad Eireann, *n.* the upper house, or senate, of the parliament of Eire. [Ir.]
séance, *n.* a session, as of a society, deliberative body etc.; a meeting for exhibiting, receiving or investigating spiritualistic manifestations. [F, a sitting, from OF *seoir,* L *sedēre,* to sit]
Sea Peoples, *n.pl.* unidentified seafaring warriors who may have been Achaeans, Etruscans, or PHILISTINES, who ravaged and settled the Mediterranean coasts in the 12th–13th centuries BC. They were defeated by Ramses III of Egypt in 1191.
SEAQ, *n.* a computerized system for recording trade and price changes in shares, used by the London Stock Exchange. From October 1987, SEAQ began displaying market maker's quotations for UK stocks, having oly been operational previously for overseas equities. [*S*tock *E*xchange *A*utomated *Q*uotations]
sear[1], sere[2], *a.* of leaves etc., dried up, withered. *v.t.* to burn or scorch the surface of to dryness and hardness; to cauterize; (*fig.*) to brand; to make callous or insensible; to wither up, to blast. **seared,** *a.* hardened, insensible, callous. **searedness,** *n.* **searing,** *a.* **searingly,** *adv.* [OE *sear* (cp. ODut. *sore,* also Gr. *auos,* for *sausos,* dry, and AUSTERE), whence *sēarian,* to sear]
sear[2], SERE[1].
†**searce,** *n.* a sieve, a strainer. *v.t.* to sift. [ME *saarce,* OF *saas* (F *sas*), ult. as SETACEOUS]
search, *v.t.* to go over and examine for what may be found or to find something; to examine (esp. a person) for concealed weapons etc.; to explore, to probe; to look for, to seek (out). *v.i.* to make a search, inquiry or investigation. *n.* the act of seeking, looking or inquiring; investigation, exploration, inquiry, quest, examination. **right of search,** the right claimed by a belligerent nation to board neutral vessels and examine their papers and cargo for contraband. **search me!** *int.* how should I know? I have no idea. **searchlight,** *n.* an electric arc-light or other powerful illuminant concentrated into a beam that can be turned in any direction for lighting channels, discovering an enemy etc. **search party,** *n.* one going out to search for a lost, concealed or abducted person or thing. **search warrant,** *n.* a warrant granted by a justice of the peace, authorizing entry into a house etc. to search for stolen property etc. **searchable,** *a.* †**searchableness,** *n.* **searcher,** *n.* **searching,** *a.* making search or inquiry; penetrating, thorough, minute, close. **searchingly,** *adv.* **searchingness,** *n.* **searchless,** *a.* [ME *serchen,* OF *cercher* (F *chercher*), L *circāre,* to go round, from CIRCUS]
Searle, *n.* **Ronald** (1920–), British cartoonist and illustrator, who created the schoolgirls of St Trinian's in 1941 and has made numerous cartoons of cats.
season, *n.* one of the four divisions of the year, spring, summer, autumn, winter; a period of time of a specified or indefinite length; the period of the greatest activity of something, or when it is in vogue, plentiful, at its best etc.; a favourable, opportune, fit, suitable or convenient time; a period when a mammal is on heat; seasoning; a season ticket. *v.t.* to make sound or fit for use by preparation, esp. by tempering, maturing, acclimatizing, inuring, habituating or hardening; to make mature or experienced; to render palatable or give a higher relish to by the addition of condiments etc.; to make more piquant or pleasant, to add zest to; to mitigate, to moderate, to qualify (justice with mercy etc.). *v.i.* to become inured, habituated, accustomed etc.; of timber, to become hard and dry. **in season,** in vogue; in condition for shooting, hatching, use, mating, eating etc.; of a mammal, on heat; at a fit or opportune time. **in season and out of season,** at all times, continuously or indiscriminately. **season ticket,** *n.* a railway or other ticket, usu. issued at a reduced rate, valid for any number of journeys etc., for the period specified. **seasonable,** *a.* occurring or done at the proper time, opportune; suitable to the season. **seasonableness,** *n.* **seasonably,** *adv.* **seasonal,** *a.* of or occurring at a particular season; required, done, etc. according to the season. **seasonally,** *adv.* **seasoner,** *n.* **seasoning,** *n.* anything added to food to make it more palatable; anything that increases enjoyment. **seasonless,** *a.* [OF *seson* (F *saison*), L *satiōnem,* nom. *-tio,* from *serere,* to sow]
seat, *n.* that on which one sits or may sit, a chair, bench, stool etc.; the part of a chair etc. on which a person's weight rests in sitting; the part of a machine or other structure on which another part or thing is supported; the buttocks or the part of trousers etc. covering them; a place for sitting or where one may sit; the place where anything is, location, site, situation; a place in which authority is vested; a country residence, a mansion; the right of sitting, esp. in a legislative body; manner or posture of sitting. *v.t.* to cause to sit down, to place or set on a seat; to assign seats to; to provide (a church etc.) with seats; to provide (a chair, trousers etc.) with a seat; to settle, to locate, to install, to establish, to fix in place. *v.i.* †to rest; to settle; of a garment, to become baggy from sitting. **in the hot seat,** having ultimate responsibility for decisions taken. **seat-back,** *n.* a loose ornamental covering for the back of a chair etc. **seat belt,** *n.* a strap to hold a person in a seat in a car, aeroplane etc. **seat-earth,** *n.* a bed of clay etc., underlying a coal-seam. **seatage,** *n.* **seated,** *a.* sitting. **seater,** *n.* (*usu. in comb.* as *two-seater*). **seating,** *n.* the provision of seats; the seats provided or their arrangement; material for seats; a support on which something rests. **seatless,** *a.* [ME *sete,* Icel. *saeti,* cogn. with SIT]
SEATO, (*abbr.*) South East Asia Treaty Organization.
Seattle, *n.* port (grain, timber, fruit, fish) of the state of Washington, US, situated between Puget Sound and Lake Washington; population (1980) 493,846, metropolitan area (with Everett) 1,601,000. It is a centre for the manufacture of jet aircraft (Boeing), and also has shipbuilding, food processing, and paper industries.
†**seax,** SAX[1].
sebaceous, *a.* fatty; made of fatty or oily matter; of glands, ducts, follicles etc., containing, conveying, or secreting fatty or oily matter. **sebacic,** *a.* **sebacic acid,** *n.* an acid derived from various oils. **sebate,** *n.* a salt of this. **sebiferous, sebific,** *a.* **seborrhoea,** (*N Am.*) **-rrhea,**), *n.* excessive secretion of sebum. **seborrhoeic,** *a.* **sebum,** *n.* the fatty matter secreted by the sebaceous glands, which lubricates the hair and skin. [L *sēbāceus,* from *sēbum,* tallow]

Sebastian, St, *n.* (died *c.* 288), Roman soldier, traditionally a member of Emperor Diocletian's bodyguard until his Christian faith was discovered. He was martyred by being shot with arrows; feast day 20 Jan.

Sebastiano del Piombo, (*c.* 1485–1547), Italian painter, born in Venice. He moved to Rome in 1511, where his friendship with Michelangelo (and rivalry with Raphael) inspired him to his greatest works, such as *The Raising of Lazarus* (1517–19; National Gallery, London). He also painted powerful portraits.

Sebat, *n.* the fifth month of the Jewish civil year and the 11th of the ecclesiastical year, corresponding to part of Jan. and Feb. [Heb. *sh'bat*]

sebesten, *n.* the drupaceous fruit of a Mesopotamian or Indian tree, *Cordia myxa* or *C. latifolia,* used medicinally. [Arab. *sebastān,* Pers. *sapistān*]

sebiferous, seborrhoea, sebum etc. SEBACEOUS.

†**sebilla,** *n.* a wooden bowl used for holding sand and water in the process of cutting marble. [F *sébile*]

sec[1], *a.* of wine, dry. [F, from L *siccus*]

sec[2], *n.* short for SECOND[1].

sec[3], (*abbr.*) secant.

sec., (*abbr.*) second, secondary; secretary; section; according to. [L *secundum*]

secability, *n.* capability of being cut or divided into parts. [late L *secābilitas,* from *secāre,* to cut]

secale, *n.* a genus of cereals containing the rye-plant. [L]

secant, *a.* cutting; dividing into two parts. *n.* a straight line intersecting a curve, esp. a radius of a circle drawn through the second extremity of an arc of this and terminating in a tangent to the first extremity; the ratio of this to the radius; the ratio of the hypotenuse to the base of a right-angled triangle formed by drawing a perpendicular to either side of the angle. [L *secans -antem,* pres.p. of *secāre,* to cut]

secateurs, *n.pl.* pruning-scissors. [F]

secco, *a.* (*Mus.*) plain, unadorned. *n.* tempera-painting. [It.]

secede, *v.i.* to withdraw from fellowship, association or communion, as with a Church. **seceder,** *n.* one who secedes; (*pl.*) those who seceded from the Scottish Church in 1733. [L *sēcēdere* (SE-, *cedere,* to go, p.p. *cessus*)]

secern, *v.t.* to separate, to distinguish; to secrete or excrete. **secernent,** *a.* secretory. *n.* a secretory organ; a drug etc. promoting secretion. **secernment,** *n.* [L *sēcernere* (SE-, *cernere,* to separate)]

secesh, secesher SECESSION.

secession, *n.* the act of seceding. **secesh,** *n., a.* (*N Am. coll.*) secessionist. **secesher.** *n.* **secessionism,** *n.* **secessionist,** *n.* a seceder or advocate of secessionism, esp. one who took part with the Southern States in the American Civil War of 1861–5. †**secessive,** *a.* retired, secluded. [L *sēcessio,* SECEDE]

sech, (*abbr.*) hyperbolic secant.

seckel, *n.* a small, pulpy variety of pear. [*Seckel,* of Pennsylvania, who introduced it]

seclude, *v.t.* to shut up or keep (a person, place etc.) apart or away from society; to cause to be solitary or retired. **secluded,** *a.* hidden from view, private; away from others, solitary. **secludedly,** *adv.* **secludedness,** *n.* †**secluse,** *a.* **seclusion,** *n.* **seclusive,** *a.* [L *sēclūdere* (SE-, *claudere,* to shut)]

second[1], *a.* immediately following the first in time, place or position; next in value, authority, rank or position; secondary, inferior; other, alternate; additional, supplementary; subordinate, derivative; (*Mus.*) lower in pitch. *n.* the next after the first in rank, importance etc.; a second class in an examination etc.; a person taking this; another or an additional person or thing; one who supports another, esp. one who attends on the principal in a duel, boxing match etc.; the 60th part of a minute of time or angular measurement; (*coll.*) a very short time; (*pl.*) goods that have a slight flaw or are of second quality; (*pl.*) coarse, inferior flour, or bread made from this; (*Mus.*) the interval of one tone between two notes, either a whole tone or a semi-tone; the next tone above or below; two tones so separated combined together; a lower part added to a melody when arranged for two voices or instruments; (*coll.*) an alto; second gear. *v.t.* to forward, to promote, to support; to support (a resolution) formally to show that the proposer is not isolated. **second advent,** *n.* the return of Christ to establish His personal reign on earth. **second-adventist,** *n.* a premillenarian. **second-best,** *a.* of second quality. **second chamber,** *n.* the upper house in a legislative body having two chambers. **second childhood,** *n.* senile dotage. **second-class,** *a.* of second or inferior quality, rank etc., second-rate; treated as inferior or second-rate; of the second class. **second class,** *n.* the category next to the first or highest; the second level of an honours degree. **second coming** SECOND ADVENT. **second floor,** *n.* the second from the ground-floor. (In the US the term is applied to the first storey.) **second gear,** *n.* the forward gear next above first gear in a car etc. **second-hand,** *a.* not primary or original; not new, sold or for sale after having been used or worn; dealing in second-hand goods. **at second hand,** indirectly, from or through another. **second nature,** *n.* something that has become effortless or instinctual through constant practice. **second-pair back** or **front,** *n.* a room in the back or front of the house on the floor two flights of stairs above the ground-floor. **second-rate,** *a.* of inferior quality, size, value etc. **second sight,** *n.* the power of seeing things at a distance in space or time as if they were present, clairvoyance. **second thoughts,** *n.pl.* reconsideration of a previous opinion or decision. **second wind,** *n.* a renewed burst of energy, stamina etc. after a concentrated effort. **secondly,** *adv.* in the second place; as the second item. [F, from L *secundus,* orig. following, from *sequī,* to follow]

second[2], *v.t.* to retire (a military officer) temporarily without pay in order that he or she may take a civil or other appointment; to transfer temporarily or release for temporary transfer to another position, branch of an organization etc.

secondary, *a.* coming next in order of place or time to the first; not primary, not original, derivative, supplementary, subordinate; of the second or of inferior rank, importance etc.; revolving round a primary planet; between the tertiary geological formation above and the primary below, Mesozoic; of or being a feather on the second joint of a bird's wing; pertaining to or carrying an induced current. *n.* a delegate or deputy; a cathedral dignitary of secondary rank; a secondary planet, a satellite; the secondary geological epoch or formation; a secondary feather; a hind wing in an insect; a secondary coil, circuit etc. **secondary cell,** *n.* a rechargeable cell or battery using reversible chemical reactions to convert chemical into electrical energy. **secondary coil** or **winding,** *n.* a coil in which the current in the primary winding induces the electric current. **secondary colours** COLOUR[1]. **secondary education** or **school,** *n.* that provided for children who have received an elementary education. **secondary electrons,** *n.pl.* the electrons emitted by secondary emission. **secondary emission,** *n.* the emission of electrons from a surface or particle bombarded by primary electrons at high velocity. **secondary picketing,** *n.* picketing of an organization by workers with whom there is no direct dispute. **secondary sex characteristics,** *n.pl.* attributes related to the sex of an individual that develop from puberty. **secondary tumour** or **growth,** *n.* a tumour occurring somewhere other than at the site of the original cancer. **secondarily,** *adv.* **secondariness,** *n.*

seconde, *n.* (*Fencing*) a position in parrying or lungeing. [F]

secondo, *n.* the second part or the second performer in a musical duet. [It.]

Second World War WORLD WAR II.

secrecy, *n.* the state of being secret, concealment; the quality of being secretive, secretiveness; solitude, retirement, seclusion.

secret, *a.* concealed from notice, kept private, hidden, not to be revealed or exposed, privy; unseen, occult, mysterious; given to secrecy, secretive, close, reserved, reticent; secluded, private. *n.* something to be kept back or concealed; a thing kept back from general knowledge; a mystery, something that cannot be explained; the explanation or key to this; secrecy; (*pl.*) the parts of the body that are usually concealed; in the Roman Catholic Church, a prayer in a low tone recited by the celebrant at Mass. **in secret,** secretly, privately. **open secret,** something known generally. **secret agent,** *n.* an agent of the secret service. **secret police,** *n.* a police force operating in secret, usu. dealing with political rather than criminal matters. **secret service,** *n.* a government service for obtaining information or other work of which no account is given to the public. **secret-service money,** money expended on this. **secretage,** *n.* a process of preparing furs. **secretly,** *adv.* **secretness,** *n.* [OF, from L *sēcrētus,* p.p. of *sēcernere,* to SECERN]

secretaire, *n.* an escritoire, a bureau. [F *secrétaire,* as foll.]

secretary, *n.* an officer appointed by a company, firm, society etc. to conduct its correspondence, keep its records and represent it in business transactions etc.; (also **private secretary**) a person employed by another to assist in literary work, correspondence etc.; Secretary of State; an escritoire; a secretary-bird; †a confidant, a confidential manager, friend etc. **secretary of an embassy, legation,** the principal assistant or deputy of an ambassador. **Secretary of State,** a minister in charge of a government department; the Foreign Secretary of the US. **under-secretary,** one of two secretaries attached to a Secretary of State. **secretary-bird,** *n.* a S African bird, *Serpentarious secretarius,* preying on snakes etc. (named from its pen-like tufts in the ear). **secretary-general,** *n.* the person in charge of the administration of an organization. **secretary hand,** *n.* (*Hist.*) a style of handwriting used for legal documents until the 17th cent. **secretarial,** *a.* **secretariat,** *n.* the post of a secretary; an administrative office headed by a Secretary; the administrative workers of an organization. **secretaryship,** *n.* [F *secrétaire,* late L *sēcrētārius,* orig. a confidential officer, as SECRET]

secrete, *v.t.* to conceal, to hide; to keep secret; to separate from the blood, sap etc. by the process of secretion. **secretion,** *n.* the act of secreting or concealing; the process of separating materials from the blood, sap etc. for the service of the body or for rejection as excreta; any matter thus secreted, as mucus, gastric juice, urine etc. **secretional, -nary,** *a.* †**secretitious,** *a.* **secretor,** *n.* **secretory,** *a.* [L *sēcrētus,* SECRET]

secretive, *a.* given to secrecy, reserved, uncommunicative;, promoting or causing secretion. **secretively,** *adv.* **secretiveness,** *n.*

secretly, secretness SECRET.

secretor, secretory SECRETE.

sect[1], *n.* a body of persons who have separated from a larger body, esp. an established church, on account of philosophical or religious differences; a religious denomination, a nonconformist church (as regarded by opponents); the body of adherents of a particular philosopher, school of thought etc.; †a party, a faction; †a class or kind. **sectarial,** *a.* **sectarian,** *n., a.* **sectarianism,** *n.* **sectarianize, -ise,** *v.t.* †**sectarist,** *n.* **sectary,** *n.* a member of a sect; (*Hist.*) a Dissenter, esp. an Independent or Presbyterian in the epoch of the Civil War. †**sectator,** *n.* a follower, adherent or disciple; a secretary. [OF *secte,* L *secta,* a following, faction (med. L, suite, suit, costume), from *sequī,* to follow]

†**sect**[2], *n.* (*Shak.*) a cutting, a scion. [prob. from L *sectum,* neut. p.p. of *secāre,* to cut]

sectant, *n.* (*Geom.*) a portion of space separated by three intersecting planes but extending to infinity. [L *sectum,* see prec., -ANT]

sectile, *a.* capable of being cut. [F, from L *sectilis,* as foll.]

section, *n.* separation by cutting; that which is cut off or separated, a part, a portion; one of a series of parts into which anything naturally separates or is constructed so as to separate for convenience in handling etc.; a division or subdivision of a book, chapter, statute etc.; a section-mark; a distinct part of a country, people, community, class etc.; (*Nat. Hist.*) a group, a sub-genus; (*Mil.*) a subdivision of a half-company; (*N Am.*) one of the portions of a square of 640 acres (259 hectares) into which public lands are divided; a thin slice of any substance prepared for microscopic examination; a cutting of a solid figure by a plane, or the figure so produced; a vertical plan of a building etc. as it would appear upon an upright plane cutting through it; a part of an orchestra consisting of all the instruments of one class. *v.t.* to divide or arrange in sections; to represent in sections. **section-mark,** *n.* the sign §, marking a reference or the beginning of a section of a book, chapter etc. **sectional,** *a.* **sectionalism,** *n.* **sectionalize, -ise,** *v.t.* **sectionally,** *adv.* [F, from L *sectio,* acc. *-ōnem,* from *secāre,* to cut, p.p. *sectus*]

sector, *n.* a portion of a circle or other curved figure included between two radii and an arc; a mathematical rule consisting of two hinged arms marked with sines, tangents etc.; a section of a battle front; a distinct part, a section. **sector of a sphere,** a solid figure generated by the revolution of a plane sector round one of the radii. **sectoral,** *a.* **sectorial,** *a.* denoting a tooth on each side of either jaw, adapted for cutting like scissors with the corresponding one, as in many Carnivora; sectoral. *n.* a sectorial tooth. [L, orig. cutter, as prec. (late L, sector)]

secular, *a.* pertaining to the present world or to things not spiritual or sacred, not ecclesiastical or monastic; worldly, temporal, profane; lasting, extending over, occurring in or accomplished during a century, an age or a very long period of time; pertaining to secularism. *n.* a layman; a Roman Catholic priest bound only by the vow of chastity and belonging to no regular order; a church official who is not ordained. **secularism,** *n.* the state of being secular; applied by George Jacob Holyoake to an ethical system founded on natural morality and opposed to religious education or ecclesiasticism. **secularist,** *n., a.* **secularity,** *n.* **secularize, -ise,** *v.t.* **secularization, -isation,** *n.* **secularly,** *adv.* †**secularness,** *n.* [OF *seculier,* L *saeculāris,* from *saeculum,* generation, age, perh. cogn. with *serere,* to sow]

secund, *a.* of flowers etc., arranged all on one side of the rachis. **secundly,** *adv.* [L, SECOND[1]]

secundine, *n.* (*often pl.*) the placenta and other parts connected with the foetus, ejected after parturition, the after-birth; (*Bot.*) the membrane immediately surrounding the nucleus. [late L *secundīnae,* pl., as prec.]

secundogeniture, *n.* the right of inheritance belonging to a second son. [L *secundō,* abl. of *secundus,* SECOND[1], GENITURE]

secundum, *prep.* (L) according to. **secundum artem,** according to art. **secundum legem,** according to law. **secundum naturam,** according to nature. **secundum regulam,** according to rule.

secure, *a.* free from danger, risk or apprehension; safe from attack, impregnable; reliable, confident, certain, sure (of); in safe keeping, safe not to escape; †overconfident, unsuspecting. *v.t.* to make safe or secure; to put into a state of safety from danger; to fasten, to close securely, to enclose or confine securely; to make safe against loss, to guarantee payment of; to get, to obtain, to gain possession of; to compress (a vein etc.) to prevent bleeding. **to secure arms,** to hold rifles muzzle downwards with the lock under the armpit as a protection from rain. **securable,** *a.* **securely,** *adv.* **securement,** *n.* **secureness,** *n.* security. **securer,** *n.* [L *sēcūrus* (SE-, *cūra,* care)]

securi-, *comb. form.* pertaining to an axe. [L *secūris,* axe]

securifer, *n.* one of the Securifera, or phyllophagous Hymenoptera, a sandfly. **securiferous,** *a.* [L *fer,* -FEROUS]

securiform, *a.* axe-shaped.

securipalp, *n.* a beetle of the division Securipalpi.

securite, *n.* a high explosive composed of nitrated hydrocarbons, used chiefly for blasting. [SECURE, -ITE]

Securities and Exchange Commission (SEC), official US agency created in 1934 to ensure full disclosure to the investing public and protection against malpractice in the securities (stocks and shares) and financial markets (such as insider trading).

Securities and Investment Board, UK body with the overall responsibility for policing financial dealings in the City of London. Introduced in 1987 following the deregulation process of the so-called BIG BANG, it acts as an umbrella organization to such self-regulating bodies as the Stock Exchange.

security, *n.* the state of being or feeling secure; freedom from danger or risk, safety; certainty, assurance, over-confidence; that which guards or secures; (an organization which sees to) the protection of premises etc. against burglary, espionage etc.; a pledge, a guarantee; something given or deposited as a pledge for payment of a loan, fulfilment of obligation etc., to be forfeited in case of non-performance; one who becomes surety for another; a document constituting evidence of debt or of property, a certificate of stock, a bond etc. **Security Council,** *n.* a body of the United Nations charged with the maintenance of international security and peace. **security guard,** *n.* one employed to guard buildings, money in transit etc. **security risk,** *n.* a person or thing considered to be a threat to (national) security. **securitization, -isation,** *n.* the putting together of a number of stocks, mortgages etc. into a single bond which is traded like a security. **securitize, -ise,** *v.t.* [F *sécurité,* L *securitās -tātem,* from *sēcūrus,* SECURE]

sedan, *n.* (also **sedan-chair**) a covered chair for one person, carried by two men by means of a pole on each side; (*N Am.*) a closed car with a single compartment for driver and passengers, a saloon car. [town in France]

sedate, *a.* composed, calm, tranquil, staid, not impulsive. *v.t.* to administer a sedative to. **sedately,** *adv.* **sedateness,** *n.* **sedation,** *n.* a state of calmness or relaxation; the administration of a sedative. **sedative,** *a.* allaying nervous irritability, soothing, assuaging pain. *n.* a sedative medicine, influence etc. [L *sēdātus,* p.p. of *sēdāre,* causal of *sedēre,* to sit]

Seddon, *n.* **Richard John** (1845–1906), New Zealand Liberal politician, prime minister from 1893–1906.

sedentary, *a.* sitting; accustomed or inclined, or obliged by occupation, to sit a great deal; involving or requiring much sitting; caused by sitting much; not migratory, attached to one place, not free-moving; belonging to the Sedentariae; †motionless, inactive, tranquil. *n.* a sedentary person; one of the Sedentariae, a group of spiders which rest motionless till the prey is entangled in the web. †**sedent,** *a.* sitting, inactive, quiet. **sedentarily,** *adv.* **sedentariness,** *n.* [F *sédentaire,* L *sedentārius,* from *sedēre,* to sit]

Seder, *n.* a ceremonial meal eaten on the first night (or the first two nights) of Passover. [Heb. *sēdher,* order]

sederunt, *v.i.* (*Sc. Law*) were present at the sitting of a court etc. *n.* a sitting of a court etc.; (*Sc.*) a long session of conversation. **Act of Sederunt,** (*Sc. Law*) an ordinance regulating procedure in the Court of Session. [L, they sat, see SEDENTARY]

sedge, *n.* a coarse grass-like plant of the genus *Carex,* usu. growing in marshes or beside water; any coarse grass growing in such spots; a sedge-fly. **sedge-bird, -warbler, -wren,** *n.* a reed-warbler, *Acrocephalus scirpaceus,* haunting sedgy places. **sedge-fly,** *n.* a caddisfly or mayfly; an imitation of this, used by anglers. †**sedged, sedgy,** *a.* [OE *secg,* cp. LG *Segge,* rel. to SAW[1], L *secāre,* to cut]

Sedgemoor, Battle of, battle which took place on 6 July 1685, on a tract of marshy land 5 km/3 miles SE of Bridgwater, Somerset, England, in which MONMOUTH's rebellion was crushed by the forces of James II of England.

sedigitate, SEXDIGITATE.

sedilia, *n.pl.* a series of (usu. three) stone seats, usu. canopied and decorated, on the south side of the chancel in churches, for the priest, deacon and sub-deacon. [L, pl. of *sedīle,* cogn. with *sedēre,* to sit]

sediment, *n.* the matter which subsides to the bottom of a liquid; lees, dregs, settlings. **sedimentary,** *a.* **sedimentary rocks,** *n.pl.* rocks or strata laid down as sediment from water. **sedementation,** *n.* [OF from L *sedimentum,* as prec.]

sedition, *n.* agitation, disorder or commotion in a state, not amounting to insurrection; conduct tending to promote treason or rebellion. **seditionary,** *n., a.* †**seditioner, -ist,** *n.* **seditious,** *a.* **seditiously,** *adv.* **seditiousness,** *n.* [OF, from L *sedītio -ōnem* (L *sed-,* SE-, *īre,* to go, supine *-itum*)]

seduce, *v.t.* to lead astray, to entice from rectitude or duty, esp. to induce a woman to a surrender of chastity; to entice or lure, esp. by offering rewards. †**seducement,** *n.* **seducer,** *n.* **seducible,** *a.* **seducing,** *a.* **seducingly,** *adv.* **seduction,** *n.* the act of seducing, esp. of persuading a woman to surrender her chastity; the state of being seduced; that which seduces, an enticement, an attraction, a tempting or attractive quality, a charm. **seductive,** *a.* **seductively,** *adv.* **seductiveness,** *n.* **seductress,** *fem. n.* [L *sēdūcere* (SE-, *dūcere,* to lead, p.p. *ductus*)]

sedulous, *a.* assiduous, constant, steady and persevering in business or endeavour; industrious, diligent. **sedulity, sedulousness,** *n.* **sedulously,** *adv.* [L *sēdulus,* from *sēdulō,* honestly, diligently (SE-, *dolō,* abl. of *dolus,* guile)]

Sedum, *n.* a genus of fleshy-leaved plants including the stonecrop, orpine etc. [L, houseleek]

see[1], *v.t.* (*past* **saw,** *p.p.* **seen**) to perceive by the eye; to discern, to descry, to observe, to look at; to perceive mentally, to understand, to apprehend, to have an idea of; to witness, to experience, to go through, to have knowledge of; to imagine, to picture to oneself; to call on, to pay a visit to, to grant an interview to, to receive; to escort, to attend, to conduct (a person home etc.); (*Poker etc.*) to accept (a challenge, bet etc., or person offering this). *v.i.* to have or exercise the power of sight; to discern, to comprehend; to inquire, to make an investigation (into); to reflect, to consider carefully; to ascertain by reading; to take heed; to give attention; to make provision for; to look out; to take care (that); (*imper.*) to refer to. **let me see,** a formula asking for time to consider or reflect. **see you (later),** goodbye for the present. **to be well** (or **ill**) **seen in,** to be versed (or not versed) in. **to see about,** to give attention to; to make preparations etc.; a polite form of refusal. **to see after,** to take care of. **to see daylight,** (*coll.*) to begin to comprehend. **to see fit, good,** to think advisable. **to see life,** to gain experience of the world, esp. by dissipation. **to see off,** to escort on departure; (*coll.*) to get rid of. **to see out,** to escort out of a house etc.; to outlive, outlast; to last to the end of. **to see over,** to inspect. **to see the light,** to be born; to realize the truth; to be converted to a religion or to any other belief. **to see through,** to penetrate, not to be deceived by; to persist (in a task etc.) until it is finished; to help through a difficulty, danger etc. **to see to,** to look after. **to see to it that,** to take care that. **see-bright,** *n.* the clary. **see-through,** *a.* (semi-)transparent, esp. of clothing. **seeable,** *a.* **seeing,** *n.* sight; (*Astron.*) atmospheric conditions for observation. *conj.* inasmuch as, since, considering (that). **seeing eye,** *n.* a guide dog for the blind. **seer,** *n.* one who sees; one who foresees, a prophet. **seership,** *n.* [OE *sēon,* cp. Dut. *zien,* G *sehen,* Icel. *sjā,* Dan. and Swed. *se*]

see[2], *n.* the diocese or jurisdiction of a bishop or archbishop. **Holy See,** the Papacy, the papal Court. [OF *se, sed,* L *sēdes,* from *sedēre,* to sit]

Seebeck effect, *n.* in physics, the generation of a voltage in a circuit containing two different metals, or semiconductors, by keeping the junctions between them at different temperatures. Discovered by the German physicist Thomas Seebeck (1770–1831), it is also called the thermoelectric effect, and is the basis of the thermocouple.

seecatch, *n.* (*pl.* **seecatchie**) an adult male fur-seal. [Alaskan or Aleutian]

seecawk, *n.* the skunk. [N Am.Ind.]

seed, *n.* the mature fertilized ovule of a flowering plant, consisting of the embryo germ or reproductive body and its covering; (*collect.*) seeds, esp. in quantity for sowing; the male fertilizing fluid, semen; the germ from which anything springs, first principle, beginning or source; (*Bibl.*) progeny, offspring, descendants, †birth, descent. *v.t.* to sow or sprinkle with seed; to put a small crystal into (a solution) to start crystallization; to scatter solid particles in (a cloud) to bring on rain; to remove the seeds from (fruit etc.); in sport, to arrange the draw in (a tournament) so that the best players do not meet in the early rounds; to classify (a good player) in this way. *v.i.* to sow seed; to run to seed. **to run to seed,** to become shabby; to lose self-respect. **seedbed,** *n.* a piece of ground where seedlings are grown; a place where anything develops. **seed-bud,** *n.* an ovule. **seedcake,** *n.* a sweet cake containing aromatic seeds, esp. caraway. **seed-coat,** *n.* the integument of a seed. **seed coral,** *n.* coral in small seed-like pieces. **seed corn, -grain,** *n.* corn set aside for sowing. **seed-eater,** *n.* a granivorous bird. **seed-fish,** *n.* one ready to spawn. **seed-lac,** *n.* lac dried. **seed-leap, lip, -lop,** *n.* the vessel in which a sower carries seed. **seed-loaf, -lobe,** *n.* a cotyledon or primary leaf. **seed money,** *n.* the money with which a project is set up. **seed oyster,** *n.* oyster-spat. **seed pearl,** *n.* a small seed-like pearl. **seed-plot,** *n.* a piece of ground on which seeds are sown; a nursery or hotbed (of seditions etc.). **seed potato,** *n.* a potato tuber used for planting. **seedsman,** *n.* one who deals in seeds. **seed-time,** *n.* the season for sowing. **seed vessel,** *n.* the pericarp. **seed wool,** *n.* raw cotton from which the seeds have not yet been removed. **seeded,** *a.* **seeder,** *n.* a seed-drill or other device for planting seeds; a device for removing the seeds from raisins etc.; a seed-fish. †**seedful,** *a.* **seedless,** *a.* **seedling,** *a.* raised from seed. *n.* a plant reared from seed; a very young plant. †**seedness,** *n.* seed-time. **seedy,** *a.* abounding in seeds; run to seed; of some French brandies, having a peculiar flavour, derived from weeds among the vines; (*coll.*) shabby, down-at-heel; off colour, as after a debauch; out of sorts. **seedily,** *adv.* **seediness,** *n.* shabbiness, near poverty; a state of poor health. [OE *saed* (cp. Dut. *zaad,* G *Saat,* Icel. *saethi,* Dan. *saed,* Swed. *säd*), cogn. with SOW[1]]

seek, *v.t.* (*past, p.p.* **sought,**) to go in search of; to try to find, to look for; to ask, to solicit (a thing of a person); to aim at, to try to gain, to pursue as an object; to search (a place etc. through), to resort to. *v.i.* to make search or inquiry (after or for); to endeavour, to try (to do). **to seek,** wanting, deficient; not found yet. **to seek out,** to search for; to cultivate the friendship of. **sought-after,** *a.* in demand, much desired or courted. **seeker,** *n.* one who seeks, an inquirer; (*Hist.*) a member of an English sect of the time of Cromwell, somewhat akin to the Quakers. **Seekerism,** *n.* [OE *sēcan* (cp. Dut. *zoekan,* G *suchen,* Icel. *saekja,* also L *sāgīre,* to perceive, Gr. *hēgeisthai,* to lead)]

†**seel,** *v.t.* to close the eyes of (a hawk), or close (its eyes) by threads drawn through the lids; to hoodwink. [OF *siller, ciller,* from *cil,* eyelid see CILIUM]

†**seely,** *a.* lucky, fortunate; blessed, pious; innocent; poor, miserable, defenceless; mean, trifling; foolish. †**seeliness,** *n.* [OE *sǣlig* in *gesǣlig,* from *sǣl,* SELE, cp. SILLY]

seem, *v.i.* to give the impression of being, to be apparently though not in reality; to appear (to do, to have done, to be true or the fact that); to be evident or apparent. †*v.t.* to befit. **I can't seem to,** (*coll.*) I am unable to. **it seems,** it appears, it is reported (that). **it would seem,** it appears, it seems to one. **seeming,** *a.* appearing, apparent, but not real; apparent and perhaps real; †becoming, seemly. *n.* appearance, semblance, esp. when false; †fair appearance; †estimation, opinion. †**seeming-virtuous,** *a.* **seemingly,** *adv.* **seemingness,** *n.* †**seemless,** *a.* unseemly. [OE *sēman,* to conciliate, cogn. with SAME]

seemly, *a.* becoming, decent; suited to the occasion, purpose etc. †*adv.* in a seemly manner. **seemliness,** *n.* [ME *semlish,* Icel. *saemiligr* (*saemr,* becoming, from *samr,* SAME, -LY)]

seen, *p.p.* SEE[1].

seep, *v.i.* to soak, to percolate, to ooze. **seepage,** *n.* [OE *sipian,* rel. to SIP]

seer SEE[1].

seer-fish, *n.* an E Indian scombroid fish. [*seer,* corr. of Port. *serra,* saw, FISH]

seersucker, *n.* a thin striped linen or cotton fabric with a puckered appearance. [corr. of Pers. *shīr o shakkar,* milk and sugar]

seesaw, *n.* a game in which two persons sit one on each end of a board balanced on a support in the middle and move alternately up and down; the board so used; alternate or reciprocating motion. *a.* moving up and down or to and fro; vacillating. *v.t.* to cause to move in a seesaw fashion. *v.i.* to play at seesaw; to move up and down or backwards and forwards; to act in a vacillating manner. [redupl. of SAW[1]]

seethe, *v.t.* (*past* **seethed,** †sod, sod *p.p.* **seethed,** †**sod, sodden**) to boil; to prepare by boiling or steeping in hot liquid. *v.i.* to be in a state of ebullition; to be agitated, to bubble over. **seether,** *n.* [OE *sēothan,* cp. Dut. *zieden,* G *sieden,* Icel. *sjotha*]

seg[1], *n.* (*dial.*) a bull castrated when full grown. [etym. unknown]

seg[2], (*dial.*) SEDGE.

segar CIGAR.

seggar, SAGGAR.

segment, *n.* a portion cut or marked off as separable, a section, a division, esp. one of a natural series (as of a limb between the joints, the body of an articulate animal, a fruit or plant organ divided by clefts); (*Geom.*) a part cut off from any figure by a line or plane. *v.i.* to divide or be divided into segments; to undergo cleavage. *v.t.* to divide into segments. **segmental, -ary, -ate,** *a.* **segmentally,** *adv.* **segmentation,** *n.* **segmented,** *a.* composed of segments; divided into segments. [L *segmentum,* from *secāre,* to cut]

segolate, segholate, *a.* (*Heb. Gram.*) disyllabic with a short unaccented vowel in the last syllable. *n.* a segolate noun. [Heb. *segōl,* name of vowel-point, -ATE]

Segrè, *n.* **Emilio** (1905–89), Italian physicist settled in the US, who in 1955 discovered antiproton, a new form of antimatter. He shared the 1959 Nobel prize for physics with Owen Chamberlain. Segrè had earlier discovered the first synthetic element technetium (atomic number 43) in 1937.

†**segreant,** *a.* (*Her.*) of a griffin, erect, rampant or salient. [etym. doubtful]

segregate[1], *v.t.* to separate from others, to set apart, to isolate; to place in a separate class; to split (a community) into separate parts on the basis of race. *v.i.* of a pair of alleles, to become separated during meiosis; (*Cryst.*) to separate from a mass and collect about nuclei and lines of fracture. **segregable,** *a.* **segregation,** *n.* the act of segregating; separation of a community on racial grounds. **segregationist,** *n.* a believer in racial segregation. **segregative,** *a.* [L *sēgregātus,* p.p. of *sēgregāre* (SE-, *grex gregis,* flock)]

segregate[2], *a.* †separate, set apart, select; (*Zool.*) simple, solitary, not compound.

seguidilla, *n.* a lively Spanish dance in triple time; the music for this. [Sp., dim. of *seguida,* a continuation, from *seguir,* L *sequī,* to follow]

seicento, *n.* the 17th cent. in Italian art, architecture or literature. [It., short for *mille seicento,* one thousand six hundred]

seiche, *n.* an undulation, somewhat resembling a tidal wave, in the water of Lake Geneva and other Swiss lakes, usu. due to disturbance of atmospheric pressure or to subterranean movements. **seichometer,** *n.* an instrument for measuring seiches. [Swiss F, prob. G *Seiche,* sinking]

Seid, *n.* a descendant of Mohammed through his

daughter Fatima and his nephew Ali. [Arab. *seyid,* prince]

Seidlitz powder, *n.* a mild aperient, composed of a mixture of Rochelle salt, bicarbonate of soda and finely powdered tartaric acid, mixed separately in water to form an effervescing drink. **Seidlitz water,** *n.* a sparkling mineral water of the same composition as that of the Seidlitz spring. [Seidlitz (mod. Sedlčancy), a village in Bohemia, Czechoslovakia, with mineral spring]

Seifert, *n.* **Jaroslav** (1901–86), Czech poet, who won state prizes, but became an original member of the Charter 77 human-rights movement. Works include *Mozart in Prague* (1970) and *Umbrella from Piccadilly* (1978). Awarded Nobel prize in 1984.

seigneur, †seignior, *n.* (*F Hist.*) a feudal lord; (*Can.*) the holder of a seigneury. **droit de seigneur,** a supposed feudal manorial right to the first night with a tenant's bride. **grand seigneur,** a great nobleman; a person of high rank. **the grand seigneur** GRAND SEIGNEUR, see GRAND. **seigneurial,** *a.* **seigneury,** *n.* (*F Hist.*) the territory or lordship of a seigneur; (*Can.*) an estate formerly held on a feudal tenure; the mansion of a seigneur. **seigniorage,** *n.* something claimed by the sovereign or by a feudal superior as a prerogative, esp. an ancient right of the Crown to a percentage on bullion brought to the mint to be coined; the profit derived from issuing coins at a rate above their intrinsic value; a royalty. **seigniorial,** SEIGNEURIAL. **†seigniorize, -ise,** *v.t., v.i.* **seigniorship, †seigniority,** *n.* **seigniory,** *n.* feudal lordship; power as sovereign lord; the territory or domain of a feudal lord; (*It. Hist.*) the municipal council of an Italian republic. [F, as SENIOR]

seil, SILE.

Seine, *n.* French river rising on the Langres plateau NW of Dijon, and flowing 774 km/472 miles in a NW direction to join the English Channel near Le Havre, passing through Paris and Rouen.

seine, *n.* a large fishing-net with floats at the top and weights at the bottom for encircling. *v.t.* to catch with this. *v.i.* to fish with it. **seine-fishing,** *n.* **seine-gang,** *n.* a body of men working a seine. **seine-roller,** *n.* a roller over which it is hauled. **seiner,** *n.* [F, from L *sagēna,* Gr. *sagēnē*]

seise, *v.t.* (*usu. in p.p.*) (*Law*) to put in possession of. **to be, stand seised of,** to have in legal possession, **seisable,** *a.* **seisin,** *n.* possession of land under a freehold; the act of taking possession; the thing possessed. **seisor,** *n.* [SEIZE]

seismic, seismal, *a.* of, pertaining to or produced by an earthquake. [Gr. *seismos,* earthquake, from *seiein,* to shake]

seismo-, *comb. form.* pertaining to an earthquake.

seismogram, *n.* a record given by a seismograph. **seismograph,** *n.* an instrument for recording the period, extent and direction of the vibrations of an earthquake. **seismographer,** *n.* **seismographic, -ical,** *a.* **seismography,** *n.*

seismology, *n.* the study or science of earthquakes. **seismological,** *a.* **seismologically,** *adv.* **seismologist,** *n.*

seismometer, *n.* a seismograph; a seismoscope. **seismometric, -ical,** *a.* **seismometry,** *n.*

seismoscope, *n.* a simple form of seismograph. **seismoscopic,** *a.*

seismotic, *a.* seismic.

seity, *n.* selfhood. [med. L *sēitas,* from L *sē,* oneself]

seize, *v.t.* to grasp or lay hold of suddenly, to snatch, to take possession of by force; to grasp mentally, to comprehend; to come upon, to affect suddenly and forcibly; (*Naut.*) to fasten, to lash with cord etc.; (*Law*) to seise; to take possession of; to impound, to confiscate. *v.i.* to lay hold (upon); to jam, to become stuck. **seizable,** *a.* **seizer,** *n.* **seizin,** etc. SEISIN, under SEISE. **seizing-up,** *n.* the locking or partial welding together of sliding surfaces from lack of lubrication. **seizure,** *n.* the act of seizing; a sudden attack, as of a disease. [OF *seisir, saisir,* to put in possession of, late L *sacīre,* to take possession of, perh. from Teut. and cogn. with SET[1]]

sejant, *a.* (*Her.*) sitting with the forelegs erect. [A-F *seiant,* pres.p. of *seier,* OF *seoir,* L *sedēre,* to sit]

sejugous, *a.* having six pairs of leaflets. [L *sējugis* (*sē-,* SEX(A)-, *jugum,* yoke)]

†sejunction, *n.* the act of disjoining; separation. [L *sējunctio* (SE-, JUNCTION)]

Sekhmet, *n.* ancient Egyptian goddess of heat and fire. She was represented with the head of a lioness, and worshipped at Memphis as the wife of Ptah.

sekos, *n.* (*Gr. Ant.*) a sacred enclosure, as the shrine or adytum of a temple. [Gr.]

sel, (*Sc.*) SELF.

selachian, *n.* a fish of the group Selachii comprising the sharks, dog-fishes etc. *a.* pertaining to this group. **selachoid,** *n., a.* [Gr. *selachos*]

Selaginella, *n.* a genus of evergreen moss-like cryptogamic plants many of which are cultivated for ornamental purposes. [L dim. of *selāgo -ginis,* club-moss]

selah, *n.* a word occurring in the Psalms and in Habakkuk, always at the end of a verse, variously interpreted as indicating a pause, a repetition, the end of a strophe etc. [Heb.]

selamlik, *n.* the part of a Muslim house assigned to the men. [Turk.]

†selcouth, *a.* rare, strange, marvellous. [OE *selcouth* (as foll., COUTH)]

seldom, *adv.* rarely, not often. *a.* rare. **†seld,** *n., a.* **†seld-shown,** *a.* **†seldomness,** *n.* [OE *seldan, -don, -dom* (*seld, -om,* dat. pl.), cp. Dut. *zelden,* G *selten,* Icel. *sjaldan*]

†sele, *n.* happiness, good fortune; occasion, opportunity. [OE *sǣl,* cp. Icel. *saell,* happy, also SILLY]

select, *a.* chosen, picked out, choice; taken as superior to or more suitable than the rest; strict in selecting new members etc., exclusive, more valuable. *v.t.* to choose, to pick out (the best etc.). **select committee,** *n.* members of parliament specially chosen to examine a particular question and to report on it. **selectman,** *n.* one of a board of officers chosen annually by the freemen of towns in New England to manage local affairs. **†selectedly,** *adv.* **selection,** *n.* the act of selecting; the right or opportunity of selecting, choice; that which is selected; a natural or artificial process of sorting out organisms suitable for survival; a range of goods (as in a shop) from which to choose; (*Austral.*) FREE SELECTION under FREE. **selective,** *a.* selecting, exercising a power or ability to choose. **selectively,** *adv.* **selectivity,** *n.* the quality of being selective; the efficiency of a wireless receiver in separating the different broadcasting stations. **selectness,** *n.* **selector,** *n.* one who or that which selects; (*Austral.*) a settler who takes up a piece of select land. [L *sēlectus,* p.p. of *sēligere,* (SE-, *legere,* to choose)]

selen- -SELENIUM, SELENO-.

Selene, *n.* in Greek mythology, the goddess of the Moon. She was the daughter of Titan, and the sister of Helios and Eos. In later times she was identified with ARTEMIS.

selenium, *n.* a non-metallic element, at. no. 34; chem. symbol Sc; obtained as a by-product in the manufacture of sulphuric acid, similar in chemical properties to sulphur and tellurium, utilized for its varying electrical resistance in light and darkness. **selenium cell,** *n.* a type of photoelectric cell using a strip of selenium. **selenate,** *n.* a salt of selenic acid. **selenic,** *a.* containing or derived from (high valency) selenium; of or derived from the moon. **selenide,** *n.* a compound of selenium with an element or radical. **selenious,** *a.* containing or derived from (low valency) selenium. **selenite,** *n.* a transparent variety of gypsum or sulphate of lime; a salt of selenious acid; an inhabitant of the moon. **selenitic,** *a.* **selenitiferous,** *a.* **†seleniuret** SELENIDE. [Gr. *Selēnē,* the moon]

selen(o)-, seleni-, *comb. form.* pertaining to or containing selenium; pertaining to the moon. [G *Selen* or SELENIUM, or Gr. *Selēnē,* the moon]

selenocentric, *a.* referred to, seen from or measured

from the moon as centre.

selenodont, *a.* of molar teeth, having crescent-shaped ridges; pertaining to the Selenodonta. *n.* a selenodont mammal. [Gr. *odous odontos,* tooth]

selenography, *n.* a description of the moon and its phenomena; the art of delineating the face of the moon. **selenograph**, *n.* **selenographer,** *n.* **selenographic, -ical**, *a.*

selenology, *n.* the branch of astronomical science treating of the moon. **selenological**, *a.* **selenologically,** *adv.* **selenologist,** *n.*

selenotropic, *a.* of plant organs, curving towards the moon. **selenotropism**, **-tropy**, *n.* [F *sélénotropique* (Gr. *tropos,* from *trepein,* to turn]

Seleucus I, *n.* **Nicator** (*c.* 358–280 BC), Macedonian general under Alexander the Great and founder of the Seleucid Empire. After Alexander's death 323 BC, Seleucus became governor, and then ruler of Babylonia in 312, founding the city of Seleucia on the river Tigris. He conquered Syria and had himself crowned king in 306, but his expansionist policies brought him into conflict with the Ptolemies, and he was assassinated by Ptolemy Ceraunus. He was succeeded by his son Antiochus I.

Seleucid, *n.* (*pl.* **-cids, -cidae**) a member of the dynasty ruling Syria *c.* 312–64 BC, founded by Seleucus. *a.* pertaining to the Seleucidae. **Seleucidan,** *a.* [L *Seleucidēs,* Gr. *Seleukidēs* (*Seleukos,*)]

self, *n.* (*pl.* **selves**) the individuality of a person or thing, as the object of reflexive consciousness or action; one's individual person; one's private interests etc.; furtherance of these; a flower of a uniform or of the original wild colour. *a.* of a colour, †same; uniform, pure, unmixed; self-coloured; of one piece or the same material throughout. *pron.* (*coll., facet.*) myself, yourself etc.) **selfdom**, **selfhood**, **selfness,** *n.* **selfish,** *a.* attentive only to one's own interests; not regarding the interests or feelings of others; actuated by or proceeding from self-interest. **selfishly,** *adv.* **selfishness,** *n.* **selfless,** *a.* having no regard for self, unselfish. **selflessness,** *n.* [OE, cp. Dut. *zelf,* G *Selbe,* Icel. *sjālfr,* Dan. *selv,* Swed. *sjelf*]

self-, *comb. form.* expressing (1) direct or indirect reflexive action, as in *self-command;* (2) action performed independently, or without external agency, as in *self-acting, self-fertilization;* (3) relation to the self, as in *self-conscious, self-suspicious;* (4) uniformity, naturalness etc. as in *self-coloured, self-glazed.* **self-abandonment** SELF- (1), *n.* **self-abasement,** SELF- (1), *n.* **self-abhorrence** SELF- (1) *n.* **self-abnegation** SELF- (1), *n.* **self-absorbed** SELF- (3), *a.* **self-absorption,** *n.* **self-abuse** SELF- (1), *n.* masturbation. **self-accusation** SELF- (1), *n.* **self-accusatory,** *a.* **self-accused,** *n., a.* **self-accuser,** *n.* **self-accusing,** *a.* **self-acting** SELF- (2), *a.* **self-action,** *n.* **self-activity,** *n.* **self-addressed** SELF- (3) *a.* of an envelope, addressed to oneself (for the sending of a reply). **self-adhesive** SELF- (3) *a.* **self-adjusting** SELF- (1), *a.* **self-adjustment,** *n.* **self-admiration** SELF- (1), *n.* **self-advancement** SELF- (1), *n.* **self-advertisement,** SELF-, *n.* †**self-affairs** SELF- (2), *n.pl.* one's own business. †**self-affected** SELF- (3), *a.* in love with oneself. †**self-affrighted** SELF- (3), *a.* frightened at oneself. **self-aggrandizement** SELF- (1), *n.* **self-amendment** SELF- (1), *n.* **self-appointed** SELF- (2) *a.* **self-appointment,** *n.* **self-appreciation** SELF- (1) *n.* **self-approval** SELF- (1), *n.* **self-approbation,** *n.* **self-asserting, -assertive** SELF- (1), *a.* **self-assertion,** *n.* **self-assumed** SELF- (2) *a.* †**self-assumption** SELF- (3), *n.* self-conceit. **self-assured,** SELF- (3), *a.* **self-begot, -begotten, -born** SELF-[1], *a.* begotten by or born of oneself or one's own powers. **self-betrayal** SELF- (1), **self-binder** SELF- (2), *n.* a reaping-machine with an automatic binding device; this device. **self-blinded** SELF- (1), *a.* †**self-bounty** SELF- (2), *n.* inherent kindness and benevolence. **self-catering** SELF- (3), *a.* of holiday accommodation, not providing meals, cleaning etc. **self-centred** SELF- (3), *a.* interested solely in oneself and one's own affairs, egotistic. †**self-charity** SELF (3), *n.* love of oneself. **self-cleaning** SELF- (1), *a.* **self-closing** SELF- (1), *a.* **self-cocking,** SELF- (1), *a.* of a gun or gun-hammer, cocking automatically. **self-collected** SELF- (3), *a.* self-possessed, composed. **self-colour** SELF - (4), *n.* a colour uniform throughout; a pure or unmixed colour; a colour not changed by cultivation. **self-coloured,** *a.* **self-command** SELF- (1), *n.* self-control. **self-communion** SELF- (3), *n.* meditation, mental converse with oneself. **self-complacent** SELF- (3), *a.* pleased with oneself. **self-complacency,** *n.* **self-conceit** SELF- (3), *n.* **self-conceited,** *a.* **self-condemned** SELF-[1], *a.* **self-condemnation,** *n.* **self-confessed** SELF- (3), *a.* openly admitting oneself to be. **self-confident** SELF- (3), *a.* **self-confidence,** *n.* **self-confidently,** *adv.* **self-conscious** SELF- (3), *a.* conscious of one's actions, behaviour, situation etc., esp. as observed by others; (*Phil.*) conscious of one's own activities, states etc.; able to reflect on these. **self-consciousness,** *n.* **self-consistent** SELF- (3), *a.* **self-consistency,** *n.* **self-constituted** SELF- (1) *a.* **self-consumed, -consuming** SELF- (1), *a.* **self-contained** SELF- (1), *a.* reserved, not communicative; complete in itself. **self-contempt** SELF- (1), *n.* **self-contemptuous,** *a.* **self-content** SELF- (3), *n.* **self-contented,** *a.* **self-contradiction** SELF- (1), *n.* **self-contradictory,** *a.* **self-control** SELF- (1), *n.* power of controlling one's feelings, impulses etc. **self-convicted** SELF- (1), *a.* **self-correcting** SELF- (1), *a.* **self-created** SELF- (1), *a.* brought into existence by one's own power or vitality. **self-creation,** *n.* **self-critical** SELF- (1), *a.* **self-criticism,** *n.* **self-culture** SELF- (1), *n.* †**self-danger** SELF- (3), *n.* danger arising from oneself. **self-deceiver** SELF- (1), *n.* **self-deceit, -deception,** *n.* **self-defence** SELF- (1), *n.* the act or art of defending one's own person, property or reputation. **the noble art of self-defence,** boxing. **self-delusion** SELF- (1), *n.* **self-denial** SELF- (1), *n.* refusal to gratify one's own appetites or desires; self-abnegation. **self-denying,** *a.* **self-dependent** SELF- (3), *a.* **self-dependence,** *n.* **self-depreciation** SELF- (1) *n.* **self-depreciative,** *a.* **self-despair** SELF- (3), *n.* **self-destroying** SELF- (1), *a.* **self-destruction,** *n.* suicide. **self-determination** SELF- (1), *n.* determination of one's own will, as opp. to fatalism; the right of a group (local or racial) to decide to what state it will adhere; the liberty of a state to determine its own form of government. **self-determined, -determining,** *a.* **self-development** SELF- (1), *n.* **self-devotion,** SELF- (1), *n.* **self-discipline** SELF- (1), *n.* **self-disparagement** SELF- (1), *n.* **self-display** SELF- (1), *n.* **self-distrust** SELF- (1), *n.*

selfdom SELF.

self-doubt SELF- (1), *n.* lack of confidence in one's abilities. **self-drive** SELF- (2), *a.* of a hired vehicle, driven by the hirer. **self-educated** SELF- (1), *a.* **self-education,** *n.* **self-effacement** SELF- (1), *n.* **self-elect, -elected,** SELF- (1), *n.* elected by oneself or (as a committee) by its own members, co-opted. **self-election,** *n.* **self-elective,** *a.* **self-employed** SELF- (1), *a.* running one's own business, or working freelance. **self-esteem** SELF- (1), *n.* **self-estimation,** *n.* **self-evident** SELF- (2), *a.* obvious of itself, not requiring proof or demonstration. **self-evidently,** *adv.* **self-examination** SELF- (1), *n.* **self-executing** SELF- (1), *a.* of a law, providing for its own enforcement independently of other legislation. **self-existent** SELF- (2), *a.* existing independently, underived, inconditioned. **self-existence,** *n.* **self-explanatory** SELF- (1), *a.* **self-expression** SELF- (1), *n.* the expression of one's own personality (through art etc.) **self-faced** SELF- (4), *a.* of stone, having its natural face, unhewn. **self-feeder** SELF- (1), *n.* a machine, furnace etc. that feeds itself. **self-feeding,** *a.* **self-fertile** SELF- (3), *a.* of plants, fertilized by their own pollen. **self-fertility,** *n.* **self-fertilized, -fertilizing,** *a.* **self-flattery** SELF- (1), *n.* **self-forgetful,** *a.* oblivious of self, unselfish. **self-forgetfulness,** *n.* **self-fulfilling** SELF- (1), *a.* **self-generating** SELF- (1), *a.* **self-glazed** SELF- (4), *a.* covered with glaze of uniform colour. **self-**

glorification SELF- (1), *n.* **self-governing** SELF- (1), *a.* controlling oneself; autonomous. **self-government,** *n.* **self-gratulation** SELF- (1), *n.* **self-heal** SELF- (1), *n.* a plant having healing virtues, esp. *Prunella vulgaris.* **self-help** SELF- (1), *n.* the act or practice of attaining one's ends without help from others. **self-helpful,** *a.*

selfhood SELF.

self-humiliation SELF- (1), *n.* **self-image** SELF- (3), *n.* one's own idea of what one is. **self-immolation** SELF- (1), *n.* sacrifice of self. **self-important** SELF- (3), *a.* important in one's own conceit, pompous. **self-importance,** *n.* **self-imposed** SELF- (2), *a.* **self-impotent** SELF- (2), *a.* (*Bot.*) unable to fertilize itself. **self-improvement** SELF- (1), *n.* improvement of one's social or economic position by one's own efforts. **self-induction** SELF- (3), *n.* production of an induced electric current in the circuit by the variation of the current in the circuit. **self-inductive,** *a.* **self-indulgent** SELF- (1), *a.* gratifying one's inclinations etc. **self-indulgence,** *n.* **self-inflicted** SELF- (3), *a.* **self-interest** SELF- (3), *n.* one's personal advantage; absorption in selfish aims. **self-interested,** *a.* **self-invited** SELF- (1), *a.* **self-involved** SELF- (3), *a.* wrapped up in oneself.

selfish etc. SELF.

self-justification SELF- (1), *n.* **self-knowing,** *a.* **self-knowledge,** *n.* **self-laudation** SELF- (1), *n.*

selfless etc. SELF.

self-loading SELF- (1), *a.* of a firearm, reloading automatically. **self-love** SELF- (1), *n.* undue regard for oneself or one's own interests; selfishness; conceit. **self-luminous** SELF- (2), *a.* shining by its own light. **self-made,** SELF- (1), *a.* successful, wealthy etc. through one's own exertions. **self-mastery** SELF- (1), *n.* **self-mortification** SELF- (1), *n.* **self-moved, -moving** SELF- (1), *a.* **self-motion,** *n.* **self-murder** SELF- (1) *n.* **self-murderer,** *n.* **self-opinion** SELF- (3), *n.* **self-opinioned, -opinionated,** *a.* conceitedly or obstinately adhering to one's own views. **self-partial** SELF- (3), *a.* **self-partiality,** *n.* **self-perpetuating** SELF (1), *a.* **self-pity** SELF- (1), *n.* **self-pleasing** SELF- (1), *a.* **self-poised** SELF- (2), *a.* **self-pollution** SELF- (1), *n.* masturbation. **self-portrait** SELF- (2), *n.* **self-possessed** SELF- (1), *a.* calm, imperturbable, having presence of mind. **self-possession,** *n.* **self-preservation** SELF- (1), *n.* preservation of oneself from injury; the instinct impelling one to this. **self-profit** SELF- (1), *n.* self-interest. **self-propagating** SELF- (1), *a.* **self-propelled** SELF- (1), *a.* **self-raising** SELF- (1), *a.* of flour, having the raising agent already added. **self-raker** SELF- (2), *n.* a reaping-machine automatically gathering corn into sheaves for binding. **self-realization** SELF- (1), *n.* full development of one's faculties. **self-recording** SELF- (2), *a.* self-registering. **self-regard** SELF- (1), *n.* consideration or respect for oneself. **self-regarding,** *a.* **self-registering** SELF- (2), *a.* of a scientific instrument etc., recording its movements etc. automatically. **self-regulating** SELF- (1), *a.* **self-reliant** SELF- (3), *a.* **self-reliance,** *n.* **self-renunciation** SELF- (1) *n.* self-sacrifice. **self-repression** SELF- (1), *n.* **self-reproach** SELF- (1), *n.* **self-reproachful,** *a.* **self-reproof** SELF- (1), *n.* **self-reproving,** *a.* **self-repugnant** SELF- (3) *a.* self-contradictory, inconsistent. **self-respect** SELF- (1), *n.* due regard for one's character and position; observing a worthy standard of conduct. **self-respectful, -respecting,** *a.* **self-restrained** SELF- (1), *a.* **self-restraint,** *n.* **self-revealing** SELF- (1), *a.* **self-revelation,** *n.* **self-reverence** SELF- (1), *n.* self-respect, esp. in a spiritual sense. **self-righteous** SELF- (3), *a.* pharisaical. **self-righteousness,** *n.* **self-righting** SELF- (1), *a.* righting itself (as when capsized). **self-sacrifice** SELF- (1), *n.* surrender or subordination of one's own interests and desires to those of others. **self-sacrificing,** *a.* **selfsame** SELF- (4), *a.* exactly the same, absolutely identical. **self-satisfaction** SELF- (3), *n.* conceit. **self-satisfied,** *a.* **self-scorn** SELF- (1), *n.* self-contempt. **self-sealing** SELF- (1), *a.* able to seal itself. **self-seeker** SELF- (3), *n.* one selfishly pursuing his or her own interests. **self-seeking,** *n., a.* **self-service,** SELF- (1), *n., a.* (a restaurant, shop etc.) where the customer helps him- or herself and pays a cashier on leaving. **self-serving,** SELF- (1), *a.* giving priority to one's own interests. **self-sown,** SELF- (1), growing from seed sown naturally by the parent plant. **self-starter** SELF- (2), *n.* an automatic device for starting a motor car. **self-sterile** SELF- (2), *a.* incapable of self-fertilization. **self-sterility,** *n.* **self-styled** SELF- (1), *a.* assuming a name or title oneself without authorization, would be, pretended. **self-substantial** SELF- (3), *a.* consisting of one's own substance. **self-sufficient, -sufficing** SELF- (3), *a.* capable of fulfilling one's own requirements, needs etc. without aid; conceited, overbearing. **self-sufficiency,** *n.* **self-suggestion** SELF- (3), *n.* suggestion arising reflexively within the self, esp. in hypnotic states. **self-support** SELF- (1), *n.* **self-supporting,** *a.* **self-surrender** SELF- (1) *n.* **self-sustained, -sustaining** SELF- (1), *a.* **self-taught** SELF- (1), *a.* **†self-tempted** SELF- (1), *a.* **self-torment, -torture** SELF- (1), *n.* **self-tormenting,** *a.* **self-tormentor,** *n.* **self-trust** SELF (1), *n.* reliance on oneself. **self-violence** SELF- (3), *n.* violence to oneself, esp. suicide. **self-will** SELF- (3), *n.* obstinacy. **self-willed,** *a.* **self-winding** SELF- (1), *a.* of a clock etc., winding itself automatically. **self-worship** SELF- (1), *n.* **†self-wrong** SELF- (3), *n.* wrong done by a person to him- or herself.

Selfridge, *n.* **Harry Gordon** (1857–1947), US entrepreneur, who in 1909 founded Selfridges in London, the first large department store in Britain.

Seljuk Empire, *n.* empire of the Turkish people, converted to Islam from the 7th century, under the leadership of the invading Tartars or Seljuk Turks. The Seljuk Empire (1055–1243) included all Anatolia and most of Syria. It was succeeded by the Ottoman Empire. **Seljukian,** *n., a.* [Turk. *seljūg*]

sell[1], *v.t.* (*past, p.p.* **sold**) to transfer or dispose of (property) to another for an equivalent in money; to yield or give up (one's life etc.) exacting some return; to be a regular dealer in; to surrender, betray or prostitute for a price, reward or bribe; (*sl.*) to disappoint, to cheat, to play a trick upon; to inspire others with a desire to possess. *v.i.* to be a shopkeeper or dealer; to be purchased, to find purchasers. *n.* (*sl.*) a disappointment, a fraud; a manner of selling (*hard,* aggressive marketing; or *soft,* gentle persuasion). **sold on,** enthusiastic about. **to sell off,** to sell the remainder of (goods); to clear out (stock), esp. at reduced prices. **to sell one a pup,** (*sl.*) to swindle. **to sell out,** to sell off (one's stock etc.); to sell completely; to dispose of (one's shares in a company etc.); to betray. **to sell up,** to sell the goods of (a debtor) to pay his debt; to sell one's business, one's house and possessions etc. **sell-out,** *n.* a betrayal; a performance etc. for which all the tickets have been sold. **seller,** *n.* **seller's market,** *n.* one in which demand exceeds supply and sellers make the price. **selling race,** *n.* a horse-race, the winner of which is sold by auction. [OE *sellan* (cp. ON *selja,* OHG *saljan*), cogn. with SALE]

sell[2], *n.* a seat, a throne; a saddle. **selliform,** *a.* saddle-shaped. [ME and OF *selle,* L *sella,* cogn. with *sedēre,* to sit]

Sellafield, *n.* site of a nuclear power station on the coast of Cumbria, NW England. It was formerly known as Windscale.

sellanders, SALLENDERS.

seller SELL[1].

Sellers, *n.* **Peter** (1925–80), English comedian and film actor, whose ability as a mimic often allowed him to take several parts. He made his name in the British radio comedy series *Goon Show* (1949–60), and his films include *Dr Strangelove* (1964), *Being There* (1979), and five *Pink Panther* films (1964–78) (as the bumbling Inspector Clouseau).

selliform SELL[2].

Sellotape®, *n.* a cellulose or plastic adhesive tape for mending, binding etc. **sellotape,** *v.t.* to fix or fasten with Sellotape.

seltzer water, *n.* an effervescing mineral water. **seltzogene**, *n.* a gazogene. [G *Selterser-wasser,* water from (Nieder-) Selters, near Wiesbaden, Germany]

selva, *n.* tropical rain forest in the Amazon basin. [Sp., Port., from L *silva,* wood]

selvage, *n.* **selvaged,** *a.* **selvagee**, *n.* (*Mil., Nav.*) a rope or ring made of spun yarns etc., laid parallel and secured by lashings. [SELVEDGE]

selvedge, *n.* the edge of cloth woven so as not to unravel; a narrow strip of different material woven along the edge of cloth etc. and removed or hidden in seaming; the edge-plate of a lock with an opening for the bolt. [MDut. *selfegge* (SELF, EDGE)]

selves, *n.pl.* SELF.

Selwyn Lloyd, *n.* **John, Baron** (1904–78), British Conservative politician. He was foreign secretary (1955–60), and chancellor of the Exchequer (1960–62), responsible for the creation of the National Economic Development Council, but the unpopularity of his policy of wage restraint in an attempt to defeat inflation forced his resignation. He was Speaker of the House of Commons from 1971–76.

Selznick, *n.* **David O(liver)** (1902–65), US film producer. His independent company Selznick International made such films as *King Kong* (1933), *Gone With the Wind* (1939), *Rebecca* (1940), and *Duel in the Sun* (1946).

Sem., (*abbr.*) Seminary; Semitic.

semantic, *a.* of or pertaining to semantics; concerned with the meaning of words and symbols. **semantically,** *adv.* **semantics,** *n.sing.* the area of linguistics concerned with meaning. **semanticist,** *n.* [Gr. *semantikos,* significant]

semaphore, *n.* an apparatus for signalling by means of oscillating arms or flags or the arrangement of lanterns etc. **semaphoric, -ical**, *a.* **semasphere**, *n.* an electric aerostatic signalling apparatus. [F *sémaphore* (Gr. *sēma,* sign, *pherein,* to bear)]

Semarang, *n.* port in N Java, Indonesia; population (1980) 1,027,000. There is a shipbuilding industry and exports include coffee, teak, sugar, tobacco, kapok, and petroleum from nearby oilfields.

semasiology, *n.* semantics. **semasiological**, *a.* **semasiologically,** *adv.* **semasiologist,** *n.* [Gr. *sēmasia,* signification, as prec.]

semasphere SEMAPHORE.

sematic, *a.* of the nature of a sign, significant, esp. pertaining to markings on animals serving to attract, to warn off enemies etc. **sematography**, *n.* the use of signs or symbols instead of letters in writing. **sematology**, *n.* the science of signs as expressions of thought etc.; semasiology. [Gr. *sēma -matos,* sign, -IC]

sematrope, *n.* a form of heliograph.

†**semblable,** *a.* like, similar, seeming. *n.* (one's) like or fellow. †**semblably,** *adv.* [OF, as foll.]

semblance, *n.* external appearance, seeming; a mere show; a likeness, an image. †**semblant,** *a.* like, resembling; apparent. *n.* resemblance, appearance; demeanour, expression; seeming, outward aspect. †**semblative,** *a.* [OF, from *sembler,* L *simulāre,* see SIMULATE]

semé, *a.* (*Her.*) applied to a field, or charge, strewn over with figures, as stars, crosses etc. [F, p.p. of *semer,* L *sēmināre,* to sow, from SEMEN]

semeiography, semeiology,, semeiotics, SEMIOGRAPHY, SEMIOLOGY, SEMIOTICS.

Semele, *n.* in Greek mythology, mother of Dionysus by Zeus. At Hera's suggestion she demanded that Zeus should appear to her in all his glory, but when he did so she was consumed by lightning.

sememe, *n.* the meaning of a morpheme. [Gr. *sēma,* a sign]

semen, *n.* the fertilizing fluid containing spermatozoa, produced by the generative organs of a male animal. [L, seed, cogn. with *serere,* to sow]

Semenov, *n.* **Nikoly** (1896–), Russian physical chemist who made significant contributions to the study of chemical chain reactions. Working mainly in Leningrad at the Institute for Chemical Physics, in 1956 he became the first Russian to gain the Nobel chemistry prize which he shared with Hinshelwood.

semester, *n.* a college half-year in German, some American and other universities. [F *semestre,* L *semestris* (*se-* sex, six, *mensis,* month)]

semi, *n.* (*coll.*) a semidetached house; a semifinal.

semi-, *pref.* half; partially, imperfectly. [L, cp. Gr. *hēmi-*, OE *sam-*, Sansk. *sāmi-*, prob. cogn. with SAME]

semiacid, *a.* subacid.

semiannual, *a.* occurring every six months; half-yearly. **semi-annually,** *adv.*

semiannular, *a.* semicircular.

Semi-Arian, *n.* one of a branch of Arians who held that the Son (of God) was of like substance with the Father, but not consubstantial with him. **semi-Arianism,** *n.*

semiarid, *a.* of a climate, less dry than a desert climate, supporting scrub vegetation.

semiattached, *a.* partially attached; semidetached.

semiautomatic, *a.* partly automatic; of a firearm, self-loading. *n.* such a firearm.

semibarbarous, *a.* half-barbarous. **semibarbarism,** *n.*

semibasement, *n.* a storey in a building which is partly below ground level.

semibreve, *n.* a note equal to half a breve, or two minims.

semibull, *n.* a bull issued by a Pope between his election and coronation.

semicentennial, *a.* happening, celebrated etc. at the end of every 50 years.

semichorous, *n.* one sung by only a half or portion of the choir; a chorus to be rendered thus. **semichoric,** *a.*

semicircle, *n.* a half circle. **semicircled,** *a.* **semicircular,** *a.* **semicircular canals,** *n.pl.* three fluid-filled tubes in the inner ear, concerned with the maintenance of balance.

semicolon, *n.* a mark (;) used in punctuation, now usu. intermediate in value between the period and the comma.

semicolumn, *n.* an engaged column of semicircular section. **semicolumnar,** *a.*

semiconductor, *n.* a substance (as silicon) whose electrical conductivity lies between those of metals and insulators and increases as its temperature rises; a device using such a substance.

semiconscious, *a.* half-conscious.

†**semicope,** *n.* a mediaeval clerical vestment; a half cloak.

semicylinder, *n.* half of a cylinder divided along the plane of its axis. **semicylindric, -ical,** *a.*

semidetached, *a.* partially detached, esp. being one of two houses built as a pair.

semidiameter, *n.* half a diameter.

semidiaphanous, *a.* imperfectly transparent.

semidiurnal, *a.* consisting of, pertaining to or lasting half a day or in half the time between the rising and setting of a heavenly body.

semidome, *n.* a half-dome, usu. a structure like a dome divided vertically.

semi-elliptical, *a.* shaped like half an ellipse divided by either axis.

semifinal, *n.* (*Sport*) the match or round before the final. **semifinalist,** *n.*

semifluid, *a.* imperfectly fluid. *n.* a semifluid substance.

semifused, *a.* a half-molten condition.

semihiant, *a.* of lips, half-open.

semi-infinite, *a.* limited in one direction and extending to infinity in the other.

semiligneous, *a.* partly woody, woody below, herbaceous above.

semiliquid, *n., a.* semifluid.

semilunar, *a.* resembling or shaped like a half-moon or crescent. *n.* a semi-lunar bone. **semilunar valve,** one of two half-moon-shaped valves in the heart. †**semilunary,** †**-nate,** *a.*

semimenstrual, *a.* half-monthly.

semimetal, *n.* an element having metallic properties but non-malleable. **semimetallic,** *a.*

semimonthly, *a.* occurring twice a month; issued at half-monthly intervals.
semimute, *a.* without the power of speech or having it poorly developed. *n.* a semimute person.
seminal, *a.* of or pertaining to semen or reproduction; germinal, propagative; important to the future development of anything; containing new ideas, original. †**seminality,** *n.* **seminally,** *adv.* [OF from L *sēminālis,* from SEMEN]
seminar, *n.* a group of students undertaking an advanced course of study or research together, usu. under the guidance of a professor; such a course; a discussion group, or a meeting of it. [G, as foll.]
seminary, *n.* a place of education, a school, academy or college, esp. a (foreign) Roman Catholic school for training priests. **seminarian,** *n., a.* **seminarist,** *n.* [L *sēminārium,* seed-plot, as foll.]
semination, *n.* the natural dispersal of seeds by plants. †**seminate,** *v.t.* **seminiferous,** *a.* bearing or producing seed; conveying semen. †**seminific, -ical,** *a.* producing seed or semen. [L *sēminātio,* from *sēmināre,* to sow, from SEMEN]
semi-official, *a.* partly or virtually official. **semi-officially,** *adv.*
semiography, *n.* the description of the symptoms of disease. [Gr. *sēmeion,* sign]
semiology, *n.* the study of the symptoms of disease; the study of signs and symbols generally. **semiological,** *a.* [Gr. *sēmeion,* sign]
semi-opal, *n.* a non-opalescent variety of opal.
semi-opaque, *a.* partly opaque. **semi-opacity,** *n.*
semi-osseous, *a.* partially ossified.
semiotics, *n.sing.* (*Linguistics*) the study of signs and symbols and their relationships in language. **semiotic,** *a.* [Gr. *sēmeiōtikos,* a. from *sēmeion,* sign]
semioval, *a.* semi-elliptical.
semioviparous, *a.* imperfectly viviparous, producing young only partially developed beyond the egg, as the marsupials.
semipalmate, *a.* half-webbed, as the toes of many shore-birds.
semiparabola, *n.* a curve of such a nature that the powers of its ordinates are to each other as the next lower powers of its abscissae. **semiparabolic,** *a.*
semiped, *n.* (*Pros.*) a half foot.
Semi-Pelagian, *n.* one of those in the 5th cent. who maintained a doctrine midway between the predestination inculcated by Augustine and the free-will taught by Pelagius. **Semi-Pelagianism,** *n.*
semipenniform, *a.* penniform on one side only.
semipermanent, *a.* long-lasting, but not permanent.
semipermeable, *a.* permeable by small molecules but not by large ones.
semipiscine, *a.* partly resembling a fish.
semipiternal, *a.* everlasting, eternal, endless. †**sempitern,** *n.* **sempiternally,** *adv.* **sempiternity,** *n.* **sempiternous,** *a.* [OF *sempiternel,* L *sempiternus* (*sempi-semper,* always), *-ternus,* cp. *nocturnus*]
semiplume,, *n.* a feather with a stiff stem but a downy web. **semiplumaceous,** *a.*
semiprecious, *a.* valuable, but not regarded as a precious stone.
semiquadrate, *n.* the aspect of two planets when distant 45° from each other.
semiquaver, *n.* (*Mus.*) a note of half the duration of a quaver.
Semiramislived, *n.* (lived *c.* 800 BC), Assyrian queen, later identified with the chief Assyrian goddess ISHTAR.
semirigid, *a.* of an airship, having a flexible gas container and a rigid keel.
semirotary, *a.* capable of turning half round.
semi-Saxon, *a.* intermediate between Anglo-Saxon and English, pertaining to the early period of Middle English, *c.* 1150–1250. *n.* the semi-Saxon language.
semisex, *n.* (*Biol.*) a group in a bisexual species capable of breeding with other groups. **semisexual,** *a.*
semisextile, *n.* the aspect of two planets when distant from each other 30° or one-twelfth of a circle.
semiskilled, *a.* of a worker, having some basic skills but not highly trained.
semismile, *n.* a half or forced smile.
semisolid, *a.* so viscous as to be almost solid.
semita, *n.* a band of minute tubercles in some sea-urchins. [L, path, way]
Semite, *n.* a descendant of Shem, or a member of one of the peoples (including Hebrews, Phoenicians, Aramaeans, Assyrians, Arabs and Abyssinians) reputed to be descended from Shem. *a.* Semitic. **Semitic,** *a.* pertaining to the Semites or their languages. *n.* one of the Semitic group of languages. **Semitic languages,** *n. pl.* a branch of the HAMITO-SEMITIC family of languages. **Semiticize, -ise, Semitize, -ise,** *v.t.* **Semitization, -isation,** *n.* **Semitism,** *n.* **Semitist,** *n.* [late L and Gr. *Sēm*]
semitone, *n.* (*Mus.*) an interval equal to half a major tone on the scale. **semitonal, semitonic,** *a.* **semitonically,** *adv.*
semitontine, *n.* a form of tontine assurance allowing surrender-value before the expiration of the tontine period.
semitrailer, *n.* a trailer which has back wheels but is supported in front by the towing vehicle.
semitransparent, *n.* almost transparent. **semitransparency,** *n.*
semitropical, *a.* partly within or bordering on the tropics.
semitubular, *a.* having the shape of a tube divided lengthwise.
semiuncial, *a.* of letters, half-uncial, between uncial and cursive.
semivitreous, *a.* partially vitreous. **semivitrify,** *v.t.* **semivitrification,** *n.*
semivowel, *n.* a sound having the character of both vowel and consonant as *w* and *y;* sometimes applied to consonants such as *l, m, r* and *z,* that are not mute; a character representing such.
semiweekly, *a.* occurring, issued etc. twice a week.
Semmelweis, *n.* **Ignaz Philipp** (1818–65), Hungarian obstetrician who pioneered asepsis.
semmit, *n.* (*Sc.*) a vest or undershirt. [var. of SAMITE]
Semnopithecus, *n.* a genus of Asiatic monkeys having long limbs and tails; a monkey of this genus. **semnopithecine,** *a.* **semnopithecoid,** *n., a.* [Gr. *semnos,* sacred, *pithekos,* ape]
semolina,, semola, *n.* the hard grains of wheat left after bolting, used for puddings etc. [It. *semolino,* dim. of *semola,* bran, L *simila,* fine wheat-flour]
semper, *adv.* (L) always. **semper fidelis,** always faithful. **semper idem,** (*pl.* **eadem**) always the same. **semper paratus,** always ready.
sempervirent, *a.* evergreen. [L *semper,* always, *virens -entem,* pres.p. of *virēre,* to be green, from *vis,* pl. *vires,* strength]
sempervivum, *n.* a genus of fleshy plants of the family Crassulaceae containing the house-leeks. [L, neut. of *sempervīvus* (as prec., *vīvus,* living)]
semple, (*Sc.*) SIMPLE.
semplice, *adv.* (*Mus.*) simply, plainly, without embellishment. [It.]
sempre, *adv.* (*Mus.*) in the same manner throughout. [It., from L *semper,* always]
†**sempster, sempstress** SEAM[1].
Semtex®, *n.* a malleable plastic explosive, manufactured in Czechoslovakia. It is safe to handle (it can only be ignited by a detonator), and difficult to trace, since it has no smell. It has been used by extremist groups in the Middle East and by the IRA in Northern Ireland.
semuncia, *n.* (*Rom. Ant.*) a coin equal to half an uncia. **semuncial,** *a.* [L (SEMI-, UNCIA)]
SEN, (*abbr.*) State Enrolled Nurse.
Sen., (*abbr.*) senate; senator; senior.
sen, *n.* a Japanese monetary unit, one-hundredth of a yen. [Jap.]
Senanayake[1], *n.* **Don Stephen** (1884–1952), first prime minister of independent Sri Lanka (formerly Ceylon) from 1947–52.
Senanayake[2], *n.* **Dudley** (1911–73), prime minister of

Sri Lanka (1952–53, 1960, and 1965–70); son of Don Senanayake.

senarius, *n.* (*L Pros.*) a verse of six feet, esp. the iambic trimeter. **senary**, *a.* containing six units; by sixes. [L, (*sēnī,* six each)]

senate, *n.* an assembly or council performing legislative or administrative functions; the state council of the ancient Roman republic and empire of ancient Athens, Lacedaemon etc., of the free cities of the Middle Ages etc.; the upper legislative house in various bicameral parliaments, as of the US and France; the governing body of the various universities; any venerable deliberative or legislative body. **senate-house,** *n.* a building in which a senate meets. **senator,** *n.* a member of a senate. **senatorial**, *a.* **senatorially,** *adv.* **senatorship,** *n.* **senatus**, *n.* the ancient Roman senate; the governing body of a university. **Senatus Consultum**, *n.* a decree of the Roman Senate; (*F Hist.*) a decree of Napoleon I. **Senatus Populusque Romanus** , the Roman Senate and People. [OF, *senat,* L *senātus,* from *sen-,* base of *senex,* old]

send, *v.t.* (*past, p.p.* **sent**) to cause or bid to go or pass or to be conveyed or transmitted to some destination; to cause to go (in, up, off, away etc.); to propel, to hurl, to cast; to cause to come or befall, to grant, to bestow, to inflict; to cause to be, to bring about. *v.i.* to dispatch a messenger; (*Naut.*) to pitch or plunge deeply into the trough of the sea. *n.* (*Naut.*) the impetus or drive of the sea; the act of sending or pitching into the trough of the sea. **to send down,** (*Univ.*) to rusticate; (*coll.*) to send to prison. **to send for,** to require the attendance of a person or the bringing of a thing; to summon; to order. **to send forth,** to put forth; to emit. **to send in,** to submit (as a competition entry). **to send off,** to dispatch; to give a send-off to one departing; in sport, to order (a player) off the field because of an infringement of the rules. **to send on,** to forward (mail); to send (luggage) in advance. **to send out,** to send forth. **to send up,** to parody; to ridicule. **send-off,** *n.* a start, as in a race; a leave-taking, a friendly demonstration to one departing on a journey. **send-up,** *n.* **sender,** *n.* [OE *sendan,* cp. Dut. *zenden,* G *senden,* Icel. *sende*]

Sendak, *n.* **Maurice** (1928–), US illustrator, born in New York, whose deliberately archaic children's book illustrations include *Where the Wild Things Are* (1963), *In the Night Kitchen* (1970), and *Outside Over There* (1981) (he also wrote the above books).

sendal, *n.* a light, thin silken fabric used in the Middle Ages for costly attire, banners etc. [OF *sendal, cendal,* low L *cendalum,* Sansk. *sindhu-,* pertaining to the Indus or Scinde]

sender, send-off SEND.

Seneca[1], *n.* **Lucius Annaeus** (*c.* 4 BC–AD 65), Roman Stoic playwright, author of essays and nine tragedies. Born at Córdoba, Spain, he was Nero's tutor, but lost favour after his accession and was ordered to commit suicide. His tragedies were accepted as classical models by 16th-century dramatists. **senecan,** *a.* of, pertaining to or in the style of Seneca.

Seneca[2], *a.* of or pertaining to Seneca Lake, New York. †**Seneca oil,** *n.* crude petroleum, so called because first found near this. [name of tribe of N Am. Indians forming one of the 'Six Nations' or Iroquois confederacy]

Senecio, *n.* a genus of composite plants, with about 500 species, containing the groundsel, ragwort etc. **senecioid**, *a.* [mod. L, from *senex,* old man]

Senefelder, *n.* **Alois** (1771–1834), German engraver, born in Prague. He is considered the founder of lithography.

senega,, -ka, *n.* the dried root of the Seneca snake-root *Polygala senega,* used as an expectorant etc. [N Am. Ind. *Seneca* Indians]

Senegal, *n.* Republic of (*République du Sénégal*), country in W Africa, on the Atlantic, bounded to the N by Mauritania, to the E by Mali, to the S by Guinea and Guinea-Bissau, and enclosing Gambia on three sides. **area** 196,200 sq km/75,753 sq miles. **capital** and chief port Dakar. **towns** Thies, Kaolack. **physical** plains; swamp and tropical forest in SW. **population** (1989) 7,704,000; annual growth rate 2.6%. **exports** groundnuts, cotton, fish, phosphates. **language** French (official). **religion** Muslim 80%, Christian 10% (chiefly Roman Catholic), animist 10%.

senescent, *a.* growing old. **senescence,** *n.* [L *senescens -ntem,* pres.p. of *senescere,* from *senex,* old]

seneschal, *n.* an officer in the houses of princes and high dignitaries in the Middle Ages having the superintendence of feasts and domestic ceremonies, sometimes dispensing justice; a steward or major-domo. **seneschalship,** *n.* [OF, from Teut]

Senghor, *n.* **Léopold** (1906–), first president of independent Senegal (1960–80).

sengreen, *n.* the houseleek or sempervivum. [OE *singrēne* (*sin,* ever, GREEN)]

senhor, *n.* a man, in a Portuguese-speaking country; the Portuguese or Brazilian title corresponding to the English Mr or sir. **senhora**, *n.* a lady; Mrs, madam. **senhorita**, *n.* a young unmarried girl; Miss. [Port.]

senile, *a.* pertaining to or proceeding from the infirmities etc. of old age; suffering from the (mental) infirmities associated with old age. **senility**, *n.* old age; the (mental) infirmity associated with old age. [L *senīlis,* see foll.]

senior, *a.* older, elder (appended to names to denote the elder of two persons with identical names, esp. father and son); older or higher in rank or service. *n.* one older than another; one older or higher in rank, service etc.; (*N Am.*) a student in his or her third or fourth year; †an aged person. **senior common room,** a common room for the use of staff at a college. **senior citizen,** *n.* an old-age pensioner. **senior service,** *n.* the Royal Navy. **senior wrangler, optime,** *n.* (*Camb. Univ.*) first in first class of mathematical tripos. **seniority**, *n.* **seniory,** *n.* [L, older, comp. of *senex senis,* old]

Senna, *n.* **Ayrton** (1960–), Brazilian motor-racing driver. He had his first Grand Prix win in the 1985 Portuguese Grand Prix, has since surpassed Jim Clark's record for most pole positions, and in 1988 was world champion, winning a championship record eight races.

senna, *n.* the dried, purgative leaflets or pods of several species of cassia. [It. *sena,* Arab. *sanā*]

Sennacherib, *n.* died 681 BC, king of Assyria from 705. Son of SARGON II, he rebuilt the city of Nineveh on a grand scale, sacked Babylon in 689, and crushed HEZEKIAH, king of Judah, though failing to take Jerusalem. He was assassinated by his sons, and one of them, Esarhaddon, succeeded him.

sennachie, *n.* (*Sc. Highlands, Ir.*) one learned in tradition and clan genealogy; a reciter of old romances. [Gael. *seanachaidh*]

Sennett, *n.* **Mack,** stage name of Michael Sinnott (1880–1960), US film producer, originally an actor, responsible for such 1920s slapstick silent comedians as the Keystone Kops, 'Fatty' Arbuckle, and Charlie Chaplin. He did not make the transition to sound with much enthusiasm and retired in 1935. His films include *Tillie's Punctured Romance (1914), The Shriek of Araby* (1923), and *The Barber Shop* (sound) (1933).

sennet, *n.* a trumpet-signal for stage entrances and exits in the Elizabethan theatre. [OF *segnet,* dim. of *seing,* L *signum,* SIGN]

†**sennight,** *n.* a week. [contr. of SEVEN-NIGHT]

sennit, *n.* (*Naut.*) braided cordage, made from three to nine strands for gaskets, packing etc. [prob. contr. of SEVEN-KNIT]

senocular, *a.* having six eyes, as some spiders. **senoculate,** *a.* [L *sēnī,* six each, OCULAR]

Senonian, *a.* (*Geol.*) a division of the upper Cretaceous in France and Belgium. [F *sénonian* (L *Senonēs,* a people in central Gaul, -IAN)]

señor, *n.* a man, in a Spanish-speaking country; the Spanish form of address equivalent to Mr or sir. **señora**, *n.* a lady; Mrs, madam. **señorita**, *n.* a young girl; Miss. [Sp.]

†**sens,** SENSE, SINCE.

sensation, *n.* the mental state of affection resulting from the excitation of an organ of sense, the primary element in perception or cognition of an external object; the content of such a mental state or affection, a state of excited feeling or interest, esp. affecting a number of people; the thing or event exciting this. **to create a sensation,** to cause surprise and excitement. **sensate**, *a.* perceived by the senses; having bodily senses. *v.t.*, to perceive by the senses. **sensational,** *a.* causing, or pertaining to, sensation; (*coll.*) very good. **sensationalism,** *n.* the employment of sensational methods in literary composition, political agitation etc.; (*Phil.*) the theory that all knowledge is derived from sensation. **sensationalist,** *n.* **sensationalistic**, *a.* **sensationalize, -ise,** *v.t.* **sensationally,** *adv.* †**sensationary,** *a.* [med. L *sensātio,* from late L *sensātus,* sensate, from L *sensus,* SENSE]

sense, *n.* one of the five faculties by which sensation is received through special bodily organs (sight, hearing, touch, taste, smell); also, the muscular sense giving a sensation of physical effort; the faculty of sensation, perception or ability to perceive through the senses, sensitiveness; bodily feeling, sensuousness; intuitive perception, comprehension, appreciation; consciousness, conviction (of); sound judgment, sagacity, common sense, good mental capacity; meaning, signification; general feeling or judgment, consensus of opinion; (*pl.*) normal command or possession of the senses, sanity. *v.t.* to be aware of, to perceive by the senses; of a computer, to detect (a signal, a hole in a punched tape etc.). **in one's senses,** sane. **out of one's senses,** insane. **to make sense,** to be intelligible. **to make sense of,** to understand. **sense-body, -capsule, -cell, -centre, -filament, -hair, -organ,** *n.* a bodily part or organ concerned in the production of sensation. **sense datum,** *n.* an item of experience received directly through a sense organ. **sense-impression,** *n.* an impression on the mind through the medium of sensation. **sense-perception,** *n.* **senseful,** *a.* significant. **senseless,** *a.* incapable of sensation, insensible; contrary to reason, foolish, nonsensical. **senselessly,** *adv.* **senselessness,** *n.* [F *sens,* L *sensus,* feeling, from *sentīre,* to feel, p.p. *sensus*]

sensible, *a.* perceptible by the senses; appreciable; acting with or characterized by good sense or judgment, judicious, reasonable; having perception (of); †capable of sensation, easily affected, sensitive (to). *n.* that which is sensible or perceptible. **sensibility**, *n.* capacity to see or feel; susceptibility of impression; (*often pl.*) acute or delicate susceptibility, over-sensitiveness. **sensibleness,** *n.* **sensibly,** *adv.* **sensify,** *v.t.* **sensifacient**, **sensific**, **sensificatory**, **sensiferous**, *a.* **sensigenous**, *a.* producing sensation. **sensile**, *a.* **sensism, -sist** SENSATIONALISM-, -IST under SENSATION. [F, from late L *sensibilis,* as prec.]

sensitive, *a.* of or depending on the senses, sensory; readily or acutely affected by external influences; impressible, delicately susceptible, excitable or responsive; (*Phot.*) susceptible to the action of light; of information, secret, classified. **sensitive plant,** *n.* a plant, *Mimosa pudica* or *M. sensitiva,* the leaves of which shrink from the touch; a sensitive person. **sensitively,** *adv.* **sensitiveness, sensitivism,** *n.* **sensitivity**, *n.* **sensitize, -ise,** *v.t.* to make sensitive; to render (paper etc.) sensitive to light; to render (a person) sensitive (to an allergen, drug etc.). **sensitization, -isation,** *n.* **sensitizer, -iser,** *n.* **sensitometer**, *n.* an apparatus for determining the sensitiveness of photographic plates, films etc. [OF *sensitif -tive,* med. L *sensitīvus,* see SENSE]

sensor, *n.* an instrument which responds to, and signals, a change in a physical stimulus, for information or control purposes. [see SENSE]

sensorium, *n.* (*pl.* **-ria**) the seat or organ of sensation, the brain; the nervous system, comprising the brain, spinal cord etc.; the grey matter of these. **sensorial,** *a.* **sensory**, *a.* sensorial; of the senses or of sensation. *n.* the sensorium. [late L, see SENSE]

sensual, *a.* pertaining to or affecting the senses, carnal as dist. from spiritual or intellectual; pertaining or devoted to the indulgence of the appetites or passions, esp. those of sex, voluptuous; (*Phil.*) pertaining or according to sensationalism; †pertaining to sense or sensation, sensory. **sensualism, sensuality**, †**sensualness,** *n.* **sensualist,** *n.* **sensualistic**, *a.* **sensualize, -ise,** *v.t.* **sensualization, -isation,** *n.* **sensually,** *adv.* [late L *sensuālis,* see SENSE]

sensuous, *a.* pertaining to or derived from the senses; abounding in or suggesting sensible images; readily affected through the senses. **sensuously,** *adv.* **sensuousness,** *n.* [L *sensus,* SENSE]

sent, *past, p.p.* SEND.

sentence, *n.* a series of words, containing a subject, predicate etc., expressing a complete thought; a penalty or declaration of penalty upon a condemned person; a judicial decision, verdict; †a decision, judgment or opinion; a pithy saying, a maxim, a proverb; two or more musical phrases forming a unit. *v.t.* to pronounce judgment on; to condemn to punishment; †to decree. **sentential**, *a.* [OF, from L *sententia,* from *sentīre,* to feel]

sententious, *a.* abounding in pithy sentences, axioms or maxims; terse, brief and energetic; pompous in tone. **sententiously,** *adv.* **sententiousness,** *n.*

sentient, *a.* having the power of sense-perception; having sense of feeling. *n.* a sentient person or thing. **sentience,** *n.* **sentiently,** *adv.* [L *sentiens -entem,* pres.p. of *sentīre,* to feel]

sentiment, *n.* mental feeling excited by aesthetic, moral or spiritual ideas; a thought, view or mental tendency derived from or characterized by emotion; susceptibility to emotion; (*often pl.*) an opinion or attitude. [ME and OF *sentement,* med. L *sentīmentum,* as prec.]

sentimental, *a.* characterized by sentiment; swayed by emotion; mawkish; displaying unbalanced tenderness. **sentimental value,** *n.* the value of an object in terms not of money but of associations, memories etc. **sentimentalism, sentimentality**, *n.* unreasonable or uncontrolled emotion; mawkishness. **sentimentalist,** *n.* **sentimentalize, -ise,** *v.i.* to affect sentimentality. *v.t.* to render sentimental. **sentimentally,** *adv.*

sentinel, *n.* one who keeps watch to prevent surprise, esp. a soldier on guard; a sentinel-crab. *v.t.* to watch over, to guard; to set sentinels at or over. **sentinel crab,** *n.* a crab with long eye-stalks found in the Indian and Pacific Oceans. [OF *sentinelle,* from It. *sentinella* or dim. of *sentine,* dim. of *sente,* L *sēmita,* path]

sentry, *n.* a sentinel; the duty of a sentinel. **sentry-box,** *n.* a shelter for a sentry. **sentry-go,** *n.* a sentry's duty of pacing to and fro. [perh. corr. of prec., or from OF *senteret,* from *sentier,* med. L *sēmītārius,* from *sēmita,* as prec.]

senza, *prep.* without. **senza tempo,** without strict time. [It.]

Seoul, Sŏul, *n.* capital of South Korea, near the Han river, and with its chief port at Inchon; population (1985) 9,646,000. Industries include engineering, textiles, and food processing.

Sep., (*abbr.*) September; Septuagint.

sepal, *n.* one of the segments, divisions or leaves of a calyx. **sepaline**, **sepaloid**, **sepalous,** *a.* **sepalody,** *n.* reversion of petals etc. into sepals by metamorphosis. [F *sépale* (L *sēpar-,* SEPARATE, assim. to PETAL)]

separate, *v.t.* to disunite, to set or keep apart; to break up into distinct parts, to disperse; to come or be between, to be the boundary of. *v.i.* to part, to be disconnected, to withdraw (from); to disperse; of a married couple, to agree to live apart. *a.*, disconnected, considered apart; distinct, individual; †disunited from the body. **separate estate,** *n.* the property of a married woman held independently of her husband. **separate maintenance,** *n.* an allowance made by a husband to a wife from whom he is separated by consent. **separability**, *n.* **separable,** *a.* †**separableness,** *n.* **separably,** *adv.* **separately,** *adv.*

separateness, *n.* **separates,** *n.pl.* women's clothes that cover part of the body and are worn together, e.g. skirts and jackets. **separation,** *n.* the act of separating or the state of being separated, esp. partial divorce, consisting of cessation of cohabitation between married persons. **separatism,** *n.* **separatist,** *n.* one who advocates secession, from a church, political party, federation etc. **separator,** *n.* one who separates; a machine that separates the cream from milk. [L *sēparātus,* p.p. of *sēparāre* (SE-, *parāre,* to arrange)]

separatrix, *n.* a separating mark, as a decimal point, or line marking off corrections in the margin of proof, the line of demarcation between light and shade in a picture etc. [L, fem. of *sēparātor,* SEPARATOR]

separatum, *n.* a reprint of one of a series of papers etc. [L *sēparātum,* neut. of *sēparātus,* see SEPARATE]

Sephardi, *n.* (*pl.* **-dim**) a Jew descended from those expelled from Spain and Portugal in the 15th century, or from those forcibly converted to Christianity (Marranos) at that time. Many settled in N Africa, and some in other Mediterranean countries or in England. **Sephardic,** *a.* [mod. Heb.]

sephen, *n.* an Arabian sting-ray, the skin of which yields shagreen. [Arab. *sapan,* shagreen]

Sephira, *n.* (*pl.* **-roth**) one of the ten intelligences, attributes or emanations of God, in the Cabbala. **Sephiric, Sephirothic,** *a.* [Heb.]

sepia, *n.* a dark brown pigment; this pigment prepared from the black secretion of the cuttlefish; a cuttlefish; (**Sepia**) a genus of cephalopodous molluscs containing this; a water-colour drawing in sepia. *a.* made in sepia; of the colour sepia. †**sepic,** *a.* [L and Gr.]

†**sepiment,** DISSEPIMENT.

sepoy, *n.* an Indian soldier disciplined in the European manner, esp. one in the former British Indian army. [perh. through Port. *sipae,* from Hind., Pers. *sipāhī,* from *sipāh,* army]

seps, *n.* a serpent-lizard, one of a genus of lizards of the family Scincidae. [L, Gr. *sēps,* from *sēpein,* to make rotten]

sepsine, *n.* a poisonous compound found in decomposing yeast and various putrid substances; a ptomaine causing septic poisoning.

sepsis, *n.* (*pl.* **sepses**) putrefaction; infection by disease-causing bacteria, e.g. from a wound, blood-poisoning. [Gr. *sēpsis,* as prec.]

sept, *n.* a clan or branch of a clan, esp. in Scotland or Ireland. [OF *septe,* var. of *secte,* SECT]

Sept., (*abbr.*) September; Septuagint.

sept-[1] SEPT(I)-[1].

sept-[2] SEPT(I)-[2].

septa, (*pl.*) SEPTUM.

septaemia, SEPTICAEMIA, under SEPTIC.

septal, *a.* of or pertaining to a septum or septa, or to a sept or septs.

septan, *a.* of fever, ague etc., recurring on the seventh day. [L *septem,* seven]

septangle, *n.* a heptagon. **septangular,** *a.* [ANGLE[2]]

septarium, *n.* (*pl.* **-ria**) a nodule of limestone, ironstone etc., with radiating fissures in the middle filled with some extraneous deposit. **septarian,** *a.*

septate, *a.* provided with or divided by a septum or septa, partitioned. **septation,** *n.* [late L *sēptatus,* see SEPTUM]

September, *n.* the ninth month of the year (the seventh after March, first month of the ancient Roman year). **Septembrist,** *n.* one of the Paris mob that massacred political prisoners in Sept. 1792. [ME and OF *Septembre,* L *September* (*septem,* seven, cp. DECEMBER)]

septempartite, *a.* divided into seven parts. [PARTITE]

septemvir, *n.* (*pl.* **-viri,**) one of seven men forming a government, committee etc. **septemvirate,** *n.* [L *vir,* man]

septenarious, *n.* (*pl.* **-rii,**) a verse of seven feet, esp. a trochaic trimeter catalectic. [L, from *septēnī,* seven apiece, from *septem,* seven]

septenary, *a.* consisting of or relating to seven; by sevens; lasting seven years. *n.* a set of seven years, things etc. **septenate, -tenous,** *a.* (*Bot.*) growing in sevens. [as prec.]

septennium, *n.* a period of seven years. **septennial,** *a.* **septennially,** *adv.* [L *annus,* year]

†**septentrion,** *n.* the north; the Great Bear. *a.* northern. **septentrional,** *a.* †**septentrionally,** *adv.* [L *septentrio,* pl. *-triōnes* (*triōnes,* pl. of *trio,* plough-ox)]

septet, *n.* a group of seven, esp. singers, voices, instruments etc.; a musical composition for seven performers. [G, from L]

septfoil, *n.* a figure of seven equal segments of a circle, used as a symbol of the seven sacraments etc.; the tormentil *Potentilla tormentilla.* [FOIL[1]]

sept(i)-[1], *comb. form.* seven. [L, *septem,* seven]

sept(i)-[2], **septo-,** *comb. form.* septum.

septic, †**-ical,** *a.* (*Path.*) causing or tending to promote putrefaction, not aseptic. *n.* a septic substance. **septic tank,** *n.* a tank in which sewage is partially purified by the action of bacteria. **septicaemia,** *n.* an abnormal state of the blood caused by the absorption of poisonous or putrid matter. **septicaemic,** *a.* **septically,** *adv.* **septicidal,** *a.* of the dehiscence of a fruit, taking place through the partitions. **septicidally,** *adv.* **septicity,** *n.* [Gr. *sēptikos,* from *sēptos,* rotten, from *sēpein,* to cause to rot]

septifarious, *a.* (*Bot.*) turned seven different ways. [late L *septifarius* (*septem,* seven, cp. MULTIFARIOUS)]

septiferous, *a.* bearing septa. [see SEPTRUM]

septiform[1], *a.* sevenfold. [SEPT(I)-[1]]

septiform[2], *a.* shaped like a septum. [SEPT(I)-[2]]

septifragal, *a.* (*Bot.*) breaking away from the partitions, pertaining to a mode of dehiscense in which the septa break away from the valves.

septilateral, *a.* seven-sided.

septillion, *n.* the seventh power of a million; (*N Am.*) the eighth power of a thousand. **septillionth,** *n., a.*

septimal, *a.* of, relating to or based on the number seven. **septime,** *n.* the seventh parry in fencing.

septimole, *n.* (*Mus.*) a group of seven notes to be played in the time of four or six.

septine SEPSINE.

septinsular, *a.* consisting of seven islands (applied to the Ionian Islands).

septisyllable, *n.* a word of seven syllables.

septo- SEPT(I)-[2].

septomaxillary, *a.* connected with a maxillary bone and a nasal septum. *n.* a small bone of this nature in some birds and fishes.

septonasal, *a.* forming a nasal septum. *n.* a septonasal bone.

septuagenarian, *n.* a person of 70 years of age, or between 69 and 80. *a.* of such an age. **septuagenary,** *a.* containing or consisting of 70. [L *septuāgēnārius,* from *septuāgēnī,* 70 each, from *septuāginta,* 70]

Septuagesima, *n.* the third Sunday before Lent, so called because about 70 days before Easter. †**septuagesimal,** *a.* consisting of 70.

Septuagint, *n.* a Greek version of the Old Testament including the Apocrypha (*c.* 3rd cent. BC), so called because, according to tradition, about 70 persons were employed on the translation. [L *septuāginta,* 70]

septum, *n.* (*pl.* **-ta**) a partition as in a chambered cell, the cell of an ovary, between the nostrils etc. **septal,** *a.* **septulum,** *n.* a small septum. **septulate,** *a.* [L, from *sē-, saepīre,* to enclose, from *sēpes, saepes,* hedge]

septuple, *a.* sevenfold. *n.* a set of seven things. *v.t., v.i.* to multiply by seven. **septuplet,** *n.* a septimole; one of seven children born at a birth. [late L *septuplus,* from *septem,* seven]

sepulchre, *n.* a tomb, esp. one hewn in the rock or built in a solid and permanent manner; a burial-vault. *v.t.* to place in a sepulchre, to entomb. **sepulchral,** *a.* pertaining to burial, the grave or to monuments raised over the dead; suggestive of a sepulchre, grave, dismal, funereal. **sepulchrally,** *adv.* [OF *sepulcre,* L *sepulcrum* (*sepelīre,* to bury, p.p. *sepultus, -crum,* suf.)]

sepulture, *n.* interment, burial; †a burial-place. [OF from L *sepultūra,* as prec.]

†**sepurture,** *a.* (*Her.*) of wings, raised about the back

and expanded. [etym. doubtful]

seq., (*abbr.*) (*sing.*) the following [L *sequens*]; and in what follows [L *sequente*]; it follows [L *sequitur*]

seqq., (*abbr.*) (*pl.*) the following [L *sequentes, sequentia*]; in the following places [L *sequentibus*]

†**sequacious,** *a.* following, inclined to follow; servile, ductile, pliant; logically consistent and coherent. **sequaciously,** *adv.* †**sequaciousness,** †**sequacity**, *n.* [L *sequax -ācis,* from *sequī,* to follow, -OUS]

sequel, *n.* that which follows; a succeeding part, a continuation (of a story etc.); the upshot, consequence or result (of an event etc.). [OF *sequele,* L SEQUELA]

sequela, *n.* (*pl.* **lae** -lē) an abnormal condition occurring as the consequence of some disease; an inference, a consequence; †an adherent. [L, from *sequī,* to follow]

sequence, †**-ency** *n.* succession, the process of coming after in space, time etc.; a series of things following one another consecutively or according to a definite principle; a set of consecutive cards; (*Mus.*) a succession of similar harmonious formations or melodic phrases at different pitches; a scene in a film. **sequent,** *a.* **sequentes**, **-tia**, *n.pl.* (and) the following. **sequential**, *a.* **sequentiality**, *n.* **sequentially,** *adv.* [OF, from L *sequentia,* from *sequens -ntis,* pres.p. of *sequī,* to follow]

sequester, *v.t.* (*esp. in p.p.*) to set apart, to isolate, to seclude; (*Law*) to separate (property etc.) from the owner temporarily; to take possession of (property in dispute) until some case is decided or claim is paid; to confiscate, to appropriate. *v.i.* (*Law*) of a widow, to renounce or decline any concern with the estate of a late husband. *n.* †the act of sequestering; seclusion, isolation. †**sequestrable,** *a.* **sequestral** SEQUESTRUM. **sequestrate**, *v.t.* (*Law*) to sequester. **sequestration**, *n.* **sequestrator,** *n.* [OF *sequestrer,* late L *sequestrāre,* to surrender, to commit, from *sequester,* agent, trustee, from *sequī,* to follow]

sequestrum, *n.* (*pl.* **-ra**) a piece of dead and separated bone remaining in place. **sequestrotomy**, *n.* the removal of this. **sequestral**, *a.* [med. L, as prec.]

sequin, *n.* (*Hist.*) a venetian gold coin; a small disc of shiny metal, jet etc., used as trimming for dresses etc. [F, from It. *zecchino,* from *zecca,* mint, Arab. *sikka,* die]

Sequoia, *n.* a Californian genus of gigantic conifers, with two species. [Cherokee]

Sequoya, *n.* **George Guess** (1770–1843), American Indian scholar and leader. After serving with the US army in the Creek War (1813–14), he made a study of his own Cherokee language and created a syllabary which was approved by the Cherokee council in 1821.

sera SERUM.

sérac, *n.* one of the large angular or tower-shaped masses into which a glacier breaks up at an ice-fall. [Swiss F, orig. a cheese in the form of a cube]

seraglio, *n.* (*pl.* **lios**) a walled palace, esp. the old palace of the Turkish Sultan, with its mosques, government offices etc. at Istanbul; a harem. [It. *serraglio,* enclosure, from *serrare,* late L *serare,* to bolt, to shut in, from L *sera,* bolt, from *serere,* to bind, to join]

serai, CARAVANSERAI.

seral SERE[3].

seralbumen, -min, *n.* a variety of albumen occurring in the serum of the blood.

serang, *n.* a boatman; leader of a lascar crew. [Hind.]

serape, *n.* a Mexican blanket or shawl. [Mex., Sp.]

seraph, *n.* (*pl.* **seraphs, seraphim**) an angel of the highest order. **seraphic,** †**-ical**, *a.* of or like a seraph; ecstatic, rapturous; (*coll.*) very good, well-behaved. **seraphically,** *adv.* [orig. *seraphin,* Heb. *serāphīm,* pl., from Arab. *sharaf,* high]

seraphina, seraphine, *n.* a form of harmonium (invented 1883) with reeds, a keyboard etc. [as prec., -INE]

Serapis, *n.* ancient Greek-Egyptian god, a combination of Hades and Osiris, invented by the Ptolemies; his finest temple was the Serapeum in Alexandria.

seraskier, *n.* (*Hist.*) a Turkish commander, esp. the commander-in-chief or minister of war. **seraskierate,** *n.* [F *sérasquieur,* Turk. *ser'asker* (Pers. *ser,* head, Arab. *'asker,* army)]

Serb, Serbian, *a.* of or pertaining to Serbia, its people, or its language. *n.* a native of Serbia; the Slav language of Serbia. [Serb. *Srb*]

Serbia, *n.* (Serbo-Croat **Srbija**) constituent republic of Yugoslavia, which includes Kosovo and Vojvodina. **area** 88,400 sq km/34,122 sq miles. **capital** Belgrade. **physical** fertile Danube plains in the north, and mountainous in the south. **population** (1986) 9,660,000. **language** the Serbian variant of Serbo-Croat, sometimes written in Cyrillic script. **religion** Serbian Orthodox.

Serbonian, *a.* (*Milton*) applied to the Egyptian lake or bog of Serbonis in the Nile delta, in which whole armies were reported to have been swallowed up; applied to a difficulty or complication from which there is no escape.

SERC, (*abbr.*) Science and Engineering Research Council.

serdab, *n.* a secret passage or cell in an ancient Egyptian tomb. [Pers.]

sere[1], *n.* the pawl or catch of a gun- or pistol-lock holding the hammer at half or full cock. [OF *serre,* grasp, lock, from *serrer,* late L *serāre,* to lock, see SERAGLIO]

sere[2] SEAR[1].

sere[3], *n.* a series of ecological communities following one another in one area. **seral,** *a.* [SERIES]

†**serecloth,** CERECLOTH.

serein, *n.* a fine rain falling from a clear sky after sunset, esp. in tropical regions. [F, as SERENE]

serenade, *n.* a song or piece of music played or sung in the open air at night, esp. by a lover beneath his lady's window; a nocturne, a serenata. *v.t.* to sing or play a serenade to or in honour of. *v.i.* to perform a serenade. **serenader,** *n.* **serenata**, *n.* a cantata or simple form of symphony, usu. with a pastoral subject, for the open air. [F *sérénade,* It. *serenata,* orig. fem. p.p. of *serenare,* to make serene, see foll.]

serendipity, *n.* the happy knack of making unexpected and delightful discoveries by accident. **serendipitous,** *a.* [coined by Horace Walpole, after the fairy tale *The Three Princes of Serendip* (an old name for Sri Lanka)]

serene, *a.* of the sky, atmosphere etc., calm, fair and clear; placid, tranquil, undisturbed; applied as a title to certain continental princes. †*n.* clearness, calmness; (*poet.*) a serene expanse of sky etc. †*v.t.* to make clear and calm. **all serene,** (*coll.*) all right. **Serene Highness,** title accorded to certain European princelings. **serenely,** *adv.* calmly, quietly, deliberately. **serenity**, †**sereneness,** *n.* [L *serēnus*]

serf, *n.* a feudal labourer attached to an estate, a villein; a slave, a drudge. **serfage**, **serfdom**, **-hood**, **-ism**, *n.* [F, from L *servus,* slave]

Serg., (*abbr.*) Sergeant.

serge, *n.* a strong and durable twilled cloth, of worsted, cotton, rayon etc. [F, from L *sērica,* fem. of *sēricus,* silken, orig. Chinese, from L and Gr. *Sēres,* the Chinese]

sergeant, (*Law*) **serjeant**, *n.* a non-commissioned military officer ranking next above corporal, teaching drill, commanding small detachments etc.; a police-officer ranking next below an inspector; a serjeant-at-law; †a bailiff, a constable. **colour-sergeant** COLOUR. **common serjeant,** a judicial officer of the Corporation of London. **Sergeant-, Serjeant-at-Arms,** *n.* an officer of the Houses of Parliament attending the Lord Chancellor or the Speaker, and carrying out arrests etc.; an officer with corresponding duties attached to other legislative bodies; one of several court and city officers with ceremonial duties. **serjeant-at-law,** *n.* formerly a member of the highest order of barristers, abolished in 1877. **sergeant-fish,** *n.* a fish with lateral stripes resembling a chevron. **sergeant-major,** *n.* the chief sergeant of a regiment, of a squadron of cavalry or of a battery of artillery. †**sergeantry,** †**-jeantry,** †**sergeanty,** †**-jeanty,** *n.* a form of feudal tenure. **grand sergeantry,** a form of tenure by special honorary service to the king. **petit, petty sergeantry,** a tenure by a rent or the rendering of some token etc. **sergeantship,** †**sergeancy, serjeancy,** *n.* [OF *sergant, serjant* (F *sergent*), late L *serviens -entem,* orig. pres.p. of *servīre,* to SERVE]

Sergel, *n.* **Johan Tobias** (1740–1814), Swedish neoclassical sculptor, active mainly in Stockholm. His portraits include *Gustaf III* (Royal Palace, Stockholm) and he made terracotta figures such as *Mars and Venus* (Nationalmuseum, Stockholm).

sergette, *n.* a thin serge. [F]

Sergius, St, *n.* **of Radonezh** (1314–92), patron saint of Russia, who founded the Eastern Orthodox monastery of the Blessed Trinity near Moscow in 1334.

Sergt., (*abbr.*) Sergeant.

serial, *a.* pertaining to, consisting of or having the nature of a series; of a novel, published in instalments in a periodical; occurring as part of a series of a set of repeated occurrences as in *serial murder*; pertaining to the computer processing of tasks one after another; of music, based on a fixed, arbitrary series of notes, not on a traditional scale. *n.* a serial story; a serial publication, a periodical. **serial number,** *n.* a number stamped on an item which identifies it in a large series of identical items. **serialism,** *n.* (*Mus.*). **serialist,** *n.* **seriality,** *n.* **serialize, -ise,** *v.t.* to publish (a novel) in instalments. **serially,** *adv.* **seriate, -ated,** *a.* arranged in a series or regular sequence. *v.t.* to arrange thus. **seriately,** *adv.* **seriatim,** *adv.* in regular order; one point etc. after the other. **seriation,** *n.*

Seric, *a.* (*poet.*) Chinese. [L *sēricus*]

sericate, -cated, sericeous, *a.* pertaining to or consisting of silk; silky, downy, soft and lustrous. [late L *sericeus,* silken, L *sericum,* silk, as prec.]

sericin, *n.* a gelatinous substance contained in silk.

sericite, *n.* (*Min.*) a silky form of muscovite. *a.* sericitic. **sericitic,** *a.*

sericterium, *n.* (*pl.* **-teria**) the silk-spinning gland in silkworms.

sericulture, *n.* the breeding of silkworms and the production of raw silk. **sericultural,** *a.* **sericulturist,** *n.*

seriema, *n.* a long-legged Brazilian and Paraguayan bird, the crested screamer. [Tupí-Guaraní]

series, *n.* (*pl.* **series**), a number, set or continued succession of things similar to each other or each bearing a definite relation to that preceding it; a sequence, a row, a set; a set of volumes, parts, articles, periodicals etc., consecutively numbered or dated or issued in the same format under one general title; (*Math.*) a number of terms, the successive pairs of which are related to each other according to a common law or mode of derivation, a progression; the connection of two or more electric circuits so that the same current traverses all the circuits; a group of allied strata forming a subdivision of a geological system. [L, from *serere,* to join together, cp. Gr. *eirein,* to bind]

serif, *n.* (*Type*) one of the fine cross-lines at the top and bottom of letters. [etym. doubtful; perh. from Dut. and Flem. *schreef,* a line]

†**Seriform,** *a.* denoting a division of the Ugro-Finnish peoples comprising the Chinese etc. [L *sēri-,* see SERIC, -FORM]

serigraph, *n.* a silk-screen print. **serigrapher,** *n.* **serigraphic,** *a.* **serigraphy,** *n.* [L *sericum,* silk, -GRAPH]

serin, *n.* a small green finch allied to the canary, *Serinus hortulanus.* **serinette,** *n.* a bird-call or bird organ. [F, etym. doubtful]

seringa, *n.* a Brazilian rubber-tree of various species; syringa. [F, Port., from L SYRINGA]

serious, *a.* grave, sober, sedate, thoughtful, earnest, not frivolous; of great importance, momentous; in earnest, not ironical or pretended, sincere; sincerely concerned about religious matters, esp. one's own salvation; having serious consequences, dangerous; (*coll.*) in large or extensive amounts as in *serious money*; (*coll.*) high-quality. **serio-comic, -comical,** *a.* mingling the serious and the comic; serious in meaning with the appearance of comedy, or comic with a grave appearance. **serioso,** *adv.* (*Mus.*) with gravity, solemnly. **seriously,** *adv.* **seriousness,** *n.* [OF *serieux,* L *serius*]

serjeant etc. SERGEANT.

†**sermocination,** *n.* (*Rhet.*) a form of prosopopoeia in which the speaker holds a dialogue with him- or herself asking and answering questions; †a conversation, discourse. [L *sermōcinātio,* from *sermōcinārī,* from *sermo,* SERMON]

sermon, *n.* a discourse founded on a text of Scripture delivered in church in exposition of doctrine or instruction in religion or morality; a similar discourse delivered elsewhere; a moral reflection; a serious exhortation or reproof. *v.t.* to deliver a sermon to; to lecture. †**sermoner,** *n.* **sermonet, sermonette,** *n.* **sermonic,** *a.* **sermonize, -ise,** *v.i., v.t.* **sermonizer, -iser,** *n.* **sermonology,** *n.* [OF, from L *sermo -ōnem,* speech, discourse]

sero-, *comb. form.* serum.

serology, *n.* the study of blood serum, its composition and properties. **serological,** *a.* **serologist,** *n.*

seron, seroon, *n.* a bale or package (of figs, almonds etc.) made up in a hide etc. [Sp. *seron,* from *sera,* basket]

seropurulent, *a.* composed of serum and pus.

serosa, *n.* serous membrane. [L, fem. of *serosus,* from SERUM]

sero-sanguinolent, *a.* composed of serum and blood.

serosity SEROUS.

Serota, *n.* **Nicholas Andrew** (1946–), British art-gallery director. He made his reputation as director of the Whitechapel Art Gallery from 1976 to 1977, when he became director of the Tate Gallery, London.

serotherapy, serum therapy.

sērotine, *n.* a small reddish bat, *Vesperugo serotinus,* flying in the evening. [F *sérotine,* L *sērōtinus,* from *sērōm,* adv., *sērus,* late]

serotinous, *a.* (*Bot.*) appearing late in the season. [from L, as prec.]

serotonin, *n.* a compound found in many body tissues which acts as a vasoconstrictor.

serous, *a.* pertaining to or resembling serum; thin, watery; like whey. **serous membrane,** *n.* a thin, transparent membrane lining certain large body cavities, and secreting a thin fluid which allows movement of the organs in the cavities. **serosity,** *n.*

Serpens, *n.* constellation of the equatorial region of the sky, representing a serpent coiled around the body of Ophiuchus. It is the only constellation divided into two halves, Serpens Caput, the head (on one side of Ophiuchus), and Serpens Cauda, the tail (on the other side). Its main feature is the Eagle Nebula.

serpent, *n.* a reptile with an elongated scaly body and no limbs, a snake; a treacherous, insinuating person; an old-fashioned wind-instrument of serpentine form; the Devil. **Pharaoh's serpent** PHARAOH. **sea-serpent** SEA. **serpent-charmer,** *n.* a snake-charmer. **serpent-charming,** *n.* **serpent-eater,** *n.* the secretary-bird. **serpent-grass,** *n.* the bistort. **serpent-lizard,** *n.* the seps. **serpent's-tongue,** *n.* the adder's tongue. **serpentaria, serpentary,** *n.* the Virginian snake-root, *Aeristolochia serpentaria,* the root of which is used for medicinal purposes. **serpentiform, serpent-like,** *a.* serpentine. **serpentine,** *a.* pertaining to, resembling or having the qualities of a serpent; coiling, winding, twisting, sinuous; subtle, wily, treacherous. *n.* a massive or fibrous rock consisting of hydrated silicate of magnesia richly coloured and variegated and susceptible of a high polish, used for making various ornamental articles. *v.i.* to wind in and out like a serpent; to meander. **serpentine-verse,** *n.* a verse beginning and ending with the same word. **serpentinely,** *adv.* †**serpentry,** *n.* [F, from L *serpens -entem,* orig. pres.p. of *serpere,* to creep, cogn. with Gr. *herpein,* to creep, and Sansk. *sarpa-,* snake]

serpette, *n.* a hooked pruning-knife. [F]

serpigo, *n.* a skin-disease, esp. a form of herpes or spreading ring-worm. **serpiginous,** *a.* [med. L *serpīgo -piginis,* from *serpere,* to creep, cp. HERPES]

serplath, (*Sc.*) SARPLIER.

serpolet, *n.* wild thyme. **serpolet oil,** *n.* a fragrant oil obtained from *Thymus serpyllum.* [F, Prov., dim. of *serpol,* L *serpullum, serpyllum*]

Serps, (*acronym*) state earnings-related pensions scheme.

serpula, *n.* (*pl.* **lae**) a brilliantly coloured marine worm living in a contorted or spiral shell. **serpulan, serpulean, serpulid, serpulidan,** *n., a.* **serpuline,** *n., a.* **serpulite,** *n.* a fossil serpula or similar formation. **serpuloid,** *a.* [late L, small serpent]

serra[1], *n.* (*pl.* **serrae**) a saw-like organ, part or structure; a saw-fish; a Californian sea-fish. [L, saw]

serra[2], Port. form of SIERRA.

serradilla, *n.* a species of clover grown for fodder. [Port., dim. of *serredo,* SERRATE[1]]

serrate[1], *a.* notched on the edge, like a saw, serrated. [L *serrātus,* from SERRA[1]]

serrate[2], *v.t.* (*usu. in p.p.*) to cut into notches and teeth, to give a saw-like edge to. **serration, serrature,** *n.* [as prec.]

serrato-, serri-, serro-, *comb. forms.* serrated.

serricorn, *a.* (*Ent.*) having serrated antennae. *n.* a serricorn beetle.

serried, *a.* close-packed, in compact order (esp. of soldiers). **serry,** *v.t.* [F *serré,* p.p. of *serrer,* to close, from late L *serāre,* see SERAGLIO]

serriped, *a.* (*Ent.*) having serrated feet.

serrirostrate, *a.* (*Ornith.*) having a serrated bill.

serro- SERRATO-.

serromotor, *n.* a reversing-gear, with cogs etc., used in marine steam-engines.

serrulate, -lated, *a.* finely serrate; having minute notches. **serrulation,** *n.*

serry SERRIED.

Sertularia, *n.* (*pl.* **-riae**) a genus of hydroids with the individual polyps set in a series of cup-like parts. [mod. L from L *sertula,* dim. of *serta,* garland]

serum, *n.* (*pl.* **serums, sera**) the thin transparent part that separates from the blood in coagulation; a constituent of milk and other animal fluids, lymph; animal serum used as an antitoxin etc. **serum hepatitis,** *n.* an acute viral infection of the liver, marked by inflammation and jaundice, spread by contact with infected blood. **serum therapy,** *n.* the treatment or prevention of disease by injecting blood containing the appropriate antibodies. [L, whey, cp. Gr. *oros,* Sansk. *saras,* flowing]

serval, *n.* an African wild cat with long legs and a black-spotted tawny coat. [F, from Port., from late L *cervālis,* from L *cervus,* a stag]

servant, *n.* a person employed by another person or body of persons to work under direction for wages, an employee, esp. one living in the house of an employer and receiving board and lodging as part of the wages, a domestic; a devoted follower, one willing to perform the will of another. **civil servant,** an employee of the state. †**your humble servant,** now usually only in ironically courteous reference to oneself. **your obedient servant,** a formal, esp. official, mode of concluding a letter, followed by the signature. **servant-girl, maid,** *n.* a female domestic servant. **servants' hall,** *n.* the room in a large domestic establishment where servants have their meals etc. together. [OF, orig. pres.p. of *servir,* to SERVE]

serve, *v.t.* to act as servant to, to be in the employment of; to be useful to, to render service to; to be subservient or subsidiary to; to satisfy, to avail, to suffice; to supply, to perform (a purpose, function etc.); to carry out the duties of, to do the work of (an office etc.); to behave towards, to treat (well, ill etc.); to dish (up), to bring to and set on table; to distribute to those at table; to furnish, to supply (a person with); to deliver (a summons, writ etc.) in the manner prescribed by law; to throw or send (a ball etc.); of a male animal, to mate with. *v.i.* to be employed, to perform the duties of or to hold an office etc.; to perform a function, to take the place of be used as, to be a satisfactory substitute (for), to suffice, to avail; to be satisfactory, favourable or suitable; to be in subjection; to deliver the ball in certain games; to attend a celebrant at the altar. *n.* the act of or turn for serving at tennis etc. **serves you right,** (*coll.*) you've got your deserts. **to serve a mare,** of a stallion, esp. one hired for the purpose, to cover her. **to serve a rope,** (*Naut.*) to lash or whip a rope with thin cord to prevent fraying. **to serve a sentence,** to undergo the punishment prescribed. **to serve at table,** to act as waiter or waitress. **to serve one's time,** to serve one's sentence; to go through an apprenticeship; to hold an office etc. for the full period. **to serve out,** to distribute portions of food to those at table; to have one's revenge on. **to serve up,** to serve out (food). **serving-maid,** *n.* a female servant. **serving-man,** *n.* a manservant. **server,** *n.* one who serves at table; a utensil (as a tray or spoon) used to serve food; in tennis etc., one who serves; one who assists the celebrant at mass. **servery,** *n.* a counter or room from which food is served. **serving,** *n.* a portion of food, a helping. [OF *servir,* L *servīre,* from *servus,* slave]

Servetus, *n.* **Michael** (1511–53) Spanish Christian theologian and Anabaptist. He was burned alive by the church reformer Calvin in Geneva, Switzerland, for his unitarian views. As a physician, he was a pioneer in the study of the circulation of the blood.

Servian, SERB.

Service, *n.* **Robert William** (1874–1938), Canadian author, born in England. He was popular for his ballads of the Yukon in the days of the Gold Rush, for example 'The Shooting of Dan McGrew' (1907).

service[1], *n.* the act of serving; work done for an employer or for the benefit of another; a benefit or advantage conferred on someone; the state of being a servant, esp. the place or position of a domestic servant; a department of state or public work or duty, the organization performing this or the persons employed in it; willingness to work or act; use, assistance; a liturgical form for worship, an office; a performance of this; a musical setting of a liturgical office or part of it; formal legal delivery, posting up or publication (of a writ, summons etc.); a set of dishes, plates etc. required for serving a meal; that which is served at table; the act of serving the ball at tennis etc.; maintenance work undertaken by the vendor after a sale; (*pl.*) the armed forces; (*pl.*) the service area of a motorway; (*pl.*) provision of water, electricity etc. to a property. *v.t.* to repair or maintain a car etc. after sale; to meet interest on (a debt); of a male animal, to serve. **on service, in active service,** engaged in actual duty in the army, navy etc. **to see service,** to have experience, esp. as a soldier or sailor. **service area,** *n.* an area served by a broadcasting station within which efficient transmission can be guaranteed; a place beside a motorway where petrol, food etc. are available. **service-book,** *n.* a book containing the church offices, esp. the Book of Common Prayer. **service car,** *n.* (*New Zealand*) a long-distance bus. **service charge,** *n.* a percentage of a bill, charged in addition to the total to pay for service. **service dress,** *n.* (*Nav., Mil.*) uniform other than full-dress. **service engineer,** *n.* one who services and repairs (electrical) equipment. **service flat,** *n.* a flat for which an inclusive sum is charged for rent and full hotel service. **service industry,** *n.* one concerned with providing a service to its customers, rather than with manufacturing. **service-line,** *n.* (*Lawn Tennis*) one of two lines marking the limit within which the serve must fall. **serviceman,** *n.* a member of the armed forces. **service-pipe,** *n.* a pipe from the water- or gas-main to a building. **service road,** *n.* a minor road running alongside a main road and carrying local traffic only. **service station,** *n.* a roadside establishment providing petrol etc. to motorists. **servicewoman,** *n., fem.* **serviceable,** *a.* able or willing to render service; useful, benificial, advantageous; durable, fit for service; †obliging, officious. **serviceability, serviceableness,** *n.* **serviceably,** *adv.* [OF, from L *servitium,* as prec.]

service[2], *n.* the service-tree. **service-berry,** *n.* the June-berry or fruit of the shad-bush. **service-tree,** *n.* a

European tree, *Pyrus sorbus,* or *domestica,* with small pear-like fruit; the wild service-tree, *Pyrus torminalis.* [ME *serves,* pl., from OE *syrpe,* ult. from L *sorbus*]

†**servient,** *a.* subordinate; (*Law*) subject to an easement or servitude. [L *serviens -ntem,* pres.p. of *servīre,* to SERVE]

serviette, *n.* a table-napkin. [F, related to *servir,* to SERVE]

servile, *a.* of, pertaining to or befitting a slave or slaves; slavish, abject, mean, cringeing, fawning, menial, dependent; of letters such as *e* in sal*e*able or in sing*e*ing, not belonging to the original root, not itself sounded but serving to modify the pronunciation of another. **servilely,** *adv.* **servility,** †**servileness,** *n.* [OF from L *servīlis,* from *servus,* slave]

serving-maid, -man SERVE.

servitor, *n.* a male servant or attendant; (*poet.*) a follower, an adherent, a henchman; (*Oxf. Univ., Hist.*) an undergraduate partly supported out of the college funds, who waited at table on the fellows and gentlemen-commoners. [OF, from late L *servītor -tōrem,* from *servīre,* to serve]

servitude, *n.* the condition of a slave, slavery, bondage; subjection to or as to a master; (*Law*) the subjection of property to an easement for the benefit of a person other than the owner or of another estate. †**serviture,** *n.* servants collectively. [F, from L *servitūdo,* as prec.]

servo, *n., a.* (*pl.* **-vos**) (of or pertaining to) a servomechanism or servomotor. **servomechanism,** *n.* an automatic device using a small amount of power which controls the performance of a much more powerful system. **servomotor,** *n.*, a motor which powers a servomechanism. [L *servus,* servant, slave]

sesame, *n.* an E Indian annual herb of the genus *Sesamum,* with oily seeds used as food, as a laxative etc. **open sesame,** a magic formula for opening a door, mentioned in the *Arabian Nights;* a key to a mystery etc.; an easy means of entry to a profession etc. **sesamoid,** *a.* shaped like a sesame-seed, nodular. *n.* a sesamoid bone, one of several small bones developed in tendons as in the knee-cap, the sole of the foot etc. [F *sésame,* ult. from Gr. *sesamon -mē,* prob. of Oriental orig.]

sesban, *n.* a tropical plant of the bean family, one species of which yields rope-fibre. [F, from Pers. *sīsabān*]

Seseli, *n.* a genus of white-flowered umbelliferous plants comprising the meadow-saxifrage. [med. L, Gr.]

sesqui-, *comb. form.* denoting a proportion of 1½ to 1 or 3 to 2; denoting combinations of three atoms of one element with two of another. [L (*semis,* half, *-que,* and), more by one half]

sesquialter, *a.* in the proportion of 1½ to 1 or 3 to 2. *n.* a sesquialtera. **sesquialtera,** *n.* (*Mus.*) an interval with the ratio of 3 to 2, a perfect fifth; a rhythm in which three minims equal two minims preceding; a compound organ-stop. **sesquialteral, -alterate, -alterous,** *a.*

sesquicentenary, *n.* a 150th anniversary. **sesquicentennial,** *n., a.*

sesquiduple,, sesquiduplicate, *a.* denoting the ratio of 2½ to 1.

sesquipedal, *a.* measuring a foot and a half; sesquipedalian. *n.* a sesquipedalian person or thing. **sesquipedalian,** *a.* of words, many-syllabled; given to using long words. *n.* a sesquipedalian word. **sesquipedalianism, sesquipedality,** *n.*

sesquiplicate, *a.* having the ratio of a cube to a square.

sesquitertia, *n.* a ratio of 1⅓ to 1; (*Mus.*) an interval having this ratio, a perfect fourth. **sesquitertial, -tian,** *a.*

sesquitone, *n.* (*Mus.*) an interval of a tone and a half, a minor third.

†**sessa,** *int.* an exclamation prob. of encouragement. [perh. from F *cessez,* CEASE]

sessile, *a.* (*Bot., Zool.*) attached by the base, destitute of a stalk or peduncle. **sessile oak,** *n.* the durmast. **sessility,** *n.* [L *sessilis* from *sess-,* see foll.]

session, *n.* the act of sitting or being assembled; a sitting or meeting of a court, council, legislature, academic body etc. for the transaction of business; the period during which such meetings are held at short intervals; the time of such meeting; the period from the meeting of Parliament till its prorogation or dissolution; the lowest court of the Presbyterian Church, called the Kirk-Session; †the enthronement of Christ on the right hand of the Father. **Court of Session,** (*Law*) the supreme civil court of justice in Scotland. **session-clerk,** *n.* the clerk of the Kirk-Session. **sessional,** *a.* [F, from L *sessio -ōnem,* from *sedēre,* to sit, p.p. *sessus*]

sesterce, sestertius, *n.* (*pl.* **-ces, -tii**) an ancient Roman silver (afterwards bronze) coin and money of account worth 2½ asses or ¼ denarius. **sestertium,** *n.* (*pl.* **-tia**) an ancient Roman money of account equivalent to 1000 sesterces. [F *sesterce,* L *sestertius,* orig. adj. (*semis,* SEMI-, TERTIUS)]

sestet, *n.* a composition for six instruments or voices; the last six lines of a sonnet. **sestetto,** *n.* (*It.*) [It. *sestetto,* dim. of *sesto,* L *sextus,* sixth]

sestina, *n.* a form of verse consisting of six six-lined stanzas with a final triplet, each stanza having the same terminal words to the lines but in different order. [It., as prec.]

Set, *n.* in Egyptian mythology, the god of night, the desert, and of all evils. He was the murderer of OSIRIS, and is portrayed as a grotesque animal.

set[1], *v.t.* (*pres.p.* **setting,** *past, p.p.* **set**) to place, to put, to stand; to fix; to plant (usu. *out*); to bring, put, place or station in a specified or right position, posture, direction or state; to arrange or dispose for use, action, display etc.; to apply (a thing to something else); to attach, to fasten, to join; to determine, to appoint, to settle, to establish; to cause to sit; to apply (oneself, one's energies etc., to), to cause (to work etc.); to present, to offer (an example, task etc.); to stud, to make insertions in (a surface etc.); to arrange, to compose (type); to fix (the hair) in waves etc.; to adapt or fit (words etc.) to music usu. composed for the purpose; (*Naut.*) to hoist, to spread (sail). *v.i.* to become solid, hard or firm from a fluid condition, to congeal, to solidify; to take shape, to become fixed; to move, tend or incline in a definite or specified direction; of flowers or fruit, to mature, to develop; of a dog, to point; to face one's partner (in dancing); to pass below the horizon; to decline, to pass away. *a.* fixed, unyielding, immovable; determined, intent (on or upon); rigid, motionless; stationary; established, prescribed; regular, in due form. **of set purpose,** intentionally, deliberately. **to set about,** to begin; to prepare or take steps (to do etc.); to attack. **to set against,** to oppose; to balance (one thing) against another; to make (a person) unfriendly to or prejudiced against. **to set apart,** to separate, to reserve (for some special purpose). **to set aside,** to reserve; to reject; to annul, to quash. **to set at defiance,** to defy. **to set at ease,** to relieve of anxiety, fear, bashfulness etc.; to make comfortable. **to set at naught** NAUGHT. **to set back,** to turn backwards, to reverse the movement of; to hinder the progress of, to impede; (*coll.*) to cost. **to set by,** to reserve; to lay by, to save. **to set by the compass,** to observe the compass bearings of. **to set by the ears** EAR[1]. **to set down,** to put on the ground; to let (a passenger) alight from a vehicle; to put in writing, to note; to attribute; to explain (as); to snub, to rebuke. **to set eyes on** EYE[1]. **to set fire to** FIRE[1]. **to set foot,** to tread (on). **to set forth,** to show, to demonstrate, to expound, to make known; to start (on a journey etc.); †to recommend. †**to set forward,** to promote, to help; to begin going forward. **to set free,** to release. **to set in,** to begin in a steady manner; to come into fashion; of the tide, to move steadily shoreward; of the weather, to become settled. **to set in order,** to arrange, to adjust; to reform. **to set little, much by,** to value little or highly. **to set off,** to make more attractive or brilliant by contrast; to act as a foil to; to beautify, to adorn; to place over, against, as an equivalent; to start (laughing etc.); to set out; to detonate. **to set on,** to incite, to instigate, to urge (to attack); to employ (on a task); to make an attack on. **to set oneself,** to apply oneself, to undertake; to resolve. **to set (one's) hand, seal etc. to,** to signal, seal etc. (a document). **to set one's hand to,** to begin (a task). **to set on foot** FOOT. **to set out,** to mark off; to assign, to allot; to display, to expound, to state at length, to publish; to equip; to adorn, to embellish; to plant out; to lay (a stone etc.) so as to project; to start (upon a journey etc.). **to set over,** to put in authority over or in control of. **to set right,** to correct. **to set sail** SAIL. **to set store by** BY. **to set the heart, mind on** HEART. **to set the teeth,** to clench them; to be obstinate or determined. **to set the teeth on edge** EDGE. **to set to,** to apply oneself vigorously; to begin to fight. **to set to work,** to begin; to cause to begin working. **to set up,** to erect, to fix up, to post up or display; to raise, to exalt, to establish; to start a business (as); to cause to develop, to occasion; to begin to utter; (*sl.*) to arrange for (someone else) to be blamed, to frame; to compose (type); to put (copy etc.) in type. **set-fair,** *a.* of the weather, fine and settled. **setter,** *n.* one who or that which sets (as type, gems, music to words etc.); a large dog trained to point at game by standing rigid. **setter-on,** *n.* an instigator. **setter-up,** *n.* one who sets up, establishes etc. **setting,** *n.* the action of one who or that which sets; the result of this; solidification, hardening, concretion; the framing etc. in which something (as a jewel) is set; the framing, surroundings or environment of a thing, event etc.; the scenery and other stage accessories of a play; a set of eggs; the music to which words, a song etc. are fitted. **setting-board,** *n.* a board for mounting entomological specimens on. **setting-box,** *n.* a case in which these are arranged as shelves. **setting-coat,** *n.* a finishing coat of plaster. **setting-stick,** *n.* a stick used in type-setting. [OE *settan,* causal of *sittan,* to SIT (cp. Dut. *zetten,* G *setzen,* Icel. *setja*)]

set[2]**,** *n.* a number of similar, related or complementary things or persons, a collection, a group, a company, a clique; a number of things intended to be used together or required to form a whole; a collection of mathematical objects, numbers etc.; a clutch or sitting of eggs; a group of games played together, counting as a unit, esp. in lawn-tennis; the direction of a current, opinion etc., drift, tendency, trend; a predisposition to respond in a certain way to a psychological stimulus; confirmation, posture, pose, carriage; the way a dress etc. sits; permanent inclination, bend, displacement, bias; the spread or deflection of the teeth of a saw alternately to right or left; the amount of this; the act of pointing at game etc. (by a setter); a young plant for setting out, a shoot, a slip for planting; the last coat of plaster on a wall; a mine or group of mines leased together; a distance set off for excavation; a timber framing for supporting the roof; the amount of margin in type determining the distance between letters; (*Theat.*) a set scene; (*Cinema*) a built-up scene; †the act of setting (of the sun etc.). **dead set** DEAD. **to have a set on,** (*Austral.*) to intend mischief to. **set-back,** *n.* a check, an arrest; an overflow, a counter-current; a relapse. **set-down,** *n.* a rebuke, a snub, a rebuff. **set-in,** *a.* of a part of a garment, made up separately and then sewn in. **set-line,** *n.* a long fishing-line with shorter lines attached to it. **set-off,** *n.* a thing set off against another, an offset, a counterpoise, a counterclaim; a decorative contrast, an embellishment; a ledge or sloping projection between the thicker part of a wall and a receding portion above; (*Print.*) an accidental transference of ink from one printed sheet to another. **set-out,** *n.* beginning, start, outset; preparations or equipment; a display. **set-piece,** *n.* a carefully prepared and usually elaborate performance; an elaborate, formalized piece of writing, painting etc.; a carefully arranged display of fireworks or a large firework built up with scaffolding; a set scene; in sport, a formal movement to put the ball back into play. **set point,** *n.* in tennis etc., a point which, if won by one of the players, will win the set. **set scene,** *n.* (*Theat.*) a scene of more or less solid and permanent construction. **set-screw,** *n.* one which secures parts of machinery together and prevents relative movement. **set-square,** *n.* a right-angled triangular piece of wood etc. used in mechanical drawing. **set theory,** *n.* a branch of mathematics which studies the properties and relationships of sets. **set-to,** *n.* a fight, esp. with the fists; a heated argument. **set-up,** *n.* an arrangement; a situation; (*N Am., sl.*) a situation which has a predetermined outcome. [OF *sette,* var. of *secte,* SECT, in some senses blended with prec.]

seta, *n.* (*pl.* **-tae**) a bristle or bristle-like plant or animal part. **setaceous,** *a.* bristly; set with, consisting of or resembling bristles. **setaceously,** *adv.* **setiferous, setigerous, setiform, setose,,** †**setous,** *a.* [L *sēta,* bristle, -ACEOUS]

seton, *n.* a twist of silk, cotton or similar material inserted in a wound to maintain drainage and as a counter irritant, esp. in veterinary surgery. [F *séton,* ult. from L *sēta,* see SETA]

setose, †**-tous** SETA.

set-out, set-square SET[2].

sett, *n.* a small rectangular block of stone used for road paving. [var. of SET[2]]

settee[1]**,** *n.* a long seat for several persons with a back; a short sofa for two. [prob. var. of SETTLE[1]]

settee[2]**,** *n.* a sharp-prowed, single-decked Mediterranean vessel with two or three masts, and lateen sails. [F *scétie,* It. *saettia,* perh. from *saetta,* L *sagitta,* arrow]

setter, setting SET[1].

setterwort, *n.* the bear's foot or stinking hellebore, *Helleborus foetidus*. [*setter,* etym. doubtful, WORT]

settle[1]**,** *n.* a long, high-backed seat or bench for several persons. [OE *setl* (cp. Dut. *zettel,* G *Sessel*), cogn. with SIT]

settle[2]**,** *v.t.* to place firmly, to put in a permanent or fixed position, to establish; to put in order; to cause to sit down or to become fixed; to determine, to decide; to plant with inhabitants, to colonize; to settle in as colonists; to cause to sink or subside, to precipitate; to clear of dregs; to deal with, to dispose of, to finish with, to do for; to adjust and liquidate (a disputed account); to pay (an account); to secure (property, an income etc., on); to arrange, to adjust, to accommodate (a quarrel, dispute etc.). *v.i.* to sit down, to alight; to cease from movement, agitation etc.; to become motionless, fixed or permanent; to take up a permanent abode, mode of life etc.; to become established, to become a colonist (in); to subside, to sink to the bottom; to become clarified; to determine, to resolve (upon); to adjust differences, claims or accounts. **to settle down,** to become regular in one's mode of life, to become established; to begin to apply oneself (to a task etc.). **to settle for,** to accept, to be content with. **to settle in,** to make or become comfortably established. **to settle up,** to pay what is owing. **settlement,** *n.* the act of settling; the state of being settled; a subsidence; a place or region newly settled, a colony; a community or group of persons living together, esp. in order to carry out social work among the poor; (*Law*) the conveyance of property or creation of an estate to make provision for the support of a person or persons or for some other object; the property so settled. **Act of Settlement,** see separate entry. **settler,** *n.* one who settles, esp. a colonist; (*sl.*) a knock-down blow, a decisive argument etc. **settler's clock,** *n.* (*Austral.*) the kookaburra. **settler's matches,** *n.pl.* (*Austral.*) pieces of dry bark used as tinder. **settling-day,** *n.* a day for the settling-up of accounts, esp. on the Stock Exchange. **settling,** *n., a.* **settlings,** *n.pl.* sediment, lees, dregs. **settlor,** *n.* (*Law*) one who makes a settlement. [OE *setlan,* as prec., combined with *sahtlian,* to reconcile, from *saht,* Icel. *saetl,* peace]

Settlement, Act of, in Britain, a law passed in 1701 during the reign of King William III, designed to ensure a Protestant succession to the throne by excluding the Roman Catholic descendants of James II in favour of the Protestant House of Hanover. Elizabeth II still reigns under this Act.

set-to SET[2].

set-up SET[1].

setwall, *n.* valerian; †root of an E Indian plant, *Curcuma zedoaria,* used as a drug. [ME *zedewal,* A-F *zedewale,* OF *citoual,* as ZEDOARY]

Seurat, *n.* **Georges** (1859–91), French artist. He originated, with SIGNAC, the neo- impressionist technique of pointillism (painting with small dabs rather than long brushstrokes), in part inspired by 19th-century theories of colour and vision. He also departed from impressionism by evolving a more formal type of composition.

seven, *n.* the number or figure 7 or vii; the age of seven; the seventh hour after midnight or midday; (*pl.*) a rugby game or tournament played with teams of seven players; a set of seven persons or things, esp. a card with seven pips. *a.* seven in number; aged seven. **seven deadly sins,** pride, covetousness, lust, gluttony, anger, envy, sloth. **seven-league boots,** magical boots enabling the wearer to travel seven leagues at a stride. **seven wise men, sages, of Greece,** seven ancient Greeks renowned for practical wisdom, Periander of Corinth, Pittacus of Mitylene, Thales of Miletus, Solon of Athens, Bias of Priene, Chilon of Sparta and Cleobulus of Lindus. **seven wonders of the world,** the Pyramids, the Hanging Gardens of Babylon, the Temple of Diana at Ephesus, the tomb of Mausolus of Caria, the Colossus of Rhodes, the statue of Zeus by Phidias and the Pharos of Alexandria. **seven-year itch,** the supposed onset of boredom, leading to infidelity, after seven years of marriage. **seven dolours,** *n.pl.* seven sorrowful experiences in the life of the Virgin Mary. **seven-knit** SENNIT. **sevennight** SENNIGHT. **seven seas,** *n.pl.* the N and S Atlantic, N and S Pacific, Arctic, Antarctic and Indian oceans. **seven-up,** *n.* (*N Am.*) a card game, all-fours. **sevenfold,** *a., adv.* **seventh,** *n.* one of seven equal parts; (*Mus.*) the interval between a given tone and the seventh above it (inclusively) on the diatonic scale; a combination of these two. *n., a.* (the) last of seven (people, things etc.); the next after the sixth. **seventh heaven,** *n.* (*coll.*) a state of perfect bliss. **seventhly,** *adv.* [OE *seofon* (cp. Dut. *zeven,* G *sieben,* Icel. *sjö,* Dan. *syv,* L *septem,* Gr. *hepta,* Sansk. *saptan*)]

seventeen, *n.* the number or figure 17 or xvii; the age of 17. *a.* 17 in number; aged 17. **seventeenth,** *n.* one of 17 equal parts. *n., a.* (the) last of 17 (people, things etc.); the next after the 16th.

Seventh Day Adventist, a member of the Protestant Christian religious sect of the same name. It has its main following in the US, and distinctive tenets are that Saturday is the Sabbath, and that Jesus' second coming is imminent.

seventy, *n.* the number or figure 70 or lxx; the age of 70. *a.* 70 in number; aged 70. **the Seventy,** the translators of the Septuagint; the 70 evangelists mentioned in Luke x.1–24; the Jewish Sanhedrin. **seventy-eight,** *n.* (*coll.*) a gramophone record playing at 78 revolutions per minute. **seventy-four,** *n.* (*Hist.*) a warship with 74 guns. **seventies,** *n.pl.* the period of time between one's 70th and 80th birthdays; the range of temperature between 70° and 80°; the period of time between the 70th and 80th years of a century. **seventieth,** *n.* one of 70 equal parts. *n., a.* (the) last of 70 (people, things etc.); the next after the 69th. [OE *seofontig* (SEVEN, -TY)]

Seven Weeks' War, a war in 1866 between Austria and Prussia, engineered by the German chancellor Bismarck. It was nominally over the possession of SCHLESWIG-HOLSTEIN, but it was actually to confirm Prussia's superseding Austria as the leading German state. The battle of SADOWA was the culmination of von Moltke's victories.

Seven Years' War, a war from 1756–63 between Britain and Prussia on the one hand, and France, Austria, Spain, and Russia on the other. Politically, Britain gained control of many of France's colonies, including Canada. Fighting against great odds, Frederick II of Prussia was eventually successful, establishing Prussia as one of the great European powers.

sever, *v.t.* to part, to separate, to disjoin; to divide, to cleave, to sunder; to cut or break off (apart from the whole); to keep distinct or apart; to conduct or carry on independently. *v.i.* to separate, to part. **severable,** *a.* **severance,** *n.* **severance pay,** *n.* a sum of money paid to a worker as compensation for loss of employment. [OF *sevrer,* L *sēparāre,* to SEPARATE]

several, *a.* separate, distinct, individual, single, particular; not common, not shared with others, pertaining to individuals; consisting of a number, more than two but not many. *n.* a few, an indefinite number, more than two but not many; an enclosed piece of ground, pasture or field; †an individual or particular person or thing. †**severality,** *n.* **severally,** *adv.* **severalty,** *n.* (*Law*) exclusive tenure or ownership. [OF, from late L *sēparāre,* as prec.]

severance SEVER.

severe, *a.* rigorous, strict, austere, harsh, merciless; trying, hard to endure or sustain; distressing, bitter, painful; grave, serious, sedate; rigidly conforming to rule, unadorned, restrained. **severely,** *adv.* **severity,** *n.* [OF, from L *sevērus*]

Severin, *n.* **Tim** (1940–), writer, historian, and traveller who re-enacted 'classic' voyages. In 1961 he led a motorcycle team along the Marco Polo route in Asia and four years later canoed the length of the Mississippi. His Brendan Voyage (1977) followed the supposed transatlantic route taken by St Brendan in the 7th century; the Sinbad Voyage took him from Oman to China (1980–81); the Jason Voyage followed the ancient route of the Argonauts in search of the Golden Fleece (1984); the Ulysses Voyage took him from Troy to Ithaca (1985); and a journey on horseback retraced the route to the Middle East taken by the Crusaders (1987–88).

Severn, *n.* river of Wales and England, rising on the NE side of Plynlimmon, N Wales, and flowing some 338 km/210 miles through Shrewsbury, Worcester, and Gloucester to the Bristol Channel. The Severn bore is a tidal wave up to 2 m/6 ft high.

Severus, *n.* **Lucius Septimus** (AD 146–211), Roman emperor. Born in N Africa, he held a command on the Danube when in AD 193 the emperor Pertinax was murdered. Proclaimed emperor by his troops, Severus proved an able administrator; he was the only African to become emperor. He died at York while campaigning in Britain against the Caledonians.

Seville, *n.* (Spanish **Sevilla**) city in Andalucia, Spain, on the Guadalquivir river, 96 km/60 miles north of Cádiz, population (1986) 668,000. Industries include machinery, spirits, porcelain, pharmaceuticals, silk, and tobacco.

Sèvres, *n.* fine porcelain produced at a factory in Sèvres, France since the early 18th century. It is characterized by the use of intensely coloured backgrounds (such as pink and royal blue), against which flowers are painted in elaborately embellished frames, often in gold.

Sèvres, Treaty of, the last of the treaties that ended World War I. Negotiated between the Allied powers and the Ottoman Empire, it was finalised in Aug. 1920 but never ratified by the Turkish government.

sew[1], *v.t.* (*p.p.* **sewn,, sewed**) to fasten together by thread worked through and through with a needle; to make, mend, close up, attach, fasten on or in etc. by sewing. *v.i.* to work with a needle and thread. **to sew up,** to mend, join etc. by sewing; (*sl.*) to exhaust, nonplus; (*sl.*) to complete satisfactorily. **sewer[1],** *n.* **sewing,** *n.* **sewing-machine,** *n.* a machine for stitching etc. driven electrically or by a treadle or a crank turned by hand. **sewing-press,** *n.* a framework used in sewing books, when binding. [OE *sīwian* (cp. Icel. *sȳja,* OHG *siwan*), cogn. with L *suere,* Gr. *kas-suein,* Sansk. *sīv*]

†**sew[2]** SUE.

sewage SEWER[1].

Sewell, *n.* **Anna** (1820–78), English author, whose only published work tells the life story of a horse, *Black Beauty* (1877). Although now read as a children's book, it was written to encourage sympathetic treatment of horses by adults.

sewer[1] SEW[1].

sewer[2], *n.* a channel, underground conduit or tunnel for carrying off the drainage and liquid refuse of a town etc. **sewer-gas,** *n.* foul air from a sewer. **sewer-rat,** *n.* the common brown rat. **sewage**, *n.* the waste matter carried off through the sewers. *v.t.* to manure with sewage. **sewage-farm,** *n.* a place where sewage is treated for use as manure. **sewage-works,** *n.sing.* a place where sewage is treated before being discharged (into the sea etc.). **sewerage**, *n.* the system of draining by means of sewers; sewers, drains etc. collectively; †sewage. [OF *seuwiere seweria,* sluice (EX-, L *aqua,* water), cp. med. L *exaquātōrium*]

†**sewer**[3], *n.* an officer who arranged the dishes at a feast, placed the guests etc. [OF *asseour, from asseoir,* L *assidēre,* (AS-, *sedēre,* to sit)]

sewin, *n.* a variety of sea or salmon-trout. [etym. doubtful]

sewing-machine, -press SEW[1].

sewn SEW[1].

sex, *n.* the sum total of the physiological, anatomical and functional characteristics which distinguish male and female; the quality of being male or female; (*collect.*) male or females, men or women; sexual intercourse. *v.t.* to determine the sex of. **the sex,** (*dated, coll.*) women. **sex appeal,** *n.* what makes a person attractive to the opposite sex. **sex chromosome**, *n.* the chromosome responsible for the initial determination of sex. **sex determination,** *n.* the factors which decide whether a particular organism will evolve into a male or a female. **sex-limited,** *a.* restricted to one sex. **sex-linked,** *a.* of a gene, located on a sex chromosome; of a character, determined by a sex-linked gene. **sex object,** *n.* a person perceived solely as an object of sexual desires and fantasies. **sexed,** *a.* **sexism,** *n.* discrimination (esp. against women) on the grounds of sex. **sexist,** *n.* **sexless,** *a.* **sexlessness,** *n.* **sexology**, *n.* the science dealing with the sexes and their relationships. **sexological**, *a.* **sexologist,** *n.* **sexy,** *a.* sexually stimulating; sexually aroused. **sexily,** *adv.* **sexiness,** *n.* [F *sexe,* L *sexus -ūs,* perh. cogn. with *secāre,* to cut]

sex(a)-, *comb. form.* containing six; sixfold. [L *sex,* six]

sexagenarian, *a.* 60 years of age or between 59 and 70. *n.* a sexagenarian person. **sexagenary**, *a.* of or pertaining to 60; sexagesimal; sexagenarian. *n.* a sexagenarian; a thing composed of 60 parts. [L *sexāgēnārius,* from *sexāgēnī,* 60 each, from *sexāginta,* 60]

Sexagesima, Sexagesima Sunday, *n.* the second Sunday before Lent, so called as being about the 60th day before Easter. **sexagesimal,** *a.* 60th; pertaining to 60; proceeding by or based on 60s. **sexagesimally,** *adv.* [L, fem. of *sexagēsimus,* 60th, from *sexāginta,* 60]

sexangle, *n.* a hexagon. **sexangled, sexangular**, *a.* **sexangularly,** *adv.*

sexcentenary, *a.* pertaining to or consisting of 600 years. *n.* a 600th anniversary.

sexdigitate, *a.* having six fingers or toes on a limb.

sexennial, *a.* occurring once every six years; lasting six years. **sexennially,** *adv.*

sexfid, sexifid, *a.* six-cleft.

sexfoil, *n.* a six-leaved flower, a six-lobed leaf; an ornament of six-lobed foliation.

sexillion, SEXTILLION.

sexism SEX.

sexisyllable, *n.* a word of six syllables. **sexisyllabic,** *a.*

sexivalent, sexvalent, *a.* having a valency or combining power of six.

sexless, sexology etc. SEX.

sexlocular, *a.* (*Bot.*) having six cells.

sexpartite, *a.* divided into six.

Sex Pistols, the, UK punk rock group (1975–78) who became notorious under the guidance of their manager, Malcolm McLaren. They released one album, *Never Mind the Bollocks, Here Come the Sex Pistols* (1977). Members included Johnny Rotten (real name John Lydon, 1956–) and Sid Vicious (John Ritchie, 1957–79).

sexploitation, *n.* the portrayal or manipulation of sex for financial profit in films, magazines etc. [*sex, exploitation*]

sext, *n.* in the Roman Catholic Church, the office for the sixth hour or noon. [F *sexte,* med. L *sexta,* orig. fem. of L *sextus,* sixth]

sextain, *n.* a stanza of six lines, a sestina. [L *sextus,* sixth, after QUATRAIN]

sextant, *n.* the sixth part of a circle; an instrument used in navigation and surveying for measuring angular distances or altitudes. **sextantal**, *a.* [L *sextans -ntem,* from *sextus,* sixth]

sextet, SESTET.

sextic, *a.* (*Math.*) of the sixth degree or order. *n.* a sextic quantic, equation or curve.

sextile, *a.* (*Astrol.*) denoting the aspect of two planets when distant from each other 60°. *n.* a sextile aspect. [L *sextilis,* from *sextus,* sixth]

sextillion, *n.* the sixth power of a million, represented by 1 followed by 36 ciphers; (*N Am., Fr.*) the seventh power of a thousand, 1 followed by 21 ciphers. [L *sex,* SIX, after MILLION]

sexto, *n.* (*pl.* **-tos**) a book formed by folding sheets into six leaves each. **sextodecimo**, *n.* a book formed by folding sheets into 16 leaves each; a sheet of paper folded thus.

Sexton, *n.* **Anne** (1928–74), US poet. She studied with Robert Lowell and wrote similarly confessional poetry, as in *All My Pretty Ones* (1962). She committed suicide, and her *Complete Poems* appeared posthumously in 1981.

sexton, *n.* an officer having the care of a church, its vessels, vestments etc., and frequently acting as parish-clerk and a grave-digger. **sexton-beetle,** *n.* a beetle that buries carrion to serve as a nidus for its eggs. **sextonship,** *n.* [ME *sekesteyn,* corr. of SACRISTAN]

sextuple, *a.* six times as many. *n.* a sextuple amount. *v.t., v.i.* to multiply by six. **sextuplet**, *n.* one of six born at one birth; (*Mus.*) a group of six notes played in the time of four. [from L *sextus,* after QUADRUPLE etc.]

sexual, *a.* of, pertaining to or based on sex or the sexes or on the distinction of sexes; pertaining to generation or copulation, venereal. **sexual intercourse,** *n.* a sexual act in which the male's erect penis is inserted into the female's vagina. **sexual harassment,** *n.* persistent unwelcome sexual advances, esp. towards a woman in her place of work. **sexual selection,** *n.* a method of selection based on the struggle for mating which, according to one school of thought, accounts for the origin of secondary sexual characteristics. **sexualist,** *n.* **sexuality**, *n.* **sexually,** *adv.* **sexualize, -ise,** *v.t.* **sexualization, -isation,** *n.* **sexually transmitted disease,** a venereal disease. [late L *sexuālis,* from *sexus,* SEX]

sexy SEX.

Seychelles, *n. pl.* country in the Indian ocean, off E Africa, N of Madagascar. **area** 453 sq km/175 sq miles. **capital** Victoria on Mahé. **physical** comprises two distinct island groups, one concentrated, the other widely scattered, totalling over 100 islands and islets. **population** (1989) 70,000; annual growth rate 0.6%. **exports** copra, cinnamon; tourism is important. **language** creole, spoken by 95%, English and French (all official). **religion** Christian (Roman Catholic 90%).

Seyfert galaxy, *n.* a type of galaxy whose small, bright centre is caused by hot gas moving at high speed around a massive central object, possibly a black hole. Almost all Seyferts are spiral galaxies. They seem to be closely related to quasars, but about 100 times fainter. They are named after discoverer Carl Seyfert (1911–60).

Seymour[1], *n.* **Jane** (*c.* 1509–37), third wife of Henry VIII, whom she married in 1536. She died soon after the birth of her son Edward VI.

Seymour[2], *n.* **Lynn** (1939–), Canadian born ballerina of rare dramatic quality. She was principal dancer of the Royal Ballet from 1959 and artistic director of the Munich State Opera Ballet from 1978–80.

sezession, *n.* various groups of German and Austrian artists in the 1890s who 'seceded' from official academic art institutions in order to found modern schools of painting. The first was in Munich in 1892; the next, linked with the paintings of Gustav KLIMT, was the Vienna sezession of 1897; the Berlin sezession followed in 1899.

SF, (*abbr.*) San Francisco; science fiction; Society of Friends.

sf., (*abbr.*) sforzando; sforzato.

SFA, (*abbr.*) Scottish Football Association; (*sl.*) Sweet Fanny Adams.

Sforza, *n.* Italian family which ruled the duchy of Milan in 1450–99 and 1522–35. Their court was a centre of Renaissance culture, and Ludovico Sforza (1451–1508) was patron of the artist LEONARDO DA VINCI.

sforzando, sforzato, *adv.* (*Mus.*) emphatically, with sudden vigour. [It., from *sforzare,* to FORCE]

SG, (*abbr.*) Solicitor General.

sg, (*abbr.*) specific gravity.

sgraffito, GRAFFITO.

sgt, (*abbr.*) sergeant.

sh, *int.* calling for silence.

Shaanxi, *n.* (formerly **Shensi**) province of NW China. **area** 195,800 sq km/75,579 sq miles. **capital** Xian. **physical** mountains; Huang He valley, one of the earliest settled areas of China. **population** (1986) 30,430,000. **products** iron, steel, mining, textiles, fruit, tea, rice, wheat.

shabby, *a.* ragged, threadbare; in ragged or threadbare clothes; mean, paltry, despicable. **shabbily,** *adv.* **shabbiness,** *n.* **shabbyish,** *a.* [OE *scæb sceab,* SCAB, -Y]

shabrack, *n.* the housing of a cavalry saddle. [G *schabracke,* Turk. *chāprāq*]

shack¹, *n.* (*dial.*) an idler, a vagabond; a worthless horse. *v.i.* to idle, to loaf; (*N Am.*) of a bear, to hibernate. [etym. doubtful]

shack², *n.* a rude cabin or shanty, esp. one built of logs. **to shack up (with),** (*sl.*) to live (with), usu. having a sexual relationship. [etym. doubtful]

shack³, *n.* (*now dial.*) grain fallen from the ear and used after harvest for feeding pigs etc.; the right to send pigs etc. to feed on this, or right of winter pasturage on another's land. *v.t.* to turn (pigs etc.) out into stubble; of animals, to feed on (stubble). [var. of SHAKE]

shackle, *n.* a fetter, gyve or handcuff; the bow of a padlock; a coupling link; an insulating spool or support for a telegraph wire; (*pl.*) fetters, restraints, impediments. *v.t.* to chain, to fetter; to restrain, to impede, to hamper; (*N Am.*) to couple (railway carriages). **shackle-bolt,** *n.* a bolt passing through holes in a shackle to fasten it; a bolt with a shackle at the end. **shackle-bone,** *n.* (*Sc.*) the wrist. **shackle-joint,** *n.* a joint composed of ring-like parts in some fishes. [OE *sceacul* rel. to SHAKE]

Shackleton, *n.* **Ernest** (1874–1922), Irish Antarctic explorer. In 1907–09, he commanded an expedition that reached 88° 23′6 S latitude, located the magnetic South Pole, and climbed Mount EREBUS.

shad, *n.* a name for several anadromous deep-bodied food-fish, esp. the American or white shad. **shadbush,** *n.* the June-berry, *Amelanchier canadensis.* [OE *sceadda* (cp. G and Gael. *sgaden*), etym. doubtful]

shaddock, *n.* the large orange-like fruit of a Malaysian and Polynesian tree, *Citrus decumana.* [Capt. *Shaddock,* who took it to the W Indies in the 17th cent.]

shade, *n.* obscurity or partial darkness caused by the interception of the rays of light; gloom, darkness; a place sheltered from the sun, a secluded retreat; the dark or darker part of a picture; a screen for protecting from or moderating light, esp. a covering for a lamp, or a shield worn over the eyes; (*N Am.*) a window blind; a glass cover for protecting an object; a colour; gradation of colour, esp. with regard to its depth or its luminosity; a scarcely perceptible degree, a small amount; something unsubstantial, unreal or delusive; the soul after its separation from the body, a spectre; (*pl.*) the abode of spirits, Hades; (*pl.*) wine and spirit or beer vaults; (*pl. coll.*) sunglasses. *v.t.* to shelter or screen from light or heat; to cover, to obscure, to darken (an object in a picture) so as to show gradations of colour or effects of light and shade; to graduate as to light and shade or colour; to cause to pass or blend with another colour. *v.i.* to pass off by degrees or blend (with another colour). **shadeless,** *a.* †**shader,** *n.* **shading,** *n.* **shady,** *a.* sheltered from the light and heat of the sun; casting shade; shunning the light, disreputable, of equivocal honesty; (*coll.*) declining, later. **shadily,** *adv.* **shadiness,** *n.* [OE *scæd, sceadu* (cp. Dut. *schaduw,* G *Schatten,* Ir. and Gael. *sgath,* also Gr. *skotos*), cogn. with SKY]

shadoof, *n.* a water-raising contrivance consisting of a long pole with bucket and counterpoise, used on the Nile etc. [Arab. *shādūf*]

shadow, *n.* shade; a patch of shade; the dark figure of a body projected on the ground etc. by the interception of light; an inseparable companion; one who follows another closely and unobtrusively; darkness, obscurity, privacy; protection, shelter; the dark part of a picture, room etc.; a reflected image; an imperfect or faint representation, an adumbration, a type; a dim foreshadowing, a premonition; a faint trace, the slightest degree; something unsubstantial or unreal; a phantom, a ghost. *v.t.* to darken, to cloud; to set (forth) dimly or in outline, to adumbrate, to typify; to watch secretly, to spy upon, to dog. **shadow boxing,** *n.* boxing against an imaginary opponent when training. **shadow cabinet,** *n.* the chief members of the British parliamentary opposition, each of whom is responsible for commenting on the policies and performance of a government ministry. **shadow mark,** *n.* (*Archaeol.*) the trace of an ancient site as observed from the air. **shadowless,** *a.* **shadowy,** *a.* **shadowiness,** *n.* [OE *sceadu,* see SHADE]

shady SHADE.

SHAEF, (*abbr.*) Supreme Headquarters Allied Expeditionary Force. World War II military centre established on 15 Feb. 1944 in London, where final plans for the Allied invasion of Europe (under US general Eisenhower) were worked out.

Shaffer, *n.* **Peter** (1926–), English playwright. His plays include *Five Finger Exercise* (1958), the historical epic *The Royal Hunt of the Sun* (1964), *Equus* (1973), and *Amadeus* (1979) about the composer Mozart.

shaft, *n.* the slender stem or stock of a spear, arrow etc.; an arrow; anything more or less resembling this, as a ray (of light), a bolt or dart (of lightning, ridicule etc.); a column between the base and the capital; a small column in a cluster or in a window-joint; a stem, a stalk, a trunk; the scape of a feather; any long, straight and more or less slender part; a penis; the handle of a tool; one of the bars between a pair of which a horse is harnessed; a large axle, arbor or long cylindrical bar, esp. rotating and transferring motion; a well-like excavation, usu. vertical, giving access to a mine; the tunnel of a blast-furnace; an upward vent to a mine, tunnel etc. *v.t.* (*N Am., sl.*) to cheat, treat unfairly; (*sl.*) to have sexual intercourse with. **shaft-horse,** *n.* a horse harnessed between the shafts. **shafted,** *a.* **shafting,** *n.* a system of shafts for the transmission of power. **shaftless,** *a.* †**shaftment¹,** *n.* the feathered part of an arrow. **shaftsman,** *n.* one employed in sinking shafts. **shafty,** *a.* of wool, long, compact and strong in the staple. [OE *sceaft,* spear-shaft, orig. shaved, from *scafan,* to SHAVE (cp. Dut. *schacht,* G *Schaft,* Icel. *skapt*)]

Shaftesbury¹, *n.* **Anthony Ashley Cooper, 1st Earl of Shaftesbury** (1621–83), English politician, a supporter of the Restoration of the monarchy. He became lord chancellor in 1672, but went into opposition in 1673 and began to organize the Whig Party. He headed the demand for the exclusion of the future James II from the succession, secured the passing of the HABEAS CORPUS Act in 1679 and, when accused of treason in 1681, fled to Holland.

Shaftesbury[2], *n.* **Anthony Ashley Cooper, 7th Earl of Shaftesbury** (1801–85), British Tory politician. He strongly supported the Ten Hours Act of 1847 and other factory legislation, including the 1842 act forbidding the employment of women and children underground in mines. He was also associated with the movement to provide free education for the poor.

shaftment[1] SHAFT.

shaftment[2], *n.* a measure of about 6 in. (15 cm); the distance from the tip of the thumb to the further side of the extended hand. [OE *sceaftmund* (SHAFT, *mund,* hand)]

shag, *n.* a rough coat of hair, a bushy mass; cloth having a long coarse nap; strong tobacco cut into fine shreds; the crested cormorant, *Phalacrocorax aristotelis, a.* shaggy, *v.t., v.i.* (*past, p.p.* **shagged**) (*taboo*) to have sexual intercourse with. †**shag-eared,** *a.* having shaggy ears. †**shag-haired,** *a.* †**shagged, shaggy,** *a.* rough-haired, hairy, hirsute; coarse, tangled, unkempt; overgrown with trees or coarse vegetation, scrubby, rugged. **shaggy dog story,** a long, inconsequential story, funny but lacking a punch-line. **shaggily,** *adv.* **shagginess,** *n.* [OE *sceacga* (cp. Icel. *skegg,* beard, *skaga,* to jut)]

shagreen, *n.* a kind of leather with a granular surface which is prepared without tanning from the skins of horses, asses, camels, sharks and seals, usu. dyed green; the skins of various sharks, rays etc., covered with hard papillae, used for polishing etc. [var. of CHAGRIN]

shagroon, *n.* (*New Zealand*) an original settler, esp. at Canterbury; one of non-European origin. [etym. doubtful]

shah, *n.* a sovereign of Iran. [Pers.]

shaheen, *n.* an Indian falcon. [from prec.]

Shah Jehan *n.* (1592–1666), Mughal emperor of India from 1627, when he succeeded his father Jehangir. From 1658 he was a prisoner of his son Aurangzeb. He built the TAJ MAHAL.

Shahn, *n.* **Ben** (1898–1969), US artist, born in Lithuania, a Social Realist painter. His work included drawings and paintings on the DREYFUS case and SACCO and VANZETTI. As a mural painter he worked at the Rockefeller Center, New York (with the Mexican artist Diego Rivera), and the Federal Security Building, Washington, (1940–42).

shaitan, *n.* the devil; an evil spirit; an evil person or animal. [Arab., from Heb. SATAN]

Shaka, Chaka *n.* (1787–1828), Zulu leader who formed a Zulu empire in S Africa. He seized power from his half-brother in 1816, and embarked on a campaign to unite the Nguni (the area that today forms the South African province of Natal), initiating the period of warfare known as the MFECANE.

shake, *v.t.* (*past* **shook,**, *p.p.* **shaken**) to move forcibly or rapidly to and fro or up and down; to cause to tremble or quiver; to shock, to convulse, to agitate, to disturb; (*lit. or fig*); to brandish, to weaken the stability of, to impair, to shatter; to trill; to upset another's composure; to cause another to doubt; (*Astral., sl.*) to steal. *v.i.* to move quickly to and fro or up and down, to tremble, to totter, to shiver; to quiver, to rock; to change the pitch or power of the voice, to make trills; (*N Am.*) to shake hands. *n.* the act or an act of shaking; a jerk, a jolt, a shock, a concussion; the state of being shaken, agitation, vibration, trembling; a trill; a milk-shake; a crack in growing timber; (*N Am., Austral.*) an earthquake. **no great shakes,** (*sl.*) of no great account. **the shakes,** (*coll.*) a fit of trembling, caused by fever, withdrawal from alcohol etc. **to shake down,** to bring down (fruit etc.) by shaking; to cause (grain etc.) to settle into a compact mass; to become compact; to settle down into a comfortable or harmonious state. **to shake hands** HAND[1]. **to shake in one's shoes,** to be very frightened. **to shake off,** to get rid of by shaking, to cast off. **to shake one's head,** to move the head from side to side in token of refusal, dissent, disapproval etc. **to shake out,** to open out or empty by shaking; (*coll.*) to shake up. **to shake up,** to mix, disturb etc. by shaking; (*coll.*) to reorganize drastically. **shake-down,** *n.* a makeshift bed. **shake-out,** *n.* **shake-up,** *n.* **shakeable,** *a.* **shaker,** *n.* a container for mixing or sprinkling by shaking; **Shaker,** see separate entry. **shaky,** *a.* liable to shake, unsteady, rickety, unstable, tottering; of doubtful integrity, solvency, ability etc. **shakily,** *adv.* **shakiness,** *n.* [OE *sceacan,* cp. Icel. and Swed. *skaka,* Dan. *skage*]

Shaker, *n.* a member of the Christian sect of the United Society of Believers in Christ's Second Appearing, so-called because of their ecstatic shakings in worship. The movement was founded by James and Jane Wardley in England about 1747, and taken to North America in 1774 by Ann Lee (1736–84). They anticipated modern spiritualist beliefs, but their doctrine of celibacy led to their virtual extinction. Shaker furniture has been admired in the 20th century for its simple and robust design.

Shakespeare, *n.* **William** (1564–1616), English dramatist and poet. Established in London by 1589 as an actor and a playwright, he was England's unrivalled dramatist until his death, and is considered the greatest English playwright. His plays, written in blank verse, can be broadly divided into lyric plays, including *Romeo and Juliet* and *Midsummer Night's Dream*; comedies, including *Comedy of Errors*, *As You Like It*, *Much Ado About Nothing*, and *Measure For Measure*; historical plays, such as *Henry VI* (in three parts), *Richard III*, and *Henry IV* (in two parts), which often showed cynical political wisdom; and tragedies, such as *Hamlet*, *Macbeth*, and *King Lear*. He also wrote numerous sonnets. **Shakespearean,** *a.* pertaining to or resembling Shakespeare or his style. *n.* a student of Shakespeare's works. **Shakespeareana,** *n.pl.* **Shakespeareanism,** *n.*

shako, *n.* (*pl.* **-kos**) a military cylindrical hat, usu. flat-topped, with a peak in front, usu. tilting forward, and decorated with a pompom, plume or tuft. [F, from Hung. *csako*]

shaky SHAKE.

shale[1], *n.* a laminated argillaceous rock resembling soft slate, often containing much bitumen. **shale oil,** *n.* oil obtained from bitumen shale. **shaly,** *a.* [G *Schale,* cogn. with obs. Eng. *shale,* shell, var. of SCALE[1]]

†**shale**[2], SHELL.

shall, *v.aux.* (*2nd sing.* **shalt**, *past, subj.* **should, shouldst, shouldest**) in the 1st pers., used to express simple futurity or a conditional statement; in the 2nd and 3rd pers., to express a command, intention, promise, permission etc., to express future or conditional obligation, duty etc., or to form a conditional protasis etc. [OE *sceal,* past of *sculan,* to owe (cp. Dut. *zal,* G *soll,* Icel. *skal*), cogn. with *scyld,* G *Schuld,* and prob. L *scelus,* guilt]

shalloon, *n.* a light worsted fabric used for linings etc. [F *Châlons*-sur-Marne, in NE France]

shallop, *n.* a light open boat. [F *chaloupe,* Dut. *sloep,* sloop]

shallot, *n.* a plant, *Allium ascalonicum,* allied to garlic with similar but milder bulbs. [OF *eschalote* (F *échalote*), corr. of *escalogne,* L *escalōnia,* fem. a. from *Ascalon* in Palestine]

shallow, *a.* not having much depth; superficial, trivial, silly. *n.* a shallow place, a shoal. *v.i.* to become shallow or shallower. *v.t.* to make shallow. **shallow-brained,** †**-pated,** *a.* weakminded. **shallow-hearted,** *a.* incapable of deep or sincere feeling. **shallowly,** *adv.* **shallowness,** *n.* [ME *schalowe,* perh. rel. to OE *sceald* (cp. Icel. *skālgr,* wry, also SHOAL[1], SHELVE[2])]

†**shalm,** †**shalmic** SHAWM.

Shalmaneser, *n.* five Assyrian kings including:

Shalmaneser III, *n.* king of Assyria (859–824 BC), who pursued an aggressive policy, and brought Babylon and Israel under the domination of Assyria.

shalt, *2nd pers. sing.* SHALL.

shaly SHALE[1].

sham, *v.t.* (*past, p.p.* **shammed**) to feign, to make a pretence of; †to cheat, to trick. *v.i.* to feign, to pretend. *n.* an imposture, a false pretence, a fraud, one who or that which pretends to be someone or something else. *a.* feigned, pretended, counterfeit. **to sham Abraham** ABRAHAMIC. **sham fight,** *n.* a mimic battle for training or showing off troops. **shammer,** *n.* [var. of SHAME]

shamanism, *n.* a form of religion based on the belief in good and evil spirits which can be influenced by shamans, prevailing among Siberian and N American tribes. **shaman,** *n.* a priest, exorcist or medicine man among shamanists. **shamanist,** *n., a.* **shamanistic,** *a.* [Rus., from Tungus (Siberian language)]

shamateur, *n.* a person classed as an amateur in sport, but who accepts payment. [*sham, am*ateur]

shamble, *v.i.* to walk in an awkward, shuffling or unsteady manner. *n.* a shambling walk or gait. **shambling,** *a.* [etym. doubtful, cp. SCAMBLE and SCAMPER]

shambles, *n.sing. or pl.* a butcher's slaughter-house; a place of carnage or execution; utter confusion; (*now dial.*) butchers' stalls, a meat-market. [pl. of obs. *shamble,* OE *scamel,* L *scamellum,* stool, dim. of *scamnum,* bench, step, cogn. with Gr. *skēptein,* to prop]

shambolic, *a.* (*coll.*) chaotic, utterly confused. [SHAMBLES]

shame, *n.* a painful feeling due to consciousness of guilt, degradation, humiliation etc.; the instinct to avoid this, the restraining sense of pride, modesty, decency, decorum; a state of disgrace, discredit or ignominy; anything that brings reproach, a disgrace; (*coll.*) an unfairness. *v.t.* to make ashamed; to bring shame on, to cause to blush or feel disgraced; to disgrace; †to mock at. †*v.i.* to be ashamed. **shame!** *int.* that is unfair! disgraceful! **shame on you,** you should be ashamed. **to put to shame,** to humiliate by exhibiting better qualities. **†shame-proof,** *a.* insensible to shame. **shameful,** *a.* **shamefully,** *adv.* **shamefulness,** *n.* **shameless,** *a.* immodest. **shamelessly,** *adv.* **shamelessness,** *n.* **†shamer,** *n.* [OE *sceamu, scamu* (cp. G *Scham,* Dan. *skam,* Icel. *skömm*) whence *sceamian scamian,* to shame]

shamefaced, †shamefast, *a.* bashful, shy, easily confused or abashed, modest, retiring. **shamefacedly,** *adv.* **shamefacedness, †shamefastness,** *n.* [OE *scamfæst* (SHAME, FAST¹)]

Shamir, *n.* **Yitzhak** (1915–), Israeli politician, born in Poland; foreign minister under Menachem Begin (1980–83), prime minister (1983–84), and again foreign minister in the PERES unity government from 1984. In Oct. 1986, he and Peres exchanged positions, Shamir becoming prime minister and Peres taking over as foreign minister. He was re-elected in 1989. Shamir was a leader of the STERN GANG guerrillas during the British mandate rule of Palestine.

shammer SHAM.

shammy,, shamoy, coll. spelling of CHAMOIS

shampoo, *v.t.* to squeeze, rub and massage (the body of) after a hot bath; to lather, wash and rub (the hair of); to wash (carpets, upholstery) with shampoo. *n.* the act of shampooing; a liquid soap or detergent used for this. [Hind. *chāmpnā,* to press, to shampoo]

shamrock, *n.* a species of trefoil forming the national emblem of Ireland. [Ir. *seamrōg*]

Shan, *n.* one of a Taic people living on the borders of N Siam, E Burma and Yunnan. *a.* pertaining to the Shans. [native name]

†shan, †shand, *n.* (*Sc.*) base coin. *a.* mean, shabby, worthless. [etym. doubtful]

Shandong, *n.* (formerly **Shantung**), province of NE China. **area** 153,300 sq km/59,174 sq miles. **capital** Jinan. **towns** ports Yantai, Weihai, Qingdao, Shigiusuo. **population** (1986) 77,760,000. **products** cereals, cotton, wild silk, varied minerals.

shandry, *n.* a light cart or trap. **shandrydan,** *n.* a kind of hooded chaise; a ramshackle conveyance. [etym. doubtful]

shandy, shandygaff, *n.* a mixture of beer and ginger-beer or lemonade. [etym. doubtful]

Shanghai, *n.* port on the Huang-pu and Wusong rivers, Jiangsu province, China, 24 km/15 miles from the Chang Jiang estuary; population (1986) 6,980,000, the largest city in China. The municipality of Shanghai has an area of 5800 sq km/2239 sq miles and a population of 12,320,000. Industries include textiles, paper, chemicals, steel, agricultural machinery, precision instruments, shipbuilding, flour and vegetable-oil milling, and oil refining. It handles about 50% of China's imports and exports.

shanghai, *v.t.* to drug and ship as a sailor while stupefied; to kidnap. *n.* (*Austral.*) a catapult. [town in China]

shank, *n.* the leg, esp. the part from the knee to the ankle; the shin-bone; a bird's tarsus; the shaft of a column; the straight part of an instrument, tool etc. connecting the acting part with the handle. *v.i.* to be affected or fall (off) with decay in the footstalks. **Shanks's mare, pony,** one's legs for walking as opp. to riding etc. **shank-painter,** *n.* a painter for fastening an anchor to the side of a vessel. **shanked,** *a.* having a shank (*esp. in comb.,* as *short-shanked*). [OE *sceanca scanca* (cp. Dut. *schonk,* Dan. and Swed. *skank*), perh. rel. to SHAKE]

Shankar, *n.* **Ravi** (1920–), Indian composer and musician. A virtuoso of the sitar, he has composed film music and founded music schools in Bombay and Los Angeles.

Shankara, *n.* (799–833), Hindu philosopher who wrote commentaries on some of the major Hindu scriptures, as well as hymns and essays on religious ideas. Shankara was responsible for the final form of the Advaita Vedanta school of Hindu philosophy, which teaches that Brahman, the supreme being, is all that exists in the universe; everything else is illusion. Shankara was fiercely opposed to Buddhism and may have influenced its decline in India.

shanker, CHANCRE.

Shannon¹, *n.* longest river in Ireland, rising in County Cavan and flowing 260 km/161 miles through Loughs Allen and Ree and past Athlone, to reach the Atlantic through a wide estuary below Limerick. It is also the major source of electric power in the republic, with hydroelectric installations at and above Ardnacrusha, 5 km/3 miles N of Limerick.

Shannon², *n.* **Claude Elwood** (1916–), US mathematician, whose paper *The Mathematical Theory of Communication* (1948) marks the beginning of the science of p information theory. He argued that information and entropy are analogous, and obtained a quantitive measure of the amount of information in a given message.

shanny, *n.* the smooth blenny. [etym. unknown]

shan't, contr. *shall not.*

shantung, *n.* a plain fabric woven in coarse silk yarns. [province in China]

shanty¹, *n.* a rude hut or cabin; a hastily built or rickety building; (*Austral.*) a low public-house, a grog-shop. **shanty-town,** *n.* a poor part of a town consisting mainly of shanties. [Can.F *chantier,* lumber camp, hut]

shanty², *n.* a song sung by sailors, esp. one with a strong rhythm sung while working. [F *chanter,* to sing, see CHANT]

Shanxi, *n.* (formerly **Shansi**), province of NE China, **area** 157,100 sq km/60,641 sq miles. **capital** Taiyuan. **population** (1986) 26,550,000. **products** coal, iron, fruit.

SHAPE, (*acronym*) *S*upreme *H*eadquarters *A*llied *P*owers *E*urope.

shape, *v.t.* (*p.p.* **shaped, †shapen**) to form, to create, to construct; to make into a particular form, mould, to fashion; to adapt, to fit, to adjust, to make conform (to); to regulate, to direct; to conceive, to conjure up. *v.i.* to take shape, to come into shape, to develop (well, ill etc.); to become fit or adapted (to). *n.* the outward form, figure, configuration or contour; outward aspect, form, guise, appearance; concrete form, embodiment, realization; definite, fit or orderly form or condition; kind, sort; an image, an appearance, an apparition; a pattern, a mould, a confection shaped in a mould. **to shape up,** to develop a shape; to develop satisfactorily. **shap(e)able,** *a.* **shaped,** *a.* having a shape (*usu. in comb.* as *square-shaped*). **shapeless,** *a.* having no regular form; lacking in symmetry; †deformed. **shapelessly,** *adv.* **shapelessness,** *n.* **shapely,** *a.* well-formed, well-proportioned; having beauty or regularity. **shapeliness,** *n.* **shaper,** *n.* [OE *scieppan* (p.p. *gescapen*) cp. G *schaffen,* to create, also -SHIP]

Shapley, *n.* **Harlow** (1885–1972), US astronomer, whose study of globular clusters showed that they were arranged in a halo around the galaxy, and that the galaxy was much larger than previously thought. He realized that the sun was not at the centre of the galaxy as then assumed, but two-thirds of the way out to the rim.

shard, sherd, *n.* a potsherd; the wing-case of a beetle; †a gap in a hedge; †a boundary. *v.t., v.i.* to break or flake off. **shard-born,** *a.* of a beetle, born in dung. †**shard-borne,** *a.* borne on wing-cases (of beetles). [OE *sceard,* cogn. with SHEAR, SHARE[1]]

share[1], *n.* a part or portion detached from a common amount or stock; a part to which one has a right or which one is obliged to contribute, a fair or just portion; a lot, an allotted part, esp. one of the equal parts into which the capital of a company is divided. *v.t.* to divide into portions, to distribute among a number, to apportion; to give away a portion of; to partake of, to have or endure with others, to participate in. *v.i.* to have a share or shares (in), to be a sharer or sharers (with), to participate. **deferred shares,** those on which a reduced or no dividend is paid until a fixed date or contingent event. **preference, preferred shares** PREFERENCE. **to go shares,** to divide equally with others. **to share out,** to divide into equal shares and distribute. **sharebroker,** *n.* a dealer in shares. **sharecropper,** *n.* (*N Am.*) a tenant farmer who pays over part of the crop as rent. **share-crop,** *v.i.* **shareholder,** *n.* one who holds a share or shares in a joint-stock company etc. **share-list,** *n.* a list of the current prices of shares. **share-out,** *n.* **sharer,** *n.* [OE *scearu,* from *sceran,* to SHEAR]

share[2], *n.* a ploughshare; a blade of a cultivator, seeder etc. **share-beam,** *n.* the part of a plough to which the share is fixed. [OE *scear,* from *sceran,* to SHEAR]

Shari'a(h), *n.* the law of Islam believed by Muslims to be based on divine revelation, and drawn from a number of sources, including the Koran, the Hadith and the consensus of the Muslim community. From the latter part of the 19th century, the role of the Shari'a courts in the majority of Muslim countries began to be taken over by secular courts, and the Shari'a to be largely restricted to family law. [Arab.]

Sharif, *n.* **Omar,** stage name of Michael Shalhoub (1932–), Egyptian actor, in international films after his successful appearance in *Lawrence of Arabia* (1962). His other films include *Dr Zhivago* (1965) and *Funny Girl* (1968).

Sharjah, Shariqah, *n.* third largest of the seven member states of the UNITED ARAB EMIRATES, situated on the Arabian Gulf NE of Dubai; area 2600 sq km/1004 sq miles; population (1985) 269,000. Since 1952 it has included the small state of Kalba. In 1974 oil was discovered offshore. Industries include ship repair, cement, paint, and metal products.

shark, *n.* a selachoid sea-fish of various species with lateral gill openings and an inferior mouth, mostly large and voracious and armed with formidable teeth; a grasping, rapacious person; a rogue, a swindler. *v.i.* to play the part of a shark or swindler. *v.t.* to gain or pick (up) by underhand, fraudulent or disreputable means; to swallow greedily. **shark-bait,** *n.* (*Austral., coll.*) a bather or surfer who goes too far out to sea. **sharkskin,** *n.* the skin of a shark; a smooth woven fabric of rayon etc. [etym. doubtful, perh. from L *carcharus* Gr. *karcharias,* from *karcharos,* jagged (in alln. to its teeth)]

sharn, *n.* the dung of cattle. [OE *scearn,* cogn. with SHARE[1], SHEAR]

sharon fruit, *n.* a kind of persimmon. [grown in the *Sharon* Valley, Israel]

Sharp, *n.* **Granville** (1735–1813), English philanthropist. He was prominent in the anti-slavery movement and in 1772 secured a legal decision 'that as soon as any slave sets foot on English territory he becomes free'.

sharp, *a.* having a keen edge or fine point; terminating in a point or edge; peaked, pointed, edged; angular, abrupt; clean-cut, clearly outlined or defined; pungent, acid, sour; of sand, gritty; shrill, biting, piercing; harsh, sarcastic, acrimonious, severe, painful, intense; acute, keen-witted; vigilant, attentive, alert, penetrating; alive to one's interests, unscrupulous, dishonest, underhand; quick, speedy, energetic, brisk, vigorous, impetuous; (*Phon.*) surd, voiceless; above the true pitch, esp. a semi-tone higher. *adv.* punctually, exactly; at a sharp angle; above the true pitch. *n.* a long and slender sewing-needle; a note a semitone above the true pitch; the sign (♯) indicating this. *v.t.* to raise the pitch of (a note); to mark with a ♯. *v.i.* to swindle, to cheat. **at the sharp end,** taking the most important or difficult part in any enterprise. **sharp-cut,** *a.* clearly outlined, well-defined. **sharp practice,** *n.* (*coll.*) underhand or questionable dealings †**sharp-set,** *a.* ravenous. **sharp-shooter,** *n.* a skilled marksman. **sharp-shooting,** *n.* **sharp-sighted,** *a.* having keen sight; sharp-witted. **sharp-witted,** *a.* having a keen wit, judgment or discernment. **sharpen,** *v.t., v.i.* to make sharp. **sharpener,** *n.* **sharper,** *n.* one who or that which sharpens; (*coll.*) a swindler, a rogue; one who lives by his wits. **sharpish,** *a.* rather sharp. *adv.* (*coll.*) rather quickly. **sharply,** *adv.* **sharpness,** *n.* [OE *scearp* (cp. Dut. *scherp,* G *scharf,* Icel. *skarpr*), perh. rel. to SCRAPE]

Sharpeville, *n.* black township in South Africa, 65 km/40 miles S of Johannesburg and N of Vereeniging; 69 people were killed there when police fired on a crowd of demonstrators on 21 Mar. 1960, during a campaign launched by the Pan-Africanist Congress against the pass laws (laws requiring nonwhite South Africans to carry identity papers).

Sharpey-Schäfer, *n.* **Edward Albert** (1850–1935), English physiologist and one of the founders of endocrinology. He made important discoveries relating to adrenaline, and to the pituitary and other endocrine or ductless glands.

shastra, shaster, *n.* any of the Vedas and other sacred scriptures of Hinduism. [Hind. *shāstr,* Sansk. *shastra*]

Shastri, *n.* **Lal Bahadur** (1904–66), Indian politician, who held various ministerial posts after independence, and succeeded Nehru as prime minister of India in 1964. He campaigned for national integration, and secured a declaration of peace with Pakistan at the Tashkent peace conference in 1966.

shat, *past, p.p.* SHIT.

Shatt-al-Arab, *n.* (Persian **Arvand**) the waterway formed by the confluence of the rivers Euphrates and Tigris; length 190 km/120 miles to the Persian Gulf. Basra, Khorramshahr, and Abadan stand on it.

shatter, *v.t.* to break up at once into many pieces; to smash, to shiver; to destroy, to dissipate, to overthrow, to ruin; to upset, distress; (*sl.*) to tire out. *v.i.* to break into fragments. †**shatter-brained, -pated,** *a.* mentally disordered. **shatter-proof,** *a.* made so as to be proof against shattering. **shatters,** *n.pl.* fragments into which anything is smashed. †**shattery,** *a.* [var. of SCATTER]

shauchle, *v.t.* (*Sc.*) to deform, to distort; to wear awry. *v.i.* to shuffle, to shamble, to limp. [cp. Icel. *skjālgr,* wry, squinting]

shave, *v.t.* to remove hair from (the face, a person etc.) with a razor; to remove (usu. off) from a surface with a razor; to pare or cut thin slices off the surface of (leather, wood etc.); to pass by closely with or without touching, to brush past, to graze. *v.i.* to shave oneself. *n.* the act of shaving or the proces of being shaved; a knife for shaving, paring or scraping, esp. a blade with a handle at each end for shaving hoops etc.; a thin slice; a narrow escape or miss; (*sl.*) a swindle; a doubtful report. **shavegrass,** *n.* the scouring-rush, *Equisetum hyemale*. †**shaveling,** *n.* a man shaved (used contemptuously for a monk or friar). **shaver,** *n.* a barber; an electric razor; (*coll.*) a young boy; a humorous fellow, a wag; **dry shaver,** *n.* an electric razor. **shavie,** *n.* (*Sc.*) a trick, a prank. **shaving,** *n.* the act of one who shaves; a thin slice pared off. **shaving-basin, -bowl, -brush, -cup,** *n.* utensils employed for lathering the face before shaving. **shaving-horse,** *n.* a bench with a clamp for holding wood, slate etc., to be shaved. [OE *sceafan, scafan* (cp. Dut. *shaven,* G *schaben,* Icel. *skafa*), cogn. with L *scabere,* to scratch, Gr. *skaptein,* to dig]

Shavian, *a.* of or in the manner of George Bernard Shaw. *n.* a follower of Shaw. [*Shavius,* mod. L form of *Shaw*]

Shaw, *n.* **George Bernard** (1856–1950), Irish dramatist. He was also a critic and novelist, and an early member of the socialist Fabian Society. His plays combine comedy with political, philosophical, and polemic aspects, aiming to make an impact on his audience's social conscience as well as their emotions. They include *Arms and the Man* (1894), *Devil's Disciple* (1897), *Man and Superman* (1905), *Pygmalion* (1913), and *St Joan* (1924). Awarded the Nobel prize for literature in 1925.

shaw[1], *n.* (*esp. Sc.*) a thicket, a small wood. [OE *scaga* (cp. Icel. *skōgr,* Swed. *skog,* Dan. *skov*), rel. to SHAG]

shaw[2], *n.* the stalk and leaves of a root-crop plant, e.g. a potato. [form of SHOW]

shawl, *n.* a square or oblong garment worn chiefly by women as a loose wrap for the upper part of the person. *v.t.* to wrap with a shawl. **shawl collar,** *n.* on a coat etc., a collar of a rolled shape that tapers down the front of the garment. **shawl-dance,** *n.* an Oriental dance in which the performer waves a shawl. **shawl-pattern,** *n.* a variegated pattern with a design characteristic of Oriental shawls. **shawlless,** *a.* [Pers. *shāl,* cp. F *châle*]

shawm, *n.* an ancient wind instrument similar to the oboe. [OF *chalemie* (cp. *chalemelle, chalumeau,* also *chaume,* straw), L *calamus,* Gr. *kalamos,* reed]

shay, *n.* (*dial., facet.*) a chaise. [from CHAISE, taken as pl.]

shaya root, CHAY ROOT.

shayk, SHEIKH.

Shchedrin, *n.* **N.,** pen name of Mikhail Evgrafovich Saltykov (1826–89), Russian writer, whose works include *Fables* (1884–85), in which he depicts misplaced 'good intentions', and the novel *The Golovlevs* (1880). He was a satirist of pessimistic outlook.

she, *pron.* (*obj.* **her,**, *poss.* **her, hers**) the female person, animal or personified thing mentioned or referred to. *n.* a female; †a woman. *a.* female (*esp. in comb.,* as *she-cat, she-devil, she-goat* etc.). [OE *sēo,* fem. of *se,* def. article (cp. Dut. *zij,* G *sie,* Icel. *sū sā,* Gr. *hē,* Sansk. *sā*)]

shea, *n.* a tropical African tree, *Bassia parkii,* yielding a kind of butter. [native name]

sheading, *n.* any one of the six divisions of the Isle of Man. [var. of SHED[1], -ING]

sheaf, *n.* (*pl.* **sheaves**) a quantity of things bound or held together lengthwise, esp. a bundle of wheat, oats, barley etc. *v.t.* to collect and bind into sheaves, to sheave. **sheafy,** *a.* [OE *scēaf* (cp. Dut. *shoof,* G *Schaub,* Icel. *skauf*), cogn. with SHOVE]

sheal, shealing etc. SHEEL, SHIEL, SHIELING.

shear, *v.t.* (*past* **sheared,** †**shore** shaw, *p.p.* **shorn** shawn, **sheared**) to cut or clip with shears; to reduce or remove nap from (cloth etc.) by clipping; to remove (wool etc.) thus; to fleece, to plunder, to strip; †to cut (usu. off) with a sword etc.; to reap. *v.i.* to use shears; to cut, to penetrate; (*Mech.*) to undergo a shear. *n.pl.* a cutting-instrument with two large blades crossing each other like scissors and joined together by a spring; a strain caused by pressure upon a solid body in which the layers of its substance move in parallel planes; (*Geol.*) alteration of structure by transverse pressure; (*pl.*) SHEERS. **shear-bill,** *n.* the scissor-bill or skimmer. **shear-legs** SHEERS. **shearman,** *n.* one employed to shear metal; †one who shears cloth. **shear steel,** *n.* blister-steel, heated, rolled etc. to improve the quality. **shearer,** *n.* one who shears sheep. **shearling,** *n.* a sheep that has been shorn once. [OE *sceran* (cp. Dut. and G *scheren,* Icel. *skera,* also Gr. *keirein*), cogn. with SCAR[1], SHARD, SHORT etc.]

Shearer, *n.* **(Edith) Norma** (1900–83), Canadian actress who starred in such 1930s films as *Private Lives* (1931), *Romeo and Juliet* (1936), and *Marie Antoinette* (1938), in which she played the title role. She was married to MGM executive Irving Thalberg.

shearwater, *n.* a bird of the genus *Procellaria,* esp. *P. puffinus,* the Manx shearwater allied to the petrels.

sheat-fish, *n.* a large catfish, *Silurus glanis,* the largest European freshwater fish. [OE *scēota,* trout, rel. to SHOOT, FISH]

sheath, *n.* a case for a blade, weapon or tool, a scabbard; (*Nat. Hist.*) an envelope, a case, a cell-covering, investing tissue, membrane etc.; a structure of loose stones for confining a river within its banks; a condom. **sheath-knife,** *n.* a large case-knife. **sheath-winged,** *a.* of insects, having the wings encased in elytra, coleopterous. **sheathe,** *v.t.* to put into a sheath; to protect by a casing or covering; to hide, to conceal. **to sheathe the sword,** the make peace. **sheathing,** *n.* that which sheathes, esp. a metal covering for a ship's bottom. **sheathless,** *a.* †**sheathy,** *a.* [OE *scæth,* cp. Dut. *scheede,* G. *Scheide,* Icel. *skeithir,* Dan. *skede*]

sheave[1], *n.* the grooved wheel in a block or pulley over which the rope runs. **sheave-hole,** *n.* (*Naut.*) a groove or channel in which to fix a sheave. [var. of SHIVE]

sheave[2], *v.t.* to gather into sheaves, to sheaf. **sheaved,** *a.* put up in sheaves; (*Shak.*) *prob.* made of straw. [from SHEAF]

sheaves, (*pl.*) SHEAF.

Sheba, *n.* ancient name for modern South YEMEN (Sha'abijah). It was once renowned for gold and spices. According to the Old Testament, its queen visited Solomon; the former Ethiopian royal house traced its descent from their union.

shebang, *n.* (*sl.*) a store, a saloon, gaming-house etc.; a brothel; business, concern, affair. [etym. unknown]

Shebat, Sebat, *n.* the fifth month in the Jewish calendar. [Heb.]

shebeen, *n.* (*Ir.*) a low public-house; an unlicenced house where excisable liquors are sold. [Ir. *síbín*]

Shechem, *n.* ancient town in Palestine, capital of Samaria. In the Old Testament, it is the traditional burial place of Joseph; nearby is Jacob's well. Shechem was destroyed about 67 AD by the Roman emperor Vespasian; on its site stands Nablus (a corruption of Neapolis) built by HADRIAN.

shechinah, SHEKINAH.

shed[1], *v.t.* (*past, p.p.* **shed**) to pour out, to let fall, to drop, to spill, to effuse; to throw off, to emit, to diffuse, to spread around; †to sprinkle, to intersperse. *v.i.* to cast off seed, a covering, clothing etc.; of an animal, to moult. *n.* a division, a parting; the ridge of a hill; a divide, a watershed; in weaving, the opening between the warp threads in a loom through which the shuttle carries the weft. **to shed light on,** to clarify (a situation etc.). **shedder,** *n.* [OE *scēadan, scādan,* to separate, to scatter (cp. G *scheiden,* also L *scindere,* Gr. *schizein,* to cleave, to split)]

shed[2], *n.* a slight simple building, usu. a roofed structure with the ends or ends and sides open; a hovel, a hut. **shedding,** *n.* [var. of SHADE]

she'd, contr. of SHE HAD, SHE WOULD.

sheeling SHIELING.

sheen, *a.* †beautiful, bright, shining. *n.* brightness, splendour, lustre, glitter. **sheeny,** *a.* [OE *scēne* (cp. Dut. *shoon,* G *schön*), not rel. to SHINE]

sheep, *n.* (*pl.* **sheep**) a gregarious ruminant animal of the genus *Ovis,* esp. the domesticated *O. aries,* or any of its numerous breeds, reared for the sake of their flesh and wool; sheepskin used as a leather; (*pl.*) God's people, as the flock of the Good Shepherd; (*pl.*) the members of a minister's flock; a timid, subservient, unoriginal person who follows the crowd; a bashful or embarrassed person. **black sheep,** a disreputable person. **sheep-biter,** *n.* a dog that worries sheep; †a petty thief, a thievish or rascally person. **sheep-bot,** *n.* a bot-fly infesting sheep. **sheep-cote** SHEEP-FOLD. **sheep-dip, -wash,** *n.* a preparation for killing vermin or preserving the wool on sheep. **sheepdog,** *n.* a breed of heavy, rough-coated, short-tailed dogs employed by shepherds; a collie. **sheep-faced,** *a.* sheepish, bashful. **sheep-fold,** *n.* a pen or enclosure for sheep. **sheep-hook,** *n.* a shepherd's crook. **sheep-louse, -tick,** *n.* an insect parasitic on sheep. **sheep-market,** *n.* a place where sheep are sold. **sheep-master,** *n.* an owner of sheep. **sheepmeat,** *n.* mutton or lamb. **sheep-pen** SHEEP-FOLD. **sheep-pox,** *n.* an eruptive contagious disease resembling smallpox, affecting sheep. **sheep-run,** *n.* a large tract of land for pasturing sheep. **sheep's-bit,** *n.* a plant with blue flowers like the scabious. **sheep's eye,** *n.* (*usu. pl.*) a bashful or diffident look; a wishful or amorose glance. **sheepshank,** *n.* a knot used to shorten a rope temporarily. **sheep's head,** *n.* the head of a sheep; an important food-fish, *Sargus ovis,* abundant on the Atlantic coasts of the US. **sheep-shearer,** *n.* one who shears sheep. **sheep-shearing,** *n.* **sheepskin,** *n.* the skin of a sheep, esp. used as a coat or rug; leather prepared therefrom, used for bookbinding etc.; parchment made therefrom or a document or diploma of this. **sheep-tick** SHEEP-LOUSE. **sheep-track,** *n.* a path trodden by the feet of sheep. **sheep-walk,** *n.* land for pasturing sheep, usu. of less extent than a sheep-run. **sheep-wash** SHEEP-DIP. **sheepish,** *a.* like a sheep; bashful, diffident, timid; ashamed. **sheepishly,** *adv.* **sheepishness,** *n.* [OE *scēap,* cp. Dut. *schaap,* G *Schaf,* OHG *scaf*]

sheer[1], *a.* pure, unmixed, simple, mere, absolute, bitter, downright; perpendicular, unbroken by a ledge or slope; of a fabric, very thin, diaphanous. *adv.* vertically, plumb; entirely, outright. **to shear off,** to break off vertically. [Icel. *skoerr,* cogn. with *skīna,* to SHINE, and OE *skir*]

sheer[2], *v.i.* (*Naut.*) to deviate from a course; of a horse, to start aside, to shy. *n.* the upward curvature of a vessel towards the bow and stern; the position of a ship riding at single anchor; a swerving or curving course. **to sheer off,** to move off, to go away. [Dut. *scheren,* to SHEAR]

sheers, *n.pl.* an apparatus consisting of two masts, or legs, secured at the top, for hoisting heavy weights, esp. in dockyards. **sheer-hulk,** *n.* a dismantled hull of a vessel fitted with sheers for hoisting out and putting in the masts of other ships etc. **sheer-legs,** *n.pl.* sheers. [var. of SHEAR]

sheerwater, SHEARWATER.

sheet, *n.* a thin, flat, broad piece of anything, esp. a rectangular piece of linen, cotton or nylon used in a bed to keep the blankets etc. from a sleeper's body; a piece of metal etc., rolled out, hammered, fused etc. into a thin sheet; a piece of paper of a regular size, esp. complete as it was made, reckoned as the 24th part of a quire; a newspaper; a broad expanse or surface; a rope attached to the clew of a sail for moving, extending it etc. *v.t.* to cover, wrap or shroud in a sheet or sheets; to form into sheets. *v.i.* of rain, to come down in sheets, very heavily. **in sheets,** of a book, not bound; of rain, very heavy. **three sheets in the wind,** (*Naut., sl.*) drunk. **to sheet home,** to secure a sail with the sheet. **sheet-anchor,** *n.* a large anchor, usu. one of two carried outside the waist of a ship for use in emergencies; a chief support, a last refuge. **sheet bend,** *n.* a kind of knot used for joining ropes of different thicknesses. **sheet-copper, -iron, -lead, -metal** etc., *n.* metal rolled out, hammered or fused into thin sheets. **sheet-glass,** *n.* **sheet-lightning,** *n.* lightning in wide extended flashes. **sheet music,** *n.* music printed on unbound sheets of paper. **sheeting,** *n.* fabric used for making sheets. [OE *scēte scyte,* rel. to and blended with *scēat,* a corner, a fold, from *scēotan,* to shoot]

Sheffield, *n.* industrial city on the Don river, South Yorkshire, England; population (1986) 538,700. From the 12th century, iron smelting was the chief industry, and by the 14th century Sheffield cutlery, silverware, and plate were famous. During the Industrial Revolution the iron and steel industries developed rapidly. It now produces alloys and special steels, cutlery of all kinds, permanent magnets, drills, and precision tools. Other industries include electroplating, type-founding, and the manufacture of optical glass.

Sheffield Outrages, *n.pl.* in British history, sensational reports in the national press in 1866 exemplifying summary justice exercised by trade unions to secure subscriptions and obtain compliance with rules by threats, removal of tools, sabotage of equipment at work, and assaults.

sheik, sheikh, *n.* the head of a Bedouin family, clan or tribe. **Sheikh ul Islam**, the grand mufti or head of the Muslim hierarchy in Turkey. **sheikdom, sheik(h)dom**, *n.* [Arab.]

sheila, *n.* (*Austral., sl.*) a girl, a young woman. [E dial. *Shaler,* assim. to girl's name *Sheila*]

shekel, *n.* a Hebrew weight of 1/60 of a mina; (*Hist.*) a silver coin of this weight; the main unit of currency of Israel; (*pl. dated sl.*) money, riches. [Heb. *sheqel,* from *shāqal,* to weigh]

Shekinah, *n.* the visible presence of Jehovah above the mercy-seat in the Tabernacle and Solomon's Temple. [Heb. from *shākan,* to dwell]

Shelburne, *n.* **William Petty FitzMaurice, 2nd Earl of Shelburne** (1737–1805), British Whig politician. He was an opponent of George III's American policy, and as prime minister in 1783, he concluded peace with the US. He was created Marquess of Lansdowne in 1784.

sheldrake, shelldrake, *n.* a large wild duck with vivid plumage of the genus *Tadorna* or *Cascarca,* esp. *T. tadorna,* breeding on sandy coasts. **sheldduck, shellduck,** *n.fem.* [OE *scild,* SHIELD (cp. G *schildern,* to paint, with alln. to plumage), DRAKE[1]]

shelf, *n.* (*pl.* **shelves**) a horizontal board or slab set in a wall or forming one of a series in a bookcase, cupboard etc., for standing vessels, books etc. on; a projecting layer of rock, a ledge; a reef, a shoal, a sandbank. **off the shelf,** available from stock. **on the shelf,** put aside, discarded; of a woman, considered too old to marry. **shelf-life,** *n.* the length of time a foodstuff or manufactured item can be stored before deteriorating. **shelf mark,** *n.* a mark on a library book indicating its place on the shelves. **shelf-ful,** *n.* [OE *scylfe,* cogn. with SCALE[1] and SHELL]

shell, *n.* a hard outside covering, as of a nut, egg, testaceous animal etc.; a husk, a pod, a wing-case or elytron, a pupa case, an exoskeleton, a carapace etc.; the framework or walls of a house, ship etc., with the interior removed or not yet built; the outline of a plan etc.; a light, long and narrow racing-boat; an inner coffin; a hollow projectile containing a bursting-charge, missiles etc., exploded by a time or percussion fuse; a case of paper or other material containing the explosive in fireworks, cartridges etc.; an intermediate form in some schools; (*poet.*) a lyre, orig. a stringed tortoise shell; mere outer form or semblance; a spherical area outside the nucleus of an atom occupied by electrons of almost equal energy. *v.t.* to strip or break off the shell from; to take out of the shell; to cover with a shell or with shells; to throw shells at, to bombard. *v.i.* to come away or fall (off) in scales; to cast the husk or shell. **to come out of one's shell,** to stop being shy or reserved. **to shell out,** (*sl.*) to pay up, to pay the required sum. **shellback,** *n.* an old sailor. **shell-bark,** *n.* either of two kinds of hickory. **shelldrake** SHELDRAKE. **shellfish,** *n.* any aquatic mollusc or crustacean having a shell. **shell-heap, -mound,** *n.* a kitchen-midden. **shell-jacket,** *n.* (*Mil.*) an undress or fatigue jacket. **shell-lime,** *n.* lime obtained by burning sea-shells. **shell-out,** *n.* a variety of pool played on the billiard-table. **shell pink,** a pale yellow-tinged pink colour. **shellproof,** *a.* impenetrable to shells, bomb-proof. **shell-shock** COMBAT FATIGUE. **shell-work,** *n.* work composed of or ornamented with shells. **shelled,** *a.* (*usu. in comb.*, as *hard-shelled*). **shell-less,** *a.* **shelly,** *a.* [OE *scell* (cp. Dut. *schel,* Icel. *skel*), cogn. with SCALE[1]]

she'll, contr. of *she shall, she will.*

shellac, *n.* a thermoplastic resin obtained by purifying the resinous excreta of certain jungle insects, used in the manufacture of varnishes. *v.t.* (*past, p.p.* **shellacked**) to varnish with this. [SHELL, LAC[1]]

Shelley[1], *n.* **Mary Wollstonecraft** (1797–1851), English writer, the daughter of Mary Wollstonecraft and William Godwin. In 1814 she eloped with the poet Percy Bysshe Shelley, whom she married in 1816. Her novels include *Frankenstein* (1818), *The Last Man* (1826), and *Valperga* (1823).

Shelley[2], *n.* **Percy Bysshe** (1792–1822), English lyric poet, a leading figure in the Romantic movement. Expelled from Oxford for atheism, he fought all his life against religion and for political freedom. This is reflected in his early poems such as *Queen Mab* (1813). He later wrote tragedies including *The Cenci* (1818), lyric dramas such as *Prometheus Unbound* (1820), and lyrical poems such as 'Ode to the West Wind'. He drowned while sailing in Italy.

Shelta, *n.* a secret jargon made up largely of Gaelic or Irish words, used by tinkers, beggars etc. [etym. doubtful]

shelter, *n.* anything that covers or shields from injury, danger, heat, wind etc.; being sheltered, security; a place of safety; a light building affording protection from the weather to persons, instruments etc.; an air-raid shelter. *v.t.* to shield from injury, danger etc.; to protect, to cover; to conceal, to screen. *v.i.* to take shelter (under). **sheltered,** *a.* protected from weather or from outside influence; of housing, providing a safe, supervised environment for the disabled or elderly. **shelterer,** *n.* **shelterless,** *a.* †**sheltery,** *a.* [ME *sheld-trume,* OE *scild-trume* (SHIELD, *truma,* hand, rel. to *trum,* firm)]

shelty, -tie, *n.* a Shetland pony; any pony; a Shetlander. [prob. from Icel. *Hjalti,* Shetlander]

shelve[1], *v.t.* to place on a shelf or shelves; to put aside, to defer indefinitely; to fit with shelves. **shelving,** *n.* shelves collectively; material for making shelves. **shelvy,** *a.* projecting, overhanging. [see SHELF]

shelve[2], *v.i.* to slope gradually. **shelving,** *a.* [cp. Icel. *skelgjask,* to be askew, also SHOAL[1]]

shelves (*pl.*) SHELF.

Shema, *n.* Jewish prayer from the Torah, recited every morning and evening, which affirms the special relationship of the Jews with God.

shemozzle, *n.* (*sl.*) an uproar, a violent row; a confused situation. [Yiddish]

shenanigan, *n.* (*often pl., sl.*) trickery, deception; noisy, boisterous behaviour. [etym. unknown]

†**shend,** *v.t.* (*past, p.p.* **shent**) to disgrace, to put to shame; to hurt, to mar, to ruin, to destroy; to surpass. [OE *scendan,* cp. Dut. *schenden,* G *shänden*]

Shenyang, *n.* industrial city and capital of Liaoning province, China; population (1986) 4,200,000. It was the capital of the Manchu emperors (1644–1912).

Shenzen, *n.* a Special Economic Zone established in 1980 opposite Hong Kong on the coast of Guangdong province, S China. Its status provided much of the driving force for its spectacular development in the 1980s when its population rose from 20,000 in 1980 to 600,000 in 1989. Part of the population is 'rotated' newcomers from other provinces who return to their homes after a few years learning foreign business techniques.

she-oak, *n.* an Australian tree of the genus *Casuarina.*

Sheol, *n.* the Hebrew place of the dead, often translated 'hell' in the Authorized Version. [Heb., from *shā'al,* to dig]

Shepard[1], *n.* **E(rnest) H(oward)** (1879–1976), British illustrator of books by A.A. Milne (*Winnie-the-Pooh,* 1926) and Kenneth Grahame (*The Wind in the Willows,* 1908).

Shepard[2], *n.* **Sam** (1943–), US dramatist and actor. His work combines colloquial American dialogue with striking visual imagery, and includes *The Tooth of Crime* (1972) and *Buried Child* (1978), for which he won the Pulitzer Prize. He has acted in a number of films, including *The Right Stuff* (1983), *Fool for Love* (1986), based on his play of the same name, and *Steel Magnolias* (1989).

shepherd, *n.* one employed to tend sheep at pasture; a pastor, a Christian minister; (*Austral.*) one who holds legal rights on a mining claim. *v.t.* to tend, as a shepherd; to drive or gather together; (*Austral.*) to preserve legal rights on (a mining claim). **Good Shepherd,** Jesus Christ. **shepherd's clock,** (*Austral.*) the kookaburra. **shepherd's crook,** *n.* a long staff armed with an iron crook, used to catch or hold sheep. **shepherd's knot,** *n.* the tormentil. **shepherd's needle,** *n.* a plant, also called Venus's comb, *Scandix pecten;* the cranesbill. **shepherd's pie,** *n.* cooked minced meat, covered with mashed potatoes and baked in an oven. **shepherd's plaid,** *n.* black and white checked cloth. **shepherd's purse,** *n.* a common cruciferous weed, *Capsella bursa-pastoris.* **shepherd's rod,** *n.* the teasel. **shepherd's staff,** *n.* the common mullein. **shepherdess,** *n.fem.* †**shepherdly,** *a.* **shepherdship,** *n.* **sheppy,** *n.* (*dial.*) a sheep-cote. [OE *scēaphyrde,* SHEEP, HERD[2]]

Sheraton, *n.* **Thomas** (*c.* 1751–1806), English designer of elegant inlaid furniture, as in his *Cabinet-maker's and Upholsterer's Drawing Book* (1791). He was influenced by his predecessors HEPPLEWHITE and CHIPPENDALE. **Sheraton,** *a.* applied to furniture of a severe style designed and introduced into England by Sheraton towards the end of the 18th cent.

sherbet, *n.* an oriental cooling drink, made of diluted fruit juices; an effervescent powder used in sweets or to make fizzy drinks; a water-ice. [Pers., from Arab. *shariba,* to drink, cp. SYRUP]

sherd SHARD.

sheria, sheriah, SHARIAH.

Sheridan[1], *n.* **Philip Henry** (1831–88), US Union general in the American Civil War. Gen. Ulysses S. Grant gave him command of his cavalry in 1864, and soon after of the army of the Shenandoah Valley, Virginia, which he cleared of Confederates. In the final stage of the war, Sheridan forced Gen. Lee to retreat to Appomattox, and surrender.

Sheridan[2], *n.* **Richard Brinsley** (1751–1816), English dramatist and politician, born in Dublin. His social comedies include *The Rivals* (1775), celebrated for the character of Mrs Malaprop, *The School for Scandal* (1777), and *The Critic* (1779). In 1776 he became lessee of the Drury Lane Theatre. He became a member of Parliament in 1780.

sherif, *n.* a descendant of Mohammed through his daughter Fatima and Hassan Ibn Ali; the chief magistrate of Mecca. [Arab. *sherif,* lofty]

sheriff, *n.* (also **high sheriff**) the chief Crown officer of a county or shire charged with the keeping of the peace, the execution of writs, sentences etc., the conduct of elections etc.; in London, Bristol, Norwich and Nottingham the sheriffs are civic authorities; (*N Am.*) an elected county official responsible for keeping the peace etc.; (*Sc.*) a judge (sheriff-principal or sheriff-substitute). **sheriff-clerk,** *n.* (*Sc.*) the registrar of the sheriff's court. **sheriff-court,** *n.* (*Sc.*) a sheriff's court, hearing civil and criminal cases. **sheriff-depute,** *n.* (*Sc., Hist.*) an officer appointed by the Crown acting as chief local judge in a county. **sheriff-principal,** *n.* (*Sc.*) the chief judge of a county or city. **sheriff's officer,** (*Sc.*) **sheriff officer,** *n.* an officer appointed to execute the sheriff's writs, to distrain etc. **sheriff-substitute,** *n.* (*Sc.*) the acting sheriff in a county or city who hears cases in the first instance subject to appeal to the sheriff-principal. **sheriffalty, sheriffdom, sheriffhood, sheriffship,** *n.* SHRIEVALTY. [OE *scīr-gerēfa* (SHIRE, REEVE[1])]

Sherman, *n.* **William Tecumseh** (1820–91), US Union

general in the American Civil War. In 1864 he captured and burned Atlanta, from where he marched to the sea, laying Georgia waste, and then drove the Confederates northwards. He was US Army Chief of Staff (1869–83).

Sherpa, *n.* a member of a people in NE Nepál of Mongolian origin, renowned for their mountaineering skill. A Sherpa, Norgay Tensing, was one of the two men to conquer Mount Everest for the first time.

Sherrington, *n.* **Charles Scott** (1857–1952), English neurophysiologist, who studied the structure and function of the nervous system. *The Integrative Action of the Nervous System* (1906) formulated the principles of reflex action. Awarded the Nobel Prize for Medicine (with E.D. Adrian) in 1932.

sherry, †sherris, *n.* a fortified Spanish white wine orig. from Xeres. **sherry-cobler** COBBLER. [*Xeres,* now Jerez de la Frontera, in S Spain]

Sherwood Forest, *n.* a hilly stretch of parkland in W Nottinghamshire, England, area about 520 sq km/200 sq miles. Formerly a royal forest, it is associated with the legendary ROBIN HOOD.

she's, contr. of *she is* or *she has.*

Shetland, *n.* a Shetland pony. **Shetland lace,** *n.* an ornamental openwork trimming made of woollen yarn. **Shetland pony,** *n.* a very small variety of the horse with flowing mane and tail, peculiar to Shetland. [Shetland Islands, see foll.]

Shetland Islands, *n. pl.* islands off N coast of Scotland. **area** 1400 sq km/541 sq miles. **towns** administrative headquarters Lerwick, on Mainland, largest of 19 inhabited islands. **physical** comprises over 100 islands; Muckle Flugga (latitude 60° 51′6 N) is the most northerly of the British Isles. **population** (1987) 22,000. **products** Europe's largest oil port is Sullom Voe, Mainland; processed fish, handknits from Fair Isle and Unst, miniature ponies. **language** the dialect is derived from Norse, the islands having been a Norse dependency from the 8th century until 1472.

sheuch, sheugh, *n.* (*Sc., North.*) a trench, ditch or drain. *v.t.* to plough, to furrow. [var. of SOUGH[2]]

sheva, *n.* the Hebrew sign (:) put under a consonant to denote the absence of a following vowel sound; SCHWA. [Rabbinic Heb. *shewā*]

Shevardnadze, *n.* **Edvard** (1928–), Soviet politician. A supporter of GORBACHEV, he was first secretary of the Georgian Communist Party from 1972, and an advocate of economic reform. In 1985 he became foreign minister and a member of the Politburo, and has worked for detente and disarmament.

shew, etc. (*Sc., Bibl.*) SHOW.

Shia, Shiah, *n.* one of the two main branches of Islam (see also SUNNA), which regards Ali (Mohammad's cousin and son-in-law) as the first rightful imam or caliph and rejects the three Sunni caliphs. *a.* belonging to, or characteristic of, the Shia sect. **Shiism,** *n.* **Shiite,** *n., a.* (a member) of the Shia sect. **Shiitic,** *a.* [Arab. *shi'a,* sect]

shibboleth, *n.* a word used as a test to distinguish the Ephraimites from the Gileadites, the former calling it *sibboleth* (Judges xii); a criterion, test or watchword of a party etc.; an old-fashioned or discredited doctrine etc. [Heb.]

shicer, *n.* (*Austral., sl.*) a crook, a welsher; a useless mine.

shicker, *n.* (*Austral., sl.*) drink, excessive drinking. **shickered,** *a.* drunk. [YIDDISH]

Shidehara, *n.* **Kijuro** (1872–1951), Japanese politician and diplomat who, as foreign minister (1924–27 and 1929–31), promoted conciliation with China, and economic rather than military expansion. In 1945 he was recognized by the US as prime minister and acted as speaker of the Japanese Diet (parliament) until his death.

shiel SHIELING.

shield, *n.* a broad piece of defensive armour made of wood, leather or metal, usu. carried on the left arm to protect the body, usu. straight across the top and tapering to a point at the bottom; a shield-shaped trophy in, e.g., a sporting competition; a wooden screen or framework or a metal plate used in tunnelling, machinery etc., as a protection when working a gun etc.; a shield-like part in an animal or a plant; (*Her.*) an escutcheon or field bearing a coat of arms; defence, a protection, a defender; (*N Am.*) a sheriff's or detective's badge; a structure of lead, concrete etc., round something highly radioactive to protect against radiation; a mass of very ancient rock at the centre of a continent. *v.t.* to screen or protect with or as with a shield. **shield-fern,** *n.* a fern of the genus *Aspidium* having shield-shaped covers protecting the fruit-dots. **shieldless,** *a.* **shieldlessly,** *adv.* **†shieldlessness,** *n.* [OE *scild,* cp. Dut. and G *Schild,* Icel. *skjöldr,* perh. rel. to SHELL and SCALE[1]]

shieling, sheeling, shealing, shiel, *n.* (*Sc.*) a hut used by shepherds, sportsmen etc.; a small house or cottage; a piece of summer pasturage. [North. ME *shāle, schele,* perh. from Icel. *skjōl,* shelter, rel. to SKY]

shier, shiest SHYER, SHYEST under SHY[1, 2].

shift, *v.t.* to move from one position to another; to change the position of; to change (one thing) for another; †to change (one's clothes); (*sl.*) to dispose of, sell. *v.i.* to move or be moved about; to change place or position; to change into a different place, form, state etc.; to change one's dress; to resort to expedients, to do the best one can, to manage, to contrive; to prevaricate, to practise evasion; (*sl.*) to move quickly. *n.* a shifting, a change of place, form or character; a substitution of one thing for another, a vicissitude; a change of clothing; a relay of workers; the period of time for which a shift works; a chemise; a woman's loose, unshaped dress; a device, a contrivance, an expedient; a dodge, a trick, an artifice, an evasion. **to make shift,** to manage, to contrive (to do, to get on etc.). **to shift about,** to turn right round, to prevaricate; to be shifted from side to side. **to shift off,** to get rid of, to defer. **shiftable,** *a.* **shifter,** *n.* **shiftingly,** *adv.* **shiftless,** *a.* incompetent, incapable, without forethought. **shiftlessly,** *adv.* **shiftlessness,** *n.* **shifty,** *a.* furtive, sly, unreliable. **shiftily,** *adv.* **shiftiness,** *n.* [OE *sciftan,* to divide (cp. Dut. *schiften,* Icel. *skipta,* Swed. *skifta*)]

Shigella, *n.* a genus of rod-shaped bacteria which cause dysentery in human beings. [K. *Shiga,* 1870–1957, Jap. bacteriologist]

Shi Huangdi, *n.* (formerly **Shih Huang Ti**) (259–210 BC), emperor of China. He succeeded to the throne of the state of Qin in 246 BC, and reunited the country as an empire by 228 BC. He burned almost all existing books in 213 BC to destroy ties with the past; built the GREAT WALL; and was buried in a tomb complex guarded by 10,000 individualized, life-size pottery warriors (excavated in the 1980s).

Shiite etc. SHIA.

shikar, *n.* hunting, sport, game. **shikari, shikaree,** *n.* a hunter. [Hind.]

Shikoku, *n.* smallest of the four main islands of Japan, S of Honshu, E of Kyushu; area 18,800 sq km/7257 sq miles; population (1986) 4,226,000; chief town Matsuyama. Products include rice, wheat, soya, sugar cane, orchard fruits, salt, and copper.

shillelagh, *n.* (*Ir.*) an oak or blackthorn sapling used as a cudgel. [place in co. Wicklow, Ireland]

shilling, *n.* a former British silver (or, later, cupronickel), coin and money of account, equal in value to 12 old pence (5 new pence); the basic monetary unit of several E African countries. **to take the King's, Queen's shilling,** to enlist (with alln. to the former practice of giving recruits a shilling as token of a contract). [OE *scilling* (cp. Dut. *schelling,* G *Schilling,* Icel. *skillingr*) perh. from Teut. *skel-,* to divide, cp. SKILL]

shilly-shally, *v.i.* to act in an irresolute manner, to hesitate; to be undecided. *n.* irresolution, hesitation; foolish trifling. [reduplicate of SHALL I]

shilpit, *a.* (*Sc.*) of drink, weak, insipid, washy; of a person, weakly, puny. [etym. doubtful]

Shilton, *n.* **Peter** (1949–), English international

footballer, an outstanding goalkeeper. His career began in the 1960s.

shily, SHYLY under SHY[1].

shim, *n.* a wedge, piece of metal etc., used to tighten up joints, fill in spaces etc. *v.t.* (*past, p.p.* **shimmed**) to fill in, wedge or fit with this. [etym. doubtful]

shimmer, *v.i.* to emit a faint or tremulous light; to glimmer, beam or glisten faintly. *n.* a faint or tremulous light. **shimmery,** *a.* [OE *scymrian,* freq. of *scīmian,* to shine (cp. Dut. *schemeren,* G *schimmern*)]

shimmy, *n.* (*coll.*) a chemise; an orig. N American dance in which the body is shaken rapidly; abnormal vibration in an aircraft or motor-vehicle. *v.i.* to dance a shimmy; of a car or aircraft, to vibrate. [CHEMISE]

shin, *n.* the forepart of the human leg between the ankle and the knee; a cut of beef, the lower foreleg. *v.i.* (*past, p.p.* **shinned**) to climb up (a tree etc.) by means of the hands and legs alone; to trudge, to trot; (*N Am., sl.*) to borrow money in a hurry. *v.t.* to kick on the shins; to climb. **shin-bone,** *n.* the tibia. **shin-guard,** *n.* a padded guard for the shin worn at football etc. [OE *scinu* (cp. Dut. *scheen,* G *Schiene*), prob. cogn. with SKIN]

shindig, *n.* a noisy or rowdy ball or dance. [SHINDY]

shindy, *n.* a row, a disturbance, a rumpus, a brawl. [perh. corr. of SHINNY OR SHINTY]

shine, *v.i.* (*past, p.p.* **shone,**) to emit or reflect rays of light; to be bright, to beam, to glow; to be brilliant, eminent or conspicuous; to be lively or animated. *v.t.* (*past, p.p.* **shined**) to cause to shine, to make bright, to polish; (*N Am.*) to clean shoes etc. *n.* (*coll.*) fair weather, sunshine, brightness, lustre; (*sl.*) a row, a shindy. **to take a shine to,** to like at first sight. **shiner,** *n.* one who or that which shines; (*sl.*) a coin, esp. a sovereign; a popular name for several silvery fishes; (*sl.*) a black eye. **shiny,** *a.* **shininess,** *n.* [OE *scīnan,* cp. Dut. *schijnen,* G *scheinen,* Icel. *skīna*]

shingle[1], *n.* a thin piece of wood laid in overlapping rows as a roof-covering; a woman's haircut in which the hair is layered like shingles, showing the shape of the head. *v.t.* to roof with shingles; to cut (hair) in a shingle. **shingler,** *n.* **shingling,** *n.* **shingly,** *a.* [corr. of *shindle,* L *scindula,* from *scindere,* to split (cp. G *Schindel*)]

shingle[2], *n.* coarse rounded gravel on the seashore. **shingle-trap,** *n.* a groin. **shingly,** *a.* [cp. Norw. *singl*]

shingles, *n. sing.* a viral infection, *Herpes zoster,* marked by pain and inflammation of the skin along the path of an affected nerve (usu. on the chest or abdomen). [OF *cengle,* L *cingulum,* girth, from *cingere,* to gird]

shingly SHINGLE[1,2].

Shinkansen, *n.* the fast railway network operated by Japanese Railways, on which the bullet trains run. The network, opened in 1964, uses specially built straight and level track, on which average speeds of 160 kph/100 mph are attained.

shinny, SHINTY.

shintiyan, -tyan, *n.* the loose trousers worn by Muslim women. [Arab.]

Shinto, *n.* the indigenous religion of Japan. It mingles an empathetic oneness with natural forces and loyalty to the reigning dynasty as descendants of the Sun goddess, Amaterasu-Omikami. Traditional Shinto stressed obedience and devotion to the emperor and an aggressive nationalistic aspect was developed by the Meiji rulers. Modern Shinto has discarded these aspects. **Shintoism,** *n.* **Shintoist,** *n.* [Jap., from Chin. *chin tao,* way of the gods]

shinty, *n.* (*Sc.*) a game somewhat resembling hockey, played by teams of 12 people. [perh. from the cry *shin (to) ye,* used in the game]

shintyan SHINTIYAN.

shiny SHINE.

ship, *n.* a large sea-going vessel, esp. one with three or more square-rigged masts; (*coll.*) an aircraft, a spacecraft. *v.t.* (*past, p.p.* **shipped**) to put on board a ship; to send, take or carry in a ship; to engage for service on board a ship; to fix (a mast, rudder etc.) in the proper place on a ship; to send (goods) by any recognized means of conveyance. *v.i.* to embark on a ship; to engage for service as a sailor. **ship of the desert,** a camel. **ship of the line,** a warship suitable for taking its place in a line of battle. **when one's ship comes in,** when one becomes rich. **ships'-biscuit,** *n.* a hard coarse kind of bread or biscuit used on board ship, hard-tack. **ship-board,** *n.* the deck or side of a ship. **on shipboard,** on board ship. **ship-breaker,** *n.* a contractor who breaks up old ships. **ship-broker,** *n.* one who transacts all necessary business for a ship when in port; a marine insurance agent. **shipbuilder,** *n.* a shipwright; a naval architect. **shipbuilding,** *n.* **ship-canal,** *n.* a canal along which ocean-going vessels can pass. **ship-chandler,** *n.* one who deals in cordage, canvas and other commodities for fitting out ships. **ship-chandlery,** *n.* **ship-fever,** *n.* typhus. **ship-load,** *n.* the quantity of cargo, passengers etc. that a ship carries. **shipman,** *n.* a sailor; the captain or master of a ship. **shipmaster,** *n.* the master, captain or commander of a vessel. **shipmate,** *n.* one who serves or sails in the same ship, esp. a fellow-sailor. **ship-money,** *n.* (*Hist.*) a tax formerly charged on the ports, towns, cities, boroughs and counties of England for providing certain ships for the navy. **shipowner,** *n.* one who owns a ship or ships or shares therein. **ship-rigged,** *n.* having three or more square-rigged masts. **shipshape,** *adv.* in a seaman-like manner, in good order. *a.* well arranged, neat, trim. **ship's husband,** *n.* one who attends to the repairs, provisioning and other necessaries of a ship, a ship-broker. **ship's papers,** *n.pl.* documents carried by a ship containing details of ownership, nationality, destination and cargo. †**ship-tire,** *n.* a head-dress either shaped like a ship or having streamers, for women. **ship-way,** *n.* a timber structure forming an inclined way for building or launching ships. **shipworm,** *n.* a bivalve that bores into ship's timbers, piles etc. **shipwreck,** *n.* the destruction or loss of a ship, by foundering, striking a rock or other cause; destruction, ruin. *v.t.* to cause to suffer shipwreck; to ruin. *v.i.* to suffer shipwreck; to be ruined. **shipwright,** *n.* a shipbuilder. **shipyard,** *n.* a yard etc. where ships are built. **shipment,** *n.* the act of shipping; goods or commodities shipped, a consignment. **shipped,** *a.* put on board a ship; †provided with ships. **shipper,** *n.* one who ships or sends goods by a common carrier. **shipping,** *a.* pertaining to ships. *n.* the act of putting on board ship, sending goods etc.; ships collectively, esp. the ships of a country or port; tonnage; sailing. **to take shipping,** to embark on board ship. **shipping-articles,** *n.pl.* articles of agreement between the captain of a vessel and the crew as to wages etc. **shipping-bill,** *n.* an invoice of goods shipped. **shipping-master,** *n.* an official superintending the signing of shipping articles, paying off of workers etc. [OE *scip* (cp. Dut. *schip,* G *Schiff,* Icel. *skip*), cogn. with SKIFF[1], Gr. *skaphos*]

-ship, *suf.* denoting state, condition, the quality of being so-and-so; status, office; tenure of office; skill in the capacity specified; the whole group of people of a specified type; as in *fellowship, friendship, judgeship, ladyship, marksmanship, scholarship.* [OE *-scipe,* cogn. with SHAPE]

shippo, *n.* Japanese cloisonné enamel ware. [Jap., from Chin. *ts'ih pao* (*ts'ih,* seven, *pao,* jewel)]

shippon, *n.* (*dial.*) a cattle-shed, a byre. [OE *scypen,* (SHOP -EN)]

shipshape, ship-way, ship-worm, shipwreck, shipwright, shipyard SHIP.

shiralee, *n.* (*Austral.*) a swag, a tramp's bundle. **to hump a shiralee,** to carry a burden. [etym. unknown]

Shiraz, *n.* a wine from Shiraz. [city in Persia, now Iran]

shire, *n.* an administrative division of England, a county, esp. one whose name ends in '-shire'; (*pl.*) the predominantly rural midland counties of England, esp. Leicestershire and Northamptonshire, noted for foxhunting. **shireman,** *n.* an inhabitant of the shires; †a sheriff. **shire-horse,** *n.* a large breed of draught horse, orig. raised in the midland shires. **shire-moot,** *n.* (*Hist.*) a deliberative assembly of the people of a shire in Anglo-Saxon times; afterwards a county court held twice a year before the ealdorman etc. †**shire-reeve,** *n.* a sheriff. [OE *scīr,* etym. doubtful; not rel. to SHEAR OR SHARE[1]]

shirk, *v.t.* to avoid or get out of unfairly. *v.i.* to avoid the performance of work or duty. *n.* one who shirks. **shirker,** *n.* †**shirky,** *a.* [prob. var. of SHARK]

shirr, *n.* an elastic cord or thread inserted in cloth etc. to make it elastic; a gathering or fulling. *v.t.* to draw (a sleeve, dress etc.) into gathers by means of elastic threads; (*N Am.*) to bake eggs in a buttered dish. **shirring,** *n.* [etym. doubtful]

shirt, *n.* a loose garment of linen, cotton, wool, silk or other material, extending from the neck to the thighs, and usu. showing at the collar and wristbands, worn by men and boys under the outer clothes; a woman's blouse with collar and cuffs; a lining or inner casing. **boiled shirt,** (*sl.*) a man's evening clothes; (*coll.*) a formal, boring person. **Black Shirts,** Italian fascists, or their British imitators. **Brown Shirts,** German Nazis. **in one's shirt sleeves,** with one's coat off. **Red Shirts,** soldiers of the Garibaldian campaigners in Italy. **to keep one's shirt on,** (*coll.*) to keep calm. **to put one's shirt on,** (*coll.*) to bet all one has. **shirt-front,** *n.* the part of a shirt covering the breast, esp. if stiffened and starched; a dicky. **shirtwaist, shirtwaister,** *n.* a woman's dress with the bodice tailored to resemble a shirt. **shirted,** *a.* **shirting,** *n.* **shirtless,** *a.* **shirty,** *a.* (*sl.*) cross, ill-tempered. [from OE, *scyrte,* from *scort,* SHORT or the cogn. Icel. *skyrta,* SKIRT]

shish kebab KEBAB.

shit, shite, *v.i.* (*past, p.p.* **shit, shat,**) (*taboo*) to empty the bowels. *n.* (*taboo*) ordure, excrement; nonsense; a worthless or despicable person or thing. *int.* (*taboo*) expressing anger, disappointment etc. **the shits,** (*taboo*) diarrhoea. **shitty,** *a.* soiled with excrement; very bad or inferior; despicable. [ON *skita,* cp. Dut. *schijten*]

shittim, *n.* the wood of the shittah tree (prob. an acacia) used in constructing the ark of the covenant and the tabernacle. **shittah,** *n.* [Heb.]

shive, *n.* (*dial.*) a thin slice; a thin fragment, a splinter, a billet etc.; a flat cork, a thin bung. [ME *schīve,* (cp. Dut. *schijf,* G *Scheibe,* Icel. *skīfa*), see also SHEAVE[1]]

shiver[1], *n.* a tiny fragment, a sliver, a shive; a species of blue slate; (*Naut.*) a sheave, a pulley. *v.t., v.i.* to break into shivers. **shiver-spar,** *n.* a slaty carbonate of lime. **shivery,** *a.* [dim. of prec.]

shiver[2], *v.i.* to tremble or shake, as with fear, cold or excitement. *n.* the act of shivering, a shivering movement. **the shivers,** a feeling or movement of horror; a chill, ague. **shiveringly,** *adv.* **shivery,** *a.* [ME *chiveren,* perh. rel. to QUIVER[2], cp. Norw. and Swed. dial., *kippa*]

shivoo, *n.* (*Austral. sl.*) a (noisy) party; an entertainment. [etym. doubtful]

shoal[1], *a.* of water, shallow, of little depth. *n.* a shallow, a submerged sand-bank. *v.i.* to become shallower. **shoaly,** *a.* **shoaliness,** *n.* [var. of SHALLOW]

shoal[2], *n.* a large number, a multitude, a crowd, esp. of fish moving together. *v.i.* of fish, to form a shoal or shoals. [OE *scolu,* cp. SCHOOL[1]]

shoat, *n.* (*N Am.*) a young hog. [Flem. *schote*]

shock[1], *n.* a violent collision of bodies, a concussion, an impact, a blow, a violent onset; a sudden and violent sensation, as that produced on the nerves by a discharge of electricity; prostration brought about by a violent and sudden disturbance of the system; (*Med., coll.*) a stroke; a sudden mental agitation, a violent disturbance (of belief, trust etc.). *v.t.* to give a violent sensation of disgust, horror or indignation to; to shake or jar by a sudden collision. *v.i.* to behave or appear in an improper or scandalous fashion; (*poet.*) to collide. **shock-absorber,** *n.* an apparatus to neutralize the shock of axle-springs on recoil. **shock-proof,** *a.* resistant to damage from shock. **shock tactics,** *n.pl.* a cavalry charge relying on weight of numbers for success; any sudden and violent action. **shock therapy, treatment,** *n.* the treatment of certain mental and other disorders by administering an electric shock. **shock troops,** *n.pl.* selected soldiers employed on tasks requiring exceptional endurance and courage. **shock wave,** *n.* a very strong sound wave, accompanied by a rise in pressure and temperature, caused by an explosion or by something travelling supersonically. **shocker,** *n.* (*coll.*) something that shocks, esp. a sensational story; a staggering specimen or example of anything. **shocking,** *a.* causing a shock; disgraceful; dreadful. **shocking pink,** *n.* a garish, intense shade of pink. **shockingly,** *adv.* **shockingness,** *n.* [prob. through F *choc,* from OHG *scoc,* (cp. Dut. *schok,* Icel. *skykkr*), cogn. with SHAKE]

shock[2], *n.* a collection of sheaves of grain, usu. 12 but varying in number. *v.i.* to collect sheaves into shocks. [cp. MDut. *schocke,* Swed. *skock,* prob. rel. to prec.]

shock[3], *n.* a thick, bushy mass or head of hair; a dog with shaggy hair, esp. a poodle. *a.* shaggy. **shock-dog,** *n.* **shock-headed,** *a.* [prob. var. of SHAG, or rel. to prec.]

shocker, shocking SHOCK[1].

Shockley, *n.* **William** (1910–89), US physicist and amateur geneticist, who worked with BARDEEN and BRATTAIN on the invention of the transistor. They were jointly awarded a Nobel prize in 1956. During the 1970s he was severely criticized for his claim that blacks were genetically inferior to whites in terms of intelligence.

shod, *past, p.p.* SHOE.

shoddy, *n.* fibre obtained from old cloth torn to pieces and shredded; inferior cloth made from a mixture of this with new wool etc.; anything of an inferior, sham or adulterated kind. *a.* made of shoddy; inferior, not genuine, sham. [prob. from OE *scēadan,* to SHED[1]]

shoe, *n.* an outer covering for the foot, esp. one distinguished from a boot by not coming up to the ankles; (*N Am.*) a boot; a metallic rim or plate nailed to the hoof of a horse, ox or ass, to preserve it from wear and damage; anything resembling a shoe in form or function, as a socket, ferrule, wheel-drag or parts fitted to implements, machinery etc. to take friction, thrust etc.; the apparatus by which a tractor collects current from a live rail. *v.t.* (*pres.p.* **shoeing,** *past, p.p.* **shod,**) to furnish (esp. a horse) with shoes; to cover at the bottom or tip. **another pair of shoes,** a different matter or state of things altogether. **dead man's shoes,** an inheritance; a position left vacant by death. **to be in another's shoes,** to be in another's place or plight. **to die in one's shoes,** to meet with a violent death, esp. by hanging. **shoe-black,** *n.* a person earning a living by cleaning the shoes of passers-by. **shoe-buckle,** *n.* a buckle for fastening a shoe over the instep. **shoe-horn,** *n.* a device to assist one in putting on a shoe. **shoe-lace,** *n.* a string of cotton etc. for fastening on a shoe. **shoe-latchet,** *n.* (*Bibl.*) a string or strap for fastening a shoe. **shoe-leather,** *n.* leather for making shoes; shoes. **shoemaker,** *n.* **shoestring,** *n.* a shoe-lace; (*coll.*) an inadequate or barely adequate sum of money. **shoe-tie,** *n.* a shoe-lace. **shoeless,** *a.* **shoer,** *n.* one who makes or puts on shoes; a farrier. [OE *scēo, scōh, scō* (cp. Dut. *schoen,* G *Schuh,* Icel. *skōr,* Swed. and Dan. *sko*)]

Shoemaker, *n.* **William Lee 'Bill'** (1931–), US jockey, whose career (1949–89) was outstandingly successful. He rode 8830 winners from nearly 40,000 mounts and his earnings exceeded $123 million.

shog, *v.t.* (*past, p.p.* **shogged**) (*dial.*) to shake, to agitate. *v.i.* to bump or jog (along); †to clear (off), *n.* a shake; a jerk. [ME *shogge,* SHOCK[1]]

shogun, *n.* the hereditary commander-in-chief of the army and virtual ruler of Japan under the feudal regime, abolished in 1868. **shogunate,** *n.* [Jap., general]

Sholokhov, *n.* **Mikhail Aleksandrovich** (1905–84), Soviet novelist. His *And Quiet Flows the Don* (1926–40) depicts the Don Cossacks through World War I and the Russian Revolution. Awarded the Nobel prize in 1965.

Shona, *n.* person of Shona culture, comprising approximately 80% of the population of Zimbabwe. They also occupy the land between the Save and Pungure rivers in Mozambique, and smaller groups are found in South Africa, Botswana, and Zambia. The Shona language belongs to the Bantu branch of the Niger-Congo family.

shone, *past, p.p.* SHINE.

shoo, *int.* begone, be off. *v.t.* to drive (fowls etc. away) by crying 'shoo'. *v.i.* to cry 'shoo'. [instinctive sound]

shook[1], *past* SHAKE.

shook[2], *n.* a set of staves and headings for a cask ready for setting up; a set of boards for a box etc. *v.t.* to pack in shooks. [prob. var. of SHOCK[2]]

†**shoon,** *n.pl.* SHOE.

shoot, *v.i.* (*past, p.p.* **shot**) to dart, rush or come (out, along, up etc.) swiftly; to sprout, to put out buds etc. to extend in growth; to protrude, to project, to jut out; to discharge a missile, esp. from a firearm; to hunt game etc. thus. *v.t.* to propel, let fly, discharge, eject or send with sudden force; to cause (a bow, firearm etc.) to discharge a missile; to hit, wound or kill with a missile from a bow, firearm etc.; to hunt thus over (ground, an estate etc.); to pass swiftly through, over or down; to protrude, to push out; to put forth; in various games, to hit or kick at a goal; to take (photographs) or record (on cine-film). *n.* a young branch, sprout or sucker; an inclined plane or trough down which water, goods etc. can slide, a chute, a rapid; a place where rubbish can be shot; a shooting-party, match or expedition, a hunt. **shoot!** *int.* (*esp. N Am.*) speak out! say it! **the whole shoot,** (*coll.*) the whole amount, everything. **to shoot ahead,** to get swiftly to the front in running, swimming etc. **to shoot a line,** (*sl.*) to boast, to exaggerate. **to shoot down,** to destroy, kill, by shooting; to defeat the argument of. **to shoot down in flames,** to criticize severely; to defeat soundly. **to shoot home,** to hit the target or mark. **to shoot one's mouth off,** (*sl.*) to brag, exaggerate. **to shoot the sun,** to take the sun's altitude at noon with a sextant. **to shoot through,** (*Austral. coll.*) to leave, to depart hurriedly. **to shoot up,** to grow rapidly; (*sl.*) to inject a drug into a vein. **shoot-out,** *n.* a fight, esp. to the death, using guns; a direct confrontation. **shootable,** *a.* **shooter,** *n.* one who or that which shoots, as *six-shooter;* (*Cricket*) a ball that darts along the ground without bouncing. **shooting,** *n.* the act of discharging firearms or arrows; a piece of land rented for shooting game; the right to shoot over an estate etc. **shooting-box,** *n.* a small house or lodge for use during the shooting season. **shooting-brake,** *n.* an estate car. **shooting-iron,** *n.* (*sl.*) a firearm; a revolver. **shooting-gallery, -range,** *n.* a piece of ground or an enclosed space with targets and measured ranges for practice with firearms. **shooting-star,** *n.* an incandescent meteor shooting across the sky. **shooting-stick,** *n.* a walking-stick that may be adapted to form a seat. [OE *scotian,* to shoot, dart, rush (intr.) *scēotan,* shoot or throw (tr.)]

shop, *n.* a building in which goods are sold by retail; a building in which a manufacture, craft or repairing is carried on; (*coll.*) one's business, profession etc. or talk about this; (*sl.*) a berth, a job. *v.i.* (*past, p.p.* **shopped**) to visit shops for the purpose of purchasing goods. *v.t.* (*coll.*) to discharge from employment; (*sl.*) to inform against to the police. **all over the shop,** (*coll.*) scattered around. **to shop around,** to try several shops to find the best value. **to shut up shop,** to give up doing something. **to talk shop,** to talk about one's occupation. **shop assistant,** *n.* one who serves in a retail shop. **shop-bell,** *n.* an automatic bell giving notice of the entry of a customer. **shop-board,** *n.* a bench on which work is done, esp. by tailors. **shop-boy, -girl,** *n.* one employed in a shop. **shop-floor,** *n.* the part of a workshop where the machinery is situated; the work-force as opposed to the management. **shopkeeper,** *n.* the owner of a shop, a trader who sells goods by retail. **shoplifter,** *n.* one who steals from a shop under pretence of purchasing. **shoplifting,** *n.* **shopman, -woman** *n.* a shopkeeper or a man employed to assist in a shop. **shop-soiled,** *a.* dirty or faded from being displayed in a shop; tarnished; hackneyed. **shop steward,** *n.* a trade union member elected from the work-force to represent them. **shopwalker,** *n.* a person employed in a large shop to direct customers etc. **shopworn** SHOP-SOILED. **shopper,** *n.* one who shops; a bag for carrying shopping. **shopping,** *n.* the act or an instance of buying goods from shops; goods purchased from shops. **shopping centre,** *n.* an area where there are many shops. **shopping mall,** *n.* a shopping centre with covered walkways. **shoppy,** *a.* [OE *sceoppa,* stall, booth (cp. LG *schup,* med. OHG *scopf,* whence F *échoppe*)]

shore[1], *n.* the land on the borders of a large body of water, the sea, a lake etc.; (*Law*) the land between high- and low-water marks. **shoreless,** *a.* **shoreward,** *a., adv.* [OE *score,* from *sceran,* to SHEAR]

shore[2], *n.* a prop, a stay; a support for a building or a vessel on the stocks. *v.t.* to support or hold (up) with shores. **shoring,** *n.* [ME *schore* (cp. MDut. *schōre,* Dut. *schoor,* Icel. *skortha*), etym. doubtful]

shore[3], *past* SHEAR.

shorl, SCHORL.

†**shorling,** *n.* (*dial.*) a newly shorn sheep; wool shorn from a living sheep, opp. to morling. [SHORE[3] or SHORN, -LING]

shorn, *p.p.* SHEAR.

short, *a.* measuring little in linear extension, not long; not extended in time or duration, brief; below the average in stature, not tall; not coming up to a certain standard; deficient, scanty, defective, in want (of); breaking off abruptly; brief, concise; abrupt, curt; brittle, friable, crumbling or breaking easily; (*coll.*) neat, undiluted; of vowels and syllables, not prolonged, unaccented; (*Comm., Stock Exchange etc.*) not having goods, stocks etc. in hand at the time of selling; of stocks etc., not in hand, sold. *adv.* abruptly, at once; to as to be short or deficient. *n.* a short syllable or vowel, or a mark (˘) indicating that a vowel is short; a short circuit; a single-reel film; the bran and coarse part of meal mixed together; (*pl.*) knee- or thigh-length trousers; (*pl., chiefly N Am.*) underpants; a drink of, or containing, spirits; (*pl.*) short-dated bonds. *v.t.* to shorten; to make of no effect; to short-circuit. **for short,** as an abbreviation. **in short,** briefly, in few words. **short for,** a shortened form of. **the long and the short of it** LONG[1]. **to be taken, caught short,** to feel a sudden need to urinate or defecate. **to come short,** to be deficient, to fail. **to cut, bring, pull up short,** to check or pause abruptly. **to fall short** FALL. **to make short work of,** to deal with quickly and expeditiously. **to run short,** to exhaust the stock in hand (of a commodity). **to sell short,** to sell (stocks) for future delivery; to cheat; to disparage. **to stop short,** to come to a sudden stop; to fail to reach the point aimed at. **shortbread, shortcake,** *n.* a brittle, dry cake like a biscuit made with much butter and sugar. **short-change,** *v.t.* to give too little change to; (*sl.*) to cheat. **short circuit,** *n.* (*Elec.*) an accidental crossing of two conductors carrying a current by another conductor of negligible resistance, which shortens the route of the current. **short-circuit,** *v.t.* to form or introduce a short circuit; to dispense with intermediaries; to take a short cut. **short-coat,** *n.* (*pl.*) clothes worn by an infant when too old for long clothes; *v.t.* to put into short-coats. **short-coming,** *n.* a failure of performance of duty etc.; a falling short of supply, produce etc. **short-cut,** *n.* a shorter route than the usual. **short-dated,** *a.* of a security etc., having only a little time to run. **shortfall,** *n.* the amount by which something falls short, deficit. **shorthand,** *n.* a system of contracted writing used for reporting etc., stenography. **short-handed,** *a.* short of workers, helpers etc. **short haul,** *n.* transport etc. over a short distance. **shorthorn,** *n.* one of a breed of cattle with short horns. **short list,** *n.* a selected list of candidates from whom a final choice will be made. **short-list,** *v.t.* **short-lived,** *a.* not living or lasting long, brief. **short measure,** *n.* less than the correct or promised amount. **short metre,** *n.* a metre for hymns, four lines of 6, 6, 8, 6 syllables. **short odds,** *n.pl.* in betting, a nearly equal chance. **short order,** *n.* an order in a restaurant for food that can be prepared quickly. **short-range,** *a.* having a small range, in time or distance. **short rib,** *n.* a false rib. **short sea,** *n.* short broken waves. **short-sight,** *n.* inability to see clearly at a distance, myopia; lack of foresight. **short-sighted,** *a.* **short-sightedly,** *adv.* **short-sightedness,** *n.* **short-sleeved,** *a.* having sleeves reaching not below the elbow. **short-spoken,** *a.* curt and abrupt in speech. **short-staffed,** *a.* short-handed. **short supply,** *n.* general shortage of a commodity. **short-tempered,** *a.* having little self-control, irascible. **short-term,** *a.* of or covering a short period of time. **short time,** *n.* the condition of working fewer than the normal number of hours per week. **short-waisted,** *a.* of a dress, having the waist high up. **short wave,** *n.* a radio wave of between 10 and 100 metres wavelength. **short-winded,** *a.* easily put out of breath. **short-windedness,** *n.* affected with shortness of breath. **shortage,** *n.* a deficiency; the amount of this. **shorten,** *v.t.* to make short in time, extent etc.; to curtail; to reduce the amount (of sail spread). *v.i.* to become short, to contract. **shortener,** *n.* **shortening,** *n.* **shortie, shorty,** *n.* (*coll.*) a shorter than average person, garment etc. **shortish,** *a.* **shortly,** *adv.* **shortness,** *n.* [OE *sceort,* cogn. with SHEAR (cp. L *curtus,* CURT, Gr. *keirein,* to cut)]

Short Parliament, *n.* the English parliament that was summoned by Charles I on 13 Apr. 1640 to raise funds for his war against the Scots. It was succeeded later in the year by the Long Parliament.

short tennis, *n.* a variation of lawn tennis. It is played on a smaller court, largely by schoolchildren. It can be played indoors or outdoors.

Shostakovich, *n.* **Dmitry (Dmitriyevich)** (1906–75), Soviet composer. His music, tonal, expressive, and sometimes highly dramatic, has not always been to official Soviet taste. He wrote 15 symphonies, chamber music, ballets, and operas, the latter including *Lady Macbeth of Mtsensk* (1934), which was suppressed as 'too divorced from the proletariat', but revived as *Katerina Izmaylova* (1963).

shot[1], *n.* a missile for a firearm, esp. a solid or non-explosive projectile; the act of shooting; the discharge of a missile from a firearm or other weapon; an attempt to hit an object with such a missile; a photographic exposure; the film taken between the starting and stopping of a cine-camera; (*coll.*) an injection by hypodermic needle; a stroke at various games; an attempt to guess etc.; the distance reached by a missile, the range of a firearm, bow etc.; a marksman; (*pl.* **shot**) a small lead pellet, a quantity of which is used in a charge or cartridge for shooting game. *a.* having a changeable colour, as shot silk. *v.t.* (*p.p.* **shotted**) to load or weight with shot. **a shot in the arm,** a hypodermic injection; something which encourages or invigorates. **a shot in the dark,** a random guess. **big shot,** *n.* (*coll.*) an important person. **like a shot,** immediately, eagerly. **to get shot of,** (*coll.*) to get rid of. **to give it one's best shot,** (*coll.*) to try one's very best. **to have shot one's bolt,** to be unable to take further action. **shot-belt,** *n.* a belt with pouches etc. for carrying shot. **shotgun,** *n.* a light gun for firing small-shot. *a.* enforced. **shot-hole,** *n.* a hole made by a shot. **shot-proof,** *a.* impenetrable to shot. **shot putting** PUTTING THE SHOT under PUT[1]. **shot silk,** *n.* silk with warp and weft of different colours, chatoyant silk. **shot-tower,** *n.* a tower in which shot is made by pouring molten lead through a rotating sieve at the top and letting it fall into water at the bottom. **shot-window,** *n.* a window projecting from a wall. [OE *gesceot,* from *scēotan,* to SHOOT]

shot[2], *n.* a reckoning. **shot-free** SCOT-FREE. [var. of SCOT[1]]

†**shotten,** *a.* of a herring etc., having ejected the spawn; (*dial.*) curdled; sour. [p.p. of SHOOT]

shough, SHOCK[3].

should, *past* SHALL.

shoulder, *n.* the part of the body at which the arm, foreleg or wing is attached to the trunk; (*pl.*) one's power to sustain burdens, responsibility etc.; (*pl.*) the upper part of the back; the fore-quarter of an animal cut up as meat; anything resembling a shoulder; a projecting part of a mountain, tool etc.; the obtuse angle formed by the face and flank of a bastion; the verge of a road. *v.t.* to push with the shoulder; to jostle, to make (one's way) thus; to take on one's shoulders; to accept a responsibility; to carry vertically (a rifle etc.) at the side of the body. **shoulder to shoulder,** (standing in rank) with shoulders nearly touching; with hearty cooperation, with mutual effort. **shoulder-belt,** *n.* a baldric, bandolier etc. passing across the shoulder. **shoulder-blade, -bone,** *n.* the scapula. **shoulder-brace,** *n.* an arrangement of straps for correcting a child's tendency to stoop. †**shoulder-clapper,** *n.* one who claps another on the shoulder, a bailiff. **shoulder-knot,** *n.* an ornamental knot of ribbons etc. worn on the shoulder by livery servants. **shoulder-of-mutton sail,** *n.* a triangular fore-and-aft sail with a boom at the bottom. †**shoulder-shotten, -slipped,** *a.* strained in the shoulder, **shoulder-slip,** *n.* **shoulder-strap,** *n.* a strap worn over the shoulder, esp. by soldiers, bearing the initials or number of the regiment etc.; one of two strips of cloth that suspend a garment from the shoulders. **shouldered,** *a.* (*usu. in comb.*) having shoulders, as *broad-shouldered.* [OE *sculdor,* (cp. Dut. *schouder,* G *Schulter,* Swed. *skuldra*), etym. doubtful]

shout, *n.* a loud, vehement and sudden call or outcry of joy, triumph or the like; (*Austral. coll.*) a round of drinks. *v.i.* to utter a loud cry or call; to speak at the top of one's voice; (*Austral. coll.*) to buy a round of drinks. *v.t.* to utter with a shout; to say at the top of one's voice. **to shout down,** to silence or render inaudible by shouting. **shouter,** *n.* [etym. doubtful]

shove, *v.t., v.i.* to push, to move forcibly along; to push against, to jostle. *v.i.* to push; to make one's way (along etc.) by pushing; to jostle. *n.* a strong or hard push. **to shove off,** to push off from the shore etc.; (*sl.*) to go away. **shove-halfpenny,** *n.* a game in which coins are slid over a flat board which is marked off into sections. [OE *scūfan,* cp. Dut. *schuiven,* G *schieven,* Icel. *skūfa*]

shovel, *n.* an implement consisting of a wide blade or scoop with a handle, used for shifting loose material. *v.t.* (*past, p.p.* **shovelled**) to shift, gather together or take up and throw with a shovel. **shovel-hat,** *n.* a hat with a broad brim turned up at the sides, worn by Anglican clergy. **shovel-head, -nose,** *n.* a popular name for kinds of sturgeon, sharks etc. **shovelful,** *n.* **shoveller,** *n.* one who shovels; (also **shoveler**) the spoon-bill duck, *Spatula clypeata.* [OE *scofl* (*scof-,* base of prec.]

shovel-board, *n.* a game played (now usu. on a ship's deck) by shoving wooden disks with the hand or a mace towards marked compartments. [orig. *shove-board*]

Shovell, *n.* **Cloudesley** (*c.* 1650–1707), English admiral who took part, with George Rooke (1650–1709), in the capture of Gibraltar in 1704. In 1707 his flagship *Association* was wrecked off the Isles of Scilly and he was strangled for his rings by an islander when he came ashore.

show, shew, *v.t.* (*past,* **showed,** *p.p.* **shown,** †**showed**) to cause or allow to be seen, to disclose, to offer to view, to exhibit, to expose, to reveal; to give, to bestow, to offer; to make clear, to point out, to explain, to demonstrate, to prove; to cause (a person) to see or understand; to conduct (round or over a house etc.). *v.i.* to become visible or noticeable, to appear; to have a specific appearance. *n.* the act of showing; outward appearance, semblance, pretence; display, ostentation, parade, pomp; a spectacle, a pageant, a display, an entertainment, an exhibition, esp. one of a petty kind shown for money; (*sl.*) an opportunity, a chance, a concern, a business. **to give**

one a fair show, to let one have a chance. **to give the show away,** to let out the real nature of something pretentious; to blab. **to show fight,** not to give in without resistance. †**to show forth,** to display, to make manifest. **to show off,** to set off, to show to advantage; to make a display of oneself, one's talents etc. **to show one's hand,** to disclose one's designs (orig. of cards). **to show up,** to expose; to be clearly visible; to be present. **show biz,** *n.* (*coll.*) show business. **showboat,** *n.* a steamboat fitted as a theatre. **showbread, shewbread,** *n.* 12 loaves (one for each tribe) displayed by the Jewish priests in the Temple, and renewed every Sabbath. **show business,** *n.* the entertainment industry, theatre, television, cinema. **showcase,** *n.* a glass case for exhibiting specimens, articles on sale etc. **showdown,** *n.* an open or final confrontation. **showgirl,** *n.* an actress working in variety theatre. **show house,** *n.* one of a group of new houses, open to the public as an example of the type. **showjumper,** *n.* **showjumping,** *n.* competitive riding over a set course containing obstacles. **showman,** *n.* the manager or proprietor of a menagerie, circus etc. **showmanship,** *n.* the showman's art; the ability to display goods etc. most attractively. **show-off,** *n.* one who shows off, an exhibitionist. **showpiece,** *n.* a particularly fine specimen, used for display. **showplace,** *n.* a place tourists etc. go to see. **showroom,** *n.* a room where goods are set out for inspection. **show-window,** *n.* **shower[1],** *n.* **showing,** *n.* **showy,** *a.* ostentatious, gaudy. **showily,** *adv.* **showiness,** *n.* [OE *scēawian,* to see, to point out (cp. Dut. *schouwen,* G *schauen,* Dan. *skue*), cogn. with L *cavēre,* to take heed, Gr. *koein,* to observe]

shower[2], *n.* a fall of rain, hail or snow of short duration; a brief fall of arrows, bullets etc.; a copious supply (of); a shower-bath; (*chiefly N Am.*) a party (e.g. for a bride-to-be or expectant mother) at which gifts are given; (*coll., derog.*) a collection of (inferior etc.) people. *v.t.* to sprinkle or wet with a shower; to discharge or deliver in a shower. *v.i.* to fall in a shower. **shower-bath,** *n.* a bath in which a stream of water is sprayed over the body. **showerless,** *a.* **showery,** *a.* **showeriness,** *n.* [OE *scūr,* cp. Dut. *schoer,* G *Schauer,* Icel. *skūr*]

shram, *v.t.* (*in p.p., dial.*) of cold, to benumb or cause to shrink. [cp. OE *scrimman,* to be drawn up (of limbs)]

shrank, *past* SHRINK.

Shrapnel, *n.* **Henry** (1761–1842), British army officer who invented shells containing bullets, first used in 1804.

shrapnel, *n.* bullets enclosed in a shell with a small charge for bursting in front of the enemy and spreading in a shower; shell-splinters from a high-explosive shell.

shred, *n.* a piece torn off; a strip, a rag, a fragment, a bit, a tiny particle. *v.t.* (*past, p.p.* **shredded**) to tear or cut into shreds. **shredder,** *n.* **shredding,** *n.* **shredless,** *a.* **shreddy,** *a.* [OE *screade* (cp. MDut. *schroode,* G *Schrot*), doublet of SCREED]

shrew, *n.* a shrewmouse; a bad-tempered, scolding woman, a virago. **shrew-mole,** *n.* a N American mole of the genus *Scalops* or *Scapanus.* **shrewmouse,** *n.* a small nocturnal insectivorous mammal, *sorex vulgaris.* **shrewish,** *a.* **shrewishly,** *adv.* **shrewishness,** *n.* [OE *screāwa,* shrew-mouse]

shrewd, *a.* astute, sagacious, discerning; †wicked, vixenish, shrewish, troublesome, spiteful. **shrewdly,** *adv.* **shrewdness,** *n.* [ME *schrewed,* p.p. of *schrewen,* to curse, as prec.]

shriek, *v.i.* to utter a sharp, shrill, inarticulate cry; to scream, to screech, as in a sudden fright; to laugh wildly. *v.t.* to utter with a shriek. *n.* a sharp, shrill, inarticulate cry. **shrieker,** *n.* [var. of SCREECH]

shrieval, *a.* of or pertaining to a sheriff. **shrievalty,** *n.* the office or jurisdiction of a sheriff; the tenure of this. [obs. *shrieve,* SHERIFF, *-alty,* as in COMMONALTY]

shrift, *n.* confession to a priest; (*fig.*) absolution, esp. of one about or appointed to die. **short shrift,** summary treatment. [OE *scrift,* from *scrīfan,* to SHRIVE]

shrike, *n.* a bird of the family Laniidae, especially *Lanius colluris,* the butcher-bird, feeding on insects and small birds and having the habit of impaling them on thorns for future use. [OE *scrīc,* cp. SCREECH, from its cry]

shrill, *a.* high-pitched and piercing in tone, sharp, acute; noisy, importunate. *n.* a shrill sound. *v.i.* to utter a piercing sound; to sound shrilly. *v.t.* to cause to utter in a shrill tone. **shrill-gorged, -tongued, -voiced,** *a.* **shrillness,** *n.* **shrilly,** *adv.* [cp. SKIRL, LG *schrell,* G dial. *schrill*]

shrimp, *n.* a slender long-tailed edible crustacean, allied to the prawn; (*coll.*) a very small person. *v.i.* to fish for shrimps. **shrimper,** *n.* [cogn. with SCRIMP and SHRINK]

shrine, *n.* a chest or casket in which sacred relics were deposited; a tomb, altar, chapel etc. of special sanctity; a place hallowed by its associations. *v.t.* to place in a shrine. [OE *scrīn,* L *scrīnium,* writing-chest, cogn. with *scrībere,* to write]

shrink, *v.i.* (*past* **shrank,** *p.p.* **shrunk,** *part.a.* **shrunken**) to grow smaller, to contract, to shrivel; to give way, to recoil; to flinch. *v.t.* to cause to shrink, to make smaller. *n.* (*sl.*) a psychiatrist. **to shrink on,** to put (a tyre etc.) on in a heated condition so that it may become firmly fixed in contracting. **shrink-wrap,** *v.t.* to wrap in plastic film, which is then shrunk, e.g. by heating, to make a tight-fitting, sealed package. *n.* **shrinkable,** *a.* **shrinkage, shrinker, shrinking,** *a.* **shrinkingly,** *adv.* [OE *scrincan,* cp. MDut. *schrinken,* Swed. *skrynka*]

shrive, *v.t.* (*past* **shrove,** shrōv, *p.p.* **shriven,**) to receive the confession of; to confess, impose penance on and absolve; to confess (oneself) and receive absolution. *v.i.* to confess, impose penance and administer absolution. **shriver,** *n.* a confessor. **shriving time,** *n.* time in which to make confession. [OE *scrīfan,* from L *scrībere,* to write]

shrivel, *v.i.* (*past, p.p.* **shrivelled**) to contract, to wither, to become wrinkled. *v.t.* to cause to contract or become wrinkled. [cogn. with Swed. dial. *skryvla*]

shriven, shriver, shriving time SHRIVE.

shroff, *n.* an E Indian banker or money-changer. *v.t.* to examine (coins) and separate the good from the debased. [Hind. *çarāf,* from *çarafa,* to exchange]

Shropshire, *n.* county in W England. **area** 3490 sq km/1347 sq miles. **towns** administrative headquarters Shrewsbury; Telford, Oswestry, Ludlow. **population** (1987) 397,000. **products** chiefly agricultural: sheep and cattle.

shroud, *n.* a winding sheet; anything that covers or conceals; (*pl.*) ropes extending from the lower mast-heads to the sides of the ship, serving to steady the masts; the ropes from a parachute to its burden. *v.t.* to dress for the grave; to cover, disguise or conceal. **shroudless,** *a.* †**shroudy,** *a.* affording shelter. [OE *scrūd* (cp. Icel. *skrūth,* Dan., Norw. and Swed. *skrud*), cogn. with SHRED]

shroud of Turin TURIN SHROUD.

shrove, *past* SHRIVE. **Shrovetide,** *n.* the period before Lent, when people went to confession and afterwards made merry. **shroving,** *n.* the festivities of Shrovetide.

Shrove Tuesday, *n.* in the Christian calendar, the day before Ash Wednesday and the beginning of Lent. It is also known as Mardi Gras and, in the UK, Pancake Tuesday, for the custom of eating rich things before the Lenten fast.

†**shrow,** SHREW.

shrub[1], *n.* a drink composed of the sweetened juice of lemons or other fruit with spirit. [Arab. *sharāb* or *shurb,* drink; see SHERBET]

shrub[2], *n.* a woody plant smaller than a tree, with branches proceeding directly from the ground without any supporting trunk. **shrubbery,** *n.* a plantation of shrubs. **shrubby,** *a.* **shrubbiness,** *n.* **shrubless,** *a.* [OE *scrybb,* cp. Norw. *skrubba,* SCRUB[2]]

shrug, *v.t.* (*past, p.p.* **shrugged**) to draw up (the shoulders) to express dislike, doubt etc. *v.i.* to draw up the shoulders. *n.* this gesture. **to shrug off,** to disregard, ignore; to throw off, get rid of. [cp. Dan. *skrugge,* Swed. *skrukka,* cogn. with SHRINK]

shrunk, *p.p.*, **shrunken,** *part.a.* SHRINK.

shuck, *n.* (*chiefly N Am.*) a shell, husk or pod; (*pl.*) something utterly valueless. *v.t.* to remove the shell etc. from. **to shuck off,** to strip off. **shucker,** *n.* **shucks,** *int.* expressive of contempt, annoyance, embarrassment etc. [etym. doubtful]

shudder, *v.i.* to shiver suddenly as with fear; to tremble, to quake, to shrink. *n.* a sudden shiver or trembling. **shudderingly,** *adv.* [ME *schuderen,* cp. MDut. *schudden,* EFris. *schüdden,* G *schüttern*]

shuffle, *v.t.* to shift or shove to and fro or from one to another; to move (cards) over each other so as to mix them up; to mix (up), to throw into disorder; to put aside to throw (off); to put or throw (on) hastily. *v.i.* to change the relative positions of cards in a pack; to shift ground; to prevaricate; to move (along) with a dragging gait. *n.* the act of shuffling; a shuffling movement of the feet etc.; the shuffling of cards; a mix-up, a general change of position; an evasive or prevaricating piece of conduct. **shuffle-cap,** *n.* a game in which money is shaken in a cap. **shuffler,** *n.* **shufflingly,** *adv.* [var. of SCUFFLE; cp. LG *schuffeln*]

shufti, -ty, *n.* (*sl.*) a (quick) look (at something). [Arab.]

Shultz, *n.* **George P** (1920–), US Republican politician, economics adviser to President REAGAN (1980–82), and secretary of state (1982–89).

shun, *v.t.* (*past, p.p.* **shunned**) to avoid, to eschew, to keep clear of. [OE *scunian,* etym. doubtful]

'shun, *int.* short for ATTENTION.

shunt, *v.t.* to turn (a train etc.) on to a side track; to get rid of, suppress or defer discussion or consideration of; to get (a person) out of the way, or keep (a person) inactive. *v.i.* of a train etc., to turn off on to a side track. *n.* the act of shunting; a conductor joining two points of a circuit through which part of an electric current may be diverted; a passage connecting two blood-vessels, diverting blood from one to the other; (*sl.*) a car crash. **shunter,** *n.* [ME *shunten,* OE *scyndan,* to hasten]

shush, *int.* calling for silence. *v.i., v.t.* to be or make quiet. [redupl. of SH]

shut, *v.t.* (*pres.p.* **shutting,** *past, p.p.* **shut**) to close by means of a door, lid, cover etc.; to cause (a door, lid, cover etc.) to close an aperture; to keep (in or out) by closing a door; to bar (out), to exclude, to keep from entering or participating in; to bring (teeth etc.) together. *v.i.* to become closed; of teeth, scissor-blades etc., to come together. **shut up!** *int.* be quiet! stop talking! **shut-off,** *n.* **to shut down,** to pull or push down (a window-sash etc.); of a factory, to stop working. **to shut in,** to confine; to encircle; to prevent egress or prospect from. (**shut-down,** *n.*) **to shut off,** to stop the inflow or escape of (gas etc.) by closing a tap etc.; to separate. **to shut out,** to exclude, to bar out; to prevent the possibility of. **to shut to,** to close (a door); of a door, to shut. **to shut up,** to close all the doors, windows etc. of a house; to close and fasten up (a box etc.); to put away in a box etc.; to confine; (*coll.*) to stop, to make an end; to confute, to silence. **shut-eye,** *n.* (*coll.*) sleep. [OE *scyttan,* cogn. with SHOOT, from shooting the bolt]

Shute, *n.* **Nevil,** pen name of Nevil Shute Norway (1899–1960), English novelist, who wrote *A Town Like Alice* (1949) and *On the Beach* (1957).

shutter, *n.* one who or that which shuts; a cover of wooden battens or panels or metal slats for sliding, folding, rolling or otherwise fastening over a window to exclude light, burglars etc.; a device for admitting and cutting off light to a photographic lens; a device in a camera which allows exposure of the film for a predetermined period; a contrivance for closing the swell-box of an organ. **shutterless,** *a.* [as prec.]

shuttle, *n.* a boat-shaped contrivance enclosing a bobbin used by weavers for passing the thread of the weft between the threads of the warp; the sliding holder carrying the lower thread for making lock-stitches in a sewing machine; a shuttle service; a vehicle used on a shuttle service or one that goes between two points. *v.i.* to move or travel regularly between two points or places. **shuttle service,** *n.* transport service running to and fro between two points. **shuttlewise,** *adv.* [OE *scyttel,* bolt, cogn. with SHUT and SHOOT]

shuttlecock, *n.* a light cone-shaped object with feathered flights, used in the games of battledore and badminton; anything repeatedly passed to and fro.

shy[1], *a.* (*comp.* **shyer, shier,** *superl.* **shyest, shiest**) easily frightened, fearful, timid; bashful, coy, shrinking from approach or familiarity; wary, cautious, suspicious; circumspect, careful, watchful (of); difficult to secure, understand etc., elusive. *adv.* short of, lacking. *v.i.* of a horse, to start or turn aside suddenly. *n.* the act of shying. **-shy,** *a.* (*in comb.*) showing reluctance or aversion, as *work-shy.* **shyly,** *adv.* **shyness,** *n.* [OE *scēoh,* cp. Dan. *shy,* Dut. *schuw,* G *scheu*]

shy[2], *v.t., v.i.* (*coll.*) to fling, to throw. *n.* the act of shying; a try, an attempt. **shyer,** *n.* [etym. doubtful]

shyster, *n.* a tricky or disreputable lawyer; (*coll.*) a tricky person.

SI, SI UNITS.

Si, (*chem. symbol*) silicon.

si, *n.* (*Mus.*) te. [perh. from initials of *Sanctus Johannes,* see GAMUT]

sial, *n.* the outer layer of the earth's crust, rock rich in silicon and aluminium. [*si*licon, *al*uminium]

sial(o-), *comb. form.* saliva. [Gr. *sialon,* saliva]

sialogenous, *a.* resembling saliva.

sialogogue, *n.* (*Med.*) a medicine promoting salivary discharge.

sialoid, *a.* resembling saliva.

sialorrhoea, *n.* excessive flow of saliva.

siamang, *n.* a large gibbon from the Malay peninsula and Sumatra. [Malay]

Siamese, *n., a.* Thai. **Siamese cat,** *n.* a breed of cat with blue eyes and dark-coloured ears, face, tail and paws. **Siamese twins,** *n.pl.* identical twins born joined together at some part of the body.

SIB, (*abbr.*) *S*ecurities and *I*nvestments *B*oard.

sib, *a.* related, akin. *n.* a brother or sister. **sibling,** *n.* one of two or more children having one or both parents in common. **sibship,** *n.* being children of the same two parents. [OE, from *sib, sibb,* relationship, peace (cp. Icel. *sif,* G *Sippe*, affinity)]

Sibelius, *n.* **Jean (Christian)** (1865–1957), Finnish composer. His works include nationalistic symphonic poems such as *En Saga* (1893) and *Finlandia* (1900), violin concerto (1904), and seven symphonies.

Siberia, *n.* Asiatic region of the USSR, extending from the Urals to the Pacific. **area** 12,050,000 sq km/ 4,650,000 sq miles. **towns** Novosibirsk, Omsk, Krasnoyarsk, Irkutsk. **products** hydroelectric power from rivers Lena, Ob, and Yenisei; forestry; mineral resources, including gold, diamonds, oil, natural gas, iron, copper, nickel, cobalt.

sibilant, *a.* hissing; having a hissing sound. *n.* a letter which is pronounced with a hissing sound, as *s* or *z.* **sibilance, -ancy,** *n.* **sibilate,** *v.t., v.i.* **sibilation,** *n.* [L *sībilans -ntem,* pres.p. of *sībilāre,* from *sībilus,* a hissing, prob. imit. in orig.]

Sibley, *n.* **Antoinette** (1939–), British dancer. Joining the Royal Ballet in 1956, she became senior soloist in 1960. Her roles included Odette/Odile, Giselle, and the betrayed girl in *The Rake's Progress*.

sibling, sibship SIB.

Sibyl, *n.* in Roman mythology, priestess of Apollo. She offered to sell TARQUINIUS nine collections of prophecies, the Sibylline Books, but the price was too high. When she had destroyed all but three, he bought those for the identical price, and these were kept for consultation in emergency at Rome.

sibyl, *n.* one of a number of women who prophesied in ancient times under the supposed inspiration of a deity; a prophetess, a sorceress; a fortune-teller, a gipsy, an old hag. **sibylline,** *a.* pertaining to or composed or uttered by a sibyl; prophetic, oracular, cryptic, mysterious. **sibyllism,** *n.* **sibyllist,** *n.* **sibyllistic,** *a.* [L *Sibylla,* Gr. *Sibulla,* prob. rel. to L *sapere,* to be wise]

sic[1], (*Sc.*) SUCH.

sic[2], *adv.* thus, so (usu. printed after a doubtful word or phrase to indicate that it is quoted exactly as in the original). [L]

sic[3], SICK[2].

Sicanian, *n.* one of the aboriginal inhabitants of Sicily, found there by the Sicels. *a.* of or pertaining to them. [L *Sīcanius,* from *Sicāni,* pl., Gr. *Sikanoi*]

siccative, *a.* drying, causing to dry; *n.* a siccative substance, esp. one used with oil-paint. **siccity,** *n.* absence of moisture; aridity, dryness. [late L *siccātivus,* from L *siccāre,* to dry, from *siccus,* dry]

sice, *n.* the number six on dice. [OF *sis,* SIX]

†**sich,** SUCH.

Sicel,, Siculian, *n.* a member of a people supposed to have entered Sicily about the 11th cent. BC, a native as dist. from a Greek ancient Sicilian. *a.* of or pertaining to the Sicels. **Siceliot,** *n.* an ancient Greek settler in Sicily; *a.* of or pertaining to the Siceliots. [Gr. *Sikeloi,* and L *Siculi,* pl.]

Sichuan, *n.* (formerly **Szechwan**), province of central China. **area** 569,000 sq km/219,634 sq miles. **capital** Chengdu. **towns** Chongqing. **population** (1986) 103,200,000. **products** rice, coal, oil, natural gas.

Sicilian, *a.* of or pertaining to Sicily or its inhabitants. *n.* a native of Sicily. **Sicilian Vespers,** *n.* a great massacre of the French in Sicily, which began at the first stroke of the vesper bell on Easter Monday in 1282. **siciliana,** *n.* a graceful dance of the Sicilian peasantry; the music (in 6/8 time) for it. **sicilienne,** *n.* a fine ribbed silk or poplin; (*Mus.*) siciliana.

Sicily, *n.* (Italian **Sicilia**) largest Mediterranean island, an autonomous region of Italy. **area** 25,700 sq km/9920 sq miles. **capital** Palermo. **towns** Catania, Messina, Syracuse, and Marsala. **population** (1988) 5,141,000. **exports** Marsala wine, olives, citrus, refined oil and petrochemicals, pharmaceuticals, potash, asphalt, and marble.

sick[1], *a.* ill, affected by some disease, in bad health; affected with nausea, inclined to vomit; tending to cause sickness; disgusted, feeling disturbed, upset, pining (for etc.); tired (of); of a ship, needing repair; of a room, quarters etc., set apart for sick persons; of humour, macabre, cruel, using subjects not usu. considered suitable for jokes. *n.* (*coll.*) vomit. **sick building syndrome,** *n.* (*Med.*) a syndrome thought to be caused by working in a fully air-conditioned building. **sick to one's stomach,** (*chiefly N Am.*) affected with nausea, vomiting. **the sick,** those who are ill. **to be, feel sick,** to vomit or be inclined to vomit. **sick-bed,** *n.* a bed occupied by one who is ill; (*fig.*) the state of being ill. †**sick-brained,** *a.* disordered in the brain. †**sick-fallen,** *a.* struck down with sickness. **sick headache,** *n.* migraine. **sick-leave,** *n.* leave of absence on account of illness. **sick-list,** *n.* a list of persons, esp. in a regiment, ship etc., laid up by sickness. **on the sick-list,** laid up by illness. **sick pay,** *n.* a benefit paid to a worker on sick-leave. **sicken,** *v.i.* to grow ill, to show symptoms of illness; to feel disgust (at). *v.t.* to make sick; to affect with nausea; to disgust. **sickener,** *n.* **sickening,** *a.* disgusting, offensive; (*coll.*) annoying. **sickeningly,** *adv.* **sickish,** *a.* **sickishly,** *adv.* **sickishness,** *n.* **sickly,** *a.* habitually indisposed, weak in health, invalid, marked by sickness; languid, faint, weakly-looking; nauseating, mawkish. *adv.* in a sick manner. *v.t.* to make sickly; to give a sickly appearance to. **sickliness,** *n.* **sickness,** *n.* [OE *sēoc,* cp. Dut. *ziek,* G *siech,* Icel. *sjūkr,* Dan. *syg*]

sick[2], *v.t.* to incite to chase or attack, to urge to set upon. [SEEK]

sicker, *a.* (*now Sc.*) sure, certain, firm. *adv.* surely; certainly. *v.t.* to make sure or certain. †**sickerly,** *adv.* [OE *sicor,* ult. from L *sēcūrus,* SECURE]

Sickert, *n.* **Walter (Richard)** (1860–1942), British artist. His impressionist cityscapes of London and Venice, portraits, and domestic interiors capture subtleties of tone and light, often with a melancholy air.

sickle, *n.* an implement with a long curved blade set on a short handle, used for reaping, lopping etc.; a reaping-hook. **sickle-bill,** *n.* a bird of various species with a sickle-shaped bill. **sickle-cell anaemia,** *n.* a severe form of anaemia marked by the presence of sickle-shaped red blood-cells. **sickle-feather,** *n.* one of the long curved feathers of a cock's tail. **sickle-man,** *n.* **sickled,** *a.* [OE *sicol,* L *secula,* cogn. with *secāre,* to cut]

sickly, sickness SICK[1].

Siculian SICEL.

Siculo-, *comb. form.* Sicel.

Sida, *n.* a genus of plants containing the Indian mallows, many of which yield fibre used for cordage etc. [Gr. *sidē*]

Siddons, *n.* **Sarah** (1755–1831), Welsh actress. Her majestic presence made her most suited to tragic and heroic roles such as Lady Macbeth, Zara in Congreve's *The Mourning Bride*, and Constance in *King John*.

side, *n.* one of the bounding surfaces (or lines) of a material object, esp. a more or less vertical inner or outer surface (as of a building, a room, a natural object etc.); such a surface as dist. from the top and bottom, back and front, or the two ends; the part of an object, region etc. to left or right of its main axis or part facing one; either surface of a plate, sheet, layer etc.; the part of a person or animal on the right hand or left, esp. that between the hip and shoulder; direction or position, esp. to right or left, in relation to a person or thing; an aspect or partial view of a thing; one of two opposing bodies, parties or sects; one of the opposing views or causes represented by them; line of descent through father or mother; a twist or spin given to a billiard ball; (*sl.*) swagger, bumptiousness, pretentiousness. *v.i.* to take part with, to put oneself on the side of. *a.* situated at or on the side, lateral; being from or towards the side, oblique, indirect. **on the side,** in addition to the main aim, occupation, (*N Am.*) dish. **to choose sides,** to select parties for competition in a game. **to take sides,** to support one side in an argument etc. **sidearms,** *n.pl.* weapons, as swords or pistols, carried at the side. **side-band,** *n.* the band of radio frequencies on either side of the carrier frequency, caused by modulation. **sideboard,** *n.* a flat-topped table or cabinet placed at the side of a room to support decanters, dining utensils etc.; (*pl.*) side-whiskers. **side-bone,** *n.* one of the small bones under the wings of a fowl, easily separated in carving; ossification of the cartilage in the pasterns of a horse. **sideburns,** *n.pl.* side-whiskers. **sidecar,** *n.* a small jaunting-car; a car with seats, attached to the side of a motor-cycle; a kind of cocktail. **side-dish,** *n.* a supplementary dish at dinner etc. **side-drum,** *n.* a small double-headed drum with snares, carried at the drummer's side. **side effect,** *n.* a secondary effect (e.g. of a drug), often adverse. **side-issue,** *a.* a subsidiary matter. **sidekick,** *n.* a close associate or assistant, often in a shady enterprise. **side-light,** *n.* light admitted into a building etc. from the side; an incidental illustration (of a subject etc.); a small light at the side of a vehicle; one of the two navigational lights carried by a ship at night. **sideline,** *n.* an incidental branch of business; a line marking the side of a sports pitch, tennis-court etc. **on the sidelines,** watching a game etc. from the side of the pitch etc.; not participating directly in an activity. **side-note,** *n.* a marginal note as dist. from a footnote. **side-piercing,** *a.* heart-rending. **side-saddle,** *n.* a saddle for sitting sideways on a horse. **sideshow,** *n.* a subordinate show, business affair etc. **side-slip,** *n.* a skid; a slip or shoot from a plant; an illegitimate child; a movement of an aeroplane downwards and outwards from its true course; a groove at the wings for moving scenery on and off the stage. *v.i.* esp. of bicycles and motor vehicles, to skid, to slip sideways. **sidesman,** *n.* a church officer assisting the churchwarden. **side-splitting,** *a.* of laughter, a joke etc., convulsing. **side-splitter,** *n.* **sidestep,** *n.* a step or movement to one side; a step at the side of a carriage etc. **side-stroke,** *n.* a stroke delivered sideways or upon the side of a thing. **sideswipe,** *n.* a glancing blow; an incidental criticism. **sidetrack,** *n.* a diversion or digression; (*N Am.*) a siding. *v.t.* to divert or distract from one's main purpose; to defer indefinitely. **side-view,** *n.* a view from the side, a profile. **sidewalk,** *n.* (*N Am.*) a pavement. **side-whiskers,** *n.pl.* hair grown by a man on the side of the face in front of the ears. **side-wind,** *n.* a wind from the side; (*fig.*) an indirect influence, agency etc. **sidewinder,** *n.* a N American rattlesnake that moves by a kind of sideways looping movement; (*N Am.*) a heavy punch from the side. **sided,** *a.* (*usu. in comb.*, as *many-sided*). **sidedly,** *adv.* **sidedness,** *n.* **sideless,** *a.* †**sideling,** *a.* sloping, slanting, inclined. *n.* a slope. *adv.* sideways; obliquely; indirectly. **sidelong,** *adv.* obliquely; laterally. *a.* oblique. **sider,** *n.* one who sides with a particular party etc. **sideward,** *adv., a.* **sidewards,** *adv.* **sideways, -wise,** *adv.* **siding,** *a.* taking sides. *n.* the act of taking sides; a short line of metals beside a railway line, used for shunting and joining this at one end. [OE *sīde* (cp. Dut. *zijde,* G *Seite,* Icel. *sītha*), prob. rel. to *sīd,* spacious]

sidereal, *a.* pertaining to the fixed stars or the constellations; starry; measured or determined by the apparent motion of the stars. **sidereal day,** *n.* the time between two successive upper culminations of a fixed star or of the vernal equinox, about 4 minutes shorter than the solar day. **sidereal month,** *n.* the mean period required by the moon to make a circuit among the stars, amounting to 27·32166 days. **sidereal time,** *n.* time as measured by the apparent diurnal motion of the stars. **sidereal year,** *n.* the time occupied by a complete revolution of the earth round the sun, longer than the tropical year. **sideral,** *a.* sidereal. [L *sīderius, from sīdus -deris,* star]

siderite, *n.* a rhombohedral carbonate of iron; an iron meteorite; a blue variety of quartz. [F, from L and Gr. *sidērītē,* from Gr. *sidēros,* iron]

sidero-, *comb. form.* iron. [Gr. *sidēros,* iron]

siderography, *n.* the art or process of engraving on steel. **siderographic, -ical,** *a.* **siderographist,** *n.*

siderolite, *n.* a meteorite consisting partly of stone and partly of iron.

sideromancy, *n.* divination by means of straws burnt on red-hot iron.

sideroscope, *n.* an instrument for detecting minute degrees of magnetism.

siderosis, *n.* a lung disease caused by breathing iron or other metal dust.

siderostat, *n.* an astronomical instrument by which a star under observation is kept within the field of the telescope. **siderostatic,** *a.*

Sideroxylon, *n.* a genus of tropical trees and shrubs of the family Sapotaceae, with very hard and heavy wood.

siding SIDE.

Siding Spring Mountain, peak 400 km/250 miles NW of Sydney, site of the 3.9 m/154 in Anglo-Australian Telescope, opened in 1974, which was the first big telescope to be fully computer controlled. It is one of the most powerful telescopes in the southern hemisphere.

sidle, *v.i.* to go or move sideways; to fawn, to cringe. [back-formation, from SIDELING under SIDE]

Sidney, *n.* **Philip** (1554–86), English poet and soldier, author of the sonnet sequence *Astrophel and Stella* (1591), *Arcadia* (1590), a prose romance, and *Apologie for Poetrie* (1595), the earliest work of English literary criticism.

siege, *n.* the process of besieging or the state of being besieged; the operations of an army before or round a fortified place to compel surrender; a seat, a fixed place or station; †excrement. **siege-basket,** *n.* a gabion. **siege-gun,** *n.* a heavy cannon adapted for breaching fortifications etc. **siege-piece,** *n.* a siege-gun; a coin issued at a place in a state of siege. **siege-train,** *n.* artillery and other materials carried by an army for siege purposes. [ME and A-F *sege,* OF *siege,* ult. from L *sedes,* seat]

Siegel, *n.* **Don(ald)** (1912–), US film director who made thrillers, Westerns, and police dramas. He also directed *Invasion of the Body Snatchers* (1956). His other films include *Madigan* (1968), *Dirty Harry* (1971), and *The Shootist* (1976).

Siegfried, *n.* legendary Germanic hero, also known as Sigurd. It is uncertain whether his story has a historical basis, but it was current about 700 AD. A version is in the German *Nibelungenlied*.

Siegfried Line, *n.* in World War I the defensive line established in 1918 by the Germans in France; in World War II the name given by the Allies to the West Wall, the German defensive line established along its western frontier, from the Netherlands to Switzerland.

Siemens, *n.* family of four brothers, creators of a vast industrial empire. The eldest, Ernst Werner von Siemens (1812–92), founded the original electrical firm of *Siemens und Halske* (1847) and made many advances in telegraphy. William (Karl Wilhelm) (1823–83) perfected the open-hearth production of steel (now superseded), pioneered the development of the electric locomotive, the laying of transoceanic cables, and improvements in the electric generator.

siemens, *n.* the SI unit of electrical conductance. [E. W. *Siemens*]

Sienese, *a.* of or pertaining to Siena, a city of Italy. *n.* a native of Siena; a member of the Sienese school of painters (13th and 14th cents.)

sienite, SYENITE.

Sienkiewicz, *n.* **Henryk** (1846–1916), Polish author. His books include *Quo Vadis?* (1895), set in Rome at the time of Nero, and the 17th-century historical trilogy *With Fire and Sword*, *The Deluge*, and *Pan Michael* (1890–93).

sienna, *n.* a pigment composed of a native clay coloured with iron and manganese, known as raw (yellowish-brown) or burnt (reddish-brown) sienna according to the mode of preparation. [It. *terra di Siena,* earth of Siena]

sierra, *n.* a long serrated mountain-chain; (*Astron.*) a chromosphere. [Sp. from L *serra,* saw]

Sierra Leone, *n.* Republic of; country in W Africa on the Atlantic, bounded to the N and E by Guinea and to the SE by Liberia. **area** 73,300 sq km/28,301 sq miles. **capital** Freetown. **towns** Bo, Kenema, Makeni. **physical** mountains in east; hills and forest; coastal mangrove swamps. **population** (1989) 4,318,000; annual growth rate 1.8%. **exports** palm kernels, cocoa, coffee, ginger, diamonds, bauxite, rutile. **language** English (official); local languages. **religion** Muslim 60%, animist 30%.

Sierra Madre, *n.* chief mountain system of Mexico, consisting of three ranges, enclosing the central plateau of the country; highest point Pico de Orizaba 5700 m/18,700 ft. The Sierra Madre del Sur ('of the south') runs along the SW Pacific coast.

siesta, *n.* a short midday sleep, esp. in hot countries. [Sp., from L *sexta (hora),* sixth (hour)]

sieve, *n.* an instrument for separating the finer particles of substances from the coarser by means of meshes or holes through which the former pass and the others are retained; a coarse-plaited basket; a talkative or indiscreet person. *v.t.* to sift. [OE *sife,* cp. Dut. *zeef,* G *Sieb*]

sievert, *n.* the SI unit of ionizing radiation, equal to 100 rems. [R. M. *Sievert,* 1896–1966, Swedish physicist]

siffle, *v.i.* to whistle; to hiss. *n.* a sibilant râle. **siffleur,** *n.* the mountain marmot; a whistling artiste. [F *siffler,* late L *siffilāre,* form of L *sibilāre,* see SIBILANT]

sift, *v.t.* to separate into finer and coarser particles by means of a sieve; to separate (from, out etc.); to sprinkle (sugar, flour etc.) as with a sieve; to examine minutely, to scrutinize, to analyse critically. *v.i.* of light snow etc., to fall or be sprinkled as from a sieve. **sifter,** *n.* (*usu. in comb.,* as *sugar-sifter*). [OE *siftan,* from SIEVE]

Sig., (*abbr.*) Signor.

sig., (*abbr.*) signature.

sigh, *v.i.* to draw a deep, long respiration, as an involuntary expression of grief, fatigue, relief etc.; to yearn (for); to make a sound like sighing. *v.t.* to utter with sighs. *n.* the act or sound of sighing. **sigher,** *n.* **sighingly,** *adv.* [OE *sīcan* (cp. Swed. *sucka,* Dan. *sukke*), prob. imit.]

sight, *n.* the faculty of seeing; the act of seeing; vision, view; range of vision; point of view, estimation; visibility; that which is seen, a spectacle, a display, a show, esp. something interesting to see; a device on a firearm, optical instrument etc. for enabling one to direct it accurately to any point; (*coll.*) a great quantity (of); a strange object, a fright. *v.t.* to get sight of, to espy, to discover by seeing; to adjust the sights of; to aim by means of sights. **at, on sight,** as soon as seen; immediately; on presentation for payment. **in sight,** visible. **out of sight,** where it cannot be seen; disappeared; forgotten. **sight unseen,** without prevous inspection (of the object to be bought etc.). **to lose sight of,** to cease to see; to overlook; to forget. **sight-read,** *v.t.* **sight-reader,** *n.* one who reads (music etc.) at sight. **sight-reading,** *n.* **sight screen,** *n.* a white screen set on the boundary of a cricket field to help the batsman see the ball. **sightseeing,** *n.* seeing the sights or notable features of a place. **sightseer,** *n.* **sightsman,** *n.* one who reads music readily at sight; a guide, a cicerone. **sighted,** *a.* having sight (*in comb.*, of a specified kind, as *short-sighted*). **sightless,** *a.* wanting sight, blind; invisible. **sightlessly,** *adv.* **sightlessness,** *n.* **sightly,** *a.* pleasing to the eye. **sightliness,** *n.* **sightworthy,** *a.* worth seeing. [OE *gesihth* from *sēon,* to SEE]

sigil, *n.* a seal, a signet; †an astrological or occult sign. **Sigillaria,** *n.* a genus of fossil cryptogamic trees found largely in coal formations. **sigillate,** *a.* marked with seal-like impressions; of pottery, decorated with stamped marks. **sigillography,** *n.* the study or science of seals. **sigillographer,** *n.* **sigillographical,** *a.* [late L *sigillum,* dim. of L *signum,* SIGN]

Sigismund, *n.* (1368–1437), Holy Roman emperor from 1411. He convened and presided over the council of Constance (1414–18), where he promised protection to the religious reformer HUSS, but imprisoned him after his condemnation for heresy, and acquiesced in his burning. King of Bohemia from 1419, he led the military campaign against the Hussites.

sigma, *n.* the name of the Greek letter Σ σ, or s, equivalent to *s.* **sigmate,** *a.* sigma- or S-shaped. *v.t.* to add *S* or a sigma to. **sigmatic,** *a.* (*Gram.*) of certain tenses etc., formed with a sigma. **sigmatism,** *n.* imperfect or peculiar utterance of the sound *s.* **sigmoid,** *a.* (*chiefly Anat.*) curved like the sigma or the letter *S;* having a double or reflexed curve; *n.* such a curve. **sigmoidal,** *a.* sigmoid. [Gr.]

Sigma Octantis, *n.* the star closest to the south celestial pole, in effect the southern equivalent of Polaris, although far less conspicuous. Situated just less than 1° from the south celestial pole, Sigma Octantis is 120 light years away.

sign, *n.* a mark expressing a particular meaning; a conventional mark used for a word or phrase to represent a mathematical process (as + or −); a symbol, a token, a symptom or proof (of), esp. a miracle as evidence of a supernatural power; a password, a secret formula, motion or gesture by which confederates etc. recognize each other; a motion, action or gesture used instead of words to convey information, commands etc.; a device, usu. painted on a board, displayed as a token or advertisement of a trade, esp. by innkeepers; one of 12 ancient divisions of the zodiac named after the constellations formerly in them but now not corresponding through the precession of the equinoxes. *v.t.* to mark with a sign, esp. with one's signature, initials or an accepted mark as an acknowledgment, guarantee, ratification etc.; to convey (away) by putting one's signature to a deed etc.; to engage or to be taken (on) as an employee by signature; to order, request or make known by a gesture; to write (one's name) as signature. *v.i.* to write one's name as signature. **to sign for,** to acknowledge receipt of by signing. **to sign in,** to record arrival by signing. **to sign off,** to stop work for the time; to discharge from employment; to stop broadcasting; to end a letter by signing. **to sign on,** (also **sign up**); to commit (oneself or another) to an undertaking or employment; to register as unemployed. **to sign out,** to record departure by signing. **signboard,** *n.* a board on which a tradesman's sign or advertisement is painted. **sign language,** *n.* a system of communication that uses visual signals rather than the spoken word. **sign manual,** *n.* a signature written by a person's own hand. **sign-painter,** *n.* one who paints signboards etc. **signpost,** *n.* a post supporting a sign, esp. as a mark of direction at crossroads etc. **signable,** *a.* **signer,** *n.* [ME and OF *signe,* L *signum*]

Signac, *n.* **Paul** (1863–1935), French artist. In 1884 he joined with SEURAT in founding the Société des Artistes Indépendants and developing the technique of pointillism.

signal, *n.* a sign agreed upon or understood as conveying information, esp. to a person or persons at a distance; an electronic transmission conveying a message, warning etc.; the apparatus by which this is conveyed; an event that is the occasion for some action; a semaphore or coloured light to indicate whether a railway line is clear or otherwise. *v.t.* (*past, p.p.* **signalled**) to make signals to; to convey, announce, order etc. by signals. *v.i.* to make signals. *a.* distinguished from the rest, conspicuous, noteworthy, extraordinary. **to signal off, on,** to signal for or against a train proceeding. **signal-box,** *n.* the cabin from which railway signals and points are worked. **signal-fire,** *n.* a fire intended to act as a signal. **signalman,** *n.* one who works the railway signals. **signal post,** *n.* a tall post bearing signalling arms. **signalize,** *v.t.* to make signal or remarkable; to point out or indicate particularly. **signaller,** *n.* **signally,** *adv.* [F, from late L *signāle* (SIGN, -AL)]

signature, *n.* the name, initials or mark of a person written or impressed with his or her own hand; a distinguishing letter or number at the bottom of the first page of each sheet of a book; such a sheet after folding; (*Mus.*) the signs of the key and rhythm placed at the beginning of a staff to the right of the clef; all such signs including the clef; a significant mark, sign or stamp. **signature tune,** *n.* a distinctive piece of music used to identify a programme, performer etc. †**signation,** *n.* a sign; a signature; signing with the cross. **signatory,** †**-tary,** *a.* having signed, bound by signature; †pertaining to a seal, used in sealing. *n.* one who signs, esp. as representing a state. [F, from med. L *signātūra,* from *signāre,* to SIGN]

signet, *n.* a small seal, esp. for use in lieu of or with a signature as a mark of authentication; such a seal used by the English or Scottish sovereigns. **signet-ring,** *n.* a finger-ring set with a seal. [F, dim of *signe,* SIGN]

signify, *v.t.* to make known by signs or words; to communicate, to announce; to be a sign of, to mean, to denote; to matter. *v.i.* to be of consequence. **significance, -ancy** *n.* the quality of being significant, expressiveness; meaning, real import; importance, moment, consequence. **significant,** *a.* meaning something; expressing or suggesting something more than appears on the surface; meaning something important, weighty, noteworthy, not insignificant. †*n.* a sign, a token. **significantly,** *adv.* **signification,** *n.* the act of signifying; that which is signified, the precise meaning, sense or implication (of a term etc.). **significative,** *a.* conveying a meaning or signification; serving as a sign or evidence (of), significant. **significatively,** *adv.* **significativeness,** *n.* **significator,** *n.* one who or that which signifies; (*Astrol.*) the planet ruling a house. **significatory,** *n., a.* [F *signifier,* L *significāre* (SIGN, -FY)]

signior, SIGNOR.

signiory, SEIGNORY.

signor, *n.* an Italian man; the Italian form of address corresponding to sir or Mr. **signora,** *n.* a lady; Mrs, madam. **signorina,** *n.* a girl; Miss. [It., as SENIOR, cp. SEIGNEUR]

Sigurd, *n.* in Norse mythology, a hero who appears in both the NIBELUNGENLIED (under his German name of

SIEGFRIED) and the EDDA.

Sihanouk, *n.* **Norodom** (1922–), Cambodian politician, king (1941–55), prime minister (1955–70), when his government was overthrown by a military coup led by Lon Nol. With Pol Pot's resistance front, he overthrew Lon Nol in 1975, and again became prime minister from 1975–76, when he was forced to resign by the Khmer Rouge.

sika, *n.* a small Japanese deer, now introduced into Britain. [Jap. *shika*]

sike, *n.* (*Sc., North.*) a small stream of water; a ditch, a channel. [OE *sīc,* cp. Icel. *sīk*]

Sikh, *n.* one of a Hindu religious (monotheistic) and military community. **Sikhism,** *n.* a religion professed by 16 million Indians, living mainly in the Punjab. Sikhism was founded by Nanak (1469–*c.* 1539). Sikhs believe in a single God who is the immortal creator of the universe and who has never been incarnate in any form, and in the equality of all human beings; Sikhism is strongly opposed to caste divisions. Their holy book is the *Guru Granth Sahib*. The *Khalsa* ('pure'), the company of the faithful, wear the five Ks: *kes*, long hair; *kangha*, a comb; *kirpan*, a sword; *kachh*, short trousers; and *kara*, a steel bracelet. Sikh men take the last name 'Singh' ('lion') and women 'Kaur' ('princess'). [Hind., from Sansk. *sishya,* disciple]

Sikh Wars, *n. pl.* two wars in India between the Sikhs and the British: First Sikh War (1845–46) following an invasion of British India by Punjabi Sikhs. The Sikhs were defeated and part of their territory annexed. Second Sikh War (1848–49) arising from a Sikh revolt in Multan. They were defeated and the British annexed the Punjab.

Sikkim, *n.* (or **Denjong**) state of NE India; formerly a protected state, it was absorbed by India in 1975, the monarchy being abolished. China does not recognize India's sovereignty. **area** 7300 sq km/2818 miles. **capital** Gangtok. **population** (1981) 316,000. **products** rice, grain, tea, fruit, soyabeans, carpets, cigarettes, lead, zinc, copper. **language** Bhutia, Lepecha, Khaskura (Nepáli) (all official). **religion** Mahayana Buddhism, Hinduism.

Sikorski, *n.* **Wladyslaw** (1881–1943), Polish general and politician. In 1909, he formed the nationalist military organization which during World War I fought for the central powers. He was prime minister (1922–23) and war minister (1923–25). In Sept. 1939 he became prime minister of the exiled Polish government, which transferred to London in 1940. He was killed in an air crash.

Sikorsky, *n.* **Igor** (1889–1972), Ukrainian engineer, who built the first successful helicopter. He emigrated to the US in 1918 where he first constructed multi-engined flying boats. His first helicopter (the VS300) flew in 1939 and a commercial version (the R3) went into production in 1943.

silage, ENSILAGE.

Silbury Hill, *n.* steep, rounded artificial mound (40 m/ 130 ft high) of the Bronze Age 2660 BC, in Wiltshire, near AVEBURY, England. Excavation has shown it not to be a barrow (grave), as was previously thought.

Silchester, *n.* archaeological site, a major town in Roman Britain. It is 10 km/6 miles N of Basingstoke, Hampshire.

sild, *n.* a young herring, esp. canned in Norway. [Norw.]

sile, *n.* (*dial.*) a strainer. *v.t.* to strain, esp. milk. [prob. from Icel., cp. Norw. and Swed. *sil*]

silence, *n.* the state of being silent, taciturnity, absence of noise, stillness; the fact of not mentioning a thing, secrecy; absence of mention, oblivion. *v.t.* to make silent, esp. by refuting with unanswerable arguments; to stop from sounding; to compel to cease firing. **silencer,** *n.* one who or that which silences; a device for reducing or muffling noise, fitted to firearms; the exhaust of a motor on a vehicle etc. [F, from L *silentium,* from *silēre,* to be silent]

Silene, *n.* a genus of caryophyllaceous plants comprising the catch-fly etc. [mod. L, from SILENUS]

silent, *a.* not speaking, not making any sound, noiseless, still; of a letter, not pronounced; not loquacious, taciturn, making no mention, saying nothing (about). †*n.* a time of silence. **silent majority,** *n.* the large majority of a population who have moderate views but do not bother to express them. **silent partner,** *n.* one having no voice in the management of a business. **silentiary,** *n.* one appointed to maintain silence in a court etc.; one sworn to secrecy in affairs of state, esp. a confidential officer of the Byzantine court. **silently,** *adv.* **silentness,** *n.*

Silenus, *n.* a riotous and drunken old man. [L, from Gr. *Seilēnos,* attendant and tutor of Bacchus and oldest of the satyrs]

Silesia, *n.* long-disputed region of Europe, Austrian from 1675–1745; Prussian/German from 1745–1919 (following its seizure by Frederick II); and in 1919 divided among newly formed Czechoslovakia, revived Poland, and Germany, which retained the major part. In 1945 all German Silesia east of the Oder-Neisse line was transferred to Polish administration; about 10 million inhabitants of German origin, both here and in Czechoslovak Silesia, were expelled.

silesia, *n.* a name for kinds of linen cloth used for blinds, dress-linings etc. [orig. made in *Silesia*]

silex, *n.* flint; silica. [L, flint]

silhouette, *n.* a portrait in profile or outline, usu. black on a white ground or cut out in paper etc.; the outline of a figure as seen against the light or cast as a shadow. *v.t.* to represent or cause to be visible in silhouette. [Etienne de *Silhouette,* 1709–67, French minister of finance, whose name became a synonym for anything cheap]

silica, *n.* a hard, crystalline silicon dioxide, occurring in various mineral forms, esp. as sand, flint, quartz etc. **silica gel,** *n.* a granular form of hydrated silica, used to absorb water and other vapours. **silicate,** *n.* a salt of silicic acid. **silicated,** *a.* combined or impregnated with silica; coated with silica. **siliceous, silicic, siliciferous,** *a.* **silicify,** *v.t.* to convert into or impregnate with silica, to petrify. *v.i.* to become or be impregnated with silica. **silicification,** *n.* **silicium,** *n.* silicon. **silicon,** *n.* a non-metallic semi-conducting element, at. no. 14; chem. symbol Si, usu. occurring in combination with oxygen as quartz or silica, and next to oxygen the most abundant of the elements. **silicon chip,** *n.* a semiconductor chip CHIP. **silicones,** *n.pl.* water-repellent oils of low melting-point, the viscosity of which changes little with temperature, used as lubricants, constituents of polish etc. **silicone rubber,** *n.* a synthetic rubber stable up to comparatively high temperatures. **silicosis,** *n.* an occupational disease of the lungs occasioned by the inhalation of silica dust. **silicotic,** *a.* [from L *silex -licis,* see SILEX]

silici-, silico-, *comb. form.* silicon.

silicle, silicula, *n.* a short siliqua or seed-pod. **siliculose,** *a.* [F *silicule* or L *silicula,* dim. of foll.]

Silicon Valley, *n.* nickname given to Santa Clara county, California, since the 1950s the site of many high-technology electronic firms, whose prosperity is based on the silicon chip.

siliqua, *n.* (*pl.* **-quae**) a dry, elongated pericarp or pod containing the seeds, as in plants of the mustard family; (*Anat.*) a podlike envelope. **silique,** *n.* (*Bot.*) a siliqua. **siliquiform,** *a.* **siliquose, siliquous,** *a.* [L]

silk, *n.* a fine, soft, glossy fibre spun by the larvae of certain moths, esp. the common silkworm, *Bombyx mori;* similar thread spun by the silk-spider and other arachnids; cloth made of silk; (*pl.*) varieties of this or garments made of it; the silky lustre seen in some gems. *a.* made of silk, silken, †silky. **to take silk,** to exchange a stuff gown for one of silk, esp. to become a KC or QC. **silk-cotton,** *n.* the silky covering of the seed-pods of the bombax and other trees. **silk-gland,** *n.* a gland in the silkworm, certain spiders etc., secreting silk. **silk hat,** *n.* a top hat. **silkman,** *n.* a maker of or dealer in silk. **silk-mercer,** *n.* **silk-mill,** *n.* **silk-reel, -winder,** *n.* a reel used for winding the raw silk from the cocoon. **silk-screen,** *a.* of a stencil method of printing in which paint or ink is forced through a screen of silk or other fine-meshed fabric. **silk-screen printing,** *n.* **silk-spider,** *n.* a spider spinning a silky substance, esp. *Nephela plumipes.* **silk-thrower, -throwster,** *n.* one who winds, twists or throws silk to prepare it for weaving. **silk-weaver,** *n.* **silkworm,** *n.* the larva of *Bombyx mori* or allied moths which enclose their chrysalis in a cocoon of silk. **silkworm gut,** *n.* a fine gut used for angling, drawn from the glands of the silkworm. **silken,** *a.* **silky,** *a.* like silk, glossy, soft; silken. **silky oak,** *n.* an Australian tree yielding wood suitable for furniture, fittings etc. **silkiness,** *n.* [OE *seolc,* L *sēricum,* see SERICATE]

Silk Road, *n.* ancient route by which silk was brought from China to Europe in return for trade goods; it ran via the Gobi Desert, Samarkand, Mount Ararat, and Transylvania.

sill, *n.* a block or timber forming a basis or foundation in a structure, esp. a slab of timber or stone at the foot of a door or window; the top level of a weir; a sheet of intrusive igneous rock between other strata. [OE *syll,* cp. Icel. *syll, svill,* Swed. *syll,* Dan. *syld*]

sillabub, SYLLABUB.

siller, *n.* (*Sc.*) silver; money.

Sillery, *n.* a sparkling, dry champagne from Sillery or the neighbourhood. [village in Marne department, France]

sillograph, *n.* a writer of satires. **sillographer, -phist,** *n.* [L *sillographus,* Gr. *sillographos* (*sillos,* satirical poem)]

sillometer, *n.* an instrument for measuring the speed of a ship, esp. without a log-line. [F *siller,* to run ahead]

sillon, *n.* a defensive work raised in the middle of a very wide ditch. [F, furrow]

silly, *a.* foolish, fatuous, weak-minded; showing want of judgment, unwise, imprudent; mentally weak, imbecile; †innocent, simple-minded, guileless; †merry, happy, blessed; (*Cricket*) close to the batsman's wicket. *n.* a silly person. **silly season,** *n.* the late summer, when newspapers are traditionally full of trivial stories, for want of anything serious to print. **sillily,** *adv.* **silliness,** *n.* [OE *sǣlig,* happy, fortunate (cp. Dut. *zalig,* G *selig,* Icel. *sæll,* blessed)]

silo, *n.* (*pl.* **-los**) a store-pit or air-tight chamber for pressing and preserving green fodder; a tall construction in which grain etc. can be stored; an underground store and launch pad for a guided missile. *v.t.* to put in a silo; to convert into ensilage. [Sp., from L *sīrus,* Gr. *siros*]

silphium, *n.* a plant of the Mediterranean region, the juice of which was used by the ancients as a condiment and as a medicine; (**Silphium**) a genus of US resinous herbs of the aster family. [L, from Gr. *silphion*]

silphology, *n.* the science of larval forms. [Gr. *silphē,* beetle]

silt, *n.* fine sediment deposited by water. *v.t.* to choke or fill (up) with silt. *v.i.* to be choked (up) with silt. **silty,** *a.* [MG *Silte,* cp. MSwed. *sylta,* mud, Dan. *sylt,* Norw. *sylta,* salt-marsh, G *Sülze,* brine]

Silures, *n.pl.* an ancient British people inhabiting S Wales. **Silurian,** *a.* of or pertaining to the Silures; of or pertaining to the Silurian system. *n.* a period of geological time 438–408 million years ago, the third period of the Palaeozoic era. Silurian sediments are mostly marine, and consist of shales and limestone. The first land plants began to evolve during this period, and there were many jawless fish. **Silurist,** *n.* one belonging to or native of the region of Wales inhabited by the Silures (applied to the poet Henry Vaughan, 1622–95). [L]

Silurus, *n.* a genus of fishes typical of the Siluridae, containing the sheat-fish. **silurid,** *n., a.* [L, from Gr. *Silouros*]

silva, sylva, *n.* a group of trees, a forest, a wood. **silvan, sylvan,** *a.* wooded; pertaining to a wood or forest; growing in woods; rural, rustic. *n.* a deity of the woods, a satyr; a rustic, a forest-dweller. **silvatic, silvestrian,** *a.* **silvicultural,** *a.* **silviculture,** *n.* the cultivation of trees, forestry. **silviculturist,** *n.*

silver, *n.* a precious ductile and malleable metallic element of a white colour, at. no. 47; chem. symbol Ag; domestic utensils, implements, ornaments etc. made of this; silver or cupronickel coin; salts of silver employed in photography; the colour or lustre of or as of silver; a silver medal. *a.* made of silver; resembling silver, white or lustrous like silver; esp. of bells, soft and clear in tone; of second-best quality or rank; a silver medal. *v.t.* to coat or plate with silver or a silver substitute; to give a silvery lustre to; to tinge (hair) with white or grey. **the silver lining (in every cloud),** the bright or compensating side of any misfortune, trouble etc. **the silver screen,** the cinema screen; cinematography. **Silver Age,** *n.* in Greek and Roman mythology, the age preceding the Golden Age; the period of Latin literature following the classical period. **silver-bath,** *n.* a solution of nitrate of silver for sensitizing photographic plates. **silver-beater,** *n.* one who beats silver into thin sheets. **silver birch,** *n.* a common variety of birch with a silvery-white trunk. **silver bream,** *n.* an edible Australian fish. **silver bromide,** *n.* a pale yellow salt used in the production of photographic emulsions. **silver chloride,** *n.* a white salt used in the production of photographic paper and emulsions, and antiseptics. **silver fir,** *n.* a tall species of fir, *Abies pectinata,* with silvery bark and two white lines on the underside of the leaves. **silver-fish,** *n.* a silvery fish of various species, esp. a white variety of goldfish; any of various small wingless insects which occur in buildings and can be destructive to books, cloth etc. **silver-foil,** *n.* silver-leaf; tin foil. **silver-fox,** *n.* a variety of common red fox in a phase during which its coat becomes black mixed with silver; the pelt of this animal. **silver-gilt,** *n.* silver or silverware gilded; an imitation gilding of silver-foil varnished with yellow lacquer. **silver grey,** *n., a.* pale luminous grey. **silver-haired,** *a.* **silver iodide,** *n.* a yellow salt used in medicine, photography, and in seeding clouds to make artificial rain. **silver-leaf,** *n.* silver beaten out into thin leaves or plates; a disease of plum trees. **silver paper,** *n.* tin-foil. **silver plate,** *n.* silver-ware; (metal articles coated with) a thin layer of silver, electroplate. *v.t.* to coat with this, to electroplate. **silver-plated,** *a.* **silver-plating,** *n.* the process of coating metal articles with a layer of silver, esp. by electroplating. **silver-point,** *n.* a silver-pointed pencil; a sketch with this; the process of drawing with it. **silver-sand,** *n.* fine, white sand. **silver service,** *n.* a set of silver dining utensils; a manner of serving food in restaurants using a fork and spoon in one hand. **silverside,** *n.* the upper and choicer part of a round of beef. **silversmith,** *n.* a maker of or worker in silver articles. **silversmithing,** *n.* **silver-stick,** *n.* a court official (a field-officer of the Life Guards) attending the sovereign on state occasions. **silver-tongued,** *a.* eloquent. **silverware,** *n.* articles of silver, esp. table utensils; silver plate. **silver wedding,** *n.* a 25th wedding anniversary. **silverweed,** *n.* any of various silvery-leaved plants, esp. *Potentilla anserina.* **silverer,** *n.* **silvering,** *n.* **silverize, -ise,** *v.t.* **silverless,** *a.* **silver-like,** *a.* **silvern,** *a.* **silvery,** *a.* having the appearance of silver; having a soft clear sound. **silveriness,** *n.* [OE *seolfor* (cp. Dut. *zilver,* G *Silber,* Icel. *silfr*), etym. doubtful]

Silverstone, *n.* Britain's premier motor-racing circuit. It is situated near Towcester, Northamptonshire, and was built on a disused airfield after World War II. It staged the first world championship Grand Prix on 13 May 1950, and became the permanent home of the British Grand Prix in 1987.

Sim, *n.* **Alistair** (1900–76), Scottish actor, usually in comedies. Possessed of a marvellously expressive face, he was ideally cast in eccentric roles, as in the title role in *Scrooge* (1951). His other films include *Inspector Hornleigh* (1939), *Green for Danger* (1945), and *The Belles of St Trinians* (1954).

sima, *n.* the inner part of the earth's crust [from *si*lica and *ma*gnesia]

simar, simarre, CYMAR.

Simaruba, *n.* a genus of tropical American trees; (**si-**

maruba) a tree of this genus; simaruba-bark. [prob. Guiana name]

Simenon, *n.* **Georges** (1903–89), Belgian crime writer. Initially a pulp fiction writer, in 1931 he created Inspector Maigret of the Paris Sûreté who appeared in a series of detective novels.

Simeonite, *n.* a Low Churchman. [Charles *Simeon,* 1759–1836, of Cambridge, distinguished for his evangelism]

Simeon Stylites, St (*c.* 390–459), Syrian Christian ascetic, who practised his ideal of self-denial by living for 37 years on a platform on top of a high pillar. Feast day is 5 Jan.

Simia, *n.* (*pl.* **-miae**) a genus of anthropoid apes containing the orangutan. **simious,** *a.* **simian,** *n., a.* (of or like) a monkey or ape. [L, ape]

similar, *a.* like, having a resemblance (to); resembling (each other); alike; (*Geom.*) made up of the same number of parts arranged in the same manner, corresponding. **similarity,** *n.* **similarly,** *adv.* [F *similaire,* L *similis,* like]

simile, *n.* a comparison of two things which have some strong point of resemblance, esp. as an illustration or poetical figure. **similitude,** *n.* likeness, resemblance, outward appearance; comparison, simile, metaphor; counterpart.

similor, *n.* a gold-coloured alloy of copper and zinc used for cheap jewelry. [F (L *similis,* SIMILAR, F *or,* gold)]

simious SIMIA.

simita, SCIMITAR.

simmer, *v.i.* to boil gently; to be just below boiling-point; to be on the point of bursting into laughter, anger etc. *v.t.* to boil gently; to keep just below boiling-point. *n.* a state of simmering; the point of breaking out. **to simmer down,** to become less agitated or excited, to calm down. [cp. Dan. *summe,* G *summen,* to hum, -ER]

Simmons, *n.* **Jean** (1929–), British actress who starred in the films *Black Narcissus* (1947), *Guys and Dolls* (1955), and *Spartacus* (1960). She worked in Hollywood from the 1950s onwards, and retired in the early 1970s.

simnel, simnel-cake, *n.* a rich cake, boiled, or boiled and baked, and ornamented with scallops, formerly eaten on Mid-Lent Sunday, Easter and Christmas Day. [OF *simenel,* late L *siminellus,* fine bread, from L *simila,* the finest wheat flour, rel. to Gr. *semidalis*]

Simon[1], *n.* **Claude** (1913–), French novelist. Originally an artist, he abandoned the 'time structure' in such novels as *La Route de Flandres/The Flanders Road* (1960), *Le Palace* (1962), and *Histoire* (1967). His later novels include *Les Géorgiques* (1981) and *L'Acacia* (1989). Awarded the Nobel Prize in (1985).

Simon[2], *n.* **Herbert** (1916–), US social scientist. He researched decision-making in business corporations, and argued that maximum profit was seldom the chief motive. Awarded the Nobel Prize for Economics in 1978.

Simon[3], *n.* **(Marvin) Neil** (1927–), US playwright. His stage plays (which were made into films) include the wryly comic *Barefoot in the Park* (1963), *The Odd Couple* (1965), and *The Sunshine Boys* (1972), and the more serious, autobiographical *Brighton Beach Memoirs* (1983) and *Biloxi Blues* (1985). He has also written screenplays and co-written musicals.

Simon[4], *n.* **Paul** (1942–), US pop singer and songwriter. In a folk-rock duo with Art Garfunkel (1942–), he had hits such as 'Mrs Robinson' (1968) and 'Bridge Over Troubled Water' (1970). His solo work includes the album *Graceland* (1986), for which he drew on Cajun and African music.

Simone, *n.* **Martini** Sienese painter; see MARTINI, SIMONE.

simoniac etc. SIMONY.

Simon Pure, *n.* the genuine article, the real person. **simon-pure,** *a.* genuine, authentic, real. [character in Mrs Centlivre's, *A Bold Stroke for a Wife,* 1718]

simony, *n.* the buying or selling of ecclesiastical preferment. **simoniac,** *n., a.* (one) guilty of simony. **simoniacal,** *a.* guilty of simony; of the nature of or obtained by simony. **simoniacally,** *adv.* †**simonious,** *a.* **simonist,** *n.* [F *simonie,* late L *simōnia,* from *Simon* Magus, who wished to buy the gift of the Holy Ghost with money (Acts viii.18)]

simoom, simoon, *n.* a hot dry wind blowing over the desert, esp. of Arabia, raising great quantities of sand and causing intense thirst. [Arab. *samūm,* from *samma,* to poison]

simp, *n.* (*coll.*) a simpleton. [SIMPLE]

simpai, *n.* a small black-crested monkey of Sumatra. [Malay]

simpatico, *n.* (*It.*) sympathetic; congenial.

simper, *v.i.* to smile in an affected manner, to smirk. *v.t.* to utter with a simper. *n.* an affected smile or smirk. **simperer,** *n.* **simpering,** *a.* **simperingly,** *adv.* [cp. Norw. *semper,* smart, Dan. dial. *semper,* Swed. *sipp,* prim]

simple, *a.* consisting of only one thing; uncompounded, unmingled, all of one kind, not analysable, not subdivided, elementary; not complicated, not complex, straightforward; not elaborate, not adorned, not sumptuous; plain, homely, humble, of low degree; insignificant, trifling; unaffected, unsophisticated, natural, artless, sincere; credulous; clear, intelligible; weak in intellect, silly, inexperienced, ignorant; absolute, mere. *n.* something not mixed or compounded; a simpleton; a medicinal herb or a medicine made from it. **simple addition,** *n.* addition of numbers all of the same denomination. **simple fraction,** *n.* a fraction having whole numbers for the denominator and numerator, a common or vulgar fraction. **simple fracture** FRACTURE. **simple-hearted,** *a.* genuine, sincere; uncomplicated, guileless. **simple interest,** *n.* interest upon the principal only. **simple machine,** *n.* any of various simple mechanisms, including the pulley, wedge, lever, wheel and axle, screw, and inclined plane, which overcome resistance at one point by applying force usu. at another point. **simple-minded,** *a.* foolish, stupid; mentally deficient, feeble-minded. **simple-mindedness,** *n.* **simple sentence,** *n.* one with only one main clause. †**simpleness,** *n.* simplicity. †**simpler,** *n.* one who gathers simples, a herbalist. †**simplesse,** *n.* simplicity. **simpleton,** *n.* a silly, gullible or feeble-minded person. **simplex,** *a.* simple, not compound; in telecommunications, allowing the transmission of a signal in only one direction at a time. *n.* the most rudimentary geometric figure of a given dimension (e.g. a line in one-dimensional space, a triangle in two-dimensional space). **simplicity,** *n.* absolutely without limitation or qualification. **simplify,** *v.t.* to make simple; to make simpler or easier to understand; to reduce to essentials. **simplification,** *n.* **simplifier,** *n.* **simplism,** *n.* affectation of simplicity; oversimplification. †**simplist,** *n.* a simpler. **simpliste,** *a.* (F) simplistic. **simplistic,** *a.* oversimplified, naive, superficial, unrealistically limited, shallow etc; oversimplifying. **simplistically,** *adv.* **simply,** *adv.* [F, from L *simplicem,* nom. *-plex,* onefold (*sim-,* cp. *semel,* once, *simul,* at once, *singulī,* one by one, *-plic-,* as in *plicāre,* to fold)]

Simpson, *n.* **Wallis Warfield, Duchess of Windsor** (1896–1986), US socialite, twice divorced, who married the Duke of Windsor (formerly EDWARD VIII) 1937, following his abdication.

simulacrum, *n.* (*pl.* **-cra**, **-crums**) an image, a shadowy or misleading representation, a semblance. [L, from *simulāre,* to SIMULATE]

simulate, *v.t.* to assume the likeness or mere appearance of; to counterfeit, to feign, to imitate, to put on, to mimic, to reproduce the structure, movement or conditions of (e.g. in an experiment, by computer etc.). **simulated,** *a.* pretended, false; of leather, fur etc., imitation; false, feigned; of the flight of an aircraft, spaceship etc., reproduced or represented (by a model). **simulation,** *n.* **simulative,** *a.* **simulatively,** *adv.* **simulator,** *n.* [L *simulātus,* p.p. of *simulāre,* from *similis,* SIMILAR]

simulcast, *n.* (the transmission of) a simultaneous broadcast on radio and television. *v.t.* to broadcast a programme in this way [*simul*taneous and broad*cast*]

simultaneous, *a.* happening, done or acting at the same time. **simultaneity**, *n.* **simultaneousness,** *n.* **simultaneously,** *adv.* [late L *simultāneus* (*simultim,* adv., from L *simul,* together, -ANEOUS)]

simurg, simurgh, **simorg**, *n.* an enormous fabulous bird of Persian mythology. [Pers. *sīmurgh*]

sin¹, *n.* transgression of duty, morality, or the law of God; wickedness, moral depravity; a transgression, an offence; a breach of etiquette, social standards etc.; †a sin-offering; †the embodiment of sin. *v.i.* (*past, p.p.* **sinned**) to commit sin; to offend (against). **mortal sin,** deliberate sin that deprives the soul of divine grace. **original sin** ORIGINAL. **seven deadly sins** SEVEN. **to live in sin,** of a couple, to cohabit without being married. **sin bin,** *n.* (*euphem.*) a brothel; (*sl.*) an area to the side of an ice-hockey pitch where players who have committed fouls are temporarily sent; (*coll.*) a special unit for unruly children. †**sin-born,** *a.* **sin-bred,** *a.* produced from sin. **sin-eater,** *n.* one who took on the sins of a deceased person by eating beside the corpse. **sin-offering,** *n.* a sacrifice to atone for sin. **sinful,** *a.* **sinfully,** *adv.* **sinfulness,** *n.* **sinless,** *a.* **sinlessly,** *adv.* **sinlessness,** *n.* **sinner,** *n.* [OE *synn,* cp. Dut. *zonde,* G *Sünde,* Icel., Dan. and Swed. *synd*]

sin², SITH.

sin³, (*abbr.*) sine.

Sinai, *n.* Egyptian peninsula, at the head of the Red Sea; area 65,000 sq km/25,000 sq miles. Resources include oil, natural gas, manganese, and coal; irrigation water from the Nile is carried under the Suez Canal. **Sinaitic,** *a.* of, pertaining to, or given at Mount Sinai or the peninsula of Sinai.

Sinai, Battle of, a battle (6–24 Oct. 1973) which took place during the Yom Kippur War between Israel and Egypt. One of the longest tank battles ever, the Israelis crossed the Suez canal on 16 Oct. cutting off the Egyptian 3rd Army.

Sinan, *n.* (1489–1588), Ottoman architect, chief architect from 1538 to SULEIMAN the Magnificent. Among the hundreds of buildings he designed are the Suleimaniye in Istanbul, a mosque complex, and the Topkapi Saray, palace of the Sultan (now a museum).

Sinanthropus, *n.* an ape-like human, the remains of whom have been discovered in China, Peking man. [Gr. *Sinae,* the Chinese, *anthropos,* a man]

Sinapis, *n.* a genus of crucifers with five species from the seeds of which mustard is prepared. **sinapic,** *a.* **sinapine**, *n.* an organic base, existing as sulphocyanate in the seed of *Sinapis alba,* white mustard. **sinapisine**, *n.* a white crystalline substance obtained from black mustard seed. **sinapism**, *n.* a mustard plaster. [L, from Gr. *sinēpi,* mustard]

Sinatra, *n.* **Frank (Francis Albert)** (1915–), US singer and film actor. He achieved fame with the Tommy Dorsey band with songs such as 'Night and Day' and 'You'd Be So Nice To Come Home To'. After a slump in his career, he established himself as an actor. *From Here to Eternity* (1953) won him an Academy Award. His later songs include 'My Way'.

Sinbad the Sailor, Sindbad, in the *Arabian Nights*, an adventurer who makes seven eventful voyages. He encounters the Old Man of the Sea and, on his second voyage, is carried aloft by the roc, a giant bird.

since, *adv.* after or from a time specified or implied till now; at some time after such a time and before now; from that time before this, before now, ago. *prep.* from the time of; throughout or during the time after; after and before now. *conj.* from the time that or when, during the time, after that; inasmuch as; because. [ME *sithens,* thence, OE *siththan* (*sith,* after, *thon,* that)]

sincere, *a.* being in reality as in appearance or profession; not feigned or put on, genuine, honest, undissembling, frank. **sincerely,** *adv.* **sincereness,** *n.* **sincerity**, *n.* [OF, from L *sincērus,* pure, sincere]

sinciput, *n.* the upper part of the head, especially from the forehead to the coronal suture. **sincipital**, *a.* [L SEMI-, *caput,* head]

Sinclair¹, *n.* **Clive** (1940–), British electronics engineer, who produced the first widely available pocket calculator, pocket and wristwatch televisions, a series of popular home computers, and the innovative but commercially disastrous 'C5' personal transport (a low cycle-like three-wheeled device powered by a washing-machine motor).

Sinclair², *n.* **Upton** (1878–1968), US novelist. His concern for social reforms is reflected in *The Jungle* (1906), which exposed the horrors of the Chicago stockyards and led to a change in food-processing laws, *Boston* (1928), and his Lanny Budd series (1940–53), including *Dragon's Teeth* (1942), which won a Pulitzer Prize.

sind, synd, *v.t.* (*Sc.*) to rinse; to wash down (drink, food etc.). *n.* a rinsing; a draught. [etym. doubtful]

sine¹, *n.* in trigonometry, orig. the straight line drawn from one extremity of an arc perpendicular to the diameter passing through the other extremity; now, of an angle, the ratio of the length of the line opposite the angle to the length of the hypotenuse in a right-angled triangle. **sinical,** *a.* pertaining to a sine or sines. [L *sinus,* curve]

sine², SYNE.

sine³, *prep.* without, lacking. **sine cura,** without duties or office. **sine die,** without any day (being fixed). **sine qua non**, an indispensable condition. [L]

sinecure, *n.* an ecclesiastical benefice without cure of souls; any paid office with few or no duties attached. **sinecurism,** *n.* **sinecurist,** *n.* [L *sine cura,* without care]

sinew, *n.* a tendon, a fibrous cord connecting muscle and bone; (*pl.*) muscles; that which gives strength or power. *v.t.* to knit strongly together; to strengthen or furnish with sinews. **the sinews of war,** money. **sinewed,** *a.* **sinewless,** *a.* **sinewy,** *a.* **sinewiness,** *n.* [OE *sinu, seono* (cp. Dut. *zenuw,* G *sehne,* Icel. *sin*), cp. HOX]

sinfonia, *n.* a symphony; a symphony orchestra. **sinfonietta,** *n.* a short or light symphony; a small symphony orchestra. [It.]

sing, *v.i.* (*past* **sang**, †**sung**, *p.p.* **sung**) to utter words in a tuneful manner, to render a song vocally, to make vocal melody; to emit sweet or melodious sounds; of a kettle etc., to make a murmuring or whistling sound; to ring, to buzz; to compose poetry. (*sl.*) to confess, to inform, to grass; to utter loudly and clearly. *v.t.* to utter (words, a song, tune etc.) in a tuneful or melodious manner; to relate, proclaim or celebrate in verse or poetry; to celebrate; to accompany with singing; to greet, acclaim, lull, usher (in or out) etc., with singing; to chant. **to sing along,** of an audience, to accompany a performer in singing popular songs. **to sing out,** to call out loudly, to shout. **singsong,** *a.* of a voice, accent etc., having a rising and falling inflection; having a monotonous rhythm. *n.* a monotonous rising and falling (of a voice etc.); an informal session of singing usu. well-known songs. *v.i., v.t.* to utter, to recite, sing etc. in a sing-song manner. **singable,** *a.* **singer,** *n.* **singing,** *n., a.* **singing-bird,** *n.* **singing-master,** *n.* one who teaches singing. **singing telegram,** *n.* a (usu. congratulatory) telegram with a message which is delivered in song (often by someone in costume). **singing-voice,** *n.* the voice as used in singing. **singingly,** *adv.* [OE *singan,* cp. Dut. *zingen,* G. *singen,* Icel. *syngja*]

sing., (*abbr.*) singular.

Singapore, *n.* Republic of; country in SE Asia, off the tip of the Malay Peninsula. **area** 620 sq km/239 sq miles. **capital** Singapore City in the south of the island, a major world port and financial centre, founded by Stamford Raffles. **physical** comprises Singapore Island, which is low and flat, and 57 small islands. **population** (1989) 2,668,000 (Chinese 75%, Malay 14%, Tamil 7%); annual growth rate 1.2%. **exports** electronics, petroleum products, rubber, machinery, vehicles. **language** Malay, Chinese, Tamil, and English (all official). **religion** Buddhist, Taoist, Muslim, Hindu, Christian.

singe, *v.t.* (*pres.p.* **singeing,** *past, p.p.* **singed**) to burn slightly; to burn the surface of or the tips of (hair etc.); to scorch; to burn bristles, nap etc. off (an animal carcase, fabric). *n.* a slight or superficial burn. [OE *sengan,* cp. Dut. *zengen,* G *sengen,* cogn. with Icel. *sangr,* burnt, singed]

Singer[1], *n.* **Isaac Bashevis** (1904–), Polish novelist and short story writer. His works, written in Yiddish, often portray traditional Jewish life in Poland, and the loneliness of old age. They include *Gimpel the Fool* (1957), *The Slave* (1960), *Shosha* (1978), and *Old Love* (1979). Awarded the Nobel Prize in 1978.

Singer[2], *n.* **Isaac Merit** (1811–75), US inventor of domestic and industrial sewing machines. Within a few years of opening his first factory in 1851, he became the world's largest manufacturer (despite charges of patent infringement by Elias HOWE), and by the late 1860s more than 100,000 Singer sewing machines were in use in the US alone. To make his machines available to the widest market, Singer became the first manufacturer to offer attractive hire-purchase terms.

Singh[1], Gobind, GOBIND SINGH.

Singh[2], *n.* **Vishwanath Pratap** (1931–), Indian politician, prime minister from 1989. As a member of the Congress (I) Party, he held ministerial posts under Indira Gandhi and Rajiv Gandhi, and from 1984 led an anti-corruption drive. When he unearthed an arms-sales scandal in 1988, he was ousted from the government and party and formed a broad-based opposition alliance, the Janata Dal.

Singhalese SINHALESE.

single, *a.* consisting of one only, sole; particular, individual, separate, solitary, alone, unaided, unaccompanied; unmarried; simple, not compound, not complicated, not combined with others; involving or performed by one or by one on each side; designed for use by or with one person, thing etc.; sincere, ingenuous, consistent; of petals or blooms, not double, not clustered. *n.* a single round, game, a hit for one run in cricket etc.; a single measure, amount or thing; an unmarried person; a flower with the usual number of petals or blooms, not a double or cluster; a gramophone record with only one track recorded on each side; a rail, bus etc ticket for a journey in one direction; (*pl.*) unmarried people; (*pl.*) a game, esp. of tennis, consisting of a single player on either side. *v.t.* to pick out from among others. **single-acting,** *a.* of an engine or pump, working by means of pressure on one side of the piston or pistons only. **single-action,** *a.* of a gun that must be cocked before firing. **single bed,** *n.* a bed intended to be used by one person. **single-breasted,** *a.* of a jacket, coat etc., having only one thickness of cloth over the breast when closed, with one central set of buttons, holes etc.; not overlapping. **single cream,** *n.* a pouring cream of a less fatty consistency than double cream. **single-deck,** *a.* of a bus, vessel etc., with accommodation on one level only. **single-decker,** *n.* (*coll.*) a bus such as this. **single-end,** *n.* (*Sc.*) a one-room dwelling. **single-entry** ENTRY. **single figures,** *n.pl.* a number etc. under 10. **single-handed,** *a.* done without assistance; unassisted, alone; of a player in certain games etc., using only one hand. *adv.* without assistance. **single-handedly,** *adv.* **single-handedness,** *n.* **single-hearted,** *a.* free from duplicity, sincere; devoted. **single-loader,** *n.* a breech-loading rifle without a magazine. **single-minded,** *a.* intent on one purpose only; dedicated. **single-mindedly,** *adv.* **single-mindedness,** *n.* **single parent,** *n.* one parent raising a child or children alone. **single-parent family,** a one-parent family. **single phase,** *n., a.* (of) an alternating current-supply using two wires. **singles bar, club,** *n.* a bar or club where unmarried people meet. **single-seater,** *a.* of a vehicle, vessel etc., having seating for only one person. **single-sex,** *a.* of a school or other institution, admitting members of one sex only. **single-stick,** *n.* a long stick formerly used in a kind of fencing; fencing with this, cudgel-play. **single-track,** *a.* of a road or railway, housing only one track. **singletree,** *n.* (*N Am., Austral.*) a swingletree. **singleness,** *n.* **singlet,** *n.* an under-shirt, a vest. **singleton,** *n.* a single-card of any particular suit in a player's hand at whist, bridge etc.; a mathematical set of one; a single object, person etc. as opposed to a group or pair. **singly,** *adv.* [late L *singulus,* from L *singulī,* one by one]

singsong SING[1].

singspiel, *n.* a dramatic entertainment in which the action is expressed alternately in dialogue and song. [G (*singen,* to SING, *spiel,* play)]

singular, *a.* single, individual, particular, standing alone, out of the usual course, strange, remarkable, extraordinary, unique, distinguished; peculiar, odd, eccentric; of a word or inflected form of a word, denoting or referring to one person or thing; not plural; of a logical proposition, referring to a specific thing or person, not general. *n.* the singular number; a word denoting this. **singularity,** *n.* **singularize, -ise,** *v.t.* to alter a word that looks like a plural (as *pease*) to the singular form (as *pea*); to make striking or eye-catching. **singularization, -isation,** *n.* **singularly,** *adv.* [ME *singuler,* F *singulier,* L *singulāris,* as SINGLE]

singultus, *n.* hiccups, hiccuping. *a.* [L]

sinh, *n.* a hyperbolic sine [*sine* and *hyperbolic*]

Sinhalese, Singhalese, Cingalese, Sinhala, *a.* of or pertaining to Sri Lanka (formerly Ceylon), or to its majority people or their language, Sri Lankan. *n.* a native or citizen of Sri Lanka; a member of the Sinhalese people largely inhabiting Sri Lanka; the official language of Sri Lanka and the Sinhalese people which belongs to the Indo-Iranian branch of the Indo-European family.

Sinic, *a.* Chinese. **Sinicism,** *n.* a Chinese idiom, custom etc. **Sinicize, -ise, Sinify,** *v.t.* **Sinicization, -isation, Sinification,** *n.* [med. L *sinicus,* from late L *Sīnae,* the Chinese]

sinical SINE[1].

sinister, *a.* (*Her.*) on the left side (of a shield etc.), the side to the right of the observer; ill-omened, inauspicious, ill-looking, malignant, malevolent, villainous. **sinisterly,** *adv.* **sinisterness,** *n.* **sinistral,** *a.* of a spiral shell, with a whorl turning to the left; sinistrous. **sinistrally,** *adv.* **sinistro-,** *comb. form.* **sinistrorse,** *a.* directed or inclining towards the left; (*Bot.*) twining to the left; sinistral. **sinistrorsal,** *a.* **sinistrorsally,** *adv.* **sinistrous,** *a.* being on, pertaining to, directed towards, or inclined to the left; ill-omened, unlucky, sinister; †wrong, perverse, absurd. **sinistrously,** *adv.* [F *sinistre,* L *sinistrum,* nom. *-tor,* left]

sink, *v.i.* (*past* **sank,** †**sunk,** *p.p.* **sunk,** *part.a.* **sunken**) to go downwards, to descend, to fall gradually; to disappear below the surface or the horizon; to fall or descend by force of gravity; to decline to a lower level of health, morals etc.; to deteriorate; to subside, to droop, to despond; to expire or come to an end by degrees; to become lower in intensity, pitch, value, price etc.; to become shrunken or hollow, to slope downwards, to recede; to go deep or deeper into, to penetrate, to be impressed into, to be absorbed. *v.t.* to cause to sink; to submerge (as) in a fluid, to send below the surface; to excavate, to make by excavating; to cause to disappear; to put out of sight, to conceal, to suppress, to lose sight of; to allow to fall or droop; to lower, to degrade, to ruin; to reduce, to diminish, to lessen the value of; to invest unprofitably, to lose, to waste, to squander; (*coll.*) to drink, to quaff. *n.* a plastic, porcelain or metal basin, usu. fitted to a water supply and drainage system in a kitchen; a sewer; a cesspool; a place of iniquity; a depression or area of ground in which water collects, a sink-hole, a swallow-hole; in physics, a device, body or process which absorbs or dissipates energy, as *heat sink.* **to sink in,** to become absorbed, to penetrate; to become understood. **to sink or swim,** to either succeed or fail (in a venture etc.). **sink-hole,** *n.* a hole for the discharge of foul waste; a hole or series of holes in limestone strata through which water sinks below the surface or a stream disappears underground, a swallow-hole. **sink-**

tidy, *n.* a receptacle with a perforated bottom for holding washing-up utensils; a small sieve placed over a plug-hole for catching refuse. **sink unit,** *n.* a sink and draining board set in a structure with a drawer and cupboards. **sinkable,** *a.* **sinkage** , *n.* the act, operation or process of sinking; the amount of sinking; a depression, a shaft, a sinking or hollow area. **sinker,** *n.* one who or that which sinks; a weight used to sink a fishing-line, net etc. **sinking,** *n., a.* **sinking-fund,** *n.* a fund set aside for the reduction of a debt. **sinky,** *a.* [OE *sincan* (cp. Dut. *zinken,* G *sinken,* Dan. *synke,* also Sansk., *sich,* to sprinkle)]

sinless, sinner etc. SIN[1].

sinnet, SENNIT.

Sinn Féin, *n.* Irish nationalist party ('We ourselves'), founded by Arthur Griffith (1872–1922) in 1905; in 1917 DE VALERA became its president. It is the political wing of the Irish Republican Army, and is similarly split between comparative moderates and extremists. In 1985 it gained representation in 17 out of 26 district councils in Northern Ireland. **Sinn Feiner,** *n.* a member of Sinn Fein. [Ir., ourselves]

Sino-, *comb. form.* Chinese.

Sino-Japanese Wars, wars waged by Japan against China to expand to the mainland. First Sino-Japanese War (1894–95): under the treaty of Shimonoseki, Japan secured the 'independence' of Korea, cession of Taiwan and the nearby Pescadores Islands, and the Liaodong peninsula (for a naval base). France, Germany, and Russia pressured Japan into returning the last-named, which Russia occupied in 1896 to establish Port Arthur (now Lüda); this led to the Russo-Japanese War of 1904–05. Second Sino-Japanese War (1931–45): in 1931–32 the Japanese occupied Manchuria, which they formed into the puppet state of Manchukuo. They also attacked Shanghai, and moved into NE China. In 1937 Chinese leaders Chiang Kai-shek and Mao Zedong allied to fight the Japanese; war was renewed as the Japanese overran NE China and seized Shanghai and Nanjing. In 1938 the Japanese capture of Wuhan and Guangzhou was followed by the transfer of the Chinese capital to Chongqing; a period of stalemate followed. The Japanese attack on the US in 1941 (see PEARL HARBOR) led to the extension of lend-lease aid to China and US entry into war against Japan and its allies. In 1944 a Japanese offensive threatened Chongqing. In 1945 the Chinese received the Japanese surrender at Nanjing in Sept., after the Allies had concluded World War II.

sinology, *n.* the study of Chinese languages, culture, literature etc. **sinological,** *a.* **sinologist, sinologue,** *n.* [Gr. *Sinae,* late L *Sinae,* see SINIC]

sinople, *n.* (*Her.*) vert, green; a red earth formerly used as a pigment. **sinopic,** *a.* [OF from L and Gr. *Sinōpis,* from *Sinōpe,* Greek colony on the Euxine]

Sino-Tibetan, *n.* a family of languages comprising most Chinese languages, Tibetan, Burmese and usu. Thai. *a.* of or pertaining to this family of languages.

sinsemilla, *n.* a specially potent type of marijuana; the (variety of) cannabis plant from which it is obtained. [N Am. Sp., without seed]

sinter, *n.* a calcareous or siliceous rock precipitated from (hot) mineral waters. *v.t.* to form (metal powder, ceramics, glass etc.) into a solid mass by pressure or heating at a temperature below melting-point. *v.i.* to be formed into such a mass. **sinterability,** *n.* **sintering,** *n.* the process of sintering. [G, CINDER]

sintoc, *n.* a tree of Sumatra, Java and Borneo, with aromatic bark. [Malay *sintoq*]

sinuate, -ated, *a.* esp. of the edges of leaves etc., bending, curving or winding in and out. †*v.i.,* to wind or creep in and out. **sinuately,** *adv.* **sinuation,** *n.* **sinuosity,** *n.* the quality of being sinuous; a bend or series of bends and curves. **sinuous,** *a.* bending in and out; winding, serpentine, tortuous. **sinuously,** *adv.* **sinuousness,** *n.* [L *sinuātus,* p.p. of *sinuāre* to bend, from SINUS]

Sinuiju, *n.* capital of North Pyongan province, near the mouth of the Yalu river, North Korea; population (1984) 754,000. It was founded in 1910.

sinupallial, -palliate, *a.* (*Conch.*) having a deeply incurved pallial line; of or pertaining to the Sinupalliata, a division of bivalves with a posterior sinus in the pallial impression for the passage to and fro of the pallial siphons.

sinus, *n.* (*pl.* **sinuses**) a cavity or pouch-like hollow, esp. in bone or tissue; the cavity in the skull which connects with the nose; a fistula; a rounded recess or curve, as in the margin of a leaf. **sinusitis,** *n.* (painful) inflammation of a nasal sinus. [L, a curve, a recess]

Sion, ZION.

Sioux, *n. pl.* principal group of the Dakota family of North American PLAINS INDIANS, now found in South Dakota and Nebraska. They defeated Gen. George Custer at Little Bighorn, Montana (under chiefs Crazy Horse and Sitting Bull); as a result, Congress abrogated the Fort Laramie treaty of 1868 (which had given the Indians a large area in the Black Hills of Dakota). Gold, uranium, coal, oil and natural gas are found there, and the Sioux were awarded $160 million compensation in 1980. *a.* pertaining to the Sioux. **Siouan,** *n.* a family of central and eastern N American languages; a Sioux. *a.* pertaining to the Sioux or their languages. [F, from N Am. Ind.]

sip, *v.t., v.i.* (*past, p.p.* **sipped**) to drink or imbibe in small quantities using the lips. *n.* a very small draught of liquid; the act of sipping. **sipper,** *n.* **sippet,** *n.* a small piece of toast or fried bread garnishing a dish of mince etc.; a small piece of bread or other food soaked in broth etc. [OE *sypian,* cogn. with *sūpan,* to SUP (cp. MDut. *sippen,* Swed. dial. *syppa*)]

sipahee, sipahi, SEPOY.

sipe, SEEP.

siphon, *n.* a curved tube having one branch longer than the other, used for conveying liquid over the edge of a cask, tank etc., through the force of atmospheric pressure; a bottle for holding aerated water, discharging through a siphon-like tube through the pressure of the gas; a soda siphon; a suctorial or other tubular organ, esp. in cephalopods, gastropods etc. *v.t.* to convey or draw off by a siphon; *v.i.* to flow or become conveyed by a siphon. **siphon bottle,** *n.* (*chiefly N Am.*) a soda siphon. **siphon-trap,** *n.* a trap in the emptying pipe of sinks, baths and water-closets in which a water seal prevents the reflux of foul gases. **siphonage,** *n.* **siphonal, siphonic,** *a.* **Siphonaptera,** *n.* an order of wingless insects represented by the fleas. **siphonet,** *n.* one of the abdominal tubes through which the honey-dew is exuded by an aphis. **siphonophore,** *n.* one of the Siphonophoridae, variously regarded as a colony of medusoid zooids or as a single individual composed of a cluster of tubular organs. **siphonophoran,** *n., a.* **siphuncle,** *n.* the tube connecting the chambers of the shell in many cephalopods; the suctorial or other tubes in insects etc. **siphuncular,** *a.* **siphunculate, -ated,** *a.* [F, from L *sīphōnem,* nom. *-pho,* Gr. *siphōn,* pipe]

sipper, sippet SIP.

sipylite, *n.* a niobite of erbium. [L *Sipyl-us,* Gr. *Sipulos,* one of the children of Niobe, -ITE]

sir, *n.* a term of courteous or formal address to a man; (**Sir**) a title prefixed to the names of baronets and knights and formerly clergymen; †a lord, a gentleman. [SIRE]

sirdar, *n.* a military leader, or commander in India; the former commander-in-chief of the Egyptian army; a leader, chief, foreman etc. [Pers. *sar,* head, *-dār,* holding]

sire, *n.* a title used in addressing a king or a sovereign prince; a father, a progenitor; the male parent of an animal, esp. a stallion. *v.t.* esp. of stallions or male domestic animals, to beget. [OF, earlier *senre,* L SENIOR]

siren, *n.* in Greek mythology, a sea-nymph, half-woman and half-bird, one of several dwelling on a rocky isle and luring sailors to shipwreck by their singing; a charming or seductive woman, esp. a dangerous temptress; a sweet singer; an apparatus for producing a loud warning sound by means of a rotating perforated disc through which steam or compressed air is emitted; an electrical warning device emitting a similarly piercing sound; one of the Sirenidae, a family of American eel-like amphibians, with two anterior feet and permanent branchiae. **siren-suit,** *n.* a suit in one piece and closed with a zip-fastening. **sirenian**, *n.* one of the Sirenia, an order of marine herbivorous mammals, allied to the whales, but having the fore limbs developed into paddles, comprising the manatees and dugongs. *a.* of or pertaining to the Sirenia. [L *sīrēn*, Gr. *seirēn*]

sirgang, *n.* a brilliant green Indian magpie or jackdaw, *Cissa chinensis*. [EInd.]

sirih, *n.* betel-leaf. [Malay]

Sirius, *n.* the brightest star in the sky, 8.7 light years away in the constellation Canis Major. Sirius is a white star with a mass of 2.35 Suns, diameter 1.8 times that of the Sun, and a luminosity of 23 Suns. It is orbited every 50 years by a white dwarf, Sirius B. **Sirian,** *a.* **siriasis**, *n.* sunstroke. [L from Gr. *seirosios*, cogn. with *seiriasis*, from *seiriân*, to be hot]

sirloin, *n.* the loin or upper part of the loin of beef. [orig. *surloine*, OF *surlonge* (*sur*, over, *longe*, LOIN)]

†**sirname,** SURNAME.

sirocco, scirocco, †**siroc**, *n.* (*pl.* **-ccos**) a hot oppressive wind blowing from N Africa across to Italy etc.; applied generally to a sultry southerly wind in Italy. [It. *sirocco*, Arab. *sharq*, east]

sirrah, *n.* fellow, sir (a term of address used in anger or contempt). [Prov. *sira*, F *sire*, SIRE]

sirree, *n.* (*N Am. coll.*) sir, sirrah (used for emphasis often with *yes* or *no*). [SIR]

†**sir-reverence,** *n.* corr. of the phrase 'save reverence' used apologetically when something distasteful is mentioned; hence, human ordure; a lump of this.

sirup, SYRUP.

sirvente, *n.* a form of lay, usu. satirical, used by the mediaeval trouvères and troubadours. [F, *servir*, L *servīre*, to SERVE]

sis, siss, *n.* (*coll.*) short for SISTER. **sissy, cissy**, *n.* an effeminate, feeble or cowardly fellow. *a.* effeminate, feeble, cowardly. [SISTER]

-sis, *suf.* (*pl.* **-ses**) denoting a process or action of, or condition caused by. [Gr.]

sisal, sisal-grass, -hemp, *n.* the fibre of the American aloe used for cordage etc. [*Sisal*, a port in Yucatan from where it was first exported]

siscowet, *n.* a great lake trout found in Lake Superior. [Ojibwa]

siskin, *n.* a small migratory song-bird, *Carduelus spinus*, allied to the goldfinch, the aberdevine. [MDut. *cijsken*, LG *zieske*, Pol. *czyzik*]

siskiwit, -kowet SISCOWET.

Sisley, *n.* **Alfred** (1839–99), French impressionist painter, known for his views of Port-Marly and the Seine, which he painted during floods in 1876.

sist, *v.t.* (*Sc. Law*) to stop, to stay; to summon. *n.* a stay of proceedings. [L *sistere*, to cause to stand, from *stāre*, to stand]

sister, *n.* a female born of the same parents as another; applied to a half-sister, a sister-in-law or a foster-sister, also to a very close female friend; a senior nurse, one in charge of a hospital ward; a female fellow-member of the same group, society, religious community etc., esp. a nun in the Roman Catholic Church; any thing, quality etc. closely resembling another. (*chiefly N Am. coll.*) a woman (usu. as a form of address). *a.* closely related, similar, of the same design, type, origins, as *sister ships*. *v.i.* to be closely allied or to have a sisterly resemblance (to). *v.t.* to be sister to; to resemble closely. **half-sister** HALF. **sister of mercy,** a member of a sisterhood. **sisterhood**, *n.* the state of being a sister, the relation of sisters; a community of women bound together by religious vows, common interests etc. **sister-hook,** *n.* one of a pair of hooks opening to receive a rope etc., and overlapping. **sister-in-law,** *n.* (*pl.* **sisters-in-law**), a husband's or wife's sister; a brother's wife. **sisterless,** *a.* **sisterlike,** *a.* **sisterliness,** *n.* **sisterly,** *a.* [OE *sweoster, swuster* (cp. Dut. *zuster*, G *schwester*, Icel. *systir*, also L *soror*, Sansk. *svasā*)]

Sistine Chapel, *n.* a chapel in the Vatican, Rome, begun under Pope Sixtus IV in 1473 by Giovanni del Dolci, and decorated by (among others) Michelangelo. It houses the conclave that meets to select a new pope.

sistrum, *n.* (*pl.* **-trums, -tra**) a jingling instrument used by the ancient Egyptians in the worship of Isis. [L, from Gr. *seistron*, from *seiein*, to shake]

Sisulu, *n.* **Walter** (1912–), South African civil-rights activist. The first full-time Secretary General of the ANC (African National Congress), in 1964, with Nelson Mandela. He was imprisoned, in the 1964 Rivonia Trial for opposition to the apartheid system and released, at the age of 77, as a gesture of reform by President F.W. De Klerk in 1989.

Sisyphus, *n.* in Greek mythology, king of Corinth who, after his evil life, was condemned in the underworld to roll a huge stone uphill, which always fell back before he could reach the top. **Sisyphean**, *a.* unceasingly or fruitlessly laborious.

Sisyrinchium, *n.* a genus of grass-like plants with blue or yellow flowers of the iris family. [Gr. *sus*, swine, *rhunchos*, snout]

sit, *v.i.* (*pres.p.* **sitting,** *past, p.p.* **sat**) to set oneself or be in a resting posture with the body nearly vertical supported on the buttocks; of birds and various animals, to be in a resting posture; to perch, to roost; to cover eggs in order to hatch, to brood; to be in a specified position, quarter etc.; to be situated; of clothes etc., to suit, to fit; to rest or weigh (on); to take a position, to pose (for one's portrait etc.); to meet, to hold a session; to hold or occupy a seat (on) a deliberative body or in a specified capacity (as in judgment); to take up a position, to encamp (before) so as to besiege; †to remain, to abide. *v.t.* to cause to sit, to set; to place (oneself) in a seat; to hold or keep a sitting position on (a horse etc.); to be a candidate for an examination; to baby-sit. *n.* an act or time of sitting; a sit-down. **to sit back,** to withdraw from active participation. **to sit by,** to observe without taking an active part. **to sit down,** to place oneself on a seat after standing; to begin a siege. **to sit for,** to take an examination; to represent a constituency in parliament; to pose for a portrait. **to sit in,** to observe, be present at, or participate in a discussion, meeting, lecture etc., as a visitor; to take part in a sit-in. **to sit on,** to hold a meeting, discussion or investigation over; (*coll.*) to repress severely, to snub; (*coll.*) to suppress. **to sit out,** to sit out of doors; to sit apart from (a dance, meeting etc.); to sit till the end of (a concert etc.); to stay longer than (other visitors). **to sit tight,** to hold firm and do nothing. **to sit under,** to attend the ministrations of (a clergyman). **to sit up,** to rise from a recumbent position; to sit with the body erect; suddenly to pay attention, take notice, become alert; not to go to bed. **sit-down,** *n.* (*coll.*) a rest, a break; a type of passive resistance offered by participants in a demonstration; a sit-down strike. *a.* of a meal, eaten while seated at a table. **sit-down strike,** *n.* a strike in which employees occupy their place of work. **sit-in,** *n.* the occupation of premises (e.g. at a university) as a form of protest. **sit-up,** *n.* a physical exercise in which the upper torso is raised from a reclining into a sitting position using the abdominal muscles. **sitter,** *n.* one who sits, esp. for a portrait; , a hen that sits on a clutch of eggs to incubate them; any other animal that sits well, badly etc.; a baby-sitter. **sitting,** *n.* a period of continuous sitting (as for a meal, a portrait); a session, a meeting for business; brooding; a seat in a church etc. allotted to one person; a clutch of eggs for hatching. *a.* seated; of a hen, brooding; holding office; occupying or in possession of; in session. **sitting duck,** an easy target, someone in a defenceless position. **sitting pretty,** in an advantageous position. **sitting-room,** *n.* a room for sitting in, a lounge; room or space for persons sitting. **sitting target,** *n.* a sitting duck. **sitting tenant,** *n.* one occupying a flat, house etc. [OE *sittan* (cp. Dut. *zitten*, G *sitzen*, Icel. *sitja*, also L *sedēre*, Gr. *hezesthai*, Sansk. *sad*)]

Sita, *n.* in Hinduism, the wife of Rama, an avatar (manifestation) of the god Vishnu; a character in the RAMAYANA epic, characterized by chastity and kindness.

sitar, *n.* an Indian stringed musical instrument with a long neck. [Hind., three-stringed]

sitcom, *n.* (*coll.*) a situation comedy. [*sit*uation *com*edy]

site, *n.* local position, situation; ground on which anything, esp. a building, stands, has stood, or will stand. *v.t.* to position, locate. †**sited,** *a.* situated; having a site. [F, from L *situs*]

†**sith,** †**sithen,** *conj.* since; seeing that. [OE, see SINCE]

sitiology, sitology, *n.* dietetics. **sit(i)ophobia,** *n.* morbid repugnance to food. [Gr. *sitos,* food, *sition,* bread, -LOGY]

sitrep, *n.* (*coll.*) a (military) report on the current situation. [*sit*uation *rep*ort]

sitter, sitting SIT.

Sitting Bull, *n.* (*c.* 1834–93), North American Indian chief who led the SIOUX onslaught against Gen. CUSTER.

situate, *v.t.* to place; to locate. *a.* situated. **situated,** *a.* placed or being in a specified situation, condition or relation. **situation,** *n.* the place in which something is situated, position, locality; position of affairs or circumstances, esp. a critical juncture in a story or play; a paid office, post or place, esp. of a domestic servant. **situation comedy,** *n.* a serialized comedy on radio or esp. television involving the same set of characters in a different comic situation in each episode. **situational,** *a.* [late L *situātus,* p.p. of *situāre,* to locate, from *situs,* SITE]

Sitwell, *n.* **Edith** (1887–1964), English poet, whose series of poems *Façade* was performed as recitations to the specially written music of WALTON from 1923.

sitz-bath, *n.* a bath in which one sits, a hip-bath; a bath taken thus. [G *Sitzbad* (*sitzen* to sit, BATH[1])]

SI units, *n. pl.* standard system of scientific units used by scientists worldwide. Originally proposed in 1960, it replaces the m.k.s., c.g.s., and f.p.s. systems. It is based on seven basic units: the metre (m) for length, kilogram (kg) for weight, second (s) for time, ampere (A) for electrical current, kelvin (K) for temperature, mole (mol) for amount of substance, and candela (cd) for luminosity. [F *S*ysteme *I*nternational d'Unités]

Siva, Shiva *n.* in Hinduism, the third chief god (with Brahma and Vishnu). As Mahadeva (great lord), he is the creator, symbolized by the phallic *lingam,* who restores what as Mahakala he destroys. He is often sculpted as Nataraja, performing his fruitful cosmic dance. His consort or female principle (*sakti*) is Parvati, otherwise known as Durga or Kali. **Sivaism,** *n.* **Sivaistic,** *a.* **Sivaite,** *n.* [Hind., from Sansk. *çiva,* auspicious]

Sivan, *n.* the third month of the Jewish ecclesiastical year comprising part of June and July. [Heb.]

Six, the, *n. pl.* the original six signatory countries to the Treaty of Rome which created the EUROPEAN COMMUNITY.

six, *n.* the number or figure 6 or vi; the age of six; the sixth in a series (e.g. a playing card); a division of a Cub Scout or Brownie pack; that which represents, amounts to or is worth six, esp. a hit for six runs in cricket; a set of six; the sixth hour after midday or midnight. *a.* six in number; aged six. **at sixes and sevens,** in disorder or confusion. **six (of one) and half a dozen (of the other),** having alternatives of equal acceptability, merit etc. **six of the best,** a severe beating, esp. with a cane. **the Six Counties,** see separate entry. **to knock for six,** to overcome completely, to defeat; to astonish; to stagger. **six-footer,** *n.* (*coll.*) a person 6 ft. tall. **six-gun,** *n.* a six-shooter. **six-pack,** *n.* a pack of six cans or bottles, esp. of beer. **sixpence,** *n.* (*formerly*) a cupronickel coin equivalent to six old pennies. **sixpenny,** *a.* worth or priced at sixpence. **six-shooter,** *n.* (*coll.*) a six-chambered revolver. **sixaine,** *n.* a six-line stanza. **sixer,** *n.* anything representing, worth or equal to six; the leader of a Cub Scout or Brownie six. **sixfold,** *a., adv.* **sixmo,** *n.* sexto. **sixth,** *n.* one of six equal parts; a sixth form; a musical interval between a tone and the sixth (inclusively) above or below it on the diatonic scale; a note separated from another by this interval; a tone and its sixth sounded together. *n., a.* (the) last of six (people, things etc.); the next after the fifth. **sixth form,** *n.* the highest form in a secondary school. **sixth-form college,** one where subjects are taught at sixth-form level. **sixth-former,** *n.* **sixth sense,** *n.* the power of intuition. **sixthly,** *adv.* [OE (cp. Dut. *zes,* G *sechs,* Icel., Dan. and Swed. *sex,* also L *sex,* Gr. *hex,* Sansk. *shash*)]

Six Acts, *n. pl.* in British history, acts of Parliament passed in 1819 by Lord Liverpool's Tory administration to curtail political radicalism in the aftermath of the Peterloo massacre and during a period of agitation for reform when habeas corpus was suspended and the powers of magistrates extended.

Six Articles, *n. pl.* an act introduced by Henry VIII in England in 1539, to settle disputes over dogma in the English Church. See ANGLICAN COMMUNION.

Six Counties, *n. pl.* the six counties which form Northern Ireland, namely Antrim, Armagh, Down, Fermanagh, Londonderry, and Tyrone.

sixte, *n.* a parry in fencing in which the hand is opposite the right breast and the point of the sword raised and a little to the right.

sixteen, *n.* the number or figure 16 or xvi; the age of 16. *a.* 16 in number; aged 16. **sixteenmo,** *n.* sextodecimo. **sixteenth,** *n.* one of 16 equal parts. *n., a.* (the) last of 16 (people, things etc.); the next after the 15th. **sixteenth note,** *n.* (*N Am.*) a semiquaver.

sixty, *n.* the number or figure 60 or lx; the age of 60; 60°F. *a.* 60 in number; aged 60. **sixties,** *n.pl.* the period of time between one's 60th and 70th birthdays; the range of temperature (fahrenheit) between 60 and 70 degrees; the period of time between the 60th and 70th years of a century. **sixtieth,** *n.* one of 60 equal parts. *n., a.* (the) last of 60 (people, things etc.); the next after the 59th. **sixtyfold,** *a., adv.*

size[1], *n.* measurement, extent, dimensions, magnitude; one of a series of standard grades or classes with which garments and other things are divided according to their relative dimensions; †a standard of weight or measurement; (*coll.*) quality, character, condition (of any one or anything). *v.t.* to sort or arrange according to size; to cut or shape to a required size. **to size up,** to form a rough estimate of the size of; to judge the capacity (of a person). **sizable, sizeable,** *a.* of considerable size. **sizableness,** *n.* **sizably,** *adv.* **sizar,** *n.* a student at Cambridge Univ. or Trinity college, Dublin, who pays lower fees than the ordinary students and formerly acted as servitor. **sized,** *a.* having a particular size (*usu. in comb.,* as *small-sized*); sorted or graded according to size. **sizer,** *n.* **sizing,** *n.* the act of sorting or arranging according to size. [orig. short for ASSIZE]

size[2], *n.* a gelatinous solution used to glaze surfaces (e.g. of paper), stiffen fabrics etc. *v.t.* to coat, glaze or prepare with size. **sized,** *a.* **sizer,** *n.* **sizing,** *n.* **sizy,** *a.* **siziness,** *n.* [It. *sisa,* short for *assisa,* painter's size, as ASSIZE]

sizel, SCISSEL.

sizer SIZE[1, 2].

sizzle, *v.i.* to make a hissing noise as of frying; (*coll.*) to be extremely hot; (*coll.*) to be in a rage. *n.* a hissing noise. **sizzler,** *n.* (*coll.*) a hot day; (*coll.*) anything which is striking or racy (e.g. a dress, a novel). **sizzling,** *a.* [imit.]

SJ, (*abbr.*) Society of Jesus.

SJA, (*abbr.*) Saint John's Ambulance (Association or Brigade).

sjambok, *n.* a short heavy whip, usu. of rhinoceros hide. *v.t.* to flog with this. [Afrikaans from Malay (*chābuk,* alert, a horse-whip)]

ska, *n.* an early form of reggae music originating in Jamaica. [etym. doubtful]

skain, SKEIN.

skald, SCALD[2].

Skara Brae, *n.* preserved Neolithic village in the Orkney Islands, Scotland, on Mainland.

skat, *n.* a three-handed card-game reminiscent of piquet. [G, from It. *scarto*]

skate[1], *n.* a fish of the genus *Raia,* distinguished by having a long pointed snout. [Icel. *skata,* cp. Norw. *skata,* Dan. *skade*]

skate[2], *n.* (a boot or shoe equipped with) a metal device fitted with a steel blade for gliding on ice, an ice-skate; a similar device with four wheels for gliding on a smooth surface, a roller-skate; the blade or runner on a skate; a period of skating. *v.i.* to move over ice or a smooth surface on skates. **to get one's skates on,** to hurry up. **to skate around,** to avoid talking about or confronting an issue, subject etc. **to skate on thin ice,** to be in a precarious or dangerous situation. **to skate over,** to avoid talking about, dealing with, or confronting an issue, subject etc., to gloss over. **skateboard,** *n.* a board mounted on roller-skate wheels on which both feet can be placed when momentum is achieved. *v.i.* to ride on a skateboard. **skateboarder,** *n.* **skateboarding,** *n.* **skater,** *n.* **skating,** *n., a.* **skating rink,** *n.* a place with an artificial floor or sheet of ice for skating. [formerly *schates, scates,* Dut. *schaats,* pl. *schaatsen,* OF *eschace* (F *échasse*), stilt, LG *schake,* SHANK]

skean, *n.* (*Ir., Sc.*) a long knife or dagger. **skean-dhu,** *n.* a knife or dagger worn with Scottish Highland dress (in the stocking). [Gael. *sgian,* knife, cp. OIr. *scīan;* Gael. *dhu,* black]

skedaddle, *v.i.* to run away, as in haste or panic. *int.* go away, beat it! *n.* a hasty flight, retreat or dispersal.

skeet, *n.* a type of clay-pigeon shooting in which targets are hurled in different directions, angles etc. from two traps [from ON *skjōta,* to shoot]

skegger, *n.* a little salmon. [etym. doubtful]

skein, *n.* a quantity of yarn, silk, wool, cotton etc., wound in a coil which is folded over and knotted; something resembling this; a flock of wild geese, swans etc. in flight; a tangle, a web. [OF *escaigne,* prob. from Celt. (cp. Ir. *sgainne,* Gael. *sgeinnidh*)]

skeleton, *n.* the bones of a person or animal dried, preserved and fastened together in the posture of the living creature; a very lean person or emaciated animal; the hard supporting or protective framework of an animal or vegetable body, comprising bones, cartilage, shell and other rigid parts; the supporting framework of any structure; the essential portions, the nucleus (of an organization); an outline or rough draft. *a.* reduced to the essential parts or a minimum. **skeleton in the cupboard,** an unpleasant or shameful secret from the past. **skeleton-key,** *n.* a key with most of the inner bits removed, used for picking locks; a pass key. **skeleton staff,** *n.* a staff reduced to the minimum number able to run a factory, office etc. **skeletal,** *a.* pertaining to the skeleton; thin, emaciated. **skeletonize, -ise,** *v.t.* to reduce to or as to a skeleton framework or outline. [Gr., a mummy, orig. neut. of *skeletos,* dried up, from *skellein,* to dry, to parch]

†**skellum,** *n.* (*S Afr.*) a rogue, a scoundrel. [Dut. *schelm,* cp. G *Schelm,* Icel. *skelmir*]

skelly[1], *n., a., v.i.* (*Sc.*) (to) squint. **skelly-eye,** *n.* **skelly-eyed,** *a.* [prob. from Icel., cp. Norw. *skjegla,* OE *sceolh,* squint]

skelly[2], (*Sc.*) SKERRY.

skelp, *n.* a blow, a smack. *v.t.* to strike, to slap. **skelping,** *n.,* a spanking. *a.* large, smacking. [Sc., from Gael. *sgealp,* a slap]

skelter, HELTER-SKELTER.

skene, SKEAN.

skep, *n.* a basket or similar receptacle or wicker, wood etc.; a beehive of straw or wicker. [Icel. *skeppa,* cp. Dut. *schepel,* G *Scheffel,* basket]

skeptic, etc. SCEPTIC.

skerrick, *n.* (*chiefly Austral., N. Zealand*) a tiny amount. **not a skerrick left,** nothing left at all.

skerry, *n.* a rocky islet in the sea; a reef. [Orkney, from Icel. *sker,* cp. SCAR[2]]

sketch, *n.* a rough, hasty, unfinished or tentative delineation; a preliminary study, a rough draft, an outline, a short account without details; a play, comic routine, descriptive essay, musical composition etc., of a brief, unelaborated or slight character. *v.t.* to make a sketch of; to present in rough draft or outline without details. *v.i.* to make a sketch or sketches. **sketch-block,** *n.* a pad of drawing-paper for making sketches on, a sketch-book. **sketch-book,** *n.* a book for sketching in; a collection of descriptive essays etc. **sketchable,** *a.* **sketcher,** *n.* **sketchy,** *a.* **sketchily,** *adv.* **sketchiness,** *n.* [Dut. *schets,* It. *schizzo,* L *schedius,* Gr. *schedios,* hasty, off-hand, cogn. with *schein,* to hold]

skew, *v.i.* to move sideways, to turn aside, to swerve; to squint, to look askance. *v.t.* to cause to skew; to distort. *a.* oblique, twisted, turned askew; distorted, unsymmetrical. *n.* an oblique course, position or movement; a squint; a sloping coping, or a stone supporting the coping of a gable. **on the skew,** skewed. **skew-back,** *n.* a stone, plate or course of masonry at the top of an abutment taking the spring of an arch. **skew-backed,** *a.* **skew bridge,** *n.* a bridge having an arch or arches set obliquely to the abutments. **skew-whiff,** *a., adv.* askew, to one side. **skewed,** *a.* **skewness,** *n.* [prob. from MDut. *schouwen,* to avoid (cp. G *scheuen,* also ESCHEW, SHY[1])]

skewbald, *a.* piebald with spots of white and a colour other than black. *n.* an animal of this colour.

skewer, *n.* a long pin of wood or metal for holding meat together; a similar implement used for various other purposes. *v.t.* to fasten with a skewer; to pierce with or as with a skewer. [var. of obs. *skiver,* SHIVER[1]]

ski, *n.* (*pl.* **ski, skis**) a long narrow runner of waxed wood, plastic etc. fastened one to each foot and used for sliding over snow or water-skiing. *v.i.* (*pres.p.* **skiing,** *past, p.p.* **skied, ski'd**) to move on skis. **skibob,** *n.* a snow vehicle with a low seat and steering device supported on two skis. **skibobber,** *n.* **skibobbing,** *n.* **skijorer,** *n.* **skijoring,** *n.* a sport in which a skier is towed by a horse or vehicle. **ski jump,** *n.* a ski-slope or run surmounted by a ramp from which skiers jump. *v.i.* to execute a jump from this. **ski jumper,** *n.* **ski-jumping,** *n.* **ski lift,** *n.* any of various forms of lifting apparatus for transporting skiers up a slope (e.g. a chair lift). **ski pants,** *n.pl.* stretch trousers with stirrups which fit under the feet. **ski-run,** a slope for skiing on. **ski stick,** *n.* one of a pair of pointed sticks used in skiing to balance or propel. **skiable,** *a.* **skier,** *n.* [Norw., from Icel. *skīth,* billet of wood, snow-shoe]

skiagraphy, *n.* the art of drawing objects with correct shading; a photograph by Röntgen rays; a sciagraph; (*Astron.*) the art of finding the hour by the shadow of the sun, moon, or stars; dialling. **skiagraph,** *n.* a photograph by Röntgen rays; a vertical section of a building showing the interior. **skiagraphic, -ical,** *a.* **skiagraphically,** *adv.* [F *sciagraphie,* L and Gr. *skiagraphia* (*skia,* shadow, -GRAPHY)]

skiamachy, *n.* a sham fight, a visionary fight; a fight with a shadow.

skiametry, *n.* the theory of eclipses; the measurement of eclipses; the science of skiagraphs mathematically considered.

skiascopy, *n.* a method of measuring the refractive power of the eye by projecting light into it from a small mirror, the shadow-test.

skid, *n.* a support or prop, usu. of wood; a ship's fender; the runner on the underside of an aircraft; a plank, log, or other device used for sliding heavy things on; a shoe or other device acting as a brake; the act of skidding, a slip on muddy ground, an icy road etc. *v.t.* (*past, p.p.* **skidded**) to cause to skid; to check or brake with a skid. *v.i.* of wheels or vehicles, to slip sideways; to revolve rapidly without progressing. **the skids,** a downward path into ruin. **skid-lid,** *n.* (*sl.*) a crash helmet. **skid pad,** *n.* a slippery area of ground for training drivers to control a skidding vehicle, a skid-pan. **skid-pan,** *n.* a shoe or drag usu. put under a wheel as a brake on a slope etc. a skid pad. **skid row,** *n.* (*sl.*) an area of a city or town inhabited by vagrants, down-and-outs etc. [cp. Icel. *skīth,* SKI, also ME *shide,* OE *scid,* a thin piece of wood, rel. to SHEATH]

skiey SKY.

skiff[1], *n.* a small light boat. *v.t.* to row or scull in a skiff. [F *esquif,* It. *schifo,* prob. from OHG *skif* (cp. G *schiff*), SHIP]

skiff[2], *a.* (*Sc.*) *v.i., v.t.* to skim (as a stone on water). *n.* a skimming action, a grazing blow.

skiffle, *n.* a type of music popular in the 1950s played on unconventional percussion instruments and guitars. **skiffle band, group,** a band composed of players who perform this music.

skill, *n.* familiar knowledge of any art or science combined with dexterity; expertness, ability, practical mastery of a craft, trade, sport etc., often attained by training. **skilful,** *a.* having, showing or requiring skill; expert, adept, clever, adroit, dexterous. **skilfully,** *adv.* **skilfulness,** *n.* **skilled,** *a.* having skill, skilful; involving or requiring skill or specialized training. [Icel. *skil,* discernment, from *skilja,* to separate, distinguish]

skillet, *n.* a metal pan with a long handle used for frying, as a saucepan etc. [OF *escuellette,* dim. of *escuelle,* L *scutella,* dim. of *scutra,* dish]

skilling, *n.* an out-house, a lean-to, a shed. [etym. doubtful]

skilly, †skilligalee, *n.* thin broth, soup or gruel. [etym. doubtful]

skim, *v.t.* (*past, p.p.* **skimmed**) to clear the scum etc. from the surface of; to take (cream etc.) from the surface of a liquid; to touch lightly or nearly touch the surface of, to graze; to throw so as to cause to graze or pass lightly over a surface; to glance over or read superficially. *v.i.* to pass lightly and rapidly over or along a surface; to glance (over) rapidly and superficially. *n.* the act or process of skimming, scum; the thick matter which forms on or is removed from, the surface of a liquid. **skim-milk, skimmed milk,** *n.* milk from which the cream has been skimmed. **skimmer,** *n.* one who or that which skims; a perforated ladle for skimming; a bird of the N American genus *Rhynchops,* which skims small fishes from the water with its lower mandible. **skimming,** *n.* **skimmingly,** *adv.* [from SCUM, cp. DINT and DENT[1], FILL[1] and FULL[1]]

Skimmia, *n.* an Asiatic genus of evergreen shrub with red berries.

skimp, *v.t.* to supply in a niggardly manner, to stint (a person, provisions etc.); to perform with insufficient attention or inadequate effort. *v.i.* to be stingy or parsimonious. **skimpingly,** *adv.* **skimpy,** *a.* **skimpily, skimpiness,** *n.* [perh. from Icel. *skemma,* to shorten, from *skamr,* short]

skin, *n.* the natural membranous outer covering of an animal body; the hide or integument of an animal removed from the body, with or without the hair; a vessel made of the skin of an animal for holding liquids (as wine); the outer layer or covering of a plant, fruit etc.; the outer layer or covering of an object, structure, liquid etc; a film; a membrane; the outer cladding of a vessel, rocket etc.; (*coll.*) a skinhead. *v.t.* (*past, p.p.* **skinned**) to strip the skin from, to flay, to peel; to graze (as the knee); to cover (over) with or as with skin; to cheat, to swindle. *v.i.* to become covered (over) with skin, to cicatrize; made of, intended for, or used on the skin. **by the skin of one's teeth,** very narrowly, by a close shave. **no skin off one's nose,** making no difference to one, not perturbing to one. **skin and bone,** extremely thin, emaciated. **to get under one's skin,** to interest or annoy one intensely. **to save one's skin,** to escape injury. **skin-deep,** *a.* superficial, not deep. **skin-diver,** *n.* one who dives deep wearing no protective clothing (orig. a pearl-diver). **skin-diving,** *n.* **skin effect,** *n.* the tendency of an alternating electric current to be diffused over the surface of a conductor instead of being equally distributed over the whole area. **skin flick,** *n.* (*coll.*) a film which features nudity and sex scenes. **skinflint,** *n.* a niggardly person, a miser. **skin graft,** *n.* the transfer of skin from a sound to a disfigured or injured part. **skin grafting,** *n.* **skinhead,** *n.* a member of a gang of aggressive and often racist youths characterized by their cropped hair, heavy-duty boots and braces; (*coll.*) someone with cropped hair. **skin test,** *n.* a test performed on the skin to determine its resistance to disease or substances liable to cause an allergic reaction. **skintight,** *a.* of garments, tight, clinging. **skinful,** *n.* (*sl.*) as much liquor as the stomach will hold. **skinless,** *a.* **skinned,** *a.* (*usu. in comb.,* as *thin-skinned*). **skinner,** *n.* one who skins; one who deals in skins, a furrier. **skinny,** *a.* of or resembling a skin; very lean or thin. **skinny-dip,** *v.i.* (*coll.*) to swim in the nude. **skinniness,** *n.* [Icel. *skinn,* cogn. with G *schinden,* to skin, to flay]

skink, *n.* a small lizard of Africa and SW Asia. [F *scinc* (now *scinque*), L *scincus,* Gr. *skinkos*]

Skinner, *n.* **B(urrhus) F(rederic)** (1903–), US psychologist, a radical behaviourist who rejects mental concepts, seeing the organism as a 'black box' where internal processes are not important in predicting behaviour. He studied operant conditioning and stressed that behaviour is shaped and maintained by its consequences.

skint, *a.* (*sl.*) hard-up for money, penniless. [var. of skinned, p.p. SKIN]

skip[1], *v.i.* (*past, p.p.* **skipped**) to move about with light bounds, hops or capers, esp. by shifting rapidly from one foot to another; to frisk, to gambol; to jump repeatedly over a skipping-rope; to pass rapidly from one thing to another; to make omissions; (*sl.*) to make off hurriedly, to bolt (off), to abscond; to go over with a bound; to pass over without notice, to omit. *v.t.* to cause to skim over a surface; of a stone etc., to skim; to omit, to miss deliberately, to absent oneself from (a meal, a class, a church service etc.); (*chiefly N Am.*) to leave (town) quickly and quietly, to abscond. *n.* a light leap or spring, esp. from one foot to the other; an act of omitting, leaving out or passing over; a belt of inaudibility in radio transmissions; a college-servant. **skip it!** forget about it! it does not matter! **skip distance,** *n.* the minimum distance around a radio transmitter at which it is possible to receive an ionospheric wave. **skipjack,** *n.* any of various kinds of fish, beetles etc., that move with skips or springs, esp. the clickbeetle and two varieties of tuna, the skipjack tuna and black skipjack. **skip zone,** *n.* an area around a broadcasting station where it is impossible to receive a transmission. **skipper**[1], *n.* one who, or that which, skips; a saury; one of the lepidopteran family Hesperidae, from their short, jerky flight. **skipping,** *n.* the act, recreation or exercise of jumping over a rope repeatedly. **skipping-rope,** *n.* a rope or cord used for skipping (over) as a game or form of physical exercise. **skippingly,** *adv.* [ME *skippen* (cp. Norw. and Swed. dial. *skopa,* also Icel. *skoppa,* to spin)]

skip[2], *n.* a container for collecting and moving refuse, building materials etc.; a box cage or bucket lift in a mine for hoisting men or materials. [var. of SKEP]

skip[3], *n.* (*coll.*) short for SKIPPER[2].

skipper[1] SKIP[1].

skipper[2], *n.* a sea captain, the master of a vessel; the captain of a team or side; an aircraft captain. *v.t.* to act as skipper (of). [Dut. *schipper* (*schip,* SHIP, -ER)]

skippet, *n.* a flat round box for holding the seal attached to a document; †a small boat. [dim. of SKIP[2]]

skippingly, skipping-rope SKIP[1].

skirl, *v.i.* (*Sc.*) to make a shrill noise like that of the bagpipes; to shriek. *n.* a shrill cry or noise; the sound of the bagpipes. [var. of SHRILL]

skirmish, *n.* a slight or irregular fight, esp. between small parties or scattered troops; a contest, clash, struggle, esp. of a preliminary, brief or minor nature. *v.i.* to engage in a skirmish. **skirmisher,** *n.* [OF *eskermiss-,* stem of *eskermir,* to fence; from OHG *scirman,* from *scirm* (cp. G *Schirm,* shelter, cover)]

skirr, *v.t.* to pass over rapidly, to range, to scour. *v.i.* to move rapidly, to scud. [prob. rel. to SCOUR[2]]

skirret, *n.* a species of water-parsnip, *Sium sisarum,* with an edible tuberous root. [ME *skyrwyt,* prob. from OF *eschervis,* Sp. *chirivia,* Arab. *karawiyā,* CARAWAY]

skirt, *n.* the part of a coat or other garment hanging below the waist; a woman's outer garment hanging from the waist; (*sl., offensive*) a woman, a girl; the edge of anything, a border, a margin; the outer flap surrounding the base of a hovercraft, racing car etc. (*pl.*) the extremities or outer parts. *v.t.* to lie or go along or by the edge of; to pass round (the edge of), to avoid; to border; to edge or border (with). *v.i.* to lie or move (along, round, on) the border or outskirts. **skirted,** *a.* **skirter,** *n.* one who skirts, esp. a dog that runs wide of the pack. **skirting,** *n.* material suitable for skirts; a skirting-board; (*pl.*) (*Austral., N. Zealand*) the inferior parts of wool trimmed from a fleece. **skirting-board,** *n.* a board running round the bottom of the wall of a room. **skirtless,** *a.* [ME *skyrt,* Icel. *skyrta,* shirt]

skit, *n.* a satirical piece, lampoon or humourous theatrical sketch. **skite,** *v.i.* (*Sc.*) to dart aside, to slip, to slide; (*Austral., N. Zealand coll.*) to boast. *v.t.* to hit with a darting blow. *n.* an act or instance of darting aside or slipping; a sharp blow, esp. in a slanting direction; (*Austral., N. Zealand coll.*) one who boasts; boastful talk. [prob. from Icel. *skȳt,* stem of *skjōta,* to SHOOT]

skitter, *v.i.* to glide, skim or skip rapidly, esp. along a surface; to fish by drawing a bait etc. along the surface; (*Sc.*) to have diarrhoea. *v.t.* to cause to skitter. *n.* an act or instance of skittering. [prob. freq. of prec.]

skittish, *a.* of horses, excitable, nervous, easily frightened; capricious, uncertain, coquettish, wanton, too lively. **skittishly,** *adv.* **skittishness,** *n.* [etym. doubtful]

skittle, *n.* one of the blocks or pins set up to be thrown at in ninepins; (*pl.*) ninepin bowling. *v.i.* to play at ninepins. **skittle-alley, -ball, -ground,** *n.* [Dan. *skyttel,* an earthen ball used in child's game, as SHUTTLE]

skive[1], *v.t.* to split (leather) into thin layers; to shave or pare (hides). **skiver,** *n.* a paring-tool for leather; a thin leather split from a sheep-skin used for book-binding. [Icel. *skīfa,* cogn. with SHIVE]

skive[2], *v.t., v.i.* (*coll.*) to avoid performing (a duty, task etc.). *n.* (*coll.*) a period of shirking or an evasion of duty etc.; (*coll.*) work etc. which is far from onerous. **skiver,** *n.*

skivvy, *n.* (*sl.*) a maid or general servant.

skoal, skol, *int.* cheers! good health! (usu. as a toast). [ON *skāl,* Dan. *skaal,* a bowl, a cup]

Skolimowski, *n.* **Jerzy** (1938–), Polish film director, formerly a writer, active both in his native country and Western Europe. His films include *Deep End* (1970), *The Shout* (1978), and *Moonlighting* (1982).

Skopje, *n.* capital and industrial city of Macedonia, Yugoslavia; population (1981) 506,547. Industries include iron, steel, chromium mining, and food processing.

Skryabin, *n.* **Alexander (Nikolayevich)** (1872–1915), Russian composer and pianist. His powerfully emotional tone poems, such as *Prometheus* (1911), and symphonies, such as *Divine Poem* (1903), employed unusual harmonies.

Skt, Skr, (*abbr.*) Sanskrit.

skua, *n.* a dark-coloured predatory sea-bird allied to the gulls. [Icel. *skūfr, skūmr* (cp. *skūmi,* shade, Norw. and Swed. *skum,* dull, dusky)]

skulduggery, skullduggery, *n.* (*coll.*) underhand trickery. [SCULDUDDERY]

skulk, *v.i.* to lurk, to withdraw and conceal oneself; to lie concealed, to move about furtively; to sneak away, esp. from duty, work, danger etc. *n.* one who skulks, a skulker. **skulker,** *n.* **skulking,** *n., a.* **skulkingly,** *adv.* [Dan. *skulk* (cp. Swed. *skolka,* Dut. *schuilen*)]

skull, *n.* the bony case enclosing the brain, the skeleton of the head, the cranium. **skullcap,** *n.* a light, brimless cap fitting closely to the head; the sinciput; a plant of the genus *Scutellaria,* with blue, helmet-shaped flowers; (*usu. derog.*) the brain, the intelligence. **skull and crossbones,** a representation of a human skull surmounting two crossed thigh-bones, used as an emblem of death or danger. **skulled,** *a.* (*usu. in comb.,* as *thick-skulled*). [ME *skulle, scolle* (cp. Swed. dial. *skulle,* Norw. *skult*), cogn. with SCALE[2]]

skunk, *n.* a N American carnivorous quadruped, *Mephitis mephitica,* with bushy tail and white stripes down the back, which when irritated ejects a fetid secretion from the anal glands; the pelt of this animal; a base or obnoxious person. **skunk-bird, -blackbird,** *n.* the bobolink. [Abenaki (Algonquin) *segongw*]

sky, *n.* the apparent vault of heaven, the firmament; the upper region of the atmosphere, the region of clouds; climate, the weather; (*pl.*) the celestial regions, the heavens. *v.t.* to hit (a ball) high into the air; to hang (a picture) in the top tier at an exhibition. **the sky is the limit,** the possibilities for achievement are unbounded. **to the skies,** lavishly, extravagantly. **sky-blue,** *n., a.* (a) pale blue. †**sky-born, -bred,** *a.* (*poet.*) of heavenly or divine origin. **skydive,** *v.i.* to jump from an aircraft and delay opening the parachute, esp. in order to execute manoeuvres. *n.* an instance of this. **skydiver,** *n.* **skydiving,** *n.* **sky-high,** *adv.* high as the sky. *a.* very high. **to blow skyhigh,** to blow up, to destroy completely. **skyjack,** *v.t.* to hijack (an aircraft). **skyjacker,** *n.* **skyjacking,** *n.* **skylark,** *n.* a lark, *Alauda arvensis,* that flies singing high into the air. *v.i.* (*coll.*) to lark, to frolic, to play practical jokes etc. **skylight,** *n.* a window set in a roof or ceiling. **skyline,** *n.* outline against the sky of the configuration of the land or buildings; the horizon. **skypilot,** *n.* (*sl.*) a clergyman, a priest, a preacher. **skyrocket,** *n.* a rocket. *v.i.* to rise rapidly to a high level. **skysail,** *n.* a light sail set above the royal in a square-rigged ship. **skyscape,** *n.* a picture or view chiefly of the sky or clouds. **skyscraper,** *n.* a very high multi-storeyed building; a triangular skysail. **sky-writing,** *n.* (the formation of) writing, traced in the sky by smoke discharged from an aeroplane. **skywriter,** *n.* **skyer, skier,** *n.* a cricket ball hit high into the air. **skyey, skiey,** *a.* **skyward,** *a., adv.* **skywards,** *adv.* [Icel. *sky* (cp. OE *scēo,* cloud, *scuwa,* shadow), cogn. with SCUM, SHOWER[2], L *obscūrus,* OBSCURE]

Skye[1], *n.* largest island of the Inner HEBRIDES, Scotland; area 1740 sq km/672 sq miles; population (1981) 8000. It is separated from the mainland by the Sound of Sleat. The chief port is Portree. The economy is based on crofting, tourism, and livestock. Bonnie Prince Charlie (Charles Edward Stuart) took refuge here after Culloden.

Skye[2], **Skye terrier,** *n.* a small rough-haired variety of Scotch terrier with long body and short legs. [Isle of *Skye*]

skyey, skylight etc. SKY.

Skylab, *n.* US space station, launched on 14 May 1973, made from the adapted upper stage of a Saturn V rocket. At 75 tonnes, it was the heaviest object ever put into space, and was 25.6 m/84 ft long. Skylab contained a workshop for carrying out experiments in weightlessness, an observatory for monitoring the Sun, and cameras for photographing Earth's surface.

skyr, *n.* a dish of curd. [Icel.]

skyscape, skyscraper etc. SKY.

slab[1], *n.* a thin, flat, regularly shaped piece of anything, esp. of stone, concrete etc.; a large slice of bread, cake etc.; the outside piece sawn from a log in squaring the side; (*Austral., N. Zealand*) a plank. *a.* (*Austral., N. Zealand*) made of rough planks. *v.t.* (*past, p.p.* **slabbed**) to saw slabs from (a log etc.); to square (a tree) in order to saw it into planks; to cut or form into a slab or slabs; to cover or line with slabs. **slabstone,** *n.* a flagstone. **slabbed,** *a.* **slabbing,** *n., a.* [etym. doubtful, cp. OF *esclape,* splinter (*es-,* EX-, LG *klappen,* to cleave noisily, cp. G *klaffen,* to split)]

slab[2], *a.* thick, slimy, viscous, sticky. *n.* ooze, mud, slime. †**slabbiness,** *n.* **slabby,** *a.* [prov. *slab,* puddle, Icel. *slabb,* mire (cp. Swed. dial. and Norw. *slabb,* MDan. *slab*)]

slabber, etc. SLOBBER.

slack[1], *a.* not drawn tight, loose; limp, relaxed, careless, listless, remiss, not zealous, eager or active; lax; tardy, sluggish, dull, slow. *adv.* in a slack manner; insufficiently. *n.* the part of a rope etc. that hangs loose; a slack period in trade etc.; a cessation of flow (of water); small coal, screenings; (*pl.*) casual trousers. *v.i.* to abate; to become loose or looser; to become slower, to fail; to become remiss or lazy. *v.t.* to slow; to lessen; to cause to abate; to loosen, to relax; to slake (lime). **to slack off,** to loosen, to reduce the tension on (a rope etc.); to shirk work. **to slack up,** to slow down (a train) before stopping; to ease off. **slack-water,** *n.* the interval between the flux and the reflux of the tide. **slacken,** *v.i.*, *v.t.* to (become) slack. **slacker,** *n.* a thing that slackens; a shirker, a lazy or remiss person. **slackly,** *adv.* **slackness,** *n.* [OE *sleac* (cp. Icel. *slakr,* Swed. and Dan. *slak,* OHG *slah*), cogn. with LAG[1] and LAX]

slack[2], *n.* (*Sc.*) a hollow, a dip, a dell; a bog, a morass. [Icel. *slakki,* cp. Norw. *slakke*]

slade, *n.* (*dial.*) a little valley or dell, a dingle; a flat piece of low moist ground. [OE *slæd,* cp. Norw. dial. *slad,* Dan. and G dial. *slade*]

slae, (*Sc.***)** SLOE.

slag, *n.* the fused refuse or dross separated in the reduction of ores, cinder; volcanic scoria; (*sl.*) a slovenly or immoral woman; a mixture of mineral dross and dust produced in coal mining. *v.i.* to form slag, to combine in a slaggy mass. *v.t.* to convert into slag; (*sl.*) to criticize, to disparage. **to slag off,** to make disparaging remarks about. **slagheap,** *n.* a hill or heap of waste material produced in coal mining. **slagger,** *n.* (*coll.*) one who disparages another. **slaggy,** *a.* [Swed. *slagg,* cp. Norw. *slagga,* to flow over, G *Schlacke,* slag]

slain, *p.p.* SLAY[1].

slaister, *n.* (*Sc.*) a dirty or repulsive mess; the act of making this. *v.t.* to plaster up, to daub. *v.i.* to do anything in a dirty, slovenly way. [etym. doubtful]

slake[1], *v.t.* to quench, to assuage, to satisfy, to appease; to mix (lime) with water so as to form a chemical combination. *v.i.* of lime, to become slaked. **slaked lime,** *n.* calcium hydroxide. **slakeable, slakable,** *a.* **slakeless,** *a.* [OE *slacian,* from *slæc, sleac,* SLACK[1]]

slake[2], *v.t.* (*Sc.*) to lick, to bedaub, to smear. *n.* a smear, a lick. [Icel. *sleikja,* also Norw.]

slalom, *n.* a ski or canoe race on a zig-zagged course marked with artificial obstacles. [Norw.]

slam, *v.t.* (*past, p.p.* **slammed**) to shut suddenly with a loud noise; to put (a thing down) thus; (*coll.*) to hit, to thrash, to defeat completely; in whist etc., to beat by winning every (a grand slam) or all but one (a little or small slam) trick; (*coll.*) to criticize severely; to put into action suddenly or violently. *v.i.* of a door, to shut violently or noisily; (*coll.*) to move, esp. to enter or leave, angrily or violently. *n.* a noise as of the violent shutting of a door; an act of slamming; in whist or bridge, a grand slam, a small or little slam. **slammer,** *n.* (*sl.*) prison. [cp. Norw. *slemba,* Icel. *slambra,* prob. imit. in orig.]

†**slammakin, -mmerkin,** *n.* a slatternly, woman. *a.* slatternly, untidy. [etym. doubtful]

slander, *n.* a false report maliciously uttered to injure a person; defamation, calumny; (*Law*) false defamatory language or statements. *v.t.* to injure by the malicious utterance of a false report, to defame falsely. **slanderer,** *n.* **slanderous,** *a.* **slanderously,** *adv.* **slanderousness,** *n.* [OF *esclander,* L *scandalum,* SCANDAL]

slang, *n.* words or language used colloquially but not regarded as correct English; the special language or dialect of a particular class, group etc., jargon. *v.i.* to use slang. *v.t.* to abuse with slang. **slanging,** *n.*, *a.* **slanging match,** *n.* a quarrel in which strong insults are exchanged. **slangily,** *adv.* **slanginess,** *n.* **slangy,** *a.* [prob. from Norw. *sleng,* slinging, from *slengja,* to SLING]

slank, SLINK.

slant, *v.i.* to slope; to incline from or be oblique to a vertical or horizontal line; to be biased (towards). *v.t.* to cause to slant; to present with a bias. *a.* sloping, oblique; inclined from a horizontal or perpendicular line. *n.* a slope; inclination from the vertical or horizontal; a solidus; an angle of approach, information concerning; a bias. **slanted,** *a.* **slanting,** *a.* **slantingly,** *adv.* **slantly, slantways, -wise,** *adv.* [prob. through ME *slenten, sclenten,* from Norw. *slenta*]

slap, *v.t.* (*past, p.p.* **slapped**) to strike with the open hand, to smack; to bring down or throw forcefully or quickly. *n.* a blow, esp. with the open hand. *adv.* as with a sudden blow, plump, bang. **slap and tickle,** sex play. **slap in the face,** a rebuff. **slap on the wrist,** a reprimand. **to slap down,** to quash. **to slap on,** to apply (paint etc.) hurriedly, carelessly, forcefully or thickly. **to slap on the back,** to congratulate. **slap-bang,** *adv.* suddenly, violently, headlong; exactly, precisely. **slap-dash,** *adv.* in a careless, rash, impetuous manner. *a.* hasty, impetuous, careless, happy-go-lucky. *n.* rough and haphazard work; rough-cast. *v.t.* to roughcast; to do hastily or carelessly. **slap-happy,** *a.* careless, irresponsible; punch-drunk; happy-go-lucky, carefree. **slap-jack,** *n.* a flap-jack. **slapstick,** *n.* a comedian's stick so constructed as to make a loud noise when striking someone; broad comedy or knockabout farce. **slap-up,** *a.* (*coll.*) first-rate; lavish. [cp. LG *slapp,* imit. of sound]

slash, *v.t.* to cut by striking violently at random; to reduce drastically; to make long incisions or narrow gashes in, to slit; (*usu. in p.p.*) to make slits in (sleeves etc.) to show the lining; to criticize severely; to lash (with a whip etc.). *v.i.* to strike (at etc.) violently and at random with a knife, sword etc.; to lash. *n.* a long cut, slit or incision; a slashing cut or stroke; a slit in a garment designed to reveal the lining as a decorative feature; a solidus; (*sl.*) the act of urinating. **slashed,** *a.* **slasher,** *n.* **slashingly,** *adv.* [OF *esclachier* (*es-*, EX-, MHG *klecken,* to break noisily, from *klac,* noise), perh. conf. with *esclicier,* to SLICE]

slat[1], *n.* a thin narrow strip, usu. of wood or metal, used in Venetian blinds, crates etc. *v.i.* (*past, p.p.* **slatted**) to make or equip with slats. **slatted,** *a.* [ME, var. of foll.]

slat[2], *v.t.* (*past, p.p.* **slatted**) to fling, to dash, to slap, to jerk; to beat, to bang. *v.i.* to beat, to bang; of sails, to flap violently. *n.* a sharp blow, a violent flap. [etym. doubtful]

slate[1], *n.* a fine-grained laminated rock easily splitting into thin, smooth, even slabs; a slab or trimmed piece of this, esp. for use as a roofing-tile; a tablet of slate, usu. framed, for writing on; (*chiefly N Am.*) a preliminary list of candidates liable to revision; the colour of slate, a dull blue-grey. *v.t.* to cover or roof with slates; (*chiefly N Am.*) to place (a candidate) on a list. *a.* made or consisting of slate; slate-coloured. **a clean slate,** an unblemished record. **a slate loose,** slightly mentally unbalanced. **on the slate,** on credit, on the tab. **to wipe the slate clean,** to start afresh, to erase past crimes, errors etc. **slate-black, -blue, -grey,** *a.* of the dark, blue or grey colour characteristic of slate. **slate-colour,** *n.* **slate-coloured,** *a.* **slate-pencil,** *n.* a piece of soft slate for writing on slates with. **slatelike,** *a.* **slater,** *n.* one who manufactures slates; one who slates roofs; a wood-louse. **slaty,** *a.* **slatiness,** *n.* **slating,** *n.* [ME *slat, sclat,* OF *esclat* (F *éclat*), from *esclater,* to break to pieces, late L *exclapitāre* (EX-, LG *klappen,* to CLAP]

slate[2], *v.t.* to criticize savagely, to abuse, to berate. [etym. unknown; prob. conn. with prec.]

slattern, *n.* an untidy or sluttish woman. **slatternly,** *a.* **slatternliness,** *n.* [from obs. *slatter,* to be wasteful or untidy, freq. of obs. *slat,* to splash, cp. Icel. *sletta*]

slaty SLATE[1].

slaughter, *n.* wholesale or indiscriminate killing, butchery, carnage; the killing of animals for market. *v.t.* to kill wantonly or ruthlessly, to massacre; to kill animals for market. **slaughterhouse,** *n.* a place where beasts are slaughtered, a shambles. **slaughterman,** *n.* one who kills livestock for market. **slaughterer,** *n.* **slaughterous,** *a.* **slaughterously,** *adv.* [Icel. *slātr,* slaughtering, meat, cogn. with SLAY[1]]

Slav, *n.* one of any of various peoples inhabiting eastern Europe who speak a Slavonic language, including the Russians, Poles, Serbo-Croatians, Bulgarians, Slovenes etc. *a.* Slavonic. **Slavic,** *n.*, *a.* Slavonic. **Slavism,** *n.* **Slavonian,** *n.*, *a.* Slovene. **Slavonic,** *a.* pertaining to a group of languages belonging to the Indo-European family including Russian, Bulgarian, Polish etc.; pertaining to the peoples who speak these. *n.* the Slavonic language(s). [F *Slave* or G *sklave,* med.

L *Slavus, Sclavus,* or late Gr. *sklabos, sklabēnos,* from Slavonic]

slave, *n.* one who is the property of and bound in obedience to another; one who is entirely under the influence (of) or a helpless victim (to); one who works like a slave, a drudge; a person of slavish mind, a mean, abject person; one device which is controlled by another, or imitates the action of a similar device. *v.i.* to toil like a slave, to drudge. †**slave-born,** *a.* born in slavery or of slave parents. **slave-driver,** *n.* an overseer of slaves; an exacting taskmaster. **slave-holder,** *n.* one who owns slaves. **slave-holding,** *n.* **slave labour,** *n.* **slave-ship,** *n.* a vessel engaged in the slave-trade. **slave state,** *n.* one of the southern States of N America in which slavery flourished prior to the Civil War. **slave-trade,** *n.* the trade of procuring, buying and transporting slaves, esp. from Africa to America in the 16th–18th cents. **slave-trader,** *n.* **slave-like,** *a.* **slaver**[1], *n.* one who deals in slaves; a slave-ship. **slavery**[1], *n.* **slavey,** *n.* (*coll.*) a maid-servant, a household drudge. **slavish,** *a.* pertaining to or characteristic of a slave; subservient, servile, base, abject, ignoble; entirely imitative, devoid of originality; consisting in drudgery. **slavishly,** *adv.* **slavishness,** *n.* **slavocracy,** *n.* slave owners collectively, esp. as a dominating political or social power. [F. *esclave,* med.L *sclavus,* a SLAV captive]

slaver[1] SLAVE.

slaver[2], *v.i.* to let saliva flow from the mouth, to slabber, to dribble; to fawn, to flatter, to drool. *v.t.* to let saliva dribble upon or over. *n.* saliva dribbling from the mouth; (*coll.*) nonsense, drivel. **slaverer,** *n.* **slavering,** *a.* **slavery**[2], *a.* [Icel. *slafra* (cp. LG *slabbern*)]

slavery[1] SLAVE.

slavery[2] SLAVER[2].

slavey SLAVE.

Slavic etc. SLAV.

Slavonian, Slavonic etc. SLAV.

Slavophil(e), *n.* a member of an intellectual and political group in 19th-century Russia which promoted the idea of an Eastern orientation for the empire in opposition to those who wanted the country to adopt Western methods and ideas of development.

slaw, *n.* sliced cabbage served as a salad, coleslaw. [Dut. *slaa,* SALAD]

slay, *v.t.* (*past* **slayed, slew,** *p.p.* **slayed, slain**) to put to death, to kill; (*coll.*) to impress powerfully; (*coll.*) to amuse to an overwhelming degree. **slayer,** *n.* [OE *slēan* (cp. Dut. *slaan,* G *schlagen,* Icel. *slā*)]

SLD, (*abbr.*) Social and Liberal Democrats.

sleaze, *n.* (*coll.*) that which is squalid, distasteful, disreputable; sleaziness. **sleazy,** *a.* thin, wanting in substance, flimsy; slatternly; squalid. **sleazily,** *adv.* **sleaziness,** *n.* [etym. doubtful]

sled, sledge[1], *n.* a vehicle on runners instead of wheels used for hauling loads etc., esp. over snow or ice; a sleigh; a toboggan. *v.t.* to carry or convey on a sled. *v.i.* to travel by sled. **sledding, sledging,** *n.* **sledger,** *n.* [ME *slede,* M Dut. *sledde* (Dut. *slede*), cp. Icel. *slethi,* Swed. *släde,* Dan *slæde,* cogn. with SLIDE (2nd form assim. to foll.)]

sledge[2], **sledgehammer**, *n.* a heavy hammer wielded by both hands. *a.* imitating the action of a sledgehammer, clumsy, hardhitting. [OE *slecge* (cp. Dut. *slegge,* Icel. *sleggja*), cogn. with SLAY[1]]

sleek, *a.* of fur, skin etc., smooth, glossy; oily, unctuous, smooth-spoken; well groomed, prosperous-looking. *v.t.* to make (hair etc.) sleek; to make pleasant or less disagreeable. **sleeken,** *v.t.* **sleekly,** *adv.* **sleekness,** *n.* **sleeky,** *a.* [Icel. *slīkr,* cp. Dut. *slijk,* G *schlick,* grease]

sleep, *v.i.* (*past, p.p.* **slept**) to take rest in sleep, to be asleep; to be or lie dormant, inactive or in abeyance; to be dead; of a top, to spin rapidly and smoothly so as to seem motionless. *v.t.* to rest in (sleep); to furnish with accommodation for sleeping, to lodge (a certain number). *n.* a state of rest in which consciousness is almost entirely suspended, the body relaxed, and the vital functions are inactive; (*coll.*) a crusty matter which collects at the corner of the eye during sleep; a spell of this; torpor, rest, quiet, death. **to sleep around,** (*coll.*) to be sexually promiscuous. **to sleep in,** to sleep on the premises; to oversleep. **to sleep off,** to rid or recover from (e.g. the effects of alcohol) by sleeping. **to sleep on it,** to postpone making a decision until the next day. **to sleep rough,** to sleep out of doors. **to sleep together, with,** to have sexual intercourse (with). **sleep-walk,** *v.i.* to walk while asleep. **sleep-walker,** *n.* a somnambulist. **sleep-walking,** *n.* **sleeper,** *n.* one who sleeps; a wooden beam or other support for the rails on a railway track; a sleeping compartment or carriage of a train; a train with these; a small stud or hoop earring worn to keep the hole in a pierced ear open; (*coll.*) (e.g. a secret agent) who lies dormant before coming into action; (*coll.*) something (e.g. a film, a book) which becomes valuable or popular after a period of being neither. **sleeping,** *n., a.* **sleeping-bag,** *n.* a bag of some warm material in which one can sleep, esp. when camping. **sleeping-car,** *n.* a railway carriage fitted with berths for sleeping in. **sleeping partner,** *n.* a partner having no share in the management of a business, a silent partner. **sleeping pill,** *n.* a sedative in tablet form for inducing sleep. **sleeping policeman,** *n.* (*coll.*) a hump in the road for slowing traffic. **sleeping sickness,** *n.* a disease characterized by fever and mental and physical lethargy, almost always fatal, endemic in tropical Africa, and caused by a parasite *Trypanosoma gambiense.* **sleepless,** *a.* **sleeplessly,** *adv.* **sleeplessness,** *n.* **sleepy,** *a.* inclined to sleep, drowsy, somnolent; dull, lazy, indolent, habitually inactive; tending to induce sleep; **sleepy-head,** *n.* a lazy or sleepy person. **sleepy sickness,** *n.* encephalitis lethargica, acute inflammation of certain portions of the brain, causing drowsiness and eventual mental disease. **sleepily,** *adv.* **sleepiness,** *n.* [OE *slǣpan, slēpan* (cp. Dut. *slapen,* G *schlafen*), from slǣp, rel. to G *schlaff,* loose]

Sleep, *n.* **Wayne** (1948–), British dancer who was principal dancer with the Royal Ballet from 1973–83 and formed his own company, Dash, in 1980.

sleet, *n.* hail or snow mingled with rain. *v.i.* to snow or hail with a mixture of rain. **sleety,** *a.* **sleetiness,** *n.* [cp. EFris. *slaite,* Norw. *slūtr,* hail, G *Schlosse,* hailstone]

sleeve, *n.* the part of a garment that covers the arm; a tube, pipe or cylindrical sheath enclosing a revolving shaft, connecting lengths of pipe etc.; the cardboard cover for a gramophone record; a wind-sock. *v.t.* to furnish with a sleeve or sleeves. **to have up one's sleeve,** to hold secretly in reserve or in readiness. **to laugh in, up one's sleeve** LAUGH. **to roll up one's sleeves,** to get ready for hard work, a fight etc. **sleeve-nut,** *n.* a long union with a right-hand and a left-hand screw-thread at the ends for drawing together and connecting pipes, shafts etc. **sleeved,** *a.* having sleeves (of a stated type). **sleeveless,** *a.* of a dress, blouse etc. without sleeves. **sleeving,** *n.* the outer insulating cover on an electric cable. [OE *slyf,* rel. to SLIP]

sleigh, *n.* a vehicle mounted on runners for driving over snow or ice, a sledge. *v.i.* to travel by sleigh. **sleigh-bell,** *n.* a small bell hung on a sleigh or its harness. **sleighing,** *n.* [form of SLED]

sleight, *n.* dexterity, skill in manipulating things; a trick or stratagem so dexterously performed as to escape detection; trickery, cunning. *a.* deceitful, artful. **sleight of hand,** legerdemain, juggling. [Icel. *slaegth,* from *slaegr,* SLY]

slender, *a.* small in circumference or width as compared with length; thin, slim; slight, scanty, meagre, inadequate, small, poor; feeble, not strong. **slenderly,** *adv.* **slenderness,** *n.* [ME *slendre,* OF *esclendre,* MDut. *slinder,* cp. G *schlendern,* to saunter (prob. cogn. with SLIDE)]

slept, *past, p.p.* SLEEP.

sleuth, *n.* (*coll.*) a detective. *v.i.* to act as a detective. *v.t.* to track. **sleuth-hound,** *n.* a bloodhound; (*coll.*) a detective. [var. of SLOT[2]]

slew¹, *past* SLAY¹.

slew², slue, *v.t., v.i.* to turn, twist or swing (round, about etc.) as on a pivot. *n.* such a turn or twist. **slewed, slued,** *a.* (*sl.*) tipsy, drunk. [etym. doubtful]

slew³, slue, *n.* (*N Am. coll.*) a great quantity or large number [Ir. *slaugh*]

slice, *n.* a broad thin piece cut off, esp. from bread etc.; a part, share etc., separated or allotted from a larger quantity; an implement used for slicing, a broad thin knife for lifting fish etc. from a frying-pan or for serving it; a slicing stroke in tennis or golf; a spatula or other similarly shaped implement. *v.t.* to cut (*usu.* up) into broad, thin pieces; to cut (off) slices from; to cut, to divide; to strike a ball with a drawing motion. *v.i.* to make a cut or motion as in slicing something. **sliceable,** *a.* **slicer,** *n.* one who or that which slices; a broad flat-bladed knife or other implement. **slicing,** *n., a.* [ME *slice,* OF *esclice, from esclicier,* to slit, from Teut., cogn. with SLIT]

slick, *a.* smooth, sleek; oily, smooth of speech etc.; polished, glossy; (*coll.*) dexterous, adroit; neatly or deftly performed; clever, smart, specious. *adv.* smoothly, deftly, smartly; quickly, immediately. *n.* a smooth or slippery surface patch, esp. of oil spilled on water. *v.t.* to make smooth or sleek. **slicker,** *n.* (*N Am.*) a waterproof, an oilskin; (*coll.*) a plausible, cunning person, a swindler. **slickly,** *adv.* **slickness,** *n.* [var. of SLEEK]

slickenside,, -sides, *n.* a specular galena found in Derbyshire limestone; (*Geol.*) a polished and grooved rock surface produced by friction, as in faults, the sides of a vein etc. [prov. *slicken,* SLICK, SIDE]

slide, *v.i.* (*past, p.p.* **slid,** †*p.p.* **slidden**) to move smoothly along a surface with continuous contact, to glide, to slip, esp. to glide over ice, snow or other slippery surface, without skates; to pass (away, into etc.) smoothly, gradually or imperceptibly to drift, to take its own course. *v.t.* to cause to move smoothly along with a slippery motion; to pass secretly or unobtrusively, to slip. *n.* an act of sliding; a slip, a thing, piece or part that slides (e.g. on a machine); a glass carrying an object to be viewed in a microscope; a photographic transparency mounted in card or plastic; the moving part on a trombone; a surface, series of grooves, guide-bars etc., on which a part slides; an inclined channel, shute etc., esp. which children slide down in play; a polished track on ice on which persons slide; a prepared slope for coasting or tobogganing; a landslip; a hairslide, a clasp; a downward turn (e.g. in value); a series of musical tones passing smoothly one into another; in guitar playing, a device fitted on the finger and pressed against the frets to produce this effect; a style of guitar playing characterized by this. **to let slide,** to leave undone, to take no positive action over, to allow to deteriorate. **slide rule,** *n.* a device, consisting of one rule sliding within another, whereby several mathematical processes can be performed mechanically. **slidable,** *a.* **slider,** *n.* **sliding,** *n., a.* **sliding-keel,** *n.* a centre-board. **sliding scale,** *n.* a scale of duties, prices etc., varying directly or inversely according to fluctuations of value or other conditions. **sliding-seat,** *n.* a seat moving on a track, esp. one in a racing boat (enabling a rower to lengthen the stroke). [OE *slīdan,* cp. LG *sliddern,* G *schlittern,* freq. from *slid-*]

slight, *a.* inconsiderable, insignificant; small in amount, intensity etc.; inadequate, paltry, superficial, negligible; slender, slim; frail, flimsy, weak. *n.* an act of disregard, disrespect or neglect. *v.t.* to treat as of little importance, to disregard; to treat disrespectfully, to snub. **slighter,** *n.* **slightingly,** *adv.* **slightish,** *a.* **slightly,** *adv.* **slightness,** *n.* [MDut. *slicht,* cp. OLG *sligt,* G *schlicht,* Icel. *slēttr*]

Sligo, *n.* county in the province of Connacht, Republic of Ireland, situated on the Atlantic coast of NW Ireland; area 1800 sq km/695 sq miles; population (1986) 56,000. The county town is Sligo; there is livestock and dairy farming.

slily SLYLY.

Slim, *n.* **William Joseph, 1st Viscount Slim** (1891–1970), British field marshal in World War II. A veteran of Gallipoli, Turkey, in World War I, he commanded the 14th 'forgotten' army from 1943–45, stemming the Japanese invasion of India at Imphal and Kohima, and then recovered Burma. He was governor general of Australia from 1953–60.

slim, *a.* (*comp.* **slimmer,** *superl.* **slimmest**) slender, thin, of slight shape or build; poor, slight; *v.i.* (*past, p.p.* **slimmed**) to adopt devices such as dieting and exercises in order to keep the body slim. *v.t.* to make slim. **slimline,** *a.* slim in shape; aiding slimness. **slimly,** *adv.* **slimmer,** *n.* one who loses or attempts to lose weight through dieting or exercise. **slimmers' disease,** *n.* anorexia nervosa. **slimming,** *n.* **slimmish,** *a.* **slimness,** *n.* [cp. MDut. *slim,* sly, G *schlimm,* bad, cunning]

slime, *n.* a soft, glutinous or viscous substance, esp. mucus or soft, moist and sticky earth. *v.t.* to smear or cover with slime. **slimy,** *a.* consisting of or of the nature of slime; covered with or abounding in slime; slippery; repulsively mean, dishonest, cringing or obsequious. **slimily,** *adv.* **sliminess,** *n.* [OE *slīm,* cp. Dut. *slijm,* G *Schleim,* Icel. *slīm,* also L *līmus,* mud]

sling¹, *v.t.* (*past, p.p.* **slung**) to throw, to hurl, esp. from a sling; (*coll.*) to cast out; to suspend in or as in a swing, to hang so as to swing; to hoist by means of a sling; (*coll.*) to throw, to hurl; (*coll.*) to pass. *v.i.* to hurl missiles with or as with a sling; to move swiftly or violently. *n.* an act of slinging; a throw; a short leather strap having a string at each end for hurling a small missile by hand; a band, loop, or other arrangement of rope, chains, straps etc., for suspending, hoisting or transferring anything; a band of cloth for supporting an injured limb. **sling your hook!** go away! **slingback,** a backless shoe with a narrow strap round the back of the ankle. **sling-shot,** *n.* a heavy weight attached to a strap or cord, used as a weapon; (*chiefly N Am.*) a catapult. **slinger,** *n.* [Icel. *slyngva,* cp. G *schlingen,* to wind, twist, sling]

sling², *n.* a sweetened drink of water mixed with spirits, esp. gin. [prob. from G *schlingen,* to swallow]

slink¹, *v.i.* (*past, p.p.* **slunk,** †*past* **slank**) to steal or sneak away in a furtive, ashamed or cowardly manner; to move sinuously and provocatively. *v.t.* of an animal, to give birth to prematurely *n.* an animal, esp. a calf, born immaturely; its flesh. **slinky,** *a.* sinuous, slender; clinging, figure-hugging. **slinkily,** *adv.* **slinkiness,** *n.* [OE *slincan,* cp. G *schleichen*]

slip¹, *v.i.* (*past, p.p.* **slipped**) to slide, to glide; to slide unintentionally or out of place, to miss one's footing; to move, go or pass unnoticed, furtively or quickly; to get away, become free, or escape thus; to commit a small mistake or oversight; to go (along) swiftly; to decline; to elapse; (*coll.*) to lose control (of a situation); of a clutch, to fail to engage; to pass from the memory; *v.t.* to cause to move in a sliding manner; to put (on or off) or to insert (into) with a sliding, stealthy, hasty or careless motion; to let loose, to unleash, to undo; to put on or remove (a garment) speedily or easily; to escape or free oneself from; of animals, to give birth to prematurely; to dislocate (a bone); to keep a clutch partially engaged; to transfer (an unworked stitch) from one knitting needle to the other. *n.* the act or state of slipping; an unintentional error, a small offence, a lapse, an indiscretion; a garment etc., easily slipped on or off, as a loose petticoat, pillow-case; a leash for a dog or hounds; an inclined ramp, dock or movable structure on which vessels are built, repaired or laid up temporarily; a landslide; in cricket, any of three off-side positions or the fielders playing these positions. (*pl.*) (*Theat.*) that part from which the scenes are slipped on, the part where actors stand before coming on the stage. **slip of the pen, tongue,** a written or spoken error. **to give the slip,** to escape from, to evade. **to let slip** LET¹. **to slip away, off,** to leave quickly or unobtrusively. **to slip up,** to make a mistake. **slipcase,** *n.* an open-ended cover for one or more books which reveals the spine(s). **slip-carriage, -coach,** *n.* a railway carriage detached at a station from an express train in motion. **slip-knot,** *n.* a knot that slips up and down the string etc. on which it is made, a running knot. **slip-on,** *n., a.* (a garment or item of footwear) which can be put on or removed easily and quickly. **slipover,** *n., a.* (a garment) easily put on over the head, a pullover. **slipped disc,** *n.* a protrusion of an intervertebral disc causing painful pressure on spinal nerves. **slipshod,** *a.* down-at-heel; careless, slovenly. **slip road,** *n.* an access or exit road from or onto a motorway. **slip stitch,** *n.* a hidden stitch used in hemming; an unworked stitch in knitting. *v.t.* to sew with a slip stitch; to slip (an unworked stitch) from one knitting needle to the other. **slipstream,** *n.* the stream of air behind an aircraft propeller; a similar stream behind any moving body, object, vehicle etc. **slip up,** *n.* an error, a blunder. **slipway,** *n.* a slip for the repair, laying up or launch of vessels. **slippage,** *n.* an act, instance, amount or degree of slipping or failure to meet a target. **slipper,** *n.* one who or that which slips or lets slip; a loose shoe easily slipped on or off, esp. for wearing indoors; a skid or shoe for braking a wheel. *v.t.* (*coll.*) to beat with a slipper. **slipper bath,** *n.* a bath with covered end, roughly resembling a slipper. **slipperwort,** *n.* a calceolaria. **slippered,** *a.* wearing slippers. **slippery,** *a.* so smooth, wet, muddy etc. as to cause slipping, not allowing a firm footing or hold; difficult to hold, elusive, not to be depended on, shifty, artful, cunning; unstable. **slipperiness,** *n.* **slippy,** *a.* (*coll.*) slippery; (*coll.*) quick, sharp, wide awake. **slippiness,** *n.* [ME *slippen* (cp. Dut. *slippen,* G *schleifen*), cogn. with OE *slūpan,* also with L *lūbricus,* slippery]

slip[2]**,** *n.* a creamy mixture of clay and water used to coat or decorate pottery. **slipware,** *n.* pottery which has been decorated with slip. [OE *slypa,* slime]

slip[3]**,** *n.* a long narrow strip of paper, wood or other material; in printing, a long gallery or a galley-proof; a cutting for grafting or planting; a scion, a descendant; a young, thin person, a stripling; *v.t.* to take a cutting from a plant. [prob. from MLG *slippe,* to strip, to cut]

slit, *v.t.* (*past, p.p.* **slit**) to cut lengthways; to cut into long pieces or strips; to make a long cut in. *n.* a long cut or narrow opening. **slit-pocket,** *n.* a pocket with a long narrow opening. **slit-trench,** *n.* a narrow trench for one or two soldiers. **slitter,** *n.* [OE *slītan,* cp. Icel. *slīta,* Dut. *slijten,* G *schleissen, schlitzen*]

slither, *v.i.* to slip, to slide unsteadily (along etc.); to move with a slipping or sliding motion (like a snake). *n.* a sliding motion. **slithery,** *a.* [OE *slēfan,* to slip on]

sliver, *n.* a piece of wood or similar material torn off, a splinter; a fleecy strand or twist pulled out from wool or other textile fibre. *v.t.* to form or divide into long, thin pieces; to cut or break into slivers. *v.i.* to split, to splinter, to break to slivers. [dim. of obs. *slive,* a slip, from OE *slīfan,* to cast off (in *tō-slāf*)]

slivovitz, slivowitz, *n.* a dry plum brandy [Serbo-Croat *šljivovica,* from *sl(j)iva,* plum]

Sloane, *n.* **Hans** (1660–1753), British physician, born in County Down, Ireland. He settled in London, and in 1721 founded the Chelsea Physic Garden. He was president of the Royal College of Physicians (1719–35), and in 1727 succeeded Newton as president of the Royal Society. His library, which he bequeathed to the nation, formed the nucleus of the British Museum.

Sloane (Ranger), *n.* a wealthy young upper-middle person with a home in central London and one in the country, characteristically wearing expensive informal country clothes. [*Sloane* Square London and Lone *Ranger,* a cowboy character]

slob, *n.* (*coll.*) a messy, slovenly or boorish person; a mire. **slobbish, slobby,** *a.*

slobber, *v.i.* to let saliva run from the mouth, to dribble; to talk or behave in a maudlin manner. *v.t.* to wet with saliva, to dribble over. *n.* saliva or spittle running from the mouth; maudlin talk or behaviour. **slobberer,** *n.* **slobbery,** *a.* **slobberiness,** *n.* [var. of SLUBBER]

sloe, *n.* the fruit of the blackthorn, *Prunus spinosa,* or the shrub bearing it. **sloe-eyed,** *a.* having dark, slanted or almond-shaped eyes. **sloe gin,** *n.* gin flavoured with sloes. [OE *sln*]

slog, *v.t., v.i.* (*past, p.p.* **slogged**) to hit vigorously and at random, esp. in batting or with the fists; to work hard; to move slowly or cumbersomely. *n.* a spell of hard work; a heavy blow; an exhausting walk. **slogger,** *n.* [etym. doubtful]

slogan, *n.* the war-cry of the old Highland clans; a political catchword; a catchy advertising phrase or word. [Gael. *sluagh-ghairm* (*sluagh,* host, *gairm,* outcry)]

sloop, *n.* a fore-and-aft rigged vessel with one mast. [Dut. *sloep,* LG *Sluup,* from *slupen,* to glide along, cogn. with SHALLOP]

sloot, *n.* (*S Afr.*) an irrigation ditch, a drainage channel. [Afrikaans, from Dut. *sluit, sluis,* SLUICE]

slop, *n.* water or other liquid carelessly thrown about; (*pl.*) liquid food refuse fed to animals, esp. pigs; dirty water, liquid refuse; (*pl.*) liquid food, weak or non-alcoholic liquors; (*pl.*) sentimental or maudlin speech or writing. *v.t.* (*past, p.p.* **slopped**) to spill or allow to overflow; to soil by spilling liquid upon; to feed liquid food refuse to; to serve (food) in a messy or clumsy way. *v.i.* to tramp through slush or mud; to show sickly sentiment, to gush; to move in a slouching, shambling manner; to become spilled, to overflow the side of a vessel. **to slop out,** of prisoners, to clean out slops from a chamber pot. **to slop over,** (*chiefly N Am.*) to be too effusive, to gush. **slop-basin, -bowl,** *n.* a basin for emptying the dregs of cups etc. into at table. **sloppy,** *a.* wet, splashed, covered with spilt water or puddles; slovenly, done carelessly; weakly sentimental, maudlin or effusive. **sloppily,** *adv.* **sloppiness,** *n.* [OE, *sloppe, slyppe,* in *cū slyppe,* see COWSLIP]

slope, *n.* an inclined surface, line or direction, an incline, a declivity or acclivity, ground whose surface makes an angle with the horizon; the degree of such inclination; the position of a rifle when carried on the shoulder. *v.i.* to be inclined at an angle to the horizon, to lie obliquely, to slant; (*sl.*) to run away, to clear off. *v.t.* to place or form with a slope, to hold or direct obliquely. **to slope arms,** to position a rifle on the shoulder with the barrel pointing up and back. **to slope off,** to leave, esp. furtively. **sloping,** *a.* **slopingly,** *adv.* **slopy,** *a.* [ME, *cogn.* with SLIP]

slops, *n.pl.* ready-made clothing, bedding etc., sold to sailors; wide loose breeches. **slop-shop,** *n.* [Icel. *sloppr,* cogn. with SLIP]

slosh, *v.t.* (*coll.*) to strike hard; (*coll.*) to splash, spread or pour (liquid); to move (something) about in liquid; to wet by splashing. *v.i.* to move or splash through slush, mud, water etc.; (*coll.*) to hit; *n.* (*coll.*) a heavy blow; slush, mud etc.; the splashing sound of liquid. **sloshed,** *a.* (*coll.*) drunk. [prob. from SLOP and SLUSH]

slot[1]**,** *n.* a groove, channel, depression or opening, esp. in timber or a machine for some part to fit into; the aperture into which coins are put in a slot-machine; a place or niche (e.g. in an organization); a (usu. regular) position in a sequence or schedule (e.g. of a television programme). *v.t.* (*past, p.p.* **slotted**) to make a slot in; to fit or place (as) into a slot. *v.i.* to fit together or into by means of a slot or slots. **slot-machine,** *n.* a machine (for gambling, dispensing sweets, drinks etc.) operated by means of coins or tokens pushed or dropped through a narrow aperture. **slotted,** *a.* **slotter,** *n.* [perh. from OF *esclot,* pit of the breast or stomach]

slot[2]**,** *n.* the track of a deer. [AF and OF *esclot,* Icel. *sloth,* cp. SLEUTH]

slot[3]**,** *n.* a bar or bolt fastening a door; a metal rod, bar etc. [ME, cp. MDut. *slot,* lock]

sloth, *n.* laziness, indolence, sluggishness; a S American arboreal mammal of the edentate group Tardigrada, characterized by its slow and awkward movements on the ground. **sloth bear,** *n.* a long-snouted bear of India and Sri Lanka which feeds on termites. **slothful,** *a.* **slothfully,** *adv.* **slothfulness,** *n.* [ME *slouthe,* OE *slæwth,* from *slāw,* SLOW]

slouch, *n.* an ungainly or negligent drooping attitude, gait, or movement; a downward bend of the hat-brim;

(*sl.*) an awkward, slovenly or incapable person; a slouch-hat. *v.i.* to droop or hang down carelessly; to stand or move in a loose, negligent or ungainly attitude. *v.t.* to bend the brim of (a hat) so that it hangs down on one side. **slouch hat,** *n.* a hat with the brim hanging down on one side. **sloucher,** *n.* **slouching,** *a.* **slouchy,** *a.* **slouchiness,** *n.* [Icel. *slōkr,* cp. Norw. *slōk,* slouching fellow, cogn. with SLACK[1]]

slough[1], *n.* a place full of mud, a bog, a quaqmire; a marsh, a swamp; a state of abject depression. **slough of despond,** extreme despondency. **sloughy,** *a.* [OE *slōh*]

slough[2], *n.* the cast skin of a snake; a covering or other part or thing cast off; dead tissue separating from a living part. *v.t.* to cast off (a skin, dead tissue etc.). *v.i.* to peel and come (off, away etc.); to cast off slough. **sloughy,** *a.* [ME *sloh,* etym. doubtful, cp. LG *slu, sluwe,* husk, covering, perh. rel. to SLEEVE]

Slovak, *n.* an inhabitant of Slovakia; the language of this people. *a.* of or pertaining to this people, their language or the region they inhabit. *a.* **Slovakian,** *n., a.* [Czech.]

Slovakia, *n.* region in the east of Czechoslovakia settled in the 5th–6th centuries by Slavs; occupied by the Magyars in the 10th century; part of the kingdom of Hungary until 1918, when it became a province of Czechoslovakia. Slovakia was a puppet state under German domination from 1939–45, and was abolished as an administrative division in 1949. Its capital and chief town was Bratislava.

sloven, *n.* one who is careless of dress or negligent of cleanliness; an untidy, careless, lazy person. **slovenly,** *a.,* †*adv.* **slovenliness,** *n.* [ME *sloveyn* (perh. MDut. *slof,* Flem. *sloef,* -EN)]

Slovene, *n.* an inhabitant of Slovenia; the language of this people. *a.* of or pertaining to this people, their language or the region they inhabit. [Gr. *Sklabēnos,* see SLAV]

Slovenia, Slovenija *n.* constituent republic of NW Yugoslavia. **area** 20,300 sq km/7836 sq miles. **capital** Ljubljana. **physical** mountainous; rivers Sava and Drava. **population** (1986) 1,930,000, including 1,710,000 Slovenes. **products** grain, sugarbeet, livestock, timber, cotton and woollen textiles, steel, vehicles. **language** Slovene, resembling Serbo-Croat, written in Roman characters. **religion** Roman Catholic. **Slovenian,** *n., a.*

slow, *a.* not quick, of small velocity, moving at a low speed; taking a long time in doing, going, proceeding, growing etc.; not prompt or willing; tardy, backward; slack; not hasty, not precipitate, behind the right time; stupid, dull; tedious, lifeless; preventing or designed to prevent fast movement. *adv.* slowly. *v.i.* to slacken speed, to go slower (*usu.* up or down). *v.t.* to reduce the speed of. **slowcoach,** *n.* one who is slow in moving, acting, deciding etc. **slow handclap,** *n.* a slow regular clapping expressing audience discontent. **slow-fuse, -match,** *n.* a fuse or match burning slowly for igniting explosives. **slow-motion,** *n.* in film and video, a technique which allows action to appear slower than normal. *a.* of or pertaining to this; operating or moving at a slower speed than is normal. **slow neutron,** *n.* a neutron with kinetic energy not greater than 10 electrovolts. **slow-witted,** *a.* **slowish,** *a.* **slowly,** *adv.* **slowness,** *n.* [OE *slāw,* cp. Dut. *sleeuw,* Icel. *sloer*]

slow-worm, *n.* a small limbless snake-like lizard, *Anguis fragilis,* the blind-worm. [OE *slā-wyrm* (prob. *slā, slah,* from *slēan,* to SLAY, WORM, from its being formerly supposed to be venomous)]

SLR, (*abbr.*) single-lens reflex, a type of camera in which the image is seen in the taking lens.

slub, *n.* a slightly twisted roll or knob in yarn. *a.* having a lumpy appearance. *v.t.* to form into slubs, in preparation for spinning. [etym. doubtful]

slubber, *v.t.* (*dial.*) to do lazily, carelessly, or bunglingly; to stain, to daub, to soil. **slubberingly,** *adv.* [cp. Dan. *slubbre,* to slaver, also LG *slubbern,* to lap up, to scamp]

sludge, *n.* mud, mire, slush; an oozy or slimy sediment, as of ore and water; a hard precipitate produced in the treatment of sewage. **sludgy,** *a.* [ME *sluche,* etym. doubtful]

slue SLEW[2,3].

slug, *n.* a shell-less air-breathing gastropod, very destructive to plants; a sea-slug; a bullet; a small, roughly rounded lump of metal; a strip of type-metal for spacing etc.; a line of type from a Linotype machine; (*coll.*) a quantity of liquor which can be gulped at one go; a unit of mass equal to 32·174 lb (14·6 kg) (*in the fps system*); (*N Am.*) a token for a slot-machine; (*coll.*) a heavy blow. *v.t.* (*past, p.p.* **slugged**) (*coll.*) to hit hard. **sluggard,** *n.* a person habitually lazy. †*a.* sluggish, lazy. **sluggardly,** *a.* **slugger,** *n.* **sluggish,** *a.* habitually lazy, dull, inactive; slow in movement or response, inert, torpid. **sluggishly,** *adv.* **sluggishness,** *n.* [orig. sluggard, from obs. *slug,* ME *sluggen* (cp. Dan. *slug,* Swed. *sloka,* Norw. *sloka,* to SLOUCH)]

sluice, *n.* a waterway with a valve or hatch by which the level of a body of water is controlled; a sluice-gate or flood-gate; the stream above, below, or passing through a flood-gate; an inclined trough or channel for washing ore, floating logs down etc. *v.t.* to flood or drench by means of a sluice or sluices; to let out or drain by a sluice; to drench, to wash thoroughly, to rinse; to furnish with a sluice. *v.i.* to pour out (as) through a sluice. **sluice-gate,** *n.* a floodgate. **sluice-way,** *n.* a channel into which water passes from a sluice. **sluicy,** *a.* [ME *scluse,* OF *escluse,* late L *exclūsa,* flood-gate, orig. fem. p.p. of *exclūdere,* to EXCLUDE]

slum[1], *n.* a squalid neighbourhood in a town; a house, flat etc. which is overcrowded, in a deteriorated condition etc. *v.i.* (*past, p.p.* **slummed**) to live in squalid or poverty-stricken conditions; to visit a place or affect a life style inferior to what one is accustomed to out of curiosity or for amusement. **slummer,** *n.* **slummy,** *a.* [Cant., etym. doubtful]

slum[2], *n.* the non-lubricating part of crude oil; the sticky residue of lubricating oil.

slumber, *v.i.* to sleep, esp. lightly; to be inactive or dormant. *v.t.* to waste (time away) in sleep. *n.* light sleep; a state of dormancy, inactivity. **slumberer,** *n. n.* **slumberingly,** *adv.* **slumberous, slumberously,** *adv.* **slumberousness,** *n.* [ME *slumeren,* freq. of *slumer* (from n. *slume,* OE *slūma,* slumber), cp. Dut. *sluimeren,* G *schlummern,* Swed. *slumra*]

slummock, *v.i.* to swallow greedily; to move or speak clumsily. *n.* a slut, a slattern. [etym. unknown]

slump, *v.i.* to fall or sink suddenly, as into a mire; of prices, prosperity etc., to come down, to collapse; to decline quickly or drastically. *n.* the act or an instance of slumping; a heavy fall or decline, a collapse (of prices etc.). [cp. Dan. *slumpe,* Norw. and Swed. *slumpa,* to fall; prob. imit.]

slung, *past, p.p.* SLING[1].

slunk, *past, p.p.* SLINK.

slur, *v.t.* (*past, p.p.* **slurred**) to soil, to sully; to calumniate; to speak slightingly of; to pass lightly over; to pronounce indistinctly; to sing or play legato. *v.i.* to speak or articulate indistinctly; to pass lightly or slightingly (over). *n.* a stain, a stigma, a reproach or disparagement; a blurred impression in printing; a slurring in pronunciation or singing; a curved line (◡ ◠) placed over or under notes, denoting that they are to be played or sung legato; the performance of this. **slurred,** *a.* [MDut. *sleuren,* to trail]

slurp, *n.* a sucking sound produced when eating or drinking noisily. *v.i.* to eat or drink noisily. [Dut. *slurpen, slorpen,* to gulp, to sip]

slurry, *n.* a thin, fluid paste made by mixing certain materials (esp. cement) with water. [obs. *slur,* fluid mud, cogn. with prec., -Y]

slush, *n.* liquid mud, sludge; half-melted snow; (*sl.*) mawkishly sentimental talk or writing, gush. *v.t.* to throw slush over, to soak or bedaub with slush; to wash thoroughly, to sluice. *v.i.* to move (as) through slush. **slush fund,** *n.* a fund of money used to finance corrupt business or political practices. **slushiness,** *n.*

slushy, *a.* [perh. from Norw. *slush* or var. of SLUDGE]

slut, *n.* a dirty, slovenly or sexually promiscuous woman. **sluttery,** *n.* **sluttish,** *a.* **sluttishly,** *adv.* **sluttishness,** *n.* [cp. Swed. dial. *slata,* Norw. *slott,* Dan. *slatte*]

Sluter, *n.* **Claus** (*c.* 1380–1406), N European sculptor, probably of Dutch origin, active in Dijon, France. His work, in an expressive Gothic style, includes the *Well of Moses* (*c.* 1395–1403) (now in the grounds of a hospital in Dijon); and the kneeling mourners, or *gisants*, for the tomb of his patron Philip the Bold, duke of Burgundy (Dijon Museum and Cleveland Museum, Ohio).

sly, *a.* (*comp.* **slyer, slier,** *superl.* **slyest, sliest**) crafty, cunning, stealthily artful; underhand, furtive, not open or frank; playfully roguish, knowing, arch. **on the sly,** slyly, in secret, on the quiet. **slyly, slily,** *adv.* **slyness,** *n.* [ME *sleigh,* Icel. *slægr,* cogn. with SLAY]

slype, *n.* a covered passage between the transept of a cathedral and the chapter-house, deanery etc. [var. of SLIP]

SM, (*abbr.*) sergeant major.

Sm, (*chem. symbol*) samarium.

smack¹, *n.* a slight taste or flavour; a suggestion, trace, tincture or dash (of); a smattering; (*sl.*) heroin. *v.i.* to have a taste, flavour or suggestion (of). [OE *smæc,* cp. MDut. *smac,* LG *smakk,* Swed. *smak,* G *geschmack*]

smack², *n.* a one-masted vessel, like a sloop or cutter, used in fishing etc. [MDut. *smacke,* cp. LG *smakk,* perh. rel. to SNAKE, cp. OE *snacc*]

smack³, *n.* a quick, smart report as of a blow with something flat, a crack of a whip etc.; a blow with the flat of the hand, a slap; a loud kiss. *v.t.* to strike with the flat of the hand, to slap; to separate (the lips) with a sharp noise; to hit, put down, crack (a whip), kiss etc. with this sound. *v.i.* of the lips, to make a sharp noise as of opening quickly; to kiss loudly. *adv.* suddenly, plump, directly. **to smack one's lips,** to gloat, to relish, to anticipate. **smacker,** *n.* a noisy kiss; a resounding blow; (*sl.*) a pound or dollar note. [prob. onomat., cp. Swed. *smacka,* Dan. *smække,* to bang, to slam]

small, *a.* deficient or relatively little in size, age, stature, degree, power, amount, number, weight etc.; of less dimensions than the standard kind, belonging to the smaller kind; in little pieces; of minor importance, slight, trifling, petty; concerned or dealing with business etc., of a restricted or minor kind; of low degree, poor, humble, plebeian; unpretentious; paltry, mean, ignoble, narrow-minded. *adv.* quietly, in a low voice; humbly, in a humiliated manner; into small pieces; †little, slightly. *n.* the slender part of anything, esp. of the back; (*pl.*) undergarments; **the small screen,** television. **to feel small,** to feel humiliated or insignificant. **small ads,** *n.pl.* classified advertisements. **small-arms,** *n.pl.* portable firearms, as rifles, pistols etc. **small beer,** *n.* beer of a mild, light quality; a trivial matter; an insignificant person. **small-bore,** *a.* of a low-calibre gun, having a chamber with a small bore. **small capitals,** *n.* capitals lower in height than the regular capitals of the same fount. **small change,** *n.* coins of low denominations. **small craft,** *n.* a vessel of small size. **small fry,** *n.* (*coll.*) an insignificant person or thing; (*pl.*) (*coll.*) children; (*pl.*) small or young fishes. **small holder,** *n.* the tenant of a small holding. **small holding,** *n.* (the working of) a portion of land of limited area and rental let, usu. by county authorities, for cultivation. **small hours,** *n.pl.* the time from midnight till 3 or 4 AM. **small intestine,** *n.* the part of the intestine comprising the duodenum, jejunum and the ileum. **small letters,** *n.pl.* lower-case letters. **small-minded,** *a.* restricted in outlook, petty. **small-mindedness,** *n.* **small potato,** *n.* (*sl.*) an insignificant person or unimportant matter. **smallpox,** *n.* variola, a contagious, feverish disease, characterized by eruptions on the skin. **small-scale,** *a.* of limited scope or extent. **small talk,** *n.* light or superficial conversation, gossip. **small-time,** *a.* (*coll.*) insignificant, unimportant; amateurish. **small-timer,** *n.* **smallish,** *a.* **smallness,** *n.* [OE *smæl,* cp. Dut., Dan. and Swed. *smal,* G. *schmal*]

smallage, *n.* wild celery, *Apium graveolens.* [small, F *ache,* L *apium,* parsley]

small-arms, smallpox etc. SMALL.

smalt, *n.* a blue glass coloured with cobalt, used in a pulverized state as a pigment. [F, from It. *smalto,* from Teut., cp. G *schmalz,* cogn. with SMELT¹]

smarm, *n.* (*coll.*) gush, fawning behaviour. *v.t.* to plaster, to flatten, (with hair oil etc.); to ingratiate oneself (with). *v.i.* to fawn, to ingratiate. **smarmy,** *a.* (*coll.*) sleek and smooth; having a wheedling manner. **smarmily,** *adv.* **smarminess,** *n.* [onomat.]

smart, *v.i.* to feel or give or cause a sharp pain or mental distress; to rankle; to feel wounded; to suffer punishment. *adv.* smartly. *n.* a sharp, lively pain, a stinging sensation; a feeling of irritation; distress, anguish; smart-money. *a.* stinging, pungent, keen, severe, poignant; vigorous, lively, brisk; astute, clever, intelligent, ingenious; quick at repartee, impertinently witty; shrewd, wide-awake, sharp; spruce, well groomed, stylish, fashionable. **to look smart,** to hurry up, be quick. **smart alec(k),** *n.* (*coll.*) a know-it-all. **smart-alecky,** *a.* **smart ass,** *n.* (*chiefly N Am. sl.*) a smart alec. **smart bomb,** *n.* one containing a device enabling it to be guided to its target. **smart-money,** *n.* money paid to buy oneself off from an unpleasant engagement etc.; money bet or invested by experienced gamblers or businessmen; in law, excessive damages. **smart set,** *n.* a fashionable social group of people. **smartweed,** *n.* the water-pepper, *Polygonum hydropiper.* **smarten,** *v.t., v.i.* **smartish,** *adv.* (*coll.*) **smartly,** *adv.* **smartness,** *n.* **smarty, smarty pants,** *n.* (*coll.*) a smart alec. [OE *smeortan* (cp. Dut. *smarten,* G *schmerzen,* Swed. *smarta,* also L *modēre,* to bite, Gr. *smerdaleos,* terrible)]

smash, *v.t.* to break to pieces by violence, to shatter, to dash, to wreck, to crash; to hit with a crushing blow; to overthrow completely, to rout, to crush; to hit (a shuttlecock, tennis ball etc.) with a forceful over-head stroke. *v.i.* to break to pieces; to go bankrupt; to collide or crash (into); to perform a smash (in badminton, tennis etc.); to come to pieces under force. *n.* an act or instance of smashing; a breaking to pieces; the sound this makes; a smash-up; in badminton, tennis etc., a forceful overhead stroke; (*coll.*) a smash-hit; a break up, a collapse; a disaster; bankruptcy, ruin. *adv.* with a smash. **smash-and-grab,** *a.* (*coll.*) descriptive of a theft where a shop window is broken and goods within hurriedly removed. **smash hit,** *n.* (*coll.*) a great success. **smash-up,** *n.* a violent collision between vehicles, a car crash. **smashable,** *a.* **smashed,** *a.* broken; (*sl.*) very drunk. **smasher,** *n.* one who or that which smashes; (*sl.*) something of staggering size, quality, effectiveness etc.; (*sl.*) an outstandingly attractive or amiable person. **smashing,** *a.* (*coll.*) very fine, wonderful. **smashing,** *adv.* [prob. onomat.]

smatter, *n.* a smattering. **smatterer,** *n.* **smattering,** *n.* a slight superficial knowledge; a small quantity. [ME *smateren,* to chatter, to prattle]

smear, *v.t.* to rub or daub with anything greasy or sticky; to rub (a screen, a lens etc.) so as to blur; to apply thickly; to soil, to pollute; to besmirch the name of someone. *v.i.* to make a smear; to become blurred, smudged etc. *n.* a stain or mark made by smearing; an attack on a person's reputation; a substance (e.g. vaginal secretion) smeared on a glass slide for examination under a microscope. **smear campaign,** *n.* a series of orchestrated attacks on the reputation of a politician, institution etc. **smear test,** *n.* a microscopic examination of a smear, e.g. for cervical cancer. **smearer,** *n.* **smeary,** *a.* **smearily,** *adv.* **smeariness,** *n.* [OE *smerien* (cp. Dut. *smeren,* G *schmieren,* Icel. *smyrja*), from *smeru,* fat, cogn. with Gr. *muron,* ointment]

smeddum, *n.* fine powder; (*Sc.*) spirit, mettle, go. [OE *smedima,* etym. doubtful]

smegma, *n.* a sebaceous soapy secretion found in the folds of the skin, esp. under the prepuce. [Gr. *smēgma,* soap, from *smēchein,* to wipe]

smell, *n.* the sense by which odours are perceived; the sensation or the act of smelling; that which affects the organs of smell, scent, odour; a bad odour, a stench; a characteristic quality, a trace, an aura. *v.t.* (*past, p.p.* **smelt**[3], †**smelled**) to perceive the odour of; to inhale the odour of anything with the nose; to detect by means of scent; to hunt, trace or find (out) by or as by the scent. *v.i.* to affect the sense of smell, to give out an odour (of etc.); to have a specified smell; to suggest, to indicate, to smack (of); to have or exercise the sense of smell; to stink. **to smell out,** to detect by instinct or prying; to pollute (e.g. a room with smoke). †**smell-feast,** *n.* a parasite, a sponger. **smelling-bottle,** *n.* a small bottle or phial for holding smelling-salts. **smelling-salts,** *n.pl.* an aromatic preparation of ammonium carbonate used in cases of faintness etc. **smeller,** *n.* one who smells; (*sl.*) the nose, a hit on the nose. **smell-less,** *a.* **smelly,** *a.* malodorous. **smelliness,** *n.* [ME *smel,* v. *smelen,* (cp. Dut. *smeulen,* LG *smelen,* to SMOULDER)]

smelt[1], *v.t.* to fuse (an ore) so as to extract the metal; to extract (metal) from ore thus. **smelter,** *n.* **smeltery,** *n.* **smelting,** *n.* **smelting-furnace,** *n.* [cp. MDut. *smelten,* G *schmelzen,* Dan. *smelta,* OHG *smelzen*]

smelt[2], *n.* (*pl.* **smelt, smelts**) a small food-fish, *Osmerus eperlanus,* allied to the salmon. [OE cp. *smeolt,* smooth]

smelt[3], *past, p.p.* SMELL.

Smersh, *n.* formerly the main administration of counter-intelligence in the USSR, established in 1942. It was a subsection of the KGB.

Smetana, *n.* **Bedřich** (1824–84), Czech composer, whose music has a distinct national character, for example, the operas *The Bartered Bride* (1866), *Dalibor* (1868), and the symphonic suite *My Country* (1875–80).

smew, *n.* a small merganser or diving-duck, *Mergus albellus*. [var. of obs. *smee, smeath,* SMOOTH]

smiddy, (*Sc.*) SMITHY.

smidgen, smidgeon, smidgin, *n.* (*coll.*) a tiny amount.

Smilax, *n.* a genus of climbing shrubs many species of which yield sarsaparilla; a S African twining plant resembling these. [Gr.]

smile, *v.i.* to express kindness, love, pleasure, amusement or contempt by an instinctive lateral and upward movement of the lips and cheeks; of the weather, fortune etc., to look bright, cheerful or favourable. *v.t.* to express by or as by a smile; to bring or drive (into, out of, away etc.) thus. *n.* the act of smiling; a gay, cheerful or favourable expression, aspect or disposition. **to come up smiling,** to end up in a favourable state, esp. after misfortune. **smileless,** *a.* **smiler,** *n.* **smiley,** *a.* **smilingly,** *adv.* [ME *smīlen* (cp. OHG *smîlen,* MHG *smielen*), cogn. with L *mīrārī,* to wonder, and Gr. *meidân,* to smile]

Smiles, *n.* **Samuel** (1812–1904), Scottish writer, author of the popular Victorian didactic work *Self Help* (1859).

smirch, *v.t.* to soil, to smear, to stain, to defile, to defame. *n.* a stain, a smear; the state of being defiled or defamed; the act of smirching. [extension of ME *smeren,* to SMEAR]

smirk, *v.i.* to smile affectedly or scornfully, to simper. *n.* an affected or scornful smile, a simper. **smirker,** *n.* **smirky,** *a.* [OE *smercian*]

Smirke, *n.* **Robert** (1780–1867), English Classical architect, designer of the British Museum, London (1823–47).

smirr SMUR.

smite, *v.t.* (*past* **smote,** †**smit** *p.p.* **smitten,** †smit) to strike, to deal a severe blow to; to inflict injury, death, defeat, damage or disaster upon; (*usu. in p.p.*) to strike or affect (with a feeling, disease etc.). *v.i.* to strike, to knock, to come (on, against etc.) with force. *n.* a blow. **smiter,** *n.* [OE *smitan*]

Smith[1], *n.* **Adam** (1723–90), Scottish economist, often regarded as the founder of modern political economy. His *The Wealth of Nations* (1776) defined national wealth in terms of labour. The cause of wealth is explained by the division of labour – dividing a production process into several repetitive operations, each carried out by different workers. Smith advocated the free working of individual enterprise, and the necessity of 'free trade'.

Smith[2], *n.* **Bessie** (1894–1937), US jazz and blues singer, born in Chattanooga, Tennessee. She established herself in the 1920s, but her popularity waned in the Depression, and she died after a car crash when she was refused admission to a whites-only hospital. She was known as the Empress of the Blues.

Smith[3], *n.* **David** (1906–65), US sculptor and painter, whose work made a lasting impact on sculpture after World War II. He trained as a steel welder in a car factory. His pieces are large openwork metal abstracts.

Smith[4], *n.* **Ian Douglas** (1919–), Rhodesian politician. He was a founder of the Rhodesian Front in 1962 and prime minister (1964–1979). In 1965 he made a unilateral declaration of Rhodesia's independence, and despite United Nations sanctions maintained his regime with tenacity. In 1979 he was succeeded as prime minister by Bishop Abel Muzorewa, when the country was renamed Zimbabwe-Rhodesia. He was suspended from the Zimbabwe parliament in Apr. 1987 and resigned in May as head of the white opposition party.

Smith[5], *n.* **John** (1580–1631), English colonist. After an adventurous early life he took part in the colonization of Virginia, acting as president of the North American colony from 1608–09. He explored New England in 1614, which he named, and published pamphlets on America and an autobiography. During an expedition among the American Indians his life is said to have been saved by Pocahontas, whom he married.

Smith[6], *n.* **John Maynard** (1920–), British biologist, whose work in evolutionary theory resulted in the theory of the evolutionarily stable strategy (ESS), which explains animal aggression as part of a ritual and suggests that evolution prevents animals from attacking each other.

Smith[7], *n.* **Joseph** (1805–44), US founder of the MORMON religious sect.

Smith[8], *n.* **Maggie (Margaret Natalie)** (1934–), English actress. Her roles include the title part (winning an Oscar) in the film *The Prime of Miss Jean Brodie* (1969). Other films include *California Suite* (1978), *A Private Function* (1984), and *A Room with a View* (1986).

Smith[9], *n.* **'Stevie' (Florence Margaret)** (1902–71), British poet, noted for eccentrically direct verse, whose books include *Novel on Yellow Paper* (1936), and the poems *A Good Time was had by All* (1937), and *Not Waving but Drowning* (1957).

Smith[10], *n.* **William** (1769–1839), British geologist, the founder of English geology. Working as a canal engineer, he noticed while supervising excavations that different beds of rock could be identified by their fossils, and so established the basis of stratigraphy. He also produced the first geological maps of England and Wales.

smith, *n.* one who works in metals, esp. one who forges iron with the hammer; a blacksmith; one who makes or effects anything. **smithery,** *n.* the craft, trade or occupation of a smith; a smithy. **smithy,** *n.* a blacksmith's workshop. [OE, cp. Dut. *smid,* G *schmied,* Icel. *smithr,* Dan. and Swed. *smed*]

smithereens, *n.pl.* little bits, tiny fragments. [dim. of dial. *smithers,* etym. doubtful]

smithery, smithy etc. SMITH.

Smiths, the, *n.pl.* English four-piece rock group (1982–87) from Manchester. Their songs, with lyrics by singer Morrissey (1959–) and tunes by guitarist Johnny Marr (1964–), drew on diverse sources such as rockabilly, Mersey beat, and the Byrds, with confessional humour and images of urban desolation.

smithsonite, *n.* (*Min.*) silicate of zinc; (*N Am.*) carbonate of zinc. [J.L.M. *Smithson,* c.1765–1829, Br. chemist]

smitten, *p.p.* (*coll.*) enamoured. [SMITE]
smock, *n.* a smock-frock; a woman's loose frock, artist's overall etc. resembling this. †a woman's undergarment, a chemise. *v.t.* to decorate with smocking; to clothe in a smock. †**smock-faced,** *a.* having an effeminate appearance or complexion. **smock-frock,** *n.* a coarse, loose garment resembling a shirt with a yoke, formerly worn by farm labourers over their other clothes. **smocking,** *n.* honeycomb work such as that decorating the front of a smock. [OE *smoc,* cogn. with *smūgan,* to creep into, cp. SMUGGLE]
smog, *n.* a smoky fog containing chemical fumes. **smoggy,** *a.* **smogless,** *a.* [comb. of SMOKE and FOG[2]]
smoke, *n.* volatile products of combustion, esp. carbonaceous and other matter in the form of visible vapour or fine particles escaping from a burning substance; a suspension of particles in gas; anything ephemeral or unsubstantial; the act of smoking a pipe, cigar etc.; (*sl.*) a cigarette. *v.i.* to emit smoke; to emit vapour, fumes etc., to reek; of a chimney etc., to send smoke into a room, to fail to draw; to draw into the mouth or inhale and exhale the smoke of tobacco etc.; *v.t.* to apply smoke to; to blacken, colour, cure, flavour, suffocate, drive out, destroy, cleanse etc., with smoke; to draw with the mouth or inhale and exhale the smoke of (tobacco etc.). **no-smoking zone, area,** part of a building, vehicle etc. where it is forbidden to smoke. **the smoke,** a (big) city; London. **to go, end up in smoke,** of a scheme, a desire, to come to nothing; to be burned to nothing. **to smoke out,** to drive out with smoke; to discover, to bring into the open. **smoke-oh, smoko,** *n.* (*Austral., New Zealand coll.*) a break from work. **smoke-ball, smoke bomb,** *n.* a projectile containing a composition that emits a dense smoke. **smoke-black,** *n.* lamp-black. **smoke box,** *n.* in a steam locomotive, the chamber through which smoke and gases pass from the boiler tubes to the funnel. **smoke-dried,** *a.* cured by smoking. **smoke-dry,** *v.t.* **smokehouse,** *n.* a building where meat, fish etc. is cured. **smoke-jack,** *n.* an apparatus for turning a roasting-spit by using the current of hot air in a chimney. **smoke-plant, -tree,** *n.* an ornamental shrub or tree with long, feathery fruit stalks. **smoke-screen,** *n.* a dense volume of smoke produced by chemicals used to conceal the movements of ships, troops etc., from the enemy; something used to obscure or deceive. **smoke signals,** *n.pl.* a method of conveying messages by a series of puffs of smoke; (*coll.*) private signals from one person to another. **smoke-stack,** *n.* a funnel, esp. on a steamer. **smokable,** *a.* **smoked,** *a.* **smoked herring,** *n.* a kipper. **smokeless,** *a.* **smokeless zone,** *n.* an area in which it is forbidden to emit smoke from chimneys. **smoker,** *n.* one who smokes tobacco; one who dries, cures, fumigates etc., with smoke; a smoking compartment. **smoking,** *n., a.* **smoking cap, jacket,** *n.* a decorated cap or (usu. velvet) jacket, formerly worn by men when smoking. **smoking carriage, compartment, room,** *n.* a railway-carriage etc., reserved for smokers. **smoky, smokey,** *a.* resembling smoke in colour, smell, flavour etc.; filled with smoke; emitting smoke; dirtied by smoke. *n.* (*Sc.*) a smoked haddock. **smokily,** *adv.* **smokiness,** *n.* [OE *smoca* (cp. Dut. *smook,* G *schmauch*), rel. to *smēocan,* cogn. with Gr. *smuchein,* to smoulder]
smolder, SMOULDER.
Smollett, *n.* **Tobias George** (1721–71), Scottish novelist, who wrote the picaresque novels *Roderick Random* (1748), *Peregrine Pickle* (1751), *Ferdinand Count Fathom* (1753), *Sir Lancelot Greaves* (1760–62), and *Humphrey Clinker* (1771).
smolt, *n.* a salmon in its second year when it acquires its silvery scales. [perh. from OE *smolt,* serene, shining]
smooch, *v.i.* (*coll.*) to kiss and cuddle, to behave amorously. [imit.]
smooth, *a.* having a continuously even surface, free from roughness, projections or indentations; not hairy; of water, unruffled; free from obstructions or impediments; offering no resistance; of sound, taste etc., not harsh; equable, calm, pleasant, bland, suave, polite, flattering. *v.t.* to make smooth; to free from harshness, discomforts, obstructions, irregularities etc.; to extenuate, to soften, to alleviate, to dispel. *v.i.* to become smooth. *n.* the act of smoothing; a smooth place or part; (*coll.*) that which is pleasant or easy. **to smooth over,** to gloss over (a difficulty). **smoothbore(d),** *a.* not rifled; *n.* a smoothbore gun. **smooth breathing,** *a.* (*Gr. Gram.*) of vowels, sounded without the aspirate. *n.* a sign marking this. **smooth-chinned,** *a.* beardless. **smooth-coated,** *a.* of an animal, having a smooth pelt or fur. **smooth-faced,** *a.* beardless; having a suave, specious, flattering appearance or expression; unwrinkled; having a smooth surface. **smooth muscle,** *n.* muscle (e.g. in the intestine, the wall of a blood vessel) capable of involuntary contractions. **smooth-spoken, -tongued,** *a.* polite, plausible, flattering. †**smoothen,** *v.t., v.i.* **smoother,** *n.* **smoothie, -thy,** *n.* (*coll., usu. derog.*) an excessively sauve or plausible person, esp. a man. **smoothing,** *n., a.* **smoothing-iron,** *n.* a polished iron implement formerly used for smoothing linen etc. **smoothing-plane,** *n.* a short plane, finely set, used for finishing. **smoothly,** *adv.* **smoothness,** *n.* [OE *smethe* (rare *smōth*)]
smorgasbord, *n.* a buffet comprising an assortment of hors d'oeuvres and other dishes. [Swed. *smörgås,* open sandwich, *bord,* table]
smorzando, smorzato, *a., adv.* (*Mus.*) with a gradual fading or dying away. [It. *pres.p.* and *p.p.* of *smorzare,* to extinguish]
smote, (*past*) SMITE.
smother, *n.* a stifling cloud of dust, smoke, vapour etc.; a smouldering state. *v.t.* to suffocate, to stifle; to kill by suffocation etc.; to keep (a fire) down by covering it with ashes etc.; to hide, to suppress, to keep from being divulged, to conceal; to overcome, to overwhelm; to cover thickly, to enclose, to envelop. *v.i.* to be suffocated, to be prevented from breathing freely. **smothered mate,** *n.* in chess, a checkmate by a knight when the king is surrounded and unable to move. **smotheringly,** *adv.* **smothery,** *a.* **smotheriness,** *n.* [ME *smorther,* from OE *smorian,* to choke, stifle, cp. Dut. *smooren,* G *schmoren,* cogn. with SMOKE and SMOULDER]
smoulder, (*esp. N Am.*) **smolder,** *v.i.* to burn in a smothered way without flame; to exist in a suppressed or latent condition; to feel or show strong repressed emotions (as anger, jealousy). *n.* a smouldering state; a smouldering fire. [ME *smolderen,* from *smolder,* smoke, cogn. with SMELL and SMOTHER]
smouse, *n.* (*S Afr.*) an itinerant trader. [Afrikaans *smous,* perh. from Yiddish *schmuoss,* news, talk, from Heb.]
smudge, *v.t.* to smear or blur (writing, drawing etc.); to make a dirty smear, blot or stain on; to soil, to smirch, to defile, to sully (purity, reputation etc.); (*N Am.*) to fumigate so as to drive mosquitoes etc. away. *v.i.* to become smeared or blurred. *n.* a dirty mark, a smear, a blur; (*N Am.*) a smouldering fire for driving away mosquitoes etc. **smudgy,** *a.* **smudginess,** *n.* [ME *smogen,* cogn. with SMUT]
smug, *a.* (*comp.* **smugger,** *superl.* **smuggest**) self-satisfied, complacent. **smugly,** *adv.* **smugness,** *n.* [cp. MDan. *smug,* smooth, LG *smuk,* G *schmuck,* neat, spruce]
smuggle, *v.t.* to import or export illegally without paying customs duties; to convey or introduce clandestinely. **smuggled,** *a.* **smuggler,** *n.* **smuggling,** *n.* [LG *smuggeln* (cp. Dan. *smöge,* Icel. *smuga,* lurking-hole), cogn. with SMOCK]
smur, smir(r), *n.* (*chiefly Sc.*) fine misty rain, drizzle. *v.i.* (*past, p.p.* **smurred**) to drizzle. **smurry, smirry,** *a.* [etym. doubtful]
smut, *n.* a particle of soot or other dirt, a mark or smudge made by this; a disease of corn due to parasitic fungi; obscene or ribald talk, language, stories etc. *v.t.* (*past, p.p.* **smutted**) to stain or mark with smut; to infect with smut. *v.i.* of corn etc., to be attacked by smut. **smutty,** *a.* **smuttily,** *adv.* **smuttiness,** *n.* [cp.

LG *Schmutt,* G *Schmutz,* Swed. *smuts*]

smutch, SMUDGE.

Smuts, *n.* **Jan Christian** (1870–1950), South African politician, field marshal, and lawyer; prime minister from 1919–24 and 1939–48. He supported the Allies in both world wars and was a member of the British imperial war cabinet (1917–18).

Smythson, *n.* **Robert** (1535–1614), English architect, freemason of the Elizabethan country houses, including Longleat (1568–75), Wollaton Hall (1580–88), and Hardwick Hall (1590–97). Their castle-like silhouettes, symmetry, and large gridded windows are a uniquely romantic, English version of classicism.

Sn, (*chem. symbol*) tin.

snack, *n.* a slight, hasty meal (often taken between main meals). *v.i.* to have a snack. **snack-bar,** *n.* a cafe, self-service restaurant or other place offering light meals or refreshments. [var. of SNATCH]

snaffle, *n.* a bridle-bit usu. with a joint in the middle. *v.t.* (*coll.*) to steal, to appropriate for oneself; to furnish or control with a snaffle. **snaffle-bit,** *n.* a snaffle. [cp. Dut. *snavel,* muzzle, G *Schnabel,* bill, snout]

snafu, *n.* (*N Am. sl.*) a state of total confusion or chaos. *a.* confused, muddled. *v.t.* to throw into confusion. [*s*ituation *n*ormal *a*ll *f*ucked *u*p]

snag, *n.* a jagged projection, as the stumpy base of a branch left in pruning, a branch broken off, a knot, a stump of a tooth; the trunk of a tree fixed at one end in the bed of a river (constituting a navigational hazard); a tear, a pull, a flaw in fabric; an unexpected or concealed difficulty, an obstacle; (*Austral. sl.*) a sausage. *v.t.* (*past, p.p.* **snagged** to run or damage on a snag; to clear of snags; to tear or catch (fabric) on a snag; (*chiefly N Am.*) to hinder, to halt, to impede; (*N Am.*) to catch, seize (an opportunity etc.), to obtain by seizing or taking quick action. *v.i.* to become snagged. **snagged, snaggy,** *a.* [prob. from Scand. (cp. Norw. dial. *snag,* Icel. *snagr*), perh. rel. to KNAG]

snail, *n.* a gasteropodous mollusc of various species, usu. bearing a shell; the sea snail; a sluggish person or thing. †**snail-paced,** *a.* slow-moving. **snail's pace,** *n.* a slow rate of progress. **snail-wheel,** *n.* a rotating part of a clock, usu. spiral or snail-shaped in outline, with notches determining the number of strokes to be given in striking. **snailery,** *n.* a place where edible snails are cultivated. **snaillike,** *a.* **snaily,** *a.* [OE *snægl,* dim. of *snaca,* SNAKE]

snake, *n.* a serpent, a limbless reptile of a venomous or non-venomous type having a forked tongue and the ability to swallow prey whole; a snake-like lizard or amphibian; a sneaking, treacherous person; anything resembling a snake in appearance or movement, esp. a tool for unblocking drains; in the EEC, a system which allows the currencies of member countries to fluctuate within narrow limits. *v.t.* to follow a snaking course, to move in the manner of a snake. *v.i.* to wind, to move quietly or snakily. **snake in the grass,** a treacherous or underhand person. **snakes and ladders,** a board game in which counters can advance more speedily up ladders or move backwards down ladders. **snake bird,** *n.* the darter. **snake bite,** *n.* the venomous bite of a snake; (*coll.*) a drink of beer and cider. **snake-charmer,** *n.* an entertainer who appears to mesmerize snakes by playing music. **snake-charming,** *n.* **snake-root,** *n.* the root of various N American plants supposed to be a specific for snake-bites; one of these plants. **snake's-head,** *n.* the fritillary. **snakeskin,** *n., a.* (made of) the skin of a snake. **snake-stone,** *n.* an ammonite. **snake-weed,** *n.* the bistort. **snakelike, snakish, snaky,** *a.* **snakily,** *adv.* **snakiness,** *n.* [OE *snaca* (cp. LG *Snake,* Icel. *snākr,* Dan. *snog*), cogn. with SNEAK]

snap, *v.t.* (*past, p.p.* **snapped**) to bite to try to bite (at); to grasp, seize or snatch (at); to make a sharp, quick sound, like a crack or slight explosion; to break, part, close or fit into place suddenly with such a noise; to collapse (with pressure, strain of work etc.), to break down; to speak sharply or irritably. *v.t.* to seize suddenly, to snatch; to take advantage of eagerly; to utter abruptly or irritably; to interrupt or take (up) in the midst of a speech etc.; to cause (a whip, the fingers etc.) to make a sharp crack or report; to break with such a noise; to shut (to) or bring (together) thus; to photograph casually. *n.* the act or an instance of snapping; the sound produced by this; the spring catch of a bracelet, purse etc.; a sudden spell of severe weather; a crisp gingerbread cake; a children's game of cards; a snapshot; vigour, briskness, dash, go; (*coll.*) something that is easy or profitable, a cinch; an abrupt response. *a.* done, taken etc., suddenly, offhand or by surprise; closing or fastening with a snap; (*coll.*) easy, profitable, cheap. *adv.* with (the sound of) a snap. *int.* uttered when playing the game of snap; hence, indicating similarity, identicalness or synchronicity. **to snap one's fingers (at),** to show contempt or defiance. **to snap out of it,** to change one's mood abruptly (for the better). **to snap someone's head, nose off,** to retort abruptly, irritably or rudely. **to snap up,** to take quick advantage of (a bargain etc), to purchase eagerly. **snap decision,** *n.* one taken without deliberation. **snapdragon,** *n.* a plant of the genus *Antirrhinum,* with a flower opening like a dragon's mouth; a game of snatching raisins from a dish of burning spirit. **snap fastener,** *n.* a press-stud. **snap-link, -ring,** *n.* a karabiner. **snap-on,** *a.* designed to be attached by a snap fastening or spring clip. **snapshot,** *n.* a photograph taken without preparation or posing. **snapper,** *n.* any of various toothed fish related to the bass which inhabit warm waters; a spotted food fish of Australia and New Zealand; a snapping turtle; one who, or that which, snaps. **snapping,** *n., a.* **snapping-turtle,** *n.* a fierce and voracious N American fresh-water turtle, *Chelydra serpentina,* a snapper. **snappingly,** *adv.* **snappish,** *a.* given to snapping or biting, given to sharp replies, spiteful, irascible. **snappishly,** *adv.* **snappishness,** *n.* **snappy,** *a.* snappish; irritable, cross; brisk, sharp, lively; smart, up-to-date, stylish. **to make it snappy,** to hurry up. **snappily,** *adv.* [prob. from MDut. *snappen,* cp. G *schnappen,* Dan. *snappe,* cogn. with SNAFFLE]

snar, SNARL[1].

snare, *n.* a trap, usu. consisting of a noose, for catching birds or other animals; a trick, trap, stratagem or allurement by which one is brought into difficulty, defeat, disgrace, sin etc.; a string of gut, wire or hide stretched inside the head of a drum making a rattling sound when the head is struck; a surgical instrument for removing tumours and other tissue matter, consisting of a wire loop. *v.t.* to catch in a snare; to ensnare, entrap or inveigle. **snare drum,** *n.* a small drum with two heads, the lower of which is fitted with a snare. **snarer,** *n.* **snary,** *a.* [OE *snear,* cp. Dut. *snaar,* G *Schnur,* Icel. *snara,* string]

snarl[1]**,** *v.i.* to growl in a sharp tone with teeth bared, as an angry dog; to speak in a harsh, surly or savage manner. *v.t.* to express or say (out) with a snarl. *n.* a sharp-toned growl; a savage remark or exclamation. **snarler,** *n.* **snarling,** *n., a.* **snarlingly,** *adv.* **snarly,** *a.* [orig. *snar,* MDut. *snarren,* to trawl, cp. G *schnarren,* Swed. *snarra,* to make guttural noises, prob. imit.]

snarl[2]**,** *n.* a tangle, a knot of hair, thread etc.; a knot in wood; (*fig.*) an entanglement, embarrassing difficulty. *v.t.* to entangle; to cause to become confused or complicated; to flute or emboss (metal-ware) by hammering the inside with a snarling-iron. *v.i.* to become entangled, muddled, complicated. **snarling-iron, -tool,** *n.* **to snarl up,** to (cause to) become tangled, disordered, inoperable, immobile etc. **snarl-up,** *n.* an instance or state of confusion, obstruction, disorder etc. (e.g. a traffic jam). **snarled,** *a.* **snarler,** *n.* [SNARE]

snatch, *v.t.* to seize suddenly, eagerly or without permission or ceremony; to remove or rescue (from, away etc.) suddenly or hurriedly; to win or gain narrowly. *v.i.* to try to seize, to make a sudden motion (at) as if to seize. *n.* an act of snatching, a grab (at); that which is snatched; a short spell of rest, work etc.; a fragment of talk, song etc.; in weightlifting, a kind of lift in which the weight is raised overhead in one motion; (*coll.*) a robbery, a kidnapping. **snatchblock,** *n.*

a single block with an opening in one side to receive a rope. **snatcher,** *n.* (*often in comb.*, as *body-snatcher*). **snatchily, snatchingly,** *adv.* **snatchy,** *a.* [ME *snacchen,* cogn. with SNACK and SNECK[1] (cp. Dut. *snakken*)]

snazzy, *a.* (*sl.*) up-to-date, showy, smart, attractive (e.g. of clothes). **snazzily,** *adv.* **snazziness,** *n.* [perh. from SNAPPY and JAZZY]

sneak, *v.i.* to creep, slink or steal (about, away, off etc.), as if afraid or ashamed to be seen; to behave in a mean, cringing, cowardly or underhand way; to tell tales. *v.t.* (*sl.*) to steal; to place or remove stealthily. *n.* one who sneaks; a tale-bearer; in cricket, a ball bowled along the ground. **to sneak away, off,** to leave unobtrusively. **sneak-thief,** *n.* a pilferer, one who steals from open windows or doors. **sneaker,** *n.* **sneakers,** *n.pl.* (*chiefly N Am.*) rubber-soled shoes. **sneakingly,** *adv.* **sneaky,** *a.* **sneakily,** *adv.* **sneakiness,** *n.* [OE *snīcan,* to creep, cogn. with SNAKE (cp. Icel. *snikja,* to hanker after)]

†**sneap,** *v.t.* to reprove, to snub; to nip, to pinch. *n.* a reprimand, a check, a snub. [earlier *snape,* Icel. *sneypa,* to outrage, to snub]

sneb(be), SNIB.

sneck[1], *n.* (*dial.*) a latch or catch. *v.t.*, *v.i.* to latch, to fasten, to lock (up). **snecked,** *a.* [cp. SNACK and SNATCH]

sneck[2], SNICK.

sneer, *v.i.* to show contempt by a smile or grin; to scoff, to jibe. *v.t.* to utter or express with a sneer; to treat or put (down etc.) with a sneer. *n.* a grimace or verbal expression of contempt or derision. **sneerer,** *n.* **sneering,** *n., a.* **sneeringly,** *adv.* **sneery,** *a.* [ME *sneren,* cp. NFris. *sneere,* MDan. *snarre,* rel. to SNARL[1]]

sneeze, *v.i.* to eject air etc. through the nostrils audibly and convulsively, owing to irritation of the inner membrane of the nose. *n.* the act of sneezing. **not to be sneezed at,** not to be despised, worth consideration. **sneezewort,** *n.* the wild pellitory, *Achillea ptarmica*. **sneezer,** *n.* **sneezy,** *a.* [ME *snesen,* OE *fnēosan* (cp. Dut. *fniezen,* Icel. *fnasa,* also Gr. *pneein,* to breathe)]

Snell, *n.* **Willebrord** (1581–1626), Dutch mathematician and physicist who devised the basic law of refraction, known as Snell's law in 1621. This states that the ratio between the sine of the angle of incidence and the sine of the angle of refraction is constant. The laws describing the reflection of light were well known in antiquity but the principles governing the refraction of light were little understood. Snell's law was published by Descartes in 1637.

snell[1], *a.* (*chiefly Sc.*) active, keen, smart, severe, stinging, pungent. [OE *snel,* cp. LG and OHG *snel,* G *schnell,* Icel. *snjallr*]

snell[2], *n.* a short line or snood, usu. of gut, for attaching fish-hooks to a line. [etym. doubtful]

snib, *n.* (*Sc.*) a bolt or catch. *v.t.* (*past, p.p.* **snibbed**) to fasten with this. [etym. doubtful]

snick, *v.t.* to cut, to nick to snip; in cricket, to hit (the ball) lightly with a glancing stroke. *n.* a slight cut, nick or notch; a light glancing hit, in cricket. [etym. doubtful]

snicker, *v.i.* to snigger; to neigh, to nicker. *v.t.* to utter with a snigger. *n.* a snigger. **snickerer,** *n.* **snickery,** *a.* [imit., cp. SNIGGER]

snickersnee, *n.* a big knife, esp. a bowie. [prob. corr. of obs. *snick or snee,* a fight with knives]

snide, *a.* sham, bogus; malicious, sneering, disparaging, sly, mean. *n.* (*sl.*) sham jewellery etc. **snidely,** *adv.* **snideness,** *n.* [etym. doubtful]

sniff, †**snift,** *v.i.* to draw air audibly up the nose in order to smell, clear the nasal passages, inhale a drug, express contempt etc. *v.t.* to draw (*usu.* up) with the breath; to smell, to perceive by sniffing. *n.* the act or sound of sniffing; that which is sniffed in (e.g. a scent). **to sniff at,** to express contempt or disdain for. **to sniff out,** to discover (as if) by sniffing. **sniffer,** *n.* **sniffer dog,** *n.* a dog trained to smell out drugs or explosives. **sniffle,** *v.i.* to sniff (as with a cold, when weeping etc.), to snuffle. *n.* an act or sound of sniffling; a snuffle. **the sniffles,** a slight head-cold. **sniffler,** *n.* **sniffly,** *a.* **sniffily,** *adv.* **sniffiness,** *n.* **sniffy,** *a.* (*coll.*) given to sniffing, disdainful. **snifter,** *n.* a short-stemmed glass with a wide bowl and narrow top (for brandy, liqueur etc.). **snifting valve,** *n.* a valve in a steam cylinder for the escape of air. [ME *sneven,* cp. Dan. *snive,* Icel. *snippa,* MDan. *snifte,* imit. in orig.]

snig, *n.* a small eel. [etym. doubtful]

snigger, *v.i.* to laugh in a half-suppressed or discourteous manner. *n.* a suppressed laugh. [var. of SNICKER]

sniggle, *v.i.* to fish for eels by thrusting the bait into their holes. *v.t.* to catch thus. [from SNIG, etym. doubtful]

snip, *v.t.* (*past, p.p.* **snipped**) to cut or clip off sharply or quickly with shears or scissors. *v.i.* to make such a cutting movement. *n.* the act, movement or sound of snipping; a cut with scissors or shears; a small piece snipped off; (*coll.*) a certainty, a cinch, a bargain; (*pl.*) shears used to cut sheet metal by hand. **snipper,** *n.* **snippet, snipping,** *n.* a small bit snipped off; (*pl.*) scraps, fragments (of news etc.). **snippety,** *a.* **snippetiness,** *n.* **snippy,** *a.* [cp. Dut. and LG *snippen,* G *schnippen,* cogn. with SNAP]

snipe, *n.* a long-billed marsh- and shore-bird of the genus *Gallinago,* esp. the British *G. coelestis;* a gunshot, usu. fired from cover; a verbal attack or criticism, usu. made from a secure position. *v.i.* to criticize, to find fault. to shoot or hunt snipe; to pick off members of the enemy, usu. from cover. *v.t.* to shoot at from cover. **sniper,** *n.* a tell-tale, an informer; a (minor) robbery. **sniping,** *n.* [Icel. *snīpa,* cp. Dut. *snip,* G *schnepfe,* cogn. with SNAP]

snipper, snippet etc. SNIP.

snitch, *v.i.* (*sl.*) to inform, to peach. *v.t.* (*sl.*) to steal, to pilfer. *n.* the nose; a tell-tale, an informer. [etym. doubtful]

snivel, *v.i.* (*past, p.p.* **snivelled**) to run at the nose; to cry or fret with snuffling, to whimper or whine; to be tearful. *n.* mucus running from the nose; audible or affected weeping; hypocrisy, cant. **sniveller,** *n.* **snivelly,** *a.* [ME *snevelen,* cogn. with OE *snofl,* mucus, cp. SNUFF[1], SNUFFLE]

SNO, (*abbr.*) Scottish National Orchestra.

snob, *n.* one who cultivates or truckles to those of higher social position, or regards the claims of wealth and position with an exaggerated and contemptible respect; one who condescends to, patronizes, or avoids those felt to be of lower standing. **snobbery, snobbishness,** *n.* **snobbish, snobby,** *a.* **snobbishly,** *adv.* [etym. doubtful]

SNOBOL, *n.* a language used in computer programming for handling strings of symbols. [acronym for *S*tri*n*g *O*rientated Sym*bo*lic *L*anguage]

Sno-Cat®, *n.* a type of vehicle designed to travel on snow.

snod, *a.* (*Sc.*) neat, tidy, trim; smooth, sleek; snug. *v.t.* (*past, p.p.* **snodded**) to make snod, to put in order. [etym. doubtful]

snoek, (*S Afr.*) SNOOK[1].

snog, *v.i.* (*coll.*) (*past, p.p.* **snogged**) to kiss and cuddle. *n.* (*coll.*) the act or an instance of this.

snood, *n.* a fillet or ribbon formerly worn round the hair in Scotland by unmarried girls; a crocheted net to contain a woman's back-hair; a gut- or hair-line by which a fish-hook is fastened to the main line. **snooded,** *a.* [OE *snōd,* from *snā-,* to spin, cogn. with SNARE]

snook[1], *n.* the tropical American fish *Centropomus undecimalis,* and various kinds of sea-fish used for food, esp. the S African and Australian pike. [Dut. *snoek,* pike]

snook[2], *n.* a gesture of derision. **to cock a snook,** to put the thumb to the nose and spread the fingers; to defy. [etym. doubtful]

snooker, *n.* a game resembling pool or pyramids played on a billiard-table; a shot or situation in this game in which the cue ball is blocked by another ball making a direct stroke impossible. *v.t.* to put (one's opponent) in this position; to place in difficulty (by presenting an obstacle), to thwart; to defeat. [etym. doubtful]

snoop, *v.i.* to go about in an inquisitive or sneaking manner, to pry. *n.* an act or instance of snooping; a snooper. **snooper,** *n.* a prying busybody. **snoopy,** *a.* [Dut. *snoepen*]

snoot, *n.* (*coll.*) the nose; an expression of disdain, contempt etc.

snooty, *a.* (*coll.*) supercilious, snobbish. **snootily,** *adv.* **snootiness,** *n.* [var. of SNOUT]

snooze, *v.i.* to take a short sleep, esp. in the day. *v.t.* to pass or waste (time) in slumber or indolence. *n.* a short sleep, a nap. **snoozer,** *n.* **snoozy,** *a.* [etym. doubtful, prob. onomat.]

snore, *v.i.* to breathe through the mouth and nostrils with a hoarse noise in sleep. *v.t.* to pass (time) in snoring or sleeping. *n.* the act or sound of snoring. **snorer,** *n.* **snoring,** *n.* [prob. imit.]

snorkel, *n.* a breathing apparatus used in diving and swimming consisting of a tube which extends from the mouth to above the surface of the water; a device on a submarine for taking in and expelling air when at periscope depth. *v.i.* (*past, p.p.* **snorkelled**) to swim with a snorkel. **snorkelling,** *n.* [from G *Schnorkel*]

snort, *v.i.* to force air violently and loudly through the nostrils like a frightened or excited horse (e.g. as an expression of contempt); to make a noise like this; to inhale drugs, esp. habitually. *v.t.* to utter or throw (out) with a snort; (*sl.*) to inhale (a drug). *n.* the act or sound of snorting; (*sl.*) an instance of inhaling a drug, or the amount inhaled in one snort; (*coll.*) a snifter. **snorter,** *n.* one who or an animal that snorts; (*coll.*) anything of extraordinary size, excellence, violence etc. (as a strong wind). **snortingly,** *adv.* [ME *snorten,* prob. imit. (cp. prec., also LG *snurten,* Dut. *snorken,* Swed. *snarka*)]

snot, *n.* mucus from the nose; (*sl.*) a low or contemptible person. **snotter,** *n.* a turkey-cock's wattles; (*Sc.*) snot. *v.i.* to snivel, to weep. **snotty,** *a.* (*coll.*) soiled with nasal mucus; (*sl.*) snobbish, snooty; (*sl.*) contemptible, low. **snotty-nosed,** *a.* **snottily,** *adv.* **snottiness,** *n.* [OE *gesnot* (cp. LG *Snotte,* Dut. and Dan. *snot*), cogn. with SNOUT]

snout, *n.* the projecting nose or muzzle of an animal; (*sl.*) the nose; a nozzle; a projecting front, as of a glacier, a cliff etc.; (*sl.*) cigarette tobacco; (*sl.*) an informant, esp. a police one. **snout beetle,** *n.* the weevil. **snouted,** *a.* (*usu. in comb.*, as *long-snouted*). **snoutish,** *a.* **snoutless,** *a.* **snoutlike,** *a.* **snouty,** *a.* [ME *snute,* cogn. with OE *snȳtan,* to blow the nose (cp. Dut. *snuit,* G *Schnauze,* Swed. *snut*)]

Snow, *n.* **C(harles) P(ercy), Baron Snow** (1905–80), English novelist and physicist. He held government scientific posts in World War II and from 1964–66. His sequence of novels *Strangers and Brothers* (1940–64) portrayed English life from 1920 onwards. His *Two Cultures* (Cambridge Rede lecture of 1959) discussed the absence of communication between literary and scientific intellectuals in the West, and added the phrase 'the two cultures' to the language.

snow, *n.* watery vapour in the atmosphere frozen into crystals and falling to the ground in flakes; (*often pl.*) a fall of this; anything resembling snow, esp. in whiteness; (*sl.*) cocaine; a mass of white dots on a television or radar screen caused by interference. *v.i.* to fall in or as snow. *v.t.* to cover, sprinkle or block (up) with snow; to send or scatter down as snow; (*chiefly N Am. coll.*) to overwhelm or charm with persuasive, glib or deceiving talk. **to snow under,** to overwhelm (with work etc.). **snowball,** *n.* a round mass of snow pressed together in the hands and flung as a missile; a round pudding or confection of various kinds; a drink of advocaat and lemonade. *v.t.* to pelt with snowballs. *v.i.* to throw snowballs; to accumulate with increasing rapidity, to accelerate. **snowball-tree,** *n.* the sterile-flowered variety of guelder-rose. **snowberry,** *n.* the N American shrub, *Symphoricarpus racemosus,* the W Indian *Chiococca racemosa,* and other white-berried ornamental shrubs; the berry of these shrubs. **snow-bird,** *n.* a small finch, bunting or sparrow, esp. the snow-bunting. **snow-blind,** *a.* partially or totally blinded, usu. temporarily, through the glare of reflected light from the surface of snow. **snow-blindness,** *n.* **snow-blink,** *n.* a luminous reflection over the horizon from snow-fields. **snowblower,** *n.* a machine which clears snow from a road by blowing it to the side. **snow-bound,** *a.* imprisoned or kept from travelling by snow. **snow-broth,** *n.* melted or melting snow. **snow-bunting,** *n.* a northern finch, *Plectrophanex nivalis,* visiting Britain in winter. **snowcap,** *n.* the cap of snow on top of a mountain. **snow-capped,** *a.* crowned with snow. **snow-drift,** *n.* a mass of snow accumulated by the wind. **snowdrop,** *n.* a bulbous plant, *Galanthus nivalis,* with a white flower appearing in early spring. **snow-fall,** *n.* a fall of snow; the amount of snow falling in a given place during a given time. **snow-field,** *n.* an expanse of snow, esp. in polar or lofty mountain regions. **snowflake,** *n.* a fleecy cluster of ice crystals falling as snow; a plant of the genus *Leucoium,* a European flower resembling the snowdrop. **snowfinch,** *n.* an Arctic bird resembling the snow-bunting. **snow-goose,** *n.* a white Arctic goose with black wing-tips. **snow-grouse,** *n.* the ptarmigan. **snow gum,** *n.* any of various types of eucalyptus growing in the mountains of SE Australia. **snow-in-summer,** *n.* a plant of S Europe and Asia cultivated as a rockery plant for its white flowers. **snow job,** *n.* (*chiefly N Am. coll.*) an instance of, or attempt to overwhelm with, persuasive, flattering or deceiving talk. **snow-leopard,** *n.* the ounce. **snow-line,** *n.* the lowest limit of perpetual snow on mountains etc. **snowman,** *n.* a large snowball shaped roughly like a human figure. **snowmobile,** *n.* a motor vehicle with runners or caterpillar tracks enabling it to travel over snow. **snow-on-the-mountains,** *n.* the arabis, N American spurge and other plants with white flowers or leaves. **snow-plough,** *n.* an implement used to clear a road or railway track of snow; a skiing position in which the tips of the skis meet to form a V shape. *v.i.* to ski in this position in order to slow or stop. **snow-shoe,** *n.* a long, light, racket- or ski-shaped frame worn to prevent sinking when walking on snow. **snow-slip,** *n.* an avalanche. **snow-storm,** *n.* a heavy fall of snow, esp. accompanied by wind. **snow tyre,** *n.* a heavy tyre with deep treads for use on snow. **snow-white,** *a.* as white or pure as snow. **snowless,** *a.* **snow-like,** *a.*, *adv.* **snowy,** *a.* white like snow; abounding with snow; covered with snow; spotless, unblemished. **snowy owl,** *n.* a white, black-barred northern owl, *Nyctea scandiaca*. **snowily,** *adv.* **snowiness,** *n.* [OE *snāw,* Dut. *sneeuw,* G *Schnee,* Dan. *snee,* Icel. *snaeo,* also L *nix nivis,* Gr. *nipha*]

Snowden, *n.* **Philip, 1st Viscount Snowden** (1864–1937), British right-wing Labour politician, chancellor of the Exchequer in 1924 and from 1929–31. He entered the coalition National Government in 1931 as Lord Privy Seal, but resigned in 1932.

Snowdon, *n.* **Anthony Armstrong-Jones, Earl of Snowdon** (1930–), English portrait photographer, who married Princess Margaret in 1960, and was divorced in 1978.

Snow White, *n.* traditional European fairy tale. Snow White is a princess persecuted by her jealous stepmother. Taking refuge in a remote cottage inhabited by seven dwarfs, she is tricked by the disguised queen into eating a poisoned apple. She is woken from apparent death by a prince.

SNP, (*abbr.*) Scottish National Party.

Snr, snr, (*abbr.*) senior.

snub, *v.t.* (*past, p.p.* **snubbed**) to check, to rebuke with sarcasm or contempt, to slight in a pointed or offensive manner; to stop (a cable, ship etc.) suddenly, esp. by tying a rope round a post; †to stunt, to nip. *n.* an act of snubbing, a check, a rebuff, a slight; a snub-nose. *a.* short, stubby. **snub-nose,** *n.* **snub-nosed,** *a.* having a short upturned nose; of a gun, having a short barrel. **snubber,** *n.* **snubbing,** *n.*, *a.* **snubbingly,** *adv.* **snubby,** *a.* [Icel. *snubba,* to chide, cp. Dan.

snubbe, to nip off]

snudge, *v.i.* to lie close and still; to save in a mean way. *n.* a miser; a sneak. [prob. rel. to SNUG]

snuff[1], *v.t.* to draw in through the nostrils, to sniff, to scent. *v.i.* to sniff; to take snuff; †to take offence. *n.* the act of snuffing; a sniff; powdered tobacco inhaled through the nose; a pinch of this; a state of resentment, a huff. **up to snuff,** knowing, sharp, not easily imposed upon; in good condition, up to scratch. **snuff-box,** *n.* a small container for carrying snuff. **snuff-mill,** *n.* a mill for grinding snuff; a snuff-box. **snuffer,** *n.* **snuffing,** *n., a.* **snuffy,** *a.* **snuffiness,** *n.* [prob. from MDut. *snuffen,* to clear the nose, prob. cogn. with MDut. *snuyven* (Dut. *snuiven*)]

snuff[2], *n.* the charred part of the wick in a candle or lamp. *v.t.* to trim (a wick, candle etc.) by removing this; to extinguish (a flame) by or as by snuffing. **to snuff it,** (*sl.*) to die. **snuffers,** *n.pl.* a scissor-like instrument for trimming away snuff from the wick of a candle; a big-handled instrument with a cone-shaped cap at the end for extinguishing candles. [etym. doubtful, cp. prov. *snop,* to crop shoots, cogn. with SNUB]

snuffle, *v.i.* to breathe noisily or make a sniffing noise as when the nose is obstructed; to talk through the nose; to snivel, to whine. *v.t.* to utter through the nose; to sniff. *n.* the act or sound of snuffling; a nasal tone or voice. **the snuffles,** obstruction of the nostrils by mucous nasal catarrh. **snuffler,** *n.* **snuffly,** *a.*

snuffy, snuffiness SNUFF[1].

snug, *a.* lying close, sheltered, and comfortable; cosy, comfortable; compact, trim, well secured; not exposed to view. *v.i.* (*past, p.p.* **snugged**) to lie close, to nestle, to snuggle. *n.* a snuggery. **snuggery,** *n.* a snug place or room, esp. in a pub or bar. **snuggle,** *v.i.* to move or lie close (up to) for warmth. *v.t.* to draw close to one, to cuddle. *n.* the act of snuggling. **snugly,** *adv.* **snugness,** *n.* [cp. LG *snügger,* Dan. *snugg,* neat, tidy, smooth, short-haired]

Snyders, *n.* **Frans** (1579–1657), Flemish painter of hunting scenes and still lifes. Based in Antwerp, he was a pupil of Brueghel the Younger and later assisted Rubens and worked with Jordaens. In 1608–09 he travelled in Italy. He excelled at painting fur, feathers, and animals fighting.

so[1], *adv.* in such a manner or to such an extent, degree etc. (with *as* expressed or understood); in the manner or to the extent, degree, intent, result etc. (with *that* or *but*); on condition or provided (that); also, in addition; indeed, certainly; as, compared; extremely, very; for this reason, therefore, consequently, accordingly; thus, this, that, then, as follows; in such a case, or state. *conj.* in order that; well; therefore; with the result that. *int.* expressing surprise, dawning awareness or dissent etc. *a.* true, corresponding; put in a set order, right. *pron.* the same. **and so forth, and so on** FORTH. **or so,** or thereabouts. **so be it,** let it be thus (in affirmation, resignation etc.). **so help me God** HELP. **so long!** *int.* au revoir, good-bye. **so much,** (of, in or to) a particular amount, degree or extent. **so much as,** however much, to whatever extent. **so much for,** there is nothing more to be said; expressing contempt at a failure. **so much so,** to such a degree, extent (that). **so what?** what about it? **so-and-so,** *n.* an indefinite person or thing (*euphem.*)an unpleasant person or disliked thing. **so-called,** *a.* usually called thus (with implication of doubt). **so-so,** *a.* indifferent, middling, mediocre. *adv.* indifferently. [OE *swā,* cp. Dut. *zoo,* G *so,* Icel. *svā,* Dan. *saa*]

so[2] SOH.

So., (*abbr.*) south, southern.

soak, *v.t.* to suck (in or up), to absorb (liquid); to put in liquid to become permeated, to steep, to wet thoroughly, to drench; to extract or remove by steeping in a liquid; (*sl.*) to overcharge, to make (a person) pay. *v.i.* to lie in liquid so as to become permeated, to steep, to penetrate, to permeate (into, through etc.); to drink excessively, to tipple. *n.* the process of soaking or being soaked; the liquid that something is immersed in or the period for which something is immersed; (*sl.*) a heavy drinker; (*Austral.*) low-lying land where water is retained. **to soak in,** to become fully understood, appreciated, felt etc. **soakaway,** *n.* a hole or depression dug in the ground to allow drainage to percolate into the soil. **soakage,** *n.* **soaker,** *n.* **soaking,** *n., a.* [OE *socian,* cogn. with SUCK]

Soames, *n.* **Christopher, Baron Soames** (1920–87), British Conservative politician. He held ministerial posts (1958–64), was vice president of the Commission of the European Communities (1973–77) and governor of (Southern) Rhodesia in the period of its transition to independence as Zimbabwe, Dec. 1979–Apr. 1980. He was created a life peer in 1978.

Soane, *n.* **John** (1753–1837), English architect, whose individual neo-classical designs anticipated modern taste. His buildings include his own house in Lincoln's Inn Fields, London, now the Soane Museum. Little remains of his extensive work at the Bank of England, London.

soap, *n.* a salt of a fatty acid; esp. an unctuous compound of a fatty acid and a base, usu. of sodium or potassium, used for washing and cleansing; (*sl.*) flattery, glib or persuasive talk; a soap opera. *v.t.* to rub or wash with soap; to flatter. **soft soap,** SOFT. **soapberry,** *n.* (*Bot.*) the fruit of *Sapindus saponaria* and related shrubs and trees which contains saponin. **soapbox,** *n.* a box for packing soap; a box or improvised stand used as a platform by an orator. **soap-bubble,** *n.* a thin inflated film of soapy water. **soap opera,** *n.* a serialized television or radio drama usu. following a regular set of characters through various domestic or sentimental situations (orig. sponsored by soap manufacturers). **soapstone,** *n.* steatite. **soap-suds,** *n.pl.* water impregnated with soap to form a foam. **soapworks,** *n. sing. or pl.* **soapwort,** *n.* a trailing herbaceous plant, *Saponaria officinalis,* the juice of which forms a lather with water. **soapy,** *a.* of the nature of or resembling soap; smeared or combined with soap; unctuous, flattering, smooth. **soapily,** *adv.* **soapiness,** *n.* [OE *sāpe,* cp. Dut. *zeep,* G Seipe, also L *sēbum,* tallow]

soar, *v.i.* to fly aloft, to rise; of a bird, aircraft etc, to sail, float at a great height; to rise or mount intellectually or in spirit, status, position etc.; to increase or rise rapidly in amount, degree etc.; to tower. *n.* a towering flight. **soarer,** *n.* **soaringly,** *adv.* [F *essorer,* prob. from a pop. L *exaurare* (EX-, *aura,* air)]

Soares, *n.* **Mario** (1924–), Portuguese politician. Exiled in 1970, he returned to Portugal in 1974, and as leader of the Portuguese Socialist Party (PSP) was prime minister from 1976–78. He resigned as party leader in 1980, but in 1986 he was elected Portugal's first socialist president.

sob, *v.i.* (*past, p.p.* **sobbed**) to catch the breath in a convulsive manner, as in violent weeping. *v.t.* to utter with a sob or sobs; to bring on (a certain state) by sobbing. *n.* a convulsive catching of the breath, as in weeping. **sob-story,** *n.* a hard-luck story intended to elicit pity. **sobstuff,** *n.* sentimental speech, writing, film etc. intended to arouse tears. **sobbingly,** *adv.* [ME *sobben,* prob. imit., perh. rel. to OE *siofian*]

sober, *a.* not drunk; temperate in the use of alcoholic liquors etc.; moderate, well-balanced, sane; self-possessed, dispassionate; serious, solemn, sedate; of colours etc., subdued, quiet. *v.t.* to make sober. *v.i.* to become calm, quiet or grave. **sober-minded,** *a.* **sobermindedness,** *n.* **sobersided,** *n.* of a sober, serious disposition. **sobersides,** *n.* a person of this disposition. **sobering,** *a.* **soberly,** *adv.* **soberness,** *n.* **sobriety,** [F *sobre,* L *sōbrius* (*sō-,* SE-, *ēbrius,* drunk), see EBRIETY]

Sobers, *n.* **'Gary' (Garfield St Aubrun)** (1936–), West Indian test cricketer. One of the game's great all-rounders, he scored more than 8000 test runs, took over 200 wickets, held more than 100 catches, and holds the record for the highest test innings, 365 not out.

Sobieski, *n.* **John** JOHN III, king of Poland.

soboles, sobole, *n.* a creeping or underground stem, a

sucker. [L]

sobriety SOBER.

sobriquet, soubriquet, *n.* a nickname; an assumed name. [F, perh. from *soubriquet,* a tap under the chin]

soc, soke, *n.* the right of holding a local court; formerly, a district under such jurisdiction. **socage,** *n.* a feudal tenure by any certain and determinate service distinct from military tenure and villainage. †**socager,** *n.* [OE *sōcn,* cogn. with SEEK (cp. Icel. *sōkn,* Norw. *sokn,* Dan. *sogn,* parish, Goth. *sōkns,* enquiry)]

Soc., soc., (*abbr.*) socialist; society.

soca, *n.* music popular in the E Caribbean which blends elements of soul and calypso. [SOUL and CALYPSO]

so-called SO[1].

soccer, *n.* (*coll.*) Association Football.

sociable, *a.* fit or inclined to associate or be friendly, companionable, affable; of a party etc., of a friendly, not stiff or formal, character. *n.* an open carriage with side seats facing each other; (*chiefly N Am.*) a social gathering. **sociability, sociableness,** *n.* **sociably,** *adv.*

social, *a.* of or pertaining to society or its divisions, or to the intercourse, behaviour or mutual relations of humans; living in communities, gregarious, not solitary, tending to associate with others, fitted for existence in an organized, cooperative system of society; of insects, organized or existing in such a community; of plants, growing in clumps; of, relating to, or conducive to shared activities or companionship; pertaining to the social services; of, characteristic of, or appropriate to a specific class (esp. the upper class or fashionable society); sociable, companionable, consisting in friendly converse, convivial. *n.* a social gathering; the social evil, prostitution. **social anthropology,** *n.* a discipline within the social sciences concerned with systems of belief and cultural organization in a society. **social climber,** *n.* one who seeks membership of a higher social class, esp. by ingratiating him- or herself. **social climbing,** *n.* **social contract,** *n.* a collective agreement between members of a society and a government that secures the rights and liberties of each individual. **social democracy,** *n.* the theories and practices of socialists who believe in transforming a capitalist society into a socialist one by democratic means. **social democrat,** *n.* a supporter of social democracy; (**Social Democrat**) a member of the Social Democratic party. **social disease,** *n.* venereal disease. **social insurance,** *n.* insurance against unemployment, sickness or old age provided by the state out of contributions from employers and wage-earners. **social science,** *n.* the study of society and the interaction and behaviour of its members, including e.g. sociology, economics, political science, anthropology and psychology; any one of these disciplines. **social scientist,** *n.* **social security,** *n.* state provision for the unemployed, aged or sick through a system of pensions or benefits. **social services,** *n.pl.* welfare services provided by the state or a local authority. **social work,** *n.* any of various types of welfare service (for the aged, disabled etc.) provided by the social services and carried out by trained employees. **social worker,** *n.* **Socialism,** *n.* the doctrine that the political and economic organization of society should be based on the subordination of the individual to the interests of the community, involving the collective ownership of the sources and instruments of production, democratic control of industries, cooperation instead of individual private gain, state distribution of the products instead of payment by wages, free education etc. **socialist,** *n., a.* **socialistic,** *a.* **socialistically,** *adv.* **socialite,** a member of or an aspirant to fashionable society. **sociality,** *n.* **socialize, -ise,** *v.t.* to prepare, make fit for social life; (*chiefly N Am.*) to constitute or transform according to socialist principles. *v.i.* to behave in a convivial or sociable manner. **socialization, -isation,** *n.* **socially,** *adv.* [L *socius,* companion, rel. to *sequī,* to follow]

Social and Liberal Democrats, official name for the British political party formed in 1988 from the former Liberal Party and most of the Social Democratic Party. Its leader (from July 1988) is Paddy ASHDOWN. The common name for the party is the Democrats, which was agreed at the party conference in Sept. 1988.

Social Democratic Federation, (SDF) in British history, a socialist society, founded as the Democratic Federation in 1881 and renamed in 1884. It was led by H.M. Hyndman (1842–1921), a former conservative journalist and stockbroker who claimed Karl Marx as his inspiration without obtaining recognition from his mentor. In 1911 it became the British Socialist Party.

Social Democratic Labour Party, (SDLP) Northern Irish left-wing political party, formed in 1970. It aims ultimately at Irish unification, but distances itself from the violent tactics of the Irish Republican Army (IRA), adopting a constitutional, conciliatory role. The SDLP, led by John Hume (1937–), was responsible for setting up the NEW IRELAND FORUM in 1983.

Social Democratic Party, (SDP) British political party formed in 1981 by Labour Members of Parliament Roy Jenkins (its first leader), David Owen (leader from 1983), Shirley Williams, and William Rodgers, who resigned from the Labour Party and took a more centrist position. The 1983 and 1987 general elections were fought in alliance with the Liberal Party as the Liberal/SDP Alliance (1983, six seats, 11.6% of the vote; 1987, five seats, 9.8% of the vote). A merger of the two parties was voted for by the SDP 1987, and the new party became the Social and Liberal Democrats. David Owen resigned the leadership during the negotiations concerning the merger and was replaced by Robert Maclennan, but continued to lead a separate SDP with two other MPs. In 1989 the SDP abandoned the attempt to operate as a national party, and planned to contest only certain electoral seats.

socialite, sociality, socialize, socially SOCIABLE.

social realism, *n.* in painting, the branch of realism concerned with poverty and deprivation. The French artist Courbet provides a 19th-century example of the genre. Subsequently, in the US, the Ashcan school and Ben Shahn are among those described as Social Realists.

society, *n.* a social community; the general body of persons, communities or nations constituting mankind regarded as a community; social organization; the privileged and fashionable classes of a community; a body of persons associated for some common object or collective interest, an association; companionship, fellowship; a group of plants of the same species or sharing the same needs, characteristics etc. *a.* of or pertaining to fashionable society. **Society of Friends,** the religious body of Quakers. **Society of Jesus,** the Roman Catholic order of Jesuits. **societal,** *a.* of or pertaining to (human) society. **societally,** *adv.* [F *société,* L *societātem,* nom. *-tas,* from *socius,* see SOCIABLE]

Society Islands, *n.pl.* (French **Archipel de la Société**) an archipelago in French Polynesia, divided into Windward Islands and Leeward Islands; **area** 1685 sq km/650 sq miles. **population** (1983) 142,000. The administrative headquarters is Papeete on Tahiti. The **Windward Islands** (French **Iles du Vent**): **area** of 1200 sq km/460 sq miles. **population** (1983) 123,000). **physical** comprises Tahiti, Moorea (area 132 sq km/51 sq miles. population 7000), Maio (or Tubuai Manu; 9 sq km/3.5 sq miles; population 200), and the smaller Tetiaroa and Mehetia. The **Leeward Islands** (French **Iles sous le Vent**): **area** 404 sq km/156 sq miles. **population** 19,000. **physical** comprises the volcanic islands of Raiatea (including the main town of Uturoa), Huahine, Bora-Bora, Maupiti, Tahaa, and four small atolls. Claimed by France in 1768, the group became a French protectorate in 1843, and a colony in 1880.

Socinianism, *n.* form of 17th-century Christian belief which rejects such traditional doctrines as the Trinity and original sin, named after Socinus, the Latinized name of Lelio Francesco Maria Sozzini (1525–62), Italian Protestant theologian. It is an early form of UNI-

TARIANISM.

socio-, *comb. form.* social; society. [L *socius,* a companion]

sociobiology, *n.* the study of human or animal behaviour from a genetic or evolutionary basis.

sociocultural, *a.* of, pertaining to or involving social and cultural factors. **socioculturally,** *adv.*

socioeconomic, *a.* of, pertaining to or involving social and economic factors. **socioeconomically,** *adv.*

sociolinguistics, *n.sing.* the study of language as it functions in society. **sociolinguist**, *n.*

sociology, *n.* the science of the organization and dynamics of human society. **sociological**, *a.* **sociologically,** *adv.* **sociologist,** *n.* [F *sociologie*]

sociometry, *n.* the study of social relationships within a group. **sociometric**, *a.* **sociometrist,** *n.*

sociopath, *n.* a psychopath. **sociopathic**, *a.* **sociopathy**, *n.*

sociopolitical, *a.* of, pertaining to or involving social and political factors.

sock[1], *n.* a short stocking; a removable inner sole; the light shoe worn by classic comic actors. **put a sock in it,** be quiet, shut up. **to pull up one's socks,** to make a vigorous effort to do better. [OE *socc,* L *soccus,* a shoe worn by comic actors]

sock[2], *v.t.* (*sl.*) to hit with a blow. *n.* a hit, a blow. **to sock it to,** to act, speak etc. with great vigour or force. [etym. doubtful]

socket, *n.* a natural or artificial hollow place or fitting adapted for receiving and holding another part or thing, esp. an implement, electric plug, revolving tool, limb, eye, head of an instrument etc.; an electric power point. *v.t.* to fit into or furnish with a socket. **socket-joint** BALL AND SOCKET JOINT under BALL[1]. **socketed,** *a.* [etym. doubtful; ME and OF *soket,* perh. dim. of *souche,* tree-stump, from Teut.]

sockeye, *n.* a Pacific blueback salmon with red flesh highly esteemed as a food. [by folk etym. from N Am. Ind. *suk-kegh*]

socle, *n.* a plain, low, rectangular block or plinth, forming a base for a statue, column etc. [G, from *zoccolo,* L *socculus,* dim. of *soccus,* SOCK[1]]

Socrates, *n.* (*c.* 469–399 BC), Athenian philosopher. He wrote nothing but was immortalized in the dialogues of his pupil, Plato. In his desire to combat the scepticism of the SOPHISTS, Socrates asserted the possibility of genuine knowledge. In ethics, he put forward the view that the good person never knowingly does wrong. True knowledge emerges through dialogue and systematic questioning, and an abandoning of uncritical claims to knowledge. **Socratic,** †**-ical,** *a.* of, pertaining to or according to Socrates. *n.* an adherent of Socrates or his philosophy. **Socratic irony,** *n.* simulation of ignorance in order to lead on and eventually confute an opponent. **Socratic method,** *n.* the dialectical method of procedure by question and answer introduced by Socrates. **Socratically,** *adv.*

sod[1], *n.* surface soil filled with the roots of grass etc., turf, sward; a piece of this cut away. *v.t.* to cover with sod. [cp. MDut. *sode,* Dut. *zode,* perh. cogn. with SEETHE, cp. foll.]

sod[2], *n.* (*sl.*) a despicable person, esp. male; a fellow, chap. *int.* used like a swear word to express annoyance. **sod all,** nothing at all. **sod off,** go away, get lost. **Sod's law**, *n.* a wry maxim that anything which can possibly go wrong will do so. [short for SODOMITE]

soda, *n.* any of various compounds of sodium, e.g. sodium carbonate, sodium hydroxide, sodium bicarbonate; soda-water; (*N Am.*) a fizzy soft drink. **soda bread, scone,** a type of bread or scone made with baking soda, esp. in Ireland. **soda-fountain,** *n.* a device for dispensing soda-water; (*N Am.*) a counter serving soft drinks, ice creams etc. **soda siphon,** *n.* a pressurized bottle for dispensing soda-water. **soda-water,** *n.* an effervescent drink composed of water charged with carbon dioxide. **sodaic,** *a.* **sodium,** *n.* a silver-white metallic element, the base of soda. **sodium bicarbonate,** *n.* a white powder used in baking powder and antacid preparations, sodium hydrogencarbonate, baking soda. **sodium carbonate,** *n.* a crystalline salt used in the manufacture of cleaning agents, glass etc., washing soda. **sodium chloride,** *n.* common salt. **sodium hydrogenglutamate,** *n.* monosodium glutamate. **sodium hydroxide,** *n.* caustic soda. **sodium lamp** SODIUM(-VAPOUR) LAMP. **sodium nitrate,** *n.* a white crystalline salt occurring naturally as Chile saltpetre, used in fertilizers, explosives etc. **sodium(-vapour) lamp,** *n.* an electric lamp used esp. in street lighting, consisting of a glass tube containing sodium vapour and neon which emits an orange light when current is passed through it. [It., prob. fem. of *sodo, solido,* glasswort, prob. from L as SOLID]

sodality, *n.* a fellowship, a confraternity, esp. a charitable association in the Roman Catholic Church. [F *sodalité,* L *sodālitas,* from *sodālis,* comrade]

sodden, *a.* soaked, saturated; of bread etc., not properly baked, heavy, doughy; bloated and stupid, esp. with drink. *v.t.* to soak, to saturate, esp. with drink. *v.i.* to become sodden. **soddenness,** *n.* [p.p. of SEETHE]

Soddy, *n.* **Frederick** (1877–1956), English physical chemist, pioneer of research into atomic disintegration, who coined the term 'isotope'. Awarded the Nobel Prize for chemistry in 1921.

Söderberg, *n.* **Hjalmar (Eric Fredrik)** (1869–1941), Swedish writer. His work includes the novels *Förvillelser* (1895), *Martin Bircks ungdom* (1901), *Doktor Glass/Dr Glass* (1906), and the play *Gertrud* (1906).

sodium SODA.

Sodom, *n.* in the Old Testament (Gen. xix.24), a corrupt city destroyed by God; hence, a place of utter wickedness or depravity. **sodomite,** *n.* an inhabitant of Sodom; one who practises sodomy. **sodomitic, -ical**, *a.* **sodomy**, *n.* anal intercourse with a man or woman, or sexual relations with an animal (supposedly the characteristic sexual behaviour of the Sodomites).

soever, *adv.* appended, sometimes as a suffix, and sometimes after an interval, to pronouns, adverbs or adjectives to give an indefinite or universal meaning.

sofa, *n.* a long stuffed couch or seat with raised back and ends. **sofa-bed,** *n.* a sofa that can be extended so as to serve as a bed, a bed-settee. [prob. through F, from Arab. *suffah*]

soffit, *n.* the under surface of a cornice, lintel, balcony, arch etc. [F *soffite,* It. *soffitta,* ceiling, fem. of *soffitto,* p.p. (SUB-, L *fīgere,* to FIX)]

Sofia, Sofiya*n.* capital of Bulgaria since 1878; population (1987) 1,129,000. Industries include textiles, rubber, machinery, and electrical equipment. It lies at the foot of the Vitosha Mountains.

soft, *a.* yielding easily to pressure, easily moulded, cut or worked, malleable, pliable, plastic, opp. to *hard;* easily magnetized and demagnetized; of radiation rays, low in energy; affecting the senses in a mild, delicate, or gentle manner; of a day, a breeze etc., balmy, gentle; low-key, non-insistent; of an image, blurred; smooth to the touch, not rough or coarse; not hot or cold, mild, genial; of colours, outlines etc., not brilliant, glaring, or abrupt; not loud or harsh, low-toned; of water, free from mineral salts that prevent lathering, suitable for washing; of a drug, relatively harmless or nonaddictive; gentle or mild in disposition, yielding, conciliatory; impressionable, sympathetic, compassionate; flaccid, out of condition, pampered; easily imposed on, lenient; weak, timorous, effeminate; silly, simple; amorous, sentimental, tender-hearted; (*Phon.*) not guttural or explosive, sibilant (as *c* in *cede* or *g* in *gem*), voiced (as *b, d,* and *g*); easy; of coal, bituminous. *n.* a soft part, object or material. *adv.* softly, gently, quietly. **soft in the head,** feeble-minded, foolish. **to be soft about, on,** to be amorously inclined towards; to be lenient or sympathetic towards. **softball,** *n.* a game resembling baseball played with a larger and softer ball. **soft-core,** *a.* of pornography, relatively inexplicit and mild. **soft-cover,** *n., a.* (a) paperback. **soft currency,** *n.* a currency that is unstable owing to the uncertainty of its gold backing. **soft drinks,** *n.pl.* non-intoxicant beverages. **soft-**

focus, *n.*, *a.* (having, designed to produce) a slightly out-offocus image with blurred edges. **soft-furnishings,** *n.pl.* textile furnishings such as carpets, curtains, chair covers etc. **soft goods,** *n.pl.* textiles. **soft-headed,** *a.* silly, stupid. **soft-headedness,** *n.* **soft-hearted,** *a.* tender-hearted, compassionate. **soft-heartedly,** *adv.* **soft-heartedness,** *n.* **soft-land,** *v.i.*, *v.t.* (to cause a spacecraft) to land gently on the moon, a planet, without incurring damage. **soft landing,** *n.* **soft option,** *n.* an option offering least difficulty. **soft palate,** *n.* the posterior part of the palate terminating in the uvula. **soft-paste,** *n.* porcelain, made from bone ash, clay etc. **soft-pedal,** *n.* a foot pedal for subduing the tone of notes played on the piano. *v.i.*, *v.t.* to play down, avoid the issue of. **soft porn(ography),** *n.* soft-core pornography. **soft sell,** *n.* selling by means of gentle persuasiveness or suggestion. **soft-shoe,** *a.* of or pertaining to a style of tap dancing performed in soft-soled shoes. **soft soap,** *n.* semi-liquid soap made with potash; (*coll.*) flattery, blarney. **soft-soap,** *v.t.* (*coll.*) to flatter for some ulterior object. **soft-spoken,** *a.* speaking softly; mild, affable, conciliatory. **soft spot,** *n.* tenderness, fondness. **soft touch,** *n.* (*sl.*) someone easily influenced or imposed upon. **software,** *n.* computer programs designed to perform various applications, e.g. word-processing. **soft water,** *n.* rain water; water free from mineral salts that prevent lathering. **softwood,** *n.* the wood of a coniferous tree; a conifer yielding this wood. **soften,** *v.t.* to make soft or softer; to palliate, to mitigate, tone down. *v.i.* to become soft or softer. **to soften up,** to make more sympathetic to; to break down the resistance of. **softener,** *n.* **softening,** *n.* **softening of the brain,** a softening of cerebral tissue resulting in mental deterioration; (*coll.*) stupidity, excessive credibility. **softly,** *adv.* **softness,** *n.* **softy, softie,** *n.* a silly, weak-minded person; one who is physically unfit or flaccid; a tender-hearted person. [OE *sōfte,* adv. (*sēfte,* a.), cp. G *sanft,* Dut. *zacht,* also Gr. *hēmeros,* mild, Sansk. *sāmen,* mildness]

softa, *n.* a student of Muslim theology and sacred law. [Turk., from Pers. *sūhtah,* lighted]

soften, softly, softy etc. SOFT.

SOGAT, (*acronym*) *So*ciety of *G*raphical and *A*llied *T*rades.

soggy, *a.* soaked, sodden, thoroughly wet; heavy with moisture; (*coll.*) dull, heavy, spiritless. **soggily,** *adv.* **sogginess,** *n.* [etym. doubtful]

soh, so, sol, *n.* the fifth tone of the diatonic scale; the syllable denoting it. [L *sol-ve,* see GAMUT]

soi-disant, *a.* self-styled, pretended, so-called. [F, *soi,* L *se,* self, *disant,* pres.p. of *dire,* L *dīcere,* to say]

soigné, (*fem.*) **soignée,** *a.* well-turned-out, elegant, exquisite in taste. [F]

soil[1], *n.* the ground, esp. the top stratum of the earth's crust whence plants derive their mineral food; land, country; that which nourishes or promotes development. **soil science,** *n.* the scientific study of soils. **soilless,** *a.* **soily,** *a.* [A-F, prob. from L *solium,* seat, or late L *solea,* sole, ground, conf. with *solum,* ground]

soil[2], *v.t.* to make dirty; to sully, to tarnish, to pollute. *v.i.* to become sullied or dirty, to tarnish. *n.* a dirty spot, stain, taint or defilement; any foul matter, filth, refuse, dung, compost. **soil-pipe,** *n.* a pipe carrying waste material and water from a toilet. **soiled,** *a.* [A-F *soyler,* OF *soillier, suillier* (F *souiller*), prob. from *soil,* a boar's soil, L *suillus,* pertaining to swine, from *sus,* pig (cp. SULLY)]

soil[3], *v.t.* to feed (cattle etc.) with green food, in order to fatten, orig. to purge. [perh. from prec., or from OF *soeler* (F *soûler*), to satiate, ult. from L *satullus*, dim. of *satur,* full]

Soil Association, *n.* pioneer British ecological organization founded in 1945, which campaigns against pesticides and promotes organic farming.

soirée, *n.* an evening party or gathering for conversation and social intercourse etc., usu. with music. [F, orig. evening, from L *sērus,* late]

soixante-neuf, *n.* sixty-nine, a sexual position or activity in which a couple engage in oral stimulation of each other's genitals at the same time. [F]

sojourn, *v.i.* to stay or reside (in, among etc.) temporarily. *n.* a temporary stay or residence. **sojourner,** *n.* [OF *sojourner* (F *séjourner*), (SUB-, L *diurnāre,* to stay, from *diurnus,* DIURNAL]

soke SOC.

soko, *n.* an anthropoid ape described by Livingstone as living west of Lake Tanganyika. [African name]

Sol, (*abbr.*) Solomon.

sol[1], (*abbr.*) soluble; solution.

sol[2], *n.* a colloidal solution. [short for SOLUTION]

sol[3], *n.* the sun; (*Her.*) or, gold. [L]

sol[4], SOH.

sola, *n.* the hat-plant or sponge-wood or its pith. **sola topee** TOPEE. [Hind. *solā,* Hindi *sholā*]

solace, *n.* comfort in grief, trouble etc., consolation, compensation; *v.t.* to comfort or console, in trouble etc.; to alleviate, to allay. **solacement,** *n.* **solacer,** *n.* [OF *solaz,* L *sōlācium,* cogn. with *sōlārī,* to console]

solan, solan goose, *n.* the gannet, *Sula bassana.* [Icel. *sūla,* perh. *ond,* goose]

solano, *n.* a hot, oppressive SE wind in Spain. [Sp., from L *Solānus,* from SOL[4]]

solanum, *n.* a large genus of plants, containing the potato, egg-plant, nightshade etc. **solanaceous,** *a.* **solanine,** *n.* a poisonous alkaloid found in several species of *Solanum.* [late L]

solar, *a.* pertaining to, proceeding from, measured by or powered by the sun. *n.* an upper room, attic, garret or loft; a platform or raised floor in a mine. **solar battery,** *n.* a battery powered by solar cells. **solar cell,** *n.* a cell that converts solar energy into electricity. **solar energy,** *n.* energy derived from the sun. **solar panel,** *n.* a panel of solar cells functioning as a power source. **solar plexus,** *n.* the epigastric plexus, a network of nerves behind the stomach. **solar power,** *n.* solar energy. **solar system,** *n.* the sun and the various heavenly bodies revolving about it. **solar wind,** *n.* streams of protons and electrons emitted by the sun. **solarium,** *n.* (*pl.* **-ria, riums**) a room or building constructed for the enjoyment of, or therapeutical exposure of the body to, the rays of the sun. **solarize, -ise,** *v.t.* to expose (photographic material) to sunlight, esp. for too long; to affect in this way. *v.i.* to be spoiled by over-exposure. **solarization, -isation,** *n.* [L *sōlāris,* from SOL[4]]

solatium, *n.* (*pl.* **-tia**) compensation for suffering or loss. [L, SOLACE]

sold, *past, p.p.* SELL[1].

solder, *n.* a fusible alloy for uniting the edges etc. of less fusible metals; anything that cements or unites. *v.t.* to unite or mend with or as with or as with solder. *v.i.* to become united or mended (as) with solder. **solderer,** *n.* **soldering,** *n.*, *a.* **soldering-iron,** *n.* a tool used hot for melting and applying solder. [ME *soudur, soudre,* OF *soudure,* from *souder,* L *solidāre,* to make firm, as foll.]

soldier, *n.* a person engaged in military service, esp. a private or non-commissioned officer; a person of military skill or experience; one who works diligently for a cause; an upright brick set in a wall; a soldier-ant, -beetle, or -crab. *v.i.* to serve as a soldier; to persevere. **soldier of fortune,** a military adventurer, a mercenary; one who lives on his or her wits. **to soldier on,** to persevere doggedly in the face of difficulty. **soldier-ant,** *n.* one of the asexual fighting ants of a community of termites. **soldier-beetle,** *n.* a reddish beetle that preys on the larvae of other insects. **soldier-crab,** *n.* a species of hermit crab. **soldier-like, -ly,** *a.*, *adv.* **soldiering,** *n.* **soldiership,** *n.* **soldiery,** *n.* soldiers collectively; a body of soldiers; the profession of soldiers, soldiership. [OF, from late L *soldārius* (SOLD[2], -ARY]

sole[1], *n.* the flat under side or bottom of the foot; the part of a boot or shoe under the foot, esp. the part in front of the heel; the bottom or lower part (of a plane, a plough, the head of a golf-club, various engines etc.). *v.t.* to furnish (a boot etc.) with a sole. **sole-plate,** *n.*

the bed-plate of a machine, an iron etc. [OE, from L *solea,* from *solum,* the ground]

sole[2], *n.* a flat-fish of various species highly esteemed as food. [L *solea,* see prec.]

sole[3], *a.* single, only, unique, alone in its kind; in law, unmarried; solitary, alone. **solely,** *adv.* **soleness,** *n.* [A-F, from OF *sol,* L *sōlum,* nom. *-lus*]

solecism, *n.* a deviation from correct idiom or grammar; any incongruity, error or absurdity; a breach of good manners, an impropriety. **solecist,** *n.* **solecistic, -ical,** *a.* **solecistically,** *adv.* †**solecize, -ise,** *v.i.* [L *solaecismus,* Gr. *soloikismos,* from *soloikos,* speaking incorrectly (*Soloi,* in Cilicia, Asia Minor, where the Attic colonists spoke bad Greek, *-oikos,* dwelling)]

solely SOLE[3].

solemn, *a.* performed with or accompanied by rites, ceremonies or due formality; awe-inspiring, impressive; grave, serious, momentous; formal, affectedly grave, self-important, pompous; dull, sombre. **solemnify,** *v.t.* to make solemn. **solemnification,** *n.* **solemnity,** *n.* solemnness, impressiveness; affected gravity or formality; (*often pl.*) a rite or ceremony, esp. one performed with religious reverence. **solemnize, -ise,** *v.t.* to dignify or to celebrate with solemn formalities or ceremonies; to make solemn. **solemnization, -isation,** *n.* **solemnizer, -iser,** *n.* **solemnly,** *adv.* **solemnness, solemness,** *n.* [ME and OF *solempne,* L *sōlemnis, sollennis,* prob. from *sollus,* whole, entire, cp. Gr. *holos*]

solenoid, *n.* a magnet consisting of a cylindrical coil traversed by an electric current. **solenoidal,** *a.* [F *solenoïde,* from Gr. *sōlēnoeides,* pipe-shaped, from *solēn,* pipe (prec., -OID]

soleus, *n.* a muscle of the calf of the leg beneath the gastrocnemius, helping to extend the foot. [from L *solea,* SOLE[1]]

sol-fa, *v.i.* to sing the notes of the musical scale up or down to the syllables *do* (or *ut*), *re, mi, fa, sol, la, si* (or *ti*). *v.t.* to sing (a musical composition) thus. *n.* solmization; tonic sol-fa. **solfège, solfeggio,** *n.* (*pl.* **-ges, -ggi, -ggios**) a singing exercise in solmization; solmization, sol-fa. [SOL[5], FA]

solfatara, *n.* a volcanic vent emitting sulphurous gases. [It., from *solfo,* sulphur]

Solferino, Battle of, Napoleon III's victory over the Austrians in 1859, at a village near Verona, N Italy, 8 km/5 miles S of Lake Garda.

solicit, *v.t.* to make earnest or importunate request for; to make earnest or persistent requests or appeals to; to entice or incite (someone) to do something illegal or immoral; of a prostitute, openly to offer sexual relations in exchange for money. *v.i.* to make earnest or importunate appeals; of a prostitute, to proposition someone as a potential client. **solicitant,** *n., a.* **solicitation,** *n.* **solicitor,** *n.* a legal practitioner authorized to advise clients and prepare causes for barristers but not to appear as advocate in the higher courts; †one who solicits. **Solicitor General,** *n.* a law officer of the British Crown ranking next to the Attorney General, appointed by the government in power to advise and represent it in legal matters. **solicitorship,** *n.* **solicitous,** *a.* anxious, concerned, apprehensive, disturbed (about, for etc.); eager (to). **solicitously,** *adv.* **solicitousness, solicitude,** *n.* [OF *soliciter,* L *sollicitāre,* from *sollicitus,* from *sollus,* whole, *citus,* aroused]

solid, *a.* composed of particles closely cohering, dense, compact; not hollow, devoid of cavities, interstices or crevices, not porous; uniform, uninterrupted; firm, unyielding, stable, rigid; sound, substantial, not flimsy; real, genuine, reliable, well-grounded; the same throughout, homogeneous; thinking, feeling or acting unanimously; (*Geom.*) of three dimensions, cubic; having no leads between the lines of printing type; of a compound word, printed or written without a hyphen. *adv.* in a solid manner; unanimously. *n.* a rigid, compact body; a body or magnitude possessing length, breadth, and thickness. **solid fuel,** *n.* fuel composed of solid matter (e.g. coal) rather than gas or liquid; solid propellant. **solid geometry,** *n.* geometry dealing with three dimensional figures. **solid propellant,** *n.* solid fuel for rockets. **solid state,** *n., a.* **solid-state physics,** *n.* a branch of physics dealing with the properties and nature of solid matter. **solidify,** *v.t., v.i.* to make or become solid. **solidifiable,** *a.* **solidification,** *n.* **solidifier,** *n.* **solidity, solidness,** *n.* **solidly,** *adv.* [OF *solide,* L *solidum,* nom. *-dus,* cogn. with Gr. *bolos,* Sansk. *sarva(s),* whole]

Solidarity, *n.* (Polish **Solidarność**) the national confederation of independent trade unions in Poland, formed under the leadership of Lech WALESA in Sept. 1980. An illegal organization from 1981 to 1989, it now heads the Polish government. Solidarity emerged from a summer of industrial disputes caused by the Polish government's attempts to raise food prices. The strikers created a trade-union movement independent of the Communist Party, and protracted negotiations with the government led to recognition of Solidarity in exchange for an acceptance of the leading role of the Communist Party in Poland. Continuing unrest and divisions in Solidarity's leadership led to the declaration of martial law in Dec. 1981; the union was banned and its leaders were arrested. Wałesa was released in Dec. 1982, and Solidarity continued to function as an underground organization. It was re-legalized in Apr. 1989 following a further wave of strikes under its direction and round-table talks with the governmemt. In the elections of June 1989 it won almost every seat open to it, and formed the senior partner in a 'grand coalition' government formed in Sept. 1989 with Tadeusz Mazowiecki as prime minister. Solidarity's achievements inspired the successful 'people power' movements in other E European countries during 1989, as well as the formation of more independent labour unions in the USSR until Apr. 1989.

solidarity, *n.* cohesion, mutual dependence; community of interests, feelings, responsibilities etc. **solidary,,** *a.* united in nature, interests, responsibility etc.

solidungulate, *a.* solid-hoofed, not cloven.

solidus, *n.* (*pl.* **-di**), the stroke (/) formerly denoting a shilling (as in 2/6); also used in writing fractions (e.g. 1/4), separating numbers (e.g. in dates) or alternative words (as in him/her) etc.; a Roman gold coin introduced by Constantine. [late L, see SOLID]

solifluction, -fluxion, *n.* a slow downwards slip of water-logged soil which usu. occurs in areas of permanent frost (e.g. tundra regions). [from L *solum,* soil, *fluctio,* an act of flowing]

soliloquy, *n.* a talking to oneself; a speech or discourse, esp. in a play, uttered to oneself, a monologue. **soliloquist,** *n.* **soliloquize, -ise,** *v.i.* **soliloquizer, -iser,** *n.* [L *sōliloquium* (as prec., *loquī,* to speak)]

solipsism, *n.* the theory that the only knowledge possible is that of oneself, absolute egoism. **solipsist,** *n., a.* **solipsistic,** *a.* [L *soli-, solus,* SOLE[3], *ipse,* self, -ISM]

solitaire, *n.* a gem, esp. a diamond, set singly, in a ring etc.; a game played by one person on a board with hollows and marbles, holes and pegs etc.; a card game for one player, patience; an American rock-thrush and other birds; an extinct bird, *Pezophaps solitarius,* allied to the dodo; †a hermit, a recluse. [F, as foll.]

solitary, *a.* living or being alone, lonely, not gregarious; of plants, growing singly; passed or spent alone; unfrequented, sequestered, secluded; single, individual, sole. *n.* one who lives in solitude a recluse. **solitary confinement,** *n.* in a prison, incarceration without the company of others, isolation. **solitarily,** *adv.* **solitariness,** *n.* **solitude,,** *n.* loneliness, solitariness, seclusion. **solitudinous,** *a.* [A-F *solitaire* (F *solitaire*), L *sōlitārius* (*sōlitas,* loneliness, from *sōlus,* SOLE[3])]

sollar, SOLAR.

solmization, -isation, *n.* the association of certain syllables with the notes of the musical scale, a recital of the notes of the gamut, sol-faing. [F, from *solmiser* (SOL[5], MI, -IZE)]

solo, *n.* (*pl.* **solos, soli**) a composition or passage played by a single instrument or sung by a single voice, usu. with an accompaniment; solo whist, a call in this game; a solo flight. *a.*, *adv.* unaccompanied, alone. *v.i.* to fly an aircraft unaccompanied. **solo flight,** *n.* a flight in an aircraft by a single person; an unaccompanied pilot. **solo whist,** *n.* a card game for four persons somewhat resembling whist. **soloist,** *n.* [It., as SOLE[3]]

Solomon[1], *n.* (*c.* 974–*c.* 937 BC), in the Old Testament or Hebrew Bible, king of Israel, son of David by Bathsheba. He was famed for his wisdom, the much later biblical Proverbs, Ecclesiastes, and Song of Songs being attributed to him. He built the temple in Jerusalem with the aid of heavy taxation and forced labour. The so-called King Solomon's Mines at Aqaba, Jordan (copper and iron), are of a later date.

Solomon[2], *n.* a very wise man (after King *Solomon* of Israel). **Solomon's seal,** *n.* a plant, *Polygonatum multiflorum,* with drooping white flowers and a rootstalk marked with scars which are said to account for the name; the Star of David. **Solomonic,** *a.*

Solomon Islands, *n.pl.* country in the W Pacific, E of New Guinea, comprising many hundreds of islands. **area** 27,600 sq km/10,656 sq miles. **capital** Honiara on Guadalcanal. **physical** comprises all but the northernmost islands (which belong to Papua New Guinea) of a Melanesian archipelago that stretches nearly 1500 km/900 mi. The largest is Guadalcanal (area 6500 sq km/2510 sq miles); others are Malaita, San Cristobal, New Georgia, Santa Isabel, Choiseul; mainly mountainous and forested. **population** (1989) 314,000 (the majority Melanesian); annual growth rate 3.9%. **exports** palm oil, copra, rice, timber. **language** English (official). **religion** Christian.

Solon, *n.* (*c.* 638–558 BC), Athenian statesman. As one of the chief magistrates about 594 BC, he carried out the revision of the constitution that laid the foundations of Athenian democracy; a sage, esp. a wise lawmaker.

so long, *int.* (*coll.*) good-bye. [possibly corr. of SALAAM]

solstice, *n.* the time (about 21 June and 22 Dec.) and point at which the sun is farthest from the celestial equator (north in summer and south in winter). **solstitial,** *a.* [F, from L *sōlstitium* (SOL[4], *-stitium,* from *statum,* neut. p.p. of *sistere,* to cause to stand)]

Solti, *n.* **Georg** (1912–), Hungarian-born British conductor. He was music director at Covent Garden from 1961–71, and became director of the Chicago Symphony Orchestra in 1969. He was also principal conductor of the London Philharmonic Orchestra from 1979–83.

soluble, *a.* capable of being dissolved in a fluid; capable of being solved. **soluble glass,** *n.* water glass. **solubility,** *n.* the quality or state of being soluble; the number of grams of substance required to saturate 100 grams of solvent. **solubilize, -ise,** *v.t.* **solute,** *n.* a dissolved substance. **solution,** *n.* the liquefaction of a solid or gaseous body by mixture with a liquid; the liquid combination so produced; the condition of being dissolved; the resolution or act or process of solving a problem, difficulty etc.; the correct answer to a problem etc.; separation, dissolution, disintegration. [F, from L *solvere,* to SOLVE]

solus,, *a.* (*fem.* **sola**, alone (used esp. in stage directions). [L, SOLE[3]]

solute, solution SOLUBLE.

Solutrean, *a.* pertaining to the period of Upper Palaeolithic culture between the Aurignacian and Magdalenian periods, including flint and bone instruments and carvings on stone. [Solutre, France]

Solvay process, *n.* industrial process for the manufacture of sodium carbonate.

solve, *v.t.* to resolve or find an answer to (a problem etc.); to clear up, to settle, to put an end to; to dissolve. **solvable,** *a.* **solvability,** *n.* **solvate,** *n.* a combination of a solute with a solvent. *v.i., v.t.* to make or become solvate. **solvation,** *n.* **solvent,** *a.* having the power to dissolve; able to pay all just debts or claims. *n.* a liquid that can dissolve a substance, a menstruum; something which solves. **solvent abuse,** *n.* the use of solvents (such as glue or petrol) as drugs, by inhaling their fumes. **solvency,** *n.* **solver,** *n.* [L *solvere*]

solver SOLVE.

Solyman I SULEIMAN.

Solzhenitsyn, *n.* **Alexander (Isayevich)** (1918–), Soviet novelist, a US citizen from 1974. After military service, he was in prison and exile from 1945–57 for anti-Stalinist comments. Much of his writing is semi-autobiographical and highly critical of the system; for example, *One Day in the Life of Ivan Denisovich* (1962) deals with the labour camps under Stalin, and *The Gulag Archipelago* (1973) is an exposé of the whole Soviet camp network. This led to his expulsion from the USSR in 1974.

Som., (*abbr.*) Somerset.

soma[1], *n.* (*pl.* **-mata**, **-mas**) the axial part of the body, i.e. without the limbs; the body as distinct from the germ cells; the body as distinguished from soul and spirit. [Gr. *soma,* the body, a dead body]

soma[2], *n.* an intoxicating liquor used in connection with ancient Vedic worship; the plant from the juice of which it was made. [Sansk.]

Somali, *n.* (*pl.* **-lis, -li**) a member of a people inhabiting Somalia; the language of this people. *a.* of or pertaining to this people, their language or their country.

Somalia, *n.* Democratic Republic of (*Jamhuriyadda Dimugradiga Somaliya*), country in the Horn of Africa, on the Indian Ocean. **area** 637,700 sq km/246,220 sq miles. **capital** Mogadishu. **towns** Hargeisa, Kismayu, port Berbera. **physical** mainly flat, with hills in the north. **population** (1989) 8,552,000 (including 1 million refugees from W Somalia); annual growth rate 4.1%. **exports** livestock, skins, hides, bananas. **language** Somali (national language), Arabic (also official), Italian, English. **religion** Sunni Muslim.

Somaliland, *n.* region of Somali-speaking peoples in E Africa including the former British Somaliland Protectorate (established in 1887), and Italian Somaliland (made a colony in 1927, conquered by Britain in 1941 and administered by Britain until 1950), which both became independent in 1960 as the Somali Democratic Republic, the official name for Somalia; and former French Somaliland which was established in 1892, became known as the Territory of the Afars and Issas in 1967, and became independent as DJIBOUTI in 1977.

somatic, *a.* pertaining to the body or the body wall, corporeal, physical. *n.pl.* somatology. **somatic cell,** *n.* a non-reproductive cell of the parent body. **somatically,** *adv.*

somato-, *comb. form.* body.

somatogenic, *a.* originating in the body of an organism, opp. to external.

somatology, *n.* the science of organic bodies, esp. human anatomy and physiology; †physics. **somatological,** *a.* **somatologist,** *n.*

somatype, *n.* a physical type (e.g. an endomorph, mesomorph, or ectomorph).

sombre, *a.* dark, gloomy; solemn, melancholy. **sombrely,** *adv.* **sombreness,** *n.* **sombrous,** *a.* [F (perh. EX-, or SUB-, L *umbra,* shade)]

sombrero, *n.* (*pl.* **-ros**) a wide-brimmed hat worn largely in Mexico. [Sp. from *sombra,* shade, as prec.]

some, *a.* an indeterminate quantity, number etc. of; an appreciable if limited amount etc. of; several; a few, a little; a considerable quantity, amount etc. of; a certain, a particular but not definitely known or specified (person or thing); (*chiefly N Am.*) striking, outstanding. *adv.* about, approximately; (*coll.*) to some extent. *pron.* a particular but undetermined part or quantity; certain not definitely known or unspecified ones. **somebody,** *pron.* some person. *n.* a person of consequence. **someday,** *adv.* at some unspecified time in the future. **somehow,** *adv.* in some indeterminate way; in some way or other; by some indeterminate means. **someone,** *pron.* somebody. **someplace,** *adv.* somewhere. **something,** *n.* some indeterminate or unspecified thing; some quantity or portion if not much; a thing of consequence or importance. *adv.* in some degree. **something else,** (*chiefly N Am., sl.*) a person or thing inspiring wonder, awe, disbelief etc. **something like** LIKE[1]. **sometime,** *adv.* once, formerly, at one time; at some unspecified time. *a.* former, late. **sometimes,** *adv.* at some times, now and then. **someway,** *adv.* in some unspecified way. **somewhat,** *adv.* to some extent, rather. *n.* a certain amount or degree; something. **somewhere,** *n., adv.* (in, at or to) some unknown or unspecified place; (in) some place or other. **to get somewhere,** to make headway, to progress. [OE *sum* (cp. Icel. *sumr,* Dan. *somme,* pl., OHG *sum*), cogn. with SAME]

-some[1], *suf.* forming adjectives, full of, as in *gladsome, troublesome, winsome;* forming nouns, denoting a group with a specified number of members, as in *threesome, foursome.* [OE *-sum* (cp. Dut. *-zaam,* G *-sam,* Icel. *-samr*), as prec.]

-some[2], *comb. form.* a body, as in *chromosome.* [Gr. *soma,* body]

somebody, -how etc. SOME.

somersault, summersault, *n.* a leap in which one turns heels over head and lands on one's feet. *v.i.* to execute a somersault. [OF *sombresaut,* Prov. *sobresaut* (L *suprā,* above, *saltum,* nom. *-tus,* a leap)]

Somerset, *n.* **Edward Seymour, 1st Duke of Somerset** (*c.* 1506–1552), English politician. Created Earl of Hertford, after Henry VIII's marriage to his sister Jane. He became Duke of Somerset and Protector (regent) for Edward VI in 1547. His attempt to check enclosure (the transfer of land from common to private ownership) offended landowners and his moderation in religion upset the Protestants, and he was beheaded on a fake treason charge in 1552.

Somerset House, *n.* government office in the Strand, London, built in 1775. It is used by the Inland Revenue, Principal Probate Registry, where wills are kept, and by the University of London. Somerset House is also the new home of the Courtauld Galleries.

Somerville, *n.* **Mary** (born Fairfax) (1780–1872), Scottish scientific writer, who produced several widely used textbooks, despite having just one year of formal education. Somerville College, Oxford, is named after her. Her main works were *Mechanism of the Heavens* (1831) (a translation of Laplace's treatise on celestial mechanics), *On the Connexion of Physical Sciences* (1834), *Physical Geography* (1848) and *On Molecular and Microscopic Science* (1869).

something, -time, -what etc. SOME.

somite, *n.* a segment of the body in an animal, esp. of an articulated or vertebrate animal. **somitic,** *a.* [Gr. *sōma,* body, -ITE]

Somme, Battle of the, Allied offensive in World War I from July–Nov. 1916 at Beaumont-Hamel-Chaulnes, on the river Somme in N France, during which severe losses were suffered by both sides. It was the first battle in which tanks were used. The German offensive around St Quentin Mar.–Apr. 1918 is sometimes called the Second Battle of the Somme.

Sommeiler, *n.* **Germain** (1815–71), French engineer who built the Mont Cenis Tunnel, 12 km/7 miles long, between Switzerland and France. The tunnel was drilled with his invention the pneumatic drill.

sommelier, *n.* a wine-waiter. [F from OF from OProvençal *saumalier,* pack-animal driver, from L *sagma,* a packsaddle, from Gr.]

Sommerfeld, *n.* **Arnold** (1868–1951), German physicist, who showed that the difficulties with the Bohr model of the atom, in which electrons move around a central nucleus in circular orbits, could be overcome by supposing that electrons adopted elliptical orbits.

somnambulance, *n.* sleep-walking. **somnambulant,** *n., a.* **somnambulate,** *v.i.* to sleep-walk. **somnambulation,** *n.* **somnambulator,** *n.* **somnambulism,** *n.* the act or condition of walking or performing other actions in sleep or a condition resembling sleep. **somnambulist,** *n.* **somnambulistic**, *a.* [L *somnus,* sleep, *ambulāre,* to walk]

somniferous, *a.* causing or inducing sleep. **somniferously,** *adv.* **somnific,** *a.* [L *somnifer* (*somni-, somnus,* see prec., -FEROUS)]

somniloquism, †**-quence, somniloquy**, *n.* the act or habit of talking in one's sleep. **somniloquist,** *n.* [L *loquī,* to talk]

somnolent, *a.* sleepy, drowsy; inducing sleep; (*Path.*) a morbid dreamy condition. **somnolence, -ency,** *n.* **somnolently,** *adv.* [earlier and OF *sompnolent,* L *somnolentus* (*somno-, somnus,* sleep, suf. *-lentus*)]

Somoza Debayle, *n.* **Anastasio** (1925–80), Nicaraguan soldier and politician, president from 1967–72 and from 1974–79. The second son of Anastasio Somoza García, he succeeded his brother Luis Somoza Debayle (1922–1967; president 1956–63) as president of Nicaragua in 1967, to head an even more oppressive regime. He was removed by Sandinista guerrillas in 1979, and assassinated in Paraguay in 1980.

Somoza García, *n.* **Anastasio** (1896–1956), Nicaraguan soldier and politician, president from 1937–47 and 1950–56. A protégé of the US, who wanted a reliable ally to protect their interests in Central America, he was virtual dictator of Nicaragua from 1937 until his assassination in 1956. He exiled most of his political opponents and amassed a considerable fortune in land and businesses. Members of his family retained control of the country until 1979, when they were overthrown by popular forces.

son, *n.* a male child in relation to a parent or parents; a male descendant; a form of address used by an old person to a youth, a priest or teacher to a disciple etc.; a native of a country; an inheritor, exponent or product of (a quality, art, occupation etc.). **son of a bitch,** a despicable or unpleasant man. **the Son (of Man),** the second person in the Trinity, Christ, the Messiah. **son-in-law,** *n.* (*pl.* **sons-in-law**) the husband of a daughter. **sonless,** *a.* **sonny,** *n.* a familiar, often patronizing or derogatory term of address to a boy or man. **sonship,** *n.* the state of being a son. [OE *sunu,* cp. Dut. *zoon,* G *Sohn,* Icel. *sunr, sonr,* OHG *sunu*]

sonant, *a.* capable of being sounded continuously, intonated, voiced, not surd (as the vowels and the consonants *b, d, g, j, m, n, v, th, z*); syllabic. *n.* a voiced letter or sound; a syllabic consonant. **sonance,** *n.* [L *sonans -ntem,* pres.p. of *sonāre,* to SOUND[2]]

sonar, *n.* a device which detects the presence and position of underwater objects by means of echo-soundings. [*so*und *na*vigation *r*anging]

sonata, *n.* an instrumental composition, esp. for the piano, usu. of three or four movements in different rhythms. **sonata form,** *n.* a musical form typically consisting of an exposition, a development and a recapitulation which is usu. included in the first movement of a sonata, symphony etc. **sonatina,** *n.* a short or simple sonata. [It., from L *sonāta,* fem. p.p. of *sonāre,* to SOUND[2]]

sondage, *n.* (*pl.* **-dages**) in archaeology, a trial excavation or inspection trench. [F, a sounding]

sonde, *n.* a scientific device for gathering information about atmospheric conditions at high altitudes. [F, sounding line]

Sondheim, *n.* **Stephen (Joshua)** (1930–), US composer and lyricist. He wrote the witty and sophisticated lyrics of Leonard Bernstein's *West Side Story* (1957) and composed musicals, including *A Little Night Music* (1973), *Pacific Overtures* (1976), *Sweeney Todd* (1979), *Into the Woods* (1987), and *Sunday in the Park with George* (1989).

son et lumière, *n.* an outdoor entertainment at a historic location which recreates past events associated with it using sound effects, a spoken narration, music, and special lighting. [F, sound and light]

song, *n.* musical or modulated utterance with the voice, singing; a melodious utterance, as the musical cry of a bird; a musical composition accompanied by words for singing; an instrumental piece of a similar character; a short poem intended or suitable for singing, esp. one set to music; poetry, verse; a trifle, a small sum; a fuss, a commotion. **going for a song,** selling for a trifle. **song and dance,** a fuss. **Song of Songs** or **of Solomon,** an Old Testament book attributed to Solomon, containing love songs. **song-bird, -sparrow, -thrush,** *n.* a bird that sings. **song cycle,** *n.* a sequence of songs concerned with the same subject or theme. **songwri-**

ter, *n.* one who composes (esp. popular) songs. **songwriting,** *n.* **songless,** *a.* **songster,** *n.* one skilled in singing; a song-bird. **songstress,** *n. fem.* [OE *sang, song,* cp. Dut. *zang,* G and Dan. *sang,* Icel. *söngr,* rel. to SING[1]]

Songhai Empire, *n.* a former kingdom of NW Africa, founded in the 8th century, which developed into a powerful Muslim empire under the rule of Sonni Ali (reigned 1464–92). It superseded Mali and extended its territory, occupying an area that includes present-day Senegal, Gambia, Mali, and parts of Mauretania, Niger, and Nigeria. In 1591 it was invaded and overthrown by Morocco.

sonic, *a.* of, pertaining to or producing sound-waves; travelling at about the speed of sound. **sonic barrier,** *n.* the sound barrier. **sonic boom,** *n.* the loud noise caused by a shock-wave produced by an aircraft or projectile travelling at supersonic speed. **sonically,** *adv.*

sonnet, *n.* a poem of 14 iambic pentameter lines, usu. consisting of an octave rhyming *a b b a a b b a,* and a sestet with three rhymes variously arranged. **sonneteer,** *n.* a writer of sonnets. *v.i.* to compose sonnets. [F, from It. *sonetto,* dim. of *sono,* L *sonus,* SOUND[2]]

sonny SON.

sonobuoy, *n.* a buoy fitted with instruments for detecting underwater sounds and communicating them by radio to surface vessels etc. [L *sonus,* sound; BUOY]

sonorous, *a.* giving out sound, resonant; loud sounding, sounding rich or full; high sounding, impressive. **sonorant,** *n.* a frictionless continuant or nasal (*l, r, m, n, ng*) which has a consonantal or vocalic function depending on its position within a syllable; either of the consonants represented by *w* or *y* which have consonantal or vocalic articulations. **sonority, sonorousness,** *n.* **sonorously,** *adv.* [L *sonōrus,* from *sonor sonōris,* sound, from *sonāre,* to SOUND[2]]

Sons of Liberty, in American colonial history, the name adopted by those colonists opposing the STAMP ACT of 1765. Merchants, lawyers, farmers, artisans and labourers joined what was an early instance of concerted resistance to British rule, causing the repeal of the Act in Mar. 1766.

sonsy, sonsie, *a.* (*chiefly Sc., Ir.*) lucky; happy or jolly-looking, buxom, well-favoured, plump; good-natured, tractable. [*sonse,* Gael. *sonas,* good fortune, -Y]

sook, *n.* (*dial.*) a baby; (*Sc.*) one who tries to ingratiate him- or herself with obsequious behaviour; (*derog.*) a timid person, a coward.

sool, *v.t.* (*Austral., New Zealand coll.*) to incite to attack (esp. a dog); to attack. **sooler,** *n.*

soon, *adv.* in a short time from now or after a specified time, early; quickly, readily, willingly. **as soon as, so soon as,** at the moment that; immediately after; not later than. **no sooner . . . than,** immediately. **sooner or later,** sometime or other; inevitably, eventually. [OE *sōna,* cp. OS and OHG *sān,* Goth. *suns*]

Soong Ching-ling, *n.* (1892–1981), Chinese politician, wife of the Guomindang founder SUN YAT-SEN; she remained a prominent figure in Chinese politics after his death, being vice chairman of the republic from 1959, but came under attack in 1967 during the Cultural Revolution. After the death of Zhu De (1886–1976), she served as acting head of state.

soot, *n.* a black substance composed of carbonaceous particles rising from fuel in a state of combustion and deposited in a chimney etc. *v.t.* to cover, manure or soil with soot. **sootless,** *a.* **sooty,** *a.* **sootily,** *adv.* **sootiness,** *n.* [OE *sōt,* cp. Icel. *sōt,* Dan. *sod,* Swed. *sot*]

sooth, *n.* truth, reality, †cajolery, blandishment. †*a.* true; truthful. **soothsay,** *v.i.* to prognosticate, to divine. **soothsayer,** *n.* a prognosticator, a diviner. [OE *sōth,* for *santh* (cp. Icel. *sannr,* Swed. *sann*), from root *es-,* to be]

soothe, *v.t.* to calm, to tranquillize; to soften, to mitigate, to assuage; to humour, to flatter, to gratify. **soother,** *n.* **soothingly,** *adv.* [OE *gesōthian,* to confirm, to assent to, as prec.]

sop, *n.* anything steeped or dipped and softened in milk, broth, gravy etc., and intended to be eaten; something given to pacify (in alln. to the legendary sop to Cerberus, the watch-dog of Hades). *v.t.* (*past, p.p.* **sopped**) to dip or steep in broth etc.; to take (*usu.* up) by absorption. *v.i.* to be thoroughly wet or soaked. **sop-, sops-in-wine,** *n.* a pink, esp. the clove-pink. **sopping,** *a.* **soppy,** *a.* wet through; maudlin, sentimental, weak-minded. **soppily,** *adv.* **soppiness,** *n.* [OE *sopp* (cp. Icel. *soppa*), cogn. with SUP]

Sophia, *n.* **Electress of Hanover** (1630–1714), twelfth child of Frederick V, elector palatine of the Rhine and king of Bohemia, and Elizabeth, daughter of James I of England. She married the Elector of Hanover in 1658. Widowed in 1698, she was recognized in the succession to the English throne in 1701, and when Queen Anne died without issue in 1714, her son George I founded the Hanoverian dynasty.

sophism, *n.* a specious but fallacious argument. **sophist,** *n.* one of a class of men in ancient Athens who taught philosophy, dialectic, rhetoric etc., for pay; a fallacious reasoner, a quibbler. **sophistic, -ical,** *a.* **sophistically,** *adv.* **sophisticate,** *v.t.* to envelop or obscure with sophistry; to mislead or delude thus; to alter or garble (a text etc.) in order to support one's arguments etc.; to make spurious by admixture, to adulterate; to deprive of simplicity, to make perverted, affected or artificial; to make more complicated or refined. *v.i.* to be sophistical. *n.*, a sophisticated person. **sophisticated,** *a.* worldly-wise, superficially; self-assured; complex, highly developed; subtle; refined; cultured; adulterated. **sophistication,** *n.* **sophisticator,** *n.* **sophistry,** *n.* a specious but fallacious argument; the art of reasoning using such argument(s); this kind of reasoning. [OF *sophisme,* L and Gr. *sophisma,* from *sophizein,* to instruct, from *sophos,* wise]

Sophocles, *n.* (495–406 BC), Greek dramatist who, with Aeschylus and Euripides, is one of the three great tragedians. He modified the form of tragedy by introducing a third actor and developing stage scenery. He wrote some 120 plays, of which seven tragedies survive. These are *Antigone* (441), *Oedipus Tyrannus, Electra, Ajax, Trachiniae, Philoctetes* (409), and *Oedipus at Colonus* (401). **Sophoclean,** *a.* pertaining to or characteristic of Sophocles. [L *Sophoclēus,* Gr. *Sophokleios* (*Sophocles,* -AN]

sophomore, *n.* (*chiefly N Am.*) a second-year student. **sophomoric, -ical,** *a.* **sophomotically,** *adv.* [from prec., -ER, or Gr. *soph-os,* wise, *mōros,* foolish]

Sophy, Sophi, *n.* (*pl.* **-phies**) (*formerly*) the title of a Persian sovereign, the shah. [from L *sophī,* wise man, from Gr. *sophos,* wise]

-sophy, *comb. form.* denoting (a branch of) knowledge.

soporific, *a.* causing or tending to cause sleep; drowsy, sleepy. *n.* a soporific medicine or agent. **soporiferous,** *a.* [L *sopor, sopōris,* sleep, -FIC]

soprano, *n.* (*pl.* **-nos, -ni**) a female or boy's voice of the highest kind; a singer having such a voice; a musical part for such voices; an instrument which has the highest range within a family of instruments. *a.* of or having a treble part, voice or pitch. **sopranino,** *n., a.* (*pl.* **-nos**) (an instrument) possessing the highest pitch in a family of instruments. **sopranist,** *n.* [It., from late L *superānus,* SOVEREIGN]

Sopwith, *n.* **Thomas Octave Murdoch** (1888–1989), English designer of the Sopwith Camel biplane, used in World War I, and joint developer of the Hawker Hurricane fighter plane used in World War II.

sora, *n.* the Carolina rail, a bird inhabiting the N American marshes and esteemed as food. [prob. from N Am. Ind.]

Sorb, *n.* one of a Slavonic people, a Wend; the language of this race, Wendish. **Sorbian,** *n., a.* [G *Sorbe,* var. of *Serbe,* SERB]

sorb, *n.* the service-tree (also **sorb-apple**); its fruit. **sorbate,** *n.* a salt of sorbic acid. **sorbic,** *a.* contained in or derived from mountain-ash or rowan berries. **sorbic acid,** *n.* **sorbitol,** *n.* a white crystalline substance obtained from sugar and often used as a sugar substitute or in the manufacture of synthetic resins. [F *sorbe*, L *sorbus*]

sorbefacient, *a.* promoting absorption. *n.* a substance or preparation promoting absorption. [L *sorbē-re*, to ABSORB, -FACIENT]

sorbet, *n.* an ice flavoured with fruit juice, spirit etc.; sherbet. [F, as SHERBET]

sorbic, sorbitol SORB.

Sorbonne, *n.* common name for the University of Paris, originally a theological institute founded in 1253 by Robert de Sorbon, chaplain to Louis IX.

sorcerer, *n.* one who uses magic, witchcraft or enchantments, a wizard. **sorceress,** *n.* **sorcerous,** *a.* **sorcery,** *n.* [ME (sorser, OF *sorcier*, late L *sortiārius*, from *sortiāre*, to cast lots, from L *sors sortis,* lot]

sordavalite, *n.* a vitreous silicate of alumina and magnesia found in diabase. [Swed. *sordawalit*, *Sordavala*, Finland]

sordid, *a.* mean, base, ignoble, vile; avaricious, niggardly; †foul, squalid. †**sordes**, *n.* foul matter, filth, esp. foul discharges, excretions, encrustations etc. **sordidly,** *adv.* **sordidness,** *n.* **sordor**, *n.* [F *sordide*, L *sordidus*, from *sordes*, dirt, filth]

sordine, -dino, *n.* (*pl.* **-dini**) a contrivance for deadening the sound of a musical instrument, a mute, a damper. **con** or **senza sordini, -dino,** to be played with or without mute. [It. *sordino*, L *surdus*, deaf, see SURD]

sore, *a.* tender and painful to the touch, esp. through disease or irritation; mentally distressed, aggrieved, vexed; easily annoyed; touchy; causing annoyance, irritating, exasperating; (*coll.*) annoyed. *adv.* sorely, grievously, severely, intensely. *n.* a sore place on the body where the surface is bruised, broken or inflamed by a boil, ulcer etc.; that which excites resentment, remorse, grief etc. **to stand out like a sore thumb,** to be highly conspicuous. **sore point,** *n.* a subject etc. which arouses irritation, annoyance, hurt feelings etc. **sorely,** *adv.* **soreness,** *n.* [OE *sār*, (cp. Dut. *zeer*, Icel. *sārr*), G *sehr*, sorely, very]

Sorel, *n.* **Georges** (1847–1922), French philosopher, who believed that socialism could only come about through a general strike; his theory of the need for a 'myth' to sway the body of the people was used by fascists.

sorel(l) SORREL[2].

Sørensen, *n.* **Søren** (1868–1939), Danish chemist, who in 1909 introduced the concept of using a pH scale as a measure of the acidity of a solution. On Sørensen's scale, still used today, a pH of 7 is neutral; higher numbers represent alkalinity, and lower numbers acidity.

sorghum, *n.* any member of a genus of plants containing the Indian millet, durra etc., much cultivated in the US for fodder etc. [mod. L, from F *sorgho*, etym. doubtful]

sorites, *n.* a series of syllogisms so connected that the predicate of one forms the subject of that which follows, the subject of the first being ultimately united with the predicate of the last; a sophistical argument in this form. **soritic, -ical**, *a.* [L, from Gr. *sōratēs*, from *sōros*. heap]

soroptimist, *n.* a member of an international organization of women's clubs, Soroptimist International. [L *soror*, sister, and OPTIMIST]

sororal, *a.* pertaining to or characteristic of a sister or sisters. **sororial,** *a.* **sororicide**, *n.* the murder of a sister; the murderer of a sister. **sorority**, *n.* a body or association of women, a sisterhood; (*N Am.*) a society of women students. **sorority house,** *n.* (*N Am.*) the residence of members of an academic sorority, usu. on the campus of a college or university. [F (L *soror*, sister, -AL)]

sorosis, *n.* a fleshy fruit formed by the cohesion of numerous flowers etc., as the pineapple. [mod. L (Gr. *sōros*, heap, -OSIS)]

sorrel[1], *n.* a herb with acid leaves, *Rumex acetosa*, allied to the dock, wood sorrel. [OF *sorel* (F *surelle*), from MHG *sūr*, SUR]

sorrel[2], *a.* of a reddish or yellowish-brown. *n.* this colour; a horse or other animal of this colour. [OF *sorel*, dim. of *sor*, sorrel horse]

sorrily, sorriness SORRY.

sorrow, *n.* mental pain or distress from loss, disappointment etc., grief, sadness; an event, thing or person causing this, an affliction, a misfortune; mourning, lamentation. *v.i.* to grieve; to lament. **sorrower,** *n.* **sorrowful,** *a.* **sorrowfully,** *adv.* **sorrowfulness,** *n.* **sorrowing,** *n., a.* [ME *sorwe*, OE *sorg* (cp. Dut. *zorg*, G. *sorge*, Icel., Dan. and Swed. *sorg*)]

sorry, *a.* feeling or showing grief or pity for some loss etc., regretful; poor, paltry, pitiful, despicable; apologetic. *int.* expressing apology. **sorrily,** *adv.* **sorriness,** *n.* [OE *sārig* (*sār,* SORE, -Y)]

sort, *n.* a number (of things etc.) having the same or similar qualities, a class, kind, type or species; an example or instance of a kind; an example or instance of something or someone sharing inadequate or remote characteristics with a kind; (*coll.*) a person, a type (of person); fashion, way, manner; a letter or other pieces of type considered as part of a fount. *v.t.* to separate into sorts, classes etc.; to select from a number; to arrange; to resolve, to deal with; to punish; to fix, to put in working order. †*v.i.* to agree or accord (with). **a good sort,** an attractive, companionable person; a decent type. **of a sort, of sorts,** of an inferior or inadequate kind. **out of sorts,** irritable, moody; slightly unwell. **sort of,** rather, to a degree, as it were. **to sort out,** to solve or resolve; to clear out; tidy up; to separate; to arrange; (*coll.*) to beat, to punish. **sortable,** *a.* **sorter,** *n.* one who or that which sorts (e.g. postal material). **sortment,** *n.* [OF *sorte*, L *sortem*, nom. *sors*, lot, chance, condition]

sortie, *n.* a sally, esp. of troops from a besieged place in order to attack or raid; a mission or attack by a single aircraft *v.i.* to sally; to make a sortie. [F, fem. p.p. of *sortir*, to go out]

sortilege, *n.* divination by drawing lots. [OF (F *sortilège*), med. L *sortilegium*, from L *sortilegus*, diviner (*sors sortis*, lot, *legere*, to choose)]

sorus, *n.* (*pl.* **sori**) a heap, group or cluster, esp. of spore-cases on the fronds of ferns. [Gr. *sōros,* heap]

S O S, *n.* an internationally recognized distress call in Morse code; any distress call or plea for help (e.g. an emergency broadcast on television or radio). *v.i.* to call for help or rescue. [Morse letters]

Sosnowiec, *n.* chief city of the Darowa coal region in the Upper Silesian province of Katowice, S Poland; population(1985) 255,000.

so-so SO.

sostenuto, *adv., a.* in a steadily sustained manner. [It., p.p. of *sostenere*, to SUSTAIN]

sot, *n.* an habitual drunkard, one habitually muddled (as if) with excessive drinking. **sottish,** *a.* [ME, prob. from OF (F *sot sotte*)]

soterial, *a.* relating to salvation. **soteriological**, *a.* **soteriology**, *n.* the doctrine of salvation. [Gr. *sōtēria*, salvation, from *sōtēr*, saviour, cogn. with *sōzein*, to save]

sotnia, *n.* a Cossack squadron. [Rus. *sotniya*, hundred, cogn. with L *centum*]

sotto voce, *adv.* in an undertone, under one's breath. [It.]

sou, *n.* a French copper coin, formerly worth 1/12 of a livre; the 5-centime piece; a very small amount of money. [F, from OF *sol*, L *solidum*, cp. SOLD[2]]

soubise, soubise sauce, *n.* a white sauce made from onions, butter, Béchamel sauce and consommé. [Prince de *Soubise*, a French Marshal, 1715–87]

soubrette, *n.* a lady's maid; an intriguing, mischievous coquettish female character in a comedy, esp. the role of a lady's maid; one who displays similar characteristics, a flirt, a coquette. [F, from Prov. *soubreto*, fem. of *soubret*, affected, from *soubra*, to put on one side]

soubriquet SOBRIQUET.

souchong, *n.* a black tea made from the youngest leaves. [F, from Chinese (Canton) *siu-chung* (*siu*, small, *chung*, sort)]

souffle, *n.* a low whispering or murmur heard in the auscultation of an organ etc. [F, from *souffler*, L *sufflare* (SUF-, *flāre*, to blow)]

soufflé, *n.* a light dish made of beaten whites of eggs etc. *a.* made light and frothy. **souffléed,** *a.* [F, p.p. of *souffler*, see prec.]

sough[1] *v.i.* to make a murmuring, sighing sound, as the wind. *n.* such a sound. [OE *swōgan*, prob. imit. in orig., cp. Goth. *ufswōgjan*]

sough[2], *n.* a drain, a sewer, a water-channel, esp. in a mine. [etym. doubtful]

sought, *past, p.p.* SEEK.

souk, *n.* an outside, often covered market in a Muslim country (esp. in N Africa and the Middle East). [Arab. *sūq*, market]

soul, *n.* the spiritual part of a person; a spiritual being; the moral and emotional part of a person; the rational part of a person, consciousness; the vital principle and mental powers possessed by humans in common with lower animals; the essential or animating or inspiring force or principle, the life, the energy in anything; one who inspires, a leader, a moving spirit; the heart; spirit, courage, nobility; a disembodied spirit; a human being, a person; an epitome, embodiment or exemplification; soul music. *a.* of or pertaining to soul music; of, relating to or characteristic of Black Americans or their culture, food etc. **my soul!** good gracious! goodness me! **the life and soul,** the liveliest or most entertaining person at a party, in company etc. **soul brother, sister,** *n.* a fellow Black person. **soul-destroying,** *a.* unrewarding, frustrating, boring. **soul food,** *n.* (*coll.*) the traditional foods of American Blacks in the south (e.g. yams, chitterlings). **soul mate,** *n.* one with whom a person feels a close affinity. **soul music,** *n.* a popular type of Black music combining elements of blues, gospel, jazz and pop. **soul-searching,** *n.* a critical and close examination of one's motives, actions etc. **souled,** *a.* (*usu. in comb.*, as *high-souled*). **soulful,** *a.* rich in, satisfying or expressing the spiritual, emotional or higher intellectual qualities. **soulfully,** *adv.* **soulfulness,** *n.* **soulless,** *a.* **soullessly,** *adv.* **soullessness,** *n.* [OE *sāwel*, *sāwl*, cp. Dut. *ziel*, G *seele*, Dan. *sjæl*, Swed. *själ*]

sound[1], *a.* whole, unimpaired, free from injury, defect or decay; (of sleep) deep, unbroken; not diseased or impaired, healthy; well-grounded, wise, well established; orthodox; trustworthy, honest; solid, stable, firm; based on truth or reason, valid, correct; solvent; thorough, complete. *adv.* soundly, fast (asleep). **soundly,** *adv.* **soundness,** *n.* [OE *sund*, cp. Dut. *gezond*, G *gesund*, Dan. and Swed. *sund*]

sound[2], *n.* the sensation produced through the organs of hearing; that which causes this sensation, the vibrations affecting the ear, esp. those of a regular and continuous nature as opp. to noise; a specific tone or note; an articulate utterance corresponding to a particular vowel or consonant; hearing distance, ear-shot; (*usu. pl.*) (*sl.*) music, esp. popular music. *a.* of or pertaining to radio as opposed to television. *v.i.* to make or give out sound; to convey a particular impression by or as by sound; to summons, to call; to resonate. *v.t.* to cause to sound, to utter audibly; to give a signal for by sound; to cause to resound, to make known, to proclaim; to test by sound. **to sound off,** to boast; to speak loudly, volubly, angrily etc. **sound barrier,** *n.* the shock wave produced when a moving body attains the speed of sound. **sound-bell,** *n.* the thick curved edge against which the tongue strikes in a bell. **sound-bite,** *n.* a succinct quote or clip from a radio or television programme. **sound board,** *n.* a board for enhancing the sounds made by various musical instruments; a sounding board. **sound-box,** *n.* a hollow cavity in the belly of some musical instruments. **sound effect,** *n.* (*often pl.*) an imitation or reproduction of a sound used in the performance of a play or on the soundtrack of a film or broadcast. **sound-film,** *n.* a combination of the projection of a film and the synchronized sounds proper to it. **sound-hole,** *n.* an opening in the belly of some stringed musical instrument, such as the guitar. **sound-post,** *n.* an upright supporting the belly of a violin etc., and transmitting sound-vibrations to the back. **sound-proof,** *a.* impenetrable to sound. *v.t.* to make impenetrable to sound, to insulate against sound. **sound-track,** *n.* the portion along the side of a film which bears the continuous recording of the accompanying sound; the synchronized sound-recording accompanying a film etc. **soundwave, sounder,** *n.* that which causes or emits a sound. **sounding,** *a.* making or giving out sound; sonorous, resonant, noisy; plausible, pompous, highflown. **sounding board,** *n.* a canopy-like structure of wood or metal placed over a pulpit etc. to reflect sound towards the audience; a sound board; *n.* a person, institution, group etc., used to test reaction to a new idea or plan. **soundless,** *a.* without a sound, silent. [ME *soun*, F *son*, L *sonus*, whence *sonāre*, F *sonner*, to sound]

sound[3], *n.* a narrow passage of water, as a strait connecting two seas; the swimming-bladder of a fish. [OE *sund*]

sound[4], *v.t.* to measure the depth of (a sea, channel, water in a ship's hold etc.) with a sounding-line or rod; to test or examine by means of a probe etc. *v.i.* to take soundings, to ascertain the depth of water; to dive deeply (as a whale etc.). *n.* an instrument for exploring cavities of the body, a probe; **to sound out,** to test, to examine, to endeavour to discover (intentions, feelings etc.); **sounder,** *n.* a device for taking soundings. **sounding,** *n.* the act of measuring the depth of water; (*pl.*) a part of the sea where the bottom can be reached by sounding; (*usu. pl.*) a measurement of depth taken thus; a test, an examination, a probe. **sounding-lead,** *n.* the weight on the end of a sounding-line. **sounding line,** *n.* a weighted wire or line for measuring the depth of water. **sounding rod,** *n.* a graduated iron rod, used to ascertain the depth of water in a ship's hold. [F *sonder*, prob. from Scand. *sund*]

sounding SOUND[2, 4].

soup, *n.* a liquid food made from meat, fish or vegetables and stock. (*coll.*) anything resembling soup in consistency etc. (e.g. a thick fog); (*coll.*) a photographic developer; (*sl.*) nitroglycerin. **in the soup,** (*sl.*) in difficulties, in trouble. **to soup-up,** to modify (the engine of a car or motorcycle) in order to increase its power. **soup-kitchen,** *n.* a public establishment for supplying soup to the poor; a mobile army kitchen. **soup-maigre,** *n.* thin soup, made without meat. **soup-plate, -spoon,** *n.* a deep plate or spoon for holding or drinking soup. **soupy,** *a.* [F *soupe*, from *souper*, to SUP]

soupçon, *n.* a mere trace, taste or flavour (of). [F, as SUSPICION]

Souphanouvong, *n.* **Prince** (1912–), Laotian politician, president from 1975–86. After an abortive revolt against French rule in 1945, he led the guerrilla organization Pathet Lao, and in 1975 became first president of the Republic of Laos. He resigned after suffering a stroke.

sour, *a.* sharp or acid to the taste, tart; tasting thus through fermentation, rancid; harsh of temper, crabbed, morose, peevish; disagreeable, jarring, inharmonious; of soil, excessively acidic or infertile; of petroleum gas etc., containing sulphur compounds. *v.t.* to make sour. *v.i.* to become sour. *n.* (*chiefly N Am.*) a cocktail usu. made with a spirit and lemon juice, sugar and ice; a solution of acid used for bleaching, curing hides etc; something sour (to the taste etc.). **sour cream,** *n.* fresh cream soured by the introduction of bacteria, used in salads, cooking etc. **sourdough,** *a.* of bread, made with fermenting yeast. **sour-dock,** *n.* the common sorrel. **sour grapes,** GRAPE. **sourpuss,** *n.* (*coll.*) a habitually morose person. **soured,** *n.*, *a.* **souring,** *n.* the process of becoming or turning sour; a process of bleaching with acid etc.; (*dial.*) a crab-apple. **sourish,** *a.* **sourly,** *adv.* **sourness,** *n.* [OE *sūr*, cp. Dut. *zuur*, G *sauer*, Icel. *sūrr*]

source, *n.* the spring or fountain-head from which a stream of water proceeds, a first cause, a generating force etc.; an origin, a beginning; one who or that which gives out, initiates or creates something; a person or thing that provides inspiration or information. **source-book,** *n.* a book containing original documents for study. **source program,** *n.* an original computer program which has been converted into machine language. [OF *sorse*, p.p. of *sordre* (F *sourdre*), L *surgere*, to rise, see SURGE]

sourdine, SORDINE.

sourock, *n.* (*Sc.*) sorrel. [SOUR, -OCK]

Sousa, *n.* **John Philip** (1854–1932), US bandmaster and composer of marches, such as 'The Stars and Stripes Forever!' (1897).

sousaphone, *n.* a brass wind-instrument resembling the tuba. **sousaphonist,** *n.* [after J.P. *Sousa*]

soutache, *n.* a narrow, ornamental braid. [F, from Hung. *szuszak*, a curl, a lock]

soutane, *n.* a cassock. [F, from It. *sottana*, L *subtus*, under]

souter, *n.* (*chiefly Sc.*) a cobbler. [OE *sūtere*, L *sūtor*, from *suere*, see SEW[1]]

south, *n.* that one of the four cardinal points of the compass directly opposite to the north; the South; a wind from the south; at cards, the player or position facing north. *a.* situated in the south; facing in the southern direction; of the wind, coming from the south. *adv.* towards the south; of the wind, from the south. **the South,** a southern part or region, esp. the area of England south of the Wash or the American states south of the Mason–Dixon Line; the less developed countries of the world, the Third World. **the South Sea(s),** the Pacific Ocean; the seas south of the equator. **southbound,** *a.* going or leading south. **Southdown,** *a.* of or pertaining to the South Downs, Sussex; *n.* a breed of hornless sheep originating here. **south-east,** *n.* the point of the compass equally distant from the south and the east; *a.* pertaining to or coming from the SE. *adv.* towards the SE. **the South-east,** the southeastern area of Britain including London. **south-easter,** *n.* a SE wind. **south-easterly,** *a., adv., n.* **south-eastern,** *a.* **southeasternmost,** *a.* **southeastwards,** *a.* in the direction of, or coming from, the SE. *n.* a south-easterly direction or southeastern area. *adv.* towards the SE. **southeastwardly,** *a., adv.* **south-eastwards,** *adv.* **southpaw,** *n., a.* (of or pertaining to) a left-hand person, esp. a left-handed boxer. **South Pole,** *n.* the most southerly point on the earth's axis or the celestial sphere; **(south-pole)** the south-seeking pole on a magnet. **south south-east, south-west,** *n.* a compass point midway between south and south-east, south and south-west. **south-west,** *n., a.* **the South-west,** the south-western part of Britain. **southwester,** *n.* a wind from the SW. **sou'wester,** *n.* a waterproof hat with a wide brim hanging down behind, worn by sailors etc. **southwesterly,** *a., adv., n.* **south-western,** *a.* **southwesternmost,** *a.* **south-westward,** *a., adv., n.* **south-westwards,** *adv.* **souther,** *n.* a south wind. **southerly**, *a., adv.* tending towards the south. *n.* a south wind. **southerliness,** *n.* **southern**, *a.* of or pertaining to or situated in or towards the south; coming from the south. *n.* a southerner. **Southern Cross** CROSS[1]. **southern lights,** *n.pl.* aurora australis. **southern-wood,** *n.* a shrubby species of wormwood, *Artemisia abrotanum*. **Southerner,** *n.* an inhabitant or native of the South, esp. of Southern England or the Southern States of the US. **southernmost,** *a.* **southing,** *n.* the act of going south or passing the meridian; the transit of the moon or a star across the meridian; difference of latitude towards the south. **southmost,** *a.* **southward** *adv., a., n.* **southwardly,** *adv.* **southwards,** *adv.* [OE *sūth* (cp. Dut. *zuid*, G *sud*, Icel. *suther*, *sunnr*, OHG *sund*), perh. rel. to SUN]

South Africa, *n.* Republic of (Afrikaans *Republiek van Suid-Afrika*), country on the S tip of Africa, bounded to the N by Namibia, Botswana and Zimbabwe, and to the NE by Swaziland and Mozambique. **area** 1,223,181 sq km/472,148 sq miles. **capital** Cape Town (legislative), Pretoria (administrative). **cities** Johannesburg, Bloemfontein; ports Cape Town, Durban, Port Elizabeth, East London. **physical** a plateau. **population** (1989) 35,625,000 (68% black, of whom the largest nations are the Zulu, Xhosa, Sotho, and Tswana, 18% white, 10% of mixed ancestry, and 3% Asiatic); annual growth rate 2.5%. **exports** maize, sugar, fruit; wool; gold, platinum (world's largest producer), diamonds. **language** Afrikaans and English (both official); various Bantu languages. **religion** Christian; largest denomination is the Nederduits Gereformeerde Kerk/Dutch Reformed Church. Congregations are segregated. **South African,** *a.* of or pertaining to the Republic of South Africa, its inhabitants or any of their languages. *n.* a native, citizen or inhabitant of South Africa.

South African Wars, two wars between the Boers (settlers of Dutch origin) and the British; essentially fought for the gold and diamonds of the Transvaal. The War of 1881 was triggered by the attempt of the Boers of the Transvaal to reassert the independence surrendered 1877 in return for British aid against African peoples. The British were defeated at Majuba, and the Transvaal again became independent. The War of 1899–1902, also known as the Boer War, was preceded by the armed Jameson Raid into the Boer Transvaal; a failed attempt, inspired by the Cape Colony prime minister Rhodes, to precipitate a revolt against Kruger, the Transvaal president. The *uitlanders* (non-Boer immigrants) were still not given the vote by the Boers, negotiations failed, and the Boers invaded British territory, besieging Ladysmith, Mafeking (now Mafikeng), and Kimberley. British Commander Kitchener countered Boer guerrilla warfare by putting the noncombatants who supported them into concentration camps (about 26,000 women and children died of sickness). The war ended with the Peace of Vereeniging when the Boers surrendered.

South America, *n.* fourth largest of the continents, nearly twice as large as Europe. **area** 17,854,000 sq km/6,893,429 sq miles. **largest cities** (over 3.5 million inhabitants) Buenos Aires, São Paulo, Rio de Janeiro, Bogotá, Santiago, Lima, Caracas. **population** (1985) 263,300,000, originally American Indians, who survive chiefly in Bolivia, Peru, and Ecuador, and are increasing in number; in addition there are many mestizo (people of mixed Spanish or Portuguese and Indian ancestry) elsewhere; many people originally from Europe, largely Spanish, Italian, and Portuguese; and many of African descent, originally imported as slaves. **exports** coffee, cocoa, sugar, bananas, oranges, wine, meat and fish products, cotton, wool, handicrafts, minerals incuding oil, silver, iron ore, copper. **language** many American Indian languages, Spanish, Portuguese is the chief language in Brazil. **religion** Roman Catholic; American Indian beliefs.

Southampton[1], *n.* port in Hampshire, England; population (1981) 204,604. Industries include engineering, chemicals, plastics, flour-milling, and tobacco; it is also a passenger and container port.

Southampton[2], *n.* **Henry Wriothesley, 3rd Earl of Southampton** (1573–1624), English courtier, patron of Shakespeare who dedicated *Venus and Adonis* and *The Rape of Lucrece* to him, and may have addressed him in the sonnets.

South Asia Regional Cooperation Committee, (SARCC) organization established in 1983 by India, Pakistan, Bangladesh, Nepál, Sri Lanka, Bhutan and the Maldives to cover agriculture, telecommunications, health, population, sport, art, and culture.

South Australia, *n.* state of the Commonwealth of Australia. **area** 984,000 sq km/379,824 sq miles. **capital** and chief port Adelaide. **towns** Whyalla, Mount Gambier. **population** (1987) 1,388,000, including 13,300 Aborigines. **products** meat and wool (80% of area cattle and sheep grazing), wines and spirits, dried and canned fruit, iron (Middleback Range), coal (Leigh Creek), copper, uranium (Roxby Downs), oil and natural gas in the NE, lead, zinc, iron, opals, household and electrical goods, vehicles.

South Carolina, *n.* state of the SE US; nickname

Palmetto State. **area** 80,600 sq km/31,112 sq miles. **capital** Columbia. **towns** Charleston, Greenville-Spartanburg. **physical** large areas of woodland; subtropical climate in coastal areas. **population** (1988) 3,493,000. **products** tobacco, cotton, fruit, soybeans, meat, textiles, clothing, paper, woodpulp, furniture, bricks, chemicals, machinery.

South Dakota, *n.* state of the US; nickname Coyote or Sunshine State. **area** 199,800 sq km/77,123 sq miles. **capital** Pierre. **towns** Sioux Falls, Rapid City, Aberdeen. **physical** Great Plains; Black Hills (which include granite Mount Rushmore, on whose face giant relief portrait heads of former presidents Washington, Jefferson, Lincoln, and T. Roosevelt are carved); Badlands. **population** (1986) 708,000. **products** cereals, livestock, gold (greatest US producer).

Southeast Asia Treaty Organization, (SEATO) former collective defence system analogous to NATO, established in 1954. Participating countries were Australia, France, New Zealand, Pakistan, the Philippines, Thailand, the UK, and the US, with Vietnam, Cambodia, and Laos as protocol states. It originated in ANZUS. After the Vietnam War, SEATO was phased out by 1977 and its nonmilitary aspects assumed by the Association of Southeast Asian Nations (ASEAN).

Southern Christian Leadership Conference, (SCLC) US civil rights organization founded in 1957 by Martin Luther KING and led by him until his assassination in 1968. It advocated nonviolence and passive resistance, and sponsored the 1963 march on Washington DC that focused national attention on the civil-rights movement.

Southern Cross CRUX.

Southerne, *n.* **Thomas** (1660–1746), English playwright and poet, author of the tragi-comedies *Oroonoko* (1695–96), and *The Fatal Marriage* (1694).

Southey, *n.* **Robert** (1774–1843), English poet and author, friend of Coleridge and Wordsworth. In 1813 he became Poet Laureate, but his verse is little read today. He is better known for his *Life of Nelson* (1813), and his letters.

South Georgia, *n.* island in the S Atlantic, a British crown colony administered with the South Sandwich Islands; area 3757 sq km/1450 sq miles. South Georgia lies 1300 km/800 miles SE of the Falkland Islands, of which it was a dependency until 1985. The British Antarctic Survey has a station on nearby Bird Island.

South Glamorgan, *n.* county in S Wales. **area** 420 sq km/162 sq miles. **towns** administrative headquarters Cardiff; Barry, Penarth. **population** (1987) 400,000. **products** dairy farming, industry (steel, plastics, engineering) in the Cardiff area. **language** 6% Welsh; English.

South Holland, *n.* (Dutch **Zuid-Holland**) low-lying coastal province of the Netherlands; area 2910 sq km/1123 sq miles; population (1988) 3,208,000. The capital is The Hague. Noted for its bulbfields and glasshouses, the province also includes part of the Randstadt conurbation with major ports at Rotterdam and the Hook of Holland. Dairy cattle are reared; there are petroleum refineries at Rotterdam, and distilleries at Schiedam.

South Korea KOREA, SOUTH.

South Sea Bubble, a financial crisis in Britain in 1720. The South Sea Company, founded in 1711, which had a monopoly of trade with South America, offered in 1719 to take over more than half the national debt in return for further concessions. Its £100 shares rapidly rose to £1000, and an orgy of speculation followed. When the 'bubble' burst, thousands were ruined. The discovery that cabinet ministers had been guilty of corruption led to a political crisis. Horace Walpole became prime minister, protected the royal family and members of the government from scandal, and restored financial confidence.

South West Africa NAMIBIA.

South Yorkshire, *n.* metropolitan county of England, created in 1976, originally administered by an elected council; its powers reverted to district councils from 1986. **area** 1,560 sq km/602 sq miles. **towns** administrative headquarters Barnsley; Sheffield, Doncaster. **population** (1987) 1,296,000. **products** all the main towns are metal-working centres; coal, dairy, sheep, arable farming.

Soutine, *n.* **Chaim** (1894–1943), Lithuanian-born French expressionist artist. He painted landscapes and portraits, including many of painters active in Paris in the 1920s and 1930s. He had a distorted style, using thick application of paint (impasto) and brilliant colours.

souvenir, *n.* a keepsake, a memento. *v.t.* (*Austral.*, *New Zealand sl.*) to pilfer, to steal. [F, orig. to remember, L *subvenīre*, (SUB-, *venīre*, to come)]

sovereign, sovran, *a.* supreme; possessing supreme power, dominion or jurisdiction; royal; efficacious, effectual, as a remedy. *n.* a supreme ruler, a king, an emperor, a monarch; a former English gold coin, worth one pound. †**sovereignly,** *adv.* **sovereignty,** *n.* [ME *soverein*, OF *soverain*, late L *superānus*, (*super*, suf. *-ānus*), assim. to REIGN]

Soviet, *a.* of or pertaining to the USSR, its government or people. *n.* (*pl.*) the government or people of the USSR; (**soviet**) a local council elected by workers and inhabitants of a district in the USSR; a regional council selected by a number of these; the national congress consisting of delegates from regional councils. *a.* of or pertaining to a soviet. **sovietic,** *a.* **sovietism,** *n.* **sovietize, -ise,** *v.t.* to transform (a country etc.) to the Soviet model of economic, social and political activity. **sovietization, -isation,** *n.* [Rus. council]

Soviet Central Asia, (formerly **Turkestan**) an area consisting of the KAZAKH, UZBEK, TADZHIK, TURKMEN, and KIRGHIZ Soviet Socialist Republics of the USSR.

Soviet Union UNION OF SOVIET SOCIALIST REPUBLICS.

sow[1], *v.t.* (*past* **sowed,** *p.p.* **sown, sowed**) to scatter (seed) for growth; to scatter seed over (ground etc.); to scatter over, to cover thickly with; to disseminate, to spread; to implant, to initiate. *v.i.* to scatter seed for growth. **to sow the seeds of,** to introduce, initiate or implant (a doubt, a suspicion etc.). **sower,** *n.* **sowing,** *n.* [OE *sāwan* (cp. Dut. *zaaïjen*, G *säen*, Icel. *sā*, also L *serere*)]

sow[2], *n.* a female pig; the main channel for molten iron leading to the pigs; a block of iron solidified in this. **sow-thistle,** *n.* a plant of the genus *Sonchus*, with toothed leaves and milky juice. [OE *sugu*, *sū* (cp. Dut. *zog*, G *sau*, Icel. *sȳr*, Dan. and Swed. *so*, also L *sūs*, Gr. *hus*, *sus*) from root *su-*, to produce, cogn. with SWINE]

sowens, *n.* (*Sc.*) a kind of flummery made from the husks of oats. [Gael. *súghan*, *súbhan*, from *súgh*, *súbh*, sap]

Soweto, *n.* township in South Africa, SW of Johannesburg; population (1983) 915,872. It has experienced civil unrest over the years due to the apartheid regime. [*So*uth *We*st *To*wnship]

sowff, sowth, *v.t.* (*Sc.*) to whistle or hum (a tune etc.) softly. [earlier *solf*, OF *solfier*, from SOL-FA]

sowl, *v.t.* to drag about, to tug, to pull by the ears. [etym. doubtful]

soya bean, *n.* a leguminous herb, *Glycine soja*, orig. cultivated in Japan as a principal ingredient of soy sauce, in more recent years grown as a source of oil or flour. **soy, soya sauce,** *n.* a thin brown sauce with a salty meaty flavour made from fermented soya beans and used extensively in Chinese cookery. [Jap. *si-yan; Chin. shi-yu*]

Soyinka, *n.* **Wole** (1934–), Nigerian author, who was a political prisoner in Nigeria from 1967–69. His works include the play *The Lion and the Jewel* (1963), his prison memoirs *The Man Died* (1972), and *Aké, The Years of Childhood* (1982), an autobiography. He was the first African to receive the Nobel prize for literature, in 1986.

Soyuz, *n.* Soviet spacecraft, capable of carrying up to three cosmonauts. Soyuz consists of three parts: a rear section containing engines; the central crew compartment; and a forward compartment that gives additional room for working and living space. They are used for ferrying crews up to space stations.

sozzled, *a.* (*coll.*) drunk. [onomat.]

Sp., (*abbr.*) Spain; Spaniard; Spanish.

sp., (*abbr.*) special; (*pl.* **spp**) species; specific; spelling.

spa, *n.* a mineral spring; a resort or place where there is such a spring. [town in Belgium]

Spaak, *n.* **Paul-Henri** (1899–1972), Belgian socialist politician. From 1936 to 1966 he held office almost continuously as foreign minister or prime minister. He was an ardent advocate of international peace.

space, *n.* continuous extension in three dimensions or any quantity or portion of this; the universe beyond the earth's atmosphere, outer space; an interval between points etc.; an interval of time; room, an unoccupied seat, an empty place; an interval between signals or characters in Morse code; a thin piece of type-metal used to separate words or lines; an interval made by this; one of the degrees between the lines of the music staff. *v.t.* to set so that there will be spaces between; to put the proper spaces between (words, lines etc.). **the space age,** the era in which space travel and exploration have become possible. **space-age,** *a.* of or pertaining to the space age; modern. **space-bar,** *n.* a bar on a typewriter or computer keyboard for making spaces (between words etc.). **spacecraft,** *n.* a manned or unmanned craft for travelling through outer space. **Space Invaders®**, *n.* a video game in which the object is to shoot down images of alien invaders from outer space. **spaceman, -woman,** (*pl.* **-men**) a space traveller. **space-platform, -station,** *n.* a platform planned in outer space to serve as a landing-stage in space travel and as a base for scientifc investigations. **space probe,** *n.* a spacecraft carrying equipment for collecting scientific measurements of conditions in space. **spaceship,** *n.* a manned spacecraft. **space shuttle,** see separate entry. **space-suit,** *n.* clothing specially adapted for space travel. **space-time (continuum),** *n.* the four-dimensional manifold for continuum which in accordance with Einstein's theory of relativity, is the result of fusing time with three-dimensional space. **spacewalk,** *n.* a trip by an astronaut outside a spacecraft when it is in space. *v.i.* to float or move in space while attached by a line to a spacecraft. **spacer,** *n.* **spacial** SPATIAL. **spacing,** *n.* **spacious,** *a.* having ample room; capacious, roomy, wide, extensive. **spaciously,** *adv.* **spaciousness,** *n.* [OF *espace*, L *spatium*]

Spacek, *n.* **'Sissy' (Mary Elizabeth)** (1949–), US film actress who starred in *Badlands* (1973) and *Carrie* (1976), in which she played a repressed telekinetic teenager. Her other films include *Coal Miner's Daughter* (1979) and *Missing* (1982).

Spacelab, *n.* a small space station built by the European Space Agency, carried in the cargo bay of the Space Shuttle, in which it remains throughout each flight, returning to Earth with the Shuttle. Spacelab consists of a pressurized module in which astronauts can work, and a series of pallets, open to the vacuum of space, on which equipment is mounted.

Space Shuttle, *n.* a reusable US crewed spacecraft, first launched on 12 Apr. 1981. It takes off vertically like a conventional rocket, but glides back to land on a runway. The Space Shuttle orbiter, the part that goes into space, is 37.2 m/122 ft long and weighs 68 tonnes. Two to eight crew members occupy the orbiter's nose section, and missions last up to ten days. In its cargo bay the orbiter can carry up to 29 tonnes of satellites, scientific equipment, Spacelab, or military payloads. In 1986 the Space Shuttle *Challenger* blew up on take-off, killing all seven crew members.

spade¹, *n.* an implement for digging, having a broad blade fitted into a long handle, and worked with both hands and one foot; a tool of similar form employed for various purposes; *v.t.* to dig with a spade; to cut out with a spade. **in spades,** in the extreme. **to call a spade a spade,** to be outspoken, not to mince matters. **spadework,** *n.* tiresome preliminary work. **spadeful,** *n.* (*pl.* **-fuls**) [OE *spædu*, *spadu*]

spade², *n.* a playing-card with a black figure or figures shaped like a heart with a small triangular handle; *pl.* this suit of cards; (*offensive*) a Negro. [Sp. *espada*, sword from L *spatha;* Gr. *spathē*, a broad blade]

spade-guinea *n.* a guinea (minted 1787–99) having a shield like the spade on cards on the reverse.

spadix, *n.* (*pl.* **-dices**), an inflorescence in which the flowers are closely arranged around a fleshy rachis and surrounded by a spathe. **spadiceous,** *a.* [L and Gr., from *spaein*, to draw out, to rend]

spaghetti, *n.* a long, thin variety of pasta. **spaghetti junction,** *n.* a road junction, esp. at a motorway, at which there are many intersecting roads and/or flyovers. **spaghetti western,** *n.* a (type of) cowboy film (pop. in the 1960s) filmed in Italy or Spain often with a violent or melodramatic content. [It., pl. dim. of *spago*, cord]

spahi, -hee, *n.* (*pl.* **-his, hees**) a Turkish irregular horse-soldier; (*formerly*) a native Algerian cavalry-soldier in the French army. [Turk. *sipāhī*, SEPOY]

Spain, *n.* (*España*), country in SW Europe, on the Iberian Peninsual between the Atlantic and the Mediterranean, bounded to the N by France and to the W by Portugal. **area** 499,700 sq km/192,884 sq miles. **capital** Madrid. **towns** Bilbao, Valencia, Zaragoza, Murcia; ports Barcelona, Seville, Málaga. **physical** a central plateau with mountain ranges; lowlands in the south. **population** (1989) 39,784,000; annual growth rate 0.6%. **exports** citrus, grapes, pomegranates, vegetables, wine (especially sherry), olive oil, tinned fruit and fish, iron ore, cork, cars and other vehicles, leather goods, ceramics. **language** Spanish (Castilian, official), but regional languages are recognized within their own boundaries (Basque, Catalan, Galician, Valencian, and Majorcan are the chief examples). **religion** Roman Catholic (there are restrictions on the practice of Protestantism).

spake, *past* SPEAK.

spall, *n.* a chip, splinter or flake. *v.t.* to break up (ore etc.) for sorting. *v.i.* to splinter, to chip. [etym. doubtful, cp. ME *speld*, splinter, Dut. *spald*, pin, MDut. *spalden*, G *spalten*, to split]

Spallanzani, *n.* **Lazzaro** (1729–99), Italian priest and biologist. He disproved the theory that microbes spontaneously generate out of rotten food, by showing that they would not grow in flasks of broth that had been boiled for 30 minutes and then sealed.

spalpeen, *n.* (*chiefly Ir.*) a scamp, a rascal. [Ir. *spailpin*]

Spam®, *n.* a tinned luncheon meat of chopped and spiced ham.

Span., (*abbr.*) Spanish.

span¹, *v.t.* (*past, p.p.* **spanned**) to extend from side to side of (a river etc.); to measure with one's hand expanded; to encompass, to cover. *n.* the space from the end of the thumb to the end of the little finger when extended, esp. as a former measure, 9 in. (23 cm); a brief space of distance or time; an entire stretch of distance or time (e.g. a lifespan, attention span); the space from end to end of a bridge etc.; the horizontal distance between the supports of an arch; a wingspan. **span-long,** *a.* of the length of a span. **span-roof,** *n.* an ordinary roof with two sloping sides. **span-worm,** *n.* the larva of the geometer moth. **spanless,** *a.* measureless. **spanner¹,** *n.* [OE *spannan* (Dut. and G *spannen*, Icel. *spenna*, also Gr. *spaein*, to draw)]

span², *n.* a pair of horses, usu. matched in colour etc., harnessed side by side; a yoke or team of oxen etc. [Dut. and G *spann*]

span³, span-new, *a.* quite new, brand new. [ON **spān**, chip, *nȳr*, new]

span⁴, *past* SPIN.

spanaemia, *n.* a blood condition in which there is a deficiency of red corpuscles. **spanaemic,** *a.* [Gr. *spanos*, *spanios*, scanty, *haima*, blood]

Spandau, *n.* suburb of West Berlin, Germany. The chief war criminals condemned at the Nuremberg Trials in 1946 were imprisoned in the fortress there. The last of them was the Nazi leader Rudolf Hess, and the prison was demolished following his death in 1987.

spandrel, -dril, *n.* the space between the shoulder of an arch and the rectangular moulding etc. enclosing it, or between the shoulders of adjoining arches and the moulding etc. [etym. doubtful]

spangle, *n.* a small disc of glittering metal or other material, used for ornamenting dresses etc.; any small sparkling object. *v.t.* to set or adorn with spangles. *v.i.* to glitter (as) with spangles. **spangled,** *a.* **spangler,** *n.* **spangly,** *a.* [ME *spangel*, dim. of obs. *spang*, OE *spang*, a metal clasp, cp. MDut. and G *Spange*, rel. to Gr. *sphingein*, to bind lightly]

Spaniard, *n.* a native or inhabitant of Spain. [alt. of ME *Spaynyell*, as foll.]

spaniel, *n.* a popular name for a class of dogs, distinguished chiefly by large drooping ears, long silky or curly coat and a gentle disposition; a servile, cringing person. [ME, from OF *espagneul*, Sp. *español*, Spanish, from *España*, L *Hispania*, Spain]

Spanish, *a.* of or pertaining to Spain, its people or their language. *n.* the Spaniards; the official language of Spain and its former colonies. **Spanish America,** *n.* the predominantly Spanish-speaking parts of Central and S America, and the West Indies (former Spanish colonies). **Spanish-American,** *n., a.* **Spanish-bayonet,** *n.* a species of yucca with lanceolate leaves. **Spanish broom,** *n.* a Mediterranean shrub, *Spartium junceum*, with rush-like branches. **Spanish-fly,** *n.* a cantharis; a (supposedly aphrodisiac) preparation made from this. **Spanish fowl,** *n.* a breed of domestic fowl of a glossy black colour. **Spanish-grass,** *n.* esparto grass. **Spanish guitar,** *n.* classical guitar music; the type of guitar this is played on. **Spanish main,** *n.* term often used to describe the Caribbean in the 16th–17th centuries, but more properly the South American mainland between the river Orinoco and Panama. **Spanish omelette,** *n.* an omelette with a filling of tomato, peppers (traditionally pimento), or other chopped vegetables. **Spanish onion,** *n.* a large variety of onion with a mild flavour.

Spanish-American War, war in 1898 by Cuban revolutionaries (with US backing) against Spanish rule. The Treaty of Paris ceded Cuba, the Philippines, Guam, and Puerto Rico to the US.

Spanish Armada, *n.* the fleet sent by Philip II of Spain against England in 1588. Consisting of 130 ships, it sailed from Lisbon, and carried on a running fight up the Channel with the English fleet of 197 small ships under Howard of Effingham and Francis DRAKE. The Armada anchored off Calais, but was forced to put to sea by fireships, and a general action followed off Gravelines. What remained of the Armada escaped round the N of Scotland and W of Ireland, suffering many losses by storm and shipwreck on the way. Only about half the original fleet returned to Spain.

Spanish Civil War CIVIL WAR, SPANISH.

Spanish Guinea EQUATORIAL GUINEA.

Spanish language, *n.* a member of the Romance branch of the Indo-European language family, traditionally known as Castilian and originally spoken only in NE Spain. As the language of the court it has been the standard and literary language of the Spanish state since the 13th century. It is now a world language, spoken in all South and Central American countries, except Brazil, Guyana, Suriname and French Guiana, as well as in the Philippines.

Spanish Sahara WESTERN SAHARA.

Spanish Succession, War of the, a war from 1701–14 between Britain, Austria, the Netherlands, Portugal, and Denmark (the Allies) and France, Spain, and Bavaria. It was caused by Louis XIV's acceptance of the Spanish throne on behalf of his grandson, Philip V of Spain, in defiance of the Partition Treaty of 1700, under which it would have passed to Archduke Charles of Austria (later Holy Roman emperor Charles VI).

spank[1], *v.t.* to strike with the open hand, to slap, esp. on the buttocks; to urge along thus. *n.* a resounding blow with the open hand, a slap, esp. on the buttocks. **spanking,** *n.* a series of such slaps. [prob. onomat.]

spank[2], *v.i.* to move briskly along, esp. at a pace between a trot and a gallop.

spanker *n.* one who spanks; a fat horse; (*coll.*) an exceptionally fine specimen, a stunner; a fore-and-aft sail set by two spars on the after-side of the mizen-mast. **spanking,** *a.* (*coll.*) dashing, brisk, stunning; of a breeze, strong. [back formation from **spanking** (etym. unknown)]

spanner[1] SPAN[1].

spanner[2], *n.* an instrument for tightening up or loosening the nuts on screws, a wrench. **to throw a spanner in the works,** to cause an impediment, to cause confusion or difficulty.

spar[1], *n.* a round timber, a pole, esp. used as a mast, yard, boom, shears etc. **spar deck,** *n.* the upper deck of a vessel stretching from stem to stern. [ME *sparre* (cp. Dut. *spar*, G *sparren*, Icel. *sparri*, Dan. and Swed. *sparre*), perh. cogn. with SPEAR]

spar[2], *n.* a name for various lustrous minerals occurring in crystalline or vitreous form. **sparry,** *a.* [OE *spær*]

spar[3], *v.i.* (*past, p.p.* **sparred**, to move the arms about in defence or offence as in boxing; of game cocks etc., to strike out, esp. with protected spurs; to engage in a contest of words etc. *n.*, a boxing-match; a cock-fight; a verbal contest, an argument. **sparrer,** *n.* **sparring,** *n.* **sparring-match,** *n.* **sparring-partner,** *n.* a boxer with whom one in training practises; a person with whom one engages in lively repartee. [perh. OF *esparer*, to strike out with the heels, perh. from Teut. and rel. to SPUR, SPURN]

sparable, *n.* a headless nail for boot-soles. [corr. of SPARROW and BILL[1]]

spare, *a.* meagre, scanty, frugal; thin, lean, wiry; concise (of style); that can be spared, kept in reserve, available for use in emergency etc. *v.t.* to use frugally, to be chary of using; to refrain from using; to dispense with; to refrain from inflicting upon; to refrain from punishing, injuring, destroying etc.; to relieve, to release; to be able to afford. †to forbear (to). *v.i.* to live sparingly or frugally. *n.* that which is surplus to immediate requirements and available for use, as *spare tyre, key, room* etc. **to go spare,** (*sl.*) to become excessively angry, agitated or distraught. **to spare,** extra, surplus, more than required. **spare part,** *n.* a replacement for a machine part which may break, wear out etc. **spare-part surgery,** *n.* surgery including the implanting of artificial organs or parts. **sparerib,** *n.* a piece of pork consisting of the ribs with only a little meat. **spare room,** *n.* a guest bedroom. **spare tyre,** *n.* a tyre carried in a vehicle as a replacement in case of a puncture; (*coll.*) a bulge of fat around the midriff. **sparely,** *adv.* **spareness,** *n.* **sparer,** *n.* **sparing,** *a.* **sparingly,** *n.* **sparingness,** *n.* [OE *spær*, whence *sparian*, to spare (cp. Icel. *sparr*, G *spärlich,* also Dut. and G *sparen*, Icel. and Swed. *spara*), prob. cogn. with L *parcere*, to spare]

sparge, *v.i.* to sprinkle. **sparger,** *n.* a sprinkling-apparatus used in brewing. [obs. *sparge*, L *spargere*, to sprinkle, -ER]

sparhawk, SPARROW-HAWK.

sparing, SPARE.

spark, *n.* an incandescent particle thrown off from a burning substance; a brilliant point, facet, gleam etc.; a flash of wit, a particle of life or energy; a trace, a hint (of kindled interest etc); a gallant, a beau; a vivacious and witty person; the luminous effect of a disruptive electrical discharge. *v.i.* to give out sparks; to produce sparks at the point of broken continuity in an electrical circuit. **to make sparks fly,** to start a violent quarrel, to cause a row. **to spark off,** to start, to kindle, to enliven. **spark coil,** *n.* an instrument for producing a high electromotive force from a supply of low EMF. **spark-plug, sparking-plug,** *n.* a device for igniting the explosive mixture in the cylinder of an internal combustion engine. **sparkish,** *a.* **sparklet**, *n.* **sparks,** *n. sing.* (*sl.*) the wireless operator on board ship; an electrician. [OE *spearca*, cp. MDut. *sparcke*, LG *sparke*, Icel. *spraka*, to crackle, prob. imit.]

Spark, *n.* **Muriel** (1918–), Scottish novelist. She is a Catholic convert, and her works have an enigmatic satire: *The Ballad of Peckham Rye* (1960), *The Prime of Miss Jean Brodie* (1961), and *The Only Problem* (1984).

sparkle, *n.* a gleam, a glittering, glitter, brilliance; vivacity, wit; effervescence. *v.i.* to emit sparks; to glisten, to glitter, to twinkle; of some wines, mineral waters etc., to emit carbon dioxide in little bubbles; to be vivacious, witty, scintillating. *v.t.* to cause to glitter, twinkle, shine etc. **sparkler,** *n.* something that sparkles; (*sl.*) a diamond; a hand-held firework that emits fizzling sparks. **sparklingly.** [dim. of SPARK]

sparre, SPAR[1].

sparrer, sparring-match SPAR[3].

sparrow, *n.* a small brownish-grey bird of the genus *Passer*, esp. *P. domesticus*, the house-sparrow; any of various other small birds resembling this, e.g. the hedge-sparrow. **sparrow-grass,** corr. of ASPARAGUS. **sparrow-hawk,** *n.* a small hawk, *Accipiter nisus*, preying on small birds etc. [OE *spearwa* (cp. Icel. *spörr*, Dan. *spurv*, Swed. *sparf*) cogn. with SPAR[3]]

sparry SPAR[2].

sparse, *a.* thinly scattered, set or occurring at considerable intervals, not dense. **sparsely,** *adv.* **sparseness, sparsity,** *n.* [L *sparsus*, p.p. of *spargere*, to scatter]

Sparta, *n.* ancient Greek city-state in the S Peloponnese (near Sparte), developed from Dorian settlements in the 10th century BC. The Spartans took part in the Persian and Peloponnesian wars. **Spartan,** *n.* a native or inhabitant of Sparta; one bearing pain, enforcing discipline etc., like a Spartan. *a.* of or pertaining to Sparta or the Spartans; like a Spartan, hardy, strict etc.; austere, rigorous, frugal.

Spartacist, *n.* member of a group of left-wing radicals in Germany at the end of World War I, founders of the Spartacus League, which became the German Communist party in 1919. The league participated in the Berlin workers' revolt of Jan. 1919 which was suppressed by the Freikorps on the orders of the socialist government. The agitation ended with the murder of Spartacist leaders Karl LIEBKNECHT and Rosa LUXEMBURG.

Spartacus, *n.* (d. 71 BC), Thracian gladiator who in 73 BC led a revolt of gladiators and slaves at Capua. He was eventually caught by CRASSUS and crucifed.

spasm, *n.* a convulsive and involuntary muscular contraction; a sudden or convulsive act, movement etc.; a violent burst of emotion or effort. **spasmodic, -ical,** *a.* **spasmodically,** *adv.* **spastic,** *a.* of, affected by, resembling or characterized by spasms; (*derog. sl.*) ineffectual, incapable. *n.* a sufferer from cerebral palsy; (*derog. sl., often considered offensive*) an ineffectual, clumsy person. **spastic paralysis,** *n.* paralysis characterized by spasms in the affected muscles. **spastically,** *adv.* **spasticity,** *n.* [F *spasme*, L *spasmus*, Gr. *spasmos*, from *spaein,* to draw out]

spat[1], *n.* the spawn of shell-fish, esp. oysters. *v.i.* to spawn. *v.t.* to deposit (spawn). [prob. from *spat*, stem of SPATTER]

spat[2], *n.* (*usu. pl.*) a short gaiter fastening over and under the shoe. [short for SPATTERDASH]

spat[3], *n.* a slap, a smack; (*chiefly N Am.*) a petty quarrel; (*chiefly N Am.*) a splash, a drop, a smattering (e.g. of rain). *v.t.* to slap. *v.i.* (*N Am., New Zealand*) to engage in a petty argument. [prob. imit.]

spat[4], *past* SPIT[2].

Spatangus, *n.* a genus of heart-shaped sea-urchins. **spatangoid,** *n., a.* [mod. L, from Gr. *spatangēs*]

spatchcock, *n.* a fowl killed and immediately cooked; a fowl opened out along the backbone and fried or grilled flat; *v.t.* to cook in this way. *v.t.* to insert or interpolate (a phrase etc.) hurriedly. [said to be short for *dispatch-cock* (perh. conf. with SPITCHCOCK)]

spate, *n.* a heavy flood, esp. in mountain stream or river; a sudden downpour; a sudden onrush or outburst. [etym. doubtful]

spathe, *n.* a large bract or pair of bracts enveloping the spadix of a plant. **spathaceous,** *a.* [L *spatha*, Gr. *spathē*, a broad blade, sword etc.]

spathic, spathose, *a.* resembling spar, esp. in cleavage. [G *spath*, spar, -IC]

spatial, spacial, *a.* of, relating to, existing or occurring in space. **spatiality,** *n.* **spatially,** *adv.* **spatiotemporal,** *a.* of space-time; of, concerned with or existing in both space and time. **spatiotemporally,** *adv.*

spatter, *v.t.* to scatter or splash (water etc.) about; to sprinkle or splash with water, mud etc.; to asperse, to defame. *v.i.* to sprinkle drops of saliva etc. about; to be scattered about thus. *n.* a shower a sprinkling, a pattering; that which is spattered or soiled. **spatterdash,** *n.* (*usu. pl.*) a legging or gaiter for protecting against mud etc. [freq. of *spat*, cogn. with prov. *spat*, to spit]

spatula, *n.* a broad knife or trowel-shaped tool used for spreading plasters, working pigments, mixing foods etc. **spatular, -late,** *a.* **spatule,** *n.* a broad, spatuliform part, as in the tail of many birds; a spatula. [L, dim. of *spatha,* SPATHE]

spavin, *n.* a disease in horses affecting the hock-joint. **blood, †bog spavin,** distension of the hock-joint by effusion of synovial fluid. **bone spavin,** a deposit of bony matter ultimately uniting the bones. **spavined,** *a.* [OF *esparvin*, prob. through a late L *sparvānus*, from OHG *sparwe*, SPARROW, with alln. to bird-like motion of a spavined horse]

†spawl, *v.i.* to eject saliva with force, to spit. [etym. doubtful]

spawn, *v.t.* of fish, amphibians etc., to deposit or produce (eggs, young etc.); (*derog.*) of human beings, to bring forth. *v.i.* of fish etc., to deposit eggs; (*derog.*) to issue, to be brought forth, esp. in abundance. *n.* the eggs of fish, frogs and molluscs; white fibrous matter from which fungi are produced; (*derog.*) offspring. **spawner,** *n.* [OF *espandre*, L *expandere*, to EXPAND]

spay, *v.t.* to destroy or remove the ovaries of female animals. [prob. through OF, from late L *spadāre,* from SPADO]

speak, *v.i.* (*past* **spoke, †spake,** *p.p.* **spoken**) to utter articulate sounds or words in the ordinary tone as dist. from singing; to talk, to converse; to deliver a speech or address; to communicate or intimate by other means; of a picture etc., to be highly expressive or lifelike; to be on speaking terms; to be a spokesman (for); to produce a (characteristic) sound. *v.t.* to utter articulately; to make known, to tell, to declare; to talk or converse in (a language); to hail and communicate with (a ship). **nothing to speak of,** insignificant, unimportant. **to speak for,** to act as an advocate for, to represent, to witness. **to speak of,** to mention. **to speak one's mind,** to speak freely and frankly. **to speak out, up,** to speak loudly; to speak without constraint, to express one's opinion freely. **to speak to,** to address; to speak in support or confirmation of. **to speak volumes,** to be of great or peculiar significance (for etc.). **to speak well of,** to furnish favourable evidence of. **speakeasy,** *n.* a premises where illicit liquor was sold during the time of Prohibition. **speakable,** *a.* **speaker,** *n.* one who speaks, esp. one who delivers a speech; a loudspeaker; (see also Speaker). **speakership,** *n.* **speaking,** *a.* animated, vivid, expressive of a likeness etc.; able to speak; (*in comb.*) able to speak a specific language; transmitting speech. **on speaking terms,** amicable. **speaking in tongues** THE GIFT OF TONGUES under TONGUE. **strictly speaking,** in the strict sense of the words. **speaking clock,** *n.* a telephone service, obtained by dialling a particular number, that tells the caller the time by means of a recorded message. **speaking-tube,** *n.* a tube for conveying the sound of the voice between parts of a building etc. **speakingly,** *adv.* [OE *sprecan*, later *specan* (cp. Dut. *spreken*, G *sprechen*, also Icel. *spraka*, SPARK[1])]

Speaker, *n.* the presiding officer charged with the preservation of order in the legislatures of various countries. In the UK the Speaker in the House of Lords is the Lord Chancellor; in the House of Commons the Speaker is elected for each parliament, usually on an agreed basis among the parties, but often holds the office for many years. The original appointment dates from 1377.

spear, *n.* a weapon with a pointed head on a long shaft; a spearman; a sharp-pointed instrument with barbs, for stabbing fish etc.; a blade or stalk of grass. *v.t.* to pierce, kill or capture with a spear. **spear-grass,** *n.* grass of various species having long, sharp leaves. **speargun,** *n.* a gun for firing spears under water. **spearhead,** *n.* the pointed end of a spear; the person or group leading a campaign, thrust or attack. *v.t.* to lead a campaign, an assault etc. **spearman,** *n.* one armed with a spear. **spearmint,** *n.* the garden mint, *Mentha viridis* **spear-thistle,** *n.* a common thistle, *Carduus lanceolatus* **spearwort,** *n.* a popular name for several species of ranunculus. [OE *spere* (cp. Dut. and G *speer*, Icel. *spjör*), perh. cogn. with SPAR[1]]

spec, *n.* (*coll.*) short for SPECULATION, SPECIFICATION *a.* (*Austral., New Zealand*) short for SPECULATIVE; **on spec,** (*coll.*) on the chance of, in the hope that, as a gamble.

spec., (*abbr.*) special.

special, *a.* particular, peculiar, not ordinary or general; additional; close, intimate; designed for a particular purpose, environment or occasion. *n.* a person or thing designed to be a special purpose etc.; a special train, constable, edition of a newspaper, item on a menu etc. **special constable** CONSTABLE. **special delivery,** *n.* express delivery. **special effect,** *n.* an extraordinary visual or sound effect, esp. one created on a film, video tape, or television or radio broadcast. **special licence,** LICENCE. **special pleading,** *n.* the allegation of special or new matter in a legal case; specious or unfair argument. **special school.** *n.* a school established to meet the educational needs of handicapped children. **special verdict,** *n.* a verdict stating the facts but leaving the decision to be determined by the court. **specialism,** *n.* a special area of expertise etc., a speciality. **specialist,** *n.* one who devotes him- or herself to a particular branch of a profession etc. **specialistic,** *a.* **speciality,**, *n.* a special characteristic or feature, a peculiarity; a special area of expertise, pursuit, occupation, service, commodity etc. **specialize, -ise,** *v.t.* to differentiate, limit, adapt or apply to a specific use, function, environment, purpose or meaning. *v.i.* to become differentiated, adapted or applied thus; to employ oneself as or train oneself to be a specialist. **specialization, -isation**, *n.* **specially,** *adv.* **specialness,** *n.* **specialty,** *n.* a legal agreement expressed in a deed; (*chiefly N Am.*) a speciality. [shortened from ESPECIAL or directly from L *speciālis*, as foll.]

Special Air Service, (SAS) specialist British regiment recruited mainly from Parachute Regiment volunteers. It has served in Malaysia, Oman, Northern Ireland, and against international terrorists, as in the siege of the Iranian embassy in London in 1980.

Special Branch, *n.* section of the British police originally established in 1883 to deal with Irish Fenian activists. All 42 police forces in Britain now have their own Special Branches. They act as the executive arm of MI5 (British intelligence) in its duty of preventing or investigating espionage, subversion and sabotage; carry out duties at air and sea ports in respect of naturalization and immigration, and provide armed bodyguards for public figures.

species, *n.* (*pl.* **species**) a group of organisms (subordinate to a genus) generally resembling each other and capable of reproduction; (*Log.*) a group of individuals having certain common attributes and designated by a common name (subordinate to a genus); a kind, a sort, a variety; the form or shape given to any material; an element in the Eucharist. **speciation,** *n.* the development of a biological species. **specie**, *n.* coin as dist. from paper money. **in specie**, in coin; in kind. [L, appearance, sort, from *specere*, to look]

specify, *v.t.* to mention expressly, to name distinctively; to include in a specification; †to distinguish from anything else. **specifiable,** *a.* **specific**, *a.* clearly specified or particularized, explicit, definite, precise; constituting, pertaining to, characterizing or particularizing a species; distinctive, peculiar, special. *n.* a medicine, remedy, agent etc. for a particular part of the body; that which is particular or specific. **specific gravity** *n.* the relative weight or density of a solid or fluid expressed by the ratio of its weight to that of an equal volume of a substance taken as a standard, water in the case of liquids and solids, air for gases. **specific heat** (**capacity**) *n.* the heat required to raise the temperature of one unit of a given substance by one degree. **specifically,** *adv.* **specificate,** *v.t.* to specify. **specification**, *n.* the act of specifying; an article or particular specified; a detailed statement of particulars, esp. of materials, work, workmanship to be undertaken or supplied by an architect, builder, manufacturer etc.; a detailed description of an invention by an applicant for a patent. **specificative**, *a.* **specificity**, **specificness,** *n.* **specified,** *a.* [F *specifique*, L *specificus* (as prec., -IC)]

specimen, *n.* a part or an individual intended to illustrate or typify the nature of a whole or a class, an example, an illustration, an instance; a sample of blood, urine etc. taken for medical analysis; (*coll., usu. derog.*) a person. [L, from *specere* to look]

speciology, *n.* the branch of biology treating of the nature and origin of species. **speciological**, *a.*

specious, *a.* apparently right or fair, plausible; deceptively pleasing to the eye, showy. **speciosity**, **speciousness,** *n.* **speciously,** *adv.* [F *specieux*, L *speciōsus*, from *specere,* to see]

speck[1], *n.* a small spot, fleck, stain or blemish; a minute particle. *v.t.* to mark with a speck or specks. **speckless,** *a.* **specky**[1], *a.* [OE *specca*, cp. LG *spaken*, to be spotted, MDut. *spickelen*, to speckle]

speck[2], *n.* bacon; blubber or fat, esp. of whales, seals etc. **specksioneer**, *n.* a chief harpooner. [Dut. *spek*, cp. G *Speck*, OE *spic*, bacon lard]

speckle, *n.* a small spot, stain or patch of colour, light etc. *v.t.* to mark (as) with speckles. **speckled,** *a.* [dim. of SPECK[1]]

specks SPECS.

specksioneer SPECK[2].

specky[1] SPECK[1].

specky[2], *n.* (*coll., usu. derog.*) one who wears spectacles.

specs, specks, *n.pl.* (*coll.*) short for SPECTACLES.

spectacle, *n.* a show, something exhibited to the view; a pageant, an object, a sight; (*coll.*) a sight attracting ridicule, laughter etc.; *pl.* an optical instrument, consisting of a lens for each eye mounted in a light frame for resting on the nose and ears, used to assist the sight. **spectacled,** *a.* **spectacular**, *a.* of the nature of a spectacle; marked by great display; dramatic; thrilling; stunning, striking. *n.* an elaborate show in a theatre, on television etc. **spectacularly,** *adv.* [F, from L *spectāculum*, from *specere*, to look]

spectator, *n.* one who looks on, esp. at a show or spectacle. *v.i.* to look on, to observe (e.g. a sport); to be an onlooker. **spectator sport,** *n.* a sport that attracts a large number of spectators. **spectatorial**, *a.* **spectatorship,** *n.* **spectatress**, **-trix**, *n. fem.* [L, from *spectāre*, to behold, from *specere*, to look]

Spector, *n.* **Phil** (1940–), US record producer, known for the Wall of Sound, created using a large orchestra, distinguishing his work in the early 1960s with vocal groups such as the Crystals and the Ronettes. He withdrew into semi-retirement in 1966.

spectre, (*esp. N Am.*) **specter**, *n.* an apparition, a ghost; a person, thought, event etc. causing alarm or threat. **spectre-bat, -crab, -insect, -lemur, -shrimp,** *n.* a bat, crab etc., having an exceedingly thin or diaphanous body. **spectral,** *a.* ghostlike, of or pertaining to ghosts. **spectrality**, *n.* **spectrally,** *adv.* [OF, from L SPECTRUM]

spectro-, *comb. form* spectrum.

spectrograph, *n.* an apparatus for photographing or otherwise reproducing spectra. **spectrogram,** *n.* **spectrographic**, *a.* **spectrographically,** *adv.*

spectrography, *n.*

spectroheliograph *n.* an instrument for photographing the sun using a particular wavelength of light. **spectroheliogram,** *n.* a photograph taken by a spectroheliograph. **spectroheliographic,** *a.* **spectroheliography,** *n.*
spectrology, *n.* the science of spectrum analysis. **spectrological**, *a.* **spectrologically,** *adv.*
spectrometer, *n.* an instrument for measuring the angular deviation of a ray of light passing through a prism. **spectrometric**, *a.* **spectrometry,** *n.*
spectrophotometer, *n.* an instrument for measuring the intensity of light radiated by various wavelengths within the spectrum. **spectrophotometric, -ical**, *a.* **spectrophotometrically,** *adv.* **spectrophotometry,** *n.*
spectroscope, *n.* an instrument for forming and analysing the spectra of rays emitted by bodies. **spectroscopic, -ical**, *a.* **spectroscopically,** *adv.* **spectroscopist**, *n.* **spectroscopy**, *n.*
spectrum, *n.* (*pl.* **-tra**) an image produced by the decomposition of rays of light or other radiant energy by means of a prism, in which the parts are arranged according to their refrangibility; an image persisting on the retina after the eyes are removed, an after image; a range, a series (of interests, activities etc.) **spectrum analysis,** *n.* chemical analysis with the spectroscope. **spectral,** *a.* of, pertaining to, or like a spectrum. [L, a vision, an image, from *specere*, to look]
speculate, *v.i.* to pursue an inquiry or form conjectures or views by consideration in the mind; to make purchases, investments etc. on the chance of profit. **speculation,** *n.* the act or practice of speculating; a mental inquiry, train of thought or series of conjectures about a subject; a speculative business transaction, investment or undertaking; a game in which the players speculate on the value of their cards. **speculative,** *a.* **speculatively,** *adv.* **speculativeness,** *n.* **speculator,** †**speculatory,** *a.* [L *speculātus*, p.p. of *speculārī*, to behold, from *specular*, a watch-tower, as foll.]
speculum, *n.* (*pl.* **-la**) a surgical instrument for dilating passages of the body, to facilitate inspection; a mirror, esp. one of polished metal used as a reflector in a telescope; a lustrous spot or coloured area on the wing of certain birds, also an ocellus. **speculum metal,** *n.* an alloy of copper and tin used for reflectors or mirrors. **specular,** *a.* of or pertaining to a mirror; mirror-like; of or pertaining to a speculum. **specular iron,** *n.* a bright crystalline variety of haematite. [L, mirror, from *specere*, to look]
sped, *past, p.p.* SPEED.
Spee, *n.* **Maximilian, Count von Spee** (1861–1914), German admiral, born in Copenhagen. He went down with his flagship in the 1914 battle of the Falkland Islands, and the *Graf Spee* battleship was named after him.
speech, *n.* the faculty or act of uttering articulate sounds or words; that which is spoken, an utterance, a remark; a public address, an oration; the language or dialect of a nation, region etc.; an individual's characteristic manner of speech; the sounding-quality of a musical instrument, esp. of an organ-pipe, inexpressible in words. **speech community,** *n.* a community sharing a common dialect or language. **speech-day,** *n.* the annual day for presenting prizes in schools etc. **speechify,** *v.i.* (*often derog.*) to make a (pompous or lengthy) speech or speeches, to harangue. **speechifier,** *n.* **speechless**, *a.* unable to speak, silent, esp. through emotion; dumb, dumb-founded. (*Linguistics*) parole. **speechlessly,** *adv.* **speechlessness,** *n.* [OE *spǣc*, *sprǣc*, see SPEAK]
speed, *n.* rapidity, swiftness, celerity, rate of motion; the ratio of the distance covered to the time taken by a moving body; †success, prosperity. (*sl.*) amphetamine; the numerical expression of the sensitivity of a photographic plate, film or paper to light; a measure of the power of a lens to take in light; a ratio of gears in a motor vehicle, on a bicycle etc. *v.i.* (*past, p.p.* **sped**) to move rapidly, to hasten; to drive, to travel at an excessively high, dangerous or illegal speed. *v.t.* to promote, to make prosperous, to cause to succeed; to cause to go fast, to urge to send at great speed; (*past, p.p.* **speeded**) to regulate the speed of, to set (an engine etc.) at a fixed rate of speed. **at speed,** quickly. **speedball,** *n.* (*sl.*) a mixture of heroin and cocaine or heroin and amphetamine. **speedboat,** *n.* a light boat driven at great speed by a motor-engine. **speed limit,** *n.* the legal limit of speed for a vehicle on a particular road in particular conditions. **speedometer,** *n.* a device attached to a vehicle to measure and indicate its speed. **speed trap,** *n.* a stretch of road monitored by police using radar devices to catch speeding drivers; **speed up,** *n.* an acceleration. **speed-way** *n.* a racecourse for motorcycles; a dirt track; the sport of motorcycle racing on a track. **speedwell,** *n.* a flowering herb, one of various species of *Veronica*. **speeder,** *n.* **speedy,** *a.* **speedily,** *adv.* **speediness,** *n.* **speeding,** *n.* an excessive, dangerous or illegal speed. *a.* travelling at such a speed. **speedo**, *n.* (*pl.* **-dos**) (*coll.*) a speedometer. **speedster**, *n.* one who speeds; a speedboat; a fast car, a sports car. [OE *spēd* (whence *spēdan*, v.), from *spōwan*, to succeed (cp. Dut. *spoed*, OHG *spuot, spōt*, success, *spuon*, to prosper, also L *spatium*, SPACE, *spēs*, hope)]
speer, speir, *v.i.*, *v.t.* (*Sc.*) to question, to inquire, to ask. [OE *spyrian*, to follow a track, cogn. with SPOOR]
speiss, *n.* a compound of arsenic, nickel, copper etc., produced in the smelting of various ores such as lead. [G *speise*, orig. food, It. *spesa*, from L as EXPENSE]
spek-boom, *n.* a large shrub, *Portulacaria afra*, the purslane-tree. [Afrikaans *spek*, fat meat, *boom*, tree]
spelaean, spelean, *a.* of or pertaining to a cave or caves; cave-dwelling. **spelaeology, speleology**, *n.* the scientific study or exploration of caves. **spel(a)eological,** *a.* **spel(a)eologist,** *n.* [L *spēlaeum*, Gr. *spēlaion*, cave, -AN]
spelding, *n.* (*Sc.*) a small fish split and dried in the sun. [OE *speld*, splinter]
spelk, *n.* (*Sc., North.*) a splint; a spike used in thatching; a rod in a loom. [OE *spelc*, cp. Dut. *spalk*]
spell[1]**,** *n.* a series of words used as a charm, an incantation; occult power, fascination, enchantment; a powerful attraction. **spellbind,** *v.t.* to put a spell on; to entrance. **spellbinder,** *n.* one or that which entrances, esp. an eloquent speaker, film, book etc. **spellbinding,** *a.* **spellbound,** *a.* under the influence of a spell; enchanted, fascinated. [OE *spel, spell*, cp. Icel. *spjall*, OHG *spel*, narrative, story, cogn. with foll.]
spell[2]**,** *v.t.* (*past, p.p.* **spelled, spelt**) to say or write the letters forming (a word); to read or decipher with difficulty; to puzzle (out or over); of letters, to form a word; to mean, to import, to portend. *v.i.* to put letters together in such a way as to (correctly) form a word. **to spell (it) out,** *n.* to utter or write letter by letter; to make clear, easy to understand; to puzzle out. **speller,** *n.* one who spells; a spelling-book. **spelling,** *n.* the act or ability of one who spells; orthography; the particular formation of letters making up a word. **spelling-bee,** *n.* a competition in spelling. **spelling-book,** *n.* a book for teaching to spell. [OF *espeler*, cp. Dut. *spelen*, OE *spellian*, from prec.]
spell[3]**,** †*v.t.* to take the turn of at work, to relieve. *n.* a turn of work or rest; a (usu. short) period of time. [OE *spelian*, perh. cogn. with *spilian*, to play, cp. G *spielan*, and *spiel*]
spelt[1]**,** *n.* a variety of wheat formerly much cultivated in S Europe etc. [OE, from late L *spelta*]
spelt[2]**,** *past, p.p.* SPELL[2].
spelter, *n.* commercial or impure zinc. [from Teut. (cp. Dut. and G *spiauter*), rel. to PEWTER]
spelunker, *n.* (*N Am.*) one who explores or studies caves as a sport or hobby. **spelunking,** *n.* [from L *spēlunca*, a cave]
Spence, *n.* **Basil** (1907–76), British architect. He was professor of architecture at the Royal Academy, London, (1961–68), and his works include Coventry Cathedral, Sussex University, and the British embassy in Rome.
Spencer, *n.* **Stanley** (1891–1959), British painter. He

was born and lived in Cookham-on-Thames, Berkshire, and recreated the Christian story in a Cookham setting. His detailed, dreamlike compositions had little regard for perspective and used generalized human figures.

spencer[1], *n.* a short overcoat or jacket, for men or women; a woman's undergarment, a vest. [Earl *Spencer*, 1758–1834]

spencer[2], *n.* a fore-and-aft set abaft the fore- or main-mast on a barque or ship. [etym. doubtful]

spend, *v.t.* (*past, p.p.* **spent**) to pay out (money etc.); to consume, to use up; to pass (time); to squander, to waste; to expand; to wear out, to exhaust; *v.i.* to expend money; to waste away, to be consumed. **spendthrift,** *a.* prodigal, wasteful. *n.* a prodigal or wasteful person. **spendable,** *a.* **spender,** *n.* **spending,** *n.* **spending money,** *n.* pocket-money, money for spending. **spent,** *a.* exhausted, burnt out, used up. **a spent force,** one who or that which is used up, exhausted, useless etc. [OE *spendan*, late L *dispendere*, to weigh out, see DISPENSE]

Spender, *n.* **Stephen (Harold)** (1909–), English poet and critic. His earlier poetry has a left-wing political content, as in *Twenty Poems* (1930), *Vienna* (1934), *The Still Centre* (1939), and *Poems of Dedication* (1946). Other works include the verse drama *Trial of a Judge* (1938), the autobiography *World within World* (1951), and translations. His *Journals 1939–83* were published in 1985.

Spenser, *n.* **Edmund** (*c.* 1552–99), English poet, who has been called the 'poet's poet' because of his rich imagery and command of versification. He is known for his moral allegory *The Faerie Queene* to Elizabeth I, of which six books survive (three published in 1590 and three in 1596). Other books include *The Shepheard's Calendar* (1579), *Astrophel* (1586), the love sonnets *Amoretti* and the *Epithalamion* (1595). **Spenserian**, *a.* of, pertaining to or in the style of the poet Edmund Spenser or his verse. *n.* one who studies Spenser; a poet writing, or poetry written, in a style resembling that of Spencer; *a.* Spensarian stanza, *a.* as used in his *Faerie Queene* or in Byron's *Childe Harold*.

sperm, *n.* the male seminal fluid of animals; a male gamete; a sperm whale or cachalot; spermaceti; sperm oil. **sperm oil,** *n.* oil from the sperm whale. **sperm whale,** *n.* a whale yielding sperm oil. [F *sperme*, from L and Gr. *sperma*, from *speirein*, to sow]

sperm- SPERMAT(O)-.

-sperm, *comb. form.* a seed.

spermaceti, *n.* a white, fatty, brittle substance, existing in solution in the oily matter in the head of the sperm-whale, used for candles, ointments etc. [L, *cētī*, gen. of *cetus*, Gr. *kētos*, whale]

spermary, spermarium, *n.* (*pl.* **-ries, -ria**) the male spermatic gland, testicle or other organ.

spermat- SPERMAT(O)-.

spermatheca, *n.* a; receptacle in female insects and other invertebrates for spermatozoa. [Gr. *thēkē*, repository]

spermatic, ical, spermic *a.* consisting of, pertaining to or conveying sperm or semen; of or pertaining to the spermary. **spermatically,** *adv.* **spematid,** *n.* any of the male gametes which develop into spermatozoa. [F *spermatique*, L *spermaticus,* from *sperma -matos,* SPERM]

spermat(o)-, sperm(o)-, *comb. form.* sperm, seed. [SPERM]

spermatoblast, *n.* a cell from which a spermatozoon develops.

spermatocyte, *n.* a cell which develops into a sperm cell.

spermatogenesis, *n.* the development of spermatozoa. **spermatogenic**, **-genic, spermatogenous,** *a.* **spermatogeny,** *n.*

spermatogonium, *n.* (*pl.* **-nia**), a primitive male germ cell which divides to form spermatophytes.

spermatophore, *n.* a capsule holding spermatozoa, in molluscs etc.

spermatophyte, *n.* a seed-bearing plant. **spermatophytic**, *a.*

spermatorrhoea, *n.* involuntary discharge of seminal fluid. [Gr. *rheein*, to flow]

spermatozoid, *n.* an antherozoid.

spermatozoon, *n.* (*pl.* **-zoa**) one of the minute living bodies in the seminal fluid essential to fecundation by the male; a male germ cell. **spermatozoal, -zoan, -zoic**, *a.*

spermic, SPERMATIC.

spermicide, *n.* a substance that kills spermatozoa. **spermicidal**, *a.*

spermism *n.* the old theory that the spermatozoon alone is the germ of the future animal. **spermist,** *n.*

sperm(o)- SPERMAT(O)-.

Sperry, *n.* **Elmer Ambrose** (1860–1930), US engineer who developed various devices using gyroscopes, such as gyrostabilizers (for ships and torpedoes) and gyro-controlled autopilots.

spew, *v.t.* to vomit; to cast out with abhorrence; to spit out; to emit or eject violently or in great quantity. *v.i.* to vomit; to stream, gush or flood out. *n.* vomit, that which is ejected with great force or in great quantity. **spewy,** *a.* [OE *speowan, spīwan* (cp. MDut. *spouwen*, G *spein*, Icel. *spȳja*, also L *spuere*, Gr. *ptuein*) imit. in orig.]

SPF, (*abbr.*) South Pacific Forum.

sp. gr., (*abbr.*) specific gravity.

sphagnum, *n.* a genus of crytograms containing the bog- or peat-mosses. **sphagnous,** *a.* [Gr. *sphagnos*]

sphen- SPHEN(O)-.

sphendone, *n.* a sling-shaped band or fillet for supporting the back-hair worn by women of ancient Greece; the curved end of a stadium. [Gr., sling]

sphene, *n.* titanite. **sphenic**, *a.* wedge-shaped. [F *sphène*, Gr. *sphēn*, *sphenos*, a wedge]

sphenethmoid, *a.* of or pertaining to the sphenoid and the ethmoid bone; applied to the girdle bone. *n.* the sphenethmoid bone or girdle bone at the base of the skull in batrachians.

sphen(o)-, *comb. form.* pertaining to or resembling a wedge.

Sphenodon, *n.* a genus of nocturnal lizard-like reptiles, now confined to New Zealand. [Gr. *odous odontos*, tooth]

sphenogram, *n.* a cuneiform character. **sphenographic**, *a.* **sphenography**, *n.*

sphenoid, *a.* wedge-shaped. *n.* a sphenoid bone; *n.* a wedge-shaped crystal enclosed by four equal isosceles triangles. **sphenoid bone,** *n.* a wedge-shaped bone lying across the base of the skull. **sphenoidal**, *a.*

sphere, *n.* a solid bounded by a surface every part of which is equally distant from a point within called the centre; a solid figure generated by the revolution of a semicircle about its diameter; a figure approximately spherical, a ball, a globe, esp. one of the heavenly bodies; a globe representing the earth or the apparent heavens; one of the spherical shells revolving round the earth as centre in which, according to ancient astronomy, the heavenly bodies were set; the sky, the heavens; area of knowledge, discipline; field of action, influence etc., scope, range, province, place, position; social class. *v.t.* to enclose in or as in a sphere; to make spherical; to put among the celestial spheres. **spheral,** *a.* spherical; of or pertaining to the celestial spheres or the music of the spheres. **spherical**, **spheric**, *a.* sphere-shaped, globular; relating to spheres. **spherical aberration,** *n.* the deterioration of an image from a lens or mirror with a spherical surface as a result of the different focal points of rays striking its edge and centre. **spherical angle,** *n.* the angle between two intersecting great circles of a sphere. **spherical coordinates,** *n.pl.* coordinates used to locate a point in space comprising a radius vector and two angles measured from a vertical and a horizontal line. **spherical triangle,** *n.* a figure on the surface of a sphere bounded by the arcs of three great circles. **spherical trigonometry,** *n.* the trigonometry concerned with spherical triangles. **spherically,** *adv.* **sphericity**, *n.* **spherics**, *n.pl.* spherical geometry and trigonometry.

spheroid, *n.* a body nearly spherical; a solid generated by the revolution of an ellipse about its minor axis (called an **oblate spheroid**) or its major axis (called a **prolate spheroid**). **spheroidal, -roidic, -ical**, *a.* **spheroidally,** *adv.* **spheroidity,, -dicity**, *n.* [ME *spere*, OF *espere*, L *sphæra*, Gr. *sphaira*, ball]
spherograph, *n.* a stereographic projection of the earth with meridians and lines of latitude, used for the mechanical solution of problems in navigation, etc.
spherometer, *n.* an instrument for measuring the radii and curvature of spherical surfaces.
spherule, *n.* a small sphere. **spherular,** *a.*
spherulite, *n.* a rounded concretion occurring in various rocks; a radiolite.
sphex, *n.* (*pl.* **spheges,**) a wasp of a genus, *Sphex*, of digger-wasps. **sphex-wasp, sphexide**, *n.* [Gr. *sphēx*]
sphincter, *n.* a ring muscle that contracts or shuts any orifice or tube. **sphincteral, -terial, -teric**, *a.* [L and Gr. *from sphingein*, to bind tight]
sphinx, *n.* in Greek mythology, a winged monster, half woman and half lion, said to have devoured the inhabitants of Thebes till a riddle she had proposed should be solved, and on its solution by Oedipus to have flung herself down and perished; an ancient Egyptian figure with the body of a lion and a human or animal head; a taciturn or enigmatic person; a hawk-moth; a variety of baboon. [L and Gr., prob. of foreign etym., pop. as prec.]
sphragistics, *n. sing.* the study of engraved seals and signets. **sphragistic,** *a.* [Gr. *sphragistikos*, from *sphragis*, seal]
sphygmic SPHYGMUS.
sphygm(o)-, *comb. form.* pertaining to a pulse.
sphygmograph, *n.* an instrument for recording the movements of the pulse. **sphygmogram**, *n.* **sphygmographic**, *a.* **sphygmography**, *n.* [Gr. *sphugmos*, pulse, from *sphuzein*, to beat, to throb]
sphygmology, *n.* the branch of physiology concerned with the pulse.
sphygmomanometer, *n.* an instrument for measuring the tension of blood in an artery.
sphygmophone, *n.* an instrument for enabling one to hear the action of the pulse.
sphygmoscope, *n.* an instrument for rendering the movements of the pulse visible.
sphygmus, *n.* a pulse, a pulsation. **sphygmic,** *a.*
†**spial, a spy, a scout; close watch.** [ESPIAL]
spic, spick, *n.* (*N Am. derog* or *offensive*) a Spanish-speaking American.
spica, *n.* (*Bot.*) a spike; a spiral surgical bandage with the turns reversed. **spicate, -ated, spiciform**, *a.* (*Bot.*) pointed, having spikes. [L, ear of corn, spike]
spiccato, *n.*, *a.* (a musical passage) played so that the bow rebounds lightly from the strings. [It. detached]
spice, *n.* any aromatic and pungent vegetable substance used for seasoning food; a flavour, a touch, a trace. something which adds zest or interest. *v.t.* to season with spice; to add interest to. **spice-bush, -wood,** *n.* the wild allspice, *Benzoin odoriferum*, an American shrub. †**spicer,** *n.* **spicery**, *n.* **spicy,** *a.* flavoured with spice; abounding in spices; pungent, piquant; suggestive, indelicate; showy, smart. **spicily,** *adv.* **spiciness,** *n.* [OF *espice*, L *speciēs*, kind, late L spice]
spick-and-span, *a.* new and fresh, clean and smart. [SPIKE, AND, SPOON]
spicknel, SPIGNEL.
spicule, *n.* a small sharp needle-shaped body, such as the calcareous or siliceous spikes in sponges etc.; (*Bot.*) a small or subsidiary spike. a spiked flare of hot gas ejected from the surface of the sun. **spicular, -late**, **spiculiform**, *a.* **spiculiferous**, **-ligerous**, *a.* **spiculum,** *n.* (*pl.* **-la**) a spicule; a needlelike process, organ etc. [L *spīculum*, dim. of SPICA]
spicy SPICE.
spider, *n.* an eight-legged arachnid of the order Araneida, usu. furnished with a spinning apparatus utilized by the most species for making webs to catch their prey; an arachnid resembling this; a spider-like thing, esp. a three-legged frying-pan, grid-iron, frame etc. an arrangement of elastic ropes with hooks attached, used for fastening loads to car roofs, motorcycles etc; a long-legged rest for a cue in snooker. **spider-catcher,** *n.* a bird of the Indian genus *Arachnothera;* the wall-creeper. **spider-crab,** *n.* a crab with long thin legs. **spider-line,** *n.* a filament of spider's web used in the reticle of astronomical instruments etc. **spider-monkey,** *n.* a monkey belonging to the American genus *Ateles* or *Eriodes* with long limbs and slender bodies. **spider plant,** *n.* a house plant having streamers of long narrow leaves with central white or yellow stripes. **spider-wasp,** *n.* a wasp that stores its nest with spiders and other insects. **spider's web, spider-web,** *n.* **spider-like,** *a.*, *adv.* **spidery,** *a.* [OE for *spinther*, *spinner*, see SPIN]
Spiegeleisen, *n.* a white variety of cast-iron containing manganese, used in making Bessemer steel. [G *Spiegel*, mirror, SPECULUM, *Eisen*, iron]
spiel, *n.* a speech, sales patter. *v.i.* to reel off patter. **spieler,** *n.* a card-sharper, a trickster. [G, a game]
Spielberg, *n.* **Steven** (1947–), US director, whose successful films include *Jaws* (1975), *Close Encounters of the Third Kind* (1977), *Raiders of the Lost Ark* (1981), and *ET* (1982).
spiffing, *a.* (*dated coll.*) excellent. **spiffy,** *a.* (*coll.*) smartly dressed, spruce. [etym. doubtful]
spiflicate, *v.t.* to smash, to crush, to do for. **spiflication,** *n.* [etym. doubtful]
spignel, *n.* an umbelliferous plant, *Meum athamanticum*, with an aromatic root used in medicine, and finely cut, ornamental leaves. [etym. doubtful]
spigot, *n.* a peg or plug for stopping the vent-hole in a cask; the turning-plug in a faucet; a faucet, a tap. [prob. from OProv. *espigot*, dim. of *espiga*, L SPICA]
spik, SPIC.
spike, *n.* a pointed piece of metal, as one of a number fixed on the top of a railing, fence, or wall, or worn on boots to prevent slipping; any pointed object, a sharp point; a large nail or pin, used in structures built of large timbers, on railways etc.; an inflorescence having flowers sessile along a common axis; spike-lavender. *v.t.* to fasten with spikes; to furnish with spikes; to sharpen to a point; to pierce or impale; to fasten on with a spike or spikes; to plug the touch-hole (of a cannon) with a spike; to lace a drink with spirits; to render useless; in volleyball, to punch the ball sharply down into the opposing court. **to spike someone's guns,** to foil someone's plans. **spike-lavender,** *n.* French lavender, *Lavandula spica.* **spike-nail,** *n.* **spikelet,** *n.* a small spike, esp. part of the inflorescence of most grasses. **spiky,** *a.* [perh. from Scand. (cp. Icel. *spīk*, Swed. *spik*), cogn. with SPOKE[1], in some senses from L SPICA]
spikenard, *n.* a herb, *Nardostachys atamansi*, related to the valerian; an ancient and costly aromatic ointment prepared chiefly from the root of this; one of various vegetable oils. [OF *spiquenare* (L SPICA, *nardī*, gen. of *nardus* NARD)]
spiky SPIKE.
spile, *n.* a small wooden plug, a spigot; a large timber driven into the ground to protect a bank etc., a pile. *v.t.* to pierce (a cask) with a hole and furnish with a spile. [cp. Dut. *spijl*, LG *spile*, bar, spile, G *Speiler*, skewer]
spill[1], *n.* a slip of paper or wood used to light a candle, pipe etc. [etym. doubtful, perh. rel. to SPILE]
spill[2], *v.t.* (*past*, *p.p.* **spilt**, **spilled**) to suffer to fall or run out of a vessel; to shed; to empty (the belly of a sail) of wind; (*coll.*) to throw out of a vehicle or from a saddle; †to ruin, to destroy. *v.i.* of liquid, to run or fall out; to be destroyed, to perish. *n.* a tumble, a fall, esp. from a vehicle or saddle. **to spill the beans,** to divulge a secret. **spillway,** *n.* a passage for the overflow of water from a reservoir etc. **spiller,** *n.* one that spills; a trawl-line; a small seine used to take the fish out of the larger one. **spilling-line,** *n.* a rope for spilling the wind out of a square sail to enable it to be reefed. †**spilth,** *n.* that which is spilt; over-plus, excess of supply. [OE *spillan*, to destroy, Icel. *spilla*, cp. Swed. *spilla*, OE

spildan, prob. cogn. with prec.]

spillikin, *n.* a small strip or pin of bone, wood etc., used in spillikins. **spillikins,** *n. sing.* a game in which players attempt to remove spillikins from a pile one at a time without disturbing the others. [prob. dim. of SPILL[1]]

spilosite, *n.* a greenish schistose rock spotted with chlorite concretions or scales. [Gr. *spilos*, spot, -ITE]

spilt, spilth SPILL[2].

spilus, *n.* a spot or mole on the skin, a naevus. [Gr. *spilos*, spot]

spin, *v.t.* (*pres. p.* **spinning** *past* **spun**, †**span**, *p.p.* **spun**) to draw out and twist (wool, cotton etc.) into threads; to make (yarn etc.) thus; of spiders etc., to produce (a web, cocoon etc.) by drawing out a thread of viscous substance; to tell, compose etc., at great length; to make (a top etc.) rotate rapidly; to shape in a lathe etc.; to fish with a revolving bait; (*sl.*) to reject after examination. *v.i.* to draw out and twist cotton etc., into threads; to make yarn etc., thus; to whirl round; to turn round quickly; to fish with a spinning bait; to go along with great swiftness. *n.* the act or motion of spinning, a whirl; a brief run in a motor car etc.; a rapid diving descent accompanied by a continued gyration of the aeroplane; (*Austral.*) fortune, luck. **in a flat spin,** extremely agitated or confused. **to spin a yarn,** to tell a story. **to spin out,** to compose or tell (a yarn etc.) at great length; to prolong, to protract; to spend (time) in tedious discussion etc. **spin-bowling,** *n.* in cricket, a style of bowling in which the ball is delivered slowly with an imparted spin to make it bounce unpredictably. **spin-bowler,** *n.* **spin-drier,** *n.* a machine that dries washing to the point of being ready for ironing by forcing out the water by centrifugal force. **spin-dry,** *v.t.* **spin-off,** *n.* a by-product, something derived from an existing idea or product. **spinner,** *n.* one who spins; a machine for spinning thread; one who shapes things in a lathe; a spider, a spinneret; (*Cricket*) a ball bowled with a sharp spin; a spin-bowler; a fishing lure designed to revolve in the water; (*Austral.*) the man who tosses the coin in two-up. **spinneret,** *n.* the spinning organ of a spider through which the silk issues; the orifice through which liquid cellulose is projected to form the threads of rayon or artificial silk. **spinnery,** *n.* a spinning-mill. **spinning,** *n.* †**spinning-house,** *n.* a house of correction in which women of loose character were obliged to spin, beat hemp etc. **spinning-jenny,** *n.* a mechanism invented by Hargreaves in 1767 for spinning several strands at once. **spinning-mill,** *n.* a factory where spinning is carried on. **spinning-wheel,** *n.* a wheel driven by the foot or hand, formerly used for spinning wool, cotton, or flax. [OE *spinnan* (cp. Dut. and G *spinnen*, Icel. and Swed. *spinna*), cogn. with SPAN[1]]

spinabifida SPINE.

spinach, *n.* an annual herb of the genus *Spinacia*, esp. *S. oleracea*, with succulent leaves cooked as food; other herbs similarly used. **spinach-beet,** *n.* a variety of beet of which the leaves are eaten as spinach. **spinaceous,** *a.* [OF *espinache*, *espinage*, Sp. *espinaca*, Arab. *aspanātch*, prob. from Pers.]

spinal SPINE.

spindle, *n.* a pin or rod in a spinning-wheel for twisting and winding the thread; a rod used for the same purpose in hand-spinning; a pin bearing the bobbin in a spinning-machine; a rod, axis, or arbor which revolves or on which anything revolves; a spindle-shaped structure formed in a cell in mitosis; a slender object or person. *v.i.* to grow into a long slender stalk, shape etc. **spindle-legged, -shanked,** *a.* having long, thin legs. **spindle-legs, -shanks,** *n.pl.* **spindle-shaped,** *a.* tapering from the middle towards both ends, fusiform. **spindle-tree,** *n.* a shrub or small tree, *Euonymus europaeus*, the hard wood of which is used for spindles, pins, skewers etc. **spindle-whorl,** *n.* a small perforated disc, usu. of baked clay, formerly used to weight a spindle. **spindly,** *a.* tall and thin; elongated. [A-S *spinl*, from *spinnan*, to SPIN]

spindrift, *n.* fine spray blown up from the surface of water. [var. of *spoon-drift*, (L *spūma*, loom, DRIFT)]

spine, *n.* the spinal column; a sharp, stiff woody process; a sharp ridge, projection, out-growth etc.; the back of a book, usu. bearing the title and the author's name. **spina bifida,** *n.* a congenital condition in which malformation of the spine causes the meninges to protrude, producing enlargement of the head and paralysis of the lower body. **spinal,** *a.* pertaining to the spine. **spinal canal,** *n.* a passage that contains the spinal cord. **spinal column,** *n.* the interconnected series of vertebrae in the skeleton which runs the length of the trunk and encloses the spinal cord. **spinal cord,** *n.* a cylindrical structure of nerve-fibres and cells within the vertebral canal and forming part of the central nervous system. **spine-chiller,** *n.* a book, film, event etc. that causes terror. **spine-chilling,** *a.* **spined,** *a.* **spineless,** *a.* without a spine; of weak character, lacking decision. **spinescent,** *a.* (*Bot.*) tending to be spinous; spinous, thorny. **spinescence,** *n.* **spiniferous**, **spinigerous**, *a.* **spinoid**, *a.* **spinose**, **spinous,** *a.* **spinosity**, *n.* **spiny,** *a.* **spininess,** *n.* [OF *espine* (F *épine*), L *spīna*, thorn, backbone]

spinel, *n.* a vitreous aluminate of magnesium, of various colours, crystallizing isometrically; other minerals of similar structure. [OF *espinel*, dim. of *espine*, prec.]

spinet, *n.* an obsolete musical instrument, similar in construction to but smaller than the harpsichord. [MF *espinette*, It. *spinetta*, perh. from Giovanni *Spinetti*, fl. 1503, supposed inventor]

spini- *comb. form.* pertaining to the spine.

spinicerebrate, *a.* having a brain and spinal cord.

spiniferous etc. SPINE.

spinifex, *n.* a coarse, spiny Australian grass growing in the sandhills etc. of the Australian steppes and often covering enormous areas of ground. [L *spīna*, SPINE, *-fex*, maker, from *facere*, to make]

spink, *n.* (*dial.*) a finch, esp. the chaffinch. [prob. imit. of cry; cp. Gr. *spingos*, from *spizein*, to chirp]

spinnaker, *n.* a large jib-shaped sail carried opposite the mainsail on the mainmast of a racing-yacht. [per. from *Sphinx*, name of a yacht]

spinner, spinneret SPIN.

spinney, *n.* a small wood with undergrowth, a copse. [OF *espinei*, *espinoye* (F *épinaie*), L *spīnētum*, from *spīna*, thorn, SPINE]

spinning-house, jenny, -mill etc. SPIN.

spinode, *n.* a stationary point on a curve, a cusp.

spinoid, spinose etc. SPINE.

Spinoza, *n.* **Benedict** or **Baruch** (1632–77), Dutch philosopher who believed in a rationalistic pantheism that owed much to Descartes' mathematical appreciation of the universe. Mind and matter are two modes of an infinite substance which he called God or Nature, good and evil being relative. He was a determinist, believing that human action was motivated by self-preservation. **Spinozism**, *n.* the monistic system of Spinoza. **Spinozist,** *n.* **Spinozistic**, *a.*

spinster, *n.* an unmarried woman. **spinsterhood**, *n.* **spinsterish,** *a.* [SPIN, -STER]

spinthariscope, *n.* an instrument for showing the rays emitted by radium by the scintillations caused by their impact against a fluorescent screen. **spinthariscopic**, *a.* [Gr. *spintharis*, spark]

†**spinthere,** *n.* (*Min.*) sphene. [F *spinthère*, Gr. *spinthēr*]

spinule, *n.* a minute spine. **spinuliferous,** *a.* **spinulose**, **-lous,** *a.* [L *spīnula*, dim. of *spīna*, SPINE]

spiny SPINE.

spiracle, *n.* a breathing-hole, a vent-hole for lava etc. **spiracular**, **-late**, **spiraculiform**, *a.* [F, from L *spīrāculum*, from *spīrāre*, to breathe]

spiraea, *n.* a flowering plant belonging to a genus of Rosaceae including the meadow-sweet. [L, from Gr. *speiraia*, meadow-sweet, from *speira*, SPIRE[2]]

spiral, *a.* forming a spire, spiral, or coil; continually winding about and receding from a centre; continually winding, as the thread of a screw. *n.* a spiral curve, formation, spring, or other object; a plane curve formed by a point revolving round a central point while continuously advancing on or receding from it; a helix; a continuous upward or downward movement, e.g. of prices; flight in a spiral motion. **spiral galaxy,** *n.* a galaxy comprising an ellipsoidal nucleus around which two arms revolve and spiral outwards. **spirality,** *n.* **spirally,** *adv.* **spiraled,** *a.* [F, from L *spīrālis, from spīra,* SPIRE[2]]

spirant, *n.* a fricative consonant. *a.* fricative. [L *spirans -ntem*, pres.p. of *spīrāre*, to breathe]

spire[1], *n.* a tapering, conical, or pyramidal structure, esp. the tapering portion of a steeple; a stalk of grass, the tapering part of a tree above the point where branching begins. *v.i.* to shoot up like a spire. *v.t.* to furnish with a spire or spires. **spiry,** *a.* [OE *spīr*, cp. Dut. and G *Spier*, Dan. *spire,* Swed. *spira*]

spire[2], *n.* a spiral, a coil; a single turn in this, a whorl, a twist. [F, from L *spīra*, Gr. *speira* coil]

spirifer, *n.* an extinct genus of brachiopods with spiral appendages. **spiriferous,** *a.* [L *spīra*, SPIRE[2], *-fer*, bearing]

spirillum, *n.* (*pl.* **-lla**) a bacterium of a genus, *Spirillum*, of bacteria having a spiral structure. **spirillar, spirilliform,** *a.* [dim. of L *spīra*, SPIRE[2]]

spirit, *n.* the immaterial part of a person, the soul; this as not connected with a physical body, a disembodied soul, a ghost; an incorporeal or supernatural being, a sprite, an elf, a fairy; a person considered with regard to his or her peculiar qualities of mind, temper, etc.; a person of great mental or moral force; vigour of mind or intellect; vivacity, energy, ardour, enthusiasm; temper, disposition; (*often pl.*) mental attitude, mood, humour; real meaning or intent; actuating principle, pervading influence, peculiar quality or tendency; (*usu. pl.*) distilled alcoholic liquors, as brandy, whisky etc.; a solution (of a volatile principle) in alcohol. *v.t.* to animate, to inspirit; to convey (away, off etc.) secretly and rapidly. **spirit, spirits of wine,** pure alcohol. **the Spirit, the Holy Spirit,** the Third Person of the Trinity. **spirit-duck,** *n.* the buffle-head and other ducks that dive with striking rapidity. **spirit-lamp,** *n.* a lamp burning methylated or other spirit. **spirit-level,** *n.* an instrument used for determining the horizontal by an air-bubble in a tube containing alcohol. **spirit-rapper,** *n.* one professing to communicate with spirits by means of raps on a table etc. **spirit-rapping,** *n.* **spirit room,** *n.* the paymaster's store-room, formerly for spirituous liquors. **spirited,** *a.* full of spirit, fire, or life, animated, lively, courageous; (*in comb.*), having a particular mental attitude, as *high-spirited.* **spiritedly,** *adv.* **spiritedness,** *n.* †**spiritful,** *a.* **spiritism** SPIRITUALISM. **spiritist** SPIRITUALIST. **spiritless,** *a.* **spiritlessly,** *adv.* **spiritlessness,** *n.* **spiritoso,** *adv.* (*Mus.*) in a spirited manner. †**spiritous,** *a.* refined, pure; ardent, active; spirituous. †**spiritousness,** *n.* **spiritual,** *a.* pertaining to or consisting of spirit; immaterial, incorporeal; pertaining to the soul or the inner nature; derived from or pertaining to God, pure, holy, sacred, divine, inspired; pertaining to sacred things, not lay or temporal. *n.* a type of hymn sung by Negroes of the southern US. **spirituality,** *n.* immateriality, incorporeity; the quality of being spiritual or unworldly; that which belongs to the church, or to an ecclesiastic on account of a spiritual office. **spiritualism,** *n.* a system of professed communication with departed spirits, chiefly through persons called mediums; (*Phil.*) the doctrine that the spirit exists as distinct from matter or as the only reality, opp. to materialism. **spiritualist,** *n.* **spiritualistic,** *a.* **spiritualize, -ise,** *v.t.* **spiritualization, -isation,** *n.* **spiritualizer, -iser,** *n.* **spiritually,** *adv.* **spiritualness,** *n.* **spirituelle,** *a.* esp. of women, characterized by refinement, grace, or delicacy of mind. **spirituous,** *a.* containing spirit, alcoholic, distilled as distinguished from fermented. **spirituousness,** *n.* **spiritus,** *n.* (*Gr. Gram.*) a breathing. **spiritus asper,** *n.* a rough breathing or aspirate, in Greek marked (ʽ). **spiritus lenis,** *n.* a smooth breathing, in Greek (ʼ), denoting the absence of an aspirate. [OF *espirit* (F *esprit*), L *spīritum*, nom. *-tus*, from *spīrāre*, to breathe]

spirket[1], *n.* (*dial.*) a stout hooked peg, esp. for hanging harness on. [E Anglian, etym. doubtful]

spirket[2], *n.* a space forward or aft between floortimbers of a ship. **spirketing,** *n.* the inside planking between the top of the water-ways and the port-sills. [etym. unknown]

spiro-[1], *comb. form.* pertaining to a coil. [Gr. *speira*, a coil]

spiro-[2], *comb. form.* pertaining to breathing. [L *spīro*, I breathe]

Spirochaeta, *n.* a genus of spiral-shaped bacteria which includes the causative agents of syphilis, relapsing fever, and epidemic jaundice.

spirograph, *n.* an instrument for recording the movement in breathing.

spirometer, *n.* an instrument for measuring the capacity of the lungs. **spirometric,** *a.* **spirometry,** *n.*

spirophore, *n.* an instrument for inducing respiration when animation is suspended.

spiroscope, *n.* a spirometer.

spirt, SPURT[1,2].

Spirula, *n.* a genus of tropical cephalopods having a flat spiral shell. [dim. of L *spīra* SPIRE[2]]

spiry SPIRE[1].

†**spissated,** *a.* thickened, inspissated. †**spissitude,** *n.* [L *spissātus* p.p. of *spissātus*, p.p. of *spissāre*, from *spissus*, thick, compact]

spit[1], *n.* a long pointed rod on which meat for roasting is rotated before a fire; a point of land or a narrow shoal extending into the sea; a spade; a spadeful. *v.t.* (*past*, *p.p.* **spitted**) to fix (meat) upon a spit; to pierce, to transfix. [OE *spitu*, cp. Dut. *spit*, G *Spiess*, Dan. *spīd*, Swed. *spētt*]

spit[2], *v.t.* (*pres. p.* **spitting,** *past*, *p.p.* **spat,**, †**spit**) to eject (saliva etc.) from the mouth; to utter in a violent or spiteful way. *v.i.* to eject saliva from the mouth; of an angry cat, to make a spitting noise; of rain, to drizzle. *n.* spittle, saliva; spitting; the spawn of certain insects; likeness, counterpart. **spit and polish,** (*coll.*) (obsessive) cleanliness, attention to details, as in the army. **to spit it out,** (*coll.*) to speak, tell immediately. **spitfire,** *n.* an irascible person. **spitter,** *n.* **spitting,** *n.* **spitting image,** *n.* (*coll.*) an exact likeness, one who or that which resembles another. **spittle[1],** *n.* saliva, esp. ejected from the mouth. **spittoon,** *n.* a receptacle for spittle. [OE *spittan*, cogn. with *spætan*, and prob. with Icel. *spyta*, Dan. *spytte*, Swed. *spotta* rel. to SPOUT]

spitch-cock, *v.t.* to split and broil (an eel etc.). *n.* an eel split and broiled. [perh. from MHG *spiz*, SPIT[1], G *kochen*, to cook]

spite, *n.* ill will, malice, malevolence; rancour, a grudge, *v.t.* to thwart maliciously; to vex or annoy. **in spite of, spite of,** notwithstanding. **spiteful,** *a.* **spitefully,** *adv.* **spitefulness,** *n.* [short for DESPITE]

spitfire SPIT[2].

Spitsbergen, *n.* the main island in the Norwegian archipelago of SVALBARD.

spitter, spittle[1] SPIT[2].

†**spittle[2]** SPITAL.

spittoon SPIT[2].

Spitz, *n.* **Mark Andrew** (1950–), US swimmer. He won a record seven gold medals at the 1972 Olympic Games, all in world record times.

spitz, *n.* a sharp-muzzled breed of dog, called also *Pomeranian*. [G]

spiv, *n.* a hanger-on in dubious circles; a man cheaply over-dressed without apparent occupation; one who dresses flashily; a petty black-market dealer. **spivvy,** *a.* [etym. unknown]

splanchnic, *a.* pertaining to the bowels. [Gr. *splanchnikos*, from *splanchna*, entrails]

splanchno-, *comb. form.* pertaining to the bowels or viscera. [see SPLANCHNIC]

splanchnography, *n.* descriptive splanchnology.

splanchnology, *n.* the branch of medical science dealing with the viscera.

splanchnoskeleton, *n.* the skeletal parts connected with the sense organs or viscera.

splanchnotomy, *n.* dissection of the viscera.
splash, *v.t.* to bespatter with water, mud etc.; to dash (liquid etc., about, over, etc.); to make (one's way) thus; to spend recklessly; to display prominently in a newspaper. *v.i.* to dash water or other liquid about; to be dashed about in drops, to dabble, to plunge; to move or to make one's way (along etc.) thus. *n.* the act of splashing; water or mud splashed about; a noise as of splashing; a spot or patch of liquid, colour etc.; a vivid display; a dash; a small amount of soda-water etc. mixed with an alcoholic drink. **to make a splash,** (*sl.*) to make a sensation, display, etc. **splash-board,** *n.* a guard in front of a vehicle to protect the occupants from mud. **splashdown,** *n.* the landing of a spacecraft on the ocean. **splash down,** *v.i.* **splasher** *n.* one who or that which splashes; a guard over the wheels of locomotives; a splash-board; a screen hung behind a wash-stand to keep splashes off the wall. **splashy** *a.* [*s*-, F *es*-, EX-, PLASH[2]]
splat[1], *n.* the slapping sound made by a soft or wet object striking a surface. [onomat.]
splat[2], *n.* a flat strip of wood forming the central part of a chair back. [rel. to ME *splātan*, to split]
splatter, *v.i.* to spatter; to make a continuous splash or splashing noise. *v.t.* to utter thus, to sputter. *n.* a spatter; a splash. **splatterdash,** *n.* a stir, a commotion; (*pl.*) spatterdashes.
splay, *v.t.* to form (a window-opening etc.) with oblique sides; to spread out. *n.* an oblique surface, side, or widening of a window etc. *a.* turned outwards. **splay-foot,** *n.* a broad, flat foot turned outwards. **splay-footed,** *a.* **splay-mouth,** *n.* a wide, distorted mouth. **splay-mouthed,** *a.* [var. of DISPLAY]
spleen, *n.* a soft vascular organ situated to the left of the stomach in most vertebrates which produces lymphocytes, antibodies, and filters the blood; spitefulness, ill temper; low spirits, melancholy. **spleen-wort,** *n.* a fern of the genus *Asplenium*, formerly supposed to be a specific for spleen. **spleenful, spleenish, spleeny,** *a.* **spleenfully, spleenishly,** *adv.* **spleenless**, *a.* [L and Gr. *splēn*]
splen-, *comb. form.* pertaining to the spleen. [Gr. *splēn*, SPLEEN]
splenalgia, *n.* pain in or near the spleen. **splenalgic**, *a.* [Gr. *algos*, pain]
splendid, *a.* magnificent, gorgeous, sumptuous; glorious, illustrious; brilliant, lustrous, dazzling; fine, excellent, first-rate. **splendent,** *a.* shining, lustrous, brilliant; very conspicuous; splendid. **splendidly,** *adv.* **splendiferous**, *a.* (*facet.*) splendid. †**splendorous,** *a.* **splendour,** *n.* [L *splendidus*, from *splendēre*, to shine]
splenetic, *a.* of or pertaining to the spleen; affected with spleen; peevish, ill-tempered. *n.* a person affected with spleen; a medicine for disease of the spleen. **splenetically,** *adv.* [late L *splēnēticus*, from L *splēn*, SPLEEN]
splenial SPLENIUS.
splenic, *a.* pertaining to or affecting the spleen. **splenitis**, inflammation of the spleen. **splenitic**, *a.* [L *splēnicus*, Gr. *splēnikos*, from *splēn*, SPLEEN]
splenius, *n.* a muscle extending in two parts on either side of the neck serving to bend the head backwards. **splenial,** *a.* of or pertaining to this; splint-like. [Gr. *splēnion*, bandage]
splenization, -isation, *n.* conversion of a portion of the lung into tissue resembling the spleen. [F *splénisation*]
splenology, *n.* scientific study of the spleen. **splenological**, *a.*
splenotomy, *n.* the dissection of or an incision into the spleen.
splent, SPLINT.
spleuchan, *n.* a small bag, pouch, or purse, esp. a tobacco-pouch. [Gael. *spliùchan*]
splice, *v.t.* to unite (two ropes etc.) by interweaving the strands of the ends; to unite (timbers etc.) by bevelling, overlapping, and fitting the ends together; (*coll.*) to unite in marriage. *n.* a union of ropes, timbers etc., by splicing; the point of juncture between two pieces of film; the joint on the handle of a cricket bat which fits into the blade. **to splice the main-brace** BRACE. **splicer,** *n.* [Dut. *splitsen*, to splice, from *splijten*, to SPLIT (cp. Dan. *splidse*, Swed. *splissa*, G *splissen*, to splice)]
spline, *n.* a flexible strip of wood or rubber used in laying down large curves in mechanical drawing; a key fitting into a slot in a shaft and wheel to make these revolve together; the slot itself. [etym. doubtful]
splint, *n.* a thin piece of wood or other material used to keep the parts of a broken bone together; a thin strip of wood used in basketmaking etc.; a splint-bone; a callous tumour on the splint-bone of a horse. *v.t.* to secure or support with splints. **splint-bone,** *n.* one of two small bones extending from the knee to the fetlock in the horse; a fibula. **splint coal,** *n.* a slaty variety of cannel coal. [MDut. *splinte*, cp. Dut., G, Dan., Swed., and Norw. *splint*]
splinter, *n.* a thin piece broken, split, or shivered off. *v.t.* to split, shiver, or rend into splinters; to support with splinters. *v.i.* to split or shiver into splinters. **splintery,** *a.* **splinter-bar,** *n.* a cross-bar in front of a horse-drawn vehicle to which the traces are attached or which supports the springs. **splinter-bone,** *n.* the splint-bone. **splinter group, party,** *n.* a small group that has broken away from its parent political etc. organization. **splinter-proof,** *a.* proof against the splinters of bursting shells or bombs. [MDut., rel. to prec.]
Split, *n.* (Italian **Spalato**) port in Yugoslavia, on the Adriatic; population (1981) 236,000. Industries include engineering, cement, and textiles, and it is also a tourist resort.
split, *v.t.* (*pres. p.* **splitting,** past, *p.p.* **split**) to break, cleave, tear, or divide, esp. longitudinally or with the grain; to divide into two or more parts, thicknesses etc.; to divide into opposed parties; to divide (one's vote or votes) between different candidates; to cause to ache or throb. *v.i.* to be broken or divided, esp. longitudinally or with the grain; to break up, to go to pieces; to divide into opposed parties; (*sl.*) to betray the secrets of, to inform (on); (*coll.*) to burst with laughter; (*sl.*) to depart. *n.* the act or result of splitting; a crack, rent, or fissure; a separation into opposed parties, a rupture, a schism; something split, a split osier for basket-work, a single thickness of split hide etc.; one of the strips or splints forming the reed of a loom; a dessert dish of sliced fruit (e.g. banana) and ice cream etc. (*pl.*) an acrobat"s feat of sitting down with the legs stretched out right and left; (*sl.*) a half bottle of soda water; a half glass of liquor. *a.* having been split; fractured; having splits. **to split hairs** HAIR. **to split one's sides,** to laugh heartily. **to split the difference,** to compromise by showing the average of two amounts. **to split the infinitive,** to insert a word between *to* and the verb, as *to completely defeat*. **split-level,** *a.* of a house, etc., divided into more than one level. **split pea,** *n.* a dried pea split in half and used in soups etc. **split personality,** *n.* a personality comprising two or more dissociated groups of attitudes and behaviour. **split pin,** *n.* a pin with a divided end which is splayed apart to keep the pin in place. **split ring,** *n.* a metal ring so constructed that keys can be put on it or taken off. **split screen,** *n.* a cinematic technique in which different images are displayed simultaneously on separate sections of the screen. **split-screen,** *a.* **split second,** *n.* an instant, a fraction of a second. **split-second,** *a.* **split shift,** *n.* a work period divided into two parts separated by a long interval. **splitter,** *n.* one who splits. **splitting,** *a.* of a headache, acute, severe. [M.Dut. *splitten*, rel. to Dut. *splijten*, G *spleissen*]
splodge, splotch, *n.* a daub, a blotch, an irregular stain. **splodgy, splotchy,** *a.* [perh. onomat.]
splore, *n.* a noisy frolic, a carousal, a spree. [etym. doubtful]
splosh, (*coll.*) SPLASH.
splotch, splotchy SPLODGE.
splurge, *v.i.* to show off, to make a blustering effort; to spend a lot of money (on). *n.* the act or an instance of splurging. [N Am., onomat.]

splutter, *v.t., v.i.* to sputter. *n.* a sputter, a noise, a fuss. **splutterer,** *n.* **spluttery,** *a.* [imit.]

Spock, *n.* **Benjamin McLane** (1903–), US paediatrician and writer on child care. His *Common Sense Book of Baby and Child Care* (1946) urged less rigidity in bringing up children than had been advised by previous generations of writers on the subject, but was misunderstood as advocating complete permissiveness.

Spode, *n.* **Josiah** (1754–1827), English potter, son of Josiah Spode the elder (an apprentice of Thomas Whieldon who started his own works at Stoke-on-Trent 1770), and his successor in the new firm in 1797. He developed bone porcelain (bone ash, china stone, and china clay) around 1800, which was produced at all English factories in the 19th century, and became potter to King George III in 1806.

spode, *n.* porcelain made by the potter Josiah Spode. **spode-ware,** *n.*

†**spodium,** *n.* fine powder obtained from calcined bone and other substances. †**spodomancy,** *n.* divination by ashes. †**spodomantic,** *a.* [L, from Gr. *spodion*, dim. of *spodos*, ashes, dust]

spodumene, *n.* a monoclinic silicate of aluminium and lithium. [F *spodumène*, G *spodumen*, Gr. *spodoumenos*, p.p. of *spodousthai*, to be turned to ashes, from *spodos*, ash]

spoffish, *a.* (*dated sl.*) fussy, officious. **spoffy,** *a.* [etym. doubtful]

spoil, *v.t.* (*past* & *p.p.* **spoilt, spoiled**) to mar, to vitiate, to impair the goodness, usefulness etc., of; to impair the character of by over-indulgence; †to plunder, to deprive (of) by violence. *v.i.* of perishable food, to decay, to deteriorate through keeping; to be eager or over-ripe (for a fight). *n.* (*usu. pl. or collect.*) plunder, booty; offices, honours, or emoluments acquired as the result of a party victory, esp. in the US; waste material obtaining in mining, quarrying, excavating etc.; pillage, spoliation, rapine. **spoil-five,** *n.* a card game in which unless a player makes three out of five possible tricks the hand is 'spoiled'. **spoilsman,** *n.* (*N Am.*) a politician working for a share of the spoils; a supporter of the spoils system. **spoilsport,** *n.* a person who interferes with another's pleasure. **spoilage,** *n.* an amount wasted or spoiled; the act of spoiling or being spoiled. **spoiler,** *n.* one who spoils; an aerodynamic device fitted to an aircraft wing to increase drag and reduce lift; a similar device fitted to the front or rear of a motor vehicle to maintain stability at high speeds. †**spoilful,** *a.* rapacious. [OF *espoiller*, L *spoliāre*, from *spolium*, a skin stripped off, (*in pl.*) booty]

spoke[1], *n.* one of the members connecting the hub with the rim of a wheel; a rung of a ladder; a stick for preventing a wheel from turning in descending a hill; one of the radial handles of a steering-wheel. *v.t.* to furnish with spokes; to check (a wheel) with a spoke. **to put a spoke in one's wheel,** to thwart someone. **spokeshave,** *n.* a plane with a handle at each end for dressing spokes, curved work etc. [OE *spāca* (cp. Dut. *speek*, G *Speiche*), rel. to SPIKE]

spoke[2],, *past*, **spoken,** *p.p.* SPEAK.

spokesman, spokeswoman, spokesperson, *n.* one who speaks for another or others.

spole SPOOL.

spoliation, *n.* robbery, pillage, the act or practice of plundering, esp. of neutral commerce, in time of war; (*Law.*) destruction, mutiliation, or alteration of a document to prevent its use as evidence; taking the emoluments of a benefice under an illegal title. †**spoliate,** *v.t.* **spoliator,** *n.* **spoliatory,** *a.*

spondee, *n.* a metrical foot of two long syllables. **spondaic,** *a.* [L *spondēus*, Gr. *spondeios*, from *spondai*, a solemn treaty, pl. of *spondē*, libation]

spondulics, *n.pl.* (*sl.*) money, cash. [etym. unknown]

spondyl, -dyle, *n.* a vertebra. [F *spondyle*, L *spondylus*, Gr. *sphondulos*]

spondylitis, *n.* inflammation of the vertebrae.

spondyl(o), *comb. form.* pertaining to vertebra(e).

sponge, *n.* a marine animal with pores in the body-wall; the skeleton or part of the skeleton of a sponge or colony of sponges, esp. of a soft, elastic kind used as an absorbent in bathing, cleansing etc.; any sponge-like substance or implement; dough for baking before it is kneaded; sponge-cake; a kind of mop for cleaning a cannon-bore after a discharge; a parasite, a sponger. *v.t.* to wipe, wet, or cleanse with a sponge; to obliterate, to wipe (out) with or as with a sponge; to absorb, to take (up) with a sponge; to extort or obtain by parasitic means. *v.i.* to suck in, as a sponge; to live parasitically or by practising mean arts (on). **to throw up the sponge:** to acknowledge oneself beaten; to give up the contest (orig. of a boxer on the tossing of the sponge into the air by his second as token of defeat). **sponge bag,** *n.* a small waterproof bag for carrying toiletries. **sponge bath,** *n.* a cleansing of the body using a wet sponge or cloth, as for bedridden persons. **sponge-cake,** *n.* a light, spongy cake. **sponge cloth,** *n.* loosely-woven fabric with a wrinkled surface. **sponging-house,** *n.* a house where persons arrested for debt were lodged temporarily before being put in prison. **spongelet,** *n.* **spongeous, spongiform, spongious, spongoid,** *a.* **sponger,** *n.* one who or that which sponges; a mean parasite. **spongy,** *a.* **sponginess,** *n.* [OE, from L *spongia*, Gr. *spongia*, *-gos*, cogn. with FUNGUS]

spongio-, spongo- *comb. form.* pertaining to sponge(s) [see SPONGE]

spongiole, *n.* (*Bot.*) the spongy extremity of a radicle, a spongelet.

spongiopiline, *n.* a substitute for a poultice, made of sponge and fibre on a rubber backing. [Gr. *pilos*, felt, -INE]

spongology, *n.* the scientific study of sponges. **spongologist,** *n.*

sponsal, *a.* pertaining to marriage. [L *sponsālis*, from *sponsus*, SPOUSE]

sponsible, (*dial.*) RESPONSIBLE.

sponsion, *n.* the act of becoming surety for another; (*International Law*) an act or engagement on behalf of a state by an agent not specially authorized. [L *sponsio*, from *spondēre*, to promise, p.p. *sponsus*]

sponson, *n.* a projection from the sides of a vessel, as before and abaft a paddle-box, for a gun on a warship, or to support a bearing etc.; a device attached to the wings of a seaplane to give it steadiness when resting on the water. [etym. doubtful]

sponsor, *n.* a surety, one who undertakes to be responsible for another; a godfather or godmother; a person or firm that pays the costs of mounting a radio or TV programme in exchange for advertising time; a person or organization that provides esp. financial support for another person or group or for some activity; a person who promises to pay a sum of money usu. to charity, the amount of which is determined by the performance of an entrant in a fund-raising event; a member who introduces a bill into a legislative assembly. *v.t.* to act as a sponsor for. **sponsorial,** *a.* **sponsorship,** *n.* [L (*spons-*, see SPONSION, -OR)]

spontaneous, *a.* arising, occurring, done, or acting without external cause; not due to external constraint or suggestion, voluntary; not due to conscious volition or motive; instinctive, automatic, involuntary; self-originated, self-generated. **spontaneity, spontaneousness,** *n.* **spontaneously,** *adv.* [L *spontāneus*, from *sponte*, of one's own accord]

spontoon, *n.* a kind of half-pike or halberd borne by British infantry officers in the 18th cent. [F *sponton*, It. *spontone*, from *punto*, point]

spoof, *v.t.* to hoax, to fool; to parody. *n.* a deception, a hoax; a parody, humorous take-off (of a play, poem etc). [after a hoaxing game invented by Arthur Roberts, 1852–1933, British comedian]

spook, *n.* a ghost; (*chiefly N Am.*) a spy *v.t.* (*chiefly N Am.*) to startle or frighten. *v.i.* (*chiefly N Am.*) to become frightened. **spookish, spooky,** *a.* ghostly; frightening. [Dut., cp. G *Spuk*]

spool, *n.* a small cylinder for winding thread, photographic film etc., on; the central bar of an angler's reel;

a reel (of cotton etc.). *v.t.* to wind on a spool. [MDut. *spoele* (perh. through ONorth.F. *espole*), cp. Dut. *spoel*, G *Spule*]

†**spoom,** *v.i.* to sail fast, to scud. **spooming,** *a.* (*Keats*) spuming, foaming. [earlier *spoon*, etym. doubtful]

spoon, *n.* a domestic utensil consisting of a shallow bowl on a stem or handle, used for conveying liquids or liquid food to the mouth etc.; an implement or other thing shaped like a spoon, as an oar with the blade curved lengthwise, a golf-club with a lofted face, a spoon-bait etc. (*dated*) a silly fellow; a mawkish or foolishly demonstrative lover. *v.t.* to take (up etc.) with a spoon; (*Cricket etc.*) to hit a ball (usu. up) with little force. *v.i.* to fish with a spoon-bait; (*dated*) to indulge in demonstrative love-making. **spoon-bait,** *n.* a spoon-shaped piece of bright metal with hooks attached used as a revolving lure in fishing. **spoon-beak, -bill,** *n.* a bird with a broad, flat bill, esp. of the genus *Platalea*. **spoon-fed,** *a.* pampered; provided with information, opinions etc. in a ready-made form which precludes the need for independent thought or effort. **spoon-food, -meat, -victuals,** *n.* liquid food, food for infants. **spoon-net,** *n.* a small landing-net used by anglers. **spoonful,** *n.* (*pl.* **spoonfuls**). **spoony, spooney,** *a.* (*dated*) mawkishly amorous. **spoonily,** *adv.* **spooniness,** *n.* [OE *spōn*, chip, splinter (cp. Dut. *spaan*, G *Span*, Icel. *spānn*, *spōnn*), also Gr. *sphēn*, wedge)]

spoonerism, *n.* accidental or facetious transposition of the initial letters or syllables of words. e.g. 'I have in my breast a half-warmed fish.'. [Rev. W.A. *Spooner* (1844–1930), Warden of New College, Oxford]

spoor, *n.* the track of a wild animal. *v.i.* to follow a spoor. [Dut., cogn. with SPEER]

sporadic, †**-ical** *a.* separate, scattered, occurring here and there or irregularly. **sporadically,** *adv.* **sporadicalness,** *n.* [Gr. *sporadikos*, from *sporas -ados* from *speirein*, to sow]

sporan, SPORRAN.

sporange, sporangium, *n.* (*Bot.*) (*pl.* **-ges, -gia**) a spore-case. **sporangial,** *a.* **sporangiferous,** *a.* [Gr. *spora*, spore, *angeion*, vessel]

spore, *n.* the reproductive body in a cryptogam, usu. composed of a single cell not containing an embryo; a minute organic body that develops into a new individual, as in protozoa etc.; a germ. **sporation,** *n.* the formation of spores. [Gr. *spora* sowing, as SPORADIC]

spor(o)- *comb. form.* pertaining to spores. [Gr. *sporu*, spore]

sporocarp, *n.* a fructification containing spores or sporangia.

sporocyst, *n.* a cyst containing spores or an encysted organism giving rise to spores. **sporocystic,** *a.*

sporogenesis, *n.* spore formation.

sporophore, *n.* a spore-bearing branch, process etc.

sporophyte, *n.* the nonsexual phase in certain plants exhibiting alternation of generations. **sporophytic,** *a.*

sporosac, *n.* a sac-shaped gonophore in certain hydrozoans.

sporozoan, *n.* any of a group of spore-producing parasitic protozoans, that includes the malaria parasite.

sporran, *n.* a pouch, usu. covered with fur, hair etc., worn by Scottish Highlanders in front of the kilt. [Gael.]

sport, *n.* diversion, amusement; fun, jest, pleasantry; game, pastime, esp. athletic or outdoor pastime, as hunting, shooting, fishing, racing, running etc.; a sportsman; a good loser; (*Austral.*) a form of address used esp. between males; an animal or plant deviating remarkably from the normal type; (*pl.*) a meeting for outdoor games etc. *v.i.* to play, to divert oneself; to trifle, to jest, to make merry (with a person's feelings etc.); to vary remarkably from the normal type. *v.t.* to wear or display in an ostentatious manner. **to make sport of,** to jeer at, to ridicule. **sporter,** *n.* †**sportful,** *a.* †**sportfully,** *adv.* †**sportfulness,** *n.* **sporting,** *a.* relating to, used in, or fond of sports; calling for sportsmanship; involving a risk, as in sports competition. **sportingly,** *adv.* **sportive,** *a.* frolicsome, playful. **sportively,** *adv.* **sportiveness,** *n.* **sportless,** *a.* **sports,** *a.* of clothing etc., suitable for sports. **sports car,** *n.* a low usu. two-seater car built for high speed performance. **sportscast,** *n.* (*N Am.*) a broadcast of sports news. **sportscaster,** *n.* **sports jacket,** *n.* a casual jacket for men, usu. made of tweed. **sportsman,** *n.* one skilled in or devoted to sports, esp. hunting, shooting, fishing etc.; one who acts fairly towards opponents or who faces good or bad luck with equanimity. **sportsmanlike,** *a.* **sportsmanship,** *n.* **sports medicine,** *n.* the medical supervision of athletes in training and in competition and the treatment of their injuries. **sportswoman,** *n.* **sporty,** *a.* taking pleasure in sports; vulgar, showy; dissipated. [short for DISPORT]

sporule, *n.* a spore, esp. a small or secondary spore. **sporular,** *a.* **sporulation,** *n.* **sporuliferous,** *a.* [F, dim. of SPORE]

spot, *n.* a small mark or stain, a speck, a blot; a stain on character or reputation; a small part of a surface of distinctive colour or texture; a small extent of space; a particular place, a definite locality; a sea-fish, esp. the red-fish, marked with a spot; a breed of domestic pigeon; (*Billiards*) a mark near the top of a billiard-table on which the red ball is placed; a spot-stroke; (*coll.*) a small amount of anything; a spotlight; a place on a television or radio programme for an entertainer; an opportunity in the interval between programmes for advertisers; *v.t.* (*past, p.p.* **spotted**) to mark, stain, or discolour with a spot or spots; to sully, to blemish (one's reputation); (*coll.*) to pick out, to notice, to detect; to place on the spot at billiards. *v.i.* to become or be liable to be marked with spots. **in a spot,** in an awkward situation. **on the spot,** at once, without change of place; alert, wideawake; in danger or difficulty, in the immediate locality. **soft spot,** a sympathetic or affectionate feeling. **tight spot,** a dangerous or complicated situation. **to change one's spots,** to reform one's ways. **to knock spots off,** to outdo easily. **weak spot,** a flaw in one's character; a gap in a person's knowledge. **spot-ball,** *n.* (*Billiards*) a white ball marked with a black spot. **spot-barred,** *a.* (*Billiards*) denoting a game in which the spot-stroke is not allowed more than twice in succession. **spot-cash,** *n.* (*coll.*) money down. **spot check,** *n.* a random examination or check without prior warning. **spot-cotton** or **wheat,** *n.* cotton or wheat on the spot for immediate delivery. **spotlight,** *n.* an apparatus for throwing a concentrated beam of light on an actor on the stage; the patch of light thus thrown. **spot-on,** *a.* (*coll.*) absolutely accurate. **spot-stroke,** *n.* (*Billiards*) a winning-hazard off the red ball when on the spot. **spot-weld,** *v.t.* to join two pieces of metal with a circular weld. *n.* a weld of this type. **spotless,** *a.* **spotlessly,** *adv.* **spotlessness,** *n.* **spotted,** *a.* **spotted dick,** *n.* a steamed suet pudding with currants. **spotted fever,** *n.* cerebrospinal meningitis, characterized by spots on the skin. **spotted gum,** *n.* (*Austral.*) a eucalyptus tree, marked on the bark with spots. **spottedness,** *n.* **spotter,** *n.* observer trained to detect the approach of enemy aircraft; one whose hobby is taking note of the registration numbers of trains, aircraft etc. **spotty,** *a.* **spottiness,** *n.* [ME (cp. EFris. *spot*, MDut. *spotten*, Icel. *spotte*, Norw. *spott*) cogn. with SPOUT]

spouse, *n.* a husband or wife. **spousal,** *a.* pertaining to marriage; nuptial, matrimonial. †*n.* (*usu. pl.*) marriage, nuptials. **spouseless,** *a.* [ME *spuse*, OF *spus*, *spuse*, var. of *éspus* (F *époux*), L *sponsus*, p.p. of *spondēre*, to promise]

spout, *v.t.* to pour out or discharge with force or in large volume; to utter or recite in a declamatory manner. *v.i.* to pour out or issue forcibly or copiously; to declaim. *n.* a short pipe, tube, or channelled projection for carrying off water from a gutter, conducting liquid from a vessel, shooting things into a receptacle etc.; a shoot or lift in a pawnbroker's shop; a continuous stream, jet, or column of water etc.; a water-spout; a whale's spiracle or spout-hole. **up the spout,** (*sl.*) at the pawnbroker's, in pawn; ruined, failed; pregnant. **spouter,** *n.* **spoutless,** *a.* [ME *spouten* (cp. Dut. *spui-*

ten, Swed. *sputa*, *spruta*), prob. by-form of SPROUT]

sprack, *a.* (*dial.*) brisk, smart, alert, sprightly, spruce. [etym. doubtful; perh. from Icel. *spraekr*, *sparkr*, lively]

sprackle, *v.i.* (*Sc.*) to clamber, to climb with difficulty. [etym. doubtful]

sprag[1], *n.* a billet of wood, esp. a prop for the roof of a mine; a chock of wood for locking the wheel of a vehicle. *v.t.* (*past*, *p.p.* **spragged**) to support with sprags. [etym. doubtful]

sprag[2], *n.* (*dial*) a young salmon; a half-grown cod. [etym. doubtful]

sprain, *v.t.* to twist or wrench the muscles or ligaments of (a joint) so as to injure without dislocation. *n.* such a twist or wrench or the injury due to it. [OF *espreindre*, L *exprimere* (EX-, *premere* to PRESS[1]]

spraints, *n.pl.* the dung of an otter. [OF *espraintes*, as prec.]

sprang,, *past* SPRING.

sprat, *n.* a small food-fish, *Clupea sprattus*, of the herring tribe; applied to the young of the herring and to other small fish. *v.i.* (*past*, *p.p.* **spratted**) to fish for sprats. **spratter** *n.* [OE *sprott*, cp. Dut. *sprot*, also OE *sprot*, *sprota*, SPROUT]

sprattle, *v.i.* (*Sc.*) to scramble, to struggle. *n.* a scramble, a struggle. [cp. Swed. *sprattla*]

sprawl, *v.i.* to lie or stretch out the body and limbs in a careless or awkward posture; to straggle, to be spread out in an irregular or ungraceful form. *v.t.* to open out or deploy (troops) irregularly. **sprawler,** *n.* **sprawling, sprawly** *a.* [OE *sprewlian*, cp. Norw. *sprala*, Dan. *spraelle*]

spray[1], *n.* water or other liquid flying in small, fine drops; a perfume or other liquid applied in fine particles with an atomizer; an appliance for spraying. *v.t.* to throw or apply in the form of spray; to treat with a spray. **spray gun,** *n.* an appliance which sprays paint etc. **sprayer,** *n.* [cp. LG *sprei*, drizzle MDut. *sprayen*, G *sprühen,* to drizzle]

spray[2], *n.* a small branch or sprig, esp. with branchlets, leaves, flowers etc., used as a decoration; an ornament resembling a sprig of leaves, flowers etc. **sprayey**, *a.* [etym. doubtful]

spread, *v.t.* (*past*, *p.p.* **spread**) to extend in length and breadth by opening, unrolling, unfolding, flattening out etc.; to scatter, to diffuse; to disseminate, to publish; to cover the surface of; to display to the eye or mind. *v.i.* to be extended in length and breadth; to be scattered, diffused, or disseminated. *n.* the act of spreading; breadth, extent, compass, expansion; diffusion, dissemination; (*coll.*) a meal set out, a feast; two facing pages in a book, magazine etc. **spreadeagle,** *n.* (*Her.*) an eagle with wings and legs extended; a seaman lashed with outstretched limbs to the rigging for punishment. *v.t.* to fix (a person) for punishment thus; to cause to stand or lie with arms and legs stretched out. *v.i.* to stand or lie thus. *a.* bombastic; bombastically patriotic (with alln. to the eagle on coins); lying or standing with the arms and legs stretched out. **spreadsheet,** *n.* a computer program which can perform rapid calculations on figures displayed on a VDU in rows and columns, used for business accounting and financial planning. **spreader,** *n.* [OE *sprædan*, cp. Dut. *spreiden*, G. *spreiten*]

spreagh, *n.* (*Sc.*) a foray, a raid; plunder, booty, esp. stolen cattle. **spreaghery,** *adv.* [var. of obs. *spreath*, Gael. *spréidh*]

spree, *n.* a lively frolic, esp. with drinking; a bout of extravagance or excess. *v.i.* to go on the sprèe. [etym. doubtful]

†**sprent,** *a.* sprinkled, besprent (with). [p.p. of obs. *sprenge*, OE *sprengan*, causal of *springan*, to SPRING]

sprig, *n.* a small branch, twig, or shoot; an ornament resembling this; a small headless nail or brad; an offshoot; (*derog.*) a scion, a young fellow. *v.t.* (*past, p.p,* **sprigged**) to ornament with sprigs; to drive small brads into. **spriggy,** *a.* [etym. doubtful]

sprightly, *a.* lively, spirited, gay, vivacious. †**spright** SPRITE. †**sprightful,** *a.* †**sprightfully,** *adv.* †**sprightless,** *a.* †**sprightliness,** *n.*

spring, *v.i.* (*past* **sprang**, *p.p.* **sprung**) to leap, to bound, to jump; to move suddenly by or as by the action of a spring; to rise, to come (up) from or as from a source, to arise, to originate, to appear, esp unexpectedly; of wood etc., to warp, to split. *v.t.* to cause to move, fly, act etc., suddenly by or as by releasing a spring; (*sl.*) to bring about the escape from prison of; to cause to explode; to cause (timber etc.) to warp, crack, or become loose; of a vessel, to develop (a leak) thus. *n.* a leap; a backward movement as from release from tension, a recoil, a rebound; the starting of a plank, seam, leak etc.; elastic force; an elastic body or structure, usu. of bent or coiled metal used to prevent jar, to convey motive power in a watch etc.; a source of energy, a cause of action, a motive; a natural issue of water from the earth, a fountain; a source, an origin; the first of the four seasons of the year, that preceding summer roughly March, April, and May in the N hemisphere; the early part, youth. **spring balance,** *n.* a balance weighing objects by the tension of a spring. **spring-beam,** *n.* a beam of wide span without intermediate support; an elastic bar used as a spring in a tilt-hammer, jig-saw etc. **spring-bed, -mattress,** *n.* one in which the mattress consists of a series of spiral springs set in a frame. **springboard,** *n.* a springy board giving impetus in leaping, diving etc.; anything that provides a starting point or initial impetus. **spring-carriage, -cart,** *n.* one mounted on springs. **spring chicken,** *n.* (*N Am.*) a tender young chicken, usu. from 2 to 10 months old; (*coll.*) a young, active, inexperienced person. **spring-clean,** *v.t.* to clean (a house) thoroughly in preparation for summer. **spring clean,** *n.* **spring-gun,** *n.* a gun fired by the stumbling of a trespasser etc., against a wire controlling its trigger. **spring-halt,** *n.* a convulsive movement of a horse's hind legs in walking. **spring loaded,** *a.* having or secured by means of a spring. **spring lock,** *n.* a lock with a spring-loaded bolt. **spring onion,** *n.* an onion with a tiny thin-skinned bulb and long leaves, eaten in salads. **spring roll,** *n.* a Chinese dish comprising a thin pancake filled with a savoury mixture and deep fried. **springtail,** *n.* an insect having bristles on its under side enabling it to leap. **spring tide,** *n.* a high tide occurring a day or two after the new or the full moon; (*poet.*) springtime. **springtime,** *n.* the season of spring. **spring washer,** *n.* a washer consisting of one or two coils of spiral-spring form, used to prevent nuts from becoming slack with vibration. **springer,** *n.* one who or that which springs; a spaniel used to rouse game; the springbok; the grampus; (*Arch.*) the part or stone where the curve of an arch begins; the rib of a groined roof; the lowest stone of a gable-coping. **springless**, *a.* **springlet**, *n.* **springlike,** *a.* **springy,** *a.* elastic, like a spring. **springiness,** *n.* [OE *springan*, *sprincan*, cp. Dut. and G *springen*, Icel. *springa*, to burst]

†**springal,** *n.* a youth. [prec., F *-ald*, OHG *-wald*, cp. HERALD]

springbok, *n.* a southern African gazelle, *Antilope euchore*, that leaps in play and when alarmed; (**Springbok**) a sportsman or sportswoman representing South Africa in international competitions. [Afrik. (SPRING, bok, BUCK[1])] .

springe, *n.* a noose, a snare, usu. for small game. *v.t.* to catch in this. [ME, var. of SPRING]

springer, springless, springy etc. SPRING.

Springsteen, *n.* **Bruce** (1949–), US rock singer, songwriter, and guitarist, born in New Jersey. His music combines melodies in traditional rock idiom and reflective lyrics of working-class life on albums such as *Born to Run* (1975) and *Born in the USA* (1984) and in concerts with the E Street Band.

sprinkle, *v.t., v.i.* to scatter in small drops or particles. *n.* a sprinkling, a light shower. **sprinkler,** *n.* that which sprinkles. **sprinkler system,** *n.* a system of fire-extinction in which a sudden rise in temperature triggers the release of water from overhead nozzles. **sprinkling,** *n.* a small quantity or number. [formerly *sprenkle*, prob. freq. from OE *sprengan*, causal of *springan*, to SPRING]

sprint, *v.i.* to run at top speed. *n.* a short burst of running, cycling etc. at top speed; a race run or cycled thus. **sprint-race,** *n.* **sprint-runner,** *n.* **sprinter,** *n.* [prob. cogn. with SPURT2]

sprit, *n.* a small spar set diagonally from the mast to the top outer corner of a sail. **spritsail,** *n.* [OE *sprēot*, pole, cogn. with SPROUT]

sprite, *n.* a fairy, an elf; a computer generated display shape that can be manipulated by a programmer to create fast and complex animation sequences. [ME, as SPIRIT]

spritely etc. SPRIGHTLY.

spritzer, *n.* a drink made from white wine and soda water. [G *spritzen*, to splash]

sprocket, *n.* one of a set of teeth on a wheel etc., engaging with the links of a chain; a sprocket-wheel; a wheel with teeth for advancing film in a camera or projector. **sprocket-wheel,** *n.* a wheel set with sprockets. [etym. doubtful]

sprod, *n.* (*dial.*) a salmon in its second year. [etym. doubtful]

sprout, *v.i.* to shoot forth, to develop shoots, to germinate; to grow, like the shoots of plants. *v.t.* to cause to put forth sprouts or to grow. *n.* a new shoot on a plant; (*pl.*) brussels sprouts. [OE *sprūtan*, cp. Dut. *spruiten*, G *spriessen*, cogn. with SPOUT and SPURT2]

spruce1, *a.* neat, trim, smart. *v.t.* to smarten (*usu. up*). **sprucely,** *adv.* **spruceness,** *n.* [prob. from OF *Pruce*, G *Preussen*, Prussia (orig. applied to Prussian leather)]

spruce2, *n.* Spruce-fir. **spruce-beer,** *n.* a fermented liquor made from the leaves and small branches of the spruce-fir. **spruce-fir,** *n.* a pine of the genus *Picea*. [G *Sprossen*, sprouts (in *Sprossen-fichte*, sprouts-fir, or fir from which sprouts-beer was brewed), assim. to prec.]

sprue1, *n.* a hole or channel through which molten metal or plastic is poured into a mould; the corresponding projection in a casting. [etym. doubtful]

sprue2, *n.* a tropical disease characterized by diarrhoea, anaemia, and wasting. [Dut. *spruw*, thrush]

sprug, *n.* (*dial.*) the common sparrow. [etym. doubtful]

spruik, *v.i.* (*Austral. coll.*) to speak in public, to make a speech. **spruiker,** *n.* a barker at a fair-booth.

spruit, *n.* (*S Afr.*) a small tributary stream, esp. one dry in summer. [*Afrik.*]

sprung, *past, p.p.* SPRING.

spry, *a.* (*comp.* **sprier, spryer,** *superl.* **spriest, spryest**) active, lively; sharp, wideawake. **spryly,** *adv.* **spryness,** *n.* [cp. Swed. dial. *sprygg*]

spud, *n.* a short spade-like tool for cutting up weeds by the root etc.; a short and thick person or thing; (*coll.*) a potato. *v.t.* to dig (up) or clear (out) with a spud. **to spud in,** to begin drilling an oil well; (*coll.*) to start work. **spud-bashing,** *n.* (*coll.*) peeling potatoes. **spuddy,** *a.* [ME *spudde*, cp. Dan. *spydd*, MDan. *spjud*, Swed. *spujt*, Icen. *spjōt*]

spue, SPEW.

spulyie, spulzie, spuilzie. (*Sc.*) SPOIL.

spume, *n.* froth, foam. *v.i.* to froth, to foam. **spumescent, spumiferous, spumous, spumy,** *a.* **spumescence, spuminess,** *n.* [L *spūma*]

spun, (*past, p.p.*) SPIN. **spun glass,** *n.* glass that is spun, when heated, into filaments that retain their pliancy when cold. **spun gold, silver,** *n.* gold or silver thread spun for weaving. **spun silk,** *n.* yarn made from silk waste and spun like woollen yarn. **spun yarn,** *n.* line made of twisted rope-yarns.

spunge, spunging-house etc. SPONGE.

spunk, *n.* mettle, spirit, pluck; touchwood, tinder; (*Sc.*) a match; (*taboo*) semen. **spunky,** *a.* plucky, spirited. [Ir. *sponc*, tinder, L and Gr. *spongia*, SPONGE]

spur, *n.* an instrument worn on a horseman's heel having a sharp or blunt point or a rowel; instigation, incentive, stimulus, impulse; a spur-shaped projection, attachment, or part, as the pointed projection on a cock's leg, or a steel point or sheath fastened on this in cock-fighting; the largest root of a tree; a ridge or buttress projecting from a mountain range; a wall crossing a rampart and connecting it to an interior work; a curved timber used in shipbuilding etc.; the projecting part of a ship's ram; a tubular projection on the columbine and other flowers; a climbing-iron etc.; a railway siding or branch line. *v.t.* (*past, p.p.* **spurred**) to prick with spurs; to urge, to incite; to furnish with spurs. *v.i.* to ride hard. **on the spur of the moment,** on impulse. **to win one's spurs;** to gain knighthood; (*fig.*) to achieve distinction, to make oneself famous. **spur-gall,** *v.t.* to wound or gall with spurring; *n.* a place galled by the spur. **spur-royal,** *n.* a gold coin of James I having on the reverse a sun with rays, somewhat resembling a rowel. **spur-wheel,** *n.* a gear-wheel with radial teeth projecting from the rim. **spurless,** *a.* **spurrer,** *n.* **spurrier,** *n.* one who makes spurs. [OE *spura, spora*, cp. Dut. *spoor,* G *Sporn*. Icel. *spori*, Dan. *spore*]

spurge, *n.* a plant of the genus *Euphorbia* with milky and usu. acrid juice. **spurge-laurel,** *n.* a bushy evergreen shrub, *Daphne laureola*, with poisonous berries. [A-F, from OF *espurge*, from *espurger*, L *expurgāre*, to EXPURGATE]

spurious, *a.* not genuine, not proceeding from the true or pretended source, false, counterfeit; like an organ in form or function but physiologically or morphologically different. **spuriously,** *adv.* **spuriousness,** *n.* [L *spurius*]

spurling-line, *n.* a line from the steering-wheel to the telltale in a ship's cabin. [etym. doubtful]

spurn, *v.t.* to thrust away, as with the foot; to reject with disdain; to treat with scorn, *v.i.* to show contempt (at). *n.* the act of spurning, scornful rejection. **spurner,** *n.* [OE *spornan spurnan* (cp. Icel. *sperna*, also L *spernere*), cogn. with SPUR]

spurrer, spurrier SPUR.

spurry, *n.* a low annual weed of the genus *Spergule* of the family Silenaceae. [OF *spurrie*, late L *spergula*, perh. from G]

spurt, *v.i.* to gush out in a jet or sudden stream; to make a sudden intense effort. *v.t.* to send or force out thus. *n.* a forcible gush or jet of liquid; a short burst of intense effort or speed. [ME *sprutten*, OE *sprytlan*, causal of *sprūtan*, to SPROUT]

spurtle, *n.* (*Sc.*) a stirring-stick for porridge. **spurtle-blade,** *n.* a broadsword. [etym. doubtful]

sputa, *pl.* SPUTUM.

Sputnik, *n.* a series of ten Soviet Earth-orbiting satellites. Sputnik 1 was the first artificial satellite, launched on 4 Oct. 1957. It weighed 84 kg/185 lb, with a 58 cm/23 in diameter, and carried only a simple radio transmitter which allowed scientists to track it as it orbited Earth. It burned up in the atmosphere 92 days later. Sputnik 2, launched on 3 Nov. 1957, weighed about 500 kg/1100 lb including the dog Laika, the first living creature in space. Unfortunately, there was no way to return the dog to Earth, and it died in space. [Rus., a travelling-companion]

sputter, *v.i.* to emit saliva in scattered particles, to splutter; to speak in a jerky, incoherent, or excited way. *v.t.* to emit with a spluttering noise; to utter rapidly and indistinctly; to remove atoms from (a surface) by bombardment with high energy ions; to coat a surface with (a metallic film) by such a process. *n.* the process or act of sputtering; confused, incoherent speech. **sputterer,** *n.* **sputteringly,** *adv.* [freq. of SPOUT]

sputum, *n.* (*pl.* **-ta**) spittle, saliva; matter expectorated in various diseases. [L, orig. p.p. or *spuere*, to spit]

spy, *v.t.* to see, to detect, to discover, esp. by close observation; to explore or search (out) secretly; to discover thus. *v.i.* to act as a spy; to search narrowly, to pry. *n.* one sent secretly into an enemy's territory, esp. in disguise, to obtain information that may be useful in the conduct of hostilities; one who keeps a constant watch on the actions, movements etc., of others. **spyglass,** *n.* a small telescope. **spy-hole,** *n.* a peephole. †**spyism,** *n.* [OF *espier*, to ESPY]

Spycatcher, *n.* the controversial memoirs (published 1987) of former UK intelligence officer Peter WRIGHT.

The Law Lords unanimously rejected the UK government's attempt to prevent allegations of MI5 misconduct being reported in the British media.

sq, (*abbr.*) square; (*pl* **sqq**) sequens (the following).

Sqd, (*abbr.*) squadron.

SQL, *n.* in computing, a language designed for use with relational databases. Although it can be used by programmers in the same way as other languages, it is often used as a means for programs to communicate among themselves. Typically, one program (called the 'client') uses SQL to request data from a database 'server'. [*S*tructured *Q*uery *L*anguage]

squab, *a.* fat, short, squat. *adv.* with a heavy fall; plump. *n.* a short, fat person; a young pigeon, esp. unfledged; a stuffed cushion, a sofa padded throughout, an ottoman. *v.i.* to fall plump. **squab-pie,** *n.* a pie made of pigeon, apples, and onions. **squabby,** †**squabbish,** *a.* [cp. Swed. dial. *squabb*, loose, fat flesh, *squabba*, fat woman]

squabble, *v.i.* to engage in a petty or noisy quarrel, to wrangle. *n.* a petty or noisy quarrel, a wrangle. **squabbler,** *n.* [cp. Swed. dial. *skvabbel*, dispute, *skvappa*, to chide, from *skvapp*, splash, imit.]

squacco, *n.* (*pl.* **-ccos)** a small crested heron of S Europe, Asia and Africa. [imit. of cry]

squad, *n.* a small number of soldiers assembled for drill or inspection; a small party of people. **awkward squad,** a body of recruits not sufficiently drilled to take their place in the regimental parade. **squad car,** *n.* a police car. **squaddy,** *n.* (*coll.*) a private soldier. [MF *esquadre* (F *escadre*), It. *squadra* SQUARE]

squadron, *n.* a main division of a cavalry regiment, usu. consisting of two troops containing 120–200 men; a detachment of several warships employed on some particular service; an air force formation of two or more flights. *v.t.* to arrange in squadrons. **squadron-leader,** *n.* a commissioned officer in an air force equivalent in rank to a major in the army. [MF *esquadron*, It. *squadrone*, as prec.]

squail, *n.* a disk used in the game of squails; (*pl.*) a game played on a small table or board with disks which are snapped from the edge towards a mark in the centre. *v.t.* to pelt with a stick etc. *v.i.* to throw a stick etc. (at). **squailer,** *n.* a stick with a leaded knob for squailing birds etc. **squail-board,** *n.* [etym. doubtful]

squalid, *a.* dirty, mean, poverty-stricken; sordid. **squalidity**, **squalidness, squalor,** *n.* **squalidly,** *adv.* [L *squālidus*, from *squālēre*, to be stiff, dirty, etc.]

squall, *v.i.*, *v.t.* to cry out; to scream discordantly. *n.* a harsh, discordant scream, esp. of a child; a sudden, violent gust or succession of gusts of wind, esp. accompanied by rain, hail, snow etc. **squaller,** *n.* **squally**[1]**,** *a.* [Icel. *skvala*, cp. Swed. *skvala*, to gush out noisily, Gael. *sjal*, loud cry]

squally[2]**,** *a.* badly or irregularly woven; (*dial.*) of a field of corn, etc., having bare patches. [prob. SCALL, -Y]

squaloid, *a.* resembling a shark; belonging to the Squalidae, a family of sharks. **squaliform**, *a.* [L *squalus*, a sea-fish, prob. a shark]

squalor SQUALID.

squama, *n.* (*pl.* **-mae**) a scale or scale-like structure, feather, part of bone etc. **Squamata**, *n.* an order of Reptilia which includes snakes and lizards. **squamiform**, **squamoid**, **squamose**, **squamous,** *a.* **squamiferous**, **squamigerous**, *a.* scalebearing. **squamulose**, *a.* covered with small scales. [L]

squander, *v.t.* to spend wastefully; to dissipate by foolish prodigality. **squanderer,** *n.* **squanderingly,** *adv.* [prob. nasalized form of prov. *squatter*, *swatter*, Dan. *sqvatte*, to splash, cp. Icel. *skvetta*, to squirt]

square, *n.* a rectangle with equal sides; any surface, area, object, part etc., of this shape; a rectangular division of a chess- or draught-board, window-pane etc.; an open quadrilateral area surrounded by buildings, usu. laid out with trees, flower-beds, lawns etc.; a block of buildings bounded by four streets; a body of infantry formed into a rectangular figure; an arrangement of words, figures etc., with as many rows as columns (usu. reading alike perpendicularly or across); an L- or T-shaped instrument for laying out and testing right angles; order, regularity, proper proportion; equity, fairness, honesty; the product of a quantity multiplied by itself; (*sl.*) a conventional, old-fashioned person, one out of keeping with modern ways of thought. *a.* having four equal sides and four right angles; rectangular; at right angles (to); broad with straight sides or outlines; (*Football etc.*) in a straight line across the pitch; just, fair, honest; in proper order; evenly balanced, even, settled, complete, thorough, absolute; full, satisfactory; (*coll.*) dull, conventional. *adv.* at right angles; honestly; fairly; evenly. *v.t.* to make square or rectangular; to adjust, to bring into conformity (with or to); to make even, to settle, to pay; (*coll.*) to bribe, to gain over thus; to multiply (a number or quantity) by itself; to lay (a vessel's yards etc.) at right angles to the plane of the keel. *v.i.* to be at right angles (with); to conform precisely, to agree, to harmonize; to put oneself in an attitude for boxing. **back to square one,** back to where one started without having made any progress. **on the square,** at right angles; fairly, honestly; descriptive of a Freemason. **square dinkum,** (*Austral. coll.*) absolutely honestly. **to square away,** (*N Am. coll.*) to put in order, tidy up. **to square off,** to assume a posture of defence or attack. **to square up,** to settle an account. **to square the circle,** to construct geometrically a square equal in area to a given circle; hence, to attempt impossibilities. **square-bashing,** *n.* (*sl.*) military drill. **square bracket,** *n.* either of a pair of written or printed characters, [ ], used to enclose a section of writing or printing, or used as a sign of aggregation in a mathematical formula. **square dance,** *n.* a dance in which the couples form squares. **square dancer, square dancing,** *n.* **square knot,** *n.* a reef knot. **square leg,** *n.* (*Cricket*) a fielder standing about 20 yd. directly behind a batsman as he receives the bowling. **square meal,** *n.* a meal which is full and satisfying. **square measure,** *n.* a system of measures expressed in square feet, metres etc. **square number,** *n.* the product of a number multiplied by itself. **square-rigged,** *a.* having the principal sails extended by horizontal yards suspended from the middle. **square root,** *n.* the quantity that, muliplied by itself, will produce the given quantity. **square-sail**, *n.* a four-cornered sail set on a yard, esp. on a fore-and-aft rigged vessel. **square-shouldered,** *a.* having the shoulders held well up and back, opp. to sloping and round shoulders. **square-toed,** *a.* having the toes (of the shoes) square; precise, prim. **square-toes,** *n.* a formal, precise person. **squarely,** *adv.* **squareness,** *n.* **squarer,** *n.* one who squares. **squarish,** *a.* [OF *esquarre*, from p.p. of nonextant late L *exquadrāre*, (EX-, L *quadrāre*, to make square, from *quadrus*, four-cornered, cogn. with *quatuor*, four)]

squarrose, -rous, *a.* rough with projecting scale-like processes. [said to be from late L *squarrōsus*, perh. *squāmōsus*]

squarson, *n.* (*facet.*) a clergyman who is also a landed proprietor. [comb. of SQUIRE and PARSON]

squash[1]**,** *v.t.* to crush, to press flat or into a pulp. *v.i.* to be crushed or beaten to pulp by a fall; to squeeze (into). *n.* a thing or mass crushed or squeezed to pulp; the fall of a soft body; the sound of this; a throng, a squeeze; a game with rackets and balls played in a court; a drink made from usu. concentrated fruit juice diluted with water. **squasher,** *n.* **squashy,** *a.* **squashiness,** *n.* [prob. from M.E. *squachen*, OF *esquacher* (EX-, late L *coacticāre*, from *coactus*, p.p. of *cōgere*, to drive together)]

squash[2]**,** *n.* the fleshy, edible, gourd-like fruit of trailing plants of the gens *Curcurbita;* (*N Am.*) a vegetable marrow. [N Am. Ind. *esquash*, green, raw]

squat, *v.i.* (*past, p.p.* **squatted**) to sit down or crouch on the haunches; chiefly of animals, to crouch, to cower; to sit; to settle on land or occupy a building without any title. *v.t.* to put (oneself) in a crouching posture; (*dial.*) to squash. *a.* short, thick, dumpy; in a squatting position. *n.* a squatting posture; a squat person; a building occupied by squatters. **squatly,** *adv.* **squatness,** *n.* **squatter,** *n.* one who sits on the haunches; one who occupies property or land without title. (*Austral.*) one who leases land for pasturage from the Government, a stock-owner. **squattocracy,** *n.* (*Austral.*) squatters as a corporate body. [OF *esquatir,* to flatten, crush (EX-, *quatir,* as SQUASH[1])]

squaw, *n.* a N American Indian woman or wife. **squaw man,** *n.* a White man married to a N American Indian. [Algonquian *squa*]

squawk, *v.i.* to utter a loud, harsh cry; (*coll.*) to protest loudly. *n.* such a cry or protest. [var. of foll.]

squeak, *v.i.* to utter a sharp, shrill, usu. short cry; to break silence or secrecy. *v.t.* to utter with a squeak. *n.* a sharp, shrill sound; (*coll.*) a narrow escape or margin, a close shave. **squeaker,** *n.* one who or that which squeaks; a young bird, esp. a pigeon; (*sl.*) an informer, a traitor. **squeaky,** *a.* **squeaky-clean,** *a.* spotless; above reproach. **squeakily,** *adv.* [cp. MSwed. *sqwæka* cp. Norw. *skvaka,* Icel. *skvakka*]

squeal, *v.i.* to utter a more or less prolonged shrill cry as in pain, etc.; (*sl.*) to turn informer; (*coll.*) to complain. *n.* a more or less prolonged shrill cry. **squealer,** *n.* [MSwed. *sqwæla,* freq. as prec.]

squeamish, *a.* easily nauseated, disgusted or offended; fastidious, finicky, hypercritical, excessively nice, prudish, unduly scrupulous. **squeamishly,** *adv.* **squeamishness,** *n.* [ME *skeymous,* A-F *escoymous,* etym. doubtful]

squeegee[1], *n.* an implement, composed of a strip of rubber fixed to a handle for cleaning windows; a similar implement, usu. with a rubber roller, used by photographers for squeezing and flattening. *v.t.* to sweep, smooth etc., with a squeegee. [formerly *squilgee,* etym. doubtful]

squeegee[2], *adv.* (*Sc.*) askew; twisted out of shape. [SKEW, AGEE]

squeeze, *v.t.* to press closely, esp. between two bodies or with the hand, so as to force juice etc., out; to extract (juice etc.) thus; to force (oneself etc., into, out of etc.); to extort money etc., from, to harass by exactions; to exact (money etc.) by extortion etc.; to put pressure on, to oppress, to constrain by arbitrary or illegitimate means. *v.i.* to press, to push, to force one's way (into, through etc.). *n.* the act of squeezing; pressure; a close embrace; a throng, a crush. **squeeze-box,** *n.* (*coll.*) an accordion. **squeezable,** *a.* **squeezability,** *n.* **squeezer,** *n.* one who or that which squeezes; (*pl.*) playing-cards marked at the top right-hand corner with the value to save spreading out in the hand. [OE *cwīesan,* cp. LG *quōsen*]

squelch, *v.t.* to crush; to silence, to extinguish, to discomfit; to make a noise as of treading in wet snow. *n.* a heavy blow; a crushing retort; a squelching noise. **squelcher,** *n.* **squelchy,** *a.* [perh. rel. to QUELL]

squib, *n.* a firework emitting sparks and exploding with a bang, usu. thrown by the hand; a tube containing gunpowder for igniting a blasting-charge; a petty lampoon; (*Austral.*) a coward, a sneak. *v.i.* (*past, p.p.* **squibbed**) to write squibs. *v.t.* to satirize in a squib. **damp squib,** something which fails to make the intended impact or impression. [perh. from ME *squippen, swippen,* to move swiftly, Icel. *svipa,* to flash, cogn. with SWEEP]

squid, *n.* (*pl.* **squid, squids**) a small kind of cuttlefish; an artificial bait roughly imitating a fish. *v.i.* (*past, p.p.* **squidded**) to fish with this. [cp. Swed. dial. *skvitta,* Icel. *skvetta,* to squirt]

squiffy, *a.* (*coll.*) slightly drunk. [onomat.]

squiggle, *v.i.* to squirm, to wriggle; (*dial.*) to shake a fluid about in the mouth; to make wriggly lines. *n.* a wriggly line. **squiggler,** *n.* **squiggly,** *a.* [prob. imit.]

squill, *n.* a liliaceous plant, *Scilla maritima,* resembling the bluebell; the sliced bulb of this used as an expectorant, diuretic etc. **squillitic,** *a.* [MF *squille,* L *squilla,* Gr. *skilla*]

squinancy-wort, *n.* the small woodruff, *Asperula cynanchica.* [obs. *squinancy,* var. of QUINSY, WORT]

squinch, *n.* an arch across the internal angle of a square tower to support the side of an octagonal spire etc. [var. of SCUNCHEON]

†**squinny,** *v.i.* (*Shak.*) to squint. [SQUINT]

squint, *v.i.* to look with the eyes differently directed; to be affected with strabismus; to look obliquely; to look with eyes half shut. *v.t.* to cause to squint; to shut or contract (the eyes) quickly; to keep (the eyes) half shut. *a.* looking obliquely; looking askance; (*coll.*) crooked. *n.* an affection of the eyes causing the axes to be differently directed, strabismus; a stealthy look, a side-long glance; (*coll.*) a look; a leaning (towards). **squint-eye,** *n.* **squint-eyed,** *a.* **squinter,** *n.* **squintingly,** *adv.* [etym. uncertain]

squire, *n.* a country gentleman, esp. the chief landowner in a place; a beau, a gallant; (*Hist.*) an attendant on a knight. *v.t.* to attend as a squire, to escort (a woman). **squirearchy,** *n.* landed proprietors collectively; the political influence of, or govenment by these. **squirearch,** *n.* **squirearchal, -archical,** *a.* **squireen,** *n.* a petty squire, esp. in Ireland. **squirehood, squireship,** *n.* [ESQUIRE]

squirm, *v.i.* to wriggle, to writhe about; to climb (up) by wriggling; to display discomfort, embarrassment etc. *n.* a wriggling movement; (*Naut.*) a twist in a rope. [perh. from M.E. *quirr,* var. of WHIRR]

squirrel, *n.* a brown or grey bushy-tailed rodent quadruped living chiefly in trees; the fur of a squirrel; (also **barking squirrel**) a prairie-dog; (*coll.*) a person who hoards things. **squirrel cage,** *n.* a small cylindrical cage with a treadmill; the rotor of an induction motor with cylindrically arranged copper bars. **squirrel-fish,** *n.* a W Indian and N American seafish. **squirrel-monkey,** *n.* a small S American monkey with soft golden fur. **squirrel-tail,** *n.* grass allied to barley with long hair-like awns. [OF *escuirel, escurel,* late L *scūrellus,* dim. of *sciūrus,* Gr. *skiouros,* perh. *shadow-tail* (*skia,* shadow, *oura,* tail)]

squirt, *v.t.* to eject in a jet or stream from a narrow orifice. *v.i.* of liquid, to be so ejected. *n.* a syringe; a jet (of liquid); (*coll.*) a pert, conceited or insignificant person. **squirter,** *n.* [cp. LG *swirtjen,* cogn. with WHIRR]

squish, *v.t.* to crush so as to make a squelching or sucking noise. *v.i.* to make a squelching or sucking sound. *n.* the sound of squishing. **squishy,** *a.*

squit, *n.* (*sl.*) an insignificant person; nonsense. [var of SQUIRT]

squitch-grass, QUITCH-GRASS.

Sr[1], (*abbr.*) Señor; Sir.

Sr[2], (*chem. symb.*) strontium.

sr, (*abbr.*) steradian.

Sra, (*abbr.*) Señora.

SRC, (*abbr.*) Science Research Council; Student Representative Council.

Sri Lanka, *n.* Democratic Socialist Republic of (former name **Ceylon**), *Prajathanrika Samajawadi Janarajaya Sri Lanka,* island in the Indian Ocean, off the SE coast of India. **area** 65,600 sq km/25,328 sq miles. **capital** and chief port Colombo. **towns** Kandy; ports Jaffna, Galle, Negombo, Trincomalee. **physical** flat in the N and around the coast; hills and mountains in the S. **population** (1989) 17,541,000 (including 2,500,000 Tamils); annual growth rate 1.8%. **exports** tea, rubber, coconut products, plumbago, sapphires, rubies, precious stones. **language** Sinhalese (official, but English and Tamil are national languages). **religion** Buddhist 67% (official), Hindu 18%.

SRN, (*abbr.*) State Registered Nurse.

SS[1], *n.* Nazi elite corps established 1925. Under Himmler its 500,000 membership included the full-time Waffen-SS (armed SS), which fought in World War II, and spare-time members. The SS performed state police duties and was brutal in its treatment of the Jews and others in the concentration camps and occupied territories. It was condemned at the Nuremberg Trials of war. [G *Schutz-Staffel,* elite guard]

SS[2], (*abbr.*) Saints; steamship.

SSE, (*abbr.*) south-southeast.

SSR, (*abbr.*) Soviet Socialist Republic.

SSW, (*abbr.*) south-southwest.
St, (*abbr.*) Saint; statute; Strait; Street.
st., (*abbr.*) stanza; stone.
stab, *v.t.* (*past, p.p.* **stabbed**) to pierce or wound with a pointed weapon; to plunge (a weapon into); to inflict pain upon or to injure by slander etc.; to roughen (a wall) with a pick to make it hold plaster. *v.i.* to aim a blow with or as with a pointed weapon (at). *n.* a blow or thrust with a pointed weapon; a wound inflicted thus; a secret malicious injury. **to have, make a stab at,** (*coll.*) to attempt. **to stab in the back,** (*fig.*) to betray; to injure the reputation of someone esp. a colleague, friend etc. **stabber,** *n.* **stabbingly,** *adv.* [ME *stabbe*, cp. Swed. dial. *stabbe*, Icel. *stabbi*, stump]
Stabat Mater, *n.* a Latin hymn reciting the seven dolours of the Virgin at the Cross, beginning with these words; a musical setting of this. [L, the Mother was standing]
stable¹, *a.* firmly fixed, established; not to be moved, shaken or destroyed easily; firm, resolute, constant, not changeable, unwavering; (*Chem.*) durable, not readily decomposed; not radioactive. **stable equilibrium,** *n.* the tendency of any body to recover equilibrium when moved. **stabile**, *a.* fixed; stable. *n.* an abstract art form similar to a mobile but stationary. **stability**, *n.* the quality of being stable; the property of mechanical, electrical or aerodynamic systems that makes them return to a state of equilibrium after disturbance. **stabilize, -ise,** *v.t.* to make stable. **stabilization, -isation,** *n.* the act of stabilizing. **stabilizer, -iser,** *n.* anything that stabilizes; a device that gives extra stability to an aircraft, vessel, children's bicycle etc., an additive which retards chemical action. **stableness,** *n.* **stably,** *adv.* [OF *estable*, L *stabilem*, nom. *-lis*, from *stāre*, to stand]
stable², *n.* a building or part of a building for horses or (sometimes) cattle; the race-horses belonging to a particular stable; a group of people with particular skills, e.g. athletes under single management; any collection or group. *v.t.* to put or keep in a stable. *v.i.* of horses, etc., to lodge in a stable. **stable-boy, -girl, -man,** *n.* one employed in a stable. **stable-companion,** *n.* a person with whom one shares rooms etc. **stable lad,** *n.* a groom in a racing stable. **stabling,** *n.* accommodation in a stable or stables. [OF *estable*, L *stabilem*, as prec.]
†**stablish,** ESTABLISH.
staccato, *n., a., adv.* (*Mus.*) (a piece of music) played with each note sharply distinct and detached, opp. to *legato*. [It. p.p. of *staccare*, to detach, from *distaccare*, to separate]
stachys, *n.* a genus of labiate plants with white or reddish spikes of flowers, also called the wound-worts. [L, from Gr. *stachus*, ear of corn]
stack, *n.* a round or rectangular pile of corn in the sheaf, hay, straw etc., usu. with a thatched top; a pile, a heap, esp. of an orderly kind; a pyramidal pile of rifles standing on their butts with the muzzles together; a measure of wood, 108 cu. ft. ($3{\cdot}05\ m^3$); (*coll.*) a great quantity; a chimney, a funnel, a smoke-stack; a towering isolated mass of rock, esp. in Scotland etc.; (*usu. pl.*) compact bookshelves, in a library, usu. with restricted public access; aircraft circling an airport at different altitudes waiting for instructions to land; a temporary storage area in a computer memory. *v.t.* to pile in a stack or stacks; to assign (waiting aircraft) to a particular altitude in preparation for landing at an airport. **to stack the cards,** to interfere with a deck of cards secretly for the purpose of cheating; to arrange (matters) to the disadvantage or advantage, of someone. **stack-stand,** *n.* a platform for supporting a stack of hay etc. **stack-yard,** *n.* a yard for stacks. [Icel. *stakkr*, Swed. *stack*, Dan. *stak*]
stacte, *n.* one of the spices used by the ancient Jews in the preparation of incense. [L and Gr., from *stazein*, to drip]
†**staddle,** *n.* a prop or support; a small tree left standing; a stack-stand. *v.t.* to leave the staddles in (a wood that is being cut down). **staddle-roof,** *n.* a covering for a stack. [OE *stathol*, foundation, base, cp. G *Stadel*]
†**stade,** STADIUM.
Stade Roland Garros, French lawn-tennis centre at Auteil, Paris, built in the 1920s for the French team to play their matches in defence of the Davis Cup. It became the home of the French Championships in 1928.
stadia, *n.* a temporary surveying-station; an instrument, usu. comprising a graduated rod and a telescope, for measuring distances. **stadiometer**, *n.* a self-recording theodolite. [late L, from foll.]
stadium, *n.* (*pl.* **-diums, -dia**) a measure of about 607 ft. (184 m), the course for foot-races at Olympia; an enclosure, usu. an amphitheatre, where games can be watched by a large number of spectators; (*Med.*) a stage in a disease. [L, from Gr. *stadion*, from *sta-*, root of *histanai*, to stand]
Stadtholder, Stadholder, *n.* (*Hist.*) a viceroy, governor, or deputy-governor of a province or town in the Netherlands; the chief magistrate of the United Provinces. **Stadtholderate**, **-ship,** *n.* [Dut. *stadhouder* (STEAD, HOLDER)]
Staël, *n.* **Anne Louise Germaine Necker, Madame de Staël** (1766–1817), French author, daughter of the financier Necker. She wrote semi-autobiographical novels such as *Delphine* (1802) and *Corinne* (1807), and the critical work *De l'Allemagne* (1810), on German literature.
staff¹, *n.* (*pl.* **staffs, staves**) a stick carried for help in walking etc., or as a weapon; support; a stick, rod, pole etc., borne as an emblem of office or authority; a shaft, pole etc., forming a support or handle, as a flagstaff; a rod used in surveying etc., a cross-staff, a Jacob's staff; a rod-like appliance, instrument, part, fitting etc.; (*Mil.*) a body of officers assisting an officer in command whose duties are concerned with a regiment or an army as a whole; a body of persons working under a manager, editor etc.; (*Mus.*) a set of five parallel lines and spaces on or between which notes are written representing the pitch of tones. *v.t.* to provide with a staff. **(the) staff of life,** staple foodstuff, esp. bread. **staff-notation,** *n.* (*Mus.*) notation by the staff as dist. from sol-fa. **staff nurse,** *n.* a qualified nurse next in rank below a sister. **staff-officer, -sergeant** etc., *n.* one serving on a staff. **staff-work,** *n.* organization. [OE *stæf*, cp. Dut. *staf*, G *Stab*, Icel. *stafr*]
staff², *n.* a composition of plaster of Paris, cement etc., used as building-material etc., esp. in temporary structures. [perh. var. of STUFF]
Staffordshire, *n.* county in W central England. **area** 2720 sq km/1050 sq miles. **towns** administrative headquarters Stafford; Stoke-on-Trent. **population** (1987) 1,028,000. **products** coal in north; china and earthenware.
Staffordshire porcelain, *n.* pottery from Staffordshire, England, one of the largest pottery producing regions in the world, built up around an area rich in clay. Different companies, the first of which was Longton, have produced stoneware and earthenware from the 17th century onwards. See also the POTTERIES.
stag, *n.* the male of the red deer, esp. from his fifth year; the male of other large deer; a bull castrated when nearly full-grown; (*sl.*) an informer; a male unaccompanied by a woman at a social function; (*Stock Exch.*) one who stags. *v.t.* (*sl.*) to watch closely, to spy. *v.i.* (*Stock Exch.*) to apply for or to purchase stock or shares in a new issue solely with the object of selling at a profit immediately on allotment. **stag-beetle,** *n.* a beetle with large mandibles, in the male branching like a stag's horns. **stag-evil,** *n.* lockjaw in horses. **staghound,** *n.* a large hound used for hunting stags. **stag party,** *n.* (*coll.*) a party for men only, esp. one given for a man about to be married. [OE *stagga*, Icel. *steggr*, he-bird, male animal]
stage, *n.* an elevated platform, as a scaffold for workers erecting or repairing a building, a shelf on which objects may be exhibited or examined etc.; a raised platform on which theatrical performances take place; the theatre, the drama, the profession of an actor, actors collectively; a scene of action; one of a series of regular

stopping-places on a route; the distance between two such stations; a definite portion of a journey; a point in a progressive movement, a definite period in development; a stagecoach; a detachable propulsion unit of a rocket; the small platform on a microscope where the slide is mounted for examination; part of a complex electronic circuit. *v.t.* to put on the stage; to plan and execute an event. **to go on the stage,** to become a professional actor or actress. **stagecoach,** *n.* a horse-drawn coach that ran regularly by stages for conveyance of parcels, passengers etc. **stage-coachman, -driver,** *n.* **stage-craft,** *n.* the art of writing or staging plays. **stage-direction,** *n.* an instruction respecting the movements etc., of actors in a play. **stage-door,** *n.* a door to a theatre for the use of actors, workmen, etc. **stage-effect,** *n.* (*lit. and fig.*), theatrical effect. **stage-fever,** *n.* intense desire to become an actor. **stagefright,** *n.* a fit of nervousness in facing an audience. **stagehand,** *n.* a worker who moves scenery etc. in a theatrical production. **stage-manage,** *v.t.* to direct or supervise (from behind the scenes). **stage-manager,** *n.* one who superintends the scenic effects etc., of a play. **stage-struck,** *a.* smitten with the theatre. **stage-whisper,** *n.* an audible aside; something meant for the ears of others than the person ostensibly addressed. **stager,** *n.* a person of long experience in anything, esp. in the compound *old-stager*. **staging,** *n.* a scaffolding; the driving or running of stage-coaches; the act of putting a play on the stage. **staging area,** *n.* an assembly point for troops in transit. **staging post,** *n.* a regular stopover point on an air route. **stagy,** *a.* theatrical, unreal. **staginess,** *n.* [OF *estage,* (F. *étage*), prob. through a L. *staticum,* from *stāre,* to stand]

stagflation, *n.* a combination of high inflation and falling industrial output and employment. [STAGNATION, INFLATION]

staggard, *n.* a stag four years old.

stagger, *v.i.* to move unsteadily in standing or walking, to totter, to reel; to begin to give way, to waver, to hesitate. *v.t.* to cause to reel; to cause to hesitate; to shock with surprise etc.; to set (the spokes of a wheel) alternately leaning in and out; to overlap, to place zigzag; of crossroads etc. to site so as not to meet opposite one another; of working hours etc., to arrange so as not to coincide with others. *n.* a staggering movement; (*pl.*) a disease affecting the brain and spinal cord in horses and cattle, characterized by vertigo etc.; giddiness, vertigo. **staggerer,** *n.* one who staggers; a staggering blow, argument etc. **staggeringly,** *adv.* [ME *stakeren,* Icel. *stakra,* freq. of *staka,* to push]

stagnant, *a.* still; without current, motionless; dull, sluggish, inert. **stagnancy,** *n.* **stagnantly,** *adv.* **stagnate,** *v.i.* to become stagnant. **stagnation,** *n.* [L *stagnāre,* from *stagnum,* pool]

Stahl, *n.* **George** (1660–1734), German chemist who produced a fallacious theory of combustion. He was professor of medicine at Halle, and physician to the king of Prussia. He argued that objects burn in so far as they contain a combustible substance, phlogiston. Substances rich in phlogiston, like wood, burn almost completely away. Metals, which are low in phlogiston, burn less well. Chemists spent much of the century evaluating Stahl's theories before they were finally overthrown by Lavoisier.

staid, *a.* sober, steady, sedate. **staidly,** *adv.* **staidness,** *n.* [STAYED, p.p. of STAY[1]]

stain, *v.t.* to discolour, to soil, to sully; to tarnish, to blemish (a reputation etc.); to colour by means of dye or other agent acting chemically or by absorption, opp. to painting; to impregnate (an object for microscopic examination) with a colouring matter affecting certain parts more powerfully than others; to dim, to obscure. *v.i.* to cause discoloration; to take stains. *n.* a discoloration; a spot of a distinct colour; a blot, a blemish. **stained glass,** *n.* glass coloured for use in windows. **stainable,** *a.* **stainer,** *n.* **stainless,** *a.* without a stain, immaculate; resistant to rust or tarnish. **stainless steel,** *n.* a rustless alloy steel used for cutlery etc. **stainlessly,** *adv.* **stainlessness,** *n.* [ME *steinen*]

stair, *n.* one of a series of steps, esp. for ascending from one storey of a house to another; (*usu. pl.*), a flight of stairs. **backstairs** BACK. **below stairs,** in the basement; in the servants' quarters or relating to their affairs; relating to the workforce as opposed to management. **flight of stairs,** a set of stairs, as from one landing to another. **stair-carpet,** *n.* a narrow carpet used to cover the stairs. **staircase,** *n.* a flight of stairs with banisters, supporting structure etc. **moving staircase** ESCALATOR. **stair-rod,** *n.* a rod for fastening a stair-carpet between two stairs. **stairway,** *n.* a staircase. **stairwell,** *n.* the vertical shaft which contains the staircase. [OE stǣger (cp. Dut. *steiger,* G *Steg,* Icel. *stigi*), from Teut. *steigan,* to climb, cogn. with Gr. *steichein,* to ascend, to go]

staith, *n.* (*dial.*) a landing-stage, a wharf, esp. a staging laid with rails from which coal-wagons etc., may discharge their loads into vessels. [OE staeth, bank, shore]

stake, *n.* a stick or post pointed at one end and set in the ground, as a support, part of a railing etc.; a post to which persons condemned to death by burning were bound; martyrdom; a prop or upright part of fitting for supporting a machine etc., a tinsmith's small anvil that may be set in a bench; anything, esp. money, wagered on a competition or contingent event, esp. deposited with a stake-holder; (*pl.*) money competed for in a race etc.; (*pl.*) a race for this; (*fig.*) anything contended for. *v.t.* to fasten, support, or protect with a stake or stakes; to mark (out or off) with stakes; to wager, to venture (on an event etc.). **at stake,** in hazard, at issue, in question. **to pull up stakes,** to move home, to move on. **to stake one's claim,** to assert one's right to possess (something). **to stake out,** *v.t.* to place under surveillance. **stake-holder,** *n.* one who holds the stakes when a wager is made. **stake-net,** *n.* a fishing-net stretched on stakes. **stakeout,** *n.* a place, person etc. under surveillance; a (police) surveillance operation covering a particular building or area. [OE *staca,* (cp. MDut. and Swed. *stake,* Icel. *stjaki,* Dan. *stage*), cogn. with STACK]

Stakhanov, *n.* **Aleksei** (1906–77), Soviet miner who exceeded production norms, and who gave his name to the Stakhanovite movement of the 1930s, when workers were encouraged to simplify and reorganize work processes in order to increase production. **Stakhanovism,** *n.* USSR system for increasing production by utilizing each worker's initiative. **Stakhanovite,** *n., a.*

stalactite, *n.* a deposit of carbonate of lime, hanging from the roof of a cave etc., in the form of a thin tube or a large icicle, produced by the evaporation of percolating water. **stalactic, stalactiform, stalactitic,** *a.* [F (Gr. *stalaktos,* dripping, from *stalazein,* to drip)]

stalag, *n.,* a German prisoner-of-war camp, esp. for men from the ranks and non-commissioned officers. [short for *Stammlager, Stamm,* base, *Lager,* Camp]

stalagmite, *n.* a deposit of the same material as in a stalactite on the floor or walls of a cave. **stalagmitic,** *a.* **stalagmitically,** *adv.* [F (Gr. *stalagos,* dripping, as prec.)]

stale[1], *a.* not fresh, dry, musty; vapid or tasteless from being kept too long; trite; in poor condition from overtraining. *n.* urine of horses etc. *v.t.* to make stale. *v.i.* of horses, to urinate. **staley,** *adv.* **staleness,** *n.* [OF *estāler,* to make water, from Teut., cogn. with STALL[1]]

†**stale[2],** *n.* a dupe; a laughing-stock. [OE *stalu,* theft, see STEAL]

stalemate, *n.* (*Chess*) the position when the king, not actually in check, is unable to move without placing himself in check, and there is no other piece that can be moved; a situation of deadlock. *v.t.* to subject to a stalemate; to bring to a standstill. [perh. from ME *stal,* OF *estal,* a fixed position, cp. STALL[1], MATE[1]]

Stalin, *n.* **Joseph,** adopted name (Russian 'steel') of Joseph Vissarionovich Djugashvili (1879–1953), Soviet politician. A member of the October Revolution Committee of 1917, Stalin became General Secretary of the Communist party in 1922. After Lenin's death in

1924, Stalin sought to create 'socialism in one country' and clashed with TROTSKY, who denied the possibility of socialism inside Russia until revolution had occurred in W Europe. Stalin won this ideological struggle by 1927, and a series of five-year plans was launched to collectivize industry and agriculture from 1928. All opposition was eliminated by the Great Purge (1936–38) by which Stalin disposed of all real and fancied enemies. During World War II, Stalin intervened in the military direction of the campaigns against Nazi Germany. His role was denounced after his death by Khrushchev and other members of the Soviet regime. **Stalinism**, *n.* the brutal authoritarian regime associated with Joseph Stalin, developed from the ideology of Marxism–Leninism. **Stalinist,** *n.*

Stalingrad, *n.* name (1925–1961) of the Soviet city of VOLGOGRAD.

stalk¹, *v.i.* to walk with high, pompous steps; to go stealthily, to steal (up to game or prey) under cover. *v.t.* to pursue stealthily by the use of cover. *n.* the act of stalking game or prey; a pompous gait. **stalker,** *n.* **stalking-horse,** *n.* a horse or figure like a horse behind which a person hides when stalking game; a mask, a pretence. [OE *stealcan*, perh. with feet uplifted, cp. *stealc*, high]

stalk², *n.* the stem or axis of a plant; the peduncle of a flower; the supporting peduncle of a barnacle etc.; the stem of a wine glass etc.; a high factory chimney. **with eyes on stalks,** (*coll.*) amazed. **stalk-eyed,** *a.* having the eyes set on peduncles (as certain crustaceans). **stalked,** *a.* (*usu. in comb.* as *thin-stalked*). **stalkless,** *a.* **stalklet,** *n.* **stalky,** *a.* [ME *stalke*, dim. of *stale*, OE *stæla*, cp. Dut. *steel*]

Stalker affair, *n.* an inquiry begun in 1984 by John Stalker, deputy chief constable in Manchester, England, into the killing of six unarmed men in 1982 by Royal Ulster Constabulary (RUC) special units in Northern Ireland. The inquiry was halted and Stalker suspended from duty in 1986. Although he was later reinstated, the inquiry did not reopen, and no reason for his suspension was given.

stall¹, *n.* a division or compartment for a horse, ox etc., in a stable or byre; a booth or shed in a market, street etc., or a bench, table etc., in a building for the sale of goods; a finger-stall; a seat in the choir of a large church, enclosed at the back and sides and usu. canopied, for a clergyman, chorister etc.; (*fig.*) a canonry etc.; one of a set of seats in a theatre, usu. in the front part of the pit; an instance of an aircraft or motor stalling. *v.t.* to put or keep in a stall (esp. cattle for fattening); to furnish with stalls. *v.i.* to stick fast (in mire etc.); of a car etc. engine, to cease working suddenly; to allow an aeroplane to lose its forward impetus and thus deprive the planes of sustaining power if there is not airspace enough underneath it for recovering lift; to play for time; to be evasive. **starting stalls,** a group of stalls from which horses emerge at the start of a race. **to stall off,** to stave off. **to stall for time,** to postpone or hold off as long as possible. **stall-feed,** *v.t.* to fatten in a stall. **stallage,** *n.* the right of erecting a stall in a fair; the rent for this; accommodation for or by stalls. [OE *steal, steall* (cp. Dut. *stal*, G *Stall*, Icel. *stallr*, OHG *stal*), cogn. with STABLE², STEAD]

stall², *n.* the confederate of a thief or pickpocket who diverts attention while the theft is committed and helpst the thief to escape. [var. of STALE²]

stallion, *n.* an uncastrated male horse, esp. one kept for breeding purposes. [OF *estalon* (F *étalon*), cogn. with STALL¹]

Stallone, *n.* **Sylvester** (1946–), US film actor. He played bit parts and occasional leads in exploitation films before starring in *Rocky* (1976), which he also wrote. His later films have mostly been based around violence, and include *F.I.S.T.* (1978), *First Blood* (1982), and *Rambo* (1985).

stalwart, *a.* strong in build, sturdy; stout, resolute. *n.* a strong, resolute dependable person. **stalwartly,** *adv.* **stalwartness,** *n.* [OE *stælwyrthe* (*stathol*, foundation, WORTH¹)]

Stamboul, *n.* the old part of the Turkish city of ISTANBUL, the area formerly occupied by BYZANTIUM.

stamen, *n.* (*pl.* **stamens, stamina**), the pollen-bearing male organ of a flower. **stamened,** *a.* **staminal, stamineous,** *a.* of or pertaining to stamens. **staminate,** *a.* having stamens (but no pistils). **staminiferous,** *a.* [L *stāmen -minis*, orig. warp in upright loom, from *stāre*, to stand]

stamina, *n.* strength, vigour, power of endurance. [L, pl. of prec.]

staminal etc. STAMEN.

stammel, *n.* (*dial.*) a woollen cloth of a dull red colour; this colour. [prob. from obs. *stamin*, OF *estamine* (F. *étamine*), L STAMEN]

stammer, *v.i., v.t.* to speak with halting articulation, nervous hesitation, or repetitions of the same sound; to stutter. *n.* a stammering utterance or vocal affection. **stammerer,** *n.* **stammeringly,** *adv.* [ME *stameren* (cp. OE *stamm*, *stamor*, stammering, Dut. *stameren*, G *stammern*), ult. from *sta-*, to stand]

stamp, *v.t.* to make a mark or impression upon with a dye, pattern etc.; to affix a stamp to; to impress (initials etc.) upon something; to impress deeply (on the memory etc.); to bring (the foot etc.) down heavily; to extinguish thus, to put (out); to crush by downward force or pressure; to destroy. *v.i.* to strike the foot forcibly on the ground. *n.* the act of stamping; an instrument for stamping marks, designs etc.; the mark made by this; an official mark set on things chargeable with some duty or tax, to show that such is paid; a small piece of paper officially stamped for affixing to letters, receipts etc.; a label, imprint, or other mark certifying ownership, quality, genuineness etc.; distinguishing mark, impress, kind, sort; a downward blow with the foot; a blow with a stamping-machine; the block for crushing ore in a stampmill. **to stamp out,** to extinguish (a fire) by stamping; to suppress, extirpate. **Stamp Act,** *n.* see separate entry. **stamp album,** *n.* a book to hold a postage-stamp collection. **stamp-collector,** *n.* one who collects specimens of postage stamps; a collector of stamp-duties. **stamp-duty,** *n.* a duty imposed on certain legal documents. **stamping-ground,** *n.* a habitual meeting place, a favourite resort. **stamp-mill,** *n.* a mill for crushing ore, fruit etc. **stamper,** *n.* [OE *stempen* (cp. Dut. *stampen*, G *stampfen*, Icel. *stappa*, Swed. *stampa*, also Gr. *stembein*)]

Stamp Act, *n.* an act of Parliament in 1765 which taxed (by requiring an official stamp) all publications and legal documents published in British colonies. A blockade of British merchant shipping proved so effective that the act was repealed the following year. It was a precursor of the War of American Independence.

stampede, *n.* a sudden fright causing horses or cattle to scatter and run; a sudden panic and flight (of troops etc.); any impulsive (unreasoning) movement on the part of a large number of persons. *v.i.* to take part in a stampede. *v.t.* to cause to do this. [Sp. and Port. *estampido*, from *estampar*, to STAMP]

stance, *n.* the position by a person adopted when standing; the position taken for a stroke in golf, cricket etc.; a personal attitude, political position etc.; (*Sc.*) place, site, station. [OF *estance*, late L *stantia*, see STANZA]

stanch¹ *v.t.* to prevent or stop the flow of (blood etc., from a wound). †*v.i.* to stop flowing. [OF *estancher*, late L *stancāre*, L. *stagnāre*, to STAGNATE]

stanch², STAUNCH².

stanchion, *n.* a prop, post, pillar etc., forming a support or part of a structure; a vertical bar or pair of bars for confining cattle in a stall. *v.t.* to fasten with a stanchion. [ONorth.F *estanchon*, (F *etançon*), dim. of *estance*, STANCE]

stand, *v.i.* (*past, p.p.* **stood,**) to be upon the feet; to be or become or remain erect; to be in a specified state, attitude, position, situation, rank etc.; to have a specified height or stature; to be or remain in a stationary position, to cease from motion, to stop, to be or remain immovable, not to give way; to remain firm or constant, to abide, to endure, to persist; to hold good, to remain valid or unimpaired; to be motionless, to lie stagnant; to move into a specified position and remain in it; to hold a specified course, to steer; of a setter, to point; to become a candidate. *v.t.* to set in an erect or a specified position; to endure, to sustain, without giving way or complaining; to undergo (a trial etc.); to sustain the expense of (a drink etc.). *n.* a cessation of motion or progress, to stop, a halt, a state of inactivity, a standstill; the act of standing, esp. with firmness, in a fixed or stationary position, place, or station; resistance, opposition, defensive effort etc.; a small frame or piece of furniture for supporting anything; a place in a town where cabs etc., stand for hire; an erection for spectators to stand or sit on; in cricket, a lengthy partnership between two batsmen at the wicket. **it stands to reason,** it is logically manifest (that). **one-night stand,** a performance given by a musical group, theatrical company etc. in one spot for one night only before moving on; (*coll.*) a sexual relationship that lasts one night only. **stand of arms,** a complete outfit of arms and ammunition for one person. **to be at a stand,** to be perplexed; to be in doubt as to further progress. **to stand by,** to be present, to be a bystander; to look on passively; to uphold, to support firmly; to abide by; to stand near in readiness to act promptly as directed. **to stand down,** to withdraw; of a committee, to be dissolved; to leave the witness box in a law court; to come off duty. **to stand fast,** to stay firm, to be unmoved. **to stand for,** to support the cause of; to represent, to imply; to offer oneself as a candidate for; to endure. **to stand good,** to remain valid. **to stand in,** to take an actor's place in a scene until the cameras are ready; to deputize for. **to stand in with,** to have an understanding or community of interest with. **to stand off,** to keep at a distance; to move away; to suspend (an employee). **to stand off and on,** (*Naut.*) to tack in and out along shore. **to stand on,** to insist on (ceremony etc.); (*Naut.*) to keep on the same course. **to stand one's ground,** to remain resolute, to stay fixed in position. **to stand on one's own feet,** to manage without the help of others. **to stand out,** to project; to be conspicuous; to persist (in opposition against); to endure without giving way. **to stand over,** to be deferred. **to stand to,** to abide by; not to desert; to fall to, to set to work. **to stand to it,** to maintain (that). **to stand up,** to rise to one's feet; to be or remain erect; to fail to keep an appointment with. **to stand up for,** to maintain, to support, to take the part of. **to stand upon,** to stand on. **stand-by,** *n.* a thing or person to be confidently relied upon; a substitute or replacement kept esp. for use in an emergency. *a.* of a ticket, not booked in advance, subject to availability. **on stand-by,** held in readiness for use in an emergency etc; of an airline passenger, awaiting an empty seat, not having booked in advance. **stand-in,** *n.* a minor actor who takes the place of a star in a scene until the cameras are ready; a substitute. **stand-off, stand-off half** FLY-HALF **stand-offish,** *a.* distant, reserved. **stand-offishly,** *adv.* **stand-offishness,** *n.* **standpipe,** *n.* an upright pipe serving as a hydrant, to provide a head of water for pressure etc. **stand-point,** *n.* a point of view. **standstill,** *n.* a stoppage, a cessation of progress. **stand-up,** *a.* of a collar, upright; manfully fought, unflinching, thorough; of a comedian, telling jokes etc. directly to the audience in a solo performance. **stand-up fight** FIGHT. **stander,** *n.* **stander-by,** *n.* **standing,** *a.* erect; not cut down; fixed, established, permanent, not temporary or for a special occasion; stagnant. *n.* the act of one that stands; station; relative place or position; repute, estimation, esp. good estimation, duration, existence. **standing army,** *n.* a peacetime army of professional soldiers. **standing order,** *n.* an instruction to a bank by a customer to pay fixed sums at regular intervals in payment of bills etc.; (*pl.*) orders made by a deliberative assembly as to the manner in which its business shall be conducted. **standing rigging,** *n.* the fixed ropes and chains by which the masts etc. on a ship, are secured. **standing room,** *n.* room for standing, esp. after all seats are filled. **standing stone,** *n.* a large erect stone set in the ground in prehistoric times. **standing wave,** *n.* a wave that has a fixed amplitude at any given point along its axis. [OE *standan, stondan*]

standard, *n.* a flag as the distinctive emblem of an army, government etc.; a measure of extent, quantity, value etc., established by law or custom as an example or criterion for others; any type, fact, thing etc., serving as a criterion; the degree of excellence required for a particular purpose; comparative degree of excellence; in coinage the proportion of gold or silver and alloy fixed by authority; a grade of classification in elementary schools; an upright pillar, post, or other support; a tree or shrub growing on a single upright stem, or supported on its own stem. *a.* recognized as a standard for imitation, comparison etc. **standard-bearer,** *n.* a soldier carrying a standard; a leader of a movement or cause. **standard deviation,** *n.* a measure of the scatter of the value of a variable about a mean in a frequency distribution. **standard lamp,** *n.* a movable lamp on a tall pedestal. **standard of living,** *n.* a level of subsistence or material welfare of an individual, group or community. **standard time,** *n.* the method of reckoning time from a conventionally-adopted meridian (for most purposes this is the meridian of Greenwich). **standardize, -ise,** *v.t.* **standardization, -isation,** *n.* [OF *estandard*, from OHG *standan*, to STAND, combined with OF *estendard*, from L as EXTEND]

standing etc. STAND.

†**standish,** *n.* a stand for ink, pens etc.

standpoint, standstill etc. STAND.

St Andrews[1], *n.* a town at the E tip of Fife, Scotland, 19 km/12 mi SE of Dundee; population (1981) 11,400. Its university (1411) is the oldest in Scotland, and the Royal and Ancient Club (1754) is the ruling body in the sporting world of golf.

St Andrews[2], *n.* Scottish golf course near the town of St Andrews in Fife. It is regarded as the home of British golf and the Royal and Ancient Club, the game's ruling body, has its headquarters there. There are four courses, all municipal; the Old Course dates from the 16th century. One of the earliest patrons was Mary Queen of Scots. The best-known hole is the 17th, the 'Road Hole'. St Andrews has been used to stage the British Open 24 times between 1873 and 1984.

Stanford, *n.* **Charles Villiers** (1852–1924), British composer and teacher, born in Ireland. A leading figure in the 19th-century renaissance of British music, his many works include operas such as *Shamus O'Brien* (1896), seven symphonies, chamber music, and church music. Among his pupils were Vaughan Williams, Holst, and Bridge.

stang[1], *n.* (*dial.*) a wooden bar, pole, or shaft, a rood of land. **to ride the stang,** to be carried on a pole in derision, an old method of punishment. [OE *steng*, rel. to *stingan*, to STING]

stang[2], *n.* (*Sc.*) STING.

Stanhope, *n.* **Hester Lucy** (1776–1839), English traveller who left England in 1810 to tour the Levant with Bedouins and eventually settled there. She adopted local dress and became involved in Eastern politics.

stanhope, *n.* a light open two- or four-wheeled carriage first built for Fitzroy Stanhope (1787–1864); an iron printing-press invented by the 3rd Earl Stanhope (1753–1816).

staniel, *n.* a kestrel. [OE *stăngiella* (STONE, *giellan*, to YELL)]

Stanislavsky, *n.* **Konstantin Sergeivich** (1863–1938), Russian actor, director, and teacher. He founded the Moscow Art Theatre (1898) and directed productions of Chekhov and Gorky. He was the originator of Method acting, described in *My Life in Art* (1924) and other works.

stank, *past* STINK.

Stanley[1], *n.* town on E Falkland, capital of the Falkland Islands; population (1986) 1200. After changing its name only once between 1843 and 1982, it was renamed five times in the space of six weeks during the Falklands War in Apr.–June 1982.

Stanley[2], *n.* family name of Earls of DERBY.
Stanley[3], *n.* **Henry Morton** (1841–1904), Welsh-born US explorer and journalist who made four expeditions in Africa. He and LIVINGSTONE met at Ujiji in 1871 and explored Lake Tanganyika. He traced the course of the river Zaïre (Congo) to the sea (1874–77), established the Congo Free State (Zaïre) in 1879–84, and charted much of the interior from 1887–89.
Stanley[4], *n.* **Wendell** (1904–71), US biochemist. Working at the Rockefeller Institute, Princeton, Stanley succeeded, in 1935, in crystallizing a virus: the tobacco mosaic Virus (TMV). He went on to demonstrate that, despite its crystalline state, TMV remained infectious. Along with John Northrop and James Sumner, Stanley received the 1946 Nobel Chemistry Prize.
stannary, *n.* a tin-mine, tin-works; a tin-mining district. *a.* pertaining to tin-mines etc. [late L *stannāria*, from *stannum*, tin]
stannic, *a.* of or containing (tetravalent) tin. **stannate,** *n.* a salt of stannic acid. **stanniferous, stannous,** *a.* of or containing (bivalent) tin.
St Anthony's fire, erysipelas.
Stanton, *n.* **Elizabeth Cady** (1815–1902), US feminist, who with Susan B ANTHONY, founded the National Woman Suffrage Association 1869, the first women's movement in the US. She and Anthony wrote and compiled the *History of Women's Suffrage* (1881–86). Stanton also worked for the abolition of slavery.
Stanwyck, *n.* **Barbara,** stage name of Ruby Stevens (1907–90), US film actress of the 1930s to 1950s. Often cast as an independently minded woman of the world, she also excelled in villainous roles, as in *Double Indemnity* (1944). Her other films include *Stella Dallas* (1937), *Ball of Fire* (1942), and *Executive Suite* (1954).
stanza, *n.* a group of rhymed lines adjusted to each other in a definite scheme. **stanzaed, stanzaic,** *a.* [It., from late L *stantia,* abode, from *stāre*, to stand]
stapes, *n.* the innermost of the three ossicles of the middle ear. **stapedial, stapediferous,** *a.* [med. L, stirrup]
staphyle, *n.* the uvula. **staphyline,** *a.* shaped like a bunch of grapes; pertaining to the uvula. **staphylitis,** *n.* inflammation of the uvula. [Gr. *staphulē*, bunch of grapes]
staphyl(o)-, *comb. form.* staphyle.
Staphylococcus, *n.* a genus of microorganisms (*cocci*) forming the bacteria most frequently found in cutaneous affections of a suppurative kind.
staphyloma, *n.* (*pl.* **-omata**) a protrusion of any of the coats of the eye. **staphylomatous,** *a.*
staphylotomy, *n.* the operation of cutting off the end of the uvula.
staple[1], *n.* a U-shaped piece of metal driven into a post, wall etc., to receive part of a fastening or to hold wire etc.; a similarly shaped piece of thin wire used to fasten papers etc.; the box-like part receiving the bolt of a lock; a bent wire used in wire-stitching; the metal tube holding the reeds of musical instruments like the oboe. *v.t.* to fasten, attach, or support with staples. **stapler,** *n.* a device for inserting staples. [OE *stapul*, cp. Dut. *stapel*, G *Staffel*, step, rung, G and Swed. *stapel*, heap, emporium, Dan. *stabel*, hinge, pile]
staple[2], *n.* the principal commodity sold or produced in any place, country etc.; the main element of diet etc.; the chief material or substance of anything; raw material; the length, strength etc., of the fibre of wool, cotton etc., as a criterion of quality. *a.* settled, marketable; chief, principal, main. *v.t.* to sort or classify (wool etc.) according to staple. [OF *estaple*, LG *stapel*, cogn. with prec.]
star, *n.* a celestial body appearing as a fixed point, esp. one of the fixed stars or those so distant that their relative position in the heavens appears constant; an object, figure, or device resembling a star, esp. one with radiating points used as an emblem or ornament; an asterisk (*); a white spot on the forehead of a horse etc.; a brilliant or prominent person, esp. an actor or singer; a heavenly body regarded as having influence over a person's life. *v.t.* (*past, p.p.* **starred**) to set, spangle, or decorate with stars; to put an asterisk against (a name etc.). *v.i.* of an actor, singer, etc., to appear as a star. **giant star** GIANT. **star-of-Bethlehem,** a bulbous plant, *Ornithogallum umbellatum*, of the lily family with star-shaped white flowers striped outside with green. **Star of David,** the emblem of Judaism and the State of Israel consisting of a six-pointed star made from two superimposed equilateral triangles. **Star of Judah,** the yellow cloth star that persons of Jewish descent were forced by the Nazi government to wear on their clothes as a distinguishing mark. **Stars and Stripes,** the national flag of the US. **to see stars,** to see small points of light as a result of e.g. a bump on the head; to be dazed. **Star-Chamber,** *n.* a court of civil and criminal jurisdiction at Westminster (abolished 1641), famous under Charles I for its arbitrary proceedings (named from the stars painted on the ceilings, or from certain Jewish covenants, called Starrs, said to have been deposited there). †**star-crossed,** *a.* unfortunate. **star-drift,** *n.* the common proper motion of stars in the same region of the heavens. **stardust,** *n.* a large concentration of distant stars appearing as dust; a romantic or magical feeling. **star-finch,** *n.* the redstart. **star fruit,** *n.* the yellow, edible fruit, star-shaped in section, of a SE Asian tree, *Averrhoa carambola*. **starfish,** *n.* an echinoderm, *Asterias rubens*, with fiver or more rays or arms. **star gaze,** *v.i.* to gaze at the stars; to daydream. **stargazer,** *n.* an astronomer or astrologer. **stargazing,** *n.* **starlight,** *n.* the light of the stars. **starlit,** *a.* **star-shell,** *n.* a shell bursting in the air and emitting luminous stars, used to light up an enemy's position. **star-spangled,** *a.* covered with stars. **Star-spangled Banner,** the Stars and Stripes; the national anthem of the US. **star- stone,** *n.* a variety of sapphire. **star-studded,** *a.* of a film, play etc., having a large proportion of famous performers; covered with stars. **Star Wars,** *n.* (*sing. in constr.*) the Strategic Defense Initiative, a proposed American defence plan involving laser-armed satellites deployed in space for destroying enemy missiles. **starwort,** *n.* a plant of the genus *Stellaria* or *Aster*. **stardom,** *n.* the state or status of being a star in films etc. **starless,** *a.* **starlet,** *n.* a young actress who is being trained and promoted as a future star performer. **starlike,** *a.* **starry,** *a.* filled, adorned with stars; shining like, or illuminated by stars. **starry-eyed,** *a.* acting or thinking in a dreamy, overoptimistic manner. **starriness,** *n.* [OE *steorra*, cp. Dut. *ster*, G *Stern*, Icel. *stjarna*, Swed. *stjerna*, also L *stella*, Gr. *astēr*]
starboard, *n.* the right-hand side of a vessel looking forward. *v.t.* to put or turn to starboard; to make (a vessel) turn to starboard. [OE *stēorbord* (*stēor*, rudder, as STEER[1])]
starch, *n.* a white, tasteless, odourless, amorphous compound, found in all plants except fungi, but esp. in cereals, potatoes, beans etc., an important constituent of vegetable foods, and used as a soluble powder to stiffen linen etc.; food, e.g. potatoes, which contains a lot of starch; stiffness, preciseness, formality. *a.* stiff, precise, prim. *v.t.* to stiffen with starch. **starch-reduced,** *a.* having the starch content reduced, as in bread etc. eaten by slimmers. **starchedly, starchly,** *adv.* **starchedness, starchness,** *n.* **starcher,** *n.* **starchy,** *a.* a pertaining to starch; stiff, unyielding. **starchiness,** *n.* [ME *sterch*, strong, cp. OE *stercan*, to stiffen, cogn. with STARK]
stare, *v.i.* to look with eyes fixed and wide open, as in admiration, surprise, horror etc.; to stand out, to be prominent. *v.t.* to affect by staring. *n.* a staring gaze. **to stare in the face,** to be obvious to. **starer,** *n.* **staringly,** *adv.* [OE *starian* (cp. Dut. *staren,* Icel. *stara*, also G *starr*, stiff), prob. rel. to Gr. *stereos*, firm]
stark, *a.* rigid, stiff; stubborn, inflexible; incomplete, downright, sheer; (*poet.*) strong. *adv.* wholly, absolutely. **starkers,** *a.* (*coll.*) stark-naked. **starkly,** *adv.* **starkness,** *n.* [OE *stearc* (cp. Dut. *sterk*, G *stark*, Icel. *sterkr*), cogn with prec.]
Stark, *n.* **Freya** (1893–), English traveller, mountaineer, and writer. She described her explorations in the

Middle East in many books, including *The Valley of the Assassins* (1934), *The Southern Gates of Arabia* (1936), and *A Winter in Arabia* (1940).

stark-naked, *a.* quite naked. [OE *steort*, tail (cp. Dut. *stert* G *Sterz*, Icel. *stertr*, also Gr. *storthē*, spike), NAKED]

starling[1], *n.* a small black and brown speckled bird of the genus *Sturnus*, esp. *S. vulgaris*. [OE *Stær* (cp. G *Star*, Icel. *stari, starri*)]

starling[2], *n.* an enclosure of piles round a bridge-pier etc. [cp. Dan. and Swed. *stor*, stake]

Starling, *n.* **Ernest Henry** (1866–1927), English physiologist who discovered secretin, and coined the word 'hormone' to describe chemicals of this sort. He formulated Starling's law, which states that the force of the heart's contraction is a function of the length of the muscle fibres.

START, (*abbr.*) Strategic Arms Reduction Talks.

start, *v.i.* to make a sudden involuntary movement, as from fear, surprise etc.; to move abruptly (aside, etc.); to shrink, to wince; of timber, rivets etc., to give way, to become loose etc.; to set out, to begin a journey; to make a beginning (on a journey etc.). *v.t.* to cause to start, to rouse; to originate, to set going; to set (people) working; to give the signal to (persons) to start in a race; to begin (work etc.); to cause (timbers etc.) to start; (*Naut.*) to draw (liquor) from, or draw liquor from (a cask). *n.* a sudden involuntary movement, as of fear, surprise etc.; (*usu. pl.*) a spasmodic effort; the beginning of a journey, enterprise etc., a setting-out; a starting-place; the amount of lead originally given to a competitor in a race etc.; advantage gained in a race, business etc. **by fits and starts** FIT[1]. **for a start,** in the first place. **to start in,** to begin. **to start on,** (*coll.*) to pick a fight with; to reprimand. **to start out,** to begin a journey; to take the first steps in a particular activity. **to start up,** to rise suddenly; to come into notice or occur to the mind suddenly; of an engine, to start. **starter,** *n.* one who starts; one who gives the signal for starting a race etc.; a horse or other competitor starting in a race; (also **self starter**) a device for starting an internal-combustion engine; anything that initiates a process; (*often pl.*) the first course of a meal. **for starters,** (*coll.*) in the first place, to begin with. †**startful,** *a.* of horses, skittish, shy. **starting,** *n., a.* **starting block,** *n.* (*usu. pl.*) a device consisting of angled wooden blocks or metal pads used by sprinters to brace their feet in crouch starts. **starting gate** GATE. **starting-point,** *n.* a point of departure. **starting-post,** *n.* a post from which competitors start in a race. **starting price,** *n.* the odds on a horse at the beginning of a race. †**startingly,** *adv.* by fits and starts. [ME *sterten*, cp. Dut. *storten*, G *sturzen*, Dan. *styrte*, Swed. *störta*, to cast down, etc.]

startle, *v.t.* to cause to start; to alarm, to shock. **startler,** *n.* **startling,** *a.* surprising, alarming. **startlingly,** *adv.* [ME *stertlen*, freq. of prec.]

starve, *v.i.* to perish or suffer severely from hunger; to be in want or penury; to suffer from the lack of mental or spiritual nutriment; (*dial.*) to die or suffer severely from cold; †to die, to perish. *v.t.* to cause to perish or be extremely distressed by lack of food; to force (into surrender etc.) thus; to deprive of physical or mental nutriment; (*dial.*) to cause to perish or suffer severely from cold. **starvation** *n.* **starveling,** *n., a.* **starvo,** *n.* (*Austral.*) a sausage, a saveloy. [OE *steorfan*, to die, cp. *sterfan*, to kill, Dut. *sterven*, G *sterben*]

stash, *v.t.* (*coll.*) to store, (money etc.) in a secret place (usu. with *away*) *n.* a secret store, a hideaway. [etym. unknown]

stasimon, *n.* (*pl.* **-ma**) (*Gr. Ant.*) an ode sung by the entire chorus after the opening ode. [Gr., as foll.]

stasis, *n.* stagnation of the blood, esp. in the small vessels or capillaries; a state of equilibrium or inaction. [Gr., from *sta-*, root of *histanai*, to stand]

-stat, *comb. form.* designating a device that causes something to remain stationary or constant, as in *thermostat*. [Gr. *-statés*, from *histanai*, to cause to stand]

state, *n.* condition, mode of existence, situation, relation to circumstances; a political community organized under a government, a commonwealth, a nation, the body politic; such a community forming part of a federal republic; civil government; dignity, pomp, splendour; †a throne, †a canopy; (*pl.*) the legislative body in Jersey or Guernsey; (*coll.*) a nervous or excited condition. *a.* of or pertaining to the state or body politic; used or reserved for ceremonial occasions. *v.t.* to set forth, esp. with explicitness and formality; to fix, to determine, to specify; to express the conditions of (a problem etc.) in mathematical symbols. **state of affairs,** a certain situation, set of circumstances. **State Registered Nurse,** a fully qualified nurse. **the States,** (*coll.*) the US. **to lie in state,** of an important dead person, to lie in a coffin in some place where the public may come to visit as a token of respect. **statecraft,** *n.* statesmanship. **State Department,** *n.* that part of the US government responsible for foreign affairs. **statehouse,** *n.* the building which houses a US state legislature. **state-of-the-art,** *a.* using the most advanced technology available at the time. **state paper,** *n.* a document relating to state affairs. **State Rights,** *n.pl.* rights reserved by the individual states of the US. **state-room,** *n.* a room reserved for ceremonial occasions; a private sleeping apartment on a liner etc. **state school,** *n.* a goverment-financed school for the provision of free education. **States General,** see separate entry. **stateside,** *a., adv.*, of, in, or towards the US. **statesman,** *n.* one skilled in the art of government; one taking a leading part in the administration of the state. **statesmanlike, statesmanly,** *a.* **statesmanship,** *n.* **stateswoman,** *n.fem.* **state socialism,** *n.* government ownership of the leading industries, financial institutions etc. in the public interest. **state trial,** *n.* a trial for offences against the state. **statable,** *a.* **statedly,** *adv.* **statehood,** *n.* **stateless,** *a.* without nationality. **stately,** *a.* grand, lofty, dignified, elevated, imposing. **stately home,** *n.* a large country mansion, usu. of historic interest and open to public view. **statement,** *n.* the act of stating; that which is stated; a formal account, recital, or narration; a formal presentation of accounts. **statism,** *n.* belief in the control of economic and social affairs by the state. **statist,** *n.* [OF *estat*, L STATUS]

stater, *n.* a coin of ancient Greece, esp. the standard gold coin of 20 drachmas. [Gr., from *sta-*, see STATIC]

States General, *n.* the former French parliament which consisted of three estates – nobility, clergy, and commons. First summoned in 1302, it declined in importance as the power of the crown grew. It was not called at all between 1614 and 1789 when the crown needed to institute fiscal reforms to avoid financial collapse. Once called, the demands made by the States General formed the first phase in the French Revolution. The term States General is also the name of the Dutch parliament.

static, *a.* pertaining to bodies at rest or in equilibrium; acting as weight without producing motion; pertaining to or causing stationary electric charges; relating to interference of radio or television signals. *n.* static electricity; atmospherics; electrical interference of radio or television signals causing crackling, hissing, and a speckled picture. **static electricity,** *n.* electrical effects caused by stationary charges, as opposed to charged particles flowing in a current. **statics,** *n. sing.* the branch of dynamics which treats the relations between forces in equilibrium. **statically,** *adv.* [Gr. *statikos*]

Statice, *n.* a genus of plants containing the sea-lavender. [Gr. *statikē*, fem. of *statikos*, STATIC]

station, *n.* the place where a person or thing stands, esp. an appointed or established place; a place where police, coastguards, naval or military forces etc., have their headquarters, a military post; a place or building at which railway-trains stop for setting down or taking up passengers or goods; position, occupation, standing, rank, esp. high rank; (*Austral.*) the ranch-house or homestead of a sheep-farmer; in the Roman Catholic Church, a church to which a procession resorts for devotion; any of a series of 14 images or pictures (in a church) representing successive scenes in Christ's passion; the area inhabited by a particular organism, a habitat; a radio or television channel. *v.t.* to assign to or place in a particular station, to post. **station-house,** *n.* a police-station. **stationmaster,** *n.* the official in charge of a railway station. **station wagon,** *n.* (*chiefly N Am.*) an estate car. **stational,** *a.* **stationary,** *a.* remaining in one place, not moving; intended to remain in one place, fixed, not portable; of planets, having no apparent movement in longitude; not changing in character, condition, magnitude etc. *n.* one who is stationary, esp. (*pl.*) stationary troops. **stationary wave** STANDING WAVE. **stationariness,** *n.* [F, from L *statiōnem*, nom. *-tio*, from *stāre*, to stand]

stationer, *n.* one who sells papers, pens, ink, and writing materials. **stationery,** *n.*.

Stationery Office, His/Her Majesty's (HMSO), office established in 1786 to supply books and stationery to British government departments, and to superintend the printing of government reports and other papers, and books and pamphlets on subjects ranging from national works of art to industrial and agricultural processes. The corresponding establishment in the US is the Government Printing Office.

Stations of the Cross, in the Christian church, a series of 14 crosses, usually each with a picture or image, depicting the 14 stages in Jesus Christ's journey to the crucifixion.

statism STATE.

statistics, *n.pl.* numerical facts, arranged and classified, esp. respecting social conditions; (*sing. in constr.*) the science of collecting, organizing, and applying statistics. **statistical,** *a.* **statistically,** *adv.* **statistician,** *n.*

stative, *a.* (*Heb. Gram.*) of some verbs, expressing past action etc., as still continuing; (*Rom. Ant.*) pertaining to a fixed camp or military post. [L *statīvus*, from *stāre*, to stand, p.p. *status*]

statoblast, *n.* an internal bud developed in freshwater sponges and polyzoa. [Gr. *statos*, fixed, from *sta-* root of *histanai*, to stand, -BLAST]

stator, *n.* the fixed part of an electrical generator. [Gr. *statos*, fixed]

statoscope, *n.* a sensitive aneroid barometer for showing minute fluctuations of pressure.

statue, *n.* a representation of a person or animal sculptured or cast, e.g. in marble or bronze, esp. about life-size. **statuary,** *a.* of or for statues. *n.* statues collectively. **statued,** *a.* **statuesque,** *a.* having the dignity or beauty of a statue. **statuesquely,** *adv.* **statuesqueness,** *n.* **statuette,** *n.* a small statue. [OF, from L *statua*, from *statuere*, to cause to stand, as foll.]

stature, *n.* the natural height of a body, esp. of a person; eminence. **statured,** *a.* [F, from L *statūra*, upright posture, from *stāre*, to stand, p.p. *status*]

status , *n.* relative standing, rank, or position in society; (*Law*) legal position or relation to others; situation, state of affairs. **status symbol,** *n.* a possession regarded as indicative of a person's elevated social rank or wealth. [L, as prec.]

status quo, *n.* the existing state of affairs. [L state in which]

statute, *n.* a law enacted by a legislative body; an ordinance of a corporation or its founder intended as a permanent law. **statute of limitations,** a statute prescribing a period of time within which proceedings must be taken to enforce a right or bring an action at law. **statute-book,** *n.* a book in which statutes are published. **statute law,** *n.* law enacted by a legislative body. **statute-roll,** *n.* a statute-book; an engrossed statute. **statutable, statutory,** *a.* enacted, regulated, enforced, or recognized by statute. **statutably,** *adv.* [L, as prec.]

Staudinger, *n.* **Hermann** (1881–1965), German organic chemist, founder of macro-molecular chemistry, who carried out pioneering research into the structure of albumen and cellulose. Awarded the Nobel prize in 1953.

Stauffenberg, *n.* **Claus von** (1907–44), German colonel in World War II, who planted a bomb in Hitler's headquarters conference room in the Wolf's Lair at Rastenburg, East Prussia, on 20 July 1944. Hitler was injured, and Stauffenberg and 200 others were later executed.

staunch[1], STANCH[1].

staunch[2], *a.* watertight; loyal, constant, trustworthy. **staunchly,** *adv.* **staunchness,** *n.* [OF *estancher*]

staurolite, *n.* (*Min.*) an orthorhombic ferrous silicate of aluminium occurring in cross-like twin crystals. **staurolitic,** *a.* **stauroscope,** *n.* an instrument for observing the effects of parallel polarized light in crystals. [Gr. *stauros*, cross, -LITE]

stave, *n.* one of the curved strips forming the side of a cask etc.; a strip of wood or other material used for a similar purpose; a stanza, a verse; (*Mus.*) a staff. *v.t.* (*past, p.p.* **staved, stove**) to break a hole in (a cask, boat etc.); to make (a hole) thus; to furnish or fit with staves; to stop, avert, or ward (off). [var. of STAFF[1], from M.E. dat. sing.]

staves, *pl.* STAFF[1], STAVE.

stavesacre, *n.* a species of larkspur, *Delphinium staphisagria*, the seeds of which were formerly used as a poison for lice etc. [OF *stavesaigre*, *staphisaigre*, L *staphisagria* (Gr. *staphis*, raisins, *agria*, wild)]

Stavropol, *n.* a territory of the Russian Soviet Federal Socialist Republic, lying N of the Caucasus mountains; area 80,600 km2/31,128 sq miles; population(1985) 2,715,000. Capital is Stavropol. Irrigated land produces grain but sheep are also reared. There are natural gas deposits.

stay[1], *v.i.* to continue in a specified place or state; to remain; to dwell or have one's abode temporarily (at, with etc.); (*Sc., S Afr.*) to live (at); to pause, to stand still; to tarry, to wait; to keep going or last out (in a race etc.). *v.t.* to hinder, to stop (the progress etc., of); to postpone, to suspend. *n.* the act of staying or dwelling; continuance in a place etc.; a check, a restraint or deterrent; suspension of judicial proceedings. **to stay over,** (*coll.*) to remain overnight. **to stay put,** to remain in one's place. **stay-at-home,** *n., a.* (one who is) unenterprising. **staying power,** *n.* stamina. **stayer**[1], *n.* [OF *ester*, L. *stāre*, STAND]

stay[2], *n.* a support, a prop; (*pl.*) a corset. *v.t.* to prop (usu. *up*), to support. **stay-bar, -rod,** *n.* one used as a stay or support in a building etc. **stay-lace,** *n.* one used in lacing a corset. **stay-maker,** *n.* a corset-maker. **stayer**[2], *n.* **stayless,** *a.* [OF *estayer*, to prop, *estaye*, prop, M. Dut. *stade*, *staeye*, OHG *stata*, fit place or time, cogn. with STEAD]

stay[3], *n.* a rope supporting a mast or spar. *v.t.* to support by stays; to put on the other tack. **(hove) in stays,** of a ship, going about from one tack to another. **to miss stays,** to fail in tacking. **staysail,** *n.* a sail extended by a stay. [perh. from OE *stæg*, etym. doubtful, or prec.]

stayer[1] STAY[1].

stayer[2], **stay-lace, -maker** etc. STAY[2].

St Bartholomew, Massacre of, religious murder of Huguenots in Paris between 24 Aug. and 17 Sept. 1572, and until 3 Oct. in the provinces. When Catherine de' Medici's plot to have Coligny assassinated failed, she resolved to have all the Huguenot leaders killed, persuading her son Charles IX it was in the interests of public safety. 25,000 people were believed to have been killed. Catherine received congratulations from all the Catholic powers, and the pope ordered a medal to be struck.

St Bernard (dog), *n.* type of dog 70 cm/2.5 ft high at the shoulder, weight about 70 kg/150 lbs. They are squarely built, with pendulous ears and lips, large feet, and drooping lower eyelids. They are usually orange and white.

St Christopher (St Kitts)-Nevis, country in the West Indies in the Leeward Islands. **area** 267 sq km/103 sq miles. **capital** Basseterre (on St Kitts). **towns** Nevis (chief town of Nevis). **physical** two islands in the Lesser Antilles. **population** (1989) 40,000; annual growth rate 2.3%. **exports** sugar, molasses, cotton; tourism is important. **language** English. **religion** Christian.

STDs, *n.* a term encompassing not only traditional venereal disease, but also a growing list of conditions, such as AIDS and scabies, which are known to be spread primarily by sexual contact. [*s*exually *t*ransmitted *d*iseases]

stead, *n.* place or room which another had or might have had. **in one's stead,** instead of one. **to stand in good stead,** to be of service to. [OE *stede* (cp. Dut. *stede*), cogn. with *stæth*, bank, Dut. *stad*, G *Stadt*, town, L *statis*, Gr. *statis*, and STAND]

steadfast, *a.* firm, resolute, unwavering. **steadfastly,** *adv.* **steadfastness,** *n.* [OE *stedefæst*]

steady, *a.* firmly fixed, not wavering; moving or acting in a regular way, uniform, constant; free from intemperance, irregularity, constant in mind, or conduct. *n.* a rest or support for keeping the hand etc., steady; (*coll.*) a regular boy friend or girl friend. **steady-state theory,** in cosmology, the theory that the Universe has always existed in a steady state, matter being created continuously as it expands. cp. BIG-BANG THEORY. **to go steady** GO[2]. *v.t.* to make steady *v.i.* to become steady. **steadily,** *adv.* **steadiness,** *n.*

steak, *n.* any of several cuts of beef such as *stewing steak, braising steak*; a slice of beef, cut for grilling etc. **steakhouse,** *n.* a restaurant that specializes in serving steaks. [ME *steike*, Icel. *steik*, from *steikja,* to roast on a spit, cogn. with STICK[2]]

steal, *v.t.* (*past* **stole**, *p.p.* **stolen**) to take away without right or permission, to take feloniously; to secure covertly or by surprise; to secure insidiously. *v.i.* to take anything feloniously; to go or come furtively or silently. *n.* (*coll.*) the act of stealing; something stolen; (*coll.*) a bargain. **to steal a march on,** to be beforehand with, to get the start of. **to steal someone's thunder,** to take the credit due to another. **stealer,** *n.* **stealingly,** *adv.* [OE *stelan,* cp. Dut. *stelen*, G *stehlen*, Icel. *stela*]

stealth, *n.* furtiveness, secrecy; secret procedure. **stealthily,** *adv.* **stealthiness,** *n.* **stealthy**, *a.*

steam, *n.* water in the form of vapour or the gaseous form to which it is changed by boiling; the visible mass of particles of water into which this condenses; any vaporous exhalation; (*coll.*) energy, force, go. *v.i.* to give off steam; to rise in steam or vapour; to move by the agency of steam. *v.t.* to treat with steam for the purpose of softening, melting etc., esp. to cook by steam. **steamed up,** of windows etc., clouded by steam; (*coll.*) angry, indignant. **to go under one's own steam,** to go by one's own efforts, to go without help. **to let off steam,** to relieve one's feelings. **steamboat,** *n.* a vessel propelled by steam. **steam-boiler,** *n.* a boiler in a steam-engine. **steam-box, -chest** *n.* the box-shaped part through which steam is conveyed from the boiler to the cylinder. **steam-engine,** *n.* an engine worked by the pressure of steam on a piston moving in a cylinder etc. **steam-gas,** *n.* superheated steam. **steam-gauge,** *n.* an instrument attached to a boiler to indicate the pressure of steam. **steam iron,** *n.* an electric iron with a compartment in which water is heated and then emitted as steam to aid pressing and ironing. **steam jacket,** *n.* a hollow casing round a cylinder etc., for receiving steam to heat the latter. **steam navvy, shovel,** *n.* a mechanical excavator consisting of a large bucket working from a long beam. **steam-power,** *n.* force applied by the agency of steam to machinery etc. **steam roller,** *n.* a heavy roller propelled by steam, used in road-making and repairing; any crushing force. *v.t.* to crush (opposition etc.) by overwhelming pressure. **steamship,** *n.* a ship propelled by steam. **steam-tug,** *n.* a small steam-vessel used for towing ships. **steam turbine,** *n.* a machine in which steam acts on moving blades attached to a drum. **steamer,** *n.* a vessel propelled by steam; a steam fire-engine; a receptacle for steaming articles, esp. for cooking food. **steamy,** *a.* of, like, full of, emitting, or covered with steam; (*sl.*) erotic. **steamily,** *adv.* **steaminess,** *n.* [OE *stēam*, cp. Dut. *stoom*]

stearin, -rine, *n.* a fatty compound contained in the more solid animal and vegetable fats; stearic acid as used for candles. **stearate,** *n.* a salt of stearic acid. **stearic,** *a.* of or pertaining to fat or stearic acid. **stearic acid,** *n.* a fatty acid obtained from solid fats and used in making candles and soap. **stearrhoea,** *n.* an abnormal increase in the secretion from the oil-glands of the skin. [F *stéarine* (Gr. *stear*, fat)]

steatite, *n.* massive talc, soapstone. **steatitic,** *a.* [F *stéatite*]

steat(o)-, *comb. form.* fat. [Gr. *stear*, steatos, fat]

steatocele, *n.* a fatty tumour of the scrotum.

steatoma, *n.* (*pl.* **-mas, -mata**) a fatty encysted tumour. **steatomatous,** *a.*

steatopygous, *a.* characterized by fat buttocks. **steatopygy,** *n.* [Gr. *pugē*, rump]

steed, *n.* a horse, esp. a war-horse. [OE *stēda*, cogn. with STUD[2]]

Steel, *n.* **David** (1938–), British politician, leader of the Liberal Party from 1976–88. He entered into a compact with the Labour government (1977–78), and into an alliance with the Social Democratic Party (SDP) in 1983. Having supported the Liberal-SDP merger (Social and Liberal Democrats), he resigned the leadership in 1988.

steel, *n.* iron combined with carbon in various proportions, remaining malleable at high temperatures and capable of being hardened by cooling; a sword; a steel rod with roughened surface for sharpening knives; a steel strip for stiffening; a quality of hardness, toughness etc. in a person. *v.t.* to cover, point, or face with steel; to harden (the heart etc.). **steel band,** *n.* a type of band (orig. from the Caribbean islands) which plays percussion instruments made from oil drums. **steel-clad,** *a.* clad in armour. **steel-engraving,** *n.* the art of engraving upon steel plates; an engraving on a steel plate; an impression from this. **steel grey,** *n., a.* bluish-grey like steel. **steel-plated,** *a.* plated with steel. **steel-wool,** *n.* fine steel shavings bunched together for cleaning and polishing. **steelworker,** *n.* **steelworks,** *n. sing.* or *pl.* a plant where steel is made. **steelify**, *v.t.* **steely, *a.* steeliness,** *n.* [OE *style*, cp. Dut. *staal*, G *Stahl*, Icel. *stal*, Dan. *staal*]

Steele, *n.* **Richard** (1672–1729), Irish essayist, who founded the journal *The Tatler* (1709–11), in which ADDISON collaborated. They continued their joint work in *The Spectator*, also founded by Steele, (1711–12), and *The Guardian* (1713). He also wrote plays, such as *The Conscious Lovers* (1722).

steelyard, *n.* a balance with unequal arms, the article weighed being hung from the shorter arm and a weight moved along the other till they balance. [mistrans. of LG *staalhof*, sample-yard (*staal*, sample, conf. with *staal*, STEEL), and YARD[2] an enclosure]

Steen, *n.* **Jan** (1626–79), Dutch painter. Born in Leiden, he was also active in The Hague, Delft, and Haarlem. He painted humorous genre scenes, mainly set in taverns or bourgeois households, as well as portraits and landscapes.

steenbok, *n.* a small S African antelope. [Dut., stone-buck, cp. G *Steinbock*]

steenkirk, *n.* a lace cravat worn loose; applied also to wigs, buckles, and other articles of attire. [battle of *Steenkerke*, 3 Aug. 1692]

steep[1], *a.* sharply inclined, sloping at a high angle; (*coll.*) of prices etc., excessive, exorbitant. *n.* a steep slope; a precipice. **steepen,** *v.t., v.i.* **steeply,** *adv.* **steepness,** *n.* **steepy,** *a.* [OE *stēap*, cp. Icel. *steypthr*, rel. to *steypa*, to overthrow, causal of *stūpa*, to stoop]

steep[2], *v.t.* to soak in liquid; to wet thoroughly. *n.* the process of steeping; a liquid for steeping. **to steep in,** to impregnate or imbue with. **steeper,** *n.* [ME *stepen*, Icel. *steypa*, to pour out or cast metals, see prec.]

steepen etc. STEEP[1].

steeper STEEP[2].

steeple, *n.* a lofty structure rising above the roof of a building, esp. a church tower with a spire. **steeple-crowned,** *a.* of a hat, having a tall, tapering crown;

steeplechase *n.* a horse-race across country in which hedges etc., have to be jumped; a track race over obstacles including hurdles and water jumps. **steeplechaser,** *n.* **steeplechasing,** *n., a.* **steeplejack,** *n.* one who climbs steeples etc., to do repairs etc. **steepled,** *a.* **steeplewise,** *adv.* [OE *stypel*, as STEEP[1]]

steer[1], *v.t.* to guide (a ship, aeroplane, motor-car etc.) by a rudder, wheel, handle etc.; to direct (one's course) thus. *v.i.* to guide a ship etc., or direct one's course by or as by this means; to be steered (easily etc.). **to steer clear of,** to avoid. **steersman,** *n.* one who steers. **steersmanship,** *n.* **steerable,** *a.* **steerage,** *n.* the part of a ship, usu. forward and on or below the main deck, allotted to passengers travelling at the lowest rate; the part of the berth-deck on a warship just forward of the ward-room, allotted as quarters to junior officers etc.; the effect of the helm on a ship; †steering; †the stern. **steerage-way,** *n.* sufficient motion of a vessel to enable her to answer the helm. **steerer,** *n.* **steering,** *n.* **steering column,** *n.* a column in a motor vehicle carrying the steering-wheel at the top. **steering committee,** *n.* a committee which determines the order of business for a legislative assembly or other body. **steering engine,** *n.* an engine for working the rudder of a ship. **steering lock,** *n.* the maximum angular amount which wheels can swivel from side to side. **steering-wheel, -gear,** *n.* the wheel or gear which controls the rudder of a ship, or the stub axles of the front wheels of a motor-car. [OE *stēoran,* cogn. with *stēor*, rudder (cp. Dut. *sturen, stuur,* G *steurern, Steuer*)]

steer[2], *n.* a young male of the ox kind, esp. a castrated bullock. **steerling,** *n.* [OE *stēor*, cp. Dut. and G *Stier*, Icel. *stjörr,* also L. *taurus*, Gr. *tauros*]

steerage etc. STEER[1].

steeve[1], *v.i.* of a bowsprit, to have a certain angle of elevation. *v.t.* to give (a bowsprit) this. *n.* such an angle. [OE *stīfian*, from *stīf*, STIFF]

steeve[2], *n.* a spar or derrick for stowing cargo. *v.t.* to stow with a steeve. [OF *estiver*, L *stīpāre*, to press, cogn. with prec.]

Stefan, *n.* **Joseph** (1835–93), Austrian physicist who established one of the basic laws of heat radiation in 1874, since known as the **Stefan–Boltzmann law**. This stated that the heat radiated by a hot body is proportional to the fourth power of its absolute temperature.

Stefan–Boltzmann constant, *n.* in physics, a constant relating the energy emitted by a black body (a hypothetical body that absorbs or emits all the energy falling on it) to its temperature. Its value is 5.6697 '3 10^{-8} W m^{-2} K^{-4}.

stegan(o)-, *comb. form.* covered; hidden; watertight. [Gr. *steganos*, covered, from *stegein,* to cover, foot]

steganography, *n.* the art of secret writing or writing in cipher. **steganographist,** *n.*

steganopod, *n.* any individual of the Steganopodes, an order of birds with all the toes webbed, as the pelicans, frigate-birds etc. *a.* pertaining to this order. **steganopodan, -dous,** *a.*

stegnosis, *n.* constriction of the pores and vessels; constipation. **stegnotic,** *n., a.*

stegosaur, -saurus, *n.* any of several quadrupedal herbivorous dinosaurs of the Jurassic period, with armour-like bony plates. [Gr. *stegos*, roof, *sauros*, lizard]

Steiermark, *n.* German name for Styria, province of Austria.

Steiger, *n.* **Rod(ney Stephen)** (1925–), US character actor, often in leading film roles. His work includes *On the Waterfront* (1954), *In the Heat of the Night* (1967), and the title role in *W. C. Fields and Me* (1976).

stein, *n.* a large, usu. earthenware beer mug, often with a hinged lid. [G]

Stein, *n.* **Gertrude** (1874–1946), US writer. She influenced writers such as HEMINGWAY and Scott FITZGERALD by her cinematic technique, use of repetition and absence of punctuation: devices to convey immediacy and realism. Her works include the self-portrait *The Autobiography of Alice B. Toklas* (1933).

Steinbeck, *n.* **John (Ernst)** (1902–68), US novelist. His work includes *Of Mice and Men* (1937), and *The Grapes of Wrath* (1939), *Cannery Row* (1945), and *East of Eden* (1952). Awarded the Nobel prize in 1962.

steinberger, *n.* a Rhenish white wine from near Wiesbaden. [G]

steinbock, STEENBOK.

Steiner, *n.* **Max(imilian Raoul)** (1888–1971), Austrian composer of film music who lived in the US from 1914. He composed his first film score in 1929 and produced some of the cinema's finest music, including the scores to *King Kong* (1933), *Gone with the Wind* (1939), and *Casablanca* (1942).

stele, (*pl.* **-lae**) an upright slab usu. with inscriptions and sculpture, for sepulchral or other purposes; the cylindrical vascular portion in the stems and roots of plants. **stelar, stelene,** *a.* [Gr. *stēlē*]

†stell, *v.t.* (*Shak.*) to place, to set. [OE *stellan*, cogn. with STALL[1]]

Stella, *n.* **Frank** (1936–), US painter, a pioneer of the hard-edged geometric trend in abstract art that succeeded abstract expressionism. From around 1960 he also experimented with the shape of his canvases.

stellar, *a.* of or pertaining to stars. **Stellaria,** *n.* a genus of tufted herbs containing the chickweeds or starworts. **stellate, -ated,** *a.* star-shaped, radiating. **stellately,** *adv.* **stelliferous,** *a.* **stelliform,** *a.* **stellular, -late,** *a.* set with or shaped like small stars. [late *stellāris*, from L *stella,* star]

stellion, *n.* a lizard belonging to the family Agamidae. [L *stellio -opis*, from *stella*, star]

St Elmo's fire, *n.* bluish, flame-like electrical discharge, which occurs above ships' masts or about an aircraft in stormy weather. Although high voltage, it is low current and therefore harmless. St Elmo (or St Erasmus) was a patron of sailors.

stem[1], *n.* the stock, stalk, or ascending axis of a tree, shrub, or other plant; the slender stalk or peduncle of a flower, leaf etc.; an analogous part, as the slender part between the body and foot of a wine glass etc., the tube of a tobacco-pipe, the part by which a watch is attached to a chain etc., the part of a noun, verb etc., to which case-endings etc., are affixed; the stock of a family, a branch of a family; the upright piece of timber or iron at the fore end of a ship to which the sides are joined. *v.t.* (*past, p.p.* **stemmed**) to remove the stem or stems of. **from stem to stern,** from one end of the ship to the other. **to stem from,** to originate in. **stem-winder,** *n.* a watch which may be wound by the stem without a key. **stemless,** *a.* **stemlet,** *n.* **stemmed,** *a.* **stemmer,** *n.* [OE *stæfn*, *stefn*, *stemn*, cp. Dut. *stam*, trunk, *steven*, prow, Icel. *stafn*, *stamn*, stem of ship, G *Stamm*, trunk, *Steven*, stem of ship]

stem[2], *v.t.* (*past, p.p.* **stemmed**) to draw up, to check, to hold back; (*fig.*) to make headway against; in skiing, to slow down by pushing the heel of one or both skis outward from the direction of travel. *n.* in skiing, the process of stemming, used to turn or slow down. [Icel. *stemma*, cp. G *stemmen*]

stemless, stemmer etc. STEM[1].

stemma, *n.* (*pl.* **stemmata**), a simple eye; one of the facets of a compound eye; an ocellus; pedigree, a family tree. [L, a wreath]

stemple, *n.* a cross-bar serving as a step or support in the shaft of a mine. [etym. doubtful]

stemson, *n.* a curved timber behind a ship's apron, supporting the scarfs. [etym. doubtful]

stench, *n.* a foul or offensive smell. **stench-trap,** *n.* a trap in a sewer to prevent the escape of noxious gas. **†stenchy,** *a.* [OE *stenc*, from *stincan*, to STINK]

stencil, *n.* a thin plate of metal or other material out of which patterns have been cut for painting through the spaces on to a surface; a decoration, etc., produced thus. *v.t.* (*past, p.p.* **stencilled**) to paint (letters, designs etc.) by means of a stencil; to decorate (a wall etc.) thus. **stenciller,** *n.* [prob. from OF *estenceler*, to sparkle, to cover with stars, from *estencele*, spark, as TINSEL]

Stendhal, *n.* pen name of Marie Henri Beyle (1783–1842), French novelist. His two major novels *Le Rouge et le Noir/The Red and the Black* (1830) and *La Chartreuse de Parme/The Charterhouse of Parme* (1839) were pioneering works in their treatment of disguise and hypocrisy; a review of the latter by Balzac in 1840 furthered his reputation.

Sten gun, *n.* a light sub-machine gun. [*S*heperd and *T*urpin, the designers, and *En*field, as in BREN GUN]

steno- *comb. form.* contracted. [Gr. *stenos*, narrow]

stenochrome, *n.* a print taken at one impression from several differently-coloured blocks. **stenochromy**, *n.*

stenograph, *n.* a character used in shorthand; a form of typewriter using stenographic characters. **stenographer**, **-graphist**, *n.* a shorthand writer. **stenography**, *n.*

stenosis, *n.* constriction of a bodily passage or orifice; constipation. **stenotic**, *a.* [Gr. *stenosis*, narrow.]

stenotype, *n.* a letter or combination of letters used in shorthand to represent a word or phrase. **stenotypic**, *a.* **stenotypy**, *n.*

†**stent,** STINT.

stentor, *n.* a person with a loud, strong voice; a howling monkey, esp. the ursine howler. **stentorian**, *a.* [L and Gr. *Stentōr*, herald in Trojan war]

step, *v.i.* (*past, p.p.* **stepped**) to lift and set down a foot or the feet alternately, to walk a short distance in a specified direction; to walk or dance slowly or with dignity. *v.t.* to go through, perform, or measure by stepping; to insert the foot of (a mast etc.) in a step. *n.* a single complete movement of one leg in the act of walking, dancing etc.; the distance traversed in this; a short distance; an action or measure taken in a series directed to some end; that on which the foot is placed in ascending or descending, a single stair or a tread in a flight of stairs; a rung of a ladder, a support for the foot in stepping in or out of a vehicle, a doorstep etc.; a footprint; a break in the outline at the bottom of a float or hull of a seaplane which assists in lifting it from the surface of the water; (*pl.*) a self-supporting stepladder with fixed or hinged prop; a degree or grade in progress, rank, or precedence; a socket supporting a frame, etc., for the end of a mast, shaft, etc. **in step,** in marching, dancing etc., in conformity or unison with others; (*coll.*) in agreement (with). **out of step,** not in step; (*coll.*) not in agreement or harmony (with others). **step by step,** *adv.* gradually, with deliberation, taking one step at a time. **step-by-step,** *a.* **to break step,** to cease marching in unison. **to step down,** to resign, retire, relinquish one's position etc.; to decrease the voltage of. **to step in,** to intervene; to visit briefly. **to step on it,** to hurry, to increase speed. **to step out,** to leave (a room etc.) briefly; to take longer, faster strides. **to step out of line,** to depart from normal or acceptable behaviour. **to step up,** to advance by one or more stages; to increase the voltage of; to come forward. **step-down,** *a.* of a transformer, reducing voltage. **step-ladder,** *n.* a ladder with flat treads or rungs. **step-up,** *a.* of a transformer, increasing the voltage. **stepped,** *a.* **stepper,** *n.* **stepping,** *n., a.* **stepping stone,** *n.* a raised stone in a stream or swampy place on which one steps in crossing; a means to an end. **stepwise,** *adv.* proceeding in steps. [OE *steppan*, cogn. with STAMP, *n. stæpe*, cp. Dut. *stap*, G *Stapfe*]

step-, (*pref.*) a prefix used to express relation only by the marriage of a parent. **stepbrother, -sister,** *n.* a stepfather's or stepmother's child by a former marriage. **stepchild, -daughter, -son,** *n.* the child of one's husband or wife by a former marriage. **stepfather, -mother, -parent,** *n.* the later husband or wife of one's parent. [OE *steop*, orphaned, cp. Dut. and G *stief*, Icel. *stjūp-*, OHG *stiufan*, to deprive of parents]

stephanite, *n.* a metallic, black sulphantimonite of silver. [Archduke *Stephan*, of Austria]

stephanotis, *n.* a tropical climbing plant with fragrant waxy flowers. [Gr. *stephanos*, wreath, *ous*, *ōtos*, *ear*]

Stephen[1]**,** *n.* (*c.* 1097–1154), king of England from 1135. A grandson of William I, he was elected king in 1135, although he had previously recognized Henry I's daughter Matilda as heiress to the throne. Matilda landed in England in 1139, and civil war disrupted the country until 1153, when Stephen acknowledged Matilda's son, Henry II, as his own heir.

Stephen[2]**,** *n.* **Leslie** (1832–1904), English critic, first editor of the *Dictionary of National Biography* and father of novelist Virginia Woolf.

Stephen, St, *n.* (died *c.* AD 35), the first Christian martyr; he was stoned to death. Feast day 26 Dec.

Stephen I, St, *n.* (975–1038), king of Hungary from 997, when he succeeded his father. He completed the conversion of Hungary to Christianity, and was canonized in 1803.

Stephenson[1]**,** *n.* **George** (1781–1848), English engineer who built the first successful steam locomotive, and who also invented a safety lamp in 1815. He was appointed engineer of the Stockton and Darlington Railway, the world's first public railway, in 1821, and of the Liverpool and Manchester Railway in 1826. In 1829 he won a £500 prize with his locomotive, *Rocket*.

Stephenson[2]**,** *n.* **Robert** (1803–59), English civil engineer, who constructed railway bridges such as the high-level bridge at Newcastle upon Tyne, England, and the Menai and Conway tubular bridges in North Wales. He was the son of George Stephenson.

stepmother etc. STEP-.

steppe, *n.* a vast plain devoid of forest, esp. in Russia and Siberia. [Rus. *stepe*]

stepping stone etc. STEP.

stepsister etc. STEP-.

Steptoe, *n.* **Patrick Christopher** (1913–88), English obstetrician who pioneered *in vitro* or 'test-tube' fertilization. Steptoe, together with biologist Robert Edwards, was the first to succeed in implanting in the womb an egg fertilized outside the body.

-ster, *suf.* denoting an agent, as in *gangster, punster, songster*. [OE *-estre* (comb. of *-es*, *-ter*, as in L *minister*)]

stercoraceous, *a.* pertaining to, composed of, or like dung. **stercoral**, *a.* **stercorary**, *n., a.* [L *stercus -coris*, dung, -ACEOUS]

stere, *n.* a cubic metre (35·147589 cu. ft.) used to measure timber. [F *stère*, as STEREO-]

Sterea Ellas-Evvoia, the region of central Greece and Euboea, occupying the southern part of the Greek mainland between the Ionian and Aegean seas and including the island of Euboea; population (1981) 1,099,800; area 24,391 km2/9421 sq miles. Chief city is Athens.

stereo[1]**,** *n.* (*pl.* **stereos**) stereophonic music reproduction; a piece of stereophonic music equipment such as a record player, tape deck etc. *a.* stereophonic.

stereo[2]**, short for** STEREOTYPE, STEREOSCOPE, STEREOSCOPIC.

stereo-, *comb. form.* solid, three-dimensional. [Gr. *stereos*, stiff, solid]

stereobate, *n.* a solid substructure or base for a building.

stereochemistry, *n.* chemistry concerned with the composition of matter as exhibited in the relations of atoms in space.

stereochromy, *n.* painting with pigments mixed with soluble or water-glass.

stereogram, *n.* a three-dimensional picture or image, a stereograph; a stereo radiogram. **stereograph**, *n.* a pair of almost identical images which when viewed together through a stereoscope give a three-dimensional effect. **stereographic**, *a.* **stereographically,** *adv.* **stereography**, *n.* the art of delineating solid forms on a plane.

stereoisomer, *n.* an isomer of a molecule in which the atoms are linked in the same order but have a different spatial arrangement. **stereoisomerism,** *n.*

stereome, *n.* a strengthening tissue in vascular plants composed of thick-walled, elongated prosenchymatous cells.

stereometer, *n.* an instrument for measuring the volume of solid bodies; an instrument for determining the specific gravity of liquids, powders etc. **stereometric, -ical,** *a.* **stereometry**, *n.*

stereophonic, *a.* of a sound recording or reproduction system involving the use of two or more separate microphones and loudspeakers to split the sound into separate channels to create a spatial effect. **stereophonically,** *adv.* **stereophony**, *n.*

stereopticon, *n.* a double magic-lantern for producing dissolving views.

stereoptics *n. sing.* the science of stereoscopy.

stereoscope, *n.* a binocular instrument for blending into one two pictures taken from slightly different positions, thus giving an effect of three dimensions. **steroscopic, -ical**, *a.* giving the effect of solidity. **stereoscopy**, *n.*

stereotrope, *n.* an optical device for bringing pictures into relief and conveying the impression of continuous motion. **stereotropic**, *a.* [Gr. *tropē*, turning, from *trepein*, to turn]

stereotype, *n.* a printing plate cast from a mould taken from movable type; a hackneyed convention, idea etc.; one who or that which conforms to a standardized image. *v.t.* to make a stereotype of; to fix or establish in a standard form. **stereotyper, -typist**, *n.* **stereotyped,** *a.* hackneyed, unoriginal. **stereotypy**, *n.* the process of making stereotype plates; meaningless, repetitive action or thought.

steric, -ical, *a.* pertaining to the spatial arrangement of atoms in a molecule.

sterigma, *n.* (*Bot.*) a stalk or support. **sterigmatic**, *a.* [Gr. *stērigma -matos*, a support]

sterile, *a.* barren, unfruitful; not producing crops, fruit, young etc.; containing no living bacteria, microbes etc., sterilized; destitute of ideas or sentiment. **sterility**, *n.* **sterilize, -ise**, *v.t.* to rid of living bacteria; to make sterile; to render incapable of procreation. **sterilization, -isation,** *n.* **sterilizer, -iser,** *n.* [OF, from L *sterilem*, nom. *-lis*, cogn. with Gr. *stereos*, STEREO-, G *starr*, rigid]

sterlet, *n.* a small sturgeon, *Acipenser ruthenus*. [F, from Rus. *sterlyadi*]

sterling, *a.* of coins and precious metals, of standard value, genuine, pure; sound, of intrinsic worth, not showy. *n.* British (as distinct from foreign) money; genuine British money. **sterling area,** *n.* a group of countries that keep their reserves in sterling rather than in gold or dollars. [perh. from OE *steorling*, little star, or as STARLING[1]]

stern[1], *a.* severe, grim, forbidding, austere; harsh, rigid, strict; ruthless, unyielding, resolute. **sternly,** *adv.* **sternness,** *n.* [OE *styrne*, perh. rel. to Gr. *stereos*, STEREO-]

stern[2], *n.* the hind part of a ship or boat; the rump or tail of an animal. **stern-chase,** *n.* a chase in which one vessel follows the other straight behind. **stern-chaser** CHASE[1]. **stern-fast,** *n.* a rope or chain mooring the stern to a wharf etc. **sternforemost,** *adv.* (moving) with the stern in front. **stern-post,** *n.* a timber or iron post forming the central upright of the stern and usu. carrying the rudder. **stern-sheets,** *n.pl.* the space in a boat between the stern and the aftermost thwart. **sternway,** *n.* the movement of a ship backwards. **stern-wheel,** *n.* a paddle-wheel at the stern of a river-steamer. **stern-wheeler,** *n.* †**sternage**, *n.* (*Shak.*) steerage; the stern. **sterned,** *a.* (*usu. in comb.*, as *flat-sterned*). **sternmost,** *a.* **sternward,** *a., adv.* **-wards,** *adv.* [ME *stēorne*, Icel. *stjörn*, steering, cogn. with STEER[1]]

Sternberg, *n.* **Josef von** (1894–1969), Austrian film director who lived in the US from childhood. He worked with Marlene Dietrich on *The Blue Angel/Der blaue Engel* (1930) and other films. He favoured striking imagery over narrative in his work, which includes *Underworld* (1927) and *Blonde Venus* (1932).

Sterne, *n.* **Laurence** (1713–68), Irish writer, creator of the comic anti-hero Tristram Shandy. *The Life and Opinions of Tristram Shandy, Gent* (1760–67), an eccentrically whimsical and bawdy novel, foreshadowed many of the techniques and devices of 20th-century novelists, including James Joyce. His other works include *A Sentimental Journey through France and Italy* (1768).

sternum, *n.* the breast-bone. **sternal,** *a.* pertaining to the sternum. **sternalgia**, *n.* pain in the chest, esp. angina pectoris. **sternebra**, *n.* one of the serial segments of the sternum of a vertebrate. **sternoclavicular**, *a.* pertaining to the sternum and the clavicle. [L, from Gr. *sternon*]

sternutation, *n.* the act of sneezing, a sneeze. **sternutative**, **-tatory,** *a.* causing (one) to sneeze. *n.* a sternutative substance, as snuff. [L *sternūtātio*, from *sternūtāre*, freq. of *sternuere*, to sneeze, cp. Gr. *ptarnusthai*]

sternward etc. STERN[2].

steroid, *n.* any of a group of compounds of similar chemical structure, including sterols, bile acids and various hormones. [STEROL, -OID]

sterol, *n.* any of various solid alcohols, such as cholesterol, ergosterol. [shortened from CHOLESTEROL etc.]

stertorous, *a.* characterized by deep snoring or snore-like sounds. **stertorously,** *adv.* **stertorousness,** *n.* [L *stertere*, to snore, -OR, -OUS]

stet, *v.t.* (*Print.*) let it stand (cancelling a previous correction); to write 'stet' against. [L, 3rd sing. pres. subj. of *stāre*, to stand]

stethoscope, *n.* an instrument used in auscultation of the chest etc. *v.t.* to examine with this. **stethoscopic,** *a.* **stethoscopically,** *adv.* **stethoscopist,** *n.* **stethoscopy,** *n.* [Gr. *stēthos*, breast, -SCOPE]

stetson, *n.* a broad-brimmed slouch hat. [from John *Stetson*, 1830–1906, hatmaker]

stevedore, *n.* one whose occupation is to load or unload ships. [Sp. *estivador*, from *estivar*, L. *stīpāre*, see STEEVE[2]]

Stevens[1], *n.* **Alfred** (1817–75), British sculptor, painter, and designer. He created the *Wellington monument* begun in 1858 (St Paul's, London). He was devoted to high renaissance art, especially to Raphael, and studied in Italy in 1833.

Stevens[2], *n.* **George** (1904–75), US film director who began as a director of photography. He made films such as *Swing Time* (1936) and *Gunga Din* (1939), and his reputation grew steadily, as did the length of his films. His later work included *A Place in the Sun* (1951), *Shane* (1953), and *Giant* 1956.

Stevens[3], *n.* **Siaka Probin** (1905–88), Sierra Leone politician, president from 1971–85. He was the leader of the moderate left-wing All People's Congress (APC), from 1978 the country's only legal political party.

Stevens[4], *n.* **Wallace** (1879–1955), US poet. His volumes of poems include *Harmonium* (1923), *The Man with the Blue Guitar* (1937), and *Transport to Summer* (1947). *The Necessary Angel* (1951) is a collection of essays. An elegant and philosophical poet, he won a Pulitzer prize in 1954 for his *Collected Poems*.

Stevenson[1], *n.* **Adlai** (1900–65), US Democrat politician. As governor of Illinois (1949–53) he campaigned vigorously against corruption in public life, and as Democratic candidate for the presidency in 1952 and 1956 was twice defeated by Eisenhower. In 1945 he was chief US delegate at the founding conference of the United Nations.

Stevenson[2], *n.* **Robert Louis** (1850–94), Scottish novelist and poet. Early works included *An Island Voyage* (1878) and *Travels with a Donkey* (1879), but he achieved fame with his adventure novel *Treasure Island* (1883). Later works included the novels *Kidnapped* (1886), *The Master of Ballantrae* (1889), *Dr Jekyll and Mr Hyde* (1886), and the anthology *A Child's Garden of Verses* (1885). In 1890 he settled at Vailima, in Samoa, where he sought a cure for the tuberculosis of which he died.

stew[1], *v.t.* to cook by boiling slowly or simmering. *v.i.* to be cooked thus; to be stifled or oppressed by a close atmosphere; (*coll.*) to be anxious, agitated. *n.* meat etc., cooked by stewing; (*coll.*) a state of mental agitation or worry; †(*pl.*) a brothel (orig. a bath- or hot-house). **to stew in one's own juice,** to suffer alone the consequences of one's actions. **stew-pan, -pot,** *n.*

a cooking-utensil for stewing. **stewed,** *a.* of meat etc, cooked by stewing; (*coll.*) drunk. [ME *stuwen* from *stuwe, stue,* OF *estuve,* bath, hot-house, cogn. with STOVE[1]]

stew[2], *n.* a fish-pond or tank for keeping fish alive for the table; an artificial oyster-bed. [ME *stewe* (cp. LG *stau,* dam, *stauen,* to dam), cogn. with STOW]

steward, *n.* a person employed to manage the property or affairs of another or other persons (esp. the paid manager of a large estate or household), or the service of provisions, etc., in a college, club etc.; an attendant on a ship, aircraft etc. in charge of provisions, cabins etc.; one of the officials superintending a ball, show, public meeting etc. **Lord High Steward,** an officer of State regulating precedence at coronations etc. **stewardess,** *n.* †**stewardry,** (*Sc.*) **stewartry, stewardship,** *n.* [OE *stigweard* (STY[1], WARD)]

Stewart, *n.* **'Jackie' (John Young)** (1939–), Scottish motor-racing driver. Until surpassed by Alain Prost (France) in 1987, Stewart held the record for the most Formula One Grand Prix wins (27).

Stewart, *n.* **James** (1908–), US film actor. Gangling and speaking with a soft drawl, he specialized in the role of the stubbornly honest, ordinary American in such films as *You Can't Take It With You* (1938), *The Philadelphia Story* (1940), *Harvey* (1950), *The Man from Laramie* (1955), and *The FBI Story* (1959).

Stewart Islander, *n.* (*New Zealand*) a fine oyster found on Stewart Island, New Zealand.

St George's, *n.* port and capital of GRENADA; population (1981) 4800, urban area 29,000.

St Helena, *n.* island in the S Atlantic, 1900 km/1200 miles W of Africa, area 122 sq km/47 sq miles; population (1985) 5900. Its capital is Jamestown, and it exports fish and timber. Ascension and Tristan da Cunha are dependencies.

sthenic, *a.* exhibiting an extreme degree of energy or vital action. [Gr. *sthenos,* strength, -IC]

stibium, *n.* (*dated*) antimony. **stibial,** *a.* **stibialism,** *n.* antimonial poisoning. **stibiated,** *a.* **stibnite,** *n.* a grey mineral consisting of antimony sulphide. [L, from Gr. *stibi*]

stich, *n.* a metrical line, a verse; a line of the Bible, esp. one of the rhythmic lines exhibiting the parallelism of the poetic books. **stichic,** *a.* [Gr. *stichos*]

stichomancy, *n.* divination by passages taken at random in a book.

stichomyth, -omythia, *n.* dialogue in alternate metrical lines, as in the ancient Greek drama. [Gr. *stochomuthia*]

†**stichometry,** *n.* measurement of books etc., by the number of lines; an appendix giving the number of stichs or lines in a book etc. †**stichometric,** *a.*

stick[1], *n.* a shoot or branch of a tree or shrub broken or cut off, or a slender piece of wood or other material used as a rod, wand, staff, baton, walking-cane etc., or as part of something; anything resembling this in shape; a drumstick, composing-stick, fiddle-stick etc.; the control-rod of an aircraft; a number of bombs dropped in succession; (*Naut.*) a mast, a spar; an awkward, incompetent or stupid person; a thrust, a stab, a dig; (*coll.*) blame, hostile criticism. *v.t.* (*past, p.p.* **sticked**) to provide (a plant) with sticks for support. **in a cleft stick,** in a difficult situation. **the sticks,** (*often derog.*) remote rural areas, the backwoods; the far-out suburbs of a town or city. **to give someone stick,** to blame or criticize someone. **wrong end of the stick,** a complete misunderstanding of a situation. **stick insect,** *n.* an insect belonging to the Phasmidoe, which resembles dry twigs. [from OE *sticca,* peg, rel. to *stician*]

stick[2], *v.t.* (*past, p.p.* **stuck**) to thrust the point of (in, through etc.); to fix or insert (into); to thrust (out or up); to protrude to fix upright; to fix on or as on a point; to pierce, to stab; to set with something pointed; to cause to adhere to; to set or compose (type); (*coll.*) to tolerate, endure (it); (*sl.*) to force something unpleasant or illegal on (one). *v.i.* to be inserted or thrust (into); to protrude project, or stand (up, out etc.); to become fixed, to adhere; to remain attached (to); to be inseparable, to be constant (to); to persist, to persevere; to be stopped, hindered, or checked; to be perplexed or embarrassed; to have scruples or misgivings, to hesitate (at). **to get stuck in(to)** GET. **to stick around,** (*coll.*) to remain in the vicinity. **to stick at nothing,** not to be deterred or feel scruples. **to stick by,** to stay close to; to remain faithful to, to support. **to stick one's neck out,** (*coll.*) to invite trouble; to take a risk. **to stick out,** to protrude; to hold out, to resist. **to stick out for,** to demand, to insist upon. **to stick to,** to adhere to; to persevere. **to stick up,** to put up, to erect; to stand up, to be prominent; to paste or post up; (*sl.*) to puzzle, to nonplus; (*Austral. sl.*) to hold up, to bail up. **to stick up for,** to take the part of, to defend. **to stick up to,** to stand up against, to resist. **sticking-place, -point,** *n.* the place where a screw etc., becomes jammed; hesitation. **sticking-plaster,** *n.* an adhesive plaster for wounds etc. **stick-in-the-mud,** *a.* dull, slow, unprogressive; *n.* such a person. **stick-up,** *n.* (*sl.*) an armed robbery. **stuck-up,** *a.* standing up, erect, of a collar, not turned down; puffed up, conceited, giving oneself airs. **sticker,** *n.* one who or that which sticks; a knife used by butchers; a bill-sticker; an adhesive label or poster; (*Organ*) a rod connecting two reciprocating levers; (*Cricket*) a batsman who stays in long, making few runs. **stickit,** *a.* (*Sc.*) stuck; spoiled. **stickit minister,** *n.* (*Sc.*) one who fails to get a pastorate. **sticky,** *a.* tending to stick, adhesive; viscous, glutinous; (*coll.*) difficult, painful. **sticky end,** *n.* (*coll.*) a disagreeable end or death. **sticky-fingered,** *a.* (*coll.*) prone to stealing. **sticky wicket,** *n.* a damp cricket pitch which is difficult to bat on; (*coll.*) a difficult situation. **stickily,** *adv.* **stickiness,** *n.* [ME *steken,* to pierce (cp. LG *steken,* G *stechen,* also Gr. *stizein,* L. *instīgāre,* to INSTIGATE), coalescing with ME *stikien,* OE *stician,* to stick, to be fixed, to prick, etc.]

stickle[1], *v.i.* to contend pertinaciously for some trifle; †to interfere, to take part with one side or the other. **stickler,** *n.* one who stands out for trifles. [prob. from M.E. *stightlen,* to be umpire, freq. from OE *stihtan,* to arrange, to regulate]

stickle[2], *n.* (*dial.*) a sharp run or shallow in a stream where the water is rough, a scour. [OE *sticol,* high, steep]

stickleback, *n.* a small spiny-backed, fresh-water fish. [OE *sticel,* prickle, from *stician,* to STICK]

stickler STICKLE[1].

sticky etc. STICK[2].

Stieglitz, *n.* **Alfred** (1864–1946), US photographer. After forming the Photo Secession group in 1903, he began the magazine *Camera Work.* Through exhibitions at his gallery '291' in New York he helped to establish photography as an art form. His works include 'Winter, Fifth Avenue' (1893) and 'Steerage' (1907). In 1924 he married the painter Georgia O'Keefe, who was the model in many of his photographs.

stiff, *a.* rigid, not easily bent or moved; not pliant, not flexible, not yielding, not working freely; obstinate, stubborn, firm, persistent; constrained, not easy, not graceful, awkward, formal, precise, affected; hard to deal with or accomplish; difficult; of liquor, strong; of prices, high; not fluid, thick and tenacious, viscous. *adv.* stiffly; (*coll.*) utterly, extremely, as in *bored stiff, frozen stiff. n.* (*sl.*) a bill of exchange, negotiable money; forged paper; a corpse; a racehorse that is sure to lose. **stiff with,** (*coll.*) packed with, full of. †**stiff-hearted,** *a.* **stiff-neck,** *n.* rheumatism affecting the muscles of the neck. **stiff-necked,** *a.* stubborn, self-willed. **stiff-neckedness,** *n.* **stiffen,** *v.t., v.i.* to make or become stiff. **stiffener,** *n.* something which stiffens; (*coll.*) a strong alcoholic drink. **stiffening,** *n.* **stiffish,** *a.* **stiffly,** *adv.* **stiffness,** *n.* [OE *stīf,* cp. Dut. *stijf,* Dan. *stiv,* Swed. *styf,* cp. STEEVE[2]]

stifle[1], *v.t., v.i.* to smother, to suffocate; to suppress; to stamp out. **stiflingly,** *adv.* [Icel. *stīfla,* freq. of *stiva,* to stiffen, cogn. with STIFF]

stifle[2], *n.* the stifle-joint; a disease affecting this or the stifle-bone. **stifle-bone,** *n.* a horse's knee-pan or patella. **stifle-joint,** *n.* the joint of a horse's hind-leg between the femur and tibia. [perh. from STIFF]

stigma, *n.* (*pl.* **-mas, -mata**) a mark formerly made with a branding-iron on slaves, criminals etc.; a mark or indication of infamy, disgrace etc.; a natural mark or spot on the skin, a pore; the part of the pistil which receives the pollen; (*Path.*) a small red spot on the skin from which blood oozes in excitement etc. **stigmata**, *n.pl.* in the Roman Catholic Church, marks miraculously developed on the body, corresponding to the wounds of Christ. **stigmatic**, *a.* pertaining to, like, or having stigmas or stigmata; anastigmatic. **stigmatiform**, *a.* **stigmatiferous**, *a.* **stigmatically,** *adv.* **stigmatism,** *n.* (*Phys.*) anastigmatism, the condition characterized by stigmata. **stigmatist,** *n.* one on whom stigmata are said to be impressed. **stigmatize, -ise,** *v.t.* to mark with a brand of disgrace etc.; to cause stigmata to appear on. **stigmatization, -isation,** *n.* **stigmatose**, *a.* (*Bot.*) stigmatic. [L, from Gr. *stigma -matos,* from *stizein,* to brand]

Stijl, de, *n.* a group of 20th-century Dutch artists and architects led by MONDRIAN from 1917. They believed in the concept of the 'designer'; that all life, work, and leisure should be surrounded by art; and that everything functional should also be aesthetic. The group had a strong influence on the Bauhaus school.

stilbite, *n.* a vitreous silicate of the zeolite group. [Gr. *stilbein,* to shine, -ITE]

stile[1], *n.* a series of steps or other contrivance by which one may get over or through a fence etc. [OE *stigel,* from *stīgan,* to climb]

stile[2], STYLE[1,2].

stiletto, *n.* (*pl.* **-ttos**) a small dagger; a pointed instrument for making eyelet-holes etc. *v.t.* to stab with a stiletto. **stiletto heel,** *n.* an excessively tapered heel for a woman's shoe. [It., dim. of *stilo,* L *stīlus,* STYLE[1]]

still[1], *a.* at rest, motionless; quiet, calm; silent, noiseless, hushed; not effervescent or sparkling. *n.* stillness, calm, quiet; (*Cinema.*) a picture made with a portrait camera for record or publicity purposes; a photograph from a single frame of a cinema film. *adv.* now, then, or for the future, as previously; even till now or then, yet; nevertheless, all the same; †continually, habitually. *v.t.* to quiet, to calm; to silence; to appease. †*v.i.* to grow calm. **still birth,** *n.* the bringing forth of a dead child; a child born dead. **stillborn,** *a.* **still life,** *n.* the representation of fruit, flowers, and other inanimate objects. †**still-vexed,** *a.* (*Shak.*) in continual agitation. †**stilly,** *adv.* **stillness,** *n.* [OE *stille,* (cp. Dut. *stil,* G *still,* Dan. *stille*), rel. to *stillan,* to rest, cogn. with *stellan,* to place]

still[2], *n.* a vessel or apparatus employed in distillation, esp. of spirits, consisting of a boiler, a tubular condenser or worm enclosed in a refrigerator, and a receiver. *v.t.* to distil. **still-room,** *n.* a room for distilling; a store-room for liquors, preserves etc. **stilliform**, *a.* drop-shaped. [L *stillāre,* to drip; sometimes short for DISTIL]

stillage, *n.* a frame, stool, bench etc., for placing things on for draining, waiting to be packed up etc. [cp. STILLING]

stilliform STILL[2].

stilling, *n.* a stand for a cask. [cp. LG *stelling,* G *Stellung,* from *stellen,* to place, cp. STILL[1]]

stillness, stilly STILL[1].

stilt, *n.* a pole having a rest for the foot, used in pairs, to raise a person above the ground in walking; any of a number of tall supports or columns for raising a building above the ground; a long-legged, three-toed, shore-bird related to the plover. **stilt-bird, -plover,** *n.* the common stilt, *Himantopus candidus*. **stilted,** *a.* raised on or as on stilts; of literary style etc., bombastic, inflated; springing from vertical masonry set on the imposts (of an arch). **stiltedly,** *adv.* **stiltedness,** *n.* [ME *stilte,* Swed. *stylta* (cp. Dut. *stelt,* G *Stelze*), prob. cogn. with OHG *stellan,* to place]

Stilton, *n.* a rich, white, veined cheese, orig. made at *Stilton,* in Cambridgeshire.

Stilwell, *n.* **Joseph Warren** (1883–1946), US general, nicknamed 'Vinegar Joe'. In 1942 he became US military representative in China, when he commanded the Chinese forces cooperating with the British (with whom he quarrelled) in Burma; he later commanded all US forces in the Chinese, Burmese, and Indian theatres until recalled to the US in 1944 after differences over nationalist policy with the Guomindang leader Chiang Kai-shek. Subsequently he commanded the US 10th Army on the Japanese island of Okinawa.

stimulus, *n.* (*pl.* **stimuli**), that which stimulates; an incitement, a spur; that which excites reaction in a living organism; (*Bot. etc.*) a sting; (*Med.*) a stimulant. **stimulant,** *a.* serving to stimulate; producing a quickly diffused and transient increase in physiological activity. *n.* anything that stimulates, such as drugs or alcohol. **stimulate,** *v.t.* to rouse to action or greater exertion; to incite; to excite organic action. *v.i.* to be a stimulus. **stimulation,** *n.* **stimulative,** *a.* **stimulator,** *n.*

stimy STYMIE.

sting, *v.t.* (*past, p.p.* **stung**) to pierce or wound with a sting; to cause acute physical or mental pain to; (*coll.*) to cheat, to overcharge. *v.i.* to have or use a sting; to have an acute and smarting pain. *n.* a sharp-pointed defensive or offensive organ, often conveying poison, with which certain insects, scorpions and plants are armed; the act of stinging; the wound or pain so caused; any acute pain, ache, smart, stimulus etc.; (*coll.*) a deception, a stratagem for extracting money etc. **sting-bull, -fish,** *n.* the greater weaver, *Trachinus draco*. **sting-ray,** *n.* a tropical ray with a venomous spine on its tail. **stingaree,** STING-RAY. **stinger,** *n.* one who, or that which, stings; a smarting blow. **stinging-nettle,** *n.* **stingless,** *a.* [OE *stingan* (cp. Icel. and Swed. *stinga,* Dan. *stinge*), perh. rel. to STICK]

stingily, stinginess STINGY.

stingo, *n.* (*sl.*) strong ale. [from STING]

stingy, *a.* tight-fisted, meanly parsimonious, niggardly. **stingily,** *adv.* **stinginess,** *n.* [STING, -Y]

stink, *v.i.* (*past* **stank**, **stunk**, *p.p.* **stunk**) to emit a strong, offensive smell; (*coll.*) to have an evil reputation. *v.t.* to annoy with an offensive smell. *n.* a strong, offensive smell; (*sl.*) a disagreeable exposure. **to raise a stink,** (*sl.*) to complain; to stir up trouble, esp. adverse publicity. **to stink out,** to drive out by creating an offensive smell; to cause to stink. **stink bomb,** *n.* a small glass sphere which releases a foul-smelling liquid when broken. **stinkhorn,** *n.* an evil-smelling fungus, esp. *Phallus impudicus*. **stink-stone,** *n.* a limestone or other rock emitting a fetid odour when struck. **stink-trap** STENCH-TRAP. **stinker,** *n.* a stinking person, animal etc.; (*sl.*) an unpleasant person or thing; the teledu; the skunk. **stinking,** *a.* emitting an offensive smell; (*coll.*) offensive, repulsive, objectionable; (*coll.*) extremely drunk. *adv.* (*coll.*) extremely, very. **stinkingly,** *adv.* [OE *stincan,* cp. Dut., G *stinken,* Dan. *stinke,* Swed. *stinka*]

stint, *v.t.* to give or allow scantily or grudgingly; to supply scantily or grudgingly (with food etc.). †*v.i.* to cease, to leave off. *n.* limit, bound, restriction; an allotted amount, quantity, turn of work etc.; a small sandpiper, esp. the dunlin. **stintedness,** *n.* †**stinter,** *n.* **stintingly,** *adv.* **stintless**, *a.* unstinted; abundant. [OE *styntan,* from *stunt,* dull, witless, cp. Icel. *stytta,* to shorten, from *stuttr,* short]

stipate, *a.* (*Bot.*) crowded, close-set. [L *stīpātus,* p.p. of *stīpāre,* to pack]

stipe, *n.* a stalk, stem or stem-like support, also **stipes**). **stipel**, *n.* a secondary stipule at the base of a leaflet. **stipellate** , **stipiform**, **stipitate**, **stipitiform**, *a.* [F, from L *stīpes -pilis*]

stipend, *n.* a periodical payment for services rendered, a salary, esp. of a clergyman. **stipendiary**, *a.* performing services for or receiving a stipend. *n.* one receiving a stipend, esp. a paid magistrate. [L *stipendium* (*stips, stipem,* gift in small coin, *pendere,* to pay)]

stipes, stipitate etc. STIPE.

stipple, *v.t.*, *v.i.* to engrave, paint or draw by means of dots or light dabs instead of lines etc. *n.* this method;

work produced thus. **stippler,** *n.* **stippling,** *n.* [Dut. *stippelen,* from *stippel,* dim. of *stip,* point, cp. G *Stift,* pin]

stipulaceous, stipular etc. STIPULE.

stipulate[1], *v.t.* to lay down or specify as essential to an agreement. *v.i.* to settle terms. **stipulation,** *n.* **stipulator,** *n.* [L *stipulātus,* p.p. of *stipulārī,* from OL *stipulus,* firm, fast, cogn. with *stīpes,* post]

stipule, *n.* a small leaf-like appendage, usu. in pairs at the base of a petiole. **stipulaceous, stipular, -lary, -late**[2], **-liform,** *a.* **stipulation,** *n.* [L *stipula,* dim. of *stipes,* STIPE]

stir, *v.t.* (*past, p.p.* **stirred**) to cause to move, to agitate, to disturb; to move vigorously, to bestir (oneself etc.); to rouse (up), to excite, to animate, to inflame. *v.i.* to move, to be in motion, not to be still. *n.* agitation, commotion, bustle, excitement; a movement; the act of stirring; (*sl.*) prison. **to stir up,** to agitate; to incite. **stir-crazy,** *a.* (*esp. N Am., sl.*) mentally unbalanced by a term in prison. **stir-frying,** *n.* a method of Chinese cooking in which food is stirred rapidly in hot oil, usu.. in a wok. **stir-fry,** *v.t., n.* **stirless,** *a.* **stirrer,** *n.* **stirring,** *a.* moving; animating, rousing, exciting, stimulating. **stirringly,** *adv.* [OE *styrian,* cp. Dut. *storen,* G *stören,* Icel. *styrr,* a stir]

stirk, *n.* (*dial.*) a yearling ox or cow. [OE *styric,* dim. of *stēor,* STEER[2]]

Stirling, *n.* **James** (1926–), British architect associated with collegiate and museum architecture. His works include the engineering building at Leicester University, and the Clore Gallery (the extension to house the Tate's TURNER collection) at the Tate Gallery, London, opened in 1987.

Stirling engine, *n.* a hot-air engine invented by Scottish priest Robert Stirling in 1876. It is a piston engine that uses hot air as a working fluid.

stirps, *n.* (*pl.* **-pes**), (*Law*) stock, family, progenitor; (*Zool.*) a classificatory group. **stirpiculture,** *n.* eugenics. **stirpicultural,** *a.* [L]

stirrup, *n.* a horseman's foot-rest, usu. consisting of an iron loop suspended from the saddle by a strap; (*Naut.*) a rope with an eye for carrying a foot-rope. **stirrup-cup,** *n.* a parting cup, esp. orig. on horseback. **stirrup-iron, -leather, -strap,** *n.* **stirrup-pump,** *n.* a portable hand-pump with a length of hose, to be worked by one or two persons. [OE *stīrāp* (*stīgan,* to climb, *rāp,* ROPE)]

stitch, *n.* a sharp intense pain in the side; a single pass of the needle in sewing; a single turn of the wool or thread round a needle in knitting; the link of thread, wool etc., thus inserted; (*coll.*) the least bit of clothing. *v.t., v.i.* to sew. **in stitches,** helpless with laughter. **to stitch up,** to sew together or mend; (*sl.*) to incriminate by informing on. **stitch-bird,** *n.* the New Zealand honey-eater. **stitchwort,** *n.* a plant of the genus *Alsine,* esp. two species with starry white flowers, common in hedges. **stitcher,** *n.* **stitchery,** *n.* [OE *stice,* from *stician,* see STICK]

†**stithy,** *n.* a forge, a smithy. *v.t.* to forge on an anvil. [ME *stith,* Icel. *stethi,* anvil]

stiver, *n.* any small coin. [Dut. *stuiver*]

St James's Palace, a palace in Pall Mall, London, a royal residence from 1698–1837.

St John, Order of, (full title Knights Hospitallers of St John of Jerusalem) oldest order of Christian chivalry, named from the hospital at Jerusalem founded about 1048 by merchants of Amalfi for pilgrims, whose travel routes the knights defended from the Muslims. Today there are about 8000 knights (male and female), and the Grand Master is the world's highest ranking Roman Catholic lay person.

St John's[1], *n.* capital and chief port of Newfoundland, Canada; population (1986) 96,000, urban area 162,000. The main industry is cod fish processing.

St John's[2], *n.* port and capital of Antigua and Barbuda, on Antigua; population (1982) 30,000.

St-John's-wort, *n.* any plant of the genus *Hypericum.*

St Kitts-Nevis ST CHRISTOPHER-NEVIS.

St Lawrence, *n.* river in E North America. From ports on the Great Lakes, it forms, with linking canals (which also give great hydroelectric capacity to the river), the St Lawrence Seaway for ocean-going ships, ending in the Gulf of St Lawrence. It is 1050 km/650 miles long, and is ice-bound for four months annually.

St Leger, *n.* horse race held at Doncaster, England every September. It is a flat race over 2.8 km/1.7 miles, and is the last of the season. First held in 1776, it is the oldest of the English classic races. Because of damage to the course, the 1989 race was held at Ayr, the first time Scotland had staged a classic.

St Louis, *n.* city in Missouri, US, on the Mississippi River; population (1980) 453,000, metropolitan area 2,356,000. Its industries include aerospace equipment, aircraft, vehicles, chemicals, electrical goods, steel, and beer.

St Lucia, *n.* country in the West Indies, one of the Windward Islands. **area** 617 sq km/238 sq miles. **capital** Castries. **physical** mountainous; mainly tropical forest. **population** (1989) 128,000; annual growth rate 1.2%. **exports** bananas, cocoa, copra; tourism is important. **language** English. **religion** Roman Catholic 90%.

St Martin's summer, a spell of mild weather in late autumn.

St Moritz, *n.* winter sports centre in SE Switzerland, which contains the Cresta Run (built in 1885) for toboggans, bobsleighs, and luges. It was the site of the Winter Olympics in 1928 and 1948.

stoa, *n.* (*pl.* **stoae, stoas**) a portico. [Gr.]

stoat, *n.* the ermine, esp. in its summer coat; applied also to the weasel, ferret etc. [ME *stot,* male animal, stoat, cp. Icel. *stūtr,* Swed., Norw. *stut,* bull, Dut. *stooten,* G *stossen,* to push]

stob, *n.* (*Coal-mining*) a steel wedge used for bringing down coal; (*Sc.*) a small post, a stake, a stump. [var. of STUB]

†**stoccade,** †**stoccado,** *n.* a movement in fencing. [It. *stoccata,* from *stocco,* rapier, G *Stock,* stick]

stochastic, *a.* random; involving chance or probability. [Gr. *stochastikos,* skilful in aiming]

stock[1], *n.* the trunk or main stem of a tree or other plant; a family, a breed, a line of descent, a distinct group of languages; (*Biol.*) a colony, an aggregate organism; a post, a butt, a stump; a stupid, senseless person; the principal supporting or holding part of anything, the handle, block, base, body etc.; liquor from boiled meat, bones etc., used as a basis for soup; the aggregate of goods, raw material etc., kept on hand for trade, manufacture etc., or as a reserve store; the beasts on a farm (called livestock), or implements of husbandry and produce; money lent to a government represented by certificates entitling the holders to fixed interest; the capital of a corporate company divided into shares entitling the holders to a proportion of the profits; (*pl.*) the shares of such capital; a stock-gillyflower; (*pl.*) a frame of timber with holes in which the ankles, and sometimes also the wrists, of petty offenders were formerly confined; (*pl.*) a timber framework on which a vessel rests during building; a band of silk, leather etc., worn as a cravat, now superseded by the collar, except in some uniforms. *a.* kept in stock; habitually used, standing, permanent. *v.t.* to provide with goods, live stock, or other requisites; to keep in stock; to furnish with a handle, butt etc.; †to put into the stocks, *v.i.* to take in supplies; to tiller. **in, out of stock,** available or not available to be sold immediately. **on the stocks,** in preparation. **to take stock,** to make an inventory of goods etc. on hand; (*fig.*) to survey one's position, prospects etc.; to examine, to form an estimate (of a person, etc.). **to take stock in,** to attach importance to. **stock-book,** *n.* a book recording quantities of goods received and disposed of. **stockbreeder,** *n.* one who raises livestock. **stockbroker,** *n.* one engaged in the purchase and sale of stocks on commission. **stockbroker belt,** *n.* (*coll., sometimes derog.*) the prosperous commuter area around London. **stock car,** *n.* a production (saloon) car modified for racing. **stock-broking,** *n.* **stock**

company, the actors working a repertory company. **stockdove,** *n.* the European wild pigeon, *Columba oenas,* smaller and darker than the ring-dove. **stock exchange,** *n.* the place where stocks or shares are publicly bought and sold. **stock-farmer,** *n.* one who raises livestock. **stock-gillyflower,** *n.* a fragrant, bright-flowered herbaceous plant, *Matthiola incana.* **stockholder,** *n.* a proprietor of stock in the public funds or shares in a stock company; (*Austral.*) a grazier. **stock-in-trade,** *n.* goods, tools and other requisites of a trade etc.; resources, capabilities. **stockjobber,** *n.* formerly, a dealer who speculated in stocks so as to profit by fluctuations of price and acted as an intermediary between buying and selling stockbrokers. **stockjobbing, -jobbery,** *n.* **stock-list,** *n.* a publication giving current prices etc., of stocks. **stockman,** *a.* one in charge of livestock, also called a **stock-keeper. stock-market,** *n.* a stock exchange or the business transacted there; a cattle-market. **stockpile,** *v.t.* to accumulate commodities, esp. reserves of raw materials. **stockpot,** *n.* a pot for making or storing stock for soup. **stock-rider,** *n.* (*Austral.*) a herdsman in charge of stock. **stock-still,** *a., adv.* motionless. **stocktaking,** *n.* **stockwhip,** *n.* a short-handled whip with a long lash for herding cattle. **stockyard,** *n.* an enclosure with pens etc., for cattle at market etc. **stockily,** *adv.* **stockiness,** *n.* †**stockish,** *a.* stupid, dull. **stockist,** *n.* one who keeps certain goods in stock. **stockless,** *a.* **stocky,** *a.* thick-set, short and stout, stumpy. [OE *stocc,* cp. Dut. *stok,* G *Stock,* Icel. *stokkr*]

†**stock**[2], STOCCADO.

stockade, *n.* a line or enclosure of posts or stakes. *v.t.* to surround or fortify with a stockade. [Sp. *estacada,* from *estaca,* MDut. *stake,* see STAKE, assim. to STOCK[1]]

stockfish, *n.* cod, ling etc. split open and dried in the sun without salting. [prob. from Dut. *stokvisch*]

Stockhausen, *n.* **Karlheinz** (1928–), German composer of avant-garde music, who has continued to explore new musical sounds and compositional techniques since the 1950s. His major works include *Gesang der Juñglinge* (1956) and *Kontakte* (1960) (electronic music); *Klavierstücke* (1952–85); *Momente* (1961–64, revised 1972), *Mikrophonie I* (1964), and *Sirius* (1977). Since 1977 all his works have been part of *Licht*, a cycle of seven musical ceremonies, intended for performance on the evenings of a week. He has completed *Donnerstag* (1980), *Samstag* (1984), and *Montag* (1988).

Stockholm, *n.* capital and industrial port of Sweden; population (1988) 667,000. It is built on a number of islands. Industries include engineering, brewing, electrical goods, paper, textiles, and pottery.

stocking, *n.* (*usu. in pl.*) a close-fitting covering for the foot and leg; an elastic covering used as a support for the leg in cases of varicose veins etc. **stocking filler,** *n.* a gift suitable for inclusion in a Christmas stocking. **stocking mask,** *n.* a nylon stocking pulled over the head as a disguise, e.g. as worn by burglars. **stocking stitch,** *n.* in knitting, alternate rows of plain and purl stitches. **stockingless,** *a.* **stockinet,** *n.* an elastic knitted material for undergarments etc. [dim. of STOCK[1], in sense of trunk or docked part, earlier *stocks,* short for *netherstocks,* the *upper-stocks* being the knee-breeches]

stockish, stocky etc. STOCK[1].

stodgy, *a.* of food, heavy, stiff, indigestible, crammed, lumpy; dull, heavy, matter-of-fact. **stodge,** *n.* (*coll.*) food, esp. stodgy food; *v.i.* to feed, to stuff. **stodginess,** *n.* [etym. doubtful]

stoep, *n.* (*S. Afr.*) an open, roofed platform in front of a house. [Afrikaans]

Stoic, *n.* a philosopher of the school founded by Zeno, *c.* 308 BC, teaching that virtue is the highest good, and that the passions and appetites should be rigidly subdued; a person who shows stoical qualities. *a.* stoical. **stoical,** *a.* resigned, impassive. **stoically,** *adv.* **stoicism,** *n.* the philosophy of the Stoics; indifference to pleasure or pain. [L *Stoicus,* Gr. *Stoikos,* from STOA, with ref. to the *Stoa Poikilē,* painted porch, at Athens, where Zeno taught]

stoichiology, *n.* the doctrine of elements of fundamental processes, laws etc. **stoichiometry,** *n.* the branch of chemistry treating of chemical combination in definite proportions, the mathematics of chemistry. **stoichiometric, -al,** *a.* [Gr. *stoicheion,* dim. of *stoichos,* post]

stoke, *v.t.* to tend (a furnace, esp. of a steam-engine). *v.i.* to act as stoker. **to stoke up,** to feed a fire or furnace with fuel; to fill oneself with food. **stokehold,** *n.* the compartment on a ship where the furnaces are tended. **stoke-hole,** *n.* the mouth of a furnace; an aperture in a blast-furnace etc. for a stirring tool and adding fuel; a stokehold. **stoker,** *n.* [back-formation from Dut., STOKER (*stoken,* to make fire, prob. from MDut. *stock,* stick or poker, -ER)]

Stoker, *n.* **Bram (Abraham)** (1847–1912), Irish novelist, actor, theatre manager, and author. His novel *Dracula* (1897) crystallized most aspects of the traditional vampire legend and became the source for all subsequent popular fiction and films on the subject.

STOL, *n.* a system by which aircraft take off and land over a short distance; an aircraft using this system, STOL craft are fitted with special devices on the wings (such as sucking flaps), which increase aerodynamic lift at low speeds, cp. VTOL. [acronym for *s*hort *t*ake-*o*ff and *l*anding]

stole[1], *n.* in ancient Rome, the outer garment of a Roman matron; a narrow band of silk etc. worn over both shoulders by priests, and by deacons over the left shoulder; a band of fur etc. worn round the neck by women. [L *stola,* Gr. *stolē,* from *stellein,* to array]

stole[2], STOLON.

stole[3], *past* **stolen**, *p.p.* STEAL.

†**stole**[4], *n.* a privy. **groom of the stole,** the first lord of the bed-chamber. [var. of STOOL]

stolid, *a.* dull, impassive, phlegmatic, stupid. **stolidity, stolidness,** *n.* **stolidly,** *adv.* [L *stolidus*]

stolon, *n.* a trailing or prostrate shoot that takes root and develops a new plant; an underground shoot in mosses developing leaves. **stolonate, stoloniferous,** *a.* [L *stolo -onis*]

stoma, *n.* (*pl.* **stomata**) a minute orifice, a pore; an aperture for respiration in a leaf. **stomatic, stomatiferous,** *a.* **stomapod,** *n.* any member of the Stomapoda, a suborder of podophthalmate crustaceans with gills attached to natatory feet. [Gr. *pous podos,* foot]

stomach, *n.* a digestive cavity formed by a dilatation of the alimentary canal, or (in certain animals) one of several such cavities; (*loosely*) the belly, the abdomen; appetite, inclination, liking; †anger, resentment, sullenness, haughtiness, arrogance. *v.t.* to accept as palatable; to put up with, to brook. **stomach-ache,** *n.* an abdominal pain. **stomach-pump,** *n.* a suction- and force-pump for withdrawing the contents of the stomach, also used as an injector. **stomach-staggers,** *n.* apoplexy in horses due to paralysis of the stomach. **stomachal,** *a.* **stomacher,** *n.* an ornamental covering for the breast and upper abdomen worn by women in the 15th–17th cents. **stomachful,** *n.* **stomachic,** *a.* pertaining to the stomach; exciting the action of the stomach or aiding digestion. *n.* a stomachic medicine. [ME *stomak,* OF *estomac,* L *stomachus,* acc. *-um,* Gr. *stomachos,* dim. of STOMA]

stomatitis, *n.* inflammation of the mouth. **stomatogastric,** *a.* pertaining to the mouth and the stomach. **stomatology,** *n.* the science of diseases of the mouth. [STOMA]

stomp, *v.t., v.i.* to stamp with the feet. *n.* an early jazz composition with a bold rhythm; a lively jazz dance involving heavy stamping of the feet. **stomper,** *n.*

Stone, *n.* **Lucy** (1818–93), US feminist orator and editor. Married to the radical Henry Blackwell in 1855 after a mutual declaration rejecting the legal superiority of the man in marriage, she gained wide publicity when she chose to retain her own surname despite her marriage. The epithet 'Lucy Stoner' was coined to mean a woman who advocated doing the same.

stone, *n.* a piece of rock, esp. a small one, a pebble, cobble, or piece used in road-making etc.; rock as material for building, paving etc.; a piece of this shaped and prepared for a specific purpose, as a millstone, grindstone, tombstone etc.; a gem, usu. called a precious stone; a calculus, the disease calculus; a testicle (*usu. in pl.*); the seed of a grape etc., the hard case of the kernel in a drupe or stonefruit, a hailstone; (*pl.* **stone**) a measure of weight 14 lb; (6·35 kg). *a.* made of stone or a hard material like stone. *v.t.* to pelt with stones; to face, wall, or pave with stone; to free (fruit) from stones. **to leave no stone unturned,** to use all available means to effect an object. **Stone Age,** see separate entry. **stone-axe,** *n.* a stonecutter's axe with two blunt edges. **stone-blind,** *a.* completely blind. **stone-borer,** *n.* a mollusc that bores into stone. **stone-break,** *n.* saxifrage. **stone-cast** STONE'S CAST. **stonechat, -chatter,** *n.* the wheatear, *Saxicola torquata.* **stone-coal,** *n.* anthracite. **stone-cold,** *a.* quite cold. **stone-coral,** *n.* massive as distinguished from branched coral. **stonecrop,** *n.* any species of *Sedum,* esp. *S. acre.* **stone-curlew,** *n.* the thick-knee curlew or any bird of the family Burhinidae. **stone-cutter,** *n.* one whose occupation is to cut stones for building, etc. **stonecutting,** *n.* **stone-dead,** *a.* dead as a stone. **stone-deaf,** *a.* completely deaf. **stone-dresser,** *n.* **stone-eater** STONE-BORER. **stone-fern,** *n.* ceterach. **stonefly,** *n.* an insect of the order Plecoptera with aquatic larvae harbouring under stones, used as bait for trout. **stonefruit,** *n.* a fruit with seeds covered by a hard shell, as peaches, plums etc., a drupe. **stone-ground,** *a.* (of flour) ground between millstones. †**stone-horse,** *n.* an uncastrated stallion. **stonemason,** *n.* one who dresses stones or builds with stone. **stone-parsley,** *n.* a hedge parsley, *Sison amomum,* the meadow saxifrage. **stonepine,** *n.* the Mediterranean pine, *Pinus pinea,* with a spreading top. **stone-pit,** *n.* a stone quarry. **stone-pitch,** *n.* hard, inspissated pitch. **stone-plover** STONE-CURLEW. **stone-rag,** *n.* a lichen, *Parmelia saxatilis.* **stone-rue,** *n.* wall-rue. **stone-snipe,** *n.* a large N American snipe. **stone's throw, stone's cast,** *n.* the distance a stone can be thrown by hand. **stone-still,** *a.* perfectly still. **stonewall,** *v.i.* (*Austral.*) to obstruct parliamentary business by making long speeches; (*Cricket*) to stay in batting without trying to make runs. **stoneware,** *n.* pottery made from clay and flint or a hard siliceous clay. **stone-washed,** *a.* of clothes, denim etc., given a faded surface by the abrasive action of small pieces of pumice. **stonework,** *n.* masonry. **stonewort,** *n.* the stone-parsley and other plants. **stoned,** *a.* (*sl.*) under the influence of drugs or alcohol. **stoneless,** *a.* **stony,** *a.* pertaining to, made or consisting of, abounding in or resembling stone; hard, cruel, pitiless; impassible; obdurate, perverse; **stony-broke,** *a.* (*sl.*) destitute or nearly destitute of money. **stony-hearted,** *a.* unfeeling. **stonily,** *adv.* **stoniness,** *n.* [OE *stān,* cp. Dut. *steen,* G *Stein,* Icel. *steinn*]

Stone Age, *n.* the period in prehistory before the use of metals, when tools and weapons were made chiefly of flint. The Stone Age is subdivided into the Old or Palaeolithic, the Middle or Mesolithic and the New or Neolithic. The people of the Old Stone Age were hunters, whereas the Neolithic people progressed to making the first steps in agriculture, domestication of animals, weaving, and pottery making.

Stonehenge, *n.* megalithic monument dating from about 2000 BC on Salisbury Plain, Wiltshire, England. It consisted originally of a circle of 30 upright stones, their tops linked by lintelstones to form a continuous circle about 30 m/100 ft across. Within the circle was a horseshoe arrangement of five trilithons (two uprights plus a lintel, set as five separate entities), and a so-called 'altar stone' – an upright pillar – on the axis of the horseshoe at the open, NE end, which faces in the direction of the rising sun. It has been suggested that it served as an observatory.

Stonehouse, *n.* **John (Thompson)** (1925–88), British Labour Party politician. An active member of the Co-operative Movement, he entered Parliament in 1957 and held junior posts under Harold Wilson before joining his cabinet in 1967. In 1974 he disappeared in Florida in mysterious circumstances, surfacing in Australia, amid suspicions of fraudulent dealings. Extradited to Britain, he was tried and imprisoned for embezzlement. He won an early release in 1979, but was unable to resume a political career.

stood, *past, p.p.* STAND.

stooge, *n.* a butt, a confederate, a decoy; a subordinate. *v.i.* to act as a stooge. [onomat.]

stook, *n.* (*chiefly Sc.*) a bundle of sheaves set up. *v.t.* to set up in stooks. [cp. LG, Dan. and Swed. dial. *stuke*]

stool, *n.* a seat without a back, for one person, usu. with three or four legs; a low bench for kneeling or resting the feet on; the seat used in evacuating the bowels; an evacuation; the stump of a timber-tree from which shoots are thrown up; a plant or stock from which young plants are produced by layering etc. *v.i.* to shoot out stems from the root; to evacuate the bowels. **stool of repentance,** a stool in a church where sinners were made to sit. **to fall between two stools** FALL. **stool ball,** *n.* a game like cricket, played in S England. **stool-pigeon,** *n.* a pigeon used as a decoy; a decoy; an informer for the police. [OE *stōl,* cp. Dut. *stoel,* G *stühl,* Icel. *stōll,* cogn. with STAND]

stoop[1], *v.i.* to bend the body downward and forward; to have an habitual forward inclination of the head and shoulders; to condescend, to lower, to bring oneself down (to); †to pounce, to swoop. *v.t.* to incline (the head, shoulders etc.) downward and forward. *n.* the act of stooping; an habitual inclination of the shoulders etc.; †the swoop of a bird on its prey. **stoopingly,** *adv.* [OE *stūpian* (cp. MDut. *stuypen,* Icel. *stūpa*), cogn. with STEEP[1 and 2]]

stoop[2], STOUP. **stoop**[3], STOEP.

stoor, *v.t.* (*prov.*) to stir up; to pour out. *v.i.* to rise in clouds (of dust or smoke). *n.* dust flying about; stir, commotion. [cogn. with STIR]

stop, *v.t.* (*past, p.p.* **stopped**) to close by filling or obstructing, to stanch, to plug (up); to fill a crack, a cavity in a tooth etc.; to impede; to cause to cease moving, going, working, or acting (or from moving etc.); to prevent the doing or performance of; to keep back, to cut off, to suspend; (*Mus.*) (of an instrument) to press a string, close an aperture etc. so as to alter the pitch. *v.i.* to come to an end, to come to rest; to discontinue, to cease or desist (from); (*coll.*) to stay, to remain temporarily, to sojourn; to punctuate. *n.* the act of stopping or the state of being stopped, a cessation, a pause, an interruption; a punctuation mark indicating a pause; a block, peg, pin etc. used to stop the movement of something at a particular point; (*Mus.*) the pressing down of a string, closing of an aperture etc., effecting a change of pitch; a key, lever or other device employed in this; a set of pipes in an organ having tones of a distinct quality; a knob bringing these into play; a perforated diaphragm for regulating the passage of light; a sound produced by closure of the mouth, a mute consonant. **to pull out all the stops,** to play at maximum volume; to make the utmost effort. **to stop a gap** GAP. **to stop at nothing,** to be ruthless, to be ready to do anything to achieve one's ends. **to stop down,** (*Phot.*) to reduce the area of (a lens) transmitting light, by means of a diaphragm. **to stop off, in, over,** to break one's journey. **stop bath,** *n.* an acidic solution used to halt the action of a developer or a photographic negative or print. **stopcock,** *n.* a small valve used to stop the flow of fluid in a pipe. **stopgap,** *n.* a temporary substitute or expedient. **stop-go,** *a.* of a policy etc., alternately active and inactive. **stopoff, stopover,** *n.* a break in a journey. **stoppress,** *a.* applied to news inserted in a paper after the printing has commenced. **stop-watch,** *n.* a watch with an additional hand which can be stopped by a special device at any second or fraction of a second, used for timing races etc. **stoppage,** *n.* the act or state of being stopped; a deduction from pay; a cessation of work, as in a strike. **stopper,** *n.* one who or that which stops; a plug, a stopple; (*Naut.*) a rope, plug, clamp etc. for checking the motion of a cable etc. *v.t.* to close or secure with a stopper. **stopping,** *n.* (*coll.*) material for filling a cavity in a tooth; the operation of stopping a tooth; plastic material for filling holes and cracks in wood etc. before painting. **stopple,** *n.* that which stops or closes the mouth of a vessel, a stopper, plug, bung etc.; *v.t.* to close with a stopple. [OE *stoppian,* in *forstoppian,* from late L *stuppāre,* from *stūpa, stuppa,* tow (cp. Gr. *stupē, stuppē*)]

Stopes, *n.* **Marie (Carmichael)** (1880–1958), Scottish birth-control campaigner. With her husband H. V. Roe (1878–1949), an aircraft manufacturer, she founded a London birth-control clinic in 1921. The Well Woman Centre in Marie Stopes House, London, commemorates her work. She wrote plays and verse as well as the best-selling manual *Married Love* (1918).

Stoppard, *n.* **Tom** (1937–), Czechoslovak-born British playwright, whose works use wit and wordplay to explore logical and philosophical ideas. He achieved fame with *Rosencrantz and Guildenstern are Dead* (1967). This was followed by comedies including *The Real Inspector Hound* (1968), *Jumpers* (1972), *Travesties* (1974), *Dirty Linen* (1976), and *The Real Thing* (1982). He has also written radio, television, and screenplays.

storage STORE.

storax, *n.* a balsamic vanilla-scented resin obtained from *Styrax officinalis,* formerly used in medicine etc.; the tree itself. [L, from Gr. *sturax*]

store, *n.* a stock laid up for drawing upon; an abundant supply, plenty, abundance (*often in pl.*); a place where things are laid up or kept for sale, a storehouse, a warehouse; a large establishment where articles of various kinds are sold; (*N Am.*) a shop; (*pl.*) articles kept on hand for special use, esp. ammunition, arms, military and naval provisions etc., a supply of such articles. *v.t.* to accumulate or lay (usu. up or away) for future use; to stock or supply (with); to deposit in a warehouse etc. for safe keeping; to hold or keep in (as water etc.); (*Comput.*) to enter data into a computer memory or in a storage device. **in store,** in reserve; ready for use; on hand; **to set store by,** to value highly. **storehouse,** *n.* a place where things are stored up, a warehouse, granary, repository, etc.; a great quantity. **storekeeper,** *n.* one who has the charge of stores; (*N Am.*) a shopkeeper. **storeroom,** *n.* **store-ship,** *n.* a supply-vessel for a fleet etc. **storable,** *a.* **storage,** *n.* the act of storing, warehousing etc.; the price paid for or the space reserved for this; (*Comput.*) the action of storing date in computer memory or on disk etc. **storage battery,** *n.* an accumulator. **storage capacity,** *n.* the maximum amount of data that can be held in a computer memory. **storage device,** *n.* a piece of computer hardware such as a magnetic tape, optical disk etc. that can store data. **storage heater,** *n.* a type of radiator which stores heat during periods of off-peak electricity. **storer,** *n.* [OF *estor,* late L *staurum, instaurum,* from *instaurāre* (IN-, *staurāre,* see RESTORE)]

storey, story, *n.* (*pl.* **-reys, -ries**) *n.* a horizontal division, a set of rooms on the same floor. **storeyed, storied,** *a.* having storeys. [L *historia,* HISTORY, but the line of sense-development is uncertain]

storiated, HISTORIATED.

storied STOREY and STORY[1].

storiology, etc. STORY[1].

stork, *n.* a long-necked, long-legged wading-bird of the genus *Ciconia,* allied to the heron, esp. the white or house-stork *C. alba,* nesting on buildings. **stork's-bill,** *n.* a plant of the genus *Erodium* allied to the crane's-bill. [OE *storc,* cp. Dut. *stork,* G *Storch,* Icel. *storkr,* also Gr. *torgos*]

storm, *n.* a violent disturbance of the atmosphere attended by wind, rain, snow, hail, or thunder and lightning, a tempest; a violent disturbance or agitation of society life, the mind etc., a tumult, commotion etc.; a violent outburst (of cheers etc.); a direct assault on a fortified place. *v.i.* to rage (of wind, rain etc.); to bluster, to fume, to behave violently. *v.t.* to take by storm. **a storm in a teacup,** a fuss about nothing. **to take by storm,** to capture by means of a violent assault; to captivate, overwhelm. **storm-beat, -beaten,** *a.* beaten or injured by storms. **storm-belt,** *n.* a zone where storms are frequent. **storm-bird,** *n.* the stormy petrel. **stormbound,** *a.* stopped or delayed by storms. **storm-centre,** *n.* the place of lowest pressure in a cyclonic storm; a place etc., liable to violent disturbance. **storm-cock,** *n.* the mistle-thrush, fieldfare, or green woodpecker. **storm-cone, storm-drum** STORM-SIGNAL. **storm-finch,** *n.* the stormy petrel. **storm-glass,** *n.* a sealed tube containing an alcoholic solution of camphor etc. which is affected by changes of temperature, and was formerly used as a weather-glass. **storm lantern** HURRICANE LAMP. **storm-proof,** *a.* storm-sail, *n.* a sail of smaller size and stouter canvas, for heavy weather. **storm-signal,** *n.* a signal usu. consisting of a hollow drum and cone of canvas, hoisted as warning of an approaching storm, the positions of the drum and cone indicating the probable direction of the wind. **storm-trooper,** *n.* a semi-military member of the Nazi party; one of a force of shock troops. **stormer,** *n.* **stormful,** *a.* **stormfulness,** *n.* **stormily,** *adv.* **storminess,** *n.* **stormless,** *a.* **stormy,** *a.* characterized by storms; tempestuous; violent, vehement, passionate. **stormy petrel,** *n.* any petrel, esp. *Hydrobates pelagicus.* [OE (cp. Dut., Swed., and Dan. *storm,* G *Sturm,* Icel. *stormr*), cogn. with STIR]

stornello, *n.* a form of improvised folk-song, usu. composed of two lines. [It.]

Storting, Storthing, *n.* the Norwegian parliament. [Norw. *stor,* great, *thing,* meeting]

story[1], *n.* a narrative or recital in prose or verse, of actual or fictitious events, a tale, short novel, romance, anecdote, legend or myth; the plot or incidents of a novel, epic or play; a series of facts of special interest connected with a person, place etc.; an account of an incident, experience etc.; a descriptive article in a newspaper; (*coll.*) a falsehood, a fib; †history. **the same old story,** (*coll.*) familiar sequence of events. **the story goes,** it is commonly said. **story-book,** *n.* a book containing a story or stories. *a.* fairy-tale. **story line,** *n.* the main plot of a book, film etc. **story-teller, -writer,** *n.* **story-telling,** *n.* **storied,** *a.* (*poet.*) adorned with scenes from or celebrated in stories or history. **storiology,** *n.* the science of folk-lore. **storiologist,** *n.* [AF *storie,* OF *estoire,* L *historia,* HISTORY]

story[2] STOREY.

stot, *n.* a bullock, a steer; †a horse, a stallion. [ME, see STOAT]

†stound, *n.* a certain length of time; a point of time, hour, season. [OE *stund,* cp. Icel. *stund,* OHG *stunt, stunta*]

stoup, *n.* †a flagon, a drinking-vessel; a basin for holy water. [Icel. *staup,* cp. Dut. *stoop,* G *Stauf,* Icel. *steap*]

†stour, *n.* a battle, a tumult; a paroxysm. [OF *estour, estor,* OHG *stōr*]

stoush, *n.* (*Austral. coll.*) a fight, a brawl. [Perh. from Sc. *stoushie,* a row, a fight]

stout, *a.* strong, sound, sturdy, stanch, well-built, lusty, vigorous, brave, resolute, intrepid; corpulent, bulky, fleshy. *n.* a malt liquor, very strong porter. **stout-hearted,** *a.* **stout-heartedly,** *adv.* **stout-heartedness,** *n.* **stoutish,** *a.* **stoutly,** *adv.* **stoutness,** *n.* [OF *estout,* MDut. *stolt,* stout (cp. G *stolz,* proud), perh. from L *stultus,* stupid]

stove[1], *n.* an apparatus, wholly or partially closed, in which fuel is burned for heating, cooking etc.; a drying-room for explosives etc.; an oven for heating the blast of a blast-furnace; a hot-house in which a high temperature is maintained. *v.t.* to heat, dry, force etc. in a stove. **stovepipe,** *n.* a pipe for conducting smoke etc., from a stove to a chimney. **stovepipe hat,** *n.* a high silk hat. [orig. a bath or hot-house, OE *stofa* (cp. MDut. *stove,* G *Stube,* Icel. *stofa, stufa*), prob. rel. to STEW[1]]

stove[2], *past* STAVE.

†stover, *n.* fodder for cattle. [OF *estover,* see ESTOVERS]

stow, *v.t.* to put or pack (often away) in a suitable or convenient place or position; to pack or fill compactly with things. **stow it,** (*sl.*) drop it! stop (joking etc.). **stowaway,** *n.* one who conceals himself on a ship, aircraft etc. in order to get a free passage. **stowage,** *n.* an area or place for stowing goods or the charge for this; the act or state of being stowed; things for stowing. **stower,** *n.* [OE *stōwigan,* from *stōw,* place, cogn. with STAND]

Stowe, *n.* **Harriet Beecher** (1811–96), US suffragist, abolitionist, and author of of the anti-slavery novel UNCLE TOM'S CABIN, first published as a serial in 1851–52.

stown, (*Sc.***)** STOLEN.

STP, *n.* in physics, a standard for comparing the properties of gases equal to a temperature of 273.15 K/0°C and a pressure of 101,325 pascals (760 mm of mercury). [*s*tandard *t*emperature and *p*ressure]

St Petersburg LENINGRAD.

St Pierre and Miquelon, territorial collectivity of France, eight small islands off the south coast of Newfoundland, Canada. **area** St Pierre group 26 sq km/10 sq miles; Miquelon-Langlade group 216 sq km/83 sq miles. **capital** St Pierre. **products** fish. **population** (1987) 6300. **language** French. **religion** Roman Catholic.

strabismus, *n.* squinting, a squint, produced by a muscular defect of the eye. **strabismal, -mic,** *a.* [Gr. *strabismos,* from *strabos,* crooked]

Strachey, *n.* **(Giles) Lytton** (1880–1932), English critic and biographer, a member of the Bloomsbury Group of writers and artists. He wrote *Landmarks in French Literature* (1912). The mocking and witty treatment of Cardinal Manning, Florence Nightingale, Thomas Arnold, and General Gordon in *Eminent Victorians* (1918) won him recognition. His biography of *Queen Victoria* (1921) was more affectionate.

strad, *n.* short for STRADIVARIUS.

straddle, *v.i.* to stand, walk or sit with the legs wide apart; to trim, to sit on the fence. *v.t.* to stand or sit astride of this; to shoot beyond and short of a target to determine the range. *n.* the act of straddling; the distance between the legs of one straddling; (*Stock Exch.*) a contract securing the right of either a put or call; a high-jumping technique in which the legs straddle the bar while the body is parallel to it. **straddle-legged,** *a.* **straddler,** *n.* [earlier *striddle,* freq. of STRIDE]

Stradivari, *n.* **Antonio,** in Latin form Stradivarius (1644–1737), Italian stringed instrument maker, generally considered the greatest of all violin makers. He was born in Cremona and studied there with Nicolo AMATI. He produced more than 1100 instruments from his family workshops. **Stradivarius,** *n.* a stringed instrument, esp. a violin, made by Antonio Stradivari. Often shortened to (*coll.*) **Strad**.

strae, *n.* (*Sc.*) straw. **strae death,** *n.* death in one's bed (orig. on one's straw), opp. to a violent death. [var. of STRAW[1]]

strafe, *v.t.* to bombard heavily; to rake with machine-gun fire from the air; to punish severely to do a serious and deliberate injury to. *n.* an attack from the air. [G *strafen,* to punish]

Strafford, *n.* **Thomas Wentworth, 1st Earl of Strafford** (1593–1641), English politician, originally an opponent of Charles I, but from 1628 on the Royalist side. He ruled despotically as Lord Deputy of Ireland (1632–39), when he returned to England as Charles's chief adviser and received an earldom. He was impeached in 1640 by Parliament, abandoned by Charles as a scapegoat, and beheaded.

straggle, *v.i.* to wander away from the main body or direct course; to get dispersed; to spread irregularly (of plants etc.). **straggler,** *n.* **stragglingly,** *adv.* **straggly,** *a.* [perh. freq. of ME *straken,* to roam]

straight, *a.* extending uniformly in one direction, not bent, curved or crooked; upright, honest, not deviating from truth or fairness, correct, accurate, right; level, even; unobstructed, uninterrupted; undiluted; reliable, trustworthy, authoritative; (of a drink) undiluted; (*sl.*) heterosexual. *n.* a straight part, piece or stretch of anything; in poker, five cards in sequence irrespective of suit; (*coll.*) a conventional person; (*sl.*) a heterosexual person; the straight part of a racetrack. *adv.* in a straight line; directly, without deviation; immediately, at once; (*coll. int.*) really? **straight away, straight off,** at once, without delay. **the straight and narrow,** the honest and virtuous way of life. **to go straight,** to abandon criminal activities and become honest. **to keep a straight face,** to refrain from smiling. **straight angle,** *n.* an angle of 180°. **straightedge,** *n.* a strip of metal or wood having one edge straight, used as a ruler etc. **straight fight,** *n.* a contest between two candidates or sides only. **straight flush,** *n.* (in poker) a hand with five cards of the same suit in sequence. **straightforward,** *a.* straight; upright, honest, frank, open; (of a task) simple, presenting no difficulties. **straightforwardly,** *adv.* **straightforwardness,** *n.* **straight man,** *n.* one who acts as a stooge to a comedian. **straight-out,** *a.* (*N Am. coll.*) outright, complete, blunt, honest. **straighten,** *v.t.* to make straight. **to straighten out,** to resolve, unscramble. **straightener,** *n.* **straightly,** *adv.* **straightness,** *n.* **†straightway,** *adv.* forthwith, at once. [OE *streht,* p.p. of *streccan,* to STRETCH]

straik[1, 2], (*Sc.***)**. STROKE[1], v., n., and p.p. of STRIKE.

strain[1], *v.t.* to stretch tight; to exert to the utmost; to weaken, injure, or distort by excessive effort or overexertion; to force beyond due limits; to apply (rules etc.) beyond the proper scope or intent; to press closely, to embrace; to constrain, to make unnatural, artificial, or uneasy; to purify from extraneous matter by passing through a colander or other strainer; to remove (solid matter) by straining (out). *v.i.* to exert oneself, to make violent efforts (after etc.); to pull or tug (at); to be filtered, to percolate. *n.* the act of straining, a violent effort, a pull, tension; an injury, distortion, or change of structure, caused by excessive effort, exertion, or tension; impulse, feeling; mental tension, fatigue from overwork etc.; a song, a tune, a melody, a piece of poetry; tone, spirit, manner, style, pitch. **strained,** *a.* unnatural; forced; tense; stressful. **strainer,** *n.* a filter; a sieve, colander. [ME *streinen,* OF *estraign-,* stem of *estraindre,* L *stringere,* see STRINGENT]

strain[2], *n.* race, stock, family, breed; natural tendency or disposition. [OE *strēon*]

strait, *a.* narrow, confined, restricted, tight; †strict, rigorous. *n.* a narrow passage of water between two seas (*usu. in pl.*); a trying position, distress, difficulty (*usu. in pl.*). **strait-jacket, -waistcoat,** *n.* a garment usu. without sleeves, for confining the arms of the violently insane etc. **strait-laced,** *a.* laced or braced tightly: puritanically strict in morals or manners. **straiten,** *v.t.* to distress; place in difficulty. **straitly,** *adv.* **straitness,** *n.* [A-F *estreit,* OF *estroict* (F *étroit*), L *strictum,* STRICT]

Straits Settlements, *n.* former province of the East India Company (1826–58), and British Crown colony from 1867–1946: it comprised Singapore, Malacca, Penang, Cocos Islands, Christmas Island, and Labuan.

strake[1], *n.* a continuous line of planking or plates from stem to stern of a vessel; part of the metal rim on a cart-wheel. [var. of STREAK]

†strake[2], *p.p.* STRIKE.

strake[3], (*Sc.***)** STROKE[2].

stramash, *n.* (*Sc.*) a disturbance, a fray, a struggle. *v.t.* to strike, beat, or bang; to break, to destroy. [etym. doubtful, cp. OF *estramaçon,* It. *stramazzone,* a cut with a sword]

stramineous, *a.* straw-coloured; consisting of straw, light, or worthless like straw. [L *strāmineus,* from *strāmen -inis,* straw, from *sternere,* to strew]

stramonium, *n.* a drug prepared from the thorn-apple, *Datura stramonium,* used for nervous complaints. [etym. doubtful]

strand[1], *n.* a shore or beach of the sea, lake, or large river. *v.t.* to run or force aground; (*in p.p.*) to bring to a standstill or into straits, esp. from lack of funds. *v.i.* to run aground. **stranded,** *p.p.* in difficulties; without resources. [OE, cp. Dut., G, Swed., Dan. *strand,* Icel. *strönd*]

strand², *n.* one of the fibres, threads, wires etc. of which a rope etc. is composed; a length of hair; a string of pearls or beads. *v.t.* to make (a rope etc.) by twisting strands together. [ONorth.F *estran,* OHG *Streno* (cp. G *Strähne),* cord]

strange, *a.* alien; not one's own; not well known, unfamiliar, new; unusual, singular, extraordinary, queer, surprising, unaccountable; fresh or unused (to), unacquainted, awkward. **strange particle,** *n.* an elementary particle (e.g. hyperon) which possesses a quantum strangeness number different from zero. **strangely,** *adv.* **strangeness,** *n.* the quality of being strange; the quantum number, conserved in strong but not in weak interactions, introduced to explain the paradoxically long lifetimes of certain elementary particles. [OF *estrange* (F *étrange*), L *extrāneus,* EXTRANEOUS]

stranger, *n.* one from another place; foreigner; a guest, a visitor; a person unknown (to one); one ignorant or unaccustomed (to); (*Law*) one not privy or party to an act.

strangle, *v.t.* to kill by compressing the windpipe, to choke, to throttle; to suppress, to stifle. **strangler,** *n.* **stranglehold,** *n.* a choking grip used in wrestling; a restrictive force or influence. **strangles,** *n.pl.* an infectious disease affecting horses etc. [OF *estrangler,* L *strangulāre,* Gr. *strangalizein,* from *strangalē,* halter, from *strangos,* twisted]

strangulate, *v.t.* to strangle; to compress a blood-vessel, intestine etc. **strangulation,** *n.* [L *strangulātus,* p.p. as prec.]

strangury, *n.* a disease characterized by pain in passing the urine, which is excreted in drops; an abnormal condition produced in plants by bandaging. **strangurious,** *a.* [L *strangū- ria,* Gr. *strangouria* (*stranxgos, ouron,* urine)]

strap, *n.* a long, narrow strip of leather, or similar material, usu. with a buckle, for fastening about things; a strip, band or plate for holding parts together; a shoulder-strap; a strop; a strap-shaped blade or part, a ligula. *v.t.* (*past, p.p.* **strapped**) to fasten (*often* down, up etc.) with a strap; to beat with a strap; to sharpen, to strop. **the strap,** chastisement with a strap. **strap-hanger,** *n.* (*coll.*) a standing passenger in a bus or train. **strap-oil,** *n.* a thrashing. **strap-shaped,** *a.* **strap-work,** *n.* ornamentation in the form of crossed or interlacing bands. **strapper,** *n.* one who uses a strap; a tall, strapping person. **strapping,** *a.* tall, lusty, strong, muscular. [OE *stropp* (cp. Dut. *strop*), L *struppus* (cp. Gr. *strophos,* cogn. with *strephein,* to twist)]

†**strappado,** *n.* the old punishment of drawing up an offender by a rope and letting him fall to the end of this. *v.t.* to torture or punish thus. [It. *strappata,* from *strappare,* to pull, GSwiss *strapfen,* prob. from Dut. *straffen,* to punish, from *straf,* severe]

strapper, etc. STRAP.

Strasberg, *n.* **Lee** (1902–82), US actor and artistic director of the ACTORS STUDIO from 1948, who developed Method acting from STANISLAVSKY's system; pupils have included Jane Fonda, John Garfield, Sidney Poitier, and Paul Newman.

Strasbourg, *n.* city on the river Ill, in Bas-Rhin *département*, capital of Alsace, France; population (1982) 373,000. Industries include car manufacture, tobacco, printing and publishing, and preserves. The Council of Europe meets here, and sessions of the European Parliament alternate between Strasbourg and Luxembourg.

strass, *n.* paste for making false gems. [Joseph *Strasser,* 18th-cent. German jeweller]

strata, *pl.,* **-stratal,** STRATUM.

stratagem, *n.* an artifice, trick or manoeuvre esp. for deceiving an enemy. [OF *stratageme,* L and Gr. *stratēgēma,* from *stratēgein,* to act as general (*stratos,* army, *agein,* to lead)]

strategic STRATEGY.

Strategic Arms Limitation Talks, (SALT) a series of US-Soviet discussions aimed at reducing the rate of nuclear-arms build-up. The talks began in 1969 between the US president Johnson and the Soviet leader Brezhnev. Neither the SALT I accord (effective 1972–77) nor SALT II called for reductions in nuclear weaponry, merely a limit on the expansion of these forces. SALT II was mainly negotiated by US president Ford before 1976 and signed by Brezhnev and Carter in 1979, but was never ratified because of the Soviet occupation of Afghanistan.

Strategic Arms Reduction Talks, (START) a phase in US-Soviet peace discussions. START began with talks in Geneva 1983, leading to the signing of the Intermediate Nuclear Forces (INF) treaty in 1987. In 1989 proposals for reductions in conventional weapons were added to the agenda.

Strategic Defense Initiative, (SDI) also called Star Wars, an attempt by the US to develop a defence system against incoming nuclear missiles, based in part outside the Earth's atmosphere. It was announced by President Reagan in Mar. 1983, and the research had by 1990 cost over $16.5 billion. In 1988, the joint chiefs of staff announced that they expected to be able to intercept no more than 30% of incoming missiles.

strategy, *n.* the art of war, generalship, esp. the art of directing military movements so as to secure the most advantageous positions and combinations of forces; a long-term plan aimed at achieving a specific goal; a strategem. **strategic, -al,** *a.* pertaining to, used in or of the nature of strategy; (of missiles etc.) for use against an enemy's homeland rather than on the battlefield. **strategically,** *adv.* **strategics,** *n.* **strategist,** *n.* an expert in strategy. **strategus,** *n.* (*pl.* **-gi**) (*Gr. Hist.*) a military commander, esp. one of the board of ten at Athens. [as prec.]

Stratford-upon-Avon, *n.* market town on the river Avon, in Warwickshire, England; population (1981) 21,000. It is the birthplace of William Shakespeare.

strath, *n.* a wide valley through which a river runs. [Gael. *srath,* rel. to STRATUM] **strathspey,** *n.* a Scottish dance slower than a reel; music in 4/4 time for this. [valley of the *Spey*]

Strathclyde, *n.* region of Scotland. **area** 13,900 sq km/ 5367 sq miles. **towns** administrative headquarters Glasgow; Paisley, Greenock, Kilmarnock, Clydebank, Hamilton, Coatbridge, Prestwick. **products** dairy, pig, and poultry products, shipbuilding, engineering, coal from Ayr and Lanark, oil-related services. **population** (1987) 2,333,000, half the population of Scotland.

strati-, *comb. form.* layer.

stratify, *v.t.* (*past, p.p.* **-fied**) to form or arrange in strata. **stratification,** *n.* **stratified,** *a.* **stratiform,** *a.*

stratify, *v.t.* to form or arrange in strata. **straticulate,** *a.* (*Geol.*) arranged in numerous thin strata. **stratification,** *n.* [F *stratifier* (STRATUM, -FY)]

stratigraphy, *n.* the branch of geology dealing with the succession, classification, nomenclature etc. of stratified rocks; the analysis of layers in archaeology. **stratigraphic,** *a.*

strato-, *comb. form.* layer; stratosphere.

stratocracy, *n.* military government; government by a military class. [Gr. *stratos,* army, -CRACY]

stratocumulus, *n.* a layer of cloud in dark round masses. **stratopause,** *n.* the upper boundary of the stratosphere. **stratosphere,** *n.* the upper layer of atmosphere extending upwards from about 6 to 50 miles (10 to 80 km) above the earth's surface in which temperature does not decrease with the height. **stratospheric,** *a.*

stratum, *n.* (*pl.* **-ta, -tums**) a horizontal layer of any material; a bed of sedimentary rock; a layer of tissue or cells; a layer of sea or atmosphere; a social level. **stratal,** *a.* [L orig. neut. p.p. of *sternere,* to strew]

stratus, *n.* (*pl.* **-ti**) a continuous horizontal sheet of cloud.

Strauss¹, *n.* **Franz-Josef** (1915–88), West German conservative politician, leader of The Bavarian Christian Social Union (CSU) party from 1961–88, premier of Bavaria from 1978–88.

Strauss², *n.* **Johann (Baptist)** (1825–99), Austrian composer, the son of Johann Strauss (1804–49), a composer of waltz music. In 1872 he gave up conducting to compose, and wrote operettas, such as *Die Fledermaus* (1874) and numerous waltzes, such as 'The Blue Danube' and 'Tales from the Vienna Woods', which gained him the title 'The Waltz King'.

Strauss³, *n.* **Richard (Georg)** (1864–1949), German composer and prominent conductor. He was influenced by the German romantic heritage but had a strongly personal style, particularly in his use of bold, colourful orchestration. His reputation was established with tone poems such as *Don Juan* (1889), *Till Eulenspiegel's Merry Pranks* (1895), and *Also Sprach Zarathustra* (1896). He then moved on to operatic success with *Salome* (1905), and *Elektra* (1909), both of which have elements of polytonality, followed by a reversion to a more traditional style with *Der Rosenkavalier* (1911).

stravaig, *v.i.* to roam about idly, to ramble. [OF *estravaguer,* late L *extrāvagārī,* see EXTRAVAGANT]

Stravinsky, *n.* **Igor** (1882–1971), Russian composer later of French (1934) and US (1945) nationality. He studied under RIMSKY-KORSAKOV and wrote the music for the Diaghilev ballets *The Firebird* (1910), *Petrushka* (1911), and *The Rite of Spring* (1913) (controversial at the time for their unorthodox rhythms and harmony). His versatility ranges from his neo-classical ballet Pulcinella (1920), the choral-orchestral *Symphony of Psalms* (1930), and his later use of serial techniques in works such as the *Canticum Sacrum* (1955) and the ballet *Agon* (1953–57).

straw¹, *n.* the dry, ripened stalk or stalks of certain species of grain, esp. wheat, rye, oats etc.; such a stalk or a piece of one; anything proverbially worthless; a long thin plastic or paper tube for sucking up a drink. †*v.t.* to strew. †**in the straw,** lying-in, in childbed. **man of straw** MAN. **straw in the wind,** a hint or indication of future events. **to clutch, grasp at a straw (or straws),** to resort to desperate remedies. **to draw the short straw,** to be the one selected for a difficult or unpleasant task. **strawboard,** *n.* a thick cardboard made from straw. **straw-colour,** *n.* a pale yellow. **straw-coloured,** *a.* **straw-hat,** *n.* a hat made of plaited straw. **straw poll,** *n.* an unofficial ballot test of opinion. **straw-worm,** *n.* the caddis-worm. **strawy,** *a.* [OE *strēaw* (cp. Dut. *stroo,* G *Stroh,* Icel. *strā*), cogn. with STRATUM]

†**straw²,** **strawed,** *past, p.p.* STREW.

strawberry, *n.* a low, stemless perennial plant of the genus *Fragaria* bearing a fleshy red fruit with small achenes on the surface; the fruit of this. *a.* of the colour (purplish-red) or flavour of strawberries. **strawberry blonde,** *a.* a woman with reddish-blonde hair. **strawberry-mark,** *n.* a soft reddish birthmark. **strawberry-tree,** *n.* an evergreen arbutus, *Arbutus unedo,* bearing a strawberry-like fruit. [as prec.]

stray, *v.i.* to wander from the direct or proper course, to go wrong, to lose one's way; to wander from the path of rectitude. *n.* any domestic animal that has gone astray; a straggler, a waif. *a.* gone astray; straggling, occasional, sporadic. **strayer,** †**strayling,** *n.* [OF *estraier,* from L *strāta,* STREET]

streak, *n.* an irregular line or long narrow mark of a distinct colour from the ground; a vein, or strip; a course or stretch, esp. of good or bad luck; *v.t.* to mark with streaks. *v.i.* (*coll.*) to run naked through a public place as a prank; to move in a straight line at speed. **yellow streak,** *n.* a strain of cowardice. **streakily,** *adv.* **streakiness,** *n.* **streaky,** *a.* marked with streaks; striped; (of bacon) having alternate layers of meat and fat. [ME *streke,* from Scand. (cp. Swed. *streck*) or OE *strica,* STROKE¹ (cp. G *Strich*), cogn. with STRIKE]

stream, *n.* a body of flowing water or other fluid; a river, a brook; a steady flow, a current, a drift; anything in a state of continuous progressive movement, a moving throng etc.; (*often in pl.*) a group of school children of the same general academic ability. *v.i.* to flow, move, or issue in or as a stream; to pour out or emit liquid abundantly; to float, hang, or wave in the wind etc. *v.t.* to pour out or flow with liquid abundantly; to group (schoolchildren) into streams. **streamline,** *n.* the direction of an air current or of the particles of air impinging on a moving body; the shape given to aircraft, vehicles etc., in order to cause the minimum of resistance. **streamer,** *n.* a long, narrow flag, strip of coloured paper or ribbon, a pennon; a column of light shooting across the sky; (*Comput.*) a device which copies data from a hard disk onto magnetic tape as a backup against accidental erasure or loss. **streamlined,** *a.* having a contoured shape to offer minimum resistance to air or liquid; effectively organized, efficient, simplified; graceful. **stream of consciousness,** *n.* the flow of thoughts and feelings forming an individual's conscious experience; a literary technique used to express the unspoken thoughts and emotions of a fictional character, without using conventional narrative or dialogue. **streamless,** *a.* **streamlet,** *n.* **streamy,** *a.* [OE (cp. Dut. *stroom,* G *Strom,* Icel. *straumr*), from Teut. *streu-,* cogn. with Sansk. *sru,* Gr. *rheein,* to flow]

Streep, *n.* **Meryl** (1949–), US actress noted for her strong character roles. Her films include *The Deer Hunter* (1978), *Kramer vs Kramer* (1979), *Out of Africa* (1985), and *Ironweed* (1988).

street, *n.* a road in a city or town with houses on one side or on both; the part of the road used by vehicles; the people living in a street. *a.* of or relating to life in urban centres. **not in the same street as,** not to be compared with. **on the streets,** living by prostitution; homeless, destitute. **streets ahead of,** far better than. **streets apart,** completely different. **up, down one's street,** ideally suited to one's talents, inclinations etc. **street arab** ARAB¹. **streetcar,** *n.* (*N Am.*) a tram. **street credibility,** *n.* knowledge of the customs, language etc. associated with the urban counterculture (also **street cred**). **street value,** *n.* the monetary value of a commodity, esp. drugs, in terms of the price paid by the ultimate user. **street-sweeper,** *n.* a person or machine that sweeps streets. **streetwalker,** *n.* a prostitute. **streetwise,** *a.* familiar with life among the poor, criminals etc. in an urban environment.

†**streight,** †**streightly,** etc. STRAIT.

strength, *n.* the quality of being strong; muscular force; firmness, solidity; power, potency; intensity; amount or proportion of the whole number (of an army, ships etc.). **from strength to strength,** with continually increasing success. **in strength,** in considerable numbers. **on the strength,** on the master-roll. **on the strength of,** in reliance on; on the faith of. **strengthen,** *v.t.* to make strong or stronger. *v.i.* to increase in strength. **strengthener,** *n.* **strengthless,** *a.* [OE *strengthu,* from *strang,* STRONG]

strenuous, *a.* energetic, vigorous, zealous, ardent; eagerly persistent. **strenuously,** *adv.* **strenuousness,** *n.* [L *strēnuus,* cp. Gr. *strēnēs,* strong, *stereos,* STEREO-]

strepitoso, *adv.* (*Mus.*) in a noisy, impetuous manner. [It., from L *strepitus,* noise, from *strepere,* to make a noise]

strepto-, *comb. form.* twisted chain; flexible. **streptococcal,** **streptococcic,** *a.* **streptococcus,** *n.* (*pl.* **-i**) a genus of bacteria consisting of spherical organisms in chains of varying length. **streptomycin,** *n.* an antibiotic obtained from soil bacterium and used in the treatment of tuberculosis and other bacterial infections. [Gr. *streptos,* twisted; *kokkus,* a grain]

stress, *n.* constraining or impelling force; physical, mental or emotional strain; tension, pressure, violence; weight, importance, or influence; emphasis accent; force exerted upon or between the parts of a body. *v.t.* to lay the stress or accent on; to subject to stress or force. **stressful,** **stressless,** *a.* [OF *estrecier,* pop. L *strictiāre,* see DISTRESS]

stretch, *v.t.* to draw out, to extend, to extend in any direction or to full length; to tighten, to draw tight; to extend lengthwise, to straighten; to cause to extend, to hit so as to prostrate; to distend, to strain; to do violence to; to exaggerate; (*sl.*) to hang by the neck. *v.i.*

to be extended in length or breadth; to have a specified extension, to reach; to be drawn out or admit of being drawn out; to extend or straighten one's body or limbs. *n.* the act of stretching or state of being stretched; extent or reach; a reach, sweep, or tract (of land, water etc.); (*Naut.*) the distance covered in one tack; period of a prison sentence. **at a stretch,** at one go; continuously. **to stretch a point,** to go beyond what might be expected. **stretcher,** *n.* one who or that which stretches; a litter or other appliance for carrying a sick, wounded or disabled person in a recumbent position; a brick or stone laid lengthwise in a course in a wall; a cross-piece in a boat for a rower to press his feet against. **stretcher-bearer,** *n.* one who helps to carry a stretcher with the wounded etc. **stretcher-bond,** *n.* a form of bond in which nothing but stretchers are used, though the joints come against the middles of the bricks in the contiguous course. **stretchy,** *a.* **stretchiness,** *n.* [OE *streccan,* from *stræc,* strong, violent (cp. Dut. *strekken,* G *strecken,* also L *stringere,* and Gr. *straggos,* twisted), cogn. with STRING, STRONG]

strew, *v.t.* (*p.p.* **strewn, strewed**) to scatter, to spread thus; to cover by scattering or by being scattered over. †**strewment,** *n.* [OE *strēowian,* from *strēaw,* STRAW[1]]

strewth, *int.* an exclamation of surprise or alarm etc. [derived from *God's truth*]

stria, *n.* (*pl.* **striae**) a superficial furrow, a thin line or groove, mark or ridge. **striate,** *a.* marked with striae. *v.t.*, **striately,** *adv.* **striation, striature,** *n.* [L]

strick, *n.* (*dial.*) a straight-edge for levelling grain, etc. [cogn. with STRIKE]

stricken, *p.p.* STRIKE.

strickle, *n.* a straightedge for levelling grain in a measure; a templet; a straightedge for sharpening curved blades. [dim. of STRICK]

strict, *a.* enforcing or observing rules precisely, not lax; rigorous, severe, stringent; defined or applied exactly, accurate, precise. **strictly,** *adv.* **strictness,** *n.* [L *strictus,* p.p. of *stringere,* see STRINGENT]

stricture, *n.* a censure, a sharp criticism; (*Path.*) a contraction of duct or channel, as of the urethra. **strictured,** *a.*

stride, *v.i.* (*past* **strode**, *p.p.* **stridden, strid**) to walk with long steps; to straddle. *v.t.* to pass over in one step; to bestride. *n.* a long or measured step or the distance covered by this; (*pl. coll. chiefly Austral.*) men's trousers. **to make great strides,** to progress or develop rapidly. **to take in one's stride,** to achieve without difficulty or effort. **stride piano,** *n.* a style of jazz piano in which the right hand plays the melody, while the left alternates in a swinging rhythm between single bass notes (on strong beats) and chords. [OE *strīdan,* cp. LG *strīden,* Dut. *strijden,* to stride, to strive, G *streiten,* to strive]

stridence, -cy, *n.* loudness or harshness of tone. **strident,** *a.* sounding harsh, grating. **stridently,** *adv.* **stridor,** *n.* a harsh, whistling noise made during respiration and caused by blockage of the air passages; a harsh high-pitched sound. **stridulate,** *v.i.* to make a shrill creaking noise (esp. of cicadas and grasshoppers by rubbing hard parts of their body together). **stridulant, stridulous, stridulatory,** *a.* **stridulation,** *n.* **stridulator,** *n.* [L *strīdens -ntem,* pres.p. of *strīdēre,* to creak]

strife, *n.* contention, conflict, hostile struggle. †**strifeful,** *a.* [OF *estrif,* Icel. *strīth,* cogn. with STRIDE]

strig, *n.* (*prov.*) the footstalk of a flower, leaf etc. *v.t.* to strip (fruit) etc. of this. [from foll.]

striga, *n.* (*pl.* **-gae**) a short stiff hair, bristle or hair-like scales; a fluting on a column. **strigose, -gous,** *a.* [L, a swath, rel. to *stringere,* to bind]

Strigidae, *n.pl.* a family of raptorial birds containing the owls. [mod. L, from L *strix strigis,* Gr. *strinx,* owl, from *strizein,* to screech]

strigil, *n.* a skin-scraper used in baths by the ancient Romans and Greeks. [L *strigilis,* rel. to *stringere,* to graze]

strike, *v.t.* (*past* **struck**, *p.p.* **struck, stricken**) to hit, to deliver a blow or blows upon; to deliver, to deal, to inflict (a blow etc.); to afflict (*usu. in p.p.*) to drive, to send (a ball etc.) with force; to attack an enemy craft, location etc.; to produce, make, form, effect, or bring into a particular state by a stroke, as to ignite (a match), to stamp or mint (a coin), to blind, to deafen etc.; to make (a bargain); to cause (a bell etc.) to sound; to notify by sound; to cause to penetrate, to thrust (into); to hook (a fish) by jerking the tackle upwards; to effect forcibly, to impress strongly; to occur suddenly to the mind of; to cause (a cutting etc.) to take root; to lower (sails, a flag, tent etc.); to surrender by lowering (a flag etc.); to leave off (work), esp. to enforce a demand for higher wages etc.; to level corn etc. in (a measure) by scraping off the surplus; to determine (a balance, average etc.); to assume (an attitude); to discover, to come across. *v.i.* to hit, to deliver a blow or blows (upon); to collide, to dash (against, upon etc.); to be driven on shore, a rock etc.; to sound (the time) by a stroke (of a bell etc.); to lower sails, flag etc. in token of surrender etc.; to take root; to leave off work to enforce a demand for higher wages etc.; to arrive suddenly, to happen (upon); to enter or turn (into a track etc.); (*Geol.*) to extend in a particular direction (of strata). *n.* the act of striking for an increase of wages etc.; an attack upon an enemy location, craft etc.; a straight-edge for levelling something, as a measure of grain; (*Geol.*) the horizontal direction of an outcrop; a discovery (as of oil); a luck find, unexpected success; in tenpin bowling, the knocking down of all ten pins with the first bowl, or the score in doing this; (*Baseball*) a good pitched ball missed by the batter and counting against him; (*Cricket*) in a position to receive the bowling; an attack on a target from the air. **to strike back,** to return a blow, retaliate. **to strike down,** to make ill or cause to die, esp. suddenly. †**to strike hands** HAND[1]. **to strike home,** to hit the intended target; to achieve the desired effect. **to strike it rich,** to find a deposit of oil, minerals etc.; to make an unexpected large financial gain. **to strike lucky,** to be fortunate. **to strike off,** to remove, separate, dislodge etc. by a blow; to erase, to strike out; to print. **to strike out,** to produce by striking; to blot out, to efface, to expunge; to devise, to contrive; to make vigorous strokes (in skating, swimming etc.); to hit from the shoulder (in boxing). **to strike up,** to drive up with a blow; to begin to play or sing; to enter into, to start (a conversation etc.). **well stricken in years,** advanced in age. **strikebound,** *a.* of a factory etc., closed or disrupted because of a strike. **strikebreaker,** *n.* a blackleg, worker brought in to replace one out on strike. **strike-pay,** *n.* an allowance for subsistence from a trade-union to workers on strike. **striker,** *n.* one who or that which strikes, esp. a worker on strike; in soccer, an attacking player, a forward. **striking,** *a.* surprising, forcible, impressive, noticeable. **striking circle,** *n.* in hockey, the semi-circular area in front of the goal from within which the ball must be struck to score. **strikingly,** *adv.* **strikingness,** *n.* [OE *strīcan,* to go (cp. Dut. *strijken,* G *streichen,* Icel. *strjūka,* to stroke, rub, smooth etc.), cogn. with L *stringere,* to graze]

Strindberg, *n.* **August** (1849–1912), Swedish playwright. His plays were influential in the development of dramatic technique, and are in a variety of styles including historical plays, symbolic dramas, and 'chamber plays'. The include *The Father* (1887), *Miss Julie* (1888), *The Dance of Death* (1901), and *The Ghost* (or *Spook*) *Sonata* (1907).

strine, *n.* used humorously, Australian English. [a rendering of *Australian* in an Australian accent]

string, *n.* twine, a fine line, usu. thicker than thread and thinner than cord; a length of this or strip of leather, tape, or other material, used for tying, fastening, binding together, connecting etc.; a string-like fibre, tendon, nerve etc.; a piece of wire, catgut etc., yielding musical sounds or notes when caused to vibrate in a piano, violin etc.; (*pl.*) the stringed instruments in an orchestra; a cord or thread upon which anything is strung, hence a series of things or persons connected together or following in close succession; (*Billiards*) the apparatus for keeping the score, the score itself; (*Racing*) the horses under training at a particular stable; (*pl.*) conditions, complications; a sequence of alphabetic or numeric characters in a computer program. *v.t.* (*past, p.p.* **strung**) to furnish with a string or strings; to fasten the string on (a bow); to make (nerves etc.) tense (*usu. in p.p.*); to thread on a string; to strip (beans etc.) of strings or fibres. *v.i.* to become stringy; (*Billiards*) to send the ball against the top cushion and back to decide which player is to begin. **on a string,** totally dependent, e.g. emotionally; held in suspense. **no strings attached,** (*coll.*) with no conditions or restrictions. **to have two strings to one's bow** BOW[1]. **to pull strings,** to exert influence unobtrusively. **to string along,** *v.i.* (*coll.*) to accompany; to agree with, go along with. *v.t.* (*coll.*) to fool, deceive. **to string up,** (*coll.*) to hang. **string-band,** *n.* a band of stringed instruments. **string-bean,** *n.* (*N Am.*) a runner bean, a french bean. **stringboard,** *n.* a timber receiving the ends of stairs in a staircase. **string-course,** *n.* a projecting horizontal band or moulding running along a building. **string-halt** SPRING-HALT. **string-piece,** *n.* a supporting timber forming the edge of a framework, esp. of a floor; a stringboard. **string quartet,** *n.* a combination of four string instruments, viz. two violins, a viola and a violoncello; music written for this combination. **string tie,** *n.* a narrow necktie. **stringed,** *a.* **stringer,** *n.* one who strings; a stringboard; a long horizontal member in a structural framework; (*coll.*) a journalist who works part-time for a newspaper or news agency in a particular area. **stringiness,** *n.* **stringless**, *a.* **stringy,** *a.* consisting of strings or small threads, fibrous, ropy, viscous. **stringy-bark,** *a.* a name for many of the Australian gum-trees, from their fibrous bark. [OE *streng,* cogn. with STRONG]

stringendo, *adv.* (*Mus.*) in accelerated time. [It., as foll.]

stringent, *a.* strict, precise, binding, rigid, hampered, tight, unaccommodating (of the money-market etc.). **stringency, stringentness,** *n.* **stringently,** *adv.* [L *stringens* acc. *-ntem,* pres.p. of *stringere,* to draw tight, p.p. *strictus*]

stringer, stringless, stringy, etc. STRING.

strip, *v.t.* (*past, p.p.* **stripped**) to pull the covering from, to denude, to skin, to peel, to husk, to clean; to deprive (of), to despoil, to plunder; to remove (clothes, bark, rigging, branches etc.); to milk (a cow) to the last drop. *v.i.* to take off one's clothes, to undress; to come away in strips; to have the thread torn off (of a screw), to be discharged without spin (of a projectile). *n.* a long, narrow piece; an airstrip; the clothes worn by a football team etc.; a striptease. **comic strip,** *n.* a row of humorous drawings in a newspaper presenting in sequence some comic incident (also called **strip cartoon**). **to strip down,** to dismantle. **to tear (someone) off a strip,** (*coll.*) to criticise severely. **strip club,** *n.* a club in which striptease artists perform. **strip lighting,** *n.* lighting by long fluorescent tubes. **stripmine,** *n.* an opencast mine. **striptease,** *n.* a cabaret turn in which an actress partially or wholly undresses herself. **stripper,** *n.* **strippings,** *n.pl.* the last milk drawn from a cow. [OE *strȳpan,* cp. Dut. *stroopen,* G *streifen*]

stripe, *n.* a long, narrow band of a distinctive colour or texture; a chevron on the sleeve of a uniform indicating rank; †a stroke with a whip, scourge etc. *v.t.* to mark with stripes; †to lash, to scourge. **stripy,** *a.* **stripiness,** *n.* [prob. from MDut. *strijpe,* cp. Norw. *stripa,* LG *Stripe,* G *Streifen*]

stripling, *n.* a youth, a lad. [dim. of STRIP]

strive, *v.i.* (*past* **strove**, *p.p.* **striven**) to make efforts, to endeavour earnestly, to struggle; to contend, to vie, to emulate; to quarrel (with each other). **striver,** *n.* **strivingly,** *adv.* [OF *estriver,* from *estrif,* STRIFE]

strobe, *n.* a stroboscope. **strobe lighting,** high-intensity flashing light; the apparatus that produces it. **stroboscope**, [-SCOPE], *n.* an instrument for observing periodic motion by making the moving body visible at certain points through the use of synchronized flashing light. **stroboscopic, -al**, *a.* **stroboscopically,** *adv.* [Gr. *strobos,* twisting, from *strephein,* to turn]

strobile, strobilus, *n.* a multiple fruit such as a pine-cone. **strobilaceous**, **strobiliform**, **strobiline**, *a.* [Gr. *strobilos,* cogn. with *strephein,* to turn]

stroboscope, etc. STROBE.

strode, *past* STRIDE.

Stroessner, *n.* **Alfredo** (1912–), military leader and president of Paraguay (1954–89). Accused by his opponents of harsh repression, his regime spent heavily on the military in order to preserve his authority. He was overthrown by a military coup and gained asylum in Brazil.

stroganoff, *n.* a dish of meat, usu. beef in strips cooked with onions and mushrooms in a sour-cream sauce (also called **beef stroganoff**). [from Count *Stroganoff,* 19th-cent. Russian diplomat]

stroke[1], *n.* the act of striking, a blow; the impact, shock, noise etc., of this; a sudden attack (of disease, affliction etc.), a sudden onset of paralysis; a single movement of something, esp. one of a series of recurring movements, as of the heart, an oar, wing, piston etc.; the length, manner, rate etc. of such a movement; a mark made by a single movement of a pen, pencil etc.; a stroke-oar. *v.t.* to act as stroke for (a boat or crew). **at a stroke,** by a single action. **off one's stroke,** not at one's best. **on the stroke,** punctually. **stroke-oar,** †strokesman, *n.* the aftermost oarsman in a boat who sets the time of the stroke for the rest. **stroke play,** *n.* in golf, scoring by counting the number of strokes played as opposed to the number of holes won. **stroker,** *n.* **strokingly,** *adv.* [OE *strāc,* from *strican,* to STRIKE]

stroke[2], *v.t.* to pass the hand over the surface of caressingly. *n.* the act of stroking. **to stroke the wrong way,** to ruffle, to annoy. [OE *strācian,* from *strāc,* see prec.]

stroll, *v.i.* to walk leisurely or idly, to saunter. *v.t.* to saunter or ramble on foot. *n.* a leisurely ramble. **stroller,** *n.* (*N Am.*) a pushchair. [Gr. *strōma,* bed, cogn. with *strōnnunai,* to spread]

stroma, *n.* (*pl.* **-mata**) the framework of tissue of an organ or cell; a dense mass of hyphae produced by some fungi, in which fructification may develop; the dense framework of a chloroplast etc. [Gr. *strōma,* bed, cogn. with *strōnnunai,* to spread]

stromb, *n.* a gasteropod of the genus *Strombus* or the family Strombidae, chiefly found in tropic seas; a shell of this used for ornament. **strombiform**, **stromboid**, *a.* **strombite,**, *n.* a fossil stromb. **strombuliform**, *a.* (*Bot.*) twisted spirally like a screw. **Strombus**, *n.* a genus of marine gasteropods. [mod. L *strombus,* Gr. *strombos,* pine-cone, cogn. with *strephein,* to turn]

strong, *a.* (*comp.* **stronger** ; *super.* **strongest**), able to exert great force, powerful, muscular, able, capable; acting with great force, vigorous, forcible, energetic; having great powers of resistance or endurance; healthy, robust, hale; firm, tough, solid; having great numbers, resources etc.; having a specified number of personnel etc.; having a powerful effect on the senses, loud and penetrating, glaring, pungent, ill-smelling, intoxicating, heady; (*Gram.*) forming inflexions by internal vowel-change, and not by addition of a syllable (*as strike, struck, stride, strode*). **going strong,** prospering, getting on famously, in good form or spirits. **to come on strong,** to act or behave in a violent, reckless, or defiant way. **strong-arm,** *a.* using or involving physical force. *v.t.* to show violence towards. **strongbox,** *n.* a safe or robust trunk for storing valuables. **strong drink,** *n.* alcoholic liquors. **stronghold,** *n.* a fortress, a fastness; a refuge. **strong interaction,** *n.* an interaction between elementary particles responsible for the forces that bind nucleons together in an atomic nucleus. **strong language,** *n.* swearing. **strong man,** *n.* one who performs muscular feats of strength; (*coll.*) an autocratic leader. **strong meat,** *n.* theories or doctrines demanding courageous thought. **strong-minded,** *a.* having a vigorous mind; resolute, determined. **strong-mindedly,** *adv.* **strong-mindedness,** *n.* **strong point,** *n.* something at which one excels. **strongroom,** *n.* a specially reinforced room for storing valuables. **strongish,** *a.* **strongly,** *adv.* [OE *strang* (cp. Dut. and Dan. *streng,* Icel. *strangr,* Swed. *sträng,* G *streng,* strict), cogn. with L *stringere,* see STRICT]

strontium, *n.* a yellowish metallic element, at. no. 38; chem. symbol Sr resembling calcium. **strontium-90,** *n.* strontium with atomic weight of 90, a radioactive product of nuclear fission which tends to accumulate in bones. **strontia,** *n.* an oxide of strontium. **strontian,** *n., a.* **strontianite,** *n.* a carbonate of strontia. [*Strontian,* Argyleshire, where first found]

†**strook,** *past* STRIKE (*Milton*).

strop, *n.* a strip of leather etc., for sharpening razors etc., on. *v.t.* (*past, p.p.* **stropped**) to sharpen with or on a strop. [var. of STRAP]

strophanthus, *n.* a genus of tropical gamopetalous small trees or shrubs. **strophanthin,** *n.* a poisonous drug made from strophanthus seeds, used as arrow-poison; its medicinal uses are similar to those of digitalis. [Gr. *strophos,* a twisted band; *anthos,* a flower]

strophe, *n.* the turning of the chorus from right to left in an ancient Greek drama; a part of the ode (consisting of strophe, antistrophe, and epode) sung whilst so turning, esp. the first part, the strophe proper. **strophic,** *a.* [Gr. *strophē,* orig. a turning, from *strephein,* to turn]

strophiole, *n.* (*Bot.*) an aril-like appendage attached to the hilum of some seeds. **strophiolate,** *a.* [L *strophiolum,* dim. of *strophium,* Gr. *strophion,* dim. of *strophos,* a band, as prec.]

stroppy, *a.* (*coll.*) rowdy, angry; awkward, quarrelsome. **stroppily,** *adv.* **stroppiness,** *n.* [perh. alteration of OBSTREPEROUS]

†**strossers,** TROUSERS.

strove, *past* STRIVE.

†**strow,** STREW.

†**stroy,** DESTROY.

struck, *past, p.p.* STRIKE.

structure, *n.* a combination of parts, as a building, machine, organism etc., esp. the supporting or essential framework; the manner in which a complex whole is constructed, put together, or organically formed; the arrangement of parts, organs, atoms etc., in a complex whole. *v.t.* to create a structure. **structural,** *a.* **structural formula,** *n.* a chemical formula showing the arrangement of atoms and bonds in a molecule. **structuralism,** *n.* an approach to the human sciences, literature, linguistics etc. as coded systems comprising self-sufficient and self-determining structures of interrelationships and rules of combination through which meaning is generated and communicated. **structuralist,** *n.* **structurally,** *adv.* **structured,** *a.* (*usu. in comb.,* as *loose-structured*) **structureless,** *a.* [F, from L *structūra,* from *struere,* to build, p.p. *structus*]

strudel, *n.* a thin pastry rolled up with a filling (e.g. apple) and baked. [G, lit. whirlpool]

struggle, *v.i.* to make violent movements; to put forth great efforts, esp. against difficulties or opposition; to strive (to); to contend (with or against); to make one's way (along etc.) against difficulties, opposition etc. *n.* an act or spell of struggling; a strenuous effort; a fight or contest, esp. of a confused character. **struggler,** *n.* **strugglingly,** *adv.* [ME *strogelen,* cp. Swed. dial. *strug,* contention, Norw. *stru,* refractory]

struldbrug, *n.* one of a class of immortals, in Swift's *Gulliver's Travels,* born with a mark on the forehead and kept at the public expense after the age of eighty. [coined by Swift]

strum, *v.t., v.i.* to play noisily or carelessly, to thrum on a stringed instrument. *n.* strumming. [imit.]

struma, *n.* (*pl.* **-mae**) (*dated*) scrofula; (*Bot.*) a cushion-like swelling on a petiole etc. **strumose, strumous,** *a.* **strumousness,** *n.* [L, from *struere,* to build]

strumpet, *n.* a prostitute, a harlot. *v.t.* to debauch. [prob. from OF *strupe, strupre,* concubinage, L *stuprum,* defilement]

strung, *past, p.p.* STRING.

strut[1], *v.i.* to walk with a pompous, conceited gait. *n.* such a gait. **strutter,** *n.* **struttingly,** *adv.* [ME *strouten,* prob. from Dan. *strutte* (cp. Swed. dial. *strutta*), cogn. with LG *strutt,* rigid]

strut[2], *n.* a timber or iron beam inserted in a framework so as to keep other members apart, a brace. *v.t.* to brace with a strut or struts. [cogn. with prec.]

Struthio, *n.* a genus of cursorial birds, containing the ostrich. **struthious,** *a.* [L, from Gr. *strouthiōn,* from *strouthos,* sparrow]

strychnine, *n.* a highly poisonous alkaloid obtained from species of *Strychnos,* esp. *S. nux vomica,* used in medicine as a stimulant etc. †**strychnia,** *n.* **strychnic,** *a.* **strychninism, strychnism,** *n.* [L *strychnos,* Gr. *struchnos,* nightshade, -INE]

St-Simonian, *n.* an adherent of the Comte de St-Simon (1760-1825), who advocated the establishment of State ownership and distribution of earnings according to capacity and labour. *a.* of or pertaining to his doctrines. **St-Simonianism, -Simonism,** *n.* **St-Simonist, -Simonite,** *n.*

St Stephen's, *n.* the British parliament (so named from the chapel within the precincts of the Houses of Parliament).

Stuart, Stewart, house of, royal family who inherited the Scottish throne in 1371 and the English throne in 1603.

stub, *n.* the stump of a tree, tooth etc.; a stump, end or remnant of anything, e.g. of a cigarette; a cheque counterfoil; (*N Am.*) a counterfoil. *v.t.* (*past, p.p.* **stubbed**) to grub up by the roots; to clear of stubs; to strike one's toe against something; to extinguish a cigarette etc. (foll. by *out*). **stubbed, stubby,** *a.* short and thickset. *n.* (*coll. Austral.*) a small squat beer bottle. **stubbedness, stubbiness,** *n.* [OE *stybb,* cp. Dut. *stobbe,* Icel. *stubbi,* Dan. *stub,* also Gr. *stupos*]

stubble, *n.* the stumps of wheat, barley etc. covering the ground after harvest; short, bristly hair, whiskers etc. **designer-stubble** DESIGN. **stubble-fed,** *a.* fed on the grass growing amongst stubble, split grain etc. **stubbly,** †**stubbled,** *a.* [ME *stobil,* OF *estoubie,* late L *stupula,* L *stipula,* see STIPULE]

stubborn, *a.* unreasonably obstinate, not to be persuaded; obdurate, inflexible, intractable, refractory. **stubbornly,** *adv.* **stubbornness,** *n.* [ME *stoburn, stiborn,* prob. from OE *stybb,* STUB]

Stubbs, *n.* **George** (1721–1806), English artist, best known for paintings of horses. After the publication of his book of engravings *The Anatomy of the Horse* (1766), he was widely commissioned as an animal painter and group portraitist.

stucco, *n.* (*pl.* **-ccoes, -ccos**) fine plaster for coating walls or moulding into decorations in relief; any plaster used for coating the outside of buildings. *v.t.* (*past, p.p.* **-ccoed**) to coat with stucco. **stuccoer,** *n.* [It., from OHG *stucchi,* crust (cp. G *Stück,* OE *stycce,* piece), cogn. with STOCK[1]]

stuck, *past, p.p.* STICK.

Stud, National, *n.* British establishment founded in 1915, and since 1964 located at Newmarket, where stallions are kept for visiting mares. It is now maintained by the Horserace Betting Levy Board.

stud[1], *n.* a large-headed nail, knob, head of a bolt etc., esp. fixed as an ornament; an ornamental button for wearing in a shirt-front etc.; a cross-piece in a link of chain-cable; a stud-bolt; a small spindle, pin, or dowel, in a lathe, watch etc.; a post or scantling to which laths are nailed in a partition. *v.t.* (*past, p.p.* **studded**) to set with studs or ornamental knobs; to set thickly, to bestrew. **stud-bolt,** *n.* a bolt with a thread for screwing into a fixed part at one end and having a nut screwed on it at the other. [OE *studu,* a post, cp. Dan. and Swed. *stöd,* Icel. *stoth,* G *Stütze,* prop.]

stud[2], *n.* a number of horses kept for riding, racing, breeding etc.; any male animal used for breeding; an animal-breeding establishment; (*sl.*) a sexually potent man. *a.* (of an animal) kept for breeding. **at stud, out**

to stud, used for breeding. **stud-book,** *n.* a register of pedigrees of horses or cattle. **stud-farm,** *n.* a farm where horses are bred. **studhorse,** *n.* a stallion. **stud poker,** *n.* a variety of poker. [OE *stōd* (cp. Icel. *stōth,* Dan. *stod,* G *gestüt*), cogn. with STAND]

studdingsail, *n.* an additional sail set beyond the sides of a square sail in light winds. [etym. doubtful]

student, *n.* a person engaged in study, esp. one receiving instruction at a university, college or other institution for higher education or technical training; (*esp. N Am.*) a schoolboy or girl; a studious person; a person receiving an annual grant for study or research from a foundation etc. **studentship,** *n.* a grant for study at a university. [L *studens -dentis,* pres.p. of *studēre,* see STUDY]

studiedly STUDY.

studio, *n.* the working-room of a sculptor, painter, photographer etc.; the room in which records, radio and television programmes are recorded, or films made; the place from which television and radio programmes are broadcast; (*pl.*) the buildings used for making films by a television or film company. [It., from L *studium,* STUDY]

studious, *a.* devoted to study; eager, diligent, anxious (to do something); careful, observant (of); studied, deliberate, intended. **studiously,** *adv.* **studiousness,** *n.* [F *studieux,* L *studiōsus,* as foll.]

study, *n.* mental application to books, art, science etc., the pursuit of knowledge; something that is studied or worth studying; a sketch or other piece of work done for practice or as a preliminary design for a picture etc.; (*Mus.*) a composition designed to test or develop technical skill; (*Theat.*) one who learns a part; a room devoted to study, literary work etc.; a reverie, a fit of musing; earnest endeavour, watchful attention; the object of this. *v.t.* to apply the mind to for the purpose of learning; to inquire into, to investigate; to contemplate, to consider attentively; to commit to memory; to apply thought and pains to, to be zealous for; (*in p.p.*) deliberate, premeditated, intentional. *v.i.* to apply oneself to study, esp. to reading; to meditate, to cogitate, to muse; to be assiduous, diligent, or anxious (to do). **studied,** *a.* deliberate, intentional. **studiedly,** *adv.* [A-F and OF *estudie,* L *studium,* eagerness, zeal, whence, med L *studiāre,* OF *estudier,* F *étudier,* to study]

stufa, *n.* a jet of steam issuing from a fissure of the earth. [It.]

stuff, *n.* the material of which anything is made or may be made; the fundamental substance, essence, or elements of anything; household goods, furniture, utensils etc.; a textile fabric, esp. woollen, as opp. to silk or linen; worthless matter, nonsense, trash. *v.t.* to cram, to pack, to fill or stop (up); to fill (a fowl etc.) with stuffing or seasoning for cooking; to fill the skin of (a dead animal) so as to restore its natural form; to fill with food; to cram, press, ram, or crowd into a receptacle, confined space etc.; to fill with ideas, notions, nonsense etc.; (*coll.*) to impose on, to hoax. *v.t.* (*taboo*) to have sexual intercourse with a woman. *v.i.* to cram oneself with food. **bit of stuff,** (*sl. derog.*) a girl or woman. **hot stuff,** (*coll.*) an attractive or potent person or thing. **that's the stuff!** just what is needed. **to do one's stuff,** (*coll.*) to act as one is expected. **to know one's stuff,** (*coll.*) to be competent in one's chosen field. **stuffed,** *a.* (of poultry etc.) filled with stuffing; having blocked nasal passages (foll. by *up*). **get stuffed!,** *int.* expressing anger, contempt etc. against another person. **stuffed shirt,** *n.* (*coll.*) a pompous person. **stuffer,** *n.* **stuffing,** *n.* material used to stuff something; a mixture of ingredients used to stuff poultry etc. before it is cooked. **to knock the stuffing out of,** to beat (an opponent thoroughly). **stuffing-box,** *n.* a chamber packed with stuffing so as to be air-tight or water-tight, in which a piston-rod etc. can work freely. **stuffy,** *a.* ill-ventilated, close, fusty; strait-laced; stuffed up. **stuffiness,** *n.* [OF *estoffe* (F *étoffe*), L *stuppa, stūpa,* see STOP]

stuggy, (*prov.*) STOCKY.

stultify, *v.t.* to render absurd, to cause to appear self contradictory, inconsistent, or ridiculous; (*Law*) to allege or prove to be insane. [L *stulti-, stultus,* foolish, -FY] **stultification,** *n.* **stultifier,** *n.* †**stultiloquence,** †**-quy,** *n.* foolish talk. †**stultiloquent,** *a.* [L *stultiloquentia* (*loqui,* to talk)]

stum, *n.* unfermented grape-juice, must. *v.t.* to prevent (wine) from fermenting by adding stum. [Dut. *stom,* orig. a., quiet, cp. G *stumm,* dumb]

stumble, *v.i.* to trip in walking or to strike the foot against something without falling, to have a partial fall; to fall into a blunder, to act, move, or speak blunderingly; to come (upon) by chance; to feel misgivings, to boggle (at). †*v.t.* to cause to stumble; to confound, to puzzle. *n.* an act of stumbling. **stumbler,** *n.* **stumbling-block,** *n.* an obstacle, an impediment, a cause of difficulty, hesitation etc. **stumblingly,** *adv.* [ME *stumblen,* freq. of *stum-,* cogn with prec. and STAMMER]

stumer, *n.* a disappointing racehorse; a failure; (*sl.*) a cheque that has no money to back it; a returned cheque. [etym. unknown]

stump, *n.* the part left in the earth after a tree has fallen or been cut down; any part left when the rest of a branch, limb, tooth etc., has been cut away, amputated, destroyed, or worn out, a stub, a butt; (*Cricket*) one of the three posts of a wicket; (*pl.*) the legs; a pointed roll of leather or paper used to rub down the strong lines of a crayon or pencil drawing etc. *v.i.* to walk stiffly, awkwardly, or noisily, as on wooden legs; to make stump-speeches, to go about doing this. *v.t.* to work upon (a drawing etc.) with a stump; to go about (a district) making stump speeches; to put out (the batsman) at cricket by touching the wicket while he is out of the crease; (*coll.*) to pose, to put at a loss; (*sl.*) to pay (up) at once. **on the stump,** going about making political speeches. **to stump up,** to pay up; to produce the money required. **stump-orator,** *n.* **stump-oratory,** *n.* **stump-speech,** *n.* a speech from some improvised platform, orig. a tree-stump; an electioneering speech. **stump-tail,** *n.* (*Austral.*) a short-tailed lizard. **stumper,** *n.* **stumpy,** *a.* short, thick-set, stocky; full of stumps, stubby. [Icel. *stumpr* (cp. Dan. and Swed. *stump,* Dut. *stomp,* G *Stumpf*), cogn. with STAMP and STUB]

stun, *v.t.* (*past, p.p.* **stunned**) to daze or deafen with noise; to render senseless with a blow; to stupefy, to overpower. **stunner,** *n.* one who or that which stuns; (*sl.*) something astonishing or first-rate. **stunning,** *a.* stupefying; (*sl.*) wonderfully good, fine etc. **stunningly,** *adv.* [OE *stunian,* to make a din, cp. Icel. *stynja,* G *stöhnen,* to groan, also Gr. *steinein*]

stung, *past, p.p.* STING.

stunk, *past, p.p.* STINK.

stunsail, stuns'l, STUDDINGSAIL.

stunt[1], *v.t.* to check in growth or development, to dwarf, to cramp. *n.* a check in growth; a stunted animal or thing. [OE, dull, obtuse (cp. Icel. *stuttr,* short), cogn. with STINT]

stunt[2], *n.* a performance serving as a display of strength, skill, or the like; a feat; a thing done to attract attention; a feat of aerobatics. **stuntman, stuntwoman,** *n.* one who performs dangerous feats (esp. as a stand-in for an actor). [etym. unknown]

stupa, *n.* a tope. [Sansk., see TOPE[2]]

stupe, *n.* a compress of flannel or other soft material used in fomentations etc. *v.t.* to treat with this, to foment. [L *stūpa,* STUFF]

stupefy, *v.t.* (*pres.p.* **stupefying,** *past, p.p.* **stupefied**) to make stupid or senseless; to deprive of sensibility. **stupefacient,** *a., n.* **stupefaction,** *n.* astonishment; the act of stupefying or state of being stupefied. **stupefactive,** *a.* **stupefier,** *n.* [F *stupéfier,* L *stupefacere* (*stupēre,* to be amazed, *facere,* to make)]

stupendous, *a.* astounding in magnitude, force, degree etc., marvellous, amazing, astonishing. **stupendously,** *adv.* **stupendousness,** *n.* [L *stupendus,* from *stupēre,* to be amazed]

stupeous, stupose, *a.* (*Nat. Hist.*) having long, loose scales or tufts of filament or hair like tow. [L *stūpeus,* from *stūpa,* STUPE]

stupid, *a.* in a state of stupor, stupefied; dull of apprehension, wit or understanding, obtuse; senseless, nonsensical. **stupidity, stupidness,** *n.* **stupidly,** *adv.* [F *stupide,* L *stupidus,* from *stupēre,* see STUPEFY]

stupor, *n.* a dazed condition, torpor, deadened sensibility. [L, as prec.]

†**stuprate,** *v.t.* to ravish, to violate, to debauch. †**stupration,** †**stuprum,** *n.* [L *stuprātus,* p.p. of *stuprāre,* to defile, from *stuprum,* dishonour, lewdness]

sturdy[1], *a.* robust, lusty, vigorous, hardy. **sturdily,** *adv.* **sturdiness,** *n.* [OF *estourdi,* p.p. of *estourdir* (F *étourdir,*) to astound, to amaze]

sturdy[2], *n.* a disease in sheep characterized by giddiness caused by a tape-worm in the brain. **sturdied,** *a.* [OF *estourdie,* giddiness, as prec.]

sturgeon, *n.* a large anadromous fish of the genus *Acipenser,* characterized by bony scales, esp. *A. sturio,* which yields caviare and isinglass. [OF *esturgeon,* med. L *sturiō,* acc. *-ōnem,* OHG *Sturjo,* cp. OE *styria,* G *Stör*]

Sturluson, *n.* **Snorri** (1179–1241), Icelandic author of the Old Norse poems called EDDAS, and the *Heimskringla,* a saga chronicle of Norwegian Kings until 1177.

sturniform, *a.* like a starling; belonging to the Sturnidae, a family of birds containing the starlings. **sturnoid,** *a.* [L *sturnus,* starling, -FORM]

stutter, *v.i.* to keep hesitating or repeating sounds spasmodically in the articulation of words. *v.t.* to utter thus (*usu.* out). *n.* this act or habit. **stutterer,** *n.* **stutteringly,** *adv.* [freq. of obs. *stut,* ME *stoten,* cp. Dut. *stottern,* G *stottern,* also G *stossen* and L *tundere,* to beat]

Stuttgart, *n.* capital of Baden-Württemberg, West Germany; population (1986) 565,000. Industries include publishing and the manufacture of vehicles and electrical goods.

St Valentine's Day Massacre, the murder in Chicago, US, of seven unarmed members of the 'Bugs' Moran gang on 14 Feb. 1929 by members of Al Capone's gang disguised as policemen. The killings testified to the intensity of gangland warfare for the control of the trade in illicit liquor during prohibition.

St Vincent and the Grenadines, country in the Windward Islands, West Indies. **area** 388 sq km/150 sq miles, including Northern Grenadines 43 sq km/17 sq miles. **capital** Kingstown. **physical** volcanic mountains, thickly forested. **population** (1987) 113,000; annual growth rate 4%. **exports** bananas, tarros, sweet potatoes, arrowroot, copra. **language** English. **religion** Christian (47% Anglican, 28% Methodist, 13% Roman Catholic).

St Vitus' dance, former name for the disease chorea. St Vitus, martyred under the Roman emperor, Diocletian, was the patron saint of dancers.

sty[1], *n.* (*pl.* **sties**) a pen or enclosure for pigs; a mean or filthy habitation; a place of debauchery. *v.t.* to shut up in or as in a sty. *v.i.* to live in or as in a sty. [OE *stīgo* (cp. Icel. *stīa, stī,* Dan. *sti,* Swed. *stia,* OHG *Stiga,* cattle-pen), prob. from *stīgan,* to climb]

sty[2], **stye,** *n.* (*pl.* **sties, styes**) a small inflamed swelling on the edge of the eyelid. [prob. from OE *stīgend,* pres.p. of *stīgan,* to rise]

Stygian, *a.* pertaining to the river Styx; of darkness, gloomy, impenetrable.

style[1], *n.* a pointed instrument used by the ancients for writing on wax-covered tablets; a writing-instrument or other thing shaped like this, an etching-needle, a graver, a blunt-pointed surgical instrument, a pointed or styloid projection, cusp, or process in a bone etc.; manner of writing, expressing ideas, speaking, behaving, doing etc., as dist. from the matter expressed or done; sort, kind, make, pattern; the general characteristics of literary diction, artistic expression, or mode of decoration, distinguishing a particular people, person, school, period etc.; the proper expression of thought in language; manner or form of a superior or fashionable character, fashion, distinction; mode of designation or address, title, description. *v.t.* to designate, to describe formally by name and title; to design or shape. **New Style,** the Gregorian method of reckoning dates (introduced 1582). **Old Style,** the Julian method, in vogue before this. **stylebook,** *n.* a book containing rules of grammar, typography etc. for printers and editors. **stylar,** *a.* of or pertaining to a style for writing etc. **styliform,** *a.* **stylish,** *a.* fashionable in style, smart, showy. **stylishly,** *adv.* **stylishness,** *n.* **stylist,** *n.* a writer having or cultivating a good style; a clothes designer; a hairdresser who styles hair. **stylistic,** *a.* **stylistics,** *n.sing.* the study of style in literary language. **stylistically,** *adv.* [ME and OF *stile,* L *stilus,* sometimes written *stylus,* assim. to foll.]

style[2], *n.* the gnomon of a sun-dial; (*Bot.*) the prolongation of an ovary, bearing the stigma. [Gr. *stulos,* pillar]

style[3], STILE[1].

stylet, *n.* a long pointed instrument, a stiletto; (*Surg.*) the stiffening wire of a catheter; a probe. [OF, from It. STILETTO]

stylist, etc. STYLE[1].

stylite, *n.* a religious recluse in ancient and mediaeval times who lived on the top of a pillar. [late Gr. *stulitēs,* from *stulos,* STYLE[2]]

stylobate, *n.* a continuous base for a range of columns. [Gr. *stulobatēs* (STYLE[2], *bainein,* to stand)]

stylograph, *n.* a pen with a tubular point fed with ink from a reservoir in the shaft. **stylographic,** *a.* **stylographically,** *adv.* **stylography,** *n.* the art, process etc. of using a style or stylograph. [see STYLE[1]]

stylohyoid, *a.* pertaining to the styloid process of the temporal bone and the hyoid bone.

styloid, *a.* style-like. *n.* the styloid process, a spine projecting from the base of the temporal bone. **stylospore,** *n.* (*Bot.*) a pycnidiospore.

stylus, *n.* a pointed instrument for writing by means of carbon paper, a style; a device attached to the cartridge in the arm of a record player that follows the groove in a record. [STYLE[1]]

stymie, *n.* (*Golf*) the position when an opponent's ball lies between the player's ball and the hole. *v.t.* to hinder by a stymie. [etym. doubtful]

styptic, *a.* that stops bleeding; †astringent. *n.* a drug that arrests bleeding. **stypticity,** *n.* [F *styptique,* L *stypticus,* Gr. *stuptikos,* from *stuphein,* to contract, prob. cogn. with STOP]

styrax, *n.* a tree or shrub of the genus *Styrax,* species of which yield benzoin and storax. **styrene,** *n.* a colourless volatile liquid derived from benzene used in the manufacture of plastics and synthetic rubber. [L, from Gr. *sturax*]

Styx, *n.* the river of Hades over which Charon ferries the departed souls. [L, from Gr. *Stux -gos*]

suable, *a.* capable of being sued. **suability,** *n.*

Suárez González, *n.* **Adolfo** (1933–), Spanish politician, prime minister (1976–81). A friend of King Juan Carlos, he worked in the National Movement for 18 years, but in 1975 became president of the newly established Unión del Pueblo Español (UPE). He took office as prime minister at the request of the king, to speed the reform programme. He suddenly resigned in 1981.

suasion, *n.* persuasion as opp. to compulsion. **suasive,** *a.* **suasively,** *adv.* [F, from L *suāsio -ōnem,* from *suādēre* to persuade, p.p. *suāsus,* cogn. with foll.]

suave, *a.* agreeable, bland, gracious, polite. **suavely,** *adv.* **suavity,** *n.* [F, from L *suāvis,* cogn. with SWEET]

sub-, *pref.* under, situated below; from below, upward; denoting inferior or subordinate position; subdivision of, part of; slightly, rather; approximately, bordering on; (*Chem.*) less than normal; containing in small proportion; (*Math.*) denoting the inverse of a ratio. In cases where no definition is given reference should be made to the unprefixed word in its proper place in the dictionary. [L *sub-,* pref., *sub,* prep., under]

sub, *n.* short for SUBALTERN, SUBEDITOR, SUBMARINE, SUBORDINATE, SUBSTITUTE; a small loan or advance payment of wages etc. *v.i.* (*past, p.p.* **subbed**) to act as a substitute or as a subeditor; to receive pay in advance on account of wages due later. *v.t.* to grant (a small loan or advance) to; to subedit.

subabdominal, *a.* situated below the abdomen.

subacid, *a.* slightly acid or sour. *n.* a subacid substance. **subacidity**, *n.*

subacrid, *a.*

†**subact,** *v.t.* to subdue, to reduce. †**subaction,** *n.*

subacute, *a.*

subaerial, *a.* (*Geol.*) being, acting or produced in the open air, as opp. to submarine, subterranean, etc. **subaerialist,** *n.* one who ascribes the chief inequalities of the earth's surface to subaerial causes. **subaerially,** *adv.*

subagent, *n.* one employed by an agent. **subagency,** *n.*

subalpine, *a.* pertaining to elevated regions not above the timber-line.

subaltern, *a.* subordinate; of inferior rank; (*Log.*) particular, ranking below universal. *n.* a junior army officer, one below the rank of captain. **subalternant, subalternate,** *n., a.* **subalternation,** *n.* (*Log.*) the relation between a particular and a universal proposition of the same quality. [F *subalterne,* med. L *subalternus* (*alternus,* see ALTERNATE)]

subantarctic, *a.* pertaining to the region bordering on the Antarctic.

subapennine, *a.* situated at the base of the Apennine mountains, in Italy.

subapostolic, *a.* pertaining to the period succeeding that of the apostles.

subaqua, *a.* pertaining to underwater sports. **subaquatic,** *a.* partially aquatic; subaqueous. **subaqueous,** *a.* being or formed under water.

subarctic, *a.* pertaining to the region bordering on the Arctic.

subassembly, *n.* an assembled unit forming part of a larger product.

subastral, *a.* terrestrial.

subatomic, *a.* of or occurring inside an atom; making up an atom; smaller than an atom.

subaudition, *n.* the act of understanding something not expressed; something implied but not expressed. [L *subauditio,* from *subaudīre* (*audīre,* to hear)]

subaxillary, *a.* situated beneath the armpit or the wing-cavity, or under the axil formed by a petiole and stem etc.

sub-base, *n.* (*Arch.*) the lowest part of a base horizontally divided; (*Elec.*) a base placed under a machine.

subbasement, *n.* **sub-branch,** *n.* **subcategory,** *n.*

subcaudal, *a.* situated under the tail.

subcelestial, *a.* terrestrial.

subcellular, *a.*

subcentral, *a.* situated under the centre; nearly central.

subcerebral, *a.* **subclass,** *n.* **subclause,** *n.*

subclavate, -clavian, -clavicular, *a.* situated under the clavicle.

subclinical, *a.* having symptoms sufficiently slight as to be undetectable clinically.

subcommission, *n.* **subcommissioner,** *n.*

subcommittee, *n.* a small committee appointed from among its members by a larger committee to consider and report on a particular matter.

subconcave, *a.* **subconical,** *a.*

subconscious, *a.* slightly or partially conscious; existing in the mind but without one's full awareness. **the subconscious,** that part of the field of consciousness which at any given moment is outside the range of one's attention; the accumulation of past conscious experiences which are forgotten or for the moment are out of one's thoughts. **subconsciously,** *adv.* **subconsciousness,** *n.*

subcontinent, *n.* a region large enough to be a continent though itself forming part of a yet larger continent.

sub-continuous, *a.*

subcontract[1], *n.* a contract sublet from another.

subcontract[2], *v.t., v.i.* to make a subcontract. **subcontractor,** *n.*

subcontrary, *a.* (*Log.*) contrary in an inferior degree. *n.* a subcontrary proposition. **subcontrariety,** *n.*

subconvex, *a.* **subcordate,** *a.* **subcostal,** *a.* **subcranial,** *a.*

subcritical, *a.* (pertaining to nuclear fuel) of insufficient mass to sustain a chain reaction.

subcrystalline, *a.*

subculture, *n.* a social or ethnic group with a characteristic culture differing from that of the national culture.

subcutaneous, *a.* **subcutaneously,** *adv.*

subcuticular, *a.* **subcylindrical,** *a.*

subdeacon, *n.* **subdeaconry, subdeaconship,** *n.* **subdiaconate,** *n.*

subdean, *n.* **subdeanery,** *n.* **subdecanal,** *a.*

subdecuple, *a.* containing one part of ten.

subdelirium, *n.* a mild or intermittent form of delirium.

subdentate, *a.* **subdermal,** *a.*

subdititious, *a.* inserted surreptitiously, foisted in. [L *subdititius, -cius,* from *subdere* (*dare,* to put)]

subdivide, *v.t., v.i.* to divide again or into smaller parts. **subdivisible,** *a.* **subdivision,** *n.*

subdominant, *n., a.* (*Mus.*) (pertaining to) the tone next below the dominant, the fourth of the scale.

subdorsal, *a.*

subdouble, *a.* in the ratio of one to two.

†**subduce,** †**subduct,** *v.t.* to withdraw, to take away, to subtract. †**subduction,** *n.* [L *subdūcere* (*dūcere,* to lead, p.p. *ductus*)]

subdue, *v.t.* to conquer, to reduce to subjection, to vanquish, to overcome; to check, to curb; to tame, to render gentle or mild; to tone down, to soften, to make less glaring. **subduable,** *a.* **subdual, subduement,** *n.* **subdued,** *a.* quiet, passive, cowed; toned down, not harsh or glaring. **subduedness,** *n.* **subduer,** *n.* [ME *soduen,* from p.p. *sodued,* OF *subduz,* pl., subdued, prob. through a late L *subdutus,* L *subditus,* p.p. of *subdere,* see SUBDITITIOUS]

subduple, *a.* in the ratio of one to two. **subduplicate,** *a.* expressed by the square root.

subedit, *v.t.* to prepare (manuscript) for printing. **subeditor,** *n.*

subentry, *n.* **subepidermal,** *a.*

subequal, *a.* nearly equal, esp. of quantities in a group of which none equals the sum of any two others.

subequatorial, *a.* **subequilateral,** *a.* **suberect,** *a.*

subereous, suberic, *a.* of the nature or texture of, pertaining to or derived from cork. **suberin,** *n.* a waxy substance found in cork. **suberization, -isation,** *n.* impregnation of plant cell walls with suberin to form cork. **suberize, -ise,** *v.* **suberose**[1], **suberous,** *a.* [L *sūber,* cork]

suberose[2], *a.* (*Bot.*) slightly erose.

subfamily, *n.* **subfebrile,** *a.* **subfile,** *n.* **subflavour,** *n.* **subflora,** *n.* **subfluvial,** *a.* **subform,** *n.* **subfreezing,** *a.*

subfusc, *a.* dusky, sombre; drab, dingy. *n.* formal academic dress at Oxford Univ. **subfuscous,** *a.* dusky. [L *fuscus,* FUSCOUS]

subgelatinous, *a.*

subgenus, *n.* (*pl.* **-genera, -genuses**). **subgeneric,** *a.*

subglacial, *a.* **subglobular** *a.* **subgranular,** *a.* **subgroup,** *n.*

subhead, -heading, *n.* a heading, often explanatory, beneath the main heading of a book, article etc.

subhepatic, *a.* **subhimalayan,** *a.*

subhuman, *a.* less than human or that which is normal to humans; pertaining to animals lower than humans. **subhumeral,** *a.*

subimago, *n.* a stage in the metamorphosis of certain insects preceding the imago.

subindicative, *a.* **subinspector,** *n.* **subintestinal,** *a.*

subintrant, *a.* characterized by paroxysms that succeed each other so rapidly as to be almost continuous. [late L *subintrans -ntem,* pres.p. of *subintrāre* (*intrāre,* ENTER)]

sub-irrigation, *n.* irrigation beneath the surface; partial irrigation.

subitamente, *adv.* (*Mus.*) suddenly. **subito,** *adv.* (*Mus.*) suddenly, immediately. [It.]

†**subitaneous,** *a.* sudden, hasty. **subitaneousness,** *n.* [L *subitāneus,* SUDDEN]

subj., (*abbr.*) subject; subjunctive.

subjacent, *a.* underlying; lower in position. [L *subjacens -ntem,* pres.p. of *subjacēre* (*jacēre,* to lie)]

subject[1], *a.* being under the power, control or authority of another; exposed, liable, prone, disposed (to); dependent, conditional; submissive; †lower in position, subjacent. *n.* one under the dominion or political rule of a person or state, one owing allegiance to a sovereign, a member of a state as related to the sovereign or government; that which is treated or to be treated in any specified way; the topic under consideration; the theme of discussion or description, or artistic expression or representation; the leading phrase or motif in music; a branch of learning or study; a dead body for dissection etc.; the cause or occasion (for); a person regarded as subject to any specific disease, mental tendency, psychic influence etc.; (*Log.*) that member of a proposition about which something is predicated; the noun or its equivalent about which something is affirmed, the nominative of a sentence; the ego, as distinguished from the object or non-ego, the mind, the conscious self; the substance or substratum to which attributes must be referred. **subject to,** conditional upon (ratification etc.); conditionally upon. **subject-heading,** *n.* a heading in an index, catalogue etc. under which references are given. **subject-matter,** *n.* the object of consideration, discussion etc. **subject-object,** *n.* the immediate object in thought as distinguished from an external thing. **subjection,** *n.* **subjective,** *a.* concerned with or proceeding from the consciousness or the mind, as opp. to objective or external things; due to or proceeding from the individual mind, personal; lacking reality, fanciful, imaginary; (*Art*) characterized by the prominence given to the individuality of the author or artist; denoting the case of the subject of a verb, nominative. *n.* the subjective case. **subjectively,** *adv.* **subjectiveness, subjectivity,** *n.* **subjectivism,** *n.* the doctrine that human knowledge is purely subjective, and therefore relative. **subjectivist,** †**subjectist,** *n.* **subjectless,** *a.* [ME and OF *suget* (F *sujet*), assim. to L *subjectus,* p.p. of *subjicere* (*jacere,* to cast)]

subject[2], *v.t.* to subdue, to reduce to subjection (to); to expose, to make liable; to cause to undergo.

subjoin, *v.t.* to add at the end, to append, to affix. **subjoinder,** *n.* **subjoint,** *n.* a secondary joint. [OF *subjoign-,* stem of *subjoindre,* L *subjungere* (*jungere,* to join, p.p. *junctus*)]

sub judice, *a.* under consideration, esp. by a court or judge. [L]

subjugate, *v.t.* to subdue, to conquer, to bring into subjection, to enslave. **subjugable,** *a.* **subjugation,** *n.* **subjugator,** *n.* [L *subjugātus,* p.p. of *subjugāre,* to bring under the yoke (*jugum,* cogn. with YOKE)]

subjunctive, *a.* denoting the mood of a verb expressing condition, hypothesis or contingency. *n.* the subjunctive mood. **subjunctively,** *adv.* [L *subjunctīvus,* from *subjunct-,* see SUBJOIN]

subkingdom, *n.* a primary division of the animal or plant kingdom.

sublanceolate, *a.*

sublapsarian, *a.* infralapsarian. **sublapsarianism,** *n.*

sublate, *v.t.* (*Log.*) to treat as untrue, to deny, opp. to posit. **sublation,** *n.* [L *sublātus* (*lātus,* p.p. of *tollere,* to take away)]

sublease, *n.* a lease of property by a tenant or lessee. *v.t.* to grant or obtain a sublease of (property). **sublessee,** *n.* **sublessor,** *n.*

sublet, *v.t.* (*pres.p.* **subletting,** *past, p.p.* **sublet**) to let property already rented or held on lease. *n.* a subletting.

sublibrarian, *n.* **sublieutenant,** *n.*

sublimate, *v.t.* to convert (a solid substance) by heat directly to vapour without passing through the liquid state (followed by an equivalent return to solidity by cooling); to refine, to purify, to etherealize; to divert by sublimation. *n.* the product of sublimation. **corrosive sublimate** CORROSIVE. **sublimation,** *n.* the result of sublimating; (*Psych.*) the diversion by the subject of certain instinctive impulses, esp. sexual, into altruistic or socially acceptable channels. **sublimatory,** *n., a.* [L *sublimātus,* p.p. of *sublimāre,* as foll.]

sublime, *a.* of the most lofty or exalted nature; characterized by grandeur, nobility or majesty; inspiring awe; unparalleled, outstanding. *v.t.* to sublimate; to elevate, to purify; to make sublime. *v.i.* to pass directly from solid to vapour, to be sublimated; to be elevated or purified; to become sublime. **Sublime Porte** PORTE. **sublimely,** *adv.* **sublimeness, sublimity,** *n.* **sublimer,** *n.* [F, from L *sublīmis* (perh. SUB-, *līmen,* lintel, reaching up to the lintel)]

subliminal, *a.* not reaching the threshold of consciousness, hardly perceived; pertaining to subconsciousness. **subliminal advertising,** *n.* advertising directed to and acting on the unconscious.

sublineation, *n.* **sublingual,** *a.* **sublittoral,** *a.*

sublunary, sublunar, *a.* situated beneath the moon, pertaining to this world, mundane.

submachine gun, *n.* a light automatic or semiautomatic rapid-firing gun fired from the hip or shoulder.

submammary, *a.*

submarine, *a.* situated, acting or growing beneath the surface of the sea. *n.* a vessel, esp. a warship, that may be submerged. **submariner,** *n.* a sailor in a submarine.

submaxilla, *n.* (*pl.* **-llae, -llas**), the lower jaw. **submaxillary,** *a.*

submedian, *a.* situated next to the median line.

submediant, *n., a.* (of) the sixth note of the diatonic scale.

submembranous, *a.*

submental, *a.* situated below the chin.

submerge, *v.t.* to put under water etc., to flood; to inundate, to overwhelm. *v.i.* to sink under water etc. **submergence,** *n.* **submerse,** *v.t.* to submerge. **submersed,** *a.* being or growing under water. **submersible,** *n., a.* (a vessel) capable of being submersed. **submersion,** *n.* [F *submerger,* L *submergere* (*mergere,* to dip, p.p. *mersus*)]

submetallic, *a.*

submicroscopic, *a.*

subminiature, *a.*

†**submiss,** *a.* submissive. **submission,** *n.* the act of submitting; the state of being submissive; compliance, obedience, resignation, meekness. **submissive,** *a.* **submissively,** *adv.* **submissiveness,** *n.* [see foll.]

submit, *v.t.* (*past, p.p.* **submitted**) to yield or surrender (oneself); to subject to a process, treatment etc.; to present or refer for consideration, decision etc.; to put forward deferentially. *v.i.* to yield, to surrender, to give in; to be submissive. **submitter,** *n.* [L *submittere* (*mittere,* to send, p.p. *missus*)]

submolecular, *a.*

submontane, *a.* situated at the foot of a mountain or range of mountains.

submultiple, *n., a.* **submuscular,** *a.* **subnarcotic,** *a.* **subnasal,** *a.* **subnatural,** *a.* **subneural,** *a.*

subnivean, *a.* situated beneath the snow.

subnodal, *a.*

subnormal, *a.* less than normal, below the normal standard; having lower intelligence than is normal. **subnormality,** *n.*

subnubilar, *a.* situated beneath the clouds.

subnuclear, *a.* **suboccipital,** *a.* **suboceanic,** *a.* **subocellate,** *a.* **suboctave,** *n.*

suboctuple, *a.* containing one part in eight.

subocular, *a.*

subopercular, *a.* **suboperculum,** *n.*

suborbital, *a.* beneath the orbit of the eye; less than a complete orbit of the earth, moon etc.

suborder, *n.* a subdivision of a taxonomic order. **subordinal,** *a.*

subordinate[1], *a.* inferior in order, rank, importance, power etc.; subject, subservient, subsidiary (to). *n.* a person working under another or inferior in official

standing. **subordinate clause,** *n.* a clause that functions as a noun, adjective or adverb rather than as a sentence. **subordinately,** *adv.* **subordinateness,** *n.* [med. L *subordinātus,* p.p. of *subordināre* (*ordo -dinem,* ORDER)]
subordinate[2], *v.t.* to make subordinate; to treat or consider as of secondary importance; to make subject or subservient (to). **subordination,** *n.* **subordinationism,** *n.* the doctrine of the priority of the first to the second and third Persons of the Trinity as regards order (the orthodox view) or as regards essence (the Arian view). **subordinative,** *a.*
suborn, *v.t.* to procure by underhand means, esp. bribery, to commit perjury or other criminal act. **subornation,** *n.* **suborner,** *n.* [F *suborner,* L *subornāre* (*ornāre,* to furnish, to incite)]
suboval, *a.* nearly oval. **subovate,** *a.*
subpanation, *n.* the doctrine that the body and blood of Christ are locally and materially present in the Eucharist under the form of the bread and wine. [cp. IMPANATION]
subparietal, *a.* **subperitoneal,** *a.* **subpermanent,** *a.* **subphylum,** *n.* **subpleural,** *a.*
subplot, *n.* a secondary or subordinate plot in a novel, play etc.
subpoena, *n.* a writ commanding a person's attendance in a court of justice under a penalty. *v.t.* (*pres.p.* **subpoenaing,** *past, p.p.* **subpoenaed**) to serve with such a writ. [L, under penalty]
subpolar, *a.* adjacent to one of the poles; lying under a celestial pole.
subprefect, *n.* **subprefecture,** *n.*
subprior, *n.* **subprovince,** *n.* **subpubic,** *a.* **subpulmonary,** *a.* **subquadrate,** *a.*
subquadruple, *a.* in the ratio of one to four.
subquintuple, *a.* **subramose,** *a.*
subreader, *n.* an assistant reader in the Inns of Court.
subregion, *n.* **subregional,** *a.*
subreption, *n.* the act of obtaining something by surprise or fraudulent representation. [L *subreptio,* from *subripere* (*rapere,* to seize)]
subrogation, *n.* the substitution of one person in the place of another with succession to his or her rights to a debt etc. **subrogate,** *v.t.*
sub rosa, *adv.* secretly; in confidence. [L, lit., under the rose, from its use as an emblem of secrecy]
subroutine, *n.* a sequence of computer instructions for a particular task that can be used at any point in a program.
sub-sacral, *a.*
sub-saturated, *a.* **sub-saturation,** *n.*
subscapular, *a.*
subscribe, *v.t.* to write (one's name etc.) at the end of a document etc.; to sign (a document, promise etc.); to contribute or pledge to contribute (an annual or other specified sum) to or for a fund, object etc.; to publish by securing subscribers beforehand; †to characterize. *v.i.* to write one's name at the end of a document; to assent or give support (to an opinion etc.); to engage to pay a contribution, to allow one's name to be entered in a list of contributors; to undertake to receive and pay for shares or a periodical, service etc.; †to yield, to surrender. **subscribable,** *a.* **subscriber,** *n.* **subscriber trunk dialling,** a telephone dialling system allowing subscribers to dial direct to any number in the system. **subscript,** *n., a.* (a character) written or printed underneath another or below the base line. **subscription,** *n.* the act of subscribing; a signature; a contribution to a fund etc.; a membership fee; a raising of money from subscribers; an advance payment for several issues of a periodical; an application to purchase shares. [L *subscrībere* (*scrībere,* to write)]
subsection, *n.* a subdivision of a section.
subsellium, *n.* (*pl.* **-llia**) a misericord. [L (*sella,* seat)]
subsensible, *a.* **subseptuple,** *a.*
subsequent, *a.* coming immediately after in time or order; following, succeeding, posterior (to). **subsequence, †-ency,** *n.* **subsequently,** *adv.* [L *subsequens -ntem,* pres.p. of *subsequī* (*sequī,* to follow)]
subserve, *v.t.* to serve as a means or instrument in promoting (an end etc.). **subservient,** *a.* useful as an instrument or means; obsequious, servile. **subservience, -ency,** *n.* **subserviently,** *adv.* [L *subservīre* (*servīre,* to SERVE)]
subsessile, *a.* nearly sessile.
subset, *n.* (*esp. Math.*) a set contained within a larger set.
subsextuple, *a.* in the ratio of one to six.
subshrub, *n.* a low-growing woody plant with non-woody tips.
subside, *v.i.* to sink, to fall in level; to settle; to sink in, to collapse; to settle down, to abate, to become tranquil. **subsidence,** *n.* [L *subsīdere* (*sīdere,* to settle, cogn. with *sedēre* to sit)]
subsidiary, *a.* aiding, auxiliary, supplemental; subordinate or secondary in importance; pertaining to or of the nature of a subsidy; tributary. *n.* a subsidiary person or thing, an auxiliary, an accessory; a company whose shares are mostly owned by another. **subsidiarily,** *adv.* [L *subsidiārius,* as foll.]
subsidy, *n.* (*Hist.*) pecuniary aid granted by parliament to the sovereign for purposes of state, a tax to defray special expenses; a sum paid by one government to another, usu. to meet the expenses of a war; a contribution by the state, a public corporation etc., to a commercial or charitable undertaking of benefit to the public; financial aid. **subsidize, -ise,** *v.t.* [ME and A-F *subsidie,* L *subsidium* (*sedēre,* to sit)]
subsist, *v.i.* to exist, to remain in existence; to live, to have means of living, to find sustenance, to be sustained (on); to inhere. **subsistence,** *n.* the state or means of subsisting; the minimum required to support life. **subsistence allowance, money,** *n.* an advance of wages, or a special payment, made to enable an employee to meet immediate needs; a payment for food etc. made in addition to salary or wages. **subsistence farming,** *n.* farming in which most of the yield is consumed by the farmer with little over for sale. **subsistence level,** *n.* an income or living standard that provides the basic necessities for life. **subsistent,** *a.* [F *subsister,* L *subsistere* (*sistere,* causal of *stāre,* to stand)]
subsoil, *n.* the stratum of earth immediately below the surface-soil.
subsonic, *a.* pertaining to or using or travelling at speeds less than that of sound.
subspecies, *n.* **subspecific,** *a.*
sub-spherical, *a.* **subspherically,** *adv.*
subspinous, *a.*
substage, *n.* an apparatus underneath the stage of a microscope carrying the condenser etc.
substance, *n.* that of which a thing consists; matter, material, as opp. to form; matter of a definite or identifiable chemical composition; the essence, the essential part, pith, gist or main purport; that which is real, solidity, firmness, solid foundation; material possessions, property, wealth, resources; (*Phil.*) the permanent substratum in which qualities and accidents are conceived to inhere, the self-existent ground of attributes and phenomena. [F, from L *substantia* (*stāre,* to stand)]
substandard, *a.* below an accepted or acceptable standard.
substantial, *a.* having physical substance; real, actually existing, not illusory; solid, stout, strongly constructed, durable; possessed of substance, having sufficient means, well-to-do, financially sound; of considerable importance, value, extent, amount etc.; material, practical, virtual. *n.* (*usu. pl.*) the essential parts, reality. **substantialism,** *n.* the doctrine that there are substantial realities underlying phenomena. **substantialist,** *n.* **substantiality,** *n.* **substantialize, -ise,** *v.t., v.i.* **substantially,** *adv.*
substantiate, *v.t.* to make real or actual; to establish, to prove, to make good (a statement etc.). **substantiation,** *n.*
substantive, *a.* expressing real existence; having substance or reality, having or pertaining to the essence or substance of anything; independently existent, not

merely implied, inferential or subsidiary; denoting or functioning as a noun; of a dye or dyeing process, not requiring a mordant; (*Mil.*) permanent (rank). *n.* a noun or part of a sentence used as a noun. **substantival**, *a.* **substantivally, substantively,** *adv.* [ME and F *substantif,* L *substantīvus,* as prec.]

substation, *n.* a subsidiary station, esp. one in which electric current from a generating station is modified before distribution.

substernal, *a.*

substitute, *n.* a person or thing put in the place of or serving for another. *v.t.* to put or use in the place of another person or thing; to replace (an atom or group in a molecule) with another; to introduce a substitute for. *v.i.* to act as a substitute. **substitution,** *n.* **substitutional, -nary, substitutive,** *a.* **substitutionally,** *adv.* [F *substitut,* L *substitūtus,* p.p. of *substituere* (*statuere,* see STATUTE)]

†**substractor,** *n.* (*Shak.*) a detractor. [erron. for SUBTRACTOR]

substratosphere, *n.*

substratum, *n.* (*pl.* **-ta**) that which underlies anything; a layer or stratum lying underneath; the subsoil; the ground or basis (of phenomena etc.), foundation. **substrate**, *n.* a substratum; the substance on which an enzyme acts; a base on which something lives or is formed. [L, neut. p.p. of *substernere* (see STRATUM)]

substructure, substruction, *n.* an under-structure or foundation. **substructural**, *a.*

substyle, *n.* the line on which the style or gnomon of a dial stands. **substylar,** *a.*

subsulphate, *n.* a basic sulphate.

subsultus, *n.* a convulsive muscular twitching. **subsultive,** *a.* [L, p.p. of *subsilīre* (*salīre,* to spring)]

subsume, *v.t.* to include under a more general class or category. **subsumption**, *n.* **subsumptive,** *a.* [L *sūmere,* to take (p.p. *sumptus*)]

subsystem, *n.*

subtangent, *n.* the portion of the axis of a curve intercepted between an ordinate and a tangent both drawn from the same point.

subtemperate, *a.* pertaining to slightly colder than temperate regions.

subtenant, *n.* a tenant holding property from one who is also a tenant. **subtenancy,** *n.*

subtend, *v.t.* to extend under or be opposite to (of a chord relatively to an arc, or the side of a triangle to an angle); (*Bot.*) to be lower than and enclose. **subtense**, *n.* that which subtends. [L *subtendere* (*tendere,* to stretch, p.p. *tensus*)]

subtepid, *a.*

subter-, *pref.* under, less than, opp. to *super-.* [L *subter*]

subterfuge, *n.* a deception, prevarication etc. employed to avoid an inference, censure etc., or to evade or conceal something. [F, from late L *subterfugium* (*fugere,* to flee)]

subterposition, *n.* position under something else, esp. of strata.

subterranean, -aneous, *a.* underground; hidden, concealed. **subterraneously,** *adv.* †**subterrene**, *a.* **subterrestrial**, *a.* [L *subterrāneus* (*terra,* earth, -ANEOUS)]

subthoracic, *a.*

subtile, *a.* tenuous, thin, extremely fine; †subtle. †**subtilely,** *adv.* **subtility**, *n.* **subtilize, -ise,** *v.t., v.i.* **subtilization, -isation,** *n.* **subtilty,** *n.* [ME *sobil,* OF *sutil,* L *subtilis,* acc. *-lem* (prob. finely-woven, SUB-, *tela,* web)]

subtitle, *n.* an additional or subsidiary title to a book etc.; a half-title, usu. placed before the title page in books; a printed explanatory caption to a silent film or a printed translation of the dialogue in a foreign film. *v.t.* to provide a subtitle for.

subtle, *a.* rarefied, attenuated, delicate, hard to seize, elusive; difficult to comprehend, not obvious, abstruse; making fine distinctions, acute, discerning; ingenious, skilful, clever; artful, cunning, crafty, insidious. **subtlety,** *n.* **subtly,** *adv.* [SUBTILE]

subtonic, *n.* (*Mus.*) the note next below the tonic. *a.* (*Phon.*) sonant.

subtopia, *n.* unsightly suburbs, ill-planned rural or urban areas. **subtopian,** *a.*

subtorrid, *a.*

subtotal, *n., v.t.*

subtract, *v.t.* to take away (a part, quantity etc.) from the rest, to deduct. **subtracter, subtractor,** *n.* **subtraction,** *n.* a subtracting; an arithmetical operation to find the difference in amount between two numbers. **subtractive,** *a.* **subtrahend,** *n.* the number or quantity to be subtracted from another. [L *subtractus,* p.p. of *subtrahere* (*trahere,* to draw)]

subtriangular, *a.* approximately triangular.

subtribe, *n.*

subtriple, *a.* containing one part of three. **subtriplicate,** *a.*

subtropical, *a.* characterized by features common to both the temperate and tropical zones; pertaining to the regions near the tropics. **subtropics,** *n.pl.*

subtype, *n.*

subulate, *a.* (*chiefly Bot.*) awl-shaped. **subuliform,** *a.* [L *subula,* awl]

subungulate, *a.* hoofed, but having several digits.

subunit, *n.*

suburb, *n.* an outlying part of a city or town; (*pl.*) the residential outskirts of a city or large town. **suburban,** *a.* pertaining to a suburb or the suburbs; (*fig.*) descriptive of an outlook on life limited by certain narrow conventions. **suburbanite,** *n.* one who lives in the suburbs. **suburbanize, -ise,** *v.t.* **suburbia,** *n.* (*often derog.*) (the inhabitants of) residential suburbs collectively; the lifestyle, culture etc. held to be characteristic of these. [A-F and OF *suburbe,* L *suburbium* (*urbs urbis,* city)]

subursine, *a.* **subvariety,** *n.*

subvene, *v.i.* to happen so as to aid or effect a result. **subvention,** *n.* a grant in aid, a subsidy. [F *subvenir,* L *subvenīre* (*venīre,* to come)]

subvert, *v.t.* to overthrow, to destroy, to overturn; to corrupt, to pervert. †**subverse,** *v.t.* **subversion,** *n.* **subversive,** *n., a.* **subverter,** *n.* **subvertible,** *a.* [F *subvertir,* L *subvertere* (*vertere,* to turn, p.p. *versus*)]

subvertebral, *a.* **subvertical,** *a.* **subvirile,** *a.* **subvitalized, -ised,** *a.* **subvitreous,** *a.*

subvocal, *n., a.* subtonic.

subway, *n.* an underground passage, tunnel, conduit etc.; (*chiefly N Am.*) an underground railway.

subzero, *a.* below zero (degrees Celsius).

suc-, *pref.* form of SUB-, used before *c.*

succades, *n.pl.* fruit candied and preserved in syrup. [L *succus,* juice]

succedaneum, *n.* (*pl.* **-nea**) that which (or *rarely* who) is used instead of something else, a substitute. **succedaneous,** *a.* [L *succēdāneus,* as foll.]

succeed, *v.t.* to follow, to come after (in time or order), to be subsequent to; to take the place previously occupied by, to be heir or successor to. *v.i.* to follow in time or order, to be subsequent (to); to be the heir or successor (to an office, estate etc.); to be successful, to attain a desired object, to end well or prosperously. †**succeeder,** *n.* [F *succéder,* L *succēdere* (*cēdere,* see CEDE, p.p. *cessus*)]

succentor, *n.* a deputy precentor; the leading bass in a choir. [late L, from L *succinere* (*canere,* to sing), p.p. *succentus*]

success, *n.* the act of succeeding, favourable result, attainment of what is desired or intended; attainment of worldly prosperity; †the issue or result of an undertaking. **successful,** *a.* **successfully,** *adv.* **successfulness,** *n.* **successless**, *a.* **successlessly,** *adv.* **successlessness,** *n.* [OF *succes,* L *successum,* nom. *-sus,* from *succēdere,* to succeed]

succession, *n.* a following in order; a series of things following in order; the act or right of succeeding to an office or inheritance; the order in which persons so succeed; the line of persons so succeeding; the order of descent in the development of species. **succession duty** DEATH DUTIES under DEATH. **successional,** *a.* **successionally,** *adv.* **successor,** *n.* one who or that which follows or succeeds another. [F, from L *successio,* acc. *-ōnem,* as prec.]

successive, *a.* following in order or uninterrupted succession, consecutive; †hereditary, legitimate. **successively,** *adv.* **successiveness,** *n.* [F *successif,* fem. *-ive,* med. L *successīvus,* from L *successus,* SUCCESS]

†**succiduous,** *a.* on the point of falling; falling. [L *succiduus,* from *succidere* (*cadere,* to fall)]

succiferous, *a.* producing or conveying sap. [L *succus,* juice]

succin, *n.* amber. **succinate,** *n.* a salt of succinic acid. **succinic,** *a.* derived from or contained in amber. **succinite,** *n.* amber; a yellow variety of garnet. [late L *succinum,* from *succus,* see prec.]

succinct, *a.* compressed into few words, brief, concise. **succinctly,** *adv.* **succinctness,** *n.* [L *succinctus,* p.p. of *succingere* (*cingere,* to gird)]

succivorous, *a.* of insects etc., feeding on sap. [L *succus,* juice, -VOROUS]

succory, *n.* chicory. [by corr.]

succose, *a.* juicy, sappy. [L *succus,* juice]

Succot, Sukkoth *n.* Jewish festival celebrated in October, also known as the Feast of Booths, which commemorates the period when the Israelites lived in the wilderness during the EXODUS from Egypt.

succotash, *n.* (*N Am.*) a dish composed of green maize and beans cooked together. [Narraganset]

succour, (*esp. N Am.*) **succor,** *v.t.* to come to the aid of; to help or relieve in difficulty or distress. *n.* aid in time of difficulty or distress; †(*pl.*) reinforcements. **succourer,** *n.* **succourless,** *a.* [OF *sucurre,* L *succurrere* (*currere,* to run, p.p. *cursus*)]

succuba, -bus, *n.* (*pl.* **-bae, -bi**) a demon believed to assume the shape of a woman and have sexual intercourse with men in their sleep. **succubate,** *v.t.* **succubine,** *a.* [L, from *succumbere* (*cumbere,* to lie)]

succulent, *a.* juicy; of a plant, stem etc., thick and fleshy. **succulence,** *n.* **succulently,** *adv.* [F, from L *succulentus,* from SUCCUS]

succumb, *v.i.* to cease to resist etc., to give way; to yield, to submit (to force etc.); to die. **succumbent,** *a.* [L *succumbere,* (*cumbere,* to lie)]

succursal, *a.* auxiliary (used esp. of an ecclesiastical building, as a chapel of ease). [F *succursale* (*église*), subsidiary (church), from med. L *succursus,* SUCCOUR]

succus, *n.* (*pl.* **succi**) a body juice of fluid secretion; the expressed juice of a plant, used medicinally. [L, also *sūcus,* juice, sap]

succuss, *v.t.* to shake suddenly, esp. in medical diagnosis. †**succussation,** *n.* a shaking, a succussion; a trot, trotting. **succussion,** *n.* a shaking; a shock; a shaking of the thorax to detect pleural effusion. **succusive,** *a.* [L *succussus,* p.p. of *succutere* (*quatere,* to shake)]

such, *a.* of that, or the same, or the like kind or degree (as); of the kind or degree mentioned or implied; being the same in quality, degree etc.; so great, intense etc. (*usu.* as *or* that). *adv.* so (in *such a nice day* etc.). *pron.* such a person, persons or things (as); suchlike. **such and such,** not known or specified, some. **such as,** of a kind like; for example. **suchlike,** *a.* of such a kind. *pron.* things of that sort. [OE *swylc,* (*swā,* so, *līc,* LIKE[1], -LY), cp. Dut. *zulk,* G *solch,* Icel. *slīkr,* Swed. *slik*]

suck, *v.t.* to draw (milk etc.) into the mouth by the action of the lips or lips and lungs; to imbibe, to drink in, to absorb (up or in), to acquire, to gain; to engulf, to draw (in); to draw liquid from with or as with the mouth; to dissolve or eat thus; to take and hold in the mouth with a sucking action. *v.i.* to draw liquid etc. in by suction; to draw milk, nourishment etc. in thus; to make the sound of sucking. *n.* an act or spell of sucking, suction; force of suction; a small draught or drink. **to suck up (to),** to act in an obsequious manner (towards), toady. **suck-in,** *n.* (*dated sl.*) a deception, a fiasco. **sucker,** *n.* one who or that which sucks; a sucking-pig; a newly-born whale; a suckling; a fish that sucks in food or has a suctorial mouth, esp. one of the N American Catostomidae; the piston of a suction-pump; a pipe or tube through which anything is drawn by suction; a sucking-disc; (*Biol.*) an organ, such as an acetabulum, acting on the same principle, a suctorial organ; a shoot from a root or a subterranean part of a stem; (*dated coll.*) a sweet, a lollipop; (*coll.*) a ready dupe, a gullible person; (*coll.*) a person who is very fond of or unable to resist a specified thing. *v.t.* to strip suckers from (a plant). *v.i.* to send out suckers. **sucking,** *a.* deriving nourishment from the breast; not yet weaned; young and inexperienced. **sucking-bottle,** *n.* an infant's feeding-bottle. **sucking-disc,** *n.* a disc of leather, rubber etc. adhering firmly to a smooth surface when wetted. **sucking-pig,** *n.* a pig not yet weaned. [OE *sūcan,* cp. L *sugere,* p.p. *suctus*]

suckle, *v.t.* to give milk from the breast or udder to. **suckling,** *n.* a child or animal not yet weaned. [freq. of SUCK]

Sucre[1], *n.* legal capital and judicial seat of Bolivia; population (1982) 80,000. It stands on the central plateau at an altitude of 2840 m/9320 ft.

Sucre[2], *n.* **Antonio Jaré de** (1795–1830), Bolivian revolutionary leader. As chief lieutenant of Simon BOLIVAR, he won several battles in freeing the colonies of South America from Spanish rule, and in 1826 became president of the new republic of Bolivia. After a mutiny by the army and invasion by Peru, he resigned in 1828 and left the country to join Bolivar. While crossing the Àndes he was killed by thieves.

sucrose, *n.* sugar as obtained from sugar cane or sugar beet. [F *sucre,* SUGAR, -OSE[2]]

suction, *n.* the act or process of sucking; the production of a vacuum in a confined space causing fluid to enter, or a body to adhere to something, under atmospheric pressure. **suction-chamber, -pipe,** *n.* **suction-pump,** *n.* the common pump, in which liquid is forced up by atmospheric pressure. **suctorial,** *a.* adapted for sucking or for adhering by suction. [F, from L *suctus,* p.p. of *sugere,* to SUCK]

sudamina, *n.pl.* minute transparent vesicles arising from a disorder of the sweatglands. **sudaminal,** *a.* [pl. of late L *sudāmen,* from L *sudāre,* to sweat]

Sudan, *n.* Democratic Republic of (*Jamhuryat es-Sudan*), country in NE Africa, S of Egypt, with a Red Sea coast, it is the largest country in Africa. **area** 2,505,800 sq km/967,489 sq miles. **capital** Khartoum. **towns** Omdurman, Juba, Wadi Medani, al-Obeid, Kassala, Atbara, al-Qadarif, Kosti; chief port Port Sudan. **physical** fertile valley of the river Nile separates Libyan Desert in west from high rocky Nubian Desert in east. **population** (1989) 25,008,000 (70% of whom are Muslim, Arab-speaking, and in the N, speakers of African languages in the S); annual growth rate 2.9%. **exports** cotton, gum arabic, sesame, groundnuts, durra. **language** 51% Arabic (official); 6% Darfurian; 18% Nilotic (Dinka and Nuer); 5% Nilo-Hamitic; 5% Sudanic. **religion** Sunni Muslim in the north, animist in the south, with a Christian minority. **Sudanese,** *a.* of or pertaining to the Republic of the Sudan. *n.* (*pl.* **Sudanese**) a native or inhabitant of the Sudan.

sudation, *n.* sweating, sweat. **sudarium,** *n.* a cloth for wiping away sweat, esp. that of St Veronica, believed to have been miraculously impressed with the face of Christ at the Crucifixion. **sudatorium,** *n.* (*pl.* **-ria**) a hot-air bath. **sudatory,** *a.* exciting perspiration. *n.* a sudatorium. [L *sūdātio,* from *sūdāre,* cogn. with SWEAT]

Sudbury, *n.* city in Ontario, Canada; population (1985) 154,000. A buried meteorite yields 90% of the world's nickel.

sudd, *n.* a floating mass of vegetation, trees etc. obstructing navigation in the White Nile. [Arab.]

sudden, *a.* happening unexpectedly, without warning; instantaneous, abrupt, swift, rapid; †precipitate, rash, choleric. **on, of a sudden,** suddenly; unexpectedly. **sudden infant death syndrome,** cot death. **sudden death,** *n.* an extended period of play to decide a tie in a game or contest, ending when one side scores. **suddenly,** *adv.* **suddenness,** *n.* [ME and OF *sodain,* L *subitāneus,* from *subitus,* sudden, from *subīre,* to come up (*īre*, to come)]

Sudetenland, *n.* mountainous region of Czechoslovakia, annexed by Germany under the MUNICH AGREEMENT (1938–45).

sudoriferous, *a.* producing or secreting perspiration. **sudorific,** *a.* causing perspiration. *n.* a sudorific drug. [L *sūdōrifer* (*sūdor -dōris*, sweat, -FEROUS)]

Sudra, *n.* a member of the lowest of the four great Hindu castes. [Hind., from Sansk. *çūdra*]

suds, *n.pl.* soapy water forming a frothy mass. [lit., things sodden, see SEETHE]

sue, *v.t.* to prosecute or to pursue a claim (for) by legal process; to entreat, to petition. *v.i.* to take legal proceedings (for); to make entreaty or petition (to or for). **to sue out,** to petition for and obtain (a writ, pardon etc.). [OF *suir* (F *suivre*), late L *sequere*, L *sequī*, to follow]

suède, *n.* undressed kid or similar leather given a nap surface by rubbing. [F, SWEDE]

suet, *n.* the hard fat about the kidneys and loins of oxen, sheep etc. **suety,** *a.* [dim. from OF *seu*, L *sebum*, tallow]

Suetonius, *n.* (**Gaius Suetonius Tranquillius**) (*c.* AD 69–140) Roman historian, author of *Lives of the Caesars* (Julius Caesar to Domitian).

Suez Canal, *n.* artificial waterway, 160 km/100 miles long, from Port Said to Suez, linking the Mediterranean and Red seas, separating Africa from Asia, and providing the shortest sea route from Europe eastwards. It was opened in 1869, nationalized in 1956, blocked by Egypt during the Arab-Israeli war of 1967, and not re-opened until 1975.

Suez Crisis, *n.* incident in Oct.–Dec. 1956 following the nationalization of the Suez Canal by President Nasser of Egypt. In an attempt to reassert international control of the canal, Israel launched an attack towards the canal, after which British and French troops landed. Widespread international censure (Soviet protest, US non-support, and considerable opposition within Britain) soon led to withdrawal of the troops and the resignation of British prime minister Eden.

suf., suff., (*abbr.*) suffix.

suf-, *pref.* SUB- (before *f*).

suffer, *v.t.* to experience, to undergo (something painful, disagreeable or unjust); to endure, to sustain, to support (unflinchingly etc.); to tolerate, to put up with; to permit, to allow. *v.i.* to undergo or endure pain, grief, injury, loss etc.; to undergo punishment, esp. to be executed; to experience damage; to be at a disadvantage. **sufferable,** *a.* **sufferableness,** *n.* **sufferably,** *adv.* **sufferance,** *n.* negative consent, toleration, allowance, tacit or passive permission; suffering; endurance, patience, submissiveness. **on sufferance,** merely tolerated. **sufferer,** *n.* **suffering,** *n.* **sufferingly,** *adv.* [OF *suffrir*, L *sufferre* (*ferre*, to bear)]

suffete, *n.* one of the two chief executive magistrates of ancient Carthage. [L *suffes*, *sūfes -ētis*, from Punic, cp. Heb. *shôphet*, judge]

suffice, *v.i.* to be enough, to be adequate or sufficient (for or to do etc.). *v.t.* to be enough for, to content, to satisfy; †to supply or provide. **sufficiency,** *n.* the quality of being sufficient; an adequate supply (of); a competence; adequate qualification, competence, efficiency. **sufficient,** *a.* enough, adequate, sufficing (for); †competent, fit, qualified (in ability, resources etc.); self-sufficient. *n.* (*coll.*) enough, a sufficiency. **sufficiently, sufficingly,** *adv.* †**suffisance,** *n.* [ME *suffisen*, OF *suffis-*, stem of *suffire*, L *sufficere* (*facere*, to make)]

suffix¹, *n.* a letter or syllable appended to the end of a word. **suffixal,** *a.* [L *suffixus*, p.p. of *suffīgere* (*fīgere*, to FIX, p.p. *fixus*)]

suffix², *v.t.* to add as a suffix, to append. **suffixion, suffixation,** *n.*

†**sufflate,** *v.t.* to blow up, to inflate; (*fig.*) to inspire. [L *sufflātus*, p.p. of *sufflāre* (*flāre*, to blow)]

suffocate, *v.t.* to choke, to kill by stopping respiration; to smother, to stifle; to cause difficulty of respiration to. *v.i.* to be or feel suffocated. †*a.* suffocated. **suffocatingly,** *adv.* **suffocation,** *n.* **suffocative,** *a.* [L *suffōcātus*, p.p. or *suffōcāre* (*fōcāre*, from *fauces*, pl., throat)]

Suffolk, *n.* county of Eastern England. **area** 3800 sq km/1467 sq miles. **towns** administrative headquarters Ipswich; Bury St Edmunds, Lowestoft, Felixstowe. **physical** low undulating surface and flat coastline; rivers Waveney, Alde, Deben, Orwell, Stour; part of the Norfolk Broads. **population** (1987) 635,000. **products** cereals, sugar beet, working horses (Suffolk punches), fertilizers, agricultural machinery.

suffragan, *a.* assisting (said of a bishop consecrated to assist another bishop or of any bishop in relation to the metropolitan). *n.* a suffragan or auxiliary bishop. **suffraganship,** *n.* [ME, from F *suffragant*, med L *suffrāgans -ntem*, pres.p., or *suffrāgāneus*, from L *suffrāgārī*, to vote for, as foll.]

suffrage, *n.* a vote in support of an opinion etc., or of a candidate for office; approval, consent; the right to vote, esp. in parliamentary elections; a short intercessory prayer by the congregation, esp. one of the responses in the Litany. **suffragette,** *n.* a female agitator for women's right to vote. **suffragist,** *n.* an advocate of extension of the right to vote, esp. to women. **suffragism,** *n.* [F, from L *suffrāgium*, perh. from *suffrāgo -gīnis*, ankle-bone (used for voting) or perh. orig. a potsherd, from *suffringere*, to break]

suffrutex, *n.* an undershrub. **suffrutescent, suffruticose,** *a.* having a woody perennial base with non-woody branches. [SUF-, L *frutex -ticis*, shrub, prob. cogn. with Gr. *bruein*, to sprout]

†**suffumigate,** *v.t.* to apply fumes or smoke to (parts of the body). †**suffumigation,** *n.* [SUF-, FUMIGATE]

suffuse, *v.t.* of a blush, fluid etc., to overspread, as from within. **suffusion,** *n.* [L *suffūsus*, p.p. of *suffundere* (*fundere*, to pour)]

Sufism, *n.* a mystical movement of Islam which originated in the 8th century. Sufis believe that deep intuition is the only real guide to knowledge. The movement has a strong strain of asceticism. The name derives from the *suf*, a rough woollen robe worn as an indication of their disregard for material things. There are a number of groups or brotherhoods within Sufism, each with its own method of meditative practice, one of which is the whirling dance of the dervishes. **sufi,** *n.* a Muslim pantheistic philosopher and mystic. **sufic,** *a.* [Arab. *sūfī*, pure, wise]

sug-, *pref.* SUB-, (before *g*).

sugar, *n.* a sweet, crystalline substance obtained from the expressed juice of various plants, esp. the sugarcane and the sugar beet; any substance resembling sugar, esp. in taste; (*Chem.*) one of various sweet or sweetish soluble carbohydrates, such as glucose, sucrose, lactose etc.; flattering or seductive words, esp. used to mitigate or disguise something distasteful; a term of affection, dear. *v.t.* to sweeten, cover or sprinkle with sugar; to mitigate, disguise or render palatable. **sugar of lead,** *n.* acetate of lead. **sugar-bean,** *n.* a variety of kidney-bean. **sugar-beet,** *n.* a variety of common beet from which sugar is extracted. **sugarberry,** *n.* (*N Am.*) the hackberry. **sugar-candy,** *n.* candy. **sugar cane,** *n.* a very tall grass, *Saccharum officinarum*, with jointed stems from 8 to 20 ft. (about 2·5 to 6 m) high, from the juice of which sugar is made. **sugar-coated,** *a.* covered with sugar; made superficially attractive, esp. to hide something less pleasant. **sugar daddy,** *n.* (*coll.*) a well-to-do usu. elderly man who spends money on a young girl. **sugar-gum,** *n.* a large Australian eucalyptus with sweet foliage. **sugarhouse,** *n.* a building in which sugar is made. **sugar loaf** LOAF¹. **sugar maple,** *n.* a N American tree, *Acer saccharum*, the sap of which yields sugar. **sugar mill,** *n.* a mill for expressing the juice from sugar-canes. **sugar-mite,** *n.* one infesting unrefined sugar. **sugar-orchard,** *n.* a small plantation of maples for making sugar. **sugar planter,** *n.* **sugarplum,** *n.* a sweetmeat, esp. boiled sugar formed into a ball etc. **sugar-refiner,** *n.* **sugar-refinery,** *n.* **sugar-squirrel,** *n.* (*Austral.*) a small opossum. **sugar tongs,** *n.pl.* a pair of small tongs for lifting lumps of sugar at table. **sugar-tree** SUGAR-MAPLE. **sugarer,** *n.* **sugarless,** *a.* **sugary,** *a.* containing or resembling sugar; (excessively) sweet-tasting; exaggeratedly charming or flattering. **sugariness,** *n.* [ME *sugre,* F *sucre,* Sp. *azucar,* Arab. *sakkar, sokkar,* Pers. *shakar,* Sansk. *çarkarā,* gravel, candy, whence Gr. *sacharon,* L *saccharum*]

Sugar, *n.* **Alan** (1947–), British entrepreneur, founder of the Amstrad electronics company in 1968 which holds a major position in the European personal-computer market.

suggest, *v.t.* to cause (an idea etc.) to arise in the mind; to propose (a plan, idea etc.) for consideration; to hint, indicate. **suggester,** *n.* **suggestible,** *a.* that may be suggested; readily yielding to (hypnotic) suggestion. **suggestion,** *n.* the act of suggesting; that which is suggested; a hint, a prompting, an insinuation; insinuation of an idea or impulse to a receptive mind or the mind of a hypnotized person; the spontaneous calling up of an associated idea in the mind. **suggestive,** *a.* containing or conveying (a) suggestion; tending to suggest thoughts etc., esp. of a prurient nature. **suggestively,** *adv.* **suggestiveness,** *n.* [L *suggestus,* p.p. of *suggerere* (*gerere,* to bring)]

Suharto, *n.* **Raden** (1921–), Indonesian politician and general. He ousted Sukarno to become president in 1967. He ended confrontation with Malaysia, invaded East Timor in 1975, and reached a cooperation agreement with Papua New Guinea in 1979. His authoritarian rule has met domestic opposition from the left. He was re-elected in 1973, 1978, 1983, and 1988.

suicide, *n.* the act of intentionally taking one's own life; any self-inflicted action of a disastrous nature; a person who takes his or her own life intentionally. **suicide pact,** *n.* an agreement between people to commit suicide at the same time. **suicidal,** *a.* **suicidally,** *adv.* †**suicidism,** *n.* [L *suī,* of oneself, gen. of *se,* self]

sui generis, *a.* unique, of its own kind. [L]

suilline, *a.* pig-like. *n.* one of the pig family. [L *suillus,* from *sus suis,* swine]

suint, *n.* the natural grease of wool. [F, from Teut., cogn. with SWEAT]

suit, *n.* the act of suing, petition, request; courtship; a legal prosecution or action for the recovery of a right etc.; one of the four sets in a pack of cards; those cards in a hand belonging to one of these; a set of outer clothes (now usu. jacket and trousers or a skirt), esp. when made of the same cloth; a set (of sails or other articles used together). *v.t.* to adapt, to accommodate, to make fitting (to); to satisfy, to please, to meet the desires etc. of; to agree with, to befit, to be appropriate to. *v.i.* to agree, to accord, to correspond (with); to be convenient. **to follow suit,** (*Cards*) to play a card of the suit led; (*fig.*) to follow an example. **suitcase,** *n.* a small travelling case. **suitable,** *a.* suited, fitting, convenient, proper, becoming. **suitability, suitableness,** *n.* **suitably,** *adv.* **suiting,** *n.* cloth for suits. [F *suite,* med. L *secūta,* from *secut-,* p.p. stem of *sequī,* to follow]

suite, *n.* a company, a retinue; a set (of connecting rooms, matching furniture etc.); a series of instrumental compositions, orig. of dance-tunes. [F, see prec.]

suitor, *n.* a petitioner, an applicant; a wooer, a lover; a party to a lawsuit.

suivez, *v.i.* (*Mus.*) follow (direction to the accompanist to adapt his or her time to the soloist). [F, imper. of *suivre*]

Sukarno, *n.* **Achmed** (1901–70), Indonesian nationalist, president (1945–67). During World War II he cooperated in the local administration set up by the Japanese, replacing Dutch rule. After the war he became the first president of the new Indonesian republic, becoming president-for-life in 1966; he was ousted by Suharto.

sukiyaki, *n.* a Japanese dish of thin slices of meat and vegetables cooked together with soy sauce, saké etc. [Jap.]

Sulawesi, *n.* (formerly **Celebes**) island in E Indonesia, one of the Sunda Islands; area (with dependent islands) 190,000 sq km/73,000 sq miles; population (1980) 10,410,000. It is mountainous and forested, and produces copra and nickel.

sulcate, †**-cated,** *a.* having longitudinal furrows, grooves or channels. **sulcus,** *n.* (*pl.* **-ci**) a groove, furrow; a furrow separating convolutions of the brain. [L *sulcātus,* p.p. of *sulcāre,* from *sulcus,* furrow]

Suleiman, Solyman, *n.* (1494–1566), Ottoman sultan from 1520, known as the Magnificent and the Lawgiver. Under his rule the Ottoman Empire flourished and reached its largest extent. He made conquests in the Balkans, the Mediterranean, Persia, and N Africa, but was defeated at Vienna in 1529 and Valletta in 1565. He was a patron of the arts, a poet, and an administrator.

sulf(o)-, sulfate, sulfur etc. SULPH(O)-, SULPHATE, SULPHUR.

sulk, *v.i.* to be sulky. *n.* (*often pl.*) a fit of sulkiness. **sulky,** *a.* sullen, morose, ill-humoured, resentful. *n.* a light, two-wheeled vehicle for a single person. **sulkily,** *adv.* **sulkiness,** *n.* [from *sulky,* from *sulkenness,* OE *solcennes* in *āsolcennes* (*solcen,* slothful)]

Sulla, *n.* **Lucius Cornelius** (138–78 BC), Roman general and politician, a leader of the senatorial party. Forcibly suppressing the democrats in 88 BC, he departed for a successful campaign against Mithridates VI of Pontus. The democrats seized power in his absence, but on his return Sulla captured Rome and massacred all opponents. As dictator, his reforms, which strengthened the Senate, were backward-looking and short-lived. He retired in 79 BC.

sullage, *n.* filth, refuse; sewage; silt. [F *souiller,* to soil]

sullen, *a.* persistently ill-humoured, morose, sour-tempered, cross; dismal, forbidding, unpropitious, baleful. *n.pl.* a fit of sullenness, the sulks. **sullenly,** *adv.* **sullenness,** *n.* [ME and OF *solain,* SOLE[3]]

Sullivan, *n.* **Arthur (Seymour)** (1842–1900), English composer who wrote operettas in collaboration with William Gilbert, including *HMS Pinafore* (1878), *The Pirates of Penzance* (1879), and *The Mikado* (1885). Their partnership broke down in 1896. Sullivan also composed serious instrumental, choral, and operatic works – for example, the opera *Ivanhoe* (1890) – which he valued more highly than the operettas.

sully, *v.t.* to soil, to tarnish; to defile, to disgrace. *v.i.* to be soiled or tarnished. *n.* a spot, a blemish. [OE *sylian,* from *sol,* mud (prob. with mixture of OF *soillier,* to SOIL[2])]

sulph- SULPH(O)-.

sulphadiazine, *n.* a sulpha drug used to treat pneumonia and meningitis.

sulpha drugs, *n.pl.* a group of sulphonamide drugs with a powerful antibacterial action.

sulphanilamide, *n.* para-aminobenzene sulphonamide, a sulphonamide drug administered orally and by injection for combating streptococcal and other bacterial diseases.

sulph-antimonic, *a.* derived from an antimonic sulphide. **sulphantimonate,** *n.* **sulph-antimonious,** *a.* **sulphantimonite,** *n.*

sulphate, *n.* a salt of sulphuric acid. **sulphate of copper,** blue vitriol; **of iron,** green vitriol; **of magnesium,** epsom salts; **of sodium,** glauber's salt; **of zinc,** white vitriol. **sulphatic,** *a.*

sulphide, *n.* a compound of sulphur, with an element or radical.

sulphite, *n.* a salt of sulphurous acid.

sulph(o)-, (*esp. N Am.*) **sulf(o)-,** *comb. form.* sulphur. [SULPHUR]

sulphonal, *n.* a crystalline compound used for hypnotic and anaesthetic purposes.

sulphonamide, *n.* an amide of a sulphonic acid; a sulpha drug.

sulphonic acid, *n.* any of a class of strong organic acids used in making dyes, drugs and detergents.

sulphovinic, *a.* denoting an acid obtained from sulphuric acid and alcohol.

sulphur, (*esp. N Am.*) **sulfur,** *n.* a pale-yellow non-metallic element, at. no. 16; chem. symbol S, insoluble in water, occurring in crystalline or amorphous forms, used in the manufacture of chemicals, gunpowder, matches etc., brimstone; one of various pale-yellow butterflies. *a.* of the colour of sulphur, pale-yellow. **sulphur bottom (whale),** *n.* the blue whale, *Sibbaldus musculus*. **sulphur dioxide,** *n.* a pungent gas used industrially and as a bleach and food preservative, that is a major source of air pollution. **sulphur ore,** *n.* iron pyrites. **sulphur spring,** *n.* a spring of water impregnated with sulphur or sulphide etc. **sulphurate,** *v.t.* to impregnate with or subject to the action of sulphur, esp. in bleaching. **sulphuration,** *n.* **sulphurator,** *n.* **sulphureous,** *a.* consisting of or having the qualities of sulphur; sulphur-coloured. **sulphureously,** *adv.* **sulphureousness,** *n.* †**sulphuret,** *n.* a sulphide. **sulphuretted,** *a.* saturated, impregnated or combined with sulphur. **sulphuric,** *a.* derived from or containing sulphur, esp. in its highest valency. **sulphuric acid,** *n.* a corrosive oily liquid acid, oil of vitriol. **sulphurize, -ise,** *v.t.* to sulphurate. **sulphurization, -isation,** *n.* **sulphurous,** *a.* containing sulphur in its lower valency; sulphureous. **sulphury,** *a.* [L]

sultan, *n.* a Muslim sovereign, esp. a former ruler of Turkey; a bird of the water-hen family with splendid blue and purple plumage; a white-crested variety of domestic fowl, orig. from Turkey. **sultana,** *n.* the wife, mother or daughter of a sultan; the mistress of a king, prince etc.; a yellow, seedless raisin grown esp. in the Mediterranean; an American purple sultan-bird. **sultanate,** *n.* **sultaness,** *n. fem.* **sultanic,** *a.* †**sultanry, sultanship,** *n.* [F, from Arab. *sultān*]

sultry, *a.* very hot, close and heavy, oppressive; passionate, sensual. **sultrily,** *adv.* **sultriness,** *n.* [var. of obs. *sweltry,* from SWELTER]

sum, *n.* the aggregate of two or more numbers, magnitudes, quantities or particulars, the total; substance, essence, summary; a particular amount of money; an arithmetical problem or the process of working it out. *v.t.* (*past, p.p.* **summed**) to add, collect or combine into one total or whole. **to sum up,** to put in a few words, to condense; to recapitulate; to form a rapid opinion or estimate of. **sumless,** *a.* innumerable, countless. [ME and F *somme,* L *summa,* orig. fem. of *summus,* super. of *superus,* higher, see SUPER-]

sumach, sumac, *n.* a tree or shrub of the genus *Rhus,* the dried and powdered leaves of which are used in tanning, dyeing etc.; a preparation of the dried leaves. [F, from Sp. *zumaque,* Arab. *summāq*]

Sumatra, Sumatera *n.* second largest island of Indonesia, one of the Sunda Islands; area 473,600 sq km/ 182,800 sq miles; population (1980) 28,016,000. East of a longitudinal volcanic mountain range is a wide plain; both are heavily forested. Products include rubber, rice, tobacco, tea, timber, tin, and petroleum.

Sumer, *n.* area of S Iraq where the Sumerian civilization was established; part of Babylonia (see BABYLON).

Sumerian, *n., a.* (a native or the language) of Sumer, an ancient region of Babylonia.

Sumerian civilization, *n.* the world's earliest civilization, which arose about 3400 BC in lower Mesopotamia (modern Iraq); it is known to have had a city-state, with priests as secular rulers, and a common culture. Cities included Lagash, Eridu, and Ur.

summary, *a.* condensed into narrow compass or few words, abridged, concise, compendious; done briefly or unceremoniously. *n.* an abridged or condensed statement, an epitome. **summary offence,** *n.* an offence tried in a magistrate's court. **summarily,** *adv.* **summarize, -ise,** *v.t.* to make or be a summary of. **summarist,** *n.* [L *summārium,* from *summa,* SUM]

summation, *n.* the act or process of making a sum, addition; a summing-up; a summary.

summer¹, *n.* that season of the year when the sun shines most directly upon a region, the warmest season of the year; (*pl.*) years of age. *a.* pertaining to or used in summer. *v.i.* to pass the summer. *v.t.* to feed or keep (cattle etc.) during the summer. **summerhouse,** *n.* a light building in a garden, for shade etc. in summer. **summer lightning,** *n.* sheet lightning seen too far off for the thunder to be heard. **summer pudding,** *n.* a pudding of soft fruit in a bread casing. **summer school,** *n.* a course of study held during the summer vacation. **summertime,** *n.* the official time of one hour in advance of Greenwich mean time that comes into force between stated dates in the summer in Britain, by virtue of the Summer Time Act of 1916. **summering,** *n.* an early variety of apple. **summerless,** *a.* **summerly, summery,** *a.* [OE *sumor* (cp. Dut. *zomer,* G *Sommer,* Icel. *sumar*), cogn. with Sansk. *samē,* year]

summer², *n.* a heavy horizontal beam or glider; a lintel, a breast-summer; a large stone laid on a column as the beginning of an arch, vault etc. [F *sommier,* L *sagmarius,* from L and Gr. *sagma,* packsaddle]

summering etc. SUMMER¹.

summersault, †**-set,** SOMERSAULT.

summit, *n.* the highest point, the top, the vertex; utmost elevation, degree etc.; a summit conference. **summit conference,** *n.* a conference between heads of states. **summit-level,** *n.* the highest level. **summitless,** *a.* [F *sommet,* dim. of OF *som,* L *summum,* neut. of *summus,* see SUM]

summon, *v.t.* to call, cite or command to meet or attend; to order by a summons to appear in court; to call upon to do something; to rouse, call up (courage etc.). **summoner,** *n.* [OF *somoner,* L *submonēre* (*monēre,* to warn)]

summons, *n.* (*pl.* **summonses**) the act of summoning; an authoritative call or citation, esp. to appear before a court or judge. *v.t.* to serve with a summons, to summon.

Sumner, *n.* **James** (1887–1955), US biochemist. In 1926 he succeeded in crystallizing the enzyme urease and demonstrating its protein nature. For this work Sumner shared the 1946 Nobel Prize for Chemistry with John Northrop and Wendell Stanley.

sumo, *n.* traditional Japanese wrestling in which a contestant attempts to force his opponent out of the designated area or to touch the ground with a part of the body other than the feet. [Jap. *sumō*]

sump, *n.* a well in the floor of a mine, to collect water for pumping; a receptacle for lubricating oil in the crank-case of an internal-combustion engine; a pit to collect metal at its first fusion; a pond at a salt-works. [cp. Swed. and Dan. *sump,* Dut. *somp,* G *Sumpf*]

sumph, *n.* (*dial., esp. Sc.*) a blockhead, a simpleton. [etym. doubtful]

sumpitan, *n.* a Malay blowpipe. **sumpit,** *n.* a poisoned arrow blown from this. [Malay]

sumpsimus, *n.* a correct expression displacing a common but inaccurate one. [L, 1st pl. perf. of *sumere,* to take]

†**sumpter,** *n.* an animal employed to carry packs, a baggage-horse etc.; a driver of this. **sumpter-horse, -mule,** *n.* [OF *sommetier,* packhorse driver, prob. through a late L *sagmatārius,* from Gr. *sagma -atos,* burden, see SUMMER²]

sumption, *n.* (*Log.*) the major premise of a syllogism. [L *sumptio,* from *sumere,* to take, p.p. *sumptus*]

sumptuary, *a.* pertaining to or regulating expenditure. **sumptuary law, edict,** *n.* one restraining private excess in dress, luxury etc. [L *sumptuārius,* as foll.]

sumptuous, *a.* costly, expensive; showing lavish expenditure; splendid, magnificent. **sumptuously,** *adv.* **sumptuousness,** *n.* [F *somptueux,* L *sumptuōsus,* from *sumptus -tūs,* expense, cost]

sun, *n.* (often **Sun**) the heavenly body round which the earth revolves and which gives light and heat to the earth and other planets of the solar system. Its diameter is 1,392,000 km/865,000 miles, its temperature at the surface about 6,000K, and at the centre 15,000,000K. It is composed of about 70% hydrogen and 30% helium, with other elements making up less than 1%. The sun generates energy by nuclear fusion reactions that turn hydrogen into helium at its centre. It is about 4700 million years old, with a predicted lifetime of 10,000 million years; the light or warmth of this, sunshine, a sunny place; a fixed star that has satellites and is the centre of a system; (*poet.*) a day, a sunrise; a sun-burner; anything splendid or luminous, or a chief source of light, honour etc. *v.t.* (*past, p.p.* **sunned**) to expose to the rays of the sun. *v.i.* to sun oneself. **a place in the sun,** a favourable situation, scope for action etc. **sun and planet** PLANET-GEAR. **Sun of righteousness,** *n.* Christ. **to have the sun in one's eyes,** to be intoxicated. **to see the sun,** to be alive. **to take,** (*sl.*) **shoot the sun,** (*Naut.*) to ascertain the sun's altitude in order to determine the latitude. **under the sun,** in the world, on earth. **sunbath,** *n.* exposure of the body to the sun or a sunlamp; insolation. **sunbathe,** *v.i.* to expose the body to the sun. **sunbather,** *n.* **sunbeam,** *n.* a ray of sunlight. **sunbed,** *n.* an array of ultraviolet-emitting light tubes under which one lies to tan the skin; a portable folding bed used for sunbathing. **sunbird,** *n.* any of the Nectariniidae, small birds of brilliant metallic plumage with a striking resemblance to humming-birds. **sunblind,** *n.* a window-shade or awning. **sunblock,** *n.* a cream, lotion etc. for the skin that blocks out the sun's ultraviolet rays; a sunscreen. **sunbonnet,** *n.* a large bonnet of light material with projections at the front and sides and a pendant at the back. **sun-bow,** *n.* a rainbow formed by sunlight on spray etc. **sunburn,** *n.* tanning or inflammation of the skin due to exposure to the sun. **sunburned, -burnt,** *a.* **sun-burner,** *n.* a concentric group of gas-jets, incandescent lamps etc., usu. with a reflector, for throwing light from a ceiling etc. **sunburst,** *n.* a strong or sudden burst of sunlight. **sundeck,** *n.* the upper deck of a passenger ship. **sundew,** *n.* a low, hairy, insectivorous bog-plant of the genus *Drosera*. **sundial,** *n.* an instrument for telling the time of day by means of the shadow of a gnomon cast on a dial etc. **sundog,** *n.* a parhelion. **sundown,** *n.* sunset. **sundowner,** *n.* (*Austral. sl.*) a tramp who times his arrival at sundown in order to get a night's lodging. **sundress,** *n.* a lightweight, lowcut, sleeveless dress for wearing in the sun. **sundried,** *a.* dried in the sun. **sun filter,** *n.* a sunscreen. **sunfish,** *n.* a large fish of various species with a body like a sphere truncated behind. **sunflower,** *n.* a plant of the genus *Helianthus,* esp. *H. annuus,* with yellow-rayed flowers. **sunglasses,** *n.pl.* darkened glasses for protecting the eyes from glare. **sun-god,** *n.* the sun worshipped as a deity. **sun-hat, -helmet,** *n.* a light hat with a broad brim etc., to protect from the sun. **sun lamp,** *n.* a lamp that gives out ultraviolet rays for curative purposes or tanning the skin. **sunlight,** *n.* **sunlit,** *a.* **sun lounge,** (*N Am.*) **parlour,** *n.* a room with large windows to admit sunlight. **sun-myth,** *n.* a solar myth. **sunproof,** *a.* **sunrise,** *n.* the first appearance of the sun above the horizon; the time of this. **sunrise industry,** *n.* a high-technology industry (with good prospects for the future). **sunroof,** *n.* a car roof with a panel that slides open. **sun-rose,** *n.* a rock-rose; a plant of the genus *Helianthemum*. **sunscreen,** *n.* a substance included in suntan preparations to protect the skin by screening out some of the ultraviolet radiation from the sun. **sunset,** *n.* the disappearance of the sun below the horizon; the time of this; the decline (of life etc.). **sunshade,** *n.* a parasol, awning, blind etc. used as a protection against the sun. **sunshine,** *n.* the light of the sun; the space illuminated by this; warmth, brightness, cheerfulness, favourable influence. **sunshine roof,** *n.* a sunroof. **sunshiny,** *a.* **sunspot,** *n.* a dark patch sometimes seen on the surface of the sun. **sunstroke,** *n.* heatstroke due to exposure to the sun in hot weather. **suntan,** *n.* a browning of the skin caused by the formation of pigment induced by exposure to the sun or a sunlamp. **suntanned,** *a.* **suntrap,** *n.* a sheltered sunny place, as in a garden. **sunup,** *n.* (*chiefly N Am.*) sunrise. **sun-worship,** *n.* **sun-worshipper,** *n.* **sunless,** *a.* **sunlessness,** *n.* **sunlike,** *a.* **sunny,** *a.* bright with or warmed by sunlight; bright, cheerful, cheery, genial; proceeding from the sun. **sunnily,** *adv.* **sunniness,** *n.* [OE *sunne* (cp. Dut. *zon,* G *Sonne,* Icel. *sunna*), cogn. with Goth. *sauil,* Icel. *sōl,* L *sōl*]

Sun., (*abbr.*) Sunday.

Sun City, *n.* alternative name for Mmabatho, resort in Bophuthatswana, South Africa.

sundae, *n.* an ice-cream containing fragments of nuts and various fruits. [etym. unknown]

Sunday, *n.* the 1st day of the week, the Lord's Day, the Christian Sabbath. **month of Sundays** MONTH. **Sunday best,** *n.* (*coll.*) best clothes for use on Sundays. **Sunday school,** *n.* a school held on Sundays for religious instruction. [OE *sunnan dæg,* day of the sun]

sunder, *v.t.* to part, to separate; to keep apart. *v.i.* to be separated. **in sunder,** apart, in two. **sunderance,** *n.* [OE *sundrian,* from *sundor,* asunder (cp. Icel. *sundra,* Dan. *söndre,* G *sondern*)]

sundew, sundown, sundowner etc. SUN.

sundry, *a.* several, various, miscellaneous. *n.pl.* matters, items or miscellaneous articles, too trifling or numerous to specify. **all and sundry** ALL. [OE *syndrig,* as SUNDER]

sung, *past, p.p.* SING.

sunk, sunken, *p.p.* SINK.

Sunna, *n.* the traditional part of the Muslim law, based on the sayings or acts of Mohammed, accepted as of equal authority to the Koran by orthodox Muslims or the Sunni but rejected by the Shiites. **Sunni,** *n.* **Sunnite,** *n., a.* [Arab.]

sunn (hemp), *n.* an E Indian plant cultivated for its fibres. [Hind. *san*]

Sunni, *n.* a member of the larger of the two main sects of Islam, with about 680 million adherents. Sunni Muslims believe that the first four caliphs were all legitimate successors of the prophet Muhammad, and that guidance on belief and life should come from the Koran and the Hadith, and from the Shari'a, not from a human authority or spiritual leader. Imams in Sunni Islam are educated lay teachers of the faith and prayer leaders.

Sunningdale Agreement, *n.* an agreement reached by the UK and Irish governments, together with the Northern Ireland executive, Dec. 1973 in Sunningdale, England. The agreement included provisions for a power-sharing executive in Northern Ireland. However, the executive lasted only five weeks before the UK government was defeated in a general election, and a subsequent general strike in May 1974 brought down the Northern Ireland government. The experiment has not been repeated.

sunny, sunrise, sunshine etc. SUN.

Sun Yat-sen, (1867–1925), Chinese nationalist politician, founder of the Guomindang in 1894, president of China in 1912 after playing a vital part in deposing the emperor, and president of a breakaway government from 1921.

Sun Zhong Shan, Pinyin transliteration of Sun Yat-sen.

sup, *v.t.* (*past, p.p.* **supped**) to take (soup etc.) in successive sips or spoonfuls. *v.i.* to take in liquid or liquid food by sips or spoonfuls; to take supper. *n.* a mouthful (of liquor, soup etc.). [OE *sūpan* (cp. Dut. *zuipen,* LG *supen,* Icel. *sūpa,* OHG *sūfan*), partly from OF *souper,* see SUPPER]

sup., (*abbr.*) superior; superlative; supine; supplement, supplementary; supra (above).

sup-, *pref.* SUB- (before *p*).

supawn, *n.* (*N Am.*) a dish or pudding composed of boiled maize. [N Am. Ind.]

super[1]**,** *n.* a supernumerary actor; (*coll.*) a (police) SUPERINTENDENT [short for SUPERNUMERARY]

super[2]**,** *a.* (*coll.*) excellent, very good, enjoyable etc. [short for SUPERFINE]

super-, *pref.* over, above; above in position, on the top of; over in degree or amount, excessive, exceeding, more than, transcending; besides, in addition; of a higher kind. In cases where no definition is given reference should be made to the unprefixed word in its proper place in the dictionary. [L *super-,* pref., *super,* prep., orig. compar. of *sub,* see SUB- (cp. Gr. *huper,* Sansk. *hupari*)]

superable, *a.* that may be overcome, conquerable. **superableness,** *n.* **superably,** *adv.* [L *superābilis,* from *superāre,* as prec.]
superabound, *v.i.* to be more than enough. **superabundance,** *n.* **superabundant,** *a.* **superabundantly,** *adv.*
superadd, *v.t.* to add over and above something else. **superaddition,** *n.*
superaltar, *n.* a consecrated slab used to place on an unconsecrated altar.
superannuate, *v.t.* to dismiss, discard, disqualify or incapacitate on account of age; to pension off on account of age. **superannuable,** *a.* **superannuated,** *a.* **superannuation,** *n.* the act of superannuating; the state of being superannuated; a regular payment made by an employee to a pension scheme; the pension paid. [SUPER-, L *annus,* year, cp. ANNUAL]
superation, *n.* the apparent passing of one planet by another in longitude. [L *superātio,* from *superāre,* to go over, from *super,* SUPER-]
superb, *a.* grand, majestic, imposing, magnificent, splendid, stately; excellent, first-rate. **superbly,** *adv.* **superbness,** *n.* [F *superbe,* L *superbus* (*super,* see SUPER-, *fu-,* stem of *fuī,* I was)]
super-calendered, *a.* of paper, highly finished.
supercargo, *n.* (*pl.* **-goes**) an officer in a merchant-ship who superintends sales etc. and has charge of the cargo.
supercelestial, *a.*
supercentre, *n.* a very large or important centre for a particular activity; a very large self-service store, a hypermarket, superstore.
supercharge, *v.t.* (*Her.*) to superimpose on another charge; to charge or fill greatly or to excess with emotion, vigour etc.; to fit a supercharger to. *n.* one charge borne upon another. **supercharger,** *n.* a mechanism in an internal-combustion engine which provides for the complete filling of the cylinder with explosive material when going at high speed.
superciliary, *a.* pertaining to or situated above the eyebrows. [as foll.]
supercilious, *a.* contemptuous, overbearing, haughtily indifferent, arrogant, disdainful. **superciliously,** *adv.* **superciliousness,** *n.* [L *superciliōsus,* from *supercilium,* see CILIUM (with alln. to raising the eyebrows)]
supercivilized, -ised, *a.*
superclass, *n.* a taxonomic category between a phylum or division and a class.
supercolumnar, *a.* having one order of columns placed over another. **supercolumniation,** *n.*
supercomputer, *n.* a very powerful computer capable of over 100 million arithmetic operations per second. **supercomputing,** *n.*
superconductivity, *n.* the total loss of electrical resistance exhibited by some metals and alloys at very low temperatures. **superconducting, superconductive,** *a.* **superconductor,** *n.*
supercool, *v.t.* to cool (a liquid) below its freezing-point without solidification.
supercritical, *a.* †**superdainty,** *a.*
superdominant, *n.* the tone above the dominant, the sixth note of the diatonic scale.
superego, *n.* (*Psych.*) the unconscious inhibitory morality in the mind which criticizes the ego and condemns the unworthy impulses of the id.
superelevation, *n.* the difference in height between the opposite sides of a curved section of road, railway track etc.
supereminent, *a.* **supereminence,** *n.* **supereminently,** *adv.*
supererogation, *n.* performance of more than duty requires. **works of supererogation,** voluntary works, besides, over and above God's Commandments. **supererogate,** *v.i.* **supererogatory,** *a.* [late L *superērogātio,* from *superērogāre,* to pay out beyond what is expected]
†**superessential,** *a.* (*Phil.*) of the absolute, transcending mere essence.
superethical, *a.*
superexalt, *v.t.* **superexaltation,** *n.*
superexcellent, *a.* **superexcellence,** *n.*
superfamily, *n.* a taxonomic category between a suborder and a family; an analogous category of languages.
superfatted, *a.* of soap, containing excess of fatty matter relatively to alkali.
superfecundation, *n.* the conception of two embryos from ova produced at one time, by separate acts of sexual intercourse.
superficial, *a.* pertaining to or lying on the surface; not penetrating deep; not deep or profound, shallow. **superficiality, superficialness,** *n.* **superficially,** *adv.* [as foll.]
superficies, *n.* (*pl.* **superficies**) a surface; its area; external appearance or form. [L]
superfine, *a.* exceedingly fine, surpassing in fineness, of extra quality; extremely fine in size; over-refined. **superfineness,** *n.*
superfluous, *a.* more than is necessary or sufficient, excessive, superabundant, redundant. **superfluity,** *n.* the state of being superfluous; something unnecessary; an excess, a superabundance. **superfluously,** *adv.* **superfluousness,** *n.* [L *superfluus* (*fluere,* to flow)]
superfoetation, -fetation, *n.* the conception of a second embryo or litter during the gestation of the first.
superfrontal, *a.* pertaining to the upper part of the frontal lobe of the brain. *n.* the part of an altar-cloth covering the top.
superfunction, *n.* **superfunctional,** *a.*
supergiant, *n.* a very large, very bright star of low density.
superglue, *n.* an adhesive that gives an extremely strong bond on contact.
supergrass, *n.* (*coll.*) a police informer whose information implicates many people or concerns major criminals or criminal activities.
superheat, *v.t.* to heat to excess, to heat (steam) above the boiling-point of water so no condensation occurs; to heat (a liquid) above boiling point without vaporization. **superheater,** *n.*
superheterodyne, *n.* a radio receiver with a high degree of selectivity.
superhighway, *n.* (*N Am.*) a motorway.
superhive, *n.* a removable upper storey to a hive.
superhuman, *a.* **superhumanly,** *adv.*
superhumeral, *n.* something worn upon the shoulders, as an archbishop's pallium, or a Jewish sacerdotal ephod.
superimpose, *v.t.* to lay upon something else. **superimposition,** *n.*
superimpregnation, *n.* superfoetation.
superincumbent, *a.* lying or resting on something.
superinduce, *v.t.* to bring in as an addition, to superadd. **superinduction,** *n.*
superinstitution, *n.* one institution upon another, as of an incumbent to a benefice already occupied.
superintend, *v.t.* to have or exercise the management or oversight of, to direct, to control. **superintendence,** *n.* superintending, supervision. **superintendency,** *n.* the office or district of a superintendent. **superintendent,** *n.* one who superintends; a police officer ranking above an inspector. [L *superintendere* (*intendere,* see INTEND)]
superior, *a.* upper, of higher position, class, grade, rank, excellence, degree etc.; better or greater relatively (to); of a quality above the average; of wider application; situated near the top, or in the higher part; (*Bot.*) growing above another, as the calyx or the ovary; above being influenced by or amenable (to); supercilious. *n.* a person superior to one or to others, one's better; the head of a monastery, convent or other religious house. **superior planet,** *n.* one further from the sun than the earth is. **superiority,** *n.* **superiority complex,** *n.* an inflated opinion of one's worth. **superiorly,** *adv.* [OF *superieur,* L *superior -ōrem,* compar. of *superus,* high (from *super,* above, see SUPER-)]

Superior, Lake, *n.* largest of the Great Lakes, and the second largest lake in the world; area 83,300 sq km/ 32,200 sq miles.
superjacent, *a.* lying on or above something. [SUPER-, JACENT]
superl., (*abbr.*) superlative.
superlative, *a.* raised to the highest degree, consummate, supreme; (*Gram.*) expressing the highest or utmost degree. *n.* the superlative degree; a word or phrase in the superlative degree; an exaggeration. **superlatively,** *adv.* **superlativeness,** *n.* [L *superlatīvus,* from *superlātus,* exaggerated (*lātus,* p.p. of *ferre,* to carry)]
superlunar, -nary, *a.* above the moon, celestial, not mundane.
Superman, *n.* comic-strip hero created 1938 in the US by writer, Jerome Siegel and artist, Joseph Shuster, later featured in television, films, and other media. In the German philosopher Nietzsche's work, his ideal future human being was the *Übermensch*, or Superman. Superman was the first comic-book superhero. Born on the planet Krypton, he has extraordinary powers and can fly; he is vulnerable only to kryptonite. Between feats of crime-fighting or rescuing accident victims, he leads an ordinary life as a bespectacled journalist, Clark Kent.
superman, *n.* a hypothetical superior being, esp. one advanced in intellect and morals; a person of outstanding ability or achievements.
supermarket, *n.* a large, self-service shop where food and domestic goods are sold.
supermedial, *n.*
supermundane, *a.* above or superior to worldly things.
supernaculum, *n.* wine or liquor of the choicest quality. *adv.* to the last drop (lit., on the nail, from the custom of pouring the last drop on the thumb-nail). †**supernacular,** *a.* [mod. L *naculum,* G *Nagel,* NAIL]
supernal, *a.* of a loftier kind, nature or region; celestial, heavenly, divine, lofty. [MF *supernel* (L *supernus*)]
supernatant, *a.* floating on the surface. **supernatation,** *n.*
supernatural, *a.* existing by, due to, or exercising powers above the usual forces of nature, outside the sphere of natural law. **supernaturalism,** *n.* belief in the supernatural. **supernaturalist,** *n.* **supernaturalistic,** *a.* **supernaturalize, -ise,** *v.t.* **supernaturally,** *adv.* **supernaturalness,** *n.*
supernormal, *a.* **supernormality,** *n.* **supernormally,** *a.*
supernova, *n.* (*pl.* **-vae, -vas**) a nova up to 100 million times brighter than the sun, produced by the eruption of a star following its implosion.
supernumerary, *a.* being in excess of a prescribed or customary number. *n.* a supernumerary person or thing, esp. a person appearing on the stage without a speaking part.
superoccipital, *a.*
superoctave, *n.* a coupler in an organ causing a note to sound an octave higher than the key struck; an organ-stop a 15th above the principal.
superorder, *n.* a taxonomic category between an order and a subclass or a class. **superordinal,** *a.*
superordinary, *a.*
superordinate, *a.* superior in rank or status; having the relation of superordination. **superordination,** *n.* the ordination of a person to fill an office not yet vacant; (*Log.*) the relation of a universal proposition to a particular proposition that it includes.
superorganic, *a.* superior or external to the organism, psychical; pertaining to a higher grade of organism, social.
superovulation, *n.* the production of large numbers of ova at a single time. **superovulate,** *v.i.*
superoxygenation, *n.*
superparasite, *n.* **superparasitic,** *a.* **superparasitism,** *n.*
superphosphate, *n.* a phosphate containing the greatest amount of phosphoric acid that can combine with the base; a mixture of phosphates used as a fertilizer.
superphysical, *a.*
superpose, *v.t.* to lay over or upon something. **superposable,** *a.* **superposition,** *n.*
superpower, *n.* a very powerful nation, esp. the US or the USSR.
†**superpraise,** *v.t.*
super-rich, *a.*
super-royal, *a.* larger than royal, denoting a size of printing paper $27\frac{1}{2} \times 20\frac{1}{2}$ in. (698 × 520 mm).
supersacral, *a.*
supersalt, *n.* an acid salt.
supersaturated, *a.* containing more material than a saturated solution or vapour. **supersaturate,** *v.t.* **supersaturation,** *n.*
superscribe, *v.t.* to write on the top or outside of something or above; to write a name, inscription, address etc. on the outside or top of. **superscript,** *a.* written at the top or outside; set above the line, superior. *n.* a superior character. **superscription,** *n.* [L *scrībere,* to write]
supersede, *v.t.* to put a person or thing in the place of, to set aside, to annul; to take the place of, to displace, to supplant. **supersedeas,** *n.* a legal writ to stay proceedings etc. **supersedence, supersedure, supersession,** *n.* [OF *superseder,* to leave off, to desist, L *supersedēre* (*sedēre,* to sit, p.p. *sessus*)]
supersensible, *a.* **supersensitive,** *a.* **supersensual, supersensuous,** *a.*
†**superserviceable,** *a.* over officious.
supersonic, *a.* pertaining to sound waves with such a high frequency that they are inaudible; above the speed of sound; travelling at or using such speeds. **supersonically,** *adv.*
superstar, *n.* a very popular film, music, sports etc. star.
superstition, *n.* credulity regarding the supernatural, the occult or the mysterious; ignorant or unreasoning dread of the unknown; a religion, particular belief or practice originating in this, esp. a belief in omens, charms etc. **superstitious,** *a.* **superstitiously,** *adv.* **superstitiousness,** *n.* [F, from L *superstitio -ōnem,* standing over, amazement (*stat-,* p.p. stem of *stāre,* to stand)]
superstore, *n.* a very large supermarket; a very large store selling goods other than food.
superstratum, *n.* (*pl.* **-ta**) a stratum resting on another.
superstructure, *n.* the part of a building above the ground; an upper part of a structure; a concept etc. based on another. **superstructural,** *a.*
supersubstantial, *a.*
supersubtle, *a.* **supersubtlety,** *n.*
supertanker, *n.* a very large tanker ship.
supertax, *n.* a tax in addition to the basic income tax, levied on incomes above a certain level.
supertelluric, *a.*
supertemporal[1], *a.* situated in the upper part of the temporal region of the head.
supertemporal[2], *a.* transcending time.
superterrene, superterrestrial, *a.*
supertonic, *n.* the note next above the tonic in the diatonic scale.
supertuberation, *n.* the production of young tubers from old ones while still growing.
supervene, *v.i.* to come or happen as something extraneous or additional **supervenient,** *a.* **supervention,** *n.* [L *sūpervenīre* (*venīre,* to come)]
supervise, *v.t.* to have oversight of, to oversee, to superintend. **supervision,** *n.* **supervisor,** *n.* **supervisory,** *a.* [L *supervīsum,* supine of *supervidēre* (*vidēre,* to see)]
supinate, *v.t.* to turn the palm of (the hand) upwards or forwards. **supinator,** *n.* either of two muscles which do this. **supination,** *n.* the placing or holding of the palm of the hand upwards or forwards. [L *supīnātus,* p.p. of *supīnāre,* as foll.]
supine, *a.* lying on the back with the face upwards;

negligent, indolent, listless, careless. *n.* a Latin verbal noun formed from the p.p. stem and ending in *-um* (1st supine) or *-u* (2nd supine). **supinely,** *adv.* **supineness,** *n.* [L *supīnus,* from *sup-, sub,* under, see SUB-]

supp., suppl., (*abbr.*) supplement.

suppedaneum, *n.* (*pl.* **-nea**) a foot-rest on a cross or crucifix. †**suppedaneous,** *a.* placed or being under the feet. [late L *sup-* (SUB-), L *pes pedis,* foot)]

supper, *n.* the last meal of the day, esp. a light one; an evening social affair including supper. **the Lord's Supper,** Holy Communion. **supperless,** *a.* [OF *soper, super* (F *souper*), from *soper,* LG *supen,* cogn. with SUP]

supplant, *v.t.* to take the place of or oust, esp. by craft or treachery. **supplantation,** *n.* **supplanter,** *n.* [OF *supplanter,* L *supplantāre* (*plantāre,* from *planta,* sole of foot)]

supple, *a.* pliant, flexible, easily bent; lithe, able to move and bend easily; yielding, compliant, soft, submissive, obsequious, servile. *v.t.* to make pliant or flexible; to make compliant. *v.i.* to become pliant. **supplejack,** *n.* a tough climbing shrub, from which walking-sticks are made. **suppleness,** *n.* **supply,** *adv.* [ME and F *souple,* L *supplex -icem* (*plic-,* base of *plicāre,* to fold)]

supplement[1]**,** *n.* an addition, esp. one that supplies a deficiency; an addition or update to a book, newspaper or periodical; the angle that added to another will make the sum two right angles. **supplemental, -ary,** *a.* **supplementary benefit,** *n.* a weekly grant of money paid by the state to people whose income falls below a certain minimum level. **suppletory,** *a.* [F *supplément,* L *supplēmentum,* from *supplēre* (*plēre,* to fill)]

supplement[2]**,** *v.t.* to make additions to; to complete by additions. **supplementation,** *n.* [as prec.]

suppliant, *a.* entreating, supplicating; expressing entreaty or supplication. *n.* a humble petitioner. **suppliance,** *n.* **suppliantly,** *adv.* [F, pres.p. of *supplier,* as foll.]

supplicate, *v.t.* to beg or ask for earnestly and humbly; to address in earnest prayer; to beg humbly (to grant etc.). *v.i.* to petition earnestly, to beseech. **supplicant,** *a.* suppliant. *n.* a suppliant. **supplicantly,** *adv.* **supplicatingly,** *adv.* **supplication,** *n.* **supplicatory,** *a.* [L *supplicātus,* p.p. of *supplicāre,* as SUPPLE]

supply[1] SUPPLE.

supply[2]**,** *v.t.* to furnish with what is wanted, to provide (with); to furnish, to provide; to satisfy; to serve instead of; to fill (the place of), to make up for (a deficiency etc.). *n.* the act of supplying things needed; that which is supplied; a sufficiency of things required or available for use; (*often pl.*) necessary stores or provisions; the quantity of goods or services offered for sale at a particular time; (*pl.*) a grant of money by Parliament to meet the expenses of government, an allowance; one who supplies a position temporarily, a substitute. **supply and demand** DEMAND. **supplier,** *n.* [OF *supploier* (F *suppléer*), L *supplēre* (*plēre,* to fill)]

support, *v.t.* to bear the weight of, to hold up, to sustain; to keep from yielding or giving way, to give strength or endurance to; to furnish with necessaries, to provide for; to give assistance to; to advocate, to defend, to back up, to second; to promote, to encourage; to bear out, to substantiate, to corroborate; to bear; to endure, to put up with; to keep up, to be able to carry on; to maintain; to act as, to represent (a character etc.); to play a secondary role to (the main character) in a film or play; to accompany (a pop group, feature film etc.) in a subordinate role. *n.* the act of supporting or the state of being supported; one who or that which supports; aid, countenance, assistance; subsistence, livelihood. **supportable,** *a.* **supportableness,** *n.* **supportably,** *adv.* †**supportance,** *n.* **supporter,** *n.* one who or that which supports or maintains; (*Her.*) a figure on each side of a shield etc., appearing to support it. **supporting,** *a.* giving support; playing or having a secondary or subordinate role. **supportive,** *a.* providing support, esp. moral or emotional encouragement. **supportless,** *a.* [F *supporter,* L *supportāre,* (*portāre,* to carry)]

suppose, *v.t.* to lay down without proof, to assume by way of argument or illustration; to imagine, to believe; to take to be the case, to accept as probable, to surmise; to believe (to exist); to involve or require as a condition, to imply; (*usu. pass.*) to require or expect, to be obliged to. **supposable,** *a.* **supposed,** *a.* believed to be so. **supposedly,** *adv.* **supposer,** *n.* **supposition,** *n.* **suppositional,** *a.* **suppositionally,** *adv.* [F *supposer* (*poser,* to POSE[1])]

supposititious, suppositious, *a.* substituted for something else, not genuine, spurious. **supposititiously,** *adv.* **supposititiousness,** *n.* [L *supposititius,* from *supposit-,* p.p. stem of *suppōnere,* to substitute (*pōnere,* to put)]

suppositive, *a.* including or implying supposition. *n.* a conjunction implying supposition. **suppositively,** *adv.* [as prec.]

suppository, *n.* a medicinal body introduced into an internal passage, as the vagina or rectum, and left to dissolve. [late L *suppositorium,* as prec.]

suppress, *v.t.* to put down, to overpower, to subdue, to quell; to keep in or back, to withhold, to stifle, to repress; to keep back from disclosure or circulation, to conceal. **suppressant,** *n.* **suppressible,** *a.* **suppression,** *n.* **suppressionist,** *n.* **suppressive,** *a.* **suppressor,** *n.* one who suppresses; a device for preventing electrical interference in a circuit. [L *suppressus,* p.p. of *supprimere* (*premere,* to press)]

suppurate, *v.i.* to generate pus, to fester. **suppuration,** *n.* **suppurative,** *a.* [L *suppūrātus,* p.p. of *suppūrāre* (*pūrāre,* from *pur-,* base of PUS)]

supra-, *pref.,* above, over, super-; beyond. [L *suprā-,* pref., *suprā,* prep. and adv., above, for *superā,* abl. of *superus,* higher, from *super,* see SUPER-]

supraciliary SUPERCILIARY.

supraclavicular, *a.* situated above the clavicle.

supradorsal, *a.* on the back; above the dorsal surface.

supralapsarian, *n.* a higher Calvinist, one believing that election and rejection were decreed before the Fall. *a.* pertaining to supralapsarianism. **supralapsarianism,** *n.* the belief and doctrines of the supralapsarians.

supramaxillary, *a.* of or pertaining to the upper jaw. *n.* the upper maxillary bone.

supramundane, *a.* above the world.

supranational, *a.* overriding national sovereignty.

supraorbital, *a.* being above the eye-socket.

supraposition SUPERPOSITION.

supraprotest, *n.* acceptance or payment of a bill of exchange by a person not a party to it after protest for non-acceptance or non-payment.

suprarenal, *a.* situated above the kidneys. **suprarenal glands,** *n.pl.* the adrenal glands.

suprascapular, -lary, *a.* situated above the shoulder-blade.

Supremacy, Acts of, two acts of the English Parliament in 1534 and 1559, which established Henry VIII and Elizabeth I respectively as head of the English church in place of the pope.

suprematism, *n.* Russian abstract-art movement developed about 1913 by Malevich. The suprematist paintings gradually became more severe, until in 1918 they reached a climax with the *White on White* series showing white geometrical shapes on a white ground.

supreme, *a.* highest in authority or power, highest in degree or importance, utmost, extreme, greatest possible; last, final. **Supreme Being,** *n.* God. **Supreme Court,** see separate entry. **Supreme Court of Judicature** JUDICATURE. **supremacist,** *n.* one who believes or promotes the supremacy of a particular group. **supremacy,** *n.* the quality or state of being supreme; the highest authority or power. **supremely,** *adv.* [F, from L *suprēmus,* superl. of *superus,* see SUPRA-]

Supreme Court, *n.* highest US judicial tribunal, composed of a chief justice (William Rehnquist from 1986) and eight associate justices. Appointments are made by the president, and members can be removed only by impeachment. In Britain, the Supreme Court of Judicature is made up of the Court of Appeal and the High Court.

Supremes, the, *n.pl.* US vocal group, pioneers of the MOTOWN sound, formed in 1959 in Detroit, from 1962 a trio comprising, initially, Diana Ross (1944–), Mary Wilson (1944–), and Florence Ballard (1943–76). The most successful female group of the 1960s, they had a string of pop hits beginning with 'Where Did Our Love Go?' (1964) and 'Baby Love' (1964). Diana Ross left for a solo career in 1969.

supremo, *n.* (*pl.* **-mos**) (*coll.*) a supreme leader or head. [Sp., from L *suprēmus,* SUPREME]

supt., (*abbr.*) superintendent.

sur-, *pref.* super-, as in *surcingle, surface, surfeit.* [OF, from L SUPER-]

sura, *n.* a chapter of the Koran. [Arab., step]

†**suraddition,** *n.* (*Shak.*) something added.

Surabaya, *n.* port on the island of Java, Indonesia; population (1980) 2,028,000. It has oil refineries and shipyards, and is a naval base.

surah, *n.* a soft, twilled, usu. self-coloured silk material. [prob. as SURAT]

Suraj-ud-Dowlah, *n.* (1728–1757), nawab of Bengal, India. He captured Calcutta from the British in 1756 and imprisoned some of the British in the BLACK HOLE of Calcutta, but was defeated in 1757 by Robert Clive, and lost Bengal to the British at the Battle of PLASSEY. He was killed in his capital, Murshidabad.

sural, *a.* pertaining to the calf of the leg. [L *sūra,* calf]

surat, *n.* coarse, short cotton grown near Surat, India; cloth made from this.

surbase, *n.* the cornice or moulding at the top of a pedestal or base. **surbased,** *a.* [SUR-, BASE[2]]

surbed, *v.t.* (*past, p.p.* **surbedded**) to set (a stone) on edge in relation to the grain.

surcease, *n.* cessation. *v.i., v.t.* to cease, desist (from). [A-F *sursise,* fem. of *sursis,* p.p. of *surseer,* F *surseoir,* L *supersedēre,* to SUPERSEDE]

surcharge, *v.t.* to overload, to overburden, to overfill; to put an extra charge on, to overcharge; to show an omission in (an account) for which credit should be allowed; to impose payment of (a sum) or on (a person) for amounts in official accounts disallowed by an auditor; to overprint (as a stamp) with a surcharge. *n.* an excessive load, burden or charge; an extra charge or cost; an overcharge; an amount surcharged on official accounts; another valuation or other matter printed on a postage- or revenue-stamp; a stamp so treated; an additional charge imposed as a penalty for false returns of income or other taxable property. †**surchargement,** *n.* **surcharger,** *n.* [A-F (SUR-, CHARGE)]

surcingle, *n.* a belt or girth put round the body of a horse etc., for holding a saddle or blanket on its back; the girdle of a cassock. *v.t.* to put a surcingle on; to fasten with this. [ME and OF *surcengle* (*cengle,* girth, L *cingula,* belt, from *cingere,* to gird)]

surcoat, *n.* an outer coat, esp. a loose robe worn over armour; an outer jacket worn by women (14th–16th cents.). [A-F *surcote*]

surculus, *n.* (*pl.* **-li**) a shoot rising from a root-stock, a sucker. **surculigerous, surculose,** *a.* [L]

surd, *a.* not capable of being expressed in rational numbers; uttered with the breath and not with the voice. *n.* (*Math.*) an irrational quantity; a surd consonant, as *p, f, s,* opp. to the vocals *b, v, z.* **surdity,** *n.* [L *surdus,* deaf]

sure, *a.* certain, confident, undoubting; free from doubts (of); positive, believing, confidently trusting (that); infallible, certain (to); safe, reliable, trustworthy, unfailing; unquestionably true; certain (of finding, gaining etc.). *adv.* (*chiefly N Am.*) surely, certainly; yes. **for sure,** surely, certainly. **sure enough,** in reality, not merely expectation. **to be sure,** (*coll.*) without doubt, certainly, of course. **to make sure,** to make certain, to ascertain; to make secure. **to make sure of,** to consider as certain. **well, I'm sure,** an exclamation of surprise. **sure-fire,** *a.* (*coll.*) bound to succeed, assured. **sure-footed,** *a.* not liable to stumble or fall. **sure thing,** *n.* something certain of success. *int.* (*coll.*) certainly, yes. **surely,** *adv.* securely, safely; certainly (frequently used by way of asseveration or to deprecate doubt); undoubtedly. **sureness,** *n.* [OF *sur, seur,* L *sēcūrus,* SECURE]

surety, *n.* a person undertaking responsibility for payment of a sum, discharge of an engagement or attendance in court by another, a guarantor; a pledge deposited as security against loss or damage or for payment or discharge of an engagement etc.; certainty. **suretyship,** *n.*

surf, *n.* the swell of the sea breaking on the shore, rocks etc.; the foam of this. *v.i.* to ride on the surf, engage in surfing. **surf-bird,** *n.* a plover-like bird of the Pacific coasts of N America, akin to the sandpiper. **surfboard,** *n.* a long narrow board used in surfing. **surfboat,** *n.* a strong and buoyant boat for use in surf. **surfboatman,** *n.* **surf-duck,** *n.* a scoter. **surfer,** *n.* one who engages in surfing. **surfie,** *n.* (*Austral., coll.*) one whose life centres round surfing. **surfing,** *n.* the sport of riding on a board on the surf of an incoming wave. **surfy,** *a.* [formerly *suffe,* prob. var. of SOUGH[1]]

surface, *n.* the exterior part of anything, the outside, the superficies; (*Geom.*) that which has length and breadth but not thickness; that which is apparent at first view or on slight consideration. *v.t.* to put a surface on; to smooth, to polish. *v.i.* to rise to the surface; (*coll. facet.*) to wake up or get out of bed. **surface-to-air,** *a.* pertaining to missiles launched from land to an airborne target. **surface-active,** *a.* capable of lessening the surface-tension of a liquid. **surface mail,** *n.* mail sent by land or sea. **surface-man,** *n.* one employed in keeping the permanent way of a railway in order; a mine-worker employed at the surface. **surface-printing,** *n.* printing from a relief surface as distinguished from an incised surface. **surface-tension,** *n.* the tension of a liquid causing it to act as an elastic enveloping membrane tending to contract to the minimum area, as seen in the bubble, the drop etc. **surface-water,** *n.* water collecting on the surface of the ground. **surfaced,** *a.* **surfacer,** *n.* **surficial,** *a.* **surficially,** *adv.* [F]

surfactant, *n.* a surface-active substance, as a detergent. [*surf*ace-*act*ive *a*ge*nt*]

surfeit, *n.* excess, esp. in eating and drinking; oppression resulting from this, satiety, nausea; an excessive supply or amount. *v.t.* to fill or feed to excess, to overload, to cloy. **surfeit water,** *n.* a highly alcoholic drink taken in small amounts to counteract the effect of over-eating. **surfeiter,** *n.* [A-F *surfet,* OF *sorfait,* p.p. of *sorfaire* (SUR-, *faire,* L *facere,* to do)]

surficial, etc. SURFACE. **surfy** SURF.

surg., (*abbr.*) surgeon, surgery, surgical.

surge, *v.i.* of waves, to swell, to heave, to move up and down; to well up, to move with a sudden rushing or swelling motion; to rise suddenly. *n.* a large wave, a billow, a swell; a heaving and rolling motion; a sudden increase or rise. †**surgeful,** †**surgent,** †**surgy,** *a.* †**surgeless,** *a.* [F *surgir,* L *surgere, surrigere* (*sur-,* SUB-, *regere,* to direct)]

surgeon, *n.* a medical practitioner treating injuries, deformities and diseases by manual procedure, often involving operations; a practitioner holding the diploma of the Royal College of Surgeons; a medical officer in the army, navy or a military hospital; a surgeonfish. **surgeon-fish,** *n.* a sea-fish of the genus *Teuthis,* with lance-like spines at the tail. **surgeon general,** *n.* the chief medical officer in the army or navy; the head of the public health service in the US. **surgeoncy, surgeonship,** *n.* [contr. of CHIRURGEON]

surgery, *n.* (the branch of medicine dealing with) the treatment of injuries, deformities or diseases by manual procedure, often operations; the office or consulting-room of a doctor, dentist etc., or its hours of opening; the time during which an MP is available for consultation. **surgical,** *a.* **surgical spirit,** *n.* methylated spirits with oil of wintergreen and castor oil used for sterilizing, cleaning the skin etc. **surgically,** *adv*.

†**surgy** SURGE.

suricate, *n*. a small S African burrowing carnivore *Suricata tetradactyla* allied to the weasel, and often domesticated as a mouser. [native name]

Suriname, *n*. Republic of, country on the N coast of South America, on the Atlantic coast, between Guyana and French Guiana. **area** 163,800 sq km/63,243 sq miles. **capital** Paramaribo. **physical** hilly and forested, with flat coast. **population** (1989) 400,000 (Creole, Chinese, Hindu, and Indonesian peoples); annual growth rate 1.1%. **exports** bauxite, rice, citrus, timber. **language** Dutch, English (both official). **religion** Christian 35%, Hindu 25%, Muslim 17%.

Surinam-toad, *n*. a S American toad-like amphibian. [*Surinam*]

surloin, SIRLOIN.

surly, *a*. churlish, rude, gruff, uncivil. **surlily,** *adv*. **surliness,** *n*. [SIR, -LY]

surmaster, *n*. a master next in rank to the headmaster in some schools.

surmise, *n*. a supposition on slight evidence, a guess, a conjecture. *v.t.* to guess, to imagine, with but little evidence; to conjecture, to suspect. *v.i.* to conjecture, to guess, to suppose. **surmisable,** *a*. **surmiser,** *n*. [OF, fem. of *surmis,* p.p. of *surmettre* (*mettre,* to put, from L *mittere,* to send, p.p. *missus*)]

surmount, *v.t.* to overcome, to vanquish, to rise above; to get or climb to the top of and beyond; to overtop, to cap; to surpass. **surmountable,** *a*. **surmountableness,** *n*. **surmounter,** *n*. [F *surmonter* (MOUNT)]

surmullet, *n*. the red mullet, *Mullus surmuletus*. [OF *surmulet* (*sur, sor,* SORREL[2], MULLET[1]]

surname, *n*. a name added to the first or Christian name; a family name; orig. an appellation signifying occupation etc., or a nickname ultimately becoming hereditary. *v.t.* to call by a surname; to give a surname to. **surnominal,** *a*. [F *surnom* (SUR-, *nom,* L *nomen,* assim. to NAME)]

surpass, *v.t.* to excel, to go beyond in amount, degree etc.; to go beyond the range or capacity of, to transcend. **surpassable,** *a*. **surpassing,** *a*. excellent in an eminent degree. **surpassingly,** *adv*. **surpassingness,** *n*. [F *surpasser*]

surplice, *n*. a loose, flowing vestment of white linen, with full sleeves, worn by the clergy and choristers in the Church of England at divine service. †**surplice-fee,** *n*. a fee paid to the clergy for occasional duties, as marriages and funerals. **surpliced,** *a*. [F *surplis,* med. L *superpelliceum* (*pelliceum,* L *pellicius,* PELISSE)]

surplus, *n*. that which remains over, excess beyond what is used or required; the balance in hand after all liabilities are paid; the residuum of an estate after all debts and legacies are paid. **surplusage,** *n*. [F]

surprise, *n*. a taking unawares or unprepared; emotion excited by something sudden or unexpected. astonishment; an event exciting this, something unexpected. *v.t.* to come or fall upon suddenly and unexpectedly, esp. to attack unawares; to strike with astonishment, to be contrary to or different from expectation; (*usu. p.p.*) to shock, to scandalize; to disconcert; to lead or drive unawares (into an act etc.). **surprisal,** *n*. **surprisedly,** *adv*. **surpriser,** *n*. **surprising,** *a*. causing surprise. **surprisingly,** *adv*. **surprisingness,** *n*. [OF, fem. of *surpris, sorpris,* p.p. of *sur-, sorprendre* (*prendre,* L *prehendere,* to take)]

surrealism, *n*. movement in art, literature, and film, which developed out of Dada around 1922. Led by André BRETON, who produced the *Surrealist Manifesto* (1924), the Surrealists were inspired by the thoughts and visions of the subconscious mind. They explored highly varied styles and techniques, and the movement was a dominant force in Western art between World Wars I and II. **surrealist,** *n*., *a*. **surrealistic,** *a*. [F *surréalisme*]

surrebut, *v.i.* to reply to a defendant's rebutter. **surrebutter,** *n*. the plaintiff's reply to the defendant's rebutter.

surrejoin, *v.i.* to reply to a defendant's rejoinder. **surrejoinder,** *n*. the plaintiff's reply to the defendant's rejoinder.

surrender, *v.t.* to yield up to the power or control of another; to give up possession of, esp. upon compulsion or demand; to yield (oneself) to any influence, habit, emotion etc. *v.i.* to yield something or to give oneself up into the power of another, esp. to an enemy in war; to give in, to yield, to submit; to appear in court in discharge of bail etc. *n*. the act of surrendering or the state of being surrendered; the voluntary relinquishing of a (life) insurance policy by its holder, usu. in return for a payment (the policy's **surrender value**). **surrenderee,** *n*. (*Law*) one to whom an estate is surrendered. **surrenderer,** *n*. †**surrendry,** *n*. [OF *surrendre*]

surreptitious, *a*. done by stealth or fraud; secret, clandestine. **surreptitiously,** *adv*. [L *surreptīcius,* from *surripere,* to purloin (*sur-,* SUB-, *rapere,* to snatch), p.p. *surreptus*]

Surrey[1], *n*. county in S England. **area** 1,660 sq km/641 sq miles. **towns** administrative headquarters Kingston upon Thames; Guildford, Woking. **population** (1987) 1,000,000. **products** market garden vegetables, agricultural products, service industries.

Surrey[2], *n*. **Henry Howard, Earl of Surrey** (*c*. 1517–47), English courtier and poet, executed on a poorly-based charge of high treason. With WYATT, he introduced the sonnet to England, and was a pioneer of blank verse.

surrogate, *n*. a deputy; a deputy of a bishop or his chancellor appointed to grant marriage licences and probates; a substitute. **surrogate mother,** *n*. a woman who bears a child for a (childless) couple, often after (artificial) insemination or embryo implantation. **surrogacy, surrogateship,** *n*. **surrogatum,** *n*. (*Sc. Law*) a substitute. [L *surrogātus,* p.p. of *surrogāre,* to elect as substitute (*sur-,* SUB-, *rogāre,* to ask)]

surround, *v.t.* to lie or be situated all round, to encompass, to environ, to encircle, to invest, to enclose; to cause to be surrounded in this way. *n*. an edging, a border; the floor-covering, or staining of floorboards, between the skirting and the carpet. **surroundings,** *n.pl.* things around a person or thing, environment, circumstances. [OF *soronder, surunder,* to overflow (SUR-, over, L *undāre,* to flow, cp. ABOUND, conf. with ROUND[2])]

†**sursize,** *n*. a penalty in feudal law for not paying castle-guard rent on the appointed day. [OF *sursise,* see SURCEASE]

sursolid, *a*. (*Math.*) of the fifth degree. *n*. the fifth power of a quantity. [SUR-, SOLID]

surtax, *n*. an additional tax; an additional graduated income tax formerly imposed in the UK in place of the supertax on all incomes above a certain amount. *v.i.* to impose a surtax.

surtitles, *n.pl.* a translation of the text of an opera etc. projected on a screen above the stage.

†**surtout,** *n*. a man's overcoat, esp. one like a frock-coat. [F (SUR-, *tout,* all, L *tōtum,* nom. *-tus,* whole)]

surv., (*abbr.*) surveyor.

surveillance, *n*. oversight, close watch, supervision. [F, from *surveiller* (*veiller,* L *vigilāre,* to watch, see VIGIL)]

survey[1], *v.t.* to look over, to take a general view of; to view with a scrutinizing eye; to examine closely; to examine and ascertain the condition, value etc. of (esp. a building); to determine by accurate observation and measurement the boundaries, extent, position, contours etc. of (a tract of country, coast, estate etc.). *v.i.* to carry out a survey. **surveyable,** *a*. **surveying,** *n*. **surveyor,** *n*. one who surveys, esp. one who measures land; an inspector (of customs, weights and measures etc.); †an overseer. **surveyorship,** *n*. [A-F *surveier* (OF *veeir,* L *vidēre,* to see)]

survey[2], *n*. the act or process of surveying; a general view; a careful examination, investigation, inspection or scrutiny; an account based on this; the operation of surveying land etc.; a department carrying this on; a map, plan etc. recording the results of this; (*N Am.*) a district for the collection of customs. [as prec.]

survive, *v.t.* to live longer than, to outlive, to outlast; to be alive after, to live through, to outlive or outlast (an event, period etc.). *v.i.* to be still alive or in existence. **survival,** *n.* the act or condition of surviving; a person, thing, custom, opinion etc. surviving into a new state of things. **survival of the fittest,** the preservation of forms of life that have proved themselves best adapted to their environment, the process or result of natural selection. **survivor,** *n.* **survivorship,** *n.* [F *survivre,* L *supervīvere* (*vīvere,* to live)]

sus[1], *n.* (*sl.*) suspicion of loitering with criminal intent. [short for SUSPICION]

sus[2] SUSS.

sus-, *pref.* SUB- (before *p, t* and some L derivatives in *c*).

susceptible, *a.* admitting (of); capable of being influenced or affected, accessible, liable (to); impressionable, sensitive. **susceptibility,** *n.* the condition or quality of being susceptible; (*pl.*) sensitive feelings, sensibilities. **susceptibleness,** *n.* **susceptibly,** *adv.* **susceptive,** *a.* readily receiving impressions etc., susceptible; receiving emotional impressions. **susceptiveness, susceptivity, susceptor,** *n.* †**suscipient,** *a.* †**suscipiency,** *n.* [F, from L *suscipere* (*capere,* to take), p.p. *susceptus*]

†**suscitate,** *v.t.* to rouse, to excite. †**susitation,** *n.* [L *suscitātus,* p.p. of *suscitāre* (*citāre,* to CITE)]

sushi, *n.* a Japanese dish of cold rice cakes with a vinegar dressing and garnishes of raw fish etc. [Jap.]

susi, *n.* an E Indian striped cotton and silk fabric. [Hind.]

suspect[1], *v.t.* to imagine to exist, to have an impression of the existence of without proof, to surmise; to be inclined to believe to be guilty but upon slight evidence, to doubt the innocence of; to hold to be uncertain, to doubt, to mistrust. *v.i.* to be suspicious. **suspectable,** *a.* **suspectedly,** *adv.* †**suspectless,** *a.* [F *suspecter,* L *suspectāre,* from *suspectus,* suspected, p.p. of *suspicere* (*specere,* to look)]

suspect[2], *a.* suspected, under suspicion, suspicious; doubtful, uncertain. *n.* a person suspected of crime etc.

suspend, *v.t.* to hang up, to hang from something above; to sustain from falling or sinking; to hold (particles) in a suspension; to render temporarily inoperative or cause to cease for a time, to intermit; to defer; to debar temporarily from a privilege, office etc. **to suspend payment,** to be unable to meet one's financial engagements. **suspended animation,** *n.* temporary ceasing of the body's vital functions. **suspended sentence,** *n.* a prison sentence that is not served unless a further crime is committed. **suspender,** *n.* one who or that which suspends; (*pl.*) attachments to hold up socks or stockings; (*N Am.*) braces. **suspender belt,** *n.* a belt with stocking suspenders attached. **suspensible,** *a.* **suspendibility,** *n.* [F *suspendre,* L *suspendere* (*pendere,* to hang), p.p. *suspensus*]

suspense, *n.* a state of uncertainty, doubt or apprehensive expectation or waiting; (*Law*) a temporary cessation of a right etc. **suspensible** etc. SUSPEND. **suspension,** *n.* the act of suspending; the state of being suspended; a dispersion of solid particles in a fluid; a system of springs etc. that supports the body of a vehicle on the axles. **suspension-bridge,** *n.* a bridge sustained by flexible supports passing over a tower or elevated pier and secured at each extremity. **suspensive, suspensory,** *a.* having power to suspend; uncertain, doubtful. **suspensively,** *adv.* **suspensor,** *n.* **suspensory, suspensorium,** *n.* (*pl.* **-ries, -riums, -ria**) a supporting ligament, part etc., esp. the bone or bones by which the lower jaw is suspended from the cranium in vertebrates. [F *suspens,* suspended, L *suspensus,* see prec.]

suspicion, *n.* the act or feeling of one who suspects; belief in the existence of wrong or guilt on inadequate proof, doubt, mistrust; a very slight amount; a trace. **suspicionless,** *a.* **suspicious,** *a.* inclined to suspect; entertaining suspicion; expressing or showing suspicion; exciting or likely to excite suspicion. **suspiciously,** *adv.* **suspiciousness,** *n.* [OF *souspeçon* (F *soupçon*), L *suspitio -ōnem,* from *suspicere,* to SUSPECT]

†**suspire,** *v.i.* to sigh; to breathe. **suspiration,** *n.* [OF *souspirer,* L *suspirāre* (SUB-, *spirāre,* to breathe)]

suss, sus, *v.t.* (*past, p.p.* **sussed**) to work out or discover the true facts of. **to suss out,** to investigate, find out about.

Sussex, *n.* former county of England, on the south coast, now divided into EAST SUSSEX and WEST SUSSEX.

sustain, *v.t.* to bear the weight of, to hold up, to keep from falling; to bear up against or under; to stand, to undergo without yielding; to experience, to suffer; to nourish, provide sustenance for; to enable to bear something, to keep from failing, to strengthen, to encourage, to keep up; to prolong; to maintain, to uphold; to establish by evidence; to support, to confirm, to bear out, to substantiate. **sustainable,** *a.* **sustainer,** *n.* a person who, or a thing that, sustains; the principal motor in a rocket. [OF *sustenir* (F *soutenir*), L *sustinēre* (*tenēre,* to hold)]

sustenance, *n.* that which sustains, the means of support or maintenance; the nourishing element in food; food, subsistence; the act of sustaining.

sustentaculum, *n.* a supporting body part, tissue etc. **sustentacular,** *a.*

sustentation, *n.* support, maintenance. **sustentation fund,** *n.* a fund to assist indigent clergy. **sustentator, sustentor,** *n.*

susurrant, -rous, *a.* whispering, rustling, murmuring. **susurration, susurrus,** *n.* [L *susurrans -ntem,* pres.p. of *susurrāre,* from *susurrus,* whisper]

Sutherland, *n.* **Graham (Vivian)** (1903–80), English painter, active mainly in the south of France from the late 1940s. He is noted for portraits, landscapes, and religious subjects. His landscapes of the 1930s show a strong surrealist influence.

†**sutile** , *a.* done or made by stitching. [L *sūtilis,* from *suere,* to sew]

sutler, *n.* a person who follows an army and sells provisions, liquor etc. **sutlership,** *n.* **sutlery,** *n.* [Dut. *zoetelaar,* from *zoetelen,* cp. G *sudeln,* to sully (cogn. with SUDS and SEETHE)]

sutor, *n.* a cobbler. **sutorial,** *a.* [L, from *suere,* to sew]

sutra, *n.* a rule, a precept, an aphorism; (*pl.*) Brahminical books of rules, doctrine etc. [Sansk.]

suttee, *n.* a Hindu custom by which the widow was burnt on the funeral pyre with her dead husband; a widow so burnt. **sutteeism,** *n.* [Sansk. *satī,* virtuous wife]

suttle, *n., a.* (the weight) taken after the tare has been deducted and the tret has yet to be allowed. [var. of SUBTLE]

Sutton Hoo, *n.* village near Woodbridge, Suffolk, England, where in 1939 a Saxon ship burial was excavated. He is the funeral monnument of Raedwald, king of the East Angles, who died about 624 or 625. The jewellery, armour, and weapons discovered were placed in the British Museum, London.

suture, *n.* the junction of two parts by their margins as if by sewing, esp. of the bones of the skull; the uniting of two body surfaces, esp. the edges of a wound, by stitching; catgut, silk etc. used in uniting body surfaces; a stitch or seam made in this way. *v.t.* to unite by a suture. **sutural, sutured,** *a.* **suturally,** *adv.* **suturation,** *n.* [F, from L *sūtūra,* from *suere,* to sew, p.p. *sūtus*]

suzerain, *n.* a feudal lord, a lord paramount; a state having sovereignty or control over another. **suzerainty,** *n.* [F, from *sus,* L *susum, sursum,* above, after *souverain,* SOVEREIGN]

Suzhou, *n.* (formerly **Soochow** and **Wuhsien** 1912–49) city on the GRAND CANAL, in Jiangsu province, China; population (1983) 670,000. It has embroidery and jade carving traditions, and Shizilin and Zhuozheng gardens. The city dates from about 1000 BC, and the name Suzhou from the 7th century AD; it was reputedly visited by Marco POLO.

Suzuki, *n.* **Zenko** (1911–), Japanese politician. Originally a socialist member of the Diet in 1947, he became a Conservative (Liberal Democrat) in 1949, and was prime minister from 1980–82.

sv, (*abbr.*) under the word or heading. [L *sub verbo* or *voce*]

Svalbard, *n.* Norwegian archipelago in the Arctic Ocean. The main island is Spitsbergen; other islands include North East Land, Edge Island, Barento Island, and Prince Charles Foreland. **area** 62,000 sq km/ 24,000 sq miles. **towns** Long Year City on Spitsbergen. **population** (1982) 4000 including 1450 Norwegians and 2500 Russians. **products** coal, phosphates, asbestos, iron ore, and galena are mined by the USSR and Norway.

svelte, *a.* esp. of a woman's figure, slender, lissom. [F, from It. *svelto*]

Sverdlovsk, *n.* (formerly **Ekaterinburg**, until 1924) industrial town in W USSR, in the E foothills of the Urals; population (1987) 1,331,000. Industries include copper, iron, platinum, engineering, and chemicals. Nicholas II and his family were murdered there in 1918.

SW, (*abbr.*) southwest, southwestern; short wave.

swab, *n.* a mop for cleaning floors, decks, the bore of a gun etc.; a small piece of cotton-wool or gauze used for removing blood, dressing wounds, taking specimens etc.; (*Naut. sl.*) an officer's epaulet; (*sl.*) a lubber, a clumsy fellow. *v.t.* (*past, p.p.* **swabbed**) to rub, wipe or clean with a swab or mop. **swabber,** *n.* [back-formation from *swabber,* Dut. *zwabber,* drudge, from *zwabberen,* to do dirty work, cp. G *schwabbern,* prob. cogn. with *schwappen,* to spill]

Swabia, *n.* (German **Schwaben**) historic region of SW Germany, an independent duchy in the Middle Ages. It includes Augsburg and Ulm, and forms part of the *Länder* (states) of Buden-Württemberg, Bavaria, and Hessen. **Swabian**, *a.* of or pertaining to Swabia. *n.* a native or inhabitant of Swabia.

swaddle, *v.t.* to wind or swathe in or as in a bandage, wrap, or wraps; to wrap in swaddling-clothes to restrict movement. **swaddler,** *n.* (*Irish sl.*) a Protestant, a Methodist. **swaddling-bands, -clothes, †-clouts,** *n.pl.* cloth bands used for swaddling an infant. [OE *swethel,* swaddling-band, from *swathu,* SWATH]

Swadeshi, *n.* a movement in India for self-government, and agitation until this was obtained. [Hind.]

swag, †*v.i.* (*past, p.p.* **swagged**) to hang loose and heavy; to sag. *v.t.* to hang or arrange in swags. *n.* an ornamental festoon; a heavy, loosely hanging fold of fabric; booty obtained by robbery, esp. burglary; a pack or bundle of personal effects, baggage. **swag-bellied,** *a.* having a large prominent belly. **swag-belly,** *n.* **swagman,** *n.* (*Austral.*) a man who carries his swag about with him in search of work. **swagshop,** *n.* (*sl.*) a shop where cheap and trashy goods are sold. [cp. Norw. *svagga,* cogn. with SWAY]

swage[1]**,** *n.* a tool for shaping wrought-iron etc. by hammering or pressure. *v.t.* to shape with a swage. **swage-block,** *n.* a heavy iron block or anvil with grooves etc. used for shaping metal. [F *suage,* etym. doubtful]

†swage[2]**, (***Milton***)** ASSUAGE.

swagger, *v.i.* to walk, strut or go (about etc.) with an air of defiance, self-confidence or superiority; to talk or behave in a blustering, boastful or hectoring manner. *v.t.* to bluster or bluff (a person into, out of etc.). *n.* a swaggering walk, gait or behaviour; bluster, dash, self-conceit. *a.* (*coll.*) smart, fashionable, swell. **swagger-cane, -stick,** *n.* a short cane with metal head carried by soldiers. **swagger-coat,** *n.* a loose coat made on full lines that sways when the wearer walks. **swaggerer,** *n.* **swaggeringly,** *adv.* [freq. of SWAG]

swagman, -shop SWAG.

Swahili, *n.* a Bantu people of Zanzibar and the adjoining coast; their language which is strongly influenced by Arabic is spoken in Kenya, Tanzania and several other parts of E Africa. [Arab. *Waswahili,* coast people]

swain, *n.* (*poet.*) a young rustic; a country gallant; a male lover. **†swainish,** *a.* **†swainishness,** *n.* [Icel. *sveinn,* cp. OE *swān*]

swallow[1]**,** *n.* a small, swift, migratory bird of the genus *Hirundo,* with long, pointed wings and forked tail; a swift or other bird resembling the swallow. **one swallow does not make summer,** a warning against jumping to conclusions. **swallow dive,** *n.* a dive with the arms outstretched. **swallow-fish,** *n.* the sapphirine gurnard, *Trigla hirundo.* **swallow tail,** *n.* a deeply-forked tail; a butterfly with such a tail, also a humming-bird; the points of a burgee; a dove-tail; (*often pl.*) a swallow-tailed coat, a dress-coat. **swallow-tailed,** *a.* with deeply-forked tail. [OE *swalewe* (cp. Dut. *zwaluw,* G *Schwalbe,* Icel. *svala*), cogn. with SWELL]

swallow[2]**,** *v.t.* to take through the mouth and throat into the stomach; to absorb, to engulf, to overwhelm, to consume (up); to accept with credulity; to accept without resentment, to put up with; to refrain from showing or expressing; to retract, to recant; to say indistinctly. *v.i.* to perform the action of swallowing. *n.* the gullet or oesophagus; the amount swallowed at once; a swallow-hole. **swallow-hole,** (*dial.*) **swallett,** *n.* an opening in limestone into which a stream or streamlet runs. **swallowable,** *a.* **swallower,** *n.* [ME *swolowen,* OE *swelgan,* cp. Dut. *zwelgen,* G *schwelgen,* Icel. *svelgja*]

swam, *past* SWIM.

swami, *n.* a Hindu religious teacher. [Sansk. *svamin,* master]

swamp, *n.* a tract of wet, spongy land, a bog, a marsh. *v.t.* to cause (a boat etc.) to be filled with or to sink in water; to plunge or sink into a bog; to overwhelm, to render helpless with difficulties, numbers etc. *v.i.* to fill with water, to sink, to founder. **swamp gum,** *n.* (*Austral.*) a variety of eucalyptus growing in swamps. **swamp oak,** *n.* the casuarina. **swamp-ore,** *n.* bog-iron ore. **swamp sparrow,** *n.* (*New Zealand*) the fern-bird. **swampy,** *a.* [cp. SUMP, Dut. *zwamp;* perh. rel. to OE *swamm,* G *Schwamm,* sponge]

Swan, *n.* **Joseph Wilson** (1828–1914), English inventor of the incandescent filament electric lamp, and of bromide paper for use in photography.

swan, *n.* a large, web-footed aquatic bird of the genus *Cygnus,* with a long neck and usu. white plumage, noted for its grace in the water; the constellation Cygnus; a poet, a singer (with alln. to the swan-song). *v.i.* to wander aimlessly (about, around etc.). **swan dive,** *n.* (*N Am.*) a swallow dive. **swan-herd,** *n.* one who tends swans, esp. a royal officer superintending swan-marks. **swan-hopping** SWAN-UPPING. **swan maiden,** *n.* in German folk-lore, a maiden able to take the shape of a swan. **swan mark,** *n.* a mark on a swan showing ownership, usu. a notch on the upper mandible. **swan marker,** *n.* **swan neck,** *n.* a pipe, tube, rail etc. curved like a swan's neck, esp. the end of a discharge-pipe. **swansdown,** *n.* down obtained from a swan; a thick cotton cloth with a downy nap on one side. **swan shot,** *n.* a large size of shot. **swanskin,** *n.* a swan's skin with the feathers on; a soft, fine-twilled flannel. **swan-song,** *n.* the song traditionally believed to be sung by a dying swan; the last or dying work, esp. of a poet; any final work, performance etc. **swan-upping,** *n.* the annual inspection and marking of Thames swans. **swanlike,** *a.* **swannery,** *n.* a place where swans are kept or bred. [OE (cp. Dut. *zwaan,* G *Schwan,* Icel. *svanr*), perh. cogn. with Sansk. *swan,* L *sonāre,* to SOUND[2]]

swank[1]**,** *v.i.* (*sl.*) to swagger, to show off, to bluster. *n.* swagger, bluster. **swanky,** *a.* showing off, showy; stylish, elegant. [etym. doubtful, perh. MG *swanken,* to sway]

swank[2]**,** *n.* (*Sc.*) slender, slim; agile, supple. **swankie,** *n.* an active fellow. [MDan. *swanc,* OE *swancor,* supple, pliant]

swap, swop, *v.t., v.i.* (*past, p.p.* **swapped**) to exchange, to barter. *n.* an exchange, a barter; something exchanged in a swap. **swapper,** *n.* **swapping,** *a.*

large, strapping. [prob. from obs. *swap,* ME *swappen,* to strike]

swape, *n.* (*dial.*) a pump-handle; a long oar or sweep; a pole for lifting water from a well, a sconce. **swape-well,** *n.* [var. of SWEEP]

SWAPO, (*abbr.*) South-West Africa People's Organization, formed in 1959 in South West Africa (NAMIBIA) to oppose South African rule. SWAPO guerrillas, led by Sam Nujoma, began attacking with support from Angola. Since 1966 SWAPO has been recognized by the United Nations as the legitimate government of Namibia.

swaraj, *n.* home rule for India; agitation to secure it. [Sansk. *svaraj,* self-ruling]

sward, *n.* a surface of land covered with thick short grass; turf. **swarded, swardy,** *a.* [OE *sweard,* skin, cp. Dut. *zwoord,* G *Schwarte,* Icel. *svörthr,* skin, hide]

†**sware,** *past* SWEAR.

swarf, *n.* grit, metal filings, chips, grindings. [ON, file-dust]

swarm[1], *n.* a large number of small animals, insects, people etc., esp. when moving in a confused mass; (*pl.*) great numbers; a cluster of honey-bees issuing from a hive with a queen-bee and seeking a new home. *v.i.* of bees, to collect together in readiness for emigrating, to leave (or go out of) a hive in a swarm; to congregate, to throng, to be exceedingly numerous; to move (about etc.) in a swarm; of places, to be thronged or overcrowded (with). **swarm-cell, -spore,** *n.* a zoospore. [OE *swearm* (cp. Dut. *zwerm,* G *Schwarm,* Icel. *svarmr*), perh. cogn. with Sansk. *svr,* to sound, L *susurrus,* see SUSURRANT]

swarm[2], *v.t., v.i.* to climb (up a tree, rope, pole etc.) by embracing it with the arms and legs. [etym. doubtful]

†**swart,** *a.* of a dark colour; swarthy. [OE *sweart* (cp. Dut. *zwart,* G *schwarz,* Icel. *svartr*), cogn. with L *sordidus,* SORDID]

swarthy, *a.* dark or dusky in complexion. **swarthily,** *adv.* **swarthiness,** *n.* [obs. *swarth,* var. of SWART]

swash, *v.i.* to make a noise as of splashing water; of liquid, to wash or splash about; to strike noisily or violently. *v.t.* to strike noisily or violently. *n.* a washing, dashing or splashing of water; a blustering noise. **swashbuckler,** *n.* a bully, a bravo; an adventurer, a dare-devil. **swash-buckling,** *a.* **swash letter,** *n.* an ornamental italic capital with tails and flourishes. **swash-plate,** *n.* an inclined disc on a revolving axis transmitting an up-and-down motion to a bar. **swasher,** *n.* [imit., cp. Swed. dial. *svasska*]

swastika, *n.* a cross with arms bent at a right angle, used as a symbol of anti-semitism or Nazism, a fylfot or gammadion. [Sansk., fortunate (*su,* well, *asti,* being)]

swat, *v.t.* (*past, p.p.* **swatted**) to hit sharply; to crush (a fly) thus. *n.* a sharp blow. **swatter,** *n.* [onomat.]

swatch, *n.* a sample of cloth. [etym. doubtful]

swath, swathe, *n.* a row or ridge of grass, corn etc. cut and left lying on the ground; the space cut by a scythe, machine etc. in one course; a broad strip or band; a space left as if by a scythe. [OE *swœth, swathu,* track (cp. Dut. *zwaad,* G *Schwad,* swath, LG *swade,* scythe, Norw. *swada,* to slice off)]

swathe[1], *v.t.* to bind or wrap in or as in a bandage, cloth etc. *n.* a bandage, a wrapping. [ME *swathen,* cp. *swethel,* SWADDLE, perh. as prec.]

swathe[2] SWATH.

sway, *v.i.* to move backwards and forwards, to swing, to oscillate irregularly; to be unsteady, to waver, to vacillate; to lean or incline to one side or in different directions; †to bear rule, to govern. *v.t.* to cause to oscillate, waver, or vacillate; to cause to incline to one side; to bias; to influence, to control, to rule. *n.* rule, dominion, control; the act of swaying, a swing. **sway-back,** *n.* a hollowed or sagging back, esp. in horses. **sway-backed, swayed,** *a.* having the back hollowed, strained or weakened. [ME *sweyen,* cp. Dan. *svaie,* Norw. *svaga,* Swed. *svaja,* to jerk]

Swazi Kingdom, *n.* southern African Kingdom, established by Sobhuza (died about 1840) as a result of the MFECANE disturbances, and named after his successor Mswati (ruled 1840–75).

Swaziland, *n.* Kingdom of, country in SE Africa, bounded by Mozambique and the Transvaal province of South Africa. **area** 17,400 sq km/6716 sq miles. **capital** Mbabane. **physical** central valley; mountains in W. **population** (1989) 757,000; annual growth rate 3%. **exports** sugar, citrus, timber, asbestos, iron ore. **language** Swazi 90%, English (both official). **religion** Christian, both Protestant and Catholic; animist.

sweal, *v.i.* (*dial.*) to burn away slowly; of a candle, to melt and run. *v.t.* to dress (a pig) by singeing the bristles off. [OE *swēlan* (cp. G *schwelen*), cogn. with SULTRY]

swear, *v.i.* (*past* **swore,** †**sware,** *p.p.* **sworn**) to affirm solemnly invoking God or some other sacred person or object as witness or pledge, to take an oath; to appeal (to) as witness of an oath; to use profane or obscene language; to give evidence on oath; to promise on oath. *v.t.* to utter or affirm with an oath, to take oath (that); to cause to take oath, to administer an oath to, to bind by an oath; to declare, to vow, to promise or testify upon oath; to utter profanely or obscenely. *n.* an act or spell of swearing; a profane oath. **to swear by,** (*coll.*) to have or profess great confidence in. **to swear in,** to induct into office with the administration of an oath. **to swear off,** to renounce solemnly. **swear-word,** *n.* an obscene or taboo word. [OE *swerian* (cp. Dut. *zweren,* G *schwören,* Icel. *sverja,* Swed. *svara,* to answer), cogn. with SWARM[1]]

sweat, *n.* the moisture exuded from the skin of an animal, perspiration; moisture exuded from or deposited in drops on any surface; the act or state of sweating (*coll.*) drudgery, toil, hard labour, exertion; (*coll.*) a state of anxiety, a flurry; (*coll.*) an old soldier. *v.i.* (*past, p.p.* **sweated, sweat**) to exude sweat, to perspire; to emit moisture; of moisture, to exude; to collect surface moisture; to be in a flurry or state of anxiety, panic etc., to smart; to toil, to labour, to drudge; to be sweated; to carry on business on the sweating-system. *v.t.* to emit as sweat; to make (an animal etc.) sweat by exertion; to employ at starvation wages, to exact the largest possible amount of labour from at the lowest pay, by utilizing competition; to bleed, to subject to extortion; to subject (hides, tobacco etc.) to fermentation; to wear away (coins) by friction etc.; to remove sweat from (horses etc.) with a scraper; to melt (solder etc.) by heating; to unite (metal pieces) in this way; to heat (esp. vegetables) in fat until the juices exude. **no sweat,** (*sl.*) no difficulty or problem, without trouble. **to sweat blood,** (*sl.*) to work or worry to an extreme degree. **to sweat out,** to remove or get rid of by sweating; (*coll.*) to endure, live through. **sweatband,** *n.* a band of absorbent material round the forehead or wrist, as worn in some sports to keep sweat out of the eyes or from the hands. **sweat-shirt,** *n.* a loose, long-sleeved sweater made from cotton jersey. **sweatshop,** *n.* a factory or other work-place that employs the sweating system. **sweated,** *a.* pertaining to or produced by the sweating system. **sweater,** *n.* a (thick) jersey, jumper or pull-over; one who or that which causes to sweat. **sweating,** *a.* causing or enduring sweat. **sweating-bath,** *n.* a vapour-bath for exciting sweat. **sweating-iron,** *n.* a scraper for removing sweat from horses. **sweating-room,** *n.* a sudatorium, esp. in a Turkish bath; a room for sweating superfluous moisture from cheese. **sweating sickness,** *n.* a form of malaria epidemic in the 15th and 16th cents. **sweating system,** *n.* the practice of employing operatives at starvation wages in unhealthy conditions and for long hours. **sweaty,** *a.* **sweatily,** *adv.* **sweatiness,** *n.* [OE *swat* cp. Dut. *zweet,* G *Schweiss,* Icel. *sveiti,* also Sansk. *svēda-,* Gr. *hidrōs,* L *sūdor*)]

Swede, *n.* a native or inhabitant of Sweden. **swede,** *n.* a Swedish turnip, *Brassica rutabaga.*

Sweden, *n.* Kingdom of (*Konungariket Sverige*), country in N Europe on the Baltic Sea, bounded to the W by Norway and to the NE by Finland. **area** 450,000 sq km/173,745 sq miles. **capital** Stockholm. **towns** Göteborg, Malmö, Uppsala, Norrköping, Västerås. **physical** mountains in the NW; plains in the south; much of the land is forested. **population** (1989) 8,371,000 (including 1,200,000 postwar immigrants from Finland, Turkey, Yugoslavia, Greece); annual growth rate 0.1%. **exports** aircraft, cars, domestic equipment, ballbearings, drills, missiles, electronics, petrochemicals, textiles, furnishings, ornamental glass. **language** Swedish. **religion** Christian (Evangelical Lutheran).

Swedenborg, *n.* **Emmanuel** (1688–1772), Swedish theologian and philosopher. He trained as a scientist, but from 1747 concentrated on scriptural study, and in *Divine Love and Wisdom* (1763) concluded that the Last Judgment had taken place in 1757, and that the New Church, of which he was the prophet, had now been inaugurated. His writings are the scriptures of the sect popularly known as Swedenborgians, and his works are kept in circulation by the Swedenborg Society, London. **Swedenborgian,** *a.* of or pertaining to Swedenborg or Swedenborgianism. *n.* a member of the Swedenborgian or New Church, or a believer in the doctrines of Swedenborg. **Swedenborgianism,** *n.*

Swedish, *a.* pertaining to Sweden or its inhabitants. *n.* the language of the Swedes.

Swedish language, *n.* a member of the Germanic branch of the Indo-European language family, spoken in Sweden and Finland and closely related to Danish and Norwegian.

sweeny, *n.* atrophy of a muscle, esp. of the shoulder in horses. [etym. doubtful]

sweep, *v.i.* (*past, p.p.* **swept**) to glide, move or pass along with a strong, swift continuous motion; of the eye, to range unchecked; of land, a curve etc., to extend continuously; to go with a stately motion. *v.t.* to carry (along, away etc.) with powerful or unchecked force; to move swiftly and powerfully over, across or along, to range, to scour; esp. of the eyes, to pass over in swift survey; to pass over destructively; to rake, to enfilade, to clear; to gain an overwhelming victory in; to dredge (the bottom of a river etc.); to wipe out, remove, destroy; to clear dirt etc. from or clean with or as with a broom etc.; to collect or gather (up) with or as with a broom; to propel with sweeps; to cause to move with a sweeping motion. *n.* the act of sweeping; a clearance, a riddance; a sweeping motion; a sweeping curve, direction, piece of road etc.; a broad expanse; the range, reach or compass of a sweeping motion or of an instrument, weapon, implement etc. having this motion; a long oar used to propel barges or sailing-vessels in a calm; a swape; a chimney-sweeper; (*dated*) a blackguard; a sweepstake. **to make a clean sweep,** to get rid of entirely. **to sweep the board,** to win everything. **sweepback,** *n.* the angle relatively to the axis at which an aircraft wing is set back. **sweepnet,** *n.* a sweep-seine; a butterfly net. **sweep (second) hand,** *n.* a watch or clock hand that registers seconds. **sweep-seine,** *n.* a long seine used for sweeping a large area. **sweeper,** *n.* one who sweeps; a carpet-sweeper; (*Austral.*) a worker in the woolsheds, a 'broomie'; (*Austral., coll.*) a slow train; a defensive player in soccer positioned behind the main defensive line. **sweeping,** *a.* that sweeps; covering a wide area; wide-ranging, comprehensive; without discrimination or qualification. *n.pl.* things collected by sweeping; (*fig.*) rubbish, refuse, litter. **sweepingly,** *adv.* **sweepingness,** *n.* [ME *swepen,* from *swǣp-,* stem of OE *swāpan,* to SWOOP]

sweepstake, sweepstakes, *n.* a lottery in which a number of persons stake sums on an event, esp. on a horse-race, the total amount staked being divided among the winning betters.

sweet, *a.* having a taste like that of honey or sugar; containing sugar or a sweetening ingredient; pleasing to the senses; fragrant; pleasant or melodious in sound; refreshing, restful; fresh, not salt or salted, not sour, bitter, stale or rancid; of butter, fresh, unsalted; free from acids or other corrosive substances; pleasant to the mind, agreeable, delightful; charming, amiable, gracious, lovable, dear, beloved. *n.* a sweet thing; a sweetmeat; a sweet dish, as a tart, pudding, ice etc.; the course at a meal after the meat; †(*pl.*) sweet scents, fragrance; the sweetness or the sweet part of anything; (*pl.*) pleasures, delights, pleasant experiences; dear one, darling. *adv.* sweetly. **†sweet-and-twenty,** young and charming. **to be sweet on,** to be in love with; to be very fond of. **to have a sweet tooth,** to be fond of sweet-tasting things. **sweet-and-sour,** *a.* cooked with sugar and vinegar or lemon juice. **sweet bay,** *n.* the laurel, bay-tree. **sweetbread,** *n.* the pancreas or thymus-gland, esp. of a calf or sheep, used as food. **sweet-brier** BRIER. **sweet chestnut** CHESTNUT. **sweet cicely** MYRRH². **sweetcorn,** *n.* a variety of maize with kernels rich in sugar; the kernels eaten as a vegetable when young. **sweet-flag** SWEET-RUSH. **sweet-gale** GALE³. **sweetheart,** *n.* a lover. *v.i.* to be love-making. **sweet-john,** *n.* the narrow-leaved variety of sweet-william. **sweetmeat,** *n.* an article of confectionery, usu. consisting wholly or principally of sugar, a sugar-plum, a bonbon; a fruit candied with sugar. **sweet-oil,** *n.* olive oil. **sweet pea,** *n.* an annual leguminous climbing plant, *Lathyrus odoratus,* with showy flowers. **sweet pepper,** *n.* a mild-flavoured capsicum fruit with a thick fleshy wall. **sweet potato,** *n.* a tropical climbing plant, *Batatas edulis,* with an edible root. **sweet root,** *n.* liquorice-root. **sweet-rush,** *n.* a flag, *Acorus calamus,* with an aromatic root-stock used in medicine, confectionery etc. **sweet-scented,** *a.* **sweet shop,** *n.* a shop where sweets are sold. **sweet sop,** *n.* a tropical American tree, *Anona squamosa*, allied to the custard-apple, with sweet, pulpy fruit. **sweet talk,** *n.* (*coll.*) flattery, blandishment. **sweet-talk,** *v.t.* to flatter, esp. in order to coax or persuade. **sweet-tempered,** *a.* **sweet violet,** *n.* the scented or wood-violet, *Viola odorata*. **sweet-water,** *n.* a sweet, watery variety of white grape. **sweet william,** *n.* a biennial species of pink, *Dianthus barbatus,* with dense clusters of showy and fragrant flowers. **sweet-willow,** *n.* the sweet-gale. **sweet wood,** *n.* the true laurel, *Laurus nobilis*; applied to other trees and shrubs of the family Lauraceae. **†sweet-wort,** *n.* any plant of a sweet taste. **sweeten,** *v.t.* to make sweet or sweeter; to make more agreeable or less unpleasant; to mollify, pacify. **sweetener,** *n.* a (sugar-free) sweetening agent; (*sl.*) a bribe. **sweetening,** *n.* **sweetie, sweety,** *n.* a sweet; a term of endearment. **sweeting,** *n.* a sweet variety of apple; †a term of endearment. **sweetish,** *a.* **sweetishness,** *n.* **sweetly,** *adv.* **sweetness,** *n.* [OE *swēte,* cp. Dut. *zoet,* G *süss*, Icel. *soetr,* Sansk. *svad,* to please, L *suāvis,* Gr. *hēdus*, sweet]

swell, *v.i.* (*p.p.* **swollen, swelled**) to dilate or increase in bulk or extent, to expand; to rise up from the surrounding surface, to bulge, to belly (out); to become greater in volume, strength or intensity; to rise in altitude; to be puffed up, to be elated, to strut, to be inflated with anger etc. *v.t.* to increase the size, bulk, volume or dimensions of; to inflate, to puff up. *n.* the act or effect of swelling; rise, increase, augmentation; a succession of long, unbroken waves in one direction, as after a storm; a bulge, a bulging part; (*Mus.*) an increase followed by a decrease in the volume of sound; a combined crescendo and diminuendo; a contrivance for gradually increasing and diminishing sound in an organ etc.; a swell-organ; (*coll.*) a person of high standing or importance, a showy, dashing or fashionable person. *a.* (*coll.*) characterized by showiness or display, smart, foppish, dandified; of distinction; (*N Am., coll.*) excellent, fine. **swell-blind,** *n.* one of the movable slats forming the front of a swell box. **swell-box,** *n.* a chamber containing the pipes of a swell organ, which is opened and closed to change the volume. **swell- organ,** *n.* an organ or partial organ with the pipes enclosed in a swell box. **swelled head,** *n.* conceit. **swelling,** *n.* the act of expanding etc., or the state of being swollen or augmented; an unnatural enlargement or tumefaction of a body part. **swellish,** *a.* (*coll.*). [OE *swellan* (cp. Dut. *zwellen,* G *schwellen,* Icel. *svella*), perh. cogn. with Gr. *saluein,* to surge]

swelter, †**swelt,** *v.i.* of the weather etc., to be hot, moist and oppressive, to cause faintness, languor or oppression; to be overcome and faint with heat; to sweat profusely. *n.* (*coll.*) a sweltering condition. **sweltering,** *a.* oppressively hot. **swelteringly,** *adv.* **sweltry,** *a.* [OE *sweltan* (cp. Icel. *svelta,* Goth. *swiltan,* OHG *schwelzan,* to be consumed), cogn. with SWEAL]

swept, *past, p.p.* SWEEP. **sweptback,** *a.* of an aircraft wing, slanting backwards, having sweepback. **sweptwing,** *a.* having sweptback wings.

swerve, *v.i.* to turn to one side, to deviate, to diverge from the direct or regular course. *v.t.* to cause to diverge, to deflect. *n.* the act of swerving, a sudden divergence or deflection. [OE *sweorfan,* to rub, file, polish (cp. Dut. *zwerven,* to swerve, Icel. *sverfa,* to file)]

SWG, (*abbr.*) standard wire gauge.

Swift, *n.* **Jonathan** (1667–1745), Irish satirist and Anglican cleric, known as the author of *Gulliver's Travels* (1726), an allegory describing travel to lands inhabited by giants, miniature people, and intelligent horses. Other works include *The Tale of the Tub* (1704), attacking corruption in religion and learning; contributions to the Tory paper *The Examiner* of which he was editor (1710–11); *A Modest Proposal* (1729) which suggested that children of the poor should be eaten; and many essays and pamphlets.

swift, *a.* moving or able to move with great rapidity, fleet, rapid, quick, speedy; ready, prompt, expeditious; passing rapidly, soon over, brief, unexpected, sudden. *adv.* swiftly. *n.* a small, long-winged insectivorous bird of the family Apodidae, esp. *Apus apus,* closely resembling the swallow; the common newt; a ghost-moth; the sail of a windmill. **swift-footed, -handed, -heeled, -winged,** *a.* running, acting, flying etc. with swiftness. **swifter,** *n.* (*Naut.*) a rope used to fasten, hold or tighten something. **swiftly,** *adv.* **swiftness,** *n.* [OE, from *swifan,* to move quickly (cp. Icel. *svīfa,* OHG *sweibōn*), cogn. with SWEEP]

swig, *v.t., v.i.* (*past, p.p.* **swigged**) (*coll.*) to drink in large draughts. *n.* (*coll.*) a large or deep draught of liquor. [perh. from OE *swelgan,* SWALLOW[2]]

swill, *v.t.* to wash, to rinse; to drink greedily. *v.i.* to drink to excess. *n.* a rinsing; liquid food for animals, esp. pigs, hog-wash; (liquid) rubbish, slops; a swig; †liquor taken in excess. **swiller,** *n.* **swillings,** *n.pl.* hogwash. [OE *swillian,* to wash, cp. Icel. *skyla*]

swim, *v.i.* (*pres.p.* **swimming,** *past* **swam,** *p.p.* **swum**) to float or be supported on water or other liquid; to move progressively in the water by the motion of the hands and feet, or fins, tail etc.; to glide along; to be drenched or flooded (with water etc.); to seem to reel or whirl round one; to have a feeling of dizziness; †to overflow, to abound. *v.t.* to pass, traverse or accomplish by swimming; to compete in (a race); to perform (a particular swimming stroke); to cause (a horse, boat etc.) to swim or float; to bear up, to float (a ship etc.). *n.* the act or a spell of swimming; a pool or run frequented by fish in a river; the swimming-bladder; the main current of life, business etc. **swim bladder** SWIMMING-BLADDER. **swimsuit** SWIMMING COSTUME. **swimmable,** *a.* **swimmer,** *n.* **swimmeret,** *n.* one of the appendages of a crustacean serving as a swimming-organ. **swimming-bath, -pool,** *n.* a bath or artificial pool for swimming in. **swimming-bell,** *n.* a bell-shaped swimming organ, as of a jellyfish. **swimming-bladder,** *n.* the air-bladder or sound of a fish. **swimming costume,** *n.* a woman's one-piece garment for swimming. **swimmingly,** *adv.* smoothly, easily, without impediment. [OE *swimman,* cp. Dut. *zwemmen,* G *schwimmen,* Icel. *svimma*), blended with OE *swīma,* a swoon (cp. Dut. *zwijm,* Icel. *svimi,* G *Schwindel*)]

Swinburne, *n.* **Algernon Charles** (1837–1909), English poet. He attracted attention with the choruses of his Greek-style tragedy *Atalanta in Calydon* (1865), but he and ROSSETTI were attached in 1871 as leaders of 'the fleshly school of poetry', and the revolutionary politics of *Songs before Sunrise* (1871) alienated others.

swindle, *v.t., v.i.* to cheat; to defraud grossly or deliberately. *n.* the act or process of swindling; a gross fraud or imposition, a fraudulent scheme; (*coll.*) a thing that is not what it pretends to be, a deception, a fraud. **swindler,** *n.* †**swindlery,** *n.* **swindlingly,** *adv.* [from *swindler,* G *Schwindler,* thoughtless person, cheat, from *schwindeln,* to be dizzy, from *Schwindel,* see prec.]

swine, *n.* (*pl.* **swine**) an ungulate omnivorous mammal of the family Suidae, esp. the genus *Sus,* a pig, a hog; a greedy, vicious or debased person; something difficult or unpleasant. **swine bread,** *n.* the truffle; the sowbread. **swine fever, -plague,** *n.* an infectious lung-disease affecting the pig. **swineherd,** *n.* one who tends swine. **swine pox,** *n.* a form of chicken-pox affecting swine. **swine's-snout,** *n.* the dandelion. **swinish,** *a.* **swinishly,** *adv.* **swinishness,** *n.* [OE *swīn* (cp. Dut. *swijn,* G *Schwein,* Icel. *svīn*), perh. orig. *a.*, cp. L *suīnus,* pertaining to swine, from *sus,* sow]

swing, *v.i.* (*past* **swung,** †**swang,** *p.p.* **swung**) to move to and fro, as a body suspended by a point or one side, to sway, hang freely as a pendulum, to oscillate, to rock; to turn on or as on a pivot, to move or wheel (round etc.) through an arc; to go with a swaying, undulating or rhythmical gait or motion; to go to and fro in a swing; (*coll.*) to hit out (at) with a swinging arm movement; to be hanged; to play swing music; to have the rhythmical quality of swing music; to fluctuate between emotions, decisions etc.; (*coll.*) to be lively or up-to-date; (*sl.*) to participate in wife-swapping. *v.t.* to cause to move to and fro, to sway, to oscillate; to wave to and fro, to brandish; to cause to turn or move around, as on a pivot or through an arc; to cause to go to and fro in a swing; to play or perform in the style of swing music; (*coll.*) to manipulate, influence; (*coll.*) to cause to happen, bring about. *n.* the act or state of swinging; a swinging or oscillating motion; a swinging gait or rhythm; the compass or sweep of a moving body; a curving or sweeping movement; a blow delivered with a sweeping arm movement; free course, unrestrained liberty; regular course of activity; a seat suspended by ropes etc., in which a person or thing may swing to and fro; a spell of swinging in this; swing music; a shift in opinion, condition etc. **in full swing,** in full activity or operation. **to swing the lead,** to trump up an excuse for evading a duty. **swing-back,** *n.* an arrangement for adjusting the screen and plate-holder at the back of a camera at different angles. **swing-boat,** *n.* a boat-shaped carriage for swinging in at fairs etc. **swing bridge,** *n.* a drawbridge opening by turning horizontally. **swing music, swing,** *n.* a style of playing jazz in which the basic melody and rhythm persist through individual interpretations of the theme, impromptu variations etc. **swingometer,** *n.* (*coll.*) a device showing the extent of swings in opinion, voting preferences etc. (in an election). **swing-plough,** *n.* a plough without wheels. **swing wheel,** *n.* the wheel driving a clock-pendulum, corresponding to the balance-wheel of a watch. **swing-wing,** *a.* of an aircraft, having movable wings allowing varying degrees of sweep-back at different speeds. **swinger,** *n.* **swinging,** *a.* that swings; (*coll.*) lively or up-to-date. **swingingly,** *adv.* [OE *swingan,* cp. Swed. *svinga,* Dan. *svinge,* G *schwingen*]

†**swinge,** *v.t.* (*pres.p.* **swingeing, swinging**) to strike hard, to beat, to thrash. *n.* the sweep of anything in motion; a heavy blow; sway, rule. †**swinge-buckler,** *n.* a bully; a swash-buckler. **swingeing,** *a.* severe, great, huge. †**swingeingly,** *adv.* [OE *swengan,* causal of *swingan,* prec.]

swingle, *v.t.* to clean (flax) by beating with a swingle. *n.* a wooden instrument for beating flax to separate the woody parts from the fibre. **swinglebar, -tree,** *n.* the cross-bar pivoted in the middle to which the ends of a horse's traces are attached. **swingling-tow,** *n.* the coarse part of flax. [ME *swingelen,* freq. from OE *swingan,* to beat, to SWING]

swinish, etc. SWINE.

†**swink,** *v.i.* to labour, to toil. *v.t.* to tire or exhaust with labour. *n.* labour, toil, drudgery. †**swinker,** *n.* [OE

swincan, perh. cogn. with SWING]

swipe, *v.t.* to hit with great force, in cricket, golf etc.; to drink off, to gulp down; (*sl.*) to pilfer. *v.i.* to hit out with a swipe; to drink the contents of a glass at one go. *n.* a hard, swiping blow, esp. at cricket; (*pl., coll.*) thin, washy or inferior beer. **swiper,** *n.* [OE *swipian,* cogn. with SWEEP]

†**swire,** *n.* a depression between two hills or peaks, a saddle, a col. [OE *swīra, swēora,* neck]

swirl, *v.i.* to form eddies, to whirl about. *v.t.* to carry (along, down etc.) with an eddying motion. *n.* a whirling motion, an eddy; the furious rush of a fish through water, or the disturbance so caused; a winding or curling pattern or figure. **swirly,** *a.* [cp. Norw. *svirla,* freq. of *sverra,* to hum, to whirl; cogn. with SWARM[1]]

swish, *v.i.* to make a whistling sound in cutting through the air; to move with such a sound. *v.t.* to make such a whistling movement with; to strike or cut (off) with such a sound; to flog, to thrash, esp. with a birch. *n.* a whistling sound, movement or blow; a stroke with a birch etc. *a.* (*coll.*) smart, elegant. [imit.]

Swiss, *a.* of or pertaining to Switzerland or its inhabitants. *n.* (*pl.* **Swiss**) a native or inhabitant of Switzerland. **Swiss chard** CHARD. **Swiss cheese plant,** common name for *Monstera,* plant of the Arum family. **Swiss Guards,** *n.pl.* mercenaries formerly employed as bodyguards in France, Naples etc., and still at the Vatican. **swiss roll,** *n.* a thin sponge cake, rolled up around a filling, esp. of jam.

switch, *n.* a small flexible twig or rod; a (false) tress of hair; a mechanism for diverting railway trains or vehicles from one line to another, or for completing or interrupting an electric circuit, transferring current from one wire to another etc.; a shift, change; an exchange. *v.t.* to lash or beat with a switch; to move, whisk or snatch (away etc.) with a jerk; to shift (a train etc.) from one line to another; to turn (on or off) with a switch; to connect or disconnect (a user of a telephone) thus; to change, divert. *v.i.* to move or swing with a careless or jerking movement, to whisk; to cut (off) connection on a telephone etc.; to make a change, to shift. **to switch off,** (*coll.*) to stop listening or paying attention, to lose interest. **to switch on,** (*coll.*) to become alive or responsive to. **switchblade,** *n.* a flick knife. **switchboard,** *n.* a board on which switches are fixed controlling electric or telephonic circuits. **switchman,** *n.* a man in charge of railway switches, a shunter. [MDut. *swick* (cp. LG *swikk,* G *Swecke,* tack, peg, *zwecken,* to prick), cogn. with TWITCH[1]]

switchback, *n.* a zigzag railway for ascending or descending steep inclines; a steeply ascending and descending road, track etc.; a railway on which the vehicles are carried over a series of ascending inclines by the momentum of previous descents, used for amusement at fairs etc.

switchel, *n.* (*N Am.*) a drink of molasses and water, flavoured with rum etc. [etym. doubtful]

swither, *v.i.* (*Sc.*) to hesitate. [etym. doubtful]

Swithun, St *n.* (d. 862), English priest, chancellor of King Ethelwolf and bishop of Winchester from 852. According to legend, the weather on his feast day (15 Jul.) is said to continue as either wet or fine for 40 days.

Switzer, *n.* a Swiss.

Switzerland, *n.* Swiss Confederation (German **Schweiz**, French **Suisse**, Romansch **Svizzera**), landlocked country in W Europe, bounded to the N by West Germany, to the E by Austria, to the S by Italy, and to the W by France. **area** 41,300 sq km/15,946 sq miles. **capital** Bern. **towns** Zürich, Geneva, Lausanne; river port Basel. **physical** most mountainous country in Europe (Alps and Jura Mountains). **population** (1989) 6,485,000; annual growth rate 0.2%. **exports** electrical goods, chemicals, pharmaceuticals, watches, precision instruments, confectionery, banking, insurance; tourism is important. **language** German 65%, French 18%, Italian 10%, Romansch 1%. **religion** Roman Catholic 50%, Protestant 48%.

swivel, *n.* a link or connection comprising a ring and pivot or other mechanism allowing the two parts to revolve independently; a support allowing free horizontal rotation; a swivel-gun. *v.i., v.t.* (*past, p.p.* **swivelled**) to turn on a swivel or pivot. **swivel chair,** *n.* a chair that revolves on its base. **swivel-eye,** *n.* a squinting eye. **swivel-eyed,** *a.* **swivel gun,** *n.* a gun mounted on a pivot. **swivel-hook, -joint** etc., *n.* [OE *swīfan,* see SWIFT, with agent suf. -LE]

swizzle, *v.t., v.i.* (*dial.*) to drink immoderately. *n.* a mixed drink of various kinds; (*coll.*) a cheat, a fraud. **swizzle-stick,** *n.* a stick with a brush-like end for frothing drinks. [perh. rel. to SWIG]

swob, etc. SWAB.

swollen, †**swoln,** *p.p.* SWELL.

swoon, *v.i.* to fall into a fainting fit; of music etc., to sink or die away. *n.* a faint. **swooningly,** *adv.* [ME *swownen, swoghenen,* from OE *swogan,* see SOUGH[1]]

swoop, *v.i.* to descend upon prey etc. suddenly, as a hawk, to come (down) upon, to attack suddenly. *v.t.* to fall on suddenly and seize, to snatch (up). *n.* a sudden plunge of or as of a bird of prey on its quarry; a sudden descent, attack, seizing or snatching; (*coll.*) a snatching up of all at once. [OE *swāpan,* to rush (cp. Icel. *sveipa,* G *schweifen,* to rove), cogn. with SWEEP]

swoosh, *v.i.* to move with or make a rushing sound. *n.* this sound.

swop SWAP.

sword, *n.* a weapon, usu. consisting of a long blade fixed in a hilt with a guard for the hand, used for cutting or thrusting; a swordlike (body) part or object; the power of the sword, military power, sovereignty; war, destruction in war, death. **sword of Damocles** DAMOCLEAN. **sword of justice,** judicial authority. **sword of State,** a sword carried before the sovereign etc. on ceremonial occasions. **Sword of the Spirit,** the word of God. **to put to the sword,** to kill (esp. those captured or defeated in war). **sword-arm,** *n.* the right arm. **sword-bayonet,** *n.* a sword-shaped bayonet. **sword bearer,** *n.* an officer who carries a sword of State. **sword belt,** *n.* a belt from which a sword is slung. **sword bill,** *n.* a S American humming-bird with a long sword-shaped bill. **sword blade,** *n.* **sword cane,** *n.* a hollow walking-stick enclosing a long, pointed blade. **sword cut,** *n.* a cut or scar inflicted by a sword. **sword dance,** *n.* a dance in which swords are brandished or clashed together or in which women pass under crossed swords; a Highland dance performed over two swords laid crosswise on the floor. **swordfish,** *n.* a sea-fish of the genus *Xiphias,* allied to the mackerel, having the upper jaw prolonged into a formidable swordlike weapon. **sword flag,** *n.* the yellow flag, *Iris pseudacorus.* **sword grass,** *n.* a species of sedge with swordlike leaves. **sword-guard,** *n.* the part of a sword-hilt protecting the hand. **sword-hand,** *n.* the right hand. **sword knot,** *n.* a ribbon or tassel tied to the hilt of a sword, orig. used for securing it to the wrist. †**sword-law,** *n.* government by the sword. **sword lily,** *n.* the gladiolus. **swordplay,** *n.* a combat between gladiators, fencing; repartee. **sword-player,** *n.* **swordproof,** *a.* **sword-shaped,** *a.* **swordsman,** *n.* one who carries a sword; one skilled in the use of the sword. **swordsmanship,** *n.* **swordstick,** *n.* a swordcane. **sworded,** *a.* wearing or armed with a sword. †**sworder,** *n.* a swordsman; a cut-throat. **swordless,** *a.* **swordlike,** *a.* [OE *sweord* (cp. Dut. *zwaard,* G *Schwert,* Icel. *sverth*), etym. doubtful]

swore, *past,* **sworn,** *p.p.* SWEAR.

swot, *v.i., v.t.* (*past, p.p.* **swotted**) (*coll.*) to study hard. *n.* hard study; a piece of hard work; one who studies hard. [var. of SWEAT]

†**swound,** SWOON.

swum, *p.p.* SWIM.

swung, *past, p.p.* SWING.

swy, *n.* (*Austral., coll.*) the game of two-up.

sybarite, *n.* a native or inhabitant of Sybaris, an ancient Greek colony in S Italy, noted for effeminacy, voluptuousness and luxury; a sensual and luxurious person. *a.* sybaritic. **sybaritic,** †**-ical** , *a.* **sybar-**

itism, *n.*
sybil, SIBYL.
sycamine, *n.* the black mulberry-tree. [L *sycamīnus,* Gr. *sukaminos,* perh. from Heb. *shiqmāh,* SYCAMORE]
sycamore, *n.* a medium-sized Eurasian tree, *Acer pseudoplatanus,* allied to the maple and plane; the sycamore-fig. **sycamore-fig,** *n.* a Syrian and Egyptian fig-tree, *Ficus sycomorus,* that is the sycamore of Scripture. **sycamore-maple,** *n.* the Eurasian sycamore. [var. of SYCOMORE]
sycee (silver), *n.* pure uncoined silver cast into ingots, usu. bearing the seal of a banker or assayer, and formerly used in China by weight as a medium of exchange. [Chin. *si sze,* fine silk]
sychnocarpous, *a.* bearing fruit more than once before dying, perennial. [Gr. *suchnos,* many, *karpos,* fruit]
sycomore (fig), *n.* the sycamore-fig. [L *sȳcomorus,* Gr. *sukomoros,* perh. as SYCAMINE, assim. to *sukon,* fig, *moron,* mulberry]
syconium, *n.* (*pl.* **-nia**) a multiple fruit developed from a fleshy receptacle having numerous flowers, as in the fig. [mod. L, from Gr. *sukon,* fig]
sycophant, *n.* a servile flatterer, a parasite; †an informer, a slanderer. *v.i., v.t.* to act or flatter in the manner of a sycophant. **sycophancy,** *n.* **sycophantic,** *a.* **sycophantish,** *a.* **sycophantism,** †**sycophantry,** *n.* **sycophantize, -ise,** *v.i.* [L *sȳcophanta,* Gr. *sukophantēs,* etym. doubtful, said to mean orig. an informer against persons exporting figs or plundering the sacred fig-trees (*sukon,* fig, *phainein,* to show)]
sycosis, *n.* a pustular eruption or inflammation of the scalp or bearded part of the face, barber's itch. [Gr. *sukōsis,* fig-like ulcer (*sukon,* fig, -OSIS)]
Sydney, *n.* capital and port of New South Wales, Australia; population (1986) 3,431,000. Industries include engineering, oil refining, electronics, scientific equipment, chemicals, clothing, and furniture. **Sydneysider,** *n.* (*Austral.*) a resident of Sydney. **Sydney silkie,** *n.* (*Austral.*) a little, long-haired dog.
syenite, *n.* a granular igneous rock consisting of orthoclase and hornblende, with or without quartz. **syenitic,** *a.* [L *Syēnītes lapis,* stone of *Syene,* Egypt]
syl-, *pref.* SYN- (before *l*).
syllable, *n.* a sound forming a word or part of a word, containing one vowel sound, with or without a consonant or consonants, and uttered at a single effort or vocal impulse; the least expression or particle of speech. *v.i.* to pronounce by syllables, to articulate; (*poet.*) to utter, to speak. **syllabary,** *n.* a catalogue of characters representing syllables; such characters collectively, serving the purpose of an alphabet in certain languages. **syllabic,** *a.* pertaining to, consisting of or based on a syllable or syllables; having each syllable distinctly articulated; representing the sound of a whole syllable, as distinct from *alphabetic.* **syllabically,** *adv.* **syllabicate, syllabify, syllabize, -ise,** *v.t.* to separate into or pronounce by syllables. **syllabication, syllabification,** *n.* **syllabled,** *a.* (*usu. in comb.*, as *two-syllabled*). [ME and OF *sillabe,* L *syllaba,* Gr. *sullabē* (*lab-,* base of *lambanein,* to take), assim. to PRINCIPLE etc.]
syllabub, *n.* a dish made by curdling cream with wine etc., adding flavouring and frothing it up.
syllabus, *n.* (*pl.* **-buses, -bi**) a list, outline, summary, abstract etc., giving the principal points or subjects of a course of lectures, teaching or study, examination requirements, hours of attendance etc.; a summary of points decided by the Curia, esp. the list of heretical doctrines etc. forming the appendix to the encyclical letter *Quanta cura* of Pius IX in 1864. [late L, from late Gr. *sullabos,* as SYLLABLE]
syllepsis, *n.* (*pl.* **-ses**) the application of a word in both the literal and the metaphorical senses at once, as in 'Doth sometimes counsel take and sometimes tea'; the connection of a verb or adjective with two nouns, with only one of which it is in syntactical agreement, as in 'Neither he nor I am there.' **sylleptic,** *a.* **sylleptically,** *adv.* [L, from Gr. *sullēpsis,* comprehension (*-lēpsis,* from *lambanein,* see SYLLABLE)]
syllogism, *n.* a form of argument consisting of three propositions, a major premise or general statement, a minor premise or instance, and a third deduced from these called the conclusion. **syllogistic,** *a.* **syllogistically,** *adv.* **syllogize, -ise,** *v.i., v.t.* to reason or deduce by syllogisms. **syllogization, -isation,** *n.* **syllogizer, -iser,** *n.* [ME and OF *silogime,* L *syllogismum,* nom. *-mus,* Gr. *sullogismos,* from *sullogizesthai,* to reason (*logos,* reason)]
sylph, *n.* an elementary being inhabiting the air, intermediate between material and immaterial beings; a graceful and slender girl; a S American humming-bird with a long, brilliantly-coloured tail. **sylphlike,** *a.* †**sylphid,** *n., a.* **sylphine,** *a.* [F *sylphe,* prob. from Gr. *silphē,* some beetle or grub]
sylvan, SILVAN.
sylvanite, *n.* a gold or silver telluride mineral. [Tran*sylvania,* where it was found]
sylviculture SILVICULTURE under SILVA.
sym-, *pref.* SYN- (before *b, m,* or *p*).
symbiont, *n.* an organism living in a state of symbiosis. **symbiontic,** *a.* **symbiosis,** *n.* the vital union or partnership of certain organisms, such as the fungus and alga in lichens. **symbiotic,** *a.* **symbiotically,** *adv.* [Gr. *sumbiōn -biountos,* pres.p. of *sumbiōnai* (*biōnai,* from *bios,* life)]
symbol, *n.* an object typifying or representing something by resemblance, association etc., a type, an emblem; a mark, character or letter accepted as representing or signifying some thing, idea, relation, process etc., as the letters of the alphabet, those representing chemical elements, the signs of mathematical relations etc. *v.t.* (*past, p.p.* **symbolled**) to symbolize. **symbolic, -ical,** *a.* pertaining to, serving as or using symbols. **symbolic logic,** *n.* logic that uses symbols to represent and clarify principles etc. **symbolically,** *adv.* **symbolicalness,** *n.* **symbolics,** *n. sing.* **symbolism,** *n.* representation by symbols or signs; a system of symbols; symbolic significance; the use of symbols, esp. in art and literature; a late 19th-cent. movement among (French) artists and writers using symbolic images to express or suggest the essential nature of things, mystical ideas, emotions etc. **symbolist,** *n.* **symbolistic,** *a.* **symbolize, -ise,** *v.t.* to be the symbol of, to typify; to represent by symbols; to treat as symbolic, not literal, to make symbolic or representative of something; †to make to agree in properties. *v.i.* to use symbols; †to agree, to harmonize. **symbolization, -isation,** *n.* **symbolizer, -iser,** *n.* **symbology,** †**-bolology,** *n.* the use of symbols as a means of expression; the study or analysis of symbols. **symbological,** *a.* **symbologist,** *n.* **symbolatry, symbololatry,** *n.* symbol-worship. [F *symbole,* L *symbolum,* Gr. *sumbolon,* token, pledge, from *sumballein* (*ballein,* to throw)]
Symington, *n.* **William** (1763–1831), Scottish engineer who built the first successful steamboat. He invented the steam road locomotive in 1787 and a steamboat engine in 1788. His steamboat, the *Charlotte Dundas* was completed in 1802.
symmetry, *n.* due proportion of the several parts of a body or any whole to each other, congruity, parity, regularity, harmony; beauty of form arising from this; arrangement of parts on either side of a dividing line or point so that the opposite parts are exactly similar in shape and size; regularity of structure so that opposite halves exactly correspond; regularity of number in sepals, petals, stamens etc., each whorl comprising the same number or multiples of this. **symmetral,** *a.* **symmetric, -ical,** *a.* **symmetrically,** *adv.* **symmetricalness,** *n.* **symmetrist,** †**symmetrian, symmetrician,** *n.* **symmetrize, -ise,** *v.t.* **symmetrization, -isation,** *n.* [F *symmetrie,* L *symmetria,* Gr. *summetria,* from *summetros,* commensurate (*metron,* measure)]
symmorph, *n.* a character differing from another or others in form but representing the same idea. [Gr. *summorphos* (*morphē,* form)]
sympathy, *n.* the quality of being affected with the same feelings as another, or of sharing emotions, affec-

tions, inclinations etc. with another person, animal etc.; fellow-feeling, agreement, harmony; (*often pl.*) a feeling of accord (with); loyalty or support; compassion (for); unity or correlation of action; response of an organ or part to an affection in another without actual transmission of the cause; the relation between inanimate bodies by which the vibration of one sets up a corresponding vibration in another; †the tendency of inanimate bodies to mutual attraction, influence etc. **sympathetic**, *a.* pertaining to, expressive of, or due to sympathy; having sympathy or common feeling with another, sympathizing; being or acting in sympathy or agreement, concordant; in accord with one's mood or disposition, congenial; proceeding from or due to pain or injury in another organ or part; pertaining to or mediated by the sympathetic nervous system; of acoustic, electrical, and other vibrations, produced by impulses from other vibrations. **sympathetic nervous system,** the part of the autonomic nervous system in which nerve impulses are transmitted chiefly by adrenalin and related substances. **sympathetic-ink,** *n.* a colourless ink, writing in which is made visible by heat or other agency. **sympathetically,** *adv.* **sympatheticism,** *n.* a morbid tendency to be sympathetic. **sympathism,** *n.* immediate communication of subjective emotions. **sympathize, -ise,** *v.i.* to have or express sympathy with another, as in pain, pleasure etc.; to be of the same disposition, opinion etc. **sympathizer, -iser, †sympathist,** *n.* **sympathomimetic,** *a.* having or causing physiological effects like those produced by the sympathetic nervous system. [F *sympathie,* L *sympathīa,* Gr. *sumpatheia,* from *sumpathēs,* sympathetic (*pathein, paschein,* to suffer)]

sympetalous, *a.* gamopetalous.

symphenomenon, *n.* (*pl.* **-na**) a phenomenon resembling or accompanying another exhibited by the same object. **symphenomenal,** *a.*

symphony, *n.* a complex and elaborate composition for an orchestra, usu. consisting of four varied movements; an instrumental passage or composition occurring as an interlude in or introduction to a vocal work; a symphony orchestra; a harmonious composition; †consonance or harmony of sounds. **symphony orchestra,** *n.* a large orchestra containing wind, string and percussion sections. **symphonic, symphonious,** *a.* **symphonic poem,** *n.* a tone-poem. **symphonist,** *n.* a composer or performer of symphonies. **†symphonize, -ise,** *v.i., v.t.* to harmonize. [OF *symphonie,* L *symphōnia,* Gr. *sumphōnia,* from *sumphōnos,* agreeing in sound (*phōnē,* sound)]

symphoricarpous, *a.* bearing several fruits clustered together. [Gr. *sumphorein,* to join together (*pherein,* to bear), *karpos,* fruit]

symphyllous, *a.* gamophyllous. [Gr. *phullon,* leaf]

symphynote, *a.* of the valves of some river mussels, soldered together at the hinge. [Gr. *sumphuēs,* grown together, *nōton,* back]

symphyogenesis, *n.* the formation of a plant organ or part by the growing together of parts previously separate. **symphyogenetic,** *a.* [Gr. *sumphuēs,* grown together (*phuein,* to grow), GENESIS]

symphysis, *n.* (*pl.* **-ses**) (the joint formed by) the union of two parts of the skeleton by growing together or the intervention of cartilage; the growing together or union of two plant parts. **symphyseal,** *a.* [Gr., as prec.]

symphytism, *n.* (*Gram.*) the coalescence of word-elements. [Gr. *sumphuein,* to grow together]

sympiesometer, *n.* an instrument for measuring the pressure or velocity of a current of water; a barometer in which atmospheric pressure is measured by the compression of a small quantity of gas behind a column of liquid. [Gr. *sumpiezein* (*piezein,* to squeeze)]

symploce, *n.* the repetition of a word or phrase at the beginning and of another at the end of successive clauses. [Gr. *sumplokē* (*plekein,* to twine)]

sympodium, *n.* (*pl.* **-dia**) a false plant axis or stem composed of superimposed branches. **sympodial,** *a.* [Gr. *pous podos,* foot]

symposiarch, *n.* the president or director of a feast; a toast-master; the leading spirit of a social or convivial meeting.

symposium, *n.* (*pl.* **-sia**, **-siums**) in ancient Greece, a drinking together, a convivial party usu. following a banquet, with music, dancing etc.; a drinking party; a series of brief articles expressing the views of different writers, in a magazine etc.; a conference or formal meeting at which several speakers give addresses on a particular topic. **symposiac, symposial,** *a.* [L, from Gr. *sumposion* (*po-,* base of *pinein,* to drink, cp. *posis,* drink)]

symptom, *n.* a perceptible change in the appearance or functions of the body indicating disease; a sign, a token, an indication. **symptomatic, -ical,** *a.* **symptomatically,** *adv.* **symptomatology,** *n.* a branch of medicine concerned with disease symptoms; the symptoms associated with a disease. [OF *symptome,* L *symptōma,* Gr. *sumptōma -matos,* a chance, a casualty, from *sumpiptein* (*piptein,* to fall)]

symptosis, *n.* (*Math.*) a meeting of polars at the same point with reference to different loci; a coming together of vowels, a hiatus. [Gr., as prec.]

syn., (*abbr.*) synonym, synonymous.

syn-, *pref.* with; together; alike. [Gr. *sun-,* pref., *sun,* prep., with]

synacmy, *n.* the simultaneous maturity of the stigmas and anthers of a flower. **synacmic,** *a.* [Gr. *akmē,* maturity]

synaeresis, syneresis, *n.* the contraction of two vowels or syllables into one; the expulsion of liquid from a gel by contraction. [L, from Gr. *sunairesis* (*haireein,* to take)]

synaesthesia, (*N Am.*) **synesthesia**, *n.* sensation experienced at a point distinct from the point of stimulation. [cp. HYPERAESTHESIA]

synagogue, *n.* a Jewish congregation for religious instruction and observances; a building or place of meeting for this. **synagogal, synagogical,** *a.* [F, from L *synagōga,* Gr. *sunagōgē* (*agein,* to bring)]

synalepha, *n.* a blending of two syllables into one, esp. by the suppression of a final vowel before an initial vowel. [Gr. *sunaloiphē* (*aleiphein,* to smear)]

synalgia, *n.* sympathetic pain. [Gr. *-algia, algos,* pain]

synallagmatic, *a.* of a contract or treaty, imposing reciprocal obligations. [Gr. *sunallagmatikos* (*allassein,* to exchange)]

synangium, *n.* (*pl.* **-gia**) the boat-shaped sorus composed of sporangia in some ferns; an arterial trunk. [Gr. *angeion,* vessel]

synantherous, *a.* having the anthers growing together.

synanthous, *a.* having flowers and leaves appearing at the same time. [Gr. *anthos,* flower]

synaphea, *n.* continuity between lines or portions of lines in verse, esp. when the last syllable of a line is made long or elided by synalepha with the initial syllable of the next. [Gr. *sunapheia* (*haptein,* to join)]

synapse, *n.* the point at which a nerve impulse is transmitted from one neuron to another. **synapsis,** *n.* (*pl.* **-ses**) the pairing of homologous chromosomes occurring at the start of cell division by meiosis; a synapse. **synaptic,** *a.* [Gr. *synapsis,* junction, from *sunaptein* (*haptein,* to fasten)]

†synarchy, *n.* joint sovereignty. [Gr. *sunarchia* (*archein,* to rule)]

synarthrosis, *n.* (*pl.* **-ses**) an articulation not permitting motion, as in sutures, symphysis etc. **synarthrodial,** *a.*

†synaxis, *n.* a congregation, esp. one assembled to partake of the Lord's Supper. [Gr. *sunaxis* (*agein,* to lead)]

syncarp, *n.* an aggregate fruit, as the blackberry. **syncarpous,** *a.* [Gr. *karpos,* fruit]

syncategorematic, *a.* (*Log.*) denoting words that can express only parts of terms, as adverbs, prepositions etc. [Gr. *sunkatēgorēmatikos*]

synch SYNC.

synchondrosis, *n.* the almost immovable articulation of bones by means of cartilage, as in the vertebrae.

[Gr. *sunchondrōsis* (*chondros*, cartilage)]

synchoresis, *n.* (*Rhet.*) a concession made for the purpose of retorting more effectively. [Gr. *sunchoresis* (*choros*, space)]

synchromesh, *a.* pertaining to a system of gearing in which the drive and driving members are automatically synchronized before engagement, thus avoiding shock and noise in changing gear.

synchronism, *n.* concurrence of two or more events in time, coincidence, simultaneousness; a tabular arrangement of historical events or personages according to their dates. **synchronal,** *a.* **synchronistic,** *a.* **synchronistically,** *adv.* **synchronize, -ise,** *v.i.* to concur in time, to happen at the same time. *v.t.* to cause to occur in unison or at the same time; to cause to agree in time or indicate the same time; to match (the sound-track of a film) exactly with the picture. **synchronized swimming,** *n.* a sport in which one or a team of swimmers perform a series of dance-like movements to music. **synchronization, -isation,** *n.* **synchronizer, -iser,** *n.* **synchronous,** *a.* occurring simultaneously; operating or recurring together at the same rate. **synchronous motor,** *n.* an electric motor whose speed is proportional to the frequency of the supply current. **synchronously,** *adv.* [Gr. *sunchronismos* (*chronos*, time, -ISM)]

synchronology, *n.* comparative chronology.

synchronology

synchysis, *n.* a diseased condition of the eye caused by cholesterol floating in the vitreous humour; †confusion, derangement; a confused arrangement of words in a sentence. [Gr. *sunchusis,* confusion (*cheein,* to pour)]

synclastic, *a.* (*Math.*) having uniform curvature, convex or concave in every direction. [Gr. *klastos,* broken]

synclinal, *a.* (*Geol.*) sloping downward towards a common point or line, opp. to *anticlinal*. **syncline,** *n.* a synclinal flexure or axis. [Gr. *klīnein,* to lean]

syncopate, *v.t.* to contract (a word) by omitting one or more letters or syllables from the middle; to modify (a musical note, rhythm etc.) by beginning on an unaccented and continuing with an accented beat. **syncopation,** *n.* [L *syncopātūs*, p.p. of *syncopāre,* orig. to swoon, as foll.]

syncope, *n.* the elision of a letter or syllable from the middle of a word; (*Med.*) a faint. **syncopal, -copic, -coptic,** *a.* **syncopist,** *n.* [L *syncopē,* Gr. *sunkopē* (*koptein,* to strike)]

syncotyledonous, *a.* having the cotyledons united.

syncretism, *n.* the attempted reconciliation of various philosophic or religious schools or systems of thought, as against a common opponent. **syncretic,** *n., a.* **syncretist,** *n.* **syncretistic,** *a.* **syncretize, -ise,** *v.t., v.i.* [Gr. *sunkrētismos,* from *sunkrētizein* (*krētizein,* etym. doubtful)]

sync, synch, *v.t., v.i., n.* short for SYNCHRONIZE, SYNCHRONIZATION under SYNCHRONISM.

synd, SIND.

syndactyl, -dactylous, *a.* having the digits united, as in webbed feet. **syndactylism,** *n.* [SYN-, Gr. *daktūlos,* finger]

syndesmosis, *n.* (*pl.* **-ses**) an articulation of bones by ligaments. **syndesmotic,** *a.* **syndesmotomy,** *n.* the dissection or anatomy of the ligaments. [Gr. *sundesmos* (*desmos,* bond, from *deein,* to bind)]

syndetic, *a.* (*Gram.*) serving to connect, copulative. [cp. ASYNDETON]

syndic, *n.* an officer or magistrate invested with varying powers in different places and times; a member of a special committee of the senate of Cambridge Univ.; a business agent of a university, corporation etc. **syndicate,** *n.* a body of syndics, esp. at Cambridge University; an association of persons or firms formed to promote some special interest or undertake a joint project; an agency that supplies material for simultaneous publication in several newspapers or periodicals. *v.t.*, to combine in a syndicate; to manage by means of a syndicate; to sell for simultaneous publication in several newspapers or periodicals; to sell (a television programme) for broadcasting by several different stations. **syndication,** *n.* [F, from L *syndicus,* Gr. *sundikos* (*dikē,* justice)]

syndicalism, *n.* the economic doctrine that all the workers in any trade or industry should participate in the management and control and in the division of the profits (and that in order to bring about this condition the workers in different trades should federate together and enforce their demands by sympathetic strikes). **syndicalist,** *n.* [see prec.]

syndrome, *n.* concurrence; the aggregate of symptoms characteristic of any disease or disorder; a pattern or set of feelings, actions etc. characteristic of a condition or problem. [Gr. *sundromē* (*dramein,* to run)]

syne, *adv.* (*Sc.*) long ago. [SINCE]

synecdoche, *n.* a rhetorical figure by which a part is put for the whole or the whole for a part. **synecdochical,** *a.* [L, from Gr. *sunekdochē* (*ek,* out, *dechesthai,* to receive)]

synechia, *n.* morbid adhesion of the iris to the cornea or to the capsule of the crystalline lens. [Gr. *sunecheia* (*echein,* to have, to hold)]

synechiology, *n.* (*Phil.*) the doctrine of connection by causation or spatial and temporal relations. **synechiological,** *a.* [as prec., -LOGY]

synecology, *n.* the ecology of plant and animal communities. **synecologic, -ical,** *a.* [SYN-, ECOLOGY]

synecphonesis, *n.* (*pl.* **-ses**) synaeresis. [Gr. *synekphōnēsis* (*ek-,* out, *phōnein,* to sound)]

synedral, -drous, *a.* growing on the angles of a stem. [Gr. *sunedros* (*hedra,* seat)]

synema, *n.* the column of combined filaments in a monadelphous flower. [Gr. *nēma,* thread]

syneresis SYNAERESIS.

synergism, *n.* the doctrine that human energy cooperates with divine grace in the work of salvation; the working together of two drugs, muscles etc. such that their combined action exceeds the sum of their individual actions. **synergic, -getic,** *a.* of muscles etc., working together, cooperative. **synergist,** *n.* something that acts with, or increases the effect of, another. **synergistic,** *a.* **synergy,** *n.* combined action between different organs etc., synergism. [Gr. *sunergos* (*ergos,* work), -ISM]

synesis, *n.* grammatical construction according to the sense rather than syntax. [Gr. *sunesis,* understanding (*hienai,* to send)]

synesthesia SYNAESTHESIA.

syngamy, *n.* sexual reproduction by union of gametes, syngenesis. **syngamic,** *a.* [SYN-, -GAMY]

Synge, *n.* **John Millington** (1871–1909), Irish playwright, a leading figure in the Irish dramatic revival of the early 20th century. His six plays reflect the speech patterns of the Aran Islands and W Ireland. They include *In the Shadow of the Glen* (1903), *Riders to the Sea* (1904), and *The Playboy of the Western World* (1907), which caused riots at the Abbey Theatre, Dublin, when first performed.

syngenesious, -ian, *a.* having the anthers cohering; of anthers, cohering into a tube. [as foll.]

syngenesis, *n.* the theory that the embryo is the product of both male and female; reproduction by the union of the ovum and the spermatozoon. **syngenetic,** *a.*

†**syngraph,** *n.* a writing signed by both or all the parties concerned.

synizesis, *n.* the combination into one syllable in pronunciation of two vowels that cannot make a diphthong; blindness caused by a closure of the pupil. [Gr. *sunizēsis* (*hizein,* to seal)]

synocha, *n.* inflammatory continued fever. **synochal, -choid,** *a.* **synochus,** *n.* a continued fever; mixed fever. [Gr. *sunochos,* lasting (*echein,* to hold)]

synod, *n.* an ecclesiastical council; (*Presbyterian*) a council intermediate between the presbyteries and the General Assembly; a deliberative assembly, a meeting for discussion; a conjunction of heavenly bodies. **synodal, synodic, -ical,** *a.* **synodically,** *adv.* [F *synode,* L *synodum,* nom. *-dus,* Gr. *sunodos* (*hodos,* way)]

synoecious, *a.* having male and female organs in the same inflorescence or receptacle. [Gr. *sunoikia* (*oikos,* house), -OUS]

†**synomosy,** *n.* in ancient Greece, a secret brotherhood or political club bound by oath, a conspiracy. [Gr. *sunōmosia* (*ommunai,* to swear)]

synonym, *n.* a word having the same meaning as another of the same language; a word denoting the same thing but differing in some senses, or in range of application. **synonymatic, synonymic, -ical,** *a.* of or pertaining to synonymy. **synonymicon,** *n.* a dictionary of synonyms. **synonymics,** *n. sing.* the study of synonyms. **synonymist,** *n.* **synonymity,** *n.* the quality of being synonymous. **synonymize, -ise,** *v.t.* to express by synonyms or a synonym. **synonymous,** *a.* expressing the same thing by a different word or words; having the same meaning, conveying the same idea. **synonymously,** *adv.* **synonymy,** *n.* a system of synonyms; a treatise on synonyms; synonymity. [F *synonime,* L *synōnyma,* Gr. *sunōnumos,* of like meaning or name (*onuma -atos,* name)]

synopsis, *n.* (*pl.* **-ses**) a general view, a conspectus, a summary. **synoptic,** *a.* of the nature of a synopsis, affording a general view. *n.* one of the synoptic gospels. **synoptic gospels,** *n.pl.* those of Matthew, Mark and Luke. **synoptical,** *a.* **synoptically,** *adv.* **synoptist,** *n.* one of the writers of the synoptic gospels. [L, from Gr. *synopsis* (*opsis,* seeing, from *op-,* to see)]

synosteography, *n.* a description of the articulations of the body. **synosteology,** *n.* the science of or a treatise on these. **synosteosis,** *n.* (*Anat.*) union of different parts of the skeleton by means of bone. **synosteotome,** *n.* a knife for the dissection of joints. **synosteotomy,** *n.* [Gr. *osteon,* bone]

synovia, *n.* an albuminous lubricating fluid secreted by the synovial membranes lining joints and tendon sheaths. **synovial,** *a.* pertaining to or secreting synovia. **synovitis,** *n.* inflammation of a synovial membrane. [L *ovum,* egg]

syntax, *n.* (the part of grammar that deals with) the due arrangement of words or the construction of sentences. **syntactic,** *a.* of, pertaining to or according to the rules of syntax. **syntactically,** *adv.* **syntactics,** *n.sing.* the branch of mathematics treating of the number of ways of putting things together, as permutations, combinations etc.; semiology dealing with the formal relations and properties of signs. [F *syntaxe,* late L *syntaxis,* Gr. *suntaxis* (*tassein,* to arrange)]

synteresis, *n.* the habit of mind which enables one to make primary moral judgments, conscience; remorse. [Gr. *sunteresis,* watching closely]

synthesis, *n.* (*pl.* **-ses**) the putting of two or more things together, combination, composition; the building up of a complex whole by the union of elements, esp. the process of forming concepts, general ideas, theories etc.; the production of a substance by chemical reaction; the formation of compound words by means of composition and inflexion, as opp. to analysis which employs prepositions etc. **synthesist, -tist,** *n.* **synthesize, -tize, -ise,** *v.t.* **synthesizer, -iser,** *n.* one who, or that which, synthesizes; a usu. keyboard-operated electronic instrument that can produce and manipulate a wide variety of sounds, imitate conventional musical instruments etc. **synthetic, -ical,** *a.* pertaining to or consisting in synthesis; artificially produced, man-made, false, sham. **synthetically,** *adv.* [L, from Gr. *sunthesis,* (*thesis,* putting, see THESIS)]

syntropic, *a.* of vertebrae etc., turning or pointing in the same direction. [Gr. *trepein,* to turn]

sypher, *v.t.* to join (planks etc.) with bevelled and overlapping edges so as to leave a flush surface. **sypher-joint,** *n.* [etym. doubtful]

syphilis, *n.* an infectious venereal disease caused by a microorganism introduced into the system by direct contact or due to heredity, having three stages: primary syphilis, affecting the genitals etc.; secondary syphilis, attacking the skin and mucous membranes; and tertiary syphilis, spreading to the muscles, bones and brain. **syphilitic, syphilous,** *a.* **syphilize, -ise,** *v.t.* **syphilization, -isation,** *n.* **syphiloid,** *a.* **syphilology,** *n.* [F, from mod. L *Syphilus,* shepherd in a poem by Frascatorio (16th cent.)]

syphon, SIPHON.

syren, SIREN.

Syria, *n.* Syrian Arab Republic (*al-Jamhuriya al-Arabya as-Suriya*), country in W Asia, on the Mediterranean, bounded to the N by Turkey, to the E by Iraq, to the S by Jordan, and to the SW by Israel and Lebanon. **area** 185,200 sq km/71,506 sq miles. **capital** Damascus. **towns** Aleppo, Homs, Hama; chief port Latakia. **physical** mountains alternate with fertile plains and desert areas; river Euphrates. **population** (1989) 12,210,000; annual growth rate 3.5%. **exports** cotton, cereals, oil, phosphates. **language** Arabic (official) 89%, Kurdish 6%, Armenian 3%. **religion** Sunni Muslim, but the ruling minority is Alawite, an Islamic sect; also Druse, again an Islamic sect.

Syriac, *a.* pertaining to Syria or its language. *n.* the language of the ancient Syrians, originally the Aramaic dialect spoken in and around Edessa (now in Turkey) and widely used in W Asia from about 700 BC–AD 700. **Syrian,** *n., a.* (a native) of Syria. [L *Syriacus,* Gr. *Suriakos,* from *Suria,* from *Suros,* Syrian]

syringa, *n.* the mock-orange, *Philadelphus;* a genus of plants containing the lilacs. [SYRINX (the stems being formerly used for the stems of Turkish pipes)]

syringe, *n.* a cylindrical instrument with a piston used to draw in a quantity of liquid by suction and eject or inject it in a stream, spray or jet, a squirt. *v.t.* to water, spray or cleanse with a syringe. **syringeful,** *n.* [OF *seringue,* L *syrinx -ingem,* from Gr. SYRINX]

syrinx, *n.* (*pl.* **syringes, syrinxes** the Eustachian tube; the organ of song in birds, the inferior larynx, a modification of the trachea where it joins the bronchi; a surgically-made passage or fistula; a Pan-pipe; a narrow gallery cut in the rock in ancient Egyptian tombs. **syringeal,** *a.* **syringitis,** *n.* inflammation of the Eustachian tube. **syringo-,** *comb.form.* [L, from Gr. *surinx -ingos,* reed, shepherd's pipe]

Syro-, *comb. form* Syriac, Syrian. [Gr. *Suros,* see SYRIAC]

Syroarabian, *a.* pertaining to or comprising Syriac and Arabic.

Syrophoenician, *a.* belonging or pertaining to Syrophoenicia, a Roman province in W Asia.

syrtis, *n.* (*pl.* **-tes**) a quicksand. **syrtic,** *a.* [L, from Gr. *surtis,* from *surein,* to draw along]

syrup, *n.* a saturated solution of sugar in water, usu. combined with fruit-juice etc. for use in cookery, as a beverage etc., or with a medicinal substance; the uncrystallizable fluid separated from sugar-cane juice in the process of refining molasses, treacle; excessive sweetness or sentimentality. **syrupy,** *a.* [OF *syrop* (F *sirop*), Arab. *sharāb,* beverage, see SHERBET]

sys-, *pref.* SYN- (before *s*).

syssarcosis, *n.* (*pl.* **-ses**) a connection of parts of the skeleton by intervening muscle. [Gr. *sussarkōsis* (*sarkoein,* from *sarx sarkos,* flesh)]

syssitia, *n.pl.* the public meals for men and youths among the Spartans and other Dorians in ancient Greece, held to promote simplicity and discipline and to inculcate patriotism. [Gr. *sussitia,* pl. of *sussition* (*sitos,* food)]

systaltic, *a.* of the heart, alternately contracting and dilating, pulsatory. [late L *systalticus,* Gr. *sustaltikos* (*stellein,* to place)]

†**systasis,** *n.* a political union or confederation. [Gr. *sustasis,* (SYN-, *histanai,* see STASIS)]

systatic, *a.* of a letter etc., commendatory; affecting several sensory faculties at the same time. [Gr. *sustatikos,* as prec.]

system, *n.* coordinated arrangement, organized combination, organization, method; an established method or procedure; a coordinated body of principles, facts, theories, doctrines etc.; a logical grouping, a method or plan of classification; a coordinated arrangement or organized combination or assembly of things or parts, for working together, performing a particular function etc. a group of related or linked natural objects, as mountains, the rocks of a geological period etc.; any complex and coordinated whole; any organic structure taken as a whole, as the animal body, the universe etc. **The System**, *n.* (*Austral. Hist.*) the whole question of transportation, including the treatment of convicts; **(the system)** (*coll., derog.*) the establishment, bureaucracy or society generally, esp. when regarded as a destroyer of individualism. **system building,** *n.* a method of building using factory-made standardized components. **system-maker, -monger,** *n.* one given to forming systems. **systems analysis,** *n.* the analysis of an industrial, medical, business etc. procedure or task in order to identify its requirements and devise a (computer) system to fulfil these. **systems analyst,** *n.* **systematic, -ical**, *a.* methodical; done, formed or arranged on a regular plan, not haphazard; taxonomic. **systematically,** *adv.* **systematics,** *n.sing.* (the study of) classification or taxonomy. **systematist,** *n.* **systematize, -ise,** *v.t.* **systematization, -isation,** *n.* **systematizer, -iser,** *n.* **systematology**, *n.* systematics. **systemic**, *a.* pertaining to or affecting the bodily system as a whole; of an insecticide etc., absorbed by the tissues of a plant etc., thus making it toxic. **systemically,** *adv.* **systemless**, *a.* [L *systēma,* Gr. *sustēma -matos* (SYN-, *stē-*, to set, from *sta-*, see STASIS)]

systole, *n.* the contraction of the heart forcing the blood outwards, alternating with diastole. **systolic**, *a.* [Gr. *sustolē,* from *sustellein,* to draw together, see SYSTALTIC]

systyle, *a.* with columns set only two diameters apart. **systylous**, *a.* (*Bot.*) having the styles united. [late L *systylos,* Gr. *sustulos* (SYN-, STYLE[2])]

†**syth, sythe**[1], SITH.

†**sythe**[2], SCYTHE.

Szczecin, *n.* (German **Stettin**) industrial (shipbuilding, fish processing, synthetic fibres, tools, iron) port on the river Oder, in NW Poland; population (1985) 391,000.

syzygy, *n.* the conjunction or opposition of any two of the heavenly bodies, esp. of a planet with the sun; (*Biol. etc.*) conjunction or union. **syzygetic**, *a.* **syzygetically,** *adv.* [L *syzygia,* Gr. *suzugia,* from *suzeugnunai,* to yoke together (SYN-, *zugon,* yoke)]

T

T, t, the 20th letter and the 16th consonant (*pl.* **Ts, T's, Tees**), is a hard voiceless dental mute; followed by *h* it has two distinct sounds, surd or breathed, as in *think, thank, thought* (shown in this dictionary by 'th'), representing the OE Þ, and sonant or vocal, as in *this that, though* (shown here by 'dh'), representing the OE ð. *n.* a T-shaped thing or part. *a.* T-shaped (*usu. in comb.*, as *T-bar, -piece, -square* etc.). **to a T,** TEE. **T-bandage,** *n.* a bandage in the shape of a 'T'. **T-bar,** *n.* a metal etc. bar in the shape of a 'T'. **T-bar lift,** *n.* a ski lift with a T-bar. **T-bone,** *n.* a bone in the shape of a 'T', as in a sirloin steak. **T-shirt,** *n.* an informal lightweight, (short-sleeved) garment for the upper-body. **T-square,** *n.* a 'T' shaped ruler.

t' , (*dial.*) the.

't, it.

T, (*chem. symbol*) tritium.

t, (*abbr.*) temperature; tempo; tense; tenor; ton(s); town; transitive.

Ta, (*chem. symbol*) tantalum.

TA, (*abbr*) territorial army.

ta, *int.* thank you. [etym. doubtful]

Taal, *n.* S African Dutch, Afrikaans. [Dut., language]

tab[1], *n.* a small flap, tag, tongue etc., as the flap of a shoe, the tag or tip of lace etc.; a small paper flap attached to a file for identification purposes; a strap, a loop; military insignia; (*N Am.*) the bill; a check, close surveillance. *v.t.* to put taps on something. **to keep tabs on,** to keep a watch on. [prob. rel. to TAPE]

tab[2], *n.* (short for) tablet, tabulator. *v.t.* tabulate.

tabard, *n.* †a coarse outer garment worn by the poorer classes; an outer garment worn over armour; a herald's sleeveless coat blazoned with the arms of the sovereign. †**tabarder,** *n.* [OF, etym. doubtful]

tabaret, *n.* a fabric of alternate satin and watered-silk stripes used for upholstery. [etym. doubtful]

Tabasco®, *n.* a hot, capsicum sauce. [*Tabasco,* Mexican State]

tabasheer, *n.* a hydrated opaline silica deposited in the joints of the bamboo, used in the E Indies as a medicine. [Hind. and Arab. *tabāshir*]

tabbinet TABINET.

tabby, *n.* silk or other stuff with a watered surface; a garment of this; a tabby-cat; a cat, esp. a female cat; (*fig.*) a gossipy old maid or old woman; a kind of concrete made with lime, shells, and gravel, or stones. *v.t.* to give a wavy or watered appearance to. *a.* wavy, watered. **tabby-cat,** *n.* a grey or brownish cat with dark stripes. [F *tabis,* Arab. *'utābī,* from *al-'attabiya,* the quarter in Baghdad where it was first made]

tabefaction, tabefy TABES.

tabellion, *n.* a notary or official scribe under the Roman empire and in France before 1761. [F, from late L *tabellio -ōnem,* from *tabella,* dim. of L *tabula,* TABLE]

taberdar, *n.* a scholar of Queen's College, Oxford. [var. of TABARDER]

tabernacle, *n.* a tent, booth, or other building of light construction, and usu. movable, used as a habitation, temple etc.; (*fig.*) the human body as the temporary abode of the soul; a tent-like structure used by the Jews as a sanctuary before settlement in Palestine; a non-conformist place of worship; an ornamental receptacle for the consecrated Elements or the pyx; a canopy, canopied stall or niche, a canopy-like structure over a tomb etc.; a socket or hinged post for unstepping the mast on a river-boat. *v.i.* to dwell in or as in a tabernacle, to sojourn. *v.t.* to give shelter to. **Feast of Tabernacles,** an autumn feast of the Jews in memory of the sojourn in the wilderness. **tabernacle-work,** *n.* carved canopies and tracery over a pulpit, stall etc. **tabernacled, tabernacular,** *a.* [F, from L *tabernāculum,* tent, dim. of *taberna,* hut]

tabes, *n.* wasting away, emaciation; a wasting disease. **tabefaction,** *n.* wasting away from disease, emaciation. **tabefy,** *v.i., v.t.* [L *tābefactio,* from *tābefacere* (*tābēre,* from TABES, *facere,* to make)] **tabes dorsalis,** *n.* an advanced form of syphilis which attacks the spinal cord. **tabescence** (təbes'əns), *n.* **tabescent, tabetic, tabic, tabid,** *a.* **tabidly,** *adv.* **tabidness, tabitude,** *n.* [L, cogn. with Gr. *tēkein,* to melt, and THAW]

tabinet, tabbinet, *n.* a watered fabric of silk and wool, used for window-curtains etc. [prob. dim. of TABBY, said by French to be from M. *Tabinet,* French refugee who introduced the manufacture to Ireland]

tabla, *n.* a pair of small Indian drums with variable pitch, played with the hands. [Hindi *tabla* from Arabic *tabla,* drum]

tablature, *n.* a painting on a wall or ceiling; a picture; (*fig.*) a vivid description, mental image etc.; a system of notation for instruments of the lute and violin class, showing string and fret position, and indicating rhythm and fingering. [F, from foll.]

table, *n.* an article of furniture consisting of a flat surface resting on one or more supports, used for serving meals upon, working, writing, playing games etc.; this used for meals; (*fig.*) the food served upon it, fare, cuisine; the company sitting at a table; a table or board adapted for a particular game (*usu. in comb.*, as *billiard-table*); either half of a back-gammon-table; (*pl.*) †the game of backgammon; a part of a machine or machine-tool on which the work is put to be operated on; any apparatus consisting of a plane surface; a slab of wood or other material; such a slab with writing or an inscription; hence, the contents of such writing etc.; a list of numbers, references, or other items arranged systematically, esp. in columns; a flat surface, a plateau; the flat face of a gem; a flat surface, usu. rectangular, a horizontal band of moulding; the sound board of a guitar, cello etc. *v.t.* to lay (a Bill etc.) on the table in front of the Speaker in the House of Commons, i.e. to submit for discussion. to fit (timbers) together with alternate feathers and grooves to prevent separation or slipping; to strengthen (a sail) with wide hems. **at table,** taking a meal. **to lay** or **lie on the table,** (*Parl.*) to defer or be deferred indefinitely. **to turn the tables,** to reverse the conditions or relations. **the twelve tables,** the Roman laws inscribed on 12 (orig. 10) tablets by the Decemvirs 451 BC, the foundation of Roman jurisprudence. **under the table,** illicit, secret; (*coll.*) drunk. **table-beer,** *n.* beer for drinking at meals. **table-book,** *n.* an ornamental book for keeping on a table. **table-cloth,** *n.* a cloth, usu. of white linen, for covering a table, esp. at mealtimes. **table-cover,** *n.* a cloth, usu. coloured, for covering a table at other times. **table-cut,** *a.* cut with a flat face (of gems). **table d'hôte,** [F, host's table], *n.* (*pl.* **tables-**) a hotel or restaurant meal at fixed price, limited to certain dishes arranged by the proprietor. **table-knife,** *n.* a knife for use at meals. **table-land,** *n.* a plateau. **table licence,** *n.* a licence which permits the holder to serve alcohol with food. **table-linen,** *n.* (*collect.*) tablecloths, napkins etc. **table-lifting, -moving, -rapping, -turning,** etc., *n.* making a table rise, move, or turn over without apparent cause, as by spiritualistic agency. **table manners,** *n.pl.* accepted behaviour during meals. **table mat,** *n.* a mat placed on a table to protect the surface from hot dishes. **table-money,** *n.* an allowance to general and flag officers for hospitality; a charge to members of clubs for use of the dining-room. **table salt,** *n.* fine, free-flowing salt used at table. **table-skittles,** *n.pl.* a game of skittles set up on a board, and knocked down by a ball suspended above the board. **tablespoon,** *n.* a large spoon, four times the size of a teaspoon and holding half a fluid ounce. **tablespoonful,** *n.* the amount contained in a tablespoon. **table-talk,** *n.* talk at table or meals; familiar conversation, miscellaneous chat. **table tennis,** *n.* a game like lawn tennis played on a table with small bats and hollow balls. **table top,** *n.* the flat top of a table; any flat top. **table-topped,** *a.* **table-turning** TABLE-LIFTING. **table-ware,** *n.* dishes, plates, knives, forks etc., for use at meals. **table wine,** *n.* an unfortified wine drunk with meals. **tabled,** *a.* **tableful,** *n.* †**tabler,** *n.* **tabling,** *n.* [OF, from L *tabula,* a board, a table]

tableau, *n.* (*pl.* **-leaux**) a picture; a striking or vivid representation or effect. **tableau vivant,** *n.* (*pl.* **tableaux vivants**) a motionless group of performers dressed and arranged to represent some scene or event. [F, dim. of prec.]

tablet, *n.* a thin flat piece of wood, ivory, or other material for writing on; (*pl.*) a set of these; a small table or slab, esp. used as a memorial; a small flat piece or cake of medicinal or other substance; (*Sc.*) a sweetmeat made from sugar and condensed milk. **tablette,** *n.* a flat, projecting coping-stone, on a wall etc. [OF *tablete* (F *tablette*), dim. of TABLE]

tablier, *n.* a small apron or apron-like part of a woman's dress. [F, from L *tabulārium,* from *tabula,* TABLE]

tabling TABLE.

tabloid, *n.* proprietary name for a compressed dose of a drug; a popular newspaper measuring about 12 in. (30 cm) by 16 in. (40 cm), informal in style with lots of photographs; (*coll. derog.*) a cheap, sensational newspaper.

taboo, tabu, *n.* a custom among the Polynesians etc., of prohibiting the use of certain persons, places or things; (*fig.*) ban, prohibition; any ritual restriction, usu. of something considered to be unclean or unholy. *a.* banned, interdicted, prohibited, by social, religious or moral convention. *v.t.* to put under taboo; to forbid the use of or intercourse with. [Maori *tapu*]

†**tabor, tabour,** *n.* a small drum used to accompany the pipe. †**taborer,** *n.* †**taboret,** †**taborine,** *n.* [OF *tabour* (F *tambour*), Arab. *tambūr,* lute, drum]

tabouret, *n.* a small seat, usu. without arms or back; an embroidery frame; a needle-case. [OF, dim. of prec.]

tabular, *a.* in the form of a table, having a broad flat surface; formed in laminae or thin plates; set forth, arranged in, or computed from tables. **tabula,** *n.* a flat surface; a writing tablet. **tabula rasa,** *n.* the mind in its original state, before any impressions have been made on it; a fresh start. †**tabularize, -ise,** *v.t.* **tabularly,** *adv.* **tabulate,** *v.t.* to reduce to or arrange (figures etc.) in tabular form; to shape with a flat surface. *a.*, table-shaped, broad and flat; arranged in laminae. **tabulation,** *n.* **tabulator,** *n.* an attachment to a typewriter to facilitate tabulation work; a machine which prints data from punched cards, producing tables etc. **tabulatory,** *a.* [L *tabula*]

tacamahac, *n.* a resinous exudation from various S American trees; the balsam poplar. [native name]

tac-au-tac, *n.* the parry combined immediately with the riposte; a series of attacks and parries in swift succession. [F, imit.]

tace, be silent! **tacet,** *imper.* a direction on a musical score indicating a certain instrument or singer is silent. [imper. L *tacere,* to be silent]

tach-, *comb. form* speed, speedy. [Gr. *tachys,* swift, *tachos,* swiftness]

tache, *n.* a freckle, a blotch on the skin; a spot, stain, or blemish; a catch, a fastening. [OF, as TACK[1]]

tacheometer TACHYMETER.

tachism(e), *n.* a form of action painting with haphazard blobs of colour. **tachist(e),** *n., a.* [F *tache,* spot]

tachistoscope, *n.* an instrument which flashes images onto a screen for very brief spaces of time, usually a fraction of a second, used in the study of learning and perception. **tachistoscopic,** *a.*

tachogram, *n.* a visual record produced by a tachograph.

tachograph, *n.* a tachometer in a motor vehicle which records its speed, and the distance travelled.

tachometer, *n.* an instrument for indicating the speed of rotation of a revolving shaft. **tachometry,** *n.* [Gr. *tachos,* speed]

tachycardia, *n.* abnormally rapid heart beat.

tachygraphy, *n.* shorthand, stenography, esp. one of the ancient Greek or Roman systems. **tachygrapher,** *n.* **tachygraphic, -al,** *a.* [Gr. *tachus,* SWIFT, cp. prec., -GRAPHY]

tachylyte, *n.* a black, vitreous basalt. **tachylytic,** *a.*

tachymeter, *n.* a surveying-instrument for measuring distances rapidly. **tachymetrical, tacheometrical,** *a.* **tachymetry, tacheometry,** *n.*

tachyon, *n.* a theoretical elementary particle which travels faster than the speed of light.

tachyphylaxis, *n.* the rapid development of tolerance or immunity to the effects of a specific drug.

tacit, *a.* implied but not expressed, understood, existing though not stated. **tacitly,** *adv.* **tacitness,** *n.* [L *tacitus,* silent, from *tacēre,* to be silent]

taciturn, *a.* habitually silent, reserved. **taciturnity,** *n.* **taciturnly,** *adv.* [F *taciturne,* from L *taciturnus,* as prec.]

Tacitus, *n.* **Publius** or **Gaius Cornelius** (*c.* AD 55–120), Roman historian. A public orator in Rome, he was consul under Nerva (AD 97) and governor of Asia AD 112–113. He wrote a life of Agricola (whose daughter he married in AD 77) and a description of the German tribes (*Germania* AD 98), but is better known for his histories of the Roman Empire, *Historiae* and *Annales*, covering the years AD 69–96 and AD 14–68 respectively.

tack[1], *n.* a small, sharp, flat-headed nail; a stitch, esp. one of a series of long, rapid stitches for fastening temporarily; a rope by which the forward lower corner of certain sails is fastened; the part of a sail to which such rope is fastened; the course of a ship as determined by the position of her sails; the act of tacking or changing direction to take advantage of a side-wind etc.; (*fig.*) course of action, policy; stickiness, tackiness; shoddiness; vulgar ostention; cheapness; seediness. (*Sc. Law*) a letting contract, a lease, land or pasturage leased; (*coll.*) food, fare. *v.t.* to fasten with tacks; to stitch together in a hasty manner; to annex, to append (to or on to); to change the course of a ship to the opposite tack. *v.i.* to change the course of a ship by shifting the tacks and position of the sails; to zigzag; (*fig.*) to alter one's conduct or policy. **hard tack,** ship's biscuit. **on the right (wrong) tack,** on the right (wrong) lines. **to come down to brass tacks,** to face realities, to state facts. **tack hammer,** *n.* a small hammer for driving in tacks. **tacker,** *n.* one who tacks; one who makes additions. **tacket,** *n.* (*Sc.*) a clout-nail. **tacky,** *a.* sticky; shoddy; vulgar and ostentatious; seedy. **tackily,** *adv.* **tackiness,** *n.* [ONorth.F *taque* (OF *tache*), fastening, nail, peg. EFris. and Dan. *takke,* pointed thing (cp. LG *takk,* G *zacke,* point, prong, Dut. *tak,* twig)]

tack[2], *n.* saddles, bridles, harness etc. [tackle]

tacking, *n.* the act of one who tacks; attaching a clause with a different object to a Bill in order to enable this to pass the House of Lords; the right of a mortgagee to priority of a subsequent mortgage over an intermediate one of which he had no notice.

tackle, *n.* apparatus, esp. of ropes, pulleys etc., for lifting, hoisting etc., or for working spars, sails etc.; a windlass or winch with its ropes etc.; the implements, gear, or outfit for carrying on any particular work or sport. *v.t.* to grapple with; to seize hold of, stop and challenge (an opponent); to collar; (*coll.*) to set to work vigorously upon; to secure or make fast with tackle. **tackler,** *n.* **tackling,** *n.* (*collect.*) tackle. [prob. from MLG or Dut. *takel,* from MLG *taken,* to TAKE, to lay hold of]

tacksman, *n.* (*Sc.*) one who holds a tack or lease of land from another.

taco, *n.* (*pl.* **-cos**) a thin pancake from Mexico, usually with a meat or spicy vegetable filling. [Spanish]

tact, *n.* an intuitive sense of what is fitting or right, or adroitness in doing or saying the proper thing; the stroke in beating time. **tactful,** *a.* **tactfully,** *adv.* **tactfulness,** *n.* **tactless,** *a.* **tactlessly,** *adv.* **tactlessness,** *n.* [L *tactus, -tūs,* touch, from *tactus,* p.p. of *tangere,* see TANGENT]

tactics, *n.* (*sing. or pl.*) the art of manoeuvring military or naval forces, esp. in actual contact with the enemy; (*pl.*) procedure or devices to attain some end. **tactical,** *a.* skilful, diplomatic. **tactical voting,** *n.* the practice of voting for the candidate most likely to defeat the favourite candidate, rather than one's preferred candidate. **tactically,** *adv.* **tactician,** *n.* [Gr. *taktika,* neut. pl. of *taktikos,* from *taktos,* ordered, from *tassein,* to arrange]

tactile, *a.* of, pertaining to, or perceived by the sense of touch. **tactility,** *n.* †**taction,** *n.* **tactual,** *a.* **tactually,** *adv.* [F, from L *tactilis* (TACT, -ILE)]

tadpole, *n.* the larva of an amphibian, esp. of a frog or toad, before the gills and tail disappear. [ME *tadpolle* (TOAD, POLL, head)]

Tadzhikistan (Russian **Tadzhikskaya**), *n.* constituent republic of the S central USSR from 1929, part of Soviet Central Asia. **area** 143,100 sq km/55,250 sq miles. **capital** Dushanbe. **population** (1984) 4,400,000, 56% Tadzhik, 23% Uzbek, 13% Russian or Ukrainian. **products** fruit, cereals, cotton, cattle, sheep, silks, carpets, coal, lead, zinc, chemicals, oil, gas. **language** Tadzhik, similar to Farsi (Persian). **religion** Sunni Muslim.

taedium vitae, *n.* weariness of life. [L]

Taegu, *n.* largest inland city of South Korea after Seoul; population (1985) 2,031,000.

Taejon, *n.* capital of South Chungchong province, central South Korea; population (1985) 866,000. Korea's tallest standing Buddha and oldest wooden building are found NE of the city at Popchusa in the Mt Songnisan National Park.

taekwondo, *n.* a form of Korean self- defence involving kicks and punches. [Korean name?]

tael, *n.* a Chinese weight of 1½ oz. (42·5g), and a silver monetary unit. **Haikwan,** or **Customs tael,** a Chinese silver coin. [Malay *tahil*]

ta'en, *contr.* TAKEN.

taenia, *n.* (*pl.* **-niae**) a band or fillet separating the Doric frieze from the architrave; a band or ribbon-like part; a genus of internal parasites containing the tapeworm. **taeniacide,** *n.* a chemical or substance which destroys tapeworms. **taeniasis,** *n.* infestation with tapeworms. **taeniate, taenioid,** *a.* [L, from Gr. *tainia,* from *teinein,* to stretch]

Tafawa Balewa, *n.* **Alhaji Abubakar** (1912–66), Nigerian politician, prime minister from 1957. He entered the House of Representatives 1952, was minister of works 1952–54, and minister of transport 1954–57. He was assassinated in the coup d'état Jan. 1966.

tafferel, *n.* the upper part of a ship's stern. [Dut. *tafereel,* dim. of *tafel,* from L as TABLE]

taffeta, *n.* a light, thin, glossy silk fabric; applied also to silk and linen or silk and wool fabrics. [F *taffetas,* It. *taffetà,* Pers. *tāftah,* from *tāftan,* to twist]

taffrail, *n.* the rail round a ship's stern. [corr. of TAFFEREL]

Taff Vale case, 1901, a legal decision that threatened the existence of trade unions in Britain. Reaction to the decision resulted in increasing the strength of the Labour Party and support of the trade union movement.

Taffy, *n.* (*coll.*) a Welshman. [Welsh pron. of *Davy,* short for *David*]

taffy, TOFFEE.

tafia, taffia, *n.* a variety of rum distilled from molasses. [native name]

Taft, *n.* **William Howard** (1857–1930), 27th president of the US 1909–13, a Republican. He was secretary of war 1904–08 in Theodore Roosevelt's administration, but as president his conservatism provoked Roosevelt to stand against him in the 1912 election. Taft served as chief justice of the Supreme Court 1921–30.

tag, *n.* any small appendage, as a metal point at the end of a lace; a loop for pulling a boot on; a label, esp. one tied on; a loose or ragged end or edge; a loose tuft of wool on a sheep; the tail or tip of the tail of an animal; anything tacked on at the end; the refrain of a song, the closing speech in a play addressed to the audience; a well-worn phrase or quotation; a children's game in which the players try to escape being touched by one; the act of tagging in wrestling. *v.t.* (*past, p.p.* **tagged**) to fit, furnish, or mark with a tag; to furnish with tags or trite phrases; to attach (to, on to or together); to touch in the game of tag; in wrestling, to touch a team-mate's hand as a signal that he may take his turn in the ring; (*coll.*) to follow closely or persistently (after); to call or name; to remove tags from (a sheep). **to tag along with,** to go along with someone, to follow. **tag day,** *n.* a flag day. **tag end,** *n.* the final part of something. **tag-rag** [RAGTAG, see RAG[1]] **tagtail,** *n.* a worm with a coloured tail; a hanger-on, a sycophant. **tagged,** *a.* **tagged atom,** *n.* the radioactive isotope of a tracer element. **tagger,** *n.* one who tags, esp. the pursuer in the game of tag; (*pl.*) thin tin-plate or sheet iron. [cp. Swed. *tagg,* prickle, Norw. *tagge,* tooth, also TACK]

Tagetes, *n.* a genus of showy American plants of the aster family comprising the French and African marigolds. [mod. L, from L *Tages,* Etruscan divinity]

Tagliacozzi, *n.* **Gaspare** (1546–99), Italian surgeon who pioneered plastic surgery. He was the first to repair noses lost in duels or through syphilis. He also carried out repair of ears. His method involved taking flaps of skin from the arm and grafting them into place.

tagliatelle, *n.* pasta in the form of thin strips. [It. *tagliare,* to cut]

Taglioni, *n.* **Marie** (1804–84), Italian dancer. The most important ballerina of the romantic era, acclaimed for her ethereal style and exceptional lightness, she was the first to use pointe work, or dancing on the toes, as an expressive part of ballet rather than as sheer technique. She created many roles, including the title role in *La Sylphide* (1832), first performed at the Paris Opéra, and choreographed by her father Filippo (1771–1871). Marie's brother Paolo (1808–84) was a choreographer and ballet master at Berlin Court Opera 1856–83, and his daughter Marie (1833–91) danced in Berlin and London, creating many roles in her father's ballets.

Tagore, *n.* **Rabindranath** (1861–1941), Bengali Indian writer, born in Calcutta. One of the most influential Indian authors of the 20th cent., he translated his own verse *Gitanjali* ('song offerings') (1912) and his verse play *Chitra* (1896) into English. Nobel prize 1913.

tahini, *n.* a thick paste made from ground sesame seeds. [Arab. tahina]

Tahiti, *n.* largest of the Society Islands, in French Polynesia; area 1042 sq km/402 sq miles; population (1983) 116,000. Its capital is Papeete. Tahiti was visited by Capt. James Cook in 1769 and by Bligh of the *Bounty* in 1788. It came under French control in 1843 and became a colony in 1880.

tahona, *n.* (*N Am.*) a grinding-mill for silver-ore, worked by means of a horse or mule. [Sp.]

tahr, thar, *n.* a beardless Himalayan goat. [Nepali *thar*].

tahsil, *n.* a division for revenue and other administrative purposes in some Indian states. **tahsildar,** *n.* a tahsil officer. [Hindi *tahsil,* from Arab.]

Tai, *n.* speakers of Tai languages, all of which belong to the Sino-Tibetan family. There are over 60 million speakers of Tai languages, the majority of whom live in Thailand. Tai peoples are also found in SW China, NW Burma, Laos, and N Vietnam.

taiaha, *n.* a chieftain's walking-stick, a wand of office. [Maori]

Taic THAI.

t'ai chi ch'uan, *n.* series of 108 complex, slow-motion movements, each named (for example, The White Crane Spreads its Wings) and designed to ensure effective circulation of the *chi* or intrinsic energy of the universe through the mind and body. It derives partly from the Shaolin martial arts of China and partly from Taoism.

taiga, *n.* the spruce-dominated coniferous forests found in subarctic North America and Eurasia. [Rus. *taiga*]

taigle, *v.t.* (*Sc.*) to hinder, to delay; to embarrass, to entangle. *v.t.* to delay, to linger, to tarry, to dawdle. [prob. from Scand., cp. Swed. dial. *taggla,* to disarrange]

taihoa, *n.* a phrase meaning 'Wait!' [Maori]

tail[1], *n.* the hindmost part of an animal, esp. when it extends beyond the rest of the body; anything resembling this in shape or position, as a prolongation of the body of or a pendant or appendage to anything, a bird's end feathers, a fish's caudal fin, the slender end or luminous train of a comet, the stem of a note in music, the skirt of a coat (*usu. in pl.*); the horizontal unit at the rear of an aeroplane; the hind or lower or inferior part of anything, as the exposed end (of a tile or slate in a roof), the unexposed end (of a brick or tile in a wall), the lower end of a stream or pool; a retinue, a suite, a queue; a person employed to follow another; (*Turkey*) a horse-tail formerly carried before a pasha; something coming from behind, e.g. a tail wind; (*sl.*) the buttocks; (*sl.*) female genitalia; (*sl.*) a woman. *v.t.* to furnish with a tail; (*coll.*) to remove the tails or ends from; to join (on to another thing); to insert one end of (a timber etc.) into a wall etc.; (*coll.*) to fasten something to the tail of a dog etc. *v.i.* to follow closely (after); (*Austral.*) to herd sheep or cattle; to fall behind or drop (away or off) in a scattered line; to swing (up and down stream) with the tide (of a vessel). **bit (piece) of tail,** (*sl. derog.*) a woman. **on someone's tail,** very close behind someone. **tail of the trenches,** the part where the advancing party begins to break ground. **to tail away, off,** to dwindle. **to turn tail,** to turn one's back; to run away. **with one's tail between one's legs,** beaten, in a state of defeat. **tailback,** *n.* a queue of traffic stretching back from an obstruction or traffic problem. **tail-board,** *n.* the hinged or sliding board at the back of a cart, wagon etc. **tail-coat,** *n.* a coat with tails or the skirt divided at the back, a morning or evening coat. **tail-coated,** *a.* **tail covert,** *n.* the covert feathers around a bird's tail. **tail-end,** *n.* the fag-end. **tail-end Charlie, tail-ender,** *n.* someone bringing up the rear. **tail-feather,** *n.* a rudder feather in a bird's tail; a feather forming a train. **tail-gate,** *n.* the lower gate of a canal-lock; a tailboard. *v.i.* to drive very closely behind another vehicle. **tail-light,** *n.* a red warning light at the rear of a motor-car. **tail-piece,** *n.* an ornamental design at the end of a chapter or section of a book; a triangular block on a violin etc., to which the strings are attached. **tail-pipe,** *n.* the suction-pipe in a pump. **tailplane,** *n.* the fixed horizontal portion of the tail of an aeroplane. **tail-race,** *n.* the part of a mill-race below a water-wheel. **tail-skid,** *n.* a device to take the weight at the rear end of an aeroplane's fuselage while taxiing. **tail-spin,** *n.* a vertical, nose-foremost dive by an aeroplane, during which it describes a spiral. **tail-stock,** *n.* an adjustable casting on a lathe which supports the free-end of a workpiece. **tail wind,** *n.* a wind blowing in the same direction as one is travelling in. **tailed,** *a.* (*usu. in comb.*, as *long-tailed*). **tailing,** *n.* the action of one that tails; the part of a stone or brick inserted into a wall; (*pl.*) the refuse part of ore, grain etc. **tail-less**, *a.* [OE *taegl, taegel,* cp. Icel. *tagl,* Swed. *tagel,* G *zegel*]

tail[2], *n.* limitation of ownership, limited ownership; an estate of inheritance limited to a person and the heirs of his body. **tailage**, TALLAGE.

tailed, tailless TAIL[1].

tailor, *n.* one whose occupation is to cut out and make clothes, esp. for men. *v.i.* to work as a tailor. *v.t.* to make clothes for (*usu. in p.p.*, as *well-tailored*); to fashion to a particular purpose or need. (*sl.*) to kill (a bird etc.) in a bungling fashion. **tailor-bird,** *n.* an oriental bird that sews together leaves to form its nest. **tailor-made,** *a.* made by a tailor, well cut and close-fitting (of women's outer clothes). *n.* a tailored article of clothing. **tailor's chalk,** *n.* pipeclay used by tailors and dressmakers to mark material. **tailor's tack,** *n.* loose tacking stitches used to transfer marks from the pattern to the material. **tailored,** *a.* well-cut, close-fitting; adapted to a specific purpose; smart. **tailoress,** *n.* **tailoring,** *n.* **tailorize, -ise,** *v.t.* [OF *tailleor, taillour,* from *tailler,* to cut, see TAIL[2]]

tailye, tailzie, (*Sc.*) TAIL[2].

tain, *n.* tin-foil for backing mirrors. [F, tinfoil, from *étain,* tin]

Taine, *n.* **Hippolyte Adolphe** (1828–93), French critic and historian. He analysed literary works as products of period and environment, for example in *Histoire de la littérature anglaise/History of English Literature* (1863) and *Philosophie de l'art/Philosophy of Art* (1865–69).

Taino, *n.* a member of an extinct American Indian race of the W Indies; their language.

taint, *n.* a trace of decay, unsoundness, disease etc.; a corrupting influence, infection; a stain, a blemish, a disgrace. *v.t.* to imbue or infect with a noxious, poisonous, or corrupting element; to sully, to tarnish. *v.i.* to be infected or affected with incipient putrefaction; to weaken. **tainted,** *a.* **taintless,** *a.* **taintlessly,** *adv.* †**tainture**, *n.* [F *teint,* p.p. of *teindre,* L *tingere,* to tinge, perh. conf. with ATTAINT]

taipan, *n.* a large and extremely venomous Australian snake. [Aborigini name]

Taipei, Taibei, *n.* capital and commercial centre of Taiwan; population (1987) 2,640,000. Industries include electronics, plastics, textiles, and machinery.

taipo, *n.* a devil, an evil spirit; a surveyor's instrument, a theodolite. [Maori]

taisch, *n.* (*Folklore*) the premonitory sound of the voice of a person about to die heard at a distance; a wraith, a vision of second sight. [Gael. *taibhs,* cp. OIr. *taidbse,* phantasm]

tait, *n.* a long-snouted phalanger, *Tarsipes,* of Western Australia. [Austral. Abor.]

Taiwan, *n.* Republic of China (*Chung Hua Min Kuo*). **area** 36,179 sq km/13,965 sq miles. **capital** Taipei. **towns** ports Keelung, Kaohsiung. **physical** island (formerly Formosa) off the coast of the People's Republic of China; mountainous, with lowlands in the W. **population** (1989) 20,283,000 (89% Taiwanese, 11% mainlanders whose dominance causes resentment); annual growth rate 1.4%. **exports** with US aid, Taiwan is highly industrialized: textiles, petrochemicals, steel, plastics, electronics. **language** Mandarin Chinese. **religion** officially atheist, but traditional religions are Taoist, Confucian, and Buddhist.

Taiyuan, *n.* capital of Shanxi province, NE China; population (1986) 1,880,000. Industries include iron, steel, agricultural machinery, and textiles.

taj, *n.* a crown, a head-dress of distinction, esp. a tall cap worn by Muslim dervishes. [Pers.]

Taj Mahal, *n.* a white marble mausoleum built on the river Jumna near Agra, India. Built by Shah Jehan to the memory of his favourite wife, it is a celebrated example of Indo-Islamic architecture, the fusion of Muslim and Hindu styles.

takahe, *n.* the notornis. [Maori]

takapu, *n.* the New Zealand gannet. [Maori]

take, *v.t.* (*past* **took**, *p.p.* **taken**) to lay hold of, to grasp, seize, capture, steal, catch, arrest, gain possession of, win, captivate, transport, escort, charm etc.; to carry off, to remove, carry away, carry with one, convey, conduct, extract, exact, withdraw, extort etc.; to go by means of; to receive, obtain, procure, acquire, consume, eat, appropriate, to assume; to accept, endure, hold, adopt, select, receive and retain, submit to, put up with; to ascertain by inquiry, weighing, measuring etc.; to follow a course of study, action; to understand, detect, apprehend, grasp, suppose, consider, infer, conclude, interpret; to be infected with, to contract, to be affected with, to feel, to experience; to bear in a specified way, to regard (as); to perform (an action etc.); to undertake the duties of; to photograph. *v.i.* to deduct something from, to derogate, to detract; to have a desired effect, to work, to operate; to come out well (in a photograph); to please, to be popular (with); to be attracted or inclined (to); to betake oneself (to); to be attracted by a bait; to make an acquisition; to fall ill. *n.* the act of taking; that which is taken; the amount (of fish etc.) taken at one catch or in one season; takings; the amount of copy taken at one time; a scene that has been filmed. **on the take,** making money dishonestly. **to take account of,** to pay attention to, to consider. **to take advantage of,** to make use of circumstances to the prejudice of; to use to advantage. **to take a fancy to** FANCY. **to take after,** to resemble, physically, mentally etc. **to take against,** to take a dislike to. **to take aim,** to direct a missile etc. **to take apart,** to separate; (*coll.*) to criticize severely. **to take as read,** to assume. **to take away,** to subtract; to remove. **to take back,** to withdraw, to retract. **to take care,** to be careful, cautious, or vigilant. **to take care of,** to look after, to provide for. **to take down,** to write down; to swallow, to gulp down; to take apart, to pull to pieces; to humiliate, to humble. **to take effect** EFFECT. **to take fire,** to ignite; (*fig.*) to become excited. **to take five,** (*coll.*) to take a few minutes' break. **to take for,** to mistake for. **to take for a ride,** to deceive, to hoodwink. **to take for granted,** to accept or assume without question; to fail to appreciate. **to take from,** to deduct from; to diminish, to lessen, to derogate. **to take heed** HEED. **to take hold of,** to seize. **to take in,** to admit, to receive; to undertake, to do (washing, typewriting etc.); to include, to comprise; to contract, to furl (sails); to understand, to receive into the mind, to accept as true; to deceive, to cheat. **to take in hand** HAND[1]. **to take into one's head,** to seize the idea or belief (that), to resolve (to). **to take it,** to accept misfortune or punishment. **to take it or leave it,** to accept with its problems, or not at all. **to take it out of,** (*coll.*) to get revenge, compensation, or satisfaction from; to exhaust the strength or freshness of. **to take it out on,** to vent one's anger on. **to take leave** LEAVE[1]. **to take notice,** to observe; to show alertness. **to take oath,** to swear (that). **to take off,** to remove; to carry away; to deduct (from); to drink off, to swallow; to mimic, to ridicule; to jump (from); to begin flight. **to take on,** to engage (workmen etc.); to undertake (work etc.); (*coll.*) to be violently affected, to be upset. **to take one up on,** to accept a person's challenge. **to take out,** to remove (a stain etc.); to bring, lead, or convey out; to obtain for oneself, to procure; to copy. **to take over,** to assume the management, ownership etc., of. **to take place,** to happen, to occur. **to take root,** to strike root. **to take someone out of themself,** to distract someone from their problems or shyness. **to take the air** AIR. **to take the field** FIELD. **to take to,** to resort to; to form a habit or liking for. **to take to heart** HEART. **to take to pieces,** to separate something into its various components; (*coll.*) to criticize severely. **to take to task,** to reprove, to call to account. **to take up,** to lift (up); to receive into a vehicle; to enter upon, to begin; to pursue; to occupy, to engage, to engross; to arrest, to take into custody; to accept; to pick up and secure; to take possession of; to criticize. **to take up on,** to argue (with someone). **to take upon,** to assume. **to take upon oneself,** to take responsibility for. **to take up with,** to associate with. **takeaway,** *n.* food bought from a restaurant for consumption at home; the restaurant or shop where such food is bought; a takeaway meal. **take-down,** *a.* made to be disassembled. *n.* a humiliation. **take-home pay,** *n.* the amount of salary left after deductions (income tax, national insurance etc.). **take-in,** *n.* a deception, a fraud, an imposition. **take-off,** *n.* caricature; the spot from which one's feet leave the ground in leaping; a stroke in croquet by which a player sends his own ball forward and touches another ball without shifting it; the rising of an aircraft into the air. **take-out,** *n.* a takeaway. **take-over,** *n.* the act of seizing control. **take-over bid,** *n.* an offer to purchase enough shares to obtain control of a company. **take-up,** *n.* the act of claiming something, especially of services or state benefit. **taker,** *n.* one who takes, esp. one who accepts a bet. **taking,** *a.* that takes; pleasing, alluring, attractive; infectious. *n.* the act of one that takes; capture, arrest; a state of agitation; (*pl.*) money taken; receipts. **takingly,** *adv.* **takingness,** *n.* [late OE *tacan,* Icel. *taka,* cogn. with TACK[1]]

Takeshita, *n.* **Noboru** (1924–), Japanese right-wing politician. Elected to parliament as a Liberal Democratic Party (LDP) deputy 1958, he became president of the LDP and prime minister Oct. 1987. His administration was undermined by the Recruit insider-trading scandal and in Apr. 1989 he resigned because of his involvement.

takhaar, *n.* a man from the wilds, an uncouth fellow. [S Afr.]

takin, *n.* a hollow-horned, goat-like antelope inhabiting the Mishmi Hills of SE Tibet. [native name]

talapoin, *n.* a Buddhist priest or monk in Burma, Ceylon etc.; an African monkey, *Cercopithecus talapoin.*

talaria, *n.pl.* the winged boots or sandals of Hermes, Iris etc. [L, pl. of *tālāris,* from TALUS]

talbot, *n.* a large variety of hound, usu. white with large pendulous ears and massive jaws, formerly used for tracking and hunting. [prob. from the surname]

Talbot, *n.* **William Henry Fox** (1800–77), English pioneer of photography. He invented the calotype process and the first negative/positive method. *The Pencil of Nature* (1844–46) by Talbot was the first book of photographs published. **talbotype,** *n.* a process invented by Fox Talbot in 1840 of producing a latent image upon sensitized paper, the basis of the photographic process.

talc, *n.* a fibrous, greasy magnesium silicate occurring in prisms and plates, used as a lubricator etc.; (*coll.*) mica; talcum powder. **talcite,** *n.* a massive variety of talc. **talcky, talcoid, -ose, -ous,** *a.* **talcum powder,** *n.* powdered magnesium silicate; a powder made from purified talc, used to absorb excess body moisture, usually perfumed. [F, from Arab. *talq*]

tale, *n.* a narrative, an account, a story, true or fictitious, esp. an imaginative or legendary story; an idle or malicious report; †a number, a total, a reckoning. **an old wive's tale** WIFE. **to tell one's (it's) own tale,** to speak for oneself (itself). **to tell tales,** to tell lies; to report malicious stories to someone in authority. **to tell tales out of school,** to give away secrets, to break confidences. **talebearer,** *n.* one who spreads malicious reports. **tale-bearing,** *n., a.* **tale-teller,** *n.* **†taleful,** *a.* [OE *tael,* number, *talu,* story (cp. TAAL, Icel. *tal,* story, *tala,* number), cogn. with TELL]

Talegalla, *n.* a genus of birds comprising the brush-turkey and allied megapods of Australia and New Guinea; a bird of this genus, esp. the brush-turkey. [F *talégalle,* Malagasy *talèva,* L *gallus,* cock]

talent, *n.* a weight and denomination of money in ancient Greece, Rome, Assyria etc. differing in various countries at different times (the later Attic talent was 56 lb. 14 oz. (29·4 kg) troy; a particular aptitude, gift, or faculty; mental capacity of a superior order; persons of talent; (*coll.*) attractive members of the opposite sex, collectively. **talent scout, spotter,** *n.* a person who is employed to discover talented people, e.g. for sports' clubs or the entertainment industry. **talent show,** *n.* a show which gives amateur entertainers the chance to show their ability. **talented,** *a.* endowed with talents or ability. **talentless,** *a.* [F, from L *talentum,* Gr. *talanton,* balance, a talent, cogn. with *talas -ntos,* enduring, cp. L. *tollere,* to lift]

tales, *n.* a writ for summoning jurors to make up a deficiency; a list of such as may be thus summoned. **to pray a tales,** to pray that the number of jurymen may be completed. **talesman,** *n.* a person thus summoned. [L, pl. of *tālis,* such (first word of writ)]

taliacotian, *a.* pertaining to the Italian anatomist Tagliacozzi (*d.* 1599). **taliacotian operation,** *n.* the operation of forming a new nose by taking a graft from the arm or forehead, dissevered only after union has taken place.

Taliesin, *n.* (lived *c.* 550), legendary Welsh poet, a bard at the court of the king of Rheged in S Scotland. Taliesin allegedly died at Taliesin (named after him) in Dyfed.

taligrade TALIPED.

talion, *n.* the law of retaliation. **talionic,** *a.* [F, from L *tāliōnem,* nom. *-lio,* from *tālis,* see TALES]

taliped, *a.* club-footed; having the feet twisted into a peculiar position (of the sloth). **taligrade,** *a.* walking on the outer side of the foot. **talipes,** *n.* club-foot; the sloth-like formation of the feet. [TAL-US, L *pes pedis,* foot]

talipot, *n.* an E Indian fan-palm. [Hind. *tālpāt*]

talisman, *n.* (*pl.* **-mans**) a charm, an amulet, a magical figure, cut or engraved under superstitious observance of the heavens, to which wonderful effects were ascribed; (*fig.*) something producing wonderful effects. **talismanic,** *a.* **talismanically,** *adv.* [F and Sp., from It. *talismano,* Arab. *tilsam,* Gr. *telesma,* payment, late Gr. mystery, from *teleein,* to accomplish, to pay, from *telos,* end]

talk, *v.i.* to speak; to utter words; to converse, to communicate ideas or exchange thoughts in spoken words; or through other means; to have the power of speech; to make sounds as in speech. *v.t.* to express in speech; to converse about, to discuss; to speak, to use (a specified language); to persuade or otherwise affect by talking. *n.* conversation, chat; a subject of conversation; gossip, rumour; a short speech or address. **to talk about,** to discuss; to gossip about. **to talk at him/her,** to address remarks too often indirectly or incessantly; to talk, esp. offensively, about (a person) in his presence. **to talk away,** to spend or use up (time) in talking. **to talk back,** to answer back, to answer impudently. **to talk big,** to boast. **tall talk,** *n.* (*coll.*) exaggeration. **to talk down,** to silence by loud or persistent talking. **to talk into,** to persuade by argument, by talking. **to talk of,** to discuss; to mention; (*coll.*) to suggest. **to talk out,** to kill a motion by discussing it until the time of adjournment. **to talk out of,** to dissuade from doing something by talking. **to talk over,** to discuss at length; to persuade or convince by talking. **to talk round,** to discuss without coming to a decision; to persuade. **to talk shop,** to talk about one's job out of work hours. **to talk tall,** to boast. **to talk through one's hat** HAT. **to talk to,** to speak to; (*coll.*) to remonstrate with, to reprove. **to talk up,** to speak loudly, boldly; to praise. **talkback,** *n.* a two-way radio system. **talk-show,** *n.* a chat-show. **talkative,** *a.* given to talking. **talkatively,** *adv.* **talkativeness,** *n.* **talker,** *n.* **talkie,** *n.* an early film with sound. **talking,** *a.* that talks; able to talk. **talking of,** concerning. **talking book,** *n.* a recording of a book for the blind. **talking head,** *n.* on the television, a person shown from the shoulder's up only, without any action or illustrative material. **talking picture,** *n.* a talkie. **talking point,** a matter to be talked about. **talking shop,** *n.* (*often derog.*) a meeting for discussion rather than action. **talking-to,** *n.* telling-off, a reproof. [ME *talken,* freq. of OE *tal-,* see TALE]

Talking Heads, *n.* US new-wave rock group formed 1975 in New York. Their nervy minimalist music was inspired by African rhythms; albums include *More Songs About Buildings and Food* (1978), *Little Creatures* (1985), and *Naked* (1988).

tall, *a.* high in stature, above the average height; having a specified height; (*sl.*) extravagant, boastful, exorbitant, excessive. **a tall man of his hands,** a dexterous worker. **tall order,** *n.* an exacting, or unreasonable, demand. **tall ship,** *n.* a square-rigged sailing ship. **tall story,** *n.* an exaggerated account. **tallish,** *a.* **tallness,** *n.* [prob. of Celtic orig., cp. W and Corn. *tal;* obs. *tall,* serviceable, valiant, is from OE *getael,* swift, prompt, cp. OHG *gizal,* quick]

tallage, talliage, *n.* (*Eng. Hist.*) a tax levied by the king (abolished 1340). [OF *taillage,* from *tailler,* to cut, see TAIL²]

tallat, tallet, *n.* a hay-loft. [W *taflawd, taflod,* med. L *tabulāta,* orig. fem. p.p. of *tabulāre,* to board, to floor, from L *tabula,* TABLE]

tallboy, *n.* a high chest of drawers, often on legs.

Talleyrand, *n.* **Charles Maurice de Talleyrand-Périgord** (1754–1838), French politician. As bishop of Autun 1789–91 he supported moderate reform in the French Revolution, and fled to the US during the Reign of Terror (persecution of anti-revolutionaries). He became foreign minister under the Directory 1797–99 and under Napoleon 1799–1807. He represented France at the Congress of Vienna 1814–15.

talliage TALLAGE. **tallier** TALLY.

Tallinn (German **Reval**), *n.* naval port and capital of Estonian Republic, NW USSR; population (1987) 478,000. Industries include electrical and oil drilling machinery, textiles, and paper. Founded 1219, it was a member of the Hanseatic League, passed to Sweden 1561, and to Russia 1750.

Tallis, *n.* **Thomas** (*c.* 1505–85), English composer in the polyphonic style. He wrote masses, anthems, and other church music.

tallith, *n.* a scarf worn by Jews during prayer. [Heb.]

tallow, *n.* a substance composed of the harder or less fusible fats, chiefly of animals, esp. beef- or mutton-fat, used for making candles, soap etc. *v.t.* to grease or smear with tallow; to fatten, to cause to have a large quantity of tallow. **tallow-candle,** *n.* **tallow-chandler** *n.* one who makes or deals in tallow-candles. **tallow-face,** *n.* a person with a pale complexion. **tallow-faced,** *a.* **tallow-tree,** *n.* one of various trees yielding vegetable tallow. **tallower,** *n.* **tallowish, tallowy,** *a.* [ME *talgh,* cp. MDut. *talgh,* Dut. *talk,* LG, Dan., and Swed. *talg,* Icel. *tōlgr*]

tally, *n.* a stick in which notches are cut as a means of keeping accounts; such a notch or mark, a score; a reckoning, an account; anything made to correspond with something else, a counterpart, a duplicate (of); a mark registering number (of things received, delivered etc.); such a number used as a unit of reckoning; a label or tag for identification. *v.t.* to score as on a tally, to record, to register; to put (a sheet etc.) aft. *v.i.* to agree, to correspond (with). **tally-clerk,** *n.* the person on the wharf who checks a ships cargo against it's cargo list. **tally-man, -woman,** *n.* one who keeps a tally; one who keeps a tally-shop; one who collects hire purchase payments. **tally-shop,** *n.* a shop at which goods are sold on the tally system. **tally system,** *n.* the system of giving and receiving goods on credit, to be paid for by regular instalments. **tallier,** *n.* [F *taille,* notch, incision, as TAIL²]

tally-ho, *n.* the huntsman's cry to hounds; a four-in-hand coach. *v.i.* to utter this cry. *v.t.* to urge on (hounds) thus. [prob. from F *taïaut*]

talma, *n.* a long cape or cloak, worn by men or women early in the 19th cent. [F.J. *Talma,* 1763–1826, F tragedian]

talmi-gold, *n.* a brass alloy, sometimes plated, used to imitate gold in cheap jewellery. [G, orig. a trade-name]

Talmud, *n.* chief work of Jewish post-Biblical literature, providing a compilation of ancient Jewish law and tradition, based on the *Mishna.* To this was added the *Gemara,* discussions centring on its texts, during the 3rd and 4th cents. AD. **Talmudic, -al,** *a.* **Talmudism,** *n.* **Talmudist,** *n.* a person learned in the Talmud. **Talmudistic,** *a.* [late Heb. from *lāmad,* to teach]

talon, *n.* a claw, esp. of a bird of prey; anything hooked or claw-like; the projection on a lock-bolt against which the key presses; the heel of a sword-blade; the cards left in the pack after dealing; an ogee moulding. **taloned,** *a.* [F, heel, late L *tālōnem,* nom. *tālo,* L TALUS]

talpa, *n.* an encysted tumour, a wen; the genus of insectivorous animals typified by the common mole. [L, mole]

talus¹, *n.* (*pl.* **-li**) the ankle bone; talipes; the slope or inclination of a wall etc., tapering towards the top. [L, *tālus,* ankle, heel]

talus², *n.* (*pl.* **-luses**) a mass or sloping heap of fragments accumulated at the base of a cliff, scree. [L *talūtium,* slope]

tam TAM-O'-SHANTER.

tamable, tamability, tamableness TAME.

tamale, *n.* a Mexican dish of maize and meat highly seasoned. [Sp. *tamal*]

tamandua, tamanoir, *n.* a genus or subgenus of tropical American ant-eaters. [Tupi-Guarani *tamandua,* whence F *tamanoir*]

tamanu, *n.* a large E Indian and Polynesian tree, *Calophyllum inophyllum,* yielding tacamahac. [Tahitian]

Tamar, *n.* in the Old Testament, the sister of Absalom. She was raped by her half-brother Amnon, who was then killed by Absalom.

tamara, *n.* a condiment used largely in Italy, consisting of powdered cinnamon, cloves, coriander, aniseed, and fennel-seeds. [E Ind.]

tamarack, *n.* the American or black larch; a N American pine, *Pinus murrayana.* [N Am.Ind.]

tamari, *n.* a concentrated sauce made from soya beans. [Jap.]

tamarillo, *n.* (a S Americann shrub bearing) an edible red fruit, the tree tomato. [Sp.]

tamarin, *n.* a S American marmoset, esp. *Midas rosalia.* [native name]

tamarind, *n.* a tropical tree, *Tamarindus indica;* its pulpy leguminous fruit, used in making cooling beverages, as a food flavouring and as a laxative, its wood. [MF, from Sp. *tamarindo,* Arab. *tamr,* ripe date, *Hind,* India]

tamarisk, *n.* an evergreen shrub of the genus *Tamarix,* with slender feathery branches and white and pink flowers. [L *tamariscus*]

tamasha, *n.* a public function.

Tambaroora, Tambaroora muster, *n.* (*Austral.*) an old game in Queensland etc., to decide who shall pay for drinks.

Tambo, *n.* **Oliver** (1917–), South African nationalist politician, in exile from 1960, president of the African National Congress (ANC) from 1977.

tambour, *n.* a drum, esp. a bass drum; a circular frame on which silk etc., is embroidered; silk or other stuff embroidered thus; a cylindrical stone, as one of the courses of the shaft of a column, a drum; a ceiled vestibule in a porch etc., for preventing draughts; a palisade defending an entrance; a sliding door, or rolling top, on cabinets and desks etc. *v.t., v.i.* to embroider with or on a tambour. **tamboura,** *n.* an eastern stringed instrument, plucked like a guitar. **tambourin,** *n.* a Provençal tabor or drum; a dance accompanied by this and the pipe; the music for such a dance. [F, see TABOR]

tambourine, *n.* a small drum-like instrument composed of a hoop with parchment stretched across one head and loose jingles in the sides, played by striking with the hand etc. **tambourinist,** *n.* [F, dim. of prec.]

tame, *a.* having lost its native wildness; domesticated, not wild; tractable, docile; subdued, spiritless; dull, insipid; (*coll.*) cultivated, produced by cultivation. *v.t.* to make tame; to domesticate, to make docile; to subdue, to humble. **tamable,** *a.* capable of being tamed. **tamability,** *n.* **tamableness,** *n.* **tameless,** *a.* **tamely,** *adv.* **tameness,** *n.* **tamer,** *n.* [OE *tam,* whence *temian,* v. (cp. Dut. *tam,* G *zahm,* Dan. and Swed. *tam,* also L *domāre,* Gr. *damaein,* to tame)]

Tamerlane, Tamburlaine, Timur i Leng, *n.* (1336–1405), Mongol ruler of Samarkand from 1369, who conquered Persia, Azerbaijan, Armenia, and Georgia. He defeated the Golden Horde 1395, sacked Delhi 1398, invaded Syria and Anatolia, and captured the Ottoman sultan in Ankara 1402. He died invading China.

Tamil, *n.* person of Tamil culture. The majority of Tamils live in the Indian state of TAMIL NADU (formerly Madras), though there are approximately 3 million Tamils in Sri Lanka. Their language belongs to the Dravidian family. **Tamil language,** *n.* a Dravidian language of SE India, spoken principally in the state of Tamil Nadu and also in N Sri Lanka. It is written in its own distinctive script.

Tamil Nadu, *n.* state of SE India; former name to 1968 Madras State. **area** 130,100 sq km/50,219 sq miles. **capital** Madras. **population** (1981) 48,297,000. **products** mainly industrial (cotton, textiles, silk, electrical machinery, tractors, rubber, sugar refining). **language** Tamil.

tamis, *n.* a sieve or strainer of cloth. [F]

tamma, *n.* a variety of wallaby. [Austral. Abor.]

Tammany, Tammany Hall, Tammany Society, *n.* Democratic Party organization in New York. It originated 1789 as the Society of St Tammany, named after an American Indian chief. It was dominant from 1800 until the 1930s and gained a reputation for gangsterism (hence its name is used figuratively for political corruption); its domination was broken by Mayor La Guardia. **Tammanyism,** *n.*

Tammuz, *n.* in Sumerian legend, a vegetation god, who died at midsummer and was brought back from the underworld in spring by his lover Ishtar. His cult spread over Babylonia, Syria, Phoenicia, and Palestine. In Greek mythology Tammuz appears as Adonis.

tammuz, *n.* the fourth month in the Jewish calendar according to bublical reckoning, the tenth in the civil year, usually falling in June and July. [Heb.]

tammy, *n.* a tam-o'-shanter.

tam-o'-shanter, tam, *n.* a cap fitted closely round the brows but wide and full above. [Burns's poem *Tam o' Shanter*]

tamp, *v.t.* to fill up (a blast-hole) with rammed clay above the charge; to ram down (railway ballast, road-metal etc.). **tamper[1],** *n.* one who or that which tamps; a reflective casing around the core of a nuclear weapon which increases its efficiency. **tamping,** *n.* the act of filling up a hole; the material used. **tampion, tompion,** *n.* a stopper for the mouth of a gun; a stopper for the top of an organ-pipe. **tampon,** *n.* a plug of lint etc. used for stopping haemorrhage and to absorb bodily secretions such as menstrual blood. *v.t.* to plug with a tampon. **tamponade, tamponage,** *n.* the surgical use of a tampon. [F *tampon,* a plug].

Tampa, *n.* port and resort in W Florida, US; population (1986) 279,000. Industries include fruit and vegetable canning, shipbuilding, and the manufacture of fertilizers, clothing, and cigars.

tampan, *n.* A S African tick with venomous bite. [native name]

tamper[2], *v.i.* to meddle (with); to interfere illegitimately, esp. to alter documents etc., to adulterate, or employ bribery. **tamperer,** *n.* **tampering,** *n.* [var. of TEMPER]

Tampere (Swedish **Tammerfors**), *n.* city in SW Finland; population (1988) 171,000, metropolitan area 258,000. It is the second largest city in Finland. Industries include textiles, paper, footwear, and turbines.

tampon TAMP.

tan[1], *n.* the bark of the oak or other trees, bruised and broken in a mill and used for tanning hides; the colour of this, yellowish brown; bronzing of the complexion. *a.* tan-coloured. *v.t.* (*past, p.p.* **tanned**) to convert (raw hide) into leather by steeping in an infusion of tannin or by the action of some mineral or chemical salt; to make brown by exposure to the sun; to subject (nets, sails, artificial marble etc.) to a hardening process; (*coll.*) to flog, to thrash. *v.i.* to become brown by exposure to the sun. **to tan someone's hide,** to beat somebody very badly, to thrash. **tan-balls,** *n.pl.* spent tan compressed into balls for fuel. **tanbark,** *n.* the bark of some trees, such as the oak, a source of tannin. **tan-bed,** *n.* a bed made of tan. **tan-coloured,** *a.* **tan-liquor, -ooze, †-pickle,** *n.* an infusion used in tanning. **tan-pit, -vat,** *n.* a vat for steeping hides in tannin. **tanstove,** *n.* a hot-house with a bark-bed. **tanyard,** *n.* a tannery. **tannable,** *a.* **tannage,** *n.* tanning; that which is tanned. **tannate,** *n.* tannic acid salt. **tanned,** *a.* **tanner[1],** *n.* **tannery,** *n.* a place where tanning is done. **tannic,** *a.* pertaining to or derived from tan. **tannic acid,** *n.* tannin. **tanniferous,** *a.* **tannin,** *n.* tannic acid, an astringent substance obtained from oak-bark etc., used in tanning leather, making writing ink etc., and in medicine. **tanning,** *n.* [F *tan* (whence *tanner,* to tan), G *Tanne,* fir-tree, OHG *Tanna,* fir, oak]

tan², (*abbr.*) tangent.

Tanabata, *n.* Japanese 'star festival' celebrated annually on 7 July, introduced from China in the 8th cent. It is dedicated to Altair and Vega, two stars in the constellation Aquila, which are united once yearly in the Milky Way. According to legend they represent two star-crossed lovers allowed by the gods to meet on that night.

tanager, *n.* an American bird of the family Tanagridoe, related to the finches, usu. with brilliant plumage. **tanagrine, tanagroid,** *a.* [Tupi-Guarani *tangara*]

Tanagra, *n.* ancient city in Boeotia, central Greece. Sparta defeated Athens there 457 BC. Terracotta statuettes called **tanagra** were excavated in 1874.

Tanaka, *n.* **Kakuei** (1918–), Japanese right-wing politician, leader of the dominant Liberal Democratic Party (LDP) and prime minister 1972–74. In 1976 he was charged with corruption and resigned from the LDP but remained a powerful faction leader.

Tananarive, *n.* former name for ANTANANARIVO.

tandem, *adv.* with two horses harnessed one behind the other; (harnessed) one behind the other. *n.* a vehicle with two horses so harnessed; a cycle for two riders one behind the other; an arrangement of two things one behind the other. *a.* harnessed or arranged thus. **in tandem,** with one thing behind another. [L, at length]

tandoori, *n.* an Indian method of cooking meat, vegetables, and bread in a clay oven. [Hindi, *tandur,* oven, from Arab, *tanur,* oven]

tanekaha, *n.* a New Zealand pine with straight-grained wood. [Maori]

tang¹, *n.* a strong taste or flavour, a twang; a distinctive quality. **tangy,** *a.* [ME, sting]

tang², *n.* a projecting piece, tongue etc., as the shank of a knife, chisel etc., inserted into the haft. *v.t.* to furnish with a tang. **tanged,** *a.* [Icel. *tangi,* cogn. with TONGS]

tang³, *v.t.* to make a ringing, twanging noise. *v.t.* to cause to sound thus; to bring (bees) together by clanging pieces of metal together. *n.* a ringing or twanging noise. [imit.]

tang⁴, *n.* one of various seaweeds. [see TANGLE]

Tanganyika¹, *n.* former British colony in E Africa, which now forms the mainland of Tanzania.

Tanganyika², Lake, *n.* lake 772 m/2534 ft. above sea level in the Great Rift Valley, E Africa, with Zaïre to the west and Tanzania and Burundi to the east. It is about 645 km/400 miles long, with an area of about 31,000 sq km/12,000 sq miles, and is the deepest lake in Africa (1435 m/4710 ft.). The mountains around its shores rise to about 2700 m/8860 ft. The chief ports are Bujumbura (Burundi), Kigoma (Tanzania), and Kalémié (Zaïre).

Tange, *n.* **Kenzo** (1913–), Japanese architect. His works include the National Gymnasium, Tokyo, for the 1964 Olympics, and the city-plan of Abuja, the capital of Nigeria.

tangelo, *n.* (*pl.* **-los**) a tangerine and pomelo hybrid. [*Tangerine Pomelo*]

tangent, *a.* meeting at a single point without intersecting it (even if produced). *n.* a straight line meeting a circle or curve without intersecting it (even if produced); in trigonometry, the ratio of the sine to the cosine; a small piece of metal in a clavichord, that strikes the string. **tangent of an angle,** (*Trig.*) the ratio of a perpendicular subtending the angle in a right-angled triangle to the base. **to go** or **fly off at a tangent,** to diverge suddenly from a course of thought or action. **tangency,** *n.* **tangential,** *a.* of a tangent; along the line of a tangent; digressive, irrelevant. **tangentiality,** *n.* **tangentially,** *adv.* [L *tangens -ntem,* pres.p. of *tangere,* to touch]

Tangerine, *a.* of or pertaining to Tangiers. *n.* a native of Tangiers; (**tangerine**) a small, loose-skinned orange from Tangiers.

tanghin, *n.* a Madagascan tree, *Tanghinia venenifera,* the fruit of which has a poisonous kernel, formerly used in trial by ordeal; this poison. [F, from Malagasy *tangena*]

tangible, *a.* perceptible by touch; definite, capable of realization, not visionary; corporeal. *n.* a tangible thing, property as opposed to goodwill. **tangibility, tangibleness,** *n.* **tangibly,** *adv.* [F, from late L *tangibilis,* from *tangere,* to touch]

Tangier, Tangiers, Tanger, *n.* port in N Morocco, on the Strait of Gibraltar; population (1982) 436,227. It was an important Phoenician trading centre in the 15th cent. BC. It was captured by the Portuguese in 1471, passed to England in 1662 as part of the dowry of Catherine of Braganza, but was abandoned in 1684 and later became a lair of Barbary pirates. From 1923, Tangier and a small surrounding enclave became an international zone, which was administered by Spain (1940–45). In 1956 it was transferred to independent Morocco, and became a free port in 1962.

tangle, *v.t.* to knot together or intertwine in a confused mass; to entangle, to ensnare, to entrap; to complicate. *v.i.* to become thus knotted together or intertwined; to come into conflict with; to embrace. *n.* a confused mass of threads, hairs etc., intertwined; (*fig.*) a state of confusion; a complicated situation or problem; a device for dredging up delicate forms of marine life; various kinds of seaweed. **tangle-foot,** *n.* (*N Am. sl.*) intoxicant, bad whisky. **tangled,** *a.* **tanglement,** *n.* **tangler,** *n.* **tanglesome,** *a.* tangling, *n., a.* **tanglingly,** *adv.* **tangly,** *a.* [conn. with Dan. *tang,* cp. Swed. *täng,* Icel. *thang,* dim. *thōngull,* seaweed]

tango, *n.* (*pl.* **-gos**) a dance of a complicated kind for couples, in 4–4 time, a development of the chica. *v.i.* to dance the tango. [Am. Sp.]

tangram, *n.* a Chinese puzzle consisting of a square cut into several differently shaped pieces which have to be fitted together. [etym. doubtful]

Tanguy, *n.* **Yves** (1900–55), French Surrealist painter, who lived in the US from 1939. His inventive canvases feature semi-abstract creatures in a barren landscape.

tangy TANG¹.

tanh, *n.* hyperbolic tangent. [*Tan*gent, *h*yperbolic]

tanist, *n.* (*Anc. Ir.*) the elected heir presumptive to a chief. **tanistry,** *n.* an ancient Irish tenure of lands and chieftainship, successors being appointed by election from the chief's kin. [Ir. *tanaiste,* heir to a prince, from *tan,* territory]

Tanizaki, *n.* **Jun-ichirō** (1886–1965), Japanese novelist. His works include a modern version of Murasaki's *The Tale of Genji* (1939–41), *The Makioka Sisters* in three volumes (1943–48), and *The Key* (1956).

tanjib, *n.* a kind of figured muslin made in Oudh. [Hind.]

tank, *n.* a cistern or vessel of large size for holding liquid, gas etc.; a reservoir for water; an excavation in which water collects; the part of a locomotive-tender containing the supply of water for the boiler. a heavily-armoured motor vehicle running on caterpillar tractors and carrying guns of various calibres. *v.t.* to store or treat in a tank; (*sl.*) to defeat. **to tank up,** to fill a vehicle with fuel; to drink, or cause to drink, a large quantity of alcohol. **tank-car, -ship, -steamer, -vessel,** *n.* one carrying a tank or tanks, one for carrying oil etc. **tank-engine,** *n.* a locomotive with a water-tank over the boiler, and without a tender. **tank farm,** *n.* an area with oil storage tanks. **tank farmer,** *n.* **tank top,** *n.* a sleeveless top with low neck, usually worn over a shirt or blouse. **tankage,** *n.* storage in tanks; a charge for this; the cubic capacity of a tank or tanks; the residuum from rendering refuse fats etc., used as a fertilizer. **tanked,** *a.* **tanked-up,** *a.* (*sl.*) drunk. **tanker,** *n.* a specially-built steamer or motor vessel fitted with tanks for carrying a cargo of oil; an aircraft for refuelling other aircraft in the air. **tankful,** *n.* **tanking,** *n.* (*sl.*) a defeat. [Port. *tanque* (cp. Sp. *estanque*), from late L as STANCH¹]

tanka¹, *n.* (*collect.*) the descendants of an aboriginal tribe now living in boats or by the waterside at Canton. **tanka-boat,** *n.* [Chin. *tan,* egg (prob. name of tribe), Cantonese *ka,* people]

tanka[2], *n.* a Japanese verse form with five lines. [Jap. *tan,* short, *ka,* verse]
tankard, *n.* a large drinking-vessel, usu. of metal and often with a cover. [F *tanquard,* MDut. *tanckaert*]
Tannenberg, Battle of, two battles, named after a village now in N Poland: 1410, the Poles and Lithuanians defeated the Teutonic Knights, establishing Poland as a major power; 1914, during World War I, when Tannenberg was part of East Prussia, Hindenburg defeated the Russians.
tanner[1] TAN[1].
tanner[2], *n.* (*old sl.*) sixpence. [etym. doubtful]
Tannoy®, *n.* a public announcement and loudspeaker system.
tanrec, tenrec, *n.* a small insectivorous mammal, *Centetes ecaudatus,* from Madagascar, allied to the hedgehog. [F *tanrec,* Malagasy *tandraka*]
tansy, *n.* a yellow-flowered perennial herb, *Tanacetum vulgare,* with much-divided, bitter, aromatic leaves. [OF *tanasie, athanasie,* L and Gr. *athanasia,* immortality, see ATHANASY]
tantalite TANTALUS.
tantalize TANTALUS.
tantalum TANTALUS.
Tantalus, *n.* (*Gr. Myth.*) a son of Zeus, condemned to stand up to his chin in water, which perpetually shrank away when he attempted to quench his thirst; a genus of wading-birds allied to the ibis; (**tantalus**) a spirit-stand in which the decanters remain in sight but are secured by a lock. **tantalus-cup,** *n.* a scientific toy consisting of a figure of a man in a cup, illustrating the principle of the siphon. **tantalate,** *n.* salt of tantalic acid. **Tantalean, Tantalian, Tantalic,** *a.* of Tantalus. **tantalic,** *a.* of tantalum. **tantalic acid,** *n.* $HTaO_3$. **tantalize, -ise,** *v.t.* to tease or torment by holding out some desirable object and continually disappointing by keeping it out of reach. **tantalization, -isation,** *n.* **tantalizer, -iser,** *n.* **tantalizing, -ising,** *a.* **tantalizingly, -isingly,** *adv.* **tantalism,** *n.* the punishment of Tantalus; torment. **tantalite,** *n.* a black mineral found in granite, an ore of tantalum. **tantalum,** *n.* a metallic element, unable to absorb water and used in surgical instruments, chem. symbol Ta, at. no. 73. [L, from Gr. *Tantalos*]
tantamount, *a.* equivalent (to) in value or effect. [A-F *tant amunter,* to amount to so much]
tantara, *n.* a quick succession of notes on a trumpet, hunting-horn etc. [imit.]
†**tantivy,** *n.* a hunting-cry, rushing movement, a furious gallop, great speed. *adv.* swiftly, speedily. *v.i.* to hasten, to rush, to speed. [prob. imit.]
tant mieux, so much the better. [Fr.]
tanto, *a.* in music, too much.
tantony, *n.* the smallest pig in a litter, usu. **tantony pig.** [corr. of *St Anthony,* patron of swine-herds]
tant pis, so much the worse. [Fr.]
Tantra, *n.* one of a class of later Sanskrit religious textbooks dealing chiefly with magical powers. **Tantric,** *a.* **Tantrism,** *n.* forms of Hinduism and Buddhism that emphasize the division of the universe into male and female forces that maintain its unity by their interaction; this gives women equal status. Tantric Hinduism is associated with magical and sexual yoga practices that imitate the union of Siva and Sakti, as described in religious books known as the *Tantras*. In Buddhism, the *Tantras* are texts attributed to the Buddha, describing methods of attaining enlightenment. **Tantrist,** *n.* [Sansk. orig. thread]
tantrum, *n.* a burst of ill-temper, a fit of passion. [perh. from W. *tant,* passion, impulse]
Tanzania, *n.* United Republic of (*Jamhuri ya Muungano wa Tanzania*), a country in E Africa, on the Indian Ocean, bounded to the N by Uganda and Kenya, to the S by Mozambique, Malawi, and Zambia, and to the W by Zaire, Burundi, and Rwanda. **area** 945,000 sq km/364,865 sq miles. **capital** Dodoma. **towns** chief port Dar es Salaam. **physical** a central plateau with lakes in the west and coastal plains. **population** (1989) 24,746,000; annual growth rate 3.5%. **exports** coffee, cotton, sisal, cloves from Zanzibar, tea, tobacco. **language** Kiswahili, English (both official). **religion** Muslim 35%, Christian 35%, traditional 30%.
tanzib, *n.* a fine variety of muslin, usu. figured, made in Oudh. [Pers. (*tan,* body, *zib,* adornment)]
Taoiseach, *n.* Gaelic name for the prime minister of the Irish Republic.
Taoism, *n.* Chinese philosophical system, traditionally founded by the Chinese philosopher Lao Zi 6th cent. BC, though the scriptures, *Tao Te Ching,* were apparently compiled 3rd cent. BC. The 'tao' or 'way' denotes the hidden Principle of the Universe, and less stress is laid on good deeds than on harmonious interaction with the environment, which automatically ensures right behaviour. The second important work is that of Zhuangzi (*c.* 389–286 BC), *The Way of Zhuangzi*. The magical side of Taoism is illustrated by the *I Ching* or *Book of Changes*, a book of divination. **Taoist,** *n.* **Taoistic,** *a.* [Chin. *tao,* way, -ISM]
tap[1], *v.t.* to strike lightly or gently; to strike lightly with; to apply leather to the heel of (a shoe). *v.i.* to strike a gentle blow. *n.* a light or gentle blow, a rap; the sound of this; a piece of leather put on the heel of a shoe; (*pl.*) a military signal for putting lights out in quarters. **tap-dance,** *n.* a step dance where the performers wear shoes with metal studs in the heels to make a rhythmic sound as they dance. *v.i.* to perform such a dance. **tap-dancer,** *n.* **tap-dancing,** *n.* **tap-shoe,** *n.* a shoe with specially fitted taps, for tap-dancing. **tapper**[1], *n.* **tapping,** *n., a.* [F *taper, tapper,* prob. from Teut. (cp. LG and G *tappen,* Icel. *tapsa*), prob. imit.]
tap[2], *n.* a cock for drawing water or other fluid through (*N Am.* a faucit or spigot); a faucet, a spigot; a plug or bung for closing a hole in a cask etc.; (*fig.*) liquor of a particular brew or quality; (*coll.*) a tap-room; a tool for cutting female or internal screw-threads; a device for listening, connected secretly to a telephone. *v.t.* (*past, p.p.* **tapped**) to pierce (a cask etc.) so as to let out a liquid; to let out or draw off (a liquid) thus; to furnish with a tap or cock; to draw (fluid) from a person's body, to draw fluid from (a person) thus; to draw upon a source of supply, usually for the first time. (*fig.*) to get into connection with (a country etc.) by way of trade etc.; to divert current from (a wire); to attach a receiver to a telephone so as to overhear private conversations; to make an internal screw in. **on tap,** tapped (of a cask etc.); ready to be drawn (of liquor). **tap-bolt,** *n.* a bolt with a head on one end and a thread on the other for screwing into some fixed part. **tap-hole,** *n.* a hole in a furnace through which molten lead can be run off. **taphouse,** *n.* an inn, a public house. **tap-room,** *a.* a room where liquor is drawn for drinking. **tap-root,** *n.* the main root of a plant penetrating straight downwards for some depth. **tap-water,** *n.* water from a tap, rather than from a bottle. **tappable,** *a.* that may be tapped (of rubber-trees etc.). **tapper**[2], *n.* **tapping,** *n.* **tapster,** [OE *taeppestre* (-STER)] *n.* one who serves liquor in a bar. [OE *taeppa,* cp. Dut. *tap,* G *zappen,* Icel. *tappi,* OHG *Zapho*]
tap[3], (*Sc.*) TOP.
tapa, *n.* a kind of tough cloth-like paper made from the bark of a tree, used by the Polynesians for clothes, nets etc. [native name]
tapadero, *n.* a leather guard worn in front of the stirrup in California. [Sp., cover, from *tapar,* to stop up, to cover]
tape, *n.* a narrow strip of woven linen, cotton etc., used for tying things together, in dressmaking, book-binding etc.; such a strip stretched across a race-course at the winning-post; a tape-line or tape-measure; a continuous strip of paper or magnetic tape on which messages are recorded by a recording machine; a strong flexible band rotating on pulleys in printing and other machines; (*sl.*) spirituous liquor. *v.t.* to furnish, fasten, or tie up with tapes; to bind (sections of a book) with tape bands; to get a measure of; to record sound on magnetic tape. **magnetic tape,** *n.* plastic tape coated with magnetic powder which can be magnetized in patterns corresponding to recorded music, speech

etc. **to breast the tape,** in a race on foot, to touch or break the tape across the course to win. **to have someone or something taped,** (*coll.*) to have a complete understanding of. **red tape** RED. **tape deck,** *n.* a machine for recording sound onto magnetic tape and which replays this sound through an independent amplifier. **tape-line, -measure,** *n.* a tape or strip of metal, marked with inches etc., for measuring, usu. coiled in a round flat case. **tape-machine,** *n.* a telegraphic instrument that records news, stock prices etc. **tape record,** *v.t.* to record sound using a tape recorder. **tape recorder,** *n.* an electronic apparatus for recording music etc., on magnetic tape. **tape recording,** *n.* a recording of sound on magnetic tape; the tape thus recorded. **tape-script,** *n.* a recording of written text. **tapeworm,** *n.* a cestoid worm infesting the alimentary canal of man and other vertebrates. **tapeless,** *a.* **taper,** *n.* [OE *taeppe,* L *tapēte,* cp. TAPPET and TAPESTRY]

taper, *n.* a small wax-candle; anything giving a very feeble light; tapering form. *a.* (*poet.*) growing smaller gradually towards one end. *v.i.* to become taper or gradually smaller towards one end; to become gradually smaller or less important. *v.t.* to make taper. **tapered,** *a.* tapering in form; lighted by tapers. **taperer,** *n.* a person who bears a taper. **tapering,** *a.* **taperingly,** *adv.* **taperness,** *n.* **taperwise,** *adv.* [OE *tapor,* cp. Ir. *tapar,* W *tampr*]

tapestry, *n.* a textile fabric in which the wool is supplied by a spindle instead of a shuttle, with designs applied by stitches across the warp; any ornamental fabric with designs applied in this manner. *v.t.* to hang with or as with tapestry. *a.* of tapestry. **tapestried,** *a.* [F *tapisserie,* from *tapisser,* to furnish with tapestry, from TAPIS]

tapetum, *n.* (*pl.* **-ta**) a layer of cells lining the cavity of anthers in flowering plants or of the sporangia in ferns; a portion of the choroid membrane of the eye in certain vertebrates. [late L, from L *tapēte,* carpet]

tapeworm TAPE.

tapioca, *n.* a starchy, granular substance produced by beating cassava, forming a light farinaceous food. [Port., from Tupi-Guarani *tipioka,* cassava-juice]

tapir, *n.* an ungulate herbivorous, swine-like mammal of the family Tapiridae, allied to the rhinoceros, with a short, flexible proboscis. **tapiroid,** *a., n.* [Tupi-Guarani *tapīra*]

tapis, *n.* tapestry (formerly used as a table-covering). **to be** or **come on the tapis,** to be or come under consideration. [F, tapestry, from med. L *tapētium,* Gr. *tapētion,* dim. of *tapēs-pētos*]

tappable TAP². **tapper** TAP¹ AND ².

tappet, *n.* a projecting arm or lever imparting intermittent motion to some part in machinery. **tappet-loom,** *n.* one in which the heddles are worked by tappets. **tappet-motion, -rod, -wheel,** *n.* [perh. dim. of TAP¹]

tapping TAP².

tappit, *a.* topped, crested. **tappit hen,** *n.* a hen with a top-knot or tuft; a drinking-vessel holding a Scotch quart or about three English quarts (about 3·4 l). [Sc. var. of *topped* (TOP, -ED)]

taps, *n.* the last bugle call at night, as a signal for lights-out; a similar call at a military funeral; a song signalling the close of a meeting in the Guide movement. [ety. doubtful, perh. from *taptoo,* an early form of tattoo]

tapsalteerie, tapsie-teerie, (*Sc.*) TOPSY-TURVY.

tapsman, (*Sc.*) TOPSMAN under TOP¹.

tapster TAP².

tapu TABOO.

tar¹, *n.* a thick, dark, viscid oily liquid produced by the dry distillation of organic bodies and bituminous minerals; coal tar. *v.t.* (*past, p.p.* **tarred**) to cover with tar. **tarred with the same brush,** having the same bad characteristics. **to tar and feather,** to smear with tar and then cover with feathers, a punishment inflicted usually by rioters. **tarbrush,** *n.* a brush used to apply tar. **tar macadam, tarmak, Tarmac®,** *n.* a mixture of tar and road metal giving a smooth, dustless surface. **tar-paper,** *n.* paper treated with tar, used in the building trade. **tar-seal,** *v.t.* to cover the surface of a road with tarmacadam; *n.* the bitumen surface of a road. **tar-sealed,** *a.* **tar-water,** *n.* a cold infusion of tar, formerly used as a medicine; a tarry ammoniacal water obtained in the process of purifying coal-gas. **tarry¹,** *a.* [OE *teoru* (cp. Dut. *teer,* Icel. *tjara,* Dan. *tjaere,* Swed. *tjära*), cogn. with TREE]

tar², *n.* (*coll.*) a sailor. [short for TARPAULIN]

tara, *n.* the tara-fern. **tara-fern,** *n.* the New Zealand and Tasmanian edible fern, *Pteris esculenta.* [native name]

taradiddle TARRADIDDLE.

taraire, *n.* a white-wood New Zealand tree. [Maori]

tarakihi, *n.* an edible fish from New Zealand waters. [Maori]

taramasalata, *n.* a pale pink creamy Greek pâté, made from grey mullet or smoked cod roe, olive oil and garlic. [Gk. *tarama,* cod roe, *salata,* salad]

tarantass, *n.* a large four-wheeled carriage without springs. [Rus. *tarantasu*]

tarantella, *n.* a rapid Neapolitan dance in triplets for one couple; the music for such a dance. [It., from *Taranto,* L *Tarentum,* S It. town]

Taranto, *n.* naval base and port in Puglia region, SE Italy; population (1988) 245,000. An important commercial centre, its steelworks are part of the new industrial complex of S Italy. It was the site of the ancient Greek *Tarentum*, founded in the 8th cent. BC by Sparta, and was captured by the Romans 272 BC.

tarantula, *n.* a large, venomous spider of S Europe, esp. *Lycosa tarantula,* whose bite was formerly supposed to produce **tarantism**, an epidemic dancing mania.

tarata, *n.* the lemon-wood tree of New Zealand. [Maori]

taratantara, *n.* the sound of a trumpet, bugle etc. [imit.]

taraxacum, *n.* a genus of plants containing the dandelion; a plant of this family; a drug prepared from this. **taraxacin,** *n.* a bitter principle believed to be the basis of this drug. [mod. L, prob. from Arab. or Pers.]

tarboosh, tarboush, tarbush, *n.* a brimless cap or fez, usu. red. [Arab. *tarbūsh*]

tardamente, *adv.* (*Mus.*) slowly. [It.]

tardigrade, *a.* slow-moving. *n.* one of the Tardigrada, a division of edentates containing the sloths. [L *tardigradus* (*tardus,* slow, *gradī,* to walk)]

tardy, *a.* moving slowly, slow, sluggish; late, behindhand, dilatory; reluctant. **tardily,** *adv.* **tardiness,** *n.* [F *tardif,* L *tardus*]

tare¹, *n.* a vetch, esp. *Vicia sativa,* the common vetch; a weed, perh. darnel. [ME, cp. MDut. *terwe,* Dut. *tarwe,* wheat]

tare², *n.* an allowance for the weight of boxes, wrapping etc. in which goods are packed; the weight of a motor vehicle without fuel, load, passengers or equipment; the weight of the vessel in which a substance is weighted. *v.t.* to ascertain the amount of tare of. [F, from Sp. *tara,* Arab. *tarhah,* rejected, from *taraha,* to fling]

†**tare³,** *p.p.* TEAR¹.

targe, *n.* a light shield. [OF *targe* from ON *targe,* shield]

target, *n.* an object set up as a mark to be fired at in archery, musketry etc., orig. a circular pad of twisted straw etc. painted with concentric bands surrounding a bull's eye; the objective of an air-raid; (*coll.*) the aim, sum of money etc., to be reached by a combined effort; the specific objective or aim of any (concerted) effort; (*fig.*) any person or thing made the object of attack, criticism etc., a butt; the anti-cathode used in a discharge-tube to set up X-rays; (*Railway*) a small signal at a switch etc.; †a shield, a buckler, esp. a small round one; the neck and breast of a lamb, as a joint of meat. *v.t.* to make a target of; to aim at. **on target,** on the right course; on schedule. **target area,** *n.* an area with a target located in it; an area which is a target. **target language,** *n.* the language into which a text etc. is to be translated. **target practice,** *n.* shooting practice to improve one's aim. **targetable,** *a.* which can be aimed at. *n.* **targeted,** *a.* **targeteer,** *n.* a soldier armed with a target. **targeting,** *n.* the art or practice of targeting, esp. in Britain the practice of directing the resources of the social services to those in most need. [OF *targuete,* dim. of *targue,* var. *targe* (cp. Icel. *targa,* OE *targe,* OHG *Zarga*)]

Targum, *n.* one of various ancient Aramaic versions or paraphrases of the Old Testament scriptures. **Targumic, Targumistic**, *a.* **Targumist,** *n.* [Chaldee, interpretation]

tariff, *n.* a list or table of duties or customs payable on the importation or export of goods; a duty on any particular kind of goods; a law imposing such duties; a table of charges; a method of charging for gas and electricity; the charges imposed on these. *v.t.* to draw up a list of duties on (goods); to price, to put a valuation on. **tariff reform,** *n.* the removal of defects or abuses in the tariff, free trade or approximation to this. **Tariff Reform League,** *n.* an organization set up in 1903 as a vehicle for the ideas of Joseph Chamberlain on protective tariffs. It aimed to unify the British Empire by promoting imperial preference in trade. [OF *tariffe,* arithmetic, Sp. *tarifa,* Arab. *ta'rīf,* information, from *'irf,* knowledge, from *'arafa,* to know]

Tarkovsky, *n.* **Andrei** (1932–86), Soviet film director, whose work is characterized by unorthodox cinematic techniques and visual beauty. His films include the science-fiction epic *Solaris* (1972), *Mirror* (1975), and *The Sacrifice* (1986).

tarlatan, *n.* a fine, transparent muslin. [F *tarlatane,* etym. doubtful]

tarn, *n.* a small mountain lake. [Icel. *tjörn,* gen. *tjarnar,* Swed. dial. *tjärn, tärn*]

tarnation, (*N Am. coll.*), *int.* expressing annoyance etc., contraction and softened form of eternal damnation.

tarnish, *v.t.* to diminish or destroy the lustre of; to sully, to stain. *v.i.* to lose lustre. *n.* loss of lustre, a stain, a blemish; the film of discoloration forming on the exposed face of a mineral. **tarnishable,** *a.* **tarnished,** *a.* **tarnisher,** *n.* [F *terniss-,* stem of *ternir,* MHG *ternen,* cp. OHG *tarnan,* to obscure, to darken, from *tarni,* secret]

taro, *n.* a tropical plant of the arum family, esp. *Colocasia esculenta* and *C. macrorhiza,* the roots of which are used as food by Pacific islanders. [native name]

taroc, tarot, *n.* a figured playing-card, one of a pack of 78, used in an old (orig. Italian) card-game; a pack of such cards, now widely used for fortune-telling; any game played with tarot cards. [F *tarots,* spotted cards, It. *tarrocchi,* etym. doubtful]

tarpan, *n.* a small wild horse of the steppes of Russia and Tartary. [Tatar]

tarpaulin, *n.* a canvas-cloth coated with tar or other waterproof compound; a sheet of this; a sailor's broad-brimmed tarred or oiled hat; (*coll.*) a sailor. [TAR[1], *palling,* covering, from PALL[1]]

Tarpeian, *a.* relating to *Tarpeia,* said to have been buried at the foot of the Tarpeian rock. **Tarpeian rock,** *n.* a cliff in ancient Rome from which state criminals were hurled.

tarpon, *n.* a large and powerful game-fish, *Megalops atlanticus,* of the herring family common in W Indian and western Atlantic waters. [etym. doubtful]

Tarquinius Superbus *n.* (lived 5th cent. BC), last king of Rome 534–510 BC. He abolished certain rights of Romans, and made the city powerful. He was deposed when his son Sextus raped Lucretia.

tarradiddle, taradiddle, *n.* (*coll.*) a lie, a fib. [etym. doubtful]

tarragon, *n.* a perennial herb, *Artemisia dracunculus,* allied to wormwood, used in cookery etc. **tarragon vinegar,** *n.* vinegar flavoured with tarragon. [Sp. *taragona,* Arab. *tarkhūn,* Gr. *drakōn,* DRAGON]

†**tarras,** *n.* a rock containing abundant fragments of pumice and other volcanic matter, found on the Rhine, used for making cement etc.; such cement used for lining cisterns etc. [Dut. *tarasse, terras,* now *tras,* cp. OF *terrace*]

†**tarre,** *v.t.* to incite; to urge (on). [as TARRY[2]]

tarrock, *n.* the young kittiwake; the tern; the guillemot. [etym. doubtful]

tarry[1] TAR[1].

tarry[2], *v.i.* to stay, to remain behind; to wait; to linger, to delay, to be late. *v.t.* to wait for. †**tarriance,** *n.* †**tarrier,** *n.* [ME *tarien,* to irritate, to delay, OE *tergan,* to vex (influenced by ME *targen,* OF *targer,* late L *tardicāre,* L *tardāre,* to delay, from *tardus,* see TARDY)]

tarsal, tarsi TARSUS.

tarsia, *n.* an Italian mosaic or inlaid woodwork. [It.]

tarsus, *n.* (*pl.* **-si**) the set of bones (seven in man) between the lower leg and the metatarsus, the ankle; the shank of a bird's leg; the terminal segment in the leg of an insect or crustacean; a plate of connective tissue in the eyelid. **tarsal,** *a.* pertaining to the tarsus or the ankle. *n.* a tarsal bone. **tarsier**, *n.* a small arboreal tarsioid lemur with very large eyes and ears, and long tarsal bones. **tarsioid**, *a.* pertaining to the tarsier. **tarso-**, *comb. form.* **tarsometatarsal**, *a.* pertaining to the tarsus and the metatarsus. **tarsometatarsus**, *n.* [Gr. *tarsos,* flat surface]

tart[1], *a.* sharp to the taste, acid; (*fig.*) biting, cutting, piercing. **tartish,** *a.* **tartly,** *adv.* **tartness,** *n.* [OE *teart,* prob. cogn. with TEAR[1]]

tart[2], *n.* a pie containing fruit; a piece of pastry with jam etc. (*N Am.*, a pie); (*coll.*) a girl, esp. one of doubtful character; a prostitute. **to tart up,** to make more showy; to dress cheaply, in a vulgar way. **tarted-up,** *a.* **tartine**, *n.* a slice of bread and butter. (Er.) **tartlet**, *n.* a small savoury or sweet tart. **tarty,** *a.* (*sl.*) cheap; promiscuous. [OF *tarte,* prob. var. of *tourte, torte,* L *torta,* fem. p.p. of *torquēre,* to twist]

tartan[1], *n.* a woollen fabric cross-barred with stripes of various colours forming patterns distinguishing the various Highland clans; the pattern on this; a garment, esp. a plaid, made of it; (*fig.*) a Highlander or a Highland regiment. *a.* consisting, made of, or like tartan. **tartaned,** *a.* dressed in tartan. [etym. doubtful]

tartan[2], tartane, *n.* a small Mediterranean one-masted vessel with bowsprit and lateen sail. [F *tartane,* perh. from Arab. *taridah*]

Tartar TATAR.

tartar[1], *n.* partially, purified argol, the impure tartrate of potassium deposited from wines; cream of tartar; a yellowish incrustation of calcium phosphate deposited on the teeth. **cream of tartar** CREAM. **tartar emetic,** *n.* a tartrate of potassium and antimony used as an emetic and purgative. **tartar sauce,** *n.* TARTAR(E) SAUCE. **tartareous**, *a.* of, or like tartar. **tartaric**, *a.* pertaining to, or containing, tartar or tartaric acid. **tartaric acid,** *n.* a crystalline acid from plants, used as a food acid (E334) and in medicines. **tartarous,** *a.* **tartarize, -ise,** *v.t.* **tartarization, -isation,** *n.* **tartrate**, *n.* a salt of tartaric acid. **tartrated,** *a.* in the form of tartrate. **tartrazine**, *n.* a yellow dye used in textiles, medicines and food (E102). [F *tartre,* late L *tartarum,* Arab. *durd,* dregs, tartar of wine]

tartar[2], *n.* a person of an intractable, irritable temper; a fearsome person. [from TARTAR]

Tartarean TARTARUS.

tartareous, -ric, tartarize, etc. TARTAR[1].

tartar(e) sauce, *n.* a relish served with fish etc. comprised of mayonnaise, chopped capers, herbs etc. [F *sauce tartare*]

Tartarus, *n.* (*Gr. Myth.*) a deep abyss below Hades where the Titans were confined; the abode of the wicked in Hades. **Tartarean,** *a.* [L, from Gr. *Tartaros*]

Tartini, *n.* **Giuseppe** (1692–1770), Italian composer and violinist. In 1728 he founded a school of violin playing in Padua. A leading exponent of violin technique, he composed the *Devil' s Trill* sonata.

tartish, tartly, etc. TART[1].

tartlet TART[2].

tartrate, tartrazine TARTAR[1].

Tartuffe, *n.* a hypocritical pretender. **Tartuffish,** *a.* **Tartuffism,** *n.* [F, a character in Molière's *Tartuffe*]

tarwhine, *n.* any of several edible Australian sea-fish, esp. the sea bream. [Aboriginal].

Tarzan, *n.* fictitious hero inhabiting the African rainforest, created by the US writer Edgar Rice Burroughs in *Tarzan of the Apes* (1914), with numerous sequels. He and his partner Jane have featured in films, comic strips, and televison serials. Tarzan, raised by apes from infancy, is in fact a British peer, Lord Greystoke. He has enormous physical strength, and the ability to communicate with animals. Jane Porter, an American, falls in love with him while on safari and elects to stay.

Tasaday, *n.* a people of the rainforests of Mindanao in the Philippines.

tash, *n.* (*coll.*) short for MOUSTACHE.

Tashkent, *n.* capital of Uzbek Republic, S central USSR; population (1987) 2,124,000. Industries include the manufacture of mining machinery, chemicals, textiles, and leather goods. Founded in the 7th cent. it was taken by the Turks in the 12th cent., and captured by Tamerlane 1361. In 1865 it was taken by the Russians. It was severely damaged by an earthquake 1966.

tasimeter, *n.* an instrument for measuring changes in atmospheric pressure. [Gk. *tasis,* a stretch, *metron,* measure]

task, *n.* a definite amount of work imposed; a lesson to be learned at school; a piece of work undertaken voluntarily. *v.t.* to impose a task upon; to strain, to overtax. **to take to task,** to reprove, to reprimand. **task force,** *n.* a group formed to carry out a specific task; a military or police group formed to undertake a specific mission. **taskmaster, taskmistress, †tasker,** *n.* one who imposes a task. **task-work,** *n.* work imposed or performed as a task. [ONorth.F *tasque,* OF *tasche* (F *tâche*), late L *tasca,* TAX]

taslet, *n.* a tasse, a tassel. [dim. of TASSE]

Tasman, *n.* **Abel Janszoon** (1603–59), Dutch navigator. In 1642, he was the first European to see Tasmania. He also made the first European sightings of New Zealand, Tonga, and Fiji.

Tasmania, *n.* island off the S coast of Australia, a state of the Commonwealth of Australia. **area** 67,800 sq km/26,171 sq miles. **capital** Hobart. **towns** chief port Launceston. **population** (1987) 448,000. **products** wool, dairy products, apples and other fruit, timber, iron, tin, coal, copper, silver. **Tasmanian,** *a.* of or pertaining to Tasmania. *n.* a native or inhabitant of Tasmania. **Tasmanian devil,** *n.* bear-like marsupial *Sarcophilus harrisii*, about 65 cm/2.1 ft. long with a 25 cm/10 in. bushy tail. It has a large head, strong teeth, and is blackish with white patches on the chest and hind parts. It is nocturnal, carnivorous, and can be ferocious, especially when cornered. It has recently become extinct in Australia, and survives only in remote parts of Tasmania. **Tasmanian tiger, wolf,** *n.* carnivorous marsupial *Thylacinus cynocephalus*; it is dog-like in appearance and can be nearly 2 m/6 ft. from nose to tail tip. It was hunted to probable extinction in the 1930s, but there are still occasional but unconfirmed reports of sightings.

tasmanite, *n.* a resinous mineral found in some Tasmanian shales.

Tass, *n.* Soviet news agency. [acronym for *T*elegrafnoye *A*gentstvo *S*ovyetskovo *S*oyuza]

tass, *n.* a cup, a goblet; a small draught. [OF *tasse,* goblet, prob. from Arab. *tass,* basin]

†tasse, *n.* (*usu. in pl.*) one of a series of overlapping plates hanging from the corslet as a sort of kirtle to protect the thighs. [OF]

tassel¹, *n.* a pendent ornament, usu. composed of a tuft of threads, cords, silk etc. attached to the corners of cushions, curtains etc.; the pendent of a flower, esp. the staminate inflorescence on Indian corn; a small ribbon of silk sewn into a book as a marker; a torsel. *v.t.* to furnish or adorn with tassels; to remove the tassels from (Indian corn) to strengthen the plant. *v.i.* to form tassels. **tasselled,** *a.* **tasselling,** *n.* **tasselly,** *adv.* [OF *tasel, tassel,* It. *tassello,* med. L *tassellus,* etym. doubtful]

†tassel², TERCEL.

Tasso, *n.* **Torquato** (1544–95), Italian poet, author of the romantic epic poem of the First Crusade *La Gerusalemme Liberata/Jerusalem Delivered* (1574), followed by the *Gerusalemme Conquistata/Jerusalem Conquered*, written during the period from 1576 when he was mentally unstable.

taste, *v.t.* to try the flavour of by taking into the mouth; to perceive the flavour of; to experience; (*coll.*) to eat a little of; †to enjoy, to relish. *v.i.* to take or eat a small portion of food etc., to partake (of); to have experience (of); to have a smack or flavour (of). *n.* the sensation excited by the contact of various soluble substances with certain organs in the mouth, flavour; the sense by which this is perceived; the act of tasting; a small quantity tasted, drunk or eaten, a bit taken as a sample; the mental faculty or power of apprehending and enjoying the beautiful and the sublime in nature and art, or of appreciating and discerning between the degrees of artistic excellence; manner, style, execution, as directed or controlled by this; an inclination, a predilection (for). **to have good taste,** to have an intuitive feeling for what is aesthetically correct. **to one's taste,** to one's liking. **taste bud,** *n.* any of the tiny organs on the tongue sensitive to taste. **tastable,** *a.* **taster,** *n.* one who tastes, esp. one employed to test the quality of teas, liquors etc., by tasting, orig. one employed to taste food and drink before it was served; an implement for cutting a small cylindrical sample from cheese, a small cup used by a wine-taster etc. **tasteful,** *a.* having, characterized by, or done with good taste; having or showing aesthetic taste. **tastefully,** *adv.* **tastefulness,** *n.* **tasteless,** *a.* having no flavour, insipid; vapid, dull; lacking aesthetic taste. **tastelessly,** *adv.* **tastelessness,** *n.* **tasty,** *a.* savoury, toothsome, pleasant to the taste; (*coll.*) in good taste. **tastily,** *adv.* **tastiness,** *n.* [OF *taster,* to handle, feel, taste (F *tâter*), L *taxāre,* from *tag-,* base of *tangere,* to touch]

tat¹, *v.t.* (*past, p.p.* **tatted**) to make by knotting. *v.i.* to make tatting. *n.* knotted work or lace used for edging etc., also called **tatting**. [cp. MSwed. *tätte,* Dan. dial. *tat,* Norw. *taatt* thread, strand]

tat², *n.* a coarse E Indian canvas or matting, esp. gunny. [Hindi]

tat³, tatt TATTY.

tat⁴, TATTOO3.

ta-ta, *int.* (*coll.*) goodbye. [instinctive sound]

Tatar, *n.* member of a Turkic, mainly Muslim people, the descendants of the followers of Genghis Khan, called the Golden Horde because of the wealth they gained by plunder. They now live mainly in Tatar and Uzbekistan (where they were deported from the Crimea in 1944) and SW Siberia, USSR. Their language belongs to the Altaic family. *a.* of or pertaining to this people, their land or language.

Tatar Autonomous Republic, autonomous republic, W central USSR. **capital** Kazan. **area** 68,000 sq km/26,250 sq miles. **population** (1986) 3,537,000. **products** oil, chemicals, textiles, timber.

tate, *n.* a small portion, tuft, handful or scrap of anything, esp. of wool, hair etc. [Sc., etym. doubtful]

Tate, *n.* **Nahum** (1652–1715), Irish poet, born in Dublin. He wrote an adaptation of Shakespeare's *King Lear* with a happy ending. He also produced a version of the psalms, and hymns; among his poems is 'While shepherds watched'. He became British Poet Laureate 1692.

tater, (*vulg.*) POTATO.

Tati, *n.* **Jacques** (stage name of Jacques Tatischeff) (1908–82), French comic actor, director, and writer. He portrayed Monsieur Hulot, a character embodying polite opposition to modern mechanization in a series of films including *Les Vacances de M Hulot/Monsieur Hulot's Holiday* (1953).

tatler, TATTLE.

Tatlin, *n.* **Vladimir** (1885–1953), Russian artist, cofounder of constructivism. After encountering cubism in Paris in 1913 he evolved his first constructivist works, using raw materials such as tin, glass, plaster, and wood to create abstract sculptures which he suspended in the air.

tatou, tatu, *n.* an armadillo. [Guarani]

tatter, *n.* a rag; a torn and hanging piece or shred. *v.i.* to fall into tatters. **tatterdemalion**, *n.* a ragged fellow. **tattered, tattering, tattery,** *a.* [cp. Icel. *tötrar,* LG *taltern,* rags, EFris. *talte,* rag]

Tattersall's, *n.* a lottery based in Melbourne; a sportsman's club. **tattersall,** *n.* material with stripes in a checked pattern. [Richard *Tattersall,* 1724–95, English horseman]

tatting TAT[1].

tattle, *v.i.* to chatter, to gossip; to tell tales or secrets. *n.* prattle, gossip, idle talk; a gossip. **tattletale,** *n., a.* a tell-tale. **tattler,** *n.* one who tattles, a gossip; a sandpiper. †**tattlery,** *n.* **tattlingly,** *adv.* [freq. of obs. *tat,* imit.]

tattoo[1], *n.* the beat of drum recalling soldiers to their quarters; a military pageant, esp. by night. *v.i.* to beat the tattoo. [Dut. *taptoe* (TAP[2], *toe,* put to, closed), signal for closing tavern taps]

tattoo[2], *v.t.* to mark (the skin) by pricking and inserting pigments. *n.* a mark or pattern so produced. **tattooage,** *n.* **tattooer,** *n.* **tattooist,** *n.* [Tahitian *tatan*]

tattoo[3], *n.* a native-bred pony. [Hind.]

tatty, *n.* a matting of cuscus-grass for hanging in doorways and other openings, usu. kept wet to cool the air. *a.* (*sl.*) untidy, unkempt; shabby, of poor quality. **tat(t),** *n.* rubbish, rags; something which is pretentious but of little real value. **tattily,** *adv.* **tattiness,** *n.* [Hind. *tatti*]

tatu TATOU.

Tatum, *n.* **Edward Lawrie** (1909–75), US microbiologist. For his work on biochemical genetics, he shared the Nobel prize with G. W. Beadle in 1958.

tau, *n.* the Greek letter τ; a tau cross; the American toad-fish *Batrachus tau.* **tau cross** a cross shaped like a T, a St Anthony's cross. [Gr.]

Taube, *n.* **Henry** (1915–), US chemist, who established the basis of modern inorganic chemistry by his study of the loss or gain of electrons by atoms during chemical reactions.

Tau Ceti, *n.* one of the nearest stars visible to the naked eye, 11.9 light years away. It has a diameter slightly less than that of the Sun, and an actual luminosity of about 45% of the Sun's. Its similarity to the Sun is sufficient to suggest that Tau Ceti may possess a planetary system, although observations have yet to reveal definite evidence of this.

taught, *past, p.p.* TEACH.

taunt[1], *v.t.* to reproach or upbraid sarcastically or contemptuously. *n.* a bitter or sarcastic reproach. **taunter,** *n.* **taunting,** *n., a.* **tauntingly,** *adv.* [from OF *tanter, tenter,* L *tentāre,* to TEMPT, or from F *tant,* L *tantum,* so much]

taunt[2], *a.* tall (of masts) ATAUNTO. [from obs. *ataunt,* in full rig, F *autant,* as much, cp. prec.]

taupe, *n.* a brownish-grey colour. *a.* of this colour. [F *taupe,* mole, L *talpa*]

Taurus, *n.* zodiac constellation in the northern hemisphere near Orion, represented as a bull. The Sun passes through Taurus from mid-May to late June. Its brightest star is Aldebaran, seen as the bull's red eye. Taurus contains the Hyades and Pleiades open star clusters, and the Crab Nebula. In astrology, the dates for Taurus are between about 20 Apr and 20 May (see precession). **Taurean,** *n.* a person born under the sign of Taurus. *a.* **tauric,** *a.* **tauriform,** *a.* having the form of a bull. **taurine,** *a.* bull-like; bovine; of or pertaining to Taurus. **tauromachy,** *n.* bull-fighting; a bull-fight. [L, from Gr. *tauros*]

Taussig, *n.* **Helen Brooke** (1898–1986), US cardiologist who developed surgery for 'blue' babies. Such babies are born with one or more congenital deformities, which cause the blood to circulate in the body without first passing through the lungs. The babies are chronically short of oxygen and may not survive.

taut[1], *a.* tight, tense, not slack; in good order, trim. **tauten,** *v.t., v.i.* to make taut, to become taut. **tautly,** *adv.* **tautness,** *n.* [ME *togt, toght,* prob. p.p. of *togen,* to TOW[1]]

taut[2], *v.t., v.i.* to tangle, to mat (esp. of hair). [Sc., etym. doubtful]

tauto-, *comb. form.* same, identical. [Gr., for *to auto,* the same]

tautochrone, *n.* a curve such that a heavy body rolling down it from a state of rest will always reach the same point in the same time from whatever point it starts. **tautochronism,** *n.* **tautochronous,** *a.* [Gr. *chronos*]

tautog, *n.* a food-fish common on the Atlantic coast of the US, the N American black-fish. [Narrangansett, *taut-anog*]

tautology, *n.* repetition of the same thing in different words; in logic, a statement that is always true. **tautologic, -al,** *a.* **tautologically,** *adv.* **tautologist,** *n.* **tautologize, -ise,** *v.i.* †**tautologous,** *a.* [L and Gr. *tautologia*]

tautomerism, *n.* the ability of two isomers to change into one another so that they may co-exist in equilibrium. **tautomer,** *n.* a readily changing isomer. **tautomeric,** *a.* [*tauto* + *isomerism*]

tautonym, *n.* a two-part name in which the specific name repeats or reflects the generic name, e.g. rattus rattus (black rat). **tautonymic, tautonymous,** *a.* **tautonymy,** *n.*

tautophony, *n.* the repetition of sounds. **tautophonical,** *a.*

Tavener, *n.* **John (Kenneth)** (1944–), English composer, whose individual and sometimes abrasive works include the dramatic cantata *The Whale* (1968) and the opera *Thérèse* (1979). He has also composed music for the Eastern Orthodox Church.

tavern, *n.* a public-house, an inn. **taverna,** *n.* a Greek hotel with its own bar; a Greek restaurant. †**taverner,** *n.* †**taverning,** *n.* [F *taverne,* L. *taberna,* hut, tavern]

Taverner, *n.* **John** (1495–1545), English organist and composer. He wrote masses and motets in polyphonic style, showing great contrapuntal skill, but as a Protestant renounced his art. He was imprisoned in 1528 for heresy, and, as an agent of Thomas Cromwell, assisted in the dissolution of the monasteries.

TAVR (*abbr.*) Territorial and Army Volunteer Reserve.

taw[1], *v.t.* to dress or make (skins) into leather with mineral agents, as alum, instead of tannin. **tawer,** *n.* **tawery,** *n.* a place where skins are dressed in this way. **tawing,** *n.* [OE *tawian,* cp. Dut. *touwen,* to curry, OHG *zouwan,* to make, to prepare]

taw[2], *n.* a game at marbles; the line from which to play in this; a marble. [etym. doubtful]

tawa, *n.* a New Zealand tree the wood of which is used for box-making. [Maori]

tawahi, *n.* the New Zealand penguin. [Maori]

tawdry, *a.* showy without taste or elegance; gaudy. *n.* tasteless or worthless finery. **tawdrily,** *adv.* **tawdriness,** *n.* [from *St Audrey* (corr. of *Etheldrida,* founder of Ely cathedral), whose fair was held in the Isle of Ely etc., on 17 Oct.]

tawer, tawery TAW[1].

tawhai, *n.* one of the New Zealand beeches. [Maori]

tawhiri, *n.* the New Zealand pittosporum. [Maori]

tawny, *a.* brownish-yellow, tan-coloured. **tawny eagle,** *n.* a tawny-coloured eagle found in Africa and Asia. **tawny owl,** *n.* a European owl with reddish-brown plumage. **tawniness,** *a.* [ME *tanny,* F *tanné,* p.p. of *tanner,* to TAN[1]]

tawpie, tawpy, *n.* (*Sc.*) a foolish, thoughtless girl or woman. *a.* foolish, silly, thoughtless. [prob. from Scand.]

taws, tawse, *n.* (*chiefly Sc.*) a leather strap, usually with the end cut into thin strips, used as an instrument of punishment; a lash. [prob. pl. of obs. *taw,* lash, from TAW[1]]

tax, *n.* a compulsory contribution levied on persons, property, or businesses to meet the expenses of government or other public services; (*fig.*) a heavy demand, requirement, strain etc. *v.t.* to impose a tax on; (*fig.*) to lay a heavy burden or strain upon, to make demands upon; to charge (with an oversight etc.) to fix amounts of (costs etc.); to register for payment of tribute; to accuse. **tax avoidance,** *n.* legal avoidance of tax. **tax-cart, taxed cart,** a light horse-drawn spring-cart for agricultural purposes etc., on which a reduced tax was charged. **tax-collector, -gatherer,** *n.* **tax deductible,** *a.* expenses which can be legally deducted before assessment for tax. **tax disk,** *n.* a paper disk on a car's windscreen showing payment of road tax. **tax evasion,** *n.* illegal avoidance of tax. **tax exile,** *n.* a person who lives abroad to avoid paying (high) taxes. **tax-free,** *a.* exempt from taxation. **tax haven,** *n.* a country where taxes are low, and which attracts tax exiles. **tax-payer,** *n.* **tax return,** *n.* a yearly statement of income and tax paid. **tax shelter,** *n.* a financial arrangement to lessen tax payable. **taxability,** *n.* **taxable,** *a.* **taxableness,** *n.* **taxably,** *adv.* **taxation,** *n.* **taxer,** *n.* **taxing master,** *n.* (*Law.*) the official who assesses costs of actions. [F *taxe,* from *taxer,* L *taxāre,* from *tag-,* base of *tangere,* to touch]

taxi, *n.* (*coll.*) a motor-cab fitted with a taximeter, also called **taxi-cab.** *v.i.* (of an aircraft) to travel along the ground. **taxi-rank, taxi-stand,** *n.* a cab rank. **taxiway,** *n.* a marked path from an airport terminal to a runway. [short for TAXIMETER]

taxidermy, *n.* the art of preparing and mounting the skins of animals so that they resemble the living forms. **taxidermal, taxidermic,** *a.* **taxidermist,** *n.* [TAXIS, DERM]

taximeter, *n.* an automatic instrument fitted in a cab for registering distances and indicating fares. [F *taximètre* (*taxe,* TAX, -METER)]

taxin, *n.* a resinous substance extracted from yew leaves. [L *tax-us,* Gr. *taxos,* yew, -IN]

taxis, *n.* (*Gr. Ant.*) a division of hoplites etc.; (*Gram. and Rhet.*) order, arrangement; (*Zool. etc.*) classification; (*Surg.*) methodical application of manual pressure to restore parts to their places. [Gr., from *tassein,* to arrange]

Taxodium, *n.* tree genus of the family Taxodiaceae. The deciduous swamp cypress, *Taxodium distichum,* grows in or near water in SE US and Mexico, and is a valuable timber tree.

taxonomy, *n.* the department of natural history treating of the principles of classification; classification; also called **taxology. taxon,** *n.* (*pl.* **-xa**) any taxonomical category or group. **taxonomic, -al,** *a.* **taxonomically,** *adv.* **taxonomist,** *n.* [F *taxonomie* (prec., Gr. *nom-,* from *nemein,* to deal out)]

†**tayout** TALLY-HO.

Tay, *n.* the longest river in Scotland; length 189 km/118 miles. Rising in NW Central region, it flows NE through Loch Tay, then E and SE past Perth to the Firth of Tay, crossed at Dundee by the Tay Bridge, before joining the North Sea. The Tay has important salmon fisheries; its main tributaries are the Tummel, Isla, and Earn.

Taylor[1], *n.* **Elizabeth** (1932–), US actress, born in England, whose films include *National Velvet* (1944), *Cat on a Hot Tin Roof* (1958), *Butterfield 8* (1960, Academy award), *Cleopatra* (1963), and *Who's Afraid of Virginia Woolf?* (1966). Her seven husbands have included the actors Michael Wilding (1912–79) and Richard Burton (twice).

Taylor[2], *n.* **Elizabeth** (born **Coles**) (1912–75), British novelist. Her books include *At Mrs Lippincote's* (1946) and *Angel* (1957).

Taylor[3], *n.* **Frederick Winslow** (1856–1915), US engineer and management consultant, the founder of scientific management. His ideas, published in *Principles of Scientific Management* (1911), were based on the breakdown of work to the simplest tasks, the separation of planning from execution of tasks, and the introduction of time and motion studies. His methods were most clearly expressed in assembly-line factories, but have been criticized for degrading and alienating workers and producing managerial dictatorship.

Tay-Sachs disease, *n.* an inherited disorder, caused by a defective gene, leading to blindness, retardation, and death in childhood. It is most common in people of Jewish descent.

Tayside, *n.* region of Scotland. **area** 7700 sq km/2973 sq miles. **towns** administrative headquarters Dundee; Perth, Arbroath, Forfar. **population** (1987) 394,000. **products** beef and dairy products, soft fruit from the fertile Carse of Gowrie (SW of Dundee).

tazza, *n.* (*pl.* **-ze**) a flattish or saucer-shaped cup, esp. one on a high foot. [It.]

TB (*abbr.*) tuberculosis.

Tb, (*chem. symbol*) terbium.

Tbilisi (formerly **Tiflis**), *n.* capital of the Georgian Republic, SW USSR; population (1985) 1,158,000. Industries include textiles, machinery, ceramics, and tobacco. Dating from the 5th cent. AD, it is a centre of Georgian culture, with fine mediaeval churches. Public demonstrations, following rejected demands for autonomy from Abkhazia enclave, were quashed here by troops in 1989, resulting in 19 deaths and 100 injured.

tbs., tbsp., (*abbr.*) tablespoon, tablespoonful.

Tc, (*chem. symbol*) technetium.

TCCB, (*abbr.*) Test and County Cricket Board.

Tchaikovsky, *n.* **Pyotr Ilyich** (1840–93), Russian composer. His strong sense of melody, personal expression and brilliant orchestration are clear throughout his large output, which includes six symphonies; three piano concertos and a violin concerto; operas, for example: *Eugene Onegin* (1879) and *The Queen of Spades* (1890); ballets, *Swan Lake* (1877), *The Sleeping Beauty* (1890), and *The Nutcracker* (1892); and orchestral fantasies, *Romeo and Juliet* (1870), *Francesca da Rimini* (1877), and *Hamlet* (1888); and chamber and vocal music.

tchick, *n.* a sound made by pressing the tongue against the palate and withdrawing it quickly. *v.i.* to make this sound, as in urging a horse. [imit.]

TD, (*abbr.*) *Teachta Dála* (Irish for a member of the Irish Parliament).

te, ti, *n.* in music, the seventh note of a scale.

tea, *n.* the dried and prepared leaves of *Thea sinensis* or *T. assamica,* a small evergreen tree or shrub of the camellia family; the tea-plant; a decoction or infusion of tea-leaves for drinking; a light afternoon or a more substantial evening meal at which tea is served; an infusion or decoction of other vegetable or animal substances for drinking, esp. for medicinal purposes. *v.i.* to take tea. *v.t.* to supply with tea. **black tea,** *n.* tea which has been allowed to ferment between the rolling and firing processes; tea without milk. **green tea,** tea roasted while fresh. **high tea, meat tea,** a cooked evening meal at which tea is drunk. **Russian tea,** tea drunk with lemon instead of milk. **tea-bag,** *n.* a small perforated bag containing tea. **tea-bread,** *n.* light, spongy fruit bread. **tea-caddy** CADDY[1]. **tea-cake,** *n.* a light cake, often toasted for eating at tea. **tea-canister,** *n.* **tea-chest,** *n.* a box lined with thin sheet-lead, in which tea is imported; †a tea-caddy. **tea-cloth,** *n.* a table-cloth for tea; a dish-cloth. **tea-cosy,** *n.* a cover for a tea-pot to keep the contents hot. **tea-cup,** *n.* a small cup for drinking tea from. **teacupful,** *n.* **tea-dealer,** *n.* **tea-drinker,** *n.* **tea-fight,** *n.* (*coll.*) a tea-party. **tea-garden,** *n.* a garden where tea and other refreshments are served to the public. **tea-gown,** *n.* a woman's loose gown for wearing at afternoon tea. **tea-kettle,** *n.* a kettle for boiling water to make tea. **tea-leaf,** *n.* a leaf of tea or the tea-plant; (*pl.* **-leaves**) such leaves after infusion. **tea meeting,** *n.* a religious meeting at which there is an interval for tea and social chatter. **tea-party,** *n.* a party at which tea is served. **tea-plant,** *n. Thea sinensis* or *T. assamica.* **teapot,** *n.* a vessel in which tea is infused. **Teapot Dome Scandal,** US political scandal which revealed the corruption of the Harding administration. It centred on the leasing of naval oil reserves in 1921 at Teapot Dome, Wyoming, without competitive bidding as a result of bribing the secretary of the interior, Albert B. Fall (1861–1944). Fall was tried and imprisoned in 1929. **tea-room,** *n.* a restaurant etc. where afternoon teas are provided. **tea rose,** *n.* a rose with scent supposed to resemble tea. **tea-saucer, -service, -set, -spoon,** *n.* utensils used in serving tea. **teaspoonful,** *n.* the quantity contained in a teaspoon; a quarter of a fluid oz. **tea-table,** *n.* **tea-taster,** *n.* one whose business it is to test and sample tea by the taste. **tea-things,** *n.pl.* (*coll.*) cups, saucers etc. for tea. **tea-time,** *n.* the time of the day when tea is had. **tea-tray,** *n.* **tea-tree,** *n.* the tea-plant or shrub; one of the Australian myrtaceous plants, *Melaleuca, Leptospermum* etc. that furnished a tea substitute for early settlers. **tea-urn,** *n.* a vessel for supplying hot water for tea, or tea in large quantities. [Chin. (Amoy) *tē* (pron. tā), *ch'a*]

teach, *v.t.* (*past, p.p.* **taught**) to cause (a person etc.) to learn (to do) or acquire knowledge or skill in, to instruct or train in; to impart knowledge or information concerning (a subject etc.), to give lessons in; to impart instruction to, to educate; to explain, to show, to disclose, to make known. *v.i.* to perform the duties of a teacher; to give instruction. **teach-in,** *n.* an informal conference on a specific subject involving specialists and students. **teachable,** *a.* that may be taught (of a subject etc.); apt to learn, docile. **teachableness,** *n.* **teacher,** *n.* **teaching,** *n.* the act of one who teaches; that which is taught, doctrine. *a.* that which teaches; instructive. **teaching aid,** *n.* any device which helps in teaching. **teaching hospital,** *n.* a hospital where medical students are trained. **teaching machine,** *n.* any machine which gives information to the user and corrects the user's answers to questions set. †**teachless,** *a.* [OE *taecan,* cogn. with TOKEN]

teagle, *n.* (*prov.*) a hoisting-apparatus, a lift. [North. var. of TACKLE]

teak, *n.* a large E Indian tree, *Tectona grandis,* yielding a heavy timber that does not crack, warp, shrink, or corrode iron, used largely for shipbuilding etc.; this timber. [Port. *teca,* Malayalam *tekka*]

teal, *n.* a small freshwater duck of the genera *Nettion* or *Querquedula.* [ME *tele,* cp. MDut. *teelingh*]

team, *n.* two or more horses, oxen etc., harnessed together; a number of persons working together, forming a side in a game etc. *v.t.* to harness or join together in a team; to haul, convey, etc., with a team; to sublet (work etc.,) to a contractor who employs teams of workmen; to match. **team-mate,** *n.* a fellow team-member. **team-spirit,** *n.* the willingness to act as a team, for the good of the team. **team-work,** *n.* co-operation with other members of a team or group. **teamster,** *n.* one who drives a team. **teamwise,** *adv.* [OE *tēam,* family, team (cp. Dut. *toom,* G *Zaum,* bridle, Icel. *taumr,* rein), cogn. with TOW[1]]

teapoy, *n.* a small three- or four-legged table for holding a tea-service etc. [Hind. *tīn, three,* Pers. *pēē, pāī,* foot, *sipāī,* assim. to TEA]

tear[1], *v.t.* (*past* **tore**, †**tare**, *p.p.* **torn**) to pull forcibly apart, to rend; to lacerate; to make (a rent, tear, wound etc.) thus; to pull violently (away, out etc.); to drag, remove, or sever thus. *v.i.* to pull violently (at); to part or separate on being pulled; to rush, move, or act with violence. *n.* a rent. **that's torn it,** (*sl.*) that's spoiled it. **to tear a strip off,** (*sl.*) to reprimand. **to tear oneself away,** to leave reluctantly. **to tear one's hair,** to be overcome with grief; to be very puzzled. **tear-away,** *n.* (*coll.*) reckless, sometimes violent, young person. *a.* reckless, impetuous. **tear sheet,** *n.* a page in a publication that is designed to be torn out. **tearer,** *n.* **tearing,** *a.* (*coll.*) violent, furious, tremendous, as in tearing hurry. [OE *teran,* cp. Goth. *gatairan,* G *zehren,* to destroy, Icel. *taera,* to consume, also Gr. *derein,* to flay]

tear[2], *n.* a drop of the saline liquid secreted by the lachrymal glands, moistening the eyes or flowing down in strong emotion etc.; a drop of liquid; a solid, transparent drop or drop-like object. **tear-drop,** *n.* **tear-duct,** *n.* the nasal duct. †**tear-falling,** *a.* shedding tears, tender, pitiful. **tear gas,** *n.* a poison gas that affects the lachrymal ducts and causes violent watering of the eyes. **tear-jerker,** *n.* a book, film or song which is excessively sentimental. **tear-shell,** *n.* a shell that on explosion liberates gases that irritate the lachrymatory glands. **tear-stained,** *a.* **tearful,** *a.* shedding tears; about to shed tears; sad. **tearfully,** *adv.* **tearfulness,** *n.* **tearless, teary,** *a.* [OE *tēar, taer* (cp. Icel. *tār,* Dan. *taar,* Goth. *tagr,* also Gr. *dakru,* L *lacrima,* OL *dacrima*)]

tease, *v.t.* to pull apart or separate the fibres of; to comb or card (wool or flax); to annoy, to irritate, to vex with petty requests, importunity, jesting, or raillery; to importune (to do something). *n.* one who teases or irritates thus. **teaser,** *n.* one who or that which teases; a machine for teasing wool etc.; (*coll.*) an awkward question, problem, or situation, a poser. **teasing,** *a.* **teasingly,** *adv.* [OE *taesan,* to pluck, pull (cp. MDut. *teesen,* Dan. *taese*)]

teasel, teazel, teazle, *n.* a plant with large burs or heads covered with stiff, hooked awns, which are used for raising a nap on cloth; this bur or head; a machine used as a substitute for this. *v.t.* to dress with teasels. **teaseler,** *n.* [OE *tasl, taesel,* from prec.]

teat, *n.* the nipple of the female breast through which milk is drawn; the pap of a woman; the dug of a beast; a projection or appliance resembling this, such as the attachment on a baby's feeding bottle through which milk etc. is sucked. **teated,** *a.* **teatlike,** *a.* [ME and OF *tete* (F *tette*), LG *titte* (cp. MDut. *titte,* G *Zitze,* OE *tit,* also Gr. *titthē*)]

Tebbit, *n.* **Norman** (1931–), British Conservative politician. His first career was an airline pilot, when he held various trade-union posts. He was minister for employment 1981–83, for trade and industry 1983–85, chancellor of the Duchy of Lancaster 1985–87, and chairman of the party 1985–87. He was injured in a bomb blast during the 1985 Conservative Party conference in Brighton.

Tebeth, *n.* the 10th month of the Jewish ecclesiastical year, comprising parts of December and January. [Heb.]

Tebilise®, *v.t.* proprietary name of a method of treating cotton and linen fabrics to prevent creasing and shrinking.

tec, (*sl.*) DETECTIVE.

tech.[1], short for TECHNICAL COLLEGE.

tech.[2], (*abbr.*) technical, technically; technology.

technetium, *n.* a chemical element, at. no. 43; chem. symbol Tc, whose radioisotope is used in radiotherapy. [Gr. *tekhnētos,* manmade]

technic, *n.* technique, technics. *a.* technical. [Gr. *technikos,* from *technē,* art]

technical, *a.* of or pertaining to the mechanical arts; of or pertaining to any particular art, science, business etc., strict interpretation within a specific field. **technical college,** *n.* a further education college which specializes in technical, secretarial and industrial skills. **technical drawing,** *n.* the study and practice of draughtsmanship. **technical knockout,** *n.* in boxing, the referee's decision to end the fight because one boxer is too badly injured to continue. **technicality,** *n.* technicalness; a technical term, expression etc., a petty, formal detail. **technically,** *adv.* **technicalness,** *n.*

technician, technicist, *n.* one skilled in the technical side of a subject, a technical expert.

Technicolor®, *n.* trade name for a film colour process using three separate negatives, invented by Daniel F. Comstock and Herbert T. Kalmus in the US in 1922. Originally, Technicolor was a two-colour process in which superimposed red and green images were thrown on to the screen by a special projector. This proved expensive and imperfect, but when the three-colour process was introduced in 1932 (producing separate negatives of blue, green, and red images) the system came to be widely adopted, culminating in its use in *Gone with the Wind* (1939). Despite increasing competition, Technicolor remains the most commonly used colour process for cinematography.

technicon, *n.* a gymnastic apparatus for training the hands of organists, pianists etc.

technics, *n.* the doctrine of arts in general; technical rules, terms, methods etc.

techniphone, *n.* a dumb piano for exercise in fingering.

technique, *n.* a mode of artistic performance or execution; mechanical skill in art, craft etc.; proficiency in some skill; a particular way of carrying out a scientific, medical etc. operation.

technocracy, *n.* government by technical experts. **technocrat,** *n.* **technocratic,** *a.*

technology, *n.* the science of the industrial arts; the practical application of science to industry and other fields; to total technical means and skills available to a particular human society; the terminology of an art or science. **technologic, technological,** *a.* **technologist,** *n.*

techy, etc. TETCHY.

tecnology, *n.* the scientific study of children; a treatise on children, their diseases etc. **tecnonymy,** [Gr. *onuma,* name] *n.* the custom of naming the parent from the child. **tecnonymous,** *a.* [Gr. *teknon,* child, -LOGY]

tectology, *n.* morphology dealing with the organism as a group of organic individuals, structural morphology. **tectological,** *a.* [G *tektologie* (Gr. *tektōn,* carpenter, -LOGY)]

tectonic, *a.* of or pertaining to building or construction; structural. **tectonics,** *n.* the art of constructing buildings, vessels, implements, etc., for use and beauty. **tectonically,** *adv.* [L *tectonicus,* Gr. *tektonikos,* from *tektōn, -tonos,* carpenter]

tectorial, *a.* forming a covering (esp. of a membrane of the ear). **tectorium,** *n.* (*pl.* **-ia**). **tectrices,** *n.pl.* the feathers covering the wing or tail. [L *tectōrius,* from *tec-,* p.p. stem of *tegere,* to cover]

Tecumseh (1768–1813), *n.* North American Indian chief of the Shawnee. He attempted to unite the Indian peoples from Canada to Florida against the encroachment of white settlers, but the defeat of his brother Tenskwatawa, 'the Prophet', at the battle of Tippecanoe in Nov. 1811 by Gov. W. H. Harrison, largely destroyed the confederacy built up by Tecumseh.

Ted, Teddy boy, Teddy girl, *n. fem.*

ted, *v.t.* (*past, p.p.* **tedded**) to turn over and spread (hay) so as to expose to the sun and air. **tedder,** *n.* an implement to do this. [prob. from an OE *teddan* (cp. Icel. *tethja,* past *tadda,* to spread manure, from *tath,* manure)]

teddy[1], TEDDY-BEAR.

teddy[2], *n.* a woman's one-piece undergarment!

teddy-bear, *n.* a stuffed toy bear; the koala. [Theodore (*Teddy*) Roosevelt, 1858–1919]

Teddy boy, *n.* an adolescent seeking self-expression by affecting clothes reminiscent of the late Edwardian period, and frequently by unruly behaviour.

Tedesco, *a., n.* (*pl.* **-chi**) German (used in connection with painting etc.). [It., from Teut., cp. OE *thēodisc,* G *deutsch*]

Te Deum, *n.* a hymn of praise sung at morning service or as a special thanksgiving; a musical setting for this; a thanksgiving service at which it is sung. [from the first words '*Te Deum* laudamus,' We praise Thee, O God]

tedious, *a.* tiresome, wearisome; monotonous, fatiguing. **tediously,** *adv.* **tediousness, tedium,** *n.* [late L *taediōsus,* from *taedium;* from *taedet,* it wearies]

tee[1], *n.* the 20th letter of the alphabet, T, t; anything shaped like this letter; a T-shaped pipe, joint etc.; a mark for quoits, curling-stones etc. **to a tee, T** exactly (right); to a nicety. *n.* **tee-shirt,** T-SHIRT. [T]

tee[2], *n.* in golf, a small pile of sand or a rubber cone from which the ball is played at the commencement of each hole. *v.t.* to put the ball on this. **to tee off,** to play from this; (*fig.*) to begin. [etym. doubtful]

tee[3], *n.* an umbrella-shaped finial surmounting a tope or pagoda. [Burmese *h'ti,* umbrella]

tee-hee, *int.* an exclamation of laughter. *n.* laughter, a chuckle. *v.i.* to laugh. [by imitation]

teem[1], †*v.t.* to bring forth (offspring); to be prolific; to be stocked to overflowing. **teemer,** *n.* **teeming,** *a.* [OE *tȳman, tīeman,* from *tēam,* or TEAM]

teem[2], *v.t.* to pour out (esp. molten metal); to empty. *v.i.* (*dial., coll.*) to pour (down) as rain etc. [Icel. *tœma,* from *tōmr,* empty, cp. TOOM]

†**teen,** *n.* grief, vexation, anger, resentment. *v.t.* to vex, to provoke. [OE *tēona,* whence *tēonian,* to irritate (cp. Icel. *tjōn,* damage)]

-teen, *suf.* denoting the addition of 10 (in numbers 13–19). **-teenth,** *suf.* forming ordinal numbers from the cardinals 13–19. [OE *-tȳne, tīen,* TEN]

teens, *n.pl.* the years of one's age from 13 to 19. **teenage, teenaged,** *a.* in the teens; pertaining to teenagers. **teenager,** *n.* an adolescent in his or her teens. **teeny-bopper,** *n.* (*coll.*) a young, usually girl, teenager, who follows the latest trends in clothes and popmusic with great enthusiasm. [from prec.]

teeny, (*childish*) TINY.

Teesside, *n.* industrial area at the mouth of the river Tees, Cleveland, NE England; population (1981) 382,700. Industries include high-technology, capital-intensive steelmaking, chemicals, an oil fuel terminal, and the main North Sea natural-gas terminal. Middlesbrough is a major port.

teetee[1], *n.* (*New Zealand*) the diving petrel. [Maori]

teetee[2], *n.* a small S American monkey of the genera *Callithrix* or *Chrysothrix.* [S Am. native]

teeter, *v.i.* to see-saw; to move to and fro unsteadily, to sway. *v.t.* to move to and fro, to tip up, to tilt. *n.* a see-saw. [var. of TITTER, ME *titer,* Icel. *titra,* to shake]

teeth, *pl.* TOOTH.

teethe, *v.i.* to cut or develop teeth. **teething,** *n., a.* **teething ring,** *n.* a ring for a teething baby to chew on. **teething troubles,** *n.pl.* the soreness and irritation caused when cutting the first teeth. [from prec.]

teetotal, TT, *a.* of, pertaining to, pledged to, or advocating total abstinence from intoxicants; (*coll.*) entire, complete. **teetotalism,** *n.* **teetotaller,** *n.* **teetotally,** *adv.* [redupl. of TOTAL]

teetotum, *n.* a toy, orig. four-sided, turning like a top, used in a game of chance. [for *T-totum,* take all (T, L *tōtum,* the whole), marked on one of the sides]

teff, *n.* the chief Ethiopian cereal, *Eragrostis abyssinica,* yielding flour used in Ethiopia for bread, elsewhere used as a fodder-plant. [Amharic]

TEFL, (*acronym*) the *T*eaching of *E*nglish as a *f*oreign *l*anguage.

Teflon®, *n.* polytetrafluoroethylene (PTFE), non-stick coating for saucepans etc.

teg, *n.* a female fallow-deer; a doe or a sheep in the second year; its fleece. [etym. doubtful, cp. Swed. *tacka,* ewe]

tegmen, *n.* (*pl.* **-mina**) a covering of an organ or part in an animal or plant; the leathery forewing in insects in the Orthoptera class. **tegmental,** *a.* **tegminal,** *a.* **tegument,** *n.* a protective covering, envelope, or membrane in animals. **tegumental, tegumentary,** *a.* **tegmentum, tegumentum,** *n.* (*pl.* **-ta**). [L, var. *tegimen, tegumen,* from *tegere,* to cover]

Tegucigalpa, *n.* capital of Honduras, population (1985) 571,400. It has textile and food processing industries, and was formerly a gold and silver mining centre.

tegular, *a.* pertaining to, resembling, or consisting of tiles. **tegularly,** *adv.* **tegulated,** *a.* [L, *tegula,* tile, as prec., -AR]

tegument TEGMEN.

tehee, *n.* a restrained laugh, a titter. *v.i.* to laugh frivolously or contemptuously; to titter. [imit.]

Tehran, *n.* capital of Iran; population (1983) 5,784,200. Industries include textiles, chemicals, engineering, and tobacco. It became the capital in 1788. **Tehran Conference,** *n.* conference held in Tehran in 1943: the first meeting of World War II Allied leaders Stalin, Roosevelt, and Churchill.

Te igitur, *n.* the first two words of the canon of the Mass; the book containing this. [L, thee, therefore]

teil, *n.* the lime-tree or linden. **teil-tree,** *n.* [OF (F *tille*), L *tilia*]

Teilhard de Chardin, *n.* **Pierre** (1881–1955), French Jesuit mystic. Publication of his *Le Phénomène humain/The Phenomenon of Man* (1955) was delayed until after his death by the embargo of his superiors. He envisaged humanity as eventually in charge of its own evolution, and developed the concept of the *noosphere,* the unconscious union of thought among human beings.

teind, *n.* (*Sc.*) a tithe. [ME *tende,* cogn. with TITHE]
teinoscope, *n.* an optical instrument, consisting of two prisms so combined that the chromatic aberration of light is corrected, and the linear dimensions of objects are increased or diminished. [Gr. *teinein,* to stretch, -SCOPE]
teknology, teknonymy, etc. TECNOLOGY.
tektite, *n.* a small, dark, glassy stone, thought to be of meteoric origin. [Gk. *tektos,* molten]
tela, *n.* (*Anat.*) a web, a web-like membrane, structure etc. **telar, telary,** *a.* [L]
telaesthesia (*esp. N Am.*) **telesthesia**, *n.* the perception of events beyond the normal range of sense perceptions. **telaesthetic, telesthetic**, *a.* [*tele* (1), Gr. *aisthesia,* sensation]
telamon, *n.* (*pl.* **-mones**) a male figure serving as a column or pilaster. [L, from Gr. *Telamōn,* mythical hero]
telangiectasis, *n.* abnormal dilation of the small arteries or capillaries. **telangiectatic**, *a.* [Gr. *telos,* end, *angeion,* vessel, *ektasis,* extension]
telautograph, *n.* a telegraph reproducing writing etc., at a distance. **telautogram**, *n.* **telautographic**, *a.* **telautography**, *n.*
Tel Aviv (Tel Aviv-Jaffa), *n.* city in Israel, on the Mediterranean Sea, with its port at Ashdod to the S; population (1982) 325,700. Industries include textiles, chemicals, sugar, printing, and publishing.
tele-, *comb. form* far, distant; television. [Gr. *tele,* far off]
tele-ad, *n.* a classified advertisement sent to a newspaper etc. by telephone.
telebarometer, *n.* an instrument showing atmospheric pressure at a distance. **telebarograph**, *n.*
telecast, *n.* a programme or item broadcast by television. *v.t.* to broadcast by television. **telecaster,** *n.*
telecom, *n.* short for TELECOMMUNICATIONS.
Telecom Tower, *n.* building in London, 189 m/620 ft. high. Completed in 1966, and formerly known as the Post Office Tower, it is a microwave relay tower capable of handling up to 150,000 simultaneous telephone conversations and over 40 television channels.
telecommunication, *n.* communication at a distance, by cable, telephone, radio etc.; (*pl.*) the science of telecommunication.
teledu, *n.* the stinking badger, Mydaus meliceps, of Java and Sumatra. [Javanese]
telefilm, *n.* a film made specifically to be shown on television.
Telefunken system, *n.* an early form of wireless on the spark system. [TELE-, G *funken,* sparks]
telega, *n.* a four-wheeled springless Russian cart. [Rus. *telêjga*]
telegenic, *a.* suitable for television.
telegnosis, *n.* knowledge of distant events not obtained through normal sense perceptions. [Gr. *tele* + *gnosis,* knowledge]
telegony, *n.* the supposed influence that a female's first mate has on her offspring by subsequent mates. **telegonic, telegonous,** *a.* [Gr. *tele,* far, *gonos,* offspring]
telegram, *n.* a communication sent by telegraph, now superseded by the telemessage.
telegraph, *n.* an apparatus or device for transmitting messages or signals to a distance, esp. by electrical agency; a telegraph-board; †a telegram. *v.t.* to transmit (a message etc.) by telegraph; to signal in any way; to give advance warning of something. *v.i.* to send a message by telegraph; to signal (to etc.). **telegraph-cable, -line, -pole, -post, -wire,** *n.* a cable, wire, support etc., used in establishing telegraphic connection. **telegraph-plant,** *n.* an E Indian plant of the bean family the leaves of which have a spontaneous jerking movement. **telegraph-table,** *n.* a board on which the names of horses in a race, cricket-scores, etc. are displayed. **telegrapher, telegraphist**, *n.* **telegraphist's cramp** MORSE-KEY PARALYSIS. **telegraphese,** *n.* jargon used in telegrams; contracted language. **telegraphic**, *a.* pertaining to the telegraph, sent by telegraph; suitable for the telegraph, brief, concisely worded. **telegraphically,** *adv.* **telegraphophone**, -PHONE, *n.* an instrument for reproducing phonographic sounds or records at a distance. **telegraphy**, *n.* the art or practice of communicating by telegraph or of constructing or managing telegraphs.
telekinesis, *n.* the movement of ponderable bodies at a distance and without the interposition of a material cause. **telekinetic**, *a.* [Gr. *kinesis,* motion, see KINESI-]
Telemann, *n.* **Georg Philipp** (1681–1767), German baroque composer, organist, and conductor at the Johanneum, Hamburg, from 1721. He composed operas, over 600 church cantatas, and other vocal and instrumental works.
telemark, *n.* a swinging turn in skiing. [district in Norway]
telemessage, *n.* a message sent by telex or telephone, superseding the telegraph.
telemeter, *n.* an instrument for determining distances, used in surveying, artillery practice etc. *v.t.* to obtain and transmit data from a distance. **telemetric**, *a.* **telemetry**, *n.* the use of radio waves to transmit data. [TELE-, -METER]
telencephalon, *n.* the front part of the brain, made up of the cerebrum, parts of the hypothalamus and the third ventricle. **telencephalic**, *a.* [*tel* + Gr. *enkephalos*]
teleology, *n.* the doctrine of final causes. **teleologic, -al**, *a.* **teleologically,** *adv.* **teleologist,** *n.* [Gr. *telos teleos,* end, -LOGY]
teleosaurus, *n.* (*Palaeont.*) a Mesozoic genus of fossil saurians. **teleostean**, [Gr. *osteon,* bone], *a.* of or belonging to the Teleostai, an order of osseous fishes. [Gr. *teleos,* complete, see prec., *saurus,* lizard]
telepathy, *n.* communication between minds at a distance without the agency of the senses, thought-transference, mind-reading. **telepathic**, *a.* **telepathically,** *adv.* **telepathist,** *n.* **telepathize, -ise,** *v.t.*, *v.i.*
telephone, *n.* an instrument for transmitting sounds to distances by a wire or cord, esp. by electrical agency. *v.t.* to transmit by means of a telephone. *v.t.* to speak thus (to). **telephone-box, -booth, -kiosk,** a call-box. *n.* **telephone directory,** *n.* a book listing names, addresses and telephone numbers in a given area. †**telepheme**, *n.* a telephonic message. **telephonic**, *a.* **telephonically,** *adv.* **telephonist**, *n.* a person who operates a telephone switchboard. **telephony**, *n.* [Gr. *phēmē,* voice]
telephote, *n.* a device for reproducing pictures at a distance. **telephotograph**, *n.* a picture reproduced at a distance, as by a telephote; a picture obtained by telephotography; *v.t.* to photograph thus. **telephotographic**, **telephoto**, *a.* **telephoto lens,** *n.* a lens of long focal length, for obtaining photographs of very distant objects. **telephotography**, *n.* the act or process of photographing objects beyond the limits of ordinary vision. [TELE-, Gr. *phōs phōtos,* light]
teleprinter, *n.* a telegraphic apparatus with a keyboard transmitter and a typeprinting receiver, whereby messages are received in printed form.
teleprompter, *n.* an apparatus which enables a speaker on television to see his/her text without this being visible to the viewers.
telerecording, *n.* a recording for broadcasting on television.
telesales, *n.pl.* the selling of items by telephone.
telescope, *n.* an optical instrument for increasing the apparent size of distant objects. *v.t.* to drive or force (sections, trains etc.) into each other, like the sliding sections of a telescope. *v.i.* to move or be forced into each other thus. **telescopic**, *a.* performed by, pertaining to, a telescope; capable of retraction and protraction. **telescopic sight,** *n.* a small telescope mounted on a rifle, used as a sight. **telescopically,** *adv.* **telescopiform**, *a.* **telescopist**, *n.* **telescopy**, *n.* [TELE-, -SCOPE]
teleseme, *n.* a system of electric transmitters with an annunciator used for signalling from different rooms in an hotel, etc. [TELE-, Gr. *sēma,* sign]
†**telesia,** *n.* a mineral composed of crystallized alumina,

a sapphire. [Gr., pl. neut. of *telesios,* completing]

telespectroscope, *n.* an instrument for spectroscopic examination of the heavenly bodies. **telestereoscope,** *n.* an optical instrument presenting distant objects in relief.

†**telestick, telestich,** *n.* a poem in which the final letters of each line make up a word or words. [Gr. *telos,* end, *stichos,* row, verse]

teletext, *n.* written data transmitted by television companies and viewable on a television screen supplied with a special adaptor.

telethermograph, *n.* a self-registering telethermometer; a record made by this. **telethermometer,** *n.* a thermometer registering at a distance by electrical means.

telethon, *n.* a very long television programme, usu. to raise funds for charities. [*tele*vision + mara*thon*]

Teletype®, *n.* the sending by direct keyboard and the type-printing of telegraph messages. **teletypewriter,** *n.* a teleprinter.

teleutospore, *n.* a spore produced at the end of the season of fructification in the rust-fungi or Uredinales. [Gr. *teleutē,* completion, from *telos,* end, SPORE]

televangelist, *n.* an evangelical preacher who hosts a television show in order to reach a wide audience. **televangelism,** *n.* [TELE-, EVANGELIST]

teleview, *v.t., v.i.* to view with a television receiver. **televiewer,** *n.* [TELE-, VIEW]

televise, *v.t.* to transmit by television.

television, *n.* the transmission by radio or other means of visual images so that they are displayed on a cathode-ray tube screen. A rapid succession of such images gives a visual impression of an event as it actually occurs. **television set,** *n.* a device designed to receive and decode incoming electrical, television signals. **televisual,** *a.* pertaining to television. **televisor,** *n.* a television receiver. [TELE-, VISION]

telex, *n.* a teleprinter-hiring service run by the Post Office; a teleprinter used for this service, the message sent. *v.t.* to send a message by telex. [*tele*-typewriter *ex*change]

Telford, *n.* **Thomas** (1757–1834), Scottish civil engineer who opened up N Scotland by building roads and waterways. He constructed many aqueducts and canals including the Caledonian (1802–23), and erected the Menai road suspension bridge (1819–26).

telic, *a.* expressing end or purpose; purposive. [Gr. *telos,* see prec., -IC]

tell, *v.t.* (*past, p.p.* **told**) to relate, to recount; to make known, to express in words, to communicate, to divulge; to inform, to assure; to order, to bid, to direct; to distinguish, to ascertain; †to count, to enumerate. *v.i.* to give information or an account (of); (*coll.*) to inform, to tattle; to produce a marked effect. **all told,** all included. **to tell apart,** to distinguish between. **to tell off,** to count off; to select or detach on some special duty; (*coll.*) to scold. **to tell on,** to give away secrets. **to tell one's beads,** to recite the rosary. **to tell the tale,** (*coll.*) to tell a piteous story. **to tell the time,** to read the time from a clock. **you're telling me,** (*coll.*) you are telling me something I know all about. **telltale,** *a.* telling tales; given to telling tales conveying information. *n.* one who tells tales, esp. about the private affairs of others; (*fig.*) a sign, an indication, a token; any automatic device for giving information as to condition, position etc.; an index in front of the wheel or in the cabin to show the position of the tiller. **tellable,** *a.* **teller,** *n.* one who tells; one who numbers or counts, esp. one of four appointed to count votes in the House of Commons; an officer in a bank etc., appointed to receive or pay out money. **tellership,** *n.* **telling,** *a.* **telling-off,** *n.* a rebuke. **tellingly,** *adv.* [OE *tellan,* from *talu,* TALE]

Tell, *n.* **Wilhelm (William)** (lived 14th cent.), legendary Swiss archer, said to have refused to salute the Hapsburg badge at Altdorf on Lake Lucerne. Sentenced to shoot an apple from his son's head, he did so, then shot the tyrannical Austrian ruler.

Tell el Amarna, *n.* site of the ancient Egyptian capital Akhetaton. The Amarna tablets were found there.

tellural, *a.* of or pertaining to the earth. **tellurian,** *n.* an inhabitant of the earth; †*a.* tellural. **telluric**[1], *a.* **tellurion,** *n.* an apparatus for illustrating the real and apparent movements of the earth, the phenomena of eclipses, day and night, the seasons etc. [L *tellus -lūris,* the earth, -AL]

tellurium, *n.* a rare silvery-white non-metallic element, at. no. 52, chem. symbol Te, found in association with gold, silver, and bismuth. **tellurate,** *n.* a salt of telluric acid. **telluret,** *n.* **telluretted,** *a.* **telluride,** *n.* **telluric**[2], **tellurous,** *a.* **telluriferous,** *a.* **tellurite,** *n.* native oxide of tellurium; a salt of tellurous acid. **tellurometer,** *n.* in surveying an electronic instrument which measures distances using radio waves. [as prec., -IUM]

telly, *n.* (*coll.*) television.

telotype, *n.* a printing electric telegraph; a telegram printed by this. [Gr. *telos,* end, TYPE]

telpher, *n.* a form of suspended monorail on which a truck runs, carrying its load hanging below the level of the truck and rail. **telpherline, -way,** *n.* **telpherage,** *n.* transportation of this nature, operated usually by electricity. [for *telephore* (TELE-, -PHORE)]

telson, *n.* the last somite or joint in the abdomen of Crustacea. [Gr., limit]

Telstar, *n.* US communications satellite, launched 10 July 1962, which relayed the first live television transmissions between the US and Europe. Telstar orbited the Earth in 158 minutes, and so had to be tracked by ground stations, unlike the geostationary satellites of today.

Telugu, *n.* (*pl.* **-gu** or **gus**) the most extensive of the Dravidian languages spoken on the Coromandel coast of India. [native name]

temenos, *n.* (*Gr. Ant.*) a sacred enclosure, esp. the precinct of a temple. [Gr., from *tem-,* base of *temnein,* to cut]

temerarious, *a.* rash, reckless, headstrong; careless, done at random. **temerariously,** *adv.* **temerity,** *n.* excessive rashness, recklessness. [L *temerārius, temere,* rashly]

temp., (*abbr.*) temperature.

temp, short for TEMPORARY, *n.* a temporary, usu. secretarial or clerical, worker. [temperary]

Tempean, *a.* of or like Tempe, a beautiful vale in Thessaly; delightful, lovely. [L and Gr. *Tempē,* -AN]

temper, *v.t.* to mix in due proportion; to bring (clay etc.,) to a proper consistency by mixing, kneading etc.; to bring (steel etc.,) to a proper degree of hardness by heating and cooling; (*fig.*) to qualify by admixture, to modify, to moderate, to tone down, to mitigate; to adjust the tones of (an instrument) according to a particular temperament. *v.i.* to be tempered. *n.* disposition of mind, esp. as regards the passions or emotions; composure, self-command; anger, irritation, passion; the state of a metal as regards hardness and elasticity; condition or consistency (of a plastic mixture as mortar). **to be out of temper,** to be irritable, to be in a bad temper. **to keep one's temper,** to remain calm and rational. **to lose one's temper,** to become angry. **bad temper,** *n.* an angry mood, a tendancy to anger. **good temper,** *n.* good-nature, calmness of mood. **temperable,** *a.* **temperative,** *a.* **tempered,** *a.* adjusted according to equal temperament; having a temper. **temperedly,** *adv.* (*usu. in comb. as hot-tempered, hot-temperedly*). **temperer,** *n.* [OE *temprian,* L *temperāre,* from *tempus -poris,* time, season]

tempera, *n.* painting in distemper. [It.]

temperament, *n.* individual character as determined by the reaction of the physical upon the mental constitution, natural disposition (formerly supposed to be determined by the relative predominance of certain humours, and classified as sanguine or full-blooded, lymphatic or phlegmatic, bilious, and melancholic); the adjustment of the tones of an instrument to fit the scale in any key, esp. by a compromise in the case of instruments of fixed intonation, as an organ or piano. **equal temperament,** *n.* a system of tuning where the octave is divided by into twelve equal intervals, or semitones.

temperamental, *a.* resulting from or connected with temperament; having an erratic or neurotic temperament. **temperamentally,** *adv.* [L *temperāmentum,* as prec.]

temperance, *n.* moderation, self-restraint, esp. in the indulgence of the appetites and passions; moderation in the use of intoxicants; (incorr.) total abstinence. *a.* advocating, promoting moderation, especially in alcoholic drinks. **temperance hotel,** *n.* one in which alcoholic liquors are not supplied. [OF, from L *temperantia,* as prec.]

temperate, *a.* moderate, self-restrained; abstemious; not liable to excess of heat or cold, mild (of climate). **temperate zone,** *n.* that part of the earth which, between the tropics and the polar circles, has a moderate climate. **temperately,** *adv.* **temperateness,** *n.* [L *temperātus,* p.p. of *temperāre,* to TEMPER]

temperative TEMPER.

temperature, *n.* degree of heat or cold in a body or the atmosphere, esp. as registered by a thermometer; (*coll.*) body temperature above normal. **temperature-humidity index,** *n.* an index which measures temperature and humidity and the effect of these on human comfort. [F, from L *temperātūra,* as TEMPERATE]

tempered, etc TEMPER.

tempest, *n.* a violent storm of wind, esp. with heavy rain, hail, or snow; (*fig.*) violent tumult or agitation. **tempestuous,** *a.* **tempestuously,** *adv.* **tempestuousness,** *n.* [OF *tempeste* (F *tempête*), L *tempestātem,* nom. *-tas,* weather, from *tempus,* time]

Templar, *n.* a member of a Christian religious and military order (the Knights of the Temple of Solomon), founded in Jerusalem in the 12th cent., for the protection of pilgrims to the Holy Land and the recovery of Palestine from the Muslims; a lawyer or a law-student having chambers in the Temple, in London; a member of the 'Good Templars'. [A-F *templer,* OF *templier,* med. L *templārius,* from *templum,* TEMPLE¹]

template TEMPLET.

temple¹, *n.* an edifice dedicated to the service of some deity or deities, esp. of the ancient Egyptians, Greeks or Romans; one of the three successive buildings that were the seat of Jewish worship at Jerusalem; a place of public Christian worship, esp. a Protestant church in France; (*London*) two Inns of Court, on the ancient site of the Temple, the establishment of the Knights Templars; (*Bibl. etc.*) a place in which the divine presence specially resides. **templar,** *a.* pertaining to a temple. [OE *templ,* L *templum,* cogn. with TEMENOS]

temple², *n.* the flat portion of the head between the forehead and ear. **temporal²,** *a.* positioned at the temples. **temporal bone,** *n.* one of the two compound bones at the sides of the skull. **temporal lobe,** *n.* one of the large lobes on either side of the cerebral hemisphere, associated with hearing and speech. [OF *temples,* L *tempora,* pl. of *tempus,* time]

temple³, *n.* an attachment in a loom for keeping the fabric stretched. [F, see foll.]

Temple, *n.* **Shirley** (1928–), US actress, who became the most successful child star of the 1930s. Her films include *Bright Eyes* (1934), in which she sang 'On the Good Ship Lollipop'. As Shirley T. Black, she was active in the Republican Party, and was US Chief of Protocol 1976–77.

templet, template, *n.* a pattern, gauge or mould, usu. of thin wood or metal, used as a guide in shaping, turning, or drilling; a short timber or stout stone placed in a wall to distribute the pressure of beams etc. [F, dim. of *temple,* L *templum,* a small timber]

tempo, *n.* (*pl.* **-pi**) quickness or rate of movement, time. [It., from L *tempus,* see foll.]

temporal¹, *a.* pertaining to this life; civil, secular; pertaining to or expressing time. **temporal lords,** *n.pl.* the peers of the realm, as distinguished from the archbishops and bishops. **temporal power,** *n.* that of the Pope or the Church in temporal as distinguished from ecclesiastical affairs. **temporally,** *adv.* **temporalness,** *n.* **temporality,** *n.* the laity; a secular possession, esp. (*pl.*) the revenues of a religious corporation or an ecclesiastic; temporalness. [OF, from L *temporālis,* from *tempus -poris,* time]

temporal² TEMPLE².

temporary, *a.* lasting or intended only for a time or a special occasion; transient. *n.* a person working on a short-term contract. **temporarily,** *adv.* **temporariness,** *n.* [L *temporārius,* as TEMPORAL¹]

temporize, -ise, *v.i.* to pursue an indecisive, procrastinating, or time-serving policy; to comply with or humour or yield to the requirements of time and occasion; to trim; to delay. **temporization, -isation,** *n.* **temporizer, -iser,** *n.* **temporizingly, -isingly,** *adv.*

tempt, *v.t.* †to put to trial or proof; to incite or entice (to something or to do); to attract, to allure, to invite; †to provoke, to defy; †to attempt. **temptable,** *a.* **temptability,** *n.* **temptation,** *n.* **tempter,** *n.* one who tempts; the devil. **tempting,** *a.* enticing, inviting. **temptingly,** *adv.* **temptress,** *n.* [OF *tenter, tempter,* L *tentāre, temptāre,* freq. of *tenēre,* to hold]

tempus fugit, time flies. [L]

†**temse,** *n.* a sieve. **temsebread, -loaf,** *n.* bread made of flour better sifted than common flour. [OE *temes* (in *temes -pile*), cp. Dut. *teems,* NFris. *tems*]

†**temulent,** *a.* intoxicated, drunk; intoxicating. †**temulence,** †**-lency,** *n.* [L *tēmulentus,* from *tēm-,* cp. *tēmētum,* strong drink]

ten, *n.* the number or figure 10 or X; the age of 10; the 10th hour after midnight or midday; a group of 10 people or things; a playing-card with 10 pips; a size of shoe or article of clothing designated by the number 10. *a.* 10 in number; aged 10. **ten minute rule,** in Parliament, a procedure where a member may make a short, ten-minute speech, introducing a bill. **Ten Commandments,** *n.pl.* in the Old Testament or Hebrew Bible, the laws given by God to the Israelite leader Moses on Mount Sinai, engraved on two tablets of stone. They are: to have no other gods besides Jehovah; to make no idols; not to misuse the name of God; to keep the sabbath holy; to honour one's parents; not to commit murder, adultery, or theft; not to give false evidence; not to be covetous. They form the basis of Jewish and Christian moral codes; the 'tablets of the Law' given to Moses are also mentioned in the Koran. **ten-gallon hat,** *n.* a wide-brimmed hat worn by American cowboys. **tenpence,** *n.* **tenpenny,** *a.* priced or sold at tenpence. **tenpenny nail,** *n.* a large nail orig. costing 10*d.* per 100. **ten-pin bowling, ten-pins,** *n.* a game played with ten pins in a skittle-alley. **tenfold,** *a., adv.* made up of 10 parts; 10 times as much. **tenth,** *n.* one of 10 equal parts. *n., a.* (the) last of 10 (people, things etc.); the next letter after the 9th. **tenthly,** *adv.* [OE *tiēn, tȳn* (Anglian *tēn*), (cp. Dut. *tien,* G *zehn,* Icel. *tīu,* also L *decem,* Gr. *deka*)]

tenable, *a.* capable of being held, retained, or maintained against attack. **tenability,** *n.* **tenableness,** *n.* [F, from *tenir,* L *tenēre,* to hold]

tenace, *n.* (*Whist, etc.*) the best and third best cards of a suit held in the same hand. **minor tenace,** the second and fourth best cards thus held. [F, as foll.]

tenacious, *a.* holding fast; inclined to hold fast, obstinate, unyielding; retentive, adhesive, sticky; highly cohesive, tough. **tenaciously,** *adv.* **tenaciousness, tenacity,** *n.* [L *tenax -ācis,* from *tenēre,* to hold]

tenaculum, *n.* (*pl.* **tenacula**) a surgeon's finely-hooked instrument for seizing blood-vessels etc.

tenail, †**tenaille,** *n.* (*Fort.*) a low outwork in the enceinte ditch in front of the curtain between two bastions. [F *tenaille,* L TENACULUM]

tena koe, *n.* a Maori greeting. [Maori]

tenant, *n.* a person holding a land or tenement from a landlord; (*Law*) one holding lands or tenements by any kind of title; a defendant in a real action; (loosely) an occupant, a dweller, an inhabitant. *v.t.* to hold as tenant; to occupy. **tenant at will,** (*Law*) one who holds possession of lands at the will of the owner or lessor. **tenant-farmer,** *n.* one cultivating land leased from the owner. **tenant-right,** *n.* the right allowed by custom to a well-behaved tenant not to be liable to injurious increase of rent or to be deprived of tenancy without compensation. **tenancy**, *n.* the holding of lands, etc.; the period of such property, or office. **tenantable,** *a.* fit for occupation by a tenant. **tenantableness,** *n.* **tenantless**, *a.* **tenantry**, *n.* (*Collect.*) tenants; the state of being a tenant. **tenantship,** *n.* [OF, pres.p. of *tenir,* see TENABLE]

tench, *n.* a freshwater fish, *Tinca tinca* or *vulgaris*, of the carp family. [OF *tenche* (F *tanche*), L *tinca*]

tend[1], *v.i.* to move, hold a course, or be directed (in a certain direction etc.); to have a bent, inclination, or attitude, to aim, to conduce (to). **tendency**, *n.* bent, drift, inclination, disposition. **tendentious**, *a.* with an underlying purpose, intended to further a cause. **tendentiously,** *adv.* **tendentiousness,** *n.* [AF *tendre,* L *tendere,* to stretch (p.p. *tensus, tentus*), cogn. with TENABLE]

tend[2], *v.t.* to attend, to watch, to look after, to take charge of; to watch (a vessel at anchor) so as to prevent her fouling the anchor and chain at the turn of the tide. *v.i.* to attend, to wait (upon). †**tendance,** *n.* **tended,** *a.* [shortened from ATTEND]

tendency, tendentious TEND[1].

tender[1], *n.* one who tends; a carriage attached to a locomotive carrying the supply of fuel, water etc.; a vessel attending a larger one, to supply provisions, carry despatches etc. [TEND[2]]

tender[2], *v.t.* to offer, to present for acceptance; to offer in payment. *v.i.* to make a tender (to do certain work or supply goods etc.). *n.* an offer for acceptance; an offer in writing to do certain work or supply certain articles, at a certain sum or rate; (*Law*) a formal offer of money or other things in satisfaction of a debt or liability; (*N Am.*) a bid. **legal tender** LEGAL. **tenderer,** *n.* **tendering,** *n.* [F *tendre,* to TEND[1]]

tender[3], *a.* easily impressed, broken, bruised etc., soft, delicate, fragile, weakly, frail; sensitive, easily pained or hurt, susceptible to pain, grief etc., impressible, sympathetic; loving, affectionate, fond; careful, solicitous, considerate (of), requiring to be treated delicately or cautiously, ticklish; easily chewed (of food). **tender-eyed,** *a.* having gentle eyes; †weak-eyed. **tenderfoot,** *n.* (*N Am., Austral. sl.*) a newcomer in the bush etc., a novice; one of the lowest grade of Scouts or Girl Guides. **tender-hearted,** *a.* having great sensibility, or susceptibility. **tender-heartedly,** *adv.* **tender-heartedness,** *n.* †**tender-hefted,** *a.* tender-hearted. **tender-loin,** *n.* the tenderest part of the loin in beef or pork; (*N Am.*) the undercut, fillet; (*N Am.*) an unsavoury quarter of New York City. **tender-minded,** *a.* **tenderize, -ise,** *v.t.* to make tender (e.g. meat) e.g. by pounding and so breaking down the fibres. **tenderization, -isation,** *n.* **tenderizer, -iser,** *n.* an instrument for pounding meat; a substance which makes (meat) tender. *a.* **tenderling,** *n.* **tenderly,** *adv.* **tenderness,** *n.* [ME and OF *tendre,* L *tenerum,* nom. *tener*]

tendon, *n.* one of the strong bands or cords of connective tissue forming the termination or connection of the fleshy part of a muscle. **tendinous, tendonous,** *a.* [F, from med. L *tendōnem,* nom. *-do,* from L *tendere,* to stretch]

tendril, *n.* a leafless organ by which a plant clings to another body for support. **tendrilled,** *a.* [etym. doubtful, prob. from L as prec.]

tenebrae, *n.pl.* in the Roman Catholic Church, the offices of matins and lauds for the last three days in Holy Week. **tenebrific**, *a.* causing or producing darkness. **tenebrism,** *n.* a 17th cent. Spanish and Neapolitan school of painting, characterized by areas of dark colour. **tenebrist,** *n.* †**tenebrosity,** *n.* †**tenebrous, tenebrious**, *a.* dark, gloomy. [L, darkness]

tenement, *n.* an apartment or set of apartments used by one family; a dwelling-house; (*esp. Sc.*) a large building divided into rooms and flats. (*fig.*) a dwelling-place, a habitation; (*Law*) any kind of permanent property that may be held, as lands, houses etc. **tenement-house,** *n.* a house let out in tenements, esp. in a poor district. **tenemental, tenementary**, *a.* [OF from med. L *tenementum,* from *tenēre,* to hold]

tenendum, *n.* (*pl.* **tenenda**) the clause in a deed in which the tenure is defined. [L]

Tenerife, *n.* largest of the Canary Islands, Spain; area 2060 sq km/795 sq miles; population (1981) 557,000. Santa Cruz is the main town, and Pico de Teide is an active volcano.

†**tenesmus,** *n.* an impotent desire, accompanied by effort and straining, to evacuate the bowels, usu. the result of inflammation in the rectum. †**tenesmic,** *a.* [med. L., from Gr. *teinesmos,* from *teinein,* to stretch, to strain]

tenet, *n.* an opinion, principle, doctrine, or dogma held by a person, school or organization. [L, he holds, see TENEMENT]

tenfold TEN.

Teng Hsiao-ping, *n.* former spelling of DENG XIAOPING.

Teniers, *n.* family of Flemish painters, active in Antwerp. The most successful was David Teniers the Younger (1610–90), who became court painter to Archduke Leopold William, governor of the Netherlands, in Brussels. He painted scenes of peasant life.

tenner, *n.* (*coll.*) a ten-pound note.

Tennessee, *n.* state of the E central US; nickname Volunteer State. **area** 109,412 sq km/42,224 sq miles. **capital** Nashville. **towns** Memphis, Jackson, Knoxville, Chattanooga. **population** (1986) 4,803,000. **products** cereals, cotton, tobacco, timber, coal, zinc, pyrites, phosphates, iron, steel, and chemicals.

Tenniel, *n.* **John** (1820–1914), British illustrator and cartoonist, known for his illustrations for Lewis Carroll's *Alice's Adventures in Wonderland* (1865) and *Through the Looking-Glass* (1872). He joined the satirical magazine *Punch* in 1850, and for over 50 years he was one of its leading cartoonists.

tennis, *n.* a game for two, three or four persons played by striking a ball to and fro with rackets over a net stretched across a walled court; now usually lawn-tennis. **lawn tennis,** *n.* a game for two (singles) or four (doubles) simpler than tennis and omitting the wall. **table tennis,** *n.* an indoor game resembling lawn tennis but played on a table; ping-pong. **tennis-arm -elbow, -knee,** *n.* an arm etc., strained or sprained in tennis- playing, or through other exercise. **tennis-ball,** *n.* **tennis-court,** *n.* **tennis-player, -racket, -shoe,** *n.* [ME *tenetz, tenys* perh. from OF *tenez,* hold, take, as foll.]

Tennyson, *n.* **Alfred, 1st Baron Tennyson** (1809–92), English poet, poet laureate 1850–96, noted for the majestic musical language of his verse. His works include 'The Lady of Shalott', 'The Lotus Eaters', 'Ulysses', 'Break, Break, Break', 'The Charge of the Light Brigade'; the longer narratives *Locksley Hall* (1832), and *Maud* (1855); the elegy *In Memoriam* (1850); and a long series of poems on the Arthurian legends *The Idylls of the King* (1857–85). **Tennysonian,** *a.* pertaining to, or in the style of, Alfred, Lord Tennyson.

tenoid TAENIOID.

tenon, *n.* the projecting end of a piece of timber fitted for insertion into a mortise etc. *v.t.* to cut a tenon on; to join by a tenon. **tenon-saw,** *n.* a thin saw with a strong brass or steel back used for cutting tenons etc. **tenon-machine,** *n.* **tenoner,** *n.* [F, from *tenir,* L *tenēre*, to hold]

tenor, *n.* a settled course, tendency, or direction; general purport or drift (of thought etc.); the exact purport or meaning, also an exact transcript or copy; the highest of male chest voices between baritone and alto; the part for this; one with a tenor voice; an instrument, esp. the viola, playing a part between bass and alto. *a.* pertaining to or adapted for singing or playing the tenor part. **tenor-clef,** *n.* the c clef placed upon the fourth line of the stave. **tenore,** [It.], *n.* (*pl.* **-ri**), **tenorino,** [It., dim. of prec.], *n.* (*pl.* **-ni**) a falsetto tenor voice or singer; an artificial soprano. **tenorist,** *n.* [ME and OF *tenour,* L *tenor, -ōrem,* a holding on, (later) melody or canto fermo, from *tenēre,* to hold]

tenosynovitis, *n.* swelling and inflammation in the tendons, usually in joints, caused by repetitive movement of the joint concerned. [Gr. *tenōn,* tendon, *itis* inflammation]

tenotomy, *n.* the cutting of a tendon. [Gr. *tenōn,* tendon, -TOMY]

tenpence, tenpenny, etc. TEN.

tenrec TANREC.

tense[1], *n.* a form taken by a verb to indicate the time, and also the continuance or completedness, of an action. **tenseless,** *a.* [OF *tens* (F *temps*), L *tempus,* time]

tense[2], *a.* stretched tight, strained to stiffness (*lit. and fig.*); under or producing emotional stress. **tensely,** *adv.* **tenseness, tensity,** *n.* **tensible,** *a.* **tensibility,** *n.* **tensile,** *a.* of or pertaining to tension; capable of extension. **tensile strength,** *n.* the greatest stress a given substance can withstand before breaking. **tensility,** *n.* **tension,** *n.* the act of stretching or the state of being stretched; strain, stress, effort; mental strain, stress, or excitement; a state of hostility, strain or anxiety; stress tending to draw asunder the particles of a body, as in a belt, sheet etc., that is being pulled; the expansive force of a gas or vapour. **tension-rod,** *n.* a rod in a structure preventing the spreading of opposite members. **tensiometry,** *n.* the branch of physics which has to do with tension and tensile strength. **tensiometer,** *n.* an instrument which measures tensile strength; an instrument for comparing vapour pressure; an instrument for measuring the surface tension of liquid; an instrument which measures the moisture content of soil. **tensional,** *a.* **tensionless,** *a.* †**tensive,** *a.* **tensor,** *n.* a muscle that stretches or tightens a part. [L *tensus,* p.p. of *tendere,* see TEND[1]]

tenson, *n.* a contention in verse between troubadours; a subdivision of a poem sung by one of them. [F, from It. *tenzone,* as TENSION]

tent[1], *n.* a portable shelter consisting of canvas or other flexible material stretched over and supported on poles. *v.t.* to cover with or lodge in a tent. *v.i.* to encamp in a tent. **bell tent,** *n.* a circular tent supported on a central pole. **tent bed,** *n.* a bed with curtains which hang from a central point, in the style of a tent. **tent-fly,** *n.* a loose piece of canvas etc., fastened over the ridge-pole to shelter a tent from sun and rain. **tent-maker,** *n.* **tent-peg, -pin,** *n.* a strong peg or pin driven into the ground to secure a tent to the ground. **tent-pole,** *n.* a pole supporting a tent. **tented,** *a.* **tenter**[1], *n.* **tentful,** *n.* **tent-wise,** *adv.* [OF *tente,* L *tenta,* pl. of *tentum* neut. p.p. of *tendere,* to stretch]

tent[2], *n.* a small roll of lint, sponge etc., inserted in a wound, ulcer etc., to keep it open. *v.t.* to keep open with a tent. [OF from *tenter,* to probe, see TEMPT]

tent[3], *n.* a Spanish wine of a deep red colour, used for sacramental purposes. [Sp. *vino tinto,* deep-coloured wine (*tinto,* L *tinctus,* see TINGE)]

tent[4], *v.i.* (*Sc., North.*) to watch, to take heed. *v.t.* to take care of, to tend. **tenter**[2], *n.* [var. of TEND[2]]

tentacle, *n.* a long slender organ of touch, prehension, or locomotion, a feeler, as an arm of a cuttle-fish; a sensitive hair. **tentacled,** *a.* **tentacular, tentaculate, -lated, -loid,** *a.* **tentaculiferous, -ligerous,** *a.* bearing, or producing, tentacles. **tentaculiform,** *a.* **tentaculum,** (*pl.* **-ula**), *n.* [from L *tentāre,* see TEMPT, after SPECTACLE etc.]

tentative, *a.* consisting or done as a trial or essay, experimental; hesitant, uncertain. *n.* an experiment, a trial, a conjecture. † **tentation,** *n.* trial, temptation, **tentatively,** *adv.* [med. L *tentātīvus,* from *tentāre,* see TEMPT]

tenter[1 and 2] TENT[1 and 4].

tenter[3], *n.* a frame or machine for stretching cloth to dry to make it set even and square; a tenter-hook. **tenter-hook,** *n.* one of a set of hooks used in stretching cloth on the tenter. **on tenter-hooks,** in a state of suspense and anxiety. [prob. through an A-F and OF *tentour,* from *tendere,* to stretch]

tenth, etc. TEN.

†**tentigo,** *n.* priapism, lecherousness. †**tentiginous,** *a.* [L]

tentorium, *n.* (*Anat.*) a membranous partition stretched across the cranium between the cerebrum and the cerebellum. [L, from *tendere,* see TENT[1]]

†**tenture,** *n.* wall-hangings, wallpaper. [F, ult. from L *tendere,* to stretch, p.p. *tentus*]

tenui-, *comb. form* slender, thin. [L *tenuis,* thin]

tenuifolious, *a.* having thin or narrow leaves.

tenuiroster, *n.* one of the Tenuirostres, a group of insessorial birds with long, slender bills. **tenuirostral,** *a.*

tenuity, *n.* thinness, slenderness; rarity; (*fig.*) meagreness. **tenuis,** *n.* (*Gr. Gram.*) one of the hard or surd mutes, *k, p, t.* [F *ténuité,* L *tēnuitātem,* nom. *-tas,* from *tenuis,* thin]

tenuous, *a.* thin, slender, small, minute; rare, rarefied, subtle, over-refined; insignificant. **tenuously,** *adv.* **tenuousness,** *a.*

tenure, *n.* the act, manner, or right of holding property, esp. real estate or office; the manner or conditions or holding; the period or term of holding; the holding of a university or college post for an assured period of time. **tenurial,** *a.* [A-F and OF, from med. L *tenitūra, tenūra,* cp. TENOR]

tenuto, *a.* sustained, held on for the full time, opp. to staccato. [It., held, from L as prec.]

teocalli, *n.* a pyramidal mound or structure, usu. surmounted by a temple, used for worship by the ancient peoples of Mexico, Central America etc. [Mex. *teotl,* god, *calli,* house]

Teotihuacán, *n.* ancient city in central Mexico, the religious centre of the Toltec civilization.

tepee, teepee, *n.* a N American Indian tent, cane-shaped, and made of animal skins. [Sioux *tipi,* dwelling]

tepefy, *v.t.* to make tepid. *v.i.* to become tepid. **tepefaction,** *n.* [L *tepefacere* (*tepēre,* see TEPID, *facere,* to make)]

tephrite, *n.* a volcanic rock allied to basalt. **tephritic, tephritoid,** *a.* **tephromancy,** *n.* divination by the inspection of sacrificial ashes. [L *tephrītis* (Gr. *tephra,* ashes, -ITE)]

tepid, *a.* moderately warm; lukewarm. **tepidarium,** *n.* (*pl.* **-ria**) (*Rom. Ant.*) the room between the frigidarium and the caldarium in a Roman bath; a boiler in which the water was heated. **tepidity, tepidness,** *n.* **tepidly,** *adv.* [L *tepidus,* from *tepēre,* to be warm]

tequila, *n.* a Mexican spirit distilled from agave which forms the basis of many drinks; the plant from which this spirit is distilled. [Mex. Sp., *Tequila* district in Mexico]

ter., (*abbr.*) terrace; territory.

ter-, *comb. form* thrice, three times. [L]

tera-, *comb. form* 10 to the power of 12. [Gr. *teras,* monster]

teraphim, *n.pl.* household gods or idols among the Jews consulted as oracles. [Heb.]

terato-, *comb. form* pertaining to a monster. [Gr. *teras-, -atos,* monster]

teratogeny, *n.* the production of monsters or abnormal growths. **teratogen,** *n.* a substance which causes abnormalities in a foetus. **teratogenic,** *a.* **teratism,** *n.* an abnormal person or animal, especially at the foetal stage.

teratology, *n.* the branch of biology dealing with monsters and malformations; a work on the marvellous, a marvellous tale etc. **teratological,** *a.* **teratologist,** *n.*

teratosis, *n.* monstrosity.

terbium, *n.* a rare metallic element, at. no. 65, chem. symbol Tb, found in association with erbium and yttrium. **terbic,** *a.* [*Ytterby,* in Sweden, cp. ERBIUM, -IUM]

Terborch, *n.* **Gerard** (1617–81), Dutch painter of small-scale portraits and genre scenes, mainly of soldiers at rest or wealthy families in their homes. He travelled widely in Europe. *The Peace of Münster* (1648) (National Gallery, London) is an official group portrait.

Terbrugghen, *n.* **Hendrik** (1588–1629), Dutch painter, a leader of the Utrecht school with Honthorst. He visited Rome around 1604 and was inspired by Caravaggio's work. He painted religious subjects and genre scenes.

terce TIERCE. **tercel** TIERCEL.
tercentenary, *a.* comprising 300 years. *n.* a 300th anniversary. **tercentennial**, *a.* of 300 years. *n.* a 300th anniversary.
tercet, *n.* a triplet. [It. *terzetto,* dim. of *terzo,* L TERTIUS]
tercine, *n.* a layer supposed to form a third coat in certain ovules. [F, from *tiers,* or L *tertius,* third]
terebene, *n.* a liquid hydrocarbon obtained by treating oil of turpentine with sulphuric acid, used as an antiseptic, disinfectant etc., **terebinthine**, *a.* pertaining to or partaking of the qualities of terebinth or turpentine. **terebic**, *a.* [-ENE]
terebinth, *n.* the turpentine-tree, *Pistacia terebinthus,* from which Chian turpentine is obtained; its resin. [L *terebinthus*, Gr. *terebinthos*]
terebra, *n.* (*pl.* **-brae**) (*Ent.*) an ovipositor adapted for boring. **terebrate,** *v.t.* to bore. **terebrant,** *a., n.* †**terebration,** *n.* **Terebratula** , *n.* (*pl.* **-lae**) (*Zool.*) a genus of brachiopods, largely extinct. **terebratular, terebratuliform**, *a.* **terebratulid**, *n.* **terebratulite**, *n.* a fossil species of Terebratula. **terebratuloid**, *a., n.* [L, borer (from *terere,* to pierce), whence *terebrāre,* to bore]
teredo, *n.* a mollusc that bores into submerged timber, the ship-worm. **teredine**, *n.* [L, from Gr. *terēdōn,* from *teirein,* to bore]
terek, *n.* a species of sandpiper, *Terekia cinerea,* with the bill curved slightly upward, frequenting E Asia. [name of river in Caucasus]
Terence, *n.* **(Publius Terentius Afer)** (190–159 BC), Roman dramatist, born in Carthage and brought as a slave to Rome, where he was freed and came under Scipio's patronage. His surviving six comedies (including *The Eunuch*, 161 BC) are subtly characterized and based on Greek models. **Terentian**, *a.* of, pertaining to, or in the style of the Roman dramatist Terence.
Teresa, St *n.* (1515–82), Spanish mystic, born in Avila. She became a Carmelite nun, and in 1562 founded a new and stricter order. She was subject to fainting fits, during which she saw visions. She wrote *The Way to Perfection* (1583), and an autobiography, *Life of the Mother Theresa of Jesus* (1611). In 1622 she was canonized, and became the first woman Doctor of the Church, 1970.
Tereshkova, *n.* **Valentina Vladimirovna** (1937–), Soviet cosmonaut, the first woman to fly in space. In June 1963 she made a three-day flight in Vostok 6, orbiting the Earth 48 times.
terete, *a.* rounded, cylindrical, and smooth. [L *teres -retis,* from *terere,* see TEREBRA]
tergal, *a.* of or pertaining to the back or a tergite. †**tergant,** †**tergiant**, *a.* showing the back part. [L *tergum,* back]
tergeminate, *a.* having a pair of leaflets on each of two secondary petioles and at the base. [L *tergeminus (*TER, *geminus,* see GEMINATE)]
tergiferous, *a.* bearing or carrying on the back, as ferns their seeds.
tergite, *n.* the upper or dorsal plate of a somite or segment of an articulate animal, also called **tergum**, (*pl.* **-ga**). **tergal,** *a.* [L *tergum*, back]
tergiversate, *v.i.* to practise evasions or subterfuges, to equivocate; to change sides. **tergiversation,** *n.* **tergiversator,** *n.* [L *tergiversatus,* p.p. of *tergiversārī* (*tergum,* back, *versārī,* freq. of *vertere,* to turn)]
tergum TERGIFEROUS.
term, *n.* a limit, a boundary; a limited period; the period during which instruction is regularly given or the courts are in session; an appointed day or date; (*Law*) an estate to be enjoyed for a fixed period; the period during which childbirth is due; a word having a definite and specific meaning; (*pl.*) language or expressions used; (*pl.*) conditions, stipulations, price, charge, rate of payment; relative position, relation, footing; a word or group of words that may be the subject or predicate of a proposition; (*Math.*) the antecedent or consequent of a ratio; one of the parts of an expression connected by the plus or minus signs. *v.t.* to designate, to call, to denominate. **to be on speaking terms,** to be well enough acquainted to speak to each other; to be friends with. **to bring to terms,** to force or induce to accept conditions. **to come to terms,** to conclude an agreement (with); to yield, to give way. **to come to terms with,** to find a way of coping and living with some difficulty. **termer, -or,** *n.* (*Law*) one who has an estate for a term of years or for life. **term insurance,** *n.* insurance of a specific period only. **terms of reference,** *n.* the specific points which a committee or other body is charged to decide. **terms of trade,** *n.* the ratio of export prices to import prices. **termtime,** *n.* †**termless**, *a.* unlimited, boundless. **termly,** *a.* occurring every term. *adv.* term by term; every term; periodically. [OF *terme,* L *terminus* limit]
terma, *n.* (*pl.* **-mata**) a thin layer of grey matter at the front of the 3rd ventricle of the brain. **termatic**, *a., n.* [Gr., see prec.]
termagant, *n.* a shrewish, abusive, violent woman, *a.* violent, boisterous, turbulent, shrewish. **termagancy,** *n.* †**termagantly,** *adv.* [ME *Tervagant,* OF *Tervagan,* It. *Trivigante* (per. L *tri-,* TER, *vagans, -ntem,* pres.p. of *vagārī,* to wander, with ref. to Selene or the moon), name of an idol or deity whom the Saracens are represented in mediaeval romances as worshipping]
termatic TERMA. **termer** TERM.
termes, *n.* (*pl.* **-mites**) a termite. [L, from *terere,* Gr. *teirein,* to rub, to bore]
terminable, etc. TERMINATE.
terminal, *a.* pertaining to or forming a boundary, limit, or terminus; forming or situated at the end of a series or part; ending in death; occurring every term. *n.* that which terminates; a limit, an extremity, an end, esp. one of the free ends of an electrical conductor from a battery etc., a rail or air terminus; a device with input and output links with a computer at a distance; a site where raw materials are unloaded, processed and distributed. **terminal illness,** *n.* a fatal disease or disorder. **terminally ill,** *a.* **terminal velocity,** *n.* the speed of an object when it reaches its target; the maximum speed attained by a rocket, missile etc., in a parabolic flight path, or by an aircraft; the maximum speed attained by an object falling through a fluid under gravity. **Terminalia**, *n.pl.* (*Rom. Ant.*) a festival celebrated annually on 23 Feb. in honour of Terminus, the god of boundaries. **terminally,** *adv.* [L *termінālis*, from TERMINUS]
terminate, *v.t.* to bound, to limit; to form the extreme point or end of; to put an end to. *v.i.* to stop, to end (in etc.). *a.* limitable, limited, bounded; (*Math.*) finite. **terminable,** *a.* capable of being terminated; having a given term or period. **terminableness,** *n.* **termination,** *n.* **terminational,** *a.* **terminative, terminatory,** *a.* **terminatively,** *adv.* **terminator,** *n.* one who or that which terminates; the dividing-line between the illuminated and the dark part of a heavenly body. [L *terminātus,* p.p. of *termināre,* from TERMINUS]
terminer OYER.
terminism, *n.* the doctrine that there is a limited period in each man's life for repentance and grace; nominalism. **terminist,** *n.*
terminology, *n.* the science or study of the (correct) use of terms; the terms used in any art, science, discipline etc. **terminological**, *a.* **terminological inexactitude,** *n.* (*facet.*) a lie. **terminologically,** *adv.* [as prec. -LOGY]
terminus, *n.* (*pl.* **-ni**) a boundary, a limit, a boundary-mark; the station at the end of a railway, bus route etc.; (*Rom. Ant.*) the god of boundaries; a figure of the upper portion of the human body, terminating in a block or pillar; †a final point, goal, or end. **terminus ad quem,** *n.* the limit to which; the terminal point; destination. **terminus a quo,** *n.* the limit from which, the starting point, beginning. [L, see TERM]
termite, *n.* a white ant. **termitarium**, **termitary**, *n.* a nest of or cage for termites. [L *termes -mitis,* wood-worm, cogn. with TEREDO]
termless, termor, etc. TERM.
tern¹, *n.* a gull-like sea-bird of the genus *Sterna,* slenderly-built, with narrow, sharp-pointed wings. **ternery,** *n.* [prob. from Dan. *terne,* cp. Icel. *therna,*

Swed. *tärna*]

tern², *a.* ternate. *n.* a set of three, esp. three lottery numbers winning a large prize if won together; the prize thus won. **ternal, ternary,** *a.* proceeding by or consisting of three. *n.* a group of three, a triad. **ternate**, *a.* arranged in threes, esp. in whorls of three (of leaflets etc.). **ternately,** *adv.* [L *ternī,* by threes, from TER]

terne, *n.* sheet-iron coated with an alloy of tin and lead; inferior tin-plate. **terne-plate,** *n.* [F, dull, tarnished]

ternery TERN¹.

terotechnology, *n.* the application of managerial, financial and engineering skills to the installation and efficient operation of equipment and machinery. [Gr. *tereo,* to watch, + technology]

terpene, *n.* one of various isomeric oily hydrocarbons derived chiefly from coniferous plants. **terpin**, *n.* a derivative of oil of turpentine and other terpenes. **terpineol**, *n.* a terpene alcohol used in perfumes. [obs. *terp-,* TURPENTINE, -ENE]

Terpsichorean, *a.* pertaining to Terpsichore the Muse of dancing; dancing.

terra, *n.* (*pl.* **rrae**) earth. **terra alba**, *n.* any of various white, earthy substances, e.g. gypsum, kaolin, pipeclay, magnesia etc. **terra-cotta**, *n.* a hard, unglazed pottery used as a decorative building-material, for statuary etc.; a statue or figure in this; the brownish-orange colour of terra-cotta. **terra firma**, *n.* dry land. **terra incognita**, *n.* unknown country. **terra japonica**, *n.* Gambier. [It. and L]

terrace¹, *n.* a raised level space or platform, artificially constructed or natural; a balcony; a paved patio; a row of houses, esp. running along the side of a slope; (*Geol.*) an old shore-line or raised beach; the open tiers around a football stadium where spectators stand. *v.t.* to form into or furnish with terraces. **terraced,** *a.* in terraces. **terraced house,** *n.* a house which forms part of a terrace. [OF, from It. *terraccia, terrazza,* from prec.]

†**terrace²,** TARRAS.

terrain, *n.* a region, a tract, an extent of land of a definite geological character; a tract of country which is the scene of operations. [F, TERRENE¹.]

terramara, *n.* (*pl.* **-re**) an earthy deposit of various kinds, usu. composed of bones, phosphates, and mineral matter, used as a fertilizer; a deposit in parts of S Europe containing prehistoric remains, analogous to that of the kitchen-middens. [It. TERRA *amara,* bitter earth (L *amārus,* bitter)]

Terramycin®, *n.* an antibiotic used to treat a wide range of bacterial infections.

terraneous, *a.* (*Bot.*) growing on land.

terrapin, *n.* a freshwater tortoise, esp. the N American saltmarsh or diamond-back terrapin, highly esteemed for food. [Algonquin]

terraqueous, *a.* consisting of land and water, as the globe. [TERRA, AQUEOUS]

terrazzo, *n.* (*pl.* **-os**) a mosaic floor-covering made by setting marble or other chips into cement, which is then polished. [It.]

terrene¹, *a.* pertaining to the earth, earthy; terrestrial. *n.* a region. **terrenely,** *adv.* [L *terrēmus,* from TERRA]

†**terrene²,** TERRINE.

terreplein, *n.* the upper surface of the rampart where guns are mounted; the level surface about a fieldwork. [F (*terre,* as prec., *plein,* PLAIN¹)]

terrestrial, *a.* pertaining to or existing on the earth, not celestial; consisting of land, not water; living on the ground, not aquatic, arboreal etc.; pertaining to this world, worldly. *n.* an inhabitant of the earth. **terrestrial magnetism,** *n.* the magnetic properties possessed by the earth as a whole, which actuate the magnetic compass. **terrestrially,** *adv.* [L *terrestris*]

terret, *n.* one of the rings or loops on harness through which the driving-reins pass; the ring on a dog's collar for attaching the lead. [etym. doubtful]

terrible, *a.* causing terror or dread; awful, formidable, terrifying, appalling, shocking; very bad, of very poor quality; (*coll.*) excessive, extreme. **terribleness,** *n.* **terribly,** *adv.* [OF, from L *terribilis,* from *terrēre,* to terrify]

terricolous, *a.* living on or in the earth; pertaining to the Terricolae, a group of annelids comprising the earthworms. [L terricola, earth-dweller (TERRA, *colere,* to dwell)]

terrier¹, *n.* a small active dog of various breeds with an instinct for pursuing its quarry underground; (*coll.*) a member of the Territorial Army. [F, from med. L *tarrārius,* from TERRA]

terrier², *n.* a book or roll in which the lands of private persons or corporations are described by site, boundaries, acreage etc. [F *papier terrier,* as prec.]

terrific, *a.* causing terror; frightful, terrible; (*coll.*) very good, excellent. **terrifically,** *adv.* frighteningly; (*coll.*) exceedingly, surprisingly. **terrify,** *v.t.* to strike with terror, to frighten. **terrifying,** *a.* **terrifyingly,** *adv.* [L *terrificus* (*terrēre,* to frighten, -FIC)]

terrigenous, *a.* produced by or derived from the earth; of geological deposits, formed in the sea from debris from land erosion. [L *terrigena,* earth-dweller]

terrine, *n.* an earthenware jar containing some table-delicacy, sold with its contents; an earthenware pot for cooking; the food, such as meat or fish, cooked in such a pot. [F, TUREEN]

territory, *n.* the extent of land within the jurisdiction of a particular sovereign, state, or other power; a large tract of land; (*US*) a division of the country not yet granted full State rights or admitted into the Union; an assigned area of jurisdiction; a field of action; the area defended by an animal or bird. **territorial,** *a.* pertaining to territory; limited to a given district; of or pertaining to the Territorial Army; (*US*) pertaining to a Territory or the Territories. *n.* (*coll.*) a member of the Territorial Army. **Territorial Army,** *n.* British force of volunteer soldiers, created from volunteer regiments (incorporated 1872) as the Territorial Force 1908. It was raised and administered by county associations, and intended primarily for home defence. It was renamed Territorial Army 1922. Merged with the Regular Army in World War II, it was revived in 1947, and replaced by a smaller, more highly trained Territorial and Army Volunteer Reserve, again renamed Territorial Army 1979. **territorial waters,** *n.pl.* the area of sea, usu. three miles out, adjoining the coast and adjudged to be under the jurisdiction of the country occupying that coast. **territorialize, -ise,** *v.t.* **territoriality,** *n.* **territorially,** *adv.* **territoried,** *a.* [L *territōrium,* from TERRA]

terror, *n.* extreme fear; an object of fear; government or revolution by terrorism; (*coll.*) an exasperating nuisance, bore, troublesome child etc. **king of terrors,** death. **Reign of Terror,** the period of the French Revolution when the Jacobins were in power (Oct. 1793–July 1794) under Maximilien Robespierre and instituted mass persecution of their opponents. About 1400 were executed, until public indignation rose and Robespierre was overthrown in July 1794. **terror-stricken, -struck,** *a.* terrified, paralysed with fear. **terrorism,** *n.* organized violence and intimidation, usu. for political ends; the act of terrorizing. **terrorist,** *n.* one who rules or advocates rule by intimidation, esp. for political reasons etc. **terroristic**, *a.* **terrorize, -ise,** *v.t.* to terrify; to coerce with threats of violence etc. **terrorization, -isation,** *n.* [ME *terrour,* F *terreur,* L *terror*, from *terrēre,* to frighten]

terry, *n.* a pile fabric in which the loops are not cut. **terry-towelling,** *n.* **terry-velvet,** *n.* [etym. doubtful]

Terry, *n.* **(John) Quinlan** (1937–), British architect. His work includes country houses in the neo-classical style, for example Merks Hall, Great Dunmow, Essex, 1982, and the larger-scale Richmond, London, riverside project, commissioned 1984.

Tersanctus, *n.* (*Eccles.*) the Trisagion. [L TER, *sanctus,* holy]

terse, *a.* concise, pithy, abrupt; of style, neat and compact. **tersely,** *adv.* **terseness,** *n.* [L *tersus,* p.p. of *tergere,* to wipe]

tertial, *a.* pertaining to the tertiary feathers. *n.* one of the tertiary feathers. [from L, as foll.]

tertian, *a.* occurring or recurring every third day. *n.* a fever or ague, the paroxysms of which recur every other day. [ME *terciane,* L *tertiānus,* from TERTIUS]

tertiary, *a.* of the third order, rank, or formation; pertaining to the Tertiary pertaining to higher education. *n.* one of the feathers attached to the proximal joint of a bird's wing; the third geological period, following the Secondary or Mesozoic, 65–1.8 million years ago, divided into into five epochs: Palaeocene, Eocene, Oligocene, Miocene, and Pliocene. In the Roman Catholic Church, a member of the 3rd order of a monastic body. **tertiary college,** *n.* a 6th-form college which teaches vocational courses. [L *tertiārius,* as prec.]

tertiate, *v.t.* †to do for the 3rd time; to examine the thickness of the metal of (a gun) by measuring at three or more points. [L *tertiātus,* p.p. of *tertiāre,* as prec.]

tertius, *a.* 3rd (of the name). **tertium quid,** *n.* a 3rd (or intermediate) something. [L, third, cp. TER]

Tertullian, *n.* **Quintus Septimius Florens** (AD 155–222), Carthaginian Father of the Church, the first important Christian writer in Latin; he became involved with Montanism AD 213.

teru-tero, *n.* the Cayenne lapwing, *Vanellus cayannensis.* [S. Am. native, imit. of cry]

tervalent, TRIVALENT.

Terylene®, *n.* trade name for a polyester synthetic fibre produced by the chemicals company ICI. It is made by polymerizing ethylene glycol and terephthalic acid. Cloth made from Terylene keeps its shape after washing and is hard-wearing.

terza rima, *n.* (*pl.* **-ze, -me**) a form of triplet in iambic decasyllables or hendecasyllables rhyming *ababcb,* employed by Dante in the *Divina Commedia.* [It., third (as TERTIUS) rhyme]

terzetto, *n.* a short composition for three performers or singers. [It., see TERCET]

TESL, (*abbr.*) teaching of English as a Second Language.

Tesla, *n.* **Nikola** (1856–1943), Croatian electrical engineer, who emigrated to the US in 1884. He invented fluorescent lighting, the Tesla induction motor, and the Tesla coil, and developed the alternating current (AC) electrical supply system. **tesla,** *n.* the unit of magnetic flux density equal to a flux of one weber per square metre. **tesla coil,** *n.* a transformer which produces high voltages at high frequencies.

tessellated, *a.* composed of tesserae, inlaid; (*Nat. Hist.*) coloured or marked in checkered squares. **tessellar,** *a.* **tessellation,** *n.* [L *tessellātus,* from *tessela,* dim. of foll.]

tessera, *n.* (*pl.* **-serae**) a small cubical piece of marble, earthenware etc., used in mosaics. **tesseral,** *a.* of or composed of tesserae; (*Cryst.*) isometric. **tessular,** *a.* (*Cryst.*) tesseral. [L, from Gr. *tessares,* four]

tessitura, *n.* the natural pitch of a voice or piece of vocal music. [It., texture]

test¹, *n.* a vessel used in refining gold and silver, a cupel; a critical trial or examination; a means of trial, a standard, a criterion; judgment, discrimination; (*Chem.*) a substance employed to detect one or more of the constituents of a compound; a removable hearth in a reverberatory furnace; an oath or declaration of loyalty or beliefs. *v.t.* to put to the test, to try, to prove by experiment; to try severely, to tax (one's endurance etc.); (*Chem.*) to examine by the application of some reagent; (*Metal.*) to refine in a cupel. **Test Act,** *n.* an Act of 1672 (repealed in 1828) requiring persons holding office, receiving pay from the Crown etc., to take the Oaths of Allegiance and Supremacy, receive the sacrament etc. **test ban,** *n.* the banning, by agreement, of the testing of nuclear weapons. **Test Ban Treaty,** a treaty signed by the US, the USSR, and the UK 5 Aug. 1963 which agreed to test nuclear weapons only underground. In the following two years 90 other nations signed the treaty, the only major non-signatories being France and China who continued underwater and ground-level tests. **test-bed,** *n.* an area for testing machinery etc. **test case,** *n.* a case taken to trial in order that the court shall decide some question that affects other cases. **test-drive,** *n.* a trial drive of a car or other motor vehicle to assess its performance, before purchase. *v.t.* **test-flight,** *n.* a trial flight of a new aircraft, **test-fly,** *v.t.* **test match,** *n.* a cricket match forming one of a series of international matches. **test-paper,** *n.* bibulous paper saturated with a chemical solution that changes colour when exposed to the action of certain chemicals. **test pilot,** *n.* a pilot who test-flies new aircraft. **test-tube,** *n.* a narrow glass tube closed at one end, used in chemical tests. **test-tube baby,** a baby born from an ovum fertilized in an artificial womb in a laboratory, then implanted into the mother's womb; a baby conceived by artificial insemination. **testable¹,** *a.* **tester¹,** *n.* one who or that which tests. **testing,** *n.* [OF (F *têt*), L *testum,* cp. TESTA]

test², *v.t.* to attest, to verify. *v.i.* (*Sc. Law*) to attest a will or other deed. [OF *tester,* L *testārī,* from *testis,* witness]

test³, *n.* a shell, a hard covering or exoskeleton. [L TESTA]

testa, *n.* (*pl.* **testae**) the outer integument of a seed; a test. [L, potsherd, tile, etc.]

testable¹ TEST¹.

testable², *a.* (*Law*) that may be given in evidence; that may be devised or bequeathed. [OF, from L *testābilis,* from *testārī,* see TESTATE]

Testacea, *n.pl.* an order of protozoans having shells, shell-bearing invertebrates excluding crustaceans. **testacean,** *a., n.* **testaceous,** *a.* **testacel,** *n.* any species of the Testacella, a group of carnivorous slugs; a member of the Testacella. **testaceology,** -LOGY, *n.* [L *testaceus,* from TESTA]

testacy, *n.* the state of being testate.

testament, *n.* that which testifies proof, attestation; a solemn instrument in writing by which a person disposes of his or her personal estate after death, a will; one of the two main divisions of the Scriptures; (*coll.*) a copy of the New Testament. **New Testament,** the portion of the Bible dealing with the Christian dispensation composed after the birth of Christ. **Old Testament,** the portion treating of the old or Mosaic dispensation. **testamentary,** †**testamental,** *a.* **testamentarily,** *adv.* †**testamentation,** *n.* **testamur,** [L, we testify], *n.* a certificate that a student has passed an examination. [OF, from L *testāmentum,* from *testārī,* to testify, see TESTATE]

testate, *a.* having made and left a will. *n.* one who has left a will in force. **testation,** *n.* **testator,** *n.* (*fem.*). **testatrix,** *n.* someone who dies testate. [L *testātus,* p.p. of *testāri,* see prec.]

tester¹ TEST¹.

tester², *n.* a canopy, esp. over a four-post bedstead. [ME and OF *testre,* L *testa,* late L, head]

†**tester³,** *n.* a shilling of Henry VIII; (*coll.*) a sixpence. †**testern,** *v.t.* (*Shak.*) to present with a tester. [corr. of earlier *teston,* OF *teston,* as prec.]

testes, *pl.* TESTIS under TESTICLE.

testicle, *n.* one of the two glands which secrete the seminal fluid in males. **testicular, testiculate,** *a.* **testis,** *n.* (*pl.* **-tes**), a testicle; a round organ or part resembling this. [L *testiculus,* dim. of TESTIS]

testify, *v.i.* to bear witness (to, against, concerning etc.); (*Law*) to give evidence; to make a solemn declaration. *v.t.* to bear witness to; to attest; to affirm or declare; to be evidence or serve as proof of. †**testificate,** *n.* (*Sc. Law*) a solemn written assertion. **testification,** *n.* **testifier,** †**testificator,** *n.* [F *testifier,* L *testificāre* (*testis,* witness, *-ficāre, facere,* to make)]

testily TESTY.

testimony, *n.* a solemn declaration or statement; (*Law*) a statement under oath or affirmation; evidence, proof, confirmation; a solemn declaration of approval or protest; (*Bibl.*) the law as set forth in the two tables, the decalogue, the word of God, the Scriptures. †*v.t.* to prove by evidence, to attest. **testimonial,** †*a.* relating to or consisting of testimony; intended as a testimonial. *n.* a certificate of character, services, qualifications etc., of a person; a formal statement of fact; a gift formally (and usu. publicly) presented to a person as a token of esteem and acknowledgement of services etc. **testimonialize, -ise,** *v.t.* to present with a testimony. [L *testimonium,* from *testis,* witness]

testiness TESTY.

testing TEST[1].

testosterone, *n.* a steroid hormone secreted by the testes. [TESTIS, STEROL]

†**testril,** (*Shak.*) corr. of TESTER[2].

testudo, *n.* (*pl.* **dos, -dines**) (*Rom. Ant.*) a screen formed by shields held above their heads and overlapping by soldiers advancing to the attack of a fortress; any similar screen, esp. one used by miners working in places liable to cave in; a genus of tortoises. **testudinal,** *a.* pertaining to or resembling the tortoise. **testudinarious,** *a.* mottled like tortoiseshell. **testudinary,** *a.* **testudinated, -dinate,** *a.* shaped or arched like the back of a tortoise. **testudineous,** *a.* resembling the shell of a tortoise. [L *testūdo -dinis* from TESTA]

testy, *a.* irritable, peevish, pettish, petulant. **testily,** *adv.* **testiness,** *n.* [ME and A-F *testif,* from OF *teste* (F *tête*), head]

tetanus, *n.* a disease marked by long-continued spasms of voluntary muscles, esp. those of the jaws, as in lock-jaw. **tetanal,** *a.* **tetanic,** *a.* pertaining to or characteristic of tetanus. *n.* a medicine acting on the muscles through the nerves, as strychnine. **tetanize, -ise,** *v.t.* **tetanization, -isation,** *n.* **tetanoid,** *a.* **tetany,** *n.* an intermittent tetanoid affection. [L, from Gr. *tetanos* redupl. from *ten-,* stem of *teinein,* to stretch]

tetchy, *a.* fretful, irritable, touchy. **tetchily,** *adv.* **tetchiness,** *n.* [etym. doubtful]

tête-á-tête, *a.* private, confidential. *adv.* in private or close confabulation. *n.* (*pl.* **têtes-à-têtes** or **tête-à-têtes**) a private interview, a close or confidential conversation; a sofa for two persons, esp. with seats facing in opposite directions so that the occupants face one another. [F, head to head]

tether, *n.* a rope or halter by which a grazing animal is prevented from moving too far; (*fig.*) prescribed range, scope. *v.t.* to confine with or as with a tether. **at the end of one's tether,** at the limit of one's strength, endurance or patience. [ME *tedir,* cp. Icel. *tjōthr,* Swed. *tjuder,* MDut. *tūder,* Dut. *tuier*]

Tet Offensive, *n.* in the Vietnam War, a prolonged attack mounted by the Vietcong against Saigon Jan.–Feb. 1968. Although the Vietcong were forced to withdraw, the attack on the South Vietnamese capital brought into question the ability of the South Vietnamese and their US allies to win the war.

tetr(a)-, *comb. form* four. [Gr., from *tettares,* four]

tetrabasic, *a.* of an acid, having four replaceable hydrogen atoms.

tetrabranchiate, *a.* having four branchiae or gills.

tetrachord, *n.* a scale series of half an octave, esp. as used in ancient music. **tetrachordal,** *a.*

tetrachotomous, *a.* separated into four branches, series etc., doubly dichotomous. **tetrachotomy,** *n.* [cp. DICHOTOMOUS]

tetract, *a.* having four rays or branches, as a sponge-spicule; *n.* a four-rayed sponge-spicule. **tetractinal, -nose,** *a.* †**tetractine,** *a., n.* [Gr. *aktis -tinos,* ray]

tetracyclic, *a.* (*Bot.*) having four circles or whorls. **tetracycline,** *n.* any of several antibiotics, some of which are derived from a bacterium, used to treat a wide range of infections.

tetrad, *n.* the number four; a collection, group, or set of four things; (*Chem.*) an atom or element that can unite with or replace four atoms of hydrogen. **tetradic,** *a.* [Gr. *tetras -ados,* as TETR(A)-]

tetradactyl, *n.* an animal having four digits on each limb. *a.* tetradactylous. **tetradactylous,** *a.* having four digits on each limb. [Gr. *tetradaktulos* (*daktūlos,* finger)]

tetradecapod, *a.* having 14 feet; of or pertaining to the Tetradecapoda, an order of crustaceans with seven pairs of feet; *n.* one of the Tetradecapoda. **tetradecapodon,** *a., n.* **tetradecapodous,** *a.*

tetraethyl, *a.* having four ethyl groups. **tetraethyl lead,** *n.* an anti-knock, insoluble liquid used in petrol.

tetragon, *n.* a plane figure having four angles. **tetragonal,** *a.* having the form of a tetragon; pertaining to the crystal system characterized by three axes at right angles, of which only two are equal. **tetragonally,** *adv.* [Gr. *tetragōnon*]

tetragram, *n.* a word of four letters; a quadrilateral figure. **tetragrammaton,** *n.* the group of four letters representing the name Jehovah or some other sacred word.

tetragynian, tetragynous, *a.* having four pistils. [Gr. *gunē,* female]

tetrahedron, *n.* a solid figure bounded by four planes, esp. equilateral, triangular faces. **tetrahedral,** *a.* **tetrahedroid,** *n.* [Gr. *hedra,* base]

tetrahexahedron, *n.* a solid bounded by 24 equal faces, four corresponding to each face of the cube. **tetrahexahedral,** *a.*

tetralogy, *n.* a collection of four dramatic works, esp. (*Gr. Ant.*) a trilogy or three tragedies, followed by a satyric piece.

tetrameral, tetramerous, *a.* consisting of four parts. [Gr. *tetramerēs* (*meros,* part)]

tetrameter, *n.* a verse consisting of four measures. [L *tetrametrus,* Gr. *tetrametros*)]

tetramorph, *n.* (*Art*) the union of the attributes of the four evangelists in one composite figure. [Gr. *morphē,* form]

tetrandrous, †**-drian,** *a.* having four stamens. [Gr. *anēr andros,* male]

tetrapetalous, *a.* having four petals.

tetraphyllous, *a.* having four leaves. [Gr. *phullon,* leaf]

tetrapla, *n.* an edition containing four versions, esp. Origen's edition of the four Greek versions of the Old Testament. [Gr. *tetraplā,* neut. of *tetraplous* (*-ploos,* -fold)]

tetraplegia, *n.* quadriplegia, paralysis of both arms and legs. **tetraplegic,** *n., a.*

tetraploid, *a.* having four times the haploid number of chromosomes; a tetraploid nucleus or cell.

tetrapod, *a.* having four feet or limbs; belonging to the Tetrapoda, a division of butterflies with only four perfect legs. *n.* a four-footed animal, esp. one of the Tetrapoda. **tetrapodous,** *a.* **tetrapody,** *n.* a group or a verse of four feet. [Gr. *pous podos,* foot]

tetrapolitan, *a.* of or pertaining to a group of four towns. **Tetrapolitan Confession,** *n.* the confession of faith submitted to the Diet of Augsburg in 1530 from Strasburg, Memmingen, Constance and Lindau. [from Gr. *tetrapolis* (*polis,* city), after METROPOLITAN]

tetrapterous, *a.* having four wings or wing-like appendages, as certain fruits. **tetrapteran,** *a.* tetrapterous; *n.* a tetrapterous insect. [Gr. *pteron,* wing]

tetraptote, *n.* a noun which has four cases only. [Gr. *ptōsis,* case]

tetrarch, *n.* a governor of the fourth part of a province under the Roman empire, also a tributary prince; the commander of a subdivision of the ancient Greek phalanx. **tetrarchate, tetrarchy,** *n.* **tetrarchical,** *a.* [late L *tetrarcha,* L and Gr. *tetrarchēs* (*archein,* to rule)]

tetraspermous, *a.* having four seeds. [Gr. *sperma,* seed]

tetraspore, *n.* a group of four spores asexually produced, as in some algae.

tetrastich, *n.* a stanza, poem, or epigram consisting of four lines of verse. [Gr. *stichos,* row]

tetrastichal, tetrastichic, *a.* **tetrastichous,** *a.* in four rows.

tetrastyle, *a.* having four pillars; *n.* a building, portico etc., having four pillars. [STYLE[2]]

tetrasyllable, *n.* a word of four syllables, **tetrasyllabic,** *a.*

tetratheism, *n.* the doctrine that the Godhead comprises four elements, the three persons of the Trinity and a divine essence from which each of these proceeds.

tetratomic, *a.* having four atoms to a molecule.

tetravalent, *a.* having a valency of four. **tetravalency,** *n.*

tetrode, *n.* a thermionic valve containing four electrodes.

tetroxide, *n.* any oxide having four oxygen atoms per molecule.

tetryl, *n.* a yellow crystalline explosive solid, used as a detonator.

†**tett,** TEAT.

tetter, *n.* a name applied to several cutaneous diseases. *v.t.* to affect with tetter. **tetterwort,** *n.* the greater celandine, *Chelidonium majus.* [OE *teter,* cp. Sansk. *dadru*]

tettix, *n.* a cicada or tree-cricket; (*Ent.*) a genus of Acridiidae or short-horned grass-hoppers; (*Gr. Ant.*) an ornament in the form of a tettix worn in the hair. [Gr.]

Tetuán, Tétouan, *n.* town in NE Morocco, near the Mediterranean coast, 64 km/40 miles SE of Tangier; population (1982) 372,000. Products include textiles, leather, and soap. It was settled by Moorish exiles from Spain in the 16th cent.

Teucrian, *a.* of ancient Troy or the Troad. *n.* an ancient Trojan. [L *Teucri,* from Gr. *Teukros,* king of Troy]

teucrium, *n.* the germander. [L, from Gr. *teukrion,* as prec.]

Teuton, *n.* orig. one of a German tribe, first mentioned as dwelling near the Elbe, *c.* 300 BC; a member of any Teutonic race. **Teuto-,** *comb. form.* **Teutonic,** *a.* pertaining to the Teutons; pertaining to the Germanic peoples, including Scandinavians, Anglo-Saxons etc., as well as the German races, *n.* the language or languages of the Teutons collectively; Germanic. **Teutonic Knight,** *n.* member of a German Christian military order, the Knights of the Teutonic Order, founded 1190 by Hermann of Salza in Palestine. They crusaded against the pagan Prussians and Lithuanians from 1228, and controlled Prussia until the 16th cent. Their capital was Marienburg (now Malbork, Poland). **Teutonic languages,** *n.pl.* a group of Aryan or Indo-European languages including High and Low German and the Scandinavian languages. **Teutonicism, Teutonism,** *n.* **Teutonize, -ise,** *v.t.* **Teutonization, -isation,** *n.* [L *Teutoni, Teutonēs,* from Teut., cp. Goth. *thiuda,* people, G *deutsch,* German]

tew TAW[1].

tewel, *n.* a pipe, a chimney, a tuyère. [ME and OF *tuel* (F *tuyau*), from Teut., cp. Dut. *tuit,* G *Tüte,* pipe]

Tex., (*abbr.*) Texas, Texan.

Texas, *n.* state of the SW US; nickname Lone Star State. **area** 691,200 sq km/266,803 sq miles. **capital** Austin. **towns** Houston, Dallas-Fort Worth, San Antonio, El Paso, Corpus Christi, Lubbock. **population** (1985) 16,370,000. **products** rice, cotton, sorghum, peanuts, pecans, vegetables, fruit, meat products, oil (one third of the needs of the US), natural gas, asphalt, graphite, sulphur, salt, helium, chemicals, oil products, processed food, machinery, transport equipment.

Tex-Mex, *a.* pertaining to or denoting the Texan version of something Mexican, such as food etc.

text, *n.* the original words of an author, esp. as opp. to a translation, commentary, or revision etc.; the actual words of a book or poem; the words of something as printed, written, or displayed on a video display unit; a verse or passage of Scripture, esp. one selected as the theme of a discourse; a subject, a topic; text-hand; any book or novel which is studied as part of an educational course. **textbook,** *n.* a standard book for a particular branch of study; a manual of instruction. *a.* conforming to textbook descriptions; ideal; typical. **textbookish,** *a.* **text-hand,** *n.* a large style of handwriting (from the practice of writing the text in a larger hand than the commentary). **textual,** *a.* pertaining to or contained in the text. **textual criticism,** *n.* the study of texts, esp. the Bible, to etablish the original text; a close reading and analysis of any literary text. **textualist,** *n.* one who adheres strictly to the text. **textualism,** *n.* **textually,** *adv.* **textuary,** *a., n.* [ME and F *texte,* L *textus -tūs,* style, later the Scriptures, from *texere,* to weave]

textile, *a.* woven; suitable for weaving; pertaining to weaving. *n.* a woven fabric; raw material suitable to be made into cloth. **textorial,** *a.* pertaining to weaving. [L *textilis,* as prec.]

textual TEXT.

texture, *n.* the particular arrangement or disposition of threads, filaments etc., in a woven fabric; the disposition of the constituent parts of any body, structure, or material; the structure of tissues, tissue; (*Art.*) the representation of the surface of objects in works of art; the quality of something as perceived by touch. *v.t.* to give texture to. **textural,** *a.* **textured,** *a.* **textureless,** *a.* **texturize, -ise,** *v.t.* **texturized vegetable protein, TVP,** *n.* a substitute made from soya beans which resembles meat in texture and taste. [F, from L *textūra,* from *textus,* TEXT]

TGV, *n.* a superfast French train that operates the world's fastest rail service between Paris and Lyon. Introduced in 1981 and electrically powered, the TGV covers the 425 km/264 mile journey in just two hours. [acronym for *t*rain à *g*rande *v*itesse]

TGWU, (*abbr.*) Transport and General Workers Union.

Th., (*abbr.*) Thomas; Thursday.

Th, (*chem. symbol*) thorium.

-th, *suf.* forming abstract names [cp. -NESS], as *filth, wealth;* forming ordinal numbers, as *fifth, fiftieth.* [from var. Teut. suffixes, in second sense from OE *-tha, -the,* cp. Gr. *-tos,* L *-tus*]

thack, *n.* (*now prov.*) thatch; (*Sc.*) the thatching on a rick or stack. **thack and rape,** (*Sc.*) the covering of straw on a rick etc., and the straw-wythes securing this. **under thack and rape,** (*fig.*) snug, comfortable. [OE *thaec* THATCH, whence, *thacian,* to thatch]

Thackeray, *n.* **William Makepeace** (1811–63), British novelist, author of *Vanity Fair.* He was a regular contributor to *Fraser's Magazine* and *Punch. Vanity Fair* (1847–48) was his first novel, followed by *Pendennis* (1848), *Henry Esmond* (1852) and its sequel *The Virginians* (1857–59), and *The Newcomes* (1853–55), in which Thackeray's tendency to sentimentality is most marked. Other works include the fairy tale *The Rose and the Ring* (1855) and *The Book of Snobs* (1848).

Thai, *a.* of or pertaining to Thailand, formerly known as Siam. *n.* the language of Thailand.

Thailand, *n.* Kingdom of (*Prathet Thai* or *Muang-Thai*), a country in SE Asia on the Gulf of Siam, bounded to the E by Laos and Cambodia, to the S by Malaysia, and to the W by Burma. **area** 513,100 sq km/198,108 sq miles. **capital** and chief port Bangkok. **towns** Chiangmai. **physical** central valley flanked by highlands; tropical rainforest. **population** (1989) 55,017,000 (Thai 75%, Chinese 14%); annual growth rate 2%. **exports** rice, sugar, rubber, teak, tin (fifth largest producer), rubies, sapphires. **language** Thai and Chinese (both official). **religion** Buddhist.

thaive THEAVE.

thalamus, *n.* (*pl.* **-mi**) (*Gr. Ant.*) an inner room, the women's apartment, a nuptial chamber; the place at which a nerve originates, or is supposed to originate, esp. the optic thalamus; the receptacle of a flower. **thalamic,** *a.* **thalamifloral,** *a.* having the petals, stamens etc., inserted on the thalamus. **thalamium,** *n.* (*pl.* **-mia**), a spore-case in algae; a form of hymenium in some fungi. [L, from Gr. *thalamos*]

thalassaemia, thalassemia, *n.* a hereditary disorder of the blood due to defects in the synthesis on haemoglobin, sometimes fatal in children. [Gr. *thalassa,* sea, + *aemia,* because of its prevalence in the eastern Mediterranean]

thalassic, *a.* of or pertaining to the sea, marine. **thalassocracy,** -CRACY, *n.* naval supremacy, sea-power, **thalassocrat,** *n.* **thalassography,** -GRAPHY, *n.* **thalassographer,** *n.* **thalassographic,** *a.* [F *thalassique* (Gr. *thalassa,* the sea, -IC)]

thaler, *n.* an old German silver coin. [G, see DOLLAR]

Thalia, *n.* the Muse of comedy and pastoral poetry. **Thalian,** *a.* [L, from Gr. *Thaleia,* from *thallein,* to bloom]

Thalictrum, *n.* a genus of ranunculaceous herbs containing the meadow-rues. [L, from Gr. *thaliktron*]

thalidomide, *n.* a drug formerly used as a sedative, withdrawn from use in 1961, as it was shown to be associated with malformation of the foetus when taken by pregnant women. **thalidomide baby,** *n.* a baby born showing the effects of thalidomide. [ph*thal*ic acid + *id* (from *imide*)]

thallium, *n.* a rare soft, white, crystalline metallic element, at. no. 81, chem. symbol Tl, the spectrum of which contains a bright-green line (whence the name), used in alloys and glass-making. **thallic, thallous,** *a.* [Gr. *thall-os,* see foll., -IUM]

thallophyte, *n.* one of a class of plants (*Thyophyta*), the lowest in organization, consisting of those whose vegetative body is a thallus, comprising the algae, fungi and lichens. **thallophytic**, *a.* [as foll.]

thallus, *n.* (*pl.* **-lusses, -lli**) a plant-body without true root, stem, or leaves. **thalliferous**, *a.* **thalloid**, *a.* **thallophyte**, *n.* any member of the lowest division of the vegetable kingdom, lacking stems, leaves and roots, and including algae, fungi, lichens and bacteria. **thallophytic**, *a.* [L, from Gr. *thallos,* from *thallein,* to bloom]

Thames, *n.* river in SE England; length 338 km/210 miles. It rises in the Cotswolds above Cirencester, and is tidal as far as Teddington. Below London there is protection from flooding by means of the **Thames barrier** a moveable barrier built across the river at Woolwich as part of London's flood defences. Completed in 1982, the barrier comprises curved flood gates which are rotated 90° into position from beneath the water to form a barrier when exceptionally high tides are expected.

thalweg, talweg *n.* the longitudinal outline of a riverbed; the line of steepest descent from a point on the land surface. [G *Thal,* or *Tal* valley, *Weg,* way]

than, *conj.* used after adjectives and adverbs expressing comparison, such as *more, better, worse, rather* etc., to introduce the second member of a comparison. [OE *thanne, thonne, thaenne,* THEN]

thanage THANE.

thanatism, *n.* the doctrine of annihilation at death. **thanatist,** *n.*

thanat(o)-, *comb. form* death. [Gr. *thanatos,* death]

thanatognomonic, *a.* indicative of death.

thanatography, *n.* an account of a person's death.

thanatoid, *a.* resembling death; apparently dead; (*Zool.*) poisonous, deadly.

thanatology, *n.* the scientific study of death.

Thanatophidia, *n.pl.* (*Zool.*) the venomous snakes. [OPHIDIA]

thanatophobia, *n.* a morbid fear of death.

thanatopsis, *n.* a view, or contemplation, of death.

thane, thegn, *n.* (*OE Hist.*) a freeman holding land by military service and ranking between ordinary freemen and the nobles. **thanage**, *n.* Thaneship; the land held by a thane; the tenure of this. **thanedom**, **thanehood**, **thaneship,** *n.* [OE *thegen, thegn* (cp. Icel. *thegn,* G *Degen,* OHG *Degan*), cogn. with Gr. *teknon,* child]

thank, *n.* (*now pl.*) an expression of gratitude; a formula of acknowledgment of a favour, kindness, benefit etc. *v.t.* to express gratitude (to or for); to make acknowledgment to for a gift, offer etc. (often used ironically, esp. as a contemp. refusal). **thanks to,** because of, owing to. **thank you,** a formula expressing thanks, polite refusal etc. **thank-offering,** *n.* an offering made as an expression of gratitude, esp. a Jewish sacrifice of thanksgiving. **thanksgiver,** *n.* **thanksgiving,** *n.* the act of returning thanks or expressing gratitude, esp. to God; a form of words expressive of this; (*Bibl.*) a thank-offering. **Thanksgiving Day,** *n.* (*N Am.*) annual national holiday for thanksgiving to God for blessings enjoyed individually and nationally, first celebrated by the Pilgrim settlers in Massachusetts on their first harvest, 1621 (last Thursday in Nov. US, second Monday in Oct. Canada). †**thank-worthy,** *a.* **thankful,** *a.* grateful; expressive of thanks. **thankfully,** *adv.* **thankfulness,** *n.* **thankless**, *a.* insensible to kindness, ungrateful; not deserving thanks, unprofitable. **thanklessly,** *adv.* **thanklessness,** *n.* [OE *thanc, thonc,* thought, grace (cp. Dut. and G *Dank,* Icel. *thökk*), whence *thancian,* cp. Dut. and G *danken*]

Thapsia, *n.* a genus of umbelliferous herbs of the Mediterranean region, comprising *Thapsia garcanica,* the deadly carrot, used by the Algerians as a panacea, and three other species. [L and Gr., prob. from *Thapsus,* in Sicily]

that, *a.* (*pl.* **those**) the (person or thing) specifically designated, pointed out, implied, or understood; (correlated with *this*) the more remote or less obvious of two things; such (usu. followed by *as*). *pron.* the person or thing specifically designated, pointed out, implied, or understood; who or which (now usu. demonstratively and introducing a restrictive or defining clause). *adv.* in such a manner, to such a degree. *conj.* introducing a clause, stating a fact or supposition; implying purpose, so that, in order that; implying result, consequence etc.; implying reason or cause, on the ground that, because, since. **and (all) that,** and everything of that sort. **at that,** at that point; moreover. **(just) like that,** effortlessly, straight off. **that away,** (*coll.*) that way, in that direction. **that is,** to be more precise, precisely. **that's that,** there is no more to be done, said etc. **thatness,** the state of being a definite thing. [OE *thaet,* orig. neut. of THE]

thatch, *n.* a roof-covering of straw, rushes, reeds etc. *v.t.* to cover with this. *v.i.* to do thatching. **thatched,** *a.* **thatcher,** *n.* **thatching,** *n.* the act of thatching; the materials used in thatching. **thatch palm,** *n.* any of several palms used in thatching. [OE *thaec* (cp. Dut. *dak,* G *Dach,* Icel. *thak,* also Gr. *tegos,* roof, L *tegere,* to cover), whence *theccan,* to thatch]

Thatcher, *n.* **Margaret Hilda** (born **Roberts**) (1925–), British Conservative politician, in Parliament from 1959, party leader from 1975, and prime minister from 1979. Landmarks of the Thatcher government include the independence of Zimbabwe; the Falklands conflict; the 1984–85 miners' strike; reduction of inflation; large-scale privatization; the attempt to suppress the publication of *Spycatcher* and other measures to limit civil liberties; the Anglo-Irish Agreement of 1985; a large rise in unemployment; depletion of the welfare state; and the introduction of the community charge or poll tax in 1989 and 1990. **Thatcherism**, *n.* the political, economic etc. philosophy and policies of Margaret Thatcher. **Thatcherite,** *n.* a supporter of Margaret Thatcher or her policies. *a.* pertaining to Margaret Thatcher or her policies.

thaumasite, *n.* a dull white, translucent compound of calcium.

thauma(t)-, *comb. form* pertaining to wonder or miracles. [Gr. *thauma,* wonder]

thaumatrope, *n.* an optical toy consisting of a disk with figures on opposite sides which appear to combine and perform movements when the disk is rotated. [Gr. *-tropos,* turning, from *trepein,* to turn]

thaumaturge, *n.* a worker of miracles; a wonder-worker, a magician or conjurer. **thaumaturgic, -al,** *a.* **thaumaturgist,** *n.* **thaumaturgy,** *n.* [med. L *thaumaturgus,* Gr. *thaumatourgos -ergos,* working)]

thaw, *v.i.* to melt, dissolve, or become liquid (of ice, snow etc.): to become so warm as to melt ice or snow (of weather); (*fig.*) to relax one's stiffness, to unbend, to become genial. *v.t.* to melt, to dissolve; to infuse warmth or into. *n.* the act of thawing or the state of being thawed; warm weather that thaws; a relaxation of tension, an in- crease in friendliness. **to thaw out,** to return to normal from a frozen condition; to become more relaxed or more friendly. **thawless,** *a.* **thawy,** *a.* [OE *thāwian,* cp. Dut. *dooijen,* G *tauen,* Icel. *theyja*]

the, *a.* applied to a person or thing or persons or things already mentioned, implied, or definitely understood; used before a singular noun to denote a species; prefixed to adjectives used absolutely, giving them the force of a substantive; before nouns expressing a unit to give distributive force (as '90p. the pint'); emphatically, to express uniqueness (as '*the* famous Duke of

Wellington'), *adv.* used before adjectives and adverbs in the comparative degree, to that extent, to that amount, by so much. [OE *the,* fem. *theo,* neut. *thaet* (earlier *sē, sēo, thaet*]

theandric, *a.* relating to or existing by the union of divine and human nature in Christ. [Gr. *theandrikos* (*anēr andros,* man)]

theanthropic, -al, *a.* being both human and divine; tending to embody deity in human forms. **theanthropism,** *n.* [Gr. *anthrōpos,* man]

thearchy, *n.* Government by God or gods; a body, class, or order of gods or deities. [Gr. *-archia,* rule, from *archein,* to rule]

theater THEATRE.

Theatine, *n.* a member of a congregation of regular clerks, founded in 1524 by John Peter Caraffa, Archbishop of Chieti. *a.* of or pertaining to this order. [mod. L *Theatīnus,* from *Theate* or *Teate,* anc. name of Chieti, a city of the Abruzzi, Italy]

theatre, (*esp. N Am*) **theater,** *n.* a building for dramatic spectacles, a play-house; a cinema; a room, hall etc.; with a platform at one end, and seats arranged in ascending tiers, used for lectures, demonstrations etc.; the room in a hospital etc. used for operations; the drama, the stage; the place or scene of an action, event etc.; matter suitable to be staged. **theatre-in-the-round,** a theatre where the seats are arranged around a central acting area; the style of producing plays in such a theatre. **theatre of cruelty,** a branch of the theatre which seeks to express pain and suffering and an awareness of evil. **theatre of the absurd,** a branch of the theatre which juxtaposes the fantastic and the bizarre with the irrationality and tragedy of human existence. **the theatre,** the world of actors, producers, theatre companies etc. **theatre-goer,** *n.* a person who goes to the theatre regularly. **theatre organ,** *n.* a type of organ usu. electrically wind-controlled, with effects of most instruments of an orchestra, employed for entertainment purposes in cinemas and theatres. †**theatric.** [OF, from Gr. *theatron,* from *theasthai,* to behold, from *thea,* view]

theatrical, *n.* of or pertaining to the theatre; befitting the stage, dramatic; suitable or calculated for display, pompous, showy; befitting or characteristic of actors, stagy, affected. **theatricalism, theatricality,** *n.* **theatricalize, -ise,** *v.t.* **theatrically,** *adv.* **theatricals,** *n.pl.* dramatic performances, esp. private.

theatrophone, *n.* a telephone connected with a theatre, etc., enabling persons to hear performances without being present.

theave, thaive, *n.* (*chiefly Midland*) a ewe of the first or second year. [etym. unknown]

thebaine, *n.* (*Chem.*) a poisonous crystalline alkaloid obtained from opium.

Thebes[1], *n.* capital of Boeotia in ancient Greece. In the Peloponnesian War it was allied with Sparta against Athens, and for a short time after 371 BC it was the most powerful state in Greece. Alexander the Great destroyed it in 336 BC and although it was restored it was never again important. **Theban**[1], *n.*, *a.*

Thebes[2], *n.* Greek name of an ancient city (Niut Ammon) in Upper Egypt, on the Nile, probably founded under the first dynasty, centre of the worship of Ammon, and the Egyptian capital under the New Kingdom about 1600 BC. Temple ruins survive near the modern villages of Karnak and Luxor, and in the nearby Valley of the Kings the 18th-20th dynasty kings, including Tutankhamen and Amenhotep III, are buried. **Theban**[2], *n.*, *a.* **Theban year,** *n.* the Egyptian year of 365¼ days. **Thebaid,** *n.* the territory of Egyptian Thebes. [L *Thēbānus,* from *Thēbae,* Gr. *Thebai*]

theca, *n.* (*pl.* **-cae**) (*Bot., Zool., etc.*) a sheath, a case. **thecal, thecate,** *a.* **theciferous,** *a.* **theciform,** *a.* [L, from Gr. *thēkē*]

thecodont, *a.* pertaining to the Thecodontia, an order of extinct saurians having the teeth in distinct sockets; *n.* one of the Thecodontia. **thecophore,** *n.* a receptacle bearing thecae; (*Bot.*) the stalk of an ovary. [Gr. *thēkē,* case, *odous odontos,* tooth]

thé dansant, *n.* (*pl.* **thés dansants**) a dance held during afternoon tea, popular in the 1920s and 1930s. [F literally dancing tea]

thee, *obj.* THOU.

theek, theik, (*Sc., North.*) THATCH.

theft, *n.* the act of thieving or stealing; larceny; that which is stolen. **theftuous,** *a.* (*Sc.*). **theftuously,** *adv.* [OE *thīefth, thēofth, thēoft*]

thegn, etc. THANE.

theic, *n.* an excessive tea-drinker. **theiform,** *a.* **theine,** *n.* an organic base occurring in tea, caffeine. **theism**[1], *n.* an abnormal condition resulting from excessive tea-drinking. [mod. L *thea,* TEA, -IC]

theik THEEK.

their, theirs, *poss.* THEY.

theism[1] THEIC.

theism[2], *n.* belief in a God, as opp. to atheism; belief in a righteous God supernaturally revealed, as opp. to Deism. **theist,** *n.* **theistic, -al,** *a.* [Gr. *theos,* god, -ISM]

them, *obj.* THEY.

theme, *n.* a subject on which a person writes or speaks; short dissertation or essay by a student, school pupil etc., on a certain subject; the part of a noun or verb remaining unchanged by inflexions; a melodic subject usu. developed with variations; (*Log.*) the subject of thought; an underlying unifying principle. **theme park,** *n.* a park designed for leisure, where all the activities are based on a single subject. **theme song,** *n.* a recurring melody in a film, musical etc. which is associated with the production or a specific character; a signature tune; (*coll.*) a person's characteristic complaint, repeated phrase etc. **thematic,** *a.* **thematic catalogue,** *n.* a catalogue giving the opening theme of each piece of music. **thematically,** *adv.* [L *thema,* Gr. *thema -atos,* from *the-,* root of *tithenai,* to put]

Themis, *n.* the Greek goddess of Justice or Law; one of the asteroids. [L and Gr., law, as prec.]

Themistocles, *n.* (525–460 BC), Greek soldier. Largely responsible for the ostracizing of Aristides in 483 BC, he held almost supreme power in Athens for ten years, created its navy and strengthened its walls, and fought with distinction in the Battle of Salamis 480 BC during the Persian War. Banished by Spartan influence about 470 BC, he fled to Asia, where Artaxerxes, the Persian king, received him with favour.

themselves, *pron.* the emphatic and reflexive form of the third plural personal pronoun. [THEM, SELVES,]

then, *adv.* at that time; afterwards, soon after, after that, next; at another time. *conj.* in that case; therefore; consequently; this being so, accordingly. *a.* (*coll.*) of or existing at that time. *n.* that time, the time mentioned or understood. **by then,** by that time. **then and there,** on the spot, immediately. **then or thenabouts,** about that time. [ME *thenne,* OE *thanne, thonne, thaenne* (cogn. with THAT, THE), cp. THAN]

thenar, *n.* the palm, the sole, the ball of the thumb. *a.* of or pertaining to the palm of the hand or the sole of the foot. [Gr. *thenar*]

thence, *adv.* from that place; for that reason, from that source; from that time. **thenceforth, thenceforward,** *adv.* from that time onward. [ME *thennes* (*thenne,* -ES), OE *thanon, thonan,* cogn. with THAT, THE]

the(o)-, *comb. form,* pertaining to God or a god. [Gr. *theos,* god]

theobroma, *n.* a genus of tropical trees, one of which, *Theobroma cacao* yields cocoa and chocolate. **theobromic,** *a.* **theobromine,** *n.* a bitter alkaloid resembling caffeine contained in the seeds of *T. cacao.* [Gr. *broma,* food]

theocracy, *n.* Government by the immediate direction of God or through a sacerdotal class; a state so governed. **theocrat,** *n.* **theocratic, theocratical,** *a.* **theocratist,** *n.*

theocrasy, *n.* mixed worship of different gods, polytheism; the union of the soul with God in contemplation. [CRASIS]

Theocritus, *n.* (b. *c.* 270 BC), Greek poet. Probably

born at Syracuse, he spent much of his life at Alexandria. His *Idylls* became models for later pastoral poetry.

Theocritean, *a.* of, pertaining to, or in the style of the Greek pastoral poet Theocritus; pastoral, idyllic, Arcadian.

theodicy, *n.* a vindication of divine justice in respect to the existence of evil. **theodicean**, *n.* [F *théodicée* (THEO-, Gr. *dikē,* justice)]

theodolite, *n.* a portable surveying instrument for measuring horizontal and vertical angles. **theodolitic**, *a.* [etym. doubtful]

Theodora, *n.* (AD 508–548), Byzantine empress from AD 527, originally the mistress of Emperor Justinian, and his consort from about AD 523. She earned a reputation for charity and courage.

Theodorakis, *n.* **Mikis** (1925–), Greek composer, imprisoned 1967–70 for attempting to overthrow the military regime.

Theodoric, *n.* **the Great** (AD 455–526), king of the Ostrogoths from AD 474 in succession to his father. He invaded Italy AD 488, overthrew King Odoacer (whom he murdered) and established his own Ostrogothic kingdom there, with its capital in Ravenna. He had no strong successor, and his kingdom eventually became part of the Byzantine Empire of Justinian.

Theodosius II, *n.* (AD 401–450), Byzantine emperor from AD 408, who defeated the Persians AD 421 and AD 441, and from AD 441 fought off Attila's Huns with tribute.

Theodosian, *a.* of or pertaining to the emperor Theodosius, esp. Theodosius II, who issued a code of Roman law (AD 438).

theogony, *n.* the genealogy of the gods; a poem treating of this. **theogonic**, *a.* **theogonist,** *n.* [L and Gr. *theogonia* (*gonia,* from *gen-,* to beget)]

theol., (*abbr.*) theologian, theological, theology.

theology, *n.* the science of God and His attributes and relations to the universe; the science of religion, esp. Christianity. **natural theology,** the science dealing with the knowledge of God as derived from His works. **theologian**, **†theologist, †theologue**, *n.* one versed in theology; a professor of theology. **theological**, *a.* **theologically,** *adv.* **theologaster**, *n.* a pretender to a knowledge of theology. **theologize, -ise,** *v.t.* to make theological. *v.i.* to speculate on theology. **†theologizer, -iser,** *n.* [ME and OF *theologie,* L and Gr. *theologia* (THEO-, -LOGY)]

theomachy, *n.* a combat against or among the gods. **theomachist,** *n.* [L and Gr. *theomachia* (*-machia,* fighting)]

theomancy, *n.* divination by oracle or by people inspired by god. [Gr. *theomanteia*]

theomania, *n.* religious insanity; a delusion that one is God. **theomaniac**, *n.*

theomorphic, *a.* having the form or semblance of God, opp. to anthropomorphic. **theomorphism,** *n.* [Gr. *morphē,* form]

theopaschite, *n.* a member of a sect who affirmed that in the crucifixion and passion the godhead had suffered. **theopaschist,** *n.* **theopaschitally,** *adv.* **theopaschitic**, **theopaschitism**, *n.* [late L *theopaschita,* Gr. *theopaschites* (*paschein,* to suffer)]

theopathy, *n.* emotion excited by the contemplation of God. **theopathetic**, *a.*

theophany, *n.* the manifestation or appearance of God to man. **theophanic**, *a.* [L *theophania,* Gr. *theophania* (*ephainein,* to show)]

theophilanthropy, *n.* a system of deism promulgated in France in 1796, based on adoration of God and love of man and intended to take the place of Roman Catholicism. **theophilanthropic**, *a.* **theophilanthropism,** *n.* **theophilanthropist,** *n.*

theopneusty, *n.* divine inspiration. **theopneustic,** *a.* [Gr. *theopneustos,* inspired (*pnein,* to blow)]

theorbo, *n.* a stringed instrument resembling a two-necked lute used in the 16th–17th cents. **theorbist,** *n.* [It. *tiorba,* etym. doubtful (cp. F *théorbe*)]

theorem, *n.* a proposition to be proved; a principle to be demonstrated by reasoning; (*Math.*) a rule or law, esp. one expressed by symbols, etc. **theorematic, -al,** *a.* **theorematist,** *n.* [late L and Gr. *theōrēma,* from *theōrein,* to behold]

theoretic, -al, *a.* pertaining to or founded on theory not facts or knowledge, not practical, speculative. **theoretically,** *adv.* **theoretics,** *n.* the speculative parts of a science. **theoretician**, *n.* a person interested in the theory rather than the practical application of a given subject. [late L *theōrēticus,* Gr. *thēōretikos,* from *theōrētos,* as foll.]

theoric, *a.* (*Gr. Ant.*) pertaining to the public spectacles; theoretic. †*n.* theory. **theorist,** etc. THEORY. [ME *theorike,* OF *theorique,* Gr. *theōrikos,* from *theōrein,* to behold, to contemplate]

theory, *n.* supposition explaining something, esp. a generalization explaining phenomena as the results of assumed natural causes; a speculative idea of something; mere hypothesis; speculation, abstract knowledge; an exposition of the general principles of a science etc.; a body of theorems illustrating a particular subject. **theorist,** *n.* one who theorizes; one given to forming theories. **theorize, -ise,** *v.i.* **theorization, -isation,** *n.* **theorizer, -iser,** *n.* [A-F *theorie,* L and Gr. *theōria,* as prec.]

theosophy, *n.* a form of speculation, mysticism, or philosophy aiming at the knowledge of God by means of intuition and contemplative illumination or by direct communion; a term commonly applied to a system founded in the US, in 1875, which claims to show the unity of all religions in their esoteric teaching, manifested by occult phenomena. **theosoph**, **theosopher, -phist,** *n.* **theosophic, -al,** *a.* **Theosophical Society,** *n.* a religious society founded in 1875 by Madame Blavatsky and others, and derived from Brahmanism and Buddhism. **theosophism,** *n.* **theosophist,** *n.* **theosophistical**, *a.* **theosophize, -ise,** *v.i.* [med. L and late Gr. *theosophia* (THEO-, *sophos,* wise)]

theotechny, *n.* the supernatural machinery of a literary composition. **theotechnic**, *a.* [THEO-, *technē,* art]

Theotokos, *n.* the God-bearer (a title of the Virgin Mary, cp. DEIPAROUS). [Gr. (THEO-, Gr. *-tokos,* bringing forth, rel. to *tiktein,* to bear)]

Therapeutae, *n.pl.* a sect of Egyptian Jews in the 1st cent. AD who gave themselves up to contemplation of God. [L, from Gr. *therapeutai,* from *therapeuein,* to wait on (also to heal), from *theraps -apos,* servant]

therapeutic, *a.* pertaining to the healing art; curative. *n.pl.* the branch of medical science dealing with the treatment of disease and the action of remedial agents in both health and disease. **therapeutical,** *a.* **therapeutically,** *adv.* **therapeutist,** *n.* **therapy**, *n.* therapeutics, the treatment of disease or physical and mental disorders from a curative and preventive point of view; physiotherapy; psychiatric or psychological therapy. **therapist,** *n.* a practitioner of therapy, esp. a psychologist or psychiatrist. [as prec.]

Theravàda, *n.* one of the two major forms of Buddhism, common in S Asia (Sri Lanka, Thailand, Cambodia, and Burma); the other is the later Mahāyāna.

there, *adv.* in or at that place, point, or stage; to that place, thither, frequently used before the verb in interrogations, negative sentences etc. *n.* that place. *int.* expressing direction, confirmation, triumph, alarm etc. **all there,** (*sl.*) wide awake; fully competent; knowing all about it; of normal intelligence. **not all there,** (*coll.*) not fully competent; mentally deficient. **here and there** HERE. **so there,** an expression of derision or triumph. **thereabout, -bouts,** *adv.* near that place, number, degree etc. **thereafter,** *adv.* after that; according to that. **thereanent,** *adv.* (*Sc.*) as regards that matter. **thereat,** *adv.* at that place; thereupon; on that account. **thereby,** *adv.* by that means; in consequence of that; thereabouts. **†therefor,** *adv.* for that object. **therefore,** *adv.* for that reason, consequently, accordingly. **therefrom,** *adv.* from this or that time, place etc. **therein,** *adv.* in that or this time, place, respect etc. **thereinafter,** *adv.* later in the same (document etc.). **thereinbefore,** *adv.* earlier in the same (document etc.). †**thereinto,** *adv.* into that place or matter. **thereof,** *adv.* of that or it. **thereon,** *adv.* on that or it. †**thereout,** *adv.* out of that or this. **thereto,** *adv.* to that or this; besides, over and above. †**thereunder,** *adv.* under that or this. †**thereunto,** *adv.* to that or this, thereto. **thereupon,** *adv.* in consequence of that; immediately after or following that; †upon that. **therewith,** *adv.* with that; thereupon. **therewithal,** *adv.* with all this, besides. [OE *thaēr, thēr* (cp. Dut. *daar,* G *da,* Icel. *thar,* Dan and Swed. *der*), cogn. with THAT, THE]

Theresa, *n.* **Mother** (born Agnes Bojaxhiu) (1910–), Indian Roman Catholic nun. She was born in Skopje, Albania and at 18 entered a Calcutta convent and became a teacher. In 1948 she became an Indian citizen, and founded the Missionaries of Charity, an order for men and women based in Calcutta, which especially helps abandoned children and the dying. Nobel Peace Prize 1979.

Thérèse of Lisieux, *n.* (1873–97), French saint. Born at Alençon, she entered a Carmelite convent at Lisieux at 15, where her holy life induced her superior to ask her to write her spiritual autobiography. She advocated the Little Way of Goodness in small things in everyday life, and is known as Little Flower of Jesus. She died of tuberculosis and was canonized in 1925.

theriac, *n.* an antidote against the bite of poisonous animals. **theriacal,** *a.* [late L *thēriaca, thēriacē,* Gr. *thēriakē,* orig. fem. a. from *thērion,* dim. of *thēr,* wild beast]

therianthropic, *a.* of or pertaining to deities represented as half man and half beast or to their worship. **therianthropism,** *n.* **theriomancy,** -MANCY, *n.* divination by observing the movements of animals. **theriomorphic, -phous,** *a.* having the form of a beast. **theriotomy,** -TOMY, *n.* zootomy. [Gr. *thērion,* see prec.]

therm, *n.* a British unit of heat, equal to 100,000 British Thermal Units. **British Thermal Unit,** *n.* 1/180th part of the quantity of heat required to raise the temperature of 1 lb (0.45 kg) of water from 32° F to 212° F (0–100°C). [Gr. *thermē,* heat]

thermae, *n.pl.* hot springs or baths, esp. the public baths of the ancient Romans. [L]

thermal, *a.* of or pertaining to heat or thermae; of clothing, insulating the body against very low temperatures. *n.* a rising current of warm air; (*pl.*) thermal (under)clothes. **thermal barrier,** *n.* the heating effect of air friction, making flight at high speeds difficult. **thermal reactor,** *n.* a nuclear reactor in which fission is induced using mainly **thermal neutrons** in thermal equilibrium with their surroundings. **thermal springs,** *n.pl.* hot springs. **thermally,** *adv.* **thermic,** *a.*

Thermidor, *n.* the 11th month of the French Republican year, 19 July–17 Aug. **Thermidorian,** *n.* one of those who aided or favoured the overthrow of Robespierre and the Jacobins on 9 Thermidor 1794. [as prec., Gr. *dōron,* gift]

thermion, *n.* an electrically charged particle emitted by an incandescent body. **thermionic,** *a.* **thermionics,** *n.* the branch of electronics dealing with the emission of electrons from hot bodies; the study of the behaviour of these electrons in a vacuum. **thermionic valve,** *n.* a vacuum tube in which a stream of electrons flows from one electrode to another and is controlled by one or more other electrodes. [Gr. *thermos,* warm, ION]

thermistor, *n.* a semi-conducting device whose resistance decreases with rising temperature. [*thermal* re*sistor*]

thermite, Thermit®, *n.* a mixture of finely-divided aluminium and a metallic oxide, esp. of iron, producing intense heat on combustion. [G *thermit* (Gr. *thermē* heat)]

thermo-, *comb. form.* heat. [Gr. *thermos,* warm, see THERM]

thermobarometer, *n.* an apparatus for measuring atmospheric pressure by the boiling-point of water.

thermochemistry, *n.* the branch of chemistry dealing with the relations between chemical reactions and the heat liberated or absorbed.

thermocline, *n.* a layer of water in a lake, etc., in which the water temperature decreases rapidly between the epilimnion and hypolimnion.

thermodynamics, *n.* the branch of physics dealing with the relations between heat and other forms of energy. **thermodynamic,** *a.*

thermoelectricity, *n.* electricity generated by differences of temperature. **thermoelectrometer,** *n.* an instrument for ascertaining the heating power of an electric current.

thermogenesis, *n.* the production of heat, esp. by physiological processes. **thermogenetic, thermogenic,** *a.*

thermograph, *n.* an instrument for automatically recording variations of temperature. **thermogram,** *n.*

thermoluminescence, *n.* phosphorescence produced by heating an irradiated substance. **thermoluminescent,** *a.*

thermomagnetism, *n.* magnetism as modified or produced by the action of heat. **thermomagnetic,** *a.*

thermometer, *n.* an instrument for measuring temperature, usu. by the expansion or contraction of a column of mercury or alcohol in a graduated tube of small bore with a bulb at one end. **thermometric, -al,,** *a.* **thermometrically,** *adv.* **thermometry,,** *n.*

thermomotive, *a.* of or relating to motion produced by heat.

thermomotor, *n.* a heat-engine, esp. one driven by hot-air.

thermonuclear, *a.* used of the fusion of nuclei, as in **thermonuclear reaction,** which is the fusion of nuclei at very high temperatures, as in the hydrogen bomb.

thermophile, -philic, *a.* (*Biol.*) thriving in a high temperature.

thermopile, *n.* a thermoelectric battery, esp. one employed to measure small quantities of radiant heat.

thermoplastic, *n., a.* (a substance) which softens under heat without undergoing any chemical change, and can therefore, be heated repeatedly.

Thermopylae, Battle of, battle during the Persian wars in 480 BC when Leonidas, king of Sparta, and 1000 men defended the pass of Thermopylae to the death against the Persians. The pass led from Thessaly to Locris in central Greece.

Thermos®, *n.* a type of a vacuum flask. **thermosetting,** *a.* of a substance which softens initially under heat but subsequently hardens and becomes infusible and insoluble.

thermoscope, *n.* an instrument for indicating differences of temperature without measuring them. **thermoscopic,** *a.*

thermosphere, *n.* the part of the earth's atmosphere above the mesosphere, from about 50 miles (80 km), in which the temperature rises steadily with height.

thermostat, *n.* a self-acting apparatus for regulating temperatures. **thermostatic,** *a.*

thermotaxis, *n.* the movement of an organism in reaction to heat stimulus. **thermotactic, -taxic,** *a.*

thermotic, *a.* of, pertaining to, or resulting from heat. **thermotics,** *n.* the science of heat.

thermotropism, *n.* the orientation of a plant in response to temperature difference. **thermotropic,** *a.*

thermotype, *n.* an impression obtained by wetting the object, as a section of wood, with dilute acid, printing from this, and developing by heat.

theroid, *a.* resembling a beast. [Gr. *thēr -ros,* wild beast, -OID]

therology, *n.* the science of mammals. **therologist,** *n.* [*thēr,* as prec., -LOGY]

THES, (*abbr.*) Times Higher Education Supplement.

thesaurus, *n.* (*pl.* **-i**) a cyclopaedia or lexicon; a collection of words, phrases etc., esp. arranged as groups of synonyms. [L, from Gr. *thēsauros,* TREASURE]

these, *pl.* THIS.

Theseus, *n.* legendary hero of Attica, supposed to have united the states of the area under a constitutional government at Athens. Ariadne, whom he later abandoned on Naxos, helped him find his way through the labyrinth to kill the Minotaur. He also fought the Amazons and was one of the Argonauts.

thesis, *n.* (*pl.* **-ses**) a proposition advanced or maintained; an essay or dissertation, esp. one submitted by a candidate for a degree, etc.; a school or college exercise; (*Log.*) an affirmation, as opp. to an hypothesis; (*Pros.*, thes'-) the unaccented part of a metrical foot, opp. to arsis. [L, from Gr. *thesis,* from the *the-,* root of *tithenai,* to set]

Thesmophoria, *n.pl.* (*Gr. Ant.*) a Greek festival celebrated by married women in honour of Demeter. **thesmophorian,** *a.* [Gr., from *thesmophoros* (*thesmos,* law, *-phoros,* bearing, rel. to *pherien,* to bear), an epithet of Demeter]

thesmothete, *n.* a lawgiver; (*Gr. Ant.*) one of the six inferior archons at Athens. [Gr. *thesmothetēs* (*thesmos,* law, *the-,* as THESIS]

Thespis, *n.* (6th cent. BC), legendary Greek poet, said to have introduced the first actor into plays (previously presented by choruses only), hence the word 'thespian' for an actor. He was also said to have invented tragedy and to have introduced the wearing of linen masks. **Thespian**, *a.* pertaining to Thespis, traditional Greek dramatic poet; (**thespian**), *a.* relating to tragedy or the drama. *n.* an actor.

Thess. (*abbr.*) Thessalonians.

Thessaloniki (English **Salonica**), *n.* port in Macedonia, NE Greece, at the head of the Gulf of Thessaloniki, the second largest city of Greece; population (1981) 706,200. Industries include textiles, shipbuilding, chemicals, brewing and tanning.

Thessaly (Greek **Thessalia**), *n.* region of E central Greece, on the Aegean; area 14,037 sq km/5395 sq miles; population (1981) 695,650. It is a major area of cereal production.

theta, *n.* the eighth letter of the Greek alphabet (θ, ϑ), transliterated by *th*. [Gr. *thēta*]

Thetford Mines, *n.* site of the world's largest asbestos deposits, Quebec, Canada.

theurgy, *n.* divine or supernatural agency, esp. in human affairs; supernatural as distinguished from natural magic. **theurgic, -al,** *a.* **theurgist,** *n.* [late L *theurgia,* Gr. *theourgia* (*theos,* god, *ergon,* work)]

thew, *n.* (*usu. in pl.*) muscles, sinews; strength, vigour; †manners, mental qualities. **thewed, thewy,** *a.* **thewless,** *a.* [OE *thēaw,* habit, cp. OHG *thau, dau,* discipline, etym. doubtful]

they, *pron.* (*obj.* **them,** *poss.* **their,** *absol.* **theirs**) the plural of the third personal pronoun (*he, she* or *it*); people in general; (*coll.*) those in authority. **they'd,** they had; they would. **they'll,** they shall; they will. **they're,** they are. **they've,** they have. [OE *thā,* pl. of THE, THAT]

thiamine, *n.* vitamin B, important for metabolism and nerve function. [Gr. *theion,* sulphur, AMINE]

thibet TIBET.

thick, *a.* having great or specified extent or depth from one surface to the opposite; arranged, set or planted closely, crowded together, close packed or abounding (with), following in quick succession; dense, inspissated, turbid, muddy, impure, cloudy, foggy; dull, stupid; of articulation etc., indistinct, muffled; (*coll.*) very friendly, familiar. *adv.* thickly; in close succession; indistinctly. *n.* the thickest part. **a bit thick,** unreasonable. **through thick and thin,** under any conditions, undauntedly, resolutely. **†thick-coming,** *a.* following in quick succession. **thick ear,** *n.* (*coll.*) a swollen ear as a result of a blow. **thickhead,** *n.* a blockhead; (*Austral.*) a bird of the Pachycephalidae family, akin to the flycatchers. **thick-headed,** *a.* **thick-knee,** *n.* the stone-curlew. **thick-lipped,** *a.* **†thick-pleached,** *a.* closely interwoven. **thick-set,** *a.* planted, set or growing close together; solidly built, stout, stumpy. *n.* a thick-set hedge; †a thicket. **thick-skinned,** *a.* not sensible to taunts, reproaches etc. **thick-skin,** *n.* **thick-skull,** *n.* **thick-skulled, -witted,** *a.* **thick 'un,** (*sl., dated*) a sovereign, one pound. **thicken,** *v.t., v.i.* **thickening,** *n.* **thicket,** *n.* a thick growth of small trees, bushes, etc. **thickish,** *a.* **thickly,** *adv.* **thickness,** *n.* the state of being thick; extent from upper surface to lower, the dimension that is neither length nor breadth; a sheet or layer of cardboard etc. **thicky,** *n.* (*sl.*) a stupid person. [OE *thicce,* cp. Dut. *dik,* G *dick,* Icel. *thykkr*]

thief, *n.* (*pl.* **thieves**) one who steals, esp. furtively and without violence; (*dial.*) a projecting piece of wick in a candle causing it to gutter. **thief-catcher, -taker,** *n.* one whose business is to arrest thieves. **thieve,** *v.i.* to practise theft; to be a thief. *v.t.* to take by theft. **thieves' Latin** LATIN. **thievery, thievishness,** *n.* **thievish,** *a.* **thievishly,** *adv.* [OE *thēof,* cp. Dut. *dief,* G *Dieb,* Icel. *thjōfr*]

Thiers, *n.* **Louis Adolphe** (1797–1877), French politician and historian. He held cabinet posts under Louis Philippe, led the parliamentary opposition to Napoleon III from 1863, and as head of the provisional government in 1871 negotiated peace with Prussia and suppressed the Paris Commune. He was first president of the Third Republic, 1871–73.

thig, *v.t.* (*Sc.*) to beg; to live by begging. **thigger,** *n.* [OE *thicgan,* to take (food, etc.), cp. OS *thiggian,* to beg, OHG *dikken*]

thigh, *n.* the thick, fleshy portion of the leg between the hip and knee in man; the corresponding part in other animals. **thigh-bone,** *n.* the principal bone in the thigh, the femur. [OE *thēok, thēo* cp. Dut. *dij,* Icel. *thjō, OHG dioh*]

†thilk, *a.* that, the same, *n.* that person or thing. [ME *thilke* (THE, ILK)]

thill, *n.* the shaft of a cart, carriage or other vehicle. **thill-horse, thiller,** *n.* the horse between the thills. [OE *thille,* plank, flooring, cogn. with DEAL[2]]

thimble, *n.* a cap of metal etc., worn to protect the end of the finger in sewing; a sleeve or short metal tube; a ferrule; an iron ring having an exterior groove worked into a rope or sail to receive another rope or lanyard. **thimble-case,** *n.* **thimbleful,** *n.* as much as a thimble holds; a very small quantity. **thimblerig,,** *n.* a sleight-of-hand trick with three nimbles and a pea, persons being challenged to bet under which cover is the pea. *v.t.* to cheat by means of thimblerigging. *v.i.* to practise this. **thimblerigger,** *n.* [OE *thȳmel,* thumbstall]

Thimbu, Thimpu, *n.* capital since 1962 of the Himalayan state of BHUTAN; population (1982) 15,000.

thin, *a.* having the opposite surfaces close together, of little thickness, slender; not close-packed, not dense; sparse, scanty, meagre; lean, not plump; not full, scant, bare; flimsy, easily seen through. *adv.* thinly. *v.t.* (*past, p.p.* **thinned**) to make thin; to make less crowded; to remove fruit, flowers etc., from (a tree or plant) to improve the rest. (also **thin out**) *v.i.* to become thin or thinner; to waste away. **thin on top,** balding. **thin-skinned,** *a.* sensitive, easily offended. **thinly,** *adv.* **thinness,** *n.* **thinner,** *n.* a solvent used to thin, e.g. paint. **thinnish,** *a.* [OE *thynne,* cp. Dut. *dun,* G *dünn,* Icel. *thunnr* also L *tenuis*]

thine THY.

thing[1], *n.* any object or thought; whatever exists or is conceived to exist as a separate entity esp. an inanimate object as distinguished from a living being; an act, a fact, affair, circumstance etc.; (*coll.*) a person or other animate object regarded with commiseration, disparagement etc.; (*pl.*) clothes, belongings, luggage etc., **one of those things,** a happening that one cannot do anything about. **the thing,** the proper thing (to do etc.). **to do one's own thing,** (*coll.*) to do what one likes or what one pleases. **to have a thing about,** to have an unaccountable prejudice or fear about. **to make a good thing of,** to make a profit out of. **thingumajig, thingummygig, thingumabob,, thingummy, thingy**, *n.* (*coll.*) a thing, what d'you call it. [OE, *thing,* cause, sake, office, reason, council (cp. Dut. *ding* and G *Ding,* Icel. *thing,* Dan. and Swed. *ting*)]

thing[2], *n.* a Scandinavian public assembly, esp. a legislative body. [Icel., as prec.]

think, *v.t.* (*past, p.p.* **thought**[1]) to regard or examine in the mind, to reflect, to ponder (over etc.); to consider, to be of opinion, to believe; to design, to intend; to effect by thinking; (*coll.*) to remember, to recollect. *v.i.* to exercise the mind actively, to reason; to meditate, to cogitate, to consider (on, about etc.). *n.* (*coll.*) an act of thinking; a thought. **to have another think coming,** (*coll.*) to be wrong about what one assumes will happen. **to think better of,** to change one's mind, to decide not to pursue (a course of action). **to think of,** to have in mind, to conceive, to imagine; to call to mind, to remember; to have a particular opinion or feeling about, to esteem. **to think out,** to devise; to solve by long thought. **to think twice,** to hesitate and consider carefully; to think again. **Think Tank,** *n.* popular name for Central Policy Review Staff, a consultative body to the UK government 1970–83, set up to provide Cabinet ministers with informed background advice on major policy decisions. **thinkable,** *a.* **thinker,** *n.* **thinking,** *a., n.* **thinkingly,** *adv.* [cp. G *denken,* Icel. *thekkja,* Dan. *tænke*) cogn. with THANK]

thinly, etc. THIN.

thio-, *comb. form.* sulphur. **thiosulphuric,** *a.* applied to an acid corresponding to sulphuric acid in which one atom of oxygen is replaced by one of sulphur. **thiosulphate,** *n.* [Gr. *theion*]

third, *n.* one of three equal parts; the 60th part of a second of time or angular measurement; (*Mus.*) an interval between a tone and the next but one on the diatonic scale; a tone separated by this interval; the consonance of two such tones; (*pl.*) the third part of a deceased husband's estate, sometimes assigned as her share to the widow; a third-class honours degree; the third gear in a motor vehicle. *n., a.* (the) last of three (people, things etc); the next after the second. †**thirdborough,** *n.* (*Shak.*) an under-constable. **third-class, -rate,** *a.* of the class coming next to the second; inferior, worthless. **third degree,** *n.* (*sl.*) intimidation or torture, esp. to extract information. **third party,** *n., a.* (a person) other than the principals (in a contract etc.). **third rail,** *n.* an extra rail through which electricity is supplied to an electric locomotive. **Third Reich,** *n.* a term coined by the German writer Moeller van den Bruck (1876–1925) in the 1920s and used by the Nazis to describe the years of Hitler's dictatorship after 1933, although they later dropped the term. The idea of the Third Reich (Third Empire) was based on the existence of two previous German empires, the mediaeval Holy Roman Empire and the second empire, 1871–1918. **Third World,** *n.* developing countries defined by the World Bank as the world's hundred poorest countries, as measured by their income per capita; they are concentrated in Asia, Africa, and Central America. They are divided into low-income countries, including China and India, and middle-income countries such as Nigeria, Indonesia, and Brazil. Problems associated with developing countries include high population growth and mortality rates, poor educational and health facilities, heavy dependence on agriculture and commodities for which prices and demand fluctuates, high levels of underemployment and, in some cases, political instability. Failure by many developing countries to meet their enormous debt obligations has led to more stringent terms being imposed on loans by industrialized countries, as well as rescheduling (deferring payment). **thirdly,** *adv.* [OE *thridda,* from *thrī,* THREE]

†**thirl,** *v.t.* to pierce through, to perforate. *n.* a hole, an aperture. [OE *thyrlian,* from *thyrel,* a hole, from *thurh,* THOROUGH]

thirst, *n.* the uneasiness or suffering caused by want of drink; desire for drink; eager longing or desire. *v.i.* to feel thirst (for or after). **thirstless,** *a.* **thirsty,** *a.* feeling thirst; dry, parched; (*coll.*) exciting thirst. **thirstily,** *adv.* **thirstiness,** *n.* [OE *thurst* (cp. Dut. *dorst,* G *Durst,* Icel. *thorsti*), whence *thyrstan,* cp. Dut. *dorsten,* G *dürsten,* cogn. with L *torrēre,* Gr. *tersesthai,* to dry up]

thirteen, *n.* the number or figure 13 or xiii; the age of 13. *a.* 13 in number; aged 13. **Thirteen Colonies,** *n.pl.* the 13 colonies of the US that signed the Declaration of Independence from Britain in 1776. Led by George Washington, they defeated the British army in the War of American Independence 1776–81 to become the original 13 United States of America. They were: Connecticut, Delaware, Georgia, Maryland, Massachusetts, New Hampshire, New Jersey, New York, North Carolina, Pennsylvania, Rhode Island, South Carolina, and Virginia. **thirteenth,** *n.* one of 13 equal parts. *n., a.* (the) last of 13 (people, things etc.); the next after the 12th. [OE *thrēotēne* (THREE, -TEEN)]

thirty, *n.* three times ten; the number or figure 30 or xxx; the age of 30. *a.* 30 in number; aged 30. **Thirty-Nine Articles,** *n.* a set of articles of faith defining the doctrine of the Anglican Church; see under Anglican Communion. **thirty-something,** *a.* referring to the lifestyle etc. of affluent people who are aged between 30 and 40. **Thirty Years' War,** a major war in central Europe 1618–48. Beginning as a conflict between Protestants and Catholics, it gradually became transformed into a struggle to determine whether the ruling Austrian Hapsburg family would gain control of all Germany. **thirties,** *n.pl.* the period of time between one's 30th and 40th birthdays; the range of temperature between 30 and 40 degrees; the period of time between the 30th and 40th years of a century. **thirtieth,**, *n.* one of 30 equal parts. *n., a.* (the) last of 30 (people, things etc.); the next after the 29th. [OE *thrītig, thrittig* (THREE, -TY)]

this, *a., pron.* (*pl.* **these**) used to denote the person or thing that is present or near in place or time, or already mentioned, implied, or familiar. *adv.* to this extent. **this and that,** (*coll.*) random and usu. unimportant subjects of conversation. **thisness,** *n.* Haecceity. [OE *thes,* fem. *theos,* neut. *this* (cp. Dut. *deze,* G *dieser,* Icel. *thessi*), cogn. with THAT, THE]

thistle, *n.* a plant of several genera of the aster family with prickly stems, leaves and involucres. **Order of the Thistle,** a Scottish order of knighthood instituted in 1687 and revived in 1703. **thistly,** *a.* [OE *thistel,* cp. Dut. *distel,* G. *distel,* Icel. *thistill*]

thither, *adv.* to that place; to that end, point or result. †**thitherward, -wards,** *adv.* [OE *thider, thyder,* cogn. with THAT, cp. HITHER]

thixotropic, *a.* of certain gels (e.g. non-drip paints), becoming fluid when shaken or stirred. **thixotropy,** *n.* [Gr. *thixis,* act of touching, *tropos,* turn]

thlipsis, *n.* constriction of blood-vessels by external compression. [Gr., from *thlibein,* to press]

tho', THOUGH.

thole[1], *n.* a pin in the gunwale of a boat serving as fulcrum for the oar, also called **thole pin**. [OE *thol,* cp. Dut. *dol,* Icel. *thollr,* tree, peg, thole]

thole[2], *v.t.* (*Sc.*) to suffer, to endure; to permit, to put up with; to bear, to undergo. [OE *tholian*]

†**tholobate,** *n.* the substructure on which a cupola is based. **tholus**, *n.* (*pl.* **-li**) a dome, cupola, or lantern. [Gr. *tholos, -balos,* from *bainein,* to go]

Thomas[1], *n.* **Dylan** (**Marlais**) (1914–53), Welsh poet. His poems include the celebration of his 30th birthday 'Poem in October' and the evocation of his youth 'Fern Hill' 1946. His radio play *Under Milk Wood* (1954) and the short stories of *Portrait of the Artist as a Young Dog* (1940) are autobiographical. He died in New York where he had made a number of reading and lecture tours.

Thomas[2], **St** *n.* in the New Testament, one of the 12 Apostles, said to have preached in S India, hence the ancient churches there were referred to as the 'Christians of St Thomas'. He is not the author of the Gospel of St Thomas, the Gnostic collection of Christ's sayings.

Thomas à Kempis, *n.* (1380–1471), German Augustinian monk who lived at the monastery of Zwolle. He took his name from his birthplace Kempen; his real surname was Hammerken. His *Die Imitatione Christi/Imitation of Christ* is probably the most widely known devotional work ever written.

Thomism, *n.* the scholastic philosophy and theology of St Thomas Aquinas (1227–74). **Thomist,** *a.*, *n.* **Thomistic,** *a.*

Thompson[1], *n.* **Flora** (1877–1948), English novelist, whose trilogy *Lark Rise to Candleford* (1945) deals with late Victorian rural life.

Thompson[2], *n.* **Francis Morgan 'Daley'** (1958–), English decathlete, who broke the world record four times, and won two Olympic titles, one world title, three European titles, and three Commonwealth titles.

Thompson[3], *n.* **John Taliaferro** (1860–1940), US colonel, and inventor of the Thompson sub-machine-gun.

Thomson[1], *n.* **Elihu** (1853–1937), US inventor. He founded, with E.J. Houston, the Thomson-Houston Electric Company in 1882, later merging with the Edison Company to form the General Electric Company. He made important advances into the nature of the electric arc, and invented the first high-frequency dynamo and transformer.

Thomson[2], *n.* **George Paget** (1892–1975), British physicist, son of Joseph Thomson. His work on interference phenomena in the scattering of electrons by crystals helped to confirm the wave-like nature of particles. He shared a Nobel Prize with C.I. Davisson 1937, and was knighted 1943.

Thomson[3], *n.* **James** (1700–48), Scottish poet, whose descriptive blank verse poem *The Seasons* (1726–30) was a forerunner of the romantic movement. He also wrote the words of 'Rule, Britannia'.

Thomson[4], *n.* **Joseph John** (1856–1940), British physicist, who discovered the electron. He was responsible for organizing the Cavendish atomic research laboratory. His work inaugurated the electrical theory of the atom, and his elucidation of positive rays and their application to an analysis of neon led to Aston's discovery of isotopes.

Thomson[5], *n.* **Virgil** (1896–1989), US composer. His large body of work, characterized by a clarity and simplicity of style, includes operas such as *Four Saints in Three Acts* (libretto by Gertrude Stein) (1934), orchestral, choral and chamber music, and film scores.

-thon, *comb. form.* a large-scale event or related series of events lasting a long time or demanding endurance of the participants (as *telethon*). [MARATHON]

thong, *n.* a strip of leather used as a whip-lash, for reins, or for fastening anything. *v.t.* to fit or furnish with a thong; to fasten or thrash with a thong. [OE *thwang* (cp. Icel. *thvengr*), cogn. with TWINGE]

Thor, *n.* the ancient Scandinavian god of thunder, war, and agriculture. **Thor's hammer,** *n.* a flint implement. [Icel. *Thorr*]

thoracic, etc. THORAX.

thoral, *a.* pertaining to the marriage-bed. [med. L *thorus,* L *torus,* bed]

thorax, *n.* (*pl.* **thoraces, thoraxes**) the part of the trunk between the neck and the abdomen; the middle division of the body of insects; (*Gr. Ant.*) a breastplate, cuirass, or corselet. **thoracic,** *a.* **thoraci(co)-, thoraco-,** *comb. form.* [L, from Gr. *thōrāx -akos*]

Thoreau, *n.* **Henry David** (1817–62), US author and naturalist. His work *Walden, or Life in the Woods* (1854) stimulated the back-to-nature movement, and he completed some 30 volumes based on his daily nature walks. His essay 'Civil Disobedience' 1849, advocating peaceful resistance to unjust laws, had a wide impact.

thorium, *n.* a radioactive metallic element, at. no. 90; chem. symbol Th; found chiefly in thorite. **thoria,** *n.* oxide of thorium, used in the manufacture of heat-resistant materials. **thoric, thorinic,** *a.* †**thorinum,** *n.* thorium. **thorite,** *n.* a massive dark hydrous silicate of thorium, found in Norway. [THOR]

thorn, *n.* a spine, a sharp-pointed process, a prickle; a thorny shrub, tree, or herb (*usu. in comb.* as *blackthorn, whitehorn*); an annoyance, a trouble, a care; the OE letter þ (th). **a thorn in one's side,** (or **flesh**), a constant source of trouble. **thorn-apple,** *n.* a plant with prickly seed-capsules, *Datura stramonium.* **thorn-back,** *n.* the British ray or skate, *Raja clavata,* the back and tail of which are covered with spines. **thorn-bill, -tail,** *n.* a name for various humming-birds. **thorn-bush,** *n.* **thornless,** *a.* **thorny,** *a.* [OE, cp. Icel. *thorn,* Dut. *doorn,* G. *Dorn*]

thorough, *a.* complete, perfect, not superficial. *n.* the uncompromising absolutist policy of Strafford, under Charles I. **thoroughbass,** *n.* (*Mus.*) a bass part accompanied by shorthand marks, usu. figures, written below the stave, to indicate the harmony; this method of indicating harmonies; the science of harmony. **thorough-brace,** *n.* a strap passing between two C-springs to support the body of a vehicle. **thoroughbred,** *a.* of pure breed; high-spirited, mettlesome. *n.* a thoroughbred animal, esp. a horse. **thoroughfare,** *n.* a passage through from one street, etc., to another, an unobstructed road or street; a road or street for public traffic. **thoroughgoing,** *a.* going or ready to go to any lengths; thorough, uncompromising. **thorough-paced,** *a.* trained to all paces (as a horse); thorough-going, out-and-out. **thorough-pin,** *n.* a dropsical swelling in the hollow of a horse's hock. **thoroughly,** *adv.* **thoroughness,** *n.* [THROUGH]

thorp, thorpe, *n.* a village, a hamlet (esp. in place-names). [OE *thorp,* cp. Dut. *dorp,* G *Dorf,* Icel. *thorp*]

Thorpe, *n.* **Jeremy** (1929–), British Liberal politician, leader of the Liberal Party 1967–76.

those, *pl.* THAT.

Thoth, *n.* in Egyptian mythology, god of wisdom and learning. He was represented as a scribe with the head of an ibis, the bird sacred to him.

Thothmes I, *n.* king of Egypt 1540–1501 BC). He founded the Egyptian empire in Syria.

Thothmes III, *n.* king of Egypt *c.* 1500–1446 BC. He extended the empire to the Euphrates and conquered Nubia. He was a grandson of Thothmes I.

thou[1], *pron.* (*obj.* **thee**) the second personal pronoun singular, denoting the person spoken to (now used only in addresses to the Deity and in poetry). *v.t.* to address as 'thou'. *v.i.* to use 'thou' instead of 'you'. [OE *thū,* cp. G, Dan., and Swed. *du,* Icel. *thū,* L *tu,* Gr. *su, tu*]

thou[2], *n.* (*pl.* **thou(s)**) (*coll.*) short for THOUSAND; a thousandth of an inch (0.0254 mm).

though, *conj.* notwithstanding that; even if; granting or supposing that; (*ellipt.*) and yet; however. **as though** AS. [ME *thogh,* Icel. *thō,* cp. Dut. and G *doch,* OE *thēah, thæh, thāh*]

thought[1], *past, p.p.* THINK.

thought[2], *n.* the act or process of thinking; reflection, serious consideration, meditation; deep concern or solicitude; the faculty of thinking or reasoning; that which is thought; a conception, an idea, a reflection, a judgment, conclusion etc.; (*pl.*) one's views, ideas, opinions, etc., **a thought,** (*coll.*) a very small degree, etc., a shade, somewhat. **happy thought,** an apposite or timely suggestion, idea etc. **thought-reader,** *n.* one who perceives by telepathy what is passing in another person's mind. **thought-reading,** *n.* †**thought-sick,** *a.* uneasy with sad reflections. **thought-transference,** *n.* telepathy. **thought-wave,** *n.* a telepathic undulation or vibration. **thoughted,** *a.* having a (usu. specified kind of) thought or thoughts. **thoughtful,** *n.* **thoughtfully,** *n.* **thoughtfully,** *adv.* **thoughtfulness,** *n.* **thoughtless,,** *a.* **thoughtlessly,** *adv.* **thoughtlessness,** *n.* [OE *thōht,* as prec.]

thousand, *a., n.* ten hundred, 1000; a great many. **thousand-legs,** *n.* a millepede or centipede. **thousand-fold,** *a.* and *adv.* **thousandth,** *a., n.* [OE *thūsend* (cp. Dut. *duizend,* G *Tausend,* Icel. *thūsund*), etym. doubtful]

†**thowel,** †**thowl** THOLE[1, 2].

thowless, (*Sc.*) THEWLESS.

Thrace (Greek **Thráki**), *n.* ancient empire (6000 BC–AD 300) in the Balkans, SE Europe, formed by parts of modern Greece and Bulgaria. It was held successively by the Greeks, Persians, Macedonians and Romans.

thrall, *n.* a slave, a serf; bondage, thraldom. *a.* in thrall. *v.t.* to enthral, to enslave. **thraldom,** *n.* [ME *thral,*

Icel. *thræll* (cp. Dan. *træl*, Swed. *trāl*), *cogn. with OE thrægan,* to run]

thrang, *a.* (*Sc.*) thronged, busy. [THRONG]

thrap, *v.t.* (*Naut.*) to bind, tie, or fasten (round, about etc.). [etym. doubtful]

thrapple, (*Sc.*) THROPPLE.

thrash, to beat soundly, esp. with a stick or whip; to overcome, to defeat, to conquer; to thresh. *v.i.* to strike out wildly and repeatedly. *n.* a thrashing; (*sl.*) a party. **to thrash out,** to discuss thoroughly in order to find a solution. **thrasher[1],** *n.* one who thrashes. **thrashing,** *n.* [THRESH]

thrasher[2], *n.* (*N Am.*) a N American songbird of the genus *Harporhyncus,* resembling the thrush, esp. the brown thrasher, *H. rufus,* common in the eastern States. [prob. var. of THRUSH[1]]

thrasonical, *a.* bragging, boastful. **thrasonically,** *adv.* [*Thraso,* the braggart in Terence's comedies, -ICAL]

thratch, etc. (*Sc.*) FRATCH.

thrave, *n.* (*Sc.*) 24 sheaves or two stooks of corn. [from Scand., cp. Icel. *threfi,* Norw. *treve,* Swed. *trafue*]

thrawn, *a.* (*Sc.*) twisted; perverse, stubborn. [THROW]

thread, *n.* a slender cord consisting of two or more yarns doubled or twisted; a single filament of cotton, silk, wool etc., esp. lisle thread; anything resembling this; a fine line of colour etc.; a thin seam or vein; the spiral on a screw; a continuous course (of life etc.); the continuing theme or linking element in an argument or story. *v.t.* to pass a thread through the eye or aperture of; to string (beads etc.) on a thread; to pick (one's way) or to go through an intricate or crowded place etc.; to streak (the hair) with grey etc.; to cut a thread on (a screw). **thread and thrum,** good and bad together, all alike. **threadbare,** *a.* worn so that the thread is visible, having the nap worn off; worn, trite, hackneyed. **threadbareness,** *n.* **thread-mark,** *n.* a mark produced by coloured silk fibres in banknotes to prevent counterfeiting. **thread-paper,** *n.* soft paper for wrapping up thread. **threadworm,** *n.* a thread-like nematode worm, esp. one infesting the rectum of children. **threader,** *n.* **threadlike,** *a., adv.* **thready,** *a.* **threadiness,** *n.* [OE *thræd,* from *thrāwan,* to THROW (cp. Dut. *draad,* G *Draht,* Icel. *thrāthr*)]

threap, *v.t.* (*Sc.* and *North.*) to assert with pertinacity; to persist; to contradict. *v.i.* to quarrel, to wrangle, *n.* persistence, stubborn insistence; contradiction. [OE *thrēapian,* to rebuke]

threat, *n.* a declaration of an intention to inflict punishment, loss, injury etc., a menace; (*Law*) such a menace as may interfere with freedom, business etc., or a menace of injury to life, property, or reputation. **threaten,** *v.t.* to use threats to; to announce intention (to inflict injury etc.); to announce one's intention to inflict (injury etc.). *v.i.* to use threats; to have a threatening appearance. **threatener,** *n.* **threateningly,** *adv.* †**threatful,** *a.* [OE *thrēat,* crowd, trouble, threat, from *āthrēotan,* to afflict (cp. Icel. *thrjōta,* cogn. with L *trūdere,* to push)]

three, *n.* the number or figure 3 or iii; the age of three; the third hour after midnight or midday; a group of three. *a.* three in number; aged three. **rule of three** RULE. †**three F's,** the demands of the Irish Land League - free sale, fixity of tenure, free rent. **three R's,** reading, writing, arithmetic. **three-colour process,** the printing of coloured illustrations by the superposition of the three primary colours. **three-cornered,** *a.* having three corners or angles. **three-decker,** *n.* a vessel carrying guns on three decks; a pulpit in three stories. **three-dimensional,** *a.* giving the effect of being seen or heard in three dimensions. **three-handed,** *a.* having three hands; of some card-games, for three players. **three-headed,** *a.* **three-master,** *n.* a vessel, esp. a schooner, with three masts. **threepence,** *n.* the sum of threepence. **threepenny,** *a.* **threepenny bit,** *n.* formerly a small coin value threepence. **three-per-cents,** *n.pl.* bonds or securities bearing interest at three per cent, esp. Government bonds. **three-phase,** *a.* a term applied to an alternating-current system in which the currents flow in three separate circuits. **three-piece,** *a.* consisting of three matching pieces, as a suit of clothes, a suite of furniture etc. †**three-pile,** *n.* the finest kind of velvet. †**three-piled,** *a.* having a thick, rich pile; of first-rate quality; exaggerated, high-flown. **three-ply,** *a.* having three strands, thicknesses etc. *n.* plywood of three layers. **three-point landing,** *n.* one in which an aeroplane touches all three wheels down simultaneously. **three-point turn,** *n.* an about-turn in a narrow space made by a vehicle moving obliquely forwards, backwards and forwards again. **three-quarter,** *a.* of three-fourths the usual size or number; of portraits, showing three-fourths of the face, or going down to the hips. **threescore,** *a.* 60. *n.* the age of 60. **three-fold,** *a., adv.* **threesome,***a.* threefold, triple. *n.* a party of three; a game for three. [OE *thrēo,* thrī, cp. Dut. *drie,* G *drei,* Icel. *thrīr,* also L *trēs,* Gr. *treis*]

thremmatology, *n.* the branch of biology dealing with the breeding of animals and plants. [Gr. *thremma -atos,* nursling from *trephein,* to nourish, -LOGY]

threnody, threnode, *n.* a song of lamentation; a poem on the death of a person. †**threne,**, *n.* a threnody. **threnetic, -al**, **threnodial**, **threnodic**, *a.* **threnodist**, *n.* [Gr. *thrēnōdia* (*thrēnos,* dirge, *ōidē,* see ODE)]

threpsology, *n.* the science of nutrition of living organisms. [Gr. *threpsis,* nutrition, from *trephein,* to nourish, -LOGY]

thresh, *v.t.* to beat out or separate the grain (from corn etc.); to thrash. *v.i.* to thresh corn; to thrash. **thresher,** *n.* one who threshes; a threshing machine. **threshing,** *n.* **threshing floor,** *n.* a floor or area on which grain is threshed. **threshing machine,** *n.* [OE *therscan,* cp. Dut. *dorschen,* G *dreschen,* Icel. *threskja*]

threshold, *n.* the stone or plank at the bottom of a doorway; an entrance, a doorway, a beginning; the minimum strength of a stimulus, etc., that will produce a response as *threshold of pain.* [OE *therscold* (THRESH, suf. doubtful)]

threw, *past* THROW.

thrice, *adv.* three times; (*fig.*) very much. **thrice-favoured,** *a.* highly favoured. [ME *thries*]

thridacium, *n.* the inspissated juice of lettuce, used as a sedative. [mod. L, from Gr. *thridax -akos,* lettuce]

thrift, *n.* frugality; good husbandry, economical management; the sea-pink, *Armeria maritima.* **thriftless,**, *a.* **thriftlessly,** *adv.* **thriftlessness,** *n.* **thrifty,** *a.* frugal, careful, economical. **thriftily,** *adv.* **thriftiness,** *n.* [Icel. *thrīfa,* to seize; see THRIVE]

thrill, *v.t.* to penetrate; to affect with emotion so as to give a sense as of vibrating or tingling; of emotion, to go through one. *v.i.* to penetrate, vibrate, or quiver (through, along etc., of emotion); to have a vibrating, shivering or tingling sense of emotion. *n.* an intense vibration, shiver or wave of emotion; a vibratory or tremulous resonance observed in auscultation; (*coll.*) anything exciting. **thriller,** *n.* a sensational or exciting novel, film etc. **thrillingly,** *adv.* **thrillingness,** *n.* [OE *thyrlian,* from *thȳrel,* bore, from *thurh,* THROUGH]

thrips, *n.* a minute insect of the genus *Thrips* or allied genus injurious to plants, esp. grain. [Gr., wood-worm]

thrive, *v.i.* (*past,* **throve**, **thrived,** *p.p.* **thriven**, **thrived**) to prosper, to be fortunate, to be successful; to grow vigorously. **thriver,** *n.* **thrivingly,** *adv.* **thrivingness,** *n.* [ME *thriven,* Icel. *thrīfask,* reflex. of *thrīfa,* to seize, cp. Swed. *trifvas,* Dan. *trives* (reflex.), to thrive]

thro', THROUGH.

throat, *n.* the front part of the neck, containing the gullet and windpipe; the gullet, the pharynx, the windpipe, the larynx; a throat-shaped inlet, opening, or entrance, a narrow passage, strait etc.; (*Naut.*) the crotch of a gaff where it rests against the mast. *v.t.* to groove or channel. **sore throat,** an inflamed condition of the membranous lining of the gullet etc., usu. due to a cold. **to be at one another's throats,** fighting or quarrelling violently. **to cut one another's throats,** to engage in a ruinous competition. **to cut one's own throat,** (*fig.*) to adopt a policy that will harm or ruin one. **to lie in one's throat,** to lie outrageously. **to ram**

something down someone's throat RAM. **throatwort** *n.* the nettle-leaved bell-flower *Campanula trachelium.* **throated,** *a.* **throaty,** *a.* guttural; hoarse; having a large or prominent throat. **throatily,** *adv.* **throatiness,** *n.* [OE *throte* (cp. G *Drossel,* OHG *drozza*), perh. cogn. with Dut. *strot,* throat, Icel. *throti,* swelling, from *thrūtna,* to swell, cp. THROPPLE]

throb, *v.i.* (*past, p.p.* **throbbed**) to beat rapidly or forcibly (of the heart or pulse); to vibrate, to quiver. *n.* a strong pulsation, a palpitation. **throbbingly,** *adv.* [ME *throbben,* prob. imit]

throe, *n.* a violent pain, a pang, esp. (*pl.*) the pains of childbirth. *v.i.* to be in agony. **in the throes of,** struggling with (a task etc.). [ME *throwe,* Icel. *thrā,* cp. OE *thrōwian,* to suffer]

Throgmorton Street, *n.* (*coll.*) the Stock Exchange; Stock Exchange operations. [street in the City of London]

thrombosis, *n.* (*pl.* **-oses**) local coagulation of the blood in the heart or a blood-vessel; (*coll.*) a coronary thrombosis. **thrombotic,** *a.* **thrombin,** *n.* an enzyme concerned in the clotting of blood. **thrombocyte,** *n.* a blood platelet. **thrombose,** *v.t., v.i.* to affect with or undergo thrombosis. **thrombosed,** *a.* **thrombus,**, *n.* the clot of blood closing a vessel in thrombosis. [Gr., from *thrombousthai,* to become clotted, from *thrombos,* thrombus]

throne, *n.* a royal seat, a chair or seat of state for a sovereign, bishop etc.; sovereign power; one of the third order of angels. *v.t.* to enthrone. *v.i.* to sit on a throne. **thronal,** *a.* **throneless,** *a.* [ME and OF *trone,* L *thronus -um,* Gr. *thronos,* seat, support]

throng, *n.* a multitude of persons or living things pressed close together, a crowd. *v.i.* to crowd or press together; to come in multitudes. *v.t.* to crowd, to fill to excess; to fill with a crowd; to press or impede by crowding upon. [OE *gethrang,* from *thringan,* to crowd (cp. Dut. *drang,* G *Drang,* Icel. *thröng*)]

thropple, *n.* the throat, the windpipe, the gullet. [etym. doubtful, cp. THROAT]

throstle, *n.* the songthrush, a machine for continuously twisting and winding wool, cotton etc. **throstling,**, *n.* a swelling in the throat in cattle. [OE, cp. MHG *trostel,* also THRUSH[1] L *turdus*]

throttle, *n.* the wind pipe, the gullet, the throat; a throttle-valve. *v.t.* to choke, to strangle; to shut off, reduce or control (the flow of steam in a steam-engine or of explosive mixture to an internal-combustion engine). **throttle-valve,** *n.* a valve regulating such flow. [dim. of THROAT]

through, *prep.* from end to end of, from side to side of, between the sides or walls of; over the whole extent of, in the midst of, throughout; by means, agency, or fault of, on account of; (*N Am.*) up to and including; during; past; at or to the end of. *adv.* from end to end or side to side, from beginning to end; to a final (successful) issue; completely. *a.* going through or to the end, proceeding right to the end or destination, esp. (of train, railway or steamboat tickets etc.) over several companies' lines; direct; completed. **all through,** all the time, throughout. **through and through,** through again and again; searchingly; completely; in everyway. **to be through,** (*coll.*) to have finished. **to carry through** CARRY. **to fall through** FALL. **to go through, to go through with** GO[1]. †**through-fare, through-going** (*Sc.*) THOROUGHFARE. **throughither** *a., adv.* (*Sc.*) confused, muddled, unmethodical. **throughput,** *n.* the amount of raw material put through or processed in e.g. a factory, computer. †**throughly** THOROUGHLY. **throughout,** *adv.* right through, in every part; from beginning to end. *prep.* right through, from beginning to end of. [OE *thurh, thuruh* (cp. Dut. *door,* G *durch*), cogn. with Goth. *thairh*]

throve, *past* THRIVE.

throw, *v.t.* (*past* **threw,** *p.p.* **thrown**) to fling, to hurl, to cast, esp. to a distance with some force; to cast down, to cause to fall, to prostrate; to drive, to impel, to dash; to make (a cast) with dice; to turn or direct quickly or suddenly (the eyes etc.); to put on (clothes etc.) hastily or carelessly; to cast off (the skin, as a snake); of rabbits etc., to bring forth (young); to twist, to wind into threads; to shape on a potter's wheel; (*coll.*) to hold (a party); to puzzle or astonish; (*sl.*) to lose (a contest) deliberately. *v.i.* to hurl or fling a missile (at etc.); to cast dice. *n.* the act of throwing, a cast; a cast of the dice; the distance to which a missile is thrown; the extent of motion (of a crank etc.); a device for giving rapid rotation to a machine; (*Geol.*) a faulting, a dislocation; the extent of dislocation; (*N Am.*) a rug or decorative cloth put over a piece of furniture. **to throw away,** to cast from one; to reject carelessly; to spend recklessly, to squander; to lose through carelessness or neglect; to fail to take advantage of. **to throw back,** to reflect, as light etc.; to revert (to ancestral traits). **to throw down,** to overturn; to lay (oneself) down prostrate. **to throw in,** to interject, to interpolate; to put in without extra charge, to add as a contribution or extra. **to throw in one's hand,** to give up a job, etc., as hopeless. **to throw off,** to cast off, to get rid of, to abandon, to discard; to produce without effort; to evade (pursuit). **to throw oneself on,** to commit oneself to the protection, favour etc., of. **to throw open,** to open suddenly and completely; to make freely accessible. **to throw out,** to cast out, to reject; to emit; to give utterance to, to suggest; to cause (a building etc.) to stand out or project; to utter (a suggestion etc.) casually; to confuse. **to throw over,** to abandon, to desert. **to throw together,** to put together hurriedly or carelessly; to bring into casual contact. **to throw up,** to raise or lift quickly; to abandon, to resign; (*coll.*) to vomit. **throwaway,** *a.* disposable; of something written or said, deliberately casually. **throwback** *n.* a reversion to an earlier type. **throw-in,** *n.* a method in soccer of putting the ball back in play from touch. **throw-off,** *n.* the start (of a race, etc.). **throw-stick,** *n.* a short curved stick for throwing, a boomerang. **thrower,** *n.* **throwing,** *n.* the operation of shaping clay on a potter's wheel. **throwster,** *n.* one who throws silk. [OE *thrāwan,* to twist, to hurl, cp. G *drehen,* Dut. *draaien,* to twist, to twirl]

thru, *prep., adv.* (*N. Am.*) THROUGH.

thrum[1], *v.i.* (*past, p.p.* **thrummed**) to play carelessly or unskilfully (on a stringed instrument); to tap, to drum monotonously (on a table etc.). *v.t.* to play (an instrument) thus; to tap or drum on. *n.* the act or sound of such drumming or playing. [Icel. *thruma,* to rattle, to thunder, cogn. with DRUM[1]]

thrum[2], *n.* the fringe of warp-threads left when the web has been cut off, or one of such threads; loose thread, fringe etc., a tassel; (*pl.*) coarse or waste yarn. *v.t.* to cover or trim with thrums. **thrummy,** *a.* [OE *tungethrum,* cp. Icel. *thrömr,* edge, Dut. *dreum,* G *Trumm*]

thrush[1], *n.* a bird of the family Turdidae, esp. the song-thrush or throstle, *Turdus philomelos.* [OE. *thrysce,* cp. G *Drosse l,* OHG *droscel,* also THROSTLE]

thrush[2], *n.* a vesicular disease of the mouth and throat, usu. affecting children, caused by the fungus *Candida albicans;* a similar infection of the vagina, caused by the same fungus; an inflammatory affection of the frog in the feet of horses. [cp. Dan. *tröske,* Swed. *törsk,* also Norw. *frosk,* prob. ident. with *frosk,* frog]

thrusher THRASHER[2].

thrust, *v.t.* (*past, p.p.* **thrust**) to push suddenly or forcibly; to stab. *v.i.* to make a sudden push (at); to stab (at); to force or squeeze (in etc.). *n.* a sudden or violent push; an attack as with a pointed weapon, a stab; force exerted by one body against another, esp. horizontal outward pressure, as of an arch against its abutments; the forceful part, or gist, of an argument etc. **to thrust oneself in,** to intrude; to interfere. **to thrust through,** to pierce. **thrust-hoe,** *n.* a hoe worked by pushing. **thruster,** *n.* [ME *thrusten, thrysten,* Icel. *thrysta,* perh. cogn. with L *trūdere*]

Thucydides, *n.* (460–400 BC), Athenian historian, who exercised command in the Peloponnesian War in 424 BC with so little success that he was banished till 404 BC. In his *History of the Peloponnesian War* he attempted a scientific impartiality.

thud, *n.* a dull sound as of a blow on something soft. *v.i.* (*past, p.p.* **thudded**) to make a thud; to fall with a thud. [cp. OE *thyddan,* to strike, to thrust]

thug, *n.* one of a fraternity of religious assassins in India (suppressed 1828–35); a cut-throat; a ruffian. **thuggee, thuggery, thuggism,** *n.* [Hindi *thag, thug*]

Thuja THUYA.

Thule, *n.* the name given by the voyager Pytheas of Massilia to the northernmost land he reached, variously identified with the Shetlands, Iceland, Norway etc. **ultima Thule,** a very remote place. **thulite,** *n.* a rose-red variety of zoisite. **thulium,** *n.* a rare silver-grey malleable metallic element at. no. 69; chem. symbol Tm; a member of the rare-earth group. [L, from Gr. *Thoulē*]

thulium THULE.

thumb, *n.* the short thick digit of the human hand; the corresponding digit in animals; the part of a glove which covers the thumb. *v.t.* to handle, perform or play awkwardly; to soil or mark with the thumb; to turn (the pages of a book) with the thumb. *v.i.* to thrum. **one's fingers all thumbs,** fumbling, clumsily. **rule of thumb,** a rough, practical method. **thumbs down,** an indication of failure or disapproval. **thumbs up** an indication of success or approval. **to thumb a lift,** to get a lift from a passing car by signalling with up-raised thumb. **under one's thumb,** completely under one's power or influence. **thumb index,** *n.* an index in a book in which the letters are printed on the fore-edge, spaces being cut away from preceding pages to expose them to sight. **thumb-latch,** *n.* one with a broad-ended lever for pressing down with the thumb. **thumb-mark,** *n.* a mark made with a (dirty) thumb. **thumb-nail sketch,** *n.* a brief, vivid description. **thumb-nut,** *n.* a nut with wings for screwing up with the thumb. **thumbscrew,** *n.* a screw adapted to be turned with the finger and thumb; an old instrument of torture for compressing the thumb. **thumb-stall,** *n.* a case, sheath, or covering for an injured or sore thumb. **thumb-tack,** *n.* (*N Am.*) a drawing-pin. **thumbed,** *a.* **thumbikins,** †**thumbkins,** *n.pl.* a thumb-screw. **thumbless,**, *a.* [OE *thūma* (cp. Dut. *duim,* G *Daumen,* Swed. *tumme*), cogn. with TUMID]

thummim URIM.

thump, *v.t.* to strike with something giving a dull sound, esp. with the fist. *v.i.* to beat, to knock, to hammer (on, at etc.). *n.* a blow giving a dull sound; the sound of this. **thumper,** *n.* one who or that which thumps; (*coll.*) anything very large, excellent, or remarkable. **thumping,** *a.* (*coll.*) very large. [imit.]

thunder, *n.* the sound following a flash of lightning, due to the disturbance of the air by the electric discharge; a thunderbolt; a loud noise; a vehement denunciation or threat. *v.i.* to make the noise of thunder; to make a loud noise; to make loud denunciations etc. *v.t.* to emit or utter as with the sound of thunder. **thunderbolt,** *n.* an electric discharge with lightning and thunder; a supposed missile or mass of heated matter formerly believed to be discharged in this; an irresistible force, hero, a daring denunciation etc. **thunder-clap, -crack, -peal,** *n.* **thunder-cloud,** *n.* a cloud from which lightning and thunder are produced. **thunder-dart,** *n.* a thunderbolt. **thunderhead,** *n.* an anvil-shaped cumulonimbus cloud indicative of thunder. **thunder-shower, -storm,** *n.* a storm with thunder. **thunder-struck,** *a.* struck by lightning; amazed, astounded. **thunderer,** *n.* one who thunders; (*facet, dated*) applied to *The Times* newspaper. **thundering,** *a.* producing thunder or a loud sound like thunder; (*sl.*) extreme, remarkable, tremendous, out-and-out. *adv.* unusually, remarkably, tremendously. **thunderingly,** *adv.* **thunderless, thunderous,** very loud; angry, threatening. **thundery,** *a.* characterized by or giving a warning of thunder. **thunderously,** *adv.* [OE *thunor* (cp. Dut. *donder,* G *Donner,* Icel. *thōrr),* whence *thunrian,* cogn. with L *tonāre,* to thunder, Gr. *stenein,* to groan]

Thurber, *n.* **James (Grover)** (1894–1961), US humourist. His short stories, written mainly for the *New Yorker* magazine, include 'The Secret Life of Walter Mitty' (1932) and his doodle drawings include fanciful impressions of dogs.

thurible, *n.* a censer. **thurifer,** *n.* one who carries a censer. **thuriferous,** *a.* producing frankincense. **thurification,** *n.* the act of burning incense. [L *thūribulum,* from *thūs, thūris,* frankincense, Gr. *thuos,* from *thuein,* to sacrifice]

Thursday, *n.* the fifth day of the week. [OE *Thūres* (*Thunres*) *dæg,* Icel. *thōrs-dagr,* Thor's day, after *dies Jovis,* Jupiter's day]

thus[1], *adv.* in this manner; in the way indicated or about to be indicated; accordingly; to this extent. **thusness,** *n.* (*facet.*). †**thuswise,** *adv.* [OE, cp. OFris. and OS *thus,* Dut. *dus,* prob. cogn. with THAT]

thus[2], *n.* resin of the spruce-fir etc.; frankincense. [L, see THURIBLE]

thuya, thuja, *n.* a genus of coniferous trees or shrubs, also called arbor-vitae. [Gr. *thuia*]

thwack WHACK.

thwaite, *n.* a piece of ground reclaimed and converted to tillage. [Icel. *thveit,* paddock, a piece cut off, cogn. with OE *thwitan,* to WHITTLE]

thwart, *a.* transverse, oblique. †*prep.* across, athwart. *n.* a transverse plank in a boat serving as seat for a rower. *v.t.* to cross, to frustrate. **thwarter,** *n.* **thwartingly,** †**thwartly,** *adv.* †**thwartness,** *n.* **thwartship,** *a., adv.* (*Naut.*) across the vessel. [ME, from Icel. *thvert,* cp. OE *thwerh, thweorh,* perverse]

thy, *pron., a.* (*before vowels usu. and absolutely* **thine**) of or pertaining to thee (poss. corresponding to THOU). [OE *thin,* gen. of thū, THOU (cp. Icel. *thinn,* Dan. and Swed. *din,* G *dein*)]

thyine, *a.* (*Bibl.*) applied to a kind of wood and a tree (Rev. xviii.12), perh. the African conifer, *Callitris quadrivalvis.* [L *thȳinus,* Gr. *thuinos,* from *thua,* THUYA]

thylacine, *n.* the Tasmanian wolf, *Thylacinus cynocephalus,* the largest predatory marsupial, poss. extinct. [F (Gr. *thulakos,* pouch)]

thyme, *n.* any plant of the genus *Thymus,* esp. the garden thyme, *T. vulgaris,* a pungent aromatic herb used in cookery. **thymy,** *a.* [OF *tym* (F *thym*), L *thymum,* nom. *-us,* Gr. *thumos*]

-thymia, *comb. form.* forming nouns indicating a mental or emotional condition. [Gr. *thūmos,* mind, soul]

thymine, *n.* one of the bases in DNA and RNA, containing nitrogen. [THYMUS, -INE]

thymol, *n.* a phenol obtained from oil of thyme, used as an antiseptic.

thymus, *n.* (*pl.* **-mi**) a gland situated in the lower region of the neck, usu. degenerating after puberty. [Gr. *thumos*]

thyroid, *a.* shield-shaped; of or connected with the thyroid gland or cartilages; (*Zool.*) having a shield-shaped marking; (*Bot.*) peltate. *n.* the thyroid body or gland; the thyroid cartilage; a thyroid artery. **thyroid body** or **gland,** *n.* a large ductless gland consisting of two lobes situated on each side of the larynx and the upper part of the windpipe, which regulates metabolism and hence growth and development. **thyroid cartilage,** a large cartilage in the larynx, called in man the Adam's apple. **thyroid extract,** *n.* an extract prepared from the thyroid glands of oxen, sheep and pigs, and employed therapeutically. **thyro-,** *comb. form.* **thyroxin,** *n.* the main hormone produced by the thyroid gland, an amino acid containing iodine. [Gr. *thureoeidēs* (*thureos,* shield, from *thura,* door, -OID)]

thyrsus, *n.* (*pl.* **-si**) (*Gr. Ant.*) a spear or shaft wrapped with ivy or vine branches and tipped with a fir-cone, an attribute of Bacchus; (*Bot.*) an inflorescence consisting of a panicle with the longest branches in the middle. **thyrse,** *n.* (*Bot.*). **thyrsoid,** *a.* [L, from Gr. *thursos*]

thysanuran, *a.* belonging to the Thysanura, a division of wingless insects comprising the springtails. *n.* one of these insects. **thysanuriform,** *a.* [Gr. *thusanos,* tassel, *oura,* tail]

thyself, *pron.* a reflexive and emphatic form used after or instead of 'thou' or 'thee'.

Ti, (*chem. symbol*) titanium.

ti, *n.* (*Mus.*) TE.
Tianjin (*formerly* **Tientsin**), *n.* port and industrial and commercial city, a special municipality in Hubei province, central China; population (1984) 5,312,000. Its handmade silk and wool carpets are renowned. Dagan oilfield is nearby. Tianjin was opened to foreign trade in 1860, and occupied by the Japanese in 1937.
Tian Shan (Chinese **Tien Shan**), *n.* mountain system on the Soviet-Chinese border. Peaks include Kongur Shan in Xinjiang, China, 7719 m/25,334 ft. and Pik Pobedy on the Kirghizia border 7439 m/24,415 ft.
tiara, *n.* the head-dress of the ancient Persian kings, resembling a lofty turban; the triple crown worn by the Pope as a symbol of his temporal, spiritual, and purgatorial power; hence, the papal dignity; a jewelled coronet or headband worn as an ornament by women. †**tiar,** *n.* **tiara'd, tiaraed,** *a.* [L and Gr., prob. from Pers.]
†**tib,** *n.* the ace of trumps in the game of gleek; a low woman, a prostitute. [short for *Isabel*]
Tiberius, *n.* **Claudius Nero** (42 BC–AD 37), Roman emperor, the stepson, adopted son, and successor of Augustus from AD 14. A distinguished soldier, he was a conscientious ruler under whom the empire prospered.
Tibet, *n.* autonomous region of SW China (Pinyin form **Xizang**). **area** 1,221,600 sq km/471,540 sq miles. **capital** Lhasa. **population** (1979) 1,700,000. **products** wool, borax, salt, horn, musk, herbs, furs, gold, iron pyrites, lapis lazuli, mercury, textiles, chemicals, agricultural machinery. Industrialization (textiles, chemicals, agricultural machinery) has been encouraged and many Chinese have settled in the country. **government** Tibet is an autonomous region of China with its own People's Government and People's Congress. The controlling force in Tibet is the Communist Party of China, represented locally by First Secretary Wu Jinghua (1985). **Tibetan,** *a.* of or pertaining to the country of Tibet or its language; *n.* an inhabitant or the language of that country.
tibet, thibet, *n.* a cloth made of goat's hair or in imitation of this; a garment of this material. [*Tibet,* in Central Asia]
tibia, *n.* (*pl.* **-biae, -bias**) the shinbone, the anterior and inner of the two bones of the leg; the fourth joint of the leg in an arthropod; a pipe or flute. **tibial,** *a.* **tibio-,** *comb. form.* [L.]
tic, *n.* a habitual convulsive twitching of muscles, esp. of the face, tic douloureux. **tic douloureux,** *n.* facial neuralgia characterized by spasmodic twitching. [F, prob. from Teut.]
tice[1], *n.* (*Cricket*) a yorker.
†**tice**[2] ENTICE.
tick[1], *n.* a name for various parasitic acarids infesting some animals and occasionally man; (*sl., dated*) an unpleasant or despicable person. **tick fever,** *n.* a disease transmitted by ticks. [OE *ticia,* cp. MDut. *teke,* G *Zecke*]
tick[2], *n.* a cover or case for the filling of mattresses and beds; the material for this, usu. strong striped cotton or linen cloth, also called **ticking**. [formerly *teke,* L *thēca*]
tick[3], *n.* (*coll.*) credit, trust. *v.i.* to give credit. [shortened from TICKET]
tick[4], *v.i.* to make a small regularly recurring sound like that of a watch or clock. *v.t.* to mark (off) with a tick. *n.* the sound made by a going watch or clock; (*coll.*) a moment; a small mark used in checking items. **to tick off,** to mark off (a series) by ticks; (*coll.*) to scold. **to tick over,** of an engine, to run slowly with gear disconnected; to operate smoothly, at a low level of activity. **what makes one tick,** (*coll.*) one's main interest or most striking characteristic. **tick-tack,** *n.* a recurring, pulsating sound; a code of signalling employed by bookmakers whereby their agents can keep them informed of the betting odds. **tick-tock,**, *n.* the noise of a clock ticking. **ticker,** *n.* (*coll.*) a watch; the heart. **ticker-tape,** *n.* continuous ribbon of paper on which some telegraphic etc. machines print out information. [ME *tek,* a light touch, prob. imit., cp. Dut. *tik,* when *tikken,* Norw. *tikka*]
ticket, *n.* a card or paper with written or printed contents entitling the holder to admission to a concert etc., conveyance by train etc., or other privilege; a tag or label giving the price etc. of a thing it is attached to; (*sl.*) a visiting-card; (*coll.*) a parking ticket; the correct thing; (*Mil. coll.*) discharge from the Army; (*Naut. coll.*) a master's certificate; (*Aviat. coll.*) a pilot's certificate; (*N Am.*) the list of candidates put up by a party, hence the principles or programme of a party. *v.t.* to put a ticket on. **the ticket, just the ticket,** (*coll.*) the right, desirable or appropriate thing. **ticket of leave,** the term formerly applied to a licence to a prisoner to be at large under certain restrictions before the expiration of the sentence. **ticket-of-leave man,** a person holding this. **ticket-day,** *n.* the day before settling-day on the Stock Exchange when the brokers and jobbers learn the amount of stocks and shares that are passing between them and are due for settlement, and the names of the actual purchasers. **ticket-porter,** *n.* a licensed porter wearing a ticket or badge of identification. **ticket-punch,** *n.* a punch for cancelling or marking tickets. **ticket-writer,** *n.* an expert in window-card lettering. [ME *etiquet,* OF *etiquet, estiquette,* ticket, bill, from G *stecken,* to STICK]
ticking TICK[2].
tickle, *v.t.* to touch lightly so as to cause a thrilling sensation usually producing laughter; to please, to gratify, to amuse. *v.i.* to feel the sensation of tickling. *n.* the act or sensation of tickling. *a.* (*prov.*) ticklish, uncertain. **tickled pink** (or **to death**), very amused, very pleased. **tickler,** *n.* one who or that which tickles; something difficult to deal with. **ticklish,** *a.* sensible to the feeling of tickling; difficult, critical, precarious, needing tact or caution. **ticklishly,** *adv.* **ticklishness,** *n.* [ME *tikelen,* freq. of TICK[4]]
tid, *n.* (*Sc.*) the right time or condition (for sowing or other agricultural operation). [TIDE]
tidal TIDE.
tidbit TITBIT.
tiddle TITTLE[2].
tiddler[1], *n.* a stickleback or other very small fish; (*coll.*) anything very small. **tiddling,** *n.* fishing for these. *a.* very small or insignificant. **tiddly**[1], *a.* [corr. of TITTLEBAT].
tiddler[2], *n.* a feather or other instrument for tickling a person in order to tease. [*tiddle,* var. of TITTLE[2]]
tiddly[2], *a.* (*coll.*) slightly drunk, drunk.
tiddlywinks, *n.* a game in which the players snap small plastic or ivory disks into a tray. [etym. doubtful]
†**tiddy,** *n.* the four of trumps in the game of gleek. [etym. doubtful]
tide, *n.* time, season, hour; a regular period of time (for a day's work etc.); the alternative rise and fall of the sea, due to the attraction of the sun and moon; a rush of water, a flood, a torrent, a stream; the course or tendency of events. *v.i.* (*Naut.*) to work in or out of a river or harbour by the help of the tide. **to tide over,** (to help) to surmount difficulties in a small way or temporarily. **tide-gate,** *n.* a gate for admitting vessels at high tide and retaining the water at low tide. **tide-gauge,** *n.* an instrument showing or registering the rise and fall of the tide. **tide-lock,** *n.* a lock between the tide-water of a harbour and an enclosed basin. **tide-mark,** *n.* a line along a shore showing the highest level of the tide; (*coll.*) a dirty line round a bath indicating the level of the bath water; (*coll.*) a line on the body showing the limit of washing. **tide-mill,** *n.* a mill driven by a wheel set in motion by the tide. **tidesman,** *n.* a tide-waiter. **tide-waiter,** *n.* a custom-house officer who boards ships entering port in order to enforce customs regulations. **tidewater,** *n.* water affected by the movement of the tide; (*N Am.*) low-lying coastal land. **tideway,** *n.* the channel in which the tide runs; the ebb or flow of the tide in this. **tidal** *a.* pertaining or relating to the tides; periodically rising and falling or ebbing and flowing, as the tides. **tidal basin, dock,** or **harbour,** *n.* one in which the level of the water rises or falls with the tide. **tidal river,** *n.* one in which the tides act a long way inland. **tidal wave,** *n.* a wave following the sun

and moon from east to west and causing the tides; (*loosely*) a large wave due to an earthquake etc.; a great movement of popular feeling. **tideless,** *a.* [OE *tīd,* time, hour, cp. Dut. *tijd,* G *Zeit,* Icel. *tīth,* Dan. and Swed. *tid*]

tidings, *n.pl.* news, intelligence, a report. [ME *tidinde* Icel. *tīthindi,* cp. OE *tiding,* as prec.]

tidy, *a.* orderly, in becoming order, neat, trim; (*coll.*) considerable, pretty large. *n.* (*N Am.*) an ornamental covering for a chair-back etc.; a receptacle for odds and ends. *v.t.* to make tidy, to put in order. **tidily,** *adv.* **tidiness,** *n.* [orig. seasonable, TIDE, -Y]

tie, *v.t.* (*pres.p.* **tying**) to fasten with a cord etc., to secure, to attach, to bind; to arrange together and draw into a knot, bow etc.; to bind together, to unite; to confine, to restrict, to bind (down etc.); (*Mus.*) to unite (notes) by a tie. *v.i.* to be exactly equal (with) in a score. *n.* something used to tie things together; a neck-tie; a bond, an obligation; a beam or rod holding parts of a structure together; (*Mus.*) a curved line placed over two or more notes to be played as one; an equality of votes, score etc., among candidates, competitors etc.; a match between any pair of a number of players or teams; (*N Am.*) a railway sleeper. **to tie in,** to agree or coordinate (with); to be associated or linked (with). **to tie up,** to fasten securely to a post etc.; to restrict, to bind by restrictive conditions; to be compatible or coordinated (with); to keep occupied to the exclusion of other activities. **tie-beam,** *n.* a horizontal beam connecting rafters. **tie-break(er),** *n.* a contest to decide the winner after a tied game etc. **tie-dyeing, tie and dye,** *n.* a method of dyeing in which parts of the fabric are knotted or tied tightly to avoid being coloured. **tie-dyed,** *a.* **tie-in,** *n.* a connection; something linked to something else, esp. a book to a film. **tie-line,** *n.* a telephone line between two branch exchanges. **tie-up,** *n.* (*N Am.*) a deadlock, a standstill, esp. in business or industry, through a strike etc. **tie-wig,** *n.* a wig tied behind with ribbon. **tied,** *a.* of a public house, bound to obtain its supplies from one brewer etc.; of a dwelling-house, owned by an employer and rented to a current employee; of a game etc., ending with an equal score on each side. **tier**[1] *n.* [ME *tigen,* OE *tīegan,* from *tēag, tēah,* bond, rope, etc., from *tēon,* to pull (cp. Icel. *tang* tie)]

Tieck, *n.* **Johann Ludwig** (1773–1853), German romantic poet and collector of folk-tales, some of which he dramatized, for example 'Puss in Boots'.

Tientsin, *n.* former name for TIANJIN.

Tiepolo, *n.* **Giovanni Battista** (1696–1770), Italian painter, born in Venice. He created monumental rococo decorative schemes in palaces and churches in NE Italy, SW Germany, and in Madrid (1762–70). The style is light-hearted, the palette light and warm, and he made great play with illusion.

tier[1] TIE.

tier[2], *n.* a row, a rank, esp. one of several rows placed one above another. *v.t.* to pile in tiers. [OF *tire,* prob. from Teut.]

tierce, *n.* a cask of 42 gallons, or one-third or a pipe; a sequence of three cards of the same suit; in fencing, the third position for guard, parry, or thrust; (*Mus.*) a third; (*Eccles.*) the office for the third hour; (*Her.*) a field divided into three parts of different tinctures. [F *tiers,* fem. *tierce,* L *tertius,* third]

tiercel, *n.* a male falcon. [OF, dim of *tiers,* prec.]

tiercet, TERCET.

Tierra del Fuego, *n.* island group divided between Chile and Argentina. It is separated from the mainland of S America by the Strait of Magellan, and Cape Horn is at the southernmost point. Ushuaia, Argentina is the chief town, and the world's most southerly town. Industries include oil and sheep farming.

tiers état, *n.* the third estate of the realm, the commonalty. [F, third estate]

tiff[1], *n.* a small draught of liquor; a fit of peevishness, a slight quarrel. *v.t.* to sip, to drink. *v.i.* to be pettish; to take tiffin. [cp Norw. *tev,* a sniff, a scent, Icel. *thefa,* to sniff]

tiff[2], *v.t.* (*dial.*) to dress, to deck, to prank. [ME *tiffen,* OF *tiffer, atiffer,* from Teut. (cp. Dut. *tippen,* to cut, to clip)]

tiffany, *n.* a kind of thin silk-like gauze. [OF *tiffanie,* THEOPHANY (orig. a Twelfth Night dress)]

Tiffany, *n.* **Louis Comfort** (1848–1933), US artist and glassmaker, son of Charles Louis Tiffany who founded the New York jewellers. He produced stained glass windows, iridescent Favrile (Latin *faber* 'craftsman') glass, and lampshades.

tiffin, *n.* among the British in India, a lunch or light repast between breakfast and dinner. *v.i.* to take this.

tig, *v.t.* to touch in the game of tig. *v.i.* (*Sc.*) to give light touches. *n.* a children's game in which one pursues and touches another who in turn pursues until he can touch someone. [perh. var. of TICK[4]]

tige, *n.* (*Arch.*) the shaft of a column; (*Bot.*) a stem or stalk. [F, from L TIBIA]

tiger, *n.* a large Asiatic carnivorous feline mammal, *Felis tigris,* tawny with black stripes; applied to other large feline animals as the American tiger or jaguar, the red tiger or cougar, etc; a fierce, relentless, very energetic and forceful or cruel person; (*coll.*) a swaggering ruffian, a bully; (*sl.*) a liveried groom attending a person in a light vehicle. **tiger-beetle,** *n.* a predaceous beetle with striped or spotted wing-cases. **tiger-cat,** *n.* a wild cat of various species; (*Austral.*) the dasyure. **tiger-flower,** *n.* a plant of the genus *Tigridia* spotted with orange and yellow. **tiger-footed,** *a.* swift as a tiger. **tiger-lily,** *n.* a lily, *Lilium tigrinum,* with orange-spotted flowers. **tiger-moth,** *n.* one of the Arctiidae, with streaked hairy wings. **tiger's-eye,** *n.* a gem with brilliant chatoyant lustre. **tiger's-foot** *n.* a plant of the genus *Ipomaea.* **tiger-wood,** *n.* a wood imported from Guyana for cabinet-making. **tigerish,** *a.* **tigress,** *n. fem.* **tigrine,,** *a.* [ME and OF *tigre,* L and Gr. *tigris,* perh. from OPers. *tighri,* arrow, in alln. to its swiftness]

tight, *a.* compactly built or put together, not leaky; impervious, impermeable (*often in comb.* as *watertight*); drawn, fastened, held, or fitting closely; tense, stretched to the full, taut; neat, trim, compact; close-fisted, parsimonious; under strict control; not easily obtainable (of money); (*coll.*) awkward, difficult; (*sl.*) drunk. *adv.* tightly. **tight-fisted,** *a.* mean, stingy. **tight-knit,** *a.* tightly integrated or organized. **tight-lipped,** *a.* having the lips pressed tightly together, in anger etc.; taciturn. **tight-rope,** *n.* a rope stretched between two points upon which an acrobat walks, dances etc. **tighten,** *v.t., v.i.* **tightener,** *n.* **tightly,** *adv.* **tightness,** *n.* **tights,** *n.pl.* a close-fitting garment made of nylon or wool etc. covering the legs and the body below the waist and worn by women, male acrobats, ballet dancers etc. [ME *tigt,* Icel. *thēttr,* cp. Swed. *tät,* Dan. *tœt* NFris. *tacht*]

tigon, *n.* the offspring of a tiger and a lioness. [*tiger, lion*]

Tigray, Tigré, *n.* region in the northern highlands of Ethiopia; area 65,900 sq km/25,444 sq miles. Chief town is Mekele. The region had an estimated population of 2.4 million in 1984, at a time when drought and famine were driving large numbers of people to fertile land in the south or into neighbouring Sudan. Since 1978 a guerrilla group known as the Tigray People's Liberation Front has been fighting for regional autonomy.

tigress, tigrine TIGER.

Tigris (Arabic **Shatt Dijla**), *n.* river flowing through Turkey and Iraq (see also MESOPOTAMIA), joining the Euphrates above Basra, where it forms the Shatt-al-Arab; length 1600 km/1000 miles.

tihore, *n.* the New Zealand flax. [Maori]

Tihuanaco, *n.* site of a Peruvian city, S of Lake Titicaca in the Andes, which gave its name to the 8th–14th-cent. civilization that preceded the Inca.

Tijuana, *n.* city and resort in NW Mexico; population (1980) 461,257; noted for horse races and casinos. San Diego adjoins it across the US border.

tika, *n.* the red mark on the forehead of a Hindu woman. [Hind.]

tike TYKE.

Tikhonov, *n.* **Nikolai** (1905–), Soviet politician. He was a close associate of President Brezhnev, joining the Politburo 1979, and was prime minister (chairman of the Council of Ministers) 1980–85. In Apr. 1989 he was removed from the central committee.

tiki, *n.* a neck ornament or figurine, a stylized representation of an ancestor etc. [Maori]

tilbury, *n.* a type of gig. [name of a London coachbuilder]

tilde, *n.* a diacritical sign (˜) in Spanish put over *n* to indicate the sound *ny;* in Portuguese put over vowels to indicate nasalization. [Sp., var. of *titulo,* TITLE]

tile, *n.* a thin slab of baked clay, used for covering roofs, paving floors, constructing drains etc.; a similar slab of porcelain or other material used for ornamental paving; (*coll.*) a silk hat. *v.t.* to cover with or as with tiles; (*freemasonry*) to secure against intrusion by stationing the tiler at the door; to bind to secrecy. **on the tiles,** enjoying oneself wildly, usu. drunkenly. **to have a tile loose,** to be eccentric, half-crazy. **tile-drain,** *n.* a drain made of tiles. **tile-kiln,** *n.* **tilestone,** *n.* an argillaceous stone, esp. from the uppermost group of the Silurian formation, used for tiling. **tiler,** *n.* one who makes or lays tiles; (*freemasonry*) the door-keeper of a lodge. **tilery,** *n.* **tiling,** *n.* [OE *tigele,* L *tēgula,* from *tegere* to cover]

tiliaceous, *a.* allied to or resembling the linden or lime-tree. [L *tilia,* linden, -ACEOUS]

tilka TIKA.

till¹, *v.t.* to cultivate. **tillable,** *a.* **tillage,** *n.* **tiller¹,** *n.* [OE *tilian, teolian,* to labour, to strive for, to till, from *til,* good, goodness]

till², *prep.* up to, up to the time of, until. *conj.* up to the time when. **till now,** up to the present time. **till then,** up to that time. [Icel. *til,* cp. Dan. *til,* Swed. *till* G. *Ziel,* purpose]

till³, *n.* a money-drawer in or on a counter; a cash-register. [earlier and dial. *tiller,* drawer, from ME *tillen,* OE *tyllan* (in *fortyllan*), to draw]

till⁴, *n.* an unstratified clay containing boulder, pebbles, sand etc., deposited by glaciers. **tilly,** *a.* [etym. doubtful]

tiller¹ TILL¹.

tiller², *n.* the lever on the head of a rudder by which this is turned. **tiller-chain, -rope** *n.* one connecting the tiller with the steering-wheel. [ME *tillen* see TILL³, -ER]

tiller³, *n.* the shoot of a plant springing from the base of the original stalk; a sucker; a sapling. *v.i.* to put forth tillers. [OE *telgor, tealgor,* from *telga,* cp. Dut. *telg*]

Tilly, *n.* **Jan Tserklaes, Count Tilly** (1559–1632), Flemish commander of the army of the Catholic League and imperial forces in the Thirty Years' War. Notorious for his storming of Magdeburg, E Germany, 1631, he was defeated by the Swedish king Gustavus Adolphus at Breitenfeld, and at the river Lech in SW Germany, where he was mortally wounded.

tilt¹, *n.* a covering for a cart or wagon; an awning over the stern-sheets of a boat etc. *v.t.* to cover with a tilt. [OE *teld,* cp. MDut. *teld, telte,* G *Zelt,* Icel. *tjald,* Dan. *telt*]

tilt², *v.i.* to heel over, to tip, to be in a slanting position; to charge with a lance, to joust, as in a tournament. *v.t.* to raise at one end, to cause to heel over, to tip, to incline; to thrust or aim (a lance); to hammer or forge with a tilt-hammer. *n.* an inclination from the vertical, a slanting position; a tilting, a tournament, a charge with the lance; a tilt-hammer; a contrivance, usu. of crossed sticks, for showing a bite in angling through ice. **at full tilt,** at full speed or full charge, with full force **tilt-hammer,** *n.* a large hammer on a pivoted lever, usu. worked by steam or waterpower. **tilt-yard,** *n.* a place for tilting. **tilter,** *n.* [ME *tilten,* from OE *tealt,* unsteady]

tilth, *n.* tillage, cultivation; the depth of soil tilled. [OE (TILL¹, -TH]

Tim., (*abbr.*) Timothy.

timbal, tymbal, *n.* a kettledrum. [F *timbale,* It. *timballo,* Arab. *tabl,* drum. cp. ATABAL]

timbale, *n.* a dish of meat or fish pounded and mixed with white of egg, cream etc., and cooked in a mould. [F]

timber, *n.* wood suitable for building, carpentry etc.; trees yielding wood suitable for constructive purposes, trees generally; a piece of wood prepared for building, esp. one of the curved pieces forming the ribs of a ship; (*Hunting*) fences, hurdles etc. *v.t.* to furnish or construct with timber. **timber-cart,** *n.* a vehicle with high wheels fitted for stringing logs and carrying lengthwise. **timber-head,** *n.* (*Naut.*) a timber rising above the deck for belaying ropes, etc. **timber line** TREE. **timber-toes,** *n.* (*coll.*) a wooden-legged person. **timberwolf,** *n.* a grey-coloured type of wolf once common in N America. **timber-yard,** *n.* a yard where timber is stored, etc. **timbered,** *a.* wooded (*usu. in comb.*, as *well-timbered*). **timbering,** *n.* the using of timber; temporary timber supports for the sides of an excavation. [OE (cp. Dut. and Swed. *timmer,* G *Zimmer,* room, timber]

timbre, *n.* the quality of tone distinguishing particular voices, instruments etc., due to the individual character of the sound-waves. [F, from F *tymbre,* L *tympanum*]

timbrel, *n.* an ancient instrument like the tambourine. [ME dim. of *timber,* as prec.]

Timbuktu, Tombouctou, *n.* a town in Mali; population (1976) 20,500. A camel caravan centre from the 11th cent. on the fringe of the Sahara, since 1960 it has been surrounded by the southward movement of the desert, and the former canal link with the Niger is dry. Products include salt.

time, *n.* the general relation of sequence or continuous or successive existence; duration or continuous existence regarded as divisible into portions or periods, a particular portion of this; a period characterized by certain events, persons, manners etc., an epoch, an era (*sometimes in pl.*); a portion of time allotted to one or to a specified purpose, the time available or at one's disposal; the period of an apprenticeship, of gestation, of a round at boxing etc.; a portion of time as characterized by circumstances, conditions of existence etc.; a point in time, a particular moment, instant, or hour; a date, a season, an occasion, an opportunity; time as reckoned by conventional standards, as sidereal time, solar time etc.; the relation of a verb as regards past, present, or future, or as regards tenses; the relative duration of a note or rest; rate of movement, tempo; style of movement, rhythm; (*Pros.*) duration of a vowel, syllable etc., in pronunciation; (*sl.*) a term of imprisonment. *v.t.* to adapt to the time or occasion; to do, begin, or perform at the proper season; to regulate as to time; to ascertain or mark the time, duration, or rate of; to measure, as in music. *v.i.* to keep time (with). **apparent time, solar time,** time as reckoned by the apparent motion of the sun. **at the same time** SAME. **at times,** at intervals, now and then. **for the time being,** for the present. **from time to time** FROM. **Greenwich time** GREENWICH. **in good time,** at the right moment; early; fortunately, happily (*often iron.*). **in no time,** very quickly. **in time,** not too late; early enough; in course of time; sometime or other, eventually; in accordance with the time, rhythm, etc. **mean time,** an average of apparent time. **on time,** punctually. **quick time** QUICK. **sidereal time,** time shown by the apparent diurnal revolutions of the stars. **time and motion study,** investigation into working methods with a view to increasing efficiency. **time and (time) again,** repeatedly. **time enough,** soon enough. **time of day,** the hour by the clock; a greeting appropriate to this; (*sl.*) the latest aspect of affairs. **time off,** time away from work. **time out of mind, time immemorial,** time beyond legal memory. **to beat time** BEAT. **to lose time,** to delay. **to pass the time of day,** to greet, to say 'good-day' to. **what time,** (*poet.*) when. **time-ball,** *n.* a ball dropped from the top of a staff at an observatory at a prescribed instant of time, usu. 1 P.M. **time-bargain,** *n.* an agreement to buy or sell stock, etc., at a certain time. †**time-bill,** *n.* a timetable. **time-**

bomb, *n.* a bomb set to explode at some prearranged time. **time-book, -card,** *n.* one specifying or recording hours of work for workmen etc. **time capsule,** *n.* a container filled with objects characteristic of a certain age or period buried in order to be dug up in the future. **time exposure,** *n.* (a photograph taken by) exposure of a film for a relatively long time. **time-expired,** *a.* applied to soldiers whose period of service is completed; **time-fuse,** *n.* a fuse in a shell, etc., graduated to ignite the charge at a certain time. **time-honoured,** *a.* of venerable age. **time-keeper,** *n.* a clock, watch, or chronometer; a person who records, time, esp. of workmen; a person considered in terms of punctuality (as a *good timekeeper*). **time lag,** *n.* the interval the elapses between cause and result. **time-lapse,** *a.* of a method of filming a slow process by taking still photographs at regular intervals and showing them as a normal-speed film. **time-limit,** *n.* the period within which a task must be completed. **time-piece,** *n.* a clock or watch. **time-server,** *n.* one who suits his conduct, opinions, and manners to those in power. **time-serving,** *a., n.* **time-serving man,** *n.* a soldier in the regular army. **time-sharing,** *n.* simultaneous access to a computer by several users on different terminals; the purchase of the use of holiday accommodation for the same period every year (also **time-share**). **time-sheet,** *n.* a sheet of paper on which hours of work are recorded. **time-signal,** *n.* a signal issued by an observatory or broadcasting station to indicate the exact time. **time signature,** *n.* an indication of time at the beginning of a piece of music. **timetable,** *n.* a printed list of the times of departure and arrival or trains etc.; a record of times of employees, school lessons etc.; a table containing the relative value of every note in music. *v.t.* to put on a timetable; to arrange in a timetable. **time-work,** *n.* work paid for by time, opp. to piece-work. **time-worn,** *a.* antiquated, dilapidated. **time zone,** *n.* a geographical region in which the same standard time is used. **timeful,** *a.* seasonable, timely, early. **timeless,**, *a.* untimely, premature; without end; ageless; not restricted to a particular period. †**timelessly,** *adv.* **timely** *a.* seasonable, opportune, early, premature. **timeliness,** *n.* **timeous, timous,**, *a.* (*Sc.*) **timeously, timously,** *adv.* **timer,** *n.* an instrument which measures or records time; one which operates a machine etc., at a preset time. **times** *prep.* multiplied by. **timing,** *n.* reckoning the time taken; the precise instant at which ignition occurs in an internal-combustion engine, and at which the valves open and close; the controlling mechanism for this; the choosing of the best time (to do something). **timist,** *n.* one who keeps time in music. [OE *tīma* (cp. Icel. *tīmi,* Dan. *time,* Swed. *tīmme*)]

†**timenoguy,** *n.* a rope or spar stretched across a place to prevent fouling of rigging. [etym. unknown]

timid, *a.* easily frightened, shy. **timidity, timidness,** *n.* habitual shyness or cowardice. **timidly,** *adv.* [F *timide,* L *timīdus,* from *timēre.* to fear]

timing, timist TIME.

Timişoara, *n.* capital of Timiş county, W Romania; population (1985) 319,000.

timocracy, *n.* a form of government in which a certain amount of property is a necessary qualification for office. **timocratic,** *a.* [Gr. *timokratia* (*timē,* honour, -CRACY]

Timon, *n.* a misanthrope. [Gr. *Timōn,* a Greek misanthrope, hero of Shakespeare's *Timon of Athens*]

†**timoneer,** *n.* a helmsman; a lookout who directs a helmsman. [F, from It. *timoniere,* from *timon,* helm, L *tēmo -ōnem,* a helm]

Timor, *n.* largest and most easterly of the Sunda Islands, part of Indonesia; area 33,610 sq km/12,973 sq miles. West Timor (capital Kupang) was formerly Dutch and was included in Indonesian independence. East Timor (capital Dili) was an overseas province of Portugal until it was annexed by Indonesia 1975. Guerrilla warfare by local people seeking independence continues. Since 1975 over 500,000 have been killed or have resettled in West Timor, according to Amnesty International. Products include coffee, maize, rice, and coconuts.

timorous, *a.* fearful, timid. **timoroso** [It.], *adv.* (*Mus.*) with hesitation. **timorously,** *adv.* **timorousness,** *n.* [med. L *timorōsus,* from L *timor,* fear, from *timēre,* to fear]

Timothy, *n.* in the New Testament, companion to St Paul, both on his missionary journeys and in prison. Two of the Pauline epistles are addressed to him.

Timothy grass, *n.* a valuable fodder-grass, *Phleum pratense.* [*Timothy* Hanson, an American through whom it first came into use, *c* 1720]

timous, etc. TIME.

timpano, *n.* (*pl.* **-ni**) an orchestral kettledrum. **timpanist,** *n.* [It., from L *tympanum*]

†**timwhisky,** *n.* a high light chaise for one horse or two horses driven tandem. [*tim,* etym. doubtful, WHISKY[2]]

tin, *n.* a lustrous white metallic element, at. no. 50; chem. symbol Sn; easily beaten into thin plates, much used for cooking utensils etc., esp. in the form of thin plates of iron coated with tin; a pot or other utensil made of this; a tinplate container that can be hermetically sealed to preserve food or drink; (*sl.*) money. *v.t.* (*past, p.p.* **tinned**) to coat or overlay with tin; to preserve (meat, fruit etc.) in tins. **(little) tin god,** a person of local, undeserved importance; a self-important person. **tin pan alley,** the world of popular music; the writers and publishers of such music. **tin can,** *n.* **tin fish,** *n.* (*Nav. sl.*) a torpedo. **tinfoil,** *n.* tin, tin alloy or aluminium beaten into foil for wrapping foodstuffs etc. *v.t.* to coat or cover with this. **tin hat,** *n.* a steel shrapnel helmet. **tin lizzie**, *n.* (*sl.*) an old or dilapidated motor car. **tinman, tinsmith,** *n.* one who makes articles of tin or tinplate. **tin-opener,** *n.* an implement for opening airtight tins of preserved meat, fruit etc. **tin-plate,** *n.* iron-plate coated with tin. *v.t.* to coat with tin. **tin-pot,** *a.* (*sl.*) worthless, rubbishy. **tin roof,** *n.* one made of corrugated iron. **tin-stone,** *n.* cassiterite, the commonest form of tin ore. **tintack,** *n.* a carpet tack, tack coated with tin. **tin-type,** *n.* ferrotype. **tinware,** *n.* vessels or utensils of tin or tin-plate. **tinner,** *n.* a tin-miner or tinsmith. **tinny,** *a.* of or like tin; making a thin, metallic sound; cheap, made of flimsy materials. **tinnily,** *adv.* [OE cp. Dut. Icel., and Dan. *tin,* G *Zinn*]

tinamou, *n.* a S American quail-like gallinaceous game-bird. [F, from Carib.]

Tinbergen, *n.* **Jan** (1903–88), Dutch economist. He shared a Nobel prize 1969 with Ragnar Frisch for his work on econometrics (the mathematical-statistical expression of economic theory).

tincal, -kal, *n.* borax in the crude state. [Malay *tingkal*]

tinchel, *n.* a circle of hunters surrounding a wide piece of ground and gradually collecting the deer. [Gael. *timchioll,* circuit, compass]

tinct, tinction, tinctorial TINCTURE.

tincture, *n.* an alcoholic or other solution of some principle, usu. vegetable, used in medicine; (*sl.*) a drink of spirits; a tinge or shade (of colour), a tint; a slight taste or flavour, a spice (of); (*Her.*) one of the colours, metals, or furs used in emblazoning. *v.t.* to imbue with a colour or tint, to tinge; to flavour; to give a flavour or tinge (of some quality etc.). **tinct,** *v.t.* †to tincture, to tint. *n.* a stain, colour, or tint. *a.* tinctured. **tinction,** *n.* colouring-material; the act or process of colouring; (*Med.*) a modification of a remedy by admixture etc. **tinctorial,** *a.* pertaining to colour or dyes; colouring. [L *tinctūra,* from *tingere,* to TINGE, p.p. *tinctus*]

tinder, *n.* any dry, very combustible substance, esp. charred linen, used to kindle fire from a spark. **tinder-box,** *n.* a box furnished with tinder, flint and steel, for this purpose. **tinder-like, tindery,** *a.* [OE *tyndre,* from *tendan,* to kindle]

tine, *n.* the prong, point, or spike of an antler, fork, harrow etc. **tined,** *a.* [OE *tind,* cp. Icel. *tindr,* Swed. *tinne,* also L *dens dentis,* tooth]

tinea, *n.* a clothes-moth; a genus of moth some species of which in the larval stage are very destructive to clothes; a fungal disease of the skin, ringworm. [L, worm, moth]

tinfoil TIN.

ting, *n.* a tinkling sound, as of a small bell. *v.i.* to make this sound. **ting-a-ling,** *n.* [imit]

Ting, *n.* **Samuel** (1936–), US high energy physicist. In 1974 he detected a new particle, known as the J particle, similar to the psi particle of Burton Richter, with whom he shared the 1976 Nobel Physics Prize.

tinge, *v.t.* to colour slightly, to stain (with); to modify the character or qualities of. *n.* a slight admixture of colour, a tint; a smack, flavour. **tinger,** *n.* **tingible, ting(e)ing,** *a.* [L *tingere,* cogn. with Gr. *tengein* to wet]

tingle, *v.t.* to feel a stinging, prickly sensation; to give this sensation. [ME *tinglen,* freq. from TING]

tinker, *n.* an itinerant mender of pots, kettles, pans etc.; a rough-and-ready worker or repairer; the act of tinkering, patching, botching. *v.t.* to mend pots, kettles etc.; to mend, alter, or patch up in a rough-and-ready way, or in a clumsy, makeshift, or ineffective manner. *v.i.* to work thus (at or with); to interfere, to meddle; to experiment (with). **not give a tinker's cuss,** not care at all. **tinkerly,** *a.* **tinkler,** *n.* (*Sc.*) [ME *tinkere,* from *tinken,* see foll.]

tinkle, *v.i.* to make a succession of sharp, metallic sounds as of a bell; (*sl.*) to urinate. *v.t.* to cause to tinkle, to ring. *n.* such a sound; (*sl.*) a telephone call. **tinkler,** *n.* one who or that which tinkles; (*sl.*) a small bell. [ME *tinklen,* freq. of *tinken,* to ring, of imit. orig.]

tinman, tinner TIN.

tinnitus, *n.* (*Med.*) ringing in the ears. [L, from *tinnīre,* to ring]

tinny, etc. TIN.

tinsel, *n.* brass, tin or other lustrous metallic substances beaten into thin sheets and used in strips, disks, or spangles to give a sparkling effect in decoration; a fabric adorned with this; a cloth composed of silk and silver; superficial brilliancy or display. *a.* gaudy, showy, superficially fine. *v.t.* to adorn with tinsel. **tinselly,** *a.* †**tinselry,** *n.* [OF *estincelle* (F *étincelle*), L *scintilla,* spark]

tin-stone TIN.

tint, *n.* a variety of colour, esp. one produced by admixture with another colour, esp. white; a pale colour; a slight tinge (of another colour); in engraving, an effect of shading texture obtained by a closed series of parallel lines. *v.t.* to give a tint or tints to; to tinge. **tint-block,** *n.* a block with a design for printing in faint colour as a background. **tint-tool,** *n.* a tool for engraving parallel lines etc. **tinter,** *n.* one who or that which tints; an engraving-tool or machine for tinting; a plain lantern-slide of one colour. **tintless,** *a.* **Tintometer**®, *n.* an instrument or a scale of colours for determining tints. **tinty,** *a.* inharmoniously tinted. [from TINCT]

tintack TIN.

tintinnabulum, *n.* (*pl.* **-la**) a bell, esp. a small tinkling one for signalling, fitting to harness etc.; a ringing, tinkling or jingling of bells, plates etc. **tintinnabular, -lary,** †**-lous,** *a.* **tintinnabulation,** *n.* [L, from *tintinnāre,* redupl. from *tinnīre*]

tintless, tintometer, etc. TINT.

Tintoretto, *n.* (real name Jacopo Robusti) (1518–94), Italian painter, active in Venice. His dramatic religious paintings are spectacularly lit and full of movement, such as his canvases of the lives of Christ and the Virgin in the Scuola di San Rocco, Venice, 1564–88.

tinware TIN.

tiny, *a.* (*comp.* **tinier,** *superl.* **tiniest**) very small. [formerly *tine, tyne,* something small, etym. doubtful]

Tiomkin, *n.* **Dimitri** (1899–1979), Russian composer who lived in the US from 1925. From 1930 he wrote Hollywood film scores including music for *Duel in the Sun* (1946), *The Thing* (1951), and *Rio Bravo* (1959). His score for *High Noon* (1952) won him an Academy Award.

-tion, *suf.* denoting action or condition, as *mention, expectation, vacation.* [L *-tiōnem,* accus. sing. of mouns in *-tio,* cp. -ION]

tip[1], *n.* the point, end, or extremity, esp. of a small or tapering thing; a small piece or part attached to anything to form a point or end, as a ferrule or shoe-tip; a brush used in laying on goldleaf. *v.t.* (*past, p.p.* **tipped**) to put a tip on; to form the tip of. **on the tip of one's tongue,** about to be uttered. **tipstaff** *n.* a metal-tipped staff carried by a sheriff's officer; a sheriff's officer. **tiptoe,** *adv.* on the tips of the toes. *v.i.* to walk or stand on tiptoe. **tip-top,** *n.* the highest point, the very best; *a.* of the very best. *adv.* in a first-rate way. **tip-topper,** *n.* [ME *typ,* cp. Dut., Dan., and Swed. *tip*]

tip[2], *v.t.* to cause to lean, to tilt (up, over etc.); to overturn, to upset; to discharge (the contents of a cart, vessel etc.) thus; to strike lightly, to tap, to touch; to give a small gratuity to; to toss or throw lightly, to give; (*coll.*) to give private information to about a horse, an investment etc. *v.i.* to lean over, to tilt; to upset. *n.* a small present in money, a gratuity; private information, esp. for betting or investment purposes; a slight touch, push or hit; a place where rubbish is dumped. **to tip in,** (*Print.*) to insert a loose plate by pasting the back margin to the page following. **to tip off,** to give a warning hint; in basketball, to start play by throwing the ball high between players of the two sides. **to tip the wink,** (*coll.*) to hint, to inform furtively. **tip-cat,** *n.* a game with a piece of wood pointed at both ends which is hit with a stick; the tapering piece of wood. **tip-off,** *n.* **tip-up,** *a.* of a (theatre) seat, able to be tilted up on a hinge or pivot. **tipper**[1], *n.* one who or that which, tips; a lorry or truck whose platform can be tilted towards the rear to empty out the load. **tipster,** *n.* one who supplies tips about races etc. [ME *tippen* (cp. Swed. *tippa*), cogn. with TAP[2]]

Tipperary, *n.* county in the Republic of Ireland, province of Munster, divided into north and south regions. North Tipperary: administrative headquarters Nenagh; area 2000 sq km/772 sq miles; population (1986) 59,000. South Tipperary: administrative headquarters Clonmel; area 2260 sq km/872 sq miles; population (1986) 77,000. It includes part of the Golden Vale, a dairy-farming region.

tippet, *n.* a fur covering for the neck and shoulders, worn by women; an ecclesiastical vestment; part of the official costume of judges etc. [OE *tæppet,* L *tapēta* Gr. *tapēs -ētos,* carpet]

Tippett, *n.* **Michael (Kemp)** (1905–), English composer whose works include the operas *The Midsummer Marriage* (1952) and *The Knot Garden* (1970); four symphonies; *Songs for Ariel* (1962); and choral music including *The Mask of Time* (1982).

tipple, *v.i.* to drink alcoholic liquors habitually. *v.t.* to sip repeatedly; to drink (alcoholic liquors) habitually. *n.* strong drink; one's favourite (alcoholic) drink. **tippler,** *n.* **tippling-house,** *n.* [freq. of TIP[1], cp. Norw. *tipla,* from *tippa,* to drip, from *tipp*]

tipsy, *a.* fuddled, partially intoxicated, proceeding from or inducing intoxication. **tipsy-cake,** *n.* a sponge cake soaked in wine served with custard. **tipsily,** *adv.* **tipsiness,** *n.* [prob. rel. to TIP[1], cp Swiss G *tipseln,* to fuddle oneself]

tiptoe, tip-top TIP[1].

Tipula, *n.* a group of dipterous insects containing the crane-flies. **tipularian, tipulid, tipulidan,** *a., n.* **tipulary, tipulideous,** *a.* [L *tippula,* water-spider]

TIR, (*abbr.*) International Road Transport (F, Transports Internationaux Routiers).

tirade, *n.* a long, vehement speech, declamation, or harangue, esp. of censure or reproof; (*Mus.*) a diatonic run filling an interval between two notes. [F, from It. *tirata,* p.p. of *tirare,* late L *tīrāre,* to draw, to pull]

tirailleur, *n.* a skirmisher, a sharpshooter. [F, from *tirailler,* to skirmish, from *tirer,* to shoot]

Tirana, Tiranë, *n.* capital (since 1920) of Albania; population (1983) 206,000. Industries include metallurgy, cotton textiles, soap, and cigarettes. It was founded in the early 17th cent. by Turks when part of the Ottoman Empire. Though now mainly modern, some older districts and mosques have been preserved.

tirasse, *n.* a pedal-coupler in an organ. [F, from *tirer,* to draw]

tire[1], *v.t.* to exhaust the strength of by toil or labour; to fatigue, to weary; to exhaust the patience or attention of. *v.i.* to become weary or exhausted. **tired,** *a.* fatigued; bored, impatient, irritated; stale, hackneyed. **tiredness,** *n.* **tireless,** *a.* unwearied, untirable. **tirelessly,** *adv.* **tiresome,**, *a.* fatiguing, tiring; wearisome, tedious, annoying. **tiresomely,** *adv.* **tiresomeness,** *n.* **tiring,** *a.* [ME *tiren, teorian,* OE *tyrigan,* etym. doubtful]

tire[2], **tyre,** *n.* a band of iron, steel, etc., placed round the rim of a wheel; (*N Am.*) a tyre. **tired,** *a.* (*usu. in comb.*, as *rubber-tired*). **tireing,** *n.* **tireless,** *a.* **tiresmith,** *n.* [etym. doubtful, perh. from foll.]

†**tire**[3], *n.* a head-dress; attire generally. *v.t.* to attire, to adorn, to dress. †**tirewoman,** *n.* one employed to dress another. †**tiring-house, -room,** *n.* a dressing-room, esp. in a theatre. [contr. of ATTIRE]

†**tire**[4], *v.t.* to pull to pieces, to rend. *v.i.* to sieze upon and tear prey; to gloat (over). [OF *tirer,* see TIRADE]

tireless, etc. TIRE[1,2].

Tiresias, Teiresias, *n.* in Greek mythology, a man blinded by the gods and given the ability to predict the future.

tirl, *v.i.* (*Sc.*) to quiver, to vibrate; to make a rattling noise. *v.t.* to strip; to lay bare; to unclothe; to unroof. *n.* a twirl, a twist; a turn; a wheel resembling a lantern-wheel used in a mill. **tirl-mill,** *n.* **tirlie-wirlie,** *n.* a whirligig; an ornament consisting of irregularly interlacing lines. *a.* tortuous, intricate, irregular. [var. of TRILL[2]]

tiro TYRO.

Tirol, *n.* federal province of Austria; area 12,600 sq km/ 4864 sq miles; population (1987) 610,000. Its capital is Innsbruck, and it produces diesel engines, optical instruments, and hydroelectric power. Tirol was formerly a province (from 1363) of the Austrian Empire, divided 1919 between Austria and Italy (see Trentino-Alto Adige). **Tirolese,** *a.* pertaining to the Tirol, in Austria. *n.* a native of Tirol.

Tironian, *a.* pertaining to a system of shorthand attributed to Tiro. [L *Tiro -ōnis,* freedman and amanuensis of Cicero]

Tirpitz, *n.* **Alfred von** (1849–1930), German admiral. As secretary for the navy 1897–1916, he created the modern German navy and planned the World War I U-boat campaign.

tirra-lirra, *n.* a warbling sound as of a lark, horn etc. [OF *tirelire,* imit.]

†**tirret** TERRET.

†**tirrit,** *n.* (*Shak.*) a fright, an upset. [prob. corr. of TERROR]

tirrivee, *n.* (*Sc.*) an ill-tempered outburst, a tantrum. [etym. doubtful]

Tirso de Molina, *n.* (pen name of Gabriel Telléz) (1571–1648), Spanish dramatist and monk, who wrote more than 400 plays, of which eight are extant, including comedies, historical and biblical dramas, and a series based on the legend of Don Juan.

tirwit, *n.* the lapwing. [imit. of cry]

Tiryns, *n.* ancient Greek city in the Peloponnese on the plain of Argos, with remains of the Mycenaean culture.

'tis, short for IT IS.

tisane, *n.* a ptisan; a medicinal infusion of dried leaves or flowers. [PTISAN]

Tishri, Tisri, *n.* the first month of the Hebrew civil and the seventh of the ecclesiastical year, corresponding to parts of September and October. [Heb. *tishrī*]

tisic, etc. PHTHISIC.

Tissot, *n.* **James (Joseph Jacques)** (1836–1902), French painter who produced detailed portraits of fashionable Victorian society during a ten-year stay in England.

tissue, *n.* any fine, gauzy, or transparent woven fabric; a fabric of cells and their products, forming the elementary substance of plant and animal organs; a fabrication, a connected series (of lies, accidents etc.); tissue paper; a paper handkerchief. *v.t.* to form into tissue; to interweave, to variegate. **tissue culture,** *n.* the growing of pieces of biological tissue in a nutritive medium in a laboratory. **tissue-paper,** *n.* a thin, gauzy, unsized paper, used for wrapping articles, protecting engravings etc. **tissue plasminogen activator (TPA),** *n.* a naturally-occurring substance in the body tissues which activates the enzyme plasmin, which is able to dissolve blood clots. Human TPA, produced in bacteria by genetic engineering, has been used to try to dissolve blood clots in the coronary arteries of heart attack victims. **tissue typing,** *n.* the ascertaining of types of body tissue, e.g. in order to match organs for transplant. **tissued,** *a.* [F *tissu,* p.p. of *tistre,* now *tisser,* L *tesere,* to weave]

Tit. (*abbr.*) Titus.

tit[1], *n.* a titmouse; a titlark; †a small horse; †a child, a girl; †a bit, a morsel. **titbit,** *n.* a delicate or dainty morsel of food or gossip. **titlark,** *n.* a small bird of the genus *Anthus,* esp. *A. pratensis,* the meadow-pipit. **titling,** *n.* a titmouse; a titlark. [Icel. *tittr,* bird, something small, cp. Norw. *tita*]

tit[2], *n.* a tap, a slight blow. **tit for tat,** blow for blow, retaliation (perh. *tip for tap*). [perh. corr. of TIP[2]]

tit[3], *n.* a teat or nipple; (*sl.*) a woman's breast. [OE, cp. TEAT]

Titan, *n.* (*Gr. Myth.*) one of the 12 children of Uranus and Gaia, of gigantic size and strength, who included Kronos, Rhea, Themis (mother of Prometheus and personification of law and order) and Oceanus; the sun-god as the offspring of Hyperion, one of the Titans; a person of superhuman strength or genius; in astronomy, largest moon of the planet Saturn, with a diameter of 5150 km/3200 miles, and a mean distance from Saturn of 1,222,000 km/759,000 miles. It was discovered in 1655 by Christiaan Huygens. *a.* Titanic. **Titanesque, Titanic,** *a.* **The Titanic,** British passenger liner, supposedly unsinkable, that struck an iceberg and sank off the Grand Banks of Newfoundland on its maiden voyage Apr. 14–15, 1912; 1513 lives were lost. In 1985 it was located by robot submarine 4 km/2.5 miles down in an ocean canyon, preserved by the ice-cold environment. In 1987 salvage operations began. **Titan rocket,** *n.* a family of US space rockets, developed from the Titan intercontinental missile. Two-stage Titan rockets launched the Gemini manned missions. More powerful Titans, with additional stages and strap-on boosters, were used to launch spy satellites and space probes, including Viking and Voyager. **Titaness,** *n. fem.* **Titano-,** *comb. form.* [L and Gr., cogn. with Sansk. *tithā,* fire]

titanium, *n.* a dark-grey metallic element, at. no. 22; chem symbol Ti; found in small quantities in various minerals. **titanium dioxide,** *n.* a white pigment. **titanate,** *n.* a salt of titanic acid. **titanic,** *a.* of quadrivalent titanium. **titaniferous,** *a.* **titanite,** *n.* an intensely hard titanosilicate of calcium, sphene. **titano-,** *comb. form.* **titanous,** *a.* [prec.]

titbit TIT[1].

titch, *n.* (*coll.*) a very small person; a very small amount. **titchy,** *a.* [Little *Tich,* d. 1928, music-hall comedian]

titfer, *n.* (*sl.*) a hat. [rhyming sl. *tit for tat*]

tithe, *n.* the 10th part of anything; a tax of one-tenth, esp. of the yearly proceeds from land and personal industry, payable for the support of the clergy and Church. *v.t.* to impose tithes upon. **tithe barn,** *n.* a barn in which the parson stored his corn and other tithes. **tithe-pig,** *n.* one pig out of 10 set apart for tithe. **tithable,** *a.* **tither,** *n.* **tithing,** *n.* the taking or levying of tithes; a civil division consisting of 10 householders living near each other bound as sureties for each other's good behaviour. †**tithing-man,** *n.* the chief man of a tithing; a peace-officer; an under-constable. [OE *tēodha* (TEN, -TH), whence *tēothian*]

titi[1], *n.* the New Zealand diving petrel. [Maori]

titi[2], *n.* a small brightly-coloured S American monkey. [Sp., from Tupi]

Titian, *n.* (**Tiziano Vecellio**) (*c.* 1487–1576), Italian painter, active in Venice, one of the greatest artists of the High Renaissance. In 1533 he became court painter to Charles V, Holy Roman emperor, whose son Philip II of Spain later became his patron. Titian's work is richly coloured, with inventive composition. He produced a vast number of portraits, religious paintings, and mythological scenes, including *Bacchus and Ariadne* (1520–23), *Venus and Adonis* (1554), and the *Entombment of Christ* (1559).

titian, *a.* reddish-brown in colour. [It. artist *Titian,* 1477–1576]

Titicaca, *n.* lake in the Andes, 3810 m/12,500 ft. above sea level; area 8300 sq km/3200 sq miles, the largest lake in S America. It is divided between Bolivia (port at Guaqui) and Peru (ports at Puno and Huancane). It has huge edible frogs.

titillate, *v.t.* to tickle; to excite or stimulate pleasurably. **titillation** *n.* [L *titallātus,* p.p of *titillāre,* to tickle]

titivate, *v.t., v.i.* to dress up, to adorn, to make smart. **titivation,** *n.* [prob. arbitrary]

titlark TIT[1].

title, *n.* an inscription serving as a name or designation, esp. of a book, chapter, poem etc.; the entire contents of the title page of a book; a book or publication; a brief part of this containing the essentials; a title page; the distinguishing formula at the head of a legal document, statute etc.; a division of a document, treatise etc., including caption and text, as arranged for reference; a personal appellation denoting office, nobility, distinction, or other qualification; (*Law*) the right to ownership of property; the legal evidence of this; a title-deed; an acknowledged claim; the grounds of this; fineness, esp. of gold, expressed in carats; (*Eccles.*) a source of income and a fixed sphere of duty required as a condition precedent to ordination; (*Rome*) a church or parish; a subtitle in a film; (*pl*). the credits in a film; in a sport, a championship. *v.t.* to give a title to. **title-deed,** *n.* a legal instrument giving the evidence of a person's right to property. **title-holder,** *n.* one holding a title in sport. **title page,** *n.* the page at the beginning of a book giving the subject, author's name etc. **title-rôle,** *n.* the character or part from whose name the title of a play is taken. **titled,** *a.* bearing a title of nobility. **titleless,**, *a.* **titling**, *n.* the act of impressing the title on the back of a book. [OF, from L *titulus*]

titling TIT[1]; TITLE.

titmouse, *n.* (*pl.* **-mice**) a small insectivorous bird of the subfamily Parinae, usu. nesting in holes in tree-trunks. [TIT[1] and OE *mase,* a name for several small birds]

Tito, *n.* (adopted name of Josip Broz) (1892–1980), Yugoslav soldier and communist politician. In World War II he organized the National Liberation Army to carry on guerrilla warfare against the German invasion 1941, and was created marshal 1943. As prime minister 1946–53 and president from 1953, he followed a foreign policy of 'positive neutralism'. **Titoism**, *n.* the kind of Communism introduced by Pres. Tito in Yugoslavia as opposed to that of Russia. **Titoist,** *n.*

Titograd (formerly **Podgorica**), *n.* capital of Montenegro, Yugoslavia; population (1981) 132,300. Industries include metal working, furniture making, and tobacco. It was damaged in World War II, and after rebuilding was renamed 1948 in honour of Tito. It was the birthplace of the Roman emperor Diocletian.

titrate, *v.t.* to determine the amount of a particular constituent in a solution by adding a known quantity of another chemical capable of reacting upon it. **titration** *n.* **titre**, *n.* the concentration of a substance in a solution, as ascertained by titration. [F *titre,* proportion of fine metal in an alloy (cp. TITLE, -ATE]

titter, *v.i.* to laugh in a restrained manner, to snigger, to giggle. *n.* a restrained laugh. **titterer,** *n.* [ME *titeren,* freq. of *tit-*, imit.]

tittie[1], *n.* (*Sc. coll.*) a sister. [perh. childish dim. of SISTER]

tittie[2], *n.* childish dim. of TIT[3].

tittle[1], *n.* any small diacritic or punctuation mark; a particle, an iota. [ME *titel,* from L *titulus,* TITLE; cp. TILDE]

tittle[2], *v.t., v.i.* (*dial.*) to tickle. [prob. var. of TICKLE]

tittlebat STICKLEBACK.

tittle-tattle, *n.* gossip. *v.i.* to gossip. [redupl. from TATTLE]

tittup, *v.i.* (*coll.*) to go, act, or behave in a lively manner, to prance, to frisk. *n.* a tittuping action or movement. **tittupy,** *a.* [etym. doubtful]

titubation, *n.* fidgeting or stumbling caused by nervous disorder. [L *titubātio,* from *titubāre,* to totter]

titular, *a.* existing in name or in title only, or holding a title without the office or duties attached, nominal; of, pertaining to, or held in virtue of a title; conferring a title. *n.* one who holds the title of an office or benefice without the authority or duties pertaining to it. **titularly,** *adv.* **titulary,** *a., n.* [F *titulaire,* from L *titulus*]

Titus, *n.* **Flavius Sabinus Vespasianus** (AD 39–81), Roman emperor from AD 79. Eldest son of Vespasian, he stormed Jerusalem AD 70 to end the Jewish revolt in Roman Palestine. He completed the Colosseum, and enjoyed a peaceful reign, except for Agricola's campaigns in Britain.

tiver, *n.* (*dial.*) a red ochre used for marking sheep. *v.t.* to mark (a sheep) with tiver. [OE *tēafor,* cp. Icel. *taufr,* secret writing, sorcery]

tizzy, *n.* (*sl.*) a sixpence; a state of extreme agitation (also **tizz**). [corr. of TESTER[3]]

Tl, (*chem. symbol*) thallium.

Tlingit, *n.* N American Indian people, living on the SE coast and nearby islands. They carved wooden totem poles bearing animals: the mythical 'thunderbird', raven, whale, octopus, beaver, bear, and wolf.

TLR camera, *n.* a twin-lens reflex camera that has a viewing lens of the same angle of view and focal length mounted above and parallel to the taking lens.

TLS, (*abbr.*) Times Literary Supplement.

TM, (*abbr.*) trademark; transcendental meditation.

Tm, (*chem. symbol*) thulium.

tmesis, *n.* (*Gram.*) the separation of the parts of a compound word by inserting one or more words between. [L and Gr., from Gr. *temnein,* to cut]

TN, (*abbr.*) Tennessee; trade name.

TNT, (*abbr.*) trinitrotoluene.

to, *prep.* in a direction towards (a place, person, thing, state or quality); as far as; no less than, in comparison with, in respect of, in correspondence with; concerning; in the relation of, for, as; against, adjoining; before; accompanied by (music); preceding the indirect object or the person or thing affected by the action etc.; the sign of the infinitive mood, expressing futurity, purpose, consequence etc., limiting the meaning of adjectiveness, or forming verbal nouns; (*ellipt.*) denoting the infinitive of a verb mentioned or understood. *adv.* towards the condition or end required; into the normal condition, esp. to a standstill or a state of adjustment; †forward, on. **as to** AS. **to and fro** FRO. **to-be,** *a.* about to be (always after the noun, as *mother-to-be*). **to-do,** *n.* fuss, commotion. [OE *tō,* cp. Dut. *toe,* G *zu,* Rus. *do*]

†**to-,** *pref.* expressing disjunction or disruption, as in *to-break, to-burst.* [OE *to-*, cp. G *zer-*, also L DIS-]

toad, *n.* a tailless amphibian like a frog, usu. with a warty body, terrestrial except during breeding; a repulsive or detestable person. **toad-eater,** *n.* an obsequious parasite, a sycophant. **toad-eating,** *a., n.* **toad-fish,** *n.* a batrachoid fish of the Atlantic coast of N America. **toad-flax,** *n.* a perennial herb of the genus *Linaria,* usu. with yellow or bluish personate flowers. **toad-in-the-hole,** *n.* a piece of beef, sausage, or the like, baked in batter. **toad-spit,** *n.* cuckoo-spit. †**toad-spotted,** *a.* spotted like a toad; polluted. **toadstool** *n.* an umbrella-shaped fungus, esp. a poisonous mushroom. [OE *tādige,* etym. doubtful]

toadstone, *n.* a stone coloured and shaped somewhat like a toad, or supposed to have been found in the body of a toad, formerly worn as a talisman; an igneous rock of Carboniferous age, occurring in veins and sheets in limestone, named from its barrenness in metalliferous ores. [G *todtes gestein,* dead stone]

toady, *n.* a toad-eater. *v.t.* to fawn upon, to play the toady to. **toadyish,** *a.* **toadyism,** *n.*

toast, *n.* a slice of bread browned at the fire, eaten dry, buttered or with some other dish; a drinking or a call for drinking to the health of some person, cause, sentiment etc., (from the old custom of putting toast in liquor perh. through an incident recorded in the *Tatler*); the person or other object of this; (*dated*) a woman often toasted. *v.t.* to brown (bread), cook (bacon etc.), or warm (the feet etc.) at an open fire; to drink to the health or in honour of. *v.i.* to be toasted. **on toast,** of food, served on a piece of toast; at one's mercy. **toast and water** or **toast-water,** *n.* a cooling drink made by pouring boiling water on toast. **toast-master, -mistress** *n.* an official who announces the toasts at public dinners etc. **toast-rack,** *n.* a table-utensil for holding slices of toast. **toaster,** *n.* **toasting-fork,** *n.* a fork to hold bread, etc., for toasting. †**toasting-iron.** *n.* (*facet.*) a sword. [ME *tost,* from *toster,* to toast, L *torrēre,* to parch, p.p. *tostus*]

toa-toa, *n.* a red-wood New Zealand tree. [Maori]

tobacco, *n.* a plant of American origin of the genus *Nicotiona,* with narcotic leaves which are used, after drying and preparing, for smoking, chewing, snuff etc.; the leaves of this, esp. prepared for smoking. **tobacco-cutter,** *n.* a knife for cutting plug-tobacco; a device for shredding tobacco. **tobacco-heart,** *n.* smoker's heart. **tobacco-pipe,** *n.* a pipe used in smoking tobacco. **tobacco-plant,** *n.* **tobacco-pouch,** *n.* a pouch for carrying a small quantity of tobacco in. **tobacco-stopper,** *n.* a plug for pressing down tobacco in a pipe. **tobacconist,** *n.* a dealer in tobacco. [Sp. *tabaco,* prob. from Taino, roll of leaves for smoking]

Tobago, *n.* island in the W Indies; part of the republic of Trinidad and Tobago.

tobine, *n.* a stout twilled silk used for dresses. [G *Tobin,* Dut. *tabijn,* TABBY]

toboggan, *n.* a long low sled used for sliding down snow- or ice-covered slopes. *v.i.* to slide on a toboggan. **toboggan-shoot, -slide,** *n.* a prepared course for tobogganing, on a hillside or a timber structure. **tobogganer,** †**ist,** *n.* **tobogganing,** *n.* [Algonquin]

Tobruk, *n.* Libyan port; population (1984) 94,000. Occupied by Italy 1911, it was taken by Britain 1941, and unsuccessfully besieged by Axis forces Apr.–Dec. 1941. It was captured by Germany June 1942 after the retreat of the main British force to Egypt, and this precipitated the replacement of Auchinleck by Montgomery as British commander.

toby, *n.* a mug or jug shaped like an old man wearing a three cornered hat. [personal name, *Tobias*]

†**toby-man,** *n.* (*sl.*) a highwayman. [prob. Shelta *tobar,* road, MAN]

toccata, *n.* a composition orig. designed to exercise the player's touch. **toccatella**, **toccatina**, *n.* a short or easy toccata. [It., p.p. of *toccare,* to TOUCH]

tocher, *n.* (*Sc.*) a woman's dowry. *v.t.* to give a dowry to. **tocherless,** *a.* [Gael. *tochar*]

toco, toko, *n.* (*sl.*) corporal punishment, castigation. [perh. Gr. *tokos,* interest on a loan (see foll.); perh. Hind. *tokna,* to castigate]

tocology, *n.* obstetrics. [Gr. *tokos,* birth, from *tiktein,* to bring forth, -LOGY]

tocopherol, *n.* vitamin E. [Gr. *tokos,* birth, *pherein,* to bear, bring, -OL]

Tocqueville, *n.* **Alexis de** (1805–59), French politician and political scientist, author of the first analytical study of the US constitution *De la Démocratie en Amérique/Democracy in America* (1835), and of a penetrating description of France before the Revolution, *L'Ancien Régime et la Révolution/The Old Regime and the Revolution* (1856).

tocsin, *n.* an alarm-bell; the ringing of an alarm-bell, an alarm-signal. [MF *toquesing* (OF *toquer,* to TOUCH, *sing,* SIGNAL)]

tod[1], *n.* **on one's tod,** (*sl.*) on one's own. [rhyming slang, *on one's Tod Sloan* (name of an American jockey)]

tod[2], *n.* a bush, esp. of thick ivy; a bunch, a mass; an old weight for wool, usu. 28 lb (12.7 kg); a fox, from his bushy tail. [Icel. *toddi,* tod or wool, cp. Dut. *todde,* G *Zolle,* rag]

today, to-day, *adv.* on or during this or the present day; at the present day. *n.* this day. [OE *todæge,* for or on (this) day]

Todd[1], *n.* **Alexander, Baron Todd** (1907–), British organic chemist, who won the Nobel prize for chemistry 1957 for his work on the role of nucleic acids in genetics. He also synthesized vitamins B_1, B_{12}, and E.

Todd[2], *n.* **'Ron' (Ronald)** (1927–), British trade union leader. The son of a London market trader, he rose from shop steward to general secretary of Britain's largest trade union, the Transport and General Workers' (TGWU). A naturally honest and forthright man, although backing the Labour Party leadership, he has openly criticized its attitude towards nuclear disarmament.

toddle, *v.i.* to walk with short unsteady steps, as a child; to walk in a careless or leisurely way, to saunter. *v.t.* to walk (a certain distance etc.) thus. *n.* a toddling walk; a stroll. **toddler,** *n.* (*coll.*) a toddling child. [var. of TOTTER[1]]

toddy, *n.* the fermented juice of various palm trees; a beverage of spirit and hot water sweetened. [Hind. *tādi, tāri,* from Hind. and Pers. *tār,* palm]

tody, *n.* a small W Indian insectivorous bird allied to the American kingfishers. [L *tōdus*]

toe, *n.* one of the five digits of the foot, the part of a boot, stocking etc., covering the toes; the fore part of the hoof of a horse etc.; the calk in the front of a horse-shoe; a projection from the foot of a buttress etc., to give it greater stability; the end of the head of a golf-club; the lower end or a projecting part in a shaft, spindle, rod, lever, organ pipe etc. *v.t.* to touch (a line, mark etc.) with the toes; to furnish (socks, shoes etc.) with toes; (*Golf*) to strike (a ball) with the toe of a club; (*sl.*) to kick. **on one's toes,** alert, ready to act. **to toe in** or **out,** to turn the toes in or out in walking etc. **to toe the line,** to conform, to bow to discipline. **to tread on someone's toes,** to offend someone. **to turn up one's toes,** (*sl.*) to die. **toecap,** *n.* a stiffened part of a boot or shoe covering the toes. **toehold,** *n.* in climbing, a small foothold; any slight or precarious means or access or progress. **toe-ragger,** *n.* (*Austral. sl.*) a tramp. (also **toe-rag**) (*British sl.*) a mean or despicable person. **toed,** *a.* (*usu. in comb.* as *three-toed*). **toeless,**, *a.* [OE *tā,* cp. Dut. *teen,* G *Zehe,* Icel. *tā,* Dan. *taa*]

toff, *n.* (*sl.*) a swell, a dandy, a person of consequence. [poss. from *tuft,* a titled undergraduate]

toffee, toffy, *n.* a sweetmeat made of boiled sugar or molasses and butter. **toffee-apple,** *n.* a toffee-coated apple on a stick. **toffee-nosed,** *a.* (*sl.*) conceited, arrogant. [F and Malay *tafia*]

to-fore, *prep., adv.* before. [OE *tōforan*]

toft, *n.* a homestead; (*Law*) a place where a messuage has stood; (*dial.*) a hillock or knoll. †**toftman,** *n.* one occupying a toft. **toftstead,** *n.* [late OE, from Icel. *topt,* pron. 'toft']

tofu, *n.* unfermented soya bean curd. [Jap.]

tog[1], *n.* (*sl.*) (*usu. in pl.*) clothes. *v.t.* (*past, p.p.* **togged**) to dress (up or out), esp. in one's best. **long togs,** (*Naut.*) shore-clothes. **toggery,** *n.* [perh. from foll.]

tog[2], *n.* a unit of measurement of the heat insulation of clothing, fabrics etc. [TOG[1]]

toga, *n.* a loose flowing robe, the principal outer garment of an ancient Roman citizen. **toga praetexta** PRAETEXTA. **toga virilis**, the toga assumed by the ancient Roman at the age of 14. **togaed**, †**togated**, †**toged,** *a.* [L, cogn. with *tegere,* to cover]

together, *adv.* in company or union, conjointly, unitedly; in the same place or at the same time; into union, so as to unite or be joined; without cessation or intermission. *a.* (*coll.*) competent, assured, composed, well-organized. **to get it together,** (*coll.*) to succeed in (doing something); to become well-organized. **togetherness,** *n.* a friendly feeling of being together as a group. [OE *tōgædere* (TO, *gador,* together, see GATHER]

toggery TOG.

toggle, *n.* a pin put through a loop or eye at the end of a rope for securing this; a cross-piece for securing a watch-chain; the barb of a toggle-iron; a toggle-joint; (*pl.*) a kind of rope ladder made with a single rope having cross-pieces fastened in the middle; (*Comput.*) a switch which is pressed to turn a feature on or off. **toggle-harpoon, iron,** *n.* a harpoon with a movable barb pivoted so as to turn in the animal's flesh. **toggle-joint,** *n.* a knee-joint formed by two plates hinged together so as to change the direction of pressure from vertical to horizontal. **toggle-press,** *n.* a press acting by means of toggle-joints. **toggle-switch,** *n.* an electric switch with a projecting lever which is pushed, usu. up or down. [prob. dim. of *tog,* cogn. with TUG]

Togliatti, *n.* **Palmiro** (1893–1964), founding member of the Italian Communist Party in 1921, and effectively leader for almost 40 years from 1926 until his death. In exile from 1926 until 1944, he returned to become a member of Badoglio's government and held office until 1946.

Togo[1], *n.* Republic of (*République Togolaise*), a country in W Africa, bounded to the W by Ghana, to the E by Benin, and to the N by Burkina Faso. **area** 56,800 sq km/21,930 sq miles. **capital** Lomé. **physical** two savanna plains, divided by a range of hills NE–SW. **population** (1986) 3,423,000; annual growth rate 3%. **exports** cocoa, coffee, coconuts, copra, phosphate, bauxite. **language** French (official), many local languages. **religion** traditional 60%, Muslim 20%, Christian 20%.

Togo[2], *n.* **Heihachiro** (1846–1934), Japanese admiral who commanded the fleet at the battle of Tsushima Strait 27 May 1905 when Japan decisively defeated the Russians and effectively ended the Russo-Japanese war of 1904–05.

togue, *n.* the great N American lake trout. [from native name]

toheroa, *n.* an edible mollusc on the New Zealand shores. [Maori]

toho, *int.* a call to a pointer or setter to halt.

Tohoku, *n.* mountainous region of N Honshu island, Japan; population (1986) 9,737,000; area 66,971 sq km/25,867 sq miles. Timber, fruit, fish, and livestock are produced. Chief city is Sendai. It is linked to the island of Hokkaido by the Seikan tunnel, the world's longest underwater tunnel.

tohu-bohu, *n.* confusion, chaos. [Heb. *thōhū wabhōhū,* emptiness and desolation]

toil[1], *v.i.* to labour with pain and fatigue of body or mind; to move or progress painfully or laboriously. *v.t.* to fatigue or wear out with toil. *n.* hard and unremitting work, labour, drudgery. **toil-worn,** *a.* worn with toil. **toiler,** *n.* **toilful, toilsome,** *a.* **toilfully, toilsomely,** *adv.* **toilless,** *a.* **toilsomeness,** *n.* [A-F *toiler,* to strive, prob. from OF *toillier,* to mix, to trouble, L *tudiculāre,* from *tudicula,* machine for bruising olives, dim. of *tudes,* mallet, cogn. with *tundere,* to beat]

toil[2], *n.* (*now in pl.*) a net or snare. [F *toile,* see foll.]

toile, *n.* cloth; a model of a garment made up in cheap cloth. [F, from L TELA]

toiler TOIL[1].

toilet, *n.* the act or process of dressing etc.; style or fashion of dress; dress, costume (also **toilette**); a toilet-table; a cover for this; a water-closet; (*Med.*) the cleansing of a part after an operation etc. **to make one's toilet,** to dress, arrange one's hair etc. **toilet-cover,** *n.* a cloth for a toilet-table. **toilet-paper,** *n.* soluble paper for use in a water-closet. **toilet-service, -set,** *n.* a set of utensils for a toilet-table. **toilet-soap,** *n.* **toilet-table,** *n.* a dressing-table with looking-glass etc. **toilet-training,** *n.* training a child to control its bowels and bladder and to use a lavatory. **toilet water,** *n.* a form of perfume lighter than an essence. **toiletry,** *n.* (*often pl.*) an article or preparation used in washing or beautifying oneself. [F *toilette,* dim of TOILE]

toilful, etc. TOIL[1].

toilinet(te), *n.* a fabric of silk and cotton with woollen filling. [dim. of TOILE]

toise, *n.* an old French measure of length = about $6\frac{1}{2}$ ft. (2 m). [F, ult. from L *tensa,* orig. neut. pl. p.p. of *tendere,* see TENSE[2]]

Toison d'or, *n.* the Golden Fleece, esp. as the Spanish and Austrian order or knighthood. [F *toison,* fleece (L *tonsio ōnem,* from *tondere,* to shear), *d'or,* of gold]

Tojo, *n.* **Hideki** (1884–1948), Japanese general and prime minister 1941–44. Promoted to chief of staff of the Guangdong army 1937, he served as minister for war 1938–39 and 1940–41. He was held responsible for defeats in the Pacific 1944 and forced to resign. He was hanged as a war criminal.

Tokay, *n.* a rich aromatic wine made at Tokaj in Hungary; a white grape from which it is made.

token, *n.* something representing or recalling another thing, event etc.; a sign, a symbol; an evidence, an indication, a symptom; a memorial of love or friendship, a keepsake; a sign proving authenticity; a piece of metal like a coin, formerly issued by tradesmen, banks etc., representing money of greater intrinsic value; a metal or plastic disk used instead of a coin, e.g. in a slot machine; a voucher that can be used as payment for goods to a certain value. *a.* serving as a token; nominal, perfunctory, done, given, invited etc. for form's sake only. †*v.t.* to make known, to betoken; to mark, to betroth. **by the same token,** in corroboration. **more by token** MORE[1]. **token payment,** *n.* a small payment made to indicate that the debt or obligation is not repudiated. **tokenism,** *n.* the practice of making only a token effort. **tokenless,** *a.* [OE *tācen, tācn* (cp. Dut. *teeken,* G *Zeichen,* Icel. *teikn*), cogn. with TEACH]

toko TOCO.

Tokyo, *n.* capital of Japan, on Honshu Island; population (1987) 8,209,000, the metropolitan area of Tokyo over 12,000,000. The Sumida river delta separates the city from its suburb of Honjo. It is Japan's main cultural and industrial centre (engineering, chemicals, textiles, electrical goods). Founded in the 16th cent. as Yedo, it was renamed when the emperor moved his court there from Kyoto 1868. An earthquake in 1923 killed 58,000 people. The city was severely damaged by Allied bombing in World War II. The subsequent rebuilding has made it into one of the world's most modern cities.

tola, *n.* a unit of weight for gold and silver, usu. about 180 grains Troy. [Hind.]

tolbooth TOLL[1].

told, *past, p.p.* TELL.

†tole TOLL[2].

Toledo[1], *n.* city on the river Tagus, Castilla–La Mancha, central Spain; population (1982) 62,000. It was the capital of the Visigoth kingdom (534–711), then became a Moorish city, and was the Castilian capital 1085–1560. **Toledo**[2], *n.* a sword or sword-blade made at Toledo in Spain. **Toledan,** *a., n.*

tolerate, *v.t.* to suffer, to endure, to permit by not preventing or forbidding; to abstain from judging harshly or condemning (persons, religions, votes, opinions etc.); to sustain, to endure (pain, toil etc.); to sustain (a drug etc.) with impunity. **tolerable,** *a.* endurable, supportable; passable, fairly good. **tolerableness,** *n.* **tolerably,** *adv.* **tolerance,** *n.* the act or state of toleration; permissible variation in weight, dimension, fitting etc. **tolerant,** *a.* showing toleration. **tolerantly,** *adv.* **toleration** *n.* the act of tolerating; the spirit of tolerance; recognition of the right of private judgment in religious matters and of freedom to exercise any forms of worship. **tolerationist,** *n.* **tolerator** *n.* [L *tolerātus,* p.p. of *tolerāre,* cogn. with *tollere,* to bear, cp. Gr. *tlēnai,* to suffer]

Tolkien, *n.* **J(ohn) R(onald) R(euel)** (1892–1973), English writer, who created the fictional world of Middle Earth in *The Hobbit* (1937) and the trilogy *The Lord of the Rings* (1954–55), fantasy novels peopled with hobbits, dwarves, and strange magical creatures. His work became a cult in the 1960s and had many imitations.

toll¹, *n.* a tax or duty charged for some privilege, service etc., esp. for the use of a road, bridge, market etc.; a portion of grain taken by a miller as compensation for grinding; damage, deaths, etc., suffered in an accident, natural disaster etc. *v.i.* to pay toll; to take toll. †*v.t.* to levy or collect (a toll). **toll-bar, -gate,** *n.* a gate or bar placed across a road to stop passengers or vehicles till toll is paid. **tolbooth, tollbooth,** *n.* (*Sc.*) a town jail; orig. a temporary structure for the collection of market-tolls. **toll-bridge,** *n.* a bridge where toll is charged for passing over it. **toll call,** *n.* (formerly) a short-distance trunk call; (*N Am.*) a long-distance telephone call. **toll-dish,** *n.* a vessel for measuring the proportion of grain paid as toll. †**toll-gatherer, -man,** *n.* **toll-house,** *n.* the house at a toll-gate occupied by a toll-collector. **tollable,** *a.* **tollage,** *n.* **toller,** *n.* [OE *toll, toln* (cp. Dut. *tol,* G *Zoll,* Icel. *tollr*), perh. from late L. *tollōnium, telōnium,* Gr. *telōnion* toll-house, from *telos,* tax]

toll², *v.t.* to cause (a bell) to sound with strokes slowly and uniformly repeated; to give out (a knell etc.) with a slow, measured sound (of a bell, clock etc.); to ring on account of. *v.i.* to sound or ring (of a bell) with slow, regular strokes. *n.* a tolling or a stroke of a bell. **toller,** *n.* [ME *tollen,* to attract, to entice, etym. doubtful]

†**toll³**, *v.t.* (*Law*) to take away; to annul. [AF *toller,* L *tollere*]

tollable, tollage, etc. TOLL¹.

toller¹, ² TOLL¹, ²

Tolpuddle Martyrs, *n.pl.* six farm labourers of Tolpuddle, near Dorchester, England, who were transported to Australia in 1834 for forming a trade union. After nationwide agitation they were pardoned two years later.

Tolstoy, *n.* **Leo Nikolaievich** (1828–1910), Russian novelist, who wrote *Tales from Sebastopol* (1856), *War and Peace* (1863–69), and *Anna Karenina* (1873–77). From 1880 Tolstoy underwent a profound spiritual crisis and took up moral positions including passive resistance to evil, rejection of authority (religious or civil) and of private ownership, and a return to basic mystical Christianity. He was excommunicated by the Orthodox Church, and his later works banned.

tolt, *n.* (*Law*) a writ transferring a cause from a court-baron to a county court. [A-F *tole,* med. L *tolta,* from *tollere,* to TOLL³]

Toltec, *n.* member of an American Indian people who ruled much of Mayan central Mexico in the 10th–12th cent., with their capital at Tula. Their religious centre was at Teotihuacán, where there are temples of the Sun and Moon, and to their serpent god Quetzalcoatl. *a.* of or pertaining to this people. **Toltecan,** *a.* [Mex. Sp. *tolteca*]

tolu, *n.* a balsam derived from a S American tree, *Myroxylon balsamum.* **toluate,** *n.* a salt of toluic acid. **toluene,** *n.* a liquid compound belonging to the aromatic series. **toluic,** *a.* [Santiago de *Tolú,* seaport in Colombia]

tom, *n.* a male animal, esp. a tom-cat. **long tom,** a long gun of large bore; a long swivel-gun carried amidships. **Old Tom,** a strong variety of gin. **Tom and Jerry,** a hot drink of rum and water with eggs beaten up etc. **Tom, Dick and Harry,** average commonplace people, any taken at random. **tom-boy,** *n.* a romping girl, a hoyden; †a boisterous boy. **tom-cat,** *n.* a male cat. **Tom Collins,** a collins made with gin. **tom-fool,** *n.* a ridiculous fool, a trifler. *a.* very foolish. *v.i.* to play the fool, to act nonsensically. **tomfoolery,** *n.* **tom-noddy,** *n.* a blockhead, a dolt; the puffin. **Tom Thumb,** *n.* a midget. **tom-tit,** *n.* a small bird, a tit, esp. a titmouse. [short for *Thomas*]

tomahawk, *n.* a N American Indian battle-axe or hatchet with a stone, horn, or steel head. *v.t.* to strike or kill with a tomahawk; to criticize or review savagely; (*Austral.*) to cut a sheep when shearing. [Algonquin]

tomalley, *n.* the soft, fatty, greenish so-called liver of the lobster. [var. of TOURMALINE]

toman, *n.* a former Persian gold coin worth about 10000 dinars. [Pers. *tūmān*]

Tomasi, Giuseppe, Prince of Lampedusa LAMPEDUSA.

tomato, *n.* (*pl.* **-toes**) the red or yellow pulpy edible fruit (used as a vegetable) of a trailing plant, *Lycopersicon esculentum,* of the nightshade family or Solanaceae, orig. S American and formerly called the love-apple; the plant itself. [Sp. and Port *tomate,* Nahuatl *tomatl*]

tomb, *n.* a grave; a vault for the dead; a sepulchral monument. *v.t.* to bury, to entomb. **tombless,** *a.* **tombstone,** *n.* a stone placed as a memorial over a grave. [OF *tumbe* (F *tombe*), L Gr. *tumba, tumbos,* prob. cogn. with TUMULUS]

tombac, tomback, *n.* one of various copper and zinc alloys. [F *tombac,* Port. *tambaca,* Malay *tambaga,* Sansk. *tāmrakam,* copper]

Tombaugh, *n.* **Clyde (William)** (1906–), US astronomer, who discovered the planet Pluto in 1930.

tombola, *n.* an instant lottery at a fête etc. [It., from *tombolare,* to TUMBLE]

tomboy, tom-cat, etc. TOM.

Tombstone, *n.* former silver-mining town in the desert of SE Arizona, US. The gunfight at the OK Corral, deputy marshal Wyatt Earp, his brothers, and 'Doc' Holliday against the Clanton gang, took place here 26 Oct. 1881.

tom-cod, *n.* a gadoid fish, esp. *Microgadus tomcod,* common on the Atlantic coast of the US; applied to other fish.

tome, *n.* a volume, esp. a ponderous one. [F, from L *tomus,* Gr. *tomos,* section, from *temnein,* to cut]

-tome, *suf.* used to form nouns, meaning a cutting instrument of a specified kind, as *microtome*. [Gr. *tomē,* a cutting, *tomos,* a slice; see also -TOMY]

tomentum, *n.* a pubescence consisting of matted woolly hairs; (*Anat.*) the inner surface of the pia mater, flocculent with tiny vessels. **tomentose, -ous,** *a.* [L wool-stuffing]

tom-fool, etc. TOM.

†**tomin,** *n.* a jeweller's weight of 12 grains. [Sp., from Arab. *tomn,* one-eighth]

tommy, *n.* a British private soldier (from *Tommy Atkins,* of disputed orig.); (*sl.*) bread, food, provisions, esp. carried by workmen or given to them in lieu of wages; this method of payment, the truck system; a form of wrench; a rod inserted in a box-spanner. **soft tommy,** (*Naut.*) soft bread, opp. to hard tack. **tommy-gun,** *n.* a short-barrelled, quick-firing firearm, popular name for Thompson submachine-gun. **tommy rot,** *n.* (*coll.*) nonsense. **tommy-shop,** *n.* a shop or other place where the truck system is in force. [fam. form. of TOM]

tomography, *n.* diagnostic radiography of plane sections of the human body. [Gr. *tomos,* a slice, -GRAPHY]

tomorrow, to-morrow, *n.* the next day after today, the morrow. *adv.* on or during this. **like there's no tomorrow,** (*coll.*) recklessly, extravagantly. [TO, MORROW, as TODAY]

tompion¹, *n.* a lithographic inking-pad; a tampon; a tampion. [var. of TAMPION under TAMP]

†**tompion²**, *n.* a watch (properly one made by Thomas *Tompion* (1639–1713) a London clockmaker, or one of the same type)

tom-tit TOM.

tom-tom, *n.* a long, narrow, hand-beaten drum used in India, Africa, etc. *v.i.* to beat this. [Hindi, *tam-tam,* imit.]

-tomy, *suf.* indicating cutting (as *anatomy*) or surgical incision (as *phlebotomy*). [Gr. *-tomia,* from *temnein,* to cut]

ton¹, *n.* a measure of weight, 20 cwt or 2240 lb. av. (1016.05 kg), also called **long ton**; (*N Am.*) 2000 lb. av. (907.18 kg) also called **short ton**; 1000 kg (2205 lb. av.), also called **metric ton, tonne**; a measure of capacity (for timber or cargo on shipboard, 40 cubic ft. (1.132 cu. m); stone, 16 cubic ft. (0.453 cu. m); wheat, 20 bushels (728 l); lime, 40 bushels (1456 l)); a measure of the displacement of a ship, 2240 lb. av. (1016.05 kg)

35 cu. ft. (0.991 cu. m) of sea water, also called **displacement ton,** a measure of the cargo space on a ship, 100 cu. ft. (2.83 cu. m), also called **register ton**; (*coll.*) an unspecified great weight; (*usu. pl., coll.*) a large quantity; (*sl.*) £100; (*sl.*) 100 mph. **-tonner,** *comb. form* a ship of a specified tonnage, as a 3000-*tonner.* [var. of TUN]

ton², *n.* the prevailing fashion or mode. **tonish,** *a.* **tonishness,** *n.* **tony¹,** *a.* (*sl.*) [F, TONE]

tonal, *a.* pertaining to tone or tonality; having tonality. **tonality,** *n.* (*Mus.*) the character or quality of a tone or tonal system; a system of tones, a key; (*Painting*) the general colour-scheme of a picture. **tonally,** *adv.*

to-name, *n.* (*Sc.*) a distinguishing name added to a surname; a nickname.

tondo, *n.* a majolica plate with a wide decorated rim. **tondeno,** *n.* a tondo with a bowl-like centre; an astragal. [It., from L *rotundus,* ROUND²]

tone, *n.* sound, with reference to pitch, quality, and volume; a musical sound; modulation or inflexion of the voice to express emotion etc.; general disposition, temper, mood, prevailing sentiment, spirit; timbre; an interval of a major second; an ancient psalm-tune, esp. one of the Gregorian tones; (*Gram.*) syllabic stress; degree of luminosity of a colour; the general effect of a picture, esp. as regards colour and luminosity, the tint or shade of colour; the shade or colour of a photographic print; healthy general condition of the bodily organs, tissues etc. *v.t.* to give tone or quality to; to tune; to modify the colour of a photographic picture by a chemical bath. *v.i.* to harmonize in colour, tint etc.; to receive a particular tone or tint. **to tone down,** to subdue, to soften (the tint, tone, pitch, intensity etc., of); to modify, to reduce, to soften (a statement, demands etc.); to become softer, less emphatic etc. **to tone up,** to become firmer, more vigorous; to heighten, intensify. **tone arm,** *n.* the pick-up arm of a record player. **tone-deaf,** *a.* unable to distinguish accurately between musical sounds of different pitch. **tone language,** *n.* a language in which variation of tone serves to distinguish between words otherwise pronounced in the same way. **tone poem,** *n.* an orchestral composition in one movement which illustrates a train of thought external to the music. **tone row,** *n.* the basic series of notes in serial music. **tone-wheel,** *n.* a high-speed commutator used for the reception of continous radio waves. **toned,** *a.* **toneless,,** *a.* **toner,** *n.* one who, or that which, tones; a lotion applied to the face to tighten the pores. **tonometer,** *n.* a tuning-fork or other instrument for determining the pitch of a tone; an instrument for measuring strains in liquids. [ME and F *ton,* L *tonus* Gr. *tonos,* from *teinein,* to stretch]

Tone, *n.* **(Theobald) Wolfe** (1763–98), Irish nationalist, called to the Bar in 1789, and prominent in the revolutionary society of the United Irishmen. In 1798 he accompanied the French invasion of Ireland, was captured and condemned to death, but slit his own throat in prison.

tong, *n.* a Chinese secret society. [Chin. *t'ang,* a meeting-place]

Tonga, *n.* Kingdom of (Friendly Islands), a country in the SW Pacific, in Polynesia. **area** 750 sq km/290 sq miles. **capital** Nuku'alofa on Tongatapu. **physical** comprises three groups of islands in the SW Pacific, mostly coral formations, but the western are actively volcanic. **population** (1988) 95,000; annual growth rate 2.4%. **language** Tongan and English. **religion** Wesleyan 47%, Roman Catholic 14%, Free Church of Tonga 14%, Mormon 9%, Church of Tonga 9%.

tonga, *n.* a light two-wheel cart for four persons. [Hindi *tanga*]

tongs, *n.pl.* an implement consisting of two limbs, usu. connected near one end by a pivot, used for grasping coals etc. (also **a pair of tongs**). [OE *tange,* sing. (cp. Dut. and Dan. *tang,* G. *Zange,* Icel. *töng*), cogn. with Gr. *daknein,* to bite]

tongue, *n.* a fleshy muscular organ in the mouth, used in tasting, swallowing and (in man) speech; the tongue of an ox, sheep etc., as food; a tongue-shaped thing or part; the clapper of a bell; the pin in a buckle; a piece of leather closing the gap in the front of a laced shoe; the index of a scale or balance; a vibrating slip in the reed of a flageolet and other instruments; a pointed rail in a railway-switch; a projecting edge for fitting into a groove in match-board; a long low promontory, a long narrow inlet; speech, utterance, the voice; manner of speech; a language; hence a nation, a race. *v.t.* to modify (the sounds of a flute etc.) with the tongue; to put a tongue on (matchboard etc.); (*poet.*) to speak; †to reproach, to reprove. *v.i.* to use the tongue in playing some wind instruments. **the gift of tongues,** the power of speaking in unknown tongues, esp. as miraculously conferred on the Apostles on the day of Pentecost. **to give tongue** GIVE¹. **to hold one's tongue** HOLD¹. **with one's tongue in one's cheek,** ironically. **tongue-bit,** *n.* a bit with a plate to prevent a horse from getting his tongue over the mouthpiece. **tongue-bone,** *n.* the hyoid bone. **tongue-lashing,** *n.* a severe scolding. **tongue-tie,** *n.* shortness of fraenum impeding movement of the tongue. **tongue-tied,** *a.* impeded in speach by this; afraid of or prevented from speaking freely. **tongue-twister,** *n.* a series of words difficult to articulate without stumbling. **tongued,** *a.* (*usu. in comb.*, as *loud-tongued*). **tongueless,** *a.* **tonguelet,** *n.* [OE *tunge* (cp. Dut. *tong,* G *Zunge.* Icel. and Swed. *tunga*), cogn. with L *lingua,* OL, *dingua*]

tonic, *a.* invigorating, bracing; of or pertaining to tones; (*Mus.*) pertaining to or founded on the key-note; (*Phonet.*) denoting a voiced sound; stressed; (*Path.*) pertaining to tension, unrelaxing (of spasms). *n.* a tonic medicine; tonic water; (*Mus.*) the key-note. **tonic sol-fa** [SOL-FA], *n.* a system of musical notation in which diatonic scales are written always in one way (the key-note being indicated), the tones being represented by syllables or initials, and time and accents by dashes and colons. **tonic sol-faist,** *n.* one versed in or advocating this system. **tonic water,** *n.* a carbonated drink flavoured with quinine often used as a mixer with alcoholic drinks. **tonically,** *adv.* **tonicity,** *n.* the state of being tonic; tone; elasticity or contractility of the muscles. [Gr. *tonikos* (TONE, -IC]

tonight, to-night, *n.* the present night; the night of today. *adv.* on or during this.

tonish, etc. TON².

tonite, *n.* a powerful explosive prepared from guncotton. [L *tonāre,* to thunder]

tonka bean, *n.* the fruit of a S American tree, *Dipterix odorata,* the fragrant seeds of which are used in perfumery. [Tupi *tonka*]

Tonkin Gulf Incident, clash that triggered US entry into the Vietnam War in Aug. 1964. Two US destroyers (USS *C Turner Joy* and USS *Maddox*) reported that they were fired on by North Vietnamese torpedo boats. It is unclear whether hostile shots were actually fired, but the reported attack was taken as a pretext for retaliatory air raids against North Vietnam. On 7 Aug. the US Congress passed the **Tonkin Resolution**, which allowed President Johnson 'to take all necessary steps, including the use of armed forces' to help SEATO (South-East Asia Treaty Organization) members 'defend their freedom'. This resolution formed the basis for the considerable increase in US military involvement in the Vietnam War; it was repealed in 1970.

tonnage, *n.* the carrying capacity or internal cubic capacity of a vessel expressed in tons; the aggregate freightage of a number of vessels, esp. of a country's merchant marine; a duty on ships, formerly assessed on tonnage, now on dimensions. **tonnage-deck,** *n.* the upper of two decks, the second from below of three or more. [TON¹]

tonne, *n.* the metric ton (see TON¹).

tonneau, *n.* the rear part of a motor-car containing the back seats. [F, cask]

-tonner TON¹.

tonometer TONE.

tonsil, *n.* either of two organs situated in the hinder part of the mouth on each side of the fauces. **tonsillar, tonsillitic,** *a.* **tonsillectomy,** *n.* surgical removal of the tonsils. **tonsillitis,** *n.* inflammation of the tonsils. [F *tonsille,* L *tonsilla,* a sharp stake, *pl.* tonsils, prob. dim. of *tonsa,* oar]

tonsorial, *a.* pertaining to a barber or his art. [L *tonsōrius,* from *tonsor -sōris,* barber, from *tondere* to shave, p.p. *tonsus*]

tonsure, *n.* the shaving of the crown (as in the Roman Catholic Church before 1972) or of the whole head (as in the Greek Church) on admission to the priesthood or a monastic order; the part of the head thus shaved; admission into holy orders. *v.t.* to shave the head of, to confer the tonsure on. [F, from L *tonsūra,* as prec.]

tontine, *n.* a form of annuity in which the shares of subscribers who die are added to the profits shared by the survivors, the last of whom receives the whole amount. [F, from Lorenzo *Tonti,* It. banker, originator, *c.* 1653]

Tonton Macoute, *n.* member of a private army of death squads on Haiti. The Tontons Macoutes were initially organized by François Duvalier, president of Haiti 1957–71.

tonus, *n.* tonicity; (*Path.*) a tonic spasm. [L, TONE]

Tony, *n.* (*pl.* **Tonys**) an annual American award by the League of New York Theaters to playwrights, performers, and technicians in Broadway plays. [Antoinette (*Tony*) Perry, d. 1946, US actress]

tony[1] TON[2].

†**tony**[2], *n.* a simpleton. [short for *Antony*]

too, *adv.* in excessive quantity, degree etc.; more than enough; as well, also, in addition, at the same time; moreover; (*coll.*) extremely, superlatively. **too-too,** *a.* (*dated*) gushing, affected. [TO]

tooart, *n.* a W Australian tree, *Eucalyptus gomphocephala,* yielding an intensely hard and durable wood valuable for ship building. [native name]

took, *past* TAKE.

tool, *n.* a simple implement, esp. one used in manual work; a machine used in the making of machines; (*fig.*) anything used as an instrument or apparatus in one's occupation or profession; a person employed as an instrument or agent, a cat's paw; (*bookbinding*) a handstamp or design used in tooling; (*sl.*) the penis. *v.t.* to impress designs on (a bookcover); (*sl.*) to drive (a coach, team of horses etc.). *v.i.* to work with a tool; (*sl.*) to drive, to ride. **tooled-up,** (*sl.*) carrying firearms. **tool-holder,** *n.* a device for pressing the tool against the work in a lathe; a handle for use with various tools. **toolmaker,** *n.* a worker who makes and repairs machine tools in a workshop, etc. **toolmaking,** *n.* **tool-post, -rest,** *n.* a device for supporting or holding the tool in a lathe. **toolroom,** *n.* the part of a workshop where tools are made or repaired. **tooler,** *n.* one who or that which tools; a stone-mason's broad chisel. **tooling,** *n.* [OE *tōl* (cp. Icel. *tōl,* pl.), cogn. with *tawian,* see TAW[1]]

toolache, *n.* (*Austral.*) Grey's wallaby, now extinct. [Abor.]

toom, *a.* (*Sc.*) empty. *v.t.* to empty. [ME *tom,* Icel. *tōmr,* cp. Swed. and Dan. *tom*]

toon, *n.* a large E Indian tree, *Toona ciliata,* with close-grained red wood. [Hind. *tun*]

toot[1], *v.i.* to make a noise with an instrument or the mouth like that of a horn; to give out such a sound; to call (of grouse). *v.t.* to sound (a horn etc.) thus; to give out (a blast etc.) on a horn. *n.* a tooting sound or blast. **tooter,** *n.* [cp. MSwed. and Norw. *tuta,* Icel. *thjōta,* LG *tuten,* MDut. *tuyten* of imit. orig.]

toot[2], *v.i.* (*obs. or dial.*) to peep about, to spy; to stand out, to be prominent. **toot-hill,** *n.* a look-out hill, a natural or artificial hillock formerly used as a watch-tower. [OE *tōtian,* see TOUT[1]]

tooth, *n.* (*pl.* **teeth**) one of the hard dense structures, originating in the epidermis, growing in the mouth or pharynx of vertebrates, and used for mastication; a false or artificial tooth made by a dentist; a tooth-like projection on the margin of a leaf etc.; a projecting pin, point, cog etc.; a discriminating taste, a palate; (*pl.*) powers, esp. to compel compliance. *v.t.* to furnish with teeth; to indent. *v.i.* to interlock. **in the teeth of,** in spite of; in direct opposition to; in the face of (the wind). **long in the tooth,** elderly, old (as in horses). **sweet tooth,** a liking for sweet things. **to cast in one's teeth** CAST[1]. **to one's teeth,** to one's face; in open opposition. **tooth and nail,** with all one's power. **to set the teeth on edge** EDGE. **to show one's teeth,** to adopt a threatening attitude. **toothache,** *n.* pain in the teeth. **tooth-bill,** *n.* the tooth-billed pigeon of Samoa. **tooth-billed,** *a.* (*Ornith.*) having tooth-like processes on the bill. **tooth-brush,** *n.* a small brush for the teeth. **tooth-comb,** *n.* a fine-toothed comb. **tooth-edge,** *n.* the tingling sensation in the teeth excited by grating sounds, etc. **toothed whale,** *n.* any of a number of whales having simple teeth, as porpoises etc. **tooth ornament** (*Arch.*) DOG'S-TOOTH. **tooth-paste, -powder,** *n.* paste or powder for cleaning the teeth. **toothpick,** *n.* a pointed instrument of bone, quill etc., for removing particles of food etc., from between the teeth. **toothwort** *n.* a herb, *Lathraea squamaria,* allied to the broom-rape, with tooth-like scales on the root-stock; the shepherd's purse, *Capsella bursa-pastoris,* and other plants. **toothful** *n.* a small draught of liquor, etc. **toothing** *n.* fitting with teeth; projecting stones or bricks left in the end of a wall for bonding it to a continuation. **toothing-plane,** *n.* a plane for scoring the under-surface of a veneer. **toothless**, *a.* **toothlet,** *n.* **toothlike,** *a.* **toothsome**, *a.* palatable, pleasing to the taste. **toothsomely,** *adv.* **toothsomeness,** *n.* **toothy,** *a.* having prominent teeth. [OE *tōth,* cp. Dut. *tand,* G *Zahn,* Icel. *tönn,* also L *dens dentis,* Gr. *odous odontos*]

tootle, *v.i.* to toot gently or continuously, as on a flute; (*coll.*) to amble, to trot. [freq. of TOOT[1]]

tootsie, *n.* a child's word for a foot.

top[1], *n.* the highest part or point of anything, the summit; the upper side or surface; the upper part of a shoe etc.; the cover of a carriage etc.; (*N Am.*) the hood of a motor-car; the head of a page in a book; the part of a plant above ground; the uppermost part of a jointed fishing-rod; the crown of the head; the upper end or head of a table; the highest position, place, rank etc.; the highest degree, the apex, the culmination, the height; (*Naut.*) a platform round the head of a lower mast, forming an extended base for securing the topmast shrouds; (*pl.*) metal buttons plated or washed only on the face. *v.t.* (*past, p.p.* **topped**) to remove the top or extremity of (a plant, etc.); to put a top or cap on; to cover the top of; to rise to the top of, to surmount; to excel, to surpass, to be higher than; to be (of a specified height); (*Naut.*) to tip (a yard) so as to bring one end above the other; (*sl.*) to execute by hanging. *a.* being on or at the top or summit; highest in position, degree etc. **big top,** a big circus tent. **off the top of one's head,** without preparation, impromptu. **on top,** in the lead; in control. **on top of,** added to; in control of. **over the top,** on the attack; to excess. **to top oneself,** (*sl.*) to commit suicide esp. by hanging onself. **to top out,** to put the last or highest stone etc., on (a building). **to top off** or **up,** to complete by putting the top or uppermost part to; to finish, to complete. **to top up,** to fill up (with petrol, oil, etc.). **top-boot,** *n.* a boot having high tops, usu. of distinctive material and colour. **top brass,** *n.* (*sl.*) the highest-ranking officials or officers. **top-coat,** *n.* an overcoat. **top dog,** *n.* (*coll.*) the uppermost fellow, the boss. **top-dress,** *v.t.* to manure on the surface, as distinguished from digging or ploughing in. **top-dressing,** *n.* **top-flight,** *a.* of the highest rank or quality. **topgallant**, *a.* (*Naut.*) applied to the mast, rigging and sail, next above the topmast. **top-hamper,** *n.* the light upper sails and rigging; tackle, anchors, casks etc., encumbering the deck. **top-hat,** *n.* a tall silk cylindrical hat. **top-heavy,** *a.* having the top or upper part too heavy for the lower; (*coll.*) intoxicated. **top-hole,** *a.* (*sl, dated*) excellent, first rate. **top-knot,** *n.* an ornamental knot or bow worn on the top of the head; a tuft or crest growing on the head. **top-lantern, -light,** *n.*

one displayed from the mizzen-top of a flagship. **top-level,** *a.* at the highest level. **topman,** *n.* (*Naut.*) a man stationed in one of the tops; a top-sawyer. **topmast,** *n.* the mast next above the lower mast. †**top-proud,** *a.* excessively proud. **topsail,** *n.* a square sail next above the lowest sail on a mast; a fore-and-aft sail above the gaff. **top-sawyer,** *n.* the one in the upper position in pit-sawing; a person in a high or superior position; a first-rate man in anything. **top secret,** *a.* requiring the highest level of secrecy. **top side,** *n.* a cut of beef from the thigh; (*pl.*) the sides of a vessel above the water-line. **topsman,** *n.* (*Sc. or dial.*) a head servant, bailiff or overseer; a chief drover; (*sl.*) a hangman. **top-soil,** *n.* the upper layer of soil. *v.t.* to remove this from (a piece of ground). **top-soiling,** *n.* †**top-ful,** *a.* high, lofty. **topless,** *a.* without a top; of women's clothing, leaving the breasts bare; of an entertainment etc., featuring women with topless clothing. **topmost,** *a.* highest, uppermost. **topper,** *n.* one who or that which tops; fruit etc., of better quality put at the top in a basket etc.; (*coll.*) a top-hat. **topping,** *a.* (*sl.*) very fine, excellent. *n.* something which forms a top layer, esp. a sauce for food. **topping-up,** *n.* the addition of distilled water to an accumulator cell to compensate for loss by evaporation. **toppingly,** *adv.* [OE, cp. Dut. and Dan. *top,* Icel. *toppr,* Swed. *topp,* G. *Zopf,* tuft, tree-top]

top[2], *n.* a wooden or metal toy, usu. conical- or pear-shaped, made to rotate with great velocity on a metal point underneath, by the rapid unwinding of a string or spring or with the hand. **to sleep like a top,** to sleep very soundly. [late OE *topp,* ult. from MHG *Topf,* cogn. with DIP]

toparch, *n.* the ruler or chief man in a place or country, a petty king. **toparchy,** *n.* a little state or country governed by a toparch. [Gr. *toparchos* (*topos,* place, *-archos,* ruler, from *archein,* to rule)]

topaz, *n.* a transparent or translucent fluosilicate of aluminium, usu. white or yellow, but sometimes green, blue, red, or colourless, valued as a gem; a large and brilliant humming-bird. **topazolite,** *n.* a yellow or green variety of garnet resembling topaz. [OF *topaze,* L *topazus, topazion,* Gr. *topazos, topazion,* cp. Sansk. *tapas,* fire, from *tap,* to shine]

top-boot, -coat, -dress, etc TOP[1].

†**topful, topgallant** TOP[1].

tope[1], *n.* a grove, esp. of mango-trees. [Tamil *toppu*]

tope[2], *n.* a Buddhist monument in the form of a dome, tower or mound, usu. containing relics. [Hindi *top,* corr. from Sansk. *stūpa,* mound]

tope[3], *v.i.* to drink alcoholic liquors excessively or habitually, to tipple. **toper,** *n.* a tippler, a heavy drinker. [perh. from F *tôpe* (from *tôper,* to cover a stake in dicing), as an int. 'accepted! agreed!' afterwards a drinking phrase; or from Teut. as TOP[1], in alln. to putting the tops of the thumbs together and crying *topp*]

tope[4], *n.* a small shark of the genus *Galeus,* the dog-fish. [prob. Cornish]

toph, tophus, *n.* calcareous matter deposited round the teeth and at the surface of the joints in gout. **tophaceous,** *a.* [L *tōphus,* TUFA]

Tophet, *n.* a place in the valley of Hinnom, SE of Jerusalem, once used for idolatrous worship, and afterwards for the deposit of the city refuse, to consume which fires were continually kept burning; (*fig.*) hell. [Heb. *tōpheth*]

topi, topee, *n.* a sun-hat, a pith helmet. **sola topi,** *n.* a helmet made of sola pith. [Hind., hat]

topia, *n.* (*Rom. Ant.*) mural decoration for interiors, usu. consisting of fanciful landscapes, trees etc. **topiary,** *a.* shaped by cutting or clipping. *n.* the art of cutting and clipping trees or shrubs etc., into fanciful shapes. **topiarian,** *a.* **topiarist,** *n.* [L, fancy gardening, from Gr. *topos,* place]

topic, *n.* the subject of a discourse, argument, literary composition, or conversation; a remedy for external application to a particular part of the body. **topical,** *a.* pertaining to or of the nature of a topic comprising or consisting of allusions, esp. to current or local topics; local, esp. of a particular part of the body. **topically,** *adv.* [F *topiques,* L *topica,* Gr. *topika,* topics, neut. pl. of *topikos,* local, from *topos,* place]

topless, topman, etc. TOP[1].

topography, *n.* the detailed description of particular places; representation of local features on maps etc.; the artificial or natural features of a place or district; the mapping of the surface or the anatomy of particular regions of the body. **topographer,** *n.* **topographic, -al,** *a.* **topographically,** *adv.* [F *topographie,* late L and Gr. *topographia* (*topos,* place, -GRAPHY)]

topolatry, *n.* excessive veneration for or attachment to a place. **topology,** *n.* topography; the study of geometrical properties and relationships which are not affected by distortion of a figure. **topological,** *a.* **toponym,** *n.* a place-name. **toponomy, toponymy,** *n.* the science of place-names; a register of place-names of a district etc.; *n.* the naming of regions of the body. (also **toponymics**) **toponymic, -ical,** *a.*

topper, topping, etc. TOP[1].

topple, *v.i.* to totter and fall; to project as if about to fall. *v.t.* to cause to topple, to overturn. [freq. of TOP[1]]

topsail, top-sawyer, etc. TOP[1]

topsy-turvy, *adv., a.* upside down; in an upset or disordered condition. *adv.* in a confused manner. *n.* a topsy-turvy state. *v.t.* to turn topsy-turvy; to throw into confusion. **topsy-turviness, topsy-turvydom, topsy-turvyism,** *n.* [acc. to Skeat from TOP[1], so, obs. *terve,* allied to OE *tearflian,* to turn, to roll over, cp. LG *tarven,* OHG *zerben*]

toque, *n.* a small, brimless, close-fitting bonnet; a cap or head-dress, usu. small and close-fitting, worn at various periods by men and women; a monkey with a cap-like bunch of hair. [F, prob. from Breton *tok,* cp. W *toc*]

tor, *n.* a prominent hill or rocky peak, esp. on Dartmoor and in Derbyshire. [OE *torr,* W *tor,* knob, cogn. with L *turris,* whence W *twr,* tower]

-tor, *suf.* denoting the agent, as in *inspector, orator.* [-OR, after *t,* L p.p. stems]

Torah, *n.* in Judaism, the first five books of the Hebrew Bible (Christian Old Testament), which are ascribed to Moses. It contains a traditional history of the world from the Creation to the death of Moses; it also includes rules and guidelines for religious observance and social conduct, including the Ten Commandments.

torc TORQUE.

torch, *n.* a light made of resinous wood, twisted flax, hemp etc., soaked in oil or tallow, for carrying in the hand; an oil, electric, or other lamp used for this purpose, esp. when raised aloft on a pole etc.; a hand-lamp containing an electric battery and bulb. **to carry a torch for,** to suffer from unrequited love for. **torch-bearer,** *n.* **torch-dance,** *n.* a dance in which each performer carries a torch. **torch-fishing** or **torching,** *n.* fishing at night by torch-light. **torch-light,** *n.* **torch-race,** *n.* a race among the ancient Greeks, in which the runners carried lighted torches. **torch-singer,** *n.* **torch-song,** *n.* a sad song about unrequited love. **torcher,** *n.* **torchère,** *n.* (F) an ornamental stand for a lamp. [ME and F *torche,* late L *tortica,* from *torquēre,* twist, p.p. *tortus*]

torchon, *n.* a dish-cloth; a kind of coarse bobbin lace. **torchon-board,** *n.* a board on which torchon-paper is stretched. **torchon-paper,** *n.* a rough-surfaced paper used for water-colours etc. [F *torcher,* to wipe, as prec.]

torcular, *n.* a surgeon's tourniquet. [L, a press, from *torquēre,* to twist]

tore[1], *past* TEAR[1].

tore[2] TORUS.

tore[3], *n.* (*dial.*) the dead grass that remains on mowing land in winter and spring. [etym. unknown]

torea, *n.* the New Zealand oyster-catcher. [Maori]

toreador, *n.* a bull-fighter, esp. one who fights on horse-back. [Sp., from *torear,* to fight bulls, from *toro,* L *taurus*]

torero, *n.* (*pl.* **-ros**) a bullfighter, esp. one who fights on foot. [Sp., from late L *taurārius,* from L *taurus,* a bull]

toreutic, *a.* pertaining to carved, chased, or embossed work, esp. in metal. **toreutics,** *n.pl.* the art of this. **toreumatography**, *n.* a description of or treatise on toreutics. †**toreumatology**, *n.* [Gr. *toreutikos,* from *toreuein,* to bore, to chase]

torfaceous, *a.* growing in bogs, mosses etc. (of some plants). [TURF, -ACEOUS]

Torgau, *n.* town in Leipzig county, East Germany; population 20,000. In 1760, during the Seven Years' War Frederick II of Prussia defeated the Austrians nearby, and in World War II the US and Soviet forces first met here.

torgoch, *n.* a red-bellied variety of char. [W. *tor,* belly, *goch,* red]

tori, toric TORUS.

torii, *n.* (*pl.* **torii**) a gateless gateway composed of two up-rights with (usu.) three superimposed cross-pieces, at the approach to a Shinto temple. [Jap.]

torment¹, *n.* extreme pain or anguish of body or mind; a source or cause of this. [OF from L *tormentum,* a machine for hurling stones, a rack, torment, from *torquēre,* to twist]

torment², *v.t.* to subject to torment, to afflict, to vex, to irritate; †to torture. **tormentingly,** *adv.* **tormentor,** *n.* one who or that which torments; a heavy harrow on wheels; (*Naut.*) a long fork for lifting meat from the coppers. **tormentress,** *n. fem.*

tormentil, *n.* a low herb, *Potentilla tormentilla,* with four-petalled yellow flowers, the astringent root-stock of which is used for medicine. [F *tormentille,* late L. *tormentilla,* perh. from prec. with ref. to curing toothache]

tormina, *n. pl.* severe griping pains in the bowels. [L, from *torquēre,* see TORMENT¹]

torn, *p.p.* TEAR¹. **that's torn it,** (*coll.*) exclamation expressing annoyance at one's plans, activities etc., having been ruined.

tornado, *n.* (*pl.* **does**) a storm of extreme violence covering a very small area at once, but progressing rapidly, usu. having a rotary motion with electric discharges; (loosely) a very strong wind, a hurricane; a person or thing of great, usu. violent, energy. **tornadic,** *a.* [Sp. *tronada,* thunder-storm, from *tronar,* to thunder]

†**torneament** TOURNAMENT.

Torness, *n.* site of an advanced gas-cooled nuclear reactor 7 km/4.5 miles SW of Dunbar, East Lothian, Scotland. It started to generate power 1987.

toroa, *n.* a species of albatross. [Maori]

toroid, *n.* a figure shaped like a torus. **toroidal,** *a.* of or like a torus.

Toronto, *n.* port on Lake Ontario, capital of Ontario, Canada; metropolitan population (1985) 3,427,000. It is Canada's main industrial and commercial centre (banking, shipbuilding, cars, farm machinery, food processing, publishing), and also a cultural centre, with theatres and a film industry. A French fort was established 1749, and the site became the provincial capital (then named York) 1793; it was renamed Toronto (N Amer. Indian 'place of meeting') 1834, when incorporated as a city.

torous, †**-ose,** *a.* muscular, knobby; (*Bot.*) cylindrical with protuberances at intervals. [L *torōsus* from TORUS]

torpedo, *n.* (*pl.* **-does**) a long, cigar-shaped apparatus charged with explosive, used for attacking a hostile ship below the water-line; a submarine mine for defending harbours etc.; a detonating fog-signal placed on a railway track to be exploded by the wheels of a train; a cartridge for exploding in an oil-well etc.; a mine or shell buried in the way of a storming-party; a mixture of fulminate and grit exploded on the ground as a toy; an electric ray, a sea-fish having an electrical apparatus for disabling or killing its prey. *v.t.* to attack, blow up, or sink with a torpedo; to destroy or wreck suddenly. **aerial torpedo,** a torpedo launched from an aircraft. **torpedo-boat,** *n.* a small swift vessel fitted for firing torpedoes. **torpedo-net,** *n.* a wire net hung round a ship to intercept torpedoes. **torpedo-tube,** *n.* (*Nav.*) a tube for the discharge of torpedoes. **torpedoist,** *n.* [L, numbness (also the fish), from *torpēre,* to be numb]

torpid, *a.* having lost the power of motion or feeling; benumbed; dormant (of a hibernating animal); dull, sluggish, inactive. *n.* a second-class racing-boat at Oxford; (*pl.*) the Lenten races in which these compete. **torpefy,** *v.t.* †**torpent,** *a.* torpid. *n.* a torpifying medicine. **torpescent,** *a.* **torpescence,** *n.* **torpidity, torpidness, torpor,** *n.* **torpidly,** *adv.* **torporific,** *a.* [L *torpidus,* from *torpēre,* to be numb]

torque, *n.* a twisted necklace of gold or other metal, worn by the ancient Gauls etc.; (also **torc**) the movement of a system of forces causing rotation. **torquate, -ated,** *a.* (*Zool.*) having a ring of distinctive colour about the neck. **torqued,** *a.* twisted; (*Her.*) wreathed. [L *torquēs,* from *torquēre,* to twist]

Torquemada, *n.* **Tomás de** (1420–98), Spanish Dominican friar, confessor to Queen Isabella I. In 1483 he revived the Inquisition on her behalf, and at least 2000 'heretics' were burned; Torquemada also expelled the Jews from Spain, with a resultant decline of the economy.

torr, *n.* a unit of pressure, equal to 1/760 of a standard atmosphere. [after E. *Torricelli* (see TORRICELLIAN)]

torrefy, *v.t.* to dry or parch; to roast (ores etc.). **torrefaction,** *n.* [L *torrefacere* (*torrēre,* to parch, *facere,* to make)]

torrent, *n.* a violent rushing stream (of water, lava etc.); a flood (of abuse, passion etc.). *a.* rushing, impetuous. **torrential,** *a.* **torrentially,** *adv.* [F, from L *torrens -rentem,* pres.p. of *torrēre,* to parch]

Torreón, *n.* industrial and agricultural city in Coahuila state, N Mexico, on the river Nazas at an altitude of 1127 m/3700 ft.; population (1986) 730,000. Before the arrival of the railway (1907) Torreón was the largest of the Laguna cotton district tri-cities (with Gómez Palacio and Ciudad Lerdo). Since then it has developed as a major thoroughfare and commercial centre.

Torricelli, *n.* **Evangelista** (1608–47), Italian physicist and pupil of Galileo, who devised the mercury barometer. **Torricellian,** *a.* pertaining to the Italian physicist E. Torricelli. **torricellian tube,** *n.* the barometer. **torricellian vacuum,** *n.* the vacuum above the mercury in this.

torrid, *a.* dried up with heat, parched, scorching, very hot; intense, passionate. **torrid zone,** *n.* the broad belt of the earth's surface included between the tropics. **torridity, torridness,** *n.* **torridly,** *adv.* [F *torride,* L *torridus,* from *torrēre,* to parch]

torsade TORSE¹.

torsal TORSE².

torse¹, *n.* (*Her.*) a wreath. **torsade,** *n.* an ornamental twisted cord, ribbon, etc. [F, also *torce,* ult. from L *tors-,* p.p. stem of *torquēre,* to twist]

torse², *n.* (*Geom.*) a surface generated by a straight line continuously moving about some point or other in its length. **torsal,** *a.* [L *torsus* p.p. of *torquēre,* see prec.]

torse³ TORSO.

torsel, *n.* a twisted ornament, as a scroll; a block of wood fixed in a wall for a beam or joist to rest on. [prob. var. of TASSEL¹]

torsion, *n.* the act of twisting or the state of being twisted; (*Mech.*) the force with which a body tends to return to its original state after being twisted; (*Surg.*) twisting of the cut end of an artery for checking haemorrhage after an operation. **torsion balance,** *n.* an instrument for estimating very minute forces by the action of a twisted wire. **torsibility,** *n.* **torsional,** *a.* **torsionally,** *adv.* **torsionless,** *a.* [F, from L *tortiōnem,* nom. *-tio,* from *torquēre,* to twist]

torsk, *n.* a food-fish, *Brosmius brosme,* allied to the cod. [Dan. and Swed., cp. Icel. *thorskr*]

torso, *n.* (*pl.* **-sos**) the trunk of a statue or body without the head and limbs. [It., stump, stalk, from L THYRSUS]

tort, *n.* (*Law*) a private or civil wrong; †mischief, injury, calamity. **tortious,** *a.* **tortiously,** *adv.* [F, wrong, harm, L *tortus,* p.p. of *torquēre,* to twist]

torte, *n.* a rich gateau or tart, with fruit, cream etc. [G, from It. *torta,* from L; see TART²]

torticollis, *n.* a spasmodic affection of the neck-muscles, stiff-neck. [L *tortus,* see prec., *collum,* neck]
tortile, *a.* twisted, wreathed, coiled, curved. **tortility,** *n.* †**tortive,** *a.* (*Shak.*) [L *tortilis,* from *tortus,* see TORT]
tortilla, *n.* in Mexican cooking, a thin flat maize cake baked on an iron plate. [Sp., dim. of *torta,* TART2]
tortious, tortiously TORT.
†**tortive** TORTILE.
tortoise, *n.* a terrestrial or freshwater turtle; (*Rom. Ant.*) a testudo; a very slow person. **tortoiseshell,** *n.* the mottled horny plates of the carapace of some sea-turtles, used for combs, ornaments, inlaying etc. *a.* made of this; resembling this in marking and colour. **tortoiseshell butterfly,** *n.* any of the genus *Nymphalis,* with mottled yellow, orange and black wings. **tortoiseshell cat,** *n.* a female domestic cat with mottled yellow, brown and black coat. [ME *tortuce, tortu,* OF *tortue,* late L *tortūca,* from *tortus,* see TORT]
tortrix, *n.* a genus of British moths typical of the family Tortricidae, called the leaf-rollers. [mod. L, fem. of *tortor,* from *tort-,* p.p. stem of *torquēre,* to twist]
tortulous, *a.* (*Nat. Hist.*) bulging out at intervals, moniliform. [from late L *tortula,* dim. of *torta,* twist, see TORT]
tortuous, *a.* twisting, winding, crooked; roundabout, devious, not open and straightforward. **tortuose,** *a.* (*Bot.*) **tortuosity,** *n.* **tortuousness,** *n.* **tortuously,** *adv.* [ME and OF *tortuos* (F *tortueux*), L *tortūosus,* from *tortus,* twist, see TORT]
torture, *n.* the infliction of extreme physical pain as a punishment or to extort confession etc.; excruciating pain or anguish of mind or body. *v.t.* to subject to torture; to wrest from the normal position; to distort; to pervert the meaning of (a statement etc.). **torturable,** *a.* **torturer,** *n.* **torturingly,** *adv.* **torturous,** *a.* [F, from L *tortura,* as prec.]
torula, *n.* a chain of spherical bacteria; (*Bot.*) a genus of microscopic yeast-like fungi. **toruliform,** *a.* **torulose, -lous,** *a.* (*Bot.*) having alternate swells and contractions like the growth of torula. [dim. of TORUS]
torus, *n.* a semi-circular projecting moulding, esp. in the base of a column; the receptacle or thalamus of a flower, the modified end of a stem supporting the floral organs; (*Anat.*) a rounded ridge; (*Geom.*) a ring-shaped surface generated by a circle rotated about a line which does not intersect the circle. **toric,** *a.* [L, a prominence, a couch]
Torvill and Dean, *n.* Jayne Torvill (1957–) and Christopher Dean (1959–), British ice-dance champions, both from Nottingham. They won the world title four times and were the 1984 Olympic champions.
Tory, *n.* one of the party opposed to the exclusion of the Duke of York (James II) from the throne and to the Revolution of 1688; a member of the Conservative party; (*pl.*) this party. *a.* pertaining to the Tories. **Tory democracy,** *n.* a concept attributed to the 19th-cent. British Conservative Party, and to the campaign of Lord Randolph Churchill against Stafford Northcote in the early 1880s. The slogan was not backed up by any specific policy proposals. 'Tory democracy' was revived in the 1980s as a rallying cry for conservatives with a social conscience. **Tory Democrat,** *n.* **Tory Party,** *n.* name applied about 1680–1830 to the forerunner of the British Conservative Party. It was the party of the squire and parson, as opposed to the Whigs (supported by the trading classes and Nonconformists). The name is still applied colloquially to the Conservative Party. In the US a Tory was an opponent of the break with Britain in the War of American Independence 1775–83. **Toryism,** *n.* [orig. an Irish moss-trooper, from Ir. *toiridhe,* from *toir,* pursuit]
-tory, *suf.* forming nouns and adjectives, as *factory, oratory, perfunctory, rotatory.* [-ORY, cp. -TOR]
Toscana, *n.* Italian name for TUSCANY.
tosh1, *n.* (*sl.*) rubbish, nonsense. [etym. doubtful, cp. TUSH]
tosh2, *v.i.* to make tidy. [OF *touse,* L *tonsus,* clipped]
toss, *v.t.* (*past, p.p.* **tossed,** *poet.* **tost**) to throw up with the hand, esp. palm upward; to throw, to pitch, to fling, with an easy or careless motion; to throw back (the head) with a jerk; to jerk; to throw about or from side to side, to cause to rise and fall, to agitate; to throw (up) a coin into the air to decide a wager etc., by seeing which way it falls; hence, to settle a wager or dispute with (a person) thus; to separate the heavy from the lighter parts of (tin ore) by agitating the slime. *v.i.* to roll and tumble about, to be agitated; to throw oneself from side to side. *n.* the act of tossing; the state of being tossed. **to take a toss,** to be thrown by a horse. **to toss off,** to swallow at a draught; to produce or do quickly or perfunctorily; (*sl.*) to masturbate. **to toss up,** to toss a coin. **to win the toss,** to have something decided in one's favour by tossing up a coin. **toss-pot,** *n.* a toper, a drunkard. **toss-up,** *n.* the tossing up of a coin; a doubtful point, an even chance. **tosser,** *n.* **tossily,** *adv.* (*coll.*) pertly, indifferently. **tossy,** *a.* [Norw. *tossa,* cp. LG *teusen*]
tot1, *n.* anything small or insignificant, esp. a small child; (*coll.*) a dram of liquor. **tottie, totty,** *n., a.* [Icel. *tottr,* cp. Dan *tot*]
tot2, *n.* a sum in simple or compound addition. *v.t.* (*past, p.p.* **totted**) to add (up) *v.i.* to mount (up). **totting-up,** *n.* adding together to make a total, esp. driving offences until there are sufficient to cause disqualification. [L, so many, or short for foll.]
tot3, *n.* (*sl.*) something re-usable salvaged from a dustbin etc. **totter,** *n.* one who scavenges from dustbins etc.; a scrap-dealer. **totting,** *n.* [etym. doubtful].
total, *a.* complete, comprising everything or constituting the whole; comprising everything; absolute, entire, thorough. *n.* the total sum or amount; the aggregate. *v.t.* (*past, p.p.* **totalled**) to ascertain the total of; to amount to as a total; (*N Am., sl.*) to wreck (a car) completely in a crash. *v.i.* to amount (to) as a total. **total abstinence,** complete abstention from intoxicating liquors. **total recall,** *n.* the ability to remember the past in great detail. **total war,** *n.* warfare in which all available resources, military and civil, are employed. **totalitarian,** *a.* permitting no rival parties or policies; controlling the entire national resources of trade, natural wealth, and manpower. **totalitarianism,** *n.* **totality,** *n.* **totalize, -ise,** *v.t.* to total. *v.i.* to use a totalizator. **totalization, -isation,** *n.* **totalizator, -isator,** *n.* a machine for showing the total amount of bets staked on a race in order to divide the whole among those betting on the winner. **totally,** *adv.* [F, from late L *tōtālis,* from *tōtus* entire]
totara, *n.* the New Zealand red pine. [Maori]
tote1, *v.t.* to carry, to bear, to lead, to haul. **to tote fair,** to act fairly. **tote bag,** *n.* a large bag for shopping etc. **tote-road,** *n.* a rough road for carriers. [etym. doubtful]
tote2, *n.* short for TOTALIZATOR.
totem, *n.* a natural object, usu. an animal, taken as a badge or emblem of an individual or clan on account of a supposed relationship; an image of this. **totem-pole,** *n.* a post on which totems are carved or hung. **totemic, totemistic,** *a.* **totemism,** *n.* **totemist,** *n.* [Algonquin]
tother, t'other, *a., pron.* the other. [ME *thet* (THAT), OTHER]
totient, *n.* the number of totitives of a given number. **totitive,** *n.* a number less than another having with this no common divisor but unity. [L *totiēs,* from *tot,* so many, after QUOTIENT]
totipalmate, *a.* wholly webbed, steganopodus. **totipalmation,** *n.* [L *tōti-, tōtus,* whole, PALMATE]
totitive TOTIENT.
Totò, *n.* **Gagliardi Ducas Comneno di Bisan zio** (stage name of Antonio Furst de Curtis) (1898–1967), Italian comedian who moved to films from the music hall. Something of a national institution, his films, such as *Totò le Moko* (1949) and *L'Oro di Napoli/Gold of Naples* (1954), made him the most famous comic actor of his generation in Italy.
totter1, *v.i.* to walk or stand unsteadily, to stagger; to be weak, to be on the point of falling. **totterer,** *n.* **totteringly,** *adv.* **tottery,** †**totty,** *a.* [for *tolter,* freq.

cognate with ME *tulten, tilten,* TILT[2]]

totter[2] TOT[3].

tottie, totty TOT[1].

toucan, *n.* a brilliantly-coloured tropical American bird with an enormous beak. [Tupi *tucana* (Port. *tucano*)]

touch, *v.t.* to meet the surface of, to have no intervening space between at one or more points, to be in contact with, to come into contact with; to bring or put the hand or other part of the body or a stick etc., into contact with; to cause (two objects) to come into contact; to put the hand to (the hat etc.); to reach, to attain; to meddle, to interfere with; to injure slightly; to approach, to compare with; to impair; to concern, to relate to; to treat of hastily or lightly; to strike lightly, to tap, to play upon lightly, to mark or delineate lightly, to put (in) fine strokes with a brush etc.; to be tangent to; to produce a mental impression on; to affect with tender feeling, to soften; to excite the anger of, to rouse, to irritate; (*sl.*) to beg or borrow money. *v.i.* to come into contact (of two or more objects); to deal with or treat of (usu. with *on*) in a slight or hasty manner; to come to land, to call (at a port etc.) *n.* the act of touching; the state of touching or being touched, contact; the junction of two bodies at the surface, so that there is no intervening space; the sense by which contact, pressure etc., are perceived; a slight effort, a light stroke with brush or pencil; (*fig.*) a stroke, a twinge; a trace, a minute quantity, a tinge; characteristic manner or method of handling, working, executing, playing on the keys or strings of a musical instrument etc.; the manner in which the keys of a piano etc., respond to this; characteristic impress; intimate correspondence, intercourse, or communication, accord, sympathy; magnetization of a steel bar by contact with magnets; a test, a proof, a touchstone; (*Med.*) the exploring of organs etc., by touch; (*Football*) the part of the field outside the touch-lines and between the goal-lines. **to touch down,** (*Rugby*) to touch the ground with the ball behind the opponent's goal; to alight. **to touch lucky,** (*sl.*) to have a stroke of luck. **to touch off,** to cause to begin, to trigger. **to touch on** or **upon,** to allude to; to deal with (a subject etc.) briefly. **to touch up,** to correct or improve by slight touches, as paint or make-up, to retouch; to strike or stimulate (a horse, etc.) gently. **touch-and-go,** *n.* a state of uncertainty. *a.* highly uncertain, very risky or hazardous. **touch-down,** *n.* a touching down. **touch-hole,** *n.* the priming hole or vent of a gun. **touch-lines,** *n.pl.* (*Football*) the two longer or side boundaries of the field. **touch-me-not,** *n.* the plant noli-me-tangere. **touch-needle,** *n.* a needle of gold alloy of known composition employed in assaying other alloys by comparison of the marks made on the touchstone. **touchpaper,** *n.* paper saturated with nitrate of potash for igniting gunpowder etc. **touchstone,** *n.* a dark stone, usu. jasper, schist, or basanite used in conjunction with touch-needles for testing the purity of gold and other alloys; a standard, a criterion. **touch-type,** *v.i.* to type without looking at the typewriter keyboard. **touch-typing,** *n.* **touchwood,** *n.* a soft white substance into which wood is converted by the action of fungi, easily ignited and burning like tinder. **touchable,** *a.* **touched,** *a.* moved by some emotion, e.g. pity or gratitude; (*coll.*) slightly insane. **toucher,** *n.* one who or that which touches; (*sl.*) a close shave, a narrow squeak. **touching,** *a.* affecting, moving, pathetic. *prep.* concerning, with regard to. **touchingly,** *adv.* **touchingness,** *n.* [ME *touchen,* OF *tuchier, tochier* (F. *toucher*), It. *toccare* prob. of imit. orig.]

touché, *int.* acknowledging a hit in fencing, or a point scored in argument. [F, p.p. in *toucher,* to TOUCH]

touchy, *a.* apt to take offence, irascible, irritable. **touchily,** *adv.* **touchiness,** *n.* [corr. of TETCHY]

tough, *a.* firm, strong, not easily broken; resilient, not brittle; able to endure hardship; viscid, stiff, tenacious; stubborn, unyielding; aggressive, violent; laborious; difficult; (*coll.*) hard, severe (of luck etc.) *n.* (*N Am.*) a rough, a bully. **toughen,** *v.t., v.i.* **toughish,** *a.* **toughly,** *adv.* **toughness,** *n.* [OE *tōh,* cp. Dut. *taai,* G *zähe*]

Toulon, *n.* port and capital of Var *département*, SE France, on the Mediterranean Sea, 48 km/30 miles SE of Marseille; population (1983) 410,000. It is the chief Mediterranean naval station of France. Industries include oil refining, chemicals, furniture, and clothing. Toulon was the Roman *Telo Martius*, and was made a port by Henry IV. It was occupied by the British 1793, and Napoleon first distinguished himself in driving them out. In World War II the French fleet was scuttled here to avoid its passing to German control.

Toulouse, *n.* capital of Haute-Garonne *département*, S France, on the river Garonne SE of Bordeaux; population (1982) 541,000. The chief industries are textiles and aircraft construction (Concorde was built here). Toulouse was the capital of the Visigoths (see GOTH), and later of Aquitaine AD 781–843. The university was founded 1229 to combat heresy.

Toulouse-Lautrec, *n.* **Henri Marie Raymond de** (1864–1901), French artist, associated with the impressionists. He was active in Paris, where he painted entertainers and prostitutes. From 1891 his lithograph posters were a great success.

toupee, toupet, *n.* an artificial lock or curl of hair; a small wig to cover a bald spot. [F *toupet,* dim. of OF *toup,* tuft, see TOP[1]]

tour, *n.* a journeying round from place to place in a district, country etc.; an extended excursion or ramble; a circuit; a shift or turn of work or duty, esp. a period of duty on a foreign station; a trip made by a theatrical company or solo performer, sports team etc., stopping at various places to play. *v.i.* to make a tour. *v.t.* to make a tour through. **Tour de France,** a French road race for professional cyclists held annually over approximately 4800 km/3000 miles of French roads. The race takes about three weeks to complete and the route varies each year, often taking in adjoining countries, but always ending in Paris. A separate stage is held every day, and the overall leader at the end of each stage wears the coveted leader's 'yellow jersey' (French *maillot jaune*). **touring car, tourer,** *n.* a large, long car with room for a lot of luggage. **tour operator,** *n.* a travel agency which organizes package tours. **tourism,** *n.* organized touring, esp. from or to a foreign country. **tourist,** *n.* a person making a tour, esp. a holidaymaker or sportsman. **tourist class,** *n.* the lowest category of passenger accommodation in a ship or aircraft. **tourist ticket,** *n.* a railway or other return or circular ticket issued on special terms. **tourist trap,** *n.* a place tawdrily got up to appeal to the ignorant tourist. **touristy,** *a.* full or tourists; designed to attract tourists. [F, from *tourner* to TURN]

touraco, *n.* a brilliantly-coloured African bird of the genus *Turacus corythaix*. [F, from native name]

tourbillion, *n.* a firework revolving in the air so as to represent a fiery scroll or spiral. [F *tourbillon,* whirlwind]

tourist TOUR.

tourmaline, *n.* a black or coloured transparent or translucent silicate with electrical properties, some varieties of which are used as gems. [F, from Sinhalese *tōramalli*]

tournament, *n.* a contest, exercise, or pageant in which mounted knights contested, usu. with blunted lances etc.; any contest of skill in which a number of persons take part. [ME *tornement,* OF *torneiement,* from *torneier,* to TOURNEY]

tournay, *n.* a printed worsted material used in upholstery. [*Tournay,* in Belgium]

tournedos, *n.* (*pl.* **-dos**) a thick round fillet steak. [F *tourner,* to TURN, *dos,* the back]

Tourneur, *n.* **Cyril** (1575–1626), English dramatist. Little is known about his life but *The Atheist's Tragedy* (1611) and *The Revenger's Tragedy* (1607) (thought by some scholars to be by Middleton) are among the most powerful of Jacobean dramas.

tourney, *n.* a tournament, *v.i.* to engage in a tournament. [ME and OF *tornei,* from *torneier,* L *tornāre,* to TURN]

tourniquet, *n.* a bandage for compressing an artery and checking haemorrhage. [F, from *tourner*, to TURN]

tournure, *n.* the curving outline or contour of a figure; a characteristic outline or contour in a drawing, etc.; a pad worn by women to give the effect of well-rounded hips; the drapery at the back of a dress. [F]

tousle, *v.t.* to pull about; to disarrange, to rumple, to dishevel, to put into disorder. *v.i.* to toss about, to rummage. *n.* a tousling, a romp; a tousled mass (of hair etc.). †**touse,** *v.t.* to tousle; to tear at, to worry. **tously, tousy,** *a.* [freq. of *touse*, ME *tūsen*, cp. G *zausen*]

tous-les-mois, *n.* a food starch got from the roots of species of Canna, esp. *C. edulis*, a perennial Peruvian herb. [F, every month]

Toussaint L'Ouverture, *n.* **Pierre Dominique** (*c.* 1743–1803), Haitian revolutionary leader, born a slave. He joined the insurrection of 1791 against the French colonizers and was made governor by the revolutionary French government. He expelled the Spanish and British, but when the French emperor Napoleon reimposed slavery he revolted, was captured, and died in prison in France. In 1983 his remains were returned to Haiti.

tout¹, *v.i.* to solicit custom in an obtrusive way; to observe secretly, to spy (esp. on horses in training for a race). *n.* one employed to tout; one who watches horses in training and supplies information; one who sells tickets (esp. for over-booked theatrical or sporting events) at very high prices (also **ticket tout**). **touter,** *n.* [ME *tūten*, var. of *toten*, OE *tōtian*, to project, to peep out, cp. TOOT²]

tout², *v.t.* (*Sc.*) to annoy, to vex, to tease. *v.i.* to have a fit of ill humour. *n.* such a fit; a slight illness. [etym. doubtful]

tout³, *a.* all, whole. *adv.* entirely. **tout à fait**, entirely. **tout de suite**, immediately. **tout ensemble**, all together. **tout le monde**, everybody.

tovaris(c)h, *n.* comrade. [Rus. *tovarishch*]

tow¹, *v.t.* to pull (a boat, ship etc.) through the water by a rope etc.; to pull a vehicle behind another; to drag (a net) over the surface of water to obtain specimens; to pull, to drag behind one. *n.* the act of towing; the state of being towed. **in tow,** being towed; following; under control or guidance. **on tow,** of a vehicle, being towed. **tow-bar,** *n.* a strong bar on the back of a vehicle for attaching a trailer. **towboat,** *n.* a tug; a boat, barge etc., that is being towed. **tow(ing)-line, -rope,** *n.* a hawser or rope used in towing. **tow(ing)-net,** *n.* one for towing along the surface of water to collect specimens. **tow(ing)-path,** *n.* a track beside a canal or river for animals towing barges etc. **towable,** *a.* **towage,** *n.* [OE *togian*, cp. Icel. *toga*, OHG *zogōn*, also L *dūcere*, to lead, and Eng. TUG]

tow², *n.* the coarse broken part of hemp or flax after heckling etc. **tow-headed,** *a.* having very pale hair. **towy,** *a.* [OE *tow-*, spinning (in *towlīc*, fit for spinning)]

towai, *n.* a tree from which bark for tanning is obtained. [Maori]

toward¹, towards, *prep.* in the direction of; as regards, with respect to; for, for the purpose of; near, about. †*adv.* in preparation, at hand. [OE *tōweard* (TO, -WARD(S))]

†**toward²,** *a.* docile, obedient; ready to learn or do, apt; †forward, advanced. †**towardly,** *a.* **towardliness,** †**towardness,** *n.* [as prec.]

towel, *n.* an absorbent cloth for wiping and drying after washing etc.; (*sl.*) a cudgel, also called an oaken towel. *v.t.* (*past, p.p.* **towelled**) to wipe with a towel; (*sl.*) to thrash. *v.i.* to wipe onself with a towel. **towel-horse,** *n.* a wooden stand on which to hang towels. **towelling,** *n.* material for making towels; (*sl.*) a thrashing. [ME *towaille*, OF *toaille* (F. *touaille*), OHG *twahila*, *dwahila* (whence G *Zwehle*), from *twahan*, to wash, cp. OE *thwēan*]

tower, *n.* a structure lofty in proportion to the area of its base, and circular, square, or polygonal in plan, frequently of several stories, insulated, or forming part of a church, castle, or other large building; (*Elec.*) a pylon; a place of defence, a protection. *v.i.* to rise to a great height, to soar; to be relatively high, to reach high (above). **Tower of London,** fortress on the Thames bank to the E of the City. The keep, or White Tower, was built about 1078 by Bishop Gundulf on the site of British and Roman fortifications. It is surrounded by two strong walls and a moat (now dry), and was for centuries a royal residence and the principal state prison. **tower block,** *n.* a very tall residential or office building. **towered,** *a.* **towering,** *a.* very high, lofty; (*fig.*) violent, outrageous (of passion etc.). **towery,** *a.* [ME *tour*, *tūr* (later OE *torr*), OF *tor* (F *tour*), Land and Gr. *turris*]

Tower, *n.* **John** (1925–), US Republican politician, a Texas senator 1961–83. Despite having been a paid arms-industry consultant, he was selected in 1989 by President Bush to serve as defence secretary, but the Senate refused to approve the appointment because of Tower's alleged heavy drinking.

town, *n.* a collection of dwelling-houses larger than a village, esp. one not constituted a city; this as contrasted with the country; the people of a town; the chief town of a district or neighbourhood, esp. London; †a collection of dwellings enclosed by a wall or other defence. **to go to town,** (*coll.*) to let oneself go, to drop all reserve. **town and gown** GOWN. **town adjutant, town major,** *n.* (*Hist.*) a garrison officer appointed to maintain discipline. **town-clerk,** *n.* formerly, the clerk to a municipal corporation; the keeper of the records of a town. **town-council,** *n.* the governing body in a town. **town-councillor,** *n.* **town-crier** CRIER. **town gas,** *n.* manufactured coal gas, opp. to *natural gas*. **town hall,** *n.* a large public building for the transaction of municipal business, public meetings, and entertainments etc. **town house,** *n.* a private residence in town, opp. to country house; a town hall; a modern urban terraced house, esp. a fashionable one. **town-planning,** *n.* the regulating of the laying out or extension of a town. **town-planner,** *n.* **townscape,** *n.* a picture of an urban scene; the visual design of an urban development. **town-talk,** *n.* the subject of general conversation. **townee,** *n.* (*sl.*) one who habituallly or for preference lives in town. **townish,** *a.* **townless,** *a.* **townlet,** *n.* **townsfolk,** *n.pl.* (*collect.*) the people of a town or city. **township,** *n.* a division of a large parish, comprising a village or town; (*Hist.*) the inhabitants of a parish, village etc., regarded as a corporate body; (*N Am.*) a territorial district subordinate to a county invested with certain administrative powers; (*Austral.*) any town or settlement, however small; in S Africa, an urban area designated for non-white people. **townsman,** *n.* an inhabitant of a town; one's fellow citizen. **townspeople,** *n.pl.* (*collect.*). **Townswomen's Guilds, National Union of,** in the UK, an urban version of the Women's Institute. It was founded 1929. **townward,** *a., adv.* **townwards,** *adv.* [OE *tūn* (cp. Dut. *tuin*, Icel. *tūn*, *G Zaun*, hedge), cogn. with DUN³]

Townes, *n.* **Charles** (1915–), US physicist who, while working at Columbia, New York, succeeded in 1953, against much competition, in designing and constructing the first maser. For this work, he shared the 1964 Nobel physics prize with Soviet physicists Basov and Prokhorov.

Townsend, *n.* **Sue** (1946–), English humorous novelist, author of *The Secret Diary of Adrian Mole, aged 13¾* (1982) and later sequels.

Townshend, *n.* **Pete** (1945–), UK rock musician, former member of the Who.

towy TOW².

toxaemia, (*esp. N Am.*) **toxemia**, *n.* blood-poisoning. [Gr. *haima*, blood]

toxanaemia, (*esp. N Am.*) **toxanemia**, *n.* anaemia due to blood-poisoning.

tox(i)-, toxico-, *comb. form* poisonous. [TOXIC]

toxic, *a.* of or pertaining to poison; poisonous. **toxically,** *adv.* **toxicant,** *a.* poisonous. *n.* a poison. **toxication,** *n.* **toxicity**, *n.* **toxicology**, *n.* the branch of medicine treating of poisons and their antibodies. **toxicologist,** *n.* **toxicological**, *a.* **toxicologically,** *adv.*

toxicomania, *n.* a morbid desire for poison. **toxicosis**, *n.* a morbid state due to the action of toxic matter. **toxigenic**, *a.* producing poison. **toxiphobia**, *n.* unreasonable fear of being poisoned. **toxic shock syndrome,** a group of symptoms including vomiting, fever and diarrhoea, attributed to the use of tampons by menstruating women, thought to be caused by a toxin arising from staphylococcal infection. [med. L *toxicus,* from L *toxicum,* Gr. *toxikon* (*pharmation*), (poisonous drug) for arrows, from *toxa,* pl., arrows, from *toxon,* bow]

toxin, *n.* a poisonous compound causing a particular disease; any poisonous ptomaine.

toxocariasis, *n.* a disease in humans caused by the larvae of a parasitic worm (*Toxocara*) found in cats and dogs, causing damage to the liver and eyes.

toxophilite, *n.* one skilled in or devoted to archery. *a.* pertaining to archery. **toxophilitic**, *a.* [Gr. *toxon,* bow]

toy, *n.* a plaything, esp. for a child; something of an amusing or trifling kind, not serious or for actual use. *v.i.* to trifle, to amuse oneself, to sport, to dally. **toyboy,** *n.* (*coll.*) a (woman's) very young lover. **toy dog, spaniel,** or **terrier** a pigmy variety of dog kept as a curiosity or pet. **toyman,** *n.* one who deals in toys. **toyshop,** *n.* a shop where toys are sold. **toyer,** *n.* **toyingly,** *adv.* **toyish,** *a.* toy-like; †trifling, wanton. †**toyishness,** *n.* †**toysome,** *a.* disposed to toy; wanton. [etym. doubtful]

Toynbee[1], *n.* **Arnold** (1852–83), English economic historian, who coined the term 'industrial revolution' in his *Lectures on the Industrial Revolution*, published 1884. Toynbee Hall, an education settlement in the east end of London, was named after him.

Toynbee[2], *n.* **Arnold Joseph** (1889–1975), English historian, whose *A Study of History* (1934–61) was an attempt to discover the laws governing the rise and fall of civilizations. He was the nephew of the economic historian Arnold Toynbee.

†**toze,** *v.t.* to pull apart, to unravel, to card (wool etc.); to search or find out; to separate tin-ore by stirring the slime. [ME *tosen,* cogn. with TEASE]

tra-, *comb. form.* as in *tradition, travesty*. [TRANS-]

trabeate, trabeated, *a.* (*Arch.*) furnished with an entablature. **trabeation,** *n.* [L *trabs -bem,* beam, -ATE]

trabecula, *n.* a band or bar of connective tissue, esp. one forming the framework of an organ; (*Bot.*) a beam-like projection, cross-bar, etc. **trabecular, trabeculate, trabeculated,** *a.*

trace[1], *n.* one of the two straps, chains, or ropes by which a vehicle is drawn by horses etc. **in the traces** in harness. **to kick over the traces,** KICK. [ME and OF *trays,* pl. of TRAIT]

trace[2], *n.* a mark left by a person or animal walking or thing moving, a track, a trail, a footprint, a rut etc. (*usu. in pl.*); a line made by a recording instrument; a token, vestige, or sign of something that has existed or taken place; a minute quanity. *v.t.* to follow the traces or track of; to note the marks and vestiges of; to ascertain the position or course of; to pursue one's way along; to delineate, to mark out; to sketch out (a plan, scheme etc.); to copy (a drawing etc.) by marking the lines on transparent paper or linen laid upon it. *v.i.* to be followed back to the origins, date back. **trace element,** *n.* a chemical element present in small quantities, esp. one that is valuable for an organism's physiological processes. **traceable,** *a.* **traceability** (-bil'-), **traceableness,** *n.* **traceably,** *adv.* **tracer,** *n.* one who makes traces; a trace-horse; an artificially produced radio-active isotope introduced into the human body where its course can be followed by its radiations. **tracer bullet, shell,** *n.* a bullet or shell whose course is marked by a smoke trail or a phosphorescent glow. **tracery,** *n.* ornamental open-work in Gothic windows etc.; any decorative work or natural markings resembling this. **traceried,** *a.* **tracing,** *n.* **tracing-paper, cloth, -linen,** *n.* a thin transparent paper or linen used for copying drawings etc., by tracing. [F, from *tracer,* OF *tracier,* L *tractus,* p.p. of *trahere,* to draw]

trachea, *n.* (*pl.* **-cheae**) the windpipe, the air-passage from the larynx to the bronchi and lungs; one of the tubes by which air is conveyed from the exterior in insects and arachnids; (*Bot.*) a duct, a vessel. **tracheal, trachean, tracheate,** *a.* **trachearian, tracheary,** *a.* belonging to the Trachearia, a division of arachnids having tracheae. *n.* one of this division. [L, from Gr. *tracheia,* orig. fem. of *trachus* rough]

trachelo-, *comb. form.* pertaining to the neck. [Gr. *trachēlos,* neck]

trachelo-occipital, *a.* pertaining to or connecting the nape of the neck and the occiput.

tracheo-, *comb. form.*

tracheocele, *n.* a tumour in the trachea, an enlargement of the thyroid gland. [-CELE]

tracheotomy, *n.* the operation of making an opening into the windpipe. [-TOMY]

trachitis, *n.* inflammation of the trachea.

trachle, trauchle, *v.t.* (*Sc.*) to tire, to fatigue, to wear out; to distress. *n.* fatiguing toil; a wearisome effort. **trachly,** *a.* [etym. doubtful]

trachoma, *n.* a disease of the eye characterized by papillary or granular excrescences on the inner surface of the lids. [Gr., roughness, from *trachus,* rough]

trachyte, *n.* a gritty-surfaced volcanic rock containing glassy feldspar crystals. **trachytic,** *a.* [Gr. *trachutēs,* roughness, as prec.]

tracing, etc. TRACE[2].

track, *n.* a series of marks left by the passage of a person, animal, or thing, a trail; a series of footprints (*usu. in pl.*); a path, esp. one not constructed but beaten by use; a course, the route followed by ships etc.; a race-course, a racing-path; a set of rails, a monorail, or a line of railway with single or double tracks; the distance between the points where a pair of wheels are in contact with the ground, or rails etc.; (*N Am.*) a railway line; the groove in a gramophone record in which the needle travels; anything, e.g. a song, recorded on a gramophone record; one of several paths on a magnetic recording device on which esp. sound from a single input channel is recorded; the endless band on which a tractor propels itself; the conveyor which carries the items being assembled in a factory. *v.t.* to follow the track or traces of; to trace, to follow out (the course of anything); to follow the flight of (a spacecraft etc.) by receiving signals emitted by or reflected from it; to film (a subject) by moving the camera along a fixed path; to tow; of the stylus of a pickup arm, to follow the groove on a record; of a camera, to move along a fixed path while shooting. **beaten track,** *n.* the usual method; the ordinary way. **in one's tracks,** where one stands. **to make tracks,** to run away, to bolt, to decamp. **to track down,** to discover by tracking. **track-clearer,** *n.* a device fixed to an engine, car, mowing-machine, etc., for clearing the track in front and behind. **track-layer,** *n.* (*N Am.*) a plate-layer. **track record,** *n.* the past achievements, performance, experience etc. of a person or thing. **track shoe,** *n.* a light running shoe with spikes on the sole to improve grip. **tracksuit,** *n.* a light, loose-fitting suit for wearing before and after vigorous exercise, or as a leisure garment. **trackage,** *n.* (*collect.*) railway-tracks; the right to use the tracks of another company; towage. **tracker,** *n.* **tracker dog,** *n.* a dog that uses its sense of smell to find e.g. drugs, persons or smuggled goods, used often by the police. **trackless,** *a.* pathless, unmarked by feet; untrodden, untravelled, leaving no track. **tracklessly,** *adv.* **tracklessness,** *n.* [OF *trac,* prob. from Teut. (cp. Dut. *treck,* TREK, from *trekken,* to pull)]

tract[1], *n.* a region or area of land or water of a considerable but undefined extent; (*Anat.*) the region of an organ or system; a period (of time). [L *tractus -tūs,* from *trahere,* to draw, p.p. *tractus*]

tract[2], *n.* a short treatise or pamphlet, esp. on religion or morals; in the Roman Catholic Church an anthem sung in place of the Alleluia. [short for TRACTATE]

tractable, *a.* that may be easily led, managed, or controlled; docile, manageable. **tractability,** *n.* **tractableness,** *n.* **tractably,** *adv.* [L *tractābilis,* from *tractāre,* to

TREAT]

Tractarian, *n.* one of the authors of *Tracts for the Times* (1833–41) a series enunciating the principles of the Oxford Movement; an adherent of this, a High Churchman. *a.* pertaining to Tractarianism. **Tractarianism,** *n.* another name for the Oxford Movement, 19th-cent. movement for Catholic revival within the Church of England.

tractate, *n.* a treatise. [L *tractātus,* orig. p.p. of *tractāre,* to TREAT]

tractile, *a.* capable of being drawn out.

traction, *n.* the act of drawing something along a surface, esp. by motive power; the state of being so drawn; contraction. **traction-engine,** *n.* a locomotive for drawing heavy loads on ordinary roads. **traction-wheel,** *n.* the wheel to which the force is applied in a locomotive etc. **tractional,** *a.* [F, from L *tractiō -onem,* from *trahere,* to draw, p.p. *tractus*]

tractor, *n.* a self-propelling vehicle capable of drawing other vehicles, farm implements etc.; the front section of an articulated lorry, consisting of a chassis, engine and driver's cab, which pulls the trailer; an aircraft with its propellor or propellors mounted in front of the engine. **tractor plane,** *n.* an aeroplane propelled by an airscrew designed to pull on its shaft. **tractor plough,** *n.* (*Agric.*) a plough with not more than five shares or coulters drawn by a tractor.

Tracy, *n.* **Spencer** (1900–67), US actor, noted for his understated, seemingly effortless natural performances. His films include *Captains Courageous* (1937) and *Boys' Town* (1938) (for both of which he won Academy Awards), and he starred with Katharine Hepburn in nine films, including *Adam's Rib* (1949) and *Guess Who's Coming to Dinner* (1967). His other films include *Bad Day at Black Rock* (1955).

trad, *a* (*coll.*) short for TRADITIONAL. *n.* traditional jazz.

trade, *n.* a business, handicraft, or mechanical or mercantile occupation carried on for subsistence or profit, distinguished from agriculture, unskilled labour, the professions etc.; the exchange of commodities, buying and selling, commerce; an exchange of one thing for another; the amount of business done in a particular year, place etc.; (*collect.*) persons engaged in a particular trade; (*coll.*) a deal, a bargain (in business or politics); (*pl.*) the trade-winds; a track, a path, a way; (*sl.*) a homosexual sexual partner. *v.i.* to buy and sell, to barter, to exchange, to traffic, to deal (in); to carry on commerce or business (with); to carry merchandise (between etc.); to buy and sell (political influence, patronage etc.) corruptly. *v.t.* to sell or exchange in commerce, to barter; to swap. **to trade in,** to give in part payment. **to trade on,** to take advantage of. **Board of Trade,** a government department dealing with commercial and industrial affairs. **domestic** or **home trade,** that carried on within a country. **foreign trade,** interchange of commodities by importation or exportation with other countries. **the Trade,** *n.* the brewing industry. **Trades Union Congress** (TUC), voluntary organization of trade unions, founded in the UK 1868, in which delegates of affiliated unions meet annually to consider matters affecting their members. In 1988 there were some 100 affiliated unions, with an aggregate membership of about 11 million. **trade cycle,** *n.* the recurrent alternation of prosperity and depression in trade. **trade gap,** *n.* the amount by which a country's visible imports exceeds its visible exports. **trade-hall,** *n.* a hall for the meetings of a trade-guild etc. **trade-in,** *n.* a transaction in which an item is given in part payment for another; the item thus given. **trademark,** *n.* a registered symbol or name used by a manufacturer or merchant to guarantee the genuineness of goods; a distinguishing feature of a person or thing. *v.t.* to provide with a trademark. **trade name,** *n.* the name by which an article is called in the trade; the name of a proprietary article. **trade-off,** *n.* the exchange of one thing for another, esp. as a compromise. **trade-price,** *n.* the price charged to dealers for articles to be sold again. **trade secret,** *n.* a process, formula etc. used to make a commercial product, known to only one manufacturer. **tradesman,** *n.* a retail dealer, a shopkeeper; a craftsman. **tradespeople,** *n.* (*collect.*) people engaged in trades, tradesmen and their families. **trade union, trades union,** *n.* an organized body of workers in any trade, formed for the promotion and protection of their common interests. **trade-unionism,** *n.* **trade-unionist,** *n.* **trade-wind,** *n.* a wind blowing from the north or south toward the thermal equator and deflected in a westerly direction by the easterly rotation of the earth; (*pl.*) these and the anti-trades. †**traded,** *a.* (*Shak.*) practised, versed, skilled. †**tradeful,** *a.* busy in traffic, commercial. **tradeless**, *a.* **trader,** *n.* a person engaged in trade; a merchant, a tradesman; a vessel employed in trade. **trading estate,** *n.* area of buildings intended for commercial or light industrial use. **trading stamp,** *n.* a stamp given free with a purchase, which can be saved and later exchanged for goods. [MLG, track, cogn. with TREAD]

Tradescant, *n.* **John** (1570–1638), English gardener and botanist, who travelled widely in Europe and may have introduced the cos lettuce to England, from the Greek island bearing the same name. He was appointed as gardener to Charles I and was succeeded by his son, John Tradescant the Younger (1608–62), after his death. The younger Tradescant undertook three plant-collecting trips to Virginia, US, and Linnaeus named the genus *Tradescantia* in his honour.

tradition, *n.* the handing down of opinions, practices, customs etc., from ancestors to posterity, esp. by oral communication; a belief, custom etc., so handed down; a doctrine believed to have divine authority but not found in Scripture, as the oral law said to have been given by God to Moses on Mt Sinai, the oral teaching of Christ not recorded in the New Testament; the acts and sayings of Mohammed not recorded in the Koran; the principles, maxims etc., derived from the usage and experience of artists, dramatists, actors etc.; (*Law*) formal delivery (of property). **traditional,** *a.* of tradition; of or concerning a type of jazz which began in New Orleans in the 1900s. **traditionalism,** *n.* adherence to tradition, esp. superstitious regard to tradition in religious matters; a philosophic system attributing human knowledge, esp. of religion and ethics, to revelation and tradition. **traditionalist, traditionist,** †**traditioner,** *n.* **traditionalistic**, *a.* **traditionally,** *adv.* [ME and OF *tradicion,* L *traditio -onem,* from *trādere,* to hand over]

traditor, *n.* one of the early Christians who, to save their lives, gave up copies of the Scriptures or the goods of the Church to the persecutors. [L, from *trādere,* see prec.]

traduce, *v.t.* to defame, to calumniate, to misrepresent. **traducement,** *n.* **traducer,** *n.* **traducible,** *a.* **traducingly,** *adv.* [L *tradūcere* (TRA-, *dūcere,* to lead)]

traducianist, *n.* one who held that souls were transmitted by parents to children. **traducianism,** *n.* [late L *trāduciānus,* from *trādux -ducis,* layer, shoot, as prec.]

traduction, *n.* the transference of conclusions from one order of reasoning or classification to another; †translation, a translation; †derivation or transmission by descent, propagation; traducement. **traductive,** *a.* [OF, from L *trāductiō -onem,* as prec.]

Trafalgar, Battle of, battle 21 Oct. 1805 in the Napoleonic Wars. The British fleet under Nelson defeated a Franco-Spanish fleet; Nelson was mortally wounded. It is named after Cape Trafalgar, a low headland in SW Spain, near the western entrance to the Straits of Gibraltar.

traffic, *n.* the exchange of goods by barter or by the medium of money; trade, commerce; the trade (in a particular commodity etc.); the transportation of persons, animals, or goods by road, rail, sea or air; the passing to and fro of persons, vehicles etc., on a road etc.; the person, vehicles etc. passing thus; amount of goods or number of persons conveyed; †intercourse, dealing (with). *v.i.* (*p.p.* **trafficked,** *pres.p.* **trafficking**) to trade, to buy and sell goods, to have business (with). *v.t.* to barter. **traffic circle,** *n.* (*N Am.*) a roundabout. **traffic jam,** *n.* vehicles that are stationary or slow-moving because of the large volume of traffic. **traffic lights,** *n.pl.* coloured lights at street intersections to control the flow and direction of traffic. **traffic warden,** *n.* a person employed to enforce observance of parking restrictions, esp. by issuing parking tickets. **trafficker,** *n.* **trafficless,** *a.* [F *trafique* (*trafiquer,* to traffic), It. *traffico,* from *trafficare,* to traffic, etym. doubtful]

trafficator, *n.* formerly, a movable arm on a car that indicates the driver's intention to turn to right or left.

tragacanth, *n.* a whitish or reddish demulcent gum obtained from species of *Astragalus,* used in pharmacy, calico-printing etc.; a low, spiny, leguminous shrub of this genus growing in SW Asia. [F *tragacanthe,* L *tragacantha,* Gr. *tragakantha* (*tragos,* goat, ACANTHUS)]

tragedian, *n.* a writer of tragedies; an actor in tragedy. **tragedienne,** *n.* an actress in tragedy.

tragedy, *n.* a drama in verse or elevated prose dealing with a lofty theme of a sad, pathetic, or terrible kind, usu. with an unhappy ending; tragedy personified, the Muse of Tragedy; a fatal or calamitous event, esp. a murder or fatal accident with dramatic accompaniments. **tragic,** *a.* of the nature or in the style of tragedy; characterized by loss of life; lamentable, sad, calamitous. **tragically,** *adv.* **tragicality, tragicalness,** *n.* **tragi-comedy,** *n.* a drama in which tragic and comic scenes or features are mingled. **tragi-comic, -ical,** *a.* **tragi-comicality,** *n.* **tragi-comically,** *adv.* [ME and OF *tragedie,* L *tragoedia* Gr. *tragōidia,* prob. *goat-song* (*tragos,* he-goat, *ōdē,* see ODE)]

tragelaph, tragelaphus, *n.* (*Myth.*) a fabulous animal, half goat, half stag; (*Zool.*) a genus of S African antelopes, an animal of this genus. **tragelaphine,** *a.* [L *tragelaphus,* Gr. *tragelaphos* (*tragos,* he-goat, *elaphos,* deer)]

tragic, tragi-comedy, etc TRAGEDY.

tragule, *n.* a ruminant of the genus *Tragulus,* a chevrotain. **traguline,** *a.* [mod. L *tragulus,* dim. of *tragus,* Gr. *tragos,* he-goat]

tragus, *n.* (*pl.* **-gi**) a small process on the front of the orifice in the external ear. [L, see prec.]

traik, *v.i.* (*Sc.*) to roam, to wander, to stray; to follow (after); to decline in health. *n.* a misfortune. [etym. doubtful]

trail, *v.t.* to drag along behind, esp. along the ground; to follow by the track or trail; to carry (a rifle, etc.) in a horizontal or oblique position in the right hand with the arm extended; to tread down (grass) to make a path; to lag behind (sb, e.g. a runner in a race). *v.i.* to be dragged along behind, to hang down loosely or grow to some length along the ground, over a wall etc.; to lag behind; to be losing in a contest etc. *n.* anything trailing behind a moving thing, a train, a floating appendage etc.; the end of a gun-carriage resting on the ground when the gun is unlimbered; a track left by an animal etc.; the scent followed in hunting; a beaten track through forest or wild country. **trail blazer,** *n.* one who blazes a trail; a pioneer in a field of endeavour. **trail-net,** *n.* a drag-net. **trailing edge,** *n.* (*Aviat.*) the rear edge of a streamlined body, or of a control surface. [ME *trailen,* prob. from OF *trailler,* to tow, prob. ult. from L *trāgula,* drag-net, sledge, from *trahere,* to draw]

trailer, *n.* one who or that which trails; a trailing plant; a light car, usu. two-wheeled, drawn behind a bicycle etc., any vehicle, sled etc., drawn behind another; (*N Am.*) a caravan; a short film giving advance publicity to a forthcoming production.

train, *n.* that which is drawn or dragged along behind; an extended part of a gown, robe etc., trailing behind the wearer; the tail of a comet; a long trailing tail or tail-feathers of a bird; the trail of a gun-carriage; a retinue, a suite; a line or long series or succession of persons or things; a series of railway carriages or trucks drawn by an engine; a line of combustible material leading fire to a charge or mine; a set of wheels, pinions etc., transmitting motion; process, orderly succession, progressive condition. *v.t.* to bring to a state of proficiency by prolonged instruction, practice etc.; to instruct, to drill, to accustom (to perform certain acts or feats); to prepare by diet and exercise (for a race etc.); to bring (a plant etc.) by pruning, manipulation etc., into a desired shape, position etc.; to bring to bear, to aim (a cannon upon); †to entice, to allure (away etc.); †to drag or draw along. *v.i.* to prepare oneself or come into a state of efficiency for (a race, match etc.); to go by train. **to train fine,** to bring or be brought to a fine pitch of efficiency by training. **train of artillery,** a seige-train. **train-, trained-band,** *n.* a company of citizen soldiers organized at various dates during the 16th-18th cents. **train-bearer,** *n.* an attendant employed to hold up the train of a robe etc. **train ferry,** *n.* a ferry on to which a train is run to be conveyed across water to a track on the farther side. **train–mile,** *n.* a mile travelled by a train, the unit of work in railway statistics. **train-spotter,** *n.* one whose hobby is to collect train numbers. **trainable,** *a.* **trainee,** *n.* a person undergoing training. **trainer,** *n.* one who trains; esp. one who prepares men, horses etc., for races etc. **training,** *n.* the preparation of a person or animal for a particular activity, occupation etc; state of being trained or physically fit. **Training Agency,** *n.* UK government-sponsored organization responsible for retraining of unemployed workers. Founded as the Manpower Services Commission 1974, the organization operated such schemes as the Training Opportunities Scheme (TOPS), the Youth Opportunities Programme (YOP) 1978, the Youth Training Scheme (YTS) 1983, and the Technical and Vocational Initiative (TVEI). **training-college, school,** *n.* one for training teachers. **training-ship,** *n.* a ship for instructing boys in navigation, seamanship, etc. [F *train,* m., retinue, series, and *traîne,* f., that which is trailed, from *trainer,* ult. from L *trahere,* to draw]

train-oil, *n.* oil obtained from the blubber or fat of whales. [formerly *train, trane,* MG, *trān,* MDut. *traen* (Dut. *traan*), orig. tear, resin]

traipse, *v.i.* to trudge, to drag along wearily. [TRAPES]

trait, *n.* a distinguishing or peculiar feature; a stroke, a touch (of). [F, orig. p.p. of *traire,* L *trahere,* to draw, p.p. *tractus*]

traitor, *n.* one who violates his allegiance; one guilty of disloyalty, treason, or treachery. †*a.* traitorous. **traitorous, †traitorly,** *a.* **traitorously,** *adv.* **traitorousness,** *n.* **traitress,** *n. fem.* [ME and OF *traitre* (A-F and OF *traitour,* acc.), L *traditor -torem,* from *trādere,* to hand over (TRA-, *-dere, dare,* to give)]

Trajan, *n.* **Marcus Ulpius (Trajanus)** (AD 52–117), Roman emperor and soldier, born in Seville. He was adopted as heir by Nerva, whom he succeeded AD 98.

trajectory, *n.* the path described by a body, comet, projectile etc., under the action of given forces; a curve or surface cutting the curves or surfaces of a given system at a constant angle. **†traject,** *v.t.* to transmit; to transport. *n.,* a ferry. **†trajection,** *n.* [L *trājectus,* p.p. of *trājicere* (TRA-, *jacere,* to throw), -ORY]

tram[1], *n.* the shaft of a cart, wagon, or truck; a four-wheeled truck or car used in coalmines; a line of beams or rails, a pair of which form a tram-way; a tramway, a tram-car. *v.t.* (*past, p.p.* **trammed**) to convey or perform (a journey) in a tram-car. *v.i.* to go in a tram-car. **tram-car, †tramway-car,** *n.* **tram-line,** *n.* a tramway; (*pl.*) the lines at the side of a tennis-court which mark the boundaries of the singles and doubles court. **tram-road,** *n.* a road laid with tracks of timber, stone, or iron. **tram-way,** *n.* a street railway on which passenger-cars are drawn by horses, or by electricity, steam, or other mechanical power. [cp. LG *traam,* balk, beam, G *Trumm,* lump, slump, Norw. *tram,* door-step, Swed. dial. *tromm,* log]

tram[2], *n.* silk thread made up of two or more strands twisted together, used for the weft of the finer kinds of silk goods. [MF *trame,* It. *trama,* L *trāma,* weft]

tram-line etc. TRAM[1].

trammel, *n.* a net of various forms for catching fish, esp. a trammel-net; a shackle or fetter, esp. one used in teaching a horse to amble; a hook in a fire-place for pots, kettles etc.; an instrument for drawing ellipses; a beam-compass; anything restraining freedom or activity (usu. in *pl.*). *v.t.* (*past, p.p.* **trammelled**) to confine, to hamper, to restrict. **trammel-net,** *n.* a net formed by a combination of three seines, in which fish become entangled. **trammelled,** *a.* confined, hampered; with white marks on the feet of one side (of a horse). **trammeller,** *n.* [ME *tramayle,* MF *tramail* (F *trémail*), pop. L *tramaculum, -la* (perh. TRI-, *macula,* mesh)]

tramontane, *a.* lying, situated or coming from beyond the Alps (as seen from Italy); hence, foreign, barbarous. *n.* a tramontane person; the tramontana. **tramontana**, *n.* a name for the north wind in the Mediterranean; a cold and blighting wind in the Greek Archipelago. [It. *tramontana* (perh. through F), L *transmontānus (*TRANS-, *mons montis,* MOUNT)]

tramp, *v.i.* to walk or tread heavily; to walk, to go on foot. *v.t.* to tread heavily on, to trample; to go over or traverse, or to perform (a journey etc.) on foot; to hike. *n.* an act of tramping, the tread of persons etc., walking or marching; the sound of this; a walk, a journey on foot; an itinerant beggar, a vagrant; (*sl.*) a promiscuous girl or woman, a harlot; a freight-vessel having no regular line; an iron plate worn to protect the sole of the boot in digging. **tramper,** *n.* [ME, LG, and G *trampen,* cp. Dan. *trampe,* Swed. and Norw. *trampa*]

trample, *v.t.* to tread under foot, esp. in scorn, triumph etc.; to tread down, to crush thus; to treat with arrogance or contemptuous indifference. *v.i.* to tread heavily (on); to tread (on) in contempt. *n.* the act or sound of trampling. **trampler,** *n.* [freq. of TRAMP]

trampoline, *n.* a sheet of canvas suspended by springs from a frame, used for bouncing on or for assisting jumps in gymnastics. [Sp. *trampolin* from It. *trampolino,* of Germanic origin: cf *trampen* to stamp]

tran-, *comb. form.* [TRANS- before *s*]

trance, *n.* a state in which the soul seems to have passed into another state of being; ecstasy, rapture; a state of insensibility to external surroundings with suspension of some of the vital functions, catalepsy; the hypnotic state. *v.t.* (*poet.*) to entrance, to enchant. **trancedly,** *adv.* [OF *transe,* from *transir,* to depart, to die, to be numbed, L *transīre* (TRANS-, *īre,* to go)]

tranche, *n.* a portion, esp. of a larger sum of money. [F, slice]

traneen, *n. Cynosurus cristatus,* crested dog's-tail grass. **not worth a traneen,** not worth a rush. [Ir. *traithnin*]

trank, *n.* an oblong piece of skin from which the parts of a glove are cut. [perh. from F *tranche,* slice]

trannie, tranny, *n.* (*coll.*) short for TRANSISTOR RADIO.

tranquil, *a.* calm, peaceful, serene, quiet, undisturbed. **tranquillity, tranquilness,** *n.* **tranquillize, -ise,** *v.t.* to make calm, esp. with a sedative drug. **tranquillization, -isation,** *n.* **tranquillizer, -iser,** *n.* that which makes tranquil; a sedative drug. **tranquillizingly, -isingly,** *adv.* **tranquilly,** *adv.* [F *tranquille,* L *tranquillus*]

trans., (*abbr.*) transitive; translated, translation, translator.

trans-, *comb. form.* across, over; beyond; through; into another state or place. [L, across, beyond]

transact, *v.t.* to do, to perform, to manage, to carry out. *v.i.* to do business, to conduct matters (with). **transaction,** *n.* the management or carrying out of a piece of business etc.; that which has been transacted, a piece of business, an affair, a proceeding; (*pl.*) the reports of the proceedings of learned societies; adjustment of a dispute by mutual concessions etc. **transactor,** *n.* [L *transactus,* p.p. of *transigere* (TRANS-, *agere,* to act)]

Trans-Alaskan Pipeline Scheme, one of the world's greatest civil engineering projects, the construction of a 1285 km/800 mile long pipeline to carry petroleum (crude oil) from N Alaska to the icefree port of Valdez. It was completed 1977 after three years' work.

transalpine, *a.* lying or situated beyond the Alps (usu. as seen from Italy). *n.* a person living beyond the Alps.

Trans-Amazonian Highway, Transamazonica, initiated as part of the Brazilian National Integration Programme (PIN) in 1970, the Trans-Amazonian Highway was designed to enhance national security, aid the development of the north of Brazil and act as a safety valve for the overpopulated coastal regions. The highway links Recife in the east with the provinces of Rondonia, Amazonas and Acre in the west.

transatlantic, *a.* lying or being beyond the Atlantic; crossing the Atlantic.

transceiver, *n.* a device for transmitting and receiving radio signals. [*trans*mitter, *re*ceiver]

transcend, *v.t., v.i.* to rise above, to surpass, to excel, to exceed; to pass or be beyond the range, sphere, or power (of human understanding etc.). **transcendence, -dency,** *n.* **transcendent,** *a.* excelling, surpassing, supremely excellent; in Scholastic philosophy, applied to concepts higher or of wider signification than the categories of Aristotle; in Kantian philosophy, beyond the sphere of knowledge or experience; above and independent of the material universe. *n.* that which is transcendent. **transcendental**, *a.* in Kantian philosophy, transcendent, beyond the sphere of experience; belonging to the a priori elements of experience, implied in and necessary to experience; explaining matter and the universe as products of mental conception; transcending ordinary ideas; abstruse, speculative, vague, obscure; (*Math.*) not capable of being produced by the fundamental operations of algebra, addition, multiplication etc. *n.* a transcendent concept. **transcendental meditation,** *n.* a technique for relieving stress, based in part on Hindu meditation. Meditators are given a mantra (a special word or phrase) to repeat over and over in the mind. The mantra is never written down or divulged to anyone else. It was introduced to the West by Maharishi Mahesh Yogi and popularized by the Beatles in the late 1960s. Practitioners claim that if even as few as 1% of the population meditated in this way, society would see much less stress. **transcendentalism,** *n.* the state of being transcendental; a transcendental philosophy, as that of Schelling. **transcendentalist,** *n.* **transcendentally,** *adv.* [OF *transcender,* L *transcendere* (TRAN-, *scandere,* to climb)]

transcontinental, *a.* extending or travelling across a continent.

transcribe, *v.t.* to copy in writing, to write out in full (shorthand notes etc.); to translate, transliterate; to transfer (data) from one recording medium to another; to record (spoken sounds) in the form of phonetic symbols; to record for broadcasting. **transcriber,** *n.* **transcript**, *n.* a written copy. **transcription,** *n.* transcribing or being transcribed; what is transcribed; (*Mus.*) the arrangement of a vocal composition for an instrument, or the readjustment of a composition for another instrument. **transcriptional, transcriptive**, *a.* [L *transcrībere* (TRAN-, *scrībere,* p.p. *scriptus*)]

transcurrent, *a.* running or passing across or transversely. [L *transcurrens -ntem,* pres.p. of *transcurrere* (TRANS-, *currere,* to run)]

transducer, *n.* a power-transforming device for which the input and output are of different kinds, electrical, acoustic, optical etc., e.g. loudspeaker, microphone, photoelectric cell, etc.

†**transduction,** *n.* a carrying or leading across. [L *transductio,* from *trans-* (*dūcere,* to lead)]

transductor, *n.* that which carries or leads across; a muscle of the great toe.

transect, *v.t.* to cut across; (*Anat.*) to dissect transversely. **transection**, *n.* [as SECT[2]]

transenna, *n.* a metal or stone lattice, etc., enclosing a shrine. [L, grating, lattice]

transept, *n.* either of the transverse arms extending north and south in a cruciform church. [TRAN-, SEPTUM]

transfer, *v.t.* (*past, p.p.* **transferred**) to convey, remove, or shift from one place or person to another; to make over the possession of; to convey (a design etc.) from one surface to another, esp. in lithography; to remove (a picture etc.) from a wall etc., to canvas or other surface. *v.i.* to move from one place to another; to change from one bus, train, etc to another. *n.* (trans′-), the removal or conveyance of a thing from one person or place to another; the act of conveying a right, property etc., from one person to another; the deed by which this is effected; that which is transferred; a design conveyed or to be conveyed from paper etc., to some other surface; a soldier transferred from one regiment, troop etc., to another; (*N Am.*) a ticket which allows a passenger on public transport to change routes. **transfer-book,** *n.* a register of transfers of stocks, shares, etc. **transfer-day,** *n.* an official day for the transfer of consols, etc., at the Bank of England. **transfer-ink,** *n.* lithograpic ink for transferable drawing, writing, etc., on lithographic stone, transfer-paper etc. **transfer list,** *n.* a list of footballers available for transfer to other clubs. **transfer-paper,** *n.* prepared paper for receiving impressions and transferring to stone. **transfer RNA,** *n.* an RNA that carries a particular amino acid to a ribosome in protein synthesis. **transferable,** *a.* **transferable vote,** *n.* in a system of proportional representation, a vote that can be transferred to a second candidate if the first loses a preliminary ballot. **transferability,** *n.* **transferee,** *n.* **transference,** *n.* **transferrer,** *n.* **transferential,** *a.* [L *transferre* (TRANS-, *ferre,* to bear)]

transferase, *n.* an enzyme that acts as a catalyst in the transfer of a chemical group from one molecule to another.

transferrin, *n.* a blood protein that transports iron. [TRANS-, L *ferrum,* iron]

transfiguration, *n.* a change of form or appearance, esp. that of Christ on the Mount (Matt. xvii.1-9); a festival on 6 Aug. in commemoration of this. **transfigure,** *v.t.* to change the outward appearance of, esp. so as to elevate and glorify. [F, from L *transfiguratio -tionem,* from *transfigūrāre* (TRANS- *figūrāre,* to change the figure of, from *figūra,* figure)]

transfix, *v.t.* to pierce through, to impale; to render motionless with shock, fear etc., **transfixion,** *n.* the act of transfixing; amputation by piercing and cutting outwards. [L *transfixus,* p.p. of *transfigere* (TRANS-, *figere,* to fix)]

†**transfluent,** *a.* flowing across or through, esp. (*Her.*) of water represented as flowing through a bridge. [L *transfluens -ntem,* pres.p. of *transfluere* (TRANS-, *fluere,* to flow)]

transform, *v.t.* to change the form, shape, or appearance of, to metamorphose; to change in disposition, character etc. *n.*, the result of a mathematical or linguistic transformation. **transformable,** *a.* **transformation,** *n.* the act of transforming; the state of being transformed, a metamorphosis, a transmutation; a change from solid to liquid or liquid to gaseous form or the reverse; (*Math.*) the change of a figure or expression with another equivalent to it; (*Physiol.*) the change in the blood in its passage through the capillaries of the vascular system; a morbid change of tissue into a form not proper to that particular part; a rule for the transforming of the underlying structures of a language into actual sentences. **transformation-scene,** *n.* a scene in a pantomime in which the principal characters are supposed to be transformed into the chief characters of the harlequinade. **transformational,** *a.* **transformational grammar,** *n.* a grammar which describes the structure of a language in terms of a set of rules for transforming the underlying structures of the language into an infinite number of actual sentences. **transformative,** *a.* **transformer,** *n.* one or that which transforms; a device which changes the current and voltage of an alternating electrical supply. The product of current and voltage remains almost unchanged. **transformism,** *n.* the theory of the development of one species from another; the theory that complex animals were developed from organisms originally free, united into a colony and then into organs of a differentiated whole. **transformist,** *n.* **transformistic,** *a.* [F *transformer,* L *transformāre* (TRANS-, *formāre,* to form)]

trans-frontier, *a.* situated, living, or done beyond the frontier.

transfuse, *v.t.* to cause to pass from one vessel etc., into another; to transfer (blood) from the veins of one person or animal to those of another; to inject (a liquid) into a blood-vessel or cavity to replace loss or wastage. †**transfusible,** *a.* **transfusion**, *n.* **transfusionist,** *n.* **transfusive,** *a.* [L *transfūsus,* p.p. of *transfundere* (TRANS-, *fundere,* to pour)]

transgress, *v.t.* to break, to violate, to infringe, *v.i.* to offend by violating a law or rule, to sin. **transgression**, *n.* **transgressive,** *a.* **transgressively,** *adv.* **transgressor,** *n.* [L *transgressus,* p.p. of *transgredī* (TRANS-, *gradī,* to walk)]

tranship, *v.t.* to transfer from one ship, vehicle etc., to another. **transhipment,** *n.*

transhume, *v.t., v.i.* to move to or from winter to summer of summer to winter pastures. **transhumance,** *n.* [TRANS-, L *humus,* ground]

transient, *a.* not lasting or durable; transitory, momentary, hasty, brief; (*Mus.*) passing, serving merely to connect or introduce; (*N Am.*) (of a hotel guest) staying one night only. *n.* a transient person or thing; a transient fluctuation in the amount of current flowing through an electrical circuit. **transience, -ency, transientness,** *n.* **transiently,** *adv.* [L *transiens,* pres.p. of *transīre* (TRANS-, *īre,* to go)]

†**transilient,** *a.* springing or extending across, spanning. †**transilience,** *n.* an abrupt transition. [L *transiliens -ntem,* pres.p. of *transilīre* (TRAN-, *salīre,* to leap)]

transilluminate, *v.t.* to send a powerful light through an organ or part in diagnosis. **transillumination,** *n.*

transire, *n.* a custom-house warrant authorizing the removal of dutiable goods. [L, TRANS-, *īre,* to go]

transisthmian, *a.* extending across an isthmus.

transistor, *n.* a device made primarily of a semiconductor (germanium or silicon) capable of giving current and power amplification. It has uses similar to a thermionic triode; (*coll.*) a transistor radio. **transistor radio,** *n.* a small portable radio. **transistorize, -ise,** *v.t.* to equip with transistors. **transistorization, -isation,** *n.*

transit, *n.* the act of passing, conveying, or being conveyed, across, over, or through; conveyance; a line of passage, a route; the apparent passage of a heavenly body over the meridian of a place; the passage of a heavenly body across the disk of another, esp. of Venus or Mercury across the sun's disk; a transit-compass or instrument. *v.t.* to pass across the disk (of the sun etc.). **in transit,** being conveyed. **transit camp,** *n.* a camp where people stay temporarily before moving on to another place. **transit-circle, -instrument,** *n.* an instrument for observing transits across a meridian. **transit-compass,** *n.* a surveying instrument for measuring horizontal angles. **transit-duty,** *n.* duty paid upon goods passing through a country. [L *transitus -tūs,* from *transīre,* see TRANSIRE]

transition, *n.* passage or change from one place, state, or action to another; a change in architecture, painting, literature etc.; a change from one musical key to another or from the major to the relative minor; in rhetoric, a passing from one subject to another. **transition stage** or **period,** *n.* the stage or period of transition in art etc. **transitional, -ary,** *a.* **transitionally,** *adv.*

transitive, *a.* of verbs, expressing an action passing over from a subject to an object, having a direct object. **transitively,** *adv.* **transitiveness,** *n.* [late L *transitivus*]

transitory, *a.* lasting but a short time, transient, not durable, short-lived. **transitorily,** *adv.* **transitoriness,** *n.* [OF *transitoire,* late L *transitōrius,* as prec.]

Transkei, *n.* largest of South Africa's Bantu Homelands, extending NE from the Great Kei River, on the coast of Cape Province, to the border of Natal; area 43,808 sq km/16,910 sq miles; population (1985) 3,000,000, including small white and Asian minorities. It became self-governing 1963, and achieved full 'independence' 1976. Its capital is Umtata, and it has a port at Mnganzana. It is one of the two homelands of the

Xhosa people, and products include livestock, coffee, tea, sugar, maize, and sorghum. Its government consists of a president (paramount chief Tutor Nyangelizwe Vulinolela Ndamase, 1986–) and single-chamber national assembly.

translate, *v.t.* to render or express the sense of (a word, passage, or work) into or in another language; to interpret, to express in clearer terms; to express, paraphrase, or convey (an idea etc.) from one art or style into another; to transform, to change; to remove from one office to another (esp. a bishop to another see); to convey to heaven without death; (*Mech.*) to move (a body) so that all parts follow the same direction, to give motion without rotation; (*Teleg.*) to retransmit (a message); †to transport, to enrapture. *v.i.* to be engaged in translation. **translatable,** *a.* **translation,** *n.* **translational,** *a.* **translator,** *n.* **translatory,** *a.* **translatress,** *n. fem.* [OF *translater,* L *translātus,* p.p. of *transferre,* to TRANSFER]

Trans-Leithan, *a.* Hungarian or Magyar, opp. to *cis-Leithan*. [TRANS-, *Leitha,* tributary of Danube, part of boundary between Austria and Hungary]

transliterate, *v.t.* to represent (words, sounds etc.) in the corresponding or approximately corresponding characters of another language. **transliteration,** *n.* **transliterator,** *n.* [TRANS-, L *litera,* LETTER]

translocation, *n.* the transfer of soluble substances from one part of a plant to another.

translucent, *a.* allowing light to pass through but not transparent; (*loosely.*) transparent. **translucence, -cency,** *n.* †**translucid,** *a.* [L *translūcens -ntem,* pres.p. of *translūcēre* (TRANS-, *lūcēre,* to shine, see LUCID)]

translunary, *a.* situated beyond the moon, opp. to sublunary; ethereal, visionary. [TRANS-, LUNARY]

transmarine, *a.* situated beyond the sea. [MARINE]

†**transmew** TRANSMUTE.

transmigrate, *v.i.* of the soul, to pass from one body into another, to undergo metempsychosis; to pass from one place, country, or jurisdiction to another, to migrate. **transmigrant,** *n.* one who transmigrates, a migrant; an alien passing through one country on the way to another. **transmigrant,** *a.* **transmigration,** *n.* **transmigrationism,** *n.* the doctrine of metempsychosis. **transmigrator,** *n.* **transmigratory,** *a.* [L *transmigrātus,* p.p. of *transmigrāre* (TRANS-, MIGRATE)]

transmit, *v.t.* (*past, p.p.* **transmitted**) to send, transfer, convey, or communicate from one person or place to another; to suffer to pass through, to act as a medium for, to conduct; to broadcast (a TV or radio programme). **transmissible,** †**-mittable,** *a.* **transmissibility,** *n.* **transmission,** *n.* the act of transmitting; the conveying of electrical energy from place to place; the radiation of ether waves; signals sent out by a transmitter; the gear by which power is conveyed from the engine to the live axle; a radio or TV broadcast. **transmissive,** *a.* **transmitter,** *n.* a person or thing that transmits: any form of machine that transmits telegraphic messages; the apparatus required for radiating a signal. [L *transmittere* (TRANS-, *mittere,* to send)]

transmogrify, *v.t.* (*coll.*) to transform, esp. as if by magical means. **transmogrification,** *n.* [TRANS-, *mogrify,* appar. an arbitrary coinage]

transmontane, *a.* situated beyond the mountains; tramontane.

†**transmove,** *v.t.* to transform, to transmute.

transmute, *v.t.* to change from one form, nature, or substance into another; to transform (into). **transmutable,** *a.* **transmutability,** *n.* **transmutably,** *adv.* **transmutative,** *a.* **transmuter,** *n.* **transmutation,** *n.* the act of transmuting; the state of being transmuted; the change of base metals into gold or silver; the change of one species into another; (*Geom.*) the reduction of one figure or body into another of the same area or content; the conversion of one element or nuclide into another either naturally or artificially. **transmutationist,** *n.* one who believes in the transmutation of species. **transmutative,** *a.* **transmuter,** *n.* [L *transmūtāre* (TRANS-, *mūtāre,* to change)]

transnormal, *a.* beyond what is normal. [TRANS-, NORMAL]

transoceanic, *a.* situated or coming from beyond the ocean; crossing the ocean. [OCEANIC]

transom, *n.* a horizontal bar of wood or stone across a window or other opening; a horizontal bar across the top of a doorway separating it from the fan-light; (*N Am.*) a fanlight; one of the beams bolted across the sternpost of a ship, supporting the after-end of the deck; a horizontal piece connecting the cheeks of a guncarriage; a beam across a saw-pit; the vane of a cross-staff. **transom-window,** *n.* a window divided by a transom; a window over the transom of a door. **transomed,** *a.* [ME *traunsum,* prob. corr. of L *transtrum,* from *trans,* see TRANS-]

transonic, *a.* relating to or being a speed near the speed of sound. [SONIC]

transpadane, *a.* situated beyond the River Po (from Rome). [L *transpadānus* (*Padus,* Po)]

transparent, *a.* having the property of transmitting rays of light without diffusion, so that objects are distinctly visible; easily seen through; plain, evident, clear; frank, sincere. **transparence, transparentness,** *n.* **transparently,** *adv.* **transparency,** *n.* transparentness; a thing that is transparent, esp. a picture, inscription, photograph etc., painted on glass, muslin, or other transparent or semi-transparent material, to be exhibited by means of light shining through it; a positive photograph on a transparent base mounted on a frame for viewing by means of a projector. [F, from med. L *transparens -ntem,* pres.p. of *transpārēre* (TRANS-, *pārēre,* to appear)]

transpierce, *v.t.* to pierce through.

transpire, *v.t.* to emit through the excretory organs (of the skin or lungs), to emit as vapour, to exhale. *v.i.* of perspiration etc. to be emitted through the excretory organs, to pass off as vapour; to leak out, become known; to happen. **transpirable,** *a.* **transpiration,** *n.* **transpiratory,** *a.* [TRAN-, L *spīrāre,* to breathe]

transplant, *v.t.* to remove and plant in another place; to remove from one place and establish in another; to transfer (living tissue) from one part or person to another. *n.*, the surgical procedure for transplanting an organ; the organ thus transplanted. **transplantable,** *a.* **transplantation,** *n.* **transplanter,** *n.* one who or that which transplants; a machine for removing trees with earth and replanting; a tool for taking up plants thus. [F *transplanter,* L *transplantāre*]

transponder, *n.* a radio or radar device which automatically transmits a signal in response to a signal received. [*trans*mitter, res- *ponder*]

transpontine, *a.* belonging to the Surrey side of London or the part across London Bridge; melodramatic, from the plays formerly in vogue there. [TRANS-, L *pons pontis,* bridge]

transport[1], *v.t.* to carry or convey from one place to another; to remove (a criminal) to a penal colony; (*chiefly in p.p.*) to carry away by powerful emotion, to entrance, to ravish. **transportable,** *a.* that may be transported; involving transportation (of an offence). **transportability,** *n.* †**transportance,** *n.* **transportedly,** *adv.* **transporter,** *n.* a large vehicle for transporting goods. **transporter bridge,** *n.* a device for carrying road traffic across a river on a moving platform. **transportingly,** *adv.* **transportation,** *n.* the act of transporting or conveying; the state of being transported; (means of) conveyance; carriage of persons or things from one place to another; banishment to a penal colony. [F *transporter,* L *transportāre* (*portāre,* carry)]

transport[2], *n.* transportation, conveyance from one place to another; a transport ship or aircraft; a vehicle, aircraft etc. used for transporting people or goods; †a transported convict or one sentenced to transportation; ecstasy. **Transport and General Workers Union (TGWU),** UK trade union founded in 1921 by the amalgamation of a number of dockers' and road-transport workers' unions, previously associated in the Transport Workers' Federation. It is the largest trade union in Britain. **transport café,** *n.* a roadside café used predominantly by lorry drivers. **transport ship** or **vessel,** *n.* one used to carry troops, munitions of war, stores, etc. **transport-worker,** *n.* a worker on any system of transport.

transpose, *v.t.* to cause to change places; to change the natural order or position of (words or a word) in a sentence; to transfer a mathematical term from one side of an equation to the other, changing the sign; (*Mus.*) to write or play in a different key. **transposal, transposition,** *n.* the act of transposing; the state of being transposed. **transpositional, transpositive,** *a.* [ME *transposen,* F *transposer* (POSE[1])]

†**transprint,** *v.t.* to reprint from another book or place; to print out of place.

transsexual, *a., n.* (of) a person who dresses and lives for all or most of the time as a member of the opposite sex; (of) a person who undergoes surgery and medical treatment to adopt the physical characteristics of the opposite sex.

trans-ship TRANSHIP.

Trans-Siberian Railway, *n.* railway line connecting the cities of European Russia with Omsk, Novosibirsk, Irkutsk, and Khabarovsk, and terminating at Vladivostok on the Pacific. It was built 1891–1905; from Leningrad to Vladivostok is about 8700 km/5400 miles. A 3102 km/1928 miles northern line was completed 1984 after ten years' work.

transubstantiate, *v.t.* to change the substance of. **transubstantiation,** *n.* change from one substance into another, a change of essence; conversion of the whole substance of the bread and wine in the Eucharist into the body and blood of Christ. **transubstantiative,** *a.* [med. L *transubstantiātus,* p.p. of *transubstantiāre* (*substantia,* SUBSTANCE)]

transude, *v.i.* to pass or ooze through the pores or interstices of a membrane etc. **transudation,** *n.* **transudatory,** *a.* [F *transsuder* (L *sūdāre,* to sweat)]

transuranic, *a.* of an atomic element, having an atomic number higher than uranium.

Transvaal, *n.* province of NE South Africa, bordering Zimbabwe in the N; area 262,499 sq km/101,325 sq miles; population (1985) 7,532,000. Its capital is Pretoria, and towns include Johannesburg, Germiston, Brakpan, Springs, Benoni, Krugersdorp, and Roodepoort. Products include diamonds, coal, iron ore, copper, lead, tin, manganese, meat, maize, tobacco, and fruit. The main rivers are the Vaal and Limpopo with their tributaries. Swaziland forms an enclave on the Natal border. It was settled by *Voortrekkers* who left Cape Colony in the Great Trek from 1831. Independence was recognized by Britain 1852, until the settlers' difficulties with the conquered Zulus led to British annexation 1877. It was made a British colony after the South African War 1899–1902, and in 1910 became a province of the Union of South Africa.

transverse, *a.* lying, being, or acting across or in a cross direction; †collateral. *n.* that which is transverse, esp. a transverse muscle. *v.t.* to lie or pass across; †to overturn; to thwart, to cross. **transversal,** *a.* transverse; running or lying across. *n.* a straight line cutting a system of lines; a transversalis. **transversalis,** *n.* a transverse muscle, one lying across other parts. **transversally, transversely,** *adv.* **transverso-,** *comb. form.* [L *transversus,* p.p. of *transvertere* (*vertere,* to turn)]

transvestism, *n.* the adoption of clothing and manners properly belonging to the opposite sex. **transvestite,** *n* one who practices this. [TRANS-, L *vestire,* to dress]

Transylvania, *n.* mountainous area of central and NW Romania, bounded to the S by the Transylvanian Alps (an extension of the Carpathians), formerly a province, with its capital at Cluj. It was part of Hungary from about AD 1000 until its people voted to unite with Romania 1918. It is the home of the vampire legends. **Transylvanian,** *a.* of or belonging to Transylvania, in Romania.

trant, *v.i.* (*dial.*) to work as a tranter. **tranter,** *n.* a local carrier, huckster, or pedlar. [from TRANTER, cp. med. L *trāvetārius,* etym. doubtful]

trap[1], *n.* a contrivance for catching game, vermin, and other animals, consisting of a pitfall, enclosure, or mechanical arrangement, esp. with a door or lid closing with a spring, often baited; a trick or artifice for misleading or betraying a person, an ambush, a stratagem; a device for suddenly releasing a bird or propelling an object into the air to be shot at; a device for hurling clay-pigeons into the air; the game of trap-ball, the wooden instrument used in this game; a U-shaped bend or other contrivance in a soil-pipe etc., for sealing this with a body of liquid and preventing the return flow of foul gas; a two-wheeled vehicle on springs; a trap-door; (*sl.*) a policeman; (*sl.*) the mouth. *v.t.* (*past, p.p.* **trapped**) to catch in or as in a trap; to retain, hold back; to furnish (a drain) with a trap; to stop or hold (gas etc.) in a trap; to make trap-doors in (a stage). *v.i.* to catch animals in traps; to be stopped or impeded (of steam etc., in a pipe). **trap-ball,** *n.* a children's game played with a wooden device having a pivoted bar for sending a ball into the air on being hit with a bat. **trap-cellar,** *n.* the space under the stage in a theatre. **trap-door,** *n.* a door in a floor or roof opening and shutting like a valve. **trapshooting,** *n.* clay-pigeon shooting. **trapper,** *n.* one who traps animals, esp. for furs; one in charge of air-doors in mines. [OE *treppe,* cp. MDut. *trappe,* WFlem. *traap,* OF *trape*]

trap[2], *n.* a dark igneous rock, esp. a variety of dolerite or basalt, presenting a columnar or stairlike aspect; (*Sc.*) a movable ladder. [Swed. *trapp,* from *trappa,* stair]

trap[3], †*n.* a cloth for a horse's back, a trapping, a caparison. *v.t.* to adorn, to comparison. **trappings,** *n.pl.* ornamental harness or housing; decorations, adornments, esp. those pertaining to an office etc., finery. **traps,** *n.pl.* one's personal belongings, luggage, baggage. [F *drap,* cloth, etym. doubtful]

trapes, *v.i.* to traipse. *n.* a slattern. [rel. to obs. *trape,* perh. from MDut. *trappen,* to tramp]

trapeze, *n.* an apparatus consisting of a suspended bar on which gymnasts perform swinging, balancing, and other feats; a trapezium. **trapezial,** *a.* trapeziform; (*Anat.*) of the trapezium. **trapezian,** *a.* (*Cryst.*). **trapeziform,** *a.* **trapezium,** *n.* (*pl.* **-zia, -ziums**) a quadrilateral figure no two or only two sides of which are parallel; (*Anat.*) the outermost bone of the distal row in the carpus. **trapezoid,** *a.* trapeziform. *n.* a quadrilateral only two or no two of whose sides are parallel. **trapezoidal,** *a.* [F *trapèze,* L *trapezium,* Gr. *trapezion,* dim of *trapeza,* table (*tra-, tetra,* four, *peza,* foot, cogn. with *pous podos*)]

trapper TRAP[1].

trappings TRAP[3].

Trappist, *n.* member of a Roman Catholic order of monks and nuns, renowned for the strictness of their rules, which includes the maintenance of silence. It originated 1664 at La Trappe, in Normandy, as a reformed version of the Cistercian order under which it is now governed once more. **Trappistine,** *n.* one of an order of nuns allied to the Trappists; a liqueur made by the Trappists. [La *Trappe*]

traps TRAP[3].

trapshooting TRAP[1].

trash[1], *n.* any waste or worthless matter, refuse, rubbish; (*N Am.*) domestic refuse; loppings of trees; bruised sugar-canes; a rubbishy article or production of any kind; a poor or worthless person or group of people. *v.t.* to lop; to subject to criticism, to denigrate. **trash-can,** (*N Am.*) a dust-bin. **trashman,** *n.* (*N Am.*) a refuse collector. **trashery, trashiness,** *n.* **trashily,** *adv.* **trashy,** *a.* **trashiness,** *n.* [etym. doubtful]

†**trash[2],** *v.t.* to check, to hold in with a leash. *n.* a leash. [etym. doubtful]

†**trash[3],** *v.t.* to tire, to wear out. [cp. Swed. *traska,* Norw. *traske*]

trass, *n.* a light-coloured type of tuff rock, often used to make hydraulic cement. [Dut., from F *terrasse,* pile of earth]

trattoria, *n.* (*pl.* **-rias, -rie**) an Italian restaurant. [It.]

trauchle TRACHLE.

trauma, *n.* a wound or external injury; the morbid condition produced by this; a psychological shock having a lasting effect on the subconscious. **traumatic,** *a.* pertaining to or adapted to the cure of wounds. *n.* a medicine for wounds. **traumatism,** *n.* **traumato-,** *comb. form.* [Gr. *trauma -atos,* wound]

travail, *n.* painful toil, painful exertion or effort; the pangs of childbirth. *v.i.* to toil painfully; to suffer the pangs of childbirth. †*v.t.* to harass, to tire. [OF, *from travailler,* to toil, prob. from late L *trepālium,* instrument of torture (*trēs,* three, *pālus,* stake, PALE[1])]

trave, *n.* †a cross-beam; a wooden frame for confining a restive horse while it is being shod. [OF, from L *trabs -bam*]

travel, *v.i.* (*past, p.p.* **travelled**) to make a journey, esp. to distant or foreign lands; of a machine or part to move (along, in, up and down etc.); to move, to go, to pass through space; to make journeys as a commercial traveller for securing orders etc.; of food or drink, to survive transportation in a specified way; (*coll.*) to move quickly. *v.t.* to journey over; to cause to travel. *n.* the act of travelling; (*pl.*) an account of travelling, usu. in distant countries; the length of stroke, the range or scope, of a piston etc. **travel agent,** *n.* one who sells holidays, air, train, bus tickets etc. **travel agency,** *n.* **travel-soiled, -stained, †-tainted, -worn,** *n.* soiled or worn with travel. **travelled,** *a.* having travelled; experienced in travelling. **traveller,** *n.* one who travels; a commercial traveller; (*Austral.*) a swag-man; a gipsy; (*Naut.*) an iron ring etc., sliding on a spar, rope etc. **traveller's cheque,** *n.* a cheque available in various denominations, sold by a financial institution for use abroad by a traveller, who signs it on receipt and countersigns it in order to cash it. **traveller's-joy,** *n.* the wild clematis, *C. vitalba.* **travelling expenses,** *n.pl.* expenses incurred by a commercial traveller etc., and paid by the employers. **travelling salesman, salesperson,** *n.* one who travels from place to place promoting and selling the products or services of his or her company. **travelogue,** *n.* a lecture or talk on travel illustrated by cinematograph films. [var. of TRAVAIL]

Traven, *n.* **Ben** (pen name of Herman Feige) (1882–1969), US novelist, born in Germany, whose true identity was unrevealed until 1979. His books include the bestseller *The Death Ship* (1926), and *The Treasure of Sierra Madre* (1934), filmed 1948 starring Humphrey Bogart.

Travers, *n.* **Morris William** (1872–1961), English chemist who, with William Ramsay, first identified the inert gases krypton, xenon, and radon (1894–1908).

traverse, *a.* lying or being across, transverse; on a zigzag track (of sailing). †*adv.* athwart, crosswise, *n.* anything, esp. a part of a building or mechanical structure, crossing something else; a gallery or loft communicating between opposite sides of a church or other large building; a mound or earthwork protecting a covered way etc., from enfilading fire; a transversal; (*Naut.*) a zigzag line described by a ship owing to contrary winds etc.; the act of traversing or travelling across; the sideways travel of part of a machine; a sideways movement of climbers on a mountain-side or precipice to avoid obstacles; (*Law.*) a denial of a formal allegation by the opposite party; the horizontal sweep of a gun; †anything that thwarts, a cross. *v.t.* , to travel across; to make a traverse along (a cliff etc.); to lie across or through; to examine, consider, or discuss thoroughly; to thwart, to frustrate, to bring to naught; to plane (wood) across the grain; (*Law.*) to deny (a plea or allegation); (*Ordnance*) to turn and point. *v.i.* to turn, as on a pivot; to make a traverse; to move or walk crosswise (of a horse). **traverse-table,** *n.* a circular board having holes and pegs to indicate the course by which a ship has been sailing during a traverse; a wheeled platform for shifting carriages, locomotives etc., from one line to another. **traversable,** *a.* **traverser,** *n.* one who or that which traverses; a traverse-table. **traversing,** *n.* a method of plane-table surveying by measured connected lines. [F *travers -rse,* L *transversus,* TRANSVERSE]

travertine, *n.* a light-yellow porous rock formed by calcareous deposit from streams, hardening on exposure, used for building. [It. *travertino,* L *Tiburtīnus,* from *Tībur,* Tivoli]

travesty, *n.* a burlesque imitation; a ridiculous misrepresentation; a parody. *v.t.* to make a travesty of, to burlesque. [F *travesti,* p.p. of *travestir,* It. *travestire,* to disguise (TRA-, L. *vestīre,* to clothe)]

travolator, *n.* a moving pavement for conveying pedestrians, e.g. at an airport. [TRAVEL, ESCALATOR]

trawl, *n.* a net, shaped like a flattened bag, for dragging along the sea-bottom; a trawl-line; the act of trawling. *v.i.* to fish with a trawl-net; to gather data etc. from a great number of different sources. **trawl-boat,** *n.* **trawl-line,** *n.* a line of great length, with short lines carrying baited hooks, buoyed up at intervals, for deep-sea fishing. **trawl-net,** *n.* **trawler,** *n.* one who trawls; a fishing-vessel using a trawl-net. **trawling,** *n.* [etym. doubtful]

tray[1], *n.* a flat shallow vessel, used for holding or carrying small articles on; a shallow coverless box, esp. one forming a compartment in a trunk etc. **trayful,** *n.* [OE *trig,* perh. cogn. with TREE]

tray[2], *n.* the third branch of a stag's horn. [var. of TREY]

treacherous, *a.* violating allegiance, disloyal, perfidious; deceptive, illusory; unreliable, unsafe. †**treacher,** †**treachetour,** *n.* **treacherously,** *n.* **treacherousness, treachery,** *n.* [OF *trecheros, tricheros,* from *trecheur,* traitor, from *trechier, trichier,* to cheat, It. *treccare,* perh. from L *trīcārī, to make difficulties,* from *trīcae,* wiles]

treacle, *n.* a syrup drained from sugar in refining; molasses; a saccharine fluid consisting of the inspissated juices or decoctions of certain plants. **treacly,** *a.* [ME and OF *triacle*]

tread, *v.i.* (*past* **trod**, **trode**, *p.p.* **trodden**) to set the foot on the ground; to walk, to step, to go; to deal (cautiously etc.); to follow (in a person's footsteps); of a male bird, to copulate with a hen. *v.t.* to step or walk on; to crush with the feet; to trample on; to walk (a distance, journey etc.); to dance (a measure etc.); of a male bird, to copulate with, to cover. *n.* the act or manner of walking; the sound of walking, a footstep; the flat part of a stair or step; a piece of rubber, metal etc., placed on this to reduce wear or noise; the part of a wheel that bears upon the ground; the outer face of a tyre that is in contact with the road; the part of a rail on which the wheels bear; the part of a sole that rests on the ground; the lateral distance between the pedals of a bicycle etc.; the act of copulating in birds; the cicatricule of an egg. **to tread down,** to press down or crush with the feet; to trample on; to destroy. **to tread in,** to press in or into with the feet. **to tread on,** to trample on; to set the foot on; to follow closely. **to tread on someone's toes,** to offend someone's susceptibilities. **to tread upon one's heels** HEEL[1]. **to tread out,** to press out (wine, etc.) with the feet; to extinguish by stamping on. **to tread under foot,** to destroy; to treat with scorn. **to tread water,** to remain upright and afloat by making walking motions with the legs; to undergo period of relative inactivity. **treadmill,** *n.* a mechanism, usu. in the form of a revolving cylinder driven by the weight of a person or persons, horses etc., treading on movable steps on the periphery, formerly used as a punishment in prisons; monotony or routine. **treader,** *n.* [OE *tredan*]

treadle, *n.* a lever worked by the foot giving motion to a lathe, sewing-machine, bicycle etc. *v.i.* to work this. [OE *tredel* (TREAD, -LE)]

treadmill TREAD.

†**treague,** *n.* a truce. [med. L *tregua,* Goth. *triggwa,* from *triggws,* true, cp. TRUCE]

Treas., (*abbr.*) treasurer; treasury.

treason, *n.* a violation of allegiance by a subject against his sovereign or government, esp. an overt attempt to subvert the government; an act of treachery, a breach of faith. **constructive treason,** an act that may be legally interpreted as treason, though not intended or realized as such. **high treason,** violation of allegiance to the sovereign or the state. **treason-felony,** *n.* the act of attempting to depose the sovereign, levying war to compel a change of measure, intimidating parliament, or stirring up foreign invasion. **treasonable,** *a.* consisting of or involving treason. **treasonableness,** *n.* **treasonably,** *adv.* †**treasonous,** *a.* [ME *trayson* A-F *treysoun,* OF *traïson* (F *trahison*), L *trāditio,* TRADITION]

treasure, *n.* precious metals in any form, or gems; a quantity of these hidden away or kept for future use, a hoard; accumulated wealth; anything highly valued, a precious or highly-prized thing, esp. if portable; a person greatly valued, a beloved person. *v.t.* to lay (up) as valuable, to hoard, to store (up); to prize, to lay (up) in the memory as valuable. **treasure-city,** *n.* a city for stores and magazines. **treasure-house,** *n.* a building in which treasures or highly-valued things are kept. **treasure hunt,** *n.* a game in which people compete to be the first to find something hidden. **treasure trove,** *n.* money, gold, silver, plate, or bullion found hidden in the earth or private place, the owner thereof being unknown, but now becoming the property of the Crown. [OF *tresor,* L THESAURUS]

treasurer, *n.* one who has charge of a treasure or treasury; an officer who receives and disburses the public revenue from taxes, duties etc.; one who has the charge of the funds of a company, society, club etc. **treasurership,** *n.*

treasury, *n.* a place or building in which treasure is stored; a place where the public revenues are kept; a government department in charge of the public revenue; the offices of this; a repository, a book etc., full of information on any subject. **treasury bench,** *n.* the front bench on the right hand of the Speaker in the House of Commons, appropriated to the First Lord of the Treasury, the Chancellor of the Exchequer, and other members of the ministry. **Treasury bill,** *n.* an instrument of credit issued by the government as an acknowledgment of money lent by a private person for three, six or twelve months. **Treasury bond,** *n.* a government promissory note running for a definite period not exceeding six years, bearing interest at a fixed rate, and redeemable at par; an Exchequer bond. **Treasury note,** *n.* a demand note issued by the Treasury; a currency note. **treasury tag,** *n.* a piece of string with a metal pin at each end, used for holding papers together. **Treasury warrant,** *n.* a warrant or order for a sum disbursed by the Exchequer.

treat, *v.t.* to act or behave to or towards; to deal with or manipulate for a particular result, to apply a particular process to, to subject to the action of a chemical agent etc.; to handle or present or express (a subject etc.) in a particular way; to supply with food, drink, or entertainment at one's expense, esp. to supply (electors) with these in order to secure votes; *v.i.* to arrange terms (with), to negotiate; to discuss, to discourse (of). *n.* an entertainment, esp. out of doors, given to school-children etc.; an unusual pleasure or gratification. **a treat,** (*coll.*) excellently, very well. **to stand treat,** (*coll.*) to pay for drinks, etc. **treatable,** *a.* **treater,** *n.* [ME *treten,* F *traiter,* L *tractāre,* to handle, freq. of *trahere,* to draw]

treatise, *n.* a literary composition expounding, discussing, and illustrating some particular subject in a thorough way.

treatment, *n.* any medical procedure intended to bring about a cure; the act or manner of treating. **the treatment,** (*coll.*) the usual way of dealing with something in a particular situation.

treaty, *n.* an agreement formally concluded and ratified between different states; an agreement between persons etc.; negotiation, the act of treating for the adjustment of differences etc. **treaty port,** *n.* a seaport kept open by treaty to foreign commerce.

treble, *a.* triple, threefold; soprano. *n.* a soprano voice, singer, or part; a high-pitched musical instrument; the higher part of the frequency range, esp. in electronic sound reproduction; a type of bet in which the stake and winnings of a bet on one race are carried forward to the next of three races. *v.t.* to multiply by three. *v.i.* to become threefold. **treble chance,** *n.* a type of bet in football pools in which one wins by accurately predicting the number of draws, and home and away wins. **treble clef,** *n.* the clef that places G above middle C on the second line of the staff. †**trebleness,** *n.* **trebly,** *adv.* [OF, from pop. L *trīplus,* TRIPLE]

trebuchet, *n.* a mediaeval military engine for hurling stones; a delicate balance for weighing small articles; a kind of trap for small birds; a cucking-stool. [OF, from *trebucher,* to overturn, to tumble (TRANS-, *buc,* trunk, OHG, *buk,* belly, cp. G *Bauch*)]

trecento, *n.* the 14th cent. as characterized by a distinctive style of Italian literature and art. [It., short for *mil trecento,* 1300]

treddle TREADLE.

†**tredille,** †**tredrille,** *n.* a card-game for three persons. [L *tre-, trēs,* three, after QUADRILLE]

tree, *n.* a perennial woody plant rising from the ground with a single supporting trunk or stem; a thing resembling a tree, esp. in having a stem and branches; a family or genealogical tree; a gibbet; a cross of crucifixion; a diagram with branching lines; a timber beam or framework, as an axle-tree, swingle-tree etc.; a boot-last. *v.t.* to drive or force to take refuge in a tree. **at the top of the tree,** having attained the highest position in a profession etc. **tree of knowledge,** a tree in the Garden of Eden, the fruit of which gave knowledge of good and evil (Gen. iii). **tree of life,** a tree in the Garden of Eden of which Adam and Eve were forbidden to eat (Gen. ii.9); the arbor-vitae. **up a tree,** in a fix, cornered. **tree-agate,** *n.* a variety of agate with dendritic markings. **tree-calf,** *n.* a brown calf binding with a conventional tree-like design. **tree-fern,** *n.* a fern with a vertical rhizome like a tree-trunk. **tree-frog,** *n.* a frog with arboreal habits. **tree surgeon,** *n.* an expert in the treatment of diseased trees. **tree surgery,** *n.* **treeless,** *a.* **treen**[1]**,** *a.* made of wood. *n.*, *a.* (of) dishes, utensils etc. made of wood. [OE *treo* (cp. Icel. *trē,* Dan. *trae,* Swed. *trä*), cogn. with Gr. *drus,* oak, *doru,* spear, Sansk. *dru,* tree]

treen[2]**,** *n.* an obsolete territorial division in the Isle of Man, the third of a tithe. [Manx]

treenail, *n.* a pin or peg of hard wood used in fastening timbers, esp. in shipbuilding.

trefle, *n.* a mine with three chambers. [F, as foll.]

trefoil, *n.* a plant with three leaflets or three-lobed leaves, esp. of the genus *Trifolium,* as the clover, the black medick etc.; a three-lobed or three-cusped ornament in window-tracery etc.; any object in this shape. **trefoiled,** *a.* [A-F *trifoil,* L *trifolium* (TRI- *folium,* leaf)]

trehala, *n.* a kind of manna formed by the substance of the cocoons of a coleopterous insect in Asia Minor, also called Turkish or Syrian manna or **trehala-manna.** [Turk. *tīqālah*]

treillage, *n.* a light frame of posts and rails to support espaliers; a trellis. [F, from *treille,* see TRELLIS]

trek, *v.i.* of oxen, to draw a vehicle or load; to travel by ox-wagon; to journey, esp. with difficulty on foot. *n.* a journey with a wagon; a stage or day's march; any long, arduous journey, esp. on foot. **trekker,** *n.* [Dut. *trekken,* cp. OHG *trechan,* to draw]

trellis, *n.* open-work of strips of wood crossing each other and nailed together, used for verandas, summer-houses etc.; a lattice, a grating; a summer-house, screen, or other structure made of this. *v.t.* to interlace into a trellis; to furnish with trellis. [ME and OF *trelis,* ult. from L *trilix -līcis* (TRI-, *līcium,* thread, thrum) combined later with OF *treille,* late L *trichila,* bower, arbour, etym. doubtful]

trematode, *a.* pertaining to the Trematoda, an order of parasitic worms containing the fluke-worms. **trematoid,** *a., n.* [Gr. *trēmatōdēs,* from *trēma,* hole]

tremble, *v.i.* to shake involuntarily, as with fear, cold, weakness etc.; to be in a state of fear or agitation; to be alarmed (for); to totter, to oscillate, to quaver. *n.* the act or state of trembling; fear. †**tremblement,** *n.* †a trembling; a trill or shake. **trembler,** *n.* one who trembles; an automatic vibrator for making or breaking an electrical circuit. **tremblingly,** *adv.* **trembly,** *a.* [F *trembler,* pop. L *tremulāre,* from *tremulus,* TREMULOUS]

tremellose, *a.* of some fungi, tremulous, jelly-like, gelatinous. [mod. L *tremella,* dim. of *tremula,* fem. of *tremulus,* see prec.]

tremendous, *a.* terrible, dreadful; of overpowering magnitude, violence etc.; (*coll.*) extraordinary, considerable. **tremendously,** *adv.* **tremendousness,** *n.* [L *tremendus,* from *tremere,* to tremble]

tremolando, *adv.* (*Mus*) tremulously. **tremolant,** *n.* TREMULANT under TREMULOUS. [It.]

tremolite, *n.* a calcium magnesium metasilicate crystallizing in the monoclinic system. **tremolitic,** *a.* [Val *Tremola,* N Italy]

tremolo, *n.* a tremulous or quavering effect in singing, playing etc.; an organ or harmonium stop producing a vibrating tone. [It.]

tremor, *n.* a trembling, shaking, or quivering; a thrill. **tremorless,** *a.* [ME and OF *tremour,* L *tremor -orem,* from *tremere,* to tremble]

tremulous, *a.* trembling, shaking, quivering; timid, irresolute, wavering. **tremulously,** *adv.* **tremulousness,** *n.* **tremulant,** *a.* tremulous. *n.* a tremolo; an organ-stop or similar device on an electronic instrument for producing this. [L *tremulus,* from *tremere,* to tremble]

trench, *n.* a long, narrow cut or deep furrow in the earth, a ditch, esp. a long narrow ditch, usu. with a parapet formed by the excavated earth, to cover besieging troops etc. *v.t.* to cut a trench or trenches in (ground etc.); to turn over (ground) by cutting a successive series of trenches and filling in with the excavated soil; to ditch; to cut a furrow or groove (in wood etc.); to cut military trenches against. *v.i.* to cut or dig a trench or trenches; to encroach (on). **to open the trenches,** to begin to dig or to form trenches or lines of approach. **trench-cart,** *n.* a low hand-cart for carrying ammunition, etc., in trenches. **trench-coat,** *n.* a heavy, lined macintosh crossing over in front and furnished with belt and storm sleeves; a similar raincoat, worn by men or women. **trench-fever,** *n.* a remittent or relapsing fever affecting men living in trenches, etc., and transmitted by the excrement of lice. **trench-foot,** *n.* a gangrenous condition of the foot caused by prolonged standing in cold water. **trench mortar,** *n.* a mortar used for throwing bombs. **trench-, trenching-plough,** *n.* a plough for cutting deep furrows. **trench warfare,** *n.* a type of warfare in which soldiers take up positions in trenches facing the enemy. **trencher**[1]**,** *n.* [ME and OF *trenche* (F *tranche*), from *trenchier* (F *trancher*), prob. ult. from L *truncāre,* to TRUNCATE]

trenchant, *a.* sharp, keen; cutting, biting, incisive. **trenchancy,** *n.* **trenchantly,** *adv.* [OF, pres.p. of *trenchier,* see prec.]

Trenchard, *n.* **Hugh Montague, 1st Viscount Trenchard** (1873–1956), British aviator and police commissioner. He commanded the Royal Flying Corps in World War I (1915–17), and 1918–29 organized the Royal Air Force, becoming first marshal of the Royal Air Force 1927. As commissioner of the Metropolitan Police, he established the Police College at Hendon and carried out the Trenchard Reforms, which introduced more scientific methods of detection.

trencher[2]**,** *n.* a wooden plate, now used for cutting bread upon; †the pleasures of the table, a trencher-cap. **trencher-cap,** *n.* a college cap with a flat top, a mortar-board. **trencher-friend, -mate,** *n.* a table-friend, a parasite. **trencher-man,** *n.* a (good or poor) feeder or eater. [A-F *trenchour* (F *tranchoir*), from *trenchier,* AS TRENCH]

trend, *v.i.* to extend or lie along in a particular direction; to incline; to bend (away etc.); to have a general tendency or direction. *n.* general tendency, bent, or inclination; mode, fashion. **trendsetter,** *n.* one who originates, dictates fashions. **trendy,** *a.* (*sometimes derog.*) following the latest trends; fashionable. *n.* a trendy person. [ME *trenden,* OE *trendan,* cp. O.Fris., Dan., and Swed. *trind,* round]

Trent, Council of, *n.* (1545–1563), council held by the Roman Catholic Church at Trento, N Italy, initiating the Counter-Reformation; see also REFORMATION.

trental, *n.* in the Roman Catholic Church, a series of thirty masses for the dead. [OF, from med. L *trentāre,* from L *trīginta,* thirty]

Trent Bridge, *n.* test cricket ground situated in Nottingham and home of the Nottinghamshire county side. One of the oldest and most celebrated cricket grounds in Britain, it was opened in 1838.

Trentino–Alto Adige, *n.* autonomous region of N Italy, comprising the provinces of Bolzano and Trento. **area** 13,600 sq km/5250 sq miles. **capital** Trento, chief towns Trento in the Italian-speaking southern area, and Bolzano-Bozen in the northern German-speaking area of South Tirol (the region was Austrian until ceded to Italy 1919); **population** (1988) 882,000.

trepan[1]**,** *n.* a surgeon's cylindrical saw for removing portions of the skull. *v.t.* to perforate with a trepan. **trepanation, trepanning,** *n.* [F *trepan,* med. L *trepanum,* Gr. *trupanon,* borer]

trepan[2]**,** *v.t.* to entrap, to ensnare; to inveigle (into); to cheat, to swindle. †*n.* a decoy; a stratagem, a snare. [formerly *trapan,* prob. a slang derivative from TRAP[1]]

trepang, *n.* the seaslug or bêche-de-mer. [Malay, *tripang*]

trephine, *n.* an improved trepan with a centre-pin. *v.t.* to operate on with this. [F *tréphine,* TREPAN[1]]

trepidation, *n.* a state of alarm, excitement, or agitation; a trembling of the limbs, as in paralysis; †a slow oscillation of the ecliptic, formerly supposed to account for the precession of the equinoxes; †vibratory motion. †**trepid,** *a.* agitated. [F, from L *trepidātio -tionem,* from *trepidāre,* to bustle, from *trepidus,* agitated]

treponema, *n.* a member of a genus of spirochetes (*Treponema*) that cause syphilis and other diseases.

trespass, *n.* a transgression against law, duty etc., an offence, a sin; a wrongful act involving injury to the person or property of another, any transgression other than treason, misprision of treason, or felony, esp. unauthorized entry into another's land. *v.i.* to commit an illegal intrusion (upon the property or personal rights of another); to intrude, encroach, or make undue claims (upon); †to transgress (against). **trespass-offering,** *n.* a sacrifice to atone for a trespass under the Mosaic law. **trespasser,** *n.* [ME and OF *trespas,* from *trespasser* (F. *trépasser*), med. L *transpassāre* (TRANS-, *passāre,* to PASS)]

tress, *n.* a lock or plait of hair, esp. from the head of a girl or woman; (*pl.*) hair. *v.t.* to arrange in tresses. **tressed, tressy,** *a.* [ME and F *tresse,* med. L *tricia, trica,* Gr. *tricha,* three-fold]

Tressell, *n.* **Robert** (pseudonym of Robert Noonan) (1868–1911), British author, whose *The Ragged Trousered Philanthropists*, published in an abridged form 1914, gave a detailed account of working people's lives.

tressure, *n.* (*Her.*) a diminutive of the orle, usually borne double and emblazoned with fleurs-de-lis. [OF, as prec.]

trestle, *n.* a movable frame for supporting a table, platform etc., usu. consisting of a pair of divergent legs, fixed or hinged; an open braced framework of timber or iron for supporting the horizontal portion of a bridge etc.; a trestle-tree; (*pl.*) the props or shores of a ship in process of building etc. **trestle-bridge,** *n.* **trestle-table,** *n.* a table formed of boards supported on movable trestles. **trestle-tree,** *n.* (*Naut.*) either of a pair of horizontal fore-and-aft timbers fixed to a lower mast to support the cross-trees. **trestlework,** *n.* [OF *trestel* (F *tréteau*), pop. L *transtellum, transtillum,* dim. of *transtrum,* TRANSOM]

tret, *n.* an allowance to purchasers of goods of certain kinds for damage or deterioration during transit, (usu. 4 lb (1.8 kg) in every 104 lb (47.2 kg). [perh. from OF *traite,* transportation, TRACT[1]]

Treurnicht, *n.* **Andries Petrus** (1921–), South African Conservative Party politician. A former minister of the Dutch Reformed Church, he was elected to the South African parliament as a National Party (NP) member but left it to form a new right-wing Conservative Party, opposed to any dilution of the apartheid system.

trevally, *n.* the silver bream.

trevet TRIVET.

Trevithick, *n.* **Richard** (1771–1833), British engineer, constructor of a steam road locomotive in 1801 and the first steam engine to run on rails in 1804.

trews, *n.pl.* trousers, esp. made of tartan. **trewsman,** *n.* a Highlander wearing these. [var. of TROUSERS]

trey, *n.* the three at cards or dice. Cp. TRAY². [A-F *treis, trei* (F *trois*), L *três*]

TRH, (*abbr.*) Their Royal Highnesses.

tri-, *comb. form.* three; three times; triple. [L and Gr. *tri-*, three, from L *três,* Gr. *treis*]

triable, *a.* that may be tried or tested. **triableness,** *n.* [AF]

triacontahedron, *n.* a solid figure or a crystal having 30 sides. **triacontahedral,** *a.* [Gr. *triakonta,* 30, *hedra,* base]

triact, *a.* having three rays, as a sponge-spicule. **triactinal, triactine,** *a.* [TRI-, Gr. *aktis -tinos,* ray]

Triad, *n.* secret society, founded in China as a Buddhist cult AD 36. It became known as the Triad because the triangle played an important part in the initiation ceremony. Today it has a reputation for organized crime (drugs, gambling, prostitution) among overseas Chinese. Its headquarters are alleged to be in Hong Kong.

triad, *n.* a collection of three; (*Welsh Lit.*) a composition in which statements etc., are grouped in threes; (*Chem.*) an element or radical with a combining power of three; (*Mus.*) a chord of three notes; a common chord. **triadic,** *a.* late L and Gr. *trias triados,* from *treie,* three]

triadelphous, *a.* of a plant having the stamens in three bundles. [TRI-, Gr. *adelphos,* brother]

triage, *n.* refuse of coffee-beans; the sorting of casualties in war etc. according to the criterion of who is most likely to survive. [F]

trial, *n.* the act or process of trying or testing; experimental treatment; a test, an examination, an experiment; that which tries or tests strength, endurance, and other qualities; hardship, trouble, suffering etc.; (*Law.*) the judicial examination and determination of the issues in a cause between parties before a judge, judge and jury, or a referee. **on trial,** undergoing a test; being tried in a lawcourt. **trial and error,** a method of solving problems by trying several solutions and choosing the most successful. **trial balance,** *n.* a comparison of the debit and credit totals in double-entry book-keeping. †**trial-fire,** *n.* (*Shak.*) a fire for trying or proving. **trial run,** *n.* a preliminary test of a new procedure etc. **trial-trip,** *n.* a test trip by a new vessel to show her capabilities. [OF (TRY, -AL)]

trialism, *n.* the doctrine or principle of threefold union, as of body, soul, and spirit in man; a union of three states, as of the German, Hungarian and Slav portions of the former Austro-Hungarian empire.

Triandria, *n.pl.* a Linnaean class consisting of plants with hermaphrodite flowers having three stamens. **triandrian, -drous,** *a.* [Gr. *anēr andros,* male]

triangle, *n.* a figure, esp. a plane figure, bounded by three lines, esp. straight lines; a drawing-implement or other thing or ornament of this shape; a combination of three spars lashed together at the top for shifting weights; a steel rod bent into a triangle and sounded by striking with a steel rod; a northern constellation; †a frame formed by three halberds to which a person was tied up to be flogged; any situation involving three people or elements. **triangular,** *a.* having the shape of a triangle; three-cornered; involving three people or elements. **triangular compasses,** *n.pl.* compasses with three legs. **triangularity,** *n.* **triangularly,** *adv.* **triangulate,** *v.t.* to make triangular; to divide into triangles. esp. (an area) in surveying; to ascertain by this means. *a.*, (*Zool.*) marked with triangles. **triangulation,** *n.* **triangulately,** *adv.* [F, from L *trangulum,* neut. adj. (*angulus,* ANGLE²)]

Trianon, *n.* two palaces in the park at Versailles, France: Le Grand Trianon built for Louis XIV, and Le Petit Trianon for Louis XV.

triapsal, -apsidal, *a.* having three apses.

triarch, *n.* the ruler of one of three divisions of a country. **triarchy,** *n.* [Gr. *triarchos -archos,* from *archein,* to rule]

†**triarian,** *a.* occupying the 3rd rank or place; in ancient Rome, denoting the veteran Roman soldiers who were stationed in the third rank from the front in order of battle. *n.* one of the triarian soldiers. [L *triārii,* pl. from TRI-, -AN]

Triassic, Trias, *n.* period of geological time 248–213 million years ago, the first period of the Mesozoic era. The continents were fused together to form the world continent Pangaea. Triassic sediments contain remains of early dinosaurs and other reptiles now extinct. By late Triassic times, the first mammals had evolved. [late L and Gr., TRIAD]

triathlon, *n.* athletic event involving three different sports (usu. swimming, cycling, running). **triathlete,** *n.* a competitor in this. [Gr. *athlon,* a contest]

triatomic, *a.* having three atoms in the molecule. [ATOMIC]

triaxal, -axial, *a.* having three axes.

tribadism, *n.* simulated heterosexual intercourse between women, lesbianism. [Gr. *tribas -ados,* a lewd woman, -ISM]

tribal, *a.* belonging or pertaining to a tribe. **tribally,** *adv.* **tribalism,** *n.* loyalty to a tribe or group. [TRIBE, -AL]

Tribal Areas, Federally administered, area of Pakistan; area 27,200 sq km/10,499 sq miles; population (1985) 2,467,000.

tribasic, *a.* having three atoms of hydrogen replaceable by a base or basic radical; of a molecule, having three monovalent basic atoms or groups.

tribble , *n.* a horizontal drying-frame used in paper-making. [etym. doubtful]

tribe, *n.* a group of people ethnologically related and forming a community or a political division; in ancient Rome, one of the three ancient divisions of the Roman people later increased to 35; a group claiming common descent or affinity, a clan or group of clans, esp. a group of savage clans under a chief; a number of persons of the same character, profession etc. (*usu. contemp.*); a family, esp. a large one; (*Bot. and Zool.*) a more or less indefinite group of plants or animals, usu. above a genus and below an order. **tribesman, tribeswoman,** *n.* [ME and OF *tribu,* L *tribus*]

triblet, *n.* a mandrel used in forging tubes, nuts, and rings etc. [formerly *tribolet,* F. *triboulet*]

triboluminescence, *n.* luminescence produced by friction. [G *tribein,* to rub]

tribometer, *n.* a sled-like apparatus for measuring sliding friction. [F *tribomètre* (Gr. *tribos,* rubbing, from *tribein,* to rub, -METER)]

tribrach, *n.* a metrical foot of three short syllables. **tribrachic,** *a.* [L *tribrachys,* Gr. *tribrachus* (*brachus,* short)]

tribrachial *n.* a three-armed tool.

tribulation, *n.* severe affliction, suffering, distress. [ME. and OF *tribulacion,* late L *tribulatio -onem,* from *trībulāre,* to rub, to oppress, from *trībulum,* threshing-sledge, from *terere,* to rub, p.p. *trītus*]

tribunal, *n.* a court of justice; a board of arbitrators etc.; a seat or bench for judges, magistrates etc., a judgment-seat. [L, from foll]

tribune¹, *n.* one of two (later ten) representatives elected by the people of ancient Rome to protect their rights and liberties against the patricians, also, one of various civil, fiscal, and military officers; a champion of popular rights and liberties. **tribunate, tribuneship,** *n.* **tribunicial, -cian, -tial,** *a.* [ME and OF *tribun,* L *tribūnus,* from *tribus,* TRIBE]

tribune², *n.* a raised floor for the curule chairs of the magistrates in the apse of a Roman basilica; a bishop's throne in an apse, hence, an apse containing this; a platform; a rostrum, a pulpit. [F, from med. L *tribūna*, tribunal, as prec.]

tributary, *a.* paying or subject to tribute; subsidiary, contributory; serving to increase a larger stream. *n.* a tributary person or state; a tributary stream. **tributarily,** *adv.* **tributariness,** *n.* [L *tribūtārius*, as foll.]

tribute, *n.* a sum of money or other valuable thing paid by one prince or state to another in token of submission, for peace or protection, or by virtue of a treaty; the state of being under obligation to pay this; a contribution, gift, or offering (of praise etc.); a share of ore paid to a miner under the system of tribute-work. **tribute-money,** *n.* **tribute-work,** *n.* (*Mining*). **tributer,** *n.* one doing tribute-work. [L *tribūtum*, neut. of *tribūtus*, p.p. of *tribuere*, to give, to pay]

tricala TREHALA.

tricapsular, *a.* having three capsules. [TRI-, CAPSULAR]

tricarpous, *a.* having three carpels. [Gr. *karpos*, fruit]

tricaudate, *a.* having three tail-like processes. [CAUDATE]

trice[1], *v.t.* (*Naut.*) to haul; to tie (up). [ME *tricen, trisen*, MDut. trîsen (cp Dut. *trijsen*, G *triezen*, to hoist]

trice[2], *n.* an instant. **in a trice,** in a moment. [prob. from prec.]

Tricel®, *n.* a partly synthetic textile fibre used in dress fabrics.

†**tricennial,** *a.* of or pertaining to 30 years; occurring once in every 30 years. [L *tricenni-um*, (TRICES, thirty times, *annus*, year)]

tricentenary TERCENTENARY.

tricephalous, *a.* three-headed.

triceps, *a.* of muscles, three-headed. *n.* a three-headed muscle, esp. the large muscle at the back of the upper arm. [L (*-ceps*, from *caput*, head)]

triceratops, *n.* a large herbivorous dinosaur of the Cretaceous period with three horns and a bony crest on the hood. [TRI-, Gr. *keras*, horn, *ops*, eye]

tricerion, *n.* a three-branched candlestick symbolizing the Trinity, used by a bishop in benediction in the Greek Orthodox Church. [late Gr. *trikērion* (*kēros*, wax)]

trichiasis, *n.* entropion or inversion of the eyelashes; a disease of the kidneys in which filamentous matter is passed in the urine; a swelling of the breasts due to obstruction of milk-excretion in child-bearing women. [Gr., as foll.]

trichina, *n.* (*pl.* **-nae**) a hair-like nematode parasitic worm, infesting the intestine or muscles of pigs, man, etc. **trichiniasis**, **trichinosis**, *n.* a disease due to the presence of trichinæ in the system. **trichinize, -ise,**, *v.t.* **trichinization, -isation,** *n.* **trichinozed**, **trichinotic**, **trichinous,** *a.* [mod. L, from Gr. *trichinos*, a. from Gr. *trichinos* a. from *thrix trichos*, hair]

trichite, *n.* a minute hair-like form occurring in certain vitreous volcanic rocks; a minute fibril found in some sponge-spicules, a spicule composed of these. [G *Trichit* (Gr. *thrix trichos* hair, -ITE)]

trichiurid, *n.* one of the Trichiuridae, a family of scombroidean fishes with a ribbon-like body and a filamentous tail. **trichiuriform**, *a.* **trichiuroid,** *a., n.* [Gr. *thrix trichos* hair, *oura*, tail]

trichocephalus, *n.* a genus of nematode worms with filamentous heads, of which *Trichocephalus dispar* affects man, residing chiefly in the caecum. **tricocephalid**, *n.* **trichocephaloid,** *a.* [Gr. *thrix trichos*, hair see CEPHAL-]

trichogenous, *a.* promoting growth of the hair. **trichogen**, *n.* [Gr. *thrix trichos*, hair, -GENOUS]

trichology, *n.* the study of the human hair. **trichological,** *a.* **trichologist,** *n.*

trichoma, *n.* one of the threads composing the thallus in filamentous algae; a disease of the hair, *plica*. **trichomatose**, *a.* affected with this. **trichome,** *n.* (*Bot.*) a hair, filament, scale, prickle, or an outgrowth. [Gr. *trichōma*, from *trichoun*, to cover with hair as prec.]

trichopter, *n.* one of the Trichoptera, a group or suborder of Neuroptera containing the caddis-flies. **trichopteran,** *a., n.* **trichopterous,** *a.* [Gr. *thrix trichos*, hair, *pteron*, wing]

trichord, *a.* esp. of pianos, having three strings to each note. *n.* a musical instrument with three strings. [Gr. *trichordos*]

trichosis, *n.* any disease of the hair. [Gr. *thrix trichos*, hair]

trichotomy, *n.* division into three, esp. of the human being into body, soul, and spirit. **trichotomize, -ise,** *v.t.* **trichotomous,** *a.* **trichotomously,** *adv.* [Gr. *tricha*, triply, from *treis*, three, -TOMY]

trichroism, *n.* the property of exhibiting different colours in three different directions when viewed by transmitted light. **trichroic,** *a.* [F *trichroïsme* (Gr. *trichroos, -chrous*, three-coloured)]

trichromatic, *a.* three-coloured, having the normal three fundamental colour-sensations (of red, green, and purple). **trichromatism,** *n.*

trick, *n.* an artifice, an artful device or stratagem; a foolish or malicious act, a prank, a practical joke; a feat of dexterity, esp. of legerdemain or sleight of hand; an ingenious or peculiar way of doing something, a knack; a particular habit or practice, a mannerism, a personal peculiarity; (*Cards.*) the whole number of cards played in one round; a round; a point gained as the result of a round; (*Naut.*) a turn or spell at the helm, usu. half a watch or two hours. *v.t.* to cheat, to deceive, to delude, to inveigle (into, out of etc.); to dress, to deck (out or up). *v.i.* to practise trickery. **to do the trick,** to achieve the required effect. **to know a trick worth two of that,** to know of some expedient. **to trick out,** to decorate, to dress up. **trick-track** TRIC-TRAC. **trick cyclist,** *n.* (*sl.*) a psychiatrist. **trick-wig,** *n.* an actor's wig so contrived that the hair can be made to stand up on end. **tricker, trickster**, *n.* **trickery,** *n.* **tricky,** *a.* (*coll.*) difficult, awkward; requiring tactful or skilful handling; deceitful. **trickishly,** *adv.* **trickishness,** *n.* **trickily,** *adv.* **trickiness,** *n.* **tricksy,** *a.* playful, sportive; excessively elaborate. [OF *trique, triche*, from *trichier, trechier* (F *tricher*), prob. from L, see TREACHEROUS]

trickle, *v.i.* to flow in drops or in a small stream. *v.t.* to cause to flow thus. *n.* a trickling; a small stream, a rill. **tricklet,** *n.* **trickly,** *a.* [ME *triklen*, acc. to Skeat for *striklen*, freq. from OE *strīcan*, to sweep along, to STRIKE]

triclinic, *a.* (*Cryst.*) having the three axes unequal and inclined at oblique angles. [TRI-, Gr. *klinein*, to lean]

triclinium, *n.* (*pl.* **-nia**) (*Rom. Ant*) a set of couches arranged round three sides of a dining-table; a dining-table furnished with this; a dining-room with this. [L, from Gr. *triklinion* (TRI-, *klinē*, couch)]

tricolour, *n.* a flag or banner having three colours, esp. arranged in equal stripes, as the national standard of France of blue, white and red, divided vertically. *a.* three-coloured. **tricoloured,** *a.* [F *tricoleur*]

triconsonantal, *a.* composed of or containing three consonants. **triconsonantalism,** *n.*

tricopathy, *n.* any disease of the hair. **tricopathic**, *a.* [-PATHY]

tricorn, *a.* having three horns. *n.* a three-cornered hat. **tricornered,** *a.* three-cornered. †**tricornigerous**, **tricornute**, *a.* [F *tricorne*, L *tricornis* (TRI-, *cornu*, horn)]

tricorporal, tricorporate, *a.* (*Her., etc.*) having three bodies. [CORPORAL[2]]

tricostate, *a.* three-ribbed. [COSTATE]

tricot, *n.* a hand-knitted woollen fabric or a machine-made imitation; a soft, ribbed cloth. [F, from *tricoter*, to knit]

tricotyledonous, *a.* having three cotyledons. [TRI-, COTYLEDONOUS]

tricrotic, *a.* of the pulse etc. having three distinct undulations for each beat, **tricrotous**, *a.* [Gr. *trikrotos*]

tric-trac, *n.* a complicated form of back-gammon. [F, imit. of clicking sound]

tricuspid, *a.* of molar teeth, a valve of the heart etc. having three cusps or points. **tricuspidate**, **-dated,** *a.* [L *tricuspis -pidis*]

tricycle, *n.* a three-wheeled cycle. *v.i.* to ride on this. **tricyclist,** *n.*

tricyclic, *a.* of a compound, having three rings in its molecule.

Tridacna, *n.* a genus of bivalve molluscs, comprising the giant clam, having an extremely hard and massive shell and attaining a greater size than any other bivalve. [mod. L, from Gr. *tridaknos,* eaten at three bites (*daknein,* to bite)]

tridactyl, -tylous, *a.* having three fingers or toes. [Gr. *tridaktulos* (*daktulos,* finger)]

tride, *a.* of a horse's pace, short and swift. [F, etym. doubtful]

trident, *n.* a three-pronged implement or weapon, esp. a fish-spear; a three-pronged sceptre or spear, the emblem of Poseidon or Neptune as god of the sea. **tridental,** *a.* **tridentate,** *a.* having three teeth or prongs. [L *tridens -ntem* (TRI-, *dens dentem* tooth)]

Tridentine, *a.* of or pertaining to Trent, or the Council held there 1545–63. *n.* one who accepts the decrees of the Council of Trent, a Roman Catholic. [med. L *Tridentīnus,* from *Tridentum,* Trent, a city of Tyrol]

tridigitate, *a.* tridactylous.

tridimensional, *a.* having three dimensions. [DIMENSIONAL]

triduo, triduum, *n.* in the Roman Catholic Church, a three days' service of prayer etc. **triduan,** *a.* lasting three days, happening every third day. [It. and Sp. *triduo,* L *triduum* (TRI-, *dies,* day)]

tridymite, *n.* a vitreous form of silica usu. occurring in small hexagonal tables composed of groups of three individual crystals. [G *tridymit* (Gr. *tridumos,* threefold)]

tried, *p.p.* TRY. *a.* shown to be effective, durable etc. by testing or use, proven.

triennial, *a.* lasting for three years; happening every three years. *n.* a triennial plant, publication, etc.; every third anniversary of an event; in the Roman Catholic Church, a mass for a dead person performed daily for three years. **triennially,** *adv.* **triennium,** *n.* (*pl.* **-nnia**) a period of three years. [L *triennium* (TRI-, *annus,* year), -AL]

trier, *n.* one who tries, examines, or tests in any way; one who keeps on endeavouring or persisting; a person appointed to determine whether a challenge to a juror or jurors is well founded.

trierarch, *n.* in ancient Greece, the commander of a trireme; a citizen appointed alone or with others to fit out and maintain a trireme. **trierarchal,** *a.* **trierarchy,** *n.* the office or duty of a trierarch; the duty of fitting out and maintaining a trireme. [L *triērarchus,* Gr. *triērarchos* (*triērēs,* trireme, *-archos,* from *archein,* to rule)]

Trieste, *n.* port on the Adriatic, opposite Venice, in Friuli-Venezia-Giulia, Italy; population (1988) 237,000, including a large Slovene minority. It is the site of the International Centre for Theoretical Physics, established 1964. Trieste was under Austrian rule from 1382 (apart from Napoleonic occupation 1809–14) until transferred to Italy 1918. It was claimed after World War II by Yugoslavia, and the city and surrounding territory were divided 1954 between Italy and Yugoslavia.

trifacial, *a.* three-fold and pertaining to the face (as the trigeminus). *n.* the trigeminus.

trifarious, *a.* (*Bot.*) arranged in three rows; facing three ways.

trifid, *a.* (*Bot. and Zool.*) divided wholly or partially into three, three-cleft. [L *trifidus* (TRI-, *fid-,* stem of *findere,* to cleave)]

trifle, *n.* a thing, matter, fact etc., of no value or importance; a small amount of money etc.; a light confection of whipped cream or white of egg, with cake, jam, wine etc.; a variety of pewter. *v.i.* to act or talk with levity; to sport, to jest, to fool. *v.t.* to waste, fritter, or fool away (time) in trifling. **to trifle with,** to treat with levity, disrespect, or lack of proper seriousness; to dally, to toy (with). **trifler,** *n.* **trifling,** *a.* insignificant, trivial. **triflingly,** *adv.* **triflingness,** *n.* [ME and OF *trufle,* var. of *truff,* mockery, cheating, cp. It. *truffa,* etym. doubtful]

trifloral, *a.* (*Bot.*) bearing three flowers. **triflorous,** *a.*

trifoliate, -ated, *a.* (*Bot.*) three-leaved, consisting of three leaflets. **trifoliolate,** *a.* having three leaflets. **Trifolium,** *n.* a genus of low herbs containing the trefoils or clovers.

trifocal, *a.* having three focusses or focal lengths.

triforium, *n.* (*pl.* **-ria**) a gallery or arcade in the wall over the arches of the nave or choir, or sometimes the transepts, in a large church. [med. L (TRI-, *foris,* door opening)]

triform, -ed, *a.* having three shapes, parts, or divisions.

trifurcate, -cated, *a.* having three branches or forks; trichotomous. *v.t., v.i.* to divide into three. [L *triformis*]

trig¹, *v.t.* to stop, check, or skid (a wheel). *n.* a wedge, block etc., used for this. [etym. doubtful]

trig², *a.* neat, trim, spruce. *n.* a dandy. **trigly,** *adv.* **trigness,** *n.* [Icel. *tryggr,* cp. Norw., Swed., and Dan. *trygg*]

trig, trigon, (*abbr.*) trigonometry.

trigamous, *a.* married three times; having three wives or three husbands at once; having male, female, and hermaphrodite flowers on the same head. **trigamist,** *n.* **trigamy,** *n.* [Gr. *trigamos* (TRI-, *gamos,* marriage)]

trigeminal, *a.* threefold; (*Anat.*) of or pertaining to the trigeminus. *n.* the trigeminus. **trigeminus,** *n.* the fifth cranial or trifacial nerve dividing into the superior and inferior maxillary and the ophthalmic nerves. [L *trigeminus* (TRI-, *geminus,* born with another)]

trigger, *n.* a catch or lever for releasing the hammer of a gun-lock; any similar device for releasing a spring, etc., in various forms of mechanism; anything that initiates a process, sequence of events etc. *v.t.* to cause to happen, to set off; to activate, to put into operation. **trigger-happy,** *a.* too eager to fire (a gun etc); too eager to take action. [formerly *tricker,* Dut. *trekker,* from *trekken,* to pull, cp. TREK]

trigla, *n.* a genus of fishes comprising the gurnard; a fish of the genus. [mod. L, from Gr. *triglē*]

Triglav, *n.* mountain in the Julian Alps, rising to 2863 m/9393 ft. It is the highest peak in Yugoslavia.

triglot, *a.* written in three languages. [TRI-, Gr. *glotta,* tongue]

triglyph, *n.* an ornament on a Doric frieze consisting of a tablet with three vertical grooves. **triglyphal, -ic, ical,** *a.* [L *triglyphus,* Gr. *trigluphos* (TRI-, *gluphein,* to carve)]

trigon, *n.* a triangle; a set of three signs of the zodiac arranged at the angles of an equilateral triangle; a triangular instrument used in dialling; in ancient Greece, a ball-game with three players; a triangular harp or lyre, also called **trigonon**. **trigonic,** *a.* **trigonal,** *a.* triangular, three-cornered; (*Math.*) denoting a system of trilinear coordinates. **trigonally,** *adv.* **trigonous,** *a.* [L *trigōnum,* Gr. *trigōnon* (TRI-, *-gōnos, gōnia,* angle)]

trigoneutic, *a.* (*Ent.*) producing three broods in a year. [TRI-, Gr. *goneuein,* to beget]

trigonic TRIGON.

trigonometry, *n.* the branch of mathematics treating of the relations of the sides and angles of triangles, and applying these to astronomy, navigation, surveying etc. **trigonometer,** *n.* an instrument for the mechanical solution of plane right-angled triangles. **trigonometric, -ical,** *a.* **trigonometric function,** *n.* any of a group of functions of an angle expressed in terms of the ratios of the sides of a right-angled triangle; the inverse of trigonometric function. **trigonometrically,** *adv.* [Gr. *trigōnon,* TRIGON, -METRY]

trigonon, etc. TRIGON

trigram, *n.* a trigraph; a set of three straight lines in one plane not all intersecting in the same point. **trigrammatic, trigrammic,** *a.*

trigraph, *n.* a group of three letters representing a single sound.

trigynous, *a.* having three pistils. [Gr. *gunē,* female]

trihedron, *n.* a figure having three sides. **trihedral,** *a.* [Gr. *hedra,* base]

trijugate, -gous *a.* (*Bot.*) having three pairs of leaflets.

trike, (*coll.*) short for TRICYCLE.

trilabe, *n.* a three-pronged grasping instrument used in

surgery. [Gr. *labein,* to hold]
trilaminar, *a.* having or consisting of three layers.
trilateral, *a.* having three sides. **trilaterally,** *adv.*
trilby, *n.* a man's soft felt hat with a dent in the middle. [heroine of George du Maurier's *Trilby*]
trilemma, *n.* a syllogism involving three alternatives. [after DILEMMA]
trilinear, *a.* consisting of three lines.
trilingual, †**-guar,** *a.* pertaining to or expressed in three languages.
triliteral, *a.* consisting of or using three letters (esp. of Semitic roots). *n.* a triliteral word or root. **triliteralism, triliterality,** *n.*
trilith, trilithon, *n.* a megalithic monument usu. consisting of two uprights supporting an impost. **trilithic,** *a.* [Gr. *trilithon,* neut. of *trilithos* (*lithos,* stone)]
trill, *v.i.* to sing or give forth a sound with a tremulous vibration. *v.i.* to sing or utter with a quavering or shake. *n.* a tremulous or quavering sound; a consonant pronounced with a trilling sound, as *r;* a shake, a rapid alternation of two notes a tone or semitone apart. [It. *trillāre,* imit.]
trilling, *n.* (*Cryst.*) a crystal composed of three individuals; any one child in a triplet. [TRI-, -LING]
trillion, *n.* the product of a million raised to the third power; (*esp. N Am.*) a million million; (*pl.*) (*coll.*) an indefinite large number. **trillionth,** *a.* [after MILLION]
trilobate , trilobated, trilobed, *a.* having three lobes. **trilobation,** *n.* [LOBATE]
trilobite, *n.* one of the Palaeozoic group of articulates with a three-lobed body. **trilobitic,** *a.*
trilocular, *a.* having three cells or chambers. [LOCULUS]
trilogy, *n.* a series of three tragedies, each complete in itself, but connected by the story or theme, and adapted for performance in immediate succession; a group of three plays, operas, novels etc., each complete in itself, but similarly connected. [Gr. *trilogia*)]
trim, *v.t.* (*past, p.p.* **trimmed**) to put in good order, to make neat and tidy; to remove irregularities, excrescences, or superfluous or unsightly parts from; to cut, lop, or clip (those) away or off; to dress, to smooth, to plane (wood, boards etc.); to put (a lamp etc.) in order by clipping or renewing a wick, carbons etc.; to reduce (e.g. costs); to decorate, to ornament (with trimmings etc.); to adjust (sails, yards etc.) to the wind; to adjust (a ship) by arranging the cargo, ballast etc.; (*coll.*) to reprove sharply, to chastise, to flog. *v.i.* to adopt a middle course, between parties, opinions etc. *a.* properly adjusted, in good order; well-equipped, neat, tidy, smart; †nice, fine. *n.* state of preparation or fitness, order, condition, esp. of a ship or her cargo, ballast, masts etc.; the angle at which an aeroplane flies in given conditions; the interior panels, decorative fascia, etc. of a vehicle; an act of trimming, esp. hair; material used to trim clothes etc; that which is removed by trimming. **trimly,** *adv.* **trimmer,** *n.* one who or that which trims; an implement or machine for clipping timber etc.; a joist into which others are framed; one who trims between parties, esp. in politics, a time-server. **trimming,** *n.* the act of one who trims; material sewn on a garment for ornament; (*coll., pl.*) accessories to a dish; (*pl.*) anything additional to the main item. **trimness,** *n.* [OE *trymian,* to make firm, to set in order, from *trum,* firm, stable]
trimaran, *n.* a sailing vessel with three hulls. [TRI-, cata*maran*]
trimensual, trimestrial, *a.* happening or issued every three months. [L *trimestus,* TRI-, *mensis,* month]
trimer, *n.* a polymer whose molecule is formed from three molecules of a monomer. **trimerous,** *a.* having three parts, joints, members etc. [Gr. *trimerēs* (*meros,* part)]
trimester, *n.* a period of three months; any of the three divisions of the academic year. [L *trimetrus,* from Gr. *trimetros*]
trimeter, *n.* a verse consisting of three measures of two feet each. *a.* consisting of three measures. **trimetric, -ical,** *a.* [L *trimetrus,* Gr. *tremetros* (-METRE)]
trimethyl, *a.* containing three methyl groups. **trimethylamine,** *n.* the tertiary amine of methyl, a frequent constituent of stale herringbrine. [METHYL]
trimonthly, *a.* occurring every three months; lasting three months.
trimorphism, *n.* the existence in certain species of plants and animals of three distinct forms, colours etc., esp. having flowers with pistils or stamens of three different relative lengths; the property of crystallizing in three distinct forms. **trimorphic, -morphous,** *a.* [TRI-, Gr. *morphē,* form]
Trimurti, *n.* the Hindu triad of gods, representing the Absolute Spirit in its three aspects: Brahma, personifying creation; Vishnu, preservation; and Siva, destruction.
trine, *a.* threefold, triple; (*Astrol.*) pertaining to or in trine. *n.* a triad, a set of three; (*Theol.*) the Trinity; (*Astrol.*) the aspect of planets distant from each other 120°. **trinal, -ary,** *a.* [L *trinus* from *trēs,* three]
trinervate, *a.* three-nerved -veined, or -ribbed.
Tringa, *n.* a genus of birds containing the sand-pipers. †**tring,** *n.* **tringine, tringoid,** *a.* [mod. L, from Gr. *trungas*]
tringle, *n.* a curtain-rod, a rod supporting the canopy of a bedstead; a small square ornament, esp. in a Doric triglyph. [F, etym. doubtful]
Trinidad and Tobago, *n.* Republic of, a country in the W Indies, off the coast of Venezuela. **area** Trinidad 4800 sq km/1853 sq miles and Tobago 300 sq km/116 sq miles. **capital** Port of Spain. **towns** San Fernando. **physical** comprises the two main islands, and some smaller ones; Trinidad has coastal swamps, and hills E–W. **population** (1988) 1,261,000 (equally divided between those of African and E Indian descent), 1.2 million on Trinidad; annual growth rate 1.6%. **exports** angostura bitters, asphalt, natural gas, oil. **language** English (official), Hindi, French, Spanish. **religion** Roman Catholic 33%, Protestant 14%, Hindu 25%, Muslim 6%.
trinitarian TRINITY.
trinitrotoluene, *n.* a chemical compound, usually known as TNT, largely used as a high explosive.
Trinity, *n.* in the Christian religion, the threefold union of three persons in one godhead, namely Father, Son, and Holy Ghost/Spirit. The precise meaning of the doctrine has been the cause of unending dispute, and was the chief cause of the split between the Orthodox and Roman Catholic churches. **trinity,** *n.* a group or union of three individuals, a triad; the state of being three or threefold; a symbolical representation of the Trinity frequent in art, as the triangle or three interlacing circles. **Trinity Brethren,** *n.pl.* Members of Trinity House. **Trinity House,** *n.* an association for licensing pilots, managing lighthouses, beacons, buoys etc., in British waters. **Trinity Sunday,** *n.* the Sunday next after Whit Sunday. **Trinity term,** *n.* the term beginning after Easter at some universities. **Trinitarian,** *a.* of or pertaining to the doctrine of the Trinity; *n.* one who believes in this. **Trinitarianism,** *n.* [OF *trinite,* late L *trinitas -tatem,* from *trīnus,* TRINE]
trinket, *n.* a small personal ornament of no great value as a jewel, esp. a ring; any small ornament or fancy article; †a small tool or implement; a topsail. †**trinketry,** *n.* [etym. unknown, perh. from ME *trenket* O.North.F *trenquet,* knife, from *trenquer,* var. of *tranchier* to cut, see TRENCH]
trinoctial, *a.* lasting or comprising three nights. [TRI-, L *nox noctis,* night, -AL]
trinodal, *a.* (*Bot., Anat., etc.*) having three nodes or joints. [NODAL]
trinomial, *a.* consisting of three terms, esp. (*Alg.*) connected by the signs + or −; *n.* a trinomial name or expression. **trinomialism,** *n.* trinomial nomenclature, esp. in biology. **trinomially,** *adv.*
trio, *n.* a set of three; a musical composition for three voices or three instruments; a set of three singers or players; the second part of a minuet, march etc.; three aces, kings, queens, knaves, or tens. [It., from L *trēs,* three]
triode, *n.* a thermionic valve with three electrodes.

[TRI-, (ELECTR)ODE]

triodion, *n.* in the Greek Orthodox Church, a book of offices for the services from Septuagesima to Easter. [Gr. *triōdion* (TRI-, *hodos,* way)]

trioecious, *a.* (*Bot.*) having male, female and hermaphrodite flowers, each on different plants of the same species. [Gr. *treis,* three; *oikos,* a house]

triole, *n.* (*Mus.*) a triplet. [F, dim. of TRIO]

triolet, *n.* a poem of eight lines with two rhymes arranged *ab a a ab ab.* [F, dim. of TRIO]

trional, *n.* a hypnotic drug prescribed in cases of mental disease and neurasthenia.

Triones, *n.pl.* the seven chief stars of the Great Bear. [L, ploughing-oxen]

trionym, *n.* a name composed of three terms. **trionymal,** *a.* [TRI-, Gr. *onoma,* Aeolic *onuma,* name]

trior TRIER.

trip, *v.i.* (*past, p.p.* **tripped**) to move, step, walk, or run lightly or nimbly; of rhythm etc. to go lightly or evenly; to make a false step, to stumble; to make a short journey; to be under the influence of a hallucinogenic drug; to catch the foot (over something) so as nearly to fall; to err, to go wrong; to be activated; †to make an excursion. *v.t.* to cause to fall by catching or obstructing the feet etc.; to catch or detect in a fault, mistake, or offence; (*Naut.*) to loosen (an anchor) from the bottom; to turn (a yard etc.) from the horizontal to the vertical position; to release (a part of a machine) by unfastening; to activate, to set off. *n.* a light nimble step; a leaping movement of the feet; a short excursion, voyage, or journey; (*sl.*) a period spent under the influence of a hallucinogenic drug; (*sl.*) an unpleasant experience; (*sl.*) a pleasurable or engrossing experience; a sudden stroke or catch by which a wrestler trips up his antagonist; a stumble; a false step; a failure, a mistake; any device for activating a mechanism; (*Naut.*) a single tack in plying to windward; the number of fish caught in one voyage. **trip-hammer,** *n.* a tilt-hammer. **trip-wire,** *n.* a wire that trips a mechanism when pulled. **trippant,** *a.* walking or trotting. **tripper,** *n.* one who trips up another; one who goes on a trip, an excursionist; a device that trips a mechanism. **trippingly,** *adv.* [ME *trippen,* OF *treper, triper, tripper,* MDut. *trippen,* cp. Swed. *trippa,* Dan. *trippe*]

tripartite, *a.* divided into three corresponding parts or copies; made or concluded between three parties. **tripartitely,** *adv.* **tripartition,** *n.* [TRI-, L *partitus,* p.p. of *partiri,* to divide, from *pars partis* PART]

tripe, *n.* a part of the stomach of ruminating animals prepared for food; (*usu. in pl.*) the entrails, the belly; (*coll.*) silly stuff; rubbish, nonsense. **tripe-de-roche,** *n.* a vegetable substance obtained from various lichens and eaten in emergency as food by hunters in N America. [F, rock-tripe] **tripe-man, tripe-seller,** *n.* **tripery,** *n.* [F (cp. Sp. and Port, *tripa,* It. *trippa*), etym. doubtful]

†**tripedal,** *a.* having three feet. [L *tripedalis* (TRI-, *pes pedis,* foot)]

tripennate, TRIPINNATE.

tripersonal, *a.* consisting of three persons (esp. of the Godhead). **tripersonalism,**, *n.* the doctrine of the Trinity. **tripersonalist,** *n.* a believer in this. **tripersonality,** *n.* [TRI-, PERSONAL]

tripetalous, *a.* having three petals.

triphane, *n.* spodumene. [Gr. *phainein,* to shine]

triphthong, *n.* a combination of three vowels forming one sound. **triphthongal,** *a.* [after DIPHTHONG]

triphyllous, *a.* three-leaved. [Gr. *phullon,* leaf]

Triphysite, *n.* one of a Spanish sect of the 7th cent. who held that Christ has three natures, human, divine and a third derived from the union of these. [Gr. *phusis,* nature]

tripinnate, *a.* triply pinnate. **tripinnately,** *adv.*

Tripitaka, *n.* the canonical texts of Theravāda Buddhism, divided into three parts.

triplane, *n.* an aeroplane with three supporting planes.

triple, *a.* consisting of three parts or three things united, threefold; multiplied by three; of musical rhythm, having three beats to the bar. *n.* a threefold quantity; three of anything. *v.t.* to treble, to make threefold; to alter (a steam-engine) to triple expansion. *v.i.* to become three times as large or as many. **Triple Alliance,** *n.* an alliance from 1882 between Germany, Austria-Hungary, and Italy to offset the power of Russia and France. It was last renewed 1912 but during World War I, Italy's initial neutrality gradually changed, and it denounced the alliance 1915. The term also refers to other alliances: 1668 – England, Holland, and Sweden; 1717 – Britain, Holland, and France (joined 1718 by Austria); 1788 – Britain, Prussia, and Holland; 1795 – Britain, Russia, and Austria. **triple crown,** the crown or tiara worn by the Pope. **triple-crowned,** *a.* **Triple Entente,** *n.* alliance of Britain, France, and Russia 1907–17. In 1911 this became a military alliance and formed the basis of the Allied powers in World War I against the Central Powers, Germany and Austria-Hungary. **triple-expansion engine,** *n.* (*Mach.*) an engine in which the steam expands successively in high, intermediate, and low pressure cylinders, all of which work on the same shaft. **triple-headed,** *a.* **triple jump,** *n.* an athletic event in which the competitor performs a hop, a step and a jump in succession. **triple point,** *n.* the temperature and pressure at which the solid, liquid and vapour phases of a substance are in equilibrium. **triplet,** *n.* a set or group of three; (*coll.*) each of three children at a birth; three verses rhyming together; (*Mus.*) three notes performed in the time of two; (*Naut., pl.*) three links of chain between the cable and the anchor-ring. **triplex,** *n.* triple-time; a composition in three parts; (**Triplex**®) a type of laminated glass. **triplicate,** *a.* made thrice as much or as many, threefold. *n.* a copy, document, or other thing corresponding to two others of the same kind. *v.t.*, to make triplicate, to treble. **in triplicate,** written out or copied three times. **triplicate ratio,** the ratio of the cubes (of two quantities). **triplication, triplicature,** *n.* **triplicity,** *n.* the state of being triple. **triply,** *adv.* [F, from L *triplus* (TRI-, *-plus,* cogn. with *plēnus,* full)]

tripod, *n.* a three-legged stand, stool, utensil, seat, table etc.; a three-legged support for a camera etc.; in ancient Greece, a bronze altar at Delphi on which the Pythian priestess sat to deliver oracles; an imitation of this, esp. offered as a prize at the Pythian games. **tripodal,** *a.* [L *tripus -podis,* Gr. *tripous -podos* (*pous podos,* foot)]

Tripoli (Arabic **Tarabolus al-Gharb**), *n.* capital and chief port of Libya, on the Mediterranean; population (1980) 980,000. Products include olive oil, fruit, fish, and textiles.

tripoli, *n.* rottenstone, a friable siliceous limestone. [*Tripoli,* Libya]

tripos, *n.* (*pl.* **-ses**) either part of the examination for an honours BA at Cambridge Univ., a printed list (arranged in three grades) of the successful candidates. [L *tripus,* TRIPOD]

tripotage, *n.* a medley, a jumble. [F]

trippant, tripper, trippingly TRIP.

triptane, *n.* (*Aviat.*) a very powerful fuel, trimethyl butane.

triptote, *n.* a noun having three cases only. [Gr. *triptōtos* (TRI-, *ptōtos,* falling, from *piptein,* to fall)]

triptych, *n.* a picture, carving, or other representation, on three panels side by side, frequently used for altarpieces; a group of three associated pictures etc.; a writing-tablet in three leaves. [Gr. *triptuchon* neut. of *triptuchos* (TRI-, *ptuchē,* fold, from *ptussein,* to fold)]

triptyque, *n.* customs pass, made out in triplicate, for importing or exporting a motor vehicle. [F]

tripudium, *n.* in ancient Rome, a religious dance; a favourable divination from the feeding of the sacred chickens. †**tripudiary,** *a.* †**tripudiation** *.n.* [L, etym. doubtful]

Tripura, *n.* state of NE India since 1972, formerly a princely state, between Bangladesh and Assam. **area** 10,500 sq km/4053 sq miles. **capital** Agartala. **population** (1981) 2,060,000. **products** rice, cotton, tea, sugar cane; steel, jute. **language** Bengali. **religion** Hindu.

tripwire TRIP.
triquetra, *n.* an ornament composed of three interlacing arcs. **triquetrous, †-tral,** *a.* three-sided, three-cornered, triangular; (*Bot.*) having three sharp angles. [L, fem. of *triquetrus,* three-cornered (*quetrus,* etym. doubtful)]
triradial, triradiate, -ated, *a.* having three rays or radiating branches.
trireme, *n.* a war-galley with three benches of oars. [L *trirēmis* (*rēmus* oar)]
trisagion, *n.* a hymn with a threefold invocation of God as holy, in the liturgies of the Greek and Eastern Churches. [Gr. *trisagios* (*tris,* thrice, from *treis,* three, *hagios* holy)]
trisect, *v.t.* to divide into three (esp. equal) parts. **trisection,** *n.* [TRI-, L *sectus,* p.p. of *secāre,* to cut]
trisepalous, *a.* having three sepals.
triserial, -ate, *a.* (*Anat., Bot., etc.*) arranged in three rows.
trishaw, *n.* a three-wheeled rickshaw. [TRI-, rick*shaw*]
trisinuate, *a.* having three sinuses (of a margin, etc.). [SINUATE]
triskaidekaphobia, *n.* fear of the number 13. [Gr. *triskaideka,* -PHOBIA]
triskelion, *n.* a form of fylfot, usu. consisting of three human legs, bent, and joined at the thigh, as in the arms of the Isle of Man. [Gr. *triskelēs* (*skelos,* leg)]
trismegistus, *a.* thrice great (epithet of Hermes). [Gr. *trismegistos* (*tris,* thrice, *megistos,* great)]
trismus, *n.* lock-jaw. [Gr. *trismos,* from *trizein,* to squeak, to creak]
trisoctahedron, *n.* a solid having 24 equal faces. [Gr. *tris,* thrice, OCTAHEDRON]
trispermous, *a.* three-seeded.
trisplanchnic, *a.* of or pertaining to the three great viscera of the body, cranial, thoracic, and abdominal. [Gr. *tris,* thrice, SPLANCHNIC]
trisporous, *a.* having three spores. **trisporic,** *a.*
†trist, *a.* sad, gloomy. **†tristful,** *a.* [OF *triste,* L *tristis*]
Tristan, *n.* hero of Celtic legend, who fell in love with Iseult, the bride he was sent to win for his uncle King Mark of Cornwall; the story became part of the Arthurian cycle, and is the subject of Wagner's opera *Tristan and Isolde.*
tristich, *n.* a strophe or set of three lines. **tristichous,** *a.* (*Bot.*) arranged in three vertical rows.
tristigmatic, *a.* (*Bot.*) having three stigmas. [Gr. *tristichos* (*tris,* thrice) from *treis,* three, *stichos,* row)]. [STIGMA]
tristylous, *a.* (*Bot.*) having three styles. [STYLE[2]]
trisulcate, *a.* (*Bot.*) having three furrows or grooves; (*Zool.*) having three digits or hoofs. [SULCATE]
trisyllable, *n.* a word of three syllables. **trisyllabic,** *a.* **trisyllabically,** *adv.* [SYLLABLE]
tritagonist, *n.* the third actor in a classical Greek play. [Gr. *tritagōnistēs* (*tritos,* third, *agōnistēs,* see AGONISTIC)]
tritanopia, *n.* a reduced ability to distinguish the colour blue. [TRI-, *anopia,* blindness, i.e. inability to see one third of the spectrum]
trite, *a.* worn out; commonplace, hackneyed, stale. **tritely,** *adv.* **triteness,** *n.* [L *trītus,* p.p. of *terere,* to rub]
triternate, *a.* thrice ternate; divided and subdivided into 27 leaflets.
tritheism, *n.* the doctrine that the three persons of the Trinity are each distinct Gods. **tritheist,** *n.* **tritheistic,** *a.*
triticum, *n.* a genus of grasses including wheat. [L, perh. from *trītus,* as TRITE]
tritium, *n.* an isotope of hydrogen with a mass three times that of ordinary hydrogen. [Gr. *tritos,* third]
tritoma, *n.* a genus of liliaceous plants comprising the flame-flowers. [Gr. *tritomos,* thrice cut (*tris,* thrice, *temnein,* to cut)]
Triton, *n.* in Greek mythology, a son of Poseidon (Neptune) by Amphitrite, or one of a race of minor sea-gods, represented as half man and half fish, and blowing a spiral shell; a genus of aquatic salamanders; a genus of gasteropod, containing the trumpet-shell; in astronomy, one of the moons of Neptune. It has a diameter of 2720 km/1690 miles, and orbits Neptune every 5.88 days in a retrograde (east to west) direction. Its surface has many fault lines and a bright polar region which reflects 90% of the sunlight it receives. Its atmosphere is comprised of methane and nitrogen, and has a pressure only 0.00001 that of the Earth at sea level. Triton was discovered 1846. **a triton among the minnows,** one greater than his fellows. [L and Gr.]
tritone, *n.* (*Mus.*) an augmented fourth, containing three whole tones.
tritubercular, *a.* of teeth, having three tubercles or cusps. **trituberculism,** *n.* [TUBERCULAR]
triturate, *v.t.* to rub or grind down to a fine powder; to masticate with the molar teeth. **triturable,** *a.* **trituration,** *n.* **triturator,** *n.* **triturium, -torium,** *n.* (*pl.* **-ia**), a vessel for separating liquids of different densities. [late L *trītūrātus,* p.p. of *trītūrāre,* from *trītūra,* rubbing, as TRITE]
triumph, *n.* in ancient Rome, a pageant in honour of a victorious general who entered the city in a solemn process, followed by religious ceremonies; the state of being victorious; victory, success; joy or exultation for success. *v.i.* to enjoy a triumph; to gain a victory, to prevail (over); to boast or exult (over); to exult. **triumphal,** *a.* of or pertaining to a triumph. †*n.* a token of victory. **triumphal arch,** *n.* an arch built to celebrate a victory or other notable event. **triumphalism,** *n.* an arrogant pride in one's own success. **triumphant,** *a.* victorious, successful; exultant. **triumphantly, triumphingly,** *adv.* **triumpher,** *n.* [ME and OF *triumphe,* L *triumphus -um,* Gr. *thriambos,* hymn to Bacchus]
triumvir, *n.* (*pl.* **triumvirs, -viri**) any one of three men united in office, esp. a member of the first or second triumvirate in ancient Rome. **triumviral,** *a.* **triumvirate,** *n.* the office of a triumvir; a group of triumvirs; a coalition of three men in office or authority, esp. the first triumvirate, of Pompey, Julius Caesar and Crassus in 60 BC, or the second, of Mark Antony, Octavian, and Lepidus, in 43 BC; a party or set of three men. **†triumviry,** *n.* [L (*trium,* gen. of *trēs,* three, *vir,* man)]
triune, *a.* three in one. **triunity,** *n.* [TRI-, L *ūnus,* one]
trivalent, *a.* having a valency or combining power of three. **trivalence, trivalency,** *n.*
trivalvular, *a.* having three valves. **trivalve,** *a., n.*
trivertebral, *a.* consisting of three vertebrae.
trivet, *n.* a three-legged stand, esp. a metal tripod or movable bracket for supporting cooking vessels at a fire. **right as a trivet,** (*coll.*) firm, stable; hence in first-rate health, circumstances, position etc. [formerly *trevet,* OE *trefet,* L *tripēs -pedem* (TRI-, *pēs pedis,* foot)]
trivia, *n.pl.* trifles, inessentials. [see foll.]
trivial, *a.* of little value or importance; trifling; inconsiderable; commonplace, ordinary; of names of plants etc., common, popular, not scientific. **trivialism, triviality, trivialness,** *n.* **trivialize, -ise,** *v.t.* to cause to seem trivial, to minimize. **trivially,** *adv.* **trivium,** *n.* in Mediaeval schools, the first three liberal arts: grammar, rhetoric, and logic. [F, from L *triviālis,* ordinary, from *trivium,* cross-roads (TRI-, *via,* way)]
tri-weekly, *a.* happening, issued or done three times a week or once every three weeks.
-trix, *suf.* denoting a feminine agent, as in *executrix, testatrix.*
trizone, *n.* the British, American and French zones of occupation in Germany after World War II. **trizonal,** *a.*
tRNA, (*abbr.*) transfer RNA.
troat, *n.* the cry of a buck in rutting time. *v.i.* to cry thus. [imit.]
trocar, *n.* an instrument for draining an internal part of fluid, used in dropsy, hydrocele etc. [F (*trois,* three, *carre,* L *quadra,* square)]
trochaic TROCHEE.
trochal TROCHE.
trochanter, *n.* any one of several bony processes on the upper part of the thigh-bone; the second joint of the leg of an insect. [Gr. from *trechein,* to run]

troche, *n.* a lozenge, usu. circular, of medicinal substance. **trochal**, *a.* wheelshaped, rotiform. [Gr. *trochos,* wheel, as prec.]

trochee, *n.* a metrical foot of two syllables, long and short. **trochaic**, *a., n.* [L *trochaeus,* Gr. *trochaios,* running, as prec.]

trochil, -us, *n.* an Egyptian plover said by the ancients to enter the mouth of crocodiles and feed on parasites; a variety of humming-bird; a crested warbler. [Gr. *trochilos,* from *trechein,* to run]

†**trochite,** *n.* the wheel-like joint of the stalk of an encrinite. [Gr. *troch-os,* wheel, as prec. -ITE]

trochiter, *n.* the greater tuberosity of the humerus for the insertion of several muscles. [var. of TROCHANTER]

trochlea, *n.* (*pl.* **-leae**) a pulley-like anatomical part or surface, esp. that of the humerus articulating with the ulna. **trochlear,** *a.* (*Anat., Bot.*). **trochleate**, *a.* (*Bot.*). [L, from Gr. *trochalia,* pulley, from *trechein,* to run]

trochoid, *a.* (*Anat.*) rotating on its own axis, pivotal; of a trochoidal. *n.* a curve generated by a point in the plane of one curve rolling upon another; (*Anat.*) a trochoid joint. **trochoidal**, *a.* (*Geom.*). [Gr. *trochoeidēs* (*trochos,* see TROCHE)]

trochometer, *n.* an hodometer.

trochophore, *n.* a free-swimming ciliate larva of many invertebrates. [Gr. *trochos,* wheel, -PHORE]

troco, *n.* an old game played on a lawn with wooden balls and a spoon-shaped cue, lawn-billiards. [Sp. *truco*]

trod, trodden, †**trode** TREAD.

trog, *v.i.* (*coll.*) to walk, often wearily, *n.* [Possibly from *tr*udge and sl*og*]

troglodyte, *n.* a cave-dweller, **troglodytic, -ical**, *a.* **troglodytism,** *n.* [F, from L *trōglodyta,* Gr. *trōglodutēs* (*trōglē,* cave, *duein,* to enter)]

trogon, *n.* one of a family of tropical American insectivorous birds, with brilliant plumage. [Gr., pres.p. of *trōgein,* to gnaw]

Troic, *a.* Trojan. [L *Trōicus,* Gr. *Trōikos,* from *Trōia,* Troy]

troika, *n.* a team of three horses harnessed abreast; a travelling-carriage drawn by this. [Rus.]

troilism, *n.* sexual activity involving three people of both sexes. [Perhaps F *trois, dualism*]

Trojan, *a.* pertaining to ancient Troy. *n.* an inhabitant of ancient Troy; a person of pluck or determination; †a boon companion. **Trojan horse,** *n.* the huge wooden horse in which the Greeks secretly entered Troy; any subterfuge intended to undermine an organization etc. from within; a computer program that appears to function normally but which, undetected by the normal user, at the same time causes damage to other files or which circumvents security procedures. The earliest appeared in the UK in about 1988. [L *Trōjānus,* from *Trōja, Trōia*]

troke, (*Sc.*) TRUCK[1].

troll[1], *v.t.* to sing the parts of (a song) in succession; to roll or reel out (a song) in a careless manner; to fish (water) by trailing or spinning a revolving bait, esp. behind a boat. *v.i.* to fish thus; to sing in a free and easy way; to walk, to stroll. *n.* a song the parts of which are sung in succession, a round, a catch; a reel on a fishing-rod; a spinning bait, a spoon-bait etc. **to troll the bowl,** to pass it round. **troller,** *n.* [OF *troller, trauler,* G *trollen,* to roll, to stroll, cp. MDut. *drollen*]

troll[2], *n.* a giant or giantess in Scandinavian mythology, endowed with supernatural powers; later, a familiar but impish dwarf. [Icel., cp. Swed. *troll,* Dan. *trold*]

troller TROLL[1].

trolley, trolly[1], *n.* a four-wheeled truck or low car, esp. one the body of which can be tilted over; a costermonger's cart; a set of shelves with wheels, used for moving things, e.g. trays of food, around; a basket on wheels used for containing goods to be purchased in a grocery shop, supermarket etc.; a grooved wheel on a pole used for conveying current to the motor on electric railways, tramways etc. **trolley bus,** *n.* an omnibus deriving its motive power through a trolley from overhead wires. **trolley-car,** *n.* (*N Am.*) a tramcar. **trolley-lace** TROLLY[2]. **trolley-pole,** *n.* **trolley-system,** *n.* the system of working electric railways, tramways etc., by means of trolleys. [TROLL[1]]

†**troll-madam,** †**trol-my-dames**, an old English game like bagatelle, also called pigeon-holes or nine-holes. [F *trou-madame*]

trollol, *v.t., v.i.* to sing in a jovial way, to troll.

trollop, *n.* a careless, slovenly woman, a slattern; a woman of bad character. **trollopy,** *a.* [etym. obscure]

Trollope, *n.* **Anthony** (1815–82), English novelist, who delineated provincial English middle-class society in his Barchester series of novels. *The Warden* (1855) began the series, which includes *Barchester Towers* (1857), *Doctor Thorne* (1858), and *The Last Chronicle of Barset* (1867).

trolly[1] TROLLEY.

trolly[2], *n.* a kind of lace with the pattern outlined by thick thread or a number of threads combined. **trolly-lace,** *n.* [cogn. with Flem. *tralje, traalje,* lattice, network]

trombone, *n.* a large and powerful wind-instrument of the trumpet kind usu. played by means of a sliding tube. **tromba**, *n.* a trumpet. **trombonist,** *n.* [It., from *tromba,* trumpet]

trommel, *n.* a rotating cylindrical sieve for cleaning and sizing ore. [G, drum]

tromometer, *n.* an instrument for measuring earth tremors. **tromometric**, *a.* [Gr. *tromos,* trembling, from *tremein,* to tremble]

Tromp, *n.* **Maarten Harpertszoon** (1597–1653), Dutch admiral. He twice defeated the occupying Spaniards 1639. He was defeated by the British admiral Blake May 1652, but in Nov. triumphed over Blake in the Strait of Dover. In Feb.–June 1653 he was defeated by Blake and Monk, and was killed off the Dutch coast. His son, Cornelius Tromp (1629–91), also an admiral, fought a battle against the English and French fleets in 1673.

trompe, *n.* an apparatus worked by a descending column of water for producing a blast in a furnace. [F, TRUMP[1]]

trompe l'oeil, *n.* (a painting etc. giving) a very deceptive appearance of reality. [F deceive the eye]

tron, *n.* (*Sc.*) a weighing-machine consisting of a beam or balance for weighing heavy goods. **tron-pound,** †**tron-weight,** *n.* an ancient Scottish standard of weight (about 21 to 28 oz. av. (595–794g)) used for certain home products. [A-F *trone,* ult. from L *trutina,* pair of scales, cp. Gr. *trutanē*]

-tron, *suf.* elementary particle, e.g. *plectron;* particle accelerator, e.g. *cyclotron.* [Gr. suffix denoting an instrument]

trona, *n.* a native hydrous carbonate of soda. [Arab.]

tronc, *n.* system whereby waiters and other employees in a restaurant share in the tips. [F, collecting box]

troop, *n.* an assemblage of persons or animals, a crowd, a company; (*pl.*) soldiers; a band or company of performers, a troupe; the unit of cavalry formation, usu. consisting of 60 troopers, commanded by a captain; a particular beat of the drum as a signal to march. *v.i.* to come together, to assemble, to come thronging (up, together etc.); to move (along a way etc.) in a troop; to hurry (off etc.). *v.t.* to form (a squadron etc.) into troops. **troop-horse,** *n.* **troop-ship,** *n.* a transport for soldiers. **trooper,** *n.* a cavalry-soldier; a private in a cavalry regiment; a troop-ship; (*Austral.*) a mounted policeman. **trooping the colour,** a ceremonial parade at which the colour is carried between the files of troops. [F *troupe,* OF *trope* (cp. Sp. *tropa,* It. *truppa*), etym. doubtful]

troopial, *n.* an American bird of the genus *Icterus,* in some respects resembling the starling. [F *troupiale,* from *troupe,* TROOP]

trop., (*abbr.*) tropical.

trop- TROPO(-).

tropaeolum, *n.* (*pl.* **-lums, -la**) one of a genus of S American climbing plants containing the Indian-cress or nasturtium. [mod. L, from Gr. *tropaios,* turning, as foll.]

trope, *n.* a figurative use of a word. [F, from L *tropus,* Gr. *tropos,* turn, trope, from *trepein,* to turn]

troph- TROPH(O)-.

trophesy, etc. TROPHIC.

trophi, *n.pl.* the parts of the mouth in insects. [mod. L, pl. of *trophus,* Gr. *trophos,* nurse, as foll.]

trophic, *a.* pertaining to nutrition. **trophesy,** *n.* (*Path.*) deranged nutrition due to nervous disorder. **trophesial,** *a.* [Gr. *trophē,* nourishment, from *trephein,* to nourish]

-trophic, *comb. form* relating to nutrition. [as prec.]

troph(o)-, *comb. form.* [as prec.]

Trophonian, *a.* pertaining or relating to the Grecian architect Trophonius, said traditionally to have built the celebrated temple of Apollo at Delphi.

trophotropism, *n.* the movement of the organs of a growing plant toward or away from nutrient substances, induced by the chemical nature of its surroundings. **trophotropic,** *a.*

trophy, *n.* in ancient Rome, a pile of arms and other spoils taken from a vanquished enemy and set up on the battlefield to commemorate a victory; in ancient Greece, a more permanent memorial imitating this decorated with captured arms, beaks of ships etc., or representations of these; anything preserved as a memorial of victory or success; an ornamental group of typical or symbolical objects placed on a wall etc. **trophied,** *a.* [F *trophée,* L *tropaeum,* Gr. *tropaion,* neut. a. from *tropē,* defeat, from *trepein,* to turn]

-trophy, *comb. form* a specified form of nourishment of growth. [Gr. *trephein,* to nourish]

tropic, *n.* either of the two parallels of latitude situated at 23° 27′ from the equator, the northern called the **tropic of Cancer,** and the southern the **tropic of Capricorn,** (*pl.*) the regions of the torrid zone between these; either of the corresponding parallels of declination on the celestial sphere. *a.* of or pertaining to the tropics, tropical. **tropic-bird,** *n.* a tern-like bird of the natatorial genus *Phaëthon.* **tropical,** *a.* pertaining to, lying within, or characteristic of the tropics; of the weather, very hot, passionate, fervent; of the nature of a trope, figurative, metaphorical. **tropical month,** *n.* the mean period of the moon's passing through 360° of longitude, i.e. 27 days, 7 hours, 43 min., 4.7 secs. **tropical year,** *n.* a solar year. **tropically,** *adv.* **tropicopolitan,** *a.* inhabiting and confined to the tropics; *n.* a tropicopolitan animal or plant. [F *tropique,* late L *tropicum* nom. *-cus,* Gr. *tropikos kuklos,* the tropic circle, from *tropē,* solstice, turning, from *trepein,* to turn]

tropism, *n.* the direction of growth in a plant or other organism that is due to an external stimulus. [Gr. *tropos,* turn]

trop(o)-, *comb. form* turn(ing); tropism. [Gr. *tropos,* turn]

tropology, *n.* the use of tropical or figurative language; interpretation of the Scriptures in a figurative sense. **tropist,** *n.* one who deals in tropes; one who explains the Scriptures by tropes. **tropological,** *a.* **tropologically,** *adv.*

tropopause, *n.* the boundary between the troposphere and the stratosphere.

troposphere, *n.* the hollow sphere of atmosphere surrounding the earth, bounded by the stratosphere, in which temperature varies and the weather functions. [Gr. *tropos,* a turn]

troppo, *adv.* (*Mus.*) too much, excessively. [It., too much]

†**trossers,** TROUSERS.

Trot, *n.* (*coll., often derog.*) a Trotskyite or other left-winger.

trot, *v.i.* (*past, p.p.* **trotted**) of a horse or other quadruped, to move at a steady rapid pace by simultaneously lifting one fore-foot and the hind-foot of the opposite side alternately with the other pair, the body being unsupported at intervals; to run with short brisk strides. *v.t.* to cause to trot; to cover (a distance etc.) by trotting. *n.* the pace, motion, or act of a horse etc., in trotting; a brisk steady pace; a dance; a toddling child; a term of endearment; †an old woman. **on the trot,** one after the other, successively. **the trots,** (*coll.*) diarrhoea. **to trot out,** (*coll.*) to utter (esp. something familiar or trite). **trotter,** *n.* one who or that which trots, esp. a horse trained for fast trotting; (*pl.*) sheep's or other animals' feet used as food. [ME *trotten,* F *trotter,* etym. doubtful, perh. from L *tolūtim,* at a trot, from *tollere,* to lift, through late L *tolūtārius,* trotting]

troth, *n.* faith, fidelity, truth. **to plight one's troth** PLIGHT[1]. **troth-plight,** *a.* betrothed, affianced. [OE *trēowth,* TRUTH]

Trotsky, *n.* **Leon** (adopted name of Lev Davidovitch Bronstein) (1879–1940), Russian revolutionary. He joined the Bolshevik party and took a leading part in the seizure of power and raising the Red Army which fought the Civil War 1918–20. In the struggle for power that followed Lenin's death 1924, Stalin defeated him, and this and other differences with the Communist Party led to his exile (1929). Trotsky settled in Mexico, where he was assassinated with an ice pick, possibly at Stalin's instigation. **Trotskyism,** *n.* the form of Marxism advocated by Leon Trotsky. Its central concept is that of permanent revolution. In his view a proletarian revolution, leading to a socialist society, could not be achieved in isolation, so it would be necessary to spark off further revolutions throughout Europe and ultimately worldwide. This was in direct opposition to the Stalinist view that socialism should be built and consolidated within individual countries.

trottoir, *n.* the pavement at the side of a street etc. [F, from *trotter,* to TROT]

troubadour, *n.* one of a class of lyric poets who flourished in Provence in the 11th cent., writing in the *langue d'oc* chiefly of love and chivalry. [F, from Prov. *trobador,* from *trobar* (F *trouver,* to find), prob. through a pop. L *tropāre,* to compose poetry, from *tropus,* TROPE]

trouble, *v.t.* to agitate, to disturb; to annoy, to molest; to distress, to afflict; to inconvenience, to put to some exertion or pains. *v.i.* to be agitated or disturbed; to take trouble or pains. *n.* affliction, distress, worry, perplexity, annoyance, misfortune; labour, exertion, inconvenience. **to ask for trouble,** (*sl.*) to lack caution. **to get into trouble,** to incur censure or punishment; to become pregnant. **troublemaker,** *n.* a person who stirs up discontent, strife, etc. **troubleshooter,** *n.* a person who finds the causes of problems and solves them. **trouble spot,** *n.* a place where there is frequent disturbance, e.g. strikes or fights. **troubler,** *n.* **troublesome,** *a.* giving trouble; annoying, vexatious; tiresome, wearisome, importunate. **troublesomely,** *adv.* **troublesomeness,** *n.* †**troublous,** *a.* full of commotion; disturbed, agitated, disorderly. [OF *troubler, trubler,* from L *turbula,* dim. of *turba,* crowd]

trough, *n.* a long, narrow, open receptacle of wood, iron etc., for holding water, fodder etc., for domestic animals, kneading dough, washing ore etc.; a deep narrow channel, furrow, or depression (in land, the sea etc.); an area of low atmospheric pressure; a hollow between the crests of a wave of radiation; a low point, e.g. in economic activity, in demand, etc.; a state of low spirits. [OE *trog* (cp. Dut., G, and Icel. *trog,* Dan. *trug,* Swed. *träg,* cogn. with TREE]

trounce, *v.t.* to beat severely; to inflict a decisive defeat upon. **trouncing,** *n.* [OF *trons,* TRUNCHEON]

troupe, *n.* a company of actors, performers etc. **trouper,** *n.* a member of such a company; a reliable person. [F, TROOP]

troupial, TROOPIAL.

trous-de-loup, *n.pl.* pits with a pointed stake in each, as a defence against cavalry. [F, wolf-holes]

trousers, *n. pl.* a two legged outer garment reaching from the waist to the ankles. **caught with one's trousers, pants down,** in a situation where one is unprepared. **to wear the trousers,** to be in the position of authority, esp. in a family. **trouser suit,** *n.* a suit of a jacket and a pair of trousers, often when worn by a woman. **trousered,** *a.* **trousering,** *n.* cloth for making trousers. [prob. Ir. *triubhas,* but cp. F *trousses,* breeches, bundles, see TRUSS]

trousse, *n.* a set of small (esp. surgical) instruments in a sheath or case. [F]

trousseau, *n.* (*pl.* **-sseaux, -sseaus**) the clothes and general outfit of a bride. [F, bundle, OF *troussel* dim. of *trousse,* TRUSS]

trout, *n.* a freshwater game-fish, *Salmo fario*, allied to but smaller than the salmon; (*coll.*) an unprepossessing woman, esp. an old one. *v.i.* to fish for trout. **trout-coloured,** *a.* white, with spots of black, bay, or sorrel. **trout-stream,** *n.* **troutlet, -ling,** *n.* **trouty,** *a.* [OE *truht,* L *tructa,* Gr. *trōkkēs,* from *trōgein,* to gnaw]

trouvere, *n.* one of the mediaeval poets of N France, composers chiefly of narrative poems. [F, from *trouver,* see TROUBADOUR]

trove SEE TREASURE.

trover, *n.* (*Law*) the acquisition of appropriation of any goods; an action for the recovery of personal property wrongfully converted by another to his own use. [OF (F *trouver*), see CONTRIVE]

†**trow,** *v.t., v.i.* to think, to suppose, to believe. [A-S *trūwian, trēowian,* cogn. with *trēowe,* TRUE]

trowel, *n.* a flat-bladed, usu. pointed, tool used by masons etc., for spreading mortar etc.; a scoop-shaped tool used in digging up plants etc. *v.t.* to apply or dress with a trowel. **to lay it on with a trowel,** to flatter grossly. [ME *truel,* F *truellle,* late L *truella,* dim. of *trua,* ladle]

Troy, (Latin **Ilium**), *n.* ancient city of Asia Minor. In the *Iliad*, the poet Homer described Troy as besieged in the ten-year Trojan War (mid-13th cent. BC), and falling to the Greeks by the stratagem of the Trojan horse.

troy, *n.* a system of weights (12 oz. av. to 1 lb. (340–454 g)) used chiefly in weighing gold, silver and gems, also called **troy weight**. [prob. from *Troyes,* town SE of Paris]

truant, *a.* shirking, idle, loitering. *n.* one who shirks or neglects duty; an idler, a loiterer; a child who stays away from school without leave. *v.i.* to play truant. **to play truant,** to stay away from school without leave. **truant-school,** *n.* an industrial school for children who habitually play truant. **truancy,** *n.* **truantly,** *adv.* [A-F *truaunt,* W *truan,* wretched, cp. Ir. *trogha,* miserable, Gael. *truaghan,* a wretched creature]

Trubenize®, *v.t.* a method to stiffen fabrics with cellulose acetate.

truce, *n.* a temporary cessation of hostilities; an agreement to cease hostilities; an armistice; a temporary intermission, alleviation, or respite. **truce-breaker,** *n.* **truceless,** *a.* [ME *triwes, treowes,* pl., from OE *trēow,* compact, faith, see TRUE]

truck[1], *v.t., v.i.* to exchange; to barter; to peddle, to hawk, *n.* exchange of commodities; barter; commodities suitable for barter, small wares; traffic; intercourse, dealings; the truck system; (*coll.*) rubbish. **to have no truck with,** to have no dealings with. **Truck Acts,** *n.pl.* UK acts of Parliament introduced 1831, 1887, 1896, and 1940 to prevent employers misusing wage payment systems to the detriment of their workers. The legislation made it illegal to pay wages with goods in kind or with tokens for use in shops owned by the employers. The 1940 act prevented employers giving canteen meals in lieu of wages. **truck farmer,** (*N Am.*) a market-gardener. **truck shop,** a shop where the truck system is carried on, a tommy shop. **truck system,** the practice of paying wages in goods instead of money. †**truckage[1],** *n.* [ME *trukken,* A-F *troquier* (F *troquer*), from OF *troque,* barter, WFlem. *trok,* sale, *trokken,* to procure goods, cogn. with TREK]

truck[2], *n.* a strong, usu. four-wheeled vehicle for conveying heavy goods; an open railway wagon; a low barrow with two small wheels used by porters etc., for moving luggage etc., at railway stations, in warehouses etc.; a framework and set of wheels for supporting the whole or part of a railway carriage etc.; (*Naut.*) a small wooden disk at the top of a mast with holes for the halyards etc.; †a small tireless wheel; (*N Am.*) a lorry. *v.t.* to convey on a truck. *v.i.* to work as a lorry-driver. **truck-bolster,** *n.* a cross-beam in a car-truck supporting one end of the car. **truckage[2],** *n.* **trucker,** *n.* a lorry-driver; one who transports goods by lorry. [L *trochus,* Gr. *trochos,* wheel, from *trechein,* to run, or perh. short for foll.]

truckle, *v.i.* orig. to sleep in a truckle-bed; hence, to give way obsequiously (to the will of another); to cringe, to be servile (to). **truckle-bed,** *n.* a low bed on castors or wheels for rolling under another; a trundle-bed. **truckler,** *n.* [from TROCHLEA; cp. prec.]

truculent, *a.* savage, ferocious, barbarous, violent. **truculence, -lency,** *n.* **truculently,** *adv.* in a truculent manner. [OF, from L *truculentum,* nom. *-tus,* from *trux trucis,* savage]

Trudeau, *n.* **Pierre (Elliott)** (1919–), Canadian Liberal politician. He was prime minister 1968–79 and won again by a landslide Feb. 1980. In 1980 his work helped to defeat the Québec independence movement in a referendum. He repatriated the constitution from Britain 1982, but by 1984 had so lost support that he resigned.

trudge, *v.i., v.t.* to travel on foot esp. with labour and fatigue. *n.* a walk of this kind. [F *trucher,* to beg, prob. from Teut. (cp. Dut. *troggelen,* also Icel. *thrūga,* Swed. *truga,* Dan. *true,* to press)]

trudgeon, trudgen, *n.* (*Swimming*) a stroke with the arms brought over the head alternately, and ordinary leg action. [John *Trudgen, fl.* 1860–70, who introduced it]

true, *a.* conformable to fact or reality, not false or erroneous; in accordance with appearance, not deceptive, counterfeit, or spurious, genuine; in accordance with right or law, legitimate, rightful; corresponding to type or standard; of a voice etc. in perfect tune; faithful, loyal, constant; of a compass bearing, determined in relation to the earth's geographical, rather than its magnetic pole. †not given to falsehood, veracious, truthful, honest. *v.t.* to make true, exact, or accurate. *adv.* truly. **in/out of true,** correctly/not correctly aligned. **not true,** (*coll.*) amazing, incredible. **true to type,** normal, what might be expected. **true bill,** a bill of indictment endorsed by a grand jury as sustained by the evidence. **true-blue,** staunch, faithful, genuine; (*Brit.*) loyal to the Conservative Party. **true-born,** *a.* of legitimate birth; such by birth or blood. **true-bred,** *a.* of genuine or right breed. **True Cross,** *n.* the instrument of Jesus's crucifixion, supposedly found by St Helena, the mother of the emperor Constantine, on Calvary AD 326. †**true-derived,** *a.* legitimate. †**true-disposing,** *a.* just. **true-hearted,** *a.* **true-heartedness,** *n.* **true-love,** *n.* one truly loved or loving; one's sweetheart. **true-love** or **true-lover's knot,** *n.* a kind of double knot with two interlacing bows on each side and two ends. †**truepenny,** *n.* an honest fellow. [OE *trēowe, trȳw,* cp. Dut. *trouw,* G *treu,* Icel. *tryggr, trūr*]

Truffaut, *n.* **François** (1932–84), French film director, whose gently comic films include *Jules et Jim* (1961), and *La Nuit américaine/Day for Night* (1973) (for which he won an Academy Award). His work was influenced by Hitchcock, and also draws on surrealist and comic traditions.

truffle, *n.* a fleshy fungus of the genus *Tuber,* used for seasoning etc.; a sweet flavoured with rum or chocolate, resembling a truffle in shape. **truffle-dog,** *n.* a dog trained to find truffles. [OF *trufle,* prob. from L TUBER]

trug, *n.* a wooden basket used by gardeners, greengrocers etc.; a wooden milk-pail; a hod for mortar. [etym. doubtful]

truism, *n.* a self-evident or unquestionable truth; an obvious statement, a platitude. **truistic,** *a.*

†**trull,** *n.* a strumpet, a drab. [G *trulle, trolle,* cogn. with TROLL[2] and DROLL]

Trujillo, *n.* city in NW Peru, with its port at Salaverry; population (1988) 491,000. Industries include engineering, copper, sugar milling, and vehicle assembly.

Trujillo Molina, *n.* **Rafael (Leónidas)** (1891–1961), dictator of the Dominican Republic from 1930. As commander of the Dominican Guard, he seized power and established a ruthless dictatorship. He was assassinated.

truly, *adv.* sincerely, in accordance with truth, accurately; genuinely; in reality; faithfully, honestly, loyally; really, indeed. **yours truly,** conventional formal ending to a letter.

Truman, *n.* **Harry S.** (1884–1972), 33rd president of the US 1945–53, a Democrat. In Jan. 1945 he became vice president to F.D. Roosevelt, and president when Roosevelt died in Apr. that year. He used the atom bombs against Japan, launched the Marshall Plan to restore W Europe's economy, and nurtured the European Community and NATO (including the rearmament of West Germany). **Truman Doctrine,** *n.* US president Harry Truman's 1947 doctrine that the US would 'support free peoples who are resisting attempted subjugation by armed minorities or by outside pressures'. It was used to justify sending US troops abroad, for example, to Korea.

trumeau, *n.* (*pl.* **-eaux**) a piece of wall, a pier or pillar, between two openings or dividing a doorway. [F]

trump[1], †*n.* a trumpet. †*v.t.* to impose (a thing) upon by fraud. **Last Trump,** the end of the world. **to trump up,** to fabricate, to concoct. [OF *trompe* (whence *tromper,* to play on this, to deceive), OHG *trumpa,* from OSlav., cp. Rus. *truba,* Pol. *trabas*]

trump[2], *n.* any card of a suit ranking for the time being above the others; (*coll.*) a good fellow; a generous or reliable person. *v.t.* to take with a trump. *v.i.* to play a trump-card; to outdo. **to come up trumps,** to be useful or helpful at an opportune moment. †**to put to one's trumps,** to reduce to one's last expedient. **trump-card,** *n.* the card turned up to determine which suit is to be trumps; any card of this suit; an infallible expedient. [F *triomphe,* a card-game, TRIUMPH]

trumpery, *n.* worthless finery; rubbish. *a.* showy but worthless, delusive, rubbishy. [OF *tromperie,* deception]

trumpet, *n.* a musical wind instrument, usu. consisting of a long, straight, curved, or coiled tube with a wide termination, usu. of brass, with a cup-shaped mouthpiece; a thing resembling this in shape, as a funnel; the horn of a gramophone; an ear-trumpet; a reed-stop in an organ; a sound of or as of a trumpet, e.g. that made by an elephant. *v.t.* to proclaim by or as by sound of trumpet. *v.i.* to make a loud sound as of a trumpet (esp. of the elephant). **to blow one's own trumpet,** to boast. **Feast of Trumpets,** a Jewish festival celebrating the beginning of the year. **trumpet-call,** *n.* a call by sound of trumpet; an imperative call to action. **trumpet-conch, -shell,** *n.* a gasteropod with a turreted shell often used as a trumpet. **trumpet-fish,** *n. Centriscus scolopax,* from its elongated tubular snout. **trumpet-flower,** *n.* a plant with large tubular flowers. **trumpet-major,** *n.* the head trumpeter in a cavalry regiment. **trumpet-tongued,** *a.* proclaiming loudly, as with the voice of a trumpet. **trumpeter,** *n.* one who sounds a trumpet, esp. a soldier giving signals on the trumpet in a cavalry regiment; one who proclaims, publishes, or denounces; a variety of the domestic pigeon, with a prolonged coo; a S American bird allied to the cranes; a N American swan; an Australian edible fish. [OF *trompette,* dim. of TRUMP[1]]

truncal TRUNK.

truncate, *v.t.* to cut the top or end from; (*Cryst.*) to replace an angle by a plane. *a.* cut short, truncated; (*Bot.*) terminating abruptly, as if a piece had been cut off. **truncately,** *adv.* **truncation, truncature,** *n.* [L *truncātus,* p.p. of *truncāre,* from *truncus,* TRUNK]

truncheon, *n.* a short staff, club, or cudgel, esp. one carried by a police officer in Britain; a baton, a staff of authority. *v.t.* to beat with a truncheon. †**truncheoneer,** *n.* [ONorth.F *tronchon,* OF *tronçon,* dim. of *tronc,* TRUNK]

trundle, *n.* a small broad wheel, a castor; a lantern-wheel; a low-wheeled vehicle, a truck; a truckle-bed. *v.t., v.i.* to move heavily (as if) on wheels. **trundle-head,** *n.* the head of a capstan. **trundle-tail,** *n.* a curled tail; a dog with a curled tail. [MF *trondeler,* LG *tröndeln,* cogn. with TREND]

trunk, *n.* the main stem of a tree, opp. to the branches or roots; the body of an animal apart from the limbs, head, and tail; the main body of anything; a trunk-line; the shaft of a column; a box or chest with a hinged lid for packing clothes etc., in for travel; (*N Am.*) the boot of a motor-car; a ventilating shaft, conduit, chute, flume etc.; a hollow cylinder in which a connecting-rod works, in marine and other steam-engines; the proboscis of an elephant or any analogous organ; (*pl.*) men's shorts for swimming; (*pl.*) trunk-hose. **trunk-call,** *n.* a long-distance telephone call. **trunk-drawers,** *n.pl.* drawers cut off at the knees. **trunk exchange,** *n.* a telephone exchange connected by trunk lines to other trunk exchanges. **trunk-hose,** *n.pl.* wide breeches extending from the waist to the middle of the thigh, worn in the 16th–17th cents. **trunk-line,** *n.* the main line of a railway, canal, telephone etc. **trunk road,** *n.* any major road for long-distance travel. **trunkful,** *n.* **trunkless,** *a.* **truncal,** *a.* [F *tronc,* L *truncus, -um,* stem, piece cut off]

trunnion, *n.* one of the cylindrical projections from the sides of a cannon or mortar; a hollow gudgeon on which the cylinder oscillates in some steam-engines, and through which the steam enters. **trunnioned,** *a.* [F *trognon,* dim. of *tron, tronc,* prec.]

truss, *v.t.* to support or brace with a truss; to fasten (a fowl or the wings of a fowl etc.) with a skewer or twine before cooking; to tie up securely, to bind; †to tie, tighten, or fasten up (one's clothes etc.); to hang (a criminal); †to seize (of hawks etc.). *n.* a timber or iron supporting and strengthening structure in a roof, bridge etc.; a large corbel; (*Naut.*) a heavy iron securing a lower yard to the mast; a padded belt or other apparatus worn round the body for preventing or compressing a hernia; a bundle (56 lb., 25·4 kg) of old, (60 lb., 27·2 kg) of new hay, or (36 lb., 16·3 kg) of straw; a compact terminal cluster of flowers. **to truss up,** to make up in to a bundle; to bind or tie up; to hang. **truss-beam,** *n.* **trussbridge,** *n.* [OF *trusser, trosser,* from L THYRSUS]

trust, *n.* confident reliance on or belief in the integrity, veracity, justice, friendship, power, protection etc., of a person or thing; confidence, firm expectation (that); the person or thing on which reliance is placed; reliance on (assumed honesty etc.) without examination; commercial credit; (*Law*) confidence reposed in a person to whom property is conveyed for the benefit of another; the right to or title in such property as distinct from its legal ownership; the property or thing held in trust; the legal relation between such property and the holder; something committed to one's charge or care; the obligation of one who has received such a charge; (*Comm.*) a combination of a number of businesses or companies under one general control for the purpose of defeating competition, creating a monopoly etc. *v.t.* to place confidence in, to believe in, to rely upon; to believe, to have a confident hope of expectation; to commit to the care of a person, to entrust; to entrust (a person with a thing); to give credit to. *v.i.* to have trust or confidence; to sell goods on credit. **trust deed,** an instrument of conveyance that creates a trust. **trust fund,** *n.* money etc. held in trust. **trust-house,** a public house owned by a trust company and not by a brewer. **trust territory,** *n.* a territory governed by another country by the authority of the United Nations. **trustable,** *a.* **trustee,** *n.* one to whom property is committed in trust for the benefit of another; one of a body of people, often elective, managing the affairs of an institution. **trusteeship,** *n.* the office of a trustee; a trust territory. **truster,** *n.* **trustful,** *a.* full of trust; trusting, confiding. **trustfully,** *adv.* **trustfulness,** *n.* **trusting,** *a.* **trustingly,** *adv.* **trustless,** *a.* not worthy of trust; faithless. **trustlessness,** *n.* **trustworthy,** *a.* deserving of trust or confidence. **trustworthiness,** *n.* **trusty,** *a.* trustworthy, reliable; not liable to fail in time of need. *n.* a prisoner trusted with a certain amount of liberty to do jobs, etc. **trustily,** *adv.* **trustiness,** *n.* [ME, cp. OFris. *trāst,*

Icel. *traust,* Dan. and Swed. *tröst,* G *trost,* comfort, consolation]

Truth, *n.* **Sojourner** (adopted name of Isabella Baumfree, subsequently Isabella Van Wagener) (1797–1883), US anti-slavery campaigner. Born a slave, she obtained her freedom and that of her son, and became involved with religious groups. In 1843 she was 'commanded in a vision' to adopt the name Sojourner Truth. She published an autobiography, *The Narrative of Sojourner Truth* (1850).

truth, *n.*(*pl.* **truths**) the state or quality of being true; conformity to fact or reality; that which is true, a fact, a verity; honesty, veracity, sincerity; fidelity, constancy; true religion. **in truth, †of a truth,** in reality, in fact, truly. **truth drug,** (*coll.*) any drug used to render a person more liable to tell the truth when being interrogated. **truth-teller,** *n.* **truth-value,** *n.* the truth or falsity of a statement. **truthful,** *a.* habitually speaking the truth, veracious, reliable, conformable to truth. **truthfully,** *adv.* **truthfulness,** *n.* **truthless,** *a.* false; faithless, unreliable. **truthlessness,** *n.* [OE *trēowthu,* from *trēowe,* TRUE]

truttaceous, *a.* related to or resembling trout.

try, *v.t.* (*past, p.p.* **tried**) to test, to examine by experiment; to determine the qualities etc., of by reference to a standard; to find out by experiment or experience; to attempt, to endeavour (to do etc.); to subject to a severe or undue test, to strain; to subject to hardship, suffering etc., as if for a test, to afflict; to investigate (a charge, issue etc.) judicially, to subject (a person) to judicial trial; to prove or settle by a test or experiment; to smooth (a roughly-planed board) with a trying-plane etc., to secure a perfectly level surface; to purify, to refine (metals etc.) by melting etc. *v.i.* to endeavour, to make an attempt, to put forth efforts. *n.* (*coll.*) an attempt; in rugby, the right to carry the ball and try to kick a goal from in front, earned by touching the ball down behind the opponents' goal line. **to try for,** to aim at; to attempt to secure; to apply for. **to try on,** to put (clothes) on to see if they fit; (*sl.*) to see how much a person will tolerate. **to try out,** to test. **try-sail,** *n.* a fore-and-aft sail set on a gaff abaft the foremast and mainmast. **triable,** *a.* **trying,** *a.* irritating, annoying. **try-, trying-square,** *n.* a carpenter's square with a wooden stock and steel limb. **tryout,** *n.* a trial, e.g. of a new method. [ME *trien,* F *trier,* late L *trītāre,* to triturate, from *trītus,* TRITE]

trygon, *n.* a genus of rays armed with a spine on the tail; a sting-ray. [Gr. *trugōn*]

tryma, *n.* (*pl.* **-mata**) a drupe-like fruit the outer wall of the pericarp of which is dehiscent, as in the walnut. [Gr. *truma,* hole, from *truein,* to rub]

tryout TRY.

trypanosome, *n.* one of the Trypanosomata, an order of flagellate infusorians infesting the blood of man and pathogenic to him. The parasite is spread by the tsetse fly and causes sleeping sickness etc. **trypanosomiasis,** *n.* a disease caused by an infection with a trypanosome. [Gr. *trupanon,* a borer; *soma,* a body]

trypograph, *n.* a stencil made by writing with a stylus on a sheet of prepared paper laid on a roughened surface so as to produce a series of minute holes. **trypographic,** *a.* [Gr. *trupan,* to bore]

trypsin, *n.* a ferment contained in the pancreatic juice etc. **tryptic,** *a.* **tryptone,** *n.* a peptone formed during digestion by the action of trypsin on proteins. **tryptophan,** *n.* an amino acid widely distributed in proteins and essential for life. [Gr., from *tribein,* to rub]

tryst, *n.* an appointed meeting, an appointment; a rendezvous. *v.i.* to agree to meet. *v.t.* to appoint (a time or place) for meeting. **trysting-day,** *n.* **trysting-place,** *n.* [OF *triste, tristre,* a watching-station in hunting, cogn. with TRUST]

Ts'ao Chan, *n.* former name for the Chinese novelist CAO CHAN.

Tsar CZAR.

TSB, (*abbr.*) Trustee Savings Bank.

tsetse, *n.* a S African fly, *Glossina morsitans,* the bite of which is often fatal to cattle, horses, dogs etc., and transmits to man the trypanosomes of sleeping-sickness. [native name]

T-shirt, T-square T.

Tsiolkovsky, *n.* **Konstantin** (1857–1935), Russian scientist. He published the first practical paper on astronautics 1903, covering rocket space travel using liquid propellants, such as liquid oxygen.

Tsumeb, *n.* the principal mining centre (diamonds, copper, lead, zinc) of N Namibia, NW of Grootfontein; population 13,500.

tsunami, *n.* a very large wave at sea caused by a submarine earthquake, volcanic eruption etc. [Jap.]

Tsung Dao Lee, *n.* (1926–), US physicist of Chinese origin. His research centred on the physics of weak interactions between particles. In 1956 Lee proposed that such interactions might disobey certain key assumptions, for instance the conservation of parity. He shared the 1957 Nobel Prize for Physics with his co-worker Chen Ning Yang (1922–).

tsung-tuh, *n.* a Chinese viceroy or governor of a province. [Chin.]

Tsvetaeva, *n.* **Marina** (1892–1941), Russian poet, born in Moscow. She wrote mythic, romantic, frenetic verse, including *The Demesne of the Swans.*

TT, (*abbr.*) teetotal(ler); Tourist Trophy; tuberculin tested.

Tuamotu Archipelago, *n.* two parallel ranges of 78 atolls, part of French Polynesia; area 690 sq km/266 sq miles; population (1983) 11,800, including the Gambier Islands to the east. The atolls stretch 2100 km/1300 miles north and east of the Society Islands. The administrative headquarters is Apataki. The largest atoll is Rangiroa, and the most important Hao; they produce pearl shell and copra. Mururoa and Fangataufa atolls to the southeast have been a French nuclear test site since 1966. Spanish explorers landed 1606, and the islands were annexed by France 1881.

tuan, *n.* a flying-squirrel. [Austral. abor.]

Tuareg, *n.* a member of a nomadic Berber tribe of the Sahara; their language.

tuart, touart, *n.* the W Australian gum, *Eucalyptus gomphocephala.* [Austral. abor.]

tuatara, *n.* the largest New Zealand reptile, the lizard-like *Sphenodon punctatus,* now the last survivor of the class Rhyncocephalia. [Maori]

tub, *n.* an open wooden (usu. round) vessel constructed of staves held together by hoops, used for washing, holding butter etc.; the amount (of butter etc.) that a packing-tub holds; a small cask; a small, usu. plastic, container for ice-cream, margarine etc.; a bath-tub, a sponge-bath, a bath in a tub; a bucket, box, or truck for bringing up ore etc. from a mine; a short clumsy boat; a boat for practising rowing in. *v.t.* (*past, p.p.* **tubbed**) to place or set in a tub; to bathe in a tub. *v.i.* to take a bath in a tub; to row in a tub. **tub-thumper,** *n.* (*coll.*) a ranting preacher. **tub-wheel,** *n.* a bowl-shaped water-wheel analogous to a turbine; a rotating drum for washing leather etc. **tubbing,** *n.* **tubbish,** *a.* **tubful,** *n.* **tubby,** *a.* tub-shaped, corpulent; (*Mus.*) sounding like an empty tub when struck, wanting resonance. [MDut. *tobbe, dobbe,* etym. doubtful]

tuba, *n.* (*pl.* **-bas, -bae**) a brass wind-instrument of the saxhorn kind, with a low pitch; a powerful reed-stop in an organ. [L, trumpet]

tube, *n.* a long hollow cylinder for the conveyance of fluids and various other purposes, a pipe; a cylindrical vessel of thin flexible metal for holding pigment, toothpaste etc.; the main body of a wind-instrument; the central portion of a heavy gun round which the jackets are fixed by shrinking; (*coll.*) a tubular electric railway; (*N Am.*) a radio valve; a tubular vessel in an animal or plant for conveying air, fluids etc.; (*esp. Austral. sl.*) a can of beer. *v.t.* to furnish with or enclose in a tube or tubes. **tube-flower,** *n.* an ornamental E Indian shrub, *Clerodendron siphonanthus,* of the vervain family. **tube foot,** *n.* a tubular growth on a echinoderm, used for locomotion and ingestion of food. **tube-railway,** *n.* an underground electric railway running in a tubular tunnel. **tubewell,** *n.* a pipe with a sharp point and perforations just above this for driving into the ground to obtain water from a depth. **tubal, tubar,** *a.* **tubeless tyre,** *n.* a type of tyre designed to be airtight without an inner tube. **tubing,** *n.* [F, from L *tubus -um,* nom. *-us,* cogn. with prec.]

tuber, *n.* a short, thick portion of an underground stem, set with eyes or modified buds, as in the potato; a genus of subterranean fungi, containing the truffle; (*Anat.*) a swelling or prominence. **tuberiferous,** *a.* **tuberiform,** *a.* **tuberosity, tuberousness,** *n.* **tuberous,** *a.* having prominent knobs or excrescences; like or bearing tubers. [L, hump, lump, swelling, tumour, truffle, cogn. with TUMID]

tubercle, *n.* a small prominence, esp. in bone; a small granular non-vascular tumour or nodule formed within the substance of an organ as the result of morbid action, due to a bacillus, tending to set up degeneration, pulmonary consumption etc.; a small tuber; a warty excrescence. **tubercled, tubercular, tuberculate, -lated, tuberculoid, tuberculose, -lous,** *a.* **tuberculation,** *n.* formation of tubercles; a system of tubercles; the state of being tuberculous. **tubercularize, -ise, tuberculize, -ise,** *v.t.* to infect with tuberculosis. **tuberculization, -isation,** *n.* **tuberculin,** *n.* a ptomaine produced by the action of the tubercle-bacillus; a fluid used hypodermically in the diagnosis of tuberculosis. **tuberculin-tested,** *a.* of milk, produced by cows tested and found free of infection and tuberculosis. **tuberculosis,** *n.* a diseased condition characterized by the presence of tubercles in the tissues, esp. pulmonary tuberculosis or consumption. **tuberculosed,** *a.* [F, from L *tūberculum,* dim. of prec.]

tuberiferous etc. TUBER.

tuberose, *a.* tuberous. *n.* a bulbous plant, *Polianthes tuberosa,* with fragrant white flowers.

tuberosity, tuberous TUBER.

tubi, *comb. form.* tube. [L *tubus,* TUBE]

†**tubicen,** *n.* (*pl.* **-cines**) a trumpeter. †**tubicinate,** *v.i.* to sound a trumpet. [L (*canere,* to sing)]

tubicolous, *a.* inhabiting a tubular case. [L *colere,* to cultivate]

tubiform, *a.* having the shape of a tube.

tubing TUBE.

Tubman[1], *n.* **Harriet Ross** (1821–1913), US abolitionist. Born a slave in Maryland, she escaped to Philadelphia (where slavery was outlawed) 1849. She set up the Underground Railroad to help slaves escape to the northern states and Canada. During the Civil War she served as a spy for the Union army. She spoke against slavery and for women's rights, and founded schools for freed slaves after the Civil War.

Tubman[2], *n.* **William V. S.** (1895–1971), Liberian politician. The descendant of US slaves, he was a lawyer in the US. After his election to the presidency of Liberia (1944) he concentrated on uniting the various ethnic groups. Re-elected several times, he died naturally in office despite frequent assassination attempts.

Tubuai Islands (**Austral Islands**), *n.pl.* chain of volcanic islands and reefs 1300 km/800 miles long, in French Polynesia, south of the Society Islands; area 148 sq km/57 sq miles; population (1983) 6300. The main settlement is Mataura on Tubuai. They were visited by Capt. Cook 1777, and annexed by France 1880.

tubular, *a.* tube-shaped; having or consisting of a tube or tubes; of breathing, sounding like air passing through a tube. **tubular bells,** *n.pl.* an orchestral percussion instrument consisting of metal tubes suspended vertically and struck to produce a bell-like sound. **tubular boiler,** *n.* one in which the water circulates in a number of pipes in contact with a fire. **tubular bridge,** *n.* one consisting of a large rectangular tube through which a roadway or railway passes. **tubulate, -lated,** *a.* **tubule,** *n.* a small pipe or fistular body. **tubuliform,** *a.* **tubulose, tubulous,** *a.* [L *tubulus,* dim. of *tubus* TUBE]

TUC, (*abbr.*) Trades Union Congress.

tuck[1], *v.t.* to press close together or press, fold, or roll the loose ends or parts of compactly (up, in etc.); to wrap or cover (up or in) closely or snugly; to gather up, to fold or draw together or into small compass; to push or press, to cram, to stuff, to stow (away, into, etc.); to gather or stitch (a dress etc.) in folds; (*sl.*) to hang (a criminal). *v.i.* to make tucks; to be got rid of by tucking away (of loose cloth etc.). *n.* a horizontal fold in a dress etc., esp. one of a series made for ornament or to dispose of loose material; a tuck-net; the after part of a ship where the ends of the bottom planks meet; (*sl.*) food, esp. sweets, pastry etc.; a type of dive in which the knees are bent and held close to the chest by embracing the shins. **tucker,** *n.* esp. (*Austral.*) food. **to tuck in,** to eat greedily, **to tuck away,** to eat heartily; to place somewhere hidden or isolated. **tuck-in, -out,** *n.* a hearty meal, a spread. **tuck-net, -seine,** *n.* a net or seine used for removing fish from a larger net. **tuck-shop,** *n.* (*sl.*) a shop, esp. in a school, where sweets and pastry are sold. [ME *tukken,* LG *tukken, tokken,* cogn. with TOUCH]

tuck[2], *n.* the beat or roll of a drum; a blast or flourish on a trumpet; a tucket. [TUCKET]

†**tuck**[3], *n.* a long, narrow sword, a rapier. [MF *étoc, estoc,* It. *stocco,* G STOCK[1]]

tuckahoe, *n.* an underground fungus dug up in parts of the southern US; an inhabitant of the poorer parts of Virginia supposed to live on this. [NAm.Ind.]

tucker[1] TUCK[1].

tucker[2], *n.* one who or that which tucks; an ornamental frilling of lace or muslin round the top of a woman's dress, covering the neck and shoulders, worn in 17th–18th cents.

tucker[3], *v.t.* (*esp. N Am. coll.*) to exhaust (often with *out*). [obs. to *tuck,* to reproach, chide]

†**tucket,** *n.* a flourish on a trumpet, a fanfare. †**tucket sonance,** (*Shak.*) the sound of the tucket. [ONorth. F *touquet,* It. *toccata,* fem. p.p. of *toccare,* to TOUCH]

tucum, *n.* a S American palm, *Astrocaryum vulgare,* yielding a fibre used for cordage etc. [Braz.]

-tude, *suf.* forming abstract nouns, as *altitude, beatitude, fortitude.* [L *-tūdinem,* nom. *-tūdo*]

Tudor, *n.* English dynasty descended from the Welsh Owen Tudor (*c.* 1400–61), the second husband of Catherine of Valois (the widow of Henry V of England). Their son Edmund married Margaret Beaufort (1443–1509), the great-granddaughter of John of Gaunt, and was the father of Henry VII, who ascended the throne 1485. *a.* pertaining to this line. **Tudor flower,** *n.* a trefoil ornament used in the Tudor style. **Tudor rose,** *n.* a five-lobed flower adopted as badge by Henry VII. **Tudor style,** *n.* the late Perpendicular style in Gothic architecture.

Tues., (*abbr.*) Tuesday.

Tuesday, *n.* the third day of the week. [OE *Tīwes dæg,* day of the god of war (*Tīw,* cogn. with L. *deus,* Gr. *Zeus*)]

tufa, *n.* a soft calcareous rock deposited by springs and streams. **tufaceous,** *a.* [It. for *tufo,* L *tōphus,* a soft, sandy stone, cp. Gr. *tophos*]

tuff, *n.* an earthy, sometimes fragmentary, deposit of volcanic materials of the most heterogeneous kind. **tuffaceous,** *a.* [F *tuf,* It. *tufo,* see prec.]

tuffet, *n.* a low mound or seat. [var. of TUFT]

tuft, *n.* a cluster, a bunch, a collection of hairs, threads, feathers etc., held or fastened together at one end; a bunch of small blood-vessels etc.: (*coll.*) a goatee, an imperial; †a young nobleman at a university, from the tuft or gold tassel formerly worn on his cap. *v.t.* to separate into tufts; to adorn with or as with tufts; to pass thread through (a mattress etc,) at regular intervals and fasten a button or tuft in the depression thus made. *v.i.* to grow in tufts. **tuft-hunter,** *n.* one who courts the society of titled persons. **tuft-hunting,** *n.* **tufted, tufty,** *a.* [F *touffe,* from Teut. (cp. Swed. dial. *tuppa,* Icel. *toppr,* G *Zopf*)]

tug, *v.t.* to pull or draw with great effort or with violence; to haul, to tow. *v.i.* (*past, p.p.* **tugged**) to pull violently (at). *n.* the act or a spell of tugging; a vigorous or violent pull; a violent effort, a severe struggle; a small powerful steam-vessel for towing others; a loop hanging from the saddle in harness supporting a shaft or trace. **tug of love,** a dispute between parents or guardians over custody of a child. **tug of war,** a contest between two sets of persons pulling a rope from opposite ends across a line marked on the ground; a struggle between two sides. **tug-carrier, -chain, -iron, -slide, -spring,** *n.* a part of the harness used in fastening the traces to the shafts etc. **tugger,** *n.* †**tuggingly,** *adv.* [ME *toggen,* perh. from Icel. *tog,* rope, cogn. with TOW[1]]

tug(h)rik, *n.* the standard unit of currency in Mongolia. [Mongolian]

tui, *n.* the parson-bird. [Maori]

†**tuille,** *n.* a steel plate protecting the thighs, hanging from the tasses. † **tuillette,** *n.* a small tuille protecting the hips. [OF (cp. F *tuile,* TILE), L *tugula,* TILE]

tuism, *n.* the theory that all thought is directed to a second person or to one's future self as such. [L *tū.* thou, -ISM]

tuition, *n.* teaching, instruction, esp. in a particular subject or group of subjects as dist. from education; a fee for this. **tuitional, tuitionary,** *a.* [F, from L *tuitiōnem,* nom. *-tio,* from *tuēri,* to watch, to guard, p.p. *tuitus*]

Tukano, *n.* indigenous people of the Vaupés Region on the Colombian-Brazilian border, numbering approximately 2000.

Tula-metal, *n.* an alloy of silver, copper, and lead, used in niello work. **Tula-work,** *n.* Niello work. [*Tula,* town in USSR, METAL]

tularaemia, (*esp. N Am.*) **-emia,** *n.* an acute infectious bacterial disease of rodents, sometimes communicated to humans by flea or tick bites, causing fever etc. [From *Tulare* County in California, where it was first discovered, -AEMIA]

tulchan, -chin, *n.* (*Sc.*) a calfskin stuffed with straw put beside a cow at milking time to induce a free flow of milk. [etym. doubtful]

tulip, *n.* any plant of the genus *Tulipa,* bulbous plants of the lily family, with gorgeous bell-shaped flowers of various colours. **tulip-tree,** *n.* a large N American tree, *Liriodendron tulipifera,* of the magnolia family, bearing greenish-yellow, tulip-like flowers. **tulip-wood,** *n.* the wood of this tree. **tulipist,** *n.* **tulipomania,** *n.* a craze for the cultivation or acquisition of tulips which arose in Holland about 1634. [F *tulippe,* It. *tulipa, tulipano,* Turk. *tulbend, dulbend,* TURBAN]

Tull, *n.* **Jethro** (1674–1741), English agriculturist who developed a drill about 1701, which enabled seeds to be sown mechanically and spaced so that cultivation between rows was possible in the growth period. His major work, *Horse-Hoeing Husbandry,* was published 1731.

tulle, *n.* a fine silk net, used for veils etc., orig. manufactured in the French city of Tulle.

Tullian, *a.* of, pertaining to, or in the style of Cicero. [Marcus *Tullius* Cicero, Roman statesman and orator]

tulwar, *n.* a curved sabre used by the Sikhs and some tribes of N India. [Hind.]

tum[1], tummy, *n.* (*coll.*) short for STOMACH.

tum[2], tum-tum, *n.* the sound of a stringed musical instrument like the banjo. [imit.]

tumata Kuru, *n.* a spiny shrub with usable wood. [Maori]

tumble, *v.i.* to fall (down etc.) suddenly or violently; to roll or toss about; to walk, run, or move about, in a careless or headlong manner; to perform acrobatic feats, esp. without special apparatus to decrease quickly. *v.t.* to toss or fling forcibly; to throw or push (down etc.); to cause to tumble or fall; to throw into disorder, to rumple; to dry (clothes) in a tumble-dryer. *n.* a fall; a state of disorder; an acrobatic feat, esp. a somersault. **to tumble home,** (*Naut.*) to incline inwards (of the sides of ships) from the line of greatest breadth. **to tumble in,** (*Carp.*) to fit (a piece of timber) into another; (*Naut.*) to tumble home; (*coll.*) to go to bed, to turn in. **to tumble to,** (*sl.*) to understand, to comprehend. **tumbledown,** *a.* dilapidated. **tumble-dry,** *v.t.* to dry (clothes) in a tumble-dryer. **tumble-dryer,** *n.* a domestic appliance with a revolving cylinder into which damp clothes are placed and dried by having warm air blown through them as they turn. **tumbleweed,** *n.* a plant that breaks away from its roofs in autumn, e.g. an amaranth and is blown around by the wind. **tumbling,** *n.* **tumbling-barrel, -box,** *n.* a revolving box etc., in which castings are cleaned by friction. **tumbly,** *a.* [ME *tumblen,* freq. from OE *tumbian,* cp. Dut. *tuimelen,* G *taumeln, tummeln,* Swed. *tumla,* Dan. *tumle*]

tumbler, *n.* one who or that which tumbles; one who performs somersaults, an acrobat; a variety of pigeon, from its habit of turning over in flight; a toy that turns somersaults; a stemless drinking-glass, orig. with a rounded base, so that it fell on the side when set down; a springlatch (usu. one of several) in a lock, that engages a bolt unless lifted by the key; a part of the lock in a fire-arm attached to the hammer and engaging with the trigger. **tumbler switch,** *n.* a simple form of switch used for electric light connections. **tumblerful,** *n.*

tumbrel, *n.* a two-wheeled cart for carrying ammunition and tools for mining and sapping; a dung-cart; (*dial.*) a large willow rack for feeding sheep in winter. [OF *tumbrel, tumberel,* from *tomber,* to fall, cogn. with prec.]

tumid, *a.* swollen, enlarged, distended; pompous, bombastic, turgid. **tumescent,** *a.* swollen, enlarged; becoming swollen or enlarged. **tumescence,** *n.* **tumidity, tumidness,** *n.* **tumidly,** *adv.* **tumefy,** *v.t.* to cause to swell; to inflate. *v.i.* to swell; to rise in or as in a tumour. **tumefacient,** *a.* **tumefaction,** *n.* [L *tumidus,* from *tumēre,* to swell]

tummy TUM[1].

tumour, (*N Am.*) **tumor,** *n.* a swelling on some part of the body, esp. if due to a morbid growth. [F *tumeur,* L *tumor -orem,* as TUMID]

tump[1], *n.* a hillock, a mound. *v.t.* (*dial.*) to form a mass of earth round (a plant). [cp. W., Gael., and Ir. *tom*]

tump[2], *v.t.* (*N Am.*) to draw (the carcass of a deer etc.) home. **tumpline,** *n.* a strap worn round the forehead or breast by Canadian voyageurs etc., to steady a load carried on the back. [etym. doubtful]

tum-tum[1], *n.* a W Indian dish of boiled plantain beaten soft; a tom-tom. [prob. imit.]

tum-tum[2] TUM[1].

tumult, *n.* the commotion, disturbance, or agitation of a multitude, esp. with a confusion of sounds; a confused outbreak or insurrection; uproar, stir, riot; excitement, agitation, or confusion of mind. **tumultuous,** *a.* **tumultuously,** *adv.* **tumultuousness,** *n.* †**tumultuation,** *n.* [F *tumulte,* L *tumultus,* as foll.]

tumulus, *n.* (*pl.* **-li**) a mound of earth, sometimes combined with masonry, usually sepulchral, a barrow. **tumular,** †**tumulary, tumulose, tumulous,** *a.* [L, from *tumēre,* to swell]

tun, *n.* a large cask, esp. for alcoholic liquors; a wine measure, 252 galls. (11·46 hl); a brewer's fermenting-vat. *v.t.* to put (liquor) into a tun. †**tun-bellied,** *a.* **tun-belly,** *n.* **tundish,** *n.* a funnel, orig. of wood. **tunnage,** *n.* a tax on imported wine levied on each cask or tun, usu. coupled with POUNDAGE. [OE *tunne,* cp. Dut. *ton,* G *tonne,* Icel. and Swed. *tunna*]

tuna[1], *n.* (*pl.*) **tuna, tunas,** (*Zool.*) any of a genus of large scombroid sea-fish found in warmer waters; (also **tuna-fish**) its flesh as food. [Am. Sp. from Sp. *atún* from Arab. *tūn,* L *thunnus,* Gr. *thunnos*]

tuna[2], *n.* a prickly-pear, plant or fruit. [Sp. from Taino]

tunable, etc. TUNE.

tundra, *n.* a marshy treeless plain in the arctic and subarctic regions, with permanently frozen subsoil and covered largely with mosses and lichens. [Rus.]

tune, *n.* a melodious succession of musical tones forming a coherent whole, an air, a melody, esp. as a setting for a song, hymn etc.; correct intonation in singing or playing; proper adjustment of an instrument for this; a distinctive intonation pattern in speech. *v.t.* to put in tune; to adjust, to adapt, to attune; (*poet.*) to sing, to produce (a song, music etc.); to adjust (an engine) for optimum performance; to adjust (a radio,

TV set) for optimum reception of an incoming signal. *v.i.* to come or be in harmony; to utter or express musically, **in, out of tune,** at, not at the correct pitch; correctly, incorrectly adjusted for pitch; (not) in harmony, sympathy, agreement (with). **to call the tune,** to give orders, to say what is to be done. **to change one's tune,** CHANGE. **to the tune of,** (*coll.*) to the sum or amount of. **to tune in,** (*Radio.*) to adjust a circuit to obtain resonance at a required frequency; to switch on a radio, TV set and start listening, watching. **to tune up,** (of a group of musicians) to adjust (instruments) to a common pitch before playing; to improve the performance of an engine by tuning. **tunable,** *a.* **tunableness,** *n.* **tunably,** *adv.* **tuneful,** *a.* melodious, musical. **tunefully,** *adv.* **tunefulness,** *n.* **tuneless,** *a.* not in tune; unmusical, inharmonious; (*fig.*) silent, without voice. **tuned circuit,** *n.* (*Radio.*) an oscillatory circuit adjusted to yield resonance at a required wavelength. **tuner,** *n.* one who tunes, esp. one whose occupation is to tune musical instruments; a knob, dial etc. by which a radio or TV set is tuned to different wavelengths. **tuning,** *n.* the act of tuning; (*Mus.*) a set of pitches to which (the strings of) stringed instruments are tuned; the state of adjustment of an engine, radio receiver etc. **tuning condenser,** *n.* (*Radio.*) a variable condenser embodied in a tuning circuit. **tuning-crook,** *n.* a hook in a cornet or other brass wind-instrument for varying the fundamental pitch. **tuning-fork,** *n.* a two pronged steel instrument giving a fixed note when struck, used to measure the pitch of musical tones, etc. **tuning-hammer,** *n.* a hammer-shaped wrench for tuning pianofortes, harps, etc. **tuning note,** *n.* (*Radio.*) a prolonged note issued by a transmitting station to enable listeners to tune in. [A-F *tun* (F *ton*), L *tonus -um* TONE]

tungsten, *n.* a heavy, greyish-white metallic element, at. no. 74; chem. symbol W (also known as **wolfram**) of unusually high melting point. **tungstic,** *a.* **tungstate,** *n.* a salt of tungstic acid. [Swed. (*tung,* heavy, *sten,* STONE)]

Tungus, *n.* (*pl.* **-gus, -guses**) a member or the language of people belonging to a Turanian group occupying parts of Siberia and China. **Tungusian**, *a.* **Tungusic**, *a., n.* [native name]

Tunguska Event, *n.* an explosion at Tunguska, central Siberia in June 1908 which devastated around 6500 sq km/2500 sq miles of forest. It is thought to have been caused by either a cometary nucleus or a fragment of Encke's comet. The magnitude of the explosion was equivalent to an atom bomb and produced a colossal shock wave; a bright falling object was seen 600 km/ 375 miles away and was heard up to 1000 km/ 625 miles away.

tunic, *n.* a short-sleeved body-garment reaching nearly to the knees, worn by the ancient Greeks and Romans; a mediaeval surcoat worn over armour; a modern loose coat or short overskirt gathered in or belted at the waist, now worn only by women and children; a military or policeman's jacket; (*Anat.*) a membrane or envelope covering some part or organ; (*Bot.*) a membranous skin. **tunicary,** *n.* a tunicate. **tunicate**, *a.* having or covered with a tunic. *n.* any individual of the order Tunicata, a division of Metazoa, forming a connecting-link between the Vertebrata and the Invertebrata, many of them in the larval state being furnished with a notochord, which atrophies in the adult. **tunicated**, *a.* **tunicle**, *n.* a small, fine, or delicate tunic, a fine integument; a close-fitting vestment worn by deacons, and by Roman Catholic cardinals, bishops, and abbots with the dalmatic. [OE *tunece,* L *tunica*]

tuning-crook, etc. TUNE.

Tunis, *n.* capital and chief port of Tunisia; population (1984) 597,000. Industries include chemicals and textiles. Founded by the Arabs, it was occupied by the French 1881, and by the Axis powers 1942–43. The ruins of ancient Carthage are to the NE.

Tunisia, *n.* Republic of, a country in N Africa, on the Mediterranean, bounded to the SE by Libya and to the W by Algeria. **area** 154,500 sq km/59,652 sq miles. **capital** and chief port Tunis. **towns** ports Sfax, Sousse, Bizerta. **physical** arable and forested land in the north graduates towards desert in the south. **population** (1989) 7,930,000; annual growth rate 2%. **exports** oil, phosphates, iron ore. **language** Arabic (official), French. **religion** Sunni Muslim, with a politically active fundamentalist opposition to the government; Jewish and Christian minorities.

tunnage TUN.

tunnel, *n.* an artificial underground passage or gallery, esp. one under a hill, river etc., for a railway, road, or canal; a passage dug by a burrowing animal; a mining level, an adit; a main flue of a chimney. *v.t.* (*past, p.p.* **tunnelled**) to make a tunnel through (a hill etc.); to shape like a tunnel; to catch in a tunnel-net. *v.i.* to cut or make a tunnel. **tunnel diode,** *n.* a semi-conductor diode capable of giving áa amplification. **tunnel-net,** *n.* a net with a wide mouth narrowing towards the other end. **tunnel vision,** *n.* a medical condition in which peripheral vision is largely lost and one can only see objects directly in front of one; extreme narrowness of viewpoint due to concentration on a single issue. [OF *tonnel* (F *tonneau,* dim. of *tonne,* TUN]

tunny TUNA.

tup, *n.* a ram or male sheep; the striking-part of a steam-hammer. *v.t., v.i.* to butt, as a ram; to cover, as a ram. [ME *tuppe,* cp. Swed. and Norw. *tupp,* cock, Dan. *top,* cock's crest, Icel. *toppr,* crest, TOP]

tupaia, *n.* a genus of small insectivorous squirrel-like mammals, the tree-shrews, from S-E Asia and Malaysia. [from Malay]

Tupamaros, *n.pl.* urban guerrilla movement operating in Uruguay, largely active in the 1960s–70s, named after the 18th-cent. revolutionary Túpac Amarú.

tupelo, *n.* a N American tree of the genus *Nyssa,* esp. the black- or sour-gum; the wood of this. [native name]

Tupi, *n.* (*pl.* **Tupis, Tupi**) a member of a S American people dwelling in the Amazon region; their language. [native name]

tupong, *n.* a variety of flat-head fish in S Australia. [Austral. Abor.]

tuppence, tuppenny, (*coll.*) TWOPENCE, TWOPENNY.

tuque, *n.* a Canadian cap made by tucking in one end of a knitted cylindrical bag both ends of which are closed. [F- Canadian, var. of TOQUE]

Turanian, *a.* applied to certain Asiatic languages that are neither Aryan nor Semitic, esp. the Ural Altaic group. [*Turan,* mythical founder of the Turkish race]

turban, *n.* an Oriental head-dress consisting of a sash or scarf wound round the cap; a woman's head-dress imitating this; a narrow-brimmed or brimless hat worn by women and children; the whorls of a univalve shell. **turban-shell,** *n.* a gasteropod of the genus *Turbo;* a shell of this. **turbaned,** *a.* [F, earlier *turbant,* It. *turbante,* Turk. *tulbend, dulbend,* Pers. *dulband,* prob. from Hindi]

turbary, *n.* (*Law*) the right of digging turf on another's land; a place where turf or peat is dug. [OF *torberie,* late L *turbāria,* from OHG *zurba,* TURF]

Turbellaria, *n.pl.* (*Zool.*) a class of flat-worms with ciliated skin and without a body-cavity, the planarians. **turbellarian,** *a., n.* **turbellariform,** *a.* [mod. L, from L *turba,* crowd]

turbid, *a.* muddy, discoloured, thick; disordered, unquiet, disturbed. **turbidity**, **turbidness,** *n.* **turbidly,** *adv.* [L *turbidus,* from *turbāre,* to disturb, from *turba,* crowd]

†**turbillion,** *n.* a vortex, a whirl. [F *tourbillon,* dim. of OF *tourbille,* ult. from L *turbo,* see TURBINE]

turbinate, *a.* top-shaped, like an inverted cone; spiral, whorled; spinning like a top. **turbinal, turbiniform**, **turbinoid**, *a.* **turbination,** *n.* [L *turbinatus,* as foll.]

turbine, *n.* a water-wheel or motor enclosed in a case or tube in which a flowing stream acts by direct impact or reaction upon a series of vanes or buckets; a similar wheel or motor driven by steam or air; a vessel propelled by a turbine. [F, from L *turbinem,* nom. *turbo,* wheel, top, whirlwind, as prec.]

turbit, *n.* a variety of domestic pigeon with a flattened head and short beak. [etym. doubtful]

Turbo, *n.* (*Zool.*) a genus of gasteropods with turbinate shells, typical of the family Turbinidae [L, see TURBINE]

turbo, *n., a.* (a model of, car etc.) incorporating a turbocharger. **turbo-**, *comb. form* having or driven by a turbine. **turbocharger**, *n.* a supercharger, esp. for motor car engines, driven by exhaust gas turbines. **turbofan**, *n.* (an aircraft powered by) a gas-turbine aero-engine with a large fan which forces air out with the exhaust gases, thus increasing thrust. **turbojet**, *n.* (an aircraft powered by) a turbojet engine. **turbojet engine,** *n.* an engine with a turbine-driven compressor for supplying compressed air to the combustion chamber. **turboprop**, *n.* (an aircraft powered by) an engine with a turbine-driven propeller.

turbot, *n.* a large European flat-fish, *Psetta maxima,* with bony tubercles, highly valued as food. [F, from L *turbo,* see TURBINE]

turbulent, *a.* disturbed, tumultuous; insubordinate, disorderly. **turbulence, †-lency,** *n.* **turbulently,** *adv.* [F, from L *turbulentus,* as TURBID]

Turcism, *n.* the religion, manners, or character of the Turks. **Turco**, *n.* an Algerian sharp-shooter in the French army. **Turcoman**, TURKOMAN. **Turcophil,** *n.* a lover of Turkey and the Turks. **Turcophilism,** *n.* **Turcophobe,** *n.*

turd, *n.* (*taboo*) a lump of excrement or dung; a contemptible person. [OE *tord*]

Turdus, *n.* a genus of passerine birds of the family Turdidae, comprising the thrush, blackbird, ring-ouzel, redwing and fieldfare. **turdiform**, **turdine**, **turdoid,** *a.* [L]

tureen, *n.* a deep covered dish or vessel for holding soup. [orig. *terreen,* TERRINE]

turf, *n.* (*pl.* **turfs, turves**) surface earth filled with the matted roots of grass and other small plants; a piece of this, a sod; greensward, growing grass; peat. *v.t.* to cover or line with turfs or sods. **the turf,** the racecourse; the occupation or profession of horse-racing. **to turf out,** (*coll.*) to throw out, to eject forcibly. **turf accountant,** *n.* a bookmaker. **turf-clad,** *a.* covered with turf. **turf-drain,** *n.* a pipe-drain constructed of turfs. **turf-man,** *n.* a turfite. **†turfen,** *a.* **turfiness,** *n.* **turfy,** *a.* **turfite**, *n.* one devoted to or making a living by horse-racing. **turfless**, *a.* [OE, cp. Dut. *turf,* Icel. and Swed. *torf,* Dan. *törv*]

Turgenev, *n.* **Ivan Sergeievich** (1818–83), Russian writer, noted for poetic realism, pessimism, and skill at characterization. His works include the play *A Month in the Country* (1849), and the novels *A Nest of Gentlefolk* (1858), *Fathers and Sons* (1862), and *Virgin Soil* (1877). His series of *A Sportsman's Sketches* (1852) criticized serfdom.

turgid, *a.* swollen, bloated, morbidly distended, tumid; pompous, inflated, bombastic. **turgescent**, *a.* **†turgent,** *a.* **turgescence,** *n.* **turgidity**, **turgidness,** *n.* **turgidly,** *adv.* [L *turgidus,* from *turgēre,* to swell]

Turin (Italian **Torino**), *n.* capital of Piedmont, NW Italy, on the river Po; population (1988) 1,025,000. Industries include iron, steel, cars, silk and other textiles, fashion goods, chocolate, and wine. It was the first capital of united Italy 1861–64. **Turin shroud,** *n.* ancient piece of linen bearing the image of a body, claimed to be that of Jesus. Independent tests carried out 1988 by scientists in Switzerland, the US, and the UK showed that the cloth of the shroud dated from between 1260 and 1390. The shroud, property of the pope, is kept in Turin Cathedral, Italy.

Turing, *n.* **Alan Mathison** (1912–54), British mathematician and logician. In 1936 he described a 'universal computing machine' that could theoretically be programmed to solve any problem capable of solution by a specially designed machine. This concept, now called the Turing Machine, foreshadowed the digital computer.

turion, *n.* a young scaly shoot rising from the ground, as in asparagus. **turioniferous,** *a.* [L *turiōnem,* nom. *-io*]

Turk, *n.* a native, inhabitant or citizen of Turkey; a native speaker of a Turkic language; a Turkish horse; a troublesome person, esp. a boy; †a Muslim. **Turk's-cap,** *n.* a martagon lily; the melon-cactus. **Turk's head,** *n.* a brush on a long handle for cleaning cornices etc.; a circular or elliptical pan for baking cakes; an ornamental knot. [F *Turc,* med. L *Turcus,* Pers. *Turk*]

Turkana, Lake (formerly **Lake Rudolf**), *n.* lake in the Great Rift Valley, 375 m/1230 ft. above sea level, with its northernmost end in Ethiopia and the rest in Kenya; area 9000 sq km/3475 sq miles. It is saline, and shrinking by evaporation. Its shores were an early human hunting ground, and valuable remains have been found which are accurately datable because of undisturbed stratification.

Turkey, *n.* Republic of, a country between the Black Sea and the Mediterranean, bounded to the E by the USSR and Iran, to the S by Iraq and Syria. **area** 779,500 sq km/300,965 sq miles. **capital** Ankara. **towns** ports Istanbul and Izmir. **physical** central plateau surrounded by mountains. **population** (1989) 55,377,000 (85% Turkish, 12% Kurdish); annual growth rate 2.1%. **exports** cotton, yarn, hazelnuts, citrus, tobacco, dried fruit, chromium ores. **language** Turkish (official; it is related to Mongolian, but is written in the Western Latin script), Kurdish Arabic. **religion** Sunni Muslim. **Turkey carpet,** *n.* a soft velvety woollen carpet, orig. made in Turkey. **Turkey leather,** *n.* leather tawed with oil before the hair is removed. **Turkey red,** *n.* a brilliant red dye orig. obtained from madder; cotton cloth dyed with this. **Turkey-rhubarb,** *n.* medicinal rhubarb. **Turkey-stone,** *n.* novaculite; turquoise. **Turkish**, *a.* pertaining to Turkey or the Turks. *n.* the Turkish language. **Turkish bath,** *n.* a hot-air bath in which one is sweated, washed, rubbed, massaged etc., and conducted through a series of cooling-rooms. **Turkish carpet** TURKEY CARPET. **Turkish delight,** *n.* a gelatinous sweetmeat. **Turkish language,** *n.* a language of central and W Asia, the national language of Turkey. Originally written in Arabic script, the Turkish of Turkey has been written in a variant of the Roman alphabet since 1928. Varieties of Turkish are spoken in NW Iran and several of the Asian republics of the USSR, and all have been influenced by Arabic and Persian.

turkey, *n.* a large gallinaceous bird of the genus *Meleagris,* allied to the pheasant, orig. introduced from America; (*Austral.*) the wild turkey, the Callegalla or brush turkey, and the mallee-bird or sand turkey. (*esp. N Am., sl.*) a flop. **to talk turkey,** (*esp. N Am.*) to come to the point, to talk business. **turkey-buzzard, -vulture,** *n.* an American vulture, *Cathartes.* **turkey-cock,** *n.* a male turkey; a conceited, pompous person. **turkey-corn,** *n.* maize. **turkey-poult,** *n.* a young turkey. **turkey-trot,** *n.* a round dance with little or no bending of the knees and a swing of the body. [as prec. (from the belief that the bird came from Turkey)]

Turki, *a.* of the Turkish, as distinct from the Tatar, branch of the Turko-Tatar languages. *n.* a Turki language or speaker. **Turkic, Turko-tatar,** *a., n.* (of) that branch of the Altaic languages to which Turkish belongs.

†turkis TURQUOISE.

†turkois TURQUOISE.

Turkmenistan, *n.* constituent republic of the USSR from 1924, part of Soviet Central Asia. **area** 488,100 sq km/188,455 sq miles. **capital** Ashkhabad. **population** (1987) 3,361,000; 69% Turkmenian, 13% Russian, 9% Uzbek, 3% Kazakh. **products** silk, sheep, astrakhan fur, carpets, oil, chemicals. **language** West Turkic, closely related to Turkish. **religion** Sunni Muslim.

Turkoman, *n.* (*pl.* **-mans**) a person of Turkoman culture. They live around the Kara Kum desert, to the E of the Caspian Sea, and straddle the borders of Afghanistan, Iran, and the USSR. Their language belongs to the Turkic branch of the Altaic family. [med L *Turco-, Turcus,* TURK, MAN]

Turks and Caicos Islands, *n.pl.* a British crown colony in the West Indies, the SE archipelago of the Bahamas. **area** 430 sq km/166 sq miles. **capital**

Cockburn Town on Grand Turk. **population** (1980) 7500, 90% of African descent. **exports** crayfish and conch (flesh and shell). **language** English, French Creole. **religion** Christian.

turlough, *n.* a hollow tract of land in Ireland liable to flooding, esp. by subterranean streams. [Ir. *turloch* (*tur*, dry, LOCH)]

†**turm,** *n.* a troop of horse. **turma,** *n.* (*pl.* **-mae**), (*Rom. Ant.*) a body of cavalry; the tenth part of the wing of a legion. [L *turma*]

turmalin TOURMALINE.

turmeric, *n.* an E Indian plant, *Curcuma longa,* of the ginger family; the powdered rhizome of this used as dye-stuff, a stimulant, or a condiment, esp. in curry. **turmeric-paper,** *n.* unsized white paper saturated with turmeric used as a test for alkalis, which change the colour from yellow to red. [corr. of F *terre-merite,* perh. corr. of Arab. *kurkum,* CURCUMA]

turmoil, *n.* commotion, disturbance, tumult. †*v.t.* to trouble, to agitate. [etym. doubtful, perh. from MOIL]

turn, *v.t.* to cause to move round on or as on an axis, to give a rotary motion to; to cause to go, move, aim, point, look etc., in a different direction; to expose the other side of, to invert, to reverse; to renew (a cuff, collar etc.) by reversing; to bring lower soil to the surface by digging or ploughing; to revolve in the mind; to perform (a somersault); to apply or devote to a different purpose or object, to give a new direction to; to bend, to adapt, to change in form, condition, nature etc.; to cause to become, to convert, to transform, to transmute; to translate, to paraphrase; to pass, go, or move to the other side of, to go round; to pass round the flank of (an army) so as to attack it from the flank or rear; to reach or pass beyond (a certain age, time); to bend back, to blunt (a knife-edge etc.); to cause to ferment, to make sour; to nauseate; to infatuate, to unsettle, to make giddy; to cause to go, to send, to put by turning; to shape in a lathe or on a potter's wheel; to give a shapely form to, to mould, to round (a sentence etc.); to cause an enemy agent to become a double agent. *v.i.* to have a circular or revolving motion, to rotate, to revolve, to move round or about; to move the body, face, or head in a different direction, to change front from right to left, etc.; to change in posture, attitude, or position; to return; to take a particular direction; to be changed in nature, form, condition etc.; to change colour; to become sour or spoiled; to become unsettled, infatuated, or giddy; to become nauseated; to result, to terminate; to undergo the process of turning on the lathe; (*Cricket*) to spin, to deviate from line; (*Cricket*) (of wicket) to assist spin bowling. *n.* the act of turning, rotary motion; a revolution; the state of being turned; a change of direction, position or tendency, a deflection; a bend, a curve, a winding, a corner; a single round or coil of a rope etc.; a change, a vicissitude; a turning-point; a point of change in time; a short walk, a stroll, a promenade; a performance, bout or spell (of doing something); an occasion, opportunity, or time (for doing something); coming in succession to each of a number of persons; succession, alternation, rotation; (*coll.*) a nervous shock; shape, form, mould, character, disposition, temper; a melodic embellishment consisting of the principal tone with those above and below it; (*Print.*) an inverted type put temporarily in place of a missing letter; (*Theat.*) (the performer of) a short, theatrical act. **a good, bad turn,** a helpful service, a disservice. **at every turn,** constantly; everywhere. **by turns,** alternately; at intervals. **done to a turn,** cooked exactly right. **ill turn** ILL. **in turn,** in order of succession, in rotation. **on the turn,** just turning (of the tide); beginning to go sour; the point of changing. **out of turn,** out of the proper order of succession; at an inappropriate time. **to serve one's turn,** to serve one's purpose; to help or suit one. **to take a turn for the better, worse,** to improve, deteriorate. **to take turns,** to alternate, to perform or participate in rotation or succession. **to turn a blind eye to,** to pretend not to see, to overlook. **to turn about,** to turn the face in another direction; to turn round. **to turn a deaf ear to,** to refuse to listen to. **to turn adrift,** to unmoor (a boat) and allow to float away; (*fig.*) to cast off. **to turn again,** to return. **to turn against,** to (cause to) become hostile to; to use against. **to turn aside,** to deviate; to divert, to avert. **to turn down,** to fold or double down; to lower (a light, the volume on a radio etc.); to lay (a card) face downwards; (*coll.*) to reject. **to turn in,** to direct or incline inwards; to fold or double in; to send, put, or drive in; to hand over, to surrender; to give, to execute (a performance etc.); (*coll.*) to go to bed. **to turn off,** to deflect; to deviate; to dismiss; to shut or switch off; to achieve, to produce, to accomplish; to hang (a criminal); to cause to lose interest in, esp. sexually. **to turn on,** to open a way to (gas etc.) by turning the tap; to switch on; to direct, to aim; to retort, to hinge or depend upon; to attack; (*coll.*) to excite, to arouse the interest of, esp. sexually; (*sl.*) to introduce to drugs; (*sl.*) to take and get high on drugs. **to turn one's hand,** to apply oneself. **to turn out,** to drive out, to expel; to point or to cause to point outwards; to turn (pockets etc.) inside out; (of a room) to clean thoroughly; to bring to view; to produce, as the result of labour; to prove to be; to switch off; to dress, to groom, to look after the appearance of; to gather, to assemble; to go out; (*coll.*) to get out of bed. **to turn over,** to change the position of, to invert, to reverse; (of an engine) to (cause to) start or run at low revolutions; to surrender, to hand over; to transfer (to), to put under other control; to cause to turn over, to upset; to do business to the amount of; to consider, to ponder; (*sl.*) to rob. **to turn round,** to face about; to adopt new views, attitude, policy etc.; to complete the processing of; to complete the unloading and reloading of (a ship, aircraft); to restore to profitability. **to turn tail,** TAIL. **to turn to,** to have recourse to; to change or be changed into; to direct towards; to find (a page) in a book; to set to work. **to turn turtle,** TURTLE[2]. **to turn up,** to bring to the surface; to unearth, to bring to light; to place (a card etc.) with the face upwards; to tilt up; to find and refer to (a passage) in a book; to point upwards; to come to light; to happen; to make one's appearance, **to turn upon,** to hinge on; to attack; to direct or aim at. **turn and turn about,** alternately, successively. **turnabout,** *n.* the act of facing in an opposite direction; a complete reversal (of opinion, policy etc.). **turnaround,** turnabout; turnround. **turnbench,** *n.* a small portable lathe, used by watchmakers. **turn-buckle,** *n.* a coupling for metal rods etc. allowing adjustment of length. **turncap,** *n.* a chimney cowl turning round with the wind. **turn-coat,** *n.* one who turns his coat; one who deserts his party or principles. **turncock,** *n.* one who turns water on or off from a main; a stopcock. **turn-down,** *a.* folded or doubled down. **turn indicator,** *n.* (*Aviat.*) a gyroscopic instrument which indicates any deviation in the course of an aircraft. **turnkey,** *n.* one who has the charge of the keys of a prison, a warder. *a.* being in its entirety the responsibility of a single contractor or supplier. **turn-out,** *n.* a turning out for duty; an assembly, a large party; a showy or well-appointed equipage; dress, get-up; a quantity of articles or products manufactured in a given time. **turn-over,** *n.* an upset; a semicircular pie or tart made by turning over half the crust; the amount of money turned over in a business in a given time; the rate at which stock in trade is sold and replenished; the rate at which employees leave and have to be replaced; an article filling a column and continued on the next page. **turnround,** *n.* (the time taken by) the process of unloading a ship, aircraft and reloading it ready for its next trip; (the time taken by) the complete processing of anything; a change to an opposite and usu. better state. **turn-screw,** *n.* a screw-driver. **turnsole** SOL[1], *n.* a plant supposed to turn with the sun. **turnspit,** *n.* a person who turns a spit; a variety of dog, allied to the terrier, formerly employed to turn spits. **turnstone,** *n.* a bird, *Arenaria interpres,* allied to the plover. **turntable,** *n.* a platform rotating in a horizontal plane used for shifting rolling-stock from one line of rails to another; the rotating table which supports a gramophone record while being played. **turn-up,** *n.* a turned-up fold at the bottom of a trouser leg; (also **a turn-up for the book**) a sudden and unexpected (fortunate) occurrence. **turner,** *n.* one who turns, esp. one who turns articles in a lathe; a variety of tumbler-pigeon. **turnery,** *n.* **turning,** *n.* the act of one who or of that which turns; a bend, a corner, the point where a road meets another; such a road. **turning circle,** *n.* the smallest circle in which a vehicle can turn round. **turning-point,** *n.* the point in place, time etc., on or at which a change takes place, the decisive point. [OE *turnian, tyrnan* (cp. OF *torner,* F *tourner*), L *tornāre,* from *tornus,* lathe, Gr. *tornos*]

Turner[1], *n.* **John Napier** (1929–), Canadian Liberal politician, prime minister 1984. He was elected to the House of Commons 1962 and served in the cabinet of Pierre Trudeau, until resigning 1975. He succeeded Trudeau as party leader and prime minister 1984, but lost the 1984 and 1988 elections. Turner resigned as leader 1989, and returned to his law practice. He was replaced as Liberal Party chief by Herbert Gray in Feb. 1990.

Turner[2], *n.* **Joseph Mallord William** (1775–1851), English landscape painter. He travelled widely in Europe, and his landscapes became increasingly romantic, with the subject often transformed in scale and flooded with brilliant, hazy light. Many later works appear to anticipate impressionism, for example *Rain, Steam and Speed* (1844, National Gallery, London).

Turner[3], *n.* **Lana (Julia Jean Mildred Frances)** (1920–), US actress who appeared in melodramatic films of the 1940s and 1950s such as *Peyton Place* (1957). Her other films include *The Postman Always Rings Twice* (1946), *The Three Musketeers* (1948), and *Imitation of Life* (1959).

Turner[4], *n.* **Nat** (1800–31), US slave and Baptist preacher, who led 60 slaves in the most important US slave revolt – the Southampton Insurrection of 1831 – in Southampton County, Virginia. Before he and 16 of the others were hanged, at least 55 people had been killed.

Turner[5], *n.* **Tina** (adopted name of Annie Mae Bullock) (1938–), US rhythm-and-blues singer who recorded 1960–76 with her husband, Ike Turner (1931–), notably *River Deep, Mountain High* (1966), produced by Phil Spector. Tina Turner had success in the 1980s as a solo performer, for example *Private Dancer* (1984).

turnip, *n.* a plant of the genus *Brassica,* with a fleshy globular root used as a vegetable and for feeding sheep. **turnip-fly,** *n.* an insect, *Athalia centifoliae* or *Anthomyia radicum,* destructive to turnips. [perh. TURN, or F TOUR, OE *næp,* L *nāpus,* turnip]

turnpike, *n.* a gate set across a road to stop carriages etc., from passing till the toll is paid, orig. a frame set with spikes to prevent passage; a turnpike road; (*N Am.*) a motorway on which a toll is payable. **turnpike-man,** *n.* a collector of tolls at a turnpike. **turnpike road,** *n.* a road on which turnpikes or toll-gates were established.

turnstile, *n.* a post with four horizontal revolving arms, set at the entrance to an enclosure, building etc., allowing persons to pass through one at a time often after a toll or fee is paid.

turpentine, *n.* an oleoresin exuding naturally or from incisions in several coniferous trees, esp. the terebinth; oil or spirit of turpentine, popularly called **turps**, used for mixing paint, varnishes etc. and in medicine; white spirit, also called **turpentine substitute**. *v.t.* to put turpentine in; to saturate with turpentine. **turpentine-tree,** *n.* the terebinth. **turpentinic**, *a.* [ME and MF *turpentine,* L *terebinthinus,* Gr. *terebinthinos,* from *terebinthos,* TEREBINTH]

turpeth, *n.* the root of an E Indian plant, *Ipomaea turpethum,* used as a drastic purgative. [OF *turbith,* Arab. and Pers. *turbid,* purge]

Turpin[1], *n.* **Ben** (1904–74), US comedian, a star of silent films. His trademark was being cross-eyed, and he parodied screen stars and their films. His work includes *The Shriek of Araby* (1923), *A Harem Knight* (1926), and *Broke in China* (1927).

Turpin[2], *n.* **Dick** (1706–39), English highwayman. The son of an innkeeper, he turned to highway robbery, cattle-thieving, and smuggling, and was hanged.

turpinite, *n.* a violent explosive containing picric acid and giving off poisonous fumes. [M. *Turpin,* manufacturer]

turpitude, *n.* baseness, depravity. [F, from L *turpitūdo,* from *turpis,* base]

turps TURPENTINE.

turquoise, *n.* a sky-blue or bluish-green translucent or opaque precious stone; a pale greenish-blue. *a.* of turquoise colour. [OF, fem. of *turquois,* Turkish, see TURK]

turret, *n.* a small tower attached to a building, and rising above it; a low flat cylindrical or conical armoured tower, usu. revolving, so that the guns command a wide radius on a warship, tank or fort; a similar structure on an aircraft; a rotatable holder for cutting tools etc. on a lathe, milling machine etc.; a high wheeled structure used for attacking a castle etc. **turret clock,** *n.* a tower clock in which the movement is separate from the dials. **turret-gun,** *n.* a gun for use in a turret. **turret-ship,** *n.* a warship with a turret or turrets. **turreted,** *a.* [F *tourette,* dim. of *tour,* TOWER]

†**turribant** TURBAN.

turriculate, -lated, *a.* having a long spire (of shells).

turtle[1], *n.* the turtle-dove. **turtle-dove,** *n.* the common wild dove, esp. *Turtur communis,* noted for its soft cooing and its affection for its mate and young. [OE, from L *turtur,* prob. imit. of coo]

turtle[2], *n.* a marine reptile encased in a carapace, like a tortoise, with flippers used in swimming; a chelonian, esp. the green turtle, *Chelonia mydes,* used for soup; turtle-soup. *v.i.* to fish or hunt for turtles. **to turn turtle,** to turn completely over, to capsize. **turtleback,** *n.* an arched covering over part of a ship's deck, esp. at the bows, and sometimes the stern, as a protection against heavy seas. **turtle-cowry,** *n.* a large dappled cowry. **turtle-neck,** *n.* (a sweater with) a round, high, close-fitting neck. **turtle-necked,** *a.* **turtle-shell,** *n.* tortoise-shell, esp. the darker and less valuable kind, used for inlaying; a turtle-cowry. **turtle-soup,** *n.* rich soup made from fatty parts of the turtle. **turtle-stone,** *n.* a septarium. **turtler,** *n.* [corr. of Port. *tartaruga* or Sp. *tortuga,* late L *tortūcu,* TORTOISE]

turves, *pl.* TURF.

Tuscany (Italian **Toscana**), *n.* region of central Italy; area 23,000 sq km/8878 sq miles; population (1988) 3,568,000. Its capital is Florence, and towns include Pisa, Livorno, and Siena. The area is mainly agricultural, with many vineyards, especially in the Chianti hills; it also has lignite and iron mines, and marble quarries. The Tuscan dialect has been adopted as the standard form of Italian. Tuscany was formerly the Roman Etruria. In mediaeval times the area was divided into small states, united under Florentine rule during the 15th–16th cents. It became part of united Italy 1861. **Tuscan**, *a.* pertaining to Tuscany. *n.* a native or the language of Tuscany; the Tuscan order. **Tuscan order,** *n.* (*Arch.*) the simplest of the five classic orders, a Roman modification of Doric.

tusche, *n.* a substance used in lithography for drawing in the design which resists the printing medium. [from G *tuschen,* to touch up]

†**tush**[1], *int.* an expression of contempt or impatience. [cp. TUT[1]]

tush[2], *n.* a long pointed tooth, esp. a horse's canine tooth. [var. of TUSK]

tush[3], *n.* (*N Am. sl.*) buttocks. [from Yiddish *toches*]

tusk, *n.* a long pointed tooth, esp. one protruding from the mouth as in the elephant, narwhal etc.; a tooth-like point, spike, projection etc., as in a harrow, lock etc. *v.t.* to gore, mangle, or root up with tusks. **tusked, tusky,** *a.* **tusker,** *n.* an elephant or wild boar with well-developed tusks. [OE *tusc, tux,* cp. OFris. *tusk, tosch,* Icel. *toskr*]

tuskar, *n.* (*Orkney and Shetland*) an iron tool with a wooden handle for cutting peat. [Icel. *torfskeri* (TURF, *skera,* to cut)]

Tussaud, *n.* **Madame (Anne Marie Grosholtz)** (1761–1850), French wax-modeller. In 1802 she established an exhibition of wax models of famous people in London. It was destroyed by fire 1925, but reopened 1928.

tussis, *n.* a cough. **tussal, tussicular, tussive,** *a.* [L, cough]

tussle, *v.i.* to struggle, to scuffle (with or for). *n.* a struggle, a scuffle. [var. of TOUSLE]

tussock, *n.* a clump, tuft, or hillock of growing grass; a tuft or lock of hair etc.; a tussock-moth. **tussock-grass,** *n.* a grass, *Dactylis caespitosa,* forming tufts 5–6 ft. (1·7–2·0 m) high, growing in Patagonia and the Falkland Islands. **tussock-moth,** *n.* a bombycid moth the larvae of which bear tufts of hair. **tussocker,** *n.* (*New Zealand*) a sun-downer. **tussocky,** *a.* [cp. Swed. dial. *tuss,* wisp of hay]

tussore, tussur, tusser, *n.* an Indian silkworm moth, *Antherea mylitta,* feeding on the jujube tree etc., or a Chinese oak-feeding silkworm moth, *A. pernyi;* a strong, coarse silk obtained from these. [Hind. *tassar,* from Sansk. *tassara,* shuttle]

tut[1], *int., n.* an exclamation of impatience, rebuke, or contempt. *v.i.* to make this exclamation. [instinctive sound]

tut[2], *n.* (*Mining*) a job. *v.i.* to work by the job, to do piece-work. **tutwork,** *n.* [etym. doubtful]

tutamen, *n.* (*pl.* **-mina**) (*Anat.*) a guard, a protection, a protecting part. [L, from *tuērī,* to look after, to keep safe]

Tutankhamen, *n.* king of Egypt of the 18th dynasty, about 1360–1350 BC. A son of Ikhnaton or of Amenhotep III, he was probably about 11 at his accession. In 1922 his tomb was discovered by the British archaeologists Lord Carnarvon and Howard Carter in the Valley of the Kings at Luxor, almost untouched by tomb robbers.

tutelage, *n.* guardianship; the state of being under a guardian; the period of this. **tutelar, -lary,** *a.* having the care or protection of a person or thing, protective; pertaining to a guardian. [L *tūtēla,* guardianship]

tutenag, *n.* a white alloy of copper; zinc or spelter from China or the E Indies. [F *tutenague,* prob. from Arab. and Pers. *tūtiyā,* TUTTY]

tutiorism, *n.* the doctrine that in cases of moral doubt the course should be followed that seems the safer or more in accord with the letter of the law; mitigated rigorism. **tutiorist,** *a., n.* [L *tūtior,* comp. of *tūtus,* safe]

tutor, *n.* a private teacher, esp. one having the general care and instruction of a pupil in preparation for a university etc.; (*Eng. Univ.*) an officer directing the studies of undergraduates in a college and charged with discipline etc.; a college or university teacher who teaches and holds discussions with students in small groups; an instruction book; (*Law*) a guardian of a minor. *v.t.* to act as a tutor to; to instruct, to teach; to train; to discipline, to correct. **tutorage,** *n.* **tutoress,,** *n. fem.* **tutorial,** *a.* of a tutor. *n.* a teaching session or conference with a tutor. **tutorially,** *adv.* **tutorship,** *n.* [ME *tutour,* F *tuteur,* L *tutor -torem,* from *tuēri,* to look after, p.p. *tūtus*]

tutsan, *n.* a species of St John's wort, *Hypericum androsaemum,* formerly held to be a panacea for wounds etc. [OF *toutesaine* (*toute,* L *tōtum,* nom. *-us,* all, *saine, sānus,* sound, SANE)]

tutti, *adv.* (*Mus. direction*) all together. *n.* a composition or passage for singing or performing thus. [It., pl. of *tutto*]

tutti-frutti, *n.* a confection, as ice-cream, made of or flavoured with different fruits. [It., all fruits, cp. prec. and FRUIT]

tutty, *n.* an impure oxide of zinc collected from the flues of smelting furnaces, used as polishing-powder. [ME and OF *tutie,* Arab. and Pers. *tūtiyā*]

tutu[1], *n.* a New Zealand shrub or small tree from the berries of which a wine like claret is obtained, the wineberry shrub. [Maori]

tutu[2], *n.* a ballet-dancer's short, stiff skirt that spreads outwards. [F]

Tutu, *n.* **Desmond (Mpilo)** (1931–), South African priest, Anglican archbishop of Cape Town and general secretary of the South African Council of Churches. He is one of the leading figures in the struggle against apartheid in the Republic of South Africa. Nobel Peace Prize 1984.

tut-work TUT[2].

tuum, *n.* thine, yours; thy or your property. [L, neut. of *tuus*]

Tuva (Russian **Tuvinskaya**), *n.* autonomous republic of the USSR, NW of Mongolian People's Republic, of which it was part until 1911. **capital** Kyzyl. **area** 170,500 sq km/65,813 sq miles. **population** (1986) 284,000.

Tuvalu, *n.* South West Pacific State of, a country in the SW Pacific, on the former Ellice Islands, part of Polynesia. **area** 25 sq km/9.5 sq miles. **capital** Funafuti. **physical** low coral atolls in Polynesia. **population** (1989) 9000 (mainly Polynesian); annual growth rate 3.4%. **exports** phosphates, copra, handicrafts, stamps. **language** Tuvaluan and English. **religion** Christian, chiefly Protestant.

tu-whit tu-whoo, *int.* an imitation of the cry of an owl.

tuxedo, *n.* (*pl.* **-dos, -does**) (*N Am.*) a dinner jacket. [New York club]

tuyère, *n.* the blast-pipe or nozzle in a furnace, forge etc. [F, from *tuyau,* TEWEL]

tuzz, *n.* (*prov.*) a tuft, a lock, a wisp (of wool, hair etc.); a posy, a nosegay. **tuzzi-muzzy,** *a.* tangled, shaggy. *n.* a posy. †**tuzzy,** *n.* [etym. doubtful, cp. TUSSOCK]

TV (*abbr.*) television. **TV dinner,** *n.* a complete, ready-packaged and frozen dinner that only needs reheating before being eaten.

TVP (*abbr.*) textured vegetable protein.

TWA (*abbr.*) Trans-World Airlines.

twa, (*Sc.*) TWO.

twaddle, *v.i.* to talk unmeaningly; to prate, to chatter. *n.* unmeaning talk, silly chatter, nonsense. **twaddler,** *n.* **twaddly,** *adv.* [formerly, *wattle,* var. of TATTLE]

twain, *a.* two. *n.* a pair, a couple. **in twain,** in two, asunder. [OE *twegen,* masc., see TWO]

Twain, *n.* **Mark** (pen name of Samuel Langhorne Clemens) (1835–1910), US humorous writer. He established his reputation with the comic *The Innocents Abroad* (1869), and two children's books, *The Adventures of Tom Sawyer* (1876) and *The Adventures of Huckleberry Finn* (1885). He also wrote satire, as in *A Connecticut Yankee at King Arthur's Court* (1889).

twal, (*Sc.*) TWELVE.

twang[1], *v.i.* to make a ringing metallic sound as by plucking the string of a musical instrument; to play (on) thus; to speak or be uttered with a nasal sound. *v.t.* to cause to sound with a twang; to play (an instrument) thus; to utter or pronounce with a nasal sound. *n.* such a ringing metallic sound; a nasal tone (in speaking etc.); (*prov.*) a tang, a disagreeable flavour. **twangle,** *v.i., v.t.* [var. of TANG[1]]

twang[2], (*Sc.*) TWINGE.

twankay, *n.* a variety of green tea. [Chin., name of river]

'twas, short for IT WAS.

twat, *n.* (*taboo*) the female genitals; (*sl.*) a stupid or contemptible person. [etym. doubtful]

twayblade, *n.* an orchid with two broad, ovate, radical leaves, and green or purplish flowers.

tweak, *v.t.* to pinch and twist or pull with a sudden jerk, to twitch. *n.* a sharp pinch or pull, a twitch. [ME *twikken,* OE *twiccian,* cp. G *zwicken* and TWITCH[1]]

twee, *a.* excessively dainty and prettified; sentimentally sweet. [from *tweet,* mincing pronunciation of *sweet*]

tweed, *n.* a twilled woollen or wool-and-cotton fabric with unfinished surface, used chiefly for outer garments. [prob. from erroneous reading of TWEEL]

tweedle, *n.* the sound of a fiddle. †*v.t.* to handle carelessly, to trifle with; to play (a fiddle). **tweedledum, and tweedledee**, distinction without difference.

[perh. var. of TWIDDLE]

tweel, (*Sc.*) TWILL.

'tween, *adv.* and *prep.* between. **'tween-decks,** *a.* between decks; *n.* space between decks. **tweeny,** *n.* a servant assisting two others, esp. the cook and housemaid. [short for BETWEEN]

tweet, tweet-tweet, *int.* imitation of the sound made by a small bird. *v.i.* make this sound. **tweeter,** *n.* loudspeaker used to produce higher frequencies. [imit.]

tweezer, *n.pl.* small pincers for picking up minute things, plucking out hairs etc., usually called a pair of tweezers. *v.t.* to pluck out or pick up with these. **tweezer-case,** *n.* [obs. *tweese,* a small case for instruments, F. *étui,* -ER]

twelfth, *a.* (*Mus.*) an interval of an octave and a fifth. *n.* one of twelve equal parts. *n., a.* the last of 12 (people, things etc.); the next after the 11th. **the glorious twelfth,** 12 Aug., when grouse-shooting begins. **Twelfth cake,** *n.* a large cake prepared for Twelfth-night festivals. **Twelfth Day,** *n.* the 12th day after Christmas, the festival of the Epiphany, 6 Jan. **Twelfth Night**[1], *n.* the eve of this, 5 Jan. **twelfthly,** *adv.* [OE *twelfta,* from foll.]

Twelfth Night[2], *n.* a comedy by William Shakespeare, performed 1601–02. The plot builds on misunderstandings and mistaken identity, leading to the successful romantic unions of Sebastian and his twin sister Viola with Olivia and Duke Orsino respectively, and the downfall of Olivia's steward Malvolio.

twelve, *n.* the number or figure 12 or XII; the age of 12; midnight or midday. *a.* 12 in number; aged 12. **the Twelve,** the twelve Apostles. **twelvemo,** *n.* Duodecimo, 12mo. **twelvemonth,** *n.* a year. †**twelvepence,** *n.* a shilling. **twelvepenny,** *a.* **Twelver,** *n.* member of a Shi'ite Muslim sect who believes that the 12th imam u (Islamic leader) did not die, but is waiting to return towards the end of the world as the Mahdi, the 'rightly guided one', to establish a reign of peace and justice on Earth. **twelvescore,** *n.* 12 times 20; 12 score yards, a common length for a shot in archery. [OE *twelf* (*twā,* TWO, *lif,* cogn. with LEAVE[2])]

twenty, *n.* the number or figure 20 or XX; the age of 20. *a.* 20 in number; aged 20; a large but indefinite number. **twentieth,** *n.* one of 20 equal parts *n., a.* the last of 20 (people, things etc.); the next after the 19th. **Twentieth Century Fox,** *n.* US film production company, formed 1935 when the Fox Company merged with Twentieth Century. Its president was Joseph Schenck (1878–1961), and Darryl Zanuck (1902–79) was vice-president in charge of production. The company made high-quality films and, despite a financial crisis in the early 1960s, is still a major studio. Recent successes include the *Star Wars* trilogy (1977–83).

twentyfold, *a., adv.* **twenty-fourmo,** *n.* a sheet folding into 24 leaves; a book etc., having 24 leaves to the sheet. **twentymo,** *n.* **twenty-pence (piece),** *n.* a British coin worth 20p. **twenty-twenty,** *a.* of vision, normal. [OE *twentig* (*twegen,* TWAIN, -TY)]

'twere, short for IT WERE.

twerp, twirp, *n.* (*sl.*) a contemptible or silly person. [etym. unknown]

twi-, *comb. form.* two; double [OE]

†**twibill,** *n.* a double-bladed battle-axe; a mattock with an axe-shaped back. [OE (*twi,* two, double, as foll., BILL[2])]

†**twiblade,** TWAYBLADE.

twice, *adv.* two times; doubly. **twice-told,** *a.* related twice; well-known, hackneyed. **twicer,** *n.* (*Print.*) one who is both compositor and pressman. [ME *twies,* OE *twiges,* gen. of *twā,* TWO]

Twickenham, *n.* England international rugby ground, laid out on 4.2 hectares of land in SW London at the suggestion of local sportsman Billy Williams. The first international was held there in 1910. The Rugby Football Union have their headquarters at Twickenham and the Harlequins club play some of their home matches there.

twiddle, *v.t.* to rotate; to twirl idly; to fiddle with. *v.i.* to twirl; to fiddle or trifle (with). **to twiddle one's thumbs,** to sit idle. **twiddling-line,** *n.* (*Naut.*) a string attached to a compass-gimbal for starting it playing freely. [cp. Norw. *tvidla,* var. of *tvilla, tvirla,* TWIRL]

twifold, *a., adv.* twofold. [*twi-,* see TWIBILL, -FOLD]

twig[1], *n.* a small shoot or branch of a tree, bush, etc., a branchlet; a divining rod; (*Anat.*) a small branch of an artery or other vessel; (*Elec.*) a small distributing conductor. **twigged,** *a.* †**twiggen,** *a.* made of twigs or wicker. **twiggy,** *a.* **twigless,** *a.* [OE (cp. Dut. *twijg,* G *zweig*), cogn. with TWO]

twig[2], *v.t.* (*past, p.p.* **twigged**) (*coll.*) to understand, to comprehend, to catch the drift of; to see, to notice. [perh. from Ir. *tuigim,* I understand]

twilight, *n.* the diffused light from the sky appearing a little before sunrise and after sunset; a faint light, shade, obscurity; indistinct or imperfect perception, revelation, or knowledge. *a.* pertaining to, happening, or done in the twilight; dim, shady, obscure. *v.t.* to illumine dimly. **twilight of the gods,** (*Norse Myth.*) a conflict in which the gods were overcome and the world destroyed. **twilight sleep,** *n.* (*Med.*) a state of semi-consciousness produced by administering scopolamine and morphine in which labour pains are mitigated and forgotten when over. **twilight zone,** *n.* a transitional or intermediate zone; a decaying urban area esp. between the commercial centre and the residential suburbs. [ME (OE *twi-,* see TWIBILL, LIGHT[1])]

twill, *n.* a fabric in which the weft-threads pass alternately over one warp-thread and then under two or more, producing diagonal ribs or lines. *v.t.* to weave thus. **twilly,** *n.* a cotton-cleaning or willowing machine. [OE *twilīc,* cogn. with G *zwillich,* two threaded (*twi-,* TWO, *-līc,* perh. from L *bilix,* BI-, *līcium,* thread)]

'twill, short for IT WILL.

twin[1], *a.* being one of two born at a birth; being one of a similar or closely related pair of things, parts etc.; double, twofold; (*Bot.*) growing in pairs or divided into two equal parts. *n.* one of two children or young produced at a birth; a person or thing very closely resembling or related to another; an exact counterpart; a compound crystal having symmetrical halves separated by a plane that is not a plane of symmetry. *v.t.* to couple, to pair (with); to pair, to mate. *v.i.* to bring forth twins; to be born at the same birth; to be mated or paired (with). **dissimilar, binovular twins,** twins proceeding from the fertilization of two oocytes. **identical, uniovular twins,** twins that have developed from a single oocyte. **the Twins,** (*Astron.*) Gemini. **twin bed,** *n.* one of a matching pair of single beds. **twin-born,** *a.* **twinflower,** *n.* a tiny creeping evergreen, *Linnaea borealis,* with thread-like stalks and fragrant flowers. **twinscrew,** *n.* a steamer with two propellers twisted in opposite directions. †**twinling,** *n.* a twin lamb. **twin set,** *n.* a jumper and cardigan made to match. **twin town,** *n.* a town which has forged close civic and cultural links with a town in a foreign country. **twin-tub,** *n.* washing machine with two separate drums, one for washing, the other for spin-drying. †**twinner,** *n.* **twinship,** *n.* [ME, from OE *getwinne* (cp. Icel. *tvinnr*), cogn. with TWO]

twin[2], *v.t.* (*Sc.*) to divide, to part in twain, to separate; to deprive of, to sever, †*v.i.* to be separated, to part; to be divided or parted in twain. [from prec.]

twine[1], *v.t.* to twist; to form (thread etc.) by twisting together; to wind or coil round, to embrace; to form by interweaving. *v.i.* to be interwoven; to entwine, to coil (about, round etc.); to wind, to meander. *n.* a twist, a convolution, a coil; the act of twining or entwining; an interlacing, a tangle; strong string made of two or three strands twisted together. **twiner,** *n.* **twiningly,** *adv.* [ME *twinen,* from OE *twīn,* twisted thread (cp. Dut. *twijn,* G *zwirn,* Icel, *tvinni*), cogn. with TWO]

†**twine**[2] TWIN[2].

twinflower TWIN[1].

twinge, *v.t.* to affect with a sharp, sudden pain. *n.* a sharp, sudden, shooting pain; a pang, as of remorse or sorrow. [OE *twengan,* cp. Dut. *dwingen,* G *zwingen,* Icel. *thvinga,* Dan. *tvinge,* to constrain, to compel]

twinkle, *v.i.* to shine with a broken quivering light, to gleam fitfully, to sparkle; to appear and disappear in rapid alternation, to move tremulously; to open and shut rapidly, to blink, to wink. *v.t.* to flash or emit (light) in rapid gleams. *n.* a tremulous gleam, a sparkle; a glimmer; a blink, a wink; a rapid tremulous movement. †**twink,** *v.i.* to twinkle; to wink; *n.* a twinkle, a wink. **twinkling,** *n.* a twinkle; the time of this, an instant. [OE *twinclian,* freq. of v. represented by obs. *twink,* var. of *twiccan,* to TWITCH]

†**twinling,** etc. TWIN[1].

twinter, *n.* (*prov.*) a beast two years old. [OE *twiwintre* (*twi-,* TWO, WINTER)]

†**twire,** *v.i.* (*Shak.*) to twinkle; to glance shyly or slyly, to peep, to peer. *n.* a sly look, a leer. [etym. obscure, cp. Bavarian *zwiren,* MHG *zwieren*]

twirk, (*Sc.*) TWITCH[1].

twirl, *v.t.* to cause to rotate rapidly, esp. with the fingers, to spin; to whirl (round); to twiddle, to twist, to curl (the moustache etc.). *v.i.* to revolve or rotate rapidly, to whirl (round). *n.* a rapid circular motion; a quick rotation; a twist, a curl, a flourish. [freq. from OE *thweran,* to turn, cp. Norw. *tvirla*]

twirp TWERP.

†**twissel,** *a.* double, twofold. *n.* a twofold fruit; anything double or twofold. **twissel-tongued,** *a.* [OE *twisel,* cogn. with TWO, cp. foll.]

twist, *v.t.* to wind a thread, filament, strand etc., round another; to form (a rope or threads etc., into a rope etc.) thus, to intertwine (with or in with); to give a spiral form to by turning the ends in opposite directions; to wrench, to distort; to pervert, to misrepresent; to twine, to wreathe; to cause (a ball) to rotate while following a curved path; to make (one's way) in a winding manner. *v.i.* to be turned or bent round and round upon itself; to be or grow in a spiral form; to move in a curving, winding, or irregular path; to writhe, to squirm; to dance the twist. *n.* the act or manner of twisting or the state of being twisted; a quick or vigorous turn, a whirling motion given to a ball etc.; a dance, popular in the 1960's in which the dancer gyrates his or her hips in time to the music while remaining more or less on the same spot; a sharp bend; a peculiar tendency, a bent, an idiosyncrasy; an unexpected development in, or conclusion to, the plot of a story; the degree of inclination of rifle grooves; (*Phys.*) a twisting strain; the angle or degree of torsion of a rod etc.; forward motion combined with rotation; thread, cord, string, rope etc., made from twisted strands, esp. strong silk thread or cotton yarn; a twisted roll of bread; twisted tobacco; a small piece of lemon rind. (*coll.*) hunger. **round the twist** (*coll.*) crazy. **to twist somebody's arm,** to use force or psychological pressure to persuade someone. **twistable,** *a.* **twister,** *n.* one who or that which twists; a ball delivered with a twist at cricket, billiards etc.; the inner part of the thigh on which a good horseman sits; (*esp. N Am. coll.*) a tornado, a waterspout; (*coll.*) a cheat, a rogue. [ME *twisten,* from OE *twist,* rope]

twit[1], *v.t.* (*past, p.p.* **twitted**) to reproach, taunt, or upbraid (with some fault etc.). **twitter**[2], **twittingly,** *adv.* [ME *atwīten,* OE *ætwītan* (AT, *wītan,* to blame, cogn. with *wītan,* to know, Goth. *wertjan,* to reproach, L. *vidēre,* to see)]

twit[2], *n.* (*coll.*) a fool. [prob. alt. of TWAT]

twitch[1], *v.t.* to pull with a sudden or sharp jerk; to snatch. *v.i.* to pull or jerk (at); to move with a spasmodic jerk or contraction. *n.* a sudden pull or jerk; a sudden involuntary contraction of a muscle etc.; a cord twisted by a stick, fastened to the upper lip of a refractory horse for controlling it. **twitcher,** *n.* one who or that which twitches; a keen bird-watcher. **twitchy,** *a.* nervous. [ME *twicchen,* var. of *twikken,* to TWEAK]

twitch[2], (*prov.*) QUITCH.

twite, *n.* the mountain-linnet, *Carduelis flavirostris.* [prob. imit. of its chirp]

twitter[1], *v.i.* to utter a succession of short, tremulous, intermittent notes; to chirp; to have a tremulous motion of the nerves, to be agitated. *v.t.* to utter with tremulous, intermittent sounds. *n.* such a succession of sounds, a chirping; (*coll.*) a state of excitement or nervous agitation (also **twitteration**). **twitter-bone,** *n.* an excrescence on a horse's hoof. [ME *twiteren,* freq. of *twit,* imit.]

twitter[2], **twittingly** TWIT.

twit-twat, *n.* a sparrow. [imit. of chirp]

'twixt, short for BETWIXT.

twizzle, *v.i.* (*prov.*) to twist round and round, to spin. [prob. cogn. with TWIST]

two, *n.* the number or figure 2 or II; the age of 2; the second hour after midnight or midday. *a.* two in number; aged 2. **in two,** into two parts; as under. **one or two, two or three,** a few. **to put two and two together,** to draw inferences. **two-bit,** *a.* (*N Am., coll.*) insignificant, small-time. **two-by-four,** *n.* untrimmed timber, 2 in. by 4 in. in cross section (somewhat less when dressed). **two-dimensional,** *a.* having two dimensions; lacking (the appearance of) depth. **two-dimensionality,** *n.* **two-edged,** *a.* having an edge on both sides (of a knife etc.); cutting both ways. **two-faced,** *a.* having two faces; deceitful, insincere. **two-fold,** *a.* double; *adv.* doubly. **two-foot,** *a.* (*coll.*) measuring two feet. **two-handed,** *a.* having two hands; having to be used with both hands; played, worked etc., by two persons; using both hands with equal dexterity, ambidextrous. **two-headed,** *a.* **two-line,** *a.* (*Print.*) having a depth of body double that of the size specified. **two-pair,** *a.* second-floor. **twopence,** *n.* the sum of two pence; a small silver coin of this value, now issued only as Maundy money. **two-pence piece,** *n.* a coin worth two pence in value. **twopenny,** *a.* worth twopence; cheap, worthless, common, vulgar. **twopenny-halfpenny,** *a.* worth or costing twopence-halfpenny; paltry, insignificant. **two-piece,** *n., a.* (a garment) consisting of two usu. matching parts. **two-ply,** *a.* having two strands (as cord) or two thicknesses (as carpets, cloth etc.). **two-sided,** *a.* having two sides or aspects. **twosome,** *n.* a couple; a dance, game of golf, etc. involving two people. **two-speed,** *a.* giving or adapted to two rates of speed. **two-step,** *n.* (*Dancing*) a kind of round dance to march or polka time. **two-stroke,** *a., n.* (being, having) an internal-combustion engine with a cycle of two strokes. **two-tier,** *a.* having an upper and a lower level, as a legislature with an upper and a lower house. **two-time,** *v.t.* (*coll.*) to be unfaithful to; to double-cross. **two-timing,** *a.* **two-timer,** *n.* **two-tone,** *a.* having two colours or shades. **two-tongued,** *a.* double-tongued, deceitful. **two-up,** *n.* an Australian gambling game in which two pennies are tossed in the air and bets made on whether they fall two heads or two tails. The game is also called swy. **two-way,** *a.* arranged to allow movement in either of two directions; of a radio, able to send and receive; reciprocal; (*Math.*) having a double mode of variation. [OE *twegen* (fem. *twā,* neut. *tu*), cp. Dut. *twee,* G *zwei,* Icel. *tveir,* also L and Gr. *duo,* Sansk. *dva*]

twyer TUYÈRE.

TX, (*abbr.*) Texas.

-ty, *suf.* forming abstract nouns as *bounty, cruelty, fealty;* as in *fifty, twenty.* [F *-té,* L *-tātem,* nom. *-tas*]. [OE *-tig,* cogn. with TEN, Goth. *tigjus,* also Gr. *dekas,* decade, from *deka,* ten]

Tyburn, *a.* of or pertaining to Tyburn. **Tyburn ticket,** *n.* a certificate exempting from certain parochial offices etc., formerly granted to a successful prosecutor for felony, then a capital crime. **Tyburn tippet,** *n.* a halter. **Tyburn tree,** *n.* the gallows. [an historic place of execution near the site of the Marble Arch, London]

Tychonic, *a.* of or pertaining to the Danish astronomer *Tycho* Brahe (1546–1601) or his system of astronomy.

tycoon, *n.* a title assumed by the shogun of Japan, from 1854 to 1868; a financial or political magnate. [Jap. *taikun,* great prince]

†**tye, tying** TIE.

tyke, *n.* a dog; a cur; (*dial.*) an ill-mannered fellow. [ME from ON *fīk*]

tylarus, *n.* (*pl.* **-ri**) (*Ornith.*) one of the fleshy pads of the toes in birds. [mod. L, from Gr. *tulos,* knot]

Tyler[1], *n.* **John** (1790–1862), 10th president of the US 1841–45, succeeding Benjamin Harrison, who died after only a month in office. His government annexed Texas in 1845.

Tyler[2], *n.* **Wat** (d. 1381), English leader of the Peasants' Revolt of 1381. He was probably born in Kent or Essex, and may have served in the French wars. After taking Canterbury he led the peasant army to Blackheath and occupied London. At Mile End King Richard II met the rebels and promised to redress their grievances, which included the imposition of a poll tax. At a further conference at Smithfield, Tyler was murdered.

tyler TILER.

tylopod, *n.* having the digits enclosed in a cutaneous pad, as the camels. *n.* a tylopod animal. **tylopodous,** *a.* [Gr. *tulos,* knot, *pous podos,* foot]

tylosis, *n.* (*Bot.*) a growth in the cavity of a duct intruding from the wall of a contiguous cell; inflammation of the eyelids with thickening and hardening of the margins. **tylotic**, *a.* [Gr., from *tuloein,* to make callous, as prec.]

tylote, *n.* a cylindrical spicule, in a sponge, knotted at each end. [Gr. *tulōtos,* as prec.]

†**tymbal** TIMBAL.

tymp, *n.* a casting or block of refractory material formerly used as the crown of the opening in front of the hearth of a blast-furnace; (*Mining*) a short horizontal roof-timber. [short for foll.]

tympan, *n.* a frame stretched with paper cloth or parchment, used for equalizing the pressure in some printing-presses; any thin sheet or membrane tightly stretched; a tympanum. [F, from L TYMPANUM]

tympanic TYMPANUM.

tympanites, *n.* (*Path.*) distension of the abdomen, due to the accumulation of air in the intestine, etc. **tympanitic,** *a.*

tympanitis, *n.* (*Path.*) inflammation of the lining membrane of the middle ear.

tympanum, *n.* (*pl.* **-na**) the middle ear; the tympanic membrane or ear-drum; the lower end of the trachea in ducks etc., modified into a resonance-cavity; (*Arch.*) a triangular area, usu. recessed, in a pediment, the space between the lintel of a doorway and the arch enclosing it; a door-panel; a form of tread-mill. **tympanic**, *a.* like a drum; acting like a drum-head; (*Anat.*) pertaining to the tympanum. †**tympany**, *n.* Tympanites; conceit, bombast. [L, from Gr. *tumpanon,* drum]

Tyndale, *n.* **William** (1492–1536), English translator of the Bible. The printing of his New Testament (basis of the Authorized Version) was begun in Cologne 1525, and, after he had been forced to flee, completed in Worms. He was strangled and burned as a heretic at Vilvorde in Belgium.

Tyndall, *n.* **John** (1820–93), Irish physicist, who in 1869 studied the scattering of light by invisibly small suspended particles. Known as the **Tyndall effect**, it was first observed with colloidal solutions, in which a beam of light is made visible when it is scattered by minute colloidal particles (whereas a pure solvent does not scatter light). Similar scattering of blue wavelengths of sunlight by particles in the atmosphere makes the sky look blue (beyond the atmosphere, the sky is black).

Tyne and Wear, a metropolitan county in NE England, created 1974, originally administered by an elected metropolitan council; its powers reverted to district councils 1986. **area** 540 sq km/208 sq miles. **towns** administrative headquarters Newcastle-upon-Tyne; South Shields, Gateshead, Sunderland. **population** (1987) 1,136,000. **products** once a centre of heavy industry, it is now being redeveloped and diversified.

Tynewald, Tynwald, *n.* the legislature of the Isle of Man. [Icel. *thingvöllr* (*thing,* assembly, *völlr,* field, cp. WEALD)]

type, *n.* a distinguishing mark, a symbol, an emblem, an image; any person or thing that stands as an illustration, pattern, characteristic example, or representative specimen of another thing or class of things; a kind, a class, a category; (*coll.*) a person (of a specified kind); a prophetic similitude; (*Biol.*) a general form or structure common to a number of individuals; an organism exhibiting the essential characteristics of its group; (*Chem.*) a compound, such as hydrochloric acid, water, ammonia or methane, illustrating other compounds by analogy; an original conception, object, or work of art, serving as a model or guide to later artists; any of a class of objects embodying the characteristics of a group or class, esp. as a model, pattern, or exponent (of beauty or other qualities); a piece of metal or hard wood bearing a letter or character usu. in relief, for printing with; (*collect.*) a set or quantity or kind of these; the device on a medal, coin etc. *v.t.* to prefigure, to be a type of; to typewrite. **-type,** *comb. form* of the kind specified, resembling. **in type,** set in type. **typebar,** *n.* a line of type cast in one piece by a linotype machine, etc.; a bar carrying a letter in a typewriter. **typecast,** *v.t.* (*past, p.p.* **typecast**) to cast (an actor) in a role for which he/she is suited by nature; to cast continually in the same kind of part. **typeface,** *n.* the printing surface of type; a design of printing type. **type-founder,** *n.* one who casts types. **type-foundry,** *n.* **type-high,** *a.* of the standard height of type or the proper height for printing. **type-metal,** *n.* an alloy of lead, antimony, and tin, used for making printing-type. **typescript,** *n.* typewritten matter. **typesetter,** *n.* a compositor; a machine for setting type. **typesetting,** *n., a.* **typewrite,** *v.i.* to write with a typewriter. **typewriter** *n.* a machine for producing printed characters as a substitute for handwriting; **typewriting,** *n.* **typewritten,** *a.* [F, from L *typus -um,* Gr. *tupos,* blow, stamp, character, from *tuptein,* to strike]

Typha, *n.* a genus of marsh plants comprising the cats'-tails. **typhaceous**, *a.* [mod. L, from Gr. *tuphē,* the plant cat's-tail]

typhlitis, *n.* (*Path.*) inflammation of the caecum. **typhlitic**, *a.* **typhlo-,** *comb. form.* [Gr. *tuphlos,* blind, -ITIS]

typhoid, *a.* pertaining to or resembling typhus. *n.* typhoid fever, an infectious fever characterized by an eruption of red spots on the chest and abdomen, severe intestinal irritation, inflammation, diarrhoea etc., enteric. **typhoidal**, *a.* **typhomalarial**, *a.* malarial with typhoidal symptoms. **typhomania**, *n.* the low muttering delirium characteristic of typhus and typhoid fever. **typhonia**, *n.* a form of sleepless and delirious stupor characteristic of typhus. [TYPHUS, -OID]

typhoon, *n.* a violent cyclonic hurricane occurring in the China Seas and the West Pacific. **typhonic**, *a.* [Chin. *tai foong,* big wind]

typhus, *n.* a contagious fever marked by an eruption of dark purple spots, great prostration, stupor and delirium. **typhous,** *a.* [L, from Gr. *tuphos,* smoke, stupor]

typic, *a.* figurative, typical. **typic fever,** a fever regular in its attacks or of a particular type. [L *typicus,* Gr. *tupikos,* from *tupos,* TYPE]

typical, *a.* of the nature of or serving as a type; representative, emblematic, symbolical (of); embodying the characters of a group, class etc.; characteristic (of). **typically,** *adv.* **typicalness,** *n.* **typify**, *v.t.* to represent by a type; to betoken, to prefigure; to be a type of, to exemplify. **typification**, *n.* **typifier,** *n.*

typist, *n.* one who types letters etc.

typ(o), (*abbr.*) TYPOGRAPHER; TYPOGRAPHIC; TYPOGRAPHY.

typo, *n.* (*pl.* **typos**) (*coll.*) a typographical error.

typography, *n.* the art of printing; the arrangement, character, or appearance of printed matter. **typograph**, *n.* a machine formerly used for making and setting type. **typographer,** *n.* **typographic, -al**, *a.* **typographically,** *adv.*

typolite, *n.* a stone impressed with the figure of a plant or animal, a fossil.

typolithography, *n.* the process of printing from lithographic stones which have previously received transferred impressions from type. **typolithographic,** *a.*

typology, *n.* the doctrine of interpretation of types, esp. those of the Scriptures. **typological**, *a.* **typologist,** *n.*

typonym, *n.* (*Biol.*) the name based on a type. **typonimal**, *a.* **typonimic**, *a.*

typtology, *n.* the practice or science of spirit-rapping. **typtological**, *a.* **typtologist,** *n.* [Gr. *tuptein,* to strike]

Tyr, *n.* in Norse mythology, the god of battles, whom the Anglo-Saxons called Týw, hence 'Tuesday'.

tyrannosauros, *n.* (*Palaeont.*) a genus of carnivorous dinosaurs, about 40 ft. (12 m) in length. [Gr. *turannos,* a tyrant; *saura,* a lizard]

tyranny TYRANT.

tyrant, *n.* an oppressive or cruel ruler or master; an oppressor, a despot, an autocrat, esp. (*Hist.*) one obtaining power by usurpation; an arbitrary or despotic ruler. **tyrannical**, *a.* acting like or characteristic of a tyrant; despotic, arbitrary, imperious. **tyrannically,** *adv.* **tyrannicalness,** *n.* **tyrannicide**, *n.* the act of killing a tyrant; one who kills a tyrant. **tyrannicidal**, *a.* **tyrannize, -ise**, *v.i.* to act the tyrant; to rule despotically or oppressively (over). *v.t.* to rule (a person etc.) despotically. **tyrannous**, *a.* **tyrannously,** *adv.* **tyranny**, *n.* arbitrary, or oppressive exercise of power; an arbitrary, despotic, or oppressive act; the office or rule of a tyrant; the period of this; harshness, severity. [TYRANT, -IZE] [ME *tirant,* OF *tiran, tirant,* L *tyranus -um,* nom. *-us,* Gr. *turannos*]

tyre, *n.* an air-filled rubber casing, a strip of solid rubber or a band of metal surrounding a wheel.

Tyrell, *n.* British motor racing team founded by Ken Tyrell 1970 although he had run the Matra and March teams in the two seasons previous. He formed a partnership with Jackie Stewart and the famous driver won all three of his world titles in Tyrell-run teams. Tyrell's only Constructor's title was in 1971.

Tyrian, *a.* pertaining to ancient Tyre; having the colour of Tyrian dye, purple. *n.* a native or inhabitant of Tyre. **Tyrian dye,** *n.* a purple dye formerly prepared from shellfish, esp. species of *Murex*.

tyriasis, *n.* (*Path.*) a form of elephantiasis; tyroma. **tyroma**, *n.* falling off of the hair through a fungoid growth at the roots. [Gr. *tur-os,* cheese, -ASIS]

tyro, *n.* (*sometimes derog.*) a beginner, a novice. **tirocinium**, *n.* apprenticeship, novitiate, pupilage. [L *tiro,* a newly enlisted soldier]

Tyrolean, Tyrolese, TIROLESE.

tyroma TYRIASIS.

Tyrone, *n.* county of Northern Ireland. **area** 3160 sq km/1220 sq miles. **towns** county town Omagh; Dungannon, Strabane, Cookstown. **population** (1981) 144,000. **products** mainly agricultural.

tyrosine, *n.* an amino acid formed by the decomposition of proteins. [from Gr. *tyros,* cheese]

tyrotoxicon, *n.* a ptomaine contained in putrid milk, cheese etc. [Gr. *turos,* cheese *toxikon,* poison, see TOXIC]

Tyrrhene, Tyrrhenian, *a.* Etruscan. *n.* an Etrurian, Etruscan, or Tuscan. [L *Tyrrhēnus,* Gr. *Turrhēnos*]

Tyrtaean, *a.* of, pertaining to or in the style of the Greek martial poet Tyrtaeus (*c.* 650 BC)

†tythe, TITHE.

Tyson, *n.* **Mike** (1966–), US heavyweight champion boxer. He won the WBC heavyweight title 1986 when he beat Trevor Berbick to become the youngest world heavyweight champion. He beat James 'Bonecrusher' Smith for the WBA title 1987 and later that year he became the first undisputed champion since 1978 when he beat Tony Tucker for the IBF title. He was undefeated until 1990 when he lost the championship to a relative outsider, James 'Buster' Douglas.

Tyuratam, *n.* site of the Baikonur Cosmodrome.

Tywi, Towy, *n.* river in Dyfed, SW Wales; length 108 km/68 miles. It rises in the Cambrian Mountains of central Wales, flowing SW to enter Carmarthen Bay.

Tzar, etc. CZAR.

tzetze, TSETSE.

Tzigany, tzigamy, *a.* of or pertaining to the Hungarian gipsies or their music. *n.* a Hungarian gipsy. [Hung. *cigány*, cp. *G. Zigeuner*]

tzimmes, tsim(m)es, *n.* a sweetened stew of vegetables and/or fruit; (*coll.*) a fuss, a to-do. [Yiddish]

Tzu-Hsi, *n.* former spelling of Zi Xi, dowager empress of China.

U

U¹, u, the twenty-first letter and the fifth vowel (*pl.* **Us, U's, Ues,**), has five principal sounds; (1) as in *rule,* ; (2) as in *bull* ; (3) as in *but* ; (4) as in *bur* ; (5) as in *due* dū. **U,** *a.* (*coll.*) of words, phrases, behaviour etc., associated with the so-called Upper Classes. **U-boat** *n.* a German submarine. [G *Unterseeboot*] **U-turn,** *n.* a turn made by a motor vehicle which takes it back along the direction from which it has come, without reversing; any complete reversal of policy etc.

U², (*abbr.*) Unionist; university; universal (of a film certified by viewing without age limit).

U³, (*chem. symbol*) uranium.

U2, *n.* Irish rock group formed 1977 by singer Bono Vox (Paul Hewson, 1960–), guitarist Dave 'The Edge' Evans (1961–), bassist Adam Clayton (1960–), and drummer Larry Mullen (1961–). Committed Christians, they play socially concerned stadium rock, and their albums include *The Unforgettable Fire* (1984), *The Joshua Tree* (1987), and the soundtrack from their documentary film *Rattle and Hum* (1988).

U-2, *n.* a US military reconnaissance aeroplane, used in clandestine flights over the USSR from 1956 to photograph military installations. In 1960 a U-2 was shot down over the USSR and the pilot, Gary Powers, was captured and imprisoned. He was exchanged for a Soviet agent two years later.

UAE, (*abbr.*) United Arab Emirates.

UAR, (*abbr.*) United Arab Republic.

UB40, *n.* a card issued to a person registered as unemployed; (*coll.*) an unemployed person.

Ubangi-Shari, *n.* former name for the CENTRAL AFRICAN REPUBLIC.

Übermensch, *n.* a superman, in the writings of Nietszche the ideal to which humans should aspire, set out in *Thus Spake Zarathustra* (1883–85). The term was popularised in George Bernard Shaw's play *Man and Superman* (1903).

†uberty, *n.* fruitfulness, fertility. **†uberous,** *a.* [L *ūbertas,* from *ūber,* rich, fertile]

ubiety, *n.* the state of being in a particular place; the relation of locality, whereness. [L *ubī,* where, -TY]

ubiquity, *n.* the quality or state of being everywhere or in an indefinite number of places at the same time, omnipresence. **ubiquitarian,** *n.* (*Theol.*) a believer in the omnipresence of Christ's body, esp. with reference to the Eucharist. *a.* of or pertaining to ubiquitarianism. **ubiquitarianism,** *n.* **ubiquitary, ubiquitous,** *a.* **ubiquitously,** *adv.* **ubiquitousness,** *n.* [F *ubiquité,* from L *ubīque,* everywhere, from *ubī,* where]

ubi supra, where mentioned above. [L]

UC, (*abbr.*) University College.

uc, (*abbr.*) upper case.

UCCA, (*abbr.*) Universities Central Council on Admissions.

Uccello, *n.* **Paolo** (1397–1475), adopted name of Paolo di Dono. Italian painter, active in Florence, celebrated for his early use of perspective. His surviving paintings date from the 1430s onwards. Decorative colour and detail dominate his later pictures. His works include *St George and the Dragon* about 1460 (National Gallery, London).

UDA, (*abbr.*) Ulster Defence Association.

udal, *n.* freehold tenure based on uninterrupted possession as in N Europe before feudalism and in Orkney and Shetland at the present day. **udaller,** *n.* the holder of such tenure. [ON *ōthal*]

Udall, *n.* **Nicholas** (1504–1556), English schoolmaster and playwright. He was the author of *Ralph Roister Doister* (about 1553), the first known English comedy.

UDC, (*abbr.*) Urban District Council.

udder, *n.* the milk-secreting organ of a cow, ewe etc.; †a teat, a dug. **uddered,** *a.* **udderless,** *a.* [OE *ūder* (cp. Dut. *uijer,* G *Euter,* Icel. *jūgr,* for *jūdr,* cogn. with L *ūber,* Gr. *outhar,* Sansk. *ūdhar*]

UDI, (*abbr.*) unilateral declaration of independence, usually applied to the declaration of Ian Smith's Rhodesian Front government on 11 Nov 1965, announcing the independence of Rhodesia (now Zimbabwe) from the British crown.

Udmurt, *n.* (Russian **Udmurtskaya**), autonomous republic in the W Ural foothills, central USSR. **area** 42,100 sq km/16,200 sq miles. **capital** Izhevsk. **products** timber, flax, potatoes, peat, quartz. **population** (1985) 1,559,000; Udmurt 33%, Tatar 7%, Russian 58%.

udometer, *n.* a rain-gauge. **udometric,** *a.* **udomograph,** *n.* a self-registering rain-gauge. [L *ūdus,* wet, moist, -METER]

UDR, (*abbr.*) Ulster Defence Regiment.

UEFA, (*abbr.*) Union of European Football Associations.

Uganda, *n.* Republic of, landlocked country in E Africa, bounded to the N by Sudan, to the E by Kenya, to the S by Tanzania and Rwanda, and to the W by Zaïre. **area** 236,600 sq km/91,351 sq miles. **capital** Kampala. **towns** Jingar, M'Bale, Entebbe. **physical** plateau with mountains in west; forest and grassland; arid in north. **exports** coffee, cotton, tea, copper. **population** (1987) 15,500,000 (the largest ethnic group is the Baganda, from whom the name of the country comes; others include the Langi and Acholi, and there are a few surviving Pygmies); annual growth rate 3.3%. **language** English (official); Swahili is a lingua franca. **religion** Christian 50%, animist 45%, Muslim 5%.

Ugarit, *n.* ancient trading city kingdom (modern **Ras Shamra**) on the Syrian coast. It was excavated by the French archaeologist Claude Schaeffer (1898–1982) from 1929, finds ranging from about 7000 to 15–13th cent. BC, including the earliest known alphabet.

UGC, (*abbr.*) University Grants Committee.

ugh, *int.* an exclamation of disgust or horror. [instinctive sound]

ugli, *n.* a cross between a grapefruit and a tangerine. [UGLY, from its wrinkled skin]

ugly, *a.* unpleasing to the sight, not beautiful; unsightly, ungraceful, not comely; morally repulsive, unpleasant; suggesting evil; awkward, cantankerous, threatening, formidable. **ugly duckling,** *n.* an unpromising person or thing which turns out surprisingly successful etc. **uglify,** *v.i.* **uglily,** *adv.* **ugliness,** *n.* [Icel. *uggligr* (*uggr,* fear, -LY)]

Ugrian, Ugric, *n.* a member of the Eastern branch of the Finno-Ugarian peoples, esp. the Magyars; their group of languages. *a.* of or relating to these peoples or their languages. [O.Rus. *Ugre,* Hungarians]

UHF (*abbr.*) ultra high frequency, referring to radio waves of very short wavelength, used, for example, for television broadcasting.

Uhlan, *n.* a cavalryman armed with a lance, in the old German and some other Continental armies. [G and Pol. *ulan,* Turk. and Tatar *oglān* son, lad]

UHT, (*abbr.*) of milk, ultra-heat treated.

uitlander, *n.* an immigrant into the Transvaal. [Dut., an outlander]

UK, (*abbr.*) United Kingdom.

UKAEA, (*abbr.*) United Kingdom Atomic Energy

Authority.

ukase, *n.* an edict or decree of the Imperial Russian Government; any arbitrary decree. [F, from Rus. *ukaz,* from *ukazat,* to show, order]

Ukraine, *n.* constituent republic of the SE USSR from 1923. **area** 603,700 sq km/233,089 sq miles. **capital** Kiev. **towns** Kharkov, Donetsk, Odessa, Dniepropetrovsk, Lvov, Zaporozhe, Krivoi Rog. **physical** Russian plain, Carpathian and Crimean Mountains; rivers Dnieper (with the Dnieper dam 1932), Donetz, and Bug. **population** (1987) 51,201,000; Ukrainian 74%, Russian 21%, Russian-speaking Jews 2%. Some 1.5 million émigrés live in the US, 750,000 in Canada. **products** grain; 60% of Soviet coal reserves; oil and other minerals. **language** Ukrainian (Slavonic), with a literature that goes back to the Middle Ages; noted writers are Ivan Kotlyarevsky (1769–1838) and Taras Shevchenko (1814–1861). **religion** traditionally Ukrainian Orthodox.

ukulele, *n.* a small four-stringed instrument resembling a guitar. [Hawaiian]

Ulaanbaatar, Ulan Bator, *n.* (until 1924 **Urga**), capital of the Mongolian Republic, a trading centre producing carpets, textiles, vodka; population (1988) 500,000.

Ulbricht, *n.* **Walter** (1893–1973), East German politician. After exile in the USSR during Hitler's rule, he became first secretary of the Socialist Unity Party in East Germany (1950) and (as chair of the Council of State from 1960) was instrumental in the building of the Berlin Wall in 1961. He established East Germany's economy and recognition outside the E European bloc.

ulcer, *n.* an open sore on the outer or inner surface of the body accompanied by a secretion of pus or other discharge; a source of corruption or moral pollution. **ulcerable,** *a.* **ulcerate,** *v.t.* to affect with or as with an ulcer *v.i.* to form an ulcer; to become ulcerous. **ulceration,** *n.* **ulcerative,** *a.* **ulcered, ulcerous,** *a.* **ulcerously,** *adv.* **ulcerousness,** *n.* [MF *ulcere,* L *ulcus -ceris,* sore, Gr. *helkos,* wound, sore]

-ule,, *dim. suf.* as in *globule, pustule.* [L *-ulus, -ula, -ulum*]

ulema, *n.* the body of Muslim doctors of law and interpreters of the Koran in a country, esp. in Turkey. [Arab., pl. of *alim* learned]

-ulent -LENT.

Ulex, *n.* a genus of thorny shrubs of the bean family including gorse. [L]

uliginose, *a.* growing in swampy or muddy places; †muddy, slimy. [L *ūlīginōsus,* from *ūliīgo ginis,* moisture]

ulitis, *n.* inflammation of the gums. [Gr. *oula, pl.* the gums]

ullage, *n.* the quantity that a cask wants of being full. [Prov. *ulhage,* from *ulha,* to fill (cp. OF *euiller, ouillier*), from L *oculus,* eye, orifice]

ulla-lulla, *n.* a cry of lamentation. [Ir.]

Ullman, *n.* **Liv** (1939–), Norwegian actress who was critically acclaimed for her roles in first Swedish and then international films. Her work includes *Persona* (1966), the title role in *Pope Joan* (1972), and *Autumn Sonata* (1978).

ulmaceous, *a.* pertaining to or characteristic of the elm. [L *ulmus,* elm]

ulmin, *n.* a black alkaline, gummy substance contained in excrescences on the elm and other trees, and in vegetable mould. **ulmic, ulmous,** *a.*

Ulmus, *n.* a genus of trees containing the elms. [L]

ulna, *n.* (*pl.* **-nae**) the larger and longer of the two bones of the fore-arm. **ulnad**, *adv.* toward the ulna. **ulnar,** *a.* **ulno-,** *comb. form.* [L, elbow, cogn. with Gr. *ōlenē*]

Ulodendron, *n.* a genus of fossil trees with lepidodendroid cortical scars and large discoid scars left by the falling cones. [Gr. *oulē,* scar, *dendron,* tree]

ulosis, *n.* cicatrization. [Gr. *oulē,* scar, -OSIS]

ulotrichous, *a.* having woolly or curly hair. **ulotrichan,** *a.* **ulotrichy,** *n.* [L *ulotrichi,* one of Huxley's divisions of mankind; Gr. *oulos,* woolly, *thrix, trichos,* hair]

Ulsan, *n.* industrial city (vehicles, shipbuilding, oil refining, petrochemicals) in South Kyongsang province, SE South Korea; population (1985) 551,000.

Ulster, *n.* former kingdom in Northern Ireland, annexed by England in 1461, from Jacobean times a centre of English, and later Scottish, settlement on land confiscated from its owners; divided in 1921 into Northern Ireland (counties Antrim, Armagh, Down, Fermanagh, Londonderry, and Tyrone) and Cavan, Donegal, and Monaghan in the Republic of Ireland.

ulster, *n.* a long, loose overcoat for men or women, usu. with a belt, originally made of Ulster frieze. [province of Ireland]

ult, (*abbr.*) ultimo.

ulterior, *a.* lying beyond or on the other side of any line or boundary; more remote or distant; not at present in view, under consideration, or pertinent; not yet disclosed, unavowed. **ulteriorly,** *adv.* [L, comp. of *ulter,* adj., whence adv. *ultra,* see ULTRA-]

ultima, *n.* the last syllable of a word. **ultima Thule,** THULE. [L, fem. of *ultimus,* last]

ultimate, *a.* last, final, beyond which there is nothing existing or possible; incapable of further analysis; fundamental, elementary, primary; †farthest, most remote. *n.* something final or fundamental. **ultimately,** *adv.* **ultimateness,** *n.* [L *ultimātus,* p.p. of *ultimāre,* from *ultimus,* superl., as prec.]

ultimatum, *n.* (*pl.* **-tums, -ta**), a final proposal, statement of conditions, or concession, the rejection of which may involve rupture of diplomatic relations and a declaration or war; anything final, essential, or fundamental. **†ultimation,** *n.*

ultimo, *adv.* last month.

ultimogeniture, *n.* inheritance by the youngest son, borough-English.

Ultra, *n.* term used by the British from spring 1940 in World War II to denote intelligence gained by deciphering German signals. [short for *Ultra* Secret]

ultra, *a.* extreme, advocating extreme views or measures; uncompromising, extravagant. *n.* an extremist. **ultraism,** *n.* **ultraist,** *n.* [see foll.]

ultra-, *pref.* beyond, on the other side of; beyond the ordinary limit or range of; beyond the reasonable, excessive(ly). **ultraclassical,** *a.* extravagantly classical in style etc. **ultraconservative,** *a.* extravagantly conservative. **ultrafiche,** *n.* a sheet of microfilm, like a microfiche but holding more microcopies. **ultrahigh,** *a.* of radio frequencies, between 300 and 3000 megahertz. **ultra-microscope,** *n.* one with a light source at the side, for examining particles too small to be seen with the ordinary microscope. **ultra-microscopic,** *a.* **ultramicroscopy,** *n.* **ultramontone,** *a.* being or lying beyond the mountains, esp. the Alps, esp. on the Italian side; hence, supporting the absolute power and infallibility of the pope. *n.* one who resides south of the Alps; a supporter of ultramontanism. **ultramontanism**, *n.* in the Roman Catholic Church, the principle that all ecclesiastical power should be concentrated in the hands of the pope, in contradistinction to the independent development of national Churches. **ultramontanist**, *n.* **ultramundane**, *a.* external to the world or the solar system; pertaining to the supernatural or another life. **ultra-Protestant,** *a.* **ultra-religious,** *a.* **ultra-sensual,** *a.* **ultra-short waves,** *n.pl.* electromagnetic waves below 10 metres in wavelength. **ultrasonic,** *a.* pertaining to, or using, sound waves of higher than audible frequency. **ultrasound,** *n.* ultrasonic waves, used esp. for medical diagnosis. **ultrastructure**, *n.* the ultramicroscopic structure of an organism or cell. **ultra-tropical,** *a.* situated beyond or hotter than the tropics. **ultraviolet,** *n., a.* (electromagnetization) having a wavelength shorter than the violet end of the visible spectrum but longer than X-rays. **ultravirus,** *n.* a very small virus that can pass through the finest of filters. [L. *ultrā,* beyond]

ultramarine, *a.* situated, being, or lying beyond the sea. *n.* a deep-blue pigment formerly obtained from lapis lazuli; the colour of this. [It. *oltra marino*]

ultra vires , *a., adv.*, beyond one's legal power or

authority. [L]

ultromotivity, *n.* the power of spontaneous movement or action. † **ultroneous**, *a.* voluntary, spontaneous. †**ultroneously,** *adv.* [L *ultro,* of one's own accord, MOTIVITY under MOTIVE]

ululate, *v.i.* to howl, as a dog or wolf, to hoot. **ululant,** *a.* **ululation,** *n.* [L *ululāre,* cp. Gr. *oluluzein,* imit.]

Ulysses, *n.* Roman name for Odysseus, Greek mythological hero.

Umar, *n.* (died AD 644), 2nd caliph (head) of Islam, noted as a strong disciplinarian. Under his rule Islam spread to Egypt and Persia. He was assassinated in Medina.

Umayyad OMAYYAD.

umbel, *n.* an inflorescence in which the flower stalks spring from one point and spread like the ribs of an umbrella forming a flattish surface, as in the parsley family. **umbellal, -lar, umbellate, -lated, umbelliferous**, *a.* **umbellet, umbellule,** *n.* **umbellifer**, *n.* [L *umbella,* parasol, dim. of *umbra,* shade]

umber, *n.* a dark yellowish-brown pigment derived from a mineral ferric oxide containing manganese; a grayling; the umber-bird or umbrette. *a.* of the colour of umber, dark, dusky. *v.t.* to colour with or as with umber. **burnt umber,** umber heated so as to produce a much redder brown. **raw umber,** umber in the natural state. **umber-bird,** *n.* the umbrette. **umbery,** *a.* [F *ombre,* in *terre d'ombre,* It. *terra d'ombra,* L *umbra,* shadow]

Umberto I, *n.* (1844–1900), king of Italy from 1878, who joined the Triple Alliance (1882) with Germany and Austria-Hungary; his colonial ventures included the defeat at Aduwa, Abyssinia, in 1896. He was assassinated by an anarchist.

Umberto II, *n.* (1904–1983), last king of Italy (1946). On the abdication of his father, Victor Emmanuel III, he ruled from 9 May to 13 June 1946, when he also abdicated and left the country.

umbilical, *a.* of, or pertaining to, or situated near the navel; central. **umbilical cord,** *n.* the rope-like structure of vessels and connective tissue connecting the foetus with the placenta; a cable carrying electricity, air etc., from a servicing point to a spacecraft, astronaut, diver etc. **umbilicate, -ed,** *a.* **umbilication,** *n.* **umbilicus**, *n.* the navel; (*Nat. Hist.*) a navel-shaped depression or other formation, the hilum; a depression at the axial base of some univalve shells; (*Rom. Ant.*) the ornamental boss at each end of the stick on which a manuscript was rolled. **umbiliferous**, *a.* **umbiliform**, *a.* [L *umbilīcus,* navel, cogn. with Gr. *omphalos,* -AL]

umbles, *n.pl.* the entrails of a deer [cp. HUMBLE-PIE]. [ME *noumbles,* OF *noumbles* corr. of *lomble,* L *lumbulus,* dim. of *lumbus,* LOIN]

umbo, *n.* (*pl.* **-bos, -bones,**) the boss or projecting point in the centre of a shield; (*Nat. Hist.*) a boss, knob, prominence, or elevation. **umbonal, umbonate**, **umbonic**, *a.* [L, cogn. with *umbilīcus,* UMBILICAL]

umbra, *n.* (*pl.* **-brae**) the part of the shadow of a planet etc., esp. the earth or moon, in which the light of the sun is entirely cut off, the dark central portion of a sun-spot; (*Rom. Ant.*) a guest brought by an invited person, a parasite. **umbral,** *a.* **umbrated,** *a.* (*Her.*) shadowed, adumbrated. **umbriferous**, †**umbrose**, *a.* †**umbrosity**, *n.* [L, shadow]

umbraculum, *n.* (*pl.* **-la**) (*Bot.*) an umbrella-shaped appendage, as the capitulum of the sporophore in some liverworts. **umbraculate, umbraculiferous**, *a.* **umbraculiform**, *a.* [L, dim. of prec.]

umbrage, *n.* a sense of injury, offence; †shade; that which affords a shade. **umbrageous**, *a.* shady, shaded. **umbrageously,** *adv.* **umbrageousness,** *n.* shadiness. [F *ombrage* from *ombre,* L UMBRA]

umbral, umbrated UMBRA.

umbrella, *n.* a light screen of silk, cotton, or other fabric, stretched on a folding frame of radiating ribs on a stick, for holding above the head as a protection against rain or sun; the umbrella-shaped disk of a medusa used as a swimming organ; an umbrella-shell; a protection, a cover; a screen of aircraft or of gunfire covering a military movement; an organization which protects or co-ordinates the activities of a number of separate groups; a general heading etc. encompassing several individual ones. **umbrella-bird,** *n.* a S American bird of the genus *Cephalopterus,* with a large erectile spreading crest. **umbrella bush,** *n.* a species of acacia. **umbrella grass,** *n.* an Australian millet. **umbrella-shell,** *n.* a tropical gasteropod with an umbrella-like shell. **umbrella-stand,** *n.* a stand for holding umbrellas, in an entrance hall etc. **umbrella-tree,** *n.* a small magnolia with flowers and leaves in an umbrella-like whorl at the ends of the branches. **umbrellaed,** *a.* [It. *umbrella, ombrella,* dim. of *ombra,* L UMBRA]

umbrette, *n.* an African bird, *Scopus umbretta,* allied to the storks and herons. [F *ombrette,* dim. of *ombre,* as prec.]

Umbrian, *a.* of or pertaining to Umbria, in Central Italy, esp. of the school of painting to which Raphael and Perugino belonged; the language of Umbria, one of the principal Italic dialects. *n.* a native of ancient Umbria.

umbriferous, †**umbrose** UMBRA.

umiak, *n.* an Eskimo boat made of skins stretched on a framework, used by women. [Eskimo]

umlaut, *n.* change of the vowel in a syllable through the influence of an *i* or *r* (usu. lost or modified) in the following syllable; (*Print.*) the diæresis mark used over German vowels. *v.t.* to sound with or modify by umlaut. [G *um,* about, *laut,* sound]

Umm al Qaiwain, *n.* one of the United Arab Emirates.

umpire, *n.* a person chosen to enforce the rules and settle disputes in a game, esp. cricket or football; a person chosen to decide a question of controversy; (*Law*) a third person called in to settle a disagreement between arbitrators. *v.t.* to act as umpire. **umpirage**, **umpireship,** *n.* [ME *nompere,* OF *nomper* (NON-, PEER[1]), peerless, odd, in the sense of odd man (cp. ADDER[2], APRON)]

umpteen, *a.* an indefinitely large number. **umpteenth,** *a.* [analogy with thirteen etc.]

umquhile, *a., adv.* (*Sc.*) formerly, late, whilom. [ME *umwhile* at times]

Umtata, *n.* capital of the South African Bantu homeland of Transkei; population (1976) 25,000.

UN, (*abbr.*) United Nations.

'un, *pron.* (*coll.*) ONE.

un-, *pref.* giving a negative sense to adjectives, adverbs, and nouns; used with verbs to denote reversal or annulment of the action of the simple verb (sometimes ambiguous, thus *unrolled* may mean 'not rolled up', or 'opened out after having been rolled up'). Since there is no limit to the use of this prefix the meaning of words not given in the following selection can be ascertained by reference to the simple verb, adjective etc. [OE *un-* (cp. G *un-,* L *in-,* Gr. *a(n)-*)]

UNA, (*abbr.*) United Nations Association.

un- (cont.) **unabashed,** *a.* not abashed; shameless. **unabated,** *a.* †**unability,** *n.* INABILITY. **unable,** *a.* not able (to); not having sufficient power or ability; incapable, incompetent; †weak, helpless. **unabolished,** *a.* **unabridged,** *a.* **unabsorbed,** *a.* **unacademic,** *a.* **unaccented,** *a.* **unacceptable,** *a.* **unacceptableness, unacceptability,** *n.* **unaccommodating,** *a.* **unaccompanied,** *a.* unattended; (*Mus.*) without accompaniment. **unaccomplished,** *a.* unfinished, not carried out or effected; lacking accomplishments. **unaccountable,** *a.* not accountable or responsible; inexplicable. **unaccountability, unaccountableness,** *n.* **unaccountability,** *adv.* **unaccounted (for),** *a.* not explained; not included in an account or list. **unaccoutred,** *a.* **unaccredited,** *a.* **unaccustomed,** *a.* not usual or familiar; not used (to). **unachievable,** *a.* **unachieved,** *a.* †**unaching,** *a.* painless. **unacknowledged,** *a.* not acknowledged, not recognized. **unacknowledging,** *a.* ungrateful.

una corda, *a., adv.* (*Mus.*) using the soft pedal. [It., one string]

un- (cont.) **unacquainted,** *a.* **unacquaintance, unacquaintedness,** *n.* **unacquirable,** *a.* **unacquired,** *a.* **unactable,** *a.* not capable of being acted; unfit for representation. **unacted,** *a.* **unadaptable,** *a.* **unadapted,** *a.* unfitted (for). **unaddicted,** *a.* **unaddressed,** *a.* **unadjudged,** *a.* **unadjusted,** *a.* **unadministered,** *a.* **unadmired,** *a.* **unadmonished,** *a.* **unadopted,** *a.* not adopted; (of road etc.) not taken over by the local authority. **unadorned,** *a.* not adorned, without decoration. **unadulterate, -ated,** *a.* not adulterated, unmixed; pure, genuine. **unadventurous,** *a.* **unadvertised,** *a.* **unadvisable,** *a.* **unadvisability, unadvisableness,** *n.* **unadvised,** *a.* not advised; not prudent or discreet, rash. **unadvisedly,** *adv.* **unadvisedness,** *n.* **unaffected,** *a.* not influenced or affected; without affectation, sincere, genuine. **unaffectedly,** *adv.* **unaffectedness,** *n.* **unaffiliated,** *a.* **unafflicted,** *a.* **unafraid,** *a.* **unaggressive,** *a.* **unaided,** *a.* **unalarmed,** *a.* **unalienable,** etc. INALIENABLE. **unaligned,** *a.*

†**unalist,** *n.* a person holding only one benefice. [L *unus,* one, after PLURALIST]

un- (cont.) **unallowable,** *a.* that cannot be allowed. **unalloyed,** *a.* **unalterable,** *a.* **unalterability, unalterableness,** *n.* **unalterably,** *adv.* **unaltered,** *a.* **unamazed,** *a.* **unambiguous,** *a.* plain, clear. **unambiguously,** *adv.* **unambiguousness,** *n.* **unambitious,** *a.* **unambitiously,** *adv.* **unambitiousness,** *n.* **unamenable,** *a.* **unamendable,** *a.* **un-American,** *a.* not American; alien to or incompatible with American ideas or principles. **unamiable,** *a.* not amiable; ill-natured; repellent, unpleasant. **unamiability, unamiableness,** *n.* **unamiably,** *adv.* **unamused,** *a.* **unamusingly,** *adv.* **unanalysable,** *a.* **unanalysed,** *a.* **unanchor,** *v.t., v.i.* †**unaneled,** *a.* not having received extreme unction. **unanimated,** *a.*

unanimous, *a.* being all of one mind, agreeing in opinion; formed, held, or expressed with one accord. **unanimity, unanimousness,** *n.* **unanimously,** *adv.* [L *ūnanimus* (*ūnus,* one, *animus,* mind)]

un- (cont.) **unannounced,** *a.* not announced. **unanswerable,** *a.* that cannot be satisfactorily answered or refuted. **unanswerability, unanswerableness,** *n.* **unanswerably,** *adv.* **unanswered,** *a.* **unanticipated,** *a.* **unapocryphal,** *a.* true, genuine. **unapologetic,** *a.* **unapostolic,** *a.* not in accordance with apostolic usage or authority. **unappalled,** *a.* **unapparel,** *v.t.* to unclothe, **unapparelled,** *a.* **unapparent,** *a.* **unappealing,** *a.* **unappeasable,** *a.* **unappeased,** *a.* **unappetizing, -ising,** *a.* **unappetizingly, -isingly,** *adv.* **unapplied,** *a.* **unappreciated,** *a.* **unappreciative,** *a.* **unapprehended,** *a.* **unapprehensible,** *a.* **unapprehensive,** *a.* **unapprehensiveness,** *n.* **unapprised,** *a.* **unapproachable,** *a.* that cannot be approached, inaccessible; reserved, distant in manner. **unapproachability, unapproachableness,** *n.* **unapproachably,** *adv.* **unappropriated,** *a.* **unapproved,** *a.* **unapproving,** *a.* **unapprovingly,** *adv.* **unapt,** *a.* **unaptly,** *adv.* **unaptness,** *n.* **unarguable,** *a.* **unarm,** *v.t., v.i.* to disarm. **unarmed,** *a.* **unarmoured,** *a.* **unarranged,** *a.* **unarrayed,** *a.* **unarrested,** *a.* †**unartful,** *a.* †**unartfully,** *adv.* **unartificial,** *a.* not artificial; natural. **unartificially,** *adv.* **unartistic,** *a.* **unascendable,** *a.* **unascended,** *a.* **unascertainable,** *a.* **unascertained,** *a.* **unashamed,** *a.* **unasked,** *a.* **unaspirated,** *a.* **unaspiring,** *a.* **unaspiringly,** *adv.* **unassailable,** *a.* incapable of being assailed; incontestable. **unassailed,** *a.* **unassayed,** *a.* **unassignable,** *a.* **unassigned,** *a.* **unassimilated,** *a.* **unassisted,** *a.* **unassuming,** *a.* not arrogant or presuming; modest. **unassured,** *a.* **unatoned,** *a.* **unattached,** *a.* not attached; (*Law*) not seized for debt; not belonging to any particular club, regiment etc. **unattainable,** *a.* **unattainableness,** *n.* **unattainted,** *a.* **unattempted,** *a.* **unattended,** *a.* **unattested,** *a.* **unattire,** *v.t., v.i.* to undress (esp. of ceremonial robes). **unattractive,** *a.* **unattractively,** *adv.* **unattractiveness,** *n.* **unaugmented,** *a.* †**unauspicious** INAUSPICIOUS. **unauthentic,** *a.* **unauthenticated,** *a.* **unauthenticity,** *n.* **unauthoritative,** *a.* **unauthorized, -ised,** *a.* **unavailable,** *a.* **unavailability, unavailableness,** *n.* **unavailing,** *a.* ineffectual; vain, useless. **unavailingly,** *adv.* **unavenged,** *a.* **unavoidable,** *a.* inevitable; that cannot be made null or void. **unavoidableness,** *n.* **unavoidably,** *adv.* **unavoided,** *a.* **unavowed,** *a.* **unaware,** *a.* not aware, ignorant (of); careless, inattentive. *adv.* (*loosely*) unawares. **unawares,** *adv.* without warning; by surprise, unexpectedly; undesignedly. **at unawares,** unexpectedly. **unbacked,** *a.* of a horse, not taught to bear a rider, unbroken; unsupported, having no backers; without a back (of seat etc.). **unbag,** *v.t.* to let out of a bag. **unbailable,** *a.* BAIL[1] **unbaked,** *a.* **unbalance,** *v.t.* to throw off one's balance. **unbalanced,** *a.* not balanced, not in equipoise; not brought to an equality of debit and credit; without mental balance, unsteady, erratic. **unballast,** *v.t.* to discharge or empty or ballast. **unballasted,** *a.* not furnished with ballast; unsteady. **unbank,** *v.t.* to remove the ashes etc., from a banked-up fire, to make it burn freely. **unbankable,** *a.* not receivable at a bank. **unbanked,** *a.* **unbaptized, -ised,** *a.* **unbar,** *v.t.* to remove a bar or bars from; to unfasten, to open. **unbarbed,** *a.* not furnished with barbs; †not shaven, untrimmed. **unbarbered,** *a.* unshaven. **unbarricade,** *v.t.* †**unbated,** *a.* unabated, undiminished, unblunted. **unbathed,** *a.* **unbattered,** *a.* †**unbay,** *v.t.* to release from restraint; to open. **unbear,** *v.t.* to take off or slacken the bearing-rein. **unbearable,** *a.* not to be borne, intolerable. **unbearably,** *adv.* **unbearded,** *a.* **unbeatable,** *a.* that cannot be beaten, unsurpassable. **unbeaten,** *a.* not beaten; not conquered or surpassed; untrodden. **unbeautiful,** *a.* not beautiful; ugly. **unbecoming,** *a.* not becoming, not suited (to); not befitting; improper, indecorous, indecent. **unbecomingly,** *adv.* **unbecomingness,** *n.* **unbed,** *v.t.* to rouse from bed. **unbedded,** *a.* not put to bed; virgin. **unbefitting,** *a.* **unbefriended,** *a.* **unbegot, unbegotten,** *a.* not begotten; self-existent. **unbeguile,** *v.t.* to undeceive. **unbegun,** *a.* †**unbeholden,** *a.* unseen. **unbeknown(st),** *a.* (*coll.*) not known; unknown (to); *adv.* without the knowledge. **unbelief,** *n.* the withholding of belief; incredulity; scepticism; disbelief (in, esp. divine revelation). **unbelievable,** *a.* **unbeliever,** *n.* one who does not believe, esp. in a religion. **unbelieving,** *a.* **unbeloved,** *a.* **unbelt,** *v.t.* **unbend,** *v.t.* (*past, p.p.* **-bent,**) to change or free from a bent position; to straighten; to relax from exertion, tension, constraint etc.; (*Naut.*) to unfasten (sails) from the yards and stays; to cast loose or untie (a cable or rope). *v.i.* to become straightened; to relax from constraint, formality etc.; to be affable, to condescend. **unbendable,** *a.* **unbending,** *a.* unyielding, resolute, inflexible; yielding oneself to relaxation or amusement; affable, condescending. **unbendingly,** *adv.* **unbendingness,** *n.* **unbeneficed,** *a.* **unbeseem,** *v.t.* to be unbecoming (to). **unbeseemingly,** *adv.* **unbesought,** *a.* **unbespoken,** *a.* **unbestowed,** *a.* **unbias,** *v.t.* to set free from bias. **unbiased,** *a.* **unbiblical,** *a.* not in or according to the Bible. †**unbid, unbidden,** *a.* not commanded; not called for, spontaneous; uninvited. **unbiddable,** *a.* **unbigoted,** *a.* **unbind,** *v.t.* (*past, p.p.* **-bound**) to untie, to unfasten; to release from a binding; to free from bonds, to release. **unbirthday,** *a.* (*coll.*) of a present, given on an occasion other than a birthday. **unbishop,** *v.t.* to depose from the office of bishop. **unbitt,** *v.t.* (*Naut.*) to remove the turns of (a rope, etc.) from the bitts. **unbitted,** *a.* not restrained with a bit, unbridled; (*Naut.*) not fastened round the bitts. **unblamable,** *a.* **unblamableness,** *n.* **unblamably,** *adv.* **unblamed,** *a.* **unbleached,** *a.* **unblemished,** *a.* †**unbless,** *v.t.* to make unhappy. **unblest,** *a.* **unblindfold,** *v.t.* **unblinking,** *a.* showing no surprise or other emotion. **unblock,** *v.t.* **unblooded,** *a.* not thoroughbred. **unbloody,** *a.* not stained with blood; not accompanied with bloodshed; not bloodthirsty. **unblotted,** *a.* not blotted; not blotted out. **unblown,** *a.* not blown (as a trumpet); yet in bud, not yet in flower; not inflated or distended with wind. **unblushing,** *a.* shameless, barefaced, impudent.

unblushingly, *adv.* **unblushingness,** *n.* **unbodied,** *a.* freed from the body; (*poet.*) incorporeal, immaterial. **unboiled,** *a.* **unbolt,** *v.t.* to undo the bolts of; to unfasten, to open. **unbolted,**[1], *a.* not fastened by a bolt. **unbolted,**[2], *a.* not bolted or sifted (of flour etc.); †(*fig.*) gross, unrefined, **unbone,** *v.t.* to remove the bones from (meat). **unbonnet,** *v.i.* to take off the cap or bonnet (esp. as a salutation); to uncover the head. *v.t.* to remove the bonnet from. **unbonneted,** *a.* **unbookish,** *a.* **unboot,** *v.t.* **unborn,** *a.* **unbosom,** *v.t.* to disclose (one's feelings etc.). *v.i.* to disclose one's secret feelings, opinions, or intentions; to open one's heart. **unbound,** *past, p.p.* UNBIND. **unbounded,** *a.* boundless, not bounded (by); infinite, not subject to check or control. **unboundedly,** *adv.* **unboundedness,** *n.* **unbowed,** *a.* not bowed; unconquered. **unbox,** *v.t.* **unbrace,** *v.t.* to remove or relax the braces of; to free from tension, to loosen, to relax. **unbraid,** *v.t.* to separate the strands of; to unweave, to disentangle. **unbreakable,** *a.* **unbreathed,** *a.* not breathed; †unexercised. **unbred,** *a.* not well bred, rude; (*Shak.*) unbegotten. **unbreech,** *v.t.* to unfasten or remove the breech of (a cannon etc.). **unbreeched,** *a.* not wearing breeches. **unbribable,** *a.* **unbridle,** *v.t.* to remove the bridle from; to set free from restraint. **unbridled,** *a.* freed from the bridle; unrestrained, unruly, ungovernable, insolent. **unbroken,** *a.* not broken; not subdued; uninterrupted, regular; not violated; not broken in, not accustomed to the saddle etc., not opened up by the plough; of a record, not bettered. **unbrotherly,** *a.* **unbrotherliness,** *n.* **unbruised,** *a.* †**unbrute,** *v.t.* to free from the nature of a brute. **unbuckle,** *v.t.* to unfasten the buckle of. **unbuild,** *v.t.* to demolish, to raze. **unbuilt,** *a.* not built; of land, not yet built upon. †**unbundle,** *v.t.* to unpack, to disclose, to reveal, to confess. **unburden,** *v.t.* to free from a load or burden; to relieve (the mind etc.) by disclosing or confession. **unburdened,** *a.* **unburied,** *a.* **unburned, -burnt,** *a.* **unbusinesslike,** *a.* **unbutton,** *v.i.* to unfasten the buttons of. *v.i.* to undo one's buttons; (*coll.*) to talk without restraint. **uncage,** *v.t.* **uncalled,** *a.* **uncalled for,** not necessary; not asked for, gratuitous, impertinent. **uncandid,** *a.* **uncanny,** *a.* not canny, weird, mysterious; incautious, rash, dangerous. **uncanonical,** *a.* **uncanonically,** *adv.* **uncanonicalness,** *n.* **uncanonized, -ised,** *a.* **uncap,** *v.t.* to remove the cap or cover from. *v.i.* to remove one's cap or hat (in salutation). **uncape,** *v.t.* to take the hood from (a hawk). **uncapped,** *a.* **uncared-for,** *a.* not cared for, neglected. **uncaring,** *a.* **uncarpeted,** *a.* **uncart,** *v.t.* to unload from a cart. **uncase,** *v.t.* to take out of a case or covering; to reveal, to disclose; to unfurl (the colours of a regiment). †*v.i.* (*Shak.*) to undress. **uncashed,** *a.* **uncastrated,** *a.* **uncatalogued,** *a.* **uncate,** SEE UNCINATE *a.* hooked. **uncaught,** *a.* **uncaused,** *a.* not caused; self-existent. **uncauterized, -ised,** *a.* **unceasing,** *a.* not ceasing, incessant, continual. **unceasingly,** *adv.* **uncensored,** *a.* **uncensured,** *a.* **unceremonious,** *a.* without ceremony, formality, or courtesy; familiar, brusque, abrupt. **unceremoniously,** *adv.* **unceremoniousness,** *n.* **uncertain,** *a.* not certain; not sure; doubtful; not certainly or precisely known; not to be relied on; undecided, changeable, fickle, capricious. **in no uncertain terms,** forcefully, unambiguously. **uncertainly,** *adv.* **uncertainty,** *n.* **uncertainty principle,** *n.* the principle that the position and velocity of a subatomic particle cannot both be ascertained at the same time. **uncertificated,** *a.* **uncertified,** *a.* **unchain,** *v.t.* **unchallengeable,** *a.* **unchallenged,** *a.* **unchancy,** *a.* (*Sc.*) unlucky; uncanny; unseasonable, inconvenient; dangerous. **unchangeable,** *a.* **unchangeableness,** *n.* **unchangeably,** *adv.* **unchanged,** *a.* **unchanging,** *a.* **unchangingly,** *adv.* **uncharacteristic,** *a.* **uncharge,** *v.t.* to free from a charge or load; to withdraw a charge from, to acquit of blame. **unchariot,** *v.t.* to turn out of a chariot. **uncharitable,** *a.* not harmonizing with Christian feeling; harsh, censorious. **uncharitableness,** *n.* **uncharitably,** *adv.* **uncharnel,** *v.t.* (*poet.*) to exhume. **uncharted,** *a.* not marked on a chart; unmapped. **unchartered,** *a.* **unchary,** *a.* **unchaste,** *a.* **unchastely,** *adv.* **unchastity,** *n.* **unchastened,** *a.* **unchecked,** *a.* not checked or repressed; unrestrained, uncontrolled; not examined. †**unchild,** *v.t.* to bereave of children; to make unfilial. **unchivalrous,** *a.* **unchivalrously,** *adv.* **unchristian,** *a.* not Christian, heathen; not according to or befitting the spirit of Christianity; (*coll.*) outrageous. †*v.t.* to make unchristian. **unchristianize, -ise,** *v.t.* **unchristianly,** *a.* **unchristianness,** *n.* **unchurch,** *v.t.* to expel from a Church; to excommunicate; to deprive of the character or standing of a Church.

uncial, *a.* denoting a kind of majuscule writing somewhat resembling modern capitals used in manuscripts of the 4-8th cents. *n.* an uncial letter or manuscript. [L *unciālis,* from *uncia* inch, ounce]

uncinate, *a.* (*Bot.*) hooked at the end; (*Anat. etc.*) having a hooked appendage. **uncinal, unciferous,, unciform,** *a.* [late L *uncinātus,* from *uncinus,* L *uncus,* hook]

un- (cont.) **uncircumcised,** *a.* not circumcised; not Jewish; heathen, unholy, profane. **uncircumcision,** *n.* **the uncircumcision,** (*Bibl.*) the Gentiles. **uncircumscribed,** not circumstantial, not given or considered in detail. **uncivil,** *a.* not civil, discourteous, ill-mannered; (*poet.*) rude, boisterous; †uncivilized. **uncivilly,** *adv.* **uncivilized,** *a.* **unclad,** *a.* **unclaimed,** *a.* **unclasp,** *v.t.* to unfasten the clasp of; to release from a grip. **unclass,** *v.t.* to degrade from one's proper class. **unclassifiable,** *a.* **unclassified,** *a.* not divided into categories; of information, not restricted.

uncle, *n.* the brother of one's father or mother; the husband of one's aunt; (*N Am.*) an elderly man (a friendly mode of address); (*sl.*) a pawnbroker. **Uncle Sam,** *n.* the government or a typical representative of the US. **Uncle Tom,** *n.* (*derog or offensive*) an American Negro considered to be servile in his manner towards white people. **uncleship,** *n.* [A-F (cp. F *oncle*), L *avunculus,* double dim. of *avus,* grandfather]

un- (cont.) **unclean,** *a.* not clean; foul, dirty; lewd, unchaste; (*Jewish Law*) not ceremonially clean. **uncleanness,** *n.* **uncleanly,** *a.* **uncleanliness,** *n.* **unclear,** *a.* **unclench,** *v.t., v.i.* **unclerical,** *a.* **unclew,** *v.t.* to unwind, untie, or undo. **unclinch,** *v.t.* **uncloak,** *v.t., v.i.* **unclog,** *v.t.* to remove a clog from; to disencumber, to free. **uncloister,** *v.t.* to release from a cloister; to set at liberty. **unclose,** *v.t., v.i.* to open. **unclothe,** *v.t.* **unclouded,** *a.* not obscured by clouds; clear, bright. **unclubbable,** *a.* **uncluttered,** *a.*

unco, *a.* (*Sc.*) strange, extraordinary. *n.* a strange or surprising person or thing. *adv.* remarkably, very. [var. of UNCOUTH]

un- (cont.) **uncock** *v.t.* to let down the hammer of (a gun, etc.) without exploding the charge. **uncoffined,** *a.* not laid in a coffin. **uncogitable,** *a.* beyond the reach of thought. **uncoif,** *v.t.* to take the coif or head-covering off. **uncoil,** *v.t., v.i.* to unwind. **uncoined,** *a.* not coined; †unfeigned, genuine. **uncoloured,** *a.* not coloured; told with simplicity or without exaggeration, unvarnished. **uncolt,** *v.t.* to unhorse. **uncombed,** *a.* **uncomeatable,** *a.* (*coll.*) that cannot be come at; not attainable, not obtainable. **uncomely,** *a.* **uncomeliness,** *n.* **uncomfortable,** *a.* **uncomfortably,** *adv.* **uncommercial,** *a.* not consistent according to commercial principles or usage. **uncommitted,** *a.* not pledged to support any particular policy, party etc. **uncommon,** *a.* not common, unusual, remarkable, extraordinary. †*adv.* uncommonly. **uncommonly,** *adv.* remarkably, to an uncommon degree. **uncommonness,** *n.* **uncommunicative,** *a.* reserved, taciturn. **uncommunicatively,** *adv.* **uncommunicativeness,** *n.* †**uncompanied,** *a.* unaccompanied; unmatched. **uncompanionable,** *a.* unsociable. **uncompensated,** *a.* **uncompetitive,** *a.* **uncomplaining,** *a.* **uncomplainingly,** *adv.* **uncomplaisant,** *a.* **uncomplaisantly,** *adv.* **uncompleted,** *a.* **uncomplicated,** *a.* **uncomplimentary,** *a.* **uncompounded,** *a.* **uncomprehending,** *a.* **uncomprehensive,** *a.* not comprehensive; †unable to comprehend; incomprehensible. **uncompromising**

a. not compromising or admitting of compromise; determined, rigid, inflexible, strict. **uncompromisingly,** *adv.* **unconcealed,** *a.* **unconcern,** *n.* absence of concern or anxiety; indifference, apathy. **unconcerned,** *a.* not concerned (in or with); free from anxiety. **unconcernedly,** *adv.* **uncondemned,** *a.* **uncondensable,** *a.* **uncondensed,** *a.* **unconditional,** *a.* not conditional; absolute. **unconditionality, unconditionalness,** *n.* **unconditionally,** *adv.* **unconditioned,** *a.* not learned or conditioned, innate. **unconfinable,** *a.* that cannot be confined; unbounded. **unconfined,** *a.* **unconfinedly,** *adv.* **unconfirmed,** *a.* **unconformable,** *a.* **unconformability, unconformableness,** *n.* **unconformably,** *adv.* **unconformity,** *n.* **uncongenial,** *a.* **uncongenially,** *adv.* **unconnected,** *a.* **unconquerable,** *a.* **unconquerably,** *adv.* **unconquered,** *a.* **unconscientious,** *a.* **unconscientiously,** *adv.* **unconscientiousness,** *n.* **unconscionable,** *a.* not reasonable, inordinate; not influenced or restrained by conscience; (*Law*) grossly unfair, inequitable. **unconscionableness,** *n.* **unconscionably,** *adv.* **unconscious,** *a.* not conscious, ignorant, unaware (of); temporarily deprived of consciousness; not perceived by the mind. *n.* (*Psych.*) a term which includes all processes which cannot be made conscious by an effort of the will. **unconsciously,** *adv.* **unconsciousness,** *n.* **unconsecrated,** *a.* **unconsenting,** *a.* **unconsidered,** *a.* not taken into consideration. †**unconstant,** INCONSTANT. **unconstitutional,** *a.* not authorized by or contrary to the principles of the constitution. **unconstitutionality,** *n.* **unconstitutionally,** *adv.* **unconstrained,** *a.* **unconstrainedly,** *adv.* **unconstricted,** *a.* **unconsumed,** *a.* **unconsummated,** *a.* **uncontainable,** *a.* **uncontaminated,** *a.* **uncontemplated,** *a.* not contemplated or expected. **uncontested,** *a.* **uncontracted,** *a.* **uncontradicted,** *a.* **uncontrollable,** *a.* unmanageable. **uncontrollableness,** *n.* **uncontrollably,** *adv.* **uncontrolled,** *a.* **uncontrolledly,** *adv.* **uncontroversial,** *a.* **uncontroversially,** *adv.* **uncontroverted,** *a.* **unconventional,** *a.* not fettered by convention or usage; informal, free and easy, bohemian. **unconventionality,** *n.* **unconventionally,** *adv.* **unconversable,** *a.* not free in conversation, reserved. **unconversant,** *a.* not conversant or familiarly acquainted (with). **unconverted,** *a.* **unconvertible,** *a.* **unconvicted,** *a.* **unconvinced,** *a.* **unconvincing,** *a.* **uncooked,** *a.* **uncool,** *a.* (*sl.*) not cool; unfashionable, unsophisticated. **uncooperative,** *a.* **uncoordinated,** *a.* **uncord,** *v.t.* to take the cord from; to unbind. **uncork,** *v.t.* to take the cork out of; to give vent to (one's feelings etc.). **uncorrected,** *a.* **uncorroborated,** *a.* **uncorroded,** *a.* **uncorrupted,** *a.* **uncorruptible,** *a.* **uncountable,** *a.* **uncounted,** *a.* not counted; innumerable. **uncountenanced,** *a.* **uncouple,** *v.t.* to disconnect; to let loose, to release. **uncourtly,** *a.* **uncourtliness,** *n.*

uncouth, *a.* awkward, clumsy; outlandish, odd, ungainly; †ignorant. **uncouthly,** *adv.* **uncouthness,** *n.* [OE *uncūth* (*cūth,* p.p of *cunman* to know, see CAN[2])]

un- (cont.) **uncovenanted,** *a.* not bound by a covenant; not promised or secured by a covenant. **Uncovenanted Civil Service,** a branch of the East Indian Civil Service the members of which passed no examination, might resign at pleasure, and received no pension. **uncover,** *v.t.* to remove a covering from; to divest of covering; to make known, to disclose; to expose (a line of troops behind) by wheeling to right or left. *v.i.* to take off the hat, in salutation. **uncovered,** *a.* **uncoveted,** *a.* **uncowl,** *v.t.* †**uncreate,** *v.t.* to blot out of existence. *a.*, uncreated. **uncreated,** *a.* not yet created; existing independently of creation. **uncreative,** *a.* **uncritical,** *a.* not critical, not inclined to criticize; not according to the rules of criticism. **uncritically,** *adv.* **uncross,** *v.t.* to change from a crossed position. **uncrossed,** *a.* not crossed (as a cheque); not opposed. **uncrowded,** *a.* **uncrown,** *v.t.* to discrown, to depose, to dethrone. **uncrowned,** *a.* discrowned; not yet crowned; having the power without the title of king. **uncrushable,** *a.* **uncrystallized, -ised,** *a.*

UNCTAD, (*abbr.*) United Nations Commission on Trade and Development.

unction, *n.* the act of anointing with oil or an unguent, as a symbol of consecration or for medical purposes; that which is used in anointing, an unguent or ointment; anything soothing or ingratiating; a quality in speech conveying deep religious or other fervour; effusive or affected emotion, gush; relish, gusto; (*Theol.*) grace. **unctuous,** *a.* greasy, oily, soapy to the touch; full of unction; oily, effusive, hypocritically or affectedly fervid. **extreme unction,** EXTREME. **unctuously,** *adv.* **unctuousness,** *n.* [F, from L *unctio -ōnem,* from *ungere,* to anoint, p.p. *unctus*]

†**uncular,** AVUNCULAR.

un- (cont.) **unculled** *a.* not culled; not separated. **uncultivable,** *a.* **uncultivated,** *a.* **uncultured,** *a.* **uncurb,** *v.t.* **uncurbed,** *a.* unrestrained. **uncured,** *a.* **uncurl,** *v.t., v.i.* **uncurtailed,** *a.* **uncurtain,** *v.t.* to remove the curtain from, to reveal.

uncus, *n.* (*pl.* **-ci**) (*Nat. Hist.*) a hook, claw, or hooklike part or appendage. [L, hook]

un- (cont.) **uncushioned,** *a.* not cushioned or padded. **uncustomed,** *a.* not subject to customs duty; not having paid duty. **uncut,** *a.* not cut; having the margins untrimmed (of leaves of a book); not shortened or abridged. **undam,** *v.t.* **undamaged,** *a.*

undate, undated,[1], *a.* having a wavy surface, undulate.

undé, *a.* (*Her.*) wavy. [L *undātus,* p.p. or *undāre,* wave]

un- (cont.) **undated**[2], not dated. **undaunted,** *a.* not daunted; fearless. **undauntedly,** *adv.* **undauntedness,** *n.* **undead,** *a.* †**undeaf,** *v.t.* (*Shak.*) to cure of deafness. **undebated,** *a.* **undebauched,** *a.*

undecagon, *n.* a plane figure having eleven angles and eleven sides. [L *undecim* eleven, Gr. *gōnia,* angle]

un- (cont.) **undeceive,** *v.t.* to free from deception or error; to open the eyes of. **undeceived,** *a.*

undecennary, undecennial, *a.* pertaining to a period of eleven years; celebrated or occurring once in every eleven years. [L *undecim* eleven, after CENTENARY and CENTENNIAL]

un- (cont.) **undecided** *a.* not decided or settled; irresolute, wavering. **undecidedly,** *adv.* **undecipherable,** *a.* †**undecisive,** INDECISIVE. †**undeck,** *v.t.* to divest of ornaments. **undecked,** *a.* not adorned; not furnished with a deck. **undeclared,** *a.* **undeeded,** *a.* (*Law*) not transferred by deed; †not signalized by any great action. **undefeated,** *a.* **undefended,** *a.* **undefiled,** *a.* not defiled; pure. **undefined,** *a.* not defined; indefinite, vague. **undeify,** *v.t.* **undelegated,** *a.* **undelivered,** *a.* **undemanded,** *a.* **undemanding,** *a.* **undemocratic,** *a.* **undemonstrated,** *a.* **undemonstrative,** *a.* not demonstrative; not exhibiting strong feelings; reserved. **undeniable,** *a.* not capable of being denied; indisputable; (*coll.*) decidedly good, excellent. **undeniably,** *adv.* **undenominational,** *a.* not sectarian. **undenounced,** *a.* **undependable,** *a.* not to be depended on. **undeplored,** *a.* **undepraved,** *a.* **undepreciated,** *a.* **undepressed,** *a.* **undeprived,** *a.*

under, *prep.* in or to a place or position lower than, below; at the foot or bottom of; covered by, on the inside of, beneath the surface of; (*fig.*) beneath the appearance or disguise of; inferior to or less than in quality, rank, degree, number, amount etc.; subject to, subordinate or subservient to; governed, controlled, or directed by; liable to, on condition or pain of, in accordance with; by virtue of; in the time of; attested by; planted or sown with; because of; in the process of; in a group consisting of. *adv.* in or into a lower or subordinate place, condition, or degree, or unconsciousness. *a.* lower, inferior, subordinate. **under age,** not of full age. **under arms,** ARM[2]. **under a cloud,** out of favour. **under fire,** FIRE[1]. **under sail,** SAIL. **under sentence,** having received sentence or judgement. **under the breath,** in a low voice; very softly. **under the rose** ROSE[1]. **under way,** WAY. **underling,** *n.* an inferior agent or assistant. **undermost,** *a.* lowest in place, position, rank etc. [OE (cp. Dut. *onder,* G *unter,* Icel. *undir,* Swed. and Dan. *under*), cogn. with L.

infrā, beneath]

under-, *pref.* under, below (the substantive to which it is prefixed); underneath, beneath, lower than, in position, rank etc., subordinate; insufficiently, incompletely, immaturely. Only a selection of compounds with this prefix is given; others can be explained by reference to the simple adjective, noun, or verb. **underachieve,** *v.i.* to fail to achieve as much (esp. academically) as expected. **underachiever,** *n.* **underact,** *v.t., v.i.* to act or to play inadequately, or in a restrained way. **underactive,** *a.* **underagent,** *n.* a subordinate agent. **underarm**, *a., adv.* (made or done) with the arm below shoulder level. **underbear,** *v.t.* to support, to endure; to face, to live. **underbearer,** *n.* one who supports the corpse at a funeral. **underbelly**, *n.* the underside of an animal, nearest to the ground and consequently less protected; any soft or vulnerable part or aspect (of an organization etc.). **underbid,** *v.t.* to bid less than (as at auction). **underbitten,** *a.* not bitten in deep enough for printing (of etched lines on a copper plate). **underblanket,** *n.* **underboard**, *adv.* secretly, underhandedly. [cp. ABOVE-BOARD] **underbred,** *a.* not thoroughbred; ill-bred. **underbrush**, *n.* undergrowth, underwood. *v.t.* to clear of this. **underbuy,** *v.t.* to buy at a lower price than that paid by others; to buy for less than the proper value. **undercapitalized, -ised,** *a.* of a business, having less capital than that needed to operate efficiently. **undercarriage**, *n.* the main alighting gear of an aircraft. **undercharge,** *v.t.* to charge less than the fair price for, or put an insufficient charge in (a gun, etc.). **underclass**, *n.* a social class falling outside the standard classification, very deprived in economic, educational etc., terms. **under-clay**, *n.* a bed of clay found under coal seams. **under-clerk,** *n.* **under-clerkship,** *n.* **under-cliff,** *n.* **underclothes**, *n.pl.* clothes worn under others, esp. next to the skin. **underclothing,** *n.* **undercoat**, *n.* a layer of fine fur underneath an animal's main coat; a coat of paint serving as a base for the main coat. **undercoat,** *v.t.* **undercover,** *a.* done in secret. †**undercrest,** *v.t.* to support or wear, as a crest. **undercroft**, *n.* a vault, esp. under a church or large building, a crypt. **undercurrent,** *n.* a current running below the surface; a secret or unapparent tendency or influence; (*Mining*) a large shallow box beside a main hydraulic sluice, with a steeper inclination, helping to save gold from the finer material. **undercut,** *v.t.* to cut under (coal etc.) so as to remove it easily; to cut away the material beneath (a carved design) to give greater relief; to make a price lower than that of a competitor; (*Golf*) to hit (a ball) so as to make it rise high. *n.*, the act or effect of undercutting; a blow upward; the underside of a sirloin, the tenderloin. **underdeveloped,** *a.* not sufficiently or adequately developed; of a country, economically backward. **underditch,** *v.t.* to cut a deep ditch in, to drain the surface. **underdo,** *v.t.* to do inadequately; to cook insufficiently. **underdog**, *n.* an oppressed person, one in an inferior position. **underdone,** *a.* insufficiently cooked. **underdose,** *v.t.* to dose insufficiently. *n.*. **underdrain**, *n.* a drain below the surface of the ground. *v.t.* to drain thus. **underdraw,** *v.t.* to draw or describe inadequately. **underdress,** *v.t., v.i.* to dress insufficiently or too plainly. **underestimate,** *v.t.* to estimate at too low a rate. *n.* an inadequate estimate. **underestimation,** *n.* **underexpose,** *v.t.* (*Phot.*). **underexposure,** *n.* **underfeed,** *v.t., v.i.* **underfelt**, *n.* a felt underlay. **underfired,** *a.* of pottery, insufficiently baked. **underfloor,** *a.* of a method of central heating using hot air piped under the floor. **underflow**, *n.* an undercurrent. **underfoot,** *adv.* under the feet; beneath; in the way. *v.t.* to shore up, to underpin. **underfunding,** *n.* **undergarment**, *n.* one worn under others. **undergear**, *n.* undergarments. **underglaze,** *a.* (*Ceramics*) suitable for painting with before the glaze is applied. *n.* such a pigment, etc. **undergo,** *v.t.* (*past* **-went,** *p.p.* **-gone**) to experience, to pass through, to suffer; to bear up against, to endure with firmness. **undergrade**, *a.* having the truss below the roadway (as in a deck-bridge). **undergraduate,** *n.* a member of a university who has not yet taken a degree. **undergraduateship,** *n.* **underground**, *a.* situated below the surface of the earth; obscure, secret, unperceived by those in authority; ignoring, or subversive of, established trends, avant-garde. *n.* that which is underground; an underground railway; a secret or subversive group or organization. *adv.* below the surface of the earth. **undergrove**, *n.* a grove or plantation overshadowed by larger trees. **undergrown,** *a.* **undergrowth**, *n.* small trees or shrubs, growing under larger ones. **underhand,** *adv.* secretly, not openly, clandestinely; slyly, unfairly, by fraud; with the hand underneath (of bowling). *a.* (*attributively*). clandestine, secret; sly, unfair, fraudulent; (of bowling) with the hand underneath both the elbow and the ball. **underhanded,** *a.* underhand. **underhandedly,** *adv.* **underhandedness,** *n.* **underhew,** *v.t.* to hew less than is proper, esp. to hew (logs etc.) so as to leave waste wood that should be cut away and convey a misleading impression of the cubic contents. **underhold,** *n.* (*Wrestling*) a hold round the body with the arms underneath one's opponent's. **underhung**, *a.* projecting beyond the upper jaw (of the lower jaw); having the lower jaw projecting before the upper. **underinsured,** *a.* **underking,** *n.* **underlap,** *v.t.* to be folded or extend under the edge of. [cp. OVERLAP] **underlay,**[1] *v.t.* (*past, p.p.* **-laid,**) to lay something under. *v.i.* (*Mining*) to incline from the perpendicular (of a vein). *n.*, inclination of a vein; a piece of paper etc., placed beneath type etc., to bring it to the proper level for printing; a thick felt or rubber sheet laid under a carpet. [LAY[1]] **underlay**[2], *past* UNDERLIE. **underlease**, *n.* a sublease. **underlet,** *v.t.* to let below the proper value; to sublet. **underletter,** *n.* **underletting,** *n.* **underlie,** *v.t.* (*past* **-lay,** *p.p.* **-lain,**) to lie under or beneath; to be the basis or foundation of. [LIE[2]] **underline,** *v.t.* to mark with a line underneath, esp. for emphasis. *n.*, an announcement of a subsequent theatrical performance at the foot of a playbill. **underlinen,** *n.* linen underclothing. **underlooker**, *n.* an underviewer. **underman,** *v.t.* to furnish (a ship) with less than the proper complement of men. **undermasted,** *a.* **undermentioned,** *a.* mentioned below or later. **undermine,** *v.t.* to dig a mine or excavation under; to render unstable by digging away the foundation of; to injure by clandestine or underhand means; to wear away (one's strength etc.) by imperceptible degrees. **underminer,** *n.* [prec.]

†**undern,** *n.* the third hour of the day, 9 A.M.; the period from this to noon, as the time of the principal meal. [OE]

under- (cont.) **underneath** *adv., prep.* beneath, below. *n.* an underside. **undernote**, *n.* a subdued note, an undertone. **undernourish,** *v.t.* **underpaid,** *a.* **underpants**, *n.pl.* a man's undergarment covering the body from the waist to the thighs. **underpart**, *n.* a lower part; a part lying underneath. **underpass**, *n.* a road passing under a railway or another road. **underpay,** *v.t.* (*past, p.p.* **-paid**) to pay inadequately. **underperform,** *v.i.* to perform less well than expected. **underpin,** *v.t.* to support (a wall etc.) by propping up with timber, masonry, etc. ; to strengthen the foundations of (a building). **underpinning,** *n.* **underplay,** *v.t.* to play (a part) inadequately. *v.i.* to play a low card whilst one holds a higher one of the same suit. *n.*, the act of underplaying. **underplot**, *n.* a subordinate plot in a play, novel, etc. **underpopulated,** *a.* **underpraise,** *v.t.* to praise less than is deserved. **underprivileged,** *a.* lacking the economic and social privileges enjoyed by most members of society. **underprize,** *v.t.* to value below one's merits. **underproduction,** *n.* lower or less production than the normal or the demand. **underproof**, *a.* containing less alcohol than proof spirit. **underprop,** *v.t.* to prop or support underneath. **underquote,** *v.t.* to offer at lower prices than; to offer (goods etc.) at lower prices than others. **underrate,** *v.t.* to rate or estimate too low. **under-reckon,** *v.t.* **underripe,** *a.* **underrun,** *v.t.* to run beneath, to pass under. **underscore,** *v.t.* to underline. **undersea,** *a.*

underseal, *v.t.* to coat the exposed underparts of (a vehicle) with a corrosion-resistant substance. *n.*, such a substance. **undersecretary,** *n.* **under-secretaryship,** *n.* **undersell,** *v.t.* to sell cheaper than. **underseller,** *n.* **under-servant,** *n.* **underset,**[1] *v.t.* to support underneath by a prop, masonry etc. **underset**[2], *n.* a current of water below the surface in a direction contrary to that of the wind or surface water. **undersexed,** *a.* having less than the normal sexual drive. **under-sheriff,** *n.* a deputy-sheriff. **undershirt,** *n.* (*N Am.*) a vest or singlet. **undershorts**, *n. pl.* **undershoot**, *n.* (*Aviat.*) falling short of the mark in landing. **undershot,** *a.* of a water-wheel, driven by water passing under it. **undershrub**, *n.* a plant of shrubby habit, but smaller than a shrub. **underside**, *n.* a lower side or surface. **undersign,** *v.t.* to sign under or at the foot of. **the undersigned,** the person or persons signing a document etc. **undersized,** *a.* below the normal or average size. †**underskinker,** *n.* an assistant tapster. **underskirt**, *n.* a skirt worn under another. **underslung,** *a.* (*Motor.*) description of a chassis with the frame below the axles. **undersoil**, *n.* subsoil. **undersong**, *n.* a subordinate strain; an underlying meaning; †the accompaniment of a song. **undersparred,** *a.* of a ship, not adequately equipped with spars. **underspend,** *v.i.* to spend less than expected or allowed for. **understaffed,** *a.*

understand, *v.t.* (*past, p.p.* **-stood**, †**-standed**) to take in, know, or perceive the meaning of; to comprehend fully, to have complete apprehension of, to perceive the force or significance of; to suppose to mean, to take as meant or implied, to gather, assume, or infer from information received; to supply (a word, explanation etc.) mentally. *v.i.* to have or exercise the power of comprehension; to be informed or told, to hear. **understandable,** *a.* **understandably,** *adv.* **understanding,** *a.* intelligent; sensible; sympathetic, tolerant. *n.* the act of one who understands; comprehension; the power or faculty of apprehension; the faculty of thinking or of apprehending relations and drawing inferences; discernment; clear insight and intelligence in practical matters; union of minds or sentiments, accord; an informal agreement or compact. **on the understanding that,** provided that. **understandingly,** *adv.* [OE *understandan* (UNDER-, STAND)]

undertake, *v.t.* (*past* **-took,**, *p.p.* **-taken,**) to take upon oneself, to assume, to engage in, to enter upon (a task, enterprise, responsibility etc.); to engage oneself, to promise (to do); to guarantee, to affirm, to answer for it (that); †to engage within combat etc. *v.i.* to promise, to be guarantee (for); (*coll.*) to manage funerals. **undertaker**, *n.* one who undertakes; a tradesman who manages funerals; (*Hist.*) a person undertaking certain political offices, esp. one of those who undertook to manage the House of Commons for the King in 1614, the settlers who undertook to hold the lands forfeited to the Crown in Ireland in the 16th-17th cents. etc. **undertaking**, *n.* the act of one who undertakes any business; that which is undertaken, a task, an enterprise, an agreement, a promise, a stipulation. [ME *undertaken*]

under- (cont.) **undertenant,** *n.* a tenant under another tenant. **undertenancy,** *n.* **underthrust,**, *n.* (*Geol.*) a fault in which rocks on a lower plane have moved underneath a more stable upper layer. **undertimed,** *a.* underexposed. **undertint**, *n.* a subdued tint. **undertone**, *n.* a low or subdued tone, esp. in speaking; an unstated meaning or emotional tone; a subdued colour, an undertint. **undertook**, *past* UNDERTAKE. **undertow**, *n.* a backward current opposite to that on the surface, an underset, esp. the backward flow under waves breaking on a shore. **undertrump,** *v.t.* to play a lower trump than (another person or another trump played). **underuse,** *n.*, *v.t.* **undervalue,** *v.t.* to value too low; to despise. **undervaluation,** *n.* **undervaluer,** *n.* **undervest**, *n.* **underviewer**, *n.* the overseer of the undergound workings in a coal-mine. **underwater,** *a.*, *adv.* **underwear**, *n.* clothes worn underneath others, underclothing; the wearing of these. **underweight,** *n.*, *a.* (being) less than the average or expected weight. **underwent,** *past* UNDERGO. **underwhelm,** *v.t.* (*coll.*) to fail to impress, to disappoint (formed from *overwhelm*). **underwing,**, *n.* a nocturnal moth with conspicuous markings on the hind or under wings. **underwood,**, *n.* undergrowth. **underwork,** *v.t.* to work for a lower price than, to undercut. *v.i.* to work inadequately. *n.*, subordinate or inferior work. **underworld,**, *n.* the nether world, the infernal regions; the antipodes; the earth as the sublunary sphere; the criminal class of society. **underwrite,** *v.t.* (*past* **-wrote,** *p.p.* **-written**) to execute and deliver (a policy of marine insurance); to engage to buy all the stock in (a new company etc.) not subscribed for by the public; to write beneath, to subscribe. *v.i.* to act as an underwriter, to practise marine insurance. **underwriter**, *n.* **underwriting**, *n.* **underwrought,** *a.* insufficiently wrought.

un- (cont.) **undescended,** *a.* not having descended; of a testis, not having descended into the scrotum. **undescried,** *a.* not descried. **undeserved,** *a.* **undeservedly**, *adv.* **undeserving,** *a.* **undeservingly,** *adv.* **undesignated,** *a.* **undesigned,** *a.* not designed, unintentional. **undesignedly**, *adv.* **undesignedness,** *n.* **undesigning,** *a.* **undesirable,** *a.* not desirable; unpleasant, inconvenient. *n.* an undesirable person. **undesirability, undesirableness,** *n.* **undesirably,** *adv.* **undesired,** *a.* not desired; not asked for. **undesirous,** *a.* not desirous (of). **undetachable,** *a.* **undetectable,** *a.* **undetected,** *a.* **undetermined,** *a.* not determined, not decided, not fixed; irresolute; indeterminate. **undeterred,** *a.* **undeveloped,** *a.* **undeviating,** *a.* **undeviatingly,** *adv.* **undevout,** *a.* **undevoutly,** *adv.* **undiagnosed,** *a.* **undid,** *past* UNDO.

undies, *n.pl.* (*coll.*) women's underwear. [short for UNDERTHINGS]

un- (cont.) **undifferentiated,** *a.* **undiffused,** *a.* **undigested,** *a.* **undignified**, *a.* not dignified; not consistent with one's dignity. **undiluted,** *a.* **undiminished,** *a.* **undimmed,** *a.*

undine, *n.* a female water sprite without a soul, but capable of obtaining one by marrying a mortal and bearing a child; (*Med.*) a form of eye-irrigator. **undinal**, *a.*

un- (cont.) **undiplomatic,** *a.* not diplomatic. **undirected,** *a.* **undiscerned,** *a.* **undiscernible,** *a.* **undiscerning,** *a.* **undiscerningly,** *adv.* **undischarged,** *a.* **undisciplined,** *a.* **undisclosed,** *a.* **undiscomfited,** *a.* **undisconcerted,** *a.* †**undiscording,** *a.* not disagreeing or discordant. **undiscouraged, undiscoverable, undiscovered,** *a.* **undiscoverably,** *adv.* **undiscriminating,** *a.* **undiscriminatingly,** *adv.* **undiscussed,** *a.* **undisguised,** *a.* not disguised; open, frank, plain. **undisguisedly**, *adv.* **undisheartened,** *a.* **undismayed,** *a.* **undispelled,** *a.* **undispersed,** *a.* **undisplayed,** *a.* **undisputed,** *a.* **undissected,** *a.* **undissembled,** *a.* **undissembling,** *a.* **undissolved,** *a.* **undistinguishable,** *a.* **undistinguishably,** *adv.* **undistinguishableness,** *n.* **undistinguished,** *a.* **undistorted,** *a.* **undistracted,** *a.* **undistressed,** *a.* **undistributed,** *a.* (*chiefly Log.*) not distributed. **undisturbed,** *a.* **undisturbedly,** *adv.* **undiversified,** *a.* **undiverted,** *a.* **undivided,** *a.* **undividedly,** *adv.* **undivorced,** *a.* **undivulged,** *a.* **undo,** *v.t.* (*past* **-did,** *p.p.* **-done**) to reverse (something that has been done) to annul; to unfasten, to untie; to unfasten the buttons, garments etc., of (a person); to bring ruin, to destroy, to corrupt. **undoer,** *n.* **undoing,** *n.* **undock,** *v.t.* to take or bring out of dock. **undocumented,** *a.* **undomesticate,** *v.t.* **undomesticated,** *a.* **undone,** *a.* not done; unfastened; ruined, destroyed. [p.p. of UNDO]

undose, *a.* wavy, undulating. [L *undōsus,* from *unda,* wave]

un- (cont.) **undoubted** *a.* not called in question, not doubted; unsuspected. **undoubtedly,** *adv.* without doubt. **undoubting,** *a.* **undoubtingly,** *adv.* **undrained,** *a.* **undramatic,** *a.* **undrape,** *v.t.* to remove drapery from, to uncover. **undraped,** *a.* **undreamed, undreamt,** *a.* **undreamed-of,** *a.* not thought of. **undress,** *v.t.* to divest of cloth, to strip; to take the dressing; bandages, etc., from (a wound etc.). *v.i.* to undress oneself. *n.* the state of being partly or completely undressed; ordinary dress, opp. to full dress or uniform; negligent attire. *a.* pertaining to everyday dress; commonplace. **undressed,** *a.* **undrinkable,** *a.*

und so weiter, usw., and so on. [G]

un- (cont.) **undue** *a.* excessive, disproportionate; not yet due; improper; illegal. **unduly,** *adv.*

undulate, *a.* wavy, bending in and out or up and down. *v.i.*, to have a wavy motion; to rise and fall (of water). **undulant,** *a.* undulating. **undulant fever,** *n.* brucellosis in human beings, so called because the fever is intermittent. **undulately,** *adv.* **undulatingly,** *adv.* **undulation,** *n.* the act of undulating; a wavy or sinuous form or motion, a gentle rise and fall, a wavelet; a wave-like movement of a fluid in a cavity of the body. **undulationist,** *n.* one who believes in the undulatory theory. **undulatory,** *a.* having an undulating character; rising and falling like waves; pertaining or due to undulation. **undulatory theory,** *n.* the theory that light is propagated through the ether by a wave-like motion imparted to the ether by the molecular vibrations of the radiant body. **undulous,** *a.* [L *undulātus,* from *unda,* wave]

UNESCO, Unesco, (*acronym*) *U*nited *N*ations *E*ducational, *S*cientific and *C*ultural *O*rganization, an agency of the UN, established 1946, with its headquarters in Paris. The US, contributor of 25% of its budget, withdrew 1984 on grounds of its overpoliticization, and Britain followed 1985.

un- (cont.) **unespied** *a.* **unessayed,** *a.* **unessential,** *a.* not essential, not absolutely necessary; not of prime importance. *n.* some thing or part not absolutely necessary or indispensable. **unestablished,** *a.* **unestimated,** *a.* **unestranged,** *a.* **unethical,** *a.* **unevangelical,** *a.* **unevaporated,** *a.* **uneven,** *a.* not even, level, or smooth; not uniform, regular, or equable. **unevenly,** *adv.* **unevenness,** *n.* **uneventful,** *a.* **unexamined,** *a.* **unexampled,** *a.* not exampled; having no parallel; unprecedented. **unexcelled,** *a.* **unexceptionable,** *a.* not exceptionable; to which no exception can be taken; unobjectionable, faultless. **unexceptionableness,** *n.* **unexceptionably,** *adv.* **unexceptional,** *a.* not exceptional, ordinary. **unexcised,** *a.* not liable to excise. **unexciting,** *a.* **unexclusive,** *a.* **unexclusively,** *adv.* **unexecuted,** *a.* **unexemplified,** *a.* **unexercised,** *a.* **unexhausted,** *a.* **unexpected,** *a.* **unexpectedly,** *adv.* **unexpectedness,** *n.* **unexpensive,** *a.* **unexpiated,** *a.* **unexpired,** *a.* not having come to an end or termination. **unexplainable,** *a.* **unexplained,** *a.* **unexploded,** *a.* **unexploited,** *a.* **unexplored,** *a.* **unexposed,** *a.* **unexpounded,** *a.* **unexpressed,** *a.* **unexpressive,** *a.* **unexpurgated,** *a.* **unextended,** *a.* not extended; occupying no assignable space; having no dimensions. **unextinguishable,** INEXTINGUISHABLE. **unface,** *v.t.* **unfadable,** *a.* **unfaded,** *a.* **unfading,** *a.* **unfadingly,** *adv.* **unfadingness,** *n.* **unfailing,** *a.* not liable to fail or run short; unerring, infallible; reliable, certain. **unfailingly,** *adv.* **unfailingness,** *n.* **unfair,** *a.* not fair; not equitable, not impartial; dishonourable, fraudulent. **unfairly,** *adv.* **unfairness,** *n.* **unfaithful,** *a.* not faithful; adulterous. **unfaith,** *n.* **unfaithfully,** *adv.* **unfaithfulness,** *n.* **unfallen,** *a.* **unfaltering,** *a.* **unfalteringly,** *adv.* **unfamiliar,** *a.* not familiar. **unfamiliarity,** *n.* **unfamiliarly,** *adv.* **unfashionable,** *a.* **unfashionableness,** *n.* **unfashionably,** *adv.* **unfashioned,** *a.* not fashioned by art; shapeless. **unfasten,** *v.t.* **unfathered,** *a.* not acknowledged by its father or author; (*poet.*) fatherless. **unfatherly,** *a.* **unfathomable,** *a.* **unfathomableness,** *n.* **unfathomably,** *adv.* **unfathomed,** *a.* **unfatigued,** *a.* not fatigued or tired. **unfavourable,** *a.* **unfavourableness,** *n.* **unfavourably,** *adv.* **unfearing,** *a.* **unfeasible,** *a.* **unfeathered,** *a.* not feathered; unfledged. **unfed,** *a.* **unfeed,** *a.* not retained by a fee. **unfeeling,** *a.* insensible; hard-hearted, cruel. **unfeelingly,** *adv.* **unfeelingness,** *n.* **unfeigned,** *a.* **unfeignedly,** *adv.* **unfelt,** *a.* not felt, not perceived. **unfeminine,** *a.* **unfenced,** *a.* not enclosed by a fence; not fortified. **unfermented,** *a.* **unfertile,** *a.* **unfertilized, -ised,** *a.* **unfetter,** *v.t.* to free from fetters or restraint. **unfettered,** *a.* **unfeudalize,** *v.t.* **unfigured,** *a.* not marked with figures. **unfile,** *v.t.* to take (a document etc.) from a file. **unfilial,**, *a.* **unfilially,** *adv.* **unfilled,** *a.* **unfiltered,** *a.* **unfinished,** *a.* not finished, incomplete; not having been through a finishing process. **unfit,** *a.* not fit (to do, to be, for etc.); improper, unsuitable. *v.t.* to make unfit or unsuitable; disqualify. **unfitly,** *adv.* **unfitness,** *n.* **unfitted,** *a.* not fitted; unfit; not fitted up, not furnished with fittings. **unfitting,** *a.* **unfittingly,** *adv.* **unfix,** *v.t.* **unfixed,** *a.* **unflagging,** *a.* **unflappable,** *a.* (*coll.*) not readily upset or agitated, imperturbable. **unflattering,** *a.* **unflatteringly,** *adv.* **unflavoured,** *a.* **unfledged,** *a.* not yet fledged; underdeveloped, immature. **unfleshed,** *a.* not having shed or tasted blood (of a sword or hound); unseasoned. **unflinching,** *a.* **unflinchingly,** *adv.* **unflustered,** *a.* **unfocus(s)ed,** *a.* **unfold,** *v.t.* to open the folds of; to spread out; to discover, to reveal; to display. *v.i.* to spread open, to expand, to develop. **unforced,** *a.* not forced, not constrained; natural, easy. **unfordable,** *a.* **unforseeable,** *a.* **unforeseen,** *a.* **unforgettable,** *a.* **unforgivable,** *a.* **unforgiven,** *a.* **unforgiving,** *a.* **unforgivingly,** *adv.* **unforgivingness,** *n.* **unforgotten,** *a.* **unform,** *v.t.* to unmake. **unformed,** *a.* devoid of form, shapeless, amorphous, structureless; not yet fully developed, immature. **unformulated,** *a.* **unforthcoming,** *a.* **unfortified,** *a.* **unfortunate,** *a.* not fortunate, unlucky, unhappy. *n.* one who is unfortunate. **unfortunately,** *adv.* **unfound,** *a.* **unfounded,** *a.* having no foundation of fact or reason, groundless; not yet established. **unframe,** *v.t.* **unfranked,** *a.* **unfreeze,** *v.t.*, *v.i.* (*past,* **froze,** *p.p.* **frozen**). **unfrequent,** *a.* **unfrequented,** *a.* †**unfriend,** *n.* an enemy. **unfriended,** *a.* without a friend or friends. **unfriendly,** *a.* **unfriendliness,** *n.* **unfrock,** *v.t.* to take the frock or gown from; hence, to deprive of the character and privileges of a priest. **unfruitful,** *a.* **unfruitfully,** *adv.* **unfruitfulness,** *n.* **unfulfilled,** *a.* **unfunded,** *a.* not funded, floating (of a debt etc.). **unfunny,** *a.* **unfurl,** *v.t.*, *v.i.* to open or spread out (a sail, banner etc.). **unfurnished,** *a.* not furnished (with); without furniture. **unfused,** *a.* not fused, not melted.

ungainly, *a.* clumsy, awkward. **ungainliness,** *n.* [ME *ungeniliche* (Icel. *gegn,* serviceable, see GAIN[2], -LY]

un- (cont.) **ungallant,** *a.* not gallant, not courteous to women. **ungalvanized, -ised,** *a.* **ungarbled,** *a.*

Ungaretti, *n.* **Giuseppe** (1888–1970), Italian poet who lived in France and Brazil. His lyrics show a cosmopolitan independence of Italian poetic tradition. His poems, such as the *Allegria di naufragi/Joy of Shipwrecks* (1919), are noted for their simplicity.

un- (cont.) **ungarnered,** *a.* **ungarnished,** *a.* not garnished, not adorned. **ungauged,** *a.* **ungear,** *v.t.* to strip of gear; to throw out of gear. **ungenerous,** *a.* **ungenerously,** *adv.* **ungenial,** *a.* **ungenteel,** *a.* **ungenteelly,** *adv.* **ungentle,** *a.* not gentle, harsh, rude, unkind; ill-bred. **ungentleness,** *n.* **ungently,** *adv.* **ungentlemanly,** *a.* not becoming a gentleman; rude, ill-bred. **ungentlemanliness,** *n.* **unget-at-able,** *a.*, *adv.* difficult of access. **ungifted,** *a.* **ungild,** *v.t.* to remove the gilding from. †**ungilded,** †**ungilt,** *a.* not gilded. **ungird,** *v.t.* (*past, p.p.* **-girt**) to undo or remove a girdle from; to unbind. **unglaze,** *v.t.* to deprive of glazing. **unglazed,** *a.* deprived of glazing; not glazed. **unglove,** *v.t.* **unglue,** *v.t.* **unglutted,** *a.* **ungodly,** *a.* not godly, heathen; wicked; (*coll.*) outrageous. **ungodlily,** *adv.* **ungodliness,** *n.* **ungovernable** *a.* not governable; unruly, wild, passionate, licentious. **ungovernably,** *adv.* **ungown,** *v.t.* **ungraceful,** *a.* not graceful; clumsy, inelegant. **ungracefully,** *adv.* **ungracefulness,** *n.* **ungracious,** *a.* wanting in graciousness; discourteous, rude, unmannerly, offensive. **ungraciously,** *adv.* **ungraduated,** *a.* **ungrammatical,** *a.* not according to the rules of grammar. **ungrammatically,** *adv.* **ungrateful,** *a.* **ungratefully,** *adv.* **ungratefulness,** *n.* **ungratified,** *a.* **ungroomed,** *a.* **ungrounded,** *a.* unfounded, baseless. **ungrudging,** *a.* **ungrudgingly,** *adv.* **unguarded,** *a.* not guarded; careless, incautious; incautiously said or done. **unguardedly,** *adv.*

unguent, *n.* any soft composition used as an ointment

or for lubrication. **unguentary,** *a.* [L *unguentum,* from *unguere,* to anoint, pres.p. *unguens -entis*]

unguis, *n.* (*pl.* **gues**), a nail, claw or hoof; the narrow base of a petal. **ungual,** *a.* of, pertaining to, or having a nail, claw, or hoof. **unguicular, unguiculated, unguiferous, unguiform,** *a.* [L *unguis*]

ungula, *n.* (*pl.* **-lae,**) a hoof, claw or talon; (*Surg.*) a hook-shaped instrument for extracting a dead foetus from the womb; (*Math.*) the portion of a cone or cylinder included between the base and a plane intersecting it obliquely. **ungular,** *a.* **Ungulata,** *n.pl.* a division of mammals comprising those with hoofs. **ungulate,,** *a.* hoofed; hoof-shaped; belonging to the Ungulata; *n.* an ungulate animal. [L, dim. of *unguis,* see UNGUIS]

un- (cont.) **ungum,** *v.t.* to loosen (a thing fastened with gum); to remove the gum from. **unhackneyed,** *a.* **unhair,** *v.t.* **unhallow,** *v.t.* to profane, to desecrate. **unhallowed,** *a.* **unhampered,** *a.* **unhand,** *v.t.* to take the hand or hands off; to let go from one's grasp. **unhandsome,** *a.* not handsome; not generous, petty, ungracious. **unhandsomely,** *adv.* **unhandsomedness,** *n.* **unhandy,** *a.* not handy; clumsy, awkward, inconvenient. **unhandily,** *adv.* **unhandiness,** *n.* **unhang,** *v.t.* to take from a hanging position; to strip of hangings. **unhanged, unhung,** *a.* not hanged; not punished by hanging. **unhappy,** *a.* not happy, miserable, wretched; unlucky, unfortunate; inappropriate. **unhappily,** *adv.* **unhappiness,** *n.* **unharmed,** *a.* **unharness,** *v.t.* to remove harness from; †to divest of armour. **unhasp,** *v.t.* to unfasten from the hasp. **unhat,** *v.t.* **unhatched,** *a.* not hatched (of eggs).

UNHCR, (*abbr.*) United Nations High Commission for Refugees.

un- (cont.) **unhealthful,** *a.* **unhealthfully,** *adv.* **unhealthfulness,** *n.* **unhealthy,** *a.* not enjoying or promoting good health; (*coll.*) dangerous. **unhealthily,** *adv.* **unhealthiness,** *n.* **unheard,** *a.* not heard. **unheard of,** not heard of; unprecedented. **unheated,** *a.* **unheeded,** *a.* not heeded; disregarded, neglected. **unheedful,** *a.* **unheedfully,** *adv.* **unheeding,** *a.* †**unhelm,** *v.t.* to divest of a helm or helmet. **unhelpful,** *a.* **unhelpfully,** *adv.* **unhemmed,** *a.* **unheralded,** *a.* **unheroic,** *a.* **unhesitating,** *a.* **unhesitatingly,** *adv.* **unhidden,** *a.* **unhindered,** *a.* **unhinge,** *v.t.* to take (a door) off the hinges; to unsettle (the mind etc.). **unhinged,** *a.* **unhistoric, -ical,** *a.* **unhitch,** *v.t.* to unfasten or release from a hitch. **unhive,** *v.t.* **unholy,** *a.* not holy, not hallowed; impious, wicked; (*coll.*) hideous, frightful. **unholily,** *adv.* **unholiness,** *n.* **unhonoured,** *a.* **unhook,** *v.t.* to remove from a hook; to open or undo by disengaging the hooks of. **unhoop,** *v.t.* **unhoped,** *a.* not hoped (for); unexpected, beyond hope. **unhorse,** *v.t.* to remove from horseback; to take the horses out of. **unhouse,** *v.t.* to drive from a house; to deprive of shelter. **unhouseled,** *a.* not having received the eucharist. **unhuman,** *a.* not human. **unhurried,** *a.* **unhurt,** *a.* **unhusk,** *v.t.* **unhygienic,** *a.*

uni-,, *comb. form.* one; single. **uniarticulate** *a.* single-jointed. [L. *unus*]

Uniat, Uniate, *n.* a member of any community of Orthodox Christians acknowledging the supremacy of the Pope but retaining its own liturgy, rites and ceremonies. *a.* of or pertaining to the Uniats. [Rus. *uniyat,* from *uniya,* union, from L *unio*]

uni- (cont.) **uniaxial, -axial,** *a.* having a single axis. **uniaxially,** *adv.* **unicameral,** *a.* consisting of a single chamber (of a legislative body). **unicameralism,** *n.* **unicameralist,** *n.* **unicapsular,** *a.* (*Bot.*) having but a single capsule.

UNICEF, Unicef, (*acronym*) *U*nited *N*ations *I*nternational *C*hildren's *E*mergency *F*und (now called United Nations Children's Fund).

uni- (cont.) **unicellular** *a.* consisting of a single cell. **unicolour, -ed,** *a.* of one colour.

unicorn, *n.* a fabulous animal like a horse, with a long, straight, tapering horn; (*Bibl.*) a two-horned animal, perh. the urus (a mistranslation of Heb. *re'em*); (*Her.*) a one-horned horse with a goat's beard and lion's tail; a unicorn-fish, -bird, -beetle, -moth, or -shell; a coaching-team consisting of a pair of horses with a third horse in front. **sea-unicorn, unicorn-fish, -whale,** *n.* the narwhal, *Monodon monoceros*. **unicorn-beetle,** *n.* a large beetle with a single horn on the prothorax. **unicorn-bird,** *n.* the horned screamer. **unicorn-moth,** *n.* a North American moth the caterpillar of which has a horn-like prominence on the back. **unicorn-shell,** *n.* a gasteropod with a prominent spine on the tip of the shell. **unicornous,** *a.* one-horned. [A-F *unicorne,* L *ūnicorne* (UNI-, *cornu,* horn)]

unification, unifier UNIFY.

uni- (cont.) **uniflorous,** *a.* bearing but a single flower. **unifoliar, unifoliate, unifoliolate,** *a.* consisting of one leaf or leaflet.

uniform, *a.* having always one and the same form, appearance, quality, character etc., always the same, not varying, not changing, homogeneous; conforming to one rule or standard, applying or operating without variation for time or place. *n.* a dress of the same kind and appearance as that worn by other members of the same body, esp. the regulation dress of soldiers, sailors etc. **uniformed,** *a.* dressed in uniform. **uniformity,** *n.* the quality or state of being uniform; consistency, sameness. **Act of Uniformity,** an Act, esp. that of 1662, prescribing the form of public prayers, administration of the sacraments, and other rites in the Church of England. **Uniformitarian,** *n.* one who believes that there has been essential uniformity of cause and effect throughout the physical history of the world, opp. to catastrophism. **Uniformitarianism,** *n.* **uniformly,** *adv.* [F *uniforme,* L *ūniformis* (UNI-, -FORM)]

unify, *v.t.* to make a unit of; to regard as one; to reduce to uniformity. **unification,** *n.* **Unification Church,** *n.* church founded in Korea in 1954 by the Reverend Sun Myung Moon. World membership is about 200,000. The theology unites Christian and Taoist ideas, and is based on Moon's book *Divine Principle* which teaches that the original purpose of creation was to set up a perfect family, in a perfect relationship with God. **unifier,** *n.* [med. L *ūnificāre* (UNI-, L *-ficāre, facere,* to make)]

Unigenitus, *n.* the bull of Clement XI, condemning Jansenism (1713), named from its initial word. **unigenital,** *a.* only-begotten. [mod. L, only-begotten (UNI-, L *genitus,* p.p. of *gignere,* to beget, cp. GENIUS]

uni- (cont.) **unilabiate,** *a.* having a single lip (of flowers). **unilateral,** *a.* arranged on or turned towards one side only; applied by one side or party only. **unilateralism, unilateralist, unilaterally,** *adv.* **uniliteral,** *a.* consisting of only one letter.

un- (cont.) **unilluminated,** *a.* not illuminated; dark; ignorant. **unillumined,** *a.* **unillustrated,** *a.*

uni- (cont.) **unilocular, -loculate,** *a.* having or consisting of a single cell or chamber.

un- (cont.) **unimaginable,** *a.* that cannot be imagined; inconceivable. **unimaginably,** *adv.* **unimaginative,** *a.* **unimaginativeness,** *n.* **unimagined,** *a.* **unimpaired,** *a.* **unimpassioned,** *a.* **unimpeachable,** *a.* **unimpeachability, unimpeachableness,** *n.* **unimpeached,** *a.* **unimpeded,** *a.* **unimportance,** *n.* **unimportant,** *a.* **unimposing,** *a.* **unimpressionable,** *a.* **unimpressed,** *a.* **unimpressive,** *a.* **unimpressively,** *adv.* **unimpressiveness,** *n.* **unimproved,** *a.* not improved; not tilled. **unimproving,** *a.* **unimpugned,** *a.* **unindexed,** *a.* **unindicated,** *a.* **uninflammable,** *a.* **uninflated,** *a.* **uninflicted,** *a.* **uninfluenced, uninfluential,** *a.* **uninformative,** *a.* **uninformed,** *a.* not informed (about); ignorant generally. **uninhabitable,** *a.* **uninhabited,** *a.* **uninhibited,** *a.* **uninitiated,** *a.* **uninjured,** *a.* **uninspired,** *a.* **uninspiring,** *a.* **uninstigated,** *a.* **uninstructed,** *a.* **uninstructive,** *a.* **uninstructively,** *adv.* **uninsulated,** *a.* **uninsurable,** *a.* **uninsured,** *a.* **unintelligent,** *a.* **unintelligently,** *adv.* **unintelligible,** *a.* **unintelligibility,** *n.* **unintelligibly,** *adv.* **unintentional,** *a.* **unintentionally,** *adv.* **uninterested,** *a.* not taking any interest. **uninteresting,** *a.* **uninterestingly,** *adv.* **unin- termittent,** *a.* **unintermittently,** *adv.*

unintermitting, *a.* **unintermittingly,** *adv.* **uninterpretable,** *a.* **uninterred,** *a.* **uninterrupted,** *a.* **uninterruptedly,** *adv.*

uni- (cont.) **uninuclear, uninucleate,** *a.*

un- (cont.) **uninventive,** *a.* **uninventively,** *adv.* **uninvestigated,** *a.* **uninvited,** *a.* **uninviting,** *a.* not inviting, not attractive, repellent. **uninvitingly,** *adv.* **uninvoked,** *a.* **uninvolved,** *a.*

Union, Act of, act of 1707 that brought about the union of England and Scotland; that of 1801 united England and Ireland. The latter was revoked when the Irish Free State was constituted in 1922.

union, *n.* the act of uniting; the state of being united; marriage; junction, coalition; a trade-union; agreement or concord of mind, will, affection, or interests; a combination of parts or members forming a whole, an amalgamation, a confederation, a league; the unit formed by such a political combination, esp. the UK, US, USSR; a students' club; (*Med.*) the growing together of parts separated by injury; (*Hist.*) two or more parishes consolidated for administration of the Poor Laws; a workhouse established by this; an amalgamation of parishes for ecclesiastical control; an association of non-conformist (esp. Congregational or Baptist) Churches for cooperative action or management; in plumbing, a device for connecting pipes; a fabric made of two different yarns, as linen and cotton; (*UK*) a device emblematic of union borne in the upper corner next the staff of a flag; this used as a flag, called a **union jack** or **union flag. Union Movement,** *n.* British political group. Founded as the New Party by Sir Oswald Mosley and a number of Labour Members of Parliament in 1931, it developed into the British Union of Fascists in 1932. In 1940 the organization was declared illegal and its leaders interned, but at the end of World War II it was revived as the Union Movement, characterized by racist doctrines including anti-Semitism. **union suit,** *n.* (*N Am.*) an undergarment combining vest and long pants, men's combinations. **unionism,** *n.* the principle of combining, esp. the system of combination among workmen engaged in the same occupation or trade, and (*Polit.*) the principles of the Unionist party. **unionist,** *n.* a member of a trade-union; a promoter or advocate of trade-unionism; a member of a political party formed to uphold the legislative union between Great Britain and Ireland and to oppose Home Rule; (*N Am.*) an opponent of secession before and during the American Civil War. **unionistic,** *a.* **unionize, -ise,** *v.t.* to organize into a trade-union. **unionization, isation,** *n.* [F, from late L *unio -ōnem,* from *ūnus,* one]

Union of Soviet Socialist Republics, a country in N Asia and E Europe, stretching from the Baltic Sea and the Black Sea to the Arctic and Pacific oceans. **area** 22,274,500 sq km/8,600,184 sq miles. **capital** Moscow. **towns** Kiev, Tashkent, Kharkov, Gorky, Novosibirsk, Minsk, Sverdlovsk, Kuibyshev, Chelyabinsk, Dnepropetrovsk, Tbilisi; ports Leningrad, Odessa, Baku, Archangel, Murmansk, Vladivostok, Vostochny, Rostov. **physical** the Ural Mountains separate the European from the Asian plain; the Caucasus Mountains are in the south between the Black Sea and the Caspian Sea, and there are mountain ranges in the south and east of the Asiatic part; the USSR covers one-sixth of the Earth's land mass and contains forest, tundra, marsh, steppe, and desert. **population** (1988) 284,500,000 (two-thirds living in towns, and of 125 different nationalities; 52% Russian, 17% Ukrainian); annual growth rate 1%. **exports** cotton, timber, iron, steel, non-ferrous metals, electrical equipment, machinery, arms, oil and natural gas and their products, asbestos, gold, manganese. The USSR has 58% of world coal reserves, 59% of oil, 41% iron, 88% manganese, 54% potassium salts, 30% phosphates (55% of trade is with communist countries). **language** Slavic (Russian, Ukrainian, Byelorussian, Polish), Altaic (Turkish, Mongolian, and others), other Indo-European, Uralian, Caucasian. **religion** 'freedom of conscience' is guaranteed under the constitution, but religious belief is discouraged and considered incompatible with party membership (17,500,000 members); the largest Christian denomination is the Orthodox Church (30 million), but the largest religious sect is Sunni Muslim (40 million), making the USSR the fifth largest Muslim nation; Jews 2,500,000

uni- (cont.) **uniparous,** *a.* bringing forth normally but one at a birth; (*Bot.*) having one axis or stem. **unipartite,** *a.* not divided. **uniped,** *a.* having only one foot. *n.* a one-footed animal. **unipersonal,** *a.* existing in one person (of the Deity); (*Gram.*) used only in one person. **uniplanar,** *a.* lying or occurring in one plane. **unipolar,** *a.* having but one pole (of nerve-cells etc.); (*Elec.*) exhibiting but one kind of polarity. **unipolarity,** *n.*

unique, *a.* having no like or equal; unmatched, unparalleled. *n.* a unique person or thing. **uniquely,** *adv.* **uniqueness,** *n.* [F, from L *ūnicus,* as prec.]

uni- (cont.) **uniradiate(d),** *a.* having only one ray or arm. **uniserial,** *a.* (*Bot.*) arranged in one row. **unisex,** *a.* that can be used, worn, etc., by both sexes. **unisexual,** *a.* of one sex only; not hermaphrodite, having only one kind of sexual organs, stamens or pistils. **unisexually,** *adv.*

un- (cont.) **unisolated** *a.* not isolated.

unison, *n.* (*Mus.*) coincidence of sounds proceeding from equality in rate of vibrations, unity of pitch; an interval of one or more octaves; the act or state of sounding together at the same pitch; concord, agreement, harmony. *a.* sounding together; coinciding in pitch; sounding alone. **unisonal, -nant, -nous,** *a.* **unisonance,** *n.* [MF *unisson,* med. L *ūnisonus* (UNI-, *sonus,* SOUND2)]

uni- (cont.) **unisulcate,** *a.* having but one groove or furrow.

unit, *n.* a single person, thing, or group, regarded as one and individual for the purposes of calculation; each one of a number of things, persons etc., forming a plurality; a quantity adopted as the standard of measurement or calculation; a part of a machine which performs a particular function; a piece of furniture which forms part of a set, designed for a particular use in a kitchen etc.; a part of a larger military formation; a quantity of a drug, vitamin etc., which produces a specific effect. **unit price,** *n.* the price of a commodity expressed per unit of weight, volume etc. **unit trust,** *n.* an investment company which purchases holdings in a range of different enterprises and allocates proportions of these holdings according to the amount invested; a quantity represented by the number one. **Unitarian,** *n.* a member of a Christian body that rejects the doctrine of the Trinity; a monotheist; one who advocates unity or unification, esp. in politics. *a.* pertaining to the Unitarians. **Unitarianism,** *n.* **Unitarianize, -ise,** *v.t.* **unitary,** *a.* of or pertaining to a unit or units; of the nature of a unit, whole, integral; (*Phil.*) monistic. **unitism,** *n.* monism. **unitize, -ise,** *v.t.* [short for UNITY]

UNITA, (*acronym*) *U*nião *N*acional por *I*ndependência *T*otal de *A*ngola (National Union for the Total Independence of Angola), an Angolan nationalist movement backed by South Africa, which continued to wage guerrilla warfare against the ruling MPLA regime after the latter gained control of the country in 1976.

Unitarianism, *n.* a Christian denomination that rejects the orthodox doctrine of the Trinity, asserts the fatherhood of God and the brotherhood of man, and gives a pre-eminent position to Jesus as a religious teacher, while denying his deity.

unite, *v.t.* to join together so as to make one; to combine, to conjoin, to amalgamate; to cause to adhere, to attach together. *v.i.* to become one; to become consolidated, to combine, to coalesce, to agree, to co-operate. **United Artists,** *n.* Hollywood film studio formed in 1919 by silent-screen stars Charles Chaplin, Mary Pickford, and Douglas Fairbanks, and director D. W. Griffiths, in order to take control of their artistic and financial affairs. Smaller than the other major studios, UA concentrated on producing adaptations of literary works in the 1930s and 1940s, including *Wuthering Heights* (1939), *Rebecca* (1940), and *Major Barbara* (1941). The company nearly collapsed after the box-office disaster of Michael Cimino's *Heaven's Gate* (1980), and UA was subsequently bought by MGM. **United Australia Party,** Australian political party formed by J. A. Lyons in 1931 from the right-wing Nationalist Party. It was led by Robert Menzies after the death of Lyons. Considered to have become too dominated by financial interests, it lost heavily to the Labor Party in 1943, and was reorganized as the Liberal Party in 1944. **United Brethren,** *n.pl.* the Moravians. **United Democratic Front,** moderate political organization in South Africa, formed in the 1980s. It was the main focus of anti-apartheid action within South Africa until 1989, while the African National Congress and Pan-Africanist Congress were illegal. **United Free Church,** a Presbyterian church in Scotland formed in 1900 by the union of the Free Church of Scotland and the United Presbyterian Church. It was united with the Church of Scotland in 1929. **United Irishmen,** *n.* a society formed in 1791 by Wolfe Tone to campaign for parliamentary reform in Ireland. It later became a secret revolutionary group. **United Nations,** *n. sing. or pl.* an association of states (successor to the League of Nations) for international peace, security, and cooperation, with its headquarters in New York. Its charter was drawn up at the San Francisco Conference 1945, based on proposals drafted at the Dumbarton Oaks conference. The original intention was that the UN's Security Council would preserve the wartime alliance of the US, USSR, and Britain (with France and China also permanent members) in order to maintain the peace. This never happened because of the outbreak of the Cold War, but the UN has played a role in many other areas such as refugees, development assistance, disaster relief, and cultural cooperation. **United Provinces,** *n. sing. or pl.* Holland, Zealand, Utrecht, Guelderland, Groningen, Friesland and Overyssel united in 1579 in the Union of Utrecht. **United Reformed,** *a.* of a church formed in 1972 from the union of the Presbyterian and Congregational churches in England and Wales. **United States,** see separate entry. **United States art,** *n.* painting and sculpture in the US from colonial times to the present. The unspoiled landscapes romantically depicted in the 18th and 19th cents. gave way to realistic city scenes in the 20th. Modern movements have flourished in the US, among them abstract expressionism and pop art. **unitedly,** *adv.* **uniter,** *n.* **unitive,** *a.* [L *ūnītus,* p.p of *ūnīre,* from *ūnus,* one]

United Arab Emirates, (UAE) federation of the emirates of Abu Dhabi, Ajman, Dubai, Fujairah, Sharjah, Umm al Qaiwain, Ras al Khaimah. **total area** 83,657 sq km/32,292 sq miles. **capital** Abu Dhabi. **towns** chief port Dubai. **physical** mainly desert; mountains in east. **population** (1986) 1,770,000 (10% are nomadic); annual growth rate 6.1%. **exports** oil, natural gas. **language** Arabic (official); Farsi, Hindi and Urdu are spoken by immigrant oilfield workers from Iran, India, and Pakistan. **religion** Muslim 90%, Christian, Hindu.

United Arab Republic, union formed 1958, broken 1961, between Egypt and Syria. Egypt continued to use the name after the breach until 1971.

United Kingdom, *n.* of Great Britain and Northern Ireland (UK), country in NW Europe off the coast of France. **area** 243,363 sq km/93,938 sq miles. **capital** London. **towns** Birmingham, Glasgow, Leeds, Sheffield, Liverpool, Manchester, Edinburgh, Bradford, Bristol, Belfast, Newcastle-upon-Tyne, Cardiff. **physical** land mass became separated from the European continent about 6000 BC; rolling landscape, becoming increasingly mountainous towards the north, with the Grampian Mountains in Scotland and Snowdon in Wales. Rivers include Thames and Severn. **population** (1985) 56,620,000; annual growth rate 0.1%. **exports** cereals, rape, sugar beet, potatoes, meat and meat products, poultry, dairy products, electronic and telecommunications equipment, engineering equipment and scientific instruments, North Sea oil and gas, petrochemicals, pharmaceuticals, fertilizers, film and television programmes; tourism is important. **religion** mainly Christian (Church of England and other Protestant sects with Roman Catholic minority); Jewish, Muslim, Hindu minorities. **language** English, Welsh, Gaelic.

United Kingdom Atomic Energy Authority, UK national authority, established in 1954, responsible for research and development of all nonmilitary aspects of nuclear energy. The authority also provides private industry with contract research and development, and specialized technical and advanced engineering services.

United Provinces of Central America, political union (1823–38) between the the Central American states of Costa Rica, El Salvador, Guatemala, Honduras, and Nicaragua. The union followed the break-up of the Spanish empire and was initially dominated by Guatemala. Its unity was more apparent than real, and the federation fell apart in 1838. Subsequent attempts at reunification foundered.

United States of America, *n.* (US), country in North America, extending from the Atlantic to the Pacific, bounded by Canada to the N and Mexico to the S, and including the outlying states of Alaska and Hawaii. **area** 9,391,900 sq km/3,626,213 sq miles. **capital** Washington DC. **towns** New York, Los Angeles, Chicago, Philadelphia, Detroit, San Francisco, Washington, Dallas, San Diego, San Antonio, Houston, Boston, Baltimore, Phoenix, Indianapolis, Memphis: all metropolitan areas over 2 million population. **physical** includes almost every kind of topography and vegetation; mountain ranges parallel with E and W coasts, and the Rocky Mountains separate rivers emptying into the Pacific from those flowing into the Gulf of Mexico; Great Lakes in north; rivers include Hudson, Mississippi, Missouri, Colorado, Columbia. **territories** the commonwealths of Puerto Rico, and Northern Marianas; the federated states of Micronesia; Guam, the US Virgin Islands, American Samoa, Wake Island, Midway Islands, Marshall Islands, Belau, and Johnston and Sand Islands. **population** (1985) 238,740,000 (ethnic minorities include 26,500,000 black, about 20,000,000 Hispanic, and 1,000,000 American Indians, of whom 50% concentrated in Arizona, California, New Mexico, North Carolina, Oklahoma); annual growth rate 0.9%. **language** English; largest minority language Spanish. **religion** 73 million Protestant, 50 million Roman Catholic, 6 million Jewish, 4 million Eastern Orthodox.

unity, *n.* the state or condition of being one or individual, oneness, as opp. to plurality or division; the state of being united, union; an agreement of parts or elements, harmonious interconnection, structural coherence; concord, agreement, harmony; a thing forming a coherent whole; (*Math.*) the number one, a factor that leaves unchanged the quantity on which it operates; (*Drama etc.*) the condition that the action of a play should be limited to the development of a single plot, that the supposed time should coincide with the actual duration of the play or to a single day, and that there should be no change of scene (called the three dramatic unities of action, time and place); (*Law*) a joint tenancy of two or more persons; joint possession by one person of two estates in the same property. [A-F *unité,* L *ūnitās -tātem,* from *ūnus,* one]

uni- (cont.) **univalent,** *a.* (*Chem.*) having a valency or combining power of one. **univalence, -ency,** *n.* **univalve,** *a.* having only one valve. *n.* a univalve mollusc. **univalvular,** *a.*

Universal, *n.* Hollywood film studio founded in 1915 by Carl Laemmle. Despite *All Quiet on the Western Front* (1930) being its most highly regarded film, the change-over to sound caused a decline in the studio's fortunes. In the 1970s–80s Universal emerged as one of the industry's leaders with box-office hits from the producer and director Steven Spielberg such as *ET the Extra-*

Terrestrial (1982) and *Back to the Future* (1985).

universal, *a.* of or pertaining to the whole world or all persons or things in the world or in the class under consideration; common to all cases, unlimited, all-embracing, general; applicable to all purposes or conditions; (*Log.*) predicable of all the individuals of a class, opp. to particular. *n.* (*Log.*) a universal proposition; (*Phil.*) a universal concept; a thing or nature predicable of many. **universal arithmetic,** *n.* algebra. **universal coupling,** or **joint,** *n.* a device for connecting two parts or things allowing freedom of movement in any direction. **universal time,** *n.* Greenwich Mean Time. **universalism,** *n.* the quality of being universal; (*Theol.*) the doctrine that all men will eventually be saved. **universalist,** *a.*, *n.* **universalistic,**, *a.* **universality,** †**universalness,** *n.* **universalize, -ise,** *v.t.* **universalization, -isation,** *n.* **universally,** *adv.* [F *universel,* L *ūniversālis,* as foll.]

Universal Postal Union, an agency of the United Nations responsible for collaboration of postal services. It was first established in 1875, with headquarters in Berne, Switzerland.

universe, *n.* the aggregate of existing things; all created things viewed as constituting one system or whole, the cosmos, including or excluding the Creator; all mankind; (*Log.*) all the objects that are the subjects of consideration. **universology,** *n.* the science dealing with everything in the universe, or with all pertaining to human relations etc. **universological,** *a.* **universologist,**, *n.* [F *univers,* L *ūniversus,* (UNI-, *versus,* p.p. of *vertere,* to turn)]

university, *n.* an educational institution for both instruction and examination in the higher branches of knowledge with the power to confer degrees, usu. comprising subordinate colleges, schools etc.; the members of this collectively; (*coll.*) a team or crew representing a university, as distinguished from a college team etc. **University Extension** EXTENSION. [A-F *université,* a school for universal knowledge, L *ūniversitās -tātem,* a whole, a universe, from prec.]

uni- (cont.) **univocal,** *a.* having only one meaning (of a word); (*Mus.*) having unison of sounds. **univocally,** *adv.* **univocation,** *n.* agreement of name and meaning.

Unix, *n.* an operating system designed for minicomputers but becoming increasingly popular on large microcomputers, workstations and supercomputers. It was developed by Bell Laboratories in the late 1960s, and is closely related to the programming language C. Its wide range of functions and flexibility have made it widely used by universities and in commercial software.

un- (cont.) **unjoin,** *v.t.* to disjoin. **unjoint,** *v.t.* to disjoint, to separate the joints. **unjust,** *a.* not just; not conformable to justice. **unjustly,** *adv.* **unjustifiable,** *a.* **unjustifiableness,** *n.* **unjustifiably,** *adv.* **unjustified,** *a.*

unkempt, *a.* uncombed; rough, unpolished. [ME *kempt, kembed,* p.p. of *kemben,* OE *cemban,* to comb]

un- (cont.) **unkennel,** *v.t.* to release or drive out from a kennel; to let loose. **unkind,** *a.* not kind, harsh, hard, cruel. **unkindly,** *adv.* **unkindness,** *n.* **unking,** *v.t.* **unkingly,** *a.* **unkink,** *v.t.*, *v.i.* **unkneaded,** *a.* **unknightly,** *a.* **unknightliness,** *n.* **unknit,** *v.t.* **unknot,** *v.t.* **unknowable,** *a.* **unknowability, unknowableness,** *n.* **unknowably,** *adv.* **unknowing,** *a.* not knowing; ignorant or unaware (of). **unknowingly,** *adv.* **unknown,** *a.* not known; untold, incalculable, inexpressible; (*Math.*) unascertained (of quantities in equations etc.). *n.* an unknown person, thing or quantity. **Unknown Soldier,** *n.* an unidentified soldier whose body is buried in a memorial as a symbol of all soldiers killed in war. **unlabelled,** *a.* **unlaboured,** *a.* not produced by labour, untilled, unworked; spontaneous, natural, easy (of style etc.). **unlace,** *v.t.* to loose or unfasten by undoing the lace or laces of. **unlade,** *v.t.* **unladylike,** *a.* **unlaid,** *a.* not laid; not having parallel watermarks (of paper); not suppressed. **unlamented,** *a.* **unlash,** *v.t.* (*Naut.*) to unfasten (something lashed). **unlatch,** *v.t.* to unfasten the latch of (a door etc.). **unlawful,** *a.* **unlawfully,** *adv.* **unlawfulness,** *n.* **unlay,** *v.t.* (*Naut.*) to untwist rope etc. **unleaded,** *a.* of petrol, without added lead compounds. **unlearn,** *v.t.* to forget the knowledge of; to expel from the mind (that which has been learned), to get rid of (a vice etc.). **unlearned**[1], **-learnt,** *a.* not learnt. **unlearned**[2], *a.* not learned. **unlearnedly,** *adv.* **unlearnedness,** *n.* **unleash,** *v.t.* **unleavened,** *a.*

unless, *conj.* if it be not the case that; except when. [formerly *onless*72(ON, LESS)]

un- (cont.) **unlettered,** *a.* illiterate. **unliberated,** *a.* **unlicensed,** *a.* **unlicked,** *a.* not licked into shape; unmannered, rough, rude. **unlike,** *a.* not like; dissimilar; †improbable. *prep.* not like; not characteristic of. **unlik(e)able,** *a.* **unlikeness,** *n.* **unlikely,** *a.* improbable; unpromising. *adv.* improbably. **unlikelihood, unlikeliness,** *n.* **unlimber,** *v.t.* **unlimited,** *a.* not limited; having no bounds, indefinite, unmeasured, unnumbered; unconfined, unrestrained. **unlimitedly,** *adv.* **unlimitedness,** *n.* **unline,** *v.t.* to remove the lining from. **unlined,** *a.* without lines. **unlink,** *v.t.* **unliquidated,** *a.* **unlisted,** *a.* not on a list; of securities, not listed on the Stock Exchange; (*N Am.*) of a telephone number, ex-directory. **unlit,** *a.* **unlived-in,** *a.* not lived in; over-tidy. **unload,** *v.t.* to discharge the load from; to discharge (a load); to withdraw the charge from (a gun etc.); *v.i.* to discharge a load or freight; **unloader,** *n.* **unlocated,** *a.* **unlock,** *v.t.* to unfasten the lock of (a door, box etc.); to disclose. **unlodge,** *v.t.* to dislodge. **unlooked-for,** *a.* not looked for, unexpected. **unloose,** *v.t.* to unfasten, to loose; to set at liberty. **unloosen,** *v.t.* **unlopped,** *a.* **unlord,** *v.t.* **unlovable,** *a.* **unloved,** *a.* **unlovely,** *a.* not lovely; not beautiful or attractive. **unloveliness,** *n.* **unloverlike,** *a.* **unloving,** *a.* **unlovingly,** *adv.* **unlucky,** *a.* not lucky or fortunate; unsuccessful, unfortunate; disastrous; inauspicious, ill-omened. **unluckily,** *adv.* **unluckiness,** *n.* **unmade,** *a.* **unmaidenly,** *a.* **unmailable,** *a.* incapable of being sent by post. **unmaimed,** *a.* **unmaintainable,** *a.* **unmake,** *v.t.* (*past, p.p.* **-made**) to destroy; to annihilate; to depose. **unmalleable,** *a.* **unmalleability,** *n.* **unman,** *v.t.* (*past, p.p.* **-manned**) to deprive of courage or fortitude; to deprive of men; to deprive of maleness or manly qualities. **unmanageable,** *a.* not manageable; not easily controlled. **unmanful,** *a.* **unmanfully,** *adv.* **unmanlike,** *a.* not like a man; effeminate, childish. **unmanly,** *a.* **unmanliness,** *n.* **unmanned,** *a.* not manned, having no crew. **unmannered,** *a.* without mannerism; lacking good manners. **unmannerly,** *a.* not mannerly; rude, ill-bred. **unmannerliness,** *n.* **unmantle,** *v.t.* **unmarked,** *a.* not marked; not noticed, unobserved. **unmarketable,** *a.* **unmarriageable,** *a.* **unmarriageableness,** *n.* **unmarried,** *a.* **unmartial,** *a.* **unmasculine,** *a.* **unmask,** *v.t.* to remove the mask from; to expose. *v.i.* to take one's mask off; to reveal one-self. **unmasticable,** *a.* **unmatchable,** *a.* **unmatched,** *a.* **unmated,** *a.* **unmatured,** *a.* **unmeaning,** *a.* having no meaning; senseless; expressionless, vacant. **unmeaningly,** *adv.* **unmeaningness,** *n.* **unmeant,** *a.* not meant, not intended. **unmeasured,** *a.* not measured; indefinite, unlimited, unmeasurable. **unmechanical,** *a.* **unmechanized, -ised,** *a.* †**unmeet,** *a.* not meet, not suitable (for, to do etc.). †**unmeetly,** *adv.* †**unmeetness,** *n.* **unmelodious,** *a.* **unmelodiously,** *adv.* **unmelodiousness,** *n.* **unmelted,** *a.* **unmemorable,** *a.* **unmendable,** *a.* **unmentionable,** *a.* not mentionable, not fit to be mentioned. *n.pl.* (*facet.*) trousers; underwear. **unmentionableness,** *n.* **unmerchantable,** *a.* **unmerciful,** *a.* **unmercifully,** *adv.* **unmercifulness,** *n.* **unmerited,** *a.* **unmethodical,** *a.* **unmetrical,** *a.* not metrical; not according to the rules or requirements of metre. **unmetrically,** *adv.* **unmew,** *v.t.* (*poet.*) to release from confinement etc.; to set free. **unmilitary,** *a.* **unmindful,** *a.* not mindful, heedless (of). **unmindfully,** *adv.* **unmindfulness,** *n.* **unminted,** *a.* **unmirthful,** *a.* **unmirthfully,** *adv.* **unmistakable,** *a.* that cannot be mistaken; manifest, plain. **unmistakably,** *adv.* **unmistaken,** *a.* **unmiti-**

gated, *a.* not mitigated; unqualified, unconscionable. **unmixed,** *a.* **unmodern,** *a.* **unmodernized, -ised,** *a.* **unmodified,** *a.* **unmodulated,** *a.* **unmolested,** *a.* **unmonk,** *v.t.* **unmoor,** *v.t.* to loose the moorings of, to unanchor; to release partially by weighing one of two or more anchors. *v.i.* to weigh anchor. **unmoral,** *a.* non-moral. **unmorality,** *n.* **unmortgaged,** *a.* **unmortise,** *v.t.* **unmotherly,** *a.* **unmotivated,** *a.* lacking in motive or incentive. **unmould,** *v.t.* to change the form of. **unmounted,** *a.* not on horseback; not mounted (of) a drawing, gem etc.). **unmourned,** *a.* **unmoved,** *a.* not moved; not changed in purpose, unshaken, firm; not affected, not having the feelings excited. **unmoving,** *a.* motionless; unaffecting. **unmown,** *a.* **unmuffle,** *v.t.* to remove a muffler from. *v.i.* to remove a muffler from one's face etc. **unmurmuring,** *a.* not complaining. **unmurmuringly,** *adv.* **unmusical,** *a.* not pleasing to the ear, discordant; not interested or skilled in music. **unmusicality,** *n.* **unmusically,** *adv.* **unmutilated,** *a.* **unmuzzle,** *v.t.* **unnail,** *v.t.* **unnameable,** *a.* **unnamed,** *a.* **unnational,** *a.* **unnatural,** *a.* not natural; contrary to nature; not in accordance with accepted standards of behaviour; monstrous, inhuman; artificial, forced, strained, affected. **unnaturalize, -ise,** *v.t.* to make unnatural. **unnaturalized, -ised,** *a.* not naturalized, alien. **unnaturally,** *adv.* **unnaturalness,** *n.* **unnavigable,** *a.* **unnecessary,** *a.* not necessary; needless, superfluous. *n.* (*usu. in pl.*) that which is unnecessary. **unnecessarily,** *adv.* **unneeded,** *a.* **unneedful,** *a.* **unnegotiable,** *a.* **unneighbourly,** *a.* **unneighbourliness,** *n.* **unnerve,** *v.t.* to deprive of nerve, strength or resolution. **unnerved,** *a.* **unnest,** *v.t.* **unnoted,** *a.* not heeded. **unnoticed,** *a.* **unnourished,** *a.* **unnumbered,** *a.* not marked with numbers; countless.

UNO, (*abbr.*) United Nations Organization.

Uno, *n.* **Sosuke,** Japanese Liberal Democrat politician. Having held various cabinet posts since 1976, he was designated prime minister in June 1989 in an attempt to restore the image of the Liberal Democrats after several scandals. He resigned after only a month in office when his affairs with geishas and prostitutes became public knowledge.

un- (cont.) **unobjectionable,** *a.* **unobjectionably,** *adv.* **unobliging,** *a.* **unobliterated,** *a.* **unobscured,** *a.* **unobservant,** *a.* **unobserved,** *a.* **unobserving,** *a.* **unobstructed,** *a.* **unobtainable,** *a.* **unobtrusive,** *a.* **unobtrusively,** *adv.* **unobtrusiveness,** *n.* **unoccupied,** *a.* **unoffending,** *a.* not offending; harmless, innocent. **unoffered,** *a.* **unofficial,** *a.* not having official character or authorization. **unofficially,** *adv.* **unofficinal,** *a.* **unopened,** *a.* **unopposed,** *a.* **unordained,** *a.* **unorganized, -ised,** *a.* not organized or arranged; not unionized. **unoriginal,** *a.* not original, derived; not possessed of originality. **unoriginated,** *a.* **unornamental,** *a.* not ornamental; plain, ugly. **unornamented,** *a.* **unorthodox,** *a.* **unostentatious,** *a.* **unostentatiously,** *adv.* **unostentatiousness,** *n.* **unowned,** *a.* **unpacified,** *a.* **unpack,** *v.t.* to open and take out the contents of; to take (things) out of a package etc. **unpaged,** *a.* not having the pages numbered. **unpaid,** *a.* not paid, not discharged (of a debt etc.); not having received the payment due; acting gratuitously. **the great unpaid,** unpaid magistrates etc. **unpaid for,** not paid for; taken on credit. **unpainted,** *a.* **unpaired,** *a.* not paired, not matched. **unpalatable,** *a.* **unpalatably,** *adv.* **unparalleled,** *a.* not paralleled; unequalled, unprecedented. **unpardonable,** *a.* **unpardonableness,,** *n.* **unpardonably,** *adv.* **unpared,** *a.***unparental,** *a.* **unparented,** *a.* **unparliamentary,** *a.* contrary to the rules or usages of Parliament (esp. of language). **unparliamentarily,** *adv.* **unparliamentariness,** *n.* **unpasteurized, -ised,** *a.* **unpatented,** *a.* **unpatriotic,** *a.* **unpatriotically,** *adv.* **unpatronized, -ised,** *a.* **unpaved,** *a.* **unpawned,** *a.* **unpeaceful,** *a.* **unpedantic,** *a.* **unpedigreed,** *a.* **unpeeled,** *a.* **unpeg,** *v.t.* to take out the pegs from; to open or unfasten thus. **unpen,** *v.t.* **unpensioned,** *a.* **unpeople,** *v.t.* to empty of inhabitants. **unperceived,** *a.* **unperch,** *v.t.* to drive from a perch. **unperforated,** *a.* **unperformed,** *a.* **unperfumed,** *a.* **unperjured,** *a.* **unperson,** *n.* a person whose existence is officially ignored or denied. **unpersuadable,** *a.* **unpersuaded,** *a.* **unpersuasive,** *a.* **unperturbed,** *a.* **unperused,** *a.* not perused; not read through. **unperverted,** *a.* **unphilosophical,** *a.* not in a philosophic way; lacking philosophy. **unphilosophically,***adv.* **unphilosophicalness,** *n.* **unpick,** *v.t.* to loosen, take out, or open, by picking; to unfasten or open with a pick. **unpicked,** *a.* not picked; not picked out or selected. **unpicturesque,** *a.* **unpiloted,** *a.* **unpin,** *v.t.* to remove the pins from; to unfasten (something held together by pins). **unpitied,** *a.* **unpitying,** *a.* **unpityingly,** *adv.* **unplaced,** *a.* not placed; not holding a place, esp. under government; not among the first three at the finish of a race. **unplagued,** *a.* **unplait,** *v.t.* **unplaned,** *a.* **unplanned,** *a.* **unplanted,** *a.* **unplastered,** *a.* **unplastic,** *a.* **unplated,** *a.* **unplausible,** *a.* **unplausibly,** *adv.* **unplayable,** *a.* **unpleasant,** *a.* not pleasant; disagreeable. **unpleasantly,** *adv.* **unpleasantness,** *n.* the quality of being unpleasant; a slight disagreement. **unpleased,** *a.* **unpleasing,** *a.* **unpleasingly,** *adv.* **unpledged,** *a.* **unpliable,** *a.* **unpliably,** *adv.* **unpliant,** *a.* **unpliantly,** *adv.* **unploughed** , *a.* **unplucked,** *a.* **unplug,** *v.t.* to remove a plug or obstruction from; to disconnect (an electrical appliance) from a source of electricity. **unplumbed,** *a.* **unpoetic, -ical,** *a.* **unpoetically,** *adv.* **unpoeticalness,** *n.* **unpointed,** *a.* not having a point; not punctuated; not having the vowel-points or diacritical marks; not pointed (of masonry). **unpolished,** *a.* **unpolitical,** *a.* not related to or interested in politics. **unpolled,** *a.* not polled, not having registered one's vote. **unpolluted,** *a.* **unpopular,** *a.* not popular; not enjoying the public favour. **unpopularity,** *n.* **unpopularly,** *adv.* **unportioned,** *a.* not portioned, portionless. **unposed,** *a.* **unpossessed,** *a.* not possessed; not in possession (of). **unposted,** *a.* not posted (of a letter etc.); not posted up; without information. **unpractical,** *a.* not practical (of a person, proposal etc.). **unpracticality,** *n.* **unpractically,** *adv.* **unpractised,** *a.* not put in practice; unskilful, inexperienced. **unpraised,** *a.* †**unpreach,** *v.t.* to recant (something preached). **unprecedented,** *a.* being without precedent, unparalleled; new. **unpredictable,** *a.* that cannot be predicted; whose behaviour cannot be predicted or relied on. **unpredicted,** *a.* **unprefaced,** *a.* **unprejudice,** *n.* freedom from prejudice. **unprejudiced,,** *a.* **unprelatical,** *a.* **unpremeditated,** *a.* not premeditated, not planned beforehand; unintentional. **unpremeditatedly,** *adv.* **unpreoccupied,** *a.* **unprepared,** *a.* not prepared, impromptu; not ready (for etc.). **unpreparedness,** *n.* **unprepossessing,** *a.* **unprescribed,** *a.* **unpresentable,** *a.* not presentable; not fit to be seen. **unpresuming,** *a.* **unpresumptuous,** *a.* **unpretending,** *a.* **unpretendingly,** *adv.* **unpretentious,** *a.* **unpretentiously,** *adv.* **unpretentiousness,** *n.* **unpreventable,** *a.* **unpriced,** *a.* having the price or prices not fixed, quoted or marked up; priceless. **unpriest,** *v.t.* to deprive of the character or position of a priest. **unpriestly,** *a.* **unprimed,** *a.* **unprince,** *v.t.* **unprincely,** *adv.* **unprincipled,** *a.* not dictated by moral principles; destitute of principle, immoral. **unprintable,** *a.* that cannot be printed (because obscene or libellous). **unprinted,** *a.* **unprivileged,** *a.* †**unprizable,** *a.* invaluable, inestimable; valueless; worthless, despised. **unprized,** *a.* **unprobed,** *a.* **unproclaimed,** *a.* **unprocurable,** *a.* **unproductive,** *a.* **unproductively,** *adv.* **unproductiveness,** *n.* **unprofaned,** *a.* **unprofessional,** *a.* not pertaining to one's profession; contrary to the rules or etiquette of a profession; not belonging to a profession. **unprofitable,** *a.* **unprofitableness,** *n.* **unprofitably,** *adv.* **unprogressive,** *a.* not progressive, conservative. **unprogressiveness,** *n.* **unprohibited,** *a.* **unprolific,** *a.* **unpromising,** *a.* not promising success. **unprompted,** *a.* of one's own free will or initiative. **unpromulgated,** *a.* **unpronounceable,** *a.* **unprop,** *v.t.* to deprive of support. **unpropagated,** *a.* **unprophetic,** *a.* **unpropi-**

tious, *a.* **unpropitiously,** *adv.* **unpropitiousness,** *n.* **unproportional,** *a.* not in proportion, disproportionate. **unproposed,** *a.* **unpropped,** *a.* **unprosperous,** *a.* **unprosperously,** *adv.* **unprosperousness,** *n.* **unprotected,** *a.* **unprotecting,** *a.* **unprotested,** *a.* **unprotesting,** *a.* **unprovable,** *a.* **unproved,** **†-proven,** *a.* **unprovided,** *a.* not provided; not furnished (with supplies etc.); †not prepared, not ready. **unprovoked,** *a.* having received no provocation; not instigated. **unpruned,** *a.* not pruned. **unpublished,** *a.* not made public; not published (of books etc.). **unpunctual,** *a.* **unpunctuality,** *n.* **unpunctually,** *adv.* **unpunctuated,** *a.* **unpunishable,** *a.* not punishable. **unpunished,** *a.* **unpurchasable,** *a.* **unpurchased,** *a.* **unpurified,** *a.* **unputdownable,** *a.* (*coll.*) of a book, too exciting to put down before it is finished. **unquailing,** *a.* **unquailingly,** *adv.* **unqualified,** *a.* not qualified; not fit, not competent; not having passed the necessary examination etc.; not qualified legally; not limited by conditions or exceptions, absolute. **unqualifiedly,** *adv.* **unquarried,** *a.* **unqueen,** *v.t.* to depose from the position of queen. **unquelled,** *a.* **unquenchable,** *a.* **unquenchably,** *adv.* **unquenched,** *a.* **unquestionable,** *a.* not to be questioned or doubted, indisputable. **unquestionably,** *adv.* **unquestioned,** *a.* not called in question, not doubted; having no questions asked, not interrogated. **unquestioning,** *a.* not questioning, not doubting; implicit. **unquestioningly,** *adv.* **unquiet,** *a.* restless, uneasy, agitated. **unquietly,** *adv.* **unquilted,** *a.* **unquotable,** *a.* **unquote,** *v.i.* to close a quotation. *int.* indicating the end of a (spoken) quotation. **unquoted,** *a.* **unransomed,** *a.* **unravaged,** *a.* **unravel,** *v.t.* to separate the threads of; to disentangle, to untwist; to solve, to clear up (the plot of a play etc.); †to throw into confusion or disorder. *v.i.* to be disentangled; to be opened up or revealed. **unravelment,** *n.* **unrazored,** *a.* unshaven; †beardless. **unreachable,** *a.* **unread,** *a.* not read; not well-read, unlearned, illiterate. **unreadable,** *a.* **unreadableness,** *n.* **unreadiness,** *n.* **unready**[1], *a.* not ready; not prompt to act, etc.

unready[2], *a.* badly or insufficiently advised (used as a nickname of Ethelred II (968–1016), king of England). [see REDE; assimilated to READY]

un- (cont.) **unreal,** *a.* not real; unsubstantial, visionary, imaginary. **unreality,** *n.* **unreally,** *adv.* **unrealizable, -isable,** *a.* **unrealized, -ised,** *a.* **unreaped,** *a.* **unreason,** *n.* want of reason; folly, absurdity. **unreasonable,** *a.* not reasonable; exorbitant, extravagant, absurd; not listening to reason; †irrational, brute. **unreasonableness,** *n.* **unreasonably,** *adv.* **unreasoned,** *a.* not reasoned or thought out rationally. **unreasoning,** *a.* not reasoning; foolish; not having reasoning faculties. **unreasoningly,** *adv.* **unrebuked,** *a.* **unrecallable,** *a.* **unrecanted,** *a.* **unreceived,** *a.* **unreciprocated,** *a.* **unreceptive,** *a.* **unreckoned,** *a.* **unreclaimed,** *a.* not reclaimed; unregenerate. **unrecognizable, -isable,** *a.* **unrecognizably, -isably,** *adv.* **unrecognized, -ised,** *a.* not recognized; not acknowledged. **unrecompensed,** *a.* **unreconciled,** *a.* **unreconstructed,** *a.* clinging to old-fashioned social or political notions. **unrecorded,** *a.* **unrectified,** *a.* not corrected. **unredeemed,** *a.* not redeemed, not fulfilled; not taken out of pawn; not recalled by payment of the value; not counterbalanced by any redeeming quality, unmitigated. **unredressed,** *a.* **unreel,** *v.t.* to unwind. *v.i.* to become unwound. **unreeve,** *v.t.* (*Naut.*) to withdraw a rope from a block, dead-eye etc.; *v.i.* to become unrove. **unrefined,** *a.* not refined; not purified; of unpolished manners, taste etc. **unreflecting,** *a.* **unreflectingly,** *adv.* **unreformable,** *a.* **unreformed,** *a.* **unrefreshed,** *a.* **unrefuted,** *a.* **unregal,** *a.* **unregarded,** *a.* **unregardful,** *a.* **unregenerate,** *a.* **unregistered,** *a.* **unregretted,** *a.* **unregulated,** *a.* not reduced to order. **unrehearsed,** *a.* **unreined,** *a.* not held in check by the rein; unrestrained, unbridled. **unrelated,** *a.* **unrelaxed,** *a.* **unrelaxing,** *a.* **unrelenting,** *a.* **unrelentingly,** *adv.* **unrelentingness,** *n.* **unreliable,** *a.* **unreliability, unreliableness,** *n.* **unreliably,** *adv.* **unrelieved,** *a.* **unreligious,** *a.* irreligious; not connected with religion, secular. **unremarkable,** *a.* **unremembered,** *a.* **unremitting,** *a.* not relaxing; incessant, continued. **unremittingly,** *adv.* **unremunerative,** *a.* not profitable. **unrenewed,** *a.* **unrenounced,** *a.* **unrepair,** *n.* disrepair, dilapidation. **unrepealed,** *a.* **unrepeatable,** *a.* that cannot be done or said again; of language, too foul to repeat. **unrepentant,** *a.* **unrepentance,** *n.* **unrepented,** *a.* **unrepining,** *a.* **unrepiningly,** *adv.* **unreplenished,** *a.* **unreported,** *a.* **unrepresentative,** *a.* **unrepresented,** *a.* **unrepressed,** *a.* **†unreproachable,** *a.* **unreproachful,** *a.* **unreproved,** *a.* **unrequited,** *a.* not requited; not recompensed. **unrescinded,** *a.* **unresented,** *a.* **unresenting,** *a.* **unresentingly,** *adv.* **unreserve,** *n.* lack of reserve, frankness, candour. **unreserved,** *a.* not reserved; open, frank; given, offered, or done without reservation. **unreservedly,** *adv.* **unreservedness,** *n.* **unresisted,** *a.* **unresisting,** *a.* **unresistingly,** *adv.* **unresolved,** *a.* not resolved, undecided, irresolute; unsolved, not cleared up. **unrespected,** *a.* **unrespited,** *a.* **unresponsive,** *a.* **unrest,** *n.* restlessness, agitation, disquiet, uneasiness, unhappiness. **unrestful,** *a.* **unrestfully,** *adv.* **unrestfulness,** *n.* **unresting,** *a.* **unrestingly,** *adv.* **unrestored,** *a.* **unrestrainable,** *a.* **unrestrainably,** *adv.* **unrestrained,** *a.* **unrestrainedly,**, *adv.* **unrestraint,** *n.* **unrestricted,** *a.* **unrestrictedly,** *adv.* **unretarded,** *a.* **unretentive,** *a.* **unretracted,** *a.* **unrevealed,** *a.* **unrevenged,** *a.* **unreversed,** *a.* **unrevised,** *a.* **unrevoked,** *a.* **unrewarded,** *a.* **unrewarding,** *a.* **unrhetorical,** *a.* **unrhymed,** *a.* **unrhythmic, -ical,** *a.* **unridable,** *a.* **unridden,** *a.* **unriddle,** *v.t.* to solve, to interpret, to explain. **unrifled,** *a.* not robbed or plundered; not rifled (of a gun etc.). **unrig,** *v.t.* to strip (a ship) of rigging. **†unright,** *n.* a wrong. *a.* unjust. **unrighted,** *a.* **unrighteous,** *a.* not righteous, not just; contrary to justice or equity; evil, wicked, sinful. **unrighteously,** *adv.* **unrighteousness,** *n.* **unrip,** *v.t.* to rip open, to undo or unfasten by ripping. **unripe,** *a.* not ripe; not mature; premature. **unripened,** *a.* **unripeness,** *n.* **unrivalled,** *a.* having no rival; unequalled, peerless. **unrivet,** *v.t.* **unrobe,** *v.t.*, *v.i.*. **unroll,** *v.t.* to unfold (a roll of cloth etc.); to display, to lay open. *v.i.* to be unrolled; to be displayed. **unromanize,** *v.t.* **unromantic,** *a.* **unromantically,** *adv.* **unroof,** *v.t.* to strip the roof off. **unroot,** *v.t.* to tear up by the roots; to extirpate, to eradicate. **unrounded,** *a.* **unroyal,** *a.* not royal; not becoming a sovereign. **unroyally,** *adv.*

UNRRA, (*abbr.*) United Nations Relief and Rehabilitation Administration.

unruffled, *a.* not ruffled, unperturbed. **unruled,** *a.* not governed; not ruled with lines (of paper etc.). **unruly,** *a.* not submitting to restraint; lawless, turbulent, ungovernable.

UNRWA, (*acronym*) *U*nited *N*ations *Re*lief and *W*orks *A*gency.

un- (cont.) **unsaddle,** *v.t.* to remove the saddle from; to unseat. *v.i.* to unsaddle one's horse. **unsafe,** *a.* dangerous, perilous, risky; not to be trusted. **unsafely,** *adv.* **unsafeness,** *n.* **unsaid,** *a.* not said, unspoken. **unsaintly,** *a.* **unsalaried,** *a.* **unsaleable,** *a.* **unsaleability, unsaleableness,** *n.* **unsalted,** *a.* **unsanctified,** *a.* **unsanctioned,** *a.* **unsanitary,** *a.* unhealthy. **unsated,** *a.* **unsatisfactory,** *a.* **unsatisfactorily,** *adv.* **unsatisfactoriness,** *n.* **unsatisfied,** *a.* **unsatisfying,** *a.* **unsatisfyingly,** *adv.* **unsaturated,** *a.* not saturated; of fats, having a high proportion of fatty acids containing double bonds. **unsaved,** *a.* **unsavoury,** *a.* unattractive, repellent, disgusting; †tasteless, insipid; morally offensive. **unsavourily,** *adv.* **unsavouriness,** *n.* **unsay,** *v.t.* to retract or withdraw (what has been said). **unsayable,** *a.* **unscalable,** *a.* that cannot be climbed. **unscannable,** *a.* that cannot be scanned. **unscared,** *a.* **unscarred,** *a.* **unscathed,** *a.* not scathed, uninjured. **unscented,** *a.* **unscheduled,** *a.* **unscholarly,** *a.* **unschooled,** *a.* **unscientific,** *a.* not in accordance with scientific principles or methods; lacking scientific knowledge. **unscientifically,** *adv.* **unscorched,** *a.* **unscoured,** *a.* **unscourged,** *a.* **unscramble,** *v.t.* to restore to order from a scrambled state; to make (a scrambled message) intelligible. **unscrambler,** *n.* **unscreened,** *a.* **unscrew,** *v.t.* to withdraw or loosen (a screw); to unfasten thus. **unscripted,** *a.* not using a script; unplanned unrehearsed. **unscriptural,** *a.* not in conformity with the Scriptures. **unscripturally,** *adv.* **unscrupulous,** *a.* having no scruples of conscience; unprincipled. **unscrupulously,** *adv.* **unscrupulousness,** *n.* **unsculptured,** *a.* not adorned with sculpture; bearing no inscription; (*Zool.*) smooth. **unseal,** *v.t.* to break or remove the seal of; to open. **unsealed,** *a.* not sealed; having the seal broken; (*Austral.*) of a road, metalled but not sealed with bitumen. **unseam,** *v.t.* to undo the seams of (a garment). **unsearchable,** *a.* incapable of being searched out, inscrutable. **unsearched,** *a.* **unseasonable,** *a.* **unseasonableness,** *n.* **unseasonably,** *adv.* **unseasoned,** *a.* **unseat,** *v.t.* to remove from one's seat; to throw from one's seat on horseback; to deprive of a parliamentary seat or political office. **unseated,** *a.* thrown from or deprived of a seat; not furnished with seats; having no seat. **unseaworthy,** *a.* **unseaworthiness,** *n.* **unseconded,** *a.* **unsectarian,** *a.* **unsectarianism,** *n.* **unsecured,** *a.* **unseduced,** *a.* **unseductive,** *a.* **unseeded,** *a.* in a sporting tournament, not put with the best players in the competition draw. **unseeing,** *a.* blind; unobservant, unsuspecting. †**unseel,** *v.t.* to open the eyes of (a hawk etc.); to enlighten. **unseem,** *v.i.* not to seem. **unseemly,** *a.* not seemly; unbefitting, unbecoming. †*adv.* in an unseemly manner. **unseemliness,** *n.* **unseen,** *a.* not seen; invisible; not seen previously (as a piece to be translated). **the unseen,** the world of spirits. **unsegregated,** *a.* **unseizable,** *a.* **unselect,** *a.* not select, mixed, miscellaneous. **unself,** *v.t.* to divest of individuality. **unselfconscious,** *a.* **unselfish,** *a.* regarding or prompted by the interests of others rather than one's own. **unselfishly,** *adv.* **unselfishness,** *n.*

unseminared, *a.* without sexual capacity, impotent, emasculated. [see SEMINARY]

un- (cont.) **unsensational,** *a.* **unsent,** *a.* **unsentenced,** *a.* **unsentimental,** *a.* **unseparated,** *a.* **unserviceable,** *a.* **unserviceableness,** *n.* **unserviceably,** *adv.* **unset,** *v.t.* to take from its setting. *a.* not set (of a gem, trap, the sun etc.). **unsettle,** *v.t.* to change from a settled state or position; to make uncertain or fluctuating; to derange, to disturb. †*v.i.* to become unsettled. **unsettled,** *a.* not settled, fixed or determined; undecided, hesitating; changeable; having no fixed abode; not occupied, uncolonized; unpaid. **unsevered,** *a.* **unsex,** *v.t.* to deprive of the qualities of sex (esp. of a woman). **unshackle,** *v.t.* **unshaded,** *a.* **unshadowed,** *a.* **unshak(e)able,** *a.* **unshaken,** †**unshaked,** *a.* not shaken; not moved in resolution; firm, steady. †**unshape,** *v.t.* to throw out of regular form; to disorder, to derange. **unshapely,** *a.* misshapen. †**unshapen,** *a.* deformed, shapeless. **unshared,** *a.* **unshaven,** *a.* **unsheathe,** *v.t.* to draw from its sheath. **unshed,** *a.* **unsheltered,** *a.* **unship,** *v.t.* to unload from a ship; to disembark; (*Naut.*) to remove from the place where it is fixed or fitted. *v.i.* to become unshipped (of an oar, tiller etc.). **unshipped,** *a.* **unshockable,** *a.* **unshocked,** *a.* **unshod,** *a.* **unshoe,** *v.t.* **unshorn,** *a.* not shorn, clipped, or shaven. **unshot,** *v.t.* to take the shot out of (a gun etc.). **unshown,** *a.* **unshrinkable,** *a.* that will not shrink (of flannel etc.). **unshrinking,** *a.* not recoiling, undaunted, unhesitating. **unshrinkingly,** *adv.* †**unshriven,** *a.* not absolved. **unshroud,** *v.t.* **unshrunk,** *a.* **unshut,** *a.* **unshuttered,** *a.* **unsifted,** *a.* **unsighted,** *a.* not sighted, not seen; invisible; not seeing; unfurnished with sights (of a gun etc.). **unsightly,** *a.* unpleasing to the sight, ugly. **unsightliness,** *n.* **unsigned,** *a.* **unsilvered,** *a.* **unsinged,** *a.* **unsinkable,** *a.* **unsinning,** *a.* **unsisterly,** *a.* **unsisterliness,** *n.* **unsized**[1], *a.* not arranged by size. **unsized**[2], *a.* not sized, not stiffened. **unskilful,** *a.* **unskilfully,** *adv.* **unskilfulness,** *n.* **unskilled,** *a.* destitute of skill or special knowledge or training; produced without or not requiring special skill or training. **unslaked,** *a.* **unsleeping,** *a.* **unsling,** *v.t.* (*past, p.p.* **-slung,**) (*Naut.*) to take (a yard, a cask etc.) off the slings. **unslumbering,** *a.* sleepless, vigilant. **unsmiling,** *a.* **unsmirched,** *a.* **unsmoked,** *a.* **unsnarl,** *v.t.* to remove a snarl or tangle from. **unsociable,** *a.* not sociable, solitary; reserved. **unsociability, unsociableness,** *n.* **unsociably,** *adv.* **unsocial,** *a.* not social, solitary; antisocial; of hours of work, falling outside the usual working day. **unsoiled,** *a.* **unsolaced,** *a.* **unsold,** *a.* **unsolder,** *v.t.* **unsoldierly,** *a.* **unsolicited,** *a.* **unsolicitous,** *a.* **unsolid,** *a.* **unsolidity,** *n.* **unsolvable,** *a.* **unsolved,** *a.* **unsoothed,** *a.* **unsophistical,** *a.* **unsophisticated,** *a.* simple, artless, free from artificiality, inexperienced; not corrupted or adulterated, pure, genuine. **unsophisticatedness,** *n.* **unsorted,** *a.* **unsought,** *a.* **unsound,** *a.* not sound; weak, decayed; unreliable; diseased; ill-founded, not valid, fallacious. **unsoundly,** *adv.* **unsoundness,** *n.* **unsounded,** *a.* not sounded or fathomed. **unsoured,** *a.* **unsown,** *a.* **unsparing,** *a.* liberal, profuse, lavish; unmerciful. **unsparingly,** *adv.* **unsparingness,** *n.* **unspeak,** *v.t.* to retract, to unsay. **unspeakable,** *a.* unutterable, inexpressible, beyond expression; inexpressibly bad or evil. **unspeakably,** *adv.* **unspeakableness,** *n.* **unspecified,** *a.* **unspeculative,** *a.* **unspent,** *a.* **unsphere,** *v.t.* to remove from its sphere. **unspilt,** *a.* **unspiritual,** *a.* **unspirituality,** *n.* **unspiritually,** *adv.* **unspliced,** *a.* **unspoiled, -spoilt,** *a.* **unspoken,** *a.* **unspontaneous,** *a.* **unsporting,** *a.* **unsportsmanlike,** *a.* unbecoming a sportsman. **unspotted,** *a.* free from spots; unblemished, uncontaminated; faultless, perfect. **unsprung,** *a.* not equipped with springs. **unsquared,** *a.* **unsquire,** *v.t.* to degrade from the rank or deprive of the title of squire. **unstable,** *a.* not stable, not firm; liable to sudden shifts of moods; decaying or decomposing rapidly or easily (of a chemical compound, atom etc.). **unstaid,** *a.* **unstained,** *a.* not stained; unblemished, unsullied. **unstamped,** *a.* not having a stamp affixed. **unstarched,** *a.* **unstartled,** *a.* **unstated,** *a.* **unstatesmanlike,** *a.* **unstatutable,** *a.* not warranted by statute law. **unstatutably,** *adv.* **unsteadfast,** *a.* **unsteadfastly,** *adv.* **unsteadfastness,** *n.* **unsteady,** *a.* not steady, not firm; changeable, variable; unstable, precarious; (*coll.*) irregular in habits or conduct. **unsteadily,** *adv.* **unsteadiness,** *n.* **unsteel,** *v.t.* to soften, to disarm. **unstep,** *v.t.* (*Naut.*) to take out of a step or socket. **unsterilized, -ised,** *a.* **unstick,** *v.t.* (*past, p.p.* **-stuck**). **unstigmatized, -ised,** *a.* **unstimulated,** *a.* **unstinted,** *a.* **unstirred, unstitch,** *v.t.* to open by unpicking the stitches of. **unstock,** *v.t.* to deplete of stock; to take the stock from (a gun etc.). **unstocked,** *a.* not stocked (with). **unstop,** *v.t.* to free from obstruction; to remove the stopper from, to open. **unstoppable,** *a.* **unstopped,** *a.* **unstopper,** *v.t.* **unstored,** *a.* **unstrained,** *a.* not strained, not filtered; not subjected to strain; not forced; easy, natural. **unstrap,** *v.t.* to unfasten or remove the strap or straps of. **unstratified,** *a.* **unstreamed,** *a.* **unstressed,** *a.* not subjected to stress; unaccented. **unstring,** *v.t.* (*past, p.p.* **-strung**) to take away the string or strings of; to loosen; to loosen the string or strings of, to relax the tension of (nerves etc.); to remove (pearls, etc.) from a string. **unstructured,** *a.* not having a formal or rigid structure; loose; relaxed, unceremonious. **unstuck,** *a.* (*sl.*) disarranged, disorganized. **to come unstuck,** (*sl.*) of a plan, course of action, to go wrong or fail. **unstudied,** *a.* not studied; easy, natural. **unstuffed,** *a.* **unstung,** *a.* **unsubdued,** *a.* **unsubjugated,** *a.* **unsubmissive,** *a.* **unsubmissively,** *adv.* **unsubmissiveness,** *n.* **unsubscribed,** *a.* **unsubstantial,** *a.* not substantial; having little solidity or validity; unreal. **unsubstantiality,** *n.* **unsubstantially,** *adv.* **unsubstantiated,** *a.* **unsubstantiation,** *n.* **unsuccess,** *n.* **unsuccessful,** *a.* **unsuccessfully,** *adv.* **unsugared,** *a.* **unsuitable,** *a.* **unsuitability, unsuitableness,** *n.* **unsuitably,** *adv.* **unsuited,** *a.* not suited, not fit or adapted (for or to). **unsullied,** *a.* **unsummed,** *a.* **unsummoned,** *a.* **unsung,** *a.* not sung; (*poet.*) not celebrated in verse. **unsunned,** *a.* not shone upon by the sun. **unsupervised,** *a.* **unsupplied,** *a.* **unsupported,**

a. **unsuppressed,** *a.* **unsure,** *a.* **unsurgical,** *a.* **unsurmised,** *a.* **unsurmountable,** *a.* **unsurmounted,** *a.* **unsurpassable,** *a.* **unsurpassably,** *adv.* **unsurpassed,** *a.* **unsurrendered,** *a.* **unsurveyed,** *a.* **unsusceptible,** *a.* **unsuspected,** *a.* **unsuspectedly,** *adv.* **unsuspecting,** *a.* **unsuspectingly,** *adv.* †**unsuspicion,** *n.* **unsuspicious,** *a.* **unsuspiciously,** *adv.* **unsuspiciousness,** *n.* **unsustainable,** *a.* **unsustained,** *a.* **unswaddle,** *v.t.* **unswallowed,** *a.* **unswathe,** *v.t.* **unswayed,** *a.* not swayed, biased, or influenced. **unswear,** *v.t.* to recant (something sworn to); to deny by oath. †**unsweet,** *a.* **unsweetened,** *a.* **unswept,** *a.* **unswerving,** *a.* **unswervingly,** *adv.* **unsworn,** *a.* not sworn; not bound by an oath. **unsymbolical,** *a.* **unsymmetrical,** *a.* out of symmetry; lacking in symmetry. **unsymmetrically,** *adv.* **unsymmetry,** *n.* **unsympathetic,** *a.* **unsystematic,** *a.* **untack,** *v.t.* to undo (something that has been tacked); to disjoin. **untainted,** *a.* **untalented,** *a.* **untam(e)able,** *a.* **untam(e)ableness,** *n.* **untamed,** *a.* **untangle,** *v.t.* to disentangle. **untanned,** *a.* **untarnishable,** *a.* **untarnished,** *a.* **untasked,** *a.* **untasted,** *a.* **untaught,** *a.* not instructed, illiterate; ignorant; natural, spontaneous. **untaxed,** *a.* **unteach,** *v.t.* to cause to be forgotten or unlearned. **unteachable,** *a.* **unteachableness,** *n.* **untearable,** *a.* **untechnical,** *a.* **untemper,** *v.t.* to take away the temper of (steel etc.). **untempered,** *a.* not moderated or controlled. **untempted,** *a.* **untenable,** *a.* **untenability, untenableness,** *n.* **untenably,** *adv.* **untenantable,** *a.* not in suitable condition for a tenant. **untenanted,** *a.* **untended,** *a.* **untender,** *a.* not tender, unkind. **untendered,** *a.* not offered. **unterrified,** *a.* **untested,** *a.* **untether,** *v.t.* **unthanked,** *a.* **unthankful,** *a.* **unthankfully,** *adv.* **unthankfulness,** *n.* **unthatched,** *a.* **unthink,** *v.t.* to retract in thought. **unthinkable,** *a.* incapable of being thought or conceived; (*coll.*) highly improbable. **unthinking,** *a.* heedless, careless; done without thought or care. **unthinkingly,** *adv.* **unthought,** *a.* not remembered or thought (of). **unthoughtful,** *a.* **unthoughtfulness,** *n.* **unthrashed,** *a.* **unthread,** *v.t.* to take a thread out of (a needle etc.); to find one's way out of (a maze etc.). **unthreaded,** *a.* not threaded. **unthreshed,** *a.* **unthrift,** *n.* unthriftiness; a prodigal, a spendthrift. *a.* unthrifty. **unthrifty,** *a.* **unthriftily,** *adv.* **unthriftiness,** *n.* **unthrone,** *v.t.* **unthwarted,** *a.* **untidy,** *a.* **untidily,** *adv.* **untidiness,** *n.* **untie,** *v.t.* to undo (a knot); to unfasten. *v.i.* to become untied. **untied,** *a.*

until, *prep.* up to the time of; as far as. *conj.* up to the time when. [ME var. of UNTO]

un- (cont.) **untiled,** *a.* not covered with tiles. **untillable,** *a.* **untilled,** *a.* **untimbered,** *a.* **untimely,** (*Sc.*) **untimeous,** *a.* unseasonable, inopportune; premature. †*adv.* unseasonably, prematurely. **untimeliness,** *n.* **untin,** *v.t.* **untinctured,** *a.* **untinged,** *a.* **untired,** *a.* not tired, not wearied. **untiring,** *a.* **untiringly,** *adv.* **untithed,** *a.* not subjected to tithes. **untitled,** *a.*

unto, *prep.* to. [OFris. and OS *und,* to, TO]

un- (cont.) **untold,** *a.* not told, revealed, or communicated; not counted, innumerable. **untormented,** *a.* **untorn,** *a.* **untortured,** *a.* **untouchable,** *n.* a Hindu belonging to one of the lowest castes or to no caste (nowadays the preferred term is HARIJAN). **untouched,** *a.* **untoward,** *a.* unlucky, unfortunate, awkward; †forward, perverse, refractory. **untowardly,** *adv.* **untraceable,** *a.* **untraced,** *a.* **untracked,** *a.* **untraded,** *a.* **untragic,** *a.* **untrained,** *a.* **untrammelled,** *a.* **untransferable,** *a.* that cannot or is not permitted to be transferred. **untranslatable,** *a.* **untranslatability, untranslatableness,** *n.* **untranslatably,** *adv.* **untranslated,** *a.* **untransportable,** *a.* **untravelled,** *a.* not having travelled; not travelled over. **untraversed,** *a.* **untreated,** *a.* **untried,** *a.* **untrimmed,** *a.* **untrod, -trodden,** *a.* **untroubled,** *a.* not disturbed by care, sorrow, business etc.; calm, unruffled. **untrue,** *a.* not in accordance with facts, false, not faithful, disloyal, inconstant; not conforming to a correct standard. **untruly,** *adv.* **untruss,** *v.t.* **untrussed,** *a.* **untrustworthy,** *a.* **untrustworthiness,** *n.* **untruth,** *n.* contrariety to truth; a falsehood, a lie; want of veracity; faithfulness. **untruthful,** *a.* **untruthfully,** *adv.* **untruthfulness,** *n.* **untuck,** *v.t.* to unfold or undo, as a tuck. **untune,** *v.t.* to put out of tune; to make discordant. **untunable,** *a.* **untuneful,** *a.* **untunefully,** *adv.* **unturned,** *a.* **untutored,** *a.* uninstructed; raw, crude. **untwine,** *v.t., v.i.* **untwist,** *v.t., v.i.* **unurged,** *a.* **unusable,** *a.* **unused,** *a.* not having been used; not accustomed (to). **unusual,** *a.* not usual; uncommon, strange, remarkable. **unusually,** *adv.* **unusualness,** †**unusuality,** *n.* **unutilized, -ised,** *a.* **unutterable,** *a.* unspeakable, inexpressible, indescribable, ineffable. **unutterably,** *adv.* **unuttered,** *a.* **unvaccinated,** *a.* **unvalued,** *a.* not esteemed; not appraised, not estimated; invaluable, inestimable. **unvanquished,** *a.* **unvaried,** *a.* **unvarnished,** *a.* not covered with varnish; not embellished, plain, simple. **unvarying,** *a.* **unvaryingly,** *adv.* **unveil,** *v.t.* to remove a veil or covering from, esp. with public ceremony from a statue etc.; to reveal, to disclose. *v.i.* to take one's veil off; to be revealed. **unveiling,** *n.* **unvenerable,** *a.* **unvenomous,** *a.* **unventilated,** *a.* **unveracious,** *a.* untruthful. **unveracity,** *n.* **unverifiable,** *a.* **unverified,** *a.* **unversed,** *a.* not versed or skilled (in). **unvexed,** *a.* **unvictualled,** *a.* **unvindicated,** *a.* **unviolated,** *a.* **unvisited,** *a.* **unvitiated,** *a.* not corrupted; pure. **unvoiced,** *a.* not spoken, not uttered; (*Phon.*) not voiced. **unvote,** *v.t.* to retract or cancel by voting. **unvouched,** *a.* not attested, not vouched (for). **unvowelled,** *a.* **unwaged,** *a.* not paid a wage; unemployed or not doing paid work. **unwaked, unwakened,** *a.* **unwalled,** *a.* **unwanted,** *a.* **unwarlike,** *a.* **unwarmed,** *a.* **unwarned,** *a.* **unwarp,** *v.t.* to restore from a warped condition. **unwarped,** *a.* **unwarrantable,** *a.* not defensible or justifiable, inexcusable; improper, illegitimate. **unwarrantableness,** *n.* **unwarrantably,** *adv.* **unwarranted,** *a.* not authorized; not guaranteed; not justified. **unwary,** *a.* **unwarily,** *adv.* **unwariness,** *n.* **unwashed,** *a.* not washed. **the great unwashed,** the mob, the rabble. **unwasted,** *a.* **unwatched,** *a.* **unwatchful,** *a.* **unwatchfulness,** *n.* **unwatered,** *a.* not watered, not furnished with water, not diluted, not irrigated. **unwavering,** *a.* steady, steadfast, firm. **unwaveringly,** *adv.* **unweaned,** *a.* **unwearable,** *a.* **unwearied,** *a.* **unweariedly,** *adv.* **unweary,** *a.* **unwearying,** *a.* **unwearyingly,** *adv.* **unweave,** *v.t.* to undo (something that has been woven); to separate the threads of. **unwed, -wedded,** *a.* **unweeded,** *a.* †**unweeting,** UNWITTING. **unweighed,** *a.* **unwelcome,** *a.* **unwelcomed,** *a.* **unwell,** *a.* not well; sick, indisposed. **unwept,** *a.* not lamented, not mourned. **unwhipped,** *a.* **unwhispered,** *a.* **unwhitened,** *a.* **unwhitewashed,** *a.* **unwholesome,** *a.* **unwholesomely,** *adv.* **unwholesomeness,** *n.* **unwieldy,** *a.* that cannot be easily wielded; bulky, ponderous, clumsy. **unwieldily,** *adv.* **unwieldiness,** *n.* **unwifely,** *a.* **unwill,** *v.t.* to will the reverse of. †**unwilled,** *a.* **unwilling,** *a.* not willing; averse, reluctant, undesirous (of, to, for, etc.); involuntary. **unwillingly,** *adv.* **unwillingness,** *n.*

Unwin, *n.* **Raymond** (1863–1940), English town planner. He put the Garden City ideals of Sir Ebenezer Howard into practice, overseeing Letchworth (begun 1903), Hampstead Garden Suburb (begun 1907) and Wythenshawe outside Manchester (begun 1927).

un- (cont.) **unwind,** *v.t.* (*past, p.p.* **-wound**) to pull out (something that has been wound); to free from entanglement. *v.i.* to become unwound; (*coll.*) to relax. **unwinged,** *a.* **unwinking,** *a.* watchful, vigilant. **unwisdom,** *n.* lack of wisdom; folly. **unwise,** *a.* not wise, without judgent; foolish. **unwisely,** *adv.* **unwished,** *a.* not desired; not sought (for). **unwithdrawn,** *a.* **unwithered,** *a.* **unwithering,** *a.* †**unwithstood,** *a.* **unwitnessed,** *a.*

unwitting, *a.* unconscious, unintentional, inadvertent. **unwittingly,** *adv.* [OE *unwitende;* see WIT[1]]

un- (cont.) **unwomanly,** *a.* **unwon,** *a.* **unwonted,** *a.* not accustomed; unusual. **unwontedly,** *adv.* **unwontedness,** *n.* **unwooded,** *a.* **unwooed,** *a.* **unwork,** *v.t.* to undo, to destroy. **unworkable,** *a.* **unworkman-**

like, *a.* **unworldly,** *a.* not worldly, spiritually minded; pertaining to spiritual things. **unworldliness,** *n.* **unworn,** *a.* never worn, new; not impaired by use. **unworshipped,** *a.* **unworthy,** *a.* not worthy, not deserving (of); not becoming, not seemly, discreditable. **unworthily,** *adv.* **unworthiness,** *n.* **unwound,** *past, p.p.* UNWIND. **unwounded,** *a.* **unwoven,** *a.* **unwrap,** *v.t.* **unwreaked,** *a.* **unwreath,** *v.t.* **unwrinkle,** *v.t., v.i.* **unwritable,** *a.* **unwritten,** *a.* not written; traditional; not distinctly expressed, not written upon, blank. **unwritten law,** *n.* one not formulated in statutes etc., esp. one based on custom and judicial decisions. **unwrought,** *a.* **unwrung,** *a.* not pinched or galled. **unyielding,** *a.* unbending, stiff; firm, obstinate. **unyieldingly,** *adv.* **unyieldingness,** *n.* **unyoke,** *v.t.* to loose from or as from a yoke. *v.i.* to give over work. **unyoked,** *a.* freed or loosed from the yoke; not yoked; †licentious, unrestrained. **unyouthful,** *a.* **unzealous,** *a.* **unzip,** *v.t.* to undo the zip of.

UP, (*abbr.*) United Presbyterian; Uttar Pradesh.

up- *pref.* up, upwards, upper. [prec.]

up, *adv.* to a higher place, position, degree, amount, rank, price, musical pitch etc.; to London, to a capital, university, a place farther north, or other place regarded as higher; at or to the time or place referred to; off the ground; to or in an erect or standing posture or a position or condition for action, out of bed, on one's legs, in the saddle; in arms, in a state of proficiency; above the horizon; so as to be level with, as high or as far as, equal (to); completely, entirely, effectually; appearing in court as a defendant. *prep.* from a lower to a higher place or point of; in an ascending direction on or along, towards the higher part of; towards the interior of; at or in a higher part of. *a.* moving, sloping, or directed towards a higher or more central part; towards the capital; finished; ready; knowledgeable (in); ahead (in a competition). *n.* that which is up; a high or higher position. *v.t.* to raise; to increase. *v.i.* to do something suddenly and unexpectedly. **on the up and up,** becoming steadily more successful; straight, honest. **time is up,** the allotted time is past; the appointed moment has arrived. **to come up with,** to overtake. **up against,** confronting, having to deal with. **up-and-coming,** enterprising, alert, keen; promising. **up and doing,** active and busy. **up and down,** here and there; in one place and another; from one place to another; in every direction. **up front,** at the front; at the forefront; (*coll., esp. N Am.*) honest, straightforward. **ups and downs,** rises and falls, undulations; vicissitudes, changes of fortune. **up the pole,** crazy; pregnant. **up to,** to an equal height with; equal to; (*sl.*) incumbent upon. **up to anything,** (*coll.*) ready for any devilment, sport, etc. **up to date,** (*coll.*) recent, abreast of the times. **up top,** (*sl.*) in one's head or brain. **up to snuff,** (*coll.*) knowing, cunning, acute, sharp. **up yours,** *int.* (*sl. offensive*) expressing contempt, defiance etc. **what's up,** what is going on? **up-and-over,** *a.* of a door, opened by pulling it upwards to a horizontal position. **upper[1],** *n.* (*sl.*) a stimulant drug. [OE *ūp, ūpp* (cp. Dut. *op,* G *auf*]

Upanishad, *n.* one of a collection of Hindu sacred treatises, written in Sanskrit, connected with the Vedas but composed later, about 800–200 BC. Metaphysical and ethical, their doctrine equated the atman (self) with the Brahman (supreme spirit): '*Tat tvam asi (Thou art that)*', and developed the theory of the transmigration of souls. [Sansk.]

upas, *n.* the upas-tree; the poisonous sap of this and other Malaysian trees; corrupting or pernicious influence. **upas-tree,** *n.* a Javanese tree, *Antiaris toxicaria,* the acrid milky juice of which contains a virulent poison, used for poisoning arrows, and formerly believed to destroy animal or vegetable life in its immediate neighbourhood. [Malay, poison]

up- (cont.) **upbear,** *v.t.* (*past* **-bore,** *p.p.*) to bear or lift up; to sustain aloft; to support. **upbeat,** *n.* (*Mus.*) an unaccented beat, on which the conductor raises his baton. *a.* (*coll.*) cheerful, optimistic. **upbind,** *v.t.* to bind or fasten up. **upblaze,** *v.i.* to blaze up.

upbraid, *v.t.* to charge; to reproach (with); to reprove with severity. *v.i.* to chide. **upbraider,** *n.* **upbraidingly,** *adv.* †**upbray,** *v.t.* to upbraid, to abuse. *n.* reproach, abuse. [OE *upbregdan,* to lay hold of, to upbraid (UP-, BRAID[2])]

up- (cont.) **upbringing,** *n.* bringing up, education. †**upbrought,** *a.* **upbuild,** *v.t.* **upburst,** *n.* a bursting up. **upby,** *adv.* (*Sc.*) a little farther up, up the way. **upcast,** *v.t.* to cast or throw up. *a.* , directed upwards, cast up. *n.* a casting or throwing upwards; the shaft by which air ascends after ventilating a mine. †**upcheer,** *v.t.* to encourage, to inspirit. †**upcoil,** *v.t., v.i.* to coil up. **up-country,** *adv., a.* towards the interior of a country, inland. †**upcurl,** *v.t., v.i.* **update,** *v.t.* to bring up to date. *n.* a bringing up to date; that which has been updated.

Updike, *n.* **John (Hoyer)** (1932–), US writer. Associated with the *New Yorker* magazine from 1955, he soon established a reputation for polished prose, poetry, and criticism. His novels include *Couples* (1968) and *Roger's Version* (1986) and deal with contemporary US middle-class life.

up- (cont.) **up-end,** *v.t.* to turn over on its end; to transform completely. †**upfill,** *v.t.* to fill up. †**upgather,** *v.t.* to gather up; to contract. **upgrade,** *v.t.* to raise (a worker or a job) to a higher grade or status. **upgrowth,** *n.* the act or process of growing up; that which grows up. †**upgrow,** *v.i.* †**upgush,** *v.t.* †**uphand,,** *a.* lifted by hand. †**upheap,** *v.t.* **upheave,** *v.t.* to lift up from beneath. *v.i.* to heave up. **upheaval,** *n.* the act or process of heaving up; (*Geol.*) an elevation of part of the crust of the earth; a violent disturbance, revolution etc. **upheld,** *past, p.p.* UPHOLD. **uphill,** *a.* leading or going up a hill; difficult, arduous, severe. *adv.,* in an ascending direction, upwards. †**uphoard,** *v.i.* **uphold,** *v.t.* to hold up, to keep erect; to support, to sustain, to maintain; to defend; to approve, to countenance. **upholder,** *n.*

upholster, *v.t.* to furnish with curtains, carpets, furniture etc.; to furnish or adorn (chairs etc.) with stuffing, cushions, coverings etc.; to cover (with etc.) **upholsterer,** *n.* **upholstery,** *n.* [from UPHOLSTERER, formerly *upholdster, upholder* (UP-, HOLDER, HOLD, -STER)]

uphroe, *n.* (*Naut.*) a long wooden block pierced with holes for reeving a cord, esp. for adjusting an awning. [Dut. *juffrouw,* young woman (*jung,* YOUNG, *vrouw,* woman)]

up- (cont.) **upkeep,** *n.* (cost of) maintenance. **upland,** *n.* the higher part of a district (*sing.* or *pl.*). *a.* situated on or pertaining to the uplands. †**uplay,** *v.t.* †**uplean,** *v.i.* **uplift,** *v.t.* to lift up, to raise. *n.,* an uplifting or upheaval; (*coll.*) spiritual improvement, edification. *a.* uplifted. †**up-lock,** *v.t.* to lock up. †**uplook,** *v.t.* **uplying,** *a.* **upmaking,** *n.* a filling of planks etc., inserted between a ship's bottom and the bilge-ways before launching. †**upmost,** *a.* uppermost, topmost.

upon, *prep., adv.* on. [OE *uppon, uppan* (UP, ON)]

upper[1] UP.

upper[2], *a.* higher in place; superior in rank, dignity etc. *n.* the part of a boot or shoe above the sole. **on one's uppers,** (*sl.*) destitute. **upper case,** *n.* (*Print.*) the case holding capitals, reference marks etc. **upper class,** *n.* the economically and socially most powerful class in a society. **upper cut,** *n.* in boxing, a punch delivered in an upwards direction with a bent arm. **upper deck,** *n.* (*Naut.*) the full-length deck of a ship above the water-level. **upper hand,** *n.* superiority, mastery. **Upper House,** *n.* The House of Lords. **the upper ten (thousand),** claimants to social superiority, the aristocracy. **upper works,** *n.* (*Naut.*) the parts above the water when a ship is in proper trim for a voyage. **uppermost,** *a.* highest in place, rank, authority etc.; predominant. *adv.* in the highest place; on, at, or to the top. [comp. of UP]

Upper Volta, *n.* former name (until 1984) of Burkina Faso.

uppish, *a.* self-assertive, pretentious, putting on airs, snobbish. **uppishly,** *adv.* **uppishness,** *n.* [UP, -ISH[1]]

uppity, (*coll.*) [UPPISH]

up- (cont.) **upraise,** *v.t.* to raise up; to lift. **uprear,** *v.t.* **uprate,** *v.t.* to raise to a higher rank, rate or power. **upright,** *a.* erect, perpendicular; righteous, honest, not deviating from moral rectitude. *adv.* erect, vertically. *n.* an upright timber, pillar, post, or other part of a structure; an upright piano etc. **upright piano,** *n.* one with a vertical case for the strings. **uprightly,** *adv.* **uprightness,** *n.* †**uprise,** *v.i.* (*past* **-rose, -risen**) to rise up. *n.*, an uprising. **uprising,** *n.* the act of rising up, esp. from bed; an insurrection, a rising, a riot. †**uprist,** *past.*

uproar, *n.* a noisy tumult, a violent disturbance, bustle and clamour. †*v.i.* to make an uproar. **uproarious,** *a.* noisy and disorderly; extremely funny. **uproariously,** *adv.* noisily; hilariously. **uproariousness,** *n.* [Dut. *oproer* (UP, *roeren,* to stir, cp. G *rühren,* OE *hreran,* Swed. *röra,* Dan. *röre,* Icel. *hrœra*)]

up- (cont.) **uproot,** *v.t.* to tear up by or as by the roots.

uprose, *past of* UPRISE.

uprush, *n.* an upward rush.

upsadaisy, UPSYDAISY.

upscale, (*esp. N Am. coll.*) *a., adv.* upmarket; trendy.

upset, *v.t.* (*past, p.p.* **upset,**) to overturn; to put out of one's normal state, to disconcert, to distress; to make slightly ill, to put out of sorts; to shorten and thicken (a tire or other metal object) by hammering or pressure. *v.i.* to be overturned. *n.*, the act of upsetting; the state of being upset. **upset price,** the lowest price at which property is offered for sale by auction, a reserve price.

upshot, *n.* the final issue, result, or conclusion (of a matter). [UP-, SHOT, p.p. of SHOOT]

upside-down, *adv., a.* with the upper part under; in complete disorder and confusion. [ME *up so down,* up as it were down]

†**upspring,** *n.* a leap in the air; an upstart. †*v.i.*, to spring up.

up- (cont.) **upstage,** *adv.* at the rear of a stage; away from a film or television camera. *a.* situated upstage; stand-offish. *v.t.* to force (an actor) to face away from the audience by taking a position upstage of him, her; to draw attention away from.

upstair, *a.* pertaining to or in an upper storey. **upstairs,** *adv., n.* (in or to) the upper storey or storeys. **to kick upstairs,** KICK.

upstanding, *a.* erect; honest, upright.

upstart, *n.* one who rises suddenly from humble origins to wealth, power or consequence; one who assumes an arrogant bearing.

upstate, *adv., a.* to or in that part of a state of the US which is away from, and usu. to the north of, the principal city.

upstream, *a., adv.* against the current; (situated) higher up a river.

upstroke, *n.* an upward line in writing.

upsurge, *n.* a sudden, rapid rise. *v.i.*, to surge up.

upswept, *a.* swept or brushed upwards.

upswing, *n.* an upward rise; an increase or improvement, esp. in economic terms.

upsydaisy, *int.* a reassuring expression to accompany the lifting up of someone, esp. a child, who has stumbled or fallen.

up- (cont.) **uptake,** *n.* the act of taking or lifting up; the process of taking, absorbing or accepting what is on offer; a pipe, shaft or flue with an upward current. **quick on the uptake,** quick to understand or learn.

up- (cont.) **up-tempo,** *a.* played or sung at a fast tempo.

upthrow, *n.* a throwing up, an upheaval; (*Geol.*) the upward displacement on one side of a fault.

upthrust, *n.* an upward thrust, esp. a geological upheaval.

uptight, *a.* tense, nervy; irritated, indignant; conventional, strait-laced.

uptime, *n.* the time during which a machine, esp. a computer, is actually working.

up-to-date, up-to-the-minute UP.

up- (cont.) **uptown,** *a., adv., n.* (*esp. N Am.*) (in or towards) the upper, or residential, part of town.

upturn, *n.* an upward trend or turn towards improved conditions, higher prices etc.; an upheaval. *v.t.* to turn up or over; to direct upwards.

UPU, (*abbr.*) Universal Postal Union.

upward, *a.* directed, turned, or moving towards a higher place. **upwardly,** *adv.* upwards. **upwardly mobile,** aspiring to improve one's lifestyle, social status etc. **upwards,** *adv.* towards a higher place, in an upward direction; towards the source or spring; more. **upwards of,** more than.

up- (cont.) **upwind,** *adv., a.* against the wind; (to or) on the windward side of.

Ur, *n.* an ancient city of the Sumerian civilization, now in S Iraq. Excavations by the British archaeologist Leonard Woolley show that it was inhabited in 3500 BC. He discovered evidence of a flood that may have inspired the biblical account, and remains of ziggurats, or step pyramids, as well as social and cultural relics.

uraemia, (*esp. N Am.*) **uremia,** *n.* a condition caused by the retention of urea and other noxious substances in the kidneys and bladder. **uraemic,** *a.* [mod. L (Gr. *ouron,* urine, *haima,* blood)]

uraeum, *n.* (*pl.* **-aea**) (*Ornith.*) the posterior half of a bird. [mod. L, from Gr. *ouraion,* neut. of *ouraios* from *oura,* tail]

uraeus, *n.* the serpent emblem worn on the head-dress of ancient Egyptian divinities and kings. [Gr. *ouraios,* from *oura,* tail]

Ural-Altaic, *a.* of or pertaining to the Ural and Altaic mountain ranges or the people inhabiting them; (*Philol.*) denoting a family of Mongoloid, Finnic and allied languages of agglutinative structure spoken in N Europe and Asia.

Uralic, *a., n.* (relating to) a language group comprising the Finno-Ugric and Samoyed languages.

uralite, *n.* (*Min.*) a pyroxene resembling hornblende in specific gravity and cleavage. **uralitic,** *a.* **uralization, -isation,** *n.* metamorphic change of pyroxene or augite to hornblende. [*Ural,* as prec., -ITE]

Ural Mountains, *n.* (Russian **Ural'skiy Khrebet**), mountain system running from the Arctic to the Caspian Sea, traditionally separating Europe from Asia. The highest peak is Naradnaya 1894 m/6214 ft. It has vast mineral wealth.

Urania, *n.* (*Gr. Myth.*) the muse of astronomy. **Uranian,** *a.* [L, from Gr. *Ourania,* the heavenly one, fem. of *ouranios,* from *ouranos,* see URANUS]

uranium, *n.* a rare, heavy, white, hexad metallic element found in pitchblende etc. It is radioactive and fissionable, as in the first atom bomb. **uranium bomb,** *n.* an atom bomb using uranium (not plutonium or hydrogen) as explosive. **uranic, uranous,** *a.* **uranite,** *n.* (*Min.*) Uranium copper phosphate, an ore of uranium. **uranitic,** *a.* [URANUS, -IUM]

urano-, *comb. form.* sky, the heavens. **uranography,** *n.* descriptive astronomy. **uranographic, -al,** *a.* **uranographist,** *n.* **uranology,** *n.* astronomy. **uranometry,** *n.* the measurement of the heavens or of stellar distances; a map of the heavens showing the relative positions and apparent magnitudes of the stars. **uranoscopy,** *n.* observation of the heavenly bodies. [see URANUS]

Uranus[1], *n.* in Greek mythology, the primeval sky god. He was responsible for both the sun and the rain, and was the son and husband of Gaia the goddess of the Earth, by whom he fathered Kronos and the Titans.

Uranus[2], *n.* the seventh planet from the Sun, discovered by William Herschel 1781. Uranus has a diameter of 50,800 km/31,600 miles and a mass 14.5 times that of Earth. It orbits the Sun in 84 years at an average distance of 2,870 million km/1,783 million miles. Uranus is thought to have a large rocky core overlain by ice, with a deep atmosphere mostly of hydrogen and helium, plus traces of methane which give the planet a greenish tinge. The spin axis of Uranus is tilted at 98°, so that at times its poles point towards the Sun, giving extreme seasons. It has 15 moons, and in 1977 astronomers discovered that Uranus has thin rings around its

equator. [Gr. *ouranos*, heaven]
urare CURARE.
urate, *n.* (*Chem.*) a salt of uric acid. **uratic,** *a.* **uratoma,** *n.* (*Path.*) a deposit of urates in the joints or tissues. **uratosis,** *n.* a morbid condition due to this.
urbacity, *n.* excess of civic pride. [as foll.]
urban, *a.* of or pertaining to, situated or living in a city or town. **urban district,** *n.* a district comprising a small town or towns with a small aggregate population or not yet incorporated as a borough. **urban guerrilla,** *n.* a terrorist who operates in cities and towns. **urban renewal,** *n.* slum redevelopment. **urbanist,** *n.* (*N Am.*) town-planner. **urbanite,** *n.* town-dweller. **urbanize, -ise,** *v.t.* [L *urbānus,* from *urbs,* city]
Urban II, *n.* (*c.* 1042–1099), pope 1088–99. He launched the First Crusade at the Council of Clermont in France in 1095.
urbane, *a.* courteous, polite, suave, refined, polished. **urbanely,** *adv.* **urbanity,** *n.* [as URBAN]
urceolus, *n.* (*pl.* **-li**) (*Bot.*) a pitcher- or urn-shaped organ; (*Zool.*) the external case or sheath of a rotifer. **urceolar, -late,** *a.* (*Bot.*) with a swelling body and contracted orifice. [L *urceolus,* dim. of *urceus,* pitcher]
urchin, *n.* a roguish, mischievous boy, a youngster, a child; a sea-urchin; †a hedgehog; †an elf, a fairy. *a.* elfin, roguish. [ME *urchon* ONorth.F *herichun* (F *hérisson*), ult. from L *ēricius,* from *ēr,* hedgehog, cogn. with Gr. *chēr*]
urd, *n.* a bean plant cultivated for its edible seed; this seed. [Hindi]
Urdu, *n.* a member of the Indo-Iranian branch of the Indo-European language family, related to Hindi and written not in Devanagari but in Arabic script. Urdu is strongly influenced by Persian and Arabic. It is the official language of Pakistan and a language used by Muslims in India.
-ure, *suf.* forming abstract nouns, as *censure, portraiture, seizure.* [F, from L *-ūra,* added to p.p stems of verbs]
urea, *n.* (*Chem.*) a soluble crystalline compound contained in urine, esp. of mammals. **ureal,** *a.* **ureameter,** -METER, *n.* an apparatus for determining the amount of urea in the urine. [Gr. *ouron,* urine]
Uredo, *n.* (*Bot.*) a form-genus or stage typical of the Uredinales, or rust-fungi, a group of higher fungi that are destitute of sexual organs and are parasitic on plants. **uredineous,** *a.* **uredospore,** *n.* a non-sexual spore in rust-fungi. **uredosporic,** *a.* **uredosporiferous,** *a.* [L *ūrēdo, -dinis,* blight, from *urere,* to burn]
ureter, *n.* the duct conveying the urine from the kidneys into the bladder. **ureteritis,** *n.* inflammation of the ureter. [Gr. *ourētēr,* from *ourein,* to make water]
urethane, *n.* a chemical compound NH_2 $COOC_2$ H_5 used esp. as a solvent or anaesthetic; polyurethane.
urethra, *n.* (*pl.* **-thrae**) the duct by which the urine is discharged from the bladder. **urethral,** *a.* **urethritis,** *n.* inflammation of the urethra. [L, from Gr. *ourēthra,* as prec.]
urethro-, *comb. form.*
urethroscope, *n.* an instrument for examining the interior of the urethra.
urethrotomy, *n.* incision of the urethra.
uretic, DIURETIC.
Urey, *n.* **Harold Clayton** (1893–1981), US chemist. In 1932 he isolated heavy water and discovered deuterium; Nobel prize 1934.
urge, *v.t.* to drive; to impel; to force onwards; to press earnestly with argument, entreaty etc. to importune; to press the acceptance or adoption of, to insist on. *n.* a strong impulse, an inner drive or compulsion. **urgency,** *n.* the quality or state of being urgent; pressure of necessity, esp. as a plea for giving a matter precedence in a deliberative assembly. **urgent,** *a.* pressing, demanding early attention; demanding or soliciting with importunity. **urgently,** *adv.* **urger,** *n.* [L *urgēre,* cogn. with Gr. *heirgein,* to repress, Eng. WREAK]
-urgy, *comb. form.* technology; technique. [Gr. *-ourgia* from *ergon,* work]
-uria, *comb. form.* diseased condition of the urine. [Gr. *-ouria* from *ouron,* wine]
uric URINE.
Urim and Thummim, *n.pl.* objects connected with the breastplate of the Jewish high-priest, apparently of oracular nature. [Heb. *ūrīm,* pl. of *ūr,* light, *tummīm,* pl. of *tom,* perfection]
urinal, *a.* toilet-vessel or fixed receptacle for the use of persons passing urine; a public or private room, building, enclosure etc. containing these; a glass receptacle for holding urine for medical inspection.
urine, *n.* a pale-yellow fluid with an acid reaction secreted from the blood by the kidneys, stored in the bladder, and discharged through the urethra, the chief means for the removal of nitrogenous and saline matters resulting from the decay of tissue. **uric,** *a.* **uric acid,** a white, tasteless and inodorous, almost insoluble compound found chiefly in excrement of birds and reptiles, and in small quantities in the urine of mammals. **urinary,** *a.* pertaining to urine. *n.* a reservoir for urine etc., for manure. **urinate,** *v.i.* to pass urine. **urination,** *n.* **urinative,** *a.* provoking the discharge of urine; diuretic. **uriniferous,** *a.* **urino-,** *comb. form.* **urinogenital,** GENITO-URINARY. **urinology,** UROLOGY. **urinometer,** *n.* an instrument for ascertaining the specific gravity of urine. **urinometric,** *a.* **urinometry,** *n.* **urinoscopy,** -SCOPY, UROSCOPY. **urinous,** *a.* [F, from L *ūrīna,* cogn. with Gr. *ouron,* Sansk. *vári,* water, OE *wœr,* the sea]
urite, *n.* the ventral portion of an abdominal segment in arthropods. [Gr. *oura,* tail, -ITE]
urman, *a.* a large tract of swampy coniferous forest country in Siberia. [Siberian]
urn, *n.* a vase with a foot and usually a rounded body used for preserving the ashes of the dead, for holding water, as a measure, and other purposes; (*fig.*) something in which the remains of the dead are preserved, a grave; a vase-shaped vessel with a tap, and usually a spirit-lamp or other heater, for keeping tea, coffee, bouillon etc., hot. *v.t.* to enclose in or as in an urn. **urn-shaped,** *a.* **urnful,** *n.* [F *urne,* L *urna*]
uro-¹, *comb. form* tail, hind part. [Gr. *oura,* tail]
uro-², *comb. form* urine. [URINO-]
urochord, *n.* the notochord of larval ascidians and some tunicates; an individual of the Urochordata or Tunicata. [URO-¹, CHORD]
urocyst, *n.* the urinary bladder. **urocystic,** *a.* [URO-², CYST]
urogenital, GENITO-URINARY.
urology, URINE.
uromancy, -MANCY, *n.* determination of disease by inspection of the urine, also called urinoscopy.
uropod, *n.* (*Zool.*) an abdominal appendage of the Malacostraca division of the Crustacea. [URO-¹, Gr. *podos,* a foot]
uropygium, *n.* (*Ornith.*) the terminal part of the body or the rump. **uropygial,** *a.* [URO-¹, Gr. *pugē,* rump]
uropyloric, PYLORIC, *n.* pertaining to the posterior part of the pyloric division of the stomach in some crustaceans.
urosacral, SACRAL, *a.* pertaining to the caudal and the sacral parts of the vertebral column.
uroscopy, *n.* the diagnostic examination of the urine.
urosome, *n.* the abdomen or post-thoracic division of the body of an arthropod; the terminal somatome of a vertebrate. [URO-¹, Gr. *sōma,* body]
urosthene, *n.* an animal with a powerful or highly developed tail, as a cetacean. **urosthenic,** *a.* [Gr. *sthenos,* strength]
urostyle, *n.* a bone forming the posterior extremity of the vertebral column in the tailless amphibians. **urostylar,** *a.*
urotoxic, *a.* denoting the poisonous nature and effects of urinary matter carried into the system. **urotoxicity,** *n.* **urotoxin,** *n.* a poison normally excreted by the urine. **urotoxy,** *n.* [URO-², TOXIC]
urry, *n.* (*prov.*) a blue or black clay lying close to a vein of coal. [cp. Gael. *uir,* earth]
Ursa, *n.* (*Astron.*) the Bear. **Ursa Major,** *n.* the third

largest constellation in the sky, in the north polar region. Its seven brightest stars make up the familiar shape of the Big Dipper or Plough. The second star of the 'handle' of the dipper, called Mizar, has a companion star, Alcor. Two stars in the 'bowl' act as pointers to the north pole star, Polaris. **Ursa Minor,** *n.* constellation in the northern sky. It is shaped like a little dipper, with the north pole star Polaris at the end of the handle. It contains the orange subgiant Kochab. **ursiform,** *a.* like a bear. **ursine,** *a.* pertaining to or resembling a bear; (*Ent.*) thickly covered with bristles (of some caterpillars). [L, she-bear]

urson, *n.* a N American porcupine, *Erethizon dorsatus.* [var. of URCHIN]

Ursuline, *n.* one of an order of nuns founded in 1537, devoted chiefly to nursing and the education of girls. *a.* belonging to this. [St *Ursula,* -INE]

urticaceous, *a.* (*Bot.*) of or having the character of nettles. **urticaria,** *n.* (*Path.*) nettle-rash. **urticate,** *v.t.* to sting with or as with nettles; to whip a benumbed or paralytic limb with nettles to restore feeling. **urtication,** *n.* [L *urtica,* nettle, -ACEOUS]

urubu, *n.* the Central American black vulture. [native name]

Uruguay, *n.* Oriental Republic of, country in South America, on the Atlantic, bounded N by Brazil and W by Argentina. **area** 176,200 sq km/68,031 sq miles. **capital** Montevideo. **physical** grassy plains (pampas). **population** (1988) 3,080,000 (mainly of Spanish and Italian descent, also mestizo, mulatto, and black); annual growth rate 0.7%. **exports** meat and meat products, leather, wool, textiles. **language** Spanish. **religion** Roman Catholic 60%.

Urumqi, *n.* (formerly **Urumchi**) industrial city and capital of Xinjiang Uygur autonomous region, China, at the N foot of the Tian Shan mountains; population (1986) 1,147,000. It produces cotton textiles, cement, chemicals, iron, and steel.

urus, *n.* an extinct wild ox, *Bos urus* or *primigenius,* the aurochs. [L, from Gr. *ouros*]

us, *pron.* the objective form of the first person plural pronoun 'we'; used for the singular 'me' in formal statements by the sovereign or a newspaper editor, or in very colloquial spoken use.

US, (*abbr.*) United States.

USA, (*abbr.*) United States Army; United States of America.

USAF, (*abbr.*) United States Air Force.

usage, *n.* the manner of using or treating, treatment; customary or habitual practice, esp. as authorizing a right etc.; (an instance of) the way a language is actually used; (*Law*) a uniform and recognized practice; †conduct, behaviour.

usance, *n.* a period of time allowed for payment of a foreign bill of exchange.

use[1], *n.* the act of using; the state of being used; employment in or application to a purpose; occasion, need, or liberty to use; the quality of being useful or serving a purpose; utility, serviceableness; custom, practice, wont, usage; a form of ritual, etc., peculiar to a church, diocese, or country; (*Law*) enjoyment of the benefit or profit of lands and tenements held by another in trust for the beneficiary. **in use,** being employed; in customary practice. **to have no use for,** to dislike, to disapprove of. **to make use of,** to use, to employ; to exploit (a person). **use and wont,** common or customary practice. **useful,** *a.* of use, serving a purpose; producing or able to produce; good, beneficial, profitable, advantageous; (*sl.*) clever, competent, highly satisfactory. **usefully,** *adv.* **usefulness,** *n.* **useless,** *a.* not of use, serving no useful end or purpose; unavailing, ineffectual; (*sl.*) out of sorts, unfit. **uselessly,** *adv.* **uselessness,** *n.* [A-F and OF *us,* L *ūsus -ūs,* from *uti,* to use (in legal senses from A-F *oes,* L *opus,* employment, need)]

use[2], *v.t.* to employ, to apply to a purpose, to put into operation; to turn to account, to avail oneself of; to treat in a specified way; to use up, to wear out; to make a practice of; (*usu. in p.p.*) to accustom, to habituate, to inure. *v.i.* (*usu. in past*) to be accustomed, to be wont, to make it one's constant practice to. **to use up,** to consume, to exhaust. **usable,** *a.* capable of being used. **used,** *a.* already made use of; secondhand; exploited. **used-up,** *a.* exhausted, finished. **user[1],** *n.* one who uses. **user[2],** *n.* (*Law*) continued use or enjoyment of a thing. **user-friendly,** *a.* easy to operate, *orig.* esp. of computers. **user-friendliness,** *n.*

Usher, *n.* **James** (1581–1656), Irish priest, archbishop of Armagh from 1625. He was responsible for the dating of creation as the year 4004 BC, a figure that was inserted in the margin of the Authorized Version of the Bible until the 19th century.

usher, *n.* an officer or servant acting as door-keeper (esp. in a court or public hall), or whose business it is to introduce strangers or to walk before a person of rank; an under-teacher or assistant in a school; a seat-attendant at a cinema, theatre etc. *v.t.* to act as usher to; to introduce, as a forerunner or harbinger, bring or show (in etc.). **usherette,** *n.* woman usher at a cinema or theatre. **ushership,** *n.* [F *huissier,* L *ostiārium,* from *ostium,* door]

Ushuaia, *n.* southernmost town in the world, at the tip of Tierra del Fuego, Argentina, less than 1,000 km/620 miles from Antarctica; population (1980) 11,000. It is a free port and naval base.

USM, (*abbr.*) unlisted securities market.

USN, (*abbr.*) United States Navy.

usquebaugh, *n.* whisky; an Irish liqueur made of brandy, spices etc. [Ir. *uisge beatha* (*uisge,* water, see WHISKY[1], *beatha,* life, cogn. with Gr. *bios,* L *vīta*)]

USS, (*abbr.*) United States Senate; United States ship.

USSR, (*abbr.*) Union of Soviet Socialist Republics.

Ustilago, *n.* a genus of parasitic fungi typical of the smut-fungi. **ustilaginous,** *a.* [late L, from *ustus,* p.p. of *ūrere,* to burn]

Ustinov, *n.* **Peter** (1921–), English stage and film actor, writer, and director. He won an Oscar for Best Supporting Actor in *Spartacus* (1960). Other films he appeared in are *Topkapi* (1964), *Death on the Nile* (1978), and *Evil under the Sun* (1981).

ustion, *n.* the act of burning; the state of being burned; (*Surg.*) cauterization. †**ustorious,** *a.* having the quality of burning. **ustulate,** *a.* scorched or coloured as if by fire. **ustulation,** *n.* the act of burning, scorching, drying etc., esp. the burning of wine. [L *ustio,* from *urere,* to burn, p.p. *ustus*]

usu., (*abbr.*) usual(ly).

usual, *a.* such as ordinarily occurs, customary, habitual, common, ordinary, frequent. **usually,** *adv.* **usualness,** *n.* [L *ūsuālis,* from *ūsus,* USE]

usucaption, -capion, *n.* (*Law*) the acquisition of the title or right to property by uninterrupted possession for a certain term of years. [L *ūsūcapio -ōnis* (*ūsū,* by use, see USE, *capere,* to take)]

usufruct, *n.* right to the use and enjoyment of property belonging to another without waste or destruction of its substance. *v.t.* to hold in or subject to usufruct. **usufructuary,** *n.* one who has usufruct. *a.* relating to or of the nature of a usufruct. [L *ūsusfructus* (USE, *fructus,* FRUIT)]

usurer, *n.* one who lends money at exorbitant interest. †**usuring, usurious,** *a.* practising usury, exacting exorbitant interest; pertaining to or of the nature of usury. **usuriously,** *adv.* **usuriousness,** *n.* **usury,** *n.* the practice of lending money at exorbitant interest, esp. higher than that allowed by law; exorbitant interest; †lending at interest or the taking of interest. [OF *usurier,* med. L *ūsūrārius,* from L *ūsūra,* use, enjoyment, interest, from *ūsus,* USE]

usurp, *v.t.* to seize or take possession of without right. †*v.i.* to encroach (upon). **usurpation,** *n.* †**usurpatory,** *a.* **usurper,** *n.* **usurping,** *adv.* [F *usurper,* L *ūsurpāre,* to employ, to acquire, etym. doubtful]

usury USURER.

USW, (*abbr.*) ultrashort wave.

UT, (*abbr.*) universal time; Utah.

ut, *n.* (*Mus.*) the first or key note in Guido's musical scale, now usu. superseded by do (see DO[2])). [L, see

GAMUT]

†**utas,** †**utis**, *n.* the octave or eighth days of a feast; merriment, festivity. [ME *utas,* A-F *utaves,* OF *oitauves,* pl. of *oitauve,* L *octava,* eight, from *octo,* eight]

Utah, *n.* state of the W US; nickname Beehive State. **area** 219,900 sq km/84,881 sq miles. **capital** Salt Lake City. **towns** Provo, Ogden. **physical** Colorado Plateau to the east; mountains in centre; Great Basin to the west; Great Salt Lake. **population** (1985) 1,645,000. **products** wool, gold, silver, uranium, coal, salt, steel.

Utamaro, *n.* **Kitagawa** (1753–1806), Japanese artist of the *ukiyo-e* ('floating world') school, who created muted colour prints of beautiful women, including informal studies of prostitutes.

UTC, (*abbr.*) Coordinated Universal Time, the standard measurement of time.

utensil, *n.* an implement, an instrument, esp. one used in cookery or domestic work. [MF *utensile,* L *ūtensilia,* utensils, from *ūtensilis,* fit for use, from *ūtī,* to USE]

uterus, *n.* (*pl.* **-ri**) the womb. **uterine,**, *a.* pertaining to the womb; born of the same mother but not the same father. **uteritis**, *n.* inflammation of the womb. **utero-,** *comb. form.* **uterogestation**, *n.* the development of the embryo within the uterus. **uteromania**, *n.* nymphomania. [L]

U (Thakin) Nu, *n.* (1907–), Burmese politician, prime minister for most of the period from 1948 to the military coup of 1962. Exiled abroad from 1966, U Nu returned to the country in 1980 and, in 1988, helped found the National League for Democracy opposition movement.

U Thant, *n.* (1909–1974), Burmese diplomat, secretary-general of the United Nations (1962–71). He helped to resolve the US-Soviet crisis over the Soviet installation of missiles in Cuba, and he made the controversial decision to withdraw the UN peacekeeping force from the Egypt–Israel border in 1967 (Arab-Israeli Wars).

utilitarian, *a.* of or pertaining to utility or to utilitarianism; concerned with, or made for, practical use rather than beauty. *n.* an advocate of utilitarianism. **utilitarianism,** *n.* the ethical doctrine that actions are right in proportion to their usefulness or as they tend to promote happiness; the doctrine that the end and criterion of public action is the greatest happiness of the greatest number.

utility, *n.* usefulness, serviceableness; that which is useful; utilitarianism, the greatest happiness of the greatest number; a public service, as the supply of water or electricity; (*Theat.*) a utility-man; a form of goods definitely planned to fit in with a rationing scheme; goods mass-produced to standard designs. *a.* designed or adapted for general use; practical, utilitarian. **utility-man,** *n.* an actor employed to take unimportant parts as required. **utility room,** *n.* a room (in a private house) used for storage, laundry etc. [F *utilité,* L *ūtilitātem,* nom. *-tas,* from *ūtilis,* useful, from *ūtī,* to USE]

utilize, -ise,, *v.t.* to make use of, to turn to account. **utilizable, -isable,** *a.* **utilization, -isation,** *n.*

utmost, *a.* being or situated at the farthest point or extremity; farthest, extreme, greatest, ultimate. *n.* the utmost extent or degree. [OE *ūtemest,* double, superlative of *ūt,* OUT]

Utopia, *n.* a place or state of ideal perfection; a book describing such. **Utopian,** *a.* pertaining to or resembling Utopia; ideal, perfect or highly desirable but impracticable. *n.* an inhabitant of Utopia; an ardent but visionary political or social reformer. **Utopianism,** *n.* [lit. nowhere, coined by Sir Thomas More as title of his book (published 1516) describing an imaginary island with a perfect social and political system (Gr. *ou,* not, *topos,* place)]

Utrecht, *n.* a province of the Netherlands lying SE of Amsterdam, Netherlands, on the Kromme Rijn (crooked Rhine); area 1330 sq km/513 sq miles; population (1988) 965,000. In rural areas livestock farming predominates. Manufactured products include textiles, chemicals, fertilizers, and electrical goods. The capital is Utrecht which forms the NE corner of the Randstad conurbation; population (1988) 522,000. **Utrecht, Treaty of,** treaty signed 1713 which ended the War of the Spanish Succession. Philip V was recognized as the legitimate king of Spain, thus founding the Spanish branch of the Bourbon dynasty; the Netherlands, Milan, and Naples were ceded to Austria; Britain gained Gibraltar; the duchy of Savoy was granted Sicily. **Utrecht, Union of,** in 1579, the union of seven provinces of the N Netherlands: Holland, Zeeland, Friesland, Groningen, Utrecht, Gelderland, and Overijssel, which became the basis of opposition to the Spanish crown and the foundation of the modern Dutch state.

utricle, *n.* (*Biol.*) a cell of an animal or plant; (*Anat.*) a sac-like cavity, esp. one in the labyrinth of the inner ear. **utricular**, *a.* [F, from L *ūtriculus,* dim. of *ūter,* leather bag or bottle]

Utrillo, *n.* **Maurice** (1883–1955), French artist. He painted townscapes of his native Paris, especially Montmartre, often from postcard photographs.

ut sup., (*abbr.*) ut supra (as mentioned above). [L]

Uttar Pradesh, *n.* state of N India. **area** 294,400 sq km/113,638 sq miles. **capital** Lucknow. **towns** Kanpur, Varanasi, Agra, Allahabad, Meerut. **population** (1981) 110,858,000. **language** Hindi. **religion** Hindu 80%, Muslim 15%.

utter¹, *a.* complete, total, perfect, entire; absolute, unconditional. **utter barrister,** *n.* a junior barrister not allowed to plead within the bar. **utterly,** *adv.* **uttermost,** *a.* **utterness,** *n.* [OE *utter a,* comp. of *ūt,* OUT]

utter², *v.t.* to give forth audibly; to give expression to; to put notes, base coin etc., into circulation; †to put forth, to give vent to, to emit. **utterable,** *a.* **utterance,** *n.* the act of uttering; vocal expression; speech, words; power of speaking. **utterer,** *n.* [ME *uttren,* as prec., cp. OE *ūtian,* from *ūt,* OUT]

UU, (*abbr.*) Ulster Unionist.

UV, (*abbr.*) ultraviolet.

uva, *n.* (*Bot.*) a succulent indehiscent fruit with a central placenta, as a grape. **uvea,** *n.* (*Anat.*) the inner coloured layer of the iris. **uveal,** *a.* **uveous,** *a.* resembling a grape; (*Anat.*) uveal. [L, bunch of grapes]

UVF, (*abbr.*) Ulster Volunteer Force.

uvula, *n.* (*pl.* **-lae**) a fleshy body hanging from the posterior margin of the soft palate; one of two similar processes in the bladder and the cerebellum. **uvular,** *a.* [mod. L, dim. of prec.]

uxorious, *a.* excessively or foolishly fond of one's wife, doting. **uxorial,** *a.* of or pertaining to a wife; uxorious. **uxoricide**, -CIDE, *n.* wife-murder; a wife-murderer. **uxoriously,** *adv.* **uxoriousness,** *n.* [L *uxōrius,* from *uxor,* wife]

Uzbek, *n.* a person of Uzbek culture. Uzbeks comprise approximately 70% of the population of Uzbekistan in the USSR. The Uzbek language belongs to the Turkic branch of the Altaic family.

Uzbekistan, *n.* constituent republic of the SE USSR, part of Soviet Central Asia. **area** 447,400 sq km/172,741 sq miles. **capital** Tashkent. **towns** Samarkand. **physical** oases in the deserts; rivers Amu Darya and Syr Darya; Fergana Valley. **population** (1987) 19,026,000; 69% Uzbek, 11% Russian, 4% Tadzhik, 4% Tatar. **products** rice, dried fruit, vines (all grown by irrigation), cotton, silk. **language** Uzbek. **religion** Sunni Muslim.

V

V¹, v, the 22nd letter, and the 17th consonant (*pl.* **Vs, V's, Vees**), is a voiced labiodental spirant or fricative, produced by the junction of the lower lip and upper teeth, corresponding to the voiceless *f*, which is similarly produced; (*Roman numeral*) 5. **V-bomb,** *n.* self-propelled rocket or bomb launched by Germany in World War II mainly against Britain, typically **V-1's** or **V-2's. V.E. Day,** *n.* the day, 8 May 1945, on which hostilities in Europe in World War II officially ceased. **V.J. Day,** *n.* the corresponding day (2 Sept. 1945) when hostilities against Japan ceased. **V-neck,** *n.* the neck of any garment when it is shaped like the letter V. **V-necked,** *a.* **V-sign,** *n.* sign made with index and middle fingers in the form of the letter V, palm outwards as a victory salute, palm inwards as a sign of contempt or derision.

V², (*chem. symbol*) vanadium.

va, *v.i.* (*Mus. direction*) go on. [It.]

vac, *n.* (*coll.*) short for vacation, esp. when applied to university holidays.

vacant, *a.* unfilled, empty, unoccupied; unemployed, at leisure; unintelligent, empty-headed, silly, inane. **vacant possession,** *n.* availability of a house or other property for immediate occupation. **vacancy,** *n.* the state of being vacant, emptiness; mental vacuity, idleness, inanity; empty space, a gap, a chasm; an unfilled or vacant post or office. **vacantly,** *adv.* [F, from L *vacans -ntem,* pres.p. of *vacāre,* to be empty]

vacate, *v.t.* to make vacant, to give up occupation or possession of; to annul, to make void.

vacation, *n.* the act of vacating; a period of cessation of legal or other business, or of studies at university etc.; a holiday.

vaccinate, *v.t.* to inoculate with vaccine to procure immunity from smallpox, or with the modified virus of any disease so as to produce a mild form of it and prevent a serious attack. **vaccination,** *n.* **vaccinationist,** *n.* **vaccinator,** *n.* **vaccine,** *a.* of, pertaining to, or obtained from cows; of or pertaining to vaccination. *n.* the virus of cowpox prepared for use in vaccination; any agent used for inoculation and immunization. **vaccine-farm,** *n.* a place where heifers are inoculated for the production of vaccine. **vaccine-point,** *n.* a sharp point used for introducing vaccine. **vaccinal, vaccinic,** *a.* **vaccinia,** *n.* cowpox, esp. as produced by inoculation. **vaccinifer,** *a.* a person or animal from whose body vaccine is obtained. [F *vaccin,* vaccine, L *vaccīnus,* a., from *vacca,* cow]

vacillate, *v.i.* to sway to and fro, to waver; to oscillate from one opinion or resolution to another, to be irresolute. †**vacillant,** *a.* **vacillatingly,** *adv.* **vacillation, vacillancy,** *n.* [L *vacillātus,* p.p. of *vacillāre*]

vacuist, *n.* one who holds the doctrine of empty spaces between the molecules of matter, opp. to a plenist.

vacuole, *n.* (*Biol.*) a minute cavity in an organ, tissue etc., containing air, fluid etc. **vacuolar, vacuolate,** *a.*

vacuous, *a.* empty, unfilled, void; unintelligent, blank, expressionless. **vacuousness,** *n.* **vacuity,** *n.* [L *vacuus,* rel. to *vacāre,* see VACANT]

vacuum, *n.* (*pl.* **-ms, -ua**) a space completely devoid of matter; a space or vessel from which the air has been exhausted to the furthest possible extent by an air-pump or analogous means; a partial diminution of pressure, as in a suction-pump, below the normal atmospheric pressure. **vacuum-brake,** *n.* a continuous train-brake in which the pressure applying the brakes is caused by the exhaustion of the air from a bellows pulling the brake-rod as it collapses. **vacuum-cleaner,** *n.* a machine for removing dirt by suction. **vacuum flask,** *n.* a flask constructed with two walls between which is a vacuum, for the purpose of keeping the contents hot or cold. **vacuum-gauge,** *n.* a gauge indicating the pressure consequent on the production of a vacuum. **vacuum packed,** *a.* sealed in a container from which most of the air has been removed. **vacuum pump,** *n.* an air-pump used to remove air or other gas, and so create a vacuum. **vacuum tube,** *n.* (*N. Am.*) an electronic valve. [L, neut. of prec.]

†**vade,** (*Shak.*) FADE.

vade-mecum, *n.* a pocket companion or manual for ready reference. [L, go with me]

vadium, *n.* (*Sc. Law*) a bailment of personal property as security for a loan. [med. L, from L *vas vadis,* surety]

Vaduz, *n.* capital of the European principality of Liechtenstein; population (1984) 5000. Industries include engineering and agricultural trade.

vagabond, *a.* wandering about, having no settled habitation, nomadic; driven or drifting to and fro, aimless. *n.* one who wanders about without any settled home, a wanderer, esp. an idle or disreputable one, a vagrant; a scamp, a rogue. **vagabondage, vagabondism,** *n.* **vagabondish,** *a.* **vagabondize, -ise,** *v.i.* [F, from late L *vagabundus,* from *vagārī,* to wander]

vagary, *n.* a whimsical idea, an extravagant notion, a freak. †**vagarious,** †**vagarish,** *a.* **vagarity,** *n.* [perh. directly from L *vagārī,* see prec.]

vagina, *n.* a sheath, a sheath-like envelope or organ; the genital passage of a female from the vulva to the uterus; (*Arch.*) the upper part of a terminus from which the figure seems to issue; a sheath or semi-tubular part, as at the base of a stem. **vaginal, vaginate, -nated,** *a.* [L]

vagini-, vagino-, *comb. form* pertaining to sheath; pertaining to the vagina. [L]

vaginipennate, *a.* sheath-winged; coleopterous.

vaginismus, *n.* spasmodic contraction of the vaginal sphincters.

vaginitis, *n.* inflammation of the vagina.

vaginotomy, *n.* incision of the vagina.

vagitus, *n.* the first cry of a new-born infant. [L]

vagrant, *a.* wandering about without a settled home; itinerant, strolling; roving, unrestrained; †unsteady, inconstant. *n.* a wanderer, an idle person, a vagabond, a tramp; (*Law*) a person wandering about begging or without visible means of subsistence. **vagrancy,** *n.* **vagrantly,** *adv.* †**vagrom,** *a.* [formerly *vagarant,* A-F *wakerant,* OF *waucrant,* pres.p. of *walcrer,* from Teut., cogn. with OHG *walkan,* to walk about, to full cloth, see WALK (confused with L *vagārī,* see VAGUE)]

vague, *a.* indistinct, of doubtful meaning or application, ambiguous, indefinite, ill-defined; †vagrant. **vaguely,** *adv.* **vagueness,** *n.* [from obs. v. to wander, F *vaguer,* L *vagārī,* from *vagus,* wandering]

vagus¹, *n.* the tenth cranial nerve which regulates the heart beat, rhythm of breathing etc.

†**vagus²,** *a.* wandering; (*Anat.*) out of place. [L, see prec.]

†**vail¹,** *v.t.* to lower (a topsail etc.) or doff (one's cap etc.), esp. in token of respect or submission. *v.i.* to yield, to give place. [shortened from AVALE]

†**vail²,** *n.* (*usu. in pl.*) money given to servants by visitors as a gratuity; a tip, esp. for a corrupt purpose. [shortened from AVAIL]

†**vail**[3], VEIL.

vain, *a.* empty, unsubstantial, unreal, worthless; fruitless, ineffectual, unavailing; unproductive, unprofitable; fallacious, deceitful; proud of petty things or of trifling attainments, conceited, self-admiring; foolish, silly. **in vain,** to no purpose; ineffectually. **to take someone's name in vain,** to use someone's name in a pejorative, insulting or blasphemous way. **vainglory,** *n.* excessive vanity; vain pomp or show; pride, boastfulness. **vainglorious,** *a.* **vaingloriously,** *adv.* **vain-gloriousness,** *n.* **vainly,** *adv.* †**vainness,** *n.* [F, from L *vānum,* nom. *-us,* empty, vain]

vair, *n.* (*Her.*) a fur represented by shield-shaped figures of argent and azure alternately. [F, from L *varius,* variegated, VARIOUS]

Vaishnava, *n.* one of the great sects of reformed Brahmins who worship Vishnu as supreme among the Hindu gods. [Sansk.]

Vaisya, *n.* the third of the four chief Hindu castes; a member of this. [Sansk. *vaiçya,* from *vīc,* settler]

vaivode VOIVODE.

valance, *n.* a short curtain; the hanging round the frame or tester of a bedstead; a damask fabric of silk etc., for covering furniture. [prob. from *Valence* in France]

Valdemar, *n.* alternative spelling of Waldemar, name of four kings of Denmark.

Valdívia, *n.* **Pedro de** (*c.* 1497–1554), Spanish explorer who travelled to Venezuela around 1530 and accompanied Francisco Pizarro on his second expedition to Peru. He then went south into Chile, where he founded the cities of Santiago (1541) and Valdívia (1544). In 1552 he crossed the Andes to explore the Negro River. He was killed by Araucanian Indians.

vale[1], *n.* a valley; a little trough or channel. **Vale of tears,** human life, existence, the world. [ME and F *val,* L *vallem,* nom. *-lis*]

vale[2], *n., int.* farewell. [L, farewell, imper. of *valēre,* to be strong]

valediction, *n.* a bidding farewell; a farewell, an adieu. **valedictorian,** *n.* (*N Am.*) a student who delivers a valedictory. **valedictory,** *a.* bidding farewell; pertaining to or of the nature of a farewell. *n.* a parting address or oration, esp. at graduation in an American university. [L *valēdictus,* p.p. of *valēdīcere* (VALE[2], *dīcere,* to say)]

valence, *n.* the combining or replacing power of an element or radical reckoned as the number of monovalent elements it can replace or combine with. **valency,** *n.* a unit of combining capacity; valence. [late L *valentia,* strength, from *valēre,* to be strong]

Valencia, *n.* industrial city (wine, fruit, chemicals, textiles, ship repair) in Valencia region, E Spain; population (1986) 739,000. The Valencian Community, consisting of Alicante, Castellón, and Valencia, has an area of 23,300 sq km/8994 sq miles, and a population of 3,772,000.

Valenciennes, *n.* Valenciennes lace: a composition used in pyrotechnics. **Valenciennes lace,** a fine variety of lace the design of which is made with and of the same thread as the ground. [*Valenciennes* in France]

Valentine, St, *n.* (died 270), according to tradition a bishop of Terni martyred at Rome, now omitted from the calendar of saints' days as probably nonexistent. His festival was 14 Feb., but the custom of sending 'valentines' to a loved one on that day seems to have arisen because the day accidentally coincided with the Roman mid-Feb festival of Lupercalia. **valentine,** *n.* a sweetheart chosen on St Valentine's day; a letter or card of an amatory or satirical kind sent to a person of the opposite sex on St Valentine's day.

Valentinian, *a.* of or pertaining to Valentinus, an Egyptian Gnostic of the 2nd cent., or his teachings. *n.* a disciple of Valentinus.

Valentino, *n.* **Rudolf** (1895–1926), Italian film actor, the archetypal romantic lover of the Hollywood silent movies. His films include *The Sheik* (1921) and *Blood and Sand* (1922).

Valera, Éamon de DE VALERA.

valerian, *n.* an herbaceous plant of the genus *Valeriana* with clusters of pink or white flowers; a preparation from the root of *V. officinalis* used as a mild stimulant etc. **valeric acid,** *n.* a fatty acid of disagreeable smell obtained from Valerian. **valerate,** *n.* a salt of valeric acid. **valeric,** *a.* [OF *valeriane,* late L *valēriana*]

Valéry, *n.* **Paul** (1871–1945), French poet and mathematician. His poems include *La Jeune Parque/The Young Fate* (1917) and *Charmes/Enchantments* (1922).

valet, *n.* a manservant who attends on his master's person; an iron-pointed stick or goad used in training horses. *v.t.* (*past.* **valeted**) to act as valet to. **valet de chambre,** a valet. **valet de place,** a courier or local guide. [F, var. of VARLET]

valeta VELETA.

valetudinarian, *a.* sickly, infirm, delicate; seeking to recover health; morbidly anxious about one's state of health. *n.* an invalid; a valetudinarian person. **valetudinarianism,** *n.* **valetudinary,** *n., a.* one who is morbidly anxious about his state of health; to be in such a condition. [F *valétudinaire,* L *valētūdinārius,* from *valētūdo -dinis,* health, from *valēre,* to be well]

valgus, *a.* twisted away from the line of the body; bow-legged or knock-kneed. [L bow-legged]

Valhalla, *n.* in Norse mythology, the palace of immortality where the souls of heroes slain in battle were carried by the Valkyries; a building used as the final resting-place of the great men of a nation, esp. the Temple of Fame, near Ratisbon, built by Louis I of Bavaria, 1830. [Icel. *valhöll,* gen. *valhallar,* hall of the slain (*valr,* slain, HALL)]

valiant, *a.* brave, courageous, intrepid. †**valiance,** †**valiantness,** *n.* **valiantly,** *adv.* [OF *valant* (F *vaillant*), pres.p. of *valoir,* to be worth, L *valēre,* to be strong]

valid, *a.* well-grounded, sound, cogent, logical, incontestable; (*Law*) legally sound, sufficient, and effective, binding. **validate,** *v.t.* to make valid, to ratify, to confirm, to make binding. **validation,** *n.* **validity, validness,** *n.* **validly,** *adv.* [F *valide,* L *validus*]

valine, *n.* an amino acid that is essential to health and growth in humans and other vertebrates. [from *val*eric acid]

valise, *n.* a bag or case, usu. of leather, for holding a traveller's clothes etc., esp. one for carrying in the hand, a small portmanteau; (*N Am.*) a suit-case. [F from late L *valisia,* etym. doubtful]

Valium®, *n.* a brand name for the tranquillizer diazepam.

Valkyrie, *n.* in Norse mythology, one of 12 maidens of Valhalla who were sent by Odin to select those destined to be slain in battle and to conduct their souls to Valhalla. **Valkyrian,** *a.* [Icel. *valkyrja,* chooser of the slain (*valr,* slain, *-kyrja,* chooser, from *kjōsa,* cogn. with CHOOSE)]

Valladolid, *n.* industrial town (food processing, vehicles, textiles, engineering), capital of Valladolid province, Spain; population (1986) 341,000.

†**vallancy,** *n.* a large wig that shaded the face, worn in the 17th cent. [VALANCE]

vallar, vallated etc. VALLUM.

vallecula, *n.* (*pl.* **lae**) (*Anat., Bot. etc.*) a groove or furrow. [late L, dim. of *vallis,* VALE[1]]

Valle d'Aosta, *n.* autonomous region of NW Italy; area 3300 sq km/1274 sq miles; population (1988) 114,000, many of whom are French-speaking. It produces wine and livestock. Its capital is Aosta.

Valletta, *n.* capital and port of Malta; population (1987) 9000, but the urban harbour area is 101,000.

valley, *n.* a depression in the earth's surface bounded by hills or mountains, and usu. with a stream flowing through it; any hollow or depression between higher ground or elevations of a surface; the internal angle formed by two inclined sides of a roof. [OF *valee* (F *vallée*), from *val,* VALE[1]]

Valley Forge, *n.* site in Pennsylvania 32 km/20 miles NW of Philadelphia, US, where Washington's army spent the winter of 1777–78 in great hardship during the War of American Independence.

Valley of Ten Thousand Smokes, *n.* valley in SW Alaska, on the Alaska Peninsula, where in 1912 Mount

Katmai erupted in one of the largest volcanic explosions ever known, though without loss of human life since the area was uninhabited. It was dedicated in 1918 as the Katmai National Monument. Thousands of fissures on the valley floor continue to emit steam and gases.

Valley of the Kings, *n.* burial place of ancient kings opposite Thebes, Egypt, on the left bank of the Nile.

vallonia, *n.* the large acorn-cup of the vallonia oak, used for dyeing, tanning, ink-making etc. **vallonia oak,** an evergreen oak, *Quercus aegiiops,* of the Greek archipelago etc. [It., from Gr. *balanos,* oak]

vallum, *n.* (*Rom. Ant.*) a rampart, an agger; an eyebrow. **vallar, †vallary, vallated,** *a.* **vallation,** *n.* [L]

Valmy, Battle of, battle in 1792 in which the army of the French Revolution under Gen. Dumouriez defeated the Prussians at a French village in the Marne *département.*

Valois, *n.* branch of the Capetian dynasty, in France, members of which occupied the French throne from Philip VI (1328) to Henry III (1589).

valonia, VALLONIA.

valorize, -ise, *v.t.* to increase or stabilize the price of an article by an officially organized scheme. [L *valere,* to be worth, -IZE]

valour, (*esp. N. Am.*) **valor,** *n.* personal bravery, courage, esp. as displayed in fighting; prowess. **valorous,** *a.* **valorously,** *adv.* [OF *valor, -lur* (F *valeur*), L *valōrem,* nom. *-or,* from *valēre,* to be strong, to be worth]

valse, *n.* a waltz. [F, WALTZ]

valuable, valuation VALUE.

value, *n.* worth, the desirability of a thing, esp. as compared with other things; the qualities that are the basis of this; worth estimated in money or other equivalent, the market price; the equivalent of a thing; valuation, estimation, appreciation of worth; meaning, signification, import; the relative duration of a tone as indicated by the note; the relation of the parts of a picture to each other with regard to light and shade, apart from colour; the amount or quantity denoted by a symbol or expression; (*Biol.*) rank in classification. *v.t.* to estimate the value of, to appraise; to esteem, to rate highly, to prize; †to be worth; †to reckon at. **commercial, economic, exchange,** or **exchangeable value, value in exchange,** the value in terms of other commodities, the purchasing power of a commodity in the open market; the market price as determined by economic laws. **valuable,** *a.* having great value, worth, or price, costly, precious; capable of being valued or appraised; worthy, estimable. **valuableness,** *n.* **valuably,** *adv.* **valuation,** *n.* the act of valuing or appraising; estimation of the value of a thing; estimated value or worth, the price placed on a thing. **valuator,** *n.* an appraiser. **valuation roll,** *n.* a list of properties and their assessed value for taxation purposes. **value-added tax,** in Britain, a tax levied at each stage of production and distribution of a commodity or service and paid by the buyer as a purchase tax. **value judgement,** a subjective and personal estimate of merit in a particular respect. **valueless,** *a.* of no value, worthless, futile. **valuelessness,** *n.* **valuer,** *n.* one who values, an appraiser, esp. of property, jewellery etc. [F, fem. of *valu,* p.p. of *valoir,* to be worth, L *valēre,* see VALOUR]

valuta, *n.* the definitive money with which it can be demanded that state payments due to individuals shall be paid; the value of one currency in terms of another. [It., value]

valve, *n.* an automatic or other contrivance for opening or closing a passage or aperture so as to permit or prevent passage of a fluid, as water, gas, or steam; a membranous part of a vessel or other organ preventing the flow of liquids in one direction and allowing it in the other; (*Bot.*) one of the segments into which a capsule dehisces, either half of an anther after its opening; a shortened form of electronic or thermionic valve; a vacuum tube or bulb containing electrodes and exhibiting sensitive control by one or more electrodes of the current flowing between the others; (*N Am.* a tube); one of the parts or divisions of a shell; †one of the leaves of a folding door. **valve box, chamber,** *n.* the chamber in which a valve works. **valve face,** *n.* the sealing surface of a valve. **valve-gear,** *n.* the mechanism operating a valve. **valve-oscillator,** *n.* (*Radio.*) an electrical circuit on which oscillations are maintained by a valve. **valve-seating,** *n.* that part of an internal-combustion engine which is in working contact with the valve face when the valve is shut. **valve voltmeter,** *n.* (*Radio.*) an electrical circuit, containing valves, used to measure voltages. **valval,** *a.* (*Bot.*) **valvar, valvate,** *a.* like a valve; descriptive of petals which meet at the margins only. **valved,** *a.* (*usu. in comb.* as *three-valved*). **valveless,** *a.* **valvelet, valvule,** *n.* a little valve. **valviferous,** *a.* **valviform, valvular,** *a.* **valvular disease,** *n.* disordered action of the heart owing to defects in the cardiac valves. [F, from L *valva,* leaf of a folding door, cogn. with *volvere,* to roll, to turn]

†vambrace, *n.* armour for the arm from the elbow to the wrist. [MF *avant-bras* (*bras,* arm)]

vamoose, vamose, *v.i.* (*sl.*) to decamp, to be gone, to be off. *v.t.* to decamp from. [Sp. *vamos,* let us go, L *vādimus,* we go, from *vādere,* to go]

vamp[1]**,** *n.* the part of a boot or shoe upper in front of the ankle seams; a patch intended to give a new appearance to an old thing; (*Mus.*) an improvised accompaniment. *v.i.* to put a new vamp on (a boot etc.); to give a new appearance to, to make more modern; (*Mus.*) to improvise an accompaniment to. *v.i.* to improvise accompaniments. **vamper,** *n.* [ME *vaumpe, vampay, vauntpe,* MF *avant-pied* (AVANT-, *pied,* foot)]

vamp[2]**,** *n.* an adventuress, a woman who exploits her charms to take advantage of men. *v.t.* to fascinate, to exploit men. [VAMPIRE]

vampire, *n.* a ghost of a heretic, criminal, or other outcast, supposed to leave the grave at night and suck the blood of sleeping persons; one who preys upon other, a blood-sucker; a bat of the genus *Desmodus,* which sucks the blood of man and the lower animals, esp. while they are asleep; (*Theat.*) a small double spring-door used for sudden entrances and exits. **vampiric,** *a.* **vampirism,** *n.* belief in vampires; blood-sucking; (*fig.*) extortion. [F, from G *vampyr,* Serbian *vampir,* prob. from Turk.]

†vamplate, *n.* an iron plate fixed on a lance as a guard for the hand. [F *avant-plate* (AVANT-, PLATE)]

van[1]**,** *n.* the foremost division of an army or fleet, the advance-guard; the front of an army or the leading ships of a fleet in battle; the leaders of a movement, the forefront; the leading position in a movement etc. [short for VANGUARD]

van[2]**,** *n.* a motor vehicle, usu. covered, for conveying goods, furniture etc.; a closed railway-carriage for luggage or for the guard. *v.t.* (*past, p.p.* **vanned**) to convey in a van. [shortened from CARAVAN]

van[3]**,** *n.* †a fan or machine for winnowing grain; †a wing; (*Mining*) a test of the quality of ore by washing on a shovel etc. *v.t.* to test (ore) thus. **vanner,** *n.* [F, from L *vannum,* nom. *-us,* FAN[1]]

vanadium, *n.* a rare, silver-white metallic element, at. no. 23; chem. symbol V, used to give tensile strength to steel and, in the form of its salts, to produce an intense permanent black colour. **vanadate,** *n.* a salt of vanadic acid. **vanadic, vanadous,** *a.* **vanadinite,** *n.* a mineral composed of vanadate and lead chloride. [mod. L, from *Vanadis,* a Scand. goddess]

Van Allen belts, *n. pl.* two doughnut-shaped zones of atomic particles around Earth, discovered 1958 by James Van Allen (1914–). The atomic particles come from the Earth's upper atmosphere and the solar wind, and are trapped by the Earth's magnetic field. The inner belt lies 1000–5000 km/620–3100 miles above the Earth, and contains protons and electrons. The outer belt lies 15,000–25,000 km/9300–15,500 miles above the equator, but is lower around the magnetic poles. It contains mostly electrons from the solar wind.

Van Basten, *n.* **Marco** (1964–), Dutch international footballer, noted as a striker. He helped the Netherlands to win the European Championship in 1988 and scored two goals for AC Milan in the European Cup final in 1989.

Vanbrugh, *n.* **John** (1664–1726), English baroque architect and dramatist. He designed Blenheim Palace, Oxfordshire, and Castle Howard, Yorkshire, and wrote the comedy plays *The Relapse* (1696) and *The Provok'd Wife* (1697).

Van Buren, *n.* **Martin** (1782–1862), 8th president of the US, a Democrat, born in Kinderhook, New York, of Dutch ancestry. He was a senator 1821–28, governor of New York State 1828–29, secretary of state 1829–31, minister to Britain 1831–33, vice president 1833–37, and president 1837–41. He initiated the independent treasury system, but his refusal to spend land revenues cost him the 1840 election. He lost the 1844 Democratic nomination to Polk, and in 1848 ran unsuccessfully for president as the Free Soil candidate.

Vance, *n.* **Cyrus** (1917–), US Democrat politician, secretary of state 1977–80. He resigned because he did not support President Carter's abortive mission to rescue the US hostages in Iran.

†**vancourier,** AVANT-COURIER, see AVANT-.

Vancouver[1], *n.* industrial city (oil refining, engineering, shipbuilding, aircraft, timber, pulp and paper, textiles, fisheries) in Canada, its chief Pacific seaport, on the mainland of British Columbia; population (1986) 1,381,000.

Vancouver[2], *n.* **George** (*c.* 1758–98), British navigator who made extensive exploration of the W coast of North America.

Vancouver Island, *n.* island off the W coast of Canada, part of British Columbia. **area** 32,136 sq km/12,404 sq miles. **towns** Victoria, Nanaimo, naval base Esquimalt. **products** coal, timber, fish.

V and A, (*abbr.*) Victoria and Albert Museum.

Vandal, *n.* one of a Teutonic people from the shores of the Baltic that overran Gaul, Spain, and N Africa and Rome in the 5th cent., destroying works of art etc.; (**vandal**) one who wilfully or ignorantly destroys or damages anything. **Vandalic,** *a.* **vandalize, -ise,** *v.t.* to destroy or damage deliberately and senselessly. **vandalism,** *n.* [L *Vandalus,* from Teut. (cp. OE *Wendle,* pl., cogn. with G *wandeln,* to WANDER)]

van de Graaff, *n.* **Robert Jemison** (1901–67), US physicist who from 1929 developed a high-voltage generator, which in its modern form can produce more than a million volts. It consists of an endless vertical conveyor belt that carries electrostatic charges (resulting from friction) up to a large hollow sphere supported on an insulated stand. The lower end of the belt is earthed, so that charge accumulates on the sphere. The size of the voltage built up in air depends on the radius of the sphere, but can be increased by enclosing the generator in an inert atmosphere, such as nitrogen.

Vandemonian, *n., a.* a native or inhabitant of or relating to Tasmania; (*Austral. hist.*) a convict in Tasmania. [Van Dieman's Land, or Tasmania]

Vanderbilt, *n.* **Cornelius** (1794–1877), US industrialist, who made a fortune in steamships and (from the age of 70) by financing railways.

Van der Post, *n.* **Laurens (Jan)** (1906–), South African writer, whose books, many of them autobiographical, are concerned with the duality of human existence. They include the novels *Flamingo Feather* (1955), *The Seed and the Sower* (1963, set in Java, Japan, Britain, and Africa) and *A Story like the Wind* (1972). His travel books include *Venture to the Interior* (1952).

Van der Waals, *n.* **Johannes Diderik** (1837–1923), Dutch physicist who was awarded a Nobel prize in 1910 for his theoretical study of gases. He emphasized the forces of attraction and repulsion between atoms and molecules in describing the behaviour of real gases, as opposed to the ideal gases dealt with in Boyle's law and Charles's law.

van Dyck, Anthony DYCK, ANTHONY VAN.

Vandyke, *n.* a picture by Sir Anthony Van DYCK (1599–1641); any one of the series of points forming an ornamental border to lace, linen etc.; a collar or cape with these points. *a.* applied to the style of dress, esp. ornamented with vandykes, worn by the figures in Van Dyck's portraits. *v.t.* to cut the edge of (linen etc.) into Vandykes. **Vandyke beard,** *n.* a pointed beard. **Vandyke brown,** *n.* a reddish-brown colour or pigment. **Vandyke cape** or **collar,** *n.* one ornamented with vandykes.

vane, *n.* a weathercock, flag or arrow pointing in the direction of the wind; a similar device on an axis turned by a current of water etc., as in a meter; a fin on a bomb to ensure its falling on its war-head; the arm of a windmill; the blade of a propeller etc.; a horizontal part on a surveyor's levelling-staff for moving up and down to the line of sight of the telescope; the sight on a quadrant, compass etc.; the broad part of a feather; (*Naut.*) a slender streamer used to show the direction of the wind, a dog-vane. **vaned,** *a.* **vaneless,** *a.* [OE *fana,* small flag (cp. Dut. *vaan,* G *Fahne,* Icel. *fāni,* Swed. *fana,* Dan. *fane*), cogn. with L *pannus,* cloth, PANE]

Vane[1], *n.* **Henry** (1613–62), English politician. In 1640 elected a member of the Long Parliament, he was prominent in the impeachment of Archbishop Laud, and 1643–53 was in effect the civilian head of the Parliamentary government. At the Restoration he was executed.

Vane[2], *n.* **John** (1923–), British pharmacologist who discovered the wide role of prostaglandins in the human body, produced in response to illness and stress. He shared a Nobel prize 1982.

Vanessa, *n.* a genus of butterflies with notched wings, comprising the Red Admiral, Camberwell Beauty etc. [etym. doubtful]

van Eyck, Jan EYCK, JAN VAN.

vang, *n.* either of a pair of guy-ropes running from the peak of a gaff to the deck to steady it. [Dut., from *vangen,* to catch, cogn. with FANG]

vangee, *n.* a contrivance comprising a barrel and crank-brakes for working a ship's pumps. [etym. doubtful]

van Gogh, Vincent GOGH, VINCENT VAN.

vanguard, *n.* the troops who march in the front or van of an army, an advance-guard, the van; the leaders or leading position in a movement etc. [OF *avant-warde, -garde* (AVANT-, GUARD)]

vanilla, *n.* a genus of tall, epiphytal orchids, natives of tropical Asia and America, bearing fragrant flowers; the fruit of *Vanilla planifolia* and other species yielding the vanilla of commerce; an extract from this used for flavouring ices, syrups etc. **vanillate,** *n.* **vanillic,** *a.* pertaining to or derived from vanilla **vanillism,** *n.* an eruptive, itching skin-disease prevalent among persons handling vanilla-pods, caused by an insect. [Sp. *vainilla,* small pod, dim. of *vaina,* case, sheath, pod, L VAGINA]

vanish, *v.i.* to disappear suddenly; to become imperceptible, to be lost to sight, to fade away, to dissolve; to pass away, to pass out of existence; (*Math.*) to become zero. **vanishing cream,** *n.* a cosmetic which is rapidly absorbed into the pores leaving no trace of grease. **vanishing fraction,** *n.* a fraction that reduces to zero for a particular value of the variable which enters it. **vanishing point,** *n.* the point in which all parallel lines in the same plane tend to meet. [ME *vanissen,* prob. through A-F *evaniss-,* pres.p. stem of *evanir,* OF *esvanir,* L *ēvānescere,* from *vānus,* empty, VAIN]

vanity, *n.* the quality or state of being vain; empty pride, conceit of one's personal attainments or attractions; ostentation, show; emptiness, futility, unreality, worthlessness; that which is visionary, unreal or deceptive. **vanity bag,** *n.* a small ornamental hand-bag carried by women, usu. containing powder-puff, mirror etc. **vanity case,** *n.* a small case used to carry a woman's make-up and toiletries. [F *vanité,* L *vānitātem,* nom. *-tas,* from *vānus,* VAIN]

vanner VAN3.

vanquish, *v.t.* to conquer, to overcome, to subdue, to

refute. **vanquishable,** *a.* **vanquisher,** *n.* †**vanquishment,** *n.* [ME *venkissen,* OF *veinquiss-,* pres.p. stem of *veinquir, veincre* (F *vaincre*), L *vincere*]

vantage, *n.* advantage; a situation, condition, or opportunity favourable to success; (*Lawn Tennis*) the point scored by either side after deuce or five all. *v.t.* to profit to advantage. **vantage-ground,** *n.* superiority of position or place. [short for ADVANTAGE]

Vanuatu, *n.* Republic of. Group of islands in the S Pacific, part of Melanesia. **area** 14,800 sq km/5714 sq miles. **capital** Vila on Efate. **physical** comprises about 70 islands, including Espiritu Santo, Malekala, and Efate; densely forested. **population** (1988) 149,400 (90% Melanesian); annual growth rate 23.6%. **exports** copra, fish, coffee; tourism is important. **language** Bislama 82%, English, French, all official. **religion** Presbyterian 40%, Roman Catholic 16%, Anglican 14%, animist 15%.

Vanwall, *n.* British motor-racing team and the first winners of the Constructor's Championship 1958. The company was started by Tony Vandervell and they launched their first car 1954. It was designed around a Ferrari chassis with a Norton engine. Stirling Moss drove for Vanwall and won the 1956 International Trophy.

†**vanward,** VANGUARD.

vapid, *a.* insipid, flat, spiritless. **vapidity, vapidness,** *n.* **vapidly,** *adv.* [L *vapidus,* cogn. with VAPOUR]

vaporable, vaporific, vaporize etc. VAPOUR.

vaporetto, *n.* a small steamship that travels the canals of Venice. [It. *vapore,* a steamboat]

vapour, *n.* moisture in the air, light mist; (*loosely*) any visible diffused substance floating in the atmosphere; the gaseous form of a substance that is normally liquid or solid; an unreal or unsubstantial thing, a vain imagination; a remedial preparation applied by inhaling; †empty brag, swagger; (*pl.*) depression of spirits, hypochondria. *v.i.* to give out vapour; to boast, to brag, to bluster. **vapour-bath,** *n.* the application of vapour or steam to the body in a close place; the room or apparatus for this. **vapour-burner,** *n.* the apparatus for vaporizing a liquid etc. **vapour density,** *n.* the density of a gas or vapour relative to hydrogen at the same temperature and pressure. **vapour-engine,** *n.* one driven by an elastic fluid other than steam. **vapour pressure,** *n.* the pressure exerted by a vapour that is in equilibrium with its solid or liquid form. **vapour trail,** *n.* a white trail of condensed vapour left in the sky after the passage of an aircraft. **vapour ware,** *n.* (*coll.*) computer hardware or software that is planned or promised but does not materialize. **vaporiferous, vaporific, vaporiform,** *a.* **vaporimeter,** *n.* an instrument for measuring the pressure of vapour. **vaporize, -ise,** *v.t.* to convert into vapour. *v.i.* to be converted into vapour. **vaporizer, -iser,** *n.* **vaporable, vaporizable, -isable,** *a.* **vaporization, -isation,** *n.* **vaporability,** *n.* **vaporole,** *n.* a thin glass capsule containing a volatile drug for inhalation or fumigation. **vaporous, vapoury,** *a.* **vaporosity, vaporousness,** *n.* **vaporously,** *adv.* †**vapourer,** *n.* a braggart, a bully. †**vapouringly,** *adv.* **vapourish,** *a.* full of vapours, hypochondriac, splenetic. **vapourishness,** *n.* [F *vapeur,* L *vapōrem,* nom. *-por* (whence *vaporāre,* to steam), cogn. with Gr. *kapnos,* smoke, and VAPID]

vapourer moth, *n.* a tussock moth, the female of which has vestigial wings and cannot fly.

vapulation, *n.* a flogging. †**vapulatory,** *a.* [L *vāpulāre,* to be flogged]

vaquero, *n.* (*Mexico, US*) a herdsman, a cowherd. [Sp., from med. L *vaccārius,* from L *vacca,* cow]

vara, *n.* a Spanish–American measure of length, about 33 in. (1 m). [Sp., VARE]

varactor, *n.* a two-electrode semi-conductor device in which capacitance varies with voltage.

Varanasi, Benares, *n.* holy city of the Hindus in Uttar Pradesh, India, on the Ganges; population (1981) 794,000. There are 1500 golden shrines, and a 5 km/3 miles frontage to the Ganges with sacred stairways (ghats) for purification by bathing.

Varangian, *n.* one of the Norse sea-rovers in the 8th to 12 cents. who ravaged the coasts of the Baltic and conquered part of Russia. **Varangian Guard,** *n.* the body-guard of the Byzantine emperors, formed partly of Varangians. [med. L *Varingus,* Icel. *Væringi,* confederate, from *vārar,* oaths, cogn. with L *vērus,* true]

Varanus, *n.* (*Zool.*) a genus of lizards comprising the monitors. [mod. L, from Arab. *waran,* lizard]

†**vare,** *n.* a wand or staff of office. [Sp. *vara,* ult. from L *vārus,* crooked]

varec, *n.* an impure carbonate of soda made in Brittany. [F *varech,* cogn. with WRECK, cp. Swed. *vrak*]

Varèse, *n.* **Edgard** (1885–1965), French composer, who settled in New York 1916 where he founded the New Symphony Orchestra 1919 to advance the cause of modern music. His work is experimental and often dissonant, combining electronic sounds with orchestral instruments, and includes *Hyperprism* (1923), *Intégrales* (1931), and *Poème Electronique* (1958).

Vargas, *n.* **Getúlio** (1883–1954), president of Brazil 1930–45 and 1951–54. He overthrew the republic 1930 and in 1937 he set up a totalitarian, pro-fascist state known as the Estado Novo. Ousted by a military coup 1945, he returned as president 1951 but, amid mounting opposition and political scandal, committed suicide 1954.

Vargas Llosa, *n.* **Mario** (1937–), Peruvian novelist and conservative politician, presidential candidate 1990. His novels include *La ciudad y los perros/The Time of the Hero* (1963) and *La guerra del fin del mundo/The War at the End of the World* (1982).

vari-, *comb. form* various, variegated. [L *varius,* VARIOUS]

variable, *a.* capable of varying, liable to change; changeable, unsteady, fickle, inconstant; able to be varied, adapted or adjusted; quantitatively indeterminate, susceptible of continuous change of value, esp. assuming different values while others remain constant; applied to stars whose apparent magnitudes are not constant; (*Biol.*) tending to variations of structure, function etc. *n.* that which is variable; (*Math.*) a variable quantity; (*Naut.*) a shifting wind, (*pl.*) the region between northerly and southerly trade-winds. **variable condenser,** *n.* a condenser whose capacity is constantly and easily adjustable. **variable mu valve,** *n.* an electronic valve in which the degree of current control varies with the amount of current. **variability, variableness,** *n.* **variably,** *adv.* [F, from late L *variābilis,* from *variāre,* to VARY]

variance, *n.* the state of being variant, disagreement, difference of opinion, dissension, discord; (*Law*) disagreement between the allegations and proof or between the writ and the declaration; (*Statistics*) a measure of the dispersion of a set of observations. **variant,** *a.* showing variation, differing in form, character, or details; tending to vary, changeable. *n.* a variant form, reading, type etc. [L *variāntia,* as prec.]

variation, *n.* the act, process or state of varying; alteration, change, modification, deviation, mutation; the extent to which a thing varies; inflexion; deviation of a heavenly body from the mean orbit or motion; the angle of deviation from true north or of declination of the magnetic needle; the deviation in structure or function from the type or parent form; (*Math.*) the relation between the changes of quantities that vary as each other; permutation; (*Mus.*) a repetition of a theme with fanciful elaborations and changes of form. **variate,** *v.t.* **variational,** *a.* **variative,** *a.* **variator,** *n.* [F, from L *variātiōnem,* nom. *-tio,* as prec.]

varicated etc. VARIX.

varicella, *n.* chicken-pox. **varicellar, varicelloid,** *a.* [dim. of VARIOLA]

varices, *n.pl.* VARIX.

varicoloured, *a.* variously coloured, variegated, particoloured. **varicorn,** *a.* having diversiform antennae. *n.* a varicorn beetle. [L *cornu,* horn]

varicose, *a.* permanently dilated, affected with varix (said of veins); intended for the cure of varices; varicated. **varicocele,** *n.* a tumour formed by varicose veins of the spermatic cord. **varicosed,** *a.* **varicosity,** *n.* †**varicous** VARICOSE. [L *varicōsus,* from VARIX]

varied VARY.

variegate, *v.t.* to diversify in colour, to mark with patches of different hues; to dapple, to chequer. **variegation,** *n.* [L *variegātus,* p.p. of *variegāre* (VARI-, *agere,* to drive, to make)]

variety, *n.* the quality or state of being various; diversity, absence of sameness or monotony, many-sidedness, versatility; a collection of diverse things; a minor class or group of things differing in some common peculiarities from the class they belong to; a kind, a sort, a thing of such a sort or kind; an individual or group differing from the type of its species in some transmittable quality but usually fertile with others of the species, a sub-species. **variety entertainment** or **show,** *n.* an entertainment consisting of singing, dancing, acrobatic turns, conjuring etc. **variety theatre,** *n.* one for variety shows, a music-hall. **varietal,** *a.* **varietally,** *adv.* **variform,** *a.* varying in form, of different shapes. †**variformed,** *a.* **varifocal lens,** *n.* a lens in a pair of spectacles which is similar to a bifocal but in which the focusing range alters more gradually from the bottom to the top of the lens. [F *varieté,* L *varietātem,* nom. *-tas,* from *varius,* VARIOUS]

variola, *n.* smallpox. **variolar, variolic, variolous,** *a.* **variolation,** *n.* inoculation with smallpox virus. **variole,** *n.* a shallow pit-like depression, a *foveola.* **variolate, -lated,** *a.* **variolite,** *n.* a variety of spherulitic basalt with a surface resembling skin marked with smallpox. **varioloid,** *a.* resembling or of the nature of smallpox. *n.* a mild form of smallpox, esp. as modified by previous inoculation. [med. L, dim. from L *varius,* VARIOUS]

variorum, *a.* with notes of various commentators inserted (of an edition of a work). **variorum edition,** *n.* an edition of a classic etc. with comparisons of texts and notes by various editors and commentators. [L, gen. of *varius,* see foll.]

various, *a.* differing from each other, diverse; divers, several; variable; uncertain, not uniform. **variously,** *adv.* **variousness,** *n.* [L *varius*]

varix, *n.* (*pl.* **-ices**) a permanent dilatation of a vein or other vessel; a varicose vessel; one of the ridges traversing the whorls of a univalve shell. **varicated,** *a.* having varices. **varication,** *n.* [L, prob. from VARUS²]

varlet, *n.* a page, an attendant preparing to be a squire; a menial; a knave, a rascal. †**varletry,** *n.* the rabble, the crowd. [OF *varlet, vaslet,* dim. of VASSAL]

varmint, *n.* (*prov.*) a troublesome or mischievous person or animal. [corr. of VERMIN]

varna, *n.* any of the four great Hindu castes. [Sansk., class]

Varna, *n.* port in Bulgaria, on an inlet of the Black Sea; population (1987) 306,000. Industries include shipbuilding and the manufacture of chemicals.

varnish, *n.* a thin resinous solution for applying to the surface of wood, metal etc., to give it a hard, transparent, shiny coating; any lustrous or glossy appearance on the surface of leaves etc.; the lustrous surface or glaze of pottery etc.; (*fig.*) superficial polish, gloss, palliation, whitewash. *v.t.* to cover with varnish; to give an improved appearance to, to gloss over, to whitewash. **varnish-tree,** *n.* any tree from which the material for varnish is obtained. **varnisher,** *n.* **varnishing-day,** *n.* a day before the opening of an exhibition when artists are allowed to varnish or retouch their pictures. [F *vernis,* etym. doubtful, whence *vernisser, vernir,* to varnish]

varry, *n.* (*Her.*) a strip of vair used as a bearing. **varriated,** *a.* crenellated, in the form of a battlement with merlons and crenelles. [var. of VAIR]

†**varsal,** *a.* (*coll.*) universal. [corr. of UNIVERSAL]

varsity, *n.* (*coll.*) university. [corr. of UNIVERSITY]

varsovienne, *n.* a dance imitating the mazurka; music for this. [F, from *Varsovie,* Warsaw]

vartabed, *n.* one of an Armenian order of teaching clergy.

Varuna, *n.* in early Hindu mythology, sky god and king of the universe.

varus¹, *n.* a variety of club-foot in which the foot is bent inwards; also called talipes varus [see TALIPES]; a knock-kneed person. [L, knock-kneed]

varus², *n.* acne. [L, blotch, pimple]

varve, *n.* a seasonal layer of clay deposited in still water, used to fix Ice Age chronology. [Swed. *varv,* layer]

†**varvel,** *n.* a metal ring bearing the owner's name attached to the jesses of a hawk. †**varveled,** *a.* (*Her.*) having varvels attached. [var. of VERVELLE]

vary, *v.t.* (*past, p.p.* **varied**) to change, to alter in appearance, form or substance; to modify, to diversify; to make variations of (a melody etc.). *v.i.* to be altered in any way; to undergo change; to be different or diverse, to differ, to be of different kinds; to increase or decrease proportionately with or inversely to the increase or decrease of another quantity. [F *varier,* L *variāre,* from *varius,* VARIOUS]

vas, *n.* (*pl.* **vasa**) a vessel or duct. **vas deferens,** *n.* the spermatic duct. **vasal,** *a.* [L, vessel]

Vasari, *n.* **Giorgio** (1511–74), Italian art historian, architect, and painter, author of *Lives of the Most Excellent Architects, Painters and Sculptors* (1550, enlarged and revised 1568), in which he proposed the theory of a renaissance of the arts beginning with Giotto and culminating with Michelangelo. He designed the Uffizi Palace, Florence.

vascular, *a.* of, consisting of, or containing vessels or ducts for the conveyance of blood, chyle, sap etc.; containing or rich in blood-vessels. **vascularity,** *n.* **vascularize, -ise,** *v.t.* **vascularization, -isation,** *n.* **vascularly,** *adv.* **vasculiform,** *a.* **vasculose,** *a.* vascular. *n.* the substance forming the chief constituent of the vessels of plants. [VASCULUM]

vasculum, *n.* (*pl.* **-la**) a botanist's collecting-case, usu. of tin; (*Anat.*) a small vessel, a vas; the penis. [L, dim. of VAS]

vase, *n.* a vessel of pottery etc., of various forms but usu. circular with a swelling body and a foot or pedestal, applied to various ornamental and other purposes; a sculptured ornament in imitation of an ancient vase, used to decorate cornices, gate-posts, monuments etc.; (*Arch.*) the bell of a Corinthian or Composite capital. **vase-painting,** *n.* the decoration of vases with pigments, esp. as practised by the ancient Greeks. **vaseful,** *a.* [F *vase,* L *vasum,* vase, vessel, cogn. with VAS]

vasectomy, *n.* excision of the vas deferens or part of it to produce sterility. [Gr. *ek,* out, *tome,* a cut]

Vaseline®, *n.* a yellow, soft, medicated paraffin jelly employed as a lubricant etc.

vasi-, vaso-, *comb. form* pertaining to a vas, vessel or duct. [VAS]

vasiform, *a.* having the form of a vas.

vaso- VASI-.

vasoconstrictor, *a.* causing constriction of a blood-vessel (of nerves). **vasoconstriction,** *n.*

vasodilator, *a.* causing dilatation of a vessel. *n.* a nerve or drug causing this. **vasodilatation,** *n.*

vasomotor, *a.* causing constriction or dilatation in a vessel. *n.* a vasomotor agent or drug. **vasomotorial,** *a.*

vasosensory, *a.* supplying sensation to the vessels.

vassal, *n.* one holding land under a superior lord by feudal tenure, a feudatory; a slave, a humble dependant, a low wretch. *a.* servile. **vassalage,** *n.* the state or condition of a vassal; the obligation of a vassal to feudal service; servitude, dependence; a fief; vassals collectively; †prowess in arms. †**vassalry,** *n.* vassals collectively. [F, from med L *vassallus vassus,* from Celt. (cp. Bret. *gwaz,* W and Corn. *gwas,* O Ir. *foss,* servant)]

Vassilou, *n.* **Georgios Vassos** (1931–), Greek-Cypriot politician and entrepreneur, president from 1988. A self-made millionaire, he entered politics as an independent and in 1988 won the presidency, with Communist Party support. He has since, with United Nations help, tried unsuccessfully to heal the rift between the Greek and Turkish communities.

vast, *a.* of great extent, immense, huge, boundless; very great in numbers, amount, degree etc. *n.* a boundless expanse. **vastly,** *adv.* **vastness, †vastidity, †vastitude,** *n.* **†vasty,** *a.* [F *vaste,* L *vastus,* empty, waste, vast]

vastus, *n.* a large muscular mass on the outer or inner surface of the thigh. [as prec.]

†vasty VAST.

VAT, (*abbr.*) VALUE-ADDED TAX.

vat, *n.* a large tub, tank, or other vessel used for holding mash or hop-liquor in brewing and in many manufacturing operations in which substances are boiled or steeped. *v.t.* (*past, p.p.* **vatted**) to put into or treat in a vat. [formerly *fat,* OE *fæt* (cp. Dut. *vat,* G *fass,* Icel. and Swed. *fat,* Dan. *fad*), cogn. with Dut. *vatten,* G *fassen,* to catch, to contain]

Vatican, *n.* the palace of the Pope on the Vatican hill in Rome; the papal government. **Vatican City,** *n.* a small area on the Vatican Hill set up as an independent state in 1929. **area** 0.4 sq km/109 acres. **physical** forms an enclave in the heart of Rome, Italy. **population** (1985) 1000. **language** Italian. **religion** Roman Catholic. **Vatican Council,** *n.* the 20th Ecumenical Council (1869–70) at which the infallibility of the Pope when speaking ex cathedra was affirmed; also **Vatican II,** a similar council held between 1962 and 1965. **Vaticanism,** *n.* the term applied by W. E. Gladstone to the pretensions of the Holy See to infallibility etc.

†vaticide, *n.* the murder or murderer of a prophet. [L *vātes vātis,* prophet, -CIDE]

vaticinate, *v.t., i.* to prophesy. **†vaticinal,** *a.* **vaticination,** *n.* a prophecy. **vaticinator,** *n.* a prophet. [L *vāticinātus,* p.p. of *vāticinārī* (*vāti-,* see prec., *canere,* to sing)]

vaudeville, *n.* a slight dramatic sketch or pantomime interspersed with songs and dances; a miscellaneous series of sketches, songs etc., a variety entertainment; a French popular song with a refrain, a topical song; orig. a comic or convivial song, such as those of Olivier Basselin, poet, born in the Val de Vire (*d.* 1418). **vaudeville theater**: (*N Am.*) a music-hall. **vaudevillian,** *n.* one who performs in vaudeville. **vaudevillist,** *n.* a writer of vaudevilles. [F, corr. of *Vau* (*Val*) *de Vire,* Valley of the Vire]

Vaudois[1], *a.* of or pertaining to the canton of Vaud. *n.* (*pl.* **Vaudois**) a native or inhabitant of Vaud (Switzerland); the Vaudois dialect. [F]

Vaudois[2], *a.* of or pertaining to the Waldenses. *n.* (*pl.* **Vaudois**) one of the Waldenses. [F, from med. L *Valdenses,* WALDENSES]

Vaughan, *n.* **Henry** (1622–95), Welsh poet and physician. He published several volumes of metaphysical religious verse and prose devotions. His mystical outlook on nature influenced later poets, including Wordsworth.

Vaughan Williams, *n.* **Ralph** (1872–1958), English composer. His style was tonal and often evocative of the English countryside through the use of folk themes. Among his works are the orchestral *Fantasia on a Theme by Thomas Tallis* (1910); the opera *Sir John in Love* (1929), featuring the Elizabethan song 'Greensleeves'; and nine symphonies 1909–57.

vault[1], *n.* an arched roof, a continuous arch or semi-cylindrical roof, a series of arches connected by radiating joints; an arched chamber, esp. underground; a cellar; a place of interment built of masonry under a church or in a cemetery; any vault-like covering or canopy, as the sky; (*Anat.*) an arched roof of a cavity. *v.t.* to cover with, or as with, a vault or vaults; to construct in the form of a vault. **vaulting,** *n.* **†vaulty,** *a.* arched; concave. [ME and OF *voute,* fem. of *volt,* vaulted, L *volūtus,* p.p. of *volvere,* to roll]

vault[2], *v.i.* to leap or spring with the hands resting on something or with the help of a pole. *v.t.* to leap over thus. *n.* such a leap. **vaulting-horse,** *n.* wooden horse or frame for vaulting over in a gymnasium. **vaulter,** *n.* [ME *volter,* as prec.]

vaunt, *v.i.* to boast, to brag. *v.t.* to boast of; †to display. *n.* a boast. **vaunter,** *n.* **†vauntful,** *a.* **vauntingly,** *adv.* [F *vanter,* late L *vānitāre,* freq. from *vānus,* VAIN]

†vaunt-courier, etc. AVANT-.

vavasour, *n.* a vassal holding land from a great vassal and having other vassals under him. **†vavasory,** *n.* the tenure or lands of a vavasour. [OF *vavassour,* med. L *vassus vassōrum,* VASSAL of vassals]

vb, (*abbr.*) verb.

VC, (*abbr.*) Victoria Cross; Vice-Chancellor; Vice-Consul; Vice-Chairman.

vc, (*abbr.*) violoncello.

VCR (*abbr.*) a video cassette recorder.

VD, (*abbr.*) venereal disease.

VDT, (*abbr.*) visual display terminal.

VDU, (*abbr.*) visual display unit, an electronic output device for displaying the data processed by a computer on a screen. The oldest and the most popular type is the cathode-ray tube (CRT), which uses essentially the same technology as a television screen. Other types use plasma display technology and liquid crystal displays.

VE, (*abbr.*) Victory in Europe. **VE Day,** *n.* the day, 8 May 1945, on which hostilities in Europe in World War II ceased.

Veader, *n.* a supplementary or intercalary month inserted by the Hebrews every third year after the month Adar. [Heb. (*ve* and ADAR)]

veal, *n.* the flesh of a calf as food. **veal-skin,** *n.* a skin-disease with shiny white tubercles, usu. on the ears, neck and face. **vealy,** *a.* [OF *veël* (F *veau*), L *vitellum,* nom. *-lus,* dim. of *vitelus,* calf, cogn. with Gr. *italos,* calf, *etos,* year, L *vetus,* old, cp. WETHER]

vector, *n.* a line in space or in a diagram representing the magnitude and direction of a quantity; as agent (such as an insect) that carries a virus disease from one host to another. *v.t.* to direct aircraft to a particular point. **vector quantity,** *n.* a quantity having both magnitude and direction (e.g. velocity), but not temperature. **vectorial,** *a.* [L, carrier, from *vehere,* to carry, p.p. *vectus*]

Veda, *n.* the ancient Hindu scriptures, divided into four portions or books (the *Rig-, Yajur-, Sâma-,* and *Artharva-Veda*). **Vedanga,** *n.* a work supplementary or auxiliary to the Veda. **Vedanta,** *n.* school of Hindu philosophy that developed the teachings of the *Upanishads.* One of its teachers was Śamkara, who lived in S India in the 8th century AD and is generally regarded as a manifestation of Siva. He taught that there is only one reality, Brahman, and that knowledge of Brahman leads finally to *moksha,* or liberation from reincarnation. **Vedantic,** *a.* **Vedantist,** *n., a.* **Vedic,** *a.* [Sansk., knowledge]

vedette, *n.* a sentinel stationed in advance of an outpost; a small vessel used for scouting purposes etc. [F, from It. *vedetta,* var. of *viduta,* fem. p.p. of *vedere,* L *vidēre,* to see]

vee, *n.* the 22nd letter of the alphabet, V, v; anything in the shape of this letter.

veer, *v.i.* to change its direction (of the wind), esp. in the direction of the sun; to shift, to change about, esp. in opinion, conduct etc. *v.t.* to let out or slacken (a rope etc.); to wear (a ship); †to shift, to change. *n.* a shift in direction or course. **to veer and haul,** to pull tight and slacken alternately. **to veer away** or **out,** to slacken and let run. **veeringly,** *adv.* [F *virer,* late L *virāre,* cp. *virola,* ring, L *viriola,* bracelet, dim. of *viria,* in *viriæ,* armlets]

veg, *n.* (*coll.*) short form of VEGETABLE.

Vega, *n.* the fifth brightest star in the sky, and the brightest in the constellation Lyra. It is a blue-white star, 27 light years away, with a luminosity of 50 Suns.

vega, *n.* a tract of flat, open land; (*Cuba*) a tobacco-field. [Sp.]

vegan, *n.* one who believes in the use for food, clothing etc. of vegetable products only, thus excluding dairy products, leather etc.; one who uses no animal products. [as foll.]

vegetable, *n.* a plant, esp. a herb used for culinary purposes or for feeding cattle etc.; one whose mental or physical capabilities are minimal as a result of injury, disease etc.; (*coll.*) an idle or passive person. *a.* pertaining to, of the nature of, or resembling, a plant; made of or pertaining to culinary vegetables. **vegetable-ivory** IVORY. **vegetable kingdom,** *n.* the division of organic nature comprising plants. **vegetable marrow,** *n.* the fruit of a species of gourd, *Curcurbita ovifera,* used as a culinary vegetable. **vegetable-mould,** *n.* mould or soil consisting to a certain extent of decaying or decayed vegetation. **vegetable oil,** *n.* an oil obtained from seeds or plants, used in cooking etc. **vegetability**, *n.* **vegetal**, *a.* pertaining to, or of the nature of plants; common to plants and animals (of the functions of nutrition, growth, circulation, secretions etc.). *n.* a plant, a vegetable. **vegetality**, *n.* **vegetaline**, *n.* a material imitating ivory, coral etc. made by treating woody fibre with sulphuric acid. **vegetarian**, *n.* one who abstains from animal food, and lives on vegetable food, and, usu. eggs, milk etc. **vegetarianism,** *n.* **vegetate**, *v.i.* to grow in the manner of a plant, to exercise the functions of a vegetable; (*fig.*) to live an idle, passive, monotonous life. **vegetation,** *n.* the act or process of vegetating; vegetables or plants collectively, plant-life; all the plants in a specified area; an excrescence on the body. **vegetative,** *a.* **vegetatively,** *adv.* **vegetativeness,** *n.* **vegeto-,** *comb. form.* [F, from late L *vegetābilis,* from *vegetāre,* to enliven, from L *vegetus,* lively, from *vegēre,* to move, to quicken, cogn. with VIGIL and VIGOUR]

veggie, *n.* short form of VEGETABLE; (*coll.*) short form of VEGETARIAN under VEGETABLE.

vehement, *a.* proceeding from or exhibiting intense fervour or passion, ardent, passionate, impetuous; acting with great force, energy or violence. **vehemently,** *adv.* **vehemence,** **†-mency,** *n.* [OF, from L *vehementem,* nom. *-ens,* perh. from *vehere,* to carry]

vehicle, *n.* any kind of carriage or conveyance for use on land, having wheels or runners; any liquid etc. serving as a medium for pigments, medicinal substances etc.; any person or thing employed as a medium for the transmission of thought, feeling etc. **vehicular, -lary, †-latory**, *a.* **†vehiculate,** *v.t., i.* [L *vehiculum,* from *vehere,* to carry]

vehmgericht, *n.* (*pl.* **-gerichte**) a system of irregular tribunals existing in Germany, esp. Westphalia, during the 14th and 15th cents., trying civil cases by day and the more serious criminal cases at night in secret sessions; such a tribunal. **vehmic,** *a.* [G *Feme,* punishment, tribunal, *Gericht,* judgment, law]

Veidt, *n.* **Conrad** (1893–1943), German film actor, memorable as the sleepwalker in *Das Kabinett des Dr Caligari/The Cabinet of Dr Caligari* (1919) and as the evil caliph in *The Thief of Bagdhad* (1940). In international films from the 1920s, he moved to Hollywood in the 1940s.

veil, *n.* a more or less transparent piece of cloth, muslin etc., usu. attached to the head-dress, worn to conceal, shade, or protect the face; a curtain or other drapery for concealing or protecting an object; a mask, a disguise, a pretext; the scarf on a pastoral staff; a velum; (*Mus.*) a slight huskiness or obscuration of voice, permanent or due to a cold etc. *v.t.* to cover with a veil; to hide, to conceal, to disguise. **veiling,** *n.* **to draw a veil over,** to conceal discretely; to refrain from mentioning. **to take the veil,** to assume the veil according to the custom of a woman when she becomes a nun; to retire to a convent. **veilless**, *a.* [ME and OF *veile,* L *vēlum*]

Veil, *n.* **Simone** (1927–), French politician. A survivor of Hitler's concentration camps, she was minister of health 1974–79, and framed the French abortion bill. In 1979–81 she was president of the European Parliament.

veilleuse, *n.* a night-lamp, shaded and usu. artistically decorated. [F, fem. of *veilleur,* from *veiller,* L *vigilāre,* to watch]

vein, *n.* one of the tubular vessels in animal bodies conveying blood to the heart; (*loosely*) any blood-vessel; a rib or nervure in an insect's wing or a leaf; a fissure in rock filled with material deposited by water; a seam of any substance; a streak or wavy stripe of different colour, in wood, marble, or stone; a distinctive trait, quality, tendency or cast of mind; particular mood or humour. *v.t.* to fill or cover with, or as with veins. **veinstone,** *n.* the non-metalliferous part in a vein, gangue. **veinage**, **veining,** *n.* **veinless**, *a.* **veinlet**, *n.* **veinlike, veiny,** *a.* [ME and F *veine,* L *vēna*]

velamen, velamentum, *n.* (*pl.* **mina, -menta**) (*Anat.*) a membraneous covering or envelope, esp. of parts of the brain. **velamentous,** *a.* **velar** VELUM. **velarium,** *n.* (*pl.* **-ia**,) the great awning stretched over the seats in a theatre or amphitheatre as a protection against rain or sun; a velum. **velation** VELUM. [L, from VELUM]

velarize, -ise, *v.t.* to sound a guttural further back than the hard palate. [L *velare,* to veil]

velatura, *n.* the glazing of pictures by rubbing on a thin coating of colour with the hand. [It. from *velare,* to VEIL]

Velázquez, *n.* **Diego Rodriguez de Silva y** (1599–1660), Spanish painter, born in Seville, the outstanding Spanish artist of the 17th cent. In 1623 he became court painter to Philip IV in Madrid, where he produced many portraits of the royal family, as well as occasional religious paintings, genre scenes, and other subjects. *Las Meninas/The Ladies-in-Waiting* (1655) (Prado, Madrid) is a complex group portrait which includes a self-portrait, but nevertheless focuses clearly on the doll-like figure of the Infanta Margareta Teresa.

Velcro®, *n.* a fastening for clothes etc. which consists of two nylon strips, one consisting of hooks the other of loops, which stick together when pressed.

veld, veldt, *n.* (*S Afr.*) open country suitable for pasturage, esp. the high treeless plains in N Transvaal and NW Natal. [Dut. *veld,* FIELD]

Velde, van de, *n.* family of Dutch artists. Both **Willem van de Velde** the Elder (1611–93) and his son **Willem van de Velde** the Younger (1633–1707) painted sea battles for Charles II and James II (having settled in London 1672). Another son **Adriaen van de Velde** (1636–72) painted landscapes.

veld-schoen, *n.* a shoe made of raw hide. [Dut. *vel,* skin, *schoen,* shoe]

veldt VELD.

veleta, *n.* a dance or dance tune in slow waltz time (also **valeta**). [Sp. weathercock]

veliferous etc. VELUM.

†velitation, *n.* a slight skirmish; a controversial skirmish, a brush. **velite,** *n.* (*Rom. Ant.*) a light-armed soldier. [L *vēlitātio,* from *vēlitārī,* to skirmish, from *vēles,* light-armed soldier, a velite]

vell, *n.* the fourth stomach of a calf used in making rennet.

†velleity, *n.* a low degree of desire or volition unaccompanied by effort. [med. L *velleitas,* from *velle,* to wish]

vellicate, *v.t., v.i.* to twitch spasmodically. **vellication,** *n.* **vellicative,** *a.* [L *vellicātus,* p.p. of *vellicāre,* from *vellere,* to pluck]

vellon, *n.* a former Spanish money of account. [Sp.]

velloped, *a.* (*Her.*) having gills or wattles. [prob. var. of DEWLAPPED]

vellum, *n.* a fine parchment orig. made of calf-skin; a manuscript written on this. **vellum-paper,** *n.* paper made to imitate vellum. **vellumy,** *a.* [ME *velim,* F *velin,* L *vitulīnus,* of a calf, from *vitulus,* see VEAL]

veloce, *adv.* (*Mus.*) with great quickness. [It.]

velocipede, *n.* any kind of carriage propelled by the feet; an early form of cycle. **†velociman,** *n.* an early vehicle resembling a velocipede, but driven by hand. **velocipedist,** *n.* [L *vēlox,* as foll.]

velocity, *n.* swiftness, rapidity, rapid motion; rate of motion, esp. of inanimate things. **velocimeter,** *n.* an apparatus for measuring velocity -METER. [F *vélocité,* L *vēlōcitātem,* nom. *-tas,* from *vēlox-lōcis,* swift, cogn. with *volāre,* to fly]

velodrome, *n.* a building containing a cycle-racing track. [F *vélodrome*]

velours, velure, *n.* velvet, velveteen or other fabric resembling velvet; a pad of velvet or silk for smoothing a

silk hat. *v.t.* to smooth with this. **velouté**, *n.* a thick creamy sauce or soup. **veloutine**, *n.* a corded fabric of merino etc. **velutinous**, *a.* (*Nat. Hist.*) velvety. [F *velours,* OF *velous,* med. L *villōsus,* shaggy, from VILLUS]
velum, *n.* (*pl.* **-la**) (*Anat. etc.*) a membrane, a membranous covering envelope etc., esp. the soft palate. **velar**, *a.* **velation**, *n.* **veliferous**, *a.* **veligerous**, *a.* [L, sail, covering, from *vehere,* to carry]
velveret, *n.* an inferior kind of velvet.
velvet, *n.* a closely-woven fabric, usu. of silk, with a short, soft nap or cut pile on one side; the furry skin covering the growing antlers of a deer; (*sl.*) money won by gambling or speculation. *a.* velvety; as soft as velvet. **cotton velvet**, velvet made with cotton back and silk face. **on velvet**, (*coll.*) in a position of comfort, luxury, wealth etc. **velvet glove**, *n.* gentleness concealing strength. †**velvet-guard**, *n.* velvet trimmings; a person wearing such trimmings. **velvet-paper**, *n.* flock wall-paper. **velvet-pile**, *n.* a pile like that of velvet; a fabric with such a pile. **velveted**, **velvety**, *a.* **velveteen**, *n.* a cotton velvet or cotton fabric with a velvet-pile; †*n.pl.* (*sl.*) a gamekeeper. **velveting**, *n.* the fine nap or pile of velvet; (*collect.*) velvet goods. [A-F from late L *velluētum,* ult. from L VILLUS]
vena, *n.* (*pl.* **venae**) a vein. **venal**[1], *a.* **venation**, *n.* the arrangement of the veins on leaves, insects' wings etc. **venational**, *a.* **venepuncture**, *n.* the piercing of a vein, esp. with a hypodermic needle. [L]
venal[2], *a.* ready to be bought over for lucre or to sacrifice honour or principle for sordid considerations; mercenary, hireling, sordid. **venality**, *n.* **venally**, *adv.* [OF, from L *vēnālis,* from *vēnus, vēnum,* sale]
venatic, -al, *a.* pertaining to or used in hunting; fond of the chase. **venatically**, *adv.* **venatorial**, *a.* [L *venāticus,* from *venātus,* hunting, see VENERY[1]]
venation VENA.
vend, *v.t.* (*chiefly legal*) to sell; to offer (small wares) for sale (as a costermonger etc.). **vending machine**, *n.* a slot machine dispensing goods, e.g. cigarettes, drinks, sweets. **vendee**, *n.* **vendor** (*Law*), **vender**, *n.* **vendible**, *a.* **vendibility**, †**vendibleness**, *n.* †**vendibly**, *adv.* in a saleable manner. †**vendition**, *n.* †**vendue**, *n.* a public auction. [F *vendre,* L *vendere* (*vēnum,* see VENAL[2], *dare,* to give)]
Venda, *n.* Black National State from 1979, near Zimbabwe border, in South Africa. **area** 6500 sq km/ 2510 sq miles. **capital** Thohoyandou. **towns** MaKearela. **population** (1980) 343,500. **products** coal, copper, graphite, construction stone. **language** Luvenda, English.
vendace, *n.* a small and delicate white-fish, *Coregonus vandesius,* found in some lakes. [OF *vendese, vandoise,* dace]
Vendéan, *a.* of or pertaining to La Vendée, a western department of France. *n.* an inhabitant or native of La Vendée; a member of the Royalist party who revolted against the French Republic in 1793–5.
Vendée, Wars of the, in the French Revolution, a series of peasant risings against the Revolutionary government that began in the Vendée *département*, W France 1793, and spread to other areas of France, lasting until 1795.
vendee etc. VEND.
Vendemiaire, *n.* the first month of the French revolutionary calendar (22 Sept.–21 Oct.). [F, from L *vindēmia,* vintage, from *vinum,* wine]
vendetta, *n.* a blood-feud, often carried on for generations, in which the family of a murdered or injured man seeks vengeance on the offender or any member of his family, prevalent, esp. in Corsica, Sardinia and Sicily; this practice; a feud, private warfare or animosity. [It., from L *vindicta,* revenge, see VINDICTIVE]
vendible, †**vendue** etc. VEND.
veneer, *v.t.* to cover with a thin layer of fine or superior wood; to coat (pottery etc.) with a thin coating; to put a superficial polish on, to disguise, to gloss over. *n.* a thin layer of superior wood for veneering; superficial polish. **veneer-cutter, -mill, -saw**, *n.* a machine etc., for cutting veneers. **veneering**, *n.* [G *furniren,* to inlay, F *fournir,* to FURNISH]
venenate, *a.* infected with poison. †**veneficial**, **-cious**, *a.* acting by poison or sorcery. **venenation**, *n.* **venenific**, **venenifluous**, *a.* [L *venēnātus,* p.p. of *venēnāre,* from *venēnum,* poison]
venerable, *a.* worthy of veneration; rendered sacred by religious or other associations; applied as a title to archdeacons in the Church of England, and to a person who has attained the first of three degrees in canonization in the Roman Catholic Church. **venerability**, **venerableness**, *n.* **venerably**, *adv.* [OF, from L *venerābilis,* as foll.]
venerate, *v.t.* to regard or treat with profound deference and respect, to revere. **veneration**, *n.* **venerative**, *a.* **venerator**, *n.* [L *venerātus,* p.p. of *venerāri,* cogn. with VENUS and with Sansk. *van,* to serve, to honour]
venereal, *a.* pertaining to, or produced by sexual intercourse. **venereal disease**, *n.* disease conveyed by sexual intercourse, viz., gonorrhoea, syphilis and chancroid. **venerean**, **venereous**, *a.* lustful, libidinous; aphrodisiac. †**venereate**, *v.t.* **venereology**, *n.* the study of venereal diseases. **venery**[1], *n.* sexual indulgence. [L *venereus,* from VENUS]
venery[2], *n.* hunting, the chase. [OF *venerie,* from *vener,* L *vēnārī,* to hunt]
venesect, *v.t., i.* to make an incision in a vein. **venesection**, *n.* [L *vēna,* VEIN, *secāre,* to cut, p.p. *sectus*]
Venetian, *a.* pertaining to the city or province of Venice, in N Italy. *n.* a native or inhabitant of Venice; (*coll.*) a venetian blind; (*pl.*) a heavy kind of tape or braid used in venetian blinds. **Venetian blind**, *n.* a blind made of thin slats on braid or webbing arranged to turn so as to admit or exclude light. **venetian chalk**, *n.* French chalk. **Venetian glass**, *n.* a delicate ornamental glass-ware made at or near Venice. **Venetian lace**, *n.* a variety of point lace. **Venetian mast**, *n.* a pole painted spirally in two or more colours, used for street decorations. **venetian window**, *n.* a window with three separate apertures. [L *Venetia,* country of the Veneti]
Veneto, *n.* region of NE Italy, comprising the provinces of Belluno, Padova (Padua), Treviso, Rovigo, Venezia (Venice), and Vicenza; area 18,400 sq km/7102 sq miles; population (1988) 4,375,000. Its capital is Venice, and towns include Padua, Verona, and Vicenza. Veneto forms part of the N Italian plain, with the delta of the Po; it includes part of the Alps and Dolomites, and Lake Garda. Products include cereals, fruit, vegetables, wine, chemicals, shipbuilding, and textiles.
†**venew, venue, veney**, *n.* a bout at fencing; a thrust or hit.
Venezuela, *n.* Republic of, country in N South America, on the Caribbean Sea, bounded E by Guyana, S by Brazil, and W by Colombia. **area** 912,100 sq km/ 352,162 sq miles. **capital** Caracas. **towns** Barquisimeto, Valencia; port Maracaibo. **physical** valleys and delta of river Orinoco flanked by mountains. **exports** coffee, cocoa, timber, oil, aluminium, iron ore, petrochemicals. **population** (1988) 18,770,000 (70% mestizos, 32,000 American Indians); annual growth rate 2.8%. **religion** Roman Catholic. **language** Spanish (official), Indian languages 2%.
vengeance, *n.* punishment inflicted in return for an injury or wrong, retribution; †mischief, evil. **with a vengeance**, forcibly, emphatically, undoubtedly, extremely. †**venge**, *v.t.* to avenge or revenge. †**vengeable**, *a.* **vengeful**, *a.* vindictive, revengeful. **vengefully**, *adv.* **vengefulness**, *n.* †**vengement**, *n.* †**venger**, *n.* †**vengeress**, *n. fem.* [F, from *venger,* to *avenge,* L *vindicāre,* see VINDICATE]
veni, vidi, vici , I came, I saw, I conquered. [L]
venial, *a.* that may be pardoned or excused; in the Roman Catholic Church, not mortal (of some sins). **veniality**, **venialness**, *n.* **venially**, *adv.* [OF, from late L *veniālis,* from *venia,* grace, pardon]
Venice[1], *n.* (Italian **Venezia**) city, port, and naval base, capital of Veneto, Italy, on the Adriatic; population

(1988) 328,000. The old city is built on piles on low-lying islands. Apart from tourism, industries include glass, jewellery, textiles, and lace. Venice was an independent trading republic from the 10th cent., ruled by a doge, or chief magistrate, and was one of the centres of the Italian Renaissance.

Venice[2], *a.* Venetian. **Venice glass,** *n.* Venetian glass. [see prec.]

Veni Creator, *n.* a hymn beginning 'Veni Creator Spiritus', 'Come Creator Spirit', used in the Anglican and Roman Catholic Churches at Whitsuntide, ordinations etc. [L]

venison, *n.* the flesh of the deer as food. [OF *veneisun* (F *venaison*), L *vēnātiōnem*, nom. *-tio,* from *vēnāri,* to hunt, see VENERY]

Venite, *n.* Psalm xcv, 'O come let us sing', used as a canticle; a musical setting of the same. [L, come ye]

Venizelos, *n.* **Eleutherios** (1864–1936), Greek politician born in Crete, leader of the Cretan movement against Turkish rule until the union of the island with Greece in 1905. He later became prime minister of the Greek state on five occasions, 1910–15, 1917–20, 1924, 1928–32 and 1933, before being exiled to France in 1935.

Venn diagram, *n.* in mathematics, a diagram representing a set or sets and the logical relationships between them. Sets are drawn as circles. An area of overlap between two circles (sets) contains elements that are common to both sets, and thus represents a third set. Circles that do not overlap represent sets with no elements in common (disjoint sets). The method is named after the British logician John Venn (1834–1923).

venom, *n.* a poisonous fluid secreted by serpents, scorpions etc., and injected by biting or stinging; spite, malignity, virulence; poison. *a.* venomous. *v.t.* to imbue with venom; to poison. **venom-mouthed,** *a.* full of venom; spiteful. **venomed, venomous,** *a.* **venomously,** *adv.* **venomousness,** *n.* [ME and OF *venim* (F *venin*), L *venēnum,* poison]

venose, -nous, *a.* pertaining to or contained in the veins; consisting of veins. **venosity,** *n.* local excess of veins or of venous blood; deficient aeration of venous blood with afflux of this to the arteries. **venously,** *adv.* [L *vēnōsus,* from *vēna,* VEIN]

vent[1], *n.* a hole or aperture, esp. for the passage of air, water etc. into or out of a confined place, as in the head of a barrel, to allow air to enter while liquid is being drawn; the flue of a chimney, a touch-hole, a finger-hole in a wind-instrument, a loophole etc.; the opening of the cloaca, the anus in animals below mammals; a means or place of passage, escape etc., an outlet, free play, utterance, expression etc.; a split in a garment as in the back of a coat or jacket. *v.t.* to make a vent in; to give vent to; to utter, to pour forth. **vent-hole,** *n.* **vent-peg,** *n.* a peg for stopping a vent-hole in a barrel. **vent-plug,** *n.* a plug for stopping the vent of a gun; a vent-peg. **vent stack,** *n.* a vertical pipe to carry sewer gas above the level of the house windows. **ventage,** *n.* **ventless,** *a.* **to give vent to,** to express freely. [formerly *fent,* F *fente,* from *fendre,* L *findere,* to cleave]

vent[2], *v.i.* to take breath (of a hunted animal, esp. an otter). *n.* the act of venting, esp. of coming to the surface to breathe, as an otter; scent, trail. [F *venter,* to blow, from *vent,* L *ventum,* nom. *-tus,* wind]

†**vent**[3], *n.* sale, market. [F *vente,* from *vendre,* L *vendere,* to VEND]

†**ventail,** AVENTAIL.

venter, *n.* the belly, the abdomen, any large cavity containing viscera; (*Nat. Hist.*) an expanded or hollowed part or surface; (*Law*) the womb, hence, a mother. **ventral** *a.* pertaining to the venter; pertaining to or situated on the anterior surface or point (of fins etc.). **ventrally,** *adv.* **ventricose,** †**-cous,** *a.* having a protruding belly; (*Bot.*) distended, inflated. [L]

ventiduct, *n.* a passage or conduit, esp. subterranean, for ventilation. [L *ventus,* wind]

ventil, *n.* a valve; a shutter for regulating the admission of air in an organ. [L *ventulus,* breeze, dim. of *ventus,* wind]

ventilate, *v.t.* to supply with fresh air, to cause a circulation of air in (a room etc.); to oxygenate (the blood); to give publicity to, to throw open for discussion etc. **ventilation,** *n.* **ventilative,** *a.* **ventilator,** *n.* [L *ventilātus,* p.p. of *ventilāre,* to blow, winnow, ventilate, from *ventus,* wind]

ventose[1], *a.* windy, flatulent. [L *ventōsus,* from *ventus,* wind]

Ventose[2], *n.* the sixth month of the French revolutionary year (19 Feb.–20 Mar.). [as prec.]

ventricle, *n.* a cavity or hollow part in an animal body, in the heart and brain. **ventricular, -lous,** *a.* [F *ventricule,* L *ventriculum,* nom. *-us,* dim of VENTER]

ventricose VENTRAL under VENTER.

ventriculite, *n.* one of a family of fossil sponges common in flint nodules. [L *ventricul-us,* see prec., -ITE]

ventriloquism, *n.* the act or art of speaking or producing sounds so that the sound appears to come not from the person speaking but from a different source. **ventriloquist,** *n.* **ventriloquy, ventrilocution,** *n.* **ventriloquize, -ise,** *v.i.* **ventriloquial, ventriloquistic, ventriloquous,** *a.* [L *ventriloquus* (*venter-tris,* see VENTER, *loquī,* to speak), -ISM]

ventr(o)-, *comb. form* pertaining to the abdomen or a venter. **ventrosity,** *n.* corpulence.

venture, *n.* the undertaking of a risk, a hazard; an undertaking of a risky nature; a commercial speculation; a stake, that which is risked; †chance, hap, contingency. *v.t.* to expose to hazard or risk, to hazard, to stake; to dare, to brave. *v.i.* to dare; to have the courage or presumption (to do etc.); to undertake a risk. **venture capital,** *n.* capital invested in a new, esp. speculative, business enterprise by people or organizations other than the owners of the business. **Venture Scout,** *n.* a senior member of the Scouts organization usu. over 15 years old. **at a venture,** at random. **to venture on** or **upon,** to dare to enter upon or engage in etc. †**venturer,** *n.* **venturesome,** *a.* **venturesomely,** *adv.* **venturesomeness,** *n.* **venturous, venturously,** *adv.* **venturousness,** *n.* [shortened from ADVENTURE]

Venturi, *n.* **Robert** (1925–), US architect. He pioneered post-modernism through his books, *Complexity and Contradiction in Architecture* (1967) and *Learning from Las Vegas* (1972). In 1986 he was commissioned to design the extension to the National Gallery, London.

venturi (tube), *n.* a tube or duct, wasp-waisted and expanding at the ends, used in measuring the flow rates of fluids, as a means of accelerating air flow, or to provide a suction source for vacuum-operated instruments. [G.B. *Venturi,* 1746–1822, Italian physicist]

venue[1], *n.* (*Law*) the place or country where a crime is alleged to have been committed and where the jury must be empanelled and the trial held; the clause in an indictment indicating this; the scene or place of an activity or event; a meeting place. **change of venue,** alteration of the place of trial etc., to avoid riot etc. [F, coming, from *venir,* L *venīre,* to come]

†**venue**[2], VENEW.

Venus[1], *n.* the second planet in order of distance from the Sun. It orbits the Sun every 225 days at an average distance of 108.2 million km/67.2 miles and can approach the Earth to within 38 million km/24 million miles, closer than any other planet. Its diameter is 12,100 km/7500 miles and its mass is 0.82 that of Earth. Venus rotates on its axis more slowly than any other planet, once every 243 days and from east to west, the opposite direction to the other planets (except Uranus). Venus is shrouded by clouds of sulphuric acid droplets which sweep across the planet from east to west every four days. The atmosphere is almost entirely carbon dioxide, which traps the Sun's heat by the greenhouse effect to raise the planet's surface temperature to 480°C, with an atmospheric pressure 90 times that at Earth's surface.

Venus[2], *n.* the goddess of love, esp. sensual love; the planet VENUS[1]. **Mount of Venus,** the female pubes, *mons veneris;* (*Palmistry*) the elevation at the base of the thumb. **Venus's basin, bath, cup,** *n.* the teasel. **Venus's comb,** *n.* an annual herb of the parsley family. **Venus's flytrap,** *n.* an insectivorous herb of the sundew family. **Venus's looking-glass,** *n.* a plant of the genus *Specularia,* esp. *S. speculum.* **Venus's slipper,** *n.* the lady's-slipper. [L]

veracious, *a.* habitually speaking or disposed to speak the truth; characterized by truth and accuracy; true. **veraciously,** *adv.* **veracity,** *n.* [L *vērax -acis,* from *vērus,* true]

veranda, verandah, *n.* a light external gallery or portico with a roof on pillars, along the front or side of a house. [Port. *varanda,* prob. from *vara,* L *vāra,* forked pole]

veratrine, *n.* a highly poisonous amorphous compound obtained from hellebore and other plants, used as a local irritant in neuralgia, rheumatism etc. **veretrate,** *n.* a salt of veratric acid. **veratric,** *a.* **veratrize, -ise,** *v.t.* [from L *veratrum,* hellebore]

veratrum, *n.* the hellebore; a genus of plants containing the hellebore. [L]

verb, *n.* that part of speech which predicates, a word that asserts something in regard to something else (the subject). **verbal,** *a.* of or pertaining to words; respecting words only, not ideas etc.; literal, word for word; pertaining to or derived from a verb; oral, spoken, not written. *n.* a verbal noun, one derived from a verb, esp. Eng. words in -ING; an oral statement; (*sl.*) an admission of guilt made by a suspect when arrested. *v.t.* (*sl.*) to attribute such an admission to someone. **verbalist,** *n.* one who deals in words only; a literal adherent to or a minute critic of words. **verbalism,** *n.* **verbalize, -ise,** *v.t.* to convert or change into a verb. *v.i.* to use many words, to be verbose. †**verbality,** *n.* **verbalization, -isation,** *n.* **verbally,** *adv.* **verbify,** *v.t.* **verbarium,** *n.* a game in which the players form words from given letters etc. [F *verbe,* L *verbum,* word, cogn. with WORD and Gr. *eirein,* to speak]

verbatim, *adv.* word for word.

verbatim et literatim, word for word and letter for letter. [L]

verbena, *n.* a large genus of plants of which *Verbena officinalis,* the common vervain, is the type. **verbenaceous,** *a.* [L, in pl. *verbēnoe,* sacred boughs, of olive etc.]

†**verberate,** *v.t.* to beat, to strike. †**verberation,** *n.* [L *verberātus,* p.p. of *verberāre,* from *verber,* rod, cogn. with prec.]

verbiage, *n.* the use of many words without necessity, verbosity, wordiness. **verbicide,** *n.* (*facet.*) word-slaughter; a word-slaughterer. [F, from *verbe,* VERB]

verbose, *a.* using or containing more words than are necessary, prolix. **verbosely,** *adv.* **verboseness, verbosity,** *n.*

verboten, *a.* forbidden by authority. [G fr. p.p. of *verbieten,* to forbid]

Vercingetorix, *n.* Gallic chieftain. Leader of a revolt against the Romans 52 BC, he was displayed in Caesar's triumph 46 BC, and later executed.

verdant, *a.* green; covered with growing plants or grass; fresh, flourishing; green, inexperienced, unsophisticated, easily taken in. **verdancy,** *n.* **verde antico,** *n.* an ornamental stone composed chiefly of serpentine, usu. green and mottled or veined; a green incrustation on ancient bronze. **verdantly,** *adv.* **verdée,** *a.* (*Her.*) charged with flowers. [OF, from L *viridans -ntem,* pres.p. of *viridāre,* from *viridis,* green]

verderer, *n.* historically, a judicial officer who has charge of the royal forests. [A-F *verder,* late L *viridārius,* forester, as prec.]

Verdi, *n.* **Giuseppe (Fortunino Francesco)** (1813–1901), Italian opera composer of the Romantic period, who took his native operatic style to new heights of dramatic expression. In 1842 he wrote the opera *Nabucco*, followed by *Ernani* (1844) and *Rigoletto* (1851). Other works include *Il Trovatore* and *La Traviata* (both 1853), *Aïda* (1871), and the masterpieces of his old age, *Otello* (1887) and *Falstaff* (1893). His *Requiem* (1874) commemorates Alessandro Manzoni.

verdict, *n.* the decision of a jury on an issue of fact submitted to them in the trial of any cause, civil or criminal; decision, judgment. **open verdict,** one reporting the commission of a crime without specifying the guilty person; of an inquest, one failing to state the cause of death. **special verdict,** one in which specific facts are placed on record but the court is left to form conclusions on the legal aspects. [ME and OF *verdit,* L *vērē dictum* (*vērē,* truly, DICTUM)]

verdigris, *n.* a green crystalline substance formed on copper by the action of dilute acetic acid, used as a pigment and in medicine; greenish rust on copper etc. [ME *verdegrees, grese,* A-F *vert de Grece,* green of Greece (VERT[1], L *Groecia,* Greece)]

verditer, *n.* a light-blue pigment prepared from copper nitrate treated with chalk or other calcium carbonate. [A-F *verd de terre,* green of earth (OF *verd,* see prec., F *terre,* L *terra,* earth)]

Verdun, *n.* fortress town in NE France on the Meuse. During World War I it became the symbol of French resistance, withstanding a German onslaught in 1916.

verdure, *n.* greenness of vegetation, fresh vegetation or foliage. **verdured, verdurous,** *a.* **verdureless,** *a.* [F, from OF *verd,* L *viridis*]

†**verecund,** *a.* bashful. **verecundity,** *n.* [L *verēcundus,* from *vereor,* to feel awe]

verge[1], *n.* the extreme edge, brink, border or margin; the grass-edging of a bed or border or alongside a road; a rod, wand or staff, carried as an emblem of authority, esp. before a bishop or other dignitary; the shaft of a column; the edge of the tiles projecting over a gable etc.; a spindle, shaft etc., in the mechanism of a watch, loom, and other machines. **on the verge of,** on the brink of. [F, from L *virga,* twig, rod]

verge[2], *v.i.* to approach, to come near, to border (on). **vergency,** *n.* the act of verging, being near; the reciprocal of the focal distance of a lens taken as a measure of the divergence or convergence of rays. †**vergent,** *a.* drawing to a close. [L *vergere,* to bend, to incline]

vergee, *n.* (*Channel Islands*) a land measure, about four-ninths of an acre (about 0.2 ha). [F, from VERGE[1]]

verger, *n.* an officer carrying the verge or staff of office before a bishop or other dignitary; an official in a church acting as usher or as pew-opener. **vergership,** *n.*

Vergil VIRGIL.

verglas, *n.* a film of ice on rock. [F *verre,* glass, *glace,* ice from OF]

veridical, *a.* truthful, veracious. **veridically,** *adv.* **veridicous,** *a.* [L *vēridicus* (*verus,* true, *dicere,* to say)]

verify, *v.t.* to confirm the truth of; to inquire into the truth of, to authenticate; to fulfil; to affirm under oath, to append an affidavit to (pleadings). **verifiable,** *a.* **verifiability,** *n.* **verification,** *n.* **verifier,** *n.* [OF *verifier,* med. L *vērificāre* (*vērus,* true, *-ficāre, facere,* to make)]

†**verily,** *adv.* in very truth, assuredly. [ME *veraily* (VERY, -LY)]

verisimilitude, *n.* the appearance of or resemblance to truth; probability, likelihood; something apparently true or a fact. †**verisimilar,** †**-lous,** *a.* [MF, from L *vērisimilitūdo,* from *verisimilis* (*vēri,* gen. of *vērus,* true, *similis,* like)]

verism, *n.* extreme naturalism in art or literature. [It. *verismo* from *vero,* true]

verity, *n.* truth, correspondence (of a statement) with fact; a true statement, truth; a thing really existent, a fact. **of a verity,** in truth, surely. **veritable,** *a.* real, genuine; actual, true. **veritably,** *adv.* [OF *verité,* L *vēritātem,* nom. *-tas,* from *vērus,* true]

verjuice, *n.* an acid liquid expressed from crab-apples, unripe grapes etc. and used in cooking and for other purposes. **verjuiced,** *a.* [F *verjus* (OF *verd,* VERT[1], JUICE)]

verkrampte, *n., a.* in S Africa, a person of Afrikaner Nationalist opinions who opposes any liberalization of government policy, esp. in matters of race. [Afrikaans, restricted]

Verlaine, *n.* **Paul** (1844–96), French lyrical poet who was influenced by the poets Baudelaire and Rimbaud. His volumes of verse include *Poèmes saturniens/Saturnine Poems* (1866), *Fêtes galantes/Amorous Entertainments* (1869) and *Romances sans paroles/Songs without Words* (1874). In 1873 he was imprisoned for attempting to shoot Rimbaud. His later works reflect his attempts to lead a reformed life and he was acknowledged as leader of the Symbolist poets.

verligte, *n., a.* in S Africa, a person of liberal political attributes, esp. towards black and coloured people. [Afrikaans, enlightened]

Vermeer, *n.* **Jan** (1632–75), Dutch painter, active in Delft. Most of his pictures are genre scenes, with a limpid clarity and distinct air of stillness, and a harmonious palette often focusing on yellow and blue. He frequently depicted single women in domestic settings, as in *The Lacemaker* (Louvre, Paris).

vermeil, *n.* silver-gilt; a transparent varnish for giving a lustre to gilt; vermilion. [F, VERMILION]

Vermes, *n.pl.* an obsolete division of animals comprising earth-worms, sea-worms, leeches, brachiopods etc. [L, pl. of *vermis,* a worm]

verm(i)- *comb. form* pertaining to worms. [L. *vermis,* a worm]

vermicelli, *n.* a wheaten paste in the form of long slender tubes or threads like macaroni. **chocolate vermicelli,** *n.* small thin pieces of chocolate used for cake decoration. [It., pl. of *vermicello,* dim. of *verme,* worm, as prec.]

vermicide, *n.* a medicine or drug that kills worms, an anthelmintic. **vermicidal,** *a.*

vermicular, *a.* of or pertaining to a worm; resembling the motion or track of a worm; tortuous, marked with intricate wavy lines (of reticulated work etc.); worm-eaten in appearance; vermiform.

vermiculate, *a.* worm-eaten; vermicular. *v.t.*, to decorate with vermicular lines or tracery. **vermiculation,** *n.* motion after the manner of a worm, as in the peristaltic motion of the intestines; the art of vermiculating; vermiculated work; the state of being worm-eaten.

vermicule, *n.* a small grub or worm. **vermiculose, †-lous,** *a.* full of or containing worms or grubs; worm-eaten; worm-shaped, vermicular.

vermiform, *a.* worm-shaped; having the form or structure of a worm; vermicular. **vermiform appendix,** *n.* a small worm-like organ of no known function situated at the extremity of the caecum.

vermifuge, *n.* a medicine or drug that destroys or expels intestinal worms, an anthelmintic. **vermifugal,** *a.*

vermigrade, *a.* moving or crawling like a worm.

vermilion, *n.* a brilliant red pigment consisting of mercuric sulphide obtained by grinding cinnabar or by the chemical treatment of mercury and sulphur; the colour of this. *a.* of a beautiful red colour. *v.t.* to colour with or as with vermilion. **†vermily,** *n., a.* [F *vermillon,* from *vermeil,* L *vermiculus,* dim. of *vermis,* worm, see VERMES]

vermin, *n.* a collective name for certain mischievous or offensive animals, as the smaller mammals or birds injurious to crops or game, noxious or offensive insects, grubs or worms, esp. lice, fleas etc.; low, despicable or repulsive persons. **vermin-killer,** *n.* **verminate,** *v.i.* to breed vermin, to become infested with parasites. **vermination,** *n.* **verminous,** *a.* **verminously,** *adv.* [F *vermine,* from L *vermis,* see VERMES]

vermis, *n.* the middle lobe connecting the two halves of the cerebellum. [VERMI-]

vermivorous, *a.* feeding on worms.

Vermont, *n.* state of the US in New England; nickname Green Mountain State. **area** 24,900 sq km/9611 sq miles. **capital** Montpelier. **towns** Burlington, Rutland. **population** (1986) 541,000. **products** apples, maple syrup, dairy products, china clay, asbestos, granite, marble, slate, business machines, furniture, paper.

vermouth, *n.* a liqueur made of white wine flavoured with wormwood and other aromatic herbs. [F *vermouth,* G *Wermuth,* wormwood]

vernacular, *a.* of architecture etc. native, indigenous, (of language, idiom etc.) belonging to the country of one's birth. *n.* one's native tongue; the native idiom or dialect of a place or country; the jargon of a particular group of people. **vernacularism,** *n.* **vernacularity,** *n.* **vernacularize, -ise,** *v.t.* **vernacularization, -isation,** *n.* **vernacularly,** *adv.* [L *vernāculus,* from *verna,* home-born slave]

vernal, *a.* pertaining to, prevailing, done, or appearing in spring; pertaining to youth. **vernal equinox** EQUINOX. **vernal grass,** *n.* a fragrant grass, *Anthoxanthum odoratum,* sown among hay. **vernally,** *adv.* **vernalization, -isation,** *n.* the wetting of seeds before sowing, in order to hasten flowering. **†vernant,** *a.* flourishing in the spring. **vernation,** *n.* the arrangement of the young leaves within the leaf-bud. [L *vernālis,* from *vernus,* pertaining to spring, from *ver,* spring, cogn. with Gr. *ear,* Icel. *vār*]

Verne, *n.* **Jules** (1828–1905), French author of tales of adventure that anticipated future scientific developments: *Five Weeks in a Balloon* (1862), *Journey to the Centre of the Earth* (1864), *Twenty Thousand Leagues under the Sea* (1870), and *Around the World in Eighty Days* (1873).

vernicle, *n.* a cloth for wiping sweat, held to have Christ's face miraculously impressed on it when St Veronica wiped his face; any representation of this; a medal or badge bearing it worn by pilgrims who have visited Rome. [from St *Veronica*]

vernier, *n.* a movable scale for measuring fractional portions of the divisions of the scale on a measuring instrument, a barometer, theodolite etc. [Pierre *Vernier* see foll.]

Vernier, *n.* **Pierre** (1580–1637), French mathematician who invented very precise measurements by the operation of what has since been called the vernier scale. He was a French government official and in 1631 published a book explaining his method called 'a new mathematical quadrant'.

Verona, *n.* industrial city (printing, paper, plastics, furniture, pasta) in Veneto, Italy, on the Adige; population (1988) 259,000.

Veronal®, *n.* a hypnotic drug, diethylbarbituric acid, also called barbitone.

Veronese¹, *a.* pertaining to Verona. *n.* a native or inhabitant of Verona.

Veronese², *n.* **Paolo** (*c.* 1528–88), Italian painter, born in Verona, active mainly in Venice (from about 1553). He specialized in grand decorative schemes, such as his ceilings in the Doge's Palace in Venice, with *trompe l'oeil* effects and inventive detail. The subjects are religious, mythological, historical, and allegorical.

veronica, *n.* a herb or shrub of the fig-wort family, with blue, purple or white flowers, the speedwell; a handkerchief or cloth bearing a portrait of Christ, esp. that of St Veronica said to have been miraculously so impressed. [name of woman said to have wiped the sweat from Christ's face on the way to Calvary, corr. of Gr. *Berenikē*]

veronique, *a.* (used after the noun) served with white grapes, e.g. *sole veronique*. [F]

verricule, *n.* a dense tuft of upright hairs. [L *verriculum,* net, from *verrere,* to sweep]

verruca, *n.* (*pl.* **-cae**) a wart; (*Nat. Hist.*) a wart-like elevation. **verruciform, verrucose, -cous, verruculose,** *a.* [L]

verrugas, *n.* a disease characterized by ulcerous tumours, endemic in Peru. [Sp.]

vers, *n.* verse. **vers libre,** free verse; **vers de société,** society verses [see SOCIETY]. [F]

†versable, *a.* capable of being turned. **†versability, †versableness,** *n.* [L *versābilis* from *versāre,* to turn round, see VERSANT]

Versailles, *n.* city in N France, capital of Les Yvelines *département*, on the outskirts of Paris; population (1982) 95,240. It grew up around the palace of Louis XV. Within the palace park are two small châteaux, Le Grand and Le Petit Trianon, built for Louis XIV (by J.-H. Mansart) and Louis XV (by J. A. Gabriel 1698–1782) respectively. **Versailles, Treaty of,** *n.* peace treaty after World War I between the Allies and Germany, signed 28 June 1919. It established the League of Nations. Germany surrendered Alsace-Lorraine to France, large areas in the east to Poland, and made smaller cessions to Czechoslovakia, Lithuania, Belgium, and Denmark. The Rhineland was demilitarized, German rearmament was restricted, and Germany agreed to pay reparations for war damage. The treaty was never ratified by the US, which made a separate peace with Germany and Austria 1921.

†**versal,** (*Shak.*) [short for UNIVERSAL].

versant, *n.* an area of land sloping in one direction; general lie or slope. *a.* †conversant, versed; (*Her.*) having the wings open. [F, from *verser,* L *versāre,* freq. of *vertere,* to turn]

versatile, *a.* turning easily, readily applying oneself to new tasks, occupations, subjects etc., many-sided; changeable, variable, inconstant; (*Bot., Zool.*) (of anthers, antennae etc.) moving freely round or to and fro on its support. **versatilely,** *adv.* **versatility,** *n.* [F *versatil,* L *versātilis,* as prec.]

verse, *n.* a metrical line consisting of a certain number of feet; a group of metrical lines, a stanza; metrical composition as distinguished from prose; a particular type of metrical composition; one of the short divisions of a chapter of the Bible; a short sentence in a liturgy etc. *v.t.* to express in verse. *v.i.* to make verses. **verseman, versemonger,** *n.* **verse-mongering,** *n.* **verselet,** *n.* †**verser,** *n.* a versifier. **verset,** *n.* a short organ interlude or prelude. **versicle,** *n.* a short verse, esp. one of a series recited in divine service by the minister alternately with the people. **versicular,** *a.* pertaining to verses; relating to division into verses. **versify,** *v.t.* to turn (prose) into verse; to narrate or express in verse. *v.i.* to make verses. **versification,** *n.* **versifier,** *n.* [OE *fers,* L *versus -sūs,* a turning, furrow, row, verse, from *vertere,* to turn, p.p. *versus*]

versed, *a.* skilled, familiar, experienced, proficient (in); (*Trig.*) turned about, reversed (of sines). [L *versātus,* p.p. of *versārī,* to turn about, see VERSANT]

verselet, verset, versicle etc. VERSE.

versicolour, -coloured, *a.* having various colours, variegated; changeable from one colour to another, with differences of light. †**versiform,** *a.* varying in form. [L *versicolor* (*versi-, versāre,* to turn, COLOUR)]

versify etc. VERSE.

version, *n.* that which is translated from one language into another, a translation; the act of translating, translation; a piece of translation, esp. the rendering of a passage into another language as a school exercise; a statement, account, or description of something from one's particular point of view; the turning of a child in the womb to facilitate delivery; the adaptation of a work of art into another medium. **versional,** *a.* [F, from med. L *versiōnem,* nom. *-sio,* from *vertere,* to turn, p.p. *versus*]

verso, *n.* a left-hand page of a book, sheet etc.; the other side of a coin or medal to that on which the head appears. [as prec.]

verst, *n.* a Russian measure of length, 3500.64 ft., nearly two-thirds of a mile (about 1 km). [Rus. *versta*]

versus, *prep.* against. [L, towards, from *vertere,* to turn, p.p. *versus*]

†**versute,** *a.* crafty, wily. [L *versūtus,* as prec.]

vert[1], *n.* (*Law*) everything in a forest that grows and bears green leaves; the right to cut green or growing wood; (*Her.*) the tincture green. [F, from L *viridem,* nom. *-dis,* green]

vert[2], *v.i.* (*coll.*) to change one's religion; to leave one Church for another. *n.* one who verts, a pervert or convert. [*-vert,* in PERVERT or CONVERT]

vertebra, *n.* (*pl.* **-brae**) one of the bony segments of which the spine or backbone consists. **vertebral,** *a.* **vertebral column,** *n.* the spinal column. **vertebrally,** *adv.* **Vertebrata,** *n.pl.* a division of animals comprising those with a backbone, including mammals, birds, reptiles, amphibians and fishes. **vertebrate,** *n., a.* **vertebrated,** *a.* **vertebration** *n.* **vertebro-,** *comb. form.* [L., from *vertere,* to turn]

vertex, *n.* (*pl.* **-tices**) the highest point, the top, summit, or apex; the point on the limb (of sun, moon or planet) furthest above the observer's horizon; the point of an angle, cone, pyramid etc.; the top of the arch of the skull. **vertical,** *a.* of, pertaining to, or situated at the vertex or highest point; situated at or passing through the zenith; perpendicular to the plane of the horizon; of or pertaining to the vertex of the head. **vertical angles,** *n.* either pair of opposite angles made by two intersecting lines. **vertical circle,** *n.* an azimuth-circle. **vertical fins,** *n.* fins situated in the median line, the dorsal, anal and caudal fins. **vertical plane,** *n.* a plane passing through the zenith perpendicular to the horizon. **vertical take-off,** the take-off of an aeroplane without a preliminary run or taxying. **verticality, verticalness,** *n.* **vertically,** *adv.* [L, whirlpool, summit, from *vertere,* to turn]

verticil, *n.* (*Bot., etc.*) a whorl, an arrangement of parts in a circle round a stem etc. **verticillate, -lated,** *a.* **verticillately,** *adv.* [L *verticillus,* dim. of VERTEX]

vertigo, *n.* giddiness, dizziness; a feeling as if one were whirling round. **vertiginous,** *a.* **vertiginously,** *adv.* **vertiginousness,** *n.* [L, as VERTEX]

vertu, VIRTU.

Verulamian, *a.* of or pertaining to Francis Bacon, Baron Verulam (1561–1626), philosopher; of or pertaining to St Albans. [L *Verulamium, Verulam,* see foll.]

Verulamium, *n.* Roman-British town whose remains have been excavated close to St Albans, Hertfordshire.

verules, *n.pl.* (*Her.*) a bearing composed of a number of concentric rings one inside the other. **veruled,** *a.* [var. of VIROLES, pl. of VIROLE]

vervain, *n.* a wild plant or weed, with small purplish flowers, of the genus *Verbena,* esp. *V. officinalis,* formerly credited with medical and other virtues. [ME and OF *verveine,* L VERBENA]

verve, *n.* spirit, enthusiasm, energy, esp. in literary or artistic creation. [F, perh. from L *verba,* words, see VERB]

†**vervel,** VARVEL.

vervet, *n.* a small S African monkey, usu. black-speckled greyish-green, with reddish-white face and abdomen. [etym. doubtful]

Verwoerd, *n.* **Hendrik (Frensch)** (1901–66), South African right-wing Nationalist Party politician, prime minister from 1958. As minister of native affairs 1950–58, he was the chief promoter of apartheid legislation. He made the country a republic 1961. He was assassinated in the House of Assembly by a parliamentary messenger, Dimitri Tsafendas.

very, *a.* real, true, actual, genuine, being what it seems or is stated to be, selfsame (now chiefly used intensively). *adv.* in a high degree; to a great extent; greatly, extremely, exceedingly. [ME *verrai,* OF *verai* (F *vrai*), L *verax -ācis,* see VERACIOUS]

Very Large Array, *n.* (VLA) the largest and most complex single-site radio telescope in the world. It is located on the Plains of San Augustine, 80 km/50 miles west of Socorro, New Mexico, US. It consists of 27 dish antennae, each 25 m/82 ft in diameter, arranged along three equally spaced arms forming a Y-shaped array. Two of the arms are 21 km/13 miles long, and the third, to the north, is 19 km/11.8 miles long. The dishes are mounted on railway tracks enabling the configuration and size of the array to be altered as required.

Very light, *n.* a firework to produce a flare for lighting up the countryside. [Edward W. *Very,* 1852–1910, US naval officer]

Very pistol, *n.* a pistol for firing Very lights.

Very Rev., (*abbr.*) Very Reverend.

Vesalius, *n.* **Andreas** (1514–64), Belgian physician

who revolutionized anatomy. His great innovations were to perform postmortem dissections, and to make use of illustrations in teaching anatomy.

vesania, *n.* (*Path.*) insanity. [L, from *vēsānus* (*vē,* not, *sānus,* SANE)]

vesica, *n.* (*pl.* **-cae**) a bladder, cyst etc., the gall-bladder, the urinary bladder. **vesica piscis**, the elliptic aureole in which the Saviour and the saints were often depicted by early painters. [L, fish-bladder] **vesical,** *a.* **vesicant,** *n.* a blister-producing counter-irritant; a poison-gas that causes blisters. **vesicate,** *v.t.* to raise vesicles or blisters on. **vesicant, vesicatory,** *n., a.* **vesication,** *n.* **vesicle**, *n.* a small bladder or cavity, sac, cyst, bubble, or hollow structure. [L]

vesico-, *comb.form.* **vesicocele**, *n.* hernia of the bladder. **vesicotomy**, *n.* **vesicular**, **-late**, **-liferous**, **-liform**, **-lose**, **-lous,** *a.* **vesiculation,** *n.* **vesiculo-,** *comb. form.*

Vespasian, *n.* **(Titus Flavius Vespasianus)** (9–79 AD), Roman emperor from 69 AD. He was the son of a moneylender, and had a distinguished military career. He was proclaimed emperor by his soldiers while he was campaigning in Palestine. He reorganized the eastern provinces, and was a capable administrator.

vesper, *n.* the evening star, Venus, appearing just after sunset; (*fig.*) evening; in the Roman Catholic and Greek Churches, (*pl.*) the sixth of the seven canonical hours; (*pl.*) the evening service. *a.* pertaining to the evening or to vespers. **Sicilian Vespers** SICILIAN. **vesper-bell,** *n.* the bell that summons to vespers. **vesperal,** *n.* the part of the antiphonary containing the chants for vespers. **vesperian**, *a.* **vespertine**, *a.* of, pertaining to, or done in the evening; (*Zool.*) flying in the evening; (*Bot.*) opening in the evening; (*Astrol.*) descending towards the horizon at sunset. [L, cogn. with HESPER]

vespertilio, *n.* a genus of Cheiroptera comprising the common bat. [L, from VESPER]

vespiary, *n.* a nest of wasps, hornets etc. **vespiform**, *a.* resembling a wasp. **vespine**, *a.* [from L *vespa,* wasp, after APIARY]

Vespucci, *n.* **Amerigo** (1454–1512), Florentine merchant. The Americas were named after him as a result of the widespread circulation of his accounts of his explorations, but recent evidence suggests that he never made the voyages.

vessel, *n.* a hollow receptacle, esp. for holding liquids, as a jug, cup, dish, bottle, barrel etc.; a ship or craft of any kind, esp. one of some size; a tube, a duct, or canal in which the blood or other fluids are conveyed; (*Bot.*) a canal or duct formed by the breaking down of the partitions between cells; (*fig.*) a person regarded as receiving or containing (grace, wrath etc.). **the weaker vessel,** (*now usu. facet.*) woman (I Peter iii.7). **vesselful,** *n.* [A-F, from OF *vaissel* (F *vaisseau*), L *vascellum,* dim. of VAS]

vessignon, *n.* a soft swelling on a horse's leg, a wind-gall. [F, from L VESICA]

vest, *n.* (*esp. N Am.*) an undergarment for the upper part of the body, a singlet, a waistcoat; a close jacket formerly worn by women, now a (usu. V-shaped) piece on the front of the body or waist of a gown; †a garment, clothing, dress. *v.t.* (*poet.*) to clothe with or as with a garment; to invest or endow (with authority, etc.); to confer an immediate fixed right of present or future possession of (property in a person). *v.i.* (of property, right etc.) to come or take effect (in a person). **vest pocket,** *a.* (*esp. N Am.*) small enough to fit into a waistcoat pocket. **vested,** *a.* wearing vestments, robed; (*Her.*) clothed; (*Law*) held by or fixed in a person, not subject to contingency. **vesting,** *n.* material for making vests. **vested interest,** *n.* a source of gain to which the owner considers himself entitled by custom and right. **vestiture**, *n.* (*Zool.*) anything covering a surface, as hair, scales etc. [L *vestis,* garment, cogn. with Gr. *esthēs,* clothing, Sansk. *vas,* to put on, and Eng. WEAR[1]]

Vesta, *n.* the goddess of the hearth and the hearth-fire; the fourth asteroid; (**vesta**) a wax match igniting by friction. **vestal,** *a.* pertaining to the goddess Vesta or the vestal virgins; pure, chaste. *n.* a vestal virgin; a woman of spotless chastity; a nun. **vestal virgin,** *n.* one of the virgin priestesses, vowed to perpetual chastity, who had charge of the temple of Vesta at Rome, and of the sacred fire which burned perpetually on her altar. [L, cogn. with Gr. *Hestia*]

vestiary, *a.* pertaining to dress. *n.* a wardrobe, a robing-room. [late L *vestiārius,* from *vestis,* VEST]

vestibule, *n.* a small hall, lobby, or ante-chamber next the outer door of a house, from which doors open into the various inner rooms; a porch; a covered passage between the cars in a corridor train; (*Anat.*) a chamber, cavity or channel communicating with others, as the central chamber of the labyrinth of the ear. **vestibule train,** *n.* a corridor train. **vestibular, -late,** *a.* (*Anat.*) **vestibuled,** *a.* [L *vestibulum*]

vestige, *n.* the mark of a foot made in passing, a footprint; a sign, a mark or trace of something no longer present or in existence; (*coll.*) an atom, a particle; (*Biol.*) an organ or part that has degenerated and become nearly or entirely useless. **vestigial, vestigiary**, *a.* [F, from L *vestīgium,* footstep, etym. doubtful]

vesting, vestiture VEST.

vestment, *n.* a garment, esp. a robe of state or office; any of the ritual garments of the clergy, choristers, etc., esp. a chasuble; an altar-cloth. [ME *vestiment,* OF *vestement,* L *vestīmentum,* from *vestīre,* to clothe, from *vestis,* see VEST]

vestry, *n.* a room or place attached to a church in which the vestments are kept and in which the clergy, choristers etc., robe; a chapel or room attached to a non-liturgical church; a meeting of the ratepayers of a parish (called a common, general or ordinary vestry) or of their elected representatives (called a select vestry) for dealing with parochial business, formerly exercising sanitary and other powers of local government, as such now superseded by the parish council. **vestry-clerk,** *n.* an officer appointed by a vestry to keep the accounts etc. **vestryman,** *n.* a member of a vestry. **vestral,** *a.* **vestrydom**, *n.* government by a vestry, esp. if corrupt or incompetent. [OF *vestiairie,* L *vestiārium,* wardrobe, neut. of *vestiārius,* VESTIARY]

vesture, *n.* (*poet.*) dress, clothes, apparel; a covering. *v.t.* to clothe, to dress. **vestural,** *a.* **vesturer,** *n.* a person in charge of church vestments; the subtreasurer of a collegiate church or cathedral. [OF *vesteure,* late L *vestītūra,* VESTITURE]

Vesuvius, *n.* (Italian **Vesuvio**) active volcano SE of Naples, Italy; height 1277 m/4190 ft. In 79 BC it destroyed the cities of Pompeii, Herculaneum, and Oplonti. **Vesuvian,** *a.* pertaining to Vesuvius; volcanic. *n.* a variety of fusee for lighting cigars etc., in the open air; vesuvianite. **vesuvianite**, *n.* a vitreous brown or green silicate first found among the ejections of Vesuvius.

vet, *n.* short form of VETERINARY SURGEON. *v.t.* **vetting,** *past, p.p.* **vetted,** to subject to careful scrutiny and appraisal. [VETERINARY]

vetch, *n.* a plant of the genus *Vicia* of the bean family, including several wild and cultivated species used for forage, esp. the common vetch or tare. **vetchling**, *n.* a plant of the genus *Lathyrus,* allied to the vetches. **vetchy,** *a.* [ME and ONorth.F *veche,* OF *vece,* L *vīcia*]

veteran, *a.* grown old or experienced, esp. in the military service; of or pertaining to veterans. *n.* one who has had long experience in any service, occupation or art, esp. as a soldier; (*N Am.*) an ex-service man. **veteran car,** *n.* a motor car built before 1916 (and, esp. before 1905). **Veterans Day,** *n.* in the US, the name adopted 1954 for Armistice Day and from 1971 observed by most states on the fourth Monday in Oct. The equivalent in the UK and Canada is Remembrance Sunday. **veteranize, -ise,** *v.t.* to render veteran. *v.i.* (*N Am.*) to re-enlist. [L *veterānus,* from *vetus -teris,* old]

veterinary, *a.* pertaining to treatment of the diseases of animals, esp. domestic animals, as cows, horses, dogs etc. as in *veterinary medicine*. *n.* a veterinary surgeon.

veterinary surgeon, *n.* a person qualified to diagnose and treat diseases and injuries in animals. **veterinarian**, *n.* [L *veterīnārius,* from *veterīnae bestiae,* beasts of burden, perh. from *vetus -teris,* see prec.]

veto, *n.* the power or right of a sovereign, president, or branch of a legislature to negative the enactments of another branch; the act of exercising such right; any authoritative prohibition, refusal, negative, or interdict. *v.t.* to refuse approval to (a Bill etc.); to prohibit, to forbid. **suspensive** or **suspensory veto,** a veto that suspends but does not necessarily prevent the ultimate completion of a measure. **vetitive**, *a.* **vetoist,** *n.* [L, I forbid]

vettura , *n.* (*pl.* **-re**) an Italian four-wheeled carriage. **vetturino**, *n.* (*pl.* **-ni**) one who lets out *vetture* for hire; one who drives a *vettura.* [It., from L *vectūra,* conveyance, from *vehere,* to convey, p.p. *vectus*]

†**vetust,** *a.* old, ancient. [L *vetustus,* from *vetus,* old]

vex, *v.t.* to cause trouble or annoyance to, to irritate; (*poet.*) to agitate, to throw (the sea etc.) into commotion; †to grieve, to afflict. **vexation,** *n.* the act of vexing or the state of being vexed, irritation, annoyance, trouble; that which causes irritation, an annoyance; a harassing by process of or under the cover of law. **vexatious,** *a.* **vexatiously,** *adv.* **vexatiousness,** *n.* **vexed,** *a.* annoyed, worried, filled with vexation; much debated or contested (of a question or doctrine). **vexedly**, *adv.* **vexing,** *a.* **vexingly,** *adv.* **vexer,** *n.* [F *vexer,* L *vexāre*]

vexillum, *n.* (*Rom. Ant.*) a square flag carried by a vexillary, forming the standard of a maniple or *turma;* a turma or other body of troops under a separate vexillum; the large upper petal of a papilionaceous flower; the web of a feather; a flag or pennon on a bishop's staff, usu. wound round it; a processional banner or cross. **vexil,** *n.* (*Bot.*) **vexillar**, **-late,** *a.* **vexillary,** *n.*, *a.* †**vexillation,** *n.* a company of troops under one standard. [L, from *vehere,* see VETTURA]

VG, (*abbr.*) Vicar-General.

VHF, (*abbr.*) very high frequency, referring to radio waves. VHF waves, which have very short wavelengths, are used for interference-free FM (frequency-modulated) transmissions. VHF transmitters have relatively short range because the waves cannot be reflected over the horizon like longer radio waves.

via, *adv.* by way of, through. **via dolorosa** , *n.* the way to Calvary. **via media** , *n.* a middle way, a mean between extremes. **Via Lactea**, *n.* The Milky Way. [L *via,* way]

viable, *a.* of a foetus etc. capable of maintaining independent existence, able to survive; (*Bot.*) able to live in a particular climate; likely to become actual or to succeed. **viability**, *n.* [F *vie,* life]

viaduct, *n.* a bridge-like structure, esp. one composed of masonry and a considerable number of arches carrying a road or railway over a valley etc. [L *via ducta* (VIA, way ducta, fem. p.p. *dūcere,* to lead, to conduct)]

vial, *n.* a small vessel, usu. cylindrical and of glass, for holding liquid medicines etc.; a vessel, a bottle. *v.t.* to put into a vial or vials. **to pour out vials of wrath,** to take vengeance (in alln. to Rev. xvi.); to give vent to one's anger or resentment. [OF *viole, fiole,* L *phiala,* PHIAL]

viameter, *n.* a hodometer. [L via, way, -METER]

viand, *n.* (*usu. in pl.*) articles of food, esp. meat, victuals. [F *viande,* L *vivenda,* things to live on, provisions, neut. pl. ger. of *vivere,* to live]

viaticum, *n.* (*Rom. Ant.*) a supply of provisions or an allowance of money for a journey granted to a magistrate, envoy etc.; the Eucharist as given to a person at the point of death. †**viatic,** *a.* pertaining to a journey or travel. **viator**, *n.* a traveller, a wayfarer. †**viatorially,** *adv.* [L, from VIA]

vibes, *n.pl.* (*sl.*) feelings, intuitions or sensations experienced or communicated. [*vibrations*]

vibex, *n.* (*pl.* **vibices**) a purple spot appearing on the skin in certain fevers. [L, weal, mark of a blow]

vibraculum, *n.* (*pl.* **-la**) one of the filamentous whip-like appendages of many polyzoa, bringing particles of food within reach by their lashing movements. **vibracular,** *a.* [mod. L, as foll.]

vibrant, *a.* vibrating, tremulous; resonant. **vibrancy,** *n.*

vibraphone, *n.* a percussion instrument similar to a xylophone but with metal bars placed over electronic resonators. [L *vibrare,* to shake, Gr. *phōnē,* voice]

vibrate, *v.i.* to move to and fro rapidly, to swing, to oscillate; to thrill, to quiver, to throb; to move to and fro ceaselessly, esp. with great rapidity. *v.t.* to cause to swing, oscillate or quiver; to measure (seconds etc.) by vibrations or oscillations. **vibratile**, *a.* **vibratility**, *n.* **vibration,** *n.* the act of vibrating; oscillation; rapid motion backward and forward, esp. of the parts of an elastic solid or of a liquid the equilibrium of which has been disturbed; one such complete movement. **vibrational,** *a.* **vibratiuncle**, *n.* a small vibration. **vibrative,** *a.* **vibrator,** *n.* one who or that which vibrates; a vibrating reed using in harmonic telegraphy; a vibrating reed used to chop a continuous current and thus produce an alternating current; a reed, as in a reed-organ; a roller with vibratory and rotary motion for distributing ink; a vibrating electrical apparatus used in massage and to provide sexual stimulation. **vibratory,** *a.* [L *vibrātus,* p.p. of *vibrāre,* to shake, to brandish]

vibrato, *n.* a pulsating effect, esp. in singing or string-playing, produced by the rapid variation of emphasis on the same tone. [It.]

vibrio, *n.* a form of bacterium more or less screw-shaped with a filament at each end, as that causing Asiatic cholera. [from L *vibro,* I vibrate]

vibrissa, *n.* (*pl.* **-sae**) a stiff coarse hair or bristle in the nostrils of man and about the mouths of most mammals; one of the bristle-like feathers about the mouths of some birds, as the flycatchers; one of the bristles about the mouths of some flies. [L, hair in the nostril, as prec.]

vibro-, *comb. form.* pertaining to vibration VIBRATE.

vibrogen, *n.* active cellular tissue in the cortex of certain tendrils, to which the movements of circumnutation are due.

vibroscope, *n.* an instrument for registering vibrations.

viburnum, *n.* a shrub or small tree of a genus containing the guelder rose and the laurustinus etc., of the honeysuckle family. [L]

vicar, *n.* the priest of a parish the greater tithes of which belong to a chapter or a layman, he himself receiving the smaller tithe or a stipend. **lay vicar,** in the Church of England, a cathedral officer who sings some portion of the service. **vicar apostolic,** *n.* in the Roman Catholic Church, a titular bishop appointed where no episcopate has been established etc. **Vicar of Bray,** a turncoat. **vicar choral,** *n.* in the Church of England, a clerical or lay assistant in the choral part of a cathedral service. **Vicar of Christ,** *n.* one of the Pope's titles. **vicar forane,** *n.* in the Roman Catholic Church, a functionary appointed by a bishop with limited (chiefly disciplinary) jurisdiction over clergy etc. **vicar-general,** *n.* in the Roman Catholic Church, an officer appointed by a bishop as his assistant, esp. in matters of jurisdiction; in the Church of England, an officer assisting a bishop or archbishop in ecclesiastical causes and visitations. **vicarage**, *n.* the benefice of a vicar; the house or residence of a vicar. †**vicarial**, *a.* **vicariate**, *a.* having delegated power, vicarious. *n.* delegated office or power; a vicarship, esp. the jurisdiction of a vicar apostolic. [OF *vicaire,* L *vicārius,* orig. a., deputed, from *vic-,* see VICE-]

vicarious, *a.* deputed, delegated; acting on behalf of another; performed, done or suffered for or instead of another. **vicariously,** *adv.* [VICAR]

vice¹, *n.* an evil or immoral practice or habit; evil conduct, gross immorality, depravity; a fault, a blemish, a defect; a bad habit or trick in a horse; †the buffoon in the old morality plays. [F, from L *vitium*]

vice², *n.* an instrument with two jaws, brought together by a screw or lever, between which an object may be clamped securely; (*fig.*) †a grip, a grasp. *v.t.* to secure in or as in a vice. [ME, spiral staircase, F *vis,* screw, L *vītis,* vine]

vice[3], *prep.* in place of. [as VICE-]

vice[4], *(coll.)* short for VICE-PRESIDENT, -CHAIRMAN etc.

vice-, *pref.* denoting one acting or qualified to act in place or as deputy of another or one next in rank. **vice-admiral,** *n.* a naval officer next in rank below an admiral, and next above a rear-admiral. **vice-admiralty,** *n.* **vice-agent,** *n.* **vice-chair,** *n.* the seat occupied by a vice-chairman, a vice-chairman. **vice-chairman,** *n.* **vice-chairmanship,** *n.* **vice-chamberlain,** *n.* the deputy of the Lord Chamberlain. **vice-chancellor,** *n.* a deputy-chancellor; an officer who discharges most of the administrative duties of a university; in the Roman Catholic Church, the head cardinal of the branch of Chancery dealing with bulls and briefs; formerly a subordinate judge in Chancery. **vice-chancellorship,** *n.* **vice-consul,** *n.* **vice-consulship,** *n.* **vice-governor,** *n.* **vice-king,** *n.* a viceroy. **vice-president,** *n.* a deputy-president. **vice-presidentship, presidency,** *n.* **vice-principal,** *n.* †**vice-queen,** *n. fem.* a woman acting as viceroy; the wife of a viceroy. **viceregal,** *a.* viceroyal. **vicereine,** *n.fem.* the wife of a viceroy. [L, abl. from gen. *vicis,* change] **viceroy,** *n.* a ruler acting with royal authority in a colony, dependency etc. **viceroyal,** *a.* **viceroyalty, viceroyship,** *n.* [VICE-, F *roi,* king]

vicegerent, *n.* (often incorr. called "viceregent"), *a.* having or exercising delegated power. *n.* an officer exercising delegated authority, a deputy. **vicegerency,** *n.* [F (L *gerens -ntem,* pres.p. of *gerere,* to carry on)]

vicenary, *a.* consisting of or pertaining to 20. [L *vīcēnārius,* from *vicēni,* twenty each, from *vīginti,* twenty]

vicennial, *a.* happening every 20 years; lasting 20 years. [L *annus,* year]

vice versa, *adv.* the order or relation being inverted, the other way round. [VICE [3], L *versa,* fem. p.p. of *vertere,* to turn]

Vichy, *n.* health resort with thermal springs, known to the Romans, on the river Allier in Allier *département*, central France. During World War II it was the seat of the French general Pétain's government 1940–44 (known also as the Vichy government), which collaborated with the Nazis. **Vichy government,** *n.* the government of unoccupied France after the defeat by the Germans in June 1940, named after the town where the cabinet under Prime Minister Pétain was based until the liberation 1944. Authoritarian and collaborationist, the Vichy regime cooperated with the Germans even after they had moved to the unoccupied zone in November 1942. **Vichy Water,** *n.* an effervescent mineral water found at Vichy. **vichyssoise,** *n.* a cream soup served chilled, with ingredients such as leeks and potatoes.

vicinage, *n.* neighbourhood, vicinity, surrounding places, environs; the state of being neighbours, neighbourliness. †**vicinal,** *a.* near, neighbouring. **vicinity,** *n.* the neighbourhood, the adjoining or surrounding district; the state of being near, proximity; near relationship (to). [F *voisinage,* from *voisin,* L *vīcīnus,* neighbouring, from *vīcus,* village, street (assim. to L)]

vicinity VICINAGE.

vicious, *a.* characterized by some vice, fault or blemish; faulty, imperfect, defective, incorrect, corrupt; contrary to moral principles or to rectitude; addicted to vice, depraved, wicked; spiteful, malignant. **viciously,** *adv.* **viciousness,** *n.* [F *vicieux,* L *vitiōsus,* from *vitium,* VICE[1]]

vicissitude, *n.* a change of condition, circumstances or fortune, a mutation, a revolution; *(poet.)* regular change or mutation. **vicissitudinary, -dinous,** *a.* [L *vicissitūdo -dinis,* from *vicissim,* by turns, as VICE[3]]

Vico, *n.* **Giambattista** (1668–1744), Italian philosopher, considered the founder of the modern philosophy of history. He rejected Descartes' emphasis on the mathematical and natural sciences, and argued that we can understand history more adequately than nature, since it is we who have made it. He believed that the study of language, ritual, and myth was a way of understanding earlier societies. His cyclical theory of history (the birth, development, and decline of human societies) was put forward in *New Science* (1725).

victim, *n.* a living creature sacrificed to some deity or in the performance of some religious rite; a person or thing destroyed or injured in the pursuit of some object; a person killed or injured in an accident, or in an epidemic; a dupe, a gull. **victimize, -ise,** *v.t.* to make a victim of; to dupe, to swindle. **victimization, -isation,** *n.* **victimizer, -iser,** *n.* [F *victime,* L *victima,* cogn. with Goth. *weihan,* to consecrate, *weihs,* holy]

victor, *n.* one who conquers in battle or wins in a contest. **victress,** *n. fem.* [L, from *vict-,* p.p. stem of *vincere,* to conquer] **victory,** *n.* the defeat of an enemy in battle, or of an opponent in a contest; a Roman or Greek goddess of victory. **Victory sign,** *n.* the first and second fingers extended in the form of a V. (see V-SIGN) [ME and OF *victorie,* L *victoria,* as VICTOR] **victorious,** *a.* having conquered in battle or any contest, triumphant, associated or connected with victory. **victoriously,** *adv.* **victoriousness,** *n.*

Victor Emmanuel II, *n.* (1820–1878), first king of united Italy from 1861. He became king of Sardinia on the abdication of his father Charles Albert 1849. In 1855 he allied Sardinia with France and the UK in the Crimean War. In 1859 in alliance with the French he defeated the Austrians and annexed Lombardy. By 1860 most of Italy had come under his rule, and in 1861 he was proclaimed king of Italy. In 1870 he made Rome his capital.

Victor Emmanuel III, *n.* (1869–1947), king of Italy from the assassination of his father Umberto I 1900. He acquiesced in the Fascist regime of Mussolini but cooperated with the Allies; he abdicated 1946.

Victoria[1], *n.* state of SE Australia. **area** 227,600 sq km/87,854 sq miles. **capital** Melbourne. **towns** Geelong, Ballarat, Bendigo. **physical** part of the Great Dividing Range runs E–W and includes the larger part of the Australian Alps; Gippsland lakes, shallow lagoons on the coast; the mallee shrub region. **population** (1987) 4,184,000; 70% live in the Melbourne area. **products** sheep, beef cattle, dairy products, tobacco, wheat; vines for wine and dried fruit, orchard fruits, vegetables, gold, brown coal (Latrobe Valley), oil and natural gas in Bass Strait.

Victoria[2], *n.* industrial port (shipbuilding, chemicals, clothing, furniture) on Vancouver Island, capital of British Columbia, Canada; population (1986) 256,000.

Victoria[3], *n.* port and capital of the Seychelles, on Mahé island; population (1985) 23,000.

Victoria[4], *n.* (1819–1901), queen of the UK from 1837, when she succeeded her uncle William IV, and empress of India from 1876. In 1840 she married Prince Albert of Saxe-Coburg and Gotha. Her relations with her prime ministers ranged from the affectionate (Melbourne and Disraeli) to the stormy (Peel, Palmerston, and Gladstone). Her golden jubilee 1887 and diamond jubilee 1897 marked a waning of republican sentiment, which had developed with her withdrawal from public life on Albert's death.

Victoria[5], **Lake,** *n.* (or **Victoria Nyanza**), largest lake in Africa, over 69,400 sq km/26,800 sq miles (410 km/255 miles long) on the equator at an altitude of 1136 m/3728 ft. It lies between Uganda, Kenya, and Tanzania, and is a source of the Nile.

victoria, *n.* a four-wheeled carriage with a raised seat for the driver, seats for two persons over the back axle and a low seat for two persons over the front axle, and a falling top; a gigantic variety of water-lily; a variety of domestic pigeon; a large red plum (also **victoria plum**). **Victoria and Albert Museum,** *n.* a museum of decorative arts in South Kensington, London, opened 1909, inspired by Henry Cole (1808–82) and Prince Albert. **Victoria Cross,** *n.* a British naval and military decoration in the shape of a Maltese cross, instituted by Queen Victoria (1856), bestowed for conspicuous bravery or devotion in the presence of the enemy. **Victoria Falls,** (or **Mosi-oa-tunya**), *n.* waterfall on the river Zambezi, on the Zambia–Zimbabwe border. The river is 1700 m/5580 ft wide, and drops 120 m/400 ft to flow through a 30 m/100 ft wide gorge. **Victorian,** *a.* of the mid- and late 19th cent. in England, covering the reign of Queen Victoria. Victorian style was often very ornate, markedly so in architecture, and Victorian Gothic harked back to the original Gothic architecture of mediaeval times. It was also an era when increasing machine mass-production threatened the existence of crafts and craft skills. *n.* a person, esp. a writer, living or flourishing then; a native of Victoria, Australia. **victoriana,** *n.* objects, ornaments etc. of the Victorian period. **Royal Victorian Order,** an order established by Queen Victoria (1896), bestowed principally for distinguished services to the sovereign. [VICTORIA[4]]

victorine, *n.* a woman's small fur tippet with long narrow ends in front; a variety of peach. [fem. name Victoria]

victress VICTOR.

victual, *n.* (*usu. in pl.*) food, provisions. *v.t.* to supply or store with provisions. *v.i.* to lay in provisions; to take food, to eat. **victualler,** *n.* one who supplies victuals, esp. an innkeeper; a victualling-ship. **licensed victualler** LICENSE. **victualless,** *a.* **victualling-bill,** *n.* a custom-house warrant for the shipment of provisions for a voyage. **victualling-department, -office,** *n.* the office managing the supply of provisions to the navy. **victualling-ship,** *n.* a ship conveying provisions to other ships or to a fleet. **victualling-yard,** *n.* one, usu. adjoining a dockyard, where warships are provisioned. [ME and OF *vitaille,* L *victuālia*, neut. pl. of *victuālis,* pertaining to nourishment from *victus,* food, from *vīvere,* to live]

vicugna, vicunia, vicuña, *n.* a S American animal, *Lama vicugna,* allied to the camel, a native of the Andean regions of Bolivia and N Chile; a fine cloth made of worsted yarn. [Sp., from Peruvian, *vicuña*]

Vidal, *n.* **Gore** (1925–), US writer and critic. Much of his work deals satirically with history and politics and includes the novels *Myra Breckinridge* (1968), *Burr* (1973), and *Empire* (1987), plays and screenplays, including *Suddenly Last Summer* (1958), and essays, such as *Armageddon?* (1987).

vidame, *n.* (*F Hist.*) a minor noble holding lands under a bishop; a bishop's deputy in secular matters. [F, corr. of med. L *vice-dominus* (VICE-, L *dominus,* lord)]

vide, *v. imper.* see (in reference to a passage in a book etc.). [L imper. of *vidēre,* to see]

videlicet, *adv.* namely, that is to say, to wit (usu. abbrev. to VIZ). [L, for *vidēre licet,* it is allowable to see, one may see]

video, *n.* a video recorder; a video recording. *a.* relating to or employed in the transmission or reception of a televised image; concerned with, or operating at video frequencies. *v.t., v.i.* to make a video recording (of). **video camera,** *n.* a camera which records its film on video tape. **video cassette,** *n.* a cassette containing video tape. **video conferencing,** *n.* meeting in conference by means of a video. **video disk,** *n.* a disk on which television picture and sound can be played back. **video frequency,** *n.* that in the range required for a video signal. **video game,** *n.* an electronically operated game played by means of a visual display unit. **video jockey** (*abbr.* VJ), *n.* one who introduces videos of popular music or similar. **video nasty,** *n.* a video film which includes horrific or gruesome scenes of violence, sexual outrage or other atrocities. **videophone, video telephone,** *n.* a telephone which can also transmit a picture of each speaker. **video (tape) recorder,** *n.* a machine for recording and playing back television broadcasts or for playing films made on videotape. **videotape,** *n.* magnetic tape used for recording a television programme or similar for subsequent transmission. **video (tape) recording,** *n.* recording both television picture and sound on magnetic tape. **video-record,** *v.t.* to record on a video recorder. **video tube,** *n.* a television tube.

vidette, VEDETTE.

vidimus, *n.* (*pl.* **-uses**) an examination or inspection of accounts etc.; an abstract or summary. [L, we have seen, as VIDE]

Vidor, *n.* **King** (1894–1982), US film director, who made epics including *The Big Parade* (1925) and *Duel in the Sun* (1946). He has been praised as a cinematic innovator, and received an honorary Academy Award in 1979. His other films include *The Crowd* (1928) and *Guerra e Pace/War and Peace* (1956).

†**viduous,** *a.* widowed. †**viduage,** †**viduity,** *n.* †**vidual,** *a.* **viduation,** *n.* [L *viduus,* separated from]

vie, *v.i.* to strive for superiority; to contend, to rival; to be equal or superior (with or in). **vying,** *a.* [ME *vien,* shortened from *envien,* OF *envier,* L *invītāre,* to INVITE]

†**vielle,** VIOL.

Vienna, *n.* (German **Wien**), capital of Austria, on the river Danube at the foot of the Wiener Wald (Vienna Woods); population (1986) 1,481,000. Industries include engineering and the production of electrical goods and precision instruments.

Vienna, Congress of, *n.* the international conference held 1814–15, which agreed the settlement of Europe after the Napoleonic Wars. National representatives included the Austrian foreign minister Metternich, Alexander I of Russia, the British foreign secretary Castlereagh and military commander Wellington, and the French politician Talleyrand.

Vienna loaf, *n.* a long round ended loaf of white bread.

Vienna steak, *n.* a meat rissole.

Viennese, *a.* pertaining to Vienna or its inhabitants. *n.* a native or the inhabitants of Vienna.

Vientiane, *n.* capital and chief port of Laos on the Mekong river; population (1985) 377,000.

Vietcong, *n.* in the Vietnam War, the members of the National Front for the Liberation of South Vietnam, founded 1960, who fought the South Vietnamese and US forces. The name was coined by the South Vietnamese government to differentiate these communist guerrillas from the Vietminh.

Viète, *n.* **François** (1540–1603), French mathematician who developed algebra and its notation. He was the first mathematician to use letters of the alphabet to denote both known and unknown quantities.

Vietminh, *n.* the Vietnam Independence League, founded 1941 to oppose the Japanese occupation of Indo-China and later directed against the French colonial power. The Vietminh were instrumental in achieving Vietnamese independence through military victory at Dien Bien Phu (1954).

Vietnam, *n.* Socialist Republic of, country in SE Asia, on the South China Sea, bounded N by China and W by Cambodia and Laos. **area** 329,600 sq km/127,259 sq miles. **capital** Hanoi. **towns** ports Ho Chi Minh City (formerly Saigon), Da Nang, and Haiphong. **physical** Red River and Mekong deltas, where cultivation and population are concentrated; some tropical rainforest; the rest is barren and mountainous. **population** (1989) 64,000,000 (750,000 refugees, the majority ethnic Chinese, left the country 1975–79, some settling in SW China, others fleeing by sea – the 'boat people' – to Hong Kong and elsewhere); annual growth rate 2%. **exports** rice, rubber, coal, iron, apatite. **language** Vietnamese, of uncertain origin but tonal like Chinese and Thai. **religion** traditionally Buddhist and Taoist. **Vietnam War,** *n.* (1954–75), war between communist North Vietnam and US-backed South Vietnam. 200,000 South Vietnamese soldiers, 1 million North Vietnamese soldiers, and 500,000 civilians were killed. 56,555 US soldiers were killed 1961–75, a fifth of whom were killed by their own troops. Cambodia, a neutral neighbour, was bombed by the US 1969–75, with 1 million killed or wounded. **Vietnamese,** *a.* of or pertaining to Vietnam; its people or their language; a native of Vietnam.

view, *n.* survey or examination by the eye; range of vision; power of seeing; that which is seen, a scene, a prospect; a picture or drawing of this; an intellectual or mental survey; the manner or mode of looking at things, considering a matter etc.; judgment, opinion, theory; intention, purpose, design; inspection by a jury etc. *v.t.* to examine with the eye; to survey mentally or intellectually; to consider, to form a mental impression or judgment of; to watch television. **in view,** in sight. **in view of,** considering, having regard to. **on view,** open to public inspection. **take a dim view of,** to regard unfavourably. †**to the view,** so as to be seen by everybody. **with a view to,** for the purpose of; with an eye to. **view-data,** *n.* a communications system by which data can be transferred through a telephone line and displayed on T.V. or video. **view-finder,** *n.* a device of mirrors in a camera which shows the view to be taken. **view-hallo,** *n.* a huntsman's shout on seeing the fox break cover. **view-phone,** another name for a video-phone. **view-point,** *n.* a point of view, as aspect. **viewable,** *a.* **viewer,** *n.* **viewless,** *a.* (*poet.*) invisible. **viewy,** *a.* having peculiar or impracticable views, faddy, visionary. **viewiness,** *n.* [A-F, from OF *veue,* fem. of *veu,* p.p. of *voir,* L. *vidēre,* to see]

vigesimal, *a.* 20th. †**vigesimation,** *n.* the putting to death of every 20th man. **vigesimo,** *n., a.* 20mo. (of books). **vigesimo-quarto,** *n., a.* 24mo. [L *vīgēsimus,* from *vīginti,* twenty]

vigia, *n.* a warning of a rock, shoal etc., on a hydrographical chart. [Sp., look out]

vigil, *n.* keeping awake during the customary hours of rest, watchfulness; devotions on the eve of a festival, orig. the watch kept on the night before a feast; the eve of a festival; (*pl.*) nocturnal devotions. **vigilance,** *n.* the state of being vigilant; (*Path.*) insomnia. **vigilance committee,** a self-organized committee for maintaining order or inflicting summary justice in an ill-ordered community or district. **vigilante,** *n.* a member of a vigilance committee. [F *vigile,* L *vigilia,* from *vigil,* awake, from *vigēre,* to be lively]

vigilant, *a.* awake and on the alert; watchful, wary, circumspect. **vigilantly,** *adv.*

vigneron, *n.* a wine-grower. [F]

vignette, *n.* an ornament of tendrils and vine leaves; an ornamental flourish round a capital letter in a manuscript; an engraving not enclosed within a definite border, esp. on the title page of a book; a photograph, drawing or other portrait showing the head and shoulders with a background shading off gradually. *v.t.* to shade off (a portrait, drawing etc.) thus; to make a photograph or portrait of in this style. **vignetter, vignettist,** *n.* [F, dim. of *vigne,* VINE]

Vigo, *n.* **Jean** (1905–34), adopted name of Jean Almereyda, French director of bizarre experimental films. He made only three feature films: *A Propos de Nice* (1930), *Zéro de conduite/Nothing for Conduct* (1933), and *L'Atalante* (1934).

vigoroso, *adv.* (*Mus.*) with energy. [It., as foll.]

vigour, *n.* active physical or mental strength or energy; abounding vitality, vital force, robustness; exertion of strength, force, activity; forcibleness, trenchancy. **vigourless,** *a.* **vigorous,** *a.* **vigorously,** *adv.* **vigorousness,** *n.* [OF *vigur, vigor,* L *vigōrem,* nom. *-or,* from *vigēre,* to be lively]

viking, *n.* a rover, freebooter or pirate, esp. one of the Scandinavian warriors of the 8th–10th cents. **Viking art,** *n.* sculpture and design of the Vikings. Viking artists are known for woodcarving and metalwork, and for an intricate interlacing ornament/similar to that found in Celtic art. **Viking probes,** *n.* two US space probes to Mars, each one consisting of an orbiter and a lander. They were launched 20 Aug. and 9 Sept. 1975. They transmitted colour pictures, and analysed the soil. **vikingism,** *n.* [Icel. *vīkingr* (prob. *vīg*, war, cogn. with *vincere,* to conquer, -ING]

Vilayet, *n.* a province of the old Turkish empire. [Turk.]

vile, *a.* worthless, morally base, depraved, despicable, abject, villainous, odious; (*coll.*) disagreeable, abominable. **vilely,** *adv.* **vileness,** *n.* [ME and OF *vil,* L *vīlis,* cheap,base]

vilify, *v.t.* to traduce, to defame; †to debase, to degrade, to make base. **vilification,** *n.* **vilifier,** *n.*

†**vilipend,** *v.t.* to speak of disparagingly or contemptuously, to depreciate. [L *vīlipendere* (VILE, L *pendere,* to weigh),]

†**vill,** *n.* a small town or village, a hamlet; a parish or part of a parish. [as foll.]

villa, *n.* a country house; a detached suburban house. **villadom,** *n.* villas collectively; (*fig.*) the middle classes. [L, farm-house, from *vīcus,* village]

village, *n.* a small assemblage of houses, smaller than a town or city and larger than a hamlet. *a.* pertaining to a village; rustic, countrified. **villager,** *n.* an inhabitant of a village. †**villagery,** *n.* **villagization, -isation,** *n.* the resettlement and rehousing of a population in new villages outside their own area, often achieved by force. **villagize, -ise,** *v.t.* [F, from L *villāticus,* pertaining to a VILLA]

villain, *n.* a person guilty or capable of crime or great wickedness; a scoundrel, a wretch; (*coll.*) a rogue, a rascal; †a rustic, a clown, a boor; a feudal serf, a bondsman attached to a feudal lord or to an estate. *a.* pertaining to, composed of, or performed by a villain or villains. **villainage,** *n.* **villainous,** *a.* worthy or characteristic of a villain; depraved, vile; very bad. †*adv.* pitifully, wretchedly. **villainously,** *adv.* **villainousness,** *n.* **villainy,** *n.* [OF and ME *vilein,* servile, base, from late L *villānus,* a farm-servant, as VILLA]

Villa-Lobos, *n.* **Heitor** (1887–1959), Brazilian composer. His style was based on folk tunes collected on travels in his country; for example, in the *Bachianas Brasileiras* (1930–44), he treats them in the manner of Bach. His works range from guitar solos to film scores to opera; he produced 2000 works, including 12 symphonies.

villanelle, *n.* a poem in five tercets and a final quatrain on two rhymes. [F, from It. *villanella,* dim. from *villano,* rustic, as prec.]

Villarsia, *n.* a genus of marsh or aquatic plants of the order Gentianaceae with yellow flowers. [Dominique *Villars,* 1745–1814, French botanist]

-ville, *comb. form* (*sl.*) a place, condition or quality with a character as specified, e.g. *dullsville, dragsville, squaresville.* [from the suffix -ville in names of towns, esp. in US, from F *ville,* a town]

villeggiatura, *n.* retirement or a stay in the country. [It., from *villegiare,* to stay at a country seat, from L VILLA]

Villehardouin, *n.* **Geoffroy de** (*c.* 1160–1213), French historian, the first to write in the French language. He was born near Troyes, and was a leader of the Fourth Crusade, of which his *Conquest of Constantinople,* about 1209, is an account.

villein, villeinage etc. VILLAIN, etc.

Villon, *n.* **François** (1431–*c.* 1465). French poet, noted for his satiric humour, pathos, and lyric power in works which used the *argot* (slang) of the time. Very little of his work survives, but it includes the *Ballade des dames du temps jadis/Ballad of the ladies of former times,* *Petit Testament* (1456), and *Grand Testament* (1461).

villus, *n.* (*pl.* **-li**) one of the short hair-like processes on certain membranes, as those on the inner surface of the small intestine; **(villi)** long, close, soft hairs. **villiform, villoid, villose, -lous,** *a.* **villosity,** *n.* [L, shaggy hair]

Vilnius, *n.* capital of Lithuanian Republic, USSR; population (1987) 566,000. Industries include engineering, and the manufacture of textiles, chemicals, and foodstuffs.

vim, *n.* (*coll.*) energy, vigour. **(full of) vim and vigour,** abounding in energy and vitality. [L, acc. of VIS]

vimana, *n.* the central shrine of an Indian temple with pyramidal roof; a temple gate. [Sansk. *vimana,* lib. a marking out]

viminal, *a.* pertaining to, producing, or consisting of twigs or shoots. **vimineous,** *a.* [L *vīminālis,* from *vīmen -minis,* twig, from *viēre,* to twist]

Vimy Ridge, *n.* hill in N France, taken in World War I by Canadian troops during the battle of Arras, Apr. 1917, at the cost of 11,285 lives. It is a spur of the ridge of Nôtre Dame de Lorette, 8 km/5 miles NE of Arras.

vin, *n.* wine. **vin blanc,** *n.* white wine. **vin ordinaire,** *n.* inexpensive table wine for daily use. **vin rosé,** *n.* rosé wine. **vin rouge,** *n.* red wine.

vina, *n.* an Indian stringed instrument with a fretted

fingerboard over two gourds. [Sansk. *vīnā*]

vinaceous, *a.* pertaining to wine or grapes; of the nature or colour of wine. [L *vīnāceus,* from *vīnum,* wine]

vinaigrette, *n.* an ornamental bottle or perforated case of gold or other metal etc. for holding aromatic vinegar etc., a smelling-bottle; a salad dressing consisting of oil, vinegar and seasoning. **vinaigrous,** *a.* sour, acid; (*fig.*) cross, crabbed. [F, dim. of *vinaigre,* VINEGAR]

vinasse, *n.* a residual product containing potassium salts from the wine-press or beets from which sugar has been extracted. [F]

Vincent de Paul, St, *n.* (*c.* 1580–1660), French Roman Catholic priest and founder of the two charitable orders of Lazarists (1625) and Sisters of Charity (1634). Born in Gascony, he was ordained 1600, then captured by Barbary pirates and was a slave in Tunis until he escaped 1607. He was canonized 1737; feast day 19 July.

Vincentian, *a.* pertaining to or founded by St Vincent de Paul. *n.* a member of a religious and charitable order founded by him, a Lazarist.

vincible, *a.* capable of being conquered, not invincible. **vincibility, vincibleness,** *n.* [L *vincibilis,* from *vincere,* to conquer]

vincristine, *n.* an alkaloid substance derived from the tropical periwinkle, used in the treatment of some types of leukaemia. [L *vinca,* genus name of the plant, and *crista,* fold]

vinculum, *n.* (*pl.* **-la**) a straight line drawn over several terms to show that they are all alike, to be added to or deducted from those preceding or following; a fraenum; (*Print.*) a brace. †**vinculate,** *v.t.* [L, a bond, from *vincire,* to bind]

vindaloo, *n.* a type of hot Indian curry.

†**vindemial,** *a.* pertaining to a vintage or grape-harvest. †**vindemiate,** *v.i.* †**vindemiation,** *n.* [late L *vindēmialis,* from *vindēmia,* grape-harvest (*vinum,* wine, *demere,* to take)]

vindicate, *v.t.* to maintain (a claim, statement etc.) against attack or denial; to defend (a person) against reproach, accusation etc.; to prove to be true or valid, to defend, to establish, to justify, to uphold. **vindicable,** *a.* **vindicability,** *n.* the state of being vindicable. **vindication,** *n.* **vindicative,** *a.* **vindicator,** *n.* **vindicatress,** *n.* **vindicatory,** *a.* tending to vindicate or justify; punitory. [L *vindicātus,* p.p. of *vindicāre* (VIM or *vēnum,* favour, *dicāre,* to assert, from *dīcere,* to say)]

vindictive, *a.* revengeful; characterized or prompted by revenge. **vindictive damages,** damages given to punish the defendant. **vindictively,** *adv.* **vindictiveness,** *n.* [shortened from VIN- DICATIVE, see prec., from conf. with L *vindicta,* revenge]

vine, *n.* a slender climbing plant of the genus *Vitis,* esp. *V. vinifera,* the common or grape-vine; any plant with a slender climbing or trailing stem. **vine-borer,** *n.* one of various insects that injure vines by boring into the stems, twigs etc. **vine-clad,** *a.* covered with vines. **vine-disease,** *n.* any disease attacking the grape-vine, esp. that caused by the phylloxera. **vine-dresser,** *n.* one who dresses, trims or prunes vines. **vine-fretter,** *n.* a small insect infesting vines. **vineyard,** *n.* a plantation of grape-vines. **vined** *a.* **vinery,** *n.* a greenhouse for vines. **viny,** *a.* pertaining to vines. **vinic,** *a.* pertaining to or derived from wine. **vinous,** †**-nose,** *a.* of, pertaining to, or having the qualities of wine. **vinosity,** *n.* [F *vigne,* L *vīnea,* vineyard, from *vīnum,* wine, cogn. with Gr. *oinos,* wine, *oinē,* vine, cp. L *vītis,* vine, *vīmen,* twig, from *viēre,* to twist]

vinegar, *n.* an acid liquid obtained by oxidation or acetous fermentation from wine, cider etc., used as a condiment and as a preservative in pickling; anything sour or soured, as a disposition etc. *v.t.* to put vinegar on or into; (*fig.*) to make sour. **vinegar-eel,** *n.* a minute worm infesting vinegar, sour paste etc. **vinegar-plant,** *n.* a microscopic fungus producing acetous fermentation. †**vinegarette,** VINAIGRETTE. **vinegarish, vinegary,** *a.* [F *vinaigre* (*vin,* L *vinum,* wine, *aigre,* see EAGER)]

vinery, vineyard VINE.

†**vinewed,** *a.* mouldy. [also *finewed,* p.p. from OE *fynegian, fynian,* from *fynig,* mouldy]

vingt-et-un, *n.* a card game in which the object is to make the aggregate number of the pips on the cards as nearly as possible 21 without exceeding this. [F, twenty-one]

vini-, *comb. form* pertaining to wine or vines. [L *vinum,* wine]

viniculture, *n.* the cultivation of grape-vines. **viniculturist,** *n.*

vinifacteur, *n.* any apparatus used for wine-making.

vinificator, *n.* an apparatus for condensing the alcoholic vapours from the fermenting must in wine-making.

†**vinolent,** *a.* full of wine (of a bottle etc.); drunk.

Vinland, *n.* Norse name for the area of North America, probably on the east coast of Nova Scotia or New England, which the Viking Leif Ericsson visited. It was named after the wild grapes that grew there.

vinometer, *n.* an instrument for measuring the percentage of alcohol in wine.

vintage, *n.* the yield of a vineyard or vine-district for a particular season; the season of gathering grapes; the product of a particular year. *a.* produced at some particular time, esp. of a past season. **vint,** *v.t.* to make (wine). **vintage car,** *n.* an old-fashioned car (esp. one built between 1919 and 1930). **vintage wine,** *n.* wine of a good vintage year. **vintager,** *n.* a grape-gatherer. [ME *vindage, vendage,* F *vendange,* L *vindēmia,* see VINDEMIAL]

vintner, *n.* a wine-merchant. **vintnery,** *n.*

vinyl, *n.* an organic radical CH_2CH; any vinyl resin or plastic, esp. PVC. *a.* of or made of a vinyl resin. **vinyl resins, plastics,** *n.* thermoplastic resins, polymers or co-polymers of vinyl compounds.

viol, *n.* a mediaeval stringed musical instrument, the predecessor of the violin; a violoncello or bass-viol. **viol class,** *n.* instruments like the violin, violoncello etc., played with a bow and having no frets, thus being capable of continuous gradation. †**viol de gamba** VIOLA DA GAMBA. [F *viole,* Prov. *viula,* late L *vitula,* cp. FIDDLE]

viola[1], *n.* an instrument like a large violin, the alto or tenor violin; a viol. [It.]

viola[2], *n.* a plant or flower of the genus containing the violet and pansy. **violaceous,** *a.* of a violet colour; of the violet family. [L, violet]

viola da gamba, an early form of bass-viol. **violist,** *n.* a player on the viol or viola. [It., leg-viol]

violate, *v.t.* to infringe or transgress, to break, to disobey (a law, obligation, duty etc.); to treat irreverently, to profane, to desecrate; to do violence to, to outrage; to deflower, by force, to ravish, to rape. **violable,** *a.* **violation,** *n.* **violative,** *a.* **violator,** *n.* [L *violatus,* p.p. of *violāre,* cogn. with VIS]

violence, *n.* the state or quality of being violent; violent exercise of power; violent treatment; injury, outrage; vehemence, intensity or impetuosity of feeling, action etc.; the illegal exercise of physical force, an act of intimidation by the show or threat of force. **to do violence to,** to do a physical injury to, to outrage, to violate. **violent,** *a.* acting with or characterized by the exertion of great physical force; vehement, impetuous, furious; intense, abrupt, immoderate; produced by or resulting from extraneous force or poison, not natural (of death etc.); based on almost conclusive evidence (of an inference or presumption). **violently,** *adv.* [F, from L *violentia,* as prec.]

violet, *n.* a plant or flower of the genus *Viola,* esp. the sweet violet, *V. odorata,* the dog violet, *V. canina,* and some other species with small blue, purple or white flowers; a colour seen at the opposite end of the spectrum to red, produced by a slight mixture of red with blue; a small violet-coloured butterfly of various species. *a.* of the colour of violet. **shrinking violet,** (*coll.*) a shy, hesitant person. **violet-wood,** *n.* one of several kinds of wood, esp. king-wood and myall-wood. **violescent,** *a.* tending to a violet colour. [F dim. of *viole,* VIOLA[2]]

violin[1], *n.* a musical instrument of the viol class with four strings, played with a bow; a player on this. **violinist,** *n.* [It. *violino,* dim. of VIOLA[1]]

violin², *n.* an emetic substance contained in the common violet. [VIOLA[2], -IN]

violinist VIOLIN[1]. **violist**. [It. VIOL]

violoncello, *n.* a four-stringed musical instrument of the viol class rested on the ground between the legs, a bass-viol. **violoncellist,** *n.*

violone, *n.* a mediaeval double-bass viol; an organ-stop of string-like tone.

VIP, (*abbr.*) very important person.

viper, *n.* a venomous snake of the family Viperidae, esp. the European viper or adder, the only poisonous British snake; a mischievous or malignant person. **viper's bugloss,** *n.* the blue weed or blue thistle, *Echium vulgare.* **viper's-grass,** *n.* a perennial plant, *Scorzonera hispanica,* of the aster family. **viperiform, viperine, viperish, viperoid, viperous,** *a.* [F *vipère,* L *vīpera,* perh. *vīvipara,* see VIVIPAROUS]

virago, *n.* an impudent, turbulent woman; a termagant; a woman of masculinestrength and courage. †**viraginian, viraginous,** *a.* †**viraginity,** *n.* [L, man-like maiden, from *vir,* man]

viral, *a.* pertaining to a virus.

†**vire,** *n.* a heavy crossbow-bolt; (*Her.*) an annulet. [OF, from L *viria,* ring]

Virchow, *n.* **Rudolf Ludwig Carl** (1821–1902), German pathologist and founder of cellular pathology. Virchow was the first to describe leukaemia (cancer of the blood). In his book *Die Cellulare Pathologie/Cellular Pathology* (1858), he proposed that disease is not due to sudden invasions or changes, but to slow processes in which normal cells give rise to abnormal ones.

virelay, *n.* an old form of French verse with two rhymes to a stanza and usu. a refrain. [OF *virelai,* from *virer,* to turn, to VEER]

virement, *n.* authorized transference of a surplus to balance a deficit. [F]

vireo, *n.* an American passerine insectivorous singing-bird. [L]

virescent, *a.* (*Bot.*) green, tending to become green, viridescent; abnormally green (of petals etc.). **virescence,** *n.* [L *virescens -ntem,* pres.p. of *virescere,* incept. of *virēre,* to be green]

virgate, *a.* long, straight, and erect, rod-like. †*n.* an old measure for land. [L *virgātus,* from *virga,* rod]

Virgil, Vergil, *n.* (**Publius Vergilius Maro**) (70–19 BC), Roman poet who wrote the *Eclogues* (37 BC), a series of pastoral poems, the *Georgics* (30 BC), four books on the art of farming and his masterpiece, the *Aeneid.* **Virgilian,** *a.* pertaining to or in the style of Virgil.

virgin, *n.* a woman who has had no sexual relations with a man, a maid; a member of an order of women under vows of chastity; a madonna; a female insect that produces eggs without fertilization; the constellation Virgo; a man who has had no carnal knowledge of woman. *a.* being a virgin; pure, chaste, undefiled; befitting a virgin; maidenly, modest; unworked, untried, not brought into cultivation; producing eggs without impregnation (of insects). †*v.i.* to be or remain chaste. **the Virgin,** the mother of Christ. **virgin-born,** *a.* born of a virgin. **Virgin Queen,** *n.* name applied to Queen Elizabeth I (1533–1603). **virgin's bower,** *n.* traveller's-joy, *Clematis vitalba.* **virginal,** *a.* pertaining to or befitting a virgin; pure, chaste, maidenly. *n.* a keyed musical instrument, shaped like a box, used in the 16th–17th cents., also called a pair of virginals. †*v.i.* to finger as on a virginal. **virginally,** *adv.* **virginhood,** †**virgin-head, virginity,** *n.* the state of being a virgin, purity, innocence. [OF *virgine,* L *virginem,* nom. *-go,* etym. doubtful]

Virginia, *n.* state of the S US; nickname Old Dominion. **area** 105,600 sq km/40,762 sq miles. **capital** Richmond. **towns** Norfolk, Virginia Beach, Newport News, Hampton, Chesapeake, Portsmouth. **population** (1986) 5,787,000. **products** sweet potatoes, corn, tobacco, apples, peanuts, coal, furniture, paper, chemicals, processed food, textiles. **Virginia,** *n.* tobacco from Virginia. **Virginia creeper,** *n.* a woody vine, *Ampelopsis hederacea,* with ornamental foliage. **Virginian,** *n., a.*

Virgin Islands, *n.pl.* group of about 100 small islands, northernmost of the Leeward Islands in the Antilles, West Indies. Tourism is the main industry. They comprise the **US Virgin Islands** St Thomas (with the capital, Charlotte Amalie), St Croix, St John, and about 50 small islets; area 350 sq km/135 sq miles; population (1985) 111,000; and the **British Virgin Islands** Tortola (with the capital, Road Town), Virgin Gorda, Anegada, Jost van Dykes, and about 40 islets; area 150 sq km/58 sq miles; population (1987) 13,250.

Virgo, *n.* constellation of the zodiac, and the second largest in the sky, representing a maiden holding an ear of wheat. The Sun passes through Virgo from late Sept. to the end of Oct. Virgo's brightest star is the first-magnitude Spica, a blue-white star about 250 light years away. Virgo contains the nearest large cluster of galaxies to us, 50 million light years away, consisting of about 3000 galaxies centred on the giant elliptical galaxy M87. Also in Virgo is the nearest quasar, 3 273, an estimated 3 billion light years distant. In astrology, the dates for Virgo are between about 23 Aug. and 22 Sept. (see PRECESSION).

virgule, *n.* a small rod, a twig; †a comma. **virgulate,** *a.* [L *virgula,* dim. of *virga,* see VIRGATE]

viridescent, *a.* greenish; becoming slightly green. **viridescence,** *n.* †**virid,** *a.* green. **viridigenous,** *a.* imparting greenness (esp. to oysters). **viridity,** *n.* greenness, the colour of fresh vegetation; greenness in oysters, due to feeding on green organisms. [late L *viridescens -ntem,* pres.p. of *viridescere,* from *viridis,* green]

virile, *a.* of or pertaining to man or the male sex, procreative; characteristic of a man, masculine, manly; of a male sexually potent. **virilism,** *n.* the development in the female of masculine characteristics, mental and physical. **virility,** *n.* [F *viril,* fem. *-ile,* L *virīlis,* from *vir,* man]

virole, *n.* a ferrule; (*Her.*) a hoop or ring encircling a horn. [OF see FERRULE]

virology etc. VIRUS.

virose, virous, *a.* poisonous; (*Bot.*) emitting a fetid odour. [L *vīrōsus,* from VIRUS]

Virtanen, *n.* **Artturi Ilmari** (1895–1973), Finnish chemist who from 1920 made discoveries in agricultural chemistry. Because green fodder tends to ferment and produce a variety of harmful acids, it cannot be preserved for long. Virtanen prevented the process from starting by acidifying the fodder. In this form it lasted longer and remained nutritious. Nobel prize 1945.

virtu, *n.* love of or taste for fine arts. **articles** or **objects of virtu,** rare, old or beautiful works of decorative art. [It. *virtù, vertù,* as VIRTUE]

virtue, *n.* moral excellence, goodness, uprightness, rectitude; conformity with or practice of morality or duty; a particular moral excellence; sexual purity, chastity, esp. in women; inherent power, goodness, or efficacy; (*pl.*) the seventh order of the celestial hierarchy. **cardinal virtues** CARDINAL. **by** or **in virtue of,** by or through the efficacy or authority of, on the strength of. **virtueless,** *a.* **virtual,** *a.* being such in essence or effect though not in name or appearance, equivalent so far as effect is concerned, in effect. **virtual memory,** *n.* (*Comput.*) a facility which allows more data to be stored than the capacity of the main memory by transferring data to and from disks. **virtuality,** *n.* **virtually,** *adv.* **virtuoso** etc. VIRTU. **virtuous,** *a.* characterized by virtue, morally good; chaste. **virtuously,** *adv.* **virtuousness,** *n.* [ME and F *vertu,* L *virtūtem,* nom. of *-tus,* from *vir,* see VIRILE]

virtuoso, *n.* (*pl.* **-osos**) a connoisseur of articles of virtu; a skilled performer in some fine art, esp. music. **virtuosity, virtuosoship,** *n.*

virulent, *a.* extremely poisonous; caused by or of the nature of virus; highly infective; having a severe effect; extremely bitter, acrimonious or malignant. **virulence,** †**-lency,** *n.* **virulently,** *adv.* **viruliferous,** *n.* (*Med.*). [F, from L *virulentus,* from foll.]

virus, *n.* a very small infective agent capable of self-propagation only in living matter, the causative agent of many diseases; a disease caused by this; corrupting influence; virulence; computer virus. **virus infection, disease,** *n.* one caused by a virus. **virology**, *n.* the study of viruses and virus diseases. **virologist,** *n.* **virological**, *a.* [L, slime, poison]

vis, *n.* (*pl.* **vires)** (*Mech.*) force, energy, potency. **vis inertiae** INERT. **vis mortua**, *n.* dead force; force doing no work. **vis viva**, *n.* living force, measured by the mass of a moving body multiplied by the square of its velocity. [L]

visa, visé, *n.* an official endorsement on a passport showing that it has been examined and found correct. *v.t.* to certify (a passport). [F *viser,* to inspect]

visage, *n.* the face, the countenance. †*v.t.* to confront, to face. **visaged,** *a.* having a visage or look of a particular type. [F, from L *vīsum,* nom. *-us,* p.p. of *vidēre,* to see]

visagiste, *n.* one who specializes in facial make-up.

visard VISOR.

vis-à-vis, *adv.* face to face, opposite to; in relation to. *n.* a person facing another as in certain dances, e.g. a quadrille; a carriage or couch for two persons sitting *vis-à-vis.* [F, face to face (*vis,* face, L *vīsum,* see VISAGE)]

Visby, *n.* historic town and bishopric on the Swedish island of Gotland in the Baltic.

viscacha, *n.* a S American burrowing rodent, *Lagostomus trichodactylus.* [Am.-Sp., from native name]

viscera, *n.pl.* the internal organs of the great cavities of the body, as the skull, thorax, and abdomen, esp. those of the abdomen, the intestines. **visceral,** *a.* **viscerate,** *v.t.* to disembowel. **visceri-, viscero-,** *comb.form.* [L, pl. of *viscus*]

viscid, *a.* sticky, adhesive; semifluid in consistency. **viscidity**, *n.* **viscin**, *n.* a viscid liquid obtained from mistletoe etc., the chief constituent of bird-lime. [F *viscide,* L *viscidus,* from *viscum,* mistletoe, bird-lime, cogn. with Gr. *ixos, ixia*]

visco-, *comb. form,* pertaining to viscosity.

viscometer, viscosimeter, *n.* an apparatus for determining the viscosity of liquids. **viscometry**, *n.*

Visconti[1], **dukes of Milan,** rulers of Milan (1277–1447). They originated as northern Italian feudal lords who attained dominance over the city as a result of their alliance with the Holy Roman emperors. By the mid-14th century, they ruled 15 other major towns in N Italy.

Visconti[2], *n.* **Luchino** (1906–76), Italian film and theatre director. The film *Ossessione* (1942) pioneers his work with neo-realist theories; later works include *The Leopard* (1963) and *Death in Venice* (1971). His powerful social comment in documentaries led to clashes with the Italian government and Roman Catholic Church.

viscose, *n.* the cellulose sodium salt used in the manufacture of artificial silk. **viscosity**, *n.* stickiness; thickness of a fluid etc.; the property of fluids, semifluids, and gases which expresses their resistance to flow, change of shape or re-arrangement of molecules; internal friction. **viscous**, **viscose,** *a.* **viscousness,** *n.* [L *viscōsus,* sticky; see VISCID]

viscount, *n.* a British peer ranking next below an earl, and above a baron. **viscountcy,** *n.* **viscountess**, *n.* **viscountship, viscounty,** *n.* [OE *visconte,* OF *viscomte* (F *vicomte*) (VICE-, COUNT[2])]

viscous, viscose VISCID.

Viscum, *n.* a genus of parasitic shrubs comprising the mistletoe. [L, see VISCID]

viscus, *n.* viscera. [L *viscus*]

Vishnu, *n.* in Hinduism, the second in the triad of gods (with Brahma and Siva) representing three aspects of the supreme spirit. He is the Preserver, and is believed to have assumed human appearance in nine *avatāras*, or incarnations, in such forms as Rama and Krishna. His worshippers are the Vaishnavas.

visible, *a.* capable of being seen, perceptible by the eye; in view, apparent, open, conspicuous. **visible Church,** *n.* the body of professing Christians. **visible horizon,** *n.* the apparent limit bounding the view. **visible means,** *n.pl.* means or resources which are apparent to or ascertainable by others. **visible radiation,** *n.* electromagnetic radiation which can be detected by the eye; light. **visible speech,** *n.* phonetic symbols representingevery possible articulate utterance. **visibility,** *n.* state of being visible, visibleness. **high, low visibility,** *n.* (*Meteor.*) clear or indistinct visibility. **visibleness,** *n.* **visibly,** *adv.* [F, from L *vīsibilis,* from *vīs-us,* see prec.]

Visigoth, *n.* one of the western Goths who settled in S Gaul and Spain in the 4th and 5th cents. **Visigothic**, *a.* [late L *Visigothī, -gothae,* from Teut. (WEST, GOTH)]

vision, *n.* the act or faculty of seeing, sight; that which is seen, an object of sight; a mental representation of a visual object, esp. in a dream or trance; a supernatural or prophetic apparition; a creation of the imagination or fancy; foresight, an appreciation of what the future may hold. *v.t.* to see in or as in a vision; to imagine; to present as in a vision. **vision mixer,** *n.* one who blends or combines different camera shots in television or films. **visional,** *a.* **visionally,** *adv.* **visionary,** *a.* existing in a vision or in the imagination only; imaginary, unreal, unsubstantial, unpractical; given to day-dreaming, fanciful theories etc. *n.* a visionary person. **visionariness,** *n.* **visionist,** *n.* **visionless**, *a.* [F, from L *vīsiōnem,* nom. *-sio,* from *vidēre,* to see, p.p. *vīsus*]

visit, *v.t.* to go or come to see, as an act of friendship, civility, business, curiosity etc.; to come or go to for the purpose of inspection, supervision, correction of abuses etc.; to come upon, to overtake, to afflict (of diseases etc.); (*Bibl.*) to chastise; to comfort, to bless. *v.i.* to call on or visit people; to keep up friendly intercourse. *n.* the act of visiting, or going to see a person, place, or thing; a call; a stay or sojourn (with or at); a formal or official call or inspection. **visitable, visitatorial**, †**visitorial,** *a.* **visiting-book,** *n.* one in which calls received or intended are entered. **visiting-card,** *n.* a small card, bearing one's name etc. to be left in making a call. **visiting professor,** *n.* a professor invited to join academic staff for a limited time. **visitant,** *n.* a migratory bird that visits a country at certain seasons; (*poet.*) a visitor, a guest; in the Roman Catholic Church, a nun of the Order of the Visitation of Our Lady, devoted to the education of young girls. **visitation,** *n.* the act of visiting; a formal or official visit for the purpose of inspection, correction etc., esp. by a bishop to the churches of his diocese; (*Internat. Law*) the boarding of a foreign vessel in time of war to ascertain her character etc.; the right to do this; a divine dispensation, esp. a chastisement or affliction; (*Her.*) the official visit of a herald to a district for the examination and verification of arms, pedigrees etc.; in the Roman Catholic Church, a festival held on 2 July in honour of the visit of the Virgin Mary to Elizabeth (Luke i.39); (*Zool.*) an abnormal and extensive irruption of animals into a region. **Nuns of the Visitation,** in the Roman Catholic Church, the order of Visitants. **visitation of the sick,** an Anglican office for the comfort and consolation of sick persons. **visitor,** *n.* one who makes a call; one who visits a place; an officer appointed to make a visitation of any institution. **visitors' book,** *n.* one in which visitors' names are entered, esp. in which visitors to an hotel, boarding-house, museum etc. write remarks. **Visitor's Passport,** *n.* a simplified short-term passport. [F *visiter,* L *vīsitāre,* freq. of *vīsere,* to behold, from *vidēre,* see prec.]

visite, *n.* a light, close-fitting outer garment worn by women early in the 19th cent. [F, VISIT]

visiting, †**visitorial** etc. VISIT.

†**visnomie,** PHYSIOGNOMY.

visor, *n.* the movable perforated part of a helmet defending the face; a projecting part on the front of a cap, for shielding the eyes; †a mask. **visored,** *a.* **visorless**, *a.* [ME and A-F *visere,* OF *visiere,* from *vis,* face, see VISAGE]

vista, *n.* a long view shut in at the sides, as between rows of trees; (*fig.*) a mental view far into the past or future. **vistaed,** *a.* [It., fem. of *visto,* p.p. of *vedere,* L *vidēre,* to see]

visual, *a.* of, pertaining to, or used in sight or seeing; serving as an organ or instrument of seeing. **visual aid,** *n.* a picture, film, photograph, diagram etc. used as an aid to teaching or imparting information. **visual arts,** *n.pl.* painting, sculpture, film etc. as opposed to music, literature etc. **visual display unit,** (*abbr.* **VDU**) *n.* a device, usu. with a keyboard, which displays characters etc. representing data stored in a computer memory. **visuality,** *n.* **visualism,** *n.* **visualist,** *n.* **visualize, -ise,** *v.t.* to make visual or visible; to make visible to the eye; to externalize or give a visible form to (an idea, mental image etc.). **visualization,** *n.* **visualizer,** *n.* **visually,** *adv.* **visually challenged,** *a.* blind or having severely impaired sight. [F, from late L *vīsuālis,* from *vīsus,* sight, from *vidēre,* to see]

vital, *a.* pertaining to, necessary to, or supporting organic life, containing life; affecting life; indispensable, essential. *n.pl.* the parts or organs of animals essential to life, as the heart, brain etc. **vital centre,** *n.* the point in the body at which a wound appears to be instantly fatal, esp. the respiratory nerve-centre in the medulla oblongata. **vital functions,** *n.pl.* the bodily functions that are essential to life such as the circulation of blood. **vital force** or **principle,** *n.* one assumed as accounting for organic life etc. **vital spark,** *n.* the principle of life, hence life or trace of life; (*coll.*) the moving spirit behind an enterprise etc. **vital statistics,** *n.pl.* those relating to birth, marriage, mortality; (*coll.*) the measurements of a woman's bust, waist and hips. **vitalism,** *n.* the doctrine that life is derived from something distinct from physical forces. **vitalist,** *n., a.* **vitalistic,** *a.* **vitality,** *n.* **vitalize, -ise,** *v.t.* to give life to; to animate, to make more lively. **vitalization,** *n.* **vitally,** *adv.* [F, from L *vītālis,* from *vīta,* life, cogn. with *vīvere,* to live, and Gr. *bios,* life]

vitamin, *n.* one of a number of naturally occurring substances which are necessary, though in minute quantities, for normal metabolism. So far as is known their functions are: Vitamin A, growth-promoting and anti-infection; B_1, or F, beneficial to nerves and bowels; B_2, or G, prevents pellagra; C, anti-scorbutic; D, prevents rickets; E, anti-sterility; H, human needs, if any, unknown; K, promotes normal blood coagulability; P, believed to help the capillary walls to resist changes of pressure. [L *vita,* life, AMINE]

vitellus, *n.* (*pl.* **-li**) yolk of egg, the protoplasmic contents of the ovum. **vitellary, vitelline,** *a.* **vitelli-, vitello-,** *comb. forms.* **vitellicle,** *n.* a yolk-sac. [L, dim. of *vitulus,* calf, see VEAL]

vitiate, *v.t.* to impair the quality of; to corrupt; to render faulty or imperfect; to render invalid or ineffectual. **vitiation,** *n.* **vitiator,** *n.* **vitiosity,** *n.* the state of being vicious; depravity, corruption; (*Scots Law*) faulty. [L *vitiāre,* from *vitium,* VICE[1]]

viticide, *n.* an insect or other vermin injurious to vines. [L *vītis,* VINE, -CIDE] **viticolous,** *a.* living on or infesting the vine. [L *colere,* to inhabit] **viticulture,** *n.* the cultivation of the grape-vine. **viticultural,** *a.* **viticulturist,** *n.*

vitiosity VITIATE.

Vitis, *n.* a genus of plants comprising the grape-vine. [L]

vitreous, *a.* consisting of or resembling glass; obtained from glass. **vitreous electricity,** *n.* electricity generated by friction on glass, formerly regarded as positive. **vitreous humour,** *n.* the jelly-like substance filling the posterior chamber of the eye, between the lens and the retina. **vitreosity, vitreousness,** *n.* **vitrescent,** *a.* **vitrescence,** *n.* **vitrescible,** *a.* vitrificable. **vitric,** *a.* of or like glass; pertaining to vitrics. *n.pl.* fused siliceous compounds, glass and glassy materials, opp. to ceramics; the science or history of glass-manufacture. **vitriform,** *a.* [L *vitreus,* from *vitrum,* glass, perh. cogn. with *vidēre,* to see]

vitric etc. VITREOUS.

vitrify, *v.t.* to convert into glass or a glassy substance by heat and fusion. *v.i.* to be converted into glass. **vitrification, vitrifaction,** *n.* †**vitrifacture,** *n.* the manufacture of glass or glass-ware. **vitrifiable,** *a.* **vitrifiability,** *n.*

vitrine, *n.* a glass show-case.

vitriol, *n.* sulphuric acid (or oil of vitriol) as made from green vitriol; any salt of this, a sulphate; malignancy, caustic criticism etc. **black vitriol,** an impure copper sulphate. **blue** or **copper vitriol,** copper sulphate. **green vitriol,** ferrous sulphate or copperas. **oil of vitriol,** sulphuric acid. **red** or **rose vitriol,** cobalt sulphate. **vitriol-throwing,** *n.* the act of throwing vitriol in the face of a person for the purpose of private vengeance. **vitriolation, -lization,** *n.* **vitriolic,** *a.* pertaining to, obtained from, or having the qualities of vitriol; caustic, bitter, malignant. **vitrioline,** *a.* **vitriolizable,** *a.* **vitriolize, -ise, vitriolate,** *v.t.* to convert into a sulphate. [ME and OF *vitriole,* med. L *vitriolus,* L *vitreolus,* dim. of *vitreus,* VITREOUS]

vitro-di-trina, *n.* white Venetian glass in which fine threads of cane form a lace like pattern. [It., glass of lace]

vitrophyre, *n.* a porphyritic-volcanic rock of a vitreous structure. **vitrophyric,** *a.* [L *vitro-, vitrum,* glass, *phyre,* from PORPHYRY]

Vitruvian, *a.* (*Arch.*) of or in the style of Marcus Vitruvius Pollio, a Roman architect of the Augustan age. **Vitruvian scroll,** *n.* a pattern consisting of convoluted undulations, used in friezes etc.

vitta, *n.* (*pl.* **-tae**) a band, fillet, or garland, worn by a priest, sacrificial victim etc.; the lappet of a mitre; an oil-tube in the fruit of the parsley family etc.; a band or stripe of colour. **vittate,** *a.* [L]

vittles, *n.pl.* an alternative or dialect form of *victuals.*

vitular, -lary, vituline, *a.* of or pertaining to a calf or calving; calf-like. [L *vitulus,* calf, see VEAL]

vituperate, *v.t.* to upbraid, to abuse, to rail at. **vituperable,** *a.* **vituperation,** *n.* **vituperative,** *a.* **vituperatively,** *adv.* **vituperator,** *n.* [L *vituperātus,* p.p. of *vituperāre* (*vitu-, vitium,* VICE[1], *parāre,* to get ready)]

Vitus, St, *n.* Christian saint, probably Sicilian, who was martyred at Rome early in the 4th cent.

viva[1], *n., int.* an exclamation of applause or joy. [It., long live, from L *vivere,* to live, as VIVACIOUS]

viva[2], VIVA VOCE.

vivace, *adv.* (*Mus.*) in a brisk, lively manner. [It., as foll.]

vivacious, *a.* lively, animated, sprightly, gay; (*Bot.*) tenacious of life, living through the winter, perennial. **vivaciously,** *adv.* **vivacity, vivaciousness,** *n.* [L *vīvax -ācis,* from *vīvere,* to live]

Vivaldi, *n.* **Antonio (Lucio)** (1678–1741), Italian baroque composer, violinist, and conductor. He wrote 23 symphonies, 75 sonatas, over 400 concertos, including the *Four Seasons* (about 1725) for violin and orchestra, over 40 operas, and much sacred music. His work was largely neglected until the 1930s.

vivandière, *n.fem.* a female sutler attached to a continental, esp. French, regiment. [F, fem. of *vivandier,* sutler, from L *vīvenda,* provisions, see VIAND]

vivarium, *n.* (*pl.* **-ria**) a park, garden or other place artificially prepared in which animals etc. are kept alive as nearly as possible in their natural state. **vivary,** *n.* [L, from *vīvus,* alive]

vivat, *n., int.* the cry 'long live'. **vivat rex** or **regina,** *int.* long live the king *or* queen. [L, may he (or she) live, from *vīvere,* to live]

viva voce, *adv., a.* by word of mouth, orally. *n.* a viva voce or oral examination. [L, with the living voice]

viverriform, *a.* having the shape or structure of the Viverridae, a family of carnivorous mammals containing the civets, mongooses etc. **viverrid,** *n.* **viverrine,** *a.* **viverroid,** *n., a.* [mod. L *viverra,* ferret, -FORM]

vivers, *n.pl.* (*Sc.*) food, provisions. [F *vivres,* from *vivre,* as VIVE]

vives, *n.* a disease of the ear-glands in horses. [OF *avives,* Sp. *avivas,* Arab. *addhība* (*al,* the, *dhība,* she-wolf)]

vivi-, *comb. form* alive, living. [L *vīvus,* living]

vivid, *a.* vigorous, lively; very bright, intense, brilliant; clear, strongly marked, highly coloured. **vividly,** *adv.*

vividness, *n.* [L *vīvidus,* from *vīvus,* living]
vivify, *v.t.* to give life to, to quicken, to animate, to enliven. †**vivific,** *a.* †**vivificate,** *v.t.* **vivification,** *n.* †**vivificative,** *a.* **vivifier,** *n.* [F *vivifier,* late L *vīvificāre* (L *vīvus,* living, *-ficāre, facere,* to make)]
viviparous, *a.* bringing forth young alive, opp. to *oviparous* and *ovoviviparous;* (*Bot.*) producing bulbs or seeds that germinate while still attached to the parent plant. **viviparously,** *adv.* **viviparity, viviparousness,** *n.* [late L *vīvaparus* (*vīvus,* alive, *parere,* to produce)]
vivisection, *n.* the dissection of or performance of inoculative or other experiments on living animals. **vivisect,** *v.t.* to dissect (a living animal). **vivisectional,** *a.* **vivisectionist,** *n.* **vivisector,** *n.* **vivisepulture,** *n.* burial alive. [F (L *vīvus,* alive, SECTION]
vivo, *adv.* (*Mus.*) with life and animation, vivace. [It.]
vixen, *n.* a she-fox; a shrewish, quarrelsome woman; a scold. **vixenish, vixenly,** *a.* having the qualities of a vixen. [OE *fyxen,* fem. of FOX, cp. G *Füschsin,* fem. of *Fuchs*]
viz, VIDELICET. †**vizard,** VISOR.
vizcacha, VISCACHA.
vizier, *n.* a high officer or minister of state in Muslim countries. **grand vizier,** the prime minister in the Turkish empire etc. **vizierate, viziership,** *n.* **vizierial,** *a.* [Arab. *wazīr,* counsellor, orig. porter, from *wazara,* to bear a burden]
vizor, VISOR.
Vizsla, *n.* a Hungarian breed of hunting dog with a smooth red or rust-coloured coat. [*Vizsla,* a town in Hungary]
vla, (*abbr.*) viola.
Vlach, *n.* a Wallachian. [Boh.]
Vladimir I, *n.* **St** (956–1015), Russian saint and prince of Kiev. Converted to Christianity 988, he married Anna, Christian sister of the Byzantine emperor Basil II, and established Orthodox Christianity as the Russian national faith. Feast day 15 July.
Vladivostok, *n.* port (naval and commercial) in E USSR at the Amur Bay on the Pacific coast; population (1987) 615,000. It is kept open by icebreakers during winter. Industries include shipbuilding, and the manufacture of precision instruments.
Vlaminck, *n.* **Maurice de** (1876–1958), French painter, who began using brilliant colour as an early member of the Fauves, mainly painting landscapes. Later he abandoned Fauve colour. He also wrote poetry, novels, and essays.
Vlei, *n.* (*S Afr.*) a swampy tract, a place where water lies in rainy seasons. [Afrikaans, prob. from Dut. *vallei,* VALLEY]
vln, (*abbr.*) violin.
VLSI, *n.* very large-scale integration, the current level of advanced technology in the microminiaturization of integrated circuits, and an order of magnitude smaller than LSI.
vocable, *n.* a word, esp. as considered phonologically. [F, from L *vocābulum,* from *vocāre,* to call, cogn. with *vox vōcis,* VOICE]
vocabulary, *n.* a list or collection of words used in a language, science, book etc., usu. arranged in alphabetical order, and explained; a word-book; the stock of words at one's command. †**vocabulist,** *n.* the compiler of a vocabulary. [F *vocabulaire,* late L *vocābulārium,* as prec.]
vocal, *a.* of or pertaining to the voice or oral utterance; having a voice; uttered or produced by the voice; resounding with or as with voices; voiced, sonant, not surd; having the character of a vowel. *n.* a vocal sound, a vowel; in the Roman Catholic Church, a person authorized to vote in certain elections. **vocal cords,** *n.pl.* the elastic folds of the lining membrane of the larynx about the opening of the glottis. **vocal music,** *n.* music composed for or produced by the voice as distinct from instrumental music. **vocal score,** *n.* a musical score showing the singing parts in full. **vocalic,** *a.* pertaining to or consisting of vowel sounds. **vocalism,** *n.* the exercise of the vocal organs; a vowel sound. **vocalist,** *n.* a singer, opp. to an instrumental performer. **vocality, vocalness,** *n.* **vocalize, -ise,** *v.t.* to form or utter with the voice, esp. to make sonant; to insert the vowel-points in (Hebrew etc.). *v.i.* to exercise the voice, to speak, to sing etc. **vocalization, -isation,** *n.* **vocally,** *adv.* [F, from L *vōcālis,* from *vox vocis,* VOICE]
vocation, *n.* a call or sense of fitness for and obligation to follow a particular career; a divine call or spiritual injunction or guidance to undertake a duty, occupation etc.; one's calling or occupation. **vocational,** *a.* **vocationally,** *adv.* [F, from L *vocātiōnem,* nom. *-tio,* from *vocāre,* see VOCABLE]
vocative, *a.* pertaining to or used in addressing a person or thing. *n.* the case of a noun used in addressing a person or thing. [F *vocatif,* fem. *-ive,* L *vocātīvus,* as prec.]
vociferate, *v.t.* to cry loudly, to bawl, to shout; to make one's views known loudly and strongly. **vociferance, vociferation,** *n.* **vociferant,** *n., a.* **vociferator,** *n.* **vociferous,** *a.* **vociferously,** *adv.* **vociferous-ness,** *n.* [L *vōciferātus,* p.p. of *vōciferāre, -ferārī* (*vox vōcis,* VOICE, *ferre,* to bear)]
vocule, *n.* the faint sound made after articulating final *k, p* or *t.* [L *vōcula,* dim. of *vox vōcis,* VOICE]
vodka, *n.* a strong spirituous liquor distilled from rye, orig. used in Russia. [Rus., dim. of *voda,* water]
voe, *n.* (*Orkney, Shetland*) a small inlet, bay or creek. [Icel. *vāgr, vogr*]
Vogel, *n.* **Hans-Jochen** (1926–), West German socialist politician, chair of the Social Democratic Party (SPD) from 1987. A former leader of the SPD in Bavaria and mayor of Munich, he served in the Brandt and Schmidt governments in the 1970s as housing and then justice minister and then, briefly, as mayor of West Berlin.
vogue, *n.* fashion prevalent at any particular time; currency, popular acceptance or usage. **vogue word,** *n.* a word much used at a particular time or period. [F, orig. sway, from *voguer,* to sail forth]
voice, *n.* the sound uttered by the mouth, esp. by a human being, in speaking, singing etc.; the faculty or power of vocal utterance, speech, language; (*fig.*) expression of the mind or will in words whether spoken or written etc.; one's opinion or judgment, one's right to express this, one's choice, vote or suffrage; one expressing the will or judgment of others, a speaker, a mouthpiece; a sound suggestive of human speech; sound produced by the breath acting on the vocal cords, sonancy; the verb-form expressing the relation of the subject to the action, as active, passive or middle. *v.t.* to give utterance to, to express; to regulate the tones of, to tune; to write the voice-parts for; to give voice or sonancy to. **with one voice,** unanimously. **voice-box,** (*coll.*) the larynx. **voicemail,** *n.* a form of electronic mail in which sounds are converted to a digital form and stored in a computer file. **voice-over,** *n.* the voice of an unseen narrator, actor etc. in a film etc. **voice-print,** *n.* an electronically recorded graphic representation of a person's voice. **voiced,** *a.* sonant; having a voice (*usu. in comb.* as *loud-voiced*). **voiceful,** *a.* vocal, sonorous. **voiceless,** *a.* having no voice or vote; speechless, mute; (*Phon.*) not voiced. **voicelessness,** *n.* [ME and OF *vois,* L *vōcem,* nom. *vox*]
void, *a.* empty, unfilled, vacant; having no holder, occupant or incumbent; free from, destitute (of); useless, ineffectual; having no legal force, null, invalid. *n.* an empty space; a vacuum. *v.t.* to invalidate, to nullify; to discharge, to emit from the bowels, †to quit, leave; to evacuate; †to avoid. **voidable,** *a.* **voidance,** *n.* the act of voiding or ejecting from a benefice; the state of being vacant; †evasion, subterfuge. **voided,** *a.* made void; (*Her.*) of a charge, having the inner part cut away so that the field shows through. **voider,** *n.* **voidly,** *adv.* **voidness,** *n.* [OF *void,* fem. *voide,* perh. from L *vacuus,* empty, or *viduus,* bereft]
Voight, *n.* **Jon** (1938–), US actor who starred with Dustin Hoffman in *Midnight Cowboy* (1969). His subsequent films include *Deliverance* (1972), *Coming Home* (1978), and *Runaway Train* (1985).

voile, *n.* a thin, semi-transparent dress material. [F, veil]
voir dire, *n.* (*Law*) an oath administered to a witness.
voivode, vaivode, *n.* orig. a military commander, a leader of an army, in Slavonic countries; formerly, a liege prince or hospodar in Rumania, Wallachia etc.; the chief of an administrative division in Poland; an inferior administrative officer in Turkey. **voivodeship,** *n.* [Pol. *wayewoda,* army leader, cp. Rus. *voevoda,* Serb. *vojvoda*]
Vojvodina, *n.* autonomous area in N Serbia, Yugoslavia; area 21,500 sq km/8299 sq miles; population (1986) 2,050,000, including 1,110,000 Serbs and 390,000 Hungarians. Its capital is Novi Sad.
vol[1], *n.* (*Her.*) two outspread wings united at the base. [F, flight, from *voler,* L *volāre,* to fly]
vol.[2], (*abbr.*) volcano; volume; volunteer.
vola, *n.* (*pl.* **-lae**,) (*Anat.*) the palm of the hand; the sole of the foot. **volar,** *a.* [L, palm, sole]
†**volable,** *a.* (*Shak.*) nimble-witted. [from L as VOL]
volant, *a.* passing through the air; flying, able to fly; current; (*poet.*) nimble, active, rapid; (*Her.*) represented as flying. [F, pres.p. of *voler,* see VOL]
volante, *n.* a two-wheeled covered horse-drawn vehicle with very long shafts and a chaise-body slung in front of the axle. [Sp.]
Volapük, *n.* a universal language invented (1879) by Johann Maria Schleyer. **Volapükist,** *n.* [Volapük (*vol,* world, *pük,* speech)]
volatile, *a.* readily evaporating; (*fig.*) lively, sprightly, brisk, gay; fickle, changeable. †**volatileness, volatility,** *n.* **volatilize, -ise,** *v.t.* to cause to pass off in vapour. *v.i.* to evaporate. **volatilizable, -sable,** *a.* **volatilization, -isation,** *n.* [F *volatil,* fem. *-tile,* L *volātilis,* from *volāre,* to fly, p.p. *volātus*]
vol au vent, *n.* a raised or puff case filled with a variety of filling, often savoury. [F]
volcano, *n.* an opening in the earth's surface through which lava, cinders, gases etc., are ejected from the interior, esp. at the top of a hill or mountain formed by the successive accumulations of ejected matter; (*fig.*) any situation where danger, upheaval etc. seems likely. **volcanic glass,** *n.* rock without a crystalline structure, as obsidian, pumice etc. produced by the rapid cooling of molten lava. **volcanic mud, sand,** *n.* volcanic ash which has been deposited under water and sorted and stratified. **volcanic rocks,** *n.pl.* those formed by volcanic agency. **volcanic,** *a.* pertaining to, produced by, or of the nature of a volcano. **volcanically,** *adv.* **volcanicity, volcanism** , *n.* **volcanist, volcanologist,** *n.* **volcanize** , *v.t.* **volcanization,** *n.* **volcanology,** -LOGY, *n.* the study of volcanoes. **volcanological,** *a.* [It., from L *volcānus,* VULCAN]
vole[1], *v.t.* (*Cards*) to win all the tricks. *n.* the act of winning all the tricks in a deal. [F *voler,* L *volāre,* to fly]
vole[2], *n.* a mouse-like rodent of the sub-family Arvicolinae, often called a water-rat. [shortened from *volemouse* (cp. Icel. *völlr,* Norw. *voll,* Swed. *vall,* field, cogn. with WOLD)]
volente Deo, God willing. [L]
volery, *n.* an aerodrome; †an aviary; a flight of birds. [F *volerie,* as VOLE[1]]
volet, *n.* a wing or panel of a triptych. [OF, shutter, from *voler,* see VOLE[1]]
Volga, *n.* longest river in Europe; 3685 km/2290 miles, 3540 km/2200 miles of which are navigable. It drains most of the central and eastern parts of European USSR, rises in the Valdai plateau and flows into the Caspian Sea 88 km/55 miles below Astrakhan.
Volgograd, *n.* industrial city (metal goods, machinery, sawmills, oil refining) in SW USSR, on the river Volga; population (1987) 988,000. It was called Tsaritsyn until 1925, and Stalingrad 1925–61.
volitant, *a.* flying, volant. †**volitation,** *n.* [L *volitans, -ntem,* pres.p. of *volitāre,* freq. of *volāre,* to fly]
volition, *n.* exercise of the will; the power of willing. **volitient,** *a.* **volitional, -ary,** *a.* **volitionally,** *adv.* **volitionless,** *a.* **volitive,** *a.* [F, from late L *volitiōnem,* nom. *-tio,* from *volo,* I wish, inf. *velle,* to wish]
Volksraad, *n.* the former legislative assemblies of the Transvaal and the Orange Free State. [Afrikaans]
Volkswagen®, *n.* German car manufacturer. The original VW, with its distinctive beetle shape, was produced in Germany 1938, a design by Ferdinand Porsche. It was still in production in Latin America in the late 1980s, by which time it had exceeded 20 million sales.
volley, *n.* a flight or simultaneous discharge of missiles; the missiles thus discharged; (*fig.*) a noisy outburst or emission of many things at once; a return of the ball at tennis and similar games before it touches the ground; (*Cricket*) a ball that flies straight at the head of the wicket after once hitting the ground. *v.t.* to discharge in or as in a volley; to return or bowl in a volley. *v.i.* to discharge a volley; to fly in a volley (of missiles etc.); to fire together (of guns); to return a ball before it touches the ground. **volley-ball,** *n.* a game in which a large ball is hit back and forward over a high net by hand, played by two teams; the ball used in this game. **half-volley,** a return immediately after the ball has touched the ground. [F *volée,* flight, from *voler,* see VOLE[1]]
volplane, *v.i.* (*Aviat.*) to fly downwards at a considerably higher angle than that of a glide. *n.* such a descending flight. [L *volāre,* to fly, PLANE[3]]
volt[1], *n.* a circular tread, the gait of a horse going sideways round a centre; a sudden leap to avoid a thrust in fencing. [F, see VAULT[2]]
volt[2], *n.* the SI unit of electric potential or potential difference, the difference of potential between two points in a conductor carrying a current of 1 ampere when the power dissipated between them is 1 watt. **voltmeter,** *n.* an instrument for measuring electromotive force directly, calibrated in volts. **volta-,** *comb. form* voltaic. *a.* **voltage,** *n.* electromotive force or potential difference as measured or expressed in volts. **voltaic,** *a.* pertaining to electricity produced by chemical action or contact, galvanic. **voltaic cell,** *n.* a primary cell. **voltaic pile,** *n.* a galvanic pile. **voltaism,** *n.* **voltite,** *n.* an insulating material for electric wires. [Alessandro *Volta,* 1745–1827, Italian physicist]
Volta[1], *n.* main river in Ghana, about 1600 km/1000 miles long, with two main upper branches, the Black and White Volta.
Volta[2], *n.* **Alessandro** (1745–1827). Italian physicist. He invented the voltaic pile (the first battery), the electrophorus (an early electrostatic generator), and an electroscope.
Volta[3], **Upper,** *n.* name until 1984 of Burkina Faso.
volta, *n.* (*pl,* **-te**) (*Mus.*) time, turn. **due volte,** twice. **prima volta,** first time. **una volta,** once. [It., see VAULT[2]]
Voltaire, *n.* pen name of François-Marie Arouet (1694–1778), French writer, who believed in deism, and devoted himself to tolerance, justice, and humanity. He was threatened with arrest for *Lettres philosophiques sur les anglais/Philosophical Letters on the English* (1733), essays in favour of English ways, thought, and political practice, and had to take refuge. Other writings include *Le Siècle de Louis XIV/The Age of Louis XIV* (1751); *Candide* (1759), a parody on Leibniz's 'best of all possible worlds'; and *Dictionnaire Philosophique* (1764). **Voltairism, Voltaireanism,** *n.* the principles or practices of Voltaire; scoffing scepticism. **Voltairean,** *n., a.*
voltaism, etc. VOLT.
volte-face, *n.* a turn round; an entire change of front in opinions, attitudes etc. [F (VOLT[1], FACE)]
voltigeur, *n.* (*Hist.*) a rifleman in a select company of a regiment of French infantry. [F, from *voltiger,* It. *volteggiare,* to vault, see VOLTA]
voltmeter VOLT.
volubilate etc. VOLUBLE.
voluble, *a.* characterized by a flow of words, fluent, glib, garrulous; (*Bot.*) twisting, volubilate. **volubilate, volubile,** *a.* (*Bot.*) twining, climbing by winding round a support; turning or rotating readily. **volubility, volubleness,** *n.* **volubly,** *adv.* [F, from L *volūbilem,*

nom. *-lis,* from *volvere,* to roll, cogn. with Goth. *walwjan,* Gr. *eiluein*]

volucrine, *a.* of or pertaining to birds. [L *volucer -cris,* bird]

volume, *n.* a collection of (usu. printed) sheets of paper, parchment etc., bound together forming a book or work or part of one; (*loosely*) a book, a tome; (*Ant.*) a roll or scroll of papyrus, vellum etc. constituting a book; a rounded, swelling mass, a wreath, a coil (*usu. in pl.*); cubical content; mass, bulk; (*Mus.*) fullness or roundness of tone; loudness, or the control for adjusting it on a radio, television etc. **to speak, express volumes,** to mean much; to be very significant. **volumed,** *a.* (*usu. in comb.* as *three-volumed*). **volumenometer,** *n.* an apparatus for measuring the volume of a solid body by the quantity of fluid that it displaces. **volumenometry,** *n.* **volumeter,** *n.* an instrument for measuring the volume of a gas; a hydrometer; a stereometer. **volumetric, -al,** *a.* **volumetrically,** *adv.* **voluminal,** *a.* pertaining to volume. [F, from L *volumen,* as VOLUBLE]

voluminous, *a.* consisting of many volumes; producing many or bulky books (of a writer); of great volume, bulk or size. **voluminosity, voluminousness,** *n.* †**volumist,** *n.* an author. **voluminously,** *adv.*

voluntary, *a.* proceeding from or determined by one's own free will or choice, not under external constraint; acting or done willingly, spontaneous, intentional, purposive, designed; endowed with or exercising the power of willing; subject to or controlled by the will (of muscles, movement etc.); brought about, established, or supported by voluntary action (of a church, school etc.); (*Law*) done without constraint or by consent, without valuable consideration; gratuitous. *n.* an organ solo played in a church etc. before, during or after service; a supporter of the principle that the Church (and usu. education) should be independent of the State and maintained by voluntary effort; †one who engages in any act of his own free will, a volunteer. **voluntarily,** †**voluntariously,** *adv.* **voluntariness,** *n.* †**voluntarious,** *a.* **voluntarism,** *n.* the reliance on voluntary subscriptions rather than on state aid for the upkeep of schools, churches etc. **voluntaryist,** *n.* **Voluntary Aid Detachment (VAD),** *n.* an official organization of men and women to render first aid in time of war and assist in hospital work etc. [MF *voluntaire, volontaire,* L *voluntārius,* from *voluntas,* free will, from *volens -ntis,* pres.p. of *velle,* to will]

volunteer, *n.* one who undertakes a job etc. voluntarily; one who enters into any service of his/her own free will, esp. orig. a member of a military body in the United Kingdom superseded by the Territorial Force in 1907. *a.* voluntary. *v.t.* to offer or undertake voluntarily. *v.i.* to offer one's services voluntarily, esp. orig. to offer to serve (for a campaign etc.) as a volunteer. [F *volontaire,* see prec.]

voluptuary, *n.* one given to luxury or sensual pleasures. *a.* pertaining to, promoting, or devoted to sensual pleasure. **voluptuous,** *a.* pertaining to, contributing to, or producing sensuous or sensual gratification; of a woman, sexually alluring because of shapeliness or fullness of figure. **voluptuously,** *adv.* **voluptuousness,** *n.* [F *voluptueux,* L *voluptuōsus,* from *voluptas -tātem,* cogn. with VOLUNTARY]]

volute, *n.* a spiral scroll used in Ionic, Corinthian and Composite capitals; a volutoid gastropod, usu. of tropical seas and having a beautiful shell. *a.* (*Bot.*) rolled up. **voluted,** *a.* **volution,** *n.* a spiral turn, a convolution; a whorl of a spiral shell. **volutoid,** *n., a.* [F, from L *volūta,* orig. fem. p.p. of *volvere,* to roll]

volvox, *n.* a genus of simple, freshwater, greenish organisms united in spherical colonies, composed of minute flagellate cells which set up a revolving motion. **volvulus,** *n.* a twisting of an intestine causing obstruction of the intestinal canal. [mod. L, from L *volvere,* to roll]

vomer, *n.* a small thin bone forming the chief portion of the partition between the nostrils in man. **vomerine,** *a.* [L, ploughshare]

vomica VOMIT.

vomit, *v.t.* to eject from the stomach by the mouth; to eject or discharge violently, to belch out. *v.i.* to eject the contents of the stomach by the mouth, to spew; to be sick. *n.* matter ejected from the stomach by the mouth; an emetic. **vomit-nut,** *n.* nux vomica. **vomica,** *n.* (*pl.* **-cae**) an encysted collection of pus, esp. in the lung. †**vomitive,** *a.* vomitory. **vomito,** *n.* the yellow fever in its worst form. **vomitory,** *a.* emetic. *n.* an emetic; (*Rom. Ant.*) one of the openings for entrance or exit in an ancient theatre or amphitheatre. **vomiturition,** *n.* an ineffectual attempt to vomit; violent or repeated vomiting of but little matter, retching. [L *vomitus,* p.p. of *vomere,* cogn. with Gr. *emein*]

von Braun, *n.* **Wernher** (1912–77), German rocket engineer who developed German military rockets (V1 and V2) during World War II, and later worked for NASA in the US.

von Gesner, *n.* **Konrad** (1516–65), Swiss naturalist who produced an encyclopaedia of the animal world, the *Historia animalium* (1551–58).

Vonnegut, *n.* **Kurt, Jr** (1922–), US writer whose work generally has a science-fiction or fantasy element; his novels include *The Sirens of Titan* (1958), *Cat's Cradle* (1963), *Slaughterhouse-Five* (1969), which draws on his World War II experience of the firebombing of Dresden, Germany, and *Galapagos* (1985).

voodoo, *n.* a system of magic orig. including snake-worship practised by Creoles and Negroes in Haiti and other parts of the W Indies and in the southern US; a sorcerer or conjurer skilled in this. *v.t.* to put a spell on or bewitch with voodoo. **voodooism,** *n.* **voodooish,** *a.* [W Afr. *vodu,* a spirit]

voortrekker, *n.* (after **Voortrekker**) one of the Dutch farmers from Cape Colony who took part in the Great Trek into the Transvaal in 1836 and following years; (without cap.) a pioneer. [Afrikaans, Dutch *voor,* before and TREK]

voracious, *a.* greedy in eating; ravenous, gluttonous, ready to swallow up or devour; insatiable, very eager. **voraciously,** *adv.* **voraciousness, voracity,** *n.* †**vorago,** *n.* a whirlpool. [L] †**voraginous,** *a.* **vorant,** *a.* (*Her.*) devouring. [L *vorax -ācis,* from *vorāre,* to devour]

-vore, *comb. form* forming corresponding nouns to the foll., as *carnivore, herbivore.* [as foll.]

-vorous, *comb. form* feeding on, living on, as *carnivorous, herbivorous.* [L *vorāre,* to devour]

Vorster, *n.* **Balthazar Johannes** (1915–83), South African Nationalist politician, prime minister 1966–78, in succession to Verwoerd, and president 1978–79. During his premiership some elements of apartheid were allowed to lapse, and attempts were made to improve relations with the outside world. He resigned when it was discovered that the Department of Information had made unauthorized use of public funds during his premiership.

vortex, *n.* (*pl.* **vortices**) a whirling or rotating mass of fluid, esp. a whirlpool; a portion of fluid the particles of which have a rotary motion. **vortex-ring,** *n.* on the axis of which is a closed curve. **vortex-theory,** *n.* the theory that matter is composed of vortices in the ether. **vortical, vorticose, vorticular,** *a.* **vortically,** *adv.* **vorticel,** *n.* a bell-shaped infusorian, a bell-animalcule. **vorticelloid,** *a.* **vorticity,** *n.* **vortiginous,** *a.* vortical, whirling. [L, var. of VERTEX]

vortical, vorticity, vortiginous etc. VORTEX.

Vorticism, *n.* a school of early 20th-cent. painting which seeks to represent nature in formal designs of straight and angular patterns. [VORTEX]

Voskhod, *n.* Soviet spacecraft used in the mid-1960s, modified from the single-seat Vostok, and the first spacecraft capable of carrying two or three cosmonauts. During the second Voskhod flight 1965, Alexei Leonov made the first space walk.

Vostok, *n.* the first Soviet spacecraft, capable of carrying one cosmonaut, used 1961–63, which made flights lasting up to five days. Vostok was a metal sphere 2.3

m/7.5 ft in diameter.

votary, *n.* one who is devoted or consecrated by a vow or promise; one who is devoted to some particular service, study, pursuit etc. **votaress,** †**votress,** *n.* [med. L *votārius,* from L *vōtum,* foll.]

vote, *n.* a formal expression of opinion, will, or choice, in regard to the election of a candidate, the passing or rejection of a resolution, law etc., usu. signified by voice, gesture, or ballot; anythinng by which this is expressed, as a ballot, ticket etc.; that which is voted, as a grant of money; the aggregate votes of a party etc.; the right to vote, the suffrage. *v.i.* to give one's vote; to express one's approval (for). *v.t.* to give one's vote for; to enact, resolve, ratify, or grant by a majority of votes; (*coll.*) to declare by general consent. **to vote down,** to defeat or suppress by vote. **to vote in,** to elect. **vote of no confidence,** the legal method of forcing the resignation of a government of governing body or person. **to vote with one's feet,** to indicate one's dissatisfaction with a situation or conditions by leaving. **votable,** *a.* **voteless,** *a.* **voter,** *n.* **voting-paper,** *n.* a paper by means of which one votes esp. by ballot in a parliamentary election. [L *vōtum,* wish, vow, orig. neut. of *vōltus,* p.p. of *vōvere,* to vow]

votive, *a.* given, paid or dedicated in fulfilment of a vow. **votively,** *adv.* [F *votif,* fem. *-ive,* L *votīvus,* from *vōtum,* prec.]

vouch, *v.t.* to uphold or guarantee by assertion, proof etc., to confirm, to substantiate. *v.i.* to give testimony, to answer (for). †*n.* warrant, attestation, testimony. **vouchee,** *n.* the person vouched or summoned in a writ of right. **voucher,** *n.* one who or that which vouches for or attests; a document etc., serving to confirm or establish something, as a payment, the correctness of an account etc.; one who vouches or acts as security for another. [OF *voucher, vocher,* L *vocare,* to call]

vouchsafe, *v.t.* to condescend to grant; to concede. *v.i.* to deign, to condescend (to). †**vouchsafement,** *n.*

voussoir, *n.* one of the wedge-shaped stones forming an arch. [F, ult. from L *volūtus,* p.p. of *volvere,* to roll]

vow, *n.* a solemn promise or pledge, esp. made to God or to a saint etc., undertaking an act, sacrifice, obligation etc.; †a votive offering. *v.t.* to promise solemnly; to dedicate by a vow; to affirm solemnly. *v.i.* to make a vow. **to take vows,** to enter a religious order and commit oneself to the vows of chastity, poverty and obedience. †**vow-fellow,** *n.* one bound by the same vow. [OF *vou* (F *voeu*), L *vōtum,* see VOTE]

vowel, *n.* a sound able to make a syllable or to be sounded alone; an open and unimpeded sound as opp. to a closed, stopped or mute sound or consonant; a letter representing this, esp. the simple vowels, *a, e, i, o, u.* **vowel-gradation,** *n.* ablaut. **vowel-mutation,** *n.* umlaut. **vowel-point,** *n.* one of the marks indicating the vowels in Hebrew etc. **vowelize, -ise,** *v.t.* to insert vowel-points. †**vowelled,** *a.* (*usu. in comb.* as *open-vowelled*). **vowelless,** *a.* **vowelly,** *a.* [OF *vouel, voiel,* L *vocālis,* VOCAL]

vox, *n.* voice. **vox humana,** an organ-stop producing tones approximating to those of the human voice. [L]

vox populi, vox pop, the voice of the people, popular feeling. [L]

voyage, *n.* a journey by water, esp. by sea to a distant place; †a project, an enterprise. *v.i.* to make a voyage. *v.t.* to travel over by water. **voyageable,** *a.* **voyager,** *n.* **Voyager probes,** *n.pl.* two US space probes, originally Mariners. Voyager 1, launched 5 Sept. 1977, passed Jupiter Mar. 1979, and reached Saturn Nov. 1980. Voyager 2 was launched earlier, 20 Aug. 1977, on a slower trajectory that took it past Jupiter July 1979, Saturn Aug. 1981, Uranus Jan. 1986, and Neptune Aug. 1989. Like the Pioneer probes, the Voyagers are on their way out of the solar system. Their tasks now include helping scientists to locate the position of the heliopause, the boundary at which the influence of the Sun gives way to the forces exerted by other stars. Both Voyagers carry long-playing records called 'Sounds of Earth' for the enlightenment of any other civilizations that might find them. **voyageur,** *n.* one of the men employed by the Hudson Bay and North West Companies to convey goods etc. between the trading posts; a Canadian boatman. [OF *voiaje,* L VIATICUM]

voyeur, *n.* one who derives gratification from watching sexual acts, people undressing etc. **voyeurism,** *n.* the act or practice of a voyeur. **voyeuristic,** *n.* [Fr. one who sees]

Voysey, *n.* **Charles Francis Annesley** (1857–1941), English architect and designer. He designed country houses which were characteristically asymmetrical with massive buttresses, long sloping roofs, and rough-cast walls. He also designed textiles and wallpaper.

VP, (*abbr.*) Vice-President.

VR, (*abbr.*) variant reading; Victoria Regina.

vraic, *n.* a seaweed used for fuel and manure, found in the Channel Islands. [F]

vraisemblance, *n.* an appearance of truth, verisimilitude. [F *vrai,* OF *verrai,* see VERY, SEMBLANCE]

Vranitzky, *n.* **Franz** (1937–), Austrian socialist politician, federal chancellor from 1986. Vranitzky first went into banking and in 1970 became adviser on economic and financial policy to the minister of finance. After a return to the banking world he entered the political arena through the Socialist Party of Austria, and became minister of finance in 1984. He succeeded Fred Sinowatz as federal chancellor in 1986, heading an SPÖ- ÖVP (Austrian People's Party) coalition.

Vries, *n.* **Hugo de** (1848–1935), Dutch botanist, who conducted important research on osmosis in plant cells and was a pioneer in the study of plant evolution. His work led to the rediscovery of Mendel's laws and the formulation of the theory of mutation.

vroom, (*coll.*) *n.* power, drive, energy (*also interj.*) *v.i.* to drive fast. [imit.]

vs., (*abbr.*) versus.

VSO, (*abbr.*) Very Superior Old, used to indicate that port or brandy is between 12 and 17 years old; in Britain, Voluntary Service Overseas, an organization which sends volunteers overseas to use and teach their skills.

VSOP, (*abbr.*) Very Special Old Pale, used to indicate that brandy or port is between 20 and 25 years old.

VTOL, (*abbr.*) vertical take-off and landing, a system by which aircraft take off and land without taxying.

Vuillard, *n.* **(Jean) Edouard** (1886–1940), French painter and printmaker, a founder member of les Nabis. His work is mainly decorative, with an emphasis on surface pattern reflecting the influence of Japanese prints. With Bonnard he produced numerous lithographs and paintings of simple domestic interiors, works that are generally categorized as *intimiste*.

Vulcan, *n.* (*Rom. Myth.*) the god of fire and metal-working. **Vulcanian,** *a.* **vulcanic, vulcanism,** etc. VOLCANIC, -ISM, etc. **Vulcanist,** *n.* an adherent of the plutonic theory. [L *Vulcānus, Volcānus,* cp. Sansk. *ulkā,* firebrand, meteor]

vulcanite, *n.* vulcanized rubber, ebonite. **vulcanize, -ise,** *v.t.* to treat rubber with sulphur at a high temperature so as to increase its strength and elasticity, producing vulcanite (the hard form) or soft and flexible rubber. **vulcanization, -isation,** *n.*

vulgar, *a.* pertaining to or characteristic of the common people, plebian, common, coarse, low, unrefined; rude, boorish; ordinary, in common use. **the vulgar,** the common people, the uneducated. **vulgar era,** *n.* the Christian era. **vulgar fraction,** *n.* a fraction having the numerator less than the denominator. **vulgar tongue,** *n.* the vernacular. **vulgarian,** *a.* vulgar. *n.* a vulgar person, esp. a rich person with low ideas, manners etc. **vulgarism,** *n.* **vulgarity,** †**vulgarness,** *n.* **vulgarize, -ise,** *v.t.* **vulgarization, -isation,** *n.* **vulgarly,** *adv.* [F *vulgaire,* L *vulgāris,* from *vulgus, volgus,* the common people, cp. Sansk. *vargas,* troop, W *gwala,* Bret. *gwalch,* fullness, Ir. *folc,* abundance]

Vulgate, *n.* the Latin translation of the Bible made by St Jerome, 383–405.

vulnerable, *a.* capable of being wounded; susceptible

of or liable to injury, attack etc. †**vuln,** *v.t.* (*Her.*) to wound. **vulnerability**, **vulnerableness,** *n.* **vulnerary,** *a.* useful in healing wounds or for the cure of external injuries. *n.* a plant, drug or composition useful in the cure of wounds. †**vulnerose**, *a.* full of wounds. [L *vulnerābilis,* from *vulnerāre,* to wound, from *vulnus -neris,* wound, cogn. with *vellere,* to pluck, and Gr. *oulē,* wound]

Vulpes, *n.* the genus which includes the common fox. **vulpine**, *a.* pertaining to or characteristic of a fox; crafty, cunning. **vulpicide**, *n.* the killing of a fox, esp. otherwise than by hunting; a fox-killer. **vulpinism**, *n.* [L *vulpīnus,* from *vulpes,* fox, cogn. with WOLF]

vulsella, *n.* a forceps with hooked teeth or claws. [mod. L, from *vulsus,* p.p. of *vellere,* to pull]

vulture, *n.* a large falconoid bird with head and neck almost naked, feeding chiefly on carrion; a rapacious person. **vulturine**, **vulturish, vulturous,** *a.* **vulturn**, *n.* an Australian turkey, *Talegallus lathami.* [L *vultur,* cogn. with *vellere* see VULNERABLE]

vulva, *n.* an opening, an entrance, esp. the external opening of the female genitals. **vulvar, vulvate**, **vulviform**, *a.* **vulvitis**, *n.* inflammation of the vulva. **vulvo-,** *comb. form.* [L, also *volva,* cogn. with *volvere,* to roll]

vying, *pres.p.* VIE.

W[1], **w**[1], the 23rd letter of the English alphabet, taking its form and name from the union of two V's, V formerly having the name and force of U. W (*pl.* **ws, w's**) has the sound of a semi-vowel, as in *was, will, forward.*

W[2], (*abbr.*) watt; West, Western; women('s size).

W[3], (*chem. symbol*) tungsten. [G *Wolfram*]

w[2], (*abbr.*) week; weight; white; wicket; wide; width; wife; with.

WA, (*abbr.*) West Africa; Western Australia.

WAAC, *n.* (a member of) the Women's Auxiliary Army Corps.

WAAF, *n.* (a member of) the Women's Auxiliary Air Force Service (later Women's Royal Air Force).

wabble, WOBBLE.

wabster, (*Sc.*) WEBSTER under WEB.

wacke, *n.* an earthy or clayey rock produced by the decomposition of igneous rocks. [G]

wacky, *a.* (*sl.*) crazy, eccentric, absurd. **wackily,** *adv.* **wackiness,** *n.* [dial. *whacky,* a fool]

wad[1], *n.* a small, compact mass of some soft material, used for stopping an opening, stuffing between things etc.; a felt or paper disk used to keep the charge in place in a gun, cartridge etc.; (*coll.*) a number of currency notes, a lot of money. *v.t.* (*past, p.p.* **wadded**) to compress into a wad; to stuff or line with wadding; to pack, stop up or secure with a wad. **wadding,** *n.* a spongy material, usu. composed of cotton or wool, used for stuffing garments, cushions etc., cottonwool; material for gun-wads. [cp. Swed. *vadd,* wadding, Icel. *vathr,* G *watte*]

wad[2], *n.* an earthy ore of manganese; (*dial.*) plumbago. [etym. doubtful]

wad[3], (*Sc.*) WOULD.

wadable WADE.

wadding WAD[1].

Waddington, *n.* **David Charles** (1929–), British Conservative politician, home secretary from 1989. A barrister, he became an MP in 1978. A Conservative whip from 1979, Waddington was a junior minister in the Department of Employment and in the Home Office before becoming chief whip in 1987.

waddle, *v.i.* to walk with an ungainly rocking or swaying motion and with short, quick steps, as a duck or goose. *n.* a waddling gait. **waddler,** *n.* **waddlingly,** *adv.* [freq. of WADE]

waddy, *n.* an Australian war-club, usu. bent like a boomerang or with a thick head. *v.t.* to hit with a waddy. **waddy wood,** *n.* a Tasmanian tree from which this is made. [Abor. name]

wade, *v.i.* to walk through water or a semi-fluid medium, as snow, mud etc.; to make one's way with difficulty and labour. *v.t.* to pass through or across by wading; to ford (a stream) on foot. **to wade in(to),** (*coll.*) to tackle or attack vigorously. **wadable,** *a.* **wader,** *n.* one who wades; a high, waterproof boot, worn by anglers etc. for wading; a wading-bird. **wading bird,** *n.* any long-legged bird that wades, esp. one of the Grallae or Grallatores, comprising the cranes, storks, herons etc. [OE *wadan* (cp. Dut. *waden,* G *waten,* Icel. *vatha,* also L *vādere,* to go, *vādum,* ford)]

wadi, wady, *n.* the valley or channel of a stream that is dry except in the rainy season. [Arab.]

†**wadset,** *n.* (*Sc. Law*) a mortgage or bond in security for a debt. †**wadsetter,** *n.* one who holds by a wadset, a mortgagee. [OE *wed,* pledge, whence *weddian,* to WED, SET[1]]

wae, etc. (*Sc.*) WOE.

Wałesa, *n.* **Lech** (1947–), Polish trade-union leader, founder of Solidarity 1980, an organization, independent of the Communist Party, which forced substantial political and economic concessions from the Polish government 1980–81 until being outlawed. In 1989 he negotiated an agreement with the Polish government that legalized Solidarity and set in place a new 'socialist pluralist' political structure. Nobel Peace Prize 1983.

wafer, *n.* a small, thin, sweet cake or biscuit; a thin disk of unleavened bread used in the Eucharist, the Host; a thin adhesive disk of dried paste for sealing letters, fastening documents etc.; a thin disk of silicon or other semiconductor material on which integrated electrical circuits are formed before being cut into individual chips. *v.t.* to seal or attach with a wafer. **wafer-cake,** *n.* **wafery,** *a.* [ME and A-F *wafre,* OF *waufre* (usu. *gaufre,* GOFER), from LG, (cp. Walloon *wafe wauffe,* G *Waffel,* Dut. *wafel,* wafer, also G *Wabe,* honeycomb), cogn. with WEAVE]

†**waff,** WAVE.

waffle[1], *n.* a thin batter cake baked on a waffle-iron. **waffle-iron,** *n.* a utensil with hinged plates for baking waffles. [Dut., see WAFER]

waffle[2], *v.i.* (*dial.*) to wave, to fluctuate; (*coll.*) to chatter or write aimlessly and at length. *n.* vague or inconsequential talk or writing. [freq. of WAFF]

waft, *v.t.* to carry or convey through the air; to carry lightly or gently along; †to signal or beckon by waving the hand etc. *v.i.* to float or be borne on the air. *n.* an act of wafting, as a sweep of a bird's wing; a breath or whiff of odour etc. †**waftage,** †**wafture,** *n.* the act of wafting; conveyance by wafting. †**wafter,** *n.* [prob. *waved,* past, p.p. of WAVE]

wag[1], *v.t.* (*past, p.p.* **wagged**) to shake up and down or backwards and forwards lightly and quickly, esp. in playfulness, reproof etc.; to move (the tongue) in chatter or gossip. *v.i.* to move up and down or to and fro, to oscillate; of the tongue, to move in chatter or gossip; to move on, to keep going, to proceed. *n.* an act or motion of wagging, a shake. **wag-at-the-wall,** *n.* a hanging clock with exposed pendulum and weights. [ME *waggen,* MSwed. *wagga* (cp. Norw. *vagga,* OE *wagian,* from *wegan,* to carry), cogn. with WAGON, WEIGH, and L *vehere,* to carry]

wag[2], *n.* a facetious fellow, a wit, a joker. **waggery, waggishness,** *n.* jocularity, playful merriment, practical joking. **waggish,** *a.* **waggishly,** *adv.* [perh. short for obs. *wag-halter,* gallows-bird]

wage, *n.* (*often pl.*) payment for work done or services rendered, esp. fixed periodical pay for labour of a manual kind; (*usul pl.*) recompense, reward, requital. *v.t.* to engage in, to carry on (a battle, war etc.); †to wager, †to engage, to employ for wages, to hire. †*v.i.* to contend in or as in battle (with). **wage-freeze,** *n.* the fixing of a wage-level for a prolonged period. **wage-, wages-fund,** *n.* the portion of the capital of a community expended in paying the wages of labour. **wage-slave,** *n.* (*coll.*) a person dependent on a wage or salary. **wagedom, wagery,** *n.* **wageless,** *a.* †**wageling,** *n.* a hireling. [OF, also *gage, guage,* from *wager, gager,* to GAGE[1]]

wager, *n.* something staked or hazarded on the event of a contest etc.; a bet; something on which bets are laid. *v.t., v.i.* to stake, to bet. **wager of battle** BATTLE. **wager of law,** a compurgation. †**wagerer,** *n.* [ME *wageoure,* OF *wageure, gageure,* low L *wadiātūra,* from *wadiāre,* to pledge, as prec.]

wagga (blanket), *n.* a rug made from corn sacks cut

open and sewn together. [Austral.]

waggery, waggish etc. WAG².

waggle, *v.t., v.i.* to wag quickly and frequently. *n.* a short, quick wagging. [freq. of WAG¹]

waggon WAGON.

Wagner¹, *n.* **Otto** (1841–1918), Viennese architect. Initially designing in the art nouveau style, for example Vienna Stadtbahn 1894–97, he later rejected ornament for rationalism, as in the Post Office Savings Bank, Vienna, 1904–06. He influenced Viennese architects such as Josef Hoffmann, Adolf Loos, and Joseph Olbrich.

Wagner², *n.* **Richard** (1813–1883), German opera composer. He revolutionized the 19th-cent. conception of opera, envisaging it as a wholly new art form in which musical, poetic, and scenic elements should be unified through such devices as the *leitmotif.* His operas include *Tannhäuser* (1845), *Lohengrin* (1850), and *Tristan und Isolde* (1865). In 1872 he founded the Festival Theatre in Bayreuth; his masterpiece *Der Ring des Nibelungen/The Ring of the Nibelung*, a sequence of four operas, was first performed there in 1876. His last work, *Parsifal*, was produced in 1882. **Wagnerian,** *a.* pertaining to or in the style of Wagner's music or musical dramas. **Wagnerianism, Wagnerism,** *n.* **Wagnerist,** *n.*

wagon, waggon, *n.* a strong four-wheeled vehicle for the transport of heavy loads, usu. with a rectangular body, often with a removable cover, usu. drawn by two or more horses; an open railway truck; †a chariot. **on (off) the wagon,** (*coll.*) abstaining (no longer abstaining) from alcohol. **wagon-ceiling, -roof, -vault,** *n.* a semi-cylindrical ceiling, a barrel-vault. **wagon-load,** *n.* **wagon-train,** *n.* a column of horse-drawn wagons carrying supplies, pioneer settlers etc. **wagonage,** *n.* money paid for the conveyance of goods in wagons; wagons collectively. **wagoner,** *n.* one who drives or leads a wagon, a charioteer; the constellation Auriga. **wagonette,** *n.* a four-wheeled pleasure carriage of light construction, for six or eight persons on seats facing each other, often with a removable cover, drawn by one or more horses. **wagonful,** *n.* [Dut. *wagen,* cogn. with WAIN]

wagon-lit, *n.* (*pl.* **wagons-lits, wagon-lits**) a sleeping-car. [F *wagon,* railway car, *lit,* bed]

Wagram, Battle of, battle in July 1809 when the French emperor Napoleon defeated the Austrians under Archduke Charles near the village of Wagram, NE of Vienna, Austria.

wagtail, *n.* any of various small, black and grey or white or yellow birds, chiefly of the genus *Motacilla,* named from the wagging of their tails.

Wahabi, *n.* (*pl.* **-bis**) the purist Saudi Islamic sect founded by Mohammed ibn-Abd-al-Wahab (1703–92), which regards all other sects as heresies whose followers are liable to the death penalty. **Wahabiism,** *n.*

wahine, *n.* a Maori or Polynesian woman. [Maori]

waif, *n.* a person or thing found astray, ownerless, or cast up by or adrift on the sea; a homeless wanderer, esp. a forsaken or unowned child. [OF, from Norse (cp. Icel. *veif,* anything flapping about), cogn. with WAIVE]

wail, *v.t.* to lament loudly over, to bewail. *v.i.* to lament, to utter wails; to make a plaintive sound (as the wind). *n.* a loud, high-pitched lamentation, a plaintive cry; a sound like this. **wailful,** *a.* **wailing,** *n., a.* **Wailing Wall,** *n.* a wall in Jerusalem, a remnant of an ancient temple, held sacred by the Jews as a place of worship and lamentation. **wailingly,** *adv.* **†wailment,** *n.* [ME *weilen,* Icel. *vœla,* from *vœ,* WOE!]

Wailing Wall, *n.* or (in Judaism) **Western Wall,** in Jerusalem, the remaining part of the Temple, a site of pilgrimage. There Jews offer prayers either aloud ('wailing') or on pieces of paper placed between the stones of the wall.

wain, *n.* (*poet.*) a four-wheeled vehicle for the transportation of goods, a wagon; Charles's Wain; †a chariot. †*v.t.* to convey in a wain. **†wain-bote,** *n.* an allowance of timber for wagons etc. **wain-rope,** *n.* a rope for fastening goods etc. on a wagon. **wainwright,** *n.* one who makes wagons. †**wainage,** *n.* [OE *wægn,* cp. Dut., G *Wagen,* Icel., Swed. *vagn,* L *vehiculum,* Sansk. *vahana-,* VEHICLE, Gr. *ochos,* car]

wainscot, *n.* a wooden, usu. panelled, lining or casing of the walls of a room; the lower part of the walls of a room when lined or finished differently from the upper part; fine-grade oak for wainscot panelling etc. *v.t.* (*past, p.p.* **wainscoted, -tted**) to line with this. **wainscoting, -tting,** *n.* (material for) a wainscot or wainscots. [Dut. *wagenschot,* a grained oak-wood, perh. MDut. *waeghe,* wave, (cp. OE *wæg, schot,* partition, wainscot), prob. cogn. with SHOT (¹,²), cp. CAMPSHOT (see CAMPSHED)]

wairepo, *n.* (*New Zealand*) grog, spirits. [Maori]

waist, *n.* that part of the human body below the ribs or thorax and above the hips; this part as normally more contracted than the rest of the trunk; the constriction between the abdomen and thorax of a wasp etc.; the middle part of an object, as an aircraft fuselage, esp. if more contracted than the other parts; the part of a ship between the quarter-deck and the forecastle; the part of a garment encircling the waist; (*N Am.*) a blouse, a shirtwaist. **waist-band,** *n.* a band or belt worn round the waist, esp. a band forming the upper part of a skirt, trousers etc. **waist-belt,** *n.* **waist-cloth,** *n.* a loincloth. **waistcoat,** *n.* a short garment, usu. without sleeves, extending from the neck to the waist. **waist-deep, -high,** *a., adv.* as deep, as high, or in (water etc.) as far as the waist. **waistline,** *n.* the waist of a dress etc., not necessarily corresponding with the wearer's natural waist. [ME *wast,* cogn. with WAX² (cp. OE *wœstm,* growth)]

wait, *v.i.* to remain inactive or in the same place until some event or time for action, to stay; to be in a state of expectation or readiness; to be on the watch (for); to be ready or in a fit state for use etc.; to act as a waiter, to attend (on persons) at table. *v.t.* to wait for, to await, to bide; to postpone, to defer, to delay. *n.* the act of waiting; time taken in waiting, delay; watching, ambush; (*pl.*) a band of singers and players performing carols in the streets etc. at Christmas-time. **to lie in wait,** to wait for in secret, to waylay. **to wait on, upon,** to attend upon as a servant; to pay a visit to deferentially; to await; of consequences etc., to follow; †to accompany, to escort, to attend; †to watch. **to wait up,** to remain out of bed waiting (for). **waiter,** *n.* one who waits; an attendant on the guests at a hotel, restaurant etc.; a dumb-waiter. **waiting,** *n., a.* **in waiting,** in attendance, esp. on the sovereign. **waiting game,** *n.* a holding back of action in the hope of more advantageous circumstances later. **waiting list,** *n.* a list of people waiting for a vacancy, treatment etc. **waiting-maid, -woman,** *n.* a female attendant. **waiting-room,** *n.* a room at a railway-station etc. where persons can rest while waiting. **waitress,** *n.fem.* [OF *waiter, gaiter* (F *guetter*), from *waite, gaite,* OHG *Wahta,* guard, watch (cp. G *Wacht,* cogn. with WAKE¹]

Waite, *n.* **'Terry' (Terence Hardy)** (1939–), British religious adviser from 1980 to the archbishop of Canterbury, Dr Robert Runcie. Waite undertook many overseas assignments but he disappeared in 1987 while making enquiries in Beirut, Lebanon, about European hostages. Worldwide efforts to secure his release, and that of his fellow hostages, have proved unsuccessful.

waive, *v.t.* to forgo, to relinquish; to refrain from using, insisting on etc.; to defer, postpone. **waiver,** *n.* (*Law*) the act of waiving a claim, right etc.; a written statement of this. [A-F *weiver,* OF *gaiver,* prob. from Icel. *veifa,* to vibrate, to swing about]

waiwode, VOIVODE.

Wajda, *n.* **Andrzej** (1926–), Polish film director, one of the major figures in postwar European cinema. His films typically deal with the predicament and disillusion of individuals caught up in political events. His works include *Ashes and Diamonds* (1958), *Man of Marble* (1977), *Man of Iron* (1981), and *Danton*

(1982).

waka, *n.* a Maori canoe. [Maori]

wake¹, *v.i.* (*past* **woke, waked,** *p.p.* **waked, woken, woke**) to be aroused from sleep, to cease to sleep; to revive from a trance, death etc.; to be awake, to be unable to sleep; to be roused or to rouse oneself from inaction, inattention etc.; †to revel or carouse at night. *v.t.* to rouse from sleep, to awake; to revive, to resuscitate, to raise from the dead; to arouse, to stir (up), to excite, to alert; to break the silence of, to disturb. *n.* the act of waking or being awake; a vigil. **wake-robin,** *n.* the wild arum, *Arum maculatum,* 'lords and ladies'. *a.* not disposed or unable to sleep, restless; passed without sleep, disturbed; watchful, alert. **wakefully,** *adv.* **wakefulness,** *n.* **waker,** *n.* [OE *wacan,* to arise, to be born, and *wacian,* to wake, to watch (cp. Dut. *waken,* G *wachen,* Icel. *vaka,* Goth. *wakan*), cogn. with VIGIL]

wake², *n.* the feast of the dedication of a church, formerly kept by watching all night; a merry-making held in connection with this; the watching of a dead body, prior to burial, by friends and neighbours of the deceased, with lamentations often followed by a merry-making. *v.t.* to hold a wake over. [from prec.]

wake³, *n.* the track left by a vessel passing through water; the track or path left after something has passed. **in the wake of,** following. [Icel. *vökr,* pl. *vaker,* a hole, an opening in ice (cp. Dut. *wak,* moist), cogn. with Gr. *hugros,* L *humidus,* HUMID]

waken, *v.t.* to rouse from sleep; to rouse to action etc.; to call forth. *v.i.* to wake, to cease from sleeping. **wakener,** *n.* [OE *wæcnan,* to arise, to be born, from *wacan,* to WAKE¹]

waker WAKE¹.

wakerife, *a.* (*Sc.*) wakeful. **wakerifely,** *adv.* **wakerifeness,** *n.*

Wakhan Salient, *n.* narrow strip of territory in Afghanistan bordered by the USSR, China, and Pakistan. It was effectively annexed by the USSR in 1980 to halt alleged arms supplies to Afghan guerrillas from China and Pakistan.

Waksman, *n.* **Selman Abraham** (1888–1973), US biochemist, born in Ukraine. He coined the word 'antibiotic' for bacteria-killing chemicals derived from microorganisms, and won the 1952 Nobel Prize for the discovery of streptomycin, an antibiotic used against tuberculosis.

Walachia, WALLACHIA.

Wald, *n.* **George** (1906–), US biochemist who explored the chemistry of vision. He found that a crucial role was played by the retinal pigment rhodopsin, derived in part from vitamin A. For this he shared the 1967 Nobel Physiology or Medicine Prize with Ragnar Granit (1900–) and Haldan Hartline (1903–).

Waldemar, Valdemar, *n.* four kings of Denmark including:

Waldemar I, *n.* **the Great** (1131–82), king of Denmark from 1157, who defeated rival claimants to the throne, and overcame the Wends on the Baltic island of Rügen in 1169.

Waldemar II, *n.* **the Conqueror** (1170–1241), king of Denmark from 1202. He was the second son of Waldemar I, and succeeded his brother Canute VI. He gained control of land N of the river Elbe (which he later lost), as well as much of Estonia, and he completed the codification of Danish law.

Waldemar IV, *n.* (1320–1375), king of Denmark from 1340, responsible for reuniting his country by capturing Skåne (S Sweden) and the island of Gotland in 1361. However, the resulting conflict with the Hanseatic League led to defeat by them, and in 1370 he was forced to submit to the Peace of Stralsund.

Walden, *n.* **Brian (Alistair)** (1932–), British journalist and, from 1977, television presenter. He was a Labour Member of Parliament 1964–77.

Waldenses, *n.pl.* (also known as **Waldensians** or **Vaudois**), Protestant religious sect, founded about 1170 by Peter Waldo, a merchant of Lyons. They were allied to the Albigenses. They lived in voluntary poverty, refused to take oaths or take part in war, and later rejected the doctrines of transubstantiation, purgatory, and the invocation of saints. Although subjected to persecution until the 17th century, they spread in France, Germany, and Italy, and still survive in Piedmont. **Waldensian,** *n., a.*

waldgrave, *n.* a German title of nobility, orig. a head forester. [G *waldgraf* (*Wald,* WOLD, forest, GRAVE⁴)]

Waldheim, *n.* **Kurt** (1918–), Austrian politician and diplomat. He was secretary general of the United Nations 1972–81, having been Austria's representative there 1964–68 and 1970–71. In 1986 he was elected president of Austria, but his tenure of office was clouded by revelations that during World War II he had been an intelligence officer in an army unit responsible for transporting Jews to death camps.

waldhorn, *n.* a hunting-horn; a french horn without valves. [G (*Wald,* see prec., HORN)]

wale¹, *n.* (*Sc., dial*) the choice, the pick. *v.t.* to choose. [ME, from Icel. *val,* choice (cp. G *Wahl*), cogn. with WILL¹]

wale², *n.* a ridge on the skin, a weal; a ridge on the surface of cloth; a wide plank extending along a ship's side. *v.t.* to weal. [OE *walu,* WEAL]

waler, *n.* (*Austral.*) a riding-horse (orig. as supplied by military authorities in New South Wales).

Wales, *n.* (Welsh *Cymru*) Principality of, part of United Kingdom. **area** 20,780 sq km/8021 sq miles. **capital** Cardiff. **towns** Swansea. **population** (1987) 2,836,000. **exports** traditional industries (coal and steel) have declined, but varied modern and high-technology ventures are being developed; Wales has the largest concentration of Japanese-owned plant in the UK. It also has the highest density of sheep in the world and a dairy industry; tourism is important. **language** Welsh 19% (1981), English. **religion** Nonconformist Protestant denominations; Roman Catholic minority.

Walhalla, VALHALLA.

walk, *v.i.* to go along by raising, advancing and setting down each foot alternately, never having both off the ground at once; of a quadruped, to go along with a slow gait keeping at least two feet on the ground at any time; to go at the ordinary pace, not to run, not to go or proceed rapidly; to go or travel on foot; of a ghost, to move about or become visible; (*coll.*) to depart, to be off, to be dismissed; †to act, conduct oneself or live in a specified way. *v.t.* to walk over, on or through, to perambulate, to tread; to cause to walk, to lead, drive or ride at a walking pace; to accompany on foot; to move (an object) by alternately lifting one side then the other. *n.* the act of walking; the pace, gait or step of a person or animal that walks; a distance walked; a stroll, a promenade; the route chosen for this; a piece of ground laid out for walking, a foot-path, a promenade etc.; the district or round of a hawker, postman etc.; a sheep-walk; one's profession, occupation, sphere of action etc. **to walk away with,** to win or gain easily. **to walk into,** (*sl.*) to thrash; to abuse; to eat heartily of. **to walk off with,** (*coll.*) to carry off, to steal; to walk away with. **to walk one's chalks, the chalk** CHALK. **to walk out with,** (*dated*) to go courting with. **to walk the plank** PLANK. **to walk the streets** STREET. **walk-about,** *n.* a wandering journey by Australian Aborigines; an informal walk to meet the public by a politician, member of royalty etc. *adv.* moving from place to place. **walk-in,** *a.* of a wardrobe etc., large enough to walk and move around in. **Walkman®,** *n.* a small portable cassette recorder with headphones. †**walk-mill,** *n.* a fulling-mill. **walk-on,** *n.* a small (non-speaking) part in a play etc. **walk-over,** *n.* an easy victory, one in which one's rivals could be beaten by walking. **walkway,** *n.* a path etc. for pedestrian use only; a place for walking, a walk. **walkable,** *a.* **walker¹,** *n.* one who walks; a shop-walker; †a fuller; a bird that steps instead of hopping; a gallinaceous bird; a frame for supporting a baby, disabled person etc. when walking. **walking,** *n., a.* **walking-dress,** *n.* a dress for wearing out of doors. **walking-gentleman, -lady,** *n.*

an actor filling subordinate parts requiring a gentlemanly or ladylike appearance. **walking-leaf,** *n.* an insect mimicking a leaf. **walking-papers,** *n.pl.* (*coll.*) notice of dismissal. **walking-stick, †-staff,** *n.* a stick carried in walking; a stick insect. [OE *wealcan,* to roll, to toss about, to rove (cp. Dut. *walken,* to press hats, G *walken,* to full, Icel. *vālka, volka,* to roll, Dan. *valke,* to full), cogn. with WALLOW]

†walker², *int.* nonsense! [old phrase Hookey *Walker*]

Walker¹, *n.* **Alice** (1944–), US poet, novelist, critic, and essay writer. She was active in the civil-rights movement in the US in the 1960s, and as a black woman has written about the double burden for women of racist and sexist oppression. Her novel *The Color Purple* (1983) won the Pulitzer Prize.

Walker², *n.* **Peter (Edward)** (1932–), British Conservative politician, energy secretary 1983–87, secretary of state for Wales from 1987.

Walker³, *n.* **William** (1824–60), US adventurer who for a short time established himself as president of a republic in NW Mexico, and was briefly president of Nicaragua 1856–57. He was eventually executed and is now regarded as a symbol of US imperialism in Central America.

walkie-talkie, *n.* a portable combined transmitter and receiver.

walkyrie, VALKYRIE.

wall, *n.* a continuous structure of stone, brick etc., narrow relatively to its height, forming an enclosure, fence, or the front, back or side, or an internal partition of a building; (*usu. pl.*) a rampart, a fortification; anything resembling a wall, as a cliff, a mountain-range etc.; the enclosing sides of a vessel, cavity etc.; a defence. *v.t.* to furnish, enclose, surround or defend with a wall; to separate or divide with a wall; to block (up) with a wall. **to give the wall to,** to allow as a courtesy to walk or pass by on the side of a pavement etc. away from the gutter. **to go to the wall,** to get the worst in a contest; to be pushed aside; to fail. **to have one's back to the wall,** to be in a desperate position. **up the wall,** (*coll.*) in or into a state of distraction or exasperation. **wall bars,** *n.pl.* horizontal bars fixed to a wall, used for gymnastics. **wall-creeper,** *n.* a bird, *Tichodroma muraria,* frequenting walls and cliffs. **wall-cress,** *n.* a plant of the genus *Arabis* growing in crevices. **wallflower,** *n.* a sweet-smelling plant of the genus *Cheiranthus,* esp. *C. cheiri,* with yellow, brown, and crimson flowers; (*coll.*) a person who is excluded from the main social activity, esp. a lady without a partner at a dance. **wall-fruit,** *n.* fruit grown on trees trained against walls. **wall game,** *n.* a kind of football played only at Eton. **wall-painting,** *n.* a painting painted on a wall, a fresco. **wallpaper,** *n.* paper, usu. with decorative patterns or texture, for pasting on the walls of rooms. **wall-pellitory** PELLITORY. **wall-pepper,** *n.* stone-crop, *Sedum acre.* **wall-plate,** *n.* a piece of timber let into a wall as a bearing for the ends of the joists etc. **wall-rue,** *n.* a small evergreen fern, *Asplenium rutamuraria,* growing on old walls, cliffs etc. **Wall Street,** *n.* the New York stock exchange and money market. **wall-tie,** *n.* a metal bond between the sides of a cavity wall. **wall-to-wall,** *a.* of carpet etc., covering all the floor; (*coll.*) continuous, nonstop. **walled,** *a.* **†waller,** *n.* one who builds walls. **walling,** *n.* [OE *weal,* L VALLUM]

wallaba, *n.* a leguminous tree, *Eperua falcata,* from Guyana, used in carpentry and building. [native name]

wallaby, *n.* one of the small species of kangaroo. **on the wallaby,** (*Austral., sl.*) tramping about looking for work etc. [Austral. Abor.]

Wallace¹, *n.* **Alfred Russel** (1823–1913), English naturalist who collected animal and plant specimens in South America and the Far East, and independently arrived at a theory of evolution by natural selection similar to that of Charles Darwin. **Wallace line,** *n.* an imaginary line running down the Lombok Strait in SE Asia, between the island of Bali and the islands of Lombok and Sulawesi. It was identified by the naturalist A. R. Wallace as separating the Asian and Australian biogeographical regions, each of which has its own distinctive animals.

Wallace², *n.* **George** (1919–), US right-wing politician, governor of Alabama 1962–66. He contested the presidency in 1968 as an independent, and in 1972 campaigned for the Democratic nomination, but was shot at a rally and became partly paralysed.

Wallace³, *n.* **William** (1272–1305), Scottish nationalist who led a revolt against English rule in 1297, won a victory at Stirling, and assumed the title 'governor of Scotland'. Edward I defeated him at Falkirk in 1298, and Wallace was captured and executed.

Wallach, *n.* a Wallachian or Vlach, a Romance-speaking inhabitant of Romania. **Wallachia,** *n.* independent mediaeval principality, under Turkish rule 1387–1861, when it was united with Moldavia to form Romania. **Wallachian,** *a.* of or pertaining to Wallachia. *n.* a native or the language of Wallachia. [G, from OHG *walh,* foreigner, cogn. with WELSH]

wallah, walla, *n.* (*often in comb. forms*) an agent, worker or any one employed in a specific type of work; (*coll., sometimes derog.*) a person, a fellow. [Hind. *-wālā,* Sansk. *-vala-,* suf. -er]

wallaroo, *n.* one of the large species of kangaroo. [Austral. Abor.]

Wallenberg, *n.* **Raoul** (1912–47), Swedish businessman who attempted to rescue several thousand Jews from German-occupied Budapest in 1944 in World War II.

Wallenstein, *n.* **Albrecht Eusebius Wenzel von** (1583–1634), German general who, until his defeat at Lützen in 1632, led the Habsburg armies in the Thirty Years' War. He was assassinated.

waller etc. WALL.

wallet, *n.* a bag or sack for carrying necessaries for a journey or march, esp. a pilgrim's or beggar's pack; a small bag or case for carrying paper money, credit cards etc.; a folder for papers, documents etc. [perh. corr. of WATTLE]

wall-eye, *n.* a condition of the eye due to opacity of the cornea or to strabismus; an eye with a very light-coloured iris, esp. due to this; a large, glaring eye, as in fish. **wall-eyed,** *a.* [from *wall-eyed,* ME *wald-eyed, vald-eygthr* (*vagl,* beam, *eygthr,* eyed, from *auga,* corr. of Icel. eye)]

wallflower WALL.

Wallis, *n.* **Barnes (Neville)** (1887–1979), British aeronautical engineer who designed the airship R-100 and during World War II perfected the 'bouncing bombs' used against the German Möhne and Eder dams in 1943 by the Royal Air Force Dambusters Squadron. He also assisted the development of the Concorde supersonic airliner, and developed the swing-wing aircraft.

Walloon, *n.* one of a French-speaking people in SE Belgium and the adjoining parts of France; their language *a.* pertaining to the Walloons or their language. [OF *Wallon,* L *Gallus,* GAUL]

wallop, *v.i.* to boil with a noisy bubbling and rolling motion; to move along in a clumsy tumbling fashion, to waddle. *v.t.* (*coll.*) to thrash, to flog; to defeat or beat decisively. *n.* (*coll.*) a blow, a punch; (*coll.*) forceful impact, power; (*sl.*) beer. **walloping,** *n.* (*coll.*) a thrashing. *a.* (*coll.*) big, thumping, whopping. **walloper,** *n.* [OF *waloper,* var. of *galoper,* see GALLOP]

wallow, *v.i.* to roll or tumble about in mire, water etc.; to revel grossly or self-indulgently (in vice etc.). *v.t.* to roll (oneself) about in mire etc. *n.* the act of wallowing; a mud-hole or other place in which animals wallow. **wallower,** *n.* [OE *wealwian,* cogn. with L *volvere*]

Wallsend, *n.* a superior kind of house coal orig. from Wallsend, on the Tyne.

Wall Street, *n.* street in Manhattan, New York, on which the stock exchange is situated, and a synonym for stock dealing in the US. It is so called from a stockade erected 1653.

wally, *n.* (*sl.*) an incompetent or stupid person. [etym. doubtful, perh. short for Sc. *wallydrag,* a feeble creature, or for *Walter*]

walnut, *n.* a tree of the genus *Juglans,* esp. *J. regia,* bearing a nut enclosed in a green fleshy covering; the unripe fruit of this used for pickling; the ripe nut; the timber of this or other species of the same genus used in cabinet-making and for gun-stocks. [ME *walnote,* OE *wealh,* foreign, (cp. WELSH, NUT)]

Walpole[1], *n.* **Robert, 1st Earl of Orford** (1676–1745), British Whig politician, the first 'prime minister' as 1st Lord of the Treasury and chancellor of the Exchequer 1715–17 and 1721–42. He encouraged trade by his peaceful foreign policy (until forced into the War of Jenkins's Ear with Spain in 1739), and received an earldom when he eventually retired in 1742.

Walpole[2], *n.* **Horace, 4th Earl of Orford** (1717–97), English novelist and politician, the son of Robert Walpole. He was a Whig Member of Parliament 1741–67. He converted his house at Strawberry Hill, Twickenham, into a Gothic castle; his *The Castle of Otranto* (1764) established the genre of the Gothic novel.

Walpurga, St, *n.* English nun who preached Christianity in Germany. **Walpurgis Night** the night before 1 May, one of her feast days, was formerly associated with witches' sabbaths. Her main feast day is 25 Feb.

walrus, *n.* a large, amphibious, long-tusked, seal-like mammal of the Arctic seas. **walrus moustache,** *n.* a thick moustache with long drooping ends. [Dut. from Scand. (cp. Swed. *vallros,* Dan. *hvalros,* Icel. *hrosshvalr,* OE *horshwæl,* horse-whale)]

Walsh, *n.* **Raoul** (1887–1981), US film director, originally an actor. He directed his first film 1914 and went on to become one of Hollywood's most prolific directors. He made a number of outstanding films, including *The Thief of Bagdad* (1924), *The Roaring Twenties* (1939), and *White Heat* (1949). He retired 1964.

Walsingham, *n.* **Francis** (*c.* 1530–90), English politician who, as secretary of state from 1573, both advocated a strong anti-Spanish policy and ran the efficient government spy system that made it work.

Walter, *n.* **Lucy** (*c.* 1630–58), mistress of Charles II, whom she met while a Royalist refugee in The Hague, Netherlands, in 1648; the Duke of Monmouth was their son.

Walters, *n.* **Sir Alan (Arthur)** (1927–), British economist and government adviser 1981–89. A believer in monetarism, he became economics adviser to Prime Minister Thatcher, but his publicly stated differences with the policies of her chancellor Nigel Lawson precipitated, in 1989, Lawson's resignation from the government as well as Walters's own departure.

Walther von der Vogelweide, (*c.* 1170–*c.* 1230), German poet, greatest of the Minnesingers. Of noble birth, he lived in his youth at the Austrian ducal court in Vienna, adopting a wandering life after the death of his patron in 1198. His lyrics deal mostly with love, but also with religion and politics.

Walton[1], *n.* **Ernest** (1903–), Irish physicist who, as a young doctoral student at the Cavendish laboratory in Cambridge, collaborated with Cockcroft on the structure of the atom. In 1932 they succeeded in splitting the atom and for this historic experiment, they shared the Nobel physics prize 1951.

Walton[2], *n.* **Izaak** (1593–1683), English author of the classic *Compleat Angler* (1653). He was born in Stafford, and settled in London as an ironmonger. He also wrote short biographies of the poets George Herbert and John Donne, and the theologian Richard Hooker.

Walton[3], *n.* **William (Turner)** (1902–83), English composer. Among his works are *Façade* (1923), a series of instrumental pieces designed to be played in conjunction with the recitation of poems by Edith Sitwell; the oratorio *Belshazzar's Feast* (1931); and *Variations on a Theme by Hindemith* (1963).

walty, *a.* (*Naut.*) unsteady, inclined to fall or roll over. [OE *wealt,* -Y]

waltz, *n.* a dance in triple time in which the partners pass round each other smoothly as they progress; the music for such a dance. *v.i.* to dance a waltz; to move quickly. **to waltz into,** (*coll.*) to rebuke severely. **waltzer,** *n.* one who waltzes; a type of fairground roundabout. [G *walzer,* from *walzen,* to revolve, to waltz, cogn. with OE *wealtan,* to WELTER[1]]

waly[1], *a.* beautiful, fine, excellent; strong, robust. [prob. cogn. with WALE[1]]

†**waly**[2], corr. of WELLAWAY.

wamble, *v.i.* of the stomach, to rumble, to heave; to be affected with nausea; to move unsteadily. *n.* a heaving; a feeling of nausea; an unsteady gait. [cp. Dan. *vamle,* imit. in orig.]

wame, (*Sc.*) WOMB.

wampee, *n.* a tree of the rice family cultivated in China and the E Indies bearing a grape-like, pulpy berry. [Chin. *hwang,* yellow, *pi,* skin]

wampum, *n.* small beads made of shells, used by the N American Indians formerly as money, or for decorating belts bracelets etc. [N Am. Ind. *wampumpeag* (*wompi,* white, *-ompeag,* string of money)]

wan, *a.* (*comp.* **wanner,** *superl.* **wannest**) pale or sickly in hue, pallid; lacking vigour or liveliness, worn; of light etc., dim, faint. †sombre, gloomy. **wanly,** *adv.* **wanness,** *n.* **wannish,** *a.* **wanny,** *a.* (*Sc.*). [OE *wann, wonn,* dark, black, etym. doubtful]

wanchancy, (*Sc.*) UNCHANCY.

wand, *n.* a long, slender rod, esp. one used by conjurers or as a staff of office; a conductor's baton; a light-pen used for reading bar codes. **wandy,** *a.* [Icel. *vöndr,* gen. *vandar,* prob. cogn. with WIND[2]]

wander, *v.i.* to travel or go here and there without any definite route or object, to rove, ramble or roam; to follow an irregular or winding course; to lose one's way, to go astray; to deviate from the right or proper course; to talk or think incoherently or senselessly, to be delirious; to digress from the subject in hand. *v.t.* to wander over, to traverse in a random way. **wanderer,** *n.* **wandering,** *n.*, *a.* (*usu. pl.*). **Wandering Jew,** *n.* a legendary character condemned, for an insult to Christ, to wander from place to place until the Day of Judgment; the Kenilworth ivy and other trailing or climbing plants. **wanderingly,** *adv.* **wanderment,** *n.* [OE *wandrian,* freq. of *wendan,* to WEND[1]]

wanderlust, *n.* the desire to travel. [G]

wanderoo, wanderu, *n.* the lion-tailed macaque, *Macacus silenus,* with a large greyish beard, of W India; a monkey from Sri Lanka. [Singalese *wanderu*]

wandoo, *n.* the white gum-tree of W Australia. [Austral. Abor.]

wane, *v.i.* to diminish in size and brilliance, as the illuminated portion of the moon; to decrease in power, strength etc., to decline. *n.* the act or process of waning, decrease, diminution; the period when the moon wanes; a defective edge or corner on timber. [OE *wanian,* from *wan,* wanting, deficient (cp. Icel. *vane,* to diminish, see WANT, WANTON)]

†**wang,** *n.* the jaw; the cheek-bone; a wang-tooth. †**wang-tooth,** *n.* a cheek-tooth or grinder. [OE *wange*]

wangle, *v.t.* (*coll.*) to manipulate, to employ cunningly; to falsify (accounts etc.); to achieve or gain by devious means. **wangler,** *n.* [etym. doubtful.]

†**wanhope,** *n.* despair, delusion. [OE *wan,* wanting, deficient in (cp. WANE), HOPE]

†**wanion,** *n.* misfortune, mischief, bad luck. †**with a wanion,** with a curse (to you). [ME *waniand,* pres.p. of *wanian,* to WANE]

wank, *v.i.* (*taboo*) to masturbate. *n.* (*taboo*) an instance of masturbating. **wanker,** *n.* (*taboo*) one who masturbates; (*sl.*) a worthless, incompetent or contemptible person. [etym. unknown]

Wankel engine, *n.* a rotary petrol engine developed by the German engineer Felix Wankel (1902–) in the 1950s. It operates according to the same stages as the four-stroke petrol engine cycle, but these stages take place in different sectors of a figure-of-eight chamber in the space between the chamber walls and a triangular rotor. Power is produced once on every turn on the rotor. The Wankel engine is simpler in construction than the normal piston petrol engine, and produces rotary power directly (instead of via a crankshaft). Problems with rotor seals have prevented its widespread use.

wankle, *a.* (*dial.*) weak, unstable; untrustworthy, unreliable. [OE *wancol*]

wanly etc. WAN.

wannabee, *n., a.* (*sl.*) (a person) anxious to become somebody or something. [want to be]

wanrestful, *a.* (*Sc.*) restless. [*wan-,* as in WANHOPE, RESTFUL]

want, *n.* the state or condition of not having, lack, deficiency, absence, need (of); need, privation, penury, poverty; a longing or desire for something that is necessary or required for happiness etc.; that which is not possessed but is so desired. *v.t.* to be without, to lack, to be deficient in; to need, to require; to be short by, to require in order to be complete; to feel a desire for, to crave; to desire or request the presence or assistance of; ought (to). *v.i.* to be in need, to be in want (for); to be deficient (in), to fall short (in); to be lacking, to have need (for). †**want-wit,** *n.* a fool. †**wantage,** *n.* deficiency. **wanter,** *n.* **wanting,** *a.* absent, missing, lacking; not meeting the required or expected standard; lacking (in), deficient (in); (*coll.*) witless, daft, deficient in intelligence. *prep.* without, less, save. **wantless,** *a.* [Icel. *vant,* neut. of *vanr,* wanting, deficient (cp. OE *wan,* WANE)]

wanton, *a.* sportive, frolicsome, playful; unrestrained, loose, wild, unruly; extravagant, luxuriant; licentious, lascivious, lewd; random, heedless, reckless, purposeless. *n.* a lewd or unchaste person, esp. a woman; a trifler; a playful, idle creature. *v.i.* to sport, to frolic; to move, act or grow at random or unrestrainedly; †to sport lasciviously. **wantonly,** *adv.* **wantonness,** *n.* [ME *wantoun, wantowen* (OE *wan-,* deficient in, *togen,* p.p. of *tēon,* to draw, to educate)]

wanty, *n.* (*dial.*) a leather band or rope, esp. a girth, belly-band etc. [etym. doubtful]

wapacut, *n.* a large white N American owl, *Nyctea scandiaca.* [N Am. Ind. *wapacuthu*]

wapens(c)haw WAPINSHAW.

wapentake, *n.* a name formerly given in certain English counties to a division corresponding to a hundred. [OE *wǣpengetǣce,* Icel. *vāpnatak,* weapon-touching (*vāpna,* gen. of *vāpn,* weapon, *taka,* to TAKE, to touch) (cp. foll.)]

wapinshaw, wapinschaw, wap(p)ens(c)haw, *n.* a review of persons under arms, made formerly in Scotland periodically in certain districts; a meeting for rifle-shooting, curling-matches etc. [Sc., weapon-show]

wapiti, *n.* a N American stag, *Cervus canadensis,* related to the red deer, erroneously called the elk. [N Am. Ind. *wapitik,* from *wapi,* white]

†**wappened,** *a.* (*Shak.*) worn out, stale. [etym. unknown]

wappens(c)haw WAPINSHAW.

wapper, *n.* (*dial.*) the gudgeon. [etym. doubtful]

Wapping, *n.* district of the Greater London borough of Tower Hamlets; situated between the Thames and the former London Docks. It replaced Fleet Street as the centre of the UK newspaper industry.

war, *n.* a contest carried on by force of arms between nations, or between parties in the same state; the state of things brought about by this, a state of hostilities with suspension of ordinary international relations; hostile operations, military or naval attack, invasion; the military art, strategy; hostility, active enmity, strife; (a) conflict, feud, struggle; †armed troops, an army. *v.i.* (*past, p.p.* **warred**) to make or carry on war; to contend, to strive, to compete; to be in opposition, to be inconsistent. **art of war,** strategy and tactics. **at war,** engaged in hostilities (with). **civil war** CIVIL. **cold war** COLD. **holy war** HOLY. **in the wars,** (*coll.*) (bruised or injured as from) fighting or quarrelling. **man-of-war,** *n.* MAN. **to be, to go on the war-path,** to be ready for or engaged in conflict; to be thoroughly roused or incensed. **War Between the States,** another (usually Southern) name for the American Civil War (now seldom used in standard histories). **war-bond** *n.* a government bond issued as a means of raising a war loan. **war-cloud,** *n.* a state of international affairs threatening war. **war correspondent,** *n.* a journalist who reports on current events from the scene of a war or battle. **war crime,** *n.* a crime committed in connection with a war. **war criminal,** *n.* **war-cry,** *n.* a name or phrase formerly shouted in charging etc.; a watchword; a party cry. **war-dance,** *n.* a dance practised, as by some N American Indian tribes, as a preparation for battle. **war footing,** *n.* a condition (of the military or naval establishments) of readiness for active hostilities. **war-game,** *n.* a simulated military battle or campaign; an enactment of a battle using models. **war-god,** *n.* a deity worshipped as giving victory, as Mars or the Greek Ares. **warhead,** *n.* the head of a torpedo, aerial bomb, rocket etc., charged with explosive, removable in peace practice. **war-horse,** *n.* a charger; (*fig.*) a veteran, a person full of warlike memories etc.; a standard, (overly-) familiar piece of music etc. **war-loan,** *n.* a loan raised to meet the cost of a war. **warlord,** *n.* a military leader or commander of (a part of) a nation. **war-marked,** *a.* bearing the marks or traces of war. **warmonger,** *n.* one who traffics in war, or promotes it by every means possible. **war neurosis** SHELL-SHOCK. **War of 1812,** *n.* a war between the US and Britain caused by British interference with US trade as part of the economic warfare against Napoleonic France. Tensions with the British in Canada led to plans for a US invasion but these were never realized and success was limited to the capture of Detroit and a few notable naval victories. In 1814, British forces occupied Washington DC and burned many public buildings. A treaty signed in Ghent, Belgium, Dec. 1814 ended the conflict. **War Office,** *n.* former British government department controlling military affairs. The Board of Ordnance, which existed in the 14th cent., was absorbed into the War Department after the Crimean War and the whole named the War Office. In 1964 its core became a subordinate branch of the newly established Ministry of Defence. **war-paint,** *n.* paint put on the face and body, esp. by N American Indians, before going into battle; full dress; (*coll.*) make-up. **war-path,** *n.* the path taken by an attacking party of N American Indians; hence a warlike expedition. **warplane,** *n.* a military aircraft for use in war. **War Powers Act,** *n.* legislation passed 1973 enabling the US president to deploy US forces abroad for combat without prior Congressional approval. The president is nevertheless required to report to both Houses of Congress within 48 hours of having taken such action. Congress may restrict the continuation of troop deployment despite any presidential veto. **war-proof,** *n.* tried or proved valour. **warship,** *n.* an armed ship for use in war. **war-song,** *n.* a song sung at a war-dance or before battle; a song on a martial theme. **wartime,** *n.* †**war-wasted,** *a.* **war-wearied,** *a.* **war-whoop,** *n.* a shout or yell raised by N American Indians in attacking. **war-worn,** *a.* exhausted by or experienced in war. **warless,** *a.* **warlike,** *a.* fit or ready for war; fond of war, martial, soldier-like, military; threatening war, hostile. †**warlikeness,** *n.* [OF *werre* (F *guerre*), from Teut. (cp. OHG *Werra,* strife, *werran,* to embroil), prob. cogn. with WORSE]

War., (*abbr.*) Warwickshire.

waratah, *n.* one of a genus of Australian proteaceous shrubs with a large, brilliant crimson flower. [Austral. Abor.]

Warbeck, *n.* **Perkin** (*c.* 1474–99), Flemish pretender to the English throne. Claiming to be Richard, brother of Edward V, he led a rising against Henry VII in 1497, and was hanged after attempting to escape from the Tower of London.

warble[1], *n.* a small hard tumour on a horse's back caused by the falling of the saddle; a small tumour produced by the larva of the bot-fly. **warble-fly,** *n.* the bot-fly. [etym. doubtful]

warble[2], *v.i.* of birds, to sing in a continuous quavering or trilling manner; of streams etc., to make a continuous melodious sound; to sing (with trills and variations etc.). *v.t.* to sing or utter thus. *n.* the act or sound of warbling; a song; a trill. **warbler,** *n.* one who, or that which, warbles; one of the Sylviidae, a family of small birds comprising the nightingale, black-cap, hedge-sparrow, robin etc. **warbling,** *a.* **warblingly,** *adv.* [ME *werblen,* OF *werbler,* freq. from Teut. (cp. MHG *werben,* G *wirbeln,* to WHIRL)]

Warburg, *n.* **Otto** (1878–1976), German biochemist, who in 1923 devised a manometer sensitive enough to measure oxygen uptake of respiring tissue. By measuring the rate at which cells absorb oxygen under differing conditions, Warburg was able to show that enzymes called cytochromes enable cells to process oxygen. Nobel Prize for Medicine 1931.

ward, *n.* watch, guard, the act of guarding, protection; an inner court of a castle; a parrying or guard in fencing; confinement, custody; guardianship, control; a minor or person under guardianship; an administrative or electoral division of a town or city; a separate division of a hospital, prison or workhouse; a projection inside a lock preventing the turning of any but the right key. *v.t.* to parry, to turn aside, to keep (off); †to guard, to watch over, to defend; †to keep safe, to imprison. **watch and ward** WATCH. **ward in Chancery,** *n.* a minor under the guardianship of the Court of Chancery. **ward-mote,** *n.* a meeting of the ratepayers of a ward. **ward-room,** *n.* a room on a warship for commissioned officers below the rank of commander. **wardship,** *n.* guardianship, tutelage. [OE *weard* (masc.), guard, watchman, (fem.) watch (whence *weardian,* to keep watch), cogn. with GUARD]

warden[1], *n.* a keeper, a guardian; a governor; the head of some colleges, schools and hostels; (*N Am.*) a prison governor; one who keeps ward, a watchman; one of the officials in a Civil Defence organization; (*Austral.*) a government official in charge of a goldfield. **Warden of the Cinque Ports,** *n.* the governor of the Cinque Ports. **wardenship,** †**wardenry,** *n.* [ME, A-F *wardein,* OF *wardain, gardein,* from *warder, garder,* to GUARD]

warden[2], *n.* a variety of cooking pear. †**warden-pie,** *n.* [prob. from *Wardon,* in Beds.]

warder, *n.* a keeper, a jailer, a prison guard; †a guard, a sentinel; †a staff of authority or baton carried by a general etc., used in giving signals. **wardress,** *n.fem.* [WARD, -ER]

wardian, *a.* applied to a close-fitting case with glass sides and top, retaining moisture, for transporting delicate plants, esp. ferns. [Nathaniel B. *Ward,* 1791–1868, inventor]

Wardour Street, *n.* the British film industry; the bogus antique language etc. of costume films. [locality in London where the cinema industry is centred]

wardrobe, *n.* a cabinet, cupboard or other place, where clothes are hung up; a person's stock of wearing apparel; the stage costumes of a theatre or company. **wardrobe dealer,** *n.* one who deals in used or second-hand clothing. [OF *warderobe, garderobe* (*warder,* see WARDEN[1], ROBE)]

-ward(s), *suf.* expressing direction as in *backward, forward, homeward, inwards, outwards* etc. [OE *-weard,* as in *tōweard,* TOWARD, from *weorthan,* to become, see WORTH[2]]

-wards -WARD.

wardship etc. WARD.

ware[1], *n.* manufactured articles of a specified kind, esp. pottery, as table-ware, stone-ware; (*pl.*) articles of merchandise, articles for sale, goods. [OE *waru* (cp. Dut. *waar,* G *Waare,* Icel. *varu,* Dan. *vare*)]

†**ware**[2], *a.* conscious, aware; cautious, wary. *v.t.* (*imper.*) beware! look out for, guard against, keep clear of. †**wareless**, *a.* †**warely,** *adv.* [OE *wœr,* whence *warian,* to watch over, to guard (cp. Icel. *varr,* G *gewahr*), cogn. with Gr. *horaein,* to perceive, L *verērī,* to regard, to dread]

†**ware**[3], *past* WEAR[1].

warehouse, *n.* a building in which goods are stored, kept for sale or in bond; a wholesale or large retail store. *v.t.*, to deposit or secure (furniture, bonded goods etc.) in a warehouse. **warehouseman,** *n.* one who keeps or is employed in a warehouse. **warehousing,** *n.* (*coll.*) the practice of anonymously building up a shareholding in a company, using nominees etc. to purchase the shares.

warfare, *n.* a state of war, hostilities; conflict, strife. *v.i.* to carry on war; to engage in war; to contend. †**warfarer,** *n.*

warfarin, *n.* a compound used as a rodent poison and to prevent blood clotting. [*W*isconsin *A*lumni *R*esearch *F*oundation, the patentee, coum*arin*]

Warhol, *n.* **Andy** (1928–87), US pop artist and film-maker. He made his name in 1962 with paintings of Campbell's soup tins, Coca-Cola bottles, and film stars. In his notorious New York studio, the Factory, he produced series of garish silk-screen prints. His films include the semi-documentary *Chelsea Girls* (1966) and *Trash* (1970).

warily etc. WARY.

†**warison,** *n.* protection; reward; (*Scott.*) a note of assault (*erron. usage*). [OF *warīson, garison,* from *warir, garir,* to protect, to heal (*F guérir*), see GARRISON]

†**wark,** WORK.

warlike etc. WAR[1].

warlock, *n.* a wizard, a sorcerer. †**warlockry,** *n.* [OE *wǣrloga,* traitor, deceiver (*wœr,* truth, cogn. with L *vērus,* true, *loga,* liar)]

warm, *a.* being at a rather high temperature; having heat in a moderate degree; promoting, emitting or conveying heat; having the sensation of rather more than ordinary heat, esp. with the temperature of the skin raised by exercise etc.; ardent, zealous, enthusiastic, cordial; sympathetic, emotional, affectionate; amorous, erotic, indelicate; animated, heated, excited, vehement, passionate, excitable; of a skirmish etc., violent, vigorous, brisk, strenuous, lively; of colours, being predominantly red or yellow; of a scent, fresh, strong; near the object sought (in children's games); (*coll.*) well off, in comfortable circumstances; (*coll.*) unpleasant, hot, uncomfortable. *v.t.* to make warm; to make ardent or enthusiastic, to excite; (*sl.*) to thrash. *v.i.* to become warm; to become animated, zealous, sympathetic or enthusiastic (to or towards). **to warm up,** to make or become warm; to reheat (cooked food); to prepare for a contest, performance etc., esp. to prepare for an athletic contest etc. by exercising and stretching; to make (an audience) more receptive to a show or main act by a preliminary entertainment. **warm-up,** *n.* **warm-blooded,** *a.* having warm blood, esp. between 98° and 112°F (36·6 and 44·4°C), as mammals and birds; emotional, passionate, excitable; amorous, erotic. **warm front,** *n.* the advancing edge of a mass of warm air. **warm-hearted,** *a.* having warm, affectionate, kindly or susceptible feelings. **warm-heartedly,** *adv.* **warm-heartedness,** *n.* **warmer,** *n.* (*usu. in comb.* as *foot-warmer*). **warming,** *a.* (*sl.*) a thrashing, a hiding. **warming-pan,** *n.* a closed pan, usu. of brass with a long handle, for holding live coals, formerly used to warm a bed; a person who holds a post temporarily till another is qualified to fill it. **warmly,** *adv.* **warmth,** †**warmness,** *n.* [OE *wearm,* (cp. Dut. and G *warm,* Icel. *varmr,* Dan. and Swed. *varm*)]

warn, *v.t.* to give notice to, to inform beforehand; to caution or put on one's guard against; to expostulate with, to admonish; to order to go or stay (away, off etc.). *v.i.* to give a warning. **warner,** *n.* **warning,** *n.* the act of cautioning or admonishing against danger etc.; previous notice, esp. to quit one's service etc.; that which serves to warn; the sound made by the partial unlocking of the striking train of a clock just before striking. **warningly,** *adv.* [OE *wearnian, warnian* (cp. G *warnen,* OHG *warnōn*), cogn. with WARY]

Warner, *n.* **Deborah** (1959–), British theatre director. Discarding period costume and furnished sets, she adopted an uncluttered approach to the classics, including productions of many Shakespeare plays and Sophocles' *Electra.*

Warner Brothers, *n.* US film production company, founded 1923 by Harry, Albert, Sam, and Jack Warner. It became one of the major Hollywood studios after releasing the first talking film, *The Jazz Singer* (1927). In the 1930s–50s, the company's stars included Humphrey Bogart, Erroll Flynn, and Bette Davis. It suffered in the 1960s through competition with television and was taken over by Seven Art Productions. In 1969 there was another takeover by Kinney National Service, and the whole company became known as Warner Communications.

warp, *n.* the threads running the long way of a woven fabric, crossed by the weft or woof; a rope, usu. smaller than a cable, used in towing a vessel; the state of being twisted, a twist or distortion in timber etc.; a perversity or aberration of mind or disposition; an alluvial deposit of water artificially introduced into low lands. *v.t.* to turn or twist out of shape, to make crooked, to distort; to pervert, to bias, to turn awry; to fertilize by means of artificial inundations; to tow or move with a line attached to a buoy, anchor or other fixed point etc.; to run (yarn) off for weaving. *v.i.* to become twisted, crooked or distorted; to turn aside; to become perverted; (*dial*) to cast young prematurely. **warper,** *n.* **warping-bank,** *n.* a bank for retaining the water let on to ground for fertilizing purposes. **warping-hook,** *n.* a rope-maker's hook used in warping. **warping mill,** *n.* a revolving wooden frame upon which fabric threads are wound when being made into a warp. **warping-post,** *n.* a post used in warping rope-yarn. [OE *wearp,* cp. Icel., Dan., and Swed. *varp,* a casting or throwing (v. from the cogn. Icel. *varpa,* to throw)]

warragal, WARRIGAL.

warrant, *v.t.* to answer or give an assurance for, to guarantee; to give authority to, to sanction; to serve as guarantee for; to attest the truth of; to serve as grounds or justification for. *n.* anything that authorizes a person to do something, authorization; sanction; reason, grounds, justification; anything that attests or bears out a statement etc.; one who or that which vouches, a voucher; a document authorizing a person to receive money etc.; an instrument giving power to arrest a person, levy a distress etc.; a certificate of office held by a warrant-officer. **warrant of attorney** ATTORNEY[2]. **warrant-officer,** *n.* an officer next below a commissioned officer, acting under a warrant from the Admiralty or War Office as a gunner, boatswain or sergeant-major. **warrantable,** *a.* justifiable, defensible; of deer, old enough to be hunted. **warrantableness,** *n.* **warrantably,** *adv.* **warrantee,** *n.* **warranter,** *n.* †**warrantise,** *n.* a warranty. †**warrantize, -ise,** *v.t.* **warrantor,** *n.* (*Law*). **warranty,** *n.* a warrant, an authorization; a promise or undertaking from a vendor to a purchaser that the thing sold is the vendor's to sell and is good and fit for use etc.; an express or implied undertaking in a contract that a fact is as stated. †*v.t.* to warrant, to guarantee. [OF *warant, guarant,* from Teut. (cp. G *gewähren,* to certify)]

†**warre,** WORSE.

warren, *n.* a piece of ground where rabbits live and breed; a place for keeping and breeding small game animals; an overcrowded district; a maze of interconnecting streets or passages. **warrener,** *n.* [ME *wareine,* OF *warenne,* from *warir,* see WARISON]

Warren[1], *n.* **Earl** (1891–1974), US jurist and politician. As Chief Justice of the US Supreme Court 1953–69 he took a stand against racial discrimination, ruling that segregation in schools was unconstitutional. He headed the commission that investigated President Kennedy's assassination 1964, which made the controversial finding that Lee Harvey Oswald acted alone.

Warren[2], *n.* **Frank** (1952–), British boxing promoter who helped bring world title-fight boxing to commercial television. His set up the London Arena in the Docklands. He survived an assassination attempt in 1989.

Warren[3], *n.* **Robert Penn** (1905–89), US poet and novelist, the only author to receive a Pulitzer prize for both prose and poetry. In 1986 he became the US's first Poet Laureate.

warrigal, *n.* (*Austral.*) the dingo; a wild native; an outlaw, a rascal. [Austral. Abor.]

warrior, *n.* a person, esp. a man, experienced or distinguished in war, a distinguished soldier. †**warrioress,** *n.fem.* [ME *werreour,* OF *guerreiur,* from *guerreier,* to make war, see WAR[1]]

Warsaw, *n.* (Polish **Warszawa**) capital of Poland, on the river Vistula; population (1985) 1,649,000. Industries include engineering, food processing, printing, clothing, and pharmaceuticals. **Warsaw Pact,** *n.* military alliance established 1955 between the USSR and E European communist states as a response to the admission of West Germany into NATO.

wart, *n.* a small hard excrescence on the skin of the hands etc. due to irregular growth of the papillae, caused by a virus; a spongy excrescence on the hind pastern of a horse; a small protuberance on the surface of a plant. **wart-hog,** *n.* an African large-headed wild pig of the genus *Phacochoerus,* with warty excrescences on the face. **warted, warty,** *a.* **wartless,** *a.* [OE *wearte* (cp. Dut. *wrat,* G *Warze,* Icel. *varta*), prob. cogn. with WORT]

Warwick, *n.* **Richard Neville, Earl of Warwick** (1428–71), English politician, called the Kingmaker. During the Wars of the Roses he fought at first on the Yorkist side, and was largely responsible for placing Edward IV on the throne. Having quarrelled with him, he restored Henry VI in 1470, but was defeated and killed by Edward at Barnet, Hertfordshire.

Warwickshire, *n.* county in central England. **area** 1980 sq km/764 sq miles. **towns** administrative headquarters Warwick; Leamington, Nuneaton, Rugby, Stratford-upon-Avon. **population** (1987) 484,000. **products** mainly agricultural, engineering, textiles.

wary, *a.* cautious, watchful against deception, dangers etc.; circumspect; done with or characterized by caution. **warily,** *adv.* **wariness,** †**wariment,** *n.* [WARE[2]]

was, wast, were, wert, past tense BE. [OE *wæs, wære, wæs, wæron* (*wæran, wærun*), *wesan,* infin. (cp. Sansk. *vas-,* to remain, dwell, live, Goth. *wisan,* to remain, continue, OFris. *wesa,* Icel. *vera*) (see also BE, AM)]

wase, *n.* (*dial.*) a wisp or pad of hay, straw etc. worn on the head by porters etc. to ease the pressure of a load. [etym. doubtful]

wase-goose WAYZGOOSE.

wash, *v.t.* to cleanse with water or other liquid; to remove or take out, off, away etc. thus; to pass water or other liquid through or over; to wash clothes, to wash (up) table utensils; to purify; of dew, waves, the sea etc., to fall upon, cover, moisten or dash against; to carry along, to sweep away etc., to scoop (out) by or as by the action of moving liquid; to separate the earthy and lighter parts from (ore); to cover with a thin coat of colour; to overlay with a thin coat of metal. *v.i.* to cleanse oneself with water etc.; to stand washing without fading or being injured in any way; (*coll.*) of a story etc., to stand examination; of water etc., to move or splash or sweep along; to drift or be carried along on water. *n.* the act or operation of washing; the state of being washed; a quantity of clothes etc. washed at one time; the motion of a body of water, esp. the swirling and foaming caused by the passage of a vessel; soil removed and accumulated by water, alluvium; land washed by the sea or a river; waste liquor from the kitchen often used as food for pigs; thin liquid food, slops; a liquid used for toilet purposes, a cosmetic, a lotion; a thin coating of colour spread over broad masses of a painting, pen-and-ink drawing etc.; a thin liquid for coating a wall etc.; a thin coat of metal; the blade of an oar; fermented wort from which spirit has been extracted; a disturbance in the air caused by the passage of an aircraft. **the wash,** the washing of clothes, linen etc. **to come right in the wash,** (*coll.*) to come right in the end. **to wash down,** to wash the whole of; to accompany (food) with a drink to aid swallowing or digestion. **to wash one's hands of,** to disclaim any responsibility for. **to wash out,** to remove by washing; to wash free of something unwanted; (*coll.*) to cancel, to annul. **to wash up,** to wash dishes etc.; (*esp. N Am.*) to wash one's hands and face. **wash-basin,** *n.* a wash-hand basin. **wash-board,** *n.* a board with a ribbed surface for scrubbing clothes on; a skirting round the lower part of the wall of a room; a board to keep the water from washing over a gun-wale or through a port etc. of a ship. **wash-boiler,** *n.* one for boiling clothes in the process of washing. **wash-bottle,** *n.* an apparatus for washing gases, precipitates etc. by passing them through a liquid. **wash-bowl,** *n.* wash-hand basin. **wash-cloth,** *n.* a piece of cloth used in washing dishes etc. **wash-day,** *n.* the day on which domestic washing is done or sent to the laundry. **washed out,** *a.* limp, exhausted, worn-out; faded, colourless. **washed-up,** *a.* (*coll.*) no longer successful or effective, finished, failed. **wash-gilding,** *n.* water-gilding. **wash-hand basin,** a basin for washing the hands etc., forming part of the furnishings of a toilet, bathroom, some (hotel) bedrooms etc. **wash-house,** *n.* a building furnished with boilers, tubs, basins etc., for washing clothes etc., a laundry; a scullery. **wash-leather,** *n.* chamois leather or an imitation of this. **wash-out,** *n.* a scooping out or sweeping away of rock, earth etc. by a rush of water; a cleansing by washing out; (*coll.*) a failure, a muddle; (*coll.*) a muddler. **wash-pot,** *n.* †a vessel in which anything is washed; a vessel used to give the final coat in tin-plating. **wash-rag,** *n.* (*N Am.*) a face-cloth, a flannel. **wash-room,** (*N Am.*) a lavatory. **wash-stand,** *n.* a piece of furniture for holding a ewer or pitcher, basin etc. for washing one's face and hands etc. **wash-tub,** *n.* a tub in which clothes etc. are washed. **washable,** *a.* **washer,** *n.* a ring or perforated disk of metal, rubber etc. for placing beneath a nut etc. to tighten the joint etc.; one who or that which washes; a washing machine. **washerman,** *n.* a laundryman. **washer-woman,** *n.* a laundress. **washing,** *n.* the act of cleansing by water etc., ablution; clothes etc. washed together or for washing. **washing-machine,** *n.* an electrical machine in which clothes are washed automatically. **washing-powder,** *n.* a preparation used in washing clothes. **washing soda,** *n.* crystalline sodium carbonate. **washing up,** *n.* the washing of dishes etc., esp. after a meal; dishes, cutlery etc. to be washed. **washy,** *a.* watery, too much diluted, weak, thin; wanting in solidity, stamina or vigour, feeble. **washily,** *adv.* **washiness,** *n.* [OE *wascan* (cp. Dut. *wasschen,* G *waschen,* Icel. and Swed. *vaska*), cogn. with WATER and WET]

Wash., (*abbr.*) Washington.

Washington¹, *n.* state of the NW US; nickname Evergreen State. **area** 176,615 sq km/68,191 sq miles. **capital** Olympia. **towns** Seattle, Spokane, Tacoma. **population** (1987) 4,481,000 including 61,000 Indians, mainly of the Yakima people. **products** apples, cereals, livestock, processed food, timber, chemicals, cement, zinc, uranium, lead, gold, silver, aircraft, ships, road transport vehicles.

Washington², *n.* **Booker T(aliaferro)** (1856–1915), US educationist, pioneer in higher education for black people in the southern US. He was the founder and first principal of Tuskegee Institute, Alabama, in 1881, originally a training college for blacks, which became a respected academic institution. He maintained that economic independence was the way for blacks to achieve social equality.

Washington³, *n.* **George** (1732–99), first president of the US 1789–97. As a strong opponent of the British government's policy, he sat in the Continental Congresses of 1774 and 1775, and on the outbreak of the War of American Independence was chosen commander in chief. After the war he retired to his Virginia estate, Mount Vernon, but in 1787 he re-entered politics as president of the Constitutional Convention. Although he attempted to draw his ministers from all factions, his aristocratic outlook alienated his secretary of state, Thomas Jefferson, with whose resignation in 1793 the two-party system originated.

Washington DC, *n.* (District of Columbia) national capital of the US, on the Potomac river. **area** 180 sq km/69 sq miles. **capital** the District of Columbia covers only the area of the city of Washington. **population** (1983) 623,000 (metropolitan area, extending outside the District of Columbia, 3 million).

Washingtonia, *n.* a gigantic Californian sequoia. [George *Washington,* 1st Pres., US, 1732–99, -IA]

WASP, *n.* an American of N European descent, considered in N America as belonging to a privileged class. [*W*hite *A*nglo-*S*axon *P*rotestant]

wasp, *n.* a predatory hymenopterous insect of solitary or social habits, esp. the common wasp, *Vespa vulgaris,* a European insect with a slender waist, black and yellow stripes and a powerful sting; a spiteful or irritable person. **wasp-bee, -beetle, -fly,** *n.* one somewhat resembling a wasp, but without a sting. **wasp-waisted,** *a.* having a very thin waist. **waspish,** *a.* snappish, petulant, irritable. **waspishly,** *adv.* **waspishness,** *n.* [OE *wæps* (cp. G *Wespe,* Lith. *wapsà*), cogn. with WEAVE (from their nests) and L *vespa*]

wassail, *n.* a festive occasion, a drinking-bout, a carouse; spiced ale or other liquor prepared for a wassail; formerly, a toast to a person's health. *v.i.* to carouse, to make merry; to go from house to house singing carols at Christmas. **wassail-bowl, -cup, -horn,** *n.* one from which wassail was drunk. **wassailer,** *n.* [OE *wæs hāl,* be thou (see WAS) of good health (*hāl,* WHOLE)]

Wassermann test, *n.* a diagnostic test for the presence of syphilis. [A. von *Wassermann,* 1866–1925]

wast, 2nd pers. sing. of past tense. [BE]

waste, *a.* desolate, desert, empty, unoccupied, untilled, devastated, made desolate; barren, unproductive; dreary, dismal, cheerless; refuse, superfluous, left over as useless or valueless. *v.t.* to devastate, to lay waste; to wear away gradually; to cause to lose weight, strength and health; to consume, to spend, to use up unnecessarily, carelessly or lavishly, to squander; to fail to use to advantage; (*Law*) to injure or impair (an estate) by neglect; (*sl.*) to kill. *v.i.* to wear away gradually, to dwindle, to wither; to lose weight, strength and health; to bring down one's weight by training. *n.* the act of wasting, squandering or throwing away to no purpose; the state or process of being wasted or used up, gradual diminution of substance, strength, value etc.; material, food etc. rejected as superfluous, useless or valueless, refuse; waste-products; a desolate or desert region, a wilderness; a dreary scene, an empty space, a void; (*Law*) damage or injury to an estate etc. caused by the act or neglect of a life-tenant etc. **to lay waste,** to render desolate; to devastate, to ruin. **waste-book,** *n.* an account book for entering transactions as they take place before carrying them over to the ledger. **waste paper,** *n.* spoiled, used or discarded paper. **waste (paper) basket,** a receptacle for waste paper. **waste-pipe,** *n.* a discharge-pipe for used or superfluous water. **waste-product,** *n.* material produced by a process as a useless by-product; an unusable product of metabolism. **wastage,** *n.* loss by use, decay, leakage etc.; avoidable loss of something useful; reduction in numbers of employees etc. by retirement, voluntary resignation etc. **wasteful,** *a.* extravagant, spending or using recklessly, unnecessarily or too lavishly; †laying waste; desolate, waste. **wastefully,** *adv.* **wastefulness,** *n.* **wasteless,** *a.* inexhaustible. †**wasteness,** *n.* the state of being waste; solitude, desolation. **waster,** *n.* one who wastes; a prodigal, a spendthrift; a good-for-nothing, a wastrel; an article spoilt and rendered unmarketable in manufacture; †a wooden sword used as a foil. **wasting,** *n., a.* **wasting asset,** a non-renewable asset that is gradually used up, as a mine. [ME and OF *wast* (var. *gast*), from MHG *Waste,* a waste, L *vastus,* VAST, whence *vastāre,* OF *waster, gaster* (F *gâter,* to spoil), to lay waste]

†**wastel,** *n.* a fine white bread made from the best wheat-flour; a round cake used as a heraldic bearing. †**wastel-bread, -cake,** *n.* [OF, pastry, from OHG *Wastel,* cake, bread]

waster, wastrel WASTE.

wastrel, *n.* an abandoned child, a waif; a profligate; a wasteful person. [WASTE]

†**wat**[1], *n.* an old name for the hare. [fam. for *Walter*]
wat[2], (*Sc., dial.*) WET.
wat[3], *n.* a Thai Buddhist temple or monastery.
watch, *n.* the act or state of watching; a state of alertness, vigilance, close observation or attention; vigil, look-out, waiting in a state of expectancy, dread etc.; a watchman or body of watchmen, a guard; a division of the night (among the Jews one-third, among the Romans a quarter); a small timepiece actuated by a spring or battery for carrying on the person; a period of or of keeping guard; the period of time during which each division of a ship's crew is alternately on duty (four hours except during the dog-watches of two hours by which the change from night to day duty is arranged); either half (starboard or port watch, from the position of the sailors' bunks in the forecastle) into which the officers and crew are divided, taking duty alternately; †wakefulness, being unable to sleep at night. *v.i.* to be on the watch, to be vigilant, observant or expectant; to look out (for); to act as a protector or guard (over); to keep awake at night, to keep vigil. *v.t.* to guard; to observe closely, to keep one's eye or eyes on; to observe with a view to detecting etc.; to look at, view; to tend, look after; to be careful of; to look out for, to await, to bide (one's time etc.). **on the watch,** vigilant, on the look-out. **to watch out,** to be on the look-out (for); to take care. **watch and ward,** *n.* continuous watch; orig. watch by night and day. **watch-box,** *n.* a sentry-box. **watch-case,** *n.* the case enclosing the works of a watch. **watch-chain,** *n.* a metal watch-guard or watch-strap. **Watch Committee,** *n.* local officials dealing with the policing etc. of the district. **watch-dog,** *n.* a dog kept to guard premises etc. and give notice of burglars etc.; a person or group that monitors the activities of an organization or in some sphere to guard against illegal or undesirable practices etc. **watch-fire,** *n.* a fire in a camp etc. at night or used as a signal. **watch-glass,** *n.* a glass covering the face of a watch; an hour- or half-hour-glass for measuring the period of a nautical watch; a curved disc of glass used in a laboratory to hold small samples etc. **watch-guard,** *n.* a chain, cord, ribbon etc. for securing a watch to the person. **watch-house,** *n.* a house occupied by a watch or guard; a lock-up. **watching brief,** *n.* a brief issued to a barrister instructed to watch a case on behalf of a client not directly concerned in the action. **watch-key,** *n.* a key for winding up a watch. **watchmaker,** *n.* **watchmaker's oil,** *n.* a fine thin oil for lubricating the works of watches etc. **watchmaking,** *n.* **watchman,** *n.* a guard, a sentinel, esp. a member of a body formerly employed to patrol; one who guards the streets of a town at night; a man so guarding a large building etc. **watch-night,** *n.* the last night of the year when services are held by Methodists etc. **watch-oil,** *n.* watchmaker's oil. **watch-spring,** *n.* the mainspring of a watch. **watch-strap,** *n.* a strap for securing a watch round the wrist. **watch-tower,** *n.* a tower of observation or one on which sentinels are placed. **watchword,** *n.* a word given to sentinels etc. as a signal that one has the right of admission etc., a password; a motto, word or phrase symbolizing or epitomizing the principles of a party etc. **watcher,** *n.* **watchful,** *a.* vigilant, observant, cautious, wary. **watchfully,** *adv.* **watchfulness,** *n.* [OE *wæcce,* from *wacian,* to watch, from *wacan,* to WAKE[1]]
†**watchet,** *a.* blue, pale blue. [etym. doubtful (cp. OF *watchet,* a sort of cloth)]
watchful, watchmaker etc. WATCH.
water, *n.* a colourless, transparent liquid, destitute of taste and smell, possessing a neutral reaction, a compound of two portions by weight of hydrogen with one of oxygen; (*often pl.*) a (natural) body of water, as a sea, a lake, a river; the surface of a body of water; a liquid consisting chiefly or partly of water, as various solutions or products of distillation; tears, sweat, urine or another secretion of animal bodies; (*usu. pl.*) the amniotic fluid surrounding a foetus; the transparency or lustre of a diamond, pearl etc.; a wavy lustrous finish on silk etc.; stock issued without any corresponding increase of paid-up capital. *v.t.* to apply water to, to moisten, sprinkle, dilute, adulterate, irrigate or supply with water; to furnish with water for drinking; to increase (nominal capital etc.) by the issue of stock without corresponding increase of assets; (*in p.p.*) to give an undulating sheen to the surface of (silk etc.) by moistening, pressing and heating in manufacture. *v.i.* of the mouth, eyes etc., to secrete, shed or run with water; to get or take in water; of cattle etc., to drink. **high water** HIGH. **in deep water, waters,** in difficulties, troubles or distress. **in hot water,** in trouble, difficulty or disgrace. **in smooth water,** out of one's troubles or difficulties. **low water** LOW[1]. **of the first water,** of the purest quality; of the highest excellence. **strong waters** STRONG. **table water** TABLE. **to go on the water wagon,** to refrain from alcoholic drink. **to hold water,** to be sound or valid, to stand scrutiny. **to keep one's head above water,** to avoid financial ruin. **to make, pass water** MAKE[2]. **to make one's mouth water,** to make one very desirous. **to take the waters,** to take a cure at a watering spa. **to throw cold water on** COLD. **troubled waters** TROUBLE. **water-bailiff,** *n.* a custom-house officer at a port; an officer employed to watch a river or other fishery to prevent poaching. **water-bed,** *n.* a bed with a rubber mattress filled with water. **water-beetle,** *n.* a beetle that lives in water. **water-bellows,** *n.* a valved vessel suspended mouth downwards in water for producing an air-current by alternate raising and lowering. **water-bird,** *n.* **water-biscuit,** *n.* a thin plain biscuit of flour and water. **water-blister,** *n.* a blister containing watery fluid without pus or blood. **water-boatman,** *n.* a water-bug with paddle-like hind legs. **water-borne,** *a.* conveyed by water. **water-brash,** *n.* a form of indigestion, with water eructations. **water-buffalo,** *n.* the common domesticated Asian buffalo. **water-bug,** *n.* an aquatic insect. **water bus,** *n.* a river craft carrying passengers on a regular service. **water-butt,** *n.* a large open-headed barrel for catching and preserving rain-water. **water cannon,** *n.* a device that ejects a jet of water at high pressure, used for quelling riots etc. **water-carriage,** *n.* conveyance by water. **water-cart,** *n.* a wheeled tank etc. for carrying a supply of water or for watering the streets. **water-cement,** *n.* hydraulic cement. **water-chute,** *n.* a structure with a slide down which water is kept running, for tobogganing down in a boat-like sled. **water-clock,** *n.* an instrument for measuring time by the passage of water, a clepsydra. **water-closet,** *n.* (a room containing) a toilet with a water-supply for flushing the basin and preventing the rise of sewer-gas. **water-colour,** *n.* a pigment ground up with water and mucilage instead of oil; a water-colour painting; (*often pl.*) the art of painting in water-colours. **water-colourist,** *n.* **water-cool,** *v.t.* to cool by (circulating) water. **water-cooled,** *a.* **water-cooler,** *n.* a device for cooling drinking water. **water-course,** *n.* a stream, a brook; a channel for the conveyance of water or in which a natural stream etc. flows. **water craft,** *n.* ships, vessels, boats etc. **water-crane,** *n.* a goose-neck apparatus for supplying water to a locomotive. **water-chestnut,** *n.* an Asian sedge, *Eleocharis tuberosa,* with an edible tuber; this tuber used in Chinese cooking; an aquatic plant, *Trapa natans,* with an edible nutlike fruit. **water-cress,** *n.* a creeping aquatic plant eaten as salad. **water-cure,** *n.* hydropathy. **water-diviner,** *n.* a dowser. **water-dog,** *n.* a dog accustomed to the water, esp. a water-spaniel. **water-drain,** *n.* **water-drainage,** *n.* **water-drop,** *n.* a drop of water, a tear etc. **water-engine,** *n.* an engine driven by water; an engine to raise water. **waterfall,** *n.* a steep or perpendicular descent of a river etc., a cascade, a cataract. **water-finder,** *n.* a dowser. **water-flag,** *n.* the yellow iris, *Iris pseudacorus.* **water-flea,** *n.* a minute freshwater crustacean. **water-flood,** *n.* an inundation. †**water-flowing,** *a.* streaming. **water-fly,** *n.* any fly of the genus *Perla,* the larvae of which lurk under stones in streams, a stone-fly. **water-fowl,** *n.* (*pl.* **waterfowl**) a bird that frequents rivers, lakes etc. **waterfront,** *n.* the part of a town facing or

bordering a sea, lake etc. **water-gall,** *n.* a cavity made by a rush of water; a secondary rainbow supposed to presage rain. **water-gas,** *n.* a gas obtained by the decomposition of water and treatment with carbon, used as a fuel. **water-gate,** *n.* a gate for confining or releasing water, a flood-gate; a gate giving access to a river etc. **water-gauge,** *n.* a glass instrument attached to a steam-boiler etc. for indicating the height of the water inside. **water-glass,** *n.* a tube with a glass end for enabling one to see objects under water; soluble glass, esp. as used for fixing a water-colour drawing on dry plaster; a water-clock; a viscous solution of sodium or potassium silicate in water, used in industry and as a preservative for eggs. **water-gruel,** *n.* gruel made with water instead of milk. **water-hammer,** *n.* a toy consisting of a glass tube from which the air has been exhausted, partly filled with water which strikes the end of the tube with a sharp shock when the tube is suddenly inverted; the concussion of water in a pipe when a tap is turned off or steam admitted. **water-hammering,** *n.* **water-hen,** *n.* the moor-hen. **water-hole,** *n.* a hole where water collects, a water pool. **water-ice,** *n.* a frozen confection made from water, sugar etc. **water-jacket,** *n.* a casing filled with water surrounding a part of a machine that is to be kept cool. **water-joint,** *n.* a water-tight joint. **water-jump,** *n.* a ditch, stream etc. to be jumped, esp. in a steeplechase. **water-junket,** *n.* (*dial.*) the sandpiper. **water-kelpie,** *n.* a malignant water-sprite. **water-laid,** *a.* of rope, cable-laid. **water-lens,** *n.* a magnifying lens formed by a glass-bottomed brass cell containing water. **water-level,** *n.* the level of the water in the sea etc., esp. used as datum; a levelling instrument in which water is employed instead of spirit. **water-lily,** *n.* a plant of the genus *Castalia* or *Nymphoea* with large floating leaves and white or coloured flowers. **water-line,** *n.* the line up to which the hull of a vessel is submerged in the water. **waterlogged,** *a.* of a vessel, flooded with water so as to lie like a log; esp. of ground, saturated with water. **water-main,** *n.* a main pipe in a system of water-supply. **waterman,** *n.* a boatman plying for hire on rivers etc.; a (good or bad) oarsman. **watermanship,** *n.* **watermark,** *n.* a mark indicating the level to which water rises in a well etc.; the limits of the rise and fall of the tide etc.; a translucent design stamped in paper in the process of manufacture to show the maker, size etc. *v.t.* to stamp with this. **water-meadow,** *n.* a meadow fertilized by being flooded at certain seasons from an adjoining stream. **water-melon,** *n.* a large trailing plant of the genus *Citrullus,* or its fruit. **water-meter,** *n.* a contrivance for measuring a water-supply. **water-mill,** *n.* a mill driven by the agency of water. **water-monkey,** *n.* an earthenware long-necked jar for drinking-water, used in hot countries. **water-motor,** *n.* a motor driven by water under pressure, a turbine, a waterwheel. **water-nymph,** *n.* a naiad. **water of crystallization,** *n.* the water that unites with salts in crystallization. **water on the brain,** *n.* hydrocephalus. **water-ouzel,** *n.* the dipper. **water-pillar,** *n.* an upright pillar or pipe with a revolving or swinging head, for feeding locomotives etc. with water. **water-pipe,** *n.* a pipe for conveying water. **water-pistol,** *n.* a toy pistol that shoots a jet of water. **water-plane,** *n.* the plane in which the water-line of a vessel lies; a hydro-aeroplane. **water-plant,** *n.* **water-plate,** *n.* a double plate containing hot water for keeping food warm. **water-polo,** *n.* a game like polo in which swimmers hit a ball with the hand. **water-pot,** *n.* **water-power,** *n.* the power of water employed or capable of being employed as a prime mover. **water-pox,** *n.* varicella, chicken-pox. **waterproof,** *a.* impervious to water. *n.* cloth rendered impervious to water; a waterproof coat or other garment. *v.t.* to render waterproof. **waterproofer,** *n.* **waterproofing,** *n.* **water-rail,** *n.* the common European rail, *Rallus aquaticus.* **water-ram,** *n.* a hydraulic ram. **water-rat** WATER-VOLE. **water-rate,** *n.* a rate or charge for the supply of water. **water-repellent, -resistant,** *a.* resistant but not impervious to water. †**water-rug,** *n.* a variety of dog. **water-sail,** *n.* a sail set in very light airs, below the lower studding-sail booms and next to the water. **water-seal,** *n.* a small body of water in a bend etc., used to prevent the escape of gas from a pipe etc. **watershed,** *n.* ridge or other line of separation between two river-basins or drainage-systems. **water-shoot,** *n.* a discharge pipe or trough for rain-water etc. **waterside,** *n.* the margin of a river, stream, lake or the sea. **water-ski,** *n.* a type of ski used for planing over water in water-skiing. **water-skiing,** *n.* the sport of being towed on skis at great speed by a motor-boat. **water-skin,** *n.* a bag or bottle of skin for carrying water. **water-snake,** *n.* **water-softener,** *n.* a device or chemical used to remove or chemically alter the substances that cause hardness in water. **water-soldier,** *n.* an aquatic plant, *Stratiotes aloides,* with long narrow leaves rising above the water. **water-spaniel,** *n.* a spaniel used in hunting waterfowl. **water-splash,** *n.* part of a road etc. always submerged by a crossing stream. **watersports,** *n.pl.* **waterspout,** *n.* a phenomenon which occurs during a tornado over the sea, in which water appears to be drawn up from the sea in a whirling column, sometimes connecting sea and cloud. **water-sprite,** *n.* †**water-standing,** *a.* filled with tears. **water-supply,** *n.* a system for storing and supplying water for the service of a town etc.; the amount of water stored for the use of a house, works etc. **water-table,** *n.* a projecting ledge or string-course for throwing off the water on a building. **water-tank,** *n.* **water-tiger,** *n.* the predatory larva of some water-beetles. **watertight,** *a.* so tightly fastened or fitted as to retain or not to admit water. **water-tower,** *n.* an elevated building carrying a large tank or reservoir for giving pressure to a water-supply. **water-tube,** *n.* a tube for containing water, esp. one of a series in a boiler in which water circulates exposed to the gases of combustion. **water-vapour,** *n.* water in gaseous form, esp. when evaporated below boiling temperature. **water-violet,** *n.* any plant of the aquatic genus *Hottonia.* **water-vole,** *n.* a large aquatic vole, the water-rat. **water-wagtail,** *n.* the pied wagtail. **waterway,** *n.* a navigable channel; a fairway; the thick planks along the edge of a deck in which a channel is hollowed for conducting water to the scuppers. **water-weed,** *n.* **water-wheel,** *n.* a wheel moved by water and employed to turn machinery. **water-wings,** *n.pl.* floats used in teaching swimming. **water-witch,** *n.* a dowser; one of various diving birds. **water-works,** *n.sing.* an establishment for the collection, preservation and distribution of water for use of communities, working of machinery etc.; an artificial fountain; (*euphem.*) the urinary system. **to turn on the waterworks,** (*sl.*) to cry, blubber. **water-worn,** *a.* worn away by the action of water. †**waterage,** *n.* money paid for transportation by water. **watered,** *a.* **watered capital,** *n.* an increase in the nominal value of stock without a corresponding increase in assets or paid-up capital. **watered-down,** *a.* diluted or weakened by or as by the addition of water; reduced in force, effect etc. **waterer,** *n.* **watering-hole,** *n.* a water-filled pool or hollow where animals can drink; (*coll.*) a pub, bar etc. **watering-can,** *n.* a vessel with a (perforated) nozzle for sprinkling water on plants etc. **watering-place,** *n.* a place where water may be procured for cattle etc.; a place to which people resort to drink mineral waters or for bathing, a spa, a seaside resort. **watering-trough,** *n.* a drinking-trough for horses or cattle. **waterless,** *a.* **watery,** *a.* containing much water; moist, sodden; suffused or running with water; thin, transparent or pale, like water; rainy-looking; consisting of water; tasteless, insipid, vapid. **wateriness,** *n.* [OE *wæter,* cp. Dut. *water,* G *Wasser,* Icel. *vatu,* Swed. *vatten,* also Gr. *hudōr,* L *unda,* Sansk. *udan*]

Waterford, *n.* county in Munster province, Republic of Ireland; area 1840 sq km/710 sq miles; population (1986) 91,000. The county town is Waterford. The county includes the rivers Suir and Blackwater, and the Comeragh and Monavallagh mountain ranges in the north and centre. Products include cattle, beer, whiskey, and glassware.

Watergate, *n.* US political scandal, named after the building in Washington DC that housed the Democrats' campaign headquarters in the 1972 presidential election. Five men, hired by the Republican Committee to Re-elect the President (CREEP), were caught inside the Watergate with electronic surveillance equipment. Over the next two years, investigation by the media and a Senate committee revealed that the White House was implicated in the break-in, and that there was a 'slush fund', used to finance unethical activities. In Aug. 1974, President Nixon was forced to surrender to Congress tape recordings of conversations he had held with administration officials, and these indicated his complicity in a cover-up. Nixon resigned, the only president to have left office through resignation.

Waterloo, Battle of, battle on 18 June 1815 in which the British commander Wellington defeated the French emperor Napoleon near the village of Waterloo, 13 km/8 miles S of Brussels, Belgium. Wellington had 68,000 men, of whom 24,000 were British, the remainder being German, Dutch, and Belgian, and Napoleon had 72,000. During the last stage of the battle Wellington was supported by the Prussians under Gen. Blücher. **waterloo,** *n.* a downfall, a decisive defeat.

Watling Street, *n.* a Roman road running from London to Wroxeter (*Viroconium*) near Chester, NW England.

Watson[1], *n.* **James Dewey** (1928–), US biologist whose researches on the molecular structure of DNA (the genetic code), in collaboration with Francis Crick, earned him a shared Nobel Prize 1962.

Watson[2], *n.* **John B(roadus)** (1878–1958), US psychologist, founder of behaviourism. He rejected introspection (observation by an individual of his or her own mental processes) and regarded psychology as the study of observable behaviour, within the scientific tradition.

Watson-Watt, *n.* **Robert Alexander** (1892–1973), Scottish physicist who developed a forerunner of radar.

watt, *n.* a unit of power or rate of doing work, equal to a rate of working of one joule per second or the power available when the electromotive force is one volt and the current is one ampere. **watt-hour,** *n.* a unit of (electrical) energy equal to a power of one watt operating for one hour. **watt-hour meter, wattmeter,** *n.* **wattage,** *n.* amount of power in watts. [James *Watt,* 1736–1819, Scottish engineer]

Watt, *n.* **James** (1736–1819), Scottish engineer who developed the steam engine. He made Newcomen's steam engine vastly more efficient by cooling the used steam in a condenser separate from the main cylinder.

Watteau, *n.* **Jean-Antoine** (1684–1721), French rococo painter. He developed a new category of genre painting known as the *fête galante*, scenes of a kind of aristocratic pastoral fantasy world. One of these pictures, *The Embarkation for Cythera* (1717, Louvre, Paris), won him membership of the French Academy. **Watteau,** *a.* denoting a style of bodice with a square-cut neck and short ruffled sleeves, as in the costumes in Watteau's pictures.

wattle, *n.* a hurdle of interwoven twigs or wicker-work; the fleshy lobe under the throat of the domestic fowl, turkey etc.; a barbel of a fish; one of various Australian and Tasmanian species of acacia, the bark of which is used in tanning; the national flower of Australia. *v.t.* to interweave, to interlace, to plait; to form or construct by plaiting etc. **wattle and daub,** *n.* a method of constructing walls of wicker-work covered with mud or clay. **Wattle Day,** *n.* 1 Aug., when the wattle begins to blossom, celebrated in Australia. **wattle-work,** *n.* wicker-work. **wattled,** *a.* **wattling,** *n.* [OE *watel*, hurdle, cogn. with *wœtla,* bandage]

Watts[1], *n.* **George Frederick** (1817–1904), English painter and sculptor. He painted allegorical, biblical, and classical subjects, investing his work with a solemn morality. Many of his portraits are in the National Portrait Gallery, London.

Watts[2], *n.* **Isaac** (1674–1748), English Nonconformist writer of hymns, including 'O God, our help in ages past'.

Waugh, *n.* **Evelyn (Arthur St John)** (1903–66), English novelist. He made his name with social satire, for example *Decline and Fall* (1928), *Vile Bodies* (1930), and *The Loved One* (1948). A Roman Catholic convert from 1930, he developed a serious concern with such issues in *Brideshead Revisited* (1945). *The Ordeal of Gilbert Pinfold* (1957) is largely autobiographical.

waukrife, (*Sc.*) WAKERIFE.

waul, *v.i.* to cry as a cat, to squall. [onomat.]

wave, *v.i.* to move to and fro with a sinuous or sweeping motion as a flag in the wind, to flutter, to undulate; to have an undulating shape or conformation to be wavy; to beckon or signal (to) by waving the hand, a handkerchief etc. *v.t.* to cause to move to and fro, to give an undulating motion to, to brandish; to give an undulating surface, conformation or appearance to, to make wavy; to indicate, direct or command by a waving signal. *n.* a moving ridge or long curved body of water or other liquid, esp. one formed on the surface of the sea, rising into an arch and breaking on the shore; (*poet., often pl.*) the sea, water; a disturbance of the equilibrium of a fluid medium continuously propagated from point to point without a corresponding advance of the particles in the same direction, by which motion, heat, light, sound, electricity etc. are transmitted; a single curve or cycle in such a motion; a curve or series of curves, an undulation; a waviness of the hair; a wave-like stripe or streak; the act or gesture of waving, as a signal etc.; a heightened volume or intensity of some force, influence, emotion, activity etc.; a movement like that of a wave on the sea; a widespread advance or influx; a prolonged spell of cold or esp. hot weather; a waveform; rhythmical electromagnetic disturbance propagated through space. **permanent wave** PERMANENT. **wave-band,** *n.* a range of frequencies or wave lengths which is allocated for radio transmissions of a particular type. **waveform,** *n.* (the shape of) the graph of a wave, showing the variation in a varying quantity against time. **waveguide,** *n.* a metal tube used for carrying and guiding electromagnetic waves, esp. microwaves. **wavelength,** *n.* the distance between the crests of two adjacent waves; the space intervening between corresponding points, as the maximum positive points of two successive waves. **wave-meter,** *n.* an instrument for measuring the wavelength or frequency of an electromagnetic wave. **wave mechanics,** *n.sing.* quantum mechanics based on the wave-like properties and behaviour of particles. **wave-motion,** *n.* **wave offering,** *n.* a Jewish offering presented by a horizontal motion of the hands, to right and left, forwards and backwards. **waveson,** *n.* (*Law*) goods floating on the sea after shipwreck. **wave-worn,** *a.* **waveless,** *a.* **wavelet,** *n.* **wave-like,** *a.* **wavy,** *a.* rising or swelling in waves; having alternately concave and convex outline etc., undulating. **Wavy Navy,** *n.* (*coll.*) the Royal Naval Volunteer Reserve (so called from the wavy gold bands indicating officers' rank). **wavily,** *adv.* **waviness,** *n.* [OE *wafian,* cogn. with WABBLE]

Wavell, *n.* **Archibald, 1st Earl Wavell** (1883–1950), British field marshal in World War II, appointed commander in chief Middle East, July 1939. He conducted the North African war against Italy, 1940–41, and achieved successes there as well as in Ethiopia. He was transferred as commander in chief in India Jul. 1941, and was viceroy 1943–47.

waver, *v.t.* to play or move to and fro; to flicker, to quiver; to begin to give way, to falter; to reel; to be in a state of indecision, to hesitate, to vacillate. **waverer,** *n.* **waveringly,** *adv.* **waveringness,** *n.* [freq. of WAVE, cp. Icel. *vafra*]

waveson WAVE.

wavey, *n.* the snow-goose. [N Am. Ind.]

wavily etc., **wavy** WAVE.

wax[1], *n.* a yellow, plastic, fatty substance excreted by bees and used for the cells of honeycombs, beeswax;

this purified and bleached, used for candles, modelling and pharmaceutical and other purposes; any one of various plant or animal substances that are principally esters of fatty acids or alcohols; a mineral substance, as ozocerite, composed of hydrocarbons; any one of various substances resembling beeswax, as cobbler's wax, sealing-wax etc.; cerumen; (*coll.*) a person who is compliant or easily influenced; (*coll.*) a gramophone record; (*sl.*) a rage. *a.* waxen. *v.t.* to smear, rub, polish, treat or join with wax. **waxberry,** *n.* the fruit of the wax-myrtle. **waxbill,** *n.* a small bird of the genus *Estrelda* with a bill resembling red sealing-wax in colour. **wax-chandler,** *n.* a maker or seller of wax candles. **wax-cloth,** *n.* a floor-cloth. **wax doll,** *n.* a doll with a face made of wax. *a.* having a face like this, pretty but devoid of expression. **wax-end, †waxed-end,** *n.* a cobbler's thread covered with wax and pointed with a bristle. **wax-insect,** *n.* an insect producing wax. **wax-light,** *n.* a taper, match etc. made of wax. **wax-moth,** *n.* a bee-moth. **wax-myrtle** CANDLEBERRY-MYRTLE. **wax-painting,** *n.* encaustic painting. **wax-palm,** *n.* a S American palm, *Ceroxylon andicola,* or *Copernicia cerifera,* the trunk or leaves of which yield wax. **wax-paper, waxed-paper,** *n.* paper waterproofed with wax. **waxpod bean,** *n.* a French bean with waxy, yellow pods. **wax-red,** *a.* bright red like sealing-wax. **wax-tree,** *n.* a tree yielding wax which exudes from it or is deposited by insects. **waxwing,** *n.* bird of the genus *Bombycilla,* the secondary and tertiary quills in some of which terminate in horny tips resembling pieces of red sealing-wax. **wax-work,** *n.* modelling in wax in close imitation of living persons; anatomical and other figures, models of fruit, flowers etc. in wax; (*pl.*) an exhibition of wax figures. **wax-worker,** *n.* **waxen,** *a.* made or consisting of wax; with a surface resembling wax; like wax, impressible, plastic. **waxy,** *a.* resembling wax; pliable, impressible, easily moulded; containing or covered with wax, waxen, like wax in consistency; pallid, wan; (*sl.*) angry, cross. **waxily,** *adv.* **waxiness,** *n.* [OE *weax* (cp. Dut. *was,* G *wachs,* Icel., Swed. *vax*)]

wax[2], *v.i.* to increase gradually in size and brilliance, as the illuminated portion of the moon between new and full; to become larger, to grow in numbers, strength, intensity etc.; to pass into a specified condition, to become gradually. [OE *weaxan* (cp. Dut. *wassen,* G *wachsen,* Icel. *vaxa,* also Gr. *auxanein,* Sansk. *vaksh,* L *augēre*)]

waxen, waxy etc. WAX[1].

way, *n.* a road, path, track or other place of passage; length of space passed over, distance to be traversed; the course or route followed or to be followed between two places or to reach a place; direction in which a thing or place lies or in which motion etc. takes place; direction; the method, plan or manner of doing something, or proceeding to carry out some purpose; a line or course of action; a usual or habitual mode of action or conduct, a personal peculiarity, an idiosyncrasy; one's line of business or occupation, sphere, range, scope; one's course of life; that which one wants; relation, respect, point; condition, state; room for passage or advance, ground over which one would proceed; onward movement, progress, advance, headway; esp. of a ship, motion, impetus; (*pl.*) the framework of timbers over which a ship is launched. *adv.* far, away. **by the way,** in passing, parenthetically; during the journey. **by way of,** by the route of, via; for the purpose of; as a form of, to serve as. **†come your way, ways,** come, come on. **each way,** *adv.* (*Racing*) for win and for place. **in a way,** to some degree; from one point of view. **in the family way** FAMILY. **in the way,** in a position or of a nature to obstruct or hinder. **in the way of,** so as to fall in with or obtain; as regards, by way of. **on the way,** in progress. **out of the way** OUT. **right of way** RIGHT. **the way of all flesh,** death. **to give way** GIVE[1]. **to go, take one's own way,** to follow one's own plan, to act independently. **to go one's way, ways,** to depart. **to have one's way,** to get what one wants. **to lead the way** LEAD[2]. **to make one's way,** to proceed; to prosper, esp. by one's own exertions. **to make way** MAKE[2]. **to pave the way for,** to prepare a way, plan or method of attaining some object. **to take one's way,** to set out; to go in some direction. **under way,** of a ship etc., in motion; in progress. **Way of the Cross,** a series of pictures in a church representing the successive stages of Christ's progress to Calvary; a series of devotions suited to each of these. **ways and means,** means of doing, esp. of providing money. **Committee of Ways and Means,** a committee of the House of Commons for considering proposed taxes etc. **way-back,** *n.* (*Austral.*) the inland areas of the continent; one who comes thence. **waybill,** *n.* a list of passengers in a public conveyance or of goods sent by a common carrier. **way-board,** *n.* a thin layer between strata of some thickness. **†wayfare,** *v.i.* **wayfarer,** *n.* a traveller, esp. on foot. **wayfaring,** *n.*, *a.* **wayfaring-tree,** *n.* a large shrub, *Viburnum lantana,* with white flowers and black berries, common by roadsides. **†waygoing,** *a.* going away, departing. **waylay,** *v.t.* to wait in the way of with a view to rob etc., to lie in wait for. **waylayer,** *n.* **wayleave,** *n.* a right of way over the land of another, esp. rented by a company etc. **†way-mark, -post,** *n.* a guide- or finger-post, a milestone etc. **way-out,** *a.* (*coll.*) out-of-the-ordinary, unconventional, experimental; (*sl.*) excellent. **wayside,** *n.* the side of the road. *a.* situated or growing by the wayside. **way-station,** *n.* (*N Am.*) a railway halt. **way-train,** *n.* (*N Am.*) a local train. **way-worn,** *a.* wearied with travel. **†wayless,** *a.* [OE *weg* (cp. Dut., G *Weg,* Icel. *vegr*), cogn. with WAIN, VEHICLE, VIADUCT]

†-way, -ways, *suf.* forming adverbs of position, direction, manner etc., as *always, †alway, lengthways, straightway.* [OE *weges,* gen. of prec.]

Wayne, *n.* **John ('Duke')** (1907–79), stage name of Marion Morrison, US film actor who was the archetypal western star. His films include *Stagecoach* (1939) and *True Grit* (1969, Academy Award).

wayward, *a.* perverse, wilful, freakish, capricious, obstinate. **waywardly,** *adv.* **waywardness,** *n.* [ME *weiward,* for *awaiward* (AWAY, -WARD)]

waywode, VOIVODE.

wayzgoose, wase-goose, *n.* (*pl.* **-gooses**) an annual dinner, picnic or other entertainment given to or held by the persons employed in a printing-office. [perh. *stubble-goose* (obs. *wayz,* stubble, GOOSE)]

Wb, (*abbr.*) weber.

WC, (*abbr.*) water closet; West Central.

WCC, (*abbr.*) World Council of Churches.

WD, (*abbr.*) War Department; Works Department.

we, *nom. pl. of* first (pers.) pron. the plural of I, denoting the person speaking and others associated with or represented by him or her; used by a sovereign, the editor of a newspaper, the writer of an unsigned article etc.; people in general. [OE *wē* (cp. Dut. *wij,* G *wir,* Icel. *vēr, voer,* Sansk. *vayam*)]

WEA, (*abbr.*) Workers' Educational Association.

weak, *a.* deficient in physical strength, not robust, vigorous or powerful; feeble, infirm, sickly, easily exhausted or fatigued; deficient in mental or moral strength, feeble-minded, of defective intelligence, lacking strength of will, resolution, or resisting power; yielding readily to temptation, easily led; characterized by or showing lack of resolution or will-power; deficient in strength, durability, force or efficiency; fragile, brittle, pliant; unreliable, ineffective, inefficacious; deficient in number, quantity, weight etc.; lacking in flavour, dilute; poor, inadequate, trivial; unsustained, unconvincing, controvertible; of verbs, inflected by the addition of *-ed, -d* or *-t* to the stem in forming the past tense and p.p., not by internal vowel-change; denoting the verse-ending in which the stress falls on a normally unaccented or proclitic word; showing a downward trend in price, characterized by falling prices. **†weak-built,** *a.* (*Shak.*) illfounded. **weak-eyed,** *a.* with eyes easily fatigued or not seeing well. **weak-headed,** *a.* weak in intellect. **†weak-hearted,** *a.* having little courage; spiritless. **weak interaction,** *n.* an interaction between elementary particles responsible for certain decay processes (cp *strong interaction*). **weak-kneed,** *a.* giving way easily; lacking in resolution. **weak-minded,** *a.* feeble in intelligence or in resolution. **weak-mindedness,** *n.* **weak side,** *n.* those traits of a person's character by which he or she is most easily influenced. **weak-sighted,** *a.* **weak-spirited,** *a.* timid, pusillanimous. **weaken,** *v.t.*, *v.i.* **weakener,** *n.* **weaker sex,** (*derog.* or *facet.*) *n.* women. **weakish,** *a.* **weakling,** *n.* a feeble person. **weakly,** *adv.* in a weak manner. *a.* not strong in constitution; feeble, infirm, sickly. **weakness,** *n.* the quality or state of being weak; a particular defect, failing or fault, one's weak point; lack of resisting power. [back-formation from *weaken,* OE *wœcan,* from *wāc,* weak (cp. Dut. *week,* G *weich,* Icel. *veikr*)]

weal[1], *n.* a sound, healthy or prosperous state of persons or things. **the public, general** or **common weal,** *n.* the welfare or prosperity of the community. †**wealsman,** *n.* (*Shak.*) a statesman, a demagogue. [OE *wela* (cp. G *Wohl,* Dan. *vel*), cogn. with WELL[1]]

weal[2], *n.* a ridge or raised streak made by a rod or whip on the flesh. *v.t.* to mark with weals by flogging. [OE *walu,* orig. a rod (cp. GUNWALE, CHANNEL[2]) (cp. OFris. *walu,* Icel. *völr*) cogn. with L *volvere,* Gr. *helissein,* to roll]

weald, *n.* a tract of open forest land, esp. the portion of Kent, Surrey, Sussex and Hants between the N and S Downs. **weald-clay,** *n.* the upper part of the Wealden strata, comprising beds of clay, iron-stone etc., rich in fossils. **Wealden,** *a.* pertaining to the Weald of Kent and Sussex, esp. geologically. **Wealden strata,** *n.* the series of lower Cretaceous freshwater strata between the oolite and the chalk, best displayed in the Weald. [ME *weeld, wald,* perh. var. of WOLD]

wealth, *n.* riches, large possessions of money, goods or lands, affluence; abundance, a profusion, great plenty (of); †weal, prosperity. **wealthy,** *a.* rich, affluent, having many possessions. **wealthily,** *adv.* **wealthiness,** *n.* [WEAL[1], -TH (cp. Dut. *weelde,* luxury, OHG *Welida,* riches)]

wean, *v.t.* to accustom (a child or animal) to nourishment other than mother's milk, to teach to feed other than from the breast; to detach or estrange from a habit, indulgence, desire etc. *n.*, (*Sc.*) a child; a weanling. **to be weaned on,** to be familiar, grow up with from an early age. **weaner,** *n.* a young animal newly weaned. **weanling,** *n.* a child or animal newly weaned; *a.* newly weaned. [OE *wenian,* to accustom (cp. Dut. *wennen,* G *gewöhnen,* Dan. *vœnne*), cogn. with WONT]

weapon, *n.* an instrument of offence or defence, a thing used to inflict bodily harm; any means used for attack or defence; a claw, sting, thorn, prickle etc. †**weapon-salve,** *n.* a salve supposed to cure a wound by being applied to the weapon. **weapon-schaw,** WAPINSHAW. †**weapon-smith,** *n.* **weaponed,** *a.* **weaponless,** *a.* **weaponry,** *n.* weapons collectively. [OE *wœpen* (cp. Dut. *wapen,* G *Wappe,* Icel. *vāpn*)]

Wear, *n.* river in NE England; length 107 km/67 miles. From its source in the Pennines it flows E past Durham to meet the North Sea at Sunderland.

wear[1], *v.t.* (*past* **wore,** *p.p.* **worn**) to carry on the person, to have on as clothing or ornament; to be dressed in, esp. habitually; to arrange (hair or clothes) in a specified manner; to bear, to carry, to maintain, to exhibit, to display; to consume, diminish, waste, impair, efface or alter by rubbing or use; to exhaust, fatigue or weary; to produce (a hole, channel etc.) by attrition; (*coll.*) to stand for, to tolerate, accept. *v.i.* to be consumed, diminished, effaced, altered etc. by rubbing or use; to be exhausted, to be tired (out); to stand continual use (well, badly etc.); to become by use, age, attrition etc.; to resist the effects of use, age, attrition etc., to endure, to last; to pass gradually (away etc.). *n.* the act of wearing; the state of being worn; that which is worn or to be worn, clothing; damage or diminution by attrition, use etc.; durability, fitness for use. **to wear down,** to overcome gradually by persistent pressure. **to wear off,** to remove, efface or diminish, or to be effaced or diminished by attrition, to rub off; to decline or pass away gradually. **to wear out,** to use until no longer of use, to consume, waste or render worthless by use; to exhaust, to tire out; to be used up, consumed or gradually wasted by attrition and use. **to wear the breeches** BREECH. **wear and tear,** *n.* waste, diminution or injury caused by ordinary use. **wearable,** *a.* **wearability,** *n.* **wearer,** *n.* **wearing,** *n.*, *a.* [OE *werian* (cp. Icel. *verja,* OHG *werian,* Goth. *wasjan*), cogn. with L *vestis,* Gr. *esthēs,* clothes, Sansk. *vas,* to dress]

wear[2], *v.t.* (*past, p.p.* **wore**) to bring (a ship) about tack by putting the helm up. *v.i.* of a ship, to come round thus. [var. of VEER]

wear[3], WEIR.

weary, *a.* tired, fatigued, exhausted; expressing weariness or exhaustion; dispirited, impatient or sick (of); tiresome, tedious, exhausting, irksome. *v.t.* to tire, to fatigue; to make weary or impatient (of). *v.i.* to become tired or fatigued; to become weary (of); (*Sc.*) to long, to be wistful, to yearn. †**weariful,** *a.* **wearifully,** *adv.* **weariless,** *a.* **wearily,** *adv.* **weariness,** *n.* **wearisome,** *a.* tedious, tiresome, causing weariness. **wearisomely,** *adv.* **wearisomeness,** *n.* [OE *wērig* (cp. OHG *wuorag,* drunk), rel. to *wōrian,* to travel]

†**weasand,** *n.* the windpipe. [OE *wāsend* (cp. MHG *Weisent,*) etym. doubtful)]

weasel, *n.* a small British reddish-brown, white-bellied quadruped related to the stoat, ferret etc., with a long lithe body and short legs, preying on small birds, mice etc. *v.i.* (*past, p.p.* **weaselled**) (*coll.*) to evade or extricate oneself from a responsibility, obligation etc.; (*chiefly N Am. coll.*) to equivocate. **weasel-faced,** *a.* having a sharp, thin face. **weasel word,** *n.* a word designed to mislead or to be evasive. [OE *wesle* (cp. Dut. *wezel,* G *Wiesel,* Icel. *vīsla,* also Gr. *ailouros*)]

†**weasen** WIZEN.

weather, *n.* the state of the atmosphere with reference to cold or heat, humidity, rain, pressure, wind, electrical conditions etc., esp. the state of the sky at any given time with reference to clouds and rain; (*usu. pl.*) change, vicissitude. *v.t.* to encounter and pass through (storms or bad weather) in safety; to endure and come through in safety; (*Naut.*) to get to windward of (a cape etc.) in spite of inclement weather; to expose to the action of the weather; (*usu. p.p.*) to wear, disintegrate or discolour (rock, cliffs, masonry etc.) by this; to slope (tiles etc.) down so as to overlap. *v.i.* to stand the effects of weather; to disintegrate or discolour by exposure to weather. *a.* situated towards the wind; windward. **stress of weather,** *n.* storms, winds etc. †**to make fair weather,** (*Shak.*) to flatter, to conciliate. **to make good, bad weather,** of a vessel, to behave well or ill in a storm. **to make heavy weather of,** to exaggerate the difficulty of doing something. **under the weather,** poorly, unwell. **weather-beaten,** †**-bitten,** *a.* seasoned, tanned by exposure to weather, storms etc. **weather-board,** *v.t.* to furnish with weather-boarding. *n.* a board used for weather-boarding. **weather-boarding,** *n.* boards fastened together so as to overlap and to throw off rain, snow etc. from roofs, walls etc. **weather-bound,** *a.* detained by bad weather. **weather-box, -house,** *n.* a toy weather-indicator worked by the effect of hygroscopic conditions on a string, the figures of a man and woman emerging at the sides of a toy house indicating wet or dry weather respectively. **weather-bureau,** *n.* a meteorological department or office. **weather-chart, -map,** *n.* a chart of a wide area showing isobars and other symbols indicating the state of the weather in different parts. **weathercock,** *n.* a revolving vane, often in the shape of a cock, mounted on the top of a steeple or other high point to show the direction of the wind; an inconstant person. **weather-contact, -cross,** *n.* a leakage from one telephone or telegraph wire to another owing to wet weather. **weather-eye,** *n.* the eye that looks at the sky to forecast the weather. **to keep one's weather-eye open,** (*coll.*) to be on the alert; to have one's wits about one. †**weather-fend,** *v.t.* to shelter from the weather. **weather-gauge**

GAUGE. **weather-glass,** *n.* a barometer. **weather-house** WEATHER-BOX. **weatherman,** *n.* a person who forecasts and reports on the weather, a meteorologist. **weather-map** WEATHER-CHART. **weather-moulding,** *n.* a dripstone or hood-moulding over a door, window etc. to throw off the rain. **weatherproof,** *a.* proof against the weather. **weather-prophet,** *n.* one who foretells the weather. **weather-report,** *n.* an official daily report of meteorological observations and probable changes in the weather. **weather-service,** *n.* a department or organization carrying out meteorological observations. **weather-ship,** *n.* a ship engaged on meteorological work. **weather-stain,** *n.* discoloration by exposure to the atmosphere. **weather-stained,** *a.* **weather-station,** *n.* a place where meteorological observations are taken or recorded. **weather-strip,** *n.* a piece of board, rubber or the like fastened across a door, window etc. to keep out draught. **weather-tiling,** *n.* tiles hung on outside walls to protect against damp. **weather-vane** WEATHER-COCK. **weather window,** *n.* a limited period of time when the weather conditions are suitable for a particular activity or project. **weather-wise,** *a.* skilful in forecasting the weather. **weathering,** *n.* an inclination for throwing off rain etc.; disintegration etc. through exposure to the weather. **weatherize, -ise,** *v.t.* to make a fabric waterproof. **weatherly,** *a.* of a ship, presenting such lateral resistance to the water as to make little leeway. **weatherliness,** *n.* **weathermost,** *a.* farthest to windward. [OE *weder* (cp. Dut. *weder,* G *Wetter,* Icel. *vethr*), cogn. with Goth. *waian,* Sansk. *va,* Gr. *aēnai,* to blow, Eng. WIND[1]]

weave, *v.t.* (*past* **wove,** *p.p.* **woven, wove**) to form (threads, yarns etc.) into a fabric by interlacing; to produce (cloth or a cloth article) thus; to construct by intertwining canes, rushes etc.; of a spider, to form (a web); to interweave (facts, details etc.) into a story, theory etc.; to construct (a scheme, plot etc.) thus. *v.i.* to make fabrics by interlacing threads etc.; to work at a loom; †to become woven or interlaced. **to get weaving** GET. **weavable,** *a.* **weaver,** *n.* one who weaves, esp. one whose occupation is to weave cloth etc.; a weaver-bird. **weaver-bird,** *n.* a finch-like bird, esp. of the family Ploceidae, of the warmer parts of Asia, Africa and Australia, that constructs elaborate nests of woven grass. [OE *wefan* (cp. Dut. *weven,* G *weben,* Icel. *vefa*), cogn. with Gr. *huphainein*]

web, *n.* a woven fabric, a piece of woven cloth; a cobweb or a similar structure woven by caterpillars etc.; an artfully contrived plot etc.; a large roll of paper for printing etc. as it comes from the mill; connective tissue; the membrane between the toes of swimming-birds etc.; the vane of a feather; the thin part of the plate in a girder connecting the upper and lower plates; the part of a railway-carriage wheel between the nave and rim; the blade of a saw etc. *v.t.* (*past, p.p.* **webbed**) to connect, furnish or cover with or as with a web. **web-eye,** *n.* a disease of the eye caused by a film. **web-eyed,** *a.* **web-fingered, -footed, -toed,** *a.* **web-fingers, -feet, -toes,** *n.pl.* those with the digits connected by a web. **web offset,** *n.* offset printing using a continuous roll of paper. **web-worm,** *n.* the gregarious larva of an insect weaving a web or tent as a shelter. **webbed,** *a.* **webbing,** *n.* a strong woven band of fibre etc., used for girths, the bottoms of seats, beds etc.; any strong woven tape or edging; a woven structure. **webby,** *a.* †**webster,** *n.* a weaver. [OE *webb.* (cp. Dut. *web,* G *Gewebe,* Icel. *vefr*), from *wefan,* to WEAVE)]

Webb[1], *n.* **(Martha) Beatrice** (born Potter) (1858–1943) and **Sidney (James), Baron Passfield** (1859–1947), English social reformers, writers, and founders of the London School of Economics 1895. They argued for social insurance in their minority report (1909) of the Poor Law Commission, and wrote many influential books, including *The History of Trade Unionism* (1894), *English Local Government* (1906), and *Soviet Communism* (1935). Sidney Webb was professor of public administration at the LSE 1912–27. He was a member of the Labour Party executive 1915–25, entered Parliament 1922, and was president of the Board of Trade 1924, dominions secretary 1929–30, and colonial secretary 1929–31. He received a peerage 1929. Beatrice also wrote *The Co-operative Movement in Great Britain* (1891), *My Apprenticeship* (1926), and *Our Partnership* (1948). They were early members of the Fabian Society, and were married 1892.

Webb[2], *n.* **Philip (Speakman)** (1831–1915), English architect. He mostly designed private houses, including the Red House, Bexley Heath, Sussex, for William Morris, and was one of the leading figures, with Richard Norman Shaw and C. F. A. Voysey, in the revival of domestic English architecture in the late 19th cent.

Webber, Andrew Lloyd LLOYD WEBBER.

weber, *n.* a unit of magnetic flux. [Wilhelm *Weber,* see WEBER[3]]

Weber[1], *n.* **Carl Maria Friedrich Ernst von** (1786–1826), German composer who established the Romantic school of opera with *Der Freischütz* (1821) and *Euryanthe* (1823). He was *Kapellmeister* at Breslau 1804–06, Prague 1813–16, and Dresden 1816. He died during a visit to London where he produced his opera *Oberon* (1826), written for the Covent Garden theatre.

Weber[2], *n.* **Max** (1864–1920), German sociologist, one of the founders of modern sociology. He emphasized cultural and political factors as key influences on economic development and individual behaviour.

Weber[3], *n.* **Wilhelm Eduard** (1804–91), German physicist, who studied magnetism and electricity. Working with Karl Gauss, he made sensitive magnetometers to measure magnetic fields, and instruments to measure direct and alternating currents. He also built an electric telegraph. The SI unit of magnetic flux, the weber, is named after him.

Webern, *n.* **Anton (Friedrich Wilhelm von)** (1883–1945), Austrian composer. A pupil of Schoenberg, whose 12-tone technique he adopted. He wrote works of extreme brevity; for example, the oratorio *Das Augenlicht* (1935), and songs to words by Stefan George and poems of Rilke.

Webster[1], *n.* **Daniel** (1782–1852), US politician and orator, born in New Hampshire. He sat in the House of Representatives from 1813 and in the Senate from 1827, at first as a Federalist and later as a Whig. He was secretary of state 1841–43 and 1850–52, and negotiated the Ashburton Treaty 1842, which fixed the Maine–Canada boundary. His celebrated 'seventh of March' speech in the Senate in 1850 helped secure a compromise on the slavery issue.

Webster[2], *n.* **John** (*c.* 1580–1634), English dramatist, who ranks after Shakespeare as the greatest tragedian of his time and is the Jacobean whose plays are most frequently performed today. His two great plays *The White Devil* (1608) and *The Duchess of Malfi* (1614) are dark, violent tragedies obsessed with death and decay and infused with poetic brilliance.

Webster[3], *n.* **Noah** (1758–1843), US lexicographer, whose books on grammar and spelling and *American Dictionary of the English Language* (1828) standardized US English.

wed, *v.t.* (*past,* **wedded,** *p.p.* **wedded, wed**) to marry; to give in marriage; to unite, to attach firmly; †to espouse; to take part with. *v.i.* to marry. †*n.* a pledge, a security. **wedded,** *a.* married, pertaining to matrimony; intimately united; strongly attached (to). **wedding,** *n.* a marriage ceremony, usu. with the accompanying festivities. **penny-wedding** PENNY. **silver wedding, golden wedding, diamond wedding,** the 25th, 20th or 60th anniversaries of a wedding. **wedding-breakfast,** *n.* a celebratory meal given after a wedding ceremony. **wedding-cake,** *n.* an iced cake distributed to the guests at a wedding, portions being afterwards sent to absent friends. **wedding-card,** *n., a.* (*pl.*) cards bearing the names of a newly-married couple sent to friends to announce the wedding. **wedding-day,** *n.* the day of a marriage or its anniversary. **wedding-favour,** *n.* a knot of white ribbons or a rosette worn at a wedding. **wedding-garment,** *n.* a garment for wearing at a wedding; something entitling one to participation etc. **wedding-ring,** *n.* a plain ring given by one partner to the other, esp. by the bridegroom to the bride, during the marriage ceremony, and worn thereafter. [OE *weddian* (cp. Dut. *wedden,* G *wetten,* Icel. *vethja,* to wager), cogn. with WAGE, WAGER, GAGE[1]]

Wed., (*abbr.*) Wednesday.

Weddell Sea, *n.* an arm of the S Atlantic Ocean that cuts into the Antarctic continent SE of Cape Horn; area 8,000,000 sq km/3,000,000 sq miles. Much of it is covered with thick pack ice for most of the year. It is named after the British explorer James Weddell.

Wedekind, *n.* **Frank** (1864–1918), German dramatist. He was a forerunner of expressionism with *Frühlings Erwachen/The Awakening of Spring* (1891), and *Der Erdgeist/The Earth Spirit* (1895) and its sequel *Der Marquis von Keith. Die Büchse der Pandora/Pandora's Box* (1904) was the source for Berg's opera *Lulu*.

wedge, *n.* a piece of wood or metal thick at one end and tapering to a thin edge at the other, used for splitting wood, rocks etc., for exerting great pressure, raising great weights etc., forming one of the mechanical powers; an object or portion of anything in the shape of a wedge; a shoe without an instep, having the heel and sole together forming a wedge; something that causes a separation or divide. *v.t.* to cleave or split with or as with a wedge; to crowd or push (in), as a wedge forces its way; to fix or fasten with a wedge or wedges. **the thin end of the wedge,** a first step, measure or change likely to have important ulterior results. **wedge-shaped,** *a.* **wedgewise,** *adv.* **wedge-tailed,** *a.* of a bird, having a wedge-shaped tail owing to the greater length of the middle feathers. [OE *wecg* (cp. Dut. *wig,* G *Wecke,* Icel. *veggr*)]

Wedgwood®, *n.* a type of fine pottery, made by Josiah Wedgwood (1730–95) and his successors, often bearing a white cameo-like design in relief. **Wedgwood blue,** *n.* a light greyish-blue.

Wedgwood, *n.* **Josiah** (1730–95), English pottery manufacturer. He set up business in Burslem, Staffordshire, in the early 1760s, to produce his unglazed blue or green stoneware decorated with white neo-classical designs, using pigments of his own invention.

wedlock, *n.* matrimony, the married state. [OE *wedlāk* (WED, pledge, *lāc,* sport, gift)]

Wednesday, *n.* the fourth day of the week. [OE *Wōdnes dœg,* Woden's or Odin's day]

wee[1], *a.* (*Sc.*) very small, tiny, little. **Wee Frees,** *n.pl.* (*Sc.*) a section of the Free Church that would not join the United Free Church in 1900. [ME, a bit, prob. var. of WAY]

wee[2], WEE-WEE.

weed, *n.* a useless or troublesome plant in cultivated land, a plant springing up where not wanted in a garden etc.; any useless or troublesome intrusive thing; a leggy, loose-bodied horse; (*coll.*) a cigar; (*coll.*) a weak or weedy person. *v.t.* to clear (ground) of weeds; to pull up (a noxious or intrusive plant); to clear of anything hurtful or offensive; to sort (out) (useless or inferior elements, members etc.); to rid of these. *v.i.* to pull up weeds from a garden etc. **the weed,** *n.* tobacco. **weeder,** *n.* one who weeds; a weeding-tool. **weed-grown,** *a.* overgrown with weeds. **weed-killer,** *n.* a chemical or other production (usu. poisonous) for destroying weeds. **weedicide,** *n.* a chemical weed-killer. **weediness,** *n.* **weeding-chisel, -fork, -hook, -tongs,** *n.* a tool used in weeding. **weedy,** *a.* containing weeds; (*coll.*) thin, weak, lacking stamina. [OE *wēod, wīod* (cp. LG *wēden,* to weed), etym. doubtful]

weeds, *n.pl.* mourning worn by a widow. [OE *wœde,* garment, cp. OFris. *wēde,* Icel. *vāth,* OHG *wāt, wōt*]

week, *n.* a period of seven days, esp. from Sunday to Saturday inclusively; the five or six working days, excluding Sunday, or Saturday and Sunday. **a week of Sundays,** (*coll.*) seven weeks; a long time. **today, tomorrow, yesterday week,** the day later or earlier by a week than the one specified. **weekday,** *n.* any day of the week except Sunday and usu. also Saturday. **weekend,** *n.* the days ending one and beginning the following week (usu. Saturday, Sunday), as a time for holiday etc. *v.i.* to make a holiday etc., on these. **weekender,** *n.* **week-night,** *n.* a night of a weekday. **weekly,** *a.* happening, issued or done once a week or every week; lasting a week; pertaining to or reckoned by the week. *adv.* once a week; week by week. *n.* a weekly periodical. [OE *wice, wuce* (cp. Dut. *week,* Icel. *vika,* OHG *Wecha*), etym. doubtful]

†**weel[1],** †**weely,** *n.* a fish-trap made of twigs or rushes; a heraldic bearing representing this. [etym. doubtful]

weel[2], (*Sc.*) WELL[1].

weem, *n.* a subterranean chamber, dwelling or passage, usu. lined with rough stones. [cp. Gael. *uamh, uamha,* cave]

†**ween,** *v.i.* to be of opinion; to think, to fancy. [OE *wēnan* (cp. Dut. *wanen,* G *wähnen,* Icel. *vāna,* to hope)]

weeny, *a.* (*coll.*) very small, tiny. **weenybopper,** *n.* a pre-adolescent fan of pop music and pop stars. [WEE[1] and *tiny*]

weep, *v.i.* (*past, p.p.* **wept**) to shed tears; to lament, mourn (for); to let fall or to be emitted; to drip, to exude, to run or be suffused with drops of moisture; (*usu. pres.p.*) to have pendulous branches. *v.t.* to shed tears over; to lament, to bewail; to shed (tears); to exude. **weeper,** *n.* one who or that which weeps; a hired mourner; a widow's white cuff or black crape veil or a man's sash-like hatband worn as a token of mourning. **weeping-ash, -birch, -willow,** *n.* an ash, birch or willow with delicate pendulous branches. **weepy,** *a.* [OE *wēpan* (OS *wōpian,* OHG *wuofan*), from *wōp,* an outcry]

†**weet,** †**weetingly** WIT[1].

weever, *n.* either of two British fishes, *Trachinus draco,* the greater and *T. vipera,* the lesser weever, inflicting painful wounds with their dorsal and opercular spines. [ME *wivere,* WYVERN]

weevil, *n.* a small beetle with the head prolonged into a rostrum or proboscis, feeding on grain, nuts, roots, leaves etc., esp. one infesting corn, a curculio. **weevilled, weevilly,** *a.* [OE *wifel* (cp. Dut. *wevel,* G *Wiebel*), cogn. with WEAVE[1]]

wee-wee, *v.i.* a child's word for urinate. *n.* an act of urinating; urine. [onom.]

weft, *n.* the threads passing through the warp from selvedge to selvedge, the woof; a web. †**weftage,** *n.* [OE, from *wefan,* to WEAVE[1]]

Wegener, *n.* **Alfred Lothar** (1880–1930), German meteorologist and geophysicist, whose theory of continental drift, expounded in *Origin of Continents and Oceans* (1915), was originally known as Wegener's hypothesis. His ideas can now be explained in terms of plate tectonics.

weigh, *v.t.* to find the weight of by means of a balance etc.; to be equivalent to in weight; to weigh out (a particular amount); to ponder, to consider carefully, to estimate the relative value or advantages of; to raise (an anchor). *v.i.* to have a specified weight; to be weighed, to ascertain one's weight; to be considered as important, to have weight or influence; to be burdensome or oppressive (on or upon); (*Naut.*) to weigh anchor, to start on a voyage. *n.* the act or process of weighing. **to weigh anchor** ANCHOR. **to weigh down,** to cause to sink by weight, to force down; to oppress. **to weigh in,** of a jockey, to be weighed before a race; (*coll.*) to intervene. **to weigh out,** to take (a particular weight of something) from a quantity; to distribute or apportion in quantities measured by scales; of a jockey, to be weighed after a race; (*sl.*) to pay (money) out. **under weigh** WAY. **weigh-beam,** *n.* a portable steelyard suspended in a frame. **weighbridge,** *n.* a machine with an iron platform, on which lorries etc. are weighed. **weigh-house,** *n.* a public building at which goods are weighed. **weighable,** *a.* **weighage,** *n.* a duty paid for weighing goods. **weigher,** *n.* **weighing-cage,** *n.* a cage in which live animals may be weighed. **weighing-machine,** *n.* a machine for weighing loaded vehicles, cattle, bales, persons etc. [OE *we-*

gan, to carry (cp. Dut. *wegen,* to weigh, G *wegen,* to move, *wägen,* to weigh, Icel. *vega,* to move, to weigh, also Sansk *vah,* L *vehere,* see VEHICLE)]

weight, *n.* the force with which bodies tend towards a centre of attraction, esp. the centre of the earth, the downward tendency caused by gravity less the centrifugal tendency due to the earth's rotation; the relative mass or quantity of matter contained in a body, heaviness, ponderosity, esp. as expressed in terms of some standard unit; the standard amount that something or someone, as a boxer, should weigh; a scale or graduated system of units of weight; a unit of weight used in such a system; a piece of metal etc. of known weight used with scales for weighing goods etc.; a heavy object or mass used for mechanical purposes, as in a clock, or for weight-training etc.; a heavy load, a burden; pressure, oppressiveness; importance, consequence, impressiveness, efficacy, preponderance; a value given to an item in a frequency distribution to represent its relative importance. *v.t.* to attach a weight or weights to; to add weight to; to burden; to treat with minerals etc., to load, to adulterate; to assign a statistical weight to; to bias. **to pull one's weight,** to take one's due share of work or responsibility. **weight (allowance),** *n.* an allowance paid in addition to basic salary to offset the higher living costs of a particular area. **weight-lifter,** *n.* **weight-lifting,** *n.* the sport of lifting barbells of increasing weight using standard lifting techniques. **weight-training,** *n.* physical training using weights to strengthen and tone muscles. **weight-watcher,** *n.* a person who is attempting to lose weight by dieting. **weight-watching,** *n.* **weightless,** *a.* **weightlessness,** *n.* the condition of having no apparent weight which exists when there are no forces opposing gravity, as in an orbiting spacecraft. **weighty,** *a.* having great weight, heavy, ponderous; important, serious, momentous; convincing, cogent, influential. **weightily,** *adv.* **weightiness,** *n.* [OE *gewiht,* as prec.]

Weil, *n.* **Simone** (1909–43), French writer, who became a practising Catholic after a mystical experience in 1938. Apart from essays, her works (advocating political passivity) were posthumously published, including *Waiting for God* (1951), *The Need for Roots* (1952), and *Notebooks* (1956).

Weill, *n.* **Kurt (Julian)** (1900–50), German composer, US citizen from 1943. He wrote chamber and orchestral music and collaborated with Brecht on operas such as *Die Dreigroschenoper/The Threepenny Opera* (1928) and *Aufsteig und Fall der Stadt Mahagonny/The Rise and Fall of the City of Mahagonny* (1930), all attacking social corruption (*Mahagonny* caused a riot at its premiere in Leipzig). He tried to evolve a new form of music theatre, using subjects with a contemporary relevance and the simplest musical means. In 1935 he left Germany for the US, where he wrote a number of successful scores for Broadway, among them the antiwar musical *Johnny Johnson* (1936, including the often covered 'September Song') and *Street Scene* (1947) based on an Elmer Rice play of the Depression.

Weil's disease, *n.* an infectious disease of animals (also known as leptospirosis) which is occasionally transmitted to human beings, usually by contact with water contaminated by rat urine. It is characterized by acute fever, and infection may spread to the liver, kidneys, and heart.

Weimar Republic, *n.* the constitutional republic in Germany 1919–33, which was crippled by the election of antidemocratic parties to the Reichstag, and then subverted by the Nazi leader Hitler after his appointment as Chancellor in 1933. It took its name from the city where in Feb. 1919 a constituent assembly met to draw up a democratic constitution.

Weinberger, *n.* **Caspar (Willard)** (1917–), US Republican politician. He served under presidents Nixon and Ford, and was Reagan's defence secretary 1981–87.

weir, *n.* a dam across a stream for raising the level of the water above it; a fence or enclosure of stakes, nets etc. set in a stream to catch fish. [OE *wer,* cogn. with *werian,* to defend]

Weir, *n.* **Peter** (1938–), Australian film director. His films have an atmospheric quality and often contain a strong spiritual element. They include *Picnic at Hanging Rock* (1975), *Witness* (1985), and *Mosquito Coast* (1986).

weird, *n.* (*chiefly Sc.*) fate, destiny; (*pl.*) the Fates. *a.* pertaining to fate or destiny; supernatural, unearthly, uncanny; strange, peculiar. **Weird Sisters,** *n.pl.* the Fates. **weirdly,** *adv.* **weirdness,** *n.* **weirdo, weirdie,** *n.* (*pl.* **-dos, -dies**) (*coll.*) a strange or eccentric person. [OE *wyrd,* from *weorthan,* to be, to become]

Weismann, *n.* **August** (1834–1914), German biologist. His failing eyesight forced him to turn from microscopy to theoretic work, proposing in 1892 that changes to the body do not in turn cause an alteration of the genetic material. **Weismannism,** *n.* (*Biol.*) the doctrines of August Weismann with regard to the continuity of the germ-plasm, and the impossibility of transmitting acquired characters.

Weismuller, *n.* **'Johnny' (Peter John)** (1904–84), US film actor, formerly an Olympic swimmer, who played Tarzan in a long-running series of films for MGM and RKO including *Tarzan the Ape Man* (1932), *Tarzan and His Mate* (1934), and *Tarzan and the Leopard Woman* (1946).

Weizmann, *n.* **Chaim** (1874–1952), Zionist leader (president of Israel 1948–52) and chemist, born in Russia. He became a naturalized British subject, and as director of the Admiralty laboratories 1916–19 discovered a process for manufacturing acetone, a solvent. He conducted the negotiations leading up to the Balfour Declaration. He was head of the Hebrew University in Jerusalem, and in 1948 became the first president of the new republic of Israel.

Weizsäcker, *n.* **Richard Freiherr Baron von** (1920–), West German Christian Democrat politician, president from 1984. He began his career as a lawyer and was also active in the German Protestant church and in Christian Democratic Union (CDU) party politics. He was elected to the Bundestag in 1969 and served as mayor of West Berlin from 1981, before being elected federal president in 1984.

weka, *n.* the New Zealand woodhen. [Maori]

welch[1], *n., a.* Welsh; spelling used for Welch Fusiliers, Welch Regiment. [WELSH[1]]

welch[2], WELSH[2].

Welch, *n.* **Raquel** (1940–), stage name of Raquel Tejada, US actress, a sex symbol of the 1960s in such films as *One Million Years* BC (1966), *Myra Breckinridge* (1970), and *The Three Musketeers* (1973).

welcome, *a.* admitted or received with pleasure and cordiality (often used ellipt. as an int. addressed to a guest etc.); producing satisfaction or gladness; gladly permitted (to do etc.). *n.* a salutation or saying of 'welcome' to a newcomer; a kind or cordial reception or entertainment of a guest etc.; a willing acceptance of an offer etc. *v.t.* to greet cordially; to receive or entertain with kindness or cordiality; to receive (news etc.) with pleasure; to greet or receive in a particular way. **to outstay, overstay one's welcome,** to stay too long. **a warm welcome,** a hearty reception, or (more generally) a very hostile one. **welcomeness,** *n.* **welcomer,** *n.* [OE *wilcuma* (*willa,* pleasure, *cuma,* comer, assim. to WELL[1], and COME)]

weld[1], *n.* dyer's-weed, *Reseda luteola,* a branched mignonette from which luteolin, a yellow dye-stuff, was formerly prepared. [prob. cogn. with WOLD]

weld[2], *v.t.* to unite or join (pieces of metal) together by heat or by compressing, esp. after they have been softened by heat; to unite (pieces of plastic) similarly; to make, produce or repair thus; to unite into a coherent mass, body etc. *v.i.* to unite (well or ill) by this process. *n.* a joint or junction made by welding. **weldable,** *a.* **weldability,** *n.* **welder,** *n.* [var. of WELL[2], to boil up]

Welensky, *n.* **Roy** (1907–), Rhodesian right-wing politician. He was instrumental in the creation of a federation of N and S Rhodesia and Nyasaland in 1953 and was prime minister 1956–63. His Federal Party was defeated by Ian Smith's Rhodesian Front in 1964.

welfare, *n.* prosperity, success; health, well-being; welfare work; financial and other aid given to those in need. **Welfare State,** *n.* (a state operating) a system in which the government promotes and assumes responsibility for the general welfare, usu. by introducing social security measures. **welfare work,** *n.* efforts to improve living conditions for the very poor, elderly etc. **welfare worker,** *n.* [WELL[1], FARE]

†**welk,** *v.t.* to fade, to wither. [Dut., G *welken,* from OHG *welk,* moist]

welkin, *n.* (*poet.*) the sky, the vault of heaven. [OE *wolcnu,* pl. of *wolcen,* cloud (cp. G *wolke,* OHG *wolka,* cloud), perh. cogn. with WALK, or with prec.]

well[1], *adv.* (*comp.* **better**, *superl.* **best**) in a good or right manner, properly, satisfactorily; happily, fortunately; skilfully; prosperously, successfully; adequately, fully, perfectly, thoroughly, abundantly, amply, sufficiently; closely, intimately; to a considerable extent; heartily, cordially, gratifyingly; with kindness, with approval, on good terms; justly, fairly, reasonably, wisely, befittingly; very possibly, indeed. *a.* (*pred. only*) in good health; in a satisfactory state, position or circumstances; sensible, advisable; fortunate. *n.* that which is well. *int.* expressing astonishment, expectation, resignation, concession etc.; often used as an expletive in resuming one's discourse. **as well,** in addition; equally, as much (as), not less than; just as reasonably, with no worse results; proper, right, not unadvisable (to). **well away,** making rapid progress; (*coll.*) drunk. **well done,** an expression of congratulation. **well-acquainted,** *a.* **well-advised,** *a.* prudent, judicious, wise. †**well-apparelled,** *a.* **well-appointed,** *a.* fully armed, furnished or equipped. **well-balanced,** *a.* sensible, sane. **well-behaved,** *a.* **well-being,** *n.* welfare. †**well-beseen,** *a.* comely, of good appearance. **well-born,** *a.* of good birth. **well-bred,** *a.* of good breeding or manners; of good or pure stock. **well-built,** *a.* sturdy, robust, muscular. **well chosen,** *n.* selected with judgment. **well-conditioned,** *a.* of good temper; in good condition. **well-conducted,** *a.* well-behaved. **well-connected,** *a.* related to good families. *a.* **well-developed,** *a.* **well-disposed,** *a.* of favourable and kindly feeling (to or towards). **well done,** *a.* of food, cooked thoroughly. **well-dressed,** *a.* **well earned,** *a.* **well enough** ENOUGH. **well-favoured,** *a.* handsome, good-looking. **well-fed,** *a.* **well-found,** *a.* well-appointed. **well-founded,** *a.* based on certain or well-authenticated grounds. **well-graced,** *a.* in favour, popular. **well-groomed,** *a.* neat and elegant in dress and appearance. **well-grounded,** *a.* well-founded; having all the basic knowledge of a subject etc. **well-heeled,** *a.* wealthy. **well-informed,** *a.* having ample information; having a knowledge of numerous subjects. **well-intentioned,** *a.* having good intentions (usu. with alln. to unsatisfactory results). **well-judged,** *a.* skilfully, tactfully or accurately done, aimed, contrived etc. **well-knit,** *a.* esp. of a person's body, compact, firmly built. **well known,** *a.* known to many people, familiar, notorious. **well-liked,** *a.* †**well-liking,** *a.* good-conditioned, plump. **well-looking,** *a.* of pleasing appearance. **well-mannered,** *a.* well-bred, polite. **well-meaning,** *a.* having good intentions. **well-meant,** *a.* well-intentioned. **well met,** *int.* hail! welcome! **well-nigh,** *adv.* almost, nearly. **well off,** *a.* in good circumstances, prosperous. **well-oiled,** *a.* (*sl.*) drunk. **well-pleasing,** *a.* **well-preserved,** *a.* young-looking for one's age. **well-proportioned,** *a.* **well-read,** *a.* having read extensively, having wide knowledge gained from books. **well-reputed,** *a.* of good reputation. **well-respected,** *a.* **well-rounded,** *a.* pleasantly curved or rounded; symmetrical, complete; broad in scope, full, varied. †**well-seeming,** *a.* having a fair outward or superficial appearance. †**well-seen,** *a.* accomplished, well-versed (in). **well set,** *a.* firmly set, well-knit, muscular. **well-spoken,** *a.* speaking well, eloquent; well-mannered, of good disposition. †**well-thewed,** *a.* well-knit. **well-thought-of,** *a.* respected, esteemed. **well-thumbed,** *a.* of a book, marked from much handling. **well-timed,** *a.* **well-to-do,** *a.* in good circumstances, well off. **well-tried,** *a.* often tried or tested with satisfactory results. **well-trod, -trodden,** *a.* much used or frequented. **well-turned,** *a.* shapely; aptly expressed. **well-upholstered,** *a.* (*facet.*) plump. **well-wisher,** *n.* a person who wishes well to one. **well-woman,** *a.* pertaining to or designed for the health and well-being of women, esp. through preventive and educative measures. **well-worn,** *a.* worn out, trite, hackneyed. [OE *wel,* (cp. Dut. *wel,* G *wohl,* Icel. *vel*) cogn. with WILL[1]]

well[2], *n.* a shaft bored in the ground to obtain water, oil, brine, gas etc.; a hole, space or cavity more or less resembling this; a space in the middle of a building enclosing the stairs or a lift or left open for light and ventilation; a space occupied by counsel etc. in a law-court; the boxed-in space enclosing the pumps of a vessel; a compartment in a fishing-vessel with a perforated bottom where fish are kept alive; the receptacle holding the ink in an inkstand; a spring, a fountain; a natural pool fed by this; a source. *v.i.* to spring or issue (forth etc.) as a fountain. **well-boat,** *n.* a fishing-boat having a well for conveying fish alive. **well-deck,** *n.* the space enclosed between the forecastle and poop on some ships. **well-dish,** *n.* one with a hollow for gravy to collect in. **well-head,** *n.* the source or fountain-head of a river etc. **well-hole,** *n.* the pit or shaft of a well; the well of a staircase etc. **well-room,** *n.* a room at a spa where the waters are served to visitors. **well-sinker,** *n.* one who digs or sinks wells. **well-sinking,** *n.* **well-spring,** *n.* a source of continual supply. **well-water,** *n.* [OE *wella,* rel. to *weallan,* to well or boil up (cp. Dut. *wel,* G *Welle,* wave, Icel. *vel,* boiling up)]

†**welladay, wellaway**, *int.* an exclamation of sorrow or despair. [OE *wā lā wā*, woe, lo! woe (see WOE, LO)]

Welles, *n.* **(George) Orson** (1915–85), US actor and director. He produced a radio version of H. G. Wells's novel *The War of the Worlds* (1938), and then produced, directed, and starred in *Citizen Kane* (1941), a landmark in the history of cinema, yet he directed very few films subsequently in Hollywood. Later films as an actor include *The Lady from Shanghai* (1948) and *The Third Man* (1949).

Wellington[1], *n.* capital and industrial port (woollen textiles, chemicals, soap, footwear, bricks) of New Zealand in North Island on Cook Strait; population (1987) 351,000. The city was founded 1840, and became the seat of government 1865.

Wellington[2], *n.* **Arthur Wellesley, 1st Duke of Wellington** (1769–1852), British soldier and Tory politician. As commander in the Peninsular War, he expelled the French from Spain in 1814. He defeated Napoleon Bonaparte at Quatre-Bras and Waterloo in 1815, and was a member of the Congress of Vienna. As prime minister 1828–30, he was forced to concede Roman Catholic emancipation. **wellington (boot),** *n.* a waterproof boot, usu. rubber, coming up to the mid-calf or knee, named after Wellington. **Wellingtonia,** *n.* a sequoia.

Wells, *n.* **H(erbert) G(eorge)** (1866–1946), English writer. He first made his name with 'scientific romances' such as *The Time Machine* (1895) and *The War of the Worlds* (1898). Later novels had an anti-establishment, anti-conventional humour remarkable in its day, for example *Kipps* (1905) and *Tono-Bungay* (1909). His many other books include *Outline of History* (1920) and *The Shape of Things to Come* (1933), from which a number of his prophecies have since been fulfilled. He also wrote many short stories.

welly, wellie, *n.* (*coll.*) a wellington boot.

wels, *n.* the sheat-fish. [G]

Welsh[1], *a.* pertaining to Wales or its inhabitants. *n.* the language of the Welsh; (*pl.*) the Welsh people. **Welsh corgi,** *n.* breed of dog with a foxlike head and pricked ears. The coat is dense, with several varieties of colouring. Corgis are about 30 cm/1 ft at the shoulder, and weigh up to 12 kg/27 lbs. **Welsh dresser,** *n.* a dresser with open shelves above drawers and cupboards. **Welsh harp,** *n.* one with three rows of strings. **Welsh language (Cymraeg),** *n.* a member of the Celtic branch of the Indo-European language family, spoken chiefly in the rural north and west of Wales; it is the strongest of the surviving Celtic languages, and in 1981 was spoken by 18.9% of the Welsh population. **Welshman, -woman,** *n.* **Welsh mutton,** *n.* mutton from a small breed of Welsh mountain sheep. **welsh rabbit, rarebit,** *n.* cheese melted and spread over toasted bread. [OE *wœlisc,* foreign, from *weahl,* foreigner, a Celt]

welsh[2]**, welch,** *v.i.* of a bookmaker, to make off from a racecourse without paying up bets; to evade an obligation, esp. to fail to pay a debt. **welsher,** *n.* [etym. doubtful]

welt, *n.* a strip of leather sewn round a boot or shoe between the upper and the sole for sewing them together; the border or trimming of a garment; a weal; (*Her.*) a narrow border to an ordinary. *v.t.* to furnish with a welt; to weal, to flog. [ME *welte,* cogn. with OE *wyllan,* to roll (cp. Icel. *velta,* Eng. WEAL[2] and WELTER[1]]

weltanschauung, *n.* (*Phil.*) a survey of the world as an entity. [G, world contemplation]

welter[1]**,** *v.i.* to roll, to tumble about, to wallow, esp. in some foul matter; of waves etc., to heave and roll about confusedly. *n.* a weltering movement, a turmoil, a confusion. [ME *weltren,* freq. of *walten,* to roll (cp. Icel. *velta,* Swed. *valtra,* G *walzen*), cogn. with WALLOW, WALTZ]

welter[2]**,** *a.* heavyweight horse-rider. **welter weight,** *n.* a welter; a boxer weighing 10st–10st 7lb (63.5–66.7 kg) if professional, 10st–10st 8lb (63.5–67.1 kg) if amateur. [etym. doubtful]

Weltpolitik, (German 'world politics'), *n.* term applied to German foreign policy after about 1890, which represented Emperor Wilhelm II's attempt to make Germany into a world power through a more aggressive foreign policy on colonies and naval building combined with an increase in nationalism at home. **weltpolitik,** *n.* a policy aiming at the predominance of a country in the affairs of the whole world.

weltschmerz, *n.* sympathy for the sorrow of the world; a pessimistic view of life. [G]

welwitschia, *n.* a genus of plants from SW tropical Africa, with one species, *Welwitschia mirabilis,* with a trunk several feet wide and only a foot high (over 1 m wide and 30 cm high), and no leaves except the two cotyledonous ones, which attain a development of 6ft (1.8 m) or more. [Dr F. *Welwitsch,* 1807–72, discoverer]

Wembley Stadium, *n.* sports ground in north London, completed 1923 for the British Empire Exhibition. The FA Cup final has been played there since that year. It is also used for concerts. Adjacent to the main stadium are the Wembley indoor arena and conference centre. Wembley Stadium holds 78,000 people.

wen, *n.* a sebaceous cyst, frequently occurring on the scalp or neck; (*fig.*) an excrescence, an abnormal growth; an overgrown city, esp. London. [OE *wenn,* (cp. Dut. *wen,* Dan. dial. *van*) prob. cogn. with Goth, *winnan,* to suffer, to WIN]

Wenceslas, St, (907–929), *n.* duke of Bohemia who attempted to Christianize his people and was murdered by his brother. He is patron saint of Czechoslovakia and the 'good King Wenceslas' of the carol. Feast day 28 Sept.

wench, *n.* (*now chiefly facet.*) a girl or young woman; a female servant; †a girl of loose character, a whore. †*v.i.* to commit fornication. **wench-like,** *a.* †**wencher,** *n.* †**wenching,** *n.* **wenchless,** *a.* [ME *wenche,* OE *wencel,* infant (as adj., weak), (cp. G *wanken,* to totter), cogn. with WINK]

wend[1]**,** *v.t.* to go or direct (one's way). *v.i.* to go. [OE *wendan,* to turn, causal of WIND[2] (orig. past WENT, now past of GO[1]]

Wend[2]**,** *n.* (a member of) the NW Slavonic peoples who settled the area east of the rivers Elbe and Saale in the 6th–8th cent. By the 12th cent. most had been forcibly Christianized and absorbed by invading Germans; a few preserved their identity and survive as the Sorbs of Lusatia (East Germany/Poland). **Wendic,** *a.* **Wendish,** *n., a.* [G *Wende,* perh. cogn. with prec., WANDER]

Wendy house®, *n.* a small toy house for children to play in. [from the house built for *Wendy* in the children's book *Peter Pan* by J. M. Barrie, 1860–1937]

Wenlock, *a.* (*Geol.*) denoting the sub-division of the Silurian system strongly developed at Wenlock, in Shropshire.

Wensleydale, *n.* a breed of long-haired sheep; a type of crumbly white cheese. [*Wensleydale* in Yorkshire]

went, *past* GO[1], see also WEND[1]

wentletrap, *n.* a univalve many-whorled shell of the family *Scalariidae.* [G *wendeltreppe* (*wendel,* turning, *Treppe,* stair)]

Wentworth, *n.* **William Charles** (1790–1872), Australian politician, the son of D'Arcy Wentworth (*c.* 1762–1827), surgeon of the penal settlement at Norfolk Island. In 1855 he was in Britain to steer the New South Wales constitution through Parliament, and campaigned for Australian federalism and self-government.

wept, *past, p.p.* WEEP.

were, WAS.

we're, contr. form of *we are.*

weren't, contr. form of *were not.*

werewolf, *n.* (*pl.* **-wolves**) a person turned or supposed to have the power of turning into a wolf. [OE *werewulf* (*wer,* see WERGILD, WOLF)]

†**wergild,** *n.* (OE and Teut. Law) a fine or monetary compensation for manslaughter and other offences against the person, paid by the kindred of the offender to the kindred of the injured person to avoid blood-feud. [OE *wer,* man, (cp. L *vir*), *gild,* payment, from *gieldan,* see YIELD]

Werner, *n.* **Abraham Gottlob** (1750–1815), German geologist, one of the first to classify minerals systematically. He also developed the later discarded theory of neptunianism – that the Earth was initially covered by water, with every mineral in suspension: as the water receded, layers of rocks 'crystallized'.

Wernerian, *a.* of or pertaining to Werner and his geological doctrines. *n.* a disciple of Werner, a Neptunist. [Abraham Gottlob *Werner,* 1750–1817, see above]

wernerite, *n.* scapolite. [*Werner,* see above, -ITE]

wersh, *a.* (*Sc.*) insipid, tasteless, unsalted. [etym. unknown]

Wertherism, *n.* morbid sentimentality, namby-pambyism. **Wertherian,** *a.* [after the hero of Goethe's *Sorrows of Werther,* 1774]

†**wesand,** WEASAND.

Wesker, *n.* **Arnold** (1932–), British playwright. His socialist beliefs were reflected in the successful trilogy *Chicken Soup with Barley*, *Roots*, *I'm Talking About Jerusalem* (1958–60). He established a catchphrase with *Chips with Everything* (1962).

Wesley[1]**,** *n.* **Charles** (1707–88), brother of John Wesley and one of the original Methodists at Oxford. He became a principal preacher and theologian of the Wesleyan Methodists. He wrote some 6500 hymns, including 'Jesu, lover of my soul'.

Wesley[2]**,** *n.* **John** (1703–1791), English founder of Methodism. When the pulpits of the established church were closed to him and his followers, he took the gospel to the people. For 50 years he rode about the country on horseback, preaching daily, largely in the open air. His sermons became the doctrinal standard of the Wesleyan Methodist Church. **Wesleyan,** *a.* of or belonging to the Church or sect founded by Wesley. *n.* a member of this, a Wesleyan Methodist. **Wesleyanism,** *n.*

Wessex, *n.* the kingdom of the West Saxons in Britain, said to have been founded by Cerdic about 500 AD, covering present-day Hampshire, Dorset, Wiltshire, Berkshire, Somerset, and Devon. In 829 Egbert established West Saxon supremacy over all England. Thomas Hardy used the term Wessex in his novels for the SW counties of England.

west, *adv.* at, in or towards the quarter opposite the east, or where the sun sets at the equinox. *n.* that one of the four cardinal points exactly opposite the east; the region or part of a country or of the world lying opposite to the east, esp. the western part of England, Europe or the US; the non-Communist countries of Europe and N America; the Occident; a wind blowing from the west *a.* being, lying or living in or towards the west; (blowing) from the west. **to go west,** to die; to be destroyed. **West African Economic Community,** *n.* international organization established 1975 to end barriers in trade and cooperation in development; members in 1988 include Burkina Faso, Ivory Coast, Mali, Mauritania, Niger, and Senegal; Benin and Togo have observer status. **west country,** *n.* the SW part of England. **west-countryman, -countrywoman,** *n.* **West End,** *n.* the fashionable part of London, immediately west of Charing Cross, where the main shops, theatres etc. are located. **West-end,** *a.* **westering,** *a.* passing to the west (of the sun). **westerly,** *a.* in, situated or directed towards the west; (blowing) from the west. *n.* a wind from the west. *adv.* towards the west. **western,** *a.* in, facing or directed towards the west; belonging to or to do with the west; (blowing) from the west. *n.* a film, a play or novel dealing with the western states of the US in the wilder periods of their history. **the Western Empire,** *n.* the western division of the Roman Empire having Rome as capital, after the division into an Eastern and Western Empire by Theodosius in 395. **Western Church,** *n.* the Latin Church which continued to acknowledge the pope after the schism of the Greek and Latin Churches in the 9th cent. **Western European Union,** *n.* organization established 1955 as a consultative forum for military issues among the W European governments: Belgium, France, Holland, Italy, Luxembourg, the UK, West Germany, and (from 1988) Spain and Portugal. **Western Powers,** *n.pl.* a loose term for the European powers (and the US) contrasted with the USSR and her satellite powers. **westerner,** *n.* **westernize, -ise,** *v.t.* **westernmost,** *a.* **westing,** *n.* distance travelled or amount of deviation towards the west. **westward,** *a., adv.* †**westwardly,** *adv.* **westwards,** *adv.* [OE (cp. Dut. and G *west,* Icel. *vestr,* Dan., Swed. *vest*), prob. cogn. with Gr. *hesperos,* L VESPER]

West[1], *n.* **Benjamin** (1738–1820), American painter, active in London from 1763. He enjoyed the patronage of George III for many years and painted historical pictures.

West[2], *n.* **Mae** (1892–1980), US vaudeville and film actress. She wrote her own dialogue, sending herself up as a sex symbol. Her films include *She Done Him Wrong* (1933); two of her often quoted lines are 'Come up and see me some time' and 'Beulah, peel me a grape'.

West[3], *n.* **Rebecca** (1892–1983), pen name of Cicily Isabel Fairfield, British journalist and novelist, an active feminist from 1911. *The Meaning of Treason* (1959) deals with the spies Burgess and Maclean. Her novels include *The Fountain Overflows* (1956).

West Bank, *n.* the area (5879 sq km/2270 sq miles) on the west bank of the river Jordan; population (1988) 866,000. The West Bank was taken by the Jordanian army 1948 at the end of the Arab-Israeli war which resulted in the creation of Israel, and was captured by Israel during the Six-Day War 5–10 June 1967. The continuing Israeli occupation has created tensions with the Arab population, especially as a result of Jewish Israeli settlements in the area.

West Bengal, *n.* state of NE India. **area** 87,900 sq km/ 33,929 sq miles. **capital** Calcutta. **towns** Asansol, Durgarpur. **physical** occupies the W part of the vast alluvial plain created by the Ganges and Brahmaputra, with the Hooghly river; annual rainfall in excess of 250 cm/100 in. **population** (1981) 54,486,000. **products** rice, jute, tea, coal, iron, steel, cars, locomotives, aluminium, fertilizers.

Western Isles, *n.pl.* island area of Scotland, comprising the Outer Hebrides (Lewis, Harris, North and South Uist, and Barra); unofficially the Inner and Outer Hebrides generally. **area** 2900 sq km/1120 sq miles. **towns** administrative headquarters Stornoway on Lewis. **population** (1987) 31,000. **products** Harris tweed, sheep, fish, cattle.

Western Sahara (formerly **Spanish Sahara**), *n.* disputed territory in NW Africa bounded to the N by Morocco, to the W and S by Mauritania, and to the E by the Atlantic Ocean. **area** 266,800 sq km/103,011 sq miles. **capital** La'Youn (Arabic *al-Aaiún*). **towns** phosphate mining town of Bou Craa. **population** (1988) 181,400; another estimated 165,000 live in refugee camps near Tindouf, SW Algeria. Ethnic composition: Sawrawis (traditionally nomadic herdsmen). **exports** phosphates. **language** Arabic. **religion** Sunni Muslim.

West Germany, GERMANY, WEST.

West Glamorgan, *n.* county in SW Wales. **area** 820 sq km/317 sq miles. **towns** administrative headquarters Swansea; Port Talbot, Neath. **population** (1987) 363,000. **products** tinplate, copper, steel, chemicals. **language** 16% Welsh, English.

West Indies, *n.pl.* archipelago of about 1200 islands, dividing the Atlantic from the Gulf of Mexico and the Caribbean. The islands are divided into: **Bahamas**; **Greater Antilles** Cuba, Hispaniola (Haiti, Dominican Republic), Jamaica, Puerto Rico; **Lesser Antilles** Aruba, Netherlands Antilles, Trinidad and Tobago, the Windward Islands (Grenada, Barbados, St Vincent, St Lucia, Martinique, Dominica, Guadeloupe), the Leeward Islands (Montserrat, Antigua, St Christopher (St Kitts)-Nevis, Barbuda, Anguilla, St Martin, British and US Virgin Islands), and many smaller islands.

West Indies, Federation of the, federal union 1958–62 comprising Antigua, Barbados, Dominica, Grenada, Jamaica, Montserrat, St Christopher (St Kitts)-Nevis and Anguilla, St Lucia, St Vincent, and Trinidad and Tobago. This federation came to an end when first Jamaica and then Trinidad and Tobago withdrew.

Westinghouse, *n.* **George** (1846–1914), US inventor and founder of the Westinghouse Corporation in 1886. After service in the Civil War he patented a powerful air brake for trains in 1869. His invention allowed trains to run more safely with greater loads at greater speeds. In the 1880s, he turned his attention to the generation of electricity. Unlike Thomas Edison, Westinghouse introduced alternating current into his power stations. **Westinghouse brake,** *n.* a brake worked by compressed air for use on railway trains and motor cars.

West Irian, *n.* former name for Irian Jaya.

Westland affair, *n.* in UK politics, the events surrounding the takeover of the British Westland helicopter company in 1985–86. There was much political acrimony in the cabinet and allegations of malpractice. The affair led to the resignation of two cabinet ministers: Michael Heseltine, minister of defence, and the secretary for trade and industry, Leon Brittan.

Westman Islands, *n.pl.* small group of islands off the south coast of Iceland. In 1973 volcanic eruption caused the population of 5200 to be temporarily evacuated, and added 2.5 sq km/1 sq mile to the islands' area. Heimaey is one of Iceland's chief fishing ports.

Westmeath, *n.* inland county of Leinster province, Republic of Ireland. **area** 1760 sq km/679 sq miles. **town** county town Mullingar. **physical** rivers Shannon, Inny, and Brosna; lakes Ree, Sheelin, and Ennell. **population** (1986) 63,000. **products** agricultural and dairy products, limestone, textiles.

West Midlands, *n.* metropolitan county in central England, created 1974, originally administered by an elected council; its powers reverted to district councils from 1986. **area** 900 sq km/347 sq miles. **towns** administrative headquarters Birmingham. **population**

(1987) 2,624,000. **products** manufacturing industrial goods.

Westminster, *n.* the British Parliament. [London borough in which the Houses of Parliament are situated]

Westminster Abbey, *n.* Gothic church in central London, officially the Collegiate Church of St Peter. It was built 1050–1745 and consecrated under Edward the Confessor in 1065. The west towers are by Hawksmoor 1740. Since William I nearly all English monarchs have been crowned in the abbey, and several are buried there; many poets are buried or commemorated there, at Poets' Corner.

Westphalia, *n.* an independent mediaeval duchy, incorporated in Prussia by the Congress of Vienna 1815, and made a province 1816 with Münster as its capital. Since 1946 it has been part of the West German *Land* (region) of North Rhine–Westphalia. **Westphalia, Treaty of,** agreement (1648) ending the Thirty Years' War.

West Point, *n.* former fort in New York State, on the Hudson River, 80 km/50 miles N of New York City, site of the US Military Academy (commonly referred to as West Point), established in 1802. Women were admitted 1976. West Point has been a military post since 1778.

West Sussex, *n.* county on the S coast of England. **area** 2020 sq km/780 sq miles. **towns** administrative headquarters Chichester; Crawley, Horsham, Haywards Heath; resorts Worthing, Littlehampton, Bognor Regis; port Shoreham. **physical** the Weald, South Downs; rivers Arun, West Rother, Adur. **population** (1987) 700,000.

West Virginia, *n.* state of the E US; nickname Mountain State. **area** 62,900 sq km/24,279 sq miles. **capital** Charleston. **towns** Huntington, Wheeling. **physical** Allegheny Mountains; Ohio river. **products** fruit, poultry, dairy and meat products, timber, coal, natural gas, oil, chemicals, synthetic fibres, plastics, steel, glass, pottery. **population** (1986) 1,919,000.

West Yorkshire, *n.* metropolitan county in NE England, created 1976, originally administered by an elected metropolitan council; its powers reverted to district councils from 1986. **area** 2040 sq km/787 sq miles. **towns** administrative headquarters Wakefield; Leeds, Bradford, Halifax, Huddersfield. **products** coal, woollen textiles. **population** (1987) 2,052,000.

wet, *a.* moistened, soaked, saturated, covered with or containing water or other liquid; rainy; not yet dry or hard; using a liquid; (*coll., dated.*) drunk; (*coll.*) sloppy, feeble, characterless, sentimental; (*N Am.*) of a state etc., allowing or favouring the sale of alcoholic beverages, opp. to prohibitionist. *n.* wetness, moisture; anything that wets, esp. rain; (*sl.*) a drink; (*coll.*) a feeble person; (*coll.*) a moderate conservative politician. *v.t.* (*past, p.p.* **wetted**) to make wet; to moisten, drench or soak with liquid; to urinate on; (*sl.*) to celebrate (a bargain etc.) with drink. **The Wet,** *n.* (*Austral.*) the monsoon season. **to wet one's whistle,** to drink. **wetback,** *n.* an illegal immigrant to the US from Mexico. **wet blanket,** *n.* (*coll.*) a person who damps enthusiasm, zeal etc. **wet bob** BOB[2]. **wet bulb** DRY-BULB THERMOMETER under DRY. **wet dock,** *n.* a dock in which vessels can float. **wet dream,** *n.* an erotic dream with emission of semen. **wetland,** *n.* (*often pl.*) swamp, marsh land. **wet-look,** *a.* (made from a material) having a shiny finish. **wet-nurse,** *n.* a woman employed to suckle a child not her own. *v.t.* to act as wet-nurse to; to coddle. **wet-pack,** *n.* (*Med.*) a wet sheet in which a patient is wrapped. **wet-shod,** *a.* having the shoes wet. **wet suit,** *n.* a tight-fitting usu. rubber garment for divers etc. that allows water in whilst retaining body heat. **wetly,** *adv.* **wetness,** *n.* **wetting,** *n.* **wettish,** *a.* [OE *wǣt* (cp. Icel. *vātr,* Dan. *vaad,* Swed. *vät*), cogn. with WATER]

wether, *n.* a castrated ram. [OE (cp. Icel. *vethr,* Dan. *væder,* G *widder*), prob. cogn. with VEAL and VETERINARY]

Wexford, *n.* county in the Republic of Ireland, province of Leinster. **area** 2350 sq km/907 sq miles. **towns** county town Wexford; Rosslare. **population** (1986) 102,000. **products** fish, livestock, oats, barley, potatoes.

wey, *n.* a certain weight or measure varying with different articles (of wool, 182 lb/82.5 kg; oats and barley, 48 bushels/1.745 m^3; cheese, 224 lb/101.6 kg; salt, 40 bushels/1.45 m^3.). [OE *wœge,* weight, from *wegan,* to WEIGH]

Weyden, *n.* **Rogier van der** (*c.* 1399–1464), Netherlandish painter, official painter to the city of Brussels from 1436. He painted portraits and religious subjects, such as *The Last Judgement* (about 1450, Hôtel-Dieu, Beaune). His refined style had considerable impact on Netherlandish painting.

Weygand, *n.* **Maxime** (1867–1965), French general. In 1940, as French commander in chief, he advised surrender to Germany, and was subsequently high commissioner of N Africa 1940–41. He was a prisoner in Germany 1942–45, and was arrested after his return to France; he was released in 1946, and in 1949 the sentence of national infamy was quashed.

whack, *v.t.* to strike heavily, to thwack; (*sl.*) to share out (plunder etc.). *n.* a heavy blow, a thwack; (*sl.*) a share, a portion; (*coll.*) an attempt. **whacked,** *a.* (*coll.*) exhausted. **whacking,** *n.* a beating, a thrashing. *a., adv.* (*coll.*) large, whopping, thumping. [onomat., cp. THWACK]

whaisle, whaizle, *v.i.* (*Sc.*) to wheeze, to breathe hard. [freq. from WHEEZE]

whale[1], *n.* a large marine fish-like mammal, of various species of *Cetacea,* several of which are hunted chiefly for their oil and whalebone; (*coll.*) something very big, exciting etc. *v.i.* to engage in whale-fishing. **whaleback,** *n.* a vessel with the main decks covered in and rounded over as a protection against rough seas. **whale-boat,** *n.* a boat sharp at both ends, such as those used in whaling. **whalebone,** *n.* a horny, elastic substance occurring in long, thin plates, found in the palate of certain whales. **whalebone whale,** *n.* **whale-calf,** *n.* a young whale. **whale-fin,** *n.* whalebone. **whale-fishery, -fishing,** *n.* **whale-line,** *n.* rope of great strength used in whaling. **whale-man,** *n.* (*chiefly N Am.*) a whaler. **whale-oil,** *n.* oil obtained from the blubber of whales; spermaceti. **whaler,** *n.* a person employed in whaling; a ship employed in whaling. **whaling,** *n.* the catching and processing of whales. **whaling-gun,** *n.* a gun for firing harpoons at whales. **whaling-master,** *n.* the captain of a whaler. [OE *hwœl* (cp. Dut. *walvisch,* G *Wal,* Icel. *hvalr,* Dan., Swed. *hval*), perh. cogn. with WHEEL]

whale[2], WEAL[2].

Whale, *n.* **James** (1886–1957), British film director. He initially went to Hollywood to film his stage success, *Journey's End* (1930), and went on to direct four horror films: *Frankenstein* (1931), *The Old Dark House* (1932), *The Invisible Man* (1933), and *Bride of Frankenstein* (1935). He also directed *Showboat* (1936).

whall, †**whally** WALL-EYE.

wham, *n.* a forceful blow; the noise of this. *v.t., v.i.* (*past, p.p.* **whammed**) to strike or crash, or cause to strike or crash with a loud, forceful blow.

whang[1], *v.t.* to beat noisily, to bang; (*Sc.*) to cut in large slices. *v.i.* of a drum etc., to make a noise as if whanged. *n.* a whanging blow, a bang; (*Sc.*) a big slice. [imit. (cp. WHACK)]

whang[2], *n.* a tough leather strap or thong. **whangee,** *n.* a flexible bamboo cane. [perh. var. of THONG]

wharf, *n.* (*pl.* **wharfs, wharves**) a landing-place for cargo beside a river, harbour, canal etc., usu. consisting of a quay of masonry or a platform, pier or quay of timber, sometimes filled in with rubble etc., (*N Am.*) a dock. *v.t.* to moor at a wharf; to deposit or store goods on a wharf. **wharf-rat,** *n.* the brown or Norway rat. **wharfage,** *n.* the charge for using a wharf; the use of a wharf. **wharfing,** *n.* **wharfinger,** *n.* a person who owns or has charge of a wharf. [OE *hwerf,* bank, dam, orig. a turning, from *wheorfan,* to turn (cp. Icel. *hvarf,* turning, Dan. *voerft,* Swed. *varf,* Dut. *werf,* wharf)]

Wharton, *n.* **Edith** (born Jones) (1862–1937), US novelist. Her work was influenced by her friend Henry James, and mostly set in New York society. It includes *The House of Mirth* (1905), the rural *Ethan Frome* (1911), *The Custom of the Country* (1913), and *The Age of Innocence* (1920).

what, *pron.* (*interrog.*) which thing or things (*often used ellipt.*); (*rel.*) that which, those which, the things that; which things, how much! (as an exclamation); (*dial.*) that or which. *a.* which thing, kind, amount, number etc. (in asking questions); how great, remarkable, ridiculous etc. (used in an exclamatory sense); (*rel.*) such as, as many or as many as, any that. *adv.* (*interrog.*) to what extent, in what respect? **what for,** for what reason, purpose? etc. **to give what for** GIVE[1]. **what for no?** (*Sc.*) why not? **what have you,** (*coll.*) anything else of the kind. **what ho!** an exclamation of greeting or accosting. **what next?** (*exclam.*) monstrous! absurd! **what not** WHAT HAVE YOU. **what of that,** no matter, never mind. **what's what,** (*coll.*) the real thing or situation; a good thing as opp. to a bad or doubtful one. **what's up?** UP. **what though,** what does it matter if? admitting that. **what time.** TIME. **what-d'ye-call-it,** *n.* (*coll.*) a phrase put for something that has slipped one's memory. **whate'er,** *pron.* (*poet.*) whatever. **whatever,** *pron.* anything soever that; all that which. *a.* no matter what (thing or things). **whatnot,** *n.* a piece of furniture with shelves for ornaments, books etc. **whatsit,** *n.* (*coll.*) a person or thing whose name is unknown or temporarily forgotten. †**whatso, whatsoever, whatsoe'er,** *pron., a.* WHATEVER. [OE *hwæt,* neut. of *hwā,* WHO]

whau, *n.* a New Zealand tree with very lightweight cork-like wood. [Maori]

whaup, *n.* (*chiefly Sc.*) the curlew. [from its cry]

wheal, *n.* (*Cornwall*) a mine (usu. a tin-mine). [Corn. *hwel*]

wheat, *n.* an annual cereal grass, *Tricicum sativum,* cultivated for its grain which is ground into flour for bread. **wheat belt,** *n.* the area east of the Rocky Mountains in Canada and the US where wheat is extensively cultivated. **wheat-ear,** *n.* an ear of wheat. **wheat-fly,** *n.* any of various flies that injure wheat, esp. the Hessian fly. **wheat germ,** *n.* the embryo of the wheat grain, rich in vitamins. **wheat-grass,** *n.* couch-grass. **wheat-meal,** *n., a.* (made from) flour containing much of the original wheat grain. **wheat-moth,** *n.* one of various moths, the larvae of which destroy wheat. **wheaten,** *a.* [OE *hwǣte,* cogn. with WHITE]

wheatear, *n.* a small white-rumped bird, *Oenanthe oenanthe.* [corr. of WHITE ARSE]

Wheatstone, *n.* **Charles** (1802–75), English physicist and inventor. With William Cooke, he patented a railway telegraph in 1837, and, developing an idea of Samuel Christie's, devised the Wheatstone bridge. Originally a musical-instrument maker, he invented the harmonica and the concertina. **Wheatstone automatic,** *n.* a mechanical system of telegraphy for transmitting and receiving high-speed signals automatically. **Wheatstone bridge,** *n.* a device for measuring an unknown electrical resistance by means of a known resistance.

whee, *int.* an exclamation of delight or excitement.

wheedle, *v.t.* to entice, to win over, to persuade by coaxing or flattery; to cajole, to humour, to cheat; to obtain from or get (out of) by coaxing and flattery. **wheedler,** *n.* **wheedling,** *a.* **wheedlingly,** *adv.* [etym. unknown; perh. from OE *wǣdlian,* to beg, *wǣdl,* poverty]

wheel, *n.* a circular frame or solid disk turning on its axis, used in vehicles, machinery etc. to reduce friction and facilitate motion; a machine, implement, device etc. consisting principally of a wheel, esp. a spinning-wheel, potter's wheel, steering-wheel etc.; (*N Am., coll.*) a cycle; (*pl., coll.*) a car; an object resembling a wheel, a disk; a catherine-wheel; an instrument of torture formerly used for breaking the limbs of criminals; torture with this; the act of wheeling, circular motion, rotation; a turn, a revolution; the turning or swinging round of a body of troops or a line of warships as on a pivot; (*pl.*) the forces controlling or activating an organization etc. *v.t.* to move or push (a wheeled vehicle etc.) in some direction; to cause to turn or swing round as on a pivot. *v.i.* to turn or swing round thus; (*lit. or fig.*) to change direction, to face another way; to go round, to gyrate; to ride a cycle etc. **to break upon the wheel** BREAK. **wheels within wheels,** concealed reasons or interdependent circumstances. **wheel and axle,** one of the mechanical powers, consisting of a cylindrical axle on which a wheel is fastened concentrically, the difference between their respective diameters supplying leverage. **wheel of life,** a scientific toy consisting of a revolving cylinder with slits through which figures depicted on the inside are seen apparently in continuous motion. **wheel-animalcule,** *n.* a rotifer. **wheelbarrow,** *n.* a barrow usu. supported on a single wheel, with two handles by which it is wheeled. **wheel-base,** *n.* the distance between the front and rear hubs of a vehicle. **wheel-brace,** *n.* a brace-shaped spanner for adjusting bolts on a wheel. **wheel-chair,** *n.* a chair on wheels, esp. for invalids. **wheel clamp,** *n.* a clamp fixed on to the wheel of an illegally parked car to prevent it from being driven away before a fine is paid. **wheel-clamp,** *v.t.* **wheel-horse,** *n.* a wheeler. **wheel-house,** *n.* a shelter for the steersman. **wheelman,** *n.* (*N Am.*) a cyclist. **wheel-seat,** *n.* the part of an axle carrying a fixed wheel and fastened into its hub. **wheel-shaped,** *a.* **wheel-spin,** *n.* the revolution of wheels without a grip of the road. **wheelstone,** *n.* an entrochite. **wheel-tread,** *n.* the part of a rim or tyre that touches the ground. **wheel-window,** *n.* a circular window with radiating tracery. **wheelwright,** *n.* a person whose occupation is to make wheels etc. **wheeled,** *a.* (*usu. in comb.,* as *four-wheeled*). **wheeler,** *n.* one who wheels; a wheelwright; a horse next to the wheels in a tandem etc. **wheeler-dealer,** *n.* one who operates shrewdly and often ruthlessly in business, politics etc. **wheeler-dealing,** *n.* **wheelie,** *n.* (*coll.*) a manoeuvre in which a bicycle or motorcycle is briefly supported on the rear wheel alone. **wheelless,** *a.* **wheely,** *a.* [OE *hwēol* (cp. Icel. *hjōl,* Dan. *huil,* also Gr. *kuklos,* see CYCLE)]

wheen, *n.* (*Sc., North.*) a little, a small quantity; a quantity. [OE *hwœne, hwōn*]

wheeze, *v.i.* to breathe hard and with an audible sound, as in asthma. *v.t.* to utter thus. *n.* a wheezing sound; (*coll., esp. dated*) a joke, a trick; (*coll.*) a design, a scheme. **wheezy,** *a.* **wheezily,** *adv.* **wheeziness,** *n.* [OE *hwēsan,* cogn. with *hwōsta,* cough (cp. G. *husten*)]

whelk[1], *n.* a marine spiral-shelled gasteropod of the genus *Buccinum,* esp. *B. undatum,* the common whelk, used for food. [ME *wilk,* OE *wiloc* (cp. Dut. *wulk*), prob. cogn. with HELIX, conf. with foll.]

whelk[2], *n.* a small pustule or pimple **whelked,** *a.* [dim. of WHEAL[1]]

†**whelm,** *v.t.* to overwhelm, to engulf, to submerge. [ME *whelmen,* prob. from a noun *whelm* (cp. MSwed. *hwalm,* hay-cock), from OE *āhwytfan,* to overwhelm (cp. Icel. *hvāfa,* to turn upside down, G *wölben,* to arch over, Gr. *kolpos,* bosom)]

whelp, *n.* the young of a dog, a pup; the young of a beast of prey, a cub; an offensive or ill-bred child or youth. *v.i.* of a bitch etc., to bring forth young. *v.t.* to bring forth (a pup or cub); (*derog.*) to give birth to or produce. **whelpless,** *a.* [OE *hwelp* (cp. Dut. *welp,* Icel. *hvelpr*)]

whemmle, *v.t.* (*Sc.*) to whelm, to overthrow. *n.* an overthrow. [freq. from WHELM]

when, *adv., conj.* (*interrog.*) at what or which time?, (*rel.*) at which (time), at the time that, at any time that, at whatever time; as soon as; at or just after the time that; after which, and then; although; considering that; while (*often ellipt. with pres.p.*). *pron.* what or which time. †**whenas,** *adv.* when; whereas, while. **whenever, whene'er,** *adv.* at whatever time. **whensoever,** *adv.* at what time soever. [OE *hwœnne,* a case of interrog. pron. WHO]

whence, *adv., conj.* (*interrog.*) from what place or

which? where from? how?; (*rel.*) from which place, origin, source etc.; for which reason, wherefore; (*ellipt.*) to or at the place from which. *pron.* what or which place or starting-point. †**whenceforth,** *adv.* †**whencesoever,** *adv., conj.* from whatsoever place or source. [ME *whennes,* OE *hwanan,* cogn. with prec. (*-an,* suf. of direction)]

whenever etc. WHEN.

where, *adv., conj.* (*interrog.*) at or in what place, situation, case, circumstances? etc.; to what place? whither? in what direction?; (*rel.*) in which (place or places), in or to the place, direction etc. in which; whereas. *pron.* what or which place. **whereabout,** *adv., conj.* about which, in regard to which; whereabouts. **whereabouts,** *adv., conj.* near what or which place roughly. *n.* the approximate locality or the locality in or near which a person or thing is. **whereas,** *conj.* the fact or case being that, considering that (in legal preambles etc.); the fact on the contrary being that, when in reality. **whereat,** *adv., conj.* at which; †at what? **whereby,** *adv.* by which (means); †by what? **where'er** WHEREVER. **wherefore,** *adv.* for what reason? why? for which reason, on which account. *n.* the reason why. **wherefrom,** *adv.* from which, whence. **wherein,** *adv., conj.* in what place, respect? etc.; in which thing, place, respect etc. **whereinsoever,** *adv.* **whereinto,** *adv.* **whereness,** *n.* **whereof,** *adv., conj.* of what? of which or whom **whereon,** *adv., conj.* **whereout,** *adv., conj.* out of which. **wheresoever,** *adv., conj.* in or to what place soever. **wherethrough,** *adv., conj.* **whereto** *adv., conj.* to which or what place or end. **whereunder,** *adv., conj.* †**whereunto,** *adv., conj.* to what end or purpose? to which. **whereupon,** *adv., conj.* upon which; in consequence of or immediately after which. **where'er,** *adv., conj.* (*poet.*) **wherever,** *adv., conj.* at, in or to whatever place. **wherewith,** *adv., conj.* with what? with which. **wherewithal,** *adv., conj.* wherewith. *n.* the necessary means or resources, esp. money. [OE *hwār* (cp. Dut. *waar,* G *warum,* Icel. *hvar*), cogn. with *hwā,* WHO, and WHEN]

wherry[1], *n.* a light shallow rowing-boat for plying on rivers. **wherryman,** *n.* [perh. rel. to WHARF and WHIR]

wherry[2], *n.* (*dial*) a liquor made from the pulp of crab-apples after the verjuice is expressed. [etym. doubtful]

whet, *v.t.* (*past, p.p.* **whetted**) to sharpen by rubbing on a stone or similar substance; to excite, to stimulate. *n.* the act of whetting; anything taken to whet or stimulate the appetite; a dram. **whetstone,** *n.* a piece of stone used for sharpening cutlery etc.; anything that sharpens or stimulates. **whetter,** *n.* [OE *hwettan,* from *hwœt,* keen, bold (cp. Dut. *wetten,* G *wetzen,* Icel. *hvetja*)]

whether, †*a., pron.* which of the two? *conj.* introducing (an indirect question in the form of) an alternative clause followed by an alternative *or, or not,* or *or whether,* or with the alternative unexpressed. [OE *hwœther*]

whethering, *n.* (*dial.*) the retention of the after-birth in cows. [etym. doubtful]

whetstone, whetter WHET.

whew, *int.* an exclamation of astonishment or consternation. [inst. sound]

Whewell, *n.* **William** (1794–1866), British physicist and philosopher who coined the term 'scientist' along with such words as eocene and miocene, electrode, cathode, and anode. Most of his career was connected with Cambridge, where he became the Master of Trinity College. His most enduring influence rests on two works of great scholarship and acuteness, *The History of the Inductive Sciences* (1837) and *The Philosophy of the Inductive Sciences* (1840), both still in print and widely read.

whey, *n.* the watery part of milk that remains after the casein etc. have formed curds and been separated **whey-face,** *n.* a pale-faced person. **whey-faced,** *a.* **whey-tub,** *n.* **wheyey, wheyish,** *a.* [OE *hwœg* (cp. Dut. *wei,* W *chwig*)]

which, *pron.* (*interrog.*) what person, thing, persons or things of a definite number; (*rel.*) representing in a subordinate clause a noun expressed or understood in the principal sentence or previous clause. *a.* (*interrog.*) what (person, thing etc.) of a definite number; (*rel.*) used with a noun defining an indefinite antecedent. **whichever,** †**whichsoever,** *a., pron.* which (person or thing) of two or more. [OE *hwilc, whilīc* (WHO, -LIKE) (cp. Dut. *welk,* G *welcher,* Icel. *hvīlīkr*)]

whicker, *v.i.* to neigh softly. [imit.]

whidah (-bird), whydah, *n.* a small W African weaver-bird, the male of which has four tail-feathers of enormous length. [*Ouidah,* in Benin]

whiff[1], *n.* a sudden expulsion of smoke etc., a puff, a light gust, esp. one carrying an odour; a small amount, a trace; a small cigar; a light outrigged sculling boat. *v.t., v.i.* to puff or blow lightly; (*coll.*) to smell (unpleasant). **whiffy,** *a.* (*coll.*) smelly. [imit.]

whiff[2], *v.i.* to fish with a hand-line, usu. from a boat, towing the bait near the surface. [perh. var. of WHIP]

whiff[3], *n.* a European or W Indian flat-fish. [etym. doubtful]

whiffle, *v.i.* of the wind etc., to veer about; to change from one opinion or course to another, to prevaricate, to equivocate. **whiffler,** *n.* [freq. from WHIFF[1]]

Whig, *n.* a member of the British political party that contended for the rights and privileges of Parliament in opp. to the Court party or Tories, supported the Revolution of 1688 and the principles it represented, and was succeeded by the Liberals; orig. a Scottish Covenanter; an American colonist who supported the cause of independence in the American Revolution; a member of an American political party from about 1834–54, representing commercial and financial interests. †**whiggarchy,** *n.* **whiggery, whiggism,** *n.* **whiggish,** *a.* **whiggishly,** *adv.* **whiggishness,** *n.* [short for obs. *whiggamore,* nickname for certain Scots who came to buy corn at Leith, from *whiggam,* a word with which they urged their horses, prob. from Sc. *whig,* to jog along]

whig, *n.* (*dial.*) sour whey, buttermilk. [var. of WHEY]

whigmaleerie, *n.* a trinket, a gewgaw; a whim. [etym. doubtful]

while, *n.* a space of time, esp. the time during which something happens or is done. *conj.* during the time that, as long as, at the same time as (*often used ellipt. with pres.p.*); at the same time that, whereas (followed by a correlative sentence bringing out a contrast); †till. **once in a while,** occasionally, †now and then, at long intervals. †**the while,** during, whilst. **to be worthwhile,** to be worth the time, labour or expense involved. **to while away,** to pass (time etc.) pleasantly or without weariness. †**whilere,** *adv.* a little time ago, erewhile. †**whiles,** *adv.* while; (*Sc.*) sometimes. **whilst,** *conj.* while. **the whilst,** the while. [OE *hwīl* (cp. Icel. *hvīla,* rest, G *weile*), prob. cogn. with QUIET]

whilk, WHICH.

†**whilom,** *adv.* formerly, once, of old. *a.* quondam. [OE *hwīlum,* instr. or dat. pl. of WHILE]

whilst WHILE.

whim, *n.* a sudden fancy, a freak, a caprice; a hoisting device, usu. consisting of a vertical winch worked by a horse, formerly used in mines for raising ore. **whimmy,** *a.* whimsical. **whimsical,** *a.* full of whims; oddly humorous; odd-looking, curious, fantastic. **whimsicality, whimsicalness,** *n.* **whimsically,** *adv.* **whimsy,** *n.* a whim, a crotchet. **whimwham,** *n.* a plaything, a whim, a fancy. [Icel. *hvima,* to wander with the eyes, from *vim,* giddiness, folly (cp. Norw. *kvim*)]

whimbrel, *n.* a small curlew, *Numenius phaeopus.* [freq. of *whim,* imit. of cry, -EL]

whimper, *v.i.* to cry with a low, broken, whining voice; to whine. *v.t.* to utter in such a tone. *n.* a low, querulous or whining cry. **whimperer,** *n.* **whimperingly,** *adv.* [freq. of *whimpe,* WHIM, prob. cogn. with WHINE]

whimsical, whimwham etc. WHIM.

whin[1], *n.* furze, gorse. **whinberry,** *n.* the bilberry. **whinchat,** *n.* a small thrush-like bird, *Saxicola rubetra.* **whinny**[1], *a.* abounding in furze or whin. [cp. Norw.

hvin]

whin[2], **whinsill, whinstone,** *n.* a very hard, resistant rock, esp. basalt, chert or quartzose sandstone. [etym. doubtful]

whine, *v.i.* to make a plaintive, long-drawn cry; to complain or find fault in a peevish way. *v.t.* to utter with a whine or in a peevish way. *n.* a whining cry, sound or tone; a peevish complaint. **whiner,** *n.* **whiningly,** *adv.* **whiny, whiney**, *a.* [OE *hwīnan* (cp. Icel. *hvīna,* to whiz, Swed. *hvina,* to whistle)]

whinge, *v.i.* (*Austral., dial.*) to cry fretfully; to complain, to whine. *n.* a complaint. **whingeing,** *n.* **whinger**[1], *n.* [OE *hwinsian,* WHINE]

whinger[2], †**whinyard,** *n.* a dirk, a short sword or hanger.

whinny[1] WHIN[1].

whinny[2], *v.i.* to neigh, esp. in a gentle or delighted way. *n.* the act or sound of whinnying. [freq. of WHINE]

whinsill, whinstone WHIN[2].

whinyard WHINGER.

whip, *v.t.* (*past, p.p.* **whipped**) to move suddenly and quickly, to snatch, to dart, to jerk (out, away etc.); to lash, to flog; to drive or urge (on) with a whip; to thrash; to beat (out of etc.); to strike forcefully as if with a whip; to beat (eggs, cream etc.) into a froth; to fish (a stream) by casting a line over the water; (*coll.*) to beat, to overcome; to manage or discipline (the members of a political party); to lash or bind with a close wrapping of twine, thread etc.; to bind (twine etc.) round a joint etc.; to oversew (a seam) with close stitches; to twist (goods etc.) with a rope passed through a pulley; (*sl.*) to steal. *v.i.* to move or start suddenly, to start, to dart (out, in etc.). *n.* an instrument for driving horses etc., or for punishing persons, consisting of a lash tied to a handle or rod; a coachman or driver; a whipper-in; a member of Parliament appointed to enforce discipline and to summon the members of the party to divisions etc.; a summons sent out by a whip to ensure such attendance; a hoisting apparatus consisting of a single rope and pulley; a whipping motion; a dessert made with whipped eggs, cream etc. **to whip up,** to excite, arouse, stimulate; to produce hurriedly. †**whip and spur,** with the greatest haste. **whip-cord,** *n.* a hard twisted cord for making a whip; a very durable corded cloth made from worsted yarns. **whip-crane,** *n.* a crane used with a whip for rapid hoisting. **whip-gin,** *n.* a block for use in hoisting. **whip-graft,** *n.* a graft made by inserting a tongue in a scion into a slit cut in the stock. *v.t.* to graft by this method. **whip-hand,** *n.* the hand holding the whip; the advantage or control. **whip-handle,** *n.* **whiplash,** *n.* **whiplash injury,** *n.* an injury to the neck caused by a sudden uncontrolled forwards and backwards movement of the unsupported head. **whip-ray,** *n.* a stingray. **whip-round,** *n.* (*coll.*) a collection of money. *v.i.* to make a collection. **whip-saw,** *n.* a narrow saw-blade with the ends fastened in a frame. *v.t.* to saw with this; (*N Am. sl.*) to beat (a person) at every point in a game or in betting. **whip-snake,** *n.* a slender whip-like snake. **whipstitch,** *n.* a small stitch used for oversewing. **whip-stock,** *n.* the rod or handle of a whip. **whip-tail,** *n.* a Tasmanian fish; a small kangaroo. **whip-top,** *n.* a top kept spinning with a whip. **whipper,** *n.* **whipper-in,** *n.* (*pl.* **whippers-in**) a person employed to assist the huntsman by looking after the hounds, now usu. called a whip; a parliamentary whip. **whipper-snapper,** *n.* a noisy, presuming, insignificant person. **whipping,** *n.* **whipping-boy,** *n.* a boy formerly educated with a young prince and taking his punishments for him; a scapegoat. †**whipping-cheer,** *n.* (*Shak.*) flogging, chastisement. **whipping-post,** *n.* a post to which offenders were tied to be whipped (usu. attached to stocks). **whipping-top** WHIP-TOP. †**whipster,** *n.* a whipper-snapper. **whippy,** *a.* flexible, springy. [(cp. Dut. *wippen,* to skip (*wip,* a moment, the strappado), Dan. *vippe,* Swed. *vippa,* to wag, G *wippen,* to see-saw, to rock), perh. cogn. with VIBRATE]

whippet, *n.* a breed of racing-dogs, similar to but smaller than the greyhound. [etym. doubtful]

Whipple[1], *n.* **Fred Lawrence** (1906–), US astronomer, whose hypothesis in 1949 that the nucleus of a comet is like a dirty snowball was confirmed 1986 by space-probe studies of Halley's comet.

Whipple[2], *n.* **George** (1878–1976), US physiologist whose research interest concerned the formation of haemoglobin. He showed that anaemic dogs, kept under restricted diets, responded well to a liver regime, and that their haemoglobin quickly regenerated. This work led to a cure for pernicious anaemia.

whipple-tree, *n.* a swingle-tree. [freq. of WHIP, TREE]

whip-poor-will, *n.* a small N American nocturnal bird, *Caprimulgus vociferus,* allied to the goat-suckers. [imit. of cry]

Whipsnade, *n.* a zoo in Bedfordshire, England, 5 km/3 miles S of Dunstable, opened 1931, where wild animals and birds are bred and exhibited in conditions resembling their natural state.

whipster WHIP.

whir, whirr, *v.i.* (*past, p.p.* **whirred**) to revolve, move or fly quickly with a buzzing or whizzing sound. *n.* a whirring sound. [ME *whirr, quirr,* cp. Dan. *hvirre,* Icel. *hverfa*]

whirl, *v.t.* to swing round and round rapidly; to cause to revolve or fly round with great velocity; to carry (away or along) rapidly; to hurl or fling. *v.i.* to turn round and round rapidly, to rotate, to gyrate, to spin; to be carried or to travel rapidly in a circular course; to move along swiftly; of the brain etc., to be giddy, to seem to spin round. *n.* a whirling motion; a confused state, giddiness; commotion, bustle; (*coll.*) an attempt, a trial. †**whirl-about,** *n.* a whirligig. †**whirl-blast,** *n.* a whirling blast, a whirlwind. **whirl-bone,** *n.* the bone of a ball-and-socket joint, esp. the patella or knee-cap. **whirligig,** *n.* a child's spinning or rotating toy; a merry-go-round; a water-beetle that darts about in a circular manner over the surface of pools etc.; something that continually moves or changes; a revolving or rotating course; †an instrument of torture consisting of a cage turning on a pivot in which the victim was whirled round. **whirlpool,** *n.* an eddy or vortex. **whirlwind,** *n.* a funnel-shaped column of air moving spirally round an axis, which at the same time has a progressive motion. **whirler,** *n.* **whirling,** *n., a.* **whirling-table,** *n.* a machine for exhibiting the effects of centrifugal and centripetal forces; a potter's wheel. [for *whirfle,* freq. from Icel. *hvirfla* (cp. G *wirbeln*), cogn. with prec. and OE *hweorfan,* to turn]

whirr WHIR.

whish[1], **whisht**, *int.* hush! silence! [onomat]

whish[2], *v.i.* to move through the air or water with a whistling sound. *n.* a whistling sound. [imit.]

whisk, *v.t.* to sweep, brush or flap (away or off); to carry off or take (away) swiftly or suddenly; to shake, flourish or wave about with a quick movement; to beat up (eggs etc.). *v.i.* to move or go swiftly or suddenly. *n.* a whisking movement; a small bunch of grass, straw, feathers, hair etc., used as a brush or for flapping away flies, dust etc.; an instrument for beating up cream, eggs etc.; †the game of whist. [(cp. Dan. *viske,* to wipe, from *visk,* a wisp, Swed. *viska,* G *wischen,* to wipe), perh. cogn. with WISP]

whisker, *n.* (*usu. pl.*) hair growing on the cheeks of a man; one of the bristly hairs growing round the mouth of a cat or other animal; a narrow margin; a very fine and strong hairlike crystal. **whiskered,** *a.* [as prec.]

whisket, *n.* (*dial.*) a basket. [etym. doubtful]

whisky[1], (*Ir., US*) **whiskey**, *n.* a spirit distilled usu. from barley, sometimes from wheat, rye etc. **whisky-liver,** *n.* cirrhosis of the liver caused by alcoholic poisoning. **whisky-toddy,** *n.* **whiskified**, *n.* (*coll.*) intoxicated by or as by whisky. [Gael. *uisgebeatha,* water of life, see USQUEBAUGH]

whisky[2], *n.* a light one-horse chaise or gig for fast travelling. [WHISK, -Y]

whisky-jack, †**whisky-dick**, **-john**, *n.* the grey or Canada jay, *Perisoreus canadensis.* [corr. of N Am. Ind. *wiss-ka-tjan*]

whisper, *v.i.* to speak with articulation but without vocal vibration; to speak in a low voice so as not to be overheard; to converse privately or in a whisper; to devise mischief, to plot, to talk slander; to rustle. *v.t.* to tell or bid in a whisper or privately; to utter or disseminate thus; to hint or suggest privately. *n.* a whispering tone or voice; a whispered remark or speech; a hint, an insinuation, a rumour. **whisperer,** *n.* **whispering,** *n.* **whispering campaign,** *n.* the organized spread of injurious rumours about a person, esp. a public figure. **whispering-gallery,** *n.* a gallery, corridor etc. in which the faintest sounds made at particular points are audible at other distant points though inaudible elsewhere. **whisperingly,** *adv.* [ONorthum. *hwisprian* (cp. MDut. *wisperen,* G *wispeln*), of imit. orig.]

whist, *n.* a card game, usu. for four persons, played with the entire pack of 52 cards. **dummy whist** DUMMY. **whist drive,** *n.* a competitive series of games of whist. [formerly WHISK in alln. to the sweeping up of the cards]

whistle, *v.i.* to make a shrill musical sound by forcing the breath through a small opening of the lips or with an instrument, an appliance on a steam-engine etc.; of an instrument, engine etc., to emit this sound; of birds etc., to make a similar sound; to make such a sound by swift motion of a missile, the wind etc. *v.t.* to emit or utter (a tune etc.) by whistling; to call or give a signal to thus. *n.* a whistling sound, note or cry; an instrument for producing such a sound; (*sl.*) the throat. †**to go whistle,** to go to ruin. **to wet one's whistle** WET. **to whistle for,** to ask for in vain, to stand little or no chance of getting. **to whistle for a wind,** the superstitious practice of old sailors in a calm. **whistle-stop,** *n.* (*N Am.*) a small station where trains stop only on signal; (*orig. N Am.*) a brief visit to a town, as by a political candidate. **whistler,** *n.* one who or that which whistles; (*N Am.*) the whistling or hoary marmot; a whistling duck or other bird; a broken-winded horse. **whistling duck,** *n.* the American widgeon. [OE *hwistlian,* freq. from *hwist-* (imit.), to make a hissing noise (cp. Dut. *hvīsla,* Dan. *hvisle*)]

Whistler, *n.* **James Abbott McNeill** (1834–1903), US painter and etcher, active in London from 1859. His riverscapes and portraits show subtle composition and colour harmonies, for example *Arrangement in Grey and Black: Portrait of the Painter's Mother* (1871, Louvre, Paris).

whit, *n.* a jot, the least particle, an iota. [OE *wiht,* WIGHT[1]]

Whitby, Synod of, council summoned by King Oswy of Northumbria in 664, which decided to adopt the Roman rather than the Celtic form of Christianity for Britain.

white, *a.* being of the colour produced by reflection of all the visible rays in sunlight, as of pure snow, common salt, foam of clear water etc.; approaching this colour, pale, pallid, bloodless, transparent, colourless; silvery, whitish-grey; belonging to a light-complexioned group or race; intended for such people; pure, clean, stainless; spotless, innocent; grey, silvery or hoary as from age etc.; of coffee, containing milk or cream; having snow; clothed in white; having white or pale fur, hair etc.; not malicious or malevolent; fair, happy, propitious. †*v.t.* to whiten. *n.* a white colour; a white paint or pigment; a white person or a member of one of the paler races, esp. a European; a white animal; a white part of anything, having the colour of snow; the sclerotic coat of the eye surrounding the iris; the albuminous material surrounding the yolk of an egg; **(White)** a counter-revolutionary, especially during the Russian civil wars 1917–21. Originally the term described the party opposing the French Revolution, when the royalists used the white lily of the French monarchy as their badge; †the central part of the butt in archery, that which is aimed at; (*pl.*) white clothes; (*pl.*) leucorrhoea. **white ant** TERMITE. **whitebait,** *n.* the fry of several clupeoid fish eaten when about 2 in. (5 cm) long. **whitebeam,** *n.* a shrub or small tree, *Sorbus aria,* with silvery undersides to the leaves. **white bear,** *n.* the polar bear. **white-beard,** *n.* a greybeard, an old man. **white blood cell,** *n.* a leucocyte. **Whiteboy,** *n.* a member of a secret agrarian organization formed in Ireland about 1760 which held nocturnal meetings and perpetrated damage to property, so called from the white shirts worn over their other garments. **Whiteboyism,** *n.* the principles or practices of the Whiteboys. **white-cap,** *n.* the redstart and other birds; a white-crested wave. **white-collar,** *a.* pertaining to non-manual employees, as office and clerical workers. **white cell, corpuscle,** *n.* a leucocyte. **white-crested, -crowned,** *a.* **white crops,** *n.pl.* wheat, barley etc., which whiten as they ripen. **white damp,** *n.* (*Mining*) carbon monoxide. **white dwarf,** *n.* a type of small, very faint, dense star. **white-eared,** *a.* **white elephant** ELEPHANT. **white ensign** NAVAL ENSIGN under ENSIGN. **white-faced,** *a.* pale-faced; having a white front or surface; of animals, having a white spot or streak on the front of the head. **white feather,** *n.* **to show the white feather** FEATHER. **white fish,** *n.* a general term for food-fish other than salmon, esp. whitings and haddocks. **whitefish,** *n.* a N American salmonoid food-fish of the genus *Coregonus;* the menhaden and other fish. **white flag** FLAG. **whitefly,** *n.* (*pl.* **-flies, -fly**) a small insect of the family Aleyrodidae, a pest of plants. **White Friar,** *n.* a Carmelite (from the white cloak). **white frost,** *n.* hoar-frost. **white gold,** *n.* a whitish alloy of gold with palladium, nickel etc. **white goods,** *n.pl.* household linen; large kitchen appliances, as freezers and cookers. **Whitehall,** *n.* street in central London, between Trafalgar Square and the Houses of Parliament, with many government offices and the Cenotaph war memorial. **white-handed,** *a.* having white hands; free from guilt or dishonesty. **white heat,** *n.* the degree of heat at which bodies become incandescent and appear white; a high pitch of excitement, passion etc. **White Horse,** *n.* any of several hill figures in England, including the one on Bratton Hill, Wiltshire, said to commemorate Alfred the Great's victory over the Danes at Ethandun 878; and the one at Uffington, Berkshire, 110 m/360 ft long, and probably a tribal totem of the Early Iron Age, 1st century BC. **white horses,** *n.pl.* foam-crested waves. **white-hot,** *a.* **White House,** *n.* official residence of the president of the US, in Washington DC. It is a plain edifice of sandstone, built in the Italian renaissance style 1792–99 to the designs of James Hoban, who also restored it after it was burned by the British 1814; it was then painted white to hide the scars. **white-iron,** *n.* thin sheet iron with a coating of tin. **white knight,** *n.* one who gives (financial) support to a person or organization in a difficult situation. **white-land,** *n.* a tough, clayey soil, of a whitish hue when dry, but blackish when wet. **white lead,** *n.* carbonate of lead, esp. used as a basis of white oil-paint. **white lie** LIE[1]. **white light,** *n.* light containing more or less equal intensities of all wavelengths in the visible spectrum. **white-limed,** *a.* whitewashed. **white-lipped,** *a.* pale to the lips, esp. with fear. **white-livered,** *a.* cowardly. **white magic,** *n.* magic not involving the devil, sorcery; magic used for good. **white man,** *n.* (*dated, coll.*) an honourable, upright man. **white man's burden,** *n.* the white man's supposed obligation to promote the welfare of the less-developed non-white races. **White Man's Grave,** *n.* the lands along the Guinea Coast of W Africa where the atmosphere was thought peculiarly unhealthy to Europeans. **white meat,** *n.* meat that appears white after cooking, as poultry, veal, pork; †dairy products. **white metal,** *n.* a tin- or sometimes lead-based alloy for bearings, domestic utensils etc. **white night,** *n.* a sleepless night. **white noise,** *n.* noise, esp. electrical, consisting of sound waves of a wide range of frequencies. **white-out,** *n.* a condition of uniform whiteness occuring in polar or similar snow-covered regions in heavy cloud. **white paper,** *n.* a government report on a matter recently investigated. **white pepper** PEPPER. **White Russia,** *n.* English translation of Byelorussia, republic of the USSR. **white sale,** *n.* a sale of household linen at reduced prices. **white satin,** *n.* the plant honestly. **white sauce,** *n.* a thick sauce made with flour and milk or a fish or white-meat stock. **white slave,** a woman or child procured, and usu. exported, for immoral purposes. **white slaver,** *n.* **white slavery,** *n.* **whitesmith,** *n.* a tinsmith; one who finishes or galvanizes iron-work. **white spirit,** *n.* a distillate of petroleum used as a paint solvent and thinner. **white squall,** *n.* a squall not preceded by clouds, as in tropic seas. **whitestone,** *n.* a fine, white granite. †**whitetail,** *n.* the wheatear. **White terror,** *n.* general term used by socialists and Marxists to describe a right-wing counter-revolution, for example, the attempts by the Chinese Guomindang to massacre the communists 1927–1931. **white thorn,** *n.* the hawthorn. **whitethroat,** *n.* a small warbler of the genus *Sylvia.* **whitewash,** *n.* a mixture of quicklime and water or of whiting and size used for whitening walls, ceilings etc.; a false colouring given to a person's character or memory to counteract disreputable allegations. *v.t.* to cover with whitewash; to cover up or conceal (a misdemeanour etc.); to clear (a person's name) thus; (*coll.*) to defeat decisively. **whitewasher,** *n.* **white water,** *n.* foaming water in breakers, rapids etc. **white wedding,** *n.* one in which the bride wears white orig. as a symbol of purity. **white whale,** *n.* the beluga. **white wine,** *n.* any wine of a light colour, as Graves, Hock etc., opp. to red. **white witch,** *n.* one using her power for beneficent purposes. **white-wood,** *n.* (any one of various trees yielding) light-coloured timber. **whited,** *a.* **whited sepulchre,** *n.* a hypocrite (from Christ's allusion to the scribes and Pharisees, Matt. xxiii.27). **whitely,** *adv.* **whiten,** *v.t., v.i.* **whitener,** *n.* **whiteness,** *n.* **whitening,** *n.* the act of making white; the state of becoming white; whiting[1]. **whitey[1],** *n.* (*derog.*) a white person; white people collectively. **whitish,** *a.* **whitishness,** *n.* [OE *hwīt* (cp. Dut. *wit,* G *weiss,* Icel. *hvītr,* Sansk. *çvēta*)]

White[1], *n.* **Gilbert** (1720–93), English cleric and naturalist, born at Selborne, Hampshire, and author of *Natural History and Antiquities of Selborne* (1789).

White[2], *n.* **Patrick** (1912–), Australian novelist. Born in London, he settled in Australia in the 1940s. His novels (with allegorical overtones) include *The Aunt's Story* (1948), *Voss* (based on the 19th-century explorer Leichhardt, 1957), and *The Twyborn Affair* (1979). Nobel Prize 1973.

Whitechapel-cart, *n.* a light two-wheeled spring-cart. [*Whitechapel,* in E London]

Whitehead, *n.* **Robert** (1823–1905), English engineer who invented the self-propelled torpedo 1866.

Whitehorse, *n.* capital of Yukon Territory, Canada; population (1986) 20,000.

Whitehouse, *n.* **Mary** (1910–), British media activist; as founder of the National Viewers' and Listeners' Association, she has campaigned to censor radio and television in their treatment of sex and violence.

Whitelaw, *n.* **William, Viscount Whitelaw** (1918–), British Conservative politician. As secretary of state for Northern Ireland he introduced the concept of power sharing. He became secretary of state for employment 1973–74, but failed to conciliate the unions. He was chair of the Conservative Party 1974, and home secretary 1979–83, when he was made a peer. He resigned 1988.

whitening, whitesmith, whitethroat, whitewash etc. WHITE.

whitey[1] WHITE.

whitey[2], *n.* (*Austral.*) a flour-and-water scone cooked in wood ashes.

whither, *adv., conj.* (*interrog.*) to what or which place, where; (*rel.*) to which; whithersoever, wheresoever. **whithersoever,** *adv., conj.* to what place soever. †**whitherward,** *adv.* [OE *hwider,* as WHETHER]

whiting[1], *n.* fine chalk pulverized and washed for use in whitewashing, polishing etc.

whiting[2], *n.* a sea-fish, *Merlangus merlangus,* used for food. **whiting-pout,** *n.* a gadoid fish resembling this with an inflatable membrane over the eyes. [as prec.]

whitish etc. WHITE.

Whitlam, *n.* **(Edward) Gough** (1916–), Australian politician, leader of the Labor Party 1967–78 and prime minister 1972–75.

whitleather, *n.* leather dressed with alum, white leather; the paxwax of the ox.

Whitley Council, *n.* an industrial council comprising employers and employees to settle disputes and promote welfare in the industry. [J.H. *Whitley,* 1866–1935, first chairman]

whitlow, *n.* a pus-filled inflammation, esp. round finger or toe nail. **whitlow-grass,** *n.* tiny white-flowered, grass-like herb of the genus *Draba.* [corr. of obs. *quick-flaw,* a flaking off of the skin round the quick, conf. with *whit,* above]

Whitman, *n.* **Walt(er)** (1819–92), US poet who published *Leaves of Grass* (1855), which contains the symbolic 'Song of Myself'. It used unconventional free verse and scandalized the public by its frank celebration of sexuality.

Whitney, *n.* **Eli** (1765–1825), US inventor who in 1793 patented the cotton gin, a device for separating cotton fibre from its seeds.

Whitsun, *a.* pertaining to Whit-Sunday or Whitsuntide. **Whit-Sunday,** *n.* the seventh Sunday after Easter, a festival commemorating the day of Pentecost. **Whit-Monday** etc., *n.* **Whitsuntide,** *n.* Whit-Sunday and the following days. **Whit-week,** *n.* [short for *Whit-Sunday* (WHITE, SUNDAY, from the white garment commonly worn at this festival which was a great season for christenings)]

whittie-whattie, *v.i.* (*Sc.*) to shilly-shally; to whisper, to mutter. *n.* shilly-shally, vague whispering, shuffling; a shuffler, a whisperer, a mutterer. [etym. doubtful]

whittle[1], †*n.* a long knife, esp. one used by butchers, sailors etc., often worn at the belt. *v.t.* to trim, shave or cut pieces or slices off with a knife; to shape thus; to thin down; to reduce, pare away or bring (down) in amount etc., gradually or by degrees. *v.i.* to keep on paring, shaving or cutting away (at a stick etc.) with a knife. [corr. of ME *thwitel,* from OE *thwītan,* to cut, to pare]

whittle[2], *n.* (*now dial.*) a blanket; a thick shawl or cloak worn by English west-country women. [OE *hwītel,* from *whīt,* WHITE (cp. Icel. *hvītill*)]

Whittle, *n.* **Frank** (1907–), British engineer who invented the jet engine in 1930. In the Royal Air Force he worked on jet propulsion 1937–46. In May 1941 the Gloster E 28/39 aircraft first flew with the Whittle jet engine.

whity, *a.* whitish, inclining to white (*usu. in comb.* as *whity-brown,* between white and brown).

whiz, whizz, *v.i.* (*past, p.p.* **whizzed**) to make or move with a hissing sound, like an arrow or ball flying through the air; to move about rapidly. *n.* a whizzing sound. **whizz-bang,** *n.* a small high-velocity shell. **whiz(z)-kid,** *n.* (*coll.*) one who is outstandingly successful or clever, esp. at a relatively young age. **whizzingly,** *adv.* [imit.]

WHO, (*abbr.*) World Health Organization.

Who, the, an English rock group, formed 1964, with a hard, aggressive sound, high harmonies, and a stage show that often included destroying their instruments. Their albums include *Tommy* (1969), *Who's Next* (1971), and *Quadrophenia* (1973). Originally a mod band, the Who comprised Pete Townshend (1945–), guitar and songwriter; Roger Daltrey (1944–), vocals; John Entwhistle (1944–), bass; Keith Moon (1947–78), drums.

who, *pron.* (*obj.* **whom,** *poss.* **whose** (*interrog.*) what or which person or persons? (*rel.*) that (identifying the subject or object in a relative clause with that of the principal clause); †he, she or they that. **whodunit,** *n.* (*coll.*) a detective or mystery story. **whoever, whoe'er** (*poet.*), †**whoso, whosoever, whosoe'er** (*poet.*), *pron.* (*obj.* **whomever, whomsoever** etc.) any one without exception who, no matter who. [OE m., f. *hwā,* neut. *hwæt,* gen. *hwæs,* dat. *hwām* (cp. Dut. *wie, wat, wiens, wien,* G *wer, was, wessen, wen* and *wem,*

Icel. *hverr, hver, hvat, hvers, hverjum,* etc.), cogn. with L *quis,* Sansk. *kas, kim, kam*]
whoa, *int.* stop! (used chiefly by drivers to horses). [var. of HO, HOA]
whole, *a.* hale and sound, in good health; unimpaired, uninjured, not broken, intact; restored to health; complete or entire; containing the total number of parts, undivided, undiminished; integral, composed of units, not fractional. *n.* a thing complete in all its parts, units etc.; all that there is of a thing, the entirety; a complete system, a complete combination of parts, an organic unity. **on the whole,** all things considered; in most cases. **whole-bound,** *a.* bound entirely in leather, opp. to half- or quarter-bound. **whole-coloured,** *a.* having the same colour throughout. **wholefood,** *n.* food that has undergone little or no processing or refining. **whole-hearted,** *a.* done or intended with all one's heart, hearty, generous, cordial, sincere. **whole-heartedly,** *adv.* **whole-heartedness,** *n.* **whole-hogger,** *n.* a thorough-paced supporter. **whole-hoofed,** *a.* having undivided hoofs. **whole-length,** *a.* of a portrait etc., exhibiting the whole figure. **wholemeal,** *n., a.* (made from) flour ground from the entire wheat grain. **whole number,** *n.* an integer. **wholeness,** *n.* [OE *hāl,* HALE[1] (cp. Dut. *heel,* G *heil,* Icel. *heill*), cogn. with HEAL[1] and HOLY]
wholesale, *n.* the sale of goods in large quantities as dist. from retail. *a.* buying or selling thus; done etc. in the mass, on the large scale, indiscriminate. *adv.* by wholesale, in large quantities; by the mass, on the large scale.
wholesome, *a.* tending to promote health, salutary, salubrious; promoting moral or mental health, not morbid; (*dial.*) clean; †healthy, sound. **wholesomely,** *adv.* **wholesomeness,** *n.*
wholly, *adv.* entirely, completely; totally, exclusively.
whom, whomsoever etc. WHO.
whoop, *v.i.* to utter the cry 'whoop'; to shout or cry out loudly in excitement, encouragement, exultation etc.; to halloo. *v.t.* to utter with a whoop; to urge (on) with whoops; to mock at with loud cries. *n.* the cry 'whoop'; a loud shout of excitement encouragement etc.; the sound made in whooping-cough. **whoopee,** *int.* an exclamation of excitement or delight. *n.* riotous enjoyment; a noisy, jolly time. **whoopee cushion,** *n.* a cushion that when sat upon emits a sound as of someone breaking wind. **whooper,** *n.* **whooper swan,** *n.* a large swan, *Cygnus cygnus,* with a whooping call. **whooping-cough,** *n.* an infectious disease, pertussis, esp. of children, characterized by a violent cough followed by a loud convulsive respiration. **whoops,** *int.* an exclamation of surprise or apology. [ME *houpen,* F *houpes,* from *houp!* a cry or int., perh. from Teut.]
whoosh, *n.* a rushing or hissing sound as of something moving swiftly through the air. *v.i.* to make or move with such a sound.
whop, *v.t.* (*past, p.p.* **whopped**) (*coll.*) to beat, to thrash; to defeat; to cause to drop with a loud noise. *v.i.* to fall with a loud noise. **whopper,** *n.* (*coll.*) anything uncommonly large etc.; a monstrous lie. **whopping,** *a.* (*coll.*) uncommonly large. [var. *whap, wap,* etym. doubtful]
whore, *n.* a prostitute, a courtesan, a strumpet; †an adulteress, an unchaste woman. *v.i.* to fornicate; (*Bibl.*) to practise idolatry. **whoredom,** *n.* fornication; idolatry. **whorehouse,** *n.* a brothel. †**whoremaster,** *n.* a pimp; a whoremonger. **whoremonger,** *n.* a fornicator. †**whoreson,** *n.* a bastard. *a.* bastard-like, mean, scurvy. †**whoring,** *n.* †**whorish,** *a.* †**whorishly,** *adv.* **whorishness,** *n.* [ME *hore,* Icel. *hōra,* adulteress (cp. Dan. *hore,* Swed. *hora,* Dut. *hoer,* G *hura*), perh. cogn. with L *cārus,* dear]
whorl, *n.* a circular set or ring of leaves, sepals or other organs on a plant; one convolution or turn of a spiral, as in a univalve shell; the disk for steadying the motion of a spindle, formerly made of stone etc.; a coil, spiral, convolution. **whorled,** *a.* [prob. shortened from *whorvel,* from OE *wheorfan,* see WHIRL]
whortleberry, *n.* the bilberry. [formerly, *hurtilberye hurtberye* (OE *horta,* BERRY)]
whose, whoso, whosoever etc. WHO.
why, *adv., conj.* (*interrog.*) for what reason or purpose? (*rel.*) on account of which. *n.* the reason, explanation or purpose of anything. *int.* expressing surprise etc. [OE *hwī,* instr. of *whā,* WHO]
whydah WHIDAH.
Whymper, *n.* **Edward** (1840–1911), English mountaineer. He made the first ascent of many Alpine peaks, including the Matterhorn 1865, and in the Andes scaled Chimborazo and other mountains.
WI, (*abbr.*) West Indies; Women's Institute.
wick[1]**,** *n.* a piece or bundle of fibrous or spongy material used in a candle or lamp to convey the melted grease or oil by capillary attraction to the flame. [OE *wice,* (cp. MDut. *wiecke,* Dan. *vœge,* Norw. *veik*)]
wick[2]**,** *v.t.* to strike (a stone) obliquely in the game of curling. *n.* such a hit. [etym. doubtful]
wick[3]**,** *n.* a town, village or municipal district (chiefly in place-names). [OE *wīc,* L *vīcus,* village]
wicked, *a.* sinful, addicted to evil or vice, wilfully transgressing against the divine or moral law, immoral, depraved; mischievous, roguish; very bad, harmful, injurious. **wickedly,** *adv.* **wickedness,** *n.* [from obs. adj. *wikke,* cogn. with WEAK and OE *wicca,* a wizard]
wicken, *n.* the rowan or mountain ash. [prob. from OE *wice,* WYNCH]
wicker, *n.* twigs, withes or osiers plaited into a material for baskets, chairs etc. *a.* made of this material. **wickerwork,** *n.* **wickered,** *a.* [orig. a pliant twig, prob. from Scand. (cp. MSwed. *wika,* to bend, Swed. *vika,* to fold, to plait, Dan. *veg,* pliant), cogn. with WEAK]
wicket, *n.* a small gate, door or other entrance, esp. one close beside or forming part of a larger one; a small aperture in a door or wall, having a grille, or opened and closed by means of a sliding panel; a set of three stumps surmounted by two bails at which the bowler directs the ball in cricket; the ground on which this is set up; the innings or turn of each batsman at the wicket; the pitch between the wickets, esp. as regards condition for bowling; (*coll.*) situation, circumstances. **to keep wicket,** in cricket, to be wicket-keeper. **wicket-door, -gate,** *n.* **wicket-keeper,** *n.* the fielder who stands behind the batsman's wicket in cricket. [OE *wiket* (F *guichet*), etym. doubtful, perh. from OHG *wisken,* to WHISK, to slip out]
Wicklow, *n.* county in the Republic of Ireland, province of Leinster. **area** 2030 sq km/784 sq miles. **towns** county town Wicklow. **physical** Wicklow Mountains; rivers Slane and Liffey. **population** (1986) 94,000.
widdershins, WITHERSHINS.
widdy, (*dial.*) WIDOW, WITHY.
wide, *a.* having a great relative extent from side to side, broad, opp. to narrow; having a specified degree of breadth; far-extending; vast, spacious, extensive; not limited or restricted, large, free, liberal, comprehensive, catholic; distant or deviating by a considerable extent or amount from a mark, point, purpose etc.; fully open or expanded; (*sl.*) crafty, shrewd. *adv.* widely; to a great distance, extensively; far from the mark or purpose. *n.* in cricket, a wide ball, one bowled too far to the side and out of the batsman's reach. **broke to the wide,** (*sl.*) absolutely penniless. **wide-angle lens,** *n.* a camera lens with an angle up to 100° used for photographing buildings etc. **wideawake,** *a.* having one's eyes open; alert, wary; keen, sharp, knowing. *n.* a soft felt hat with a broad brim. **wideawakeness,** *n.* **wide boy,** *n.* a crafty, shrewd fellow, inclined to sharp practice. **wide-eyed,** *a.* surprised, astonished; naive. **wide open,** *a.* open to attack; of indeterminate or unpredictable outcome; (*N Am.*) lawless, disorderly. **widespread,** *a.* widely disseminated. †**wide-stretched,** *a.* **widely,** *adv.* **widen,** *v.t., v.i.* **wideness,** *n.* **widish,** *a.* [OE *wīd* (cp. Dut. *wijd,* G *weit,* far, Icel. *vīthr*)]
-wide, *comb. form.* extending throughout, as in *nationwide.*
widgeon, wigeon, *n.* a wild duck of the genus *Anas,*

esp. the European *A. penelope*. [cp. F *vigeon, vingeon,* L *vipio, vipiōnem,* a small crane]

widget, *n.* a gadget; a thingumajig, a whatsit. [alteration of GADGET]

Widmark, *n.* **Richard** (1914–), US actor who made his film debut in *Kiss of Death* (1947) as a psychopath. He subsequently appeared in a great variety of roles in films including *The Alamo* (1960), *Madigan* (1968), and *Coma* (1978).

widow, *n.* a woman who has lost her husband by death and remains unmarried; a woman whose husband devotes much time to a (sporting) activity that takes him away from home; a short final line of a paragraph etc. at the top of a printed column or page. *v.t.* to bereave of a husband; to make a widow or widower; to bereave, to deprive (of). **grass-widow** GRASS. †**widow-bench,** *n.* (*Law*) the share allowed to a widow of her husband's estate beside her jointure. **widow-hunter,** *n.* one who courts a widow for her fortune. **widow's cruse,** *n.* an unfailing source of supply (I Kings xvii.16). **widow's mite,** *n.* a small but ill-afforded contribution (Mark xii.42). **widow's peak,** *n.* the natural growth of hair to a point in the middle of the forehead. **widow's weeds,** *n.pl.* deep mourning with a flowing veil of black crepe. **widower,** *n.* a man who has lost his wife by death and remains unmarried. **widow-hood,** *n.* [OE *widwe* (cp. Dut. *weduwe,* G *Wittwe* OHG *wituwa*), cogn. with L *viduus,* bereft (whence F *veuve*), Sansk. *vidhavā,* widow, Gr. *ēitheos,* bachelor]

width, *n.* extent of a thing from side to side, breadth, wideness; a piece of material cut from the full width of a roll etc.; comprehensiveness of mind, liberality, catholicity. **widthways, -wise,** *adv.* in a crosswise direction.

wield, *v.t.* to have the management or control of; to sway; to handle, to use or employ. **to wield the sceptre,** to rule with supreme command. **wieldable,** *a.* **wielder,** *n.* †**wieldless,** *a.* †**wieldy,** *a.* that may be wielded, manageable. [OE *geweldan, -wyldan,* from *wealdan,* to govern, to rule, (cp. Icel. *valda,* G *walten*)]

Wien, *n.* **Wilhelm** (1864–1928), German physicist who worked with radiation and established the principle, since known as Wien's law, that the wave length carrying the maximum energy is inversely proportional to the body's absolute temperature. That is, the hotter the body, the shorter the wavelength. For this, and other work on radiation, he was awarded the 1911 Nobel physics prize.

Wiene, *n.* **Robert** (1880–1938), German film director of the bizarre expressionist film *Das Kabinett des Dr Caligari/The Cabinet of Dr Caligari* (1919). He also directed *Orlacs Hände/The Hands of Orlac* (1924), *Der Rosenkavalier* (1926), and *Ultimatum* (1938).

wiener, *n.* (*N Am.*) a type of frankfurter. [G, Viennese (sausage)]

Wiener, *n.* **Norbert** (1894–1964), US mathematician, credited with the establishment of the science of cybernetics in his book *Cybernetics* (1948). In mathematics, he laid the foundation of the study of stochastic processes (those dependent on random events), particularly Brownian movement.

Wiener schnitzel, *n.* a cutlet of veal or pork, coated with a breadcrumb mixture. [G, Viennese cutlet]

Wien's law, WIEN.

Wiesel, *n.* **Elie** (1928–), US academic and human-rights campaigner, born in Romania. He was held in Buchenwald concentration camp during World War II, and has assiduously documented wartime atrocities against the Jews in an effort to alert the world to the dangers of racism and violence. Nobel Peace Prize 1986.

wife, *n.* (*pl.* **wives**) a married woman, esp. in relation to her husband; (*dial.*) a woman; (in comb. and usu. denoting some humble occupation as in *fish-wife*) a woman; (*dial.*) an elderly or humble woman. **old wives' tale,** a legend, a foolish story. **wife-swapping,** *n.* the temporary exchange of spouses for sexual activity. **wifehood,** *n.* **wifeless,** *n.* **wifelike, wifely,** *a.* **wifie,** *n.* [OE *wīf,* (cp. Dut. *wijf,* G *Weib,* Icel. *vīf,* neut.)]

wig[1], *n.* a covering for the head composed of false hair, worn to conceal baldness, as a disguise, for ornament or as part of an official costume, esp. by judges, lawyers, servants in livery etc. **wigged,** *a.* †**wiggery,** *n.* false hair; empty formality; red-tapeism. **wigless,** *a.* **wigmaker,** *n.* [shortened from PERIWIG]

wig[2], *v.t.* (*past, p.p.* **wigged**) to rate, to reprimand, to scold. **wigging,** *n.* a scolding. [etym. doubtful]

wigan, *n.* an open canvas-like fabric used for stiffening. [*Wigan,* town in Lancashire]

wigeon WIDGEON.

wiggle, *v.t., v.i.* to move jerkily, esp. from side to side. *n.* an act of wiggling.

wight[1], *n.* a person; †a supernatural being, an elf, a sprite. [OE *wiht,* see WHIT]

†**wight**[2], *a.* nimble, active, strong, brave, doughty. **wightly,** *adv.* [Icel. *vīgr,* (cp. Swed. *vig,* OE *wīglīc,* warlike, from *wīg,* war)]

Wight, Isle of, island and county in S England. **area** 380 sq km/147 sq miles. **towns** administrative headquarters Newport; resorts Ryde, Sandown, Shanklin, Ventnor. **economy** agriculture, tourism. **population** (1987) 127,000.

Wightman Cup, *n.* annual lawn-tennis competition between international women's teams from the US and the UK. The trophy, first contested in 1923, was donated by Hazel Wightman (born Hotchkiss; 1886–1974), a former US lawn-tennis player who won singles, doubles, and mixed doubles titles at the US Championships 1909–1911.

Wigner, *n.* **Eugene** (1902–), US physicist, born in Hungary, who introduced the notion of parity into nuclear physics with the consequence that all nuclear processes should be indistinguishable from their mirror images. For this, and other work on nuclear structure, he shared the 1963 Nobel physics prize with Goeppert-Mayer and Jensen.

wigwag, *v.t.* to wag to and fro. *v.i.* to move to and fro, to wag; to signal by waving flags. [redupl. of WAG[1]]

wigwam, *n.* a N American Indian hut or cabin, usu. consisting of a framework covered with bark, matting, hides etc. [Algonquin, *weekouomut,* in his house, inflected from *week,* house]

Wilander, *n.* **Mats** (1964–), Swedish lawn-tennis player. He won his first Grand Slam event 1982 when he beat Guillermo Vilas to win the French Open, and had won eight Grand Slam titles by 1990. He played a prominent role in Sweden's rise to the forefront of men's tennis in the 1980s, including Davis Cup successes.

Wilberforce, *n.* **William** (1759–1833), English reformer who was instrumental in abolishing slavery in the British Empire. He began his attacks on slavery while at school, and from 1788 devoted himself to its abolition. He entered Parliament in 1780; in 1807 his bill for the abolition of the slave trade was passed, and in 1833, largely through his efforts, slavery was abolished throughout the empire.

wilco, *int.* used in radio communications etc. to indicate that a message received will be complied with. [*will comply*]

wild, *a.* living in a state of nature, esp. inhabiting or growing in the forest or open country; esp. of animals and plants, not tamed, domesticated or cultivated; not civilized, savage; unsettled, uncultivated, irregular, desert, uninhabited; wayward, loose or disorderly in conduct, lawless, reckless, incautious, rash; ill-considered, ill-armed, imprudent, extravagant, inordinate; ungoverned, unchecked, unrestrained; turbulent, stormy, furious; anxiously eager, passionate, mad (with etc.); excited, enthusiastic (about etc.); of horses etc., shy, easily startled, given to shying; (*Bot.*) growing in a state of nature; having a certain resemblance to some other plant but inferior to it in appearance; of a playing card, able to represent any card the holder chooses. *n.* a desert or uninhabited and uncultivated tract. **wild-boar,** *n.* **wild-born,** *a.* born in a wild state. **wildcat,** *n.* an undomesticated species of cat native to Europe; a quick-tempered, fierce person; an exploratory drilling for oil or natural gas. *a.* speculative or risky as *wildcat scheme.* **wildcat scheme,** *n.* a rash and risky speculation or other scheme. **wildcat strike,** *n.* a strike not approved by the relevant union, or undertaken in breach of a contract. **wild-duck, wild-fire** FIRE. **to spread like wildfire,** to spread very quickly. **wildfowl,** *n.* (*collect.*) birds of various species pursued as game, esp. waterfowl. **wild-fowling,** *n.* **wild-goose chase,** a foolish or hopeless enterprise. **wildlife,** *n.* wild animals. **wild oats,** *n.pl.* youthful excesses, esp. sexual ones, as in *sow one's wild oats.* **Wild West,** *n.* the N American West during the lawless period of its early settlement. **wild-wood,** *n.* a tract of natural wood or forest. *a.* consisting of or pertaining to this. **wilding,** *n.* a plant that springs up by natural agency, esp. a wild fruit-tree; the fruit of such a plant; †*a.* growing wild; wild. **wildish,** *a.* **wildly** *adv.* **wildness,** *n.* [OE *wilde* (cp. Dut., G *wild,* Icel. *villr*), prob. cogn. with WILL[1]]

Wild, *n.* **Jonathan** (*c.* 1682–1725), English criminal who organized the thieves of London and ran an office which, for a payment, returned stolen goods to their owners. He was hanged at Tyburn.

Wilde[1], *n.* **Cornel(ius Louis)** (1915–89), US actor and film director, born in Austria-Hungary. He starred in *A Song to Remember* (1945), and directed *The Naked Prey* (1966) (in which he also acted) and *No Blade of Grass* (1970).

Wilde[2], *n.* **Oscar (Fingal O'Flahertie Wills)** (1854–1900), Irish writer. With his flamboyant style and quotable conversation, he dazzled London society and, on his lecture tour in 1882, the US. He published his only novel *The Picture of Dorian Gray* (1891), followed by witty plays including *A Woman of No Importance* (1893) and *The Importance of Being Earnest* (1895). In 1895 he was imprisoned for two years for homosexual offences; he died in exile.

wildebeest, *n.* a gnu. [S Afr. Dut. (WILD, BEAST)]

†**wilder,** *v.t.* to bewilder. [shortened from *wilderne,* see foll. or BEWILDER]

Wilder[1], *n.* **Billy** (1906–), US film director, born in Austria. He directed and collaborated on the script of *Double Indemnity* (1944), *The Lost Weekend* (1945), *Sunset Boulevard* (1950), and *Some Like it Hot* (1959).

Wilder[2], *n.* **Thornton (Niven)** (1897–1975), US playwright and novelist. He won the Pulitzer Prize for the novel *The Bridge of San Luis Rey* (1927), and for the plays *Our Town* (1938) and *The Skin of Our Teeth* (1942). His play *The Matchmaker* appeared at the Edinburgh Festival in 1954, and as the hit musical entitled *Hello Dolly!* in New York in 1964, and in London the following year.

wilderness, *n.* an uninhabited or uncultivated land, a desert; a waste, a scene of disorder or confusion; a portion of a garden left to run wild; a confused mass or quantity (of). **in the wilderness,** out of office; not wielding power. [ME *wilderne,* desert, OE *wilder,* wild animal, -NESS]

wildgrave, *n.* a German title of nobility; orig. the head keeper of a forest. [G *Wild,* game, GRAVE[4]]

wilding, wildish etc. WILD.

wile, *n.* a trick, an artifice, a stratagem or deception. *v.t.* to entice, to cajole (into, away etc.) [OE *wil,* prob. cogn. with OF GUILE]

wilful, *a.* intentional, voluntary, deliberate; done of one's own free will, without compulsion, not accidental; due to malice or evil intent; obstinate, self-willed, headstrong, perverse; †willing, ready. **wilfully,** *adv.* **wilfulness,** *n.*

wilga, *n.* the dogwood tree. [Austral. Abor.]

Wilhelm I, (1797–1888), *n.* king of Prussia from 1861 and emperor of Germany from 1871; the son of Friedrich Wilhelm III. He served in the Napoleonic Wars 1814–15 and helped to crush the 1848 revolution. After he succeeded his brother Friedrich Wilhelm IV to the throne of Prussia, his policy was largely dictated by his chancellor Bismarck, who secured his proclamation as emperor.

Wilhelm II, *n.* (1859–1941), emperor of Germany from 1888, the son of Frederick III and Victoria, daughter of Queen Victoria. In 1890 he forced Chancellor Bismarck to resign and began to direct foreign policy himself, which proved disastrous. In 1914 he first approved Austria's ultimatum to Serbia and then, when he realized war was inevitable, tried in vain to prevent it. In 1918 he fled to Holland.

wilily, wiliness WILY.

Wilkes, *n.* **John** (1727–97), British Radical politician, imprisoned for his political views; Member of Parliament 1757–64 and from 1774. He championed parliamentary reform, religious toleration, and US independence.

Wilkie, *n.* **David** (1785–1841), Scottish genre and portrait painter, active in London from 1805. His paintings are in the 17th-cent. Dutch tradition.

Wilkins[1], *n.* **Maurice Hugh Frederick** (1916–), New Zealand scientist. In 1962 he shared the Nobel Prize for Medicine and Physiology with Francis Crick and James Watson for his work on the molecular structure of nucleic acids, particularly DNA, using X-ray diffraction.

Wilkins[2], *n.* **William** (1778–1839), English architect. He pioneered the Greek revival in England with his design for Downing College, Cambridge. Other works include the main block of University College London, 1827–28, and the National Gallery, London, 1834–38.

will[1], *v.t.* (*past, cond.* **would,** *coll. neg.* **won't, wouldn't**) *v.t.* to desire, to wish, to choose, to want (a thing, that etc.); to be induced, to consent, to agree (to etc.); to be in the habit or accustomed (to); to be able (to). *v.aux* (*in second and third pers., or in first pers. in reported statement*) to be about or going to (expressing simple futurity or conditional action); (*in first pers.*) to intend, desire or have a mind to; to be certain or probable as a natural consequence, must. **willer,** *n.* **willing,** *a.* inclined, ready, not averse or reluctant (to); cheerfully acting, done, given etc. **to show willing,** to indicate a readiness to help, comply etc. **willingly,** *adv.* **willingness,** *n.* **would-be,** *pref.* desirous, vainly aspiring to be. [OE *willan* (cp. Dut. *willen,* G *wollen,* Icel. *vilja*), cogn. with L *velle,* and Eng. WELL[1] and WILD]

will[2], *n.* the mental power or faculty by which one initiates or controls one's activities, opp. to external causation and to impulse or instinct; the exercise of this power, an act of willing, a choice of volition, an intention; a fixed or authoritative purpose; determination, energy of character, power of carrying out one's intentions or dominating others; that which is willed, resolved or determined upon; arbitrary disposal, discretion or sufferance; inclination or disposition towards others; the legal declaration of one's intentions as to the disposal of one's property (esp. freehold or landed) after one's death, embodied in a written instrument. **at will,** at one's pleasure or discretion. **with a will,** heartily, zealously. **will-worship,** *n.* (*Bibl.*) a religion devised by or imposed on oneself. **willed,** *a.* (*usu. in comb.* as *strong-willed*). **will-less,** *a.* [OE *willa,* from prec. (cp. Dut. *wil,* G *Wille,* Icel. *vili*)]

will[3], *v.t.* to intend or bring about by the exercise of one's will, to resolve, to determine; to direct, control or cause to act in a specified way by the exercise of one's will-power; to bequeath or devise by will. *v.i.* to exercise will-power. **will-power,** *n.* control exercised deliberately over impulse or inclinations. [from WILL[1,2]]

willet, *n.* a N American sandpiper, *Symphemia semipalmata,* allied to the snipe. [imit. of cry]

William, *n.* four kings of England:

William I, *n.* **the Conqueror** (*c.* 1027–87), king of England from 1066. He was the illegitimate son of Duke Robert the Devil, and succeeded his father as duke of Normandy 1035. Claiming that his relative Edward the Confessor had bequeathed him the English throne, William invaded the country 1066, defeating Harold II at Hastings, Sussex, and was crowned king of England (as depicted in the Bayeux Tapestry).

William II, *n.* **Rufus, 'the Red'** (*c.* 1056–1100), king of England from 1087, the third son of William I. He spent most of his reign attempting to capture Normandy from his brother Robert II, duke of Normandy. His extortion of money led his barons to revolt and caused confrontation with Bishop Anselm. He was killed while hunting in the New Forest, and was succeeded by his brother Henry I.

William III, *n.* (**William of Orange**) (1650–1702), king of Great Britain and Ireland from 1688, the son of William II of Orange and Mary, daughter of Charles I. He was offered the English crown by the parliamentary opposition to James II. He invaded England 1688 and in 1689 became joint sovereign with his wife Mary. He spent much of his reign campaigning, first in Ireland, where he defeated James II at the Boyne 1690, and later against the French in Flanders. He was succeeded by Anne.

William IV, *n.* (1765–1837), king of the United Kingdom from 1830, when he succeeded his brother George IV, and third son of George III. He was created duke of Clarence 1789, and married Adelaide of Saxe-Meiningen (1792–1849) in 1818. During the Reform Bill crisis he secured its passage by agreeing to create new peers to overcome the hostile majority in the House of Lords. He was succeeded by Victoria.

William, *n.* three kings of the Netherlands:

William I, *n.* (1772–1844), king of the Netherlands 1815–40. He lived in exile during the French occupation 1795–1813, and fought against the emperor Napoleon at Jena and Wagram. The Austrian Netherlands were added to his kingdom by the Allies 1815, but secured independence (recognized by the major European states, 1839) by the revolution of 1830. William's unpopularity led to his abdication 1840.

William II, *n.* (1792–1849), king of the Netherlands 1840–49, son of William I. He served with the British army in the Peninsular War and at Waterloo. In 1848 he averted revolution by conceding a liberal constitution.

William III, *n.* (1817–90), king of the Netherlands 1849–90, the son of William II. In 1862 he abolished slavery in the Dutch East Indies.

William[1], *n.* (full name **William Arthur Philip Louis**) (1982–), prince of the United Kingdom, first child of the Prince and Princess of Wales.

William[2], *n.* (1143–1214), king of Scotland from 1165, known as William the Lion. He was captured by Henry II while invading England 1174, and forced to do homage, but Richard I abandoned the English claim to suzerainty for a money payment 1189. In 1209 William was forced by John I to renounce his claim to Northumberland.

William[3], *n.* (1533–84), prince of Orange from 1544, known as William the Silent because of his absolute discretion. He was appointed governor of Holland by Philip II of Spain in 1559, but joined the revolt of 1572 against Spain's oppressive rule, and, as a Protestant from 1573, became the national leader. He briefly succeeded in uniting the Catholic south and Protestant northern provinces.

William[4], *n.* the badly behaved schoolboy hero of a series of children's books by British author Richmal Crompton, published 1922–70. William rebels against conventional English family life and, with his fellow 'Outlaws', Henry, Douglas, and Ginger, has many mishaps from which there is no honourable escape. Violet Elizabeth Bott, a 'soppy' girl, is an unwelcome addition to the Outlaws.

William of Malmesbury, *n.* (*c.* 1080–*c.* 1143), English historian and monk. He compiled the *Gesta regum/ Deeds of the Kings* about 1120–40 and *Historia novella*, which together formed a history of England to 1142.

Williams[1], *n.* British racing-car manufacturing company started by Frank Williams in 1969 when he modified a Brabham BT26A. The first Williams Grand Prix car was designed by Patrick Head in 1978 and since then the team has been one of the most successful in Grand Prix racing.

Williams[2], *n.* **Roger** (*c.* 1604–1684), British founder of Rhode Island colony in North America 1636, on a basis of democracy and complete religious freedom.

Williams[3], *n.* **Shirley** (1930–), British Social Democrat Party politician. She was Labour minister for prices and consumer protection 1974–76, and education and science 1976–79. She became a founder member of the SDP 1981 and its president 1982. In 1983 she lost her parliamentary seat. She is the daughter of the socialist writer Vera Brittain.

Williams[4], *n.* **Tennessee (Thomas Lanier)** (1911–83), US playwright, born in Mississippi. His work is characterized by fluent dialogue and searching analysis of the psychological deficiencies of his characters. His plays, usually set in the Deep South against a background of decadence and degradation, include *The Glass Menagerie* (1945) and *A Streetcar Named Desire* (1947).

Williams[5], *n.* **William Carlos** (1883–1963), US poet. His spare images and language reflect everyday speech. His epic poem *Paterson* (1946–58) celebrates his home town in New Jersey. *Pictures from Brueghel* (1963) won a Pulitzer Prize. His work had great impact on younger US poets.

Williamson[1], *n.* **Henry** (1895–1977), English author, known for stories of animal life such as *Tarka the Otter* (1927).

Williamson[2], *n.* **Malcolm (Benjamin Graham Christopher)** (1931–), Australian composer, pianist, and organist, who settled in Britain in 1953. His works include operas (*Our Man in Havana*, 1963), symphonies, and chamber music.

willie, *n.* (*coll.*) a childish or facetious word for PENIS. [short for *William*]

willies, *n.pl.* (*coll.*) nervousness, apprehensiveness. [etym. unknown]

willing etc. WILL[1].

Willis, *n.* **Norman David** (1933–), British trade-union leader. A trade union official since leaving school, he succeeded Len Murray as the general secretary of the Trades Union Congress (TUC) in 1984.

will-o'-the-wisp, *n.* an ignis fatuus; an illusory hope, goal etc. [*Will,* short for *William,* WISP (of lighted tow etc.)]

willow[1], *n.* any tree or shrub of the genus *Salix,* usu. growing near water, characterized by long, slender, pliant branches, largely yielding osiers and timber used for cricket-bats etc.; hence, a cricket-bat. **willow-herb,** *n.* a plant of the genus *Epilobium,* esp. the rose-bay, *E. angustifolium.* **willow-pattern,** *n.* a decorative pattern of Chinese style in blue on a white ground for china, introduced in 1780. **willow-warbler, -wren,** *n.* the chiff-chaff. **willowed, willowy,** *a.* abounding with willows; lithe, slender or graceful, like a willow. [OE *welig* (cp. Dut. *wilg*), perh. cogn. with HELIX]

willow[2], **willy,** *n.* a machine for the preliminary process of beating, picking and cleaning wool. *v.t.* to treat (wool) thus. [from prec.]

willy-nilly, *adv.* willingly or unwillingly; randomly, haphazardly. *a.* happening whether it is desired or not; random, haphazard. [*will he, nill he,* see NILL]

willy-willy, *n.* (*Austral.*) the tropical cyclone that sweeps over NW Australia in the late summer.

Wilson[1], *n.* **Angus (Frank Johnstone)** (1913–), British novelist, whose acidly humorous books include *Anglo-Saxon Attitudes* (1956) and *The Old Men at the Zoo* (1961).

Wilson[2], *n.* **Edward O.** (1929–), US zoologist, whose books have stimulated interest in biogeography and the evolution of behaviour, or sociobiology. His works include *Sociobiology* (1975) and *On Human Nature* (1978).

Wilson[3], *n.* **(James) Harold, Baron Wilson of Rievaulx** (1916–), British Labour politician, party leader from 1963, prime minister 1964–70 and 1974–76. His premiership was dominated by the issue of UK admission to EEC membership, the social contract (unofficial agreement with the trade unions), and economic difficulties.

Wilson[4], *n.* **Richard** (1714–82), British painter, whose English and Welsh landscapes are infused with an Italianate atmosphere and recomposed in a Classical manner. They influenced the development of an English landscape-painting tradition.

Wilson[5], *n.* **(Thomas) Woodrow** (1856–1924), 28th president of the US 1913–21, a Democrat. He kept the US out of World War I until 1917, and in Jan. 1918 issued his Fourteen Points as a basis for a just peace settlement. At the peace conference in Paris he secured the inclusion of the League of Nations in individual peace treaties, but these were not ratified by Congress, so the US did not join the League. Nobel Peace prize 1919.

wilt, *v.i.* to wither, to droop; to lose freshness or vigour. *v.t.* to cause to wilt. [perh. var. of WELK]

Wilton, *n.* a carpet resembling Brussels, but with the loops cut open into an elastic velvet-pile, orig. manufactured at Wilton, in Wiltshire, and also called **Wilton Carpet**.

Wiltshire, *n.* county in SW England. **area** 3480 sq km/ 1343 sq miles. **towns** administrative headquarters Trowbridge; Salisbury, Swindon, Wilton. **physical** Marlborough Downs, Savernake Forest; rivers Kennet, and Salisbury and Bristol Avons; Salisbury Plain, including Stonehenge. **population** (1987) 551,000. **products** wheat, cattle, carpets, rubber, engineering. **Wiltshire**, *n.* a breed of pigs; a kind of mild-cured bacon; a kind of cheese.

wily, *a.* using or full of wiles; cunning, crafty. **wilily,** *adv.* **wiliness,** *n.*

†**wimble,** *n.* a boring-instrument, a gimlet, brace-and-bit etc. *v.t.* to bore with this. [(cp. MDut. *wemelen* to bore with a wimble, LG *wemel, wemmel,* Dan. *vimmel,* a boring-tool), perh. cogn. with WHIM]

Wimbledon, *n.* English lawn-tennis centre used for world tennis matches, situated in south London. There are currently 18 courts.

WIMP, *n.* windows, icons, menus, pointing device, in computing, a type of user interface, in which programs and files appear as icons, menus drop down from a bar along the top of the screen, and data are displayed in rectangular areas, called windows, which the operator can manipulate in various ways. The operator uses a pointing device, typically a mouse, to make selections and initiate actions.

wimp, *n.* (*coll.*) a feeble, ineffectual person, esp. a man. [etym. unknown]

wimple, *n.* a covering of silk, linen etc., worn over the head, neck and sides of the face formerly by women and still by some nuns. †*v.t.* to cover with a wimple; to fold in plaits etc.; to hoodwink. *v.i.* to be folded in plaits etc.; to ripple. [OE *winpel* (perh. WIND[2], *pell, pœll,* L PALLIUM), (cp. Dut., G *Wimpel,* Icel. *vimpill,* pennon, streamer)]

Wimpy®, *n.* a type of hamburger inside a bread roll.

Wimshurst machine, *n.* a friction machine by which static electricity can be generated and stored. [British engineer James *Wimshurst,* 1832–1903]

win, *v.t.* (*past, p.p.* **won**[1]) to gain, obtain, achieve or attain by fighting, struggling or superiority in a contest, competition, wager etc.; to gain by toil etc., to earn; to be victorious in; to make one's way to, to reach; to attract, to charm (*in pres.p*); to persuade, to secure the support, favour or assent of, to gain over; to get or extract (ore etc.) by mining, smelting etc.; (*sl.*) to steal. *v.i.* to be successful or victorious in a fight, contest, wager etc.; to make one's way by struggle or effort (to etc.); to produce an attractive effect (upon). *n.* a success, a victory. **to win one's spurs** SPURS. **to win out,** to be successful, to prevail. **you can't win,** *int.* used to express resignation when one has failed, been defeated etc. **winner,** *n.* a person or thing that wins; a person or thing that is bound to succeed. **winning,** *a.* that wins; attractive, charming. *n.pl.* the amount won at racing, in a game of cards etc. **winning hazard** HAZARD. **winning post,** *n.* a post marking the end of a race. **winningly,** *adv.* [OE *winnan,* to fight, to labour (cp. Dut. *winnen,* G *gewinnen,* Icel. *vinna*), cogn. with L *venus,* desire, and WISH]

wince, *v.i.* to shrink, start back, recoil or flinch, as from pain, trouble or a blow. *n.* the act of wincing. **wincer,** *n.* [prob. from a non-extant OF *wencir,* from OF *guincir,* OS *wenkian,* cogn. with WINK]

wincey, *n.* a cotton cloth with wool filling. **winceyette,** *n.* a light-weight cotton cloth raised on both sides. [perh. corr. of LINSEY-WOOLSEY]

winch, *n.* a windlass, a hoisting-machine; a crank or handle for turning an axle etc. [OE *wince,* cogn. with WINKLE]

Winchester disk, *n.* an alternative name for hard disk.

wind[1], *n.* air in motion, a natural air-current, a breeze, a gale; air set in motion artificially; air used or stored for use in a musical instrument, machine etc.; (*collect.*) (those playing the) wind-instruments in an orchestra etc.; breath as acquired by the body in exertion; power of breathing in exertion, lung power; a part of the body near the stomach a blow on which causes temporary inability to breathe; breath expended in words, meaningless talk or rhetoric; the gas produced in the stomach during digestion etc., flatulence; scent or odour carried on the wind; hence, a hint, suggestion or indication (of); the windward position, the weather-gauge (of). *v.t.* (*past, p.p.* **winded**) to perceive the presence of by scent; to cause to be out of breath; to enable to recover breath by resting etc.; to bring the wind up from the stomach of (a baby), e.g. by patting his/her back; to expose to the wind, to ventilate. **how the wind blows,** the position or state of affairs. **in the wind,** showing signs of occurring. **in the wind's eye,** towards the precise point from which the wind blows. **it's an ill wind,** few situations are so bad that nobody at all benefits from them. **to get the wind up,** to get nervous, frightened. **to get wind of,** to find out about. **the four winds,** the four cardinal points. **to break wind,** to discharge wind from the anus. **to raise the wind,** to procure the necessary amount of cash. **to sail close to the wind,** to keep the vessel's head as near the quarter from which the wind is blowing as possible while keeping the sails filled; to take risks. **to take the wind out of someone's sails,** to sail to the windward of; to frustrate someone's plans, to disconcert. **windbag,** *n.* a bag inflated with wind; a person of mere words, a long-winded speaker. **wind-blown,** *a.* blown by the wind, said esp. of trees deformed by a prevailing wind. **wind-bound,** *a.* prevented from sailing by contrary winds. **windburn,** *n.* skin irritation caused by the wind. **wind-cheater,** *n.* a close-knitted pullover or close-textured garment to keep out the wind; an anorak. **wind-chest,** *n.* the box or reservoir for compressed air in an organ. **windchill,** *n.* a measure of the combined chilling effect of low-temperature and wind, as in *windchill factor*. **wind-colic,** *n.* pain in the abdomen caused by flatulence. **wind cone, sock,** *n.* an open-ended fabric sleeve flying from a mast, serving as an indicator of the strength and direction of the wind. **wind-egg,** *n.* an imperfect egg, esp. an unfertilized, addled or shell-less one. **windfall,** *n.* something blown down by the wind; (*N Am.*) the track of a whirlwind by which trees are laid prostrate; unexpected good fortune. **windfallen,** *a.* blown down by the wind. **wind-fanner,** *n.* a windhover. **wind-flower,** *n.* the wood-anemone. **wind-gall,** *n.* a soft tumour on the fetlock joint of a horse. **wind-gauge,** *n.* an anemometer; an instrument for showing the pressure in the wind-chest of an organ; a contrivance attached to the sight of a gun to show the allowance necessary for deflection due to the wind. **windhover,** *n.* the kestrel. **wind-instrument,** *n.* a musical instrument in which the tones are produced by the vibration of an air-column forced into the pipes, reeds etc. by a bellows or the mouth. **windjammer,** *n.* a merchant sailing-ship as dist. from a steamer; one of the crew of this. **wind machine,** *n.* a machine used in cinema films, the theatre etc. for producing an airstream. **windmill,** *n.* a mill driven by the action of the wind on sails; (*pl.*) imaginary adversaries, chimeras (with alln. to Don Quixote); a device for generating power to drive fuel pumps, wireless generators etc. by a small propeller blade placed in the slip-stream of an aircraft. *v.t., v.i.* to (cause to) move like a windmill. **windpipe,** *n.* the breathing passage, the trachea. **wind power,** *n.* electrical power produced by harnessing wind energy, e.g. by means of a windmill. **wind-pump,** *n.* a pump operated by the force of the wind on a propeller. **windrose,** *n.* a diagram with radiating lines indicating the velocity and direction of winds affecting a place. **windrow,** *n.* a row of hay raked together, corn-sheaves, peats etc. set up for drying. **wind-sail,** *n.* (*Naut.*) a canvas tube used to convey a current of air into the lower parts of a ship. **wind sock** WIND CONE. **windscreen,** *n.* a glass screen in the front of a car to protect the driver and passengers from the wind caused by the speed of the car. **windshaken,** *a.* **windshield,** *n.* (*N Am.*) a windscreen. **wind-surfing,** *n.* the sport of sailing standing upright on a surfboard fitted with a sail. **wind-swept,** *a.* exposed to the wind. **wind-tight,** *a.* airtight, excluding the wind. **wind-tunnel,** *n.* a tunnel-like device for producing an air-stream of known velocity for testing the effect of wind on the structure of model vehicles, aircraft etc. **windage,** *n.* the difference between the diameter of the bore of a muzzle-loading rifled gun and that of the projectile; the influence of wind deflecting a projectile; allowance for this. **windless,** *a.* **windward,** *n.* the direction from which the wind blows. *a.* lying in or directed towards this. *adv.* in the direction from which the wind blows. **to get to the windward of,** to get to this side of, to get the weather-gauge of; to get the advantage over. **windy,** *a.* characterized by wind, stormy, boisterous; exposed to the wind; flatulent, caused by flatulence; verbose, loquacious, empty; (*coll.*) scared, frightened, apprehensive. **windily,** *adv.* **windiness,** *n.* [OE, (cp. Dut., G *Wind,* Icel. *vindr,* also L *ventus,* Sansk. *vātas,*) cogn. with WEATHER]

wind², *v.i.* (*past, p.p.* **wound**) to turn, move, go or be twisted or coiled in a spiral, curved or tortuous course or shape; to be circular, spiral, tortuous or crooked; to meander; to proceed circuitously, to twist one's way or insinuate oneself (into etc.); to be wrapped spirally (round, into etc.); to sound a horn by blowing. *v.t.* to cause to turn spirally, to wrap, twine or coil; to encircle, to coil round, to entwine; to pursue (one's course) in a spiral, sinuous or circuitous way; to hoist or move by means of a windlass, capstan etc. **to wind down,** to reduce gradually; to relax. **winding-down,** *n.* **to wind off,** to unwind; to stop talking. **to wind up,** to coil up; to coil or tighten up the spring of (a watch etc.); to put into a state of tension or readiness for activity; (*coll.*) to irritate, to annoy; (*coll.*) to find oneself in a certain state or situation; to bring or come to a conclusion, to conclude; to arrange the final settlement of the affairs of (a business etc.); to go into liquidation. **winding-up,** *n.* **winder,** *n.* **winding,** *n.*, *a.* material wound or coiled round something, e.g. wire in an electric motor. **winding-drum,** *n.* a mechanically-driven drum on which a haulage rope is wound. **winding-engine,** *n.* a hoisting engine. **winding-sheet,** *n.* the sheet in which a corpse is wrapped. **winding-stair,** *n.* a stair built around a newel. **winding-tackle,** *n.* **windingly,** *adv.* [OE *windan* (cp. Dut., G *winden,* Icel. *vinda*), perh. cogn. with WITHY]

windage, windhover etc. WIND¹.

Windermere, *n.* largest lake in England, in Cumbria, 17 km/10.5 miles long and 1.6 km/1 mile wide.

Windhoek, *n.* capital of Namibia; population (1988) 115,000. It is just north of the Tropic of Capricorn, 290 km/180 miles from the W coast.

windlass¹, *n.* a machine consisting of a cylinder on an axle turned by a crank, used for hoisting or hauling. *v.t.* to hoist or haul with this. [ME *windelas,* Icel. *vindilāss* (*vindill,* winder, from *vinda,* to WIND², *āss,* pole, beam)]

†**windlass²,** *n.* (*Shak.*) a circuit, an indirect or crafty course. [prob. corr. of ME *wanlace,* OF *wanelace,* deceit, artifice]

windle, *n.* (*dial.*) a reel, a spindle; †an old dry measure of about 3½ bushels (127 l). [OE *windel,* from *windan,* to WIND²]

windless, windmill WIND¹.

windlestraw, *n.* the old stalks of various grasses. [OE *windel-strēaw* (*windel,* basket, from *windan,* to WIND², STRAW¹)]

window, *n.* an opening in the wall or roof of a building, vehicle or other structure, usu. with the wooden or metal glazed framework filling it, for the admission of light or of light and air; the sash of a window-frame; a brief period of time when the conditions allow a particular activity; (*Comput.*) a rectangular area on a VDU where information can be displayed. **window-bar,** *n.* the bar of a sash or window-frame; †(*pl.*) lattice-work on a woman's stomacher. **window-blind,** *n.* **window-box,** *n.* the casing in which a sash-weight slides; a flower-box for a window-sill. **window-curtain,** *n.* **window-dressing,** *n.* the arrangement of goods for display in a shop window; deceptive display, insincere argument. **window-envelope,** *n.* an envelope with an open or transparent panel through which the address can be seen. **window-frame,** *n.* the framework in a window holding the sashes. **window-glass,** *n.* **window-sash,** *n.* a frame in which panes of glass for windows are set. **window-seat,** *n.* a seat in the recess of a window. **window-shop,** *v.i.* to gaze idly at the displays in shop-windows. **window-shopper,** *n.* **window shopping,** *n.* **windowed,** *a.* (*usu. in comb.* as *many-windowed*). **windowless,** *a.* †**windowy,** *a.* [Icel. *vindauga* (*vindr,* WIND¹, *auga* (cp. OE *ēage,* EYE))]

windpipe, windrow WIND¹.

Windscale, *n.* former name of Sellafield in Cumbria.

Windsor, *n.* a town in Berks, England. **brown Windsor,** *n.* Windsor soup; a common, tasteless soup. **Duchess of Windsor,** title of Wallis Warfield Simpson. **Duke of Windsor,** title of Edward VIII. **House of Windsor,** official name of the British royal family since 1917, adopted in place of Saxe-Coburg-Gotha. Since 1960 those descendants of Elizabeth II not entitled to the prefix HRH have borne the surname Mountbatten-Windsor. **Windsor Castle,** *n.* British royal residence in Windsor, founded by William the Conqueror on the site of an earlier fortress. It includes the Perpendicular Gothic St George's Chapel and the Albert Memorial Chapel, beneath which George III, George IV, and William IV are buried. In the Home Park adjoining the castle is the Royal Mausoleum where Queen Victoria and Prince Albert are buried. **Windsor chair,** *n.* a strong, plain wooden chair with a back curved into supports for the arms. **Windsor soap,** *n.* a brown scented soap formerly made at Windsor.

windward, windy etc. WIND¹.

Windward Islands, *n.pl.* islands in the path of the prevailing wind, notably: **West Indies** see ANTILLES; **Cape Verde Islands; French Polynesia** (Tahiti, Moorea, and Makatea).

wine, *n.* the fermented juice of grapes; the juice of certain fruits etc. prepared in imitation of this; intoxication; (*Univ.*) a wine party; a medicinal preparation in wine as medium. **spirit of wine** SPIRIT. **to wine and dine,** to entertain with food and alcohol. **winebag,** *n.* a skin for holding wine; a wine-bibber. **wine bar,** *n.* a bar that serves mostly wine, esp. with food. **wine-bibber,** *n.* a wine-drinker, a tippler. **wine-bibbing,** *n.* **wine-bottle,** *n.* **wine-bowl,** *n.* **wine-box,** *n.* a cardboard box with a plastic lining, usu. with a three-litre capacity, fitted with a tap for dispensing wine. **wine-carriage,** *n.* a wheeled receptacle for circulating a wine-bottle at table. **wine-cask,** *n.* **wine-cellar,** *n.* **wine-cooler,** *n.* a vessel for cooling wine in bottles with ice. **wine-cup,** *n.* †**winefat,** *n.* a winepress. **wine-glass,** *n.* a small glass for drinking wine from. **wine-glassful,** *n.* about 2 fl oz (6 cl). **winegrower,** *n.* **wine-measure,** *n.* an old English measure by which wine and spirits were sold. **wine-merchant,** *n.* **wine-palm,** *n.* a palm tree from which palm-wine is obtained. **winepress,** *n.* an apparatus in which grapes are pressed; the place in which this is done. **wineskin,** *n.* a skin, usu. of a goat, sewn into a bag for holding wine. **wine-stone,** *n.* a deposit of crude tartar or argal in wine-casks. **wine-tasting,** *n.* an occasion when people can sample various wines. **wine-vault,** *n.* a vault in which wine is stored; a bar or tap-room where wine is retailed. **wineless,** *a.* **winy,** *a.* [OE *wīn,* L *vīnum* (cp. Dut. *wijn,* G *Wein,* also Gr. *oinos*), cogn. with WITHE, from *wei-,* to twine]

wing, *n.* one of the limbs or organs of flight in birds, insects etc.; one of the supporting parts of a flying-machine; motion by means of wings, flight, power of flight; (*coll.*) an arm; a part of a building, fortification, army, bone, implement etc. projecting laterally; an RAF unit of three squadrons; in football and similar games, a player on one or other extreme flank; the position in which such a player plays; one of the extreme factions of a party, group etc.; one of the front-wheel mudguards of a car; the sides of a stage or pieces of scenery placed there; two lateral petals of a papilionaceous flower which stand opposite each other; (*pl.*) the mark of proficiency a pilot qualified in the RAF is entitled to wear on his uniform. *v.t.* to furnish with wings; to enable to fly or move with swiftness; to traverse or travel on wings; to wound in the wing or (*coll.*) the arm. *v.i.* to fly. **in the wings,** waiting in readiness. **on the wing,** flying; in motion. **to take under one's wing,** to take under one's protection. **to take wing,** to begin flying, to fly away; to disappear. **wing and wing,** said of a fore-and-aft vessel going before the wind with her fore-sail hauled over to one side and main-sail to the other. **wingbeat,** *n.* a complete stroke of the wing in flying. **wing-case,** *n.* the horny cover or case, consisting of a modified wing, protecting the flying wings of coleopterous insects. **wing-collar,** *n.* a stiff upright shirt-collar with the points turned down. **wind-commander,** *n.* a commissioned officer in the RAF equivalent to a lieutenant-colonel. **wing-covert,** *n.* one of the small feathers covering the insertion of a bird's flight-feathers. **wing-footed,** *a.* as if having wings on the feet; swift. **wing nut,** *n.* a nut that is tightened by two flat wings on its sides. **wing-sheath,** *n.* a wing-case. **wingspan,** *n.* the distance from one wing-tip of a bird, aircraft etc. to the other. **wing-stroke,** *n.* a wing-beat. **winged,** *a.* furnished with wings; (*poet.,* wing'id) going straight to the mark, powerful, rousing (of words etc.). **winger,** *n.* a football-player etc. positioned on the wing. **wingless,** *a.* **winglet,** *n.* †**wingy,** *a.* [ME *winge, wenge,* Norw. *vengja* (cp. Icel. *vœngr,* Dan., Swed. *vinge*), cogn. with Sansk. *vā,* to blow]

wink, *v.i.* to close and open the eyes quickly, to blink; of an eye, to close and open; to give a sign or signal by such a motion of the eye; to twinkle, to flicker. *v.t.* to close and open (an eye or the eyes). *n.* the act of winking, esp. as a signal; a hint, a private intimation; a moment, an instant. **forty winks,** (*coll.*) a nap. **to tip one the wink,** to give one a hint privately. **to wink at,** to affect not to see; to connive at. **winker,** *n.* **winking,** *n.* **like winking,** very rapidly; with great vigour. **winkingly,** *adv.* [OE *wincian* (cp. MDut. *wincken,* G *winken,* Icel. *vanka*), cogn. with WINCE and WINKLE]

winkle, *n.* an edible sea-snail, a periwinkle. **to winkle out,** to extract sharpshooters and small bodies of enemy troops from hiding-places; (*coll.*) to extract with difficulty; to elicit (information etc.) with difficulty. **winkle-pickers,** *n.pl.* shoes with pointed toes. [OE *-wincla,* in *wine-wincla,* cogn. with prec. and WINCH]

winna, (*Sc.*) WILL NOT.

winning etc. WIN

Winnipeg, *n.* capital and industrial city (sawmills, textiles, meat packing) in Manitoba, Canada, on the Red River, south of Lake Winnipeg; population (1986) 623,000. **Lake Winnipeg,** *n.* lake in S Manitoba, Canada, draining much of the Canadian prairies; area 24,500 sq km/9460 sq miles.

winnow, *v.t.* to separate and drive the chaff from (grain); to fan chaff (away, out etc.); to sift, to sort, to examine or analyse thoroughly; to blow on, to stir (hair etc.); (*poet.*) to beat or flap (wings). **winnower,** *n.* **winnowing,** *n.* [OE *windwian,* from WIND[1]]

wino, *n.* (*pl.* **winos**) (*coll.*) an alcoholic, esp. one who drinks mainly wine.

winsey, WINCEY.

winsome, *a.* engaging, winning, charming, attractive; graceful, lovely. **winsomely,** *adv.* **winsomeness,** *n.* [OE *wynsum* (*wynn,* joy, cogn. with WIN, -SOME)]

winter, *n.* the cold season of the year, astronomically in northern latitudes from the December solstice to the March equinox. usu. regarded as including December, January, February; a period of inactivity, a cheerless or depressing state of things; (*poet.*) a year of life. *a.* pertaining, suitable to or lasting for the winter. *v.i.* to pass the winter; to hibernate. *v.t.* to keep, manage or maintain through the winter. **winter-apple,** *n.* an apple that keeps well or ripens in winter. **winter-barley, -wheat,** *n.* varieties of cereal sown in autumn. **winterberry,** *n.* a N American shrub of the genus *Ilex,* bearing bright red berry-like drupes. **winter-cough,** *n.* chronic bronchitis. **winter-cress,** *n.* a herb of the mustard family grown in the winter as a salad. **winter-crop,** *n.* **winter-garden,** *n.* a large conservatory or glass-house for plants not hardy enough to withstand the climate outside during winter. **wintergreen,** *n.* a low herb of the genus *Pyrola,* keeping green throughout the winter. **winter-lodge,** *n.* a bud or bulb protecting an embryo or very young shoot during the winter. **winter-quarters,** *n.pl.* the quarters occupied by an army etc. during the winter. **winter sport,** *n.* sport practised on snow and ice, usu. outdoors, e.g. skiing, skating. **Winter War,** *n.* the USSR's invasion of Finland 30 Nov. 1939–12 Mar. 1940. **winterless,** *a.* **wintry,** *a.* of or like winter, e.g. of a smile, look etc., cold and cheerless. **wintriness,** *n.* [OE, (cp. Dut., G *Winter,* Dan., Swed. *vinter,*) perh. cogn. with L *unda,* wave, Eng. WET and WATER]

Winters-bark, *n.* a tree of the magnolia family, *Drimys winteri,* brought from the Straits of Magellan by Capt. John *Winter* in 1579; the aromatic bark of this.

winy WINE.

winze, *n.* (*Mining*) a shaft sunk from one level to another for communication or ventilation. [prob. cogn. with WINNOW]

wipe, *v.t.* to rub with something soft in order to clean or dry; to apply solder to with something soft; to clear (a magnetic tape or videotape) of recorded material; to apply (grease etc.) by wiping. *v.i.* to strike (at). *n.* the act of wiping; a sweeping blow. **to wipe away,** to remove by wiping; to get rid of. **to wipe off,** to clear away. **to wipe one's eyes,** to cease weeping. **to wipe out,** to clean out by wiping; to efface, to obliterate; to destroy, to annihilate. **to wipe the floor with,** (*sl.*) to defeat utterly. **wipe-out,** *n.* an act or instance of wiping out; interference that renders impossible the reception of other signals. **wipe-out area,** *n.* the vicinity of a transmitting station where wipe-out occurs. **wiper,** *n.* cloth etc. used for wiping; an automatically operated arm to keep a portion of the windscreen free from rain. [OE *wipian* (cp. EFris. *wīp,* LG *wiep*)]

wire, *n.* metal drawn out into a slender and flexible rod or thread of uniform diameter; such a slender rod, thread or strand of metal; the electric telegraph, a telegraphic message; a wire barrier or fence. *v.t.* to apply wire to, to fasten, secure, bind or stiffen with wire; to string (beads) on a wire; to snare with wire; (*coll.*) to telegraph to. *v.i.* to send a telegram. **to pull the wires,** to manipulate puppets; to control politics etc. by clandestine means. **to wire in,** (*sl.*) to apply oneself vigorously. **wire brush,** *n.* a brush with wire bristles used, e.g. for scraping rust off metal. **wire-cloth, -gauze, -netting,** *n.* a fabric of woven wire. **wire-cutter,** *n.* an implement for cutting wire. **wire-dancer,** *n.* an acrobat performing on a tight wire. **wiredraw,** *v.t.* (*p.p.* **-drawn**) to form (metal) into wire by forcibly drawing through a series of gradually diminishing holes; to overstrain or over-refine (an argument etc.). **wiredrawer,** *n.* **wire-edge,** *n.* an edge turned back like wire, on a knife etc., by over-sharpening. **wire-entanglement,** *n.* an obstruction composed of interlacing barbed wire defending the front of an entrenchment etc. against a rapid assault. **wire gauge,** *n.* an instrument for measuring the diameter of wire. **wire-gun,** *n.* a heavy gun constructed of steel wire of rectangular section coiled round a tube. **wire-haired,** *a.* having stiff, wiry hair (esp. of terriers). **wire-heel,** *n.* a disease of the foot in horses. **wire-puller,** *n.* a politician etc. working behind the scenes. **wire-pulling,** *n.* **wire-rope,** *n.* a rope made by twisting strands of wire. **wire-tap,** *v.t.* to tap (a telephone). **wire-wool,** *n.* abrasive material consisting of a mass of very fine wires, used for cleaning etc. **wireworm,** *n.* a vermiform larva of a click-beetle, destructive to roots of vegetables, cereals etc. **wirer,** *n.* **wiring,** *n.* a system of wires, esp. one carrying electric current. **wiry,** *a.* made of or resembling wire; tough and flexible; lean but sinewy; stiff (of hair etc.). **wirily,** *adv.* **wiriness,** *n.* [OE *wīr* (cp. Icel. *vīrr,* Swed. *vira,* to twist, also L *viriae,* armlets), cogn. with WITHE]

wireless, *n.* wireless telegraphy, radio; any process or method whereby messages, music or other sounds can be transmitted in the ether by electromagnetic waves without the intervention of wires; an instrument for receiving such messages etc.; the programmes of entertainment etc. thus transmitted; radio. *v.t., v.i.* (*coll.*) to communicate with or inform by this.

wirrycow, *n.* (*Sc.*) a hobgoblin, a bogy; the devil. [etym. doubtful]

†**wis,** *v.i. first sing.* (I) know. [supposed pres. of WIT[1], evolved from *iwis, ywis,* OE *gewis,* certain]

†**wisard,** WIZARD.

Wisconsin, *n.* state of the north central US; nickname Badger State. **area** 145,500 sq km/56,163 sq miles. **capital** Madison. **towns** Milwaukee, Green Bay, Racine. **population** (1988) 4,816,000. **products** premier dairying state, cereals, coal, iron, zinc, lead, agricultural machinery, precision instruments, plumbing equipment.

wisdom, *n.* the quality or state of being wise; knowledge and experience together with ability to make use of them rightly, practical discernment, sagacity, judgment, common sense; †a collection of wise sayings. **wisdom-tooth,** *n.* the third molar appearing about the age of 20. [OE]

wise[1], *a.* having or characterized by the power or faculty of discerning or judging rightly, or by knowledge and experience together with ability to apply them rightly, sagacious, sensible, discreet, prudent, judicious; experienced, understanding; informed, aware; (*N Am. coll.*) insolent, cocksure; †having occult knowledge. **to put someone wise,** to inform someone. **to wise up,** (*esp. N Am. coll.*) to (cause to) be aware or informed. **wisecrack,** *n.* (*coll.*) a smart but not profound epigram; a witty comment. **wise guy,** *n.* (*esp. N Am. coll.*) an insolent or cocksure person. †**wise man,** *n.* a wizard. **wise woman,** *n.* a witch, a fortune-teller; (*Sc.*) a midwife. †**wiseling,** *n.* a wiseacre. **wisely,** *adv.* †**wiseness,** *n.* [OE *wīs* (cp. Dut. *wijs,* G *weise,* Icel. *vīss*), cogn. with WIT[1]]

wise[2], *n.* manner, way, mode of acting, behaving etc., guise. [OE (cp. Dut. *wijs,* G *Weise,* Dan. *viis,* Swed. *vis*), from *wīsian,* to show the way, orig. to make WISE[1]]

Wise, *n.* **Robert** (1914–), US film director who began as a film editor. His debut was a horror film, *Curse of the Cat People* (1944); he progressed to such large-scale projects as *The Sound of Music* (1965) and *Star* (1968). His other films include *The Body Snatcher* (1945) and *Star Trek: The Motion Picture* (1979).

-wise, *suf.* forming adverbs of manner, as *anywise, lengthwise, likewise, otherwise;* with regard to, concerning, as in *jobwise, weatherwise.* [WIZE[2]]

wiseacre, *n.* one pretending to learning or wisdom. [MDut. *wijs-sagger,* G *Weissager,* from MHG *wīzago,* a prophet (cp. OE *wītiga,* prophet, from *wītan,* to see, cogn. with *witan,* to WIT[1])]

wish, *v.t.* to have a strong desire, aspiration or craving (that etc.), to crave, to covet, to want; to frame or express a desire or wish concerning, to invoke, to bid. *v.i.* to have a strong desire (for); to make a wish. *n.* a desire, a longing, an aspiration; an expression of this, a request, a petition, an invocation; that which is desired. **to wish someone, something on someone,** to foist someone or something on someone. **wishbone, wishing-bone,** *n.* the merrythought, the longer part of which when broken by two persons is supposed to entitle the holder to the fulfilment of some wish. **wisher,** *n.* (*usu. in comb.* as *well-wisher).* **wishful,** *a.* **wishful thinking,** *n.* belief based on desires rather than facts. **wishfully,** *adv.* **wishfulness,** *n.* **wishing-cap,** *n.* a magic cap conferring the power of realizing one's wishes. [OE *wȳscan* (cp. Dut. *wenschen,* G *wunschen,* Icel. *æskja*), cogn. with WIN]

wishtonwish, *n.* the N American prairie-dog. [N Am. Ind.]

wish-wash, *n.* thin weak liquor or drink; feeble talk, claptrap. **wishy-washy,** *a.* vague, ill-defined; lacking strength, forcefulness etc. [redupl. of WASH]

†**wisket,** WHISKET.

wisp, *n.* a small bunch or handful of straw, hay etc.; a tuft; a thin band or streak; a slim or delicate person, esp. a girl. **wispy,** *a.* [ME, var. *wips* (cp. LG *Wiep,* Norw. *vippa*), cogn. with WIPE]

wist, *past* WIT[1].

wistaria, wisteria, *n.* a leguminous climbing shrub with racemes of lilac-coloured flowers. [after US anatomist Caspar *Wistar* 1761–1818]

wistful, *a.* full of vague yearnings, esp. for unattainable things, sadly longing; thoughtful in a melancholy way, pensive. **wistfully,** *adv.* **wistfulness,** *n.* [etym. doubtful (perh. WHIST[1], -FUL, conf. with WISHFUL)]

wistiti, ouistiti, *n.* the marmoset. [S Am. native]

†**wit[1],** *v.t., v.i.* (*first sing.* **wot**, *second sing.* **wottest**, *past* **wist** ; *no other parts used*) to know (esp. in the infinitive 'to wit', namely). **witting,** *a.* **wittingly,** *adv.* consciously, knowingly, intentionally. [OE *witan* (cp. Dut. *weten,* G *wissen,* Icel. *vita*), cogn. with L *vidēre,* Gr. *idein,* to see, *oida,* I know, Sansk, *vēda*]

wit[2], *n.* intelligence, understanding, sense, sagacity (*often in pl.*); (*pl.*) sanity; the power of perceiving analogies and other relations between apparently incongruous ideas or of forming unexpected, striking or ludicrous combinations of them; a person distinguished for this power, a witty person; †a wise man. **at one's wits' end,** at a complete loss what further steps to take. †**the five wits,** the five senses; the mental faculties. **to have one's wits about one,** to be alert. **witless,** *a.* **witlessly,** *adv.* **witlessness,** *n.* †**witling,** *n.* one with little wit or understanding. **witted,** *a.* **witticism,** *n.* a witty phrase or saying, a jest. **witty,** *a.* **wittily,** *adv.* **wittiness,** *n.* (*usu. in comb.* as *slow-witted*). [OE *witt,* knowledge, from *witan,* see prec.]

witan, WITENAGEMOT.

witch[1], *n.* a woman having dealings with evil spirits or practising the black art or sorcery; a bewitching or fascinating woman; an old and ugly woman, a hag. *v.t.* to bewitch, fascinate, to enchant. **witchcraft,** *n.* the practices of witches; sorcery, magic. **witch-doctor,** *n.* in some tribal societies, a man who invokes supernatural powers, esp. to cure people. **witch-finder,** *n.* (*Hist.*) one whose business was to discover witches. **witch hunt,** *n.* the searching out and public exposure of opponents accused of disloyalty to a state, political party etc. **witchery,** *n.* **witching,** *a.* **witchingly,** *adv.* [OE masc. *wicca,* fem. *wicce,* rel. to *wiccian,* to practise sorcery (cp. Icel. *vikja,* to turn aside, to exorcize, OE *wīcan,* to give way), cogn. with WEAK]

witch[2], witch-elm, witch-hazel, WYCH.

witchetty, *n.* the edible grub of a longicorn beetle. [Austral. Abor.]

†**wite,** *v.t.* to blame, to censure. *n.* blame, reproach. †**witeless,** *a.* [OE *wītan,* cogn. with *witan,* see WIT[1]]

witenagemot, *n.* the Anglo-Saxon national assembly or parliament. [OE *witena,* gen. pl. of WITAN, GEMOTE]

with, *prep.* in or into company of or the relation of accompaniment, association, simultaneousness, cooperation, harmoniousness etc.; having, possessed of, marked or characterized by; in the possession, care or guardianship of; by the means, instrumentality, use or aid of; by the addition or supply of; because of, owing to, in consequence of; in regard to, in respect of, concerning, in the case of; in separation from; in opposition to, against; in spite of, notwithstanding. **with child,** *adv.* pregnant. **with it,** *a.* (*coll.*) up-to-date, fashionable; alert to what is being done or said. **with young,** *adv.* (of a mammal) pregnant. [OE, from *wither,* against (cp. Icel. *vith,* Dan. *ved,* Swed. *vid*), superseding OE and ME *mid,* with]

withal, *adv.* with the rest, in addition, at the same time, further, moreover. †*prep.* (*used after its obj.*) with.

withdraw, *v.t.* (*past* **-drew**, *p.p.* **-drawn**) to draw back, aside or apart; to take away, to remove, to retract. *v.i.* to retire from a presence or place; to go apart or aside; to retract a statement, accusation etc.; to isolate oneself socially, emotionally etc. **withdrawal,** *n.* **withdrawer,** *n.* †**withdrawing-room,** *n.* a drawing-room. **withdrawn,** *a.* very reserved, socially isolated etc.

withe, *n.* a tough, flexible branch, esp. of willow or osier, used in binding things together; a band or tie made of osiers, twigs, straw etc. [WITHY]

wither, *v.t.* to cause to fade, shrivel or dry, to shrivel and dry (up); to cause to lose freshness, soundness, vitality or vigour; (*fig.*) to blight, to blast; to make abashed. *v.i.* to become dry and wrinkled; to dry and shrivel (up); to lose freshness, soundness, vigour etc.; to fade away, to languish, to droop. **witheredness,** *n.* **withering,** *a.* **witheringly,** *adv.* [ME *widren, wederen,* to expose to the weather, from *weder,* WEATHER]

withers, *n.pl.* the ridge between the shoulder-blades of a horse. **wither-wrung,** *a.* injured or hurt in the withers. [OE *wither,* against (because it is against the collar or load), see WITH]

withershins, *adv.* anti-clockwise, in the contrary direction, esp. to the left or opposite to the direction of the sun, opp. to deiseal. [Icel. *vithr,* against (cp. Dan., Swed. *veder,* OE *wither,* Dut. *weder,* G *Wieder*), Icel. *sinni,* walk, movement, cogn. with OE *sīth*]

withhold, *v.t.* (*past, p.p.* **-held**) to keep from action, to hold back, to refuse to grant, to refrain; †to maintain. †**withholden,** *p.p.* withheld. **withholder,** *n.* **withholdment,** *n.*

within, *adv.* inside, in or to the inside, in the inner part or parts, internally, indoors, in the mind, heart or spirit. *n.* the inside. *prep.* in or to the inner or interior part or parts of, inside; in the limits, range, scope or compass of; not beyond, not outside of, not farther off than; in no longer a time than. [OE *widhinnan,* on the inside]

without, *adv.* in, at or to the outside, outside, outwardly, externally, out of doors. *n.* the outside. *prep.* not having, not with, having no, destitute of, lacking, free from; outside of; out of the limits, compass or range of, beyond. *conj.* (*dial.*) unless, except. †**withoutdoor,** *a.* outdoor; outward, external. [OE *withūtan*]

withstand, *v.t.* (*past, p.p.* **-stood**) to stand up against, to resist, to oppose. *v.i.* (*poet.*) to make a stand or resistance (against). **withstander,** *n.* [OE *withstandan*]

withwind, *n.* (*dial.*) the bindweed and other climbing weeds. [WITHE, WIND[2]]

withy, *n.* a withe; a willow. [OE *withig* (cp. MDut. *wiede,* G *Weide,* Icel. *vithja*), cogn. with Gr. *itea,* willow, L *vitis,* vine]

witless etc. WIT[2].

witness, *n.* attestation of a fact etc., testimony, evidence; a thing that constitutes evidence or proof, confirmation; a thing or person serving as testimony to or proof of; one who has seen or known an incident etc., a spectator, a person present at an event; one who gives evidence in a law-court or for judicial purposes, esp. on oath; one who affixes his name to a document to testify to the genuineness of the signature. *v.t.* to see or know by personal presence, to be a spectator of; to attest, to sign as witness; to indicate, to show, to prove; †to state in evidence. *v.i.* to bear testimony, to testify, to give evidence; to serve as evidence (against, for etc.); †to be a witness (in invocations etc.). **to bear witness,** to give testimony; to be a sign (of). **witness-box,** *n.* an enclosure in a law-court for witnesses (*esp. N Am.* witness-stand). **witnessable,** *a.* [OE *witnes* (WIT[1], -NESS)]

Witt, *n.* **Johann de** (1625–72), Dutch politician, Grand Pensionary of Holland and virtual prime minister from 1653. His skilful diplomacy ended the Dutch Wars of 1652–54 and 1665–67, and in 1668 he formed a triple alliance with England and Sweden against Louis XIV of France. He was murdered by a rioting mob.

Wittelsbach, *n.* Bavarian dynasty, who ruled Bavaria as dukes from 1180, electors from 1623, and kings 1806–1918.

Wittgenstein, *n.* **Ludwig** (1889–1951), Austrian philosopher. *Tractatus Logico-Philosophicus* (1922) postulated the 'picture theory' of language: that words represent things according to social agreement. He subsequently rejected this idea, and developed the idea that usage was more important than convention.

witticism etc. WIT[2].

witting etc. WIT[1].

wittol, *n.* one who puts up with his wife's infidelity. †**wittolly,** *a.* [perh. corr. of WITWALL]

witty WIT[2].

†**witwall,** *n.* the green or the greater spotted woodpecker; the golden oriole. [var. of obs. *woodwall, wodewale* (cp. MDut. *weduwael,* OHG *Witewal*)]

Witwatersrand, *n.* (or **the Rand**), the economic heartland of S Transvaal, South Africa. Its gold-bearing reef, which streches nearly 100 km/62 miles, produces over half the world's gold. The chief city of the region is Johannesburg.

†**wive,** *v.t.* to take for a wife; to provide with a wife. *v.i.* to marry a wife. [OE *wīfian,* from *wīf,* WIFE]

wiver, wivern, WYVERN.

wives WIFE.

wiwi, *n.* a small, fine grass. [Maori]

wiz, *n., a.* (*coll.*) short for WIZARD.

wizard, *n.* a sorcerer, an enchanter, a magician; one who works wonders. *a.* magic, enchanting, enchanted; (*sl.*) wonderful, marvellous. **Wizard of the North,** Sir Walter Scott. **wizardry,** *n.* [ME *wisard* (*wīs,* WISE[1], -ARD)]

wizen, *v.t., v.i.* to wither, to dry up, to shrivel. *a.* wizened. [OE *wisnian* (cp. Icel. *visna,* from *visinn,* withered), cogn. with L VIRUS, Sansk. *visha-*]

wk, (*abbr.*) week.

wkly, (*abbr.*) weekly.

wkt, (*abbr.*) wicket.

WNP, (*abbr.*) Welsh National Party.

WO, (*abbr.*) Warrant Officer.

wo[1], WHOA.

†**wo[2],** etc. WOE.

woad, *n.* a plant, *Isatis tinctoria,* yielding a blue dye; this dye formerly in use for staining the body, esp. by the ancient Britons. **woaded,** *a.* [OE *wād* (cp. Dut. *weede,* G *Waid,* OF *waide,* F *guède*), cogn. with L *vitrum,* Gr. *isatis*]

wobbegong, *n.* a mottle-skin shark also known as the carpet shark. [Austral. Abor.]

wobble, *v.i.* to incline to one side and then the other alternately, as a rotating body when not properly balanced; to oscillate; to go unsteadily, to stagger; to waver, to be inconsistent or inconstant. *v.t.* to cause to wobble. *n.* a rocking, uneven motion, a stagger, a swerve; an act of hesitation, inconsistency or vacillation. **wobbler,** *n.* **wobbly,** *a.* inclined to wobble; unsteady. *n.* (*coll.*) a tantrum.

wobbles, *n.* (*Austral.*) a W Australian horse- and cattle-disease caused by eating poisonous palm-leaves.

Wodehouse, *n.* **P(elham) G(renville)** (1881–1975), English novelist, a US citizen from 1955, whose humorous novels portray the accident-prone world of such characters as the socialite Bertie Wooster and his invaluable and impeccable manservant Jeeves, and Lord Emsworth of Blandings Castle with his prize pig, the Empress of Blandings.

Woden, Wodan, *n.* the foremost Anglo-Saxon god, whose Norse counterpart is Odin.

wodge, *n.* (*sl.*) a thick slice or chunk. [var. of WEDGE]

woe, *n.* sorrow, affliction, distress, calamity, overwhelming grief. **woe worth the day** WORTH[2]. **woebegone,** *a.* overcome with woe, sorrowful-looking, dismal. **woeful,** *a.* sorrowful, miserable; pitiful, inadequate. **woefully,** *adv.* **woefulness,** *n.* [OE *wā*, int. (cp. Dut. *wee,* G *Weh,* Icel. *vei,* L *vae*)]

wog, *n.* (*offensive*) any dark-skinned person. [prob. from GOLLIWOG]

woggle, *n.* a leather ring used to tie a Boy Scout's kerchief at the front. [etym. doubtful]

Wöhler, *n.* **Friedrich** (1800–82), German chemist who synthesized the first organic compound (urea) from an inorganic compound (ammonium cyanate). He also isolated the elements aluminium, beryllium, yttrium, and titanium.

wok, *n.* a large metal bowl with curved sides and handles used in Chinese cooking. [Cantonese]

woke, woken WAKE[1].

wold, *n.* a tract of open country, esp. downland or moorland. [OE *weald* (*wald,* forest, cp. Dut. *woud,* G *Wald,* Icel. *völlr*), cp. WEALD]

wolf, *n.* (*pl.* **wolves**) a grey, tawny-grey, reddish or white carnivorous quadruped, closely allied to the dog, preying on sheep, calves etc., and hunting larger animals in packs; a rapacious, ravenous, greedy or cruel person; (*coll.*) a man who is rapacious in the pursuit of women for sexual purposes; (*Mus.*) a discordant sound in certain chords of a keyboard instrument, esp. an organ, due to unequal temperament. *v.t.* to devour ravenously, gulp or swallow (down) greedily. **to cry wolf,** to raise a false alarm. **to keep the wolf from the door,** to keep off starvation. **wolf in sheep's clothing,** a person who disguises malicious intentions behind a pretence of innocence. **wolf-cub,** *n.* a member of the junior branch of the Boy Scouts. **wolf-dog,** *n.* a large dog used for guarding sheep against wolves; a cross between a wolf and a dog. **wolf-fish,** *n.* a large voracious fish, also called a sea-wolf. **wolf-hound,** *n.* a large powerful dog of Russian or Irish breed. **wolf's-bane,** *n.* a species of aconite or monk's-hood. *Aconitum lycoctonum.* **wolf's-claw, -foot,** *n.* club-moss, *Lycopodium clavatum.* **wolf's-fist,** *n.* a puff-ball. **wolf-tooth,** *n.* a small additional pre-molar in horses. **wolf-whistle,** *n.* a whistle made by a male at the sight of an attractive girl. **wolfish,** *a.* **wolfishly,** *adv.* **wolfishness,** *n.* [OE *wulf* (cp. Dut. and G *Wolf,* Icel. *ūlfr,* L *lupus,* Gr. *lukos,* Sansk. *vrka-*), from *welq-,* to tear]

Wolf, *n.* **Hugo (Filipp Jakob)** (1860–1903), Austrian composer, whose songs are in the German *Lieder* tradition. He also composed the opera *Der Corregidor* (1895) and orchestral works, such as *Italian Serenade* (1892).

Wolfe[1], *n.* **James** (1727–59), British soldier. He fought at the battles of Dettingen, Falkirk, and Culloden. In 1758 he served in Canada, and played a conspicuous part in the siege of the French stronghold of Louisburg. He was promoted to major-general 1759 and commanded a victorious expedition against Québec, in which he was killed.

Wolfe[2], *n.* **Thomas** (1900–38), US novelist. He wrote four long and powerful autobiographical novels: *Look Homeward, Angel* (1929), *Of Time and the River* (1935), and the posthumous *The Web and the Rock* (1939) and *You Can't Go Home Again* (1940).

Wolfe[3], *n.* **Tom** (1931–), US journalist and novelist. In the 1960s a founder of the 'New Journalism', which brought fiction's methods to reportage, Wolfe recorded US mores and fashions in Pop style in *The Kandy-Kolored Tangerine-Flake Streamline Baby* (1965). His sharp social eye is applied to the New York of the 1980s in his novel *The Bonfire of the Vanities* (1988).

wolfram, *n.* a native tungsten ore composed of tungstate of iron and manganese; tungsten. [G, wolf-cream]

Wollaston, *n.* **William** (1766–1828), British chemist and physicist. Wollaston amassed a large fortune through his discovery in 1804 of how to make malleable platinum. He went on to discover the new elements palladium in 1804 and rhodium in 1805.

wollomai, *n.* an edible fish, sometimes known as the snapper. [Austral. Abor.]

Wollongong, *n.* industrial city (iron, steel) in New South Wales, Australia, 65 km/40 miles south of Sydney; population (1985, with Port Kembla) 238,000.

Wollstonecraft, *n.* **Mary** (1759–97), British feminist, member of a group of radical intellectuals called the English Jacobins, whose book *Vindication of the Rights of Women* (1792) demanded equal educational opportunities for women. She married William Godwin and died in giving birth to a daughter, Mary (see MARY SHELLEY).

Wolsey, *n.* **Thomas** (*c.* 1475–1530), English cardinal and politician. Under Henry VIII he became both cardinal and lord chancellor 1515, and began the dissolution of the monasteries. His reluctance to further Henry's divorce from Catherine of Aragon, partly because of his ambitions to be pope, led to his downfall 1529. He was charged with high treason 1530 but died before being tried.

Wolverhampton, *n.* industrial city (metalworking, chemicals, tyres, aircraft, commercial vehicles) in West Midlands, England, 20 km/12 miles NW of Birmingham; population (1984) 254,000.

wolverine, *n.* a small N American carnivorous animal, *Gulo luscus,* also called the glutton or carcajou. [dim. of WOLF, after MHG *wölfelin*]

woman, *n.* (*pl.* **women**) an adult human female; womankind, the female sex; womanly feeling, womanliness, an effeminate or timid and tender man; (*coll., often offensive*) a mistress or girlfriend; †a female attendant on a person of rank, a lady-in-waiting, *a.* female. *v.t.* to cause to act or behave like a woman; to address or speak of as 'woman'. **to make an honest woman of** HONEST. **to play the woman,** to weep; to give vent to emotion, esp. fear. **woman of the world,** a woman knowledgeable about in the ways of the world; a society woman. **woman-born,** *a.* born of a woman. **woman-hater,** *n.* a misogynist. **womankind,** *n.* women collectively, the female sex; the women of a household. †**woman-post,** *n.* (*Shak.*) a female messenger. **woman suffrage,** *n.* the exercise of the electoral franchise by or its extension to women. †**woman-tired,** *a.* (*Shak.*) henpecked. **womanhood,** *n.* **womanish,** *a.* having the character or qualities of a woman, effeminate. †**womanishly,** *adv.* **womanishness,** *n.* **womanize, -ise,** *v.t.* to make effeminate, to unman. *v.i.* of a man, to have casual sexual relationships with many women. **womanizer, -iser,** *n.* **womanless,** *a.* **womanlike,** *a., adv.* **womanly,** *a.* having the qualities becoming a woman, truly feminine. *adv.* in the manner of a woman. **womanliness,** *n.* **women,** *n.pl.* **womenfolk,** *n.* one's womenkind; women collectively. **Women's Institute,** *n.* a rural organization of women in Britain, non-political and nonsectarian, for mutual training and improvement in domestic and social life. **Women's Land Army,** an organization founded 1916 for the recruitment of women to work on farms during World War I. At its peak in Sept. 1918 it had 16,000 members. It re-formed June 1939, before the outbreak of World War II. Many 'Land Girls' joined up to help the war effort and by Aug. 1943, 87,000 were employed in farm work. **women's liberation, women's lib,** *n.* a movement (women's movement) which began in the 1960s and advocated the social, sexual and psychological emancipation of women from the dominance of men. **Women's Social and Political Union (WSPU),** a British political movement founded 1903 by Emmeline Pankhurst to organize a militant crusade for female suffrage. [OE *wīfman* (WIFE, MAN)]

womb, *n.* the organ in a woman or other female mammal in which the young is developed before birth, the uterus; the place where anything is engendered or brought into existence; †a deep cavity. **wombed,** *a.* having a womb; capacious. †**womby,** *a.* deep hollow, capacious. [OE *wamb* (cp. Dut. *wam.* G *Wampe, Wamme,* Icel. *vomb*)]

wombat, *n.* an Australian nocturnal marsupial mammal, *Phascolomys ursinus,* resembling a small bear. [Austral. Abor.]

women, *pl.* WOMAN.

womenfolk WOMAN.
womerah, *n.* a throwing-stick. [Austral. Abor.]
won[1], *past, p.p.* WIN.
†**won[2],** *v.t.* to dwell, to abide; to be accustomed. *n.* a dwelling, an abode; custom, habit. †**woning,** *n.* a dwelling. [OE *gewunian* (cp. G *gewohnen,* to be used to, Icel. *venja,* to accustom), cogn. with WONT]
won[3], *n.* the standard monetary unit in N and S Korea. [Korean]
wonder, *n.* a strange, remarkable or marvellous thing, event, action, incident etc., a miracle, a prodigy; the emotion excited by that which is unexpected, strange, extraordinary or inexplicable, or which arrests by its grandeur; surprise mingled with admiration. *v.i.* to be struck with wonder or surprise; to look with or feel wonder; to feel doubt or curiosity (about etc.). *v.t.* to speculate about. **nine days' wonder** NINE. **no small wonder,** it is not surprising (that etc.); quite natural, of course. **seven wonders of the world** SEVEN. **wonder-struck, -stricken,** *a.* †**wonder-worker,** *n.* one who performs wonders. **wonder-working,** *a.* **wonder-wounded,** *a.* (*Shak.*) struck with wonder. †**wondered,** *a.* (*Shak.*) having performed wonders; wonder-working. **wonderer,** *n.* **wonderful** *a.* astonishing, strange, admirable; exciting wonder or astonishment. **wonderfully,** *adv.* admirably; strangely; greatly. **wonderfulness,** *n.* **wondering,** *n., a.* **wonderingly,** *adv.* **wonderland,** *n.* a land of marvels, fairyland. **wonderment,** *n.* amazement, awe; curiosity. **wondrous,** *a.* wonderful, marvellous, strange. *adv.* wonderfully, exceedingly. **wondrously,** *adv.* [OE *wunder,* a portent (cp. Dut. *wonder,* G *Wunder,* Icel. *undr*), perh. cogn. with *wandiian,* to turn aside from, to reverse]
Wonder, *n.* **Stevie** (1950–), stage name of Steveland Judkins Morris, US pop musician, singer, and songwriter, associated with Motown Records. His hits include 'My Cherie Amour' (1973), 'Master Blaster (Jammin')' (1980), and the album *Innervisions* (1973).
wonga-wonga, *n.* the large Australian white-faced pigeon, *Leucosarcia picata.* [Austral. Abor.]
wonky, *a.* (*sl.*) unsteady, shaky.
wont, *a.* used, accustomed (to); using or doing habitually. *n.* custom, habit, use. *v.aux.* to be accustomed or used (to). **wonted,** *a.* customary, habitual, usual. †**wontedness,** *n.* [ME *woned,* p.p. of *wonen,* to dwell, to be accustomed, in sense to *wone,* OE *gewun,* used, accustomed (cp. WON[2])]
woo, *v.t.* to court, to solicit in marriage; to seek to gain or attain; to solicit, to coax, to importune. *v.i.* to go courting. **wooer,** *n.* [ME *wowen, wogen,* OE *wōgian,* in *awōgian,* from *wōh,* bent]
wood[1], *n.* a large and thick collection of growing trees, a forest (*often pl.*); the fibrous substance of a tree between the bark and the pith; trees, timber; (*Bowls*) a bowl; a golf-club with a wooden head; (*Mus.*) the woodwind. **from the wood,** from the cask. **not to see the wood for the trees,** to be prevented by excessive details from getting an overall view. **out of the wood,** out of danger. **wood-agate,** *n.* an agate derived from wood by silicification and still showing the woody structure. **wood alcohol,** *n.* methyl alcohol, formerly produced by the distillation of wood, now synthesized. **wood-anemone,** *n.* the wild anemone, *Anemone nemorosa.* **wood-ashes,** *n.pl.* the ashes of burnt wood or plants. **woodbine,** *n.* the wild honeysuckle. [OE *wudebinde* BIND] **woodblock,** *n.* a die cut in box or other wood for striking impressions from; a wood-cut. **woodchat,** *n.* a type of shrike of Europe and N Africa. **woodchuck,** *n.* a N American marmot, *Arctomys monax.* [corr. of N Am. Ind. *wejack*] **wood-coal,** *n.* charcoal; lignite. **woodcock,** *n.* a game-bird of the genus *Scolopax* or *Philohela,* related to the snipe. **woodcraft,** *n.* skill in anything pertaining to life in the woods or forest, esp. in hunting. **woodcut,** *n.* an engraving on wood, a wood-block; a print or impression from this. **wood-cutter,** *n.* one who cuts wood or timber; an engraver on wood. **wood-engraver,** *n.* an engraver on wood; a beetle that bores under the bark of trees. **wood-engraving,** *n.* **wood-fibre,** *n.* fibre obtained from wood, used for paper-making etc. **wood-fretter,** *n.* an insect that eats into wood. **wood-gas,** *n.* illuminating gas produced by dry distillation of wood. **wood-grouse,** *n.* the capercailzie, *Tetrao urogallus.* **wood-hole,** *n.* a place where wood is stored. **wood-house,** *n.* **wood-ibis,** *n.* a variety of stork from the southern US. **woodland,** *n.* land covered with woods, wooded country; *a.* pertaining to this, sylvan. **wood-lark,** *n.* a European lark, *Alauda arborea,* smaller than the skylark. **wood-layer,** *n.* a young oak or other timber plant laid down among bushes etc., planted to make hedges. **wood-leopard,** *n.* a moth the caterpillars of which live in the wood of fruit trees. **wood-louse,** *n.* a wingless isopod insect of the family Oniseidae, infesting decayed wood etc. **woodman,** *n.* a forester; one who fells timber; a wood-cutter. **wood-note,** *n.* a wild or natural note or song; artless poetry. **wood-nymph,** *n.* a dryad; a brilliantly-coloured moth of the genus *Endryas;* a variety of humming-bird. **wood- offering,** *n.* (*Bibl.*) wood burnt on the altar. **wood-opal,** *n.* silicified wood. **wood-paper,** *n.* paper made from wood-fibre. **wood-pavement,** *n.* paving composed of blocks of wood. **woodpecker,** *n.* a bird of the genus *Picus* living in woods and tapping trees to discover insects. **wood-pie,** *n.* the great spotted woodpecker. **wood-pigeon,** *n.* the ringdove, *Columba palumbus,* a European pigeon whose neck is nearly encircled by a ring of whitish-coloured feathers. **wood-pile,** *n.* a pile of wood. **a nigger in the wood-pile** NIGGER. **wood-pulp,** *n.* wood-fibre pulped in the process of manufacturing paper. **wood-reeve,** *n.* a steward or overseer of a wood. **woodruff,** *n.* a woodland plant with fragrant flowers of the genus *Asperula,* esp. *A. odorata.* [OE *wuderōfe*] **wood-screw,** *n.* a metal screw for fastening pieces of wood together. **woodshed,** *n.* a shed for storing wood, esp. firewood. **woodsman,** *n.* one who lives in the woods; a woodman. **woodsorrel,** *n.* a creeping woodland plant of the genus *Oxalis,* with acid juice and small white flowers. **wood-tar,** *n.* tar obtained from wood. **wood-vetch,** *n.* a climbing vetch, *Vicia sylvatica.* †**wood-wale,** *n.* the witwall. **wood-warbler,** *n.* an American warbler; a wood-wren. †**woodward,** *n.* a wood-reeve, a forester. **wood-wasp,** *n.* a wasp that makes its cells in wood or hangs its nest to the branches of trees. **woodwind,** *n.* (*Mus.*) the wooden wind instruments in an orchestra etc. **wood-wool,** *n.* fine shavings, esp. of pine, used for dressing wounds, for packing etc. **woodwork,** *n.* things made of wood; the part of a building or other structure which is composed of wood. **wood-worker,** *n.* **woodworm,** *n.* any of various insect larvae that bore into furniture, wooden beams etc. **wood-wren,** *n.* a European warbler, *Phylloscopus sibilatrix.* **wooded,** *a.* (*usu. in comb.* as *well-wooded*). **wooden,** *a.* made of wood; (*fig.*) stiff, clumsy, ungainly, awkward; spiritless, expressionless. **wooden-head,** *n.* (*coll.*) a stupid person, a blockhead. **wooden-headed,** *a.* **wooden-headedness,** *n.* **wooden spoon,** *n.* a spoon made of wood, used in cooking; a booby prize, esp. in sports competitions. **woodenly,** *adv.* **woodenness,** *n.* **woodie,** *n.* (*Sc.*) the gallows. **woodless,** *a.* **woodlessness,** *n.* **woody,** *a.* abounding in woods, well-wooded; of the nature of or consisting of wood; †pertaining to or found in woods. **woody fibre, tissue,** *n.* fibre or tissue consisting of wood-cells; the tissue of which wood is composed. **woody-nightshade** NIGHTSHADE. **woodiness,** *n.* [OE *wudu* (cp. Icel. *vithr,* Dan., Swed. *ved,* OHG *Witu*]
†**wood[2],** *a.* mad, furious. †**woodness,** *n.* [OE *wōd* (cp. Dut. *woede,* G *wuth,* Icel. *ōthr*), perh. cogn. with L *vates,* a soothsayer]
Wood[1], *n.* **Grant** (1892–1942), US painter based mainly in his native Iowa. Though his work is highly stylized, he struck a note of hard realism in his studies of farmers, such as *American Gothic* (1930, Art Institute, Chicago).
Wood[2], *n.* **Henry (Joseph)** (1869–1944), English conductor, from 1895 until his death, of the London Pro-

menade Concerts, now named after him. He promoted a national interest in music and encouraged many young composers.

Wood[3], *n.* **Natalie** (1938–81), stage name of Natasha Gurdin, US film actress who began as a child star. Her films include *Miracle on 34th Street* (1947), *The Searchers* (1956), and *Bob and Carol and Ted and Alice* (1969).

woodchuck, -cut, -man etc. WOOD[1].

Woodstock, *n.* the first free rock festival, held near Bethel, New York State, US, over three days in Aug. 1969. It was attended by 400,000 people, and performers included the Band, Country Joe and the Fish, the Grateful Dead, Jimi Hendrix, the Jefferson Airplane, and the Who. The festival was a landmark in the youth culture of the 1960s.

Woodward[1], *n.* **Joanne** (1930–), US actress, active in film, television, and theatre. She was directed by Paul Newman in the film *Rachel Rachel* (1968), and also starred in *The Three Faces of Eve* (1957), *They Might Be Giants* (1971), and *Harry and Son* (1984).

Woodward[2], *n.* **Robert** (1917–79), US chemist who worked on synthesizing a large number of complex molecules. These included quinine, 1944, cholesterol, 1951, chlorophyll, 1960, and vitamin B_{12}, 1971. Nobel prize 1965.

wooer woo.

woof[1], *n.* the threads that cross the warp, the weft; cloth; texture. [ME *oof*, OE *ōwef* (A-, *wef*, WEB)]

woof[2], *n.* the sound of a dog barking or growling. *v.i.* to produce this sound. **woofer,** *n.* a large loud-speaker used for low-frequency sounds. [imit.]

Wookey Hole, *n.* natural cave near Wells, Somerset, England, in which flint implements of Old Stone Age people and bones of extinct animals have been found.

wool, *n.* the fine, soft, crisp or curly hair, forming the fleece of sheep, goats and some other animals, used as the raw material of cloth etc.; short, thick hair, underfur or down, resembling this; woollen yarn, worsted; fibrous or fleecy substance resembling wool. **dyed in the wool,** extremely committed to specified beliefs, opinions, politics etc. **great cry and little wool,** much ado about nothing, a fiasco. **to pull the wool over someone's eyes,** to deceive. **wool-ball,** *n.* a ball or mass of wool, esp. a lump of concreted wool frequently found in the stomach of sheep etc. **wool-bearing,** *a.* **wool-carding, -combing,** *n.* a process in the preparation of wool for spinning. **wool-classer,** *n.* (*Austral.*) a grader of wool. **wool-clip,** *n.* (*Austral.*) the annual amount of wool shorn. **wool-fat, -oil,** *n.* lanolin. **wool-fell,** *n.* a skin from which the wool has not been removed. **wool-gathering,** *a.* in a brown study, absent-minded. *n.* absent-mindedness, inattention. **wool-grower,** *n.* **wool-hall,** *n.* a market or exchange where wool-merchants do their business. **woolpack,** *n.* a pack or bale of wool, formerly one weighing 240 lb. (109 kg); a fleecy cloud. **woolshed,** *n.* (*Austral.*) the building for shearing, packing and storing wool. **woolsorter,** *n.* a person who sorts wool according to quality etc. **woolsorter's disease,** *n.* pulmonary anthrax due to the inhalation of dust from infected wool. **wool-staple,** *n.* the fibre of wool. **wool-trade,** *n.* †**woolward,** *a.* dressed in wool only, without linen. †**to go woolward,** (*Shak.*) to wear woollen fabrics next the skin as a penance. **woollen,** *a.* made or consisting of wool. *n.* cloth made of wool; (*pl.*) woollen goods. **woollen-draper,** *n.* one retailing woollens. **woollenette,** *n.* **woolly,** *a.* consisting of or resembling, bearing or naturally covered with wool, or with a hair resembling wool; like wool in appearance, fleecy; (*Painting*) lacking clear definition, firmness or incisiveness; (*coll.*) with hazy ideas, muddled. *n.* a woollen pullover etc. **woolly-bear,** *n.* a hairy caterpillar, esp. of *Arctia virgo* or the tiger-moth. **woolly-but,** *n.* the popular name for two valuable Australian timber-trees, *Eucalyptus longifolia* and *E. viminalis.* **woolly-haired, -headed,** *a.* **woolliness,** *n.* [OE *wull* (cp. Dut. *wol*, G *Wolle*, Icel. *ull*), perh. cogn. with L *lāna*, Gr. *lēnos*]

woold, *v.t.* (*Naut.*) to wind, esp. to wind (a rope etc.) round a mast or yard made of two or more pieces, at a place where they are fished. **woolder,** *n.* a stick used for woolding. [prob. from Dut. *woelen*]

Woolf, *n.* **Virginia** (born **Virginia Stephen)** (1882–1941), English novelist and critic. Her first novel, *The Voyage Out* (1915), explored the tensions experienced by women who want marriage and a career. In *Mrs Dalloway* (1925) she perfected her 'stream of consciousness' technique. Among her later books are *To the Lighthouse* (1927), *Orlando* (1928), and *The Years* (1937), which considers the importance of economic independence for women.

woollen, woolly, wool-pack etc. WOOL.

Woolsack, *n.* the seat of the Lord Chancellor in the House of Lords, consisting of a large square cushion without back or arms; the post of Lord Chancellor.

woolsey, short for LINSEY-WOOLSEY.

Woolworth, *n.* **Frank Winfield** (1852–1919), US entrepreneur. He opened his first successful 'five and ten cent' store in Lancaster, Pennsylvania, 1879, and, together with his brother C. S. Woolworth (1856–1947), built up a chain of similar shops throughout the US, Canada, the UK, and Europe.

woomera, WOMERAH.

woopie, *n.* (*coll., facet.*) a well-off older person. [acronym]

wootz, *n.* a fine quality of E Indian steel imported into Europe and America for edge-tools. [etym. doubtful]

woozy, *a.* (*coll.*) suffering from giddiness, nausea etc.; dazed, fuddled, e.g. with drink. **woozily,** *adv.* **wooziness,** *n.* [etym. unknown]

wop, *n.* (*offensive*) any person with a dark complexion, esp. an Italian. [etym. unknown]

Worcester Porcelain Factory, English porcelain factory, since 1862 the Royal Worcester Porcelain Factory. The factory was founded 1751, and produced a hard-wearing type of softpaste porcelain, mainly as tableware and decorative china.

Worcestershire, *n.* former Midland county of England, merged 1974 with Herefordshire in the new county of Hereford and Worcester, except for a small projection in the north, which went to West Midlands. Worcester was the county town. **Worcestershire** (also **Worcester**) **sauce,** *n.* a dark sauce made by mixing soy sauce, vinegar, spices etc.

word, *n.* an articulate sound or combination of sounds uttered by the human voice or written, printed etc., expressing an idea or ideas and forming a constituent part, or the whole of or a substitute for a sentence; speech, discourse, talk; news, intelligence, information, a message; a command, an order, an injunction; a password, a watchword, a motto; one's assurance, promise or definite affirmation; (*coll., pl.*) terms interchanged expressive of anger, contention or reproach; (*Comput.*) a set of bits processed as one unit by a computer. *v.t.* to express in words, to phrase, to select words to express. **a man** etc. **of his word,** a man etc. who can be relied upon to do what he says he will do. **as good as one's word,** reliable enough to do what one has said one will do. **big words,** boasting, bluff, exaggeration. **by word of mouth,** by actual speaking, orally. **good word,** a favourable account or mention, a commendation. **in a, one word,** briefly, in short; to sum up. **in word and deed,** not in speech or profession only. **last word,** the latest improvement. **my word,** used to express surprise, indignation etc. **the, God's Word,** the Scriptures, or any part of them; Christ as the Logos. **to eat one's words,** to retract what one has said. **to have a word with,** to have a brief conversation with. **to have words with,** to have a dispute with. **to take someone at his, her word,** to assume that someone means what he, she says. **word for word,** in exactly the same words, verbatim. **word-blind, deaf,** *a.* unable to understand words owing to a cerebral lesion. **word-book,** *n.* a vocabulary. **word-break,** *n.* the place where a word is divided when it runs from one line to another in printing. **word order,** *n.* the order in which words are arranged in a sentence etc. **word-painter,** *n.* a writer who depicts scenes or events in a vivid and picturesque manner. **word-painting,** *n.* **word-perfect,** *a.* able to repeat something without a mistake. **word-picture,** *n.* a vivid description. **word-play,** *n.* a discussion or dispute hingeing on the definition given to certain words; a play upon words, a pun. **word processor,** *n.* an electronic device used for the automatic typing, editing and often printing of texts in various formats, usu. equipped with a VDU. **word processing,** *n.* **wordsmith,** *n.* a person skilled in the use of words, esp. a writer. **word-square,** *n.* a series of words so arranged that the letters spell the same words when read across or downwards. **wording,** *n.* choice of words, phrasing etc.; letterpress; contents of a document, advertisement etc. **wordless,** *a.* **wordy,** *a.* verbose, diffuse, prolix, consisting of words, verbal. **wordily,** *adv.* **wordiness,** *n.* †**wordish,** *adv.* †**wordishness,** *n.* [OE]

Wordsworth, *n.* **William** (1770–1850), English Romantic poet. In 1797 he moved with his sister Dorothy to Somerset to be near Coleridge, collaborating with him on *Lyrical Ballads* (1798, which included 'Tintern Abbey'). From 1799 he lived in the Lake District, and later works include *Poems* (1807, including 'Intimations of Immortality') and *The Prelude* (written by 1805, published 1850). He was appointed poet laureate 1843. **Wordsworthian,** *a.* of, pertaining to or after the manner or spirit of Wordsworth or his poetry. *n.* a devotee of Wordsworth.

wore, *past* WEAR[1].

work, *n.* exertion of energy (physical or mental), effort or activity directed to some purpose; labour, toil; that upon which labour is expended, an undertaking, a task; the materials used or to be used in this; employment as a means of livelihood, occupation; that which is done, an action, deed, performance or achievement; a thing made; a product of nature or art; a large engineering structure, esp. a piece of fortification; a place of employment; a book or other literary composition, a musical or other artistic production; (*Phys.*) the exertion of force in producing or maintaining motion against the action of a resisting force; (*pl.*) an industrial establishment, a manufactory (*often as sing.*); building operations, esp. carried out under the management of a public authority; the working part or mechanism (of a watch etc.); (*Theol.*) moral duties or the performance of meritorious acts, as opp. to grace. *v.i.* (*past, p.p.* **worked,** †**wrought**) to exert physical or mental energy for some purpose, to be engaged in labour, toil or effort, to be employed or occupied (at, in, on etc.); to be in continuous activity, to do the work or perform the motions appointed, to act, to operate; to take effect, to be effective, to exercise influence; to be in a state of motion or agitation, to ferment; to make way with effort or difficulty; to reach a certain condition gradually. *v.t.* to exert energy in or upon; to cause to do work, to keep in operation, to employ, to keep busy; to make or embroider with needlework; to carry on, to manage, to run; to bring about, to effect, to produce as a result; to prepare or alter the condition, shape or consistency of by some process, to knead, to mould, to fashion; to earn through paid work; to treat, to investigate, to solve; to excite. **in, out of work,** employed or not employed. **the works,** (*coll.*) everything; the appropriate treatment; a violent beating. **to have one's work cut out,** to have a hard task. **to make short work of** SHORT. **to set to work,** to employ; to start working; **to work in,** to introduce or combine by manipulation; to intermix or admit of being introduced. **to work off,** to get rid of; to produce; to pay off (a debt etc.) by working; to find customers for, to palm off. **to work out,** to compute, to solve, to find out; to exhaust; to accomplish, to effect; to expiate; to undertake a series of physical exercises to get fit. **to work over,** to examine carefully; to beat severely, to mug. **to work up,** to elaborate, to bring gradually into shape or efficiency; to excite gradually, to stir up, to rouse; to mingle together, to study (a subject) perseveringly. **work-to-rule,** *n.* a form of industrial action in which employees follow regulations very strictly and thus slow down the usual rate of work. **workaday,** *a.* pertaining to or suitable for workdays, everyday, common, practical. **work-bag, -basket, -box,** *n.* one used for holding materials etc. for work, articles to be repaired etc., esp. for sewing. **workbench,** *n.* a bench specially designed for woodworking, metalworking etc. **workbook,** *n.* an exercise book with spaces for answers to printed problems; a book for recording work done. **work-day,** *n.* a working-day. †**work-fellow,** *n.* **workfolk, -folks,** *n.pl.* work-people. **work-force,** *n.* total number of workers employed or employable. **workhorse,** *n.* a person or thing that does or is capable of doing a great deal of work. **workhouse,** *n.* (*formerly*) a public establishment maintained by a parish or union for paupers. **work-in,** *n.* a form of protest, e.g. against the closure of a factory etc., in which workers occupy it and continue working. **workload,** *n.* the amount of work expected from or done by a person, machine etc. **workman,** *n.* any man employed in manual labour, an operative. **workmanlike,** *a.* done in the manner of a good workman. †**workmanly,** *a.*, *adv.* **workmanship,** *n.* comparative skill, finish or execution shown in making something or in the thing made; the result of working or making. **workmate,** *n.* a person with whom one works. **workout,** *n.* a series of exercises for physical fitness. **work-people,** *n.pl.* workmen or workwomen. **workpiece,** *n.* any item on which work is being done. **workplace,** *n.* the place where one works. **workroom,** *n.* a room in which work is done. **workshop,** *n.* a room or building in which a handicraft or other work is carried on. **work-shy,** *a.* with a repugnance to work. **work station,** *n.* the place in an office, factory etc. where one person works; (*Comput.*) a unit consisting of a VDU and keyboard for use by one worker. **work study,** *n.* the investigation of the methods and practice of particular work with a view to getting the best results for all concerned. **work-table,** *n.* a table with drawers and other conveniences for keeping sewing-materials etc. in. **worktop,** *n.* a flat board covered with laminate and often fixed to the top of kitchen units, used to prepare food. **workwoman,** *n.fem.* **workable,** *a.* capable of being worked, practicable; that will work or operate; worth working or developing. **workaholic,** *n.* (*coll.*) a person addicted to working. **worker,** *n.* a person who works, esp. a member of the working-class; a sterile female insect in a colony of insects which specializes in gathering food, caring for the young etc. **worker-bee,** *n.* a partially developed female bee doing the work of the hive. **workless,** *a.* [OE *weorc* (cp. Dut., G *Werk*, Icel. *verk*, Gr. *ergon*), whence *wiercan, wyrcan*, to work, past *worhte*]

Workers' Educational Association (WEA), *n.* British organization founded 1913 to provide adult education. It had its origins in classes on cooperation organized by Albert Mansbridge, a clerk at a cooperative store near Toynbee Hall, where meetings were held.

working, *a.* engaged in work, esp manual labour; during which work is done or business discussed; able to function; taking an active part in a business. *n.* the act of labouring; operation, mode of operation; a mine or quarry or a portion of it which has been worked or in which work is going on; fermentation, movement. **working capital,** *n.* funds employed for the actual carrying on of a business. **working-class,** *n.* those who earn their living by manual labour. **working-day,** *n.* any day upon which work is ordinarily performed, as dist. from Sundays and holidays; the period daily devoted to work. **work drawing, plan,** a drawing or plan of a work prepared to guide a builder, engineer etc. in executing work. **working-out,** *n.* the act of working out, calculating, elaborating etc. **working party,** *n.* a committee set up specifically to investigate a particular issue.

Workmen's Compensation Act, British legislation (1897) that conferred on workers a right to compensation for the loss of earnings resulting from an injury at work.

world, *n.* the whole system of things, the universe, everything; a system of things, an orderly or organic whole, a cosmos; the earth with its lands and seas; a celestial body regarded as similar to this; a large natural or other division of the earth; the human inhabitants of the world, mankind; human society, the public; fashionable or prominent people; human affairs, the ways, customs, opinions etc. of people, active life, social life and intercourse; a particular section, department or class of people, animals or things, a realm, a domain, a sphere; a vast quantity, amount, number, degree etc. (of); all things external to oneself as related to the individual; man as a microcosm, man's inner life; any time, state or sphere of existence; the present state of existence as dist. from the future life; secular interest as opp. to spiritual; the ungodly or unregenerate portion of mankind. **all the world,** everybody. **for all the world,** exactly, precisely. **for the world,** on any account. **in the world,** at all, possibly. **out of this world,** (*coll.*) remarkable, striking; excellent. **to think the world of,** to love or respect greatly. **world without end,** to all eternity, everlastingly. **World Bank,** *n.* an agency of the United Nations set up in 1945 to lend money at moderate rates to poorer countries seeking to develop their resources. **World Court,** *n.* popular name for the Permanent Court of International Justice at the Hague set up in 1921 by the League of Nations to settle disputes between states. **World Cup,** *n.* competitions in football, cricket, rugby union, and other sports, held every four years. The 1990 World Cup of football was won by W Germany, the 1987 cricket World Cup by Australia, and the 1987 rugby World Cup by New Zealand. **world-hardened,** *a.* hardened by the love of worldly things. **World Health Organization (WHO)**, a specialized agency of the United Nations dating from 1948 with the object of helping countries to develop their health administration. **World Intellectual Property Organization (WIPO),** specialist agency of the United Nations, established 1974, to coordinate the international protection (initiated by the Paris convention 1883) of inventions, trademarks, and industrial designs, and also literary and artistic works (as initiated by the Berne convention 1886). **World Meteorological Organization,** an agency, part of the United Nations since 1950, that promotes the international exchange of weather information through the establishment of a worldwide network of meteorological stations. It was founded as the International Meteorological Organization, 1873, and its headquarters are now in Geneva, Switzerland. **world power,** *n.* (*Polit.*) a sovereign state so strong as to be able to affect the policy of every civilized state in the world. **World Series,** *n.* a series of baseball games played in the US between the winners of major leagues to decide the professional championship. **world-view** WELTANSCHAUUNG. **world war,** *n.* a war involving most of the earth's major nations, see WORLD WAR I, WORLD WAR II. **world-wearied, -weary,** *a.* tired of existence. **world-wide,** *a.* spread over the whole world; existing everywhere. **World Wide Fund for Nature, (WWF,** formerly **the World Wildlife Fund**), an international organization established 1961 to raise funds for conservation by public appeal. Its headquarters are in Gland, Switzerland. Projects include conservation of particular species (for example, the tiger and giant panda) and special areas (such as the Simen Mountains, Ethiopia). [OE *weoruld* (*wer,* man, cp. Icel. *verr,* L *vir,* ELD), (cp. Dut. *wereld,* G *Welt,* Icel. *veröld*)]

worldly, *a.* pertaining to the present, temporal or material world; earthly, secular, material, not spiritual. **worldly-minded,** *a.* devoted to worldly things. **worldly-mindedness,** *n.* **worldly-wise,** *a.* wise in the things of this world. **worldliness,** *n.* **worldling,** *n.* a worldly person.

World War I, *n.* (1914–18), war between the Central Powers (Germany, Austria-Hungary, and allies) on one side and the Triple Entente (Britain and the British Empire, France, and Russia) and their allies, including the US (which entered 1917), on the other side. An estimated 10 million lives were lost and twice that number were wounded.

World War II, *n.* (1939–45), war between Germany, Italy, and Japan (the Axis powers) on one side, and Britain, the Commonwealth, France, the US, the USSR, and China (the Allied powers) on the other. An estimated 55 million lives were lost, 20 million of them citizens of the USSR.

WORM, *n.* write once, read many times, in computing, a storage device, similar to CD-ROM. The computer can write to the disk directly, but cannot subsequently erase or overwrite the same area. WORMs are mainly used for archiving and backup copies.

worm, *n.* an invertebrate creeping animal with a long limbless segmented body, belonging to the genus *Vermes;* an intestinal parasite, a tapeworm, a fluke; any small creeping animal with very small or undeveloped feet, as larvae, grubs, caterpillars, maggots etc.; (*pl.*) any disease caused by parasitic worms, esp. in the intestine; a poor, grovelling, debased or despised person; a vermicular or spiral part or thing; the spiral part of a screw; a spiral tool for boring rock; a spiral device for extracting cartridges etc.; the spiral condensing-pipe of a still; a ligament under a dog's tongue. *v.i.* to crawl, creep, wriggle or progress with a worm-like motion; to work stealthily or underhandedly. *v.t.* to insinuate (oneself), to make (one's way) in a worm-like manner; to draw (out) or extract by craft and perseverance; to free (a dog etc.) from worms; to cut the worm from under the tongue of (a dog). **worm-cast,** *n.* a cylindrical mass of earth voided by an earth-worm. **worm-eaten,** *a.* gnawed or bored by worms. **worm-fishing,** *n.* fishing with worms for bait. **worm-gear,** *n.* gear having a toothed or cogged wheel engaging with a revolving spiral. **worm-hole,** *n.* a hole made by a worm in wood, fruit, the ground etc. **worm-holed,** *a.* **worm-powder,** *n.* a powder used as vermifuge. **worm-seed,** *n.* a Levantine plant the seed of which is used as an anthelmintic. **worm's eye view,** a view from below, low down or from a humble position. **worm-wheel,** *n.* the toothed wheel of worm-gear. **wormless,** *a.* **worm-like,** *a.* **wormy,** *a.* [OE *wyrm* (cp. Dut. *worm,* G *Wurm,* Icel. *ormr*), cogn. with Gr. *rhomos,* L *vermis,* see VERMICULAR]

Worms, *n.* industrial town in Rhineland-Palatinate, West Germany, on the Rhine; population (1984) 73,000. Liebfraumilch wine is produced here. The Protestant reformer Luther appeared before the Diet (Assembly) of Worms 1521, and was declared an outlaw by the Roman Catholic church.

wormul, -mil, *n.* a warble. [corr. of WARBLE[2]]

wormwood, *n.* a perennial herb, *Artemisia absinthium,* having bitter and tonic properties, used in the manufacture of vermouth and absinthe and in medicine; bitterness, gall, mortification. [OE *wermōd* (cp. Dut. *wermoet,* G *Wermuth,* see VERMOUTH), assim. to WORM, WOOD]

worn, *p.p.* **worn-out,** *a.* rendered useless by long wear; (*coll.*) exhausted, tired. [WEAR[1]]

Worner, *n.* **Manfred** (1934–), West German politician, NATO Secretary-General from 1988. He was elected for the conservative Christian Democratic Union (CDU) to the Bundestag (parliament) in 1965 and, as a specialist in strategic affairs, served as defence minister under Chancellor Kohl 1982–88. A proponent of closer European military collaboration, he succeeded Peter Carrington as secretary general of NATO in July 1988.

Worrall, *n.* **Denis John** (1935–), South African politician, member of the white opposition to apartheid.

worry, *v.t.* of dogs fighting, molesting sheep etc., to bite or keep on biting, to mangle, choke or pull about with the teeth; to tease, harass, bother, persecute or wear out with importunity etc.; to cause mental distress to. *v.i.* of dogs fighting etc., to bite, pull about etc.; to be unduly anxious or troubled, to fret. *n.* the act of worrying; a worrying person; the state of being worried, care, anxiety, solicitude, vexation, fret (*often in pl.*).

not to worry, (*coll.*) there's no need to worry. **to worry along,** to get along somehow in spite of trouble and difficulty. **to worry oneself,** to put oneself to needless trouble or anxiety. **worry beads,** *n.pl.* a string of beads that are fingered in order to relieve tension. **worriedly,** *adv.* **worrier,** *n.* **worriless,** *a.* **worriment,** *n.* **worrisome,** *a.* **worryingly,** *adv.* [OE *wrygan* (cp. Dut. *worgen,* G *würgen,* to strangle), cogn. with WRING]

worse, *a.* (*comp. of* BAD) more bad; (*predicatively*) in a poorer state of health; in a less favourable state, position or circumstances. *adv.* more badly; into a poorer state of health etc.; less. *n.* a worse thing or things; loss, disadvantage, defeat. **the worse for,** damaged or harmed by. **the worse for drink,** (*coll.*) drunk. **the worse for wear,** shabby, worn; (*coll.*) tired, untidy etc. **worse off,** in a poorer condition or financial situation. **worsen,** *v.t., v.i.* to (cause to) grow worse. [OE *wyrs,* adv., adj. *wyrsa, wirsa,* prob. cogn. with G *wirren,* to twist, to confuse, see WAR[1]]

worship, *n.* †the quality of being worthy, merit, excellence; †honour; deference, respect (used as a title of respect or honour in addressing certain magistrates etc., esp. mayors); the act of paying divine honour to God, esp. in religious services; an act or feeling of adoration or loving or admiring devotion or submissive respect (to a person, principle etc.). *v.t.* (*past, p.p.* **worshipped**) to pay divine honours to; to perform religious service to; to reverence with supreme respect and admiration; to treat as divine. *v.i.* to take part in a religious service. **place of worship,** Church, chapel etc., where religious services are held. †**worshipable,** *a.* **worshipful,** *a.* deserving of worship (phrase applied to certain magistrates etc.). **worshipfully,** *adv.* **worshipfulness,** *n.* **worshipper,** *n.* one who worships; an attender at a place of worship. [OE *weorthschipe*]

worst, *a.* bad in the highest degree. *adv.* most badly. *n.* that which is most bad; the most bad, evil, severe or calamitous part, event, state etc. *v.t.* to get the better of in a contest etc., to defeat, to overthrow, to best. **at worst,** in the worst circumstances; in the least favourable view. **if the worst comes to the worst,** if the worst of all possible things happens. **to come off worst, to get the worst of it,** to be defeated. [OE *wyrst,* adv., adj. *wyrsta,* shortened from *wyrsesta* (WORSE, -EST)]

worsted, *n.* woollen yarn used for knitting stockings, carpets etc. *a.* made of worsted. [*Worsted* (now Worstead), Norfolk, where first manufactured]

wort, *a.* a plant, a herb (*usu. in comb.,* as *moneywort, soapwort*); an infusion of malt for fermenting into beer. [OE *wyrt* (cp. G *Wurz,* Icel. *urt*), cogn. with ROOT]

worth[1], *a.* equal in value or price to; deserving, worthy of; having property to the value of, possessed of; †estimable, valuable. *n.* that which a person or thing is worth, value, the equivalent of anything, esp. in money; merit, desert, high character, excellence. **for all one is worth,** (*coll.*) with all one's strength, energy etc. **worthless,** *a.* **worthlessly,** *adv.* **worthlessness,** *n.* [OE *wyrthe,* from *wyrth, weorth,* value (cp. Dut. *waard, waarde,* Icel. *verthr, verth,* G *Werth*), cogn. with W *gwerth,* value, price, L *verērī,* see REVERE and Eng. WARE[2]]

worthless etc. WORTH[1].

worthwhile, *a.* worth the time, expense or effort involved.

worthy, *a.* having worth, estimable; deserving of respect, praise or honour, respectable; deserving (of, to be etc.); fit, suitable, adequate, appropriate, equivalent or adequate to the worth (of); †of high rank, noble, honourable. *n.* a person of eminent worth; a person of some note or distinction in his or her time, locality etc. **the Nine Worthies,** Hector of Troy, Alexander the Great, Julius Caesar, Joshua, David, Judas Maccabaeus, King Arthur, Charlemagne and Godfrey of Bouillon. **worthily,** *adv.* **worthiness,** *n.* [WORTH[1], -Y]

-worthy, *comb. form.* safe or suitable for, as in *seaworthy;* deserving of, as in *praiseworthy.*

†**wot,** *first and second sing.* WIT[1].

wotcher, *int.* (*sl.*) a form of greeting. [Cockney pronunciation of archaic greeting *what cheer?*]

would, *past, cond.* WILL[1].

would-be WILL[1].

Woulfe bottle, *n.* a bottle with three or more necks used in the handling and washing of gases. [British chemist P. *Woulfe,* 1727–1803]

wound[1], *n.* an injury caused by violence to the skin and flesh of an animal or the bark or substance of plants, esp. one involving disruption of the tissues; any damage, hurt or pain to feelings, reputation etc., esp. the pangs of love. *v.t.* to inflict a wound on. *v.i.* to cause a wound. **woundwort,** *n.* a plant of the genus *Stachys,* and other plants supposed to heal wounds. **woundable,** *a.* **wounder,** *n.* **woundless,** *a.* †**woundy,** *a.* causing wounds; excessive. †**woundily,** *adv.* [OE *wund* (cp. Dut. *wond,* G *Wunde,* Icel. *und*), prob. cogn. with WIN]

wound[2], *past, p.p.* WIND[1,2].

Wounded Knee, *n.* site on the Oglala Sioux Reservation, South Dakota, US, of a confrontation between the US Army and American Indians. Sitting Bull was killed, supposedly resisting arrest, on 15 Dec. 1890, and on 29 Dec. a group of Indians involved with him in the Ghost Dance Movement (aimed at resumption of Indian control of North America with the aid of the spirits of dead braves) were surrounded and 153 killed.

wourali, CURARE.

wove, *past, p.p.,* **woven,** *p.p.* WEAVE.

wow[1], *int.* an exclamation of astonishment, wonder etc. *n.* a sensational or spectacular success. *v.t.* (*coll.*) to cause to feel great enthusiasm. [instinctive sound]

wow[2], *n.* a variation in pitch occurring at low frequencies in sound-reproducing systems. [imit.]

wowser, *n.* (*Austral. sl.*) a spoil-sport, a puritan. **wowserism,** *n.* [onomat.]

wow-wow, *n.* the silvery gibbon, *Hylobates leuciscus,* of Java and Sumatra. [imit.]

WP, (*abbr.*) word processor.

W particle, *n.* type of elementary particle.

WPC, (*abbr.*) woman police constable.

wpm, (*abbr.*) words per minute.

WRAC, (*abbr.*) Woman's Royal Army Corps.

wrack, *n.* seaweed thrown upon the shore; cloud-rack; wreck, destruction, ruin. †**wrackful,** *a.* ruinous, destructive. [var. of WRECK]

WRAF, (*abbr.*) Women's Royal Air Force.

wraith, *n.* the double or phantom of a living person; an apparition, a ghost appearing after death. [perh. var. of WREATH, or cogn. with Norw. *vardyvle* (WARD, EVIL)]

wrangle, *v.i.* to dispute, argue or quarrel angrily, peevishly or noisily, to brawl; †to engage in public discussion and disputation. *n.* an angry or noisy dispute or quarrel, an altercation, a brawl. **wrangler,** *n.* one who wrangles; (*esp. N Am.*) a cowboy; a horse-breaker; (*Camb. Univ.*) one of those who are placed in the first class in the mathematical tripos. **senior wrangler,** formerly the student who took the first place in this. **wranglership,** *n.* †**wranglesome,** *a.* [freq. from OE *wrang,* cogn. with WRING]

wrap[1], *v.t.* (*past, p.p.* **wrapped**) to fold or arrange so as to cover or enclose something; to enfold, envelop, muffle, pack, surround or conceal in some soft material; to enfold or muffle (up) thus; to hide, to conceal, to disguise; (*in p.p.*) to absorb, to engross, to comprise (with *up*). *v.i.* to fold, to lap. *n.* something intended to wrap, as a cloak, shawl, rug etc. (*usu. in pl.*). **to wrap up,** to dress warmly; (*coll.*) to bring to a conclusion; (*sl.*) to fall silent. **under wraps,** secret. **wraparound,** *a.* of a skirt etc., designed to be wrapped around the body; of a windscreen etc., curving round at the sides. **wrappage,** *n.* the act of wrapping; that which wraps or envelops, a wrapping or wrappings. **wrapper,** *n.* one who wraps; that in which anything is wrapped, esp. an outer covering for a new book, and for a newspaper for posting; a woman's loose outer garment for indoor wear. **wrapping,** *n.* that which wraps; that in which something is wrapped or packaged; a wrapper, a cloak, a shawl, a rug. [perh. rel. to WARP]

†**wrap**[2], RAP3.

†**wrapt**, RAPT.

wrasse, *n.* an acanthopterygian sea-fish of numerous species of the genus *Labrus* or *Crenilabrus*, haunting coasts and rocks. [cp. W. *gwrachen*]

wrath, *n.* deep or violent anger, indignation, rage; †impetuosity. **wrathful**, *a.* **wrathfully**, *adv.* **wrathfulness**, *n.* **wrathless**, *a.* **wrathy**, *a.* **wrathily**, *adv.* [OE *wrætho*, from *wrāth*, WROTH]

†**wrawl**, *v.i.* to cry as a cat, to whine. [imit.]

wraxling, (*Sc.*) WRESTLING.

Wray, *n.* **Fay** (1907–), US film actress who starred in *King Kong* (1933) after playing the lead in Erich von Stroheim's *The Wedding March* (1928) and starring in *Doctor X* (1932) and *The Most Dangerous Game* (1932).

wreak[1], *v.t.* to carry out, to inflict, to execute; †to avenge. **wreaker**, *n.* †**wreakful**, *a.* †**wreakless**, *a.* [OE *wrecan* (cp. Dut. *wrecken*, G *rächen*, Icel. *reka*), cogn. with L *urgēre*, to urge, Gr. *eirgein*, to shut in, and WRACK, WRECK]

†**wreak**[2], RECK.

wreath, *n.* a band or ring of flowers or leaves tied, woven or twisted together for wearing on the head, decorating statues, walls, graves etc.; a representation of this in wood, stone etc.; a similar circlet of twisted silk etc.; a ring, a twist, a curl (of cloud, smoke etc.); a garland, a chaplet. [OE *wrǣth*, cogn. with WRITHE]

wreathe, *v.t.* to form (flowers, leaves etc.) into a wreath; to surround, encircle, entwine (as if) with a wreath or with anything twisted; to form a wreath round; to cause (the face) to take on a certain expression, esp. a smiling one. *v.i.* to be curled, folded or entwined (round etc.). †**wreathen**, *a.* wreathed. **wreather**, *n.* **wreathless**, *a.* †**wreathy**, *a.*

wreck, *n.* destruction, ruin, esp. of a ship; a vessel dashed against rocks or otherwise destroyed, seriously crippled or shattered; the remains of anything irretrievably shattered or ruined; a dilapidated or worn-out person or thing; wreckage. *v.t.* to destroy or cast away (a vessel etc.) by collision, driving ashore etc.; to involve in shipwreck; to ruin or destroy. *v.i.* to suffer shipwreck. **wreck-master**, *n.* an official appointed to take charge of goods etc. cast ashore after a shipwreck. **wreckage**, *n.* the debris, fragments or material from a wreck. **wrecker**, *n.* a plunderer from wrecks; one who wrecks or causes shipwreck, esp. one who lures vessels to shipwreck with intent to plunder; a person or ship employed in recovering a wreck or a wrecked cargo; a person or thing that brings about ruin or destruction; (*esp. N Am.*) a recovery vehicle. **wrecking-car**, *n.* (*N Am.*) a railway-car carrying appliances for removing wreckage and obstructions from the line. [OE *wræc*, expulsion, perh. modified in sense through Icel. *rek*, anything cast ashore (cp. Dut. *wrak*) cogn. with WREAK[1]]

WREN, (*abbr.*) a member of the Women's Royal Naval Service.

wren, *n.* a small insessorial bird of the genus *Troglodytes* with a short erect tail and short wings. **wrenning-day**, *n.* St Stephen's Day, 26 Dec., on which it was formerly the custom to stone a wren to death to commemorate his martyrdom. [OE *wrenna* (cp. Icel. *rindill*)]

Wren, *n.* **Christopher** (1632–1723), English architect, designer of St Paul's Cathedral, London, built 1675–1710; many London churches including St Bride's, Fleet Street, and St Mary-le-Bow, Cheapside; the Royal Exchange; Marlborough House; and the Sheldonian Theatre, Oxford.

wrench, *n.* a violent twist or sideways pull; an injury caused by twisting, a sprain; pain or distress caused by a parting, loss etc.; a tool for twisting or untwisting screws, bolts, nuts etc., a spanner. *v.t.* to pull, wrest or twist with force or violence; to pull (off or away) thus; to strain, to sprain; to pervert, to distort. [OE *wrenc* (deceit, guile, cp. G *Rank*), cogn. with WRONG, WRINKLE[1]]

wrest, *v.t.* to twist, to turn aside by a violent effort; to pull, extort or wrench (away) forcibly; to pervert, to distort, to twist or deflect from its natural meaning. *n.* a violent wrench or twist; a turning instrument, esp. a tuning-key for a harp etc. **wrester**, *n.* [OE *wrǣstan* (cp. Icel. *reista*, Dan. *vriste*), cogn with WRITHE, WRIST]

wrestle, *v.i.* to contend by grappling with and trying to throw one's opponent, esp. in a match under recognized rules; to struggle, to contend, to strive vehemently; †to make earnest supplication. *v.t.* to contend with in a wrestling-match; to move with difficulty, to manhandle. *n.* a bout at wrestling, a wrestling-match; a struggle. **wrestler**, *n.* **wrestling**, *n.* [freq. of prec.]

wretch, *n.* a miserable or unfortunate person; a despicable, mean, base or vile person (often used to express ironical pity or contempt or even tenderness and compassion). **wretched**, *a.* miserable, unhappy, sunk in deep affliction or distress; calamitous, pitiable, afflictive; worthless, paltry, contemptible; (*coll.*) extremely unsatisfactory, uncomfortable or unpleasant. **wretchedly**, *adv.* **wretchedness**, *n.* [OE *wrecca*, an outcast, from *wrecan*, to drive out, to WREAK[1]]

wrick, *v.t.* to sprain or strain. *n.* a sprain or strain.

wriggle, *v.i.* to turn, twist or move the body to and fro with short motions like an eel; to move or go (along, in, out etc.) with writhing contortions or twistings; to manoeuvre by clever or devious means. *v.t.* to move (one's body etc.) with a wriggling motion; to effect or make (one's way etc.) by wriggling. *n.* a wriggling motion. **wriggler**, *n.* [freq. of obs. *wrīg* (cp. Dut. *wriggelen*, LG *wriggeln*), cogn. with prec. and WRY, WRING]

wright, *n.* one who is occupied in some mechanical business, an artificer, a workman, (*esp. in comb.*, as *shipwright, wheelwright*, etc.). [OE *wyrhta*, from *wyrht*, work, from *wyrcan*, to WORK]

Wright[1], *n.* **Frank Lloyd** (1869–1959), US architect who rejected neo-classicist styles for 'organic architecture', in which buildings reflected their natural surroundings. Among his buildings are his Wisconsin home Taliesin East, 1925; Falling Water, Pittsburgh, Pennsylvania, 1936; and the Guggenheim Museum, New York, 1959.

Wright[2], *n.* **Joseph** (1855–1930), English philologist. He was professor of comparative philology at Oxford 1901–25, and recorded English local speech in his six-volume *English Dialect Dictionary* (1896–1905).

Wright[3], *n.* **Joseph** (1734–97), British painter, known as Wright of Derby from his birthplace. He painted portraits, landscapes, and scientific experiments. His work is often dramatically lit, by fire, candlelight, or even volcanic explosion.

Wright[4], *n.* **Judith** (1915–), Australian poet, author of *The Moving Image* (1946) and *Alive* (1972).

Wright[5], *n.* **Orville** (1871–1948) and **Wilbur** (1867–1912), US brothers who pioneered powered flight. Inspired by Lilienthal's gliding, they perfected their piloted glider 1902. In 1903 they built a powered machine and became the first to make a successful powered flight, near Kitty Hawk, North Carolina.

Wright[6], *n.* **Peter** (1917–), British intelligence agent. His book *Spycatcher* (1987), written after his retirement, caused an international stir when the British government tried unsuccessfully to block its publication anywhere in the world because of its damaging revelations about the secret service.

Wright[7], *n.* **Richard** (1908–60), US novelist. He was one of the first to depict the condition of black people in 20th-century US society with *Native Son* (1940) and the autobiography *Black Boy* (1945).

Wright[8], *n.* **Sewall** (1889–1988), US geneticist and statistician. During the 1920s he helped modernize Darwin's theory of evolution, using statistics to model the behaviour of populations of genes.

wring, *v.t.* (*past, p.p.* **wrung**) to twist and squeeze or compress; to turn, twist or strain forcibly; to press or squeeze (water etc. out) thus; to pervert, to distort (a meaning etc.); to pain, to torture, to distress; to extract, to extort. *n.* a press, a squeeze, **to wring one's withers,** to appeal passionately to one's pity. **to wring the hands,** to press the hands together convulsively, as in great distress. **wringer,** *n.* one who or that which wrings; a wringing-machine. **wringing,** *n., a.* **wringing-machine,** *n.* a machine for wringing water out of newly-washed clothes etc. **wringing-wet,** *a.* so wet that moisture can be wrung out. [OE *wringan* (cp. Dut. *wringen,* G *ringen*), cogn. with WRIGGLE]

wrinkle[1], *n.* a small ridge, crease or furrow caused by the folding or contraction of a flexible surface. *v.t., v.i.* to fold or contract into furrows, creases or ridges. *v.i.* to fold or shrink into furrows and ridges. **wrinkly,** *a.* [freq. or dim., cogn. with prec.]

wrinkle[2], *n.* a useful bit of information or advice, a bright idea, a tip, a dodge. [dim. of OE *wrenc,* trick, cogn. with WRENCH and prec.]

wrist, *n.* the joint uniting the hand to the forearm; the part of a sleeve over the wrist; a wrist-pin. **wristband,** *n.* a band or part of a sleeve, esp. a shirt-sleeve, covering the wrist, usu. of starched linen, a cuff. **wrist-drop,** *n.* paralysis of the muscles of the forearm through lead-poisoning. **wrist-pin,** *n.* a pin or stud projecting from a crank for a connecting-rod to turn on. **wrist-watch,** *n.* a watch worn on a strap round the wrist. **wristlet,** *n.* a band worn round the wrist to strengthen it, hold up a glove, carry a watch etc.; a bracelet; a handcuff. [OE, from *wrīthan,* to WRITHE (cp. Icel., G *Rist,* Dan., Swed. *vrist,* instep]

writ[1], *n.* that which is written, a writing; a written command or precept issued by a court in the name of the sovereign to an officer or other person commanding him to do or refrain from doing some particular act therein specified. **holy writ** HOLY. [OE *gewrit,* a writing, cogn. with WRITE]

†**writ**[2], *past, p.p.* WRITE.

write, *v.t.* (*past* **wrote**, †**writ**, *p.p.* **written**, †**writ**) to form or trace (esp. words, a sentence etc.) in letters or symbols, with a pen, pencil or the like on paper or other material; to trace (signs, characters etc.) thus, to set (down), to record, to describe, to state or convey by writing; to compose or produce as an author; to cover or fill with writing; to impress or stamp (disgrace etc.) on a person's face; to designate, to call, to put (oneself down as etc.) in writing; (*coll.*) to send a letter to, to communicate in writing; (*Comput.*) to record (data) in a storage device. *v.i.* to trace letters or symbols representing words on paper etc.; to write or send a letter; to compose or produce articles, books etc., as an author. **to write down,** to put in writing, to record; to depreciate, to criticize unfavourably; to write in such a way that one appeals to low standards of taste, intelligence etc. **to write off,** to record the cancelling of (a debt etc.); to compose rapidly and easily; to discard as useless, damaged etc.; to damage (a car) beyond repair; to write and send a letter etc. **to write oneself out,** to exhaust one's powers of literary production. **to write out,** to write the whole of; to remove (a character) from a drama series. **to write up,** to praise in writing, to puff; to post up (account-books etc.); to give full details in writing. **writ large,** set down or recorded in large letters; magnified, emphasized. **writer,** *n.* one who writes; an author, a journalist etc.; a clerk, an amanuensis; (*Sc.*) a solicitor, an attorney. **writer to the signet,** (*Sc.*) a solicitor. **writer's cramp,** *n.* a spasmodic pain in the fingers or hand caused by prolonged writing. **writership,** *n.* **writing,** *n.* the act of one who writes; that which is written; an inscription; a book, article or other literary composition; a legal instrument. **writing on the wall,** a solemn warning. **writing-case,** *n.* a portable case for writing materials etc. **writing desk,** *n.* a portable desk with space for papers etc. **writing-ink,** *n.* ink for writing, opp. to printer's ink. **writing-master,** *n.* one who teaches penmanship. **writing-paper,** *n.* paper with a smooth surface for writing on. **writing-school,** *n.* a school where penmanship is taught. **writing-table,** *n.* a table used for writing on, usu. with a knee-hole, drawers etc. [OE *wrītan,* (cp. Dut. *rijten,* G *reissen,* Icel. *rīta,* to tear, cut, draw, scratch out etc.)]

writhe, *v.i.* to twist, turn or roll the body about, as in pain; to shrink, to squirm (at, with shame etc.). *v.t.* to twist or distort (the limbs etc.). *n.* an act of writhing. †**writhen,** *a.* twisted, distorted. **writhingly,** *adv.* †**writhle,** *v.t.* to wrinkle. [OE *wrīthan* (cp. Icel. *rītha,* Dan. *vride,* OHG *rīdan*)]

writing WRITE.

written, etc. WRITE.

WRNS, (*abbr.*) Women's Royal Naval Service.

†**wroke,** *past,* †**wroken,** *p.p.* WREAK[1].

Wrocław, *n.* industrial river port in Poland, on the river Oder; population (1985) 636,000. Under the German name of Breslau, it was the capital of former German Silesia. Industries include shipbuilding, engineering, textiles, and electronics.

wrong, *a.* not morally right, contrary to morality, conscience or law, wicked; not the right (one etc.), not that which is required, intended, proper, best etc.; not according to truth or reality; out of order, in bad condition, not suitable etc.; false, inaccurate, mistaken, erroneous. *adv.* wrongly, unjustly. *n.* that which is wrong; a wrong act, an injustice, a trespass, an injury, hurt or pain; deviation from what is right; wrongness, error. *v.t.* to treat unjustly, to do wrong to; to impute evil motives to unjustly; to seduce (a woman). **in the wrong,** in a wrong position; in error. **to get on the wrong side of,** to fall into disfavour with. **to go wrong,** to fail morally, to fall into sin; to fail to operate correctly; to fall into error. **wrong side out,** inside out. **wrong-foot,** *v.t.* to cause to be off-balance; to gain an advantage over. **wrong fount,** *a.* of type, not of the right fount, size or pattern. **wrongdoer,** *n.* **wrongdoing,** *n.* **wrong-headed,** *a.* perverse, obstinate, crotchety. **wrong-headedness,** *n.* **wronger,** *n.* **wrongful,** *a.* injurious, unjust, wrong. **wrongfully,** *adv.* **wrongfulness,** *n.* †**wrongless**, *a.* †**wronglessly,** *adv.* **wrongly,** *adv.* **wrongness,** *n.* **wrongous**, *a.* (*Sc. Law*) not right, illegal. [OE *wrang,* a wrong thing, from Scand. (cp. Icel. *rangr,* awry, Dan. *vrang,* wrong), cogn. with WRING]

wrote, *past* WRITE.

wroth, *a.* (*poet.*) angry, wrathful. [OE *wrāth,* perverted, from *wrīthan* to WRITHE, (cp. Dut. *wread,* Icel. *reithr*)]

wrought, *a.* worked; (*often in comb.*) formed or fashioned; decorated or ornamented. **wrought iron,** *n.* iron made malleable by having non-metallic impurities burned out of it; iron made malleable by forging or rolling. **wrought-up,** *a.* very tense or excited. [*past, p.p.* WORK]

wrung, *past, p.p.* WRING.

WRVS, (*abbr.*) Women's Royal Voluntary Service.

wry, †*v.i.* to swerve, to go wrong or astray. †*v.t.* to distort. *a.* twisted, distorted, crooked, skew; showing distaste, disgust etc.; wrong, false, perverted. **wrybill,** *n.* a species of the plover. **wry-mouth,** *n.* an eel-like sea-fish with a vertical mouth. **wry-mouthed,** *a.* having a distorted mouth or a cynical or distorted expression. **wry-neck,** *n.* a bird, *Junx torquīlla,* allied to the woodpeckers, with a habit of twisting its head round as on a pivot; stiff-neck. **wrynecked,** *a.* **wryness,** *n.* **wryly,** *adv.* [ME *wrien,* OE *wrigian,* cogn. with WRIGGLE]

WSW, (*abbr.*) west south-west.

Wuhan, *n.* river port and capital of Hubei province, China, at the confluence of the Han and Chang Jiang, formed 1950 as one of China's greatest industrial areas by the amalgamation of Hankou, Hanyang, and Wuchang; population (1986) 3,400,000. It produces iron, steel, machine tools, textiles, and fertilizer.

Wundt, *n.* **Wilhelm Max** (1832–1920), German physiologist, who regarded psychology as the study of internal experience or consciousness. His main psychological method was introspection; he also studied sensation, perception of space and time, and reaction times.

wyandotte, *n.* a breed of domestic fowl. [name of a N Am. Ind. people]

wych, *pref.* drooping. **wych-elm,** *n.* the Scotch elm,

Ulmus montana. **wych-hazel,** *n.* a N American shrub, *Hamamelis virginea,* with several large branching trunks. [OE *wice,* cogn. with WICKER]

Wycherley, *n.* **William** (1640–1710), English Restoration playwright. His first comedy *Love in a Wood* won him court favour 1671, and later bawdy works include *The Country Wife* (1675) and *The Plain Dealer* (1676).

Wycliffe, *n.* **John** (*c.* 1320–84), English religious reformer. Allying himself with the party of John of Gaunt, which was opposed to ecclesiastical influence at court, he attacked abuses in the church, maintaining that the Bible rather than the church was the supreme authority. About 1378 he criticized such fundamental doctrines as priestly absolution, confession, and indulgences. He set disciples to work on translating the Bible into English. **Wycliffite**, *a.* pertaining to Wycliffe, his tenets or his followers. *n.* a follower of Wycliffe.

Wye, *n.* river in Wales and England; length 208 km/130 miles. It rises on Plynlimmon, NE Dyfed, flowing SE and E through Powys, and Hereford and Worcester, then follows the Gwent/Gloucestershire border before joining the river Severn S of Chepstow. Other rivers of the same name in the UK are found in Buckinghamshire (15 km/9 miles) and Derbyshire (32 km/20 miles).

wye, *n.* a Y-shaped thing. [letter Y]

Wyeth, *n.* **Andrew (Newell)** (1917–), US painter, based in Maine. His portraits and landscapes, usually in watercolour or tempera, are naturalistic and minutely detailed and often have a strong sense of the isolation of the countryside, for example *Christina's World* (1948).

Wykehamist, *n.* a member (past or present) of Winchester College founded by William of Wykeham (1324–1404) Bishop of Winchester. *a.* of or pertaining to this.

Wyler, *n.* **William** (1902–81), German-born film director who lived in the US from 1922. He directed *Wuthering Heights* (1939), *Mrs Miniver* (1942), *Ben-Hur* (1959) and *Funny Girl* (1968), among others.

wynd, *n.* (*Sc.*) an alley. [prob. var. of WIND[2]]

Wyndham, *n.* **John** (1903–69), pen name of John Wyndham Parkes Lucas Beynon Harris, English science-fiction writer who wrote *The Day of the Triffids* (1951), *The Chrysalids* (1955), and *The Midwich Cuckoos* (1957). A recurrent theme in his work is people's response to disaster, whether caused by nature, aliens, or human error.

Wynne-Edwards, *n.* **Vera** (1906–), English zoologist who argued that animal behaviour is often altruistic and that animals will behave for the good of the group, even if this entails individual sacrifice. Her study *Animal Dispersal in Relation to Social Behaviour* was published in 1962.

Wyoming, *n.* state of W US; nickname Equality State. **area** 253,400 sq km/97,812 sq miles. **capital** Cheyenne. **towns** Casper, Laramie. **population** (1988) 477,000. **products** oil, natural gas, tin, sodium salts, coal, phosphates, sulphur, uranium, sheep, beef.

WYSIWYG, *n.* what you see is what you get, in computing, a program that attempts to display on the screen a faithful representation of the final printed output. For example, a WYSIWYG word processor would show actual line widths, page breaks, and the sizes and styles of type.

Wyss, *n.* **Johann David** (1743–1818), Swiss author of the children's classic *Swiss Family Robinson* (1813).

wyvern, *n.* (*Her.*) a two-legged dragon with erect wings and barbed tail. [OE *wyvre,* OF *wivre,* L *vīpera,* VIPER (cp. *n.* in BITTERN)]

X

X, x, the 24th letter, and the 18th consonant, of the English alphabet (**Xs, X's, Exes**), as a medial letter has the sound of *ks*, as in *axis, taxes*, or of *gz*, as in *exhaust, exult*; as an initial (chiefly in words of Greek origin) it has the sound of *z*; (Roman numeral), 10 (xx, 20, xxx, 30, xc, 90); (*Alg.*, *x*) the first unknown quantity or variable; an unknown thing or person; Christ, Christian (first letter of Christ in Greek); before 1982, a film for over 18-year-olds only; a kiss; a choice; an error. **x-axis,** *n.* the horizontal axis, along which **x-coordinates** are plotted in the Cartesian coordinate system. **X chromosome,** *n.* a sex chromosome which is found paired in women, and paired with the Y chromosome in men. **X-ray,** *n.* electromagnetic radiation in the wavelength range 10^{-11} to 10^{-9} m (shorter wavelengths are gamma rays; see ELECTROMAGNETIC WAVES). Applications of X-rays make use of their short wavelength (such as X-ray crystallography) or their penetrating power (as in medical X-rays of internal body tissues). High doses of X-rays are dangerous, and can cause cancer; a picture thus produced. *v.t.* to produce such an image of part of the body; to treat with X-rays. **X-ray astronomy,** *n.* detection of X-rays from intensely hot gas in the universe. Such X-rays are prevented from reaching the Earth's surface by the atmosphere, so detectors must be placed in rockets and satellites. The first celestial X-ray source, Scorpius X-1, was discovered by a rocket flight in 1962. **X-ray diffraction,** *n.* method of studying the atomic and molecular structure of crystalline substances by using X-rays. X-rays directed at such substances spread out as they pass through the crystals owing to diffraction (the slight spreading of waves around the edge of an opaque object) of the rays around the atoms. By using measurements of the position and intensity of the diffracted waves, it is possible to calculate the shape and size of the atoms in the crystal. The method has been used to study substances such as DNA that are found in living material. **X-ray tube,** *n.* an evacuated tube in which electrons are beamed onto a metal target to produce X-rays. **xx** or **double-x, xxx** or **triple-x,** marks indicating the strength of ale etc. placed on brewers' casks.

Xanthian, *a.* of Xanthus, an ancient town of Asia Minor. **Xanthian marbles** or **sculptures,** *n.pl.* a collection of marble sculptures from Xanthus placed in the British Museum (1838).

xanthic, *a.* of a yellowish colour. **xanthic acid,** *n.* a colourless oily liquid, prepared by decomposing xanthate of potassium with sulphuric or hydrochloric acid. **xanthic flowers,** *n.pl.* flowers having yellow as their type and passing into red and white, opp. to *cyanic*, having blue as the type. **xanthin, -thine,** *n.* the part of the yellow colouring-matter of flowers that is insoluble in water; a yellow colouring-matter obtained from madder; a crystalline compound found in blood, urine, the liver etc.; a gaseous product of the decomposition of xanthate. [XANTH(O)-]

xanthium, *n.* a genus of hardy composite plants. [Gr. *xanthion*]

xanth(o)-, *comb. form.* yellow. **xanthate,** *n.* a salt of xanthic acid. **xanthein,** *n.* the part of the yellow colouring-matter of flowers that is soluble in water. [Gr. *xanthos*]

Xanthochroi, *n.pl.* fair whites or blonds, those having yellow or red hair, blue eyes and fair complexion. **xanthochroic, -chroous,** *a.* **xanthochroism,** *n.* a condition where all skin pigments apart from yellow disappear, as in some goldfish. [XANTH(O)-, cp. MELANOCHROI]

xanthoma, *n.* a skin disease characterized by a growth of yellowish tubercles, usu. in flat patches, on the eyelids. **xanthomatous,** *a.*

xanthomelanous, *a.* having black hair and yellow or brownish skin. [Gr. *melas melanos,* black]

xanthophyll, *n.* the yellow colouring-matter of withered leaves. **xanthophyllous,** *a.* [Gr. *phullon,* leaf]

xanthopsia, *n.* (*Path.*) an affection of the sight in which objects appear yellowish. [Gr. *opsis,* sight]

xanthosis, *n.* yellow discoloration of the skin, as in cancerous tumours. **xanthous,** *a.* belonging to one of the Asiatic races; †xanthochroic.

xanthoxylene, *n.* a volatile oily compound obtained from the fruit of the Japanese pepper, *Xanthoxylon piperitum.*

xanthoxylum, -lon, *n.* a genus of tropical or subtropical trees with prickly stems, several of which yield valuable timber. [Gr. *xulon,* wood]

Xantippe, *n.* a shrewish wife, a scold. [wife of Socrates]

Xavier, St Francis, *n.* (1506–52), Spanish Jesuit missionary. He went as a Catholic missionary to the Portuguese colonies in the Indies, arriving at Goa in 1542. He was in Japan 1549–51, establishing a Christian mission which lasted for 100 years. He returned to Goa in 1552, and sailed for China, but died of fever there. He was canonized in 1622.

xd, (*abbr.*) ex dividend.

Xe, (*chem. symbol*) xenon.

xebec, *n.* a small three-masted vessel with lateen and square sails, used in the Mediterranean. [Sp. *xabeque* (cp. Port. *zabeco,* F *chebdec,* It. *sciabecco*), Turk. *sumbakī,* cp. Arab. *sumbūk*]

xen-, XEN(O)-.

xenarthral, *a.* (*Anat.*) peculiarly jointed (of certain vertebrae). [Gr. *arthron,* joint, -AL]

xenelasia, *n.* (*Gr. Hist.*) exclusion of foreigners from a country, as in Sparta. [Gr. (XEN-, *elaunein,* to drive)]

xenial, *a.* of or pertaining to hospitality or the relations between host and guest.

xenium, *n.* (*Class. Ant.*) a present given to a guest, ambassador etc.; a picture of still life on the walls of a guest-chamber.

xen(o)-, *comb. form.* strange, foreign. [Gr. *xenos,* strange, stranger]

xenogamy, *n.* cross-fertilization. **xenogamous,** *a.*

xenogenesis, *n.* heterogenesis.

xenogenous, *a.* arising from external causes.

xenoglossia, *n.* in psychical research the knowledge of a language one has not learned, claimed by some mediums.

xenograft, *n.* a tissue graft from a member of a different species.

xenolith, *n.* a fragment of rock enclosed in a different type of rock.

xenomania, *n.* inordinate liking for everything foreign.

xenomenia, *n.* loss of menstrual blood elsewhere than from the uterus, e.g. from the nose; vicarious menstruation.

xenomorphic, *a.* (*Petrol.*) not having its own proper form but an irregular shape due to surrounding minerals.

xenon, *n.* an inert gaseous element, at. no. 54; chem. symbol Xe, found in the atmosphere and solidifying at the temperature of liquid air.

xenophile, *n.* someone who likes foreign people and

things.

xenophobia, *n.* fear of, or aversion from, strangers or foreigners. **xenophobe,** *n.* **xenophobic,** *a.*

Xenophon, *n.* (*c.* 430–354 BC), Greek historian, philosopher, and soldier. He was a disciple of Socrates (described in Xenophon's *Symposium*). In 401 BC he joined a Greek mercenary army aiding the Persian prince Cyrus, and on Cyrus' death, took command. His *Anabasis* describes how he led 10,000 Greeks in a 1,000-mile march home across enemy territory. His other works include *Memorabilia* and *Apology*.

xeransis, *n.* the state of being dried up, desiccation. **xerantic,** *a.* [Gr. *xēros,* dry]

xeranthemum, *n.* an annual plant of the order Compositae with everlasting flowers. [Gr. *anthemon, anthos,* flower]

xerasia, *n.* a disease of the hair in which it becomes dry and powdery.

xer(o)-, *comb. form.* dry.

xerodermia, *n.* morbid dryness of the skin. **xerodermatic, xerodermatous,** *a.* [Gr. *derma,* skin]

xerography, *n.* a photographic process in which the plate is sensitized electrically, and the latent image developed by a resinous powder. **xerographic,** *a.*

xeromyron, *n.* a dry ointment.

xerophagy, *n.* the Christian rule of fasting; the act or habit of living on dry food or a meagre diet.

xerophilous, *a.* adapted to living in a hot, dry climate. **xerophile,** *n.* **xerophily,** *n.*

xerophthalmia, *n.* a dry inflammation of the lining membrane of the eye, caused by a deficiency of vitamin A. **xeropthalmic,** *a.*

xerophyte, *n.* a plant adapted to living in a region of little moisture, such as a cactus. **xerophytic,** *a.* **xerophytism,** *n.*

xerostomia, *n.* abnormal dryness of the mouth.

xerotes, *n.* a dry habit or disposition of the body. **xerotic,** *a.*

Xerox®, *n.* a xerographic copying process; the copy produced by this process; the machine used for this process. *v.t.* to produce a copy of an original document by this process.

Xerxes, *n.* (*c.* 519 BC–465 BC), king of Persia from 485 BC, when he succeeded his father Darius and, continued the Persian invasion of Greece. In 480 BC, at the head of an army of some 400,000 men and supported by a fleet of 800 ships, he crossed the Hellespont strait over a bridge of boats. He defeated the Greek fleet at Artemisium and captured and burned Athens, but Themistocles annihilated the Persian fleet at Salamis and Xerxes was forced to retreat. He spent his later years working on a grandiose extension of the capital Persepolis and was eventually murdered in a court intrigue.

Xhosa, *n.* a member of one of the Bantu-speaking peoples in the Cape district of S Africa; their language, which is characterized by a sound system involving a series of clicks. **Xhosan,** *a.*

xi, *n.* the 14th letter of the Greek alphabet.

Xian¹, *n.* industrial city and capital of Shaanxi province, China; population (1986) 2,330,000. It produces chemicals, electrical equipment, and fertilizers.

Xian², (*abbr.*) CHRISTIAN.

Xi Jiang (formerly **Si-Kiang**), *n.* river in China, which rises in Yunnan and flows into the South China Sea; length 1900 km/1200 miles. Guangzhou lies on the N arm of its delta, and Hong Kong island at its mouth. The name means West River.

Xingú, *n.* river (Amazon tributary) and region in Pará, Brazil. In 1989 Xingú Indians protested at the creation of a huge, intrusive lake for the Babaquara and Kararao dams of the Altamira complex.

Xinhua, *n.* official Chinese news agency.

Xining (formerly **Sining**), *n.* industrial city, capital of Qinghai province, China; population (1982) 873,000.

Xinjiang Uygur (formerly **Sinkiang Uighur**), *n.* autonomous region of NW China. **area** 1,646,800 sq km/ 635,665 sq miles. **capital** Urumqi. **products** cereals, cotton, fruit in valleys and oases; uranium, coal, iron, copper, tin, oil. **population** (1986) 13,840,000. **religion** 50% Muslim.

xiph-, xiphi-, xipho- *comb. form.* sword. **Xiphias,** *n.* the swordfish genus of fishes. **xiphisternum,** *n.* the lower segment or xiphoid process of the sternum. **xiphoid,** *a.* sword-shaped. **xiphoid appendage, cartilage** or **process,** *n.* the xiphisternum. [Gr. *xiphos,* sword]

Xmas, CHRISTMAS.

Xn, Xnty, (*abbr.*) CHRISTIAN, CHRISTIANITY.

X-ray X.

Xt. (*abbr.*) CHRIST.

xylanthrax, *n.* wood coal, or charcoal, opp. to mineral coal. [Gr. *anthrax,* coal]

xylem, *n.* woody tissue, wood parenchyma, opp. to phloem.

xylene, *n.* any one of three isomeric colourless, volatile, liquid hydrocarbons distilled from coal- or wood-tar. [-ENE]

xyl(o)-, *comb. form.* wood. [Gr. *xulon,* wood]

xylobalsamum, *n.* the wood of or a balsam obtained by decoction of the twigs and leaves of the Balm of Gilead tree. [see BALSAM]

xylocarp, *n.* a hard, woody fruit, or a tree bearing this. **xylocarpous,** *a.* [Gr. *karpos,* fruit]

xylograph, *n.* an engraving on wood, esp. in a primitive style, or an impression from such an engraving; an impression obtained from the grain of wood used for surface decoration. **xylographer,** *n.* **xylographic,** *a.* **xylography,** *n.* [-GRAPH]

xyloid, *a.* woody, ligneous.

xyloidine, *n.* a high explosive prepared by the action of nitric acid on starch or wood-fibre.

Xylonite®, *n.* celluloid.

xylophagous, *a.* boring into wood (of insects). **xylophagan,** *n., a.*

xylophilous, *a.* living or growing on wood.

xylophone, *n.* a musical instrument consisting of a graduated series of wooden bars vibrating when struck or rubbed. **xylophonic,** *a.* **xylophonist,** *n.*

xylose, *n.* wood sugar.

xylotomous, *a.* describing an insect that bores into wood.

xyster, *n.* an instrument for scraping bones. [Gr. *xustēr,* from *xuein,* to scrape]

xystus, *n.* (*pl.* **-ti**) in antiquity, a long covered portico or colonnade used for athletic exercises; a garden walk or terrace. [L, from Gr. *xustos,* orig. polished, as prec.]

Y

Y, y, the 25th letter of the English alphabet (**Y's, Ys, wyes**) is both a vowel and a palatal semi-vowel; as a vowel it has the same value as *i;* at the beginning of syllables and followed by a vowel, it corresponds to the L. *i* or *j,* as in *ye, you;* (*Alg., y*) the second unknown quantity or variable; a Y-shaped branch, pipe, fork, coupling, figure etc. **y-axis,** *n.* the vertical axis along which *y*-coordinates are plotted in the Cartesian co-ordinate system. **Y-chromosome,** *n.* a sex chromosome which is found paired with the X chromosome in men, and is not present at all in women. **Y-cross,** *n.* a Y-shaped cross on chasubles etc. **y-fronts®,** *n.pl.* men's or boys' underpants with an inverted Y-shaped front opening. **Y-level,** *n.* a surveying level mounted on a pair of Ys. **Y-moth,** *n.* the gamma moth, from the Y-shaped mark on its wings.

y., (*abbr.*) year.

y-, *pref.* as in Y-CLEPT, YWIS. [ME, from OE *ge-,* cp. Dut. and G *ge-,* pref. of p.p. etc., cp. *a-* in *alike, among* etc.]

-y, *comb. form* forming abstract nouns etc., as in *memory, remedy* [L *-ius, -ia, -ium* (sometimes through F *-ie*)], forming adjectives as in *mighty, trusty* [OE *-ig;* forming diminutives of proper names etc., as *Jimmy, sonny;* forming nouns as *army, treaty* [F *-é, -ée,* L *-ātus, -āta, -ātum,* p.p. suf.]

Y, (*chem. symbol*) yttrium.

yabber, *v.i.* to talk, to chatter. *n.* Aboriginal talk. [Austral. Abor.]

yabbie, yabby, *n.* a fresh-water crayfish. [Austral. Abor.]

yacca, *n.* either of two W Indian evergreen trees of the yew family yielding wood used for cabinet work. [local name]

yacht, *n.* a light sailing-vessel specially designed for racing; a vessel, propelled by steam, sails, electricity or other motive power, used for pleasure trips, cruising, travel or as a state vessel to convey royal personages or government officials. *v.i.* to sail or cruise about in a yacht. **yacht-built,** *a.* built on the lines of a yacht. **yacht-club,** *n.* a club for yacht-racing etc. **yachtsman, -woman,** *n.* one who keeps or sails a yacht. **yachtsmanship,** *n.* **yachter,** *n.* **yachting,** *n.* [Dut. *jacht* (now *jagt*), from *jagen,* to hunt]

yack, yak, *n.* noisy, unceasing, trivial chatter. *v.t.* to talk in this way. **yackety-yak,** *n.* trivial, persistent chatter. [imit.]

yaffle, yaffingale, after NIGHTINGALE, *n.* the green woodpecker. [imit. of cry]

Yager, *n.* a member of certain German corps of light infantry, esp. of sharp-shooters. [G *Jäger,* orig. huntsman, from *jagen,* to hunt, cp. YACHT]

yah, *int.* an exclamation of derision; (*coll.*) yes. [instinctive sound]

yahoo, *n.* one of a race of brutes in human shape; a coarse, brutish or vicious and degraded person. [coined by Swift in *Gulliver's Travels*]

Yahveh, Yahvist etc. JEHOVAH

Yahya Khan, *n.* **Agha Mohammed** (1917–80), former Pakistani leader, president 1969–71. His mishandling of the Bangladesh separatist issue led to civil war, and he was forced to resign.

yak¹, *n.* a long-haired ruminant, *Bosgrunniens,* from the mountainous regions of Central Asia, intermediate between the ox and the bison. [Tibetan *gyak*]

yak² YACK.

Yakut (Russian **Yakutskaya**), *n.* Autonomous Soviet Socialist Republic in NE USSR. **area** 3,103,000 sq km/1,197,760 sq miles. **capital** Yakutsk. **products** furs; gold, natural gas, some agriculture in the south. **population** (1986) 1,009,000; Yakuts 37%, Russians 50%.

Yale® lock, *n.* a pin-tumbler lock invented by Linus Yale Jr (1821–68) in 1865 and still widely used.

Yalta Conference, *n.* in 1945, a conference at which the Allied leaders Churchill, Roosevelt, and Stalin completed plans for the defeat of Germany in World War II and the foundation of the United Nations. It took place in Yalta, a Soviet holiday resort in the Crimea.

yam, *n.* the fleshy edible tuber of various species of *Dioscorea,* a tropical climber orig. from India; the plant. **yam-stick,** *n.* a hard-wood stick for digging yams. [Port. *inhame,* from W Afr. word]

Yama, *n.* the Hindu god of the dead and judge and chastiser of souls. [Sansk.]

Yamagata, *n.* **Aritomo** (1838–1922), Japanese soldier and politician, prime minister 1890–91 and 1898–1900. As chief of the imperial general staff in the 1870s and 1880s he was largely responsible for the modernization of the military system. He returned as chief of staff during the Russo-Japanese war (1904–05) and remained an influential political figure until he was disgraced 1921 for having meddled in the marriage arrangements of the crown prince.

Yamamoto, *n.* **Gombei** (1852–1933), Japanese admiral and politician. As prime minister 1913–14, he began Japanese expansion on the Chinese mainland and initiated reforms in the political system. He was briefly again premier in the aftermath of the Tokyo earthquake 1923.

yamen, YAMUN.

yammer, *v.i.* (*prov.*) to cry out, to whine, to complain peevishly. *n.* a complaint; nonsense; a whining sound. **yammerer,** *n.* **yammering,** *n., a.* [OE *gēomerian,* from *gēomor,* sad, mournful]

Yamoussoukro, *n.* capital designate of Ivory Coast (Côte d'Ivoire); population (1986) 120,000. The economy is based on tourism and agricultural trade.

yamun, *n.* the office or official residence of a Chinese mandarin. [Chin.]

yang, *n.* the masculine, positive, bright principle in nature, according to Chinese philosophy, which interacts with its complement, yin. [Chin. *yang,* bright]

Yangon (former name (until 1989) **Rangoon**), *n.* capital and chief port of Myanmar (Burma), on the Rangoon River, 32 km/20 miles from the Indian Ocean; population (1983) 2,459,000. Products include timber, oil, and rice. The city Dagon was founded on the site AD 746; it was given the name Rangoon (meaning 'end of conflict') by King Alaungpaya 1755.

Yang Shangkun, *n.* (1907–), Chinese communist politician. He held a senior position in the party 1956–66, but was demoted during the Cultural Revolution. He was rehabilitated 1978, elected to the Politburo 1982, and to the position of state president 1988.

Yangtze-Kiang, *n.* former name for Chang Jiang, greatest Chinese river.

yank¹, *v.t.* to pull sharply, to twitch, to jerk (off, out of etc.). *v.i.* to jerk vigorously. *n.* a sharp jerk, a twitch. [cp. Swed. dial. *jakka,* to wander, Icel. *jaga,* to move about, Dut. and G *jagen,* see YACHT, YAGER]

Yank², (*sl.*) YANKEE.

Yankee, *n.* an inhabitant of New England (applied by foreigners to all the inhabitants of the US), (*sometimes* *derog.*) an American; (*Hist.*) a Federal soldier or Northerner in the American Civil War (1861–5). *a.* pertaining to America or the Yankees. **Yankee Doodle,** *n.* a tune (probably of English origin) and song regarded as a national air of the US; an American. **Yankee shout,** *n.* (*Austral. sl.*) everyone pays for his own drinks. **Yank,** *n.* (*sometimes derog.*) short form of YANKEE. **Yankeedom, Yankeeism,** *n.* **Yankeefied,** *a.* [perh. from *Yengees,* pl. Am. Ind., corr. of F *Anglais,* the English]

Yaoundé, *n.* capital of Cameroon, 210 km/130 miles E of the port of Douala; population (1984) 552,000. Industry includes tourism, oil refining, and cigarette manufacturing.

yap, *v.i.* to yelp or bark snappishly; to talk constantly in a shrill, foolish manner; to scold. *n.* such a bark; foolish chatter. **yapper,** *n.* **yappy,** *a.* **yapster,** *n.* a dog. [imit.]

yapok, *n.* a small opossum, *Cheironectes variegatus,* with webbed hind feet and aquatic habits. [river *Oyapok* separating Guiana from Brazil]

yapon, *n.* an evergreen shrub, *Ilex vomitoria,* growing in the southern US, the leaves of which are used for tea and by the Indians for their 'black drink', an emetic and purgative medicine. [Am. Ind.]

yapp, *n.* a style of book-binding, usu. in leather, with flaps at the edges. [etym. unknown]

yarborough, *n.* (*Whist etc.*) a hand containing no card higher than a nine. [2nd Earl of *Yarborough,* who bet £1000 that no one could hold such a hand]

yard[1], *n.* a unit of length, 3 ft. or 36 in. (0·9144 m); a measuring rod of this length, or this length of material; a cylindrical spar tapering each way from the middle slung horizontally or slantwise on a mast to extend a sail; †the male organ of generation. **to man the yards,** to place men, or (of sailors) to stand along the yards, as a salute at reviews etc. **yard of ale,** a tall, narrow drinking glass for beer or ale; the amount of beer or ale in such a glass. **yard-arm,** *n.* either half of a sail-yard from the centre to the end. **yardland,** *n.* an old measurement of area, varying in different countries from 15 acres to 40 acres (6–16 ha). **yard-measure, -stick, -wand,** *n.* a tape or stick, 3 ft. in length and usu. graduated in feet, inches, etc., used for measuring. **yardage,** *n.* (*Eng.*) the amount of excavation in cubic yards. [OE *gyrd, gerd,* stick, cp. Dut. *garde,* G *Gerte*]

yard[2], *n.* a small piece of enclosed ground, esp. enclosed by, enclosing or adjoining a house or other building; a garden; such an enclosure used for some specified manufacture or other purpose, as a dockyard, graveyard, timber-yard etc.; a series of tracks near a railway used for the storage and maintenance of rolling-stock. *v.t.* to collect or pen (cattle etc.) in a yard. **Scotland Yard, The Yard,** headquarters in London of the Metropolitan Police. **stock yard,** place where cattle are penned. **yard-man,** *n.* a man employed in a railway-yard. **yard-master,** *n.* the manager of this. **yardage,** *n.* a railway yard used as a cattle enclosure; the charge levied for such a use. [OE *geard* (cp. Dut. *gaard,* G *Garten,* Icel. *garthr,* L *hortus,* Gr. *chortos*), doublet of GARDEN]

†**yare,** *a.* ready, prepared; quick, dexterous; (*Naut.*) answering readily to the helm. *adv.* soon. †**yarely,** *adv.* quickly, smartly. [OE *gearu, gearo,* cp. Dut. *gaar,* Icel. *görr,* G *gar,* wholly, cogn. with GAR[2], GEAR]

yarmulka, yarmulke, *n.* a skullcap worn all the time by Orthodox male Jews, and during prayer by others. [Yiddish, from Ukrainian and Pol. *yarmulka,* small cap]

yarn, *n.* any spun fibre prepared for weaving, knitting, rope-making etc.; (*coll.*) a story or tale told by a sailor, a long or rambling story, esp. one of doubtful truth or accuracy. *v.i.* to tell a yarn, to spin yarns. **yarn-dye,** *v.t.* to dye the yarn before it is spun or woven. **yarn-dyed,** *a.* [OE *gearn* (cp. Dut. *garen,* G, Icel., Dan. and Swed. *garn*), cogn. with Gr. *chordē,* CORD]

yarrah, *n.* the river-gum eucalyptus. [Austral. Abor.]

yarrow, *n.* a perennial herb, *Achillea millefolium,* with white flowers, pungent odour and astringent properties, the milfoil. [OE *gæruwe* (cp. Dut. *gerw,* G *Garbe*), perh. cogn. with YARE]

yashmak, *n.* the veil worn by Muslim women in public. [Arab.]

Yasht, *n.* one of a collection of hymns and prayers in the Zend-Avesta. [Avestan]

yataghan, *n.* a Turkish sword or scimitar with double-curved blade and without a guard or cross-piece. [Turk.]

yate, (*prov.*) GATE[1].

yaup, (*Sc.*) var. of YAP.

yaupon, YAPON.

yaw, *v.i.* to steer out of the direct course, to move unsteadily (of a ship); (of a ship, aircraft etc.) to turn about its vertical axis. *v.t.* to cause to deviate from its course. *n.* an unsteady motion or temporary deviation from a course; the motion of an aircraft about its vertical axis. **yawing,** *n.* the unstable motion of an aircraft about its normal axis. [Icel. *jaga,* to hunt, cp. Dut. and G *jagen,* see YACHT, YAGER]

yawl[1], *v.i.* to howl, to yell. *n.* a howl or yell. [ME *goulen,* cp. Dut. *jolen,* Icel. and Norw. *gaula,* of imit. orig., cp. YELL]

yawl[2], *n.* a small boat, esp. a ship's jolly-boat; a small sailing-vessel cutter-rigged and having a jigger-mast. [Dut. *jol* (cp. Dan. *jolle,* Swed. *julle*), cp. JOLLYBOAT]

yawn, *v.i.* to gape, to be or stand wide open; to open the mouth wide or to have the mouth open involuntarily through drowsiness, boredom, bewilderment etc., to stand agape. *v.t.* to express or utter by or with a yawn. *n.* the act of yawning. **yawner,** *n.* **yawning,** *n.* **yawningly,** *adv.* **yawn,** *a.* [OE *gānian, gīnan* (cp. Icel. *gīna,* MDut. *gienen,* Dut. *geeuwen,* also L *hiāre*)]

yaws, *n.pl.* (*Med.*) an infectious tropical disease whose symptoms include sores; framboesia. [perh. from Afr. native *yaw,* raspberry]

Yb, (*chem. symbol*) ytterbium.

†**y-clad,** *a.* clad, clothed. [Y-, CLAD]

†**y-clept,** *a.* called, named. [Y-, p.p. of CLEPE]

Y-cross, *n.* Y.

yd., (*abbr.*) yard, yards.

ye[1], *pron., 2nd pers. pl.* properly the nominative of *you,* for which it is now often used. [OE *gē,* cp. Dut. *gij,* G *ihr,* Icel. *ēr, ier,* Dan. and Swed. *i,* Gr. *humeis,* Sansk. *yūyam*]

ye[2], **y**[e], the old method of printing THE, but never pron. yee, from a confusion between the letters þ (th) and y.

yea, *adv.* yes; verily, truly, indeed; not only so but also. *n.* an affirmative; one who votes in the affirmative. [OE *gēa,* cp. Dut., G, Dan. and Swed. *ja,* Icel. *jā,* Gr. *ē,* truly]

yeah, *int.* (*coll.*) yes. **oh yeah!** an expression of incredulity.

yean, *v.t., v.i.* to bring forth (of sheep and goats). **yeanling,** *n.* a lamb or kid. [OE *ēanian,* see EAN]

year, *n.* the period of time occupied by the revolution of the earth round the sun (the astronomical, equinoctial, natural, solar or tropical year, the time taken by the sun in returning to the same equinox, in mean length, 365 days, 5 hrs, 48 min. and 46 sec.; the astral or sidereal year, in which the sun apparently returns to the same place in relation to the fixed stars, 365 days, 6 hrs, 9 min. and 9 sec.; the Platonic, great or perfect year, estimated by early Greek and Hindu astronomers at about 26,000 years, at the end of which all the heavenly bodies were imagined to return to the same places as they occupied at the Creation); the period of 365 days, from 1 Jan. to 31 Dec., divided into 12 months, adopted as the calendar, legal or civil year, one day being added every fourth year (with the exception of centuries not divisible by 400), called bissextile or leap year; any period of this length taken as a unit of time; a body of students who enter a school or university in the same year; (*pl.*) age, length or time of life, (*coll.*) a long time; old age. **historical year,** 12 months beginning on 1 Jan.; **Marian year,** beginning on 25 Mar. **regnal year** REGNAL. **since the year dot,** since as long ago as can be remembered. **year by year,** as the years go by. **year of grace,** a year of the Christian era. **year in year out,** right through the year, without cessation. **yearbook,** *n.* a book published annually giving information up to date on some subject liable to change. **year-end,** *n.* the end of the (fiscal) year. **year-long,** *a.* lasting a year. **year-round,** *a.* open, operating, all year. **yearly,** *a.* happening or recurring once a year or every year, annual; lasting a year. *adv.* annually; once a year, by the year. [OE *gēar, gēr* (cp. Dut. *jaar,* G *Jahr,* Icel. *ār*), cogn. with Gr. *hōros,* a season, L *hōra,* HOUR]

yearling, *n.* an animal more than one and less than two years old; a colt a year old dating from 1 Jan. of the year of foaling. *a.* being one year old.

yearn[1], *v.i.* to feel a longing desire, tenderness, compassion etc. (for, after etc.); †to grieve, to be pained or distressed. †**it yearns my heart,** it vexes or grieves me. **yearner,** *n.* †**yearnful,** *a.* **yearning,** *n., a.* **yearningly,** *adv.* [OE *giernan* (cp. Icel. *girna,* G *begehren,* OHG *gerōn*), cogn. with Gr. *chairein,* to rejoice, L *hortārī,* to exhort]

†**yearn**[2], EARN.

yeast, *n.* a yellowish, viscous substance consisting of a growth of fungous cells developed in contact with saccharine liquids and producing alcoholic fermentation by means of enzymes, used in brewing, distilling etc., for raising dough for bread etc.; (*fig.*) mental or moral ferment. **yeast-plant,** *n.* any of several single-celled fungi that produce alcoholic fermentation in saccharine liquids. **yeast-powder,** *n.* a baking-powder used as a substitute for yeast. **yeasty,** *a.* containing or resembling yeast, esp. in causing or being characterized by fermentation; (*fig.*) frothy, foamy; unsubstantial, empty, superficial. **yeastily,** *adv.* **yeastiness,** *n.* [OE *gist* (cp. Dut. *gest,* G *Gischt,* Icel. *jast, jastr*), cogn. with Gr. *zeein,* to boil]

Yeats, *n.* **W(illiam) (B)utler** (1865–1939), Irish poet. He was a leader of the Celtic revival and a founder of the Abbey Theatre in Dublin. His early work was romantic and lyrical, as in the poem 'The Lake Isle of Innisfree' and plays *The Countess Cathleen* (1892) and *The Land of Heart's Desire* (1894). His later books of poetry include *The Wild Swans at Coole* (1917) and *The Winding Stair* (1929). He was a senator of the Irish Free State 1922–28. Nobel prize 1923.

Yedo, Edo, *n.* former name of Tokyo, Japan, until 1868.

yegg, *n.* (*N Am. sl.*) a safe-breaker; a dangerous criminal. [etym. doubtful, perh. the name of a US safe-breaker]

yeld, *a.* (*Sc.*) barren, not giving milk. [var. of GELD[1]]

yeldring, YOWLEY.

yelk, YOLK.

yell, *v.i.* to cry out with a loud, sharp, or inarticulate cry as in rage, agony, terror or uncontrollable laughter. *v.t.* to utter or express thus. *n.* such a cry or shout, esp. the war-cry of some savages; (*N Am.*) a distinctive shout used by college students etc. for encouragement, applause etc. **yeller,** *n.* **yelling,** *a.* [OE *gellan, giellan,* cp. Dut. *gillen,* G *gellen,* Icel. *gella*]

yelloch, (*Sc.*) YELL.

yellow, *a.* of a colour like that between green and orange in the spectrum or like that of gold, brass, sulphur, lemon; (*fig.*) jaundiced, jealous, envious; (*coll.*) cowardly; (*offensive*) of one of the Asiatic peoples of mongoloid ancestry. *n.* this colour, a yellow pigment, dye etc.; a sulphur butterfly (and other yellow butterflies and moths); (*pl.*) jaundice, jealousy; (*N Am., pl.*) a disease of unknown origin attacking peach-trees etc.; egg yolk; the yellow ball in snooker. *v.t.* to make yellow. *v.i.* to turn yellow. **yellow-back,** *n.* a cheap railway-novel. **yellow-backed, -bellied, -billed, -headed, -legged** etc., *a.* having a yellow back, belly etc as specified. **yellow-belly, -bill, -head, -legs, -poll, -rump, -seed,** *n.* used as a name for animals, birds, fish and plants. **yellow bile,** *n.* in mediaeval physiology, one of the four humours, choler. **yellow-bird,** *n.* the American goldfinch, the yellow warbler, the golden oriole and other birds. **yellow blight,** *n.* the wilt disease in potatoes. **yellow-blossomed,** *a.* **yellow-boy,** *n.* (*sl.*) a gold coin. **yellow card,** *n.* a yellow card shown by a referee to a competitor who has violated a rule. **yellow cartilage** or **tissue,** *n.* elastic tissue. **yellow-earth,** *n.* a yellow ochre, sometimes used as a pigment. **yellow fever,** *n.* a malignant tropical fever caused by the bite of the mosquito, attended with jaundice and black vomit. **yellow flag,** *n.* a flag hoisted by a ship in quarantine or with an infectious disease on board. **yellow-gum,** *n.* infants' black jaundice. **yellow-hammer,** *n.* a bunting, *Emberiza citrinella,* with yellow head, neck and breast. **yellow jack,** *n.* yellow fever. **yellow-jacket,** *n.* a species of social wasp. **yellow line,** *n.* a line on a road showing parking restrictions. **yellow men,** *n.* the Xanthochroi. **yellow metal,** *n.* an alloy of three parts of copper and two of zinc. **yellow pages,**® *n.pl.* that part of a telephone directory, printed on yellow paper, which lists subscribers according to business. **yellow peril,** *n.* the alleged danger that the Asiatic races may overwhelm the Western civilizations. **yellow pine,** *n.* a soft even-grained Canadian wood. **Yellow Press,** *n.* journalism or the newspaper press of sensational and jin goist tendencies. **yellow-rattle,** *n.* an annual herb of the genus *Rhinanthus cristagalli,* with yellow flowers and winged seeds that rattle in the capsules when ripe. **yellow spot,** *n.* the area at the centre of the retina in vertebrates where vision is acutest in daylight. **yellow streak,** *n.* a tendency toward cowardice. **yellow-wort,** *n.* an annual, *Chlora perfoliata,* of the gentian family, used for dyeing yellow. **yellowish, yellowy,** *a.* **yellowly,** *adv.* **yellowness,** *n.* [OE *geolo, geolu* (cp. Dut. *geel,* G *gelb,* L *helvus*), cogn. with Gr. *chlōros,* see CHLOR-, Sansk. *harī,* green, yellow, GALL[1]]

Yellowknife, *n.* capital of Northwest Territories, Canada, on the north shore of Great Slave Lake; population (1984) 11,000. It was founded 1935 when gold was discovered in the area, and became the capital 1967.

Yellow River, *n.* English name for the Huang He river, China.

Yellow Sea, *n.* gulf of the Pacific Ocean between China and Korea; area 466,200 sq km/180,000 sq miles. It receives the Huang He (Yellow River) and Chang Jiang.

Yellowstone National Park, largest US nature reserve, established 1872, on a broad plateau in the Rocky Mountains, Wyoming. 1 million of its 2.2 million acres have been destroyed by fire since July 1988.

yelp, *v.i.* to utter a sharp, quick cry, as a dog in pain, fear or anticipation. *n.* such a bark or cry. **yelper,** *n.* **yelping,** *n.* [OE *gilpan,* to boast, cp. Icel. *gjālpa*]

Yeltsin, *n.* **Boris Nikolayevich** (1931–), Soviet communist politician, Moscow party chief 1985–87, when he was dismissed after criticizing the slow pace of political and economic reform. He was re-elected in Mar. 1989 with a 89% share of the vote, defeating an 'official Communist Party' candidate, and was elected to the Supreme Soviet in May 1989.

Yemen, North, *n.* Yemen Arab Republic. **area** 195,000 sq km/75,290 sq miles. **capital** San'a. **towns** Ta'iz, and chief port Hodeida. **physical** hot moist coastal plain, rising to plateau. **population** (1989) 6,937,000; annual growth rate 2.7%. **exports** cotton, coffee, grapes. **language** Arabic. **religion** Sunni Muslim 50%, Shi'ite Muslim 50%.

Yemen, South, *n.* People's Democratic Republic of Yemen. **area** 336,900 sq km/130,077 sq miles. **capital** Aden. **physical** desert and mountains; very hot and dry. **population** (1989) 2,488,000; annual growth rate 2.8%. **exports** cotton goods, coffee. **language** Arabic. **religion** Sunni Muslim 91%.

yen[1], *n.* (*pl.* **yen**) the Japanese monetary unit. [Jap., from Chin. *yuen,* round, dollar]

yen[2], *n.* ambition, yearning, desire, longing. *v.i.* to yearn. [Chin., opium]

Yenisei, *n.* river in Asiatic USSR, rising in Tuva region and flowing across the Siberian plain into the Arctic Ocean; length 4100 km/2550 miles.

yeoman, *n.* (*pl.* **-men**) a freeholder not ranking as one of the gentry; (*formerly*) a man qualified to serve on juries and to vote etc., as holding free land of £2 annual value; a farmer, esp. a freeholder; a small landowner; a member of the yeomanry force; †an assistant, a journeyman; a petty or non-commissioned officer who carries out signalling or clerical duties in the navy. **Yeomen of the Guard,** English military corps, popularly known as Beefeaters, the sovereign's bodyguard since the corps was founded by Henry VII in 1485. Its duties are now purely ceremonial. **yeoman's service,** *n.* good service, hearty support. **yeomanlike,** *a.* **yeomanly,** *a.* **yeomanry**, *n.* (*collect.*) yeomen; a British force of volunteer cavalry consisting largely of country gentlemen and farmers, now forming part of the Territorial Army. [ME *yeman, yoman,* (prob. OE *gā,* district or village, MAN)]

yep, (*coll.*) yes.

-yer, *comb. form.* denoting an agent, as in *lawyer, sawyer.* [var. of -ER, arising from the use of ME *-ien,* instead of *-en,* in causal verbs and those derived from nouns]

yerba, *n.* Paraguay tea, maté. [Sp., from L *herba,* HERB]

Yerevan, *n.* industrial city (tractor parts, machine tools, chemicals, bricks, bicycles, wine, fruit canning), capital of Armenian Republic, USSR, a few miles north of the Turkish border; population (1987) 1,168,000. It was founded in the 7th cent., and was alternately Turkish and Persian from the 15th cent. until ceded to Russia 1828.

†yerk, JERK.

Yerkes Observatory, *n.* astronomical centre in Wisconsin, US, founded by George Hale in 1897. It houses the world's largest refracting optical telescope, with a lens of diameter 102 cm/40 in.

Yersin, *n.* **Alexandre Emile Jean** (1863–1943), Swiss bacteriologist, who discovered the bubonic plague bacillus in Hong Kong in 1894 and prepared a serum against it.

yes, *adv.* as you say, it is true, agreed (indicating affirmation or consent); I hear (in answer to a summons etc.). *n.* (*pl.* **yeses**) the word 'yes'; an affirmative reply. **yes-man,** *n.* (*coll.*) an unquestioning follower, a sycophant. [OE *gise, gese* (prob. *gēa swā,* YEA, SO)]

yeshiva(h), *n.* (*pl.* **-va(h)s** or **-voth**) a Jewish school devoted to the study of the Talmud; an Orthodox Jewish day school providing religious and secular instruction. [Heb. *yĕshībhāh,* seat, academy]

yester-, *pref.* of or pertaining to the day preceding today. **yesterday**, *n.* the day immediately before today; (*fig.*) time in the immediate past. *adv.* on or during yesterday; in the recent past. **†yester-eve, †-even, †-evening,** (*Sc.*) **yestreen**, *n.*, *adv.* yesterday evening. **yestermorn,** *n.*, *adv.* **yesternight,** *n.*, *adv.* last night. **yester-year,** *n.*, *adv.* (*poet.*) last year; the recent past. [OE *geostra, giestra,* usu. in acc. *geostran dæg,* yesterday (cp. Dut. *gisteren,* G *Gestern,* also L *hesternus,* Gr. *chthes,* Sansk *hyas*)]

yet, *adv.* still, up to this or that time; by this or that time, so soon or early as the present, so far, in addition, further, besides; eventually, at some future time, before all is over; even (*with compar.*); nevertheless, in spite of that. *conj.* nevertheless, notwithstanding, but still. **as yet,** up to this or that time, so far. **just yet,** in the immediate future (*with neg.*). **not yet,** not up to the present time. [OE *git, get, giet,* cp. Fris. *jiette,* G *jetzt*]

yeti, *n.* the hypothetical creature whose tracks are alleged to have been found in the snows of the Himalayas, also called 'The Abominable Snowman'. [Tibetan]

yett, (*Sc.*) GATE[1].

Yevele, *n.* **Henry** (died 1400) English architect, mason of the naves of Westminster Abbey (begun 1375), Canterbury Cathedral, and Westminster Hall (1394), with its majestic hammerbeam roof.

Yevtushenko, *n.* **Yevgeny Aleksandrovich** (1933–), Soviet poet, born in Siberia. He aroused controversy by his anti-Stalinist 'Stalin's Heirs' (1956), published with Khrushchev's support, and 'Babi Yar' (1961). His *Autobiography* was published in 1963.

yew, *n.* a dark-leaved evergreen shrub or tree of the genus *Taxus,* esp. *T. baccata,* a large tree with spreading branches, the wood of which has long been valued for making bows; its wood. **yew-tree,** *n.* [OE *īw,* cp. G *Eibe,* Icel. *ȳr*]

Yggdrasil, *n.* in Scandinavian mythology, the world tree, a sacred ash that spans heaven and hell. It is evergreen and tended by the Norns, goddesses of past, present, and future.

YHA, (*abbr.*) Youth Hostels Association.

YHVH, YHWH, *n.* Yahweh, the tetragrammaton.

Yiddish, *n.* a language spoken by Jews of E Europe and N America, based on a Hebraicized Middle German, with an admixture of Polish, French and English, and usually written in Hebrew characters. *a.* pertaining to this language. **Yid,** *n.* (*offensive*) a Jew. **Yiddisher,** *n.* a Yiddish speaker, a Jew. *a.* pertaining to Yiddish; Jewish.

yield, *v.t.* to produce, to bear, to bring forth as fruit, reward or result; to give up, to surrender, to concede, to relinquish, to resign. *v.i.* to give a return, to repay one's labour in cultivation etc., to bear, produce or bring forth (well or ill); to give way, to assent, to submit, to comply, to surrender; to make submission (to); to give place, to yield precedence or admit inferiority (to). *n.* that which is yielded or produced, output, return; annual return from an investment. **yield point,** *n.* the stress point at which a material, under increasing stress, ceases to behave elastically. **yieldable,** *a.* **†yieldance,** *n.* **yielder,** *n.* **yielding,** *a.* compliant; pliable. **yieldingly,** *adv.* **yieldingness,** *n.* [OE *gieldan,* to pay, cp. Dut. *gelden,* G *gelten,* Icel. *gjalda,* Swed. *gälla,* to be worth]

yill, (*Sc.*) ALE.

yin, *n.* the feminine, negative, dark principle in nature, according to Chinese philosophy, which interacts with its complement and opposite, yang. [Chin. *yin,* dark]

Yinchuan, *n.* capital of Ningxia autonomous region, NW China; population (1984) 383,000.

yip, *n.* a short, sudden cry, yell. *v.t.* to give a short, sudden cry. [imit.]

yippee, *int.* an exclamation of delight, pleasure, exuberant anticipation.

Yippie, *n.* member of the Youth International Party (YIP), led by Abbie Hoffmann and Jerry Rubin, known for their antics during the 1960s as they mocked the US political process.

-yl, *comb.form* (*chem.*) denoting a radical; as in *ethyl, methyl.* [Gr. *hulē,* wood, material]

ylang-ylang, *n.* a Malayan tree, *Canangium odoratum,* of the custard-apple family; an oil from the flowers of this tree, used in perfumes. [Malay, flower of flowers]

YMCA, (*abbr.*) Young Men's Christian Association.

Ymir, *n.* in Scandinavian mythology, the first living being, a giant who grew from melting frost. Among his descendants, the god Odin with two brothers killed Ymir and created heaven and earth from parts of his body.

Ynca, INCA.

-yne, *comb.form* (*Chem.*) denoting a triple bond, as in *alkyne.* [form of -INE]

yob, *n.* a raw recruit; an aggressive, loutish youth; a hooligan. **yobbish,** *a.* **yobbo**, *n.* [back slang, *boy*]

yodel, *v.t.*, *v.i.* to sing or shout in a musical fashion with alternation from the natural voice to the falsetto. *n.* such a shout or musical cry, peculiar to Swiss and Tyrolese mountaineers; a yodelling contest. **yodeller,** *n.* [G dial. *jodeln*]

yoga, *n.* a Hindu system of abstract meditation and rigid asceticism by which the soul is supposed to become united with the eternal spirit of the universe; certain exercises and practices assisting this. **hatha yoga**, that form of yoga most common in the West, which emphasizes the importance of physical exercises and breathing control. **yogi**, *n.* a devotee or adept of yoga. **yogic,** *a.* **yogism,** *n.* [Hind., from Sansk., union]

yogourt, yoghourt, yogurt, yoghurt, *n.* a dish of milk fermented in a special way. [Turk.]
yo-heave-ho, *int.* (*Naut.*) a sailor's cry while heaving the anchor etc. [inst. sound]
yo-ho, *int.* an exclamation calling attention. [redupl. of HO]
yoicks, *n., int.* a foxhunter's hallo cry. **yoick,** *n. int.* yoicks; *v.i.* to cry 'yoicks'. *v.t.* to urge (hounds) on thus. [etym. doubtful]
yojan, *n.* an E Indian measure of distance, usu. about 5 miles (8 km). [Hind.]
yoke, *n.* a frame or cross-bar fitting over the necks of two oxen or other draught animals and attaching them to a plough or vehicle; a device resembling this; a frame fitting a person's shoulders for carrying a pair of buckets suspended from the ends; a frame or cross-bar on which a bell swings; the cross-bar of a rudder to which the steering-lines are fastened; a coupling for two pipes discharging into one; a coupling, guiding or controlling piece in a machine; a tie-beam, tie-rod etc.; a part of a garment made to support the rest, as at the shoulders or hips; (*fig.*) a bond, a link, a tie, esp. that of love or wedlock; a pair of draught animals, esp. oxen yoked together; (*Rom. Hist.*) two upright spears with a third resting across them at the top, under which vanquished enemies were made to pass; hence, servitude, slavery, submission. *v.t.* to put a yoke upon; to unite by a yoke; to couple, esp. in marriage; to join, to link; to enslave. *v.i.* to go or work (well or ill together etc.). †**yoke of land,** as much land as might be ploughed by a yoke of oxen in a day. **yoke-bone,** *n.* the malar or cheek-bone connecting the bones at the side of the head with those of the face. **yoke-fellow, -mate,** *n.* a person associated with one in marriage, work etc., a companion, a partner. **yoke-line, -rope,** *n.* one of the pair of ropes by which a rudder-yoke is worked. [OE *geoc* (cp. Dut. *juk,* G *Joch,* Icel. and Swed. *ok,* L *jugum,* Gr. *zugon,* Sansk. *yuga-*), cogn. with JOIN]
yokel, *n.* a rustic, a country bumpkin. **yokelish,** *a.* [prob. from prec., ploughman]
Yokohama, *n.* Japanese port on Tokyo Bay; population (1987) 3,072,000. Industries include shipbuilding, oil refining, engineering, textiles, glass, and clothing.
yolding, yoldring, YOWLEY.
yolk, *n.* the yellow part of an egg, the contents of the ovum, esp. that nourishing the embryo, the vitellus; the unctuous secretion from the sebaceous glands of sheep, wool-oil. **yolk-sac,** *n.* the thin, membranous bag enclosing the yolk in an egg. **yolked, yolky,** *a.* [OE *geolca,* YELLOW]
Yom Kippur, *n.* the Day of Atonement, a Jewish day of fasting. **Yom Kippur War,** *n.* the 1973 October War between the Arabs and Israelis. [Heb.]
yomp, *v.i.* to trek, often with heavy equipment, over heavy terrain. [etym. doubtful]
yon, *a., adv.* (*Sc.*) yonder. *pron.* (*prov.*) yonder person, thing or place; that. **yond,** *a.* the most distant. *adv.* yonder. [OE *geon* (cp. Icel. *enn,* G *jener*)]
yonder, *a.* that over there; being at a distance, but in the direction looked at or pointed out; distant but within view. *adv.* over there; at a distance but within view, or where one is looking or pointing. **the yonder,** the most distant, farthest. [ME, from prec.]
yoni, *n.* the Hindu symbol of the fertility of nature under which the consort of a male deity is worshipped, represented by an oval figure (the female organ). [Sansk]
yonks, *n.pl.* (*coll.*) a long time, ages. [etym. unknown]
yoo-hoo, *int.* a call to attract someone's attention.
YOP, *n.* a former training scheme in Britain. [acronym for *Y*outh *O*pportunity *P*rogramme]
yore, *n.* long ago, old time. *adv.* long ago. **of yore,** formerly of old time, long ago. [OE *geāra,* orig. gen. pl. of *gēar,* YEAR]
York[1], *n.* English dynasty founded by Richard, duke of York (1411–60). He claimed the throne through his descent from Lionel, duke of Clarence (1338–68), third son of Edward III, whereas the reigning monarch, Henry VI of the rival house of Lancaster, was descended from the fourth son. The argument was fought out in the Wars of the Roses. York was killed at the Battle of Wakefield 1460, but next year his son became king as Edward IV, in turn succeeded by his son Edward V and then by his brother Richard III, with whose death at Bosworth the line ended. The Lancastrian victor in that battle became king as Henry VII, and consolidated his claim by marrying Edward IV's eldest daughter, Elizabeth. **Yorkist,** *a.* of or pertaining to the house descended from Edmund Duke of York, son of Edward III, or the White Rose party supporting this in the Wars of the Roses. *n.* an adherent of this house or party.
York[2]**, archbishop of,** *n.* metropolitan of the northern province of the Anglican Church in England, hence Primate of England.
York[3]**, Duke of,** ANDREW.
York[4], *n.* **Frederick Augustus, Duke of York** (1763–1827), second son of George III. He was an unsuccessful commander in the Netherlands 1793–99, and British commander in chief 1798–1809.
yorker, *n.* (*Cricket*) a ball bowled so as to pitch immediately in front of the bat. **york,** *v.t.* to bowl with a yorker. [prob. from being first used by a Yorkshire player]
yorkie, *n.* a Yorkshire terrier.
Yorks., (*abbr.*) Yorkshire.
Yorkshire, *n.* county in NE England on the North Sea, formerly divided into north, east, and west ridings (thirds), but in 1974 reorganized to form a number of new counties: the major part of Cleveland and Humberside; North Yorkshire, South Yorkshire, and West Yorkshire. Small outlying areas also went to Durham, Cumbria, Lancashire, and Greater Manchester. South and West Yorkshire are both former metropolitan counties. *a.* of or derived from Yorkshire. **Yorkshire flannel,** *n.* flannel of undyed wool. **Yorkshire grit,** *n.* a grit used for polishing. **Yorkshire pudding,** *n.* batter baked under meat, esp. beef. **Yorkshire terrier,** *n.* a small shaggy variety of toy terrier. [county in N England]
Yoruba, *n.* a member of the people living in the coastal regions of W Africa, esp. SW Nigeria; the Kwa language of this people. **Yoruban,** *a.*
Yoshida, *n.* **Shigeru** (1878–1967), Japanese politician and prime minister. He held various diplomatic posts in the 1920s and 1930s before becoming leader of the Liberal party and serving as prime minister for most of the 1946–54 period.
you, *2nd pers. pron., sing. and pl.* (*pl. v.*) the person, animal, thing, or persons, etc., addressed; (*reflex.*) yourself. yourselves; (*indef.*) one, anyone, people generally. **you-all,** (*N Am. pl; coll*) you. **you-know-what, -who,** someone unspecified known to both the speaker and the hearer. **you're another,** (*coll.*) a retort to abuse etc. [OE *ēow,* dat. and acc. of *gē, ye* (see also YE), sing. **thou,** obj. **thee,** poss. **your, yours**]
you'd, *contr.* you had, you would.
you'll, *contr.* you shall, you will.
young, *a.* being in the early stage of life, growth or development; of recent birth or beginning, newly formed, produced, come into action or operation etc.; not infirm or decayed with age, vigorous, fresh; immature, raw, inexperienced; pertaining to or characteristic of youth. *n.* offspring, esp. of animals; those who are young. **with young,** pregnant. **young blood,** *n.* a new accession of vigour or enterprise. **Young Ireland,** *n.* Irish nationalist organization, founded 1840 by William Smith O'Brien (1803–64), who rejected the nonviolent policies of Daniel O'Connell's Repeal Association. It attempted an abortive insurrection of the peasants against the British at Tipperary in 1848. O'Brien was sentenced to death, but later pardoned. **Young Italy,** *n.* Italian nationalist organization, founded 1831 by Giuseppe Mazzini while in exile in Marseille. The movement, which was immediately popular, was followed the next year by Young Germany, Young Poland, and similar organizations. All the groups were

linked by Mazzini in his Young Europe movement, but none achieved much practical success; attempted uprisings by Young Italy in 1834 and 1844 failed miserably. **young man, woman,** *n.* a sweetheart. **young person,** *n.* somebody aged between 14 and 17. **Young Pretender,** *n.* nickname of Charles Edward Stuart, claimant to the Scottish and English thrones. **Young Turk,** *n.* member of a reformist movement of young army officers in the Ottoman Empire founded 1889. The movement was instrumental in the constitutional changes of 1908 and gained prestige during the Balkan Wars 1912–13; it also encouraged Turkish links with the German empire. Its influence diminished after 1918. The term is now used for a member of any radical or rebellious faction within a party or organization. **Young Women's Christian Association, (YWCA)** *n.* organization for women and girls, formed in 1887 when two organizations, both founded in 1855 – the one by Emma Robarts and the other by Lady Kinnaird – combined their work. **younger,** *a.* **youngish,** *a.* **youngling,** *n.* †**youngly,** *a.* and *adv.* **youngness,** *n.* **youngster,** *n.* a young person, a child, a lad; a young animal, such as a young horse. [OE *geong,* cp. Dut. *jong,* G *jung,* Icel. *ungr,* Dan. and Swed. *ung,* L *juvenis,* Sansk. *yuvan*]

Young[1], *n.* **Arthur** (1741–1820), English writer and publicizer of the new farm practices associated with the agricultural revolution. When the Board of Agriculture was established 1792, Young was appointed secretary, and was the guiding force behind the production of a county-by-county survey of British agriculture.

Young[2], *n.* **Brigham** (1801–77), US Mormon religious leader, born in Vermont. He joined the Mormon Church 1832, and three years later was appointed an apostle. After a successful recruiting mission in Liverpool, he returned to the US, and as successor of Joseph Smith, who had been murdered, led the Mormon migration to the Great Salt Lake in Utah 1846, founded Salt Lake City, and ruled the colony until his death.

Young[3], *n.* **David Ivor (Baron Young of Graffham)** (1932–), British Conservative politician, chair of the Manpower Services Commission (MSC) 1982–84, secretary for employment from 1985, trade and industry secretary 1987–89.

Young[4], *n.* **John Watts** (1930–), US astronaut. His first flight was on Gemini 3 in 1965. He landed on the Moon with Apollo 16 in 1972, and was commander of the first flight of the space shuttle in 1981.

Young[5], *n.* **Lester (Willis) 'Pres'** (1909–59), US tenor saxophonist and jazz composer. He was a major figure in the development of his instrument for jazz music from the 1930s, and was an accompanist to the singer Billie Holiday.

Young[6], *n.* **Thomas** (1773–1829), British physicist who revived the wave theory of light and in 1801 identified the phenomenon of interference. A child prodigy and man of universal genius, he had mastered most European languages and many of the Eastern tongues by the age of 20. He had also absorbed the physics of Newton, and the chemistry of Lavoisier. He further displayed his versatility by publishing an account of the Rosetta stone which played a crucial role in its eventual decipherment by Champollion.

younker, *n.* (*coll.*) a youngster; †a stripling; a junker. [Dut. *jonker* (*jong,* YOUNG, *heer,* SIR, cp. HERR)]

your, *a.* (often used indefinitely with a suggestion of disparagement). pertaining or belonging to you. **yours,** *pron.* that or those belonging or pertaining to you. *a.* belonging to you; at your service. **you and yours,** you and your family or belongings. **yours faithfully, obediently, truly,** etc., formal expressions preceding the signature in a letter. **yours truly,** (*coll.*) I, this person. **yourself,** *pron* (*pl.* **-selves**) you and not another or others, you alone; you in your own person or in particular; you in your normal condition, health etc.; also used reflexively. **by yourself,** alone; unaided. [OE *ēower,* gen. pl. of YE]

Yourcenar, *n.* **Marguerite** (pen name of Marguerite de Crayencour) (1903–1987), French writer, born in Belgium. She achieved a reputation as a novelist in France in the 1930s (for example with *La Nouvelle Euridyce/The New Euridyce* (1931)), but after World War II she settled in the US. Novels such as *Les Mémoires d'Hadrien/The Memoirs of Hadrian* (1951) won her acclaim as a historical novelist. In 1980 she became the first woman to be elected to the French Academy.

you're, contr. form of *you are.*

youth, *n.* (*pl.* **youths,**) the state of being young; the period of life from infancy to manhood or womanhood, youthfulness, the vigour, freshness, inexperience etc. of this period; a young man; young men and women collectively. **youth club,** *n.* a club which provides leisure time and social activities for young people. **Youth Hostel,** *n.* an organized establishment where hikers etc. may put up for the night. **youth hosteller,** *n.* **youth hostelling,** *n.* **youth leader,** *n.* a social worker who works with young people in a particular community. **Youth Training Scheme,** *n.* a government-funded scheme of in-firm job training for otherwise unemployed school leavers. **youthful,** *a.* **youthfully,** *adv.* **youthfulness,** *n.* †**youthly,** *a.* †**youthhood,** *n.* †**youthsome,** *a.* [OE *geoguth* (YOUNG, -TH), cp. Dut. *jeugd,* G *jugend,* L *juventa*]

you've, contr. form of *you have.*

yowl, var. of YAWL[1].

yowley, *n.* (*dial.*) the yellow-hammer. [OE *geole, georwe,* yellow]

yo-yo, *n.* a toy which consists of a spool winding up and down on a string, originally a trade-name.

Ypres (Flemish **Ieper**), *n.* Belgian town in W Flanders, 40 km/25 miles S of Ostend, a centre of fighting in World War I. The Menin Gate 1927 is a memorial to British soldiers lost in the great battles fought around the town 1914–18.

ypsilon, *n.* the 20th letter of the Greek alphabet.

yr. (*abbr.*) year; younger; your.

yrs. (*abbr.*) years; yours.

YTS, (*abbr.*) Youth Training Scheme, in the UK, a mandatory one- or two-year course of training and work experience for unemployed school leavers aged 16 and 17. Opponents argue that it is a form of extremely cheap forced labour for employers, does not provide young people with the high-technology skills that will be needed in the future, and does not pay well enough.

ytterbium, *n.* a rare metallic element, at. no. 70; chem. symbol Yb, discovered spectroscopically in gadolinite. **ytterbia,** *n.* ytterbium oxide. **ytterbic,** *a.* [*Ytterby,* town in Sweden, -IUM]

yttrium, *n.* a rare metallic element, at. no. 39; chem. symbol Y, belonging to the cerium group. **yttria,** *n.* a white earth, peroxide of yttrium. **yttric, yttrious, yttriferous,** *a.*

yttro-, *comb.form* yttrium. **yttrocerite,** *n.* a violet-blue fluoride of yttrium. **yttrotantalite,** *n.* an orthorhombic tantalite of yttrium.

yuan, *n.* (*pl.* **yuan**) the standard monetary unit of the People's Republic of China. [Chin. *yüan,* round object]

Yucatán, *n.* peninsula in Central America, divided between Mexico, Belize, and Guatemala; area 180,000 sq km/70,000 sq miles. Tropical crops are grown. It is inhabited by Maya Indians and contains the remains of their civilization.

yucca, *n.* a liliaceous subtropical American flowering-plant, with rigid lanceolate leaves and an erect panicle of white flowers, many species of which are grown for ornament. [Sp. *yuca,* from Haytian]

yuck, *v.i.* (*dial.*) to itch. *n.* the itch; an exclamation of disgust; something unpleasant. **yucky,** *a.* (*coll.*) disgusting, unpleasant. [etym. doubtful]

yuga, *n.* one of the Hindu ages or cycles of the world. [Sansk]

Yugoslavia, *n.* Socialist Federal Republic of, country in SE Europe. **area** 255,800 sq km/98,739 sq miles. **capital** Belgrade. **towns** Zagreb, Skopje, Ljubljana; ports Split, Rijeka. **physical** mountainous; river Danube plains in north and east. **population** (1989) 23,753,000 (Serbs 36%, Croats 20%, Muslims 9%, Slovenes 8%, Albanians 8%, Macedonians 6%, Montenegrins 3%, Hungarians 2%, 5.5% declared themselves to be 'Yugoslavs'); annual growth rate 0.8%. **exports** machinery, electrical goods, chemicals. **language** individual national languages have equality, but Serbo-Croat is the most widespread. **religion** Orthodox (Serbs), Roman Catholic (Croats), Muslim (50% in Bosnia). **Yugoslav, Jugoslav,** *a.* of or pertaining to the southern Slav peoples or countries, esp. Yugoslavia. *n.* a native or inhabitant of Yugoslavia. [Serb., south Slav]

Yukon, *n.* territory of NW Canada. **area** 483,500 sq km/186,631 sq miles. **towns** capital Whitehorse; Dawson City. **products** oil, natural gas, gold, silver, coal. **population** (1986) 24,000. **Yukon River,** *n.* a river rising in the Yukon Territory of NW Canada. It flows 3680 km/2300 miles from Lake Tagish into Alaska where it empties into the Bering Sea in a great delta.

yulan, *n.* a Chinese tree, *Magnolia yulan,* with large, brilliant, snow-white or rosy flowers. [Chin. (*yu,* gem, *lan,* plant)]

yule, *n.* Christmas time or the festival of Christmas. **yule-log,** *n.* a log formerly burned on Christmas Eve. **yule-tide,** *n.* [OE *gēola*]

yum-yum, *int.* (*coll.*) an expression of pleasure, especially anticipation of delicious food. **yummy,** *int. a.* delicious. [imit.]

Yunnan, *n.* province of SW China, adjoining Burma, Laos, and Vietnam. **area** 436,200 sq km/168,373 sq miles. **capital** Kunming. **physical** Chang Jiang, Salween, and Mekong rivers; crossed by the Burma Road; mountainous and well forested. **population** (1986) 34,560,000. **products** rice, tea, timber, wheat, cotton, rubber, tin, copper, lead, zinc, coal, salt.

Yunx, *n.* a genus of birds containing the wrynecks; a wryneck. [Gr. *iunx*]

Yuppie, yuppie, *n.* (*sometimes derog.*) a young financially successful professional person who spends much money on his/her life style. *a.* pertaining to, designed to appeal to these. **Yuppie, yuppie flu,** (*often derog.*) myalgic encephalomyelitis, ME. **yuppi(e)fy,** *v.t.* to make suitable for or typical of yuppies. **yuppification,** *n.* [acronym for *y*oung *u*pwardly-mobile (or *u*rban) *p*rofessional]

yurt, yourt, *n.* a circular, collapsible tent made of skins and used by nomads in Central Asia. [Rus. *yurta,* dwelling, from Turkic]

YWCA, (*abbr.*) Young Women's Christian Association.

ywis, *adv.* certainly, verily, truly. [OE *gewis* (cp. Dut. *gewis,* G. *gewiss,* Icel. and Swed. *viss*), cogn. with WIT[1]]

Z

Z, z, the last letter of the English alphabet (*pl.* **Zs, Z's, zeds**) has the sound of a voiced or sonant *s*, as in *zeal, lazy, reason,* or of a voiced *sh,* as in *azure;* (*Alg., z*) the third unknown quantity or variable; (*Chem.*) atomic number; (*Phys.*) impedance; something in the shape of a z. **z-axis,** *n.* a reference axis in the Cartesian coordinate system.

z, (*abbr.*) zero; zone.

zabaglione, zabaione, *n.* a warm whipped dessert of egg yolks, sugar and marsala. [It.]

Zabian etc. SABIAN.

zabra, *n.* a small sailing vessel formerly used on the coasts of the Iberian Peninsula. [Sp.]

Zadkine, *n.* **Ossip** (1890–1967), French cubist sculptor, born in Russia, active in Paris from 1909. He represented the human form in dramatic, semi-abstract terms, as in the monument *To a Destroyed City* (1953, Rotterdam).

zaffre, zaffer, *n.* impure oxide of cobalt used for enamelling and as a blue pigment for painting on glass, porcelain etc. [F *zafre,* from Arab.]

Zagreb, *n.* industrial city (leather, linen, carpets, paper, and electrical goods), capital of Croatia, Yugoslavia, on the Sava river; population (1981) 1,174,512.

Zahir, *n.* **ud-din Mohammed** (1483–1530), first Great Mogul of India from 1526, called Baber (Arabic 'lion'). He was the great-grandson of the Mongol conqueror Tamerlane and, at the age of 12, succeeded his father, Omar Sheikh Mirza, as ruler of Ferghana (Turkestan). In 1526 he defeated the emperor of Delhi at Panipat in the Punjab, captured Delhi and Agra, and established a dynasty which lasted until 1858.

Zahir Shah, *n.* **Mohammed** (1914–), king of Afghanistan 1933–73. Zahir, educated in Kabul and Paris, served in the government 1932–33 before being crowned king. He was overthrown in 1973 by a republican coup and went into exile. He has been a symbol of national unity for the mujaheddin resistance groups.

zaibatsu, *n.* an elite group of wealthy families dominating Japanese industry and commerce. [Jap. *zai,* wealth, *batsu,* family]

Zaïre[1]**,** *n.* Republic of, country in Central Africa. **area** 2,344,900 sq km/905,366 sq miles. **capital** Kinshasa. **towns** Lubumbashi, Kananga, Kisangani; ports Matadi, Boma. **physical** Zaïre river basin has tropical rainforest and savanna; mountains in east and west. **population** (1988) 33,991,000; annual growth rate 2.9%. **exports** palm oil, coffee, tea, rubber, timber, copper, cobalt (80% of world output), zinc, cadmium, industrial diamonds. **language** French (official), Swahili, Lingala. **religion** 70% Christian, 10% Muslim. **Zairean,** *n.* a native or inhabitant of the republic of Zaïre. *a.* of or pertaining to Zaïre.

Zaïre[2]**,** (formerly (until 1971) **Congo**), *n.* second longest river in Africa, rising near the Zambia-Zaïre border (and known as the Lualaba river in the upper reaches) and flowing 4500 km/2800 miles to the Atlantic, running in a great curve which crosses the Equator twice, and discharging a volume of water second only to the Amazon. The chief tributaries are the Ubangi, Sangha, and Kasai.

zakuska, *n.* (*pl.* **-ski**) a snack, an hors d'oeuvre. [Rus.]

Zama, Battle of, battle fought in 202 BC in Numidia (now Algeria), in which the Carthaginians under Hannibal were defeated by the Romans under Scipio, so ending the Second Punic War.

Zambezi, *n.* river in central and SE Africa; length 2650 km/1650 miles from NW Zambia through Mozambique to the Indian Ocean, with a wide delta near Chinde. Major tributaries include the Kafue in Zambia.

Zambia, *n.* Republic of, landlocked country in Central Africa. **area** 752,600 sq km/290,579 sq miles. **capital** Lusaka. **towns** Kitwe, Ndola, Kabwe, Chipata, Livingstone. **physical** a forested plateau cut through by rivers. **population** (1989) 7,770,000; annual growth rate 3.3%. **exports** copper, emeralds, tobacco. **language** English (official); the majority speak Bantu languages. **religion** mainly animist, 21% Roman Catholic, also Protestant, Hindu, and Muslim minorities. **Zambian,** *n.* a native or inhabitant of the republic of Zambia. *a.* of or pertaining to Zambia.

zambomba, *n.* a toy musical instrument made by stretching a piece of parchment over a wide-mouthed jar and inserting a stick through it which is rubbed with the fingers. [Sp.]

Zamia, *n.* a genus of palm-like trees or low shrubs of the cyad family, from the W Indies and America, from the seeds of some of which Florida arrow-root is prepared. [L and Gr., hurt, damage]

zamindar ZEMINDAR.

zamouse, *n.* the W African short-horned buffalo, *Bos brachyceros.* [native name]

zampogna, *n.* an Italian bagpipe. [It.]

zanje, *n.* a canal for irrigation. **zanjero,** *n.* a person employed in working this. [Sp. Am.]

Zante, Zante-wood,, *n.* the wood of the smoke-tree, *Rhus cotinus,* satinwood. [one of the Ionian islands]

ZANU, *n.* (Zimbabwe African National Union) political organization founded in Aug. 1963 by Ndabaningi Sithole with Robert Mugabe as secretary general. It was banned 1964 by Ian Smith's Rhodesian Front government, against which it conducted a guerrilla war from Zambia until the free elections of 1980, when the ZANU (PF) party, led by Mugabe, won 63% of the vote. In 1987 it merged with ZAPU in preparation for making Zimbabwe a one-party state.

zany, *n.* a buffoon in old theatrical entertainments who mimicked the clown; a simpleton, a fool; one who acts the fool. *a.* outrageous, fantastical, comical, absurd (e.g. of a comedy show). **zanily,** *adv.* **zaniness,** *n.* **zanyism,** *n.* [F *zani,* It. *zanni,* fam. for *Giovanni,* John]

Zanzibar, *n.* island region of Tanzania. **area** 1658 sq km/640 sq miles (80 km/50 miles long). **towns** Zanzibar. **products** cloves, copra. **population** (1985) 571,000.

zap, *v.t.* (*coll.*) to hit, smack, strike; to overwhelm; to kill or destroy; to cause to go quickly. *v.i.* to move suddenly or quickly; to switch rapidly between television channels using a remote-control device. *n.* energy, go, vitality. *int.* expressing a sudden action. **zapper,** *n.* (*coll.*) one who habitually switches rapidly between television channels. **zappy,** *a.* (*coll.*) energetic, fast-moving; punchy, snappy. [imit.]

Zapata, *n.* **Emiliano** (1879–1919), Mexican Indian revolutionary leader. He led a revolt against dictator Porfirio Díaz (1830–1915) from 1911 under the slogan 'Land and Liberty', to repossess for the indigenous Mexicans the land taken by the Spanish. He was driven into retreat by 1915, and was assassinated.

zapateado, *n.* (*pl.* **-dos**) a Spanish dance characterized by much clicking of the heels, and stamping and tapping of the feet. [from Sp. *zapatear,* to tap with the shoe, from *zapato,* shoe]

Zapotec, *n.* indigenous American people of S Mexico, numbering approximately 250,000, living mainly in

Oaxaca. The Zapotec language, which belongs to the Oto-Mangean family, has nine dialects. The ancestors of the Zapotec built the city of Monte Albán 1000–500 BC.

zapotilla, SAPODILLA.

ZAPU, *n.* (Zimbabwe African People's Union) political organization founded by Joshua Nkomo in 1961 and banned 1962 by the Rhodesian government. It engaged in a guerrilla war in alliance with ZANU against the Rhodesian regime until late 1979. In the 1980 elections ZAPU was defeated and was then persecuted by the ruling ZANU (PF) party. In 1987 the two parties merged.

Zara, *n.* Italian name for Zadar, port on the Adriatic coast of Yugoslavia.

Zaragoza (English **Saragossa**), *n.* industrial city in Aragon, Spain; population (1986) 596,000. It produces iron, steel, chemicals, plastics, canned food, and electrical goods. The mediaeval city walls and bridges over the Ebro survive, and there is a 15th-cent. university.

Zarathustrian etc. ZOROASTRIAN.

zaratite, *n.* a hydrous carbonate of nickel, usu. occurring as an incrustation. [Señor *Zarate*]

zareba, zareeba, zariba, *n.* a stockade, hedge or other enclosure for a camp or village in the Sudan. [Arab. *zarība, -bat*]

zarf, *n.* an ornamental cup-shaped holder for a hot coffee-cup. [Arab.]

zarzuela, *n.* a traditional Spanish form of vaudeville or comic opera. [La *Zarzuela,* the Spanish royal palace where it was first performed]

zastruga, sastruga, *n.* (*pl.* **-gi**) a ridge of snow caused by the wind. [Rus.]

zax, *n.* a slater's hatchet with a sharp point for perforating the slate, a sax. [OE *seax*]

zea, *n.* a genus of tall, half-hardy grasses, with but one species, *Zen mays,* Indian corn or maize. [L and Gr., spelt]

zeal, *n.* ardour, earnestness, enthusiasm, intense and eager pursuit or endeavour to attain or accomplish some object. **zealot,** *n.* one full of zeal, esp. one carried away by excess of zeal; a fanatical partisan. **zealotism, zealotry**, *n.* **zealous**, *a.* **zealously,** *adv.* **zealousness,** *n.* [OF *zele,* L *zēlum,* nom. *-us,* Gr. *zēlos*]

zebec, zebeck, XEBEC.

Zebedee, *n.* in the New Testament, the father of the apostles John and James.

zebra, *n.* (*pl.* **-bra, -bras**) a black and white striped, ass-like mammal of the genus *Equus,* esp. *E. zebra,* the true or mountain zebra from the mountainous regions of S Africa; any of various kinds or species of plant, bird, fish or mammal with similar markings, including the **zebra-antelope, -caterpillar, -finch, -fish, -mouse, -wolf, -wood, -woodpecker zebra crossing,** *n.* a street-crossing marked by stripes where pedestrians have precedence over all other traffic. **zebrine**, **zebroid**, *a.* [Port., from Afr. name]

zebu, *n.* the humped Indian ox, *Bos indicus.* [F *zébu,* Tibetan *mdzopo*]

zebub, *n.* an E African fly similar to the tsetse, a zimb. [Arab. *zubāb,* fly]

zecchino, zechino, SEQUIN.

Zech., (*abbr.*) Zechariah.

Zechariah, *n.* an Old Testament book named after the Hebrew prophet to whom it is attributed. [Heb. *Zĕkharyāh*]

zechstein, *n.* (*Geol.*) a German magnesian limestone. [G (*Zeche,* mine, *Stein,* stone)]

zed, *n.* the letter Z. [F *zède,* L and Gr. *zēta*]

Zedekiah, *n.* in the Old Testament, last king of Judah, 597–586 BC. Placed on the throne by Nebuchadnezzar, he died a blinded captive in Babylon.

zedoary, *n.* a substance made from the root-stock of some species of curcuma, used in medicine, dyeing, perfumery etc. [MF *zedoaire,* med. L *zedoāria,* Pers. *zadwār*]

zee, *n.* (*N Am.*) zed.

Zeebrugge, *n.* small Belgian ferry port on the North Sea, linked to Bruges by 14 km/9 miles canal (built 1896–1907). In Mar. 1987 it was the scene of a disaster in which over 180 passengers lost their lives when the car ferry *Herald of Free Enterprise* put to sea from Zeebrugge with its car loading doors not properly closed.

Zeeland, *n.* province of the SW Netherlands; capital Middelburg; area 1,790 sq km/691 sq miles; population (1988) 356,000. It includes the estuary of the Scheldt and the island of Walcheren and North and South Beveland. Most of Zeeland is below sea level.

Zeeman, *n.* **Pieter** (1865–1943), Dutch physicist who discovered in 1896 that when light from certain elements, such as sodium or lithium flame, was passed through a spectroscope in the presence of a strong magnetic field, the spectrum split into a number of distinct lines. This is known as the Zeeman effect and won him a share of the 1902 Nobel physics prize.

Zeffirelli, *n.* **Franco** (1923–), Italian theatre and film director and designer, noted for his stylish designs and lavish productions. His films include *Jesus of Nazareth* (1977) and *La Traviata* (1983).

zein, *n.* a protein found in Indian corn, used in the manufacture of inks, coatings, adhesives etc. [G *zeia,* spelt]

Zeiss, *n.* **Carl** (1816–88), German optician. He opened his first workshop in Jena in 1846, and in 1866 joined forces with Ernst Abbe (1840–1905) producing cameras, microscopes, and field glasses.

zeitgeist, *n.* the spirit, or moral and intellectual tendency, of a period. [G, time-spirit]

Zelanian, *a.* (*Zool.*) of or pertaining to New Zealand. [mod. L *Zelania,* -AN]

zeloso, *adv.* (*Mus.*) with energy. [It., as ZEALOUS]

zemindar, zamindar, *n.* one of a class of Bengali landowners formerly paying a certain land-tax to the British government; orig. a local governor and farmer of the revenue under the Mogul empire paying a fixed sum for his district. **zemindary**, *n.* [Pers. *zemin,* land, *-dār,* holding]

zemstvo, *n.* a Russian elective local assembly dealing with economic affairs. [Rus.]

Zen, *n.* a Japanese Buddhist sect teaching that truth is in one's heart and can be learned only by meditation and self-mastery. **Zenic,** *a.* **Zenist,** *n.* [Jap., from Chin. *ch'an,* from Pali *jhana,* from Sansk. *dhyāna,* religious meditation]

zenana, *n.* in the East (esp. India or Iran), the portion of the house in a Hindu or Muslim household which is reserved for the women. **Zenana Mission,** *n.* a mission undertaken by women for spreading educational, medical and religious reforms among the inmates of zenanas. [Hind. *zanāna,* from Pers. *zanān,* pl. of *zan,* woman.]

Zend, *n.* a former name for the ancient Iranian language, closely allied to Sanskrit, in which the sacred writings of the Zoroastrians are set down, now usu. called Avestan; a name for the Zend-Avesta. **Zend-Avesta**, **Zendavesta,** *n.* the sacred scriptures of Zoroastrianism, today practised by the Parsees. They comprise the *Avesta* (liturgical books for the priests); the *Gathas* (the discourses and revelations of Zoroaster); and the *Zend* (commentary upon them). [Pers. *Avesta'-va-zend, -zand,* Avesta with commentary (Pers. *Zend*, a commentary, *Avesta* a text)]

zenith, *n.* the point in the heavens directly overhead to an observer, opp. to nadir; the highest or culminating point. **zenith-distance,** *n.* the angular distance of a heavenly body from the zenith. **zenithal,** *a.* **zenithal projection,** *n.* [ME *senith,* OF *cenith* (F *zénith*), OSp. *zenith,* Arab. *samt* (pron. semt), way, road]

Zenobia, *n.* Queen of Palmyra (266–272 AD), she assumed the crown in the Syrian desert as regent for her sons, after the death of her husband Odaenathus, and in 272 was defeated at Homs by Aurelian and taken as a captive to Rome.

Zeno of Elea, *n.* (*c.* 490–430 BC), Greek philosopher, whose paradoxes raised 'modern' problems of space and time. For example, motion is an illusion, since an arrow in flight must occupy a determinate space at each instant, and therefore must be at rest.

zeolite, *n.* any one of a group of hydrous silicates found in cavities of eruptive rocks, which gelatinize in acid owing to the liberation of silica; any of various synthetic silicates resembling this. **zeolithiform, zeolitic,** *a.* [Gr. *zeein,* to boil, -LITE]

Zeph., (*abbr.*) Zephaniah.

Zephaniah, *n.* an Old Testament book named after the Hebrew prophet to whom it is attributed. [Heb. *Sĕphanyāh*]

zephyr, *n.* the west wind personified; any soft, gentle breeze; a light, gauzy fabric or worsted or woollen yarn, used for shawls, jerseys etc.; a jersey or other garment made of this. [F *zéphyr,* L *zephyrus,* Gr. *zephuoros*]

Zeppelin, *n.* **Ferdinand, Count von Zeppelin** (1838–1917), German airship pioneer. On retiring from the army in 1891, he devoted himself to the study of aeronautics, and his first airship was built and tested in 1900. During World War I a number of Zeppelin airships bombed England. They were also used for luxury passenger transport but the construction of hydrogen-filled airships with rigid keels was abandoned after several disasters in the 1920s and 1930s. Zeppelin also helped to pioneer large multi-engine bomber planes.

zerda, *n.* the fennec. [Afr. native]

Zernicke, *n.* **Frits** (1888–1966), Dutch physicist who developed the phase-contrast microscope 1935. Earlier microscopes allowed many specimens to be examined only after they had been transformed by heavy staining and other treatment. The phase-contrast microscope allowed living cells to be directly observed by depending on the difference in refractive indices between specimens and medium. Nobel physics prize 1953.

zero, *n.* (*pl.* **-oes**) the figure 0, a cipher, nothing, nought, nil; the point on a scale from which positive or negative quantities are reckoned, esp. on a thermometer (e.g. in Fahrenheit's thermometer 32° below the freezing point of water; in the Centigrade and Réaumur's scales zero is the freezing-point); the lowest point in any scale or standard of comparison, the nadir, nullity. *a.* having no measurable quantity, size etc.; of a cloud ceiling, limiting visibility to 15 m (approx. 50 ft.) or less; of horizontal visibility, limited to 50 m (approx. 165 ft.) or less; (*coll.*) not any, nothing. *v.t.* to adjust or set to zero (of an instrument, scale, gauge etc.). **absolute zero** ABSOLUTE. **to zero in on,** (*coll.*) to focus attention on, to fix on; to aim for; to converge upon, to home in on. **zero hour,** *n.* the precise hour for the commencement of a prearranged military movement or other action, operation etc. **zero option,** *n.* a proposal that both sides in international nuclear arms negotiations agree to limit or remove shorter-range nuclear missiles. **zero-rated,** *a.* referring to goods on which the buyer need pay no value-added tax, but on which the seller can claim back any value-added tax he/she has already paid. **zeroth,** *a.* referring to a term in a series of terms which precedes what is usu. regarded as the first term. [OF and It., for *zefiro,* Arab. *cipr,* CIPHER]

zest, *n.* a piece of lemon or orange peel, or the oil extracted from this, used to give a flavour to soups, wines etc.; hence, that which makes a thing enjoyable, piquancy, relish; keen enjoyment. **zestful,** *a.* **zestfully,** *adv.* **zestfulness,** *n.* **zesty,** *a.* [OF, the woody skin dividing the kernel of a walnut, from L and Gr. *schistos,* cleft, from *schizein,* to divide]

ZETA, *n.* a British apparatus used in investigating the controlled production of nuclear energy by the fusion of hydrogen. [acronym for Zero Energy Thermonuclear Apparatus]

zeta[1], *n.* the sixth letter of the Greek alphabet (Z, ζ).

zeta[2], *n.* a little closet or chamber; a sexton's room over the porch of a church, where church documents etc. were kept. [late L, from Gr. *diaita,* dwelling, see DIET[1]]

zetetic, *a.* proceeding by enquiry. *n.* a seeker (a name adopted by some of the Pyrrhonists); an enquiry, a search. [Gr. *zētētikos,* from *zēteein,* to seek]

Zeuglodon, *n.* a genus of extinct whales from the Eocene. **zeuglodon,** *n.* any individual of such genus. [Gr. *zeuglē,* strap of a yoke, from *zeugnunai,* to yoke, *odous odontos,* tooth]

zeugma, *n.* a figure in which a verb or adjective governs or modifies two nouns to only one of which it is logically applicable. **zeugmatic,** *a.* [Gr. *zeugma -matos,* yoke, see prec.]

Zeus, *n.* in Greek mythology, chief of the gods (Roman Jupiter). He was the son of Kronos, whom he overthrew; his brothers included Hades and Poseidon, his sisters Demeter and Hera. As the supreme god he dispensed good and evil and was the father and ruler of all humankind. His emblems are the thunderbolt and aegis (shield), representing the thunder cloud.

zeuxite, *n.* a variety of tourmaline. [Gr. *zeuxis,* joining, from *zeugnunai,* to yoke, -ITE]

Zhangjiakou, *n.* (formerly *Changchiakow*) historic town and trade centre in Hebei province, China, 160 km/100 miles NW of Beijing, on the Great Wall; population (1980) 1,100,000. Zhangjiakou is on the border of Inner Mongolia (its Mongolian name is Kalgan, 'gate') and on the road and railway to Ulaanbaatar in Mongolia. It developed under the Manchu dynasty, and was the centre of the tea trade from China to Russia.

Zhao Ziyang, *n.* (1918–), Chinese politician, prime minister from 1980, and secretary of the Chinese Communist Party (CCP) 1987–89. His reforms included self-management and incentives for workers and factories. He lost his secretaryship and other posts after the Tiananmen Square massacre in Beijing, June 1989.

Zhejiang (formerly **Chekiang**), *n.* province of SE China. **area** 101,800 sq km/39,295 sq miles. **capital** Hangzhou. **population** (1986) 40,700,000. **products** rice, cotton, sugar, jute, maize; timber on the uplands.

Zhengzhou (formerly **Chengchow**), *n.* industrial city (light engineering, cotton textiles, foods), capital of Henan province (from 1954), China, on the Huang Ho; population (1986) 1,590,000.

Zhivkov, *n.* **Todor** (1911–), Bulgarian Communist Party leader from 1954, prime minister 1962–71, president 1971–89. His period in office was one of caution and conservatism.

zho, zo, dso, dzo, *n.* (*pl.* **-s**) a hybrid breed of Himalayan cattle developed from crossing the yak with common horned cattle. [Tibetan *mdzo*]

Zhou Enlai (formerly **Chou En-lai**), *n.* (1898–1976), Chinese politician. Zhou, a member of the Chinese Communist Party from the 1920s, was prime minister 1949–76 and foreign minister 1949–58. He was a moderate Maoist, and weathered the Cultural Revolution. He played a key role in foreign affairs.

Zhubov scale, *n.* scale for measuring ice coverage, used in the USSR. The unit is the ball; 1 ball is 10% coverage, 2 balls 20%, and so on.

Zhu De (formerly **Chu Teh**), *n.* (1886–1976), Chinese Red Army leader from 1931. He devised the tactic of mobile guerrilla warfare and organized the Long March to Shaanxi 1934–36. He was made a marshal 1955.

Zhukov, *n.* **Grigory Konstantinovich** (1896–1974), marshal of the USSR in World War II and minister of defence 1955–57. As chief of staff from 1941, he defended Moscow 1941, counterattacked at Stalingrad, organized the relief of Leningrad 1943, and led the offensive from Ukraine Mar. 1944 which ended in the fall of Berlin. He subsequently commanded the Soviet occupation forces in Germany.

Zia ul-Haq, *n.* **Mohammad** (1924–88), Pakistani general, in power from 1977 until his assassination. He was a career soldier from a middle-class Punjabi Muslim family, and became army chief of staff 1976. He led the military coup against Zulfiqar Ali Bhutto 1977 and became president 1978. Zia introduced a fundamentalist Islamic regime and restricted political activity.

zibel(l)ine, *a.* of, pertaining to or resembling the sable.

n. the sable or its fur; a thick woollen fabric with a soft deep nap. [F, from It. *zibellino,* prob. from Slav.]

zibet, *n.* the Indian or Asiatic civet, *Viverra zibetha.* [It. *zibello,* CIVET]

zidovudine, *n.* an alternative name for the drug AZT, used in the treatment of AIDS.

ZIFT (*abbr.*) zygote inter-fallopian transfer, a modified form of in vitro fertilization in which the fertilized ovum is reintroduced into the mother's fallopian tube before it has undergone its first cell division. This mimics the natural processes of fertilization (which normally occurs in the fallopian tube) and implantation more effectively than older techniques do.

ziggurat, *n.* an ancient Mesopotamian temple-tower of a rectangular or tiered design. [Assyrian *ziqquratu,* peak, summit]

zigzag, *a.* having or taking sharp alternate turns or angles to left and right; of a sewing machine, capable of executing zigzag stitches. *n.* a zigzag line, road, path, pattern, moulding, series of trenches, stitches etc. *adv.* in a zigzag course or manner. *v.t.* (*past, p.p.* **zigzagged**) to form or do in a zigzag fashion. *v.i.* to move in a zigzag course. **zigzaggery,** *n.* **zigzaggy,** *a.* [F, from G *Zickzack,* redupl. from *Zacke,* tooth, prong]

zilch, *n.* (*sl.*) nothing, zero; a dice game in which a player's score may fall sharply to zero.

zilla(h), zila, *n.* an administrative district in India or Bangladesh. [Hind. from Arab. *dila,* a part, a district].

zillion, *n.* (*coll.*) a huge unspecified amount, quantity or number. [in imit. of MILLION]

zimb, *n.* a dipterous insect common in Ethiopia resembling the tsetse, and hurtful to cattle. [Arab.]

Zimbabwe[1], *n.* extensive ruins near Victoria in Mashonaland, Zimbabwe. They were probably the work of a highly advanced Bantu-speaking people from Zaïre or Ethiopia, smelters of iron, who were in the area before 300 AD. The new state of Zimbabwe took its name from these ruins, and the national emblem is a bird derived from soapstone sculptures of fish eagles found in them.

Zimbabwe[2], *n.* Republic of, landlocked country in Central Africa. **area** 390,300 sq km/150,695 sq miles. **capital** Harare. **towns** Bulawayo, Gweru, Kwekwe, Mutare, Hwange. **physical** a high plateau with mountains in the east. **population** (1989) 9,987,000 (Shona 80%, Ndbele, of Zulu descent, 19%; before independence there were some 275,000 whites, in 1985 about 100,000); annual growth rate 3.5%. **exports** tobacco, citrus, tea, coffee, gold, silver. **language** English (official); Shona, Ndbele, Nyanja. **religion** Christian. **Zimbabwean,** *n.* a native or inhabitant of the republic of Zimbabwe. *a.* of or pertaining to Zimbabwe.

zimmer®, *n.* a metal walking-frame used as a means of support by those with walking difficulties.

zimocca, *n.* a soft, fine, cup-shaped bath-sponge from the Mediterranean. [It.]

zinc, *n.* a bluish-white metallic element, at. no. 30; chem. symbol Zn, used in the manufacture of brass and German silver, for coating sheet-iron, as roofing-material, for printing-blocks etc. *v.t.* to coat or cover with zinc. *a.* of or containing zinc. **flowers of zinc,** zinc oxide. **zinc-blende,** *n.* native sulphide of zinc, sphalerite. **zinc ointment,** *n.* a medical preparation of zinc oxide in an ointment base such as petroleum jelly. **zinc oxide,** *n.* white powdery oxide of zinc used as a white pigment, and in cements, ointments etc. **zinc sulphate,** *n.* white vitriol. **zinc-white,** *n.* oxide of zinc used as a pigment. **zinc-worker,** *n.* **zincic, zinciferous, zinkiferous,** *a.* **zincite,** *n.* a native oxide of zinc. **zincograph,** *n.* a zinc plate on which a picture or design has been etched in relief for printing; an impression from this. **zincographer,** *n.* **zincographic, -ical,** *a.* **zincography,** *n.* **zincoid,** *a.* **zincous,** *a.* **zincy, zin(c)ky,** *a.* [G *Zingk,* etym. doubtful]

zincic, zincoid etc. ZINC.

zing, *n.* (*coll.*) a shrill buzzing noise as of a bullet or a vibrating rope; energy, go, zest. *v.i.* (*coll.*) to move very quickly esp. (as) with a high-pitched humming sound. **zingy,** *a.* (*coll.*). [imit.]

zingaro, *n.* (*pl.* **-ri**) a gipsy. [It.]

zingiber, *n.* a genus of monocotyledonous tropical herbs with creeping, jointed, woody root-stocks, of which the common ginger, *Zingiber officinale,* is the type. **zingiberaceous,** *a.* [L, ginger]

Zinjanthropus, *n.* name given to the man-like fossil found in Tanzania in 1959 now known as *Australopithecus boisei.* [Arab. *zinj,* E Africa, Gr. *anthrōpos,* man]

zinke, *n.* (*pl.* **-ken**) an old wind instrument consisting of a leather-covered tube with seven finger-holes, the precursor of the cornet. [G]

zinky ZINC.

Zinneman, *n.* **Fred(erick)** (1907–), Austrian film director, in the US from 1921. His films include *High Noon* (1952), *The Nun's Story* (1959), *The Day of the Jackal* (1973), and *Five Days One Summer* (1982).

zinnia, *n.* a plant of the aster family with showy-rayed flowers in single terminal heads. [J G *Zinn,* 1727-59, German botanist]

Zinoviev, *n.* **Grigory** (1883–1936), Russian politician. A prominent Bolshevik, he returned to Russia in 1917 with Lenin and played a leading part in the Revolution. As head of the Communist International 1919, his name was attached to a forgery, the Zinoviev letter, inciting Britain's communists to rise, which helped to topple the Labour government in 1924. As one of the 'Old Bolsheviks', he was seen by Stalin as a threat. He was accused of complicity in the murder of the Bolshevik leader Kirov, and shot.

Zion, Sion, *n.* a hill in ancient Jerusalem, the royal residence of David and his successors; the ancient Hebrew theocracy, the Church of Christ, the heavenly Jerusalem, heaven; the Jewish homeland or people; the modern Jewish nation of Israel; used as a name for a Nonconformist chapel. **Zionism,** *n.* orig. a movement for establishing the resettlement of Palestine as the Jewish homeland, and the development of the state of Israel. **Zionist,** *n., a.* **Zionistic,** *a.* [Gr., from Heb. *tsīyōn,* hill]

zip, *n.* a zip-fastener, a zipper; the sharp sound made by a bullet or other missile striking an object or flying through the air; (*coll.*) energy, zest. *v.i.* (*past, p.p.* **zipped**) to move or fly (as) with such a sound. **to zip along, through,** to move swiftly; to rush, to finish quickly. **to zip up,** to fasten by means of a zip. **zip-fastener, zipper,** *n.* a fastening device, with interlocking teeth, which opens or closes with a single motion. **zippy,** *a.* (*coll.*) energetic, speedy. [imit.]

zip code, *n.* (*N Am.*) postal code. [acronym for zone improvement plan]

zircon, *n.* a translucent, variously-coloured silicate of zirconium, some varieties of which are cut into gems. **zircalloy,** *n.* an alloy of zirconium and small quantities of nickel, chromium and tin used in nuclear reactors. **zirconate,** *n.* a salt of zirconic acid. **zirconic,** *a.* **zirconium,** *n.* an earthy metallic element found chiefly in zircon. [Arab. *zarqūn,* Pers. *zargūn,* gold-coloured]

zit, zitch, *n.* (*sl.*) a spot, a pimple. **zitty, zitchy,** *a.* [etym. doubtful]

zither, *n.* a simple stringed instrument consisting of a flat sounding-board and strings plucked by the fingers. **zitherist,** *n.* [G, from L *cithara,* CITHER]

Zi Xi (formerly **Tzu-Hsi**), *n.* (1836–1908), dowager empress of China. She was presented as a concubine to the emperor Hsien-Feng. On his death 1861 she became regent for her son T'ung Chih, and, when he died in 1875, for her nephew Guang Xu (1871–1908).

Zizania, *n.* a genus of tall aquatic grasses comprising the different species of rice. [Gr. *zizanion,* a weed, perh. darnel]

zizz, *n.* (*coll.*) a nap. *v.i.* to doze. [imit.]

zloty, *n.* (*pl.* **zloty, -s**) a coin and monetary unit of Poland. [Pol. golden]

Zn, (*chem. symbol*) zinc.

zo ZHO.

zo-, *comb. form.* zoo; as in *zoology.* [zoo-]

zoa, *pl.* of ZOON.

-zoa, *comb. form* animals, as in *Metazoa, Protozoa.* [L from Gr. *zōia,* animals]

Zoantharia, *n.* an order of Actinozoa which includes sea-anemones etc. [Gr. *zōon,* an animal, *anther,* a flower]

zoanthropy, *n.* a mental disorder in which the patient believes himself transformed into one of the lower animals. **zoanthropic,** *a.* [Gr. *zōon,* animal, *anthrōpos,* man]

zoarium, *n.* (*pl.* **-ia**) a polyzoan colony, a polyzoary. [Gr. *zōarion,* dim. of *zōon,* animal]

zobo, ZEBU.

zocco, zoccolo, *n.* (*pl.* **-ccos, -ccolos**) a socle. [It.]

zodiac, *n.* the zone or broad belt of the heavens, extending about 8° to each side of the ecliptic, which the sun traverses during the year, anciently divided into 12 equal parts called the **signs of the zodiac,** which orig. corresponded to the **zodiacal constellations** bearing the same names, but now, through the precession of the equinoxes, coinciding with the constellations bearing the names next in order; **zodiacal,** *a.* pertaining to the zodiac. **zodiacal light,** *n.* a triangular tract or pillar of light sometimes seen, esp. in the tropics, rising from the point at which the sun is just about to rise or has just set. [F *zodiaque,* L *zōdiacus,* Gr. *zōdiakos,* orig. adj., pertaining to animals, from *zōdion,* dim. of *zōon,* animal]

zoetic, *a.* pertaining to or of the nature of life, vital. [Gr. *zōē,* life, -IC]

Zog, *n.* **Ahmed Beg Zogu** (1895–1961), king of Albania 1928–39. He became prime minister of Albania in 1922, president of the republic in 1925, and proclaimed himself king in 1928. He was driven out by the Italians in 1939, and settled in England.

zoic, *a.* of or pertaining to animals or animal life; of rocks, containing fossils or other evidences of plant or animal life. [Gr. *zōikos,* from *zōon,* animal]

-zoic, *comb. form.* indicating a geological era, as in *Mesozoic, Palaeozoic.* [Gr. *zōē,* life, -IC]

zoilean, *a.* like or pertaining to Zoilus, a Greek grammarian of the 4th cent. BC, who severely criticised Homer, Plato and Socrates; bitter, severe, malignant (of criticism or critics). **zoilism,** *n.*

zoisite, *n.* a translucent silicate of calcium and aluminium, first found in Carinthia. [Baron von *Zois,* 1747–1819, Slovenian geologist]

zoism, *n.* the doctrine that life originates from a specific principle, and is not merely the resultant of various forces. **zoist,** *n.* **zoistic,** *a.*

Zola, *n.* **Emile Edouard Charles Antoine** (1840–1902), French novelist and social reformer. With *La Fortune des Rougon/The Fortune of the Rougons* (1867) he began a series of some 20 naturalistic novels, portraying the fortunes of a French family under the Second Empire. They include *Le Ventre de Paris/The Underbelly of Paris* (1873), *Nana* (1880), and *La Débâcle/The Debacle* (1892). In 1898 he published *J'accuse/I Accuse,* a pamphlet indicting the persecutors of Dreyfus, for which he was prosecuted but later pardoned. **Zolaism,** *n.* excessive naturalism, unshrinking realism dealing with the sordid and repulsive aspects of life. **Zolaesque, Zolaistic,** *a.* **Zolaist,** *n.*

Zollverein, *n.* a customs union among states maintaining a tariff against imports and usu. having free trade with each other; a customs union among German states in the early 1830s led by Prussia. [G (*Zoll,* duty, *Verein,* union)]

zombi(e), *n.* orig. an African snake god; in W Indian voodooism, a reanimated dead person capable of slow automatic movements; the supernatural spirit animating the dead person's body; a stupid, apathetic or slow moving person. **zombielike,** *a.* **zombiism,** *n.* [W Afr. *zumbi,* fetish]

zonal, zonary etc. ZONE.

zonda, *n.* a hot dry west wind blowing from the Andes, usu. during July and August, in the Argentine. [village in Argentina]

zone, *n.* †a girdle, a belt; a well-marked band or stripe encircling an object; any one of the five great divisions of the earth bounded by circles parallel to the equator (the **torrid zone** between the tropics extending $23\frac{1}{2}$° on each side of the equator, the **temperate zones** between the tropics and the polar circles and the **frigid zones** situated within the polar circles); any well-defined belt or tract of land distinguished by climate, the character of its organisms etc.; the part of the surface of a sphere or of a cone or cylinder enclosed between two parallel planes perpendicular to the axis; a stratum or area of rock distinguished by particular fossil remains; an area sectioned off for a particular function (e.g. a smoke-free zone); an area characterized by a particular form of government, business practice etc. (e.g. a duty-free zone). *v.t.* to encircle with or as with a zone; to allocate to certain districts or zones; to divide into zones. **zonetime,** *n.* local time for any longitude. **zonal, zonary,** *a.* **zonally,** *adv.* **zonate, -ated,** *a.* marked with zones or concentric bands of colour. **zonation,** *n.* arrangement or division into zones. **zoned,** *a.* †**zoneless,** *a.* destitute of a zone; ungirded. **zoner,** *n.* **zoning,** *n.* division into, or allocation to, zones; the marking off in town-planning of certain areas for specific purposes, e.g. residence, shopping etc. [F, from L *zōna,* Gr. *zōnē,* girdle, from *zōnnunai,* to gird]

zonked, *a.* (*sl.*) intoxicated by drugs or alcohol, extremely drunk or stoned; (*sl.*) tired out, exhausted. [etym. unknown]

zoo, *n.* a zoological garden or a collection of living wild animals, orig. the Zoological Gardens in London.

zoo-, *comb. form.* pertaining to animals or to animal life. [Gr. *zōon,* animal, neut. of *zōos,* living, from *zaein* (Ionic *zōein*), to live]

zooblast, *n.* an animal cell. [Gr. *blastos,* germ]

zoochemistry, *n.* the chemistry of the substances occurring in the animal body. **zoochemical,** *a.* **zoodynamics,** *n.* the science of the vital power of animals.

zooecium, *n.* (*pl.* **-cia**), one of the cells forming the investment of polyzoans. [Gr. *oikos,* house]

zoogamy, *n.* sexual reproduction of animals. **zoogamous,** *a.* relating to zoogamy. [Gr. *gamos,* marriage]

zoogeny, zoogenic, -genous, *a.* produced from animals. [-GENY]

zoogeography, *n.* the study of the distribution of animals, faunal geography. **zoogeographer,** *n.* **zoogeographic, -ical,** *a.* **zoogeographically,** *adv.* **zoography,** *n.* descriptive zoology. **zoographer,** *n.* **zoographic, -ical,** *a.*

zoogony, *n.* the formation of animal organs. [Gr. *-gonia,* begetting, from *-gon-,* stem of *gignesthai,* to beget]

zooid, *a.* having the nature of an animal, having organic life and motion. *n.* a more or less independent organism developed by fission or gemmation; a member of a compound organism; an organic body or cell capable of independent motion. **zooidal,** *a.*

zool., (*abbr.*) zoological; zoology.

zoolatry, *n.* animal-worship. **zoolater,** *n.* an animal-worshipper. **zoolatrous,** *a.* [ZOO-, -LATRY]

zoolite, zoolith, *n.* a fossil animal or animal substance. **zoolithic, -litic,** *a.* [-LITE]

zoology, *n.* the natural history of animals, the branch of biology dealing with the structure, physiology, classification, habits and distribution of animals. **zoological,** *a.* **zoological garden,** *n.* a public garden or park in which a collection of wild and other animals is kept. **zoologically,** *adv.* **zoologist,** *n.*

zoom, *v.i.* to turn an aircraft upwards suddenly at a very sharp angle; to make a continuous, deep, loud buzzing noise; to move quickly (as) with this noise; to rise rapidly, to soar (e.g. of prices). *n.* an act, instance or sound of zooming; a zoom lens; in cinematography, a shot taken with a lens whose focal length is adjusted during the shot. **to zoom in** or **out,** to increase or decrease rapidly the focal length of a zoom lens when taking a photograph, a film shot etc. in order to change the size of the image. **zoom lens,** *n.* a lens in a camera or microscope which has a variable focal length and can increase or decrease the size of an image continuously without changing position. [onomat.]

zoomagnetism, *n.* animal magnetism.

zoomancy, *n.* divination by means of observation of the movements and behaviour of animals. [-MANCY]

zoometry, *n.* comparative measurement of the parts of animals. **zoometric, -ical,** *a.* [-METRY]

zoomorphic, *a.* pertaining to or exhibiting animal forms; of religious symbolism representing animals; of gods represented under the form of animals. **zoomorphism, -morphy,** *n.* [Gr. *morphē,* form]

-zoon, *comb. form.* animal, as in *spermatozoon.* [Gr. *zōon,* animal]

zoon, *n.* (*pl.* **zoa**) the total product of a fertilized ovum; a developed individual of a compound organism. **zoonal,** *a.* **zoonic,** *a.* derived from or contained in animal substances. **zoonomy,** *n.* the science of the laws of animal life. **zoonomic,** *a.* **zoonomist,** *n.*

zoonosis, *n.* a disease which can be transmitted to humans by animals, e.g. rabies. **zoonotic,** *a.*

zoopathology, *n.* animal pathology.

†**zoopathy,** *n.* zoopathology.

zoophagous, *a.* feeding on animals, carnivorous. **zoophagan,** *n., a.*

zoophile, *n.* an animal lover; a defender of animal rights and welfare. **zoophilia, zoophilism, zoophily,** *n.* love of animals; sexual attraction towards animals. **zoophilist,** *n.* **zoophilous,** *a.*

zoophobia, *n.* abnormal fear or hatred of animals. **zoophobous,** *a.*

zoophorus, *n.* a continuous frieze carved with figures of men and animals in relief. **zoophoric,** *a.* [Gr. *pherein,* to bear]

zoophyte, *n.* (*dated*) an invertebrate animal presenting many external resemblances to a plant, as a coral sea-anemone, holothurian, sponge etc. **zoophytic, -ical,** *a.* **zoophytoid,** *a.* **zoophytology,** *n.* the natural history of zoophytes. **zoophytological,** *a.* **zoophytologist,** *n.*

zooplankton, *n.* the minute floating animal life of a body of water. **zooplanktonic,** *a.*

zooscopy, *n.* a form of hallucination involving visions of animals. [-SCOPY]

zoospore, *n.* a spore having the power of independent motion, usu. by means of cilia. **zoosporic, -sporous,** *a.*

zootaxy, *n.* the classification of animals. [see TAXIS]

zootechnics, *n.* the science of breeding and of the domestication of animals. [TECHNIC]

zootheism, *n.* the attribution of divine qualities to animals. **zootheistic,** *a.* [THEISM]

zootomy, *n.* the dissection or anatomy of animals. **zootomic, -ical,** *a.* **zootomically,** *adv.* **zootomist,** *n.* [-TOMY]

zootoxin, *n.* a toxin produced by an animal, e.g. snake venom.

zootrophic, *a.* pertaining to the nourishment of animals. [TROPHIC]

zoot suit, *n.* a man's baggy suit popular in the late 1940s, consisting of a long jacket with fitted waist and padded shoulders, and wide trousers tapering into narrow cuffs. [etym. unknown; prob. rhyming with SUIT]

zopilote, *n.* a turkey-buzzard, esp. the urubu. [Mex. Sp. *tzopilotl*]

zoril, zorilla, zorille, *n.* a small carnivorous quadruped, *Zorilla striata,* allied to the skunks and polecats, found in Africa and Asia Minor. **zorra, zorillo** *n.* a S American skunk. **zorro,** *n.* a S American fox-wolf. [F *zorille,* Sp. *zorilla,* dim. of *zorra,* fox]

Zoroaster, Zarathustra *n.* (*c.* 628–*c.* 551 BC), Persian prophet and religious teacher, founder of Zoroastrianism. **Zoroastrian,** *a.* pertaining to Zoroaster or the religious system set forth by him and his followers in the Zend-Avesta, based on the dual principle of Ormazd, the god of light and good, and Ahriman, the god of darkness and evil, the ancient Persian religion of the Magi and still held by the Parsees, sometimes called fire-worshippers. *n.* a follower of Zoroaster; an adherent of Zoroastrianism. **Zoroastrianism,** *n.* [L *Zoroastres,* OPers. *Zarathustra*]

zorra, zorro ZORIL.

zoster, *n.* an ancient Greek girdle or belt, worn esp. by men; shingles; herpes zoster. [Gr. *zōstēr,* girdle, from *zōnnunai,* to gird]

Zouave, *n.* a soldier belonging to a French light infantry corps, orig. composed of Algerian recruits and still wearing an Oriental uniform; a zouave jacket. **zouave jacket,** *n.* a short, round-fronted jacket, usu. sleeveless, worn by women. [F, MAfr. *Zuawa,* name of a Kabyle tribe]

ZOUK, *n.* a kind of lively music originating in the French Caribbean.

zounds, *int.* an exclamation of anger, surprise etc. [contr. from *God's wounds,* an obsolete oath]

Z particle, *n.* type of elementary particle.

Zsigmondy, *n.* **Richard** (1865–1929), Austrian chemist who devised and built an ultramicroscope in 1903. The microscope's illumination was placed at right angles to the axis. (In a conventional microscope the light source is placed parallel to the instrument's axis.) Zsigmondy's arrangement made it possible to observe gold particles with a diameter of 10-millionth of a millimetre. Nobel chemistry prize 1925.

ZST, (*abbr.*) Zone Standard Time.

zucchini, *n.* (*chiefly N Am. and Austral.*) (*pl.* **-ni, -nis**) a courgette. [It., pl. of *zucchino,* dim. of *zucca,* gourd]

zuchetto, zuchetta, *n.* (*pl.* **-os**) the skull-cap of a Roman Catholic ecclesiastic, black for priest, purple for bishop, red for cardinal, white for pope. [It., small gourd]

zugzwang, *n.* a blocking position in chess making any move by an opponent disadvantageous. *v.t.* to place an opponent in this position. [G]

Zuider Zee, *n.* former sea inlet in Holland, cut off from the North Sea by the closing of a dyke in 1932, much of which has been reclaimed as land. The remaining lake is called the IJsselmeer.

Zulu, *n.* person of Zulu culture from Natal, South Africa. The modern homeland, Kwazulu, represents the nucleus of the old Zulu kingdom. The Zulu language belongs to the Bantu branch of the Niger-Congo family. *a.* of or pertaining to this people or their language.

Zululand, *n.* region in Natal, South Africa, largely corresponding to the Black National State, Kwazulu. It was formerly a province, annexed to Natal 1897.

Zuñi, *n.* a member of an American Indian people of New Mexico; the language of this people. **Zuñian,** *n., a..*

Zurbarán, *n.* **Francisco de** (1598–1664), Spanish painter, based in Seville. He painted religious subjects in a powerful, austere style, often focusing on a single figure in prayer.

Zürich, *n.* financial centre and industrial city (machinery, electrical goods, textiles) on Lake Zürich, capital of Zürich canton, the largest city in Switzerland; population (1987) 840,000.

Zweig, *n.* **Stefan** (1881–1942), Austrian writer, noted for plays, poems, and many biographies of writers (Balzac, Dickens) and historical figures (Marie Antoinette, Mary Stuart). He and his wife, exiles from the Nazis from 1934, despairing at what they saw as the end of civilization and culture, committed suicide in Brazil.

zwieback, *n.* a type of biscuit or rusk. [G twice-baked]

Zwingli, *n.* **Ulrich** (1484–1531), Swiss Protestant, born in St Gallen. He was ordained a Roman Catholic priest 1506, but by 1519 was a Reformer, and led the Reformation in Switzerland with his insistence on the sole authority of the Scriptures. In a war against the cantons that had not accepted the Reformation he was killed in a skirmish at Kappel. **Zwinglian,** *a.* of or pertaining to Zwingli or his doctrines (esp. the denial of 'real presence' in the Eucharist). *n.* a believer in Zwinglian doctrine; a follower of Zwingli.

zwitterion, *n.* an ion that carries both a positive and negative electric charge. [G *Zwitter,* bisexual, ION]

Zworykin, *n.* **Vladimir Kosma** (1889–1982), Russian electronics engineer, in the US from 1919. He invented a television camera tube and the electron microscope.

zyg-, zygo- *comb. form.* yoke, union. **zygal**, *a.* H-shaped, of the nature of a zygon.

zygapophysis, *n.* (*pl.* **-physes**) one of the processes by which a vertebra articulates with another. [Gr. *apophusis,* process (APO-, *phuein,* to grow)]

zygobranchiate, *a.* having the right and the left gills alike (of certain gasteropods). **zygobranch**, *n.* one of the Zygobranchia, an order of zygobranchiate gasteropods. [BRANCHIATE]

zygodactyl, *a.* of birds, having the toes disposed in pairs, two in front and two behind; belonging to the Zygodactylae, a group of birds with two toes pointed forwards and two backwards, as in the parrots. *n.* one of the Zygodactylae. **zygodactylic**, **zygodactylous,** *a.* [Gr. *daktulos,* digit]

zygoma, *n.* (*pl.* **-mata**) the arch joining the malar and temporal bones, the yoke-bone, the zygomatic arch. **zygomatic**, *a.* **zygomatic arch,** *n.* the zygoma. **zygomatic bone,** *n.* the cheekbone.

zygomorphic, zygomorphous, *a.* of flowers, divisible into similar halves only in one plane. **zygomorphism, -morphy**, *n.* [Gr. *morphē,* form]

zygon, *n.* a connecting bar, as the cross-bar of an H-shaped fissure of the brain.

Zygophyllum, *n.* a genus of trees or shrubs comprising the bean-caper. **zygophyllaceous**, *a.* [Gr. *phullon,* leaf]

zygophyte, *n.* a plant reproduced by means of zygospores.

zygopleural, *a.* bilaterally symmetrical.

zygosis, *n.* (*Biol.*) conjugation. **zygose**, *a.* relating to zygosis.

zygospore, *n.* a spore formed by conjugation of two similar gametes. **zygosporic**, *a.*

zygote, *n.* the product of the fusion between the oocyte and the spermatozoon; the fertilized ovum. **zygotic**, *a.* [Gr. *zugon,* yoke]

zyme, *n.* a ferment, a disease-germ, the supposed cause of a zymotic disease. **zymase**, *n.* an enzyme. **zymic,** *a.* relating to fermentation. [Gr. *zumē,* leaven, from *zeein,* to boil]

zym(o)-, *comb. form.* indicating fermentation.

zymogen, *n.* a substance developing by internal change into a ferment or enzyme.

zymology, *n.* the science of fermentation. **zymologic, -ical**, *a.* **zymologist,** *n.*

zymolysis, *n.* zymosis.

zymometer, zymosimeter, *n.* an instrument for measuring the degree of fermentation.

zymosis, *n.* the process of fermentation, esp. that by which disease is introduced into the system; any zymotic disease. **zymotic**, *a.* of, pertaining to or produced by fermentation. **zymotic disease,** *n.* an epidemic, endemic or contagious disease produced by the multiplication of germs introduced from without. **zymotically,** *adv.*

zymurgy, *n.* the department of technological chemistry treating of processes in which fermentation plays the principal part. [Gr. *zumé,* leaven, *ergon,* work]

zythum, *n.* a malt beverage of the ancient Egyptians. [Gr. *zuthos*]

Appendix I
Gazetteer

COUNTRIES, CAPITALS, LANGUAGES, CURRENCIES

Country	*Capital*	*Language*	*Currency*
Afghanistan	Kabul	Pushtoo, Dari Persian	afghani = 100 puls
Albania	Tiranë	Albanian	lek = 100 qindarka
Algeria	Algiers	Arabic, French	dinar = 10 centimes
Andorra	Andorra la Vella	Catalan	franc = 100 centimes peseta = 100 céntimos
Angola	Luanda	Portuguese	kwanza = 100 lweis
Antigua and Barbuda	St Johns	English	dollar = 100 cents
Argentina	Buenos Aires	Spanish	austral = 100 centavos
Australia	Canberra	English	dollar = 100 cents
Austria	Vienna	German	Schilling = 100 Groschen
Bahamas	Nassau	English	dollar = 100 cents
Bahrain	Manama	Arabic	dinar = 1000 fils
Bangladesh	Dhaka	Bengali	taka = 100 paisa
Barbados	Bridgetown	English	dollar = 100 cents
Belgium	Brussels	French, Flemish, German	franc = 100 centimes
Belize	Belmopan	English	dollar = 100 cents
Benin	Porto Novo	French	franc CFA
Bermuda	Hamilton	English	dollar = 100 cents
Bhutan	Thimphu	Dzongkha	ngultrum = 100 chetrums
Bolivia	La Paz	Spanish	peso = 100 centavos
Botswana	Gaborone	English	pula = 100 thebe
Brazil	Brasilia	Portuguese	cruzacio = 1000 cruzeiro
Brunei	Bandar Seri Begawan	Malay	dollar = 100 sen
Bulgaria	Sofia	Bulgarian	lev = 100 stotinki
Burkina Faso	Ouagadougou	French	franc CFA
Burma	Rangoon	Burmese	kyat = 100 pyas
Burundi	Bujumbura	French	franc = 100 centimes
Cambodia	Phnom Penh	Khmer	riel = 100 sen
Cameroon	Yaounde	French, English	franc CFA
Canada	Ottawa	English, French	dollar = 100 cents
Cape Verde Islands	Praia	Portuguese	escudo = 100 centavos
Cayman Islands	Georgetown	English	dollar = 100 cents
Central African Republic	Bangui	French, Sango	franc CFA
Chad	N'Djamena	French	franc CFA
Chile	Santiago	Spanish	peso = 100 centavos
China, People's Republic	Beijing (Peking)	Mandarin Chinese	yuan = 10 jiao, 100 fen
Colombia	Bogotá	Spanish	peso = 100 centavos
Comoro Islands	Moroni	French	franc CFA
Congo	Brazzaville	French	franc CFA
Costa Rica	San José	Spanish	colón = 100 céntimos
Cuba	Havana	Spanish	peso = 100 centavos
Cyprus	Nicosia	Turkish, Greek	pound = 1000 mils
Czechoslovakia	Prague	Czech, Slovak	koruna = 100 haléru

Country	*Capital*	*Language*	*Currency*
Denmark	Copenhagen	Danish	krone = 100 öre
Djibouti	Djibouti	French	franc = 100 centimes
Dominica	Roseau	English	dollar = 100 cents
Dominican Republic	Santo Domingo	Spanish	peso = 100 centavos
Ecuador	Quito	Spanish	sucre = centavos
Egypt	Cairo	Arabic	pound = 100 piastries, 1000 millièmes
El Salvador	San Salvador	Spanish	colón = 100 centavos
Equatorial Guinea	Malabo	Spanish	ekuele = 100 centimos
Ethiopia	Addis Ababa	Amharic	birr = 100 cents
Falkland Islands	Stanley	English	pound = 100 pence
Fiji	Suva	English	dollar = 100 cents
Finland	Helsinki	Finnish, Swedish	markka = 100 penniä
France	Paris	French	franc = 100 centimes
Gabon	Libreville	French	franc CFA
Gambia	Banjul	English	dalasi = 100 bututs
Germany Democratic Republic	East Berlin	German	Deutschmark = 100 Pfennig
Federal Republic	Bonn	German	Deutschmark = 100 Pfennig
Ghana	Accra	English	cedi = 100 pesewa
Greece	Athens	Greek	drachma = 100 lepta
Grenada	St George's	English	dollar = 100 cents
Guatemala	Guatemala	Spanish	quetzal = 100 centavos
Guinea	Conakry	French	syli = 100 cauris
Guinea-Bissau	Bissau	Portuguese	peso = 100 centavos
Guyana	Georgetown	English	dollar = 100 cents
Haiti	Port-au-Prince	French, Creole	gourde = 100 centimes
Honduras	Tegucigalpa	Spanish	lempira = 100 centavos
Hong Kong	Victoria	English	dollar = 100 cents
Hungary	Budapest	Hungarian (Magyar)	forint = 100 fillér
Iceland	Reykjavik	Icelandic	króna = 100 aurar
India	New Delhi	Hindi, English	rupee = 100 paise
Indonesia	Djakarta	Bahasa Indonesian	rupiah = 100 sen
Iran	Teheran	Farsi Parsian	rial = 100 dinars
Iraq	Baghdad	Arabic	dinar = 1000 fils
Ireland, Republic of	Dublin	Irish Gaelic, English	punt (pound) = 100 pence
Israel	Jerusalem	Hebrew, Arabic	shekel = 100 agorot
Italy	Rome	Italian	lira
Ivory Coast	Abidjan	French	franc CFA
Jamaica	Kingston	English	dollar = 100 cents
Japan	Tokyo	Japanese	yen = 100 sen
Jordan	Amman	Arabic	dinar = 1000 fils
Kampuchea – see CAMBODIA			
Kenya	Nairobi	English, Swahili	shilling = 100 cents
Kiribati	Tarawa	English	dollar = 100 cents
Korea, North	Pyongyang	Korean	won = 100 chon or jun
Korea, South	Seoul	Korean	won = 100 chon or jeon
Kuwait	Kuwait	Arabic	dinar = 1000 fils

Country	*Capital*	*Language*	*Currency*
Laos	Vientiane	Lao	kip = 100 ats
Lebanon	Beirut	Arabic	pound = 100 piastres
Lesotho	Maseru	Sesotho, English	loti = 100 licente
Liberia	Monrovia	English	dollar = 100 cents
Libya	Tripoli	Arabic	dinar = 1000 dirhams
Liechtenstein	Vaduz	German	franc = 100 centimes
Luxemburg	Luxembourg	French	franc = 100 centimes
Macao	Macao	Portuguese	pataca = 100 avos
Madagascar	Antananarivo	French	franc = 100 centimes
Malawi	Lilongwe	English	kwacha = 100 tambala
Malaysia	Kuala Lumpur	Malay	ringgit (dollar) = 100 cents
Maldives	Malé	Divehi	rufiyaa = 100 laris
Mali	Bamako	French	franc = 100 centimes
Malta	Valletta	Maltese	pound = 100 cents
Mauritania	Nouakchott	Arabic, French	ouguiya = 5 khoums
Mauritius	Port Louis	English	rupee = 100 cents
Mexico	Mexico City	Spanish	peso = 100 centavos
Monaco	Monaco	French	franc = 100 centimes
Mongolia	Ulan Bátor	Khalkha Mongolian	tugrik = 100 mongo
Montserrat	Plymouth	English	dollar = 100 cents
Morocco	Rabat; summer capital Tangier	Arabic	dirham = 100 centimes
Mozambique	Maputo	Portuguese	metical = 100 centavos
Namibia	Windhoek	Afrikaans, English	rand = 100 cents
Nauru	Yaren	Nauruan, English	dollar = 100 cents
Nepal	Kathmandu	Nepali	rupee = 100 paisa
Netherlands	Amsterdam; seat of government The Hague	Dutch	gulder, guilder or florin = 100 cents
New Zealand	Wellington	English	dollar = 100 cents
Nicaragua	Managua	Spanish	córdoba = 100 centavos
Niger	Niamey	French	franc CFA
Nigeria	Lagos	English	naira = 100 kobo
Norway	Oslo	Norwegian	krone = 100 öre
Oman	Muscat	Arabic	rial = 1000 baiza
Pakistan	Islamabad	Urdu, English	rupee = 100 paisa
Panama	Panama	Spanish	balboa = 100 cents
Papua New Guinea	Port Moresby	Papuan, English	kina = 100 toea
Paraguay	Asunción	Spanish	guarani = 100 centimos
Peru	Lima	Spanish	sol = 100 centavos
Philippines	Manila	Pilipino, English	peso = 100 centavos
Poland	Warsaw	Polish	zloty = 100 groszy
Portugal	Lisbon	Portuguese	escudo = 100 centavos
Puerto Rico	San Juan	Spanish, English	dollar = 100 cents
Qatar	Doha	Arabic	riyal = 100 dirhams
Rumania	Bucharest	Rumanian	leu = 100 bani
Rwanda	Kigali	Kinyarwanda, French	franc = 100 centimes
St Helena	Jamestown	English	pound = 100 pence

Country	Capital	Language	Currency
St Kitts–Nevis	Basseterre	English	dollar = 100 cents
St Lucia	Castries	English	dollar = 100 cents
St Vincent	Kingstown	English	dollar = 100 cents
San Marino	San Marino	Italian	lira
São Tomé and Principe	São Tomé	Portuguese	dobra = 100 centavos
Saudi Arabia	Riyadh	Arabic	riyal = 20 qursh, 100 halalas
Senegal	Dakar	French	franc CFA
Seychelles	Victoria	English	rupee = 100 cents
Sierra Leone	Freetown	English	leone = 100 cents
Singapore	Singapore	Malay, English, Tamil, Chinese	dollar = 100 cents
Somalia	Mogadishu	Somali, Arabic	shilling = 100 cents
South Africa	Pretoria (administrative), Cape Town (legislative)	Afrikaans, English	rand = 100 cents
South-West Africa – see NAMIBIA			
Spain	Madrid	Spanish	peseta = 100 centimos
Sri Lanka	Colombo	Sinhala, Tamil, English	rupee = 100 cents
Sudan	Khartoum	Arabic	pound = 100 piastres, 1000 millièmes
Suriname	Paramaribo	Dutch	guilder or florin = 100 cents
Swaziland	Mbabane	siSwati, English	lilangeni = 100 cents
Sweden	Stockholm	Swedish	krona = 100 öre
Switzerland	Berne	French, German, Italian	franc = 100 centimes
Syria	Damascus	Arabic	pound = 100 piastres
Taiwan, Republic of China	Taipei	Mandarin Chinese	New Taiwan dollar = 100 cents
Tanzania	Dodoma, Dar-es-Salaam	Swahili, English	shilling = 100 cents
Thailand	Bangkok	Thai	baht = 100 stangs
Togo	Lomé	French	franc CFA
Tonga	Nukualofa	Tongan	pa'anga = 100 seniti
Trinidad and Tobago	Port of Spain	English	dollar = 100 cents
Tunisia	Tunis	Arabic	dinar = 1000 millimes
Turkey	Ankara	Turkish	lira = 100 kurus
Tuvalu	Funafuti	English, French	dollar = 100 cents
Uganda	Kampala	Swahili, English	shilling = 100 cents
Union of Soviet Socialist Republics	Moscow	Russian	rouble = 100 kopecks
United Arab Emirates	Abu Dhabi	Arabic	dirham = 100 fils
United Kingdom:	London	English	pound = 100 pence
England	London		
Northern Ireland	Belfast		
Scotland	Edinburgh		
Wales	Cardiff	English, Welsh	
United States of America	Washington, DC	English	dollar = 100 cents
Uruguay	Montevideo	Spanish	peso = 100 centésimos

Country	*Capital*	*Language*	*Currency*
Vanuatu	Vila	English, French	vatu (Vanuatuan franc)
Venezuela	Caracas	Spanish	bolivar = 100 cétimos
Vietnam	Hanoi	Vietnamese	dong = 10 hào, 100 xu
Western Samoa	Apia	English, Samoan	tala = 100 sene
Yemen Arab Republic	San'a	Arabic	riyal = 100 fils
Yemen, People's Democratic Republic of	Aden	Arabic	dinar = 1000 fils
Yugoslavia	Belgrade	Serbo-Croat, Slovene, Macedonian	dinar = 100 paras
Zaïre	Kinshasa	French	zaire = 100 makuta, 10,000 senghi
Zambia	Lusaka	English	kwacha = 100 ngwee
Zimbabwe	Harare	English, Shona, Ndebele	dollar = 100 cents

WORLD STANDARD TIMES

Standard time in different parts of the world is based on Greenwich mean time (GMT), which is the time shown at Greenwich, England through which the prime meridian of longitude passes. The world is divided into 24 time zones, each one hour apart. Zones to the east of that containing the prime meridian progressively add one hour to GMT to arrive at standard time, while zones to the west progressively lose one hour. The theoretical line at which the two sets of zones meet is called the International Date Line. The date is advanced one day when crossing the Date Line in a westerly direction and set back one day when crossing in an easterly direction.

The following table shows the time in various cities of the world when GMT is 12:00 noon.

Addis Ababa	15:00(+3)	Hong Kong	20:00(+8)
Alexandria	14:00(+2)	Istanbul	14:00(+2)
Amsterdam	13:00(+1)	Jakarta	19:00(+7)
Ankara	14:00(+2)	Jerusalem	14:00(+2)
Athens	14:00(+2)	Johannesburg	14:00(+2)
Auckland	24:00(+12)	Karachi	17:00(+5)
Baghdad	15:00(+3)	Kuala Lumpur	20:00(+8)
Bangkok	19:00(+7)	Kuwait	15:00(+3)
Beijing (Peking)	20:00(+8)	Lagos	13:00(+1)
Belfast	GMT	Leningrad	15:00(+3)
Belgrade	13:00(+1)	Lima	07:00(−5)
Berlin	13:00(+1)	London	GMT
Berne	13:00(+1)	Los Angeles	04:00(−8)
Bogota	07:00(−5)	Madrid	13:00(+1)
Bombay	17:30(+5½)	Manila	20:00(+8)
Bonn	13:00(+1)	Mecca	15:00(+3)
Brasilia	09:00(−3)	Melbourne	22:00(+10)
Brussels	13:00(+1)	Mexico City	06:00(−6)
Bucharest	14:00(+2)	Montevideo	09:00(−3)
Budapest	13:00(+1)	Montreal	07:00(−5)
Buenos Aires	09:00(−3)	Moscow	15:00(+3)
Cairo	14:00(+2)	Muscat	16:00(+4)
Calcutta	17:30(+5½)	Nagasaki	21:00(+9)
Cape Town	14:00(+2)	Nairobi	15:00(+3)
Caracas	08:00(−4)	New York	07:00(−5)
Casablanca	GMT	Oslo	13:00(+1)
Chicago	06:00(−6)	Ottawa	07:00(−5)
Copenhagen	13:00(+1)	Paris	13:00(+1)
Dar-es-Salaam	15:00(+3)	Perth	20:00(+8)
Darwin	21:30(+9½)	Prague	13:00(+1)
Delhi	17:30(+5½)	Pretoria	14:00(+2)
Dhaka	18:00(+6)	Quebec	07:00(−5)
Dublin	GMT	Rangoon	18:30(+6½)
Gdansk	13:00(+1)	Rio de Janeiro	09:00(−3)
Geneva	13:00(+1)	Riyadh	15:00(+3)
Havana	07:00(−5)	Rome	13:00(+1)
Helsinki	14:00(+2)	San Francisco	04:00(−8)

Santiago (Chile)	08:00(−4)	Tripoli	14:00(+2)
Seoul	21:00(+9)	Vancouver	04:00(−8)
Shanghai	20:00(+8)	Vienna	13:00(+1)
Singapore	20:00(+8)	Vladivistok	22:00(+10)
Stockholm	13:00(+1)	Warsaw	13:00(+1)
Sydney	22:00(+10)	Washington	07:00(−5)
Teheran	15:30(+3½)	Wellington	24:00(+12)
Tel Aviv	14:00(+2)	Yokohama	21:00(+9)
Tokyo	21:00(+9)	Zurich	13:00(+1)

Appendix II
Politics

SOVEREIGNS OF ENGLAND AND OF THE UNITED KINGDOM

Saxon Kings

Edwy	955
Edgar	959
Edward the Martyr	975
Ethelred the Unready	978
Edmund Ironside	1016

Danish Kings

Canute (Cnut)	1017
Harold I	1035
Hardicanute (Harthacnut)	1040

Saxon Kings (restored)

Edward the Confessor	1042
Harold II	1066

House of Normandy

William I (the Conqueror)	1066
William II	1087
Henry I	1100
Stephen	1135

House of Plantagenet

Henry II	1154
Richard I	1189
John	1199
Henry III	1216
Edward I	1272
Edward II	1307
Edward III	1327
Richard II	1377

House of Lancaster

Henry IV	1399
Henry V	1413
Henry VI	1422

House of York

Edward IV	1461
Edward V	1483
Richard III	1483

House of Tudor

Henry VII	1485
Henry VIII	1509
Edward VI	1547
Mary I	1553
Elizabeth I	1558

House of Stuart

James I (James VI of Scotland)	1603
Charles I	1625

The Commonwealth (declared in 1649)

Oliver Cromwell, Lord Protector	1653
Richard Cromwell	1658

House of Stuart (restored)

Charles II	1660
James II	1685
William III and Mary II	1689
Anne	1702

House of Hanover

George I	1714
George II	1727
George III	1760
George IV	1820
William IV	1830
Victoria	1837

House of Saxe-Coburg-Gotha

Edward VII	1901

House of Windsor

George V	1910
Edward VIII	1936
George VI	1936
Elizabeth II	1952–

PRIME MINISTERS OF GREAT BRITAIN

Name	Party	Year
Sir Robert Walpole	Whig	1721
Earl of Wilmington	Whig	1742
Henry Pelham	Whig	1743
Duke of Newcastle	Whig	1754
Duke of Devonshire	Whig	1756
Duke of Newcastle	Whig	1757
Earl of Bute	Tory	1762
George Grenville	Whig	1763
Marquis of Rockingham	Whig	1765
Earl of Chatham	Whig	1766
Duke of Grafton	Whig	1768
Lord North	Tory	1770
Marquis of Rockingham	Whig	1782
Earl of Shelburne	Whig	1782
Duke of Portland	Coalition	1783
William Pitt	Tory	1783
Henry Addington	Tory	1801
William Pitt	Tory	1804
Lord William Grenville	Whig	1806
Duke of Portland	Tory	1807
Spencer Perceval	Tory	1809
Earl of Liverpool	Tory	1812
George Canning	Tory	1827
Viscount Goderich	Tory	1827
Duke of Wellington	Tory	1828
Earl Grey	Whig	1830
Viscount Melbourne	Whig	1834
Duke of Wellington	Tory	1834
Sir Robert Peel	Conservative	1834
Viscount Melbourne	Whig	1835
Sir Robert Peel	Conservative	1841
Lord John Russell	Liberal	1846
Earl of Derby	Conservative	1852
Earl of Aberdeen	Peelite	1852
Viscount Palmerston	Liberal	1855
Earl of Derby	Conservative	1858
Viscount Palmerston	Liberal	1859
Earl Russell	Liberal	1865
Earl of Derby	Conservative	1866
Benjamin Disraeli	Conservative	1868
William Ewart Gladstone	Liberal	1868
Benjamin Disraeli	Conservative	1874
William Ewart Gladstone	Liberal	1880
Marquis of Salisbury	Conservative	1885
William Ewart Gladstone	Liberal	1886
Marquis of Salisbury	Conservative	1886
William Ewart Gladstone	Liberal	1892
Earl of Rosebery	Liberal	1894
Marquis of Salisbury	Conservative	1895
Arthur James Balfour	Conservative	1902
Sir Henry Campbell-Bannerman	Liberal	1905
Herbert Henry Asquith	Liberal	1908
Herbert Henry Asquith	Coalition	1915
David Lloyd George	Coalition	1916
Andrew Bonar Law	Conservative	1922
Stanley Baldwin	Conservative	1923
James Ramsay MacDonald	Labour	1924
Stanley Baldwin	Conservative	1924
James Ramsay MacDonald	Labour	1929
James Ramsay MacDonald	National	1931
Stanley Baldwin	National	1935
Neville Chamberlain	National	1937
Winston Spencer Churchill	Coalition	1940
Clement Richard Attlee	Labour	1945
Sir Winston Spencer Churchill	Conservative	1951
Sir Anthony Eden	Conservative	1955
Harold Macmillan	Conservative	1957
Sir Alexander Douglas-Home	Conservative	1963
Harold Wilson	Labour	1964
Edward Heath	Conservative	1970
Harold Wilson	Labour	1974
James Callaghan	Labour	1976
Margaret Thatcher	Conservative	1979–

PRIME MINISTERS OF AUSTRALIA

Name	Year
Edmund Barton	1901
Alfred Deakin	1903
John C. Watson	1904
George Houstoun Reid	1904
Alfred Deakin	1905
Andrew Fisher	1908
Alfred Deakin	1909
Andrew Fisher	1910
Joseph Cook	1913
Andrew Fisher	1914
William M. Hughes	1915
Stanley M. Bruce	1923
James H. Scullin	1929
Joseph A. Lyons	1932
Robert Gordon Menzies	1939
Arthur William Fadden	1941
John Curtin	1941
Joseph Benedict Chifley	1945
Robert Gordon Menzies	1949
Harold Edward Holt	1966
John Grey Gorton	1968
William McMahon	1971
Gough Whitlam	1972
J. Malcolm Fraser	1975
Robert J.L. Hawke	1983–

PRIME MINISTERS OF CANADA

Name	Year
John A. Macdonald	1867
Alexander Mackenzie	1873
John A. Macdonald	1878
John J.C. Abbott	1891
John S.D. Thompson	1892
Mackenzie Bowell	1894

Charles Tupper 1896
Wilfrid Laurier 1896
Robert L. Borden 1911
Arthur Meighen 1920
W.L. Mackenzie King 1921
Arthur Meighen 1926
W.L. Mackenzie King 1926
Richard B. Bennett 1930
W.L. Mackenzie King 1935
Louis Stephen St Laurent 1948
John George Diefenbaker 1957
Lester B. Pearson 1963
Pierre Elliott Trudeau 1968
Joseph Clark 1979
Pierre Elliott Trudeau 1980
John Turner 1984
Brian Mulroney 1984–

PRIME MINISTERS OF NEW ZEALAND

Henry Sewell 1856
William Fox 1856
Edward William Stafford 1856
William Fox 1861
Alfred Domett 1862
Frederick Whitaker 1863
Frederick Aloysius Weld 1864
Edward William Stafford 1865
William Fox 1869
Edward William Stafford 1872
George Marsden Waterhouse 1872
William Fox 1873
Julius Vogel 1873
Daniel Pollen 1875
Julius Vogel 1876
Harry Albert Atkinson 1876
George Grey 1877
John Hall 1879
Frederick Whitaker 1882
Harry Albert Atkinson 1883
Robert Stout 1884
Harry Albert Atkinson 1884
Robert Stout 1884
Harry Albert Atkinson 1887
John Ballance 1891
Richard John Seddon 1893
William Hall-Jones 1906
Joseph George Ward 1906
Thomas Mackenzie 1912
William Ferguson Massey 1912
Francis Henry Dillon Bell 1925
Joseph Gordon Coates 1925
Joseph George Ward 1928
George William Forbes 1930
Michael J. Savage 1935
Peter Fraser 1940
Sidney G. Holland 1949
Walter Nash 1957
Keith J. Holyoake 1960
John R. Marshall 1972
Norman Kirk 1972
Wallace Rowling 1974
Robert D. Muldoon 1975
Hon. David Lange 1984
Geoffrey Palmer 1989–

PRESIDENTS OF THE UNITED STATES OF AMERICA

George Washington Federalist 1789
John Adams Federalist 1797
Thomas Jefferson Democratic-Republican 1801
James Madison Democratic-Republican 1809
James Monroe Democratic-Republican 1817
John Quincy Adams Independent 1825
Andrew Jackson Democrat 1829
Martin Van Buren Democrat 1837
William Henry Harrison Whig 1841
John Tyler Whig 1841
James Knox Polk Democrat 1845
Zachary Taylor Whig 1849
Millard Fillmore Whig 1850
Franklin Pierce Democrat 1853
James Buchanan Democrat 1857
Abraham Lincoln Republican 1861
Andrew Johnson Democrat 1865
Ulysses Simpson Grant Republican 1869
Rutherford Birchard Hayes Republican 1877
James Abram Garfield Republican 1881
Chester Alan Arthur Republican 1881
Grover Cleveland Democrat 1885
Benjamin Harrison Republican 1889
Grover Cleveland Democrat 1893
William McKinley Republican 1897
Theodore Roosevelt Republican 1901
William Howard Taft Republican 1909
Woodrow Wilson Democrat 1913
Warren Gamaliel Harding Republican 1921
Calvin Coolidge Republican 1923
Herbert Hoover Republican 1929
Franklin Delano Roosevelt Democrat 1933
Harry S. Truman Democrat 1945
Dwight D. Eisenhower Republican 1953
John F. Kennedy Democrat 1961
Lyndon B. Johnson Democrat 1963
Richard M. Nixon Republican 1969
Gerald R. Ford Republican 1974
James Earl Carter Democrat 1977
Ronald W. Reagan Republican 1981
George H.W. Bush Republican 1989–

Appendix III
Science
WEIGHTS AND MEASURES

1. IMPERIAL WITH METRIC EQUIVALENTS

Linear Measure

1 inch	= 25.4 millimetres exactly
1 foot = 12 inches	= 0.3048 metre exactly
1 yard = 3 feet	= 0.9144 metre exactly
1 (statute) mile = 1,760 yards	= 1.609 kilometres

Square Measure

1 square inch	= 6.45 sq. centimetres
1 square foot = 144 sq. in.	= 9.29 sq. decimetres
1 square yard = 9 sq. ft.	= 0.836 sq. metre
1 acre = 4,840 sq. yd.	= 0.405 hectare
1 square mile = 640 acres	= 259 hectares

Cubic Measure

1 cubic inch	= 16.4 cu. centimetres
1 cubic foot = 1,728 cu. in.	= 0.0283 cu. metre
1 cubic yard = 27 cu. ft.	= 0.765 cu. metre

Capacity Measure

British

1 pint = 20 fluid oz. = 34.68 cu. in.	= 0.568 litre
1 quart = 2 pints	= 1.136 litres
1 gallon = 4 quarts	= 4.546 litres
1 peck = 2 gallons	= 9.092 litres
1 bushel = 4 pecks	= 36.4 litres
1 quarter = 8 bushels	= 2.91 hectolitres

Avoirdupois Weight

1 grain	= 0.065 gram
1 dram	= 1.772 grams
1 ounce = 16 drams	= 28.35 grams
1 pound = 16 ounces = 7,000 grains	= 0.4536 kilogram
1 stone = 14 pounds	= 6.35 kilograms
1 quarter = 2 stones	= 12.70 kilograms
1 hundredweight = 4 quarters	= 50.80 kilograms
1 (long) ton = 20 hundredweight	= 1.016 tonnes
1 short ton = 2,000 pounds	= 0.907 tonne

2. METRIC, WITH IMPERIAL EQUIVALENTS

Linear Measure

1 millimetre	= 0.039 inch
1 centimetre = 10 mm	= 0.394 inch
1 decimetre = 10 cm	= 3.94 inches
1 metre = 10 dm	= 1.094 yards
1 decametre = 10 m	= 10.94 yards
1 hectometre = 100 m	= 109.4 yards
1 kilometre = 1,000 m	= 0.6214 mile

Square Measure

1 square centimetre	= 0.155 sq. inch
1 square metre = 10,000 sq. cm	= 1.196 sq. yards
1 are = 100 sq. metres	= 119.6 sq. yards
1 hectare = 100 ares	= 2.471 acres
1 square kilometre = 100 hectares	= 0.386 sq. mile

Cubic Measure

1 cubic centimetre	= 0.061 cu. inch
1 cubic metre = 1,000,000 cu. cm	= 1.308 cu. yards

Capacity Measure

1 millilitre	= 0.002 pint (British)
1 centilitre = 10 ml	= 0.018 pint
1 decilitre = 10 cl	= 0.176 pint
1 litre = 10 dl	= 1.76 pints
1 decalitre = 10 l	= 2.20 gallons
1 hectolitre = 100 l	= 2.75 bushels
1 kilolitre = 1,000 l	= 3.44 quarters

Weight

1 milligram	= 0.015 grain
1 centigram = 10 mg	= 0.154 grain
1 decigram = 10 cg	= 1.543 grain
1 gram = 10 dg	= 15.43 grain
1 decagram = 10 g	= 5.64 drams
1 hectogram = 100 g	= 3.527 ounces
1 kilogram = 1,000 g	= 2.205 pounds
1 tonne (metric ton) = 1,000 kg	= 0.984 (long) ton

THE CHEMICAL ELEMENTS

Element	*Symbol*	*Atomic number*
actinium	Ac	89
aluminium	Al	13
americium	Am	95
antimony	Sb	51
argon	Ar	18
arsenic	As	33
astatine	At	85
barium	Ba	56
berkelium	Bk	97
beryllium	Be	4
bismuth	Bi	83
boron	B	5
bromine	Br	35
cadmium	Cd	48
caesium	Cs	55
calcium	Ca	20
californium	Cf	98
carbon	C	6
cerium	Ce	58
chlorine	Cl	17
chromium	Cr	24
cobalt	Co	27
copper	Cu	29
curium	Cm	96
dysprosium	Dy	66
einsteinium	Es	99
erbium	Er	68
europium	Eu	63
fermium	Fm	100
fluorine	F	9
francium	Fr	87
gadolinium	Gd	64
gallium	Ga	31
germanium	Ge	32
gold	Au	79
hafnium	Hf	72
helium	He	2
holmium	Ho	67
hydrogen	H	1
indium	In	49
iodine	I	53
iridium	Ir	77
iron	Fe	26
krypton	Kr	36
lanthanum	La	57
lawrencium	Lr	103
lead	Pb	82
lithium	Li	3
lutetium	Lu	71
magnesium	Mg	12
manganese	Mn	25
mendelevium	Md	101
mercury	Hg	80
molybdenum	Mo	42
neodymium	Nd	60
neon	Ne	10
neptunium	Np	93
nickel	Ni	28
niobium	Nb	41
nitrogen	N	7
nobelium	No	102
osmium	Os	76
oxygen	O	8
palladium	Pd	46
phosphorus	P	15
platinum	Pt	78
plutonium	Pu	94
polonium	Po	84
potassium	K	19
praseodymium	Pr	59
promethium	Pm	61
protactinium	Pa	91
radium	Ra	88
radon	Rn	86
rhenium	Re	75
rhodium	Rh	45
rubidium	Rb	37
ruthenium	Ru	44
samarium	Sm	62
scandium	Sc	21
selenium	Se	34
silicon	Si	14
silver	Ag	47
sodium	Na	11
strontium	Sr	38
sulphur	S	16
tantalum	Ta	73
technetium	Tc	43
tellurium	Te	52
terbium	Tb	65
thallium	Tl	81
thorium	Th	90
thulium	Tm	69
tin	Sn	50
titanium	Ti	22
tungsten	W	74
unnilhexium	Unh	106
unnilquadium	Unq	104
unnilpentium	Unp	105
unnilseptium	Uns	107
uranium	U	92
vanadium	V	23
xenon	Xe	54
ytterbium	Yb	70
yttrium	Y	39
zinc	Zn	30
zirconium	Zr	40

Appendix IV

Signs and Symbols

ROMAN NUMERALS

I *or* i = 1	V *or* v = 5	X *or* x = 10	L *or* l = 50
C *or* c = 100	D *or* d = 500	M *or* m = 1000	

1	=	I	30	=	XXX
2	=	II	31	=	XXXI
3	=	III	32, etc.	=	XXXII
4	=	IV (also IIII[1])	40	=	XL (also XXXX)
5	=	V	41	=	XLI
6	=	VI	42, etc.	=	XLII
7	=	VII	50	=	L
8	=	VIII	60	=	LX
9	=	IX	70	=	LXX
10	=	X	80	=	LXXX
11	=	XI	90	=	XC (also LXXXX)
12	=	XII	100	=	C
13	=	XIII	101	=	CI
14	=	XIV	102, etc.	=	CII
15	=	XV	150	=	CL
16	=	XVI	200	=	CC
17	=	XVII	300	=	CCC
18	=	XVIII	400	=	CD (also CCCC)
19	=	XIX	500	=	D (also IↃ[2])
20	=	XX	600	=	DC (also IↃC)
21	=	XXI	700	=	DCC (also IↃCC)
22	=	XXII	800	=	DCCC (also IↃCCC)
23	=	XXIII	900	=	CM
24	=	XXIV	1000	=	M
25	=	XXV	2000	=	MM
26	=	XXVI	5000	=	$\underline{\mathrm{V}}$[3]
27	=	XXVII	10,000	=	$\underline{\mathrm{X}}$
28	=	XXVIII	100,000	=	$\underline{\mathrm{C}}$
29	=	XXIX	1,000,000	=	$\underline{\mathrm{M}}$

[1] In modern use IV is preferred to IIII although IIII can still be seen on clock faces, etc.

[2] In ancient and medieval times the symbol Ↄ, called the *apostrophus*, was used after I to express the number 500 and repeated after IↃ to express numbers ten times greater, as IↃↃ=5000, IↃↃↃ=50,000. Preceding such a number with the symbol C, repeated as many times as the symbol Ↄ appeared, multiplied the number by two, thus CCIↃↃ=10,000, CCCIↃↃↃ=100,000.

[3] In medieval times and later, a line over a symbol indicated a multiple of a thousand.

GREEK ALPHABET

Α	α	alpha	a
Β	β	beta	b
Γ	γ	gamma	g
Δ	δ	delta	d
Ε	ε	epsilon	e
Ζ	ζ	zeta	z
Η	η	eta	ē
Θ	θ	theta	th
Ι	ι	iota	i
Κ	ϰ	kappa	k
Λ	λ	lambda	l
Μ	μ	mu	m
Ν	ν	nu	n
Ξ	ξ	xi	x
Ο	ο	omicron	o
Π	π	pi	p
Ρ	ϱ	rho	r
Σ	σ	sigma	s
Τ	τ	tau	t
Υ	υ	upsilon	u
Φ	ϕ	phi	ph
Χ	χ	chi	ch/kh (pronounced hh as in loch)
Ψ	ψ	psi	ps
Ω	ω	omega	ō

RUSSIAN ALPHABET

А	а	a
Б	б	b
В	в	v
Г	г	g
Д	д	d
Е	е	e/ye (as in yet)
Ё	ё	ë/yo (as in yawn)
Ж	ж	zh
З	з	z
И	и	i (pronounced ee as in sheep)
Й	й	ĭ/y
К	к	k
Л	л	l
М	м	m
Н	н	n
О	о	o
П	п	p
Р	р	r
С	с	s
Т	т	t
У	у	u (pronounced oo as in boot)
Ф	ф	f
Х	х	kh (pronounced *hh* as in loch)
Ц	ц	ts
Ч	ч	ch
Ш	ш	sh
Щ	щ	shch
Ъ	ъ	indicates that the preceding consonant is not palatalized
Ы	ы	i/ȳ
Ь	ь	indicates that the preceding consonant is palatalized
Э	э	e (as in led)
Ю	ю	yu (as in universal)
Я	я	ya (as in yard)

ARITHMETIC, ALGEBRA, GEOMETRY

+	plus, the sign of addition: also of positive (*Elec. and Mag.*), and compression (*Eng.*)
−	minus, the sign of subtraction; also of negative (*Elec. and Mag.*), and tension (*Eng.*)
×	the sign of multiplication.
÷	the sign of division.
:	is to } the signs of proportion.
::	as } the signs of proportion.
:	is to } the signs of proportion.
∵	because.
∴	therefore.
=	equals; the sign of equality.
≡	equivalent to, representing, varies as.
α	infinity.
$\sqrt{}$	square root.
$\sqrt[3]{}$	cube root.
$\sqrt[4]{}$	fourth root, etc.
$\sqrt[n]{}$	n^{th} root.
≠	is unequal to.
>	is greater than.
≯	is not greater than.
<	is less than.
≮	is not less than.
∥	is parallel to.
∦	is not parallel to.
⊥	is perpendicular to.
±	equilateral.
∠	angle.
∠s	angles.
∟	right angle.
≚	equiangular.
△	triangle.
□	square.
▭	rectangle, or parallelogram.
⊙	circle.
○	circumference.
⌓	semicircle.
◔	quadrant.
⌒	arc.
∼	difference.
0	the cipher, zero.
°	degrees, ′minutes, ″seconds, ‴thirds.
′	feet, ″inches.
c	constant.
d	differential (in calculus).
f	integration (in calculus).
E	modulus of elasticity.
F *or f*	functions.
g	gravity.
k	coefficient.
M	modulus.
n	any number.
δ	variation.
Δ	finite difference.
ϵ	base of hyperbolic logarithms.
λ	latitude.
π	ratio of circumference to diameter = 3·14159.
R, *r*, ϱ	radius.
Σ	sum of finite quantities.

ASTRONOMY

⊙	the sun.
●	new moon.
☽	first quarter of the moon.
○	full moon.
☾	last quarter of the moon.
☿	Mercury.
♀	Venus.
⊕ *or* ♁	earth.
♂	Mars.
♃	Jupiter.
♄	Saturn.
♅	Uranus.
♆	Neptune.
⦵	planet.
☄	comet.
①, ②,	etc., *or* *1, *2, etc. asteroids, in order of discovery.
✻	fixed star.
☌	conjunction.
☍	opposition.
△	trine.
□	quadrature.
☊	ascending node.
☋	descending node.
+	north.
−	south.
a	right ascension.
ß	celestial latitude.
δ	declination.
e	eccentricity.
i	inclination to the ecliptic.
λ	longitude.
μ	mean daily motion.
π	longitude of perihelion.
q	perihelion distance of a comet.
ø	latitude.
°	degree of arc.
′	minute(s) of arc.
″	second(s) of arc.

THE ZODIAC

Spring

♈ Aries, the ram (March).
♉ Taurus, the bull (April).
♊ Gemini, the twins (May).

Summer

♋ Cancer, the crab (June).
♌ Leo, the lion (July).
♍ Virgo, the virgin (August).

Autumn

♎ Libra, the scales (September).
♏ Scorpio, the scorpion (October).
♐ Sagittarius, the archer (November).

Winter

♑ Capricornus, the goat (December).
♒ Aquarius, the water-carrier (January).
♓ Pisces, the fishes (February).

BOTANY

0 absent.
① annual.
② biennial.
⌒ climbing plant.
Δ evergreen.
♂ male.
♀ female.
☿ hermaphrodite.
× hybrid.
∞ number indefinite.
⚥ *or* ♂–♀ monœcious.
♀ ♂ *or* ⚲:♀ diœcious.
⊙ monocarpous.
§ naturalised plant.
0 none.
† ornamental plant.
♃ perennial.
? doubtful.
! personally verified.
♀☿♂ *or* ♀⚲♀ polygamous.
) winding to left.
(winding to right.
♄ woody-stem plant.
‡ useful plant.

CHEMICAL

<> *or* ♁ antimony.
⚩ *or* o-o arsenic.
☍ cobalt.
♀ copper.
⊙ gold.
♂ iron.
♄ lead.
☿ mercury.
☽ silver.
♃ tin.
♃ zinc.

Appendix V
Names

THE PLAYS OF SHAKESPEARE

Estimated date of writing	
1589–92	1, 2, 3 Henry VI
	Richard III
	The Comedy of Errors
1593–4	Titus Andronicus
	The Taming of the Shrew
	The Two Gentlemen of Verona
	Love's Labour's Lost
1595–6	Romeo and Juliet
	A Midsummer Night's Dream
	Richard II
	King John
	The Merchant of Venice
1597–8	1, 2 Henry IV
	The Merry Wives of Windsor
	Much Ado About Nothing

Estimated date of writing	
1599–1600	Henry V
	Julius Caesar
	As You Like It
	Twelfth Night
1601–2	Hamlet
	Troilus and Cressida
1603–4	All's Well That Ends Well
	Measure for Measure
	Othello
1605–6	King Lear
	Macbeth
1607–8	Antony and Cleopatra
	Timon of Athens
	Coriolanus
	Pericles
1609–10	Cymbeline
1611–12	The Winter's Tale
	The Tempest
1613	Henry VIII
	Two Noble Kinsmen

BOOKS OF THE BIBLE

OLD TESTAMENT

Protestant canon	*Roman Catholic canon*
Genesis	Genesis
Exodus	Exodus
Leviticus	Leviticus
Numbers	Numbers
Deuteronomy	Deuteronomy
Joshua	Joshua
Judges	Judges
Ruth	Ruth
1 Samuel	1 Samuel
2 Samuel	2 Samuel
1 Kings	1 Kings
2 Kings	2 Kings
1 Chronicles	1 Chronicles
2 Chronicles	2 Chronicles
Ezra	Ezra
Nehemiah	Nehemiah
	Tobit
	Judith
Esther	Esther
	1 Maccabees
	2 Maccabees
Job	Job
Psalms	Psalms
Proverbs	Proverbs
Ecclesiastes	Ecclesiastes
Song of Solomon	Song of Songs
	Wisdom
	Ecclesiasticus
Isaiah	Isaiah
Jeremiah	Jeremiah
Lamentations	Lamentations
	Baruch
Ezekiel	Ezekiel
Daniel	Daniel
Hosea	Hosea
Joel	Joel
Amos	Amos
Obadiah	Obadiah
Jonah	Jonah
Micah	Micah
Nahum	Nahum
Habakkuk	Habakkuk
Zephaniah	Zephaniah
Haggai	Haggai
Zechariah	Zechariah
Malachi	Malachi

Protestant apocrypha

1 Esdras
2 Esdras
Tobit
Judith
Additions to Esther
Wisdom of Solomon
Ecclesiasticus
Baruch
Prayer of Azariah and the Song of the Three Holy Children
Susanna
Bel and the Dragon
The Prayer of Manasses
1 Maccabees
2 Maccabees

NEW TESTAMENT

Matthew
Mark
Luke
John
Acts of the Apostles
Romans
1 Corinthians
2 Corinthians
Galatians
Ephesians
Philippians
Colossians
1 Thessalonians
2 Thessalonians
1 Timothy
2 Timothy
Titus
Philemon
Hebrews
James
1 Peter
2 Peter
1 John
2 John
3 John
Jude
Revelation

AN ETYMOLOGICAL TABLE OF FIRST NAMES

Aaron *m.* perh. mountaineer [Heb.] or of Egypt. origin.
Abel *m.* breath. [Heb.]
Abigail *f.* father of exaltation (also **abb(e)y, Abbie, Gail, Gale, Gayle**). [Heb.]
Abner *m.* father of light. [Heb.]
Abraham *m.* father of a multitude (also **Abe, Abie, Abram, Bram**). [Heb.]
Absalom *m.* father of peace (also **Axel**). [Heb.]
Ada *f.* perh. happy, joyful or form of ADÈLE or ADELAIDE (also **Addie, Addy, Aida**). [Teut.]
Adam *m.* earth. [Heb.]
Adelaide *f.* noble sort. [Norm. from Teut.]
Adèle *f.* noble (also **Adela, Adelina, Adeline, Addy**). [F. from Teut.]
Adolf *m.* noble wolf (also **Adolph(e), Adolphus**). [Teut.]
Adrian *m.* man from Adria, a former town in Italy (also **Adrien, Hadrian**). [L.]
Adrienne *f.* fem. of ADRIAN (also **Adrian(n)a, Adrien(n)e**).
Agatha *f.* good (also **Aggie, Aggy**). [Gr.]
Agnes *f.* pure, chaste (also **Aggie, Aggy, Annis, Ines, Inez, Nessa, Nessie, Nesta, Ynes**). [Gr.]
Aileen *f.* EILEEN, HELEN. [Ang.-Ir.]
Alan *m.* prob. harmony (also **Al, Allan, Allen, Allyn, Alun**). [Celt.]
Alana *f.* fem. of ALAN.
Alasdair, Alastair *m.* ALEXANDER.
Albert *m.* noble and famous (also **Al, Bert**). [Teut.]
Alberta *f.* fem. of ALBERT (also **Albertina, Albertine**).
Aldous *m.* old (also **Aldis, Aldus**). [Norm.]
Alethea *f.* truth. [Gr.]
Alexander *m.* defender of mankind (also **Alasdair, Alastair, Alister, Alec(k), Alex, Sandy, Sa(u)nders, Sasha, Sacha**). [Gr.]
Alexandra *f.* fem. of ALEXANDER (also **Alex, Alexa, Sandie, Sandy, Sandra, Zandra**).
Alexis *m., f.* to defend, help (also **Alex, Alexa** (*f.*), **Alexia** (*f.*)). [Gr.]
Alfonso *m.* ALPHONSUS.
Alfred *m.* elf (wise) counsel (also **Al, Alf, Alfie**). [A.-S.]
Alfreda *f.* fem. of ALFRED.
Algernon *m.* moustached (also **Algie, Algy**). [Norm.]
Alice *f.* nobility (also **Alicia, Alisa, Alissa, Allis, Al(l)ys, Al(l)ison, Allie, Ally**). [Norm. from Teut.]
Alison *f.* ALICE.
Allan, Allen *m.* ALAN.
Alma *f.* nourishing, fostering. [L.]
Aloysius *m.* LOUIS (also **Aloys**).
Alphonsus *m.* noble and ready (also **Alphonse, Alphonso, Alfonso, Alonso**). [Teut.]
Althea *f.* healer. [Gr.]
Alvin *m.* noble friend (also **Alwin, Alwyn, Aylwin**). [A.-S.]
Amanda *f.* worthy of being loved (also **Mandy**). [L.]
Ambrose *m.* of the immortals. [Gr.]
Amelia *f.* industrious, labouring (also **Amalia**). [Teut.]
Amos *m.* carrying a burden, strong. [Heb.]
Amy *f.* beloved (also **Aimee**). [F.]
Anastasia *f.* resurrection (also **Stac(e)y, Stacie**). [Gr.]
Andrea *f.* fem. of ANDREW (also **Andri(a)na, Andree**).
Andrew *m.* manly (also **Andre, Andie, Andy, Drew**). [Gr.]
Aneurin *m.* perh. honour, from L. *Honorius* (also **Nye**). [W.]
Angela *f.* angel, messenger (also **Angelina, Angeline, Angelita, Angie**). [Gr.]
Angelica *f.* angelic (also **Angelique**). [L.]
Angharad *f.* most dear. [W.]
Angus *m.* one choice. [Celt.]
Anita *f.* ANNE. [Sp.]
Annabel *f.* prob. from *Amabel*, lovable (also **Annabella, Annabelle, Bel, Bella, Belle**). [O.F. from L.]
Anne *f.* grace (also **Ann, Anna, Annie, Anita, Annette, Annika, Hannah, Nan, Nan(n)a, Nancy, Nanette, Nina, Ninette, Ninon**). [Heb.]
Annis *f.* AGNES.
Anselm *m.* divine helmet. [Teut.]
Anthea *f.* flowery. [Gr.]
Anthony *m.* from the Rom. family name *Antonius*. (also **Antony, Anton, Antoine, Antonio, Tony**). [L.]
Antonia *f.* fem. of ANTHONY (also **Antoinette, Antonina, Netta, Nettie, Netty, Toni**).
Arabella *f.* prob. from *Annabella* (see ANNABEL) (also **Bel, Bella, Belle**).
Archibald *m.* genuine and brave (also **Archie, Archy**). [Teut.]
Arlene *f.* perh. from *Adeline* (see ADÈLE) or MARLENE.
Arnold *m.* eagle strength (also **Arne, Arnie**). [Teut.]
Arthur *m.* perh. bear, bearkeeper, or stone (also **Art, Artie**) [Celt.]
Asa *m.* healer. [Heb.]
Ashley *m.* ash wood. [A.-S.]
Astrid *f.* god-strength. [O.-N.]
Auberon *m.* prob. from AUBREY.
Aubrey *m.* elf ruler. [Teut.]
Audrey *f.* noble strength (also **Audrie, Audra**). [A.-S.]
Augusta *f.* fem. of AUGUSTUS.
Augustus *m.* magnificent, exalted (also **Augustine, Gus, Gussie**) [L.]
Aurelia *f.* golden. [L.]
Aurora *f.* dawn. [L.]
Austin, Austen *m.* contr. forms of *Augustine* (see AUGUSTUS).
Avril *f.* perh. boar slayer [A.-S.]; April [F.] (also **Averil**).
Axel *m.* Scand. form of ABSALOM.
Aylwin *m.* ALVIN.

Barbara *f.* foreign woman (also **Barbra, Barbie, Bab, Babs**). [Gr.]
Barnabas *m.* son of consolation (also **Barnaby, Barn(e)y**). [Aram.]
Barry *m.* spear. [Gael.]
Bartholomew *m.* son of Talmai (also **Barthelmey, Bartley, Bart, Bat**). [Heb.]
Basil *m.* royal, kingly. [Gr.]
Beatrix *f.* bringer of joy (also **Beatrice, Bea, Bee, Trix, Trixie**). [L.]
Becky *f.* REBECCA.
Belinda *f.* from a compound word, the second element meaning snake. [Teut.]
Bella, Belle *f.* short for *Isabella* (see ISABEL), *Annabella* (see ANNABEL), ARABELLA; It. *bella* beautiful.
Benedict *m.* blessed (also **Benedick, Bennett, Bennet, Benito, Ben**). [L.]

Benjamin *m.* son of the right hand (also **Ben, Benny, Benjy**). [Heb.]
Berenice *f.* bringer of victory (also **Bernice, Bunny, Veronica**). [Gr.]
Bernadette *f.* fem. of BERNARD.
Bernard *m.* strong as a bear (also **Barnard, Barn(e)y, Bernie**). [Teut.]
Bert *m.* short for ALBERT, BERTRAM, EGBERT, HERBERT, ROBERT.
Bertha *f.* bright. [Teut.]
Bertram *m.* bright raven (also **Bertrand, Bert, Bertie**). [Teut.]
Beryl *f.* from the precious green stone. [Gr.]
Bess, Bessie, Bet, Beth *f.* ELIZABETH.
Bethany *f.* house of dates. [Heb.]
Betsy, Bette, Betty *f.* ELIZABETH.
Beverley *m., f.* beaver stream (also **Beverly, Bev**). [A.-S.]
Bianca *f.* white. [It.]
Biddy *f.* BRIDGET.
Bill, Billie[1], **Billy** *m.* WILLIAM.
Billie[2] *f.* WILHELMINA.
Blake *m.* black, dark-complexioned or pale, fair. [A.-S.]
Blanche *f.* white, fair. [F.]
Blodwen *f.* white flowers (also **Blodwyn**). [W.]
Bob, Bobby *m.* ROBERT.
Bonnie *f.* pretty. [Sc.]
Boris *m.* fight. [Rus.]
Bram *m.* ABRAHAM.
Brenda *f.* fiery sword [Scand.] or fem. of BRENDAN.
Brendan *m.* perh. stinking hair or form of BRIAN. [Gael.]
Brent *m.* hill. [A.-S.]
Brett *m.* Breton. [M.E.]
Brian *m.* perh. hill (also **Brien, Bryan, Briant, Bryant**). [Celt.]
Bridget *f.* strength (also **Bride, Bridie, Brigid, Brigit, Briggite, Biddy**). [Ir.]
Bronwen *f.* white breast. [W.]
Bruce *m.* from the surname. [Norm.]
Bruno *m.* brown. [Teut.]
Bryan(t) *m.* BRIAN.
Bryony *f.* from the plant (also **Briony**). [Gr.]
Bunny *f.* BERENICE.

Caitlin *f.* Ir. form of KATHERINE.
Caleb *m.* dog or intrepid (also **Cal**). [Heb.]
Cal(l)um *m.* dove. [L.]
Calvin *m.* bald (also **Cal**). [F.]
Cameron *m.* crooked nose. [Gael.]
Camilla *f.* origin unknown, acc. to Virgil the name of a queen of the Volsci (also **Camille**).
Campbell *m.* crooked mouth. [Gael.]
Candida *f.* white (also **Candy**). [L.]
Cara *f.* dear, beloved (also **Carina, Carita**). [It.]
Carl *m.* CHARLES (also **Karl**).
Carla *f.* fem. of *Carl* (see CHARLES).
Carlotta *f.* CHARLOTTE.
Carmel *f.* garden (also **Carmel(l)a, Carmelita**). [Heb.]
Carmen *f.* song (also **Charmaine**). [L.]
Carol *m., f.* CHARLES, CAROLINE.
Caroline *f.* fem. of CHARLES (also **Carol, Carole, Carolyn, Carline, Caro, Carrie**).
Cary *m.* from the Eng. surname.
Cassandra *f.* name of a legendary Trojan princess (see dictionary entry) (also **Cass, Cassie**).
Catharine, Catherine, Cathleen, Cathy *f.* KATHERINE.
Catriona *f.* KATHERINE. [Gael.]
Cecil *m.* blind. [L.]
Cecilia *f.* fem. of CECIL (also **Cecily, Cicely, Celia, Sisley, Ciss, Cissy, Sis, Sissy**).
Cedric *m.* from Sir Walter Scott's character in *Ivanhoe*, perh. a mistake for Cerdic, king of W. Saxony.
Celeste *f.* heavenly (also **Celestine**). [L.]
Celia *f.* from the Rom. family name *Caelius*, perh. meaning of heaven; CECILIA (also **Sheila, Shelagh**).
Chad *m.* warlike or battle. [A.-S.]
Charity *f.* charity, Christian love (also **Cherry, Cheryl**). [Eng. from L.]
Charlene *f.* fem. of CHARLES (also **Charleen, Charline**).
Charles *m.* man (also **Carl, Karl, Carol, Charley, Charlie, Chas, Chay, Chuck**). [Teut.]
Charlotte *f.* fem. of CHARLES (also **Carlotta, Charlie, Lottie, Lotty**).
Charmaine *f.* CARMEN.
Cherie *f.* darling (also **Cherry, Cheryl, Sherry, Sherrie**). [F.]
Cherry *f.* CHARITY, CHERIE (also **Cheryl, Cher**).
Chloe *f.* green shoot. [Gr.]
Christabel *f.* beautiful Christian. [L.]
Christian *m.* follower of Christ (also **Chris, Christie, Christy**). [L.]
Christine *f.* follower of Christ (also **Christina, Christiana, Chris, Chrissy, Kirsten, Kirsty**). [L.]
Christopher *m.* Christ bearer (also **Chris, Kris, Kit**). [Gr.]
Chuck *m.* CHARLES.
Cicely *f.* CECILIA.
Cilla *f.* PRISCILLA.
Clara *f.* bright, clear (also **Clare, Claire, Clarinda, Clarice, Klarissa, Clarrie**). [L.]
Claud *m.* lame (also **Claude, Claudius**). [L.]
Claudia *f.* fem. of CLAUD (also **Claudette, Claudine**).
Clemence *f.* fem. of CLEMENT (also **Clemency, Clementine, Clementina**).
Clement *m.* merciful (also **Clem, Clemmie**). [L.]
Clive *m.* cliff. [A.-S.]
Clyde *m.* from the Scottish river.
Colin *m.* orig. F. dim. of NICHOLAS; Gael. *caileann* pup, youth.
Colleen *f.* girl. [Ir.]
Conrad *m.* bold counsellor (also **Konrad, Curt, Kurt**). [Teut.]
Constance *f.* constancy (also **Constantina, Connie**). [L.]
Constantine *m.* firm, steadfast. [L.]
Cora *f.* maiden, girl (also **Corrine, Corrinna**). [Gr.]
Cordelia *f.* perh. warm-hearted [L.] or jewel of the sea [W.]
Cornelia *f.* fem. of CORNELIUS.
Cornelius *m.* horn (also **Cornel, Corn(e)y**). [L.]
Cosmo *m.* order (also **Cosimo**). [Gr.]
Craig *m.* from the surname, Crag, rock. [Gael.]
Crispin *m.* curly, curly-haired. (also **Crispian, Crispen**). [L.]
Crystal *f.* from the glass (also **Krystal, Krystle**). [Eng.]
Curt *m.* CONRAD.
Curtis *m.* courteous. [F.]
Cuthbert *m.* known, famous, bright. [A.-S.]
Cynthia *f.* of Mount Cynthus, a title of the Gr. moon goddess Artemis (also **Cyn, Cindy, Sindy**). [Gr.]
Cyril *m.* lord (also **Cy**). [Gr.]
Cyrus *m.* sun or throne (also **Cy**). [Pers.]

Dafydd *m.* W. form of DAVID (also **Dai**).
Daisy *f.* from the flower; used as a name for MARGARET (from F. *Marguerite*, daisy). [Eng.]
Dale *m., f.* valley. [A.-S.]
Damian *m.* tamer (also **Damien**). [Gr.]
Damon *m.* to subdue, tame. [Gr.]
Daniel *m.* the Lord is my judge (also **Dan, Danny**). [Heb.]
Danielle *f.* fem. of DANIEL (also **Daniel(l)a**).
Daphne *f.* laurel. [Gr.]
Darrell *esp.m.* darling (also **Darrel, Darryl, Daryl**). [Norm.]
Darren *m.* of uncertain meaning and origin.
David *m.* beloved (also **Dave, Davie, Davy**). [Heb.]
Davina *f.* fem. of DAVID (also **Davida, Davinia**).
Dawn *f.* dawn, daybreak. [Eng.]
Dean *m.* valley dweller. [A.-S.]
Deborah *f.* bee (also **Debbie, Debby, Debra**). [Heb.]
Deirdre *f.* perh. sorrowful. [Ir.]
Delia *f.* of Delos, birthplace of the Gr. moon goddess Artemis. [Gr.]
Delilah *f.* delicate (also **Delila**). [Heb.]
Del(l) *m.* DEREK.
Della *f.* perh. from DELIA OR ADELAIDE.
Delmar *m.* perh. of the sea [Sp.] or form of ELMER.
Delroy *m.* (servant) of the king. [F.]
Denise *f.* fem. of DENNIS (also **Denice, Denys**).
Dennis *m.* follower of *Dionysos*, Gr. god of wine (also **Denis, Den, Denny**). [Gr.]
Denzil *m.* from the Cornish surname *Denzell*.
Derek *m.* from *Theodoric*, people's ruler (also **Derrick, Dirk, Derry, Del**). [G.]
Desmond *m.* man from S Munster (also **Des, Desi**). [Ir.]
Diana *f.* from the Rom. goddess of the moon and hunting (also **Diane, Dianne, Deanna, Deanne, Dyan, Di**). [L.]
Dick *m.* RICHARD.
Dinah *f.* judged, vindicated. [Heb.]
Dionne *f.* fem. of DENNIS (also **Dion**).
Dolly *f.* DOLORES, DOROTHY.
Dolores *f.* sorrows (also **Dolly, Lola, Lolita**). [Sp.]
Dominic *m.* of the Lord (also **Dominick**). [L.]
Donald *m.* world ruler (also **Donnell, Don, Donny**). [Celt.]
Donna *f.* lady. [It.]
Dora *f.* DOROTHY, THEODORA.
Doreen *f.* perh. from DOROTHY or sullen (also **Dorene, Dorine, Dorrie**). [Ir.]
Doris *f.* woman from Doria, in ancient Greece. [Gr.]
Dorothy *f.* gift of god (also **Dorothea, Dora, Dolly, Dot, Dotty, Dodie**). [Gr.]
Dougal *m.* dark stranger (also **Dugal, Dugald**). [Gael.]
Douglas *m.* dark water (also **Doug, Douggie, Duggy**). [Gael.]
Drew *m.* ANDREW.
Duane *m.* small dark one (also **Dwayne**). [Ir.]
Dudley *m.* from the surname, orig. [A.-S.] wood of Dudda (also **Dud**).
Duke *m.* from the title or short for MARMADUKE.
Dulcie *f.* sweet. [L.]
Duncan *m.* brown warrior. [Celt.]
Dustin *m.* perh. Thor's stone. [prob. Norm. from O.N.]
Dyan *f.* DIANA.

Eamon(n) *m.* Ir. form of EDMUND.
Earl *m.* from the title, orig. meaning nobleman, warrior (also **Erle**). [A.-S.]
Ebenezer *m.* stone of help. [Heb.]
Edgar *m.* fortunate spear (also **Ed, Eddie, Ned, Neddy**). [A.-S.]
Edith *f.* prosperous battle (also **Edie, Edy**). [A.-S.]
Edmund *m.* prosperous protection (also **Edmond, Eamon(n), Ed, Eddie, Ned, Neddy**). [A.-S.]
Edna *f.* perh. rejuvenation [Heb.], or fire [Celt.]
Edward *m.* rich guardian (also **Ed, Eddie, Ned, Neddy, Ted, Teddy**). [A.-S.]
Edwin *m.* prosperous friend (also **Ed, Eddie**). [A.-S.]
Edwina *f.* fem. of EDWIN.
Egbert *m.* sword bright (also **Bert**). [A.-S.]
Eileen *f.* perh. pleasant or light [Gael.] or form of EVELYN; Ir. form of HELEN (also **Aileen**).
Elaine *f.* O.F. form of HELEN.
Eleanor *f.* med. form of HELEN (also **Eleanora, Eleanore, Elinor, Leonora, Leonore, Lenora, Lenore, Nell, Nellie, Nora(h)**). [F.]
Eli *m.* height. [Heb.]
Elias *m.* Jehovah is God (also **Elijah, Ellis, Eliot, Elliot(t)**). [Heb.]
Elizabeth *f.* God's oath (also **Elisabeth, Elise, Eliza, Elsa, Elsie, Elspeth, Elspie, Bess, Bessie, Bet, Beth, Betsy, Bette, Betty, Libby, Lisa, Lisbeth, Liz, Lisette, Liza, Lizzie, Lizzy, Isabel(la)**). [Heb.]
Ella *f.* all or foreign [Teut.]; ELLEN.
Ellen *f.* HELEN (also **Ella, Nell**).
Elliot, Ellis *m.* ELIAS.
Elmer *m.* from the Eng. surname, [A.-S.] noble.
Elroy *m.* LEROY.
Elsa, Elsie, Elspeth *f.* ELIZABETH.
Elton *m.* from the Eng. surname, perh. [A.-S.] Ella's settlement.
Elvira *f.* perh. elf-counsel or foreign and true. [Sp. from Teut.]
Elvis origin unknown, perh. from the Ir. saint Ailbhe, or all-wise [Scand.]
Emily *f.* from *Aemilius*, Roman family name (also **Emilia**). [L.]
Emma *f.* universal, whole (also **Em(m), Emmy, Irma**). [Teut.]
Emmanuel *m.* God with us (also **Immanuel, Manuel, Manny**). [Heb.]
Enid *f.* life, soul. [W.]
Enoch *m.* perh. skilled, trained or consecrated, dedicated. [Heb.]
Eric *m.* forever ruler. [O.N.]
Erica *f.* fem. of ERIC.
Ernest *m.* earnest (also **Ernie**). [Teut.]
Errol *m.* perh. a form of EARL.
Esmeralda *f.* emerald. [Sp.]
Estelle *f.* STELLA (also **Estella**).
Esther *f.* perh. myrtle (also **Hester, Ess(ie)**). [Pers.]
Ethel *f.* noble. [Teut.]
Eugene *m.* well-born (also **Gene**). [Gr.]
Eunice *f.* good victory. [Gr.]
Eustace *m.* fruitful (also **Stac(e)y**). [Gr.]
Evan *m.* W. form of JOHN.
Eve *f.* life (also **Eva, Evie, Evita**). [Heb.]
Evelyn *m., f.* from the surname.
Everard *m.* boar-brave. [Teut.]
Ezra *m.* help. [Heb.]

Faith *f.* faith, trust in God (also **Fay(e)**). [Eng.]
Fanny *f.* FRANCES.
Fay *f.* fairy [F.]; FAITH (also **Faye**).
Felicia *f.* fem. of FELIX (also **Felice**).
Felicity *f.* happiness. [L.]
Felix *m.* happy, lucky. [L.]
Fenella *f.* fair shoulder (also **Fi(o)nola, Fionnuala,**

Nola, Nuala). [Gael.]
Ferdinand *m.* journey venture (also **Fernando, Ferrant(e), Ferrand, Ferdie**). [Teut.]
Fergus *m.* best choice (also **Fearg(h)us**). [Gael.]
Finlay *m.* fair warrior (also **Findlay, Finley**). [Gael.]
Fiona *f.* fair, white. [Gael.]
Fionola *f.* FENELLA.
Flavia *f.* yellow-haired. [L.]
Flora *f.* flower (also **Flo, Florrie**). [L.]
Florence *f.* blossoming (also **Flo, Florrie, Flossie**). [L.]
Floyd *m.* LLOYD.
Frances *f.* fem. of FRANCIS (also **Francesca, Francine, Fran, Franny, Francie, Frankie, Fanny**).
Francis *m.* Frenchman (also **Frank, Frankie**). [L.]
Franklin *m.* free. [M.E.]
Fraser *m.* from the Sc. surname.
Freda *f.* WINIFRED, FREDERICA (also **Frieda**).
Frederica *f.* fem. of FREDERICK (also **Freda**).
Frederick *m.* peaceful ruler (also **Frederic, Fred, Freddie, Freddy**). [Teut.]

Gabriel *m.* man of God. [Heb.]
Gabrielle *f.* fem. of GABRIEL (also **Gabriella, Gaby**).
Gail, Gale *f.* ABIGAIL.
Gareth *m.* perh. gentle (also **Gar(r)y**). [W.]
Gary *m.* spear, spearman [Teut.]; short for *Garfield* (spearfield), GARETH (also **Garry**).
Gavin *m.* white hawk or hawk of the field (also **Gawain**). [W.]
Gayle *f.* ABIGAIL.
Gaynor *f.* GUINEVERE.
Gemma *f.* gem (also **Jemma**). [It.]
Gene *m.* EUGENE.
Genevieve *f.* perh. woman of the tribe. [F. from Celt.]
Geoffrey *m.* district peace, stranger peace, or pledge peace (also **Jeffrey, Jeffery, Geoff, Jeff**). [Teut.]
George *m.* farmer (also **Geordie**). [Gr.]
Georgina *f.* fem of GEORGE (also **Georgia, Georgette, Georgine, Georgiana, Gina**).
Gerald *m.* spear rule (also **Gerry, Jerry**). [Teut.]
Geraldine *f.* fem. of GERALD (also **Gerry, Jerry**).
Gerard *m.* spear strong (also **Gerrard, Gerry, Jerry**). [Teut.]
Germaine *f.* perh. German. [L.]
Gertrude *f.* spear strength or spear beloved (also **Gert, Gertie, Trudie, Trudy**). [Teut.]
Gervase *m.* spear bearer (also **Gervais(e), Jarvis**). [Teut.]
Gideon *m.* hewer. [Heb.]
Gilbert *m.* pledge bright (also **Gib, Gil**). [Teut.]
Giles *m.* kid (young goat) (also **Gyles**). [Gr.]
Gillian *f.* fem. of JULIAN (also **Jillian, Gill, Jill**).
Gina *f.* GEORGINA.
Ginny *f.* VIRGINIA.
Gladys *f.* W. form of CLAUDIA.
Glen *m.* valley (also **Glenn, Glyn(n)**). [Celt.]
Glenda *f.* pure good. [W.]
Gloria *f.* glory [L.]
Glynis *f.* little valley. [W.]
Godfrey *m.* God's peace. [Teut.]
Gordon *m.* orig. a Sc. place-name.
Grace *f.* grace (also **Gracie**). [L.]
Graham *m.* orig. an Eng. place-name (also **Grahame, Graeme**).
Grant *m.* tall. [F.]
Gregory *m.* watcher (also **Gregor, Greg(g)**). [Gr.]
Greta, Gretel *f.* MARGARET.
Griselda *f.* perh. grey battle or grey battle-heroine (also **Grizelda, Grizel, Zelda**). [Teut.]
Guinevere *f.* fair and soft (also **Guenevere, Gaynor, Jennifer**). [W.]
Gus, Gussie *m.* AUGUSTUS.
Guy *m.* perh. wood or wide. [Norm. from Teut.]
Gwendoline *f.* white ring (also **Gwendolen, Gwendolyn, Gwen, Gwenda**). [W.]
Gwilym *m.* W. form of WILLIAM.
Gwyneth *f.* blessed (also **Gwyn**). [W.]

Hadrian *m.* ADRIAN.
Hal *m.* HENRY.
Hamish *m.* Sc. form of JAMES.
Hank *m.* HENRY.
Hannah *f.* ANNE.
Harold *m.* army rule (also **Harry**). [A.-S.]
Harriet *f.* fem. of *Harry* (see HENRY) (also **Harriot, Hattie, Hatty**).
Harry *m.* HAROLD, HENRY.
Harvey *m.* battle-worthy [F.]
Hayley *f.* hay field. [A.-S.]
Hazel, Heather *f.* from the plants.
Hector *m.* hold fast, restrain. [Gr.]
Helen *f.* bright, light (also **Helena, Aileen, Eileen, Elaine, Eleanor, Ellen, Ilona, Lena, Nell, Nellie**). [Gr.]
Helga *f. (also* **Olga**). [Norse].
Henrietta *f.* fem. of HENRY (also **Hetty, Etta, Ettie**).
Henry *m.* home ruler (also **Harry, Hal, Hank**). [Teut.]
Herbert *m.* army-famous (also **Herb, Bert**). [Teut.]
Herman(n) *m.* army-man. [Teut.]
Hermione *f.* from *Hermes*, messenger of the gods. [Gr.]
Hester *f.* ESTHER.
Hew *m.* HUGH.
Hilary *m., f.* cheerful (also **Hillary**). [L.]
Hilda *f.* battle. [Teut.]
Hiram *m.* perh. noble brother. [Heb.]
Holly *esp. f.* from the plant (also **Hollie**).
Honor *f.* honour (also **Honora, Honoria, Nora(h)**). [L.]
Hope *f.* hope. [Eng.]
Horace *m.* from the Roman family name *Horatius* (also **Horatio**). [L.]
Howard *m.* from the surname, perh. [Scand.] high guard.
Hubert *m.* spirit-bright (also **Huey**). [Teut.]
Hugh *m.* mind, spirit (also **Hew, Huw, Hughie, Huey, Hugo**). [Teut.]
Humphrey *m.* warrior peace (also **Humphry**). [Teut.]
Hywel *m.* eminent. [W.]

Ian *m.* orig. Sc. form of JOHN (also **Iain**).
Ida *f.* work, labour. [Teut.]
Ignatius *m.* from the Roman family name *Egnatius* (also **Inigo**). [L.]
Immanuel *m.* EMMANUEL.
Imogen *f.* perh. maiden [Gael.] or beloved child [Gr.]
Ines, Inez *f.* AGNES.
Ingrid *f.* beautiful Ing (God of fertility) or ride of Ing (also **Inga, Inge**). [O.N.]
Irene *f.* peace (also **Rene**). [Gr.]
Iris *f.* rainbow. [Gr.]
Irma *f.* EMMA.
Isaac *m.* laughter (also **Izaak, Ike, Zak**). [Heb.]
Isabel *f.* orig. Sp. form of ELIZABETH (also **Isabelle, Isabella, Isobel, Belle, Bella**).
Isaiah *m.* God is salvation. [Heb.]
Isolde *f.* perh. fair one (also **Isolda, Ysolde**). [W.]
Ivan *m.* JOHN. [Rus.]

Ivor *m.* perh. yew, yew bow. [Norse.]

Jack *m.* orig. from *Jankin*, Flemish dim. of JOHN (also **Jackie, Jock, Jake**).
Jacob *m.* perh. supplanter (also **Jake**). [Heb.]
Jacqueline *f.* fem. of *Jacques*, F. form of JAMES (also **Jacquelyn, Jacklyn, Jacquetta, Jacqui, Jackie, Jacky**).
James *m.* orig. a form of JACOB (also **Jim, Jimmy, Jamie, Hamish, Seamus, Shamus**).
Jan *m., f.* JOHN, JANET.
Jane *f.* fem. of JOHN (also **Janet(te), Janice, Janis, Jayne, Janey, Janie, Sìan, Sìne, Shenna, Shona**); see also JEAN, JOAN.
Janet *f.* dim. of JANE (also **Janette, Jan, Jessie, Netta, Sinéad**).
Jarvis *m.* GERVASE.
Jasmine *f.* from the flower (also **Jasmin, Jessamine, Yasmin(e)**). [Pers.]
Jason *m.* perh. healer or form of JOSHUA. [Gr.]
Jasper *m.* bringer of treasure. [Pers.]
Jean *f.* fem. of JOHN (also **Janine, Jeanette, Jean(n)ie, Jennie, Jenny**); see also JANE, JOAN.
Jeffrey, Jeff *m.* GEOFFREY.
Jemima *f.* dove. [Heb.]
Jemma *f.* GEMMA.
Jennifer *f.* Cornish form of GUINEVERE (also **Jenny, Jenni(e)**).
Jenny *f.* JENNIFER, JEAN.
Jeremy *m.* exalted or appointed by God (also **Jeremiah, Jeremias, Jerry**). [Heb.]
Jerome *m.* holy name. [Gr.]
Jerry *m., f.* GERALD, GERALDINE, GERARD, JEREMY.
Jesse *m.* God is or God's gift (also **Jess**). [Heb.]
Jessica *f.* perh. God sees (also **Jessie**). [Heb.]
Jessie *f.* JANET, JESSICA.
Jethro *m.* excellence [Heb.]
Jill, Jillian *f.* GILLIAN.
Jim, Jimmy *m.* JAMES.
Jo *f., m.* short for Joanne (see JOAN), JOSEPH, JOSEPHINE.
Joan *f.* fem. of JOHN (also **Joanne, Joanna, Johanna, Joanie, Joni, Jo, Siobhan, Shevaun**); see also JANE, JEAN.
Job *m.* persecuted. [Heb.]
Jocelyn *m., f.* perh. from the *Gauts*, a Germanic people or a form of JUSTIN (also **Jocelin(e), Joscelin(e)**).
Jock *m.* Sc. form of JACK.
Jodie, Jody *f.* JUDITH.
Joe, Joey *m.* JOSEPH.
Joel *m.* Jehovah is God. [Heb.]
John *m.* God is gracious (also **Johnnie, Johnny, Jon, Jack, Evan, Ia(i)n, Ivan, Sean, Shaun, Shawn, Shane**). [Heb.]
Jonah *m.* dove (also **Jonas**). [Heb.]
Jonathan *m.* God has given (also **Jonathon, Jon**). [Heb.]
Joni *f.* JOAN.
Joseph *m.* God adds (a son to the family) (also **Joe, Joey, José**). [Heb.]
Josephine *f.* fem. of JOSEPH (also **Jo, Josie**).
Joshua *m.* God is salvation (also **Josh**). [Heb.]
Joy *f.* joy. [Eng.]
Joyce *f.* perh. champion or lord. [Celt.]
Jude *m.* perh. praised (also **Judah, Judas**). [Heb.]
Judith *f.* Jewess (also **Judy, Jodie, Jody**). [Heb.]
Julia *f.* fem. of JULIUS (also **Julie, Juliet(te), Juliana**).
Julius *m.* from the Rom. family name, perh. meaning clean-shaven (also **Julian, Jolyon, Jule, Jules**). [L.]
Justin *m.* just. [L.]
Justine *f.* fem. of JUSTIN (also **Justina**).

Karl *m.* CHARLES.
Katherine *f.* origin unknown, associated with Gr. *Katharos*, pure (also **Katharine, Kathryn, Catherine, Catharine, Katrine, Kat(e)rina, Catriona, Caitlin, Kathleen, Cathleen, Kath(y), Cath(y), Kate, Katie, Katy, Kitty, Kay(e), Karen, Karin**). [Gr.]
Keith *m.* from the Sc. surname or place-name, prob. [Gael.] wood.
Kelly *m., f.* from the Ir. surname, [Gael.] strife or warlike.
Kelvin *m.* from the Sc. river.
Kenneth *m.* handsome (also **Ken, Kenny**). [Gael.]
Kent *m.* from the Eng. surname, person from the county of Kent.
Kenton *m.* from the place name, royal estate.
Kerry *f., m.* perh. from the Ir. county or a form of KELLY.
Kevin *m.* handsome birth (also **Kev**). [Ir.]
Kieran *m.* small dark one (also **Keiran**). [Ir.]
Kimberley *f., m.* from the S. Afr. town, orig. an A.-S. place-name (also **Kim**).
King *m.* from the title.
Kingsley *m.* king's wood. [A.-S.]
Kirk *m.* church. [O.N.]
Kirsten, Kirsty *f.* CHRISTINE.
Kit *m.* CHRISTOPHER.
Kitty *f.* KATHERINE.
Kristal, Krystle *f.* CRYSTAL.
Kurt *m.* CONRAD.
Kylie *f.* perh. curl [Abor.] or from KELLY.

Lana *f.* perh. from ALANA.
Lance *m.* land (also **Lancelot, Launcelot**). [Teut.]
Laura *f.* laurel (also **Lauretta, Loretta, Laurissa, Laurel, Lauren, Laurie, Lori, Lora, Lolly**). [L.]
Laurence *m.* of Laurentum, a town in Latium (also **Lawrence, Laurie, Larry, Laurie, Lawrie**). [L.]
Lavinia *f.* origin unknown, in Rom. mythology the wife of Aeneas. [L.]
Leah *f.* cow or languid (also **Lea**). [Heb.]
Lee *m., f.* from the surname, [A.-S.] wood or field (also **Leigh, Lea**).
Leila *f.* night-dark. [Pers. or Arab.]
Lena *f.* short for *Helena* (see HELEN).
Leo *m.* lion (also **Leon**). [L.]
Leonard *m.* lion brave (also **Len, Lennie, Lenny, Lennard**). [Teut.]
Leonie *f.* fem. of LEO.
Le(o)nora, Le(o)nore *f.* ELEANOR.
Leopold *m.* people bold. [Teut.]
Leroy *m.* the king. [F.]
Lesley *esp. f.* from the Sc. surname.
Leslie *esp. m.* usual masc. form of LESLIE (also **Les**).
Lester *m.* from the town of Leicester.
Lettice *f.* happiness (also **L(a)etitia, Lettie, Letty**). [L.]
Levi *m.* associate. [Heb.]
Lewis *m.* Eng. form of LOUIS (also **Lew, Lewie**).
Liam *m.* Ir. form of WILLIAM.
Libby *f.* ELIZABETH.
Lilian *f.* prob. from ELIZABETH (also **Lillian, Lil, Lili**).
Lily *f.* from the flower; short for LILIAN.
Linda *f.* snake; short for BELINDA (also **Lynda, Lindy, Lin, Linn, Lyn, Lynn, Lynne**). [Teut.]
Lindsey *m., f.* from the Sc. surname, [A.-S.] pool

island (also **Lindsay**).
Lin(n)ette *f.* LYNETTE.
Lionel *m.* young lion. [F. from L.]
Lisa, Lisbeth, Lisette, Liz, Liza, Lizzie *f.* ELIZABETH.
Llewellyn *m.* perh. lionlike. [W.]
Lloyd *m.* grey (also **Floyd**). [W.]
Lois *f.* origin unknown. [prob. Gr.]
Lola, Lolita *f.* DOLORES.
Lolly, Lora, Loretta *f.* LAURA.
Lorna *f.* invented by R.D. Blackmore, author of *Lorna Doone*.
Lorne *m.* masc. of LORNA.
Lorraine *f.* from the F. province of *Lorraine* (also **Loraine, Laraine, Lori**).
Lottie *f.* CHARLOTTE.
Louella *f.* perh. famous elf [A.-S.] or LOUISE + ELLA (also **Luella**).
Louis *m.* famous warrior (also **Lou, Louie, Lewis, Lew(ie), Aloysius, Ludovic(k)**). [F. from Teut.]
Louise *f.* fem. of LOUIS (also **Louisa, Lou, Louie, Lulu**).
Lucas *m.* LUKE.
Lucius *m.* prob. light (also **Lucien, Lucian**). [L.]
Lucretia *f.* perh. riches, gain. [L.]
Lucy *f.* fem. of LUCIUS (also **Lucia, Lucie, Luce, Lucilla, Lucille, Lucinda, Lucette**).
Ludovic(k) *m.* LOUIS (also **Ludo**). [L. from Teut.]
Luke *m.* man from Lucania in Italy (also **Lucas**). [Gr.]
Luther *m.* famous warrior. [Teut.]
Lydia *f.* woman from Lydia, district of Asia Minor. [Gr.]
Lyn, Lynda *f.* LINDA.
Lynette *f.* idol, image [W.]; form of LYN (also **Lynette, Lin(n)ette**).
Lynn(e) *f.* LINDA.

Mabel *f.* from *Amabel*, lovable. [O.F. from L.]
Madel(e)ine *f.* MAGDALEN.
Madge *f.* MARGARET.
Mae *f.* MAY.
Maeve *f.* joy, the name of a legendary warrior queen. [Ir.]
Magdalene *f.* of Magdala, a town on the Sea of Galilee (also **Magdalen, Magdalena, Madel(e)ine, Maudlin, Maddie, Maddy, Magda**). [Heb.]
Mag(gie) *f.* MARGARET.
Magnus *m.* great. [L.]
Maisie *f.* MARGARET.
Malcolm *m.* follower of St Columba. [Gael.]
Mamie *f.* MARGARET, MARY.
Mandy *f.* AMANDA.
Manfred *m.* man peace, much peace, or strength peace. [Teut.]
Manny, Manuel *m.* EMMANUEL.
Marc, Marcel, Marcus *m.* MARK.
Marcia *f.* from the Rom. family name *Marcius*; used as fem. form of MARK (also **Marcie, Marcy, Marsha**). [L.]
Margaret *f.* pearl (also **Margarita, Marg(h)anita, Margaretta, Marguerite, Margot, Margery, Marjorie, Marg(ie), Mag, Maggie, Madge, Mamie, May, Meg, Megan, Peg, Peggy, Pearl, Greta, Gretel, Rita, Daisy**). [Gr.]
Maria, Marie, Marietta, Marilyn *f.* MARY.
Marion *f.* orig. a form of *Marie* (see MARY) (also **Marian, Marianne, Mary Ann(e)**).
Marisa *f.* MARY.
Marius *m.* prob. from *Mars*, Rom. god of war (also **Mario**). [L.]
Marjorie *f.* MARGARET (also **Marjory, Margery, Marg, Margie**).
Mark *m.* perh. from *Mars* (see MARIUS) (also **Marcus, Marc, Marcel**). [L.]
Marlene *f.* contr. form of *Maria Magdalene*. [G.]
Marlon *m.* origin unknown.
Marmaduke *m.* servant of Madoc. [Celt.]
Marsha *f.* MARCIA.
Martha *f.* lady (also **Marta, Marty, Marti(e), Matty, Mattie**). [Aram.]
Marti *f.* MARTY.
Martin *m.* prob. of Mars, warlike (also **Martyn, Marty**). [L.]
Martina *f.* fem. of MARTIN (also **Martine, Marti, Marty, Tina**).
Marty *f., m.* MARTHA, MARTINA, MARTIN.
Marvin *m.* prob. form of MERVYN.
Mary *f.* perh. wished-for child (also **Maria, Marie, Marietta, Marilyn, Marion, Marissa, Maureen, Miriam, Moira, Mamie, May, Moll(y), Mimi, Minnie, Mitzi, Polly**). [Heb.]
Matilda *f.* mighty battle-maiden (also **Mathilda, Maud(e), Mattie, Matty, Tilly**). [Teut.]
Matthew *m.* gift of God (also **Matthais, Matt**). [Heb.]
Mattie, Matty *f.* MARTHA, MATILDA.
Maud(e) *f.* MATILDA.
Maureen *f.* from *Maire*, Gael. form of MARY (also **Maura**).
Maurice *m.* Moor (also **Morris, Morrie**). [L.]
Mavis *f.* song-thrush. [O.-F.]
Maximilian *m.* from *maximus*, greatest (also **Max**). [L.]
Maxine *f.* fem. of *Max* (see MAXIMILIAN, MAXWELL).
Maxwell *m.* great stream or stream of Mack (also **Max**). [A.-S.]
May *f.* MARGARET, MARY (also **Mae**).
Meg, Megan *f.* MARGARET.
Melanie *f.* black (also **Melany, Mel, Mellie**). [Gr.]
Melissa *f.* bee (also **Mel**). [Gr.]
Melody *f.* melody, singing of songs. [Gr.]
Melvin *m.* perh. polished chief [Ir.] or sword friend [A.-S.] (also **Melvyn, Mel**).
Mercy *f.* mercy (also **Merry**). [Eng.]
Meredith *f., m.* great lord (also **Merry**). [Celt.]
Meriel *f.* MURIEL.
Merle *f.* blackbird [O.F.] or contr. form of MERIEL (also **Meryl**).
Mervyn *m.* sea hill (also **Merlin, Merlyn**) [Celt.]; or famous friend [A.-S.] (also **Mervin**).
Meryl *f.* MERLE, MURIEL.
Michael *m.* who is like the Lord? (also **Micah, Mick, Mickey, Micky, Mike**). [Heb.]
Michelle *f.* fem. of MICHAEL (also **Michaela, Micaela, Mick(e)y, Micki(e)**).
Mildred *f.* gentle strength. [A.-S.]
Miles *m.* perh. merciful [Slav.], beloved [Teut.], or soldier [L.] (also **Myles, Milo**).
Millicent *f.* hardworking, strong worker (also **Millie, Milly**). [Teut.]
Mimi *f.* MARY.
Minnie *f.* MARY, WILHEMINA.
Mirabelle *f.* wonderful (also **Mirabel, Mirabella**). [L.]
Miranda *f.* to be admired. [L.]
Miriam, Mitzi *f.* MARY.
Moira *f.* Anglicization of *Maire*, Gael. form of MARY (also **Moyra**).
Molly *f.* MARY (also **Moll, Mollie**).
Mona *f.* noble. [Gael.]
Monica *f.* origin unknown, perh. connected with Gr. *monos*, alone or L. *monēre* to counsel (also

Monique).
Montagu(e) *m.* pointed hill (also **Monty**). [O.F.]
Montgomery *m.* hill of the powerful man (also **Monty**). [O.F.]
Morag *f.* great. [Gael.]
Morgan *m., f.* sea-bright. [Celt.]
Morris *m.* MAURICE.
Mortimer *m.* from the Eng. surname, [O.F.] dead sea (also **Mort**).
Moses *m.* origin and meaning uncertain (also **Moshe, Moss**).
Mungo *m.* beloved friend. [Gael.]
Murdoch *m.* seaman (also **Murdo**). [Gael.]
Muriel *f.* sea-bright (also **Meriel, Merrill, Meryl**). [Celt.]
Murray *m.* from the Sc. surname.
Myfanwy *f.* my fine one. [W.]
Myra *f.* invented by the 16th-cent. poet Fulke Greville.
Myrna *f.* beloved (also **Morna**). [Gael.]

Nadine *f.* hope (also **Nadia**). [Rus.]
Nan, Nan(n)a, Nanette *f.* ANNE.
Nancy *f.* orig. a form of ANNE.
Naomi *f.* pleasant [Heb.]
Natalie *f.* birthday (of the Lord), form of NOEL (also **Natalia, Natasha**). [L.]
Nathan *m.* gift (also **Nat**). [Heb.]
Nathaniel *m.* gift of God (also **Nat**). [Heb.]
Ned, Neddy *m.* EDMUND, EDWARD.
Neil *m.* champion (also **Neal, Niall**). [Ir.]
Nell *f.* ELEANOR, ELLEN, HELEN (also **Nelly, Nellie**).
Nelson *m.* from the Eng. surname, Neil's son.
Nerys *f.* lady. [W.]
Nessa, Nessie, Nesta *f.* AGNES.
Netta, Nettie *f.* JANET, Antoinette (see ANTONIA).
Neville *m.* from the surname, [F.] new town.
Niall *m.* NEIL.
Nicholas *m.* victory of the people (also **Nicolas, Nicol, Nichol, Nick, Nicky, Colin**). [Gr.]
Nicola *f.* fem. of NICHOLAS (also **Nicole, Nicolette, Nicky, Nikki**).
Nigel *m.* NEIL, confused with L. *niger*, black.
Nina, Ninette, Ninon *f.* ANNE.
Noah *m.* perh. rest. [Heb.]
Noel *m.* birthday (of the Lord), Christmas. [L.]
Noelle *m.* fem. of NOEL.
Nola *f.* *Finola* (see FENELLA).
Nora(h) *f.* HONOR, ELEANOR (also **Noreen**).
Norma *f.* perh. rule, standard. [L.]
Norman *m.* Northman (also **Norrie, Norm**). [Teut.]
Nuala *f.* *Fionnuala* (see FENELLA).
Nye *m.* ANUERIN.

Odette, Odile *f.* OTTILIE.
Olaf *m.* relics of ancestors. [Scand.]
Olga *f.* Rus. form of HELGA.
Olive *f.* Olive (also **Olivia**). [L.]
Oliver *m.* olive tree [L.] or perh. form of OLAF (also **Ol, Ollie**).
Olwen *m.* white footprint (also **Olwyn**). [W.]
Omar *m.* eloquent. [Heb.]
Oona, Oonagh *f.* UNA. [Ir.]
Ophelia *f.* help. [Gr.]
Orlando *m.* It. form of ROLAND.
Orson *m.* little bear. [O.F. from L.]
Osbert *m.* god-bright (also **Oz, Ozzie**). [A.-S.]
Oscar *m.* god-spear. [A.-S.]
Oswald *m.* god-rule (also **Oz, Ozzie**). [A.-S.]
Ottilie *f.* perh. of the fatherland or fem. of OTTO (also **Ottilia, Ottoline, Odette, Odile**). [Teut.]
Otto *m.* riches, fortune. [Teut.]
Owen *m.* perh. youth (also **Owain**). [W.]

Paddy *m.* PATRICK, PATRICIA.
Pamela *f.* invented by the Eng. poet Sir Philip Sidney (1554–86), perh. meaning all honey [Gr.] (also **Pam**).
Pansy *f.* from the flower, from O.F. *pensee* thought.
Pat *m., f.* PATRICK, PATRICIA.
Patience *f.* patience. [Eng.]
Patricia *f.* fem. of PATRICK (also **Pat, Patti(e), Patsy, Paddy, Tricia**).
Patrick *m.* patrician, nobleman (also **Pat**). [L.]
Paul *m.* small. [L.]
Paula *f.* fem. of PAUL (also **Pauline, Paulina, Paulette**).
Pearl *f.* from the gem; MARGARET.
Peg, Peggy *f.* MARGARET.
Penelope *f.* perh. weaver or duck (also **Pen, Penny**). [Gr.]
Percival *m.* perh. pierce valley (also **Perceval, Perce, Percy**). [O.F.]
Percy *m.* from the Eng. surname derived from the name of a Normandy village; PERCIVAL.
Perdita *f.* lost. [L.]
Peregrine *m.* traveller, pilgrim (also **Perry**). [L.]
Peter *m.* rock (also **Piers, Pete**). [Gr.]
Petra *f.* fem. of PETER.
Petula *f.* perh. seeker, supplicant. [L.]
Philip *m.* lover of horses (also **Phillip, Phil, Pip**). [Gr.]
Philippa *f.* fem. of PHILIP (also **Phillip(p)a, Pippa**).
Philomena *f.* strongly loved or strong friendship. [Gr.]
Phoebe *f.* shining, bright. [Gr.]
Phyllis *f.* leafy, foliage (also **Phillis, Phyllida, Phyl**). [Gr.]
Pia *f.* pious. [L.]
Piers *m.* PETER.
Pip *m., f.* PHILIP, PHILIPPA (also **Pippa** *f.*).
Polly *f.* MARY.
Poppy *f.* from the flower.
Prince *m.* from the title.
Priscilla *f.* ancient (also **Prissy, Cilla**). [L.]
Prudence *f.* prudence (also **Prue**). [L.]
Prunella *f.* plum-coloured [F.] or plum [L.]

Queenie *f.* from *queen*.
Quentin *m.* fifth (-born) (also **Quintin, Quinton**). [L.]
Quincy *m.* from the Eng. surname derived from a Normandy place-name (also **Quincey**).

Rab, Rabbie *m.* Sc. form of ROBERT.
Rachel *f.* ewe (also **Rachael, Rachelle, Raquel, Rochelle, Rae, Ray**). [Heb.]
Raelene *f.* from *Rae* (see RACHEL).
Raine, Raina *f.* REGINA.
Ralph *m.* counsel-wolf (also **Ralf, Rafe, Raoul**). [O.N.]
Ramon *m.* Sp. form of RAYMOND.
Ramona *f.* fem. of RAMON.
Ranald *m.* REGINALD.
Randolph *m.* shield-wolf (also **Randolf, Randal(l), Ranulf, Randy**). [Teut.]
Raoul *m.* RALPH.
Racquel *f.* RACHEL.
Ray *m., f.* RAYMOND, RACHEL.
Raymond *m.* counsel protection or might protection (also **Raimond, Raymund, Ramon, Ray**).

Rana, Rani *f.* REGINA.
Rebecca *f.* noose (also **Becky**). [Heb.]
Regina *f.* queen (also **Raina, Raine, Rana, Rani, Ranee**). [L.]
Reginald *m.* might rule (also **Reynold, Ranald, Ronald, Reg, Reggie, Rex**). [Teut.]
Rene *f.* IRENE.
Renée *f.* reborn (also **Renata**). [F.]
Reuben *m.* prob. behold a son. [Heb.]
Rex *m.* king [L.]; REGINALD.
Reynold *m.* REGINALD.
Rhiannon *f.* nymph, goddess. [W.]
Rhoda *f.* rose [Gr.]
Rhys *m.* ardour, rashness. [W.]
Richard *m.* hard ruler (also **Rich, Richie, Ritchie, Rick, Rickie, Dick, Dickie**). [Teut.]
Rita *f.* MARGARET.
Robert *m.* fame-bright (also **Roberto, Rupert, Robbie, Rob, Robin, Rab, Rabbie, Bob, Bobby, Bert**). [Teut.]
Roberta *f.* fem. of ROBERT (also **Robina, Robin, Robyn**).
Rochelle *f.* RACHEL.
Roderick *m.* fame-rule (also **Rodrigo, Rod, Roddy, Rory**). [Teut.]
Rodney *m.* from the Eng. surname or place name, perh. meaning reed island (also **Rod, Roddy**).
Roger *m.* fame-spear. [Teut.]
Roland *m.* fame-land (also **Rowland, Orlando**). [Teut.]
Rolf *m.* fame-wolf (also **Rollo, Rudolph, Rudolf**). [Teut.]
Ronald *m.* REGINALD (also **Ron, Ronnie**).
Rory *m.* red [Celt.]; RODERICK (also **Rorie**).
Rosalind *f.* horse-snake (also **Rosalyn, Rosaline, Rose, Ros, Roz**). [Teut.]
Rosamund *f.* horse protection (also **Rosamond, Rose, Ros, Roz**). [Teut.]
Rose *f.* horse [Teut.]; rose [L.] (also **Rosa, Rosabel(la), Rosalie, Ros(e)anna, Rosetta, Rosina, Rosie**).
Rosemary *f.* from the plant, meaning sea dew [L.]; ROSE+MARY (also **Rosemarie, Rosie**).
Ross *m.* peninsula, headland. [Gael.]
Rowan *m.* little red one. [Ir.]
Rowena *f.* perh. from W. *Rhonwen*, fair lance.
Roxanne *f.* brilliant one or dawn. (also **Roxan(n)a, Roxane**). [Pers.]
Roy *m.* red. [Gael.]
Royston *m.* from the Eng. place name.
Roz *f.* ROSALIND, ROSAMUND.
Ruby *f.* from the gemstone.
Rudolph *m.* ROLF (also **Rudolf, Rudy**).
Rufus *m.* red (-haired). [L.]
Rupert *m.* ROBERT.
Russell *m.* little red one (also **Russ**). [O.F. from L.]
Ruth *f.* perh. friendship or beautiful vision. [Heb.]
Ryan *m.* from the Ir. surname.

Sabina *f.* Sabine woman (also **Sabine**). [L.]
Sabrina *f.* prob. from the L. name of the River Severn.
Sacha *esp. m.* ALEXANDER (also **Sasha, Sascha**).
Sadie *f.* SARAH.
Sal, Sally *f.* SARAH.
Salome *f.* peace. [Heb.]
Sam *m., f.* SAMUEL, SAMANTHA.
Samantha *f.* perh. listener [Aram.], or fem. of SAMUEL (also **Sam, Sammie**).
Samson *m.* of the sun (also **Sampson**). [Heb.]
Samuel *m.* heard by God (also **Sam, Sammy**). [Heb.]
Sandra *f.* ALEXANDRA (also **Sandie, Sandy**).
Sandy *m., f.* ALEXANDER, ALEXANDRA, SANDRA.
Sarah *f.* princess (also **Sara, Sal, Sally, Sadie**). [Heb.]
Saul *m.* asked for. [Heb.]
Scott *m.* from the surname, person from Scotland.
Seamus *m.* Ir. form of JAMES (also SHAMUS).
Sean *m.* Ir. form of JOHN (also **Shaun, Shawn, Shane**).
Sebastian *m.* man from Sebastia (town in Asia Minor named from the Gr. *sebastos*, venerable) (also **Seb**). [L. from Gr.]
Selina *f.* perh. from moon [Gr.] or form of CELIA [L.]
Serena *f.* calm, serene. [L.]
Seth *m.* substitute. [Heb.]
Shamus *m.* *Seamus* (see JAMES).
Shane *m.* Anglicized form of *Sean* (see JOHN).
Sharon *f.* plain, field. [Heb.]
Shaun, Shawn *m.* Anglicized forms of Sean (see JOHN).
Sheena *f.* Anglicized form of *Sine* (see JANE).
Sheila, Shelagh *f.* Anglicized forms of *Sile*, Ir. form of CELIA.
Shelley *esp. f.* from the surname, [A.-S.] sloping meadow; SHIRLEY.
Sherrie, Sherry *f.* CHERIE.
Shevaun *f.* Anglicized form of *Siobhan* (see JOAN).
Shirley *f.* from the surname or place-name, [A.-S.] county meadow (also **Shelley**).
Shona *f.* JANE.
Sìan *f.* W. form of JANE.
Sibyl *f.* SYBIL.
Sidney *esp. m.* from the Eng. surname, perh. [A.-S.] wide meadow or derived from St Denis, France (also **Sydney, Sid**).
Sidony *f.* person from Sidon, Phoenicia (also **Sidonie**). [L.]
Siegfried *m.* victory peace. [Teut.]
Silvester *m.* of the woods, wood-dweller (also **Sylvester, Silas, Si**). [L.]
Silvia *f.* of the woods (also **Sylvia, Silvie, Syl**).
Simon *m.* listening (also **Simeon**). [Heb.]
Simone *f.* fem. of SIMON.
Sindy *f.* CYNTHIA.
Sine *f.* Sc. Gael. form of JANE (also **Sheena**).
Sinéad *f.* Ir. Gael. form of JANET.
Siobhan *f.* Ir. form of JOAN (also **Shevaun**).
Sis, Sissie, Sissy *f.* CECILIA.
Solomon *m.* peaceable (also **Sol, Solly**). [Heb.]
Sonia *f.* SOPHIA (also **Sonya**). [Rus.]
Sophia *f.* wisdom (also **Sophie, Sophy, Sonia**). [Gr.]
Spencer *m.* from the Eng. surname, dispenser (of supplies in feudal times).
Stacey *f., m.* ANASTASIA, EUSTACE (also **Stacy**).
Stanley *m.* from the surname or place name, [A.-S.] stony meadow (also **Stan**).
Stella *f.* star (also **Estella, Estelle**). [L.]
Stephanie *f.* fem. of STEPHEN.
Stephen *m.* garland, crown (also **Stephan, Stefan, Steven, Steve, Stevie**). [Gr.]
Stewart *m.* from the surname, orig. given to a steward in a manor house etc. (also **Stuart**).
Susan *f.* lily (also **Susanna, Susannah, Suzanne, Suzette, Susie, Susy, Suzie, Sue, Sukie**). [Heb.]
Sybil *f.* one of a class of ancient Greek prophetesses (see dictionary entry at SIBYL) (also **Sibyl, Sybille, Sybilla**). [Gr.]
Sydney *m.* SIDNEY.
Sylvester *m.* SILVESTER.
Sylvia *f.* SILVIA.

Tabitha *f.* gazelle (also **Tabatha**). [Aram.]
Tamara *f.* palm tree (also **Tammy**). [Heb.]
Tamsin *f.* THOMASINA (also **Tammy**).
Tania *f.* short for Rus. *Tatiana* (also **Tanya**).
Tansy *f.* from the flower.
Tara *f.* from the name (meaning hill) of the seat of the High Kings of Ireland [Ir.]; star [Sansk.]
Ted, Teddy *m.* EDWARD, THEODORE.
Tel *m.* TERENCE, TERRY.
Terence *m.* from the Rom. name *Terentius* (also **Terry, Tel**). [L.]
Teresa *f.* THERESA.
Terri, Terry[1] *f.* THERESA.
Terry[2] *m.* from *Theororic*, people's ruler (see DEREK). [G.]; TERENCE (also **Tel**).
Tess(a) *f.* THERESA.
Thea *f.* short for *Dorothea* (see DOROTHY), THEODORA.
Thelma *f.* perh. will, wish. [Gr.]
Theobald *m.* people-bold (also **Tybalt, Theo**). [Teut.]
Theodora *f.* fem. of THEODORE (also **Thea, Theor, Dora**).
Theodore *m.* gift of God (also **Theo, Teddy, Tudor**). [Gr.]
Theophilus *m.* beloved of God (also **Theo**). [Gr.]
Theresa *f.* origin unknown, perh. from the ancient Gr. island of Therasia (also **Teresa, Terri, Terry, Tess, Tessa, Tessie, Trac(e)y**).
Thomas *m.* twin (also **Tom, Tommy, Tam, Tammie**). [Aram.]
Thomasina *f.* fem. of THOMAS (also **Thomasine, Tamsin, Tammy**).
Thora *f.* dedicated to Thor (Norse god of thunder). [O.N.]
Tiffanny *f.* from *Theophania*, Epiphany, manifestation of God. [Gr.]
Tilly *f.* MATILDA.
Timothy *m.* honour God (also **Tim, Timmy**).
Tina *f.* short for *Christina* (see CHRISTINE), MARTINA etc.
Titus *m.* origin unknown. [L.]
Toby *m.* God is good (also **Tobias**). [Heb.]
Todd *m.* from the surname, [M.E.] fox.
Toni *f.*, **Tony** *m.* ANTONIA, ANTHONY.
Tracy *esp. f.* THERESA; orig. from the Eng. surname derived from *Tracy*, place in France (also **Tracey, Tracie**).
Travis *m.* from the Eng. surname, [Norm.] crossroads.
Trevor *m.* from the W. surname or place name meaning large settlement.
Tricia *f.* PATRICIA (also **Trisha**).
Tristram *m.* perh. tumult (also **Tristan**). [Celt.]
Trix, Trixie *f.* BEATRIX.
Trudie, Trudy *f.* GERTRUDE.
Tyrone *m.* from the Ir. county.

Ulric *m.* wolf-rule. [Teut.]
Ulrike *f.* fem. of ULRIC (also **Ulrika**).
Ulysses *m.* angry one, hater. [L. from Gr.]
Una *f.* origin unknown (also **Oona, Oonagh**). [Ir.]
Uriah *m.* God is light. [Heb.]
Ursula *f.* little she-bear. [L.]

Valentine *esp. m.* strong, healthy (also **Val**). [L.]
Valerie *f.* from the Rom. family name *Valerius*, in good health (also **Valery, Val, Valerie**). [L.]
Vanessa *f.* invented by the 18th-cent. Eng. satirist Jonathan Swift.
Vaughan *m.* small one. [W.]
Venetia *f.* of Venice. [L.]
Vera *f.* faith [Rus.]; true [L.]
Verity *f.* truth. [Eng.]
Vernon *m.* from the Eng. surname, orig. F. place name meaning place of alders.
Veronica *f.* BERENICE; true image. [L.]
Vi *f.* VIOLA.
Victor *m.* conqueror (also **Vic**). [L.]
Victoria *f.* victory [L.]; fem. of VICTOR (also **Vicki, Vicky, Vikki, Vita**).
Vincent *m.* conquering (also **Vince**). [L.]
Viola *f.* violet (flower) (also **Violet, Violette, Violetta, Vi**). [L.]
Virgil *m.* prob. from the Rom. poet Publius Vergilius Maro. [L.]
Virginia *f.* from the Rom. family name or after Elizabeth I the 'virgin queen' (also **Ginny**).
Vita *f.* life [L.]; VICTORIA.
Vivian *m.*, *f.* lively (also **Vivien, Vivienne** (*f.*), **Vivyan, Viv**). [L.]

Wallace *m.* foreign (also **Wallis, Wally**). [A.-S.]
Walter *m.* rule-army (also **Walt, Wal, Wally**). [Teut.]
Wanda *f.* perh. vandal or stern, stock. [Teut.]
Ward *m.* guardian, watcher. [A.-S.]
Warren *m.* perh. guard or defender. [Teut.]
Wayne *m.* from the Eng. surname, [A.-S.] cart or cartmaker.
Wendy *f.* invented by J.M. Barrie for *Peter Pan* (1904). [Eng.]
Wesley *m.* from John Wesley, founder of the Methodist church, orig. west meadow (also **Wes**). [A.-S.]
Wilbur *m.* perh. resolute protection [Teut.] or will-fortress [A.-S.]
Wilfred *m.* will-peace (also **Wilfrid, Wilf**). [Teut.]
Wilhelmina *f.* fem. of WILLIAM (also **Wilma, Willa, Minnie**).
William *m.* will helmet (protection) (also **Will, Willie, Willy, Bill, Billie, Billy, Gwilym, Liam**). [Teut.]
Winifred *f.* from W. *Gwenfrewi*, fair reconciliation; later associated with Eng. masc. name *Winfrith*, friend of peace (also **Win, Winnie, Wyn, Wynne, Freda**).
Winston *m.* from the place-name, perh. [A.-S.] friend's settlement.

Xavier *m.* from St Francis Xavier, perh. from Sp. place name meaning new house, or Arab. splendid, bright.
Xaviera *f.* fem. of XAVIER.

Yasmin(e) *f.* JASMINE.
Ynes *f.* AGNES.
Yolande *f.* perh. violet (flower) (also **Yolanda**). [Gr.]
Yves *m.* yew. [F. from Teut.]
Yvonne *f.* fem. of YVES (also **Yvette**).

Zachary *m.* God has remembered (also **Zachariah, Zechariah, Zak**). [Heb.]
Zandra *f.* ALEXANDRA.
Zara *f.* dawn splendour, brightness. [Arab.]
Zelda *f.* GRISELDA.
Zena *f.* perh. woman. [Pers.]
Zillah *f.* shade. [Heb.]
Zoe *f.* life. [Gr.]
Zola *f.* from the F. novelist Emile *Zola*.
Zuleika *f.* fair beauty. [Pers. or Arab.]